THE AMERICAN EPHEMERIS

for the

20th CENTURY

1900 to 2000
at Midnight

Revised Fifth Edition

compiled and programmed by
Neil F. Michelsen
revisions by Rique Pottenger

International Standard Book Number: 0-935127-19-4

Printed in the United States of America

Published by ACS Publications
5521 Ruffin Rd
San Diego, California 92123-1314

PHENOMENA SECTION EXPLANATION

The phenomena data at the bottom of each page is listed in six sections (samples below) Sections 1, 2, 5 and 6 separate the first month from the second month by a blank line. All the sections except 6 list the astrological events by day, hour and minute of occurence with the headings of these 3 columns shown as Dy Hr Mn.

Astro Data	Dy	Hr Mn
♃ ✶ ♄	5	15:40
☿ D	5	14:02
☽ 0 S	12	2:40
♄ ♅°	12	19:13
☽ 0 N	25	23:09
♃ ♅°	27	12:31
☽ 0 S	8	9:16
♃ ✶ ♄	8	11:02
♂ D	19	18:15
☽ 0 N	22	7:04

SECTION 1 provides three types of information that should be interpreted as follows:

a) **STATIONS** are indicated by a planet glyph followed by D or an R indicating whether the planet is going direct or retrograde in its motion.

b) Planets at **0° DECLINATION** are indicated by a planet glyph, a zero and an N or S indicating whether the planet is moving North or South as it crosses the celestial equator.

c) **ASPECTS** between the **OUTER** planets, Jupiter through Pluto, are indicated.

Planet Ingress		Dy	Hr Mn
♀	♉	2	4:53
☿	♉	15	12:33
♇	♎	18	14:32
☉	♊	20	20:58
♀	♊	26	14:40
☿	♊	7	15:45
♀	♋	20	0:48
☉	♋	21	5:02
☿	♋	22	6:39
♆	♐	23	1:15

SECTION 2 The **PLANET INGRESS** tables gives the day and time each planet enters a new sign of the zodiac.

☽ Phases & Eclipses Dy	Hr Mn		
3	21:43	●	12♑08
3	21:45:13	● T	4'14"
10	13.53	☽	18♈57
18	13.37	μ	27♋05
18	13.21	♪ A	0.537
26	15.01	≤	5♏17

SECTION 5 contains the **MOON PHASES** and **ECLIPSE** data. The day, hour, minute and zodiacal position of the Moon is given for each:

● New Moon
☽ First Quarter Moon
○ Full Moon
☾ Third Quarter Moon

♪ indicates a **LUNAR ECLIPSE**. The three types of lunar eclipses are indicated as follows:

A = an **APPULSE**, a penumbral eclipse where the ☽ enters only the penumbra of the Earth.
P = a **PARTIAL** eclipse where the ☽ enters the umbra without being totally immersed in it.
T = a **TOTAL** eclipse, where the ☽ is entirely immersed within the umbra.

The time of the greatest obscuration is given which, in general, is not the exact time of the opposition in longitude. The magnitude of the lunar eclipse, which is the fraction of the ☽'s diameter obscured by the shadow of the Earth at the greatest phase, is also given.

● indicates a **SOLAR ECLIPSE**. The six types are:

P = a **PARTIAL** eclipse where the ☽ does not completely cover the solar disk.
T = a **TOTAL** eclipse where the ☽ completely covers the solar disk as seen from a shadow path on the Earth's surface.
A = an **ANNULAR** eclipse, a 'total' but the ☽ is too far from the Earth for the apex of its shadow to reach the Earth's surface. Therefore, the ☽ will not entirely hide the ☉ so a narrow ring of light will surround the dark new ☽.
AT = an **ANNULAR-TOTAL** eclipse, total for part of its path, annular for the rest.
A non-C = a rare **ANNULAR** eclipse where the central line does not touch the Earth's surface.
T non-C = a rare **TOTAL** eclipse where the central line does not touch the Earth's surface.

The time of greatest eclipse is given to the second which, in general, is not the exact time of conjunction in longitude. For partial eclipses the magnitude is given; for total and annular ones the duration in minutes and seconds is given.

SECTION 3 shows the **VOID** of **COURSE** ☽ data for the first month; **SECTION 4**, the second. The void period starts with the last major aspect (☌ ✶ □ △ ☍) to the ☽ whose day, hour and minute are given and ends when the ☽ enters the next sign indicated by the sign glyph and day, hour and minute of entry. The Void period may begin in the preceding month.

Last Aspect Dy Hr Mn			☽ Ingress	Dy Hr Mn	Last Aspect Dy Hr Mn			☽ Ingress	Dy Hr Mn
2 4:38	♂	☍	♊	2 16: 2	1 5:22	♇	△	♋	1 5:54
4 16:46	☿	✶	♋	4 23:26	3 9:44	♇	□	∞	3 10:19
6 22:23	☿	□	∞	7 4:32	5 12:49	♇	✶	♍	5 13:27
9 2:37	☿	△	♍	9 8: 2	6 16:42	☉	□	♎	7 16: 3
10 19: 7	♂	✶	♎	11 9:54	9 18: 3	♇	☌	♏	9 18:48
13 9: 4	☿	☍	♏	13 11:22	10 15:45	♂	☌	♐	11 22:26
15 4:29	☉	☍	♐	15 13:50	14 2:52	♇	✶	♑	14 3:48
16 11: 2	°	☌	♑	17 18:43	16 10:39	♇	□	♒	16 11:41
20 2:51	♇	□	♒	20 2:55	18 21:10	♇	△	≠	18 22:18
22 13:57	♇	△	≠	22 14: 9	21 6: 9	☿	□	♈	21 10:40
24 22:31	♀	✶	♈	25 2:39	23 22:35	♆	△	♉	23 22:38
27 13:50	♇	☍	♉	27 14:13	24 21:45	♂	☍	♊	26 8: 4
28 19: 2	♂	☍	♊	29 23:23	28 13:53	♆	☍	♋	28 14: 9
					30 16:23	♇	□	∞	30 17:30

Astro Data
1 MAY 1984
Julian Day # 30802
Delta T 54.0 sec
SVP 05≠29'00"
Obliquity 23°26'32"
∫ Chiron 1♊03.2
☽ Mean ☊8♊07.2
1 JUNE 1984
Julian Day # 30833
Delta T 54.0 sec
SVP 05≠28'55"
Obliquity 23°26'32"
∫ Chiron 3♊20.5
☽ Mean ☊ 6♊28.7

SECTION 6 contains six items of Astro Data for the first day of each month:

a) The **"JULIAN DAY'** is the count of the number of days elapsed since December 31, 1899, at Greenwich noon. January 1, 1900, is Julian Day 1; January 1, 1901, Julian Day 366; etc. This information can be used to calculate the midpoint in time between two events. For the astronomical Julian Day number counted from January 1, 4713 BC, add 2,415,020 to the number given for noon on the first day of the month.

b) **DELTA T** is the time in seconds that one must add to Universal Time to arrive at Ephemeris Time (see inside front cover).

c) **SVP** (the **SYNETIC VERNAL POINT**) is the tropical 0° point in the sidereal zodiac, as defined by Cyril Fagan. The tropical and sidereal zodiacs coincided in AD 221 and have diverged at the rate of one degree every 71 1/2 years as the tropical zodiac's starting point continues its retrograde movement on the ecliptic because of the precession of the equinoxes. Tropical positions are converted to sidereal by adding the degree, minutes, and seconds of the SVP to the tropical longitude and subtracting one sign.

d) The value of the **TRUE OBLIQUITY** of the **ECLIPTIC** is given.

e) **A MONTHLY POSITION** is given for the planetoid **CHIRON** ⚷, whose 51-year orbit around the ☉ is between Saturn and Uranus. Suggested keywords for Chiron are teacher and healer, related to the sign of Sagittarius.

f) **The MEAN LUNAR NODE** (☽ MEAN ☊) is so regular in its motion it can be accurately calculated for any day in the month for noon from the position given in this section on the 1st of the month. Use the ☽ Mean ☊ Interpolation table on the inside front cover. Enter the table using the day of the month for which you want the mean ☊. The minutes or degrees and minutes obtained must then be subtracted from the first of the month position. **Example:** birthday of May 16, 1901. Entering the table at 16 gives 47.7' so, 23♏28.7' – 47.7' = 22 ♏ 41.0'.

LONGITUDE — JANUARY 1900

Day	Sid.Time	☉	0 hr ☽	Noon ☽	True ☊	☿	♀	♂	♃	♄	♅	♆	♇
1 M	6 40 45	10♑ 9 12	2♑24 59	9♑36 59	20♐16.4	18♐59.9	6♒22.5	13♑52.1	1♐ 8.2	27♐43.0	10♐ 8.4	25♊13.1	15♊15.1
2 Tu	6 44 42	11 10 23	16 53 9	24 12 40	20R 14.9	20 17.2	7 37.1	14 38.3	1 19.9	27 50.0	10 11.7	25R 11.5	15R 14.1
3 W	6 48 38	12 11 35	1♒34 38	8♒58 8	20 12.4	21 36.0	8 51.6	15 24.6	1 31.5	27 56.9	10 14.9	25 9.9	15 13.1
4 Th	6 52 35	13 12 46	16 22 8	23 45 43	20 9.2	22 56.1	10 6.2	16 10.9	1 43.0	28 3.9	10 18.2	25 8.3	15 12.0
5 F	6 56 31	14 13 57	1♓ 7 57	8♓28 0	20 5.8	24 17.4	11 20.7	16 57.3	1 54.5	28 10.8	10 21.4	25 6.7	15 11.0
6 Sa	7 0 28	15 15 7	15 45 10	22 58 49	20 2.8	25 39.7	12 35.2	17 43.6	2 5.9	28 17.7	10 24.6	25 5.1	15 10.1
7 Su	7 4 25	16 16 17	0♈ 8 31	7♈13 55	20 0.7	27 3.0	13 49.7	18 30.1	2 17.3	28 24.5	10 27.8	25 3.5	15 9.1
8 M	7 8 21	17 17 27	14 14 49	21 11 8	19D 59.8	28 27.2	15 4.2	19 16.5	2 28.5	28 31.4	10 31.0	25 2.0	15 8.1
9 Tu	7 12 18	18 18 36	28 2 51	4♉50 4	20 0.1	29 52.3	16 18.6	20 3.0	2 39.7	28 38.2	10 34.1	25 0.4	15 7.2
10 W	7 16 14	19 19 44	11♉32 55	18 11 36	20 1.3	1♑18.1	17 33.0	20 49.5	2 50.8	28 45.0	10 37.2	24 58.9	15 6.2
11 Th	7 20 11	20 20 52	24 46 19	1♊17 19	20 3.0	2 44.6	18 47.3	21 36.1	3 1.8	28 51.8	10 40.2	24 57.4	15 5.3
12 F	7 24 7	21 22 0	7♊44 49	14 9 2	20R 4.5	4 11.8	20 1.6	22 22.7	3 12.7	28 58.5	10 43.3	24 55.9	15 4.4
13 Sa	7 28 4	22 23 6	20 30 12	26 48 30	20 5.1	5 39.7	21 15.9	23 9.3	3 23.6	29 5.3	10 46.3	24 54.4	15 3.5
14 Su	7 32 0	23 24 13	3♋ 4 6	9♋17 10	20 4.3	7 8.2	22 30.2	23 55.9	3 34.3	29 11.9	10 49.2	24 53.0	15 2.6
15 M	7 35 57	24 25 18	15 27 50	21 36 16	20 1.7	8 37.4	23 44.4	24 42.6	3 45.0	29 18.6	10 52.2	24 51.5	15 1.7
16 Tu	7 39 54	25 26 23	27 42 34	3♌46 53	19 57.2	10 7.1	24 58.6	25 29.3	3 55.6	29 25.2	10 55.1	24 50.1	15 0.9
17 W	7 43 50	26 27 28	9♌49 21	15 50 9	19 51.1	11 37.4	26 12.7	26 16.0	4 6.1	29 31.8	10 57.9	24 48.7	15 0.0
18 Th	7 47 47	27 28 32	21 49 26	27 47 25	19 43.9	13 8.3	27 26.8	27 2.8	4 16.5	29 38.4	11 0.8	24 47.3	14 59.2
19 F	7 51 43	28 29 36	3♍44 22	9♍40 32	19 36.3	14 39.8	28 40.9	27 49.5	4 26.8	29 44.9	11 3.6	24 45.9	14 58.4
20 Sa	7 55 40	29 30 39	15 36 16	21 31 54	19 29.0	16 11.9	29 54.9	28 36.4	4 37.0	29 51.4	11 6.3	24 44.6	14 57.6
21 Su	7 59 36	0♒31 41	27 27 52	3♎24 36	19 22.8	17 44.6	1♓ 8.9	29 23.2	4 47.1	29 57.8	11 9.1	24 43.3	14 56.8
22 M	8 3 33	1 32 43	9♎22 35	15 22 22	19 18.2	19 17.8	2 22.9	0♒10.1	4 57.1	0♑ 4.2	11 11.7	24 42.0	14 56.1
23 Tu	8 7 29	2 33 45	21 24 29	27 29 33	19 15.5	20 51.7	3 36.8	0 57.0	5 7.0	0 10.6	11 14.4	24 40.7	14 55.3
24 W	8 11 26	3 34 46	3♏38 8	9♏50 51	19D 14.7	22 26.1	4 50.6	1 43.9	5 16.8	0 16.9	11 17.0	24 39.4	14 54.6
25 Th	8 15 23	4 35 46	16 8 20	22 31 8	19 15.3	24 1.2	6 4.5	2 30.8	5 26.5	0 23.2	11 19.6	24 38.2	14 53.9
26 F	8 19 19	5 36 46	28 59 48	5♐34 49	19 16.7	25 36.9	7 18.2	3 17.8	5 36.1	0 29.5	11 22.1	24 37.0	14 53.2
27 Sa	8 23 16	6 37 46	12♐16 35	19 5 23	19R 17.8	27 13.2	8 32.0	4 4.8	5 45.5	0 35.7	11 24.6	24 35.8	14 52.5
28 Su	8 27 12	7 38 44	26 1 22	3♑ 4 30	19 17.8	28 50.2	9 45.7	4 51.9	5 54.9	0 41.8	11 27.1	24 34.6	14 51.9
29 M	8 31 9	8 39 42	10♑14 36	17 31 13	19 15.9	0♒27.8	10 59.3	5 38.9	6 4.2	0 47.9	11 29.5	24 33.5	14 51.3
30 Tu	8 35 5	9 40 40	24 53 46	2♒21 24	19 11.7	2 6.1	12 12.9	6 26.0	6 13.3	0 54.0	11 31.9	24 32.4	14 50.6
31 W	8 39 2	10 41 36	9♒53 3	17 27 34	19 5.2	3 45.1	13 26.5	7 13.1	6 22.3	0 60.0	11 34.2	24 31.3	14 50.1

LONGITUDE — FEBRUARY 1900

Day	Sid.Time	☉	0 hr ☽	Noon ☽	True ☊	☿	♀	♂	♃	♄	♅	♆	♇
1 Th	8 42 58	11♒42 31	25♒ 3 38	2♓39 53	18♐57.2	5♒24.9	14♓40.0	8♒ 0.2	6♐31.2	1♑ 6.0	11♐36.5	24♊30.3	14♊49.5
2 F	8 46 55	12 43 25	10♓14 58	17 47 36	18R 48.5	7 5.3	15 53.4	8 47.3	6 40.0	1 11.9	11 38.7	24R 29.2	14R 48.9
3 Sa	8 50 52	13 44 17	25 16 38	2♈41 3	18 40.4	8 46.5	17 6.8	9 34.4	6 48.7	1 17.7	11 40.9	24 28.2	14 48.4
4 Su	8 54 48	14 45 9	10♈ 0 5	17 13 8	18 33.8	10 28.4	18 20.2	10 21.6	6 57.2	1 23.5	11 43.1	24 27.3	14 47.9
5 M	8 58 45	15 45 58	24 19 51	1♉20 3	18 29.4	12 11.0	19 33.4	11 8.7	7 5.6	1 29.3	11 45.2	24 26.3	14 47.4
6 Tu	9 2 41	16 46 47	8♉13 44	15 1 3	18D 27.3	13 54.5	20 46.6	11 55.9	7 13.9	1 35.0	11 47.3	24 25.4	14 46.9
7 W	9 6 38	17 47 34	21 42 17	28 17 47	18 27.1	15 38.7	21 59.8	12 43.1	7 22.1	1 40.6	11 49.3	24 24.5	14 46.4
8 Th	9 10 34	18 48 19	4♊47 59	11♊13 19	18 27.7	17 23.7	23 12.9	13 30.3	7 30.1	1 46.2	11 51.2	24 23.7	14 46.0
9 F	9 14 31	19 49 3	17 34 18	23 51 22	18R 28.3	19 9.4	24 25.9	14 17.5	7 38.0	1 51.7	11 53.2	24 22.9	14 45.6
10 Sa	9 18 27	20 49 45	0♋ 5 0	6♋15 37	18 27.6	20 56.0	25 38.8	15 4.8	7 45.7	1 57.1	11 55.1	24 22.1	14 45.2
11 Su	9 22 24	21 50 25	12 23 39	18 29 25	18 24.7	22 43.3	26 51.7	15 52.0	7 53.4	2 2.5	11 56.9	24 21.3	14 44.8
12 M	9 26 21	22 51 4	24 33 16	0♌35 29	18 19.1	24 31.3	28 4.5	16 39.3	8 0.9	2 7.9	11 58.7	24 20.6	14 44.5
13 Tu	9 30 17	23 51 42	6♌36 19	12 35 59	18 10.7	26 20.1	29 17.2	17 26.5	8 8.2	2 13.2	12 0.4	24 19.9	14 44.1
14 W	9 34 14	24 52 17	18 34 39	24 32 30	17 59.7	28 9.6	0♈29.9	18 13.8	8 15.4	2 18.4	12 2.1	24 19.2	14 43.8
15 Th	9 38 10	25 52 52	0♍29 42	6♍26 23	17 46.9	29 59.7	1 42.4	19 1.0	8 22.5	2 23.5	12 3.7	24 18.5	14 43.5
16 F	9 42 7	26 53 25	12 22 43	18 18 53	17 33.3	1♓50.4	2 54.9	19 48.3	8 29.4	2 28.6	12 5.3	24 17.9	14 43.3
17 Sa	9 46 3	27 53 56	24 15 5	0♎11 30	17 20.1	3 41.5	4 7.3	20 35.6	8 36.2	2 33.6	12 6.9	24 17.4	14 43.0
18 Su	9 50 0	28 54 26	6♎ 8 26	12 6 10	17 8.2	5 33.1	5 19.6	21 22.9	8 42.8	2 38.5	12 8.4	24 16.8	14 42.8
19 M	9 53 56	29 54 54	18 5 2	24 5 26	16 58.6	7 25.0	6 31.9	22 10.2	8 49.3	2 43.4	12 9.8	24 16.3	14 42.6
20 Tu	9 57 53	0♓55 21	0♏ 7 47	6♏12 35	16 51.8	9 17.0	7 44.1	22 57.5	8 55.7	2 48.2	12 11.2	24 15.8	14 42.4
21 W	10 1 50	1 55 47	12 20 20	18 31 35	16 47.9	11 8.9	8 56.1	23 44.8	9 1.9	2 53.0	12 12.5	24 15.4	14 42.2
22 Th	10 5 46	2 56 12	24 46 55	1♐ 6 55	16D 46.2	13 0.6	10 8.1	24 32.1	9 7.9	2 57.6	12 13.8	24 15.0	14 42.1
23 F	10 9 43	3 56 35	7♐32 11	14 3 15	16R 46.0	14 51.9	11 20.0	25 19.5	9 13.8	3 2.2	12 15.1	24 14.6	14 42.0
24 Sa	10 13 39	4 56 57	20 40 39	27 24 51	16 46.1	16 42.3	12 31.9	26 6.8	9 19.5	3 6.7	12 16.2	24 14.2	14 41.9
25 Su	10 17 36	5 57 17	4♑16 11	11♑14 53	16 45.1	18 31.6	13 43.6	26 54.1	9 25.1	3 11.2	12 17.4	24 13.9	14 41.8
26 M	10 21 32	6 57 36	18 20 58	25 34 19	16 42.1	20 19.4	14 55.2	27 41.4	9 30.5	3 15.6	12 18.5	24 13.6	14 41.8
27 Tu	10 25 29	7 57 53	2♒54 32	10♒21 2	16 36.4	22 5.4	16 6.8	28 28.8	9 35.7	3 19.9	12 19.5	24 13.4	14D 41.8
28 W	10 29 25	8 58 9	17 52 56	25 29 10	16 27.9	23 49.0	17 18.2	29 16.1	9 40.8	3 24.1	12 20.5	24 13.2	14 41.8

Astro Data

	Dy Hr Mn
☽0N	6 3:26
☽0S	20 4:51
☽0N	2 12:34
♀0N	14 22:38
☽0S	16 12:01
♇ D	27 14:50

Planet Ingress

	Dy Hr Mn
☿ ♑	9 2:10
☉ ♒	20 11:33
♀ ♓	20 1:39
♂ ♒	21 18:51
♄ ♑	21 8:10
☿ ♒	28 17:11
♀ ♈	13 14:08
☿ ♓	15 0:04
☉ ♓	19 2:01
♂ ♓	28 22:15

Last Aspect / ☽ Ingress

Last Aspect Dy Hr Mn	☽ Ingress Dy Hr Mn
1 20:06 ♂ ☌	♒ 2 21:26
4 19:09 ♄ ⚹	♓ 4 22:09
6 21:04 ♄ □	♈ 6 23:46
9 1:03 ♄ △	♉ 9 3:26
10 17:50 ♂ △	♊ 11 9:37
13 16:30 ♄ ☍	♋ 13 18:06
15 19:20 ♂ ☍	♌ 16 4:31
18 15:52 ♄ △	♍ 18 16:27
21 5:06 ♄ □	♎ 21 5:07
23 6:27 ♆ △	♏ 23 16:55
25 16:53 ♆ ⚹	♐ 26 1:50
27 21:31 ♆ ☍	♑ 28 6:48
29 1:21 ♀ ⚹	♒ 30 8:13

Last Aspect / ☽ Ingress

Last Aspect Dy Hr Mn	☽ Ingress Dy Hr Mn
31 23:07 ♆ △	♓ 1 7:48
2 22:42 ♆ □	♈ 3 7:38
5 0:11 ♆ ⚹	♉ 5 9:42
7 0:35 ♀ ⚹	♊ 7 15:08
9 14:31 ♀ □	♋ 9 23:50
12 7:46 ♀ △	♌ 12 10:49
14 22:48 ♀ ☍	♍ 14 23:00
17 0:05 ♆ □	♎ 17 11:37
19 12:21 ♆ △	♏ 19 23:45
21 23:30 ♂ □	♐ 22 9:54
24 10:18 ♂ ⚹	♑ 24 16:33
26 3:46 ☿ ⚹	♒ 26 19:16
28 18:55 ♂ ☌	♓ 28 19:05

☽ Phases & Eclipses

Dy Hr Mn	
1 13:52	● 10♑45
8 5:40	☽ 17♈32
15 19:07	○ 25♋14
23 23:53	☽ 3♏34
31 1:23	● 10♒45
6 16:23	☽ 17♉28
14 13:50	○ 25♌27
22 16:44	☽ 3♐38

Astro Data

1 JANUARY 1900
Julian Day # 1
Delta T -2.7 sec
SVP 06♓39'04"
Obliquity 23°27'06"
⚷ Chiron 18♐53.7
☽ Mean ☊ 19♐09.7

1 FEBRUARY 1900
Julian Day # 32
Delta T -2.6 sec
SVP 06♓38'59"
Obliquity 23°27'06"
⚷ Chiron 22♐02.6
☽ Mean ☊ 17♐31.2

MARCH 1900 — LONGITUDE

Day	Sid.Time	☉	0 hr ☽	Noon ☽	True ☊	☿	♀	♂	♃	♄	♅	♆	♇
1 Th	10 33 22	9♓58 23	3♓ 8 25	10♓49 17	16♐17.4	25♓29.7	18♈29.6	0♓ 3.4	9♐45.7	3♑28.2	12♐21.4	24♊13.0	14♊41.8
2 F	10 37 19	10 58 35	18 30 15	26 9 48	16R 5.8	27 7.1	19 40.9	0 50.8	9 50.5	3 32.3	12 22.3	24R 12.9	14 41.8
3 Sa	10 41 15	11 58 46	3♈46 28	11♈18 57	15 54.6	28 40.6	20 52.0	1 38.1	9 55.1	3 36.2	12 23.1	24 12.7	14 41.9
4 Su	10 45 12	12 58 54	18 46 7	26 7 4	15 45.2	0♈ 9.6	22 3.0	2 25.4	9 59.5	3 40.1	12 23.8	24 12.7	14 42.0
5 M	10 49 8	13 59 1	3♉21 11	10♉28 1	15 38.3	1 33.6	23 14.0	3 12.7	10 3.7	3 44.0	12 24.6	24D 12.6	14 42.1
6 Tu	10 53 5	14 59 5	17 27 24	24 19 22	15 34.2	2 51.9	24 24.8	3 60.0	10 7.8	3 47.7	12 25.2	24 12.6	14 42.2
7 W	10 57 1	15 59 7	1♊ 4 6	7♊41 58	15 32.5	4 4.1	25 35.5	4 47.3	10 11.7	3 51.3	12 25.8	24 12.6	14 42.4
8 Th	11 0 58	16 59 7	14 13 23	20 38 53	15 32.1	5 9.6	26 46.1	5 34.6	10 15.4	3 54.9	12 26.4	24 12.7	14 42.5
9 F	11 4 54	17 59 5	26 59 3	3♋14 27	15 32.0	6 7.9	27 56.6	6 21.8	10 19.0	3 58.4	12 26.9	24 12.8	14 42.7
10 Sa	11 8 51	18 59 1	9♋25 41	15 33 21	15 30.9	6 58.6	29 6.9	7 9.1	10 22.4	4 1.8	12 27.3	24 12.9	14 43.0
11 Su	11 12 48	19 58 55	21 38 1	27 40 12	15 27.6	7 41.4	0♉17.1	7 56.3	10 25.6	4 5.1	12 27.7	24 13.1	14 43.2
12 M	11 16 44	20 58 46	3♌40 24	9♌39 3	15 21.6	8 16.0	1 27.2	8 43.6	10 28.6	4 8.3	12 28.0	24 13.3	14 43.5
13 Tu	11 20 41	21 58 35	15 36 33	21 33 16	15 12.7	8 42.1	2 37.2	9 30.8	10 31.4	4 11.4	12 28.3	24 13.5	14 43.8
14 W	11 24 37	22 58 22	27 29 29	3♍25 30	15 1.1	8 59.7	3 47.0	10 18.0	10 34.1	4 14.5	12 28.6	24 13.8	14 44.1
15 Th	11 28 34	23 58 7	9♍21 31	15 17 44	14 47.6	9R 8.7	4 56.7	11 5.2	10 36.6	4 17.4	12 28.7	24 14.1	14 44.4
16 F	11 32 30	24 57 49	21 14 20	27 11 29	14 33.2	9 9.1	6 6.2	11 52.4	10 38.9	4 20.3	12 28.9	24 14.4	14 44.7
17 Sa	11 36 27	25 57 30	3♎ 9 19	9♎ 8 0	14 19.1	9 1.4	7 15.6	12 39.5	10 41.0	4 23.1	12R 28.9	24 14.8	14 45.1
18 Su	11 40 23	26 57 9	15 7 41	21 8 34	14 6.4	8 45.6	8 24.8	13 26.7	10 43.0	4 25.8	12 28.9	24 15.2	14 45.5
19 M	11 44 20	27 56 46	27 10 51	3♏14 46	13 56.0	8 22.5	9 33.9	14 13.8	10 44.7	4 28.4	12 28.9	24 15.6	14 45.9
20 Tu	11 48 16	28 56 21	9♏20 36	15 28 39	13 48.5	7 52.5	10 42.8	15 0.9	10 46.3	4 30.9	12 28.8	24 16.1	14 46.4
21 W	11 52 13	29 55 54	21 39 18	27 52 56	13 43.9	7 16.3	11 51.6	15 48.0	10 47.7	4 33.3	12 28.7	24 16.6	14 46.8
22 Th	11 56 10	0♈55 26	4♐ 9 58	10♐30 52	13D 41.9	6 35.0	13 0.2	16 35.1	10 48.9	4 35.6	12 28.5	24 17.1	14 47.3
23 F	12 0 6	1 54 55	16 56 7	23 26 11	13 41.6	5 49.3	14 8.7	17 22.2	10 49.9	4 37.8	12 28.2	24 17.7	14 47.8
24 Sa	12 4 3	2 54 23	0♑ 1 33	6♑42 37	13R 41.9	5 0.4	15 17.0	18 9.2	10 50.7	4 39.9	12 27.9	24 18.3	14 48.3
25 Su	12 7 59	3 53 49	13 29 47	20 23 20	13 41.6	4 9.3	16 25.2	18 56.3	10 51.4	4 42.0	12 27.6	24 18.9	14 48.9
26 M	12 11 56	4 53 14	27 23 25	4♒30 4	13 39.6	3 17.1	17 33.1	19 43.3	10 51.8	4 43.9	12 27.2	24 19.6	14 49.4
27 Tu	12 15 52	5 52 37	11♒43 8	19 2 15	13 35.3	2 24.9	18 40.9	20 30.3	10R 52.1	4 45.8	12 26.7	24 20.3	14 50.0
28 W	12 19 49	6 51 57	26 26 52	3♓56 10	13 28.5	1 33.8	19 48.5	21 17.3	10 52.2	4 47.5	12 26.2	24 21.1	14 50.6
29 Th	12 23 45	7 51 16	11♓29 12	19 4 46	13 19.8	0 44.7	20 56.0	22 4.2	10 52.0	4 49.2	12 25.7	24 21.8	14 51.2
30 F	12 27 42	8 50 33	26 41 36	4♈18 17	13 10.0	29♓58.4	22 3.2	22 51.2	10 51.7	4 50.7	12 25.1	24 22.6	14 51.9
31 Sa	12 31 39	9 49 48	11♈53 27	19 25 47	13 0.4	29 15.6	23 10.3	23 38.1	10 51.2	4 52.2	12 24.4	24 23.4	14 52.5

APRIL 1900 — LONGITUDE

Day	Sid.Time	☉	0 hr ☽	Noon ☽	True ☊	☿	♀	♂	♃	♄	♅	♆	♇
1 Su	12 35 35	10♈49 1	26♈54 2	4♉17 9	12♐52.2	28♓37.1	24♉17.2	24♓24.9	10♐50.5	4♑53.5	12♐23.7	24♊24.3	14♊53.2
2 M	12 39 32	11 48 12	11♉34 16	18 44 46	12R 46.1	28R 3.3	25 23.8	25 11.8	10R 49.7	4 54.8	12R 22.9	24 25.2	14 53.9
3 Tu	12 43 28	12 47 21	25 48 14	2♊44 26	12 42.6	27 34.4	26 30.3	25 58.6	10 48.6	4 56.0	12 22.1	24 26.1	14 54.6
4 W	12 47 25	13 46 28	9♊33 22	16 15 11	12D 41.4	27 10.9	27 36.5	26 45.4	10 47.4	4 57.0	12 21.3	24 27.1	14 55.3
5 Th	12 51 21	14 45 32	22 50 12	29 18 49	12 41.7	26 52.9	28 42.6	27 32.2	10 45.9	4 58.0	12 20.4	24 28.1	14 56.1
6 F	12 55 18	15 44 34	5♋41 32	11♋58 54	12R 42.5	26 40.4	29 48.4	28 18.9	10 44.3	4 58.9	12 19.4	24 29.1	14 56.9
7 Sa	12 59 14	16 43 34	18 11 30	24 19 59	12 42.9	26D 33.4	0♊53.9	29 5.6	10 42.5	4 59.6	12 18.4	24 30.1	14 57.7
8 Su	13 3 11	17 42 31	0♌24 56	6♌26 58	12 41.9	26 31.8	1 59.3	29 52.3	10 40.5	5 0.3	12 17.4	24 31.2	14 58.5
9 M	13 7 8	18 41 26	12 26 40	18 24 36	12 38.9	26 35.6	3 4.4	0♈38.9	10 38.4	5 0.9	12 16.3	24 32.3	14 59.3
10 Tu	13 11 4	19 40 19	24 21 17	0♍17 13	12 33.7	26 44.6	4 9.2	1 25.5	10 36.0	5 1.3	12 15.2	24 33.5	15 0.2
11 W	13 15 1	20 39 9	6♍12 50	12 8 31	12 26.4	26 58.7	5 13.8	2 12.1	10 33.5	5 1.7	12 14.0	24 34.6	15 1.0
12 Th	13 18 57	21 37 57	18 4 38	24 1 30	12 17.6	27 17.6	6 18.0	2 58.6	10 30.8	5 2.0	12 12.7	24 35.8	15 1.9
13 F	13 22 54	22 36 43	29 59 23	5♎58 30	12 8.1	27 41.2	7 22.1	3 45.1	10 27.9	5 2.2	12 11.5	24 37.1	15 2.8
14 Sa	13 26 50	23 35 27	11♎59 4	18 1 16	11 58.6	28 9.2	8 25.8	4 31.6	10 24.8	5R 2.2	12 10.1	24 38.3	15 3.7
15 Su	13 30 47	24 34 9	24 5 14	0♏11 7	11 50.2	28 41.5	9 29.3	5 18.0	10 21.6	5 2.2	12 8.8	24 39.6	15 4.6
16 M	13 34 43	25 32 49	6♏19 4	12 29 12	11 43.5	29 17.9	10 32.4	6 4.4	10 18.2	5 2.1	12 7.4	24 40.9	15 5.6
17 Tu	13 38 40	26 31 28	18 41 40	24 56 38	11 38.8	29 58.1	11 35.3	6 50.8	10 14.6	5 1.9	12 5.9	24 42.2	15 6.5
18 W	13 42 36	27 30 4	1♐14 17	7♐34 48	11D 36.4	0♈42.0	12 37.8	7 37.1	10 10.9	5 1.6	12 4.5	24 43.6	15 7.5
19 Th	13 46 33	28 28 39	13 58 24	20 25 20	11 35.8	1 29.5	13 40.0	8 23.4	10 7.0	5 1.2	12 2.9	24 45.0	15 8.5
20 F	13 50 30	29 27 11	26 55 52	3♑30 15	11 36.7	2 20.3	14 41.9	9 9.7	10 2.9	5 0.7	12 1.4	24 46.4	15 9.5
21 Sa	13 54 26	0♉25 43	10♑ 8 45	16 51 36	11 38.1	3 14.4	15 43.5	9 55.9	9 58.7	5 0.1	11 59.8	24 47.8	15 10.5
22 Su	13 58 23	1 24 12	23 39 2	0♒31 13	11R 39.2	4 11.5	16 44.7	10 42.1	9 54.3	4 59.4	11 58.1	24 49.3	15 11.6
23 M	14 2 19	2 22 40	7♒28 15	14 30 9	11 39.4	5 11.5	17 45.5	11 28.3	9 49.7	4 58.6	11 56.4	24 50.8	15 12.6
24 Tu	14 6 16	3 21 7	21 36 48	28 48 0	11 38.0	6 14.3	18 46.0	12 14.4	9 45.0	4 57.7	11 54.7	24 52.3	15 13.7
25 W	14 10 12	4 19 32	6♓ 3 21	13♓22 23	11 35.0	7 19.9	19 46.1	13 0.5	9 40.1	4 56.7	11 53.0	24 53.8	15 14.8
26 Th	14 14 9	5 17 55	20 44 24	28 8 39	11 30.7	8 28.0	20 45.8	13 46.5	9 35.1	4 55.6	11 51.2	24 55.4	15 15.9
27 F	14 18 5	6 16 16	5♈34 12	13♈ 0 4	11 25.6	9 38.7	21 45.2	14 32.5	9 29.9	4 54.4	11 49.3	24 57.0	15 17.0
28 Sa	14 22 2	7 14 36	20 25 14	27 48 39	11 20.5	10 51.8	22 44.1	15 18.5	9 24.6	4 53.1	11 47.5	24 58.6	15 18.1
29 Su	14 25 59	8 12 55	5♉ 9 18	12♉26 18	11 16.2	12 7.2	23 42.6	16 4.4	9 19.2	4 51.8	11 45.6	25 0.2	15 19.2
30 M	14 29 55	9 11 11	19 38 48	26 46 8	11 13.1	13 24.9	24 40.6	16 50.3	9 13.6	4 50.3	11 43.7	25 1.9	15 20.4

Astro Data (Dy Hr Mn)	Planet Ingress (Dy Hr Mn)	Last Aspect (Dy Hr Mn)	☽ Ingress (Dy Hr Mn)	Last Aspect (Dy Hr Mn)	☽ Ingress (Dy Hr Mn)	☽ Phases & Eclipses (Dy Hr Mn)	Astro Data
☽0N 1 23:47	☿ ♈ 3 21:21	2 15:03 ☿ ☌	♈ 2 18:02	31 19:58 ♆ ⚹	♉ 1 5:01	1 11:25 ● 10♓27	1 MARCH 1900
☿0N 2 21:25	♀ ♉ 10 18:08	4 8:52 ♆ ⚹	♉ 4 18:25	3 2:57 ☿ ⚹	♊ 3 7:14	8 5:34 ☽ 17♊13	Julian Day # 60
♆ D 5 16:54	☉ ♈ 21 1:39	5 19:24 ☉ ⚹	♊ 6 22:05	5 9:15 ♂ □	♋ 5 13:17	16 8:12 ○ 25♍18	Delta T -2.5 sec
☽0S 15 18:17	☿ ♓ 29 23:07	9 2:01 ♀ ⚹	♋ 9 5:46	7 22:51 ♂ △	♌ 7 23:11	24 5:36 ☽ 3♑08	SVP 06♓38'56"
☿ R 15 13:22		10 20:26 ☉ △	♌ 11 16:39	10 0:25 ♆ ⚹	♍ 10 11:25	30 20:30 ● 9♈41	Obliquity 23°27'07"
♅ R 17 19:27	♀ ♊ 6 4:15	13 17:24 ♆ ⚹	♍ 14 5:04	12 19:12 ☿ ☍	♎ 13 0:01		⚷ Chiron 24♐03.2
♃ R 27 21:18	♂ ♈ 8 3:58	16 8:12 ☉ ☍	♎ 16 17:39	15 1:08 ♆ △	♏ 15 11:38	6 20:55 ☽ 16♋36	☽ Mean ☊ 16♐02.3
☽0N 29 10:46	☿ ♈ 17 1:05	18 18:12 ♆ △	♏ 19 5:35	15 21:30 ♄ ⚹	♐ 17 21:39	15 1:02 ○ 24♎37	
☿0S 3 2:53	☉ ♉ 20 13:27	20 11:51 ♂ △	♐ 21 16:03	20 4:59 ☉ △	♑ 20 5:37	22 14:33 ☽ 1♒60	1 APRIL 1900
☿ D 7 18:51		23 13:35 ♆ ☍	♑ 23 23:57	20 23:36 ♂ □	♒ 22 11:06	29 5:23 ● 8♉26	Julian Day # 91
♂0N 11 0:39		25 10:03 ♂ ⚹	♒ 26 4:26	24 5:28 ♆ △	♓ 24 14:00		Delta T -2.4 sec
☽0S 12 0:14		27 20:37 ♆ △	♓ 28 5:42	26 6:48 ♆ □	♈ 26 15:00		SVP 06♓38'53"
♄ R 14 6:59		30 4:56 ☿ ☌	♈ 30 5:13	28 7:24 ♆ ⚹	♉ 28 15:34		Obliquity 23°27'06"
☿0N 23 22:49	☽0N 25 19:35			29 5:23 ☉ ☌	♊ 30 17:30		⚷ Chiron 24♐58.9
							☽ Mean ☊ 14♐23.7

LONGITUDE MAY 1900

Day	Sid.Time	☉	0 hr ☽	Noon ☽	True ☊	☿	♀	♂	♃	♄	♅	♆	♇
1 Tu	14 33 52	10♉ 9 26	3♊47 47	10♊43 23	11♐11.6	14♈44.8	25♊38.2	17♈36.1	9♐ 7.9	4♑48.8	11♐41.7	25♊ 3.6	15♊21.5
2 W	14 37 48	11 7 39	17 32 43	24 15 44	11D11.5	16 7.0	26 35.4	18 21.9	9R 2.0	4R47.1	11R39.7	25 5.3	15 22.7
3 Th	14 41 45	12 5 50	0♋52 31	7♋23 16	11 12.6	17 31.2	27 32.0	19 7.6	8 56.0	4 45.4	11 37.7	25 7.0	15 23.9
4 F	14 45 41	13 3 59	13 48 18	20 8 0	11 14.2	18 57.6	28 28.1	19 53.3	8 50.0	4 43.6	11 35.6	25 8.8	15 25.1
5 Sa	14 49 38	14 2 6	26 22 51	2♌33 21	11 15.7	20 26.0	29 23.8	20 39.0	8 43.7	4 41.6	11 33.6	25 10.5	15 26.3
6 Su	14 53 34	15 0 11	8♌40 4	14 43 34	11R16.7	21 56.4	0♋18.8	21 24.6	8 37.4	4 39.6	11 31.5	25 12.3	15 27.5
7 M	14 57 31	15 58 15	20 44 26	26 43 16	11 16.8	23 28.9	1 13.3	22 10.1	8 31.0	4 37.6	11 29.3	25 14.1	15 28.7
8 Tu	15 1 28	16 56 16	2♍40 38	8♍37 6	11 15.7	25 3.5	2 7.2	22 55.6	8 24.4	4 35.4	11 27.2	25 15.9	15 30.0
9 W	15 5 24	17 54 15	14 33 13	20 29 30	11 13.7	26 40.0	3 0.5	23 41.1	8 17.8	4 33.1	11 25.0	25 17.8	15 31.2
10 Th	15 9 21	18 52 13	26 26 24	2♎24 24	11 10.8	28 18.5	3 53.2	24 26.5	8 11.0	4 30.8	11 22.8	25 19.7	15 32.4
11 F	15 13 17	19 50 8	8♎23 54	14 25 14	11 7.4	29 59.0	4 45.2	25 11.8	8 4.2	4 28.4	11 20.6	25 21.5	15 33.7
12 Sa	15 17 14	20 48 3	20 28 45	26 34 43	11 4.1	1♉41.6	5 36.6	25 57.1	7 57.3	4 25.9	11 18.3	25 23.4	15 35.0
13 Su	15 21 10	21 45 55	2♏43 22	8♏54 53	11 1.2	3 26.1	6 27.3	26 42.4	7 50.3	4 23.3	11 16.0	25 25.3	15 36.3
14 M	15 25 7	22 43 46	15 9 26	21 27 8	10 58.9	5 12.7	7 17.2	27 27.6	7 43.2	4 20.6	11 13.7	25 27.3	15 37.5
15 Tu	15 29 3	23 41 35	27 48 4	4♐12 16	10 57.6	7 1.2	8 6.4	28 12.8	7 36.1	4 17.9	11 11.4	25 29.2	15 38.8
16 W	15 33 0	24 39 23	10♐39 48	17 10 39	10D57.1	8 51.8	8 54.8	28 57.9	7 28.9	4 15.1	11 9.1	25 31.2	15 40.1
17 Th	15 36 57	25 37 10	23 44 51	0♑22 21	10 57.5	10 44.4	9 42.4	29 43.0	7 21.6	4 12.2	11 6.8	25 33.2	15 41.5
18 F	15 40 53	26 34 55	7♑ 3 8	13 47 10	10 58.4	12 39.0	10 29.1	0♉28.0	7 14.2	4 9.2	11 4.4	25 35.2	15 42.8
19 Sa	15 44 50	27 32 39	20 34 26	27 24 50	10 59.5	14 35.5	11 15.1	1 12.9	7 6.8	4 6.2	11 2.0	25 37.2	15 44.1
20 Su	15 48 46	28 30 22	4♒18 20	11♒14 50	11 0.5	16 34.0	12 0.1	1 57.9	6 59.4	4 3.1	10 59.7	25 39.2	15 45.4
21 M	15 52 43	29 28 4	18 14 12	25 16 18	11R 1.1	18 34.3	12 44.2	2 42.7	6 51.9	3 59.9	10 57.3	25 41.2	15 46.8
22 Tu	15 56 39	0♊25 45	2♓20 55	9♓27 49	11 1.3	20 36.5	13 27.3	3 27.5	6 44.4	3 56.7	10 54.8	25 43.3	15 48.1
23 W	16 0 36	1 23 25	16 36 42	23 47 12	11 1.0	22 40.5	14 9.4	4 12.3	6 36.8	3 53.4	10 52.4	25 45.4	15 49.5
24 Th	16 4 32	2 21 4	0♈58 55	8♈11 22	11 0.4	24 46.0	14 50.5	4 57.0	6 29.2	3 50.0	10 50.0	25 47.4	15 50.8
25 F	16 8 29	3 18 42	15 24 1	22 36 19	10 59.5	26 53.1	15 30.6	5 41.7	6 21.6	3 46.6	10 47.5	25 49.5	15 52.2
26 Sa	16 12 26	4 16 19	29 47 40	6♉57 26	10 58.7	29 1.6	16 9.5	6 26.3	6 14.0	3 43.1	10 45.1	25 51.6	15 53.5
27 Su	16 16 22	5 13 55	14♉ 5 3	21 9 54	10 58.1	1♊11.2	16 47.3	7 10.8	6 6.3	3 39.5	10 42.6	25 53.7	15 54.9
28 M	16 20 19	6 11 30	28 11 26	5♊ 9 11	10D57.7	3 21.8	17 23.9	7 55.3	5 58.7	3 35.9	10 40.2	25 55.9	15 56.3
29 Tu	16 24 15	7 9 4	12♊ 2 43	18 51 42	10 57.6	5 33.1	17 59.2	8 39.8	5 51.0	3 32.2	10 37.7	25 58.0	15 57.6
30 W	16 28 12	8 6 37	25 35 53	2♋15 6	10 57.7	7 44.9	18 33.3	9 24.2	5 43.4	3 28.5	10 35.2	26 0.1	15 59.0
31 Th	16 32 8	9 4 8	8♋49 17	15 18 29	10 57.9	9 57.0	19 6.0	10 8.5	5 35.8	3 24.7	10 32.7	26 2.3	16 0.4

LONGITUDE JUNE 1900

Day	Sid.Time	☉	0 hr ☽	Noon ☽	True ☊	☿	♀	♂	♃	♄	♅	♆	♇
1 F	16 36 5	10♊ 1 39	21♋42 49	28♋ 2 28	10♐58.1	12♊ 9.0	19♋37.3	10♉52.8	5♐28.2	3♑20.9	10♐30.3	26♊ 4.5	16♊ 1.8
2 Sa	16 40 2	10 59 8	4♌17 45	10♌29 0	10R58.1	14 20.7	20 7.1	11 37.0	5R20.6	3R17.0	10R27.8	26 6.6	16 3.2
3 Su	16 43 58	11 56 36	16 36 37	22 41 3	10 58.1	16 31.8	20 35.5	12 21.2	5 13.0	3 13.1	10 25.3	26 8.8	16 4.6
4 M	16 47 55	12 54 3	28 42 50	4♍42 28	10 58.0	18 42.0	21 2.2	13 5.3	5 5.4	3 9.1	10 22.8	26 11.0	16 6.0
5 Tu	16 51 51	13 51 28	10♍40 30	16 37 32	10D57.9	20 51.2	21 27.3	13 49.3	4 57.9	3 5.1	10 20.4	26 13.2	16 7.3
6 W	16 55 48	14 48 53	22 34 6	28 30 48	10 57.9	22 59.0	21 50.8	14 33.3	4 50.5	3 1.0	10 17.9	26 15.4	16 8.7
7 Th	16 59 44	15 46 16	4♎28 11	10♎26 50	10 58.2	25 5.3	22 12.5	15 17.2	4 43.1	2 57.0	10 15.4	26 17.6	16 10.1
8 F	17 3 41	16 43 38	16 27 15	22 29 57	10 58.6	27 9.9	22 32.3	16 1.1	4 35.7	2 52.8	10 13.0	26 19.8	16 11.5
9 Sa	17 7 37	17 40 59	28 35 24	4♏44 1	10 59.3	29 12.6	22 50.4	16 44.9	4 28.4	2 48.7	10 10.5	26 22.0	16 12.9
10 Su	17 11 34	18 38 19	10♏56 12	17 12 15	10 60.0	1♋13.3	23 6.4	17 28.6	4 21.2	2 44.5	10 8.1	26 24.2	16 14.3
11 M	17 15 30	19 35 39	23 32 26	29 56 57	11 0.6	3 11.9	23 20.5	18 12.3	4 14.0	2 40.3	10 5.6	26 26.4	16 15.7
12 Tu	17 19 27	20 32 57	6♐25 54	12♐59 21	11R 1.0	5 8.4	23 32.5	18 56.0	4 6.9	2 36.0	10 3.2	26 28.6	16 17.1
13 W	17 23 24	21 30 15	19 37 17	26 19 33	11 0.9	7 2.6	23 42.4	19 39.5	3 59.9	2 31.7	10 0.8	26 30.9	16 18.5
14 Th	17 27 20	22 27 32	3♑ 6 1	9♑56 24	11 0.3	8 54.5	23 50.2	20 23.1	3 53.0	2 27.4	9 58.4	26 33.1	16 19.9
15 F	17 31 17	23 24 48	16 50 25	23 47 42	10 59.1	10 44.1	23 55.8	21 6.5	3 46.1	2 23.1	9 56.0	26 35.3	16 21.2
16 Sa	17 35 13	24 22 5	0♒47 50	7♒50 24	10 57.6	12 31.3	23R59.0	21 49.9	3 39.4	2 18.8	9 53.6	26 37.6	16 22.6
17 Su	17 39 10	25 19 20	14 54 57	22 1 2	10 55.9	14 16.1	24 0.0	22 33.2	3 32.7	2 14.4	9 51.3	26 39.8	16 24.0
18 M	17 43 6	26 16 35	29 8 11	6♓15 59	10 54.3	15 58.5	23 58.7	23 16.5	3 26.1	2 10.1	9 48.9	26 42.1	16 25.4
19 Tu	17 47 3	27 13 50	13♓24 2	20 31 55	10 53.2	17 38.5	23 55.0	23 59.7	3 19.6	2 5.7	9 46.6	26 44.3	16 26.7
20 W	17 51 0	28 11 5	27 39 20	4♈45 56	10D52.8	19 16.1	23 49.0	24 42.9	3 13.3	2 1.3	9 44.3	26 46.5	16 28.1
21 Th	17 54 56	29 8 20	11♈51 26	18 55 33	10 53.1	20 51.3	23 40.5	25 26.0	3 7.0	1 56.9	9 42.0	26 48.8	16 29.5
22 F	17 58 53	0♋ 5 34	25 58 4	2♉58 45	10 54.1	22 24.0	23 29.7	26 9.1	3 0.9	1 52.4	9 39.7	26 51.0	16 30.8
23 Sa	18 2 49	1 2 49	9♉57 22	16 53 42	10 55.4	23 54.2	23 16.5	26 52.0	2 54.9	1 48.0	9 37.5	26 53.2	16 32.2
24 Su	18 6 46	2 0 3	23 47 34	0♊38 44	10 56.6	25 21.9	23 0.9	27 35.0	2 49.0	1 43.6	9 35.2	26 55.5	16 33.5
25 M	18 10 42	2 57 17	7♊27 1	14 12 12	10R57.3	26 47.2	22 43.1	28 17.8	2 43.2	1 39.2	9 33.0	26 57.7	16 34.9
26 Tu	18 14 39	3 54 32	20 54 8	27 32 39	10 57.0	28 9.8	22 22.9	29 0.6	2 37.5	1 34.8	9 30.8	26 59.9	16 36.2
27 W	18 18 35	4 51 46	4♋ 7 35	10♋38 51	10 55.6	29 29.9	22 0.6	29 43.4	2 32.0	1 30.4	9 28.7	27 2.1	16 37.6
28 Th	18 22 32	5 49 0	17 6 23	23 30 8	10 53.0	0♌47.4	21 36.1	0♊26.1	2 26.7	1 26.0	9 26.5	27 4.4	16 38.9
29 F	18 26 29	6 46 13	29 50 9	6♌ 6 31	10 49.3	2 2.2	21 9.6	1 8.7	2 21.4	1 21.6	9 24.4	27 6.6	16 40.2
30 Sa	18 30 25	7 43 26	12♌19 20	18 28 50	10 45.1	3 14.3	20 41.1	1 51.2	2 16.4	1 17.2	9 22.3	27 8.8	16 41.5

Astro Data

	Dy Hr Mn
☽0S	9 6:45
☽0N	23 2:00
☽0S	5 14:20
♀ R	16 22:20
☽0N	19 7:28

Planet Ingress

	Dy Hr Mn
♀ ♋	5 15:46
☿ ♉	11 0:14
♂ ♉	17 9:05
☉ ♊	21 13:17
☿ ♊	26 10:51
☿ ♋	9 9:23
☉ ♋	21 21:40
☿ ♌	27 9:13
♂ ♊	27 9:21

Last Aspect / ☽ Ingress

Last Aspect Dy Hr Mn		☽ Ingress Dy Hr Mn
2 17:27	♀ ☌	♋ 2 22:24
4 12:17	♂ □	♌ 5 7:01
7 9:02	♆ ⚹	♍ 7 18:36
9 21:45	♆ □	♎ 10 7:10
12 11:29	♂ ☍	♏ 12 18:42
14 15:37	☉ ☍	♐ 15 4:08
17 3:17	♆ ☍	♑ 17 11:20
19 13:09	☉ △	♒ 19 16:31
21 12:44	♆ △	♓ 21 20:02
23 15:19	♆ □	♈ 23 22:22
25 17:25	♆ ⚹	♉ 26 0:21
27 4:47	♀ ⚹	♊ 28 3:06
30 0:44	♆ ☌	♋ 30 7:55

Last Aspect / ☽ Ingress

Last Aspect Dy Hr Mn		☽ Ingress Dy Hr Mn
31 19:54	♀ ☌	♌ 1 15:45
3 18:56	♆ ⚹	♍ 4 2:34
6 7:28	♆ □	♎ 6 15:00
9 1:27	☿ △	♏ 9 2:46
10 23:37	♀ △	♐ 11 12:06
13 12:22	♆ ☍	♑ 13 18:31
15 12:17	♀ ☍	♒ 15 22:38
17 19:53	♆ △	♓ 18 1:27
20 0:57	☉ □	♈ 20 3:57
22 1:31	♆ ⚹	♉ 22 6:54
24 7:00	♂ ☌	♊ 24 10:52
26 11:03	♆ ☌	♋ 26 16:28
28 8:09	♀ ☌	♌ 29 0:19

☽ Phases & Eclipses

Dy Hr Mn	
6 13:39	☽ 15♌33
14 15:37	○ 23♏21
21 20:31	☽ 0♓17
28 14:50	● 6♊47
28 14:53:56	● T 2'10"
5 6:59	☽ 14♍08
13 3:39	○ 21♐39
13 3:28	○ A 1.001
20 0:57	☽ 28♓13
27 1:27	● 4♋55

Astro Data

1 MAY 1900
Julian Day # 121
Delta T -2.3 sec
SVP 06♓38'50"
Obliquity 23°27'05"
⚷ Chiron 24♐27.7R
☽ Mean ☊ 12♐48.4

1 JUNE 1900
Julian Day # 152
Delta T -2.2 sec
SVP 06♓38'45"
Obliquity 23°27'05"
⚷ Chiron 22♐46.3R
☽ Mean ☊ 11♐09.9

JULY 1900 — LONGITUDE

Day	Sid.Time	☉	0 hr ☽	Noon ☽	True ☊	☿	♀	♂	♃	♄	♅	♆	♇
1 Su	18 34 22	8♋40 39	24♌35 15	0♍38 55	10♐40.7	4♌23.6	20♋10.9	2♊33.7	2♐11.4	1♑12.8	9♐20.3	27♊11.0	16♊42.9
2 M	18 38 18	9 37 52	6♍40 10	12 39 26	10R 36.7	5 30.0	19R 39.1	3 16.1	2R 6.6	1R 8.4	9R 18.3	27 13.2	16 44.2
3 Tu	18 42 15	10 35 4	18 37 10	24 33 52	10 33.5	6 33.4	19 5.8	3 58.4	2 2.0	1 4.1	9 16.3	27 15.4	16 45.4
4 W	18 46 11	11 32 16	0♎30 6	6♎26 23	10 31.6	7 33.9	18 31.3	4 40.7	1 57.5	0 59.8	9 14.3	27 17.6	16 46.7
5 Th	18 50 8	12 29 28	12 23 20	18 21 33	10D 30.9	8 31.1	17 55.7	5 22.9	1 53.2	0 55.5	9 12.3	27 19.7	16 48.0
6 F	18 54 4	13 26 40	24 21 37	0♏24 10	10 31.5	9 25.2	17 19.3	6 5.1	1 49.0	0 51.2	9 10.4	27 21.9	16 49.3
7 Sa	18 58 1	14 23 51	6♏29 46	12 39 0	10 32.8	10 15.9	16 42.2	6 47.2	1 45.0	0 47.0	9 8.6	27 24.1	16 50.5
8 Su	19 1 58	15 21 2	18 52 24	25 10 27	10 34.5	11 3.1	16 4.8	7 29.2	1 41.2	0 42.8	9 6.7	27 26.2	16 51.8
9 M	19 5 54	16 18 14	1♐33 34	8♐ 2 6	10R 35.7	11 46.7	15 27.2	8 11.1	1 37.5	0 38.6	9 4.9	27 28.4	16 53.0
10 Tu	19 9 51	17 15 25	14 36 19	21 16 21	10 36.0	12 26.6	14 49.7	8 53.0	1 34.0	0 34.5	9 3.1	27 30.5	16 54.3
11 W	19 13 47	18 12 36	28 2 15	4♑53 53	10 34.7	13 2.6	14 12.6	9 34.8	1 30.7	0 30.4	9 1.4	27 32.6	16 55.5
12 Th	19 17 44	19 9 48	11♑51 2	18 53 19	10 31.8	13 34.6	13 36.0	10 16.6	1 27.5	0 26.3	8 59.7	27 34.8	16 56.7
13 F	19 21 40	20 6 59	26 0 13	3♒11 6	10 27.2	14 2.4	13 0.3	10 58.3	1 24.5	0 22.3	8 58.0	27 36.9	16 57.9
14 Sa	19 25 37	21 4 11	10♒25 14	17 41 48	10 21.5	14 26.0	12 25.6	11 39.9	1 21.7	0 18.3	8 56.4	27 39.0	16 59.1
15 Su	19 29 33	22 1 24	24 59 57	2♓18 49	10 15.3	14 45.0	11 52.2	12 21.4	1 19.0	0 14.3	8 54.8	27 41.0	17 0.3
16 M	19 33 30	22 58 36	9♓37 32	16 55 20	10 9.5	14 59.6	11 20.2	13 2.9	1 16.6	0 10.4	8 53.3	27 43.1	17 1.4
17 Tu	19 37 27	23 55 50	24 11 30	1♈25 25	10 4.9	15 9.4	10 49.9	13 44.4	1 14.3	0 6.6	8 51.8	27 45.2	17 2.6
18 W	19 41 23	24 53 4	8♈36 34	15 44 36	10 2.0	15R 14.4	10 21.3	14 25.7	1 12.2	0 2.8	8 50.3	27 47.2	17 3.7
19 Th	19 45 20	25 50 19	22 49 14	29 50 17	10D 0.8	15 14.6	9 54.7	15 7.0	1 10.2	29♐59.0	8 48.9	27 49.2	17 4.9
20 F	19 49 16	26 47 35	6♉47 40	13♉41 24	10 1.1	15 9.9	9 30.1	15 48.3	1 8.5	29 55.3	8 47.5	27 51.2	17 6.0
21 Sa	19 53 13	27 44 51	20 31 30	27 18 3	10 2.2	15 0.3	9 7.6	16 29.4	1 6.9	29 51.6	8 46.1	27 53.2	17 7.1
22 Su	19 57 9	28 42 9	4♊ 1 11	10♊40 59	10R 3.2	14 45.8	8 47.4	17 10.5	1 5.5	29 48.0	8 44.8	27 55.2	17 8.2
23 M	20 1 6	29 39 27	17 17 35	23 51 5	10 3.1	14 26.5	8 29.4	17 51.6	1 4.3	29 44.5	8 43.5	27 57.2	17 9.3
24 Tu	20 5 2	0♌36 46	0♋21 33	6♋49 6	10 1.2	14 2.6	8 13.8	18 32.5	1 3.2	29 41.0	8 42.3	27 59.2	17 10.3
25 W	20 8 59	1 34 6	13 13 44	19 35 32	9 57.0	13 34.4	8 0.6	19 13.4	1 2.4	29 37.6	8 41.1	28 1.1	17 11.4
26 Th	20 12 56	2 31 27	25 54 32	2♌10 44	9 50.5	13 2.1	7 49.7	19 54.3	1 1.7	29 34.3	8 40.0	28 3.0	17 12.4
27 F	20 16 52	3 28 48	8♌24 13	14 35 2	9 42.0	12 26.2	7 41.2	20 35.0	1 1.3	29 31.0	8 38.9	28 4.9	17 13.4
28 Sa	20 20 49	4 26 10	20 43 14	26 48 58	9 32.2	11 47.1	7 35.1	21 15.7	1 1.0	29 27.7	8 37.9	28 6.8	17 14.5
29 Su	20 24 45	5 23 33	2♍52 23	8♍53 39	9 21.9	11 5.4	7 31.4	21 56.3	1D 0.8	29 24.6	8 36.9	28 8.7	17 15.5
30 M	20 28 42	6 20 57	14 53 1	20 50 48	9 12.2	10 21.9	7D 30.0	22 36.8	1 0.9	29 21.5	8 35.9	28 10.6	17 16.4
31 Tu	20 32 38	7 18 21	26 47 19	2♎42 58	9 3.8	9 37.1	7 30.9	23 17.3	1 1.2	29 18.5	8 35.0	28 12.4	17 17.4

AUGUST 1900 — LONGITUDE

Day	Sid.Time	☉	0 hr ☽	Noon ☽	True ☊	☿	♀	♂	♃	♄	♅	♆	♇
1 W	20 36 35	8♌15 45	8♎38 12	14♎33 30	8♐57.5	8♌51.8	7♋34.1	23♊57.7	1♐ 1.6	29♐15.5	8♐34.2	28♊14.2	17♊18.3
2 Th	20 40 31	9 13 11	20 29 25	26 26 30	8R 53.4	8R 7.0	7 39.5	24 38.0	1 2.2	29R 12.7	8R 33.4	28 16.0	17 19.3
3 F	20 44 28	10 10 37	2♏25 22	8♏26 39	8D 51.5	7 23.4	7 47.1	25 18.3	1 3.1	29 9.9	8 32.6	28 17.8	17 20.2
4 Sa	20 48 25	11 8 4	14 30 59	20 39 1	8 51.2	6 41.8	7 56.8	25 58.4	1 4.1	29 7.2	8 31.9	28 19.5	17 21.1
5 Su	20 52 21	12 5 31	26 51 24	3♐ 8 45	8R 51.8	6 3.1	8 8.6	26 38.5	1 5.2	29 4.5	8 31.2	28 21.3	17 22.0
6 M	20 56 18	13 2 59	9♐31 37	16 0 33	8 52.2	5 28.0	8 22.4	27 18.6	1 6.6	29 2.0	8 30.6	28 23.0	17 22.8
7 Tu	21 0 14	14 0 29	22 35 57	29 18 9	8 51.4	4 57.3	8 38.2	27 58.5	1 8.1	28 59.5	8 30.1	28 24.7	17 23.7
8 W	21 4 11	14 57 59	6♑ 7 20	13♑ 3 32	8 48.6	4 31.5	8 55.9	28 38.4	1 9.9	28 57.1	8 29.5	28 26.3	17 24.5
9 Th	21 8 7	15 55 29	20 6 36	27 16 11	8 43.4	4 11.4	9 15.5	29 18.2	1 11.8	28 54.8	8 29.1	28 28.0	17 25.3
10 F	21 12 4	16 53 1	4♒31 45	11♒52 33	8 35.8	3 57.3	9 36.8	29 57.9	1 13.8	28 52.6	8 28.7	28 29.6	17 26.1
11 Sa	21 16 0	17 50 34	19 17 40	26 46 1	8 26.4	3D 49.6	9 59.9	0♋37.6	1 16.1	28 50.4	8 28.3	28 31.2	17 26.9
12 Su	21 19 57	18 48 8	4♓16 26	11♓47 41	8 16.3	3 48.7	10 24.7	1 17.2	1 18.5	28 48.3	8 28.0	28 32.8	17 27.7
13 M	21 23 54	19 45 43	19 18 33	26 47 51	8 6.7	3 54.8	10 51.2	1 56.7	1 21.1	28 46.4	8 27.7	28 34.4	17 28.4
14 Tu	21 27 50	20 43 20	4♈14 31	11♈37 38	7 58.6	4 8.1	11 19.1	2 36.1	1 23.9	28 44.5	8 27.5	28 35.9	17 29.1
15 W	21 31 47	21 40 58	18 56 27	26 10 24	7 52.8	4 28.6	11 48.7	3 15.5	1 26.9	28 42.7	8 27.3	28 37.4	17 29.9
16 Th	21 35 43	22 38 37	3♉19 7	10♉22 22	7 49.5	4 56.4	12 19.7	3 54.8	1 30.0	28 41.0	8 27.2	28 38.9	17 30.5
17 F	21 39 40	23 36 19	17 20 8	24 12 27	7D 48.3	5 31.5	12 52.1	4 34.0	1 33.3	28 39.3	8D 27.1	28 40.3	17 31.2
18 Sa	21 43 36	24 34 2	0♊59 32	7♊41 36	7R 48.2	6 13.8	13 25.8	5 13.1	1 36.8	28 37.8	8 27.1	28 41.8	17 31.9
19 Su	21 47 33	25 31 46	14 18 58	20 51 59	7 48.2	7 3.1	14 0.9	5 52.2	1 40.4	28 36.3	8 27.2	28 43.2	17 32.5
20 M	21 51 29	26 29 33	27 20 58	3♋46 15	7 46.9	7 59.3	14 37.2	6 31.2	1 44.2	28 35.0	8 27.2	28 44.6	17 33.1
21 Tu	21 55 26	27 27 21	10♋ 8 11	16 27 3	7 43.5	9 2.1	15 14.8	7 10.1	1 48.2	28 33.7	8 27.4	28 45.9	17 33.7
22 W	21 59 23	28 25 10	22 43 6	28 56 34	7 37.2	10 11.3	15 53.5	7 48.9	1 52.4	28 32.6	8 27.6	28 47.3	17 34.3
23 Th	22 3 19	29 23 2	5♌ 7 39	11♌16 32	7 28.1	11 26.6	16 33.3	8 27.7	1 56.7	28 31.5	8 27.8	28 48.6	17 34.8
24 F	22 7 16	0♍20 54	17 23 21	23 28 13	7 16.4	12 47.6	17 14.2	9 6.4	2 1.2	28 30.5	8 28.1	28 49.8	17 35.4
25 Sa	22 11 12	1 18 49	29 31 17	5♍32 39	7 3.1	14 13.9	17 56.1	9 45.0	2 5.8	28 29.6	8 28.5	28 51.1	17 35.9
26 Su	22 15 9	2 16 44	11♍32 27	17 30 50	6 49.0	15 45.2	18 39.1	10 23.5	2 10.6	28 28.8	8 28.9	28 52.3	17 36.4
27 M	22 19 5	3 14 42	23 27 58	29 24 4	6 35.5	17 20.9	19 22.9	11 1.9	2 15.6	28 28.1	8 29.3	28 53.5	17 36.9
28 Tu	22 23 2	4 12 40	5♎19 21	11♎14 8	6 23.6	19 0.6	20 7.8	11 40.2	2 20.7	28 27.5	8 29.8	28 54.7	17 37.3
29 W	22 26 58	5 10 41	17 8 44	23 3 32	6 14.2	20 43.9	20 53.5	12 18.5	2 26.0	28 27.0	8 30.4	28 55.8	17 37.7
30 Th	22 30 55	6 8 42	28 58 58	4♏55 30	6 7.5	22 30.2	21 40.0	12 56.7	2 31.5	28 26.6	8 31.0	28 56.9	17 38.1
31 F	22 34 52	7 6 45	10♏53 41	16 54 5	6 3.6	24 19.1	22 27.4	13 34.7	2 37.1	28 26.3	8 31.6	28 58.0	17 38.5

Astro Data	Planet Ingress	Last Aspect	☽ Ingress	Last Aspect	☽ Ingress	☽ Phases & Eclipses	Astro Data
Dy Hr Mn	Dy Hr Mn	Dy Hr Mn	Dy Hr Mn	Dy Hr Mn	Dy Hr Mn	Dy Hr Mn	1 JULY 1900
☽0S 2 22:41	♄ ♐ 18 17:32	1 5:09 ♆ ⚹	♍ 1 10:43	2 17:30 ♄ ⚹	♏ 2 19:09	5 0:13 ☽ 12♎30	Julian Day # 182
☽0N 16 14:00	☉ ♌ 23 8:36	3 17:30 ♆ □	♎ 3 22:59	3 16:46 ☉ □	♐ 5 6:01	12 13:22 ○ 19♑42	Delta T -2.1 sec
☿ R 18 12:54		6 6:00 ♆ △	♏ 6 11:12	7 11:25 ♄ ☌	♑ 7 13:14	19 5:31 ☽ 26♈03	SVP 06♓38'40"
♃ D 29 2:23	♂ ♋ 10 1:15	7 18:53 ♀ △	♐ 8 21:05	8 5:00 ♀ ☍	♒ 9 16:32	26 13:43 ● 3♌04	Obliquity 23°27'04"
☽0S 30 6:56	☉ ♍ 23 15:20	10 23:08 ♆ ☍	♑ 11 3:27	11 15:17 ♄ ⚹	♓ 11 17:10		⚷ Chiron 20♐46.1R
♀ D 30 2:30		12 13:22 ☉ ☍	♒ 13 6:41	13 15:09 ♄ □	♈ 13 17:09	3 16:46 ☽ 10♏51	☽ Mean ☊ 9♐34.6
		15 4:25 ♆ △	♓ 15 8:12	15 16:13 ♄ △	♉ 15 18:24	10 21:30 ○ 17♒45	
☿ D 11 15:10		17 5:55 ♆ □	♈ 17 9:38	17 11:46 ☉ □	♊ 17 22:14	17 11:46 ☽ 24♉05	1 AUGUST 1900
☽0N 12 22:41		19 12:12 ♄ △	♉ 19 12:17	20 2:36 ♆ ☌	♋ 20 4:56	25 3:53 ● 1♍28	Julian Day # 213
♄☍♆ 16 16:01		21 13:46 ☉ ⚹	♊ 21 16:49	21 10:13 ♀ ☌	♌ 22 14:03		Delta T -2.0 sec
♅ D 17 18:17		23 22:45 ♄ ☍	♋ 23 23:20	24 22:40 ♆ ⚹	♍ 25 0:57		SVP 06♓38'35"
☽0S 26 14:15		24 14:23 ♀ ☌	♌ 26 7:49	27 10:59 ♆ □	♎ 27 13:13		Obliquity 23°27'05"
		28 17:10 ♄ △	♍ 28 18:18	29 23:56 ♆ △	♏ 30 2:03		⚷ Chiron 19♐15.4R
		31 5:05 ♄ □	♎ 31 6:30				☽ Mean ☊ 7♐56.1

LONGITUDE SEPTEMBER 1900

Day	Sid.Time	☉	0 hr ☽	Noon ☽	True ☊	☿	♀	♂	♃	♄	♅	♆	♇
1 Sa	22 38 48	8♍ 4 50	22♏57 17	29♏ 3 55	6♐ 1.9	26♌10.1	23♋15.6	14♋12.7	2♐42.8	28♐26.1	8♐32.3	28♊59.0	17♊38.9
2 Su	22 42 45	9 2 56	5♐14 39	11♐30 6	6R 1.6	28 2.8	24 4.6	14 50.7	2 48.7	28D 26.0	8 33.1	29 0.0	17 39.3
3 M	22 46 41	10 1 3	17 50 56	24 17 45	6 1.5	29 56.9	24 54.3	15 28.5	2 54.8	28 26.0	8 33.9	29 1.0	17 39.6
4 Tu	22 50 38	10 59 12	0♑51 5	7♑31 25	6 0.5	1♍51.9	25 44.7	16 6.2	3 1.0	28 26.1	8 34.8	29 2.0	17 39.9
5 W	22 54 34	11 57 22	14 19 5	21 14 18	5 57.6	3 47.5	26 35.8	16 43.9	3 7.4	28 26.2	8 35.7	29 2.9	17 40.2
6 Th	22 58 31	12 55 34	28 17 6	5♒27 19	5 52.2	5 43.4	27 27.7	17 21.4	3 13.9	28 26.5	8 36.6	29 3.8	17 40.4
7 F	23 2 27	13 53 48	12♒44 33	20 8 12	5 44.2	7 39.3	28 20.1	17 58.9	3 20.5	28 26.9	8 37.7	29 4.7	17 40.7
8 Sa	23 6 24	14 52 2	27 37 22	5♓11 0	5 34.4	9 35.1	29 13.2	18 36.3	3 27.3	28 27.4	8 38.7	29 5.5	17 40.9
9 Su	23 10 21	15 50 19	12♓47 50	20 26 29	5 23.5	11 30.6	0♌ 6.9	19 13.6	3 34.3	28 27.9	8 39.8	29 6.3	17 41.1
10 M	23 14 17	16 48 37	28 5 32	5♈43 31	5 13.0	13 25.5	1 1.2	19 50.8	3 41.3	28 28.6	8 41.0	29 7.1	17 41.3
11 Tu	23 18 14	17 46 57	13♈19 6	20 51 3	5 4.1	15 19.9	1 56.1	20 27.9	3 48.5	28 29.4	8 42.2	29 7.8	17 41.4
12 W	23 22 10	18 45 19	28 18 20	5♉40 5	4 57.6	17 13.4	2 51.6	21 4.9	3 55.9	28 30.2	8 43.5	29 8.5	17 41.6
13 Th	23 26 7	19 43 44	12♉55 44	20 4 52	4 53.8	19 6.2	3 47.6	21 41.8	4 3.4	28 31.2	8 44.8	29 9.2	17 41.7
14 F	23 30 3	20 42 10	27 7 18	4♊ 3 2	4D 52.3	20 58.1	4 44.1	22 18.7	4 11.0	28 32.2	8 46.1	29 9.8	17 41.8
15 Sa	23 34 0	21 40 39	10♊52 13	17 35 6	4R 52.2	22 49.1	5 41.2	22 55.4	4 18.7	28 33.4	8 47.6	29 10.4	17 41.9
16 Su	23 37 56	22 39 10	24 12 2	0♋43 28	4 52.3	24 39.1	6 38.7	23 32.1	4 26.6	28 34.7	8 49.0	29 11.0	17 41.9
17 M	23 41 53	23 37 43	7♋ 9 51	13 31 38	4 51.6	26 28.1	7 36.7	24 8.7	4 34.6	28 36.0	8 50.5	29 11.5	17R 41.9
18 Tu	23 45 49	24 36 18	19 49 19	26 3 22	4 48.9	28 16.1	8 35.2	24 45.1	4 42.8	28 37.4	8 52.1	29 12.1	17 41.9
19 W	23 49 46	25 34 56	2♌14 12	8♌22 14	4 43.6	0♎ 3.1	9 34.1	25 21.5	4 51.0	28 39.0	8 53.7	29 12.5	17 41.9
20 Th	23 53 43	26 33 35	14 27 50	20 31 21	4 35.7	1 49.1	10 33.5	25 57.8	4 59.4	28 40.6	8 55.3	29 13.0	17 41.9
21 F	23 57 39	27 32 17	26 33 4	2♍33 15	4 25.4	3 34.1	11 33.2	26 33.9	5 7.9	28 42.3	8 57.0	29 13.4	17 41.8
22 Sa	0 1 36	28 31 1	8♍32 9	14 29 56	4 13.5	5 18.1	12 33.4	27 10.0	5 16.6	28 44.2	8 58.8	29 13.8	17 41.7
23 Su	0 5 32	29 29 47	20 26 50	26 23 1	4 0.9	7 1.1	13 34.0	27 45.9	5 25.3	28 46.1	9 0.6	29 14.1	17 41.6
24 M	0 9 29	0♎28 34	2♎18 39	8♎13 56	3 48.8	8 43.1	14 34.9	28 21.8	5 34.2	28 48.1	9 2.4	29 14.4	17 41.5
25 Tu	0 13 25	1 27 24	14 9 2	20 4 11	3 38.1	10 24.2	15 36.3	28 57.5	5 43.2	28 50.2	9 4.3	29 14.7	17 41.4
26 W	0 17 22	2 26 16	25 59 38	1♏55 39	3 29.6	12 4.4	16 37.9	29 33.1	5 52.3	28 52.4	9 6.2	29 14.9	17 41.2
27 Th	0 21 18	3 25 10	7♏52 32	13 50 39	3 23.8	13 43.6	17 40.0	0♌ 8.7	6 1.6	28 54.7	9 8.2	29 15.2	17 41.0
28 F	0 25 15	4 24 5	19 50 23	25 52 11	3 20.6	15 21.9	18 42.3	0 44.1	6 10.9	28 57.1	9 10.2	29 15.3	17 40.8
29 Sa	0 29 12	5 23 3	1♐56 31	8♐ 3 53	3D 19.5	16 59.4	19 45.0	1 19.4	6 20.4	28 59.6	9 12.2	29 15.5	17 40.6
30 Su	0 33 8	6 22 2	14 14 51	20 29 57	3 19.9	18 35.9	20 48.1	1 54.5	6 29.9	29 2.1	9 14.4	29 15.6	17 40.3

LONGITUDE OCTOBER 1900

Day	Sid.Time	☉	0 hr ☽	Noon ☽	True ☊	☿	♀	♂	♃	♄	♅	♆	♇
1 M	0 37 5	7♎21 4	26♐49 46	3♑14 51	3♐20.9	20♎11.6	21♌51.4	2♌29.6	6♐39.6	29♐ 4.8	9♐16.5	29♊15.7	17♊40.0
2 Tu	0 41 1	8 20 6	9♑45 45	16 22 56	3R 21.3	21 46.5	22 55.0	3 4.6	6 49.4	29 7.5	9 18.7	29R 15.7	17R 39.7
3 W	0 44 58	9 19 11	23 6 50	29 57 45	3 20.3	23 20.5	23 59.0	3 39.4	6 59.3	29 10.4	9 20.9	29 15.7	17 39.4
4 Th	0 48 54	10 18 18	6♒55 51	14♒ 1 10	3 17.3	24 53.7	25 3.2	4 14.1	7 9.3	29 13.3	9 23.2	29 15.7	17 39.1
5 F	0 52 51	11 17 26	21 13 32	28 32 32	3 12.4	26 26.1	26 7.7	4 48.7	7 19.4	29 16.3	9 25.5	29 15.6	17 38.7
6 Sa	0 56 47	12 16 35	5♓57 36	13♓27 52	3 5.7	27 57.7	27 12.5	5 23.1	7 29.6	29 19.4	9 27.9	29 15.5	17 38.4
7 Su	1 0 44	13 15 47	21 2 19	28 39 44	2 58.1	29 28.6	28 17.5	5 57.5	7 39.8	29 22.6	9 30.3	29 15.4	17 38.0
8 M	1 4 41	14 15 1	6♈18 48	13♈58 6	2 50.6	0♏58.6	29 22.9	6 31.7	7 50.2	29 25.9	9 32.7	29 15.2	17 37.5
9 Tu	1 8 37	15 14 16	21 36 13	29 11 50	2 44.2	2 27.8	0♍28.4	7 5.8	8 0.7	29 29.3	9 35.2	29 15.0	17 37.1
10 W	1 12 34	16 13 34	6♉43 41	14♉10 44	2 39.7	3 56.2	1 34.3	7 39.8	8 11.3	29 32.7	9 37.7	29 14.8	17 36.6
11 Th	1 16 30	17 12 54	21 32 6	28 47 8	2D 37.3	5 23.9	2 40.4	8 13.6	8 21.9	29 36.2	9 40.2	29 14.6	17 36.2
12 F	1 20 27	18 12 16	5♊55 23	12♊56 37	2 36.9	6 50.7	3 46.7	8 47.4	8 32.7	29 39.9	9 42.8	29 14.3	17 35.7
13 Sa	1 24 23	19 11 41	19 50 47	26 37 58	2 37.8	8 16.7	4 53.3	9 21.0	8 43.5	29 43.6	9 45.5	29 13.9	17 35.1
14 Su	1 28 20	20 11 8	3♋18 26	9♋52 32	2 39.1	9 41.9	6 0.1	9 54.4	8 54.5	29 47.3	9 48.1	29 13.6	17 34.6
15 M	1 32 16	21 10 37	16 20 40	22 43 20	2R 40.2	11 6.2	7 7.2	10 27.7	9 5.5	29 51.2	9 50.8	29 13.2	17 34.0
16 Tu	1 36 13	22 10 9	29 1 3	5♌14 21	2 40.0	12 29.6	8 14.4	11 0.9	9 16.6	29 55.1	9 53.5	29 12.8	17 33.5
17 W	1 40 10	23 9 42	11♌23 47	17 29 52	2 38.3	13 52.1	9 21.9	11 34.0	9 27.8	29 59.1	9 56.3	29 12.3	17 32.9
18 Th	1 44 6	24 9 18	23 33 7	29 34 1	2 34.7	15 13.6	10 29.6	12 6.9	9 39.1	0♑ 3.2	9 59.1	29 11.8	17 32.3
19 F	1 48 3	25 8 57	5♍33 2	11♍30 35	2 29.5	16 34.1	11 37.5	12 39.6	9 50.4	0 7.4	10 2.0	29 11.3	17 31.6
20 Sa	1 51 59	26 8 37	17 27 3	23 22 47	2 23.2	17 53.5	12 45.6	13 12.2	10 1.9	0 11.7	10 4.8	29 10.7	17 31.0
21 Su	1 55 56	27 8 20	29 18 7	5♎13 21	2 16.4	19 11.7	13 53.8	13 44.7	10 13.4	0 16.0	10 7.7	29 10.2	17 30.3
22 M	1 59 52	28 8 5	11♎ 8 43	17 4 29	2 9.8	20 28.7	15 2.3	14 17.0	10 25.0	0 20.4	10 10.7	29 9.5	17 29.6
23 Tu	2 3 49	29 7 51	23 0 51	28 58 4	2 4.1	21 44.3	16 10.9	14 49.1	10 36.6	0 24.9	10 13.6	29 8.9	17 28.9
24 W	2 7 45	0♏ 7 40	4♏56 18	10♏55 48	1 59.7	22 58.4	17 19.8	15 21.1	10 48.4	0 29.4	10 16.6	29 8.2	17 28.2
25 Th	2 11 42	1 7 31	16 56 46	22 59 25	1 57.0	24 11.0	18 28.8	15 52.9	11 0.2	0 34.0	10 19.7	29 7.5	17 27.4
26 F	2 15 38	2 7 24	29 4 2	5♐10 53	1D 55.9	25 21.8	19 37.9	16 24.5	11 12.1	0 38.7	10 22.7	29 6.7	17 26.7
27 Sa	2 19 35	3 7 19	11♐20 14	17 32 25	1 56.2	26 30.7	20 47.2	16 56.0	11 24.1	0 43.5	10 25.8	29 6.0	17 25.9
28 Su	2 23 32	4 7 15	23 47 46	0♑ 6 39	1 57.5	27 37.5	21 56.7	17 27.3	11 36.1	0 48.3	10 28.9	29 5.2	17 25.1
29 M	2 27 28	5 7 13	6♑29 27	12 56 31	1 59.2	28 41.9	23 6.4	17 58.5	11 48.2	0 53.2	10 32.1	29 4.3	17 24.3
30 Tu	2 31 25	6 7 13	19 28 14	26 4 57	2 0.7	29 43.8	24 16.1	18 29.4	12 0.3	0 58.2	10 35.3	29 3.5	17 23.5
31 W	2 35 21	7 7 14	2♒46 57	9♒34 32	2R 1.6	0♐42.7	25 26.1	19 0.2	12 12.6	1 3.3	10 38.4	29 2.6	17 22.7

Astro Data	Planet Ingress	Last Aspect	☽ Ingress	Last Aspect	☽ Ingress	☽ Phases & Eclipses	Astro Data
Dy Hr Mn	Dy Hr Mn	Dy Hr Mn	Dy Hr Mn	Dy Hr Mn	Dy Hr Mn	Dy Hr Mn	1 SEPTEMBER 1900
♄ D 2 15:16	☿ ♍ 3 0:39	1 7:28 ☿ □	♐ 1 13:49	1 4:34 ♆ ☍	♑ 1 5:57	2 7:56 ☽ 9♐22	Julian Day # 244
☽0N 9 9:11	♀ ♌ 8 20:55	3 20:41 ♆ ☍	♑ 3 22:27	3 0:27 ☿ □	♒ 3 12:04	9 5:06 ○ 16♓03	Delta T -1.9 sec
♇ R 17 19:23	☿ ♎ 18 23:18	5 22:31 ♀ ☍	♒ 6 2:53	5 13:14 ♄ ⚹	♓ 5 14:22	15 20:57 ☽ 22♊32	SVP 06♓38'32"
☿0S 20 8:53	☉ ♎ 23 12:20	8 2:20 ♆ △	♓ 8 3:47	7 13:10 ♄ □	♈ 7 14:06	23 19:57 ● 0♎19	Obliquity 23°27'05"
☽0S 22 20:23	♂ ♌ 26 18:08	10 1:37 ♆ □	♈ 10 3:00	9 12:31 ♄ △	♉ 9 13:16		⚷ Chiron 18♐58.7
		12 1:21 ♆ ⚹	♉ 12 2:45	10 1:33 ♂ □	♊ 11 14:02	1 21:10 ☽ 8♑13	☽ Mean ☊ 6♐17.6
♆ R 2 17:47	☿ ♏ 7 8:22	13 15:25 ♂ ⚹	♊ 14 4:58	13 17:37 ♄ ☍	♋ 13 18:02	8 13:18 ○ 14♈48	
♄☍♆ 4 18:30	♀ ♍ 8 13:36	16 9:09 ♆ ☌	♋ 16 10:40	15 9:51 ☉ □	♌ 16 1:53	15 9:51 ☽ 21♋35	1 OCTOBER 1900
☽0N 6 20:02	♄ ♑ 17 5:03	18 19:02 ☿ ⚹	♌ 18 19:39	18 11:15 ♆ ⚹	♍ 18 12:52	23 13:27 ● 29♎41	Julian Day # 274
☽0S 20 1:58	☉ ♏ 23 20:55	21 5:20 ♆ ⚹	♍ 21 6:53	20 23:44 ♆ □	♎ 21 1:25	31 8:17 ☽ 7♒28	Delta T -1.8 sec
♃☌♅ 20 8:15	☿ ♐ 30 6:29	23 17:47 ♆ □	♎ 23 19:19	23 13:27 ☉ ☌	♏ 23 14:05		SVP 06♓38'29"
		26 7:35 ♂ □	♏ 26 8:06	25 15:55 ☿ ☌	♐ 26 1:50		Obliquity 23°27'05"
		27 21:31 ♀ □	♐ 28 20:10	28 10:03 ♆ ☍	♑ 28 11:47		⚷ Chiron 20♐03.3
				30 9:34 ♀ △	♒ 30 19:02		☽ Mean ☊ 4♐42.3

NOVEMBER 1900 LONGITUDE

Day	Sid.Time	☉	0 hr ☽	Noon ☽	True ☊	☿	♀	♂	♃	♄	♅	♆	♇
1 Th	2 39 18	8♏ 7 17	16♒27 51	23♒26 58	2♐ 1.4	1♐38.4	26♍36.2	19♌30.8	12♐24.8	1♑ 8.4	10♐41.7	29♊ 1.7	17♊21.8
2 F	2 43 14	9 7 22	0♓31 52	7♓42 22	2R 0.1	2 30.5	27 46.4	20 1.2	12 37.2	1 13.5	10 44.9	29R 0.7	17R20.9
3 Sa	2 47 11	10 7 28	14 58 6	22 18 36	1 57.9	3 18.6	28 56.7	20 31.4	12 49.6	1 18.8	10 48.2	28 59.8	17 20.1
4 Su	2 51 7	11 7 35	29 43 10	7♈11 1	1 55.2	4 2.2	0♎ 7.2	21 1.4	13 2.0	1 24.1	10 51.5	28 58.8	17 19.2
5 M	2 55 4	12 7 45	14♈41 11	22 12 36	1 52.5	4 40.8	1 17.8	21 31.2	13 14.6	1 29.4	10 54.8	28 57.7	17 18.3
6 Tu	2 59 1	13 7 55	29 44 9	7♉14 42	1 50.1	5 13.8	2 28.6	22 0.9	13 27.1	1 34.8	10 58.1	28 56.7	17 17.3
7 W	3 2 57	14 8 8	14♉43 6	22 8 19	1 48.6	5 40.6	3 39.5	22 30.3	13 39.8	1 40.3	11 1.5	28 55.6	17 16.4
8 Th	3 6 54	15 8 23	29 29 22	6♊45 27	1D48.0	6 0.6	4 50.5	22 59.6	13 52.4	1 45.8	11 4.9	28 54.5	17 15.5
9 F	3 10 50	16 8 39	13♊55 55	21 0 15	1 48.3	6R13.0	6 1.7	23 28.6	14 5.2	1 51.4	11 8.3	28 53.3	17 14.5
10 Sa	3 14 47	17 8 57	27 58 7	4♋49 22	1 49.2	6 17.2	7 12.9	23 57.4	14 17.9	1 57.1	11 11.7	28 52.2	17 13.5
11 Su	3 18 43	18 9 17	11♋34 0	18 12 7	1 50.4	6 12.5	8 24.3	24 26.0	14 30.8	2 2.8	11 15.2	28 51.0	17 12.5
12 M	3 22 40	19 9 39	24 43 58	1♌ 9 53	1 51.5	5 58.3	9 35.8	24 54.4	14 43.6	2 8.6	11 18.6	28 49.8	17 11.5
13 Tu	3 26 36	20 10 3	7♌30 18	13 45 42	1 52.3	5 34.1	10 47.5	25 22.6	14 56.6	2 14.4	11 22.1	28 48.6	17 10.5
14 W	3 30 33	21 10 29	19 56 35	26 3 32	1R52.7	4 59.7	11 59.2	25 50.6	15 9.5	2 20.2	11 25.6	28 47.3	17 9.5
15 Th	3 34 30	22 10 57	2♍ 7 5	8♍ 7 51	1 52.5	4 15.1	13 11.0	26 18.3	15 22.5	2 26.2	11 29.1	28 46.0	17 8.5
16 F	3 38 26	23 11 26	14 6 22	20 3 12	1 51.8	3 20.6	14 23.0	26 45.7	15 35.6	2 32.1	11 32.6	28 44.7	17 7.4
17 Sa	3 42 23	24 11 57	25 58 54	1♎53 58	1 50.9	2 17.1	15 35.0	27 12.9	15 48.7	2 38.1	11 36.2	28 43.4	17 6.4
18 Su	3 46 19	25 12 31	7♎48 53	13 44 7	1 49.9	1 6.0	16 47.2	27 39.9	16 1.8	2 44.2	11 39.7	28 42.1	17 5.3
19 M	3 50 16	26 13 5	19 40 3	25 37 5	1 49.1	29♏48.9	17 59.4	28 6.6	16 15.0	2 50.3	11 43.3	28 40.7	17 4.3
20 Tu	3 54 12	27 13 42	1♏35 33	7♏35 46	1 48.4	28 28.3	19 11.7	28 33.1	16 28.2	2 56.5	11 46.9	28 39.3	17 3.2
21 W	3 58 9	28 14 20	13 37 59	19 42 28	1 48.0	27 6.7	20 24.1	28 59.3	16 41.4	3 2.7	11 50.5	28 37.9	17 2.1
22 Th	4 2 5	29 15 0	25 49 23	1♐58 57	1D47.8	25 46.8	21 36.6	29 25.2	16 54.7	3 8.9	11 54.1	28 36.5	17 1.0
23 F	4 6 2	0♐15 41	8♐11 17	14 26 32	1 47.8	24 31.3	22 49.2	29 50.8	17 8.0	3 15.2	11 57.7	28 35.0	16 59.9
24 Sa	4 9 59	1 16 23	20 44 49	27 6 13	1R47.8	23 22.6	24 1.9	0♍16.1	17 21.3	3 21.6	12 1.3	28 33.6	16 58.8
25 Su	4 13 55	2 17 7	3♑30 51	9♑58 47	1 47.8	22 22.6	25 14.6	0 41.2	17 34.7	3 27.9	12 5.0	28 32.1	16 57.7
26 M	4 17 52	3 17 52	16 30 7	23 4 55	1 47.7	21 32.8	26 27.5	1 6.0	17 48.1	3 34.4	12 8.6	28 30.6	16 56.6
27 Tu	4 21 48	4 18 39	29 43 15	6♒25 12	1 47.5	20 54.2	27 40.3	1 30.4	18 1.5	3 40.8	12 12.2	28 29.1	16 55.5
28 W	4 25 45	5 19 26	13♒10 47	20 0 4	1 47.2	20 27.1	28 53.3	1 54.6	18 14.9	3 47.3	12 15.9	28 27.6	16 54.3
29 Th	4 29 41	6 20 14	26 53 3	3♓49 41	1D47.0	20D11.6	0♏ 6.3	2 18.4	18 28.4	3 53.8	12 19.6	28 26.0	16 53.2
30 F	4 33 38	7 21 3	10♓49 55	17 53 37	1 46.9	20 7.2	1 19.4	2 41.9	18 41.9	4 0.4	12 23.2	28 24.5	16 52.0

DECEMBER 1900 LONGITUDE

Day	Sid.Time	☉	0 hr ☽	Noon ☽	True ☊	☿	♀	♂	♃	♄	♅	♆	♇
1 Sa	4 37 34	8♐21 52	25♓ 0 35	2♈10 32	1♐47.1	20♏13.5	2♏32.6	3♍ 5.1	18♐55.4	4♑ 7.0	12♐26.9	28♊22.9	16♊50.9
2 Su	4 41 31	9 22 43	9♈23 10	16 38 0	1 47.7	20 29.6	3 45.8	3 28.0	19 8.9	4 13.6	12 30.6	28R21.3	16R49.8
3 M	4 45 28	10 23 35	23 54 32	1♉12 12	1 48.4	20 54.7	4 59.1	3 50.5	19 22.5	4 20.3	12 34.2	28 19.7	16 48.6
4 Tu	4 49 24	11 24 27	8♉30 18	15 48 9	1 49.2	21 27.8	6 12.4	4 12.7	19 36.1	4 27.0	12 37.9	28 18.1	16 47.4
5 W	4 53 21	12 25 20	23 4 59	0♊20 3	1R49.7	22 8.3	7 25.8	4 34.5	19 49.6	4 33.7	12 41.6	28 16.5	16 46.3
6 Th	4 57 17	13 26 15	7♊32 35	14 41 53	1 49.8	22 55.2	8 39.3	4 56.0	20 3.2	4 40.4	12 45.3	28 14.9	16 45.1
7 F	5 1 14	14 27 10	21 47 18	28 48 14	1 49.2	23 47.7	9 52.8	5 17.1	20 16.8	4 47.2	12 48.9	28 13.3	16 44.0
8 Sa	5 5 10	15 28 6	5♋44 14	12♋34 55	1 47.9	24 45.3	11 6.4	5 37.9	20 30.5	4 54.0	12 52.6	28 11.6	16 42.8
9 Su	5 9 7	16 29 4	19 20 3	25 59 30	1 46.0	25 47.1	12 20.0	5 58.2	20 44.1	5 0.8	12 56.3	28 10.0	16 41.7
10 M	5 13 4	17 30 2	2♌33 14	9♌ 1 23	1 43.7	26 52.8	13 33.7	6 18.2	20 57.7	5 7.7	12 60.0	28 8.3	16 40.5
11 Tu	5 17 0	18 31 1	15 24 9	21 41 50	1 41.4	28 1.8	14 47.5	6 37.8	21 11.4	5 14.6	13 3.6	28 6.6	16 39.3
12 W	5 20 57	19 32 2	27 54 49	4♍ 3 33	1 39.4	29 13.6	16 1.2	6 56.9	21 25.0	5 21.5	13 7.3	28 5.0	16 38.2
13 Th	5 24 53	20 33 3	10♍ 8 32	16 10 20	1D38.2	0♐28.0	17 15.1	7 15.7	21 38.7	5 28.4	13 10.9	28 3.3	16 37.0
14 F	5 28 50	21 34 5	22 9 32	28 6 44	1 37.7	1 44.5	18 29.0	7 34.0	21 52.4	5 35.3	13 14.6	28 1.6	16 35.9
15 Sa	5 32 46	22 35 9	4♎ 2 32	9♎57 35	1 38.2	3 2.9	19 42.9	7 51.9	22 6.0	5 42.3	13 18.2	27 59.9	16 34.7
16 Su	5 36 43	23 36 13	15 52 29	21 47 50	1 39.5	4 22.9	20 56.9	8 9.3	22 19.7	5 49.2	13 21.9	27 58.2	16 33.6
17 M	5 40 39	24 37 19	27 44 12	3♏42 10	1 41.2	5 44.4	22 10.9	8 26.3	22 33.4	5 56.2	13 25.5	27 56.5	16 32.4
18 Tu	5 44 36	25 38 25	9♏42 12	15 44 48	1 43.0	7 7.1	23 25.0	8 42.8	22 47.0	6 3.2	13 29.1	27 54.8	16 31.3
19 W	5 48 33	26 39 32	21 50 23	27 59 19	1R44.3	8 30.9	24 39.1	8 58.8	23 0.7	6 10.2	13 32.7	27 53.1	16 30.1
20 Th	5 52 29	27 40 39	4♐11 53	10♐28 21	1 44.7	9 55.7	25 53.2	9 14.3	23 14.4	6 17.3	13 36.3	27 51.4	16 29.0
21 F	5 56 26	28 41 48	16 48 51	23 13 30	1 43.7	11 21.3	27 7.4	9 29.4	23 28.0	6 24.3	13 39.9	27 49.7	16 27.8
22 Sa	6 0 22	29 42 57	29 42 20	6♑15 16	1 41.3	12 47.7	28 21.6	9 43.9	23 41.7	6 31.4	13 43.5	27 48.0	16 26.7
23 Su	6 4 19	0♑44 6	12♑52 12	19 32 58	1 37.5	14 14.8	29 35.8	9 57.9	23 55.3	6 38.4	13 47.1	27 46.3	16 25.6
24 M	6 8 15	1 45 15	26 17 19	3♒ 5 0	1 32.8	15 42.5	0♐50.1	10 11.3	24 9.0	6 45.5	13 50.6	27 44.6	16 24.5
25 Tu	6 12 12	2 46 25	9♒55 42	16 49 5	1 27.6	17 10.7	2 4.4	10 24.2	24 22.6	6 52.6	13 54.2	27 42.9	16 23.4
26 W	6 16 8	3 47 35	23 44 50	0♓42 38	1 22.7	18 39.4	3 18.7	10 36.6	24 36.2	6 59.6	13 57.7	27 41.2	16 22.3
27 Th	6 20 5	4 48 45	7♓42 10	14 43 8	1 18.7	20 8.6	4 33.1	10 48.4	24 49.8	7 6.7	14 1.2	27 39.5	16 21.2
28 F	6 24 2	5 49 55	21 45 16	28 48 21	1 16.2	21 38.2	5 47.4	10 59.6	25 3.4	7 13.8	14 4.7	27 37.8	16 20.1
29 Sa	6 27 58	6 51 4	5♈52 9	12♈56 28	1D15.4	23 8.3	7 1.8	11 10.3	25 16.9	7 20.9	14 8.2	27 36.1	16 19.0
30 Su	6 31 55	7 52 14	20 1 7	27 5 54	1 15.9	24 38.7	8 16.2	11 20.3	25 30.5	7 28.0	14 11.6	27 34.5	16 17.9
31 M	6 35 51	8 53 23	4♉10 37	11♉15 3	1 17.3	26 9.5	9 30.7	11 29.8	25 44.0	7 35.1	14 15.1	27 32.8	16 16.8

Astro Data

	Dy Hr Mn
☽0N	3 5:24
♀0S	7 0:03
☿ R	9 23:37
☽0S	16 8:15
♃☍♇	22 10:34
☿ D	29 21:34
☽0N	30 12:29
☽0S	13 16:10
☽0N	27 18:21

Planet Ingress

	Dy Hr Mn
♀ ♎	3 21:33
☿ ♏	18 20:38
☉ ♐	22 17:48
♂ ♍	23 8:41
♀ ♏	28 21:55
☿ ♐	12 15:03
☉ ♑	22 6:42
♀ ♐	23 7:48

Last Aspect / ☽ Ingress

Last Aspect Dy Hr Mn		☽ Ingress Dy Hr Mn
1 21:27	♆ △	♓ 1 23:06
3 22:48	♆ □	♈ 4 0:27
5 22:44	♆ ✶	♉ 6 0:25
7 13:02	♂ □	♊ 8 0:50
10 1:34	♆ ☌	♋ 10 3:32
11 12:54	☉ △	♌ 12 9:49
14 17:22	♆ ✶	♍ 14 19:48
17 5:33	♆ □	♎ 17 8:09
19 18:07	♆ △	♏ 19 20:48
22 7:17	☉ ☌	♐ 22 8:09
24 14:42	♆ ☍	♑ 24 17:26
26 19:56	♀ □	♒ 27 0:30
29 2:41	♆ △	♓ 29 5:24

Last Aspect / ☽ Ingress

Last Aspect Dy Hr Mn		☽ Ingress Dy Hr Mn
1 5:39	♆ □	♈ 1 8:22
3 7:16	♆ ✶	♉ 3 10:01
4 22:21	☿ ☍	♊ 5 11:27
7 10:59	♆ ☌	♋ 7 14:04
9 12:40	☿ △	♌ 9 19:19
12 2:50	☿ □	♍ 12 4:04
14 11:48	♆ □	♎ 14 15:49
17 0:25	♆ △	♏ 17 4:34
19 6:07	♀ ☌	♐ 19 15:54
22 0:01	☉ ☌	♑ 22 0:33
22 18:39	♂ △	♒ 24 6:34
26 6:47	♆ △	♓ 26 10:47
28 9:59	♆ □	♈ 28 14:02
30 12:47	♆ ✶	♉ 30 16:55

☽ Phases & Eclipses

Dy Hr Mn	
6 23:00	○ 14♉06
14 2:37	☽ 21♌17
22 7:17	● 29♏33
22 7:19:43	● A 6'42"
29 17:35	☽ 7♓05
6 10:38	○ 13♊53
6 10:26	● A 0.818
13 22:42	☽ 21♍31
22 0:01	● 29♐43
29 1:48	☽ 6♈56

Astro Data

1 NOVEMBER 1900
Julian Day # 305
Delta T -1.7 sec
SVP 06♓38'26"
Obliquity 23°27'04"
⚷ Chiron 22♐21.5
☽ Mean ☊ 3♐03.8

1 DECEMBER 1900
Julian Day # 335
Delta T -1.6 sec
SVP 06♓38'22"
Obliquity 23°27'03"
⚷ Chiron 25♐20.9
☽ Mean ☊ 1♐28.4

LONGITUDE JANUARY 1901

Day	Sid.Time	☉	0 hr ☽	Noon ☽	True ☊	☿	♀	♂	♃	♄	♅	♆	♇
1 Tu	6 39 48	9♑54 33	18♉18 59	25♉22 6	1♐18.7	27♐40.8	10♐45.1	11♍38.6	25♐57.5	7♑42.1	14♐18.5	27♊31.1	16♊15.8
2 W	6 43 44	10 55 42	2♊24 7	9♊24 42	1R 19.3	29 12.3	11 59.6	11 46.8	26 11.0	7 49.2	14 21.9	27R 29.5	16R 14.7
3 Th	6 47 41	11 56 51	16 23 27	23 19 58	1 18.3	0♑44.3	13 14.1	11 54.4	26 24.4	7 56.3	14 25.2	27 27.8	16 13.7
4 F	6 51 37	12 57 59	0♋13 52	7♋ 4 44	1 15.2	2 16.6	14 28.6	12 1.4	26 37.9	8 3.4	14 28.6	27 26.2	16 12.7
5 Sa	6 55 34	13 59 8	13 52 11	20 35 51	1 9.9	3 49.3	15 43.2	12 7.6	26 51.3	8 10.4	14 31.9	27 24.6	16 11.7
6 Su	6 59 31	15 0 17	27 15 27	3♌50 45	1 2.9	5 22.4	16 57.7	12 13.3	27 4.6	8 17.5	14 35.2	27 23.0	16 10.7
7 M	7 3 27	16 1 25	10♌21 34	16 47 50	0 54.6	6 55.9	18 12.3	12 18.2	27 18.0	8 24.6	14 38.5	27 21.4	16 9.7
8 Tu	7 7 24	17 2 33	23 9 35	29 26 52	0 46.1	8 29.7	19 26.9	12 22.4	27 31.3	8 31.6	14 41.8	27 19.8	16 8.7
9 W	7 11 20	18 3 41	5♍39 56	11♍49 1	0 38.2	10 4.0	20 41.5	12 25.9	27 44.6	8 38.6	14 45.0	27 18.2	16 7.7
10 Th	7 15 17	19 4 49	17 54 29	23 56 45	0 31.7	11 38.7	21 56.1	12 28.8	27 57.8	8 45.6	14 48.2	27 16.7	16 6.8
11 F	7 19 13	20 5 57	29 56 20	5♎53 45	0 27.1	13 13.9	23 10.8	12 30.9	28 11.1	8 52.6	14 51.4	27 15.1	16 5.8
12 Sa	7 23 10	21 7 5	11♎49 36	17 44 31	0D 24.6	14 49.5	24 25.4	12 32.2	28 24.2	8 59.6	14 54.6	27 13.6	16 4.9
13 Su	7 27 6	22 8 13	23 39 7	29 34 7	0 24.0	16 25.6	25 40.1	12R 32.8	28 37.4	9 6.6	14 57.7	27 12.1	16 4.0
14 M	7 31 3	23 9 21	5♏30 9	11♏27 54	0 24.7	18 2.1	26 54.8	12 32.6	28 50.5	9 13.6	15 0.8	27 10.6	16 3.1
15 Tu	7 35 0	24 10 28	17 28 2	23 31 10	0 25.9	19 39.2	28 9.5	12 31.7	29 3.6	9 20.5	15 3.8	27 9.1	16 2.2
16 W	7 38 56	25 11 36	29 37 54	5♐48 48	0R 26.6	21 16.7	29 24.2	12 30.0	29 16.6	9 27.4	15 6.9	27 7.6	16 1.3
17 Th	7 42 53	26 12 43	12♐ 4 19	18 24 52	0 25.8	22 54.8	0♑39.0	12 27.5	29 29.6	9 34.3	15 9.9	27 6.1	16 0.4
18 F	7 46 49	27 13 50	24 50 46	1♑22 12	0 22.9	24 33.5	1 53.7	12 24.3	29 42.5	9 41.2	15 12.9	27 4.7	15 59.6
19 Sa	7 50 46	28 14 56	7♑59 16	14 41 56	0 17.4	26 12.6	3 8.5	12 20.2	29 55.4	9 48.1	15 15.8	27 3.3	15 58.8
20 Su	7 54 42	29 16 2	21 30 0	28 23 9	0 9.6	27 52.4	4 23.3	12 15.3	0♑ 8.3	9 54.9	15 18.7	27 1.9	15 57.9
21 M	7 58 39	0♒17 7	5♒20 58	12♒22 54	29♏59.8	29 32.7	5 38.0	12 9.7	0 21.1	10 1.7	15 21.6	27 0.5	15 57.1
22 Tu	8 2 35	1 18 11	19 28 18	26 36 27	29 49.2	1♒13.6	6 52.8	12 3.2	0 33.8	10 8.5	15 24.5	26 59.2	15 56.4
23 W	8 6 32	2 19 15	3♓46 36	10♓58 1	29 39.0	2 55.1	8 7.6	11 55.9	0 46.5	10 15.3	15 27.3	26 57.8	15 55.6
24 Th	8 10 29	3 20 17	18 9 58	25 21 47	29 30.2	4 37.2	9 22.4	11 47.8	0 59.1	10 22.0	15 30.0	26 56.5	15 54.9
25 F	8 14 25	4 21 18	2♈32 51	9♈42 42	29 23.8	6 19.9	10 37.1	11 38.9	1 11.7	10 28.7	15 32.8	26 55.2	15 54.1
26 Sa	8 18 22	5 22 19	16 50 54	23 57 10	29 20.0	8 3.1	11 51.9	11 29.2	1 24.2	10 35.4	15 35.5	26 54.0	15 53.4
27 Su	8 22 18	6 23 18	1♉ 1 16	8♉ 3 5	29D 18.6	9 46.9	13 6.7	11 18.8	1 36.7	10 42.0	15 38.1	26 52.7	15 52.7
28 M	8 26 15	7 24 16	15 2 34	21 59 40	29 18.6	11 31.3	14 21.5	11 7.5	1 49.1	10 48.6	15 40.8	26 51.5	15 52.0
29 Tu	8 30 11	8 25 13	28 54 26	5♊46 52	29R 18.9	13 16.2	15 36.3	10 55.5	2 1.5	10 55.2	15 43.3	26 50.3	15 51.4
30 W	8 34 8	9 26 8	12♊37 0	19 24 50	29 18.2	15 1.6	16 51.1	10 42.7	2 13.7	11 1.7	15 45.9	26 49.2	15 50.7
31 Th	8 38 4	10 27 2	26 10 22	2♋53 33	29 15.4	16 47.5	18 5.9	10 29.2	2 26.0	11 8.2	15 48.4	26 48.0	15 50.1

LONGITUDE FEBRUARY 1901

Day	Sid.Time	☉	0 hr ☽	Noon ☽	True ☊	☿	♀	♂	♃	♄	♅	♆	♇
1 F	8 42 1	11♒27 55	9♋34 17	16♋12 29	29♏ 9.8	18♒33.7	19♑20.7	10♍14.9	2♑38.1	11♑14.7	15♐50.9	26♊46.9	15♊49.5
2 Sa	8 45 58	12 28 47	22 48 0	29 20 40	29R 1.2	20 20.2	20 35.5	9R 59.9	2 50.2	11 21.1	15 53.3	26R 45.8	15R 48.9
3 Su	8 49 54	13 29 37	5♌50 22	12♌16 56	28 49.9	22 7.0	21 50.3	9 44.1	3 2.2	11 27.5	15 55.7	26 44.7	15 48.4
4 M	8 53 51	14 30 27	18 40 14	25 0 12	28 36.8	23 53.8	23 5.1	9 27.7	3 14.1	11 33.9	15 58.0	26 43.7	15 47.8
5 Tu	8 57 47	15 31 15	1♍16 46	7♍29 57	28 23.1	25 40.6	24 19.9	9 10.6	3 26.0	11 40.2	16 0.3	26 42.7	15 47.3
6 W	9 1 44	16 32 1	13 39 49	19 46 30	28 10.0	27 27.2	25 34.7	8 52.8	3 37.8	11 46.4	16 2.6	26 41.7	15 46.8
7 Th	9 5 40	17 32 47	25 50 12	1♎51 13	27 58.6	29 13.4	26 49.5	8 34.4	3 49.5	11 52.6	16 4.8	26 40.8	15 46.3
8 F	9 9 37	18 33 32	7♎49 54	13 46 38	27 49.7	0♓58.9	28 4.3	8 15.4	4 1.2	11 58.8	16 7.0	26 39.8	15 45.9
9 Sa	9 13 33	19 34 15	19 41 54	25 36 15	27 43.6	2 43.5	29 19.1	7 55.8	4 12.8	12 4.9	16 9.1	26 38.9	15 45.4
10 Su	9 17 30	20 34 58	1♏30 14	7♏24 30	27 40.2	4 26.9	0♒34.0	7 35.7	4 24.3	12 11.0	16 11.2	26 38.1	15 45.0
11 M	9 21 27	21 35 39	13 19 41	19 16 30	27D 38.9	6 8.6	1 48.8	7 15.0	4 35.7	12 17.0	16 13.2	26 37.2	15 44.6
12 Tu	9 25 23	22 36 20	25 15 37	1♐17 45	27R 38.7	7 48.2	3 3.6	6 53.8	4 47.0	12 23.0	16 15.2	26 36.4	15 44.2
13 W	9 29 20	23 36 59	7♐23 35	13 33 49	27 38.6	9 25.4	4 18.4	6 32.2	4 58.3	12 29.0	16 17.2	26 35.6	15 43.9
14 Th	9 33 16	24 37 37	19 49 3	26 9 53	27 37.2	10 59.5	5 33.2	6 10.2	5 9.4	12 34.8	16 19.1	26 34.9	15 43.5
15 F	9 37 13	25 38 14	2♑36 47	9♑10 10	27 33.7	12 29.9	6 48.0	5 47.7	5 20.5	12 40.7	16 20.9	26 34.2	15 43.2
16 Sa	9 41 9	26 38 49	15 50 17	22 37 15	27 27.4	13 56.2	8 2.9	5 25.0	5 31.5	12 46.4	16 22.8	26 33.5	15 42.9
17 Su	9 45 6	27 39 24	29 31 1	6♒31 22	27 18.5	15 17.6	9 17.7	5 1.9	5 42.4	12 52.2	16 24.5	26 32.8	15 42.6
18 M	9 49 2	28 39 56	13♒37 51	20 49 52	27 7.3	16 33.4	10 32.5	4 38.6	5 53.2	12 57.8	16 26.2	26 32.2	15 42.4
19 Tu	9 52 59	29 40 28	28 6 38	5♓27 15	26 55.1	17 43.0	11 47.3	4 15.0	6 3.9	13 3.4	16 27.9	26 31.6	15 42.2
20 W	9 56 56	0♓40 57	12♓50 39	20 15 44	26 43.0	18 45.7	13 2.1	3 51.3	6 14.5	13 9.0	16 29.5	26 31.0	15 42.0
21 Th	10 0 52	1 41 25	27 41 25	5♈ 6 37	26 32.5	19 40.9	14 16.9	3 27.5	6 25.0	13 14.5	16 31.1	26 30.5	15 41.8
22 F	10 4 49	2 41 52	12♈30 21	19 51 44	26 24.5	20 27.8	15 31.7	3 3.6	6 35.4	13 19.9	16 32.6	26 30.0	15 41.6
23 Sa	10 8 45	3 42 16	27 10 2	4♉24 42	26 19.5	21 6.1	16 46.5	2 39.7	6 45.8	13 25.3	16 34.1	26 29.5	15 41.5
24 Su	10 12 42	4 42 38	11♉35 19	18 41 38	26 17.2	21 35.2	18 1.2	2 15.8	6 56.0	13 30.6	16 35.5	26 29.1	15 41.3
25 M	10 16 38	5 42 59	25 43 30	2♊40 56	26 16.7	21 54.8	19 16.0	1 52.0	7 6.1	13 35.8	16 36.8	26 28.7	15 41.3
26 Tu	10 20 35	6 43 17	9♊34 0	16 22 51	26 16.7	22R 4.7	20 30.7	1 28.3	7 16.1	13 41.0	16 38.2	26 28.4	15 41.2
27 W	10 24 31	7 43 34	23 7 41	29 48 41	26 15.9	22 4.8	21 45.5	1 4.8	7 26.0	13 46.1	16 39.4	26 28.0	15 41.1
28 Th	10 28 28	8 43 48	6♋26 7	13♋ 0 10	26 13.2	21 55.3	23 0.2	0 41.5	7 35.7	13 51.2	16 40.6	26 27.7	15D 41.1

Astro Data	Planet Ingress	Last Aspect	☽ Ingress	Last Aspect	☽ Ingress	☽ Phases & Eclipses	Astro Data
Dy Hr Mn	Dy Hr Mn	Dy Hr Mn	Dy Hr Mn	Dy Hr Mn	Dy Hr Mn	Dy Hr Mn	1 JANUARY 1901
♃☍♆ 7 5:28	☿ ♑ 2 12:27	31 12:33 ♂ △	♊ 1 19:54	1 19:33 ♀ ☍	♌ 2 13:12	5 0:13 ○ 13♋60	Julian Day # 366
☽0S 10 1:28	♀ ♑ 16 11:29	3 19:08 ♆ ☌	♋ 3 23:36	4 15:16 ♆ ⚹	♍ 4 21:33	12 20:38 ☽ 21♎60	Delta T -1.5 sec
♂ R 13 7:04	♃ ♑ 19 8:33	5 0:13 ☉ ☍	♌ 6 4:59	7 2:12 ♀ △	♎ 7 8:18	20 14:36 ● 29♑53	SVP 06♓38'16"
☽0N 24 1:13	☉ ♒ 20 17:17	8 8:28 ♃ △	♍ 8 13:04	9 14:06 ♆ △	♏ 9 20:56	27 9:52 ☽ 6♉48	Obliquity 23°27'03"
♅☍♇ 31 13:26	☊ ♏ 20 23:36	10 20:25 ♃ □	♎ 11 0:07	11 18:12 ☉ □	♐ 12 9:26		⚷ Chiron 28♐43.4
	☿ ♒ 21 6:30	13 10:16 ♃ ⚹	♏ 13 12:52	14 12:46 ♆ ☍	♑ 14 19:10	3 15:30 ○ 14♌09	☽ Mean ☊ 29♏50.0
☽0S 6 10:42		15 14:30 ☉ ⚹	♐ 16 0:43	15 20:12 ☿ ⚹	♒ 17 0:50	11 18:12 ☽ 22♏22	
☽0N 20 10:22	☿ ♓ 7 10:35	18 9:07 ♃ ☌	♑ 18 9:30	19 2:45 ☉ ☌	♓ 19 3:06	19 2:45 ● 29♒47	1 FEBRUARY 1901
☿ R 26 12:18	♀ ♒ 9 13:07	20 14:36 ☉ ☌	♒ 20 14:48	20 22:05 ♆ □	♈ 21 3:44	25 18:38 ☽ 6♊30	Julian Day # 397
♇ D 28 18:18	☉ ♓ 19 7:45	22 12:37 ♆ △	♓ 22 17:41	22 22:53 ♆ ⚹	♉ 23 4:41		Delta T -1.4 sec
		24 14:37 ♆ □	♈ 24 19:45	24 17:21 ☿ ⚹	♊ 25 7:22		SVP 06♓38'11"
		26 16:58 ♆ ⚹	♉ 26 22:16	27 5:59 ♆ ☌	♋ 27 12:20		Obliquity 23°27'03"
		27 22:42 ♀ △	♊ 29 1:54				⚷ Chiron 1♑51.2
		31 1:07 ♆ ☌	♋ 31 6:50				☽ Mean ☊ 28♏11.5

MARCH 1901 LONGITUDE

Day	Sid.Time	☉	0 hr ☽	Noon☽	True☊	☿	♀	♂	♃	♄	♅	♆	♇
1 F	10 32 25	9♓44 1	19♋31 1	25♋58 52	26♏ 7.8	21♓36.5	24♒15.0	0♍18.5	7♑45.4	13♑56.2	16♐41.8	26♊27.5	15♊41.1
2 Sa	10 36 21	10 44 11	2♌23 49	8♌46 1	25R 59.5	21R 8.8	25 29.7	29♌55.7	7 55.0	14 1.1	16 42.9	26R 27.2	15 41.1
3 Su	10 40 18	11 44 19	15 5 31	21 22 23	25 48.5	20 33.0	26 44.4	29R 33.3	8 4.4	14 5.9	16 44.0	26 27.1	15 41.2
4 M	10 44 14	12 44 25	27 36 41	3♍48 28	25 35.9	19 50.1	27 59.1	29 11.2	8 13.8	14 10.7	16 45.0	26 26.9	15 41.2
5 Tu	10 48 11	13 44 30	9♍57 45	16 4 36	25 22.5	19 1.1	29 13.8	28 49.6	8 23.0	14 15.4	16 45.9	26 26.8	15 41.3
6 W	10 52 7	14 44 32	22 9 7	28 11 25	25 9.6	18 7.2	0♓28.5	28 28.4	8 32.1	14 20.0	16 46.8	26 26.7	15 41.4
7 Th	10 56 4	15 44 33	4♎11 38	10♎ 9 58	24 58.3	17 9.8	1 43.2	28 7.6	8 41.0	14 24.6	16 47.7	26 26.6	15 41.5
8 F	11 0 0	16 44 32	16 6 39	22 2 0	24 49.4	16 10.3	2 57.8	27 47.4	8 49.9	14 29.1	16 48.5	26D 26.6	15 41.7
9 Sa	11 3 57	17 44 29	27 56 22	3♏50 8	24 43.2	15 10.2	4 12.5	27 27.7	8 58.6	14 33.5	16 49.2	26 26.6	15 41.8
10 Su	11 7 53	18 44 24	9♏43 45	15 37 44	24 39.8	14 10.7	5 27.2	27 8.6	9 7.2	14 37.8	16 49.9	26 26.6	15 42.0
11 M	11 11 50	19 44 18	21 32 38	27 29 3	24D 38.5	13 13.1	6 41.8	26 50.0	9 15.7	14 42.1	16 50.5	26 26.7	15 42.2
12 Tu	11 15 47	20 44 9	3♐27 34	9♐28 53	24 38.8	12 18.6	7 56.5	26 32.1	9 24.1	14 46.3	16 51.1	26 26.8	15 42.5
13 W	11 19 43	21 44 0	15 33 38	21 42 30	24R 39.4	11 28.0	9 11.1	26 14.9	9 32.3	14 50.4	16 51.7	26 27.0	15 42.7
14 Th	11 23 40	22 43 48	27 56 9	4♑15 13	24 39.4	10 42.3	10 25.7	25 58.2	9 40.4	14 54.4	16 52.1	26 27.2	15 43.0
15 F	11 27 36	23 43 35	10♑40 17	17 11 53	24 37.9	10 1.9	11 40.4	25 42.3	9 48.4	14 58.4	16 52.6	26 27.4	15 43.3
16 Sa	11 31 33	24 43 20	23 50 25	0♒36 12	24 34.3	9 27.4	12 55.0	25 27.1	9 56.2	15 2.2	16 52.9	26 27.6	15 43.6
17 Su	11 35 29	25 43 4	7♒29 22	14 29 54	24 28.4	8 58.9	14 9.6	25 12.6	10 3.9	15 6.0	16 53.3	26 27.9	15 44.0
18 M	11 39 26	26 42 45	21 37 34	28 51 57	24 20.6	8 36.7	15 24.2	24 58.8	10 11.4	15 9.7	16 53.5	26 28.2	15 44.4
19 Tu	11 43 22	27 42 25	6♓12 24	13♓38 2	24 11.6	8 20.8	16 38.8	24 45.8	10 18.8	15 13.3	16 53.7	26 28.6	15 44.8
20 W	11 47 19	28 42 3	21 7 52	28 40 41	24 2.7	8 11.1	17 53.4	24 33.6	10 26.1	15 16.9	16 53.9	26 28.9	15 45.2
21 Th	11 51 16	29 41 39	6♈15 15	13♈50 15	23 54.9	8D 7.5	19 7.9	24 22.1	10 33.2	15 20.3	16 54.0	26 29.4	15 45.6
22 F	11 55 12	0♈41 12	21 24 26	28 56 34	23 49.0	8 9.8	20 22.5	24 11.4	10 40.2	15 23.7	16R 54.0	26 29.8	15 46.0
23 Sa	11 59 9	1 40 44	6♉25 36	13♉50 38	23 45.5	8 17.8	21 37.0	24 1.4	10 47.0	15 27.0	16 54.0	26 30.3	15 46.5
24 Su	12 3 5	2 40 14	21 10 55	28 25 54	23D 44.3	8 31.2	22 51.6	23 52.3	10 53.7	15 30.2	16 54.0	26 30.8	15 47.0
25 M	12 7 2	3 39 41	5♊35 14	12♊38 42	23 44.7	8 49.9	24 6.1	23 44.0	11 0.2	15 33.3	16 53.9	26 31.4	15 47.5
26 Tu	12 10 58	4 39 6	19 36 17	26 28 7	23 45.7	9 13.4	25 20.6	23 36.5	11 6.6	15 36.3	16 53.7	26 32.0	15 48.1
27 W	12 14 55	5 38 28	3♋14 10	9♋54 53	23R 46.5	9 41.6	26 35.1	23 29.7	11 12.8	15 39.2	16 53.5	26 32.6	15 48.6
28 Th	12 18 51	6 37 48	16 30 31	23 1 24	23 46.0	10 14.2	27 49.5	23 23.8	11 18.8	15 42.1	16 53.3	26 33.2	15 49.2
29 F	12 22 48	7 37 6	29 27 54	5♌50 21	23 43.7	10 50.9	29 4.0	23 18.6	11 24.8	15 44.8	16 52.9	26 33.9	15 49.8
30 Sa	12 26 45	8 36 22	12♌ 9 6	18 24 29	23 39.3	11 31.6	0♈18.4	23 14.2	11 30.5	15 47.5	16 52.6	26 34.7	15 50.4
31 Su	12 30 41	9 35 35	24 36 49	0♍46 23	23 33.1	12 16.0	1 32.9	23 10.6	11 36.1	15 50.1	16 52.2	26 35.4	15 51.1

APRIL 1901 LONGITUDE

Day	Sid.Time	☉	0 hr ☽	Noon☽	True☊	☿	♀	♂	♃	♄	♅	♆	♇
1 M	12 34 38	10♈34 46	6♍53 27	12♍58 15	23♏25.7	13♓ 4.0	2♈47.3	23♌ 7.8	11♑41.5	15♑52.5	16♐51.7	26♊36.2	15♊51.7
2 Tu	12 38 34	11 33 54	19 1 1	25 1 57	23R 17.7	13 55.2	4 1.7	23R 5.7	11 46.8	15 54.9	16R 51.2	26 37.0	15 52.4
3 W	12 42 31	12 33 1	1♎ 1 15	6♎59 8	23 9.9	14 49.6	5 16.1	23 4.4	11 51.9	15 57.2	16 50.6	26 37.8	15 53.1
4 Th	12 46 27	13 32 5	12 55 47	18 51 25	23 3.2	15 46.9	6 30.4	23D 3.8	11 56.8	15 59.4	16 50.0	26 38.7	15 53.8
5 F	12 50 24	14 31 8	24 46 15	0♏40 33	22 58.1	16 47.1	7 44.8	23 4.0	12 1.6	16 1.5	16 49.3	26 39.6	15 54.5
6 Sa	12 54 20	15 30 8	6♏34 35	12 28 38	22 54.8	17 49.9	8 59.2	23 4.9	12 6.2	16 3.5	16 48.6	26 40.6	15 55.3
7 Su	12 58 17	16 29 7	18 23 4	24 18 14	22D 53.3	18 55.4	10 13.5	23 6.5	12 10.7	16 5.5	16 47.8	26 41.5	15 56.1
8 M	13 2 14	17 28 3	0♐14 34	6♐12 29	22 53.5	20 3.2	11 27.8	23 8.8	12 14.9	16 7.3	16 47.0	26 42.5	15 56.8
9 Tu	13 6 10	18 26 58	12 12 28	18 15 2	22 54.7	21 13.5	12 42.1	23 11.8	12 19.0	16 9.0	16 46.1	26 43.6	15 57.7
10 W	13 10 7	19 25 51	24 20 43	0♑30 3	22 56.5	22 26.0	13 56.4	23 15.5	12 23.0	16 10.6	16 45.2	26 44.6	15 58.5
11 Th	13 14 3	20 24 43	6♑43 37	13 1 58	22 58.0	23 40.6	15 10.7	23 19.8	12 26.7	16 12.2	16 44.3	26 45.7	15 59.3
12 F	13 18 0	21 23 32	19 25 37	25 55 6	22R 58.8	24 57.4	16 25.0	23 24.9	12 30.3	16 13.6	16 43.3	26 46.8	16 0.2
13 Sa	13 21 56	22 22 20	2♒30 51	9♒13 14	22 58.3	26 16.2	17 39.3	23 30.6	12 33.7	16 15.0	16 42.2	26 48.0	16 1.1
14 Su	13 25 53	23 21 6	16 2 30	22 58 49	22 56.6	27 37.0	18 53.5	23 36.9	12 36.9	16 16.2	16 41.1	26 49.2	16 2.0
15 M	13 29 49	24 19 50	0♓ 2 9	7♓12 18	22 53.7	28 59.7	20 7.8	23 43.9	12 39.9	16 17.4	16 40.0	26 50.4	16 2.9
16 Tu	13 33 46	25 18 33	14 28 54	21 51 22	22 50.0	0♈24.3	21 22.0	23 51.5	12 42.8	16 18.4	16 38.8	26 51.6	16 3.8
17 W	13 37 42	26 17 14	29 18 56	6♈50 39	22 46.2	1 50.7	22 36.3	23 59.7	12 45.5	16 19.4	16 37.5	26 52.9	16 4.7
18 Th	13 41 39	27 15 53	14♈25 25	22 2 1	22 42.8	3 18.9	23 50.5	24 8.6	12 48.0	16 20.2	16 36.3	26 54.2	16 5.7
19 F	13 45 36	28 14 30	29 39 13	7♉15 42	22 40.4	4 49.0	25 4.7	24 18.0	12 50.3	16 21.0	16 34.9	26 55.5	16 6.7
20 Sa	13 49 32	29 13 5	14♉50 15	22 21 44	22D 39.2	6 20.8	26 18.9	24 28.0	12 52.4	16 21.6	16 33.6	26 56.8	16 7.7
21 Su	13 53 29	0♉11 39	29 49 7	7♊11 33	22 39.2	7 54.3	27 33.0	24 38.6	12 54.4	16 22.2	16 32.2	26 58.2	16 8.7
22 M	13 57 25	1 10 10	14♊28 22	21 39 4	22 40.0	9 29.6	28 47.2	24 49.8	12 56.1	16 22.7	16 30.7	26 59.6	16 9.7
23 Tu	14 1 22	2 8 39	28 43 20	5♋41 1	22 41.4	11 6.6	0♉ 1.3	25 1.5	12 57.7	16 23.0	16 29.2	27 1.0	16 10.7
24 W	14 5 18	3 7 7	12♋32 6	19 16 43	22 42.7	12 45.4	1 15.5	25 13.8	12 59.1	16 23.3	16 27.7	27 2.5	16 11.8
25 Th	14 9 15	4 5 31	25 55 6	2♌27 34	22R 43.5	14 25.9	2 29.6	25 26.6	13 0.3	16 23.5	16 26.1	27 4.0	16 12.8
26 F	14 13 11	5 3 54	8♌54 29	15 16 17	22 43.7	16 8.1	3 43.7	25 39.9	13 1.3	16R 23.5	16 24.5	27 5.5	16 13.9
27 Sa	14 17 8	6 2 15	21 33 24	27 46 20	22 43.0	17 52.0	4 57.8	25 53.7	13 2.1	16 23.5	16 22.9	27 7.0	16 15.0
28 Su	14 21 5	7 0 33	3♍55 31	10♍ 1 25	22 41.6	19 37.7	6 11.8	26 8.1	13 2.7	16 23.4	16 21.2	27 8.6	16 16.1
29 M	14 25 1	7 58 50	16 4 31	22 5 12	22 39.8	21 25.2	7 25.9	26 22.9	13 3.2	16 23.1	16 19.5	27 10.1	16 17.2
30 Tu	14 28 58	8 57 4	28 3 55	4♎ 1 2	22 37.7	23 14.4	8 39.9	26 38.2	13R 3.4	16 22.8	16 17.7	27 11.7	16 18.4

Astro Data Dy Hr Mn	Planet Ingress Dy Hr Mn	Last Aspect Dy Hr Mn	☽ Ingress Dy Hr Mn	Last Aspect Dy Hr Mn	☽ Ingress Dy Hr Mn	☽ Phases & Eclipses Dy Hr Mn	Astro Data
☽0S 5 18:26	♂ ♌ 1 19:28	1 3:45 ☿ △	♌ 1 19:30	2 15:11 ♆ □	♎ 2 21:57	5 8:04 ○ 14♍05	1 MARCH 1901
♆ D 8 6:24	♀ ♓ 5 14:51	4 2:57 ♂ ☌	♍ 4 4:37	5 3:51 ♆ △	♏ 5 10:38	13 13:06 ☽ 22♐17	Julian Day # 425
☽0N 19 21:03	☉ ♈ 21 7:24	6 8:31 ♆ □	♎ 6 15:37	7 9:36 ♂ □	♐ 7 23:31	20 12:53 ● 29♓14	Delta T -1.3 sec
☿ D 21 2:31	♀ ♈ 29 18:03	8 23:03 ♂ ⚹	♏ 9 4:12	10 4:42 ♆ ☍	♑ 10 11:02	27 4:39 ☽ 5♋50	SVP 06♓38'08"
♅ R 22 11:26		11 10:26 ♂ □	♐ 11 17:04	12 11:22 ☿ ⚹	♒ 12 19:27		Obliquity 23°27'03"
♄⚻♇ 31 13:01	☿ ♈ 15 17:10	13 21:09 ♆ ☍	♑ 14 3:56	14 18:35 ♆ △	♓ 14 23:56	4 1:20 ○ 13♎35	⚷ Chiron 4♑01.9
♀0N 1 10:10	☉ ♉ 20 19:14	16 1:42 ☉ ⚹	♒ 16 10:56	16 20:05 ♆ □	♈ 17 1:06	12 3:57 ☽ 21♑33	☽ Mean ☊ 26♏42.5
☽0S 2 0:26	♀ ♉ 22 23:34	18 8:03 ♆ △	♓ 18 13:52	18 21:37 ☉ ☌	♉ 19 0:33	18 21:37 ● 28♈09	
♂ D 4 6:52		20 12:53 ☉ ☌	♈ 20 14:06	20 15:34 ♂ □	♊ 21 0:18	25 16:15 ☽ 4♌45	1 APRIL 1901
☽0N 16 7:31		22 8:06 ♆ ⚹	♉ 22 13:41	22 21:05 ♆ ☌	♋ 23 2:11		Julian Day # 456
☿0N 19 19:54		24 4:24 ♂ □	♊ 24 14:37	24 6:50 ♄ ☍	♌ 25 7:28		Delta T -1.2 sec
♄⚺♅ 26 14:25		26 12:08 ♆ ☌	♋ 26 18:15	27 10:45 ♆ ⚹	♍ 27 16:20		SVP 06♓38'05"
♄ R 26 4:34	♅☍♇ 29 18:24	28 23:10 ♀ △	♌ 29 1:00	29 22:15 ♆ □	♎ 30 3:54		Obliquity 23°27'03"
☽0S 29 5:51	♃ R 30 20:41	31 3:51 ♆ ⚹	♍ 31 10:29				⚷ Chiron 5♑19.6
							☽ Mean ☊ 25♏04.0

LONGITUDE — MAY 1901

Day	Sid.Time	☉	0 hr ☽	Noon ☽	True ☊	☿	♀	♂	♃	♄	♅	♆	♇
1 W	14 32 54	9♉55 16	9♎56 56	15♎51 56	22♏35.7	25♈ 5.3	9♉53.9	26♌53.9	13♑ 3.5	16♑22.4	16♐15.9	27♊13.3	16♊19.5
2 Th	14 36 51	10 53 27	21 46 22	27 40 33	22R 34.1	26 58.1	11 7.9	27 10.1	13R 3.4	16R 21.9	16R 14.1	27 15.0	16 20.7
3 F	14 40 47	11 51 36	3♏34 45	9♏29 16	22 32.9	28 52.6	12 21.9	27 26.8	13 3.1	16 21.3	16 12.2	27 16.7	16 21.8
4 Sa	14 44 44	12 49 43	15 24 21	21 20 17	22D 32.3	0♉48.8	13 35.9	27 43.9	13 2.6	16 20.6	16 10.3	27 18.3	16 23.0
5 Su	14 48 40	13 47 48	27 17 21	3♐15 48	22 32.3	2 46.8	14 49.9	28 1.4	13 1.9	16 19.8	16 8.4	27 20.1	16 24.2
6 M	14 52 37	14 45 52	9♐15 56	15 18 3	22 32.6	4 46.5	16 3.8	28 19.3	13 1.0	16 18.9	16 6.4	27 21.8	16 25.4
7 Tu	14 56 34	15 43 55	21 22 28	27 29 30	22 33.2	6 47.9	17 17.8	28 37.6	12 60.0	16 17.9	16 4.4	27 23.5	16 26.6
8 W	15 0 30	16 41 55	3♑39 29	9♑52 48	22 33.9	8 50.9	18 31.7	28 56.4	12 58.7	16 16.8	16 2.4	27 25.3	16 27.9
9 Th	15 4 27	17 39 55	16 9 47	22 30 49	22 34.5	10 55.4	19 45.7	29 15.5	12 57.3	16 15.6	16 0.4	27 27.1	16 29.1
10 F	15 8 23	18 37 53	28 56 16	5♒26 28	22 34.8	13 1.3	20 59.6	29 35.0	12 55.7	16 14.3	15 58.3	27 28.9	16 30.3
11 Sa	15 12 20	19 35 50	12♒ 1 46	18 42 27	22R 35.0	15 8.6	22 13.5	29 54.9	12 53.9	16 13.0	15 56.2	27 30.8	16 31.6
12 Su	15 16 16	20 33 45	25 28 44	2♓20 48	22 35.1	17 17.0	23 27.4	0♍15.2	12 51.9	16 11.5	15 54.1	27 32.6	16 32.8
13 M	15 20 13	21 31 39	9♓18 42	16 22 25	22 35.0	19 26.5	24 41.3	0 35.8	12 49.7	16 10.0	15 51.9	27 34.5	16 34.1
14 Tu	15 24 9	22 29 32	23 31 45	0♈46 26	22D 35.0	21 36.7	25 55.1	0 56.8	12 47.4	16 8.3	15 49.7	27 36.4	16 35.4
15 W	15 28 6	23 27 24	8♈ 6 0	15 29 50	22 35.0	23 47.5	27 9.0	1 18.1	12 44.8	16 6.6	15 47.5	27 38.3	16 36.7
16 Th	15 32 3	24 25 14	22 57 13	0♉27 15	22 35.1	25 58.7	28 22.9	1 39.8	12 42.1	16 4.8	15 45.3	27 40.2	16 38.0
17 F	15 35 59	25 23 4	7♉58 57	15 31 16	22R 35.3	28 10.0	29 36.7	2 1.8	12 39.2	16 2.9	15 43.1	27 42.1	16 39.3
18 Sa	15 39 56	26 20 52	23 3 5	0♊33 19	22 35.4	0♊21.1	0♊50.6	2 24.1	12 36.1	16 0.9	15 40.8	27 44.1	16 40.6
19 Su	15 43 52	27 18 38	8♊ 0 52	15 24 46	22 35.2	2 31.7	2 4.4	2 46.8	12 32.8	15 58.8	15 38.5	27 46.1	16 41.9
20 M	15 47 49	28 16 24	22 44 8	29 58 14	22 34.8	4 41.5	3 18.2	3 9.8	12 29.4	15 56.6	15 36.2	27 48.0	16 43.2
21 Tu	15 51 45	29 14 7	7♋ 6 28	14♋ 8 25	22 34.2	6 50.3	4 32.1	3 33.1	12 25.8	15 54.4	15 33.9	27 50.0	16 44.6
22 W	15 55 42	0♊11 50	21 3 48	27 52 33	22 33.4	8 57.8	5 45.9	3 56.7	12 22.0	15 52.0	15 31.6	27 52.1	16 45.9
23 Th	15 59 38	1 9 30	4♌34 40	11♌10 19	22 32.5	11 3.8	6 59.6	4 20.6	12 18.1	15 49.6	15 29.2	27 54.1	16 47.3
24 F	16 3 35	2 7 10	17 39 48	24 3 27	22 31.8	13 8.0	8 13.4	4 44.8	12 14.0	15 47.1	15 26.8	27 56.1	16 48.6
25 Sa	16 7 32	3 4 47	0♍21 44	6♍35 7	22D 31.5	15 10.3	9 27.2	5 9.3	12 9.7	15 44.5	15 24.5	27 58.2	16 50.0
26 Su	16 11 28	4 2 23	12 44 9	18 49 22	22 31.6	17 10.4	10 40.9	5 34.1	12 5.3	15 41.9	15 22.1	28 0.3	16 51.3
27 M	16 15 25	4 59 58	24 51 20	0♎50 38	22 32.3	19 8.3	11 54.7	5 59.1	12 0.7	15 39.1	15 19.6	28 2.3	16 52.7
28 Tu	16 19 21	5 57 31	6♎47 48	12 43 24	22 33.3	21 3.7	13 8.4	6 24.4	11 55.9	15 36.3	15 17.2	28 4.4	16 54.1
29 W	16 23 18	6 55 3	18 37 57	24 31 56	22 34.6	22 56.6	14 22.1	6 50.0	11 51.0	15 33.4	15 14.8	28 6.5	16 55.4
30 Th	16 27 14	7 52 33	0♏25 49	6♏20 4	22 35.9	24 46.9	15 35.8	7 15.8	11 46.0	15 30.5	15 12.4	28 8.7	16 56.8
31 F	16 31 11	8 50 3	12 15 3	18 11 10	22R 36.8	26 34.6	16 49.5	7 41.9	11 40.8	15 27.4	15 9.9	28 10.8	16 58.2

LONGITUDE — JUNE 1901

Day	Sid.Time	☉	0 hr ☽	Noon ☽	True ☊	☿	♀	♂	♃	♄	♅	♆	♇
1 Sa	16 35 7	9♊47 31	24♏ 8 44	0♐ 8 4	22♏37.0	28♊19.6	18♊ 3.2	8♍ 8.2	11♑35.4	15♑24.3	15♐ 7.5	28♊12.9	16♊59.6
2 Su	16 39 4	10 44 58	6♐ 9 27	12 13 5	22R 36.5	0♋ 1.8	19 16.9	8 34.8	11R 30.0	15R 21.2	15R 5.0	28 15.1	17 1.0
3 M	16 43 1	11 42 25	18 19 14	24 28 3	22 35.0	1 41.2	20 30.5	9 1.6	11 24.3	15 17.9	15 2.6	28 17.2	17 2.4
4 Tu	16 46 57	12 39 50	0♑39 44	6♑54 25	22 32.7	3 17.8	21 44.2	9 28.6	11 18.6	15 14.6	15 0.1	28 19.4	17 3.7
5 W	16 50 54	13 37 14	13 12 15	19 33 22	22 29.7	4 51.5	22 57.8	9 55.9	11 12.7	15 11.3	14 57.6	28 21.5	17 5.1
6 Th	16 54 50	14 34 38	25 57 52	2♒25 54	22 26.5	6 22.4	24 11.5	10 23.4	11 6.7	15 7.9	14 55.2	28 23.7	17 6.5
7 F	16 58 47	15 32 1	8♒57 33	15 32 56	22 23.3	7 50.4	25 25.1	10 51.1	11 0.6	15 4.4	14 52.7	28 25.9	17 7.9
8 Sa	17 2 43	16 29 23	22 12 9	28 55 17	22 20.8	9 15.4	26 38.7	11 19.0	10 54.3	15 0.8	14 50.2	28 28.1	17 9.3
9 Su	17 6 40	17 26 45	5♓42 25	12♓33 36	22D 19.2	10 37.5	27 52.3	11 47.2	10 48.0	14 57.2	14 47.8	28 30.3	17 10.7
10 M	17 10 36	18 24 6	19 28 52	26 28 10	22 18.8	11 56.6	29 6.0	12 15.5	10 41.5	14 53.5	14 45.3	28 32.5	17 12.1
11 Tu	17 14 33	19 21 27	3♈31 25	10♈38 30	22 19.3	13 12.7	0♋19.6	12 44.1	10 34.9	14 49.8	14 42.8	28 34.7	17 13.5
12 W	17 18 30	20 18 47	17 49 11	25 3 8	22 20.6	14 25.7	1 33.2	13 12.9	10 28.2	14 46.1	14 40.4	28 36.9	17 14.9
13 Th	17 22 26	21 16 7	2♉19 58	9♉39 9	22 22.0	15 35.6	2 46.7	13 41.8	10 21.4	14 42.2	14 37.9	28 39.1	17 16.3
14 F	17 26 23	22 13 27	17 0 5	24 22 4	22R 22.8	16 42.2	4 0.3	14 11.0	10 14.5	14 38.4	14 35.5	28 41.4	17 17.7
15 Sa	17 30 19	23 10 46	1♊44 19	9♊ 6 0	22 22.7	17 45.6	5 13.9	14 40.4	10 7.6	14 34.4	14 33.1	28 43.6	17 19.1
16 Su	17 34 16	24 8 4	16 26 16	23 44 12	22 21.0	18 45.6	6 27.5	15 10.0	10 0.5	14 30.5	14 30.6	28 45.8	17 20.5
17 M	17 38 12	25 5 23	0♋59 0	8♋ 9 52	22 17.8	19 42.3	7 41.1	15 39.7	9 53.4	14 26.5	14 28.2	28 48.1	17 21.8
18 Tu	17 42 9	26 2 40	15 16 6	22 17 7	22 13.3	20 35.3	8 54.6	16 9.7	9 46.2	14 22.4	14 25.8	28 50.3	17 23.2
19 W	17 46 6	26 59 57	29 12 28	6♌ 1 51	22 8.1	21 24.8	10 8.2	16 39.8	9 38.9	14 18.3	14 23.4	28 52.5	17 24.6
20 Th	17 50 2	27 57 14	12♌45 4	19 22 7	22 2.8	22 10.6	11 21.7	17 10.2	9 31.5	14 14.2	14 21.0	28 54.8	17 26.0
21 F	17 53 59	28 54 29	25 53 4	2♍18 9	21 58.0	22 52.5	12 35.3	17 40.7	9 24.1	14 10.0	14 18.7	28 57.0	17 27.4
22 Sa	17 57 55	29 51 44	8♍37 42	14 52 8	21 54.5	23 30.5	13 48.8	18 11.4	9 16.7	14 5.9	14 16.3	28 59.2	17 28.7
23 Su	18 1 52	0♋48 58	21 1 55	27 7 37	21D 52.5	24 4.4	15 2.3	18 42.2	9 9.2	14 1.6	14 14.0	29 1.5	17 30.1
24 M	18 5 48	1 46 12	3♎ 9 49	9♎ 9 7	21 51.9	24 34.1	16 15.8	19 13.2	9 1.6	13 57.4	14 11.7	29 3.7	17 31.5
25 Tu	18 9 45	2 43 25	15 6 10	21 1 36	21 52.7	24 59.6	17 29.3	19 44.4	8 54.0	13 53.1	14 9.4	29 5.9	17 32.8
26 W	18 13 41	3 40 38	26 56 3	2♏50 9	21 54.1	25 20.8	18 42.8	20 15.8	8 46.4	13 48.8	14 7.1	29 8.2	17 34.2
27 Th	18 17 38	4 37 50	8♏44 28	14 39 36	21 55.5	25 37.4	19 56.2	20 47.3	8 38.8	13 44.5	14 4.8	29 10.4	17 35.5
28 F	18 21 35	5 35 1	20 36 4	26 34 22	21R 56.3	25 49.5	21 9.7	21 19.0	8 31.1	13 40.1	14 2.6	29 12.6	17 36.8
29 Sa	18 25 31	6 32 13	2♐34 58	8♐38 15	21 55.7	25 57.0	22 23.1	21 50.8	8 23.4	13 35.8	14 0.3	29 14.8	17 38.2
30 Su	18 29 28	7 29 24	14 44 33	20 54 8	21 53.2	25R 59.9	23 36.6	22 22.8	8 15.8	13 31.4	13 58.1	29 17.1	17 39.5

Astro Data	Planet Ingress	Last Aspect	☽ Ingress	Last Aspect	☽ Ingress	☽ Phases & Eclipses	Astro Data
Dy Hr Mn	Dy Hr Mn	Dy Hr Mn	Dy Hr Mn	Dy Hr Mn	Dy Hr Mn	Dy Hr Mn	1 MAY 1901
♄⊼♇ 2 16:35	☿ ♉ 3 13:58	2 12:35 ☿ ☍	♏ 2 16:44	31 6:28 ♄ ⚹	♐ 1 11:44	3 18:19 ○ 12♏36	Julian Day # 486
☽0N 13 16:21	♂ ♍ 11 6:05	5 1:31 ♂ □	♐ 5 5:27	3 19:28 ♆ ☍	♑ 3 22:43	3 18:31 ◐ A 1.043	Delta T -1.0 sec
☽0S 26 12:19	☿ ♊ 17 20:08	7 14:35 ♂ △	♑ 7 16:54	5 3:45 ♄ ☌	♒ 6 7:30	11 14:38 ☽ 20♒11	SVP 06♓38'02"
	♀ ♊ 17 7:34	9 7:33 ♀ △	♒ 10 1:58	8 11:13 ♆ △	♓ 8 13:55	18 5:38 ● 26♉34	Obliquity 23°27'02"
☽0N 9 23:22	☉ ♊ 21 19:05	12 3:38 ♆ △	♓ 12 7:55	10 15:35 ♆ □	♈ 10 18:01	18 5:33:48 ◐ T 6'29"	⚷ Chiron 5♑15.3R
♄⊻♅ 15 21:36		14 6:47 ♆ □	♈ 14 10:43	12 17:56 ♆ ⚹	♉ 12 20:10	25 5:40 ☽ 3♍18	☽ Mean ☊ 23♏28.7
☽0S 22 20:34	☿ ♋ 1 23:35	16 7:34 ♆ ⚹	♉ 16 11:17	13 23:29 ☿ ⚹	♊ 14 21:10		
☿ R 30 2:52	♀ ♋ 10 17:37	18 5:38 ☉ ☌	♊ 18 11:07	16 20:22 ♆ ☌	♋ 16 22:22	2 9:53 ○ 11♐09	1 JUNE 1901
	☉ ♋ 22 3:28	20 8:24 ♆ ☌	♋ 20 12:03	18 9:40 ☿ ☌	♌ 19 1:23	9 22:00 ☽ 18♓19	Julian Day # 517
		21 15:00 ♄ ☍	♌ 22 15:47	21 6:05 ☉ ⚹	♍ 21 7:40	16 13:33 ● 24♊40	Delta T -0.9 sec
		24 19:25 ♆ ⚹	♍ 24 23:18	23 15:49 ♆ □	♎ 23 17:42	23 20:59 ☽ 1♎39	SVP 06♓37'58"
		27 6:23 ♆ □	♎ 27 10:18	26 4:29 ♆ △	♏ 26 6:14		Obliquity 23°27'01"
		29 19:20 ♆ △	♏ 29 23:07	28 10:38 ☿ △	♐ 28 18:51		⚷ Chiron 3♑57.0R
							☽ Mean ☊ 21♏50.2

JULY 1901 LONGITUDE

Day	Sid.Time	☉	0 hr ☽	Noon ☽	True ☊	☿	♀	♂	♃	♄	♅	♆	♇
1 M	18 33 24	8♋26 35	27♐ 7 15	3♑24 2	21♏48.8	25♋58.1	24♋50.0	22♍54.9	8♑ 8.1	13♑27.0	13♐56.0	29♊19.3	17♊40.8
2 Tu	18 37 21	9 23 45	9♑44 35	16 8 54	21R 42.4	25R 51.8	26 3.4	23 27.2	8R 0.4	13R 22.6	13R 53.8	29 21.5	17 42.1
3 W	18 41 17	10 20 56	22 37 0	29 8 46	21 34.7	25 40.9	27 16.8	23 59.6	7 52.7	13 18.2	13 51.7	29 23.7	17 43.4
4 Th	18 45 14	11 18 6	5♒44 6	12♒22 49	21 26.3	25 25.6	28 30.2	24 32.2	7 45.0	13 13.8	13 49.6	29 25.9	17 44.7
5 F	18 49 10	12 15 17	19 4 47	25 49 46	21 18.3	25 6.1	29 43.6	25 4.9	7 37.4	13 9.4	13 47.5	29 28.1	17 46.0
6 Sa	18 53 7	13 12 28	2♓37 36	9♓28 5	21 11.3	24 42.6	0♌57.0	25 37.8	7 29.7	13 5.0	13 45.5	29 30.3	17 47.3
7 Su	18 57 4	14 9 39	16 21 2	23 16 18	21 6.2	24 15.5	2 10.3	26 10.8	7 22.1	13 0.6	13 43.4	29 32.5	17 48.6
8 M	19 1 0	15 6 51	0♈13 45	7♈13 13	21 3.2	23 45.1	3 23.7	26 43.9	7 14.5	12 56.2	13 41.5	29 34.6	17 49.9
9 Tu	19 4 57	16 4 3	14 14 36	21 17 47	21D 2.2	23 11.8	4 37.0	27 17.2	7 7.0	12 51.7	13 39.5	29 36.8	17 51.1
10 W	19 8 53	17 1 15	28 22 38	5♉28 59	21 2.6	22 36.1	5 50.3	27 50.6	6 59.5	12 47.3	13 37.6	29 39.0	17 52.4
11 Th	19 12 50	17 58 28	12♉36 39	19 45 24	21R 3.3	21 58.7	7 3.7	28 24.2	6 52.0	12 42.9	13 35.7	29 41.1	17 53.6
12 F	19 16 46	18 55 41	26 54 55	4♊ 4 52	21 3.4	21 20.1	8 17.0	28 57.9	6 44.6	12 38.5	13 33.8	29 43.3	17 54.8
13 Sa	19 20 43	19 52 56	11♊14 48	18 24 15	21 1.8	20 41.0	9 30.3	29 31.7	6 37.3	12 34.2	13 32.0	29 45.4	17 56.0
14 Su	19 24 39	20 50 10	25 32 38	2♋39 23	20 57.9	20 1.9	10 43.6	0♎ 5.7	6 30.0	12 29.8	13 30.2	29 47.5	17 57.3
15 M	19 28 36	21 47 25	9♋43 54	16 45 31	20 51.4	19 23.7	11 56.9	0 39.8	6 22.8	12 25.5	13 28.4	29 49.6	17 58.5
16 Tu	19 32 33	22 44 41	23 43 42	0♌37 52	20 42.8	18 47.0	13 10.2	1 14.0	6 15.7	12 21.2	13 26.7	29 51.7	17 59.6
17 W	19 36 29	23 41 57	7♌27 34	14 12 24	20 32.8	18 12.4	14 23.5	1 48.4	6 8.6	12 16.9	13 25.0	29 53.8	18 0.8
18 Th	19 40 26	24 39 13	20 52 7	27 26 32	20 22.4	17 40.6	15 36.7	2 22.9	6 1.6	12 12.6	13 23.3	29 55.9	18 2.0
19 F	19 44 22	25 36 29	3♍55 36	10♍19 25	20 12.7	17 12.2	16 50.0	2 57.5	5 54.8	12 8.3	13 21.7	29 58.0	18 3.1
20 Sa	19 48 19	26 33 46	16 38 8	22 52 3	20 4.7	16 47.6	18 3.2	3 32.2	5 48.0	12 4.1	13 20.1	0♋ 0.0	18 4.3
21 Su	19 52 15	27 31 3	29 1 33	5♎ 7 5	19 58.8	16 27.5	19 16.4	4 7.1	5 41.3	11 59.9	13 18.6	0 2.0	18 5.4
22 M	19 56 12	28 28 20	11♎ 9 11	17 8 25	19 55.3	16 12.1	20 29.6	4 42.1	5 34.7	11 55.8	13 17.1	0 4.1	18 6.5
23 Tu	20 0 8	29 25 38	23 5 24	29 0 48	19D 53.8	16 1.9	21 42.8	5 17.2	5 28.2	11 51.7	13 15.6	0 6.1	18 7.6
24 W	20 4 5	0♌22 56	4♏55 17	10♏49 31	19 53.7	15D 57.1	22 56.0	5 52.4	5 21.9	11 47.6	13 14.2	0 8.1	18 8.7
25 Th	20 8 2	1 20 14	16 44 12	22 39 59	19R 54.1	15 58.0	24 9.1	6 27.8	5 15.6	11 43.5	13 12.8	0 10.0	18 9.8
26 F	20 11 58	2 17 33	28 37 32	4♐37 26	19 53.8	16 4.8	25 22.2	7 3.2	5 9.5	11 39.5	13 11.5	0 12.0	18 10.8
27 Sa	20 15 55	3 14 52	10♐40 16	16 46 34	19 52.0	16 17.5	26 35.4	7 38.8	5 3.5	11 35.6	13 10.2	0 14.0	18 11.9
28 Su	20 19 51	4 12 12	22 56 46	29 11 16	19 47.9	16 36.4	27 48.4	8 14.5	4 57.6	11 31.7	13 8.9	0 15.9	18 12.9
29 M	20 23 48	5 9 32	5♑30 21	11♑54 13	19 41.3	17 1.4	29 1.5	8 50.3	4 51.9	11 27.8	13 7.7	0 17.8	18 13.9
30 Tu	20 27 44	6 6 54	18 22 58	24 56 37	19 32.3	17 32.6	0♍14.6	9 26.2	4 46.3	11 24.0	13 6.6	0 19.7	18 14.9
31 W	20 31 41	7 4 15	1♒35 3	8♒18 3	19 21.4	18 9.9	1 27.6	10 2.2	4 40.8	11 20.2	13 5.4	0 21.6	18 15.9

AUGUST 1901 LONGITUDE

Day	Sid.Time	☉	0 hr ☽	Noon ☽	True ☊	☿	♀	♂	♃	♄	♅	♆	♇
1 Th	20 35 37	8♌ 1 38	15♒ 5 19	21♒56 28	19♏ 9.6	18♋53.3	2♍40.6	10♎38.3	4♑35.5	11♑16.5	13♐ 4.4	0♋23.4	18♊16.9
2 F	20 39 34	8 59 1	28 51 3	5♓48 35	18R 58.1	19 42.8	3 53.6	11 14.6	4R 30.3	11R 12.9	13R 3.3	0 25.3	18 17.8
3 Sa	20 43 31	9 56 26	12♓48 33	19 50 25	18 48.0	20 38.2	5 6.6	11 50.9	4 25.2	11 9.3	13 2.3	0 27.1	18 18.8
4 Su	20 47 27	10 53 51	26 53 43	3♈57 59	18 40.3	21 39.5	6 19.6	12 27.4	4 20.4	11 5.7	13 1.4	0 28.9	18 19.7
5 M	20 51 24	11 51 18	11♈ 2 49	18 7 52	18 35.3	22 46.6	7 32.5	13 3.9	4 15.6	11 2.2	13 0.5	0 30.7	18 20.6
6 Tu	20 55 20	12 48 46	25 12 52	2♉17 35	18 32.8	23 59.1	8 45.4	13 40.6	4 11.0	10 58.8	12 59.6	0 32.5	18 21.5
7 W	20 59 17	13 46 15	9♉21 50	16 25 30	18 32.1	25 17.1	9 58.3	14 17.3	4 6.6	10 55.5	12 58.8	0 34.2	18 22.3
8 Th	21 3 13	14 43 46	23 28 28	0♊30 37	18 32.1	26 40.3	11 11.2	14 54.2	4 2.4	10 52.2	12 58.1	0 35.9	18 23.2
9 F	21 7 10	15 41 19	7♊31 53	14 32 7	18 31.4	28 8.4	12 24.1	15 31.2	3 58.3	10 48.9	12 57.4	0 37.6	18 24.0
10 Sa	21 11 6	16 38 52	21 31 10	28 28 50	18 28.9	29 41.1	13 36.9	16 8.3	3 54.3	10 45.8	12 56.7	0 39.3	18 24.9
11 Su	21 15 3	17 36 27	5♋24 53	12♋19 4	18 23.7	1♌18.2	14 49.8	16 45.5	3 50.6	10 42.7	12 56.1	0 41.0	18 25.7
12 M	21 19 0	18 34 4	19 11 2	26 0 29	18 15.7	2 59.4	16 2.6	17 22.8	3 47.0	10 39.7	12 55.6	0 42.6	18 26.5
13 Tu	21 22 56	19 31 41	2♌47 3	9♌30 24	18 5.2	4 44.2	17 15.4	18 0.2	3 43.6	10 36.7	12 55.1	0 44.3	18 27.2
14 W	21 26 53	20 29 20	16 10 13	22 46 12	17 52.9	6 32.3	18 28.2	18 37.7	3 40.4	10 33.8	12 54.6	0 45.8	18 28.0
15 Th	21 30 49	21 27 1	29 18 9	5♍45 54	17 40.2	8 23.3	19 40.9	19 15.3	3 37.3	10 31.0	12 54.2	0 47.4	18 28.7
16 F	21 34 46	22 24 42	12♍ 9 21	18 28 31	17 28.1	10 16.8	20 53.7	19 53.0	3 34.4	10 28.3	12 53.8	0 49.0	18 29.4
17 Sa	21 38 42	23 22 24	24 43 28	0♎54 24	17 17.8	12 12.3	22 6.4	20 30.8	3 31.7	10 25.7	12 53.5	0 50.5	18 30.1
18 Su	21 42 39	24 20 8	7♎ 1 33	13 5 17	17 9.9	14 9.6	23 19.1	21 8.7	3 29.2	10 23.1	12 53.2	0 52.0	18 30.8
19 M	21 46 35	25 17 53	19 6 0	25 4 11	17 4.7	16 8.2	24 31.7	21 46.7	3 26.9	10 20.6	12 53.0	0 53.5	18 31.5
20 Tu	21 50 32	26 15 39	1♏ 0 21	6♏55 7	17 2.0	18 7.7	25 44.4	22 24.9	3 24.7	10 18.2	12 52.9	0 54.9	18 32.1
21 W	21 54 29	27 13 27	12 49 5	18 42 55	17D 1.2	20 7.8	26 57.0	23 3.1	3 22.7	10 15.9	12 52.8	0 56.3	18 32.7
22 Th	21 58 25	28 11 15	24 37 18	0♐32 54	17R 1.2	22 8.2	28 9.5	23 41.4	3 21.0	10 13.6	12D 52.7	0 57.7	18 33.3
23 F	22 2 22	29 9 5	6♐30 26	12 30 35	17 1.0	24 8.7	29 22.1	24 19.8	3 19.4	10 11.5	12 52.7	0 59.1	18 33.9
24 Sa	22 6 18	0♍ 6 56	18 33 59	24 41 17	16 59.7	26 8.9	0♎34.6	24 58.2	3 18.0	10 9.4	12 52.8	1 0.4	18 34.5
25 Su	22 10 15	1 4 48	0♑53 2	7♑ 9 45	16 56.3	28 8.7	1 47.1	25 36.8	3 16.8	10 7.4	12 52.9	1 1.7	18 35.0
26 M	22 14 11	2 2 41	13 31 52	19 59 42	16 50.5	0♍ 7.9	2 59.6	26 15.5	3 15.8	10 5.5	12 53.0	1 3.0	18 35.5
27 Tu	22 18 8	3 0 36	26 33 29	3♒13 17	16 42.3	2 6.4	4 12.0	26 54.3	3 14.9	10 3.7	12 53.2	1 4.3	18 36.0
28 W	22 22 4	3 58 32	9♒59 4	16 50 37	16 32.3	4 4.0	5 24.4	27 33.1	3 14.3	10 2.0	12 53.5	1 5.5	18 36.5
29 Th	22 26 1	4 56 30	23 47 36	0♓49 32	16 21.2	6 0.7	6 36.8	28 12.1	3 13.8	10 0.4	12 53.8	1 6.7	18 37.0
30 F	22 29 58	5 54 29	7♓55 49	15 5 45	16 10.4	7 56.3	7 49.1	28 51.1	3D 13.6	9 58.9	12 54.1	1 7.9	18 37.4
31 Sa	22 33 54	6 52 29	22 18 32	29 33 23	16 0.9	9 50.8	9 1.4	29 30.2	3 13.5	9 57.4	12 54.5	1 9.1	18 37.8

Astro Data	Planet Ingress	Last Aspect	☽ Ingress	Last Aspect	☽ Ingress	☽ Phases & Eclipses	Astro Data
Dy Hr Mn	Dy Hr Mn	Dy Hr Mn	Dy Hr Mn	Dy Hr Mn	Dy Hr Mn	Dy Hr Mn	1 JULY 1901
☽0N 7 5:32	♀ ♌ 5 5:22	1 4:14 ♆ ☍	♑ 1 5:31	1 5:37 ♇ △	♓ 2 1:59	1 23:18 ○ 9♑22	Julian Day # 547
♂0S 15 5:26	♂ ♎ 13 19:59	3 9:28 ♀ ☍	♒ 3 13:34	3 14:23 ☿ △	♈ 4 5:16	9 3:20 ☽ 16♈12	Delta T -0.8 sec
☽0S 20 6:01	♆ ♋ 19 23:59	5 18:29 ♆ △	♓ 5 19:22	5 21:43 ☿ □	♉ 6 8:07	15 22:10 ● 22♋40	SVP 06♓37'53"
☿ D 24 8:17	☉ ♌ 23 14:24	7 22:53 ♆ □	♈ 7 23:36	8 6:04 ☿ ⚹	♊ 8 11:08	23 13:58 ☽ 29♎59	Obliquity 23°27'01"
	♀ ♍ 29 19:13	10 2:09 ♆ ⚹	♉ 10 2:45	9 18:39 ♇ ☌	♋ 10 14:38	31 10:34 ○ 7♒30	⚷ Chiron 2♑03.3R
☽0N 3 12:19		12 3:34 ♂ △	♊ 12 5:10	11 20:41 ♂ □	♌ 12 19:04		☽ Mean ☊ 20♏14.9
☽0S 16 15:19	☿ ♌ 10 4:45	14 7:11 ♆ ☌	♋ 14 7:31	14 8:27 ☉ ☌	♍ 15 1:17	7 8:02 ☽ 14♉06	
♅ D 22 13:55	☉ ♍ 23 21:08	15 22:10 ☉ ☌	♌ 16 10:54	16 18:25 ♀ ☌	♎ 17 10:14	14 8:27 ● 20♌50	1 AUGUST 1901
♀0S 25 3:21	♀ ♎ 23 12:33	18 16:38 ♆ ⚹	♍ 18 16:43	19 13:34 ☉ ⚹	♏ 19 21:58	22 7:52 ☽ 28♏30	Julian Day # 578
☽0N 30 20:41	☿ ♍ 25 22:24	20 20:48 ☉ ⚹	♎ 21 1:55	22 7:59 ♀ ⚹	♐ 22 10:54	29 20:21 ○ 5♓46	Delta T -0.7 sec
♃ D 30 21:46	♂ ♏ 31 18:13	23 13:58 ☉ □	♏ 23 14:00	24 17:42 ☿ △	♑ 24 22:18		SVP 06♓37'48"
		25 16:42 ♀ □	♐ 26 2:45	27 0:40 ♂ □	♒ 27 6:13		Obliquity 23°27'01"
		28 10:22 ♀ △	♑ 28 13:33	29 7:54 ♂ △	♓ 29 10:36		⚷ Chiron 0♑18.3R
		29 22:23 ☿ ☍	♒ 30 21:09	30 17:53 ♇ □	♈ 31 12:44		☽ Mean ☊ 18♏36.4

LONGITUDE — SEPTEMBER 1901

Day	Sid.Time	☉	0 hr ☽	Noon ☽	True ☊	☿	♀	♂	♃	♄	♅	♆	♇
1 Su	22 37 51	7♍50 32	6♈49 27	14♈ 5 58	15♏53.6	11♍44.2	10♎13.7	0♏ 9.5	3♑13.6	9♑56.1	12♐55.0	1♋10.2	18♊38.2
2 M	22 41 47	8 48 36	21 22 11	28 37 27	15R 49.0	13 36.5	11 25.9	0 48.8	3 13.9	9R 54.8	12 55.5	1 11.3	18 38.6
3 Tu	22 45 44	9 46 42	5♉51 12	13♉ 3 0	15D 46.9	15 27.5	12 38.1	1 28.2	3 14.4	9 53.6	12 56.0	1 12.3	18 39.0
4 W	22 49 40	10 44 50	20 12 28	27 19 22	15 46.6	17 17.4	13 50.3	2 7.6	3 15.1	9 52.6	12 56.7	1 13.4	18 39.3
5 Th	22 53 37	11 43 0	4♊23 30	11♊24 47	15R 47.1	19 6.0	15 2.4	2 47.2	3 15.9	9 51.6	12 57.3	1 14.4	18 39.6
6 F	22 57 33	12 41 12	18 23 10	25 18 37	15 47.1	20 53.5	16 14.5	3 26.9	3 17.0	9 50.7	12 58.0	1 15.3	18 39.9
7 Sa	23 1 30	13 39 27	2♋11 8	9♋ 0 45	15 45.6	22 39.8	17 26.6	4 6.6	3 18.2	9 49.9	12 58.8	1 16.3	18 40.2
8 Su	23 5 26	14 37 43	15 47 27	22 31 15	15 41.9	24 24.9	18 38.7	4 46.5	3 19.7	9 49.2	12 59.6	1 17.2	18 40.4
9 M	23 9 23	15 36 2	29 12 6	5♌50 0	15 35.7	26 8.8	19 50.7	5 26.4	3 21.3	9 48.6	13 0.5	1 18.1	18 40.7
10 Tu	23 13 20	16 34 22	12♌24 52	18 56 38	15 27.3	27 51.6	21 2.7	6 6.5	3 23.1	9 48.1	13 1.4	1 18.9	18 40.9
11 W	23 17 16	17 32 44	25 25 14	1♍50 37	15 17.5	29 33.3	22 14.7	6 46.6	3 25.1	9 47.7	13 2.4	1 19.7	18 41.0
12 Th	23 21 13	18 31 8	8♍12 42	14 31 29	15 7.1	1♎13.9	23 26.6	7 26.8	3 27.3	9 47.4	13 3.4	1 20.5	18 41.2
13 F	23 25 9	19 29 35	20 46 57	26 59 9	14 57.2	2 53.3	24 38.5	8 7.1	3 29.7	9 47.2	13 4.4	1 21.3	18 41.4
14 Sa	23 29 6	20 28 3	3♎ 8 9	9♎14 7	14 48.8	4 31.7	25 50.3	8 47.5	3 32.2	9D 47.1	13 5.6	1 22.0	18 41.5
15 Su	23 33 2	21 26 32	15 17 13	21 17 43	14 42.5	6 8.9	27 2.2	9 28.0	3 35.0	9 47.1	13 6.7	1 22.7	18 41.6
16 M	23 36 59	22 25 4	27 15 55	3♏12 11	14 38.5	7 45.2	28 13.9	10 8.5	3 37.9	9 47.2	13 8.0	1 23.4	18 41.6
17 Tu	23 40 55	23 23 37	9♏ 6 55	15 0 36	14D 36.8	9 20.4	29 25.7	10 49.2	3 41.0	9 47.4	13 9.2	1 24.0	18 41.7
18 W	23 44 52	24 22 12	20 53 45	26 46 55	14 36.8	10 54.5	0♏37.4	11 29.9	3 44.3	9 47.7	13 10.5	1 24.6	18 41.7
19 Th	23 48 49	25 20 49	2♐40 42	8♐35 43	14 37.9	12 27.7	1 49.0	12 10.7	3 47.8	9 48.1	13 11.9	1 25.1	18R 41.7
20 F	23 52 45	26 19 28	14 32 37	20 32 3	14 39.2	13 59.8	3 0.7	12 51.6	3 51.4	9 48.6	13 13.3	1 25.7	18 41.7
21 Sa	23 56 42	27 18 8	26 34 41	2♑41 10	14R 39.8	15 30.9	4 12.2	13 32.6	3 55.3	9 49.2	13 14.8	1 26.2	18 41.7
22 Su	0 0 38	28 16 50	8♑52 8	15 8 11	14 39.1	17 1.0	5 23.8	14 13.7	3 59.3	9 49.8	13 16.3	1 26.6	18 41.6
23 M	0 4 35	29 15 34	21 29 51	27 57 36	14 36.7	18 30.1	6 35.3	14 54.8	4 3.5	9 50.6	13 17.9	1 27.0	18 41.6
24 Tu	0 8 31	0♎14 19	4♒31 47	11♒12 41	14 32.5	19 58.1	7 46.7	15 36.0	4 7.8	9 51.5	13 19.5	1 27.4	18 41.5
25 W	0 12 28	1 13 6	18 0 24	24 54 54	14 26.8	21 25.1	8 58.1	16 17.3	4 12.3	9 52.5	13 21.1	1 27.8	18 41.4
26 Th	0 16 24	2 11 55	1♓56 0	9♓ 3 18	14 20.2	22 51.1	10 9.4	16 58.7	4 17.0	9 53.6	13 22.8	1 28.1	18 41.2
27 F	0 20 21	3 10 46	16 16 15	23 34 10	14 13.6	24 16.1	11 20.7	17 40.2	4 21.9	9 54.7	13 24.6	1 28.4	18 41.0
28 Sa	0 24 18	4 9 39	0♈56 11	8♈21 20	14 7.8	25 39.9	12 31.9	18 21.7	4 26.9	9 56.0	13 26.4	1 28.7	18 40.9
29 Su	0 28 14	5 8 33	15 48 36	23 16 54	14 3.5	27 2.7	13 43.1	19 3.3	4 32.1	9 57.4	13 28.2	1 28.9	18 40.7
30 M	0 32 11	6 7 30	0♉45 12	8♉12 30	14D 1.0	28 24.3	14 54.2	19 45.0	4 37.5	9 58.8	13 30.1	1 29.1	18 40.4

LONGITUDE — OCTOBER 1901

Day	Sid.Time	☉	0 hr ☽	Noon ☽	True ☊	☿	♀	♂	♃	♄	♅	♆	♇
1 Tu	0 36 7	7♎ 6 29	15♉37 51	23♉ 0 29	14♏ 0.4	29♎44.8	16♏ 5.3	20♏26.8	4♑43.0	10♑ 0.4	13♐32.0	1♋29.3	18♊40.2
2 W	0 40 4	8 5 30	0♊19 41	7♊34 57	14 1.1	1♏ 4.0	17 16.3	21 8.7	4 48.7	10 2.0	13 34.0	1 29.4	18R 39.9
3 Th	0 44 0	9 4 34	14 45 51	21 52 7	14 2.6	2 21.9	18 27.3	21 50.6	4 54.6	10 3.8	13 36.0	1 29.5	18 39.6
4 F	0 47 57	10 3 40	28 53 36	5♋50 13	14R 3.8	3 38.6	19 38.2	22 32.6	5 0.6	10 5.6	13 38.1	1 29.5	18 39.3
5 Sa	0 51 53	11 2 48	12♋42 1	19 29 6	14 4.3	4 53.8	20 49.1	23 14.7	5 6.8	10 7.6	13 40.2	1R 29.6	18 39.0
6 Su	0 55 50	12 1 58	26 11 34	2♌49 38	14 3.4	6 7.5	21 59.9	23 56.9	5 13.1	10 9.6	13 42.3	1 29.6	18 38.6
7 M	0 59 46	13 1 11	9♌23 29	15 53 20	14 1.1	7 19.6	23 10.6	24 39.2	5 19.6	10 11.8	13 44.5	1 29.5	18 38.3
8 Tu	1 3 43	14 0 26	22 19 22	28 41 49	13 57.4	8 30.0	24 21.3	25 21.5	5 26.2	10 14.0	13 46.8	1 29.4	18 37.9
9 W	1 7 40	14 59 44	5♍ 0 53	11♍16 45	13 52.8	9 38.5	25 32.0	26 3.9	5 33.0	10 16.3	13 49.0	1 29.3	18 37.4
10 Th	1 11 36	15 59 3	17 29 36	23 39 37	13 47.9	10 45.1	26 42.6	26 46.4	5 40.0	10 18.7	13 51.4	1 29.2	18 37.0
11 F	1 15 33	16 58 25	29 46 59	5♎51 52	13 43.3	11 49.5	27 53.1	27 29.0	5 47.1	10 21.2	13 53.7	1 29.0	18 36.6
12 Sa	1 19 29	17 57 49	11♎54 27	17 54 56	13 39.5	12 51.6	29 3.5	28 11.6	5 54.3	10 23.8	13 56.1	1 28.8	18 36.1
13 Su	1 23 26	18 57 15	23 53 31	29 50 27	13 36.7	13 51.1	0♐13.9	28 54.3	6 1.7	10 26.5	13 58.5	1 28.6	18 35.6
14 M	1 27 22	19 56 43	5♏45 57	11♏40 20	13D 35.3	14 47.8	1 24.3	29 37.1	6 9.2	10 29.3	14 1.0	1 28.3	18 35.1
15 Tu	1 31 19	20 56 13	17 33 53	23 26 58	13 35.1	15 41.4	2 34.5	0♐20.0	6 16.9	10 32.2	14 3.5	1 28.0	18 34.5
16 W	1 35 15	21 55 45	29 19 58	5♐13 16	13 35.9	16 31.7	3 44.7	1 3.0	6 24.7	10 35.1	14 6.1	1 27.6	18 34.0
17 Th	1 39 12	22 55 19	11♐ 7 21	17 2 41	13 37.4	17 18.2	4 54.8	1 46.0	6 32.7	10 38.2	14 8.7	1 27.2	18 33.4
18 F	1 43 9	23 54 55	22 59 46	28 59 10	13 39.0	18 0.7	6 4.9	2 29.1	6 40.8	10 41.3	14 11.3	1 26.8	18 32.8
19 Sa	1 47 5	24 54 32	5♑ 1 25	11♑ 7 6	13 40.5	18 38.6	7 14.9	3 12.3	6 49.0	10 44.5	14 14.0	1 26.4	18 32.2
20 Su	1 51 2	25 54 12	17 16 48	23 31 5	13R 41.5	19 11.6	8 24.7	3 55.5	6 57.4	10 47.9	14 16.7	1 25.9	18 31.6
21 M	1 54 58	26 53 53	29 50 30	6♒15 34	13 41.6	19 39.1	9 34.5	4 38.8	7 5.9	10 51.3	14 19.4	1 25.4	18 30.9
22 Tu	1 58 55	27 53 35	12♒46 44	19 24 25	13 41.1	20 0.5	10 44.2	5 22.2	7 14.5	10 54.7	14 22.2	1 24.9	18 30.3
23 W	2 2 51	28 53 20	26 8 54	3♓ 0 21	13 39.8	20 15.5	11 53.8	6 5.7	7 23.3	10 58.3	14 25.0	1 24.3	18 29.6
24 Th	2 6 48	29 53 6	9♓58 50	17 4 11	13 38.2	20R 23.2	13 3.4	6 49.2	7 32.2	11 2.0	14 27.8	1 23.7	18 28.9
25 F	2 10 44	0♏52 53	24 16 10	1♈34 16	13 36.5	20 23.2	14 12.8	7 32.8	7 41.2	11 5.7	14 30.7	1 23.1	18 28.1
26 Sa	2 14 41	1 52 43	8♈57 51	16 26 4	13 35.0	20 15.0	15 22.1	8 16.4	7 50.3	11 9.5	14 33.6	1 22.4	18 27.4
27 Su	2 18 38	2 52 34	23 57 59	1♉32 28	13 34.0	19 58.0	16 31.3	9 0.2	7 59.6	11 13.4	14 36.5	1 21.7	18 26.7
28 M	2 22 34	3 52 28	9♉ 8 20	16 44 23	13D 33.6	19 31.9	17 40.4	9 44.0	8 9.0	11 17.4	14 39.5	1 21.0	18 25.9
29 Tu	2 26 31	4 52 23	24 19 25	1♊52 16	13 33.7	18 56.5	18 49.4	10 27.8	8 18.5	11 21.4	14 42.5	1 20.2	18 25.1
30 W	2 30 27	5 52 20	9♊21 53	16 47 20	13 34.1	18 11.8	19 58.3	11 11.8	8 28.1	11 25.6	14 45.5	1 19.4	18 24.3
31 Th	2 34 24	6 52 20	24 7 51	1♋22 50	13 34.8	17 18.2	21 7.1	11 55.8	8 37.8	11 29.8	14 48.6	1 18.6	18 23.5

Astro Data Dy Hr Mn	Planet Ingress Dy Hr Mn	Last Aspect Dy Hr Mn	☽ Ingress Dy Hr Mn	Last Aspect Dy Hr Mn	☽ Ingress Dy Hr Mn	☽ Phases & Eclipses Dy Hr Mn	Astro Data
☽0S 12 23:11	☿ ♎ 11 6:21	1 19:30 ♇ ⚹	♉ 2 14:17	1 8:13 ♂ ☍	♊ 1 23:28	5 13:27 ☽ 12♊16	1 SEPTEMBER 1901
☿0S 12 1:46	♀ ♏ 17 11:29	3 18:23 ☿ △	♊ 4 16:32	3 6:34 ♇ ☌	♋ 4 1:54	12 21:19 ● 19♍23	Julian Day # 609
♄ D 14 14:09	☉ ♎ 23 18:09	6 4:58 ☿ □	♋ 6 20:11	5 19:45 ♂ △	♌ 6 6:52	21 1:33 ☽ 27♐22	Delta T -0.5 sec
♇ R 19 0:36		8 17:41 ☿ ⚹	♌ 9 1:26	8 6:02 ♂ □	♍ 8 14:28	28 5:36 ○ 4♈23	SVP 06♓37'45"
☽0N 27 6:38	☿ ♏ 1 4:35	10 17:30 ♀ ⚹	♍ 11 8:33	10 19:52 ♀ ⚹	♎ 11 0:26		Obliquity 23°27'02"
	♀ ♐ 12 19:15	12 21:19 ☉ ☌	♎ 13 17:52	12 13:22 ♇ △	♏ 13 12:19	4 20:52 ☽ 10♋55	⚷ Chiron 29♐31.6R
♆ R 5 6:56	♂ ♐ 14 12:48	16 2:10 ♀ ☌	♏ 16 5:31	14 19:53 ☿ ☌	♐ 16 1:22	12 13:11 ● 18♎30	☽ Mean ☊ 16♏57.9
☽0S 10 5:20	☉ ♏ 24 2:46	18 7:44 ☉ ⚹	♐ 18 18:33	18 2:01 ☉ ⚹	♑ 18 14:01	20 17:58 ☽ 26♑39	
☽0N 24 17:07		21 1:33 ☉ □	♑ 21 6:44	20 17:58 ☉ □	♒ 21 0:18	27 15:06 ○ 3♉30	1 OCTOBER 1901
☿ R 24 12:10		23 15:33 ☉ △	♒ 23 15:45	23 5:12 ☉ △	♓ 23 6:46	27 15:15 P 0.221	Julian Day # 639
		25 6:39 ☿ △	♓ 25 20:43	24 17:34 ☿ △	♈ 25 9:26		Delta T -0.4 sec
		27 3:59 ♇ □	♈ 27 22:29	26 15:13 ♇ ⚹	♉ 27 9:34		SVP 06♓37'42"
		29 19:51 ☿ ☍	♉ 29 22:47	28 15:49 ☿ ☍	♊ 29 9:01		Obliquity 23°27'02"
				30 18:38 ♀ ☍	♋ 31 9:42		⚷ Chiron 0♑02.1
							☽ Mean ☊ 15♏22.5

NOVEMBER 1901 LONGITUDE

Day	Sid.Time	☉	0 hr ☽	Noon ☽	True ☊	☿	♀	♂	♃	♄	♅	♆	♇
1 F	2 38 20	7♏52 22	8♋31 51	15♋34 37	13♏35.3	16♏16.4	22♐15.8	12♐39.8	8♑47.7	11♑34.1	14♐51.7	1♋17.8	18♊22.6
2 Sa	2 42 17	8 52 25	22 31 0	29 21 3	13 35.8	15R 7.6	23 24.3	13 24.0	8 57.7	11 38.4	14 54.8	1R 16.9	18R 21.8
3 Su	2 46 13	9 52 31	6♌ 4 52	12♌42 42	13R 35.9	13 53.4	24 32.7	14 8.2	9 7.7	11 42.9	14 57.9	1 16.0	18 20.9
4 M	2 50 10	10 52 39	19 14 50	25 41 39	13 35.9	12 35.8	25 41.0	14 52.4	9 17.9	11 47.4	15 1.1	1 15.1	18 20.1
5 Tu	2 54 7	11 52 49	2♍ 3 32	8♍20 54	13 35.8	11 17.0	26 49.2	15 36.8	9 28.2	11 52.0	15 4.3	1 14.1	18 19.2
6 W	2 58 3	12 53 1	14 34 12	20 43 51	13D 35.7	9 59.6	27 57.2	16 21.2	9 38.6	11 56.7	15 7.5	1 13.1	18 18.3
7 Th	3 2 0	13 53 16	26 50 16	2♎53 53	13 35.6	8 46.1	29 5.2	17 5.6	9 49.1	12 1.4	15 10.8	1 12.1	18 17.3
8 F	3 5 56	14 53 32	8♎55 4	14 54 12	13 35.7	7 38.8	0♑12.9	17 50.2	9 59.7	12 6.2	15 14.0	1 11.0	18 16.4
9 Sa	3 9 53	15 53 50	20 51 38	26 47 41	13 35.9	6 39.6	1 20.6	18 34.8	10 10.4	12 11.1	15 17.3	1 10.0	18 15.5
10 Su	3 13 49	16 54 10	2♏42 40	8♏36 53	13R 36.1	5 50.3	2 28.0	19 19.4	10 21.3	12 16.0	15 20.6	1 8.9	18 14.5
11 M	3 17 46	17 54 31	14 30 37	20 24 7	13 36.2	5 11.9	3 35.4	20 4.2	10 32.2	12 21.0	15 24.0	1 7.8	18 13.5
12 Tu	3 21 42	18 54 55	26 17 40	2♐11 32	13 36.1	4 45.1	4 42.5	20 48.9	10 43.2	12 26.1	15 27.3	1 6.6	18 12.5
13 W	3 25 39	19 55 20	8♐ 6 0	14 1 19	13 35.6	4D 29.9	5 49.5	21 33.8	10 54.3	12 31.3	15 30.7	1 5.4	18 11.5
14 Th	3 29 36	20 55 47	19 57 49	25 55 47	13 34.7	4 26.3	6 56.4	22 18.7	11 5.5	12 36.5	15 34.1	1 4.2	18 10.5
15 F	3 33 32	21 56 15	1♑55 33	7♑57 28	13 33.6	4 33.7	8 3.0	23 3.7	11 16.8	12 41.7	15 37.5	1 3.0	18 9.5
16 Sa	3 37 29	22 56 44	14 1 56	20 9 19	13 32.3	4 51.4	9 9.5	23 48.7	11 28.2	12 47.1	15 41.0	1 1.8	18 8.5
17 Su	3 41 25	23 57 15	26 20 2	2♒34 30	13 31.0	5 18.7	10 15.8	24 33.8	11 39.7	12 52.5	15 44.4	1 0.5	18 7.4
18 M	3 45 22	24 57 48	8♒53 11	15 16 29	13 30.0	5 54.6	11 21.8	25 19.0	11 51.2	12 57.9	15 47.9	0 59.2	18 6.4
19 Tu	3 49 18	25 58 21	21 44 49	28 18 37	13D 29.5	6 38.3	12 27.7	26 4.2	12 2.9	13 3.5	15 51.4	0 57.9	18 5.3
20 W	3 53 15	26 58 56	4♓58 12	11♓43 53	13 29.6	7 28.8	13 33.3	26 49.4	12 14.6	13 9.0	15 54.9	0 56.6	18 4.3
21 Th	3 57 11	27 59 32	18 35 53	25 34 19	13 30.3	8 25.3	14 38.7	27 34.8	12 26.4	13 14.7	15 58.4	0 55.2	18 3.2
22 F	4 1 8	29 0 9	2♈39 10	9♈50 19	13 31.4	9 27.1	15 43.9	28 20.1	12 38.3	13 20.4	16 2.0	0 53.8	18 2.1
23 Sa	4 5 5	0♐ 0 47	17 7 25	24 30 1	13 32.7	10 33.5	16 48.8	29 5.5	12 50.3	13 26.1	16 5.5	0 52.4	18 1.0
24 Su	4 9 1	1 1 27	1♉57 27	9♉28 55	13R 33.6	11 43.9	17 53.5	29 51.0	13 2.3	13 31.9	16 9.1	0 51.0	17 59.9
25 M	4 12 58	2 2 7	17 3 24	24 39 48	13 33.8	12 57.7	18 57.9	0♑36.5	13 14.5	13 37.8	16 12.6	0 49.6	17 58.8
26 Tu	4 16 54	3 2 49	2♊16 54	9♊53 26	13 33.1	14 14.3	20 2.1	1 22.1	13 26.7	13 43.7	16 16.2	0 48.1	17 57.7
27 W	4 20 51	4 3 33	17 28 10	24 59 53	13 31.3	15 33.5	21 5.9	2 7.8	13 38.9	13 49.6	16 19.8	0 46.7	17 56.6
28 Th	4 24 47	5 4 17	2♋27 27	9♋49 56	13 28.6	16 54.7	22 9.5	2 53.4	13 51.3	13 55.7	16 23.4	0 45.2	17 55.4
29 F	4 28 44	6 5 4	17 6 30	24 16 34	13 25.4	18 17.8	23 12.8	3 39.2	14 3.7	14 1.7	16 27.0	0 43.7	17 54.3
30 Sa	4 32 40	7 5 51	1♌19 42	8♌15 41	13 22.3	19 42.4	24 15.8	4 25.0	14 16.2	14 7.8	16 30.7	0 42.2	17 53.2

DECEMBER 1901 LONGITUDE

Day	Sid.Time	☉	0 hr ☽	Noon ☽	True ☊	☿	♀	♂	♃	♄	♅	♆	♇
1 Su	4 36 37	8♐ 6 40	15♌ 4 27	21♌46 9	13♏19.6	21♏ 8.3	25♑18.4	5♑10.8	14♑28.8	14♑14.0	16♐34.3	0♋40.6	17♊52.0
2 M	4 40 34	9 7 30	28 21 0	4♍49 22	13D 17.9	22 35.3	26 20.7	5 56.7	14 41.4	14 20.2	16 37.9	0R 39.1	17R 50.9
3 Tu	4 44 30	10 8 22	11♍11 44	17 28 35	13 17.4	24 3.2	27 22.7	6 42.6	14 54.1	14 26.4	16 41.6	0 37.5	17 49.7
4 W	4 48 27	11 9 15	23 40 29	29 48 2	13 18.1	25 31.8	28 24.3	7 28.6	15 6.8	14 32.7	16 45.2	0 36.0	17 48.6
5 Th	4 52 23	12 10 10	5♎51 50	11♎52 28	13 19.6	27 1.1	29 25.6	8 14.7	15 19.6	14 39.0	16 48.9	0 34.4	17 47.4
6 F	4 56 20	13 11 5	17 50 32	23 46 36	13 21.5	28 31.0	0♒26.5	9 0.7	15 32.5	14 45.4	16 52.5	0 32.8	17 46.3
7 Sa	5 0 16	14 12 2	29 41 11	5♏34 48	13 23.1	0♐ 1.4	1 27.0	9 46.9	15 45.4	14 51.8	16 56.2	0 31.2	17 45.1
8 Su	5 4 13	15 13 1	11♏27 54	17 20 56	13R 24.0	1 32.1	2 27.1	10 33.1	15 58.4	14 58.3	16 59.8	0 29.5	17 44.0
9 M	5 8 9	16 14 0	23 14 17	29 8 17	13 23.4	3 3.2	3 26.8	11 19.3	16 11.4	15 4.8	17 3.5	0 27.9	17 42.8
10 Tu	5 12 6	17 15 0	5♐ 3 15	10♐59 27	13 21.2	4 34.6	4 26.0	12 5.6	16 24.5	15 11.3	17 7.1	0 26.3	17 41.6
11 W	5 16 3	18 16 2	16 57 9	22 56 32	13 17.2	6 6.2	5 24.8	12 51.9	16 37.7	15 17.9	17 10.8	0 24.6	17 40.5
12 Th	5 19 59	19 17 4	28 57 48	5♑ 1 9	13 11.5	7 38.1	6 23.1	13 38.3	16 50.9	15 24.5	17 14.5	0 22.9	17 39.3
13 F	5 23 56	20 18 7	11♑ 6 42	17 14 38	13 4.7	9 10.1	7 20.9	14 24.7	17 4.2	15 31.1	17 18.2	0 21.3	17 38.1
14 Sa	5 27 52	21 19 10	23 25 6	29 38 16	12 57.3	10 42.3	8 18.2	15 11.1	17 17.5	15 37.8	17 21.8	0 19.6	17 37.0
15 Su	5 31 49	22 20 14	5♒54 19	12♒13 26	12 50.3	12 14.7	9 15.0	15 57.6	17 30.8	15 44.5	17 25.5	0 17.9	17 35.8
16 M	5 35 45	23 21 19	18 35 48	25 1 41	12 44.2	13 47.3	10 11.2	16 44.1	17 44.2	15 51.2	17 29.1	0 16.2	17 34.7
17 Tu	5 39 42	24 22 24	1♓31 18	8♓ 4 55	12 39.8	15 20.0	11 6.8	17 30.7	17 57.6	15 57.9	17 32.8	0 14.6	17 33.5
18 W	5 43 38	25 23 29	14 42 46	21 25 8	12D 37.4	16 52.9	12 1.9	18 17.3	18 11.1	16 4.7	17 36.4	0 12.9	17 32.4
19 Th	5 47 35	26 24 35	28 12 12	5♈ 4 12	12 36.8	18 26.0	12 56.3	19 3.9	18 24.6	16 11.5	17 40.1	0 11.2	17 31.2
20 F	5 51 32	27 25 41	12♈ 1 16	19 3 27	12 37.6	19 59.2	13 50.0	19 50.6	18 38.2	16 18.4	17 43.7	0 9.5	17 30.1
21 Sa	5 55 28	28 26 47	26 10 44	3♉22 57	12 38.9	21 32.5	14 43.0	20 37.3	18 51.8	16 25.2	17 47.3	0 7.8	17 28.9
22 Su	5 59 25	29 27 53	10♉39 50	18 0 57	12R 39.7	23 6.1	15 35.4	21 24.0	19 5.4	16 32.1	17 50.9	0 6.1	17 27.8
23 M	6 3 21	0♑29 0	25 25 40	2♊53 16	12 39.0	24 39.9	16 27.0	22 10.8	19 19.1	16 39.0	17 54.5	0 4.4	17 26.6
24 Tu	6 7 18	1 30 7	10♊22 50	17 53 20	12 36.2	26 13.8	17 17.8	22 57.6	19 32.8	16 45.9	17 58.1	0 2.7	17 25.5
25 W	6 11 14	2 31 14	25 23 39	2♋52 38	12 31.0	27 48.0	18 7.8	23 44.5	19 46.5	16 52.9	18 1.7	0 1.0	17 24.4
26 Th	6 15 11	3 32 21	10♋19 6	17 41 58	12 23.8	29 22.5	18 57.0	24 31.3	20 0.3	16 59.8	18 5.3	29♊59.3	17 23.3
27 F	6 19 7	4 33 29	25 0 12	2♌12 56	12 15.2	0♑57.1	19 45.3	25 18.2	20 14.1	17 6.8	18 8.8	29 57.6	17 22.2
28 Sa	6 23 4	5 34 37	9♌19 29	16 19 20	12 6.3	2 32.1	20 32.7	26 5.1	20 27.9	17 13.8	18 12.4	29 55.9	17 21.1
29 Su	6 27 1	6 35 45	23 12 10	29 57 51	11 58.2	4 7.3	21 19.1	26 52.1	20 41.8	17 20.8	18 15.9	29 54.2	17 20.0
30 M	6 30 57	7 36 54	6♍36 26	13♍ 8 8	11 51.8	5 42.8	22 4.6	27 39.1	20 55.6	17 27.9	18 19.4	29 52.5	17 18.9
31 Tu	6 34 54	8 38 3	19 33 18	25 52 23	11 47.5	7 18.6	22 49.1	28 26.1	21 9.5	17 34.9	18 22.9	29 50.8	17 17.8

Astro Data Dy Hr Mn	Planet Ingress Dy Hr Mn	Last Aspect Dy Hr Mn	☽ Ingress Dy Hr Mn	Last Aspect Dy Hr Mn	☽ Ingress Dy Hr Mn	☽ Phases & Eclipses Dy Hr Mn	Astro Data
☽0S 6 10:46	♀ ♑ 7 19:25	1 12:13 ☿ △	♌ 2 13:09	1 12:11 ☿ □	♍ 2 3:02	3 7:24 ☽ 10♌11	1 NOVEMBER 1901
☿ D 13 19:42	☉ ♐ 22 23:41	4 13:09 ♀ △	♍ 4 20:06	4 10:06 ♀ △	♎ 4 12:24	11 7:34 ● 18♏14	Julian Day # 670
☽0N 21 2:40	♂ ♑ 24 4:44	7 4:54 ♀ □	♎ 7 6:15	5 23:51 ♇ △	♏ 7 0:38	11 7:28:21 ☌ A 11'01"	Delta T -0.3 sec
♃☌♄ 28 16:29		8 19:06 ♂ ⚹	♏ 9 18:30	8 9:22 ♃ ⚹	♐ 9 13:45	19 8:23 ☽ 26♒20	SVP 06♓37'39"
	♀ ♒ 5 13:32	11 7:34 ☉ ☌	♐ 12 7:32	11 2:53 ☉ ☌	♑ 12 2:04	26 1:18 ○ 3♊06	Obliquity 23°27'01"
☽0S 3 17:21	☿ ♐ 6 23:38	14 5:03 ♂ ☌	♑ 14 20:09	13 11:52 ♃ ☌	♒ 14 12:42		⚷ Chiron 1♑47.7
♃⚺♅ 14 10:50	☉ ♑ 22 12:37	16 18:59 ☉ ⚹	♒ 17 7:04	16 9:39 ☉ ⚹	♓ 16 21:12	2 21:50 ☽ 10♍03	☽ Mean ☊ 13♏44.0
♃⚻♇ 15 8:16	♆ ♊ 25 13:27	19 8:24 ♂ ⚹	♓ 19 15:04	18 20:35 ☉ □	♈ 19 3:09	11 2:53 ● 18♐23	
♅☍♇ 17 3:36	☿ ♑ 26 9:31	21 17:22 ☉ △	♈ 21 19:32	21 4:05 ☉ △	♉ 21 6:23	18 20:35 ☽ 26♓16	1 DECEMBER 1901
☽0N 18 10:24		23 20:26 ♂ △	♉ 23 20:52	22 18:28 ♂ △	♊ 23 7:22	25 12:16 ○ 3♋02	Julian Day # 700
♄⚻♇ 28 21:29		25 3:15 ♀ △	♊ 25 20:24	25 4:18 ☿ ☍	♋ 25 7:23		Delta T -0.1 sec
☽0S 31 2:17		27 0:45 ♇ ☌	♋ 27 20:02	27 0:31 ♂ ☍	♌ 27 8:18		SVP 06♓37'35"
		29 11:01 ♀ ☍	♌ 29 21:43	29 11:52 ♆ ⚹	♍ 29 12:04		Obliquity 23°27'00"
				31 19:36 ♆ □	♎ 31 19:56		⚷ Chiron 4♑22.4
							☽ Mean ☊ 12♏08.7

LONGITUDE — JANUARY 1902

Day	Sid.Time	☉	0 hr ☽	Noon ☽	True ☊	☿	♀	♂	♃	♄	♅	♆	♇
1 W	6 38 50	9♑39 12	2♎ 5 55	8♎14 31	11♏45.4	8♑54.8	23♒32.5	29♑13.1	21♑23.5	17♑41.9	18♐26.4	29♊49.1	17♊16.7
2 Th	6 42 47	10 40 22	14 18 50	20 19 33	11D45.2	10 31.3	24 14.8	0♒ 0.2	21 37.4	17 49.0	18 29.9	29R47.5	17R15.7
3 F	6 46 43	11 41 32	26 17 22	2♏12 58	11 45.9	12 8.1	24 56.0	0 47.3	21 51.4	17 56.1	18 33.3	29 45.8	17 14.6
4 Sa	6 50 40	12 42 42	8♏ 7 1	14 0 10	11R46.6	13 45.4	25 36.0	1 34.4	22 5.4	18 3.2	18 36.8	29 44.1	17 13.6
5 Su	6 54 36	13 43 53	19 53 3	25 46 15	11 46.3	15 22.9	26 14.8	2 21.6	22 19.4	18 10.2	18 40.2	29 42.5	17 12.6
6 M	6 58 33	14 45 4	1♐40 17	7♐35 39	11 44.0	17 0.9	26 52.3	3 8.7	22 33.4	18 17.3	18 43.6	29 40.9	17 11.5
7 Tu	7 2 30	15 46 14	13 32 47	19 32 1	11 39.2	18 39.3	27 28.4	3 55.9	22 47.4	18 24.4	18 47.0	29 39.2	17 10.5
8 W	7 6 26	16 47 25	25 33 42	1♑38 4	11 31.6	20 18.0	28 3.2	4 43.2	23 1.5	18 31.5	18 50.3	29 37.6	17 9.5
9 Th	7 10 23	17 48 36	7♑45 18	13 55 31	11 21.4	21 57.2	28 36.5	5 30.4	23 15.6	18 38.6	18 53.7	29 36.0	17 8.5
10 F	7 14 19	18 49 46	20 8 49	26 25 13	11 9.3	23 36.7	29 8.4	6 17.7	23 29.6	18 45.7	18 57.0	29 34.4	17 7.6
11 Sa	7 18 16	19 50 56	2♒44 43	9♒ 7 15	10 56.3	25 16.7	29 38.6	7 5.0	23 43.7	18 52.8	19 0.3	29 32.8	17 6.6
12 Su	7 22 12	20 52 6	15 32 46	22 1 13	10 43.5	26 57.0	0♓ 7.3	7 52.3	23 57.8	18 60.0	19 3.5	29 31.3	17 5.7
13 M	7 26 9	21 53 15	28 32 30	5♓ 6 36	10 32.3	28 37.6	0 34.2	8 39.6	24 11.9	19 7.1	19 6.7	29 29.7	17 4.7
14 Tu	7 30 5	22 54 24	11♓43 28	18 23 5	10 23.4	0♒18.6	0 59.4	9 26.9	24 26.0	19 14.2	19 10.0	29 28.2	17 3.8
15 W	7 34 2	23 55 32	25 5 29	1♈50 43	10 17.4	1 59.8	1 22.8	10 14.3	24 40.1	19 21.2	19 13.1	29 26.6	17 2.9
16 Th	7 37 59	24 56 39	8♈38 52	15 30 0	10 14.3	3 41.3	1 44.2	11 1.6	24 54.2	19 28.3	19 16.3	29 25.1	17 2.0
17 F	7 41 55	25 57 45	22 24 12	29 21 34	10D13.3	5 22.9	2 3.7	11 49.0	25 8.3	19 35.4	19 19.4	29 23.6	17 1.1
18 Sa	7 45 52	26 58 51	6♉22 9	13♉25 55	10R13.4	7 4.7	2 21.2	12 36.4	25 22.5	19 42.5	19 22.5	29 22.2	17 0.2
19 Su	7 49 48	27 59 55	20 32 48	27 42 39	10 13.2	8 46.4	2 36.6	13 23.8	25 36.6	19 49.5	19 25.6	29 20.7	16 59.4
20 M	7 53 45	29 0 59	4♊55 11	12♊10 1	10 11.3	10 28.0	2 49.8	14 11.2	25 50.7	19 56.6	19 28.6	29 19.3	16 58.6
21 Tu	7 57 41	0♒ 2 2	19 26 38	26 44 22	10 6.8	12 9.3	3 0.8	14 58.6	26 4.8	20 3.6	19 31.7	29 17.8	16 57.7
22 W	8 1 38	1 3 4	4♋ 2 31	11♋20 13	9 59.4	13 50.3	3 9.6	15 46.0	26 18.9	20 10.7	19 34.6	29 16.4	16 56.9
23 Th	8 5 35	2 4 5	18 36 36	25 50 44	9 49.2	15 30.6	3 15.9	16 33.4	26 33.0	20 17.7	19 37.6	29 15.1	16 56.2
24 F	8 9 31	3 5 5	3♌ 1 43	10♌ 8 45	9 37.2	17 10.0	3 19.9	17 20.9	26 47.0	20 24.7	19 40.5	29 13.7	16 55.4
25 Sa	8 13 28	4 6 5	17 11 4	24 8 3	9 24.5	18 48.3	3R21.4	18 8.3	27 1.1	20 31.7	19 43.4	29 12.4	16 54.6
26 Su	8 17 24	5 7 3	0♍59 14	7♍44 18	9 12.6	20 25.2	3 20.5	18 55.7	27 15.2	20 38.6	19 46.2	29 11.0	16 53.9
27 M	8 21 21	6 8 1	14 23 6	20 55 39	9 2.5	22 0.2	3 17.1	19 43.2	27 29.2	20 45.6	19 49.1	29 9.7	16 53.2
28 Tu	8 25 17	7 8 58	27 22 4	3♎42 39	8 55.0	23 32.9	3 11.2	20 30.6	27 43.2	20 52.5	19 51.8	29 8.5	16 52.5
29 W	8 29 14	8 9 55	9♎57 48	16 8 0	8 50.3	25 2.9	3 2.7	21 18.1	27 57.3	20 59.4	19 54.6	29 7.2	16 51.8
30 Th	8 33 10	9 10 50	22 13 48	28 15 51	8 48.1	26 29.7	2 51.7	22 5.5	28 11.3	21 6.3	19 57.3	29 6.0	16 51.1
31 F	8 37 7	10 11 45	4♏14 47	10♏11 20	8 47.5	27 52.5	2 38.2	22 53.0	28 25.3	21 13.1	19 60.0	29 4.8	16 50.5

LONGITUDE — FEBRUARY 1902

Day	Sid.Time	☉	0 hr ☽	Noon ☽	True ☊	☿	♀	♂	♃	♄	♅	♆	♇
1 Sa	8 41 3	11♒12 39	16♏ 6 10	22♏ 0 2	8♏47.4	29♒10.8	2♓22.3	23♒40.5	28♑39.2	21♑20.0	20♐ 2.6	29♊ 3.6	16♊49.9
2 Su	8 45 0	12 13 33	27 53 36	3♐47 34	8R46.8	0♓23.8	2R 3.9	24 27.9	28 53.2	21 26.8	20 5.2	29R 2.4	16R49.3
3 M	8 48 57	13 14 25	9♐42 34	15 39 15	8 44.4	1 30.8	1 43.2	25 15.4	29 7.1	21 33.6	20 7.8	29 1.3	16 48.7
4 Tu	8 52 53	14 15 17	21 38 8	27 39 46	8 39.5	2 31.0	1 20.2	26 2.9	29 21.0	21 40.3	20 10.3	29 0.2	16 48.1
5 W	8 56 50	15 16 8	3♑44 34	9♑52 55	8 31.8	3 23.6	0 55.0	26 50.4	29 34.9	21 47.1	20 12.8	28 59.1	16 47.6
6 Th	9 0 46	16 16 57	16 5 7	22 21 20	8 21.4	4 7.8	0 27.8	27 37.8	29 48.8	21 53.8	20 15.2	28 58.1	16 47.0
7 F	9 4 43	17 17 46	28 41 43	5♒ 6 18	8 8.9	4 43.0	29♒58.6	28 25.3	0♒ 2.6	22 0.5	20 17.6	28 57.0	16 46.5
8 Sa	9 8 39	18 18 34	11♒35 1	18 7 44	7 55.3	5 8.5	29 27.7	29 12.8	0 16.4	22 7.1	20 20.0	28 56.1	16 46.0
9 Su	9 12 36	19 19 20	24 44 15	1♓24 19	7 41.9	5R23.7	28 55.3	0♓ 0.2	0 30.2	22 13.7	20 22.3	28 55.1	16 45.6
10 M	9 16 32	20 20 4	8♓ 7 37	14 53 51	7 30.0	5 28.3	28 21.4	0 47.7	0 43.9	22 20.3	20 24.6	28 54.1	16 45.1
11 Tu	9 20 29	21 20 48	21 42 42	28 33 49	7 20.6	5 22.1	27 46.4	1 35.1	0 57.6	22 26.8	20 26.8	28 53.2	16 44.7
12 W	9 24 26	22 21 30	5♈26 55	12♈21 45	7 14.1	5 5.3	27 10.4	2 22.5	1 11.3	22 33.3	20 29.0	28 52.3	16 44.3
13 Th	9 28 22	23 22 10	19 18 5	26 15 46	7 10.6	4 38.2	26 33.7	3 10.0	1 24.9	22 39.8	20 31.1	28 51.5	16 43.9
14 F	9 32 19	24 22 48	3♉14 39	10♉14 38	7D 9.5	4 1.3	25 56.5	3 57.4	1 38.5	22 46.2	20 33.3	28 50.7	16 43.5
15 Sa	9 36 15	25 23 25	17 15 39	24 17 37	7R 9.6	3 15.7	25 19.1	4 44.8	1 52.1	22 52.6	20 35.3	28 49.9	16 43.2
16 Su	9 40 12	26 24 0	1♊20 28	8♊24 7	7 9.6	2 22.6	24 41.7	5 32.1	2 5.6	22 58.9	20 37.3	28 49.1	16 42.9
17 M	9 44 8	27 24 33	15 28 26	22 33 13	7 8.4	1 23.3	24 4.7	6 19.5	2 19.1	23 5.2	20 39.3	28 48.4	16 42.6
18 Tu	9 48 5	28 25 5	29 38 14	6♋43 10	7 4.8	0 19.6	23 28.2	7 6.9	2 32.5	23 11.5	20 41.2	28 47.7	16 42.3
19 W	9 52 1	29 25 34	13♋47 38	20 51 11	6 58.5	29♒13.1	22 52.5	7 54.2	2 45.9	23 17.7	20 43.1	28 47.0	16 42.0
20 Th	9 55 58	0♓26 2	27 53 19	4♌53 31	6 49.8	28 5.7	22 17.8	8 41.5	2 59.3	23 23.8	20 44.9	28 46.4	16 41.8
21 F	9 59 55	1 26 28	11♌51 13	18 45 53	6 39.3	26 59.0	21 44.4	9 28.8	3 12.6	23 29.9	20 46.7	28 45.8	16 41.6
22 Sa	10 3 51	2 26 52	25 37 1	2♍24 9	6 28.1	25 54.6	21 12.5	10 16.1	3 25.8	23 36.0	20 48.4	28 45.2	16 41.4
23 Su	10 7 48	3 27 15	9♍ 6 53	15 44 57	6 17.5	24 53.9	20 42.2	11 3.4	3 39.0	23 42.0	20 50.1	28 44.6	16 41.2
24 M	10 11 44	4 27 36	22 18 9	28 46 23	6 8.4	23 58.1	20 13.8	11 50.6	3 52.2	23 48.0	20 51.7	28 44.1	16 41.1
25 Tu	10 15 41	5 27 55	5♎ 9 41	11♎28 10	6 1.7	23 8.0	19 47.4	12 37.9	4 5.3	23 53.9	20 53.3	28 43.7	16 41.0
26 W	10 19 37	6 28 13	17 42 4	23 51 41	5 57.5	22 24.3	19 23.1	13 25.1	4 18.4	23 59.8	20 54.9	28 43.2	16 40.9
27 Th	10 23 34	7 28 29	29 57 27	5♏59 50	5D55.6	21 47.5	19 1.1	14 12.3	4 31.4	24 5.6	20 56.4	28 42.8	16 40.8
28 F	10 27 30	8 28 43	11♏59 21	17 56 35	5 55.6	21 17.7	18 41.3	14 59.5	4 44.3	24 11.4	20 57.8	28 42.4	16 40.7

Astro Data Dy Hr Mn	Planet Ingress Dy Hr Mn	Last Aspect Dy Hr Mn	☽ Ingress Dy Hr Mn	Last Aspect Dy Hr Mn	☽ Ingress Dy Hr Mn	☽ Phases & Eclipses Dy Hr Mn	Astro Data
♄⚺♅ 12 22:05	♂ ♒ 1 23:54	3 7:01 ♆ △	♏ 3 7:30	2 2:04 ♃ ✶	♐ 2 4:17	1 16:08 ☽ 10♎20	1 JANUARY 1902
☽0N 14 16:56	♀ ♓ 11 17:47	5 13:42 ♀ □	♐ 5 20:36	4 14:38 ♆ ☍	♑ 4 16:38	9 21:14 ● 18♑43	Julian Day # 731
♀ R 25 3:03	☿ ♒ 13 19:35	8 8:01 ♆ ☍	♑ 8 8:47	6 11:13 ♄ ☌	♒ 7 2:27	17 6:38 ☽ 26♈15	Delta T 0.0 sec
☽0S 27 12:52	☉ ♒ 20 23:12	10 7:39 ☿ ☌	♒ 10 18:48	9 7:32 ♆ △	♓ 9 9:29	24 0:06 ○ 3♌05	SVP 06♓37'29"
		13 1:45 ♆ △	♓ 13 2:40	11 12:33 ♆ □	♈ 11 14:30	31 13:08 ☽ 10♏45	Obliquity 23°27'00"
♃⚻♆ 2 14:45	☿ ♓ 1 15:58	15 7:44 ♆ □	♈ 15 8:44	13 16:27 ♆ ✶	♉ 13 18:26		⚷ Chiron 7♑28.9
☿ R 9 22:18	♀ ♒ 6 22:55	17 12:02 ♆ ✶	♉ 17 13:06	15 14:56 ☉ □	♊ 15 21:43	8 13:21 ● 18♒52	☽ Mean ☊ 10♏30.2
☽0N 10 23:54	♃ ♒ 6 19:31	19 13:26 ☉ △	♊ 19 15:49	17 22:34 ♆ ☌	♋ 18 0:37	15 14:56 ☽ 26♉01	
♃⚼♇ 14 8:38	♂ ♓ 8 23:54	21 16:11 ♆ ☌	♋ 21 17:21	19 16:17 ♄ ☍	♌ 20 3:37	22 13:03 ○ 2♍60	1 FEBRUARY 1902
☽0S 23 23:02	☿ ♒ 18 7:09	23 13:23 ♃ ☍	♌ 23 18:56	22 5:32 ♆ ✶	♍ 22 7:44		Julian Day # 762
	☉ ♓ 19 13:40	25 20:50 ♆ ✶	♍ 25 22:16	24 11:55 ♆ □	♎ 24 14:18		Delta T 0.1 sec
		28 3:20 ♆ □	♎ 28 4:57	26 21:33 ♆ △	♏ 27 0:05		SVP 06♓37'25"
		30 13:39 ♆ △	♏ 30 15:28				Obliquity 23°27'00"
							⚷ Chiron 10♑31.3
							☽ Mean ☊ 8♏51.7

MARCH 1902 LONGITUDE

Day	Sid.Time	☉	0 hr ☽	Noon ☽	True ☊	☿	♀	♂	♃	♄	♅	♆	♇
1 Sa	10 31 27	9♓28 56	23♏52 11	29♏46 45	5♏56.5	20♒55.1	18♒24.0	15♓46.6	4♒57.2	24♑17.1	20♐59.2	28♊42.1	16♊40.7
2 Su	10 35 24	10 29 8	5♐41 0	11♐35 35	5R 57.4	20R 39.7	18R 9.1	16 33.8	5 10.0	24 22.7	21 0.5	28R 41.8	16D 40.7
3 M	10 39 20	11 29 18	17 31 11	23 28 28	5 57.3	20D 31.1	17 56.6	17 20.9	5 22.8	24 28.3	21 1.8	28 41.5	16 40.7
4 Tu	10 43 17	12 29 27	29 28 4	5♑30 36	5 55.5	20 29.2	17 46.7	18 8.0	5 35.5	24 33.9	21 3.1	28 41.2	16 40.7
5 W	10 47 13	13 29 34	11♑36 37	17 46 39	5 51.6	20 33.8	17 39.2	18 55.1	5 48.1	24 39.4	21 4.3	28 41.0	16 40.8
6 Th	10 51 10	14 29 39	24 1 6	0♒20 22	5 45.6	20 44.4	17 34.3	19 42.1	6 0.7	24 44.8	21 5.4	28 40.8	16 40.9
7 F	10 55 6	15 29 43	6♒44 41	13 14 13	5 38.0	21 0.7	17D 31.8	20 29.1	6 13.2	24 50.2	21 6.5	28 40.7	16 41.0
8 Sa	10 59 3	16 29 44	19 49 3	26 29 6	5 29.3	21 22.4	17 31.7	21 16.1	6 25.7	24 55.5	21 7.5	28 40.6	16 41.1
9 Su	11 2 59	17 29 45	3♓14 12	10♓ 4 5	5 20.6	21 49.2	17 34.0	22 3.1	6 38.1	25 0.7	21 8.5	28 40.5	16 41.2
10 M	11 6 56	18 29 43	16 58 21	23 56 34	5 12.8	22 20.7	17 38.7	22 50.1	6 50.4	25 5.9	21 9.4	28D 40.5	16 41.4
11 Tu	11 10 53	19 29 39	0♈58 10	8♈ 2 36	5 6.8	22 56.6	17 45.6	23 37.0	7 2.6	25 11.0	21 10.3	28 40.5	16 41.6
12 W	11 14 49	20 29 33	15 9 16	22 17 34	5 2.9	23 36.6	17 54.8	24 23.9	7 14.8	25 16.0	21 11.1	28 40.5	16 41.8
13 Th	11 18 46	21 29 26	29 26 56	6♉36 49	5D 1.3	24 20.4	18 6.1	25 10.7	7 26.9	25 21.0	21 11.9	28 40.5	16 42.0
14 F	11 22 42	22 29 16	13♉46 45	20 56 16	5 1.4	25 7.9	18 19.5	25 57.6	7 38.9	25 25.9	21 12.6	28 40.6	16 42.3
15 Sa	11 26 39	23 29 4	28 5 2	5♊12 44	5 2.6	25 58.8	18 35.0	26 44.4	7 50.8	25 30.7	21 13.3	28 40.8	16 42.5
16 Su	11 30 35	24 28 50	12♊19 6	19 23 56	5R 3.9	26 52.8	18 52.5	27 31.1	8 2.7	25 35.5	21 13.9	28 40.9	16 42.8
17 M	11 34 32	25 28 33	26 27 3	3♋28 18	5 4.4	27 49.7	19 11.9	28 17.9	8 14.4	25 40.2	21 14.5	28 41.1	16 43.2
18 Tu	11 38 28	26 28 14	10♋27 32	17 24 37	5 3.5	28 49.5	19 33.2	29 4.5	8 26.1	25 44.8	21 15.0	28 41.4	16 43.5
19 W	11 42 25	27 27 53	24 19 25	1♌11 47	5 0.9	29 51.8	19 56.2	29 51.2	8 37.7	25 49.3	21 15.4	28 41.6	16 43.9
20 Th	11 46 22	28 27 29	8♌ 1 33	14 48 35	4 56.6	0♓56.7	20 21.0	0♈37.8	8 49.2	25 53.8	21 15.8	28 41.9	16 44.3
21 F	11 50 18	29 27 4	21 32 41	28 13 41	4 51.3	2 3.9	20 47.5	1 24.4	9 0.7	25 58.2	21 16.2	28 42.3	16 44.7
22 Sa	11 54 15	0♈26 36	4♍51 26	11♍25 47	4 45.4	3 13.3	21 15.6	2 11.0	9 12.0	26 2.5	21 16.5	28 42.6	16 45.1
23 Su	11 58 11	1 26 5	17 56 36	24 23 48	4 39.8	4 24.9	21 45.2	2 57.5	9 23.2	26 6.8	21 16.7	28 43.0	16 45.5
24 M	12 2 8	2 25 33	0♎47 20	7♎ 7 12	4 35.1	5 38.5	22 16.4	3 44.0	9 34.4	26 11.0	21 16.9	28 43.5	16 46.0
25 Tu	12 6 4	3 24 59	13 23 25	19 36 7	4 31.7	6 54.1	22 49.0	4 30.4	9 45.5	26 15.1	21 17.1	28 44.0	16 46.5
26 W	12 10 1	4 24 22	25 45 26	1♏51 35	4D 29.9	8 11.5	23 23.0	5 16.8	9 56.4	26 19.1	21 17.1	28 44.5	16 47.0
27 Th	12 13 57	5 23 44	7♏54 52	13 55 34	4 29.6	9 30.8	23 58.3	6 3.2	10 7.3	26 23.0	21R 17.2	28 45.0	16 47.6
28 F	12 17 54	6 23 4	19 54 6	25 50 53	4 30.5	10 51.8	24 34.9	6 49.5	10 18.1	26 26.9	21 17.2	28 45.6	16 48.1
29 Sa	12 21 50	7 22 22	1♐46 22	7♐41 6	4 32.1	12 14.6	25 12.8	7 35.8	10 28.8	26 30.7	21 17.1	28 46.2	16 48.7
30 Su	12 25 47	8 21 38	13 35 36	19 30 26	4 33.9	13 39.0	25 51.8	8 22.1	10 39.4	26 34.3	21 17.0	28 46.8	16 49.3
31 M	12 29 44	9 20 52	25 26 14	1♑23 34	4 35.4	15 5.0	26 32.0	9 8.3	10 49.8	26 38.0	21 16.8	28 47.5	16 49.9

APRIL 1902 LONGITUDE

Day	Sid.Time	☉	0 hr ☽	Noon ☽	True ☊	☿	♀	♂	♃	♄	♅	♆	♇
1 Tu	12 33 40	10♈20 5	7♑23 4	13♑25 21	4♏36.2	16♓32.6	27♒13.3	9♈54.5	11♒ 0.2	26♑41.5	21♐16.6	28♊48.2	16♊50.5
2 W	12 37 37	11 19 16	19 31 0	25 40 37	4R 36.0	18 1.9	27 55.6	10 40.6	11 10.5	26 44.9	21R 16.3	28 48.9	16 51.2
3 Th	12 41 33	12 18 25	1♒54 43	8♒13 48	4 34.7	19 32.6	28 39.0	11 26.7	11 20.7	26 48.3	21 16.0	28 49.7	16 51.8
4 F	12 45 30	13 17 32	14 38 17	21 8 30	4 32.5	21 4.9	29 23.3	12 12.8	11 30.7	26 51.6	21 15.6	28 50.5	16 52.5
5 Sa	12 49 26	14 16 37	27 44 43	4♓27 4	4 29.8	22 38.7	0♓ 8.5	12 58.8	11 40.7	26 54.8	21 15.2	28 51.3	16 53.3
6 Su	12 53 23	15 15 41	11♓15 33	18 10 3	4 26.9	24 14.0	0 54.6	13 44.8	11 50.5	26 57.9	21 14.7	28 52.1	16 54.0
7 M	12 57 19	16 14 43	25 10 18	2♈15 56	4 24.4	25 50.8	1 41.6	14 30.7	12 0.2	27 0.9	21 14.1	28 53.0	16 54.7
8 Tu	13 1 16	17 13 42	9♈26 23	16 41 1	4 22.5	27 29.2	2 29.4	15 16.6	12 9.8	27 3.8	21 13.6	28 54.0	16 55.5
9 W	13 5 13	18 12 40	23 59 5	1♉19 46	4D 21.4	29 9.0	3 17.9	16 2.5	12 19.3	27 6.7	21 12.9	28 54.9	16 56.3
10 Th	13 9 9	19 11 36	8♉42 11	16 5 27	4 21.2	0♈50.3	4 7.2	16 48.3	12 28.7	27 9.4	21 12.2	28 55.9	16 57.1
11 F	13 13 6	20 10 30	23 28 42	0♊51 5	4 21.8	2 33.2	4 57.3	17 34.0	12 37.9	27 12.1	21 11.5	28 56.9	16 57.9
12 Sa	13 17 2	21 9 21	8♊11 50	15 30 15	4 22.7	4 17.6	5 48.0	18 19.8	12 47.0	27 14.6	21 10.7	28 58.0	16 58.8
13 Su	13 20 59	22 8 10	22 45 46	29 57 54	4 23.7	6 3.5	6 39.4	19 5.4	12 56.0	27 17.1	21 9.9	28 59.0	16 59.6
14 M	13 24 55	23 6 58	7♋ 6 14	14♋10 31	4 24.5	7 51.0	7 31.4	19 51.1	13 4.9	27 19.5	21 9.0	29 0.1	17 0.5
15 Tu	13 28 52	24 5 42	21 10 32	28 6 12	4R 24.9	9 40.0	8 24.0	20 36.6	13 13.6	27 21.8	21 8.1	29 1.3	17 1.4
16 W	13 32 48	25 4 25	4♌57 29	11♌44 24	4 24.7	11 30.5	9 17.3	21 22.2	13 22.3	27 24.0	21 7.1	29 2.4	17 2.3
17 Th	13 36 45	26 3 5	18 27 2	25 5 29	4 24.2	13 22.6	10 11.1	22 7.6	13 30.7	27 26.1	21 6.1	29 3.6	17 3.2
18 F	13 40 42	27 1 43	1♍39 54	8♍10 24	4 23.4	15 16.3	11 5.4	22 53.1	13 39.1	27 28.1	21 5.0	29 4.9	17 4.2
19 Sa	13 44 38	28 0 18	14 37 11	21 0 25	4 22.6	17 11.6	12 0.3	23 38.4	13 47.3	27 30.0	21 3.9	29 6.1	17 5.1
20 Su	13 48 35	28 58 52	27 20 15	3♎36 52	4 21.8	19 8.4	12 55.7	24 23.8	13 55.4	27 31.8	21 2.8	29 7.4	17 6.1
21 M	13 52 31	29 57 23	9♎50 28	16 1 12	4 21.3	21 6.7	13 51.6	25 9.1	14 3.3	27 33.5	21 1.6	29 8.7	17 7.1
22 Tu	13 56 28	0♉55 53	22 9 16	28 14 51	4 21.0	23 6.6	14 48.0	25 54.3	14 11.2	27 35.2	21 0.3	29 10.0	17 8.1
23 W	14 0 24	1 54 20	4♏18 10	10♏19 25	4D 20.9	25 7.9	15 44.9	26 39.5	14 18.8	27 36.7	20 59.0	29 11.4	17 9.1
24 Th	14 4 21	2 52 46	16 18 50	22 16 41	4 20.9	27 10.7	16 42.2	27 24.6	14 26.4	27 38.1	20 57.7	29 12.8	17 10.1
25 F	14 8 17	3 51 10	28 13 15	4♐ 8 50	4R 21.0	29 14.8	17 39.9	28 9.7	14 33.7	27 39.5	20 56.3	29 14.2	17 11.2
26 Sa	14 12 14	4 49 32	10♐ 3 46	15 58 24	4 21.0	1♉20.1	18 38.1	28 54.7	14 41.0	27 40.7	20 54.9	29 15.6	17 12.3
27 Su	14 16 10	5 47 53	21 53 9	27 48 25	4 20.9	3 26.6	19 36.7	29 39.7	14 48.1	27 41.9	20 53.5	29 17.1	17 13.3
28 M	14 20 7	6 46 12	3♑44 40	9♑42 22	4 20.7	5 34.1	20 35.6	0♉24.7	14 55.0	27 42.9	20 52.0	29 18.6	17 14.4
29 Tu	14 24 4	7 44 29	15 42 1	21 44 10	4 20.4	7 42.4	21 35.0	1 9.6	15 1.9	27 43.9	20 50.4	29 20.1	17 15.5
30 W	14 28 0	8 42 45	27 49 19	3♒58 1	4D 20.1	9 51.4	22 34.7	1 54.4	15 8.5	27 44.8	20 48.9	29 21.6	17 16.6

Astro Data	Dy Hr Mn
♇ D	2 1:06
☿ D	3 18:51
♃ ∠ ♅	6 9:49
♀ D	7 12:46
☽ 0 N	10 8:21
♆ D	10 18:14
♂ 0 N	21 11:38
☽ 0 S	23 7:10
♅ R	27 3:49
☽ 0 N	6 18:07
☿ 0 N	12 12:57
☽ 0 S	19 13:17
♃ □ ♆	21 19:46

Planet Ingress	Dy Hr Mn
☿ ♓	19 3:04
♂ ♈	19 4:31
☉ ♈	21 13:17
♀ ♓	4 19:31
☿ ♈	9 12:07
☉ ♉	21 1:04
☿ ♉	25 8:41
♂ ♉	27 10:49

Last Aspect Dy Hr Mn		☽ Ingress Dy Hr Mn
1 0:51	♄ ⚹	♐ 1 12:27
3 22:27	♆ ☍	♑ 4 1:04
6 1:24	♄ ☌	♒ 6 11:22
8 15:55	♆ △	♓ 8 18:16
10 20:05	♆ □	♈ 10 22:21
12 22:42	♆ ⚹	♉ 13 0:55
14 21:37	♂ ⚹	♊ 15 3:13
17 3:49	♆ ☌	♋ 17 6:04
19 5:54	☉ △	♌ 19 9:54
21 12:52	♆ ⚹	♍ 21 15:12
23 20:07	♆ □	♎ 23 22:31
26 5:52	♆ △	♏ 26 8:20
28 13:17	♄ ⚹	♐ 28 20:24
31 6:46	♆ ☍	♑ 31 9:12

Last Aspect Dy Hr Mn		☽ Ingress Dy Hr Mn
2 14:08	♄ ☌	♒ 2 20:20
5 2:00	♆ △	♓ 5 4:03
7 6:18	♆ □	♈ 7 8:11
9 8:04	♆ ⚹	♉ 9 9:50
11 6:04	♄ △	♊ 11 10:37
13 10:22	♆ ☌	♋ 13 12:04
15 10:44	♄ ☍	♌ 15 15:18
17 19:16	♆ ⚹	♍ 17 20:57
20 3:25	♆ □	♎ 20 5:05
22 13:51	♆ △	♏ 22 15:28
24 22:52	♄ ⚹	♐ 25 3:36
27 15:01	♆ ☍	♑ 27 16:26
29 23:51	♄ ☌	♒ 30 4:16

☽ Phases & Eclipses Dy Hr Mn	
2 10:39	☽ 10♐56
10 2:50	● 18♓37
16 22:13	☽ 25♊24
24 3:21	○ 2♎34
1 6:24	☽ 10♑36
8 13:50	● 17♈48
8 14:05:02	☌ P 0.064
15 5:25	☽ 24♋19
22 18:49	○ 1♏42
22 18:53	☍ T 1.333
30 22:58	☽ 9♒38

Astro Data

1 MARCH 1902
Julian Day # 790
Delta T 0.2 sec
SVP 06♓37'22"
Obliquity 23°27'00"
⚷ Chiron 12♑46.8
☽ Mean ☊ 7♏22.8

1 APRIL 1902
Julian Day # 821
Delta T 0.3 sec
SVP 06♓37'19"
Obliquity 23°27'00"
⚷ Chiron 14♑19.8
☽ Mean ☊ 5♏44.2

Day	Sid.Time	☉	0 hr ☽	Noon ☽	True ☊	☿	♀	♂	♃	♄	♅	♆	♇
1 Th	14 31 57	9♉40 59	10♒10 48	16♒28 12	4♏20.0	12♉ 0.7	23♓34.7	2♉39.2	15♒15.0	27♑45.5	20♐47.2	29♊23.2	17♊17.8
2 F	14 35 53	10 39 12	22 50 43	29 18 48	4 20.2	14 10.3	24 35.1	3 24.0	15 21.4	27 46.2	20R45.6	29 24.8	17 18.9
3 Sa	14 39 50	11 37 23	5♓52 51	12♓33 11	4 20.6	16 19.8	25 35.8	4 8.7	15 27.5	27 46.8	20 43.9	29 26.4	17 20.1
4 Su	14 43 46	12 35 33	19 20 2	26 13 30	4 21.3	18 28.9	26 36.8	4 53.3	15 33.6	27 47.2	20 42.2	29 28.0	17 21.2
5 M	14 47 43	13 33 41	3♈13 36	10♈20 8	4 22.1	20 37.3	27 38.2	5 37.9	15 39.5	27 47.6	20 40.4	29 29.7	17 22.4
6 Tu	14 51 39	14 31 48	17 32 46	24 51 0	4 22.7	22 44.8	28 39.8	6 22.5	15 45.2	27 47.9	20 38.6	29 31.3	17 23.6
7 W	14 55 36	15 29 54	2♉14 12	9♉41 30	4R23.0	24 51.0	29 41.7	7 7.0	15 50.7	27 48.0	20 36.8	29 33.0	17 24.8
8 Th	14 59 33	16 27 57	17 11 58	24 44 31	4 22.8	26 55.7	0♈43.9	7 51.4	15 56.1	27R48.1	20 34.9	29 34.7	17 26.0
9 F	15 3 29	17 26 0	2♊18 1	9♊51 19	4 22.0	28 58.6	1 46.3	8 35.8	16 1.3	27 48.1	20 33.0	29 36.5	17 27.3
10 Sa	15 7 26	18 24 0	17 23 15	24 52 44	4 20.6	0♊59.4	2 49.0	9 20.2	16 6.4	27 48.0	20 31.1	29 38.3	17 28.5
11 Su	15 11 22	19 21 59	2♋18 46	9♋40 31	4 18.8	2 57.9	3 51.9	10 4.5	16 11.3	27 47.7	20 29.1	29 40.0	17 29.7
12 M	15 15 19	20 19 56	16 57 16	24 8 29	4 17.0	4 53.9	4 55.1	10 48.7	16 16.0	27 47.4	20 27.1	29 41.8	17 31.0
13 Tu	15 19 15	21 17 52	1♌13 48	8♌13 0	4 15.5	6 47.3	5 58.4	11 32.9	16 20.5	27 47.0	20 25.1	29 43.7	17 32.3
14 W	15 23 12	22 15 45	15 6 1	21 52 55	4D14.7	8 37.8	7 2.1	12 17.0	16 24.9	27 46.5	20 23.1	29 45.5	17 33.5
15 Th	15 27 8	23 13 37	28 33 53	5♍ 9 10	4 14.6	10 25.4	8 5.9	13 1.1	16 29.1	27 45.9	20 21.0	29 47.4	17 34.8
16 F	15 31 5	24 11 26	11♍39 5	18 4 2	4 15.4	12 9.8	9 9.9	13 45.1	16 33.1	27 45.2	20 18.9	29 49.2	17 36.1
17 Sa	15 35 2	25 9 14	24 24 25	0♎40 38	4 16.7	13 51.2	10 14.1	14 29.0	16 36.9	27 44.4	20 16.8	29 51.1	17 37.4
18 Su	15 38 58	26 7 1	6♎53 7	13 2 17	4 18.2	15 29.3	11 18.6	15 12.9	16 40.6	27 43.5	20 14.6	29 53.0	17 38.7
19 M	15 42 55	27 4 46	19 8 32	25 12 15	4 19.6	17 4.1	12 23.2	15 56.8	16 44.1	27 42.5	20 12.4	29 55.0	17 40.0
20 Tu	15 46 51	28 2 29	1♏13 48	7♏13 32	4R20.3	18 35.6	13 28.0	16 40.6	16 47.4	27 41.4	20 10.2	29 56.9	17 41.3
21 W	15 50 48	29 0 11	13 11 45	19 8 46	4 20.0	20 3.6	14 33.0	17 24.3	16 50.5	27 40.2	20 8.0	29 58.9	17 42.7
22 Th	15 54 44	29 57 51	25 4 51	1♐ 0 15	4 18.5	21 28.2	15 38.2	18 8.0	16 53.5	27 39.0	20 5.8	0♋ 0.9	17 44.0
23 F	15 58 41	0♊55 30	6♐55 15	12 50 6	4 15.7	22 49.4	16 43.6	18 51.6	16 56.3	27 37.6	20 3.5	0 2.8	17 45.3
24 Sa	16 2 37	1 53 8	18 45 2	24 40 19	4 11.8	24 6.9	17 49.1	19 35.2	16 58.9	27 36.2	20 1.2	0 4.9	17 46.7
25 Su	16 6 34	2 50 45	0♑36 12	6♑32 59	4 7.0	25 21.0	18 54.8	20 18.7	17 1.3	27 34.6	19 58.9	0 6.9	17 48.0
26 M	16 10 31	3 48 21	12 30 57	18 30 26	4 2.0	26 31.3	20 0.6	21 2.2	17 3.5	27 33.0	19 56.6	0 8.9	17 49.4
27 Tu	16 14 27	4 45 55	24 31 46	0♒35 20	3 57.1	27 38.0	21 6.7	21 45.6	17 5.5	27 31.3	19 54.3	0 11.0	17 50.8
28 W	16 18 24	5 43 29	6♒41 32	12 50 46	3 53.1	28 41.0	22 12.8	22 29.0	17 7.4	27 29.5	19 51.9	0 13.0	17 52.1
29 Th	16 22 20	6 41 2	19 3 29	25 20 9	3 50.2	29 40.1	23 19.2	23 12.3	17 9.0	27 27.6	19 49.6	0 15.1	17 53.5
30 F	16 26 17	7 38 34	1♓41 13	8♓ 7 8	3D48.8	0♋35.3	24 25.6	23 55.6	17 10.5	27 25.6	19 47.2	0 17.2	17 54.9
31 Sa	16 30 13	8 36 5	14 38 21	21 15 17	3 48.8	1 26.6	25 32.3	24 38.8	17 11.8	27 23.5	19 44.8	0 19.3	17 56.3

LONGITUDE JUNE 1902

Day	Sid.Time	☉	0 hr ☽	Noon ☽	True ☊	☿	♀	♂	♃	♄	♅	♆	♇
1 Su	16 34 10	9♊33 35	27♓58 17	4♈47 38	3♏49.8	2♋13.9	26♈39.0	25♉22.0	17♒12.9	27♑21.3	19♐42.4	0♋21.4	17♊57.6
2 M	16 38 6	10 31 4	11♈43 32	18 46 2	3 51.3	2 57.0	27 45.9	26 5.1	17 13.8	27R19.1	19R40.0	0 23.5	17 59.0
3 Tu	16 42 3	11 28 33	25 55 5	3♉10 25	3R52.4	3 36.0	28 52.9	26 48.1	17 14.5	27 16.8	19 37.6	0 25.6	18 0.4
4 W	16 46 0	12 26 1	10♉31 37	17 58 4	3 52.4	4 10.7	0♉ 0.0	27 31.1	17 15.0	27 14.4	19 35.1	0 27.8	18 1.8
5 Th	16 49 56	13 23 28	25 28 58	3♊ 3 19	3 50.8	4 41.0	1 7.3	28 14.1	17 15.3	27 11.9	19 32.7	0 29.9	18 3.2
6 F	16 53 53	14 20 55	10♊39 59	18 17 41	3 47.4	5 6.9	2 14.7	28 57.0	17R15.5	27 9.3	19 30.2	0 32.1	18 4.6
7 Sa	16 57 49	15 18 21	25 55 6	3♋30 55	3 42.4	5 28.3	3 22.2	29 39.8	17 15.4	27 6.6	19 27.8	0 34.2	18 6.0
8 Su	17 1 46	16 15 46	11♋ 3 51	18 32 43	3 36.3	5 45.2	4 29.8	0♊22.6	17 15.1	27 3.9	19 25.3	0 36.4	18 7.4
9 M	17 5 42	17 13 10	25 56 30	3♌14 22	3 30.0	5 57.6	5 37.5	1 5.3	17 14.7	27 1.1	19 22.9	0 38.6	18 8.8
10 Tu	17 9 39	18 10 32	10♌25 40	17 30 1	3 24.4	6 5.3	6 45.3	1 48.0	17 14.1	26 58.2	19 20.4	0 40.8	18 10.2
11 W	17 13 35	19 7 54	24 27 10	1♍17 7	3 20.2	6R 8.5	7 53.2	2 30.6	17 13.2	26 55.3	19 18.0	0 43.0	18 11.6
12 Th	17 17 32	20 5 15	8♍ 0 0	14 36 5	3 17.7	6 7.1	9 1.2	3 13.1	17 12.2	26 52.2	19 15.5	0 45.2	18 13.0
13 F	17 21 29	21 2 35	21 5 46	27 29 30	3D17.0	6 1.3	10 9.4	3 55.6	17 11.0	26 49.1	19 13.0	0 47.4	18 14.4
14 Sa	17 25 25	21 59 53	3♎47 51	10♎ 1 20	3 17.6	5 51.1	11 17.6	4 38.1	17 9.6	26 46.0	19 10.6	0 49.6	18 15.8
15 Su	17 29 22	22 57 11	16 10 35	22 16 9	3 18.7	5 36.9	12 25.9	5 20.5	17 8.0	26 42.7	19 8.1	0 51.8	18 17.2
16 M	17 33 18	23 54 28	28 18 38	4♏18 35	3R19.7	5 18.7	13 34.3	6 2.8	17 6.2	26 39.4	19 5.7	0 54.0	18 18.6
17 Tu	17 37 15	24 51 44	10♏16 31	16 12 56	3 19.5	4 56.9	14 42.8	6 45.1	17 4.2	26 36.1	19 3.2	0 56.3	18 20.0
18 W	17 41 11	25 49 0	22 8 16	28 2 58	3 17.6	4 31.8	15 51.3	7 27.3	17 2.1	26 32.6	19 0.8	0 58.5	18 21.3
19 Th	17 45 8	26 46 15	3♐57 23	9♐51 51	3 13.5	4 3.8	17 0.0	8 9.5	16 59.7	26 29.1	18 58.4	1 0.7	18 22.7
20 F	17 49 4	27 43 29	15 46 41	21 42 7	3 7.0	3 33.3	18 8.8	8 51.6	16 57.2	26 25.6	18 55.9	1 2.9	18 24.1
21 Sa	17 53 1	28 40 43	27 38 24	3♑35 45	2 58.5	3 0.8	19 17.7	9 33.6	16 54.5	26 22.0	18 53.5	1 5.2	18 25.5
22 Su	17 56 58	29 37 56	9♑34 21	15 34 23	2 48.5	2 27.0	20 26.6	10 15.6	16 51.6	26 18.3	18 51.1	1 7.4	18 26.9
23 M	18 0 54	0♋35 9	21 36 1	27 39 26	2 37.8	1 52.3	21 35.6	10 57.6	16 48.6	26 14.6	18 48.7	1 9.6	18 28.3
24 Tu	18 4 51	1 32 22	3♒44 51	9♒52 26	2 27.5	1 17.3	22 44.8	11 39.5	16 45.3	26 10.8	18 46.3	1 11.9	18 29.6
25 W	18 8 47	2 29 35	16 2 26	22 15 6	2 18.4	0 42.6	23 54.0	12 21.3	16 41.9	26 7.0	18 44.0	1 14.1	18 31.0
26 Th	18 12 44	3 26 47	28 30 43	4♓49 35	2 11.3	0 8.8	25 3.2	13 3.1	16 38.3	26 3.2	18 41.6	1 16.3	18 32.3
27 F	18 16 40	4 23 59	11♓12 2	17 38 26	2 6.6	29♊36.6	26 12.6	13 44.9	16 34.5	25 59.2	18 39.3	1 18.6	18 33.7
28 Sa	18 20 37	5 21 12	24 9 8	0♈44 30	2D 4.2	29 6.4	27 22.1	14 26.5	16 30.6	25 55.3	18 36.9	1 20.8	18 35.1
29 Su	18 24 33	6 18 24	7♈24 54	14 10 40	2 3.6	28 38.9	28 31.6	15 8.2	16 26.4	25 51.3	18 34.6	1 23.0	18 36.4
30 M	18 28 30	7 15 37	21 2 3	27 59 16	2R 4.0	28 14.4	29 41.2	15 49.8	16 22.1	25 47.2	18 32.3	1 25.3	18 37.7

Astro Data	Planet Ingress	Last Aspect	☽ Ingress	Last Aspect	☽ Ingress	☽ Phases & Eclipses	Astro Data
Dy Hr Mn	Dy Hr Mn	Dy Hr Mn	Dy Hr Mn	Dy Hr Mn	Dy Hr Mn	Dy Hr Mn	1 MAY 1902
☽0N 4 4:06	♀ ♈ 7 7:05	2 12:12 ♆ △	♓ 2 13:16	31 22:55 ♄ ⚹	♈ 1 3:35	7 22:45 ● 16♉25	Julian Day # 851
♄ R 8 6:18	☿ ♊ 9 12:09	4 17:37 ♆ □	♈ 4 18:30	3 5:20 ♀ ☌	♉ 3 6:46	7 22:34:15 P 0.859	Delta T 0.4 sec
♀0N 10 3:20	♆ ♋ 21 13:37	6 19:38 ♆ ⚹	♉ 6 20:23	5 4:35 ♂ ☌	♊ 5 7:10	14 13:40 ☽ 22♌49	SVP 06♓37'16"
☽0S 16 18:56	☉ ♊ 22 0:54	8 17:54 ☿ ☌	♊ 8 20:21	6 13:52 ♅ ☍	♋ 7 6:26	22 10:46 ○ 0♐24	Obliquity 23°27'00"
☽0N 31 13:13	☿ ♋ 29 8:28	10 19:43 ♆ ☌	♋ 10 20:15	9 1:45 ♄ ☍	♌ 9 6:39	30 12:00 ☽ 8♓07	⚷ Chiron 14♑37.1R
		12 18:09 ♄ ☍	♌ 12 21:54	10 15:07 ♅ △	♍ 11 9:44		☽ Mean ☊ 4♏08.9
♃ R 6 4:31	♀ ♉ 3 23:59	15 2:13 ♆ ⚹	♍ 15 2:36	13 10:41 ♄ △	♎ 13 16:45	6 6:11 ● 14♊36	
☿ R 11 4:42	♂ ♊ 7 11:20	17 10:26 ♆ □	♎ 17 10:42	15 20:43 ♄ □	♏ 16 3:22	12 23:54 ☽ 21♍02	1 JUNE 1902
☽0S 13 1:55	☉ ♋ 22 9:15	19 21:26 ♆ △	♏ 19 21:33	18 8:54 ♄ ⚹	♐ 18 15:58	21 2:17 ○ 28♐46	Julian Day # 882
☽0N 27 20:57	☿ ♊ 26 6:27	22 5:12 ♄ ⚹	♐ 22 9:58	21 2:17 ☉ ☍	♑ 21 4:46	28 21:52 ☽ 6♈13	Delta T 0.5 sec
♅☍♇ 28 12:24	♀ ♊ 30 6:28	24 12:09 ☿ ☍	♑ 24 22:47	23 9:09 ♄ ☌	♒ 23 16:37		SVP 06♓37'12"
♃⚻♆ 29 12:35		27 5:55 ♄ ☌	♒ 27 10:50	25 16:43 ♀ □	♓ 26 2:50		Obliquity 23°26'59"
		29 8:57 ♀ ⚹	♓ 29 20:50	28 8:43 ☿ □	♈ 28 10:39		⚷ Chiron 13♑40.7R
				30 12:07 ☿ ⚹	♉ 30 15:26		☽ Mean ☊ 2♏30.4

JULY 1902 LONGITUDE

Day	Sid.Time	☉	0 hr ☽	Noon ☽	True ☊	☿	♀	♂	♃	♄	♅	♆	♇
1 Tu	18 32 27	8♋12 49	5♉ 2 24	12♉11 26	2♏ 4.2	27♊53.4	0♊50.9	16♊31.3	16♒17.7	25♑43.1	18♐30.1	1♋27.5	18♊39.1
2 W	18 36 23	9 10 2	19 26 10	26 46 15	2R 3.2	27R36.3	2 0.7	17 12.8	16R13.1	25R39.0	18R27.8	1 29.7	18 40.4
3 Th	18 40 20	10 7 15	4♊11 8	11♊40 3	1 60.0	27 23.4	3 10.5	17 54.2	16 8.3	25 34.8	18 25.6	1 31.9	18 41.7
4 F	18 44 16	11 4 29	19 12 6	26 46 10	1 54.2	27 14.9	4 20.4	18 35.6	16 3.3	25 30.6	18 23.4	1 34.2	18 43.0
5 Sa	18 48 13	12 1 42	4♋21 3	11♋55 26	1 46.0	27D11.2	5 30.4	19 16.9	15 58.2	25 26.4	18 21.2	1 36.4	18 44.3
6 Su	18 52 9	12 58 56	19 28 1	26 57 32	1 36.3	27 12.4	6 40.5	19 58.2	15 53.0	25 22.2	18 19.0	1 38.6	18 45.6
7 M	18 56 6	13 56 10	4♌22 47	11♌42 47	1 26.0	27 18.5	7 50.6	20 39.4	15 47.6	25 17.9	18 16.9	1 40.8	18 46.9
8 Tu	19 0 3	14 53 23	18 56 39	26 3 48	1 16.5	27 29.8	9 0.8	21 20.5	15 42.0	25 13.6	18 14.7	1 43.0	18 48.2
9 W	19 3 59	15 50 37	3♍ 3 48	9♍56 28	1 8.7	27 46.2	10 11.0	22 1.6	15 36.4	25 9.2	18 12.7	1 45.1	18 49.5
10 Th	19 7 56	16 47 50	16 41 47	23 19 56	1 3.2	28 7.8	11 21.3	22 42.7	15 30.5	25 4.9	18 10.6	1 47.3	18 50.7
11 F	19 11 52	17 45 3	29 51 13	6♎16 6	1 0.2	28 34.6	12 31.7	23 23.7	15 24.6	25 0.5	18 8.5	1 49.5	18 52.0
12 Sa	19 15 49	18 42 16	12♎35 5	18 48 46	0D 59.0	29 6.6	13 42.1	24 4.6	15 18.5	24 56.1	18 6.5	1 51.7	18 53.2
13 Su	19 19 45	19 39 29	24 57 48	1♏ 2 49	0R59.0	29 43.8	14 52.6	24 45.5	15 12.3	24 51.7	18 4.6	1 53.8	18 54.5
14 M	19 23 42	20 36 43	7♏ 4 30	13 3 30	0 58.9	0♋26.1	16 3.2	25 26.3	15 5.9	24 47.3	18 2.6	1 55.9	18 55.7
15 Tu	19 27 38	21 33 56	19 0 28	24 55 59	0 57.8	1 13.6	17 13.8	26 7.1	14 59.5	24 42.9	18 0.7	1 58.1	18 56.9
16 W	19 31 35	22 31 9	0♐50 38	6♐44 57	0 54.7	2 6.1	18 24.5	26 47.8	14 52.9	24 38.5	17 58.8	2 0.2	18 58.1
17 Th	19 35 32	23 28 23	12 39 25	18 34 29	0 49.1	3 3.5	19 35.3	27 28.4	14 46.2	24 34.0	17 57.0	2 2.3	18 59.3
18 F	19 39 28	24 25 37	24 30 30	0♑27 50	0 40.7	4 5.9	20 46.1	28 9.1	14 39.4	24 29.6	17 55.1	2 4.4	19 0.5
19 Sa	19 43 25	25 22 51	6♑26 44	12 27 27	0 29.8	5 13.2	21 57.0	28 49.6	14 32.6	24 25.2	17 53.3	2 6.5	19 1.6
20 Su	19 47 21	26 20 6	18 30 9	24 35 0	0 17.2	6 25.2	23 7.9	29 30.1	14 25.6	24 20.8	17 51.6	2 8.6	19 2.8
21 M	19 51 18	27 17 21	0♒42 6	6♒51 33	0 3.7	7 42.0	24 18.9	0♋10.6	14 18.5	24 16.3	17 49.9	2 10.7	19 3.9
22 Tu	19 55 14	28 14 36	13 3 25	19 17 46	29♎50.6	9 3.3	25 30.0	0 51.0	14 11.4	24 11.9	17 48.2	2 12.7	19 5.1
23 W	19 59 11	29 11 52	25 34 39	1♓54 9	29 39.0	10 29.1	26 41.1	1 31.3	14 4.1	24 7.5	17 46.6	2 14.8	19 6.2
24 Th	20 3 7	0♌ 9 9	8♓16 22	14 41 24	29 29.7	11 59.2	27 52.3	2 11.6	13 56.8	24 3.1	17 44.9	2 16.8	19 7.3
25 F	20 7 4	1 6 27	21 9 24	27 40 32	29 23.1	13 33.6	29 3.6	2 51.8	13 49.4	23 58.7	17 43.4	2 18.8	19 8.4
26 Sa	20 11 1	2 3 45	4♈14 59	10♈52 58	29 19.4	15 11.9	0♋14.9	3 32.0	13 42.0	23 54.3	17 41.8	2 20.8	19 9.5
27 Su	20 14 57	3 1 5	17 34 44	24 20 29	29D17.9	16 54.1	1 26.3	4 12.2	13 34.5	23 50.0	17 40.3	2 22.8	19 10.5
28 M	20 18 54	3 58 25	1♉10 27	8♉ 4 47	29R17.7	18 39.9	2 37.7	4 52.3	13 26.9	23 45.6	17 38.9	2 24.8	19 11.6
29 Tu	20 22 50	4 55 47	15 3 37	22 7 0	29 17.5	20 28.9	3 49.3	5 32.3	13 19.3	23 41.3	17 37.5	2 26.7	19 12.6
30 W	20 26 47	5 53 9	29 14 50	6♊26 59	29 16.1	22 21.0	5 0.8	6 12.3	13 11.6	23 37.0	17 36.1	2 28.7	19 13.6
31 Th	20 30 43	6 50 33	13♊43 4	21 2 38	29 12.7	24 15.9	6 12.5	6 52.2	13 3.9	23 32.8	17 34.8	2 30.6	19 14.7

AUGUST 1902 LONGITUDE

Day	Sid.Time	☉	0 hr ☽	Noon ☽	True ☊	☿	♀	♂	♃	♄	♅	♆	♇
1 F	20 34 40	7♌47 58	28♊25 1	5♋49 27	29♎ 6.5	26♋13.1	7♋24.2	7♋32.1	12♒56.2	23♑28.5	17♐33.5	2♋32.5	19♊15.7
2 Sa	20 38 36	8 45 24	13♋14 59	20 40 36	28R57.9	28 12.4	8 35.9	8 12.0	12R48.4	23R24.3	17R32.3	2 34.4	19 16.6
3 Su	20 42 33	9 42 51	28 5 12	5♌27 44	28 47.5	0♌13.4	9 47.7	8 51.8	12 40.6	23 20.2	17 31.1	2 36.3	19 17.6
4 M	20 46 30	10 40 20	12♌47 6	20 2 20	28 36.5	2 15.7	10 59.6	9 31.5	12 32.8	23 16.0	17 29.9	2 38.1	19 18.5
5 Tu	20 50 26	11 37 48	27 12 35	4♍17 9	28 26.1	4 19.0	12 11.5	10 11.2	12 25.0	23 11.9	17 28.8	2 40.0	19 19.5
6 W	20 54 23	12 35 18	11♍15 32	18 7 22	28 17.4	6 22.9	13 23.5	10 50.8	12 17.2	23 7.9	17 27.7	2 41.8	19 20.4
7 Th	20 58 19	13 32 49	24 52 31	1♎30 59	28 11.1	8 27.2	14 35.5	11 30.4	12 9.3	23 3.8	17 26.7	2 43.6	19 21.3
8 F	21 2 16	14 30 20	8♎ 2 57	14 28 42	28 7.4	10 31.6	15 47.6	12 9.9	12 1.5	22 59.9	17 25.7	2 45.4	19 22.2
9 Sa	21 6 12	15 27 53	20 48 39	27 3 18	28D 5.8	12 35.8	16 59.8	12 49.3	11 53.7	22 55.9	17 24.8	2 47.1	19 23.0
10 Su	21 10 9	16 25 26	3♏13 14	9♏19 4	28 5.7	14 39.5	18 12.0	13 28.7	11 45.9	22 52.1	17 23.9	2 48.9	19 23.9
11 M	21 14 5	17 23 0	15 21 27	21 21 2	28R 6.0	16 42.6	19 24.2	14 8.1	11 38.2	22 48.2	17 23.1	2 50.6	19 24.7
12 Tu	21 18 2	18 20 35	27 18 31	3♐14 32	28 5.6	18 44.9	20 36.5	14 47.4	11 30.5	22 44.4	17 22.3	2 52.3	19 25.5
13 W	21 21 59	19 18 11	9♐ 9 45	15 4 46	28 3.7	20 46.3	21 48.8	15 26.6	11 22.8	22 40.7	17 21.5	2 53.9	19 26.3
14 Th	21 25 55	20 15 48	21 0 9	26 56 27	27 59.6	22 46.6	23 1.2	16 5.8	11 15.1	22 37.0	17 20.8	2 55.6	19 27.1
15 F	21 29 52	21 13 26	2♑54 10	8♑53 42	27 53.0	24 45.7	24 13.7	16 44.9	11 7.5	22 33.4	17 20.2	2 57.2	19 27.8
16 Sa	21 33 48	22 11 5	14 55 28	20 59 45	27 44.2	26 43.6	25 26.2	17 24.0	10 60.0	22 29.9	17 19.6	2 58.8	19 28.6
17 Su	21 37 45	23 8 45	27 6 50	3♒16 53	27 33.7	28 40.2	26 38.8	18 3.0	10 52.5	22 26.4	17 19.0	3 0.4	19 29.3
18 M	21 41 41	24 6 26	9♒30 3	15 46 24	27 22.4	0♍35.6	27 51.4	18 42.0	10 45.1	22 22.9	17 18.5	3 2.0	19 30.0
19 Tu	21 45 38	25 4 9	22 5 59	28 28 45	27 11.3	2 29.5	29 4.1	19 20.9	10 37.7	22 19.6	17 18.1	3 3.5	19 30.7
20 W	21 49 34	26 1 52	4♓54 41	11♓23 41	27 1.5	4 22.1	0♌16.8	19 59.8	10 30.4	22 16.2	17 17.7	3 5.0	19 31.4
21 Th	21 53 31	26 59 38	17 55 41	24 30 35	26 53.8	6 13.3	1 29.6	20 38.6	10 23.2	22 13.0	17 17.3	3 6.5	19 32.0
22 F	21 57 27	27 57 24	1♈ 8 17	7♈48 45	26 48.6	8 3.1	2 42.4	21 17.4	10 16.1	22 9.8	17 17.0	3 7.9	19 32.6
23 Sa	22 1 24	28 55 13	14 31 54	21 17 43	26D45.8	9 51.6	3 55.3	21 56.1	10 9.0	22 6.7	17 16.8	3 9.4	19 33.2
24 Su	22 5 21	29 53 3	28 6 10	4♉57 16	26 45.2	11 38.7	5 8.2	22 34.8	10 2.1	22 3.7	17 16.6	3 10.8	19 33.8
25 M	22 9 17	0♍50 54	11♉51 1	18 47 25	26 45.8	13 24.4	6 21.2	23 13.4	9 55.3	22 0.7	17 16.4	3 12.2	19 34.4
26 Tu	22 13 14	1 48 48	25 46 29	2♊48 9	26R46.6	15 8.8	7 34.3	23 51.9	9 48.5	21 57.8	17 16.3	3 13.5	19 34.9
27 W	22 17 10	2 46 44	9♊52 20	16 58 53	26 46.5	16 51.9	8 47.4	24 30.4	9 41.9	21 55.0	17D16.3	3 14.9	19 35.5
28 Th	22 21 7	3 44 41	24 7 34	1♋18 4	26 44.7	18 33.7	10 0.6	25 8.9	9 35.4	21 52.3	17 16.3	3 16.2	19 36.0
29 F	22 25 3	4 42 40	8♋29 59	15 42 49	26 40.9	20 14.1	11 13.8	25 47.3	9 28.9	21 49.6	17 16.3	3 17.4	19 36.5
30 Sa	22 29 0	5 40 41	22 55 58	0♌ 8 48	26 35.0	21 53.3	12 27.0	26 25.6	9 22.7	21 47.0	17 16.4	3 18.7	19 36.9
31 Su	22 32 56	6 38 44	7♌20 35	14 30 35	26 27.7	23 31.2	13 40.3	27 3.9	9 16.5	21 44.6	17 16.6	3 19.9	19 37.4

Astro Data Dy Hr Mn	Planet Ingress Dy Hr Mn	Last Aspect Dy Hr Mn	☽ Ingress Dy Hr Mn	Last Aspect Dy Hr Mn	☽ Ingress Dy Hr Mn	☽ Phases & Eclipses Dy Hr Mn	Astro Data
☿ D 5 6:26	☿ ♋ 13 9:31	2 10:08 ♄ △	♊ 2 17:14	31 9:04 ♇ ☌	♋ 1 2:34	5 12:59 ● 12♋33	1 JULY 1902
☽0S 10 10:56	♂ ♋ 20 17:44	4 12:41 ☿ ☌	♋ 4 17:07	2 16:20 ♄ ☍	♌ 3 3:06	12 12:46 ☽ 19♎13	Julian Day # 912
☽0N 25 3:36	☊ ♎ 21 6:43	6 9:24 ♄ ☍	♌ 6 16:54	4 10:48 ♇ ⚹	♍ 5 4:43	20 16:45 ○ 27♑00	Delta T 0.6 sec
	☉ ♌ 23 20:10	8 14:43 ♄ ⚹	♍ 8 18:43	6 20:47 ♄ △	♎ 7 9:15	28 5:15 ☽ 4♉11	SVP 06♓37'07"
☽0S 6 21:13	♀ ♋ 25 18:59	10 21:33 ☿ □	♎ 11 0:16	9 4:02 ♄ □	♏ 9 17:43		Obliquity 23°26'59"
☽0N 21 10:13		12 23:48 ♄ □	♏ 13 9:56	11 14:51 ♄ ⚹	♐ 12 5:26	3 20:17 ● 10♌31	⚷ Chiron 11♑58.2R
♅ D 27 10:19	☿ ♌ 2 21:22	15 11:29 ♄ ⚹	♐ 15 22:17	14 4:19 ☿ △	♑ 14 18:10	11 4:24 ☽ 17♏34	☽ Mean ☊ 0♏55.1
	☿ ♍ 17 16:34	18 7:47 ♂ ☍	♑ 18 11:04	16 22:59 ♀ ☍	♒ 17 5:38	19 6:03 ○ 25♒19	
	♀ ♌ 19 18:28	20 16:45 ☉ ☍	♒ 20 22:38	19 6:03 ☉ ☍	♓ 19 14:51	26 11:04 ☽ 2♊16	1 AUGUST 1902
	☉ ♍ 24 2:53	23 2:20 ♀ △	♓ 23 8:24	21 7:48 ♄ ⚹	♈ 21 21:57		Julian Day # 943
		25 15:59 ♀ □	♈ 25 16:15	23 13:47 ♂ □	♉ 24 3:20		Delta T 0.7 sec
		27 11:03 ♄ □	♉ 27 21:57	25 20:34 ♂ ⚹	♊ 26 7:13		SVP 06♓37'02"
		29 14:35 ♄ △	♊ 30 1:16	27 16:24 ♇ ☌	♋ 28 9:50		Obliquity 23°26'59"
				30 6:05 ♂ ☌	♌ 30 11:45		⚷ Chiron 10♑07.8R
							☽ Mean ☊ 29♎16.6

LONGITUDE SEPTEMBER 1902

Day	Sid.Time	☉	0 hr ☽	Noon ☽	True ☊	☿	♀	♂	♃	♄	♅	♆	♇
1 M	22 36 53	7♍36 49	21♌38 5	28♌42 22	26♎19.8	25♍ 7.9	14♌53.7	27♋42.2	9♒10.5	21♑42.1	17♐16.8	3♋21.1	19♊37.8
2 Tu	22 40 50	8 34 55	5♍42 47	12♍38 47	26R12.3	26 43.3	16 7.1	28 20.4	9R 4.6	21R39.8	17 17.1	3 22.3	19 38.2
3 W	22 44 46	9 33 3	19 29 54	26 15 49	26 6.1	28 17.5	17 20.6	28 58.5	8 58.8	21 37.5	17 17.4	3 23.4	19 38.6
4 Th	22 48 43	10 31 13	2♎56 18	9♎31 16	26 1.7	29 50.4	18 34.1	29 36.6	8 53.2	21 35.4	17 17.7	3 24.5	19 39.0
5 F	22 52 39	11 29 24	16 0 46	22 24 55	25D59.4	1♎22.1	19 47.6	0♌14.6	8 47.7	21 33.3	17 18.2	3 25.6	19 39.3
6 Sa	22 56 36	12 27 37	28 43 59	4♏58 20	25 59.0	2 52.5	21 1.2	0 52.5	8 42.4	21 31.3	17 18.6	3 26.6	19 39.6
7 Su	23 0 32	13 25 51	11♏ 8 22	17 14 34	25 59.8	4 21.7	22 14.8	1 30.4	8 37.3	21 29.4	17 19.1	3 27.7	19 39.9
8 M	23 4 29	14 24 7	23 17 30	29 17 44	26 1.3	5 49.7	23 28.5	2 8.3	8 32.3	21 27.6	17 19.7	3 28.6	19 40.2
9 Tu	23 8 25	15 22 24	5♐15 52	11♐12 33	26R 2.7	7 16.4	24 42.2	2 46.0	8 27.4	21 25.9	17 20.3	3 29.6	19 40.5
10 W	23 12 22	16 20 43	17 8 23	23 4 2	26 3.2	8 41.9	25 56.0	3 23.8	8 22.7	21 24.3	17 21.0	3 30.5	19 40.7
11 Th	23 16 19	17 19 4	29 0 6	4♑57 11	26 2.4	10 6.0	27 9.8	4 1.4	8 18.2	21 22.7	17 21.7	3 31.4	19 40.9
12 F	23 20 15	18 17 26	10♑55 53	16 56 42	25 59.9	11 28.9	28 23.6	4 39.0	8 13.9	21 21.3	17 22.5	3 32.3	19 41.1
13 Sa	23 24 12	19 15 50	23 0 8	29 6 39	25 55.9	12 50.4	29 37.5	5 16.6	8 9.7	21 19.9	17 23.3	3 33.1	19 41.3
14 Su	23 28 8	20 14 15	5♒16 37	11♒30 21	25 50.7	14 10.5	0♍51.4	5 54.1	8 5.7	21 18.7	17 24.2	3 33.9	19 41.4
15 M	23 32 5	21 12 42	17 48 6	24 10 3	25 44.9	15 29.1	2 5.4	6 31.5	8 1.9	21 17.5	17 25.1	3 34.7	19 41.5
16 Tu	23 36 1	22 11 11	0♓36 16	7♓ 6 48	25 39.1	16 46.3	3 19.4	7 8.9	7 58.2	21 16.5	17 26.1	3 35.4	19 41.6
17 W	23 39 58	23 9 41	13 41 35	20 20 30	25 34.0	18 2.0	4 33.5	7 46.2	7 54.8	21 15.5	17 27.1	3 36.1	19 41.7
18 Th	23 43 54	24 8 14	27 3 20	3♈49 52	25 30.1	19 16.0	5 47.5	8 23.5	7 51.5	21 14.6	17 28.2	3 36.8	19 41.8
19 F	23 47 51	25 6 48	10♈39 49	17 32 50	25 27.7	20 28.4	7 1.7	9 0.7	7 48.4	21 13.8	17 29.3	3 37.5	19 41.8
20 Sa	23 51 48	26 5 24	24 28 37	1♉26 48	25D26.9	21 39.0	8 15.8	9 37.8	7 45.5	21 13.1	17 30.5	3 38.1	19R41.8
21 Su	23 55 44	27 4 3	8♉27 2	15 29 0	25 27.4	22 47.7	9 30.0	10 14.9	7 42.7	21 12.6	17 31.7	3 38.6	19 41.8
22 M	23 59 41	28 2 43	22 32 22	29 36 49	25 28.7	23 54.5	10 44.3	10 51.9	7 40.2	21 12.1	17 33.0	3 39.2	19 41.8
23 Tu	0 3 37	29 1 26	6♊42 5	13♊47 53	25 30.2	24 59.1	11 58.6	11 28.9	7 37.9	21 11.7	17 34.3	3 39.7	19 41.8
24 W	0 7 34	0♎ 0 11	20 53 58	28 0 3	25R31.3	26 1.5	13 12.9	12 5.8	7 35.7	21 11.4	17 35.7	3 40.2	19 41.7
25 Th	0 11 30	0 58 59	5♋ 5 53	12♋11 13	25 31.5	27 1.5	14 27.3	12 42.6	7 33.7	21 11.2	17 37.1	3 40.6	19 41.6
26 F	0 15 27	1 57 48	19 15 46	26 19 15	25 30.6	27 58.8	15 41.7	13 19.4	7 32.0	21D11.1	17 38.6	3 41.0	19 41.5
27 Sa	0 19 23	2 56 40	3♌21 22	10♌21 47	25 28.6	28 53.3	16 56.1	13 56.2	7 30.4	21 11.1	17 40.1	3 41.4	19 41.4
28 Su	0 23 20	3 55 35	17 20 11	24 16 14	25 26.0	29 44.9	18 10.6	14 32.8	7 29.0	21 11.2	17 41.7	3 41.8	19 41.2
29 M	0 27 16	4 54 31	1♍ 9 37	7♍59 59	25 23.0	0♏33.1	19 25.1	15 9.4	7 27.8	21 11.4	17 43.3	3 42.1	19 41.0
30 Tu	0 31 13	5 53 30	14 47 4	21 30 35	25 20.1	1 17.7	20 39.6	15 46.0	7 26.8	21 11.7	17 45.0	3 42.4	19 40.8

LONGITUDE OCTOBER 1902

Day	Sid.Time	☉	0 hr ☽	Noon ☽	True ☊	☿	♀	♂	♃	♄	♅	♆	♇
1 W	0 35 10	6♎52 30	28♍10 19	4♎46 4	25♎17.8	1♏58.4	21♍54.2	16♌22.4	7♒26.0	21♑12.1	17♐46.7	3♋42.6	19♊40.6
2 Th	0 39 6	7 51 33	11♎17 44	17 45 14	25R16.4	2 34.9	23 8.8	16 58.8	7R25.4	21 12.6	17 48.4	3 42.8	19R40.4
3 F	0 43 3	8 50 38	24 8 36	0♏27 53	25D15.9	3 6.8	24 23.5	17 35.2	7 25.0	21 13.2	17 50.2	3 43.0	19 40.1
4 Sa	0 46 59	9 49 45	6♏43 14	12 54 50	25 16.2	3 33.7	25 38.1	18 11.4	7D 24.8	21 13.9	17 52.1	3 43.1	19 39.8
5 Su	0 50 56	10 48 53	19 2 59	25 7 59	25 17.1	3 55.1	26 52.8	18 47.6	7 24.8	21 14.7	17 54.0	3 43.2	19 39.5
6 M	0 54 52	11 48 4	1♐10 13	7♐10 8	25 18.4	4 10.7	28 7.5	19 23.8	7 25.0	21 15.6	17 55.9	3 43.3	19 39.2
7 Tu	0 58 49	12 47 17	13 8 10	19 4 51	25 19.6	4R19.9	29 22.3	19 59.8	7 25.5	21 16.6	17 57.9	3R43.4	19 38.8
8 W	1 2 45	13 46 31	25 0 43	0♑56 20	25 20.6	4 22.2	0♎37.1	20 35.8	7 26.1	21 17.7	17 59.9	3 43.4	19 38.5
9 Th	1 6 42	14 45 47	6♑52 16	12 49 8	25R21.2	4 17.3	1 51.9	21 11.7	7 26.9	21 18.9	18 2.0	3 43.3	19 38.1
10 F	1 10 39	15 45 5	18 47 30	24 47 58	25 21.4	4 4.7	3 6.7	21 47.6	7 27.9	21 20.2	18 4.1	3 43.3	19 37.7
11 Sa	1 14 35	16 44 25	0♒51 7	6♒57 30	25 21.0	3 44.1	4 21.5	22 23.3	7 29.1	21 21.6	18 6.2	3 43.2	19 37.2
12 Su	1 18 32	17 43 46	13 7 37	19 21 57	25 20.4	3 15.2	5 36.4	22 59.0	7 30.5	21 23.1	18 8.4	3 43.1	19 36.8
13 M	1 22 28	18 43 9	25 40 56	2♓ 4 54	25 19.6	2 37.9	6 51.3	23 34.7	7 32.1	21 24.7	18 10.7	3 42.9	19 36.3
14 Tu	1 26 25	19 42 34	8♓34 8	15 8 49	25 18.8	1 52.5	8 6.2	24 10.2	7 33.9	21 26.4	18 13.0	3 42.7	19 35.8
15 W	1 30 21	20 42 1	21 49 2	28 34 46	25 18.1	0 59.3	9 21.1	24 45.7	7 35.8	21 28.2	18 15.3	3 42.5	19 35.3
16 Th	1 34 18	21 41 30	5♈25 53	12♈22 8	25 17.8	29♎59.0	10 36.1	25 21.1	7 38.0	21 30.1	18 17.6	3 42.2	19 34.8
17 F	1 38 14	22 41 0	19 23 9	26 28 29	25D17.6	28 52.8	11 51.0	25 56.4	7 40.4	21 32.1	18 20.0	3 41.9	19 34.2
18 Sa	1 42 11	23 40 33	3♉37 34	10♉49 45	25 17.6	27 41.9	13 6.0	26 31.7	7 43.0	21 34.1	18 22.5	3 41.6	19 33.6
19 Su	1 46 8	24 40 8	18 4 22	25 20 40	25R17.7	26 28.2	14 21.0	27 6.8	7 45.7	21 36.3	18 25.0	3 41.2	19 33.1
20 M	1 50 4	25 39 45	2♊37 55	9♊55 22	25 17.7	25 13.7	15 36.1	27 41.9	7 48.7	21 38.6	18 27.5	3 40.8	19 32.5
21 Tu	1 54 1	26 39 24	17 12 20	24 28 9	25 17.6	24 0.5	16 51.1	28 17.0	7 51.8	21 40.9	18 30.0	3 40.4	19 31.8
22 W	1 57 57	27 39 5	1♋42 14	8♋54 5	25 17.4	22 50.9	18 6.2	28 51.9	7 55.1	21 43.4	18 32.6	3 40.0	19 31.2
23 Th	2 1 54	28 38 49	16 3 17	23 9 28	25D17.2	21 47.0	19 21.3	29 26.8	7 58.7	21 45.9	18 35.3	3 39.5	19 30.5
24 F	2 5 50	29 38 35	0♌12 22	7♌11 50	25 17.2	20 50.7	20 36.5	0♍ 1.6	8 2.4	21 48.5	18 37.9	3 38.9	19 29.8
25 Sa	2 9 47	0♏38 23	14 7 42	20 59 56	25 17.3	20 3.5	21 51.6	0 36.3	8 6.3	21 51.3	18 40.6	3 38.4	19 29.1
26 Su	2 13 43	1 38 14	27 48 29	4♍33 23	25 17.7	19 26.6	23 6.8	1 10.9	8 10.3	21 54.1	18 43.4	3 37.8	19 28.4
27 M	2 17 40	2 38 6	11♍14 40	17 52 24	25 18.3	19 0.8	24 22.0	1 45.4	8 14.6	21 57.0	18 46.1	3 37.2	19 27.7
28 Tu	2 21 37	3 38 1	24 26 38	0♎57 27	25 19.1	18D46.5	25 37.2	2 19.9	8 19.0	22 0.0	18 48.9	3 36.5	19 26.9
29 W	2 25 33	4 37 58	7♎24 55	13 49 9	25 19.8	18 43.6	26 52.4	2 54.3	8 23.6	22 3.1	18 51.8	3 35.8	19 26.2
30 Th	2 29 30	5 37 57	20 10 12	26 28 10	25R20.3	18 51.8	28 7.6	3 28.5	8 28.4	22 6.3	18 54.7	3 35.1	19 25.4
31 F	2 33 26	6 37 58	2♏43 10	8♏55 18	25 20.2	19 10.7	29 22.8	4 2.7	8 33.4	22 9.5	18 57.6	3 34.4	19 24.6

Astro Data	Planet Ingress	Last Aspect	☽ Ingress	Last Aspect	☽ Ingress	☽ Phases & Eclipses	Astro Data
Dy Hr Mn	Dy Hr Mn	Dy Hr Mn	Dy Hr Mn	Dy Hr Mn	Dy Hr Mn	Dy Hr Mn	1 SEPTEMBER 1902
☽0S 3 7:17	☿ ♎ 4 2:30	31 20:37 ♇ ✶	♍ 1 14:12	30 11:33 ♀ ☌	♎ 1 3:19	2 5:19 ● 8♍48	Julian Day # 974
☿0S 4 1:52	♂ ♌ 4 14:48	3 17:42 ♂ ✶	♎ 3 18:42	2 18:29 ♄ □	♏ 3 11:07	9 22:15 ☽ 16♐16	Delta T 0.8 sec
☽0N 17 17:54	♀ ♍ 13 7:18	5 10:21 ♄ □	♏ 6 2:25	5 17:14 ♀ ✶	♐ 5 21:40	17 18:23 ○ 23♓55	SVP 06♓36'59"
♇ R 20 6:48	☉ ♎ 23 23:55	8 0:24 ♀ □	♐ 8 13:25	7 14:35 ♂ △	♑ 8 10:06	24 16:31 ☽ 0♋41	Obliquity 23°26'59"
♄ D 26 10:54	☿ ♏ 28 7:22	10 19:51 ♀ △	♑ 11 2:01	10 5:06 ♄ ☌	♒ 10 22:19		⚷ Chiron 9♑00.2R
☽0S 30 15:46		12 20:42 ♄ ☌	♒ 13 13:44	12 19:49 ♂ ☍	♓ 13 8:07	1 17:09 ● 7♎35	☽ Mean ☊ 27♎38.1
	♀ ♎ 7 12:06	15 3:35 ♇ △	♓ 15 22:53	14 23:23 ♄ ✶	♈ 15 14:30	9 17:21 ☽ 15♑29	
♃ D 4 11:13	☿ ♎ 15 23:38	17 18:23 ☉ ☍	♈ 18 5:14	17 14:50 ☿ ☍	♉ 17 17:56	17 6:01 ○ 22♈56	1 OCTOBER 1902
☿ R 7 20:00	♂ ♍ 23 22:55	19 18:40 ☿ ☍	♉ 20 9:31	19 15:32 ♂ □	♊ 19 19:40	17 6:03 ☍ T 1.456	Julian Day # 1004
♆ R 7 17:36	☉ ♏ 24 8:36	22 10:02 ☉ △	♊ 22 12:39	21 19:05 ♂ ✶	♋ 21 21:10	23 22:58 ☽ 29♋36	Delta T 0.9 sec
♀0S 10 5:25	♀ ♏ 31 11:51	24 9:20 ☿ △	♋ 24 15:23	23 22:58 ☉ □	♌ 23 23:39	31 8:14 ● 6♏59	SVP 06♓36'56"
☽0N 15 3:06		26 15:52 ☿ □	♌ 26 18:16	25 14:53 ♀ ✶	♍ 26 3:53	31 8:00:16 ☌ P 0.696	Obliquity 23°26'59"
☽0S 27 22:22		28 4:04 ♇ ✶	♍ 28 21:58	27 19:30 ♄ △	♎ 28 10:14		⚷ Chiron 9♑02.7
☿ D 28 18:06				30 16:52 ♀ ☌	♏ 30 18:46		☽ Mean ☊ 26♎02.8

NOVEMBER 1902 LONGITUDE

Day	Sid.Time	☉	0 hr ☽	Noon ☽	True ☊	☿	♀	♂	♃	♄	♅	♆	♇
1 Sa	2 37 23	7♏38 1	15♏ 4 42	21♏11 31	25♎19.5	19♎39.5	0♏38.1	4♍36.8	8♒38.6	22♑12.9	19♐ 0.5	3♋33.6	19♊23.8
2 Su	2 41 19	8 38 6	27 15 55	3♐18 7	25R 18.1	20 17.3	1 53.4	5 10.8	8 43.9	22 16.3	19 3.5	3R 32.8	19R 22.9
3 M	2 45 16	9 38 12	9♐18 20	15 16 52	25 16.1	21 3.4	3 8.7	5 44.7	8 49.4	22 19.9	19 6.5	3 32.0	19 22.1
4 Tu	2 49 12	10 38 21	21 14 1	27 10 7	25 13.7	21 56.8	4 23.9	6 18.5	8 55.1	22 23.5	19 9.5	3 31.1	19 21.2
5 W	2 53 9	11 38 31	3♑ 5 34	9♑ 0 47	25 11.2	22 56.8	5 39.3	6 52.2	9 0.9	22 27.2	19 12.6	3 30.2	19 20.4
6 Th	2 57 5	12 38 42	14 56 14	20 52 24	25 8.9	24 2.3	6 54.6	7 25.7	9 7.0	22 31.0	19 15.6	3 29.3	19 19.5
7 F	3 1 2	13 38 55	26 49 49	2♒49 2	25 7.1	25 12.8	8 9.9	7 59.2	9 13.2	22 34.8	19 18.8	3 28.4	19 18.6
8 Sa	3 4 59	14 39 10	8♒50 36	14 55 7	25D 6.2	26 27.6	9 25.2	8 32.6	9 19.5	22 38.8	19 21.9	3 27.4	19 17.6
9 Su	3 8 55	15 39 26	21 3 9	27 15 17	25 6.2	27 45.9	10 40.5	9 5.9	9 26.0	22 42.8	19 25.1	3 26.4	19 16.7
10 M	3 12 52	16 39 44	3♓32 5	9♓54 3	25 7.0	29 7.3	11 55.9	9 39.1	9 32.7	22 46.9	19 28.3	3 25.3	19 15.8
11 Tu	3 16 48	17 40 2	16 21 41	22 55 23	25 8.4	0♏31.3	13 11.2	10 12.1	9 39.6	22 51.1	19 31.5	3 24.3	19 14.8
12 W	3 20 45	18 40 23	29 35 29	6♈22 10	25 10.0	1 57.5	14 26.6	10 45.1	9 46.6	22 55.4	19 34.7	3 23.2	19 13.8
13 Th	3 24 41	19 40 45	13♈15 34	20 15 35	25R 11.3	3 25.4	15 42.0	11 18.0	9 53.7	22 59.7	19 38.0	3 22.1	19 12.8
14 F	3 28 38	20 41 8	27 22 1	4♉34 29	25 11.7	4 54.8	16 57.3	11 50.7	10 1.0	23 4.2	19 41.3	3 21.0	19 11.8
15 Sa	3 32 34	21 41 33	11♉52 24	19 15 2	25 10.8	6 25.4	18 12.7	12 23.3	10 8.5	23 8.7	19 44.6	3 19.8	19 10.8
16 Su	3 36 31	22 41 59	26 41 29	4♊10 43	25 8.6	7 57.0	19 28.1	12 55.8	10 16.1	23 13.2	19 47.9	3 18.6	19 9.8
17 M	3 40 28	23 42 27	11♊41 38	19 13 4	25 5.1	9 29.3	20 43.5	13 28.3	10 23.9	23 17.9	19 51.3	3 17.4	19 8.8
18 Tu	3 44 24	24 42 57	26 43 51	4♋12 50	25 0.8	11 2.3	21 58.9	14 0.5	10 31.8	23 22.6	19 54.7	3 16.2	19 7.8
19 W	3 48 21	25 43 29	11♋39 2	19 1 31	24 56.5	12 35.8	23 14.3	14 32.7	10 39.8	23 27.4	19 58.0	3 14.9	19 6.7
20 Th	3 52 17	26 44 2	26 19 33	3♌32 34	24 52.6	14 9.6	24 29.7	15 4.8	10 48.0	23 32.2	20 1.5	3 13.6	19 5.7
21 F	3 56 14	27 44 37	10♌40 8	17 42 1	24 50.0	15 43.7	25 45.1	15 36.7	10 56.4	23 37.2	20 4.9	3 12.3	19 4.6
22 Sa	4 0 10	28 45 14	24 38 8	1♍28 32	24D 48.8	17 18.0	27 0.5	16 8.5	11 4.9	23 42.2	20 8.3	3 11.0	19 3.5
23 Su	4 4 7	29 45 52	8♍13 22	14 52 51	24 49.0	18 52.5	28 16.0	16 40.2	11 13.5	23 47.2	20 11.8	3 9.7	19 2.4
24 M	4 8 3	0♐46 32	21 27 19	27 57 5	24 50.2	20 27.0	29 31.4	17 11.7	11 22.2	23 52.4	20 15.3	3 8.3	19 1.3
25 Tu	4 12 0	1 47 14	4♎22 32	10♎44 3	24 51.9	22 1.5	0♐46.8	17 43.1	11 31.1	23 57.6	20 18.8	3 6.9	19 0.2
26 W	4 15 57	2 47 57	17 1 59	23 16 42	24R 53.2	23 36.1	2 2.3	18 14.4	11 40.2	24 2.8	20 22.3	3 5.5	18 59.1
27 Th	4 19 53	3 48 42	29 28 32	5♏37 48	24 53.4	25 10.7	3 17.7	18 45.5	11 49.4	24 8.1	20 25.8	3 4.1	18 58.0
28 F	4 23 50	4 49 29	11♏44 45	17 49 40	24 51.8	26 45.2	4 33.2	19 16.5	11 58.7	24 13.5	20 29.4	3 2.6	18 56.9
29 Sa	4 27 46	5 50 16	23 52 45	29 54 14	24 48.1	28 19.7	5 48.7	19 47.3	12 8.1	24 19.0	20 32.9	3 1.2	18 55.8
30 Su	4 31 43	6 51 5	5♐54 17	11♐53 5	24 42.4	29 54.1	7 4.2	20 18.0	12 17.6	24 24.5	20 36.5	2 59.7	18 54.6

DECEMBER 1902 LONGITUDE

Day	Sid.Time	☉	0 hr ☽	Noon ☽	True ☊	☿	♀	♂	♃	♄	♅	♆	♇
1 M	4 35 39	7♐51 56	17♐50 48	23♐47 39	24♎34.8	1♐28.5	8♐19.6	20♍48.6	12♒27.3	24♑30.1	20♐40.1	2♋58.2	18♊53.5
2 Tu	4 39 36	8 52 47	29 43 47	5♑39 26	24R 25.9	3 2.8	9 35.1	21 18.9	12 37.1	24 35.7	20 43.7	2R 56.7	18R 52.3
3 W	4 43 32	9 53 40	11♑34 50	17 30 15	24 16.7	4 37.1	10 50.6	21 49.2	12 47.1	24 41.4	20 47.3	2 55.2	18 51.2
4 Th	4 47 29	10 54 33	23 25 58	29 22 21	24 7.9	6 11.3	12 6.1	22 19.2	12 57.1	24 47.2	20 50.9	2 53.6	18 50.1
5 F	4 51 26	11 55 28	5♒19 45	11♒18 36	24 0.4	7 45.5	13 21.5	22 49.1	13 7.3	24 53.0	20 54.5	2 52.1	18 48.9
6 Sa	4 55 22	12 56 23	17 19 23	23 22 34	23 54.8	9 19.7	14 37.0	23 18.9	13 17.6	24 58.8	20 58.1	2 50.5	18 47.7
7 Su	4 59 19	13 57 19	29 28 42	5♓38 20	23 51.3	10 53.9	15 52.5	23 48.4	13 28.0	25 4.8	21 1.7	2 48.9	18 46.6
8 M	5 3 15	14 58 16	11♓52 3	18 10 26	23D 50.0	12 28.0	17 8.0	24 17.8	13 38.5	25 10.7	21 5.4	2 47.3	18 45.4
9 Tu	5 7 12	15 59 13	24 34 4	1♈ 3 29	23 50.3	14 2.2	18 23.4	24 47.0	13 49.1	25 16.7	21 9.0	2 45.7	18 44.3
10 W	5 11 8	17 0 11	7♈39 14	14 21 43	23 51.3	15 36.4	19 38.9	25 16.1	13 59.9	25 22.8	21 12.6	2 44.1	18 43.1
11 Th	5 15 5	18 1 9	21 11 17	28 8 9	23R 52.1	17 10.7	20 54.4	25 44.9	14 10.7	25 28.9	21 16.3	2 42.5	18 41.9
12 F	5 19 1	19 2 9	5♉12 23	12♉23 50	23 51.6	18 45.0	22 9.8	26 13.6	14 21.7	25 35.1	21 19.9	2 40.8	18 40.8
13 Sa	5 22 58	20 3 8	19 42 11	27 6 51	23 48.9	20 19.4	23 25.3	26 42.1	14 32.7	25 41.3	21 23.6	2 39.2	18 39.6
14 Su	5 26 55	21 4 9	4♊37 2	12♊11 44	23 43.8	21 53.8	24 40.8	27 10.4	14 43.9	25 47.5	21 27.2	2 37.5	18 38.4
15 M	5 30 51	22 5 10	19 49 43	27 29 38	23 36.3	23 28.4	25 56.2	27 38.5	14 55.1	25 53.8	21 30.9	2 35.9	18 37.3
16 Tu	5 34 48	23 6 12	5♋10 2	12♋49 25	23 27.2	25 3.1	27 11.7	28 6.4	15 6.5	26 0.2	21 34.5	2 34.2	18 36.1
17 W	5 38 44	24 7 14	20 26 23	27 59 35	23 17.6	26 37.9	28 27.1	28 34.1	15 17.9	26 6.6	21 38.2	2 32.5	18 34.9
18 Th	5 42 41	25 8 18	5♌27 54	12♌50 23	23 8.8	28 12.9	29 42.6	29 1.6	15 29.5	26 13.0	21 41.8	2 30.9	18 33.8
19 F	5 46 37	26 9 22	20 6 20	27 15 16	23 1.7	29 48.1	0♑58.1	29 28.9	15 41.1	26 19.4	21 45.5	2 29.2	18 32.6
20 Sa	5 50 34	27 10 27	4♍16 58	11♍11 23	22 57.0	1♑23.4	2 13.5	29 56.0	15 52.8	26 25.9	21 49.1	2 27.5	18 31.5
21 Su	5 54 31	28 11 32	17 58 39	24 39 4	22D 54.7	2 58.9	3 29.0	0♎22.9	16 4.6	26 32.5	21 52.7	2 25.8	18 30.3
22 M	5 58 27	29 12 39	1♎13 2	7♎41 2	22 54.2	4 34.5	4 44.4	0 49.5	16 16.5	26 39.1	21 56.4	2 24.1	18 29.2
23 Tu	6 2 24	0♑13 46	14 3 36	20 21 17	22R 54.7	6 10.4	5 59.9	1 15.9	16 28.5	26 45.7	21 60.0	2 22.4	18 28.0
24 W	6 6 20	1 14 54	26 34 40	2♏44 20	22 54.8	7 46.5	7 15.3	1 42.1	16 40.6	26 52.3	22 3.6	2 20.7	18 26.9
25 Th	6 10 17	2 16 3	8♏50 48	14 54 36	22 53.5	9 22.7	8 30.8	2 8.0	16 52.8	26 59.0	22 7.2	2 19.0	18 25.8
26 F	6 14 13	3 17 12	20 56 12	26 56 1	22 49.9	10 59.2	9 46.2	2 33.7	17 5.0	27 5.7	22 10.8	2 17.3	18 24.6
27 Sa	6 18 10	4 18 22	2♐54 28	8♐51 51	22 43.4	12 35.8	11 1.7	2 59.2	17 17.4	27 12.4	22 14.4	2 15.6	18 23.5
28 Su	6 22 6	5 19 32	14 48 29	20 44 37	22 33.8	14 12.5	12 17.1	3 24.3	17 29.8	27 19.2	22 18.0	2 13.9	18 22.4
29 M	6 26 3	6 20 42	26 40 28	2♑36 13	22 21.6	15 49.4	13 32.6	3 49.3	17 42.3	27 26.0	22 21.6	2 12.2	18 21.3
30 Tu	6 30 0	7 21 53	8♑32 3	14 28 7	22 7.5	17 26.4	14 48.0	4 13.9	17 54.8	27 32.9	22 25.2	2 10.5	18 20.2
31 W	6 33 56	8 23 4	20 24 35	26 21 34	21 52.7	19 3.4	16 3.5	4 38.3	18 7.5	27 39.7	22 28.7	2 8.8	18 19.1

Astro Data Dy Hr Mn	Planet Ingress Dy Hr Mn	Last Aspect Dy Hr Mn	☽ Ingress Dy Hr Mn	Last Aspect Dy Hr Mn	☽ Ingress Dy Hr Mn	☽ Phases & Eclipses Dy Hr Mn	Astro Data
♅☍♇ 6 22:49	☿ ♏ 10 15:08	1 14:05 ♄ ⚹	♐ 2 5:26	1 6:14 ♂ □	♑ 2 0:33	8 12:30 ☽ 15♒11	1 NOVEMBER 1902
☽0N 11 13:18	☉ ♐ 23 5:36	4 1:34 ☿ ⚹	♑ 4 17:44	4 2:46 ♄ ☌	♒ 4 13:16	15 17:06 ○ 22♉25	Julian Day # 1035
☽0S 24 4:17	♀ ♐ 24 9:06	6 20:23 ☿ □	♒ 7 6:22	6 7:16 ♅ ⚹	♓ 7 1:01	22 7:47 ☽ 29♌05	Delta T 1.0 sec
	☿ ♐ 30 1:30	9 14:33 ☿ △	♓ 9 17:16	9 1:20 ♄ ⚹	♈ 9 10:03	30 2:04 ● 6♐56	SVP 06♓36'54"
☽0N 8 23:09		11 11:56 ♄ ⚹	♈ 12 0:44	11 7:30 ♄ □	♉ 11 15:11		Obliquity 23°26'59"
☽0S 21 11:31	♀ ♑ 18 5:32	13 16:44 ♄ □	♉ 14 4:24	13 11:42 ♂ △	♊ 13 16:38	8 6:27 ☽ 15♓15	⚷ Chiron 10♑19.3
♃□♆ 26 20:57	☿ ♑ 19 3:01	15 18:23 ♄ △	♊ 16 5:19	15 12:37 ♂ □	♋ 15 15:55	15 3:47 ○ 22♊15	☽ Mean ☊ 24♎24.2
♃△♇ 31 20:15	♂ ♎ 20 3:33	17 13:04 ♅ ☍	♋ 18 5:14	17 13:20 ♂ ⚹	♌ 17 15:13	21 20:00 ☽ 29♍02	
	☉ ♑ 22 18:36	20 0:44 ☉ △	♌ 20 6:05	19 10:56 ☉ △	♍ 19 16:40	29 21:25 ● 7♑15	1 DECEMBER 1902
		22 7:47 ☉ □	♍ 22 9:24	21 20:00 ☉ □	♎ 21 21:46		Julian Day # 1065
		24 4:29 ♄ △	♎ 24 15:49	24 0:35 ♄ □	♏ 24 6:39		Delta T 1.1 sec
		26 13:35 ♄ □	♏ 27 1:01	26 12:26 ♄ ⚹	♐ 26 18:09		SVP 06♓36'50"
		29 10:11 ☿ ☌	♐ 29 12:12	28 15:14 ♅ ☌	♑ 29 6:44		Obliquity 23°26'58"
				31 14:46 ♄ ☌	♒ 31 19:20		⚷ Chiron 12♑30.6
							☽ Mean ☊ 22♎48.9

LONGITUDE — JANUARY 1903

Day	Sid.Time	☉	0 hr ☽	Noon ☽	True ☊	☿	♀	♂	♃	♄	♅	♆	♇
1 Th	6 37 53	9♑24 15	2♒19 16	8♒17 53	21♎38.4	20♑40.4	17♑18.9	5♎ 2.4	18♒20.2	27♑46.6	22♐32.3	2♋ 7.1	18♊18.0
2 F	6 41 49	10 25 25	14 17 36	20 18 43	21R 25.7	22 17.4	18 34.3	5 26.2	18 33.0	27 53.5	22 35.8	2R 5.4	18R 17.0
3 Sa	6 45 46	11 26 36	26 21 30	2♓26 18	21 15.5	23 54.2	19 49.7	5 49.7	18 45.8	28 0.4	22 39.3	2 3.7	18 15.9
4 Su	6 49 42	12 27 46	8♓33 31	14 43 33	21 8.4	25 30.8	21 5.2	6 12.9	18 58.8	28 7.4	22 42.8	2 2.1	18 14.8
5 M	6 53 39	13 28 57	20 56 53	27 14 1	21 4.2	27 7.0	22 20.6	6 35.8	19 11.7	28 14.4	22 46.3	2 0.4	18 13.8
6 Tu	6 57 35	14 30 6	3♈35 29	10♈ 1 48	21D 2.5	28 42.7	23 36.0	6 58.3	19 24.8	28 21.3	22 49.7	1 58.7	18 12.8
7 W	7 1 32	15 31 16	16 33 30	23 11 5	21R 2.2	0♒17.7	24 51.3	7 20.6	19 37.9	28 28.3	22 53.2	1 57.1	18 11.7
8 Th	7 5 29	16 32 25	29 55 1	6♉45 39	21 2.1	1 51.9	26 6.7	7 42.6	19 51.1	28 35.4	22 56.6	1 55.4	18 10.7
9 F	7 9 25	17 33 33	13♉43 15	20 47 56	21 0.9	3 24.9	27 22.1	8 4.2	20 4.3	28 42.4	23 0.0	1 53.8	18 9.7
10 Sa	7 13 22	18 34 42	27 59 38	5♊18 5	20 57.4	4 56.5	28 37.4	8 25.5	20 17.6	28 49.5	23 3.4	1 52.2	18 8.7
11 Su	7 17 18	19 35 49	12♊42 48	20 13 2	20 51.1	6 26.4	29 52.8	8 46.4	20 31.0	28 56.5	23 6.8	1 50.6	18 7.7
12 M	7 21 15	20 36 56	27 47 48	5♋25 55	20 42.1	7 54.3	1♒ 8.1	9 7.0	20 44.4	29 3.6	23 10.1	1 49.0	18 6.8
13 Tu	7 25 11	21 38 3	13♋ 6 3	20 46 42	20 31.0	9 19.6	2 23.4	9 27.2	20 57.8	29 10.7	23 13.5	1 47.4	18 5.8
14 W	7 29 8	22 39 9	28 26 23	6♌ 3 34	20 19.2	10 41.9	3 38.7	9 47.1	21 11.3	29 17.8	23 16.8	1 45.8	18 4.9
15 Th	7 33 4	23 40 15	13♌36 55	21 5 11	20 8.0	12 0.6	4 54.0	10 6.6	21 24.9	29 24.9	23 20.1	1 44.3	18 4.0
16 F	7 37 1	24 41 20	28 27 24	5♍42 45	19 58.6	13 15.1	6 9.3	10 25.8	21 38.5	29 32.0	23 23.3	1 42.7	18 3.1
17 Sa	7 40 58	25 42 25	12♍50 45	19 51 7	19 51.9	14 24.8	7 24.6	10 44.5	21 52.1	29 39.1	23 26.6	1 41.2	18 2.2
18 Su	7 44 54	26 43 30	26 43 46	3♎28 52	19 48.0	15 28.7	8 39.9	11 2.8	22 5.8	29 46.3	23 29.8	1 39.7	18 1.3
19 M	7 48 51	27 44 34	10♎ 6 43	16 37 43	19D 46.4	16 26.3	9 55.1	11 20.7	22 19.6	29 53.4	23 33.0	1 38.2	18 0.4
20 Tu	7 52 47	28 45 38	23 2 24	29 21 22	19R 46.2	17 16.5	11 10.4	11 38.2	22 33.4	0♒ 0.5	23 36.1	1 36.7	17 59.5
21 W	7 56 44	29 46 42	5♏35 15	11♏44 40	19 46.2	17 58.5	12 25.6	11 55.3	22 47.2	0 7.7	23 39.2	1 35.2	17 58.7
22 Th	8 0 40	0♒47 45	17 50 18	23 52 47	19 45.0	18 31.5	13 40.9	12 12.0	23 1.1	0 14.8	23 42.3	1 33.8	17 57.9
23 F	8 4 37	1 48 48	29 52 43	5♐50 42	19 41.8	18 54.6	14 56.1	12 28.1	23 15.0	0 21.9	23 45.4	1 32.4	17 57.1
24 Sa	8 8 33	2 49 51	11♐47 15	17 42 51	19 35.8	19R 7.2	16 11.3	12 43.9	23 28.9	0 29.1	23 48.5	1 30.9	17 56.3
25 Su	8 12 30	3 50 53	23 37 58	29 32 59	19 26.9	19 8.7	17 26.5	12 59.1	23 42.9	0 36.2	23 51.5	1 29.6	17 55.5
26 M	8 16 27	4 51 54	5♑28 13	11♑23 59	19 15.3	18 58.9	18 41.7	13 13.9	23 57.0	0 43.3	23 54.5	1 28.2	17 54.7
27 Tu	8 20 23	5 52 55	17 20 30	23 18 1	19 1.9	18 37.5	19 56.8	13 28.2	24 11.0	0 50.4	23 57.4	1 26.8	17 54.0
28 W	8 24 20	6 53 54	29 16 40	5♒16 36	18 47.7	18 5.0	21 12.0	13 42.0	24 25.1	0 57.6	24 0.4	1 25.5	17 53.3
29 Th	8 28 16	7 54 53	11♒17 58	17 20 51	18 33.8	17 22.0	22 27.1	13 55.2	24 39.2	1 4.7	24 3.3	1 24.2	17 52.6
30 F	8 32 13	8 55 51	23 25 24	29 31 43	18 21.6	16 29.5	23 42.2	14 8.0	24 53.4	1 11.8	24 6.1	1 22.9	17 51.9
31 Sa	8 36 9	9 56 48	5♓39 58	11♓50 18	18 11.7	15 29.0	24 57.4	14 20.2	25 7.6	1 18.9	24 8.9	1 21.6	17 51.2

LONGITUDE — FEBRUARY 1903

Day	Sid.Time	☉	0 hr ☽	Noon ☽	True ☊	☿	♀	♂	♃	♄	♅	♆	♇
1 Su	8 40 6	10♒57 43	18♓ 2 55	24♓18 4	18♎ 4.8	14♒22.2	26♒12.4	14♎31.8	25♒21.8	1♒25.9	24♐11.7	1♋20.4	17♊50.6
2 M	8 44 2	11 58 38	0♈36 1	6♈57 3	18R 0.8	13R 11.1	27 27.5	14 42.9	25 36.0	1 33.0	24 14.5	1R 19.2	17R 49.9
3 Tu	8 47 59	12 59 31	13 21 31	19 49 47	17D 59.3	11 57.8	28 42.6	14 53.5	25 50.3	1 40.1	24 17.2	1 18.0	17 49.3
4 W	8 51 56	14 0 22	26 22 13	2♉59 13	17 59.4	10 44.4	29 57.6	15 3.4	26 4.5	1 47.1	24 19.9	1 16.8	17 48.7
5 Th	8 55 52	15 1 13	9♉41 7	16 28 14	17R 60.0	9 32.9	1♓12.6	15 12.8	26 18.8	1 54.1	24 22.5	1 15.7	17 48.2
6 F	8 59 49	16 2 1	23 20 51	0♊19 8	17 59.8	8 25.1	2 27.6	15 21.6	26 33.2	2 1.1	24 25.1	1 14.6	17 47.6
7 Sa	9 3 45	17 2 49	7♊23 8	14 32 45	17 58.0	7 22.6	3 42.5	15 29.8	26 47.5	2 8.1	24 27.7	1 13.5	17 47.1
8 Su	9 7 42	18 3 35	21 47 46	29 7 43	17 53.8	6 26.4	4 57.4	15 37.4	27 1.8	2 15.1	24 30.2	1 12.4	17 46.6
9 M	9 11 38	19 4 19	6♋31 59	13♋59 45	17 47.3	5 37.4	6 12.4	15 44.3	27 16.2	2 22.0	24 32.7	1 11.4	17 46.1
10 Tu	9 15 35	20 5 2	21 30 3	29 1 45	17 39.0	4 56.2	7 27.2	15 50.6	27 30.6	2 29.0	24 35.2	1 10.4	17 45.6
11 W	9 19 31	21 5 43	6♌33 39	14♌ 4 28	17 29.9	4 23.0	8 42.1	15 56.3	27 45.0	2 35.9	24 37.6	1 9.4	17 45.1
12 Th	9 23 28	22 6 23	21 32 59	28 58 2	17 21.1	3 58.0	9 56.9	16 1.3	27 59.4	2 42.8	24 40.0	1 8.5	17 44.7
13 F	9 27 25	23 7 1	6♍18 33	13♍33 39	17 13.7	3 40.9	11 11.7	16 5.7	28 13.8	2 49.6	24 42.3	1 7.5	17 44.3
14 Sa	9 31 21	24 7 38	20 42 39	27 45 1	17 8.5	3D 31.6	12 26.5	16 9.4	28 28.2	2 56.4	24 44.6	1 6.6	17 43.9
15 Su	9 35 18	25 8 13	4♎40 29	11♎28 56	17D 5.6	3 29.7	13 41.2	16 12.3	28 42.6	3 3.2	24 46.8	1 5.8	17 43.5
16 M	9 39 14	26 8 48	18 10 24	24 45 8	17 4.9	3 34.8	14 56.0	16 14.6	28 57.1	3 10.0	24 49.0	1 4.9	17 43.2
17 Tu	9 43 11	27 9 21	1♏13 27	7♏35 48	17 5.6	3 46.5	16 10.7	16 16.2	29 11.5	3 16.8	24 51.2	1 4.1	17 42.9
18 W	9 47 7	28 9 53	13 52 43	20 4 45	17 6.9	4 4.3	17 25.3	16R 17.0	29 25.9	3 23.5	24 53.3	1 3.3	17 42.6
19 Th	9 51 4	29 10 24	26 12 32	2♐16 42	17R 7.7	4 27.9	18 40.0	16 17.1	29 40.4	3 30.2	24 55.4	1 2.6	17 42.3
20 F	9 55 0	0♓10 53	8♐17 53	14 16 42	17 7.4	4 56.7	19 54.6	16 16.5	29 54.8	3 36.8	24 57.4	1 1.9	17 42.0
21 Sa	9 58 57	1 11 21	20 13 48	26 9 45	17 5.2	5 30.4	21 9.2	16 15.1	0♓ 9.3	3 43.5	24 59.4	1 1.2	17 41.8
22 Su	10 2 54	2 11 48	2♑ 5 7	8♑ 0 26	17 1.0	6 8.6	22 23.8	16 13.0	0 23.7	3 50.0	25 1.4	1 0.5	17 41.6
23 M	10 6 50	3 12 13	13 56 9	19 52 43	16 55.0	6 51.0	23 38.3	16 10.1	0 38.2	3 56.6	25 3.3	0 59.9	17 41.4
24 Tu	10 10 47	4 12 37	25 50 31	1♒49 54	16 47.5	7 37.3	24 52.8	16 6.4	0 52.6	4 3.1	25 5.1	0 59.3	17 41.2
25 W	10 14 43	5 12 59	7♒51 7	13 54 25	16 39.4	8 27.1	26 7.3	16 1.9	1 7.1	4 9.6	25 6.9	0 58.8	17 41.0
26 Th	10 18 40	6 13 20	20 0 1	26 8 3	16 31.4	9 20.2	27 21.8	15 56.7	1 21.5	4 16.0	25 8.7	0 58.2	17 40.9
27 F	10 22 36	7 13 39	2♓18 38	8♓31 53	16 24.3	10 16.4	28 36.2	15 50.6	1 35.9	4 22.4	25 10.4	0 57.7	17 40.8
28 Sa	10 26 33	8 13 56	14 47 49	21 6 32	16 18.8	11 15.4	29 50.6	15 43.8	1 50.3	4 28.8	25 12.0	0 57.3	17 40.7

Astro Data Dy Hr Mn	Planet Ingress Dy Hr Mn	Last Aspect Dy Hr Mn	☽ Ingress Dy Hr Mn	Last Aspect Dy Hr Mn	☽ Ingress Dy Hr Mn	☽ Phases & Eclipses Dy Hr Mn	Astro Data
♂0S 2 7:37	☿ ♒ 6 19:31	2 16:37 ♅ ∗	♓ 3 7:12	1 11:51 ♅ □	♈ 1 22:52	6 21:57 ☽ 15♈26	1 JANUARY 1903
☽0N 5 7:28	♀ ♒ 11 2:18	5 14:02 ♄ ∗	♈ 5 17:14	3 23:27 ♃ ∗	♉ 4 6:36	13 14:17 ○ 22♋14	Julian Day # 1096
☽0S 17 21:13	♄ ♒ 19 22:15	7 21:38 ♄ □	♉ 8 0:09	6 5:38 ♃ □	♊ 6 11:27	20 11:49 ☽ 29♎16	Delta T 1.2 sec
☿ R 24 15:15	☉ ♒ 21 5:14	10 1:23 ♄ △	♊ 10 3:19	8 8:43 ♃ △	♋ 8 13:25	28 16:38 ● 7♒36	SVP 06♓36'44"
♃∗♅ 25 18:37		11 16:39 ♅ ☍	♋ 12 3:28	9 14:54 ♂ □	♌ 10 13:33		Obliquity 23°26'58"
♄⚻♆ 31 8:00	♀ ♓ 4 0:47	14 1:21 ♄ ☍	♌ 14 2:27	12 10:35 ♃ ☍	♍ 12 13:41	5 10:12 ☽ 15♉27	⚷ Chiron 15♑20.3
	☉ ♓ 19 19:41	15 15:42 ♅ △	♍ 16 2:32	14 6:52 ♅ □	♎ 14 15:53	12 0:58 ○ 22♌09	☽ Mean ☊ 21♎10.5
☽0N 1 14:19	♃ ♓ 20 8:35	18 5:26 ♄ △	♎ 18 5:47	16 20:08 ♃ △	♏ 16 21:43	19 6:23 ☽ 29♏26	
♄⚼♇ 12 6:27	♀ ♈ 28 3:03	20 11:49 ☉ □	♏ 20 13:14	19 6:58 ♃ □	♐ 19 7:29	27 10:19 ● 7♓40	1 FEBRUARY 1903
☽0S 14 8:27		22 10:29 ♃ □	♐ 23 0:15	21 9:39 ♅ ☌	♑ 21 19:46		Julian Day # 1127
☿ D 14 18:20		25 0:28 ♅ ☌	♑ 25 12:55	23 21:51 ♀ ∗	♒ 24 8:20		Delta T 1.4 sec
♂ R 18 15:34		26 16:02 ♂ □	♒ 28 1:27	26 10:06 ♅ ∗	♓ 26 19:31		SVP 06♓36'39"
♃△♆ 24 10:43		30 2:57 ♃ ☌	♓ 30 12:55				Obliquity 23°26'58"
☽0N 28 20:53							⚷ Chiron 18♑15.0
							☽ Mean ☊ 19♎32.0

MARCH 1903 LONGITUDE

Day	Sid.Time	☉	0 hr ☽	Noon ☽	True ☊	☿	♀	♂	♃	♄	♅	♆	♇
1 Su	10 30 29	9♓14 12	27♓28 4	3♈52 27	16♎15.1	12♒17.1	1♈ 4.9	15♎36.2	2♓ 4.7	4♒35.1	25♐13.6	0♋56.9	17♊40.7
2 M	10 34 26	10 14 25	10♈19 45	16 50 2	16D 13.5	13 21.2	2 19.2	15R 27.8	2 19.1	4 41.4	25 15.2	0R 56.5	17R 40.6
3 Tu	10 38 22	11 14 37	23 23 21	29 59 49	16 13.5	14 27.7	3 33.5	15 18.7	2 33.5	4 47.6	25 16.7	0 56.1	17D 40.6
4 W	10 42 19	12 14 47	6♉39 32	13♉22 35	16 14.7	15 36.3	4 47.8	15 8.8	2 47.9	4 53.8	25 18.2	0 55.8	17 40.6
5 Th	10 46 16	13 14 54	20 9 5	26 59 6	16 16.3	16 47.0	6 2.0	14 58.0	3 2.2	4 59.9	25 19.6	0 55.5	17 40.6
6 F	10 50 12	14 15 0	3♊52 44	10♊49 59	16R 17.6	17 59.6	7 16.1	14 46.6	3 16.5	5 6.0	25 20.9	0 55.2	17 40.7
7 Sa	10 54 9	15 15 3	17 50 50	24 55 10	16 18.0	19 14.1	8 30.3	14 34.4	3 30.9	5 12.0	25 22.3	0 55.0	17 40.7
8 Su	10 58 5	16 15 4	2♋ 2 48	9♋13 27	16 17.0	20 30.3	9 44.3	14 21.4	3 45.2	5 18.0	25 23.5	0 54.8	17 40.8
9 M	11 2 2	17 15 4	16 26 43	23 42 8	16 14.7	21 48.2	10 58.4	14 7.8	3 59.4	5 23.9	25 24.7	0 54.6	17 41.0
10 Tu	11 5 58	18 15 0	0♌59 5	8♌16 53	16 11.4	23 7.7	12 12.4	13 53.4	4 13.7	5 29.8	25 25.9	0 54.5	17 41.1
11 W	11 9 55	19 14 55	15 34 48	22 51 59	16 7.4	24 28.8	13 26.3	13 38.3	4 27.9	5 35.7	25 27.0	0 54.4	17 41.3
12 Th	11 13 51	20 14 47	0♍ 7 39	7♍20 58	16 3.6	25 51.4	14 40.2	13 22.5	4 42.1	5 41.4	25 28.1	0 54.4	17 41.5
13 F	11 17 48	21 14 38	14 31 11	21 37 33	16 0.4	27 15.4	15 54.1	13 6.1	4 56.3	5 47.1	25 29.1	0D 54.3	17 41.7
14 Sa	11 21 45	22 14 26	28 39 30	5♎36 30	15 58.3	28 40.9	17 7.9	12 49.0	5 10.4	5 52.8	25 30.0	0 54.4	17 41.9
15 Su	11 25 41	23 14 13	12♎28 12	19 14 20	15D 57.4	0♓ 7.7	18 21.7	12 31.3	5 24.5	5 58.4	25 30.9	0 54.4	17 42.1
16 M	11 29 38	24 13 57	25 54 47	2♏29 33	15 57.7	1 36.0	19 35.4	12 12.9	5 38.6	6 4.0	25 31.8	0 54.5	17 42.4
17 Tu	11 33 34	25 13 40	8♏58 45	15 22 36	15 58.7	3 5.5	20 49.1	11 54.0	5 52.6	6 9.5	25 32.6	0 54.6	17 42.7
18 W	11 37 31	26 13 21	21 41 25	27 55 35	16 0.3	4 36.5	22 2.8	11 34.6	6 6.7	6 14.9	25 33.3	0 54.7	17 43.0
19 Th	11 41 27	27 13 0	4♐ 5 33	10♐11 49	16 1.8	6 8.7	23 16.4	11 14.6	6 20.7	6 20.3	25 34.0	0 54.9	17 43.4
20 F	11 45 24	28 12 38	16 14 57	22 15 30	16 2.9	7 42.2	24 29.9	10 54.1	6 34.6	6 25.6	25 34.7	0 55.1	17 43.7
21 Sa	11 49 20	29 12 14	28 14 3	4♑11 13	16R 3.3	9 17.1	25 43.4	10 33.2	6 48.5	6 30.8	25 35.3	0 55.4	17 44.1
22 Su	11 53 17	0♈11 48	10♑ 7 34	16 3 42	16 3.0	10 53.2	26 56.9	10 11.9	7 2.4	6 36.0	25 35.8	0 55.7	17 44.5
23 M	11 57 14	1 11 20	22 0 12	27 57 35	16 2.0	12 30.6	28 10.3	9 50.1	7 16.3	6 41.1	25 36.3	0 56.0	17 44.9
24 Tu	12 1 10	2 10 50	3♒56 23	9♒57 5	16 0.4	14 9.4	29 23.7	9 28.0	7 30.1	6 46.2	25 36.7	0 56.3	17 45.4
25 W	12 5 7	3 10 19	16 0 7	22 5 54	15 58.6	15 49.4	0♉37.0	9 5.6	7 43.8	6 51.2	25 37.1	0 56.7	17 45.8
26 Th	12 9 3	4 9 46	28 14 44	4♓26 57	15 56.7	17 30.8	1 50.3	8 42.9	7 57.6	6 56.1	25 37.4	0 57.1	17 46.3
27 F	12 13 0	5 9 10	10♓42 45	17 2 19	15 55.2	19 13.5	3 3.5	8 20.0	8 11.3	7 0.9	25 37.7	0 57.6	17 46.8
28 Sa	12 16 56	6 8 33	23 25 46	29 53 8	15 54.0	20 57.5	4 16.7	7 57.0	8 24.9	7 5.7	25 37.9	0 58.1	17 47.4
29 Su	12 20 53	7 7 54	6♈24 27	12♈59 38	15D 53.4	22 42.9	5 29.8	7 33.7	8 38.5	7 10.4	25 38.1	0 58.6	17 47.9
30 M	12 24 49	8 7 13	19 38 34	26 21 8	15 53.3	24 29.6	6 42.9	7 10.4	8 52.0	7 15.1	25 38.2	0 59.1	17 48.5
31 Tu	12 28 46	9 6 30	3♉ 7 8	9♉56 20	15 53.6	26 17.7	7 55.9	6 47.1	9 5.5	7 19.6	25R 38.3	0 59.7	17 49.1

APRIL 1903 LONGITUDE

Day	Sid.Time	☉	0 hr ☽	Noon ☽	True ☊	☿	♀	♂	♃	♄	♅	♆	♇
1 W	12 32 42	10♈ 5 44	16♉48 31	23♉43 26	15♎54.1	28♓ 7.2	9♉ 8.9	6♎23.8	9♓18.9	7♒24.1	25♐38.3	1♋ 0.3	17♊49.7
2 Th	12 36 39	11 4 57	0♊40 47	7♊40 20	15 54.6	29 58.1	10 21.8	6R 0.5	9 32.3	7 28.5	25R 38.3	1 1.0	17 50.3
3 F	12 40 36	12 4 7	14 41 47	21 44 51	15 55.0	1♈50.3	11 34.7	5 37.3	9 45.7	7 32.9	25 38.2	1 1.7	17 51.0
4 Sa	12 44 32	13 3 15	28 49 16	5♋54 45	15 55.3	3 44.0	12 47.5	5 14.3	9 58.9	7 37.1	25 38.0	1 2.4	17 51.6
5 Su	12 48 29	14 2 20	13♋ 1 0	20 7 44	15R 55.3	5 39.0	14 0.2	4 51.5	10 12.2	7 41.3	25 37.8	1 3.1	17 52.3
6 M	12 52 25	15 1 24	27 14 37	4♌21 22	15D 55.3	7 35.4	15 12.9	4 28.9	10 25.3	7 45.4	25 37.6	1 3.9	17 53.0
7 Tu	12 56 22	16 0 24	11♌27 39	18 33 5	15 55.3	9 33.2	16 25.5	4 6.6	10 38.4	7 49.5	25 37.3	1 4.7	17 53.8
8 W	13 0 18	16 59 23	25 37 21	2♍40 4	15 55.4	11 32.3	17 38.1	3 44.6	10 51.5	7 53.4	25 36.9	1 5.6	17 54.5
9 Th	13 4 15	17 58 19	9♍40 52	16 39 21	15 55.5	13 32.7	18 50.5	3 23.0	11 4.4	7 57.3	25 36.5	1 6.5	17 55.3
10 F	13 8 11	18 57 13	23 35 12	0♎28 2	15 55.7	15 34.3	20 3.0	3 1.7	11 17.4	8 1.1	25 36.1	1 7.4	17 56.1
11 Sa	13 12 8	19 56 5	7♎17 33	14 3 27	15R 55.9	17 37.1	21 15.3	2 40.9	11 30.2	8 4.8	25 35.6	1 8.3	17 56.9
12 Su	13 16 5	20 54 54	20 45 31	27 23 32	15 56.0	19 40.9	22 27.6	2 20.6	11 43.0	8 8.4	25 35.0	1 9.3	17 57.7
13 M	13 20 1	21 53 42	3♏57 24	10♏27 1	15 55.7	21 45.8	23 39.8	2 0.7	11 55.7	8 12.0	25 34.4	1 10.3	17 58.5
14 Tu	13 23 58	22 52 28	16 52 24	23 13 37	15 55.1	23 51.4	24 52.0	1 41.4	12 8.4	8 15.4	25 33.8	1 11.3	17 59.4
15 W	13 27 54	23 51 12	29 30 48	5♐44 9	15 54.2	25 57.7	26 4.1	1 22.6	12 21.0	8 18.8	25 33.1	1 12.4	18 0.2
16 Th	13 31 51	24 49 54	11♐53 56	18 0 28	15 53.0	28 4.4	27 16.1	1 4.4	12 33.5	8 22.1	25 32.3	1 13.5	18 1.1
17 F	13 35 47	25 48 34	24 4 8	0♑ 5 22	15 51.8	0♉11.4	28 28.1	0 46.8	12 45.9	8 25.3	25 31.6	1 14.6	18 2.0
18 Sa	13 39 44	26 47 13	6♑ 4 38	12 2 26	15 50.7	2 18.3	29 40.0	0 29.9	12 58.3	8 28.4	25 30.7	1 15.7	18 3.0
19 Su	13 43 40	27 45 50	17 59 18	23 55 49	15D 49.9	4 24.9	0♊51.8	0 13.6	13 10.6	8 31.5	25 29.8	1 16.9	18 3.9
20 M	13 47 37	28 44 25	29 52 32	5♒50 3	15 49.7	6 31.0	2 3.6	29♍57.9	13 22.8	8 34.4	25 28.9	1 18.1	18 4.9
21 Tu	13 51 34	29 42 59	11♒48 56	17 49 48	15 50.1	8 36.1	3 15.3	29 43.0	13 35.0	8 37.3	25 27.9	1 19.3	18 5.8
22 W	13 55 30	0♉41 30	23 53 11	29 59 38	15 51.0	10 40.1	4 26.9	29 28.8	13 47.0	8 40.0	25 26.9	1 20.6	18 6.8
23 Th	13 59 27	1 40 1	6♓ 9 39	12♓23 42	15 52.2	12 42.4	5 38.4	29 15.3	13 59.0	8 42.7	25 25.8	1 21.9	18 7.8
24 F	14 3 23	2 38 29	18 42 12	25 5 29	15 53.6	14 42.9	6 49.9	29 2.6	14 10.9	8 45.3	25 24.7	1 23.2	18 8.8
25 Sa	14 7 20	3 36 56	1♈33 48	8♈ 7 21	15 54.7	16 41.3	8 1.3	28 50.6	14 22.7	8 47.8	25 23.5	1 24.5	18 9.9
26 Su	14 11 16	4 35 21	14 46 12	21 30 20	15R 55.2	18 37.1	9 12.7	28 39.4	14 34.5	8 50.2	25 22.3	1 25.9	18 10.9
27 M	14 15 13	5 33 45	28 19 36	5♉13 46	15 54.8	20 30.3	10 23.9	28 29.0	14 46.1	8 52.5	25 21.0	1 27.3	18 12.0
28 Tu	14 19 9	6 32 6	12♉12 29	19 15 16	15 53.4	22 20.4	11 35.1	28 19.4	14 57.7	8 54.7	25 19.7	1 28.7	18 13.1
29 W	14 23 6	7 30 26	26 21 37	3♊30 53	15 51.0	24 7.4	12 46.2	28 10.6	15 9.1	8 56.9	25 18.4	1 30.2	18 14.2
30 Th	14 27 3	8 28 44	10♊42 25	17 55 31	15 48.0	25 50.9	13 57.2	28 2.6	15 20.5	8 58.9	25 17.0	1 31.7	18 15.3

Astro Data Dy Hr Mn	Planet Ingress Dy Hr Mn	Last Aspect Dy Hr Mn	☽ Ingress Dy Hr Mn	Last Aspect Dy Hr Mn	☽ Ingress Dy Hr Mn	☽ Phases & Eclipses Dy Hr Mn	Astro Data
♀0N 2 3:04	☿ ♓ 14 21:52	28 19:46 ♅ □	♈ 1 4:45	1 22:35 ☿ ✶	♊ 1 22:50	6 19:14 ☽ 15♊03	1 MARCH 1903
♇ D 3 7:12	☉ ♈ 21 19:15	3 3:27 ♅ △	♉ 3 12:00	3 18:36 ♅ ☍	♋ 4 2:00	13 12:13 ○ 21♍45	Julian Day # 1155
☽0S 13 19:09	♀ ♉ 24 11:53	4 17:28 ☿ □	♊ 5 17:16	5 1:51 ☉ □	♌ 6 4:39	21 2:08 ☽ 29♐18	Delta T 1.5 sec
♆ D 13 5:33		7 12:47 ♅ ☍	♋ 7 20:34	7 23:59 ♅ △	♍ 8 7:27	29 1:26 ● 7♈11	SVP 06♓36'36"
♃⚺♄ 18 22:54	☿ ♈ 2 0:25	9 1:26 ☉ △	♌ 9 22:23	10 3:30 ♅ □	♎ 10 11:11	29 1:35:20 ☄ A 1'53"	Obliquity 23°26'58"
☽0N 28 4:26	☿ ♉ 16 21:51	11 16:17 ♅ △	♍ 11 23:47	12 8:43 ♅ ✶	♏ 12 16:45		⚷ Chiron 20♑31.8
♂0N 29 21:52	♀ ♊ 18 6:41	13 18:35 ♅ □	♎ 14 2:18	14 16:43 ♀ ☍	♐ 15 0:56	5 1:51 ☽ 14♋07	☽ Mean ☊ 18♎03.0
♅ R 31 17:50	♂ ♍ 19 20:46	15 23:18 ♅ ✶	♏ 16 7:26	17 3:46 ☉ △	♑ 17 11:49	12 0:18 ○ 20♎56	
	☉ ♉ 21 6:59	18 9:28 ☉ △	♐ 18 16:01	20 0:11 ♂ △	♒ 20 0:15	12 0:13 ☄ P 0.968	1 APRIL 1903
☿0N 4 6:36		21 2:08 ☉ □	♑ 21 3:33	22 3:04 ♅ ✶	♓ 22 12:01	19 21:30 ☽ 28♑38	Julian Day # 1186
☽0S 10 3:50		23 13:51 ♀ □	♒ 23 16:06	24 19:03 ♅ ☍	♈ 24 21:07	27 13:31 ● 6♉07	Delta T 1.6 sec
☽0N 24 13:21		25 18:54 ♅ ✶	♓ 26 3:24	26 18:47 ♅ △	♉ 27 2:55		SVP 06♓36'34"
		28 4:07 ♅ □	♈ 28 12:13	29 3:01 ♂ △	♊ 29 6:07		Obliquity 23°26'58"
		30 10:44 ♅ △	♉ 30 18:29				⚷ Chiron 22♑15.1
							☽ Mean ☊ 16♎24.5

LONGITUDE — MAY 1903

Day	Sid.Time	☉	0 hr ☽	Noon ☽	True ☊	☿	♀	♂	♃	♄	♅	♆	♇
1 F	14 30 59	9♉27 0	25♊ 9 28	2♋23 36	15♎44.8	27♉30.9	15♊ 8.2	27♍55.3	15♓31.8	9♒ 0.8	25♐15.6	1♋33.2	18♊16.4
2 Sa	14 34 56	10 25 14	9♋37 17	16 49 54	15R42.0	29 7.2	16 19.1	27R48.9	15 43.0	9 2.7	25R14.1	1 34.7	18 17.5
3 Su	14 38 52	11 23 27	24 0 58	1♌10 2	15 40.0	0♊39.6	17 29.8	27 43.3	15 54.1	9 4.4	25 12.6	1 36.2	18 18.7
4 M	14 42 49	12 21 37	8♌16 45	15 20 51	15D39.0	2 8.1	18 40.5	27 38.5	16 5.1	9 6.1	25 11.1	1 37.8	18 19.8
5 Tu	14 46 45	13 19 44	22 22 7	29 20 25	15 39.2	3 32.5	19 51.1	27 34.5	16 16.0	9 7.6	25 9.5	1 39.4	18 21.0
6 W	14 50 42	14 17 50	6♍15 40	13♍ 7 49	15 40.3	4 52.8	21 1.6	27 31.3	16 26.8	9 9.1	25 7.9	1 41.0	18 22.2
7 Th	14 54 38	15 15 54	19 56 51	26 42 46	15 41.9	6 8.9	22 12.0	27 28.9	16 37.4	9 10.4	25 6.2	1 42.7	18 23.4
8 F	14 58 35	16 13 56	3♎25 34	10♎ 5 17	15R43.2	7 20.7	23 22.3	27 27.2	16 48.0	9 11.7	25 4.5	1 44.3	18 24.6
9 Sa	15 2 32	17 11 56	16 41 54	23 15 27	15 43.7	8 28.2	24 32.6	27D26.4	16 58.5	9 12.9	25 2.8	1 46.0	18 25.8
10 Su	15 6 28	18 9 55	29 45 55	6♏13 19	15 42.8	9 31.3	25 42.7	27 26.2	17 8.9	9 14.0	25 1.0	1 47.7	18 27.0
11 M	15 10 25	19 7 52	12♏37 38	18 58 55	15 40.4	10 29.9	26 52.7	27 26.9	17 19.1	9 14.9	24 59.2	1 49.4	18 28.2
12 Tu	15 14 21	20 5 47	25 17 9	1♐32 24	15 36.3	11 24.0	28 2.6	27 28.3	17 29.3	9 15.8	24 57.4	1 51.2	18 29.5
13 W	15 18 18	21 3 41	7♐44 45	13 54 18	15 30.8	12 13.5	29 12.4	27 30.4	17 39.3	9 16.6	24 55.5	1 53.0	18 30.7
14 Th	15 22 14	22 1 33	20 1 10	26 5 35	15 24.5	12 58.3	0♋22.1	27 33.3	17 49.3	9 17.3	24 53.6	1 54.8	18 32.0
15 F	15 26 11	22 59 24	2♑ 7 45	8♑ 7 57	15 17.9	13 38.4	1 31.7	27 36.9	17 59.1	9 17.9	24 51.7	1 56.6	18 33.3
16 Sa	15 30 7	23 57 14	14 6 31	20 3 50	15 11.8	14 13.7	2 41.2	27 41.1	18 8.8	9 18.4	24 49.7	1 58.4	18 34.6
17 Su	15 34 4	24 55 2	26 0 19	1♒56 26	15 6.8	14 44.3	3 50.6	27 46.1	18 18.4	9 18.8	24 47.7	2 0.2	18 35.8
18 M	15 38 1	25 52 49	7♒52 42	13 49 38	15 3.3	15 9.9	4 59.9	27 51.8	18 27.9	9 19.1	24 45.7	2 2.1	18 37.1
19 Tu	15 41 57	26 50 35	19 47 50	25 47 53	15D 1.5	15 30.7	6 9.0	27 58.1	18 37.2	9 19.2	24 43.7	2 4.0	18 38.5
20 W	15 45 54	27 48 20	1♓50 23	7♓55 58	15 1.3	15 46.6	7 18.1	28 5.2	18 46.5	9R19.3	24 41.6	2 5.9	18 39.8
21 Th	15 49 50	28 46 3	14 5 15	20 18 48	15 2.2	15 57.7	8 27.0	28 12.8	18 55.6	9 19.3	24 39.5	2 7.8	18 41.1
22 F	15 53 47	29 43 46	26 37 11	3♈ 0 57	15 3.6	16R 3.9	9 35.9	28 21.2	19 4.5	9 19.3	24 37.4	2 9.7	18 42.4
23 Sa	15 57 43	0♊41 28	9♈30 30	16 6 14	15R 4.6	16 5.4	10 44.6	28 30.1	19 13.4	9 19.1	24 35.2	2 11.7	18 43.8
24 Su	16 1 40	1 39 8	22 48 23	29 37 5	15 4.4	16 2.3	11 53.1	28 39.7	19 22.1	9 18.8	24 33.0	2 13.7	18 45.1
25 M	16 5 36	2 36 48	6♉32 19	13♉33 54	15 2.5	15 54.7	13 1.6	28 50.0	19 30.7	9 18.4	24 30.8	2 15.6	18 46.4
26 Tu	16 9 33	3 34 26	20 41 28	27 54 29	14 58.5	15 42.8	14 9.9	29 0.8	19 39.2	9 17.9	24 28.6	2 17.6	18 47.8
27 W	16 13 30	4 32 3	5♊12 15	12♊33 55	14 52.6	15 26.9	15 18.2	29 12.3	19 47.5	9 17.3	24 26.4	2 19.7	18 49.2
28 Th	16 17 26	5 29 39	19 58 30	27 24 56	14 45.3	15 7.2	16 26.2	29 24.3	19 55.7	9 16.6	24 24.1	2 21.7	18 50.5
29 F	16 21 23	6 27 14	4♋52 7	12♋18 57	14 37.5	14 44.1	17 34.2	29 36.9	20 3.7	9 15.8	24 21.8	2 23.7	18 51.9
30 Sa	16 25 19	7 24 48	19 44 22	27 7 26	14 30.2	14 18.0	18 42.0	29 50.1	20 11.6	9 15.0	24 19.5	2 25.8	18 53.3
31 Su	16 29 16	8 22 20	4♌27 20	11♌43 22	14 24.4	13 49.4	19 49.7	0♎ 3.9	20 19.4	9 14.0	24 17.2	2 27.9	18 54.7

LONGITUDE — JUNE 1903

Day	Sid.Time	☉	0 hr ☽	Noon ☽	True ☊	☿	♀	♂	♃	♄	♅	♆	♇
1 M	16 33 12	9♊19 51	18♌55 3	26♌ 2 0	14♎20.6	13♊18.7	20♋57.2	0♎18.2	20♓27.0	9♒12.9	24♐14.9	2♋29.9	18♊56.0
2 Tu	16 37 9	10 17 21	3♍ 4 2	10♍ 1 4	14D18.9	12R46.5	22 4.5	0 33.0	20 34.5	9R11.8	24R12.5	2 32.0	18 57.4
3 W	16 41 5	11 14 49	16 53 10	23 40 27	14 18.7	12 13.3	23 11.7	0 48.4	20 41.8	9 10.5	24 10.2	2 34.1	18 58.8
4 Th	16 45 2	12 12 16	0♎23 7	7♎ 1 26	14 19.5	11 39.7	24 18.8	1 4.3	20 49.0	9 9.2	24 7.8	2 36.2	19 0.2
5 F	16 48 59	13 9 42	13 35 40	20 6 5	14R20.0	11 6.3	25 25.7	1 20.7	20 56.0	9 7.8	24 5.4	2 38.4	19 1.6
6 Sa	16 52 55	14 7 6	26 33 0	2♏56 40	14 19.3	10 33.7	26 32.4	1 37.5	21 2.9	9 6.2	24 3.0	2 40.5	19 3.0
7 Su	16 56 52	15 4 30	9♏17 20	15 35 13	14 16.6	10 2.3	27 38.9	1 54.9	21 9.7	9 4.6	24 0.6	2 42.6	19 4.4
8 M	17 0 48	16 1 52	21 50 30	28 3 21	14 11.3	9 32.8	28 45.2	2 12.7	21 16.2	9 2.9	23 58.2	2 44.8	19 5.8
9 Tu	17 4 45	16 59 14	4♐13 56	10♐22 22	14 3.5	9 5.7	29 51.4	2 31.0	21 22.7	9 1.1	23 55.8	2 46.9	19 7.2
10 W	17 8 41	17 56 34	16 28 45	22 33 14	13 53.5	8 41.3	0♌57.4	2 49.8	21 28.9	8 59.2	23 53.3	2 49.1	19 8.6
11 Th	17 12 38	18 53 54	28 35 55	4♑36 57	13 42.0	8 20.2	2 3.2	3 9.0	21 35.1	8 57.3	23 50.9	2 51.3	19 10.0
12 F	17 16 34	19 51 13	10♑36 29	16 34 41	13 30.1	8 2.6	3 8.8	3 28.6	21 41.0	8 55.2	23 48.5	2 53.5	19 11.4
13 Sa	17 20 31	20 48 32	22 31 49	28 28 6	13 18.6	7 48.8	4 14.2	3 48.6	21 46.8	8 53.1	23 46.0	2 55.7	19 12.8
14 Su	17 24 28	21 45 50	4♒23 52	10♒19 27	13 8.7	7 39.1	5 19.4	4 9.1	21 52.4	8 50.8	23 43.6	2 57.9	19 14.2
15 M	17 28 24	22 43 7	16 15 16	22 11 45	13 0.9	7D33.6	6 24.4	4 30.0	21 57.9	8 48.5	23 41.1	3 0.1	19 15.6
16 Tu	17 32 21	23 40 25	28 9 24	4♓ 8 45	12 55.6	7 32.6	7 29.2	4 51.2	22 3.2	8 46.1	23 38.7	3 2.3	19 17.0
17 W	17 36 17	24 37 41	10♓10 21	16 14 50	12 52.8	7 36.1	8 33.8	5 12.9	22 8.3	8 43.6	23 36.2	3 4.5	19 18.4
18 Th	17 40 14	25 34 58	22 22 48	28 34 53	12D51.8	7 44.3	9 38.2	5 35.0	22 13.3	8 41.1	23 33.8	3 6.7	19 19.8
19 F	17 44 10	26 32 14	4♈51 43	11♈13 56	12R51.9	7 57.0	10 42.3	5 57.4	22 18.1	8 38.4	23 31.3	3 8.9	19 21.2
20 Sa	17 48 7	27 29 30	17 42 3	24 16 38	12 52.0	8 14.4	11 46.2	6 20.2	22 22.7	8 35.7	23 28.9	3 11.1	19 22.6
21 Su	17 52 3	28 26 45	0♉58 4	7♉46 40	12 50.9	8 36.4	12 49.9	6 43.4	22 27.1	8 32.9	23 26.4	3 13.4	19 24.0
22 M	17 56 0	29 24 1	14 42 36	21 45 50	12 47.7	9 3.0	13 53.3	7 7.0	22 31.4	8 30.1	23 24.0	3 15.6	19 25.3
23 Tu	17 59 57	0♋21 16	28 56 10	6♊13 10	12 42.1	9 34.2	14 56.5	7 30.9	22 35.5	8 27.1	23 21.5	3 17.8	19 26.7
24 W	18 3 53	1 18 32	13♊36 10	21 4 18	12 33.9	10 9.9	15 59.4	7 55.2	22 39.4	8 24.1	23 19.1	3 20.1	19 28.1
25 Th	18 7 50	2 15 47	28 36 29	6♋11 30	12 24.0	10 50.0	17 2.0	8 19.8	22 43.1	8 21.0	23 16.7	3 22.3	19 29.5
26 F	18 11 46	3 13 1	13♋47 59	21 24 34	12 13.3	11 34.5	18 4.4	8 44.7	22 46.7	8 17.8	23 14.3	3 24.5	19 30.9
27 Sa	18 15 43	4 10 16	28 59 53	6♌32 38	12 3.1	12 23.3	19 6.5	9 10.0	22 50.1	8 14.6	23 11.9	3 26.8	19 32.2
28 Su	18 19 39	5 7 30	14♌ 1 41	21 26 4	11 54.7	13 16.3	20 8.4	9 35.6	22 53.2	8 11.3	23 9.5	3 29.0	19 33.6
29 M	18 23 36	6 4 43	28 45 2	5♍58 2	11 48.6	14 13.5	21 9.9	10 1.6	22 56.2	8 8.0	23 7.1	3 31.2	19 34.9
30 Tu	18 27 32	7 1 56	13♍ 4 44	20 5 0	11 45.2	15 14.9	22 11.1	10 27.8	22 59.1	8 4.5	23 4.8	3 33.5	19 36.3

Astro Data (Dy Hr Mn)	Planet Ingress (Dy Hr Mn)	Last Aspect (Dy Hr Mn)	☽ Ingress (Dy Hr Mn)	Last Aspect (Dy Hr Mn)	☽ Ingress (Dy Hr Mn)	☽ Phases & Eclipses (Dy Hr Mn)	Astro Data
☽0S 7 10:34	☿ ♊ 2 13:36	1 4:33 ♂ □	♋ 1 8:02	1 8:57 ♅ △	♍ 1 18:45	4 7:26 ☽ 12♌40	1 MAY 1903
♂ D 9 15:26	♀ ♋ 13 16:23	3 6:10 ♂ ✶	♌ 3 10:02	3 12:51 ♅ □	♎ 3 23:18	11 13:18 ○ 19♏40	Julian Day # 1216
♃□♇ 19 3:41	☉ ♊ 22 6:45	5 4:47 ♅ △	♍ 5 13:08	5 23:59 ♀ □	♏ 6 6:28	19 15:18 ☽ 27♒27	Delta T 1.7 sec
♄ R 20 12:08	♂ ♎ 30 17:21	7 13:20 ♂ ☌	♎ 7 17:52	8 14:40 ♀ △	♐ 8 15:46	26 22:50 ● 4♊29	SVP 06♓36'31"
☽0N 21 23:04		9 15:47 ♀ △	♏ 10 0:26	10 14:36 ♅ ☌	♑ 11 2:47		Obliquity 23°26'58"
☿ R 22 19:39	♀ ♌ 9 3:07	12 4:12 ♂ ✶	♐ 12 9:02	12 22:28 ♃ ✶	♒ 13 15:06	2 13:24 ☽ 10♍49	⚷ Chiron 22♑49.4R
	☉ ♋ 22 15:05	14 14:58 ♂ □	♑ 14 19:46	15 14:57 ♅ ✶	♓ 16 3:42	10 3:08 ○ 18♐04	☽ Mean ☊ 14♎49.1
♄∠♅ 2 16:12		17 3:36 ♂ △	♒ 17 8:05	18 6:44 ☉ □	♈ 18 14:43	18 6:44 ☽ 25♓51	
☽0S 3 16:47		19 15:18 ☉ □	♓ 19 20:21	20 19:09 ☉ ✶	♉ 20 22:17	25 6:11 ● 2♋31	1 JUNE 1903
♂0S 4 15:12		22 6:20 ☉ ✶	♈ 22 6:22	22 13:21 ♃ ✶	♊ 23 1:46		Julian Day # 1247
☿ D 15 17:24		24 3:05 ♅ △	♉ 24 12:40	24 15:33 ♅ ☍	♋ 25 2:12		Delta T 1.8 sec
☽0N 18 8:28		26 14:00 ♂ △	♊ 26 15:27	26 14:13 ♃ △	♌ 27 1:35		SVP 06♓36'27"
♄∠♅ 29 18:34		28 15:25 ♂ △	♋ 28 16:10	28 14:47 ♅ △	♍ 29 2:04		Obliquity 23°26'57"
♃∠♄ 30 21:27		30 16:41 ♂ ✶	♌ 30 16:42				⚷ Chiron 22♑12.4R
							☽ Mean ☊ 13♎10.6

JULY 1903 LONGITUDE

Day	Sid.Time	☉	0 hr ☽	Noon ☽	True ☊	☿	♀	♂	♃	♄	♅	♆	♇
1 W	18 31 29	7♋59 9	26♍58 51	3♎46 27	11♎43.8	16♊20.3	23♌12.0	10♎54.4	23♓ 1.7	8♒ 1.0	23♐ 2.4	3♋35.7	19♊37.6
2 Th	18 35 26	8 56 21	10♎28 6	17 4 9	11R43.6	17 29.8	24 12.5	11 21.2	23 4.1	7R57.5	23R 0.1	3 37.9	19 39.0
3 F	18 39 22	9 53 33	23 35 0	0♏ 1 7	11 43.4	18 43.2	25 12.7	11 48.4	23 6.4	7 53.9	22 57.8	3 40.1	19 40.3
4 Sa	18 43 19	10 50 45	6♏22 57	12 40 56	11 42.0	20 0.6	26 12.6	12 15.8	23 8.4	7 50.2	22 55.5	3 42.4	19 41.6
5 Su	18 47 15	11 47 56	18 55 30	25 7 5	11 38.4	21 21.8	27 12.1	12 43.6	23 10.3	7 46.5	22 53.2	3 44.6	19 43.0
6 M	18 51 12	12 45 7	1♐16 1	7♐22 40	11 32.1	22 46.9	28 11.2	13 11.6	23 12.0	7 42.7	22 50.9	3 46.8	19 44.3
7 Tu	18 55 8	13 42 18	13 27 18	19 30 12	11 23.0	24 15.7	29 9.9	13 39.9	23 13.5	7 38.9	22 48.7	3 49.0	19 45.6
8 W	18 59 5	14 39 29	25 31 35	1♑31 40	11 11.5	25 48.2	0♍ 8.2	14 8.4	23 14.7	7 35.0	22 46.5	3 51.2	19 46.9
9 Th	19 3 1	15 36 40	7♑30 37	13 28 36	10 58.3	27 24.3	1 6.2	14 37.2	23 15.9	7 31.1	22 44.3	3 53.4	19 48.1
10 F	19 6 58	16 33 51	19 25 47	25 22 20	10 44.6	29 4.0	2 3.6	15 6.3	23 16.8	7 27.1	22 42.1	3 55.6	19 49.4
11 Sa	19 10 55	17 31 2	1♒18 25	7♒14 15	10 31.4	0♋47.1	3 0.7	15 35.6	23 17.5	7 23.1	22 39.9	3 57.8	19 50.7
12 Su	19 14 51	18 28 14	13 10 2	19 6 3	10 19.8	2 33.5	3 57.3	16 5.1	23 18.0	7 19.0	22 37.8	3 60.0	19 52.0
13 M	19 18 48	19 25 26	25 2 33	0♓59 55	10 10.5	4 23.0	4 53.4	16 34.9	23 18.3	7 15.0	22 35.7	4 2.2	19 53.2
14 Tu	19 22 44	20 22 38	6♓58 29	12 58 41	10 4.0	6 15.5	5 49.0	17 5.0	23R18.5	7 10.8	22 33.6	4 4.3	19 54.4
15 W	19 26 41	21 19 50	19 1 0	25 5 56	10 0.2	8 10.8	6 44.2	17 35.3	23 18.4	7 6.6	22 31.6	4 6.5	19 55.7
16 Th	19 30 37	22 17 4	1♈14 0	7♈25 48	9D 58.6	10 8.6	7 38.8	18 5.8	23 18.2	7 2.4	22 29.5	4 8.6	19 56.9
17 F	19 34 34	23 14 18	13 41 53	20 2 53	9R 58.4	12 8.7	8 32.9	18 36.5	23 17.7	6 58.2	22 27.5	4 10.8	19 58.1
18 Sa	19 38 30	24 11 32	26 29 20	3♉ 1 48	9 58.5	14 10.8	9 26.4	19 7.5	23 17.0	6 53.9	22 25.6	4 12.9	19 59.3
19 Su	19 42 27	25 8 48	9♉40 46	16 26 37	9 57.8	16 14.6	10 19.4	19 38.7	23 16.2	6 49.6	22 23.6	4 15.0	20 0.5
20 M	19 46 24	26 6 4	23 19 39	0♊20 1	9 55.2	18 19.8	11 11.8	20 10.2	23 15.2	6 45.3	22 21.7	4 17.1	20 1.7
21 Tu	19 50 20	27 3 21	7♊27 39	14 42 19	9 50.4	20 26.0	12 3.6	20 41.8	23 13.9	6 41.0	22 19.8	4 19.2	20 2.8
22 W	19 54 17	28 0 38	22 3 33	29 30 40	9 43.2	22 33.0	12 54.7	21 13.7	23 12.5	6 36.6	22 18.0	4 21.3	20 4.0
23 Th	19 58 13	28 57 57	7♋ 2 42	14♋38 33	9 34.2	24 40.4	13 45.3	21 45.8	23 10.9	6 32.2	22 16.2	4 23.4	20 5.1
24 F	20 2 10	29 55 16	22 16 55	29 56 23	9 24.3	26 48.0	14 35.1	22 18.1	23 9.0	6 27.8	22 14.4	4 25.5	20 6.2
25 Sa	20 6 6	0♌52 36	7♌35 30	15♌12 51	9 14.8	28 55.4	15 24.3	22 50.6	23 7.0	6 23.4	22 12.7	4 27.5	20 7.4
26 Su	20 10 3	1 49 56	22 47 6	0♍17 4	9 6.8	1♌ 2.5	16 12.7	23 23.3	23 4.8	6 19.0	22 11.0	4 29.6	20 8.5
27 M	20 13 59	2 47 17	7♍41 45	15 0 24	9 1.1	3 8.9	17 0.3	23 56.3	23 2.4	6 14.5	22 9.3	4 31.6	20 9.5
28 Tu	20 17 56	3 44 39	22 12 27	29 17 34	8 57.9	5 14.5	17 47.2	24 29.4	22 59.8	6 10.1	22 7.6	4 33.6	20 10.6
29 W	20 21 53	4 42 1	6♎15 38	13♎ 6 41	8D 56.8	7 19.2	18 33.3	25 2.7	22 57.0	6 5.6	22 6.0	4 35.6	20 11.7
30 Th	20 25 49	5 39 23	19 50 57	26 28 43	8 57.1	9 22.7	19 18.5	25 36.3	22 54.0	6 1.1	22 4.5	4 37.6	20 12.7
31 F	20 29 46	6 36 46	3♏ 0 26	9♏26 32	8R 57.6	11 25.0	20 2.8	26 10.0	22 50.9	5 56.7	22 3.0	4 39.5	20 13.7

AUGUST 1903 LONGITUDE

Day	Sid.Time	☉	0 hr ☽	Noon ☽	True ☊	☿	♀	♂	♃	♄	♅	♆	♇
1 Sa	20 33 42	7♌34 10	15♏47 33	22♏ 4 1	8♎57.3	13♌25.9	20♍46.2	26♎43.9	22♓47.5	5♒52.2	22♐ 1.5	4♋41.5	20♊14.8
2 Su	20 37 39	8 31 34	28 16 28	4♐25 25	8R55.4	15 25.5	21 28.6	27 17.9	22R44.0	5R47.8	22R 0.0	4 43.4	20 15.8
3 M	20 41 35	9 28 59	10♐31 22	16 34 48	8 51.2	17 23.6	22 10.0	27 52.2	22 40.3	5 43.3	21 58.7	4 45.3	20 16.7
4 Tu	20 45 32	10 26 24	22 36 9	28 35 49	8 44.7	19 20.2	22 50.4	28 26.6	22 36.4	5 38.9	21 57.3	4 47.2	20 17.7
5 W	20 49 28	11 23 50	4♑34 11	10♑31 33	8 36.1	21 15.3	23 29.7	29 1.3	22 32.3	5 34.5	21 56.0	4 49.1	20 18.7
6 Th	20 53 25	12 21 18	16 28 14	22 24 29	8 26.1	23 8.8	24 7.9	29 36.1	22 28.1	5 30.1	21 54.7	4 51.0	20 19.6
7 F	20 57 22	13 18 46	28 20 33	4♒16 38	8 15.7	25 0.8	24 45.0	0♏11.0	22 23.7	5 25.7	21 53.5	4 52.8	20 20.5
8 Sa	21 1 18	14 16 14	10♒12 56	16 9 40	8 5.6	26 51.2	25 20.8	0 46.1	22 19.1	5 21.3	21 52.3	4 54.6	20 21.4
9 Su	21 5 15	15 13 44	22 7 0	28 5 10	7 56.8	28 40.0	25 55.4	1 21.4	22 14.4	5 16.9	21 51.1	4 56.4	20 22.3
10 M	21 9 11	16 11 16	4♓ 4 21	10♓ 4 49	7 49.9	0♍27.3	26 28.6	1 56.9	22 9.5	5 12.6	21 50.0	4 58.2	20 23.2
11 Tu	21 13 8	17 8 48	16 6 49	22 10 38	7 45.3	2 13.1	27 0.6	2 32.5	22 4.4	5 8.3	21 49.0	5 0.0	20 24.0
12 W	21 17 4	18 6 21	28 16 36	4♈25 5	7D 42.9	3 57.3	27 31.1	3 8.3	21 59.2	5 4.0	21 48.0	5 1.7	20 24.9
13 Th	21 21 1	19 3 56	10♈36 26	16 51 7	7 42.5	5 40.1	28 0.1	3 44.2	21 53.8	4 59.7	21 47.0	5 3.5	20 25.7
14 F	21 24 57	20 1 32	23 9 32	29 32 9	7 43.3	7 21.3	28 27.7	4 20.3	21 48.3	4 55.5	21 46.1	5 5.2	20 26.5
15 Sa	21 28 54	20 59 10	5♉59 24	12♉31 45	7 44.6	9 1.0	28 53.7	4 56.5	21 42.6	4 51.3	21 45.2	5 6.9	20 27.3
16 Su	21 32 51	21 56 49	19 9 36	25 53 18	7R45.4	10 39.3	29 18.1	5 32.9	21 36.8	4 47.1	21 44.4	5 8.5	20 28.1
17 M	21 36 47	22 54 30	2♊43 8	9♊39 17	7 44.9	12 16.1	29 40.8	6 9.5	21 30.8	4 43.0	21 43.6	5 10.2	20 28.8
18 Tu	21 40 44	23 52 13	16 41 48	23 50 34	7 42.9	13 51.4	0♎ 1.8	6 46.2	21 24.7	4 38.9	21 42.9	5 11.8	20 29.5
19 W	21 44 40	24 49 57	1♋ 5 20	8♋25 38	7 39.1	15 25.3	0 21.0	7 23.1	21 18.4	4 34.8	21 42.2	5 13.4	20 30.2
20 Th	21 48 37	25 47 43	15 50 48	23 20 0	7 33.8	16 57.7	0 38.4	8 0.1	21 12.0	4 30.8	21 41.6	5 15.0	20 30.9
21 F	21 52 33	26 45 31	0♌52 13	8♌26 18	7 27.9	18 28.6	0 53.9	8 37.3	21 5.5	4 26.9	21 41.0	5 16.5	20 31.6
22 Sa	21 56 30	27 43 20	16 1 2	23 35 8	7 22.1	19 58.1	1 7.4	9 14.6	20 58.9	4 22.9	21 40.4	5 18.0	20 32.3
23 Su	22 0 26	28 41 10	1♍ 7 20	8♍36 29	7 17.2	21 26.1	1 18.9	9 52.1	20 52.2	4 19.1	21 39.9	5 19.5	20 32.9
24 M	22 4 23	29 39 2	16 1 29	23 21 27	7 13.9	22 52.6	1 28.3	10 29.7	20 45.3	4 15.3	21 39.5	5 21.0	20 33.5
25 Tu	22 8 20	0♍36 55	0♎35 39	7♎43 33	7D 12.3	24 17.6	1 35.6	11 7.4	20 38.3	4 11.5	21 39.1	5 22.5	20 34.1
26 W	22 12 16	1 34 50	14 44 47	21 39 12	7 12.3	25 41.0	1 40.6	11 45.3	20 31.3	4 7.8	21 38.8	5 23.9	20 34.7
27 Th	22 16 13	2 32 45	28 26 48	5♏ 7 44	7 13.5	27 2.9	1R43.5	12 23.4	20 24.1	4 4.1	21 38.5	5 25.3	20 35.2
28 F	22 20 9	3 30 43	11♏42 16	18 10 45	7 15.0	28 23.2	1 44.0	13 1.6	20 16.8	4 0.5	21 38.2	5 26.6	20 35.8
29 Sa	22 24 6	4 28 41	24 33 38	0♐51 25	7R16.3	29 41.9	1 42.2	13 39.9	20 9.5	3 57.0	21 38.0	5 28.0	20 36.3
30 Su	22 28 2	5 26 41	7♐ 4 38	13 13 49	7 16.7	0♎58.8	1 38.1	14 18.3	20 2.1	3 53.6	21 37.9	5 29.3	20 36.8
31 M	22 31 59	6 24 42	19 19 33	25 22 22	7 15.8	2 14.0	1 31.5	14 56.9	19 54.5	3 50.2	21 37.8	5 30.6	20 37.3

Astro Data	Planet Ingress	Last Aspect	☽ Ingress	Last Aspect	☽ Ingress	☽ Phases & Eclipses	Astro Data
Dy Hr Mn	Dy Hr Mn	Dy Hr Mn	Dy Hr Mn	Dy Hr Mn	Dy Hr Mn	Dy Hr Mn	1 JULY 1903
☽0S 1 0:07	♀ ♍ 7 20:36	30 17:09 ♅ □	♎ 1 5:19	1 13:20 ♃ △	♐ 2 3:21	1 21:02 ☽ 8♎49	Julian Day # 1277
♃□♅ 1 3:42	☿ ♋ 10 13:08	3 3:17 ♀ ⚹	♏ 3 11:58	4 12:17 ♂ ⚹	♑ 4 14:49	9 17:43 ○ 16♑19	Delta T 1.9 sec
♃ R 14 4:20	☉ ♌ 24 1:59	5 17:27 ♀ □	♐ 5 21:31	6 16:20 ♀ △	♒ 7 3:21	17 19:24 ☽ 24♈01	SVP 06♓36'22"
☽0N 15 16:39	☿ ♌ 25 12:11	8 0:38 ☿ ☍	♑ 8 8:56	9 15:29 ☿ ☍	♓ 9 15:50	24 12:46 ● 0♌26	Obliquity 23°26'57"
☽0S 28 9:19		10 7:47 ♃ ⚹	♒ 10 21:21	11 22:27 ♀ ☍	♈ 12 3:23	31 7:15 ☽ 6♏54	⚷ Chiron 20♑43.0R
♀0S 5 23:48	♂ ♏ 6 16:27	12 19:04 ♅ ⚹	♓ 13 9:59	13 21:22 ♅ △	♉ 14 12:52		☽ Mean ☊ 11♎35.3
♄⊼♇ 7 23:18	☿ ♍ 9 17:51	15 8:28 ♃ ☌	♈ 15 21:36	16 18:32 ♀ △	♊ 16 19:15	8 8:54 ○ 14♒38	
☽0N 11 23:27	♀ ♎ 17 21:51	17 19:24 ☉ □	♉ 18 6:28	18 12:54 ☉ ⚹	♋ 18 22:12	16 5:23 ☽ 22♉10	1 AUGUST 1903
♄⊼♆ 12 8:52	☉ ♍ 24 8:42	20 5:07 ☉ ⚹	♊ 20 11:26	20 8:32 ♃ △	♌ 20 22:37	22 19:51 ● 28♌31	Julian Day # 1308
♃□♅ 14 11:02	☿ ♎ 29 5:36	22 1:51 ♃ □	♋ 22 12:47	22 19:51 ☉ ☌	♍ 22 22:13	29 20:34 ☽ 5♐18	Delta T 2.1 sec
☽0S 24 19:51		24 8:13 ☿ ☌	♌ 24 12:06	24 12:25 ☿ ☌	♎ 24 23:00		SVP 06♓36'18"
♃□♇ 25 13:15		26 1:00 ♂ ⚹	♍ 26 11:33	26 11:59 ♅ ⚹	♏ 27 2:46		Obliquity 23°26'57"
☿0S 27 17:43		28 1:19 ♃ ☍	♎ 28 13:13	28 15:47 ♃ △	♐ 29 10:21		⚷ Chiron 18♑53.1R
♀ R 27 17:36		30 10:52 ♂ ☌	♏ 30 18:27	31 4:34 ♅ ☌	♑ 31 21:14		☽ Mean ☊ 9♎56.8

LONGITUDE — SEPTEMBER 1903

Day	Sid.Time	☉	0 hr ☽	Noon ☽	True ☊	☿	♀	♂	♃	♄	♅	♆	♇
1 Tu	22 35 55	7♍22 45	1♑22 49	7♑21 26	7♎13.6	3♎27.4	1♎22.6	15♏35.6	19♓47.0	3♒46.8	21♐37.8	5♋31.9	20♊37.7
2 W	22 39 52	8 20 49	13 18 41	19 15 3	7R10.2	4 39.0	1R11.2	16 14.4	19R39.3	3R43.5	21D37.8	5 33.1	20 38.2
3 Th	22 43 49	9 18 54	25 10 57	1♒ 6 47	7 5.9	5 48.5	0 57.5	16 53.4	19 31.6	3 40.3	21 37.9	5 34.3	20 38.6
4 F	22 47 45	10 17 1	7♒ 2 56	12 59 42	7 1.3	6 56.0	0 41.4	17 32.5	19 23.9	3 37.2	21 38.0	5 35.5	20 39.0
5 Sa	22 51 42	11 15 9	18 57 23	24 56 15	6 56.8	8 1.3	0 23.0	18 11.7	19 16.1	3 34.2	21 38.2	5 36.6	20 39.3
6 Su	22 55 38	12 13 19	0♓56 33	6♓58 30	6 53.0	9 4.4	0 2.3	18 51.0	19 8.3	3 31.2	21 38.4	5 37.8	20 39.7
7 M	22 59 35	13 11 31	13 2 17	19 8 6	6 50.1	10 5.0	29♍39.4	19 30.4	19 0.4	3 28.3	21 38.6	5 38.9	20 40.0
8 Tu	23 3 31	14 9 44	25 16 9	1♈26 34	6D48.5	11 3.0	29 14.4	20 10.0	18 52.5	3 25.4	21 39.0	5 39.9	20 40.3
9 W	23 7 28	15 8 0	7♈39 35	13 55 21	6 48.0	11 58.4	28 47.4	20 49.7	18 44.5	3 22.7	21 39.3	5 40.9	20 40.6
10 Th	23 11 24	16 6 17	20 14 4	26 35 57	6 48.5	12 50.8	28 18.6	21 29.5	18 36.6	3 20.0	21 39.8	5 41.9	20 40.9
11 F	23 15 21	17 4 36	3♉ 1 12	9♉30 1	6 49.7	13 40.1	27 48.0	22 9.4	18 28.6	3 17.4	21 40.2	5 42.9	20 41.1
12 Sa	23 19 17	18 2 57	16 2 39	22 39 17	6 51.1	14 26.1	27 16.0	22 49.4	18 20.6	3 14.9	21 40.8	5 43.9	20 41.3
13 Su	23 23 14	19 1 20	29 20 8	6♊ 5 21	6 52.4	15 8.6	26 42.6	23 29.6	18 12.7	3 12.4	21 41.3	5 44.8	20 41.5
14 M	23 27 11	19 59 46	12♊55 4	19 49 22	6R53.1	15 47.2	26 8.0	24 9.9	18 4.7	3 10.1	21 42.0	5 45.7	20 41.7
15 Tu	23 31 7	20 58 14	26 48 15	3♋51 38	6 53.2	16 21.7	25 32.5	24 50.3	17 56.7	3 7.8	21 42.7	5 46.5	20 41.9
16 W	23 35 4	21 56 44	10♋59 20	18 11 5	6 52.5	16 51.7	24 56.3	25 30.8	17 48.8	3 5.6	21 43.4	5 47.3	20 42.0
17 Th	23 39 0	22 55 16	25 26 28	2♌44 57	6 51.2	17 17.1	24 19.6	26 11.4	17 40.8	3 3.6	21 44.2	5 48.1	20 42.1
18 F	23 42 57	23 53 50	10♌ 5 53	17 28 33	6 49.7	17 37.3	23 42.7	26 52.1	17 32.9	3 1.6	21 45.0	5 48.9	20 42.2
19 Sa	23 46 53	24 52 26	24 52 5	2♍15 37	6 48.2	17 52.1	23 5.7	27 33.0	17 25.1	2 59.6	21 45.9	5 49.6	20 42.3
20 Su	23 50 50	25 51 5	9♍38 14	16 58 59	6 47.0	18R 1.0	22 29.0	28 13.9	17 17.2	2 57.8	21 46.8	5 50.3	20 42.3
21 M	23 54 46	26 49 45	24 17 1	1♎31 30	6D46.3	18 3.8	21 52.8	28 55.0	17 9.5	2 56.1	21 47.8	5 51.0	20R42.3
22 Tu	23 58 43	27 48 27	8♎41 43	15 47 2	6 46.1	18 0.0	21 17.2	29 36.2	17 1.7	2 54.4	21 48.8	5 51.6	20 42.3
23 W	0 2 40	28 47 12	22 46 59	29 41 12	6 46.4	17 49.4	20 42.6	0♐17.4	16 54.1	2 52.9	21 49.9	5 52.2	20 42.3
24 Th	0 6 36	29 45 58	6♏29 29	13♏11 46	6 46.9	17 31.7	20 9.1	0 58.8	16 46.5	2 51.4	21 51.1	5 52.7	20 42.3
25 F	0 10 33	0♎44 46	19 48 4	26 18 33	6 47.5	17 6.6	19 36.9	1 40.3	16 38.9	2 50.1	21 52.3	5 53.3	20 42.2
26 Sa	0 14 29	1 43 36	2♐43 30	9♐ 3 14	6 48.1	16 34.2	19 6.3	2 21.9	16 31.5	2 48.8	21 53.5	5 53.8	20 42.1
27 Su	0 18 26	2 42 27	15 18 11	21 28 48	6 48.5	15 54.6	18 37.3	3 3.6	16 24.1	2 47.6	21 54.8	5 54.2	20 42.0
28 M	0 22 22	3 41 21	27 35 38	3♑39 13	6R48.7	15 7.9	18 10.2	3 45.5	16 16.8	2 46.6	21 56.1	5 54.7	20 41.9
29 Tu	0 26 19	4 40 16	9♑40 6	15 38 52	6 48.7	14 14.8	17 45.0	4 27.4	16 9.6	2 45.6	21 57.5	5 55.0	20 41.7
30 W	0 30 15	5 39 13	21 36 6	27 32 22	6 48.6	13 15.9	17 21.9	5 9.4	16 2.6	2 44.7	21 58.9	5 55.4	20 41.6

LONGITUDE — OCTOBER 1903

Day	Sid.Time	☉	0 hr ☽	Noon ☽	True ☊	☿	♀	♂	♃	♄	♅	♆	♇
1 Th	0 34 12	6♎38 11	3♒28 13	9♒24 11	6♎48.6	12♎12.4	17♍ 1.1	5♐51.5	15♓55.6	2♒44.0	22♐ 0.4	5♋55.7	20♊41.4
2 F	0 38 9	7 37 11	15 20 46	21 18 27	6D48.6	11R 5.4	16R42.4	6 33.7	15R48.7	2R43.3	22 1.9	5 56.0	20R41.1
3 Sa	0 42 5	8 36 14	27 17 41	3♓18 51	6 48.8	9 56.6	16 26.2	7 16.0	15 41.9	2 42.7	22 3.5	5 56.3	20 40.9
4 Su	0 46 2	9 35 18	9♓22 20	15 28 26	6 49.0	8 47.6	16 12.3	7 58.3	15 35.3	2 42.2	22 5.1	5 56.5	20 40.7
5 M	0 49 58	10 34 23	21 37 25	27 49 31	6 49.3	7 40.4	16 0.9	8 40.8	15 28.8	2 41.8	22 6.8	5 56.7	20 40.4
6 Tu	0 53 55	11 33 31	4♈ 4 55	10♈23 45	6R49.4	6 36.7	15 51.8	9 23.4	15 22.4	2 41.5	22 8.5	5 56.9	20 40.1
7 W	0 57 51	12 32 41	16 46 6	23 12 0	6 49.3	5 38.4	15 45.3	10 6.0	15 16.1	2 41.4	22 10.3	5 57.0	20 39.7
8 Th	1 1 48	13 31 53	29 41 29	6♉14 30	6 48.9	4 47.1	15 41.2	10 48.8	15 10.0	2D41.3	22 12.1	5 57.1	20 39.4
9 F	1 5 44	14 31 7	12♉51 0	19 30 55	6 48.2	4 4.3	15D39.5	11 31.6	15 4.0	2 41.3	22 13.9	5 57.1	20 39.0
10 Sa	1 9 41	15 30 23	26 14 7	3♊ 0 30	6 47.1	3 31.0	15 40.3	12 14.5	14 58.1	2 41.4	22 15.8	5R57.2	20 38.7
11 Su	1 13 37	16 29 42	9♊49 56	16 42 16	6 46.0	3 8.0	15 43.4	12 57.5	14 52.4	2 41.6	22 17.8	5 57.2	20 38.2
12 M	1 17 34	17 29 3	23 37 19	0♋34 57	6 44.9	2D55.9	15 48.8	13 40.6	14 46.9	2 41.9	22 19.8	5 57.1	20 37.8
13 Tu	1 21 31	18 28 26	7♋34 58	14 37 11	6D44.2	2 54.7	15 56.6	14 23.8	14 41.5	2 42.4	22 21.8	5 57.1	20 37.4
14 W	1 25 27	19 27 52	21 41 22	28 47 18	6 44.0	3 4.3	16 6.5	15 7.1	14 36.3	2 42.9	22 23.9	5 56.9	20 36.9
15 Th	1 29 24	20 27 20	5♌54 43	13♌ 3 18	6 44.4	3 24.4	16 18.7	15 50.5	14 31.2	2 43.5	22 26.0	5 56.8	20 36.4
16 F	1 33 20	21 26 50	20 12 43	27 22 37	6 45.3	3 54.4	16 33.0	16 33.9	14 26.3	2 44.2	22 28.2	5 56.6	20 35.9
17 Sa	1 37 17	22 26 22	4♍32 33	11♍42 6	6 46.5	4 33.8	16 49.3	17 17.5	14 21.6	2 45.0	22 30.4	5 56.4	20 35.4
18 Su	1 41 13	23 25 57	18 50 45	25 58 1	6 47.6	5 21.7	17 7.7	18 1.1	14 17.0	2 46.0	22 32.6	5 56.2	20 34.8
19 M	1 45 10	24 25 34	3♎ 3 22	10♎ 6 17	6R48.2	6 17.3	17 27.9	18 44.8	14 12.6	2 47.0	22 34.9	5 55.9	20 34.3
20 Tu	1 49 6	25 25 13	17 6 16	24 2 49	6 47.9	7 19.9	17 50.0	19 28.6	14 8.4	2 48.1	22 37.2	5 55.6	20 33.7
21 W	1 53 3	26 24 54	0♏55 32	7♏44 1	6 46.7	8 28.5	18 14.0	20 12.4	14 4.4	2 49.3	22 39.6	5 55.2	20 33.1
22 Th	1 57 0	27 24 37	14 27 59	21 7 13	6 44.4	9 42.5	18 39.7	20 56.4	14 0.5	2 50.7	22 42.0	5 54.9	20 32.5
23 F	2 0 56	28 24 22	27 41 34	4♐11 1	6 41.3	11 1.1	19 7.0	21 40.4	13 56.9	2 52.1	22 44.4	5 54.4	20 31.8
24 Sa	2 4 53	29 24 9	10♐35 37	16 55 31	6 37.7	12 23.7	19 36.0	22 24.6	13 53.4	2 53.6	22 46.9	5 54.0	20 31.2
25 Su	2 8 49	0♏23 58	23 10 56	29 22 12	6 34.1	13 49.6	20 6.5	23 8.7	13 50.2	2 55.2	22 49.4	5 53.5	20 30.5
26 M	2 12 46	1 23 48	5♑29 40	11♑33 48	6 31.1	15 18.2	20 38.6	23 53.0	13 47.1	2 57.0	22 52.0	5 53.0	20 29.8
27 Tu	2 16 42	2 23 41	17 35 5	23 34 3	6 28.9	16 49.2	21 12.1	24 37.4	13 44.2	2 58.8	22 54.6	5 52.5	20 29.1
28 W	2 20 39	3 23 34	29 31 18	5♒27 24	6D27.9	18 22.1	21 47.0	25 21.8	13 41.5	3 0.7	22 57.2	5 51.9	20 28.4
29 Th	2 24 35	4 23 30	11♒22 59	17 18 40	6 28.1	19 56.5	22 23.3	26 6.2	13 39.0	3 2.7	22 59.9	5 51.3	20 27.6
30 F	2 28 32	5 23 27	23 15 4	29 12 48	6 29.2	21 32.0	23 0.8	26 50.8	13 36.7	3 4.8	23 2.6	5 50.7	20 26.8
31 Sa	2 32 29	6 23 26	5♓12 28	11♓14 36	6 30.9	23 8.5	23 39.7	27 35.4	13 34.7	3 7.0	23 5.4	5 50.0	20 26.1

Astro Data Dy Hr Mn	Planet Ingress Dy Hr Mn	Last Aspect Dy Hr Mn	☽ Ingress Dy Hr Mn	Last Aspect Dy Hr Mn	☽ Ingress Dy Hr Mn	☽ Phases & Eclipses Dy Hr Mn
♅ D 1 4:19	♀ ♍ 6 2:28	2 12:41 ♃ ✶	♒ 3 9:45	2 13:29 ♅ ✶	♓ 3 5:24	7 0:20 ○ 13♓12
☽0N 8 5:40	♂ ♐ 22 13:52	5 5:23 ♅ ✶	♓ 5 22:07	5 0:57 ♅ □	♈ 5 16:11	14 13:14 ☽ 20♊32
♃∠♄ 13 0:55	☉ ♎ 24 5:44	8 7:28 ♀ ☍	♈ 8 9:12	7 10:07 ♅ △	♉ 8 0:34	21 4:31 ● 27♍01
☿ R 20 22:21		10 2:42 ♅ △	♉ 10 18:22	9 5:04 ♀ △	♊ 10 6:41	21 4:39:48 ● T 2'12"
☽0S 21 6:26	☉ ♏ 24 14:23	12 19:29 ♀ △	♊ 13 1:11	11 21:45 ♅ ☍	♋ 12 11:00	28 13:08 ☽ 4♑14
♇ R 21 12:39		14 21:56 ♀ □	♋ 15 5:27	13 19:57 ☉ □	♌ 14 14:03	
		17 1:18 ♂ △	♌ 17 7:30	16 3:47 ♅ △	♍ 16 16:24	6 15:23 ○ 12♈11
☽0N 5 12:38		19 4:34 ♂ □	♍ 19 8:20	18 6:14 ♅ □	♎ 18 18:49	6 15:17 ● P 0.865
♀0N 6 5:55		21 8:03 ♂ ✶	♎ 21 9:28	20 15:30 ☉ ☌	♏ 20 22:23	13 19:57 ☽ 19♋18
♄ D 8 8:06		22 22:22 ♅ ✶	♏ 23 12:33	22 7:49 ♀ ✶	♐ 23 4:15	20 15:30 ● 26♎04
♀ D 9 4:36		24 23:40 ♀ ✶	♐ 25 18:53	24 23:56 ♂ ☌	♑ 25 13:14	28 8:33 ☽ 3♒45
♆ R 10 6:36		27 12:52 ♅ ☌	♑ 28 4:45	27 7:37 ♀ △	♒ 28 0:58	
☿ D 12 14:40		29 15:43 ♀ △	♒ 30 16:59	30 7:43 ♂ ✶	♓ 30 13:35	
☽0S 18 15:44						

Astro Data

1 SEPTEMBER 1903
Julian Day # 1339
Delta T 2.2 sec
SVP 06♓36'14"
Obliquity 23°26'58"
⚷ Chiron 17♑31.6R
☽ Mean ☊ 8♎18.3

1 OCTOBER 1903
Julian Day # 1369
Delta T 2.3 sec
SVP 06♓36'12"
Obliquity 23°26'58"
⚷ Chiron 17♑12.1
☽ Mean ☊ 6♎43.0

NOVEMBER 1903 LONGITUDE

Day	Sid.Time	☉	0 hr ☽	Noon ☽	True ☊	☿	♀	♂	♃	♄	♅	♆	♇
1 Su	2 36 25	7♏23 26	17♓19 46	23♓28 25	6♎32.7	24♎45.7	24♍19.7	28♐20.1	13♓32.8	3♒ 9.3	23♐ 8.1	5♋49.3	20♊25.3
2 M	2 40 22	8 23 28	29 41 1	5♈57 53	6R33.9	26 23.4	25 0.9	29 4.9	13R31.1	3 11.7	23 10.9	5R48.6	20R24.4
3 Tu	2 44 18	9 23 32	12♈19 21	18 45 35	6 34.0	28 1.5	25 43.2	29 49.7	13 29.6	3 14.2	23 13.8	5 47.8	20 23.6
4 W	2 48 15	10 23 37	25 16 42	1♉52 45	6 32.5	29 39.8	26 26.6	0♑34.6	13 28.3	3 16.8	23 16.7	5 47.0	20 22.8
5 Th	2 52 11	11 23 45	8♉33 36	15 19 6	6 29.2	1♏18.2	27 11.1	1 19.5	13 27.3	3 19.5	23 19.6	5 46.2	20 21.9
6 F	2 56 8	12 23 54	22 8 57	29 2 47	6 24.5	2 56.5	27 56.6	2 4.5	13 26.4	3 22.3	23 22.5	5 45.4	20 21.0
7 Sa	3 0 4	13 24 5	6♊ 0 10	13♊ 0 36	6 18.7	4 34.9	28 43.1	2 49.6	13 25.7	3 25.1	23 25.5	5 44.5	20 20.1
8 Su	3 4 1	14 24 18	20 3 32	27 8 25	6 12.5	6 13.1	29 30.5	3 34.8	13 25.3	3 28.1	23 28.5	5 43.6	20 19.2
9 M	3 7 58	15 24 33	4♋14 41	11♋21 49	6 6.7	7 51.1	0♎18.8	4 20.0	13D25.0	3 31.1	23 31.5	5 42.6	20 18.3
10 Tu	3 11 54	16 24 49	18 29 17	25 36 41	6 2.2	9 29.0	1 8.0	5 5.2	13 25.0	3 34.3	23 34.6	5 41.7	20 17.4
11 W	3 15 51	17 25 8	2♌43 36	9♌49 42	5 59.3	11 6.6	1 58.0	5 50.5	13 25.1	3 37.5	23 37.6	5 40.7	20 16.5
12 Th	3 19 47	18 25 29	16 54 46	23 58 32	5D58.3	12 43.9	2 48.8	6 35.9	13 25.5	3 40.8	23 40.8	5 39.7	20 15.5
13 F	3 23 44	19 25 52	1♍ 0 53	8♍ 1 40	5 58.8	14 21.0	3 40.4	7 21.4	13 26.1	3 44.2	23 43.9	5 38.6	20 14.5
14 Sa	3 27 40	20 26 17	15 0 47	21 58 8	6 0.1	15 57.9	4 32.8	8 6.9	13 26.8	3 47.7	23 47.1	5 37.6	20 13.5
15 Su	3 31 37	21 26 43	28 53 36	5♎47 7	6R 1.2	17 34.5	5 25.9	8 52.4	13 27.8	3 51.3	23 50.3	5 36.5	20 12.5
16 M	3 35 33	22 27 12	12♎38 30	19 27 38	6 1.2	19 10.8	6 19.7	9 38.1	13 29.0	3 55.0	23 53.5	5 35.3	20 11.5
17 Tu	3 39 30	23 27 42	26 14 21	2♏58 25	5 59.3	20 46.9	7 14.1	10 23.7	13 30.4	3 58.7	23 56.7	5 34.2	20 10.5
18 W	3 43 26	24 28 14	9♏39 40	16 17 52	5 55.0	22 22.7	8 9.2	11 9.5	13 32.0	4 2.6	23 60.0	5 33.0	20 9.5
19 Th	3 47 23	25 28 48	22 52 49	29 24 21	5 48.3	23 58.2	9 4.9	11 55.3	13 33.8	4 6.5	24 3.3	5 31.8	20 8.5
20 F	3 51 20	26 29 23	5♐52 18	12♐16 34	5 39.7	25 33.5	10 1.2	12 41.1	13 35.8	4 10.5	24 6.6	5 30.6	20 7.4
21 Sa	3 55 16	27 30 0	18 37 5	24 53 52	5 29.8	27 8.7	10 58.0	13 27.0	13 38.0	4 14.6	24 9.9	5 29.4	20 6.3
22 Su	3 59 13	28 30 38	1♑ 6 58	7♑16 34	5 19.7	28 43.6	11 55.5	14 13.0	13 40.4	4 18.7	24 13.3	5 28.1	20 5.3
23 M	4 3 9	29 31 17	13 22 51	19 26 7	5 10.4	0♐18.3	12 53.4	14 59.0	13 43.0	4 23.0	24 16.6	5 26.8	20 4.2
24 Tu	4 7 6	0♐31 58	25 26 44	1♒25 6	5 2.6	1 52.8	13 51.9	15 45.0	13 45.8	4 27.3	24 20.0	5 25.5	20 3.1
25 W	4 11 2	1 32 40	7♒21 43	13 17 6	4 57.0	3 27.2	14 50.8	16 31.1	13 48.8	4 31.7	24 23.4	5 24.1	20 2.0
26 Th	4 14 59	2 33 22	19 11 49	25 6 31	4 53.8	5 1.4	15 50.3	17 17.2	13 52.0	4 36.2	24 26.9	5 22.8	20 0.9
27 F	4 18 56	3 34 6	1♓ 1 50	6♓58 25	4D52.6	6 35.5	16 50.2	18 3.4	13 55.4	4 40.8	24 30.3	5 21.4	19 59.8
28 Sa	4 22 52	4 34 51	12 56 58	18 58 8	4 52.9	8 9.4	17 50.5	18 49.6	13 59.0	4 45.4	24 33.8	5 20.0	19 58.7
29 Su	4 26 49	5 35 37	25 2 37	1♈11 3	4R53.7	9 43.3	18 51.3	19 35.9	14 2.8	4 50.1	24 37.3	5 18.6	19 57.6
30 M	4 30 45	6 36 24	7♈24 2	13 42 6	4 54.0	11 17.1	19 52.5	20 22.2	14 6.8	4 54.9	24 40.8	5 17.2	19 56.5

DECEMBER 1903 LONGITUDE

Day	Sid.Time	☉	0 hr ☽	Noon ☽	True ☊	☿	♀	♂	♃	♄	♅	♆	♇
1 Tu	4 34 42	7♐37 12	20♈ 5 46	26♈35 23	4♎52.8	12♐50.8	20♎54.1	21♑ 8.5	14♓11.0	4♒59.7	24♐44.3	5♋15.7	19♊55.3
2 W	4 38 38	8 38 1	3♉11 14	9♉53 27	4R49.4	14 24.4	21 56.1	21 54.9	14 15.3	5 4.6	24 47.8	5R14.2	19R54.2
3 Th	4 42 35	9 38 51	16 42 2	23 36 49	4 43.3	15 58.0	22 58.5	22 41.3	14 19.9	5 9.6	24 51.3	5 12.8	19 53.0
4 F	4 46 31	10 39 41	0♊37 28	7♊43 29	4 34.7	17 31.6	24 1.3	23 27.8	14 24.6	5 14.7	24 54.9	5 11.3	19 51.9
5 Sa	4 50 28	11 40 33	14 54 13	22 8 51	4 24.4	19 5.1	25 4.4	24 14.3	14 29.5	5 19.8	24 58.4	5 9.7	19 50.7
6 Su	4 54 25	12 41 27	29 26 30	6♋46 13	4 13.3	20 38.6	26 7.9	25 0.8	14 34.6	5 25.0	25 2.0	5 8.2	19 49.6
7 M	4 58 21	13 42 21	14♋ 7 0	21 27 52	4 2.7	22 12.1	27 11.7	25 47.4	14 39.9	5 30.3	25 5.6	5 6.7	19 48.4
8 Tu	5 2 18	14 43 16	28 47 55	6♌ 6 19	3 53.9	23 45.6	28 15.9	26 34.0	14 45.3	5 35.6	25 9.1	5 5.1	19 47.3
9 W	5 6 14	15 44 13	13♌22 22	20 35 32	3 47.6	25 19.0	29 20.3	27 20.6	14 51.0	5 41.0	25 12.7	5 3.5	19 46.1
10 Th	5 10 11	16 45 10	27 45 22	4♍51 35	3 44.0	26 52.4	0♏25.1	28 7.2	14 56.8	5 46.5	25 16.3	5 1.9	19 44.9
11 F	5 14 7	17 46 9	11♍54 1	18 52 38	3D42.6	28 25.8	1 30.2	28 53.9	15 2.8	5 52.0	25 20.0	5 0.3	19 43.8
12 Sa	5 18 4	18 47 9	25 47 28	2♎38 37	3R42.6	29 59.1	2 35.6	29 40.6	15 8.9	5 57.6	25 23.6	4 58.7	19 42.6
13 Su	5 22 0	19 48 10	9♎26 13	16 10 27	3 42.6	1♑32.4	3 41.2	0♒27.4	15 15.2	6 3.2	25 27.2	4 57.1	19 41.4
14 M	5 25 57	20 49 12	22 51 28	29 29 27	3 41.3	3 5.5	4 47.1	1 14.2	15 21.7	6 8.9	25 30.8	4 55.5	19 40.3
15 Tu	5 29 54	21 50 15	6♏ 4 31	12♏36 48	3 37.6	4 38.5	5 53.3	2 1.0	15 28.4	6 14.6	25 34.4	4 53.8	19 39.1
16 W	5 33 50	22 51 20	19 6 21	25 33 15	3 30.9	6 11.3	6 59.7	2 47.8	15 35.2	6 20.5	25 38.1	4 52.2	19 37.9
17 Th	5 37 47	23 52 25	1♐57 31	8♐19 7	3 21.1	7 43.8	8 6.4	3 34.7	15 42.2	6 26.3	25 41.7	4 50.5	19 36.8
18 F	5 41 43	24 53 31	14 38 3	20 54 18	3 8.6	9 16.1	9 13.3	4 21.6	15 49.4	6 32.2	25 45.4	4 48.9	19 35.6
19 Sa	5 45 40	25 54 37	27 7 51	3♑18 42	2 54.4	10 47.9	10 20.4	5 8.5	15 56.7	6 38.2	25 49.0	4 47.2	19 34.4
20 Su	5 49 36	26 55 44	9♑26 53	15 32 28	2 39.7	12 19.2	11 27.7	5 55.5	16 4.2	6 44.2	25 52.6	4 45.5	19 33.3
21 M	5 53 33	27 56 52	21 35 34	27 36 21	2 25.7	13 49.9	12 35.2	6 42.4	16 11.8	6 50.3	25 56.3	4 43.8	19 32.1
22 Tu	5 57 29	28 58 0	3♒35 2	9♒31 55	2 13.6	15 19.7	13 43.0	7 29.4	16 19.6	6 56.5	25 59.9	4 42.1	19 31.0
23 W	6 1 26	29 59 8	15 27 20	21 21 42	2 4.2	16 48.7	14 50.9	8 16.4	16 27.6	7 2.6	26 3.5	4 40.4	19 29.8
24 Th	6 5 23	1♑ 0 16	27 15 28	3♓ 9 9	1 57.8	18 16.4	15 59.0	9 3.4	16 35.7	7 8.9	26 7.2	4 38.7	19 28.7
25 F	6 9 19	2 1 25	9♓ 3 19	14 58 35	1 54.2	19 42.8	17 7.3	9 50.5	16 43.9	7 15.1	26 10.8	4 37.0	19 27.5
26 Sa	6 13 16	3 2 33	20 55 36	26 55 2	1 52.8	21 7.4	18 15.8	10 37.5	16 52.3	7 21.5	26 14.4	4 35.3	19 26.4
27 Su	6 17 12	4 3 42	2♈57 36	9♈ 3 59	1 52.6	22 30.1	19 24.4	11 24.6	17 0.8	7 27.8	26 18.0	4 33.6	19 25.3
28 M	6 21 9	5 4 51	15 14 54	21 31 0	1 52.4	23 50.3	20 33.2	12 11.7	17 9.5	7 34.2	26 21.6	4 31.9	19 24.2
29 Tu	6 25 5	6 5 59	27 52 55	4♉21 13	1 51.0	25 7.7	21 42.2	12 58.8	17 18.3	7 40.7	26 25.2	4 30.2	19 23.0
30 W	6 29 2	7 7 8	10♉56 22	17 38 42	1 47.5	26 21.8	22 51.3	13 45.9	17 27.3	7 47.1	26 28.8	4 28.5	19 21.9
31 Th	6 32 58	8 8 16	24 28 27	1♊25 37	1 41.3	27 31.9	24 0.6	14 33.0	17 36.4	7 53.7	26 32.4	4 26.8	19 20.8

Astro Data Dy Hr Mn	Planet Ingress Dy Hr Mn
☽0N 1 21:15	♂ ♑ 3 5:31
♀0S 8 21:12	☿ ♏ 4 4:56
♃ D 9 17:32	♀ ♎ 8 14:44
☽0S 14 23:11	☿ ♐ 22 19:22
☽0N 29 7:14	☉ ♐ 23 11:22
♄Q♇ 30 6:21	
	♀ ♏ 9 14:42
♄⊼♆ 3 11:27	☿ ♑ 12 0:14
☽0S 12 5:42	♂ ♒ 12 9:56
☽0N 26 17:11	☉ ♑ 23 0:21

Last Aspect Dy Hr Mn	☽ Ingress Dy Hr Mn	Last Aspect Dy Hr Mn	☽ Ingress Dy Hr Mn
1 22:46 ♂ □	♈ 2 0:36	1 8:38 ♅ △	♉ 1 18:14
3 20:19 ♅ △	♉ 4 8:36	3 11:01 ♂ △	♊ 3 22:56
6 10:41 ♀ △	♊ 6 13:39	5 18:08 ♀ △	♋ 6 0:55
8 5:49 ♅ ☍	♋ 8 16:50	7 23:03 ♀ □	♌ 8 1:58
9 20:14 ☉ △	♌ 10 19:24	9 22:20 ☿ △	♍ 10 3:47
12 11:32 ♅ △	♍ 12 22:16	12 7:12 ♂ △	♎ 12 7:21
14 15:12 ♅ □	♎ 15 1:55	14 4:49 ♅ ✶	♏ 14 12:56
16 19:55 ♅ ✶	♏ 17 6:41	15 17:26 ♃ △	♐ 16 20:19
19 5:10 ☉ ☌	♐ 19 13:06	18 21:27 ♅ ☌	♑ 19 5:34
21 10:39 ♅ ☌	♑ 21 21:50	20 13:11 ♃ ✶	♒ 21 16:48
23 3:23 ♂ ☌	♒ 24 9:09	23 21:40 ♅ ✶	♓ 24 5:35
26 10:43 ♅ ✶	♓ 26 21:55	26 10:42 ♅ □	♈ 26 18:08
28 23:10 ♅ □	♈ 29 9:42	28 21:15 ♅ △	♉ 29 3:57
		31 5:46 ☿ △	♊ 31 9:33

☽ Phases & Eclipses Dy Hr Mn	
5 5:27	○ 11♉37
12 2:46	☽ 18♌32
19 5:10	● 25♏42
27 5:37	☽ 3♓48
4 18:13	○ 11♊26
11 10:53	☽ 18♍14
18 21:26	● 25♐48
27 2:22	☽ 4♈10

Astro Data

1 NOVEMBER 1903
Julian Day # 1400
Delta T 2.4 sec
SVP 06♓36'09"
Obliquity 23°26'57"
⚷ Chiron 18♑03.4
☽ Mean ☊ 5♎04.5

1 DECEMBER 1903
Julian Day # 1430
Delta T 2.5 sec
SVP 06♓36'05"
Obliquity 23°26'57"
⚷ Chiron 19♑53.1
☽ Mean ☊ 3♎29.1

LONGITUDE JANUARY 1904

Day	Sid.Time	☉	0 hr ☽	Noon ☽	True ☊	☿	♀	♂	♃	♄	♅	♆	♇
1 F	6 36 55	9♑ 9 25	8♊30 2	15♊41 20	1♎32.4	28♑37.6	25♏10.0	15♒20.1	17♓45.6	8♒ 0.2	26♐36.0	4♋25.1	19♊19.7
2 Sa	6 40 52	10 10 33	22 58 54	0♋21 55	1R21.4	29 37.9	26 19.6	16 7.2	17 55.0	8 6.8	26 39.6	4R23.4	19R18.6
3 Su	6 44 48	11 11 42	7♋49 23	15 20 8	1 9.5	0♒32.3	27 29.3	16 54.4	18 4.5	8 13.5	26 43.1	4 21.8	19 17.6
4 M	6 48 45	12 12 50	22 52 54	0♌26 23	0 58.0	1 19.7	28 39.2	17 41.5	18 14.1	8 20.2	26 46.7	4 20.1	19 16.5
5 Tu	6 52 41	13 13 59	7♌59 18	15 30 25	0 48.3	1 59.4	29 49.2	18 28.6	18 23.8	8 26.9	26 50.2	4 18.4	19 15.4
6 W	6 56 38	14 15 7	22 58 38	0♍23 3	0 41.1	2 30.4	0♐59.3	19 15.8	18 33.7	8 33.6	26 53.7	4 16.7	19 14.4
7 Th	7 0 34	15 16 15	7♍42 54	14 57 39	0 36.8	2 51.9	2 9.5	20 2.9	18 43.7	8 40.4	26 57.2	4 15.1	19 13.4
8 F	7 4 31	16 17 24	22 6 56	29 10 36	0D35.1	3R 2.9	3 19.9	20 50.1	18 53.8	8 47.2	27 0.7	4 13.4	19 12.3
9 Sa	7 8 27	17 18 33	6♎ 8 35	13♎ 1 1	0R34.9	3 2.9	4 30.4	21 37.2	19 4.1	8 54.0	27 4.2	4 11.7	19 11.3
10 Su	7 12 24	18 19 41	19 48 5	26 30 4	0 35.1	2 51.2	5 41.0	22 24.4	19 14.4	9 0.8	27 7.6	4 10.1	19 10.3
11 M	7 16 21	19 20 50	3♏ 7 17	9♏40 4	0 34.3	2 27.7	6 51.7	23 11.6	19 24.9	9 7.7	27 11.1	4 8.5	19 9.3
12 Tu	7 20 17	20 21 59	16 8 47	22 33 46	0 31.4	1 52.5	8 2.5	23 58.7	19 35.5	9 14.6	27 14.5	4 6.8	19 8.3
13 W	7 24 14	21 23 8	28 55 20	5♐13 48	0 25.8	1 6.2	9 13.5	24 45.9	19 46.2	9 21.6	27 17.9	4 5.2	19 7.3
14 Th	7 28 10	22 24 16	11♐29 24	17 42 24	0 17.4	0 9.7	10 24.5	25 33.1	19 57.0	9 28.5	27 21.3	4 3.6	19 6.4
15 F	7 32 7	23 25 25	23 52 58	0♑ 1 16	0 6.5	29♑ 4.7	11 35.6	26 20.2	20 7.9	9 35.5	27 24.7	4 2.0	19 5.4
16 Sa	7 36 3	24 26 33	6♑ 7 29	12 11 42	29♍53.9	27 52.9	12 46.8	27 7.4	20 19.0	9 42.5	27 28.0	4 0.4	19 4.5
17 Su	7 40 0	25 27 41	18 14 5	24 14 43	29 40.9	26 36.7	13 58.1	27 54.6	20 30.1	9 49.6	27 31.4	3 58.9	19 3.6
18 M	7 43 56	26 28 48	0♒13 46	6♒11 21	29 28.4	25 18.4	15 9.5	28 41.7	20 41.3	9 56.6	27 34.7	3 57.3	19 2.7
19 Tu	7 47 53	27 29 55	12 7 39	18 2 52	29 17.6	24 0.6	16 20.9	29 28.9	20 52.7	10 3.7	27 38.0	3 55.8	19 1.8
20 W	7 51 50	28 31 1	23 57 16	29 51 6	29 9.1	22 45.4	17 32.5	0♓16.0	21 4.1	10 10.7	27 41.2	3 54.3	19 0.9
21 Th	7 55 46	29 32 6	5♓44 44	11♓38 31	29 3.4	21 35.0	18 44.1	1 3.2	21 15.7	10 17.8	27 44.5	3 52.8	19 0.1
22 F	7 59 43	0♒33 10	17 32 54	23 28 21	29D 0.4	20 30.9	19 55.8	1 50.3	21 27.3	10 24.9	27 47.7	3 51.3	18 59.2
23 Sa	8 3 39	1 34 13	29 25 23	5♈24 34	28 59.6	19 34.5	21 7.5	2 37.4	21 39.1	10 32.1	27 50.8	3 49.8	18 58.4
24 Su	8 7 36	2 35 16	11♈26 30	17 31 49	29 0.2	18 46.5	22 19.3	3 24.5	21 50.9	10 39.2	27 54.0	3 48.3	18 57.6
25 M	8 11 32	3 36 17	23 41 8	29 55 7	29R 1.2	18 7.4	23 31.2	4 11.6	22 2.8	10 46.3	27 57.1	3 46.9	18 56.8
26 Tu	8 15 29	4 37 18	6♉14 23	12♉39 33	29 1.6	17 37.5	24 43.1	4 58.7	22 14.8	10 53.5	28 0.2	3 45.5	18 56.0
27 W	8 19 25	5 38 17	19 11 11	25 49 43	29 0.6	17 16.5	25 55.1	5 45.8	22 26.9	11 0.6	28 3.3	3 44.1	18 55.2
28 Th	8 23 22	6 39 15	2♊35 34	9♊28 55	28 57.5	17D 4.3	27 7.2	6 32.8	22 39.1	11 7.8	28 6.4	3 42.7	18 54.5
29 F	8 27 19	7 40 12	16 29 52	23 38 16	28 52.3	17 0.4	28 19.3	7 19.8	22 51.3	11 15.0	28 9.4	3 41.4	18 53.8
30 Sa	8 31 15	8 41 8	0♋53 47	8♋15 52	28 45.4	17 4.2	29 31.5	8 6.9	23 3.7	11 22.1	28 12.4	3 40.0	18 53.1
31 Su	8 35 12	9 42 2	15 43 41	23 16 15	28 37.6	17 15.4	0♑43.7	8 53.9	23 16.1	11 29.3	28 15.3	3 38.7	18 52.4

LONGITUDE FEBRUARY 1904

Day	Sid.Time	☉	0 hr ☽	Noon ☽	True ☊	☿	♀	♂	♃	♄	♅	♆	♇
1 M	8 39 8	10♒42 56	0♌52 24	8♌30 47	28♍29.8	17♑33.3	1♑56.0	9♓40.8	23♓28.6	11♒36.5	28♐18.3	3♋37.4	18♊51.7
2 Tu	8 43 5	11 43 48	16 10 3	23 48 47	28R23.2	17 57.5	3 8.4	10 27.8	23 41.2	11 43.7	28 21.2	3R36.1	18R51.0
3 W	8 47 1	12 44 39	1♍25 37	8♍59 20	28 18.4	18 27.3	4 20.8	11 14.7	23 53.8	11 50.9	28 24.0	3 34.9	18 50.4
4 Th	8 50 58	13 45 29	16 28 50	23 53 15	28D15.9	19 2.3	5 33.2	12 1.6	24 6.5	11 58.0	28 26.9	3 33.7	18 49.8
5 F	8 54 54	14 46 19	1♎11 51	8♎24 10	28 15.4	19 42.1	6 45.7	12 48.5	24 19.3	12 5.2	28 29.6	3 32.5	18 49.2
6 Sa	8 58 51	15 47 7	15 29 56	22 29 0	28 16.2	20 26.3	7 58.2	13 35.4	24 32.2	12 12.4	28 32.4	3 31.3	18 48.6
7 Su	9 2 48	16 47 54	29 21 26	6♏ 7 24	28 17.6	21 14.4	9 10.8	14 22.2	24 45.1	12 19.6	28 35.1	3 30.1	18 48.0
8 M	9 6 44	17 48 40	12♏47 11	19 21 9	28R18.7	22 6.1	10 23.5	15 9.1	24 58.1	12 26.7	28 37.8	3 29.0	18 47.5
9 Tu	9 10 41	18 49 26	25 49 42	2♐13 16	28 18.5	23 1.1	11 36.2	15 55.9	25 11.2	12 33.9	28 40.5	3 27.9	18 47.0
10 W	9 14 37	19 50 10	8♐32 19	14 47 18	28 16.7	23 59.2	12 48.9	16 42.7	25 24.4	12 41.0	28 43.1	3 26.8	18 46.5
11 Th	9 18 34	20 50 54	20 58 40	27 6 51	28 13.1	25 0.1	14 1.7	17 29.4	25 37.6	12 48.2	28 45.7	3 25.8	18 46.0
12 F	9 22 30	21 51 36	3♑12 15	9♑15 15	28 8.0	26 3.5	15 14.5	18 16.2	25 50.8	12 55.3	28 48.2	3 24.8	18 45.5
13 Sa	9 26 27	22 52 17	15 16 13	21 15 26	28 1.7	27 9.3	16 27.3	19 2.9	26 4.1	13 2.4	28 50.7	3 23.8	18 45.1
14 Su	9 30 23	23 52 57	27 13 13	3♒ 9 50	27 55.0	28 17.3	17 40.2	19 49.6	26 17.5	13 9.6	28 53.2	3 22.8	18 44.7
15 M	9 34 20	24 53 36	9♒ 5 32	15 0 33	27 48.6	29 27.3	18 53.1	20 36.2	26 31.0	13 16.7	28 55.6	3 21.9	18 44.3
16 Tu	9 38 17	25 54 13	20 55 7	26 49 27	27 43.1	0♒39.2	20 6.0	21 22.9	26 44.4	13 23.7	28 58.0	3 21.0	18 43.9
17 W	9 42 13	26 54 49	2♓43 48	8♓38 22	27 39.0	1 52.9	21 19.0	22 9.5	26 58.0	13 30.8	29 0.3	3 20.1	18 43.6
18 Th	9 46 10	27 55 23	14 33 26	20 29 16	27 36.5	3 8.3	22 32.0	22 56.1	27 11.6	13 37.8	29 2.7	3 19.2	18 43.2
19 F	9 50 6	28 55 55	26 26 10	2♈24 27	27D35.6	4 25.2	23 45.0	23 42.6	27 25.2	13 44.9	29 4.9	3 18.4	18 42.9
20 Sa	9 54 3	29 56 26	8♈24 29	14 26 39	27 36.1	5 43.7	24 58.1	24 29.1	27 38.9	13 51.9	29 7.1	3 17.6	18 42.6
21 Su	9 57 59	0♓56 55	20 31 22	26 39 5	27 37.5	7 3.6	26 11.1	25 15.6	27 52.7	13 58.9	29 9.3	3 16.8	18 42.4
22 M	10 1 56	1 57 22	2♉50 15	9♉ 5 21	27 39.3	8 24.8	27 24.2	26 2.1	28 6.5	14 5.8	29 11.4	3 16.1	18 42.1
23 Tu	10 5 52	2 57 47	15 24 54	21 49 21	27 40.9	9 47.4	28 37.3	26 48.5	28 20.3	14 12.8	29 13.5	3 15.4	18 41.9
24 W	10 9 49	3 58 11	28 19 10	4♊54 47	27R41.8	11 11.2	29 50.5	27 34.9	28 34.2	14 19.7	29 15.6	3 14.8	18 41.7
25 Th	10 13 46	4 58 33	11♊36 34	18 24 47	27 41.7	12 36.3	1♒ 3.6	28 21.2	28 48.1	14 26.6	29 17.6	3 14.1	18 41.5
26 F	10 17 42	5 58 52	25 19 38	2♋21 9	27 40.7	14 2.5	2 16.8	29 7.5	29 2.0	14 33.5	29 19.5	3 13.5	18 41.4
27 Sa	10 21 39	6 59 10	9♋29 14	16 43 37	27 38.7	15 29.9	3 30.0	29 53.8	29 16.0	14 40.3	29 21.4	3 12.9	18 41.2
28 Su	10 25 35	7 59 25	24 3 51	1♌29 16	27 36.2	16 58.5	4 43.2	0♈40.1	29 30.1	14 47.1	29 23.3	3 12.4	18 41.1
29 M	10 29 32	8 59 39	8♌59 4	16 32 16	27 33.6	18 28.2	5 56.4	1 26.3	29 44.1	14 53.9	29 25.1	3 11.9	18 41.0

Astro Data	Dy Hr Mn
☽ 0 S	8 13:10
☿ R	8 11:56
♃ □ ♇	9 15:18
☽ 0 N	23 1:41
☿ D	28 23:48
☽ 0 S	4 22:47
☽ 0 N	19 8:28
♄ ∠ ♅	23 3:35
♃ □ ♅	27 10:39
♂ 0 N	28 22:48

Planet Ingress	Dy Hr Mn
☿ ♒	2 9:24
♀ ♐	5 3:43
☿ ♑	14 3:47
☊ ♍	15 12:40
♂ ♓	19 15:50
☉ ♒	21 10:58
♀ ♑	30 9:28
☿ ♒	15 10:59
☉ ♓	20 1:25
♀ ♒	24 3:08
♂ ♈	27 3:12

Last Aspect Dy Hr Mn		☽ Ingress Dy Hr Mn
2 6:01	♅ ☍	♋ 2 11:25
4 9:56	♀ △	♌ 4 11:18
6 6:22	♅ △	♍ 6 11:22
8 8:20	♅ □	♎ 8 13:25
10 13:11	♅ ✶	♏ 10 18:19
12 15:38	♂ □	♐ 13 2:03
15 6:55	♅ ☌	♑ 15 11:58
17 15:47	☉ ☌	♒ 17 23:32
20 7:38	♅ ✶	♓ 20 12:18
22 20:49	♅ □	♈ 23 1:10
25 8:16	♅ △	♉ 25 12:09
27 6:01	♃ ✶	♊ 27 19:26
29 21:33	♀ ☍	♋ 29 22:32
31 12:10	♃ △	♌ 31 22:38

Last Aspect Dy Hr Mn		☽ Ingress Dy Hr Mn
2 19:12	♅ △	♍ 2 21:45
4 19:32	♅ □	♎ 4 22:01
6 22:38	♅ ✶	♏ 7 1:08
8 22:47	♃ △	♐ 9 7:49
11 15:17	♅ ☌	♑ 11 17:41
14 2:23	☿ ☌	♒ 14 5:36
16 16:25	♅ ✶	♓ 16 18:27
19 5:20	♅ □	♈ 19 7:10
21 16:55	♅ △	♉ 21 18:31
24 3:04	♀ △	♊ 24 3:05
26 6:53	♂ □	♋ 26 8:00
28 8:56	♃ △	♌ 28 9:36

☽ Phases & Eclipses Dy Hr Mn	
3 5:47	○ 11♋26
9 21:10	☽ 18♎12
17 15:47	● 26♑08
25 20:41	☽ 4♉29
1 16:33	○ 11♌25
8 9:56	☽ 18♏14
16 11:05	● 26♒22
24 11:08	☽ 4♊26

Astro Data

1 JANUARY 1904
Julian Day # 1461
Delta T 2.6 sec
SVP 06♓36'00"
Obliquity 23°26'56"
⚷ Chiron 22♑26.4
☽ Mean ☊ 1♎50.7

1 FEBRUARY 1904
Julian Day # 1492
Delta T 2.7 sec
SVP 06♓35'55"
Obliquity 23°26'57"
⚷ Chiron 25♑12.2
☽ Mean ☊ 0♎12.2

MARCH 1904 LONGITUDE

Day	Sid.Time	☉	0 hr ☽	Noon ☽	True ☊	☿	♀	♂	♃	♄	♅	♆	♇
1 Tu	10 33 28	9♓59 50	24♌ 7 43	1♍44 14	27♍31.4	19♒59.0	7♒ 9.7	2♈12.4	29♓58.2	15♒ 0.7	29♐26.9	3♋11.4	18♊41.0
2 W	10 37 25	11 0 0	9♍20 34	16 55 27	27R29.9	21 30.9	8 22.9	2 58.5	0♈12.4	15 7.4	29 28.6	3R11.0	18R40.9
3 Th	10 41 21	12 0 8	24 27 41	1♎56 12	27D29.3	23 3.9	9 36.2	3 44.6	0 26.5	15 14.1	29 30.3	3 10.6	18D40.9
4 F	10 45 18	13 0 14	9♎20 2	16 38 23	27 29.6	24 38.0	10 49.5	4 30.7	0 40.7	15 20.7	29 31.9	3 10.2	18 40.9
5 Sa	10 49 14	14 0 18	23 50 39	0♏56 23	27 30.4	26 13.2	12 2.9	5 16.7	0 54.9	15 27.4	29 33.5	3 9.8	18 40.9
6 Su	10 53 11	15 0 21	7♏55 20	14 47 26	27 31.4	27 49.5	13 16.2	6 2.6	1 9.2	15 33.9	29 35.0	3 9.5	18 41.0
7 M	10 57 8	16 0 22	21 32 43	28 11 23	27 32.4	29 27.0	14 29.6	6 48.6	1 23.5	15 40.5	29 36.5	3 9.3	18 41.0
8 Tu	11 1 4	17 0 21	4♐43 44	11♐10 8	27 33.1	1♓ 5.5	15 42.9	7 34.5	1 37.8	15 47.0	29 37.9	3 9.0	18 41.1
9 W	11 5 1	18 0 19	17 31 2	23 46 55	27R33.4	2 45.2	16 56.3	8 20.3	1 52.1	15 53.5	29 39.3	3 8.8	18 41.2
10 Th	11 8 57	19 0 15	29 58 19	6♑ 5 45	27 33.2	4 26.0	18 9.7	9 6.1	2 6.4	15 59.9	29 40.7	3 8.6	18 41.4
11 F	11 12 54	20 0 10	12♑ 9 46	18 10 54	27 32.7	6 8.0	19 23.2	9 51.9	2 20.8	16 6.3	29 41.9	3 8.5	18 41.5
12 Sa	11 16 50	21 0 3	24 9 40	0♒ 6 34	27 31.9	7 51.1	20 36.6	10 37.6	2 35.2	16 12.7	29 43.2	3 8.4	18 41.7
13 Su	11 20 47	21 59 54	6♒ 2 5	11 56 39	27 31.1	9 35.4	21 50.0	11 23.3	2 49.6	16 19.0	29 44.4	3 8.3	18 41.9
14 M	11 24 43	22 59 44	17 50 42	23 44 37	27 30.4	11 20.8	23 3.5	12 9.0	3 4.0	16 25.2	29 45.5	3D 8.3	18 42.1
15 Tu	11 28 40	23 59 31	29 38 45	5♓33 27	27 29.8	13 7.5	24 17.0	12 54.6	3 18.5	16 31.5	29 46.6	3 8.3	18 42.4
16 W	11 32 37	24 59 17	11♓29 1	17 25 43	27 29.6	14 55.4	25 30.5	13 40.2	3 32.9	16 37.6	29 47.6	3 8.3	18 42.6
17 Th	11 36 33	25 59 0	23 23 50	29 23 36	27D29.5	16 44.4	26 43.9	14 25.7	3 47.4	16 43.7	29 48.6	3 8.3	18 42.9
18 F	11 40 30	26 58 42	5♈25 15	11♈29 1	27R29.5	18 34.7	27 57.4	15 11.2	4 1.9	16 49.8	29 49.5	3 8.4	18 43.2
19 Sa	11 44 26	27 58 22	17 35 7	23 43 45	27 29.5	20 26.3	29 10.9	15 56.6	4 16.4	16 55.8	29 50.4	3 8.6	18 43.6
20 Su	11 48 23	28 57 59	29 55 10	6♉ 9 35	27 29.4	22 19.1	0♓24.4	16 42.0	4 30.9	17 1.8	29 51.2	3 8.7	18 43.9
21 M	11 52 19	29 57 34	12♉27 13	18 48 19	27 29.1	24 13.0	1 37.9	17 27.4	4 45.4	17 7.7	29 52.0	3 8.9	18 44.3
22 Tu	11 56 16	0♈57 8	25 13 6	1♊41 50	27 28.7	26 8.2	2 51.5	18 12.7	4 59.9	17 13.6	29 52.7	3 9.2	18 44.7
23 W	12 0 12	1 56 39	8♊14 44	14 52 2	27 28.3	28 4.6	4 5.0	18 57.9	5 14.5	17 19.4	29 53.4	3 9.4	18 45.1
24 Th	12 4 9	2 56 7	21 33 54	28 20 32	27D28.0	0♈ 2.2	5 18.5	19 43.1	5 29.0	17 25.2	29 54.0	3 9.7	18 45.6
25 F	12 8 6	3 55 34	5♋12 2	12♋ 8 26	27 27.9	2 0.8	6 32.0	20 28.3	5 43.5	17 30.9	29 54.6	3 10.1	18 46.0
26 Sa	12 12 2	4 54 58	19 9 44	26 15 50	27 28.1	4 0.5	7 45.5	21 13.4	5 58.0	17 36.5	29 55.1	3 10.4	18 46.5
27 Su	12 15 59	5 54 19	3♌26 29	10♌41 22	27 28.6	6 1.2	8 59.0	21 58.5	6 12.6	17 42.1	29 55.5	3 10.8	18 47.0
28 M	12 19 55	6 53 39	18 0 2	25 21 55	27 29.4	8 2.7	10 12.6	22 43.5	6 27.1	17 47.6	29 56.0	3 11.3	18 47.6
29 Tu	12 23 52	7 52 56	2♍46 18	10♍12 25	27 30.2	10 5.0	11 26.1	23 28.5	6 41.6	17 53.1	29 56.3	3 11.8	18 48.1
30 W	12 27 48	8 52 10	17 39 21	25 6 11	27R30.8	12 7.9	12 39.6	24 13.4	6 56.1	17 58.5	29 56.6	3 12.3	18 48.7
31 Th	12 31 45	9 51 23	2♎31 56	9♎55 37	27 30.8	14 11.3	13 53.2	24 58.2	7 10.7	18 3.9	29 56.9	3 12.8	18 49.3

APRIL 1904 LONGITUDE

Day	Sid.Time	☉	0 hr ☽	Noon ☽	True ☊	☿	♀	♂	♃	♄	♅	♆	♇
1 F	12 35 41	10♈50 33	17♎16 18	24♎33 8	27♍30.3	16♈14.8	15♓ 6.7	25♈43.1	7♈25.2	18♒ 9.1	29♐57.1	3♋13.4	18♊49.9
2 Sa	12 39 38	11 49 42	1♏45 20	8♏52 15	27R29.0	18 18.4	16 20.2	26 27.8	7 39.7	18 14.4	29 57.2	3 14.0	18 50.5
3 Su	12 43 34	12 48 48	15 53 24	22 48 24	27 27.1	20 21.7	17 33.8	27 12.5	7 54.2	18 19.5	29 57.3	3 14.6	18 51.1
4 M	12 47 31	13 47 53	29 37 3	6♐19 16	27 25.0	22 24.4	18 47.3	27 57.2	8 8.7	18 24.6	29R57.3	3 15.3	18 51.8
5 Tu	12 51 28	14 46 56	12♐55 9	19 24 52	27 22.8	24 26.3	20 0.9	28 41.8	8 23.1	18 29.6	29 57.3	3 16.0	18 52.5
6 W	12 55 24	15 45 57	25 48 44	2♑ 7 7	27 21.0	26 27.0	21 14.4	29 26.4	8 37.6	18 34.6	29 57.3	3 16.7	18 53.2
7 Th	12 59 21	16 44 56	8♑20 29	14 29 22	27D19.9	28 26.1	22 28.0	0♉11.0	8 52.1	18 39.5	29 57.2	3 17.5	18 53.9
8 F	13 3 17	17 43 53	20 34 19	26 35 55	27 19.7	0♉23.2	23 41.6	0 55.4	9 6.5	18 44.3	29 57.0	3 18.3	18 54.7
9 Sa	13 7 14	18 42 49	2♒34 47	8♒31 31	27 20.4	2 18.1	24 55.1	1 39.9	9 20.9	18 49.0	29 56.8	3 19.1	18 55.4
10 Su	13 11 10	19 41 43	14 26 43	20 20 58	27 21.7	4 10.3	26 8.7	2 24.3	9 35.3	18 53.7	29 56.5	3 19.9	18 56.2
11 M	13 15 7	20 40 35	26 14 52	2♓ 8 57	27 23.4	5 59.5	27 22.3	3 8.6	9 49.7	18 58.3	29 56.2	3 20.8	18 57.0
12 Tu	13 19 3	21 39 26	8♓ 3 44	13 59 41	27 25.0	7 45.3	28 35.8	3 52.9	10 4.1	19 2.9	29 55.9	3 21.7	18 57.8
13 W	13 23 0	22 38 14	19 57 15	25 56 51	27R26.1	9 27.5	29 49.4	4 37.1	10 18.5	19 7.3	29 55.4	3 22.7	18 58.7
14 Th	13 26 57	23 37 1	1♈58 48	8♈ 3 25	27 26.3	11 5.9	1♈ 3.0	5 21.3	10 32.8	19 11.7	29 55.0	3 23.7	18 59.5
15 F	13 30 53	24 35 46	14 10 58	20 21 39	27 25.1	12 40.0	2 16.6	6 5.5	10 47.1	19 16.0	29 54.4	3 24.7	19 0.4
16 Sa	13 34 50	25 34 29	26 35 37	2♉52 59	27 22.6	14 9.8	3 30.1	6 49.6	11 1.4	19 20.2	29 53.9	3 25.7	19 1.3
17 Su	13 38 46	26 33 10	9♉13 50	15 38 11	27 18.8	15 34.9	4 43.7	7 33.6	11 15.7	19 24.4	29 53.3	3 26.8	19 2.2
18 M	13 42 43	27 31 48	22 6 2	28 37 22	27 14.1	16 55.4	5 57.3	8 17.6	11 29.9	19 28.5	29 52.6	3 27.9	19 3.1
19 Tu	13 46 39	28 30 25	5♊12 7	11♊50 13	27 9.0	18 10.8	7 10.8	9 1.6	11 44.1	19 32.5	29 51.9	3 29.0	19 4.0
20 W	13 50 36	29 29 0	18 31 37	25 16 13	27 4.2	19 21.3	8 24.4	9 45.5	11 58.3	19 36.4	29 51.1	3 30.2	19 5.0
21 Th	13 54 32	0♉27 33	2♋ 3 55	8♋54 40	27 0.3	20 26.6	9 38.0	10 29.3	12 12.5	19 40.2	29 50.3	3 31.4	19 6.0
22 F	13 58 29	1 26 4	15 48 21	22 44 54	26 57.7	21 26.6	10 51.5	11 13.1	12 26.6	19 44.0	29 49.4	3 32.6	19 7.0
23 Sa	14 2 26	2 24 32	29 44 13	6♌46 10	26D56.7	22 21.3	12 5.1	11 56.8	12 40.7	19 47.7	29 48.5	3 33.9	19 8.0
24 Su	14 6 22	3 22 58	13♌50 37	20 57 23	26 57.1	23 10.5	13 18.6	12 40.5	12 54.7	19 51.2	29 47.6	3 35.1	19 9.0
25 M	14 10 19	4 21 22	28 6 16	5♍16 58	26 58.3	23 54.2	14 32.1	13 24.1	13 8.8	19 54.7	29 46.6	3 36.5	19 10.0
26 Tu	14 14 15	5 19 44	12♍29 10	19 42 26	26 59.6	24 32.3	15 45.7	14 7.7	13 22.7	19 58.2	29 45.5	3 37.8	19 11.1
27 W	14 18 12	6 18 4	26 56 19	4♎10 15	27R 0.3	25 4.9	16 59.2	14 51.2	13 36.7	20 1.5	29 44.5	3 39.1	19 12.1
28 Th	14 22 8	7 16 21	11♎23 40	18 35 53	26 59.4	25 31.8	18 12.7	15 34.7	13 50.6	20 4.7	29 43.3	3 40.5	19 13.2
29 F	14 26 5	8 14 37	25 46 14	2♏54 3	26 56.7	25 53.1	19 26.2	16 18.1	14 4.5	20 7.9	29 42.1	3 41.9	19 14.3
30 Sa	14 30 1	9 12 51	9♏58 41	16 59 30	26 52.1	26 8.9	20 39.8	17 1.5	14 18.3	20 11.0	29 40.9	3 43.4	19 15.4

Astro Data	Dy Hr Mn
♃∠♄	1 7:56
☽0S	3 9:59
♇ D	3 13:41
♃0N	11 17:05
♃□♆	14 7:00
♆ D	14 17:03
☽0N	17 14:34
☿0N	25 13:39
☽0S	30 21:00
♄⚻♆	1 21:55
♅ R	4 9:09
♄△♇	10 15:35
☽0N	13 21:26
♀0N	16 1:19

Planet Ingress		Dy Hr Mn
♃	♈	1 3:00
☿	♓	7 8:05
♀	♓	19 16:01
☉	♈	21 0:59
☿	♈	23 23:34
♂	♉	6 18:06
☿	♉	7 19:13
♀	♈	13 3:27
☉	♉	20 12:42
☽0S		27 6:24

Last Aspect Dy Hr Mn			☽ Ingress	Dy Hr Mn
1 8:24	♅	△	♍	1 9:16
3 8:06	♅	□	♎	3 8:53
5 9:40	♅	⚹	♏	5 10:24
6 13:29	♄	□	♐	7 15:18
9 23:26	♅	☌	♑	10 0:03
11 17:04	☉	⚹	♒	12 11:47
15 0:16	♅	⚹	♓	15 0:43
17 12:51	♅	□	♈	17 13:13
19 23:52	♅	△	♉	20 0:09
22 2:01	☿	⚹	♊	22 8:52
24 14:45	♅	☍	♋	24 14:55
26 3:42	♂	□	♌	26 18:16
28 19:25	♅	△	♍	28 19:31
30 19:49	♅	□	♎	30 19:54

Last Aspect Dy Hr Mn			☽ Ingress	Dy Hr Mn
1 20:59	♅	⚹	♏	1 21:04
3 4:14	♄	□	♐	4 0:41
6 7:52	♅	☌	♑	6 7:57
8 6:54	♀	⚹	♒	8 18:49
11 7:30	♅	⚹	♓	11 7:38
13 19:54	♅	□	♈	13 20:04
16 6:19	♅	△	♉	16 6:31
17 19:07	♄	□	♊	18 14:31
20 20:05	♅	☍	♋	20 20:22
22 10:27	☿	⚹	♌	23 0:27
25 2:48	♅	△	♍	25 3:10
27 4:39	♅	□	♎	27 5:05
29 6:36	♅	⚹	♏	29 7:06

☽ Phases & Eclipses Dy Hr Mn	
2 2:48	○ 11♍07
2 3:02	☍ A 0.175
9 1:01	☽ 18♐03
17 5:39	● 26♓13
17 5:40:40	☌ A 8'07"
24 21:37	☽ 3♋50
31 12:44	○ 10♎23
31 12:32	☍ A 0.704
7 17:53	☽ 17♑29
15 21:53	● 25♈29
23 4:54	☽ 2♌36
29 22:36	○ 9♏09

Astro Data
1 MARCH 1904
Julian Day # 1521
Delta T 2.8 sec
SVP 06♓35'52"
Obliquity 23°26'57"
⚷ Chiron 27♑32.4
☽ Mean ☊ 28♍40.0
1 APRIL 1904
Julian Day # 1552
Delta T 2.9 sec
SVP 06♓35'50"
Obliquity 23°26'58"
⚷ Chiron 29♑20.7
☽ Mean ☊ 27♍01.5

LONGITUDE MAY 1904

Day	Sid.Time	☉	0 hr ☽	Noon ☽	True ☊	☿	♀	♂	♃	♄	♅	♆	♇
1 Su	14 33 58	10♉11 3	23♏55 57	0♐47 34	26♍45.8	26♉19.1	21♈53.3	17♉44.8	14♈32.1	20♒14.0	29♐39.7	3♋44.8	19♊16.5
2 M	14 37 55	11 9 13	7♐34 1	14 15 1	26R38.5	26R23.9	23 6.8	18 28.1	14 45.8	20 16.9	29R38.3	3 46.3	19 17.6
3 Tu	14 41 51	12 7 22	20 50 29	27 20 24	26 31.1	26 23.4	24 20.3	19 11.3	14 59.5	20 19.7	29 37.0	3 47.8	19 18.8
4 W	14 45 48	13 5 30	3♑44 52	10♑ 4 6	26 24.4	26 17.7	25 33.9	19 54.5	15 13.2	20 22.4	29 35.6	3 49.3	19 19.9
5 Th	14 49 44	14 3 36	16 18 27	22 28 18	26 19.1	26 7.2	26 47.4	20 37.6	15 26.8	20 25.0	29 34.2	3 50.9	19 21.1
6 F	14 53 41	15 1 40	28 34 8	4♒36 29	26 15.6	25 52.0	28 0.9	21 20.7	15 40.3	20 27.6	29 32.7	3 52.5	19 22.3
7 Sa	14 57 37	15 59 43	10♒35 57	16 33 8	26D14.0	25 32.6	29 14.4	22 3.7	15 53.9	20 30.0	29 31.2	3 54.1	19 23.5
8 Su	15 1 34	16 57 45	22 28 42	28 23 17	26 14.0	25 9.3	0♉28.0	22 46.6	16 7.3	20 32.4	29 29.6	3 55.7	19 24.7
9 M	15 5 30	17 55 45	4♓17 34	10♓12 11	26 14.9	24 42.5	1 41.5	23 29.6	16 20.7	20 34.7	29 28.1	3 57.4	19 25.9
10 Tu	15 9 27	18 53 44	16 7 48	22 5 0	26R16.0	24 12.9	2 55.0	24 12.4	16 34.1	20 36.8	29 26.4	3 59.0	19 27.1
11 W	15 13 24	19 51 41	28 4 22	4♈ 6 27	26 16.5	23 40.8	4 8.6	24 55.3	16 47.4	20 38.9	29 24.8	4 0.7	19 28.4
12 Th	15 17 20	20 49 37	10♈11 43	16 20 37	26 15.4	23 7.0	5 22.1	25 38.0	17 0.7	20 40.9	29 23.1	4 2.5	19 29.6
13 F	15 21 17	21 47 32	22 33 29	28 50 35	26 12.2	22 31.9	6 35.6	26 20.8	17 13.8	20 42.8	29 21.3	4 4.2	19 30.9
14 Sa	15 25 13	22 45 26	5♉12 8	11♉38 13	26 6.6	21 56.4	7 49.1	27 3.4	17 27.0	20 44.6	29 19.5	4 6.0	19 32.1
15 Su	15 29 10	23 43 18	18 8 52	24 43 59	25 58.9	21 20.8	9 2.7	27 46.1	17 40.1	20 46.3	29 17.7	4 7.7	19 33.4
16 M	15 33 6	24 41 8	1♊23 25	8♊ 6 55	25 49.7	20 46.0	10 16.2	28 28.6	17 53.1	20 47.9	29 15.9	4 9.5	19 34.7
17 Tu	15 37 3	25 38 58	14 54 11	21 44 51	25 39.7	20 12.4	11 29.7	29 11.2	18 6.0	20 49.4	29 14.0	4 11.3	19 36.0
18 W	15 40 59	26 36 45	28 38 30	5♋34 43	25 30.0	19 40.7	12 43.3	29 53.7	18 18.9	20 50.8	29 12.1	4 13.2	19 37.3
19 Th	15 44 56	27 34 32	12♋33 5	19 33 12	25 21.8	19 11.3	13 56.8	0♊36.1	18 31.7	20 52.1	29 10.2	4 15.0	19 38.6
20 F	15 48 53	28 32 16	26 34 41	3♌37 11	25 15.8	18 44.7	15 10.3	1 18.5	18 44.5	20 53.4	29 8.2	4 16.9	19 39.9
21 Sa	15 52 49	29 29 59	10♌40 25	17 44 8	25 12.2	18 21.3	16 23.8	2 0.8	18 57.2	20 54.5	29 6.2	4 18.8	19 41.2
22 Su	15 56 46	0♊27 41	24 48 8	1♍52 15	25D10.8	18 1.4	17 37.3	2 43.1	19 9.8	20 55.5	29 4.2	4 20.7	19 42.6
23 M	16 0 42	1 25 20	8♍56 19	16 0 14	25 10.8	17 45.4	18 50.8	3 25.3	19 22.4	20 56.4	29 2.1	4 22.7	19 43.9
24 Tu	16 4 39	2 22 58	23 3 50	0♎ 6 59	25R11.2	17 33.5	20 4.4	4 7.5	19 34.8	20 57.2	29 0.1	4 24.6	19 45.2
25 W	16 8 35	3 20 35	7♎ 9 29	14 11 9	25 10.7	17 25.8	21 17.9	4 49.6	19 47.2	20 58.0	28 58.0	4 26.5	19 46.6
26 Th	16 12 32	4 18 10	21 11 43	28 10 52	25 8.3	17D22.5	22 31.4	5 31.7	19 59.6	20 58.6	28 55.8	4 28.5	19 47.9
27 F	16 16 28	5 15 44	5♏ 8 16	12♏ 3 33	25 3.4	17 23.6	23 44.9	6 13.7	20 11.8	20 59.1	28 53.7	4 30.5	19 49.3
28 Sa	16 20 25	6 13 16	18 56 18	25 46 8	24 55.7	17 29.2	24 58.4	6 55.6	20 24.0	20 59.6	28 51.5	4 32.5	19 50.7
29 Su	16 24 22	7 10 47	2♐32 40	9♐15 31	24 45.7	17 39.4	26 11.9	7 37.6	20 36.1	20 59.9	28 49.3	4 34.5	19 52.0
30 M	16 28 18	8 8 18	15 54 22	22 28 58	24 34.3	17 54.0	27 25.4	8 19.4	20 48.1	21 0.2	28 47.1	4 36.6	19 53.4
31 Tu	16 32 15	9 5 47	28 59 10	5♑24 51	24 22.4	18 13.0	28 38.9	9 1.3	21 0.0	21R 0.3	28 44.9	4 38.6	19 54.8

LONGITUDE JUNE 1904

Day	Sid.Time	☉	0 hr ☽	Noon ☽	True ☊	☿	♀	♂	♃	♄	♅	♆	♇
1 W	16 36 11	10♊ 3 15	11♑46 0	18♑ 2 45	24♍11.3	18♉36.4	29♉52.5	9♊43.0	21♈11.9	21♒ 0.3	28♐42.6	4♋40.7	19♊56.2
2 Th	16 40 8	11 0 42	24 15 16	0♒23 49	24R 1.9	19 4.1	1♊ 6.0	10 24.8	21 23.7	21R 0.3	28R40.3	4 42.7	19 57.6
3 F	16 44 4	11 58 9	6♒28 46	12 30 32	23 54.9	19 36.1	2 19.5	11 6.5	21 35.4	21 0.1	28 38.0	4 44.8	19 59.0
4 Sa	16 48 1	12 55 34	18 29 37	24 26 34	23 50.4	20 12.1	3 33.0	11 48.1	21 47.0	20 59.9	28 35.7	4 46.9	20 0.4
5 Su	16 51 57	13 52 59	0♓22 0	6♓16 31	23 48.1	20 52.2	4 46.6	12 29.7	21 58.5	20 59.5	28 33.4	4 49.0	20 1.8
6 M	16 55 54	14 50 23	12 10 49	18 5 33	23 47.5	21 36.3	6 0.1	13 11.2	22 9.9	20 59.1	28 31.0	4 51.1	20 3.2
7 Tu	16 59 51	15 47 47	24 1 24	29 59 5	23 47.5	22 24.1	7 13.7	13 52.8	22 21.2	20 58.6	28 28.7	4 53.3	20 4.6
8 W	17 3 47	16 45 10	5♈59 14	12♈ 2 31	23 47.1	23 15.8	8 27.2	14 34.2	22 32.5	20 57.9	28 26.3	4 55.4	20 6.0
9 Th	17 7 44	17 42 33	18 9 32	24 20 50	23 45.3	24 11.1	9 40.8	15 15.6	22 43.6	20 57.2	28 23.9	4 57.5	20 7.4
10 F	17 11 40	18 39 55	0♉36 54	6♉58 8	23 41.3	25 10.0	10 54.4	15 57.0	22 54.7	20 56.4	28 21.5	4 59.7	20 8.8
11 Sa	17 15 37	19 37 16	13 24 51	19 57 13	23 34.6	26 12.4	12 8.0	16 38.3	23 5.6	20 55.4	28 19.1	5 1.9	20 10.2
12 Su	17 19 33	20 34 37	26 35 19	3♊19 6	23 25.5	27 18.3	13 21.6	17 19.6	23 16.5	20 54.4	28 16.7	5 4.0	20 11.6
13 M	17 23 30	21 31 57	10♊ 8 20	17 2 43	23 14.5	28 27.5	14 35.1	18 0.8	23 27.2	20 53.3	28 14.3	5 6.2	20 13.0
14 Tu	17 27 26	22 29 17	24 1 45	1♋ 4 53	23 2.6	29 40.1	15 48.8	18 42.0	23 37.9	20 52.1	28 11.9	5 8.4	20 14.4
15 W	17 31 23	23 26 36	8♋11 27	15 20 44	22 51.1	0♊56.0	17 2.4	19 23.2	23 48.4	20 50.8	28 9.4	5 10.6	20 15.8
16 Th	17 35 20	24 23 55	22 31 58	29 44 25	22 41.1	2 15.2	18 16.0	20 4.3	23 58.9	20 49.4	28 7.0	5 12.8	20 17.2
17 F	17 39 16	25 21 13	6♌57 22	14♌10 10	22 33.5	3 37.5	19 29.6	20 45.3	24 9.2	20 47.9	28 4.6	5 15.0	20 18.6
18 Sa	17 43 13	26 18 30	21 22 13	28 33 4	22 28.8	5 3.1	20 43.2	21 26.3	24 19.4	20 46.3	28 2.1	5 17.2	20 20.0
19 Su	17 47 9	27 15 46	5♍42 18	12♍49 38	22 26.5	6 31.8	21 56.8	22 7.3	24 29.5	20 44.6	27 59.7	5 19.4	20 21.4
20 M	17 51 6	28 13 1	19 54 52	26 57 50	22 26.0	8 3.6	23 10.4	22 48.2	24 39.5	20 42.9	27 57.2	5 21.6	20 22.8
21 Tu	17 55 2	29 10 16	3♎58 28	10♎56 45	22 25.9	9 38.5	24 24.1	23 29.1	24 49.4	20 41.0	27 54.8	5 23.9	20 24.2
22 W	17 58 59	0♋ 7 30	17 52 38	24 46 6	22 25.1	11 16.4	25 37.7	24 9.9	24 59.2	20 39.0	27 52.3	5 26.1	20 25.6
23 Th	18 2 55	1 4 43	1♏37 10	8♏25 46	22 22.5	12 57.4	26 51.3	24 50.7	25 8.8	20 37.0	27 49.9	5 28.3	20 27.0
24 F	18 6 52	2 1 55	15 11 52	21 55 22	22 17.3	14 41.4	28 5.0	25 31.4	25 18.4	20 34.9	27 47.4	5 30.5	20 28.4
25 Sa	18 10 49	2 59 8	28 36 10	5♐14 8	22 9.3	16 28.3	29 18.6	26 12.1	25 27.8	20 32.7	27 45.0	5 32.8	20 29.7
26 Su	18 14 45	3 56 19	11♐49 8	18 21 1	21 59.0	18 18.0	0♋32.3	26 52.7	25 37.1	20 30.4	27 42.6	5 35.0	20 31.1
27 M	18 18 42	4 53 31	24 49 39	1♑14 55	21 47.1	20 10.5	1 46.0	27 33.3	25 46.2	20 28.0	27 40.1	5 37.2	20 32.5
28 Tu	18 22 38	5 50 42	7♑36 44	13 55 2	21 34.8	22 5.6	2 59.6	28 13.9	25 55.3	20 25.6	27 37.7	5 39.5	20 33.9
29 W	18 26 35	6 47 53	20 9 51	26 21 14	21 23.2	24 3.2	4 13.3	28 54.4	26 4.2	20 23.0	27 35.3	5 41.7	20 35.2
30 Th	18 30 31	7 45 4	2♒29 19	8♒34 17	21 13.2	26 3.1	5 27.0	29 34.8	26 13.0	20 20.4	27 32.9	5 43.9	20 36.6

Astro Data	Planet Ingress	Last Aspect	☽ Ingress	Last Aspect	☽ Ingress	☽ Phases & Eclipses	Astro Data
Dy Hr Mn	Dy Hr Mn	Dy Hr Mn	Dy Hr Mn	Dy Hr Mn	Dy Hr Mn	Dy Hr Mn	1 MAY 1904
☿ R 2 9:34	♀ ♉ 7 14:52	1 4:12 ☿ ☍	♐ 1 10:36	1 18:22 ♃ □	♒ 2 11:13	7 11:50 ☽ 16♒28	Julian Day # 1582
☽0N 11 5:46	♂ ♊ 18 3:35	3 16:13 ♅ ☌	♑ 3 16:58	4 20:20 ♅ ⚹	♓ 4 23:15	15 10:58 ● 24♉10	Delta T 3.0 sec
☽0S 24 13:55	☉ ♊ 21 12:29	5 22:47 ♀ □	♒ 6 2:50	7 8:57 ♅ □	♈ 7 12:02	22 10:18 ☽ 0♍52	SVP 06♓35'47"
♃⚹♇ 24 22:37		8 14:13 ♅ ⚹	♓ 8 15:17	9 19:43 ♅ △	♉ 9 22:50	29 8:55 ○ 7♐32	Obliquity 23°26'57"
☿ D 26 5:57	♀ ♊ 1 2:28	11 2:40 ♅ □	♈ 11 3:51	12 1:24 ☿ ☌	♊ 12 6:06		⚷ Chiron 0♒06.1
♃⚹♄ 31 0:31	☿ ♊ 14 6:23	13 12:56 ♅ △	♉ 13 14:12	14 7:05 ♅ ☍	♋ 14 10:10	6 5:53 ☽ 15♓04	☽ Mean ☊ 25♍26.2
♄ R 31 23:27	☉ ♋ 21 20:51	15 18:28 ♂ ☌	♊ 15 21:30	16 2:27 ♃ □	♌ 16 12:26	13 21:10 ● 22♊23	
	♀ ♋ 25 13:29	18 0:58 ♅ ☍	♋ 18 2:21	18 11:06 ♅ △	♍ 18 14:26	20 15:10 ☽ 28♍49	1 JUNE 1904
☽0N 7 15:12	♂ ♋ 30 14:56	20 3:35 ☉ ⚹	♌ 20 5:50	20 15:10 ☉ □	♎ 20 17:11	27 20:23 ○ 5♑42	Julian Day # 1613
☽0S 20 20:29		22 7:14 ♅ △	♍ 22 8:49	22 17:23 ♅ ⚹	♏ 22 21:09		Delta T 3.1 sec
♄⚻♆ 24 23:37		24 10:05 ♅ □	♎ 24 11:48	24 9:34 ♄ □	♐ 25 2:31		SVP 06♓35'42"
♄△♇ 25 19:20		26 13:15 ♅ ⚹	♏ 26 15:08	27 5:22 ♂ ☍	♑ 27 9:39		Obliquity 23°26'56"
		28 11:39 ♀ ☍	♐ 28 19:29	29 11:35 ♃ □	♒ 29 19:07		⚷ Chiron 29♑43.9R
		30 23:34 ♅ ☌	♑ 31 1:53				☽ Mean ☊ 23♍47.7

JULY 1904 LONGITUDE

Day	Sid.Time	☉	0 hr ☽	Noon ☽	True ☊	☿	♀	♂	♃	♄	♅	♆	♇
1 F	18 34 28	8♋42 14	14♒36 24	20♒35 59	21♍ 5.6	28♊ 5.2	6♋40.7	0♋15.3	26♈21.7	20♒17.7	27♐30.5	5♋46.2	20♊37.9
2 Sa	18 38 24	9 39 25	26 33 25	2♓29 9	21R 0.6	0♋ 9.2	7 54.4	0 55.7	26 30.2	20R15.0	27R28.2	5 48.4	20 39.3
3 Su	18 42 21	10 36 36	8♓23 41	14 17 33	20 58.0	2 14.9	9 8.1	1 36.0	26 38.6	20 12.1	27 25.8	5 50.6	20 40.6
4 M	18 46 18	11 33 47	20 11 20	26 5 41	20D57.2	4 22.0	10 21.9	2 16.3	26 46.9	20 9.2	27 23.4	5 52.8	20 41.9
5 Tu	18 50 14	12 30 58	2♈ 1 14	7♈58 40	20R57.5	6 30.3	11 35.6	2 56.6	26 55.0	20 6.2	27 21.1	5 55.1	20 43.3
6 W	18 54 11	13 28 10	13 58 39	20 1 51	20 57.8	8 39.4	12 49.4	3 36.8	27 3.0	20 3.1	27 18.8	5 57.3	20 44.6
7 Th	18 58 7	14 25 22	26 8 56	2♉20 32	20 57.1	10 49.0	14 3.1	4 17.0	27 10.9	19 59.9	27 16.5	5 59.5	20 45.9
8 F	19 2 4	15 22 34	8♉37 15	14 59 34	20 54.7	12 59.0	15 16.9	4 57.1	27 18.6	19 56.7	27 14.2	6 1.7	20 47.2
9 Sa	19 6 0	16 19 47	21 27 56	28 2 42	20 50.1	15 8.8	16 30.7	5 37.3	27 26.1	19 53.4	27 11.9	6 3.9	20 48.5
10 Su	19 9 57	17 17 0	4♊44 2	11♊32 1	20 43.2	17 18.4	17 44.5	6 17.3	27 33.6	19 50.1	27 9.7	6 6.1	20 49.8
11 M	19 13 53	18 14 14	18 26 33	25 27 21	20 34.7	19 27.5	18 58.3	6 57.4	27 40.8	19 46.7	27 7.4	6 8.3	20 51.0
12 Tu	19 17 50	19 11 28	2♋33 59	9♋45 51	20 25.2	21 35.8	20 12.1	7 37.4	27 48.0	19 43.2	27 5.2	6 10.5	20 52.3
13 W	19 21 47	20 8 43	17 2 12	24 22 8	20 15.9	23 43.1	21 26.0	8 17.3	27 54.9	19 39.6	27 3.0	6 12.7	20 53.6
14 Th	19 25 43	21 5 57	1♌44 42	9♌ 8 53	20 7.8	25 49.3	22 39.8	8 57.2	28 1.8	19 36.0	27 0.8	6 14.9	20 54.8
15 F	19 29 40	22 3 12	16 33 42	23 58 8	20 1.8	27 54.3	23 53.7	9 37.1	28 8.4	19 32.4	26 58.7	6 17.1	20 56.1
16 Sa	19 33 36	23 0 28	1♍21 19	8♍42 25	19 58.3	29 57.8	25 7.5	10 17.0	28 14.9	19 28.6	26 56.6	6 19.2	20 57.3
17 Su	19 37 33	23 57 43	16 0 48	23 15 53	19D56.9	1♌59.8	26 21.4	10 56.7	28 21.3	19 24.9	26 54.5	6 21.4	20 58.5
18 M	19 41 29	24 54 58	0♎27 17	7♎34 43	19 57.2	4 0.2	27 35.3	11 36.5	28 27.5	19 21.0	26 52.4	6 23.5	20 59.7
19 Tu	19 45 26	25 52 14	14 37 59	21 37 2	19R58.0	5 59.0	28 49.1	12 16.2	28 33.5	19 17.1	26 50.4	6 25.7	21 0.9
20 W	19 49 22	26 49 30	28 31 52	5♏22 32	19 58.4	7 56.2	0♌ 3.0	12 55.9	28 39.4	19 13.2	26 48.3	6 27.8	21 2.1
21 Th	19 53 19	27 46 46	12♏ 9 8	18 51 49	19 57.4	9 51.6	1 16.9	13 35.5	28 45.1	19 9.2	26 46.4	6 29.9	21 3.2
22 F	19 57 16	28 44 2	25 30 42	2♐ 5 56	19 54.4	11 45.3	2 30.8	14 15.1	28 50.6	19 5.2	26 44.4	6 32.0	21 4.4
23 Sa	20 1 12	29 41 19	8♐37 40	15 6 1	19 49.4	13 37.2	3 44.7	14 54.7	28 56.0	19 1.1	26 42.5	6 34.1	21 5.5
24 Su	20 5 9	0♌38 36	21 31 6	27 53 2	19 42.5	15 27.4	4 58.7	15 34.2	29 1.2	18 57.0	26 40.6	6 36.2	21 6.7
25 M	20 9 5	1 35 54	4♑11 53	10♑27 46	19 34.4	17 15.9	6 12.6	16 13.7	29 6.2	18 52.9	26 38.7	6 38.2	21 7.8
26 Tu	20 13 2	2 33 12	16 40 47	22 51 0	19 25.9	19 2.6	7 26.5	16 53.1	29 11.1	18 48.7	26 36.9	6 40.3	21 8.9
27 W	20 16 58	3 30 31	28 58 32	5♒ 3 33	19 18.0	20 47.6	8 40.5	17 32.5	29 15.8	18 44.5	26 35.1	6 42.4	21 10.0
28 Th	20 20 55	4 27 50	11♒ 6 10	17 6 35	19 11.2	22 30.9	9 54.4	18 11.9	29 20.3	18 40.2	26 33.3	6 44.4	21 11.1
29 F	20 24 51	5 25 10	23 5 2	29 1 46	19 6.2	24 12.4	11 8.4	18 51.2	29 24.6	18 35.9	26 31.6	6 46.4	21 12.1
30 Sa	20 28 48	6 22 31	4♓57 5	10♓51 21	19 3.2	25 52.3	12 22.3	19 30.5	29 28.8	18 31.6	26 29.9	6 48.4	21 13.2
31 Su	20 32 45	7 19 53	16 44 55	22 38 15	19D 2.0	27 30.4	13 36.3	20 9.7	29 32.8	18 27.3	26 28.3	6 50.4	21 14.2

AUGUST 1904 LONGITUDE

Day	Sid.Time	☉	0 hr ☽	Noon ☽	True ☊	☿	♀	♂	♃	♄	♅	♆	♇
1 M	20 36 41	8♌17 16	28♓31 49	4♈26 6	19♍ 2.4	29♌ 6.8	14♌50.3	20♋49.0	29♈36.6	18♒22.9	26♐26.6	6♋52.4	21♊15.3
2 Tu	20 40 38	9 14 41	10♈21 40	16 19 6	19 3.8	0♍41.5	16 4.3	21 28.2	29 40.2	18R18.5	26R25.0	6 54.3	21 16.3
3 W	20 44 34	10 12 6	22 18 59	28 21 55	19 5.3	2 14.6	17 18.2	22 7.3	29 43.6	18 14.1	26 23.5	6 56.3	21 17.3
4 Th	20 48 31	11 9 32	4♉28 33	10♉39 28	19R 6.5	3 45.9	18 32.3	22 46.4	29 46.9	18 9.7	26 22.0	6 58.2	21 18.2
5 F	20 52 27	12 7 0	16 55 18	23 16 34	19 6.6	5 15.5	19 46.3	23 25.5	29 50.0	18 5.2	26 20.5	7 0.1	21 19.2
6 Sa	20 56 24	13 4 29	29 43 49	6♊17 27	19 5.3	6 43.4	21 0.3	24 4.6	29 52.9	18 0.8	26 19.1	7 2.0	21 20.1
7 Su	21 0 20	14 2 0	12♊57 49	19 45 8	19 2.5	8 9.5	22 14.3	24 43.6	29 55.5	17 56.3	26 17.7	7 3.9	21 21.1
8 M	21 4 17	14 59 31	26 39 28	3♋40 45	18 58.6	9 33.9	23 28.4	25 22.6	29 58.0	17 51.8	26 16.4	7 5.7	21 22.0
9 Tu	21 8 14	15 57 4	10♋48 42	18 2 53	18 53.9	10 56.5	24 42.5	26 1.6	0♉ 0.4	17 47.3	26 15.1	7 7.6	21 22.9
10 W	21 12 10	16 54 39	25 22 41	2♌47 16	18 49.2	12 17.3	25 56.5	26 40.5	0 2.5	17 42.8	26 13.8	7 9.4	21 23.8
11 Th	21 16 7	17 52 15	10♌15 43	17 46 56	18 45.1	13 36.2	27 10.6	27 19.4	0 4.4	17 38.3	26 12.6	7 11.2	21 24.6
12 F	21 20 3	18 49 51	25 19 48	2♍53 9	18 42.2	14 53.1	28 24.7	27 58.2	0 6.1	17 33.8	26 11.4	7 13.0	21 25.5
13 Sa	21 24 0	19 47 29	10♍25 48	17 56 41	18D40.7	16 8.2	29 38.8	28 37.0	0 7.6	17 29.4	26 10.3	7 14.7	21 26.3
14 Su	21 27 56	20 45 8	25 24 47	2♎49 14	18 40.6	17 21.1	0♍52.8	29 15.8	0 9.0	17 24.9	26 9.2	7 16.5	21 27.1
15 M	21 31 53	21 42 48	10♎ 9 20	17 24 30	18 41.6	18 32.0	2 6.9	29 54.6	0 10.1	17 20.4	26 8.1	7 18.2	21 27.9
16 Tu	21 35 49	22 40 29	24 34 20	1♏38 35	18 43.0	19 40.7	3 21.0	0♌33.3	0 11.0	17 15.9	26 7.1	7 19.9	21 28.7
17 W	21 39 46	23 38 11	8♏37 7	15 29 55	18 44.2	20 47.1	4 35.1	1 11.9	0 11.8	17 11.5	26 6.2	7 21.5	21 29.4
18 Th	21 43 43	24 35 55	22 17 6	28 58 49	18R44.9	21 51.2	5 49.2	1 50.6	0 12.3	17 7.0	26 5.3	7 23.2	21 30.2
19 F	21 47 39	25 33 39	5♐35 20	12♐ 6 53	18 44.5	22 52.7	7 3.3	2 29.2	0 12.7	17 2.6	26 4.4	7 24.8	21 30.9
20 Sa	21 51 36	26 31 24	18 33 49	24 56 26	18 43.2	23 51.7	8 17.4	3 7.8	0R12.8	16 58.2	26 3.6	7 26.4	21 31.6
21 Su	21 55 32	27 29 11	1♑15 4	7♑30 3	18 40.9	24 47.9	9 31.5	3 46.3	0 12.8	16 53.8	26 2.8	7 28.0	21 32.3
22 M	21 59 29	28 26 59	13 41 43	19 50 22	18 38.0	25 41.2	10 45.6	4 24.8	0 12.5	16 49.5	26 2.1	7 29.6	21 32.9
23 Tu	22 3 25	29 24 48	25 56 18	1♒59 49	18 35.0	26 31.4	11 59.7	5 3.3	0 12.1	16 45.1	26 1.4	7 31.1	21 33.6
24 W	22 7 22	0♍22 38	8♒ 1 10	14 0 38	18 32.1	27 18.4	13 13.8	5 41.7	0 11.4	16 40.8	26 0.8	7 32.6	21 34.2
25 Th	22 11 18	1 20 30	19 58 29	25 54 58	18 29.8	28 2.0	14 27.9	6 20.1	0 10.5	16 36.5	26 0.3	7 34.1	21 34.8
26 F	22 15 15	2 18 23	1♓50 20	7♓44 52	18 28.3	28 42.0	15 42.0	6 58.5	0 9.5	16 32.3	25 59.7	7 35.6	21 35.4
27 Sa	22 19 12	3 16 18	13 38 49	19 32 29	18D27.6	29 18.0	16 56.1	7 36.8	0 8.3	16 28.1	25 59.3	7 37.0	21 35.9
28 Su	22 23 8	4 14 14	25 26 10	1♈20 11	18 27.6	29 50.0	18 10.2	8 15.1	0 6.8	16 23.9	25 58.8	7 38.4	21 36.5
29 M	22 27 5	5 12 12	7♈14 54	13 10 41	18 28.3	0♎17.6	19 24.3	8 53.4	0 5.2	16 19.8	25 58.4	7 39.8	21 37.0
30 Tu	22 31 1	6 10 11	19 7 55	25 7 3	18 29.3	0 40.5	20 38.4	9 31.6	0 3.3	16 15.7	25 58.1	7 41.2	21 37.5
31 W	22 34 58	7 8 13	1♉ 8 30	7♉12 46	18 30.5	0 58.5	21 52.6	10 9.8	0 1.3	16 11.6	25 57.8	7 42.5	21 38.0

Astro Data Dy Hr Mn	Planet Ingress Dy Hr Mn	Last Aspect Dy Hr Mn	☽ Ingress Dy Hr Mn	Last Aspect Dy Hr Mn	☽ Ingress Dy Hr Mn	☽ Phases & Eclipses Dy Hr Mn	Astro Data
☽0N 5 0:36	☿ ♋ 1 22:14	2 1:50 ♅ ⚹	♓ 2 6:58	31 19:46 ♅ □	♈ 1 2:59	5 22:54 ☽ 13♈26	1 JULY 1904
♃△♅ 7 13:25	☿ ♌ 16 0:26	4 14:35 ♅ □	♈ 4 19:55	3 14:45 ♃ ☌	♉ 3 15:13	13 5:27 ● 20♋22	Julian Day # 1643
☽0S 18 3:36	♀ ♌ 19 23:01	7 2:11 ♅ △	♉ 7 7:29	5 12:56 ♂ ⚹	♊ 6 0:30	19 20:48 ☽ 26♎42	Delta T 3.2 sec
	☉ ♌ 23 7:50	8 21:07 ♄ □	♊ 9 15:32	8 5:42 ♃ ⚹	♋ 8 5:44	27 9:42 ○ 3♒54	SVP 06♓35'38"
☽0N 1 8:50		11 15:54 ♃ ⚹	♋ 11 19:41	10 2:12 ♂ ☌	♌ 10 7:30		Obliquity 23°26'56"
☽0S 14 12:18	☿ ♍ 1 13:25	13 17:55 ♃ □	♌ 13 21:10	12 5:20 ♀ ☌	♍ 12 7:25	4 14:03 ☽ 11♉43	⚷ Chiron 28♑26.3R
♃ R 20 5:28	♃ ♉ 8 20:11	15 18:55 ♃ △	♍ 15 21:48	14 6:31 ♂ ⚹	♎ 14 7:25	11 12:58 ● 18♌23	☽ Mean ☊ 22♍12.4
☿0S 21 3:05	♀ ♍ 13 6:53	17 18:45 ♀ ⚹	♎ 17 23:14	16 2:37 ♅ ⚹	♏ 16 9:12	18 4:27 ☽ 24♏47	
☽0N 28 15:33	♂ ♌ 15 3:22	20 0:13 ♃ ☍	♏ 20 2:34	18 4:27 ☉ □	♐ 18 13:50	26 1:02 ○ 2♓21	1 AUGUST 1904
	☉ ♍ 23 14:36	22 6:19 ☉ △	♐ 22 8:10	20 16:14 ☉ △	♑ 20 21:37		Julian Day # 1674
	☿ ♎ 28 8:17	24 14:15 ♃ △	♑ 24 16:01	23 1:14 ☿ △	♒ 23 8:02		Delta T 3.4 sec
	♃ ♈ 31 13:54	27 0:34 ♃ □	♒ 27 2:01	25 12:10 ♅ ⚹	♓ 25 20:16		SVP 06♓35'33"
		29 12:51 ♃ ⚹	♓ 29 13:58	28 1:06 ♅ □	♈ 28 9:17		Obliquity 23°26'57"
				30 13:42 ♅ △	♉ 30 21:44		⚷ Chiron 26♑40.3R
							☽ Mean ☊ 20♍33.9

LONGITUDE SEPTEMBER 1904

Day	Sid.Time	☉	0 hr ☽	Noon ☽	True ☊	☿	♀	♂	♃	♄	♅	♆	♇
1 Th	22 38 54	8♍ 6 16	13♉20 18	19♉31 38	18♍31.4	1♎11.4	23♍ 6.7	10♌48.0	29♈59.0	16♒ 7.6	25♐57.6	7♋43.8	21♊38.5
2 F	22 42 51	9 4 22	25 47 15	2♊ 7 39	18 32.1	1R 18.7	24 20.8	11 26.2	29R 56.6	16R 3.7	25R 57.4	7 45.1	21 38.9
3 Sa	22 46 47	10 2 29	8♊33 17	15 4 36	18R 32.4	1 20.4	25 34.9	12 4.3	29 54.0	15 59.8	25 57.3	7 46.3	21 39.3
4 Su	22 50 44	11 0 38	21 41 58	28 25 42	18 32.3	1 16.0	26 49.0	12 42.4	29 51.2	15 55.9	25D 57.2	7 47.6	21 39.7
5 M	22 54 40	11 58 50	5♋16 2	12♋13 2	18 31.8	1 5.4	28 3.1	13 20.4	29 48.1	15 52.1	25 57.2	7 48.8	21 40.1
6 Tu	22 58 37	12 57 3	19 16 41	26 26 47	18 31.3	0 48.4	29 17.3	13 58.5	29 44.9	15 48.3	25 57.2	7 49.9	21 40.5
7 W	23 2 34	13 55 19	3♌42 59	11♌ 4 45	18 30.7	0 25.0	0♎31.4	14 36.5	29 41.5	15 44.6	25 57.3	7 51.1	21 40.8
8 Th	23 6 30	14 53 36	18 31 23	26 2 1	18 30.3	29♍55.1	1 45.5	15 14.4	29 37.9	15 41.0	25 57.4	7 52.2	21 41.1
9 F	23 10 27	15 51 55	3♍35 38	11♍11 8	18 30.1	29 18.9	2 59.6	15 52.4	29 34.2	15 37.4	25 57.6	7 53.3	21 41.4
10 Sa	23 14 23	16 50 16	18 47 20	26 23 0	18D 30.0	28 36.6	4 13.7	16 30.3	29 30.2	15 33.9	25 57.9	7 54.3	21 41.7
11 Su	23 18 20	17 48 39	3♎56 57	11♎28 4	18R 30.0	27 48.7	5 27.9	17 8.1	29 26.1	15 30.5	25 58.1	7 55.3	21 41.9
12 M	23 22 16	18 47 4	18 55 18	26 17 47	18 30.0	26 55.8	6 42.0	17 46.0	29 21.7	15 27.1	25 58.5	7 56.3	21 42.2
13 Tu	23 26 13	19 45 30	3♏34 47	10♏45 45	18 30.0	25 58.7	7 56.1	18 23.8	29 17.2	15 23.8	25 58.9	7 57.3	21 42.4
14 W	23 30 9	20 43 58	17 50 17	24 48 12	18 29.8	24 58.4	9 10.2	19 1.5	29 12.6	15 20.5	25 59.3	7 58.2	21 42.5
15 Th	23 34 6	21 42 28	1♐39 24	8♐24 0	18 29.5	23 56.2	10 24.3	19 39.3	29 7.7	15 17.4	25 59.8	7 59.1	21 42.7
16 F	23 38 3	22 40 59	15 2 10	21 34 13	18D 29.4	22 53.3	11 38.4	20 17.0	29 2.7	15 14.3	26 0.3	7 60.0	21 42.8
17 Sa	23 41 59	23 39 32	28 0 31	4♑21 30	18 29.3	21 51.4	12 52.5	20 54.6	28 57.5	15 11.2	26 0.9	8 0.8	21 43.0
18 Su	23 45 56	24 38 7	10♑37 37	16 49 23	18 29.6	20 51.8	14 6.6	21 32.3	28 52.2	15 8.3	26 1.6	8 1.6	21 43.1
19 M	23 49 52	25 36 43	22 57 17	29 1 50	18 30.1	19 56.1	15 20.7	22 9.9	28 46.7	15 5.4	26 2.3	8 2.4	21 43.1
20 Tu	23 53 49	26 35 21	5♒ 3 31	11♒ 2 50	18 30.9	19 5.8	16 34.7	22 47.4	28 41.0	15 2.6	26 3.0	8 3.1	21 43.2
21 W	23 57 45	27 34 1	17 0 13	22 56 7	18 31.8	18 22.1	17 48.8	23 25.0	28 35.2	14 59.9	26 3.8	8 3.8	21R 43.2
22 Th	0 1 42	28 32 43	28 50 56	4♓45 3	18 32.6	17 46.2	19 2.9	24 2.5	28 29.2	14 57.3	26 4.6	8 4.5	21 43.2
23 F	0 5 38	29 31 26	10♓38 49	16 32 35	18R 33.2	17 19.0	20 16.9	24 39.9	28 23.1	14 54.7	26 5.5	8 5.1	21 43.2
24 Sa	0 9 35	0♎30 11	22 26 39	28 21 18	18 33.3	17 1.3	21 30.9	25 17.4	28 16.9	14 52.3	26 6.5	8 5.8	21 43.2
25 Su	0 13 32	1 28 58	4♈16 50	10♈13 28	18 32.7	16D 53.4	22 45.0	25 54.8	28 10.5	14 49.9	26 7.5	8 6.3	21 43.1
26 M	0 17 28	2 27 47	16 11 30	22 11 9	18 31.5	16 55.6	23 59.0	26 32.1	28 4.0	14 47.6	26 8.5	8 6.9	21 43.0
27 Tu	0 21 25	3 26 39	28 12 41	4♉16 21	18 29.6	17 7.9	25 13.0	27 9.5	27 57.4	14 45.4	26 9.6	8 7.4	21 42.9
28 W	0 25 21	4 25 32	10♉22 25	16 31 8	18 27.3	17 30.2	26 27.0	27 46.8	27 50.6	14 43.3	26 10.8	8 7.9	21 42.8
29 Th	0 29 18	5 24 28	22 42 49	28 57 45	18 24.8	18 2.0	27 41.0	28 24.1	27 43.7	14 41.2	26 12.0	8 8.3	21 42.7
30 F	0 33 14	6 23 25	5♊16 13	11♊38 34	18 22.4	18 43.0	28 55.0	29 1.3	27 36.7	14 39.3	26 13.2	8 8.7	21 42.5

LONGITUDE OCTOBER 1904

Day	Sid.Time	☉	0 hr ☽	Noon ☽	True ☊	☿	♀	♂	♃	♄	♅	♆	♇
1 Sa	0 37 11	7♎22 26	18♊ 5 5	24♊36 5	18♍20.6	19♍32.5	0♏ 9.0	29♌38.5	27♈29.6	14♒37.4	26♐14.5	8♋ 9.1	21♊42.3
2 Su	0 41 7	8 21 28	1♋11 53	7♋52 44	18D 19.6	20 29.8	1 23.0	0♍15.7	27R 22.4	14R 35.7	26 15.9	8 9.5	21R 42.1
3 M	0 45 4	9 20 33	14 38 54	21 30 31	18 19.5	21 34.4	2 37.0	0 52.9	27 15.1	14 34.0	26 17.3	8 9.8	21 41.9
4 Tu	0 49 1	10 19 40	28 27 43	5♌30 30	18 20.3	22 45.4	3 51.0	1 30.0	27 7.7	14 32.5	26 18.7	8 10.1	21 41.6
5 W	0 52 57	11 18 50	12♌38 47	19 52 20	18 21.6	24 2.2	5 5.0	2 7.1	27 0.2	14 31.0	26 20.2	8 10.3	21 41.4
6 Th	0 56 54	12 18 1	27 10 48	4♍33 38	18 23.0	25 23.9	6 19.0	2 44.1	26 52.6	14 29.6	26 21.7	8 10.5	21 41.1
7 F	1 0 50	13 17 15	12♍ 0 12	19 29 41	18R 23.9	26 50.0	7 32.9	3 21.1	26 44.9	14 28.3	26 23.3	8 10.7	21 40.7
8 Sa	1 4 47	14 16 32	27 1 7	4♎33 28	18 23.8	28 19.8	8 46.9	3 58.1	26 37.2	14 27.1	26 24.9	8 10.8	21 40.4
9 Su	1 8 43	15 15 50	12♎ 5 36	19 36 24	18 22.4	29 52.8	10 0.9	4 35.1	26 29.4	14 26.0	26 26.6	8 10.9	21 40.0
10 M	1 12 40	16 15 10	27 4 42	4♏29 27	18 19.6	1♎28.3	11 14.8	5 12.0	26 21.5	14 25.1	26 28.3	8 11.0	21 39.7
11 Tu	1 16 36	17 14 33	11♏49 40	19 4 31	18 15.7	3 5.8	12 28.7	5 48.9	26 13.6	14 24.2	26 30.1	8R 11.1	21 39.3
12 W	1 20 33	18 13 57	26 13 21	3♐15 38	18 11.2	4 45.1	13 42.7	6 25.7	26 5.6	14 23.4	26 31.9	8 11.1	21 38.8
13 Th	1 24 29	19 13 24	10♐11 6	16 59 35	18 6.8	6 25.7	14 56.6	7 2.5	25 57.6	14 22.7	26 33.8	8 11.0	21 38.4
14 F	1 28 26	20 12 52	23 41 8	0♑15 54	18 3.1	8 7.2	16 10.5	7 39.3	25 49.6	14 22.1	26 35.7	8 11.0	21 37.9
15 Sa	1 32 23	21 12 22	6♑44 13	13 6 27	18 0.7	9 49.5	17 24.4	8 16.0	25 41.5	14 21.6	26 37.7	8 10.9	21 37.5
16 Su	1 36 19	22 11 53	19 23 8	25 34 47	17D 59.6	11 32.2	18 38.3	8 52.7	25 33.4	14 21.2	26 39.7	8 10.8	21 37.0
17 M	1 40 16	23 11 27	1♒42 1	7♒45 26	17 59.9	13 15.3	19 52.2	9 29.3	25 25.3	14 21.0	26 41.7	8 10.6	21 36.4
18 Tu	1 44 12	24 11 2	13 45 39	19 43 20	18 1.3	14 58.4	21 6.1	10 5.9	25 17.2	14 20.8	26 43.8	8 10.4	21 35.9
19 W	1 48 9	25 10 39	25 39 4	1♓33 27	18 3.0	16 41.5	22 19.9	10 42.5	25 9.0	14D 20.7	26 45.9	8 10.2	21 35.3
20 Th	1 52 5	26 10 17	7♓27 4	13 20 26	18R 4.5	18 24.4	23 33.8	11 19.0	25 0.9	14 20.7	26 48.1	8 9.9	21 34.7
21 F	1 56 2	27 9 58	19 14 3	25 8 23	18 5.1	20 7.1	24 47.6	11 55.5	24 52.8	14 20.8	26 50.3	8 9.6	21 34.1
22 Sa	1 59 58	28 9 40	1♈ 3 50	7♈ 0 46	18 4.0	21 49.6	26 1.4	12 32.0	24 44.7	14 21.1	26 52.6	8 9.3	21 33.5
23 Su	2 3 55	29 9 24	12 59 31	19 0 20	18 1.1	23 31.6	27 15.2	13 8.4	24 36.6	14 21.4	26 54.8	8 8.9	21 32.9
24 M	2 7 52	0♏ 9 10	25 3 28	1♉ 9 5	17 56.2	25 13.3	28 29.0	13 44.8	24 28.6	14 21.8	26 57.2	8 8.5	21 32.2
25 Tu	2 11 48	1 8 58	7♉17 21	13 28 22	17 49.5	26 54.5	29 42.7	14 21.1	24 20.5	14 22.4	26 59.5	8 8.1	21 31.6
26 W	2 15 45	2 8 48	19 42 14	25 59 2	17 41.5	28 35.3	0♐56.5	14 57.4	24 12.6	14 23.0	27 2.0	8 7.6	21 30.9
27 Th	2 19 41	3 8 40	2♊18 47	8♊41 34	17 33.1	0♏15.6	2 10.2	15 33.7	24 4.6	14 23.7	27 4.4	8 7.2	21 30.2
28 F	2 23 38	4 8 34	15 7 25	21 36 23	17 25.0	1 55.4	3 24.0	16 9.9	23 56.8	14 24.6	27 6.9	8 6.6	21 29.4
29 Sa	2 27 34	5 8 31	28 8 32	4♋43 58	17 18.2	3 34.8	4 37.7	16 46.1	23 48.9	14 25.5	27 9.4	8 6.1	21 28.7
30 Su	2 31 31	6 8 29	11♋22 45	18 5 0	17 13.3	5 13.6	5 51.4	17 22.2	23 41.2	14 26.5	27 12.0	8 5.5	21 27.9
31 M	2 35 27	7 8 30	24 50 49	1♌40 19	17D 10.5	6 52.0	7 5.1	17 58.3	23 33.5	14 27.7	27 14.6	8 4.9	21 27.2

Astro Data	Dy Hr Mn
☿ R	2 18:37
♅ D	4 23:11
♀0S	8 16:59
☽0S	10 22:38
☿0N	16 5:02
♇ R	21 20:45
☽0N	24 21:32
☿ D	25 6:46
☽0S	8 9:38
♃△♅	9 6:53
☿0S	11 20:38
♆ R	11 17:47
♄ D	19 6:57
☽0N	22 4:08

Planet Ingress	Dy Hr Mn
♀ ♎	6 13:50
☿ ♍	7 20:25
☉ ♎	23 11:40
♀ ♏	30 21:04
♂ ♍	1 13:52
☿ ♎	9 1:51
☉ ♏	23 20:19
♀ ♐	25 5:37
☿ ♏	26 20:16

Last Aspect Dy Hr Mn		☽ Ingress Dy Hr Mn
1 20:57	♀ △	♊ 2 7:59
4 14:28	♃ ⚹	♋ 4 14:46
6 17:24	♃ □	♌ 6 17:53
8 17:39	♃ △	♍ 8 18:18
10 14:46	☿ ☌	♎ 10 17:44
12 16:57	♃ ☍	♏ 12 18:05
14 11:27	☿ ⚹	♐ 14 21:05
17 1:46	♃ △	♑ 17 3:45
19 11:25	♃ □	♒ 19 13:55
21 23:16	♃ ⚹	♓ 22 2:20
24 7:27	♅ □	♈ 24 15:20
26 23:30	♃ ☌	♉ 27 3:33
29 11:30	♂ □	♊ 29 13:59

Last Aspect Dy Hr Mn		☽ Ingress Dy Hr Mn
1 17:07	♃ ⚹	♋ 1 21:50
3 21:44	♃ □	♌ 4 2:38
5 23:30	♃ △	♍ 6 4:36
8 2:19	☿ ☌	♎ 8 4:45
9 23:01	♅ ⚹	♏ 10 4:43
11 4:15	♄ □	♐ 12 6:25
14 5:18	♅ ☌	♑ 14 11:31
16 11:50	♃ □	♒ 16 20:39
19 2:16	♅ ⚹	♓ 19 8:50
21 15:30	♅ □	♈ 21 21:51
24 3:45	♅ △	♉ 24 9:44
25 14:24	♂ △	♊ 26 19:38
28 22:12	♅ ☍	♋ 29 3:24
30 21:45	♃ □	♌ 31 9:04

☽ Phases & Eclipses Dy Hr Mn	
3 2:58	☽ 10♊10
9 20:43	● 16♍42
9 20:44:16	☍ T 6'20"
16 15:13	☽ 23♐18
24 17:50	○ 1♈14
24 17:35	☍ A 0.544
2 13:52	☽ 8♋56
9 5:25	● 15♎29
16 5:54	☽ 22♑27
24 10:56	○ 0♉36
31 23:13	☽ 8♌07

Astro Data

1 SEPTEMBER 1904
Julian Day # 1705
Delta T 3.5 sec
SVP 06♓35'30"
Obliquity 23°26'57"
⚷ Chiron 25♑11.6R
☽ Mean ☊ 18♍55.4

1 OCTOBER 1904
Julian Day # 1735
Delta T 3.6 sec
SVP 06♓35'28"
Obliquity 23°26'57"
⚷ Chiron 24♑36.8R
☽ Mean ☊ 17♍20.0

NOVEMBER 1904 LONGITUDE

Day	Sid.Time	☉	0 hr ☽	Noon ☽	True ☊	☿	♀	♂	♃	♄	♅	♆	♇
1 Tu	2 39 24	8♏ 8 33	8♌33 35	15♌30 43	17♍ 9.7	8♏30.0	8♐18.8	18♍34.4	23♈25.9	14♒28.9	27♐17.2	8♋ 4.2	21♊26.4
2 W	2 43 21	9 8 37	22 31 42	29 36 33	17 10.3	10 7.4	9 32.5	19 10.4	23R18.3	14 30.3	27 19.9	8R 3.5	21R25.6
3 Th	2 47 17	10 8 45	6♍45 7	13♍57 12	17R11.3	11 44.5	10 46.1	19 46.4	23 10.9	14 31.7	27 22.6	8 2.8	21 24.7
4 F	2 51 14	11 8 54	21 12 29	28 30 32	17 11.6	13 21.0	11 59.8	20 22.3	23 3.5	14 33.3	27 25.4	8 2.1	21 23.9
5 Sa	2 55 10	12 9 5	5♎50 46	13♎12 30	17 10.1	14 57.2	13 13.4	20 58.2	22 56.2	14 34.9	27 28.2	8 1.3	21 23.0
6 Su	2 59 7	13 9 18	20 34 57	27 57 11	17 6.2	16 33.0	14 27.0	21 34.1	22 49.1	14 36.7	27 31.0	8 0.5	21 22.1
7 M	3 3 3	14 9 33	5♏18 17	12♏37 16	16 59.8	18 8.4	15 40.6	22 9.9	22 42.0	14 38.5	27 33.8	7 59.7	21 21.3
8 Tu	3 7 0	15 9 50	19 53 11	27 5 8	16 51.2	19 43.4	16 54.2	22 45.6	22 35.1	14 40.4	27 36.7	7 58.8	21 20.4
9 W	3 10 56	16 10 9	4♐12 19	11♐14 4	16 41.3	21 18.1	18 7.8	23 21.3	22 28.3	14 42.5	27 39.6	7 57.9	21 19.4
10 Th	3 14 53	17 10 29	18 9 52	24 59 21	16 31.2	22 52.4	19 21.4	23 57.0	22 21.6	14 44.6	27 42.6	7 57.0	21 18.5
11 F	3 18 50	18 10 51	1♑42 20	8♑18 47	16 22.0	24 26.4	20 34.9	24 32.6	22 15.0	14 46.9	27 45.5	7 56.1	21 17.6
12 Sa	3 22 46	19 11 15	14 48 50	21 12 45	16 14.7	26 0.1	21 48.4	25 8.1	22 8.6	14 49.2	27 48.5	7 55.1	21 16.6
13 Su	3 26 43	20 11 40	27 30 53	3♒43 44	16 9.7	27 33.5	23 1.9	25 43.6	22 2.3	14 51.7	27 51.6	7 54.1	21 15.6
14 M	3 30 39	21 12 6	9♒51 52	15 55 52	16 7.1	29 6.6	24 15.4	26 19.1	21 56.2	14 54.2	27 54.6	7 53.0	21 14.7
15 Tu	3 34 36	22 12 34	21 56 24	27 54 9	16D 6.4	0♐39.5	25 28.9	26 54.5	21 50.2	14 56.8	27 57.7	7 52.0	21 13.7
16 W	3 38 32	23 13 2	3♓49 49	9♓44 5	16 6.7	2 12.1	26 42.3	27 29.8	21 44.4	14 59.6	28 0.8	7 50.9	21 12.7
17 Th	3 42 29	24 13 33	15 37 39	21 31 10	16R 7.1	3 44.4	27 55.7	28 5.1	21 38.7	15 2.4	28 4.0	7 49.8	21 11.6
18 F	3 46 25	25 14 4	27 25 17	3♈20 35	16 6.5	5 16.5	29 9.1	28 40.3	21 33.2	15 5.3	28 7.1	7 48.6	21 10.6
19 Sa	3 50 22	26 14 37	9♈17 37	15 16 54	16 3.9	6 48.4	0♑22.4	29 15.5	21 27.8	15 8.3	28 10.3	7 47.5	21 9.6
20 Su	3 54 19	27 15 11	21 18 50	27 23 50	15 58.7	8 20.0	1 35.7	29 50.6	21 22.6	15 11.4	28 13.5	7 46.3	21 8.5
21 M	3 58 15	28 15 46	3♉32 9	9♉44 3	15 50.6	9 51.4	2 49.0	0♎25.7	21 17.6	15 14.6	28 16.8	7 45.1	21 7.5
22 Tu	4 2 12	29 16 23	15 59 40	22 19 4	15 40.1	11 22.6	4 2.3	1 0.7	21 12.8	15 17.8	28 20.0	7 43.9	21 6.4
23 W	4 6 8	0♐17 1	28 42 15	5♊ 9 10	15 27.7	12 53.5	5 15.5	1 35.7	21 8.1	15 21.2	28 23.3	7 42.6	21 5.3
24 Th	4 10 5	1 17 40	11♊39 40	18 13 36	15 14.5	14 24.1	6 28.7	2 10.6	21 3.6	15 24.7	28 26.6	7 41.3	21 4.2
25 F	4 14 1	2 18 21	24 50 44	1♋30 51	15 1.7	15 54.5	7 41.9	2 45.4	20 59.3	15 28.2	28 30.0	7 40.0	21 3.2
26 Sa	4 17 58	3 19 4	8♋13 44	14 59 7	14 50.7	17 24.6	8 55.0	3 20.2	20 55.2	15 31.8	28 33.3	7 38.7	21 2.1
27 Su	4 21 54	4 19 48	21 46 49	28 36 39	14 42.1	18 54.4	10 8.1	3 55.0	20 51.2	15 35.6	28 36.7	7 37.4	21 0.9
28 M	4 25 51	5 20 33	5♌28 29	12♌22 11	14 36.6	20 23.8	11 21.1	4 29.7	20 47.5	15 39.4	28 40.1	7 36.0	20 59.8
29 Tu	4 29 48	6 21 20	19 17 42	26 15 0	14 33.8	21 52.8	12 34.2	5 4.3	20 43.9	15 43.3	28 43.5	7 34.6	20 58.7
30 W	4 33 44	7 22 8	3♍14 2	10♍14 47	14 32.9	23 21.4	13 47.2	5 38.8	20 40.6	15 47.2	28 46.9	7 33.2	20 57.6

DECEMBER 1904 LONGITUDE

Day	Sid.Time	☉	0 hr ☽	Noon ☽	True ☊	☿	♀	♂	♃	♄	♅	♆	♇
1 Th	4 37 41	8♐22 58	17♍17 13	24♍21 17	14♍32.9	24♐49.4	15♑ 0.1	6♎13.3	20♈37.4	15♒51.3	28♐50.3	7♋31.8	20♊56.4
2 F	4 41 37	9 23 50	1♎26 51	8♎33 45	14R32.3	26 16.8	16 13.1	6 47.7	20R34.4	15 55.4	28 53.8	7R30.3	20R55.3
3 Sa	4 45 34	10 24 42	15 41 44	22 50 27	14 29.8	27 43.6	17 25.9	7 22.1	20 31.7	15 59.6	28 57.3	7 28.9	20 54.2
4 Su	4 49 30	11 25 36	29 59 29	7♏ 8 18	14 24.4	29 9.5	18 38.8	7 56.4	20 29.1	16 3.9	29 0.8	7 27.4	20 53.0
5 M	4 53 27	12 26 32	14♏16 20	21 22 56	14 16.1	0♑34.5	19 51.6	8 30.6	20 26.7	16 8.3	29 4.3	7 25.9	20 51.9
6 Tu	4 57 23	13 27 28	28 27 25	5♐29 6	14 5.0	1 58.4	21 4.4	9 4.8	20 24.6	16 12.8	29 7.8	7 24.4	20 50.7
7 W	5 1 20	14 28 26	12♐27 21	19 21 32	13 52.2	3 21.0	22 17.1	9 38.8	20 22.6	16 17.3	29 11.3	7 22.9	20 49.5
8 Th	5 5 17	15 29 25	26 11 9	2♑55 47	13 39.0	4 42.1	23 29.8	10 12.8	20 20.9	16 21.9	29 14.8	7 21.3	20 48.4
9 F	5 9 13	16 30 24	9♑35 8	16 9 1	13 26.7	6 1.5	24 42.4	10 46.8	20 19.3	16 26.6	29 18.4	7 19.8	20 47.2
10 Sa	5 13 10	17 31 25	22 37 25	29 0 23	13 16.4	7 18.9	25 55.0	11 20.6	20 18.0	16 31.4	29 22.0	7 18.2	20 46.0
11 Su	5 17 6	18 32 26	5♒18 10	11♒31 3	13 8.8	8 33.8	27 7.6	11 54.4	20 16.9	16 36.2	29 25.5	7 16.6	20 44.9
12 M	5 21 3	19 33 28	17 39 27	23 43 52	13 4.1	9 46.1	28 20.0	12 28.1	20 16.0	16 41.2	29 29.1	7 15.0	20 43.7
13 Tu	5 24 59	20 34 30	29 44 51	5♓43 2	13 1.8	10 55.1	29 32.5	13 1.7	20 15.3	16 46.1	29 32.7	7 13.4	20 42.5
14 W	5 28 56	21 35 32	11♓39 3	17 33 37	13 1.3	12 0.4	0♒44.8	13 35.2	20 14.8	16 51.2	29 36.3	7 11.8	20 41.4
15 Th	5 32 52	22 36 35	23 27 24	29 21 8	13 1.3	13 1.5	1 57.1	14 8.7	20D14.5	16 56.3	29 39.9	7 10.2	20 40.2
16 F	5 36 49	23 37 39	5♈15 31	11♈11 14	13 0.8	13 57.6	3 9.3	14 42.0	20 14.4	17 1.5	29 43.5	7 8.5	20 39.0
17 Sa	5 40 46	24 38 43	17 8 57	23 9 17	12 58.7	14 48.1	4 21.5	15 15.3	20 14.6	17 6.8	29 47.1	7 6.9	20 37.9
18 Su	5 44 42	25 39 47	29 12 49	5♉20 4	12 54.2	15 32.2	5 33.6	15 48.5	20 14.9	17 12.1	29 50.7	7 5.2	20 36.7
19 M	5 48 39	26 40 52	11♉31 28	17 47 23	12 46.9	16 9.0	6 45.6	16 21.6	20 15.5	17 17.5	29 54.3	7 3.6	20 35.5
20 Tu	5 52 35	27 41 57	24 8 6	0♊33 45	12 37.1	16 37.7	7 57.6	16 54.6	20 16.3	17 23.0	29 58.0	7 1.9	20 34.4
21 W	5 56 32	28 43 2	7♊ 4 26	13 40 3	12 25.3	16 57.3	9 9.4	17 27.5	20 17.2	17 28.5	0♑ 1.6	7 0.2	20 33.2
22 Th	6 0 28	29 44 8	20 20 29	27 5 25	12 12.7	17R 7.0	10 21.2	18 0.3	20 18.4	17 34.1	0 5.2	6 58.5	20 32.0
23 F	6 4 25	0♑45 14	3♋54 33	10♋47 24	12 0.4	17 6.0	11 32.9	18 33.1	20 19.8	17 39.7	0 8.8	6 56.9	20 30.9
24 Sa	6 8 21	1 46 21	17 43 30	24 42 19	11 49.7	16 53.6	12 44.6	19 5.7	20 21.4	17 45.4	0 12.4	6 55.2	20 29.8
25 Su	6 12 18	2 47 28	1♌43 19	8♌45 58	11 41.4	16 29.5	13 56.1	19 38.3	20 23.2	17 51.2	0 16.1	6 53.5	20 28.6
26 M	6 16 15	3 48 35	15 49 48	22 54 21	11 36.1	15 53.6	15 7.5	20 10.7	20 25.2	17 57.0	0 19.7	6 51.8	20 27.5
27 Tu	6 20 11	4 49 43	29 59 14	7♍ 4 8	11D33.5	15 6.2	16 18.9	20 43.1	20 27.4	18 2.9	0 23.3	6 50.1	20 26.3
28 W	6 24 8	5 50 51	14♍ 8 48	21 13 2	11 33.1	14 8.3	17 30.2	21 15.4	20 29.8	18 8.8	0 26.9	6 48.4	20 25.2
29 Th	6 28 4	6 52 0	28 16 40	5♎19 36	11R33.5	13 1.3	18 41.3	21 47.5	20 32.4	18 14.8	0 30.5	6 46.7	20 24.1
30 F	6 32 1	7 53 9	12♎21 44	19 22 58	11 33.6	11 47.0	19 52.4	22 19.6	20 35.2	18 20.8	0 34.1	6 45.0	20 23.0
31 Sa	6 35 57	8 54 19	26 23 12	3♏22 19	11 32.2	10 27.8	21 3.4	22 51.5	20 38.2	18 26.9	0 37.7	6 43.3	20 21.9

Astro Data Dy Hr Mn	Planet Ingress Dy Hr Mn
☽0S 4 19:49	☿ ♐ 14 13:47
☽0N 18 12:20	♀ ♑ 18 16:40
♃✶♇ 23 19:22	♂ ♎ 20 6:24
♂0S 26 10:47	☉ ♐ 22 17:16
☽0S 2 4:04	☿ ♑ 4 14:14
☽0N 15 21:56	♀ ♒ 13 9:08
♃ D 15 19:58	♅ ♑ 20 13:35
☿ R 22 9:50	☉ ♑ 22 6:14
♃✶♇ 26 16:25	
☽0S 29 10:47	

Last Aspect Dy Hr Mn	☽ Ingress Dy Hr Mn	Last Aspect Dy Hr Mn	☽ Ingress Dy Hr Mn
2 8:11 ♅ △	♍ 2 12:40	1 19:40 ♅ □	♎ 1 21:33
4 10:15 ♅ □	♎ 4 14:27	3 22:27 ☿ ✶	♏ 4 0:01
6 11:19 ♅ ✶	♏ 6 15:20	5 10:18 ♀ ✶	♐ 6 2:38
8 4:59 ♂ ✶	♐ 8 16:54	8 5:27 ♅ ☌	♑ 8 6:46
10 16:54 ♅ ☌	♑ 10 20:56	10 6:49 ♀ ☌	♒ 10 13:53
13 0:06 ☿ ✶	♒ 13 4:47	12 23:36 ♅ ✶	♓ 13 0:30
15 12:10 ♅ ✶	♓ 15 16:14	15 12:42 ♅ □	♈ 15 13:19
18 3:55 ♀ □	♈ 18 5:14	18 1:15 ♅ △	♉ 18 1:33
20 13:41 ♅ △	♉ 20 17:06	19 11:08 ♄ □	♊ 20 10:57
21 22:40 ♄ □	♊ 23 2:25	22 0:21 ♇ ☌	♋ 22 17:08
25 6:37 ♅ ☍	♋ 25 9:17	24 4:33 ♃ □	♌ 24 21:04
26 22:23 ♃ □	♌ 27 14:26	26 7:50 ♇ ✶	♍ 27 0:01
29 16:19 ♅ △	♍ 29 18:27	28 10:38 ♇ □	♎ 29 2:56
		30 17:43 ♂ ☌	♏ 31 6:12

☽ Phases & Eclipses Dy Hr Mn	
7 15:37	● 14♏49
15 0:35	☽ 22♒14
23 3:12	○ 0♊25
30 7:38	☽ 7♍41
7 3:46	● 14♐38
14 22:07	☽ 22♓32
22 18:01	○ 0♋30
29 15:46	☽ 7♎32

Astro Data

1 NOVEMBER 1904
Julian Day # 1766
Delta T 3.7 sec
SVP 06♓35'24"
Obliquity 23°26'57"
⚷ Chiron 25♑08.9
☽ Mean ☊ 15♍41.5

1 DECEMBER 1904
Julian Day # 1796
Delta T 3.8 sec
SVP 06♓35'20"
Obliquity 23°26'57"
⚷ Chiron 26♑40.8
☽ Mean ☊ 14♍06.2

LONGITUDE JANUARY 1905

Day	Sid.Time	☉	0 hr ☽	Noon ☽	True ☊	☿	♀	♂	♃	♄	♅	♆	♇
1 Su	6 39 54	9♑55 29	10♏20 10	17♏16 34	11♍28.5	9♑ 6.4	22♒14.3	23♎23.3	20♈41.4	18♒33.1	0♑41.3	6♋41.6	20♊20.8
2 M	6 43 50	10 56 40	24 11 16	1♐ 4 0	11R 22.2	7R 45.4	23 25.0	23 55.0	20 44.8	18 39.3	0 44.9	6R 39.9	20R 19.7
3 Tu	6 47 47	11 57 51	7♐54 28	14 42 22	11 13.5	6 27.4	24 35.7	24 26.6	20 48.4	18 45.5	0 48.5	6 38.2	20 18.6
4 W	6 51 44	12 59 2	21 27 20	28 9 6	11 3.3	5 14.7	25 46.3	24 58.1	20 52.2	18 51.8	0 52.0	6 36.5	20 17.5
5 Th	6 55 40	14 0 13	4♑47 20	11♑21 47	10 52.6	4 9.1	26 56.7	25 29.5	20 56.2	18 58.1	0 55.6	6 34.8	20 16.5
6 F	6 59 37	15 1 24	17 52 15	24 18 36	10 42.5	3 12.1	28 7.0	26 0.7	21 0.4	19 4.5	0 59.2	6 33.1	20 15.4
7 Sa	7 3 33	16 2 34	0♒40 45	6♒58 45	10 34.1	2 24.6	29 17.2	26 31.8	21 4.8	19 10.9	1 2.7	6 31.5	20 14.4
8 Su	7 7 30	17 3 45	13 12 40	19 22 42	10 27.9	1 46.9	0♓27.3	27 2.8	21 9.3	19 17.4	1 6.2	6 29.8	20 13.3
9 M	7 11 26	18 4 55	25 29 6	1♓32 11	10 24.3	1 19.3	1 37.3	27 33.6	21 14.1	19 23.9	1 9.7	6 28.1	20 12.3
10 Tu	7 15 23	19 6 5	7♓32 23	13 30 8	10D 22.9	1 1.5	2 47.1	28 4.3	21 19.0	19 30.5	1 13.2	6 26.5	20 11.3
11 W	7 19 19	20 7 14	19 25 59	25 20 29	10 23.2	0D 53.2	3 56.7	28 34.9	21 24.1	19 37.1	1 16.7	6 24.8	20 10.3
12 Th	7 23 16	21 8 22	1♈14 15	7♈ 7 55	10 24.5	0 53.7	5 6.2	29 5.3	21 29.4	19 43.7	1 20.2	6 23.2	20 9.3
13 F	7 27 13	22 9 30	13 2 8	18 57 35	10R 25.8	1 2.5	6 15.6	29 35.6	21 34.9	19 50.4	1 23.6	6 21.5	20 8.3
14 Sa	7 31 9	23 10 38	24 54 57	0♉54 52	10 26.2	1 19.0	7 24.8	0♏ 5.7	21 40.5	19 57.1	1 27.1	6 19.9	20 7.4
15 Su	7 35 6	24 11 44	6♉58 2	13 5 1	10 25.1	1 42.4	8 33.8	0 35.7	21 46.3	20 3.8	1 30.5	6 18.3	20 6.4
16 M	7 39 2	25 12 50	19 16 26	25 32 45	10 22.1	2 12.1	9 42.7	1 5.5	21 52.3	20 10.6	1 33.9	6 16.7	20 5.5
17 Tu	7 42 59	26 13 55	1♊54 27	8♊21 51	10 17.2	2 47.6	10 51.4	1 35.2	21 58.5	20 17.4	1 37.3	6 15.1	20 4.5
18 W	7 46 55	27 15 0	14 55 12	21 34 37	10 10.8	3 28.3	11 59.9	2 4.8	22 4.8	20 24.2	1 40.6	6 13.6	20 3.6
19 Th	7 50 52	28 16 3	28 20 5	5♋11 27	10 3.6	4 13.6	13 8.2	2 34.1	22 11.3	20 31.1	1 44.0	6 12.0	20 2.7
20 F	7 54 48	29 17 6	12♋ 8 25	19 10 34	9 56.4	5 3.2	14 16.4	3 3.4	22 18.0	20 38.0	1 47.3	6 10.5	20 1.9
21 Sa	7 58 45	0♒18 8	26 17 21	3♌28 4	9 50.1	5 56.5	15 24.3	3 32.4	22 24.9	20 44.9	1 50.6	6 9.0	20 1.0
22 Su	8 2 42	1 19 10	10♌42 1	17 58 22	9 45.5	6 53.3	16 32.0	4 1.3	22 31.8	20 51.9	1 53.9	6 7.4	20 0.2
23 M	8 6 38	2 20 10	25 16 18	2♍35 0	9 42.7	7 53.2	17 39.6	4 30.0	22 39.0	20 58.8	1 57.2	6 5.9	19 59.3
24 Tu	8 10 35	3 21 10	9♍53 42	17 11 40	9D 41.9	8 55.8	18 46.9	4 58.6	22 46.3	21 5.8	2 0.4	6 4.5	19 58.5
25 W	8 14 31	4 22 10	24 28 16	1♎42 55	9 42.6	10 1.1	19 54.0	5 27.0	22 53.8	21 12.8	2 3.6	6 3.0	19 57.7
26 Th	8 18 28	5 23 8	8♎55 12	16 4 43	9 44.0	11 8.6	21 0.8	5 55.1	23 1.4	21 19.9	2 6.8	6 1.6	19 56.9
27 F	8 22 24	6 24 6	23 11 13	0♏14 29	9 45.4	12 18.3	22 7.5	6 23.2	23 9.2	21 27.0	2 9.9	6 0.1	19 56.1
28 Sa	8 26 21	7 25 4	7♏14 23	14 10 52	9R 46.0	13 29.9	23 13.9	6 51.0	23 17.1	21 34.0	2 13.1	5 58.7	19 55.4
29 Su	8 30 17	8 26 1	21 3 53	27 53 26	9 45.3	14 43.3	24 20.0	7 18.6	23 25.2	21 41.1	2 16.2	5 57.3	19 54.7
30 M	8 34 14	9 26 57	4♐39 32	11♐22 13	9 43.2	15 58.4	25 26.0	7 46.0	23 33.4	21 48.3	2 19.3	5 56.0	19 53.9
31 Tu	8 38 11	10 27 53	18 1 29	24 37 24	9 39.7	17 14.9	26 31.6	8 13.2	23 41.8	21 55.4	2 22.3	5 54.6	19 53.2

LONGITUDE FEBRUARY 1905

Day	Sid.Time	☉	0 hr ☽	Noon ☽	True ☊	☿	♀	♂	♃	♄	♅	♆	♇
1 W	8 42 7	11♒28 48	1♑ 9 58	7♑39 14	9♍35.2	18♑32.9	27♓37.0	8♏40.2	23♈50.3	22♒ 2.6	2♑25.3	5♋53.3	19♊52.6
2 Th	8 46 4	12 29 42	14 5 12	20 27 56	9R 30.5	19 52.3	28 42.2	9 7.0	23 58.9	22 9.7	2 28.3	5R 52.0	19R 51.9
3 F	8 50 0	13 30 34	26 47 27	3♒ 3 48	9 26.0	21 12.9	29 47.0	9 33.6	24 7.7	22 16.9	2 31.3	5 50.7	19 51.3
4 Sa	8 53 57	14 31 26	9♒17 4	15 27 20	9 22.4	22 34.7	0♈51.6	9 59.9	24 16.6	22 24.1	2 34.2	5 49.5	19 50.6
5 Su	8 57 53	15 32 17	21 34 45	27 39 27	9 19.9	23 57.6	1 55.8	10 26.0	24 25.7	22 31.3	2 37.1	5 48.2	19 50.0
6 M	9 1 50	16 33 6	3♓41 39	9♓41 35	9D 18.7	25 21.6	2 59.8	10 51.9	24 34.9	22 38.5	2 40.0	5 47.0	19 49.4
7 Tu	9 5 46	17 33 54	15 39 31	21 35 48	9 18.7	26 46.6	4 3.4	11 17.5	24 44.2	22 45.7	2 42.8	5 45.8	19 48.9
8 W	9 9 43	18 34 41	27 30 46	3♈24 51	9 19.7	28 12.6	5 6.7	11 42.9	24 53.7	22 53.0	2 45.6	5 44.7	19 48.3
9 Th	9 13 40	19 35 26	9♈18 29	15 12 9	9 21.3	29 39.6	6 9.7	12 8.0	25 3.3	23 0.2	2 48.4	5 43.5	19 47.8
10 F	9 17 36	20 36 10	21 6 23	27 1 43	9 23.0	1♒ 7.6	7 12.3	12 32.9	25 13.0	23 7.4	2 51.1	5 42.4	19 47.3
11 Sa	9 21 33	21 36 52	2♉58 45	8♉58 2	9 24.4	2 36.5	8 14.5	12 57.5	25 22.8	23 14.7	2 53.8	5 41.3	19 46.8
12 Su	9 25 29	22 37 33	15 0 13	21 5 52	9R 25.3	4 6.3	9 16.4	13 21.8	25 32.7	23 21.9	2 56.5	5 40.3	19 46.4
13 M	9 29 26	23 38 12	27 15 35	3♊29 58	9 25.4	5 37.0	10 17.8	13 45.9	25 42.8	23 29.1	2 59.1	5 39.2	19 45.9
14 Tu	9 33 22	24 38 49	9♊49 31	16 14 45	9 24.8	7 8.6	11 18.9	14 9.7	25 53.0	23 36.4	3 1.7	5 38.2	19 45.5
15 W	9 37 19	25 39 24	22 46 4	29 23 47	9 23.6	8 41.1	12 19.5	14 33.2	26 3.3	23 43.6	3 4.2	5 37.2	19 45.1
16 Th	9 41 15	26 39 58	6♋ 8 9	12♋59 14	9 22.0	10 14.6	13 19.7	14 56.4	26 13.7	23 50.9	3 6.8	5 36.3	19 44.7
17 F	9 45 12	27 40 30	19 57 0	27 1 14	9 20.4	11 48.9	14 19.5	15 19.4	26 24.2	23 58.1	3 9.2	5 35.4	19 44.4
18 Sa	9 49 9	28 41 0	4♌11 34	11♌27 29	9 19.0	13 24.1	15 18.7	15 42.0	26 34.9	24 5.3	3 11.7	5 34.5	19 44.0
19 Su	9 53 5	29 41 29	18 48 16	26 13 7	9 18.0	15 0.2	16 17.5	16 4.3	26 45.6	24 12.5	3 14.1	5 33.6	19 43.7
20 M	9 57 2	0♓41 56	3♍41 4	11♍11 6	9D 17.6	16 37.3	17 15.8	16 26.3	26 56.5	24 19.8	3 16.4	5 32.8	19 43.4
21 Tu	10 0 58	1 42 21	18 42 7	26 13 3	9 17.6	18 15.2	18 13.6	16 48.0	27 7.4	24 27.0	3 18.7	5 32.0	19 43.1
22 W	10 4 55	2 42 45	3♎42 49	11♎10 26	9 18.0	19 54.1	19 10.8	17 9.4	27 18.5	24 34.2	3 21.0	5 31.2	19 42.9
23 Th	10 8 51	3 43 7	18 35 2	25 55 49	9 18.5	21 34.0	20 7.5	17 30.4	27 29.6	24 41.4	3 23.2	5 30.5	19 42.7
24 F	10 12 48	4 43 28	3♏12 10	10♏23 36	9 19.0	23 14.9	21 3.6	17 51.1	27 40.8	24 48.5	3 25.4	5 29.8	19 42.4
25 Sa	10 16 44	5 43 47	17 29 45	24 30 26	9 19.3	24 56.7	21 59.1	18 11.5	27 52.2	24 55.7	3 27.5	5 29.1	19 42.3
26 Su	10 20 41	6 44 5	1♐25 34	8♐15 10	9R 19.5	26 39.5	22 54.1	18 31.4	28 3.6	25 2.8	3 29.6	5 28.4	19 42.1
27 M	10 24 38	7 44 22	14 59 20	21 38 16	9 19.5	28 23.4	23 48.4	18 51.0	28 15.1	25 10.0	3 31.7	5 27.8	19 42.0
28 Tu	10 28 34	8 44 37	28 12 12	4♑41 26	9D 19.5	0♓ 8.2	24 42.0	19 10.2	28 26.8	25 17.1	3 33.7	5 27.2	19 41.8

Astro Data	Planet Ingress	Last Aspect	☽ Ingress	Last Aspect	☽ Ingress	☽ Phases & Eclipses	Astro Data
Dy Hr Mn	Dy Hr Mn	Dy Hr Mn	Dy Hr Mn	Dy Hr Mn	Dy Hr Mn	Dy Hr Mn	1 JANUARY 1905
☿ D 11 10:26	♀ ♓ 7 14:38	1 22:32 ♀ □	♐ 2 10:08	2 18:53 ♃ □	♒ 3 6:08	5 18:17 ● 14♑47	Julian Day # 1827
☽0N 12 7:35	♂ ♏ 13 19:26	4 8:28 ♀ ✶	♑ 4 15:20	5 5:41 ♃ ✶	♓ 5 16:39	13 20:11 ☽ 23♈01	Delta T 3.9 sec
♄△♇ 15 8:04	☉ ♒ 20 16:52	6 15:50 ♂ □	♒ 6 22:43	8 1:37 ☿ ✶	♈ 8 5:03	21 7:14 ○ 0♌37	SVP 06♓35'15"
♄♇♆ 23 20:09		9 4:17 ♂ △	♓ 9 8:57	10 8:27 ♃ ☌	♉ 10 18:00	28 0:20 ☽ 7♏26	Obliquity 23°26'57"
☽0S 25 17:47	♀ ♈ 3 4:49	11 1:32 ☉ ✶	♈ 11 21:29	12 16:36 ♄ □	♊ 13 5:17		⚷ Chiron 28♑59.5
	☿ ♒ 9 5:35	13 20:11 ☉ □	♉ 14 10:11	15 6:03 ♃ ✶	♋ 15 13:05	4 11:06 ● 14♒60	☽ Mean ☊ 12♍27.7
♀0N 2 15:02	☉ ♓ 19 7:21	16 12:22 ☉ △	♊ 16 20:25	17 11:06 ♃ □	♌ 17 17:00	12 16:20 ☽ 23♉19	
☽0N 8 15:57	☿ ♓ 27 22:07	18 13:00 ♃ ✶	♋ 19 2:56	19 13:02 ♃ △	♍ 19 18:05	19 18:52 ○ 0♍29	1 FEBRUARY 1905
☽0S 22 2:42		20 17:25 ♃ □	♌ 21 6:13	21 1:37 ♇ □	♎ 21 18:03	19 18:60 ☍P 0.405	Julian Day # 1858
		22 19:39 ♃ △	♍ 23 7:46	23 14:46 ♃ ☍	♏ 23 18:42	26 10:04 ☽ 7♐09	Delta T 4.0 sec
		24 16:34 ♇ □	♎ 25 9:09	25 14:33 ☿ □	♐ 25 21:31		SVP 06♓35'11"
		26 23:57 ♃ ☍	♏ 27 11:35	28 0:27 ♃ △	♑ 28 3:19		Obliquity 23°26'57"
		29 6:14 ♀ △	♐ 29 15:44				⚷ Chiron 1♒36.0
		31 16:53 ♀ □	♑ 31 21:51				☽ Mean ☊ 10♍49.2

MARCH 1905 — LONGITUDE

Day	Sid.Time	☉	0 hr ☽	Noon ☽	True ☊	☿	♀	♂	♃	♄	♅	♆	♇
1 W	10 32 31	9♓44 51	11♑ 6 15	17♑26 59	9♍19.5	1♓54.1	25♈35.0	19♏29.1	28♈38.5	25♒24.2	3♑35.7	5♋26.7	19♊41.7
2 Th	10 36 27	10 45 3	23 43 58	29 57 30	9 19.6	3 41.1	26 27.3	19 47.5	28 50.3	25 31.3	3 37.6	5R 26.1	19R 41.7
3 F	10 40 24	11 45 14	6♒ 7 54	12♒15 29	9 19.8	5 29.1	27 18.9	20 5.5	29 2.2	25 38.4	3 39.5	5 25.6	19 41.6
4 Sa	10 44 20	12 45 22	18 20 33	24 23 20	9 20.1	7 18.2	28 9.7	20 23.1	29 14.1	25 45.4	3 41.3	5 25.2	19D 41.6
5 Su	10 48 17	13 45 30	0♓24 8	6♓23 12	9R 20.3	9 8.3	28 59.7	20 40.3	29 26.2	25 52.4	3 43.1	5 24.8	19 41.6
6 M	10 52 13	14 45 35	12 20 46	18 17 6	9 20.4	10 59.5	29 49.0	20 57.0	29 38.3	25 59.4	3 44.9	5 24.4	19 41.6
7 Tu	10 56 10	15 45 38	24 12 26	0♈ 7 3	9 20.1	12 51.7	0♉37.4	21 13.2	29 50.6	26 6.4	3 46.6	5 24.0	19 41.6
8 W	11 0 7	16 45 40	6♈ 1 11	11 55 9	9 19.5	14 45.0	1 24.9	21 29.1	0♉ 2.8	26 13.4	3 48.2	5 23.7	19 41.7
9 Th	11 4 3	17 45 39	17 49 15	23 43 48	9 18.5	16 39.3	2 11.6	21 44.4	0 15.2	26 20.3	3 49.8	5 23.4	19 41.8
10 F	11 8 0	18 45 36	29 39 9	5♉35 41	9 17.1	18 34.5	2 57.2	21 59.3	0 27.7	26 27.2	3 51.3	5 23.1	19 41.9
11 Sa	11 11 56	19 45 32	11♉33 48	17 33 56	9 15.6	20 30.7	3 42.0	22 13.7	0 40.2	26 34.1	3 52.8	5 22.9	19 42.0
12 Su	11 15 53	20 45 25	23 36 33	29 42 7	9 14.2	22 27.7	4 25.7	22 27.5	0 52.8	26 40.9	3 54.3	5 22.7	19 42.2
13 M	11 19 49	21 45 16	5♊51 8	12♊ 4 7	9 13.2	24 25.4	5 8.3	22 40.9	1 5.4	26 47.7	3 55.7	5 22.5	19 42.4
14 Tu	11 23 46	22 45 5	18 21 33	24 43 56	9D 12.6	26 23.9	5 49.8	22 53.8	1 18.1	26 54.5	3 57.1	5 22.4	19 42.6
15 W	11 27 42	23 44 52	1♋11 44	7♋45 24	9 12.7	28 22.8	6 30.2	23 6.1	1 30.9	27 1.3	3 58.4	5 22.3	19 42.8
16 Th	11 31 39	24 44 36	14 25 18	21 11 44	9 13.4	0♈22.2	7 9.4	23 17.9	1 43.8	27 8.0	3 59.6	5 22.3	19 43.0
17 F	11 35 35	25 44 18	28 4 52	5♌ 4 49	9 14.6	2 21.7	7 47.3	23 29.2	1 56.7	27 14.7	4 0.8	5D 22.3	19 43.3
18 Sa	11 39 32	26 43 58	12♌11 30	19 24 40	9 15.8	4 21.1	8 24.0	23 39.9	2 9.7	27 21.3	4 2.0	5 22.3	19 43.6
19 Su	11 43 29	27 43 36	26 43 56	4♍ 8 42	9R 16.8	6 20.3	8 59.3	23 50.1	2 22.7	27 27.9	4 3.1	5 22.3	19 43.9
20 M	11 47 25	28 43 11	11♍38 11	19 11 26	9 17.1	8 18.9	9 33.2	23 59.6	2 35.8	27 34.5	4 4.1	5 22.4	19 44.2
21 Tu	11 51 22	29 42 44	26 47 23	4♎24 48	9 16.5	10 16.7	10 5.7	24 8.6	2 48.9	27 41.0	4 5.1	5 22.5	19 44.6
22 W	11 55 18	0♈42 15	12♎ 2 26	19 38 59	9 14.7	12 13.1	10 36.7	24 17.0	3 2.1	27 47.5	4 6.1	5 22.7	19 44.9
23 Th	11 59 15	1 41 44	27 13 12	4♏43 56	9 12.1	14 8.0	11 6.1	24 24.8	3 15.4	27 53.9	4 7.0	5 22.8	19 45.3
24 F	12 3 11	2 41 12	12♏10 8	19 30 56	9 8.9	16 0.8	11 33.9	24 31.9	3 28.7	28 0.3	4 7.8	5 23.1	19 45.7
25 Sa	12 7 8	3 40 37	26 45 39	3♐53 48	9 5.7	17 51.2	12 0.0	24 38.4	3 42.0	28 6.7	4 8.6	5 23.3	19 46.2
26 Su	12 11 4	4 40 1	10♐55 5	17 49 24	9 3.1	19 38.8	12 24.4	24 44.3	3 55.5	28 13.0	4 9.4	5 23.6	19 46.6
27 M	12 15 1	5 39 23	24 36 46	1♑17 24	9D 1.4	21 23.1	12 47.1	24 49.5	4 8.9	28 19.3	4 10.1	5 23.9	19 47.1
28 Tu	12 18 58	6 38 44	7♑51 36	14 19 44	9 1.0	23 3.6	13 7.9	24 54.0	4 22.4	28 25.5	4 10.7	5 24.3	19 47.6
29 W	12 22 54	7 38 2	20 42 17	26 59 44	9 1.6	24 40.1	13 26.8	24 57.9	4 36.0	28 31.7	4 11.3	5 24.6	19 48.1
30 Th	12 26 51	8 37 19	3♒12 37	9♒21 29	9 3.1	26 12.1	13 43.7	25 1.1	4 49.6	28 37.9	4 11.9	5 25.1	19 48.7
31 F	12 30 47	9 36 34	15 26 51	21 29 14	9 4.8	27 39.2	13 58.6	25 3.5	5 3.2	28 43.9	4 12.4	5 25.5	19 49.2

APRIL 1905 — LONGITUDE

Day	Sid.Time	☉	0 hr ☽	Noon ☽	True ☊	☿	♀	♂	♃	♄	♅	♆	♇
1 Sa	12 34 44	10♈35 47	27♒29 8	3♓27 2	9♍ 6.3	29♈ 1.1	14♉11.4	25♏ 5.2	5♉16.9	28♒50.0	4♑12.8	5♋26.0	19♊49.8
2 Su	12 38 40	11 34 58	9♓23 22	15 18 32	9R 6.9	0♉17.6	14 22.1	25R 6.2	5 30.6	28 56.0	4 13.2	5 26.5	19 50.4
3 M	12 42 37	12 34 7	21 12 55	27 6 51	9 6.1	1 28.4	14 30.6	25 6.5	5 44.3	29 1.9	4 13.5	5 27.1	19 51.1
4 Tu	12 46 33	13 33 15	3♈ 0 38	8♈54 34	9 3.6	2 33.2	14 36.9	25 6.0	5 58.1	29 7.8	4 13.8	5 27.7	19 51.7
5 W	12 50 30	14 32 20	14 48 54	20 43 53	8 59.4	3 31.8	14 40.8	25 4.8	6 12.0	29 13.6	4 14.0	5 28.3	19 52.4
6 Th	12 54 27	15 31 23	26 39 44	2♉36 40	8 53.6	4 24.1	14R 42.4	25 2.8	6 25.8	29 19.4	4 14.2	5 28.9	19 53.0
7 F	12 58 23	16 30 24	8♉34 55	14 34 42	8 46.8	5 10.0	14 41.6	25 0.1	6 39.7	29 25.1	4 14.3	5 29.6	19 53.8
8 Sa	13 2 20	17 29 24	20 36 16	26 39 50	8 39.5	5 49.3	14 38.3	24 56.6	6 53.7	29 30.7	4R 14.4	5 30.3	19 54.5
9 Su	13 6 16	18 28 20	2♊45 42	8♊54 10	8 32.6	6 21.9	14 32.6	24 52.4	7 7.6	29 36.3	4 14.4	5 31.1	19 55.2
10 M	13 10 13	19 27 15	15 5 31	21 20 8	8 26.7	6 47.9	14 24.4	24 47.3	7 21.6	29 41.9	4 14.4	5 31.8	19 56.0
11 Tu	13 14 9	20 26 8	27 38 20	4♋ 0 33	8 22.4	7 7.3	14 13.8	24 41.6	7 35.6	29 47.3	4 14.3	5 32.7	19 56.8
12 W	13 18 6	21 24 58	10♋27 7	16 58 29	8D 20.0	7 20.0	14 0.7	24 35.0	7 49.7	29 52.7	4 14.1	5 33.5	19 57.6
13 Th	13 22 2	22 23 46	23 34 59	0♌16 59	8 19.4	7R 26.3	13 45.1	24 27.7	8 3.7	29 58.1	4 14.0	5 34.4	19 58.4
14 F	13 25 59	23 22 32	7♌ 4 47	13 58 38	8 20.1	7 26.2	13 27.1	24 19.6	8 17.8	0♓ 3.4	4 13.7	5 35.3	19 59.2
15 Sa	13 29 55	24 21 16	20 58 39	28 4 53	8 21.3	7 19.9	13 6.7	24 10.8	8 31.9	0 8.6	4 13.4	5 36.2	20 0.1
16 Su	13 33 52	25 19 57	5♍17 12	12♍35 20	8R 22.2	7 7.9	12 44.0	24 1.2	8 46.0	0 13.7	4 13.1	5 37.2	20 0.9
17 M	13 37 49	26 18 36	19 58 47	27 26 56	8 21.7	6 50.3	12 19.1	23 50.9	9 0.2	0 18.8	4 12.7	5 38.2	20 1.8
18 Tu	13 41 45	27 17 12	4♎58 56	12♎33 44	8 19.2	6 27.7	11 52.1	23 39.8	9 14.3	0 23.9	4 12.3	5 39.2	20 2.7
19 W	13 45 42	28 15 47	20 10 12	27 47 3	8 14.5	6 0.5	11 23.2	23 28.1	9 28.5	0 28.8	4 11.8	5 40.3	20 3.6
20 Th	13 49 38	29 14 20	5♏22 58	12♏56 37	8 7.9	5 29.3	10 52.4	23 15.6	9 42.7	0 33.7	4 11.2	5 41.4	20 4.6
21 F	13 53 35	0♉12 51	20 26 45	27 52 14	8 0.1	4 54.7	10 20.0	23 2.4	9 56.9	0 38.5	4 10.7	5 42.5	20 5.5
22 Sa	13 57 31	1 11 20	5♐12 5	12♐25 33	7 52.1	4 17.5	9 46.2	22 48.5	10 11.2	0 43.3	4 10.0	5 43.6	20 6.5
23 Su	14 1 28	2 9 47	19 32 2	26 31 13	7 44.8	3 38.3	9 11.1	22 33.9	10 25.4	0 47.9	4 9.4	5 44.8	20 7.5
24 M	14 5 24	3 8 13	3♑22 57	10♑ 7 16	7 39.2	2 57.9	8 34.9	22 18.6	10 39.7	0 52.5	4 8.6	5 46.0	20 8.5
25 Tu	14 9 21	4 6 37	16 44 23	23 14 40	7 35.6	2 17.1	7 58.0	22 2.7	10 53.9	0 57.1	4 7.8	5 47.2	20 9.5
26 W	14 13 18	5 5 0	29 38 33	5♒56 35	7D 34.0	1 36.6	7 20.5	21 46.2	11 8.2	1 1.5	4 7.0	5 48.5	20 10.5
27 Th	14 17 14	6 3 21	12♒ 9 22	18 17 31	7 34.0	0 57.0	6 42.8	21 29.1	11 22.5	1 5.9	4 6.1	5 49.8	20 11.6
28 F	14 21 11	7 1 41	24 21 43	0♓22 36	7 34.8	0 19.2	6 4.9	21 11.4	11 36.8	1 10.2	4 5.2	5 51.1	20 12.6
29 Sa	14 25 7	7 59 59	6♓20 48	12 16 57	7R 35.4	29♈43.6	5 27.3	20 53.2	11 51.0	1 14.4	4 4.3	5 52.4	20 13.7
30 Su	14 29 4	8 58 15	18 11 38	24 5 24	7 34.7	29 10.9	4 50.1	20 34.4	12 5.3	1 18.6	4 3.2	5 53.8	20 14.8

Astro Data Dy Hr Mn	Planet Ingress Dy Hr Mn	Last Aspect Dy Hr Mn	☽ Ingress Dy Hr Mn	Last Aspect Dy Hr Mn	☽ Ingress Dy Hr Mn	☽ Phases & Eclipses Dy Hr Mn
♇ D 4 18:30	♀ ♉ 6 5:26	2 10:00 ♃ □	♒ 2 12:05	1 3:28 ☿ ✱	♓ 1 5:03	6 5:19 ● 14♓59
☽0N 7 22:42	♃ ♉ 7 18:28	4 22:02 ♃ ✱	♓ 4 23:12	3 7:55 ♂ △	♈ 3 17:52	6 5:12:20 ● A 7'58"
☿0N 16 17:21	☿ ♈ 15 19:33	6 17:48 ♂ △	♈ 7 11:46	6 5:25 ♄ ✱	♉ 6 6:44	14 8:59 ☽ 23♊07
♆ D 17 2:33	☉ ♈ 21 6:58	9 17:28 ♄ ✱	♉ 10 0:42	8 17:45 ♄ □	♊ 8 18:34	21 4:55 ○ 29♍55
☽0S 21 13:29		12 6:07 ♄ □	♊ 12 12:35	11 4:06 ♄ △	♋ 11 4:28	27 21:35 ☽ 6♑33
♃△♅ 27 2:11	☿ ♉ 1 18:19	14 17:51 ♄ △	♋ 14 21:48	13 1:34 ♂ △	♌ 13 11:30	
♃∠♇ 29 22:24	♄ ♓ 13 8:39	16 19:37 ☉ △	♌ 17 3:19	15 6:09 ☉ △	♍ 15 15:13	4 23:23 ● 14♈31
♃✱♆ 1 16:36	☉ ♉ 20 18:44	19 1:12 ♄ ☍	♍ 19 5:18	17 6:09 ♂ ✱	♎ 17 16:04	12 21:41 ☽ 22♋18
♂ R 2 20:46	☿ ♈ 28 12:43	21 4:55 ☉ ☍	♎ 21 5:03	19 13:38 ☉ ☍	♏ 19 15:30	19 13:38 ○ 28♎49
☽0N 4 4:43		23 1:05 ♄ △	♏ 23 4:26	21 4:07 ♂ ☌	♐ 21 15:28	26 11:13 ☽ 5♒32
♀ R 6 3:54		25 2:16 ♄ □	♐ 25 5:25	23 1:00 ♇ ☍	♑ 23 18:03	
♅ R 8 21:20		27 6:42 ♄ ✱	♑ 27 9:40	25 9:34 ♂ ✱	♒ 26 0:41	
☿ R 13 11:35		29 8:37 ☿ □	♒ 29 17:47	27 17:52 ♂ □	♓ 28 11:15	
☽0S 18 0:41						

Astro Data

1 MARCH 1905
Julian Day # 1886
Delta T 4.1 sec
SVP 06♓35'07"
Obliquity 23°26'58"
⚷ Chiron 3♒48.8
☽ Mean ☊ 9♍20.2

1 APRIL 1905
Julian Day # 1917
Delta T 4.2 sec
SVP 06♓35'05"
Obliquity 23°26'58"
⚷ Chiron 5♒41.8
☽ Mean ☊ 7♍41.7

LONGITUDE — MAY 1905

Day	Sid.Time	☉	0 hr ☽	Noon ☽	True ☊	☿	♀	♂	♃	♄	♅	♆	♇
1 M	14 33 0	9♉56 30	29♓58 45	5♈52 11	7♍32.2	28♈41.5	4♉13.5	20♏15.2	12♉19.6	1♓22.7	4♑ 2.2	5♋55.2	20♊15.9
2 Tu	14 36 57	10 54 43	11♈46 4	17 40 48	7R27.1	28R15.9	3R37.9	19R55.5	12 34.0	1 26.6	4R 1.1	5 56.6	20 17.0
3 W	14 40 53	11 52 55	23 36 42	29 34 2	7 19.4	27 54.3	3 3.4	19 35.4	12 48.3	1 30.6	3 59.9	5 58.1	20 18.2
4 Th	14 44 50	12 51 5	5♉33 3	11♉33 54	7 9.4	27 37.0	2 30.2	19 14.9	13 2.6	1 34.4	3 58.7	5 59.5	20 19.3
5 F	14 48 47	13 49 13	17 36 47	23 41 49	6 57.7	27 24.2	1 58.5	18 54.1	13 16.9	1 38.1	3 57.5	6 1.0	20 20.5
6 Sa	14 52 43	14 47 20	29 49 6	5♊58 46	6 45.3	27 16.1	1 28.5	18 33.1	13 31.2	1 41.8	3 56.2	6 2.5	20 21.6
7 Su	14 56 40	15 45 25	12♊10 54	18 25 36	6 33.3	27D 12.6	1 0.3	18 11.8	13 45.5	1 45.4	3 54.9	6 4.1	20 22.8
8 M	15 0 36	16 43 28	24 43 0	1♋ 3 14	6 22.8	27 13.9	0 34.1	17 50.2	13 59.7	1 48.9	3 53.5	6 5.7	20 24.0
9 Tu	15 4 33	17 41 29	7♋26 28	13 52 53	6 14.5	27 19.8	0 10.0	17 28.6	14 14.0	1 52.3	3 52.1	6 7.3	20 25.2
10 W	15 8 29	18 39 29	20 22 41	26 56 7	6 8.9	27 30.4	29♈48.0	17 6.8	14 28.3	1 55.6	3 50.7	6 8.9	20 26.4
11 Th	15 12 26	19 37 27	3♌33 26	10♌14 54	6 6.0	27 45.6	29 28.3	16 45.0	14 42.6	1 58.8	3 49.2	6 10.5	20 27.6
12 F	15 16 22	20 35 23	17 0 45	23 51 14	6D 5.0	28 5.2	29 10.9	16 23.2	14 56.8	2 2.0	3 47.7	6 12.2	20 28.9
13 Sa	15 20 19	21 33 17	0♍46 31	7♍46 43	6R 5.1	28 29.2	28 55.9	16 1.4	15 11.1	2 5.1	3 46.1	6 13.9	20 30.1
14 Su	15 24 16	22 31 9	14 51 52	22 1 54	6 5.0	28 57.5	28 43.3	15 39.7	15 25.3	2 8.0	3 44.5	6 15.6	20 31.4
15 M	15 28 12	23 28 59	29 16 34	6♎35 30	6 3.4	29 29.8	28 33.1	15 18.1	15 39.5	2 10.9	3 42.9	6 17.3	20 32.7
16 Tu	15 32 9	24 26 48	13♎58 10	21 23 50	5 59.5	0♉ 6.2	28 25.3	14 56.7	15 53.7	2 13.7	3 41.2	6 19.0	20 33.9
17 W	15 36 5	25 24 35	28 51 40	6♏20 38	5 52.9	0 46.4	28 19.9	14 35.5	16 7.9	2 16.4	3 39.5	6 20.8	20 35.2
18 Th	15 40 2	26 22 21	13♏49 38	21 17 30	5 43.9	1 30.3	28D 16.9	14 14.5	16 22.1	2 19.0	3 37.8	6 22.6	20 36.5
19 F	15 43 58	27 20 5	28 43 5	6♐ 5 14	5 33.2	2 17.9	28 16.3	13 53.9	16 36.2	2 21.6	3 36.0	6 24.4	20 37.8
20 Sa	15 47 55	28 17 48	13♐22 57	20 35 20	5 22.0	3 8.9	28 18.1	13 33.6	16 50.4	2 24.0	3 34.2	6 26.2	20 39.1
21 Su	15 51 51	29 15 29	27 41 40	4♑41 26	5 11.6	4 3.3	28 22.1	13 13.7	17 4.5	2 26.3	3 32.3	6 28.1	20 40.4
22 M	15 55 48	0♊13 10	11♑34 19	18 20 9	5 3.1	5 1.0	28 28.4	12 54.1	17 18.6	2 28.6	3 30.5	6 29.9	20 41.8
23 Tu	15 59 45	1 10 49	24 59 1	1♒31 5	4 57.0	6 1.9	28 37.0	12 35.1	17 32.6	2 30.8	3 28.5	6 31.8	20 43.1
24 W	16 3 41	2 8 27	7♒56 43	14 16 21	4 53.4	7 5.9	28 47.6	12 16.5	17 46.7	2 32.8	3 26.6	6 33.7	20 44.4
25 Th	16 7 38	3 6 4	20 30 31	26 39 50	4 51.9	8 12.9	29 0.4	11 58.4	18 0.7	2 34.8	3 24.6	6 35.6	20 45.8
26 F	16 11 34	4 3 41	2♓44 57	8♓46 31	4 51.6	9 22.9	29 15.2	11 40.9	18 14.7	2 36.7	3 22.6	6 37.6	20 47.1
27 Sa	16 15 31	5 1 16	14 45 15	20 41 48	4 51.5	10 35.7	29 31.9	11 23.9	18 28.7	2 38.4	3 20.6	6 39.5	20 48.5
28 Su	16 19 27	5 58 50	26 36 52	2♈31 5	4 50.4	11 51.4	29 50.6	11 7.6	18 42.6	2 40.1	3 18.6	6 41.5	20 49.9
29 M	16 23 24	6 56 24	8♈25 3	14 19 22	4 47.5	13 9.8	0♉11.1	10 51.9	18 56.5	2 41.7	3 16.5	6 43.4	20 51.2
30 Tu	16 27 20	7 53 56	20 14 32	26 11 2	4 42.0	14 30.9	0 33.3	10 36.9	19 10.4	2 43.2	3 14.4	6 45.4	20 52.6
31 W	16 31 17	8 51 28	2♉ 9 18	8♉ 9 41	4 33.9	15 54.8	0 57.3	10 22.5	19 24.3	2 44.6	3 12.2	6 47.4	20 54.0

LONGITUDE — JUNE 1905

Day	Sid.Time	☉	0 hr ☽	Noon ☽	True ☊	☿	♀	♂	♃	♄	♅	♆	♇
1 Th	16 35 14	9♊48 59	14♉12 29	20♉17 56	4♍23.2	17♉21.3	1♉22.9	10♏ 8.9	19♉38.1	2♓45.9	3♑10.1	6♋49.5	20♊55.4
2 F	16 39 10	10 46 29	26 26 14	2♊37 30	4R10.8	18 50.4	1 50.1	9R56.0	19 51.9	2 47.1	3R 7.9	6 51.5	20 56.8
3 Sa	16 43 7	11 43 58	8♊51 48	15 9 10	3 57.6	20 22.2	2 18.8	9 43.9	20 5.7	2 48.2	3 5.7	6 53.6	20 58.1
4 Su	16 47 3	12 41 26	21 29 35	27 53 1	3 44.7	21 56.6	2 49.0	9 32.6	20 19.4	2 49.2	3 3.5	6 55.6	20 59.5
5 M	16 51 0	13 38 53	4♋19 25	10♋48 43	3 33.4	23 33.5	3 20.6	9 22.0	20 33.1	2 50.1	3 1.2	6 57.7	21 0.9
6 Tu	16 54 56	14 36 20	17 20 53	23 55 52	3 24.4	25 13.1	3 53.5	9 12.3	20 46.7	2 50.9	2 59.0	6 59.8	21 2.3
7 W	16 58 53	15 33 45	0♌33 39	7♌14 15	3 18.2	26 55.2	4 27.8	9 3.3	21 0.3	2 51.6	2 56.7	7 1.9	21 3.7
8 Th	17 2 49	16 31 9	13 57 40	20 43 59	3 14.9	28 39.8	5 3.3	8 55.2	21 13.9	2 52.2	2 54.4	7 4.0	21 5.2
9 F	17 6 46	17 28 32	27 33 16	4♍25 34	3D 13.7	0♊27.0	5 40.0	8 47.9	21 27.4	2 52.7	2 52.1	7 6.1	21 6.6
10 Sa	17 10 43	18 25 54	11♍20 59	18 19 32	3R 13.7	2 16.7	6 17.8	8 41.5	21 40.9	2 53.1	2 49.8	7 8.2	21 8.0
11 Su	17 14 39	19 23 14	25 21 16	2♎26 5	3 13.7	4 8.8	6 56.8	8 35.9	21 54.3	2 53.4	2 47.4	7 10.4	21 9.4
12 M	17 18 36	20 20 34	9♎33 53	16 44 25	3 12.4	6 3.3	7 36.8	8 31.1	22 7.7	2 53.6	2 45.1	7 12.5	21 10.8
13 Tu	17 22 32	21 17 53	23 57 22	1♏12 17	3 9.1	8 0.2	8 17.9	8 27.1	22 21.0	2R 53.7	2 42.7	7 14.7	21 12.2
14 W	17 26 29	22 15 11	8♏28 35	15 45 37	3 3.2	9 59.3	8 60.0	8 24.0	22 34.3	2 53.8	2 40.3	7 16.9	21 13.6
15 Th	17 30 25	23 12 28	23 2 37	0♐18 44	2 55.1	12 0.6	9 43.0	8 21.7	22 47.5	2 53.7	2 37.9	7 19.0	21 15.0
16 F	17 34 22	24 9 44	7♐33 9	14 44 58	2 45.3	14 3.8	10 27.0	8 20.2	23 0.7	2 53.5	2 35.5	7 21.2	21 16.4
17 Sa	17 38 18	25 7 0	21 53 24	28 57 41	2 35.0	16 8.9	11 11.8	8D 19.6	23 13.8	2 53.2	2 33.1	7 23.4	21 17.8
18 Su	17 42 15	26 4 15	5♑57 12	12♑51 24	2 25.4	18 15.6	11 57.6	8 19.7	23 26.9	2 52.8	2 30.7	7 25.6	21 19.2
19 M	17 46 12	27 1 29	19 39 55	26 22 33	2 17.4	20 23.8	12 44.1	8 20.7	23 39.9	2 52.4	2 28.3	7 27.8	21 20.6
20 Tu	17 50 8	27 58 44	2♒59 11	9♒29 53	2 11.6	22 33.1	13 31.4	8 22.4	23 52.9	2 51.8	2 25.9	7 30.0	21 22.0
21 W	17 54 5	28 55 57	15 54 51	22 14 22	2 8.3	24 43.4	14 19.5	8 25.0	24 5.8	2 51.1	2 23.4	7 32.2	21 23.4
22 Th	17 58 1	29 53 11	28 28 51	4♓38 46	2D 7.0	26 54.4	15 8.4	8 28.3	24 18.6	2 50.4	2 21.0	7 34.4	21 24.8
23 F	18 1 58	0♋50 25	10♓44 40	16 47 8	2 7.2	29 5.7	15 58.0	8 32.4	24 31.4	2 49.5	2 18.6	7 36.6	21 26.2
24 Sa	18 5 54	1 47 38	22 46 48	28 44 20	2R 7.9	1♋17.2	16 48.2	8 37.2	24 44.2	2 48.5	2 16.1	7 38.9	21 27.6
25 Su	18 9 51	2 44 51	4♈40 22	10♈35 35	2 8.2	3 28.5	17 39.1	8 42.8	24 56.8	2 47.5	2 13.7	7 41.1	21 29.0
26 M	18 13 47	3 42 5	16 30 36	22 26 6	2 7.3	5 39.4	18 30.7	8 49.2	25 9.5	2 46.3	2 11.2	7 43.3	21 30.4
27 Tu	18 17 44	4 39 18	28 22 38	4♉20 48	2 4.4	7 49.5	19 22.8	8 56.3	25 22.0	2 45.1	2 8.8	7 45.5	21 31.8
28 W	18 21 41	5 36 31	10♉21 6	16 24 1	1 59.4	9 58.8	20 15.6	9 4.1	25 34.5	2 43.7	2 6.4	7 47.8	21 33.2
29 Th	18 25 37	6 33 45	22 29 56	28 39 14	1 52.3	12 7.0	21 8.9	9 12.7	25 46.9	2 42.3	2 3.9	7 50.0	21 34.5
30 F	18 29 34	7 30 58	4♊52 10	11♊ 8 56	1 43.7	14 13.8	22 2.8	9 22.0	25 59.2	2 40.8	2 1.5	7 52.2	21 35.9

Astro Data Dy Hr Mn	Planet Ingress Dy Hr Mn
☽0N 1 11:18	♀ ♈ 9 10:37
☿ D 7 5:35	☿ ♉ 15 20:06
☽0S 15 10:42	☉ ♊ 21 18:31
♀ D 18 18:04	♀ ♉ 28 11:18
♃□♅ 26 11:53	
☽0N 28 19:11	☿ ♊ 8 18:00
	☉ ♋ 22 2:51
♃⊻♇ 7 6:47	☿ ♋ 23 9:54
♄⚹♅ 8 18:40	
☽0S 11 18:42	
♃∠♆ 12 10:28	
♄ R 13 15:10	
♂ D 17 7:24	
☽0N 25 4:08	

Last Aspect Dy Hr Mn	☽ Ingress Dy Hr Mn	Last Aspect Dy Hr Mn	☽ Ingress Dy Hr Mn
30 4:43 ♂ △	♈ 1 0:03	1 10:54 ♃ ☌	♊ 2 6:55
3 8:26 ☿ ☌	♉ 3 12:52	3 23:03 ♇ ☌	♋ 4 15:57
5 2:29 ♂ ☍	♊ 6 0:21	6 16:26 ☿ ⚹	♌ 6 22:59
8 4:48 ☿ ⚹	♋ 8 10:01	8 13:06 ♃ □	♍ 9 4:17
10 16:47 ♀ □	♌ 10 17:34	10 18:02 ♃ △	♎ 11 7:53
12 20:52 ♀ △	♍ 12 22:40	12 19:25 ♇ △	♏ 13 10:01
14 13:44 ☉ △	♎ 15 1:12	14 23:35 ♃ ☍	♐ 15 11:29
16 23:09 ♀ ☍	♏ 17 1:50	17 5:51 ☉ ☍	♑ 17 13:46
18 21:36 ☉ ☍	♐ 19 2:05	19 7:15 ♃ △	♒ 19 18:33
21 1:09 ♀ △	♑ 21 3:56	21 20:19 ☿ △	♓ 22 2:57
23 6:44 ♀ □	♒ 23 9:12	24 4:00 ♃ ⚹	♈ 24 14:33
25 16:56 ♀ ⚹	♓ 25 18:34	26 10:08 ♇ ⚹	♉ 27 3:16
27 12:15 ♇ □	♈ 28 6:53	29 6:31 ♃ ☌	♊ 29 14:37
30 1:17 ♇ ⚹	♉ 30 19:41		

☽ Phases & Eclipses Dy Hr Mn		Astro Data
4 15:50	● 13♉29	1 MAY 1905
12 6:46	☽ 20♌52	Julian Day # 1947
18 21:36	○ 27♏14	Delta T 4.4 sec
26 2:50	☽ 4♓10	SVP 06♓35'02"
		Obliquity 23°26'57"
3 5:56	● 11♊58	⚷ Chiron 6♒37.7
10 13:04	☽ 18♍57	☽ Mean ☊ 6♍06.4
17 5:51	○ 25♐21	
24 19:46	☽ 2♈35	1 JUNE 1905
		Julian Day # 1978
		Delta T 4.5 sec
		SVP 06♓34'58"
		Obliquity 23°26'57"
		⚷ Chiron 6♒29.9R
		☽ Mean ☊ 4♍27.9

JULY 1905 — LONGITUDE

Day	Sid.Time	☉	0 hr ☽	Noon ☽	True ☊	☿	♀	♂	♃	♄	♅	♆	♇
1 Sa	18 33 30	8♋28 11	17♊29 40	23♊54 25	1♍34.4	16♋19.3	22♉57.1	9♏31.9	26♉11.5	2♓39.1	1♑59.1	7♋54.5	21♊37.3
2 Su	18 37 27	9 25 25	0♋23 10	6♋55 50	1R 25.2	18 23.1	23 52.0	9 42.6	26 23.7	2R 37.4	1R 56.7	7 56.7	21 38.6
3 M	18 41 23	10 22 38	13 32 15	20 12 15	1 17.2	20 25.3	24 47.4	9 54.0	26 35.8	2 35.6	1 54.2	7 58.9	21 40.0
4 Tu	18 45 20	11 19 52	26 55 35	3♌42 1	1 11.0	22 25.7	25 43.3	10 6.0	26 47.9	2 33.7	1 51.8	8 1.2	21 41.3
5 W	18 49 16	12 17 5	10♌31 17	17 23 7	1 7.0	24 24.3	26 39.6	10 18.7	26 59.9	2 31.7	1 49.5	8 3.4	21 42.7
6 Th	18 53 13	13 14 18	24 17 17	1♍13 31	1D 5.2	26 21.1	27 36.3	10 32.1	27 11.8	2 29.7	1 47.1	8 5.6	21 44.0
7 F	18 57 10	14 11 31	8♍11 37	15 11 24	1 5.2	28 15.9	28 33.5	10 46.0	27 23.6	2 27.5	1 44.7	8 7.9	21 45.3
8 Sa	19 1 6	15 8 44	22 12 41	29 15 17	1 6.2	0♌ 8.8	29 31.1	11 0.7	27 35.3	2 25.2	1 42.3	8 10.1	21 46.6
9 Su	19 5 3	16 5 57	6♎19 3	13♎23 49	1R 7.3	1 59.8	0♊29.0	11 15.9	27 47.0	2 22.9	1 40.0	8 12.3	21 47.9
10 M	19 8 59	17 3 9	20 29 23	27 35 33	1 7.6	3 48.8	1 27.4	11 31.7	27 58.5	2 20.5	1 37.7	8 14.5	21 49.2
11 Tu	19 12 56	18 0 22	4♏42 4	11♏48 36	1 6.4	5 35.8	2 26.1	11 48.2	28 10.0	2 18.0	1 35.4	8 16.7	21 50.5
12 W	19 16 52	18 57 34	18 54 51	26 0 25	1 3.4	7 20.9	3 25.2	12 5.2	28 21.4	2 15.4	1 33.1	8 18.9	21 51.8
13 Th	19 20 49	19 54 47	3♐ 4 52	10♐ 7 44	0 58.8	9 4.0	4 24.7	12 22.8	28 32.7	2 12.7	1 30.8	8 21.1	21 53.1
14 F	19 24 45	20 51 59	17 8 32	24 6 48	0 53.1	10 45.2	5 24.5	12 40.9	28 43.9	2 10.0	1 28.5	8 23.3	21 54.3
15 Sa	19 28 42	21 49 12	1♑ 2 4	7♑53 52	0 46.9	12 24.4	6 24.6	12 59.6	28 55.0	2 7.2	1 26.3	8 25.5	21 55.6
16 Su	19 32 39	22 46 25	14 41 50	21 25 38	0 41.2	14 1.7	7 25.1	13 18.8	29 6.1	2 4.3	1 24.1	8 27.7	21 56.8
17 M	19 36 35	23 43 38	28 5 0	4♒39 46	0 36.4	15 37.0	8 25.9	13 38.5	29 17.0	2 1.3	1 21.9	8 29.9	21 58.1
18 Tu	19 40 32	24 40 52	11♒ 9 52	17 35 17	0 33.2	17 10.3	9 27.0	13 58.8	29 27.9	1 58.2	1 19.7	8 32.0	21 59.3
19 W	19 44 28	25 38 6	23 56 8	0♓12 34	0D 31.6	18 41.7	10 28.4	14 19.5	29 38.6	1 55.1	1 17.5	8 34.2	22 0.5
20 Th	19 48 25	26 35 20	6♓24 53	12 33 23	0 31.6	20 11.0	11 30.1	14 40.7	29 49.3	1 51.9	1 15.4	8 36.3	22 1.7
21 F	19 52 21	27 32 36	18 38 29	24 40 38	0 32.7	21 38.4	12 32.1	15 2.4	29 59.8	1 48.6	1 13.3	8 38.5	22 2.9
22 Sa	19 56 18	28 29 52	0♈40 20	6♈38 8	0 34.3	23 3.8	13 34.4	15 24.6	0♊10.3	1 45.3	1 11.2	8 40.6	22 4.1
23 Su	20 0 14	29 27 9	12 34 35	18 30 17	0 35.9	24 27.1	14 36.9	15 47.2	0 20.6	1 41.9	1 9.1	8 42.7	22 5.2
24 M	20 4 11	0♌24 27	24 25 52	0♉21 54	0R 37.0	25 48.3	15 39.7	16 10.3	0 30.9	1 38.4	1 7.1	8 44.8	22 6.4
25 Tu	20 8 8	1 21 45	6♉19 2	12 17 51	0 37.0	27 7.4	16 42.8	16 33.9	0 41.0	1 34.9	1 5.1	8 46.9	22 7.5
26 W	20 12 4	2 19 5	18 18 57	24 22 51	0 35.9	28 24.4	17 46.1	16 57.9	0 51.1	1 31.3	1 3.1	8 49.0	22 8.7
27 Th	20 16 1	3 16 26	0♊30 6	6♊41 9	0 33.6	29 39.1	18 49.7	17 22.3	1 1.0	1 27.6	1 1.2	8 51.1	22 9.8
28 F	20 19 57	4 13 47	12 56 24	19 16 12	0 30.3	0♍51.6	19 53.5	17 47.2	1 10.8	1 23.9	0 59.3	8 53.2	22 10.9
29 Sa	20 23 54	5 11 10	25 40 49	2♋10 24	0 26.6	2 1.7	20 57.5	18 12.4	1 20.5	1 20.1	0 57.4	8 55.2	22 12.0
30 Su	20 27 50	6 8 34	8♋45 4	15 24 48	0 22.8	3 9.3	22 1.7	18 38.1	1 30.1	1 16.3	0 55.5	8 57.3	22 13.0
31 M	20 31 47	7 5 58	22 9 29	28 58 54	0 19.5	4 14.5	23 6.2	19 4.2	1 39.5	1 12.4	0 53.7	8 59.3	22 14.1

AUGUST 1905 — LONGITUDE

Day	Sid.Time	☉	0 hr ☽	Noon ☽	True ☊	☿	♀	♂	♃	♄	♅	♆	♇
1 Tu	20 35 43	8♌ 3 24	5♌52 47	12♌50 44	0♍17.1	5♍17.1	24♊10.9	19♏30.7	1♊48.9	1♓ 8.5	0♑51.9	9♋ 1.3	22♊15.1
2 W	20 39 40	9 0 50	19 52 19	26 57 1	0D 15.7	6 16.9	25 15.8	19 57.6	1 58.1	1R 4.5	0R 50.2	9 3.3	22 16.2
3 Th	20 43 37	9 58 17	4♍ 4 19	11♍13 38	0 15.5	7 13.9	26 20.9	20 24.8	2 7.2	1 0.4	0 48.5	9 5.3	22 17.2
4 F	20 47 33	10 55 45	18 24 25	25 36 5	0 16.1	8 8.0	27 26.2	20 52.5	2 16.2	0 56.4	0 46.8	9 7.3	22 18.2
5 Sa	20 51 30	11 53 14	2♎48 7	10♎ 0 1	0 17.3	8 58.9	28 31.6	21 20.5	2 25.1	0 52.2	0 45.1	9 9.2	22 19.2
6 Su	20 55 26	12 50 43	17 11 18	24 21 34	0 18.5	9 46.6	29 37.3	21 48.9	2 33.8	0 48.1	0 43.5	9 11.1	22 20.1
7 M	20 59 23	13 48 13	1♏30 26	8♏37 34	0R 19.4	10 30.8	0♋43.1	22 17.6	2 42.4	0 43.9	0 41.9	9 13.1	22 21.1
8 Tu	21 3 19	14 45 44	15 42 42	22 45 34	0 19.7	11 11.5	1 49.1	22 46.7	2 50.8	0 39.6	0 40.4	9 15.0	22 22.0
9 W	21 7 16	15 43 16	29 45 56	6♐43 39	0 19.3	11 48.4	2 55.3	23 16.1	2 59.2	0 35.3	0 38.9	9 16.8	22 23.0
10 Th	21 11 12	16 40 49	13♐38 31	20 30 24	0 18.2	12 21.3	4 1.7	23 45.8	3 7.4	0 31.0	0 37.5	9 18.7	22 23.9
11 F	21 15 9	17 38 22	27 19 9	4♑ 4 39	0 16.8	12 50.0	5 8.2	24 15.9	3 15.4	0 26.7	0 36.1	9 20.6	22 24.8
12 Sa	21 19 6	18 35 57	10♑46 49	17 25 33	0 15.3	13 14.3	6 15.0	24 46.3	3 23.4	0 22.3	0 34.7	9 22.4	22 25.6
13 Su	21 23 2	19 33 32	24 0 47	0♒32 27	0 13.9	13 34.1	7 21.8	25 17.0	3 31.1	0 17.9	0 33.4	9 24.2	22 26.5
14 M	21 26 59	20 31 8	7♒ 0 33	13 25 5	0 12.8	13 48.9	8 28.9	25 48.0	3 38.8	0 13.5	0 32.1	9 26.0	22 27.3
15 Tu	21 30 55	21 28 46	19 46 4	26 3 36	0D 12.2	13 58.8	9 36.1	26 19.3	3 46.3	0 9.1	0 30.8	9 27.8	22 28.1
16 W	21 34 52	22 26 25	2♓17 45	8♓28 42	0 12.1	14R 3.3	10 43.4	26 50.8	3 53.7	0 4.6	0 29.6	9 29.5	22 28.9
17 Th	21 38 48	23 24 5	14 36 37	20 41 44	0 12.3	14 2.5	11 51.0	27 22.7	4 0.9	0 0.1	0 28.5	9 31.2	22 29.7
18 F	21 42 45	24 21 47	26 44 20	2♈44 44	0 12.8	13 56.1	12 58.7	27 54.9	4 7.9	29♒55.6	0 27.3	9 32.9	22 30.5
19 Sa	21 46 41	25 19 30	8♈43 16	14 40 21	0 13.3	13 44.0	14 6.5	28 27.3	4 14.9	29 51.1	0 26.3	9 34.6	22 31.2
20 Su	21 50 38	26 17 14	20 36 24	26 31 55	0 13.8	13 26.1	15 14.5	28 60.0	4 21.6	29 46.6	0 25.2	9 36.3	22 31.9
21 M	21 54 35	27 15 1	2♉27 21	8♉23 16	0 14.2	13 2.6	16 22.6	29 33.0	4 28.2	29 42.1	0 24.2	9 37.9	22 32.7
22 Tu	21 58 31	28 12 48	14 20 11	20 18 40	0 14.4	12 33.4	17 30.9	0♐ 6.2	4 34.7	29 37.6	0 23.3	9 39.5	22 33.3
23 W	22 2 28	29 10 38	26 19 18	2♊22 38	0 14.4	11 58.7	18 39.3	0 39.7	4 41.0	29 33.0	0 22.4	9 41.1	22 34.0
24 Th	22 6 24	0♍ 8 29	8♊29 15	14 39 41	0 14.4	11 19.0	19 47.9	1 13.4	4 47.2	29 28.5	0 21.6	9 42.7	22 34.7
25 F	22 10 21	1 6 23	20 54 28	27 14 4	0 14.5	10 34.6	20 56.6	1 47.4	4 53.1	29 23.9	0 20.8	9 44.3	22 35.3
26 Sa	22 14 17	2 4 18	3♋38 55	10♋ 9 22	0 14.6	9 46.2	22 5.4	2 21.7	4 59.0	29 19.4	0 20.0	9 45.8	22 35.9
27 Su	22 18 14	3 2 14	16 45 41	23 28 4	0 14.8	8 54.4	23 14.4	2 56.2	5 4.6	29 14.9	0 19.3	9 47.3	22 36.5
28 M	22 22 10	4 0 13	0♌16 33	7♌11 6	0 15.2	8 0.2	24 23.5	3 30.9	5 10.1	29 10.4	0 18.7	9 48.8	22 37.1
29 Tu	22 26 7	4 58 13	14 11 29	21 17 24	0 15.5	7 4.6	25 32.7	4 5.9	5 15.4	29 5.9	0 18.1	9 50.2	22 37.6
30 W	22 30 4	5 56 15	28 28 21	5♍43 44	0R 15.6	6 8.5	26 42.1	4 41.1	5 20.6	29 1.4	0 17.5	9 51.7	22 38.2
31 Th	22 34 0	6 54 19	13♍ 2 49	20 24 48	0 15.5	5 13.4	27 51.6	5 16.6	5 25.6	28 56.9	0 17.0	9 53.1	22 38.7

Astro Data Dy Hr Mn	Planet Ingress Dy Hr Mn	Last Aspect Dy Hr Mn	☽ Ingress Dy Hr Mn	Last Aspect Dy Hr Mn	☽ Ingress Dy Hr Mn	☽ Phases & Eclipses Dy Hr Mn	Astro Data
☽0S 9 1:11	☿ ♌ 7 22:07	1 7:45 ♇ ☌	♋ 1 23:17	2 9:54 ♀ ✶	♍ 2 17:09	2 17:50 ● 10♋08	1 JULY 1905
☽0N 22 13:12	♀ ♊ 8 12:00	3 23:46 ♃ ✶	♌ 4 5:27	4 16:18 ♀ □	♎ 4 19:20	9 17:46 ☽ 16♎48	Julian Day # 2008
♃⊼♅ 27 0:25	♃ ♊ 21 0:23	6 6:10 ♀ □	♍ 6 9:53	6 8:37 ♇ △	♏ 6 21:28	16 15:32 ○ 23♑23	Delta T 4.6 sec
♃□♄ 28 23:21	☉ ♌ 23 13:46	8 9:18 ♃ △	♎ 8 13:16	8 12:28 ♂ ☌	♐ 9 0:24	24 13:08 ☽ 0♉56	SVP 06♓34'53"
	☿ ♍ 27 6:51	10 2:15 ♇ △	♏ 10 16:04	10 15:20 ♇ ☍	♑ 11 4:45		Obliquity 23°26'57"
☽0S 5 7:36		12 16:12 ♃ ☍	♐ 12 18:46	13 2:25 ♂ ✶	♒ 13 11:00	1 4:02 ● 8♌13	⚷ Chiron 5♒25.0R
♄✶♅ 7 16:57	♀ ♋ 6 8:17	14 8:12 ♇ ☍	♑ 14 22:12	15 13:03 ♂ □	♓ 15 19:34	7 22:16 ☽ 14♏42	☽ Mean ☊ 2♍52.6
☿ R 16 8:22	♄ ♒ 17 0:41	17 2:13 ♃ △	♒ 17 3:29	18 2:27 ♂ △	♈ 18 6:30	15 3:31 ○ 21♒37	
☽0N 18 21:22	♂ ♐ 21 19:33	19 11:04 ♃ □	♓ 19 11:36	20 18:27 ♄ ✶	♉ 20 19:02	15 3:41 P 0.287	1 AUGUST 1905
	☉ ♍ 23 20:29	21 19:16 ♃ ✶	♈ 21 22:39	23 6:22 ♄ □	♊ 23 7:18	23 6:10 ☽ 29♉25	Julian Day # 2039
		24 3:08 ☿ △	♉ 24 11:16	25 15:58 ♄ △	♋ 25 17:12	30 13:13 ● 6♍28	Delta T 4.7 sec
		26 22:09 ☿ □	♊ 26 23:01	27 12:40 ♀ ✶	♌ 27 23:31	30 13:07:19 T 3'46"	SVP 06♓34'48"
		28 17:30 ♇ ☌	♋ 29 8:00	30 0:55 ♄ ☍	♍ 30 2:32		Obliquity 23°26'57"
		30 18:20 ♂ △	♌ 31 13:47				⚷ Chiron 3♒44.8R
							☽ Mean ☊ 1♍14.1

LONGITUDE SEPTEMBER 1905

Day	Sid.Time	☉	0 hr ☽	Noon ☽	True ☊	☿	♀	♂	♃	♄	♅	♆	♇
1 F	22 37 57	7♍52 24	27♍48 45	5♎13 45	0♍15.0	4♍20.2	29♋ 1.2	5♐52.2	5♊30.4	28♒52.4	0♑16.5	9♋54.4	22♊39.2
2 Sa	22 41 53	8 50 30	12♎38 51	20 3 7	0R 14.2	3R 30.3	0♌10.9	6 28.1	5 35.0	28R 48.0	0R 16.1	9 55.8	22 39.6
3 Su	22 45 50	9 48 38	27 25 42	4♏45 48	0 13.2	2 44.7	1 20.7	7 4.3	5 39.5	28 43.6	0 15.7	9 57.1	22 40.1
4 M	22 49 46	10 46 48	12♏ 2 44	19 15 56	0 12.1	2 4.6	2 30.6	7 40.6	5 43.7	28 39.2	0 15.4	9 58.4	22 40.5
5 Tu	22 53 43	11 44 59	26 24 58	3♐29 31	0 11.3	1 31.0	3 40.7	8 17.2	5 47.8	28 34.8	0 15.2	9 59.7	22 40.9
6 W	22 57 39	12 43 12	10♐29 22	17 24 25	0D 10.9	1 4.7	4 50.8	8 53.9	5 51.8	28 30.5	0 15.0	10 0.9	22 41.3
7 Th	23 1 36	13 41 26	24 14 39	1♑ 0 10	0 11.1	0 46.2	6 1.1	9 30.9	5 55.5	28 26.2	0 14.8	10 2.1	22 41.7
8 F	23 5 33	14 39 41	7♑41 5	14 17 35	0 11.9	0D 36.3	7 11.5	10 8.0	5 59.0	28 21.9	0 14.7	10 3.3	22 42.0
9 Sa	23 9 29	15 37 58	20 49 51	27 18 9	0 13.0	0 35.2	8 21.9	10 45.4	6 2.4	28 17.7	0D 14.6	10 4.4	22 42.3
10 Su	23 13 26	16 36 17	3♒42 41	10♒ 3 43	0 14.3	0 43.1	9 32.5	11 22.9	6 5.6	28 13.5	0 14.6	10 5.6	22 42.6
11 M	23 17 22	17 34 37	16 21 29	22 36 12	0 15.4	1 0.1	10 43.2	12 0.6	6 8.6	28 9.3	0 14.7	10 6.7	22 42.9
12 Tu	23 21 19	18 32 59	28 48 7	4♓57 25	0R 15.9	1 26.1	11 54.0	12 38.5	6 11.4	28 5.2	0 14.8	10 7.7	22 43.2
13 W	23 25 15	19 31 23	11♓ 4 19	17 9 2	0 15.5	2 1.0	13 4.9	13 16.6	6 14.0	28 1.2	0 14.9	10 8.8	22 43.4
14 Th	23 29 12	20 29 48	23 11 45	29 12 40	0 14.1	2 44.3	14 15.9	13 54.9	6 16.5	27 57.1	0 15.1	10 9.8	22 43.6
15 F	23 33 8	21 28 15	5♈12 2	11♈10 2	0 11.7	3 35.8	15 27.0	14 33.3	6 18.7	27 53.2	0 15.4	10 10.7	22 43.8
16 Sa	23 37 5	22 26 44	17 6 56	23 2 59	0 8.4	4 35.0	16 38.2	15 11.9	6 20.7	27 49.2	0 15.6	10 11.7	22 44.0
17 Su	23 41 1	23 25 16	28 58 30	4♉53 47	0 4.6	5 41.3	17 49.5	15 50.7	6 22.6	27 45.4	0 16.0	10 12.6	22 44.1
18 M	23 44 58	24 23 49	10♉49 12	16 45 7	0 0.6	6 54.2	19 0.9	16 29.6	6 24.2	27 41.6	0 16.4	10 13.5	22 44.2
19 Tu	23 48 55	25 22 25	22 41 58	28 40 12	29♌56.9	8 13.0	20 12.4	17 8.7	6 25.7	27 37.8	0 16.8	10 14.3	22 44.4
20 W	23 52 51	26 21 2	4♊40 16	10♊42 42	29 54.0	9 37.1	21 24.0	17 47.9	6 27.0	27 34.1	0 17.3	10 15.2	22 44.4
21 Th	23 56 48	27 19 42	16 48 2	22 56 47	29D 52.3	11 5.9	22 35.7	18 27.4	6 28.0	27 30.5	0 17.9	10 15.9	22 44.5
22 F	0 0 44	28 18 24	29 9 32	5♋26 47	29 51.8	12 38.8	23 47.5	19 6.9	6 28.9	27 26.9	0 18.5	10 16.7	22 44.5
23 Sa	0 4 41	29 17 9	11♋49 7	18 17 0	29 52.4	14 15.3	24 59.4	19 46.7	6 29.6	27 23.4	0 19.2	10 17.4	22R 44.6
24 Su	0 8 37	0♎15 55	24 50 54	1♌31 11	29 53.7	15 54.6	26 11.4	20 26.5	6 30.0	27 20.0	0 19.9	10 18.1	22 44.5
25 M	0 12 34	1 14 44	8♌18 9	15 11 58	29 55.3	17 36.4	27 23.5	21 6.6	6R 30.3	27 16.6	0 20.6	10 18.8	22 44.5
26 Tu	0 16 30	2 13 35	22 12 40	29 20 8	29R 56.5	19 20.1	28 35.6	21 46.8	6 30.4	27 13.3	0 21.4	10 19.4	22 44.5
27 W	0 20 27	3 12 29	6♍34 4	13♍53 56	29 56.5	21 5.4	29 47.8	22 27.1	6 30.2	27 10.1	0 22.3	10 20.0	22 44.4
28 Th	0 24 24	4 11 24	21 19 5	28 48 37	29 55.0	22 51.9	1♍ 0.2	23 7.6	6 29.9	27 6.9	0 23.2	10 20.6	22 44.3
29 F	0 28 20	5 10 21	6♎21 29	13♎56 32	29 51.8	24 39.1	2 12.5	23 48.2	6 29.3	27 3.8	0 24.2	10 21.1	22 44.2
30 Sa	0 32 17	6 9 21	21 32 28	29 8 1	29 47.2	26 26.9	3 25.0	24 28.9	6 28.6	27 0.8	0 25.2	10 21.6	22 44.0

LONGITUDE OCTOBER 1905

Day	Sid.Time	☉	0 hr ☽	Noon ☽	True ☊	☿	♀	♂	♃	♄	♅	♆	♇
1 Su	0 36 13	7♎ 8 22	6♏41 54	14♏12 54	29♌41.7	28♍15.0	4♍37.6	25♐ 9.8	6♊27.6	26♒57.9	0♑26.2	10♋22.1	22♊43.9
2 M	0 40 10	8 7 26	21 39 58	29 2 10	29R 36.2	0♎ 3.2	5 50.2	25 50.9	6R 26.5	26R 55.0	0 27.4	10 22.5	22R 43.7
3 Tu	0 44 6	9 6 31	6♐18 48	13♐29 20	29 31.4	1 51.4	7 2.9	26 32.1	6 25.1	26 52.3	0 28.5	10 22.9	22 43.5
4 W	0 48 3	10 5 38	20 33 26	27 30 58	29 28.1	3 39.2	8 15.7	27 13.4	6 23.5	26 49.6	0 29.7	10 23.3	22 43.3
5 Th	0 51 59	11 4 47	4♑21 56	11♑ 6 30	29D 26.4	5 26.8	9 28.5	27 54.8	6 21.8	26 47.0	0 31.0	10 23.6	22 43.0
6 F	0 55 56	12 3 57	17 44 57	24 17 38	29 26.3	7 13.9	10 41.4	28 36.4	6 19.8	26 44.5	0 32.3	10 23.9	22 42.8
7 Sa	0 59 53	13 3 10	0♒44 58	7♒ 7 24	29 27.4	9 0.4	11 54.4	29 18.0	6 17.7	26 42.0	0 33.7	10 24.1	22 42.5
8 Su	1 3 49	14 2 24	13 25 27	19 39 33	29 28.8	10 46.4	13 7.4	29 59.8	6 15.3	26 39.7	0 35.1	10 24.4	22 42.2
9 M	1 7 46	15 1 40	25 50 12	1♓57 50	29R 29.8	12 31.8	14 20.5	0♑41.7	6 12.8	26 37.5	0 36.5	10 24.6	22 41.8
10 Tu	1 11 42	16 0 57	8♓ 2 54	14 5 46	29 29.4	14 16.5	15 33.7	1 23.7	6 10.0	26 35.3	0 38.0	10 24.7	22 41.5
11 W	1 15 39	17 0 17	20 6 49	26 6 21	29 27.1	16 0.6	16 47.0	2 5.9	6 7.1	26 33.2	0 39.6	10 24.9	22 41.1
12 Th	1 19 35	17 59 38	2♈ 4 40	8♈ 2 1	29 22.6	17 43.9	18 0.3	2 48.1	6 3.9	26 31.2	0 41.2	10 24.9	22 40.7
13 F	1 23 32	18 59 1	13 58 40	19 54 48	29 15.7	19 26.6	19 13.7	3 30.4	6 0.6	26 29.4	0 42.8	10 25.0	22 40.3
14 Sa	1 27 28	19 58 27	25 50 37	1♉46 20	29 7.0	21 8.6	20 27.1	4 12.9	5 57.1	26 27.6	0 44.5	10R 25.0	22 39.8
15 Su	1 31 25	20 57 54	7♉42 7	13 38 11	28 56.9	22 49.9	21 40.6	4 55.4	5 53.4	26 25.9	0 46.3	10 25.0	22 39.4
16 M	1 35 21	21 57 24	19 34 45	25 32 3	28 46.5	24 30.5	22 54.2	5 38.1	5 49.5	26 24.3	0 48.0	10 25.0	22 38.9
17 Tu	1 39 18	22 56 56	1♊30 20	7♊29 55	28 36.5	26 10.4	24 7.8	6 20.8	5 45.4	26 22.8	0 49.9	10 24.9	22 38.4
18 W	1 43 15	23 56 30	13 31 7	19 34 19	28 28.0	27 49.7	25 21.5	7 3.7	5 41.2	26 21.4	0 51.7	10 24.8	22 37.9
19 Th	1 47 11	24 56 6	25 39 54	1♋48 20	28 21.6	29 28.3	26 35.3	7 46.6	5 36.7	26 20.0	0 53.7	10 24.6	22 37.4
20 F	1 51 8	25 55 44	8♋ 0 4	14 15 37	28 17.6	1♏ 6.3	27 49.1	8 29.6	5 32.1	26 18.8	0 55.6	10 24.5	22 36.8
21 Sa	1 55 4	26 55 25	20 35 30	27 0 15	28D 15.8	2 43.6	29 2.9	9 12.8	5 27.3	26 17.7	0 57.6	10 24.3	22 36.2
22 Su	1 59 1	27 55 8	3♌30 22	10♌ 6 21	28 15.7	4 20.4	0♎16.9	9 56.0	5 22.4	26 16.7	0 59.7	10 24.0	22 35.6
23 M	2 2 57	28 54 53	16 48 38	23 37 35	28R 16.4	5 56.6	1 30.8	10 39.3	5 17.2	26 15.8	1 1.8	10 23.7	22 35.0
24 Tu	2 6 54	29 54 41	0♍33 27	7♍36 23	28 16.7	7 32.3	2 44.9	11 22.7	5 11.9	26 15.0	1 3.9	10 23.4	22 34.4
25 W	2 10 50	0♏54 31	14 46 19	22 3 2	28 15.6	9 7.3	3 59.0	12 6.2	5 6.5	26 14.3	1 6.1	10 23.1	22 33.7
26 Th	2 14 47	1 54 23	29 26 5	6♎54 46	28 12.2	10 41.9	5 13.1	12 49.8	5 0.8	26 13.6	1 8.3	10 22.7	22 33.1
27 F	2 18 44	2 54 17	14♎28 11	22 5 14	28 6.1	12 15.9	6 27.3	13 33.5	4 55.0	26 13.1	1 10.6	10 22.3	22 32.4
28 Sa	2 22 40	3 54 13	29 44 37	7♏24 55	27 57.7	13 49.5	7 41.5	14 17.2	4 49.1	26 12.7	1 12.9	10 21.9	22 31.7
29 Su	2 26 37	4 54 11	15♏ 4 39	22 42 22	27 47.7	15 22.5	8 55.8	15 1.1	4 43.0	26 12.4	1 15.2	10 21.4	22 30.9
30 M	2 30 33	5 54 11	0♐16 40	7♐46 19	27 37.4	16 55.1	10 10.1	15 45.0	4 36.8	26 12.2	1 17.6	10 20.9	22 30.2
31 Tu	2 34 30	6 54 13	15 10 17	22 27 43	27 28.0	18 27.2	11 24.5	16 29.0	4 30.4	26D 12.1	1 20.0	10 20.3	22 29.4

Astro Data	Planet Ingress	Last Aspect	☽ Ingress	Last Aspect	☽ Ingress	☽ Phases & Eclipses
Dy Hr Mn	Dy Hr Mn	Dy Hr Mn	Dy Hr Mn	Dy Hr Mn	Dy Hr Mn	Dy Hr Mn
☽0S 1 15:30	♀ ♌ 1 20:16	1 2:07 ♀ ⚹	♎ 1 3:32	2 8:31 ♄ □	♐ 2 13:35	6 4:09 ☽ 12♐53
☿ D 8 15:01	☊ ♌ 18 3:28	3 2:06 ♄ △	♏ 3 4:12	4 12:06 ♂ ☌	♑ 4 16:20	13 18:10 ○ 20♓16
♅ D 9 15:17	☉ ♎ 23 17:30	5 3:38 ♄ □	♐ 5 6:04	5 12:54 ☉ □	♒ 6 22:36	21 22:13 ☽ 28♊14
☽0N 15 4:17	♀ ♍ 27 4:02	7 7:23 ♄ ⚹	♑ 7 10:13	9 1:32 ♄ ☌	♓ 9 8:09	28 21:59 ● 5♎05
♇ R 23 7:12		8 13:41 ☉ △	♒ 9 17:02	11 5:08 ♇ □	♈ 11 19:49	
♃ R 25 19:20	☿ ♎ 1 23:17	11 22:37 ♄ ☌	♓ 12 2:20	14 1:15 ♄ ⚹	♉ 14 8:25	5 12:54 ☽ 11♑37
☽0S 29 1:31	♂ ♑ 8 0:06	13 23:04 ♇ □	♈ 14 13:35	16 13:43 ♄ □	♊ 16 20:59	13 11:02 ○ 19♈26
	☿ ♏ 19 7:45	16 21:33 ♄ ⚹	♉ 17 2:05	19 2:01 ♀ □	♋ 19 8:29	21 12:50 ☽ 27♋27
☿0S 4 3:04	♀ ♎ 21 18:32	19 9:52 ♄ □	♊ 19 14:40	21 17:27 ♀ ⚹	♌ 21 17:33	28 6:58 ● 4♏12
☽0N 12 10:31	☉ ♏ 24 2:08	21 22:13 ☉ □	♋ 22 1:37	23 22:48 ☉ ⚹	♍ 23 23:03	
♆ R 14 5:21		23 5:12 ♄ ⚹	♌ 24 9:17	25 12:49 ♇ □	♎ 26 0:55	
♀0S 24 17:12		26 11:44 ♀ ☌	♍ 26 13:07	27 18:28 ♄ △	♏ 28 0:24	
☽0S 26 12:49		28 3:03 ♂ □	♎ 28 13:54	29 17:32 ♄ □	♐ 29 23:33	
♄ D 31 9:03		30 8:37 ♄ △	♏ 30 13:22			

Astro Data

1 SEPTEMBER 1905
Julian Day # 2070
Delta T 4.9 sec
SVP 06♓34'45"
Obliquity 23°26'58"
⚷ Chiron 2♒11.2R
☽ Mean ☊ 29♌35.6

1 OCTOBER 1905
Julian Day # 2100
Delta T 5.0 sec
SVP 06♓34'43"
Obliquity 23°26'58"
⚷ Chiron 1♒22.9R
☽ Mean ☊ 28♌00.2

NOVEMBER 1905 LONGITUDE

Day	Sid.Time	☉	0 hr ☽	Noon ☽	True ☊	☿	♀	♂	♃	♄	♅	♆	♇
1 W	2 38 26	7♏54 16	29♐38 4	6♑40 58	27♌20.6	19♏58.9	12♎38.9	17♑13.1	4♊23.9	26♒12.2	1♑22.5	10♋19.8	22♊28.7
2 Th	2 42 23	8 54 21	13♑36 19	20 24 11	27R 15.7	21 30.1	13 53.3	17 57.2	4R 17.2	26 12.3	1 25.0	10R 19.2	22R 27.9
3 F	2 46 19	9 54 28	27 4 49	3♒38 35	27 13.2	23 0.8	15 7.8	18 41.4	4 10.4	26 12.5	1 27.5	10 18.5	22 27.1
4 Sa	2 50 16	10 54 36	10♒ 5 58	16 27 32	27D 12.5	24 31.1	16 22.3	19 25.7	4 3.6	26 12.8	1 30.1	10 17.9	22 26.3
5 Su	2 54 13	11 54 46	22 43 53	28 55 38	27R 12.7	26 1.0	17 36.9	20 10.1	3 56.5	26 13.2	1 32.7	10 17.2	22 25.4
6 M	2 58 9	12 54 57	5♓ 3 24	11♓ 7 49	27 12.6	27 30.4	18 51.4	20 54.5	3 49.4	26 13.8	1 35.4	10 16.4	22 24.6
7 Tu	3 2 6	13 55 10	17 9 29	23 8 56	27 10.9	28 59.3	20 6.1	21 39.0	3 42.2	26 14.4	1 38.1	10 15.7	22 23.7
8 W	3 6 2	14 55 24	29 6 41	5♈ 3 14	27 6.9	0♐27.8	21 20.7	22 23.6	3 34.8	26 15.1	1 40.8	10 14.9	22 22.8
9 Th	3 9 59	15 55 40	10♈59 0	16 54 21	26 59.9	1 55.7	22 35.4	23 8.2	3 27.4	26 16.0	1 43.5	10 14.1	22 21.9
10 F	3 13 55	16 55 57	22 49 37	28 45 5	26 50.0	3 23.2	23 50.1	23 52.8	3 19.9	26 16.9	1 46.3	10 13.2	22 21.0
11 Sa	3 17 52	17 56 16	4♉41 0	10♉37 33	26 37.6	4 50.1	25 4.8	24 37.5	3 12.3	26 18.0	1 49.1	10 12.3	22 20.1
12 Su	3 21 48	18 56 37	16 34 56	22 33 17	26 23.4	6 16.4	26 19.6	25 22.3	3 4.6	26 19.1	1 52.0	10 11.4	22 19.1
13 M	3 25 45	19 56 59	28 32 45	4♊33 27	26 8.6	7 42.1	27 34.4	26 7.1	2 56.8	26 20.4	1 54.9	10 10.5	22 18.2
14 Tu	3 29 42	20 57 23	10♊35 32	16 39 8	25 54.4	9 7.1	28 49.3	26 52.0	2 49.0	26 21.8	1 57.8	10 9.5	22 17.2
15 W	3 33 38	21 57 49	22 44 27	28 51 39	25 42.0	10 31.4	0♏ 4.2	27 36.9	2 41.1	26 23.2	2 0.7	10 8.5	22 16.2
16 Th	3 37 35	22 58 17	5♋ 0 59	11♋12 42	25 32.1	11 54.9	1 19.1	28 21.9	2 33.2	26 24.8	2 3.7	10 7.5	22 15.2
17 F	3 41 31	23 58 46	17 27 8	23 44 37	25 25.3	13 17.5	2 34.0	29 6.9	2 25.2	26 26.4	2 6.7	10 6.5	22 14.2
18 Sa	3 45 28	24 59 17	0♌ 5 32	6♌30 18	25 21.4	14 39.0	3 48.9	29 52.0	2 17.1	26 28.2	2 9.7	10 5.4	22 13.2
19 Su	3 49 24	25 59 50	12 59 21	19 33 6	25 19.9	15 59.4	5 3.9	0♒37.1	2 9.1	26 30.1	2 12.8	10 4.3	22 12.2
20 M	3 53 21	27 0 25	26 12 0	2♍56 26	25 19.7	17 18.6	6 19.0	1 22.3	2 0.9	26 32.0	2 15.9	10 3.2	22 11.1
21 Tu	3 57 17	28 1 1	9♍46 44	16 43 9	25 19.5	18 36.3	7 34.0	2 7.5	1 52.8	26 34.1	2 19.0	10 2.0	22 10.1
22 W	4 1 14	29 1 39	23 45 49	0♎54 44	25 18.0	19 52.4	8 49.1	2 52.8	1 44.6	26 36.3	2 22.1	10 0.9	22 9.0
23 Th	4 5 11	0♐ 2 19	8♎ 9 42	15 30 21	25 14.1	21 6.6	10 4.1	3 38.1	1 36.4	26 38.5	2 25.3	9 59.7	22 8.0
24 F	4 9 7	1 3 1	22 56 3	0♏26 2	25 7.4	22 18.7	11 19.3	4 23.4	1 28.2	26 40.9	2 28.5	9 58.4	22 6.9
25 Sa	4 13 4	2 3 44	7♏59 15	15 34 33	24 58.1	23 28.4	12 34.4	5 8.8	1 20.0	26 43.4	2 31.7	9 57.2	22 5.8
26 Su	4 17 0	3 4 28	23 10 35	0♐45 59	24 46.9	24 35.3	13 49.5	5 54.2	1 11.9	26 45.9	2 35.0	9 55.9	22 4.7
27 M	4 20 57	4 5 14	8♐19 22	15 49 24	24 35.2	25 39.1	15 4.7	6 39.7	1 3.7	26 48.6	2 38.2	9 54.6	22 3.6
28 Tu	4 24 53	5 6 2	23 14 54	0♑34 51	24 24.2	26 39.3	16 19.9	7 25.2	0 55.5	26 51.3	2 41.5	9 53.3	22 2.5
29 W	4 28 50	6 6 50	7♑48 25	14 55 1	24 15.2	27 35.4	17 35.1	8 10.7	0 47.4	26 54.2	2 44.8	9 52.0	22 1.4
30 Th	4 32 46	7 7 40	21 54 18	28 46 6	24 8.9	28 26.7	18 50.3	8 56.3	0 39.3	26 57.1	2 48.2	9 50.6	22 0.3

DECEMBER 1905 LONGITUDE

Day	Sid.Time	☉	0 hr ☽	Noon ☽	True ☊	☿	♀	♂	♃	♄	♅	♆	♇
1 F	4 36 43	8♐ 8 30	5♒30 30	12♒ 7 43	24♌ 5.4	29♐12.8	20♏ 5.6	9♒41.9	0♊31.2	27♒ 0.2	2♑51.5	9♋49.3	21♊59.1
2 Sa	4 40 40	9 9 22	18 38 6	25 2 9	24D 4.1	29 52.8	21 20.8	10 27.5	0R 23.2	27 3.3	2 54.9	9R 47.9	21R 58.0
3 Su	4 44 36	10 10 14	1♓20 25	7♓33 31	24R 4.1	0♑26.1	22 36.1	11 13.2	0 15.3	27 6.5	2 58.3	9 46.4	21 56.9
4 M	4 48 33	11 11 7	13 42 6	19 46 52	24 4.3	0 51.7	23 51.3	11 58.9	0 7.4	27 9.9	3 1.7	9 45.0	21 55.7
5 Tu	4 52 29	12 12 1	25 48 26	1♈47 31	24 3.3	1 8.9	25 6.6	12 44.6	29♉59.5	27 13.3	3 5.1	9 43.6	21 54.6
6 W	4 56 26	13 12 55	7♈44 42	13 40 36	24 0.4	1R 16.7	26 21.9	13 30.3	29 51.7	27 16.8	3 8.5	9 42.1	21 53.4
7 Th	5 0 22	14 13 50	19 35 47	25 30 44	23 54.9	1 14.5	27 37.2	14 16.0	29 44.0	27 20.4	3 12.0	9 40.6	21 52.2
8 F	5 4 19	15 14 46	1♉25 57	7♉21 50	23 46.6	1 1.6	28 52.5	15 1.8	29 36.4	27 24.0	3 15.4	9 39.1	21 51.1
9 Sa	5 8 15	16 15 43	13 18 43	19 16 56	23 35.9	0 37.3	0♐ 7.8	15 47.6	29 28.9	27 27.8	3 18.9	9 37.6	21 49.9
10 Su	5 12 12	17 16 41	25 16 42	1♊18 15	23 23.6	0 1.7	1 23.1	16 33.4	29 21.5	27 31.6	3 22.4	9 36.0	21 48.7
11 M	5 16 9	18 17 39	7♊21 44	13 27 16	23 10.6	29♐14.7	2 38.4	17 19.2	29 14.1	27 35.6	3 25.9	9 34.5	21 47.6
12 Tu	5 20 5	19 18 39	19 34 57	25 44 52	22 58.1	28 17.2	3 53.8	18 5.0	29 6.9	27 39.6	3 29.4	9 32.9	21 46.4
13 W	5 24 2	20 19 39	1♋57 2	8♋11 33	22 47.2	27 10.2	5 9.1	18 50.8	28 59.8	27 43.7	3 33.0	9 31.4	21 45.2
14 Th	5 27 58	21 20 39	14 28 28	20 47 51	22 38.6	25 55.7	6 24.5	19 36.7	28 52.8	27 47.9	3 36.5	9 29.8	21 44.1
15 F	5 31 55	22 21 41	27 9 48	3♌34 28	22 32.8	24 35.7	7 39.9	20 22.5	28 45.9	27 52.2	3 40.1	9 28.2	21 42.9
16 Sa	5 35 51	23 22 44	10♌ 1 58	16 32 31	22D 29.8	23 13.0	8 55.3	21 8.4	28 39.1	27 56.5	3 43.6	9 26.6	21 41.7
17 Su	5 39 48	24 23 47	23 6 18	29 43 34	22 29.0	21 50.4	10 10.6	21 54.3	28 32.4	28 1.0	3 47.2	9 24.9	21 40.5
18 M	5 43 44	25 24 51	6♍24 32	13♍ 9 27	22 29.6	20 30.5	11 26.0	22 40.2	28 25.9	28 5.5	3 50.8	9 23.3	21 39.4
19 Tu	5 47 41	26 25 56	19 58 32	26 51 56	22R 30.4	19 16.1	12 41.4	23 26.1	28 19.5	28 10.1	3 54.4	9 21.7	21 38.2
20 W	5 51 38	27 27 2	3♎49 49	10♎52 10	22 30.4	18 9.0	13 56.9	24 12.0	28 13.3	28 14.7	3 57.9	9 20.0	21 37.0
21 Th	5 55 34	28 28 9	17 58 55	25 9 54	22 28.6	17 11.1	15 12.3	24 57.9	28 7.2	28 19.5	4 1.5	9 18.4	21 35.9
22 F	5 59 31	29 29 16	2♏24 44	9♏42 57	22 24.6	16 23.3	16 27.7	25 43.8	28 1.3	28 24.3	4 5.1	9 16.7	21 34.7
23 Sa	6 3 27	0♑30 25	17 3 55	24 26 50	22 18.4	15 46.2	17 43.1	26 29.7	27 55.5	28 29.2	4 8.7	9 15.0	21 33.5
24 Su	6 7 24	1 31 34	1♐50 49	9♐14 51	22 10.7	15 19.9	18 58.6	27 15.7	27 49.8	28 34.2	4 12.3	9 13.3	21 32.4
25 M	6 11 20	2 32 43	16 37 54	23 58 56	22 2.3	15 4.3	20 14.0	28 1.6	27 44.4	28 39.2	4 16.0	9 11.7	21 31.2
26 Tu	6 15 17	3 33 53	1♑16 55	8♑30 56	21 54.4	14D 58.8	21 29.5	28 47.6	27 39.1	28 44.3	4 19.6	9 10.0	21 30.1
27 W	6 19 14	4 35 3	15 40 11	22 44 0	21 48.0	15 2.8	22 44.9	29 33.5	27 33.9	28 49.5	4 23.2	9 8.3	21 29.0
28 Th	6 23 10	5 36 14	29 41 52	6♒33 28	21 43.5	15 15.6	24 0.4	0♓19.5	27 29.0	28 54.8	4 26.8	9 6.6	21 27.8
29 F	6 27 7	6 37 24	13♒18 38	19 57 22	21D 41.3	15 36.5	25 15.8	1 5.4	27 24.2	29 0.1	4 30.4	9 4.9	21 26.7
30 Sa	6 31 3	7 38 34	26 29 48	2♓56 12	21 41.1	16 4.6	26 31.3	1 51.4	27 19.6	29 5.5	4 34.0	9 3.2	21 25.6
31 Su	6 35 0	8 39 45	9♓16 58	15 32 31	21 42.2	16 39.4	27 46.7	2 37.3	27 15.2	29 10.9	4 37.6	9 1.5	21 24.4

Astro Data	Planet Ingress	Last Aspect	☽ Ingress	Last Aspect	☽ Ingress	☽ Phases & Eclipses	Astro Data
Dy Hr Mn	Dy Hr Mn	Dy Hr Mn	Dy Hr Mn	Dy Hr Mn	Dy Hr Mn	Dy Hr Mn	1 NOVEMBER 1905
☽0N 8 17:05	☿ ♐ 7 16:27	31 18:14 ♄ ✶	♑ 1 0:37	2 15:54 ♄ ☌	♓ 2 21:26	4 1:39 ☽ 10♒59	Julian Day # 2131
♃⚻♅ 18 15:57	♀ ♏ 14 22:40	2 15:44 ☿ ✶	♒ 3 5:19	5 8:18 ♃ ✶	♈ 5 8:24	12 5:11 ○ 19♉10	Delta T 5.1 sec
☽0S 22 23:33	♂ ♒ 18 4:15	5 7:13 ☿ □	♓ 5 14:05	7 15:47 ♄ ✶	♉ 7 21:06	20 1:34 ☽ 27♌04	SVP 06♓34'40"
	☉ ♐ 22 23:05	7 10:28 ♇ □	♈ 8 1:48	10 8:03 ♃ ☌	♊ 10 9:24	26 16:47 ● 3♐47	Obliquity 23°26'58"
☽0N 6 0:50		10 7:01 ♄ ✶	♉ 10 14:32	12 15:48 ♄ △	♋ 12 20:14		⚷ Chiron 1♒36.8
☿ R 6 6:57	☿ ♑ 2 4:46	12 19:35 ♄ □	♊ 13 2:54	15 2:59 ♃ ✶	♌ 15 5:19	3 18:37 ☽ 10♓57	☽ Mean ☊ 26♌21.7
♃□♄ 19 20:51	♃ ♉ 4 22:31	15 7:10 ♄ △	♋ 15 14:14	17 9:47 ♃ □	♍ 17 12:30	11 23:25 ○ 19♊17	
☽0S 20 8:02	♀ ♐ 8 21:31	17 23:33 ♂ ☍	♌ 17 23:50	19 14:25 ♃ △	♎ 19 17:25	19 12:08 ☽ 26♍57	1 DECEMBER 1905
☿ D 26 1:35	☿ ♐ 10 0:57	20 1:34 ☉ □	♍ 20 6:47	21 18:48 ☉ ✶	♏ 21 20:01	26 4:04 ● 3♑44	Julian Day # 2161
	☉ ♑ 22 12:04	22 9:31 ☉ ✶	♎ 22 10:29	23 18:39 ♄ □	♐ 23 21:00		Delta T 5.2 sec
	♂ ♓ 27 13:50	24 6:01 ♄ △	♏ 24 11:19	25 19:47 ♄ ✶	♑ 25 21:53		SVP 06♓34'35"
		26 5:41 ♄ □	♐ 26 10:47	27 20:11 ♃ △	♒ 28 0:31		Obliquity 23°26'57"
		28 5:57 ☿ ☌	♑ 28 11:03	30 4:51 ♄ ☌	♓ 30 6:30		⚷ Chiron 2♒51.3
		29 18:11 ♀ ✶	♒ 30 14:11				☽ Mean ☊ 24♌46.4

LONGITUDE JANUARY 1906

Day	Sid.Time	☉	0 hr ☽	Noon ☽	True ☊	☿	♀	♂	♃	♄	♅	♆	♇
1 M	6 38 56	9♑40 55	21♓43 26	27♓50 15	21♌43.8	17♐20.0	29♐ 2.2	3♓23.2	27♉11.0	29♒16.5	4♑41.2	8♋59.8	21♊23.3
2 Tu	6 42 53	10 42 5	3♈53 37	9♈54 8	21R 45.0	18 5.8	0♑17.6	4 9.1	27R 6.9	29 22.0	4 44.8	8R 58.1	21R 22.2
3 W	6 46 49	11 43 14	15 52 29	21 49 16	21 45.1	18 56.3	1 33.1	4 55.1	27 3.1	29 27.7	4 48.4	8 56.4	21 21.1
4 Th	6 50 46	12 44 23	27 45 7	3♉40 40	21 43.7	19 51.0	2 48.5	5 41.0	26 59.4	29 33.4	4 52.0	8 54.7	21 20.0
5 F	6 54 43	13 45 33	9♉36 27	15 33 1	21 40.5	20 49.4	4 3.9	6 26.9	26 55.9	29 39.2	4 55.6	8 53.0	21 19.0
6 Sa	6 58 39	14 46 41	21 30 53	27 30 29	21 35.7	21 51.1	5 19.4	7 12.7	26 52.6	29 45.0	4 59.1	8 51.3	21 17.9
7 Su	7 2 36	15 47 50	3♊32 12	9♊36 24	21 29.7	22 55.7	6 34.8	7 58.6	26 49.6	29 50.9	5 2.7	8 49.6	21 16.8
8 M	7 6 32	16 48 58	15 43 21	21 53 18	21 23.1	24 2.9	7 50.2	8 44.5	26 46.7	29 56.8	5 6.3	8 47.9	21 15.8
9 Tu	7 10 29	17 50 5	28 6 24	4♋22 47	21 16.7	25 12.5	9 5.7	9 30.3	26 44.0	0♓ 2.8	5 9.8	8 46.3	21 14.7
10 W	7 14 25	18 51 13	10♋42 31	17 5 36	21 11.2	26 24.2	10 21.1	10 16.1	26 41.5	0 8.9	5 13.4	8 44.6	21 13.7
11 Th	7 18 22	19 52 20	23 32 2	0♌ 1 44	21 7.0	27 37.8	11 36.5	11 1.9	26 39.3	0 15.0	5 16.9	8 42.9	21 12.7
12 F	7 22 18	20 53 27	6♌34 40	13 10 42	21 4.5	28 53.1	12 51.9	11 47.7	26 37.2	0 21.1	5 20.4	8 41.3	21 11.7
13 Sa	7 26 15	21 54 33	19 49 45	26 31 43	21D 3.6	0♑ 9.9	14 7.4	12 33.5	26 35.3	0 27.3	5 23.9	8 39.6	21 10.7
14 Su	7 30 12	22 55 39	3♍16 29	10♍ 3 58	21 4.1	1 28.2	15 22.8	13 19.3	26 33.6	0 33.6	5 27.4	8 38.0	21 9.7
15 M	7 34 8	23 56 45	16 54 4	23 46 42	21 5.4	2 47.7	16 38.2	14 5.0	26 32.2	0 39.9	5 30.9	8 36.4	21 8.8
16 Tu	7 38 5	24 57 51	0♎41 48	7♎39 16	21 7.1	4 8.4	17 53.6	14 50.7	26 30.9	0 46.2	5 34.3	8 34.7	21 7.8
17 W	7 42 1	25 58 56	14 39 0	21 40 53	21R 8.3	5 30.3	19 9.0	15 36.4	26 29.9	0 52.6	5 37.8	8 33.1	21 6.9
18 Th	7 45 58	27 0 1	28 44 45	5♏50 25	21 8.7	6 53.1	20 24.4	16 22.1	26 29.0	0 59.1	5 41.2	8 31.5	21 5.9
19 F	7 49 54	28 1 6	12♏57 36	20 6 2	21 8.0	8 16.9	21 39.9	17 7.8	26 28.4	1 5.6	5 44.6	8 29.9	21 5.0
20 Sa	7 53 51	29 2 11	27 15 18	4♐25 1	21 6.2	9 41.7	22 55.3	17 53.4	26 27.9	1 12.1	5 48.0	8 28.4	21 4.1
21 Su	7 57 47	0♒ 3 15	11♐34 40	18 43 44	21 3.6	11 7.3	24 10.7	18 39.0	26D 27.7	1 18.7	5 51.4	8 26.8	21 3.2
22 M	8 1 44	1 4 19	25 51 38	2♑57 48	21 0.7	12 33.7	25 26.1	19 24.6	26 27.7	1 25.3	5 54.8	8 25.2	21 2.4
23 Tu	8 5 41	2 5 22	10♑ 1 37	17 2 33	20 57.9	14 0.9	26 41.5	20 10.2	26 27.9	1 32.0	5 58.1	8 23.7	21 1.5
24 W	8 9 37	3 6 25	24 0 4	0♒53 41	20 55.7	15 28.8	27 56.9	20 55.8	26 28.3	1 38.7	6 1.4	8 22.2	21 0.7
25 Th	8 13 34	4 7 27	7♒43 1	14 27 46	20D 54.3	16 57.5	29 12.3	21 41.3	26 28.9	1 45.4	6 4.7	8 20.7	20 59.8
26 F	8 17 30	5 8 28	21 7 41	27 42 40	20 53.9	18 26.9	0♒27.6	22 26.9	26 29.7	1 52.2	6 8.0	8 19.2	20 59.0
27 Sa	8 21 27	6 9 28	4♓12 42	10♓37 50	20 54.3	19 57.0	1 43.0	23 12.4	26 30.7	1 59.0	6 11.3	8 17.7	20 58.2
28 Su	8 25 23	7 10 27	16 58 15	23 14 11	20 55.3	21 27.8	2 58.4	23 57.8	26 31.9	2 5.8	6 14.5	8 16.3	20 57.5
29 M	8 29 20	8 11 25	29 25 58	5♈33 59	20 56.5	22 59.3	4 13.7	24 43.3	26 33.3	2 12.7	6 17.7	8 14.8	20 56.7
30 Tu	8 33 16	9 12 21	11♈38 40	17 40 32	20 57.7	24 31.5	5 29.1	25 28.7	26 34.9	2 19.6	6 20.9	8 13.4	20 56.0
31 W	8 37 13	10 13 17	23 40 6	29 37 56	20 58.6	26 4.4	6 44.4	26 14.0	26 36.7	2 26.6	6 24.1	8 12.0	20 55.2

LONGITUDE FEBRUARY 1906

Day	Sid.Time	☉	0 hr ☽	Noon ☽	True ☊	☿	♀	♂	♃	♄	♅	♆	♇
1 Th	8 41 10	11♒14 11	5♉34 37	11♉30 44	20♌59.1	27♑38.0	7♒59.7	26♓59.4	26♉38.8	2♓33.5	6♑27.2	8♋10.7	20♊54.5
2 F	8 45 6	12 15 4	17 26 55	23 23 43	20R 59.1	29 12.3	9 15.1	27 44.7	26 41.0	2 40.5	6 30.3	8R 9.3	20R 53.9
3 Sa	8 49 3	13 15 55	29 21 45	5♊21 35	20 58.7	0♒47.3	10 30.4	28 30.0	26 43.4	2 47.5	6 33.4	8 8.0	20 53.2
4 Su	8 52 59	14 16 45	11♊23 45	17 28 44	20 58.1	2 23.1	11 45.7	29 15.3	26 46.0	2 54.6	6 36.4	8 6.7	20 52.5
5 M	8 56 56	15 17 34	23 37 1	29 49 1	20 57.3	3 59.5	13 0.9	0♈ 0.5	26 48.9	3 1.6	6 39.4	8 5.4	20 51.9
6 Tu	9 0 52	16 18 21	6♋ 5 3	12♋25 26	20 56.6	5 36.8	14 16.2	0 45.7	26 51.9	3 8.7	6 42.4	8 4.1	20 51.3
7 W	9 4 49	17 19 7	18 50 22	25 19 58	20 56.1	7 14.7	15 31.5	1 30.8	26 55.1	3 15.8	6 45.4	8 2.9	20 50.7
8 Th	9 8 45	18 19 52	1♌54 18	8♌33 19	20 55.8	8 53.5	16 46.7	2 15.9	26 58.5	3 23.0	6 48.3	8 1.6	20 50.1
9 F	9 12 42	19 20 35	15 16 55	22 4 52	20D 55.7	10 33.0	18 2.0	3 1.0	27 2.0	3 30.1	6 51.2	8 0.4	20 49.6
10 Sa	9 16 39	20 21 17	28 56 55	5♍52 42	20R 55.7	12 13.4	19 17.2	3 46.0	27 5.8	3 37.3	6 54.1	7 59.3	20 49.1
11 Su	9 20 35	21 21 57	12♍51 49	19 53 48	20 55.7	13 54.5	20 32.4	4 31.1	27 9.8	3 44.5	6 56.9	7 58.1	20 48.6
12 M	9 24 32	22 22 36	26 58 11	4♎ 4 27	20 55.6	15 36.5	21 47.6	5 16.0	27 13.9	3 51.7	6 59.7	7 57.0	20 48.1
13 Tu	9 28 28	23 23 14	11♎12 5	18 20 37	20 55.4	17 19.4	23 2.8	6 1.0	27 18.2	3 58.9	7 2.5	7 55.9	20 47.6
14 W	9 32 25	24 23 51	25 29 33	2♏38 26	20 55.1	19 3.1	24 18.0	6 45.9	27 22.7	4 6.1	7 5.2	7 54.8	20 47.1
15 Th	9 36 21	25 24 26	9♏46 53	16 54 29	20 54.7	20 47.7	25 33.2	7 30.7	27 27.4	4 13.4	7 7.9	7 53.8	20 46.7
16 F	9 40 18	26 25 1	24 0 57	1♐ 5 57	20D 54.6	22 33.1	26 48.3	8 15.5	27 32.3	4 20.6	7 10.6	7 52.8	20 46.3
17 Sa	9 44 14	27 25 34	8♐ 9 16	15 10 39	20 54.7	24 19.5	28 3.5	9 0.3	27 37.3	4 27.9	7 13.2	7 51.8	20 45.9
18 Su	9 48 11	28 26 6	22 9 55	29 6 53	20 55.1	26 6.7	29 18.6	9 45.1	27 42.5	4 35.2	7 15.8	7 50.8	20 45.6
19 M	9 52 8	29 26 37	6♑ 1 23	12♑53 16	20 55.8	27 54.9	0♓33.8	10 29.8	27 47.9	4 42.5	7 18.4	7 49.9	20 45.2
20 Tu	9 56 4	0♓27 7	19 42 24	26 28 38	20 56.7	29 43.9	1 48.9	11 14.5	27 53.5	4 49.8	7 20.9	7 49.0	20 44.9
21 W	10 0 1	1 27 35	3♒11 49	9♒51 51	20 57.5	1♓33.8	3 4.0	11 59.2	27 59.2	4 57.1	7 23.4	7 48.1	20 44.6
22 Th	10 3 57	2 28 1	16 28 37	23 2 0	20R 58.0	3 24.5	4 19.1	12 43.8	28 5.1	5 4.4	7 25.8	7 47.2	20 44.3
23 F	10 7 54	3 28 26	29 31 57	5♓58 24	20 57.8	5 16.0	5 34.2	13 28.4	28 11.2	5 11.7	7 28.2	7 46.4	20 44.1
24 Sa	10 11 50	4 28 50	12♓21 21	18 40 48	20 57.0	7 8.3	6 49.3	14 12.9	28 17.4	5 19.0	7 30.6	7 45.6	20 43.8
25 Su	10 15 47	5 29 11	24 56 50	1♈ 9 32	20 55.4	9 1.2	8 4.3	14 57.4	28 23.8	5 26.3	7 32.9	7 44.9	20 43.6
26 M	10 19 43	6 29 31	7♈19 5	13 25 42	20 53.6	10 54.8	9 19.4	15 41.9	28 30.3	5 33.6	7 35.2	7 44.2	20 43.4
27 Tu	10 23 40	7 29 49	19 29 37	25 31 10	20 50.6	12 49.0	10 34.4	16 26.3	28 37.0	5 40.9	7 37.4	7 43.5	20 43.2
28 W	10 27 36	8 30 5	1♉30 42	7♉28 38	20 47.9	14 43.5	11 49.4	17 10.7	28 43.9	5 48.2	7 39.6	7 42.8	20 43.1

Astro Data	Planet Ingress	Last Aspect	☽ Ingress	Last Aspect	☽ Ingress	☽ Phases & Eclipses	Astro Data
Dy Hr Mn	Dy Hr Mn	Dy Hr Mn	Dy Hr Mn	Dy Hr Mn	Dy Hr Mn	Dy Hr Mn	1 JANUARY 1906
☽0N 2 9:47	♀ ♑ 1 18:23	1 16:02 ♀ □	♈ 1 16:16	2 22:09 ♂ ✱	♊ 3 1:17	2 14:52 ☽ 11♈20	Julian Day # 2192
☽0S 16 14:21	♄ ♓ 8 12:47	4 3:41 ♄ ✱	♉ 4 4:33	4 18:38 ♇ ☌	♋ 5 12:21	10 16:36 ○ 19♋34	Delta T 5.4 sec
♃ D 21 14:25	☿ ♑ 12 20:56	6 16:36 ♄ □	♊ 6 16:58	7 14:58 ♃ ✱	♌ 7 20:32	17 20:49 ☽ 26♎52	SVP 06♓34'30"
☽0N 29 19:02	☉ ♒ 20 22:43	8 17:50 ☿ ☍	♋ 9 3:38	9 20:46 ♃ □	♍ 10 1:50	24 17:09 ● 3♒50	Obliquity 23°26'58"
	♀ ♒ 25 15:12	11 5:46 ♃ ✱	♌ 11 11:57	12 0:27 ♃ △	♎ 12 5:07		⚷ Chiron 4♒55.5
♂0N 6 8:15		13 12:05 ♃ □	♍ 13 18:11	13 22:01 ☉ △	♏ 14 7:34	1 12:31 ☽ 11♉46	☽ Mean ☊ 23♌07.9
☽0S 12 20:33	☿ ♒ 2 12:04	15 16:46 ♃ △	♎ 15 22:48	16 6:00 ♃ ☍	♐ 16 10:08	9 7:45 ○ 19♌40	
☽0N 26 3:30	♂ ♈ 4 23:45	17 20:49 ☉ □	♏ 18 2:07	18 11:40 ☉ ✱	♑ 18 13:32	9 7:47 ☍T 1.625	1 FEBRUARY 1906
	♀ ♓ 18 13:13	20 3:13 ☉ ✱	♐ 20 4:36	20 14:37 ♃ △	♒ 20 18:17	16 4:22 ☽ 26♏36	Julian Day # 2223
	☉ ♓ 19 13:15	21 15:53 ♇ ☍	♑ 22 6:59	22 21:29 ♃ □	♓ 23 0:52	23 7:57 ● 3♓48	Delta T 5.4 sec
	☿ ♓ 20 3:32	24 7:33 ♀ ☌	♒ 24 10:26	25 6:43 ♃ ✱	♈ 25 9:45	23 7:43:13 ● P 0.539	SVP 06♓34'26"
		26 9:47 ♃ □	♓ 26 16:12	27 2:26 ♇ ✱	♉ 27 20:58		Obliquity 23°26'58"
		28 18:24 ♃ ✱	♈ 29 1:06				⚷ Chiron 7♒22.8
		31 5:34 ☿ □	♉ 31 12:44				☽ Mean ☊ 21♌29.4

MARCH 1906 LONGITUDE

Day	Sid.Time	☉	0 hr ☽	Noon ☽	True ☊	☿	♀	♂	♃	♄	♅	♆	♇
1 Th	10 31 33	9♓30 19	13♉25 24	19♉21 31	20♌45.5	16♓38.3	13♓ 4.4	17♈55.0	28♉50.9	5♓55.5	7♑41.8	7♋42.2	20♊43.0
2 F	10 35 30	10 30 31	25 17 30	1♊13 54	20R43.8	18 33.2	14 19.3	18 39.3	28 58.1	6 2.8	7 43.9	7R41.6	20R42.9
3 Sa	10 39 26	11 30 41	7♊11 17	13 10 16	20D42.9	20 27.9	15 34.3	19 23.5	29 5.4	6 10.1	7 46.0	7 41.0	20 42.8
4 Su	10 43 23	12 30 49	19 11 25	25 15 21	20 43.0	22 22.3	16 49.2	20 7.7	29 12.9	6 17.4	7 48.0	7 40.4	20 42.7
5 M	10 47 19	13 30 55	1♋22 40	7♋33 54	20 44.0	24 16.1	18 4.1	20 51.9	29 20.5	6 24.7	7 50.0	7 39.9	20D42.7
6 Tu	10 51 16	14 30 58	13 49 36	20 10 16	20 45.5	26 8.9	19 19.0	21 36.0	29 28.3	6 32.0	7 51.9	7 39.5	20 42.7
7 W	10 55 12	15 31 0	26 36 18	3♌ 8 2	20 47.2	28 0.4	20 33.9	22 20.1	29 36.2	6 39.2	7 53.8	7 39.0	20 42.7
8 Th	10 59 9	16 31 0	9♌45 45	16 29 33	20R48.5	29 50.2	21 48.7	23 4.1	29 44.3	6 46.5	7 55.7	7 38.6	20 42.8
9 F	11 3 5	17 30 57	23 19 29	0♍15 23	20 48.8	1♈37.9	23 3.6	23 48.1	29 52.5	6 53.7	7 57.5	7 38.3	20 42.8
10 Sa	11 7 2	18 30 52	7♍17 1	14 23 56	20 47.9	3 23.0	24 18.4	24 32.1	0♊ 0.8	7 0.9	7 59.2	7 37.9	20 42.9
11 Su	11 10 59	19 30 46	21 35 35	28 51 15	20 45.6	5 5.0	25 33.1	25 15.9	0 9.2	7 8.1	8 0.9	7 37.6	20 43.0
12 M	11 14 55	20 30 37	6♎10 9	13♎31 21	20 41.9	6 43.4	26 47.9	25 59.8	0 17.8	7 15.3	8 2.6	7 37.3	20 43.1
13 Tu	11 18 52	21 30 27	20 53 56	28 16 55	20 37.5	8 17.8	28 2.6	26 43.6	0 26.5	7 22.5	8 4.2	7 37.1	20 43.3
14 W	11 22 48	22 30 14	5♏39 22	13♏ 0 24	20 32.9	9 47.5	29 17.4	27 27.4	0 35.4	7 29.6	8 5.8	7 36.9	20 43.4
15 Th	11 26 45	23 30 0	20 19 13	27 35 8	20 28.7	11 12.2	0♈32.1	28 11.1	0 44.3	7 36.8	8 7.3	7 36.7	20 43.6
16 F	11 30 41	24 29 45	4♐47 36	11♐56 12	20 25.8	12 31.3	1 46.8	28 54.7	0 53.4	7 43.9	8 8.7	7 36.6	20 43.8
17 Sa	11 34 38	25 29 27	19 0 38	26 0 43	20D24.3	13 44.3	3 1.4	29 38.4	1 2.7	7 51.0	8 10.2	7 36.5	20 44.1
18 Su	11 38 34	26 29 9	2♑56 23	9♑47 41	20 24.3	14 51.0	4 16.1	0♉22.0	1 12.0	7 58.1	8 11.5	7 36.4	20 44.3
19 M	11 42 31	27 28 48	16 34 41	23 17 33	20 25.4	15 50.8	5 30.7	1 5.5	1 21.5	8 5.1	8 12.9	7D36.3	20 44.6
20 Tu	11 46 28	28 28 26	29 56 28	6♒31 37	20 26.9	16 43.5	6 45.3	1 49.0	1 31.0	8 12.2	8 14.2	7 36.3	20 44.9
21 W	11 50 24	29 28 1	13♒ 3 14	19 31 30	20R28.1	17 28.7	7 59.9	2 32.5	1 40.7	8 19.2	8 15.4	7 36.4	20 45.2
22 Th	11 54 21	0♈27 36	25 56 38	2♓18 47	20 28.2	18 6.4	9 14.5	3 15.9	1 50.5	8 26.1	8 16.6	7 36.4	20 45.6
23 F	11 58 17	1 27 8	8♓38 8	14 54 48	20 26.5	18 36.3	10 29.1	3 59.2	2 0.5	8 33.1	8 17.7	7 36.5	20 46.0
24 Sa	12 2 14	2 26 38	21 8 55	27 20 35	20 22.8	18 58.4	11 43.6	4 42.6	2 10.5	8 40.0	8 18.8	7 36.7	20 46.3
25 Su	12 6 10	3 26 6	3♈29 56	9♈37 3	20 17.0	19 12.6	12 58.1	5 25.9	2 20.6	8 46.9	8 19.8	7 36.8	20 46.8
26 M	12 10 7	4 25 32	15 42 4	21 45 6	20 9.4	19R19.0	14 12.6	6 9.1	2 30.9	8 53.8	8 20.8	7 37.0	20 47.2
27 Tu	12 14 3	5 24 56	27 46 19	3♉45 55	20 0.8	19 17.7	15 27.0	6 52.3	2 41.2	9 0.6	8 21.7	7 37.2	20 47.6
28 W	12 18 0	6 24 18	9♉44 5	15 41 6	19 51.8	19 9.1	16 41.5	7 35.4	2 51.7	9 7.4	8 22.5	7 37.5	20 48.1
29 Th	12 21 56	7 23 38	21 37 17	27 32 57	19 43.4	18 53.5	17 55.9	8 18.6	3 2.3	9 14.1	8 23.4	7 37.8	20 48.6
30 F	12 25 53	8 22 55	3♊28 31	9♊24 24	19 36.3	18 31.3	19 10.3	9 1.6	3 12.9	9 20.9	8 24.1	7 38.2	20 49.1
31 Sa	12 29 50	9 22 11	15 21 7	21 19 9	19 31.1	18 3.0	20 24.6	9 44.6	3 23.7	9 27.5	8 24.9	7 38.5	20 49.7

APRIL 1906 LONGITUDE

Day	Sid.Time	☉	0 hr ☽	Noon ☽	True ☊	☿	♀	♂	♃	♄	♅	♆	♇
1 Su	12 33 46	10♈21 24	27♊19 5	3♋21 30	19♌28.1	17♈29.5	21♈39.0	10♉27.6	3♊34.5	9♓34.2	8♑25.5	7♋38.9	20♊50.2
2 M	12 37 43	11 20 35	9♋26 59	15 36 12	19D27.0	16R51.3	22 53.3	11 10.5	3 45.5	9 40.8	8 26.1	7 39.4	20 50.8
3 Tu	12 41 39	12 19 43	21 49 44	28 8 13	19 27.4	16 9.3	24 7.6	11 53.4	3 56.5	9 47.4	8 26.7	7 39.8	20 51.4
4 W	12 45 36	13 18 49	4♌32 13	11♌ 2 16	19 28.4	15 24.5	25 21.8	12 36.2	4 7.6	9 53.9	8 27.2	7 40.3	20 52.0
5 Th	12 49 32	14 17 53	17 38 48	24 22 12	19R29.1	14 37.7	26 36.1	13 19.0	4 18.8	10 0.4	8 27.7	7 40.9	20 52.7
6 F	12 53 29	15 16 55	1♍12 41	8♍10 20	19 28.5	13 49.9	27 50.3	14 1.7	4 30.1	10 6.8	8 28.1	7 41.4	20 53.3
7 Sa	12 57 25	16 15 54	15 15 5	22 26 36	19 25.9	13 2.1	29 4.4	14 44.4	4 41.5	10 13.2	8 28.4	7 42.0	20 54.0
8 Su	13 1 22	17 14 51	29 44 25	7♎ 7 49	19 20.9	12 15.1	0♉18.6	15 27.0	4 53.0	10 19.6	8 28.7	7 42.7	20 54.7
9 M	13 5 19	18 13 46	14♎35 53	22 7 32	19 13.7	11 29.9	1 32.7	16 9.6	5 4.5	10 25.9	8 29.0	7 43.3	20 55.4
10 Tu	13 9 15	19 12 38	29 41 33	7♏16 37	19 4.9	10 47.1	2 46.8	16 52.2	5 16.2	10 32.2	8 29.2	7 44.0	20 56.2
11 W	13 13 12	20 11 29	14♏51 24	22 24 37	18 55.7	10 7.5	4 0.8	17 34.7	5 27.9	10 38.4	8 29.3	7 44.8	20 56.9
12 Th	13 17 8	21 10 19	29 55 2	7♐21 38	18 47.2	9 31.6	5 14.9	18 17.1	5 39.6	10 44.6	8 29.4	7 45.5	20 57.7
13 F	13 21 5	22 9 6	14♐43 29	21 59 57	18 40.3	8 60.0	6 28.9	18 59.5	5 51.5	10 50.7	8R29.5	7 46.3	20 58.5
14 Sa	13 25 1	23 7 52	29 10 32	6♑14 58	18 35.7	8 32.9	7 42.9	19 41.9	6 3.4	10 56.8	8 29.5	7 47.1	20 59.3
15 Su	13 28 58	24 6 36	13♑13 9	20 5 8	18D33.5	8 10.7	8 56.8	20 24.2	6 15.4	11 2.8	8 29.4	7 48.0	21 0.2
16 M	13 32 54	25 5 18	26 51 7	3♒31 23	18 33.0	7 53.6	10 10.8	21 6.5	6 27.5	11 8.7	8 29.3	7 48.9	21 1.0
17 Tu	13 36 51	26 3 59	10♒ 6 18	16 36 16	18R33.4	7 41.6	11 24.7	21 48.7	6 39.6	11 14.7	8 29.2	7 49.8	21 1.9
18 W	13 40 48	27 2 38	23 1 43	29 23 5	18 33.5	7D34.8	12 38.6	22 30.9	6 51.9	11 20.5	8 29.0	7 50.8	21 2.8
19 Th	13 44 44	28 1 15	5♓40 49	11♓55 17	18 32.2	7 33.2	13 52.4	23 13.0	7 4.1	11 26.3	8 28.7	7 51.7	21 3.7
20 F	13 48 41	28 59 50	18 6 53	24 15 57	18 28.6	7 36.7	15 6.2	23 55.2	7 16.5	11 32.1	8 28.4	7 52.8	21 4.6
21 Sa	13 52 37	29 58 24	0♈22 48	6♈27 42	18 22.2	7 45.2	16 20.1	24 37.2	7 28.9	11 37.7	8 28.1	7 53.8	21 5.5
22 Su	13 56 34	0♉56 56	12 30 53	18 32 32	18 13.0	7 58.6	17 33.8	25 19.2	7 41.4	11 43.4	8 27.6	7 54.9	21 6.5
23 M	14 0 30	1 55 26	24 32 51	0♉32 0	18 1.3	8 16.7	18 47.6	26 1.2	7 53.9	11 48.9	8 27.2	7 56.0	21 7.4
24 Tu	14 4 27	2 53 55	6♉30 8	12 27 24	17 48.1	8 39.4	20 1.3	26 43.1	8 6.5	11 54.4	8 26.7	7 57.1	21 8.4
25 W	14 8 23	3 52 21	18 23 58	24 20 0	17 34.3	9 6.4	21 15.0	27 25.0	8 19.1	11 59.9	8 26.1	7 58.3	21 9.4
26 Th	14 12 20	4 50 46	0♊15 42	6♊11 19	17 21.2	9 37.7	22 28.7	28 6.9	8 31.8	12 5.3	8 25.5	7 59.4	21 10.4
27 F	14 16 17	5 49 9	12 7 7	18 3 24	17 9.7	10 13.1	23 42.4	28 48.7	8 44.6	12 10.6	8 24.9	8 0.7	21 11.5
28 Sa	14 20 13	6 47 29	24 0 32	29 58 54	17 0.6	10 52.3	24 56.0	29 30.4	8 57.4	12 15.8	8 24.2	8 1.9	21 12.5
29 Su	14 24 10	7 45 48	5♋58 58	12♋ 1 13	16 54.3	11 35.3	26 9.6	0♊12.2	9 10.3	12 21.0	8 23.4	8 3.2	21 13.6
30 M	14 28 6	8 44 5	18 6 12	24 14 27	16 50.8	12 21.8	27 23.1	0 53.8	9 23.2	12 26.1	8 22.6	8 4.5	21 14.6

Astro Data	Dy Hr Mn
♅☍♆	1 3:10
♇ D	5 21:26
☿0N	8 2:17
☽0S	12 4:40
♄△♆	14 23:45
♀0N	16 22:50
♆ D	19 15:17
♄✶♅	20 8:17
☽0N	25 10:42
☿ R	26 8:03
☽0S	8 14:59
♅ R	13 11:54
☿ D	18 19:32
☽0N	21 17:06

Planet Ingress	Dy Hr Mn
☿ ♈	8 2:10
♃ ♊	9 21:48
♀ ♈	14 13:42
♂ ♉	17 11:54
☉ ♈	21 12:53
♀ ♉	7 17:59
☉ ♉	21 0:39
♂ ♊	28 17:00
♃⚺♆	23 4:21
♃⚻♅	25 12:38

Last Aspect Dy Hr Mn		☽ Ingress Dy Hr Mn
2 7:30	♃ ☌	♊ 2 9:31
4 7:29	☿ □	♋ 4 21:19
7 5:35	♃ ✶	♌ 7 6:16
9 11:27	♃ □	♍ 9 11:34
11 7:10	☿ ☍	♎ 11 13:53
13 9:58	♂ ☍	♏ 13 14:48
15 5:38	☉ △	♐ 15 16:01
17 11:57	☉ □	♑ 17 18:54
19 21:08	☉ ✶	♒ 20 0:06
21 14:18	♇ △	♓ 22 7:38
23 23:16	♇ □	♈ 24 17:10
26 10:05	♇ ✶	♉ 27 4:27
27 22:45	♄ ✶	♊ 29 16:58

Last Aspect Dy Hr Mn		☽ Ingress Dy Hr Mn
31 11:21	♀ ✶	♋ 1 5:20
3 4:52	♀ □	♌ 3 15:31
5 17:31	♀ △	♍ 5 21:53
7 9:27	♇ □	♎ 8 0:25
9 10:06	♇ △	♏ 10 0:29
11 4:32	♂ ☍	♐ 12 0:08
13 13:09	☉ △	♑ 14 1:23
15 20:37	☉ □	♒ 16 5:39
18 8:12	☉ ✶	♓ 18 13:10
20 12:00	♂ ✶	♈ 20 23:15
22 17:09	♇ ✶	♉ 23 10:56
25 19:23	♂ ☌	♊ 25 23:28
27 18:21	♇ ☌	♋ 28 12:02
30 20:05	♀ ✶	♌ 30 23:09

☽ Phases & Eclipses Dy Hr Mn	
3 9:28	☽ 11♊54
10 20:17	○ 19♍21
17 11:57	☽ 25♐59
24 23:52	● 3♈26
2 4:02	☽ 11♋31
9 6:12	○ 18♎29
15 20:37	☽ 24♑57
23 16:06	● 2♉35

Astro Data

1 MARCH 1906
Julian Day # 2251
Delta T 5.5 sec
SVP 06♓34'23"
Obliquity 23°26'59"
⚷ Chiron 9♒32.6
☽ Mean ☊ 20♌00.5

1 APRIL 1906
Julian Day # 2282
Delta T 5.6 sec
SVP 06♓34'20"
Obliquity 23°26'59"
⚷ Chiron 11♒28.4
☽ Mean ☊ 18♌21.9

LONGITUDE MAY 1906

Day	Sid.Time	☉	0 hr ☽	Noon ☽	True ☊	☿	♀	♂	♃	♄	♅	♆	♇
1 Tu	14 32 3	9♉42 20	0♌26 34	6♌43 11	16♌49.4	13♈11.8	28♉36.6	1♊35.5	9♊36.1	12♓31.2	8♑21.8	8♋ 5.8	21♊15.7
2 W	14 35 59	10 40 32	13 4 52	19 32 14	16R 49.2	14 5.0	29 50.1	2 17.0	9 49.2	12 36.2	8R 20.9	8 7.2	21 16.8
3 Th	14 39 56	11 38 43	26 5 49	2♍46 7	16 49.1	15 1.4	1♊ 3.6	2 58.6	10 2.2	12 41.1	8 19.9	8 8.5	21 18.0
4 F	14 43 52	12 36 52	9♍33 30	16 28 15	16 47.8	16 0.8	2 17.0	3 40.1	10 15.3	12 45.9	8 18.9	8 9.9	21 19.1
5 Sa	14 47 49	13 34 58	23 30 29	0♎40 7	16 44.5	17 3.1	3 30.4	4 21.5	10 28.4	12 50.7	8 17.9	8 11.4	21 20.2
6 Su	14 51 46	14 33 3	7♎56 51	15 20 9	16 38.5	18 8.2	4 43.8	5 2.9	10 41.6	12 55.4	8 16.8	8 12.8	21 21.4
7 M	14 55 42	15 31 6	22 49 16	0♏23 12	16 30.1	19 16.0	5 57.1	5 44.3	10 54.8	13 0.0	8 15.7	8 14.3	21 22.5
8 Tu	14 59 39	16 29 7	8♏ 0 44	15 40 31	16 19.8	20 26.5	7 10.4	6 25.6	11 8.1	13 4.6	8 14.6	8 15.8	21 23.7
9 W	15 3 35	17 27 6	23 21 5	1♐ 0 56	16 8.9	21 39.5	8 23.7	7 6.9	11 21.4	13 9.1	8 13.4	8 17.4	21 24.9
10 Th	15 7 32	18 25 4	8♐38 38	16 12 50	15 58.6	22 55.0	9 36.9	7 48.1	11 34.7	13 13.5	8 12.1	8 18.9	21 26.1
11 F	15 11 28	19 23 1	23 42 21	1♑ 6 14	15 50.0	24 13.0	10 50.1	8 29.3	11 48.1	13 17.8	8 10.8	8 20.5	21 27.3
12 Sa	15 15 25	20 20 56	8♑23 45	15 34 24	15 43.9	25 33.3	12 3.3	9 10.4	12 1.5	13 22.1	8 9.5	8 22.1	21 28.6
13 Su	15 19 21	21 18 50	22 37 56	29 34 16	15 40.5	26 56.0	13 16.4	9 51.6	12 14.9	13 26.2	8 8.1	8 23.7	21 29.8
14 M	15 23 18	22 16 42	6♒23 31	13♒ 5 56	15D 39.2	28 21.0	14 29.6	10 32.6	12 28.4	13 30.3	8 6.7	8 25.4	21 31.1
15 Tu	15 27 15	23 14 34	19 41 55	26 11 54	15R 39.0	29 48.3	15 42.6	11 13.7	12 41.9	13 34.3	8 5.3	8 27.0	21 32.3
16 W	15 31 11	24 12 24	2♓36 25	8♓55 58	15 38.9	1♉17.8	16 55.7	11 54.7	12 55.4	13 38.3	8 3.8	8 28.7	21 33.6
17 Th	15 35 8	25 10 13	15 11 8	21 22 28	15 37.6	2 49.5	18 8.7	12 35.6	13 9.0	13 42.1	8 2.2	8 30.4	21 34.9
18 F	15 39 4	26 8 1	27 30 28	3♈35 39	15 34.1	4 23.5	19 21.7	13 16.5	13 22.6	13 45.9	8 0.7	8 32.2	21 36.1
19 Sa	15 43 1	27 5 47	9♈38 28	15 39 21	15 28.0	5 59.6	20 34.7	13 57.4	13 36.2	13 49.6	7 59.0	8 33.9	21 37.4
20 Su	15 46 57	28 3 33	21 38 40	27 36 47	15 19.1	7 38.0	21 47.6	14 38.2	13 49.8	13 53.2	7 57.4	8 35.7	21 38.7
21 M	15 50 54	29 1 17	3♉33 58	9♉30 29	15 7.8	9 18.5	23 0.5	15 19.1	14 3.5	13 56.7	7 55.7	8 37.5	21 40.0
22 Tu	15 54 50	29 59 0	15 26 35	21 22 28	14 55.0	11 1.3	24 13.4	15 59.8	14 17.2	14 0.2	7 54.0	8 39.3	21 41.4
23 W	15 58 47	0♊56 42	27 18 19	3♊14 18	14 41.5	12 46.2	25 26.3	16 40.6	14 30.9	14 3.5	7 52.2	8 41.1	21 42.7
24 Th	16 2 44	1 54 22	9♊10 37	15 7 25	14 28.7	14 33.3	26 39.1	17 21.2	14 44.6	14 6.8	7 50.5	8 43.0	21 44.0
25 F	16 6 40	2 52 2	21 4 56	27 3 21	14 17.4	16 22.5	27 51.8	18 1.9	14 58.3	14 9.9	7 48.6	8 44.9	21 45.4
26 Sa	16 10 37	3 49 40	3♋ 2 55	9♋ 3 56	14 8.4	18 14.0	29 4.6	18 42.5	15 12.1	14 13.0	7 46.8	8 46.8	21 46.7
27 Su	16 14 33	4 47 17	15 6 41	21 11 33	14 2.3	20 7.6	0♋17.3	19 23.1	15 25.9	14 16.0	7 44.9	8 48.7	21 48.1
28 M	16 18 30	5 44 52	27 18 55	3♌29 13	13 58.8	22 3.2	1 30.0	20 3.6	15 39.7	14 18.9	7 43.0	8 50.6	21 49.4
29 Tu	16 22 26	6 42 26	9♌42 54	16 0 29	13D 57.5	24 1.0	2 42.6	20 44.1	15 53.5	14 21.8	7 41.0	8 52.5	21 50.8
30 W	16 26 23	7 39 59	22 22 27	28 49 19	13 57.6	26 0.8	3 55.2	21 24.6	16 7.3	14 24.5	7 39.1	8 54.5	21 52.2
31 Th	16 30 19	8 37 30	5♍21 35	11♍59 43	13R 58.1	28 2.5	5 7.8	22 5.0	16 21.1	14 27.1	7 37.1	8 56.5	21 53.6

LONGITUDE JUNE 1906

Day	Sid.Time	☉	0 hr ☽	Noon ☽	True ☊	☿	♀	♂	♃	♄	♅	♆	♇
1 F	16 34 16	9♊35 0	18♍44 6	25♍35 3	13♌57.7	0♊ 6.1	6♋20.3	22♊45.4	16♊34.9	14♓29.7	7♑35.0	8♋58.4	21♊54.9
2 Sa	16 38 13	10 32 29	2♎32 47	9♎37 21	13R 55.8	2 11.4	7 32.8	23 25.8	16 48.8	14 32.1	7R 33.0	9 0.4	21 56.3
3 Su	16 42 9	11 29 56	16 48 38	24 6 18	13 51.6	4 18.3	8 45.2	24 6.1	17 2.6	14 34.5	7 30.9	9 2.5	21 57.7
4 M	16 46 6	12 27 22	1♏29 50	8♏58 30	13 45.3	6 26.6	9 57.6	24 46.3	17 16.5	14 36.7	7 28.8	9 4.5	21 59.1
5 Tu	16 50 2	13 24 47	16 31 19	24 7 10	13 37.4	8 36.1	11 10.0	25 26.6	17 30.3	14 38.9	7 26.6	9 6.5	22 0.5
6 W	16 53 59	14 22 11	1♐44 45	9♐22 42	13 28.7	10 46.7	12 22.3	26 6.8	17 44.2	14 41.0	7 24.5	9 8.6	22 1.9
7 Th	16 57 55	15 19 34	16 59 38	24 34 11	13 20.4	12 58.0	13 34.6	26 46.9	17 58.1	14 43.0	7 22.3	9 10.6	22 3.3
8 F	17 1 52	16 16 56	2♑ 5 6	9♑31 18	13 13.6	15 9.8	14 46.8	27 27.1	18 11.9	14 44.8	7 20.1	9 12.7	22 4.7
9 Sa	17 5 48	17 14 18	16 51 51	24 6 4	13 8.8	17 21.9	15 59.0	28 7.2	18 25.8	14 46.6	7 17.9	9 14.8	22 6.1
10 Su	17 9 45	18 11 38	1♒13 27	8♒13 45	13D 6.3	19 34.0	17 11.2	28 47.2	18 39.7	14 48.3	7 15.7	9 16.9	22 7.5
11 M	17 13 42	19 8 59	15 6 52	21 52 53	13 5.7	21 45.7	18 23.3	29 27.2	18 53.5	14 49.9	7 13.4	9 19.0	22 9.0
12 Tu	17 17 38	20 6 18	28 32 5	5♓ 4 46	13 6.4	23 56.9	19 35.3	0♋ 7.2	19 7.4	14 51.4	7 11.1	9 21.2	22 10.4
13 W	17 21 35	21 3 38	11♓31 25	17 52 31	13R 7.3	26 7.2	20 47.4	0 47.2	19 21.3	14 52.8	7 8.8	9 23.3	22 11.8
14 Th	17 25 31	22 0 56	24 8 38	0♈20 19	13 7.7	28 16.5	21 59.4	1 27.1	19 35.1	14 54.1	7 6.5	9 25.4	22 13.2
15 F	17 29 28	22 58 15	6♈28 10	12 32 45	13 6.6	0♋24.5	23 11.3	2 7.0	19 49.0	14 55.4	7 4.2	9 27.6	22 14.6
16 Sa	17 33 24	23 55 33	18 34 38	24 34 20	13 3.7	2 31.0	24 23.2	2 46.9	20 2.8	14 56.5	7 1.8	9 29.7	22 16.0
17 Su	17 37 21	24 52 51	0♉32 21	6♉29 10	12 58.7	4 35.9	25 35.1	3 26.7	20 16.7	14 57.5	6 59.5	9 31.9	22 17.4
18 M	17 41 17	25 50 8	12 25 11	18 20 50	12 52.0	6 39.1	26 46.9	4 6.6	20 30.5	14 58.4	6 57.1	9 34.1	22 18.8
19 Tu	17 45 14	26 47 25	24 16 25	0♊12 17	12 44.0	8 40.4	27 58.7	4 46.3	20 44.3	14 59.2	6 54.7	9 36.3	22 20.3
20 W	17 49 11	27 44 42	6♊ 8 42	12 5 54	12 35.5	10 39.7	29 10.4	5 26.1	20 58.1	14 59.9	6 52.4	9 38.5	22 21.7
21 Th	17 53 7	28 41 59	18 4 8	24 3 35	12 27.3	12 37.0	0♌22.1	6 5.8	21 11.9	15 0.5	6 50.0	9 40.7	22 23.1
22 F	17 57 4	29 39 15	0♋ 4 27	6♋ 6 55	12 20.3	14 32.1	1 33.8	6 45.5	21 25.7	15 1.0	6 47.6	9 42.9	22 24.5
23 Sa	18 1 0	0♋36 30	12 11 9	18 17 22	12 14.8	16 25.2	2 45.4	7 25.2	21 39.5	15 1.4	6 45.1	9 45.1	22 25.9
24 Su	18 4 57	1 33 46	24 25 44	0♌36 28	12 11.3	18 16.0	3 56.9	8 4.8	21 53.3	15 1.8	6 42.7	9 47.3	22 27.3
25 M	18 8 53	2 31 1	6♌49 50	13 6 3	12D 9.8	20 4.7	5 8.4	8 44.4	22 7.0	15 2.0	6 40.3	9 49.5	22 28.7
26 Tu	18 12 50	3 28 15	19 25 26	25 48 14	12 9.9	21 51.2	6 19.9	9 23.9	22 20.7	15R 2.1	6 37.9	9 51.7	22 30.1
27 W	18 16 46	4 25 29	2♍14 48	8♍45 26	12 11.0	23 35.4	7 31.3	10 3.5	22 34.4	15 2.1	6 35.4	9 53.9	22 31.5
28 Th	18 20 43	5 22 42	15 20 27	22 0 9	12 12.5	25 17.4	8 42.6	10 43.0	22 48.1	15 2.0	6 33.0	9 56.2	22 32.9
29 F	18 24 40	6 19 55	28 44 46	5♎34 33	12R 13.6	26 57.2	9 53.9	11 22.5	23 1.8	15 1.8	6 30.6	9 58.4	22 34.2
30 Sa	18 28 36	7 17 8	12♎29 36	19 29 59	12 13.7	28 34.7	11 5.1	12 1.9	23 15.4	15 1.5	6 28.1	10 0.6	22 35.6

Astro Data	Planet Ingress	Last Aspect	☽ Ingress	Last Aspect	☽ Ingress	☽ Phases & Eclipses	Astro Data
Dy Hr Mn	Dy Hr Mn	Dy Hr Mn	Dy Hr Mn	Dy Hr Mn	Dy Hr Mn	Dy Hr Mn	1 MAY 1906
☽0S 6 2:08	♀ ♊ 2 3:13	2 15:14 ♇ ✶	♍ 3 7:03	1 7:26 ♂ □	♎ 1 19:38	1 19:07 ☽ 10♌29	Julian Day # 2312
♅☍♆ 7 12:45	☿ ♉ 15 3:10	4 20:19 ♇ □	♎ 5 10:53	3 12:34 ♂ △	♏ 3 21:35	8 14:09 ○ 17♏03	Delta T 5.6 sec
☽0N 18 23:35	☉ ♊ 22 0:25	6 21:41 ♇ △	♏ 7 11:23	4 21:01 ♄ △	♐ 5 21:15	15 7:03 ☽ 23♒32	SVP 06♓34'17"
♃□♄ 20 8:03	♀ ♋ 26 18:17	8 14:09 ☉ ☍	♐ 9 10:24	7 16:15 ♂ ☍	♑ 7 20:40	23 8:01 ● 1♊16	Obliquity 23°26'59"
	☿ ♊ 31 22:49	11 0:54 ☿ △	♑ 11 10:12	8 22:25 ♀ ☍	♒ 9 21:55	31 6:23 ☽ 8♍53	⚷ Chiron 12♒32.6
☽0S 2 12:13		13 8:15 ☿ □	♒ 13 12:45	11 14:05 ☿ △	♓ 12 2:40		☽ Mean ☊ 16♌46.6
☽0N 15 6:55	♂ ♋ 11 19:39	15 7:03 ☉ □	♓ 15 19:06	14 9:40 ☿ □	♈ 14 11:20	6 21:12 ○ 15♐13	
♃☌♇ 26 18:14	☿ ♋ 14 19:24	17 21:04 ☉ ✶	♈ 18 4:54	16 12:55 ♀ □	♉ 16 22:55	13 19:34 ☽ 21♓50	1 JUNE 1906
♄ R 26 14:36	♀ ♌ 20 16:36	20 0:20 ♀ ✶	♉ 20 16:49	19 8:20 ♀ ✶	♊ 19 11:35	21 23:05 ● 29♊37	Julian Day # 2343
☽0S 29 20:08	☉ ♋ 22 8:42	21 21:04 ♄ ✶	♊ 23 5:27	21 23:05 ☉ ☌	♋ 21 23:51	29 14:19 ☽ 6♎54	Delta T 5.7 sec
	☿ ♌ 30 21:27	25 15:09 ♀ ☌	♋ 25 17:54	23 9:49 ☿ ☌	♌ 24 10:49		SVP 06♓34'13"
		27 11:45 ☿ ✶	♌ 28 5:14	26 5:49 ♇ ✶	♍ 26 19:50		Obliquity 23°26'58"
		30 8:03 ☿ □	♍ 30 14:10	28 20:23 ☿ ✶	♎ 29 2:13		⚷ Chiron 12♒37.2R
							☽ Mean ☊ 15♌08.1

JULY 1906 LONGITUDE

Day	Sid.Time	☉	0 hr ☽	Noon ☽	True ☊	☿	♀	♂	♃	♄	♅	♆	♇
1 Su	18 32 33	8♋14 20	26♎35 38	3♏46 20	12♌12.5	0♌10.0	12♌16.3	12♋41.3	23♊29.0	15♓ 1.1	6♑25.7	10♋ 2.9	22♊37.0
2 M	18 36 29	9 11 31	11♏ 1 45	18 21 22	12R 9.8	1 43.0	13 27.4	13 20.7	23 42.6	15R 0.7	6R23.3	10 5.1	22 38.4
3 Tu	18 40 26	10 8 43	25 44 33	3♐10 28	12 6.1	3 13.7	14 38.5	14 0.1	23 56.1	15 0.1	6 20.8	10 7.3	22 39.7
4 W	18 44 22	11 5 54	10♐38 14	18 6 48	12 1.8	4 42.2	15 49.4	14 39.4	24 9.7	14 59.4	6 18.4	10 9.5	22 41.1
5 Th	18 48 19	12 3 5	25 35 6	3♑ 2 4	11 57.7	6 8.3	17 0.4	15 18.7	24 23.2	14 58.6	6 16.0	10 11.8	22 42.4
6 F	18 52 15	13 0 15	10♑26 37	17 47 46	11 54.3	7 32.1	18 11.2	15 57.9	24 36.7	14 57.7	6 13.6	10 14.0	22 43.8
7 Sa	18 56 12	13 57 26	25 4 40	2♒16 32	11 52.2	8 53.5	19 22.0	16 37.2	24 50.1	14 56.8	6 11.2	10 16.2	22 45.1
8 Su	19 0 9	14 54 37	9♒22 47	16 23 0	11D51.3	10 12.5	20 32.7	17 16.4	25 3.5	14 55.7	6 8.8	10 18.5	22 46.4
9 M	19 4 5	15 51 49	23 16 55	0♓ 4 24	11 51.7	11 29.1	21 43.4	17 55.6	25 16.9	14 54.5	6 6.4	10 20.7	22 47.8
10 Tu	19 8 2	16 49 0	6♓45 31	13 20 23	11 52.8	12 43.1	22 54.0	18 34.8	25 30.2	14 53.3	6 4.0	10 22.9	22 49.1
11 W	19 11 58	17 46 12	19 49 18	26 12 37	11 54.4	13 54.5	24 4.5	19 13.9	25 43.5	14 51.9	6 1.6	10 25.1	22 50.4
12 Th	19 15 55	18 43 25	2♈30 46	8♈44 15	11 55.7	15 3.4	25 15.0	19 53.0	25 56.8	14 50.5	5 59.3	10 27.4	22 51.7
13 F	19 19 51	19 40 37	14 53 34	20 59 17	11R56.5	16 9.5	26 25.4	20 32.1	26 10.0	14 48.9	5 56.9	10 29.6	22 53.0
14 Sa	19 23 48	20 37 51	27 1 59	3♉ 2 13	11 56.4	17 12.8	27 35.7	21 11.2	26 23.2	14 47.3	5 54.6	10 31.8	22 54.2
15 Su	19 27 44	21 35 5	9♉ 0 34	14 57 34	11 55.4	18 13.2	28 46.0	21 50.2	26 36.4	14 45.5	5 52.3	10 34.0	22 55.5
16 M	19 31 41	22 32 20	20 53 45	26 49 38	11 53.6	19 10.6	29 56.2	22 29.2	26 49.5	14 43.7	5 50.0	10 36.2	22 56.8
17 Tu	19 35 38	23 29 35	2♊45 42	8♊42 22	11 51.2	20 4.9	1♍ 6.3	23 8.2	27 2.6	14 41.8	5 47.7	10 38.4	22 58.0
18 W	19 39 34	24 26 51	14 40 4	20 39 9	11 48.5	20 56.0	2 16.4	23 47.2	27 15.6	14 39.8	5 45.4	10 40.6	22 59.3
19 Th	19 43 31	25 24 7	26 39 58	2♋42 49	11 45.9	21 43.7	3 26.3	24 26.2	27 28.6	14 37.7	5 43.2	10 42.7	23 0.5
20 F	19 47 27	26 21 24	8♋47 56	14 55 33	11 43.8	22 27.9	4 36.2	25 5.1	27 41.5	14 35.5	5 40.9	10 44.9	23 1.7
21 Sa	19 51 24	27 18 42	21 5 52	27 19 2	11 42.2	23 8.5	5 46.1	25 44.0	27 54.4	14 33.2	5 38.7	10 47.1	23 2.9
22 Su	19 55 20	28 16 1	3♌35 11	9♌54 26	11D41.4	23 45.3	6 55.8	26 22.9	28 7.3	14 30.9	5 36.5	10 49.2	23 4.1
23 M	19 59 17	29 13 19	16 16 52	22 42 33	11 41.3	24 18.1	8 5.5	27 1.8	28 20.1	14 28.4	5 34.4	10 51.4	23 5.3
24 Tu	20 3 13	0♌10 39	29 11 35	5♍43 59	11 41.8	24 46.8	9 15.1	27 40.6	28 32.8	14 25.9	5 32.2	10 53.5	23 6.5
25 W	20 7 10	1 7 58	12♍19 50	18 59 8	11 42.6	25 11.2	10 24.6	28 19.5	28 45.5	14 23.2	5 30.1	10 55.6	23 7.7
26 Th	20 11 7	2 5 19	25 41 56	2♎28 16	11 43.5	25 31.1	11 34.0	28 58.3	28 58.1	14 20.5	5 28.0	10 57.8	23 8.8
27 F	20 15 3	3 2 39	9♎18 5	16 11 23	11 44.2	25 46.4	12 43.3	29 37.0	29 10.7	14 17.8	5 25.9	10 59.9	23 9.9
28 Sa	20 19 0	4 0 0	23 8 7	0♏ 8 9	11R44.7	25 57.0	13 52.5	0♌15.8	29 23.2	14 14.9	5 23.9	11 1.9	23 11.1
29 Su	20 22 56	4 57 22	7♏11 21	14 17 30	11 44.8	26R 2.5	15 1.6	0 54.5	29 35.7	14 11.9	5 21.9	11 4.0	23 12.2
30 M	20 26 53	5 54 44	21 26 19	28 37 29	11 44.6	26 3.1	16 10.7	1 33.2	29 48.1	14 8.9	5 19.9	11 6.1	23 13.3
31 Tu	20 30 49	6 52 6	5♐50 33	13♐ 5 2	11 44.2	25 58.5	17 19.6	2 11.9	0♋ 0.4	14 5.8	5 17.9	11 8.2	23 14.3

AUGUST 1906 LONGITUDE

Day	Sid.Time	☉	0 hr ☽	Noon ☽	True ☊	☿	♀	♂	♃	♄	♅	♆	♇
1 W	20 34 46	7♌49 30	20♐20 24	27♐36 1	11♌43.8	25♌48.8	18♍28.4	2♌50.6	0♋12.7	14♓ 2.7	5♑16.0	11♋10.2	23♊15.4
2 Th	20 38 42	8 46 54	4♑51 14	12♑ 5 24	11R43.5	25R33.8	19 37.2	3 29.2	0 24.9	13R59.4	5R14.1	11 12.2	23 16.5
3 F	20 42 39	9 44 18	19 17 48	26 27 47	11 43.3	25 13.8	20 45.8	4 7.9	0 37.0	13 56.1	5 12.2	11 14.3	23 17.5
4 Sa	20 46 36	10 41 44	3♒34 42	10♒37 59	11D43.2	24 48.8	21 54.3	4 46.5	0 49.1	13 52.7	5 10.4	11 16.3	23 18.5
5 Su	20 50 32	11 39 10	17 37 7	24 31 40	11R43.2	24 19.0	23 2.7	5 25.0	1 1.1	13 49.3	5 8.6	11 18.3	23 19.5
6 M	20 54 29	12 36 37	1♓21 18	8♓ 5 48	11 43.1	23 44.7	24 10.9	6 3.6	1 13.1	13 45.8	5 6.8	11 20.2	23 20.5
7 Tu	20 58 25	13 34 5	14 45 2	21 18 58	11 43.0	23 6.3	25 19.1	6 42.2	1 24.9	13 42.2	5 5.1	11 22.2	23 21.5
8 W	21 2 22	14 31 35	27 47 42	4♈11 22	11 42.8	22 24.4	26 27.1	7 20.7	1 36.8	13 38.6	5 3.4	11 24.1	23 22.5
9 Th	21 6 18	15 29 5	10♈30 15	16 44 40	11 42.4	21 39.6	27 35.1	7 59.2	1 48.5	13 34.9	5 1.7	11 26.1	23 23.4
10 F	21 10 15	16 26 38	22 55 1	29 1 44	11 41.9	20 52.5	28 42.9	8 37.7	2 0.1	13 31.1	5 0.1	11 28.0	23 24.3
11 Sa	21 14 11	17 24 11	5♉ 5 19	11♉ 6 17	11 41.6	20 4.0	29 50.6	9 16.2	2 11.7	13 27.3	4 58.5	11 29.9	23 25.2
12 Su	21 18 8	18 21 46	17 5 13	23 2 39	11D41.4	19 14.9	0♎58.1	9 54.6	2 23.2	13 23.4	4 56.9	11 31.7	23 26.1
13 M	21 22 5	19 19 22	28 59 11	4♊55 23	11 41.5	18 26.1	2 5.6	10 33.1	2 34.6	13 19.4	4 55.4	11 33.6	23 27.0
14 Tu	21 26 1	20 17 0	10♊51 50	16 49 6	11 42.0	17 38.6	3 12.9	11 11.5	2 46.0	13 15.5	4 53.9	11 35.4	23 27.9
15 W	21 29 58	21 14 39	22 47 42	28 48 10	11 42.8	16 53.3	4 20.1	11 49.9	2 57.2	13 11.4	4 52.5	11 37.3	23 28.7
16 Th	21 33 54	22 12 20	4♋50 58	10♋56 32	11 43.8	16 11.2	5 27.1	12 28.3	3 8.4	13 7.3	4 51.1	11 39.1	23 29.6
17 F	21 37 51	23 10 3	17 5 16	23 17 30	11 44.8	15 33.2	6 34.0	13 6.7	3 19.5	13 3.2	4 49.7	11 40.8	23 30.4
18 Sa	21 41 47	24 7 46	29 33 32	5♌53 34	11R45.5	15 0.1	7 40.8	13 45.1	3 30.5	12 59.0	4 48.4	11 42.6	23 31.2
19 Su	21 45 44	25 5 32	12♌17 46	18 46 12	11 45.8	14 32.5	8 47.4	14 23.5	3 41.4	12 54.8	4 47.1	11 44.3	23 31.9
20 M	21 49 40	26 3 18	25 18 55	1♍55 51	11 45.4	14 11.2	9 53.9	15 1.8	3 52.3	12 50.6	4 45.9	11 46.1	23 32.7
21 Tu	21 53 37	27 1 6	8♍36 52	15 21 48	11 44.3	13 56.7	11 0.2	15 40.1	4 3.0	12 46.3	4 44.7	11 47.8	23 33.4
22 W	21 57 34	27 58 55	22 10 25	29 2 25	11 42.5	13D49.4	12 6.4	16 18.4	4 13.6	12 41.9	4 43.6	11 49.4	23 34.1
23 Th	22 1 30	28 56 46	5♎57 29	12♎55 17	11 40.3	13 49.6	13 12.4	16 56.7	4 24.2	12 37.5	4 42.5	11 51.1	23 34.8
24 F	22 5 27	29 54 38	19 55 25	26 57 32	11 38.0	13 57.7	14 18.3	17 35.0	4 34.6	12 33.1	4 41.4	11 52.7	23 35.5
25 Sa	22 9 23	0♍52 31	4♏ 1 15	11♏ 6 11	11 35.9	14 13.6	15 23.9	18 13.3	4 45.0	12 28.7	4 40.4	11 54.3	23 36.2
26 Su	22 13 20	1 50 25	18 12 1	25 18 23	11 34.5	14 37.4	16 29.4	18 51.5	4 55.2	12 24.3	4 39.4	11 55.9	23 36.8
27 M	22 17 16	2 48 21	2♐25 0	9♐31 32	11D34.0	15 9.2	17 34.7	19 29.8	5 5.4	12 19.8	4 38.5	11 57.5	23 37.4
28 Tu	22 21 13	3 46 18	16 37 45	23 43 20	11 34.5	15 48.8	18 39.9	20 8.0	5 15.4	12 15.3	4 37.6	11 59.0	23 38.0
29 W	22 25 9	4 44 16	0♑48 3	7♑51 37	11 35.6	16 36.0	19 44.8	20 46.2	5 25.4	12 10.8	4 36.8	12 0.5	23 38.6
30 Th	22 29 6	5 42 16	14 53 46	21 54 14	11 37.0	17 30.6	20 49.5	21 24.4	5 35.2	12 6.2	4 36.0	12 2.0	23 39.2
31 F	22 33 3	6 40 16	28 52 45	5♒49 1	11R38.2	18 32.2	21 54.1	22 2.5	5 44.9	12 1.7	4 35.3	12 3.5	23 39.7

Astro Data Dy Hr Mn	Planet Ingress Dy Hr Mn	Last Aspect Dy Hr Mn	☽ Ingress Dy Hr Mn	Last Aspect Dy Hr Mn	☽ Ingress Dy Hr Mn	☽ Phases & Eclipses Dy Hr Mn	Astro Data
☽0N 12 15:13	♀ ♍ 16 1:18	30 18:40 ♃ △	♏ 1 5:43	1 8:55 ☿ △	♑ 1 15:58	6 4:27 ○ 13♑11	1 JULY 1906
☽0S 27 2:05	☉ ♌ 23 19:33	2 6:32 ♄ △	♐ 3 6:53	3 2:40 ♀ △	♒ 3 17:57	13 10:13 ☽ 20♈05	Julian Day # 2373
☿ R 29 14:38	♂ ♌ 27 14:13	4 22:03 ♃ ☍	♑ 5 7:06	5 11:11 ☿ ☍	♓ 5 21:36	21 12:59 ● 27♋50	Delta T 5.8 sec
	♃ ♋ 30 23:12	6 9:25 ♂ ☍	♒ 7 8:11	7 21:16 ♀ ☍	♈ 8 4:07	21 13:14:14 ✔ P 0.336	SVP 06♓34'08"
☽0N 8 24:00		9 3:34 ♃ △	♓ 9 11:52	10 0:57 ♇ ✶	♉ 10 13:55	28 19:56 ☽ 4♏48	Obliquity 23°26'58"
♀0S 11 13:20	♀ ♎ 11 3:21	11 11:17 ♃ □	♈ 11 19:12	12 4:04 ☿ □	♊ 13 2:03		⚷ Chiron 11♒44.1R
☿ D 22 11:16	☉ ♍ 24 2:14	14 1:14 ♀ △	♉ 14 5:55	15 1:22 ♇ ☌	♋ 15 14:23		☽ Mean ☊ 13♌32.8
☽0S 23 7:44		16 3:37 ☉ ✶	♊ 16 18:25	16 16:11 ♄ △	♌ 18 0:50	4 13:00 ○ 11♒13	
♃☍♅ 24 14:15		19 1:39 ♃ ☌	♋ 19 6:37	20 1:27 ☉ ☌	♍ 20 8:31	4 13:00 ☍ T 1.780	1 AUGUST 1906
♄△♆ 30 16:50		21 12:59 ☉ ☌	♌ 21 17:09	22 2:27 ♇ □	♎ 22 13:40	12 2:47 ☽ 18♉28	Julian Day # 2404
		23 22:47 ♃ ✶	♍ 24 1:29	24 6:16 ♇ △	♏ 24 17:10	20 1:27 ● 26♌07	Delta T 5.8 sec
		26 6:06 ♂ ✶	♎ 26 7:38	26 1:10 ♂ □	♐ 26 19:55	20 1:12:41 ✔ P 0.315	SVP 06♓34'03"
		28 10:53 ♃ △	♏ 28 11:46	28 11:52 ♇ ☍	♑ 28 22:38	27 0:42 ☽ 2♐50	Obliquity 23°26'59"
		30 7:41 ☿ □	♐ 30 14:17	30 11:00 ♀ □	♒ 31 1:56		⚷ Chiron 10♒10.9R
							☽ Mean ☊ 11♌54.3

LONGITUDE — SEPTEMBER 1906

Day	Sid.Time	☉	0 hr ☽	Noon ☽	True ☊	☿	♀	♂	♃	♄	♅	♆	♇
1 Sa	22 36 59	7♍38 19	12♒42 44	19♒33 38	11♌38.7	19♌40.6	22♎58.4	22♌40.7	5♋54.5	11♓57.1	4♑34.6	12♋ 4.9	23♊40.2
2 Su	22 40 56	8 36 22	26 21 25	3♓ 5 50	11R37.9	20 55.3	24 2.4	23 18.8	6 4.0	11R52.6	4R34.0	12 6.3	23 40.7
3 M	22 44 52	9 34 28	9♓46 39	16 23 40	11 35.8	22 15.8	25 6.3	23 56.9	6 13.4	11 48.0	4 33.4	12 7.7	23 41.2
4 Tu	22 48 49	10 32 35	22 56 43	29 25 43	11 32.3	23 41.7	26 9.9	24 35.1	6 22.7	11 43.4	4 32.8	12 9.1	23 41.7
5 W	22 52 45	11 30 43	5♈50 38	12♈11 28	11 27.8	25 12.6	27 13.3	25 13.2	6 31.8	11 38.8	4 32.3	12 10.4	23 42.1
6 Th	22 56 42	12 28 54	18 28 19	24 41 22	11 22.6	26 47.7	28 16.5	25 51.2	6 40.9	11 34.2	4 31.9	12 11.7	23 42.5
7 F	23 0 38	13 27 7	0♉50 50	6♉57 2	11 17.5	28 26.7	29 19.4	26 29.3	6 49.8	11 29.7	4 31.5	12 13.0	23 42.9
8 Sa	23 4 35	14 25 21	13 0 17	19 1 2	11 13.0	0♍ 9.1	0♏22.1	27 7.4	6 58.6	11 25.1	4 31.2	12 14.3	23 43.3
9 Su	23 8 32	15 23 38	24 59 45	0♊56 57	11 9.5	1 54.2	1 24.4	27 45.5	7 7.3	11 20.5	4 30.9	12 15.5	23 43.6
10 M	23 12 28	16 21 56	6♊53 9	12 48 58	11D 7.6	3 41.7	2 26.6	28 23.5	7 15.8	11 15.9	4 30.6	12 16.7	23 44.0
11 Tu	23 16 25	17 20 17	18 45 0	24 41 51	11 7.0	5 31.0	3 28.4	29 1.5	7 24.3	11 11.4	4 30.4	12 17.9	23 44.3
12 W	23 20 21	18 18 40	0♋40 9	6♋40 32	11 7.8	7 21.8	4 30.0	29 39.6	7 32.5	11 6.8	4 30.3	12 19.0	23 44.6
13 Th	23 24 18	19 17 4	12 43 36	18 49 56	11 9.2	9 13.7	5 31.3	0♍17.6	7 40.7	11 2.3	4 30.2	12 20.1	23 44.8
14 F	23 28 14	20 15 31	25 0 6	1♌14 36	11 10.8	11 6.3	6 32.3	0 55.6	7 48.7	10 57.8	4D30.1	12 21.2	23 45.1
15 Sa	23 32 11	21 14 1	7♌33 52	13 58 18	11R11.8	12 59.3	7 32.9	1 33.6	7 56.6	10 53.3	4 30.1	12 22.3	23 45.3
16 Su	23 36 7	22 12 32	20 28 9	27 3 36	11 11.4	14 52.5	8 33.3	2 11.6	8 4.4	10 48.9	4 30.2	12 23.3	23 45.5
17 M	23 40 4	23 11 5	3♍44 44	10♍31 28	11 9.3	16 45.7	9 33.3	2 49.6	8 12.0	10 44.4	4 30.3	12 24.3	23 45.7
18 Tu	23 44 0	24 9 40	17 23 38	24 20 52	11 5.2	18 38.6	10 33.0	3 27.5	8 19.5	10 40.0	4 30.5	12 25.2	23 45.8
19 W	23 47 57	25 8 17	1♎22 46	8♎28 43	10 59.3	20 31.2	11 32.3	4 5.5	8 26.8	10 35.6	4 30.7	12 26.2	23 46.0
20 Th	23 51 54	26 6 56	15 38 5	22 50 7	10 52.3	22 23.2	12 31.3	4 43.4	8 34.0	10 31.3	4 30.9	12 27.1	23 46.1
21 F	23 55 50	27 5 37	0♏ 4 2	7♏19 2	10 45.0	24 14.7	13 29.8	5 21.4	8 41.1	10 27.0	4 31.3	12 27.9	23 46.2
22 Sa	23 59 47	28 4 19	14 34 21	21 49 15	10 38.4	26 5.4	14 28.0	5 59.3	8 48.0	10 22.7	4 31.6	12 28.8	23 46.2
23 Su	0 3 43	29 3 4	29 3 4	6♐15 16	10 33.2	27 55.3	15 25.8	6 37.2	8 54.7	10 18.5	4 32.0	12 29.6	23 46.3
24 M	0 7 40	0♎ 1 50	13♐25 20	20 32 57	10 29.9	29 44.5	16 23.1	7 15.1	9 1.3	10 14.3	4 32.5	12 30.3	23R46.3
25 Tu	0 11 36	1 0 38	27 37 50	4♑39 48	10D 28.7	1♎32.7	17 20.0	7 53.0	9 7.8	10 10.2	4 33.0	12 31.1	23 46.3
26 W	0 15 33	1 59 27	11♑38 45	18 34 41	10 29.0	3 20.1	18 16.5	8 30.9	9 14.0	10 6.1	4 33.6	12 31.8	23 46.3
27 Th	0 19 29	2 58 19	25 27 35	2♒17 29	10 30.0	5 6.7	19 12.4	9 8.7	9 20.2	10 2.0	4 34.2	12 32.5	23 46.2
28 F	0 23 26	3 57 12	9♒ 4 27	15 48 32	10R30.6	6 52.3	20 7.9	9 46.6	9 26.1	9 58.0	4 34.9	12 33.1	23 46.2
29 Sa	0 27 23	4 56 6	22 29 47	29 8 13	10 30.0	8 37.0	21 2.8	10 24.4	9 32.0	9 54.1	4 35.6	12 33.7	23 46.1
30 Su	0 31 19	5 55 3	5♓43 51	12♓16 39	10 27.2	10 20.8	21 57.2	11 2.3	9 37.6	9 50.2	4 36.4	12 34.3	23 46.0

LONGITUDE — OCTOBER 1906

Day	Sid.Time	☉	0 hr ☽	Noon ☽	True ☊	☿	♀	♂	♃	♄	♅	♆	♇
1 M	0 35 16	6♎54 1	18♓46 37	25♓13 42	10♌21.9	12♎ 3.7	22♏51.0	11♍40.1	9♋43.1	9♓46.4	4♑37.2	12♋34.9	23♊45.8
2 Tu	0 39 12	7 53 1	1♈37 51	7♈59 2	10R14.1	13 45.7	23 44.3	12 17.9	9 48.4	9R42.6	4 38.1	12 35.4	23R45.7
3 W	0 43 9	8 52 3	14 17 12	20 32 21	10 4.2	15 26.9	24 37.0	12 55.7	9 53.6	9 38.9	4 39.0	12 35.8	23 45.5
4 Th	0 47 5	9 51 8	26 44 32	2♉53 47	9 53.1	17 7.3	25 29.0	13 33.5	9 58.6	9 35.2	4 40.0	12 36.3	23 45.3
5 F	0 51 2	10 50 14	9♉ 0 15	15 4 5	9 41.9	18 46.8	26 20.4	14 11.3	10 3.4	9 31.7	4 41.1	12 36.7	23 45.1
6 Sa	0 54 58	11 49 23	21 5 30	27 4 49	9 31.4	20 25.4	27 11.1	14 49.0	10 8.0	9 28.1	4 42.1	12 37.1	23 44.8
7 Su	0 58 55	12 48 33	3♊ 2 20	8♊58 29	9 22.6	22 3.3	28 1.1	15 26.8	10 12.5	9 24.7	4 43.3	12 37.4	23 44.6
8 M	1 2 52	13 47 47	14 53 43	20 48 31	9 16.1	23 40.5	28 50.4	16 4.6	10 16.8	9 21.3	4 44.4	12 37.8	23 44.3
9 Tu	1 6 48	14 47 2	26 43 27	2♋39 8	9 12.1	25 16.8	29 39.0	16 42.3	10 20.9	9 18.0	4 45.7	12 38.0	23 44.0
10 W	1 10 45	15 46 20	8♋36 10	14 35 12	9D 10.3	26 52.4	0♐26.7	17 20.1	10 24.9	9 14.8	4 46.9	12 38.3	23 43.7
11 Th	1 14 41	16 45 40	20 36 55	26 42 0	9 10.1	28 27.3	1 13.7	17 57.8	10 28.6	9 11.6	4 48.3	12 38.5	23 43.3
12 F	1 18 38	17 45 2	2♌51 5	9♌ 4 51	9R10.5	0♏ 1.5	1 59.8	18 35.5	10 32.2	9 8.6	4 49.6	12 38.7	23 43.0
13 Sa	1 22 34	18 44 27	15 23 54	21 48 45	9 10.5	1 35.0	2 45.1	19 13.3	10 35.6	9 5.6	4 51.1	12 38.8	23 42.6
14 Su	1 26 31	19 43 54	28 19 54	4♍57 42	9 8.9	3 7.8	3 29.4	19 51.0	10 38.8	9 2.6	4 52.5	12 38.9	23 42.2
15 M	1 30 27	20 43 23	11♍42 22	18 34 0	9 5.1	4 39.9	4 12.8	20 28.7	10 41.9	8 59.8	4 54.0	12 39.0	23 41.7
16 Tu	1 34 24	21 42 54	25 32 29	2♎37 34	8 58.5	6 11.3	4 55.3	21 6.4	10 44.7	8 57.0	4 55.6	12R39.0	23 41.3
17 W	1 38 20	22 42 27	9♎48 44	17 5 19	8 49.5	7 42.1	5 36.7	21 44.1	10 47.3	8 54.4	4 57.2	12 39.1	23 40.8
18 Th	1 42 17	23 42 3	24 26 29	1♏51 13	8 38.8	9 12.2	6 17.0	22 21.8	10 49.8	8 51.8	4 58.9	12 39.0	23 40.3
19 F	1 46 14	24 41 41	9♏18 23	16 46 49	8 27.4	10 41.6	6 56.2	22 59.4	10 52.1	8 49.3	5 0.6	12 39.0	23 39.8
20 Sa	1 50 10	25 41 20	24 15 21	1♐42 50	8 16.8	12 10.4	7 34.3	23 37.1	10 54.1	8 46.9	5 2.3	12 38.9	23 39.3
21 Su	1 54 7	26 41 2	9♐ 8 13	16 30 36	8 8.1	13 38.6	8 11.2	24 14.7	10 56.0	8 44.6	5 4.1	12 38.7	23 38.7
22 M	1 58 3	27 40 45	23 49 14	1♑ 3 33	8 2.1	15 6.0	8 46.7	24 52.4	10 57.7	8 42.3	5 6.0	12 38.6	23 38.1
23 Tu	2 2 0	28 40 30	8♑13 9	15 17 48	7 58.7	16 32.7	9 21.0	25 30.0	10 59.2	8 40.2	5 7.9	12 38.4	23 37.5
24 W	2 5 56	29 40 17	22 17 25	29 12 2	7D 57.5	17 58.8	9 53.9	26 7.6	11 0.5	8 38.2	5 9.8	12 38.2	23 36.9
25 Th	2 9 53	0♏40 5	6♒ 1 47	12♒46 55	7R 57.5	19 24.0	10 25.4	26 45.2	11 1.6	8 36.2	5 11.8	12 37.9	23 36.3
26 F	2 13 49	1 39 55	19 27 39	26 4 17	7 57.2	20 48.6	10 55.4	27 22.8	11 2.5	8 34.4	5 13.8	12 37.6	23 35.7
27 Sa	2 17 46	2 39 47	2♓37 8	9♓ 6 27	7 55.4	22 12.3	11 23.8	28 0.4	11 3.2	8 32.6	5 15.9	12 37.3	23 35.0
28 Su	2 21 43	3 39 40	15 32 32	21 55 37	7 51.2	23 35.1	11 50.6	28 37.9	11 3.7	8 31.0	5 18.0	12 36.9	23 34.3
29 M	2 25 39	4 39 35	28 15 53	4♈33 33	7 44.0	24 57.0	12 15.7	29 15.5	11 4.0	8 29.4	5 20.1	12 36.5	23 33.6
30 Tu	2 29 36	5 39 32	10♈48 43	17 1 31	7 33.9	26 18.0	12 39.1	29 53.1	11R 4.1	8 27.9	5 22.3	12 36.1	23 32.9
31 W	2 33 32	6 39 30	23 12 4	29 20 24	7 21.2	27 37.9	13 0.7	0♎30.6	11 4.0	8 26.6	5 24.6	12 35.6	23 32.1

Astro Data

	Dy Hr Mn
☽0N	5 8:31
♅ D	14 8:12
☽0S	19 15:00
♇ R	24 14:12
☿0S	25 19:55
♃△♄	1 8:35
☽0N	2 16:13
♆ R	16 16:57
☽0S	17 0:44
☽0N	29 23:04
♃ R	30 0:16

Planet Ingress

	Dy Hr Mn
☿ ♍	7 21:54
♀ ♏	7 15:32
♂ ♍	12 12:53
☉ ♎	23 23:15
☿ ♎	24 3:26
♀ ♐	9 10:31
☿ ♏	11 23:37
☉ ♏	24 7:55
♂ ♎	30 4:26

Last Aspect / ☽ Ingress

Last Aspect Dy Hr Mn		☽ Ingress Dy Hr Mn
1 19:33	♀ △	♓ 2 6:28
4 1:23	♇ □	♈ 4 13:04
6 20:45	♀ ☍	♉ 6 22:21
9 5:52	♂ □	♊ 9 10:05
11 21:52	♂ ✶	♋ 11 22:39
13 14:00	☉ ✶	♌ 14 9:37
16 6:01	♇ ✶	♍ 16 17:18
18 12:33	☉ ☌	♎ 18 21:39
20 13:33	♇ △	♏ 20 23:53
22 24:00	☉ ✶	♐ 23 1:35
24 17:27	♇ ☍	♑ 25 4:02
26 12:18	♀ ✶	♒ 27 7:58
29 2:17	♇ △	♓ 29 13:34

Last Aspect / ☽ Ingress

Last Aspect Dy Hr Mn		☽ Ingress Dy Hr Mn
1 9:16	♇ □	♈ 1 20:56
3 18:13	♇ ✶	♉ 4 6:20
6 13:08	♀ ☍	♊ 6 17:52
8 20:37	☿ △	♋ 9 6:38
11 17:42	☿ □	♌ 11 18:27
13 15:30	♇ ✶	♍ 14 3:02
15 20:50	♇ □	♎ 16 7:34
17 22:45	♇ △	♏ 18 9:00
19 22:56	♂ ✶	♐ 20 9:14
22 6:51	☉ ✶	♑ 22 10:14
24 6:58	♂ △	♒ 24 13:24
26 7:29	♇ △	♓ 26 19:11
29 1:59	♂ ☍	♈ 29 3:18
31 0:39	♇ ✶	♉ 31 13:18

☽ Phases & Eclipses

Dy Hr Mn		
2 23:36	○	9♓34
10 20:53	☽	17♊13
18 12:33	●	24♍40
25 6:11	☽	1♑16
2 12:48	○	8♈25
10 15:39	☽	16♋25
17 22:43	●	23♎39
24 13:50	☽	0♒15

Astro Data

1 SEPTEMBER 1906
Julian Day # 2435
Delta T 5.9 sec
SVP 06♓33'59"
Obliquity 23°27'00"
⚷ Chiron 8♒35.2R
☽ Mean ☊ 10♌15.8

1 OCTOBER 1906
Julian Day # 2465
Delta T 5.9 sec
SVP 06♓33'57"
Obliquity 23°27'00"
⚷ Chiron 7♒36.7R
☽ Mean ☊ 8♌40.5

NOVEMBER 1906

LONGITUDE

Day	Sid.Time	☉	0 hr ☽	Noon ☽	True ☊	☿	♀	♂	♃	♄	♅	♆	♇
1 Th	2 37 29	7♏39 31	5♉26 38	11♉30 50	7♌ 7.0	28♏56.7	13♐20.5	1♎ 8.1	11♋ 3.7	8♓25.3	5♑26.8	12♋35.1	23♊31.4
2 F	2 41 25	8 39 33	17 33 5	23 33 31	6R 52.4	0♐14.3	13 38.3	1 45.6	11R 3.2	8R 24.2	5 29.1	12R 34.6	23R 30.6
3 Sa	2 45 22	9 39 37	29 32 16	5♊29 32	6 38.7	1 30.5	13 54.1	2 23.2	11 2.5	8 23.1	5 31.5	12 34.1	23 29.8
4 Su	2 49 18	10 39 43	11♊25 33	17 20 36	6 26.8	2 45.3	14 7.9	3 0.7	11 1.6	8 22.1	5 33.9	12 33.5	23 29.0
5 M	2 53 15	11 39 51	23 15 0	29 9 8	6 17.7	3 58.3	14 19.5	3 38.2	11 0.5	8 21.3	5 36.3	12 32.9	23 28.2
6 Tu	2 57 12	12 40 1	5♋ 3 28	10♋58 27	6 11.5	5 9.6	14 29.0	4 15.6	10 59.2	8 20.5	5 38.8	12 32.2	23 27.4
7 W	3 1 8	13 40 13	16 54 40	22 52 40	6 8.0	6 18.9	14 36.3	4 53.1	10 57.7	8 19.9	5 41.3	12 31.5	23 26.5
8 Th	3 5 5	14 40 28	28 53 5	4♌56 33	6D 6.8	7 25.8	14 41.4	5 30.6	10 56.0	8 19.3	5 43.8	12 30.8	23 25.6
9 F	3 9 1	15 40 44	11♌ 3 46	17 15 23	6R 6.7	8 30.3	14R 44.1	6 8.0	10 54.1	8 18.9	5 46.4	12 30.1	23 24.8
10 Sa	3 12 58	16 41 2	23 32 4	29 54 29	6 6.6	9 31.9	14 44.4	6 45.5	10 52.0	8 18.6	5 49.0	12 29.3	23 23.9
11 Su	3 16 54	17 41 22	6♍23 13	12♍58 46	6 5.3	10 30.3	14 42.4	7 22.9	10 49.7	8 18.3	5 51.7	12 28.5	23 22.9
12 M	3 20 51	18 41 44	19 41 34	26 31 53	6 1.9	11 25.1	14 37.9	8 0.4	10 47.2	8D 18.2	5 54.4	12 27.7	23 22.0
13 Tu	3 24 47	19 42 8	3♎29 50	10♎35 21	5 56.0	12 15.8	14 31.1	8 37.8	10 44.6	8 18.2	5 57.1	12 26.8	23 21.1
14 W	3 28 44	20 42 34	17 48 7	25 7 38	5 47.5	13 2.0	14 21.8	9 15.2	10 41.7	8 18.3	5 59.9	12 25.9	23 20.1
15 Th	3 32 41	21 43 1	2♏33 6	10♏ 3 34	5 37.1	13 43.1	14 10.0	9 52.6	10 38.6	8 18.5	6 2.7	12 25.0	23 19.2
16 F	3 36 37	22 43 31	17 37 51	25 14 37	5 25.9	14 18.4	13 55.9	10 30.0	10 35.3	8 18.8	6 5.5	12 24.0	23 18.2
17 Sa	3 40 34	23 44 2	2♐52 29	10♐30 1	5 15.3	14 47.3	13 39.4	11 7.3	10 31.9	8 19.2	6 8.4	12 23.1	23 17.2
18 Su	3 44 30	24 44 34	18 5 51	25 38 44	5 6.5	15 9.1	13 20.5	11 44.7	10 28.2	8 19.7	6 11.2	12 22.0	23 16.2
19 M	3 48 27	25 45 8	3♑ 7 34	10♑31 27	5 0.3	15 23.0	12 59.4	12 22.0	10 24.4	8 20.3	6 14.2	12 21.0	23 15.2
20 Tu	3 52 23	26 45 44	17 49 42	25 1 50	4 56.8	15R 28.2	12 36.1	12 59.4	10 20.3	8 21.0	6 17.1	12 20.0	23 14.1
21 W	3 56 20	27 46 21	2♒ 7 36	9♒ 6 55	4D 55.7	15 24.0	12 10.6	13 36.7	10 16.1	8 21.9	6 20.1	12 18.9	23 13.1
22 Th	4 0 16	28 46 58	15 59 52	22 46 38	4 56.0	15 9.9	11 43.2	14 14.0	10 11.8	8 22.8	6 23.1	12 17.8	23 12.1
23 F	4 4 13	29 47 37	29 27 31	6♓ 2 55	4R 56.3	14 45.2	11 14.0	14 51.3	10 7.2	8 23.8	6 26.2	12 16.6	23 11.0
24 Sa	4 8 10	0♐48 17	12♓33 12	18 58 51	4 55.6	14 9.8	10 43.1	15 28.5	10 2.5	8 25.0	6 29.2	12 15.5	23 9.9
25 Su	4 12 6	1 48 58	25 20 17	1♈37 56	4 52.9	13 23.6	10 10.7	16 5.8	9 57.5	8 26.2	6 32.3	12 14.3	23 8.9
26 M	4 16 3	2 49 40	7♈52 12	14 3 29	4 47.7	12 27.3	9 37.1	16 43.0	9 52.5	8 27.6	6 35.4	12 13.1	23 7.8
27 Tu	4 19 59	3 50 23	20 12 8	26 18 27	4 39.8	11 21.8	9 2.3	17 20.2	9 47.2	8 29.0	6 38.6	12 11.8	23 6.7
28 W	4 23 56	4 51 7	2♉22 43	8♉25 11	4 29.7	10 8.6	8 26.8	17 57.4	9 41.8	8 30.6	6 41.7	12 10.6	23 5.6
29 Th	4 27 52	5 51 53	14 26 4	20 25 33	4 18.3	8 49.7	7 50.6	18 34.6	9 36.3	8 32.3	6 44.9	12 9.3	23 4.5
30 F	4 31 49	6 52 39	26 23 50	2♊21 3	4 6.5	7 27.7	7 14.2	19 11.8	9 30.6	8 34.0	6 48.2	12 8.0	23 3.3

DECEMBER 1906

LONGITUDE

Day	Sid.Time	☉	0 hr ☽	Noon ☽	True ☊	☿	♀	♂	♃	♄	♅	♆	♇
1 Sa	4 35 45	7♐53 27	8♊17 25	14♊13 4	3♌55.4	6♐ 5.2	6♐37.6	19♎49.0	9♋24.7	8♓35.9	6♑51.4	12♋ 6.7	23♊ 2.2
2 Su	4 39 42	8 54 16	20 8 13	26 3 3	3R 45.8	4R 45.0	6R 1.3	20 26.1	9R 18.7	8 37.9	6 54.7	12R 5.3	23R 1.1
3 M	4 43 39	9 55 6	1♋57 50	7♋52 49	3 38.6	3 29.8	5 25.4	21 3.2	9 12.5	8 39.9	6 57.9	12 3.9	22 60.0
4 Tu	4 47 35	10 55 58	13 48 19	19 44 41	3 33.8	2 21.8	4 50.1	21 40.4	9 6.2	8 42.1	7 1.3	12 2.6	22 58.8
5 W	4 51 32	11 56 51	25 42 19	1♌41 38	3D 31.5	1 23.1	4 15.9	22 17.5	8 59.8	8 44.4	7 4.6	12 1.2	22 57.7
6 Th	4 55 28	12 57 44	7♌43 8	13 47 19	3 31.3	0 34.7	3 42.7	22 54.5	8 53.2	8 46.8	7 7.9	11 59.7	22 56.5
7 F	4 59 25	13 58 40	19 54 44	26 5 57	3 32.2	29♏57.5	3 11.0	23 31.6	8 46.5	8 49.2	7 11.3	11 58.3	22 55.4
8 Sa	5 3 21	14 59 36	2♍21 32	8♍42 6	3 33.5	29 31.7	2 40.9	24 8.7	8 39.7	8 51.8	7 14.7	11 56.8	22 54.2
9 Su	5 7 18	16 0 33	15 8 12	21 40 21	3R 34.2	29D 17.1	2 12.5	24 45.7	8 32.8	8 54.5	7 18.1	11 55.4	22 53.0
10 M	5 11 14	17 1 32	28 19 2	5♎ 4 38	3 33.6	29 13.4	1 46.0	25 22.7	8 25.7	8 57.3	7 21.5	11 53.9	22 51.9
11 Tu	5 15 11	18 2 32	11♎57 25	18 57 29	3 31.0	29 19.9	1 21.6	25 59.8	8 18.5	9 0.1	7 24.9	11 52.3	22 50.7
12 W	5 19 8	19 3 33	26 4 48	3♏19 6	3 26.5	29 35.8	0 59.3	26 36.7	8 11.3	9 3.1	7 28.4	11 50.8	22 49.5
13 Th	5 23 4	20 4 35	10♏39 55	18 6 34	3 20.5	0♐ 0.2	0 39.4	27 13.7	8 3.9	9 6.1	7 31.8	11 49.3	22 48.3
14 F	5 27 1	21 5 38	25 38 8	3♐13 31	3 13.8	0 32.4	0 21.8	27 50.7	7 56.4	9 9.3	7 35.3	11 47.7	22 47.2
15 Sa	5 30 57	22 6 42	10♐51 28	18 30 39	3 7.3	1 11.5	0 6.5	28 27.6	7 48.9	9 12.5	7 38.8	11 46.2	22 46.0
16 Su	5 34 54	23 7 47	26 9 38	3♑47 3	3 1.8	1 56.7	29♏53.8	29 4.5	7 41.3	9 15.9	7 42.3	11 44.6	22 44.8
17 M	5 38 50	24 8 53	11♑21 36	18 52 8	2 58.1	2 47.3	29 43.5	29 41.4	7 33.6	9 19.3	7 45.8	11 43.0	22 43.6
18 Tu	5 42 47	25 9 59	26 17 39	3♒37 22	2D 56.4	3 42.8	29 35.6	0♏18.2	7 25.8	9 22.9	7 49.4	11 41.4	22 42.5
19 W	5 46 44	26 11 5	10♒50 41	17 57 14	2 56.5	4 42.4	29 30.3	0 55.1	7 17.9	9 26.5	7 52.9	11 39.8	22 41.3
20 Th	5 50 40	27 12 12	24 56 51	1♓49 29	2 57.7	5 45.7	29D 27.4	1 31.9	7 10.0	9 30.2	7 56.4	11 38.1	22 40.1
21 F	5 54 37	28 13 19	8♓35 19	15 14 35	2 59.3	6 52.3	29 26.9	2 8.7	7 2.1	9 34.0	7 60.0	11 36.5	22 39.0
22 Sa	5 58 33	29 14 26	21 47 38	28 14 55	3R 0.5	8 1.7	29 28.9	2 45.4	6 54.1	9 37.9	8 3.6	11 34.8	22 37.8
23 Su	6 2 30	0♑15 34	4♈36 54	10♈54 6	3 0.7	9 13.5	29 33.2	3 22.2	6 46.1	9 41.8	8 7.1	11 33.2	22 36.6
24 M	6 6 26	1 16 41	17 7 1	23 16 10	2 59.4	10 27.6	29 39.9	3 58.9	6 38.0	9 45.9	8 10.7	11 31.5	22 35.5
25 Tu	6 10 23	2 17 49	29 22 4	5♉25 13	2 56.6	11 43.6	29 48.9	4 35.5	6 29.9	9 50.0	8 14.3	11 29.9	22 34.3
26 W	6 14 19	3 18 56	11♉26 3	17 25 1	2 52.5	13 1.3	0♐ 0.1	5 12.2	6 21.8	9 54.3	8 17.9	11 28.2	22 33.1
27 Th	6 18 16	4 20 4	23 22 31	29 18 55	2 47.5	14 20.5	0 13.5	5 48.8	6 13.7	9 58.6	8 21.4	11 26.5	22 32.0
28 F	6 22 13	5 21 12	5♊14 34	11♊ 9 45	2 42.3	15 41.0	0 29.0	6 25.4	6 5.5	10 3.0	8 25.0	11 24.8	22 30.8
29 Sa	6 26 9	6 22 20	17 4 46	22 59 51	2 37.4	17 2.8	0 46.6	7 2.0	5 57.4	10 7.5	8 28.6	11 23.1	22 29.7
30 Su	6 30 6	7 23 28	28 55 17	4♋51 17	2 33.3	18 25.6	1 6.2	7 38.6	5 49.3	10 12.0	8 32.2	11 21.4	22 28.6
31 M	6 34 2	8 24 37	10♋48 3	16 45 49	2 30.3	19 49.3	1 27.7	8 15.1	5 41.2	10 16.6	8 35.8	11 19.7	22 27.4

Astro Data Dy Hr Mn	Planet Ingress Dy Hr Mn	Last Aspect Dy Hr Mn	☽ Ingress Dy Hr Mn	Last Aspect Dy Hr Mn	☽ Ingress Dy Hr Mn	☽ Phases & Eclipses Dy Hr Mn	Astro Data
♂0S 3 16:03	☿ ♐ 1 19:33	1 14:07 ♆ ⚹	♊ 3 0:56	2 5:50 ♇ ☌	♋ 2 20:01	1 4:46 ○ 7♉51	1 NOVEMBER 1906
♀ R 9 15:36	☉ ♐ 23 4:54	5 0:27 ♇ ☌	♋ 5 13:43	4 16:45 ♂ □	♌ 5 8:37	9 9:45 ☽ 16♌05	Julian Day # 2496
♄ D 12 17:09		6 16:51 ☉ △	♌ 8 2:13	7 18:44 ☿ □	♍ 7 19:30	16 8:36 ● 23♏05	Delta T 6.0 sec
☽0S 13 11:58	☿ ♏ 6 22:06	9 23:44 ♇ ⚹	♍ 10 12:10	10 1:37 ☿ ⚹	♎ 10 3:00	23 0:39 ☽ 29♒49	SVP 06♓33'54"
☿ R 20 1:40	☿ ♐ 12 23:49	12 6:28 ♇ □	♎ 12 18:00	12 0:56 ♂ ☌	♏ 12 6:31	30 23:07 ○ 7♊51	Obliquity 23°27'00"
☽0N 26 5:36	♀ ♏ 15 11:42	14 9:04 ♇ △	♏ 14 19:54	13 1:52 ♆ △	♐ 14 6:55		⚷ Chiron 7♒35.2
	♂ ♏ 17 12:07	16 8:36 ☉ ☌	♐ 16 19:29	16 4:46 ♂ ⚹	♑ 16 6:02	9 1:45 ☽ 16♍05	☽ Mean ☊ 7♌01.9
♃△♄ 6 16:54	☉ ♑ 22 17:53	18 8:12 ♇ ☍	♑ 18 18:58	18 5:21 ♀ ⚹	♒ 18 6:03	15 18:54 ● 22♐55	
☿ D 9 20:29	♀ ♐ 25 23:49	20 16:03 ☉ ⚹	♒ 20 20:23	20 7:50 ♀ □	♓ 20 8:48	22 15:04 ☽ 29♓53	1 DECEMBER 1906
☽0S 10 22:29		23 0:39 ☉ □	♓ 23 0:59	22 15:04 ☉ □	♈ 22 15:17	30 18:44 ○ 8♋11	Julian Day # 2526
♃☍♅ 15 21:44		24 19:51 ♇ □	♈ 25 8:53	24 10:39 ♇ ⚹	♉ 25 1:15		Delta T 6.1 sec
♀ D 20 16:26		27 5:42 ♇ ⚹	♉ 27 19:17	26 0:04 ♆ ⚹	♊ 27 13:23		SVP 06♓33'50"
☽0N 23 12:42		28 19:27 ♆ ⚹	♊ 30 7:15	29 10:58 ♇ ☌	♋ 30 2:11		Obliquity 23°26'59"
							⚷ Chiron 8♒34.1
							☽ Mean ☊ 5♌26.6

LONGITUDE — JANUARY 1907

Day	Sid.Time	☉	0 hr ☽	Noon ☽	True ☊	☿	♀	♂	♃	♄	♅	♆	♇
1 Tu	6 37 59	9♑25 45	22♋44 50	28♋45 19	2♌28.7	21♐14.0	1♐51.1	8♏51.6	5♋33.1	10♓21.4	8♑39.4	11♋18.1	22♊26.3
2 W	6 41 55	10 26 54	4♌47 31	10♌51 43	2D 28.3	22 39.4	2 16.3	9 28.1	5R 25.0	10 26.1	8 43.0	11R 16.4	22R 25.2
3 Th	6 45 52	11 28 2	16 58 11	23 7 15	2 29.0	24 5.6	2 43.3	10 4.5	5 16.9	10 31.0	8 46.6	11 14.7	22 24.1
4 F	6 49 48	12 29 11	29 19 15	5♍34 32	2 30.3	25 32.4	3 12.0	10 40.9	5 8.9	10 36.0	8 50.2	11 13.0	22 23.0
5 Sa	6 53 45	13 30 20	11♍53 28	18 16 26	2 31.9	26 59.9	3 42.3	11 17.3	5 0.9	10 41.0	8 53.8	11 11.3	22 21.9
6 Su	6 57 42	14 31 29	24 43 49	1♎15 58	2 33.3	28 28.0	4 14.1	11 53.7	4 53.0	10 46.1	8 57.4	11 9.6	22 20.8
7 M	7 1 38	15 32 38	7♎53 14	14 35 55	2R 34.2	29 56.6	4 47.5	12 30.0	4 45.1	10 51.2	9 0.9	11 7.9	22 19.7
8 Tu	7 5 35	16 33 48	21 24 16	28 18 26	2 34.3	1♑25.8	5 22.3	13 6.3	4 37.3	10 56.4	9 4.5	11 6.2	22 18.7
9 W	7 9 31	17 34 57	5♏18 27	12♏24 17	2 33.6	2 55.5	5 58.5	13 42.6	4 29.5	11 1.7	9 8.1	11 4.5	22 17.6
10 Th	7 13 28	18 36 7	19 35 42	26 52 22	2 32.3	4 25.8	6 36.0	14 18.8	4 21.8	11 7.1	9 11.7	11 2.8	22 16.6
11 F	7 17 24	19 37 16	4♐13 43	11♐39 5	2 30.7	5 56.5	7 14.8	14 55.0	4 14.2	11 12.5	9 15.2	11 1.1	22 15.5
12 Sa	7 21 21	20 38 26	19 7 39	26 38 26	2 29.1	7 27.7	7 54.8	15 31.2	4 6.7	11 18.1	9 18.8	10 59.4	22 14.5
13 Su	7 25 17	21 39 35	4♑10 23	11♑42 21	2 27.9	8 59.4	8 36.1	16 7.3	3 59.2	11 23.6	9 22.3	10 57.8	22 13.5
14 M	7 29 14	22 40 45	19 13 12	26 41 50	2D 27.1	10 31.7	9 18.4	16 43.4	3 51.9	11 29.3	9 25.8	10 56.1	22 12.5
15 Tu	7 33 11	23 41 53	4♒ 7 10	11♒28 17	2 26.9	12 4.4	10 1.8	17 19.5	3 44.6	11 35.0	9 29.4	10 54.5	22 11.5
16 W	7 37 7	24 43 2	18 44 21	25 54 43	2 27.2	13 37.6	10 46.3	17 55.5	3 37.5	11 40.7	9 32.9	10 52.8	22 10.6
17 Th	7 41 4	25 44 9	2♓58 54	9♓56 34	2 27.7	15 11.3	11 31.7	18 31.5	3 30.4	11 46.6	9 36.4	10 51.2	22 9.6
18 F	7 45 0	26 45 16	16 47 34	23 31 54	2 28.4	16 45.5	12 18.1	19 7.4	3 23.5	11 52.4	9 39.9	10 49.6	22 8.6
19 Sa	7 48 57	27 46 22	0♈ 9 41	6♈41 10	2 28.9	18 20.3	13 5.4	19 43.3	3 16.7	11 58.4	9 43.3	10 47.9	22 7.7
20 Su	7 52 53	28 47 27	13 6 43	19 26 43	2 29.2	19 55.6	13 53.5	20 19.1	3 10.0	12 4.4	9 46.8	10 46.3	22 6.8
21 M	7 56 50	29 48 31	25 41 42	1♉52 9	2R 29.4	21 31.4	14 42.6	20 54.9	3 3.5	12 10.4	9 50.2	10 44.7	22 5.9
22 Tu	8 0 46	0♒49 34	7♉58 39	14 1 46	2 29.4	23 7.8	15 32.4	21 30.6	2 57.0	12 16.6	9 53.6	10 43.2	22 5.0
23 W	8 4 43	1 50 36	20 2 4	26 0 8	2D 29.3	24 44.8	16 23.0	22 6.3	2 50.8	12 22.7	9 57.0	10 41.6	22 4.1
24 Th	8 8 40	2 51 38	1♊56 31	7♊51 45	2 29.3	26 22.3	17 14.4	22 42.0	2 44.6	12 28.9	10 0.4	10 40.0	22 3.2
25 F	8 12 36	3 52 38	13 46 22	19 40 49	2 29.4	28 0.5	18 6.5	23 17.6	2 38.6	12 35.2	10 3.8	10 38.5	22 2.4
26 Sa	8 16 33	4 53 37	25 35 34	1♋31 3	2 29.7	29 39.3	18 59.2	23 53.2	2 32.8	12 41.5	10 7.2	10 37.0	22 1.6
27 Su	8 20 29	5 54 35	7♋27 37	13 25 38	2 30.0	1♒18.7	19 52.7	24 28.7	2 27.1	12 47.9	10 10.5	10 35.5	22 0.8
28 M	8 24 26	6 55 33	19 25 24	25 27 11	2 30.3	2 58.8	20 46.8	25 4.2	2 21.6	12 54.3	10 13.8	10 34.0	21 60.0
29 Tu	8 28 22	7 56 29	1♌31 14	7♌37 45	2R 30.5	4 39.6	21 41.5	25 39.6	2 16.2	13 0.8	10 17.1	10 32.5	21 59.2
30 W	8 32 19	8 57 24	13 46 55	19 58 53	2 30.3	6 21.0	22 36.9	26 15.0	2 11.0	13 7.3	10 20.4	10 31.0	21 58.4
31 Th	8 36 15	9 58 18	26 13 47	2♍31 45	2 29.8	8 3.1	23 32.8	26 50.3	2 5.9	13 13.8	10 23.6	10 29.6	21 57.7

LONGITUDE — FEBRUARY 1907

Day	Sid.Time	☉	0 hr ☽	Noon ☽	True ☊	☿	♀	♂	♃	♄	♅	♆	♇
1 F	8 40 12	10♒59 11	8♍52 53	15♍17 16	2♌28.9	9♒46.0	24♐29.3	27♏25.6	2♋ 1.1	13♓20.4	10♑26.9	10♋28.2	21♊57.0
2 Sa	8 44 9	12 0 4	21 45 0	28 16 9	2R 27.6	11 29.5	25 26.3	28 0.8	1R 56.4	13 27.1	10 30.1	10R 26.8	21R 56.2
3 Su	8 48 5	13 0 55	4♎50 48	11♎29 1	2 26.2	13 13.7	26 23.8	28 36.0	1 51.8	13 33.7	10 33.3	10 25.4	21 55.5
4 M	8 52 2	14 1 45	18 10 53	24 56 26	2 25.0	14 58.6	27 21.8	29 11.1	1 47.5	13 40.5	10 36.4	10 24.0	21 54.9
5 Tu	8 55 58	15 2 35	1♏45 43	8♏38 44	2 24.0	16 44.2	28 20.3	29 46.1	1 43.3	13 47.2	10 39.5	10 22.7	21 54.2
6 W	8 59 55	16 3 24	15 35 29	22 35 52	2D 23.7	18 30.5	29 19.3	0♐21.2	1 39.3	13 54.0	10 42.6	10 21.4	21 53.6
7 Th	9 3 51	17 4 11	29 39 48	6♐47 5	2 24.0	20 17.5	0♑18.7	0 56.1	1 35.5	14 0.9	10 45.7	10 20.1	21 53.0
8 F	9 7 48	18 4 58	13♐57 27	21 10 35	2 24.9	22 5.1	1 18.5	1 31.0	1 31.8	14 7.7	10 48.8	10 18.8	21 52.4
9 Sa	9 11 44	19 5 44	28 26 2	5♑43 18	2 26.1	23 53.2	2 18.8	2 5.8	1 28.4	14 14.6	10 51.8	10 17.5	21 51.8
10 Su	9 15 41	20 6 29	13♑ 1 48	20 20 50	2 27.3	25 41.9	3 19.4	2 40.6	1 25.2	14 21.6	10 54.8	10 16.3	21 51.2
11 M	9 19 38	21 7 13	27 39 41	4♒57 35	2R 28.0	27 31.0	4 20.5	3 15.3	1 22.1	14 28.5	10 57.8	10 15.1	21 50.7
12 Tu	9 23 34	22 7 56	12♒13 44	19 27 21	2 27.8	29 20.5	5 21.8	3 49.9	1 19.2	14 35.5	11 0.7	10 13.9	21 50.2
13 W	9 27 31	23 8 37	26 37 41	3♓44 3	2 26.5	1♓10.3	6 23.6	4 24.5	1 16.6	14 42.6	11 3.6	10 12.7	21 49.7
14 Th	9 31 27	24 9 17	10♓45 49	17 42 31	2 24.2	3 0.1	7 25.6	4 59.0	1 14.1	14 49.6	11 6.5	10 11.6	21 49.2
15 F	9 35 24	25 9 55	24 33 46	1♈19 16	2 20.9	4 49.9	8 28.0	5 33.4	1 11.8	14 56.7	11 9.3	10 10.5	21 48.8
16 Sa	9 39 20	26 10 31	7♈58 56	14 32 44	2 17.2	6 39.5	9 30.7	6 7.7	1 9.7	15 3.8	11 12.1	10 9.4	21 48.3
17 Su	9 43 17	27 11 6	21 0 47	27 23 19	2 13.5	8 28.5	10 33.7	6 42.0	1 7.8	15 11.0	11 14.9	10 8.4	21 47.9
18 M	9 47 13	28 11 39	3♉40 40	9♉53 12	2 10.4	10 16.9	11 36.9	7 16.2	1 6.2	15 18.1	11 17.6	10 7.3	21 47.5
19 Tu	9 51 10	29 12 11	16 1 26	22 5 53	2 8.3	12 4.1	12 40.5	7 50.3	1 4.7	15 25.3	11 20.3	10 6.3	21 47.1
20 W	9 55 7	0♓12 40	28 7 7	4♊ 5 45	2D 7.5	13 49.9	13 44.3	8 24.3	1 3.4	15 32.5	11 23.0	10 5.3	21 46.8
21 Th	9 59 3	1 13 8	10♊ 2 24	15 57 41	2 7.9	15 34.0	14 48.4	8 58.2	1 2.3	15 39.7	11 25.6	10 4.4	21 46.5
22 F	10 3 0	2 13 34	21 52 16	27 46 44	2 9.2	17 15.7	15 52.8	9 32.1	1 1.4	15 47.0	11 28.2	10 3.5	21 46.2
23 Sa	10 6 56	3 13 57	3♋41 43	9♋37 47	2 11.0	18 54.7	16 57.3	10 5.9	1 0.8	15 54.2	11 30.8	10 2.6	21 45.9
24 Su	10 10 53	4 14 19	15 35 28	21 35 18	2 12.8	20 30.3	18 2.2	10 39.6	1 0.3	16 1.5	11 33.3	10 1.7	21 45.6
25 M	10 14 49	5 14 40	27 37 44	3♌43 11	2R 13.8	22 2.1	19 7.2	11 13.2	1D 0.0	16 8.8	11 35.8	10 0.9	21 45.4
26 Tu	10 18 46	6 14 58	9♌51 59	16 4 25	2 13.6	23 29.5	20 12.5	11 46.7	0 59.9	16 16.1	11 38.3	10 0.1	21 45.2
27 W	10 22 42	7 15 14	22 20 44	28 41 4	2 11.8	24 51.7	21 18.0	12 20.2	1 0.0	16 23.4	11 40.7	9 59.3	21 45.0
28 Th	10 26 39	8 15 29	5♍ 5 30	11♍34 2	2 8.2	26 8.3	22 23.7	12 53.5	1 0.4	16 30.8	11 43.0	9 58.6	21 44.8

Astro Data Dy Hr Mn	Planet Ingress Dy Hr Mn	Last Aspect Dy Hr Mn	☽ Ingress Dy Hr Mn	Last Aspect Dy Hr Mn	☽ Ingress Dy Hr Mn	☽ Phases & Eclipses Dy Hr Mn	Astro Data
☽0S 7 6:24	☿ ♑ 7 0:55	31 1:04 ♆ ☌	♌ 1 14:29	2 12:04 ♂ ✶	♎ 2 15:10	7 14:47 ☽ 16♎10	1 JANUARY 1907
♄△♆ 9 9:21	☉ ♒ 21 4:31	3 15:44 ♇ △	♍ 4 1:18	4 17:32 ♀ ✶	♏ 4 20:55	14 5:57 ● 22♑56	Julian Day # 2557
☽0N 19 21:00	☿ ♒ 26 5:00	6 7:45 ♆ □	♎ 6 9:41	6 5:44 ☿ □	♐ 7 0:34	14 6:05:37 ● T 2'25"	Delta T 6.1 sec
		8 1:35 ♇ △	♏ 8 14:55	8 15:25 ☿ ✶	♑ 9 2:35	21 8:42 ☽ 0♉11	SVP 06♓33'44"
♅☍♆ 1 6:50	♂ ♐ 5 9:29	9 22:14 ☉ ✶	♐ 10 17:07	10 2:12 ♄ ✶	♒ 11 3:50	29 13:45 ○ 8♌31	Obliquity 23°26'59"
☽0S 3 11:59	♀ ♑ 6 16:28	12 4:58 ♇ ☍	♑ 12 17:21	12 17:43 ☉ ☌	♓ 13 5:41	29 13:38 ○ P 0.711	⚷ Chiron 10♒24.8
☽0N 16 6:13	☿ ♓ 12 8:38	14 5:57 ☉ ☌	♒ 14 17:20	14 19:10 ♇ □	♈ 15 9:38		☽ Mean ☊ 3♌48.2
♃ D 25 21:40	☉ ♓ 19 18:58	16 5:43 ♇ △	♓ 16 18:55	17 12:37 ☉ ✶	♉ 17 16:58	6 0:52 ☽ 16♏06	
☿0N 28 17:06		18 19:18 ☉ ✶	♈ 18 23:42	18 22:48 ♄ ✶	♊ 20 3:46	12 17:43 ● 22♒53	1 FEBRUARY 1907
		20 17:05 ♇ ✶	♉ 21 8:21	21 23:48 ♇ ☌	♋ 22 16:30	20 4:35 ☽ 0♊24	Julian Day # 2588
		23 10:58 ☿ △	♊ 23 20:04	24 11:18 ☿ △	♌ 25 4:41	28 6:23 ○ 8♍31	Delta T 6.3 sec
		25 16:46 ♇ ☌	♋ 26 8:56	26 22:52 ♇ ✶	♍ 27 14:28		SVP 06♓33'39"
		28 11:49 ♂ △	♌ 28 21:00				Obliquity 23°27'00"
		31 1:13 ♂ □	♍ 31 7:12				⚷ Chiron 12♒43.0
							☽ Mean ☊ 2♌09.7

MARCH 1907 — LONGITUDE

Day	Sid.Time	☉	0 hr ☽	Noon ☽	True ☊	☿	♀	♂	♃	♄	♅	♆	♇
1 F	10 30 36	9♓15 41	18♍ 6 36	24♍43 4	2♌ 3.0	27♓18.5	23♑29.6	13♐26.8	1♋ 0.9	16♓38.1	11♑45.4	9♋57.9	21♊44.6
2 Sa	10 34 32	10 15 52	1♎23 17	8♎ 6 59	1R56.7	28 21.9	24 35.7	13 60.0	1 1.6	16 45.4	11 47.7	9R57.2	21R44.5
3 Su	10 38 29	11 16 2	14 53 55	21 43 49	1 50.0	29 17.8	25 42.0	14 33.0	1 2.5	16 52.8	11 49.9	9 56.6	21 44.4
4 M	10 42 25	12 16 9	28 36 20	5♏31 13	1 43.7	0♈ 5.8	26 48.5	15 6.0	1 3.6	17 0.2	11 52.1	9 55.9	21 44.3
5 Tu	10 46 22	13 16 15	12♏28 8	19 26 51	1 38.6	0 45.5	27 55.2	15 38.9	1 4.9	17 7.5	11 54.3	9 55.4	21 44.2
6 W	10 50 18	14 16 20	26 27 6	3♐28 39	1 35.2	1 16.4	29 2.1	16 11.7	1 6.4	17 14.9	11 56.4	9 54.8	21 44.2
7 Th	10 54 15	15 16 23	10♐31 19	17 34 56	1D33.8	1 38.4	0♒ 9.1	16 44.3	1 8.1	17 22.3	11 58.5	9 54.3	21D44.2
8 F	10 58 11	16 16 24	24 39 17	1♑44 14	1 33.9	1R51.4	1 16.3	17 16.9	1 9.9	17 29.7	12 0.5	9 53.8	21 44.2
9 Sa	11 2 8	17 16 24	8♑49 36	15 55 11	1 35.1	1 55.3	2 23.7	17 49.3	1 12.0	17 37.1	12 2.5	9 53.3	21 44.2
10 Su	11 6 5	18 16 22	23 0 45	0♒ 6 1	1R36.2	1 50.2	3 31.2	18 21.7	1 14.3	17 44.5	12 4.5	9 52.9	21 44.3
11 M	11 10 1	19 16 19	7♒10 42	14 14 25	1 36.3	1 36.5	4 38.8	18 53.9	1 16.7	17 51.9	12 6.4	9 52.5	21 44.4
12 Tu	11 13 58	20 16 14	21 16 46	28 17 20	1 34.6	1 14.5	5 46.6	19 26.0	1 19.4	17 59.2	12 8.2	9 52.2	21 44.5
13 W	11 17 54	21 16 7	5♓15 37	12♓11 11	1 30.6	0 44.9	6 54.6	19 58.0	1 22.2	18 6.6	12 10.0	9 51.8	21 44.6
14 Th	11 21 51	22 15 58	19 3 34	25 52 19	1 24.2	0 8.4	8 2.6	20 29.8	1 25.2	18 14.0	12 11.8	9 51.6	21 44.7
15 F	11 25 47	23 15 47	2♈37 3	9♈17 27	1 15.8	29♓25.9	9 10.8	21 1.5	1 28.4	18 21.4	12 13.5	9 51.3	21 44.9
16 Sa	11 29 44	24 15 34	15 53 16	22 24 21	1 6.3	28 38.4	10 19.1	21 33.1	1 31.8	18 28.7	12 15.2	9 51.1	21 45.1
17 Su	11 33 40	25 15 19	28 50 38	5♉12 10	0 56.6	27 47.1	11 27.5	22 4.5	1 35.3	18 36.1	12 16.8	9 50.9	21 45.3
18 M	11 37 37	26 15 2	11♉29 4	17 41 36	0 47.8	26 53.2	12 36.1	22 35.8	1 39.1	18 43.5	12 18.4	9 50.7	21 45.5
19 Tu	11 41 33	27 14 42	23 50 3	29 54 51	0 40.6	25 57.8	13 44.7	23 6.9	1 43.0	18 50.8	12 20.0	9 50.6	21 45.8
20 W	11 45 30	28 14 21	5♊56 26	11♊55 22	0 35.6	25 2.2	14 53.5	23 38.0	1 47.1	18 58.1	12 21.4	9 50.5	21 46.0
21 Th	11 49 27	29 13 57	17 52 13	23 47 36	0 32.9	24 7.5	16 2.3	24 8.8	1 51.4	19 5.5	12 22.9	9 50.5	21 46.3
22 F	11 53 23	0♈13 31	29 42 10	5♋36 35	0D32.1	23 14.9	17 11.3	24 39.5	1 55.8	19 12.8	12 24.3	9D50.4	21 46.7
23 Sa	11 57 20	1 13 3	11♋31 32	17 27 41	0 32.5	22 25.2	18 20.3	25 10.1	2 0.4	19 20.1	12 25.6	9 50.4	21 47.0
24 Su	12 1 16	2 12 32	23 25 43	29 26 16	0R33.3	21 39.3	19 29.5	25 40.5	2 5.2	19 27.3	12 26.9	9 50.5	21 47.4
25 M	12 5 13	3 11 59	5♌29 57	11♌37 19	0 33.4	20 57.8	20 38.7	26 10.7	2 10.2	19 34.6	12 28.1	9 50.6	21 47.8
26 Tu	12 9 9	4 11 24	17 48 55	24 5 9	0 31.8	20 21.3	21 48.0	26 40.8	2 15.3	19 41.8	12 29.3	9 50.7	21 48.2
27 W	12 13 6	5 10 47	0♍26 23	6♍52 53	0 28.0	19 50.2	22 57.4	27 10.7	2 20.6	19 49.1	12 30.5	9 50.8	21 48.6
28 Th	12 17 2	6 10 7	13 24 47	20 2 7	0 21.6	19 24.7	24 7.0	27 40.5	2 26.1	19 56.3	12 31.6	9 51.0	21 49.0
29 F	12 20 59	7 9 25	26 44 48	3♎32 37	0 12.9	19 5.0	25 16.5	28 10.0	2 31.7	20 3.5	12 32.6	9 51.2	21 49.5
30 Sa	12 24 56	8 8 41	10♎25 12	17 22 8	0 2.4	18 51.2	26 26.2	28 39.4	2 37.4	20 10.6	12 33.6	9 51.5	21 50.0
31 Su	12 28 52	9 7 55	24 22 51	1♏26 43	29♋51.2	18D43.1	27 36.0	29 8.7	2 43.4	20 17.8	12 34.6	9 51.8	21 50.5

APRIL 1907 — LONGITUDE

Day	Sid.Time	☉	0 hr ☽	Noon ☽	True ☊	☿	♀	♂	♃	♄	♅	♆	♇
1 M	12 32 49	10♈ 7 7	8♏33 6	15♏41 19	29♋40.5	18♓40.8	28♒45.8	29♐37.7	2♋49.4	20♓24.9	12♑35.4	9♋52.1	21♊51.0
2 Tu	12 36 45	11 6 17	22 50 40	0♐ 0 31	29R31.5	18 44.1	29 55.7	0♑ 6.5	2 55.7	20 32.0	12 36.3	9 52.4	21 51.6
3 W	12 40 42	12 5 25	7♐10 19	14 19 33	29 24.9	18 52.8	1♓ 5.7	0 35.2	3 2.1	20 39.0	12 37.1	9 52.8	21 52.2
4 Th	12 44 38	13 4 32	21 27 47	28 34 43	29 20.9	19 6.7	2 15.8	1 3.7	3 8.6	20 46.1	12 37.8	9 53.2	21 52.8
5 F	12 48 35	14 3 37	5♑40 6	12♑43 44	29D19.3	19 25.5	3 26.0	1 31.9	3 15.3	20 53.1	12 38.5	9 53.7	21 53.4
6 Sa	12 52 31	15 2 40	19 45 33	26 45 27	29R19.2	19 49.2	4 36.2	1 60.0	3 22.1	21 0.1	12 39.2	9 54.2	21 54.0
7 Su	12 56 28	16 1 42	3♒43 26	10♒39 26	29 19.2	20 17.4	5 46.5	2 27.8	3 29.1	21 7.0	12 39.8	9 54.7	21 54.7
8 M	13 0 25	17 0 41	17 33 28	24 25 27	29 18.2	20 49.9	6 56.8	2 55.4	3 36.2	21 14.0	12 40.3	9 55.2	21 55.4
9 Tu	13 4 21	17 59 39	1♓15 21	8♓ 3 2	29 15.0	21 26.6	8 7.2	3 22.7	3 43.5	21 20.8	12 40.8	9 55.8	21 56.1
10 W	13 8 18	18 58 35	14 48 22	21 31 13	29 8.9	22 7.1	9 17.7	3 49.9	3 50.9	21 27.7	12 41.2	9 56.4	21 56.8
11 Th	13 12 14	19 57 29	28 11 22	4♈48 37	28 59.9	22 51.3	10 28.2	4 16.8	3 58.4	21 34.5	12 41.6	9 57.1	21 57.5
12 F	13 16 11	20 56 22	11♈22 47	17 53 39	28 48.5	23 39.0	11 38.8	4 43.4	4 6.1	21 41.3	12 41.9	9 57.8	21 58.3
13 Sa	13 20 7	21 55 12	24 21 3	0♉44 52	28 35.5	24 30.1	12 49.4	5 9.8	4 13.9	21 48.1	12 42.2	9 58.5	21 59.0
14 Su	13 24 4	22 54 0	7♉ 5 1	13 21 29	28 22.1	25 24.3	14 0.1	5 35.9	4 21.9	21 54.8	12 42.4	9 59.2	21 59.8
15 M	13 28 0	23 52 46	19 34 18	25 43 37	28 9.5	26 21.5	15 10.8	6 1.7	4 29.9	22 1.5	12 42.6	10 0.0	22 0.6
16 Tu	13 31 57	24 51 31	1♊49 36	7♊52 31	27 58.8	27 21.6	16 21.6	6 27.3	4 38.1	22 8.1	12 42.7	10 0.8	22 1.5
17 W	13 35 53	25 50 13	13 52 44	19 50 38	27 50.7	28 24.5	17 32.4	6 52.6	4 46.5	22 14.7	12R42.8	10 1.7	22 2.3
18 Th	13 39 50	26 48 53	25 46 42	1♋41 28	27 45.4	29 30.0	18 43.3	7 17.6	4 54.9	22 21.2	12 42.8	10 2.5	22 3.2
19 F	13 43 47	27 47 31	7♋35 30	13 29 25	27 42.6	0♈38.0	19 54.2	7 42.3	5 3.5	22 27.7	12 42.8	10 3.4	22 4.1
20 Sa	13 47 43	28 46 6	19 23 52	25 19 32	27 41.7	1 48.4	21 5.2	8 6.8	5 12.2	22 34.2	12 42.7	10 4.4	22 5.0
21 Su	13 51 40	29 44 40	1♌17 6	7♌17 17	27 41.6	3 1.2	22 16.2	8 30.9	5 21.0	22 40.6	12 42.6	10 5.3	22 5.9
22 M	13 55 36	0♉43 11	13 20 45	19 28 10	27 41.2	4 16.3	23 27.2	8 54.7	5 30.0	22 47.0	12 42.4	10 6.3	22 6.8
23 Tu	13 59 33	1 41 40	25 40 10	1♍57 21	27 39.6	5 33.5	24 38.3	9 18.2	5 39.0	22 53.3	12 42.2	10 7.4	22 7.8
24 W	14 3 29	2 40 7	8♍20 11	14 49 5	27 35.8	6 52.9	25 49.4	9 41.4	5 48.2	22 59.6	12 41.9	10 8.4	22 8.7
25 Th	14 7 26	3 38 32	21 24 23	28 6 13	27 29.4	8 14.4	27 0.5	10 4.2	5 57.5	23 5.8	12 41.6	10 9.5	22 9.7
26 F	14 11 22	4 36 54	4♎54 37	11♎49 25	27 20.6	9 37.9	28 11.7	10 26.7	6 6.8	23 12.0	12 41.2	10 10.6	22 10.7
27 Sa	14 15 19	5 35 15	18 50 19	25 56 48	27 9.8	11 3.4	29 23.0	10 48.9	6 16.3	23 18.1	12 40.7	10 11.8	22 11.7
28 Su	14 19 16	6 33 34	3♏ 8 15	10♏23 51	26 58.3	12 30.9	0♈34.2	11 10.7	6 25.9	23 24.2	12 40.3	10 12.9	22 12.8
29 M	14 23 12	7 31 51	17 42 42	25 3 50	26 47.2	14 0.3	1 45.5	11 32.2	6 35.6	23 30.2	12 39.7	10 14.1	22 13.8
30 Tu	14 27 9	8 30 6	2♐26 15	9♐48 56	26 37.7	15 31.7	2 56.9	11 53.2	6 45.4	23 36.2	12 39.2	10 15.4	22 14.9

Astro Data	Planet Ingress	Last Aspect	☽ Ingress	Last Aspect	☽ Ingress	☽ Phases & Eclipses	Astro Data
Dy Hr Mn	Dy Hr Mn	Dy Hr Mn	Dy Hr Mn	Dy Hr Mn	Dy Hr Mn	Dy Hr Mn	1 MARCH 1907
☽0S 2 17:33	☿ ♈ 3 20:52	1 18:08 ☿ ☍	♎ 1 21:31	1 20:06 ♄ △	♐ 2 11:59	7 8:42 ☽ 15♐38	Julian Day # 2616
♇ D 7 4:17	♀ ♒ 6 20:44	3 20:36 ♀ □	♏ 4 2:26	4 0:42 ♇ ☍	♑ 4 14:24	14 6:05 ● 22♓31	Delta T 6.4 sec
☿ R 8 22:19	☿ ♓ 14 4:59	6 4:48 ♀ ⚹	♐ 6 6:04	6 2:09 ♄ ⚹	♒ 6 17:35	22 1:10 ☽ 0♋16	SVP 06♓33'36"
☽0N 15 15:22	☉ ♈ 21 18:33	7 19:03 ♇ ☍	♑ 8 9:03	8 7:38 ♇ △	♓ 8 21:47	29 19:44 ○ 7♎58	Obliquity 23°27'01"
☿0S 21 19:11	☊ ♋ 30 5:08	9 15:22 ☉ ⚹	♒ 10 11:50	10 13:49 ☿ ☌	♈ 11 3:16		⚷ Chiron 14♒49.3
♆ D 22 1:59		12 0:47 ♇ △	♓ 12 14:56	12 19:35 ♇ ⚹	♉ 13 10:35	5 15:20 ☽ 14♑41	☽ Mean ☊ 0♌40.7
☽0S 30 1:09	♂ ♑ 1 18:33	14 18:37 ☿ ☌	♈ 14 19:20	15 14:24 ☿ ⚹	♊ 15 20:24	12 19:06 ● 21♈43	
☿ D 31 21:51	♀ ♓ 2 1:28	16 10:52 ♂ △	♉ 17 2:10	18 8:20 ☿ □	♋ 18 8:34	20 20:38 ☽ 29♋36	1 APRIL 1907
☽0N 11 23:29	☿ ♈ 18 10:42	19 7:19 ☉ ⚹	♊ 19 12:10	20 20:38 ☉ □	♌ 20 21:25	28 6:04 ○ 6♏48	Julian Day # 2647
♄□♇ 14 20:41	☉ ♉ 21 6:17	21 13:18 ♂ ☍	♋ 22 0:36	22 17:10 ♇ ⚹	♍ 23 8:17		Delta T 6.5 sec
♅ R 17 22:43	♀ ♈ 27 12:29	23 20:39 ☿ △	♌ 24 13:07	25 11:01 ♀ ☍	♎ 25 15:22		SVP 06♓33'33"
☿0N 23 14:44		26 17:37 ♂ △	♍ 26 23:10	27 5:42 ♇ △	♏ 27 18:47		Obliquity 23°27'01"
☽0S 26 10:57		29 2:37 ♂ □	♎ 29 5:46	29 9:31 ♄ △	♐ 29 20:02		⚷ Chiron 16♒46.7
♀0N 30 15:07		31 8:23 ♂ ⚹	♏ 31 9:33				☽ Mean ☊ 29♋02.2

LONGITUDE — MAY 1907

Day	Sid.Time	☉	0 hr ☽	Noon ☽	True ☊	☿	♀	♂	♃	♄	♅	♆	♇
1 W	14 31 5	9♉28 20	17♐10 59	24♐31 32	26♋30.7	17♈ 5.0	4♈ 8.2	12♑13.9	6♋55.3	23♓42.1	12♑38.5	10♋16.6	22♊15.9
2 Th	14 35 2	10 26 32	1♑49 51	9♑ 5 22	26R 26.4	18 40.1	5 19.7	12 34.3	7 5.3	23 48.0	12R 37.9	10 17.9	22 17.0
3 F	14 38 58	11 24 43	16 17 36	23 26 13	26D 24.6	20 17.2	6 31.1	12 54.2	7 15.4	23 53.8	12 37.1	10 19.2	22 18.1
4 Sa	14 42 55	12 22 52	0♒31 2	7♒31 58	26R 24.3	21 56.1	7 42.6	13 13.7	7 25.7	23 59.5	12 36.4	10 20.5	22 19.3
5 Su	14 46 51	13 21 0	14 28 58	21 22 7	26 24.5	23 36.9	8 54.1	13 32.7	7 35.9	24 5.2	12 35.6	10 21.9	22 20.4
6 M	14 50 48	14 19 7	28 11 31	4♓57 17	26 23.8	25 19.7	10 5.7	13 51.4	7 46.3	24 10.9	12 34.7	10 23.3	22 21.5
7 Tu	14 54 45	15 17 12	11♓39 34	18 18 30	26 21.2	27 4.3	11 17.3	14 9.5	7 56.8	24 16.4	12 33.8	10 24.7	22 22.7
8 W	14 58 41	16 15 15	24 54 12	1♈26 47	26 16.1	28 50.8	12 28.9	14 27.3	8 7.4	24 21.9	12 32.8	10 26.2	22 23.8
9 Th	15 2 38	17 13 17	7♈56 19	14 22 53	26 8.2	0♉39.2	13 40.5	14 44.5	8 18.0	24 27.4	12 31.8	10 27.6	22 25.0
10 F	15 6 34	18 11 18	20 46 30	27 7 12	25 58.2	2 29.5	14 52.2	15 1.3	8 28.8	24 32.8	12 30.8	10 29.1	22 26.2
11 Sa	15 10 31	19 9 17	3♉25 1	9♉39 59	25 46.7	4 21.7	16 3.9	15 17.5	8 39.6	24 38.1	12 29.7	10 30.6	22 27.4
12 Su	15 14 27	20 7 15	15 52 6	22 1 28	25 34.8	6 15.8	17 15.6	15 33.3	8 50.5	24 43.3	12 28.6	10 32.2	22 28.6
13 M	15 18 24	21 5 11	28 8 8	4♊12 13	25 23.6	8 11.7	18 27.4	15 48.6	9 1.5	24 48.5	12 27.4	10 33.7	22 29.9
14 Tu	15 22 20	22 3 6	10♊13 54	16 13 22	25 14.0	10 9.5	19 39.1	16 3.3	9 12.6	24 53.6	12 26.2	10 35.3	22 31.1
15 W	15 26 17	23 1 0	22 10 53	28 6 46	25 6.7	12 9.2	20 50.9	16 17.5	9 23.8	24 58.7	12 24.9	10 36.9	22 32.4
16 Th	15 30 14	23 58 51	4♋ 1 21	9♋55 5	25 2.0	14 10.6	22 2.7	16 31.1	9 35.0	25 3.6	12 23.6	10 38.6	22 33.6
17 F	15 34 10	24 56 41	15 48 24	21 41 49	24D 59.7	16 13.7	23 14.6	16 44.2	9 46.3	25 8.5	12 22.2	10 40.2	22 34.9
18 Sa	15 38 7	25 54 30	27 35 53	3♌31 12	24 59.3	18 18.4	24 26.5	16 56.7	9 57.7	25 13.4	12 20.9	10 41.9	22 36.2
19 Su	15 42 3	26 52 16	9♌28 24	15 28 6	24 60.0	20 24.7	25 38.3	17 8.7	10 9.2	25 18.1	12 19.4	10 43.6	22 37.5
20 M	15 46 0	27 50 2	21 30 58	27 37 40	25R 0.8	22 32.3	26 50.2	17 20.0	10 20.7	25 22.8	12 18.0	10 45.3	22 38.7
21 Tu	15 49 56	28 47 45	3♍48 52	10♍ 5 11	25 0.8	24 41.1	28 2.2	17 30.8	10 32.3	25 27.4	12 16.5	10 47.1	22 40.1
22 W	15 53 53	29 45 27	16 27 11	22 55 23	24 59.3	26 51.1	29 14.1	17 41.0	10 44.0	25 32.0	12 14.9	10 48.9	22 41.4
23 Th	15 57 49	0♊43 7	29 30 14	6♎12 2	24 55.9	29 1.8	0♉26.1	17 50.5	10 55.7	25 36.4	12 13.3	10 50.6	22 42.7
24 F	16 1 46	1 40 46	13♎ 0 59	19 57 4	24 50.4	1♊13.2	1 38.0	17 59.4	11 7.5	25 40.8	12 11.7	10 52.4	22 44.0
25 Sa	16 5 43	2 38 23	27 0 10	4♏ 9 54	24 43.4	3 24.9	2 50.1	18 7.7	11 19.4	25 45.1	12 10.0	10 54.3	22 45.3
26 Su	16 9 39	3 35 59	11♏25 44	18 46 57	24 35.6	5 36.7	4 2.1	18 15.4	11 31.3	25 49.4	12 8.4	10 56.1	22 46.7
27 M	16 13 36	4 33 33	26 12 37	3♐41 42	24 28.0	7 48.3	5 14.1	18 22.3	11 43.3	25 53.5	12 6.6	10 58.0	22 48.0
28 Tu	16 17 32	5 31 6	11♐13 3	18 45 30	24 21.5	9 59.5	6 26.2	18 28.7	11 55.3	25 57.6	12 4.9	10 59.8	22 49.4
29 W	16 21 29	6 28 39	26 17 50	3♑48 56	24 16.8	12 10.0	7 38.3	18 34.3	12 7.4	26 1.6	12 3.1	11 1.7	22 50.8
30 Th	16 25 25	7 26 10	11♑17 44	18 43 19	24D 14.3	14 19.4	8 50.4	18 39.3	12 19.6	26 5.5	12 1.3	11 3.6	22 52.1
31 F	16 29 22	8 23 40	26 4 56	3♒21 59	24 13.7	16 27.6	10 2.6	18 43.5	12 31.8	26 9.3	11 59.4	11 5.6	22 53.5

LONGITUDE — JUNE 1907

Day	Sid.Time	☉	0 hr ☽	Noon ☽	True ☊	☿	♀	♂	♃	♄	♅	♆	♇
1 Sa	16 33 18	9♊21 10	10♒34 1	17♒40 45	24♋14.4	18♊34.4	11♉14.7	18♑47.1	12♋44.0	26♓13.1	11♑57.5	11♋ 7.5	22♊54.9
2 Su	16 37 15	10 18 39	24 42 3	1♓37 53	24 15.6	20 39.5	12 26.9	18 49.9	12 56.4	26 16.7	11R 55.6	11 9.5	22 56.3
3 M	16 41 12	11 16 7	8♓28 20	15 13 34	24R 16.4	22 42.8	13 39.2	18 52.0	13 8.7	26 20.3	11 53.6	11 11.5	22 57.7
4 Tu	16 45 8	12 13 34	21 53 47	28 29 14	24 16.0	24 44.0	14 51.4	18 53.3	13 21.2	26 23.8	11 51.7	11 13.4	22 59.1
5 W	16 49 5	13 11 0	5♈ 0 13	11♈27 1	24 13.9	26 43.1	16 3.7	18R 53.9	13 33.6	26 27.2	11 49.6	11 15.5	23 0.5
6 Th	16 53 1	14 8 26	17 49 54	24 9 11	24 10.0	28 40.0	17 16.0	18 53.7	13 46.1	26 30.5	11 47.6	11 17.5	23 1.9
7 F	16 56 58	15 5 52	0♉25 7	6♉37 57	24 4.7	0♋34.5	18 28.3	18 52.8	13 58.7	26 33.7	11 45.5	11 19.5	23 3.3
8 Sa	17 0 54	16 3 16	12 47 57	18 55 18	23 58.3	2 26.7	19 40.6	18 51.1	14 11.3	26 36.9	11 43.5	11 21.5	23 4.7
9 Su	17 4 51	17 0 40	25 0 16	1♊ 3 1	23 51.6	4 16.4	20 53.0	18 48.6	14 24.0	26 39.9	11 41.3	11 23.6	23 6.1
10 M	17 8 47	17 58 3	7♊ 3 46	13 2 43	23 45.4	6 3.7	22 5.3	18 45.4	14 36.7	26 42.9	11 39.2	11 25.7	23 7.5
11 Tu	17 12 44	18 55 26	19 0 6	24 56 7	23 40.1	7 48.4	23 17.7	18 41.5	14 49.4	26 45.8	11 37.0	11 27.8	23 8.9
12 W	17 16 41	19 52 48	0♋51 2	6♋45 6	23 36.3	9 30.5	24 30.1	18 36.7	15 2.2	26 48.6	11 34.9	11 29.9	23 10.3
13 Th	17 20 37	20 50 9	12 38 36	18 31 54	23D 34.2	11 10.1	25 42.6	18 31.2	15 15.0	26 51.3	11 32.7	11 32.0	23 11.7
14 F	17 24 34	21 47 29	24 25 19	0♌19 15	23 33.6	12 47.1	26 55.0	18 25.0	15 27.9	26 53.8	11 30.4	11 34.1	23 13.2
15 Sa	17 28 30	22 44 49	6♌14 8	12 10 25	23 34.2	14 21.6	28 7.5	18 18.0	15 40.8	26 56.3	11 28.2	11 36.2	23 14.6
16 Su	17 32 27	23 42 7	18 8 36	24 9 11	23 35.7	15 53.3	29 20.0	18 10.4	15 53.7	26 58.8	11 25.9	11 38.4	23 16.0
17 M	17 36 23	24 39 25	0♍12 44	6♍19 48	23 37.4	17 22.5	0♊32.5	18 1.9	16 6.7	27 1.1	11 23.7	11 40.5	23 17.4
18 Tu	17 40 20	25 36 42	12 30 56	18 46 42	23 38.8	18 49.0	1 45.0	17 52.8	16 19.7	27 3.3	11 21.4	11 42.7	23 18.8
19 W	17 44 16	26 33 58	25 7 40	1♎34 18	23R 39.4	20 12.7	2 57.6	17 43.1	16 32.7	27 5.4	11 19.0	11 44.8	23 20.3
20 Th	17 48 13	27 31 14	8♎ 7 6	14 46 26	23 39.0	21 33.8	4 10.2	17 32.6	16 45.7	27 7.4	11 16.7	11 47.0	23 21.7
21 F	17 52 10	28 28 28	21 32 35	28 25 44	23 37.5	22 52.1	5 22.7	17 21.5	16 58.7	27 9.4	11 14.4	11 49.2	23 23.1
22 Sa	17 56 6	29 25 42	5♏25 53	12♏32 56	23 35.0	24 7.5	6 35.4	17 9.8	17 11.9	27 11.2	11 12.0	11 51.4	23 24.5
23 Su	18 0 3	0♋22 55	19 46 31	27 6 10	23 32.1	25 20.1	7 48.0	16 57.5	17 25.1	27 12.9	11 9.7	11 53.5	23 25.9
24 M	18 3 59	1 20 8	4♐31 11	12♐ 0 42	23 29.1	26 29.7	9 0.6	16 44.6	17 38.2	27 14.6	11 7.3	11 55.7	23 27.3
25 Tu	18 7 56	2 17 21	19 33 42	27 9 4	23 26.6	27 36.4	10 13.3	16 31.1	17 51.4	27 16.1	11 4.9	11 57.9	23 28.7
26 W	18 11 52	3 14 33	4♑45 34	12♑21 58	23 24.9	28 40.0	11 26.0	16 17.1	18 4.6	27 17.6	11 2.5	12 0.2	23 30.1
27 Th	18 15 49	4 11 44	19 57 3	27 29 41	23D 24.2	29 40.4	12 38.7	16 2.6	18 17.9	27 18.9	11 0.1	12 2.4	23 31.5
28 F	18 19 46	5 8 56	4♒58 49	12♒23 33	23 24.5	0♌37.6	13 51.5	15 47.7	18 31.1	27 20.2	10 57.7	12 4.6	23 32.9
29 Sa	18 23 42	6 6 7	19 43 9	26 57 1	23 25.3	1 31.4	15 4.3	15 32.2	18 44.4	27 21.3	10 55.3	12 6.8	23 34.3
30 Su	18 27 39	7 3 19	4♓ 4 47	11♓ 6 12	23 26.5	2 21.8	16 17.1	15 16.4	18 57.7	27 22.4	10 52.9	12 9.0	23 35.7

Astro Data	Planet Ingress	Last Aspect	☽ Ingress	Last Aspect	☽ Ingress	☽ Phases & Eclipses	Astro Data
Dy Hr Mn	Dy Hr Mn	Dy Hr Mn	Dy Hr Mn	Dy Hr Mn	Dy Hr Mn	Dy Hr Mn	
☽0N 9 6:20	☿ ♉ 8 15:23	1 10:43 ♄ □	♑ 1 20:59	1 20:58 ♇ △	♓ 2 9:10	4 21:53 ☽ 13♒16	1 MAY 1907
♃☌♆ 22 11:47	☉ ♊ 22 6:03	3 12:52 ♄ ⚹	♒ 3 23:07	4 8:13 ♄ ☌	♈ 4 14:46	12 8:59 ● 20♉29	Julian Day # 2677
☽0S 23 21:30	♀ ♉ 22 15:18	5 18:13 ☿ ⚹	♓ 6 3:12	6 9:53 ♇ ⚹	♉ 6 23:12	20 13:27 ☽ 28♌22	Delta T 6.7 sec
♃☍♅ 28 16:32	☿ ♊ 23 10:39	7 23:01 ♄ ☌	♈ 8 9:20	9 3:18 ♄ ⚹	♊ 9 9:55	27 14:18 ○ 5♐08	SVP 06♓33'30"
		10 3:08 ♇ ⚹	♉ 10 17:29	11 15:46 ♄ □	♋ 11 22:16		Obliquity 23°27'01"
☽0N 5 12:34	☿ ♋ 6 16:43	12 17:25 ♄ ⚹	♊ 13 3:41	14 5:40 ♀ ⚹	♌ 14 11:21	3 5:20 ☽ 11♓29	⚷ Chiron 17♒57.6
♂ R 5 6:42	♀ ♊ 16 13:14	15 5:41 ♄ □	♋ 15 15:50	16 12:03 ☉ ⚹	♍ 16 23:35	10 23:50 ● 18♊55	☽ Mean ☊ 27♋26.8
♅☍♆ 13 3:50	☉ ♋ 22 14:23	17 20:16 ☉ ⚹	♌ 18 4:52	19 3:41 ♄ ☍	♎ 19 9:05	19 2:55 ☽ 26♍41	
☽0S 20 6:57	☿ ♌ 27 8:05	20 13:27 ☉ □	♍ 20 16:37	21 12:58 ☉ △	♏ 21 14:43	25 21:27 ○ 3♑08	1 JUNE 1907
		22 22:58 ☿ △	♎ 23 0:54	23 12:12 ♄ △	♐ 23 16:42		Julian Day # 2708
		24 16:47 ♇ △	♏ 25 5:03	25 12:12 ♄ □	♑ 25 16:30		Delta T 6.8 sec
		26 23:29 ♄ △	♐ 27 6:05	27 11:44 ♄ ⚹	♒ 27 16:00		SVP 06♓33'25"
		28 23:34 ♄ □	♑ 29 5:54	29 6:23 ♇ △	♓ 29 17:07		Obliquity 23°27'00"
		31 0:07 ♄ ⚹	♒ 31 6:26				⚷ Chiron 18♒12.9R
							☽ Mean ☊ 25♋48.4

JULY 1907 LONGITUDE

Day	Sid.Time	☉	0 hr ☽	Noon ☽	True ☊	☿	♀	♂	♃	♄	♅	♆	♇
1 M	18 31 35	8♋ 0 30	18♓ 1 10	24♓49 45	23♋27.6	3♌ 8.6	17♊29.9	15♑ 0.2	19♋11.0	27♓23.3	10♑50.5	12♋11.3	23♊37.1
2 Tu	18 35 32	8 57 42	1♈32 5	8♈ 8 26	23R28.2	3 51.8	18 42.7	14R43.6	19 24.3	27 24.2	10R48.0	12 13.5	23 38.5
3 W	18 39 28	9 54 54	14 39 6	21 4 29	23 28.3	4 31.1	19 55.6	14 26.8	19 37.6	27 24.9	10 45.6	12 15.7	23 39.8
4 Th	18 43 25	10 52 6	27 24 57	3♉40 58	23 27.8	5 6.6	21 8.5	14 9.6	19 51.0	27 25.6	10 43.2	12 17.9	23 41.2
5 F	18 47 21	11 49 18	9♉52 57	16 1 22	23 26.7	5 38.0	22 21.4	13 52.3	20 4.3	27 26.1	10 40.8	12 20.2	23 42.6
6 Sa	18 51 18	12 46 31	22 6 37	28 9 8	23 25.4	6 5.2	23 34.4	13 34.8	20 17.7	27 26.6	10 38.3	12 22.4	23 43.9
7 Su	18 55 15	13 43 44	4♊ 9 19	10♊ 7 33	23 24.0	6 28.1	24 47.4	13 17.1	20 31.1	27 26.9	10 35.9	12 24.6	23 45.3
8 M	18 59 11	14 40 57	16 4 12	21 59 36	23 22.7	6 46.6	26 0.4	12 59.4	20 44.5	27 27.2	10 33.5	12 26.9	23 46.6
9 Tu	19 3 8	15 38 11	27 54 6	3♋47 59	23 21.8	7 0.5	27 13.4	12 41.6	20 57.9	27R27.3	10 31.1	12 29.1	23 48.0
10 W	19 7 4	16 35 24	9♋41 34	15 35 7	23 21.2	7 9.8	28 26.5	12 23.9	21 11.3	27 27.3	10 28.6	12 31.3	23 49.3
11 Th	19 11 1	17 32 38	21 28 57	27 23 21	23D21.0	7R14.4	29 39.6	12 6.2	21 24.7	27 27.3	10 26.2	12 33.6	23 50.6
12 F	19 14 57	18 29 52	3♌18 35	9♌14 57	23 21.1	7 14.3	0♋52.7	11 48.7	21 38.2	27 27.1	10 23.8	12 35.8	23 51.9
13 Sa	19 18 54	19 27 7	15 12 46	21 12 21	23 21.3	7 9.4	2 5.8	11 31.3	21 51.6	27 26.9	10 21.4	12 38.0	23 53.2
14 Su	19 22 50	20 24 21	27 14 1	3♍18 9	23 21.7	6 59.7	3 19.0	11 14.1	22 5.0	27 26.5	10 19.1	12 40.2	23 54.5
15 M	19 26 47	21 21 36	9♍25 5	15 35 13	23 22.0	6 45.4	4 32.2	10 57.2	22 18.5	27 26.0	10 16.7	12 42.4	23 55.8
16 Tu	19 30 44	22 18 50	21 48 57	28 6 39	23 22.1	6 26.5	5 45.4	10 40.6	22 31.9	27 25.5	10 14.3	12 44.6	23 57.1
17 W	19 34 40	23 16 5	4♎28 45	10♎55 37	23R22.2	6 3.2	6 58.6	10 24.4	22 45.3	27 24.8	10 12.0	12 46.9	23 58.4
18 Th	19 38 37	24 13 20	17 27 37	24 5 5	23D22.2	5 35.9	8 11.9	10 8.5	22 58.7	27 24.0	10 9.6	12 49.0	23 59.6
19 F	19 42 33	25 10 35	0♏48 18	7♏37 29	23 22.2	5 4.8	9 25.2	9 53.1	23 12.1	27 23.2	10 7.3	12 51.2	24 0.9
20 Sa	19 46 30	26 7 50	14 32 45	21 34 6	23 22.3	4 30.3	10 38.5	9 38.2	23 25.6	27 22.2	10 5.0	12 53.4	24 2.1
21 Su	19 50 26	27 5 5	28 41 28	5♐54 34	23 22.5	3 52.9	11 51.8	9 23.7	23 39.0	27 21.2	10 2.7	12 55.6	24 3.3
22 M	19 54 23	28 2 21	13♐13 2	20 36 17	23 22.9	3 13.3	13 5.1	9 9.8	23 52.4	27 20.0	10 0.4	12 57.8	24 4.5
23 Tu	19 58 19	28 59 37	28 3 38	5♑34 14	23 23.3	2 32.0	14 18.5	8 56.5	24 5.8	27 18.8	9 58.2	12 60.0	24 5.7
24 W	20 2 16	29 56 54	13♑ 7 5	20 41 8	23R23.7	1 49.7	15 31.9	8 43.8	24 19.2	27 17.4	9 56.0	13 2.1	24 6.9
25 Th	20 6 13	0♌54 11	28 15 15	5♒48 16	23 23.7	1 7.1	16 45.3	8 31.7	24 32.5	27 16.0	9 53.7	13 4.3	24 8.1
26 F	20 10 9	1 51 28	13♒19 4	20 46 35	23 23.4	0 25.0	17 58.8	8 20.3	24 45.9	27 14.4	9 51.5	13 6.4	24 9.3
27 Sa	20 14 6	2 48 47	28 9 51	5♓28 2	23 22.6	29♋44.2	19 12.3	8 9.5	24 59.3	27 12.8	9 49.4	13 8.5	24 10.4
28 Su	20 18 2	3 46 6	12♓40 28	19 46 38	23 21.5	29 5.4	20 25.8	7 59.5	25 12.6	27 11.1	9 47.2	13 10.7	24 11.6
29 M	20 21 59	4 43 26	26 46 12	3♈38 59	23 20.2	28 29.4	21 39.3	7 50.1	25 25.9	27 9.2	9 45.1	13 12.8	24 12.7
30 Tu	20 25 55	5 40 47	10♈24 59	17 4 17	23 19.0	27 56.8	22 52.9	7 41.5	25 39.2	27 7.3	9 43.0	13 14.9	24 13.8
31 W	20 29 52	6 38 9	23 37 9	0♉ 3 55	23 18.1	27 28.3	24 6.5	7 33.6	25 52.5	27 5.3	9 40.9	13 17.0	24 14.9

AUGUST 1907 LONGITUDE

Day	Sid.Time	☉	0 hr ☽	Noon ☽	True ☊	☿	♀	♂	♃	♄	♅	♆	♇
1 Th	20 33 48	7♌35 32	6♉24 59	12♉40 51	23♋17.7	27♋ 4.4	25♋20.1	7♑26.5	26♋ 5.8	27♓ 3.2	9♑38.8	13♋19.0	24♊16.0
2 F	20 37 45	8 32 57	18 52 2	24 59 5	23D18.0	26R45.7	26 33.8	7R20.2	26 19.1	27R 1.0	9R36.8	13 21.1	24 17.1
3 Sa	20 41 42	9 30 22	1♊ 2 33	7♊ 3 0	23 18.8	26 32.6	27 47.5	7 14.7	26 32.3	26 58.7	9 34.8	13 23.1	24 18.2
4 Su	20 45 38	10 27 49	13 1 1	18 57 7	23 20.2	26D25.5	29 1.2	7 10.0	26 45.5	26 56.4	9 32.8	13 25.2	24 19.2
5 M	20 49 35	11 25 17	24 51 50	0♋45 39	23 21.6	26 24.7	0♌15.0	7 6.1	26 58.7	26 53.9	9 30.9	13 27.2	24 20.2
6 Tu	20 53 31	12 22 46	6♋39 4	12 32 29	23 22.9	26 30.3	1 28.7	7 3.0	27 11.9	26 51.4	9 29.0	13 29.2	24 21.3
7 W	20 57 28	13 20 17	18 26 19	24 20 57	23R23.7	26 42.5	2 42.5	7 0.8	27 25.0	26 48.7	9 27.1	13 31.2	24 22.3
8 Th	21 1 24	14 17 48	0♌16 43	6♌13 55	23 23.6	27 1.4	3 56.4	6 59.4	27 38.2	26 46.0	9 25.2	13 33.2	24 23.2
9 F	21 5 21	15 15 21	12 12 49	18 13 41	23 22.5	27 27.2	5 10.2	6D58.8	27 51.3	26 43.2	9 23.4	13 35.2	24 24.2
10 Sa	21 9 17	16 12 54	24 16 44	0♍22 11	23 20.2	27 59.7	6 24.1	6 59.1	28 4.3	26 40.3	9 21.6	13 37.1	24 25.2
11 Su	21 13 14	17 10 29	6♍30 13	12 41 1	23 17.1	28 39.0	7 38.0	7 0.3	28 17.4	26 37.4	9 19.8	13 39.1	24 26.1
12 M	21 17 11	18 8 5	18 54 44	25 11 34	23 13.2	29 25.0	8 51.9	7 2.3	28 30.4	26 34.3	9 18.1	13 41.0	24 27.0
13 Tu	21 21 7	19 5 41	1♎31 39	7♎55 11	23 9.2	0♌17.5	10 5.9	7 5.1	28 43.3	26 31.2	9 16.4	13 42.9	24 27.9
14 W	21 25 4	20 3 19	14 22 18	20 53 11	23 5.4	1 16.4	11 19.9	7 8.8	28 56.3	26 28.0	9 14.8	13 44.8	24 28.8
15 Th	21 29 0	21 0 58	27 28 1	4♏ 6 57	23 2.5	2 21.6	12 33.9	7 13.3	29 9.2	26 24.7	9 13.2	13 46.6	24 29.7
16 F	21 32 57	21 58 38	10♏50 8	17 37 42	23D 0.8	3 32.8	13 47.9	7 18.6	29 22.0	26 21.4	9 11.6	13 48.5	24 30.5
17 Sa	21 36 53	22 56 18	24 29 44	1♐26 19	23 0.3	4 49.7	15 1.9	7 24.8	29 34.9	26 18.0	9 10.0	13 50.3	24 31.4
18 Su	21 40 50	23 54 0	8♐27 26	15 33 1	23 1.0	6 12.2	16 16.0	7 31.8	29 47.7	26 14.5	9 8.6	13 52.1	24 32.2
19 M	21 44 46	24 51 43	22 42 52	29 56 45	23 2.3	7 39.7	17 30.1	7 39.5	0♌ 0.4	26 10.9	9 7.1	13 53.9	24 33.0
20 Tu	21 48 43	25 49 27	7♑14 17	14♑34 57	23 3.6	9 12.1	18 44.2	7 48.1	0 13.1	26 7.3	9 5.7	13 55.7	24 33.8
21 W	21 52 40	26 47 12	21 58 8	29 23 6	23R 4.3	10 48.9	19 58.4	7 57.4	0 25.8	26 3.7	9 4.3	13 57.5	24 34.5
22 Th	21 56 36	27 44 59	6♒49 1	14♒14 58	23 3.7	12 29.7	21 12.5	8 7.5	0 38.4	25 59.9	9 3.0	13 59.2	24 35.3
23 F	22 0 33	28 42 46	21 39 59	29 3 4	23 1.4	14 14.0	22 26.7	8 18.3	0 51.0	25 56.1	9 1.7	14 0.9	24 36.0
24 Sa	22 4 29	29 40 35	6♓23 16	13♓39 40	22 57.4	16 1.5	23 40.9	8 29.9	1 3.5	25 52.2	9 0.4	14 2.6	24 36.7
25 Su	22 8 26	0♍38 25	20 51 27	27 57 56	22 52.1	17 51.7	24 55.1	8 42.2	1 16.0	25 48.3	8 59.2	14 4.2	24 37.4
26 M	22 12 22	1 36 17	4♈58 33	11♈52 55	22 46.2	19 44.1	26 9.4	8 55.2	1 28.4	25 44.4	8 58.0	14 5.9	24 38.1
27 Tu	22 16 19	2 34 11	18 40 48	25 22 6	22 40.3	21 38.4	27 23.6	9 8.9	1 40.8	25 40.3	8 56.9	14 7.5	24 38.7
28 W	22 20 15	3 32 6	1♉56 55	8♉25 26	22 35.3	23 34.1	28 37.9	9 23.2	1 53.1	25 36.2	8 55.8	14 9.1	24 39.3
29 Th	22 24 12	4 30 4	14 47 58	21 4 57	22 31.7	25 30.8	29 52.3	9 38.3	2 5.4	25 32.1	8 54.8	14 10.7	24 39.9
30 F	22 28 9	5 28 3	27 16 52	3♊24 17	22D29.7	27 28.2	1♍ 6.6	9 54.0	2 17.6	25 27.9	8 53.8	14 12.2	24 40.5
31 Sa	22 32 5	6 26 4	9♊27 48	15 28 3	22 29.4	29 26.1	2 21.0	10 10.4	2 29.8	25 23.7	8 52.8	14 13.8	24 41.1

Astro Data	Planet Ingress	Last Aspect	☽ Ingress	Last Aspect	☽ Ingress	☽ Phases & Eclipses	Astro Data
Dy Hr Mn	Dy Hr Mn	Dy Hr Mn	Dy Hr Mn	Dy Hr Mn	Dy Hr Mn	Dy Hr Mn	1 JULY 1907
☽0N 2 19:12	♀ ♋ 11 6:42	1 16:35 ♄ ☌	♈ 1 21:14	2 16:49 ♀ ⚹	♊ 2 21:56	2 14:34 ☽ 9♈32	Julian Day # 2738
♄ R 9 22:15	☉ ♌ 24 1:18	3 16:55 ♇ ⚹	♉ 4 4:56	5 4:07 ♄ □	♋ 5 10:27	10 15:17 ● 17♋12	Delta T 6.9 sec
☿ R 11 11:17	☿ ♋ 26 14:36	6 10:36 ♄ ⚹	♊ 6 15:41	7 18:33 ♃ ☌	♌ 7 23:26	10 15:24:26 • A 7'22"	SVP 06♓33'20"
☽0S 17 14:10		8 23:06 ♄ □	♋ 9 4:16	10 0:17 ♇ ⚹	♍ 10 11:16	18 13:11 ☽ 24♎45	Obliquity 23°27'01"
♃⚺♇ 22 23:56	♀ ♌ 4 19:08	11 12:08 ♄ △	♌ 11 17:18	12 18:36 ♃ ⚹	♎ 12 21:07	25 4:29 ○ 1♒05	⚷ Chiron 17♒30.7R
☽0N 30 2:58	☿ ♌ 12 16:20	13 17:23 ♇ ⚹	♍ 14 5:29	15 3:06 ♃ □	♏ 15 4:35	25 4:22 • P 0.615	☽ Mean ☊ 24♋13.1
	♃ ♌ 18 23:15	16 10:41 ♄ ☍	♎ 16 15:34	17 8:56 ♃ △	♐ 17 9:31		
♃△♄ 4 16:37	☉ ♍ 24 8:03	18 13:11 ☉ □	♏ 18 22:34	19 5:45 ♄ □	♑ 19 12:05	1 2:25 ☽ 7♉41	1 AUGUST 1907
☿ D 4 15:18	♀ ♍ 29 2:30	20 21:46 ♄ △	♐ 21 2:11	21 6:36 ♄ ⚹	♒ 21 13:00	9 6:36 ● 15♌31	Julian Day # 2769
♂ D 9 3:28	☿ ♍ 31 6:54	22 22:48 ♄ □	♑ 23 3:06	23 12:15 ☉ ☍	♓ 23 13:33	16 21:05 ☽ 22♏49	Delta T 7.1 sec
☽0S 13 19:30		24 22:26 ♄ ⚹	♒ 25 2:46	25 8:18 ♄ ☌	♈ 25 15:28	23 12:15 ○ 29♒12	SVP 06♓33'16"
☽0N 26 11:55		26 17:30 ♇ △	♓ 27 3:00	27 17:18 ♀ △	♉ 27 20:26	30 17:28 ☽ 6♊10	Obliquity 23°27'01"
		29 2:52 ☿ △	♈ 29 5:37	30 0:26 ☿ □	♊ 30 5:19		⚷ Chiron 16♒04.9R
		31 6:55 ☿ □	♉ 31 11:53				☽ Mean ☊ 22♋34.6

LONGITUDE — SEPTEMBER 1907

Day	Sid.Time	☉	0 hr ☽	Noon ☽	True ☊	☿	♀	♂	♃	♄	♅	♆	♇
1 Su	22 36 2	7♍24 7	21♊25 41	27♊21 20	22♋30.2	1♍24.0	3♍35.4	10♑27.4	2♌41.9	25♓19.4	8♑51.9	14♋15.3	24♊41.6
2 M	22 39 58	8 22 12	3♋15 41	9♋ 9 19	22 31.6	3 21.9	4 49.8	10 45.0	2 54.0	25R 15.1	8R 51.1	14 16.7	24 42.2
3 Tu	22 43 55	9 20 18	15 2 52	20 56 53	22R 32.8	5 19.4	6 4.2	11 3.3	3 6.0	25 10.8	8 50.3	14 18.2	24 42.7
4 W	22 47 51	10 18 27	26 51 56	2♌48 28	22 33.0	7 16.4	7 18.7	11 22.2	3 17.9	25 6.4	8 49.5	14 19.6	24 43.2
5 Th	22 51 48	11 16 38	8♌46 58	14 47 48	22 31.5	9 12.8	8 33.2	11 41.6	3 29.8	25 2.0	8 48.8	14 21.0	24 43.6
6 F	22 55 44	12 14 50	20 51 18	26 57 45	22 27.8	11 8.4	9 47.7	12 1.7	3 41.6	24 57.5	8 48.1	14 22.4	24 44.1
7 Sa	22 59 41	13 13 4	3♍ 7 23	9♍20 19	22 22.0	13 3.1	11 2.2	12 22.3	3 53.4	24 53.1	8 47.5	14 23.8	24 44.5
8 Su	23 3 37	14 11 20	15 36 42	21 56 32	22 14.1	14 57.0	12 16.7	12 43.6	4 5.0	24 48.6	8 46.9	14 25.1	24 44.9
9 M	23 7 34	15 9 38	28 19 51	4♎46 35	22 5.0	16 49.8	13 31.3	13 5.3	4 16.6	24 44.0	8 46.4	14 26.4	24 45.3
10 Tu	23 11 31	16 7 57	11♎16 41	17 50 3	21 55.4	18 41.6	14 45.8	13 27.6	4 28.2	24 39.5	8 45.9	14 27.6	24 45.6
11 W	23 15 27	17 6 18	24 26 33	1♏ 6 6	21 46.3	20 32.4	16 0.4	13 50.5	4 39.6	24 34.9	8 45.5	14 28.9	24 46.0
12 Th	23 19 24	18 4 41	7♏48 35	14 33 53	21 38.7	22 22.0	17 15.0	14 13.9	4 51.0	24 30.3	8 45.1	14 30.1	24 46.3
13 F	23 23 20	19 3 6	21 21 57	28 12 41	21 33.3	24 10.6	18 29.6	14 37.8	5 2.3	24 25.7	8 44.8	14 31.3	24 46.6
14 Sa	23 27 17	20 1 32	5♐ 6 4	12♐ 2 3	21 30.2	25 58.1	19 44.3	15 2.1	5 13.6	24 21.1	8 44.5	14 32.4	24 46.9
15 Su	23 31 13	20 59 59	19 0 35	26 1 38	21D 29.1	27 44.5	20 58.9	15 27.0	5 24.7	24 16.4	8 44.3	14 33.6	24 47.1
16 M	23 35 10	21 58 29	3♑ 5 8	10♑10 59	21 29.5	29 29.8	22 13.6	15 52.4	5 35.8	24 11.8	8 44.1	14 34.7	24 47.3
17 Tu	23 39 6	22 57 0	17 19 1	24 29 1	21R 30.1	1♎14.0	23 28.2	16 18.2	5 46.8	24 7.2	8 44.0	14 35.7	24 47.6
18 W	23 43 3	23 55 32	1♒40 41	8♒53 37	21 29.7	2 57.2	24 42.9	16 44.4	5 57.8	24 2.5	8D 43.9	14 36.8	24 47.7
19 Th	23 47 0	24 54 6	16 7 20	23 21 16	21 27.5	4 39.3	25 57.6	17 11.1	6 8.6	23 57.9	8 43.9	14 37.8	24 47.9
20 F	23 50 56	25 52 42	0♓34 46	7♓47 8	21 22.7	6 20.4	27 12.3	17 38.2	6 19.3	23 53.2	8 43.9	14 38.7	24 48.0
21 Sa	23 54 53	26 51 20	14 57 38	22 5 31	21 15.3	8 0.4	28 27.0	18 5.8	6 30.0	23 48.6	8 44.0	14 39.7	24 48.2
22 Su	23 58 49	27 49 59	29 10 2	6♈10 32	21 5.7	9 39.5	29 41.7	18 33.7	6 40.6	23 44.0	8 44.1	14 40.6	24 48.3
23 M	0 2 46	28 48 40	13♈ 6 25	19 57 12	20 54.8	11 17.6	0♎56.5	19 2.0	6 51.1	23 39.3	8 44.3	14 41.5	24 48.3
24 Tu	0 6 42	29 47 24	26 42 31	3♉22 7	20 43.8	12 54.8	2 11.2	19 30.7	7 1.4	23 34.7	8 44.6	14 42.3	24 48.4
25 W	0 10 39	0♎46 9	9♉55 56	16 23 59	20 33.8	14 31.0	3 26.0	19 59.8	7 11.7	23 30.1	8 44.8	14 43.2	24R 48.4
26 Th	0 14 35	1 44 57	22 46 26	29 3 35	20 25.8	16 6.2	4 40.8	20 29.2	7 21.9	23 25.6	8 45.2	14 44.0	24 48.4
27 F	0 18 32	2 43 47	5♊15 47	11♊23 31	20 20.2	17 40.6	5 55.6	20 59.0	7 32.1	23 21.0	8 45.6	14 44.7	24 48.4
28 Sa	0 22 29	3 42 39	17 27 20	23 27 50	20 17.0	19 14.0	7 10.4	21 29.2	7 42.1	23 16.5	8 46.0	14 45.4	24 48.4
29 Su	0 26 25	4 41 34	29 25 39	5♋21 26	20D 15.7	20 46.6	8 25.2	21 59.7	7 52.0	23 11.9	8 46.5	14 46.1	24 48.3
30 M	0 30 22	5 40 31	11♋15 55	17 9 45	20R 15.7	22 18.3	9 40.0	22 30.5	8 1.8	23 7.5	8 47.0	14 46.8	24 48.2

LONGITUDE — OCTOBER 1907

Day	Sid.Time	☉	0 hr ☽	Noon ☽	True ☊	☿	♀	♂	♃	♄	♅	♆	♇
1 Tu	0 34 18	6♎39 30	23♋ 3 40	28♋58 18	20♋15.8	23♎49.0	10♎54.8	23♑ 1.7	8♌11.5	23♓ 3.0	8♑47.6	14♋47.4	24♊48.1
2 W	0 38 15	7 38 31	4♌54 20	10♌52 22	20R 15.0	25 19.0	12 9.7	23 33.2	8 21.1	22R 58.6	8 48.3	14 48.0	24R 48.0
3 Th	0 42 11	8 37 35	16 52 59	22 56 42	20 12.2	26 48.0	13 24.5	24 5.0	8 30.6	22 54.2	8 48.9	14 48.6	24 47.9
4 F	0 46 8	9 36 41	29 3 57	5♍15 8	20 6.9	28 16.1	14 39.4	24 37.1	8 40.0	22 49.8	8 49.7	14 49.1	24 47.7
5 Sa	0 50 4	10 35 49	11♍30 33	17 50 24	19 58.8	29 43.4	15 54.3	25 9.5	8 49.3	22 45.5	8 50.5	14 49.6	24 47.5
6 Su	0 54 1	11 34 59	24 14 47	0♎43 45	19 48.2	1♏ 9.7	17 9.2	25 42.2	8 58.4	22 41.2	8 51.3	14 50.1	24 47.3
7 M	0 57 58	12 34 12	7♎17 12	13 54 57	19 35.9	2 35.2	18 24.1	26 15.2	9 7.5	22 37.0	8 52.2	14 50.5	24 47.0
8 Tu	1 1 54	13 33 26	20 36 47	27 22 21	19 22.9	3 59.7	19 39.0	26 48.5	9 16.4	22 32.8	8 53.2	14 50.9	24 46.8
9 W	1 5 51	14 32 42	4♏11 17	11♏ 3 10	19 10.5	5 23.2	20 53.9	27 22.1	9 25.2	22 28.7	8 54.2	14 51.3	24 46.5
10 Th	1 9 47	15 32 1	17 57 35	24 54 7	18 59.9	6 45.7	22 8.8	27 55.9	9 33.9	22 24.6	8 55.2	14 51.6	24 46.2
11 F	1 13 44	16 31 21	1♐52 22	8♐51 57	18 51.9	8 7.2	23 23.7	28 30.0	9 42.5	22 20.5	8 56.3	14 51.9	24 45.9
12 Sa	1 17 40	17 30 43	15 52 35	22 53 59	18 46.9	9 27.6	24 38.7	29 4.4	9 50.9	22 16.6	8 57.5	14 52.2	24 45.5
13 Su	1 21 37	18 30 8	29 55 57	6♑58 20	18 44.6	10 46.8	25 53.6	29 39.0	9 59.2	22 12.6	8 58.7	14 52.4	24 45.2
14 M	1 25 33	19 29 33	14♑ 1 0	21 3 51	18 44.0	12 4.9	27 8.5	0♒13.9	10 7.4	22 8.8	8 59.9	14 52.6	24 44.8
15 Tu	1 29 30	20 29 1	28 6 48	5♒ 9 46	18 43.9	13 21.6	28 23.5	0 48.9	10 15.5	22 5.0	9 1.2	14 52.8	24 44.4
16 W	1 33 27	21 28 30	12♒12 37	19 15 14	18 43.0	14 37.0	29 38.4	1 24.3	10 23.4	22 1.2	9 2.5	14 52.9	24 44.0
17 Th	1 37 23	22 28 1	26 17 23	3♓18 50	18 40.1	15 51.0	0♏53.3	1 59.8	10 31.2	21 57.6	9 3.9	14 53.0	24 43.5
18 F	1 41 20	23 27 34	10♓19 18	17 18 23	18 34.3	17 3.3	2 8.3	2 35.5	10 38.9	21 53.9	9 5.4	14 53.0	24 43.1
19 Sa	1 45 16	24 27 8	24 15 43	1♈10 50	18 25.7	18 13.9	3 23.2	3 11.5	10 46.4	21 50.4	9 6.9	14R 53.1	24 42.6
20 Su	1 49 13	25 26 44	8♈ 3 17	14 52 38	18 14.7	19 22.6	4 38.2	3 47.7	10 53.8	21 46.9	9 8.4	14 53.1	24 42.1
21 M	1 53 9	26 26 22	21 38 26	28 20 19	18 2.1	20 29.3	5 53.1	4 24.0	11 1.0	21 43.5	9 10.0	14 53.0	24 41.5
22 Tu	1 57 6	27 26 2	4♉57 58	11♉31 8	17 49.3	21 33.8	7 8.1	5 0.5	11 8.1	21 40.2	9 11.6	14 52.9	24 41.0
23 W	2 1 2	28 25 45	17 59 40	24 23 30	17 37.5	22 35.8	8 23.0	5 37.3	11 15.1	21 37.0	9 13.3	14 52.8	24 40.4
24 Th	2 4 59	29 25 29	0♊42 43	6♊57 25	17 27.7	23 35.0	9 38.0	6 14.2	11 21.9	21 33.8	9 15.0	14 52.7	24 39.8
25 F	2 8 55	0♏25 16	13 7 53	19 14 25	17 20.5	24 31.3	10 52.9	6 51.2	11 28.6	21 30.7	9 16.8	14 52.5	24 39.2
26 Sa	2 12 52	1 25 4	25 17 26	1♋17 24	17 16.0	25 24.3	12 7.9	7 28.5	11 35.1	21 27.7	9 18.6	14 52.3	24 38.6
27 Su	2 16 49	2 24 55	7♋14 54	13 10 29	17D 14.0	26 13.6	13 22.8	8 5.9	11 41.5	21 24.8	9 20.4	14 52.0	24 38.0
28 M	2 20 45	3 24 48	19 4 48	24 58 32	17 13.6	26 58.8	14 37.8	8 43.5	11 47.7	21 21.9	9 22.3	14 51.8	24 37.3
29 Tu	2 24 42	4 24 43	0♌52 20	6♌46 56	17R 13.8	27 39.4	15 52.8	9 21.2	11 53.8	21 19.2	9 24.3	14 51.5	24 36.6
30 W	2 28 38	5 24 41	12 43 0	18 41 14	17 13.6	28 15.1	17 7.8	9 59.1	11 59.7	21 16.5	9 26.3	14 51.1	24 35.9
31 Th	2 32 35	6 24 40	24 42 18	0♍46 50	17 12.0	28 45.1	18 22.8	10 37.2	12 5.4	21 13.9	9 28.3	14 50.7	24 35.2

Astro Data (Dy Hr Mn)	Planet Ingress (Dy Hr Mn)	Last Aspect (Dy Hr Mn)	☽ Ingress (Dy Hr Mn)	Last Aspect (Dy Hr Mn)	☽ Ingress (Dy Hr Mn)	☽ Phases & Eclipses (Dy Hr Mn)	Astro Data
♄□♇ 8 17:47	☿ ♎ 16 6:56	1 7:50 ♄ □	♋ 1 17:22	1 1:46 ☿ □	♌ 1 14:05	7 21:04 ● 14♍04	1 SEPTEMBER 1907
☽0S 10 0:43	♀ ♎ 22 5:52	3 20:28 ♄ △	♌ 4 6:20	3 22:14 ☿ ✶	♍ 4 1:49	15 3:40 ☽ 21♐09	Julian Day # 2800
☿0S 17 11:05	☉ ♎ 24 5:09	6 7:38 ♇ ✶	♍ 6 17:56	6 2:50 ♂ △	♎ 6 10:39	21 21:34 ○ 27♓44	Delta T 7.2 sec
♅ D 18 22:04		8 17:18 ♄ ☍	♎ 9 3:07	8 11:28 ♂ □	♏ 8 16:38	29 11:37 ☽ 5♋10	SVP 06♓33'12"
☽0N 22 21:21	☿ ♏ 5 4:36	11 0:35 ♇ △	♏ 11 10:01	10 17:57 ♂ ✶	♐ 10 20:47		Obliquity 23°27'02"
♀0S 24 16:53	♂ ♒ 13 14:29	13 5:41 ☿ ✶	♐ 13 15:07	12 16:26 ♀ ✶	♑ 13 0:07	7 10:20 ● 12♎60	⚷ Chiron 14♒29.2R
♇ R 25 20:53	♀ ♏ 16 6:55	15 17:03 ☿ □	♑ 15 18:46	15 0:31 ♀ □	♒ 15 3:13	14 10:02 ☽ 19♑54	☽ Mean ☊ 20♋56.1
♃⚼♄ 30 9:35	☉ ♏ 24 13:52	17 11:20 ♄ ✶	♒ 17 21:12	16 21:20 ♇ △	♓ 17 6:20	21 9:17 ○ 26♈49	
		19 14:24 ♇ △	♓ 19 23:02	19 0:46 ♇ □	♈ 19 9:57	29 7:51 ☽ 4♌44	1 OCTOBER 1907
♃⚻♅ 5 3:30		22 0:59 ♀ ☍	♈ 22 1:25	21 9:17 ☉ ☍	♉ 21 15:00		Julian Day # 2830
☽0S 7 7:42		23 20:36 ♇ ✶	♉ 24 5:55	23 9:21 ☿ ☍	♊ 23 22:38		Delta T 7.3 sec
♃∠♇ 11 9:21		26 1:14 ♄ ✶	♊ 26 13:49	25 22:43 ♇ ☌	♋ 26 9:25		SVP 06♓33'09"
♆ R 19 4:32		28 14:42 ♇ ☌	♋ 29 1:09	28 17:05 ☿ △	♌ 28 22:14		Obliquity 23°27'02"
☽0N 20 6:11				31 8:18 ☿ □	♍ 31 10:28		⚷ Chiron 13♒23.1R
							☽ Mean ☊ 19♋20.7

NOVEMBER 1907 LONGITUDE

Day	Sid.Time	☉	0 hr ☽	Noon ☽	True ☊	☿	♀	♂	♃	♄	♅	♆	♇
1 F	2 36 31	7♏24 42	6♍55 25	13♍ 8 34	17♋ 8.1	29♏ 9.0	19♏37.7	11♒15.4	12♌11.0	21♓11.4	9♑30.4	14♋50.3	24♊34.5
2 Sa	2 40 28	8 24 46	19 26 43	25 50 14	17R 1.7	29 26.1	20 52.7	11 53.8	12 16.5	21R 9.0	9 32.5	14R49.9	24R33.7
3 Su	2 44 24	9 24 51	2♎19 22	8♎54 13	16 52.9	29R35.8	22 7.7	12 32.3	12 21.7	21 6.7	9 34.7	14 49.4	24 32.9
4 M	2 48 21	10 24 59	15 34 48	22 20 59	16 42.4	29 37.4	23 22.7	13 10.9	12 26.8	21 4.5	9 36.9	14 48.9	24 32.1
5 Tu	2 52 18	11 25 9	29 12 28	6♏ 8 53	16 31.1	29 30.3	24 37.7	13 49.7	12 31.8	21 2.3	9 39.1	14 48.4	24 31.3
6 W	2 56 14	12 25 21	13♏ 9 41	20 14 17	16 20.2	29 14.0	25 52.7	14 28.6	12 36.5	21 0.3	9 41.4	14 47.8	24 30.5
7 Th	3 0 11	13 25 34	27 21 59	4♐32 3	16 10.9	28 48.1	27 7.7	15 7.6	12 41.1	20 58.4	9 43.7	14 47.2	24 29.7
8 F	3 4 7	14 25 50	11♐43 47	18 56 26	16 4.0	28 12.3	28 22.7	15 46.8	12 45.6	20 56.5	9 46.1	14 46.5	24 28.8
9 Sa	3 8 4	15 26 7	26 9 21	3♑21 55	15 59.9	27 26.7	29 37.7	16 26.1	12 49.8	20 54.8	9 48.5	14 45.9	24 28.0
10 Su	3 12 0	16 26 25	10♑33 37	17 44 0	15D58.3	26 31.7	0♐52.7	17 5.5	12 53.9	20 53.2	9 51.0	14 45.2	24 27.1
11 M	3 15 57	17 26 45	24 52 44	1♒59 33	15 58.4	25 28.0	2 7.7	17 45.1	12 57.8	20 51.6	9 53.4	14 44.4	24 26.2
12 Tu	3 19 53	18 27 7	9♒ 4 16	16 6 44	15R59.1	24 17.1	3 22.7	18 24.7	13 1.5	20 50.2	9 56.0	14 43.7	24 25.3
13 W	3 23 50	19 27 29	23 6 53	0♓ 4 40	15 59.4	23 0.7	4 37.7	19 4.5	13 5.0	20 48.9	9 58.5	14 42.9	24 24.4
14 Th	3 27 47	20 27 53	7♓ 0 1	13 52 55	15 58.0	21 40.9	5 52.7	19 44.4	13 8.4	20 47.6	10 1.1	14 42.1	24 23.4
15 F	3 31 43	21 28 19	20 43 19	27 31 9	15 54.4	20 20.3	7 7.7	20 24.3	13 11.5	20 46.5	10 3.8	14 41.2	24 22.5
16 Sa	3 35 40	22 28 45	4♈16 21	10♈58 47	15 48.5	19 1.6	8 22.6	21 4.4	13 14.5	20 45.5	10 6.4	14 40.3	24 21.5
17 Su	3 39 36	23 29 13	17 38 22	24 14 57	15 40.6	17 47.2	9 37.6	21 44.5	13 17.3	20 44.6	10 9.1	14 39.4	24 20.5
18 M	3 43 33	24 29 43	0♉48 25	7♉18 37	15 31.4	16 39.7	10 52.6	22 24.7	13 19.9	20 43.8	10 11.9	14 38.5	24 19.5
19 Tu	3 47 29	25 30 13	13 45 28	20 8 51	15 22.0	15 40.9	12 7.5	23 5.0	13 22.4	20 43.0	10 14.6	14 37.5	24 18.5
20 W	3 51 26	26 30 46	26 28 44	2♊45 7	15 13.2	14 52.3	13 22.5	23 45.4	13 24.6	20 42.4	10 17.4	14 36.5	24 17.5
21 Th	3 55 22	27 31 20	8♊58 2	15 7 35	15 6.1	14 14.9	14 37.4	24 25.9	13 26.7	20 41.9	10 20.3	14 35.5	24 16.5
22 F	3 59 19	28 31 55	21 13 56	27 17 17	15 0.9	13 49.2	15 52.4	25 6.5	13 28.5	20 41.6	10 23.1	14 34.5	24 15.5
23 Sa	4 3 16	29 32 32	3♋17 57	9♋16 15	14D58.0	13D35.1	17 7.4	25 47.1	13 30.2	20 41.3	10 26.0	14 33.4	24 14.4
24 Su	4 7 12	0♐33 11	15 12 36	21 7 25	14 57.2	13 32.3	18 22.3	26 27.8	13 31.7	20 41.1	10 28.9	14 32.3	24 13.3
25 M	4 11 9	1 33 51	27 1 15	2♌54 36	14 57.9	13 40.3	19 37.3	27 8.6	13 33.0	20D41.0	10 31.9	14 31.2	24 12.3
26 Tu	4 15 5	2 34 33	8♌48 4	14 42 16	14 59.4	13 58.3	20 52.2	27 49.4	13 34.1	20 41.1	10 34.9	14 30.0	24 11.2
27 W	4 19 2	3 35 16	20 37 50	26 35 25	15 1.0	14 25.4	22 7.2	28 30.3	13 35.0	20 41.2	10 37.9	14 28.9	24 10.1
28 Th	4 22 58	4 36 1	2♍35 41	8♍39 16	15R 1.9	15 0.8	23 22.1	29 11.3	13 35.7	20 41.4	10 40.9	14 27.7	24 9.0
29 F	4 26 55	5 36 47	14 46 51	20 59 0	15 1.4	15 43.5	24 37.0	29 52.3	13 36.2	20 41.8	10 44.0	14 26.4	24 7.9
30 Sa	4 30 51	6 37 35	27 16 17	3♎39 13	14 59.3	16 32.8	25 52.0	0♓33.4	13 36.5	20 42.3	10 47.1	14 25.2	24 6.8

DECEMBER 1907 LONGITUDE

Day	Sid.Time	☉	0 hr ☽	Noon ☽	True ☊	☿	♀	♂	♃	♄	♅	♆	♇
1 Su	4 34 48	7♐38 25	10♎ 8 13	16♎43 35	14♋55.5	17♏27.7	27♐ 6.9	1♓14.6	13♌36.6	20♓42.8	10♑50.2	14♋23.9	24♊ 5.7
2 M	4 38 45	8 39 15	23 25 32	0♏14 7	14R50.4	18 27.7	28 21.9	1 55.8	13R36.5	20 43.5	10 53.4	14R22.6	24R 4.6
3 Tu	4 42 41	9 40 8	7♏ 9 13	14 10 37	14 44.6	19 32.1	29 36.8	2 37.0	13 36.3	20 44.3	10 56.6	14 21.3	24 3.4
4 W	4 46 38	10 41 1	21 17 52	28 30 24	14 38.9	20 40.2	0♑51.7	3 18.4	13 35.8	20 45.2	10 59.7	14 20.0	24 2.3
5 Th	4 50 34	11 41 56	5♐47 30	13♐ 8 19	14 34.0	21 51.6	2 6.6	3 59.8	13 35.1	20 46.2	11 3.0	14 18.6	24 1.1
6 F	4 54 31	12 42 52	20 31 54	27 57 18	14 30.5	23 5.8	3 21.6	4 41.2	13 34.2	20 47.3	11 6.2	14 17.2	23 60.0
7 Sa	4 58 27	13 43 49	5♑23 29	12♑49 28	14D28.8	24 22.5	4 36.5	5 22.7	13 33.1	20 48.5	11 9.5	14 15.8	23 58.8
8 Su	5 2 24	14 44 47	20 14 20	27 37 15	14 28.6	25 41.2	5 51.4	6 4.2	13 31.8	20 49.9	11 12.8	14 14.4	23 57.7
9 M	5 6 21	15 45 45	4♒57 28	12♒14 23	14 29.6	27 1.8	7 6.3	6 45.8	13 30.4	20 51.3	11 16.1	14 13.0	23 56.5
10 Tu	5 10 17	16 46 44	19 27 30	26 36 29	14 31.1	28 23.9	8 21.2	7 27.5	13 28.7	20 52.8	11 19.4	14 11.5	23 55.4
11 W	5 14 14	17 47 44	3♓41 5	10♓41 8	14 32.5	29 47.3	9 36.1	8 9.1	13 26.8	20 54.5	11 22.8	14 10.1	23 54.2
12 Th	5 18 10	18 48 44	17 36 36	24 27 31	14R33.1	1♐11.9	10 50.9	8 50.9	13 24.8	20 56.2	11 26.1	14 8.6	23 53.0
13 F	5 22 7	19 49 45	1♈13 57	7♈56 2	14 32.6	2 37.5	12 5.8	9 32.6	13 22.5	20 58.1	11 29.5	14 7.1	23 51.8
14 Sa	5 26 3	20 50 46	14 33 54	21 7 45	14 31.0	4 4.0	13 20.6	10 14.4	13 20.0	21 0.0	11 32.9	14 5.6	23 50.7
15 Su	5 30 0	21 51 48	27 37 44	4♉ 4 4	14 28.3	5 31.2	14 35.5	10 56.2	13 17.4	21 2.1	11 36.3	14 4.0	23 49.5
16 M	5 33 56	22 52 50	10♉26 54	16 46 26	14 24.9	6 59.0	15 50.3	11 38.0	13 14.6	21 4.2	11 39.7	14 2.5	23 48.3
17 Tu	5 37 53	23 53 53	23 2 49	29 16 14	14 21.4	8 27.4	17 5.1	12 19.9	13 11.5	21 6.5	11 43.2	14 0.9	23 47.1
18 W	5 41 50	24 54 56	5♊26 50	11♊34 46	14 18.2	9 56.4	18 19.9	13 1.8	13 8.3	21 8.9	11 46.7	13 59.3	23 46.0
19 Th	5 45 46	25 56 0	17 40 14	23 43 23	14 15.7	11 25.8	19 34.7	13 43.7	13 4.9	21 11.3	11 50.1	13 57.7	23 44.8
20 F	5 49 43	26 57 5	29 44 25	5♋43 32	14 14.1	12 55.6	20 49.4	14 25.6	13 1.4	21 13.9	11 53.6	13 56.2	23 43.6
21 Sa	5 53 39	27 58 10	11♋40 59	17 37 1	14D13.4	14 25.8	22 4.2	15 7.6	12 57.6	21 16.6	11 57.1	13 54.5	23 42.4
22 Su	5 57 36	28 59 15	23 31 54	29 25 58	14 13.7	15 56.3	23 18.9	15 49.5	12 53.7	21 19.3	12 0.6	13 52.9	23 41.2
23 M	6 1 32	0♑ 0 21	5♌19 34	11♌13 5	14 14.6	17 27.2	24 33.6	16 31.5	12 49.5	21 22.2	12 4.1	13 51.3	23 40.1
24 Tu	6 5 29	1 1 28	17 6 57	23 1 35	14 15.8	18 58.3	25 48.4	17 13.5	12 45.2	21 25.2	12 7.7	13 49.7	23 38.9
25 W	6 9 25	2 2 35	28 57 30	4♍55 13	14 17.1	20 29.8	27 3.0	17 55.6	12 40.8	21 28.2	12 11.2	13 48.0	23 37.7
26 Th	6 13 22	3 3 43	10♍55 15	16 58 10	14 18.3	22 1.5	28 17.7	18 37.6	12 36.1	21 31.4	12 14.7	13 46.3	23 36.6
27 F	6 17 19	4 4 51	23 3 43	29 14 57	14R19.0	23 33.6	29 32.4	19 19.7	12 31.3	21 34.6	12 18.3	13 44.7	23 35.4
28 Sa	6 21 15	5 6 0	5♎29 56	11♎50 3	14 19.2	25 5.9	0♒47.0	20 1.7	12 26.3	21 38.0	12 21.8	13 43.0	23 34.3
29 Su	6 25 12	6 7 9	18 15 48	24 47 39	14 19.0	26 38.5	2 1.7	20 43.8	12 21.2	21 41.4	12 25.4	13 41.3	23 33.1
30 M	6 29 8	7 8 19	1♏25 56	8♏10 59	14 18.4	28 11.4	3 16.3	21 25.9	12 15.9	21 44.9	12 29.0	13 39.6	23 32.0
31 Tu	6 33 5	8 9 29	15 2 55	22 1 46	14 17.7	29 44.6	4 30.9	22 8.0	12 10.4	21 48.6	12 32.6	13 38.0	23 30.8

Astro Data	Planet Ingress	Last Aspect	☽ Ingress	Last Aspect	☽ Ingress	☽ Phases & Eclipses	Astro Data
Dy Hr Mn	Dy Hr Mn	Dy Hr Mn	Dy Hr Mn	Dy Hr Mn	Dy Hr Mn	Dy Hr Mn	1 NOVEMBER 1907
☽0S 3 17:04	♀ ♐ 9 7:08	2 18:56 ☿ ⚹	♎ 2 19:43	2 9:36 ♀ ⚹	♏ 2 11:35	5 22:39 ● 12♏22	Julian Day # 2861
☿ R 3 16:39	☉ ♐ 23 10:52	4 15:49 ♇ △	♏ 5 1:23	3 23:05 ♄ △	♐ 4 14:28	12 17:14 ☽ 19♒10	Delta T 7.5 sec
☽0N 16 13:35	♂ ♓ 29 4:30	7 2:19 ☿ ☌	♐ 7 4:25	6 5:36 ♇ ☍	♑ 6 15:18	20 0:04 ○ 26♉31	SVP 06♓33'06"
☿ D 23 17:56		8 21:12 ♇ ☍	♑ 9 6:24	8 9:44 ☿ ⚹	♒ 8 15:53	28 4:21 ☽ 4♍47	Obliquity 23°27'02"
♄ D 25 4:06	♀ ♑ 3 7:26	11 0:55 ☿ ⚹	♒ 11 8:38	10 16:39 ☿ □	♓ 10 17:44		⚷ Chiron 13♒08.4
	☿ ♐ 11 3:37	13 2:13 ♇ △	♓ 13 11:52	12 10:58 ♇ □	♈ 12 21:48	5 10:22 ● 12♐08	☽ Mean ☊ 17♋42.2
☽0S 1 3:33	☉ ♑ 22 23:52	15 6:26 ♇ □	♈ 15 16:24	14 16:58 ♇ ⚹	♉ 15 4:24	12 2:16 ☽ 18♓54	
♃ R 1 1:20	♀ ♒ 27 8:53	17 12:09 ♇ ⚹	♉ 17 22:31	16 20:16 ♄ ⚹	♊ 17 13:25	19 17:55 ○ 26♊42	1 DECEMBER 1907
☽0N 13 19:44	☿ ♑ 31 3:57	20 0:04 ☉ ☍	♊ 20 6:43	19 17:55 ☉ ☍	♋ 20 0:31	27 23:10 ☽ 5♎04	Julian Day # 2891
☽0S 28 12:56		22 8:07 ♂ △	♋ 22 17:24	21 23:31 ♀ ☍	♌ 22 13:09		Delta T 7.6 sec
♃⊼♅ 28 12:23		24 11:06 ♄ △	♌ 25 6:04	24 13:14 ♇ ⚹	♍ 25 2:06		SVP 06♓33'02"
		27 16:48 ♂ ☍	♍ 27 18:50	27 1:05 ☿ □	♎ 27 13:27		Obliquity 23°27'02"
		29 21:02 ♀ □	♎ 30 5:09	29 17:24 ☿ ⚹	♏ 29 21:26		⚷ Chiron 13♒53.5
							☽ Mean ☊ 16♋06.9

LONGITUDE — JANUARY 1908

Day	Sid.Time	☉	0 hr ☽	Noon ☽	True ☊	☿	♀	♂	♃	♄	♅	♆	♇
1 W	6 37 1	9♑10 40	29♏ 7 26	6♐19 34	14♋17.0	1♑18.1	5♒45.5	22♓50.1	12♌ 4.8	21♓52.3	12♑36.1	13♋36.3	23♊29.7
2 Th	6 40 58	10 11 51	13♐37 43	21 1 13	14R 16.5	2 52.0	7 0.0	23 32.3	11R 59.0	21 56.1	12 39.7	13R 34.6	23R 28.6
3 F	6 44 54	11 13 3	28 29 14	6♑ 0 48	14 16.2	4 26.1	8 14.6	24 14.4	11 53.1	21 60.0	12 43.3	13 32.9	23 27.4
4 Sa	6 48 51	12 14 14	13♑34 48	21 10 5	14D 16.1	6 0.6	9 29.1	24 56.6	11 47.1	22 4.0	12 46.9	13 31.2	23 26.3
5 Su	6 52 48	13 15 25	28 45 25	6♒19 38	14 16.2	7 35.5	10 43.6	25 38.7	11 40.9	22 8.0	12 50.5	13 29.5	23 25.2
6 M	6 56 44	14 16 37	13♒51 34	21 20 11	14R 16.2	9 10.7	11 58.1	26 20.9	11 34.5	22 12.2	12 54.1	13 27.8	23 24.1
7 Tu	7 0 41	15 17 48	28 44 34	6♓ 3 57	14 16.2	10 46.3	13 12.5	27 3.1	11 28.1	22 16.4	12 57.6	13 26.1	23 23.0
8 W	7 4 37	16 18 58	13♓17 47	20 25 37	14 16.0	12 22.3	14 26.9	27 45.3	11 21.5	22 20.8	13 1.2	13 24.4	23 22.0
9 Th	7 8 34	17 20 8	27 27 11	4♈22 26	14 15.8	13 58.7	15 41.3	28 27.5	11 14.8	22 25.2	13 4.8	13 22.7	23 20.9
10 F	7 12 30	18 21 17	11♈11 21	17 54 7	14D 15.6	15 35.5	16 55.7	29 9.6	11 8.0	22 29.7	13 8.4	13 21.0	23 19.8
11 Sa	7 16 27	19 22 26	24 30 58	1♉ 2 13	14 15.6	17 12.8	18 10.0	29 51.8	11 1.0	22 34.3	13 11.9	13 19.3	23 18.8
12 Su	7 20 23	20 23 34	7♉28 15	13 49 28	14 15.8	18 50.5	19 24.3	0♈34.0	10 54.0	22 38.9	13 15.5	13 17.6	23 17.7
13 M	7 24 20	21 24 42	20 6 17	26 19 9	14 16.4	20 28.6	20 38.6	1 16.2	10 46.8	22 43.7	13 19.1	13 15.9	23 16.7
14 Tu	7 28 17	22 25 49	2♊28 30	8♊34 45	14 17.2	22 7.3	21 52.8	1 58.3	10 39.6	22 48.5	13 22.6	13 14.3	23 15.7
15 W	7 32 13	23 26 56	14 38 18	20 39 32	14 18.2	23 46.4	23 7.0	2 40.5	10 32.3	22 53.4	13 26.2	13 12.6	23 14.7
16 Th	7 36 10	24 28 2	26 38 50	2♋36 31	14 19.0	25 26.1	24 21.2	3 22.7	10 24.9	22 58.3	13 29.7	13 10.9	23 13.7
17 F	7 40 6	25 29 7	8♋32 55	14 28 19	14R 19.6	27 6.2	25 35.3	4 4.8	10 17.4	23 3.4	13 33.2	13 9.3	23 12.7
18 Sa	7 44 3	26 30 12	20 23 1	26 17 16	14 19.5	28 46.9	26 49.4	4 46.9	10 9.8	23 8.5	13 36.7	13 7.6	23 11.8
19 Su	7 47 59	27 31 16	2♌11 19	8♌ 5 27	14 18.8	0♒28.0	28 3.4	5 29.1	10 2.2	23 13.7	13 40.3	13 6.0	23 10.8
20 M	7 51 56	28 32 19	13 59 54	19 54 57	14 17.4	2 9.7	29 17.4	6 11.2	9 54.5	23 19.0	13 43.8	13 4.4	23 9.9
21 Tu	7 55 52	29 33 22	25 50 50	1♍47 52	14 15.3	3 51.8	0♓31.3	6 53.3	9 46.8	23 24.3	13 47.2	13 2.7	23 8.9
22 W	7 59 49	0♒34 25	7♍46 21	13 46 35	14 12.6	5 34.5	1 45.3	7 35.4	9 39.0	23 29.7	13 50.7	13 1.1	23 8.0
23 Th	8 3 46	1 35 26	19 48 56	25 53 46	14 9.9	7 17.5	2 59.1	8 17.5	9 31.1	23 35.2	13 54.2	12 59.5	23 7.1
24 F	8 7 42	2 36 28	2♎ 1 28	8♎12 28	14 7.3	9 1.0	4 12.9	8 59.5	9 23.2	23 40.7	13 57.6	12 58.0	23 6.2
25 Sa	8 11 39	3 37 28	14 27 11	20 46 4	14 5.3	10 44.9	5 26.7	9 41.6	9 15.3	23 46.3	14 1.1	12 56.4	23 5.4
26 Su	8 15 35	4 38 28	27 9 33	3♏38 3	14D 4.1	12 29.1	6 40.5	10 23.6	9 7.3	23 52.0	14 4.5	12 54.8	23 4.5
27 M	8 19 32	5 39 28	10♏12 1	16 51 47	14 4.0	14 13.6	7 54.2	11 5.7	8 59.4	23 57.7	14 7.9	12 53.3	23 3.7
28 Tu	8 23 28	6 40 27	23 37 41	0♐29 56	14 4.8	15 58.2	9 7.8	11 47.7	8 51.4	24 3.5	14 11.3	12 51.7	23 2.9
29 W	8 27 25	7 41 26	7♐28 41	14 33 56	14 6.2	17 42.8	10 21.4	12 29.7	8 43.3	24 9.4	14 14.6	12 50.2	23 2.1
30 Th	8 31 21	8 42 24	21 45 32	29 3 11	14 7.7	19 27.4	11 35.0	13 11.7	8 35.3	24 15.3	14 18.0	12 48.7	23 1.3
31 F	8 35 18	9 43 21	6♑26 25	13♑54 31	14R 8.8	21 11.8	12 48.5	13 53.7	8 27.3	24 21.3	14 21.3	12 47.2	23 0.5

LONGITUDE — FEBRUARY 1908

Day	Sid.Time	☉	0 hr ☽	Noon ☽	True ☊	☿	♀	♂	♃	♄	♅	♆	♇
1 Sa	8 39 15	10♒44 17	21♑26 40	29♑ 1 50	14♋ 8.8	22♒55.7	14♓ 1.9	14♈35.6	8♌19.3	24♓27.3	14♑24.6	12♋45.8	22♊59.7
2 Su	8 43 11	11 45 12	6♒38 52	14♒16 30	14R 7.4	24 39.0	15 15.3	15 17.6	8R 11.3	24 33.4	14 27.9	12R 44.3	22R 59.0
3 M	8 47 8	12 46 7	21 53 26	29 28 22	14 4.5	26 21.3	16 28.7	15 59.6	8 3.3	24 39.6	14 31.2	12 42.9	22 58.3
4 Tu	8 51 4	13 47 0	7♓ 0 4	14♓27 25	14 0.5	28 2.4	17 42.0	16 41.5	7 55.4	24 45.8	14 34.5	12 41.5	22 57.6
5 W	8 55 1	14 47 52	21 49 25	29 5 18	13 55.8	29 42.0	18 55.2	17 23.4	7 47.5	24 52.1	14 37.7	12 40.1	22 56.9
6 Th	8 58 57	15 48 42	6♈14 29	13♈16 34	13 51.3	1♓19.5	20 8.4	18 5.3	7 39.6	24 58.4	14 40.9	12 38.7	22 56.3
7 F	9 2 54	16 49 31	20 11 23	26 58 55	13 47.4	2 54.6	21 21.5	18 47.2	7 31.7	25 4.8	14 44.1	12 37.4	22 55.6
8 Sa	9 6 50	17 50 18	3♉39 19	10♉12 55	13 44.9	4 26.7	22 34.5	19 29.0	7 23.9	25 11.2	14 47.2	12 36.0	22 55.0
9 Su	9 10 47	18 51 4	16 40 5	23 1 19	13D 43.9	5 55.2	23 47.5	20 10.9	7 16.2	25 17.6	14 50.3	12 34.7	22 54.4
10 M	9 14 44	19 51 48	29 17 10	5♊28 13	13 44.3	7 19.6	25 0.3	20 52.7	7 8.5	25 24.2	14 53.4	12 33.4	22 53.8
11 Tu	9 18 40	20 52 31	11♊35 4	17 38 19	13 45.7	8 39.2	26 13.2	21 34.5	7 0.9	25 30.7	14 56.5	12 32.2	22 53.2
12 W	9 22 37	21 53 12	23 38 35	29 36 26	13 47.5	9 53.2	27 25.9	22 16.3	6 53.4	25 37.3	14 59.6	12 30.9	22 52.7
13 Th	9 26 33	22 53 52	5♋32 26	11♋27 5	13R 48.9	11 0.9	28 38.6	22 58.0	6 45.9	25 44.0	15 2.6	12 29.7	22 52.2
14 F	9 30 30	23 54 30	17 20 54	23 14 19	13 49.2	12 1.7	29 51.2	23 39.7	6 38.6	25 50.7	15 5.6	12 28.5	22 51.7
15 Sa	9 34 26	24 55 6	29 7 44	5♌ 1 31	13 47.8	12 54.7	1♈ 3.7	24 21.4	6 31.3	25 57.4	15 8.5	12 27.3	22 51.2
16 Su	9 38 23	25 55 41	10♌55 59	16 51 26	13 44.3	13 39.4	2 16.1	25 3.1	6 24.1	26 4.2	15 11.5	12 26.2	22 50.7
17 M	9 42 19	26 56 14	22 48 6	28 46 13	13 38.8	14 15.1	3 28.5	25 44.7	6 17.0	26 11.0	15 14.4	12 25.1	22 50.3
18 Tu	9 46 16	27 56 45	4♍45 58	10♍47 32	13 31.4	14 41.3	4 40.8	26 26.4	6 10.0	26 17.9	15 17.3	12 24.0	22 49.9
19 W	9 50 13	28 57 15	16 51 3	22 56 43	13 22.7	14 57.5	5 52.9	27 8.0	6 3.1	26 24.7	15 20.1	12 22.9	22 49.5
20 Th	9 54 9	29 57 44	29 4 39	5♎15 1	13 13.6	15R 3.7	7 5.0	27 49.5	5 56.3	26 31.7	15 22.9	12 21.9	22 49.1
21 F	9 58 6	0♓58 11	11♎28 0	17 43 47	13 5.0	14 59.6	8 17.1	28 31.1	5 49.6	26 38.6	15 25.7	12 20.9	22 48.7
22 Sa	10 2 2	1 58 37	24 2 36	0♏24 40	12 57.6	14 45.4	9 29.0	29 12.6	5 43.1	26 45.6	15 28.4	12 19.9	22 48.4
23 Su	10 5 59	2 59 1	6♏50 14	13 19 35	12 52.2	14 21.5	10 40.8	29 54.1	5 36.7	26 52.6	15 31.1	12 18.9	22 48.1
24 M	10 9 55	3 59 24	19 53 1	26 30 49	12 49.0	13 48.6	11 52.5	0♉35.6	5 30.4	26 59.7	15 33.8	12 18.0	22 47.8
25 Tu	10 13 52	4 59 45	3♐13 16	10♐ 0 38	12D 47.9	13 7.3	13 4.2	1 17.0	5 24.2	27 6.8	15 36.4	12 17.1	22 47.5
26 W	10 17 48	6 0 6	16 53 8	23 50 56	12 48.3	12 19.0	14 15.7	1 58.4	5 18.2	27 13.9	15 39.0	12 16.2	22 47.3
27 Th	10 21 45	7 0 24	0♑54 6	8♑ 2 36	12R 49.3	11 24.7	15 27.2	2 39.8	5 12.3	27 21.1	15 41.6	12 15.4	22 47.0
28 F	10 25 42	8 0 42	15 16 15	22 34 44	12 49.7	10 25.9	16 38.6	3 21.2	5 6.6	27 28.2	15 44.1	12 14.5	22 46.8
29 Sa	10 29 38	9 0 58	29 57 35	7♒24 6	12 48.4	9 24.2	17 49.8	4 2.6	5 1.0	27 35.4	15 46.6	12 13.8	22 46.7

Astro Data	Dy Hr Mn
☽0N	10 2:03
♂0N	12 2:42
♅☍♆	12 9:41
♄□♇	18 12:41
☽0S	24 19:47
♃⚻♄	27 2:51
♃∠♇	3 16:39
☽0N	6 10:04
♀0N	15 10:46
☿ R	20 2:21
☽0S	21 0:53

Planet Ingress	Dy Hr Mn
♂ ♈	11 4:39
☿ ♒	18 17:22
♀ ♓	20 13:50
☉ ♒	21 10:28
☿ ♓	5 4:24
♀ ♈	14 2:55
☉ ♓	20 0:54
♂ ♉	23 3:25

Last Aspect Dy Hr Mn		☽ Ingress Dy Hr Mn
31 12:49	♂ △	♐ 1 1:28
2 16:51	♂ □	♑ 3 2:25
4 18:50	♂ ⚹	♒ 5 1:58
6 15:19	♇ △	♓ 7 2:03
9 1:49	♂ ☌	♈ 9 4:24
10 21:48	♇ ⚹	♉ 11 10:05
13 5:05	♄ ⚹	♊ 13 19:10
15 18:52	♀ △	♋ 16 6:45
18 13:37	☉ ☍	♌ 18 19:33
20 18:33	♇ ⚹	♍ 21 8:23
23 7:31	♄ ☍	♎ 23 20:03
25 16:21	♇ △	♏ 26 5:17
28 0:46	♄ △	♐ 28 11:08
30 4:09	♄ □	♑ 30 13:33

Last Aspect Dy Hr Mn		☽ Ingress Dy Hr Mn
1 4:48	♄ ⚹	♒ 1 13:32
3 7:57	☿ ☌	♓ 3 12:50
5 5:03	♄ ☌	♈ 5 13:31
7 4:48	♇ ⚹	♉ 7 17:24
9 16:29	♄ ⚹	♊ 10 1:23
12 8:29	♀ □	♋ 12 12:48
14 17:29	♄ △	♌ 15 1:46
17 9:05	☉ ☍	♍ 17 14:28
19 18:58	♄ ☍	♎ 20 1:48
22 10:18	♂ ☍	♏ 22 11:14
24 12:59	♄ △	♐ 24 18:15
26 17:56	♄ □	♑ 26 22:28
28 20:08	♄ ⚹	♒ 29 0:04

☽ Phases & Eclipses Dy Hr Mn	
3 21:43	● 12♑08
3 21:45:13	☌ T 4'14"
10 13:53	☽ 18♈57
18 13:37	○ 27♋05
18 13:21	☍ A 0.537
26 15:01	☽ 5♏17
2 8:36	● 12♒07
9 4:27	☽ 19♉02
17 9:05	○ 27♌19
25 3:24	☽ 5♐08

Astro Data

1 JANUARY 1908
Julian Day # 2922
Delta T 7.8 sec
SVP 06♓32'56"
Obliquity 23°27'02"
⚷ Chiron 15♒31.7
☽ Mean ☊ 14♋28.4

1 FEBRUARY 1908
Julian Day # 2953
Delta T 7.9 sec
SVP 06♓32'51"
Obliquity 23°27'02"
⚷ Chiron 17♒41.2
☽ Mean ☊ 12♋50.0

MARCH 1908 — LONGITUDE

Day	Sid.Time	☉	0 hr ☽	Noon ☽	True ☊	☿	♀	♂	♃	♄	♅	♆	♇
1 Su	10 33 35	10♓ 1 12	14♒53 28	22♒24 42	12♋44.9	8♓21.0	19♈ 1.0	4♉43.9	4♌55.5	27♓42.7	15♑49.1	12♋13.0	22♊46.5
2 M	10 37 31	11 1 25	29 56 41	7♓28 13	12R 38.7	7R 18.0	20 12.0	5 25.2	4R 50.3	27 49.9	15 51.5	12R 12.3	22R 46.4
3 Tu	10 41 28	12 1 35	14♓58 4	22 25 3	12 30.4	6 16.5	21 23.0	6 6.5	4 45.1	27 57.2	15 53.9	12 11.6	22 46.3
4 W	10 45 24	13 1 44	29 48 1	7♈ 5 57	12 20.7	5 17.8	22 33.8	6 47.7	4 40.2	28 4.5	15 56.2	12 10.9	22 46.2
5 Th	10 49 21	14 1 51	14♈18 2	21 23 36	12 10.8	4 23.1	23 44.5	7 28.9	4 35.3	28 11.8	15 58.5	12 10.3	22 46.1
6 F	10 53 17	15 1 56	28 22 12	5♉13 36	12 1.9	3 33.3	24 55.2	8 10.1	4 30.7	28 19.1	16 0.8	12 9.7	22 46.1
7 Sa	10 57 14	16 1 59	11♉57 45	18 34 45	11 54.9	2 49.0	26 5.6	8 51.3	4 26.2	28 26.5	16 3.0	12 9.1	22D 46.0
8 Su	11 1 11	17 2 0	25 4 54	1♊28 35	11 50.3	2 10.8	27 16.0	9 32.5	4 21.9	28 33.8	16 5.2	12 8.6	22 46.0
9 M	11 5 7	18 1 58	7♊46 20	13 58 42	11D 48.0	1 39.0	28 26.3	10 13.6	4 17.8	28 41.2	16 7.3	12 8.1	22 46.1
10 Tu	11 9 4	19 1 55	20 6 21	26 9 56	11 47.4	1 13.8	29 36.4	10 54.7	4 13.9	28 48.6	16 9.4	12 7.6	22 46.1
11 W	11 13 0	20 1 49	2♋10 8	8♋ 7 39	11R 47.8	0 55.2	0♉46.3	11 35.7	4 10.1	28 56.0	16 11.4	12 7.2	22 46.2
12 Th	11 16 57	21 1 41	14 3 10	19 57 19	11 48.1	0 43.2	1 56.2	12 16.8	4 6.5	29 3.4	16 13.4	12 6.8	22 46.3
13 F	11 20 53	22 1 31	25 50 45	1♌44 2	11 47.1	0D 37.6	3 5.9	12 57.8	4 3.1	29 10.8	16 15.4	12 6.4	22 46.4
14 Sa	11 24 50	23 1 18	7♌37 44	13 32 20	11 44.0	0 38.2	4 15.4	13 38.7	3 59.9	29 18.3	16 17.3	12 6.1	22 46.5
15 Su	11 28 46	24 1 4	19 28 16	25 25 56	11 38.2	0 44.8	5 24.8	14 19.7	3 56.9	29 25.7	16 19.2	12 5.7	22 46.7
16 M	11 32 43	25 0 47	1♍25 40	7♍27 43	11 29.7	0 57.1	6 34.1	15 0.6	3 54.0	29 33.2	16 21.0	12 5.5	22 46.9
17 Tu	11 36 40	26 0 28	13 32 19	19 39 36	11 18.6	1 14.7	7 43.2	15 41.4	3 51.3	29 40.6	16 22.8	12 5.2	22 47.1
18 W	11 40 36	27 0 7	25 49 42	2♎ 2 39	11 5.9	1 37.5	8 52.2	16 22.3	3 48.9	29 48.1	16 24.5	12 5.0	22 47.3
19 Th	11 44 33	27 59 44	8♎18 31	14 37 16	10 52.4	2 5.1	10 0.9	17 3.1	3 46.6	29 55.5	16 26.2	12 4.8	22 47.5
20 F	11 48 29	28 59 19	20 58 54	27 23 23	10 39.4	2 37.2	11 9.6	17 43.9	3 44.5	0♈ 3.0	16 27.9	12 4.7	22 47.8
21 Sa	11 52 26	29 58 52	3♏50 41	10♏20 49	10 28.1	3 13.6	12 18.0	18 24.6	3 42.5	0 10.5	16 29.5	12 4.6	22 48.1
22 Su	11 56 22	0♈58 24	16 53 47	23 29 36	10 19.3	3 54.1	13 26.3	19 5.3	3 40.8	0 17.9	16 31.0	12 4.5	22 48.4
23 M	12 0 19	1 57 53	0♐ 8 20	6♐50 5	10 13.4	4 38.2	14 34.5	19 46.0	3 39.3	0 25.4	16 32.5	12D 4.5	22 48.8
24 Tu	12 4 15	2 57 21	13 34 57	20 23 4	10 10.3	5 26.0	15 42.4	20 26.7	3 37.9	0 32.9	16 34.0	12 4.5	22 49.1
25 W	12 8 12	3 56 47	27 14 34	4♑ 9 32	10 9.2	6 17.0	16 50.2	21 7.3	3 36.8	0 40.3	16 35.4	12 4.5	22 49.5
26 Th	12 12 8	4 56 11	11♑ 8 6	18 10 16	10 9.2	7 11.3	17 57.8	21 47.9	3 35.8	0 47.8	16 36.7	12 4.6	22 49.9
27 F	12 16 5	5 55 34	25 16 0	2♒25 12	10 8.7	8 8.5	19 5.2	22 28.5	3 35.0	0 55.2	16 38.1	12 4.7	22 50.3
28 Sa	12 20 2	6 54 55	9♒37 36	16 52 51	10 6.7	9 8.5	20 12.5	23 9.1	3 34.4	1 2.7	16 39.3	12 4.8	22 50.8
29 Su	12 23 58	7 54 14	24 10 27	1♓29 47	10 2.1	10 11.1	21 19.5	23 49.6	3 34.0	1 10.1	16 40.5	12 5.0	22 51.2
30 M	12 27 55	8 53 31	8♓50 4	16 10 28	9 54.6	11 16.3	22 26.3	24 30.1	3D 33.8	1 17.6	16 41.7	12 5.2	22 51.7
31 Tu	12 31 51	9 52 46	23 30 3	0♈47 51	9 44.5	12 23.9	23 33.0	25 10.6	3 33.8	1 25.0	16 42.8	12 5.4	22 52.2

APRIL 1908 — LONGITUDE

Day	Sid.Time	☉	0 hr ☽	Noon ☽	True ☊	☿	♀	♂	♃	♄	♅	♆	♇
1 W	12 35 48	10♈51 59	8♈ 2 54	15♈14 19	9♋32.8	13♓33.8	24♉39.4	25♉51.0	3♌34.0	1♈32.4	16♑43.9	12♋ 5.7	22♊52.8
2 Th	12 39 44	11 51 10	22 21 14	29 22 59	9R 20.6	14 45.9	25 45.6	26 31.4	3 34.4	1 39.8	16 44.9	12 6.0	22 53.3
3 F	12 43 41	12 50 20	6♉19 0	13♉ 8 53	9 9.4	16 0.1	26 51.7	27 11.8	3 35.0	1 47.2	16 45.8	12 6.3	22 53.9
4 Sa	12 47 37	13 49 27	19 52 26	26 29 33	9 0.2	17 16.3	27 57.4	27 52.2	3 35.7	1 54.6	16 46.8	12 6.7	22 54.5
5 Su	12 51 34	14 48 31	3♊ 0 22	9♊25 6	8 53.5	18 34.5	29 3.0	28 32.5	3 36.7	2 1.9	16 47.6	12 7.1	22 55.1
6 M	12 55 31	15 47 34	15 44 6	21 57 50	8 49.6	19 54.6	0♊ 8.3	29 12.8	3 37.8	2 9.3	16 48.4	12 7.5	22 55.7
7 Tu	12 59 27	16 46 34	28 6 49	4♋11 41	8D 47.9	21 16.5	1 13.4	29 53.1	3 39.1	2 16.6	16 49.2	12 8.0	22 56.4
8 W	13 3 24	17 45 32	10♋13 3	16 11 36	8R 47.6	22 40.2	2 18.2	0♊33.4	3 40.6	2 23.9	16 49.9	12 8.5	22 57.1
9 Th	13 7 20	18 44 28	22 8 1	28 3 1	8 47.6	24 5.7	3 22.7	1 13.6	3 42.3	2 31.2	16 50.6	12 9.0	22 57.8
10 F	13 11 17	19 43 21	3♌57 16	9♌51 26	8 46.8	25 32.9	4 27.0	1 53.8	3 44.2	2 38.5	16 51.2	12 9.6	22 58.5
11 Sa	13 15 13	20 42 13	15 46 9	21 42 3	8 44.3	27 1.8	5 31.0	2 33.9	3 46.3	2 45.7	16 51.7	12 10.2	22 59.2
12 Su	13 19 10	21 41 1	27 39 40	3♍39 30	8 39.3	28 32.4	6 34.8	3 14.0	3 48.5	2 52.9	16 52.2	12 10.8	22 60.0
13 M	13 23 6	22 39 48	9♍42 1	15 47 36	8 31.8	0♈ 4.7	7 38.2	3 54.1	3 50.9	3 0.1	16 52.7	12 11.5	23 0.7
14 Tu	13 27 3	23 38 32	21 56 32	28 9 4	8 21.8	1 38.6	8 41.3	4 34.2	3 53.5	3 7.3	16 53.1	12 12.2	23 1.5
15 W	13 31 0	24 37 15	4♎25 22	10♎45 30	8 10.1	3 14.1	9 44.1	5 14.2	3 56.3	3 14.4	16 53.4	12 12.9	23 2.3
16 Th	13 34 56	25 35 55	17 9 29	23 37 16	7 57.6	4 51.3	10 46.6	5 54.2	3 59.3	3 21.6	16 53.8	12 13.7	23 3.1
17 F	13 38 53	26 34 33	0♏ 8 44	6♏43 42	7 45.6	6 30.1	11 48.8	6 34.2	4 2.4	3 28.6	16 54.0	12 14.4	23 4.0
18 Sa	13 42 49	27 33 9	13 21 58	20 3 18	7 35.1	8 10.5	12 50.6	7 14.1	4 5.7	3 35.7	16 54.2	12 15.3	23 4.8
19 Su	13 46 46	28 31 44	26 47 29	3♐34 16	7 26.9	9 52.6	13 52.1	7 54.1	4 9.2	3 42.7	16 54.4	12 16.1	23 5.7
20 M	13 50 42	29 30 17	10♐23 26	17 14 47	7 21.5	11 36.3	14 53.3	8 33.9	4 12.8	3 49.7	16 54.5	12 17.0	23 6.6
21 Tu	13 54 39	0♉28 48	24 8 10	1♑ 3 26	7D 18.8	13 21.7	15 54.0	9 13.8	4 16.7	3 56.7	16R 54.5	12 17.9	23 7.5
22 W	13 58 35	1 27 17	8♑ 0 29	14 59 15	7 18.1	15 8.7	16 54.4	9 53.6	4 20.7	4 3.7	16 54.5	12 18.9	23 8.5
23 Th	14 2 32	2 25 45	21 59 38	29 1 34	7R 18.5	16 57.5	17 54.5	10 33.4	4 24.8	4 10.6	16 54.5	12 19.9	23 9.4
24 F	14 6 29	3 24 11	6♒ 4 58	13♒ 9 43	7 18.8	18 47.8	18 54.1	11 13.2	4 29.1	4 17.4	16 54.4	12 20.9	23 10.4
25 Sa	14 10 25	4 22 36	20 15 40	27 22 34	7 17.7	20 39.9	19 53.3	11 53.0	4 33.6	4 24.3	16 54.2	12 21.9	23 11.4
26 Su	14 14 22	5 20 59	4♓30 9	11♓38 3	7 14.6	22 33.7	20 52.1	12 32.7	4 38.3	4 31.1	16 54.0	12 23.0	23 12.4
27 M	14 18 18	6 19 20	18 45 51	25 53 1	7 9.0	24 29.1	21 50.5	13 12.4	4 43.1	4 37.8	16 53.7	12 24.1	23 13.4
28 Tu	14 22 15	7 17 40	2♈59 3	10♈ 3 19	7 1.3	26 26.2	22 48.4	13 52.1	4 48.1	4 44.5	16 53.4	12 25.2	23 14.4
29 W	14 26 11	8 15 58	17 5 14	24 4 12	6 52.1	28 24.9	23 45.9	14 31.7	4 53.2	4 51.2	16 53.1	12 26.3	23 15.4
30 Th	14 30 8	9 14 15	0♉59 40	7♉51 6	6 42.4	0♉25.2	24 42.9	15 11.4	4 58.5	4 57.9	16 52.7	12 27.5	23 16.5

Astro Data

	Dy Hr Mn
☽0N	4 19:50
♇ D	7 11:14
☿ D	13 9:32
☽0S	19 6:23
♆ D	23 15:01
♃ D	30 13:16
☽0N	1 5:59
☽0S	15 13:42
☿0N	16 13:12
♅ R	21 12:18
☽0N	28 14:55
♄0N	29 17:09
♃△♄	30 12:14

Planet Ingress

	Dy Hr Mn
♀ ♉	10 8:06
♄ ♈	19 14:23
☉ ♈	21 0:27
♀ ♊	5 20:57
♂ ♊	7 4:06
☿ ♈	12 22:48
☉ ♉	20 12:11
☿ ♉	29 19:00

Last Aspect / ☽ Ingress (March)

Last Aspect Dy Hr Mn		☽ Ingress Dy Hr Mn
1 12:35	♇ △	♓ 2 0:05
3 21:10	♄ ☌	♈ 4 0:20
5 17:30	♀ ☌	♉ 6 2:50
8 6:34	♄ ⚹	♊ 8 9:13
10 17:27	♄ □	♋ 10 19:39
13 6:52	♄ △	♌ 13 8:28
15 6:40	♇ ⚹	♍ 15 21:09
18 7:45	♄ ☍	♎ 18 8:04
20 3:25	♇ △	♏ 20 16:52
22 4:13	♂ ☍	♐ 22 23:45
24 16:17	♂ ☍	♑ 25 4:48
26 19:03	♂ △	♒ 27 7:57
28 23:24	♂ □	♓ 29 9:33
31 2:53	♂ ⚹	♈ 31 10:41

Last Aspect / ☽ Ingress (April)

Last Aspect Dy Hr Mn		☽ Ingress Dy Hr Mn
2 0:54	♇ ⚹	♉ 2 13:04
4 16:01	♀ ☌	♊ 4 18:26
6 13:53	♇ ☌	♋ 7 3:43
9 4:31	☿ △	♌ 9 15:58
11 14:37	♇ ⚹	♍ 12 4:41
14 2:06	♇ □	♎ 14 15:33
16 16:55	☉ ☍	♏ 16 23:44
18 6:21	♅ ⚹	♐ 19 5:41
20 22:15	♇ ☍	♑ 21 10:10
22 15:18	♅ ☌	♒ 23 13:40
25 4:57	♇ △	♓ 25 16:25
27 7:31	♇ □	♈ 27 18:57
29 12:19	♀ ⚹	♉ 29 22:16

☽ Phases & Eclipses

Dy Hr Mn		
2 18:57	●	11♓49
9 21:42	☽	18♊56
18 2:28	○	27♍06
25 12:31	☽	4♑28
1 5:02	●	11♈04
8 16:31	☽	18♋26
16 16:55	○	26♎17
23 19:07	☽	3♒12
30 15:33	●	9♉52

Astro Data

1 MARCH 1908
Julian Day # 2982
Delta T 8.0 sec
SVP 06♓32'47"
Obliquity 23°27'03"
⚷ Chiron 19♒48.0
☽ Mean ☊ 11♋17.8

1 APRIL 1908
Julian Day # 3013
Delta T 8.1 sec
SVP 06♓32'45"
Obliquity 23°27'04"
⚷ Chiron 21♒45.1
☽ Mean ☊ 9♋39.3

LONGITUDE — MAY 1908

Day	Sid.Time	☉	0 hr ☽	Noon ☽	True ☊	☿	♀	♂	♃	♄	♅	♆	♇
1 F	14 34 4	10♉12 30	14♉38 6	21♉20 20	6♋33.5	2♉27.1	25♊39.4	15♊51.0	5♌ 3.9	5♈ 4.4	16♑52.2	12♋28.7	23♊17.6
2 Sa	14 38 1	11 10 43	27 57 34	4♊29 40	6R26.1	4 30.6	26 35.4	16 30.6	5 9.5	5 11.0	16R51.7	12 30.0	23 18.7
3 Su	14 41 58	12 8 54	10♊56 38	17 18 36	6 20.8	6 35.4	27 30.9	17 10.1	5 15.3	5 17.5	16 51.2	12 31.3	23 19.8
4 M	14 45 54	13 7 4	23 35 44	29 48 21	6 17.9	8 41.6	28 25.8	17 49.7	5 21.2	5 24.0	16 50.6	12 32.6	23 20.9
5 Tu	14 49 51	14 5 12	5♋56 51	12♋ 1 40	6D17.0	10 48.9	29 20.2	18 29.2	5 27.2	5 30.4	16 49.9	12 33.9	23 22.0
6 W	14 53 47	15 3 17	18 3 19	24 2 23	6 17.6	12 57.4	0♋14.0	19 8.6	5 33.4	5 36.7	16 49.2	12 35.2	23 23.2
7 Th	14 57 44	16 1 21	29 59 27	5♌55 10	6 18.8	15 6.6	1 7.2	19 48.1	5 39.7	5 43.1	16 48.5	12 36.6	23 24.3
8 F	15 1 40	16 59 23	11♌50 10	17 45 5	6R19.7	17 16.6	1 59.7	20 27.5	5 46.2	5 49.3	16 47.7	12 38.0	23 25.5
9 Sa	15 5 37	17 57 23	23 40 37	29 37 21	6 19.7	19 27.1	2 51.6	21 6.9	5 52.9	5 55.5	16 46.9	12 39.4	23 26.7
10 Su	15 9 33	18 55 21	5♍35 57	11♍36 59	6 18.0	21 37.7	3 42.8	21 46.3	5 59.6	6 1.7	16 46.0	12 40.9	23 27.9
11 M	15 13 30	19 53 18	17 41 0	23 48 30	6 14.5	23 48.2	4 33.3	22 25.6	6 6.5	6 7.8	16 45.1	12 42.4	23 29.1
12 Tu	15 17 27	20 51 12	29 59 54	6♎15 36	6 9.2	25 58.5	5 23.1	23 5.0	6 13.5	6 13.9	16 44.1	12 43.9	23 30.3
13 W	15 21 23	21 49 5	12♎35 52	19 0 53	6 2.6	28 8.1	6 12.1	23 44.3	6 20.7	6 19.9	16 43.1	12 45.4	23 31.5
14 Th	15 25 20	22 46 56	25 30 48	2♏ 5 35	5 55.3	0♊16.8	7 0.3	24 23.5	6 28.0	6 25.8	16 42.0	12 46.9	23 32.7
15 F	15 29 16	23 44 45	8♏45 10	15 29 23	5 48.1	2 24.2	7 47.7	25 2.8	6 35.4	6 31.7	16 40.9	12 48.5	23 34.0
16 Sa	15 33 13	24 42 33	22 17 57	29 10 32	5 41.9	4 30.3	8 34.2	25 42.0	6 43.0	6 37.5	16 39.7	12 50.1	23 35.2
17 Su	15 37 9	25 40 20	6♐ 6 43	13♐ 6 3	5 37.2	6 34.6	9 19.9	26 21.2	6 50.7	6 43.3	16 38.5	12 51.7	23 36.5
18 M	15 41 6	26 38 5	20 8 5	27 12 17	5 34.4	8 37.0	10 4.7	27 0.4	6 58.5	6 49.0	16 37.3	12 53.4	23 37.8
19 Tu	15 45 2	27 35 49	4♑18 11	11♑25 19	5D33.5	10 37.2	10 48.5	27 39.5	7 6.4	6 54.7	16 36.0	12 55.1	23 39.1
20 W	15 48 59	28 33 32	18 33 14	25 41 32	5 34.0	12 35.1	11 31.3	28 18.6	7 14.5	7 0.3	16 34.7	12 56.7	23 40.4
21 Th	15 52 56	29 31 14	2♒49 51	9♒57 50	5 35.3	14 30.6	12 13.2	28 57.7	7 22.7	7 5.8	16 33.4	12 58.5	23 41.7
22 F	15 56 52	0♊28 55	17 5 13	24 11 44	5 36.6	16 23.5	12 54.0	29 36.8	7 31.0	7 11.3	16 32.0	13 0.2	23 43.0
23 Sa	16 0 49	1 26 34	1♓17 8	8♓21 12	5R37.2	18 13.6	13 33.7	0♋15.9	7 39.4	7 16.7	16 30.5	13 1.9	23 44.3
24 Su	16 4 45	2 24 13	15 23 43	22 24 28	5 36.5	20 1.0	14 12.2	0 54.9	7 47.9	7 22.0	16 29.0	13 3.7	23 45.7
25 M	16 8 42	3 21 50	29 23 15	6♈19 49	5 34.4	21 45.5	14 49.6	1 34.0	7 56.5	7 27.3	16 27.5	13 5.5	23 47.0
26 Tu	16 12 38	4 19 27	13♈13 57	20 5 26	5 31.0	23 27.1	15 25.8	2 13.0	8 5.3	7 32.5	16 26.0	13 7.3	23 48.3
27 W	16 16 35	5 17 3	26 54 1	3♉39 29	5 26.7	25 5.7	16 0.7	2 51.9	8 14.1	7 37.6	16 24.4	13 9.1	23 49.7
28 Th	16 20 31	6 14 38	10♉21 37	17 0 14	5 22.1	26 41.3	16 34.3	3 30.9	8 23.1	7 42.7	16 22.7	13 11.0	23 51.1
29 F	16 24 28	7 12 12	23 35 11	0♊ 6 19	5 17.8	28 13.8	17 6.6	4 9.9	8 32.2	7 47.7	16 21.1	13 12.8	23 52.4
30 Sa	16 28 25	8 9 44	6♊33 36	12 56 58	5 14.4	29 43.3	17 37.5	4 48.8	8 41.4	7 52.6	16 19.4	13 14.7	23 53.8
31 Su	16 32 21	9 7 16	19 16 29	25 32 14	5 12.2	1♋ 9.7	18 6.8	5 27.7	8 50.7	7 57.5	16 17.6	13 16.6	23 55.2

LONGITUDE — JUNE 1908

Day	Sid.Time	☉	0 hr ☽	Noon ☽	True ☊	☿	♀	♂	♃	♄	♅	♆	♇
1 M	16 36 18	10♊ 4 47	1♋44 20	7♋53 2	5♋11.2	2♋32.9	18♋34.7	6♋ 6.6	9♌ 0.1	8♈ 2.3	16♑15.9	13♋18.6	23♊56.6
2 Tu	16 40 14	11 2 17	13 58 35	20 1 18	5D11.5	3 53.0	19 1.0	6 45.5	9 9.6	8 7.0	16R14.1	13 20.5	23 57.9
3 W	16 44 11	11 59 45	26 1 33	1♌59 46	5 12.6	5 9.8	19 25.6	7 24.3	9 19.2	8 11.6	16 12.2	13 22.4	23 59.3
4 Th	16 48 7	12 57 13	7♌56 25	13 52 0	5 14.1	6 23.3	19 48.6	8 3.2	9 28.9	8 16.1	16 10.4	13 24.4	24 0.7
5 F	16 52 4	13 54 39	19 47 2	25 42 5	5 15.8	7 33.5	20 9.7	8 42.0	9 38.7	8 20.6	16 8.5	13 26.4	24 2.1
6 Sa	16 56 0	14 52 4	1♍37 45	7♍34 36	5 17.0	8 40.3	20 29.1	9 20.8	9 48.5	8 25.0	16 6.5	13 28.4	24 3.5
7 Su	16 59 57	15 49 27	13 33 15	19 34 17	5R17.5	9 43.6	20 46.5	9 59.5	9 58.5	8 29.3	16 4.6	13 30.4	24 5.0
8 M	17 3 54	16 46 50	25 38 18	1♎45 50	5 17.3	10 43.4	21 2.0	10 38.3	10 8.6	8 33.6	16 2.6	13 32.4	24 6.4
9 Tu	17 7 50	17 44 12	7♎57 26	14 13 35	5 16.3	11 39.6	21 15.5	11 17.0	10 18.7	8 37.7	16 0.6	13 34.5	24 7.8
10 W	17 11 47	18 41 32	20 34 43	27 1 10	5 14.6	12 32.1	21 27.0	11 55.7	10 29.0	8 41.8	15 58.5	13 36.5	24 9.2
11 Th	17 15 43	19 38 52	3♏33 14	10♏11 4	5 12.6	13 20.9	21 36.3	12 34.4	10 39.3	8 45.8	15 56.5	13 38.6	24 10.6
12 F	17 19 40	20 36 11	16 54 45	23 44 14	5 10.6	14 5.7	21 43.4	13 13.1	10 49.7	8 49.7	15 54.4	13 40.7	24 12.0
13 Sa	17 23 36	21 33 28	0♐39 21	7♐39 48	5 8.8	14 46.6	21 48.2	13 51.8	11 0.2	8 53.6	15 52.3	13 42.7	24 13.4
14 Su	17 27 33	22 30 46	14 45 11	21 54 56	5 7.7	15 23.4	21R50.8	14 30.4	11 10.8	8 57.3	15 50.1	13 44.8	24 14.9
15 M	17 31 29	23 28 2	29 8 27	6♑25 2	5D 7.1	15 56.1	21 51.1	15 9.0	11 21.5	9 1.0	15 48.0	13 47.0	24 16.3
16 Tu	17 35 26	24 25 18	13♑43 53	21 4 13	5 7.2	16 24.5	21 49.0	15 47.6	11 32.2	9 4.6	15 45.8	13 49.1	24 17.7
17 W	17 39 23	25 22 34	28 25 13	5♒46 5	5 7.6	16 48.6	21 44.6	16 26.2	11 43.0	9 8.1	15 43.6	13 51.2	24 19.1
18 Th	17 43 19	26 19 49	13♒ 6 4	20 24 29	5 8.4	17 8.2	21 37.7	17 4.8	11 53.9	9 11.5	15 41.4	13 53.4	24 20.6
19 F	17 47 16	27 17 4	27 40 42	4♓54 11	5 9.0	17 23.4	21 28.5	17 43.4	12 4.9	9 14.8	15 39.1	13 55.5	24 22.0
20 Sa	17 51 12	28 14 18	12♓ 4 30	19 11 17	5 9.5	17 34.0	21 16.8	18 21.9	12 15.9	9 18.0	15 36.9	13 57.7	24 23.4
21 Su	17 55 9	29 11 33	26 14 16	3♈13 16	5R 9.8	17R40.0	21 2.8	19 0.5	12 27.0	9 21.2	15 34.6	13 59.8	24 24.8
22 M	17 59 5	0♋ 8 47	10♈ 8 12	16 58 59	5 9.7	17 41.5	20 46.5	19 39.0	12 38.2	9 24.2	15 32.3	14 2.0	24 26.2
23 Tu	18 3 2	1 6 1	23 45 38	0♉28 11	5 9.4	17 38.4	20 27.8	20 17.5	12 49.4	9 27.2	15 30.0	14 4.2	24 27.7
24 W	18 6 58	2 3 15	7♉ 6 44	13 41 21	5 9.1	17 30.9	20 6.9	20 56.0	13 0.7	9 30.0	15 27.6	14 6.4	24 29.1
25 Th	18 10 55	3 0 29	20 12 11	26 39 21	5 8.8	17 19.0	19 43.8	21 34.5	13 12.1	9 32.8	15 25.3	14 8.5	24 30.5
26 F	18 14 52	3 57 43	3♊ 2 59	9♊23 14	5 8.6	17 3.0	19 18.6	22 13.0	13 23.6	9 35.5	15 22.9	14 10.7	24 31.9
27 Sa	18 18 48	4 54 57	15 40 14	21 54 10	5D 8.6	16 42.9	18 51.4	22 51.4	13 35.1	9 38.1	15 20.6	14 13.0	24 33.3
28 Su	18 22 45	5 52 11	28 5 11	4♋13 28	5R 8.6	16 19.2	18 22.4	23 29.9	13 46.7	9 40.6	15 18.2	14 15.2	24 34.7
29 M	18 26 41	6 49 25	10♋19 12	16 22 36	5 8.6	15 52.1	17 51.6	24 8.3	13 58.3	9 43.0	15 15.8	14 17.4	24 36.1
30 Tu	18 30 38	7 46 38	22 23 52	28 23 17	5 8.5	15 22.1	17 19.3	24 46.8	14 10.0	9 45.3	15 13.4	14 19.6	24 37.5

Astro Data (Dy Hr Mn)	Planet Ingress (Dy Hr Mn)	Last Aspect (Dy Hr Mn)	☽ Ingress (Dy Hr Mn)	Last Aspect (Dy Hr Mn)	☽ Ingress (Dy Hr Mn)	☽ Phases & Eclipses (Dy Hr Mn)	Astro Data
☽0S 12 22:42	♀ ♋ 5 17:44	1 3:59 ♅ △	♊ 2 3:44	2 10:22 ♀ ☌	♌ 3 7:59	8 11:23 ☽ 17♌27	1 MAY 1908
♃△♄ 12 7:02	☿ ♊ 13 20:52	4 10:04 ♀ ☌	♋ 4 12:23	5 8:38 ♇ ✶	♍ 5 20:42	16 4:32 ○ 24♏53	Julian Day # 3043
☽0N 25 21:55	☉ ♊ 21 11:58	5 21:32 ♅ ☍	♌ 7 0:01	7 20:58 ♇ □	♎ 8 8:33	23 0:17 ☽ 1♓27	Delta T 8.2 sec
♃∠♇ 31 13:29	♂ ♋ 22 14:14	8 23:32 ♇ ✶	♍ 9 12:46	10 6:42 ♇ △	♏ 10 17:30	30 3:14 ● 8♊18	SVP 06♓32'42"
	☿ ♋ 30 4:34	11 14:33 ☿ △	♎ 12 0:00	12 8:32 ♀ △	♐ 12 22:52		Obliquity 23°27'03"
☽0S 9 8:04		13 21:50 ♂ △	♏ 14 8:12	14 15:55 ♇ ☍	♑ 15 1:25	7 4:56 ☽ 16♍01	⚷ Chiron 22♒59.8
♀ R 14 14:51	☉ ♋ 21 20:19	16 4:32 ☉ ☍	♐ 16 13:26	16 13:10 ♀ ☍	♒ 17 2:35	14 13:55 ○ 23♐04	☽ Mean ☊ 8♋04.0
☿ R 21 19:46		18 12:14 ♂ ☍	♑ 18 16:44	18 23:18 ☉ △	♓ 19 3:51	14 14:06 ☍ A 0.813	
☽0N 22 3:38		20 18:02 ☉ △	♒ 20 19:14	21 5:26 ☉ □	♈ 21 6:27	21 5:26 ☽ 29♓25	1 JUNE 1908
		22 11:13 ♇ △	♓ 22 21:49	23 1:15 ♇ ✶	♉ 23 11:09	28 16:31 ● 6♋32	Julian Day # 3074
		24 14:21 ♇ □	♈ 25 1:03	25 2:40 ♂ ✶	♊ 25 18:16	28 16:29:41 ☌ A 3'60"	Delta T 8.3 sec
		26 20:23 ☿ ✶	♉ 27 5:30	27 17:10 ♇ ☌	♋ 28 3:44		SVP 06♓32'37"
		28 11:42 ♀ ✶	♊ 29 11:48	30 5:02 ♂ ☌	♌ 30 15:14		Obliquity 23°27'03"
		31 8:54 ♇ ☌	♋ 31 20:37				⚷ Chiron 23♒22.4R
							☽ Mean ☊ 6♋25.5

JULY 1908 LONGITUDE

Day	Sid.Time	☉	0 hr ☽	Noon ☽	True ☊	☿	♀	♂	♃	♄	♅	♆	♇
1 W	18 34 34	8♋43 52	4♌21 6	10♌17 37	5♋ 8.2	14♋49.5	16♋45.7	25♋25.2	14♌21.8	9♈47.5	15♑11.0	14♋21.8	24♊38.9
2 Th	18 38 31	9 41 5	16 13 11	22 8 9	5R 7.7	14R 14.9	16R 10.8	26 3.6	14 33.6	9 49.6	15R 8.6	14 24.0	24 40.3
3 F	18 42 27	10 38 17	28 2 54	3♍57 52	5 7.0	13 38.9	15 35.0	26 42.0	14 45.5	9 51.6	15 6.2	14 26.3	24 41.7
4 Sa	18 46 24	11 35 30	9♍53 31	15 50 19	5 6.3	13 2.1	14 58.4	27 20.4	14 57.4	9 53.6	15 3.8	14 28.5	24 43.0
5 Su	18 50 21	12 32 42	21 48 46	27 49 24	5 5.6	12 25.0	14 21.2	27 58.7	15 9.4	9 55.4	15 1.4	14 30.7	24 44.4
6 M	18 54 17	13 29 55	3♎52 44	9♎59 21	5D 5.1	11 48.3	13 43.7	28 37.1	15 21.4	9 57.1	14 59.0	14 33.0	24 45.8
7 Tu	18 58 14	14 27 6	16 9 46	22 24 31	5 5.0	11 12.6	13 6.2	29 15.4	15 33.5	9 58.7	14 56.5	14 35.2	24 47.1
8 W	19 2 10	15 24 18	28 44 8	5♏ 9 4	5 5.3	10 38.6	12 28.9	29 53.8	15 45.6	10 0.2	14 54.1	14 37.4	24 48.5
9 Th	19 6 7	16 21 30	11♏39 46	18 16 34	5 5.9	10 6.9	11 51.9	0♌32.1	15 57.8	10 1.6	14 51.7	14 39.6	24 49.8
10 F	19 10 3	17 18 42	24 59 45	1♐49 28	5 6.9	9 38.0	11 15.7	1 10.4	16 10.0	10 3.0	14 49.3	14 41.9	24 51.1
11 Sa	19 14 0	18 15 53	8♐45 46	15 48 32	5 7.9	9 12.5	10 40.3	1 48.7	16 22.3	10 4.2	14 46.9	14 44.1	24 52.5
12 Su	19 17 56	19 13 5	22 57 31	0♑12 18	5R 8.7	8 50.9	10 5.9	2 27.0	16 34.6	10 5.3	14 44.5	14 46.3	24 53.8
13 M	19 21 53	20 10 17	7♑32 17	14 56 45	5 8.9	8 33.4	9 32.9	3 5.3	16 46.9	10 6.3	14 42.1	14 48.6	24 55.1
14 Tu	19 25 50	21 7 29	22 24 46	29 55 22	5 8.4	8 20.6	9 1.4	3 43.6	16 59.3	10 7.3	14 39.7	14 50.8	24 56.4
15 W	19 29 46	22 4 42	7♒27 27	14♒59 52	5 7.1	8 12.7	8 31.6	4 21.8	17 11.8	10 8.1	14 37.3	14 53.0	24 57.7
16 Th	19 33 43	23 1 54	22 31 30	0♓ 1 14	5 5.2	8D 10.0	8 3.5	5 0.1	17 24.2	10 8.8	14 34.9	14 55.2	24 59.0
17 F	19 37 39	23 59 8	7♓28 4	14 51 6	5 2.9	8 12.6	7 37.4	5 38.3	17 36.7	10 9.4	14 32.5	14 57.4	25 0.3
18 Sa	19 41 36	24 56 22	22 9 35	29 22 56	5 0.6	8 20.8	7 13.5	6 16.6	17 49.3	10 9.9	14 30.1	14 59.6	25 1.5
19 Su	19 45 32	25 53 36	6♈30 43	13♈32 38	4 58.9	8 34.5	6 51.6	6 54.8	18 1.9	10 10.3	14 27.7	15 1.8	25 2.8
20 M	19 49 29	26 50 52	20 28 36	27 18 37	4D 57.9	8 53.9	6 32.1	7 33.0	18 14.5	10 10.6	14 25.4	15 4.0	25 4.0
21 Tu	19 53 26	27 48 8	4♉ 2 48	10♉41 22	4 57.9	9 19.1	6 14.8	8 11.3	18 27.1	10 10.9	14 23.1	15 6.2	25 5.2
22 W	19 57 22	28 45 25	17 14 36	23 42 51	4 58.8	9 50.0	5 59.9	8 49.5	18 39.8	10R 11.0	14 20.7	15 8.4	25 6.5
23 Th	20 1 19	29 42 43	0♊ 6 28	6♊25 51	5 0.2	10 26.6	5 47.4	9 27.7	18 52.5	10 11.0	14 18.4	15 10.6	25 7.7
24 F	20 5 15	0♌40 2	12 41 23	18 53 29	5 1.8	11 8.9	5 37.3	10 5.9	19 5.3	10 10.9	14 16.1	15 12.8	25 8.9
25 Sa	20 9 12	1 37 22	25 2 30	1♋ 8 47	5R 3.0	11 56.8	5 29.6	10 44.1	19 18.1	10 10.7	14 13.8	15 14.9	25 10.1
26 Su	20 13 8	2 34 43	7♋12 42	13 14 34	5 3.4	12 50.3	5 24.3	11 22.4	19 30.9	10 10.4	14 11.6	15 17.1	25 11.3
27 M	20 17 5	3 32 4	19 14 39	25 13 15	5 2.5	13 49.3	5D 21.3	12 0.6	19 43.7	10 10.0	14 9.3	15 19.2	25 12.4
28 Tu	20 21 1	4 29 26	1♌10 37	7♌ 7 0	5 0.2	14 53.8	5 20.7	12 38.8	19 56.6	10 9.4	14 7.1	15 21.4	25 13.6
29 W	20 24 58	5 26 49	13 2 39	18 57 47	4 56.4	16 3.5	5 22.4	13 17.0	20 9.4	10 8.8	14 4.9	15 23.5	25 14.7
30 Th	20 28 55	6 24 13	24 52 41	0♍47 34	4 51.5	17 18.4	5 26.3	13 55.2	20 22.3	10 8.1	14 2.7	15 25.6	25 15.8
31 F	20 32 51	7 21 38	6♍42 42	12 38 23	4 45.8	18 38.3	5 32.5	14 33.3	20 35.3	10 7.3	14 0.5	15 27.7	25 16.9

AUGUST 1908 LONGITUDE

Day	Sid.Time	☉	0 hr ☽	Noon ☽	True ☊	☿	♀	♂	♃	♄	♅	♆	♇
1 Sa	20 36 48	8♌19 3	18♍34 56	24♍32 40	4♋39.9	20♋ 3.0	5♋40.8	15♌11.5	20♌48.2	10♈ 6.4	13♑58.4	15♋29.8	25♊18.0
2 Su	20 40 44	9 16 29	0♎31 57	6♎33 10	4R 34.5	21 32.5	5 51.2	15 49.7	21 1.2	10R 5.4	13R 56.3	15 31.9	25 19.1
3 M	20 44 41	10 13 55	12 36 47	18 43 12	4 30.2	23 6.4	6 3.7	16 27.9	21 14.1	10 4.2	13 54.2	15 34.0	25 20.2
4 Tu	20 48 37	11 11 23	24 52 55	1♏ 6 25	4 27.3	24 44.5	6 18.2	17 6.1	21 27.1	10 3.0	13 52.1	15 36.0	25 21.2
5 W	20 52 34	12 8 51	7♏24 12	13 46 47	4D 25.9	26 26.5	6 34.6	17 44.2	21 40.1	10 1.7	13 50.1	15 38.1	25 22.3
6 Th	20 56 30	13 6 19	20 14 38	26 48 14	4 26.0	28 12.1	6 52.9	18 22.4	21 53.2	10 0.3	13 48.1	15 40.1	25 23.3
7 F	21 0 27	14 3 49	3♐27 58	10♐14 12	4 27.1	0♌ 1.0	7 13.1	19 0.6	22 6.2	9 58.8	13 46.1	15 42.1	25 24.3
8 Sa	21 4 24	15 1 20	17 7 10	24 6 59	4 28.5	1 52.9	7 35.0	19 38.7	22 19.3	9 57.2	13 44.1	15 44.1	25 25.3
9 Su	21 8 20	15 58 51	1♑13 40	8♑27 0	4R 29.4	3 47.3	7 58.6	20 16.9	22 32.3	9 55.5	13 42.2	15 46.1	25 26.3
10 M	21 12 17	16 56 23	15 46 37	23 11 56	4 28.9	5 43.9	8 23.9	20 55.0	22 45.4	9 53.7	13 40.3	15 48.1	25 27.3
11 Tu	21 16 13	17 53 56	0♒42 11	8♒16 22	4 26.7	7 42.4	8 50.7	21 33.2	22 58.5	9 51.8	13 38.4	15 50.1	25 28.2
12 W	21 20 10	18 51 30	15 53 22	23 31 53	4 22.5	9 42.2	9 19.2	22 11.3	23 11.6	9 49.8	13 36.6	15 52.0	25 29.1
13 Th	21 24 6	19 49 6	1♓10 35	8♓48 5	4 16.7	11 43.2	9 49.1	22 49.5	23 24.6	9 47.7	13 34.8	15 53.9	25 30.0
14 F	21 28 3	20 46 42	16 23 2	23 54 13	4 9.9	13 44.8	10 20.5	23 27.6	23 37.7	9 45.5	13 33.0	15 55.8	25 30.9
15 Sa	21 31 59	21 44 20	1♈20 34	8♈41 9	4 3.2	15 46.9	10 53.3	24 5.8	23 50.8	9 43.3	13 31.3	15 57.7	25 31.8
16 Su	21 35 56	22 42 0	15 55 19	23 2 34	3 57.3	17 49.1	11 27.4	24 43.9	24 3.9	9 40.9	13 29.6	15 59.6	25 32.7
17 M	21 39 53	23 39 40	0♉ 2 40	6♉55 33	3 53.0	19 51.1	12 2.8	25 22.1	24 17.1	9 38.5	13 27.9	16 1.5	25 33.5
18 Tu	21 43 49	24 37 23	13 41 20	20 20 15	3D 50.7	21 52.8	12 39.5	26 0.3	24 30.2	9 35.9	13 26.3	16 3.3	25 34.3
19 W	21 47 46	25 35 7	26 52 41	3♊19 6	3 50.1	23 54.0	13 17.3	26 38.4	24 43.3	9 33.3	13 24.7	16 5.1	25 35.2
20 Th	21 51 42	26 32 53	9♊40 0	15 55 56	3 50.7	25 54.4	13 56.4	27 16.6	24 56.4	9 30.6	13 23.1	16 6.9	25 35.9
21 F	21 55 39	27 30 41	22 7 30	28 15 14	3R 51.7	27 54.0	14 36.5	27 54.8	25 9.5	9 27.8	13 21.6	16 8.7	25 36.7
22 Sa	21 59 35	28 28 30	4♋19 43	10♋21 29	3 52.3	29 52.6	15 17.7	28 32.9	25 22.6	9 25.0	13 20.1	16 10.5	25 37.5
23 Su	22 3 32	29 26 21	16 21 2	22 18 50	3 51.4	1♍50.1	15 59.9	29 11.1	25 35.7	9 22.0	13 18.7	16 12.2	25 38.2
24 M	22 7 28	0♍24 14	28 15 20	4♌10 55	3 48.4	3 46.5	16 43.1	29 49.3	25 48.8	9 19.0	13 17.3	16 13.9	25 38.9
25 Tu	22 11 25	1 22 8	10♌ 5 55	16 0 39	3 42.9	5 41.7	17 27.3	0♍27.5	26 1.9	9 15.8	13 15.9	16 15.7	25 39.6
26 W	22 15 22	2 20 4	21 55 24	27 50 25	3 35.0	7 35.7	18 12.4	1 5.7	26 14.9	9 12.6	13 14.6	16 17.3	25 40.3
27 Th	22 19 18	3 18 2	3♍45 54	9♍42 3	3 25.0	9 28.4	18 58.4	1 43.8	26 28.0	9 9.4	13 13.3	16 19.0	25 41.0
28 F	22 23 15	4 16 1	15 39 4	21 37 8	3 13.7	11 19.9	19 45.2	2 22.0	26 41.1	9 6.0	13 12.0	16 20.6	25 41.6
29 Sa	22 27 11	5 14 1	27 36 25	3♎37 8	3 1.9	13 10.1	20 32.8	3 0.2	26 54.1	9 2.6	13 10.9	16 22.2	25 42.2
30 Su	22 31 8	6 12 3	9♎39 28	15 43 41	2 50.8	14 59.0	21 21.2	3 38.4	27 7.1	8 59.1	13 9.7	16 23.8	25 42.8
31 M	22 35 4	7 10 7	21 50 3	27 58 50	2 41.3	16 46.6	22 10.4	4 16.6	27 20.1	8 55.5	13 8.6	16 25.4	25 43.4

Astro Data	Planet Ingress	Last Aspect	☽ Ingress	Last Aspect	☽ Ingress	☽ Phases & Eclipses	Astro Data
Dy Hr Mn	Dy Hr Mn	Dy Hr Mn	Dy Hr Mn	Dy Hr Mn	Dy Hr Mn	Dy Hr Mn	1 JULY 1908
♃⊻♆ 1 0:06	♂ ♌ 8 3:54	2 17:11 ♇ ⚹	♍ 3 3:58	1 13:32 ♇ □	♎ 1 22:56	6 20:25 ☽ 14♎19	Julian Day # 3104
♃⊼♅ 4 10:42	☉ ♌ 23 7:14	5 13:00 ♂ ⚹	♎ 5 16:19	4 0:55 ♇ △	♏ 4 9:53	13 21:48 ○ 21♑02	Delta T 8.4 sec
☽0S 6 16:20		8 2:18 ♂ □	♏ 8 2:23	6 16:49 ☿ △	♐ 6 17:47	13 21:34 ☍ A 0.229	SVP 06♓32'31"
♅☍♆ 11 14:16	☿ ♌ 6 23:47	9 9:12 ☉ △	♐ 10 8:49	8 14:14 ♇ ☍	♑ 8 21:57	20 12:02 ☽ 27♈20	Obliquity 23°27'03"
☿ D 16 0:22	☿ ♍ 22 1:31	12 3:14 ♇ ☍	♑ 12 11:40	10 0:02 ♆ ☍	♒ 10 22:53	28 7:17 ● 4♌47	⚷ Chiron 22♒48.6R
☽0N 19 9:36	☉ ♍ 23 13:57	13 21:48 ☉ ☍	♒ 14 12:07	12 15:05 ♇ △	♓ 12 22:09		☽ Mean ☊ 4♋50.2
♄ R 22 12:46	♂ ♍ 24 6:44	16 3:56 ♇ △	♓ 16 11:58	14 14:36 ♇ □	♈ 14 21:49	5 9:40 ☽ 12♏32	
♀ D 27 18:25		18 4:56 ☉ △	♈ 18 13:02	16 16:17 ♇ ⚹	♉ 16 23:55	12 4:59 ○ 19♒03	1 AUGUST 1908
		20 12:02 ☉ □	♉ 20 16:46	18 23:32 ♂ □	♊ 19 5:48	18 21:25 ☽ 25♉29	Julian Day # 3135
☽0S 2 22:44		22 23:12 ☉ ⚹	♊ 22 23:48	21 13:30 ☿ ⚹	♋ 21 15:26	26 22:59 ● 3♍16	Delta T 8.6 sec
☽0N 15 17:12		25 0:15 ♇ ☌	♋ 25 9:44	22 23:42 ♆ ☌	♌ 24 3:32		SVP 06♓32'26"
♃Q♄ 18 8:51		26 16:07 ♆ ☌	♌ 27 21:38	26 8:56 ♃ ☌	♍ 26 16:23		Obliquity 23°27'04"
♃⚹♇ 23 4:54		30 0:47 ♇ ⚹	♍ 30 10:24	28 20:11 ♇ □	♎ 29 4:47		⚷ Chiron 21♒29.3R
☽0S 30 3:52				31 10:56 ♃ ⚹	♏ 31 15:55		☽ Mean ☊ 3♋11.7

LONGITUDE — SEPTEMBER 1908

Day	Sid.Time	☉	0 hr ☽	Noon ☽	True ☊	☿	♀	♂	♃	♄	♅	♆	♇
1 Tu	22 39 1	8♍ 8 11	4♏10 23	10♏25 4	2♋34.1	18♍33.0	23♋ 0.4	4♍54.8	27♌33.1	8♈51.9	13♑ 7.5	16♋26.9	25♊43.9
2 W	22 42 57	9 6 18	16 43 16	23 5 24	2R29.5	20 18.1	23 51.0	5 33.0	27 46.1	8R48.2	13R 6.5	16 28.4	25 44.5
3 Th	22 46 54	10 4 26	29 31 55	6♐ 3 15	2D27.3	22 2.0	24 42.3	6 11.3	27 59.1	8 44.4	13 5.5	16 29.9	25 45.0
4 F	22 50 50	11 2 35	12♐39 50	19 22 4	2 26.8	23 44.7	25 34.3	6 49.5	28 12.0	8 40.6	13 4.6	16 31.4	25 45.5
5 Sa	22 54 47	12 0 46	26 10 17	3♑ 4 47	2R27.1	25 26.2	26 26.9	7 27.7	28 24.9	8 36.7	13 3.7	16 32.8	25 45.9
6 Su	22 58 44	12 58 58	10♑ 5 43	17 13 7	2 27.0	27 6.4	27 20.1	8 5.9	28 37.8	8 32.7	13 2.9	16 34.3	25 46.4
7 M	23 2 40	13 57 12	24 26 50	1♒46 34	2 25.4	28 45.5	28 14.0	8 44.2	28 50.7	8 28.7	13 2.1	16 35.6	25 46.8
8 Tu	23 6 37	14 55 27	9♒11 47	16 41 45	2 21.4	0♎23.4	29 8.4	9 22.4	29 3.6	8 24.6	13 1.4	16 37.0	25 47.2
9 W	23 10 33	15 53 44	24 15 30	1♓51 53	2 14.8	2 0.2	0♌ 3.4	10 0.6	29 16.4	8 20.5	13 0.7	16 38.3	25 47.6
10 Th	23 14 30	16 52 2	9♓29 39	17 7 25	2 5.8	3 35.8	0 58.9	10 38.9	29 29.2	8 16.4	13 0.0	16 39.7	25 48.0
11 F	23 18 26	17 50 22	24 43 45	2♈17 18	1 55.4	5 10.3	1 55.0	11 17.1	29 42.0	8 12.1	12 59.4	16 40.9	25 48.3
12 Sa	23 22 23	18 48 44	9♈46 46	17 11 3	1 44.8	6 43.7	2 51.6	11 55.4	29 54.7	8 7.9	12 58.9	16 42.2	25 48.7
13 Su	23 26 19	19 47 8	24 29 13	1♉40 35	1 35.1	8 16.0	3 48.7	12 33.6	0♍ 7.4	8 3.6	12 58.4	16 43.4	25 49.0
14 M	23 30 16	20 45 34	8♉44 39	15 41 12	1 27.5	9 47.2	4 46.3	13 11.9	0 20.1	7 59.2	12 57.9	16 44.6	25 49.3
15 Tu	23 34 13	21 44 3	22 30 12	29 11 47	1 22.4	11 17.2	5 44.4	13 50.2	0 32.7	7 54.8	12 57.5	16 45.8	25 49.5
16 W	23 38 9	22 42 33	5♊46 16	12♊14 4	1 19.7	12 46.2	6 42.9	14 28.5	0 45.3	7 50.4	12 57.2	16 46.9	25 49.7
17 Th	23 42 6	23 41 6	18 35 44	24 51 51	1D18.8	14 14.0	7 41.9	15 6.8	0 57.9	7 45.9	12 56.9	16 48.0	25 50.0
18 F	23 46 2	24 39 41	1♋ 3 3	7♋ 9 59	1R18.8	15 40.8	8 41.3	15 45.1	1 10.4	7 41.5	12 56.6	16 49.1	25 50.2
19 Sa	23 49 59	25 38 18	13 13 19	19 13 43	1 18.5	17 6.4	9 41.2	16 23.4	1 22.9	7 36.9	12 56.4	16 50.2	25 50.3
20 Su	23 53 55	26 36 57	25 11 47	1♌ 8 9	1 16.7	18 30.9	10 41.4	17 1.7	1 35.4	7 32.4	12 56.2	16 51.2	25 50.5
21 M	23 57 52	27 35 38	7♌ 3 22	12 57 57	1 12.6	19 54.1	11 42.0	17 40.1	1 47.8	7 27.8	12 56.1	16 52.2	25 50.6
22 Tu	0 1 48	28 34 22	18 52 21	24 47 0	1 5.7	21 16.2	12 43.0	18 18.4	2 0.2	7 23.2	12D56.1	16 53.2	25 50.7
23 W	0 5 45	29 33 7	0♍42 16	6♍38 27	0 55.9	22 37.0	13 44.4	18 56.8	2 12.5	7 18.5	12 56.1	16 54.1	25 50.8
24 Th	0 9 42	0♎31 55	12 35 50	18 34 37	0 43.7	23 56.6	14 46.2	19 35.1	2 24.8	7 13.9	12 56.1	16 55.0	25 50.9
25 F	0 13 38	1 30 45	24 35 0	0♎37 8	0 29.9	25 14.8	15 48.2	20 13.5	2 37.1	7 9.2	12 56.2	16 55.9	25 50.9
26 Sa	0 17 35	2 29 37	6♎41 6	12 47 3	0 15.5	26 31.7	16 50.7	20 51.9	2 49.3	7 4.5	12 56.4	16 56.7	25R50.9
27 Su	0 21 31	3 28 30	18 55 2	25 5 10	0 1.8	27 47.0	17 53.4	21 30.3	3 1.4	6 59.8	12 56.6	16 57.5	25 50.9
28 M	0 25 28	4 27 26	1♏17 33	7♏32 19	29♊50.0	29 0.9	18 56.5	22 8.7	3 13.5	6 55.1	12 56.8	16 58.3	25 50.9
29 Tu	0 29 24	5 26 24	13 49 35	20 9 32	29 40.8	0♏13.1	19 59.8	22 47.1	3 25.6	6 50.4	12 57.1	16 59.0	25 50.8
30 W	0 33 21	6 25 23	26 32 23	2♐58 22	29 34.5	1 23.6	21 3.5	23 25.5	3 37.5	6 45.7	12 57.5	16 59.7	25 50.7

LONGITUDE — OCTOBER 1908

Day	Sid.Time	☉	0 hr ☽	Noon ☽	True ☊	☿	♀	♂	♃	♄	♅	♆	♇
1 Th	0 37 17	7♎24 25	9♐27 46	16♐ 0 52	29♊31.2	2♏32.3	22♌ 7.5	24♍ 4.0	3♍49.5	6♈41.0	12♑57.9	17♋ 0.4	25♊50.6
2 F	0 41 14	8 23 28	22 37 58	29 19 24	29D30.0	3 38.9	23 11.7	24 42.4	4 1.3	6R36.3	12 58.4	17 1.0	25R50.5
3 Sa	0 45 11	9 22 33	6♑ 5 26	12♑56 21	29R29.9	4 43.5	24 16.3	25 20.9	4 13.2	6 31.6	12 58.9	17 1.7	25 50.4
4 Su	0 49 7	10 21 40	19 52 19	26 53 29	29 29.7	5 45.8	25 21.1	25 59.3	4 24.9	6 26.9	12 59.4	17 2.2	25 50.2
5 M	0 53 4	11 20 48	3♒59 50	11♒11 14	29 28.1	6 45.6	26 26.2	26 37.8	4 36.6	6 22.2	13 0.1	17 2.8	25 50.0
6 Tu	0 57 0	12 19 58	18 27 23	25 47 50	29 24.3	7 42.6	27 31.5	27 16.2	4 48.2	6 17.6	13 0.7	17 3.3	25 49.8
7 W	1 0 57	13 19 10	3♓11 56	10♓38 52	29 17.7	8 36.8	28 37.1	27 54.7	4 59.8	6 12.9	13 1.4	17 3.8	25 49.6
8 Th	1 4 53	14 18 24	18 7 40	25 37 13	29 8.8	9 27.8	29 42.9	28 33.2	5 11.3	6 8.3	13 2.2	17 4.2	25 49.3
9 F	1 8 50	15 17 40	3♈ 6 21	10♈33 52	28 58.2	10 15.2	0♍49.0	29 11.7	5 22.7	6 3.7	13 3.0	17 4.6	25 49.1
10 Sa	1 12 46	16 16 57	17 58 34	25 19 23	28 47.3	10 58.8	1 55.3	29 50.2	5 34.1	5 59.1	13 3.9	17 5.0	25 48.8
11 Su	1 16 43	17 16 17	2♉35 19	9♉45 34	28 37.3	11 38.3	3 1.9	0♎28.8	5 45.4	5 54.5	13 4.8	17 5.4	25 48.5
12 M	1 20 39	18 15 38	16 49 31	23 46 45	28 29.2	12 13.1	4 8.7	1 7.3	5 56.6	5 49.9	13 5.8	17 5.7	25 48.1
13 Tu	1 24 36	19 15 2	0♊37 2	7♊20 19	28 23.7	12 42.9	5 15.7	1 45.9	6 7.8	5 45.4	13 6.8	17 6.0	25 47.8
14 W	1 28 33	20 14 29	13 56 45	20 26 35	28 20.7	13 7.2	6 22.9	2 24.4	6 18.9	5 40.9	13 7.9	17 6.2	25 47.4
15 Th	1 32 29	21 13 57	26 50 14	3♋ 8 10	28D19.8	13 25.5	7 30.4	3 3.0	6 29.9	5 36.5	13 9.0	17 6.4	25 47.0
16 F	1 36 26	22 13 28	9♋20 59	15 29 16	28 20.1	13 37.2	8 38.0	3 41.6	6 40.8	5 32.1	13 10.1	17 6.6	25 46.6
17 Sa	1 40 22	23 13 1	21 33 42	27 34 55	28R20.5	13R41.9	9 45.9	4 20.2	6 51.6	5 27.7	13 11.4	17 6.8	25 46.1
18 Su	1 44 19	24 12 37	3♌33 36	9♌30 26	28 20.1	13 39.1	10 54.0	4 58.9	7 2.4	5 23.4	13 12.6	17 6.9	25 45.7
19 M	1 48 15	25 12 15	15 26 2	21 21 1	28 17.8	13 28.1	12 2.2	5 37.5	7 13.1	5 19.1	13 13.9	17 6.9	25 45.2
20 Tu	1 52 12	26 11 55	27 15 58	3♍11 24	28 13.2	13 8.7	13 10.7	6 16.1	7 23.7	5 14.8	13 15.3	17R 7.0	25 44.7
21 W	1 56 8	27 11 37	9♍ 7 50	15 5 41	28 6.1	12 40.6	14 19.3	6 54.8	7 34.2	5 10.6	13 16.7	17 7.0	25 44.2
22 Th	2 0 5	28 11 21	21 5 19	27 7 3	27 56.9	12 3.5	15 28.1	7 33.5	7 44.6	5 6.5	13 18.2	17 7.0	25 43.6
23 F	2 4 2	29 11 7	3♎11 11	9♎17 52	27 46.1	11 17.7	16 37.1	8 12.2	7 55.0	5 2.4	13 19.7	17 6.9	25 43.1
24 Sa	2 7 58	0♏10 56	15 27 18	21 39 33	27 34.8	10 23.4	17 46.3	8 50.9	8 5.2	4 58.3	13 21.2	17 6.8	25 42.5
25 Su	2 11 55	1 10 46	27 54 41	4♏12 44	27 24.0	9 21.6	18 55.6	9 29.6	8 15.3	4 54.4	13 22.8	17 6.7	25 41.9
26 M	2 15 51	2 10 39	10♏33 41	16 57 30	27 14.7	8 13.3	20 5.1	10 8.3	8 25.4	4 50.4	13 24.5	17 6.5	25 41.2
27 Tu	2 19 48	3 10 33	23 24 9	29 53 37	27 7.6	7 0.1	21 14.7	10 47.1	8 35.4	4 46.6	13 26.2	17 6.3	25 40.6
28 W	2 23 44	4 10 30	6♐25 53	13♐ 0 55	27 3.1	5 43.8	22 24.5	11 25.8	8 45.2	4 42.8	13 27.9	17 6.1	25 39.9
29 Th	2 27 41	5 10 28	19 38 45	26 19 26	27D 1.0	4 26.8	23 34.4	12 4.6	8 55.0	4 39.1	13 29.7	17 5.8	25 39.3
30 F	2 31 37	6 10 28	3♑ 3 0	9♑49 32	27 0.9	3 11.3	24 44.5	12 43.4	9 4.6	4 35.4	13 31.5	17 5.5	25 38.6
31 Sa	2 35 34	7 10 30	16 39 6	23 31 48	27 1.9	1 59.8	25 54.7	13 22.2	9 14.2	4 31.8	13 33.4	17 5.2	25 37.9

Astro Data

	Dy Hr Mn
♃⚼♅	3 11:09
☿0S	8 6:19
☽0N	12 2:48
♃∠♆	21 9:09
♅ D	22 13:26
☽0S	26 9:16
♇ R	26 2:04
♄0S	7 9:21
☽0N	9 13:22
♃⚻♄	11 13:48
♂0S	13 20:08
☿ R	17 3:10
♆ R	20 17:12
☽0S	23 16:12

Planet Ingress

	Dy Hr Mn
☿ ♎	7 18:14
♀ ♌	8 22:32
♃ ♍	12 10:02
☉ ♎	23 10:58
☊ ♊	27 3:28
☿ ♏	28 19:36
♀ ♍	8 6:13
♂ ♎	10 6:05
☉ ♏	23 19:37

Last Aspect / ☽ Ingress (September)

Last Aspect Dy Hr Mn		☽ Ingress Dy Hr Mn
2 21:05	♃ □	♐ 3 0:52
5 3:59	♃ △	♑ 5 6:40
7 7:58	☿ △	♒ 7 9:06
9 8:02	♃ ☍	♓ 9 9:04
11 1:42	♇ □	♈ 11 8:21
13 2:12	♇ ⚹	♉ 13 9:11
14 22:32	☉ △	♊ 15 13:27
17 13:52	♇ ☌	♋ 17 21:57
20 3:07	☉ ⚹	♌ 20 9:42
22 14:09	♇ ⚹	♍ 22 22:34
25 2:31	♇ □	♎ 25 10:46
27 19:08	☿ ☌	♏ 27 21:30
29 17:51	♂ ⚹	♐ 30 6:28

Last Aspect / ☽ Ingress (October)

Last Aspect Dy Hr Mn		☽ Ingress Dy Hr Mn
2 5:46	♇ ☍	♑ 2 13:12
4 10:58	♂ △	♒ 4 17:16
6 15:59	♀ ☍	♓ 6 18:49
8 17:27	♂ ☍	♈ 8 19:01
10 12:48	♇ ⚹	♉ 10 19:42
12 0:28	♆ ⚹	♊ 12 22:55
14 22:01	♇ ☌	♋ 15 6:00
17 3:35	☉ □	♌ 17 16:51
19 21:38	☉ ⚹	♍ 20 5:32
22 9:14	♇ □	♎ 22 17:43
24 19:46	♇ △	♏ 25 3:59
26 19:36	♀ ⚹	♐ 27 12:12
29 10:47	♇ ☍	♑ 29 18:34
31 17:38	♀ △	♒ 31 23:12

☽ Phases & Eclipses

Dy Hr Mn	
3 20:50	☽ 10♐55
10 12:23	○ 17♓22
17 10:33	☽ 24♊07
25 14:59	● 2♎07
3 6:13	☽ 9♑38
9 21:03	○ 16♈10
17 3:35	☽ 23♋22
25 6:46	● 1♏28

Astro Data

1 SEPTEMBER 1908
Julian Day # 3166
Delta T 8.7 sec
SVP 06♓32'23"
Obliquity 23°27'05"
⚷ Chiron 19♒55.1R
☽ Mean ☊ 1♋33.2

1 OCTOBER 1908
Julian Day # 3196
Delta T 8.8 sec
SVP 06♓32'20"
Obliquity 23°27'05"
⚷ Chiron 18♒44.5R
☽ Mean ☊ 29♊57.8

NOVEMBER 1908 LONGITUDE

Day	Sid.Time	☉	0 hr ☽	Noon ☽	True ☊	☿	♀	♂	♃	♄	♅	♆	♇
1 Su	2 39 31	8♏10 33	0♒27 39	7♒26 42	27♊ 2.9	0♏54.4	27♍ 5.1	14♎ 1.0	9♍23.6	4♈28.3	13♑35.3	17♋ 4.8	25♊37.1
2 M	2 43 27	9 10 37	14 28 54	21 34 9	27R 3.0	29♎57.2	28 15.5	14 39.8	9 33.0	4R24.9	13 37.3	17R 4.5	25R36.4
3 Tu	2 47 24	10 10 44	28 42 16	5♓52 59	27 1.5	29R 9.7	29 26.2	15 18.7	9 42.2	4 21.5	13 39.3	17 4.0	25 35.6
4 W	2 51 20	11 10 51	13♓ 5 52	20 20 28	26 57.9	28 32.9	0♎36.9	15 57.5	9 51.3	4 18.2	13 41.3	17 3.6	25 34.8
5 Th	2 55 17	12 11 0	27 36 8	4♈52 13	26 52.5	28 7.6	1 47.8	16 36.3	10 0.3	4 15.0	13 43.4	17 3.1	25 34.0
6 F	2 59 13	13 11 11	12♈ 7 56	19 22 28	26 45.8	27D53.9	2 58.8	17 15.2	10 9.2	4 11.9	13 45.6	17 2.5	25 33.2
7 Sa	3 3 10	14 11 23	26 35 2	3♉44 48	26 38.7	27 51.8	4 9.9	17 54.1	10 18.0	4 8.9	13 47.8	17 2.0	25 32.4
8 Su	3 7 6	15 11 38	10♉51 1	17 53 2	26 32.2	28 0.7	5 21.1	18 33.0	10 26.7	4 5.9	13 50.0	17 1.4	25 31.5
9 M	3 11 3	16 11 53	24 50 17	1♊42 18	26 27.0	28 20.0	6 32.5	19 11.9	10 35.2	4 3.0	13 52.2	17 0.8	25 30.7
10 Tu	3 15 0	17 12 11	8♊28 49	15 9 36	26 23.6	28 49.0	7 44.0	19 50.8	10 43.6	4 0.3	13 54.5	17 0.1	25 29.8
11 W	3 18 56	18 12 31	21 44 40	28 14 3	26D22.2	29 26.7	8 55.5	20 29.8	10 51.9	3 57.6	13 56.9	16 59.4	25 28.9
12 Th	3 22 53	19 12 52	4♋37 58	10♋56 43	26 22.4	0♏12.3	10 7.3	21 8.7	11 0.1	3 55.0	13 59.3	16 58.7	25 28.0
13 F	3 26 49	20 13 15	17 10 41	23 20 20	26 23.7	1 4.9	11 19.1	21 47.7	11 8.2	3 52.5	14 1.7	16 58.0	25 27.1
14 Sa	3 30 46	21 13 40	29 26 11	5♌28 48	26 25.4	2 3.6	12 31.0	22 26.7	11 16.1	3 50.0	14 4.1	16 57.2	25 26.1
15 Su	3 34 42	22 14 7	11♌28 46	17 26 43	26 26.9	3 7.7	13 43.0	23 5.7	11 23.9	3 47.7	14 6.6	16 56.4	25 25.2
16 M	3 38 39	23 14 36	23 23 16	29 19 4	26R27.5	4 16.4	14 55.1	23 44.7	11 31.5	3 45.5	14 9.2	16 55.6	25 24.2
17 Tu	3 42 35	24 15 6	5♍14 43	11♍10 51	26 26.8	5 29.1	16 7.3	24 23.8	11 39.1	3 43.3	14 11.7	16 54.7	25 23.2
18 W	3 46 32	25 15 39	17 8 1	23 6 47	26 24.7	6 45.3	17 19.7	25 2.8	11 46.4	3 41.3	14 14.3	16 53.8	25 22.2
19 Th	3 50 29	26 16 13	29 7 40	5♎11 8	26 21.1	8 4.3	18 32.1	25 41.9	11 53.7	3 39.3	14 17.0	16 52.9	25 21.2
20 F	3 54 25	27 16 49	11♎17 34	17 27 21	26 16.6	9 25.8	19 44.6	26 21.0	12 0.8	3 37.5	14 19.7	16 51.9	25 20.2
21 Sa	3 58 22	28 17 26	23 40 45	29 57 59	26 11.7	10 49.4	20 57.1	27 0.1	12 7.8	3 35.7	14 22.4	16 50.9	25 19.2
22 Su	4 2 18	29 18 5	6♏19 13	12♏44 32	26 6.9	12 14.7	22 9.8	27 39.2	12 14.6	3 34.1	14 25.1	16 49.9	25 18.1
23 M	4 6 15	0♐18 46	19 13 54	25 47 18	26 2.8	13 41.5	23 22.5	28 18.4	12 21.3	3 32.6	14 27.9	16 48.9	25 17.1
24 Tu	4 10 11	1 19 28	2♐24 36	9♐ 5 38	25 59.9	15 9.5	24 35.3	28 57.5	12 27.8	3 31.1	14 30.7	16 47.8	25 16.0
25 W	4 14 8	2 20 12	15 50 11	22 37 59	25D58.3	16 38.5	25 48.2	29 36.7	12 34.2	3 29.8	14 33.5	16 46.8	25 15.0
26 Th	4 18 4	3 20 57	29 28 48	6♑22 18	25 58.0	18 8.4	27 1.2	0♏15.8	12 40.4	3 28.6	14 36.4	16 45.6	25 13.9
27 F	4 22 1	4 21 43	13♑18 13	20 16 16	25 58.7	19 38.9	28 14.2	0 55.0	12 46.5	3 27.5	14 39.3	16 44.5	25 12.8
28 Sa	4 25 58	5 22 30	27 16 9	4♒17 36	26 0.0	21 10.0	29 27.3	1 34.2	12 52.4	3 26.4	14 42.3	16 43.3	25 11.7
29 Su	4 29 54	6 23 18	11♒20 22	18 24 11	26 1.5	22 41.6	0♏40.5	2 13.5	12 58.2	3 25.5	14 45.2	16 42.2	25 10.6
30 M	4 33 51	7 24 7	25 28 49	2♓34 1	26R 2.5	24 13.5	1 53.7	2 52.7	13 3.8	3 24.7	14 48.2	16 40.9	25 9.5

DECEMBER 1908 LONGITUDE

Day	Sid.Time	☉	0 hr ☽	Noon ☽	True ☊	☿	♀	♂	♃	♄	♅	♆	♇
1 Tu	4 37 47	8♐24 57	9♓39 33	16♓45 8	26♊ 2.9	25♏45.7	3♏ 7.0	3♏31.9	13♍ 9.3	3♈24.0	14♑51.2	16♋39.7	25♊ 8.4
2 W	4 41 44	9 25 48	23 50 32	0♈55 26	26R 2.4	27 18.2	4 20.4	4 11.2	13 14.5	3R23.5	14 54.3	16R38.4	25R 7.3
3 Th	4 45 40	10 26 39	7♈59 32	15 2 30	26 1.1	28 50.8	5 33.8	4 50.4	13 19.7	3 23.0	14 57.4	16 37.2	25 6.1
4 F	4 49 37	11 27 31	22 4 0	29 3 38	25 59.3	0♐23.6	6 47.2	5 29.7	13 24.6	3 22.6	15 0.5	16 35.8	25 5.0
5 Sa	4 53 33	12 28 25	6♉ 1 4	12♉55 56	25 57.4	1 56.5	8 0.7	6 9.0	13 29.4	3 22.4	15 3.6	16 34.5	25 3.8
6 Su	4 57 30	13 29 19	19 47 51	26 36 31	25 55.7	3 29.6	9 14.3	6 48.3	13 34.0	3D22.2	15 6.8	16 33.2	25 2.7
7 M	5 1 27	14 30 14	3♊21 37	10♊ 2 54	25 54.4	5 2.7	10 27.9	7 27.6	13 38.5	3 22.2	15 9.9	16 31.8	25 1.5
8 Tu	5 5 23	15 31 9	16 40 10	23 13 17	25D53.7	6 35.9	11 41.6	8 7.0	13 42.8	3 22.2	15 13.1	16 30.4	25 0.4
9 W	5 9 20	16 32 6	29 42 10	6♋ 6 49	25 53.6	8 9.2	12 55.3	8 46.3	13 46.9	3 22.4	15 16.4	16 29.0	24 59.2
10 Th	5 13 16	17 33 4	12♋27 17	18 43 43	25 53.9	9 42.5	14 9.1	9 25.7	13 50.9	3 22.7	15 19.6	16 27.6	24 58.0
11 F	5 17 13	18 34 3	24 56 19	1♌ 5 20	25 54.6	11 16.0	15 23.0	10 5.1	13 54.6	3 23.1	15 22.9	16 26.2	24 56.9
12 Sa	5 21 9	19 35 3	7♌11 7	13 14 2	25 55.3	12 49.5	16 36.9	10 44.5	13 58.2	3 23.6	15 26.2	16 24.7	24 55.7
13 Su	5 25 6	20 36 3	19 14 32	25 13 4	25 56.0	14 23.0	17 50.8	11 23.9	14 1.7	3 24.2	15 29.5	16 23.2	24 54.5
14 M	5 29 3	21 37 5	1♍10 10	7♍ 6 22	25 56.5	15 56.7	19 4.8	12 3.4	14 4.9	3 24.9	15 32.8	16 21.7	24 53.3
15 Tu	5 32 59	22 38 8	13 2 15	18 58 23	25R56.8	17 30.5	20 18.8	12 42.8	14 8.0	3 25.7	15 36.1	16 20.2	24 52.2
16 W	5 36 56	23 39 11	24 55 22	0♎53 49	25 56.8	19 4.4	21 32.8	13 22.3	14 10.8	3 26.7	15 39.5	16 18.7	24 51.0
17 Th	5 40 52	24 40 16	6♎54 17	12 57 23	25 56.8	20 38.4	22 46.9	14 1.8	14 13.5	3 27.7	15 42.9	16 17.1	24 49.8
18 F	5 44 49	25 41 21	19 3 39	25 13 36	25D56.7	22 12.5	24 1.1	14 41.3	14 16.0	3 28.9	15 46.3	16 15.6	24 48.6
19 Sa	5 48 45	26 42 27	1♏27 42	7♏46 22	25 56.8	23 46.8	25 15.3	15 20.8	14 18.3	3 30.1	15 49.7	16 14.0	24 47.4
20 Su	5 52 42	27 43 34	14 9 58	20 38 45	25 56.9	25 21.3	26 29.5	16 0.3	14 20.5	3 31.5	15 53.1	16 12.4	24 46.2
21 M	5 56 38	28 44 42	27 12 55	3♐52 31	25 57.2	26 56.0	27 43.7	16 39.9	14 22.4	3 33.0	15 56.6	16 10.8	24 45.1
22 Tu	6 0 35	29 45 50	10♐37 33	17 27 52	25 57.4	28 30.8	28 58.0	17 19.4	14 24.2	3 34.6	16 0.0	16 9.2	24 43.9
23 W	6 4 32	0♑46 59	24 23 13	1♑23 13	25R57.6	0♑ 5.9	0♐12.3	17 59.0	14 25.7	3 36.3	16 3.5	16 7.6	24 42.7
24 Th	6 8 28	1 48 9	8♑27 26	15 35 17	25 57.5	1 41.2	1 26.7	18 38.6	14 27.1	3 38.1	16 7.0	16 6.0	24 41.5
25 F	6 12 25	2 49 19	22 46 9	29 59 20	25 57.0	3 16.7	2 41.0	19 18.2	14 28.3	3 40.0	16 10.5	16 4.3	24 40.4
26 Sa	6 16 21	3 50 29	7♒14 6	14♒29 45	25 56.2	4 52.5	3 55.4	19 57.8	14 29.3	3 42.0	16 14.0	16 2.7	24 39.2
27 Su	6 20 18	4 51 39	21 45 33	29 0 49	25 55.1	6 28.5	5 9.9	20 37.4	14 30.1	3 44.1	16 17.5	16 1.0	24 38.0
28 M	6 24 14	5 52 48	6♓14 57	13♓27 23	25 54.1	8 4.8	6 24.3	21 17.1	14 30.7	3 46.3	16 21.0	15 59.4	24 36.9
29 Tu	6 28 11	6 53 58	20 37 38	27 45 21	25 53.2	9 41.4	7 38.8	21 56.7	14 31.1	3 48.7	16 24.5	15 57.7	24 35.7
30 W	6 32 7	7 55 8	4♈50 11	11♈51 55	25D52.8	11 18.3	8 53.2	22 36.4	14R31.3	3 51.1	16 28.1	15 56.0	24 34.6
31 Th	6 36 4	8 56 17	18 50 25	25 45 34	25 52.9	12 55.5	10 7.7	23 16.1	14 31.3	3 53.6	16 31.6	15 54.4	24 33.4

Astro Data Dy Hr Mn	Planet Ingress Dy Hr Mn	Last Aspect Dy Hr Mn	☽ Ingress Dy Hr Mn	Last Aspect Dy Hr Mn	☽ Ingress Dy Hr Mn	☽ Phases & Eclipses Dy Hr Mn
☽0N 5 23:04	☿ ♎ 1 22:44	3 0:44 ☿ △	♓ 3 2:10	2 6:35 ☿ △	♈ 2 10:26	1 14:16 ☽ 8♒46
♀0S 6 13:53	♀ ♎ 3 11:29	4 20:38 ♇ □	♈ 5 3:58	4 5:10 ♇ ✶	♉ 4 13:37	8 7:58 ○ 15♉32
☿ D 6 16:32	☿ ♏ 11 17:53	7 2:09 ☿ ☍	♉ 7 5:43	5 18:20 ♆ ✶	♊ 6 18:01	15 23:41 ☽ 23♌14
☽0S 20 0:46	☉ ♐ 22 16:35	8 10:31 ♆ ✶	♊ 9 9:00	8 15:16 ♇ ☌	♋ 9 0:33	23 21:53 ● 1♐14
	♂ ♏ 25 14:18	11 15:08 ☿ △	♋ 11 15:18	10 7:38 ♆ ☌	♌ 11 9:52	30 21:44 ☽ 8♓19
☽0N 3 6:27	♀ ♏ 28 10:43	13 9:29 ♂ □	♌ 14 1:07	13 11:22 ♇ ✶	♍ 13 21:38	
♄ D 6 21:04		16 4:04 ♇ ✶	♍ 16 13:23	15 23:51 ♇ □	♎ 16 10:12	7 21:44 ○ 15♊25
☽0S 17 9:47	☿ ♐ 3 17:54	18 17:47 ☉ ✶	♎ 19 1:44	18 14:03 ☉ ✶	♏ 18 21:12	7 21:55 ☍ A 1.034
♅☍♆ 23 19:21	☉ ♑ 22 5:34	21 6:42 ♂ ☌	♏ 21 12:04	21 1:02 ♀ ☌	♐ 21 5:02	15 21:12 ☽ 23♍32
☽0N 30 11:54	☿ ♑ 22 22:31	22 19:33 ♆ △	♐ 23 19:39	23 0:34 ♇ ☍	♑ 23 9:38	23 11:50 ● 1♑17
♃ R 30 14:22	♀ ♐ 22 20:01	25 19:17 ♀ ✶	♑ 26 0:54	24 17:56 ♂ ✶	♒ 25 12:01	23 11:44:17 ● AT 0'12"
		28 4:06 ♀ □	♒ 28 4:40	27 4:45 ♇ △	♓ 27 13:38	30 5:40 ☽ 8♈10
		29 23:27 ♇ △	♓ 30 7:39	29 6:40 ♇ □	♈ 29 15:48	
				31 9:54 ♇ ✶	♉ 31 19:24	

Astro Data

1 NOVEMBER 1908
Julian Day # 3227
Delta T 8.9 sec
SVP 06♓32'16"
Obliquity 23°27'05"
⚷ Chiron 18♒20.7
☽ Mean ☊ 28♊19.3

1 DECEMBER 1908
Julian Day # 3257
Delta T 9.0 sec
SVP 06♓32'12"
Obliquity 23°27'04"
⚷ Chiron 18♒55.3
☽ Mean ☊ 26♊44.0

LONGITUDE — JANUARY 1909

Day	Sid.Time	☉	0 hr ☽	Noon ☽	True ☊	☿	♀	♂	♃	♄	♅	♆	♇
1 F	6 40 1	9♑57 27	2♉37 18	9♉25 39	25♊53.7	14♑33.0	11♐22.2	23♏55.7	14♍31.2	3♈56.3	16♑35.2	15♋52.7	24♊32.3
2 Sa	6 43 57	10 58 36	16 10 36	22 52 12	25 54.9	16 10.8	12 36.8	24 35.4	14R30.8	3 59.0	16 38.7	15R51.0	24R31.1
3 Su	6 47 54	11 59 45	29 30 30	6♊ 5 33	25 56.2	17 48.9	13 51.3	25 15.1	14 30.2	4 1.8	16 42.3	15 49.3	24 30.0
4 M	6 51 50	13 0 53	12♊37 23	19 6 5	25 57.3	19 27.3	15 5.9	25 54.9	14 29.5	4 4.8	16 45.8	15 47.6	24 28.9
5 Tu	6 55 47	14 2 2	25 31 41	1♋54 13	25R57.7	21 6.0	16 20.5	26 34.6	14 28.5	4 7.8	16 49.4	15 45.9	24 27.8
6 W	6 59 43	15 3 10	8♋13 46	14 30 23	25 57.3	22 44.9	17 35.1	27 14.3	14 27.4	4 10.9	16 53.0	15 44.2	24 26.7
7 Th	7 3 40	16 4 18	20 44 9	26 55 9	25 55.7	24 24.1	18 49.7	27 54.1	14 26.1	4 14.1	16 56.5	15 42.5	24 25.6
8 F	7 7 36	17 5 26	3♌ 3 30	9♌ 9 22	25 53.1	26 3.5	20 4.4	28 33.9	14 24.5	4 17.5	17 0.1	15 40.8	24 24.5
9 Sa	7 11 33	18 6 34	15 12 55	21 14 21	25 49.5	27 43.0	21 19.0	29 13.7	14 22.8	4 20.9	17 3.7	15 39.1	24 23.4
10 Su	7 15 30	19 7 42	27 13 58	3♍12 3	25 45.4	29 22.6	22 33.7	29 53.5	14 20.9	4 24.4	17 7.2	15 37.4	24 22.4
11 M	7 19 26	20 8 49	9♍ 8 55	15 5 0	25 41.3	1♒ 2.3	23 48.4	0♐33.3	14 18.8	4 28.0	17 10.8	15 35.7	24 21.3
12 Tu	7 23 23	21 9 57	21 0 42	26 56 29	25 37.6	2 41.8	25 3.1	1 13.2	14 16.5	4 31.7	17 14.4	15 34.0	24 20.3
13 W	7 27 19	22 11 4	2♎52 53	8♎50 24	25 34.7	4 21.2	26 17.8	1 53.0	14 14.1	4 35.5	17 17.9	15 32.3	24 19.2
14 Th	7 31 16	23 12 11	14 49 38	20 51 9	25D33.1	6 0.3	27 32.6	2 32.9	14 11.4	4 39.4	17 21.5	15 30.7	24 18.2
15 F	7 35 12	24 13 18	26 55 33	3♏ 3 26	25 32.8	7 38.9	28 47.3	3 12.8	14 8.5	4 43.3	17 25.0	15 29.0	24 17.2
16 Sa	7 39 9	25 14 24	9♏15 24	15 32 2	25 33.6	9 16.9	0♑ 2.1	3 52.6	14 5.5	4 47.4	17 28.6	15 27.3	24 16.2
17 Su	7 43 5	26 15 31	21 53 52	28 21 24	25 35.1	10 54.0	1 16.9	4 32.6	14 2.3	4 51.5	17 32.1	15 25.6	24 15.2
18 M	7 47 2	27 16 37	4♐55 2	11♐35 5	25 36.9	12 29.9	2 31.6	5 12.5	13 58.9	4 55.8	17 35.7	15 24.0	24 14.2
19 Tu	7 50 59	28 17 43	18 21 47	25 15 13	25R38.1	14 4.4	3 46.4	5 52.4	13 55.3	5 0.1	17 39.2	15 22.3	24 13.3
20 W	7 54 55	29 18 49	2♑15 16	9♑21 44	25 38.1	15 37.1	5 1.3	6 32.4	13 51.5	5 4.5	17 42.7	15 20.7	24 12.3
21 Th	7 58 52	0♒19 54	16 34 9	23 51 56	25 36.5	17 7.6	6 16.1	7 12.3	13 47.6	5 9.0	17 46.2	15 19.1	24 11.4
22 F	8 2 48	1 20 58	1♒14 18	8♒40 18	25 33.1	18 35.4	7 30.9	7 52.3	13 43.5	5 13.6	17 49.8	15 17.4	24 10.5
23 Sa	8 6 45	2 22 2	16 8 53	23 38 55	25 28.1	19 59.9	8 45.7	8 32.3	13 39.2	5 18.2	17 53.2	15 15.8	24 9.6
24 Su	8 10 41	3 23 4	1♓ 9 12	8♓38 36	25 22.3	21 20.7	10 0.5	9 12.2	13 34.7	5 23.0	17 56.7	15 14.2	24 8.7
25 M	8 14 38	4 24 6	16 6 0	23 30 25	25 16.3	22 36.9	11 15.4	9 52.2	13 30.1	5 27.8	18 0.2	15 12.6	24 7.8
26 Tu	8 18 35	5 25 7	0♈51 1	8♈ 7 6	25 11.0	23 48.0	12 30.2	10 32.2	13 25.3	5 32.7	18 3.6	15 11.0	24 7.0
27 W	8 22 31	6 26 6	15 18 9	22 23 51	25 7.3	24 53.1	13 45.0	11 12.2	13 20.4	5 37.6	18 7.1	15 9.5	24 6.1
28 Th	8 26 28	7 27 4	29 24 0	6♉18 35	25D 5.4	25 51.4	14 59.9	11 52.3	13 15.3	5 42.7	18 10.5	15 7.9	24 5.3
29 F	8 30 24	8 28 1	13♉ 7 41	19 51 29	25 5.1	26 42.1	16 14.7	12 32.3	13 10.0	5 47.8	18 13.9	15 6.4	24 4.5
30 Sa	8 34 21	9 28 57	26 30 16	3♊ 4 20	25 6.2	27 24.4	17 29.5	13 12.3	13 4.6	5 53.0	18 17.3	15 4.9	24 3.7
31 Su	8 38 17	10 29 52	9♊34 1	15 59 41	25 7.6	27 57.5	18 44.4	13 52.3	12 59.0	5 58.3	18 20.7	15 3.4	24 2.9

LONGITUDE — FEBRUARY 1909

Day	Sid.Time	☉	0 hr ☽	Noon ☽	True ☊	☿	♀	♂	♃	♄	♅	♆	♇
1 M	8 42 14	11♒30 45	22♊21 42	28♊40 25	25♊ 8.5	28♒20.7	19♑59.2	14♐32.4	12♍53.3	6♈ 3.7	18♑24.1	15♋ 1.9	24♊ 2.1
2 Tu	8 46 10	12 31 37	4♋56 7	11♋ 9 8	25R 8.0	28R33.4	21 14.0	15 12.5	12R47.5	6 9.1	18 27.4	15R 0.4	24R 1.4
3 W	8 50 7	13 32 28	17 19 43	23 28 5	25 5.4	28 35.1	22 28.9	15 52.5	12 41.5	6 14.6	18 30.7	14 58.9	24 0.7
4 Th	8 54 4	14 33 17	29 34 29	5♌39 3	25 0.4	28 25.8	23 43.7	16 32.6	12 35.4	6 20.1	18 34.0	14 57.5	23 60.0
5 F	8 58 0	15 34 5	11♌41 59	17 43 25	24 53.1	28 5.4	24 58.5	17 12.7	12 29.2	6 25.7	18 37.3	14 56.1	23 59.3
6 Sa	9 1 57	16 34 52	23 43 31	29 42 24	24 43.7	27 34.4	26 13.4	17 52.8	12 22.8	6 31.4	18 40.6	14 54.7	23 58.6
7 Su	9 5 53	17 35 38	5♍40 16	11♍37 16	24 33.1	26 53.4	27 28.2	18 32.9	12 16.3	6 37.2	18 43.8	14 53.3	23 58.0
8 M	9 9 50	18 36 22	17 33 38	23 29 34	24 22.2	26 3.5	28 43.0	19 13.1	12 9.8	6 43.0	18 47.0	14 51.9	23 57.4
9 Tu	9 13 46	19 37 6	29 25 23	5♎21 22	24 11.9	25 6.0	29 57.9	19 53.2	12 3.0	6 48.9	18 50.2	14 50.6	23 56.7
10 W	9 17 43	20 37 48	11♎17 53	17 15 20	24 3.2	24 2.6	1♒12.7	20 33.4	11 56.2	6 54.8	18 53.4	14 49.3	23 56.1
11 Th	9 21 39	21 38 29	23 14 11	29 14 54	23 56.6	22 55.0	2 27.6	21 13.5	11 49.3	7 0.8	18 56.6	14 48.0	23 55.6
12 F	9 25 36	22 39 9	5♏18 3	11♏24 9	23 52.5	21 45.3	3 42.4	21 53.7	11 42.3	7 6.9	18 59.7	14 46.7	23 55.0
13 Sa	9 29 32	23 39 47	17 33 50	23 47 41	23D50.8	20 35.1	4 57.2	22 33.9	11 35.2	7 13.0	19 2.8	14 45.4	23 54.5
14 Su	9 33 29	24 40 25	0♐ 6 19	6♐30 19	23 50.7	19 26.5	6 12.1	23 14.1	11 28.0	7 19.2	19 5.9	14 44.2	23 54.0
15 M	9 37 26	25 41 2	13 0 17	19 36 41	23R51.3	18 21.0	7 26.9	23 54.3	11 20.7	7 25.4	19 8.9	14 43.0	23 53.5
16 Tu	9 41 22	26 41 37	26 20 0	3♑10 30	23 51.7	17 20.1	8 41.8	24 34.5	11 13.3	7 31.7	19 11.9	14 41.8	23 53.0
17 W	9 45 19	27 42 11	10♑ 8 24	17 13 42	23 50.5	16 24.8	9 56.6	25 14.7	11 5.9	7 38.0	19 14.9	14 40.7	23 52.6
18 Th	9 49 15	28 42 44	24 26 13	1♒45 32	23 47.1	15 36.0	11 11.5	25 54.9	10 58.4	7 44.4	19 17.9	14 39.5	23 52.2
19 F	9 53 12	29 43 15	9♒11 0	16 41 44	23 40.9	14 54.3	12 26.3	26 35.1	10 50.8	7 50.9	19 20.8	14 38.4	23 51.7
20 Sa	9 57 8	0♓43 45	24 16 40	1♓54 31	23 32.4	14 20.0	13 41.1	27 15.4	10 43.2	7 57.4	19 23.7	14 37.4	23 51.4
21 Su	10 1 5	1 44 14	9♓33 52	17 13 15	23 22.2	13 53.2	14 55.9	27 55.6	10 35.6	8 3.9	19 26.6	14 36.3	23 51.0
22 M	10 5 1	2 44 40	24 51 14	2♈26 25	23 11.7	13 33.9	16 10.8	28 35.8	10 27.8	8 10.5	19 29.5	14 35.3	23 50.7
23 Tu	10 8 58	3 45 5	9♈57 33	17 23 34	23 2.0	13 22.0	17 25.6	29 16.0	10 20.1	8 17.2	19 32.3	14 34.3	23 50.3
24 W	10 12 55	4 45 28	24 43 40	1♉57 12	22 54.3	13D17.2	18 40.4	29 56.3	10 12.3	8 23.9	19 35.0	14 33.3	23 50.0
25 Th	10 16 51	5 45 49	9♉ 3 50	16 3 23	22 49.2	13 19.1	19 55.2	0♑36.5	10 4.5	8 30.6	19 37.8	14 32.4	23 49.8
26 F	10 20 48	6 46 8	22 55 55	29 41 36	22 46.6	13 27.5	21 10.0	1 16.8	9 56.6	8 37.4	19 40.5	14 31.4	23 49.5
27 Sa	10 24 44	7 46 25	6♊20 46	12♊53 50	22D45.9	13 41.9	22 24.7	1 57.0	9 48.8	8 44.2	19 43.2	14 30.6	23 49.3
28 Su	10 28 41	8 46 40	19 21 17	25 43 40	22R46.0	14 2.0	23 39.5	2 37.3	9 40.9	8 51.0	19 45.8	14 29.7	23 49.1

Astro Data Dy Hr Mn	Planet Ingress Dy Hr Mn	Last Aspect Dy Hr Mn	☽ Ingress Dy Hr Mn	Last Aspect Dy Hr Mn	☽ Ingress Dy Hr Mn	☽ Phases & Eclipses Dy Hr Mn
☽0S 13 17:43	☿ ♒ 10 9:00	2 15:53 ♂ ☍	♊ 3 0:54	1 11:37 ☿ △	♋ 1 14:32	6 14:12 ○ 15♋39
♄0N 24 0:15	♂ ♐ 10 3:55	4 22:00 ♇ ☌	♋ 5 8:24	3 11:12 ♀ ☍	♌ 4 0:50	14 18:11 ☽ 23♎58
☽0N 26 17:41	♀ ♑ 15 23:20	7 14:42 ♂ △	♌ 7 18:01	6 7:20 ☿ ☍	♍ 6 12:35	22 0:12 ● 1♒21
	☉ ♒ 20 16:11	9 18:17 ♇ ⚹	♍ 10 5:34	8 12:56 ♇ □	♎ 9 1:10	28 15:07 ☽ 8♉05
☿ R 2 15:51		12 9:08 ♀ □	♎ 12 18:11	11 1:23 ♇ △	♏ 11 13:30	
☽0S 9 23:59	♀ ♒ 9 0:41	15 4:04 ♀ ⚹	♏ 15 6:02	13 12:47 ☉ □	♐ 13 23:48	5 8:24 ○ 15♌55
☽0N 23 1:53	☉ ♓ 19 6:38	17 8:49 ☉ ⚹	♐ 17 15:01	16 0:41 ☉ ⚹	♑ 16 6:27	13 12:47 ☽ 24♏12
☿ D 24 4:54	♂ ♑ 24 2:13	19 10:12 ♇ ☍	♑ 19 20:09	17 15:26 ♅ ☌	♒ 18 9:08	20 10:52 ● 1♓11
		21 2:00 ♅ ☌	♒ 21 22:00	20 4:54 ♂ ⚹	♓ 20 9:00	27 2:49 ☽ 7♊53
		23 12:48 ♇ △	♓ 23 22:09	22 6:11 ♂ □	♈ 22 8:08	
		25 13:00 ♇ □	♈ 25 22:36	23 22:32 ♇ ⚹	♉ 24 8:44	
		27 17:29 ☿ ⚹	♉ 28 1:02	25 20:35 ♀ □	♊ 26 12:33	
		30 1:43 ☿ □	♊ 30 6:22	28 8:58 ♀ △	♋ 28 20:08	

Astro Data

1 JANUARY 1909
Julian Day # 3288
Delta T 9.1 sec
SVP 06♓32'06"
Obliquity 23°27'04"
⚷ Chiron 20♒23.3
☽ Mean ☊ 25♊05.6

1 FEBRUARY 1909
Julian Day # 3319
Delta T 9.2 sec
SVP 06♓32'01"
Obliquity 23°27'05"
⚷ Chiron 22♒25.2
☽ Mean ☊ 23♊27.1

MARCH 1909 LONGITUDE

Day	Sid.Time	☉	0 hr ☽	Noon ☽	True ☊	☿	♀	♂	♃	♄	♅	♆	♇
1 M	10 32 37	9♓46 53	2♋ 1 29	8♋15 19	22♊45.8	14♒27.4	24♒54.3	3♑17.5	9♍33.1	8♈57.9	19♑48.4	14♋28.9	23♊48.9
2 Tu	10 36 34	10 47 4	14 25 40	20 33 2	22R44.0	14 57.8	26 9.0	3 57.8	9R25.2	9 4.9	19 51.0	14R28.1	23R48.7
3 W	10 40 30	11 47 13	26 37 53	2♌40 39	22 39.7	15 32.7	27 23.7	4 38.0	9 17.4	9 11.9	19 53.5	14 27.3	23 48.6
4 Th	10 44 27	12 47 20	8♌41 42	14 41 22	22 32.5	16 11.9	28 38.5	5 18.3	9 9.5	9 18.9	19 56.0	14 26.6	23 48.5
5 F	10 48 24	13 47 25	20 39 57	26 37 41	22 22.3	16 55.1	29 53.2	5 58.5	9 1.7	9 25.9	19 58.5	14 25.9	23 48.4
6 Sa	10 52 20	14 47 27	2♍34 48	8♍31 29	22 9.6	17 42.0	1♓ 7.9	6 38.8	8 53.9	9 33.0	20 0.9	14 25.2	23 48.3
7 Su	10 56 17	15 47 28	14 27 55	20 24 15	21 55.3	18 32.3	2 22.6	7 19.1	8 46.1	9 40.1	20 3.3	14 24.5	23 48.2
8 M	11 0 13	16 47 27	26 20 37	2♎17 13	21 40.5	19 25.8	3 37.3	7 59.3	8 38.4	9 47.2	20 5.6	14 23.9	23D48.2
9 Tu	11 4 10	17 47 24	8♎14 11	14 11 44	21 26.4	20 22.4	4 52.0	8 39.6	8 30.7	9 54.4	20 7.9	14 23.3	23 48.2
10 W	11 8 6	18 47 20	20 10 5	26 9 30	21 14.1	21 21.7	6 6.7	9 19.9	8 23.1	10 1.6	20 10.2	14 22.8	23 48.2
11 Th	11 12 3	19 47 13	2♏10 16	8♏12 45	21 4.4	22 23.7	7 21.3	10 0.2	8 15.5	10 8.8	20 12.4	14 22.3	23 48.3
12 F	11 15 59	20 47 5	14 17 20	20 24 26	20 57.7	23 28.2	8 36.0	10 40.4	8 7.9	10 16.0	20 14.6	14 21.8	23 48.3
13 Sa	11 19 56	21 46 55	26 34 32	2♐48 9	20 53.9	24 35.0	9 50.6	11 20.7	8 0.4	10 23.3	20 16.8	14 21.3	23 48.4
14 Su	11 23 53	22 46 43	9♐ 5 49	15 28 4	20D52.4	25 44.0	11 5.3	12 1.0	7 53.0	10 30.6	20 18.9	14 20.9	23 48.5
15 M	11 27 49	23 46 30	21 55 27	28 28 32	20R52.2	26 55.2	12 19.9	12 41.3	7 45.7	10 38.0	20 20.9	14 20.5	23 48.6
16 Tu	11 31 46	24 46 15	5♑ 7 47	11♑53 37	20 52.0	28 8.3	13 34.6	13 21.6	7 38.4	10 45.3	20 22.9	14 20.2	23 48.8
17 W	11 35 42	25 45 58	18 46 22	25 46 15	20 50.6	29 23.3	14 49.2	14 1.9	7 31.2	10 52.7	20 24.9	14 19.8	23 49.0
18 Th	11 39 39	26 45 40	2♒53 17	10♒ 7 18	20 47.1	0♓40.2	16 3.8	14 42.1	7 24.1	11 0.1	20 26.8	14 19.5	23 49.2
19 F	11 43 35	27 45 20	17 27 56	24 54 33	20 40.8	1 58.8	17 18.4	15 22.4	7 17.1	11 7.5	20 28.7	14 19.3	23 49.4
20 Sa	11 47 32	28 44 58	2♓26 19	10♓ 2 10	20 32.0	3 19.2	18 33.0	16 2.7	7 10.2	11 14.9	20 30.6	14 19.1	23 49.6
21 Su	11 51 28	29 44 34	17 40 48	25 20 51	20 21.4	4 41.1	19 47.6	16 42.9	7 3.4	11 22.3	20 32.4	14 18.9	23 49.9
22 M	11 55 25	0♈44 8	3♈ 0 47	10♈39 10	20 10.1	6 4.7	21 2.2	17 23.2	6 56.7	11 29.8	20 34.1	14 18.7	23 50.2
23 Tu	11 59 22	1 43 40	18 14 33	25 45 39	19 59.6	7 29.8	22 16.8	18 3.4	6 50.1	11 37.3	20 35.8	14 18.6	23 50.5
24 W	12 3 18	2 43 10	3♉11 22	10♉30 51	19 51.0	8 56.4	23 31.3	18 43.7	6 43.6	11 44.8	20 37.5	14 18.5	23 50.8
25 Th	12 7 15	3 42 38	17 43 26	24 48 43	19 45.1	10 24.5	24 45.8	19 23.9	6 37.3	11 52.3	20 39.1	14 18.4	23 51.2
26 F	12 11 11	4 42 3	1♊46 33	8♊36 57	19 41.8	11 54.1	26 0.4	20 4.1	6 31.0	11 59.8	20 40.6	14D18.4	23 51.6
27 Sa	12 15 8	5 41 27	15 20 6	21 56 21	19D40.7	13 25.1	27 14.9	20 44.3	6 24.9	12 7.3	20 42.1	14 18.4	23 52.0
28 Su	12 19 4	6 40 48	28 26 9	4♋50 2	19R40.8	14 57.6	28 29.4	21 24.5	6 18.9	12 14.8	20 43.6	14 18.5	23 52.4
29 M	12 23 1	7 40 6	11♋ 8 32	17 22 18	19 40.9	16 31.5	29 43.9	22 4.6	6 13.1	12 22.3	20 45.0	14 18.6	23 52.8
30 Tu	12 26 57	8 39 22	23 31 55	29 38 0	19 39.8	18 6.8	0♈58.3	22 44.8	6 7.4	12 29.9	20 46.4	14 18.7	23 53.3
31 W	12 30 54	9 38 36	5♌41 8	11♌41 53	19 36.7	19 43.5	2 12.8	23 24.9	6 1.9	12 37.4	20 47.7	14 18.8	23 53.8

APRIL 1909 LONGITUDE

Day	Sid.Time	☉	0 hr ☽	Noon ☽	True ☊	☿	♀	♂	♃	♄	♅	♆	♇
1 Th	12 34 51	10♈37 48	17♌40 45	23♌38 14	19♊31.1	21♓21.6	3♈27.2	24♑ 5.1	5♍56.4	12♈45.0	20♑49.0	14♋19.0	23♊54.3
2 F	12 38 47	11 36 57	29 34 45	5♍30 42	19R22.8	23 1.2	4 41.6	24 45.2	5R51.2	12 52.5	20 50.2	14 19.2	23 54.8
3 Sa	12 42 44	12 36 4	11♍26 26	17 22 15	19 12.3	24 42.1	5 56.0	25 25.3	5 46.1	13 0.1	20 51.4	14 19.5	23 55.4
4 Su	12 46 40	13 35 9	23 18 23	29 15 6	19 0.3	26 24.5	7 10.4	26 5.4	5 41.1	13 7.6	20 52.6	14 19.8	23 55.9
5 M	12 50 37	14 34 12	5♎12 34	11♎10 58	18 47.7	28 8.3	8 24.8	26 45.5	5 36.3	13 15.2	20 53.6	14 20.1	23 56.5
6 Tu	12 54 33	15 33 13	17 10 28	23 11 12	18 35.8	29 53.6	9 39.1	27 25.6	5 31.6	13 22.7	20 54.7	14 20.4	23 57.1
7 W	12 58 30	16 32 11	29 13 20	5♏17 2	18 25.4	1♈40.4	10 53.5	28 5.6	5 27.1	13 30.2	20 55.6	14 20.8	23 57.8
8 Th	13 2 26	17 31 8	11♏22 29	17 29 52	18 17.3	3 28.6	12 7.8	28 45.7	5 22.8	13 37.8	20 56.6	14 21.2	23 58.4
9 F	13 6 23	18 30 3	23 39 26	29 51 26	18 11.9	5 18.3	13 22.1	29 25.7	5 18.6	13 45.3	20 57.5	14 21.7	23 59.1
10 Sa	13 10 19	19 28 56	6♐ 6 10	12♐23 58	18D 9.0	7 9.4	14 36.5	0♒ 5.7	5 14.6	13 52.8	20 58.3	14 22.1	23 59.8
11 Su	13 14 16	20 27 47	18 45 11	25 10 12	18 8.3	9 2.1	15 50.8	0 45.7	5 10.8	14 0.4	20 59.1	14 22.7	24 0.5
12 M	13 18 13	21 26 36	1♑39 25	8♑13 13	18 8.8	10 56.3	17 5.0	1 25.7	5 7.2	14 7.9	20 59.8	14 23.2	24 1.2
13 Tu	13 22 9	22 25 24	14 51 59	21 36 3	18R 9.7	12 51.9	18 19.3	2 5.7	5 3.7	14 15.4	21 0.5	14 23.8	24 2.0
14 W	13 26 6	23 24 10	28 25 42	5♒21 10	18 9.8	14 49.1	19 33.6	2 45.6	5 0.4	14 22.9	21 1.1	14 24.4	24 2.7
15 Th	13 30 2	24 22 54	12♒22 30	19 29 42	18 8.3	16 47.7	20 47.9	3 25.5	4 57.2	14 30.4	21 1.7	14 25.1	24 3.5
16 F	13 33 59	25 21 37	26 42 32	4♓ 0 38	18 4.8	18 47.7	22 2.1	4 5.4	4 54.3	14 37.9	21 2.2	14 25.7	24 4.3
17 Sa	13 37 55	26 20 18	11♓23 26	18 50 11	17 59.2	20 49.2	23 16.3	4 45.3	4 51.5	14 45.3	21 2.7	14 26.5	24 5.1
18 Su	13 41 52	27 18 57	26 19 58	3♈51 43	17 52.1	22 51.9	24 30.5	5 25.1	4 48.9	14 52.8	21 3.1	14 27.2	24 6.0
19 M	13 45 48	28 17 34	11♈24 14	18 56 17	17 44.5	24 55.9	25 44.8	6 4.9	4 46.4	15 0.2	21 3.5	14 28.0	24 6.8
20 Tu	13 49 45	29 16 10	26 26 39	3♉54 6	17 37.2	27 1.0	26 59.0	6 44.6	4 44.2	15 7.6	21 3.8	14 28.8	24 7.7
21 W	13 53 42	0♉14 43	11♉17 34	18 36 7	17 31.3	29 7.2	28 13.1	7 24.3	4 42.1	15 15.0	21 4.1	14 29.6	24 8.6
22 Th	13 57 38	1 13 15	25 48 58	2♊55 32	17 27.3	1♉14.2	29 27.3	8 4.0	4 40.3	15 22.4	21 4.3	14 30.5	24 9.5
23 F	14 1 35	2 11 45	9♊55 27	16 48 29	17D25.4	3 22.0	0♉41.5	8 43.7	4 38.6	15 29.7	21 4.5	14 31.4	24 10.5
24 Sa	14 5 31	3 10 13	23 34 39	0♋14 4	17 25.3	5 30.2	1 55.6	9 23.3	4 37.1	15 37.1	21 4.6	14 32.3	24 11.4
25 Su	14 9 28	4 8 38	6♋47 0	13 13 50	17 26.4	7 38.8	3 9.7	10 2.9	4 35.8	15 44.4	21R 4.7	14 33.3	24 12.4
26 M	14 13 24	5 7 2	19 35 0	25 51 3	17 27.8	9 47.3	4 23.8	10 42.4	4 34.6	15 51.7	21 4.7	14 34.3	24 13.3
27 Tu	14 17 21	6 5 23	2♌ 2 32	8♌10 3	17R28.7	11 55.6	5 37.9	11 21.9	4 33.7	15 59.0	21 4.7	14 35.3	24 14.3
28 W	14 21 17	7 3 43	14 14 11	20 15 33	17 28.5	14 3.4	6 52.0	12 1.3	4 32.9	16 6.2	21 4.6	14 36.4	24 15.4
29 Th	14 25 14	8 2 0	26 14 44	2♍12 17	17 26.7	16 10.3	8 6.1	12 40.7	4 32.4	16 13.4	21 4.5	14 37.4	24 16.4
30 F	14 29 11	9 0 15	8♍ 8 46	14 4 42	17 23.2	18 16.1	9 20.1	13 20.0	4 32.0	16 20.6	21 4.3	14 38.5	24 17.4

Astro Data	Dy Hr Mn
♃⚻♄	3 8:54
♇ D	8 19:55
☽0S	9 5:26
☽0N	22 12:22
♆ D	26 2:12
♀0N	31 21:07
♃⚼♅	2 3:28
☽0S	5 11:20
☿0N	8 17:59
♄□♆	14 5:18
☽0N	18 23:14
♅ R	25 22:27

Planet Ingress	Dy Hr Mn
♀ ♓	5 2:11
☿ ♓	17 11:31
☉ ♈	21 6:13
♀ ♈	29 5:12
☿ ♈	6 1:27
♂ ♒	9 20:34
☉ ♉	20 17:58
☿ ♉	21 10:00
♀ ♉	22 10:35

Last Aspect Dy Hr Mn		☽ Ingress Dy Hr Mn
2 10:40	♅ ☍	♌ 3 6:41
5 6:19	♇ ⚹	♍ 5 18:48
7 18:52	♇ □	♎ 8 7:23
10 7:17	♇ △	♏ 10 19:40
12 19:45	☿ □	♐ 13 6:37
15 10:06	☿ ⚹	♑ 15 14:46
17 12:54	☉ ⚹	♒ 17 19:09
19 10:16	♇ △	♓ 19 20:08
21 9:38	♇ □	♈ 21 19:17
23 8:56	♇ ⚹	♉ 23 18:50
25 13:05	♀ ⚹	♊ 25 20:55
28 0:07	♀ □	♋ 28 2:55
29 22:22	♂ ☍	♌ 30 12:43

Last Aspect Dy Hr Mn		☽ Ingress Dy Hr Mn
1 12:33	♇ ⚹	♍ 2 0:51
4 7:19	☿ ☍	♎ 4 13:31
6 21:38	♂ □	♏ 7 1:33
9 11:48	♂ ⚹	♐ 9 12:17
11 9:51	♇ ☍	♑ 11 20:57
13 14:30	☉ □	♒ 14 2:44
15 21:36	☉ ⚹	♓ 16 5:26
17 20:26	♇ □	♈ 18 5:51
20 4:51	☉ ☌	♉ 20 5:43
21 16:05	♅ △	♊ 22 7:02
24 1:06	♇ ☌	♋ 24 11:34
26 2:51	♅ ☍	♌ 26 20:02
28 20:02	♇ ⚹	♍ 29 7:33

☽ Phases & Eclipses Dy Hr Mn	
7 2:56	○ 15♍55
15 3:41	☽ 23♐56
21 20:11	● 0♈35
28 16:49	☽ 7♋22
5 20:28	○ 15♎25
13 14:30	☽ 23♑01
20 4:51	● 29♈28
27 8:36	☽ 6♌26

Astro Data

1 MARCH 1909
Julian Day # 3347
Delta T 9.3 sec
SVP 06♓31'57"
Obliquity 23°27'06"
⚷ Chiron 24♒23.8
☽ Mean ☊ 21♊58.1

1 APRIL 1909
Julian Day # 3378
Delta T 9.5 sec
SVP 06♓31'54"
Obliquity 23°27'06"
⚷ Chiron 26♒21.2
☽ Mean ☊ 20♊19.6

LONGITUDE MAY 1909

Day	Sid.Time	☉	0 hr ☽	Noon ☽	True ☊	☿	♀	♂	♃	♄	♅	♆	♇
1 Sa	14 33 7	9♉58 28	20♍ 0 31	25♍56 40	17♊18.2	20♉20.4	10♉34.1	13♒59.4	4♍31.8	16♈27.8	21♑ 4.1	14♋39.7	24♊18.5
2 Su	14 37 4	10 56 39	1♎53 33	7♎51 31	17R 12.2	22 23.0	11 48.1	14 38.6	4D 31.7	16 34.9	21R 3.8	14 40.9	24 19.5
3 M	14 41 0	11 54 48	13 50 51	19 51 51	17 5.8	24 23.5	13 2.1	15 17.8	4 31.9	16 42.0	21 3.5	14 42.0	24 20.6
4 Tu	14 44 57	12 52 55	25 54 43	1♏59 40	16 59.6	26 21.7	14 16.1	15 57.0	4 32.3	16 49.0	21 3.1	14 43.3	24 21.7
5 W	14 48 53	13 51 1	8♏ 6 53	14 16 28	16 54.3	28 17.4	15 30.1	16 36.1	4 32.8	16 56.1	21 2.7	14 44.5	24 22.8
6 Th	14 52 50	14 49 5	20 28 35	26 43 21	16 50.3	0♊10.4	16 44.0	17 15.2	4 33.5	17 3.1	21 2.2	14 45.8	24 24.0
7 F	14 56 46	15 47 7	3♐ 0 51	9♐21 12	16 47.9	2 0.5	17 58.0	17 54.2	4 34.4	17 10.0	21 1.7	14 47.1	24 25.1
8 Sa	15 0 43	16 45 8	15 44 32	22 10 57	16D 47.1	3 47.4	19 11.9	18 33.1	4 35.5	17 17.0	21 1.1	14 48.4	24 26.3
9 Su	15 4 40	17 43 7	28 40 34	5♑13 32	16 47.6	5 31.2	20 25.8	19 12.0	4 36.7	17 23.9	21 0.5	14 49.8	24 27.4
10 M	15 8 36	18 41 5	11♑49 58	18 30 2	16 48.9	7 11.5	21 39.8	19 50.9	4 38.1	17 30.7	20 59.8	14 51.2	24 28.6
11 Tu	15 12 33	19 39 2	25 13 51	2♒ 1 31	16 50.5	8 48.5	22 53.7	20 29.7	4 39.8	17 37.5	20 59.1	14 52.6	24 29.8
12 W	15 16 29	20 36 57	8♒53 8	15 48 44	16R 51.7	10 21.9	24 7.6	21 8.4	4 41.6	17 44.3	20 58.3	14 54.0	24 31.0
13 Th	15 20 26	21 34 51	22 48 17	29 51 42	16 52.1	11 51.7	25 21.4	21 47.0	4 43.5	17 51.0	20 57.5	14 55.5	24 32.2
14 F	15 24 22	22 32 44	6♓58 49	14♓ 9 21	16 51.5	13 17.9	26 35.3	22 25.6	4 45.7	17 57.7	20 56.7	14 57.0	24 33.5
15 Sa	15 28 19	23 30 35	21 22 55	28 39 2	16 49.8	14 40.4	27 49.2	23 4.1	4 48.0	18 4.4	20 55.8	14 58.5	24 34.7
16 Su	15 32 15	24 28 26	5♈57 6	13♈16 26	16 47.3	15 59.0	29 3.0	23 42.5	4 50.5	18 11.0	20 54.8	15 0.0	24 36.0
17 M	15 36 12	25 26 15	20 36 18	27 55 50	16 44.4	17 13.9	0♊16.9	24 20.9	4 53.1	18 17.6	20 53.8	15 1.6	24 37.2
18 Tu	15 40 9	26 24 3	5♉14 14	12♉30 38	16 41.7	18 24.8	1 30.7	24 59.1	4 56.0	18 24.1	20 52.8	15 3.2	24 38.5
19 W	15 44 5	27 21 49	19 44 14	26 54 16	16 39.6	19 31.9	2 44.5	25 37.3	4 59.0	18 30.6	20 51.7	15 4.8	24 39.8
20 Th	15 48 2	28 19 35	4♊ 0 7	11♊ 1 11	16D 38.3	20 34.9	3 58.4	26 15.4	5 2.2	18 37.0	20 50.6	15 6.4	24 41.0
21 F	15 51 58	29 17 19	17 57 4	24 47 26	16 37.9	21 33.9	5 12.2	26 53.3	5 5.5	18 43.4	20 49.4	15 8.1	24 42.4
22 Sa	15 55 55	0♊15 2	1♋32 7	8♋11 4	16 38.4	22 28.7	6 26.0	27 31.2	5 9.0	18 49.7	20 48.2	15 9.8	24 43.7
23 Su	15 59 51	1 12 43	14 44 20	21 12 6	16 39.4	23 19.4	7 39.7	28 9.0	5 12.7	18 56.0	20 47.0	15 11.5	24 45.0
24 M	16 3 48	2 10 23	27 34 37	3♌52 14	16 40.6	24 5.7	8 53.5	28 46.7	5 16.6	19 2.2	20 45.7	15 13.2	24 46.3
25 Tu	16 7 44	3 8 1	10♌ 5 22	16 14 30	16 41.8	24 47.8	10 7.3	29 24.3	5 20.6	19 8.4	20 44.3	15 14.9	24 47.6
26 W	16 11 41	4 5 38	22 20 8	28 22 48	16 42.6	25 25.4	11 21.0	0♓ 1.7	5 24.8	19 14.5	20 43.0	15 16.7	24 49.0
27 Th	16 15 38	5 3 13	4♍23 4	10♍21 32	16R 42.9	25 58.5	12 34.8	0 39.1	5 29.1	19 20.5	20 41.6	15 18.5	24 50.3
28 F	16 19 34	6 0 47	16 18 44	22 15 16	16 42.6	26 27.1	13 48.5	1 16.3	5 33.6	19 26.5	20 40.1	15 20.3	24 51.7
29 Sa	16 23 31	6 58 19	28 11 41	4♎ 8 31	16 42.0	26 51.1	15 2.2	1 53.5	5 38.2	19 32.5	20 38.6	15 22.1	24 53.0
30 Su	16 27 27	7 55 50	10♎ 6 17	16 5 28	16 41.0	27 10.4	16 15.9	2 30.5	5 43.0	19 38.3	20 37.1	15 23.9	24 54.4
31 M	16 31 24	8 53 20	22 6 30	28 9 49	16 40.0	27 25.1	17 29.6	3 7.4	5 48.0	19 44.2	20 35.5	15 25.8	24 55.8

LONGITUDE JUNE 1909

Day	Sid.Time	☉	0 hr ☽	Noon ☽	True ☊	☿	♀	♂	♃	♄	♅	♆	♇
1 Tu	16 35 20	9♊50 48	4♏15 45	10♏24 38	16♊39.0	27♊35.1	18♊43.2	3♓44.2	5♍53.1	19♈49.9	20♑33.9	15♋27.6	24♊57.2
2 W	16 39 17	10 48 16	16 36 44	22 52 16	16R 38.2	27R 40.5	19 56.9	4 20.8	5 58.4	19 55.6	20R 32.3	15 29.5	24 58.5
3 Th	16 43 13	11 45 42	29 11 24	5♐34 15	16 37.8	27 41.2	21 10.6	4 57.4	6 3.8	20 1.3	20 30.6	15 31.4	24 59.9
4 F	16 47 10	12 43 7	12♐ 0 53	18 31 18	16D 37.6	27 37.5	22 24.2	5 33.8	6 9.4	20 6.9	20 28.9	15 33.4	25 1.3
5 Sa	16 51 7	13 40 32	25 5 29	1♑43 22	16 37.6	27 29.4	23 37.8	6 10.0	6 15.1	20 12.4	20 27.1	15 35.3	25 2.7
6 Su	16 55 3	14 37 55	8♑24 50	15 9 44	16 37.7	27 17.1	24 51.4	6 46.2	6 20.9	20 17.8	20 25.3	15 37.3	25 4.1
7 M	16 59 0	15 35 18	21 57 54	28 49 10	16 37.9	27 0.8	26 5.1	7 22.2	6 26.9	20 23.2	20 23.5	15 39.2	25 5.5
8 Tu	17 2 56	16 32 40	5♒43 18	12♒40 4	16R 37.9	26 40.8	27 18.7	7 58.0	6 33.1	20 28.5	20 21.7	15 41.2	25 7.0
9 W	17 6 53	17 30 2	19 39 15	26 40 35	16 37.9	26 17.5	28 32.3	8 33.7	6 39.3	20 33.8	20 19.8	15 43.2	25 8.4
10 Th	17 10 49	18 27 23	3♓43 48	10♓48 39	16 37.8	25 51.2	29 45.9	9 9.2	6 45.7	20 39.0	20 17.9	15 45.2	25 9.8
11 F	17 14 46	19 24 43	17 54 49	25 2 1	16D 37.7	25 22.3	0♋59.4	9 44.6	6 52.3	20 44.1	20 16.0	15 47.3	25 11.2
12 Sa	17 18 43	20 22 3	2♈ 9 55	9♈18 12	16 37.8	24 51.4	2 13.0	10 19.8	6 59.0	20 49.1	20 14.0	15 49.3	25 12.6
13 Su	17 22 39	21 19 23	16 26 29	23 34 25	16 38.0	24 18.9	3 26.6	10 54.8	7 5.8	20 54.1	20 12.0	15 51.4	25 14.1
14 M	17 26 36	22 16 42	0♉41 36	7♉47 36	16 38.5	23 45.4	4 40.1	11 29.6	7 12.7	20 59.0	20 10.0	15 53.4	25 15.5
15 Tu	17 30 32	23 14 1	14 52 2	21 54 27	16 39.0	23 11.5	5 53.7	12 4.3	7 19.8	21 3.8	20 8.0	15 55.5	25 16.9
16 W	17 34 29	24 11 19	28 54 26	5♊51 36	16 39.6	22 37.7	7 7.3	12 38.7	7 27.0	21 8.6	20 5.9	15 57.6	25 18.3
17 Th	17 38 25	25 8 37	12♊45 34	19 35 59	16R 39.9	22 4.7	8 20.8	13 13.0	7 34.4	21 13.3	20 3.8	15 59.7	25 19.8
18 F	17 42 22	26 5 55	26 22 33	3♋ 5 1	16 39.8	21 32.9	9 34.3	13 47.0	7 41.9	21 17.9	20 1.7	16 1.8	25 21.2
19 Sa	17 46 18	27 3 12	9♋43 12	16 17 0	16 39.2	21 3.0	10 47.9	14 20.8	7 49.5	21 22.4	19 59.5	16 4.0	25 22.6
20 Su	17 50 15	28 0 29	22 46 20	29 11 16	16 38.0	20 35.4	12 1.4	14 54.4	7 57.2	21 26.8	19 57.4	16 6.1	25 24.0
21 M	17 54 12	28 57 45	5♌31 53	11♌48 21	16 36.5	20 10.6	13 14.9	15 27.8	8 5.0	21 31.2	19 55.2	16 8.2	25 25.5
22 Tu	17 58 8	29 55 0	18 0 55	24 9 54	16 34.7	19 49.0	14 28.4	16 1.0	8 13.0	21 35.5	19 53.0	16 10.4	25 26.9
23 W	18 2 5	0♋52 15	0♍15 39	6♍18 35	16 32.9	19 31.1	15 41.9	16 33.9	8 21.1	21 39.7	19 50.7	16 12.6	25 28.3
24 Th	18 6 1	1 49 29	12 19 10	18 17 54	16 31.5	19 17.0	16 55.4	17 6.6	8 29.3	21 43.8	19 48.5	16 14.7	25 29.7
25 F	18 9 58	2 46 43	24 15 20	0♎12 0	16D 30.6	19 7.2	18 8.8	17 39.0	8 37.6	21 47.8	19 46.2	16 16.9	25 31.2
26 Sa	18 13 54	3 43 56	6♎ 8 29	12 5 23	16 30.4	19D 1.8	19 22.3	18 11.2	8 46.0	21 51.8	19 43.9	16 19.1	25 32.6
27 Su	18 17 51	4 41 8	18 3 15	24 2 42	16 30.9	19 0.9	20 35.7	18 43.1	8 54.5	21 55.7	19 41.6	16 21.3	25 34.0
28 M	18 21 47	5 38 20	0♏ 4 17	6♏ 8 33	16 32.0	19 4.8	21 49.2	19 14.7	9 3.2	21 59.4	19 39.3	16 23.5	25 35.4
29 Tu	18 25 44	6 35 32	12 16 1	18 27 8	16 33.5	19 13.4	23 2.6	19 46.1	9 11.9	22 3.1	19 37.0	16 25.7	25 36.8
30 W	18 29 41	7 32 43	24 42 21	1♐ 2 0	16 34.9	19 27.0	24 16.0	20 17.3	9 20.8	22 6.8	19 34.7	16 27.9	25 38.2

Astro Data

	Dy Hr Mn
♃ D	1 14:51
☽0S	2 18:18
☽0N	16 8:26
♃⚻♅	29 1:24
☽0S	30 2:07
☿ R	2 16:03
♄□♅	7 1:05
☽0N	12 15:09
☽0S	26 10:03
☿ D	26 16:25

Planet Ingress

	Dy Hr Mn
☿ ♊	5 21:46
♀ ♊	16 18:31
☉ ♊	21 17:45
♂ ♓	25 22:54
♀ ♋	10 4:37
☉ ♋	22 2:06

Last Aspect / ☽ Ingress

Last Aspect Dy Hr Mn		☽ Ingress Dy Hr Mn
1 8:42	♇ □	♎ 1 20:11
3 20:56	♇ △	♏ 4 8:04
6 1:05	♅ ⚹	♐ 6 18:16
8 16:12	♇ ☍	♑ 9 2:26
10 19:26	♀ △	♒ 11 8:26
13 4:46	♀ □	♓ 13 12:14
15 11:37	♀ ⚹	♈ 15 14:13
17 6:35	♇ ⚹	♉ 17 15:24
19 13:42	☉ ☌	♊ 19 17:13
21 16:29	♂ △	♋ 21 21:15
23 11:12	♅ ☍	♌ 24 4:36
26 6:26	☿ ⚹	♍ 26 15:14
28 21:12	☿ □	♎ 29 3:39
31 10:42	☿ △	♏ 31 15:37

Last Aspect / ☽ Ingress

Last Aspect Dy Hr Mn		☽ Ingress Dy Hr Mn
2 7:31	♅ ⚹	♐ 3 1:32
5 4:18	☿ ☍	♑ 5 8:54
6 21:14	♅ ☌	♒ 7 14:03
9 16:37	♀ △	♓ 9 17:40
11 12:17	♇ □	♈ 11 20:21
13 14:49	♇ ⚹	♉ 13 22:50
15 8:57	♅ △	♊ 16 1:53
17 23:28	☉ ☌	♋ 18 6:28
19 21:31	♄ □	♌ 20 13:32
22 14:33	♇ ⚹	♍ 22 23:29
25 2:33	♇ □	♎ 25 11:36
27 15:04	♇ △	♏ 27 23:51
29 23:04	♀ △	♐ 30 10:03

☽ Phases & Eclipses

Dy Hr Mn	
5 12:08	○ 14♏20
12 21:45	☽ 21♒29
19 13:42	● 27♉55
27 1:27	☽ 5♍07
4 1:24	○ 12♐46
4 1:29	☊T 1.158
11 2:43	☽ 19♓31
17 23:28	● 26♊05
17 23:18:26	☽ AT 0'24"
25 18:43	☽ 3♎31

Astro Data

1 MAY 1909
Julian Day # 3408
Delta T 9.6 sec
SVP 06♓31'51"
Obliquity 23°27'06"
⚷ Chiron 27♒40.4
☽ Mean ☊ 18♊44.3

1 JUNE 1909
Julian Day # 3439
Delta T 9.7 sec
SVP 06♓31'46"
Obliquity 23°27'06"
⚷ Chiron 28♒11.1
☽ Mean ☊ 17♊05.8

JULY 1909 — LONGITUDE

Day	Sid.Time	☉	0 hr ☽	Noon ☽	True ☊	☿	♀	♂	♃	♄	♅	♆	♇
1 Th	18 33 37	8♋29 54	7♐26 24	13♐55 46	16♊35.9	19♊45.4	25♋29.4	20♓48.1	9♍29.7	22♈10.3	19♑32.3	16♋30.1	25♊39.6
2 F	18 37 34	9 27 5	20 30 12	27 9 44	16R 36.1	20 8.8	26 42.8	21 18.7	9 38.8	22 13.7	19R 30.0	16 32.3	25 41.0
3 Sa	18 41 30	10 24 16	3♑54 19	10♑43 44	16 35.2	20 37.1	27 56.1	21 48.9	9 48.0	22 17.1	19 27.6	16 34.5	25 42.4
4 Su	18 45 27	11 21 26	17 37 44	24 35 56	16 33.2	21 10.2	29 9.5	22 18.9	9 57.2	22 20.3	19 25.2	16 36.7	25 43.8
5 M	18 49 23	12 18 37	1♒37 52	8♒43 0	16 30.2	21 48.2	0♌22.8	22 48.5	10 6.6	22 23.5	19 22.8	16 39.0	25 45.2
6 Tu	18 53 20	13 15 48	15 50 45	23 0 29	16 26.6	22 31.0	1 36.2	23 17.8	10 16.1	22 26.6	19 20.4	16 41.2	25 46.6
7 W	18 57 16	14 12 59	0♓11 34	7♓23 22	16 22.8	23 18.5	2 49.5	23 46.8	10 25.6	22 29.6	19 18.0	16 43.4	25 47.9
8 Th	19 1 13	15 10 10	14 35 17	21 46 45	16 19.6	24 10.8	4 2.8	24 15.5	10 35.3	22 32.5	19 15.6	16 45.6	25 49.3
9 F	19 5 10	16 7 21	28 57 17	6♈ 6 27	16 17.3	25 7.6	5 16.1	24 43.8	10 45.0	22 35.3	19 13.2	16 47.9	25 50.6
10 Sa	19 9 6	17 4 33	13♈13 52	20 19 16	16D 16.3	26 9.1	6 29.4	25 11.7	10 54.8	22 38.0	19 10.8	16 50.1	25 52.0
11 Su	19 13 3	18 1 46	27 22 24	4♉23 5	16 16.5	27 15.1	7 42.7	25 39.3	11 4.8	22 40.6	19 8.4	16 52.3	25 53.3
12 M	19 16 59	18 58 59	11♉21 13	18 16 40	16 17.6	28 25.5	8 55.9	26 6.5	11 14.8	22 43.1	19 6.0	16 54.5	25 54.7
13 Tu	19 20 56	19 56 13	25 9 23	1♊59 18	16 19.1	29 40.4	10 9.2	26 33.2	11 24.9	22 45.5	19 3.6	16 56.8	25 56.0
14 W	19 24 52	20 53 27	8♊46 22	15 30 31	16R 20.2	0♋59.5	11 22.5	26 59.6	11 35.1	22 47.9	19 1.1	16 59.0	25 57.3
15 Th	19 28 49	21 50 42	22 11 43	28 49 54	16 20.3	2 23.0	12 35.7	27 25.6	11 45.4	22 50.1	18 58.7	17 1.2	25 58.6
16 F	19 32 45	22 47 57	5♋24 59	11♋56 55	16 18.8	3 50.5	13 49.0	27 51.1	11 55.7	22 52.2	18 56.3	17 3.5	25 59.9
17 Sa	19 36 42	23 45 13	18 25 39	24 51 7	16 15.5	5 22.2	15 2.2	28 16.1	12 6.2	22 54.3	18 53.9	17 5.7	26 1.2
18 Su	19 40 39	24 42 30	1♌13 18	7♌32 12	16 10.5	6 57.7	16 15.4	28 40.8	12 16.7	22 56.2	18 51.5	17 7.9	26 2.5
19 M	19 44 35	25 39 46	13 47 51	20 0 20	16 4.1	8 37.1	17 28.6	29 4.9	12 27.3	22 58.0	18 49.1	17 10.1	26 3.8
20 Tu	19 48 32	26 37 3	26 9 46	2♍16 20	15 57.0	10 20.1	18 41.8	29 28.6	12 38.0	22 59.8	18 46.7	17 12.3	26 5.0
21 W	19 52 28	27 34 21	8♍20 15	14 21 47	15 49.8	12 6.5	19 54.9	29 51.8	12 48.7	23 1.4	18 44.3	17 14.5	26 6.3
22 Th	19 56 25	28 31 38	20 21 18	26 19 10	15 43.4	13 56.2	21 8.1	0♈14.5	12 59.6	23 2.9	18 42.0	17 16.7	26 7.5
23 F	20 0 21	29 28 56	2♎15 49	8♎11 45	15 38.3	15 48.9	22 21.2	0 36.7	13 10.5	23 4.4	18 39.6	17 18.9	26 8.8
24 Sa	20 4 18	0♌26 15	14 7 28	20 3 33	15 34.9	17 44.3	23 34.3	0 58.4	13 21.5	23 5.7	18 37.2	17 21.1	26 10.0
25 Su	20 8 14	1 23 34	26 0 34	1♏59 8	15D 33.4	19 42.1	24 47.4	1 19.5	13 32.5	23 6.9	18 34.9	17 23.3	26 11.2
26 M	20 12 11	2 20 53	7♏59 53	14 3 27	15 33.4	21 42.1	26 0.5	1 40.1	13 43.6	23 8.0	18 32.6	17 25.5	26 12.4
27 Tu	20 16 8	3 18 13	20 10 26	26 21 28	15 34.4	23 43.9	27 13.6	2 0.2	13 54.8	23 9.1	18 30.3	17 27.6	26 13.6
28 W	20 20 4	4 15 33	2♐37 7	8♐57 54	15 35.6	25 47.1	28 26.6	2 19.7	14 6.0	23 10.0	18 28.0	17 29.8	26 14.7
29 Th	20 24 1	5 12 54	15 24 18	21 56 40	15R 36.2	27 51.5	29 39.6	2 38.7	14 17.4	23 10.8	18 25.7	17 31.9	26 15.9
30 F	20 27 57	6 10 15	28 35 17	5♑20 20	15 35.4	29 56.6	0♍52.6	2 57.0	14 28.7	23 11.5	18 23.4	17 34.1	26 17.0
31 Sa	20 31 54	7 7 37	12♑11 47	19 9 31	15 32.7	2♌ 2.2	2 5.6	3 14.8	14 40.2	23 12.1	18 21.2	17 36.2	26 18.2

AUGUST 1909 — LONGITUDE

Day	Sid.Time	☉	0 hr ☽	Noon ☽	True ☊	☿	♀	♂	♃	♄	♅	♆	♇
1 Su	20 35 50	8♌ 5 0	26♑13 13	3♒22 23	15♊27.8	4♌ 8.0	3♍18.5	3♈32.0	14♍51.7	23♈12.6	18♑18.9	17♋38.3	26♊19.3
2 M	20 39 47	9 2 24	10♒36 25	17 54 29	15R 21.0	6 13.7	4 31.5	3 48.5	15 3.2	23 13.0	18R 16.7	17 40.4	26 20.4
3 Tu	20 43 44	9 59 48	25 15 42	2♓39 4	15 12.9	8 19.1	5 44.4	4 4.4	15 14.9	23 13.3	18 14.5	17 42.5	26 21.5
4 W	20 47 40	10 57 13	10♓ 3 32	17 28 4	15 4.6	10 23.8	6 57.3	4 19.7	15 26.5	23 13.5	18 12.4	17 44.6	26 22.6
5 Th	20 51 37	11 54 40	24 51 40	2♈13 26	14 57.0	12 27.9	8 10.2	4 34.2	15 38.2	23R 13.6	18 10.2	17 46.7	26 23.6
6 F	20 55 33	12 52 8	9♈32 33	16 48 22	14 51.1	14 31.0	9 23.0	4 48.2	15 50.0	23 13.6	18 8.1	17 48.8	26 24.7
7 Sa	20 59 30	13 49 37	24 0 22	1♉ 8 11	14 47.4	16 33.1	10 35.8	5 1.4	16 1.9	23 13.5	18 6.0	17 50.8	26 25.7
8 Su	21 3 26	14 47 7	8♉11 36	15 10 31	14D 45.7	18 34.0	11 48.7	5 13.9	16 13.8	23 13.3	18 3.9	17 52.9	26 26.7
9 M	21 7 23	15 44 39	22 4 56	28 54 57	14 45.7	20 33.7	13 1.4	5 25.6	16 25.7	23 13.0	18 1.8	17 54.9	26 27.7
10 Tu	21 11 19	16 42 12	5♊40 43	12♊22 26	14R 46.3	22 32.0	14 14.2	5 36.7	16 37.7	23 12.6	17 59.8	17 56.9	26 28.7
11 W	21 15 16	17 39 47	19 0 20	25 34 37	14 46.5	24 29.0	15 27.0	5 47.0	16 49.7	23 12.0	17 57.8	17 58.9	26 29.7
12 Th	21 19 13	18 37 23	2♋ 5 31	8♋33 15	14 45.1	26 24.6	16 39.7	5 56.5	17 1.8	23 11.4	17 55.8	18 0.9	26 30.6
13 F	21 23 9	19 35 1	14 57 58	21 19 52	14 41.5	28 18.8	17 52.4	6 5.2	17 14.0	23 10.7	17 53.9	18 2.9	26 31.6
14 Sa	21 27 6	20 32 40	27 39 3	3♌55 38	14 35.1	0♍11.5	19 5.1	6 13.1	17 26.1	23 9.8	17 52.0	18 4.8	26 32.5
15 Su	21 31 2	21 30 20	10♌ 9 42	16 21 20	14 26.2	2 2.8	20 17.8	6 20.3	17 38.4	23 8.9	17 50.1	18 6.8	26 33.4
16 M	21 34 59	22 28 1	22 30 37	28 37 37	14 15.1	3 52.6	21 30.5	6 26.6	17 50.6	23 7.8	17 48.2	18 8.7	26 34.3
17 Tu	21 38 55	23 25 44	4♍42 27	10♍45 12	14 2.7	5 40.9	22 43.1	6 32.1	18 2.9	23 6.7	17 46.4	18 10.6	26 35.2
18 W	21 42 52	24 23 28	16 46 2	22 45 7	13 50.1	7 27.9	23 55.7	6 36.8	18 15.3	23 5.4	17 44.6	18 12.5	26 36.0
19 Th	21 46 48	25 21 13	28 42 42	4♎39 2	13 38.4	9 13.3	25 8.3	6 40.7	18 27.7	23 4.1	17 42.9	18 14.3	26 36.9
20 F	21 50 45	26 19 0	10♎34 27	16 29 20	13 28.6	10 57.4	26 20.8	6 43.7	18 40.1	23 2.6	17 41.2	18 16.2	26 37.7
21 Sa	21 54 41	27 16 48	22 24 5	28 19 11	13 21.1	12 40.1	27 33.3	6 45.9	18 52.5	23 1.1	17 39.5	18 18.0	26 38.5
22 Su	21 58 38	28 14 37	4♏15 10	10♏12 35	13 16.3	14 21.4	28 45.8	6 47.2	19 5.0	22 59.4	17 37.8	18 19.8	26 39.2
23 M	22 2 35	29 12 27	16 12 3	22 14 10	13 14.0	16 1.3	29 58.3	6R 47.7	19 17.6	22 57.7	17 36.2	18 21.6	26 40.0
24 Tu	22 6 31	0♍10 18	28 19 37	4♐29 3	13D 13.3	17 39.8	1♎10.7	6 47.4	19 30.1	22 55.8	17 34.6	18 23.4	26 40.7
25 W	22 10 28	1 8 11	10♐43 6	17 2 26	13R 13.4	19 17.0	2 23.1	6 46.2	19 42.7	22 53.9	17 33.1	18 25.1	26 41.5
26 Th	22 14 24	2 6 5	23 27 38	29 59 13	13 13.1	20 52.8	3 35.5	6 44.2	19 55.3	22 51.9	17 31.6	18 26.9	26 42.2
27 F	22 18 21	3 4 0	6♑37 40	13♑23 16	13 11.4	22 27.3	4 47.8	6 41.3	20 8.0	22 49.7	17 30.1	18 28.6	26 42.9
28 Sa	22 22 17	4 1 57	20 16 15	27 16 35	13 7.4	24 0.5	6 0.1	6 37.7	20 20.7	22 47.5	17 28.7	18 30.3	26 43.5
29 Su	22 26 14	4 59 55	4♒24 7	11♒38 26	13 0.9	25 32.3	7 12.4	6 33.2	20 33.4	22 45.2	17 27.3	18 32.0	26 44.2
30 M	22 30 10	5 57 54	18 58 56	26 24 46	12 51.9	27 2.8	8 24.6	6 27.9	20 46.1	22 42.8	17 26.0	18 33.6	26 44.8
31 Tu	22 34 7	6 55 55	3♓54 54	11♓28 9	12 41.3	28 31.9	9 36.8	6 21.7	20 58.8	22 40.3	17 24.7	18 35.2	26 45.4

Astro Data Dy Hr Mn	Planet Ingress Dy Hr Mn
☽0N 9 20:15	♀ ♌ 4 16:32
☽0S 23 17:20	☿ ♋ 13 6:04
	♂ ♈ 21 8:36
♄ R 5 9:32	☉ ♌ 23 13:01
☽0N 6 1:49	♀ ♍ 29 6:42
♅☍♆ 10 17:24	☿ ♌ 30 0:39
♃△♅ 15 19:57	
♃✶♆ 17 17:34	☿ ♍ 13 21:32
☽0S 19 23:41	☉ ♍ 23 19:44
♂ R 23 2:31	♀ ♎ 23 0:34
♀0S 24 14:55	
☿0S 31 11:37	

Last Aspect Dy Hr Mn	☽ Ingress Dy Hr Mn	Last Aspect Dy Hr Mn	☽ Ingress Dy Hr Mn
2 9:22 ♇ ☍	♑ 2 17:04	31 18:54 ♄ □	♒ 1 6:22
4 8:23 ♂ ✶	♒ 4 21:14	3 1:47 ♇ △	♓ 3 7:42
6 16:39 ♇ △	♓ 6 23:41	5 2:30 ♇ □	♈ 5 8:22
8 18:47 ♇ □	♈ 9 1:45	7 4:04 ♇ ✶	♉ 7 10:05
10 23:46 ☿ □	♉ 11 4:29	8 20:54 ☿ □	♊ 9 13:55
13 2:32 ♂ ✶	♊ 13 8:30	11 13:42 ♇ ☌	♋ 11 20:08
15 9:46 ♂ □	♋ 15 14:07	13 15:29 ♄ □	♌ 14 4:29
17 19:02 ♂ △	♌ 17 21:41	16 7:58 ♇ ✶	♍ 16 14:42
19 23:51 ♇ ✶	♍ 20 7:32	18 19:46 ♇ □	♎ 19 2:36
22 17:53 ☉ ✶	♎ 22 19:26	21 10:46 ☉ ✶	♏ 21 15:24
25 0:21 ♇ △	♏ 25 8:01	23 6:16 ♃ ✶	♐ 24 3:16
27 15:09 ♀ □	♐ 27 19:00	26 5:59 ♇ ☍	♑ 26 12:01
29 19:51 ♇ ☍	♑ 30 2:32	28 7:13 ☿ △	♒ 28 16:37
		30 12:33 ♇ △	♓ 30 17:45

☽ Phases & Eclipses Dy Hr Mn	
3 12:17	○ 10♑54
10 6:58	☽ 17♈21
17 10:45	● 24♋11
25 11:45	☽ 1♏52
1 21:14	○ 8♒56
8 12:10	☽ 15♉16
15 23:54	● 22♌28
24 3:55	☽ 0♐20
31 5:08	○ 7♓08

Astro Data

1 JULY 1909
Julian Day # 3469
Delta T 9.8 sec
SVP 06♓31'41"
Obliquity 23°27'06"
⚷ Chiron 27♒46.5R
☽ Mean ☊ 15♊30.5

1 AUGUST 1909
Julian Day # 3500
Delta T 9.9 sec
SVP 06♓31'35"
Obliquity 23°27'06"
⚷ Chiron 26♒34.8R
☽ Mean ☊ 13♊52.0

LONGITUDE SEPTEMBER 1909

Day	Sid.Time	☉	0 hr ☽	Noon ☽	True ☊	☿	♀	♂	♃	♄	♅	♆	♇
1 W	22 38 4	7♍53 57	19♓ 3 12	26♓38 43	12♊30.3	29♍59.7	10♎49.0	6♈14.8	21♍11.6	22♈37.7	17♑23.4	18♋36.8	26♊46.0
2 Th	22 42 0	8 52 1	4♈13 20	11♈45 47	12R 20.1	1♎26.1	12 1.1	6R 7.1	21 24.4	22R 35.0	17R 22.2	18 38.4	26 46.6
3 F	22 45 57	9 50 7	19 14 58	26 39 53	12 11.8	2 51.2	13 13.2	5 58.7	21 37.2	22 32.3	17 21.0	18 39.9	26 47.1
4 Sa	22 49 53	10 48 15	3♉59 46	11♉14 5	12 6.1	4 14.9	14 25.3	5 49.4	21 50.0	22 29.4	17 19.9	18 41.5	26 47.6
5 Su	22 53 50	11 46 24	18 22 27	25 24 43	12 3.1	5 37.1	15 37.3	5 39.4	22 2.9	22 26.5	17 18.8	18 43.0	26 48.1
6 M	22 57 46	12 44 36	2♊20 51	9♊11 1	12 2.0	6 57.9	16 49.3	5 28.7	22 15.8	22 23.5	17 17.8	18 44.5	26 48.6
7 Tu	23 1 43	13 42 50	15 55 25	22 34 25	12 1.9	8 17.2	18 1.2	5 17.3	22 28.6	22 20.4	17 16.8	18 45.9	26 49.1
8 W	23 5 39	14 41 7	29 8 21	5♋37 38	12 1.5	9 35.0	19 13.2	5 5.2	22 41.5	22 17.2	17 15.8	18 47.3	26 49.5
9 Th	23 9 36	15 39 25	12♋ 2 41	18 23 53	11 59.6	10 51.2	20 25.1	4 52.4	22 54.5	22 13.9	17 14.9	18 48.8	26 49.9
10 F	23 13 33	16 37 45	24 41 39	0♌56 20	11 55.3	12 5.7	21 36.9	4 39.1	23 7.4	22 10.6	17 14.1	18 50.1	26 50.3
11 Sa	23 17 29	17 36 7	7♌ 8 14	13 17 40	11 48.1	13 18.5	22 48.8	4 25.1	23 20.3	22 7.1	17 13.2	18 51.5	26 50.7
12 Su	23 21 26	18 34 31	19 24 54	25 30 7	11 38.1	14 29.5	24 0.6	4 10.6	23 33.3	22 3.7	17 12.5	18 52.8	26 51.1
13 M	23 25 22	19 32 57	1♍33 32	7♍35 19	11 25.7	15 38.6	25 12.3	3 55.6	23 46.2	22 0.1	17 11.8	18 54.1	26 51.4
14 Tu	23 29 19	20 31 26	13 35 37	19 34 34	11 11.9	16 45.7	26 24.0	3 40.1	23 59.2	21 56.4	17 11.1	18 55.4	26 51.7
15 W	23 33 15	21 29 55	25 32 21	1♎29 5	10 57.9	17 50.7	27 35.7	3 24.2	24 12.2	21 52.7	17 10.5	18 56.6	26 52.0
16 Th	23 37 12	22 28 27	7♎24 58	13 20 11	10 44.7	18 53.5	28 47.4	3 7.9	24 25.2	21 49.0	17 9.9	18 57.8	26 52.3
17 F	23 41 8	23 27 1	19 14 59	25 9 37	10 33.5	19 53.8	29 59.0	2 51.3	24 38.1	21 45.1	17 9.3	18 59.0	26 52.5
18 Sa	23 45 5	24 25 36	1♏ 4 24	6♏59 42	10 24.8	20 51.6	1♏10.5	2 34.4	24 51.1	21 41.2	17 8.9	19 0.2	26 52.7
19 Su	23 49 2	25 24 14	12 55 55	18 53 31	10 19.1	21 46.6	2 22.0	2 17.3	25 4.1	21 37.2	17 8.4	19 1.3	26 52.9
20 M	23 52 58	26 22 53	24 52 58	0♐54 50	10 16.0	22 38.7	3 33.5	2 0.0	25 17.1	21 33.2	17 8.1	19 2.4	26 53.1
21 Tu	23 56 55	27 21 33	6♐59 41	13 8 7	10D 15.0	23 27.5	4 44.9	1 42.6	25 30.1	21 29.1	17 7.7	19 3.5	26 53.3
22 W	0 0 51	28 20 16	19 20 46	25 38 15	10R 15.1	24 13.0	5 56.3	1 25.1	25 43.0	21 25.0	17 7.4	19 4.5	26 53.4
23 Th	0 4 48	29 19 0	2♑ 1 12	8♑30 11	10 15.2	24 54.7	7 7.7	1 7.5	25 56.0	21 20.8	17 7.2	19 5.5	26 53.5
24 F	0 8 44	0♎17 46	15 5 43	21 48 17	10 14.3	25 32.4	8 18.9	0 50.0	26 9.0	21 16.6	17 7.0	19 6.5	26 53.6
25 Sa	0 12 41	1 16 34	28 38 12	5♒35 39	10 11.4	26 5.7	9 30.2	0 32.6	26 22.0	21 12.3	17 6.9	19 7.4	26 53.7
26 Su	0 16 37	2 15 23	12♒40 38	19 53 0	10 6.2	26 34.3	10 41.4	0 15.3	26 34.9	21 7.9	17 6.8	19 8.3	26 53.7
27 M	0 20 34	3 14 14	27 12 18	4♓37 54	9 58.6	26 57.8	11 52.5	29♓58.1	26 47.9	21 3.5	17D 6.8	19 9.2	26R 53.7
28 Tu	0 24 31	4 13 7	12♓ 8 54	19 44 12	9 49.4	27 15.8	13 3.5	29 41.2	27 0.8	20 59.1	17 6.8	19 10.1	26 53.7
29 W	0 28 27	5 12 2	27 22 32	5♈ 2 29	9 39.7	27 27.9	14 14.5	29 24.5	27 13.7	20 54.7	17 6.9	19 10.9	26 53.7
30 Th	0 32 24	6 10 59	12♈42 37	20 21 28	9 30.6	27R 33.7	15 25.5	29 8.1	27 26.6	20 50.1	17 7.0	19 11.7	26 53.7

LONGITUDE OCTOBER 1909

Day	Sid.Time	☉	0 hr ☽	Noon ☽	True ☊	☿	♀	♂	♃	♄	♅	♆	♇
1 F	0 36 20	7♎ 9 57	27♈57 40	5♉29 59	9♊23.2	27♎32.7	16♏36.4	28♓52.0	27♍39.5	20♈45.6	17♑ 7.2	19♋12.5	26♊53.6
2 Sa	0 40 17	8 8 58	12♉57 22	20 19 0	9R 18.2	27R 24.5	17 47.2	28R 36.3	27 52.4	20R 41.0	17 7.4	19 13.2	26R 53.5
3 Su	0 44 13	9 8 1	27 34 15	4♊42 44	9D 15.6	27 8.9	18 58.0	28 21.0	28 5.3	20 36.4	17 7.7	19 13.9	26 53.4
4 M	0 48 10	10 7 7	11♊44 16	18 38 49	9 15.1	26 45.5	20 8.7	28 6.2	28 18.1	20 31.8	17 8.0	19 14.5	26 53.3
5 Tu	0 52 6	11 6 15	25 26 35	2♋ 7 48	9 15.7	26 14.3	21 19.4	27 51.8	28 31.0	20 27.2	17 8.4	19 15.2	26 53.1
6 W	0 56 3	12 5 25	8♋42 52	15 12 13	9R 16.4	25 35.2	22 30.0	27 38.0	28 43.8	20 22.5	17 8.8	19 15.8	26 52.9
7 Th	1 0 0	13 4 38	21 36 18	27 55 40	9 16.1	24 48.4	23 40.5	27 24.7	28 56.6	20 17.8	17 9.3	19 16.3	26 52.7
8 F	1 3 56	14 3 53	4♌10 48	10♌22 13	9 13.9	23 54.5	24 51.0	27 12.0	29 9.4	20 13.1	17 9.9	19 16.9	26 52.5
9 Sa	1 7 53	15 3 10	16 30 23	22 35 46	9 9.5	22 54.2	26 1.5	26 60.0	29 22.1	20 8.3	17 10.4	19 17.4	26 52.3
10 Su	1 11 49	16 2 29	28 38 47	4♍39 49	9 2.8	21 48.5	27 11.8	26 48.5	29 34.9	20 3.6	17 11.1	19 17.8	26 52.0
11 M	1 15 46	17 1 51	10♍39 13	16 37 19	8 54.1	20 39.0	28 22.1	26 37.8	29 47.6	19 58.8	17 11.8	19 18.3	26 51.7
12 Tu	1 19 42	18 1 14	22 34 23	28 30 41	8 44.3	19 27.1	29 32.3	26 27.7	0♎ 0.2	19 54.1	17 12.5	19 18.7	26 51.4
13 W	1 23 39	19 0 40	4♎26 26	10♎21 51	8 34.3	18 15.0	0♐42.5	26 18.3	0 12.9	19 49.3	17 13.3	19 19.0	26 51.1
14 Th	1 27 35	20 0 8	16 17 8	22 12 29	8 24.8	17 4.5	1 52.6	26 9.7	0 25.5	19 44.5	17 14.1	19 19.4	26 50.7
15 F	1 31 32	20 59 38	28 8 6	4♏ 4 12	8 16.9	15 57.7	3 2.6	26 1.9	0 38.1	19 39.7	17 15.0	19 19.6	26 50.3
16 Sa	1 35 28	21 59 10	10♏ 1 0	15 58 46	8 10.9	14 56.7	4 12.5	25 54.8	0 50.6	19 35.0	17 15.9	19 19.9	26 49.9
17 Su	1 39 25	22 58 44	21 57 47	27 58 21	8 7.2	14 3.2	5 22.4	25 48.5	1 3.1	19 30.2	17 16.9	19 20.1	26 49.5
18 M	1 43 22	23 58 20	4♐ 0 48	10♐ 5 33	8D 5.7	13 18.7	6 32.2	25 43.0	1 15.6	19 25.5	17 18.0	19 20.3	26 49.1
19 Tu	1 47 18	24 57 58	16 12 59	22 23 34	8 5.9	12 44.2	7 41.9	25 38.3	1 28.1	19 20.7	17 19.1	19 20.5	26 48.6
20 W	1 51 15	25 57 38	28 37 46	4♑56 4	8 7.2	12 20.6	8 51.5	25 34.4	1 40.5	19 16.0	17 20.2	19 20.6	26 48.1
21 Th	1 55 11	26 57 20	11♑18 58	17 46 58	8 8.7	12D 8.3	10 1.0	25 31.3	1 52.8	19 11.3	17 21.4	19 20.7	26 47.7
22 F	1 59 8	27 57 3	24 20 30	1♒ 0 0	8R 9.6	12 7.2	11 10.5	25 29.0	2 5.2	19 6.6	17 22.6	19 20.8	26 47.1
23 Sa	2 3 4	28 56 48	7♒45 49	14 38 12	8 9.3	12 17.1	12 19.8	25 27.6	2 17.4	19 1.9	17 23.9	19R 20.8	26 46.6
24 Su	2 7 1	29 56 34	21 37 17	28 43 3	8 7.4	12 37.5	13 29.0	25D 26.9	2 29.7	18 57.3	17 25.3	19 20.8	26 46.0
25 M	2 10 57	0♏56 22	5♓55 19	13♓13 41	8 3.8	13 7.9	14 38.1	25 27.1	2 41.9	18 52.7	17 26.6	19 20.7	26 45.5
26 Tu	2 14 54	1 56 12	20 37 36	28 6 15	7 59.1	13 47.3	15 47.2	25 28.0	2 54.0	18 48.1	17 28.1	19 20.7	26 44.9
27 W	2 18 51	2 56 4	5♈38 42	13♈13 50	7 53.8	14 35.1	16 56.1	25 29.8	3 6.1	18 43.5	17 29.5	19 20.5	26 44.2
28 Th	2 22 47	3 55 57	20 50 24	28 27 5	7 48.8	15 30.3	18 4.8	25 32.3	3 18.1	18 39.0	17 31.1	19 20.4	26 43.6
29 F	2 26 44	4 55 52	6♉ 2 36	13♉35 41	7 44.7	16 32.1	19 13.5	25 35.6	3 30.1	18 34.5	17 32.6	19 20.2	26 42.9
30 Sa	2 30 40	5 55 49	21 5 10	28 30 0	7 42.2	17 39.6	20 22.1	25 39.7	3 42.0	18 30.1	17 34.3	19 20.0	26 42.3
31 Su	2 34 37	6 55 48	5♊49 23	13♊ 2 37	7D 41.3	18 52.2	21 30.5	25 44.5	3 53.9	18 25.7	17 35.9	19 19.8	26 41.6

Astro Data Dy Hr Mn	Planet Ingress Dy Hr Mn
☽0N 2 9:38	☿ ♎ 1 0:05
♃⊼♄ 6 11:35	♀ ♏ 17 0:21
☽0S 16 5:30	☉ ♎ 23 16:45
♃□♇ 27 10:53	♂ ♓ 26 21:19
♅ D 27 1:29	
♇ R 27 10:44	♃ ♎ 11 23:33
☽0N 29 19:56	♀ ♐ 12 9:28
☿ R 30 8:34	☉ ♏ 24 1:23
☽0S 13 11:29	
♄□♆ 19 1:09	
☿ D 21 14:21	
♆ R 23 5:03	
♃0S 24 6:41	
♂ D 24 7:15	☽0N 27 7:12

Last Aspect Dy Hr Mn	☽ Ingress Dy Hr Mn	Last Aspect Dy Hr Mn	☽ Ingress Dy Hr Mn
1 12:12 ♇ □	♈ 1 17:18	30 23:21 ☿ ☍	♉ 1 3:14
3 12:12 ♇ ✶	♉ 3 17:26	3 1:17 ♂ ✶	♊ 3 4:04
5 6:20 ♃ △	♊ 5 19:55	5 5:35 ♃ □	♋ 5 8:09
7 19:45 ♇ ☌	♋ 8 1:35	7 14:11 ♃ ✶	♌ 7 15:58
9 20:57 ♃ ✶	♌ 10 10:11	9 20:49 ♀ □	♍ 10 2:42
12 14:40 ♇ ✶	♍ 12 20:54	12 8:39 ♇ □	♎ 12 15:01
15 2:41 ♇ □	♎ 15 9:00	14 21:23 ♇ △	♏ 15 3:46
17 15:29 ♇ △	♏ 17 21:49	17 7:37 ♂ △	♐ 17 16:02
20 3:15 ☉ ✶	♐ 20 10:11	19 20:30 ♇ ☍	♑ 20 2:37
22 18:31 ☉ □	♑ 22 20:13	22 7:03 ☉ □	♒ 22 10:13
24 19:58 ♃ △	♒ 25 2:22	24 8:43 ♇ △	♓ 24 14:09
26 23:36 ♃ ☍	♓ 27 4:32	26 9:49 ♇ □	♈ 26 15:02
29 3:08 ♂ ☌	♈ 29 4:07	28 9:16 ♇ ✶	♉ 28 14:27
		30 7:26 ♂ ✶	♊ 30 14:27

☽ Phases & Eclipses Dy Hr Mn	
6 19:44	☽ 13♊33
14 15:08	● 21♍08
22 18:31	☽ 29♐06
29 13:05	○ 5♈44
6 6:44	☽ 12♋22
14 8:13	● 20♎21
22 7:03	☽ 28♑15
28 22:07	○ 4♉51

Astro Data

1 SEPTEMBER 1909
Julian Day # 3531
Delta T 10.0 sec
SVP 06♓31'31"
Obliquity 23°27'07"
⚷ Chiron 25♒02.6R
☽ Mean ☊ 12♊13.5

1 OCTOBER 1909
Julian Day # 3561
Delta T 10.1 sec
SVP 06♓31'29"
Obliquity 23°27'07"
⚷ Chiron 23♒47.7R
☽ Mean ☊ 10♊38.2

NOVEMBER 1909 LONGITUDE

Day	Sid.Time	☉	0 hr ☽	Noon ☽	True ☊	☿	♀	♂	♃	♄	♅	♆	♇
1 M	2 38 33	7♏55 49	20♊ 9 16	27♊ 9 3	7♊41.7	20♎ 9.1	22♐38.8	25♓50.1	4♎ 5.8	18♈21.3	17♑37.7	19♋19.5	26♊40.9
2 Tu	2 42 30	8 55 53	4♋ 1 52	10♋47 47	7 43.1	21 29.7	23 47.0	25 56.4	4 17.5	18R 17.0	17 39.4	19R 19.2	26R 40.1
3 W	2 46 26	9 55 58	17 27 0	23 59 51	7 44.7	22 53.4	24 55.0	26 3.4	4 29.2	18 12.8	17 41.2	19 18.8	26 39.4
4 Th	2 50 23	10 56 6	0♌26 42	6♌48 2	7R46.0	24 19.7	26 2.9	26 11.2	4 40.9	18 8.6	17 43.1	19 18.4	26 38.6
5 F	2 54 20	11 56 15	13 4 22	19 16 13	7 46.4	25 48.2	27 10.7	26 19.6	4 52.5	18 4.4	17 45.0	19 18.0	26 37.9
6 Sa	2 58 16	12 56 27	25 24 9	1♍28 43	7 45.7	27 18.4	28 18.3	26 28.8	5 4.0	18 0.3	17 46.9	19 17.6	26 37.1
7 Su	3 2 13	13 56 41	7♍30 29	13 29 57	7 43.9	28 50.1	29 25.8	26 38.6	5 15.5	17 56.3	17 48.9	19 17.1	26 36.2
8 M	3 6 9	14 56 56	19 27 38	25 24 1	7 41.0	0♏22.9	0♑33.1	26 49.1	5 26.9	17 52.3	17 50.9	19 16.6	26 35.4
9 Tu	3 10 6	15 57 14	1♎19 32	7♎14 36	7 37.5	1 56.7	1 40.3	27 0.3	5 38.2	17 48.3	17 53.0	19 16.1	26 34.6
10 W	3 14 2	16 57 33	13 9 35	19 4 50	7 33.8	3 31.2	2 47.3	27 12.2	5 49.5	17 44.5	17 55.1	19 15.5	26 33.7
11 Th	3 17 59	17 57 55	25 0 41	0♏57 23	7 30.4	5 6.2	3 54.1	27 24.7	6 0.7	17 40.7	17 57.2	19 14.9	26 32.8
12 F	3 21 55	18 58 18	6♏55 13	12 54 24	7 27.6	6 41.7	5 0.8	27 37.8	6 11.8	17 37.0	17 59.4	19 14.2	26 31.9
13 Sa	3 25 52	19 58 43	18 55 10	24 57 42	7 25.7	8 17.4	6 7.3	27 51.5	6 22.8	17 33.3	18 1.7	19 13.6	26 31.0
14 Su	3 29 49	20 59 9	1♐ 2 13	7♐ 8 54	7D24.7	9 53.3	7 13.6	28 5.9	6 33.8	17 29.7	18 3.9	19 12.9	26 30.1
15 M	3 33 45	21 59 38	13 17 57	19 29 35	7 24.7	11 29.3	8 19.7	28 20.8	6 44.7	17 26.2	18 6.3	19 12.1	26 29.2
16 Tu	3 37 42	23 0 7	25 44 0	2♑ 1 25	7 25.4	13 5.4	9 25.7	28 36.4	6 55.5	17 22.8	18 8.6	19 11.4	26 28.2
17 W	3 41 38	24 0 39	8♑22 5	14 46 13	7 26.5	14 41.4	10 31.4	28 52.5	7 6.2	17 19.5	18 11.0	19 10.6	26 27.2
18 Th	3 45 35	25 1 11	21 14 5	27 45 57	7 27.7	16 17.4	11 36.9	29 9.2	7 16.8	17 16.2	18 13.5	19 9.8	26 26.3
19 F	3 49 31	26 1 45	4♒22 1	11♒ 2 32	7 28.7	17 53.3	12 42.1	29 26.4	7 27.4	17 13.0	18 15.9	19 8.9	26 25.3
20 Sa	3 53 28	27 2 20	17 47 41	24 37 37	7R29.3	19 29.1	13 47.2	29 44.2	7 37.9	17 10.0	18 18.4	19 8.0	26 24.3
21 Su	3 57 24	28 2 56	1♓32 25	8♓32 5	7 29.5	21 4.7	14 52.0	0♈ 2.5	7 48.3	17 6.9	18 21.0	19 7.1	26 23.3
22 M	4 1 21	29 3 34	15 36 33	22 45 38	7 29.1	22 40.2	15 56.5	0 21.3	7 58.5	17 4.0	18 23.6	19 6.2	26 22.2
23 Tu	4 5 18	0♐ 4 12	29 58 59	7♈16 12	7 28.5	24 15.6	17 0.7	0 40.6	8 8.7	17 1.2	18 26.2	19 5.2	26 21.2
24 W	4 9 14	1 4 51	14♈36 43	21 59 50	7 27.7	25 50.8	18 4.7	1 0.3	8 18.8	16 58.5	18 28.8	19 4.2	26 20.1
25 Th	4 13 11	2 5 32	29 24 45	6♉50 36	7 27.0	27 25.8	19 8.4	1 20.6	8 28.8	16 55.8	18 31.5	19 3.2	26 19.1
26 F	4 17 7	3 6 14	14♉16 26	21 41 16	7 26.6	29 0.8	20 11.9	1 41.3	8 38.8	16 53.2	18 34.3	19 2.1	26 18.0
27 Sa	4 21 4	4 6 57	29 4 9	6♊24 8	7D26.3	0♐35.6	21 15.0	2 2.4	8 48.6	16 50.8	18 37.0	19 1.1	26 16.9
28 Su	4 25 0	5 7 41	13♊40 23	20 52 8	7 26.3	2 10.2	22 17.8	2 24.0	8 58.3	16 48.4	18 39.8	18 60.0	26 15.9
29 M	4 28 57	6 8 27	27 58 45	4♋59 43	7 26.4	3 44.8	23 20.2	2 46.0	9 7.9	16 46.1	18 42.6	18 58.8	26 14.8
30 Tu	4 32 54	7 9 14	11♋54 43	18 43 30	7R26.5	5 19.3	24 22.3	3 8.4	9 17.4	16 44.0	18 45.5	18 57.7	26 13.7

DECEMBER 1909 LONGITUDE

Day	Sid.Time	☉	0 hr ☽	Noon ☽	True ☊	☿	♀	♂	♃	♄	♅	♆	♇
1 W	4 36 50	8♐10 2	25♋26 1	2♌ 2 20	7♊26.5	6♐53.7	25♑24.1	3♈31.1	9♎26.8	16♈41.9	18♑48.4	18♋56.5	26♊12.5
2 Th	4 40 47	9 10 52	8♌32 37	14 57 9	7R26.3	8 28.0	26 25.5	3 54.3	9 36.1	16R39.9	18 51.3	18R55.3	26R11.4
3 F	4 44 43	10 11 43	21 16 19	27 30 33	7 26.1	10 2.3	27 26.6	4 17.9	9 45.3	16 38.1	18 54.2	18 54.1	26 10.3
4 Sa	4 48 40	11 12 36	3♍40 21	9♍46 16	7D25.9	11 36.5	28 27.2	4 41.8	9 54.4	16 36.3	18 57.2	18 52.8	26 9.2
5 Su	4 52 36	12 13 29	15 48 52	21 48 44	7 25.9	13 10.7	29 27.5	5 6.1	10 3.4	16 34.6	19 0.2	18 51.6	26 8.0
6 M	4 56 33	13 14 24	27 46 28	3♎42 39	7 26.1	14 44.9	0♒27.3	5 30.8	10 12.3	16 33.0	19 3.2	18 50.3	26 6.9
7 Tu	5 0 29	14 15 21	9♎37 52	15 32 41	7 26.6	16 19.1	1 26.8	5 55.7	10 21.0	16 31.6	19 6.3	18 49.0	26 5.7
8 W	5 4 26	15 16 18	21 27 39	27 23 16	7 27.4	17 53.3	2 25.7	6 21.1	10 29.6	16 30.2	19 9.3	18 47.6	26 4.6
9 Th	5 8 23	16 17 17	3♏20 1	9♏18 21	7 28.4	19 27.6	3 24.3	6 46.7	10 38.1	16 29.0	19 12.5	18 46.3	26 3.4
10 F	5 12 19	17 18 17	15 18 38	21 21 15	7 29.3	21 1.9	4 22.3	7 12.7	10 46.5	16 27.8	19 15.6	18 44.9	26 2.2
11 Sa	5 16 16	18 19 17	27 26 30	3♐34 38	7R30.0	22 36.3	5 19.8	7 39.0	10 54.8	16 26.8	19 18.7	18 43.5	26 1.1
12 Su	5 20 12	19 20 19	9♐45 52	16 0 23	7 30.2	24 10.7	6 16.9	8 5.7	11 2.9	16 25.9	19 21.9	18 42.1	25 59.9
13 M	5 24 9	20 21 22	22 18 16	28 39 38	7 29.7	25 45.3	7 13.3	8 32.6	11 10.9	16 25.0	19 25.1	18 40.6	25 58.7
14 Tu	5 28 5	21 22 25	5♑ 4 29	11♑32 50	7 28.5	27 19.9	8 9.3	8 59.8	11 18.8	16 24.3	19 28.4	18 39.2	25 57.5
15 W	5 32 2	22 23 30	18 4 39	24 39 52	7 26.7	28 54.6	9 4.6	9 27.3	11 26.5	16 23.7	19 31.6	18 37.7	25 56.3
16 Th	5 35 58	23 24 34	1♒18 25	8♒ 0 13	7 24.4	0♑29.5	9 59.4	9 55.1	11 34.2	16 23.3	19 34.9	18 36.2	25 55.2
17 F	5 39 55	24 25 39	14 45 8	21 33 6	7 21.9	2 4.4	10 53.5	10 23.2	11 41.6	16 22.9	19 38.2	18 34.7	25 54.0
18 Sa	5 43 52	25 26 45	28 23 58	5♓17 38	7 19.8	3 39.4	11 46.9	10 51.5	11 49.0	16 22.6	19 41.5	18 33.2	25 52.8
19 Su	5 47 48	26 27 51	12♓13 58	19 12 50	7 18.3	5 14.5	12 39.6	11 20.1	11 56.2	16D 22.5	19 44.8	18 31.6	25 51.6
20 M	5 51 45	27 28 57	26 14 5	3♈17 34	7D17.8	6 49.7	13 31.7	11 48.9	12 3.2	16 22.4	19 48.2	18 30.1	25 50.4
21 Tu	5 55 41	28 30 3	10♈23 4	17 30 22	7 18.1	8 24.9	14 22.9	12 18.0	12 10.2	16 22.5	19 51.5	18 28.5	25 49.2
22 W	5 59 38	29 31 9	24 39 12	1♉49 14	7 19.3	10 0.2	15 13.4	12 47.3	12 16.9	16 22.7	19 54.9	18 26.9	25 48.0
23 Th	6 3 34	0♑32 15	9♉ 0 6	16 11 23	7 20.8	11 35.5	16 3.1	13 16.8	12 23.6	16 22.9	19 58.3	18 25.4	25 46.9
24 F	6 7 31	1 33 22	23 22 36	0♊33 14	7R22.1	13 10.7	16 51.9	13 46.6	12 30.1	16 23.3	20 1.7	18 23.8	25 45.7
25 Sa	6 11 27	2 34 29	7♊42 43	14 50 28	7 22.6	14 45.8	17 39.9	14 16.5	12 36.4	16 23.9	20 5.1	18 22.1	25 44.5
26 Su	6 15 24	3 35 36	21 55 54	28 58 25	7 21.9	16 20.8	18 26.9	14 46.7	12 42.6	16 24.5	20 8.6	18 20.5	25 43.3
27 M	6 19 21	4 36 44	5♋57 30	12♋52 37	7 19.7	17 55.6	19 12.9	15 17.1	12 48.6	16 25.2	20 12.0	18 18.9	25 42.2
28 Tu	6 23 17	5 37 51	19 43 20	26 29 19	7 16.2	19 30.0	19 58.0	15 47.6	12 54.5	16 26.1	20 15.5	18 17.3	25 41.0
29 W	6 27 14	6 38 59	3♌10 18	9♌46 7	7 11.5	21 4.0	20 42.0	16 18.4	13 0.3	16 27.0	20 19.0	18 15.6	25 39.8
30 Th	6 31 10	7 40 7	16 16 43	22 42 11	7 6.3	22 37.4	21 25.0	16 49.3	13 5.8	16 28.1	20 22.5	18 14.0	25 38.7
31 F	6 35 7	8 41 16	29 2 38	5♍18 19	7 1.2	24 10.1	22 6.8	17 20.4	13 11.3	16 29.2	20 26.0	18 12.3	25 37.5

Astro Data	Dy Hr Mn
♄□♅	8 5:27
☽0S	9 18:06
☽0N	23 17:00
♂0N	25 20:58
♅☍♆	2 23:16
☽0S	7 1:25
♄ D	19 21:51
☽0N	20 23:47

Planet Ingress	Dy Hr Mn
☿ ♏	7 18:06
♀ ♑	7 12:11
♂ ♈	20 20:48
☉ ♐	22 22:20
☿ ♐	26 14:59
♀ ♒	5 13:01
☿ ♑	15 16:33
☉ ♑	22 11:20

Last Aspect Dy Hr Mn		☽ Ingress Dy Hr Mn
1 11:11	♇ ☌	♋ 1 16:57
3 15:58	♂ △	♌ 3 23:10
6 6:18	♀ △	♍ 6 9:04
8 15:06	♂ ☍	♎ 8 21:19
11 3:06	♇ △	♏ 11 10:04
13 18:05	♂ △	♐ 13 21:57
16 5:37	♂ □	♑ 16 8:09
18 14:51	♂ ✶	♒ 18 16:05
20 17:29	☉ □	♓ 20 21:20
22 17:59	♇ □	♈ 23 0:02
24 19:00	♇ ✶	♉ 25 0:57
26 10:19	♀ △	♊ 27 1:31
28 21:04	♇ ☌	♋ 29 3:26

Last Aspect Dy Hr Mn		☽ Ingress Dy Hr Mn
30 23:56	♀ ☍	♌ 1 8:17
3 9:24	♇ ✶	♍ 3 16:50
5 20:40	♇ □	♎ 6 4:30
8 9:20	♇ △	♏ 8 17:17
10 7:53	♅ ✶	♐ 11 5:01
13 7:27	☿ ☌	♑ 13 14:31
15 2:40	♅ ☌	♒ 15 21:39
17 19:36	♇ △	♓ 18 2:48
20 2:17	☉ □	♈ 20 6:25
22 8:46	☉ △	♉ 22 8:57
23 18:23	♅ △	♊ 24 11:04
26 6:26	♇ ☌	♋ 26 13:45
28 0:57	♅ ☍	♌ 28 18:17
30 17:31	♇ ✶	♍ 31 1:49

☽ Phases & Eclipses Dy Hr Mn	
4 21:38	☽ 11♌50
13 2:18	● 20♏05
20 17:29	☽ 27♒46
27 8:52	○ 4♊29
27 8:54	☍ T 1.366
4 16:12	☽ 11♍54
12 19:58	● 20♐11
12 19:44:35	☌ P 0.542
20 2:17	☽ 27♓35
26 21:30	○ 4♋30

Astro Data

1 NOVEMBER 1909
Julian Day # 3592
Delta T 10.2 sec
SVP 06♓31'25"
Obliquity 23°27'07"
⚷ Chiron 23♒14.5R
☽ Mean ☊ 8♊59.7

1 DECEMBER 1909
Julian Day # 3622
Delta T 10.3 sec
SVP 06♓31'20"
Obliquity 23°27'07"
⚷ Chiron 23♒37.9
☽ Mean ☊ 7♊24.4

LONGITUDE — JANUARY 1910

Day	Sid.Time	☉	0 hr ☽	Noon ☽	True ☊	☿	♀	♂	♃	♄	♅	♆	♇
1 Sa	6 39 3	9♑42 24	11♍29 36	17♍36 53	6♊56.9	25♑41.9	22♒47.4	17♈51.7	13♎16.5	16♈30.5	20♑29.5	18♋10.6	25♊36.4
2 Su	6 43 0	10 43 33	23 40 37	29 41 22	6R 53.7	27 12.5	23 26.9	18 23.2	13 21.6	16 31.9	20 33.0	18R 8.9	25R 35.2
3 M	6 46 56	11 44 42	5♎39 42	11♎36 12	6D 52.1	28 41.7	24 5.1	18 54.8	13 26.5	16 33.4	20 36.5	18 7.3	25 34.1
4 Tu	6 50 53	12 45 52	17 31 32	23 26 19	6 52.0	0♒ 9.2	24 42.0	19 26.6	13 31.3	16 35.0	20 40.0	18 5.6	25 32.9
5 W	6 54 50	13 47 1	29 21 13	5♏16 52	6 53.1	1 34.6	25 17.5	19 58.5	13 35.9	16 36.7	20 43.6	18 3.9	25 31.8
6 Th	6 58 46	14 48 11	11♏13 53	17 12 54	6 54.9	2 57.4	25 51.6	20 30.7	13 40.3	16 38.5	20 47.1	18 2.2	25 30.7
7 F	7 2 43	15 49 21	23 14 28	29 19 7	6 56.5	4 17.4	26 24.3	21 2.9	13 44.6	16 40.5	20 50.6	18 0.5	25 29.6
8 Sa	7 6 39	16 50 32	5♐27 20	11♐39 31	6R 57.4	5 33.8	26 55.4	21 35.3	13 48.7	16 42.5	20 54.2	17 58.8	25 28.5
9 Su	7 10 36	17 51 42	17 56 2	24 17 8	6 56.7	6 46.0	27 24.9	22 7.9	13 52.6	16 44.6	20 57.7	17 57.1	25 27.4
10 M	7 14 32	18 52 52	0♑42 59	7♑13 40	6 54.1	7 53.5	27 52.8	22 40.6	13 56.4	16 46.9	21 1.3	17 55.4	25 26.3
11 Tu	7 18 29	19 54 2	13 49 10	20 29 21	6 49.4	8 55.4	28 19.0	23 13.5	13 59.9	16 49.2	21 4.9	17 53.7	25 25.3
12 W	7 22 26	20 55 11	27 14 0	4♒ 2 48	6 42.9	9 50.9	28 43.4	23 46.5	14 3.3	16 51.7	21 8.4	17 52.0	25 24.2
13 Th	7 26 22	21 56 20	10♒55 23	17 51 18	6 35.1	10 39.2	29 6.0	24 19.6	14 6.5	16 54.3	21 12.0	17 50.3	25 23.1
14 F	7 30 19	22 57 29	24 50 2	1♓51 4	6 27.0	11 19.4	29 26.7	24 52.8	14 9.6	16 56.9	21 15.5	17 48.6	25 22.1
15 Sa	7 34 15	23 58 37	8♓53 54	15 58 1	6 19.5	11 50.5	29 45.4	25 26.2	14 12.4	16 59.7	21 19.1	17 46.9	25 21.1
16 Su	7 38 12	24 59 44	23 2 56	0♈ 8 15	6 13.6	12 11.8	0♓ 2.0	25 59.7	14 15.1	17 2.6	21 22.6	17 45.2	25 20.1
17 M	7 42 8	26 0 51	7♈13 35	14 18 38	6 9.8	12R 22.4	0 16.5	26 33.3	14 17.6	17 5.5	21 26.2	17 43.6	25 19.1
18 Tu	7 46 5	27 1 56	21 23 8	28 26 54	6D 8.1	12 21.9	0 28.9	27 7.1	14 19.9	17 8.6	21 29.7	17 41.9	25 18.1
19 W	7 50 1	28 3 1	5♉29 47	12♉31 40	6 8.2	12 9.7	0 39.0	27 40.9	14 22.0	17 11.8	21 33.3	17 40.2	25 17.1
20 Th	7 53 58	29 4 5	19 32 26	26 31 59	6 9.1	11 45.9	0 46.8	28 14.8	14 23.9	17 15.0	21 36.8	17 38.5	25 16.1
21 F	7 57 55	0♒ 5 8	3♊30 14	10♊27 1	6R 9.9	11 10.7	0 52.2	28 48.9	14 25.7	17 18.4	21 40.4	17 36.9	25 15.2
22 Sa	8 1 51	1 6 10	17 22 13	24 15 37	6 9.3	10 24.7	0R 55.2	29 23.0	14 27.2	17 21.8	21 43.9	17 35.3	25 14.2
23 Su	8 5 48	2 7 11	1♋ 7 1	7♋56 9	6 6.6	9 29.2	0 55.8	29 57.3	14 28.6	17 25.4	21 47.4	17 33.6	25 13.3
24 M	8 9 44	3 8 11	14 42 45	21 26 33	6 1.2	8 25.5	0 53.8	0♉31.6	14 29.8	17 29.0	21 50.9	17 32.0	25 12.4
25 Tu	8 13 41	4 9 10	28 7 14	4♌44 32	5 53.3	7 15.6	0 49.4	1 6.1	14 30.8	17 32.8	21 54.4	17 30.4	25 11.5
26 W	8 17 37	5 10 9	11♌18 14	17 48 7	5 43.2	6 1.6	0 42.4	1 40.6	14 31.6	17 36.6	21 57.9	17 28.8	25 10.6
27 Th	8 21 34	6 11 6	24 14 3	0♍35 57	5 31.8	4 45.8	0 32.8	2 15.2	14 32.2	17 40.5	22 1.4	17 27.2	25 9.7
28 F	8 25 30	7 12 3	6♍53 50	13 7 46	5 20.4	3 30.5	0 20.8	2 49.8	14 32.7	17 44.6	22 4.9	17 25.6	25 8.9
29 Sa	8 29 27	8 12 59	19 17 55	25 24 31	5 9.9	2 17.6	0 6.2	3 24.6	14R 32.9	17 48.7	22 8.3	17 24.0	25 8.1
30 Su	8 33 24	9 13 54	1♎27 55	7♎28 29	5 1.3	1 9.2	29♒49.2	3 59.4	14 33.0	17 52.8	22 11.8	17 22.5	25 7.2
31 M	8 37 20	10 14 48	13 26 41	19 23 2	4 55.1	0 6.7	29 29.8	4 34.3	14 32.8	17 57.1	22 15.2	17 20.9	25 6.4

LONGITUDE — FEBRUARY 1910

Day	Sid.Time	☉	0 hr ☽	Noon ☽	True ☊	☿	♀	♂	♃	♄	♅	♆	♇
1 Tu	8 41 17	11♒15 41	25♎18 7	1♏12 32	4♊51.4	29♑11.3	29♒ 8.0	5♉ 9.3	14♎32.5	18♈ 1.5	22♑18.6	17♋19.4	25♊ 5.7
2 W	8 45 13	12 16 34	7♏ 6 56	13 1 59	4D 49.9	28R 23.7	28R 44.0	5 44.4	14R 32.0	18 5.9	22 22.0	17R 17.9	25R 4.9
3 Th	8 49 10	13 17 26	18 58 23	24 56 50	4 49.9	27 44.5	28 17.9	6 19.5	14 31.2	18 10.5	22 25.4	17 16.4	25 4.1
4 F	8 53 6	14 18 17	0♐58 1	7♐ 2 35	4R 50.3	27 13.8	27 49.8	6 54.7	14 30.3	18 15.1	22 28.8	17 14.9	25 3.4
5 Sa	8 57 3	15 19 7	13 11 11	19 24 25	4 50.1	26 51.6	27 19.9	7 30.0	14 29.2	18 19.8	22 32.1	17 13.4	25 2.7
6 Su	9 0 59	16 19 56	25 42 48	2♑ 6 46	4 48.1	26 37.7	26 48.2	8 5.3	14 28.0	18 24.6	22 35.5	17 12.0	25 2.0
7 M	9 4 56	17 20 45	8♑36 40	15 12 44	4 43.7	26D 31.7	26 15.1	8 40.7	14 26.5	18 29.4	22 38.8	17 10.6	25 1.3
8 Tu	9 8 53	18 21 32	21 55 1	28 43 29	4 36.5	26 33.2	25 40.8	9 16.2	14 24.8	18 34.4	22 42.1	17 9.1	25 0.7
9 W	9 12 49	19 22 18	5♒37 54	12♒37 53	4 26.8	26 41.9	25 5.3	9 51.7	14 23.0	18 39.4	22 45.4	17 7.8	25 0.0
10 Th	9 16 46	20 23 3	19 42 53	26 52 14	4 15.2	26 57.1	24 29.0	10 27.3	14 20.9	18 44.5	22 48.6	17 6.4	24 59.4
11 F	9 20 42	21 23 46	4♓ 5 9	11♓20 44	4 3.1	27 18.4	23 52.2	11 3.0	14 18.7	18 49.7	22 51.9	17 5.0	24 58.8
12 Sa	9 24 39	22 24 28	18 38 4	25 56 14	3 51.7	27 45.3	23 15.0	11 38.7	14 16.3	18 54.9	22 55.1	17 3.7	24 58.2
13 Su	9 28 35	23 25 8	3♈14 22	10♈31 37	3 42.2	28 17.4	22 37.7	12 14.5	14 13.7	19 0.3	22 58.3	17 2.4	24 57.7
14 M	9 32 32	24 25 47	17 47 18	25 0 48	3 35.4	28 54.3	22 0.5	12 50.3	14 10.9	19 5.7	23 1.5	17 1.1	24 57.1
15 Tu	9 36 28	25 26 24	2♉11 40	9♉19 33	3 31.5	29 35.6	21 23.8	13 26.2	14 7.9	19 11.1	23 4.6	16 59.8	24 56.6
16 W	9 40 25	26 26 59	16 24 14	23 25 36	3D 30.0	0♒20.9	20 47.7	14 2.1	14 4.8	19 16.7	23 7.7	16 58.6	24 56.1
17 Th	9 44 22	27 27 33	0♊23 39	7♊18 24	3R 29.8	1 10.0	20 12.6	14 38.1	14 1.4	19 22.3	23 10.8	16 57.4	24 55.7
18 F	9 48 18	28 28 5	14 9 57	20 58 23	3 29.6	2 2.4	19 38.5	15 14.1	13 57.9	19 28.0	23 13.9	16 56.2	24 55.2
19 Sa	9 52 15	29 28 35	27 43 52	4♋26 28	3 28.1	2 58.0	19 5.8	15 50.1	13 54.3	19 33.7	23 17.0	16 55.0	24 54.8
20 Su	9 56 11	0♓29 3	11♋ 6 19	17 43 26	3 24.1	3 56.5	18 34.7	16 26.3	13 50.4	19 39.5	23 20.0	16 53.9	24 54.4
21 M	10 0 8	1 29 29	24 17 54	0♌49 41	3 17.1	4 57.7	18 5.3	17 2.4	13 46.4	19 45.4	23 23.0	16 52.8	24 54.0
22 Tu	10 4 4	2 29 53	7♌18 46	13 45 7	3 7.2	6 1.4	17 37.8	17 38.6	13 42.2	19 51.3	23 25.9	16 51.7	24 53.6
23 W	10 8 1	3 30 16	20 8 40	26 29 22	2 54.7	7 7.4	17 12.3	18 14.8	13 37.9	19 57.3	23 28.9	16 50.6	24 53.3
24 Th	10 11 57	4 30 37	2♍47 8	9♍ 1 58	2 40.8	8 15.6	16 49.0	18 51.1	13 33.4	20 3.4	23 31.8	16 49.6	24 52.9
25 F	10 15 54	5 30 56	15 13 52	21 22 51	2 26.6	9 25.9	16 27.9	19 27.3	13 28.7	20 9.5	23 34.6	16 48.6	24 52.6
26 Sa	10 19 51	6 31 14	27 29 0	3♎32 29	2 13.3	10 38.1	16 9.2	20 3.7	13 23.9	20 15.7	23 37.5	16 47.6	24 52.3
27 Su	10 23 47	7 31 29	9♎33 30	15 32 18	2 2.1	11 52.1	15 52.9	20 40.0	13 18.9	20 21.9	23 40.3	16 46.6	24 52.1
28 M	10 27 44	8 31 44	21 29 12	27 24 37	1 53.5	13 7.8	15 39.1	21 16.4	13 13.8	20 28.2	23 43.1	16 45.7	24 51.8

Astro Data	Dy Hr Mn
☽0S	3 9:00
☽0N	17 4:32
☿ R	17 10:52
♀ R	22 17:24
♄□♆	24 13:15
♃ R	29 18:10
☽0S	30 16:25
☿ D	7 6:52
☽0N	13 10:14
☽0S	26 23:25

Planet Ingress	Dy Hr Mn
☿ ♒	3 21:27
♀ ♓	15 20:56
☉ ♒	20 21:59
♂ ♉	23 1:54
♀ ♒	29 9:12
☿ ♑	31 2:44
☿ ♒	15 13:10
☉ ♓	19 12:28

Last Aspect Dy Hr Mn		☽ Ingress Dy Hr Mn
2 8:02	☿ △	♎ 2 12:37
4 16:15	♇ △	♏ 5 1:19
7 6:33	♀ □	♐ 7 13:20
9 18:32	♀ ✱	♑ 9 22:40
11 17:36	♂ □	♒ 12 4:53
14 8:05	♀ ☌	♓ 14 8:50
16 3:52	♇ □	♈ 16 11:46
18 10:20	☉ □	♉ 18 14:38
20 17:39	☉ △	♊ 20 17:58
22 21:52	♂ ✱	♋ 22 22:02
24 12:47	♅ ☍	♌ 25 3:24
27 1:44	♇ ✱	♍ 27 10:52
29 11:27	♇ □	♎ 29 21:05

Last Aspect Dy Hr Mn		☽ Ingress Dy Hr Mn
1 7:32	♀ △	♏ 1 9:33
3 18:00	♀ □	♐ 3 22:05
6 1:58	♀ ✱	♑ 6 8:03
8 8:15	☿ ☌	♒ 8 14:14
10 8:51	♇ △	♓ 10 17:13
12 15:32	☿ ✱	♈ 12 18:40
14 19:25	☿ □	♉ 14 20:19
16 18:32	☉ □	♊ 16 23:19
19 3:22	☉ △	♋ 19 4:03
20 22:19	♅ ☍	♌ 21 10:28
23 8:58	♇ ✱	♍ 23 18:41
25 18:51	♇ □	♎ 26 4:58
28 6:50	♇ △	♏ 28 17:16

☽ Phases & Eclipses Dy Hr Mn	
3 13:27	☽ 12♎19
11 11:51	● 20♑24
18 10:20	☽ 27♈28
25 11:50	○ 4♌39
2 11:27	☽ 12♏46
10 1:13	● 20♒26
16 18:32	☽ 27♉14
24 3:36	○ 4♍40

Astro Data

1 JANUARY 1910
Julian Day # 3653
Delta T 10.5 sec
SVP 06♓31'14"
Obliquity 23°27'07"
⚷ Chiron 24♒55.3
☽ Mean ☊ 5♊45.9

1 FEBRUARY 1910
Julian Day # 3684
Delta T 10.6 sec
SVP 06♓31'09"
Obliquity 23°27'08"
⚷ Chiron 26♒49.4
☽ Mean ☊ 4♊07.4

MARCH 1910 LONGITUDE

Day	Sid.Time	☉	0 hr ☽	Noon ☽	True ☊	☿	♀	♂	♃	♄	♅	♆	♇
1 Tu	10 31 40	9♓31 56	3♏18 58	9♏12 47	1♊47.8	14♒25.2	15♒27.7	21♉52.8	13♎ 8.5	20♈34.5	23♑45.8	16♋44.8	24♊51.6
2 W	10 35 37	10 32 7	15 6 35	21 1 0	1R 44.8	15 44.1	15R 18.8	22 29.2	13R 3.1	20 40.9	23 48.5	16R 43.9	24R 51.4
3 Th	10 39 33	11 32 17	26 56 39	2♐54 11	1D 43.8	17 4.6	15 12.5	23 5.7	12 57.5	20 47.4	23 51.2	16 43.1	24 51.3
4 F	10 43 30	12 32 25	8♐54 20	14 57 45	1R 43.8	18 26.5	15 8.6	23 42.2	12 51.8	20 53.9	23 53.9	16 42.3	24 51.1
5 Sa	10 47 26	13 32 32	21 5 9	27 17 12	1 43.7	19 49.8	15D 7.2	24 18.8	12 46.0	21 0.5	23 56.5	16 41.5	24 51.0
6 Su	10 51 23	14 32 37	3♑34 33	9♑57 46	1 42.3	21 14.4	15 8.2	24 55.3	12 40.0	21 7.1	23 59.0	16 40.7	24 50.9
7 M	10 55 20	15 32 40	16 27 23	23 3 46	1 38.7	22 40.4	15 11.6	25 31.9	12 33.9	21 13.7	24 1.6	16 40.0	24 50.8
8 Tu	10 59 16	16 32 42	29 47 14	6♒37 52	1 32.6	24 7.7	15 17.3	26 8.5	12 27.7	21 20.4	24 4.1	16 39.3	24 50.8
9 W	11 3 13	17 32 42	13♒35 37	20 40 15	1 24.0	25 36.3	15 25.3	26 45.2	12 21.3	21 27.2	24 6.6	16 38.6	24 50.7
10 Th	11 7 9	18 32 40	27 51 19	5♓ 8 8	1 13.5	27 6.1	15 35.6	27 21.9	12 14.9	21 34.0	24 9.0	16 38.0	24D 50.7
11 F	11 11 6	19 32 37	12♓29 53	19 55 33	1 2.3	28 37.1	15 47.9	27 58.6	12 8.3	21 40.8	24 11.4	16 37.4	24 50.7
12 Sa	11 15 2	20 32 31	27 24 1	4♈54 6	0 51.6	0♓ 9.4	16 2.4	28 35.3	12 1.6	21 47.7	24 13.7	16 36.8	24 50.7
13 Su	11 18 59	21 32 24	12♈24 34	19 54 16	0 42.7	1 42.9	16 18.9	29 12.0	11 54.9	21 54.6	24 16.0	16 36.3	24 50.8
14 M	11 22 55	22 32 14	27 22 6	4♉47 6	0 36.3	3 17.6	16 37.3	29 48.8	11 48.0	22 1.5	24 18.3	16 35.8	24 50.9
15 Tu	11 26 52	23 32 3	12♉ 8 29	19 25 37	0 32.6	4 53.5	16 57.7	0♊25.6	11 41.0	22 8.5	24 20.5	16 35.3	24 51.0
16 W	11 30 48	24 31 49	26 38 2	3♊45 28	0D 31.4	6 30.6	17 19.8	1 2.4	11 34.0	22 15.6	24 22.7	16 34.9	24 51.1
17 Th	11 34 45	25 31 33	10♊47 45	17 44 53	0 31.5	8 8.9	17 43.7	1 39.3	11 26.8	22 22.6	24 24.9	16 34.5	24 51.3
18 F	11 38 42	26 31 15	24 36 57	1♋24 8	0R 32.0	9 48.5	18 9.4	2 16.1	11 19.6	22 29.8	24 27.0	16 34.1	24 51.4
19 Sa	11 42 38	27 30 54	8♋ 6 39	14 44 46	0 31.5	11 29.3	18 36.6	2 53.0	11 12.3	22 36.9	24 29.1	16 33.8	24 51.6
20 Su	11 46 35	28 30 31	21 18 45	27 48 54	0 29.1	13 11.3	19 5.5	3 29.9	11 5.0	22 44.1	24 31.1	16 33.5	24 51.8
21 M	11 50 31	29 30 6	4♌15 28	10♌38 42	0 24.2	14 54.6	19 35.9	4 6.8	10 57.6	22 51.3	24 33.1	16 33.2	24 52.1
22 Tu	11 54 28	0♈29 39	16 58 50	23 16 4	0 16.8	16 39.1	20 7.7	4 43.7	10 50.1	22 58.5	24 35.0	16 33.0	24 52.3
23 W	11 58 24	1 29 9	29 30 35	5♍42 32	0 7.4	18 24.9	20 41.0	5 20.6	10 42.6	23 5.8	24 36.9	16 32.8	24 52.6
24 Th	12 2 21	2 28 37	11♍52 2	17 59 14	29♉56.7	20 12.0	21 15.6	5 57.6	10 35.0	23 13.1	24 38.7	16 32.6	24 52.9
25 F	12 6 17	3 28 3	24 4 16	0♎ 7 13	29 45.6	22 0.4	21 51.6	6 34.5	10 27.4	23 20.4	24 40.5	16 32.5	24 53.3
26 Sa	12 10 14	4 27 27	6♎ 8 16	12 7 32	29 35.4	23 50.1	22 28.8	7 11.5	10 19.8	23 27.7	24 42.3	16 32.3	24 53.6
27 Su	12 14 11	5 26 48	18 5 13	24 1 31	29 26.7	25 41.2	23 7.2	7 48.4	10 12.1	23 35.1	24 44.0	16 32.3	24 54.0
28 M	12 18 7	6 26 8	29 56 42	5♏51 2	29 20.1	27 33.5	23 46.7	8 25.4	10 4.5	23 42.5	24 45.7	16D 32.2	24 54.4
29 Tu	12 22 4	7 25 26	11♏44 52	17 38 34	29 16.0	29 27.2	24 27.4	9 2.4	9 56.7	23 49.9	24 47.3	16 32.2	24 54.8
30 W	12 26 0	8 24 42	23 32 34	29 27 19	29D 14.2	1♈22.2	25 9.2	9 39.4	9 49.0	23 57.3	24 48.9	16 32.3	24 55.2
31 Th	12 29 57	9 23 56	5♐23 20	11♐21 10	29 14.2	3 18.5	25 52.0	10 16.4	9 41.3	24 4.8	24 50.4	16 32.3	24 55.7

APRIL 1910 LONGITUDE

Day	Sid.Time	☉	0 hr ☽	Noon ☽	True ☊	☿	♀	♂	♃	♄	♅	♆	♇
1 F	12 33 53	10♈23 9	17♐21 23	23♐24 37	29♉15.3	5♈16.1	26♒35.8	10♊53.5	9♎33.6	24♈12.2	24♑51.9	16♋32.4	24♊56.2
2 Sa	12 37 50	11 22 19	29 31 28	5♑42 33	29 16.6	7 15.0	27 20.6	11 30.5	9R 25.8	24 19.7	24 53.3	16 32.5	24 56.7
3 Su	12 41 46	12 21 28	11♑58 32	18 19 58	29R 17.2	9 15.1	28 6.3	12 7.5	9 18.1	24 27.3	24 54.7	16 32.7	24 57.2
4 M	12 45 43	13 20 35	24 47 26	1♒21 24	29 16.5	11 16.3	28 52.8	12 44.6	9 10.4	24 34.8	24 56.1	16 32.9	24 57.7
5 Tu	12 49 40	14 19 41	8♒ 2 16	14 50 20	29 14.0	13 18.5	29 40.2	13 21.7	9 2.7	24 42.3	24 57.4	16 33.1	24 58.3
6 W	12 53 36	15 18 44	21 45 43	28 48 23	29 9.7	15 21.8	0♓28.4	13 58.7	8 55.0	24 49.9	24 58.6	16 33.4	24 58.9
7 Th	12 57 33	16 17 46	5♓58 6	13♓14 27	29 4.0	17 25.9	1 17.4	14 35.8	8 47.4	24 57.4	24 59.8	16 33.7	24 59.5
8 F	13 1 29	17 16 46	20 36 48	28 4 17	28 57.6	19 30.6	2 7.1	15 12.9	8 39.8	25 5.0	25 1.0	16 34.0	25 0.1
9 Sa	13 5 26	18 15 44	5♈35 54	13♈10 29	28 51.3	21 35.9	2 57.6	15 50.0	8 32.2	25 12.6	25 2.1	16 34.4	25 0.7
10 Su	13 9 22	19 14 40	20 46 46	28 23 28	28 46.1	23 41.5	3 48.7	16 27.1	8 24.7	25 20.2	25 3.1	16 34.8	25 1.4
11 M	13 13 19	20 13 34	5♉59 17	13♉33 0	28 42.5	25 47.2	4 40.5	17 4.3	8 17.2	25 27.8	25 4.1	16 35.2	25 2.1
12 Tu	13 17 15	21 12 26	21 3 30	28 29 50	28D 40.7	27 52.6	5 32.8	17 41.4	8 9.8	25 35.4	25 5.1	16 35.7	25 2.8
13 W	13 21 12	22 11 16	5♊51 14	13♊ 7 6	28 40.7	29 57.6	6 25.8	18 18.5	8 2.5	25 43.1	25 6.0	16 36.2	25 3.5
14 Th	13 25 9	23 10 4	20 17 0	27 20 43	28 41.8	2♉ 1.8	7 19.4	18 55.7	7 55.2	25 50.7	25 6.8	16 36.7	25 4.3
15 F	13 29 5	24 8 49	4♋18 9	11♋ 9 22	28 43.3	4 4.9	8 13.6	19 32.8	7 48.0	25 58.3	25 7.6	16 37.3	25 5.1
16 Sa	13 33 2	25 7 32	17 54 31	24 33 51	28R 44.4	6 6.5	9 8.2	20 10.0	7 40.9	26 5.9	25 8.4	16 37.9	25 5.8
17 Su	13 36 58	26 6 13	1♌ 7 41	7♌36 23	28 44.4	8 6.3	10 3.4	20 47.2	7 33.8	26 13.6	25 9.1	16 38.5	25 6.6
18 M	13 40 55	27 4 52	14 0 19	20 19 55	28 43.2	10 4.0	10 59.1	21 24.3	7 26.9	26 21.2	25 9.7	16 39.2	25 7.5
19 Tu	13 44 51	28 3 28	26 35 35	2♍47 41	28 40.5	11 59.3	11 55.3	22 1.5	7 20.0	26 28.8	25 10.3	16 39.9	25 8.3
20 W	13 48 48	29 2 3	8♍56 37	15 2 45	28 36.6	13 51.8	12 52.0	22 38.7	7 13.2	26 36.5	25 10.9	16 40.6	25 9.2
21 Th	13 52 44	0♉ 0 35	21 6 26	27 7 58	28 31.9	15 41.2	13 49.1	23 15.9	7 6.5	26 44.1	25 11.4	16 41.4	25 10.0
22 F	13 56 41	0 59 5	3♎ 7 40	9♎ 5 48	28 27.0	17 27.3	14 46.6	23 53.0	6 60.0	26 51.7	25 11.8	16 42.2	25 10.9
23 Sa	14 0 38	1 57 32	15 2 39	20 58 28	28 22.5	19 9.9	15 44.6	24 30.2	6 53.5	26 59.3	25 12.2	16 43.0	25 11.8
24 Su	14 4 34	2 55 58	26 53 30	2♏47 59	28 18.7	20 48.7	16 43.0	25 7.4	6 47.2	27 6.9	25 12.5	16 43.8	25 12.8
25 M	14 8 31	3 54 23	8♏42 12	14 36 24	28 16.1	22 23.6	17 41.7	25 44.6	6 40.9	27 14.5	25 12.8	16 44.7	25 13.7
26 Tu	14 12 27	4 52 45	20 30 51	26 25 50	28D 14.7	23 54.4	18 40.9	26 21.8	6 34.8	27 22.1	25 13.1	16 45.6	25 14.7
27 W	14 16 24	5 51 6	2♐21 41	8♐18 43	28 14.6	25 21.0	19 40.4	26 58.9	6 28.8	27 29.7	25 13.3	16 46.6	25 15.6
28 Th	14 20 20	6 49 25	14 17 20	20 17 53	28 15.3	26 43.2	20 40.3	27 36.1	6 22.9	27 37.3	25 13.4	16 47.5	25 16.6
29 F	14 24 17	7 47 42	26 20 48	2♑26 31	28 16.7	28 0.9	21 40.5	28 13.3	6 17.2	27 44.8	25 13.5	16 48.6	25 17.6
30 Sa	14 28 13	8 45 58	8♑35 31	14 48 15	28 18.3	29 14.1	22 41.1	28 50.5	6 11.6	27 52.4	25R 13.6	16 49.6	25 18.7

Astro Data	Planet Ingress	Last Aspect	☽ Ingress	Last Aspect	☽ Ingress	☽ Phases & Eclipses	Astro Data
Dy Hr Mn	Dy Hr Mn	Dy Hr Mn	Dy Hr Mn	Dy Hr Mn	Dy Hr Mn	Dy Hr Mn	1 MARCH 1910
♀ D 5 1:55	☿ ♓ 11 21:34	2 17:44 ♅ ⚹	♐ 3 6:10	1 19:27 ♀ ⚹	♑ 2 0:56	4 7:52 ☽ 12♐52	Julian Day # 3712
♇ D 10 1:16	♂ ♊ 14 7:17	5 7:18 ♇ ☍	♑ 5 17:12	4 0:16 ♅ ☌	♒ 4 9:32	11 12:12 ● 20♓03	Delta T 10.6 sec
☽0N 12 18:49	☉ ♈ 21 12:03	7 17:13 ♂ △	♒ 8 0:23	6 5:31 ♇ △	♓ 6 14:01	18 3:37 ☽ 26♊40	SVP 06♓31'05"
☽0S 26 5:56	☊ ♉ 23 16:41	9 23:09 ♂ □	♓ 10 3:33	8 7:06 ♅ ⚹	♈ 8 15:05	25 20:21 ○ 4♎18	Obliquity 23°27'08"
♆ D 28 16:14	☿ ♈ 29 6:52	12 1:59 ♂ ⚹	♈ 12 4:10	10 7:15 ♄ ☌	♉ 10 14:32		⚷ Chiron 28♒44.1
☿0N 31 6:11		13 19:56 ♇ ⚹	♉ 14 4:15	12 6:29 ♅ △	♊ 12 14:26	3 0:47 ☽ 12♑23	☽ Mean ☊ 2♊38.4
	♀ ♓ 5 9:53	15 20:13 ☉ ⚹	♊ 16 5:39	14 9:31 ♄ ⚹	♋ 14 16:33	9 21:25 ● 19♈08	
♅⊼♇ 6 10:19	☿ ♉ 13 0:28	18 3:37 ☉ □	♋ 18 9:31	16 14:56 ♄ □	♌ 16 21:56	16 14:04 ☽ 25♋42	1 APRIL 1910
♄⚹♇ 7 7:01	☉ ♉ 20 23:46	20 14:24 ☉ △	♌ 20 16:03	19 3:04 ☉ △	♍ 19 6:35	24 13:22 ○ 3♏29	Julian Day # 3743
♄□♅ 7 8:50	☿ ♊ 30 15:54	22 15:05 ♇ ⚹	♍ 23 0:57	21 8:08 ♅ △	♎ 21 17:44		Delta T 10.7 sec
☽0N 9 5:37		25 1:37 ♇ □	♎ 25 11:46	24 0:28 ♄ ☍	♏ 24 6:19		SVP 06♓31'02"
☽0S 22 12:10		27 13:47 ♇ △	♏ 28 0:07	26 9:33 ♅ ⚹	♐ 26 19:14		Obliquity 23°27'08"
♅⊼♇ 23 15:29		30 3:29 ♀ □	♐ 30 13:06	29 3:54 ♂ ☍	♑ 29 7:12		⚷ Chiron 0♓41.3
♅ R 30 10:51							☽ Mean ☊ 0♊59.9

LONGITUDE — MAY 1910

Day	Sid.Time	☉	0 hr ☽	Noon ☽	True ☊	☿	♀	♂	♃	♄	♅	♆	♇
1 Su	14 32 10	9♉44 12	21♑ 5 12	27♑26 50	28♉19.6	0♊22.6	23♓42.0	29♊27.7	6♎ 6.1	27♈59.9	25♑13.6	16♋50.7	25♊19.7
2 M	14 36 7	10 42 25	3♒53 38	10♒26 0	28R 20.4	1 26.5	24 43.2	0♋ 4.9	6R 0.8	28 7.4	25R 13.5	16 51.8	25 20.8
3 Tu	14 40 3	11 40 36	17 4 20	23 48 56	28 20.4	2 25.5	25 44.7	0 42.1	5 55.6	28 14.9	25 13.4	16 52.9	25 21.8
4 W	14 44 0	12 38 45	0♓40 0	7♓37 38	28 19.8	3 19.7	26 46.5	1 19.4	5 50.6	28 22.4	25 13.3	16 54.0	25 22.9
5 Th	14 47 56	13 36 54	14 41 48	21 52 19	28 18.5	4 8.9	27 48.6	1 56.6	5 45.7	28 29.9	25 13.1	16 55.2	25 24.0
6 F	14 51 53	14 35 1	29 8 50	6♈30 47	28 16.8	4 53.2	28 51.0	2 33.8	5 40.9	28 37.3	25 12.8	16 56.4	25 25.1
7 Sa	14 55 49	15 33 6	13♈57 28	21 28 2	28 15.2	5 32.4	29 53.6	3 11.0	5 36.4	28 44.8	25 12.5	16 57.6	25 26.3
8 Su	14 59 46	16 31 10	29 1 27	6♉36 35	28 14.0	6 6.6	0♈56.5	3 48.2	5 31.9	28 52.2	25 12.1	16 58.9	25 27.4
9 M	15 3 42	17 29 12	14♉12 16	21 47 16	28D 13.2	6 35.6	1 59.6	4 25.5	5 27.7	28 59.6	25 11.7	17 0.2	25 28.6
10 Tu	15 7 39	18 27 13	29 20 25	6♊50 36	28 12.9	6 59.6	3 2.9	5 2.7	5 23.5	29 6.9	25 11.3	17 1.5	25 29.7
11 W	15 11 36	19 25 13	14♊16 48	21 38 9	28 13.2	7 18.3	4 6.5	5 40.0	5 19.6	29 14.3	25 10.8	17 2.9	25 30.9
12 Th	15 15 32	20 23 10	28 53 57	6♋ 3 40	28 13.8	7 32.0	5 10.2	6 17.2	5 15.8	29 21.6	25 10.2	17 4.2	25 32.1
13 F	15 19 29	21 21 6	13♋ 6 56	20 3 32	28 14.4	7 40.6	6 14.2	6 54.5	5 12.2	29 28.9	25 9.7	17 5.7	25 33.3
14 Sa	15 23 25	22 19 1	26 53 27	3♌36 46	28 15.0	7R 44.2	7 18.4	7 31.7	5 8.8	29 36.2	25 9.0	17 7.1	25 34.5
15 Su	15 27 22	23 16 53	10♌13 41	16 44 31	28 15.3	7 42.9	8 22.8	8 9.0	5 5.5	29 43.4	25 8.3	17 8.5	25 35.8
16 M	15 31 18	24 14 44	23 9 39	29 29 30	28R 15.5	7 36.8	9 27.4	8 46.3	5 2.4	29 50.6	25 7.6	17 10.0	25 37.0
17 Tu	15 35 15	25 12 32	5♍44 33	11♍55 18	28 15.4	7 26.3	10 32.2	9 23.5	4 59.5	29 57.8	25 6.8	17 11.5	25 38.3
18 W	15 39 11	26 10 19	18 2 16	24 5 58	28 15.2	7 11.4	11 37.1	10 0.8	4 56.7	0♉ 4.9	25 6.0	17 13.0	25 39.5
19 Th	15 43 8	27 8 5	0♎ 6 55	6♎ 5 35	28 15.1	6 52.6	12 42.2	10 38.0	4 54.1	0 12.0	25 5.1	17 14.6	25 40.8
20 F	15 47 5	28 5 48	12 2 28	17 58 0	28D 15.0	6 30.1	13 47.5	11 15.3	4 51.7	0 19.1	25 4.2	17 16.1	25 42.1
21 Sa	15 51 1	29 3 31	23 52 37	29 46 43	28 15.0	6 4.4	14 53.0	11 52.5	4 49.5	0 26.1	25 3.2	17 17.7	25 43.3
22 Su	15 54 58	0♊ 1 12	5♏40 40	11♏34 50	28 15.2	5 36.0	15 58.6	12 29.8	4 47.5	0 33.1	25 2.2	17 19.4	25 44.6
23 M	15 58 54	0 58 51	17 29 33	23 25 5	28R 15.3	5 5.3	17 4.4	13 7.1	4 45.6	0 40.1	25 1.1	17 21.0	25 46.0
24 Tu	16 2 51	1 56 29	29 21 45	5♐19 49	28 15.4	4 32.9	18 10.4	13 44.3	4 43.9	0 47.0	25 0.0	17 22.7	25 47.3
25 W	16 6 47	2 54 6	11♐19 32	17 21 9	28 15.3	3 59.4	19 16.5	14 21.6	4 42.4	0 53.9	24 58.9	17 24.3	25 48.6
26 Th	16 10 44	3 51 42	23 24 55	29 31 4	28 14.9	3 25.4	20 22.8	14 58.9	4 41.1	1 0.7	24 57.7	17 26.0	25 49.9
27 F	16 14 40	4 49 16	5♑39 51	11♑51 31	28 14.2	2 51.4	21 29.2	15 36.1	4 39.9	1 7.6	24 56.5	17 27.8	25 51.3
28 Sa	16 18 37	5 46 50	18 6 20	24 24 31	28 13.3	2 18.1	22 35.8	16 13.4	4 39.0	1 14.3	24 55.2	17 29.5	25 52.6
29 Su	16 22 34	6 44 23	0♒46 22	7♒12 6	28 12.3	1 45.9	23 42.5	16 50.7	4 38.2	1 21.1	24 53.9	17 31.3	25 54.0
30 M	16 26 30	7 41 54	13 42 0	20 16 19	28 11.3	1 15.5	24 49.3	17 27.9	4 37.6	1 27.7	24 52.6	17 33.1	25 55.4
31 Tu	16 30 27	8 39 25	26 55 15	3♓39 0	28D 10.7	0 47.4	25 56.3	18 5.2	4 37.2	1 34.4	24 51.2	17 34.9	25 56.7

LONGITUDE — JUNE 1910

Day	Sid.Time	☉	0 hr ☽	Noon ☽	True ☊	☿	♀	♂	♃	♄	♅	♆	♇
1 W	16 34 23	9♊36 55	10♓27 44	17♓21 31	28♉10.4	0♊22.0	27♈ 3.4	18♋42.5	4♎36.9	1♉41.0	24♑49.8	17♋36.7	25♊58.1
2 Th	16 38 20	10 34 25	24 20 24	1♈24 19	28 10.7	29♉59.7	28 10.6	19 19.8	4D 36.8	1 47.5	24R 48.3	17 38.6	25 59.5
3 F	16 42 16	11 31 53	8♈33 5	15 46 27	28 11.5	29R 40.9	29 18.0	19 57.1	4 36.9	1 54.0	24 46.8	17 40.4	26 0.9
4 Sa	16 46 13	12 29 21	23 4 0	0♉25 14	28 12.5	29 25.8	0♉25.4	20 34.4	4 37.2	2 0.5	24 45.2	17 42.3	26 2.3
5 Su	16 50 9	13 26 48	7♉49 29	15 16 0	28 13.5	29 14.7	1 33.0	21 11.7	4 37.7	2 6.9	24 43.6	17 44.2	26 3.7
6 M	16 54 6	14 24 15	22 43 54	0♊12 15	28R 14.1	29 7.9	2 40.7	21 49.0	4 38.4	2 13.2	24 42.0	17 46.1	26 5.1
7 Tu	16 58 3	15 21 41	7♊40 3	15 6 17	28 14.0	29D 5.3	3 48.5	22 26.3	4 39.2	2 19.5	24 40.4	17 48.0	26 6.5
8 W	17 1 59	16 19 6	22 29 59	29 50 11	28 13.0	29 7.2	4 56.4	23 3.7	4 40.2	2 25.7	24 38.7	17 50.0	26 7.9
9 Th	17 5 56	17 16 30	7♋ 6 4	14♋16 54	28 11.1	29 13.6	6 4.4	23 41.0	4 41.4	2 31.9	24 37.0	17 52.0	26 9.3
10 F	17 9 52	18 13 53	21 22 5	28 21 10	28 8.6	29 24.5	7 12.5	24 18.3	4 42.8	2 38.1	24 35.2	17 53.9	26 10.7
11 Sa	17 13 49	19 11 16	5♌13 53	12♌ 0 6	28 5.8	29 39.9	8 20.7	24 55.7	4 44.3	2 44.1	24 33.4	17 55.9	26 12.1
12 Su	17 17 45	20 8 37	18 39 49	25 13 11	28 3.1	29 59.8	9 29.0	25 33.0	4 46.1	2 50.2	24 31.6	17 57.9	26 13.6
13 M	17 21 42	21 5 57	1♍40 27	8♍ 1 59	28 1.0	0♊24.1	10 37.4	26 10.4	4 48.0	2 56.1	24 29.7	17 60.0	26 15.0
14 Tu	17 25 38	22 3 17	14 18 13	20 29 39	27D 59.8	0 52.9	11 45.9	26 47.7	4 50.0	3 2.0	24 27.8	18 2.0	26 16.4
15 W	17 29 35	23 0 35	26 36 50	2♎40 20	27 59.6	1 26.0	12 54.5	27 25.1	4 52.3	3 7.8	24 25.9	18 4.0	26 17.9
16 Th	17 33 32	23 57 52	8♎40 46	14 38 44	28 0.4	2 3.3	14 3.1	28 2.4	4 54.7	3 13.6	24 24.0	18 6.1	26 19.3
17 F	17 37 28	24 55 9	20 34 49	26 29 37	28 1.9	2 44.9	15 11.9	28 39.8	4 57.3	3 19.3	24 22.0	18 8.2	26 20.7
18 Sa	17 41 25	25 52 25	2♏23 42	8♏17 37	28 3.6	3 30.6	16 20.7	29 17.2	5 0.1	3 25.0	24 20.0	18 10.3	26 22.1
19 Su	17 45 21	26 49 40	14 11 52	20 6 57	28 5.1	4 20.3	17 29.6	29 54.5	5 3.0	3 30.6	24 18.0	18 12.4	26 23.6
20 M	17 49 18	27 46 55	26 3 18	2♐ 1 20	28R 5.8	5 14.0	18 38.6	0♌31.9	5 6.1	3 36.1	24 15.9	18 14.5	26 25.0
21 Tu	17 53 14	28 44 9	8♐ 1 23	14 3 47	28 5.4	6 11.7	19 47.7	1 9.3	5 9.4	3 41.5	24 13.9	18 16.6	26 26.4
22 W	17 57 11	29 41 22	20 8 47	26 16 38	28 3.5	7 13.2	20 56.8	1 46.7	5 12.8	3 46.9	24 11.8	18 18.7	26 27.9
23 Th	18 1 8	0♋38 35	2♑27 30	8♑41 32	28 0.2	8 18.5	22 6.1	2 24.1	5 16.4	3 52.3	24 9.6	18 20.8	26 29.3
24 F	18 5 4	1 35 48	14 58 49	21 19 27	27 55.5	9 27.5	23 15.4	3 1.5	5 20.2	3 57.5	24 7.5	18 23.0	26 30.7
25 Sa	18 9 1	2 33 1	27 43 27	4♒10 50	27 50.0	10 40.2	24 24.8	3 38.9	5 24.1	4 2.7	24 5.3	18 25.1	26 32.2
26 Su	18 12 57	3 30 13	10♒41 37	17 15 47	27 44.2	11 56.6	25 34.3	4 16.3	5 28.1	4 7.8	24 3.1	18 27.3	26 33.6
27 M	18 16 54	4 27 25	23 53 19	0♓34 10	27 38.9	13 16.5	26 43.9	4 53.7	5 32.4	4 12.9	24 0.9	18 29.5	26 35.0
28 Tu	18 20 50	5 24 37	7♓18 21	14 5 50	27 34.7	14 40.1	27 53.5	5 31.1	5 36.8	4 17.8	23 58.7	18 31.7	26 36.4
29 W	18 24 47	6 21 49	20 56 34	27 50 32	27 32.0	16 7.1	29 3.2	6 8.5	5 41.3	4 22.7	23 56.4	18 33.8	26 37.8
30 Th	18 28 43	7 19 1	4♈47 42	11♈47 59	27D 31.0	17 37.7	0♊13.0	6 46.0	5 46.0	4 27.5	23 54.2	18 36.0	26 39.3

Astro Data

	Dy Hr Mn
☽0N	6 16:25
♀0N	9 23:38
☿ R	14 5:30
☽0S	19 18:24
♃ D	1 21:14
☽0N	3 1:10
☿ D	7 1:50
☽0S	16 1:00
☽0N	30 7:14

Planet Ingress

	Dy Hr Mn
♂ ♋	1 20:49
♀ ♈	7 2:27
♄ ♉	17 7:30
☉ ♊	21 23:30
☿ ♉	1 23:39
♀ ♉	3 14:58
☿ ♊	12 0:14
♂ ♌	19 3:30
☉ ♋	22 7:49
♀ ♊	29 19:32

Last Aspect / ☽ Ingress

Last Aspect Dy Hr Mn		☽ Ingress Dy Hr Mn
1 13:10	♄ □	♒ 1 16:46
3 19:58	♄ ✶	♓ 3 22:50
5 23:28	♀ ☌	♈ 6 1:24
7 23:45	♄ ☌	♉ 8 1:33
9 17:24	♅ △	♊ 10 1:03
12 0:46	♄ ✶	♋ 12 1:50
14 4:52	♄ □	♌ 14 5:32
16 12:48	♄ △	♍ 16 12:58
18 17:32	☉ △	♎ 18 23:46
21 3:45	♀ ☍	♏ 21 12:27
23 15:13	♅ ✶	♐ 24 1:17
26 4:46	♇ ☍	♑ 26 12:57
28 12:57	♅ ☌	♒ 28 22:33
30 22:15	♇ △	♓ 31 5:31

Last Aspect / ☽ Ingress

Last Aspect Dy Hr Mn		☽ Ingress Dy Hr Mn
2 9:24	☿ ✶	♈ 2 9:37
4 4:52	♇ ✶	♉ 4 11:19
6 10:14	☿ ☌	♊ 6 11:40
8 5:56	♇ ☌	♋ 8 12:16
10 14:05	☿ ✶	♌ 10 14:51
12 13:53	♇ ✶	♍ 12 20:52
15 1:40	♂ ✶	♎ 15 6:42
17 17:19	♂ □	♏ 17 19:08
19 20:24	♅ ✶	♐ 20 7:56
22 12:23	♇ ☍	♑ 22 19:14
24 17:13	♅ ☌	♒ 25 4:15
27 5:36	♀ □	♓ 27 10:59
29 15:23	♀ ✶	♈ 29 15:44

☽ Phases & Eclipses

Dy Hr Mn		
2 13:29	☽	11♒15
9 5:33	●	17♉43
9 5:42:02	☊ T	4'15"
16 2:13	☽	24♌20
24 5:39	○	2♐10
24 5:34	☋ T	1.095
31 22:24	☽	9♓33
7 13:16	●	15♊53
14 16:19	☽	22♍42
22 20:12	○	0♑30
30 4:39	☽	7♈30

Astro Data

1 MAY 1910
Julian Day # 3773
Delta T 10.8 sec
SVP 06♓30'58"
Obliquity 23°27'08"
⚷ Chiron 2♓04.3
☽ Mean ☊ 29♉24.6

1 JUNE 1910
Julian Day # 3804
Delta T 10.9 sec
SVP 06♓30'53"
Obliquity 23°27'08"
⚷ Chiron 2♓42.3
☽ Mean ☊ 27♉46.1

JULY 1910 LONGITUDE

Day	Sid.Time	☉	0 hr ☽	Noon ☽	True ☊	☿	♀	♂	♃	♄	♅	♆	♇
1 F	18 32 40	8♋16 14	18♈51 17	25♈57 29	27♉31.3	19♊11.6	1♊22.9	7♌23.4	5♎50.9	4♉32.3	23♑51.9	18♋38.2	26♊40.7
2 Sa	18 36 37	9 13 26	3♉ 6 23	10♉17 43	27 32.5	20 49.0	2 32.8	8 0.9	5 55.9	4 36.9	23R49.6	18 40.4	26 42.1
3 Su	18 40 33	10 10 39	17 31 9	24 46 16	27R33.6	22 29.6	3 42.8	8 38.3	6 1.1	4 41.5	23 47.3	18 42.6	26 43.5
4 M	18 44 30	11 7 52	2♊ 2 34	9♊19 28	27 33.9	24 13.5	4 52.9	9 15.8	6 6.4	4 46.1	23 45.0	18 44.8	26 44.9
5 Tu	18 48 26	12 5 6	16 36 19	23 52 23	27 32.5	26 0.5	6 3.1	9 53.3	6 11.8	4 50.5	23 42.6	18 47.1	26 46.3
6 W	18 52 23	13 2 19	1♋ 6 54	8♋19 8	27 29.1	27 50.6	7 13.3	10 30.8	6 17.4	4 54.8	23 40.3	18 49.3	26 47.7
7 Th	18 56 19	13 59 33	15 28 19	22 33 43	27 23.6	29 43.5	8 23.6	11 8.3	6 23.2	4 59.1	23 37.9	18 51.5	26 49.0
8 F	19 0 16	14 56 47	29 34 44	6♌30 48	27 16.6	1♋39.1	9 33.9	11 45.8	6 29.1	5 3.3	23 35.5	18 53.7	26 50.4
9 Sa	19 4 12	15 54 0	13♌21 30	20 6 32	27 8.7	3 37.2	10 44.3	12 23.4	6 35.2	5 7.4	23 33.2	18 56.0	26 51.8
10 Su	19 8 9	16 51 14	26 45 43	3♍19 3	27 1.0	5 37.6	11 54.8	13 0.9	6 41.3	5 11.4	23 30.8	18 58.2	26 53.2
11 M	19 12 6	17 48 28	9♍46 37	16 8 37	26 54.2	7 40.0	13 5.4	13 38.4	6 47.7	5 15.4	23 28.4	19 0.4	26 54.5
12 Tu	19 16 2	18 45 41	22 25 23	28 37 19	26 49.0	9 44.2	14 15.9	14 16.0	6 54.1	5 19.2	23 26.0	19 2.7	26 55.9
13 W	19 19 59	19 42 55	4♎44 54	10♎48 42	26 45.8	11 49.9	15 26.6	14 53.6	7 0.7	5 23.0	23 23.6	19 4.9	26 57.2
14 Th	19 23 55	20 40 8	16 49 17	22 47 18	26D44.5	13 56.8	16 37.3	15 31.1	7 7.5	5 26.6	23 21.2	19 7.1	26 58.5
15 F	19 27 52	21 37 22	28 43 24	4♏38 14	26 44.7	16 4.6	17 48.1	16 8.7	7 14.3	5 30.2	23 18.8	19 9.3	26 59.9
16 Sa	19 31 48	22 34 36	10♏32 29	16 26 46	26 45.6	18 13.0	18 58.9	16 46.3	7 21.3	5 33.7	23 16.4	19 11.6	27 1.2
17 Su	19 35 45	23 31 50	22 21 45	28 18 1	26R46.4	20 21.6	20 9.8	17 23.9	7 28.5	5 37.1	23 13.9	19 13.8	27 2.5
18 M	19 39 41	24 29 4	4♐16 8	10♐16 39	26 46.2	22 30.2	21 20.7	18 1.5	7 35.7	5 40.5	23 11.5	19 16.0	27 3.8
19 Tu	19 43 38	25 26 18	16 20 1	22 26 40	26 44.2	24 38.6	22 31.8	18 39.1	7 43.1	5 43.7	23 9.1	19 18.2	27 5.1
20 W	19 47 35	26 23 33	28 36 56	4♑51 5	26 40.0	26 46.4	23 42.8	19 16.8	7 50.6	5 46.8	23 6.7	19 20.5	27 6.3
21 Th	19 51 31	27 20 48	11♑ 9 21	17 31 49	26 33.4	28 53.5	24 54.0	19 54.4	7 58.2	5 49.9	23 4.3	19 22.7	27 7.6
22 F	19 55 28	28 18 4	23 58 31	0♒29 26	26 24.8	0♌59.7	26 5.2	20 32.0	8 6.0	5 52.8	23 1.9	19 24.9	27 8.9
23 Sa	19 59 24	29 15 20	7♒ 4 26	13 43 18	26 14.7	3 4.7	27 16.4	21 9.7	8 13.9	5 55.7	22 59.5	19 27.1	27 10.1
24 Su	20 3 21	0♌12 37	20 25 50	27 11 43	26 4.2	5 8.6	28 27.7	21 47.4	8 21.9	5 58.4	22 57.2	19 29.3	27 11.4
25 M	20 7 17	1 9 54	4♓ 0 38	10♓52 15	25 54.4	7 11.2	29 39.1	22 25.1	8 30.0	6 1.1	22 54.8	19 31.5	27 12.6
26 Tu	20 11 14	2 7 12	17 46 14	24 42 17	25 46.2	9 12.3	0♋50.5	23 2.8	8 38.2	6 3.7	22 52.4	19 33.7	27 13.8
27 W	20 15 10	3 4 31	1♈40 6	8♈39 25	25 40.2	11 11.9	2 2.0	23 40.5	8 46.5	6 6.1	22 50.0	19 35.9	27 15.0
28 Th	20 19 7	4 1 51	15 40 1	22 41 43	25 36.8	13 10.0	3 13.6	24 18.2	8 55.0	6 8.5	22 47.7	19 38.0	27 16.2
29 F	20 23 4	4 59 12	29 44 21	6♉47 48	25D35.6	15 6.5	4 25.2	24 55.9	9 3.5	6 10.8	22 45.3	19 40.2	27 17.4
30 Sa	20 27 0	5 56 34	13♉51 55	20 56 35	25R35.6	17 1.4	5 36.9	25 33.7	9 12.2	6 13.0	22 43.0	19 42.4	27 18.6
31 Su	20 30 57	6 53 58	28 1 40	5♊ 6 58	25 35.8	18 54.7	6 48.6	26 11.5	9 21.0	6 15.0	22 40.7	19 44.5	27 19.7

AUGUST 1910 LONGITUDE

Day	Sid.Time	☉	0 hr ☽	Noon ☽	True ☊	☿	♀	♂	♃	♄	♅	♆	♇
1 M	20 34 53	7♌51 22	12♊12 17	19♊17 21	25♉34.9	20♌46.3	8♋ 0.4	26♌49.3	9♎29.9	6♉17.0	22♑38.4	19♋46.7	27♊20.8
2 Tu	20 38 50	8 48 48	26 21 49	3♋25 18	25R31.9	22 36.3	9 12.3	27 27.1	9 38.9	6 18.9	22R36.1	19 48.8	27 22.0
3 W	20 42 46	9 46 15	10♋27 23	17 27 35	25 26.2	24 24.7	10 24.2	28 4.9	9 48.0	6 20.7	22 33.8	19 50.9	27 23.1
4 Th	20 46 43	10 43 43	24 25 24	1♌20 19	25 17.7	26 11.5	11 36.2	28 42.7	9 57.2	6 22.4	22 31.6	19 53.0	27 24.2
5 F	20 50 39	11 41 12	8♌11 52	14 59 36	25 7.1	27 56.7	12 48.2	29 20.6	10 6.5	6 23.9	22 29.3	19 55.2	27 25.3
6 Sa	20 54 36	12 38 42	21 43 6	28 22 4	24 55.2	29 40.2	14 0.3	29 58.5	10 15.9	6 25.4	22 27.1	19 57.3	27 26.4
7 Su	20 58 33	13 36 13	4♍56 16	11♍25 35	24 43.3	1♍22.2	15 12.4	0♍36.4	10 25.4	6 26.8	22 24.9	19 59.3	27 27.4
8 M	21 2 29	14 33 44	17 50 0	24 9 35	24 32.4	3 2.6	16 24.6	1 14.3	10 35.0	6 28.0	22 22.7	20 1.4	27 28.5
9 Tu	21 6 26	15 31 17	0♎24 32	6♎35 8	24 23.5	4 41.4	17 36.8	1 52.2	10 44.7	6 29.2	22 20.6	20 3.5	27 29.5
10 W	21 10 22	16 28 50	12 41 45	18 44 51	24 17.1	6 18.6	18 49.1	2 30.1	10 54.5	6 30.2	22 18.4	20 5.5	27 30.5
11 Th	21 14 19	17 26 25	24 44 55	0♏42 32	24 13.3	7 54.3	20 1.4	3 8.1	11 4.4	6 31.2	22 16.3	20 7.5	27 31.5
12 F	21 18 15	18 24 0	6♏38 20	12 32 57	24 11.6	9 28.4	21 13.8	3 46.0	11 14.4	6 32.0	22 14.2	20 9.6	27 32.5
13 Sa	21 22 12	19 21 36	18 27 4	24 21 21	24 11.3	11 0.9	22 26.3	4 24.0	11 24.5	6 32.8	22 12.2	20 11.6	27 33.4
14 Su	21 26 8	20 19 14	0♐16 31	6♐13 15	24 11.2	12 31.9	23 38.8	5 2.0	11 34.6	6 33.4	22 10.1	20 13.6	27 34.4
15 M	21 30 5	21 16 52	12 12 11	18 13 59	24 10.4	14 1.2	24 51.3	5 40.0	11 44.9	6 33.9	22 8.1	20 15.5	27 35.3
16 Tu	21 34 2	22 14 31	24 19 14	0♑28 28	24 7.8	15 29.0	26 3.9	6 18.0	11 55.2	6 34.4	22 6.1	20 17.5	27 36.2
17 W	21 37 58	23 12 12	6♑42 9	13 0 42	24 2.9	16 55.2	27 16.6	6 56.1	12 5.6	6 34.7	22 4.2	20 19.4	27 37.1
18 Th	21 41 55	24 9 53	19 24 22	25 53 23	23 55.3	18 19.8	28 29.3	7 34.2	12 16.1	6 34.9	22 2.2	20 21.4	27 38.0
19 F	21 45 51	25 7 36	2♒27 49	9♒ 7 36	23 45.4	19 42.7	29 42.0	8 12.2	12 26.7	6R35.0	22 0.4	20 23.3	27 38.9
20 Sa	21 49 48	26 5 20	15 52 34	22 42 27	23 33.8	21 3.9	0♌54.8	8 50.3	12 37.3	6 35.0	21 58.5	20 25.2	27 39.7
21 Su	21 53 44	27 3 5	29 36 50	6♓35 12	23 21.7	22 23.4	2 7.6	9 28.4	12 48.1	6 34.9	21 56.7	20 27.1	27 40.5
22 M	21 57 41	28 0 52	13♓36 59	20 41 35	23 10.2	23 41.2	3 20.6	10 6.6	12 58.9	6 34.7	21 54.9	20 28.9	27 41.3
23 Tu	22 1 37	28 58 40	27 48 18	4♈56 32	23 0.6	24 57.1	4 33.5	10 44.7	13 9.7	6 34.4	21 53.1	20 30.8	27 42.1
24 W	22 5 34	29 56 29	12♈ 5 38	19 15 3	22 53.5	26 11.2	5 46.5	11 22.9	13 20.7	6 34.0	21 51.3	20 32.6	27 42.9
25 Th	22 9 31	0♍54 21	26 24 16	3♉32 53	22 49.2	27 23.3	6 59.6	12 1.1	13 31.7	6 33.4	21 49.6	20 34.4	27 43.6
26 F	22 13 27	1 52 14	10♉40 32	17 46 58	22D47.4	28 33.4	8 12.7	12 39.3	13 42.8	6 32.8	21 48.0	20 36.2	27 44.4
27 Sa	22 17 24	2 50 9	24 51 59	1♊55 26	22R47.1	29 41.4	9 25.9	13 17.5	13 54.0	6 32.1	21 46.3	20 37.9	27 45.1
28 Su	22 21 20	3 48 6	8♊57 14	15 57 19	22 47.1	0♎47.2	10 39.1	13 55.8	14 5.2	6 31.2	21 44.7	20 39.7	27 45.8
29 M	22 25 17	4 46 5	22 55 37	29 52 3	22 46.1	1 50.8	11 52.4	14 34.1	14 16.5	6 30.3	21 43.2	20 41.4	27 46.5
30 Tu	22 29 13	5 44 5	6♋46 34	13♋39 2	22 43.0	2 51.9	13 5.7	15 12.4	14 27.9	6 29.2	21 41.7	20 43.1	27 47.1
31 W	22 33 10	6 42 8	20 29 19	27 17 16	22 37.3	3 50.4	14 19.1	15 50.7	14 39.3	6 28.1	21 40.2	20 44.8	27 47.8

Astro Data Dy Hr Mn	Planet Ingress Dy Hr Mn	Last Aspect Dy Hr Mn	☽ Ingress Dy Hr Mn	Last Aspect Dy Hr Mn	☽ Ingress Dy Hr Mn	☽ Phases & Eclipses Dy Hr Mn	Astro Data
☽0S 13 8:05	☿ ♋ 7 3:28	1 13:14 ♇ ✶	♉ 1 18:48	2 1:56 ♂ ✶	♋ 2 6:11	6 21:20 ● 13♋53	1 JULY 1910
☽0N 27 11:54	☿ ♌ 21 12:38	3 10:21 ♅ △	♊ 3 20:38	3 20:44 ♅ ☍	♌ 4 9:40	14 8:24 ☽ 21♎00	Julian Day # 3834
	☉ ♌ 23 18:43	5 17:46 ☿ ☌	♋ 5 22:09	6 10:20 ♇ ✶	♍ 6 14:58	22 8:37 ○ 28♑39	Delta T 11.0 sec
☽0S 9 15:32	♀ ♋ 25 7:01	7 13:47 ♅ ☍	♌ 8 0:43	8 18:22 ♇ □	♎ 8 23:13	29 9:34 ☽ 5♉22	SVP 06♓30'48"
♄ R 19 12:50		10 0:14 ♇ ✶	♍ 10 5:54	11 5:35 ♇ △	♏ 11 10:34		Obliquity 23°27'08"
☽0N 23 17:28	☿ ♍ 6 4:37	12 8:44 ♇ □	♎ 12 14:41	13 9:02 ♀ △	♐ 13 23:27	5 6:37 ● 11♌57	⚷ Chiron 2♓26.0R
☿0S 24 15:15	♂ ♍ 6 0:58	14 20:30 ♇ △	♏ 15 2:35	16 6:26 ♇ ☍	♑ 16 11:05	13 2:01 ☽ 19♏26	☽ Mean ☊ 26♉10.8
	♀ ♌ 19 5:56	17 2:34 ☉ △	♐ 17 15:25	18 18:28 ♀ ☍	♒ 18 19:31	20 19:14 ○ 26♒52	
	☉ ♍ 24 1:27	19 21:04 ♇ ☍	♑ 20 2:41	20 20:38 ♇ △	♓ 21 0:40	27 14:33 ☽ 3♊25	1 AUGUST 1910
	☿ ♎ 27 6:42	22 8:37 ☉ ☍	♒ 22 11:06	22 23:50 ♇ □	♈ 23 3:42		Julian Day # 3865
		24 15:36 ♀ △	♓ 24 16:57	25 2:13 ♇ ✶	♉ 25 6:02		Delta T 11.1 sec
		26 16:23 ♇ □	♈ 26 21:08	26 18:46 ♅ △	♊ 27 8:43		SVP 06♓30'43"
		28 19:49 ♇ ✶	♉ 29 0:27	29 8:23 ♇ ☌	♋ 29 12:14		Obliquity 23°27'08"
		30 20:45 ♂ □	♊ 31 3:20	31 2:05 ♅ ☍	♌ 31 16:48		⚷ Chiron 1♓21.7R
							☽ Mean ☊ 24♉32.4

LONGITUDE — SEPTEMBER 1910

Day	Sid.Time	☉	0 hr ☽	Noon ☽	True ☊	☿	♀	♂	♃	♄	♅	♆	♇
1 Th	22 37 6	7♍40 13	4♌ 2 40	10♌45 19	22♉28.9	4♎46.2	15♌32.5	16♍29.1	14♎50.9	6♉26.8	21♑38.8	20♋46.4	27♊48.4
2 F	22 41 3	8 38 19	17 25 0	24 1 28	22R 18.3	5 39.2	16 46.0	17 7.4	15 2.4	6R 25.5	21R 37.3	20 48.1	27 49.0
3 Sa	22 45 0	9 36 27	0♍34 31	7♍ 3 59	22 6.3	6 29.1	17 59.5	17 45.8	15 14.0	6 24.0	21 36.0	20 49.7	27 49.5
4 Su	22 48 56	10 34 36	13 29 42	19 51 37	21 54.2	7 15.7	19 13.0	18 24.3	15 25.7	6 22.5	21 34.7	20 51.3	27 50.1
5 M	22 52 53	11 32 48	26 9 40	2♎23 55	21 43.1	7 58.9	20 26.6	19 2.7	15 37.5	6 20.8	21 33.4	20 52.8	27 50.6
6 Tu	22 56 49	12 31 1	8♎34 29	14 41 33	21 33.9	8 38.3	21 40.3	19 41.2	15 49.3	6 19.0	21 32.1	20 54.4	27 51.1
7 W	23 0 46	13 29 15	20 45 21	26 46 16	21 27.2	9 13.8	22 54.0	20 19.6	16 1.1	6 17.2	21 30.9	20 55.9	27 51.6
8 Th	23 4 42	14 27 31	2♏44 39	8♏40 59	21 23.2	9 45.0	24 7.7	20 58.1	16 13.1	6 15.2	21 29.8	20 57.4	27 52.1
9 F	23 8 39	15 25 49	14 35 47	20 29 37	21D 21.4	10 11.7	25 21.5	21 36.7	16 25.0	6 13.1	21 28.7	20 58.9	27 52.5
10 Sa	23 12 35	16 24 9	26 23 4	2♐16 48	21 21.3	10 33.5	26 35.3	22 15.2	16 37.0	6 11.0	21 27.6	21 0.3	27 53.0
11 Su	23 16 32	17 22 30	8♐11 27	14 7 42	21R 21.9	10 50.1	27 49.1	22 53.8	16 49.1	6 8.7	21 26.6	21 1.7	27 53.4
12 M	23 20 29	18 20 52	20 6 15	26 7 47	21 22.2	11 1.2	29 3.0	23 32.4	17 1.2	6 6.4	21 25.6	21 3.1	27 53.7
13 Tu	23 24 25	19 19 17	2♑12 56	8♑22 20	21 21.2	11R 6.4	0♍17.0	24 11.0	17 13.4	6 4.0	21 24.7	21 4.5	27 54.1
14 W	23 28 22	20 17 43	14 36 36	20 56 12	21 18.4	11 5.5	1 31.0	24 49.6	17 25.6	6 1.4	21 23.8	21 5.8	27 54.5
15 Th	23 32 18	21 16 10	27 21 37	3♒53 10	21 13.3	10 58.2	2 45.0	25 28.3	17 37.9	5 58.8	21 23.0	21 7.1	27 54.8
16 F	23 36 15	22 14 39	10♒31 4	17 15 23	21 6.1	10 44.1	3 59.0	26 7.0	17 50.2	5 56.1	21 22.2	21 8.4	27 55.1
17 Sa	23 40 11	23 13 10	24 6 5	1♓ 2 55	20 57.4	10 23.2	5 13.1	26 45.7	18 2.5	5 53.3	21 21.5	21 9.7	27 55.3
18 Su	23 44 8	24 11 42	8♓ 5 30	15 13 17	20 48.1	9 55.3	6 27.2	27 24.4	18 14.9	5 50.4	21 20.8	21 10.9	27 55.6
19 M	23 48 4	25 10 17	22 25 37	29 41 42	20 39.2	9 20.4	7 41.4	28 3.2	18 27.3	5 47.4	21 20.1	21 12.1	27 55.8
20 Tu	23 52 1	26 8 53	7♈ 0 38	14♈21 30	20 31.8	8 38.8	8 55.6	28 42.0	18 39.8	5 44.3	21 19.5	21 13.2	27 56.0
21 W	23 55 58	27 7 31	21 43 23	29 5 21	20 26.5	7 50.8	10 9.8	29 20.8	18 52.3	5 41.2	21 19.0	21 14.4	27 56.2
22 Th	23 59 54	28 6 11	6♉26 35	13♉46 17	20D 23.6	6 57.0	11 24.1	29 59.6	19 4.8	5 38.0	21 18.5	21 15.5	27 56.4
23 F	0 3 51	29 4 54	21 3 50	28 18 40	20 22.8	5 58.3	12 38.4	0♎38.5	19 17.4	5 34.7	21 18.0	21 16.6	27 56.5
24 Sa	0 7 47	0♎ 3 38	5♊30 22	12♊38 39	20 23.4	4 55.6	13 52.8	1 17.4	19 30.0	5 31.3	21 17.6	21 17.6	27 56.6
25 Su	0 11 44	1 2 26	19 43 17	26 44 10	20R 24.5	3 50.3	15 7.2	1 56.3	19 42.6	5 27.8	21 17.2	21 18.7	27 56.7
26 M	0 15 40	2 1 15	3♋41 14	10♋34 32	20 24.9	2 43.8	16 21.6	2 35.2	19 55.3	5 24.3	21 16.9	21 19.7	27 56.8
27 Tu	0 19 37	3 0 7	17 24 4	24 9 56	20 23.9	1 37.7	17 36.1	3 14.2	20 8.0	5 20.7	21 16.7	21 20.6	27 56.9
28 W	0 23 33	3 59 1	0♌52 13	7♌31 0	20 20.9	0 33.9	18 50.6	3 53.2	20 20.7	5 17.0	21 16.5	21 21.6	27R 56.9
29 Th	0 27 30	4 57 57	14 6 22	20 38 23	20 15.9	29♍34.0	20 5.2	4 32.2	20 33.5	5 13.2	21 16.3	21 22.5	27 56.9
30 F	0 31 27	5 56 56	27 7 7	3♍32 38	20 9.2	28 39.5	21 19.7	5 11.3	20 46.3	5 9.4	21 16.2	21 23.3	27 56.9

LONGITUDE — OCTOBER 1910

Day	Sid.Time	☉	0 hr ☽	Noon ☽	True ☊	☿	♀	♂	♃	♄	♅	♆	♇
1 Sa	0 35 23	6♎55 56	9♍54 59	16♍14 11	20♉ 1.6	27♍52.1	22♍34.3	5♎50.4	20♎59.1	5♉ 5.5	21♑16.1	21♋24.2	27♊56.9
2 Su	0 39 20	7 54 59	22 30 20	28 43 27	19R 53.7	27R 13.0	23 49.0	6 29.5	21 11.9	5R 1.5	21D 16.1	21 25.0	27R 56.8
3 M	0 43 16	8 54 4	4♎53 39	11♎ 1 2	19 46.6	26 43.1	25 3.6	7 8.6	21 24.8	4 57.5	21 16.2	21 25.7	27 56.7
4 Tu	0 47 13	9 53 11	17 5 44	23 7 55	19 40.8	26 23.3	26 18.3	7 47.8	21 37.7	4 53.4	21 16.3	21 26.5	27 56.6
5 W	0 51 9	10 52 19	29 7 47	5♏ 5 37	19 36.7	26D 13.9	27 33.0	8 27.0	21 50.6	4 49.3	21 16.4	21 27.2	27 56.5
6 Th	0 55 6	11 51 30	11♏ 1 41	16 56 21	19D 34.6	26 15.1	28 47.8	9 6.2	22 3.5	4 45.1	21 16.6	21 27.9	27 56.3
7 F	0 59 2	12 50 43	22 49 59	28 43 2	19 34.3	26 26.8	0♎ 2.6	9 45.5	22 16.5	4 40.8	21 16.9	21 28.5	27 56.2
8 Sa	1 2 59	13 49 58	4♐35 58	10♐29 19	19 35.2	26 48.8	1 17.4	10 24.8	22 29.4	4 36.5	21 17.2	21 29.1	27 56.0
9 Su	1 6 55	14 49 15	16 23 36	22 19 26	19 36.9	27 20.6	2 32.2	11 4.1	22 42.4	4 32.1	21 17.5	21 29.7	27 55.7
10 M	1 10 52	15 48 33	28 17 23	4♑18 7	19 38.7	28 1.6	3 47.0	11 43.4	22 55.4	4 27.7	21 17.9	21 30.3	27 55.5
11 Tu	1 14 49	16 47 53	10♑22 13	16 30 21	19R 39.8	28 51.0	5 1.9	12 22.8	23 8.4	4 23.3	21 18.4	21 30.8	27 55.3
12 W	1 18 45	17 47 16	22 43 6	29 1 4	19 39.9	29 48.2	6 16.8	13 2.2	23 21.4	4 18.8	21 18.9	21 31.3	27 55.0
13 Th	1 22 42	18 46 39	5♒24 46	11♒54 40	19 38.6	0♎52.4	7 31.7	13 41.6	23 34.4	4 14.3	21 19.5	21 31.7	27 54.7
14 F	1 26 38	19 46 5	18 31 8	25 14 28	19 36.0	2 2.8	8 46.6	14 21.1	23 47.4	4 9.7	21 20.1	21 32.1	27 54.3
15 Sa	1 30 35	20 45 32	2♓ 4 46	9♓ 2 3	19 32.4	3 18.6	10 1.6	15 0.6	24 0.5	4 5.1	21 20.7	21 32.5	27 54.0
16 Su	1 34 31	21 45 1	16 6 6	23 16 35	19 28.3	4 39.1	11 16.6	15 40.1	24 13.5	4 0.5	21 21.5	21 32.8	27 53.6
17 M	1 38 28	22 44 32	0♈32 57	7♈54 30	19 24.3	6 3.6	12 31.6	16 19.6	24 26.6	3 55.8	21 22.2	21 33.2	27 53.2
18 Tu	1 42 24	23 44 5	15 20 21	22 49 31	19 20.9	7 31.6	13 46.6	16 59.2	24 39.6	3 51.1	21 23.0	21 33.4	27 52.8
19 W	1 46 21	24 43 39	0♉20 54	7♉53 23	19 18.7	9 2.4	15 1.6	17 38.8	24 52.7	3 46.4	21 23.9	21 33.7	27 52.4
20 Th	1 50 18	25 43 16	15 25 49	22 57 6	19D 17.8	10 35.5	16 16.6	18 18.4	25 5.7	3 41.6	21 24.8	21 33.9	27 51.9
21 F	1 54 14	26 42 55	0♊26 11	7♊52 11	19 18.1	12 10.6	17 31.7	18 58.1	25 18.8	3 36.9	21 25.8	21 34.1	27 51.5
22 Sa	1 58 11	27 42 36	15 14 18	22 31 54	19 19.1	13 47.3	18 46.8	19 37.8	25 31.8	3 32.1	21 26.8	21 34.2	27 51.0
23 Su	2 2 7	28 42 20	29 44 29	6♋51 44	19 20.5	15 25.1	20 1.9	20 17.5	25 44.9	3 27.3	21 27.8	21 34.3	27 50.5
24 M	2 6 4	29 42 6	13♋53 27	20 49 32	19 21.7	17 3.8	21 17.1	20 57.2	25 58.0	3 22.5	21 29.0	21 34.4	27 49.9
25 Tu	2 10 0	0♏41 54	27 40 3	4♌25 6	19R 22.3	18 43.3	22 32.2	21 37.0	26 11.0	3 17.7	21 30.1	21R 34.4	27 49.4
26 W	2 13 57	1 41 44	11♌ 4 52	17 39 37	19 22.1	20 23.1	23 47.4	22 16.9	26 24.1	3 12.9	21 31.3	21 34.4	27 48.8
27 Th	2 17 53	2 41 37	24 9 37	0♍35 11	19 21.0	22 3.3	25 2.6	22 56.7	26 37.1	3 8.0	21 32.6	21 34.4	27 48.2
28 F	2 21 50	3 41 31	6♍56 36	13 14 13	19 19.3	23 43.6	26 17.8	23 36.6	26 50.1	3 3.2	21 33.9	21 34.4	27 47.6
29 Sa	2 25 47	4 41 28	19 28 19	25 39 14	19 17.2	25 24.0	27 33.0	24 16.5	27 3.2	2 58.4	21 35.3	21 34.3	27 47.0
30 Su	2 29 43	5 41 27	1♎47 15	7♎52 38	19 15.0	27 4.3	28 48.2	24 56.5	27 16.2	2 53.6	21 36.7	21 34.1	27 46.3
31 M	2 33 40	6 41 27	13 55 39	19 56 35	19 13.1	28 44.4	0♏ 3.5	25 36.5	27 29.2	2 48.7	21 38.1	21 34.0	27 45.6

Astro Data	Planet Ingress	Last Aspect	☽ Ingress	Last Aspect	☽ Ingress	☽ Phases & Eclipses	Astro Data
Dy Hr Mn	Dy Hr Mn	Dy Hr Mn	Dy Hr Mn	Dy Hr Mn	Dy Hr Mn	Dy Hr Mn	1 SEPTEMBER 1910
☽0S 5 23:00	♀ ♍ 12 18:29	2 18:57 ♇ ⚹	♍ 2 22:57	2 10:30 ♇ □	♎ 2 14:28	3 18:06 ● 10♍20	Julian Day # 3896
☿ R 13 8:36	♂ ♎ 22 0:15	5 3:14 ♇ □	♎ 5 7:22	4 21:37 ♇ △	♏ 5 1:45	11 20:10 ☽ 18♐12	Delta T 11.2 sec
☽0N 20 1:37	☉ ♎ 23 22:31	7 14:12 ♇ △	♏ 7 18:29	7 7:34 ☿ ⚹	♐ 7 14:37	19 4:52 ○ 25♓22	SVP 06♓30'38"
♅☍♆ 23 23:12	☿ ♍ 28 13:20	10 0:28 ♀ □	♐ 10 7:22	9 23:26 ☿ □	♑ 10 3:25	25 20:54 ☽ 1♋54	Obliquity 23°27'09"
♂0S 24 23:21		12 15:30 ♇ ☍	♑ 12 19:39	12 1:15 ♃ □	♒ 12 13:51		⚷ Chiron 29♒52.4R
♇ R 28 20:28	♀ ♎ 6 23:11	14 20:18 ♂ △	♒ 15 4:53	14 16:42 ♇ △	♓ 14 20:22	3 8:32 ● 9♎15	☽ Mean ☊ 22♉53.9
☿0N 1 8:21	☿ ♎ 12 4:36	17 6:37 ♇ △	♓ 17 10:12	16 19:38 ♇ □	♈ 16 23:06	11 13:40 ☽ 17♑22	
♅ D 1 15:05	☉ ♏ 24 7:11	19 9:44 ♂ ☍	♈ 19 12:30	18 20:03 ♇ ⚹	♉ 18 23:27	18 14:24 ○ 24♈20	1 OCTOBER 1910
♃□♅ 2 7:52	♀ ♏ 30 22:53	21 10:07 ♇ ⚹	♉ 21 13:29	20 9:47 ♆ ⚹	♊ 20 23:18	25 5:48 ☽ 0♌56	Julian Day # 3926
☽0S 3 6:02	☿ ♏ 31 18:09	23 14:15 ☉ △	♊ 23 14:49	22 22:08 ☉ △	♋ 23 0:26		Delta T 11.3 sec
♃□♆ 3 1:53	☽0N 17 12:11	25 14:05 ♇ ☌	♋ 25 17:37	24 21:21 ♃ □	♌ 25 4:08		SVP 06♓30'35"
☿ D 5 9:16	♆ R 25 17:30	27 6:59 ♆ ☌	♌ 27 22:26	27 6:47 ♇ ⚹	♍ 27 10:54		Obliquity 23°27'10"
♀0S 9 16:17	♅☍♆ 28 7:42	30 1:33 ♇ ⚹	♍ 30 5:22	29 16:08 ♇ □	♎ 29 20:30		⚷ Chiron 28♒34.4R
☿0S 15 21:55	☽0S 30 12:21						☽ Mean ☊ 21♉18.5

NOVEMBER 1910 LONGITUDE

Day	Sid.Time	☉	0 hr ☽	Noon ☽	True ☊	☿	♀	♂	♃	♄	♅	♆	♇
1 Tu	2 37 36	7♏41 30	25♎55 39	1♏53 8	19♉11.6	0♏24.4	1♏18.7	26♎16.5	27♎42.1	2♉43.9	21♑39.6	21♋33.8	27♊44.9
2 W	2 41 33	8 41 35	7♏49 14	13 44 15	19D10.7	2 4.0	2 34.0	26 56.6	27 55.1	2R39.1	21 41.2	21R33.5	27R44.2
3 Th	2 45 29	9 41 42	19 38 24	25 31 59	19 10.5	3 43.4	3 49.3	27 36.7	28 8.1	2 34.4	21 42.8	21 33.3	27 43.5
4 F	2 49 26	10 41 50	1♐25 16	7♐18 35	19 10.7	5 22.5	5 4.6	28 16.8	28 21.0	2 29.6	21 44.4	21 33.0	27 42.8
5 Sa	2 53 22	11 42 1	13 12 16	19 6 40	19 11.3	7 1.2	6 19.9	28 56.9	28 33.9	2 24.9	21 46.1	21 32.6	27 42.0
6 Su	2 57 19	12 42 13	25 2 11	0♑59 13	19 12.1	8 39.6	7 35.2	29 37.1	28 46.8	2 20.1	21 47.8	21 32.3	27 41.2
7 M	3 1 16	13 42 26	6♑58 13	12 59 40	19 12.8	10 17.6	8 50.6	0♏17.3	28 59.7	2 15.4	21 49.6	21 31.9	27 40.4
8 Tu	3 5 12	14 42 42	19 4 2	25 11 51	19 13.3	11 55.3	10 5.9	0 57.6	29 12.5	2 10.8	21 51.4	21 31.4	27 39.6
9 W	3 9 9	15 42 58	1♒23 37	7♒39 51	19 13.6	13 32.6	11 21.3	1 37.9	29 25.4	2 6.2	21 53.3	21 31.0	27 38.8
10 Th	3 13 5	16 43 16	14 1 4	20 27 45	19R13.8	15 9.5	12 36.6	2 18.2	29 38.2	2 1.6	21 55.2	21 30.5	27 37.9
11 F	3 17 2	17 43 36	27 0 19	3♓39 11	19 13.7	16 46.1	13 52.0	2 58.5	29 50.9	1 57.0	21 57.2	21 30.0	27 37.1
12 Sa	3 20 58	18 43 57	10♓24 37	17 16 50	19D13.7	18 22.3	15 7.3	3 38.9	0♏ 3.7	1 52.5	21 59.2	21 29.4	27 36.2
13 Su	3 24 55	19 44 19	24 15 54	1♈21 45	19 13.7	19 58.3	16 22.7	4 19.3	0 16.4	1 48.0	22 1.2	21 28.8	27 35.3
14 M	3 28 51	20 44 43	8♈34 10	15 52 43	19 13.8	21 33.9	17 38.1	4 59.7	0 29.1	1 43.6	22 3.3	21 28.2	27 34.4
15 Tu	3 32 48	21 45 8	23 16 51	0♉45 46	19 14.0	23 9.2	18 53.4	5 40.2	0 41.7	1 39.2	22 5.5	21 27.5	27 33.5
16 W	3 36 45	22 45 34	8♉18 32	15 54 7	19R14.1	24 44.2	20 8.8	6 20.7	0 54.3	1 34.8	22 7.6	21 26.8	27 32.5
17 Th	3 40 41	23 46 2	23 31 18	1♊ 8 51	19 14.2	26 19.0	21 24.2	7 1.2	1 6.9	1 30.6	22 9.8	21 26.1	27 31.6
18 F	3 44 38	24 46 32	8♊45 31	16 20 4	19 14.0	27 53.5	22 39.6	7 41.8	1 19.4	1 26.3	22 12.1	21 25.4	27 30.6
19 Sa	3 48 34	25 47 3	23 51 22	1♋18 23	19 13.4	29 27.8	23 55.0	8 22.4	1 31.9	1 22.2	22 14.4	21 24.6	27 29.7
20 Su	3 52 31	26 47 37	8♋40 14	15 56 14	19 12.6	1♐ 1.9	25 10.4	9 3.1	1 44.4	1 18.0	22 16.7	21 23.8	27 28.7
21 M	3 56 27	27 48 11	23 5 52	0♌ 8 48	19 11.7	2 35.8	26 25.8	9 43.7	1 56.8	1 14.0	22 19.1	21 23.0	27 27.7
22 Tu	4 0 24	28 48 48	7♌ 4 52	13 54 5	19 10.8	4 9.5	27 41.2	10 24.5	2 9.2	1 10.0	22 21.5	21 22.1	27 26.7
23 W	4 4 21	29 49 26	20 36 35	27 12 36	19D10.2	5 43.0	28 56.7	11 5.2	2 21.5	1 6.1	22 24.0	21 21.2	27 25.6
24 Th	4 8 17	0♐50 6	3♍42 30	10♍ 6 42	19 10.0	7 16.4	0♐12.1	11 46.0	2 33.8	1 2.2	22 26.4	21 20.3	27 24.6
25 F	4 12 14	1 50 47	16 25 40	22 39 53	19 10.4	8 49.6	1 27.5	12 26.8	2 46.1	0 58.4	22 29.0	21 19.3	27 23.6
26 Sa	4 16 10	2 51 30	28 49 54	4♎56 14	19 11.4	10 22.7	2 43.0	13 7.7	2 58.3	0 54.7	22 31.5	21 18.3	27 22.5
27 Su	4 20 7	3 52 15	10♎59 22	16 59 49	19 12.7	11 55.7	3 58.4	13 48.6	3 10.4	0 51.0	22 34.1	21 17.3	27 21.4
28 M	4 24 3	4 53 1	22 58 4	28 54 34	19 14.2	13 28.5	5 13.9	14 29.5	3 22.5	0 47.4	22 36.8	21 16.3	27 20.3
29 Tu	4 28 0	5 53 48	4♏49 44	10♏43 57	19 15.3	15 1.3	6 29.4	15 10.5	3 34.5	0 43.9	22 39.4	21 15.2	27 19.3
30 W	4 31 56	6 54 37	16 37 36	22 31 0	19R15.9	16 33.9	7 44.8	15 51.5	3 46.5	0 40.5	22 42.1	21 14.1	27 18.2

DECEMBER 1910 LONGITUDE

Day	Sid.Time	☉	0 hr ☽	Noon ☽	True ☊	☿	♀	♂	♃	♄	♅	♆	♇
1 Th	4 35 53	7♐55 27	28♏24 27	4♐18 15	19♉15.7	18♐ 6.5	9♐ 0.3	16♏32.5	3♏58.4	0♉37.2	22♑44.9	21♋13.0	27♊17.0
2 F	4 39 50	8 56 19	10♐12 40	16 7 56	19R14.3	19 38.9	10 15.8	17 13.6	4 10.3	0R33.9	22 47.6	21R11.9	27R15.9
3 Sa	4 43 46	9 57 12	22 4 19	28 2 1	19 11.9	21 11.2	11 31.2	17 54.7	4 22.1	0 30.8	22 50.4	21 10.7	27 14.8
4 Su	4 47 43	10 58 5	4♑ 1 17	10♑ 2 22	19 8.6	22 43.3	12 46.7	18 35.8	4 33.9	0 27.7	22 53.3	21 9.5	27 13.7
5 M	4 51 39	11 59 0	16 5 31	22 10 58	19 4.7	24 15.4	14 2.2	19 17.0	4 45.6	0 24.7	22 56.1	21 8.3	27 12.5
6 Tu	4 55 36	12 59 56	28 19 2	4♒30 0	19 0.6	25 47.2	15 17.7	19 58.2	4 57.2	0 21.8	22 59.0	21 7.1	27 11.4
7 W	4 59 32	14 0 52	10♒44 11	17 1 55	18 56.9	27 18.8	16 33.1	20 39.5	5 8.7	0 19.0	23 2.0	21 5.8	27 10.3
8 Th	5 3 29	15 1 49	23 23 33	29 49 26	18 54.1	28 50.4	17 48.6	21 20.7	5 20.2	0 16.2	23 4.9	21 4.5	27 9.1
9 F	5 7 25	16 2 47	6♓19 56	12♓55 22	18D52.4	0♑21.3	19 4.1	22 2.0	5 31.6	0 13.6	23 7.9	21 3.2	27 7.9
10 Sa	5 11 22	17 3 45	19 36 5	26 22 20	18 52.0	1 52.1	20 19.5	22 43.4	5 43.0	0 11.1	23 10.9	21 1.9	27 6.8
11 Su	5 15 19	18 4 44	3♈14 22	10♈12 17	18 52.8	3 22.4	21 35.0	23 24.7	5 54.3	0 8.7	23 13.9	21 0.5	27 5.6
12 M	5 19 15	19 5 44	17 16 9	24 25 53	18 54.2	4 52.2	22 50.5	24 6.1	6 5.5	0 6.3	23 17.0	20 59.1	27 4.4
13 Tu	5 23 12	20 6 44	1♉41 14	9♉ 1 49	18 55.8	6 21.5	24 5.9	24 47.6	6 16.6	0 4.1	23 20.1	20 57.8	27 3.2
14 W	5 27 8	21 7 44	16 27 5	23 56 18	18R56.6	7 50.0	25 21.4	25 29.1	6 27.6	0 2.0	23 23.2	20 56.3	27 2.1
15 Th	5 31 5	22 8 46	1♊28 33	9♊ 2 50	18 56.0	9 17.6	26 36.8	26 10.6	6 38.6	29♈59.9	23 26.3	20 54.9	27 0.9
16 F	5 35 1	23 9 47	16 37 58	24 12 44	18 53.8	10 44.2	27 52.3	26 52.1	6 49.5	29 58.0	23 29.5	20 53.5	26 59.7
17 Sa	5 38 58	24 10 50	1♋45 52	9♋16 11	18 49.8	12 9.5	29 7.7	27 33.7	7 0.3	29 56.2	23 32.7	20 52.0	26 58.5
18 Su	5 42 54	25 11 53	16 42 30	24 3 50	18 44.5	13 33.4	0♑23.2	28 15.3	7 11.0	29 54.5	23 35.9	20 50.5	26 57.3
19 M	5 46 51	26 12 57	1♌19 18	8♌28 16	18 38.6	14 55.6	1 38.6	28 57.0	7 21.7	29 52.8	23 39.1	20 49.0	26 56.1
20 Tu	5 50 48	27 14 2	15 30 16	22 25 1	18 32.7	16 15.7	2 54.1	29 38.7	7 32.2	29 51.3	23 42.4	20 47.5	26 55.0
21 W	5 54 44	28 15 7	29 12 27	5♍52 40	18 27.9	17 33.4	4 9.5	0♐20.4	7 42.7	29 49.9	23 45.7	20 46.0	26 53.8
22 Th	5 58 41	29 16 13	12♍25 55	18 52 34	18 24.6	18 48.3	5 25.0	1 2.2	7 53.1	29 48.6	23 48.9	20 44.5	26 52.6
23 F	6 2 37	0♑17 19	25 13 5	1♎28 1	18D23.0	19 59.8	6 40.4	1 44.0	8 3.3	29 47.4	23 52.3	20 42.9	26 51.4
24 Sa	6 6 34	1 18 27	7♎37 58	13 43 35	18 23.0	21 7.5	7 55.8	2 25.8	8 13.5	29 46.3	23 55.6	20 41.3	26 50.2
25 Su	6 10 30	2 19 35	19 45 31	25 44 24	18 24.2	22 10.7	9 11.3	3 7.7	8 23.6	29 45.4	23 58.9	20 39.7	26 49.0
26 M	6 14 27	3 20 43	1♏40 54	7♏35 37	18 25.8	23 8.7	10 26.7	3 49.6	8 33.6	29 44.5	24 2.3	20 38.1	26 47.8
27 Tu	6 18 23	4 21 53	13 29 10	19 22 7	18R26.9	24 0.8	11 42.1	4 31.5	8 43.5	29 43.7	24 5.7	20 36.5	26 46.6
28 W	6 22 20	5 23 2	25 14 57	1♐ 8 11	18 26.8	24 46.1	12 57.6	5 13.5	8 53.3	29 43.1	24 9.1	20 34.9	26 45.5
29 Th	6 26 17	6 24 12	7♐ 2 13	12 57 27	18 24.7	25 23.8	14 13.0	5 55.5	9 3.0	29 42.6	24 12.5	20 33.3	26 44.3
30 F	6 30 13	7 25 23	18 54 12	24 52 45	18 20.2	25 52.9	15 28.4	6 37.6	9 12.6	29 42.2	24 15.9	20 31.7	26 43.1
31 Sa	6 34 10	8 26 34	0♑53 20	6♑56 9	18 13.4	26 12.6	16 43.9	7 19.7	9 22.1	29 41.9	24 19.3	20 30.0	26 42.0

Astro Data Dy Hr Mn	Planet Ingress Dy Hr Mn	Last Aspect Dy Hr Mn	☽ Ingress Dy Hr Mn	Last Aspect Dy Hr Mn	☽ Ingress Dy Hr Mn	☽ Phases & Eclipses Dy Hr Mn	Astro Data
♃△♇ 1 4:54	♂ ♏ 6 13:39	1 3:40 ♇ △	♏ 1 8:12	30 12:26 ♅ ⚹	♐ 1 3:15	2 1:56 ● 8♏46	1 NOVEMBER 1910
☽0N 13 23:12	♃ ♏ 11 17:04	3 4:14 ♅ ⚹	♐ 3 21:06	3 10:24 ♇ ☍	♑ 3 15:57	2 2:08:20 ● P 0.852	Julian Day # 3957
♃☍♄ 18 9:55	☿ ♐ 19 8:12	6 9:48 ♂ ⚹	♑ 6 10:01	5 13:32 ♅ ☌	♒ 6 3:17	10 5:29 ☽ 16♒57	Delta T 11.4 sec
☽0S 26 18:12	☉ ♐ 23 4:11	8 20:08 ♃ □	♒ 8 21:19	8 11:31 ☿ ⚹	♓ 8 12:20	17 0:25 ○ 23♉47	SVP 06♓30'32"
	♀ ♐ 23 20:09	11 5:14 ♃ △	♓ 11 5:26	10 13:17 ♇ □	♈ 10 18:22	17 0:21 ● T 1.125	Obliquity 23°27'09"
☽0N 11 8:08		13 5:38 ♇ □	♈ 13 9:43	12 16:22 ♇ ⚹	♉ 12 21:13	23 18:13 ☽ 0♍35	⚷ Chiron 27♒53.1R
☽0S 24 0:22	☿ ♑ 8 18:22	15 6:52 ♇ ⚹	♉ 15 10:47	14 15:10 ♂ ☍	♊ 14 21:39		☽ Mean ☊ 19♉40.0
	♄ ♈ 14 23:08	17 4:54 ☿ ☍	♊ 17 10:12	16 21:06 ♄ ⚹	♋ 16 21:11	1 21:10 ● 8♐49	
	♀ ♑ 17 16:38	19 5:50 ♇ ☌	♋ 19 9:53	18 21:37 ♄ □	♌ 18 21:48	9 19:05 ☽ 16♓51	1 DECEMBER 1910
	♂ ♐ 20 12:16	21 8:37 ☉ △	♌ 21 11:45	21 1:07 ♄ △	♍ 21 1:25	16 11:05 ○ 23♊38	Julian Day # 3987
	☉ ♑ 22 17:12	23 16:48 ♀ □	♍ 23 17:08	23 3:08 ♇ □	♎ 23 9:10	23 10:36 ☽ 0♎44	Delta T 11.4 sec
		25 21:09 ♇ □	♎ 26 2:17	25 20:05 ♄ ☍	♏ 25 20:36	31 16:21 ● 9♑08	SVP 06♓30'27"
		28 8:49 ♇ △	♏ 28 14:12	27 22:57 ☿ ⚹	♐ 28 9:41		Obliquity 23°27'09"
				30 21:38 ♄ △	♑ 30 22:14		⚷ Chiron 28♒06.6
							☽ Mean ☊ 18♉04.7

LONGITUDE JANUARY 1911

Day	Sid.Time	☉	0 hr ☽	Noon ☽	True ☊	☿	♀	♂	♃	♄	♅	♆	♇
1 Su	6 38 6	9♑27 44	13♑ 1 21	19♑ 9 3	18♉ 4.6	26♑21.9	17♑59.3	8♐ 1.8	9♏31.5	29♈41.7	24♑22.8	20♋28.4	26♊40.8
2 M	6 42 3	10 28 55	25 19 21	1♒32 19	17R 54.4	26R 20.2	19 14.7	8 44.0	9 40.8	29D 41.6	24 26.3	20R 26.7	26R 39.7
3 Tu	6 45 59	11 30 6	7♒48 1	14 6 30	17 43.8	26 6.9	20 30.1	9 26.2	9 49.9	29 41.6	24 29.7	20 25.0	26 38.5
4 W	6 49 56	12 31 17	20 27 50	26 52 7	17 33.8	25 41.7	21 45.5	10 8.4	9 59.0	29 41.8	24 33.2	20 23.3	26 37.4
5 Th	6 53 53	13 32 27	3♓19 25	9♓49 53	17 25.4	25 4.8	23 0.9	10 50.7	10 7.9	29 42.0	24 36.7	20 21.7	26 36.2
6 F	6 57 49	14 33 37	16 23 37	23 0 47	17 19.3	24 16.6	24 16.3	11 32.9	10 16.7	29 42.4	24 40.2	20 20.0	26 35.1
7 Sa	7 1 46	15 34 47	29 41 35	6♈26 11	17 15.7	23 18.2	25 31.7	12 15.3	10 25.4	29 42.9	24 43.7	20 18.3	26 34.0
8 Su	7 5 42	16 35 56	13♈14 45	20 7 27	17D 14.5	22 11.1	26 47.0	12 57.6	10 33.9	29 43.4	24 47.2	20 16.6	26 32.9
9 M	7 9 39	17 37 5	27 4 26	4♉ 5 44	17 14.7	20 57.3	28 2.4	13 40.0	10 42.4	29 44.2	24 50.7	20 14.9	26 31.7
10 Tu	7 13 35	18 38 13	11♉11 22	18 21 13	17R 15.4	19 39.2	29 17.7	14 22.4	10 50.7	29 45.0	24 54.3	20 13.2	26 30.7
11 W	7 17 32	19 39 21	25 35 3	2♊52 32	17 15.2	18 19.2	0♒33.1	15 4.9	10 58.9	29 45.9	24 57.8	20 11.5	26 29.6
12 Th	7 21 28	20 40 28	10♊13 9	17 36 14	17 13.1	16 60.0	1 48.4	15 47.4	11 7.0	29 46.9	25 1.3	20 9.8	26 28.5
13 F	7 25 25	21 41 35	25 1 0	2♋26 32	17 8.4	15 43.9	3 3.7	16 29.9	11 14.9	29 48.1	25 4.9	20 8.1	26 27.4
14 Sa	7 29 22	22 42 41	9♋51 49	17 15 48	17 1.0	14 33.0	4 19.0	17 12.5	11 22.7	29 49.4	25 8.4	20 6.4	26 26.4
15 Su	7 33 18	23 43 47	24 37 23	1♌55 34	16 51.2	13 29.1	5 34.3	17 55.0	11 30.4	29 50.7	25 12.0	20 4.7	26 25.3
16 M	7 37 15	24 44 52	9♌ 9 21	16 17 57	16 40.2	12 33.4	6 49.5	18 37.7	11 38.0	29 52.2	25 15.5	20 3.0	26 24.3
17 Tu	7 41 11	25 45 57	23 20 39	0♍16 58	16 29.0	11 46.7	8 4.8	19 20.3	11 45.4	29 53.8	25 19.0	20 1.3	26 23.3
18 W	7 45 8	26 47 1	7♍ 6 34	13 49 20	16 19.0	11 9.4	9 20.1	20 3.0	11 52.7	29 55.5	25 22.6	19 59.7	26 22.3
19 Th	7 49 4	27 48 5	20 25 17	26 54 36	16 11.1	10 41.6	10 35.3	20 45.8	11 59.8	29 57.3	25 26.1	19 58.0	26 21.3
20 F	7 53 1	28 49 8	3♎17 38	9♎34 49	16 5.7	10 23.1	11 50.5	21 28.5	12 6.8	29 59.2	25 29.7	19 56.3	26 20.3
21 Sa	7 56 57	29 50 11	15 46 40	21 53 49	16 2.9	10D 13.7	13 5.7	22 11.4	12 13.6	0♉ 1.2	25 33.2	19 54.6	26 19.3
22 Su	8 0 54	0♒51 14	27 56 53	3♏56 35	16D 2.0	10 12.7	14 20.9	22 54.2	12 20.4	0 3.4	25 36.8	19 53.0	26 18.3
23 M	8 4 51	1 52 16	9♏53 37	15 48 41	16R 2.1	10 19.7	15 36.1	23 37.1	12 26.9	0 5.6	25 40.3	19 51.3	26 17.4
24 Tu	8 8 47	2 53 18	21 42 28	27 35 41	16 2.0	10 34.1	16 51.3	24 20.0	12 33.3	0 7.9	25 43.8	19 49.7	26 16.5
25 W	8 12 44	3 54 19	3♐28 59	9♐22 57	16 0.7	10 55.2	18 6.5	25 2.9	12 39.6	0 10.4	25 47.3	19 48.0	26 15.5
26 Th	8 16 40	4 55 20	15 18 11	21 15 11	15 57.2	11 22.5	19 21.6	25 45.9	12 45.7	0 12.9	25 50.9	19 46.4	26 14.6
27 F	8 20 37	5 56 20	27 14 26	3♑16 19	15 51.0	11 55.5	20 36.8	26 28.9	12 51.7	0 15.6	25 54.4	19 44.8	26 13.7
28 Sa	8 24 33	6 57 19	9♑21 9	15 29 13	15 41.7	12 33.6	21 51.9	27 12.0	12 57.5	0 18.4	25 57.9	19 43.1	26 12.9
29 Su	8 28 30	7 58 18	21 40 40	27 55 39	15 29.9	13 16.3	23 7.0	27 55.1	13 3.1	0 21.2	26 1.4	19 41.5	26 12.0
30 M	8 32 26	8 59 16	4♒14 11	10♒36 15	15 16.4	14 3.3	24 22.1	28 38.2	13 8.6	0 24.2	26 4.8	19 40.0	26 11.2
31 Tu	8 36 23	10 0 12	17 1 46	23 30 37	15 2.2	14 54.1	25 37.2	29 21.3	13 14.0	0 27.3	26 8.3	19 38.4	26 10.4

LONGITUDE FEBRUARY 1911

Day	Sid.Time	☉	0 hr ☽	Noon ☽	True ☊	☿	♀	♂	♃	♄	♅	♆	♇
1 W	8 40 20	11♒ 1 8	0♓ 2 40	6♓37 42	14♉48.7	15♑48.4	26♒52.3	0♑ 4.5	13♏19.1	0♉30.4	26♑11.8	19♋36.8	26♊ 9.5
2 Th	8 44 16	12 2 3	13 15 34	19 56 5	14R 37.1	16 45.9	28 7.3	0 47.7	13 24.1	0 33.7	26 15.2	19R 35.3	26R 8.8
3 F	8 48 13	13 2 56	26 39 6	3♈24 30	14 28.2	17 46.3	29 22.3	1 30.9	13 29.0	0 37.0	26 18.7	19 33.7	26 8.0
4 Sa	8 52 9	14 3 47	10♈12 10	17 2 3	14 22.5	18 49.3	0♓37.3	2 14.2	13 33.6	0 40.5	26 22.1	19 32.2	26 7.2
5 Su	8 56 6	15 4 38	23 54 7	0♉48 23	14 19.6	19 54.7	1 52.3	2 57.5	13 38.1	0 44.1	26 25.5	19 30.7	26 6.5
6 M	9 0 2	16 5 27	7♉44 52	14 43 35	14 18.8	21 2.4	3 7.3	3 40.8	13 42.5	0 47.7	26 28.9	19 29.2	26 5.8
7 Tu	9 3 59	17 6 14	21 44 32	28 47 42	14 18.7	22 12.1	4 22.2	4 24.2	13 46.6	0 51.5	26 32.3	19 27.7	26 5.1
8 W	9 7 55	18 7 0	5♊52 59	13♊ 0 14	14 18.1	23 23.8	5 37.1	5 7.5	13 50.6	0 55.3	26 35.6	19 26.3	26 4.4
9 Th	9 11 52	19 7 45	20 9 15	27 19 40	14 15.5	24 37.2	6 52.0	5 51.0	13 54.5	0 59.2	26 39.0	19 24.8	26 3.7
10 F	9 15 49	20 8 28	4♋31 4	11♋42 56	14 10.2	25 52.3	8 6.9	6 34.4	13 58.1	1 3.3	26 42.3	19 23.4	26 3.1
11 Sa	9 19 45	21 9 9	18 54 37	26 5 27	14 2.0	27 8.9	9 21.7	7 17.9	14 1.6	1 7.4	26 45.6	19 22.0	26 2.5
12 Su	9 23 42	22 9 49	3♌14 41	10♌21 34	13 51.3	28 27.0	10 36.5	8 1.4	14 4.9	1 11.6	26 48.9	19 20.7	26 1.9
13 M	9 27 38	23 10 27	17 25 21	24 25 21	13 39.1	29 46.4	11 51.3	8 44.9	14 8.0	1 15.9	26 52.2	19 19.3	26 1.3
14 Tu	9 31 35	24 11 4	1♍20 56	8♍11 35	13 26.6	1♒ 7.2	13 6.0	9 28.5	14 11.0	1 20.2	26 55.5	19 18.0	26 0.7
15 W	9 35 31	25 11 39	14 56 55	21 36 40	13 15.2	2 29.3	14 20.7	10 12.1	14 13.7	1 24.7	26 58.7	19 16.6	26 0.2
16 Th	9 39 28	26 12 13	28 10 42	4♎39 3	13 5.8	3 52.6	15 35.4	10 55.7	14 16.3	1 29.2	27 1.9	19 15.4	25 59.6
17 F	9 43 24	27 12 46	11♎ 1 51	17 19 22	12 59.1	5 17.0	16 50.1	11 39.4	14 18.7	1 33.9	27 5.1	19 14.1	25 59.1
18 Sa	9 47 21	28 13 17	23 31 57	29 40 4	12 55.2	6 42.6	18 4.7	12 23.1	14 20.9	1 38.6	27 8.3	19 12.8	25 58.6
19 Su	9 51 18	29 13 47	5♏44 14	11♏45 4	12D 53.6	8 9.3	19 19.3	13 6.8	14 23.0	1 43.4	27 11.4	19 11.6	25 58.2
20 M	9 55 14	0♓14 16	17 43 11	23 39 16	12 53.4	9 37.0	20 33.9	13 50.5	14 24.8	1 48.3	27 14.5	19 10.4	25 57.7
21 Tu	9 59 11	1 14 43	29 33 59	5♐28 2	12R 53.7	11 5.8	21 48.4	14 34.3	14 26.5	1 53.2	27 17.6	19 9.2	25 57.3
22 W	10 3 7	2 15 9	11♐22 8	17 16 57	12 53.3	12 35.7	23 3.0	15 18.1	14 28.0	1 58.3	27 20.7	19 8.1	25 56.9
23 Th	10 7 4	3 15 34	23 13 9	29 11 21	12 51.3	14 6.6	24 17.5	16 2.0	14 29.3	2 3.4	27 23.8	19 6.9	25 56.5
24 F	10 11 0	4 15 57	5♑12 9	11♑16 4	12 46.9	15 38.5	25 31.9	16 45.9	14 30.4	2 8.6	27 26.8	19 5.8	25 56.2
25 Sa	10 14 57	5 16 19	17 23 35	23 35 4	12 40.0	17 11.4	26 46.4	17 29.8	14 31.3	2 13.8	27 29.8	19 4.7	25 55.9
26 Su	10 18 53	6 16 40	29 50 51	6♒11 10	12 30.6	18 45.4	28 0.8	18 13.7	14 32.1	2 19.2	27 32.7	19 3.7	25 55.6
27 M	10 22 50	7 16 59	12♒36 7	19 5 44	12 19.6	20 20.3	29 15.2	18 57.7	14 32.6	2 24.6	27 35.7	19 2.7	25 55.3
28 Tu	10 26 47	8 17 16	25 39 57	2♓18 37	12 8.0	21 56.3	0♈29.5	19 41.6	14 33.0	2 30.1	27 38.6	19 1.7	25 55.0

Astro Data	Planet Ingress	Last Aspect	☽ Ingress	Last Aspect	☽ Ingress	☽ Phases & Eclipses	Astro Data
Dy Hr Mn	Dy Hr Mn	Dy Hr Mn	Dy Hr Mn	Dy Hr Mn	Dy Hr Mn	Dy Hr Mn	1 JANUARY 1911
☿ R 1 8:26	♀ ♒ 10 13:28	2 8:27 ♄ □	♒ 2 9:02	2 23:23 ♅ ⚹	♈ 3 5:57	8 6:20 ☽ 16♈52	Julian Day # 4018
♄ D 2 5:19	♄ ♉ 20 9:22	4 17:16 ♄ ⚹	♓ 4 17:50	5 4:25 ♅ □	♉ 5 10:36	14 22:26 ○ 23♋40	Delta T 11.5 sec
☽0N 7 13:58	☉ ♒ 21 3:51	6 18:24 ♇ □	♈ 7 0:33	7 8:12 ♅ △	♊ 7 14:03	22 6:21 ☽ 1♏07	SVP 06♓30'21"
♃□♇ 14 9:56	♂ ♑ 31 21:30	9 4:34 ♄ ☌	♉ 9 5:01	9 9:53 ♇ ☌	♋ 9 16:28	30 9:44 ● 9♒24	Obliquity 23°27'09"
☽0S 20 7:42		10 22:58 ♅ △	♊ 11 7:17	11 15:08 ☿ ☍	♌ 11 18:33		⚷ Chiron 29♒14.0
☿ D 21 14:44	♀ ♓ 3 12:03	13 7:45 ♄ ⚹	♋ 13 8:03	13 14:45 ♇ ⚹	♍ 13 21:39	6 15:27 ☽ 16♉45	☽ Mean ☊ 16♉26.3
♅×♇ 31 11:25	☿ ♒ 13 4:03	15 8:35 ♄ □	♌ 15 8:49	15 21:53 ♅ △	♎ 16 3:22	13 10:37 ○ 23♌37	
	☉ ♓ 19 18:20	17 11:21 ♄ △	♍ 17 11:30	18 9:59 ☉ △	♏ 18 12:39	21 3:44 ☽ 1♐24	1 FEBRUARY 1911
☽0N 3 18:27	♀ ♈ 27 14:29	19 14:51 ☉ △	♎ 19 17:47	20 19:22 ♅ ⚹	♐ 21 0:53		Julian Day # 4049
☽0S 16 16:11		21 20:44 ♇ △	♏ 22 4:06	23 5:29 ♇ ☍	♑ 23 13:37		Delta T 11.7 sec
		24 8:14 ♅ ⚹	♐ 24 16:54	25 20:07 ♀ ⚹	♒ 26 0:17		SVP 06♓30'15"
		26 22:23 ♂ ☌	♑ 27 5:30	28 0:27 ♇ △	♓ 28 7:51		Obliquity 23°27'10"
		29 8:24 ♅ ☌	♒ 29 15:57				⚷ Chiron 1♓00.6
		31 17:34 ♀ ☌	♓ 31 23:55				☽ Mean ☊ 14♉47.8

MARCH 1911 — LONGITUDE

Day	Sid.Time	☉	0 hr ☽	Noon ☽	True ☊	☿	♀	♂	♃	♄	♅	♆	♇
1 W	10 30 43	9♓17 31	9♓ 1 28	15♓48 12	11♉56.7	23♒33.3	1♈43.8	20♑25.6	14♏33.1	2♉35.6	27♑41.4	19♋ 0.7	25♊54.7
2 Th	10 34 40	10 17 45	22 38 24	29 31 41	11R47.1	25 11.4	2 58.1	21 9.7	14R33.1	2 41.3	27 44.3	18R59.8	25R54.5
3 F	10 38 36	11 17 56	6♈27 36	13♈25 43	11 39.9	26 50.4	4 12.3	21 53.7	14 32.9	2 47.0	27 47.1	18 58.8	25 54.3
4 Sa	10 42 33	12 18 6	20 25 35	27 26 51	11 35.4	28 30.6	5 26.5	22 37.8	14 32.5	2 52.7	27 49.9	18 58.0	25 54.1
5 Su	10 46 29	13 18 14	4♉29 8	11♉32 9	11D33.4	0♓11.7	6 40.7	23 21.9	14 31.9	2 58.6	27 52.6	18 57.1	25 54.0
6 M	10 50 26	14 18 20	18 35 39	25 39 24	11 33.4	1 54.0	7 54.8	24 6.0	14 31.1	3 4.5	27 55.3	18 56.3	25 53.9
7 Tu	10 54 22	15 18 24	2♊43 14	9♊47 1	11R34.2	3 37.4	9 8.9	24 50.2	14 30.2	3 10.4	27 58.0	18 55.5	25 53.7
8 W	10 58 19	16 18 25	16 50 36	23 53 51	11 34.7	5 21.8	10 22.9	25 34.3	14 29.0	3 16.4	28 0.7	18 54.7	25 53.7
9 Th	11 2 16	17 18 25	0♋56 38	7♋58 46	11 33.8	7 7.4	11 36.9	26 18.5	14 27.7	3 22.5	28 3.3	18 54.0	25 53.6
10 F	11 6 12	18 18 22	15 0 3	22 0 14	11 30.8	8 54.1	12 50.8	27 2.7	14 26.1	3 28.7	28 5.9	18 53.3	25 53.6
11 Sa	11 10 9	19 18 17	28 59 3	5♌56 10	11 25.6	10 41.9	14 4.7	27 47.0	14 24.4	3 34.9	28 8.4	18 52.6	25D53.5
12 Su	11 14 5	20 18 9	12♌51 14	19 43 54	11 18.4	12 30.9	15 18.6	28 31.2	14 22.5	3 41.2	28 10.9	18 52.0	25 53.6
13 M	11 18 2	21 18 0	26 33 46	3♍20 30	11 10.0	14 21.0	16 32.4	29 15.5	14 20.4	3 47.5	28 13.4	18 51.3	25 53.6
14 Tu	11 21 58	22 17 48	10♍ 3 44	16 43 10	11 1.3	16 12.3	17 46.2	29 59.8	14 18.2	3 53.8	28 15.8	18 50.8	25 53.6
15 W	11 25 55	23 17 35	23 18 34	29 49 45	10 53.3	18 4.7	18 59.9	0♒44.1	14 15.7	4 0.3	28 18.2	18 50.2	25 53.7
16 Th	11 29 51	24 17 19	6♎16 37	12♎39 8	10 46.8	19 58.3	20 13.6	1 28.4	14 13.1	4 6.8	28 20.6	18 49.7	25 53.8
17 F	11 33 48	25 17 2	18 57 22	25 11 28	10 42.4	21 53.1	21 27.2	2 12.8	14 10.3	4 13.3	28 22.9	18 49.2	25 53.9
18 Sa	11 37 45	26 16 42	1♏21 39	7♏28 14	10D40.0	23 48.9	22 40.8	2 57.2	14 7.3	4 19.9	28 25.2	18 48.7	25 54.1
19 Su	11 41 41	27 16 21	13 31 33	19 32 4	10 39.6	25 45.8	23 54.3	3 41.6	14 4.2	4 26.5	28 27.4	18 48.3	25 54.2
20 M	11 45 38	28 15 58	25 30 15	1♐26 39	10 40.5	27 43.7	25 7.8	4 26.0	14 0.8	4 33.2	28 29.6	18 47.9	25 54.4
21 Tu	11 49 34	29 15 33	7♐21 50	13 16 24	10 42.1	29 42.6	26 21.2	5 10.5	13 57.3	4 39.9	28 31.8	18 47.6	25 54.6
22 W	11 53 31	0♈15 7	19 10 59	25 6 14	10 43.5	1♈42.3	27 34.6	5 55.0	13 53.7	4 46.7	28 33.9	18 47.3	25 54.8
23 Th	11 57 27	1 14 39	1♑ 2 48	7♑ 1 18	10R44.2	3 42.8	28 48.0	6 39.5	13 49.8	4 53.5	28 35.9	18 47.0	25 55.1
24 F	12 1 24	2 14 9	13 2 24	19 6 40	10 43.5	5 44.0	0♉ 1.2	7 24.0	13 45.8	5 0.4	28 38.0	18 46.7	25 55.4
25 Sa	12 5 20	3 13 37	25 14 42	1♒27 0	10 41.2	7 45.6	1 14.5	8 8.5	13 41.6	5 7.3	28 40.0	18 46.5	25 55.7
26 Su	12 9 17	4 13 4	7♒44 3	14 6 11	10 37.3	9 47.5	2 27.7	8 53.1	13 37.3	5 14.3	28 41.9	18 46.3	25 56.0
27 M	12 13 14	5 12 28	20 33 45	27 6 54	10 32.2	11 49.4	3 40.8	9 37.6	13 32.8	5 21.2	28 43.8	18 46.1	25 56.3
28 Tu	12 17 10	6 11 51	3♓45 44	10♓30 12	10 26.5	13 51.2	4 53.9	10 22.2	13 28.1	5 28.3	28 45.7	18 46.0	25 56.7
29 W	12 21 7	7 11 12	17 20 9	24 15 18	10 21.0	15 52.5	6 7.0	11 6.8	13 23.3	5 35.4	28 47.5	18 45.9	25 57.1
30 Th	12 25 3	8 10 31	1♈15 14	8♈19 28	10 16.2	17 53.1	7 20.0	11 51.4	13 18.3	5 42.5	28 49.3	18 45.9	25 57.5
31 F	12 29 0	9 9 48	15 27 23	22 38 21	10 12.8	19 52.5	8 32.9	12 36.0	13 13.2	5 49.6	28 51.0	18D45.9	25 57.9

APRIL 1911 — LONGITUDE

Day	Sid.Time	☉	0 hr ☽	Noon ☽	True ☊	☿	♀	♂	♃	♄	♅	♆	♇
1 Sa	12 32 56	10♈ 9 2	29♈51 40	7♉ 6 35	10♉10.9	21♈50.5	9♉45.8	13♒20.6	13♏ 7.9	5♉56.8	28♑52.7	18♋45.9	25♊58.4
2 Su	12 36 53	11 8 15	14♉22 25	21 38 28	10D10.6	23 46.6	10 58.6	14 5.3	13R 2.5	6 4.0	28 54.3	18 45.9	25 58.9
3 M	12 40 49	12 7 26	28 54 5	6♊ 8 43	10 11.5	25 40.5	12 11.4	14 49.9	12 57.0	6 11.2	28 55.9	18 46.0	25 59.4
4 Tu	12 44 46	13 6 34	13♊21 51	20 33 3	10 12.9	27 31.7	13 24.1	15 34.6	12 51.3	6 18.5	28 57.5	18 46.1	25 59.9
5 W	12 48 42	14 5 40	27 41 56	4♋48 15	10 14.3	29 20.0	14 36.8	16 19.2	12 45.5	6 25.8	28 58.9	18 46.3	26 0.4
6 Th	12 52 39	15 4 44	11♋51 45	18 52 15	10R15.0	1♉ 4.9	15 49.3	17 3.9	12 39.6	6 33.2	29 0.4	18 46.4	26 1.0
7 F	12 56 36	16 3 45	25 49 39	2♌43 50	10 14.7	2 46.0	17 1.9	17 48.6	12 33.5	6 40.5	29 1.8	18 46.7	26 1.6
8 Sa	13 0 32	17 2 44	9♌34 44	16 22 19	10 13.3	4 23.1	18 14.3	18 33.3	12 27.3	6 47.9	29 3.2	18 46.9	26 2.2
9 Su	13 4 29	18 1 41	23 6 32	29 47 22	10 11.0	5 55.8	19 26.7	19 18.0	12 21.0	6 55.4	29 4.5	18 47.2	26 2.8
10 M	13 8 25	19 0 35	6♍24 48	12♍58 49	10 8.0	7 23.8	20 39.0	20 2.7	12 14.6	7 2.8	29 5.7	18 47.5	26 3.4
11 Tu	13 12 22	19 59 27	19 29 26	25 56 38	10 4.9	8 47.0	21 51.3	20 47.4	12 8.1	7 10.3	29 6.9	18 47.8	26 4.1
12 W	13 16 18	20 58 17	2♎20 27	8♎40 55	10 2.0	10 5.1	23 3.5	21 32.1	12 1.5	7 17.7	29 8.1	18 48.2	26 4.8
13 Th	13 20 15	21 57 5	14 58 7	21 12 7	9 59.8	11 17.8	24 15.6	22 16.8	11 54.8	7 25.2	29 9.2	18 48.6	26 5.5
14 F	13 24 11	22 55 51	27 23 2	3♏31 2	9 58.5	12 25.2	25 27.7	23 1.5	11 48.0	7 32.8	29 10.3	18 49.1	26 6.2
15 Sa	13 28 8	23 54 35	9♏36 18	15 39 3	9D58.0	13 26.9	26 39.6	23 46.2	11 41.1	7 40.3	29 11.3	18 49.6	26 7.0
16 Su	13 32 5	24 53 17	21 39 33	27 38 6	9 58.4	14 22.9	27 51.6	24 31.0	11 34.1	7 47.9	29 12.3	18 50.1	26 7.7
17 M	13 36 1	25 51 57	3♐35 4	9♐30 49	9 59.3	15 13.1	29 3.4	25 15.7	11 27.0	7 55.5	29 13.2	18 50.6	26 8.5
18 Tu	13 39 58	26 50 35	15 25 47	21 20 24	10 0.5	15 57.3	0♊15.2	26 0.5	11 19.9	8 3.1	29 14.0	18 51.2	26 9.3
19 W	13 43 54	27 49 12	27 15 12	3♑10 40	10 1.7	16 35.7	1 26.9	26 45.2	11 12.7	8 10.7	29 14.9	18 51.8	26 10.1
20 Th	13 47 51	28 47 47	9♑ 7 22	15 5 50	10 2.7	17 8.0	2 38.5	27 30.0	11 5.4	8 18.3	29 15.6	18 52.5	26 10.9
21 F	13 51 47	29 46 20	21 6 41	27 10 28	10R 3.3	17 34.2	3 50.1	28 14.7	10 58.1	8 25.9	29 16.4	18 53.2	26 11.8
22 Sa	13 55 44	0♉44 52	3♒17 45	9♒29 8	10 3.5	17 54.5	5 1.5	28 59.5	10 50.7	8 33.6	29 17.0	18 53.9	26 12.7
23 Su	13 59 40	1 43 22	15 45 6	22 6 11	10 3.2	18 8.8	6 12.9	29 44.2	10 43.3	8 41.2	29 17.7	18 54.6	26 13.6
24 M	14 3 37	2 41 51	28 32 48	5♓ 5 19	10 2.6	18R17.2	7 24.3	0♓29.0	10 35.8	8 48.9	29 18.2	18 55.4	26 14.5
25 Tu	14 7 34	3 40 17	11♓44 1	18 29 5	10 1.8	18 19.8	8 35.5	1 13.7	10 28.2	8 56.6	29 18.8	18 56.2	26 15.4
26 W	14 11 30	4 38 42	25 20 32	2♈18 18	10 1.1	18 16.8	9 46.7	1 58.5	10 20.7	9 4.3	29 19.2	18 57.0	26 16.3
27 Th	14 15 27	5 37 6	9♈22 10	16 31 44	10 0.6	18 8.5	10 57.8	2 43.2	10 13.1	9 12.0	29 19.6	18 57.9	26 17.3
28 F	14 19 23	6 35 27	23 46 29	1♉ 5 44	10 0.3	17 55.1	12 8.9	3 27.9	10 5.4	9 19.6	29 20.0	18 58.8	26 18.3
29 Sa	14 23 20	7 33 48	8♉28 42	15 54 28	10D 0.2	17 36.9	13 19.8	4 12.6	9 57.8	9 27.3	29 20.3	18 59.7	26 19.3
30 Su	14 27 16	8 32 6	23 22 5	0♊50 31	10 0.2	17 14.3	14 30.7	4 57.3	9 50.1	9 35.0	29 20.6	19 0.7	26 20.3

Astro Data Dy Hr Mn	Planet Ingress Dy Hr Mn	Last Aspect Dy Hr Mn	☽ Ingress Dy Hr Mn	Last Aspect Dy Hr Mn	☽ Ingress Dy Hr Mn	☽ Phases & Eclipses Dy Hr Mn	Astro Data
♀0N 1 14:12	☿ ♓ 4 21:14	2 8:55 ♅ ⚹	♈ 2 12:49	31 22:22 ♅ □	♉ 1 0:14	1 0:31 ● 9♓19	1 MARCH 1911
♃ R 1 8:49	♂ ♒ 14 0:07	4 15:41 ☿ ⚹	♉ 4 16:21	3 0:03 ♅ △	♊ 3 1:49	7 23:01 ☽ 16♊16	Julian Day # 4077
☽0N 3 0:28	☉ ♈ 21 17:54	6 15:54 ♅ △	♊ 6 19:23	5 3:09 ☿ ⚹	♋ 5 3:53	14 23:58 ○ 23♍17	Delta T 11.8 sec
♇ D 11 5:18	☿ ♈ 21 3:30	8 15:24 ♇ ☌	♋ 8 22:24	7 5:34 ♅ ☍	♌ 7 7:15	23 0:26 ☽ 1♑16	SVP 06♓30'11"
☽0S 16 0:44	♀ ♉ 23 23:35	10 22:33 ♅ ☍	♌ 11 1:45	9 5:16 ♇ ⚹	♍ 9 12:23	30 12:38 ● 8♈42	Obliquity 23°27'10"
☿0N 22 11:00		12 22:49 ♇ ⚹	♍ 13 6:04	11 17:58 ♅ △	♎ 11 19:36		⚷ Chiron 2♓51.6
☽0N 30 9:12	☿ ♉ 5 9:04	15 9:13 ♅ △	♎ 15 12:19	14 3:30 ♅ □	♏ 14 5:06	6 5:55 ☽ 15♋19	☽ Mean ☊ 13♉18.8
♆ D 31 4:41	♀ ♊ 17 18:56	17 18:15 ♅ □	♏ 17 21:21	16 15:11 ♅ ⚹	♐ 16 16:46	13 14:36 ○ 22♎33	
	☉ ♉ 21 5:36	20 6:05 ☉ △	♐ 20 9:05	19 1:15 ☉ △	♑ 19 5:34	21 18:35 ☽ 0♒32	1 APRIL 1911
☽0S 12 8:13	♂ ♓ 23 8:28	22 18:57 ♀ △	♑ 22 21:53	21 16:09 ♅ ☌	♒ 21 17:33	28 22:25 ● 7♉30	Julian Day # 4108
♃⚻♇ 19 7:40		25 6:39 ♅ ☌	♒ 25 9:13	23 19:43 ♇ △	♓ 24 2:41	28 22:27:09 • T 4'57"	Delta T 12.0 sec
☿ R 24 23:09		27 9:52 ♇ △	♓ 27 17:14	26 6:53 ♅ ⚹	♈ 26 8:03		SVP 06♓30'08"
☽0N 26 19:31		29 19:50 ♅ ⚹	♈ 29 21:52	28 9:07 ♅ □	♉ 28 10:13		Obliquity 23°27'10"
♃☍♄ 30 23:35				30 9:36 ♅ △	♊ 30 10:39		⚷ Chiron 4♓48.2
							☽ Mean ☊ 11♉40.3

LONGITUDE — MAY 1911

Day	Sid.Time	☉	0 hr ☽	Noon ☽	True ☊	☿	♀	♂	♃	♄	♅	♆	♇
1 M	14 31 13	9♉30 22	8♊18 46	15♊45 51	10♉ 0.3	16♉47.8	15♊41.5	5♓42.0	9♏42.5	9♉42.7	29♑20.8	19♋ 1.7	26♊21.3
2 Tu	14 35 9	10 28 37	23 10 49	0♋32 53	10R 0.3	16R 18.0	16 52.2	6 26.7	9R 34.8	9 50.5	29 21.0	19 2.7	26 22.3
3 W	14 39 6	11 26 50	7♋51 20	15 5 33	10 0.2	15 45.3	18 2.8	7 11.3	9 27.2	9 58.2	29 21.1	19 3.7	26 23.4
4 Th	14 43 3	12 25 1	22 15 6	29 19 41	10 0.1	15 10.4	19 13.3	7 56.0	9 19.5	10 5.9	29R 21.2	19 4.8	26 24.5
5 F	14 46 59	13 23 9	6♌19 4	13♌13 12	9D 59.9	14 34.0	20 23.7	8 40.6	9 11.9	10 13.6	29 21.2	19 5.9	26 25.6
6 Sa	14 50 56	14 21 16	20 2 6	26 45 50	9 59.9	13 56.7	21 34.0	9 25.2	9 4.3	10 21.2	29 21.1	19 7.1	26 26.7
7 Su	14 54 52	15 19 20	3♍24 36	9♍58 36	10 0.1	13 19.1	22 44.3	10 9.8	8 56.7	10 28.9	29 21.1	19 8.2	26 27.8
8 M	14 58 49	16 17 23	16 28 6	22 53 23	10 0.6	12 42.0	23 54.4	10 54.4	8 49.1	10 36.6	29 20.9	19 9.4	26 28.9
9 Tu	15 2 45	17 15 24	29 14 42	5♎32 24	10 1.3	12 6.0	25 4.4	11 38.9	8 41.6	10 44.3	29 20.7	19 10.6	26 30.0
10 W	15 6 42	18 13 23	11♎46 44	17 58 1	10 2.0	11 31.7	26 14.3	12 23.5	8 34.1	10 51.9	29 20.5	19 11.9	26 31.2
11 Th	15 10 38	19 11 20	24 6 31	0♏12 29	10 2.7	10 59.6	27 24.2	13 8.0	8 26.7	10 59.6	29 20.2	19 13.2	26 32.4
12 F	15 14 35	20 9 15	6♏16 13	12 17 56	10R 3.0	10 30.3	28 33.9	13 52.5	8 19.3	11 7.2	29 19.9	19 14.5	26 33.5
13 Sa	15 18 32	21 7 9	18 17 54	24 16 21	10 2.9	10 4.1	29 43.5	14 37.0	8 11.9	11 14.9	29 19.5	19 15.8	26 34.7
14 Su	15 22 28	22 5 2	0♐13 33	6♐ 9 44	10 2.2	9 41.6	0♋53.0	15 21.4	8 4.7	11 22.5	29 19.1	19 17.1	26 35.9
15 M	15 26 25	23 2 53	12 5 11	18 0 9	10 0.9	9 22.9	2 2.3	16 5.8	7 57.5	11 30.1	29 18.6	19 18.5	26 37.2
16 Tu	15 30 21	24 0 42	23 54 58	29 49 56	9 59.1	9 8.4	3 11.6	16 50.3	7 50.3	11 37.7	29 18.1	19 19.9	26 38.4
17 W	15 34 18	24 58 30	5♑45 23	11♑41 41	9 56.9	8 58.2	4 20.8	17 34.7	7 43.3	11 45.3	29 17.5	19 21.4	26 39.6
18 Th	15 38 14	25 56 18	17 39 16	23 38 30	9 54.6	8D 52.4	5 29.8	18 19.0	7 36.3	11 52.8	29 16.9	19 22.8	26 40.9
19 F	15 42 11	26 54 3	29 39 52	5♒43 49	9 52.5	8 51.1	6 38.7	19 3.4	7 29.4	12 0.4	29 16.3	19 24.3	26 42.1
20 Sa	15 46 7	27 51 48	11♒50 51	18 1 27	9 51.0	8 54.4	7 47.5	19 47.7	7 22.6	12 7.9	29 15.5	19 25.8	26 43.4
21 Su	15 50 4	28 49 32	24 16 9	0♓35 25	9D 50.2	9 2.3	8 56.2	20 32.0	7 15.8	12 15.4	29 14.8	19 27.4	26 44.7
22 M	15 54 1	29 47 14	6♓59 46	13 29 38	9 50.3	9 14.7	10 4.7	21 16.2	7 9.2	12 22.9	29 14.0	19 28.9	26 46.0
23 Tu	15 57 57	0♊44 55	20 5 25	26 47 29	9 51.1	9 31.6	11 13.2	22 0.4	7 2.7	12 30.3	29 13.1	19 30.5	26 47.3
24 W	16 1 54	1 42 36	3♈36 5	10♈31 21	9 52.5	9 52.9	12 21.5	22 44.6	6 56.3	12 37.8	29 12.2	19 32.1	26 48.6
25 Th	16 5 50	2 40 15	17 33 18	24 41 49	9 53.8	10 18.4	13 29.6	23 28.7	6 50.0	12 45.2	29 11.3	19 33.7	26 49.9
26 F	16 9 47	3 37 53	1♉56 35	9♉17 7	9R 54.8	10 48.2	14 37.7	24 12.8	6 43.8	12 52.6	29 10.3	19 35.4	26 51.2
27 Sa	16 13 43	4 35 31	16 42 46	24 12 41	9 54.8	11 22.1	15 45.6	24 56.9	6 37.7	12 60.0	29 9.3	19 37.1	26 52.6
28 Su	16 17 40	5 33 7	1♊45 53	9♊21 13	9 53.6	12 0.0	16 53.4	25 40.9	6 31.7	13 7.3	29 8.2	19 38.7	26 53.9
29 M	16 21 36	6 30 42	16 57 28	24 33 23	9 51.2	12 41.8	18 1.0	26 24.9	6 25.9	13 14.6	29 7.1	19 40.5	26 55.3
30 Tu	16 25 33	7 28 17	2♋ 7 42	9♋39 15	9 47.9	13 27.3	19 8.5	27 8.8	6 20.2	13 21.9	29 5.9	19 42.2	26 56.6
31 W	16 29 30	8 25 50	17 6 56	24 29 49	9 44.0	14 16.6	20 15.8	27 52.7	6 14.6	13 29.2	29 4.7	19 44.0	26 58.0

LONGITUDE — JUNE 1911

Day	Sid.Time	☉	0 hr ☽	Noon ☽	True ☊	☿	♀	♂	♃	♄	♅	♆	♇
1 Th	16 33 26	9♊23 21	1♌47 8	8♌58 20	9♉40.3	15♉ 9.3	21♋23.0	28♓36.5	6♏ 9.2	13♉36.4	29♑ 3.5	19♋45.7	26♊59.4
2 F	16 37 23	10 20 51	16 3 0	23 0 57	9R 37.2	16 5.6	22 30.0	29 20.3	6R 3.9	13 43.6	29R 2.2	19 47.5	27 0.8
3 Sa	16 41 19	11 18 20	29 52 9	6♍36 44	9D 35.4	17 5.2	23 36.8	0♈ 4.0	5 58.7	13 50.7	29 0.9	19 49.4	27 2.2
4 Su	16 45 16	12 15 48	13♍14 55	19 47 2	9 34.9	18 8.2	24 43.5	0 47.7	5 53.7	13 57.8	28 59.5	19 51.2	27 3.5
5 M	16 49 12	13 13 14	26 13 30	2♎34 47	9 35.5	19 14.4	25 50.0	1 31.3	5 48.8	14 4.9	28 58.1	19 53.0	27 4.9
6 Tu	16 53 9	14 10 39	8♎51 22	15 3 45	9 36.9	20 23.8	26 56.4	2 14.8	5 44.1	14 12.0	28 56.6	19 54.9	27 6.3
7 W	16 57 6	15 8 3	21 12 28	27 17 59	9 38.5	21 36.3	28 2.5	2 58.4	5 39.6	14 19.0	28 55.2	19 56.8	27 7.7
8 Th	17 1 2	16 5 26	3♏20 47	9♏21 19	9R 39.7	22 51.9	29 8.5	3 41.8	5 35.2	14 25.9	28 53.6	19 58.7	27 9.2
9 F	17 4 59	17 2 48	15 20 2	21 17 18	9 39.7	24 10.4	0♌14.2	4 25.2	5 30.9	14 32.9	28 52.1	20 0.6	27 10.6
10 Sa	17 8 55	18 0 9	27 13 28	3♐ 8 54	9 38.1	25 32.0	1 19.8	5 8.5	5 26.8	14 39.8	28 50.5	20 2.6	27 12.0
11 Su	17 12 52	18 57 29	9♐ 3 52	14 58 39	9 34.7	26 56.6	2 25.1	5 51.8	5 22.9	14 46.6	28 48.8	20 4.5	27 13.4
12 M	17 16 48	19 54 48	20 53 31	26 48 42	9 29.5	28 24.1	3 30.3	6 35.0	5 19.1	14 53.4	28 47.2	20 6.5	27 14.8
13 Tu	17 20 45	20 52 7	2♑44 25	8♑40 54	9 22.8	29 54.5	4 35.3	7 18.2	5 15.5	15 0.2	28 45.5	20 8.5	27 16.3
14 W	17 24 41	21 49 25	14 38 22	20 37 4	9 15.2	1♊27.8	5 40.0	8 1.2	5 12.1	15 6.9	28 43.8	20 10.5	27 17.7
15 Th	17 28 38	22 46 43	26 37 13	2♒39 7	9 7.3	3 3.9	6 44.5	8 44.3	5 8.8	15 13.6	28 42.0	20 12.5	27 19.1
16 F	17 32 35	23 44 0	8♒43 2	14 49 16	8 60.0	4 42.9	7 48.8	9 27.2	5 5.7	15 20.2	28 40.2	20 14.5	27 20.6
17 Sa	17 36 31	24 41 16	20 58 11	27 10 8	8 53.9	6 24.8	8 52.8	10 10.1	5 2.8	15 26.8	28 38.4	20 16.5	27 22.0
18 Su	17 40 28	25 38 32	3♓25 30	9♓44 42	8 49.6	8 9.4	9 56.6	10 52.9	5 0.0	15 33.3	28 36.5	20 18.6	27 23.4
19 M	17 44 24	26 35 48	16 8 10	22 36 18	8D 47.3	9 56.8	11 0.2	11 35.7	4 57.5	15 39.8	28 34.6	20 20.7	27 24.9
20 Tu	17 48 21	27 33 4	29 9 33	5♈48 17	8 46.7	11 46.8	12 3.5	12 18.3	4 55.0	15 46.2	28 32.7	20 22.7	27 26.3
21 W	17 52 17	28 30 19	12♈32 53	19 23 36	8 47.4	13 39.5	13 6.6	13 0.9	4 52.8	15 52.6	28 30.7	20 24.8	27 27.7
22 Th	17 56 14	29 27 34	26 20 40	3♉24 8	8R 48.4	15 34.7	14 9.4	13 43.4	4 50.7	15 58.9	28 28.7	20 26.9	27 29.2
23 F	18 0 10	0♋24 50	10♉33 58	17 49 56	8 48.8	17 32.4	15 12.0	14 25.8	4 48.9	16 5.2	28 26.7	20 29.0	27 30.6
24 Sa	18 4 7	1 22 5	25 11 36	2♊38 24	8 47.8	19 32.3	16 14.2	15 8.2	4 47.2	16 11.4	28 24.7	20 31.1	27 32.0
25 Su	18 8 4	2 19 20	10♊ 9 29	17 43 53	8 44.6	21 34.4	17 16.2	15 50.4	4 45.6	16 17.6	28 22.6	20 33.3	27 33.5
26 M	18 12 0	3 16 35	25 20 27	2♋57 52	8 39.2	23 38.5	18 17.9	16 32.6	4 44.3	16 23.7	28 20.5	20 35.4	27 34.9
27 Tu	18 15 57	4 13 49	10♋34 50	18 9 58	8 31.9	25 44.3	19 19.3	17 14.6	4 43.1	16 29.7	28 18.4	20 37.6	27 36.4
28 W	18 19 53	5 11 4	25 41 58	3♌ 9 40	8 23.6	27 51.6	20 20.4	17 56.6	4 42.2	16 35.7	28 16.3	20 39.7	27 37.8
29 Th	18 23 50	6 8 18	10♌32 1	17 48 12	8 15.3	0♋ 0.1	21 21.2	18 38.5	4 41.4	16 41.6	28 14.2	20 41.9	27 39.2
30 F	18 27 46	7 5 31	24 57 35	1♍59 46	8 8.0	2 9.6	22 21.6	19 20.2	4 40.7	16 47.5	28 12.0	20 44.1	27 40.6

Astro Data	Planet Ingress	Last Aspect	☽ Ingress	Last Aspect	☽ Ingress	☽ Phases & Eclipses	Astro Data
Dy Hr Mn	Dy Hr Mn	Dy Hr Mn	Dy Hr Mn	Dy Hr Mn	Dy Hr Mn	Dy Hr Mn	1 MAY 1911
♅ R 4 20:17	♀ ♋ 13 5:42	2 5:12 ♇ ☌	♋ 2 11:06	2 19:00 ♇ ✶	♍ 3 0:14	5 13:14 ☽ 13♌55	Julian Day # 4138
☽0S 9 14:17	☉ ♊ 22 5:19	4 12:03 ♅ ☍	♌ 4 13:09	5 5:09 ♅ △	♎ 5 7:07	13 6:09 ○ 21♏22	Delta T 12.1 sec
♄∠♇ 16 2:38		6 11:27 ♇ ✶	♍ 6 17:49	7 15:10 ♅ □	♏ 7 17:21	13 5:56 • A 0.799	SVP 06♓30'05"
☿ D 18 18:36	♂ ♈ 2 21:48	9 0:11 ♅ △	♎ 9 1:26	10 3:16 ♅ ✶	♐ 10 5:37	21 9:23 ☽ 29♒12	Obliquity 23°27'10"
☽0N 24 5:20	♀ ♌ 8 18:48	11 10:17 ♅ □	♏ 11 11:35	12 12:55 ♇ ☍	♑ 12 18:27	28 6:24 ● 5♊48	⚷ Chiron 6♓14.4
	☿ ♊ 13 1:26	13 22:10 ♅ ✶	♐ 13 23:33	15 4:08 ♅ ☌	♒ 15 6:44		☽ Mean ☊ 10♉05.0
☽0S 5 19:39	☉ ♋ 22 13:36	16 5:32 ♇ ☍	♑ 16 12:20	17 12:24 ♇ △	♓ 17 17:27	3 22:04 ☽ 12♍11	
♂0N 9 5:18	☿ ♋ 28 23:59	18 23:13 ♅ ☌	♒ 19 0:40	19 22:53 ♅ ✶	♈ 20 1:32	11 21:50 ○ 19♐50	1 JUNE 1911
☽0N 20 13:02		21 9:23 ☉ □	♓ 21 10:53	22 5:42 ☉ ✶	♉ 22 6:14	19 20:50 ☽ 27♓26	Julian Day # 4169
		23 16:17 ♅ ✶	♈ 23 17:41	24 5:11 ♅ △	♊ 24 7:46	26 13:19 ● 3♋48	Delta T 12.3 sec
		25 19:26 ♅ □	♉ 25 20:48	26 3:32 ♇ ☌	♋ 26 7:20		SVP 06♓29'59"
		27 19:50 ♅ △	♊ 27 21:12	28 4:07 ♅ ☍	♌ 28 6:54		Obliquity 23°27'10"
		29 15:46 ♇ ☌	♋ 29 20:37	30 4:37 ♇ ✶	♍ 30 8:34		⚷ Chiron 6♓58.8
		31 19:30 ♅ ☍	♌ 31 21:03				☽ Mean ☊ 8♉26.5

JULY 1911 — LONGITUDE

Day	Sid.Time	☉	0 hr ☽	Noon ☽	True ☊	☿	♀	♂	♃	♄	♅	♆	♇
1 Sa	18 31 43	8♋ 2 44	8♍54 35	15♍42 1	8♉ 2.6	4♋19.8	23♌21.7	20♈ 1.9	4♏40.3	16♉53.3	28♑ 9.8	20♋46.3	27♊42.1
2 Su	18 35 39	8 59 57	22 22 15	28 55 36	7R59.3	6 30.4	24 21.5	20 43.4	4D40.1	16 59.0	28R 7.6	20 48.4	27 43.5
3 M	18 39 36	9 57 9	5♎22 31	11♎43 30	7D57.9	8 41.1	25 20.9	21 24.9	4 40.0	17 4.7	28 5.3	20 50.6	27 44.9
4 Tu	18 43 33	10 54 21	17 59 7	24 10 0	7 58.0	10 51.6	26 19.8	22 6.2	4 40.1	17 10.3	28 3.1	20 52.8	27 46.3
5 W	18 47 29	11 51 33	0♏16 46	6♏20 3	7R58.6	13 1.7	27 18.4	22 47.4	4 40.4	17 15.9	28 0.8	20 55.0	27 47.7
6 Th	18 51 26	12 48 45	12 20 28	18 18 36	7 58.7	15 11.1	28 16.6	23 28.6	4 40.9	17 21.3	27 58.5	20 57.2	27 49.1
7 F	18 55 22	13 45 56	24 15 3	0♐10 19	7 57.4	17 19.7	29 14.4	24 9.6	4 41.5	17 26.7	27 56.2	20 59.5	27 50.5
8 Sa	18 59 19	14 43 7	6♐ 4 53	11 59 12	7 53.9	19 27.2	0♍11.8	24 50.4	4 42.3	17 32.1	27 53.9	21 1.7	27 51.9
9 Su	19 3 15	15 40 19	17 53 40	23 48 37	7 47.8	21 33.4	1 8.6	25 31.2	4 43.4	17 37.4	27 51.6	21 3.9	27 53.3
10 M	19 7 12	16 37 30	29 44 22	5♑41 11	7 39.2	23 38.3	2 5.1	26 11.9	4 44.5	17 42.6	27 49.3	21 6.1	27 54.6
11 Tu	19 11 9	17 34 41	11♑39 16	17 38 50	7 28.4	25 41.6	3 1.0	26 52.4	4 45.9	17 47.7	27 46.9	21 8.3	27 56.0
12 W	19 15 5	18 31 53	23 40 2	29 43 0	7 16.2	27 43.4	3 56.5	27 32.9	4 47.5	17 52.7	27 44.6	21 10.6	27 57.4
13 Th	19 19 2	19 29 5	5♒47 54	11♒54 51	7 3.6	29 43.5	4 51.4	28 13.1	4 49.2	17 57.7	27 42.2	21 12.8	27 58.7
14 F	19 22 58	20 26 17	18 3 58	24 15 26	6 51.7	1♌41.8	5 45.8	28 53.3	4 51.1	18 2.6	27 39.8	21 15.0	28 0.1
15 Sa	19 26 55	21 23 29	0♓29 22	6♓46 0	6 41.5	3 38.4	6 39.7	29 33.4	4 53.1	18 7.5	27 37.4	21 17.2	28 1.4
16 Su	19 30 51	22 20 42	13 5 31	19 28 11	6 33.7	5 33.2	7 33.0	0♉13.3	4 55.4	18 12.2	27 35.0	21 19.5	28 2.7
17 M	19 34 48	23 17 56	25 54 16	2♈24 4	6 28.6	7 26.2	8 25.8	0 53.0	4 57.8	18 16.9	27 32.6	21 21.7	28 4.1
18 Tu	19 38 44	24 15 10	8♈57 53	15 36 3	6 26.0	9 17.4	9 17.9	1 32.7	5 0.4	18 21.5	27 30.2	21 23.9	28 5.4
19 W	19 42 41	25 12 24	22 18 53	29 6 39	6D25.3	11 6.7	10 9.4	2 12.2	5 3.1	18 26.0	27 27.8	21 26.2	28 6.7
20 Th	19 46 38	26 9 40	5♉59 36	12♉57 54	6R25.3	12 54.3	11 0.3	2 51.5	5 6.1	18 30.4	27 25.4	21 28.4	28 8.0
21 F	19 50 34	27 6 57	20 1 38	27 10 44	6 24.9	14 40.0	11 50.5	3 30.7	5 9.1	18 34.8	27 23.0	21 30.6	28 9.3
22 Sa	19 54 31	28 4 14	4♊25 1	11♊44 7	6 22.9	16 23.8	12 40.0	4 9.7	5 12.4	18 39.1	27 20.6	21 32.8	28 10.6
23 Su	19 58 27	29 1 32	19 7 30	26 34 25	6 18.4	18 5.9	13 28.9	4 48.6	5 15.9	18 43.3	27 18.2	21 35.0	28 11.8
24 M	20 2 24	29 58 51	4♋ 3 59	11♋35 9	6 11.2	19 46.2	14 17.0	5 27.3	5 19.5	18 47.4	27 15.8	21 37.3	28 13.1
25 Tu	20 6 20	0♌56 11	19 6 44	26 37 32	6 1.8	21 24.7	15 4.3	6 5.9	5 23.2	18 51.4	27 13.4	21 39.5	28 14.3
26 W	20 10 17	1 53 32	4♌ 6 16	11♌31 46	5 50.9	23 1.3	15 50.8	6 44.3	5 27.2	18 55.3	27 11.0	21 41.7	28 15.6
27 Th	20 14 13	2 50 53	18 52 55	26 8 47	5 39.8	24 36.2	16 36.5	7 22.5	5 31.3	18 59.2	27 8.6	21 43.9	28 16.8
28 F	20 18 10	3 48 15	3♍18 35	10♍21 45	5 29.8	26 9.2	17 21.4	8 0.5	5 35.5	19 2.9	27 6.2	21 46.1	28 18.0
29 Sa	20 22 7	4 45 37	17 17 55	24 6 57	5 21.9	27 40.5	18 5.3	8 38.4	5 39.9	19 6.6	27 3.9	21 48.3	28 19.2
30 Su	20 26 3	5 43 0	0♎48 50	7♎23 48	5 16.5	29 9.9	18 48.3	9 16.0	5 44.5	19 10.2	27 1.5	21 50.4	28 20.4
31 M	20 30 0	6 40 23	13 52 9	20 14 21	5 13.6	0♍37.4	19 30.4	9 53.5	5 49.3	19 13.7	26 59.1	21 52.6	28 21.6

AUGUST 1911 — LONGITUDE

Day	Sid.Time	☉	0 hr ☽	Noon ☽	True ☊	☿	♀	♂	♃	♄	♅	♆	♇
1 Tu	20 33 56	7♌37 47	26♎30 55	2♏42 27	5♉12.6	2♍ 3.1	20♍11.4	10♉30.8	5♏54.1	19♉17.1	26♑56.8	21♋54.8	28♊22.7
2 W	20 37 53	8 35 11	8♏49 37	14 53 3	5R12.5	3 26.9	20 51.4	11 7.9	5 59.2	19 20.4	26R54.4	21 56.9	28 23.9
3 Th	20 41 49	9 32 36	20 53 27	26 51 28	5 12.2	4 48.8	21 30.3	11 44.8	6 4.4	19 23.6	26 52.1	21 59.1	28 25.0
4 F	20 45 46	10 30 2	2♐47 46	8♐42 57	5 10.7	6 8.7	22 8.1	12 21.5	6 9.8	19 26.7	26 49.8	22 1.2	28 26.1
5 Sa	20 49 42	11 27 29	14 37 37	20 32 20	5 7.0	7 26.6	22 44.7	12 58.0	6 15.3	19 29.7	26 47.5	22 3.3	28 27.3
6 Su	20 53 39	12 24 56	26 27 35	2♑23 49	5 0.8	8 42.5	23 20.0	13 34.3	6 20.9	19 32.6	26 45.2	22 5.5	28 28.3
7 M	20 57 36	13 22 24	8♑21 27	14 20 47	4 51.9	9 56.2	23 54.1	14 10.3	6 26.7	19 35.5	26 42.9	22 7.6	28 29.4
8 Tu	21 1 32	14 19 53	20 22 9	26 25 45	4 40.7	11 7.8	24 26.8	14 46.2	6 32.7	19 38.2	26 40.6	22 9.7	28 30.5
9 W	21 5 29	15 17 24	2♒31 46	8♒40 20	4 28.1	12 17.2	24 58.2	15 21.9	6 38.8	19 40.9	26 38.4	22 11.8	28 31.5
10 Th	21 9 25	16 14 55	14 51 32	21 5 25	4 15.0	13 24.1	25 28.2	15 57.3	6 45.0	19 43.4	26 36.2	22 13.9	28 32.6
11 F	21 13 22	17 12 27	27 22 2	3♓41 22	4 2.6	14 28.7	25 56.6	16 32.5	6 51.4	19 45.8	26 34.0	22 15.9	28 33.6
12 Sa	21 17 18	18 10 0	10♓ 3 26	16 28 15	3 52.0	15 30.8	26 23.5	17 7.5	6 57.9	19 48.2	26 31.8	22 18.0	28 34.6
13 Su	21 21 15	19 7 34	22 55 49	29 26 11	3 43.8	16 30.2	26 48.9	17 42.3	7 4.5	19 50.4	26 29.6	22 20.0	28 35.6
14 M	21 25 11	20 5 10	5♈59 24	12♈35 33	3 38.4	17 26.8	27 12.6	18 16.8	7 11.3	19 52.6	26 27.5	22 22.0	28 36.6
15 Tu	21 29 8	21 2 47	19 14 45	25 57 8	3 35.7	18 20.5	27 34.6	18 51.0	7 18.3	19 54.6	26 25.3	22 24.0	28 37.5
16 W	21 33 5	22 0 26	2♉42 51	9♉32 1	3D35.0	19 11.2	27 54.8	19 25.1	7 25.3	19 56.6	26 23.2	22 26.0	28 38.5
17 Th	21 37 1	22 58 6	16 24 47	23 21 15	3R35.2	19 58.6	28 13.2	19 58.8	7 32.5	19 58.4	26 21.2	22 28.0	28 39.4
18 F	21 40 58	23 55 49	0♊21 28	7♊25 25	3 35.2	20 42.7	28 29.8	20 32.3	7 39.8	20 0.1	26 19.1	22 30.0	28 40.3
19 Sa	21 44 54	24 53 32	14 33 0	21 43 59	3 33.8	21 23.1	28 44.4	21 5.5	7 47.3	20 1.8	26 17.1	22 32.0	28 41.2
20 Su	21 48 51	25 51 18	28 58 3	6♋14 42	3 30.2	21 59.8	28 57.0	21 38.5	7 54.9	20 3.3	26 15.1	22 33.9	28 42.0
21 M	21 52 47	26 49 5	13♋33 21	20 53 16	3 24.1	22 32.4	29 7.6	22 11.2	8 2.6	20 4.7	26 13.1	22 35.8	28 42.9
22 Tu	21 56 44	27 46 54	28 13 38	5♌33 32	3 15.9	23 0.8	29 16.1	22 43.5	8 10.4	20 6.1	26 11.2	22 37.7	28 43.7
23 W	22 0 40	28 44 44	12♌52 1	20 8 9	3 6.2	23 24.7	29 22.5	23 15.6	8 18.4	20 7.3	26 9.3	22 39.6	28 44.6
24 Th	22 4 37	29 42 36	27 21 1	4♍29 46	2 56.3	23 43.9	29 26.6	23 47.4	8 26.5	20 8.4	26 7.4	22 41.5	28 45.4
25 F	22 8 34	0♍40 29	11♍33 43	18 32 15	2 47.4	23 58.0	29R28.5	24 18.9	8 34.7	20 9.4	26 5.6	22 43.3	28 46.1
26 Sa	22 12 30	1 38 23	25 24 58	2♎11 34	2 40.2	24 6.9	29 28.1	24 50.0	8 43.0	20 10.3	26 3.7	22 45.2	28 46.9
27 Su	22 16 27	2 36 19	8♎51 56	15 26 8	2 35.4	24R10.3	29 25.4	25 20.8	8 51.5	20 11.1	26 2.0	22 47.0	28 47.6
28 M	22 20 23	3 34 17	21 54 19	28 16 47	2D32.9	24 8.0	29 20.3	25 51.3	9 0.1	20 11.8	26 0.2	22 48.8	28 48.4
29 Tu	22 24 20	4 32 15	4♏33 55	10♏46 13	2 32.4	23 59.8	29 12.9	26 21.4	9 8.7	20 12.3	25 58.5	22 50.5	28 49.1
30 W	22 28 16	5 30 15	16 54 13	22 58 31	2 33.0	23 45.5	29 3.0	26 51.2	9 17.5	20 12.8	25 56.8	22 52.3	28 49.7
31 Th	22 32 13	6 28 17	28 59 44	4♐58 31	2R33.9	23 25.0	28 50.7	27 20.7	9 26.4	20 13.2	25 55.2	22 54.0	28 50.4

Astro Data Dy Hr Mn	Planet Ingress Dy Hr Mn
♃ D 2 21:30	♀ ♍ 7 19:04
☽0S 3 1:34	☿ ♌ 13 3:20
♅⊼♇ 8 13:13	♂ ♉ 15 16:01
☽0N 17 18:28	☉ ♌ 24 0:29
☽0S 30 8:58	☿ ♍ 30 13:41
♀0S 6 7:46	☉ ♍ 24 7:13
☽0N 13 23:07	
☿0S 21 4:38	
♀ R 25 7:54	
☽0S 26 17:43	
☿ R 27 2:25	

Last Aspect Dy Hr Mn	☽ Ingress Dy Hr Mn	Last Aspect Dy Hr Mn	☽ Ingress Dy Hr Mn
2 10:30 ♅ △	♎ 2 13:59	1 3:36 ♇ △	♏ 1 6:44
4 19:33 ♅ □	♏ 4 23:27	3 11:59 ♅ ✶	♐ 3 18:21
7 11:00 ♀ □	♐ 7 11:39	6 4:05 ♇ ☍	♑ 6 7:10
9 20:18 ♇ ☍	♑ 10 0:32	8 12:27 ♅ ☌	♒ 8 19:02
12 9:39 ☿ ☍	♒ 12 12:34	11 2:16 ♇ △	♓ 11 5:00
14 22:06 ♂ ✶	♓ 14 23:04	13 10:28 ♇ □	♈ 13 13:02
17 4:01 ♇ □	♈ 17 7:35	15 16:47 ♇ ✶	♉ 15 19:12
19 10:16 ♇ ✶	♉ 19 13:34	17 20:46 ♀ △	♊ 17 23:23
21 12:44 ☉ ✶	♊ 21 16:42	19 23:58 ♀ □	♋ 20 1:42
23 14:37 ♇ ☌	♋ 23 17:30	22 1:43 ♀ ✶	♌ 22 2:54
25 12:55 ♅ ☍	♌ 25 17:24	24 4:14 ☉ ☌	♍ 24 4:26
27 15:35 ♇ ✶	♍ 27 18:26	26 7:08 ♀ ☌	♎ 26 8:06
29 19:32 ♇ □	♎ 29 22:32	28 13:01 ♇ △	♏ 28 15:16
		30 23:42 ♀ ✶	♐ 31 2:01

☽ Phases & Eclipses Dy Hr Mn	Astro Data
3 9:20 ☽ 10♎19	1 JULY 1911
11 12:53 ○ 18♑05	Julian Day # 4199
19 5:31 ☽ 25♈26	Delta T 12.4 sec
25 20:12 ● 1♌44	SVP 06♓29'53"
	Obliquity 23°27'10"
1 23:29 ☽ 8♏34	⚷ Chiron 6♓50.4R
10 2:54 ○ 16♒22	☽ Mean ☊ 6♉51.2
17 12:10 ☽ 23♉27	
24 4:14 ● 29♌53	1 AUGUST 1911
31 16:20 ☽ 7♐08	Julian Day # 4230
	Delta T 12.6 sec
	SVP 06♓29'48"
	Obliquity 23°27'10"
	⚷ Chiron 5♓53.2R
	☽ Mean ☊ 5♉12.7

LONGITUDE SEPTEMBER 1911

Day	Sid.Time	☉	0 hr ☽	Noon ☽	True ☊	☿	♀	♂	♃	♄	♅	♆	♇
1 F	22 36 9	7♍26 20	10♐55 32	16♐51 25	2♉34.1	22♍58.4	28♍36.1	27♉49.8	9♏35.5	20♉13.4	25♑53.6	22♋55.7	28♊51.0
2 Sa	22 40 6	8 24 24	22 46 49	28 42 22	2R 32.8	22R 25.8	28R 19.1	28 18.6	9 44.6	20R 13.6	25R 52.0	22 57.4	28 51.7
3 Su	22 44 3	9 22 30	4♑38 38	10♑36 10	2 29.5	21 47.3	27 59.8	28 46.9	9 53.8	20 13.6	25 50.4	22 59.1	28 52.3
4 M	22 47 59	10 20 37	16 35 28	22 37 1	2 24.1	21 3.4	27 38.3	29 14.9	10 3.2	20 13.5	25 48.9	23 0.7	28 52.9
5 Tu	22 51 56	11 18 46	28 41 11	4♒48 18	2 16.9	20 14.5	27 14.6	29 42.5	10 12.6	20 13.4	25 47.5	23 2.4	28 53.4
6 W	22 55 52	12 16 56	10♒58 39	17 12 27	2 8.5	19 21.4	26 48.8	0♊ 9.8	10 22.2	20 13.1	25 46.1	23 4.0	28 54.0
7 Th	22 59 49	13 15 8	23 29 49	29 50 50	1 59.5	18 24.9	26 21.1	0 36.6	10 31.8	20 12.7	25 44.7	23 5.5	28 54.5
8 F	23 3 45	14 13 21	6♓15 31	12♓43 48	1 51.0	17 26.1	25 51.5	1 3.0	10 41.5	20 12.2	25 43.4	23 7.1	28 55.0
9 Sa	23 7 42	15 11 36	19 15 37	25 50 50	1 43.8	16 26.2	25 20.3	1 29.0	10 51.4	20 11.6	25 42.1	23 8.6	28 55.5
10 Su	23 11 38	16 9 53	2♈29 17	9♈10 48	1 38.5	15 26.4	24 47.7	1 54.6	11 1.3	20 10.9	25 40.8	23 10.1	28 55.9
11 M	23 15 35	17 8 11	15 55 12	22 42 18	1 35.3	14 28.1	24 13.7	2 19.8	11 11.4	20 10.1	25 39.6	23 11.6	28 56.3
12 Tu	23 19 32	18 6 32	29 31 56	6♉23 56	1D 34.2	13 32.7	23 38.7	2 44.5	11 21.5	20 9.1	25 38.4	23 13.1	28 56.8
13 W	23 23 28	19 4 55	13♉18 10	20 14 29	1 34.6	12 41.6	23 2.7	3 8.7	11 31.7	20 8.1	25 37.3	23 14.5	28 57.2
14 Th	23 27 25	20 3 20	27 12 48	4♊11 59	1 35.9	11 56.0	22 26.2	3 32.5	11 42.0	20 7.0	25 36.2	23 15.9	28 57.5
15 F	23 31 21	21 1 47	11♊14 55	18 18 26	1R 37.1	11 17.1	21 49.3	3 55.8	11 52.4	20 5.7	25 35.2	23 17.3	28 57.9
16 Sa	23 35 18	22 0 17	25 23 25	2♋29 37	1 37.4	10 45.9	21 12.2	4 18.6	12 2.9	20 4.4	25 34.2	23 18.6	28 58.2
17 Su	23 39 14	22 58 48	9♋36 49	16 44 40	1 36.2	10 23.2	20 35.3	4 40.9	12 13.5	20 3.0	25 33.2	23 20.0	28 58.5
18 M	23 43 11	23 57 22	23 52 50	1♌ 0 53	1 33.4	10D 9.6	19 58.6	5 2.7	12 24.2	20 1.4	25 32.3	23 21.3	28 58.8
19 Tu	23 47 7	24 55 58	8♌ 8 21	15 14 41	1 29.1	10 5.4	19 22.6	5 24.0	12 34.9	19 59.8	25 31.4	23 22.5	28 59.1
20 W	23 51 4	25 54 36	22 19 22	29 21 50	1 23.8	10 10.9	18 47.3	5 44.7	12 45.7	19 58.0	25 30.6	23 23.8	28 59.3
21 Th	23 55 1	26 53 16	6♍21 33	13♍17 58	1 18.2	10 26.1	18 13.1	6 4.9	12 56.7	19 56.1	25 29.9	23 25.0	28 59.5
22 F	23 58 57	27 51 59	20 10 38	26 59 9	1 13.2	10 50.9	17 40.1	6 24.5	13 7.6	19 54.2	25 29.1	23 26.2	28 59.7
23 Sa	0 2 54	28 50 43	3♎43 11	10♎22 30	1 9.3	11 24.9	17 8.5	6 43.5	13 18.7	19 52.1	25 28.5	23 27.3	28 59.9
24 Su	0 6 50	29 49 29	16 56 57	23 26 30	1 6.9	12 7.8	16 38.5	7 2.0	13 29.9	19 50.0	25 27.8	23 28.4	29 0.0
25 M	0 10 47	0♎48 17	29 51 12	6♏11 12	1D 6.0	12 59.0	16 10.2	7 19.8	13 41.1	19 47.7	25 27.3	23 29.5	29 0.2
26 Tu	0 14 43	1 47 7	12♏26 44	18 38 7	1 6.5	13 57.9	15 43.9	7 37.0	13 52.4	19 45.3	25 26.7	23 30.6	29 0.3
27 W	0 18 40	2 45 59	24 45 44	0♐50 1	1 7.9	15 4.0	15 19.5	7 53.7	14 3.8	19 42.9	25 26.3	23 31.6	29 0.3
28 Th	0 22 36	3 44 53	6♐51 29	12 50 39	1 9.7	16 16.5	14 57.3	8 9.6	14 15.2	19 40.4	25 25.8	23 32.7	29 0.4
29 F	0 26 33	4 43 48	18 48 5	24 44 24	1 11.3	17 34.8	14 37.3	8 25.0	14 26.7	19 37.7	25 25.5	23 33.6	29 0.4
30 Sa	0 30 29	5 42 45	0♑40 10	6♑36 2	1R 12.2	18 58.2	14 19.6	8 39.6	14 38.3	19 35.0	25 25.1	23 34.6	29R 0.5

LONGITUDE OCTOBER 1911

Day	Sid.Time	☉	0 hr ☽	Noon ☽	True ☊	☿	♀	♂	♃	♄	♅	♆	♇
1 Su	0 34 26	6♎41 44	12♑32 36	18♑30 27	1♉12.1	20♍26.0	14♍ 4.2	8♊53.6	14♏50.0	19♉32.2	25♑24.9	23♋35.5	29♊ 0.5
2 M	0 38 23	7 40 45	24 30 11	0♒32 20	1R 11.0	21 57.6	13R 51.3	9 7.0	15 1.7	19R 29.3	25R 24.6	23 36.4	29R 0.4
3 Tu	0 42 19	8 39 48	6♒37 27	12 45 59	1 8.9	23 32.4	13 40.7	9 19.6	15 13.5	19 26.3	25 24.4	23 37.2	29 0.4
4 W	0 46 16	9 38 52	18 58 22	25 14 57	1 6.0	25 9.9	13 32.6	9 31.5	15 25.3	19 23.2	25 24.3	23 38.1	29 0.3
5 Th	0 50 12	10 37 58	1♓36 0	8♓ 1 46	1 2.8	26 49.6	13 26.9	9 42.7	15 37.2	19 20.0	25 24.2	23 38.8	29 0.2
6 F	0 54 9	11 37 6	14 32 20	21 7 45	0 59.8	28 31.0	13D 23.7	9 53.2	15 49.2	19 16.7	25D 24.2	23 39.6	29 0.1
7 Sa	0 58 5	12 36 16	27 47 58	4♈32 51	0 57.3	0♎13.7	13 22.9	10 3.0	16 1.2	19 13.4	25 24.2	23 40.3	28 59.9
8 Su	1 2 2	13 35 28	11♈22 8	18 15 34	0 55.5	1 57.4	13 24.4	10 12.0	16 13.3	19 10.0	25 24.3	23 41.0	28 59.8
9 M	1 5 58	14 34 42	25 12 43	2♉13 12	0D 54.7	3 41.9	13 28.3	10 20.2	16 25.4	19 6.5	25 24.4	23 41.7	28 59.6
10 Tu	1 9 55	15 33 58	9♉16 32	16 22 11	0 54.8	5 26.8	13 34.5	10 27.7	16 37.6	19 2.9	25 24.6	23 42.3	28 59.4
11 W	1 13 52	16 33 16	23 29 41	0♊38 29	0 55.5	7 12.0	13 43.0	10 34.3	16 49.9	18 59.3	25 24.8	23 42.9	28 59.1
12 Th	1 17 48	17 32 36	7♊48 6	14 58 4	0 56.5	8 57.2	13 53.7	10 40.2	17 2.2	18 55.5	25 25.1	23 43.5	28 58.9
13 F	1 21 45	18 31 59	22 7 54	29 17 14	0 57.6	10 42.4	14 6.6	10 45.2	17 14.5	18 51.8	25 25.4	23 44.0	28 58.6
14 Sa	1 25 41	19 31 25	6♋25 40	13♋32 53	0 58.3	12 27.4	14 21.5	10 49.4	17 26.9	18 47.9	25 25.8	23 44.5	28 58.3
15 Su	1 29 38	20 30 52	20 38 34	27 42 29	0R 58.6	14 12.1	14 38.5	10 52.8	17 39.4	18 44.0	25 26.2	23 45.0	28 58.0
16 M	1 33 34	21 30 22	4♌44 21	11♌44 0	0 58.3	15 56.4	14 57.5	10 55.3	17 51.9	18 40.0	25 26.7	23 45.4	28 57.7
17 Tu	1 37 31	22 29 54	18 41 12	25 35 48	0 57.7	17 40.3	15 18.4	10 57.0	18 4.4	18 35.9	25 27.3	23 45.8	28 57.3
18 W	1 41 27	23 29 29	2♍27 37	9♍16 29	0 56.8	19 23.7	15 41.2	10R 57.7	18 17.0	18 31.8	25 27.8	23 46.2	28 56.9
19 Th	1 45 24	24 29 5	16 2 17	22 44 52	0 55.9	21 6.6	16 5.8	10 57.6	18 29.6	18 27.6	25 28.5	23 46.5	28 56.5
20 F	1 49 21	25 28 44	29 24 6	5♎59 55	0 55.2	22 49.0	16 32.0	10 56.6	18 42.3	18 23.3	25 29.2	23 46.8	28 56.1
21 Sa	1 53 17	26 28 25	12♎32 12	19 0 55	0 54.7	24 30.8	16 60.0	10 54.7	18 55.0	18 19.0	25 29.9	23 47.0	28 55.6
22 Su	1 57 14	27 28 8	25 26 3	1♏47 35	0D 54.5	26 12.0	17 29.5	10 51.8	19 7.8	18 14.7	25 30.7	23 47.3	28 55.2
23 M	2 1 10	28 27 53	8♏ 5 36	14 20 11	0 54.6	27 52.7	18 0.6	10 48.1	19 20.6	18 10.3	25 31.5	23 47.5	28 54.7
24 Tu	2 5 7	29 27 40	20 31 28	26 39 38	0 54.7	29 32.8	18 33.2	10 43.5	19 33.4	18 5.8	25 32.4	23 47.6	28 54.2
25 W	2 9 3	0♏27 30	2♐44 56	8♐47 38	0R 54.7	1♏12.3	19 7.2	10 38.0	19 46.3	18 1.3	25 33.3	23 47.7	28 53.6
26 Th	2 13 0	1 27 20	14 48 5	20 46 38	0 54.7	2 51.2	19 42.6	10 31.6	19 59.2	17 56.8	25 34.3	23 47.8	28 53.1
27 F	2 16 56	2 27 13	26 43 43	2♑39 46	0 54.6	4 29.6	20 19.3	10 24.3	20 12.1	17 52.2	25 35.4	23 47.9	28 52.5
28 Sa	2 20 53	3 27 8	8♑35 18	14 30 49	0 54.4	6 7.5	20 57.3	10 16.1	20 25.1	17 47.6	25 36.5	23R 47.9	28 51.9
29 Su	2 24 50	4 27 4	20 26 52	26 24 1	0 54.1	7 44.8	21 36.6	10 7.1	20 38.1	17 42.9	25 37.6	23 47.9	28 51.3
30 M	2 28 46	5 27 1	2♒22 51	8♒23 57	0D 54.0	9 21.6	22 17.0	9 57.1	20 51.1	17 38.2	25 38.8	23 47.9	28 50.7
31 Tu	2 32 43	6 27 1	14 27 53	20 35 16	0 54.0	10 58.0	22 58.6	9 46.3	21 4.1	17 33.5	25 40.0	23 47.8	28 50.0

Astro Data Dy Hr Mn	Planet Ingress Dy Hr Mn	Last Aspect Dy Hr Mn	☽ Ingress Dy Hr Mn	Last Aspect Dy Hr Mn	☽ Ingress Dy Hr Mn	☽ Phases & Eclipses Dy Hr Mn	Astro Data
♄ R 2 20:57	♂ ♊ 5 15:21	2 12:19 ♇ ☍	♑ 2 14:37	2 1:49 ♅ ☌	♒ 2 10:56	8 15:56 ○ 14♓52	1 SEPTEMBER 1911
☿0N 5 5:53	☉ ♎ 24 4:18	5 2:05 ♂ △	♒ 5 2:35	4 19:07 ♇ △	♓ 4 20:59	15 17:51 ☽ 21♊45	Julian Day # 4261
☽0N 10 5:01		7 10:14 ♇ △	♓ 7 12:17	7 2:09 ♇ □	♈ 7 3:56	22 14:37 ● 28♍28	Delta T 12.7 sec
☿ D 18 22:23	☿ ♎ 6 20:49	9 17:35 ♇ □	♈ 9 19:31	9 6:29 ♇ ✶	♉ 9 8:12	30 11:08 ☽ 6♑10	SVP 06♓29'44"
☽0S 23 2:45	☉ ♏ 24 12:58	11 22:58 ♇ ✶	♉ 12 0:49	11 3:14 ♅ △	♊ 11 10:55		Obliquity 23°27'11"
♃♇♇ 26 16:43	☿ ♏ 24 6:33	13 21:14 ♅ △	♊ 14 4:47	13 11:29 ♇ ☌	♋ 13 13:12	8 4:11 ○ 13♈46	⚷ Chiron 4♓27.3R
♇ R 30 4:37		16 6:03 ♇ ☌	♋ 16 7:47	15 8:09 ♅ ☍	♌ 15 15:54	14 23:46 ☽ 20♋30	☽ Mean ☊ 3♉34.2
♀0N 1 1:35		18 2:47 ♅ ☍	♌ 18 10:18	17 17:51 ♇ ✶	♍ 17 19:41	22 4:09 ● 27♎38	
♀ D 6 20:24		20 11:22 ♇ ✶	♍ 20 13:05	19 23:09 ♇ □	♎ 20 1:05	22 4:12:48 ☄ A 3'47"	1 OCTOBER 1911
♅ D 6 1:53		22 15:34 ♇ □	♎ 22 17:21	22 6:34 ♇ △	♏ 22 8:36	30 6:41 ☽ 5♒44	Julian Day # 4291
☽0N 7 13:16		24 22:24 ♇ △	♏ 25 0:17	24 9:49 ♅ ✶	♐ 24 18:34		Delta T 12.9 sec
☿0S 9 8:11		27 1:20 ♅ ✶	♐ 27 10:21	27 4:20 ♇ ☍	♑ 27 6:37		SVP 06♓29'41"
♃☍♄ 18 21:05	☽0S 20 10:42	29 20:38 ♇ ☍	♑ 29 22:39	29 10:28 ♅ ☌	♒ 29 19:14		Obliquity 23°27'11"
♂ R 18 8:37	♆ R 28 4:02						⚷ Chiron 3♓07.3R
							☽ Mean ☊ 1♉58.9

NOVEMBER 1911 LONGITUDE

Day	Sid.Time	☉	0 hr ☽	Noon ☽	True ☊	☿	♀	♂	♃	♄	♅	♆	♇
1 W	2 36 39	7♏27 2	26♒46 36	3♓ 2 26	0♉54.4	12♏33.8	23♍41.2	9♊34.7	21♏17.2	17♉28.8	25♑41.3	23♋47.7	28♊49.4
2 Th	2 40 36	8 27 4	9♓23 14	15 49 23	0 55.0	14 9.2	24 25.0	9R 22.3	21 30.3	17R 24.0	25 42.7	23R 47.5	28R 48.7
3 F	2 44 32	9 27 8	22 21 15	28 59 4	0 55.8	15 44.2	25 9.8	9 9.0	21 43.4	17 19.2	25 44.0	23 47.3	28 48.0
4 Sa	2 48 29	10 27 14	5♈42 57	12♈32 56	0 56.6	17 18.7	25 55.5	8 55.0	21 56.6	17 14.4	25 45.5	23 47.1	28 47.2
5 Su	2 52 25	11 27 22	19 28 55	26 30 38	0R 57.3	18 52.8	26 42.2	8 40.2	22 9.7	17 9.5	25 46.9	23 46.9	28 46.5
6 M	2 56 22	12 27 31	3♉37 41	10♉49 32	0 57.4	20 26.5	27 29.9	8 24.6	22 22.9	17 4.7	25 48.5	23 46.6	28 45.7
7 Tu	3 0 19	13 27 42	18 5 32	25 24 55	0 57.0	21 59.8	28 18.4	8 8.4	22 36.1	16 59.8	25 50.0	23 46.3	28 45.0
8 W	3 4 15	14 27 55	2♊46 47	10♊10 16	0 55.9	23 32.8	29 7.8	7 51.4	22 49.3	16 55.0	25 51.7	23 45.9	28 44.2
9 Th	3 8 12	15 28 9	17 34 22	24 58 10	0 54.2	25 5.4	29 58.1	7 33.8	23 2.6	16 50.1	25 53.3	23 45.5	28 43.4
10 F	3 12 8	16 28 26	2♋20 47	9♋41 22	0 52.2	26 37.7	0♎49.1	7 15.6	23 15.8	16 45.2	25 55.0	23 45.1	28 42.5
11 Sa	3 16 5	17 28 45	16 59 12	24 13 41	0 50.3	28 9.6	1 40.9	6 56.7	23 29.1	16 40.3	25 56.8	23 44.7	28 41.7
12 Su	3 20 1	18 29 6	1♌24 18	8♌30 42	0 48.9	29 41.2	2 33.5	6 37.3	23 42.4	16 35.5	25 58.6	23 44.2	28 40.9
13 M	3 23 58	19 29 28	15 32 39	22 30 0	0D 48.2	1♐12.5	3 26.7	6 17.3	23 55.7	16 30.6	26 0.5	23 43.7	28 40.0
14 Tu	3 27 54	20 29 53	29 22 43	6♍10 51	0 48.3	2 43.4	4 20.7	5 56.9	24 9.0	16 25.7	26 2.3	23 43.1	28 39.1
15 W	3 31 51	21 30 19	12♍54 32	19 33 55	0 49.3	4 14.1	5 15.3	5 36.0	24 22.3	16 20.9	26 4.3	23 42.6	28 38.2
16 Th	3 35 48	22 30 47	26 9 10	2♎40 33	0 50.8	5 44.4	6 10.6	5 14.7	24 35.6	16 16.0	26 6.3	23 41.9	28 37.3
17 F	3 39 44	23 31 17	9♎ 8 15	15 32 30	0 52.3	7 14.4	7 6.5	4 53.1	24 48.9	16 11.2	26 8.3	23 41.3	28 36.3
18 Sa	3 43 41	24 31 49	21 53 31	28 11 30	0R 53.5	8 44.0	8 2.9	4 31.1	25 2.2	16 6.4	26 10.3	23 40.6	28 35.4
19 Su	3 47 37	25 32 23	4♏26 39	10♏39 7	0 53.7	10 13.3	8 60.0	4 8.9	25 15.6	16 1.6	26 12.5	23 39.9	28 34.4
20 M	3 51 34	26 32 58	16 49 7	22 56 46	0 52.7	11 42.2	9 57.6	3 46.5	25 28.9	15 56.8	26 14.6	23 39.2	28 33.4
21 Tu	3 55 30	27 33 35	29 2 14	5♐ 5 41	0 50.2	13 10.7	10 55.7	3 24.0	25 42.2	15 52.1	26 16.8	23 38.4	28 32.4
22 W	3 59 27	28 34 13	11♐ 7 18	17 7 14	0 46.4	14 38.7	11 54.3	3 1.4	25 55.5	15 47.4	26 19.0	23 37.6	28 31.4
23 Th	4 3 23	29 34 53	23 5 43	29 2 58	0 41.4	16 6.2	12 53.4	2 38.7	26 8.9	15 42.7	26 21.3	23 36.8	28 30.4
24 F	4 7 20	0♐35 34	4♑59 14	10♑54 49	0 35.8	17 33.2	13 53.0	2 16.1	26 22.2	15 38.1	26 23.6	23 36.0	28 29.4
25 Sa	4 11 17	1 36 17	16 50 3	22 45 18	0 30.2	18 59.5	14 53.1	1 53.5	26 35.5	15 33.5	26 26.0	23 35.1	28 28.4
26 Su	4 15 13	2 37 0	28 40 59	4♒37 31	0 25.1	20 25.2	15 53.6	1 31.1	26 48.8	15 28.9	26 28.4	23 34.2	28 27.3
27 M	4 19 10	3 37 45	10♒35 25	16 35 11	0 21.2	21 50.0	16 54.5	1 8.9	27 2.1	15 24.4	26 30.8	23 33.2	28 26.3
28 Tu	4 23 6	4 38 30	22 37 21	28 42 31	0 18.8	23 13.9	17 55.8	0 46.8	27 15.4	15 19.9	26 33.3	23 32.2	28 25.2
29 W	4 27 3	5 39 17	4♓51 14	11♓ 4 7	0D 18.0	24 36.8	18 57.5	0 25.1	27 28.7	15 15.5	26 35.8	23 31.2	28 24.1
30 Th	4 30 59	6 40 4	17 21 44	23 44 40	0 18.5	25 58.5	19 59.7	0 3.6	27 42.0	15 11.1	26 38.3	23 30.2	28 23.0

DECEMBER 1911 LONGITUDE

Day	Sid.Time	☉	0 hr ☽	Noon ☽	True ☊	☿	♀	♂	♃	♄	♅	♆	♇
1 F	4 34 56	7♐40 53	0♈13 25	6♈48 27	0♉19.9	27♐18.8	21♎ 2.2	29♉42.6	27♏55.2	15♉ 6.8	26♑40.9	23♋29.2	28♊21.9
2 Sa	4 38 52	8 41 42	13 30 10	20 18 50	0 21.5	28 37.6	22 5.0	29R 21.9	28 8.5	15R 2.5	26 43.5	23R 28.1	28R 20.8
3 Su	4 42 49	9 42 32	27 14 36	4♉17 27	0R 22.4	29 54.5	23 8.2	29 1.8	28 21.7	14 58.3	26 46.1	23 27.0	28 19.7
4 M	4 46 46	10 43 24	11♉27 11	18 43 26	0 21.9	1♑ 9.4	24 11.8	28 42.1	28 34.9	14 54.2	26 48.8	23 25.8	28 18.6
5 Tu	4 50 42	11 44 16	26 5 36	3♊32 53	0 19.6	2 21.8	25 15.7	28 22.9	28 48.1	14 50.1	26 51.5	23 24.7	28 17.4
6 W	4 54 39	12 45 9	11♊ 4 18	18 38 41	0 15.2	3 31.4	26 19.9	28 4.3	29 1.2	14 46.1	26 54.3	23 23.5	28 16.3
7 Th	4 58 35	13 46 3	26 14 48	3♋51 17	0 9.1	4 37.8	27 24.5	27 46.3	29 14.4	14 42.2	26 57.1	23 22.3	28 15.2
8 F	5 2 32	14 46 59	11♋26 49	19 0 6	0 2.1	5 40.5	28 29.3	27 28.9	29 27.5	14 38.3	26 59.9	23 21.1	28 14.0
9 Sa	5 6 28	15 47 55	26 29 58	3♌55 24	29♈55.1	6 38.9	29 34.4	27 12.1	29 40.6	14 34.5	27 2.7	23 19.8	28 12.9
10 Su	5 10 25	16 48 53	11♌15 33	18 29 49	29 49.1	7 32.4	0♏39.9	26 56.0	29 53.7	14 30.7	27 5.6	23 18.6	28 11.7
11 M	5 14 22	17 49 52	25 37 45	2♍39 9	29 44.9	8 20.4	1 45.6	26 40.7	0♐ 6.7	14 27.1	27 8.5	23 17.3	28 10.5
12 Tu	5 18 18	18 50 51	9♍33 58	16 22 18	29D 42.6	9 2.1	2 51.6	26 26.0	0 19.8	14 23.5	27 11.4	23 16.0	28 9.4
13 W	5 22 15	19 51 52	23 4 25	29 40 37	29 42.2	9 36.6	3 57.8	26 12.0	0 32.8	14 20.0	27 14.4	23 14.6	28 8.2
14 Th	5 26 11	20 52 54	6♎11 21	12♎37 2	29 43.0	10 3.1	5 4.3	25 58.9	0 45.7	14 16.5	27 17.4	23 13.2	28 7.0
15 F	5 30 8	21 53 57	18 58 9	25 15 11	29R 44.2	10 20.8	6 11.0	25 46.5	0 58.6	14 13.2	27 20.4	23 11.9	28 5.8
16 Sa	5 34 4	22 55 1	1♏28 37	7♏38 54	29 44.6	10R 28.6	7 18.0	25 34.8	1 11.5	14 9.9	27 23.5	23 10.5	28 4.6
17 Su	5 38 1	23 56 6	13 46 26	19 51 37	29 43.4	10 26.0	8 25.2	25 24.0	1 24.4	14 6.8	27 26.5	23 9.0	28 3.4
18 M	5 41 57	24 57 12	25 54 48	1♐56 18	29 39.9	10 12.1	9 32.6	25 14.0	1 37.2	14 3.7	27 29.6	23 7.6	28 2.3
19 Tu	5 45 54	25 58 18	7♐56 22	13 55 15	29 33.7	9 46.7	10 40.2	25 4.8	1 50.0	14 0.7	27 32.7	23 6.1	28 1.1
20 W	5 49 51	26 59 25	19 53 11	25 50 19	29 24.9	9 9.6	11 48.0	24 56.4	2 2.7	13 57.8	27 35.9	23 4.7	27 59.9
21 Th	5 53 47	28 0 33	1♑46 52	7♑42 57	29 13.9	8 21.1	12 56.0	24 48.9	2 15.4	13 55.0	27 39.1	23 3.2	27 58.7
22 F	5 57 44	29 1 41	13 38 46	19 34 30	29 1.7	7 22.1	14 4.2	24 42.2	2 28.1	13 52.3	27 42.3	23 1.7	27 57.5
23 Sa	6 1 40	0♑ 2 50	25 30 18	1♒26 26	28 49.1	6 14.1	15 12.6	24 36.3	2 40.7	13 49.6	27 45.5	23 0.2	27 56.3
24 Su	6 5 37	1 3 59	7♒23 8	13 20 40	28 37.4	4 58.8	16 21.2	24 31.3	2 53.3	13 47.1	27 48.7	22 58.6	27 55.1
25 M	6 9 33	2 5 8	19 19 23	25 19 38	28 27.5	3 38.7	17 29.9	24 27.0	3 5.8	13 44.7	27 52.0	22 57.1	27 53.9
26 Tu	6 13 30	3 6 17	1♓21 51	7♓26 29	28 20.1	2 16.4	18 38.8	24 23.7	3 18.3	13 42.4	27 55.2	22 55.5	27 52.7
27 W	6 17 26	4 7 27	13 34 2	19 45 2	28 15.4	0 54.7	19 47.8	24 21.1	3 30.7	13 40.2	27 58.5	22 53.9	27 51.5
28 Th	6 21 23	5 8 36	26 0 1	2♈19 36	28D 13.2	29♐36.2	20 57.0	24 19.3	3 43.1	13 38.0	28 1.9	22 52.3	27 50.3
29 F	6 25 20	6 9 45	8♈44 19	15 14 45	28 12.8	28 23.4	22 6.4	24D 18.4	3 55.4	13 36.0	28 5.2	22 50.7	27 49.2
30 Sa	6 29 16	7 10 54	21 51 25	28 34 46	28R 13.2	27 18.1	23 15.9	24 18.3	4 7.6	13 34.1	28 8.5	22 49.1	27 48.0
31 Su	6 33 13	8 12 3	5♉25 11	12♉22 54	28 13.2	26 21.7	24 25.5	24 18.9	4 19.8	13 32.3	28 11.9	22 47.5	27 46.8

Astro Data	Dy Hr Mn
☽0N	3 23:15
♀0S	9 22:34
♃△♆	12 3:10
☽0S	16 16:47
♃⚹♅	24 3:06
☽0N	1 8:56
♃⊼♇	2 20:40
☽0S	13 21:45
☿ R	16 6:10
♅⊼♇	25 10:24
☽0N	28 16:25
♂ D	29 16:25

Planet Ingress	Dy Hr Mn
♀ ♎	9 0:55
☿ ♐	12 4:56
☉ ♐	23 9:56
♂ ♉	30 4:07
☿ ♑	3 1:44
☊ ♈	8 7:06
♀ ♏	9 9:23
♃ ♐	10 11:35
☉ ♑	22 22:53
☿ ♐	27 16:35

Last Aspect Dy Hr Mn		☽ Ingress	Dy Hr Mn
1 3:56	♇ △	♓	1 6:12
3 11:39	♇ □	♈	3 13:49
5 15:49	♇ ⚹	♉	5 17:54
7 17:42	♀ △	♊	7 19:29
9 18:05	♇ ☌	♋	9 20:11
11 20:46	☿ △	♌	11 21:39
13 22:44	♇ ⚹	♍	14 1:05
16 4:31	♇ □	♎	16 7:04
18 12:45	♇ △	♏	18 15:28
20 20:49	☉ ☌	♐	21 1:54
23 10:53	♇ ☍	♑	23 13:55
25 20:09	♃ ⚹	♒	26 2:40
28 11:25	♇ △	♓	28 14:32
30 23:05	♂ ⚹	♈	30 23:35

Last Aspect Dy Hr Mn		☽ Ingress	Dy Hr Mn
3 1:51	♇ ⚹	♉	3 4:43
5 4:26	♃ ☍	♊	5 6:18
7 3:10	♇ ☌	♋	7 5:55
9 5:21	♀ □	♌	9 5:39
11 4:19	♇ ⚹	♍	11 7:27
13 9:10	♇ □	♎	13 12:35
15 17:26	♇ △	♏	15 21:09
18 3:09	♅ ⚹	♐	18 8:08
20 16:20	♇ ☍	♑	20 20:24
23 4:35	♅ ☌	♒	23 9:05
25 17:06	♇ △	♓	25 21:18
28 6:14	☿ □	♈	28 7:36
30 11:16	♅ □	♉	30 14:31

☽ Phases & Eclipses Dy Hr Mn	
6 15:48	○ 13♉07
6 15:36	☊ A 0.815
13 7:19	☽ 19♌48
20 20:49	● 27♏26
29 1:42	☽ 5♓44
6 2:52	○ 12♊52
12 17:46	☽ 19♍36
20 15:40	● 27♐39
28 18:47	☽ 5♈56

Astro Data

1 NOVEMBER 1911
Julian Day # 4322
Delta T 13.1 sec
SVP 06♓29'37"
Obliquity 23°27'11"
⚷ Chiron 2♓19.1R
☽ Mean ☊ 0♉20.4

1 DECEMBER 1911
Julian Day # 4352
Delta T 13.2 sec
SVP 06♓29'32"
Obliquity 23°27'10"
⚷ Chiron 2♓23.4
☽ Mean ☊ 28♈45.1

LONGITUDE — JANUARY 1912

Day	Sid.Time	☉	0 hr ☽	Noon ☽	True ☊	☿	♀	♂	♃	♄	♅	♆	♇
1 M	6 37 9	9♑13 12	19♉28 1	26♉40 25	28♈11.4	25♐35.2	25♏35.3	24♉20.3	4♐32.0	13♉30.6	28♑15.3	22♋45.8	27♊45.6
2 Tu	6 41 6	10 14 21	3♊59 48	11♊25 36	28R 7.3	24R 59.0	26 45.2	24 22.5	4 44.1	13R 29.0	28 18.7	22R 44.2	27R 44.5
3 W	6 45 2	11 15 30	18 57 1	26 33 2	28 0.3	24 33.2	27 55.3	24 25.4	4 56.1	13 27.5	28 22.1	22 42.6	27 43.3
4 Th	6 48 59	12 16 38	4♋12 23	11♋53 41	27 50.8	24 17.5	29 5.4	24 29.1	5 8.0	13 26.2	28 25.5	22 40.9	27 42.2
5 F	6 52 56	13 17 47	19 35 25	27 16 3	27 39.8	24D 11.5	0♐15.7	24 33.5	5 19.9	13 24.9	28 28.9	22 39.2	27 41.0
6 Sa	6 56 52	14 18 55	4♌54 5	12♌28 10	27 28.6	24 14.6	1 26.1	24 38.6	5 31.8	13 23.7	28 32.4	22 37.6	27 39.9
7 Su	7 0 49	15 20 4	19 57 5	27 19 52	27 18.5	24 26.1	2 36.7	24 44.4	5 43.5	13 22.7	28 35.8	22 35.9	27 38.7
8 M	7 4 45	16 21 12	4♍35 47	11♍44 21	27 10.6	24 45.4	3 47.3	24 50.9	5 55.2	13 21.8	28 39.3	22 34.2	27 37.6
9 Tu	7 8 42	17 22 20	18 45 21	25 38 44	27 5.3	25 11.6	4 58.1	24 58.1	6 6.8	13 20.9	28 42.8	22 32.5	27 36.5
10 W	7 12 38	18 23 29	2♎24 41	9♎ 3 30	27 2.7	25 44.3	6 9.0	25 5.9	6 18.4	13 20.2	28 46.3	22 30.8	27 35.4
11 Th	7 16 35	19 24 37	15 35 37	22 1 34	27 1.9	26 22.6	7 19.9	25 14.4	6 29.9	13 19.6	28 49.8	22 29.1	27 34.3
12 F	7 20 31	20 25 45	28 21 56	4♏37 19	27 1.9	27 6.1	8 31.0	25 23.5	6 41.3	13 19.1	28 53.3	22 27.4	27 33.2
13 Sa	7 24 28	21 26 54	10♏48 20	16 55 37	27 1.4	27 54.2	9 42.2	25 33.2	6 52.6	13 18.7	28 56.8	22 25.7	27 32.1
14 Su	7 28 25	22 28 2	22 59 45	29 1 19	26 59.2	28 46.5	10 53.5	25 43.6	7 3.9	13 18.5	29 0.3	22 24.0	27 31.0
15 M	7 32 21	23 29 10	5♐ 0 49	10♐58 44	26 54.4	29 42.4	12 4.8	25 54.5	7 15.0	13D 18.3	29 3.8	22 22.3	27 30.0
16 Tu	7 36 18	24 30 18	16 55 30	22 51 30	26 46.5	0♑41.7	13 16.3	26 6.1	7 26.1	13 18.3	29 7.3	22 20.7	27 28.9
17 W	7 40 14	25 31 26	28 47 4	4♑42 30	26 35.6	1 44.0	14 27.8	26 18.2	7 37.2	13 18.3	29 10.9	22 19.0	27 27.9
18 Th	7 44 11	26 32 33	10♑38 1	16 33 51	26 22.2	2 48.9	15 39.4	26 30.9	7 48.1	13 18.5	29 14.4	22 17.3	27 26.8
19 F	7 48 7	27 33 40	22 30 9	28 27 6	26 7.2	3 56.3	16 51.1	26 44.2	7 58.9	13 18.8	29 17.9	22 15.6	27 25.8
20 Sa	7 52 4	28 34 46	4♒24 50	10♒23 28	25 51.8	5 5.9	18 2.8	26 58.0	8 9.7	13 19.2	29 21.5	22 13.9	27 24.8
21 Su	7 56 0	29 35 51	16 23 10	22 24 5	25 37.2	6 17.4	19 14.7	27 12.3	8 20.3	13 19.8	29 25.0	22 12.2	27 23.8
22 M	7 59 57	0♒36 56	28 26 23	4♓30 17	25 24.7	7 30.8	20 26.5	27 27.2	8 30.9	13 20.4	29 28.5	22 10.5	27 22.8
23 Tu	8 3 54	1 38 0	10♓36 2	16 43 54	25 14.9	8 45.8	21 38.5	27 42.5	8 41.4	13 21.2	29 32.1	22 8.8	27 21.9
24 W	8 7 50	2 39 3	22 54 14	29 7 23	25 8.4	10 2.4	22 50.5	27 58.4	8 51.7	13 22.0	29 35.6	22 7.2	27 20.9
25 Th	8 11 47	3 40 4	5♈23 45	11♈43 47	25 4.8	11 20.3	24 2.6	28 14.7	9 2.0	13 23.0	29 39.1	22 5.5	27 20.0
26 F	8 15 43	4 41 5	18 7 58	24 36 45	25D 3.5	12 39.6	25 14.7	28 31.6	9 12.2	13 24.1	29 42.6	22 3.9	27 19.1
27 Sa	8 19 40	5 42 5	1♉10 37	7♉50 2	25R 3.4	14 0.1	26 26.9	28 48.8	9 22.3	13 25.3	29 46.2	22 2.2	27 18.1
28 Su	8 23 36	6 43 3	14 35 23	21 27 1	25 3.2	15 21.7	27 39.1	29 6.6	9 32.2	13 26.6	29 49.7	22 0.6	27 17.2
29 M	8 27 33	7 44 1	28 25 10	5♊29 54	25 1.8	16 44.5	28 51.4	29 24.8	9 42.1	13 28.1	29 53.2	21 58.9	27 16.4
30 Tu	8 31 29	8 44 57	12♊41 10	19 58 41	24 58.1	18 8.2	0♑ 3.8	29 43.4	9 51.9	13 29.6	29 56.7	21 57.3	27 15.5
31 W	8 35 26	9 45 52	27 21 59	4♋50 20	24 51.6	19 32.9	1 16.2	0♊ 2.4	10 1.5	13 31.2	0♒ 0.2	21 55.7	27 14.7

LONGITUDE — FEBRUARY 1912

Day	Sid.Time	☉	0 hr ☽	Noon ☽	True ☊	☿	♀	♂	♃	♄	♅	♆	♇
1 Th	8 39 23	10♒46 45	12♋22 51	19♋58 22	24♈42.7	20♑58.6	2♑28.6	0♊21.8	10♐11.1	13♉33.0	0♒ 3.7	21♋54.1	27♊13.8
2 F	8 43 19	11 47 38	27 35 38	5♌13 15	24R 32.1	22 25.1	3 41.1	0 41.6	10 20.5	13 34.9	0 7.2	21R 52.6	27R 13.0
3 Sa	8 47 16	12 48 29	12♌49 48	20 23 53	24 21.1	23 52.6	4 53.7	1 1.8	10 29.9	13 36.8	0 10.6	21 51.0	27 12.2
4 Su	8 51 12	13 49 19	27 54 10	5♍19 32	24 11.0	25 20.9	6 6.3	1 22.3	10 39.1	13 38.9	0 14.1	21 49.4	27 11.4
5 M	8 55 9	14 50 8	12♍39 1	19 51 52	24 2.9	26 50.1	7 18.9	1 43.2	10 48.2	13 41.1	0 17.6	21 47.9	27 10.7
6 Tu	8 59 5	15 50 56	26 57 34	3♎55 52	23 57.5	28 20.0	8 31.6	2 4.5	10 57.2	13 43.4	0 21.0	21 46.4	27 9.9
7 W	9 3 2	16 51 43	10♎46 40	17 30 6	23 54.6	29 50.8	9 44.3	2 26.1	11 6.0	13 45.8	0 24.4	21 44.9	27 9.2
8 Th	9 6 58	17 52 29	24 6 26	0♏36 4	23D 53.9	1♒22.5	10 57.1	2 48.1	11 14.8	13 48.3	0 27.8	21 43.4	27 8.5
9 F	9 10 55	18 53 14	6♏59 31	13 17 20	23 54.3	2 54.9	12 9.9	3 10.3	11 23.4	13 50.9	0 31.2	21 41.9	27 7.8
10 Sa	9 14 52	19 53 58	19 30 8	25 38 34	23R 54.7	4 28.2	13 22.8	3 32.9	11 31.9	13 53.6	0 34.6	21 40.4	27 7.1
11 Su	9 18 48	20 54 40	1♐43 17	7♐44 56	23 54.1	6 2.3	14 35.7	3 55.9	11 40.3	13 56.4	0 38.0	21 39.0	27 6.5
12 M	9 22 45	21 55 22	13 44 9	19 41 30	23 51.4	7 37.2	15 48.6	4 19.1	11 48.5	13 59.4	0 41.4	21 37.5	27 5.9
13 Tu	9 26 41	22 56 3	25 37 35	1♑32 54	23 46.4	9 12.9	17 1.6	4 42.6	11 56.7	14 2.4	0 44.7	21 36.1	27 5.2
14 W	9 30 38	23 56 43	7♑27 55	13 23 6	23 38.7	10 49.5	18 14.6	5 6.4	12 4.7	14 5.5	0 48.0	21 34.8	27 4.7
15 Th	9 34 34	24 57 21	19 18 47	25 15 19	23 29.0	12 26.9	19 27.6	5 30.5	12 12.5	14 8.7	0 51.4	21 33.4	27 4.1
16 F	9 38 31	25 57 58	1♒12 58	7♒11 59	23 17.8	14 5.2	20 40.6	5 54.9	12 20.2	14 12.1	0 54.6	21 32.0	27 3.5
17 Sa	9 42 27	26 58 34	13 12 34	19 14 52	23 6.3	15 44.4	21 53.7	6 19.6	12 27.8	14 15.5	0 57.9	21 30.7	27 3.0
18 Su	9 46 24	27 59 8	25 19 1	1♓25 9	22 55.3	17 24.5	23 6.8	6 44.5	12 35.3	14 19.0	1 1.2	21 29.4	27 2.5
19 M	9 50 21	28 59 40	7♓33 20	13 43 42	22 45.9	19 5.4	24 20.0	7 9.7	12 42.6	14 22.6	1 4.4	21 28.1	27 2.0
20 Tu	9 54 17	0♓ 0 11	19 56 20	26 11 22	22 38.7	20 47.3	25 33.1	7 35.2	12 49.7	14 26.3	1 7.6	21 26.9	27 1.5
21 W	9 58 14	1 0 40	2♈28 55	8♈49 9	22 34.1	22 30.1	26 46.3	8 0.9	12 56.8	14 30.1	1 10.8	21 25.6	27 1.1
22 Th	10 2 10	2 1 7	15 12 17	21 38 29	22D 32.0	24 13.8	27 59.5	8 26.8	13 3.6	14 34.0	1 14.0	21 24.4	27 0.6
23 F	10 6 7	3 1 33	28 8 1	4♉41 8	22 31.9	25 58.5	29 12.7	8 53.0	13 10.4	14 38.0	1 17.1	21 23.2	27 0.2
24 Sa	10 10 3	4 1 57	11♉18 6	17 59 10	22 32.9	27 44.2	0♒26.0	9 19.4	13 17.0	14 42.1	1 20.2	21 22.0	26 59.9
25 Su	10 14 0	5 2 19	24 44 36	1♊34 37	22R 34.0	29 30.8	1 39.2	9 46.0	13 23.4	14 46.3	1 23.3	21 20.9	26 59.5
26 M	10 17 56	6 2 39	8♊29 21	15 28 54	22 34.4	1♓18.4	2 52.5	10 12.9	13 29.7	14 50.5	1 26.4	21 19.8	26 59.2
27 Tu	10 21 53	7 2 56	22 33 14	29 42 13	22 33.3	3 7.0	4 5.8	10 40.0	13 35.8	14 54.9	1 29.4	21 18.7	26 58.8
28 W	10 25 50	8 3 12	6♋55 34	14♋12 52	22 30.2	4 56.6	5 19.1	11 7.2	13 41.8	14 59.3	1 32.4	21 17.6	26 58.5
29 Th	10 29 46	9 3 26	21 33 31	28 56 48	22 25.3	6 47.2	6 32.4	11 34.7	13 47.6	15 3.8	1 35.4	21 16.6	26 58.3

Astro Data Dy Hr Mn	Planet Ingress Dy Hr Mn	Last Aspect Dy Hr Mn	☽ Ingress Dy Hr Mn	Last Aspect Dy Hr Mn	☽ Ingress Dy Hr Mn	☽ Phases & Eclipses Dy Hr Mn	Astro Data
☿ D 5 3:33	♀ ♐ 4 18:38	1 14:40 ♅ △	♊ 1 17:28	1 15:01 ♆ ☌	♌ 2 3:47	4 13:29 ○ 12♋51	1 JANUARY 1912
☽0S 10 3:42	☿ ♑ 15 7:15	3 13:49 ♇ ☌	♋ 3 17:25	3 22:51 ♇ ⚹	♍ 4 3:23	11 7:43 ☽ 19♎44	Julian Day # 4383
♃□♆ 15 13:41	☉ ♒ 21 9:29	5 13:57 ♅ ☍	♌ 5 16:17	6 2:38 ☿ △	♎ 6 5:12	19 11:10 ● 28♑02	Delta T 13.4 sec
♄ D 15 20:23	♀ ♑ 29 22:45	7 12:30 ♇ ⚹	♍ 7 16:23	8 5:35 ♇ △	♏ 8 10:53	27 8:51 ☽ 6♉05	SVP 06♓29'26"
☽0N 24 21:38	♂ ♊ 30 21:02	9 17:29 ♅ △	♎ 9 19:42	10 4:13 ♆ △	♐ 10 20:35		Obliquity 23°27'10"
	♅ ♒ 30 22:40	12 1:00 ♅ □	♏ 12 3:07	13 2:57 ♇ ☍	♑ 13 8:52	2 23:58 ○ 12♌48	⚷ Chiron 3♓21.6
☽0S 6 12:06		14 12:01 ♅ ⚹	♐ 14 13:57	15 4:32 ♆ ☍	♒ 15 21:33	10 0:50 ☽ 19♏56	☽ Mean ☊ 27♈06.6
☽0N 21 2:30	☿ ♒ 7 2:24	16 21:20 ♇ ☍	♑ 17 2:28	18 5:44 ☉ ☌	♓ 18 9:13	18 5:44 ● 28♒14	
	☉ ♓ 19 23:56	19 13:46 ♅ ☌	♒ 19 15:07	20 13:35 ♇ □	♈ 20 19:17	25 19:26 ☽ 5♊51	1 FEBRUARY 1912
	♀ ♒ 23 15:29	21 22:00 ♂ □	♓ 22 3:06	23 2:11 ♇ □	♉ 23 3:26		Julian Day # 4414
	☿ ♓ 25 6:32	24 12:58 ♅ ⚹	♈ 24 13:41	24 18:00 ♆ ⚹	♊ 25 9:15		Delta T 13.5 sec
		26 21:26 ♅ □	♉ 26 21:52	27 7:26 ♇ ☌	♋ 27 12:30		SVP 06♓29'20"
		29 2:31 ♅ △	♊ 29 2:42	28 23:32 ♆ ☌	♌ 29 13:42		Obliquity 23°27'11"
		30 23:48 ♇ ☌	♋ 31 4:15				⚷ Chiron 5♓01.1
							☽ Mean ☊ 25♈28.2

MARCH 1912 LONGITUDE

Day	Sid.Time	☉	0 hr ☽	Noon ☽	True ☊	☿	♀	♂	♃	♄	♅	♆	♇
1 F	10 33 43	10♓ 3 38	6♌21 52	13♌47 43	22♈19.2	8♓38.7	7♒45.8	12♊ 2.4	13♐53.3	15♉ 8.4	1♒38.4	21♋15.6	26♊58.0
2 Sa	10 37 39	11 3 48	21 13 21	28 37 40	22R 12.6	10 31.2	8 59.1	12 30.2	13 58.8	15 13.1	1 41.3	21R 14.6	26R 57.8
3 Su	10 41 36	12 3 55	5♍59 38	13♍18 15	22 6.4	12 24.6	10 12.5	12 58.3	14 4.1	15 17.9	1 44.2	21 13.7	26 57.6
4 M	10 45 32	13 4 1	20 32 37	27 42 0	22 1.6	14 18.8	11 25.9	13 26.5	14 9.3	15 22.8	1 47.1	21 12.7	26 57.4
5 Tu	10 49 29	14 4 5	4♎45 46	11♎43 28	21 58.4	16 13.9	12 39.3	13 54.9	14 14.3	15 27.7	1 49.9	21 11.8	26 57.2
6 W	10 53 25	15 4 7	18 34 51	25 19 47	21D 57.2	18 9.7	13 52.7	14 23.4	14 19.2	15 32.7	1 52.8	21 11.0	26 57.1
7 Th	10 57 22	16 4 8	1♏58 19	8♏30 36	21 57.5	20 6.2	15 6.1	14 52.1	14 23.9	15 37.8	1 55.5	21 10.1	26 57.0
8 F	11 1 19	17 4 7	14 56 56	21 17 43	21 58.9	22 3.1	16 19.6	15 21.0	14 28.4	15 43.0	1 58.3	21 9.3	26 56.9
9 Sa	11 5 15	18 4 4	27 33 24	3♐44 30	22 0.6	24 0.5	17 33.0	15 50.1	14 32.8	15 48.2	2 1.0	21 8.5	26 56.8
10 Su	11 9 12	19 4 0	9♐51 36	15 55 17	22R 1.9	25 58.1	18 46.5	16 19.3	14 37.0	15 53.5	2 3.7	21 7.8	26 56.8
11 M	11 13 8	20 3 54	21 56 10	27 54 52	22 2.3	27 55.6	20 0.0	16 48.7	14 41.0	15 58.9	2 6.3	21 7.1	26D 56.7
12 Tu	11 17 5	21 3 46	3♑51 59	9♑48 7	22 1.4	29 53.0	21 13.5	17 18.2	14 44.8	16 4.4	2 9.0	21 6.4	26 56.7
13 W	11 21 1	22 3 37	15 43 51	21 39 42	21 59.1	1♈49.9	22 27.0	17 47.9	14 48.5	16 9.9	2 11.5	21 5.7	26 56.8
14 Th	11 24 58	23 3 26	27 36 12	3♒33 48	21 55.6	3 45.9	23 40.6	18 17.7	14 52.0	16 15.5	2 14.1	21 5.1	26 56.8
15 F	11 28 54	24 3 13	9♒32 57	15 34 0	21 51.1	5 40.9	24 54.1	18 47.6	14 55.3	16 21.2	2 16.6	21 4.5	26 56.9
16 Sa	11 32 51	25 2 59	21 37 18	27 43 8	21 46.4	7 34.2	26 7.6	19 17.7	14 58.5	16 27.0	2 19.1	21 3.9	26 57.0
17 Su	11 36 48	26 2 42	3♓51 43	10♓ 3 15	21 41.8	9 25.7	27 21.2	19 47.9	15 1.4	16 32.8	2 21.5	21 3.4	26 57.1
18 M	11 40 44	27 2 23	16 17 52	22 35 40	21 37.9	11 14.8	28 34.8	20 18.3	15 4.2	16 38.7	2 23.9	21 2.9	26 57.2
19 Tu	11 44 41	28 2 3	28 56 42	5♈21 0	21 35.1	13 1.1	29 48.3	20 48.8	15 6.8	16 44.6	2 26.3	21 2.4	26 57.4
20 W	11 48 37	29 1 40	11♈48 35	18 19 24	21D 33.6	14 44.2	1♓ 1.9	21 19.4	15 9.2	16 50.6	2 28.6	21 2.0	26 57.6
21 Th	11 52 34	0♈ 1 16	24 53 26	1♉30 38	21 33.4	16 23.5	2 15.5	21 50.2	15 11.4	16 56.7	2 30.9	21 1.6	26 57.8
22 F	11 56 30	1 0 49	8♉10 58	14 54 23	21 34.0	17 58.7	3 29.0	22 21.1	15 13.5	17 2.8	2 33.1	21 1.2	26 58.0
23 Sa	12 0 27	2 0 20	21 40 49	28 30 13	21 35.3	19 29.2	4 42.6	22 52.1	15 15.4	17 9.0	2 35.3	21 0.9	26 58.2
24 Su	12 4 23	2 59 49	5♊22 32	12♊17 41	21 36.7	20 54.7	5 56.2	23 23.2	15 17.0	17 15.3	2 37.5	21 0.6	26 58.5
25 M	12 8 20	3 59 16	19 15 35	26 16 7	21 37.8	22 14.8	7 9.8	23 54.4	15 18.5	17 21.6	2 39.6	21 0.3	26 58.8
26 Tu	12 12 17	4 58 41	3♋19 8	10♋24 25	21R 38.3	23 29.1	8 23.4	24 25.7	15 19.9	17 28.0	2 41.7	21 0.1	26 59.1
27 W	12 16 13	5 58 3	17 31 44	24 40 47	21 38.0	24 37.3	9 37.0	24 57.2	15 21.0	17 34.4	2 43.7	20 59.8	26 59.5
28 Th	12 20 10	6 57 22	1♌51 11	9♌ 2 30	21 37.0	25 39.1	10 50.5	25 28.7	15 21.9	17 40.9	2 45.7	20 59.7	26 59.8
29 F	12 24 6	7 56 39	16 14 16	23 25 55	21 35.5	26 34.3	12 4.1	26 0.4	15 22.7	17 47.4	2 47.7	20 59.5	27 0.2
30 Sa	12 28 3	8 55 54	0♍36 53	7♍46 34	21 33.9	27 22.7	13 17.7	26 32.1	15 23.2	17 54.0	2 49.6	20 59.4	27 0.6
31 Su	12 31 59	9 55 7	14 54 21	21 59 37	21 32.4	28 4.1	14 31.3	27 3.9	15 23.6	18 0.7	2 51.5	20 59.4	27 1.0

APRIL 1912 LONGITUDE

Day	Sid.Time	☉	0 hr ☽	Noon ☽	True ☊	☿	♀	♂	♃	♄	♅	♆	♇
1 M	12 35 56	10♈54 17	29♍ 1 49	6♎ 0 26	21♈31.3	28♈38.5	15♓44.9	27♊35.9	15♐23.8	18♉ 7.3	2♒53.3	20♋59.3	27♊ 1.5
2 Tu	12 39 52	11 53 25	12♎55 0	19 45 9	21D 30.7	29 5.6	16 58.5	28 7.9	15R 23.8	18 14.1	2 55.1	20D 59.3	27 2.0
3 W	12 43 49	12 52 32	26 30 35	3♏11 6	21 30.6	29 25.6	18 12.0	28 40.0	15 23.6	18 20.9	2 56.8	20 59.3	27 2.4
4 Th	12 47 45	13 51 36	9♏46 37	16 17 8	21 31.0	29 38.5	19 25.6	29 12.2	15 23.2	18 27.7	2 58.5	20 59.4	27 3.0
5 F	12 51 42	14 50 38	22 42 43	29 3 35	21 31.5	29R 44.4	20 39.2	29 44.5	15 22.7	18 34.6	3 0.2	20 59.5	27 3.5
6 Sa	12 55 39	15 49 39	5♐19 57	11♐32 10	21 32.2	29 43.4	21 52.8	0♋16.8	15 21.9	18 41.5	3 1.8	20 59.6	27 4.1
7 Su	12 59 35	16 48 38	17 40 37	23 45 46	21 32.7	29 35.8	23 6.4	0 49.3	15 21.0	18 48.4	3 3.3	20 59.8	27 4.6
8 M	13 3 32	17 47 35	29 48 5	5♑48 7	21 33.1	29 21.9	24 20.1	1 21.8	15 19.9	18 55.4	3 4.8	20 60.0	27 5.2
9 Tu	13 7 28	18 46 30	11♑46 23	17 43 30	21R 33.3	29 2.1	25 33.7	1 54.5	15 18.6	19 2.5	3 6.3	21 0.2	27 5.8
10 W	13 11 25	19 45 24	23 40 0	29 36 30	21 33.3	28 36.9	26 47.3	2 27.1	15 17.1	19 9.6	3 7.7	21 0.5	27 6.5
11 Th	13 15 21	20 44 16	5♒33 34	11♒31 46	21D 33.3	28 6.9	28 0.9	2 59.9	15 15.4	19 16.7	3 9.1	21 0.8	27 7.1
12 F	13 19 18	21 43 6	17 31 39	23 33 44	21 33.3	27 32.8	29 14.5	3 32.8	15 13.6	19 23.8	3 10.4	21 1.1	27 7.8
13 Sa	13 23 14	22 41 54	29 38 30	5♓46 24	21 33.3	26 55.1	0♈28.1	4 5.7	15 11.5	19 31.0	3 11.7	21 1.5	27 8.5
14 Su	13 27 11	23 40 40	11♓57 50	18 13 7	21 33.5	26 14.7	1 41.7	4 38.7	15 9.3	19 38.3	3 12.9	21 1.9	27 9.2
15 M	13 31 8	24 39 25	24 32 34	0♈56 21	21 33.8	25 32.5	2 55.4	5 11.8	15 6.9	19 45.5	3 14.1	21 2.3	27 10.0
16 Tu	13 35 4	25 38 7	7♈24 38	13 57 28	21 34.1	24 49.1	4 9.0	5 44.9	15 4.3	19 52.8	3 15.2	21 2.8	27 10.7
17 W	13 39 1	26 36 48	20 34 49	27 16 37	21R 34.2	24 5.5	5 22.6	6 18.2	15 1.5	20 0.1	3 16.3	21 3.3	27 11.5
18 Th	13 42 57	27 35 27	4♉ 2 39	10♉52 43	21 34.1	23 22.5	6 36.2	6 51.5	14 58.5	20 7.5	3 17.3	21 3.8	27 12.3
19 F	13 46 54	28 34 4	17 46 29	24 43 36	21 33.6	22 40.7	7 49.8	7 24.8	14 55.4	20 14.9	3 18.3	21 4.4	27 13.1
20 Sa	13 50 50	29 32 39	1♊43 38	8♊46 11	21 32.8	22 1.0	9 3.4	7 58.3	14 52.1	20 22.3	3 19.3	21 5.0	27 14.0
21 Su	13 54 47	0♉31 12	15 50 45	22 56 53	21 31.8	21 23.9	10 17.0	8 31.8	14 48.6	20 29.7	3 20.1	21 5.6	27 14.8
22 M	13 58 43	1 29 43	0♋ 4 8	7♋12 3	21 30.7	20 50.0	11 30.6	9 5.3	14 45.0	20 37.2	3 21.0	21 6.3	27 15.7
23 Tu	14 2 40	2 28 12	14 20 12	21 28 12	21 29.8	20 19.8	12 44.2	9 39.0	14 41.2	20 44.7	3 21.8	21 6.9	27 16.6
24 W	14 6 37	3 26 39	28 35 40	5♌42 18	21D 29.4	19 53.7	13 57.8	10 12.7	14 37.2	20 52.2	3 22.5	21 7.7	27 17.5
25 Th	14 10 33	4 25 3	12♌47 48	19 51 53	21 29.4	19 32.0	15 11.3	10 46.4	14 33.0	20 59.8	3 23.2	21 8.4	27 18.4
26 F	14 14 30	5 23 25	26 54 18	3♍54 50	21 30.1	19 14.8	16 24.9	11 20.2	14 28.7	21 7.3	3 23.8	21 9.2	27 19.4
27 Sa	14 18 26	6 21 45	10♍53 17	17 49 26	21 31.1	19 2.5	17 38.5	11 54.1	14 24.3	21 14.9	3 24.4	21 10.0	27 20.3
28 Su	14 22 23	7 20 3	24 43 5	1♎34 4	21 32.3	18 54.9	18 52.0	12 28.0	14 19.6	21 22.5	3 25.0	21 10.9	27 21.3
29 M	14 26 19	8 18 19	8♎22 12	15 7 18	21R 33.2	18D 52.3	20 5.6	13 1.9	14 14.9	21 30.1	3 25.4	21 11.8	27 22.3
30 Tu	14 30 16	9 16 33	21 49 12	28 27 47	21 33.6	18 54.6	21 19.2	13 36.0	14 9.9	21 37.7	3 25.9	21 12.7	27 23.3

Astro Data	Planet Ingress	Last Aspect	☽ Ingress	Last Aspect	☽ Ingress	☽ Phases & Eclipses	Astro Data
Dy Hr Mn	Dy Hr Mn	Dy Hr Mn	Dy Hr Mn	Dy Hr Mn	Dy Hr Mn	Dy Hr Mn	1 MARCH 1912
☽0S 4 22:16	☿ ♈ 12 1:26	2 9:18 ♇ ⚹	♍ 2 14:14	31 21:27 ♂ □	♎ 1 1:40	3 10:42 ○ 12♍31	Julian Day # 4443
♇ D 11 12:46	♀ ♓ 19 3:49	4 10:45 ♇ □	♎ 4 15:53	3 5:20 ☿ ☍	♏ 3 6:15	10 19:55 ☽ 19♐54	Delta T 13.6 sec
☿0N 12 15:28	☉ ♈ 20 23:29	6 14:55 ♇ △	♏ 6 20:25	4 20:46 ♆ △	♐ 5 13:47	18 22:08 ● 27♓57	SVP 06♓29'16"
☽0N 19 8:56		8 15:55 ☿ △	♐ 9 4:43	7 23:09 ☿ △	♑ 8 0:24	26 3:02 ☽ 5♋06	Obliquity 23°27'11"
	♂ ♋ 5 11:31	11 14:23 ☿ □	♑ 11 16:12	10 9:37 ☿ □	♒ 10 12:47		⚷ Chiron 6♓52.2
☽0S 1 8:04	♀ ♈ 12 14:50	13 13:59 ☉ ⚹	♒ 14 4:50	12 19:04 ♇ △	♓ 13 0:42	1 22:04 ○ 11♎49	☽ Mean ☊ 23♈56.0
♃ R 1 12:12	☉ ♉ 20 11:12	16 10:30 ♇ △	♓ 16 16:28	15 4:57 ♇ □	♈ 15 10:15	1 22:14 ☍ P 0.182	
♆ D 1 16:36		18 22:08 ☉ ☌	♈ 19 1:59	17 11:52 ♇ ⚹	♉ 17 16:51	9 15:23 ☽ 19♑24	1 APRIL 1912
☿ R 5 8:26		21 3:46 ♇ ⚹	♉ 21 9:16	19 5:42 ♆ ⚹	♊ 19 21:03	17 11:40 ● 27♈05	Julian Day # 4474
☽0N 15 17:12		22 22:49 ♆ ⚹	♊ 23 14:37	21 19:16 ♇ ☌	♋ 21 23:53	17 11:34:07 ☌ AT 0'02"	Delta T 13.7 sec
♀0N 15 12:29		25 13:13 ♇ ☌	♋ 25 18:22	23 11:25 ♆ ☌	♌ 24 2:22	24 8:47 ☽ 3♌48	SVP 06♓29'13"
♄⚹♆ 26 6:45		27 12:51 ☿ □	♌ 27 20:54	26 0:43 ♇ ⚹	♍ 26 5:18		Obliquity 23°27'12"
☽0S 28 15:48		29 18:17 ☿ △	♍ 29 22:58	28 4:37 ♇ □	♎ 28 9:15		⚷ Chiron 8♓47.6
☿ D 29 0:53				30 10:04 ♇ △	♏ 30 14:47		☽ Mean ☊ 22♈17.5

LONGITUDE — MAY 1912

Day	Sid.Time	☉	0 hr ☽	Noon ☽	True ☊	☿	♀	♂	♃	♄	♅	♆	♇
1 W	14 34 12	10♉14 45	5♏ 2 53	11♏34 26	21♈33.1	19♈ 1.7	22♈32.7	14♋10.0	14♐ 4.9	21♉45.4	3♒26.3	21♋13.6	27♊24.3
2 Th	14 38 9	11 12 56	18 2 22	24 26 38	21R31.7	19 13.5	23 46.3	14 44.2	13R59.6	21 53.0	3 26.6	21 14.6	27 25.3
3 F	14 42 6	12 11 4	0♐47 16	7♐ 4 19	21 29.2	19 30.0	24 59.8	15 18.3	13 54.3	22 0.7	3 26.9	21 15.6	27 26.4
4 Sa	14 46 2	13 9 12	13 17 55	19 28 15	21 26.1	19 50.9	26 13.4	15 52.5	13 48.8	22 8.4	3 27.1	21 16.6	27 27.5
5 Su	14 49 59	14 7 17	25 35 30	1♑40 0	21 22.5	20 16.3	27 26.9	16 26.8	13 43.2	22 16.1	3 27.3	21 17.7	27 28.5
6 M	14 53 55	15 5 21	7♑42 2	13 42 1	21 19.0	20 45.9	28 40.5	17 1.1	13 37.4	22 23.8	3 27.5	21 18.8	27 29.6
7 Tu	14 57 52	16 3 24	19 40 22	25 37 33	21 15.9	21 19.7	29 54.0	17 35.5	13 31.5	22 31.5	3 27.6	21 19.9	27 30.8
8 W	15 1 48	17 1 25	1♒34 5	7♒30 30	21 13.8	21 57.3	1♉ 7.6	18 9.9	13 25.5	22 39.3	3R27.6	21 21.1	27 31.9
9 Th	15 5 45	17 59 25	13 27 22	19 25 17	21D12.7	22 38.8	2 21.2	18 44.4	13 19.4	22 47.0	3 27.6	21 22.2	27 33.0
10 F	15 9 41	18 57 24	25 24 49	1♓26 36	21 12.8	23 23.9	3 34.7	19 18.9	13 13.1	22 54.7	3 27.5	21 23.4	27 34.2
11 Sa	15 13 38	19 55 21	7♓31 11	13 39 11	21 13.8	24 12.5	4 48.3	19 53.5	13 6.7	23 2.5	3 27.4	21 24.7	27 35.3
12 Su	15 17 35	20 53 17	19 51 8	26 7 32	21 15.4	25 4.6	6 1.8	20 28.1	13 0.3	23 10.2	3 27.3	21 25.9	27 36.5
13 M	15 21 31	21 51 11	2♈28 51	8♈55 28	21 17.0	25 59.9	7 15.4	21 2.7	12 53.7	23 18.0	3 27.1	21 27.2	27 37.7
14 Tu	15 25 28	22 49 5	15 27 42	22 5 44	21R18.0	26 58.3	8 28.9	21 37.4	12 47.0	23 25.8	3 26.8	21 28.5	27 38.9
15 W	15 29 24	23 46 56	28 49 40	5♉39 29	21 17.9	27 59.9	9 42.5	22 12.2	12 40.2	23 33.5	3 26.5	21 29.9	27 40.1
16 Th	15 33 21	24 44 47	12♉34 59	19 35 53	21 16.3	29 4.4	10 56.0	22 47.0	12 33.3	23 41.3	3 26.1	21 31.2	27 41.4
17 F	15 37 17	25 42 37	26 41 42	3♊51 53	21 13.2	0♉11.7	12 9.6	23 21.8	12 26.4	23 49.0	3 25.7	21 32.6	27 42.6
18 Sa	15 41 14	26 40 25	11♊ 5 42	18 22 24	21 8.7	1 21.9	13 23.2	23 56.7	12 19.3	23 56.8	3 25.3	21 34.1	27 43.9
19 Su	15 45 10	27 38 11	25 41 5	3♋ 0 52	21 3.3	2 34.8	14 36.7	24 31.7	12 12.2	24 4.5	3 24.8	21 35.5	27 45.1
20 M	15 49 7	28 35 56	10♋20 53	17 40 16	20 57.9	3 50.3	15 50.3	25 6.6	12 5.0	24 12.3	3 24.2	21 37.0	27 46.4
21 Tu	15 53 4	29 33 40	24 58 14	2♌14 6	20 53.3	5 8.4	17 3.8	25 41.7	11 57.8	24 20.0	3 23.6	21 38.5	27 47.7
22 W	15 57 0	0♊31 22	9♌27 17	16 37 18	20 49.9	6 29.1	18 17.4	26 16.7	11 50.5	24 27.8	3 23.0	21 40.0	27 49.0
23 Th	16 0 57	1 29 2	23 43 49	0♍46 35	20D48.2	7 52.4	19 30.9	26 51.8	11 43.1	24 35.5	3 22.3	21 41.6	27 50.3
24 F	16 4 53	2 26 41	7♍45 30	14 40 30	20 48.1	9 18.1	20 44.4	27 26.9	11 35.7	24 43.2	3 21.6	21 43.1	27 51.6
25 Sa	16 8 50	3 24 18	21 31 36	28 18 55	20 49.0	10 46.2	21 58.0	28 2.1	11 28.2	24 50.9	3 20.8	21 44.7	27 52.9
26 Su	16 12 46	4 21 53	5♎ 2 31	11♎42 34	20 50.3	12 16.9	23 11.5	28 37.3	11 20.7	24 58.6	3 20.0	21 46.3	27 54.3
27 M	16 16 43	5 19 27	18 19 13	24 52 36	20R51.1	13 49.9	24 25.1	29 12.6	11 13.2	25 6.3	3 19.1	21 48.0	27 55.6
28 Tu	16 20 39	6 17 0	1♏22 50	7♏50 4	20 50.6	15 25.4	25 38.6	29 47.8	11 5.6	25 14.0	3 18.2	21 49.6	27 56.9
29 W	16 24 36	7 14 31	14 14 24	20 35 54	20 48.2	17 3.2	26 52.1	0♌23.2	10 58.0	25 21.6	3 17.2	21 51.3	27 58.3
30 Th	16 28 33	8 12 2	26 54 39	3♐10 44	20 43.7	18 43.5	28 5.7	0 58.5	10 50.4	25 29.3	3 16.2	21 53.0	27 59.7
31 F	16 32 29	9 9 31	9♐24 13	15 35 10	20 37.0	20 26.2	29 19.2	1 33.9	10 42.8	25 36.9	3 15.1	21 54.7	28 1.0

LONGITUDE — JUNE 1912

Day	Sid.Time	☉	0 hr ☽	Noon ☽	True ☊	☿	♀	♂	♃	♄	♅	♆	♇
1 Sa	16 36 26	10♊ 6 59	21♐43 41	27♐49 52	20♈28.7	22♉11.3	0♊32.7	2♌ 9.3	10♐35.1	25♉44.5	3♒14.0	21♋56.5	28♊ 2.4
2 Su	16 40 22	11 4 26	3♑53 51	9♑55 48	20R19.5	23 58.7	1 46.3	2 44.8	10R27.5	25 52.1	3R12.9	21 58.2	28 3.8
3 M	16 44 19	12 1 53	15 55 57	21 54 31	20 10.1	25 48.5	2 59.8	3 20.3	10 19.9	25 59.7	3 11.7	22 0.0	28 5.2
4 Tu	16 48 15	12 59 18	27 51 51	3♒48 15	20 1.6	27 40.6	4 13.4	3 55.8	10 12.2	26 7.2	3 10.5	22 1.8	28 6.6
5 W	16 52 12	13 56 43	9♒44 9	15 39 58	19 54.6	29 35.1	5 27.0	4 31.4	10 4.6	26 14.8	3 9.3	22 3.6	28 8.0
6 Th	16 56 9	14 54 7	21 36 11	27 33 21	19 49.7	1♊31.7	6 40.5	5 7.0	9 57.0	26 22.3	3 8.0	22 5.5	28 9.4
7 F	17 0 5	15 51 30	3♓32 2	9♓32 47	19 46.8	3 30.6	7 54.1	5 42.6	9 49.4	26 29.7	3 6.6	22 7.3	28 10.8
8 Sa	17 4 2	16 48 53	15 36 16	21 43 5	19D45.9	5 31.5	9 7.7	6 18.3	9 41.8	26 37.2	3 5.2	22 9.2	28 12.2
9 Su	17 7 58	17 46 15	27 53 52	4♈ 9 14	19 46.3	7 34.4	10 21.3	6 54.0	9 34.3	26 44.6	3 3.8	22 11.1	28 13.6
10 M	17 11 55	18 43 37	10♈29 47	16 56 3	19R47.1	9 39.2	11 34.8	7 29.7	9 26.8	26 52.1	3 2.3	22 13.0	28 15.0
11 Tu	17 15 51	19 40 58	23 28 32	0♉ 7 35	19 47.3	11 45.6	12 48.4	8 5.5	9 19.4	26 59.4	3 0.8	22 14.9	28 16.5
12 W	17 19 48	20 38 19	6♉53 30	13 46 24	19 46.0	13 53.5	14 2.0	8 41.3	9 12.0	27 6.8	2 59.3	22 16.9	28 17.9
13 Th	17 23 44	21 35 39	20 46 15	27 52 50	19 42.6	16 2.7	15 15.7	9 17.2	9 4.6	27 14.1	2 57.7	22 18.8	28 19.3
14 F	17 27 41	22 32 59	5♊ 5 43	12♊24 19	19 36.7	18 13.0	16 29.3	9 53.0	8 57.3	27 21.4	2 56.1	22 20.8	28 20.8
15 Sa	17 31 38	23 30 18	19 47 48	27 15 10	19 28.8	20 24.1	17 42.9	10 29.0	8 50.1	27 28.7	2 54.5	22 22.8	28 22.2
16 Su	17 35 34	24 27 37	4♋45 19	12♋17 1	19 19.5	22 35.7	18 56.5	11 4.9	8 43.0	27 35.9	2 52.8	22 24.8	28 23.6
17 M	17 39 31	25 24 55	19 49 1	27 20 5	19 10.0	24 47.5	20 10.2	11 40.9	8 35.9	27 43.1	2 51.1	22 26.8	28 25.1
18 Tu	17 43 27	26 22 13	4♌49 4	12♌14 54	19 1.4	26 59.3	21 23.8	12 17.0	8 28.9	27 50.3	2 49.3	22 28.9	28 26.5
19 W	17 47 24	27 19 30	19 36 44	26 53 52	18 54.7	29 10.8	22 37.4	12 53.0	8 22.0	27 57.4	2 47.5	22 30.9	28 28.0
20 Th	17 51 20	28 16 46	4♍ 5 47	11♍12 9	18 50.3	1♋21.8	23 51.1	13 29.1	8 15.1	28 4.5	2 45.7	22 33.0	28 29.4
21 F	17 55 17	29 14 1	18 12 50	25 7 50	18D48.2	3 31.9	25 4.7	14 5.3	8 8.4	28 11.6	2 43.9	22 35.1	28 30.8
22 Sa	17 59 13	0♋11 15	1♎57 15	8♎41 18	18 47.8	5 41.0	26 18.4	14 41.4	8 1.8	28 18.6	2 42.0	22 37.1	28 32.3
23 Su	18 3 10	1 8 29	15 20 18	21 54 35	18R48.1	7 48.9	27 32.0	15 17.6	7 55.2	28 25.5	2 40.1	22 39.2	28 33.7
24 M	18 7 7	2 5 42	28 24 30	4♏50 25	18 47.8	9 55.4	28 45.7	15 53.8	7 48.8	28 32.5	2 38.2	22 41.3	28 35.2
25 Tu	18 11 3	3 2 54	11♏12 42	17 31 43	18 45.9	12 0.3	29 59.4	16 30.1	7 42.5	28 39.4	2 36.2	22 43.4	28 36.6
26 W	18 15 0	4 0 6	23 47 46	0♐ 1 7	18 41.6	14 3.5	1♋13.0	17 6.4	7 36.3	28 46.2	2 34.2	22 45.6	28 38.0
27 Th	18 18 56	4 57 18	6♐12 3	12 20 47	18 34.6	16 4.9	2 26.7	17 42.7	7 30.2	28 53.0	2 32.2	22 47.7	28 39.5
28 F	18 22 53	5 54 30	18 27 30	24 32 22	18 24.8	18 4.5	3 40.4	18 19.0	7 24.2	28 59.8	2 30.2	22 49.8	28 40.9
29 Sa	18 26 49	6 51 41	0♑35 32	6♑37 9	18 12.9	20 2.1	4 54.1	18 55.4	7 18.4	29 6.5	2 28.1	22 52.0	28 42.4
30 Su	18 30 46	7 48 52	12 37 21	18 36 17	17 59.7	21 57.8	6 7.8	19 31.8	7 12.7	29 13.1	2 26.0	22 54.2	28 43.8

Astro Data Dy Hr Mn	Planet Ingress Dy Hr Mn	Last Aspect Dy Hr Mn	☽ Ingress Dy Hr Mn	Last Aspect Dy Hr Mn	☽ Ingress Dy Hr Mn	☽ Phases & Eclipses Dy Hr Mn
♅ R 8 7:34	♀ ♉ 7 1:57	2 7:16 ♄ ☍	♐ 2 22:30	1 12:26 ♇ ☍	♑ 1 16:17	1 10:19 ○ 10♏40
☽0N 13 2:12	☿ ♉ 16 19:54	5 4:04 ♀ △	♑ 5 8:42	3 23:33 ☿ △	♒ 4 4:19	9 9:56 ☽ 18♒23
☽0S 25 21:20	☉ ♊ 21 10:57	7 5:49 ♄ △	♒ 7 20:50	6 13:14 ♇ △	♓ 6 16:55	16 22:13 ● 25♉38
	♂ ♌ 28 8:16	10 4:18 ♇ △	♓ 10 9:08	9 0:38 ♇ □	♈ 9 4:03	23 14:11 ☽ 2♍03
☽0N 9 10:26	♀ ♊ 31 13:19	12 14:50 ♇ □	♈ 12 19:20	11 8:42 ♇ ⚹	♉ 11 11:46	30 23:29 ○ 9♐08
☽0S 22 2:08		14 22:24 ☿ ☌	♉ 15 2:04	13 11:01 ♄ ☌	♊ 13 15:33	
♄⚺♇ 24 11:52	☿ ♊ 5 5:10	16 22:13 ☉ ☌	♊ 17 5:33	15 13:49 ♇ ☌	♋ 15 16:24	8 2:35 ☽ 16♓55
♃⚻♆ 24 21:18	☿ ♋ 19 9:00	19 3:24 ♇ ☌	♋ 19 7:04	17 12:43 ♄ ⚹	♌ 17 16:16	15 6:23 ● 23♊46
	☉ ♋ 21 19:17	21 8:07 ☉ ⚹	♌ 21 8:18	19 14:38 ♇ ⚹	♍ 19 17:09	21 20:39 ☽ 0♎03
	♀ ♋ 25 0:12	23 7:00 ♇ ⚹	♍ 23 10:40	21 17:58 ♇ □	♎ 21 20:33	29 13:33 ○ 7♑24
		25 12:02 ♂ ⚹	♎ 25 15:00	24 0:44 ♀ △	♏ 24 2:58	
		27 20:56 ♂ □	♏ 27 21:27	26 9:40 ♄ ☍	♐ 26 11:58	
		30 2:30 ♀ ☍	♐ 30 5:54	28 20:15 ♇ ☍	♑ 28 22:49	

Astro Data

1 MAY 1912
Julian Day # 4504
Delta T 13.8 sec
SVP 06♓29'09"
Obliquity 23°27'11"
⚷ Chiron 10♓15.4
☽ Mean ☊ 20♈42.2

1 JUNE 1912
Julian Day # 4535
Delta T 13.9 sec
SVP 06♓29'04"
Obliquity 23°27'11"
⚷ Chiron 11♓04.0
☽ Mean ☊ 19♈03.7

JULY 1912 LONGITUDE

Day	Sid.Time	☉	0 hr ☽	Noon ☽	True ☊	☿	♀	♂	♃	♄	♅	♆	♇
1 M	18 34 43	8♋46 2	24♑34 6	0♒30 59	17♈46.3	23♋51.5	7♋21.5	20♌ 8.3	7♐ 7.1	29♉19.8	2♒23.9	22♋56.3	28♊45.2
2 Tu	18 38 39	9 43 13	6♒27 8	12 22 49	17R 33.9	25 43.1	8 35.2	20 44.7	7R 1.7	29 26.3	2R 21.8	22 58.5	28 46.6
3 W	18 42 36	10 40 24	18 18 19	24 13 58	17 23.3	27 32.7	9 49.0	21 21.2	6 56.4	29 32.8	2 19.6	23 0.7	28 48.1
4 Th	18 46 32	11 37 35	0♓10 8	6♓ 7 14	17 15.1	29 20.2	11 2.7	21 57.8	6 51.2	29 39.3	2 17.4	23 2.9	28 49.5
5 F	18 50 29	12 34 46	12 5 46	18 6 14	17 9.8	1♌ 5.7	12 16.5	22 34.3	6 46.2	29 45.7	2 15.2	23 5.1	28 50.9
6 Sa	18 54 25	13 31 57	24 9 11	0♈15 12	17 6.9	2 49.1	13 30.2	23 10.9	6 41.3	29 52.1	2 13.0	23 7.3	28 52.3
7 Su	18 58 22	14 29 9	6♈24 54	12 38 54	17 5.9	4 30.4	14 44.0	23 47.6	6 36.6	29 58.4	2 10.8	23 9.5	28 53.7
8 M	19 2 18	15 26 21	18 57 51	25 22 19	17 5.9	6 9.7	15 57.8	24 24.2	6 32.0	0♊ 4.6	2 8.5	23 11.7	28 55.1
9 Tu	19 6 15	16 23 33	1♉52 54	8♉30 5	17 5.5	7 46.9	17 11.5	25 0.9	6 27.6	0 10.8	2 6.2	23 13.9	28 56.5
10 W	19 10 11	17 20 46	15 14 17	22 5 48	17 3.8	9 22.1	18 25.4	25 37.7	6 23.3	0 17.0	2 3.9	23 16.1	28 57.8
11 Th	19 14 8	18 17 59	29 4 45	6♊11 7	16 59.9	10 55.1	19 39.2	26 14.4	6 19.2	0 23.0	2 1.6	23 18.3	28 59.2
12 F	19 18 5	19 15 13	13♊24 38	20 44 49	16 53.4	12 26.1	20 53.0	26 51.3	6 15.2	0 29.1	1 59.3	23 20.5	29 0.6
13 Sa	19 22 1	20 12 28	28 10 58	5♋42 8	16 44.6	13 55.0	22 6.8	27 28.1	6 11.5	0 35.0	1 57.0	23 22.8	29 2.0
14 Su	19 25 58	21 9 43	13♋17 10	20 54 46	16 34.2	15 21.7	23 20.7	28 5.0	6 7.9	0 40.9	1 54.7	23 25.0	29 3.3
15 M	19 29 54	22 6 58	28 33 33	6♌12 2	16 23.4	16 46.3	24 34.5	28 41.9	6 4.4	0 46.8	1 52.3	23 27.2	29 4.7
16 Tu	19 33 51	23 4 14	13♌48 51	21 22 39	16 13.5	18 8.8	25 48.4	29 18.8	6 1.2	0 52.5	1 50.0	23 29.5	29 6.0
17 W	19 37 47	24 1 29	28 52 17	6♍16 48	16 5.5	19 29.0	27 2.3	29 55.8	5 58.1	0 58.2	1 47.6	23 31.7	29 7.4
18 Th	19 41 44	24 58 45	13♍35 26	20 47 41	16 0.2	20 46.9	28 16.2	0♍32.8	5 55.1	1 3.9	1 45.2	23 33.9	29 8.7
19 F	19 45 41	25 56 1	27 53 14	4♎51 58	15 57.4	22 2.5	29 30.0	1 9.9	5 52.4	1 9.4	1 42.8	23 36.1	29 10.0
20 Sa	19 49 37	26 53 17	11♎43 58	18 29 26	15D 56.5	23 15.7	0♌43.9	1 47.0	5 49.8	1 15.0	1 40.4	23 38.4	29 11.3
21 Su	19 53 34	27 50 34	25 8 40	1♏42 6	15R 56.5	24 26.5	1 57.8	2 24.1	5 47.4	1 20.4	1 38.0	23 40.6	29 12.6
22 M	19 57 30	28 47 51	8♏10 11	14 33 23	15 56.3	25 34.8	3 11.7	3 1.2	5 45.2	1 25.7	1 35.6	23 42.8	29 13.9
23 Tu	20 1 27	29 45 8	20 52 12	27 7 7	15 54.6	26 40.5	4 25.6	3 38.4	5 43.2	1 31.0	1 33.3	23 45.0	29 15.1
24 W	20 5 23	0♌42 25	3♐18 39	9♐27 12	15 50.7	27 43.5	5 39.6	4 15.6	5 41.3	1 36.3	1 30.9	23 47.3	29 16.4
25 Th	20 9 20	1 39 43	15 33 12	21 37 1	15 44.2	28 43.7	6 53.5	4 52.8	5 39.7	1 41.4	1 28.5	23 49.5	29 17.7
26 F	20 13 16	2 37 2	27 39 1	3♑39 29	15 35.1	29 41.0	8 7.4	5 30.1	5 38.2	1 46.5	1 26.1	23 51.7	29 18.9
27 Sa	20 17 13	3 34 21	9♑38 40	15 36 51	15 23.8	0♍35.3	9 21.3	6 7.4	5 36.9	1 51.5	1 23.7	23 53.9	29 20.1
28 Su	20 21 10	4 31 40	21 34 12	27 30 55	15 11.4	1 26.5	10 35.3	6 44.7	5 35.8	1 56.4	1 21.3	23 56.1	29 21.4
29 M	20 25 6	5 29 1	3♒27 13	9♒23 14	14 58.7	2 14.4	11 49.2	7 22.1	5 34.8	2 1.3	1 18.9	23 58.3	29 22.6
30 Tu	20 29 3	6 26 22	15 19 11	21 15 15	14 46.9	2 58.8	13 3.2	7 59.5	5 34.1	2 6.0	1 16.5	24 0.5	29 23.8
31 W	20 32 59	7 23 44	27 11 39	3♓ 8 38	14 36.8	3 39.6	14 17.2	8 36.9	5 33.5	2 10.7	1 14.1	24 2.7	29 25.0

AUGUST 1912 LONGITUDE

Day	Sid.Time	☉	0 hr ☽	Noon ☽	True ☊	☿	♀	♂	♃	♄	♅	♆	♇
1 Th	20 36 56	8♌21 7	9♓ 6 27	15♓ 5 26	14♈29.1	4♍16.6	15♌31.1	9♍14.4	5♐33.1	2♊15.3	1♒11.7	24♋ 4.8	29♊26.1
2 F	20 40 52	9 18 30	21 5 56	27 8 19	14R 24.1	4 49.7	16 45.1	9 51.9	5D 32.9	2 19.9	1R 9.3	24 7.0	29 27.3
3 Sa	20 44 49	10 15 55	3♈13 2	9♈20 32	14D 21.6	5 18.7	17 59.1	10 29.4	5 32.9	2 24.3	1 7.0	24 9.2	29 28.4
4 Su	20 48 45	11 13 21	15 31 20	21 45 57	14 21.0	5 43.3	19 13.1	11 7.0	5 33.1	2 28.7	1 4.6	24 11.3	29 29.6
5 M	20 52 42	12 10 48	28 4 55	4♉28 47	14 21.5	6 3.4	20 27.1	11 44.6	5 33.4	2 33.0	1 2.3	24 13.5	29 30.7
6 Tu	20 56 39	13 8 17	10♉58 4	17 33 16	14R 22.0	6 18.8	21 41.1	12 22.2	5 33.9	2 37.2	0 59.9	24 15.6	29 31.8
7 W	21 0 35	14 5 47	24 14 49	1♊ 3 4	14 21.5	6 29.3	22 55.1	12 59.9	5 34.6	2 41.3	0 57.6	24 17.7	29 32.9
8 Th	21 4 32	15 3 18	7♊58 15	15 0 27	14 19.4	6R 34.8	24 9.1	13 37.6	5 35.5	2 45.3	0 55.3	24 19.8	29 34.0
9 F	21 8 28	16 0 51	22 9 36	29 25 24	14 15.0	6 35.0	25 23.2	14 15.4	5 36.6	2 49.3	0 53.0	24 21.9	29 35.0
10 Sa	21 12 25	16 58 25	6♋47 23	14♋14 48	14 8.7	6 29.8	26 37.2	14 53.2	5 37.9	2 53.1	0 50.7	24 24.0	29 36.1
11 Su	21 16 21	17 56 1	21 46 45	29 22 7	14 0.9	6 19.2	27 51.3	15 31.0	5 39.3	2 56.9	0 48.5	24 26.1	29 37.1
12 M	21 20 18	18 53 38	6♌59 37	14♌37 54	13 52.6	6 3.2	29 5.3	16 8.9	5 41.0	3 0.6	0 46.2	24 28.2	29 38.1
13 Tu	21 24 14	19 51 16	22 15 34	29 51 15	13 44.9	5 41.7	0♍19.4	16 46.8	5 42.8	3 4.1	0 44.0	24 30.3	29 39.1
14 W	21 28 11	20 48 55	7♍23 42	14♍51 45	13 38.8	5 14.8	1 33.5	17 24.7	5 44.8	3 7.6	0 41.8	24 32.3	29 40.1
15 Th	21 32 8	21 46 35	22 14 28	29 31 8	13 34.8	4 42.8	2 47.6	18 2.7	5 46.9	3 11.0	0 39.6	24 34.3	29 41.1
16 F	21 36 4	22 44 16	6♎41 11	13♎44 20	13D 33.1	4 5.9	4 1.6	18 40.7	5 49.3	3 14.3	0 37.4	24 36.4	29 42.0
17 Sa	21 40 1	23 41 59	20 40 26	27 29 33	13 33.1	3 24.6	5 15.7	19 18.8	5 51.8	3 17.5	0 35.2	24 38.4	29 42.9
18 Su	21 43 57	24 39 42	4♏11 53	10♏47 44	13 34.0	2 39.4	6 29.8	19 56.9	5 54.5	3 20.6	0 33.1	24 40.4	29 43.8
19 M	21 47 54	25 37 27	17 17 31	23 41 41	13R 35.1	1 50.9	7 43.9	20 35.0	5 57.4	3 23.7	0 31.0	24 42.3	29 44.7
20 Tu	21 51 50	26 35 13	0♐ 0 46	6♐15 19	13 35.3	0 59.9	8 57.9	21 13.1	6 0.5	3 26.6	0 28.9	24 44.3	29 45.6
21 W	21 55 47	27 32 59	12 25 51	18 32 55	13 34.0	0 7.4	10 12.0	21 51.3	6 3.7	3 29.4	0 26.9	24 46.2	29 46.5
22 Th	21 59 43	28 30 48	24 37 4	0♑38 47	13 30.9	29♌14.3	11 26.1	22 29.6	6 7.1	3 32.1	0 24.8	24 48.2	29 47.3
23 F	22 3 40	29 28 37	6♑38 33	12 36 48	13 25.9	28 21.6	12 40.2	23 7.8	6 10.7	3 34.8	0 22.8	24 50.1	29 48.2
24 Sa	22 7 37	0♍26 27	18 33 56	24 30 20	13 19.3	27 30.5	13 54.3	23 46.1	6 14.5	3 37.3	0 20.9	24 52.0	29 49.0
25 Su	22 11 33	1 24 19	0♒26 20	6♒22 13	13 11.8	26 42.1	15 8.3	24 24.5	6 18.4	3 39.7	0 18.9	24 53.9	29 49.8
26 M	22 15 30	2 22 13	12 18 17	18 14 46	13 4.0	25 57.3	16 22.4	25 2.8	6 22.5	3 42.0	0 17.0	24 55.7	29 50.5
27 Tu	22 19 26	3 20 7	24 11 53	0♓ 9 52	12 56.8	25 17.3	17 36.5	25 41.3	6 26.7	3 44.3	0 15.1	24 57.6	29 51.3
28 W	22 23 23	4 18 3	6♓ 8 54	12 9 12	12 50.8	24 42.9	18 50.6	26 19.7	6 31.2	3 46.4	0 13.2	24 59.4	29 52.0
29 Th	22 27 19	5 16 1	18 10 58	24 14 24	12 46.5	24 15.0	20 4.6	26 58.2	6 35.8	3 48.4	0 11.4	25 1.2	29 52.7
30 F	22 31 16	6 14 0	0♈19 45	6♈27 16	12 43.9	23 54.2	21 18.7	27 36.7	6 40.5	3 50.3	0 9.6	25 3.0	29 53.4
31 Sa	22 35 12	7 12 1	12 37 12	18 49 52	12D 43.1	23 41.1	22 32.8	28 15.3	6 45.4	3 52.1	0 7.8	25 4.7	29 54.1

Astro Data

	Dy Hr Mn
☽0N	6 17:06
☽0S	19 8:13
♄△♅	23 6:57
☽0N	2 22:27
♃ D	2 14:56
☿ R	8 12:58
☽0S	15 16:39
☽0N	30 3:40

Planet Ingress

	Dy Hr Mn
☿ ♌	4 9:00
♄ ♊	7 6:13
♂ ♍	17 2:43
♀ ♌	19 9:44
☉ ♌	23 6:14
☿ ♍	26 8:13
♀ ♍	12 17:43
☿ ♌	21 3:21
☉ ♍	23 13:01

Last Aspect / ☽ Ingress

Last Aspect Dy Hr Mn		☽ Ingress Dy Hr Mn
1 9:42	♄ △	♒ 1 10:57
3 22:57	♄ □	♓ 3 23:40
6 11:21	♄ ⚹	♈ 6 11:30
8 18:36	♇ ⚹	♉ 8 20:33
10 18:55	♂ □	♊ 11 1:34
13 1:22	♇ ☌	♋ 13 2:55
14 17:12	♀ ☌	♌ 15 2:16
17 1:47	♂ ☌	♍ 17 1:49
19 3:01	♀ ⚹	♎ 19 3:37
21 7:26	♇ △	♏ 21 8:52
23 12:11	☿ △	♐ 23 17:34
26 4:24	☿ △	♑ 26 4:41
28 4:47	♆ ☍	♒ 28 17:01
31 4:29	♇ △	♓ 31 5:40

Last Aspect / ☽ Ingress

Last Aspect Dy Hr Mn		☽ Ingress Dy Hr Mn
2 16:37	♇ □	♈ 2 17:40
5 2:42	♇ ⚹	♉ 5 3:37
7 0:05	♆ ⚹	♊ 7 10:10
9 12:17	♇ ☌	♋ 9 12:57
11 4:13	♆ ☌	♌ 11 13:00
13 11:42	♇ ⚹	♍ 13 12:14
15 12:17	♇ □	♎ 15 12:48
17 15:59	♇ △	♏ 17 16:28
19 16:56	☉ □	♐ 19 23:59
22 10:18	♇ ☍	♑ 22 10:43
24 12:46	♆ ☍	♒ 24 23:07
27 11:23	♇ △	♓ 27 11:40
29 23:08	♇ □	♈ 29 23:21

☽ Phases & Eclipses

Dy Hr Mn	
7 16:47	☽ 15♈09
14 13:13	● 21♋41
21 5:18	☽ 28♎03
29 4:28	○ 5♒40
6 4:17	☽ 13♉19
12 19:57	● 19♌42
19 16:56	☽ 26♏18
27 19:58	○ 4♓08

Astro Data

1 JULY 1912
Julian Day # 4565
Delta T 14.0 sec
SVP 06♓28'58"
Obliquity 23°27'10"
⚷ Chiron 11♓01.2R
☽ Mean ☊ 17♈28.4

1 AUGUST 1912
Julian Day # 4596
Delta T 14.1 sec
SVP 06♓28'53"
Obliquity 23°27'11"
⚷ Chiron 10♓09.6R
☽ Mean ☊ 15♈50.0

LONGITUDE SEPTEMBER 1912

Day	Sid.Time	☉	0 hr ☽	Noon ☽	True ☊	☿	♀	♂	♃	♄	♅	♆	♇
1 Su	22 39 9	8♍10 4	25♈ 5 35	1♉24 40	12♈43.7	23♌36.2	23♍46.9	28♍53.9	6♐50.5	3♊53.9	0♒ 6.1	25♋ 6.5	29♊54.7
2 M	22 43 6	9 8 9	7♉47 29	14 14 23	12 45.2	23D 39.7	25 0.9	29 32.5	6 55.7	3 55.5	0R 4.4	25 8.2	29 55.4
3 Tu	22 47 2	10 6 16	20 45 44	27 21 52	12 46.7	23 51.7	26 15.0	0♎11.2	7 1.1	3 57.0	0 2.7	25 9.9	29 56.0
4 W	22 50 59	11 4 24	4♊ 3 6	10♊49 41	12R47.8	24 12.4	27 29.1	0 49.9	7 6.6	3 58.4	0 1.1	25 11.6	29 56.6
5 Th	22 54 55	12 2 35	17 41 49	24 39 36	12 47.9	24 41.7	28 43.2	1 28.7	7 12.3	3 59.7	29♑59.5	25 13.2	29 57.1
6 F	22 58 52	13 0 48	1♋43 1	8♋51 55	12 46.7	25 19.3	29 57.3	2 7.5	7 18.2	4 0.8	29 58.0	25 14.9	29 57.7
7 Sa	23 2 48	13 59 3	16 6 0	23 24 49	12 44.2	26 5.1	1♎11.3	2 46.3	7 24.2	4 1.9	29 56.5	25 16.5	29 58.2
8 Su	23 6 45	14 57 20	0♌47 44	8♌14 0	12 40.8	26 58.7	2 25.4	3 25.2	7 30.4	4 2.9	29 55.0	25 18.1	29 58.7
9 M	23 10 41	15 55 39	15 42 41	23 12 46	12 37.1	27 59.7	3 39.5	4 4.2	7 36.7	4 3.7	29 53.6	25 19.6	29 59.2
10 Tu	23 14 38	16 54 0	0♍43 9	8♍12 42	12 33.6	29 7.6	4 53.6	4 43.1	7 43.1	4 4.5	29 52.2	25 21.2	29 59.7
11 W	23 18 35	17 52 23	15 40 18	23 4 55	12 30.9	0♍22.0	6 7.7	5 22.2	7 49.7	4 5.1	29 50.8	25 22.7	0♋ 0.1
12 Th	23 22 31	18 50 47	0♎25 34	7♎41 26	12D 29.3	1 42.2	7 21.7	6 1.2	7 56.5	4 5.7	29 49.5	25 24.2	0 0.6
13 F	23 26 28	19 49 14	14 51 51	21 56 18	12 28.9	3 7.7	8 35.8	6 40.3	8 3.4	4 6.1	29 48.2	25 25.7	0 1.0
14 Sa	23 30 24	20 47 42	28 54 26	5♏46 4	12 29.5	4 38.0	9 49.9	7 19.5	8 10.4	4 6.4	29 47.0	25 27.1	0 1.3
15 Su	23 34 21	21 46 12	12♏31 12	19 9 55	12 30.8	6 12.4	11 3.9	7 58.6	8 17.6	4 6.6	29 45.8	25 28.5	0 1.7
16 M	23 38 17	22 44 43	25 42 27	2♐ 9 7	12 32.3	7 50.5	12 18.0	8 37.9	8 24.9	4R 6.7	29 44.6	25 29.9	0 2.0
17 Tu	23 42 14	23 43 17	8♐30 21	14 46 36	12 33.5	9 31.5	13 32.1	9 17.1	8 32.4	4 6.7	29 43.5	25 31.3	0 2.4
18 W	23 46 10	24 41 52	20 58 23	27 6 15	12R34.1	11 15.1	14 46.1	9 56.4	8 40.0	4 6.5	29 42.5	25 32.6	0 2.6
19 Th	23 50 7	25 40 28	3♑10 44	9♑12 25	12 34.0	13 0.7	16 0.1	10 35.8	8 47.7	4 6.3	29 41.4	25 33.9	0 2.9
20 F	23 54 4	26 39 7	15 11 52	21 9 38	12 33.1	14 48.0	17 14.2	11 15.2	8 55.6	4 6.0	29 40.5	25 35.2	0 3.2
21 Sa	23 58 0	27 37 47	27 6 13	3♒ 2 10	12 31.5	16 36.5	18 28.2	11 54.6	9 3.6	4 5.5	29 39.6	25 36.5	0 3.4
22 Su	0 1 57	28 36 28	8♒57 55	14 53 56	12 29.6	18 25.8	19 42.2	12 34.0	9 11.7	4 5.0	29 38.7	25 37.7	0 3.6
23 M	0 5 53	29 35 12	20 50 37	26 48 21	12 27.6	20 15.7	20 56.2	13 13.6	9 19.9	4 4.3	29 37.8	25 38.9	0 3.8
24 Tu	0 9 50	0♎33 57	2♓47 28	8♓48 17	12 25.7	22 6.0	22 10.2	13 53.1	9 28.3	4 3.5	29 37.1	25 40.1	0 3.9
25 W	0 13 46	1 32 44	14 51 3	20 56 2	12 24.3	23 56.3	23 24.2	14 32.7	9 36.8	4 2.6	29 36.3	25 41.2	0 4.1
26 Th	0 17 43	2 31 33	27 3 24	3♈13 21	12 23.4	25 46.5	24 38.2	15 12.3	9 45.4	4 1.6	29 35.6	25 42.3	0 4.2
27 F	0 21 39	3 30 24	9♈26 3	15 41 38	12D23.0	27 36.5	25 52.1	15 52.0	9 54.2	4 0.5	29 35.0	25 43.4	0 4.3
28 Sa	0 25 36	4 29 17	22 0 12	28 21 52	12 23.1	29 26.1	27 6.1	16 31.7	10 3.0	3 59.3	29 34.4	25 44.4	0 4.3
29 Su	0 29 32	5 28 12	4♉46 45	11♉14 56	12 23.5	1♎15.2	28 20.0	17 11.5	10 12.0	3 58.0	29 33.8	25 45.5	0 4.4
30 M	0 33 29	6 27 9	17 46 30	24 21 32	12 24.1	3 3.7	29 34.0	17 51.3	10 21.1	3 56.6	29 33.3	25 46.5	0R 4.4

LONGITUDE OCTOBER 1912

Day	Sid.Time	☉	0 hr ☽	Noon ☽	True ☊	☿	♀	♂	♃	♄	♅	♆	♇
1 Tu	0 37 26	7♎26 9	1♊ 0 6	7♊42 16	12♈24.7	4♎51.6	0♏47.9	18♎31.1	10♐30.3	3♊55.1	29♑32.9	25♋47.4	0♋ 4.4
2 W	0 41 22	8 25 11	14 28 6	21 17 36	12 25.1	6 38.8	2 1.9	19 11.0	10 39.6	3R 53.5	29R 32.5	25 48.4	0R 4.4
3 Th	0 45 19	9 24 15	28 10 47	5♋ 7 37	12R25.3	8 25.2	3 15.8	19 50.9	10 49.1	3 51.7	29 32.1	25 49.3	0 4.3
4 F	0 49 15	10 23 22	12♋ 8 0	19 11 48	12 25.4	10 11.0	4 29.7	20 30.9	10 58.6	3 49.9	29 31.8	25 50.1	0 4.3
5 Sa	0 53 12	11 22 31	26 18 48	3♌28 43	12 25.3	11 55.9	5 43.7	21 11.0	11 8.3	3 48.0	29 31.6	25 51.0	0 4.2
6 Su	0 57 8	12 21 42	10♌41 12	17 55 46	12D25.3	13 40.1	6 57.6	21 51.0	11 18.1	3 45.9	29 31.4	25 51.8	0 4.1
7 M	1 1 5	13 20 56	25 11 55	2♍29 3	12 25.3	15 23.5	8 11.5	22 31.2	11 27.9	3 43.8	29 31.2	25 52.6	0 3.9
8 Tu	1 5 2	14 20 11	9♍46 30	17 3 34	12 25.5	17 6.1	9 25.4	23 11.3	11 37.9	3 41.5	29 31.1	25 53.3	0 3.8
9 W	1 8 58	15 19 29	24 19 30	1♎33 34	12 25.7	18 47.9	10 39.3	23 51.5	11 48.0	3 39.2	29D 31.1	25 54.0	0 3.6
10 Th	1 12 55	16 18 50	8♎45 2	15 53 15	12R25.8	20 29.0	11 53.2	24 31.8	11 58.2	3 36.8	29 31.0	25 54.7	0 3.4
11 F	1 16 51	17 18 12	22 57 33	29 57 26	12 25.7	22 9.3	13 7.1	25 12.1	12 8.5	3 34.2	29 31.1	25 55.3	0 3.2
12 Sa	1 20 48	18 17 36	6♏52 27	13♏42 15	12 25.4	23 48.9	14 20.9	25 52.5	12 18.9	3 31.6	29 31.2	25 55.9	0 2.9
13 Su	1 24 44	19 17 3	20 26 38	27 5 28	12 24.7	25 27.8	15 34.8	26 32.9	12 29.4	3 28.9	29 31.3	25 56.5	0 2.6
14 M	1 28 41	20 16 31	3♐38 47	10♐ 6 40	12 23.7	27 6.0	16 48.6	27 13.3	12 39.9	3 26.0	29 31.6	25 57.1	0 2.4
15 Tu	1 32 37	21 16 1	16 29 20	22 47 6	12 22.6	28 43.4	18 2.5	27 53.8	12 50.6	3 23.1	29 31.8	25 57.6	0 2.0
16 W	1 36 34	22 15 33	29 0 19	5♑ 9 26	12 21.6	0♏20.2	19 16.3	28 34.3	13 1.4	3 20.1	29 32.1	25 58.1	0 1.7
17 Th	1 40 30	23 15 7	11♑14 56	17 17 20	12 20.8	1 56.4	20 30.2	29 14.9	13 12.3	3 17.0	29 32.5	25 58.5	0 1.4
18 F	1 44 27	24 14 42	23 17 14	29 15 11	12D20.5	3 31.9	21 44.0	29 55.5	13 23.2	3 13.9	29 32.9	25 58.9	0 1.0
19 Sa	1 48 24	25 14 20	5♒11 47	11♒ 7 39	12 20.8	5 6.7	22 57.8	0♏36.2	13 34.3	3 10.6	29 33.3	25 59.3	0 0.6
20 Su	1 52 20	26 13 59	17 3 21	22 59 28	12 21.6	6 41.0	24 11.5	1 16.9	13 45.4	3 7.2	29 33.9	25 59.6	0 0.2
21 M	1 56 17	27 13 39	28 56 33	4♓55 10	12 22.8	8 14.7	25 25.3	1 57.6	13 56.6	3 3.8	29 34.4	25 59.9	29♊59.7
22 Tu	2 0 13	28 13 22	10♓55 46	16 58 51	12 24.2	9 47.8	26 39.1	2 38.4	14 7.9	3 0.3	29 35.0	26 0.2	29 59.3
23 W	2 4 10	29 13 6	23 4 49	29 14 1	12 25.5	11 20.3	27 52.8	3 19.3	14 19.2	2 56.7	29 35.7	26 0.5	29 58.8
24 Th	2 8 6	0♏12 52	5♈26 45	11♈43 17	12R26.3	12 52.3	29 6.5	4 0.2	14 30.7	2 53.1	29 36.4	26 0.7	29 58.3
25 F	2 12 3	1 12 40	18 3 48	24 28 23	12 26.4	14 23.7	0♐20.2	4 41.1	14 42.2	2 49.3	29 37.2	26 0.8	29 57.7
26 Sa	2 15 59	2 12 30	0♉57 6	7♉29 55	12 25.4	15 54.5	1 33.9	5 22.1	14 53.8	2 45.5	29 38.0	26 1.0	29 57.2
27 Su	2 19 56	3 12 21	14 6 45	20 47 28	12 23.5	17 24.9	2 47.6	6 3.1	15 5.5	2 41.6	29 38.8	26 1.1	29 56.6
28 M	2 23 53	4 12 15	27 31 50	4♊19 37	12 20.6	18 54.7	4 1.2	6 44.2	15 17.3	2 37.7	29 39.8	26 1.2	29 56.0
29 Tu	2 27 49	5 12 11	11♊10 33	18 4 18	12 17.2	20 23.9	5 14.9	7 25.3	15 29.1	2 33.6	29 40.7	26R 1.2	29 55.4
30 W	2 31 46	6 12 9	25 0 34	1♋59 0	12 13.8	21 52.6	6 28.5	8 6.5	15 41.0	2 29.5	29 41.7	26 1.2	29 54.8
31 Th	2 35 42	7 12 10	8♋59 17	16 1 7	12 10.9	23 20.8	7 42.1	8 47.7	15 53.0	2 25.4	29 42.8	26 1.2	29 54.2

Astro Data	Planet Ingress	Last Aspect	☽ Ingress	Last Aspect	☽ Ingress	☽ Phases & Eclipses	Astro Data
Dy Hr Mn	Dy Hr Mn	Dy Hr Mn	Dy Hr Mn	Dy Hr Mn	Dy Hr Mn	Dy Hr Mn	1 SEPTEMBER 1912
☿ D 1 2:11	♂ ♎ 2 17:04	1 9:10 ♇ ⚹	♉ 1 9:20	2 8:44 ♂ △	♋ 3 3:09	4 13:23 ☽ 11♊37	Julian Day # 4627
♂0S 5 3:55	♅ ♑ 4 16:51	3 11:01 ♀ △	♊ 3 16:45	5 5:23 ♅ ☍	♌ 5 6:11	11 3:48 ● 18♍02	Delta T 14.2 sec
♅⚻♇ 6 3:15	♀ ♎ 6 0:53	5 21:02 ♇ ☌	♋ 5 21:06	6 19:22 ♂ ⚹	♍ 7 7:55	18 7:54 ☽ 25♐01	SVP 06♓28'49"
♀0S 8 3:47	☿ ♍ 10 17:07	7 22:35 ♅ ☍	♌ 7 22:43	9 8:36 ♅ △	♎ 9 9:24	26 11:34 ○ 2♈60	Obliquity 23°27'12"
☽0S 12 2:52	♇ ♋ 10 16:08	9 22:50 ♇ ⚹	♍ 9 22:51	11 11:15 ♅ □	♏ 11 12:04	26 11:45 • P 0.118	⚷ Chiron 8♓46.8R
♄ R 16 8:36	☉ ♎ 23 10:08	11 23:01 ♅ △	♎ 11 23:18	13 16:26 ♅ ⚹	♐ 13 17:18		☽ Mean ☊ 14♈11.5
☽0N 26 9:57	☿ ♎ 28 7:27	14 1:31 ♅ □	♏ 14 1:54	15 23:07 ♂ ⚹	♑ 16 1:56	3 20:48 ☽ 10♋15	
☿0S 30 6:28	♀ ♏ 30 8:26	16 7:29 ♅ ⚹	♐ 16 7:58	18 12:36 ♅ ☌	♒ 18 13:30	10 13:40 ● 16♎53	1 OCTOBER 1912
♇ R 30 13:09		18 7:54 ☉ □	♑ 18 17:42	21 2:07 ♇ △	♓ 21 2:08	10 13:35:58 • T 1'55"	Julian Day # 4657
♃□♆ 3 0:31	☿ ♏ 15 18:58	21 5:10 ♅ ☌	♒ 21 5:51	23 13:26 ♇ □	♈ 23 13:29	18 2:06 ☽ 24♑20	Delta T 14.3 sec
☽0S 9 13:02	♂ ♏ 18 2:39	23 0:13 ♀ △	♓ 23 18:25	25 22:10 ♇ ⚹	♉ 25 22:15	26 2:30 ○ 2♉19	SVP 06♓28'45"
♅ D 9 13:43	♇ ♊ 20 8:40	26 4:57 ♅ ⚹	♈ 26 5:44	28 3:47 ♅ △	♊ 28 4:22		Obliquity 23°27'12"
☽0N 23 17:41	☉ ♏ 23 18:50	28 14:15 ♅ □	♉ 28 15:04	30 8:26 ♇ ☌	♋ 30 8:36		⚷ Chiron 7♓26.1R
♃∠♅ 24 12:43	♀ ♐ 24 17:25	30 21:23 ♅ △	♊ 30 22:12				☽ Mean ☊ 12♈36.1

NOVEMBER 1912 LONGITUDE

Day	Sid.Time	☉	0 hr ☽	Noon ☽	True ☊	☿	♀	♂	♃	♄	♅	♆	♇
1 F	2 39 39	8♏12 12	23♋ 4 11	0♌ 8 13	12♈ 8.9	24♏48.4	8♐55.7	9♏28.9	16♐ 5.0	2♊21.2	29♑43.9	26♋ 1.1	29♊53.5
2 Sa	2 43 35	9 12 16	7♌12 56	14 18 8	12D 8.0	26 15.4	10 9.3	10 10.3	16 17.2	2R16.9	29 45.1	26R 1.0	29R52.8
3 Su	2 47 32	10 12 23	21 23 33	28 28 57	12 8.4	27 41.8	11 22.9	10 51.6	16 29.3	2 12.6	29 46.3	26 0.9	29 52.1
4 M	2 51 28	11 12 32	5♍34 6	12♍38 47	12 9.7	29 7.6	12 36.5	11 33.0	16 41.6	2 8.2	29 47.6	26 0.7	29 51.4
5 Tu	2 55 25	12 12 43	19 42 42	26 45 36	12 11.2	0♐32.7	13 50.0	12 14.5	16 53.9	2 3.8	29 48.9	26 0.5	29 50.7
6 W	2 59 22	13 12 55	3♎47 10	10♎47 4	12R12.4	1 57.0	15 3.6	12 56.0	17 6.2	1 59.3	29 50.2	26 0.3	29 49.9
7 Th	3 3 18	14 13 10	17 44 57	24 40 27	12 12.5	3 20.6	16 17.1	13 37.5	17 18.7	1 54.7	29 51.6	26 0.0	29 49.1
8 F	3 7 15	15 13 27	1♏33 13	8♏22 53	12 11.1	4 43.4	17 30.6	14 19.2	17 31.2	1 50.2	29 53.1	25 59.7	29 48.3
9 Sa	3 11 11	16 13 46	15 9 6	21 51 34	12 7.9	6 5.2	18 44.1	15 0.8	17 43.7	1 45.5	29 54.6	25 59.4	29 47.5
10 Su	3 15 8	17 14 6	28 30 2	5♐ 4 17	12 3.0	7 26.0	19 57.6	15 42.5	17 56.3	1 40.9	29 56.1	25 59.0	29 46.7
11 M	3 19 4	18 14 28	11♐34 12	17 59 43	11 56.8	8 45.7	21 11.0	16 24.3	18 9.0	1 36.2	29 57.7	25 58.6	29 45.9
12 Tu	3 23 1	19 14 52	24 20 52	0♑37 45	11 50.1	10 4.2	22 24.5	17 6.1	18 21.7	1 31.5	29 59.4	25 58.2	29 45.0
13 W	3 26 57	20 15 17	6♑50 33	12 59 33	11 43.5	11 21.3	23 37.9	17 47.9	18 34.5	1 26.7	0♒ 1.1	25 57.7	29 44.1
14 Th	3 30 54	21 15 44	19 5 4	25 7 32	11 37.8	12 36.9	24 51.3	18 29.8	18 47.3	1 21.9	0 2.8	25 57.2	29 43.3
15 F	3 34 51	22 16 12	1♒ 7 24	7♒ 5 12	11 33.6	13 50.7	26 4.6	19 11.7	19 0.2	1 17.1	0 4.6	25 56.7	29 42.4
16 Sa	3 38 47	23 16 42	13 1 30	18 56 53	11D31.2	15 2.6	27 18.0	19 53.7	19 13.1	1 12.3	0 6.4	25 56.1	29 41.4
17 Su	3 42 44	24 17 12	24 52 0	0♓47 28	11 30.5	16 12.2	28 31.3	20 35.7	19 26.0	1 7.4	0 8.3	25 55.5	29 40.5
18 M	3 46 40	25 17 44	6♓43 57	12 42 7	11 31.2	17 19.4	29 44.6	21 17.8	19 39.0	1 2.5	0 10.2	25 54.9	29 39.6
19 Tu	3 50 37	26 18 17	18 42 34	24 45 58	11 32.6	18 23.7	0♑57.8	21 59.9	19 52.1	0 57.6	0 12.2	25 54.2	29 38.6
20 W	3 54 33	27 18 52	0♈52 52	7♈ 3 49	11R34.0	19 24.8	2 11.0	22 42.1	20 5.2	0 52.7	0 14.2	25 53.5	29 37.6
21 Th	3 58 30	28 19 27	13 19 18	19 39 45	11 34.5	20 22.3	3 24.2	23 24.3	20 18.3	0 47.8	0 16.2	25 52.8	29 36.6
22 F	4 2 26	29 20 4	26 5 27	2♉36 39	11 33.3	21 15.6	4 37.4	24 6.6	20 31.5	0 42.9	0 18.3	25 52.1	29 35.6
23 Sa	4 6 23	0♐20 43	9♉13 27	15 55 50	11 30.0	22 4.2	5 50.5	24 48.9	20 44.7	0 38.0	0 20.4	25 51.3	29 34.6
24 Su	4 10 20	1 21 22	22 43 40	29 36 41	11 24.5	22 47.5	7 3.6	25 31.2	20 57.9	0 33.1	0 22.6	25 50.5	29 33.6
25 M	4 14 16	2 22 3	6♊34 28	13♊36 29	11 17.0	23 24.8	8 16.7	26 13.6	21 11.2	0 28.1	0 24.8	25 49.6	29 32.6
26 Tu	4 18 13	3 22 46	20 42 9	27 50 45	11 8.3	23 55.5	9 29.7	26 56.1	21 24.5	0 23.2	0 27.1	25 48.8	29 31.5
27 W	4 22 9	4 23 29	5♋ 1 33	12♋13 47	10 59.4	24 18.6	10 42.7	27 38.6	21 37.9	0 18.3	0 29.4	25 47.9	29 30.5
28 Th	4 26 6	5 24 15	19 26 42	26 39 35	10 51.3	24 33.4	11 55.6	28 21.1	21 51.2	0 13.4	0 31.7	25 46.9	29 29.4
29 F	4 30 2	6 25 1	3♌51 49	11♌ 2 50	10 45.1	24R39.2	13 8.5	29 3.7	22 4.6	0 8.6	0 34.1	25 46.0	29 28.3
30 Sa	4 33 59	7 25 50	18 12 10	25 19 29	10 41.1	24 35.1	14 21.4	29 46.3	22 18.1	0 3.7	0 36.5	25 45.0	29 27.2

DECEMBER 1912 LONGITUDE

Day	Sid.Time	☉	0 hr ☽	Noon ☽	True ☊	☿	♀	♂	♃	♄	♅	♆	♇
1 Su	4 37 56	8♐26 39	2♍24 31	9♍27 6	10♈39.4	24♐20.4	15♑34.2	0♐29.0	22♐31.5	29♉58.8	0♒38.9	25♋44.0	29♊26.1
2 M	4 41 52	9 27 30	16 27 8	23 24 34	10D39.4	23R54.8	16 47.0	1 11.8	22 45.0	29R54.0	0 41.4	25R43.0	29R25.0
3 Tu	4 45 49	10 28 23	0♎19 25	7♎11 43	10R40.1	23 18.0	17 59.8	1 54.6	22 58.5	29 49.2	0 43.9	25 41.9	29 23.9
4 W	4 49 45	11 29 16	14 1 29	20 48 46	10 40.4	22 30.2	19 12.5	2 37.4	23 12.1	29 44.4	0 46.5	25 40.8	29 22.8
5 Th	4 53 42	12 30 12	27 33 34	4♏15 53	10 39.0	21 32.0	20 25.2	3 20.3	23 25.6	29 39.7	0 49.1	25 39.7	29 21.6
6 F	4 57 38	13 31 8	10♏55 39	17 32 49	10 35.2	20 24.7	21 37.8	4 3.2	23 39.2	29 35.0	0 51.7	25 38.5	29 20.5
7 Sa	5 1 35	14 32 6	24 7 17	0♐38 56	10 28.5	19 9.9	22 50.4	4 46.2	23 52.8	29 30.3	0 54.4	25 37.4	29 19.3
8 Su	5 5 31	15 33 5	7♐ 7 40	13 33 21	10 19.0	17 49.8	24 2.9	5 29.2	24 6.5	29 25.7	0 57.1	25 36.2	29 18.2
9 M	5 9 28	16 34 4	19 55 53	26 15 12	10 7.3	16 27.0	25 15.4	6 12.3	24 20.1	29 21.1	0 59.8	25 35.0	29 17.0
10 Tu	5 13 25	17 35 5	2♑31 14	8♑44 1	9 54.5	15 4.4	26 27.9	6 55.5	24 33.8	29 16.5	1 2.6	25 33.7	29 15.9
11 W	5 17 21	18 36 7	14 53 37	21 0 9	9 41.6	13 44.8	27 40.3	7 38.6	24 47.4	29 12.0	1 5.4	25 32.4	29 14.7
12 Th	5 21 18	19 37 9	27 3 48	3♒ 4 50	9 29.9	12 30.6	28 52.6	8 21.8	25 1.1	29 7.5	1 8.2	25 31.2	29 13.5
13 F	5 25 14	20 38 12	9♒ 3 35	15 0 25	9 20.2	11 24.1	0♒ 4.9	9 5.1	25 14.8	29 3.1	1 11.1	25 29.9	29 12.3
14 Sa	5 29 11	21 39 15	20 55 49	26 50 16	9 13.2	10 26.9	1 17.1	9 48.4	25 28.5	28 58.8	1 13.9	25 28.5	29 11.2
15 Su	5 33 7	22 40 19	2♓44 20	8♓38 38	9 8.9	9 40.1	2 29.2	10 31.8	25 42.2	28 54.5	1 16.9	25 27.2	29 10.0
16 M	5 37 4	23 41 23	14 33 47	20 30 29	9D 6.9	9 4.2	3 41.3	11 15.2	25 55.9	28 50.2	1 19.8	25 25.8	29 8.8
17 Tu	5 41 0	24 42 27	26 29 25	2♈31 17	9 6.6	8 39.5	4 53.3	11 58.6	26 9.6	28 46.1	1 22.8	25 24.4	29 7.6
18 W	5 44 57	25 43 32	8♈36 45	14 46 32	9R 6.7	8D25.6	6 5.2	12 42.1	26 23.4	28 42.0	1 25.8	25 23.0	29 6.4
19 Th	5 48 54	26 44 37	21 1 16	27 21 32	9 6.2	8 22.1	7 17.0	13 25.6	26 37.1	28 37.9	1 28.8	25 21.5	29 5.2
20 F	5 52 50	27 45 43	3♉47 52	10♉20 40	9 4.0	8 28.3	8 28.8	14 9.2	26 50.8	28 33.9	1 31.9	25 20.1	29 4.0
21 Sa	5 56 47	28 46 49	17 0 15	23 46 45	8 59.2	8 43.5	9 40.5	14 52.8	27 4.5	28 30.0	1 34.9	25 18.6	29 2.8
22 Su	6 0 43	29 47 55	0♊40 12	7♊40 22	8 51.7	9 6.8	10 52.1	15 36.4	27 18.3	28 26.2	1 38.0	25 17.2	29 1.6
23 M	6 4 40	0♑49 2	14 46 54	21 59 12	8 41.6	9 37.5	12 3.6	16 20.1	27 32.0	28 22.4	1 41.2	25 15.7	29 0.4
24 Tu	6 8 36	1 50 8	29 16 31	6♋37 55	8 29.8	10 14.9	13 15.0	17 3.9	27 45.7	28 18.8	1 44.3	25 14.1	28 59.2
25 W	6 12 33	2 51 16	14♋ 2 22	21 28 44	8 17.6	10 58.1	14 26.3	17 47.7	27 59.4	28 15.2	1 47.5	25 12.6	28 58.0
26 Th	6 16 30	3 52 23	28 55 51	6♌22 36	8 6.3	11 46.6	15 37.6	18 31.5	28 13.1	28 11.6	1 50.7	25 11.1	28 56.8
27 F	6 20 26	4 53 31	13♌47 55	21 10 52	7 57.2	12 39.7	16 48.7	19 15.4	28 26.8	28 8.2	1 53.9	25 9.5	28 55.6
28 Sa	6 24 23	5 54 39	28 30 39	5♍46 38	7 50.9	13 37.0	17 59.7	19 59.4	28 40.5	28 4.8	1 57.2	25 7.9	28 54.5
29 Su	6 28 19	6 55 48	12♍58 22	20 5 33	7 47.4	14 37.9	19 10.7	20 43.3	28 54.2	28 1.6	2 0.4	25 6.4	28 53.3
30 M	6 32 16	7 56 57	27 8 1	4♎ 5 47	7 46.2	15 42.0	20 21.5	21 27.4	29 7.9	27 58.4	2 3.7	25 4.8	28 52.1
31 Tu	6 36 12	8 58 7	10♎58 54	17 47 33	7 46.0	16 49.0	21 32.2	22 11.4	29 21.5	27 55.3	2 7.0	25 3.2	28 50.9

Astro Data	Planet Ingress	Last Aspect	☽ Ingress	Last Aspect	☽ Ingress	☽ Phases & Eclipses	Astro Data
Dy Hr Mn	Dy Hr Mn	Dy Hr Mn	Dy Hr Mn	Dy Hr Mn	Dy Hr Mn	Dy Hr Mn	1 NOVEMBER 1912
☽0S 5 21:08	☿ ♐ 4 14:46	1 11:20 ♅ ☍	♌ 1 11:46	2 23:08 ♄ △	♎ 2 23:26	2 3:38 ☽ 9♌21	Julian Day # 4688
♅⚻♇ 5 20:26	♅ ♒ 12 8:41	3 14:20 ♇ ⚹	♍ 3 14:34	5 3:13 ♇ △	♏ 5 4:22	9 2:05 ● 16♏19	Delta T 14.4 sec
☽0N 20 2:09	♀ ♑ 18 5:03	5 17:15 ♇ □	♎ 5 17:32	7 9:50 ♄ ☍	♐ 7 10:48	16 22:43 ☽ 24♒14	SVP 06♓28'41"
♄△♅ 25 11:09	☉ ♐ 22 15:48	7 21:05 ♅ □	♏ 7 21:17	9 17:46 ♇ ☍	♑ 9 19:10	24 16:12 ○ 2♊02	Obliquity 23°27'11"
☿ R 29 2:15	♂ ♐ 30 7:41	10 2:37 ♅ ⚹	♐ 10 2:44	12 4:05 ♄ △	♒ 12 5:51		⚷ Chiron 6♓33.3R
	♄ ♉ 30 18:18	12 10:18 ♇ ☍	♑ 12 10:48	14 16:45 ♇ △	♓ 14 18:26	1 11:05 ☽ 8♍55	☽ Mean ☊ 10♈57.6
☽0S 3 2:36		14 13:39 ♆ ☍	♒ 14 21:45	17 5:15 ♇ □	♈ 17 7:00	8 17:06 ● 16♐17	
♄⚺♇ 10 4:32	♀ ♒ 12 22:23	17 9:44 ♇ △	♓ 17 10:24	19 15:13 ♇ ⚹	♉ 19 16:57	16 20:06 ☽ 24♓33	1 DECEMBER 1912
♃⚻♆ 14 0:02	☉ ♑ 22 4:45	19 21:33 ♇ □	♈ 19 22:17	21 20:09 ♄ ☌	♊ 21 22:51	24 4:30 ○ 2♋02	Julian Day # 4718
☽0N 17 10:03		22 6:28 ♇ ⚹	♉ 22 7:13	23 23:32 ♇ ☌	♋ 24 1:11	30 20:12 ☽ 8♎48	Delta T 14.5 sec
☿ D 18 20:24		24 5:26 ♆ ⚹	♊ 24 12:40	25 22:49 ♄ ⚹	♌ 26 1:43		SVP 06♓28'36"
♃⚻♄ 25 21:55		26 14:48 ♇ ☌	♋ 26 15:36	28 0:39 ♇ ⚹	♍ 28 2:27		Obliquity 23°27'11"
♃☍♇ 28 22:31		28 15:35 ♂ △	♌ 28 17:34	30 3:29 ♃ □	♎ 30 4:55		⚷ Chiron 6♓31.1
☽0S 30 7:11		30 19:54 ♄ □	♍ 30 19:55				☽ Mean ☊ 9♈22.3

LONGITUDE JANUARY 1913

Day	Sid.Time	☉	0 hr ☽	Noon ☽	True ☊	☿	♀	♂	♃	♄	♅	♆	♇
1 W	6 40 9	9♑59 17	24♎31 57	1♏12 20	7♈45.7	17♐58.5	22♒42.9	22♐55.5	29♐35.2	27♉52.3	2♒10.3	25♋ 1.5	28♊49.7
2 Th	6 44 5	11 0 27	7♏48 59	14 22 8	7R43.7	19 10.2	23 53.4	23 39.7	29 48.8	27R49.3	2 13.6	24R59.9	28R48.6
3 F	6 48 2	12 1 38	20 52 3	27 18 55	7 39.1	20 24.0	25 3.8	24 23.9	0♑ 2.4	27 46.5	2 17.0	24 58.3	28 47.4
4 Sa	6 51 59	13 2 49	3♐42 55	10♐ 4 12	7 31.4	21 39.5	26 14.0	25 8.2	0 16.0	27 43.8	2 20.3	24 56.6	28 46.2
5 Su	6 55 55	14 4 0	16 22 54	22 39 4	7 20.7	22 56.7	27 24.2	25 52.4	0 29.6	27 41.2	2 23.7	24 55.0	28 45.1
6 M	6 59 52	15 5 11	28 52 47	5♑ 4 6	7 7.6	24 15.2	28 34.2	26 36.8	0 43.1	27 38.6	2 27.1	24 53.3	28 43.9
7 Tu	7 3 48	16 6 22	11♑13 4	17 19 43	6 53.1	25 35.1	29 44.1	27 21.2	0 56.7	27 36.2	2 30.5	24 51.6	28 42.8
8 W	7 7 45	17 7 33	23 24 8	29 26 25	6 38.5	26 56.2	0♓53.9	28 5.6	1 10.2	27 33.9	2 34.0	24 50.0	28 41.7
9 Th	7 11 41	18 8 44	5♒26 41	11♒25 5	6 24.9	28 18.3	2 3.5	28 50.0	1 23.7	27 31.7	2 37.4	24 48.3	28 40.5
10 F	7 15 38	19 9 54	17 21 52	23 17 16	6 13.5	29 41.4	3 13.0	29 34.6	1 37.1	27 29.5	2 40.8	24 46.6	28 39.4
11 Sa	7 19 34	20 11 4	29 11 37	5♓ 5 18	6 4.9	1♑ 5.4	4 22.3	0♑19.1	1 50.5	27 27.5	2 44.3	24 44.9	28 38.3
12 Su	7 23 31	21 12 13	10♓58 44	16 52 24	5 59.4	2 30.3	5 31.5	1 3.7	2 3.9	27 25.6	2 47.8	24 43.2	28 37.2
13 M	7 27 28	22 13 22	22 46 51	28 42 39	5 56.5	3 56.0	6 40.5	1 48.3	2 17.3	27 23.8	2 51.2	24 41.5	28 36.1
14 Tu	7 31 24	23 14 30	4♈40 26	10♈40 50	5D55.7	5 22.4	7 49.4	2 32.9	2 30.6	27 22.1	2 54.7	24 39.8	28 35.0
15 W	7 35 21	24 15 37	16 44 32	22 52 14	5R55.9	6 49.5	8 58.0	3 17.6	2 43.9	27 20.5	2 58.2	24 38.1	28 34.0
16 Th	7 39 17	25 16 44	29 4 37	5♉22 19	5 56.0	8 17.4	10 6.5	4 2.4	2 57.1	27 19.0	3 1.7	24 36.4	28 32.9
17 F	7 43 14	26 17 49	11♉46 0	18 16 13	5 54.9	9 45.9	11 14.8	4 47.1	3 10.4	27 17.7	3 5.2	24 34.7	28 31.9
18 Sa	7 47 10	27 18 54	24 53 27	1♊38 2	5 51.6	11 15.0	12 23.0	5 32.0	3 23.5	27 16.4	3 8.7	24 33.0	28 30.8
19 Su	7 51 7	28 19 59	8♊30 12	15 29 59	5 45.9	12 44.7	13 30.9	6 16.8	3 36.7	27 15.2	3 12.2	24 31.3	28 29.8
20 M	7 55 3	29 21 2	22 37 13	29 51 30	5 37.8	14 15.1	14 38.6	7 1.7	3 49.8	27 14.2	3 15.7	24 29.6	28 28.8
21 Tu	7 59 0	0♒22 5	7♋12 14	14♋38 35	5 28.0	15 46.1	15 46.1	7 46.6	4 2.8	27 13.3	3 19.2	24 28.0	28 27.8
22 W	8 2 57	1 23 6	22 9 30	29 43 46	5 17.6	17 17.7	16 53.4	8 31.6	4 15.9	27 12.5	3 22.8	24 26.3	28 26.8
23 Th	8 6 53	2 24 7	7♌20 6	14♌57 6	5 7.9	18 49.9	18 0.5	9 16.6	4 28.8	27 11.8	3 26.3	24 24.6	28 25.8
24 F	8 10 50	3 25 7	22 33 24	0♍ 7 44	4 60.0	20 22.8	19 7.3	10 1.6	4 41.7	27 11.2	3 29.8	24 22.9	28 24.9
25 Sa	8 14 46	4 26 7	7♍38 55	15 5 57	4 54.6	21 56.2	20 13.9	10 46.7	4 54.6	27 10.7	3 33.3	24 21.2	28 23.9
26 Su	8 18 43	5 27 5	22 28 2	29 44 33	4D51.8	23 30.3	21 20.3	11 31.8	5 7.4	27 10.3	3 36.8	24 19.6	28 23.0
27 M	8 22 39	6 28 3	6♎55 8	13♎59 33	4 51.2	25 5.0	22 26.4	12 16.9	5 20.2	27 10.1	3 40.4	24 17.9	28 22.1
28 Tu	8 26 36	7 29 1	20 57 46	27 49 51	4 51.8	26 40.3	23 32.2	13 2.1	5 32.9	27D 9.9	3 43.9	24 16.3	28 21.2
29 W	8 30 32	8 29 57	4♏36 1	11♏16 34	4R52.5	28 16.3	24 37.8	13 47.4	5 45.6	27 9.9	3 47.4	24 14.6	28 20.3
30 Th	8 34 29	9 30 53	17 51 50	24 22 12	4 52.3	29 53.0	25 43.2	14 32.6	5 58.2	27 10.0	3 50.9	24 13.0	28 19.4
31 F	8 38 26	10 31 49	0♐48 4	7♐ 9 50	4 50.1	1♒30.4	26 48.2	15 17.9	6 10.8	27 10.2	3 54.4	24 11.4	28 18.6

LONGITUDE FEBRUARY 1913

Day	Sid.Time	☉	0 hr ☽	Noon ☽	True ☊	☿	♀	♂	♃	♄	♅	♆	♇
1 Sa	8 42 22	11♒32 44	13♐27 53	19♐42 36	4♈45.5	3♒ 8.4	27♓53.0	16♑ 3.3	6♑23.2	27♉10.5	3♒57.9	24♋ 9.8	28♊17.7
2 Su	8 46 19	12 33 38	25 54 19	2♑ 3 21	4R38.7	4 47.2	28 57.5	16 48.7	6 35.7	27 10.9	4 1.4	24R 8.2	28R16.9
3 M	8 50 15	13 34 30	8♑ 9 57	14 14 25	4 29.9	6 26.7	0♈ 1.7	17 34.1	6 48.1	27 11.5	4 4.9	24 6.6	28 16.1
4 Tu	8 54 12	14 35 22	20 16 57	26 17 45	4 20.0	8 6.9	1 5.6	18 19.5	7 0.4	27 12.1	4 8.4	24 5.0	28 15.3
5 W	8 58 8	15 36 13	2♒17 1	8♒14 56	4 9.9	9 47.9	2 9.1	19 5.0	7 12.6	27 12.9	4 11.9	24 3.5	28 14.5
6 Th	9 2 5	16 37 3	14 11 40	20 7 24	4 0.5	11 29.7	3 12.4	19 50.5	7 24.8	27 13.8	4 15.3	24 1.9	28 13.8
7 F	9 6 2	17 37 51	26 2 20	1♓56 42	3 52.8	13 12.2	4 15.2	20 36.0	7 36.9	27 14.8	4 18.8	24 0.4	28 13.1
8 Sa	9 9 58	18 38 39	7♓50 43	13 44 39	3 47.1	14 55.5	5 17.8	21 21.6	7 49.0	27 15.9	4 22.2	23 58.9	28 12.3
9 Su	9 13 55	19 39 24	19 38 50	25 33 37	3 43.7	16 39.6	6 19.9	22 7.2	8 0.9	27 17.1	4 25.7	23 57.4	28 11.6
10 M	9 17 51	20 40 8	1♈29 21	7♈26 30	3D42.4	18 24.5	7 21.7	22 52.8	8 12.8	27 18.4	4 29.1	23 55.9	28 11.0
11 Tu	9 21 48	21 40 51	13 25 30	19 26 53	3 42.9	20 10.3	8 23.1	23 38.5	8 24.6	27 19.9	4 32.5	23 54.4	28 10.3
12 W	9 25 44	22 41 32	25 31 9	1♉38 55	3 44.3	21 56.8	9 24.1	24 24.2	8 36.4	27 21.4	4 35.9	23 52.9	28 9.7
13 Th	9 29 41	23 42 12	7♉50 42	14 7 8	3 45.9	23 44.1	10 24.6	25 9.9	8 48.1	27 23.1	4 39.3	23 51.5	28 9.0
14 F	9 33 37	24 42 50	20 28 46	26 56 9	3R46.9	25 32.3	11 24.8	25 55.6	8 59.6	27 24.9	4 42.6	23 50.1	28 8.4
15 Sa	9 37 34	25 43 26	3♊29 47	10♊10 6	3 46.7	27 21.2	12 24.4	26 41.4	9 11.2	27 26.7	4 46.0	23 48.7	28 7.9
16 Su	9 41 30	26 44 0	16 57 26	23 51 59	3 44.9	29 10.8	13 23.6	27 27.2	9 22.6	27 28.7	4 49.3	23 47.3	28 7.3
17 M	9 45 27	27 44 33	0♋53 48	8♋ 2 46	3 41.5	1♓ 1.1	14 22.3	28 13.0	9 33.9	27 30.8	4 52.7	23 46.0	28 6.8
18 Tu	9 49 24	28 45 4	15 18 34	22 40 39	3 36.9	2 52.1	15 20.5	28 58.8	9 45.2	27 33.0	4 56.0	23 44.6	28 6.3
19 W	9 53 20	29 45 33	0♌ 8 17	7♌40 31	3 31.7	4 43.6	16 18.2	29 44.7	9 56.4	27 35.4	4 59.2	23 43.3	28 5.8
20 Th	9 57 17	0♓46 0	15 16 15	22 54 14	3 26.8	6 35.7	17 15.3	0♒30.6	10 7.4	27 37.8	5 2.5	23 42.0	28 5.3
21 F	10 1 13	1 46 25	0♍33 8	8♍11 35	3 22.8	8 28.1	18 11.9	1 16.5	10 18.4	27 40.3	5 5.8	23 40.8	28 4.8
22 Sa	10 5 10	2 46 49	15 48 17	23 21 59	3 20.2	10 20.7	19 7.9	2 2.5	10 29.3	27 42.9	5 9.0	23 39.5	28 4.4
23 Su	10 9 6	3 47 11	0♎51 36	8♎16 13	3D19.2	12 13.5	20 3.3	2 48.4	10 40.1	27 45.7	5 12.2	23 38.3	28 4.0
24 M	10 13 3	4 47 32	15 35 4	22 47 38	3 19.6	14 6.1	20 58.1	3 34.4	10 50.9	27 48.5	5 15.4	23 37.1	28 3.6
25 Tu	10 16 59	5 47 51	29 53 33	6♏52 38	3 20.9	15 58.5	21 52.2	4 20.5	11 1.5	27 51.4	5 18.5	23 35.9	28 3.2
26 W	10 20 56	6 48 9	13♏44 55	20 30 30	3 22.5	17 50.2	22 45.7	5 6.5	11 12.0	27 54.5	5 21.7	23 34.8	28 2.9
27 Th	10 24 53	7 48 25	27 9 38	3♐42 39	3R23.7	19 41.1	23 38.5	5 52.6	11 22.4	27 57.6	5 24.8	23 33.6	28 2.5
28 F	10 28 49	8 48 40	10♐ 9 58	16 32 1	3 24.1	21 30.7	24 30.6	6 38.7	11 32.8	28 0.9	5 27.9	23 32.5	28 2.2

Astro Data Dy Hr Mn	Planet Ingress Dy Hr Mn
☽0 N 13 16:37	♃ ♑ 2 19:46
♃⊻♅ 16 11:11	♀ ♓ 7 5:27
☽0 S 26 13:49	☿ ♑ 10 5:20
♄ D 28 18:13	♂ ♑ 10 13:43
	☉ ♒ 20 15:19
♀0 N 2 6:36	☿ ♒ 30 1:44
☽0 N 9 22:17	
☽0 S 22 23:33	♀ ♈ 2 23:22
♄⊻♇ 28 9:11	☿ ♓ 16 10:43
	☉ ♓ 19 5:44
	♂ ♒ 19 8:00

Last Aspect Dy Hr Mn	☽ Ingress Dy Hr Mn	Last Aspect Dy Hr Mn	☽ Ingress Dy Hr Mn
1 9:14 ♃ ✶	♏ 1 9:49	2 6:31 ♀ □	♑ 2 7:59
3 12:49 ♄ ☍	♐ 3 17:01	4 13:50 ♄ △	♒ 4 19:25
5 23:43 ♇ ☍	♑ 6 2:10	7 4:25 ♇ △	♓ 7 8:03
8 8:14 ♄ △	♒ 8 13:07	9 17:19 ♇ □	♈ 9 20:59
10 22:52 ♇ △	♓ 11 1:38	12 5:11 ♇ ✶	♉ 12 8:47
13 11:46 ♇ □	♈ 13 14:36	14 12:55 ♄ ☌	♊ 14 17:38
15 22:59 ♇ ✶	♉ 16 1:46	16 19:16 ♇ ☌	♋ 16 22:29
18 4:42 ☉ △	♊ 18 9:07	18 23:20 ♂ ☍	♌ 18 23:47
20 9:43 ♇ ☌	♋ 20 12:14	20 20:07 ♇ ✶	♍ 20 23:08
22 8:00 ♄ ✶	♌ 22 12:26	22 19:31 ♇ □	♎ 22 22:37
24 9:16 ♇ ✶	♍ 24 11:48	24 20:53 ♇ △	♏ 25 0:11
26 9:44 ♇ □	♎ 26 12:26	27 1:28 ♄ ☍	♐ 27 5:11
28 12:54 ♇ △	♏ 28 15:50		
30 17:12 ♄ ☍	♐ 30 22:30		

☽ Phases & Eclipses Dy Hr Mn	
7 10:28	● 16♑33
15 16:01	☽ 24♈56
22 15:40	○ 2♌03
29 7:34	☽ 8♏49
6 5:22	● 16♒51
14 8:33	☽ 25♉04
21 2:03	○ 1♍52
27 21:15	☽ 8♐42

Astro Data

1 JANUARY 1913
Julian Day # 4749
Delta T 14.7 sec
SVP 06♓28'30"
Obliquity 23°27'11"
⚷ Chiron 7♓22.3
☽ Mean ☊ 7♈43.9

1 FEBRUARY 1913
Julian Day # 4780
Delta T 14.8 sec
SVP 06♓28'25"
Obliquity 23°27'11"
⚷ Chiron 8♓55.9
☽ Mean ☊ 6♈05.4

MARCH 1913

LONGITUDE

Day	Sid.Time	☉	0 hr ☽	Noon ☽	True ☊	☿	♀	♂	♃	♄	♅	♆	♇
1 Sa	10 32 46	9♓48 53	22♐49 17	29♐ 2 15	3♈23.4	23♓18.7	25♈21.9	7♒24.8	11♑43.0	28♉ 4.2	5♒30.9	23♋31.5	28♊ 2.0
2 Su	10 36 42	10 49 5	5♑11 26	11♑17 18	3R 21.6	25 4.7	26 12.5	8 10.9	11 53.1	28 7.6	5 34.0	23R 30.4	28R 1.7
3 M	10 40 39	11 49 16	17 20 19	23 20 56	3 18.9	26 48.2	27 2.3	8 57.1	12 3.1	28 11.2	5 37.0	23 29.4	28 1.5
4 Tu	10 44 35	12 49 24	29 19 35	5♒16 40	3 15.6	28 28.7	27 51.3	9 43.3	12 13.0	28 14.8	5 40.0	23 28.4	28 1.3
5 W	10 48 32	13 49 31	11♒12 31	17 7 30	3 12.2	0♈ 5.6	28 39.5	10 29.5	12 22.8	28 18.5	5 42.9	23 27.4	28 1.1
6 Th	10 52 28	14 49 37	23 1 56	28 56 6	3 9.1	1 38.5	29 26.8	11 15.7	12 32.5	28 22.3	5 45.9	23 26.5	28 0.9
7 F	10 56 25	15 49 40	4♓50 16	10♓44 43	3 6.6	3 6.7	0♉13.1	12 2.0	12 42.1	28 26.3	5 48.8	23 25.6	28 0.7
8 Sa	11 0 22	16 49 42	16 39 42	22 35 27	3 4.9	4 29.8	0 58.5	12 48.2	12 51.5	28 30.3	5 51.7	23 24.7	28 0.6
9 Su	11 4 18	17 49 41	28 32 14	4♈30 18	3D 4.2	5 47.2	1 43.0	13 34.5	13 0.9	28 34.4	5 54.5	23 23.8	28 0.5
10 M	11 8 15	18 49 39	10♈29 55	16 31 22	3 4.2	6 58.3	2 26.4	14 20.8	13 10.1	28 38.6	5 57.3	23 23.0	28 0.4
11 Tu	11 12 11	19 49 35	22 34 56	28 40 57	3 5.0	8 2.7	3 8.7	15 7.1	13 19.2	28 42.8	6 0.1	23 22.2	28 0.4
12 W	11 16 8	20 49 28	4♉49 45	11♉ 1 41	3 6.0	8 59.9	3 49.9	15 53.4	13 28.2	28 47.2	6 2.8	23 21.4	28D 0.3
13 Th	11 20 4	21 49 20	17 17 7	23 36 26	3 7.2	9 49.6	4 30.0	16 39.7	13 37.0	28 51.6	6 5.6	23 20.7	28 0.3
14 F	11 24 1	22 49 9	0♊ 0 1	6♊28 13	3 8.1	10 31.4	5 8.9	17 26.0	13 45.8	28 56.2	6 8.2	23 20.0	28 0.4
15 Sa	11 27 57	23 48 56	13 1 25	19 39 56	3R 8.7	11 5.1	5 46.5	18 12.4	13 54.4	29 0.8	6 10.9	23 19.3	28 0.4
16 Su	11 31 54	24 48 41	26 24 3	3♋13 57	3 8.9	11 30.5	6 22.8	18 58.7	14 2.9	29 5.5	6 13.5	23 18.7	28 0.5
17 M	11 35 51	25 48 24	10♋ 9 47	17 11 32	3 8.7	11 47.5	6 57.7	19 45.1	14 11.2	29 10.3	6 16.1	23 18.1	28 0.5
18 Tu	11 39 47	26 48 4	24 19 6	1♌32 14	3 8.2	11R 56.2	7 31.3	20 31.5	14 19.4	29 15.2	6 18.7	23 17.5	28 0.7
19 W	11 43 44	27 47 42	8♌50 32	16 13 25	3 7.6	11 56.5	8 3.3	21 17.9	14 27.5	29 20.2	6 21.2	23 17.0	28 0.8
20 Th	11 47 40	28 47 18	23 40 11	1♍ 9 58	3 7.0	11 48.8	8 33.9	22 4.3	14 35.5	29 25.2	6 23.6	23 16.4	28 0.9
21 F	11 51 37	29 46 51	8♍41 48	16 14 35	3 6.7	11 33.3	9 2.9	22 50.7	14 43.3	29 30.3	6 26.1	23 16.0	28 1.1
22 Sa	11 55 33	0♈46 22	23 47 13	1♎18 33	3D 6.5	11 10.6	9 30.2	23 37.1	14 51.0	29 35.5	6 28.5	23 15.5	28 1.3
23 Su	11 59 30	1 45 51	8♎47 30	16 13 1	3 6.5	10 41.3	9 55.8	24 23.5	14 58.5	29 40.7	6 30.9	23 15.1	28 1.5
24 M	12 3 26	2 45 19	23 34 11	0♏50 13	3R 6.5	10 6.0	10 19.7	25 9.9	15 5.9	29 46.1	6 33.2	23 14.7	28 1.8
25 Tu	12 7 23	3 44 44	8♏ 0 27	15 4 26	3 6.5	9 25.6	10 41.8	25 56.3	15 13.2	29 51.5	6 35.5	23 14.3	28 2.0
26 W	12 11 20	4 44 7	22 1 52	28 52 35	3 6.4	8 41.0	11 1.9	26 42.8	15 20.3	29 57.0	6 37.7	23 14.0	28 2.3
27 Th	12 15 16	5 43 29	5♐36 36	12♐14 3	3 6.1	7 53.2	11 20.2	27 29.2	15 27.3	0♊ 2.5	6 39.9	23 13.7	28 2.6
28 F	12 19 13	6 42 49	18 45 10	25 10 20	3 5.9	7 3.3	11 36.5	28 15.7	15 34.1	0 8.2	6 42.1	23 13.5	28 3.0
29 Sa	12 23 9	7 42 7	1♑29 57	7♑44 30	3D 5.7	6 12.3	11 50.7	29 2.2	15 40.8	0 13.9	6 44.2	23 13.3	28 3.3
30 Su	12 27 6	8 41 23	13 54 31	20 0 34	3 5.7	5 21.3	12 2.8	29 48.6	15 47.3	0 19.6	6 46.3	23 13.1	28 3.7
31 M	12 31 2	9 40 38	26 3 12	2♒ 3 0	3 5.9	4 31.1	12 12.8	0♓35.1	15 53.7	0 25.5	6 48.4	23 12.9	28 4.1

APRIL 1913

LONGITUDE

Day	Sid.Time	☉	0 hr ☽	Noon ☽	True ☊	☿	♀	♂	♃	♄	♅	♆	♇
1 Tu	12 34 59	10♈39 51	8♒ 0 31	13♒56 20	3♈ 6.5	3♈42.9	12♉20.5	1♓21.6	15♑59.9	0♊31.4	6♒50.4	23♋12.8	28♊ 4.5
2 W	12 38 55	11 39 1	19 50 57	25 44 55	3 7.4	2R 57.4	12 25.9	2 8.0	16 6.0	0 37.3	6 52.4	23R 12.7	28 5.0
3 Th	12 42 52	12 38 10	1♓38 40	7♓32 41	3 8.3	2 15.4	12R 29.1	2 54.5	16 11.9	0 43.3	6 54.3	23 12.6	28 5.4
4 F	12 46 49	13 37 18	13 27 22	19 23 6	3 9.2	1 37.4	12 29.9	3 41.0	16 17.6	0 49.4	6 56.2	23D 12.6	28 5.9
5 Sa	12 50 45	14 36 23	25 20 14	1♈19 4	3R 9.8	1 3.9	12 28.2	4 27.4	16 23.2	0 55.6	6 58.0	23 12.6	28 6.4
6 Su	12 54 42	15 35 26	7♈19 54	13 22 58	3 9.9	0 35.3	12 24.2	5 13.9	16 28.6	1 1.8	6 59.8	23 12.7	28 7.0
7 M	12 58 38	16 34 27	19 28 30	25 36 40	3 9.3	0 11.9	12 17.6	6 0.4	16 33.9	1 8.1	7 1.5	23 12.7	28 7.5
8 Tu	13 2 35	17 33 26	1♉47 40	8♉ 1 37	3 8.0	29♓53.9	12 8.7	6 46.8	16 39.0	1 14.4	7 3.2	23 12.9	28 8.1
9 W	13 6 31	18 32 23	14 18 41	20 39 0	3 6.1	29 41.3	11 57.2	7 33.3	16 43.9	1 20.8	7 4.9	23 13.0	28 8.7
10 Th	13 10 28	19 31 18	27 2 39	3♊29 45	3 3.8	29D 34.1	11 43.3	8 19.7	16 48.7	1 27.2	7 6.5	23 13.2	28 9.3
11 F	13 14 24	20 30 11	10♊ 0 26	16 34 46	3 1.3	29 32.3	11 27.0	9 6.1	16 53.3	1 33.7	7 8.1	23 13.4	28 9.9
12 Sa	13 18 21	21 29 2	23 12 52	29 54 49	2 59.1	29 35.8	11 8.2	9 52.5	16 57.7	1 40.3	7 9.6	23 13.7	28 10.6
13 Su	13 22 18	22 27 51	6♋40 41	13♋30 31	2 57.6	29 44.4	10 47.1	10 39.0	17 2.0	1 46.9	7 11.1	23 13.9	28 11.3
14 M	13 26 14	23 26 37	20 24 21	27 22 9	2D 56.9	29 58.1	10 23.8	11 25.4	17 6.1	1 53.5	7 12.5	23 14.3	28 12.0
15 Tu	13 30 11	24 25 21	4♌23 51	11♌29 20	2 57.1	0♈16.6	9 58.2	12 11.7	17 10.0	2 0.2	7 13.9	23 14.6	28 12.7
16 W	13 34 7	25 24 2	18 38 24	25 50 46	2 58.1	0 39.7	9 30.6	12 58.1	17 13.7	2 7.0	7 15.2	23 15.0	28 13.4
17 Th	13 38 4	26 22 41	3♍ 6 3	10♍23 47	2 59.5	1 7.2	9 1.1	13 44.5	17 17.3	2 13.8	7 16.5	23 15.4	28 14.2
18 F	13 42 0	27 21 18	17 43 24	25 4 16	3 0.7	1 39.0	8 29.8	14 30.8	17 20.7	2 20.6	7 17.8	23 15.8	28 14.9
19 Sa	13 45 57	28 19 53	2♎25 38	9♎46 43	3R 1.3	2 14.9	7 56.9	15 17.1	17 23.9	2 27.5	7 18.9	23 16.3	28 15.7
20 Su	13 49 53	29 18 26	17 6 41	24 24 42	3 0.7	2 54.7	7 22.6	16 3.5	17 26.9	2 34.5	7 20.1	23 16.8	28 16.6
21 M	13 53 50	0♉16 57	1♏39 55	8♏51 34	2 58.8	3 38.2	6 47.1	16 49.8	17 29.7	2 41.4	7 21.2	23 17.4	28 17.4
22 Tu	13 57 47	1 15 26	15 58 57	23 1 25	2 55.5	4 25.2	6 10.7	17 36.1	17 32.4	2 48.5	7 22.2	23 18.0	28 18.2
23 W	14 1 43	2 13 53	29 58 31	6♐49 51	2 51.3	5 15.6	5 33.5	18 22.4	17 34.9	2 55.5	7 23.2	23 18.6	28 19.1
24 Th	14 5 40	3 12 18	13♐35 11	20 14 27	2 46.7	6 9.3	4 55.8	19 8.6	17 37.2	3 2.6	7 24.2	23 19.2	28 20.0
25 F	14 9 36	4 10 42	26 47 40	3♑15 0	2 42.3	7 6.0	4 17.9	19 54.9	17 39.3	3 9.8	7 25.1	23 19.9	28 20.9
26 Sa	14 13 33	5 9 4	9♑36 42	15 53 9	2 38.6	8 5.8	3 40.0	20 41.1	17 41.3	3 16.9	7 26.0	23 20.6	28 21.8
27 Su	14 17 29	6 7 25	22 4 47	28 12 7	2 36.1	9 8.3	3 2.4	21 27.3	17 43.0	3 24.1	7 26.8	23 21.3	28 22.8
28 M	14 21 26	7 5 44	4♒15 43	10♒16 9	2D 35.1	10 13.6	2 25.4	22 13.5	17 44.6	3 31.4	7 27.5	23 22.1	28 23.7
29 Tu	14 25 22	8 4 2	16 14 4	22 10 5	2 35.4	11 21.5	1 49.1	22 59.7	17 46.0	3 38.7	7 28.2	23 22.9	28 24.7
30 W	14 29 19	9 2 17	28 4 50	3♓58 58	2 36.6	12 32.0	1 13.7	23 45.9	17 47.2	3 46.0	7 28.9	23 23.7	28 25.7

Astro Data	Dy Hr Mn
☿0N	4 7:31
☽0N	9 4:02
♇ D	12 20:19
♃□♄	16 17:54
☿ R	18 12:57
☽0S	22 10:47
♀ R	3 19:46
♆ D	4 4:57
☽0N	5 10:28
☿0S	9 0:49
☿ D	10 20:05
☽0S	18 20:54
♃□♄	18 0:08
☿0N	23 14:13

Planet Ingress	Dy Hr Mn
☿ ♈	4 22:35
♀ ♉	6 17:09
☉ ♈	21 5:18
♄ ♊	26 13:07
♂ ♓	30 5:53
☿ ♓	7 15:02
☿ ♈	14 2:49
☉ ♉	20 17:03

Last Aspect Dy Hr Mn		☽ Ingress Dy Hr Mn
1 10:03	♇ ☍	♑ 1 13:52
3 22:01	☿ ⚹	♒ 4 1:21
6 13:57	♀ ⚹	♓ 6 14:10
9 0:04	♄ ⚹	♈ 9 2:57
11 10:40	♇ ⚹	♉ 11 14:35
13 22:00	♄ ☌	♊ 13 24:00
16 2:50	♇ ☌	♋ 16 6:21
18 8:16	♄ ⚹	♌ 18 9:27
20 9:16	♄ □	♍ 20 10:08
22 9:19	♄ △	♎ 22 9:54
24 7:21	♇ △	♏ 24 10:37
26 8:41	♂ □	♐ 26 13:59
28 19:00	♂ ⚹	♑ 28 21:08
30 18:21	♆ ☍	♒ 31 7:53

Last Aspect Dy Hr Mn		☽ Ingress Dy Hr Mn
2 16:46	♇ △	♓ 2 20:39
5 5:34	♇ □	♈ 5 9:22
7 16:54	♇ ⚹	♉ 7 20:32
10 4:41	☿ ⚹	♊ 10 5:31
12 11:32	☿ □	♋ 12 12:09
14 5:39	☉ □	♌ 14 16:30
16 15:57	♇ ⚹	♍ 16 18:53
18 17:12	♇ □	♎ 18 20:02
20 18:24	♇ △	♏ 20 21:14
22 12:29	♆ △	♐ 23 0:03
25 2:53	♇ ☍	♑ 25 5:56
27 2:30	♆ ☍	♒ 27 15:33
30 0:42	♇ △	♓ 30 3:54

☽ Phases & Eclipses Dy Hr Mn	
8 0:22	● 16♓51
15 20:58	☽ 24♊41
22 11:56	○ 1♎16
22 11:58	☍T 1.568
29 12:57	☽ 8♑14
6 17:48	● 16♈19
6 17:32:50	☌P 0.424
14 5:39	☽ 23♋40
20 21:32	○ 0♏11
28 6:09	☽ 7♒21

Astro Data

1 MARCH 1913
Julian Day # 4808
Delta T 14.9 sec
SVP 06♓28'21"
Obliquity 23°27'12"
⚷ Chiron 10♓39.7
☽ Mean ☊ 4♈36.4

1 APRIL 1913
Julian Day # 4839
Delta T 15.0 sec
SVP 06♓28'17"
Obliquity 23°27'12"
⚷ Chiron 12♓34.4
☽ Mean ☊ 2♈57.9

LONGITUDE — MAY 1913

Day	Sid.Time	☉	0 hr ☽	Noon ☽	True ☊	☿	♀	♂	♃	♄	♅	♆	♇
1 Th	14 33 16	10♉ 0 32	9♓53 4	15♓47 45	2♈38.3	13♈44.9	0♉39.6	24♓32.0	17♑48.2	3♊53.3	7♒29.5	23♋24.6	28♊26.7
2 F	14 37 12	10 58 45	21 43 34	27 41 3	2R 39.8	15 0.3	0R 6.9	25 18.1	17 49.0	4 0.7	7 30.0	23 25.5	28 27.7
3 Sa	14 41 9	11 56 56	3♈40 41	9♈42 53	2 40.3	16 17.9	29♈35.7	26 4.2	17 49.6	4 8.1	7 30.6	23 26.4	28 28.7
4 Su	14 45 5	12 55 5	15 48 2	21 56 29	2 39.4	17 37.8	29 6.4	26 50.3	17 50.1	4 15.6	7 31.0	23 27.4	28 29.8
5 M	14 49 2	13 53 14	28 8 27	4♉24 9	2 36.6	18 60.0	28 38.9	27 36.3	17R 50.3	4 23.0	7 31.4	23 28.4	28 30.8
6 Tu	14 52 58	14 51 20	10♉43 42	17 7 9	2 31.9	20 24.3	28 13.4	28 22.3	17 50.4	4 30.5	7 31.8	23 29.4	28 31.9
7 W	14 56 55	15 49 25	23 34 32	0♊ 5 45	2 25.5	21 50.8	27 50.1	29 8.3	17 50.2	4 38.0	7 32.1	23 30.4	28 33.0
8 Th	15 0 51	16 47 29	6♊40 42	13 19 14	2 18.1	23 19.4	27 28.9	29 54.3	17 49.9	4 45.6	7 32.3	23 31.5	28 34.1
9 F	15 4 48	17 45 30	20 1 9	26 46 14	2 10.5	24 50.0	27 10.1	0♈40.2	17 49.4	4 53.1	7 32.6	23 32.6	28 35.3
10 Sa	15 8 45	18 43 30	3♋34 15	10♋24 59	2 3.5	26 22.8	26 53.6	1 26.1	17 48.7	5 0.7	7 32.7	23 33.8	28 36.4
11 Su	15 12 41	19 41 29	17 18 12	24 13 41	1 57.9	27 57.6	26 39.5	2 11.9	17 47.8	5 8.3	7 32.8	23 34.9	28 37.6
12 M	15 16 38	20 39 25	1♌11 15	8♌10 43	1 54.2	29 34.5	26 27.8	2 57.7	17 46.7	5 16.0	7R 32.9	23 36.1	28 38.7
13 Tu	15 20 34	21 37 19	15 11 55	22 14 42	1D 52.5	1♉13.4	26 18.4	3 43.5	17 45.4	5 23.6	7 32.9	23 37.3	28 39.9
14 W	15 24 31	22 35 12	29 18 55	6♍24 24	1 52.5	2 54.3	26 11.5	4 29.3	17 44.0	5 31.3	7 32.9	23 38.6	28 41.1
15 Th	15 28 27	23 33 3	13♍31 0	20 38 28	1 53.4	4 37.3	26 7.0	5 15.0	17 42.3	5 38.9	7 32.8	23 39.9	28 42.3
16 F	15 32 24	24 30 52	27 46 35	4♎55 1	1R 54.2	6 22.4	26D 4.9	6 0.7	17 40.5	5 46.6	7 32.6	23 41.1	28 43.5
17 Sa	15 36 20	25 28 39	12♎ 3 26	19 11 24	1 53.8	8 9.5	26 5.1	6 46.3	17 38.5	5 54.3	7 32.4	23 42.5	28 44.8
18 Su	15 40 17	26 26 25	26 18 27	3♏24 5	1 51.5	9 58.6	26 7.7	7 31.9	17 36.3	6 2.1	7 32.2	23 43.8	28 46.0
19 M	15 44 14	27 24 9	10♏27 44	17 28 52	1 46.8	11 49.8	26 12.5	8 17.4	17 33.9	6 9.8	7 31.9	23 45.2	28 47.3
20 Tu	15 48 10	28 21 52	24 26 55	1♐21 22	1 39.8	13 43.1	26 19.6	9 3.0	17 31.4	6 17.5	7 31.6	23 46.6	28 48.5
21 W	15 52 7	29 19 33	8♐11 44	14 57 37	1 31.0	15 38.3	26 28.8	9 48.5	17 28.7	6 25.3	7 31.2	23 48.0	28 49.8
22 Th	15 56 3	0♊17 13	21 38 43	28 14 49	1 21.2	17 35.6	26 40.2	10 33.9	17 25.7	6 33.0	7 30.8	23 49.5	28 51.1
23 F	16 0 0	1 14 52	4♑45 47	11♑11 38	1 11.5	19 34.8	26 53.7	11 19.3	17 22.7	6 40.8	7 30.3	23 51.0	28 52.4
24 Sa	16 3 56	2 12 30	17 32 28	23 48 30	1 2.9	21 35.9	27 9.1	12 4.7	17 19.4	6 48.6	7 29.8	23 52.5	28 53.7
25 Su	16 7 53	3 10 7	0♒ 0 3	6♒ 7 29	0 56.0	23 38.8	27 26.5	12 50.0	17 16.0	6 56.4	7 29.2	23 54.0	28 55.0
26 M	16 11 49	4 7 43	12 11 17	18 11 58	0 51.4	25 43.4	27 45.8	13 35.3	17 12.3	7 4.2	7 28.6	23 55.6	28 56.3
27 Tu	16 15 46	5 5 18	24 10 7	0♓ 6 22	0 49.0	27 49.7	28 6.9	14 20.6	17 8.6	7 12.0	7 27.9	23 57.2	28 57.7
28 W	16 19 43	6 2 52	6♓ 1 21	11 55 44	0D 48.3	29 57.4	28 29.8	15 5.8	17 4.6	7 19.8	7 27.2	23 58.8	28 59.0
29 Th	16 23 39	7 0 25	17 50 12	23 45 25	0 48.6	2♊ 6.4	28 54.3	15 50.9	17 0.5	7 27.6	7 26.4	24 0.4	29 0.3
30 F	16 27 36	7 57 57	29 42 4	5♈40 46	0R 49.0	4 16.5	29 20.5	16 36.1	16 56.2	7 35.3	7 25.6	24 2.0	29 1.7
31 Sa	16 31 32	8 55 28	11♈42 8	17 46 44	0 48.5	6 27.4	29 48.3	17 21.1	16 51.7	7 43.1	7 24.8	24 3.7	29 3.1

LONGITUDE — JUNE 1913

Day	Sid.Time	☉	0 hr ☽	Noon ☽	True ☊	☿	♀	♂	♃	♄	♅	♆	♇
1 Su	16 35 29	9♊52 59	23♈55 5	0♉ 7 37	0♈46.2	8♊39.1	0♉17.6	18♈ 6.1	16♑47.1	7♊50.9	7♒23.9	24♋ 5.4	29♊ 4.4
2 M	16 39 25	10 50 28	6♉24 42	12 46 37	0R 41.4	10 51.1	0 48.3	18 51.1	16R 42.4	7 58.7	7R 22.9	24 7.1	29 5.8
3 Tu	16 43 22	11 47 57	19 13 33	25 45 33	0 34.1	13 3.2	1 20.4	19 36.0	16 37.4	8 6.5	7 22.0	24 8.8	29 7.2
4 W	16 47 18	12 45 25	2♊22 36	9♊ 4 33	0 24.6	15 15.1	1 53.9	20 20.9	16 32.4	8 14.3	7 20.9	24 10.6	29 8.6
5 Th	16 51 15	13 42 53	15 51 8	22 41 59	0 13.6	17 26.6	2 28.6	21 5.7	16 27.2	8 22.1	7 19.9	24 12.3	29 10.0
6 F	16 55 12	14 40 19	29 36 41	6♋34 43	0 2.1	19 37.4	3 4.6	21 50.5	16 21.8	8 29.9	7 18.7	24 14.1	29 11.4
7 Sa	16 59 8	15 37 45	13♋35 32	20 38 35	29♓51.4	21 47.3	3 41.8	22 35.2	16 16.3	8 37.6	7 17.6	24 16.0	29 12.8
8 Su	17 3 5	16 35 9	27 43 16	4♌49 4	29 42.6	23 55.9	4 20.1	23 19.8	16 10.6	8 45.4	7 16.4	24 17.8	29 14.2
9 M	17 7 1	17 32 32	11♌55 29	19 2 6	29 36.3	26 3.2	4 59.5	24 4.4	16 4.9	8 53.2	7 15.2	24 19.6	29 15.6
10 Tu	17 10 58	18 29 55	26 8 32	3♍14 29	29 32.6	28 8.8	5 40.0	24 48.9	15 58.9	9 0.9	7 13.9	24 21.5	29 17.1
11 W	17 14 54	19 27 16	10♍19 42	17 24 3	29D 31.2	0♋12.7	6 21.5	25 33.4	15 52.9	9 8.6	7 12.5	24 23.4	29 18.5
12 Th	17 18 51	20 24 36	24 27 22	1♎29 33	29R 31.0	2 14.7	7 3.9	26 17.8	15 46.7	9 16.3	7 11.2	24 25.3	29 19.9
13 F	17 22 47	21 21 55	8♎30 31	15 30 11	29 30.9	4 14.7	7 47.3	27 2.1	15 40.5	9 24.0	7 9.8	24 27.2	29 21.4
14 Sa	17 26 44	22 19 13	22 28 26	29 25 9	29 29.5	6 12.6	8 31.6	27 46.4	15 34.1	9 31.7	7 8.3	24 29.1	29 22.8
15 Su	17 30 41	23 16 30	6♏20 11	13♏13 18	29 26.0	8 8.3	9 16.8	28 30.6	15 27.6	9 39.4	7 6.9	24 31.1	29 24.2
16 M	17 34 37	24 13 47	20 4 19	26 52 56	29 19.6	10 1.7	10 2.8	29 14.7	15 21.0	9 47.0	7 5.3	24 33.1	29 25.7
17 Tu	17 38 34	25 11 3	3♐38 53	10♐21 53	29 10.5	11 52.9	10 49.6	29 58.8	15 14.3	9 54.6	7 3.8	24 35.0	29 27.1
18 W	17 42 30	26 8 18	17 1 38	23 37 53	28 59.3	13 41.8	11 37.3	0♉42.9	15 7.5	10 2.2	7 2.2	24 37.0	29 28.6
19 Th	17 46 27	27 5 33	0♑10 23	6♑38 59	28 46.8	15 28.4	12 25.6	1 26.8	15 0.6	10 9.8	7 0.6	24 39.0	29 30.0
20 F	17 50 23	28 2 47	13 3 33	19 24 3	28 34.3	17 12.6	13 14.7	2 10.7	14 53.6	10 17.4	6 58.9	24 41.1	29 31.5
21 Sa	17 54 20	29 0 1	25 40 30	1♒53 2	28 22.9	18 54.5	14 4.5	2 54.6	14 46.5	10 24.9	6 57.2	24 43.1	29 32.9
22 Su	17 58 17	29 57 14	8♒ 1 49	14 7 9	28 13.4	20 34.0	14 55.0	3 38.4	14 39.4	10 32.5	6 55.5	24 45.2	29 34.4
23 M	18 2 13	0♋54 27	20 9 22	26 8 53	28 6.6	22 11.1	15 46.1	4 22.1	14 32.2	10 40.0	6 53.7	24 47.2	29 35.8
24 Tu	18 6 10	1 51 40	2♓ 6 12	8♓ 1 50	28 2.3	23 45.8	16 37.9	5 5.7	14 24.9	10 47.4	6 51.9	24 49.3	29 37.2
25 W	18 10 6	2 48 53	13 56 23	19 50 28	28 0.3	25 18.1	17 30.3	5 49.3	14 17.5	10 54.9	6 50.1	24 51.4	29 38.7
26 Th	18 14 3	3 46 6	25 44 44	1♈39 51	27 59.8	26 48.0	18 23.2	6 32.8	14 10.1	11 2.3	6 48.3	24 53.5	29 40.1
27 F	18 17 59	4 43 19	7♈36 32	13 35 26	27 59.8	28 15.5	19 16.7	7 16.2	14 2.6	11 9.7	6 46.4	24 55.6	29 41.6
28 Sa	18 21 56	5 40 32	19 37 15	25 42 38	27 59.2	29 40.5	20 10.8	7 59.6	13 55.1	11 17.1	6 44.4	24 57.7	29 43.0
29 Su	18 25 52	6 37 45	1♉52 11	8♉ 6 29	27 57.1	1♌ 3.0	21 5.4	8 42.9	13 47.6	11 24.4	6 42.5	24 59.8	29 44.5
30 M	18 29 49	7 34 58	14 26 1	20 51 12	27 52.7	2 23.0	22 0.5	9 26.1	13 40.0	11 31.7	6 40.5	25 2.0	29 45.9

Astro Data	Dy Hr Mn
☽0N	2 17:34
♃ R	5 19:02
♂0N	12 5:32
♅ R	12 16:33
☽0S	16 4:17
♀ D	16 9:38
♄△♅	28 20:54
☽0N	30 0:53
☽0S	12 9:19
♄∠♆	13 13:18
☽0N	26 7:57

Planet Ingress	Dy Hr Mn
♀ ♈	2 5:12
♂ ♈	8 3:00
☿ ♉	12 6:15
☉ ♊	21 16:50
☿ ♊	28 0:30
♀ ♉	31 9:45
☊ ♓	6 4:31
☿ ♋	10 21:31
♂ ♉	17 0:38
☉ ♋	22 1:10
☿ ♌	28 5:37

Last Aspect Dy Hr Mn		☽ Ingress Dy Hr Mn
2 13:35	♇ □	♈ 2 16:39
5 0:57	♀ ☌	♉ 5 3:35
7 10:53	♂ ⚹	♊ 7 11:49
9 15:14	♇ ☌	♋ 9 17:43
11 20:51	☿ □	♌ 11 21:57
13 22:56	♇ ⚹	♍ 14 1:10
16 1:36	♇ □	♎ 16 3:44
18 4:10	♇ △	♏ 18 6:14
20 7:18	☉ ☍	♐ 20 9:38
22 13:08	♇ ☍	♑ 22 15:13
24 18:54	♀ □	♒ 24 24:00
27 9:42	♇ △	♓ 27 11:47
29 22:39	♇ □	♈ 30 0:36

Last Aspect Dy Hr Mn		☽ Ingress Dy Hr Mn
1 10:00	♇ ⚹	♉ 1 11:45
3 9:04	♆ ⚹	♊ 3 19:42
5 23:16	♇ ☌	♋ 6 0:40
7 18:11	♆ ☌	♌ 8 3:51
10 5:19	♇ ⚹	♍ 10 6:31
12 8:20	♇ □	♎ 12 9:27
14 11:57	♇ △	♏ 14 13:00
16 7:54	♆ △	♐ 16 17:31
18 22:45	♇ ☍	♑ 18 23:41
20 22:09	♆ ☍	♒ 21 8:21
23 18:59	♇ △	♓ 23 19:45
26 7:59	♇ □	♈ 26 8:38
28 19:52	♇ ⚹	♉ 28 20:22

☽ Phases & Eclipses Dy Hr Mn	
6 8:24	● 15♉12
13 11:45	☽ 22♌06
20 7:18	○ 28♏39
28 0:03	☽ 6♓03
4 19:57	● 13♊33
11 16:37	☽ 20♍07
18 17:53	○ 26♐51
26 17:40	☽ 4♈28

Astro Data

1 MAY 1913
Julian Day # 4869
Delta T 15.1 sec
SVP 06♓28'13"
Obliquity 23°27'11"
⚷ Chiron 14♓04.6
☽ Mean ☊ 1♈22.6

1 JUNE 1913
Julian Day # 4900
Delta T 15.2 sec
SVP 06♓28'09"
Obliquity 23°27'11"
⚷ Chiron 14♓58.6
☽ Mean ☊ 29♓44.1

JULY 1913 LONGITUDE

Day	Sid.Time	☉	0 hr ☽	Noon☽	True☊	☿	♀	♂	♃	♄	♅	♆	♇
1 Tu	18 33 46	8♋32 11	27♉22 19	3♊59 34	27♓45.9	3♌40.4	22♉56.0	10♉ 9.3	13♑32.3	11♊39.0	6♒38.5	25♋ 4.1	29♊47.3
2 W	18 37 42	9 29 24	10♊42 59	17 32 27	27R36.7	4 55.1	23 52.1	10 52.3	13R24.7	11 46.2	6R36.5	25 6.3	29 48.8
3 Th	18 41 39	10 26 38	24 27 44	1♋28 25	27 25.9	6 7.2	24 48.6	11 35.3	13 17.0	11 53.4	6 34.4	25 8.4	29 50.2
4 F	18 45 35	11 23 52	8♋33 57	15 43 40	27 14.7	7 16.6	25 45.5	12 18.2	13 9.3	12 0.6	6 32.4	25 10.6	29 51.6
5 Sa	18 49 32	12 21 5	22 56 45	0♌12 25	27 4.1	8 23.1	26 42.9	13 1.1	13 1.6	12 7.7	6 30.3	25 12.8	29 53.1
6 Su	18 53 28	13 18 19	7♌29 45	14 47 54	26 55.3	9 26.8	27 40.6	13 43.8	12 53.9	12 14.8	6 28.1	25 15.0	29 54.5
7 M	18 57 25	14 15 32	22 6 2	29 23 24	26 49.0	10 27.4	28 38.8	14 26.5	12 46.1	12 21.8	6 26.0	25 17.2	29 55.9
8 Tu	19 1 21	15 12 45	6♍39 21	13♍53 19	26 45.5	11 25.0	29 37.3	15 9.0	12 38.4	12 28.8	6 23.8	25 19.4	29 57.3
9 W	19 5 18	16 9 58	21 4 52	28 13 40	26D44.1	12 19.3	0♊36.2	15 51.5	12 30.7	12 35.8	6 21.6	25 21.6	29 58.7
10 Th	19 9 15	17 7 11	5♎19 30	12♎22 12	26R44.2	13 10.4	1 35.4	16 33.9	12 23.1	12 42.7	6 19.4	25 23.8	0♋ 0.1
11 F	19 13 11	18 4 24	19 21 44	26 18 3	26 44.4	13 58.0	2 35.0	17 16.2	12 15.4	12 49.6	6 17.2	25 26.0	0 1.5
12 Sa	19 17 8	19 1 37	3♏11 11	10♏ 1 12	26 43.6	14 42.1	3 34.9	17 58.5	12 7.8	12 56.4	6 15.0	25 28.2	0 2.9
13 Su	19 21 4	19 58 50	16 48 6	23 31 58	26 40.9	15 22.4	4 35.2	18 40.6	12 0.2	13 3.2	6 12.7	25 30.4	0 4.2
14 M	19 25 1	20 56 3	0♐12 49	6♐50 39	26 35.7	15 58.9	5 35.8	19 22.6	11 52.7	13 10.0	6 10.4	25 32.6	0 5.6
15 Tu	19 28 57	21 53 16	13 25 28	19 57 15	26 28.1	16 31.4	6 36.7	20 4.6	11 45.2	13 16.7	6 8.1	25 34.8	0 7.0
16 W	19 32 54	22 50 29	26 25 58	2♑51 35	26 18.5	16 59.8	7 37.9	20 46.5	11 37.7	13 23.3	6 5.8	25 37.1	0 8.3
17 Th	19 36 50	23 47 42	9♑14 3	15 33 21	26 7.8	17 23.8	8 39.3	21 28.3	11 30.3	13 29.9	6 3.5	25 39.3	0 9.7
18 F	19 40 47	24 44 56	21 49 30	28 2 30	25 57.1	17 43.5	9 41.1	22 9.9	11 23.0	13 36.5	6 1.2	25 41.5	0 11.0
19 Sa	19 44 44	25 42 10	4♒12 26	10♒19 25	25 47.2	17 58.5	10 43.2	22 51.5	11 15.7	13 43.0	5 58.9	25 43.8	0 12.4
20 Su	19 48 40	26 39 25	16 23 35	22 25 10	25 39.2	18 8.9	11 45.5	23 33.0	11 8.5	13 49.4	5 56.5	25 46.0	0 13.7
21 M	19 52 37	27 36 40	28 24 25	4♓21 40	25 33.3	18R14.4	12 48.1	24 14.5	11 1.4	13 55.8	5 54.2	25 48.2	0 15.0
22 Tu	19 56 33	28 33 56	10♓17 16	16 11 41	25 29.9	18 15.0	13 51.0	24 55.8	10 54.3	14 2.1	5 51.8	25 50.4	0 16.3
23 W	20 0 30	29 31 12	22 5 22	27 58 50	25D28.6	18 10.7	14 54.1	25 37.0	10 47.4	14 8.4	5 49.4	25 52.7	0 17.6
24 Th	20 4 26	0♌28 30	3♈52 40	9♈47 27	25 28.8	18 1.4	15 57.5	26 18.1	10 40.5	14 14.6	5 47.0	25 54.9	0 18.9
25 F	20 8 23	1 25 48	15 43 49	21 42 24	25 29.8	17 47.1	17 1.1	26 59.1	10 33.7	14 20.8	5 44.6	25 57.1	0 20.2
26 Sa	20 12 19	2 23 7	27 43 52	3♉48 51	25R30.6	17 28.0	18 5.0	27 40.1	10 27.0	14 26.9	5 42.3	25 59.3	0 21.4
27 Su	20 16 16	3 20 27	9♉58 2	16 12 1	25 30.5	17 4.2	19 9.0	28 20.9	10 20.4	14 33.0	5 39.9	26 1.5	0 22.7
28 M	20 20 13	4 17 49	22 31 22	28 56 36	25 28.8	16 35.9	20 13.3	29 1.6	10 14.0	14 39.0	5 37.5	26 3.7	0 23.9
29 Tu	20 24 9	5 15 11	5♊28 8	12♊ 6 19	25 25.1	16 3.4	21 17.9	29 42.2	10 7.6	14 44.9	5 35.1	26 5.9	0 25.1
30 W	20 28 6	6 12 34	18 51 19	25 43 12	25 19.7	15 27.1	22 22.6	0♊22.8	10 1.4	14 50.7	5 32.7	26 8.2	0 26.4
31 Th	20 32 2	7 9 59	2♋41 50	9♋46 56	25 12.8	14 47.6	23 27.6	1 3.2	9 55.2	14 56.6	5 30.3	26 10.4	0 27.6

AUGUST 1913 LONGITUDE

Day	Sid.Time	☉	0 hr ☽	Noon☽	True☊	☿	♀	♂	♃	♄	♅	♆	♇
1 F	20 35 59	8♌ 7 24	16♋58 2	24♋14 29	25♓ 5.5	14♌ 5.3	24♊32.7	1♊43.5	9♑49.2	15♊ 2.3	5♒27.9	26♋12.6	0♋28.8
2 Sa	20 39 55	9 4 51	1♌35 29	9♌ 0 6	24R58.5	13R21.0	25 38.0	2 23.6	9R43.4	15 8.0	5R25.5	26 14.7	0 30.0
3 Su	20 43 52	10 2 18	16 27 17	23 55 58	24 52.7	12 35.3	26 43.6	3 3.7	9 37.6	15 13.6	5 23.1	26 16.9	0 31.1
4 M	20 47 49	10 59 46	1♍25 3	8♍53 29	24 48.8	11 49.2	27 49.3	3 43.6	9 32.0	15 19.1	5 20.7	26 19.1	0 32.3
5 Tu	20 51 45	11 57 15	16 20 16	23 44 33	24D46.9	11 3.3	28 55.2	4 23.5	9 26.6	15 24.5	5 18.3	26 21.3	0 33.4
6 W	20 55 42	12 54 45	1♎ 5 34	8♎22 43	24 46.8	10 18.6	0♋ 1.2	5 3.2	9 21.2	15 29.9	5 15.9	26 23.4	0 34.5
7 Th	20 59 38	13 52 15	15 35 31	22 43 41	24 47.8	9 35.9	1 7.5	5 42.8	9 16.1	15 35.2	5 13.6	26 25.6	0 35.7
8 F	21 3 35	14 49 47	29 46 59	6♏45 22	24 49.1	8 56.0	2 13.9	6 22.2	9 11.1	15 40.5	5 11.2	26 27.7	0 36.8
9 Sa	21 7 31	15 47 19	13♏38 48	20 27 24	24R49.8	8 19.9	3 20.5	7 1.6	9 6.2	15 45.7	5 8.9	26 29.8	0 37.8
10 Su	21 11 28	16 44 52	27 11 17	3♐50 39	24 49.3	7 48.1	4 27.2	7 40.8	9 1.5	15 50.8	5 6.5	26 32.0	0 38.9
11 M	21 15 24	17 42 26	10♐25 41	16 56 37	24 47.2	7 21.4	5 34.1	8 19.9	8 56.9	15 55.8	5 4.2	26 34.1	0 40.0
12 Tu	21 19 21	18 40 0	23 23 41	29 47 5	24 43.6	7 0.5	6 41.2	8 58.9	8 52.5	16 0.7	5 1.9	26 36.2	0 41.0
13 W	21 23 18	19 37 36	6♑ 7 3	12♑23 46	24 38.6	6 45.7	7 48.4	9 37.7	8 48.3	16 5.6	4 59.6	26 38.3	0 42.0
14 Th	21 27 14	20 35 13	18 37 27	24 48 16	24 32.9	6D37.5	8 55.8	10 16.4	8 44.3	16 10.4	4 57.3	26 40.3	0 43.0
15 F	21 31 11	21 32 51	0♒56 25	7♒ 2 4	24 27.2	6 36.3	10 3.3	10 55.0	8 40.4	16 15.1	4 55.1	26 42.4	0 44.0
16 Sa	21 35 7	22 30 30	13 5 25	19 6 38	24 21.9	6 42.2	11 11.0	11 33.5	8 36.7	16 19.7	4 52.8	26 44.5	0 45.0
17 Su	21 39 4	23 28 10	25 5 57	1♓ 3 34	24 17.8	6 55.5	12 18.8	12 11.8	8 33.1	16 24.2	4 50.6	26 46.5	0 46.0
18 M	21 43 0	24 25 51	6♓59 44	12 54 43	24 15.0	7 16.2	13 26.8	12 50.0	8 29.7	16 28.7	4 48.3	26 48.5	0 46.9
19 Tu	21 46 57	25 23 34	18 48 49	24 42 22	24D13.7	7 44.4	14 34.9	13 28.0	8 26.5	16 33.1	4 46.1	26 50.5	0 47.8
20 W	21 50 53	26 21 18	0♈35 44	6♈29 18	24 13.7	8 20.0	15 43.2	14 6.0	8 23.5	16 37.4	4 44.0	26 52.5	0 48.7
21 Th	21 54 50	27 19 4	12 23 32	18 18 52	24 14.8	9 2.9	16 51.6	14 43.8	8 20.7	16 41.6	4 41.8	26 54.5	0 49.6
22 F	21 58 46	28 16 52	24 15 48	0♉14 53	24 16.4	9 53.0	18 0.1	15 21.4	8 18.0	16 45.7	4 39.7	26 56.5	0 50.5
23 Sa	22 2 43	29 14 41	6♉16 39	12 21 39	24 18.1	10 50.1	19 8.8	15 58.9	8 15.5	16 49.8	4 37.5	26 58.4	0 51.3
24 Su	22 6 40	0♍12 32	18 30 29	24 43 42	24 19.3	11 53.9	20 17.6	16 36.3	8 13.2	16 53.7	4 35.5	27 0.4	0 52.2
25 M	22 10 36	1 10 24	1♊ 1 51	7♊25 29	24R19.8	13 4.1	21 26.6	17 13.5	8 11.1	16 57.6	4 33.4	27 2.3	0 53.0
26 Tu	22 14 33	2 8 19	13 55 4	20 30 59	24 19.3	14 20.4	22 35.7	17 50.6	8 9.2	17 1.3	4 31.3	27 4.2	0 53.8
27 W	22 18 29	3 6 15	27 13 36	4♋ 3 5	24 17.9	15 42.4	23 44.9	18 27.5	8 7.4	17 5.0	4 29.3	27 6.1	0 54.6
28 Th	22 22 26	4 4 13	10♋59 32	18 2 52	24 15.8	17 9.6	24 54.3	19 4.2	8 5.9	17 8.6	4 27.3	27 8.0	0 55.4
29 F	22 26 22	5 2 13	25 12 50	2♌29 1	24 13.3	18 41.7	26 3.7	19 40.8	8 4.5	17 12.1	4 25.4	27 9.8	0 56.1
30 Sa	22 30 19	6 0 15	9♌50 47	17 17 23	24 10.8	20 18.1	27 13.3	20 17.3	8 3.3	17 15.5	4 23.4	27 11.7	0 56.8
31 Su	22 34 16	6 58 18	24 47 52	2♍21 10	24 8.9	21 58.4	28 23.0	20 53.5	8 2.4	17 18.8	4 21.5	27 13.5	0 57.5

Astro Data Dy Hr Mn	Planet Ingress Dy Hr Mn	Last Aspect Dy Hr Mn	☽ Ingress Dy Hr Mn	Last Aspect Dy Hr Mn	☽ Ingress Dy Hr Mn	☽ Phases & Eclipses Dy Hr Mn	Astro Data
♃⊼♄ 8 15:42	♀ ♊ 8 9:16	30 19:46 ♆ ⚹	♊ 1 4:47	1 15:16 ♆ ☌	♌ 1 21:25	4 5:06 ● 11♋36	1 JULY 1913
☽0S 9 14:03	♇ ♋ 9 22:18	3 9:14 ♇ ☌	♋ 3 9:29	3 17:47 ♀ ⚹	♍ 3 21:44	10 21:37 ☽ 17♎59	Julian Day # 4930
☿ R 21 15:03	☉ ♌ 23 12:04	5 6:41 ♀ ⚹	♌ 5 11:40	5 22:06 ♀ □	♎ 5 22:13	18 6:06 ○ 24♑59	Delta T 15.3 sec
☽0N 23 14:32	♂ ♊ 29 10:31	7 12:55 ♇ ⚹	♍ 7 13:00	7 18:19 ♆ ⚹	♏ 8 0:22	26 9:58 ☽ 2♉47	SVP 06♓28'03"
		9 14:59 ♇ □	♎ 9 14:59	9 22:49 ♆ △	♐ 10 5:03		Obliquity 23°27'10"
☽0S 5 20:44	♀ ♋ 5 23:33	11 10:31 ♆ □	♏ 11 18:26	11 14:29 ☉ △	♑ 12 12:24	2 12:58 ● 9♌36	⚷ Chiron 15♓02.7R
☿ D 14 16:14	☉ ♍ 23 18:48	13 15:35 ♆ △	♐ 13 23:37	14 15:41 ♆ ☍	♒ 14 22:09	9 4:03 ☽ 15♏57	☽ Mean ☊ 28♓08.8
☽0N 19 20:44		15 5:55 ☿ △	♑ 16 6:39	16 20:27 ☉ ☍	♓ 17 9:52	16 20:27 ○ 23♒20	
		18 7:29 ♆ ☍	♒ 18 15:48	19 16:24 ♆ △	♈ 19 22:47	25 0:17 ☽ 1♊11	1 AUGUST 1913
		20 15:08 ♂ □	♓ 21 3:12	22 8:46 ☉ △	♉ 22 11:30	31 20:38 ● 7♍48	Julian Day # 4961
		23 7:44 ♆ △	♈ 23 16:07	24 16:24 ♆ ⚹	♊ 24 22:03	31 20:51:52 ● P 0.151	Delta T 15.4 sec
		25 20:32 ♆ □	♉ 26 4:29	26 7:31 ♂ ☌	♋ 27 4:54		SVP 06♓27'57"
		28 12:49 ♂ ☌	♊ 28 13:57	29 3:14 ♆ ☌	♌ 29 7:55		Obliquity 23°27'11"
		30 6:42 ♀ ☌	♋ 30 19:23	30 18:55 ☿ ☌	♍ 31 8:16		⚷ Chiron 14♓17.8R
							☽ Mean ☊ 26♓30.4

LONGITUDE — SEPTEMBER 1913

Day	Sid.Time	☉	0 hr ☽	Noon ☽	True ☊	☿	♀	♂	♃	♄	♅	♆	♇
1 M	22 38 12	7♍56 23	9♍56 7	17♍31 32	24♓ 7.7	23♌42.1	29♋32.8	21♊29.6	8♑ 1.6	17♊22.0	4♒19.7	27♋15.3	0♋58.2
2 Tu	22 42 9	8 54 30	25 6 13	2♎39 1	24D 7.3	25 28.7	0♌42.8	22 5.6	8R 1.0	17 25.1	4R17.8	27 17.0	0 58.9
3 W	22 46 5	9 52 38	10♎ 8 53	17 34 51	24 7.7	27 17.7	1 52.8	22 41.3	8 0.6	17 28.1	4 16.0	27 18.8	0 59.5
4 Th	22 50 2	10 50 48	24 56 9	2♏12 9	24 8.5	29 8.7	3 3.0	23 16.9	8D 0.3	17 31.1	4 14.2	27 20.5	1 0.1
5 F	22 53 58	11 49 0	9♏22 22	16 26 32	24 9.6	1♍ 1.3	4 13.2	23 52.3	8 0.3	17 33.9	4 12.5	27 22.2	1 0.7
6 Sa	22 57 55	12 47 12	23 24 27	0♐16 8	24 10.4	2 55.0	5 23.6	24 27.5	8 0.5	17 36.6	4 10.8	27 23.9	1 1.3
7 Su	23 1 51	13 45 27	7♐ 1 41	13 41 16	24R10.9	4 49.6	6 34.0	25 2.5	8 0.8	17 39.2	4 9.1	27 25.6	1 1.9
8 M	23 5 48	14 43 43	20 15 11	26 43 46	24 10.9	6 44.6	7 44.6	25 37.4	8 1.4	17 41.7	4 7.5	27 27.2	1 2.4
9 Tu	23 9 44	15 42 0	3♑ 7 22	9♑26 24	24 10.5	8 39.8	8 55.3	26 12.1	8 2.1	17 44.1	4 5.9	27 28.9	1 2.9
10 W	23 13 41	16 40 19	15 41 16	21 52 24	24 9.8	10 35.1	10 6.1	26 46.5	8 3.1	17 46.4	4 4.3	27 30.5	1 3.4
11 Th	23 17 38	17 38 39	28 0 12	4♒ 5 4	24 9.0	12 30.1	11 16.9	27 20.8	8 4.2	17 48.7	4 2.8	27 32.0	1 3.9
12 F	23 21 34	18 37 1	10♒ 7 23	16 7 31	24 8.1	14 24.7	12 27.9	27 54.9	8 5.5	17 50.8	4 1.3	27 33.6	1 4.4
13 Sa	23 25 31	19 35 25	22 5 50	28 2 38	24 7.5	16 18.8	13 39.0	28 28.8	8 7.0	17 52.8	3 59.8	27 35.1	1 4.8
14 Su	23 29 27	20 33 50	3♓58 16	9♓53 1	24 7.1	18 12.2	14 50.1	29 2.5	8 8.7	17 54.6	3 58.4	27 36.6	1 5.2
15 M	23 33 24	21 32 18	15 47 10	21 41 1	24D 6.9	20 4.9	16 1.4	29 36.0	8 10.6	17 56.4	3 57.0	27 38.1	1 5.6
16 Tu	23 37 20	22 30 47	27 34 50	3♈28 54	24 6.9	21 56.7	17 12.8	0♋ 9.3	8 12.7	17 58.1	3 55.7	27 39.6	1 6.0
17 W	23 41 17	23 29 17	9♈23 30	15 18 56	24R 6.9	23 47.7	18 24.2	0 42.3	8 14.9	17 59.7	3 54.4	27 41.0	1 6.3
18 Th	23 45 13	24 27 50	21 15 29	27 13 30	24 6.9	25 37.8	19 35.8	1 15.2	8 17.4	18 1.2	3 53.1	27 42.4	1 6.6
19 F	23 49 10	25 26 25	3♉13 17	9♉15 13	24 6.8	27 26.9	20 47.4	1 47.9	8 20.0	18 2.5	3 51.9	27 43.8	1 6.9
20 Sa	23 53 7	26 25 2	15 19 40	21 27 1	24 6.6	29 15.0	21 59.2	2 20.3	8 22.8	18 3.8	3 50.8	27 45.1	1 7.2
21 Su	23 57 3	27 23 42	27 37 41	3♊52 5	24 6.2	1♎ 2.2	23 11.0	2 52.5	8 25.8	18 4.9	3 49.6	27 46.4	1 7.5
22 M	0 1 0	28 22 23	10♊10 38	16 33 46	24 5.9	2 48.4	24 23.0	3 24.5	8 29.0	18 6.0	3 48.6	27 47.7	1 7.7
23 Tu	0 4 56	29 21 7	23 1 49	29 35 20	24D 5.7	4 33.6	25 35.0	3 56.2	8 32.3	18 6.9	3 47.5	27 49.0	1 7.9
24 W	0 8 53	0♎19 53	6♋14 30	12♋59 39	24 5.7	6 17.9	26 47.1	4 27.7	8 35.8	18 7.7	3 46.5	27 50.3	1 8.1
25 Th	0 12 49	1 18 42	19 50 58	26 48 35	24 6.0	8 1.1	27 59.3	4 59.0	8 39.6	18 8.5	3 45.6	27 51.5	1 8.3
26 F	0 16 46	2 17 32	3♌52 27	11♌ 2 26	24 6.6	9 43.5	29 11.6	5 30.0	8 43.5	18 9.1	3 44.7	27 52.7	1 8.4
27 Sa	0 20 42	3 16 25	18 18 14	25 39 23	24 7.3	11 24.9	0♍23.9	6 0.7	8 47.5	18 9.6	3 43.8	27 53.8	1 8.5
28 Su	0 24 39	4 15 20	3♍ 5 15	10♍35 2	24 8.0	13 5.4	1 36.4	6 31.2	8 51.8	18 9.9	3 43.0	27 55.0	1 8.6
29 M	0 28 36	5 14 17	18 7 48	25 42 28	24R 8.5	14 44.9	2 48.9	7 1.4	8 56.2	18 10.2	3 42.3	27 56.0	1 8.7
30 Tu	0 32 32	6 13 17	3♎17 55	10♎52 57	24 8.4	16 23.6	4 1.5	7 31.4	9 0.8	18R10.4	3 41.5	27 57.1	1 8.8

LONGITUDE — OCTOBER 1913

Day	Sid.Time	☉	0 hr ☽	Noon ☽	True ☊	☿	♀	♂	♃	♄	♅	♆	♇
1 W	0 36 29	7♎12 18	18♎26 20	25♎56 57	24♓ 7.7	18♎ 1.5	5♍14.1	8♋ 1.1	9♑ 5.6	18♊10.4	3♒40.9	27♋58.2	1♋ 8.8
2 Th	0 40 25	8 11 21	3♏23 42	10♏45 41	24R 6.3	19 38.4	6 26.9	8 30.4	9 10.5	18R10.3	3R40.3	27 59.2	1R 8.8
3 F	0 44 22	9 10 27	18 2 5	25 12 19	24 4.5	21 14.6	7 39.7	8 59.5	9 15.6	18 10.2	3 39.7	28 0.1	1 8.8
4 Sa	0 48 18	10 9 34	2♐15 56	9♐12 41	24 2.4	22 49.9	8 52.6	9 28.3	9 20.9	18 9.9	3 39.2	28 1.1	1 8.7
5 Su	0 52 15	11 8 43	16 2 29	22 45 25	24 0.6	24 24.4	10 5.5	9 56.8	9 26.3	18 9.5	3 38.7	28 2.0	1 8.7
6 M	0 56 11	12 7 54	29 21 41	5♑51 35	23 59.4	25 58.2	11 18.6	10 25.0	9 32.0	18 9.0	3 38.3	28 2.9	1 8.6
7 Tu	1 0 8	13 7 6	12♑15 32	18 34 0	23D 58.9	27 31.1	12 31.7	10 52.9	9 37.7	18 8.4	3 37.9	28 3.7	1 8.5
8 W	1 4 5	14 6 21	24 47 32	0♒56 38	23 59.2	29 3.3	13 44.8	11 20.5	9 43.7	18 7.6	3 37.6	28 4.6	1 8.4
9 Th	1 8 1	15 5 37	7♒ 1 55	13 3 55	24 0.4	0♏34.7	14 58.0	11 47.8	9 49.8	18 6.8	3 37.3	28 5.4	1 8.2
10 F	1 11 58	16 4 54	19 3 14	25 0 23	24 2.0	2 5.3	16 11.3	12 14.7	9 56.0	18 5.9	3 37.1	28 6.1	1 8.1
11 Sa	1 15 54	17 4 14	0♓55 55	6♓50 19	24 3.7	3 35.2	17 24.6	12 41.3	10 2.4	18 4.8	3 36.9	28 6.8	1 7.9
12 Su	1 19 51	18 3 35	12 44 3	18 37 33	24R 5.0	5 4.3	18 38.0	13 7.6	10 9.0	18 3.6	3 36.8	28 7.5	1 7.6
13 M	1 23 47	19 2 59	24 31 13	0♈25 26	24 5.5	6 32.6	19 51.5	13 33.5	10 15.7	18 2.4	3D 36.7	28 8.2	1 7.4
14 Tu	1 27 44	20 2 24	6♈20 30	12 16 43	24 4.8	8 0.2	21 5.0	13 59.1	10 22.6	18 1.0	3 36.7	28 8.8	1 7.1
15 W	1 31 40	21 1 51	18 14 22	24 13 41	24 2.8	9 27.0	22 18.6	14 24.3	10 29.6	17 59.5	3 36.7	28 9.4	1 6.8
16 Th	1 35 37	22 1 20	0♉14 53	6♉18 10	23 59.4	10 53.1	23 32.3	14 49.1	10 36.8	17 57.9	3 36.8	28 10.0	1 6.5
17 F	1 39 34	23 0 52	12 23 42	18 31 41	23 54.9	12 18.3	24 46.0	15 13.6	10 44.1	17 56.2	3 36.9	28 10.5	1 6.2
18 Sa	1 43 30	24 0 25	24 42.17	0♊55 41	23 49.6	13 42.6	25 59.8	15 37.7	10 51.6	17 54.4	3 37.1	28 11.0	1 5.9
19 Su	1 47 27	25 0 1	7♊12 3	13 31 34	23 44.3	15 6.1	27 13.6	16 1.5	10 59.2	17 52.5	3 37.3	28 11.4	1 5.5
20 M	1 51 23	25 59 39	19 54 27	26 20 54	23 39.5	16 28.7	28 27.5	16 24.8	11 7.0	17 50.5	3 37.6	28 11.9	1 5.1
21 Tu	1 55 20	26 59 19	2♋51 8	9♋25 22	23 35.8	17 50.3	29 41.4	16 47.7	11 14.9	17 48.4	3 38.0	28 12.3	1 4.7
22 W	1 59 16	27 59 1	16 3 50	22 46 45	23D 33.6	19 11.0	0♎55.4	17 10.2	11 22.9	17 46.2	3 38.3	28 12.6	1 4.3
23 Th	2 3 13	28 58 46	29 34 16	6♌26 35	23 32.9	20 30.5	2 9.5	17 32.3	11 31.1	17 43.9	3 38.8	28 13.0	1 3.8
24 F	2 7 9	29 58 33	13♌23 46	20 25 52	23 33.6	21 48.9	3 23.6	17 53.9	11 39.4	17 41.5	3 39.3	28 13.3	1 3.3
25 Sa	2 11 6	0♏58 22	27 32 48	4♍44 24	23 34.9	23 6.1	4 37.7	18 15.1	11 47.8	17 39.0	3 39.8	28 13.5	1 2.8
26 Su	2 15 3	1 58 14	12♍ 0 24	19 20 22	23R36.2	24 21.9	5 51.9	18 35.8	11 56.4	17 36.3	3 40.4	28 13.7	1 2.3
27 M	2 18 59	2 58 7	26 43 43	4♎ 9 44	23 36.6	25 36.3	7 6.2	18 56.1	12 5.1	17 33.6	3 41.0	28 13.9	1 1.8
28 Tu	2 22 56	3 58 3	11♎37 35	19 6 18	23 35.4	26 49.1	8 20.4	19 15.9	12 14.0	17 30.8	3 41.7	28 14.1	1 1.2
29 W	2 26 52	4 58 1	26 34 51	4♏ 2 8	23 32.1	28 0.1	9 34.8	19 35.2	12 22.9	17 27.9	3 42.5	28 14.2	1 0.6
30 Th	2 30 49	5 58 0	11♏27 4	18 48 36	23 26.9	29 9.2	10 49.2	19 54.0	12 32.0	17 24.9	3 43.3	28 14.3	1 0.0
31 F	2 34 45	6 58 2	26 5 47	3♐17 46	23 20.2	0♐16.2	12 3.6	20 12.2	12 41.3	17 21.9	3 44.1	28 14.4	0 59.4

Astro Data Dy Hr Mn	Planet Ingress Dy Hr Mn	Last Aspect Dy Hr Mn	☽ Ingress Dy Hr Mn	Last Aspect Dy Hr Mn	☽ Ingress Dy Hr Mn	☽ Phases & Eclipses Dy Hr Mn	Astro Data
☽0S 2 6:08	♀ ♌ 1 9:19	2 3:28 ♆ ⚹	♎ 2 7:47	1 15:16 ♆ □	♏ 1 18:31	7 13:05 ☽ 14♐17	1 SEPTEMBER 1913
♃ D 4 14:56	☿ ♍ 4 10:58	4 7:58 ♆ ⚹	♏ 4 8:21	3 16:45 ♆ △	♐ 3 20:08	15 12:46 ○ 22♓03	Julian Day # 4992
☽0N 16 2:49	♂ ♋ 15 17:18	6 6:58 ♆ △	♐ 6 11:32	5 16:59 ♆ ⚹	♑ 6 1:10	15 12:48 T 1.430	Delta T 15.6 sec
☿0S 21 21:40	☿ ♎ 20 10:03	8 10:24 ♂ ☍	♑ 8 18:07	8 9:29 ♆ □	♒ 8 10:09	23 12:30 ☽ 29♊52	SVP 06♓27'52"
☽0S 29 17:10	☉ ♎ 23 15:53	10 23:05 ♆ ☍	♒ 11 3:56	9 22:05 ♄ △	♓ 10 22:07	30 4:57 ● 6♎25	Obliquity 23°27'11"
♄ R 30 21:49	♀ ♍ 26 16:04	13 13:31 ♂ △	♓ 13 15:57	13 7:22 ♆ △	♈ 13 11:08	30 4:45:32 P 0.825	⚷ Chiron 12♓58.8R
		16 0:10 ♆ △	♈ 16 4:55	15 19:51 ♆ □	♉ 15 23:30		Mean ☊ 24♓51.9
♇ R 1 19:27	☿ ♏ 8 14:53	18 12:59 ♆ □	♉ 18 17:34	18 6:43 ♆ ⚹	♊ 18 10:13	7 1:46 ☽ 13♑11	1 OCTOBER 1913
☽0N 13 9:03	♀ ♎ 21 6:02	21 0:17 ♆ ⚹	♊ 21 4:35	20 17:34 ♀ □	♋ 20 18:45	15 6:06 ○ 21♈17	Julian Day # 5022
♅ D 13 23:23	☉ ♏ 24 0:35	23 12:30 ☉ □	♋ 23 12:45	22 22:53 ☉ □	♌ 23 0:45	22 22:53 ☽ 28♋56	Delta T 15.7 sec
♀0S 24 4:30	☿ ♐ 30 18:07	25 13:49 ♆ ☌	♌ 25 17:26	24 15:47 ♆ □	♍ 25 4:06	29 14:29 ● 5♏34	SVP 06♓27'49"
☽0S 27 3:30		26 23:46 ♄ ⚹	♍ 27 19:02	27 2:26 ♆ ⚹	♎ 27 5:17		Obliquity 23°27'12"
		29 15:32 ♆ ⚹	♎ 29 18:47	29 2:40 ♆ □	♏ 29 5:30		⚷ Chiron 11♓37.3R
				31 3:33 ♆ △	♐ 31 6:29		Mean ☊ 23♓16.5

NOVEMBER 1913 LONGITUDE

Day	Sid.Time	☉	0 hr ☽	Noon ☽	True ☊	☿	♀	♂	♃	♄	♅	♆	♇
1 Sa	2 38 42	7♏58 6	10♐23 52	17♐23 34	23♓12.8	1♐20.8	13♎18.0	20♋30.0	12♑50.6	17♊18.7	3♒45.0	28♋14.4	0♋58.8
2 Su	2 42 38	8 58 11	24 16 32	1♑ 2 37	23R 5.7	2 22.8	14 32.5	20 47.2	13 0.1	17R15.4	3 45.9	28R14.4	0R58.1
3 M	2 46 35	9 58 18	7♑41 49	14 14 19	22 59.8	3 21.8	15 47.1	21 3.9	13 9.7	17 12.1	3 46.9	28 14.3	0 57.4
4 Tu	2 50 32	10 58 26	20 40 24	27 0 30	22 55.6	4 17.6	17 1.7	21 20.1	13 19.4	17 8.7	3 48.0	28 14.2	0 56.7
5 W	2 54 28	11 58 36	3♒15 5	9♒24 45	22D53.4	5 9.6	18 16.3	21 35.7	13 29.2	17 5.2	3 49.1	28 14.1	0 56.0
6 Th	2 58 25	12 58 48	15 30 7	21 31 49	22 53.0	5 57.6	19 30.9	21 50.7	13 39.2	17 1.6	3 50.2	28 14.0	0 55.3
7 F	3 2 21	13 59 1	27 30 32	3♓26 55	22 53.8	6 40.9	20 45.6	22 5.1	13 49.2	16 57.9	3 51.4	28 13.8	0 54.5
8 Sa	3 6 18	14 59 15	9♓21 39	15 15 23	22 55.0	7 19.1	22 0.3	22 19.0	13 59.4	16 54.2	3 52.7	28 13.6	0 53.8
9 Su	3 10 14	15 59 31	21 8 42	27 2 12	22R55.8	7 51.5	23 15.0	22 32.2	14 9.7	16 50.3	3 54.0	28 13.3	0 53.0
10 M	3 14 11	16 59 49	2♈56 27	8♈51 54	22 55.2	8 17.6	24 29.7	22 44.8	14 20.0	16 46.5	3 55.3	28 13.0	0 52.2
11 Tu	3 18 7	18 0 8	14 49 2	20 48 13	22 52.5	8 36.6	25 44.5	22 56.9	14 30.5	16 42.5	3 56.7	28 12.7	0 51.3
12 W	3 22 4	19 0 28	26 49 48	2♉54 3	22 47.4	8R47.9	26 59.3	23 8.2	14 41.1	16 38.5	3 58.1	28 12.3	0 50.5
13 Th	3 26 1	20 0 50	9♉ 1 10	15 11 20	22 39.8	8 50.6	28 14.2	23 18.9	14 51.8	16 34.4	3 59.6	28 12.0	0 49.6
14 F	3 29 57	21 1 14	21 24 39	27 41 9	22 30.1	8 44.2	29 29.1	23 29.0	15 2.6	16 30.2	4 1.1	28 11.5	0 48.8
15 Sa	3 33 54	22 1 40	4♊ 0 51	10♊23 43	22 19.1	8 28.1	0♏44.0	23 38.4	15 13.5	16 26.0	4 2.7	28 11.1	0 47.9
16 Su	3 37 50	23 2 7	16 49 43	23 18 46	22 7.8	8 1.7	1 58.9	23 47.1	15 24.5	16 21.7	4 4.3	28 10.6	0 47.0
17 M	3 41 47	24 2 36	29 50 47	6♋25 42	21 57.3	7 25.0	3 13.9	23 55.1	15 35.6	16 17.4	4 6.0	28 10.1	0 46.1
18 Tu	3 45 43	25 3 7	13♋ 3 28	19 44 1	21 48.6	6 38.0	4 28.9	24 2.4	15 46.8	16 13.0	4 7.7	28 9.5	0 45.1
19 W	3 49 40	26 3 39	26 27 22	3♌13 30	21 42.3	5 41.1	5 43.9	24 9.0	15 58.1	16 8.5	4 9.5	28 9.0	0 44.2
20 Th	3 53 36	27 4 13	10♌ 2 26	16 54 14	21 38.7	4 35.4	6 58.9	24 14.8	16 9.4	16 4.0	4 11.3	28 8.4	0 43.2
21 F	3 57 33	28 4 49	23 48 56	0♍46 34	21D37.4	3 22.4	8 14.0	24 19.9	16 20.9	15 59.5	4 13.1	28 7.7	0 42.3
22 Sa	4 1 30	29 5 27	7♍47 11	14 50 43	21R37.5	2 3.9	9 29.1	24 24.2	16 32.4	15 54.9	4 15.0	28 7.0	0 41.3
23 Su	4 5 26	0♐ 6 6	21 57 8	29 6 14	21 37.8	0 42.5	10 44.2	24 27.7	16 44.1	15 50.2	4 17.0	28 6.3	0 40.3
24 M	4 9 23	1 6 47	6♎17 48	13♎31 27	21 37.0	29♏20.7	11 59.3	24 30.5	16 55.8	15 45.6	4 18.9	28 5.6	0 39.3
25 Tu	4 13 19	2 7 29	20 46 45	28 3 4	21 34.1	28 1.4	13 14.5	24 32.4	17 7.6	15 40.8	4 21.0	28 4.8	0 38.2
26 W	4 17 16	3 8 14	5♏19 46	12♏36 3	21 28.2	26 47.1	14 29.7	24R33.6	17 19.5	15 36.1	4 23.0	28 4.0	0 37.2
27 Th	4 21 12	4 8 59	19 51 6	27 4 3	21 19.6	25 40.2	15 44.9	24 33.9	17 31.5	15 31.3	4 25.1	28 3.2	0 36.2
28 F	4 25 9	5 9 47	4♐14 3	11♐20 17	21 8.6	24 42.4	17 0.1	24 33.4	17 43.5	15 26.5	4 27.3	28 2.3	0 35.1
29 Sa	4 29 5	6 10 35	18 22 2	25 18 41	20 56.4	23 55.2	18 15.3	24 32.0	17 55.7	15 21.7	4 29.5	28 1.4	0 34.0
30 Su	4 33 2	7 11 25	2♑ 9 44	8♑54 52	20 44.3	23 19.2	19 30.6	24 29.8	18 7.9	15 16.8	4 31.7	28 0.5	0 32.9

DECEMBER 1913 LONGITUDE

Day	Sid.Time	☉	0 hr ☽	Noon ☽	True ☊	☿	♀	♂	♃	♄	♅	♆	♇
1 M	4 36 59	8♐12 16	15♑33 53	22♑ 6 46	20♓33.5	22♏54.8	20♏45.8	24♋26.8	18♑20.2	15♊11.9	4♒34.0	27♋59.6	0♋31.9
2 Tu	4 40 55	9 13 7	28 33 37	4♒54 41	20R25.0	22D41.8	22 1.1	24R22.9	18 32.5	15R 7.0	4 36.3	27R58.6	0R30.8
3 W	4 44 52	10 14 0	11♒10 20	17 21 1	20 19.2	22 39.8	23 16.4	24 18.2	18 45.0	15 2.1	4 38.7	27 57.6	0 29.7
4 Th	4 48 48	11 14 53	23 27 16	29 29 43	20 16.0	22 48.1	24 31.7	24 12.6	18 57.5	14 57.2	4 41.1	27 56.6	0 28.5
5 F	4 52 45	12 15 48	5♓28 59	11♓25 46	20D14.9	23 6.1	25 47.0	24 6.2	19 10.0	14 52.2	4 43.5	27 55.5	0 27.4
6 Sa	4 56 41	13 16 42	17 20 46	23 14 42	20R14.8	23 32.7	27 2.3	23 58.9	19 22.7	14 47.3	4 46.0	27 54.5	0 26.3
7 Su	5 0 38	14 17 38	29 8 16	5♈ 2 9	20 14.6	24 7.1	28 17.6	23 50.8	19 35.4	14 42.3	4 48.5	27 53.3	0 25.1
8 M	5 4 34	15 18 34	10♈57 1	16 53 30	20 13.2	24 48.5	29 32.9	23 41.8	19 48.1	14 37.4	4 51.0	27 52.2	0 24.0
9 Tu	5 8 31	16 19 32	22 52 11	28 53 36	20 9.6	25 36.2	0♐48.2	23 32.0	20 0.9	14 32.4	4 53.6	27 51.0	0 22.8
10 W	5 12 28	17 20 29	4♉58 12	11♉ 6 25	20 3.3	26 29.2	2 3.6	23 21.3	20 13.8	14 27.5	4 56.2	27 49.9	0 21.7
11 Th	5 16 24	18 21 28	17 18 31	23 34 47	19 54.1	27 27.1	3 18.9	23 9.8	20 26.8	14 22.5	4 58.8	27 48.7	0 20.5
12 F	5 20 21	19 22 27	29 55 19	6♊20 11	19 42.4	28 29.2	4 34.3	22 57.6	20 39.8	14 17.6	5 1.5	27 47.4	0 19.3
13 Sa	5 24 17	20 23 27	12♊49 20	19 22 39	19 29.0	29 35.0	5 49.7	22 44.5	20 52.8	14 12.7	5 4.2	27 46.2	0 18.1
14 Su	5 28 14	21 24 28	25 59 55	2♋40 52	19 15.3	0♐43.9	7 5.0	22 30.6	21 5.9	14 7.8	5 7.0	27 44.9	0 17.0
15 M	5 32 10	22 25 30	9♋25 12	16 12 32	19 2.4	1 55.6	8 20.4	22 15.9	21 19.1	14 2.9	5 9.7	27 43.6	0 15.8
16 Tu	5 36 7	23 26 32	23 2 31	29 54 48	18 51.5	3 9.8	9 35.8	22 0.5	21 32.3	13 58.1	5 12.6	27 42.3	0 14.6
17 W	5 40 4	24 27 35	6♌49 0	13♌44 50	18 43.4	4 26.0	10 51.2	21 44.3	21 45.6	13 53.2	5 15.4	27 40.9	0 13.4
18 Th	5 44 0	25 28 39	20 42 2	27 40 23	18 38.5	5 44.1	12 6.6	21 27.4	21 58.9	13 48.4	5 18.3	27 39.6	0 12.2
19 F	5 47 57	26 29 44	4♍39 43	11♍39 54	18 36.2	7 3.8	13 22.1	21 9.8	22 12.3	13 43.7	5 21.2	27 38.2	0 11.0
20 Sa	5 51 53	27 30 49	18 40 51	25 42 30	18 35.7	8 25.0	14 37.5	20 51.5	22 25.7	13 38.9	5 24.1	27 36.8	0 9.8
21 Su	5 55 50	28 31 56	2♎44 47	9♎47 37	18 35.8	9 47.3	15 52.9	20 32.5	22 39.1	13 34.2	5 27.0	27 35.4	0 8.6
22 M	5 59 46	29 33 3	16 50 56	23 54 35	18 34.8	11 10.8	17 8.3	20 12.9	22 52.6	13 29.5	5 30.0	27 33.9	0 7.4
23 Tu	6 3 43	0♑34 11	0♏58 22	8♏ 2 1	18 31.8	12 35.2	18 23.8	19 52.7	23 6.2	13 24.9	5 33.0	27 32.5	0 6.2
24 W	6 7 39	1 35 19	15 5 13	22 7 34	18 26.0	14 0.5	19 39.2	19 32.0	23 19.8	13 20.3	5 36.1	27 31.0	0 5.0
25 Th	6 11 36	2 36 29	29 8 38	6♐ 7 55	18 17.3	15 26.6	20 54.7	19 10.8	23 33.4	13 15.8	5 39.1	27 29.5	0 3.8
26 F	6 15 33	3 37 39	13♐ 4 53	19 59 1	18 6.2	16 53.3	22 10.2	18 49.0	23 47.1	13 11.3	5 42.2	27 28.0	0 2.6
27 Sa	6 19 29	4 38 49	26 49 48	3♑36 46	17 53.7	18 20.7	23 25.6	18 26.8	24 0.8	13 6.9	5 45.3	27 26.5	0 1.4
28 Su	6 23 26	5 40 0	10♑19 30	16 57 43	17 41.2	19 48.7	24 41.1	18 4.3	24 14.5	13 2.5	5 48.5	27 24.9	0 0.2
29 M	6 27 22	6 41 10	23 31 8	29 59 40	17 29.9	21 17.2	25 56.6	17 41.4	24 28.3	12 58.2	5 51.6	27 23.4	29♊59.0
30 Tu	6 31 19	7 42 21	6♒23 17	12♒42 5	17 20.8	22 46.2	27 12.0	17 18.2	24 42.1	12 53.9	5 54.8	27 21.8	29 57.8
31 W	6 35 15	8 43 32	18 56 15	25 6 5	17 14.3	24 15.7	28 27.5	16 54.7	24 55.9	12 49.7	5 58.0	27 20.2	29 56.6

Astro Data Dy Hr Mn	Planet Ingress Dy Hr Mn	Last Aspect Dy Hr Mn	☽ Ingress Dy Hr Mn	Last Aspect Dy Hr Mn	☽ Ingress Dy Hr Mn	☽ Phases & Eclipses Dy Hr Mn	Astro Data
♆ R 1 3:01	♀ ♏ 14 9:55	1 11:49 ♄ ☍	♑ 2 10:08	1 22:55 ♆ ☍	♒ 2 2:42	5 18:34 ☽ 12♒45	1 NOVEMBER 1913
☽0N 9 15:34	☉ ♐ 22 21:35	4 14:21 ♆ ☍	♒ 4 17:44	4 2:22 ♀ □	♓ 4 13:00	13 23:11 ○ 20♉59	Julian Day # 5053
☿ R 12 19:28	☿ ♏ 23 12:26	6 8:54 ♀ △	♓ 7 5:01	6 22:05 ♀ △	♈ 7 1:45	21 7:56 ☽ 28♌25	Delta T 15.8 sec
♃⚻♄ 19 15:52		9 14:24 ♆ △	♈ 9 18:02	9 9:55 ♆ □	♉ 9 14:12	28 1:41 ● 5♐14	SVP 06♓27'46"
☽0S 23 11:07	♀ ♐ 8 8:38	12 2:44 ♆ □	♉ 12 6:17	11 21:03 ☿ ☍	♊ 12 0:09		Obliquity 23°27'11"
♂ R 26 21:11	☿ ♐ 13 8:51	14 12:57 ♆ ⚹	♊ 14 16:24	13 15:00 ☉ ☍	♋ 14 7:12	5 14:58 ☽ 12♓54	⚷ Chiron 10♓39.3R
	☉ ♑ 22 10:35	15 23:08 ♄ ☌	♋ 17 0:17	16 8:08 ♆ ☌	♌ 16 12:09	13 15:00 ○ 21♊02	☽ Mean ☊ 21♓38.0
☿ D 2 16:26	♇ ♊ 28 4:26	19 3:00 ♆ ☌	♌ 19 6:18	18 8:52 ☉ △	♍ 18 16:00	20 16:15 ☽ 28♍12	
☽0N 6 22:24		21 7:56 ☉ □	♍ 21 10:40	20 16:15 ☉ □	♎ 20 19:19	27 14:58 ● 5♑17	1 DECEMBER 1913
☽0S 20 16:03		23 13:24 ☿ ⚹	♎ 23 13:30	22 18:11 ♆ □	♏ 22 22:21		Julian Day # 5083
		25 12:02 ♆ □	♏ 25 15:13	24 21:11 ♆ △	♐ 25 1:28		Delta T 15.9 sec
		27 13:38 ♆ △	♐ 27 16:54	26 17:25 ♀ ☌	♑ 27 5:36		SVP 06♓27'40"
		28 18:53 ♄ ☍	♑ 29 20:12	29 7:08 ♆ ☍	♒ 29 12:01		Obliquity 23°27'10"
				31 21:29 ♇ △	♓ 31 21:38		⚷ Chiron 10♓29.5
							☽ Mean ☊ 20♓02.7

LONGITUDE JANUARY 1914

Day	Sid.Time	☉	0 hr ☽	Noon ☽	True ☊	☿	♀	♂	♃	♄	♅	♆	♇
1 Th	6 39 12	9♑44 42	1♓11 58	7♓14 22	17♓10.7	25♐45.6	29♐42.9	16♋31.0	25♑ 9.8	12♊45.6	6♒ 1.3	27♋18.6	29♊55.5
2 F	6 43 8	10 45 53	13 13 47	19 10 48	17D 9.3	27 15.9	0♑58.4	16R 7.2	25 23.7	12R41.5	6 4.5	27R17.0	29R54.3
3 Sa	6 47 5	11 47 3	25 6 4	1♈ 0 13	17 9.5	28 46.6	2 13.9	15 43.3	25 37.6	12 37.5	6 7.8	27 15.4	29 53.1
4 Su	6 51 2	12 48 13	6♈53 56	12 47 55	17R10.1	0♑17.8	3 29.3	15 19.3	25 51.5	12 33.5	6 11.0	27 13.8	29 51.9
5 M	6 54 58	13 49 23	18 42 52	24 39 28	17 10.1	1 49.3	4 44.8	14 55.3	26 5.5	12 29.7	6 14.3	27 12.2	29 50.8
6 Tu	6 58 55	14 50 32	0♉38 24	6♉40 17	17 8.5	3 21.3	6 0.2	14 31.3	26 19.5	12 25.9	6 17.7	27 10.5	29 49.6
7 W	7 2 51	15 51 41	12 45 43	18 55 15	17 4.8	4 53.6	7 15.7	14 7.5	26 33.5	12 22.2	6 21.0	27 8.9	29 48.5
8 Th	7 6 48	16 52 49	25 9 21	1♊28 25	16 58.7	6 26.4	8 31.1	13 43.8	26 47.5	12 18.6	6 24.3	27 7.2	29 47.3
9 F	7 10 44	17 53 58	7♊52 44	14 22 29	16 50.4	7 59.6	9 46.5	13 20.3	27 1.6	12 15.0	6 27.7	27 5.5	29 46.2
10 Sa	7 14 41	18 55 5	20 57 44	27 38 27	16 40.6	9 33.2	11 2.0	12 57.0	27 15.6	12 11.5	6 31.1	27 3.9	29 45.0
11 Su	7 18 37	19 56 13	4♋24 27	11♋15 26	16 30.2	11 7.2	12 17.4	12 34.0	27 29.7	12 8.2	6 34.5	27 2.2	29 43.9
12 M	7 22 34	20 57 20	18 10 59	25 10 37	16 20.4	12 41.7	13 32.8	12 11.3	27 43.8	12 4.9	6 37.9	27 0.5	29 42.8
13 Tu	7 26 31	21 58 27	2♌13 44	9♌19 42	16 12.2	14 16.6	14 48.3	11 49.0	27 57.9	12 1.7	6 41.3	26 58.8	29 41.7
14 W	7 30 27	22 59 33	16 27 51	23 37 33	16 6.3	15 52.0	16 3.7	11 27.1	28 12.0	11 58.6	6 44.7	26 57.1	29 40.6
15 Th	7 34 24	24 0 39	0♍48 8	7♍59 3	16 2.9	17 27.9	17 19.1	11 5.6	28 26.1	11 55.5	6 48.2	26 55.5	29 39.5
16 F	7 38 20	25 1 44	15 9 44	22 19 46	16D 1.9	19 4.2	18 34.5	10 44.6	28 40.3	11 52.6	6 51.6	26 53.8	29 38.4
17 Sa	7 42 17	26 2 49	29 28 44	6♎36 21	16 2.4	20 41.1	19 50.0	10 24.1	28 54.4	11 49.8	6 55.1	26 52.1	29 37.4
18 Su	7 46 13	27 3 54	13♎42 23	20 46 38	16 3.5	22 18.6	21 5.4	10 4.1	29 8.6	11 47.0	6 58.6	26 50.4	29 36.3
19 M	7 50 10	28 4 59	27 48 58	4♏49 16	16R 4.2	23 56.5	22 20.8	9 44.7	29 22.7	11 44.4	7 2.0	26 48.7	29 35.3
20 Tu	7 54 7	29 6 4	11♏47 28	18 43 28	16 3.4	25 35.1	23 36.2	9 26.0	29 36.9	11 41.8	7 5.5	26 47.0	29 34.2
21 W	7 58 3	0♒ 7 8	25 37 12	2♐28 32	16 0.6	27 14.2	24 51.6	9 7.8	29 51.0	11 39.4	7 9.0	26 45.3	29 33.2
22 Th	8 2 0	1 8 12	9♐17 22	16 3 35	15 55.7	28 53.9	26 7.0	8 50.3	0♒ 5.2	11 37.0	7 12.5	26 43.6	29 32.2
23 F	8 5 56	2 9 15	22 47 1	29 27 32	15 49.1	0♒34.2	27 22.4	8 33.5	0 19.4	11 34.8	7 16.0	26 41.9	29 31.2
24 Sa	8 9 53	3 10 18	6♑ 4 56	12♑39 5	15 41.4	2 15.1	28 37.8	8 17.4	0 33.5	11 32.6	7 19.5	26 40.2	29 30.3
25 Su	8 13 49	4 11 20	19 9 51	25 37 6	15 33.7	3 56.6	29 53.2	8 2.0	0 47.7	11 30.6	7 23.0	26 38.5	29 29.3
26 M	8 17 46	5 12 21	2♒ 0 46	8♒20 48	15 26.6	5 38.7	1♒ 8.6	7 47.4	1 1.8	11 28.7	7 26.5	26 36.9	29 28.3
27 Tu	8 21 42	6 13 22	14 37 13	20 50 5	15 21.0	7 21.5	2 24.0	7 33.6	1 16.0	11 26.8	7 30.0	26 35.2	29 27.4
28 W	8 25 39	7 14 21	26 59 31	3♓ 5 44	15 17.3	9 4.8	3 39.4	7 20.5	1 30.1	11 25.1	7 33.6	26 33.5	29 26.5
29 Th	8 29 36	8 15 20	9♓ 8 56	15 9 29	15D 15.5	10 48.8	4 54.7	7 8.2	1 44.3	11 23.5	7 37.1	26 31.9	29 25.6
30 F	8 33 32	9 16 17	21 7 42	27 4 2	15 15.5	12 33.4	6 10.1	6 56.7	1 58.4	11 22.0	7 40.6	26 30.2	29 24.7
31 Sa	8 37 29	10 17 13	2♈58 56	8♈52 56	15 16.7	14 18.5	7 25.4	6 46.0	2 12.5	11 20.6	7 44.1	26 28.6	29 23.8

LONGITUDE FEBRUARY 1914

Day	Sid.Time	☉	0 hr ☽	Noon ☽	True ☊	☿	♀	♂	♃	♄	♅	♆	♇
1 Su	8 41 25	11♒18 8	14♈46 35	20♈40 28	15♓18.6	16♒ 4.2	8♒40.8	6♋36.1	2♒26.6	11♊19.3	7♒47.6	26♋26.9	29♊22.9
2 M	8 45 22	12 19 1	26 35 12	2♉31 25	15 20.3	17 50.4	9 56.1	6R27.0	2 40.7	11R18.2	7 51.1	26R25.3	29R22.1
3 Tu	8 49 18	13 19 54	8♉29 45	14 30 52	15R21.4	19 37.1	11 11.4	6 18.8	2 54.7	11 17.1	7 54.6	26 23.7	29 21.2
4 W	8 53 15	14 20 44	20 35 22	26 43 52	15 21.3	21 24.1	12 26.7	6 11.4	3 8.8	11 16.2	7 58.1	26 22.1	29 20.4
5 Th	8 57 11	15 21 34	2♊56 58	9♊15 11	15 19.8	23 11.5	13 42.0	6 4.7	3 22.8	11 15.3	8 1.6	26 20.5	29 19.6
6 F	9 1 8	16 22 22	15 38 57	22 8 40	15 17.0	24 59.1	14 57.3	5 58.9	3 36.8	11 14.6	8 5.1	26 18.9	29 18.9
7 Sa	9 5 5	17 23 9	28 44 37	5♋26 56	15 13.3	26 46.7	16 12.6	5 53.9	3 50.8	11 14.0	8 8.5	26 17.3	29 18.1
8 Su	9 9 1	18 23 54	12♋15 40	19 10 40	15 9.0	28 34.2	17 27.8	5 49.7	4 4.8	11 13.5	8 12.0	26 15.8	29 17.4
9 M	9 12 58	19 24 38	26 11 42	3♌18 20	15 4.9	0♓21.5	18 43.1	5 46.2	4 18.7	11 13.1	8 15.5	26 14.3	29 16.6
10 Tu	9 16 54	20 25 20	10♌30 1	17 46 2	15 1.5	2 8.3	19 58.3	5 43.6	4 32.6	11 12.9	8 18.9	26 12.7	29 15.9
11 W	9 20 51	21 26 0	25 5 37	2♍27 51	14 59.2	3 54.4	21 13.5	5 41.7	4 46.5	11D 12.7	8 22.4	26 11.2	29 15.3
12 Th	9 24 47	22 26 40	9♍51 50	17 16 37	14D 58.2	5 39.5	22 28.7	5D 40.6	5 0.4	11 12.7	8 25.8	26 9.7	29 14.6
13 F	9 28 44	23 27 18	24 41 16	2♎ 4 55	14 58.3	7 23.2	23 43.9	5 40.2	5 14.2	11 12.7	8 29.2	26 8.3	29 13.9
14 Sa	9 32 40	24 27 54	9♎26 45	16 46 4	14 59.3	9 5.1	24 59.1	5 40.6	5 28.0	11 12.9	8 32.7	26 6.8	29 13.3
15 Su	9 36 37	25 28 30	24 2 17	1♏14 55	15 0.7	10 44.8	26 14.3	5 41.7	5 41.8	11 13.2	8 36.1	26 5.4	29 12.7
16 M	9 40 34	26 29 4	8♏23 34	15 28 0	15 1.9	12 21.9	27 29.4	5 43.6	5 55.6	11 13.6	8 39.4	26 3.9	29 12.1
17 Tu	9 44 30	27 29 38	22 28 3	29 23 37	15R 2.6	13 55.7	28 44.6	5 46.2	6 9.3	11 14.2	8 42.8	26 2.5	29 11.5
18 W	9 48 27	28 30 10	6♐14 43	13♐ 1 24	15 2.5	15 25.8	29 59.7	5 49.4	6 22.9	11 14.8	8 46.2	26 1.1	29 11.0
19 Th	9 52 23	29 30 41	19 43 45	26 21 55	15 1.7	16 51.4	1♓14.9	5 53.4	6 36.6	11 15.6	8 49.5	25 59.8	29 10.5
20 F	9 56 20	0♓31 10	2♑56 3	9♑26 17	15 0.1	18 12.0	2 30.0	5 58.0	6 50.2	11 16.4	8 52.9	25 58.4	29 10.0
21 Sa	10 0 16	1 31 38	15 52 50	22 15 51	14 58.2	19 26.8	3 45.1	6 3.3	7 3.8	11 17.4	8 56.2	25 57.1	29 9.5
22 Su	10 4 13	2 32 5	28 35 30	4♒51 58	14 56.3	20 35.2	5 0.2	6 9.3	7 17.3	11 18.5	8 59.5	25 55.8	29 9.0
23 M	10 8 9	3 32 30	11♒ 5 25	17 16 0	14 54.6	21 36.6	6 15.3	6 16.0	7 30.8	11 19.7	9 2.8	25 54.5	29 8.6
24 Tu	10 12 6	4 32 54	23 23 56	29 29 21	14 53.4	22 30.4	7 30.4	6 23.3	7 44.2	11 21.0	9 6.0	25 53.3	29 8.2
25 W	10 16 3	5 33 16	5♓32 27	11♓33 27	14D 52.7	23 15.9	8 45.4	6 31.2	7 57.6	11 22.4	9 9.3	25 52.0	29 7.8
26 Th	10 19 59	6 33 36	17 32 33	23 30 1	14 52.6	23 52.7	10 0.5	6 39.7	8 10.9	11 24.0	9 12.5	25 50.8	29 7.4
27 F	10 23 56	7 33 54	29 26 6	5♈21 6	14 52.9	24 20.4	11 15.5	6 48.8	8 24.2	11 25.6	9 15.7	25 49.6	29 7.0
28 Sa	10 27 52	8 34 11	11♈15 21	17 9 11	14 53.4	24 38.7	12 30.5	6 58.6	8 37.5	11 27.4	9 18.9	25 48.5	29 6.7

Astro Data Dy Hr Mn	Planet Ingress Dy Hr Mn	Last Aspect Dy Hr Mn	☽ Ingress Dy Hr Mn	Last Aspect Dy Hr Mn	☽ Ingress Dy Hr Mn	☽ Phases & Eclipses Dy Hr Mn	Astro Data
☽0N 3 5:32	♀ ♑ 1 5:25	3 9:43 ♇ □	♈ 3 9:57	2 5:37 ♇ ⚹	♉ 2 6:54	4 13:09 ☽ 13♈22	1 JANUARY 1914
♃☍♆ 9 6:04	☿ ♑ 3 19:20	5 22:23 ♇ ⚹	♉ 5 22:43	4 11:16 ♆ ⚹	♊ 4 18:20	12 5:09 ○ 21♋10	Julian Day # 5114
♃⚼♄ 9 18:24	☉ ♒ 20 21:12	8 3:44 ♆ ⚹	♊ 8 9:13	7 1:00 ♇ ☌	♋ 7 2:16	19 0:30 ☽ 28♎06	Delta T 16.0 sec
♄∠♆ 15 1:24	♃ ♒ 21 15:13	10 15:44 ♇ ☌	♋ 10 16:12	9 0:04 ♆ ☌	♌ 9 6:26	26 6:34 ● 5♒29	SVP 06♓27'34"
☽0S 16 20:52	☿ ♒ 22 15:51	12 16:38 ♃ ☍	♌ 12 20:13	11 6:47 ♇ ⚹	♍ 11 8:00		Obliquity 23°27'10"
♃⚻♇ 19 19:51	♀ ♒ 25 2:09	14 22:05 ♇ ⚹	♍ 14 22:40	13 7:22 ♇ □	♎ 13 8:37	3 10:32 ☽ 13♉47	⚷ Chiron 11♓12.5
☽0N 30 12:47		17 0:15 ♇ □	♎ 17 0:53	15 8:36 ♇ △	♏ 15 9:55	10 17:34 ○ 21♌10	☽ Mean ☊ 18♓24.3
	☿ ♓ 8 19:11	19 3:02 ♇ △	♏ 19 3:44	17 11:57 ♀ □	♐ 17 13:03	17 9:23 ☽ 27♏53	
♄∠♆ 9 21:28	♀ ♓ 18 0:05	21 7:32 ♃ ⚹	♐ 21 7:40	19 17:06 ♇ ☍	♑ 19 18:38	25 0:02 ● 5♓33	1 FEBRUARY 1914
♄ D 11 20:52	☉ ♓ 19 11:38	23 12:06 ♇ ☍	♑ 23 12:59	21 18:57 ♆ ☍	♒ 22 2:41	25 0:12:42 ✔ A 5'35"	Julian Day # 5145
♂ D 12 23:35		25 13:53 ♆ ☍	♒ 25 20:13	24 11:18 ♇ △	♓ 24 13:01		Delta T 16.1 sec
☽0S 13 4:23		28 4:48 ♇ △	♓ 28 5:54	26 23:21 ♇ □	♈ 27 1:09		SVP 06♓27'29"
☽0N 26 19:48		30 16:44 ♇ □	♈ 30 17:57				Obliquity 23°27'11"
☿0N 27 4:18							⚷ Chiron 12♓39.6
							☽ Mean ☊ 16♓45.8

MARCH 1914 LONGITUDE

Day	Sid.Time	☉	0 hr ☽	Noon ☽	True ☊	☿	♀	♂	♃	♄	♅	♆	♇
1 Su	10 31 49	9♓34 26	23♈ 3 2	28♈57 18	14♓54.1	24♓47.4	13♓45.5	7♋ 8.9	8♒50.7	11♊29.3	9♒22.0	25♋47.3	29♊ 6.4
2 M	10 35 45	10 34 38	4♉52 26	10♉48 55	14 54.6	24R46.5	15 0.4	7 19.8	9 3.8	11 31.2	9 25.2	25R46.2	29R 6.1
3 Tu	10 39 42	11 34 49	16 47 17	22 48 4	14 55.1	24 36.3	16 15.4	7 31.2	9 16.9	11 33.3	9 28.3	25 45.1	29 5.8
4 W	10 43 38	12 34 58	28 51 47	4♊59 2	14 55.3	24 16.9	17 30.3	7 43.2	9 30.0	11 35.5	9 31.4	25 44.1	29 5.6
5 Th	10 47 35	13 35 4	11♊10 20	17 26 16	14R55.4	23 49.0	18 45.2	7 55.8	9 42.9	11 37.8	9 34.4	25 43.0	29 5.4
6 F	10 51 32	14 35 9	23 47 20	0♋14 2	14D55.3	23 13.3	20 0.1	8 8.8	9 55.9	11 40.2	9 37.5	25 42.0	29 5.2
7 Sa	10 55 28	15 35 11	6♋46 47	13 25 56	14 55.4	22 30.6	21 15.0	8 22.4	10 8.7	11 42.7	9 40.5	25 41.1	29 5.0
8 Su	10 59 25	16 35 12	20 11 44	27 4 20	14 55.5	21 42.2	22 29.8	8 36.4	10 21.5	11 45.3	9 43.5	25 40.1	29 4.8
9 M	11 3 21	17 35 10	4♌ 3 45	11♌ 9 49	14 55.7	20 49.0	23 44.7	8 51.0	10 34.3	11 48.1	9 46.4	25 39.2	29 4.7
10 Tu	11 7 18	18 35 6	18 22 14	25 40 31	14 56.0	19 52.6	24 59.5	9 6.0	10 46.9	11 50.9	9 49.4	25 38.3	29 4.6
11 W	11 11 14	19 34 59	3♍ 4 0	10♍31 51	14R56.3	18 54.2	26 14.2	9 21.4	10 59.5	11 53.8	9 52.3	25 37.4	29 4.5
12 Th	11 15 11	20 34 51	18 3 7	25 36 43	14 56.3	17 55.1	27 29.0	9 37.4	11 12.1	11 56.8	9 55.1	25 36.6	29 4.5
13 F	11 19 7	21 34 41	3♎11 30	10♎46 15	14 56.1	16 56.8	28 43.7	9 53.7	11 24.5	11 60.0	9 58.0	25 35.8	29 4.4
14 Sa	11 23 4	22 34 28	18 19 49	25 51 3	14 55.5	16 0.4	29 58.4	10 10.5	11 37.0	12 3.2	10 0.8	25 35.0	29D 4.4
15 Su	11 27 1	23 34 14	3♏18 57	10♏42 35	14 54.6	15 6.9	1♈13.1	10 27.7	11 49.3	12 6.5	10 3.6	25 34.2	29 4.4
16 M	11 30 57	24 33 59	18 1 14	25 14 18	14 53.5	14 17.4	2 27.8	10 45.3	12 1.6	12 9.9	10 6.3	25 33.5	29 4.4
17 Tu	11 34 54	25 33 41	2♐21 23	9♐22 15	14 52.5	13 32.5	3 42.5	11 3.3	12 13.8	12 13.4	10 9.0	25 32.8	29 4.5
18 W	11 38 50	26 33 22	16 16 48	23 5 4	14D51.8	12 52.9	4 57.1	11 21.7	12 25.9	12 17.0	10 11.7	25 32.2	29 4.6
19 Th	11 42 47	27 33 2	29 47 14	6♑23 31	14 51.6	12 19.0	6 11.7	11 40.5	12 37.9	12 20.7	10 14.4	25 31.6	29 4.7
20 F	11 46 43	28 32 39	12♑54 17	19 19 52	14 52.0	11 51.0	7 26.3	11 59.7	12 49.9	12 24.5	10 17.0	25 31.0	29 4.8
21 Sa	11 50 40	29 32 15	25 40 42	1♒57 12	14 53.0	11 29.2	8 40.9	12 19.2	13 1.8	12 28.4	10 19.6	25 30.4	29 5.0
22 Su	11 54 36	0♈31 49	8♒ 9 48	14 18 57	14 54.3	11 13.6	9 55.5	12 39.1	13 13.6	12 32.4	10 22.2	25 29.9	29 5.1
23 M	11 58 33	1 31 21	20 25 2	26 28 29	14 55.7	11 4.0	11 10.0	12 59.4	13 25.3	12 36.5	10 24.7	25 29.4	29 5.3
24 Tu	12 2 30	2 30 51	2♓29 40	8♓28 56	14 56.8	11D 0.5	12 24.5	13 19.9	13 37.0	12 40.7	10 27.2	25 28.9	29 5.5
25 W	12 6 26	3 30 20	14 26 37	20 23 2	14R57.2	11 2.8	13 39.0	13 40.9	13 48.5	12 44.9	10 29.6	25 28.5	29 5.8
26 Th	12 10 23	4 29 46	26 18 28	2♈13 12	14 56.8	11 10.7	14 53.5	14 2.1	13 60.0	12 49.3	10 32.0	25 28.1	29 6.0
27 F	12 14 19	5 29 10	8♈ 7 30	14 1 37	14 55.2	11 24.0	16 7.9	14 23.7	14 11.4	12 53.7	10 34.4	25 27.7	29 6.3
28 Sa	12 18 16	6 28 32	19 55 47	25 50 17	14 52.7	11 42.5	17 22.4	14 45.6	14 22.6	12 58.2	10 36.7	25 27.3	29 6.6
29 Su	12 22 12	7 27 52	1♉45 23	7♉41 20	14 49.2	12 5.8	18 36.8	15 7.8	14 33.8	13 2.8	10 39.0	25 27.0	29 6.9
30 M	12 26 9	8 27 10	13 38 26	19 37 0	14 45.1	12 33.8	19 51.1	15 30.3	14 44.9	13 7.5	10 41.3	25 26.8	29 7.3
31 Tu	12 30 5	9 26 26	25 37 23	1♊39 55	14 41.0	13 6.2	21 5.5	15 53.2	14 56.0	13 12.3	10 43.5	25 26.5	29 7.7

APRIL 1914 LONGITUDE

Day	Sid.Time	☉	0 hr ☽	Noon ☽	True ☊	☿	♀	♂	♃	♄	♅	♆	♇
1 W	12 34 2	10♈25 40	7♊45 1	13♊53 4	14♓37.3	13♓42.7	22♈19.8	16♋16.3	15♒ 6.9	13♊17.1	10♒45.7	25♋26.3	29♊ 8.1
2 Th	12 37 58	11 24 51	20 4 30	26 19 47	14R34.5	14 23.2	23 34.1	16 39.6	15 17.7	13 22.1	10 47.8	25R26.2	29 8.5
3 F	12 41 55	12 24 1	2♋39 21	9♋ 3 40	14D32.8	15 7.4	24 48.4	17 3.3	15 28.4	13 27.1	10 49.9	25 26.0	29 8.9
4 Sa	12 45 52	13 23 7	15 33 10	22 8 17	14 32.4	15 55.1	26 2.6	17 27.2	15 39.0	13 32.2	10 52.0	25 25.9	29 9.4
5 Su	12 49 48	14 22 12	28 49 22	5♌36 44	14 33.1	16 46.1	27 16.8	17 51.4	15 49.5	13 37.3	10 54.0	25 25.9	29 9.9
6 M	12 53 45	15 21 14	12♌30 36	19 31 5	14 34.5	17 40.3	28 31.0	18 15.8	15 59.9	13 42.6	10 55.9	25D25.8	29 10.4
7 Tu	12 57 41	16 20 14	26 38 10	3♍51 38	14 36.0	18 37.4	29 45.1	18 40.5	16 10.2	13 47.9	10 57.9	25 25.8	29 10.9
8 W	13 1 38	17 19 11	11♍11 10	18 36 12	14R36.9	19 37.4	0♉59.3	19 5.4	16 20.4	13 53.3	10 59.8	25 25.8	29 11.4
9 Th	13 5 34	18 18 6	26 6 0	3♎39 40	14 36.4	20 40.1	2 13.4	19 30.6	16 30.5	13 58.8	11 1.6	25 25.9	29 12.0
10 F	13 9 31	19 16 59	11♎16 5	18 54 4	14 34.4	21 45.4	3 27.4	19 56.0	16 40.5	14 4.3	11 3.4	25 26.0	29 12.6
11 Sa	13 13 27	20 15 50	26 32 18	4♏ 9 27	14 30.7	22 53.2	4 41.5	20 21.6	16 50.3	14 9.9	11 5.2	25 26.1	29 13.2
12 Su	13 17 24	21 14 39	11♏44 12	19 15 20	14 25.8	24 3.3	5 55.5	20 47.4	17 0.1	14 15.6	11 6.9	25 26.3	29 13.8
13 M	13 21 21	22 13 27	26 41 45	4♐ 2 31	14 20.2	25 15.8	7 9.4	21 13.5	17 9.7	14 21.3	11 8.5	25 26.5	29 14.5
14 Tu	13 25 17	23 12 12	11♐16 55	18 24 26	14 14.8	26 30.4	8 23.4	21 39.7	17 19.2	14 27.1	11 10.2	25 26.7	29 15.2
15 W	13 29 14	24 10 56	25 24 44	2♑17 43	14 10.3	27 47.2	9 37.3	22 6.2	17 28.6	14 33.0	11 11.8	25 27.0	29 15.9
16 Th	13 33 10	25 9 38	9♑ 3 26	15 42 7	14 7.4	29 6.0	10 51.2	22 32.8	17 37.9	14 39.0	11 13.3	25 27.3	29 16.6
17 F	13 37 7	26 8 18	22 14 6	28 39 49	14D 6.1	0♈26.9	12 5.1	22 59.7	17 47.1	14 45.0	11 14.8	25 27.6	29 17.3
18 Sa	13 41 3	27 6 57	4♒59 46	11♒14 33	14 6.3	1 49.7	13 19.0	23 26.8	17 56.1	14 51.0	11 16.2	25 28.0	29 18.1
19 Su	13 45 0	28 5 34	17 24 44	23 30 54	14 7.5	3 14.4	14 32.8	23 54.0	18 5.0	14 57.2	11 17.6	25 28.4	29 18.8
20 M	13 48 56	29 4 9	29 33 41	5♓33 38	14 8.9	4 41.0	15 46.6	24 21.5	18 13.8	15 3.4	11 19.0	25 28.8	29 19.6
21 Tu	13 52 53	0♉ 2 43	11♓31 20	17 27 18	14R 9.6	6 9.4	17 0.4	24 49.1	18 22.5	15 9.6	11 20.3	25 29.3	29 20.4
22 W	13 56 50	1 1 15	23 22 2	29 15 58	14 9.3	7 39.7	18 14.1	25 16.9	18 31.0	15 15.9	11 21.5	25 29.8	29 21.3
23 Th	14 0 46	1 59 45	5♈ 9 33	11♈ 3 7	14 6.9	9 11.8	19 27.8	25 44.9	18 39.4	15 22.3	11 22.7	25 30.3	29 22.1
24 F	14 4 43	2 58 13	16 57 2	22 51 34	14 2.3	10 45.6	20 41.5	26 13.0	18 47.7	15 28.7	11 23.9	25 30.8	29 23.0
25 Sa	14 8 39	3 56 39	28 46 59	4♉43 31	13 55.4	12 21.3	21 55.2	26 41.4	18 55.8	15 35.2	11 25.0	25 31.4	29 23.8
26 Su	14 12 36	4 55 4	10♉41 22	16 40 45	13 46.8	13 58.7	23 8.8	27 9.9	19 3.8	15 41.7	11 26.1	25 32.1	29 24.7
27 M	14 16 32	5 53 27	22 41 48	28 44 44	13 37.0	15 37.9	24 22.5	27 38.6	19 11.6	15 48.3	11 27.1	25 32.7	29 25.7
28 Tu	14 20 29	6 51 48	4♊49 41	10♊56 52	13 26.9	17 18.8	25 36.0	28 7.4	19 19.3	15 55.0	11 28.1	25 33.4	29 26.6
29 W	14 24 25	7 50 7	17 6 27	23 18 41	13 17.5	19 1.5	26 49.6	28 36.4	19 26.9	16 1.7	11 29.0	25 34.1	29 27.6
30 Th	14 28 22	8 48 24	29 33 48	5♋52 4	13 9.7	20 46.1	28 3.1	29 5.5	19 34.3	16 8.4	11 29.8	25 34.9	29 28.5

Astro Data	Dy Hr Mn
☿ R	1 9:48
♃☌♅	4 3:24
☿0S	8 5:36
☽0S	12 14:47
♇ D	14 5:02
♀0N	16 9:26
♃△♄	16 23:05
☿ D	24 2:24
☽0N	26 2:11
♃⚼♇	26 13:03
♆ D	6 14:48
☽0S	9 1:59
☿0N	21 0:27
☽0N	22 7:59

Planet Ingress	Dy Hr Mn
♀ ♈	14 0:30
☉ ♈	21 11:11
♀ ♉	7 4:48
☿ ♈	16 16:06
☉ ♉	20 22:53

Last Aspect Dy Hr Mn		☽ Ingress Dy Hr Mn
1 12:18	♇ ⚹	♉ 1 14:07
3 17:50	♆ ⚹	♊ 4 2:14
6 9:52	♇ ☌	♋ 6 11:34
8 9:33	♆ ☌	♌ 8 17:03
10 17:32	♇ ⚹	♍ 10 19:02
12 17:29	♇ □	♎ 12 18:57
14 17:10	♇ △	♏ 14 18:39
16 12:32	♆ △	♐ 16 20:01
18 22:43	♇ ☍	♑ 19 0:23
21 8:00	☉ ⚹	♒ 21 8:15
23 17:12	♇ △	♓ 23 19:01
26 5:40	♇ □	♈ 26 7:30
28 18:39	♇ ⚹	♉ 28 20:26
30 23:38	♆ ⚹	♊ 31 8:42

Last Aspect Dy Hr Mn		☽ Ingress Dy Hr Mn
2 17:22	♇ ☌	♋ 2 18:59
4 20:58	♀ □	♌ 5 2:06
7 4:15	♇ ⚹	♍ 7 5:37
9 4:56	♇ □	♎ 9 6:12
11 4:13	♇ △	♏ 11 5:27
12 21:58	♆ △	♐ 13 5:23
15 6:42	♇ ☍	♑ 15 7:58
17 7:52	☉ □	♒ 17 14:31
19 23:32	♇ △	♓ 20 0:52
22 12:12	♇ □	♈ 22 13:30
25 1:15	♇ ⚹	♉ 25 2:28
27 10:13	♂ ⚹	♊ 27 14:29
29 23:50	♇ ☌	♋ 30 0:50

☽ Phases & Eclipses Dy Hr Mn	
5 5:02	☽ 13♊48
12 4:18	○ 20♍46
12 4:13	☍ P 0.911
18 19:39	☽ 27♐22
26 18:09	● 5♈15
3 19:41	☽ 13♋12
10 13:28	○ 19♎50
17 7:52	☽ 26♑28
25 11:21	● 4♉24

Astro Data

1 MARCH 1914
Julian Day # 5173
Delta T 16.2 sec
SVP 06♓27'25"
Obliquity 23°27'11"
⚷ Chiron 14♓19.9
☽ Mean ☊ 15♓16.8

1 APRIL 1914
Julian Day # 5204
Delta T 16.3 sec
SVP 06♓27'22"
Obliquity 23°27'11"
⚷ Chiron 16♓13.6
☽ Mean ☊ 13♓38.3

LONGITUDE MAY 1914

Day	Sid.Time	☉	0 hr ☽	Noon ☽	True ☊	☿	♀	♂	♃	♄	♅	♆	♇
1 F	14 32 19	9♉46 40	12♋13 46	18♋39 13	13♓ 4.0	22♈32.3	29♉16.6	29♋34.8	19♒41.6	16♊15.2	11♒30.7	25♋35.7	29♊29.5
2 Sa	14 36 15	10 44 53	25 8 46	1♌42 44	13R 0.7	24 20.4	0♊30.1	0♌ 4.3	19 48.7	16 22.0	11 31.4	25 36.5	29 30.5
3 Su	14 40 12	11 43 4	8♌21 29	15 5 17	12D59.5	26 10.3	1 43.5	0 33.9	19 55.7	16 28.9	11 32.2	25 37.4	29 31.6
4 M	14 44 8	12 41 13	21 54 28	28 49 13	12 59.7	28 1.9	2 56.9	1 3.6	20 2.6	16 35.8	11 32.8	25 38.2	29 32.6
5 Tu	14 48 5	13 39 20	5♍49 40	12♍55 53	13R 0.3	29 55.4	4 10.2	1 33.5	20 9.3	16 42.8	11 33.5	25 39.1	29 33.6
6 W	14 52 1	14 37 25	20 7 44	27 24 58	13 0.3	1♉50.6	5 23.5	2 3.5	20 15.8	16 49.8	11 34.0	25 40.1	29 34.7
7 Th	14 55 58	15 35 28	4♎47 8	12♎13 38	12 58.6	3 47.6	6 36.8	2 33.7	20 22.2	16 56.8	11 34.5	25 41.1	29 35.8
8 F	14 59 54	16 33 29	19 43 39	27 16 12	12 54.4	5 46.4	7 50.1	3 3.9	20 28.4	17 3.9	11 35.0	25 42.1	29 36.9
9 Sa	15 3 51	17 31 29	4♏50 10	12♏24 20	12 47.8	7 46.9	9 3.3	3 34.3	20 34.4	17 11.1	11 35.4	25 43.1	29 38.0
10 Su	15 7 48	18 29 27	19 57 25	27 28 7	12 39.1	9 49.0	10 16.5	4 4.8	20 40.4	17 18.2	11 35.8	25 44.1	29 39.1
11 M	15 11 44	19 27 23	4♐55 14	12♐17 40	12 29.3	11 52.7	11 29.6	4 35.5	20 46.1	17 25.4	11 36.2	25 45.2	29 40.3
12 Tu	15 15 41	20 25 18	19 34 28	26 44 54	12 19.5	13 58.0	12 42.8	5 6.3	20 51.7	17 32.7	11 36.4	25 46.4	29 41.4
13 W	15 19 37	21 23 11	3♑48 25	10♑44 41	12 10.9	16 4.7	13 55.9	5 37.1	20 57.1	17 39.9	11 36.7	25 47.5	29 42.6
14 Th	15 23 34	22 21 4	17 33 35	24 15 11	12 4.3	18 12.6	15 8.9	6 8.2	21 2.4	17 47.2	11 36.8	25 48.7	29 43.8
15 F	15 27 30	23 18 55	0♒49 42	7♒17 29	11 60.0	20 21.7	16 21.9	6 39.3	21 7.5	17 54.6	11 37.0	25 49.9	29 45.0
16 Sa	15 31 27	24 16 44	13 39 2	19 54 54	11D57.9	22 31.7	17 34.9	7 10.5	21 12.4	18 2.0	11 37.1	25 51.1	29 46.2
17 Su	15 35 23	25 14 33	26 5 41	2♓12 3	11 57.5	24 42.3	18 47.9	7 41.8	21 17.2	18 9.4	11R37.1	25 52.4	29 47.4
18 M	15 39 20	26 12 20	8♓14 40	14 14 12	11R57.7	26 53.5	20 0.8	8 13.3	21 21.8	18 16.8	11 37.1	25 53.7	29 48.6
19 Tu	15 43 17	27 10 6	20 11 19	26 6 41	11 57.5	29 5.0	21 13.7	8 44.9	21 26.2	18 24.2	11 37.0	25 55.0	29 49.9
20 W	15 47 13	28 7 51	2♈ 0 54	7♈54 33	11 55.8	1♊16.3	22 26.6	9 16.6	21 30.4	18 31.7	11 36.9	25 56.3	29 51.1
21 Th	15 51 10	29 5 35	13 48 10	19 42 15	11 51.9	3 27.4	23 39.5	9 48.3	21 34.5	18 39.2	11 36.7	25 57.7	29 52.4
22 F	15 55 6	0♊ 3 18	25 37 13	1♉33 27	11 45.3	5 37.9	24 52.3	10 20.2	21 38.4	18 46.8	11 36.5	25 59.1	29 53.7
23 Sa	15 59 3	1 0 59	7♉31 18	13 31 2	11 36.0	7 47.5	26 5.0	10 52.2	21 42.1	18 54.3	11 36.2	26 0.5	29 54.9
24 Su	16 2 59	1 58 40	19 32 53	25 37 1	11 24.4	9 56.0	27 17.8	11 24.3	21 45.7	19 1.9	11 35.9	26 1.9	29 56.2
25 M	16 6 56	2 56 19	1♊43 35	7♊52 40	11 11.3	12 3.0	28 30.5	11 56.6	21 49.0	19 9.5	11 35.6	26 3.4	29 57.5
26 Tu	16 10 52	3 53 57	14 4 20	20 18 39	10 57.9	14 8.5	29 43.2	12 28.9	21 52.2	19 17.2	11 35.2	26 4.9	29 58.9
27 W	16 14 49	4 51 34	26 35 40	2♋55 23	10 45.2	16 12.1	0♋55.8	13 1.3	21 55.2	19 24.8	11 34.7	26 6.4	0♋ 0.2
28 Th	16 18 46	5 49 10	9♋17 52	15 43 12	10 34.4	18 13.8	2 8.4	13 33.8	21 58.0	19 32.5	11 34.2	26 7.9	0 1.5
29 F	16 22 42	6 46 45	22 11 25	28 42 40	10 26.2	20 13.2	3 21.0	14 6.4	22 0.6	19 40.2	11 33.6	26 9.5	0 2.9
30 Sa	16 26 39	7 44 18	5♌17 3	11♌54 45	10 20.9	22 10.4	4 33.5	14 39.1	22 3.1	19 47.9	11 33.0	26 11.1	0 4.2
31 Su	16 30 35	8 41 49	18 35 56	25 20 47	10 18.2	24 5.2	5 46.0	15 11.9	22 5.3	19 55.6	11 32.4	26 12.7	0 5.6

LONGITUDE JUNE 1914

Day	Sid.Time	☉	0 hr ☽	Noon ☽	True ☊	☿	♀	♂	♃	♄	♅	♆	♇
1 M	16 34 32	9♊39 20	2♍ 9 30	9♍ 2 14	10♓17.4	25♊57.4	6♋58.5	15♌44.8	22♒ 7.4	20♊ 3.3	11♒31.7	26♋14.3	0♋ 7.0
2 Tu	16 38 28	10 36 48	15 59 8	23 0 15	10R17.3	27 47.1	8 10.9	16 17.7	22 9.2	20 11.1	11R31.0	26 16.0	0 8.3
3 W	16 42 25	11 34 16	0♎ 5 35	7♎15 2	10 16.8	29 34.2	9 23.2	16 50.8	22 10.9	20 18.8	11 30.2	26 17.7	0 9.7
4 Th	16 46 21	12 31 42	14 28 21	21 45 9	10 14.5	1♋18.5	10 35.6	17 23.9	22 12.4	20 26.6	11 29.3	26 19.4	0 11.1
5 F	16 50 18	13 29 7	29 4 57	6♏27 3	10 9.7	3 0.2	11 47.8	17 57.2	22 13.7	20 34.3	11 28.5	26 21.1	0 12.5
6 Sa	16 54 15	14 26 31	13♏50 40	21 14 51	10 2.3	4 39.2	13 0.1	18 30.5	22 14.9	20 42.1	11 27.5	26 22.8	0 13.9
7 Su	16 58 11	15 23 54	28 38 38	6♐ 0 56	9 52.6	6 15.3	14 12.3	19 3.9	22 15.8	20 49.9	11 26.6	26 24.6	0 15.3
8 M	17 2 8	16 21 17	13♐20 44	20 37 1	9 41.6	7 48.7	15 24.4	19 37.3	22 16.6	20 57.7	11 25.6	26 26.4	0 16.7
9 Tu	17 6 4	17 18 38	27 48 54	4♑55 35	9 30.5	9 19.3	16 36.5	20 10.9	22 17.1	21 5.5	11 24.5	26 28.2	0 18.1
10 W	17 10 1	18 15 59	11♑56 27	18 51 5	9 20.5	10 47.1	17 48.6	20 44.5	22 17.5	21 13.3	11 23.4	26 30.0	0 19.6
11 Th	17 13 57	19 13 18	25 39 10	2♒20 38	9 12.6	12 12.0	19 0.6	21 18.2	22R17.7	21 21.1	11 22.3	26 31.8	0 21.0
12 F	17 17 54	20 10 38	8♒55 33	15 24 7	9 7.1	13 33.9	20 12.6	21 52.0	22 17.6	21 29.0	11 21.1	26 33.7	0 22.4
13 Sa	17 21 51	21 7 57	21 46 40	28 3 38	9 4.2	14 53.0	21 24.5	22 25.9	22 17.4	21 36.8	11 19.9	26 35.6	0 23.8
14 Su	17 25 47	22 5 15	4♓15 34	10♓23 2	9D 3.1	16 9.1	22 36.4	22 59.8	22 17.0	21 44.6	11 18.6	26 37.5	0 25.3
15 M	17 29 44	23 2 33	16 26 41	22 27 10	9R 3.1	17 22.2	23 48.2	23 33.8	22 16.4	21 52.4	11 17.3	26 39.4	0 26.7
16 Tu	17 33 40	23 59 50	28 25 10	4♈21 21	9 3.2	18 32.2	25 0.0	24 7.9	22 15.6	22 0.2	11 16.0	26 41.3	0 28.2
17 W	17 37 37	24 57 7	10♈16 24	16 10 56	9 2.1	19 39.0	26 11.8	24 42.1	22 14.7	22 8.0	11 14.6	26 43.2	0 29.6
18 Th	17 41 33	25 54 24	22 5 37	28 0 59	8 59.2	20 42.7	27 23.5	25 16.3	22 13.5	22 15.8	11 13.2	26 45.2	0 31.1
19 F	17 45 30	26 51 41	3♉57 37	9♉55 58	8 53.9	21 43.0	28 35.2	25 50.7	22 12.1	22 23.6	11 11.7	26 47.1	0 32.5
20 Sa	17 49 26	27 48 57	15 56 30	21 59 34	8 46.1	22 40.0	29 46.8	26 25.1	22 10.6	22 31.4	11 10.2	26 49.1	0 34.0
21 Su	17 53 23	28 46 14	28 5 30	4♊14 31	8 36.1	23 33.5	0♌58.3	26 59.5	22 8.8	22 39.2	11 8.7	26 51.1	0 35.4
22 M	17 57 20	29 43 30	10♊26 48	16 42 29	8 24.7	24 23.5	2 9.9	27 34.1	22 6.9	22 47.0	11 7.1	26 53.2	0 36.9
23 Tu	18 1 16	0♋40 45	23 1 35	29 24 8	8 12.9	25 9.8	3 21.4	28 8.7	22 4.8	22 54.8	11 5.5	26 55.2	0 38.3
24 W	18 5 13	1 38 1	5♋50 4	12♋19 18	8 1.8	25 52.4	4 32.8	28 43.4	22 2.5	23 2.6	11 3.9	26 57.2	0 39.8
25 Th	18 9 9	2 35 16	18 51 43	25 27 11	7 52.3	26 31.0	5 44.2	29 18.2	21 60.0	23 10.3	11 2.2	26 59.3	0 41.2
26 F	18 13 6	3 32 30	2♌ 5 34	8♌46 44	7 45.2	27 5.7	6 55.5	29 53.0	21 57.3	23 18.1	11 0.5	27 1.4	0 42.7
27 Sa	18 17 2	4 29 44	15 30 35	22 17 1	7 40.7	27 36.2	8 6.8	0♍27.9	21 54.4	23 25.8	10 58.8	27 3.4	0 44.1
28 Su	18 20 59	5 26 58	29 5 57	5♍57 20	7D38.7	28 2.5	9 18.0	1 2.9	21 51.4	23 33.5	10 57.0	27 5.5	0 45.6
29 M	18 24 55	6 24 11	12♍51 9	19 47 22	7 38.5	28 24.4	10 29.1	1 38.0	21 48.1	23 41.2	10 55.2	27 7.6	0 47.0
30 Tu	18 28 52	7 21 24	26 45 58	3♎46 53	7R39.1	28 41.9	11 40.2	2 13.1	21 44.7	23 48.9	10 53.3	27 9.7	0 48.5

Astro Data	Planet Ingress	Last Aspect	☽ Ingress	Last Aspect	☽ Ingress	☽ Phases & Eclipses	Astro Data
Dy Hr Mn	Dy Hr Mn	Dy Hr Mn	Dy Hr Mn	Dy Hr Mn	Dy Hr Mn	Dy Hr Mn	1 MAY 1914
☽0S 6 11:31	♀ ♊ 1 14:11	2 0:51 ♆ ☌	♌ 2 8:53	2 23:00 ☿ □	♎ 2 23:51	3 6:29 ☽ 11♌59	Julian Day # 5234
♅ R 17 2:40	♂ ♌ 1 20:31	4 13:16 ♇ ✶	♍ 4 14:02	4 19:32 ♆ □	♏ 5 1:30	9 21:30 ○ 18♏23	Delta T 16.4 sec
☽0N 19 13:45	☿ ♉ 5 0:58	6 15:33 ♇ □	♎ 6 16:13	6 20:22 ♆ △	♐ 7 2:12	16 22:12 ☽ 25♒10	SVP 06♓27'18"
	☿ ♊ 19 10:03	8 15:44 ♇ △	♏ 8 16:20	8 14:46 ♃ ✶	♑ 9 3:40	25 2:34 ● 3♊03	Obliquity 23°27'10"
☽0S 2 18:17	☉ ♊ 21 22:38	10 9:14 ♆ △	♐ 10 16:04	11 1:34 ♆ ☍	♒ 11 7:46		⚷ Chiron 17♓46.0
♃ R 11 9:56	♀ ♋ 26 5:34	12 17:00 ♇ ☍	♑ 12 17:30	13 1:18 ♂ ☍	♓ 13 15:44	1 14:03 ☽ 10♍13	☽ Mean ☊ 12♓03.0
☽0N 15 20:07	♇ ♋ 26 20:36	14 14:51 ♆ ☍	♒ 14 22:29	15 20:30 ♆ △	♈ 16 3:11	8 5:18 ○ 16♐34	
♃△♄ 17 17:47		17 7:15 ♇ △	♓ 17 7:40	18 11:56 ♀ □	♉ 18 16:01	15 14:20 ☽ 23♓37	1 JUNE 1914
☽0S 29 23:06	☿ ♋ 3 5:53	19 19:35 ♇ □	♈ 19 19:54	20 21:44 ♂ □	♊ 21 3:44	23 15:33 ● 1♋18	Julian Day # 5265
	♀ ♌ 20 4:26	22 8:39 ♇ ✶	♉ 22 8:51	23 10:06 ♂ ✶	♋ 23 13:07	30 19:24 ☽ 8♎08	Delta T 16.5 sec
	☉ ♋ 22 6:55	24 12:51 ♆ ✶	♊ 24 20:37	25 14:49 ♆ ☌	♌ 25 20:14		SVP 06♓27'12"
	♂ ♍ 26 4:48	26 15:03 ♃ △	♋ 27 6:28	27 14:10 ♄ ✶	♍ 28 1:35		Obliquity 23°27'10"
		29 7:20 ♆ ☌	♌ 29 14:22	30 3:22 ☿ ✶	♎ 30 5:32		⚷ Chiron 18♓44.9
		31 11:21 ☿ ✶	♍ 31 20:13				☽ Mean ☊ 10♓24.5

JULY 1914

LONGITUDE

Day	Sid.Time	☉	0 hr ☽	Noon ☽	True ☊	☿	♀	♂	♃	♄	♅	♆	♇
1 W	18 32 49	8♋18 36	10♎50 3	17♎55 22	7♓39.4	28♋54.8	12♌51.2	2♍48.3	21♒41.1	23♊56.6	10♒51.4	27♋11.9	0♋49.9
2 Th	18 36 45	9 15 48	25 2 38	2♏11 37	7R38.3	29 3.2	14 2.2	3 23.5	21R37.4	24 4.2	10R49.5	27 14.0	0 51.4
3 F	18 40 42	10 13 0	9♏21 59	16 33 18	7 35.3	29R 6.9	15 13.1	3 58.8	21 33.4	24 11.9	10 47.6	27 16.1	0 52.8
4 Sa	18 44 38	11 10 11	23 45 4	0♐56 42	7 30.0	29 5.9	16 24.0	4 34.2	21 29.3	24 19.5	10 45.7	27 18.3	0 54.2
5 Su	18 48 35	12 7 22	8♐ 7 33	15 16 58	7 22.9	29 0.3	17 34.7	5 9.6	21 25.0	24 27.1	10 43.7	27 20.4	0 55.7
6 M	18 52 31	13 4 33	22 24 12	29 28 37	7 14.6	28 50.0	18 45.4	5 45.1	21 20.6	24 34.6	10 41.7	27 22.6	0 57.1
7 Tu	18 56 28	14 1 44	6♑29 31	13♑26 22	7 6.1	28 35.3	19 56.1	6 20.7	21 16.0	24 42.2	10 39.6	27 24.8	0 58.5
8 W	19 0 25	14 58 55	20 18 38	27 5 57	6 58.5	28 16.3	21 6.7	6 56.3	21 11.2	24 49.7	10 37.6	27 27.0	0 60.0
9 Th	19 4 21	15 56 6	3♒48 2	10♒24 44	6 52.5	27 53.2	22 17.2	7 32.0	21 6.3	24 57.2	10 35.5	27 29.2	1 1.4
10 F	19 8 18	16 53 17	16 56 2	23 21 59	6 48.6	27 26.3	23 27.6	8 7.8	21 1.3	25 4.7	10 33.4	27 31.3	1 2.8
11 Sa	19 12 14	17 50 29	29 42 49	5♓58 48	6D46.7	26 55.9	24 37.9	8 43.6	20 56.0	25 12.1	10 31.2	27 33.5	1 4.2
12 Su	19 16 11	18 47 41	12♓10 19	18 17 49	6 46.6	26 22.5	25 48.2	9 19.5	20 50.6	25 19.5	10 29.1	27 35.7	1 5.6
13 M	19 20 7	19 44 53	24 21 49	0♈22 52	6 47.6	25 46.6	26 58.4	9 55.4	20 45.1	25 26.9	10 26.9	27 37.9	1 7.0
14 Tu	19 24 4	20 42 6	6♈21 34	12 18 32	6 48.9	25 8.7	28 8.6	10 31.4	20 39.5	25 34.3	10 24.7	27 40.2	1 8.4
15 W	19 28 0	21 39 19	18 14 25	24 9 49	6R49.8	24 29.5	29 18.7	11 7.5	20 33.6	25 41.6	10 22.5	27 42.4	1 9.7
16 Th	19 31 57	22 36 34	0♉ 5 25	6♉ 1 48	6 49.5	23 49.6	0♍28.6	11 43.6	20 27.7	25 48.9	10 20.3	27 44.6	1 11.1
17 F	19 35 54	23 33 48	11 59 36	17 59 21	6 47.7	23 9.6	1 38.6	12 19.8	20 21.6	25 56.1	10 18.0	27 46.8	1 12.5
18 Sa	19 39 50	24 31 4	24 1 36	0♊ 6 51	6 44.1	22 30.3	2 48.4	12 56.0	20 15.4	26 3.3	10 15.8	27 49.0	1 13.8
19 Su	19 43 47	25 28 20	6♊15 29	12 27 54	6 38.9	21 52.5	3 58.2	13 32.4	20 9.1	26 10.5	10 13.5	27 51.3	1 15.2
20 M	19 47 43	26 25 37	18 44 22	25 5 7	6 32.7	21 16.6	5 7.9	14 8.7	20 2.6	26 17.7	10 11.2	27 53.5	1 16.5
21 Tu	19 51 40	27 22 54	1♋30 17	7♋59 55	6 26.0	20 43.6	6 17.5	14 45.2	19 56.1	26 24.8	10 8.9	27 55.7	1 17.9
22 W	19 55 36	28 20 13	14 33 59	21 12 23	6 19.6	20 13.8	7 27.0	15 21.7	19 49.4	26 31.9	10 6.6	27 57.9	1 19.2
23 Th	19 59 33	29 17 32	27 54 55	4♌41 22	6 14.3	19 47.9	8 36.4	15 58.3	19 42.6	26 38.9	10 4.2	28 0.2	1 20.5
24 F	20 3 29	0♌14 51	11♌31 25	18 24 44	6 10.5	19 26.5	9 45.8	16 34.9	19 35.7	26 45.9	10 1.9	28 2.4	1 21.8
25 Sa	20 7 26	1 12 11	25 20 58	2♍19 42	6D 8.4	19 9.9	10 55.1	17 11.6	19 28.7	26 52.8	9 59.5	28 4.6	1 23.1
26 Su	20 11 23	2 9 31	9♍20 36	16 23 15	6 8.0	18 58.5	12 4.2	17 48.3	19 21.6	26 59.7	9 57.2	28 6.8	1 24.4
27 M	20 15 19	3 6 52	23 27 20	0♎32 29	6 8.8	18D52.7	13 13.3	18 25.2	19 14.5	27 6.6	9 54.8	28 9.1	1 25.7
28 Tu	20 19 16	4 4 14	7♎38 24	14 44 48	6 10.2	18 52.7	14 22.3	19 2.0	19 7.2	27 13.4	9 52.4	28 11.3	1 26.9
29 W	20 23 12	5 1 35	21 51 23	28 57 55	6 11.5	18 58.6	15 31.2	19 39.0	18 59.9	27 20.2	9 50.0	28 13.5	1 28.2
30 Th	20 27 9	5 58 58	6♏ 4 7	13♏ 9 45	6R12.0	19 10.7	16 40.0	20 15.9	18 52.5	27 26.9	9 47.6	28 15.7	1 29.4
31 F	20 31 5	6 56 21	20 14 33	27 18 15	6 11.4	19 29.1	17 48.6	20 53.0	18 45.0	27 33.6	9 45.3	28 17.9	1 30.6

AUGUST 1914

LONGITUDE

Day	Sid.Time	☉	0 hr ☽	Noon ☽	True ☊	☿	♀	♂	♃	♄	♅	♆	♇
1 Sa	20 35 2	7♌53 44	4♐20 32	11♐21 9	6♓ 9.5	19♋53.7	18♍57.2	21♍30.1	18♒37.5	27♊40.2	9♒42.9	28♋20.1	1♋31.9
2 Su	20 38 58	8 51 8	18 19 45	25 16 2	6R 6.5	20 24.7	20 5.6	22 7.3	18R29.9	27 46.7	9R40.5	28 22.3	1 33.1
3 M	20 42 55	9 48 33	2♑ 9 41	9♑ 0 23	6 2.9	21 1.9	21 14.0	22 44.5	18 22.3	27 53.3	9 38.1	28 24.5	1 34.3
4 Tu	20 46 52	10 45 59	15 47 51	22 31 49	5 59.1	21 45.5	22 22.2	23 21.8	18 14.6	27 59.7	9 35.7	28 26.7	1 35.4
5 W	20 50 48	11 43 25	29 12 4	5♒48 23	5 55.7	22 35.2	23 30.3	23 59.1	18 6.9	28 6.1	9 33.3	28 28.9	1 36.6
6 Th	20 54 45	12 40 52	12♒20 40	18 48 50	5 53.2	23 31.0	24 38.3	24 36.5	17 59.2	28 12.5	9 30.9	28 31.1	1 37.7
7 F	20 58 41	13 38 21	25 12 53	1♓32 52	5D51.7	24 32.8	25 46.1	25 13.9	17 51.4	28 18.8	9 28.5	28 33.3	1 38.9
8 Sa	21 2 38	14 35 50	7♓48 54	14 1 11	5 51.4	25 40.5	26 53.9	25 51.4	17 43.6	28 25.0	9 26.1	28 35.4	1 40.0
9 Su	21 6 34	15 33 20	20 9 58	26 15 33	5 51.9	26 53.7	28 1.5	26 29.0	17 35.8	28 31.2	9 23.8	28 37.6	1 41.1
10 M	21 10 31	16 30 52	2♈18 19	8♈18 39	5 53.2	28 12.5	29 9.0	27 6.6	17 27.9	28 37.3	9 21.4	28 39.7	1 42.2
11 Tu	21 14 27	17 28 25	14 17 1	20 13 56	5 54.7	29 36.4	0♎16.3	27 44.3	17 20.1	28 43.4	9 19.0	28 41.8	1 43.3
12 W	21 18 24	18 25 59	26 9 54	2♉ 5 29	5 56.1	1♌ 5.3	1 23.5	28 22.0	17 12.3	28 49.4	9 16.6	28 44.0	1 44.3
13 Th	21 22 21	19 23 35	8♉ 1 15	13 57 47	5 57.1	2 38.8	2 30.6	28 59.8	17 4.4	28 55.3	9 14.3	28 46.1	1 45.4
14 F	21 26 17	20 21 12	19 55 42	25 55 34	5R57.4	4 16.7	3 37.5	29 37.6	16 56.6	29 1.2	9 12.0	28 48.2	1 46.4
15 Sa	21 30 14	21 18 51	1♊57 57	8♊ 3 26	5 57.1	5 58.5	4 44.3	0♎15.5	16 48.8	29 7.0	9 9.6	28 50.3	1 47.5
16 Su	21 34 10	22 16 31	14 12 33	20 25 45	5 56.2	7 43.9	5 51.0	0 53.5	16 41.0	29 12.8	9 7.3	28 52.4	1 48.5
17 M	21 38 7	23 14 13	26 43 30	3♋ 6 10	5 54.8	9 32.5	6 57.5	1 31.5	16 33.3	29 18.5	9 5.0	28 54.4	1 49.4
18 Tu	21 42 3	24 11 57	9♋34 3	16 7 21	5 53.3	11 23.8	8 3.8	2 9.6	16 25.6	29 24.1	9 2.7	28 56.5	1 50.4
19 W	21 46 0	25 9 42	22 46 11	29 30 34	5 51.8	13 17.5	9 10.1	2 47.8	16 17.9	29 29.6	9 0.4	28 58.6	1 51.4
20 Th	21 49 56	26 7 28	6♌20 23	13♌15 26	5 50.7	15 13.1	10 16.1	3 26.0	16 10.2	29 35.1	8 58.2	29 0.6	1 52.3
21 F	21 53 53	27 5 16	20 15 22	27 19 46	5 49.9	17 10.3	11 22.0	4 4.3	16 2.7	29 40.5	8 55.9	29 2.6	1 53.2
22 Sa	21 57 50	28 3 6	4♍28 5	11♍39 44	5D49.7	19 8.7	12 27.7	4 42.6	15 55.1	29 45.8	8 53.7	29 4.6	1 54.1
23 Su	22 1 46	29 0 56	18 54 1	26 10 14	5 49.8	21 7.8	13 33.3	5 21.0	15 47.7	29 51.1	8 51.5	29 6.6	1 55.0
24 M	22 5 43	29 58 48	3♎27 38	10♎45 29	5 50.2	23 7.5	14 38.6	5 59.4	15 40.3	29 56.3	8 49.3	29 8.6	1 55.9
25 Tu	22 9 39	0♍56 42	18 3 6	25 19 47	5 50.7	25 7.3	15 43.8	6 38.0	15 33.0	0♋ 1.4	8 47.1	29 10.5	1 56.7
26 W	22 13 36	1 54 36	2♏34 58	9♏48 5	5 51.1	27 7.1	16 48.8	7 16.5	15 25.7	0 6.4	8 45.0	29 12.5	1 57.5
27 Th	22 17 32	2 52 32	16 58 42	24 6 25	5 51.3	29 6.6	17 53.6	7 55.1	15 18.6	0 11.4	8 42.9	29 14.4	1 58.3
28 F	22 21 29	3 50 30	1♐10 57	8♐12 3	5R51.4	1♍ 5.6	18 58.2	8 33.8	15 11.5	0 16.2	8 40.8	29 16.3	1 59.1
29 Sa	22 25 25	4 48 28	15 9 35	22 3 25	5 51.4	3 3.9	20 2.6	9 12.6	15 4.5	0 21.0	8 38.7	29 18.2	1 59.9
30 Su	22 29 22	5 46 28	28 53 31	5♑39 52	5D51.4	5 1.5	21 6.8	9 51.3	14 57.7	0 25.7	8 36.6	29 20.1	2 0.7
31 M	22 33 19	6 44 29	12♑22 28	19 1 22	5 51.4	6 58.2	22 10.8	10 30.2	14 50.9	0 30.4	8 34.6	29 22.0	2 1.4

Astro Data (Dy Hr Mn)

☿ R 3 6:58
☽0N 13 3:23
♄□♅ 13 0:01
☽0S 27 4:11
☿ D 27 12:10

☽0N 9 11:11
♄⊻♆ 10 14:25
♀0S 11 2:45
♃□♇ 15 3:42
♂0S 16 13:47
☽0S 23 11:26
♃□♄ 27 14:26

Planet Ingress (Dy Hr Mn)

♀ ♍ 15 14:10
☉ ♌ 23 17:47

♀ ♎ 10 18:11
☿ ♌ 11 6:30
♂ ♎ 14 14:10
☉ ♍ 24 0:30
♄ ♋ 24 17:28
☿ ♍ 27 10:46

Last Aspect Dy Hr Mn		☽ Ingress Dy Hr Mn
2 6:47	☿ □	♏ 2 8:19
4 8:53	☿ △	♐ 4 10:25
6 3:43	♄ ☍	♑ 6 12:53
8 13:43	☿ ☍	♒ 8 17:10
10 15:22	♄ △	♓ 11 0:33
13 6:32	♆ △	♈ 13 11:14
15 19:14	♆ □	♉ 15 23:49
18 7:30	♆ ⚹	♊ 18 11:47
20 14:24	♄ ☌	♋ 20 21:12
23 2:38	☉ ☌	♌ 23 3:42
25 2:40	♄ ⚹	♍ 25 8:00
27 7:59	♆ ⚹	♎ 27 11:05
29 10:47	♆ □	♏ 29 13:45
31 13:44	♆ △	♐ 31 16:35

Last Aspect Dy Hr Mn		☽ Ingress Dy Hr Mn
2 16:30	♄ ☍	♑ 2 20:14
4 22:42	♆ ☍	♒ 5 1:27
7 5:54	♄ △	♓ 7 9:03
9 17:05	♀ ☍	♈ 9 19:25
12 5:26	♄ ⚹	♉ 12 7:46
14 17:47	♆ ⚹	♊ 14 20:06
17 4:55	♄ ☌	♋ 17 6:11
19 11:05	♆ ☌	♌ 19 12:52
21 16:03	♄ ⚹	♍ 21 16:30
23 18:10	♄ □	♎ 23 18:18
25 18:24	♆ □	♏ 25 19:43
27 20:45	♆ △	♐ 27 21:59
29 9:12	♀ ⚹	♑ 30 1:57

☽ Phases & Eclipses (Dy Hr Mn)

7 13:59 ○ 14♑35
15 7:31 ☽ 21♈57
23 2:38 ● 29♋24
29 23:51 ☽ 5♏59

6 0:40 ○ 12♒42
14 0:56 ☽ 20♉23
21 12:26 ● 27♌35
21 12:34:08 • T 2'15"
28 4:52 ☽ 4♐02

Astro Data

1 JULY 1914
Julian Day # 5295
Delta T 16.6 sec
SVP 06♓27'07"
Obliquity 23°27'10"
⚷ Chiron 18♓55.4R
☽ Mean ☊ 8♓49.2

1 AUGUST 1914
Julian Day # 5326
Delta T 16.7 sec
SVP 06♓27'01"
Obliquity 23°27'10"
⚷ Chiron 18♓17.1R
☽ Mean ☊ 7♓10.8

LONGITUDE SEPTEMBER 1914

Day	Sid.Time	☉	0 hr ☽	Noon ☽	True ☊	☿	♀	♂	♃	♄	♅	♆	♇
1 Tu	22 37 15	7♍42 32	25♑36 38	2♒ 8 19	5♓51.5	8♍54.0	23♎14.5	11♎ 9.1	14♒44.3	0♋34.9	8♒32.6	29♋23.8	2♋ 2.1
2 W	22 41 12	8 40 36	8♒36 31	15 1 18	5 51.8	10 48.6	24 18.0	11 48.1	14R37.7	0 39.4	8R30.7	29 25.6	2 2.8
3 Th	22 45 8	9 38 41	21 22 48	27 41 5	5 52.0	12 42.2	25 21.2	12 27.1	14 31.3	0 43.8	8 28.7	29 27.4	2 3.5
4 F	22 49 5	10 36 48	3♓56 18	10♓ 8 34	5R52.2	14 34.7	26 24.2	13 6.1	14 25.0	0 48.1	8 26.8	29 29.2	2 4.1
5 Sa	22 53 1	11 34 57	16 18 3	22 24 54	5 52.1	16 26.0	27 27.0	13 45.3	14 18.8	0 52.3	8 24.9	29 31.0	2 4.8
6 Su	22 56 58	12 33 7	28 29 19	4♈31 31	5 51.6	18 16.2	28 29.5	14 24.4	14 12.8	0 56.4	8 23.1	29 32.7	2 5.4
7 M	23 0 54	13 31 19	10♈31 45	16 30 19	5 50.8	20 5.2	29 31.7	15 3.7	14 6.9	1 0.4	8 21.2	29 34.5	2 6.0
8 Tu	23 4 51	14 29 33	22 27 30	28 23 40	5 49.7	21 53.0	0♏33.6	15 43.0	14 1.1	1 4.4	8 19.4	29 36.2	2 6.5
9 W	23 8 48	15 27 49	4♉19 12	10♉14 31	5 48.4	23 39.7	1 35.3	16 22.3	13 55.5	1 8.2	8 17.7	29 37.8	2 7.1
10 Th	23 12 44	16 26 7	16 10 4	22 6 19	5 47.1	25 25.2	2 36.6	17 1.8	13 50.0	1 12.0	8 15.9	29 39.5	2 7.6
11 F	23 16 41	17 24 27	28 3 47	4♊ 3 0	5 45.9	27 9.5	3 37.7	17 41.2	13 44.6	1 15.7	8 14.3	29 41.1	2 8.1
12 Sa	23 20 37	18 22 50	10♊ 4 30	16 8 51	5D45.2	28 52.8	4 38.4	18 20.8	13 39.5	1 19.2	8 12.6	29 42.7	2 8.6
13 Su	23 24 34	19 21 14	22 16 37	28 28 21	5 45.1	0♎34.9	5 38.9	19 0.4	13 34.4	1 22.7	8 11.0	29 44.3	2 9.1
14 M	23 28 30	20 19 41	4♋44 36	11♋ 5 51	5 45.5	2 15.9	6 39.0	19 40.0	13 29.6	1 26.1	8 9.4	29 45.9	2 9.5
15 Tu	23 32 27	21 18 9	17 32 36	24 5 13	5 46.5	3 55.8	7 38.7	20 19.7	13 24.9	1 29.4	8 7.9	29 47.5	2 9.9
16 W	23 36 23	22 16 40	0♌44 2	7♌29 16	5 47.8	5 34.7	8 38.2	20 59.5	13 20.3	1 32.6	8 6.3	29 49.0	2 10.3
17 Th	23 40 20	23 15 13	14 21 2	21 19 18	5 49.0	7 12.5	9 37.2	21 39.4	13 16.0	1 35.7	8 4.9	29 50.5	2 10.7
18 F	23 44 17	24 13 48	28 23 53	5♍34 26	5R49.8	8 49.3	10 35.9	22 19.2	13 11.8	1 38.7	8 3.4	29 51.9	2 11.1
19 Sa	23 48 13	25 12 25	12♍50 28	20 11 17	5 49.8	10 25.1	11 34.2	22 59.2	13 7.7	1 41.6	8 2.0	29 53.4	2 11.4
20 Su	23 52 10	26 11 4	27 36 5	5♎ 3 54	5 48.8	11 59.9	12 32.1	23 39.2	13 3.9	1 44.4	8 0.7	29 54.8	2 11.7
21 M	23 56 6	27 9 44	12♎33 41	20 4 20	5 46.8	13 33.7	13 29.6	24 19.3	13 0.2	1 47.1	7 59.4	29 56.2	2 12.0
22 Tu	0 0 3	28 8 27	27 34 44	5♏ 3 46	5 44.0	15 6.4	14 26.6	24 59.4	12 56.7	1 49.7	7 58.1	29 57.5	2 12.3
23 W	0 3 59	29 7 12	12♏30 26	19 53 47	5 40.9	16 38.2	15 23.3	25 39.6	12 53.4	1 52.2	7 56.9	29 58.9	2 12.5
24 Th	0 7 56	0♎ 5 58	27 13 4	4♐27 37	5 38.0	18 9.1	16 19.4	26 19.9	12 50.3	1 54.6	7 55.7	0♌ 0.2	2 12.7
25 F	0 11 52	1 4 46	11♐37 0	18 40 53	5 35.8	19 38.9	17 15.1	27 0.2	12 47.4	1 56.9	7 54.6	0 1.5	2 12.9
26 Sa	0 15 49	2 3 36	25 39 6	2♑31 39	5D34.6	21 7.8	18 10.2	27 40.6	12 44.7	1 59.1	7 53.5	0 2.7	2 13.1
27 Su	0 19 46	3 2 28	9♑18 36	16 0 8	5 34.6	22 35.7	19 4.8	28 21.0	12 42.1	2 1.2	7 52.4	0 4.0	2 13.3
28 M	0 23 42	4 1 21	22 36 30	29 8 1	5 35.6	24 2.6	19 58.9	29 1.5	12 39.8	2 3.1	7 51.4	0 5.2	2 13.4
29 Tu	0 27 39	5 0 16	5♒35 1	11♒57 51	5 37.2	25 28.5	20 52.4	29 42.0	12 37.6	2 5.0	7 50.4	0 6.3	2 13.5
30 W	0 31 35	5 59 12	18 16 53	24 32 28	5 38.8	26 53.3	21 45.4	0♏22.6	12 35.7	2 6.8	7 49.5	0 7.5	2 13.6

LONGITUDE OCTOBER 1914

Day	Sid.Time	☉	0 hr ☽	Noon ☽	True ☊	☿	♀	♂	♃	♄	♅	♆	♇
1 Th	0 35 32	6♎58 11	0♓44 57	6♓54 40	5♓39.8	28♎17.1	22♏37.7	1♏ 3.3	12♒33.9	2♋ 8.4	7♒48.7	0♌ 8.6	2♋13.6
2 F	0 39 28	7 57 11	13 1 54	19 6 55	5R39.6	29 39.8	23 29.3	1 44.0	12R32.3	2 9.9	7R47.8	0 9.7	2 13.7
3 Sa	0 43 25	8 56 13	25 10 0	1♈11 23	5 37.9	1♏ 1.5	24 20.3	2 24.7	12 31.0	2 11.4	7 47.0	0 10.7	2R13.7
4 Su	0 47 21	9 55 17	7♈11 17	13 9 54	5 34.5	2 21.9	25 10.6	3 5.6	12 29.8	2 12.7	7 46.3	0 11.7	2 13.7
5 M	0 51 18	10 54 23	19 7 28	25 4 10	5 29.4	3 41.2	26 0.2	3 46.4	12 28.8	2 13.9	7 45.6	0 12.7	2 13.7
6 Tu	0 55 14	11 53 32	1♉ 0 13	6♉55 52	5 23.1	4 59.2	26 49.1	4 27.4	12 28.0	2 15.0	7 45.0	0 13.7	2 13.6
7 W	0 59 11	12 52 42	12 51 20	18 46 55	5 16.0	6 15.9	27 37.2	5 8.4	12 27.4	2 16.0	7 44.4	0 14.6	2 13.5
8 Th	1 3 8	13 51 55	24 42 53	0♊39 36	5 8.9	7 31.2	28 24.5	5 49.4	12 27.0	2 16.9	7 43.9	0 15.5	2 13.4
9 F	1 7 4	14 51 9	6♊37 24	12 36 43	5 2.5	8 45.0	29 11.0	6 30.6	12D26.9	2 17.7	7 43.4	0 16.4	2 13.3
10 Sa	1 11 1	15 50 27	18 37 57	24 41 36	4 57.5	9 57.3	29 56.6	7 11.7	12 26.9	2 18.4	7 42.9	0 17.2	2 13.2
11 Su	1 14 57	16 49 46	0♋48 9	6♋58 8	4 54.2	11 7.8	0♐41.3	7 53.0	12 27.1	2 18.9	7 42.5	0 18.0	2 13.0
12 M	1 18 54	17 49 8	13 12 5	19 30 34	4D52.7	12 16.5	1 25.1	8 34.3	12 27.5	2 19.4	7 42.2	0 18.8	2 12.8
13 Tu	1 22 50	18 48 32	25 54 6	2♌23 13	4 52.8	13 23.2	2 7.9	9 15.6	12 28.1	2 19.7	7 41.9	0 19.6	2 12.6
14 W	1 26 47	19 47 58	8♌58 24	15 40 3	4 53.9	14 27.7	2 49.7	9 57.1	12 28.9	2 20.0	7 41.6	0 20.3	2 12.4
15 Th	1 30 43	20 47 27	22 28 32	29 24 2	4R55.2	15 29.9	3 30.5	10 38.5	12 29.9	2R20.1	7 41.4	0 20.9	2 12.1
16 F	1 34 40	21 46 58	6♍26 38	13♍36 15	4 55.7	16 29.6	4 10.1	11 20.1	12 31.1	2 20.1	7 41.3	0 21.6	2 11.9
17 Sa	1 38 37	22 46 31	20 52 35	28 15 8	4 54.6	17 26.4	4 48.7	12 1.7	12 32.5	2 20.0	7 41.2	0 22.2	2 11.6
18 Su	1 42 33	23 46 6	5♎43 11	13♎15 48	4 51.4	18 20.1	5 26.1	12 43.3	12 34.1	2 19.7	7D41.2	0 22.8	2 11.2
19 M	1 46 30	24 45 43	20 51 53	28 30 9	4 46.0	19 10.3	6 2.2	13 25.1	12 35.9	2 19.4	7 41.2	0 23.3	2 10.9
20 Tu	1 50 26	25 45 23	6♏ 9 14	13♏47 42	4 38.8	19 56.8	6 37.1	14 6.9	12 37.9	2 18.9	7 41.2	0 23.8	2 10.5
21 W	1 54 23	26 45 4	21 24 10	28 57 19	4 30.6	20 39.2	7 10.6	14 48.7	12 40.1	2 18.4	7 41.3	0 24.3	2 10.1
22 Th	1 58 19	27 44 48	6♐25 59	13♐49 13	4 22.7	21 16.9	7 42.8	15 30.6	12 42.5	2 17.7	7 41.5	0 24.7	2 9.7
23 F	2 2 16	28 44 33	21 6 15	28 16 32	4 16.0	21 49.5	8 13.5	16 12.6	12 45.1	2 16.9	7 41.7	0 25.2	2 9.3
24 Sa	2 6 12	29 44 20	5♑19 45	12♑15 49	4 11.2	22 16.6	8 42.6	16 54.6	12 47.9	2 16.0	7 42.0	0 25.5	2 8.8
25 Su	2 10 9	0♏44 8	19 4 47	25 46 53	4D 8.6	22 37.5	9 10.3	17 36.7	12 50.9	2 15.0	7 42.3	0 25.9	2 8.4
26 M	2 14 6	1 43 59	2♒22 28	8♒51 58	4 7.9	22 51.6	9 36.2	18 18.8	12 54.1	2 13.9	7 42.7	0 26.2	2 7.9
27 Tu	2 18 2	2 43 51	15 15 53	21 34 46	4 8.4	22R58.4	10 0.5	19 1.0	12 57.4	2 12.7	7 43.1	0 26.5	2 7.4
28 W	2 21 59	3 43 44	27 49 11	3♓59 41	4R 9.2	22 57.3	10 23.0	19 43.2	13 1.0	2 11.3	7 43.5	0 26.7	2 6.8
29 Th	2 25 55	4 43 39	10♓ 6 49	16 11 6	4 9.2	22 47.7	10 43.7	20 25.5	13 4.7	2 9.9	7 44.1	0 26.9	2 6.3
30 F	2 29 52	5 43 36	22 13 2	28 13 3	4 7.4	22 29.1	11 2.5	21 7.9	13 8.6	2 8.3	7 44.6	0 27.1	2 5.7
31 Sa	2 33 48	6 43 34	4♈11 35	10♈ 8 58	4 3.1	22 1.2	11 19.3	21 50.3	13 12.8	2 6.7	7 45.2	0 27.2	2 5.1

Astro Data	Planet Ingress	Last Aspect	☽ Ingress	Last Aspect	☽ Ingress	☽ Phases & Eclipses	Astro Data
Dy Hr Mn	Dy Hr Mn	Dy Hr Mn	Dy Hr Mn	Dy Hr Mn	Dy Hr Mn	Dy Hr Mn	1 SEPTEMBER 1914
☽0N 5 18:44	♀ ♏ 7 10:58	1 6:58 ♆ ☍	♒ 1 8:03	2 22:14 ♀ △	♈ 3 9:38	4 14:01 ○ 11♓11	Julian Day # 5357
☿0S 13 13:53	☿ ♎ 12 15:47	3 8:14 ♀ △	♓ 3 16:26	4 10:38 ♃ ⚹	♉ 5 21:58	4 13:55 P 0.859	Delta T 16.8 sec
☽0S 19 21:10	☉ ♎ 23 21:34	6 2:06 ♆ △	♈ 6 3:00	8 7:59 ♀ ☍	♊ 8 10:40	12 17:48 ☽ 19♊06	SVP 06♓26'57"
	♆ ♌ 23 20:25	8 14:29 ♆ □	♉ 8 15:15	9 17:57 ☉ △	♋ 10 22:26	19 21:33 ● 26♍05	Obliquity 23°27'10"
☽0N 3 1:21	♂ ♏ 29 10:38	11 3:16 ♆ ⚹	♊ 11 3:53	12 9:33 ☉ □	♌ 13 7:36	26 12:03 ☽ 2♑33	⚷ Chiron 17♓02.2R
♇ R 3 3:15		12 17:48 ☉ □	♋ 13 14:56	14 20:49 ☉ ⚹	♍ 15 13:02		☽ Mean ☊ 5♓32.3
♄☌♇ 4 18:39	☿ ♏ 2 5:54	15 22:21 ♆ ☌	♌ 15 22:41	16 17:58 ☿ ⚹	♎ 17 14:49	4 5:59 ○ 10♈10	
♃ D 9 10:25	♀ ♐ 10 1:49	17 13:12 ♂ ⚹	♍ 18 2:42	19 6:33 ☉ ☌	♏ 19 14:21	12 9:33 ☽ 18♋13	1 OCTOBER 1914
♄ R 15 11:41	☉ ♏ 24 6:17	20 3:44 ♆ ⚹	♎ 20 3:52	20 22:46 ☿ ☌	♐ 21 13:40	19 6:33 ● 25♎02	Julian Day # 5387
☽0S 17 7:59		22 3:49 ♆ □	♏ 22 3:53	23 13:45 ☉ ⚹	♑ 23 14:55	25 22:44 ☽ 1♒41	Delta T 16.9 sec
♅ D 18 9:40		23 4:59 ♀ ☌	♐ 24 4:36	25 6:27 ☿ ⚹	♒ 25 19:39		SVP 06♓26'53"
☿ R 27 8:47		26 3:42 ♂ ⚹	♑ 26 7:34	27 14:41 ☿ □	♓ 28 4:13		Obliquity 23°27'10"
☽0N 30 6:55		28 12:27 ♂ □	♒ 28 13:36	30 0:31 ☿ △	♈ 30 15:34		⚷ Chiron 15♓40.5R
		30 18:37 ☿ △	♓ 30 22:33				☽ Mean ☊ 3♓56.9

NOVEMBER 1914 LONGITUDE

Day	Sid.Time	☉	0 hr ☽	Noon ☽	True ☊	☿	♀	♂	♃	♄	♅	♆	♇
1 Su	2 37 45	7♏43 35	16♈ 5 34	22♈ 1 37	3♓56.1	21♏23.9	11♐34.1	22♏32.8	13♒17.0	2♋ 4.9	7♒45.9	0♌27.3	2♋ 4.5
2 M	2 41 41	8 43 37	27 57 24	3♉53 8	3R 46.5	20R 37.1	11 46.9	23 15.3	13 21.5	2R 3.1	7 46.6	0 27.4	2R 3.8
3 Tu	2 45 38	9 43 40	9♉48 59	15 45 9	3 34.7	19 41.5	11 57.4	23 57.9	13 26.2	2 1.1	7 47.4	0R 27.4	2 3.2
4 W	2 49 35	10 43 46	21 41 47	27 39 4	3 21.7	18 37.7	12 5.8	24 40.5	13 31.0	1 59.0	7 48.2	0 27.4	2 2.5
5 Th	2 53 31	11 43 54	3♊37 9	9♊36 14	3 8.5	17 27.1	12 12.0	25 23.2	13 36.0	1 56.8	7 49.1	0 27.4	2 1.8
6 F	2 57 28	12 44 3	15 36 32	21 38 17	2 56.2	16 11.5	12 15.8	26 6.0	13 41.2	1 54.6	7 50.0	0 27.3	2 1.1
7 Sa	3 1 24	13 44 15	27 41 45	3♋47 16	2 45.9	14 52.8	12R 17.3	26 48.8	13 46.6	1 52.2	7 51.0	0 27.2	2 0.4
8 Su	3 5 21	14 44 28	9♋55 11	16 5 53	2 38.2	13 33.6	12 16.4	27 31.7	13 52.1	1 49.7	7 52.0	0 27.1	1 59.6
9 M	3 9 17	15 44 44	22 19 49	28 37 25	2 33.3	12 16.4	12 13.2	28 14.6	13 57.8	1 47.1	7 53.1	0 26.9	1 58.9
10 Tu	3 13 14	16 45 1	4♌59 12	11♌25 39	2 30.9	11 3.6	12 7.4	28 57.6	14 3.7	1 44.4	7 54.2	0 26.7	1 58.1
11 W	3 17 10	17 45 21	17 57 16	24 34 32	2D 30.4	9 57.6	11 59.3	29 40.6	14 9.8	1 41.7	7 55.4	0 26.5	1 57.3
12 Th	3 21 7	18 45 42	1♍17 54	8♍ 7 42	2R 30.5	9 0.4	11 48.7	0♐23.8	14 16.0	1 38.8	7 56.6	0 26.2	1 56.5
13 F	3 25 4	19 46 6	15 4 13	22 7 36	2 30.1	8 13.3	11 35.7	1 6.9	14 22.4	1 35.8	7 57.9	0 25.9	1 55.6
14 Sa	3 29 0	20 46 31	29 17 48	6♎34 37	2 27.8	7 37.4	11 20.3	1 50.2	14 28.9	1 32.8	7 59.2	0 25.6	1 54.8
15 Su	3 32 57	21 46 58	13♎57 35	21 26 5	2 23.0	7 13.1	11 2.6	2 33.4	14 35.6	1 29.6	8 0.6	0 25.2	1 53.9
16 M	3 36 53	22 47 27	28 59 10	6♏35 46	2 15.3	7D 0.5	10 42.6	3 16.8	14 42.5	1 26.4	8 2.0	0 24.8	1 53.0
17 Tu	3 40 50	23 47 58	14♏14 35	21 54 11	2 5.2	6 59.4	10 20.3	4 0.2	14 49.5	1 23.1	8 3.4	0 24.4	1 52.1
18 W	3 44 46	24 48 30	29 33 7	7♐ 9 54	1 53.6	7 9.1	9 56.0	4 43.6	14 56.7	1 19.7	8 5.0	0 23.9	1 51.2
19 Th	3 48 43	25 49 4	14♐43 9	22 11 37	1 42.1	7 28.8	9 29.6	5 27.2	15 4.1	1 16.2	8 6.5	0 23.4	1 50.3
20 F	3 52 39	26 49 40	29 34 16	6♑50 17	1 31.9	7 57.9	9 1.4	6 10.7	15 11.6	1 12.6	8 8.1	0 22.9	1 49.4
21 Sa	3 56 36	27 50 16	13♑59 4	21 0 18	1 24.0	8 35.2	8 31.4	6 54.4	15 19.2	1 8.9	8 9.8	0 22.3	1 48.4
22 Su	4 0 33	28 50 54	27 53 53	4♒39 54	1 18.9	9 20.1	7 59.8	7 38.0	15 27.1	1 5.2	8 11.5	0 21.7	1 47.4
23 M	4 4 29	29 51 33	11♒18 36	17 50 23	1 16.3	10 11.5	7 26.8	8 21.8	15 35.0	1 1.4	8 13.2	0 21.1	1 46.4
24 Tu	4 8 26	0♐52 14	24 15 45	0♓35 18	1 15.5	11 8.8	6 52.7	9 5.6	15 43.1	0 57.5	8 15.0	0 20.4	1 45.4
25 W	4 12 22	1 52 55	6♓49 39	12 59 26	1 15.5	12 11.1	6 17.6	9 49.4	15 51.4	0 53.6	8 16.8	0 19.7	1 44.4
26 Th	4 16 19	2 53 37	19 5 20	25 8 0	1 14.9	13 17.8	5 41.8	10 33.3	15 59.8	0 49.5	8 18.7	0 19.0	1 43.4
27 F	4 20 15	3 54 20	1♈ 8 2	7♈ 6 4	1 12.6	14 28.3	5 5.6	11 17.2	16 8.3	0 45.4	8 20.6	0 18.2	1 42.4
28 Sa	4 24 12	4 55 5	13 2 37	18 58 14	1 7.7	15 42.0	4 29.1	12 1.2	16 17.0	0 41.3	8 22.6	0 17.5	1 41.3
29 Su	4 28 8	5 55 50	24 53 22	0♉48 25	0 59.9	16 58.5	3 52.6	12 45.3	16 25.8	0 37.1	8 24.6	0 16.6	1 40.3
30 M	4 32 5	6 56 37	6♉43 44	12 39 39	0 49.2	18 17.5	3 16.4	13 29.4	16 34.7	0 32.8	8 26.6	0 15.8	1 39.2

DECEMBER 1914 LONGITUDE

Day	Sid.Time	☉	0 hr ☽	Noon ☽	True ☊	☿	♀	♂	♃	♄	♅	♆	♇
1 Tu	4 36 2	7♐57 24	18♉36 25	24♉34 14	0♓36.1	19♏38.4	2♐40.8	14♐13.5	16♒43.8	0♋28.4	8♒28.7	0♌14.9	1♋38.1
2 W	4 39 58	8 58 13	0♊33 18	6♊33 45	0R 21.7	21 1.1	2R 6.0	14 57.7	16 53.0	0R 24.0	8 30.9	0R 14.0	1R 37.0
3 Th	4 43 55	9 59 3	12 35 43	18 39 18	0 6.9	22 25.3	1 32.2	15 42.0	17 2.4	0 19.6	8 33.0	0 13.1	1 35.9
4 F	4 47 51	10 59 54	24 44 35	0♋51 42	29♒53.2	23 50.8	0 59.7	16 26.3	17 11.9	0 15.1	8 35.3	0 12.1	1 34.8
5 Sa	4 51 48	12 0 47	7♋ 0 46	13 11 54	29 41.5	25 17.3	0 28.6	17 10.7	17 21.5	0 10.6	8 37.5	0 11.1	1 33.7
6 Su	4 55 44	13 1 40	19 25 18	25 41 8	29 32.6	26 44.7	29♏59.2	17 55.1	17 31.2	0 6.0	8 39.8	0 10.1	1 32.6
7 M	4 59 41	14 2 35	1♌59 40	8♌21 9	29 26.8	28 13.0	29 31.6	18 39.6	17 41.0	0 1.3	8 42.1	0 9.1	1 31.4
8 Tu	5 3 38	15 3 30	14 45 55	21 14 16	29 23.8	29 41.8	29 6.0	19 24.1	17 51.0	29♊56.6	8 44.5	0 8.0	1 30.3
9 W	5 7 34	16 4 27	27 46 36	4♍23 15	29D 23.0	1♐11.2	28 42.6	20 8.7	18 1.1	29 51.9	8 46.9	0 6.9	1 29.1
10 Th	5 11 31	17 5 25	11♍ 4 35	17 50 56	29R 23.2	2 41.2	28 21.3	20 53.3	18 11.3	29 47.2	8 49.4	0 5.8	1 28.0
11 F	5 15 27	18 6 25	24 42 34	1♎39 42	29 23.1	4 11.5	28 2.4	21 38.0	18 21.6	29 42.4	8 51.9	0 4.7	1 26.8
12 Sa	5 19 24	19 7 25	8♎42 24	15 50 39	29 21.6	5 42.2	27 45.9	22 22.7	18 32.1	29 37.6	8 54.4	0 3.5	1 25.7
13 Su	5 23 20	20 8 26	23 4 15	0♏22 49	29 17.8	7 13.2	27 31.8	23 7.5	18 42.6	29 32.7	8 56.9	0 2.3	1 24.5
14 M	5 27 17	21 9 29	7♏45 47	15 12 24	29 11.3	8 44.5	27 20.2	23 52.3	18 53.3	29 27.8	8 59.5	0 1.1	1 23.3
15 Tu	5 31 13	22 10 33	22 41 45	0♐12 44	29 2.4	10 16.0	27 11.0	24 37.2	19 4.1	29 22.9	9 2.2	29♋59.8	1 22.1
16 W	5 35 10	23 11 38	7♐44 9	15 14 45	28 52.1	11 47.8	27 4.4	25 22.2	19 15.0	29 18.0	9 4.8	29 58.6	1 20.9
17 Th	5 39 7	24 12 43	22 43 17	0♑ 8 33	28 41.6	13 19.8	27 0.3	26 7.2	19 26.0	29 13.1	9 7.5	29 57.3	1 19.7
18 F	5 43 3	25 13 49	7♑29 27	14 45 3	28 32.2	14 52.0	26D 58.6	26 52.2	19 37.1	29 8.2	9 10.3	29 56.0	1 18.5
19 Sa	5 47 0	26 14 56	21 54 35	28 57 32	28 24.8	16 24.3	26 59.3	27 37.3	19 48.3	29 3.2	9 13.0	29 54.6	1 17.4
20 Su	5 50 56	27 16 3	5♒53 33	12♒42 28	28 19.9	17 56.9	27 2.5	28 22.4	19 59.6	28 58.2	9 15.8	29 53.3	1 16.2
21 M	5 54 53	28 17 10	19 24 20	25 59 22	28D 17.6	19 29.7	27 8.0	29 7.6	20 11.0	28 53.3	9 18.6	29 51.9	1 14.9
22 Tu	5 58 49	29 18 18	2♓27 52	8♓50 18	28 17.3	21 2.6	27 15.8	29 52.8	20 22.5	28 48.3	9 21.5	29 50.5	1 13.7
23 W	6 2 46	0♑19 25	15 7 11	21 19 7	28 18.1	22 35.8	27 25.9	0♑38.1	20 34.1	28 43.3	9 24.4	29 49.1	1 12.5
24 Th	6 6 42	1 20 33	27 26 43	3♈30 39	28R 18.9	24 9.2	27 38.2	1 23.4	20 45.7	28 38.4	9 27.3	29 47.7	1 11.3
25 F	6 10 39	2 21 41	9♈31 35	15 30 10	28 18.6	25 42.7	27 52.6	2 8.7	20 57.5	28 33.4	9 30.2	29 46.2	1 10.1
26 Sa	6 14 36	3 22 49	21 27 2	27 22 47	28 16.6	27 16.5	28 9.1	2 54.1	21 9.4	28 28.5	9 33.2	29 44.7	1 8.9
27 Su	6 18 32	4 23 57	3♉18 2	9♉13 18	28 12.2	28 50.6	28 27.7	3 39.6	21 21.3	28 23.5	9 36.2	29 43.3	1 7.7
28 M	6 22 29	5 25 5	15 9 5	21 5 50	28 5.6	0♑24.9	28 48.2	4 25.1	21 33.4	28 18.6	9 39.2	29 41.8	1 6.5
29 Tu	6 26 25	6 26 14	27 3 56	3♊ 3 43	27 57.1	1 59.4	29 10.6	5 10.6	21 45.5	28 13.7	9 42.3	29 40.2	1 5.3
30 W	6 30 22	7 27 22	9♊ 5 30	15 9 29	27 47.4	3 34.3	29 34.8	5 56.2	21 57.7	28 8.9	9 45.3	29 38.7	1 4.1
31 Th	6 34 18	8 28 30	21 15 52	27 24 47	27 37.3	5 9.4	0♐ 0.8	6 41.8	22 10.0	28 4.0	9 48.4	29 37.2	1 2.9

Astro Data	Planet Ingress	Last Aspect	☽ Ingress	Last Aspect	☽ Ingress	☽ Phases & Eclipses	Astro Data
Dy Hr Mn	Dy Hr Mn	Dy Hr Mn	Dy Hr Mn	Dy Hr Mn	Dy Hr Mn	Dy Hr Mn	1 NOVEMBER 1914
♄☌♇ 1 8:48	♂ ♐ 11 10:47	31 18:17 ♃ ✶	♉ 2 4:08	1 2:21 ☿ ☍	♊ 1 22:53	2 23:48 ○ 9♉43	Julian Day # 5418
♆ R 3 13:17	☉ ♐ 23 3:20	4 6:23 ♂ ☍	♊ 4 16:44	3 8:55 ♃ △	♋ 4 10:19	10 23:36 ☽ 17♌44	Delta T 17.0 sec
♀ R 7 3:11		5 20:08 ♃ △	♋ 7 4:33	6 19:29 ♀ △	♌ 6 20:13	17 16:02 ● 24♏28	SVP 06♓26'50"
☽0S 13 17:35	☊ ♒ 3 11:47	9 11:57 ♂ △	♌ 9 14:36	9 3:47 ♄ ✶	♍ 9 4:03	24 13:38 ☽ 1♓27	Obliquity 23°27'10"
☿ D 16 14:28	♀ ♏ 5 23:20	10 23:36 ☉ □	♍ 11 21:42	11 8:35 ♄ □	♎ 11 9:09		⚷ Chiron 14♓37.8R
♃⚻♄ 25 4:15	♄ ♊ 7 6:48	13 8:37 ☉ ✶	♎ 14 1:10	13 10:35 ♄ △	♏ 13 11:23	2 18:20 ○ 9♊45	☽ Mean ☊ 2♓18.4
☽0N 26 12:15	☿ ♐ 8 4:53	15 1:02 ♃ △	♏ 16 1:36	15 11:38 ♆ △	♐ 15 11:40	10 11:31 ☽ 17♍35	
♃⚻♇ 30 10:32	♆ ♋ 14 20:37	17 16:02 ☉ ☌	♐ 18 0:42	17 10:27 ♄ ☍	♑ 17 11:46	17 2:35 ● 24♐19	1 DECEMBER 1914
	☉ ♑ 22 16:22	19 0:34 ♃ ✶	♑ 20 0:42	19 13:37 ♆ ☍	♒ 19 13:47	24 8:24 ☽ 1♈42	Julian Day # 5448
♄⚺♆ 4 20:02	♂ ♑ 22 3:49	22 1:48 ☉ ✶	♒ 22 3:42	21 18:53 ♂ ✶	♓ 21 19:25		Delta T 17.1 sec
☽0S 11 0:25	☿ ♑ 27 17:40	23 7:55 ♃ ☌	♓ 24 10:53	24 4:37 ♆ △	♈ 24 5:02		SVP 06♓26'45"
♀ D 18 4:29	♀ ♐ 30 23:15	25 11:27 ☿ △	♈ 26 21:44	26 16:46 ♆ □	♉ 26 17:19		Obliquity 23°27'09"
☽0N 23 18:41		28 6:38 ♃ ✶	♉ 29 10:22	29 5:13 ♆ ✶	♊ 29 5:53		⚷ Chiron 14♓21.0
				31 13:11 ♄ ☌	♋ 31 17:01		☽ Mean ☊ 0♓43.1

LONGITUDE JANUARY 1915

Day	Sid.Time	☉	0 hr ☽	Noon ☽	True ☊	☿	♀	♂	♃	♄	♅	♆	♇
1 F	6 38 15	9♑29 39	3♋36 19	9♋50 33	27♒27.9	6♑44.9	0♐28.6	7♑27.4	22♒22.4	27♊59.2	9♒51.6	29♋35.6	1♋ 1.7
2 Sa	6 42 12	10 30 47	16 7 30	22 27 11	27R20.0	8 20.7	0 58.0	8 13.1	22 34.8	27R54.4	9 54.7	29R34.0	1R 0.5
3 Su	6 46 8	11 31 56	28 49 38	5♌14 51	27 14.2	9 56.8	1 29.0	8 58.9	22 47.4	27 49.7	9 57.9	29 32.5	0 59.4
4 M	6 50 5	12 33 4	11♌42 51	18 13 39	27 10.8	11 33.3	2 1.5	9 44.6	22 60.0	27 44.9	10 1.1	29 30.9	0 58.2
5 Tu	6 54 1	13 34 13	24 47 18	1♍23 53	27D 9.5	13 10.1	2 35.5	10 30.5	23 12.6	27 40.3	10 4.3	29 29.2	0 57.0
6 W	6 57 58	14 35 21	8♍ 3 29	14 46 11	27 9.9	14 47.4	3 11.0	11 16.3	23 25.4	27 35.6	10 7.5	29 27.6	0 55.8
7 Th	7 1 54	15 36 30	21 32 6	28 21 20	27 11.3	16 25.0	3 47.8	12 2.2	23 38.2	27 31.0	10 10.7	29 26.0	0 54.7
8 F	7 5 51	16 37 39	5♎13 58	12♎10 4	27R12.7	18 3.1	4 25.9	12 48.2	23 51.1	27 26.5	10 14.0	29 24.4	0 53.5
9 Sa	7 9 47	17 38 48	19 9 38	26 12 38	27 13.2	19 41.5	5 5.3	13 34.2	24 4.0	27 21.9	10 17.3	29 22.7	0 52.4
10 Su	7 13 44	18 39 57	3♏18 54	10♏28 13	27 12.2	21 20.4	5 45.9	14 20.2	24 17.0	27 17.5	10 20.6	29 21.1	0 51.2
11 M	7 17 41	19 41 7	17 40 15	24 54 33	27 9.4	22 59.7	6 27.7	15 6.3	24 30.1	27 13.1	10 23.9	29 19.4	0 50.1
12 Tu	7 21 37	20 42 16	2♐10 34	9♐27 38	27 5.1	24 39.5	7 10.6	15 52.4	24 43.3	27 8.7	10 27.3	29 17.7	0 48.9
13 W	7 25 34	21 43 25	16 45 1	24 1 54	26 59.8	26 19.6	7 54.5	16 38.5	24 56.5	27 4.5	10 30.6	29 16.1	0 47.8
14 Th	7 29 30	22 44 34	1♑17 28	8♑30 51	26 54.2	28 0.2	8 39.5	17 24.7	25 9.8	27 0.2	10 34.0	29 14.4	0 46.7
15 F	7 33 27	23 45 43	15 41 16	22 47 57	26 49.1	29 41.2	9 25.5	18 10.9	25 23.1	26 56.1	10 37.4	29 12.7	0 45.6
16 Sa	7 37 23	24 46 52	29 50 16	6♒47 40	26 45.2	1♒22.5	10 12.3	18 57.2	25 36.5	26 52.0	10 40.8	29 11.0	0 44.5
17 Su	7 41 20	25 47 59	13♒39 44	20 26 11	26D42.8	3 4.2	11 0.1	19 43.5	25 49.9	26 47.9	10 44.2	29 9.3	0 43.4
18 M	7 45 16	26 49 7	27 6 52	3♓41 47	26 42.1	4 46.2	11 48.8	20 29.8	26 3.4	26 44.0	10 47.6	29 7.6	0 42.4
19 Tu	7 49 13	27 50 13	10♓11 1	16 34 49	26 42.8	6 28.4	12 38.2	21 16.1	26 17.0	26 40.1	10 51.0	29 5.9	0 41.3
20 W	7 53 10	28 51 18	22 53 28	29 7 24	26 44.3	8 10.8	13 28.5	22 2.5	26 30.6	26 36.3	10 54.4	29 4.2	0 40.3
21 Th	7 57 6	29 52 23	5♈17 3	11♈22 58	26 46.1	9 53.3	14 19.5	22 48.9	26 44.2	26 32.5	10 57.9	29 2.5	0 39.2
22 F	8 1 3	0♒53 27	17 25 42	23 25 50	26 47.7	11 35.8	15 11.3	23 35.4	26 57.9	26 28.9	11 1.3	29 0.8	0 38.2
23 Sa	8 4 59	1 54 30	29 23 59	5♉20 46	26R48.4	13 18.1	16 3.8	24 21.8	27 11.7	26 25.3	11 4.8	28 59.1	0 37.2
24 Su	8 8 56	2 55 31	11♉16 49	17 12 43	26 48.1	15 0.2	16 56.9	25 8.3	27 25.4	26 21.8	11 8.3	28 57.4	0 36.2
25 M	8 12 52	3 56 32	23 9 3	29 6 23	26 46.7	16 41.8	17 50.7	25 54.9	27 39.3	26 18.4	11 11.8	28 55.7	0 35.2
26 Tu	8 16 49	4 57 32	5♊ 5 15	11♊ 6 9	26 44.2	18 22.7	18 45.2	26 41.4	27 53.1	26 15.1	11 15.2	28 54.1	0 34.2
27 W	8 20 45	5 58 31	17 9 30	23 15 43	26 41.2	20 2.7	19 40.2	27 28.0	28 7.1	26 11.9	11 18.7	28 52.4	0 33.3
28 Th	8 24 42	6 59 28	29 25 9	5♋38 2	26 37.8	21 41.5	20 35.9	28 14.6	28 21.0	26 8.7	11 22.2	28 50.7	0 32.3
29 F	8 28 39	8 0 25	11♋54 38	18 15 4	26 34.7	23 18.7	21 32.1	29 1.3	28 35.0	26 5.7	11 25.7	28 49.0	0 31.4
30 Sa	8 32 35	9 1 21	24 39 27	1♌ 7 47	26 32.2	24 54.0	22 28.8	29 47.9	28 49.0	26 2.7	11 29.2	28 47.4	0 30.5
31 Su	8 36 32	10 2 15	7♌40 3	14 16 9	26 30.4	26 26.8	23 26.1	0♒34.6	29 3.1	25 59.9	11 32.7	28 45.7	0 29.6

LONGITUDE FEBRUARY 1915

Day	Sid.Time	☉	0 hr ☽	Noon ☽	True ☊	☿	♀	♂	♃	♄	♅	♆	♇
1 M	8 40 28	11♒ 3 8	20♌55 58	27♌39 17	26♒29.6	27♒56.8	24♐23.9	1♒21.3	29♒17.1	25♊57.1	11♒36.2	28♋44.1	0♋28.7
2 Tu	8 44 25	12 4 1	4♍25 55	11♍15 37	26D29.7	29 23.3	25 22.2	2 8.1	29 31.3	25R54.4	11 39.7	28R42.4	0R27.8
3 W	8 48 21	13 4 52	18 8 8	25 3 12	26 30.4	0♓45.6	26 20.9	2 54.8	29 45.4	25 51.9	11 43.2	28 40.8	0 27.0
4 Th	8 52 18	14 5 42	2♎ 0 33	8♎59 53	26 31.4	2 3.3	27 20.1	3 41.6	29 59.6	25 49.4	11 46.7	28 39.1	0 26.1
5 F	8 56 14	15 6 32	16 0 59	23 3 33	26 32.5	3 15.4	28 19.8	4 28.4	0♓13.8	25 47.0	11 50.2	28 37.5	0 25.3
6 Sa	9 0 11	16 7 20	0♏ 7 20	7♏12 5	26 33.2	4 21.3	29 19.8	5 15.3	0 28.0	25 44.7	11 53.7	28 35.9	0 24.5
7 Su	9 4 8	17 8 8	14 17 32	21 23 25	26R33.6	5 20.2	0♑20.3	6 2.1	0 42.3	25 42.6	11 57.2	28 34.3	0 23.7
8 M	9 8 4	18 8 55	28 29 28	5♐35 23	26 33.5	6 11.3	1 21.2	6 49.0	0 56.5	25 40.5	12 0.7	28 32.7	0 22.9
9 Tu	9 12 1	19 9 41	12♐40 52	19 45 34	26 33.0	6 53.9	2 22.4	7 35.9	1 10.8	25 38.5	12 4.2	28 31.2	0 22.2
10 W	9 15 57	20 10 25	26 49 10	3♑51 17	26 32.3	7 27.3	3 24.0	8 22.9	1 25.2	25 36.7	12 7.6	28 29.6	0 21.5
11 Th	9 19 54	21 11 9	10♑51 34	17 49 39	26 31.6	7 50.9	4 26.0	9 9.8	1 39.5	25 34.9	12 11.1	28 28.1	0 20.8
12 F	9 23 50	22 11 52	24 45 8	1♒37 40	26 31.0	8R 4.2	5 28.3	9 56.8	1 53.9	25 33.3	12 14.6	28 26.5	0 20.1
13 Sa	9 27 47	23 12 34	8♒26 56	15 12 39	26 30.7	8 7.0	6 30.9	10 43.8	2 8.3	25 31.8	12 18.0	28 25.0	0 19.4
14 Su	9 31 43	24 13 14	21 54 31	28 32 22	26D30.5	7 59.3	7 33.8	11 30.8	2 22.7	25 30.4	12 21.5	28 23.5	0 18.7
15 M	9 35 40	25 13 52	5♓ 6 4	11♓35 30	26 30.5	7 41.0	8 37.0	12 17.8	2 37.1	25 29.0	12 24.9	28 22.0	0 18.1
16 Tu	9 39 37	26 14 29	18 0 42	24 21 41	26R30.6	7 12.6	9 40.5	13 4.8	2 51.5	25 27.8	12 28.4	28 20.6	0 17.5
17 W	9 43 33	27 15 4	0♈38 38	6♈51 43	26 30.6	6 34.9	10 44.3	13 51.9	3 5.9	25 26.7	12 31.8	28 19.1	0 16.9
18 Th	9 47 30	28 15 38	13 1 12	19 7 25	26 30.4	5 48.8	11 48.3	14 39.0	3 20.4	25 25.8	12 35.2	28 17.7	0 16.3
19 F	9 51 26	29 16 10	25 10 45	1♉11 37	26 30.1	4 55.5	12 52.6	15 26.0	3 34.8	25 24.9	12 38.6	28 16.3	0 15.8
20 Sa	9 55 23	0♓16 40	7♉10 31	13 7 56	26 29.7	3 56.5	13 57.1	16 13.1	3 49.3	25 24.1	12 42.0	28 14.9	0 15.2
21 Su	9 59 19	1 17 9	19 4 26	25 0 35	26 29.4	2 53.3	15 1.9	17 0.2	4 3.7	25 23.5	12 45.3	28 13.5	0 14.7
22 M	10 3 16	2 17 35	0♊56 57	6♊54 7	26D29.2	1 47.7	16 6.9	17 47.3	4 18.2	25 23.0	12 48.7	28 12.2	0 14.2
23 Tu	10 7 12	3 18 0	12 52 42	18 53 17	26 29.4	0 41.3	17 12.1	18 34.4	4 32.7	25 22.6	12 52.0	28 10.8	0 13.7
24 W	10 11 9	4 18 23	24 56 26	1♋ 2 41	26 29.8	29♒35.8	18 17.6	19 21.5	4 47.1	25 22.3	12 55.4	28 9.5	0 13.3
25 Th	10 15 6	5 18 44	7♋12 33	13 26 31	26 30.6	28 32.8	19 23.2	20 8.7	5 1.6	25 22.1	12 58.7	28 8.2	0 12.9
26 F	10 19 2	6 19 3	19 44 59	26 8 18	26 31.6	27 33.4	20 29.1	20 55.8	5 16.1	25D22.0	13 2.0	28 7.0	0 12.5
27 Sa	10 22 59	7 19 20	2♌36 44	9♌10 27	26 32.5	26 38.8	21 35.2	21 42.9	5 30.6	25 22.0	13 5.2	28 5.7	0 12.1
28 Su	10 26 55	8 19 35	15 49 33	22 34 1	26R33.2	25 49.9	22 41.4	22 30.1	5 45.0	25 22.2	13 8.5	28 4.5	0 11.7

Astro Data	Planet Ingress	Last Aspect	☽ Ingress	Last Aspect	☽ Ingress	☽ Phases & Eclipses	Astro Data
Dy Hr Mn	Dy Hr Mn	Dy Hr Mn	Dy Hr Mn	Dy Hr Mn	Dy Hr Mn	Dy Hr Mn	1 JANUARY 1915
☽0S 7 5:14	☿ ♒ 15 4:28	3 1:20 ♆ ☌	♌ 3 2:12	1 15:10 ♃ ☍	♍ 1 16:10	1 12:20 ○ 10♋01	Julian Day # 5479
☽0N 20 2:51	☉ ♒ 21 3:00	5 5:13 ♄ ⚹	♍ 5 9:28	3 18:14 ♆ ⚹	♎ 3 20:32	8 21:12 ☽ 17♎32	Delta T 17.2 sec
♃△♄ 20 7:52	♂ ♒ 30 6:12	7 13:52 ♆ ⚹	♎ 7 14:53	5 22:33 ♀ ⚹	♏ 5 23:48	15 14:42 ● 24♑23	SVP 06♓26'39"
♄Q♅ 25 23:32		9 17:20 ♆ □	♏ 9 18:25	8 0:06 ♆ △	♐ 8 2:33	23 5:32 ☽ 2♉09	Obliquity 23°27'08"
♃⚻♆ 29 21:30	☿ ♓ 2 10:33	11 19:15 ♆ △	♐ 11 20:25	9 21:57 ♄ ☍	♑ 10 5:25	31 4:41 ○ 10♌14	⚷ Chiron 14♓56.3
	♃ ♓ 4 0:44	13 16:56 ♄ ☍	♑ 13 21:52	12 6:25 ♆ ☍	♒ 12 9:09	31 4:57 • A 0.045	☽ Mean ☊ 29♒04.7
☽0S 3 10:42	♀ ♑ 6 15:57	15 22:53 ♆ ☍	♒ 16 0:17	14 6:29 ♄ △	♓ 14 14:40		
♃△♇ 5 18:24	☉ ♓ 19 17:23	17 23:19 ♄ △	♓ 18 5:14	16 19:33 ♆ △	♈ 16 22:46	7 5:11 ☽ 17♏21	1 FEBRUARY 1915
☿ R 12 18:23	☿ ♒ 23 15:04	20 12:31 ☉ ⚹	♈ 20 13:42	19 8:54 ☉ ⚹	♉ 19 9:37	14 4:31 ● 24♒25	Julian Day # 5510
☽0N 16 11:53		22 23:10 ♆ □	♉ 23 1:13	21 18:28 ♆ ⚹	♊ 21 22:05	14 4:33:02 • A 2'03"	Delta T 17.3 sec
♄ D 26 3:25		25 11:37 ♆ ⚹	♊ 25 13:48	24 8:26 ☿ △	♋ 24 9:57	22 2:58 ☽ 2♊25	SVP 06♓26'33"
		27 21:53 ♃ △	♋ 28 1:08	26 15:39 ♆ ☌	♌ 26 19:11		Obliquity 23°27'09"
		30 7:39 ♆ ☌	♌ 30 9:55				⚷ Chiron 16♓17.1
							☽ Mean ☊ 27♒26.2

MARCH 1915 LONGITUDE

Day	Sid.Time	☉	0 hr ☽	Noon ☽	True ☊	☿	♀	♂	♃	♄	♅	♆	♇
1 M	10 30 52	9♓19 48	29♌23 42	6♍18 22	26♒33.4	25♒ 7.4	23♑47.9	23♒17.2	5♓59.5	25♊22.5	13♒11.7	28♋ 3.3	0♋11.4
2 Tu	10 34 48	10 19 59	13♍17 39	20 21 6	26R32.9	24R31.5	24 54.5	24 4.4	6 13.9	25 22.8	13 14.9	28R 2.1	0R11.1
3 W	10 38 45	11 20 9	27 28 10	4♎38 14	26 31.6	24 2.6	26 1.3	24 51.5	6 28.4	25 23.3	13 18.1	28 1.0	0 10.8
4 Th	10 42 41	12 20 16	11♎50 36	19 4 34	26 29.8	23 40.7	27 8.3	25 38.7	6 42.8	25 23.9	13 21.3	27 59.9	0 10.5
5 F	10 46 38	13 20 23	26 19 25	3♏34 27	26 27.5	23 25.8	28 15.5	26 25.9	6 57.2	25 24.6	13 24.5	27 58.8	0 10.2
6 Sa	10 50 35	14 20 27	10♏48 59	18 2 25	26 25.4	23D17.7	29 22.8	27 13.0	7 11.7	25 25.5	13 27.6	27 57.7	0 10.0
7 Su	10 54 31	15 20 30	25 14 13	2♐23 55	26 23.6	23 16.2	0♒30.2	28 0.2	7 26.1	25 26.4	13 30.7	27 56.6	0 9.8
8 M	10 58 28	16 20 31	9♐31 9	16 35 38	26D22.7	23 20.9	1 37.9	28 47.4	7 40.5	25 27.5	13 33.8	27 55.6	0 9.6
9 Tu	11 2 24	17 20 31	23 37 7	0♑35 30	26 22.7	23 31.7	2 45.7	29 34.6	7 54.9	25 28.6	13 36.8	27 54.6	0 9.5
10 W	11 6 21	18 20 30	7♑30 39	14 22 33	26 23.5	23 48.1	3 53.6	0♓21.7	8 9.2	25 29.9	13 39.9	27 53.7	0 9.3
11 Th	11 10 17	19 20 26	21 11 11	27 56 35	26 24.9	24 9.9	5 1.6	1 8.9	8 23.6	25 31.3	13 42.9	27 52.7	0 9.2
12 F	11 14 14	20 20 21	4♒38 45	11♒17 43	26 26.4	24 36.6	6 9.8	1 56.1	8 37.9	25 32.8	13 45.9	27 51.8	0 9.1
13 Sa	11 18 10	21 20 15	17 53 33	24 26 16	26R27.5	25 8.0	7 18.2	2 43.3	8 52.2	25 34.4	13 48.8	27 51.0	0 9.1
14 Su	11 22 7	22 20 6	0♓55 52	7♓22 25	26 27.7	25 43.9	8 26.6	3 30.5	9 6.5	25 36.1	13 51.8	27 50.1	0 9.0
15 M	11 26 4	23 19 55	13 45 56	20 6 26	26 26.6	26 23.8	9 35.2	4 17.6	9 20.8	25 37.9	13 54.7	27 49.3	0D 9.0
16 Tu	11 30 0	24 19 43	26 23 57	2♈38 34	26 24.0	27 7.6	10 43.8	5 4.8	9 35.0	25 39.8	13 57.6	27 48.5	0 9.0
17 W	11 33 57	25 19 28	8♈50 20	14 59 23	26 20.0	27 54.9	11 52.6	5 52.0	9 49.3	25 41.9	14 0.4	27 47.7	0 9.0
18 Th	11 37 53	26 19 12	21 5 50	27 9 52	26 14.9	28 45.7	13 1.5	6 39.1	10 3.5	25 44.0	14 3.2	27 47.0	0 9.1
19 F	11 41 50	27 18 53	3♉11 43	9♉11 39	26 9.3	29 39.6	14 10.5	7 26.2	10 17.6	25 46.3	14 6.0	27 46.3	0 9.1
20 Sa	11 45 46	28 18 32	15 9 58	21 7 1	26 3.7	0♓36.4	15 19.5	8 13.4	10 31.8	25 48.6	14 8.7	27 45.6	0 9.2
21 Su	11 49 43	29 18 9	27 3 13	2♊59 2	25 58.8	1 36.1	16 28.7	9 0.5	10 45.9	25 51.1	14 11.5	27 45.0	0 9.3
22 M	11 53 39	0♈17 44	8♊54 55	14 51 26	25 55.1	2 38.4	17 38.0	9 47.6	10 60.0	25 53.7	14 14.2	27 44.4	0 9.5
23 Tu	11 57 36	1 17 17	20 49 6	26 48 32	25D52.9	3 43.2	18 47.3	10 34.7	11 14.0	25 56.3	14 16.8	27 43.8	0 9.6
24 W	12 1 33	2 16 47	2♋50 19	8♋55 4	25 52.3	4 50.4	19 56.8	11 21.8	11 28.0	25 59.1	14 19.4	27 43.2	0 9.8
25 Th	12 5 29	3 16 15	15 3 23	21 15 53	25 52.9	5 59.8	21 6.3	12 8.8	11 42.0	26 2.0	14 22.0	27 42.7	0 10.0
26 F	12 9 26	4 15 40	27 33 8	3♌55 41	25 54.4	7 11.4	22 15.9	12 55.9	11 56.0	26 5.0	14 24.6	27 42.3	0 10.3
27 Sa	12 13 22	5 15 4	10♌23 58	16 58 25	25 55.9	8 25.1	23 25.6	13 42.9	12 9.9	26 8.0	14 27.1	27 41.8	0 10.5
28 Su	12 17 19	6 14 25	23 39 19	0♍26 51	25R56.7	9 40.7	24 35.4	14 30.0	12 23.7	26 11.2	14 29.6	27 41.4	0 10.8
29 M	12 21 15	7 13 43	7♍21 3	14 21 48	25 56.2	10 58.2	25 45.3	15 17.0	12 37.5	26 14.5	14 32.0	27 41.0	0 11.1
30 Tu	12 25 12	8 13 0	21 28 47	28 41 33	25 53.8	12 17.5	26 55.2	16 3.9	12 51.3	26 17.9	14 34.5	27 40.6	0 11.4
31 W	12 29 8	9 12 14	5♎59 25	13♎21 36	25 49.4	13 38.7	28 5.2	16 50.9	13 5.1	26 21.3	14 36.8	27 40.3	0 11.8

APRIL 1915 LONGITUDE

Day	Sid.Time	☉	0 hr ☽	Noon ☽	True ☊	☿	♀	♂	♃	♄	♅	♆	♇
1 Th	12 33 5	10♈11 26	20♎47 6	28♎14 53	25♒43.4	15♓ 1.6	29♒15.3	17♓37.9	13♓18.7	26♊24.9	14♒39.2	27♋40.0	0♋12.1
2 F	12 37 1	11 10 37	5♏43 47	13♏12 41	25R36.5	16 26.1	0♓25.4	18 24.8	13 32.4	26 28.5	14 41.5	27R39.8	0 12.5
3 Sa	12 40 58	12 9 45	20 40 27	28 6 2	25 29.5	17 52.4	1 35.6	19 11.7	13 46.0	26 32.3	14 43.7	27 39.6	0 12.9
4 Su	12 44 55	13 8 52	5♐28 32	12♐47 10	25 23.5	19 20.2	2 45.9	19 58.6	13 59.6	26 36.1	14 45.9	27 39.4	0 13.4
5 M	12 48 51	14 7 57	20 1 21	27 10 37	25 19.1	20 49.7	3 56.3	20 45.5	14 13.1	26 40.1	14 48.1	27 39.2	0 13.8
6 Tu	12 52 48	15 7 0	4♑14 42	11♑13 29	25D16.8	22 20.7	5 6.7	21 32.4	14 26.5	26 44.1	14 50.3	27 39.1	0 14.3
7 W	12 56 44	16 6 1	18 6 58	24 55 16	25 16.2	23 53.3	6 17.2	22 19.2	14 40.0	26 48.2	14 52.4	27 39.0	0 14.8
8 Th	13 0 41	17 5 1	1♒38 35	8♒17 12	25 16.9	25 27.5	7 27.8	23 6.1	14 53.3	26 52.4	14 54.5	27 39.0	0 15.3
9 F	13 4 37	18 3 59	14 51 23	21 21 28	25R17.9	27 3.2	8 38.4	23 52.9	15 6.6	26 56.7	14 56.5	27D38.9	0 15.9
10 Sa	13 8 34	19 2 55	27 47 47	4♓10 39	25 18.3	28 40.4	9 49.1	24 39.7	15 19.9	27 1.1	14 58.5	27 39.0	0 16.5
11 Su	13 12 30	20 1 49	10♓30 20	16 47 9	25 17.1	0♈19.2	10 59.8	25 26.4	15 33.1	27 5.5	15 0.4	27 39.0	0 17.0
12 M	13 16 27	21 0 41	23 1 18	29 13 2	25 13.6	1 59.5	12 10.6	26 13.2	15 46.2	27 10.1	15 2.3	27 39.1	0 17.6
13 Tu	13 20 24	21 59 32	5♈22 32	11♈29 57	25 7.5	3 41.4	13 21.4	26 59.9	15 59.3	27 14.7	15 4.2	27 39.2	0 18.3
14 W	13 24 20	22 58 20	17 35 26	23 39 7	24 58.9	5 24.8	14 32.2	27 46.5	16 12.3	27 19.4	15 6.0	27 39.3	0 18.9
15 Th	13 28 17	23 57 7	29 41 9	5♉41 40	24 48.5	7 9.8	15 43.2	28 33.2	16 25.2	27 24.2	15 7.7	27 39.5	0 19.6
16 F	13 32 13	24 55 52	11♉40 48	17 38 44	24 36.9	8 56.3	16 54.1	29 19.8	16 38.1	27 29.1	15 9.5	27 39.7	0 20.3
17 Sa	13 36 10	25 54 34	23 35 39	29 31 49	24 25.2	10 44.4	18 5.1	0♈ 6.4	16 50.9	27 34.1	15 11.1	27 40.0	0 21.0
18 Su	13 40 6	26 53 15	5♊27 28	11♊22 56	24 14.5	12 34.1	19 16.2	0 53.0	17 3.7	27 39.1	15 12.8	27 40.3	0 21.7
19 M	13 44 3	27 51 53	17 18 34	23 14 47	24 5.6	14 25.4	20 27.3	1 39.5	17 16.4	27 44.2	15 14.4	27 40.6	0 22.5
20 Tu	13 47 59	28 50 30	29 12 2	5♋10 48	23 59.0	16 18.3	21 38.4	2 26.0	17 29.0	27 49.4	15 15.9	27 40.9	0 23.2
21 W	13 51 56	29 49 4	11♋11 39	17 15 7	23 55.0	18 12.7	22 49.5	3 12.5	17 41.5	27 54.7	15 17.4	27 41.3	0 24.0
22 Th	13 55 53	0♉47 36	23 21 50	29 32 24	23D53.2	20 8.8	24 0.7	3 58.9	17 54.0	28 0.1	15 18.9	27 41.7	0 24.8
23 F	13 59 49	1 46 6	5♌47 27	12♌ 7 36	23 53.0	22 6.4	25 12.0	4 45.3	18 6.4	28 5.5	15 20.3	27 42.2	0 25.7
24 Sa	14 3 46	2 44 34	18 33 27	25 5 32	23R53.4	24 5.6	26 23.2	5 31.7	18 18.7	28 11.0	15 21.6	27 42.6	0 26.5
25 Su	14 7 42	3 42 59	1♍44 19	8♍30 12	23 53.3	26 6.3	27 34.5	6 18.0	18 31.0	28 16.5	15 22.9	27 43.2	0 27.4
26 M	14 11 39	4 41 22	15 23 24	22 24 2	23 51.5	28 8.5	28 45.9	7 4.3	18 43.1	28 22.1	15 24.2	27 43.7	0 28.2
27 Tu	14 15 35	5 39 44	29 31 59	6♎46 57	23 47.5	0♉12.0	29 57.2	7 50.5	18 55.2	28 27.8	15 25.4	27 44.3	0 29.1
28 W	14 19 32	6 38 3	14♎ 8 23	21 35 32	23 40.9	2 16.9	1♈ 8.6	8 36.7	19 7.2	28 33.6	15 26.6	27 44.9	0 30.1
29 Th	14 23 28	7 36 20	29 7 24	6♏42 49	23 32.0	4 23.1	2 20.1	9 22.9	19 19.2	28 39.4	15 27.7	27 45.5	0 31.0
30 F	14 27 25	8 34 35	14♏20 27	21 58 54	23 21.7	6 30.3	3 31.5	10 9.1	19 31.0	28 45.3	15 28.8	27 46.2	0 31.9

Astro Data Dy Hr Mn	Planet Ingress Dy Hr Mn	Last Aspect Dy Hr Mn	☽ Ingress Dy Hr Mn	Last Aspect Dy Hr Mn	☽ Ingress Dy Hr Mn	☽ Phases & Eclipses Dy Hr Mn	Astro Data
☽0S 2 18:42	♀ ♒ 6 13:15	28 16:57 ♄ ⚹	♍ 1 1:03	1 14:46 ♀ △	♏ 1 14:49	1 18:32 ○ 10♍06	1 MARCH 1915
☿ D 6 17:42	♂ ♓ 9 12:56	3 0:55 ♆ ⚹	♎ 3 4:15	3 11:17 ♆ △	♐ 3 15:05	1 18:19 ☍ A 0.555	Julian Day # 5538
☽0N 15 20:04	☿ ♓ 19 8:46	5 3:28 ♀ □	♏ 5 6:05	5 11:12 ♄ ☍	♑ 5 16:47	8 12:27 ☽ 16♐52	Delta T 17.4 sec
♇ D 15 12:31	☉ ♈ 21 16:51	7 4:54 ♂ □	♐ 7 7:58	7 16:51 ♆ ☍	♒ 7 21:03	15 19:42 ● 24♓09	SVP 06♓26'29"
♃ Q ♆ 29 5:52		9 10:52 ♂ ⚹	♑ 9 10:59	9 22:32 ♄ △	♓ 10 4:08	23 22:48 ☽ 2♋14	Obliquity 23°27'09"
☽0S 30 4:45	♀ ♓ 1 15:19	11 11:52 ♆ ☍	♒ 11 15:40	12 8:58 ♆ △	♈ 12 13:31	31 5:37 ○ 9♎26	⚷ Chiron 17♓53.8
♃ ⚻ ♅ 8 2:26	☿ ♈ 10 19:22	13 14:07 ♄ △	♓ 13 22:16	14 19:58 ♆ □	♉ 15 0:38		☽ Mean ☊ 25♒57.2
♆ D 9 3:32	♂ ♈ 16 20:42	16 2:42 ♆ △	♈ 16 6:55	17 8:14 ♆ ⚹	♊ 17 12:57	6 20:12 ☽ 15♑57	
☽0N 12 2:25	☉ ♉ 21 4:29	18 16:23 ☿ ⚹	♉ 18 17:38	19 23:13 ☉ ⚹	♋ 20 1:36	14 11:35 ● 23♈27	1 APRIL 1915
☿0N 13 23:42	☿ ♉ 26 21:40	21 4:58 ☉ ⚹	♊ 21 5:58	22 8:26 ♆ ☌	♌ 22 12:53	22 15:39 ☽ 1♌26	Julian Day # 5569
♄ ⚻ ♆ 18 5:40	♀ ♈ 27 0:56	23 10:18 ♄ ☌	♋ 23 18:22	24 17:44 ♄ ⚹	♍ 24 20:53	29 14:19 ○ 8♏11	Delta T 17.5 sec
♂0N 19 23:49		26 0:17 ♆ ☌	♌ 26 4:38	27 0:46 ♀ ☍	♎ 27 0:47		SVP 06♓26'26"
☽0S 26 14:53		28 4:31 ♄ ⚹	♍ 28 11:13	28 23:15 ♄ △	♏ 29 1:23		Obliquity 23°27'09"
♀0N 30 3:24		30 10:19 ♆ ⚹	♎ 30 14:10				⚷ Chiron 19♓46.5
							☽ Mean ☊ 24♒18.7

LONGITUDE — MAY 1915

Day	Sid.Time	☉	0 hr ☽	Noon ☽	True ☊	☿	♀	♂	♃	♄	♅	♆	♇
1 Sa	14 31 22	9♉32 49	29♏36 43	7♐12 32	23♒11.3	8♉38.4	4♈43.0	10♈55.2	19♓42.8	28♊51.3	15♒29.8	27♋46.9	0♋32.9
2 Su	14 35 18	10 31 1	14♐45 4	22 13 13	23R 1.9	10 47.3	5 54.6	11 41.2	19 54.4	28 57.3	15 30.8	27 47.7	0 33.9
3 M	14 39 15	11 29 12	29 36 3	6♑52 53	22 54.6	12 56.8	7 6.2	12 27.3	20 6.0	29 3.4	15 31.8	27 48.4	0 34.9
4 Tu	14 43 11	12 27 21	14♑ 3 16	21 6 55	22 49.8	15 6.6	8 17.8	13 13.3	20 17.5	29 9.5	15 32.6	27 49.2	0 35.9
5 W	14 47 8	13 25 29	28 3 49	4♒54 3	22 47.4	17 16.4	9 29.4	13 59.2	20 28.9	29 15.7	15 33.5	27 50.1	0 37.0
6 Th	14 51 4	14 23 35	11♒37 51	18 15 35	22 46.7	19 26.1	10 41.1	14 45.2	20 40.3	29 22.0	15 34.3	27 50.9	0 38.0
7 F	14 55 1	15 21 40	24 47 39	1♓14 32	22 46.8	21 35.2	11 52.8	15 31.0	20 51.5	29 28.3	15 35.0	27 51.8	0 39.1
8 Sa	14 58 57	16 19 43	7♓36 43	13 54 42	22 46.2	23 43.6	13 4.5	16 16.9	21 2.6	29 34.7	15 35.7	27 52.7	0 40.2
9 Su	15 2 54	17 17 45	20 8 59	26 20 0	22 43.9	25 50.9	14 16.3	17 2.7	21 13.6	29 41.1	15 36.3	27 53.7	0 41.3
10 M	15 6 51	18 15 46	2♈28 12	8♈33 59	22 39.2	27 56.9	15 28.0	17 48.4	21 24.6	29 47.6	15 36.9	27 54.7	0 42.4
11 Tu	15 10 47	19 13 45	14 37 41	20 39 39	22 31.5	0♊ 1.1	16 39.8	18 34.2	21 35.4	29 54.1	15 37.5	27 55.7	0 43.5
12 W	15 14 44	20 11 43	26 40 8	2♉39 23	22 21.0	2 3.5	17 51.7	19 19.8	21 46.1	0♋ 0.7	15 38.0	27 56.7	0 44.6
13 Th	15 18 40	21 9 39	8♉37 37	14 35 1	22 8.3	4 3.8	19 3.5	20 5.5	21 56.8	0 7.4	15 38.4	27 57.8	0 45.8
14 F	15 22 37	22 7 34	20 31 46	26 28 1	21 54.3	6 1.7	20 15.4	20 51.0	22 7.3	0 14.1	15 38.8	27 58.9	0 46.9
15 Sa	15 26 33	23 5 27	2♊23 56	8♊19 42	21 40.1	7 57.1	21 27.3	21 36.6	22 17.7	0 20.8	15 39.1	28 0.0	0 48.1
16 Su	15 30 30	24 3 19	14 15 31	20 11 35	21 26.9	9 49.8	22 39.2	22 22.1	22 28.0	0 27.6	15 39.4	28 1.2	0 49.3
17 M	15 34 26	25 1 10	26 8 9	2♋ 5 32	21 15.6	11 39.7	23 51.2	23 7.5	22 38.2	0 34.4	15 39.7	28 2.4	0 50.5
18 Tu	15 38 23	25 58 59	8♋ 4 2	14 4 1	21 7.0	13 26.7	25 3.2	23 52.9	22 48.3	0 41.3	15 39.9	28 3.6	0 51.8
19 W	15 42 20	26 56 46	20 5 55	26 10 11	21 1.3	15 10.6	26 15.1	24 38.2	22 58.3	0 48.2	15 40.0	28 4.9	0 53.0
20 Th	15 46 16	27 54 32	2♌17 20	8♌27 52	20 58.3	16 51.4	27 27.1	25 23.5	23 8.2	0 55.2	15 40.1	28 6.1	0 54.2
21 F	15 50 13	28 52 16	14 42 23	21 1 25	20D 57.3	18 29.1	28 39.2	26 8.7	23 17.9	1 2.2	15R 40.2	28 7.4	0 55.5
22 Sa	15 54 9	29 49 58	27 25 34	3♍55 23	20R 57.2	20 3.5	29 51.2	26 53.9	23 27.5	1 9.3	15 40.2	28 8.7	0 56.8
23 Su	15 58 6	0♊47 39	10♍31 23	17 14 1	20 57.0	21 34.6	1♉ 3.3	27 39.1	23 37.0	1 16.4	15 40.1	28 10.1	0 58.0
24 M	16 2 2	1 45 18	24 3 39	1♎ 0 31	20 55.5	23 2.4	2 15.3	28 24.1	23 46.4	1 23.5	15 40.0	28 11.5	0 59.3
25 Tu	16 5 59	2 42 55	8♎ 4 42	15 16 5	20 51.8	24 26.9	3 27.4	29 9.2	23 55.7	1 30.7	15 39.9	28 12.9	1 0.6
26 W	16 9 55	3 40 31	22 34 20	29 58 53	20 45.6	25 47.9	4 39.5	29 54.1	24 4.8	1 37.9	15 39.7	28 14.3	1 1.9
27 Th	16 13 52	4 38 6	7♏28 58	15♏ 3 34	20 37.2	27 5.5	5 51.7	0♉39.0	24 13.8	1 45.1	15 39.4	28 15.8	1 3.2
28 F	16 17 49	5 35 39	22 41 27	0♐21 16	20 27.3	28 19.6	7 3.8	1 23.9	24 22.7	1 52.4	15 39.1	28 17.2	1 4.6
29 Sa	16 21 45	6 33 12	8♐ 1 33	15 40 50	20 17.1	29 30.1	8 16.0	2 8.7	24 31.5	1 59.7	15 38.8	28 18.7	1 5.9
30 Su	16 25 42	7 30 43	23 17 42	0♑50 50	20 7.8	0♋37.0	9 28.2	2 53.5	24 40.1	2 7.0	15 38.4	28 20.3	1 7.3
31 M	16 29 38	8 28 13	8♑19 5	15 41 33	20 0.5	1 40.3	10 40.4	3 38.2	24 48.6	2 14.4	15 38.0	28 21.8	1 8.6

LONGITUDE — JUNE 1915

Day	Sid.Time	☉	0 hr ☽	Noon ☽	True ☊	☿	♀	♂	♃	♄	♅	♆	♇
1 Tu	16 33 35	9♊25 42	22♑57 31	0♒ 6 31	19♒55.6	2♋39.8	11♉52.7	4♉22.9	24♓57.0	2♋21.8	15♒37.5	28♋23.4	1♋10.0
2 W	16 37 31	10 23 11	7♒ 8 17	14 2 48	19D 53.2	3 35.6	13 4.9	5 7.5	25 5.2	2 29.2	15R 37.0	28 25.0	1 11.4
3 Th	16 41 28	11 20 38	20 50 10	27 30 40	19 52.6	4 27.4	14 17.2	5 52.1	25 13.3	2 36.7	15 36.4	28 26.6	1 12.7
4 F	16 45 25	12 18 5	4♓ 4 41	10♓32 40	19R 52.9	5 15.3	15 29.5	6 36.6	25 21.3	2 44.2	15 35.8	28 28.3	1 14.1
5 Sa	16 49 21	13 15 31	16 55 9	23 12 41	19 53.1	5 59.2	16 41.9	7 21.0	25 29.1	2 51.7	15 35.1	28 29.9	1 15.5
6 Su	16 53 18	14 12 57	29 25 50	5♈35 9	19 51.9	6 38.9	17 54.2	8 5.4	25 36.8	2 59.2	15 34.4	28 31.6	1 16.9
7 M	16 57 14	15 10 21	11♈41 13	17 44 31	19 48.8	7 14.5	19 6.6	8 49.7	25 44.3	3 6.8	15 33.6	28 33.3	1 18.3
8 Tu	17 1 11	16 7 46	23 45 35	29 44 50	19 43.2	7 45.7	20 19.0	9 34.0	25 51.7	3 14.3	15 32.8	28 35.0	1 19.7
9 W	17 5 7	17 5 9	5♉42 42	11♉39 33	19 35.1	8 12.6	21 31.4	10 18.2	25 59.0	3 21.9	15 31.9	28 36.8	1 21.1
10 Th	17 9 4	18 2 32	17 35 44	23 31 32	19 25.2	8 35.0	22 43.9	11 2.4	26 6.1	3 29.6	15 31.0	28 38.6	1 22.5
11 F	17 13 0	18 59 55	29 27 12	5♊23 0	19 14.1	8 53.0	23 56.3	11 46.5	26 13.0	3 37.2	15 30.1	28 40.3	1 24.0
12 Sa	17 16 57	19 57 16	11♊19 7	17 15 45	19 2.7	9 6.4	25 8.8	12 30.6	26 19.8	3 44.9	15 29.1	28 42.2	1 25.4
13 Su	17 20 54	20 54 37	23 13 6	29 11 21	18 52.2	9 15.2	26 21.3	13 14.6	26 26.5	3 52.6	15 28.1	28 44.0	1 26.8
14 M	17 24 50	21 51 58	5♋10 40	11♋11 17	18 43.3	9R 19.5	27 33.8	13 58.5	26 32.9	4 0.3	15 27.0	28 45.8	1 28.3
15 Tu	17 28 47	22 49 17	17 13 25	23 17 19	18 36.7	9 19.3	28 46.4	14 42.4	26 39.3	4 8.0	15 25.9	28 47.7	1 29.7
16 W	17 32 43	23 46 36	29 23 15	5♌31 33	18 32.5	9 14.5	29 58.9	15 26.2	26 45.4	4 15.7	15 24.7	28 49.6	1 31.2
17 Th	17 36 40	24 43 54	11♌42 32	17 56 37	18D 30.6	9 5.5	1♊11.5	16 9.9	26 51.4	4 23.4	15 23.5	28 51.5	1 32.6
18 F	17 40 36	25 41 12	24 14 9	0♍35 37	18 30.5	8 52.2	2 24.1	16 53.6	26 57.3	4 31.2	15 22.3	28 53.4	1 34.1
19 Sa	17 44 33	26 38 28	7♍ 1 24	13 31 57	18 31.4	8 34.9	3 36.7	17 37.2	27 2.9	4 39.0	15 21.0	28 55.3	1 35.5
20 Su	17 48 29	27 35 44	20 7 42	26 49 0	18R 32.3	8 13.8	4 49.3	18 20.7	27 8.5	4 46.7	15 19.7	28 57.3	1 37.0
21 M	17 52 26	28 32 59	3♎36 12	10♎29 30	18 32.4	7 49.4	6 2.0	19 4.2	27 13.8	4 54.5	15 18.3	28 59.2	1 38.4
22 Tu	17 56 23	29 30 13	17 29 4	24 34 51	18 31.0	7 21.8	7 14.7	19 47.6	27 19.0	5 2.3	15 16.9	29 1.2	1 39.9
23 W	18 0 19	0♋27 27	1♏46 41	9♏ 4 14	18 27.7	6 51.7	8 27.3	20 31.0	27 24.0	5 10.1	15 15.4	29 3.2	1 41.4
24 Th	18 4 16	1 24 39	16 26 56	23 54 4	18 22.6	6 19.4	9 40.0	21 14.3	27 28.8	5 17.9	15 14.0	29 5.2	1 42.8
25 F	18 8 12	2 21 52	1♐24 43	8♐57 47	18 16.4	5 45.4	10 52.8	21 57.5	27 33.5	5 25.7	15 12.5	29 7.2	1 44.3
26 Sa	18 12 9	3 19 4	16 32 6	24 6 25	18 9.7	5 10.4	12 5.5	22 40.6	27 38.0	5 33.5	15 10.9	29 9.3	1 45.7
27 Su	18 16 5	4 16 16	1♑39 26	9♑ 9 57	18 3.7	4 35.0	13 18.3	23 23.7	27 42.3	5 41.3	15 9.3	29 11.3	1 47.2
28 M	18 20 2	5 13 27	16 36 49	23 59 2	17 59.0	3 59.6	14 31.1	24 6.8	27 46.5	5 49.1	15 7.7	29 13.4	1 48.7
29 Tu	18 23 58	6 10 38	1♒15 46	8♒26 24	17 56.0	3 25.1	15 43.9	24 49.7	27 50.4	5 57.0	15 6.0	29 15.5	1 50.1
30 W	18 27 55	7 7 49	15 30 28	22 27 43	17D 54.9	2 51.8	16 56.8	25 32.7	27 54.2	6 4.8	15 4.3	29 17.5	1 51.6

Astro Data	Planet Ingress	Last Aspect	☽ Ingress	Last Aspect	☽ Ingress	☽ Phases & Eclipses
Dy Hr Mn	Dy Hr Mn	Dy Hr Mn	Dy Hr Mn	Dy Hr Mn	Dy Hr Mn	Dy Hr Mn
☽0N 9 7:24	☿ ♊ 10 23:47	30 21:07 ♆ △	♐ 1 0:37	1 9:07 ♆ ☍	♒ 1 11:49	6 5:22 ☽ 14♒37
♄□♅ 17 18:54	♄ ♋ 11 21:23	2 23:06 ♄ ☍	♑ 3 0:39	2 14:45 ♅ ☌	♓ 3 16:32	14 3:31 ● 22♉16
♄☌♇ 19 19:55	☉ ♊ 22 4:10	4 23:36 ♆ ☍	♒ 5 3:23	5 22:15 ♆ △	♈ 6 1:06	22 4:49 ☽ 0♍02
♅ R 21 10:48	♀ ♉ 22 2:56	7 8:46 ♄ △	♓ 7 9:41	8 9:41 ♆ □	♉ 8 12:30	28 21:33 ○ 6♐27
☽0S 23 23:21	♂ ♉ 26 3:08	9 18:42 ♄ □	♈ 9 19:10	10 22:25 ♆ ✶	♊ 11 1:06	
	☿ ♋ 29 10:34	12 2:34 ♆ □	♉ 12 6:40	13 6:32 ♃ □	♋ 13 13:38	4 16:32 ☽ 12♓58
☽0N 5 12:33		14 15:05 ♆ ✶	♊ 14 19:09	15 22:54 ♆ ☌	♌ 16 1:12	12 18:57 ● 20♊43
☿ R 14 10:38	♀ ♊ 16 0:21	16 18:53 ♀ ✶	♋ 17 7:47	18 2:58 ☉ ✶	♍ 18 10:53	20 14:24 ☽ 28♍10
☽0S 20 5:35	☉ ♋ 22 12:29	19 15:47 ♆ ☌	♌ 19 19:31	20 15:50 ♆ ✶	♎ 20 17:39	27 4:27 ○ 4♑27
		21 22:57 ♂ △	♍ 22 4:47	22 19:28 ♆ □	♏ 22 21:03	
		24 7:10 ♆ ✶	♎ 24 10:16	24 20:20 ♆ △	♐ 24 21:45	
		26 9:12 ♆ □	♏ 26 12:02	26 17:41 ♃ □	♑ 26 21:22	
		28 8:47 ♆ △	♐ 28 11:27	28 20:40 ♆ ☍	♒ 28 21:54	
		30 2:12 ♃ □	♑ 30 10:39			

Astro Data

1 MAY 1915
Julian Day # 5599
Delta T 17.5 sec
SVP 06♓26'23"
Obliquity 23°27'08"
⚷ Chiron 21♓20.8
☽ Mean ☊ 22♒43.4

1 JUNE 1915
Julian Day # 5630
Delta T 17.6 sec
SVP 06♓26'17"
Obliquity 23°27'08"
⚷ Chiron 22♓24.4
☽ Mean ☊ 21♒04.9

JULY 1915 LONGITUDE

Day	Sid.Time	☉	0 hr ☽	Noon ☽	True ☊	☿	♀	♂	♃	♄	♅	♆	♇
1 Th	18 31 52	8♋ 5 0	29♒18 5	6♓ 1 38	17♒55.4	2♋20.5	18♊ 9.6	26♉15.5	27♓57.9	6♋12.6	15♒ 2.6	29♋19.6	1♋53.0
2 F	18 35 48	9 2 11	12♓38 35	19 9 16	17 56.6	1R51.7	19 22.5	26 58.3	28 1.3	6 20.4	15R 0.9	29 21.7	1 54.5
3 Sa	18 39 45	9 59 23	25 34 5	1♈53 32	17 58.1	1 25.8	20 35.5	27 41.0	28 4.5	6 28.2	14 59.1	29 23.9	1 55.9
4 Su	18 43 41	10 56 34	8♈ 8 9	14 18 28	17R58.9	1 3.4	21 48.4	28 23.6	28 7.6	6 36.0	14 57.2	29 26.0	1 57.4
5 M	18 47 38	11 53 46	20 25 4	26 28 32	17 58.5	0 44.9	23 1.4	29 6.2	28 10.5	6 43.8	14 55.4	29 28.1	1 58.8
6 Tu	18 51 34	12 50 58	2♉29 26	8♉28 17	17 56.7	0 30.5	24 14.4	29 48.7	28 13.2	6 51.6	14 53.5	29 30.3	2 0.3
7 W	18 55 31	13 48 10	14 25 38	20 21 58	17 53.4	0 20.6	25 27.4	0♊31.2	28 15.7	6 59.4	14 51.6	29 32.4	2 1.7
8 Th	18 59 27	14 45 23	26 17 45	2♊13 23	17 48.9	0D 15.4	26 40.5	1 13.5	28 18.0	7 7.2	14 49.6	29 34.6	2 3.1
9 F	19 3 24	15 42 36	8♊ 9 18	14 5 48	17 43.6	0 15.2	27 53.5	1 55.8	28 20.1	7 14.9	14 47.7	29 36.7	2 4.6
10 Sa	19 7 21	16 39 50	20 3 14	26 1 53	17 38.0	0 20.1	29 6.6	2 38.1	28 22.0	7 22.7	14 45.7	29 38.9	2 6.0
11 Su	19 11 17	17 37 3	2♋ 1 58	8♋ 3 45	17 32.9	0 30.2	0♋19.8	3 20.2	28 23.8	7 30.4	14 43.6	29 41.1	2 7.4
12 M	19 15 14	18 34 17	14 7 25	20 13 8	17 28.7	0 45.5	1 32.9	4 2.3	28 25.3	7 38.2	14 41.6	29 43.3	2 8.8
13 Tu	19 19 10	19 31 31	26 21 6	2♌31 28	17 25.7	1 6.1	2 46.1	4 44.4	28 26.7	7 45.9	14 39.5	29 45.5	2 10.2
14 W	19 23 7	20 28 46	8♌44 25	15 0 5	17D 24.1	1 32.1	3 59.3	5 26.3	28 27.8	7 53.6	14 37.4	29 47.7	2 11.6
15 Th	19 27 3	21 26 0	21 18 40	27 40 21	17 23.9	2 3.4	5 12.5	6 8.2	28 28.8	8 1.3	14 35.3	29 49.9	2 13.0
16 F	19 31 0	22 23 15	4♍ 5 18	10♍33 43	17 24.7	2 40.0	6 25.8	6 50.0	28 29.6	8 8.9	14 33.2	29 52.1	2 14.4
17 Sa	19 34 57	23 20 30	17 5 49	23 41 47	17 26.1	3 21.9	7 39.1	7 31.7	28 30.1	8 16.6	14 31.0	29 54.3	2 15.8
18 Su	19 38 53	24 17 45	0♎21 50	7♎ 6 6	17 27.5	4 9.0	8 52.4	8 13.4	28 30.5	8 24.2	14 28.8	29 56.5	2 17.2
19 M	19 42 50	25 15 0	13 54 44	20 47 50	17R28.6	5 1.3	10 5.7	8 54.9	28R30.7	8 31.8	14 26.6	29 58.7	2 18.5
20 Tu	19 46 46	26 12 16	27 45 24	4♏47 25	17 29.0	5 58.7	11 19.0	9 36.4	28 30.7	8 39.4	14 24.4	0♌ 1.0	2 19.9
21 W	19 50 43	27 9 31	11♏53 43	19 4 3	17 28.4	7 1.2	12 32.4	10 17.9	28 30.5	8 47.0	14 22.1	0 3.2	2 21.2
22 Th	19 54 39	28 6 47	26 18 3	3♐35 14	17 27.0	8 8.7	13 45.8	10 59.2	28 30.1	8 54.5	14 19.9	0 5.4	2 22.6
23 F	19 58 36	29 4 3	10♐55 1	18 16 41	17 25.0	9 21.0	14 59.2	11 40.5	28 29.5	9 2.1	14 17.6	0 7.6	2 23.9
24 Sa	20 2 32	0♌ 1 20	25 39 26	3♑ 2 24	17 22.8	10 38.1	16 12.6	12 21.7	28 28.7	9 9.6	14 15.3	0 9.9	2 25.2
25 Su	20 6 29	0 58 37	10♑24 42	17 45 24	17 20.8	11 60.0	17 26.1	13 2.8	28 27.7	9 17.0	14 13.0	0 12.1	2 26.5
26 M	20 10 26	1 55 55	25 3 38	2♒18 34	17 19.3	13 26.3	18 39.6	13 43.8	28 26.5	9 24.5	14 10.7	0 14.3	2 27.9
27 Tu	20 14 22	2 53 13	9♒29 27	16 35 40	17D 18.5	14 57.1	19 53.1	14 24.8	28 25.1	9 31.9	14 8.4	0 16.6	2 29.1
28 W	20 18 19	3 50 32	23 36 41	0♓32 8	17 18.5	16 32.1	21 6.6	15 5.7	28 23.5	9 39.3	14 6.1	0 18.8	2 30.4
29 Th	20 22 15	4 47 51	7♓21 46	14 5 28	17 19.0	18 11.2	22 20.2	15 46.5	28 21.8	9 46.6	14 3.7	0 21.0	2 31.7
30 F	20 26 12	5 45 12	20 43 14	27 15 13	17 19.9	19 54.0	23 33.8	16 27.3	28 19.8	9 53.9	14 1.4	0 23.2	2 33.0
31 Sa	20 30 8	6 42 33	3♈41 38	10♈ 2 47	17 20.9	21 40.4	24 47.4	17 7.9	28 17.6	10 1.2	13 59.0	0 25.4	2 34.2

AUGUST 1915 LONGITUDE

Day	Sid.Time	☉	0 hr ☽	Noon ☽	True ☊	☿	♀	♂	♃	♄	♅	♆	♇
1 Su	20 34 5	7♌39 56	16♈19 5	22♈30 59	17♒21.7	23♋30.1	26♋ 1.1	17♊48.5	28♓15.3	10♋ 8.5	13♒56.6	0♌27.6	2♋35.4
2 M	20 38 1	8 37 20	28 38 58	4♉43 34	17R22.3	25 22.7	27 14.8	18 29.0	28R12.7	10 15.7	13R54.2	0 29.9	2 36.7
3 Tu	20 41 58	9 34 45	10♉45 20	16 44 50	17 22.4	27 17.9	28 28.5	19 9.5	28 10.0	10 22.9	13 51.9	0 32.1	2 37.9
4 W	20 45 55	10 32 11	22 42 39	28 39 20	17 22.2	29 15.5	29 42.2	19 49.8	28 7.1	10 30.0	13 49.5	0 34.3	2 39.1
5 Th	20 49 51	11 29 38	4♊35 28	10♊31 33	17 21.8	1♌14.9	0♌56.0	20 30.1	28 4.0	10 37.2	13 47.1	0 36.5	2 40.3
6 F	20 53 48	12 27 7	16 28 7	22 25 39	17 21.2	3 15.9	2 9.8	21 10.3	28 0.7	10 44.2	13 44.7	0 38.7	2 41.4
7 Sa	20 57 44	13 24 37	28 24 36	4♋25 23	17 20.7	5 18.1	3 23.6	21 50.4	27 57.2	10 51.3	13 42.3	0 40.8	2 42.6
8 Su	21 1 41	14 22 8	10♋28 23	16 33 56	17 20.2	7 21.2	4 37.5	22 30.5	27 53.5	10 58.3	13 39.9	0 43.0	2 43.8
9 M	21 5 37	15 19 40	22 42 18	28 53 45	17 20.0	9 24.8	5 51.3	23 10.4	27 49.7	11 5.2	13 37.5	0 45.2	2 44.9
10 Tu	21 9 34	16 17 14	5♌ 8 28	11♌26 37	17 19.8	11 28.6	7 5.3	23 50.3	27 45.7	11 12.1	13 35.1	0 47.4	2 46.0
11 W	21 13 30	17 14 48	17 48 18	24 13 35	17 19.8	13 32.4	8 19.2	24 30.1	27 41.5	11 19.0	13 32.7	0 49.5	2 47.1
12 Th	21 17 27	18 12 24	0♍42 30	7♍15 1	17 19.8	15 35.8	9 33.1	25 9.8	27 37.1	11 25.8	13 30.3	0 51.7	2 48.2
13 F	21 21 24	19 10 1	13 51 7	20 30 43	17 19.7	17 38.8	10 47.1	25 49.4	27 32.5	11 32.6	13 28.0	0 53.8	2 49.3
14 Sa	21 25 20	20 7 39	27 13 43	4♎ 0 0	17 19.5	19 41.1	12 1.1	26 28.9	27 27.8	11 39.3	13 25.6	0 55.9	2 50.3
15 Su	21 29 17	21 5 17	10♎49 27	17 41 54	17 19.1	21 42.5	13 15.1	27 8.3	27 22.9	11 45.9	13 23.2	0 58.1	2 51.4
16 M	21 33 13	22 2 57	24 37 11	1♏35 8	17 18.7	23 43.0	14 29.2	27 47.6	27 17.9	11 52.6	13 20.9	1 0.2	2 52.4
17 Tu	21 37 10	23 0 38	8♏35 31	15 38 10	17 18.3	25 42.4	15 43.3	28 26.9	27 12.7	11 59.1	13 18.5	1 2.3	2 53.4
18 W	21 41 6	23 58 20	22 42 48	29 49 11	17D 18.1	27 40.6	16 57.3	29 6.0	27 7.3	12 5.7	13 16.2	1 4.4	2 54.4
19 Th	21 45 3	24 56 4	6♐57 0	14♐ 5 57	17 18.3	29 37.5	18 11.5	29 45.1	27 1.8	12 12.1	13 13.8	1 6.4	2 55.4
20 F	21 48 59	25 53 48	21 15 39	28 25 44	17 18.7	1♍33.2	19 25.6	0♋24.1	26 56.1	12 18.5	13 11.5	1 8.5	2 56.4
21 Sa	21 52 56	26 51 33	5♑35 46	12♑45 17	17 19.5	3 27.6	20 39.7	1 3.0	26 50.3	12 24.9	13 9.2	1 10.6	2 57.3
22 Su	21 56 53	27 49 20	19 53 50	27 0 54	17 20.3	5 20.7	21 53.9	1 41.8	26 44.3	12 31.2	13 6.9	1 12.6	2 58.2
23 M	22 0 49	28 47 7	4♒ 5 59	11♒ 8 36	17R21.0	7 12.3	23 8.1	2 20.5	26 38.3	12 37.4	13 4.6	1 14.6	2 59.1
24 Tu	22 4 46	29 44 56	18 8 16	25 4 32	17 21.2	9 2.7	24 22.3	2 59.1	26 32.0	12 43.6	13 2.4	1 16.7	3 0.0
25 W	22 8 42	0♍42 47	1♓57 1	8♓45 22	17 20.8	10 51.7	25 36.6	3 37.6	26 25.7	12 49.7	13 0.1	1 18.7	3 0.9
26 Th	22 12 39	1 40 38	15 29 18	22 8 38	17 19.8	12 39.3	26 50.8	4 16.0	26 19.2	12 55.8	12 57.9	1 20.6	3 1.8
27 F	22 16 35	2 38 32	28 43 14	5♈13 4	17 18.0	14 25.6	28 5.1	4 54.3	26 12.6	13 1.8	12 55.7	1 22.6	3 2.6
28 Sa	22 20 32	3 36 26	11♈38 11	17 58 44	17 15.8	16 10.6	29 19.4	5 32.6	26 5.8	13 7.7	12 53.5	1 24.6	3 3.4
29 Su	22 24 28	4 34 23	24 14 54	0♉27 0	17 13.3	17 54.3	0♍33.7	6 10.7	25 59.0	13 13.6	12 51.3	1 26.5	3 4.2
30 M	22 28 25	5 32 22	6♉35 22	12 40 25	17 11.1	19 36.6	1 48.1	6 48.8	25 52.1	13 19.4	12 49.1	1 28.4	3 5.0
31 Tu	22 32 22	6 30 22	18 42 37	24 42 28	17 9.3	21 17.7	3 2.5	7 26.7	25 45.0	13 25.1	12 47.0	1 30.3	3 5.8

Astro Data	Dy Hr Mn
☽0N	2 19:20
☿ D	8 13:03
☽0S	17 10:38
♃ R	19 9:49
☽0N	30 3:58
☽0S	13 16:15
☽0N	26 13:23
♄⚻♅	26 6:09

Planet Ingress	Dy Hr Mn
♂ ♊	6 6:23
♀ ♋	10 17:31
♆ ♌	19 13:34
☉ ♌	23 23:26
☿ ♌	4 9:00
♀ ♌	4 5:47
☿ ♍	19 4:38
♂ ♋	19 9:10
☉ ♍	24 6:15
♀ ♍	28 13:06

Last Aspect Dy Hr Mn		☽ Ingress	Dy Hr Mn
30 18:20	♂ □	♓	1 1:14
3 7:16	♆ △	♈	3 8:24
5 18:01	♆ □	♉	5 19:01
8 6:40	♆ ⚹	♊	8 7:30
10 16:43	♃ □	♋	10 19:56
13 6:39	♆ ☌	♌	13 7:06
14 11:15	♅ ☍	♍	15 16:22
17 23:15	♆ ⚹	♎	17 23:21
19 21:08	☉ □	♏	20 3:50
22 3:38	♃ △	♐	22 6:06
24 4:35	♃ □	♑	24 7:03
26 5:35	♃ ⚹	♒	26 8:10
27 8:43	♂ △	♓	28 11:04
30 13:57	♃ ☌	♈	30 17:06

Last Aspect Dy Hr Mn		☽ Ingress	Dy Hr Mn
1 20:56	♀ □	♉	2 2:39
4 10:52	♃ ⚹	♊	4 14:43
6 23:05	♃ □	♋	7 3:11
9 9:53	♃ △	♌	9 14:08
11 13:11	♂ ⚹	♍	11 22:42
14 0:25	♃ ☍	♎	14 4:55
16 5:45	♂ △	♏	16 9:17
18 9:43	☿ □	♐	18 12:18
20 9:26	♃ □	♑	20 14:38
22 11:27	♃ ⚹	♒	22 17:03
24 11:50	♀ ☍	♓	24 20:35
26 19:26	♃ ☌	♈	27 2:21
28 2:50	♄ □	♉	29 11:08
31 13:57	♃ ⚹	♊	31 22:38

☽ Phases & Eclipses Dy Hr Mn	
4 5:54	☽ 11♈11
12 9:30	● 18♋57
19 21:08	☽ 26♎05
26 12:11	○ 2♒25
26 12:24	☍ A 0.354
2 21:27	☽ 9♉29
10 22:52	● 17♌12
10 22:52:06	☌ A 1'33"
18 2:17	☽ 24♏04
24 21:40	○ 0♓37
24 21:27	☍ A 0.575

Astro Data

1 JULY 1915
Julian Day # 5660
Delta T 17.7 sec
SVP 06♓26'11"
Obliquity 23°27'08"
⚷ Chiron 22♓41.1R
☽ Mean ☊ 19♒29.6

1 AUGUST 1915
Julian Day # 5691
Delta T 17.8 sec
SVP 06♓26'06"
Obliquity 23°27'08"
⚷ Chiron 22♓09.2R
☽ Mean ☊ 17♒51.1

LONGITUDE — SEPTEMBER 1915

Day	Sid.Time	☉	0 hr ☽	Noon ☽	True ☊	☿	♀	♂	♃	♄	♅	♆	♇
1 W	22 36 18	7♍28 25	0♊40 30	6♊37 19	17♒ 8.3	22♍57.6	4♍16.9	8♋ 4.6	25♓37.8	13♋30.8	12♒44.9	1♌32.2	3♋ 6.5
2 Th	22 40 15	8 26 29	12 33 29	18 29 35	17D 8.1	24 36.2	5 31.3	8 42.4	25R30.6	13 36.4	12R42.8	1 34.1	3 7.2
3 F	22 44 11	9 24 35	24 26 15	0♋24 3	17 8.9	26 13.5	6 45.7	9 20.0	25 23.3	13 41.9	12 40.8	1 35.9	3 7.9
4 Sa	22 48 8	10 22 43	6♋23 34	12 25 23	17 10.3	27 49.6	8 0.2	9 57.6	25 15.8	13 47.4	12 38.7	1 37.8	3 8.6
5 Su	22 52 4	11 20 53	18 30 0	24 37 55	17 12.0	29 24.6	9 14.7	10 35.0	25 8.3	13 52.8	12 36.7	1 39.6	3 9.3
6 M	22 56 1	12 19 6	0♌49 35	7♌ 5 22	17 13.4	0♎58.3	10 29.2	11 12.4	25 0.7	13 58.1	12 34.7	1 41.4	3 9.9
7 Tu	22 59 57	13 17 19	13 25 35	19 50 29	17R14.3	2 30.8	11 43.7	11 49.6	24 53.1	14 3.4	12 32.8	1 43.2	3 10.6
8 W	23 3 54	14 15 35	26 20 12	2♍54 49	17 14.0	4 2.1	12 58.2	12 26.8	24 45.4	14 8.5	12 30.8	1 44.9	3 11.2
9 Th	23 7 51	15 13 53	9♍34 18	16 18 31	17 12.4	5 32.2	14 12.8	13 3.8	24 37.6	14 13.6	12 28.9	1 46.6	3 11.7
10 F	23 11 47	16 12 12	23 7 13	0♎ 0 8	17 9.5	7 1.1	15 27.4	13 40.7	24 29.8	14 18.7	12 27.1	1 48.4	3 12.3
11 Sa	23 15 44	17 10 33	6♎56 50	13 56 52	17 5.4	8 28.8	16 42.0	14 17.5	24 21.9	14 23.6	12 25.2	1 50.0	3 12.8
12 Su	23 19 40	18 8 56	20 59 43	28 4 51	17 0.8	9 55.3	17 56.6	14 54.2	24 14.0	14 28.5	12 23.4	1 51.7	3 13.4
13 M	23 23 37	19 7 21	5♏11 42	12♏19 42	16 56.1	11 20.6	19 11.2	15 30.8	24 6.1	14 33.2	12 21.6	1 53.4	3 13.9
14 Tu	23 27 33	20 5 47	19 28 19	26 37 4	16 52.2	12 44.5	20 25.8	16 7.2	23 58.1	14 37.9	12 19.9	1 55.0	3 14.3
15 W	23 31 30	21 4 15	3♐45 30	10♐53 15	16 49.6	14 7.2	21 40.5	16 43.6	23 50.2	14 42.6	12 18.2	1 56.6	3 14.8
16 Th	23 35 26	22 2 45	17 59 57	25 5 21	16D48.4	15 28.6	22 55.1	17 19.8	23 42.2	14 47.1	12 16.5	1 58.2	3 15.2
17 F	23 39 23	23 1 16	2♑ 9 12	9♑11 21	16 48.6	16 48.6	24 9.8	17 55.9	23 34.2	14 51.5	12 14.9	1 59.7	3 15.6
18 Sa	23 43 20	23 59 49	16 11 38	23 9 55	16 49.8	18 7.3	25 24.5	18 31.9	23 26.2	14 55.9	12 13.3	2 1.3	3 16.0
19 Su	23 47 16	24 58 23	0♒ 6 5	7♒ 0 2	16 51.3	19 24.4	26 39.2	19 7.7	23 18.2	15 0.2	12 11.7	2 2.8	3 16.4
20 M	23 51 13	25 56 59	13 51 38	20 40 45	16R52.1	20 40.1	27 53.9	19 43.5	23 10.2	15 4.4	12 10.2	2 4.2	3 16.7
21 Tu	23 55 9	26 55 37	27 27 15	4♓10 58	16 51.7	21 54.2	29 8.6	20 19.1	23 2.2	15 8.5	12 8.7	2 5.7	3 17.0
22 W	23 59 6	27 54 17	10♓51 46	17 29 28	16 49.4	23 6.6	0♎23.3	20 54.6	22 54.3	15 12.5	12 7.3	2 7.1	3 17.3
23 Th	0 3 2	28 52 58	24 3 56	0♈35 1	16 45.0	24 17.2	1 38.0	21 30.0	22 46.4	15 16.4	12 5.9	2 8.5	3 17.6
24 F	0 6 59	29 51 41	7♈ 2 36	13 26 37	16 38.8	25 26.0	2 52.8	22 5.2	22 38.5	15 20.2	12 4.5	2 9.9	3 17.9
25 Sa	0 10 55	0♎50 26	19 47 2	26 3 51	16 31.2	26 32.9	4 7.5	22 40.3	22 30.6	15 23.9	12 3.2	2 11.3	3 18.1
26 Su	0 14 52	1 49 14	2♉17 11	8♉27 8	16 22.9	27 37.6	5 22.3	23 15.3	22 22.8	15 27.6	12 1.9	2 12.6	3 18.3
27 M	0 18 48	2 48 3	14 33 55	20 37 48	16 14.8	28 40.1	6 37.1	23 50.2	22 15.1	15 31.1	12 0.7	2 13.9	3 18.5
28 Tu	0 22 45	3 46 55	26 39 7	2♊38 15	16 7.8	29 40.1	7 51.9	24 24.9	22 7.4	15 34.6	11 59.5	2 15.1	3 18.7
29 W	0 26 42	4 45 49	8♊35 38	14 31 47	16 2.3	0♏37.6	9 6.7	24 59.5	21 59.8	15 38.0	11 58.3	2 16.4	3 18.8
30 Th	0 30 38	5 44 46	20 27 13	26 22 32	15 58.9	1 32.2	10 21.5	25 34.0	21 52.2	15 41.2	11 57.2	2 17.6	3 18.9

LONGITUDE — OCTOBER 1915

Day	Sid.Time	☉	0 hr ☽	Noon ☽	True ☊	☿	♀	♂	♃	♄	♅	♆	♇
1 F	0 34 35	6♎43 44	2♋18 19	8♋15 14	15♒57.4	2♏23.7	11♎36.3	26♋ 8.3	21♓44.7	15♋44.4	11♒56.1	2♌18.8	3♋19.0
2 Sa	0 38 31	7 42 45	14 13 55	20 15 2	15D57.5	3 12.0	12 51.1	26 42.5	21R37.3	15 47.5	11R55.1	2 20.0	3 19.1
3 Su	0 42 28	8 41 48	26 19 12	2♌27 5	15 58.5	3 56.6	14 6.0	27 16.5	21 30.0	15 50.4	11 54.1	2 21.1	3 19.1
4 M	0 46 24	9 40 54	8♌39 16	14 56 18	15R59.5	4 37.3	15 20.8	27 50.4	21 22.8	15 53.3	11 53.2	2 22.2	3R19.2
5 Tu	0 50 21	10 40 1	21 18 41	27 46 50	15 59.5	5 13.7	16 35.7	28 24.1	21 15.6	15 56.1	11 52.3	2 23.2	3 19.2
6 W	0 54 17	11 39 11	4♍21 2	11♍ 1 30	15 57.9	5 45.4	17 50.6	28 57.7	21 8.6	15 58.7	11 51.4	2 24.3	3 19.1
7 Th	0 58 14	12 38 23	17 48 16	24 41 15	15 53.9	6 12.0	19 5.5	29 31.2	21 1.7	16 1.3	11 50.6	2 25.3	3 19.1
8 F	1 2 11	13 37 38	1♎40 10	8♎44 37	15 47.6	6 33.1	20 20.3	0♌ 4.4	20 54.9	16 3.7	11 49.9	2 26.3	3 19.0
9 Sa	1 6 7	14 36 54	15 54 1	23 7 38	15 39.2	6 48.1	21 35.2	0 37.5	20 48.2	16 6.1	11 49.2	2 27.2	3 18.9
10 Su	1 10 4	15 36 13	0♏24 37	7♏44 2	15 29.7	6R56.7	22 50.1	1 10.5	20 41.6	16 8.3	11 48.5	2 28.1	3 18.8
11 M	1 14 0	16 35 33	15 4 56	22 26 19	15 20.1	6 58.3	24 5.1	1 43.3	20 35.1	16 10.5	11 47.9	2 29.0	3 18.7
12 Tu	1 17 57	17 34 55	29 47 14	7♐ 6 50	15 11.6	6 52.5	25 20.0	2 15.9	20 28.8	16 12.5	11 47.3	2 29.9	3 18.5
13 W	1 21 53	18 34 20	14♐24 20	21 39 7	15 5.1	6 38.8	26 34.9	2 48.3	20 22.7	16 14.4	11 46.8	2 30.7	3 18.4
14 Th	1 25 50	19 33 46	28 50 40	5♑58 38	15 1.0	6 16.9	27 49.8	3 20.6	20 16.6	16 16.3	11 46.4	2 31.5	3 18.2
15 F	1 29 46	20 33 14	13♑ 2 48	20 3 4	14D59.3	5 46.6	29 4.7	3 52.7	20 10.8	16 18.0	11 46.0	2 32.2	3 17.9
16 Sa	1 33 43	21 32 43	26 59 19	3♒51 43	14 59.1	5 7.8	0♏19.7	4 24.6	20 5.0	16 19.6	11 45.6	2 33.0	3 17.7
17 Su	1 37 40	22 32 15	10♒40 22	17 25 25	14R59.6	4 20.7	1 34.6	4 56.4	19 59.4	16 21.1	11 45.3	2 33.7	3 17.4
18 M	1 41 36	23 31 48	24 7 2	0♓45 24	14 59.3	3 25.8	2 49.5	5 27.9	19 54.0	16 22.5	11 45.0	2 34.3	3 17.1
19 Tu	1 45 33	24 31 22	7♓20 40	13 52 58	14 57.2	2 23.8	4 4.4	5 59.3	19 48.8	16 23.7	11 44.8	2 34.9	3 16.8
20 W	1 49 29	25 30 59	20 22 26	26 49 9	14 52.6	1 16.0	5 19.4	6 30.5	19 43.7	16 24.9	11 44.6	2 35.5	3 16.5
21 Th	1 53 26	26 30 37	3♈13 10	9♈34 31	14 45.0	0 3.8	6 34.3	7 1.5	19 38.7	16 26.0	11 44.5	2 36.1	3 16.1
22 F	1 57 22	27 30 17	15 53 14	22 9 19	14 34.6	28♎49.1	7 49.2	7 32.3	19 34.0	16 26.9	11D44.5	2 36.6	3 15.7
23 Sa	2 1 19	28 29 59	28 22 47	4♉33 39	14 22.2	27 33.9	9 4.1	8 2.9	19 29.4	16 27.7	11 44.4	2 37.1	3 15.3
24 Su	2 5 15	29 29 43	10♉41 58	16 47 49	14 8.7	26 20.6	10 19.1	8 33.3	19 25.0	16 28.5	11 44.5	2 37.6	3 14.9
25 M	2 9 12	0♏29 29	22 51 17	28 52 33	13 55.2	25 11.4	11 34.0	9 3.5	19 20.7	16 29.1	11 44.6	2 38.0	3 14.4
26 Tu	2 13 9	1 29 17	4♊51 48	10♊49 19	13 43.0	24 8.4	12 49.0	9 33.5	19 16.7	16 29.6	11 44.7	2 38.4	3 14.0
27 W	2 17 5	2 29 8	16 45 25	22 40 28	13 32.9	23 13.4	14 3.9	10 3.3	19 12.8	16 30.0	11 44.9	2 38.7	3 13.5
28 Th	2 21 2	3 29 0	28 34 53	4♋29 11	13 25.5	22 28.0	15 18.8	10 32.9	19 9.1	16 30.2	11 45.2	2 39.1	3 13.0
29 F	2 24 58	4 28 55	10♋23 53	16 19 34	13 20.9	21 53.2	16 33.8	11 2.2	19 5.6	16R30.4	11 45.4	2 39.4	3 12.5
30 Sa	2 28 55	5 28 52	22 16 52	28 16 25	13 18.7	21 29.7	17 48.7	11 31.3	19 2.3	16 30.5	11 45.8	2 39.6	3 11.9
31 Su	2 32 51	6 28 51	4♌18 54	10♌25 0	13 18.1	21D17.8	19 3.7	12 0.2	18 59.2	16 30.4	11 46.2	2 39.8	3 11.3

Astro Data

	Dy Hr Mn
☿0S	5 12:25
☽0S	9 23:41
☽0N	22 21:58
♀0S	24 3:21
♇ R	4 14:45
☽0S	7 8:54
☿ R	10 17:22
☽0N	20 4:33
♅ D	22 18:11
♄ R	29 22:58
☿ D	31 13:00

Planet Ingress

	Dy Hr Mn
☿ ♎	5 9:02
♀ ♎	21 16:31
☉ ♎	24 3:24
☿ ♏	28 8:11
♂ ♌	7 20:48
♀ ♏	15 17:42
☿ ♎	21 1:13
☉ ♏	24 12:10

Last Aspect / ☽ Ingress

Last Aspect Dy Hr Mn	☽ Ingress Dy Hr Mn	Last Aspect Dy Hr Mn	☽ Ingress Dy Hr Mn
3 4:10 ☿ □	♋ 3 11:12	3 1:58 ♂ ☌	♌ 3 7:13
5 12:51 ♃ △	♌ 5 22:24	4 14:10 ♀ ⚹	♍ 5 16:04
6 22:21 ♅ ☍	♍ 8 6:42	7 5:36 ♃ ☍	♎ 7 21:09
10 2:23 ♃ ☍	♎ 10 12:00	9 10:21 ♀ ☌	♏ 9 23:20
11 13:10 ♂ □	♏ 12 15:14	11 8:55 ♃ △	♐ 12 0:21
14 7:29 ♃ △	♐ 14 17:41	13 22:08 ♀ ⚹	♑ 14 1:56
16 9:34 ♃ □	♑ 16 20:20	15 13:51 ☉ □	♒ 16 5:15
18 17:26 ♀ △	♒ 18 23:49	17 22:51 ☉ △	♓ 18 10:38
20 13:11 ☿ △	♓ 21 4:32	19 22:49 ♃ ☌	♈ 20 17:57
23 9:35 ☉ ☍	♈ 23 10:55	23 0:15 ☉ ☍	♉ 23 3:08
25 14:10 ☿ ☍	♉ 25 19:35	24 17:05 ♃ ⚹	♊ 25 14:15
27 19:19 ♂ ⚹	♊ 28 6:42	27 12:17 ☿ △	♋ 28 2:53
30 2:50 ♃ □	♋ 30 19:20	29 22:28 ☿ □	♌ 30 15:26

☽ Phases & Eclipses

Dy Hr Mn	
1 14:56	☽ 8♊05
9 10:52	● 15♍40
16 7:21	☽ 22♐21
23 9:35	○ 29♓16
1 9:44	☽ 7♋08
8 21:42	● 14♎31
15 13:51	☽ 21♑08
23 0:15	○ 28♈31
31 4:39	☽ 6♌40

Astro Data

1 SEPTEMBER 1915
Julian Day # 5722
Delta T 17.9 sec
SVP 06♓26'02"
Obliquity 23°27'08"
⚷ Chiron 20♓58.4R
☽ Mean ☊ 16♒12.7

1 OCTOBER 1915
Julian Day # 5752
Delta T 18.0 sec
SVP 06♓25'59"
Obliquity 23°27'08"
⚷ Chiron 19♓36.9R
☽ Mean ☊ 14♒37.3

NOVEMBER 1915 LONGITUDE

Day	Sid.Time	☉	0 hr ☽	Noon ☽	True ☊	☿	♀	♂	♃	♄	♅	♆	♇
1 M	2 36 48	7♏28 52	16♌35 24	22♌50 46	13♒18.1	21♎17.3	20♏18.7	12♌28.9	18♓56.3	16♋30.2	11♒46.6	2♌40.0	3♋10.8
2 Tu	2 40 44	8 28 55	29 11 45	5♍38 55	13R 17.4	21 27.9	21 33.6	12 57.3	18R 53.6	16R 29.9	11 47.1	2 40.2	3R 10.1
3 W	2 44 41	9 29 0	12♍12 44	18 53 37	13 15.1	21 48.9	22 48.6	13 25.5	18 51.0	16 29.5	11 47.7	2 40.3	3 9.5
4 Th	2 48 38	10 29 8	25 41 48	2♎37 22	13 10.2	22 19.6	24 3.5	13 53.5	18 48.7	16 29.0	11 48.3	2 40.4	3 8.9
5 F	2 52 34	11 29 17	9♎40 12	16 49 59	13 2.5	22 59.1	25 18.5	14 21.2	18 46.6	16 28.4	11 48.9	2R 40.4	3 8.2
6 Sa	2 56 31	12 29 29	24 6 12	1♏28 4	12 52.4	23 46.6	26 33.5	14 48.6	18 44.7	16 27.6	11 49.6	2 40.5	3 7.5
7 Su	3 0 27	13 29 42	8♏54 40	16 24 50	12 40.8	24 41.2	27 48.5	15 15.7	18 42.9	16 26.8	11 50.4	2 40.4	3 6.8
8 M	3 4 24	14 29 57	23 57 21	1♐30 55	12 28.9	25 42.0	29 3.4	15 42.6	18 41.4	16 25.8	11 51.2	2 40.4	3 6.1
9 Tu	3 8 20	15 30 15	9♐ 4 11	16 35 55	12 18.1	26 48.3	0♐18.4	16 9.2	18 40.1	16 24.8	11 52.0	2 40.3	3 5.3
10 W	3 12 17	16 30 33	24 4 58	1♑30 21	12 9.6	27 59.2	1 33.4	16 35.5	18 39.0	16 23.6	11 52.9	2 40.2	3 4.6
11 Th	3 16 13	17 30 54	8♑51 15	16 7 5	12 4.0	29 14.2	2 48.4	17 1.6	18 38.1	16 22.3	11 53.9	2 40.0	3 3.8
12 F	3 20 10	18 31 15	23 17 26	0♒22 5	12 1.1	0♏32.6	4 3.3	17 27.3	18 37.4	16 20.9	11 54.9	2 39.9	3 3.0
13 Sa	3 24 7	19 31 38	7♒20 58	14 14 10	12 0.2	1 54.0	5 18.3	17 52.8	18 37.0	16 19.4	11 56.0	2 39.6	3 2.2
14 Su	3 28 3	20 32 2	21 1 53	27 44 23	12 0.2	3 17.8	6 33.3	18 17.9	18D 36.7	16 17.7	11 57.1	2 39.4	3 1.4
15 M	3 32 0	21 32 28	4♓21 59	10♓55 2	11 59.7	4 43.6	7 48.2	18 42.7	18 36.6	16 16.0	11 58.2	2 39.1	3 0.5
16 Tu	3 35 56	22 32 55	17 23 56	23 49 2	11 57.5	6 11.2	9 3.2	19 7.3	18 36.8	16 14.2	11 59.4	2 38.8	2 59.6
17 W	3 39 53	23 33 23	0♈10 41	6♈29 11	11 52.8	7 40.1	10 18.1	19 31.5	18 37.1	16 12.2	12 0.7	2 38.4	2 58.8
18 Th	3 43 49	24 33 53	12 44 51	18 57 54	11 45.1	9 10.3	11 33.0	19 55.3	18 37.7	16 10.2	12 2.0	2 38.0	2 57.9
19 F	3 47 46	25 34 24	25 8 35	1♉17 4	11 34.5	10 41.3	12 48.0	20 18.9	18 38.4	16 8.0	12 3.3	2 37.6	2 56.9
20 Sa	3 51 42	26 34 56	7♉23 31	13 28 4	11 21.8	12 13.2	14 2.9	20 42.1	18 39.4	16 5.8	12 4.7	2 37.2	2 56.0
21 Su	3 55 39	27 35 30	19 30 50	25 31 57	11 8.0	13 45.6	15 17.8	21 4.9	18 40.6	16 3.4	12 6.2	2 36.7	2 55.1
22 M	3 59 36	28 36 5	1♊31 31	7♊29 42	10 54.1	15 18.5	16 32.8	21 27.4	18 42.0	16 1.0	12 7.7	2 36.1	2 54.1
23 Tu	4 3 32	29 36 42	13 26 38	19 22 31	10 41.5	16 51.8	17 47.7	21 49.6	18 43.5	15 58.4	12 9.2	2 35.6	2 53.1
24 W	4 7 29	0♐37 20	25 17 34	1♋12 3	10 30.9	18 25.3	19 2.6	22 11.4	18 45.3	15 55.8	12 10.8	2 35.0	2 52.2
25 Th	4 11 25	1 38 0	7♋ 6 16	13 0 35	10 23.1	19 59.1	20 17.5	22 32.8	18 47.3	15 53.1	12 12.4	2 34.4	2 51.2
26 F	4 15 22	2 38 41	18 55 23	24 51 9	10 18.1	21 33.0	21 32.4	22 53.8	18 49.5	15 50.2	12 14.1	2 33.8	2 50.2
27 Sa	4 19 18	3 39 24	0♌48 22	6♌47 36	10D 15.8	23 7.1	22 47.3	23 14.4	18 51.9	15 47.3	12 15.8	2 33.1	2 49.1
28 Su	4 23 15	4 40 8	12 49 24	18 54 25	10 15.4	24 41.2	24 2.3	23 34.6	18 54.5	15 44.3	12 17.6	2 32.4	2 48.1
29 M	4 27 11	5 40 54	25 3 17	1♍16 37	10R 15.9	26 15.3	25 17.2	23 54.4	18 57.3	15 41.1	12 19.4	2 31.6	2 47.1
30 Tu	4 31 8	6 41 41	7♍35 6	13 59 20	10 16.2	27 49.4	26 32.1	24 13.8	19 0.3	15 37.9	12 21.3	2 30.9	2 46.0

DECEMBER 1915 LONGITUDE

Day	Sid.Time	☉	0 hr ☽	Noon ☽	True ☊	☿	♀	♂	♃	♄	♅	♆	♇
1 W	4 35 5	7♐42 30	20♍29 54	27♍ 7 17	10♒15.4	29♏23.5	27♐47.0	24♌32.8	19♓ 3.4	15♋34.6	12♒23.2	2♌30.1	2♋44.9
2 Th	4 39 1	8 43 20	3♎51 55	10♎44 3	10R 12.5	0♐57.7	29 1.9	24 51.3	19 6.8	15R 31.2	12 25.1	2R 29.2	2R 43.8
3 F	4 42 58	9 44 11	17 43 49	24 51 8	10 7.3	2 31.8	0♑16.7	25 9.3	19 10.4	15 27.8	12 27.1	2 28.4	2 42.8
4 Sa	4 46 54	10 45 5	2♏ 5 41	9♏26 57	9 59.9	4 5.9	1 31.6	25 26.9	19 14.2	15 24.2	12 29.1	2 27.5	2 41.7
5 Su	4 50 51	11 45 59	16 54 11	24 26 24	9 50.9	5 40.0	2 46.5	25 44.1	19 18.1	15 20.6	12 31.2	2 26.6	2 40.5
6 M	4 54 47	12 46 55	2♐ 2 25	9♐40 53	9 41.6	7 14.0	4 1.4	26 0.7	19 22.3	15 16.9	12 33.3	2 25.6	2 39.4
7 Tu	4 58 44	13 47 52	17 20 25	24 59 34	9 33.0	8 48.1	5 16.3	26 16.8	19 26.6	15 13.1	12 35.5	2 24.6	2 38.3
8 W	5 2 41	14 48 49	2♑36 56	10♑11 14	9 26.2	10 22.1	6 31.2	26 32.5	19 31.2	15 9.2	12 37.7	2 23.6	2 37.2
9 Th	5 6 37	15 49 48	17 41 19	25 6 16	9 21.9	11 56.2	7 46.0	26 47.6	19 35.9	15 5.3	12 39.9	2 22.6	2 36.0
10 F	5 10 34	16 50 47	2♒25 20	9♒38 2	9D 20.0	13 30.3	9 0.9	27 2.2	19 40.8	15 1.3	12 42.2	2 21.6	2 34.9
11 Sa	5 14 30	17 51 47	16 44 4	23 43 18	9 20.0	15 4.4	10 15.7	27 16.3	19 45.9	14 57.2	12 44.5	2 20.5	2 33.7
12 Su	5 18 27	18 52 48	0♓35 48	7♓21 47	9 21.0	16 38.6	11 30.6	27 29.8	19 51.2	14 53.1	12 46.9	2 19.4	2 32.6
13 M	5 22 23	19 53 49	14 1 30	20 35 22	9R 21.9	18 12.8	12 45.4	27 42.7	19 56.6	14 48.8	12 49.3	2 18.2	2 31.4
14 Tu	5 26 20	20 54 50	27 3 49	3♈27 17	9 21.9	19 47.1	14 0.2	27 55.1	20 2.3	14 44.6	12 51.7	2 17.1	2 30.2
15 W	5 30 16	21 55 52	9♈46 16	16 1 15	9 20.1	21 21.5	15 15.0	28 7.0	20 8.1	14 40.2	12 54.2	2 15.9	2 29.0
16 Th	5 34 13	22 56 55	22 12 40	28 21 0	9 16.1	22 56.0	16 29.8	28 18.2	20 14.0	14 35.9	12 56.7	2 14.7	2 27.8
17 F	5 38 10	23 57 58	4♉26 39	10♉29 59	9 10.1	24 30.7	17 44.5	28 28.9	20 20.2	14 31.4	12 59.2	2 13.4	2 26.6
18 Sa	5 42 6	24 59 1	16 31 21	22 31 5	9 2.5	26 5.4	18 59.3	28 38.9	20 26.5	14 26.9	13 1.8	2 12.2	2 25.4
19 Su	5 46 3	26 0 5	28 29 28	4♊26 45	8 53.9	27 40.3	20 14.0	28 48.3	20 33.0	14 22.4	13 4.4	2 10.9	2 24.2
20 M	5 49 59	27 1 9	10♊23 10	16 18 56	8 45.3	29 15.4	21 28.8	28 57.1	20 39.7	14 17.8	13 7.1	2 9.6	2 23.0
21 Tu	5 53 56	28 2 14	22 14 16	28 9 22	8 37.5	0♑50.7	22 43.5	29 5.3	20 46.5	14 13.2	13 9.7	2 8.3	2 21.8
22 W	5 57 52	29 3 19	4♋ 4 26	9♋59 41	8 31.1	2 26.2	23 58.2	29 12.8	20 53.5	14 8.5	13 12.4	2 6.9	2 20.6
23 Th	6 1 49	0♑ 4 25	15 55 22	21 51 42	8 26.6	4 1.8	25 12.8	29 19.6	21 0.7	14 3.8	13 15.2	2 5.6	2 19.4
24 F	6 5 45	1 5 31	27 48 59	3♌47 31	8D 24.0	5 37.7	26 27.5	29 25.8	21 8.0	13 59.1	13 18.0	2 4.2	2 18.2
25 Sa	6 9 42	2 6 38	9♌47 39	15 49 46	8 23.4	7 13.8	27 42.1	29 31.3	21 15.5	13 54.3	13 20.8	2 2.8	2 17.0
26 Su	6 13 39	3 7 45	21 54 15	28 1 35	8 24.2	8 50.1	28 56.8	29 36.1	21 23.1	13 49.5	13 23.6	2 1.4	2 15.8
27 M	6 17 35	4 8 53	4♍12 11	10♍26 35	8 25.8	10 26.6	0♒11.4	29 40.1	21 30.9	13 44.6	13 26.5	1 59.9	2 14.6
28 Tu	6 21 32	5 10 1	16 45 16	23 8 44	8 27.6	12 3.4	1 26.0	29 43.5	21 38.8	13 39.8	13 29.4	1 58.5	2 13.4
29 W	6 25 28	6 11 10	29 37 29	6♎11 57	8R 28.8	13 40.3	2 40.5	29 46.1	21 46.9	13 34.9	13 32.3	1 57.0	2 12.2
30 Th	6 29 25	7 12 19	12♎52 32	19 39 35	8 28.8	15 17.5	3 55.1	29 47.9	21 55.1	13 30.0	13 35.3	1 55.5	2 11.0
31 F	6 33 21	8 13 29	26 33 17	3♏33 45	8 27.5	16 54.8	5 9.6	29R 49.0	22 3.5	13 25.0	13 38.2	1 54.0	2 9.8

Astro Data Dy Hr Mn	Planet Ingress Dy Hr Mn	Last Aspect Dy Hr Mn	☽ Ingress Dy Hr Mn	Last Aspect Dy Hr Mn	☽ Ingress Dy Hr Mn	☽ Phases & Eclipses Dy Hr Mn	Astro Data
☽0S 3 18:35	♀ ♐ 8 18:07	1 9:07 ☿ ✶	♍ 2 1:30	1 14:32 ♀ □	♎ 1 17:09	7 7:52 ● 13♏49	1 NOVEMBER 1915
♆ R 5 23:53	☿ ♏ 11 14:08	3 20:50 ♀ ✶	♎ 4 7:29	3 12:46 ♂ ✶	♏ 3 20:33	13 23:03 ☽ 20♒30	Julian Day # 5783
♃ D 14 19:30	☉ ♐ 23 9:14	5 23:26 ☿ ☌	♏ 6 9:37	5 14:19 ♂ □	♐ 5 20:47	21 17:36 ○ 28♉20	Delta T 18.1 sec
☽0N 16 9:24		8 8:50 ♀ ☌	♐ 8 9:36	7 14:16 ♂ △	♑ 7 19:53	29 22:10 ☽ 6♍37	SVP 06♓25'55"
	☿ ♐ 1 9:18	10 6:52 ☿ ✶	♑ 10 9:33	9 3:06 ♃ ✶	♒ 9 20:01		Obliquity 23°27'07"
☽0S 1 2:58	♀ ♑ 2 18:38	11 16:11 ♃ ✶	♒ 12 11:22	11 18:29 ♂ ☍	♓ 11 22:57	6 18:03 ● 13♐33	⚷ Chiron 18♓30.3R
☽0N 13 14:29	☿ ♑ 20 11:14	13 23:03 ☉ □	♓ 14 16:05	13 11:38 ☉ □	♈ 14 5:30	13 11:38 ☽ 20♓23	☽ Mean ☊ 12♒58.8
☽0S 28 9:18	☉ ♑ 22 22:16	16 10:26 ☉ △	♈ 16 23:40	16 12:05 ♂ △	♉ 16 15:14	21 12:52 ○ 28♊35	
♄⊼♅ 29 7:53	♀ ♒ 26 20:21	18 14:18 ♂ △	♉ 19 9:29	19 0:38 ♂ □	♊ 19 3:02	29 12:58 ☽ 6♎44	1 DECEMBER 1915
♂ R 31 22:29		21 17:36 ☉ ☍	♊ 21 20:56	21 14:02 ♂ ✶	♋ 21 15:44		Julian Day # 5813
		23 17:30 ♂ ✶	♋ 24 9:34	23 20:57 ♀ ☍	♌ 24 4:23		Delta T 18.2 sec
		26 6:08 ☿ △	♌ 26 22:23	26 15:09 ♂ ☌	♍ 26 15:51		SVP 06♓25'50"
		29 2:40 ☿ □	♍ 29 9:33	28 9:18 ♃ ☍	♎ 29 0:41		Obliquity 23°27'07"
				31 5:37 ♂ ✶	♏ 31 5:55		⚷ Chiron 18♓06.8
							☽ Mean ☊ 11♒23.5

LONGITUDE JANUARY 1916

Day	Sid.Time	☉	0 hr ☽	Noon ☽	True ☊	☿	♀	♂	♃	♄	♅	♆	♇
1 Sa	6 37 18	9♑14 39	10♏40 54	17♏54 30	8♒24.8	18♑32.3	6♒24.1	29♌49.4	22♓12.0	13♋20.1	13♒41.2	1♌52.5	2♋ 8.6
2 Su	6 41 14	10 15 50	25 14 8	2♐39 8	8R21.1	20 9.9	7 38.6	29R48.9	22 20.7	13R15.2	13 44.3	1R50.9	2R 7.4
3 M	6 45 11	11 17 1	10♐ 8 44	17 41 53	8 17.1	21 47.6	8 53.1	29 47.7	22 29.5	13 10.2	13 47.3	1 49.4	2 6.2
4 Tu	6 49 8	12 18 12	25 17 28	2♑54 15	8 13.3	23 25.3	10 7.6	29 45.7	22 38.5	13 5.2	13 50.4	1 47.8	2 5.0
5 W	6 53 4	13 19 23	10♑30 55	18 6 11	8 10.3	25 2.9	11 22.0	29 42.9	22 47.5	13 0.3	13 53.5	1 46.2	2 3.8
6 Th	6 57 1	14 20 35	25 38 49	3♒ 7 42	8D 8.6	26 40.4	12 36.5	29 39.3	22 56.8	12 55.3	13 56.7	1 44.6	2 2.6
7 F	7 0 57	15 21 46	10♒31 50	17 50 26	8 8.2	28 17.6	13 50.8	29 34.8	23 6.1	12 50.4	13 59.8	1 43.0	2 1.5
8 Sa	7 4 54	16 22 56	25 2 51	2♓ 8 39	8 8.9	29 54.5	15 5.2	29 29.6	23 15.6	12 45.4	14 3.0	1 41.4	2 0.3
9 Su	7 8 50	17 24 6	9♓ 7 37	15 59 40	8 10.2	1♒30.8	16 19.5	29 23.5	23 25.3	12 40.5	14 6.2	1 39.8	1 59.1
10 M	7 12 47	18 25 16	22 44 52	29 23 27	8 11.7	3 6.5	17 33.8	29 16.6	23 35.0	12 35.5	14 9.4	1 38.2	1 58.0
11 Tu	7 16 43	19 26 25	5♈55 42	12♈22 2	8 12.9	4 41.2	18 48.1	29 9.0	23 44.9	12 30.6	14 12.6	1 36.5	1 56.8
12 W	7 20 40	20 27 34	18 42 54	24 58 49	8R13.4	6 14.7	20 2.3	29 0.5	23 54.9	12 25.7	14 15.9	1 34.9	1 55.7
13 Th	7 24 37	21 28 42	1♉10 19	7♉17 56	8 13.1	7 46.8	21 16.5	28 51.2	24 5.0	12 20.8	14 19.2	1 33.2	1 54.5
14 F	7 28 33	22 29 49	13 22 14	19 23 43	8 12.0	9 17.1	22 30.7	28 41.1	24 15.2	12 16.0	14 22.5	1 31.5	1 53.4
15 Sa	7 32 30	23 30 56	25 22 55	1♊20 19	8 10.3	10 45.1	23 44.8	28 30.2	24 25.6	12 11.2	14 25.8	1 29.9	1 52.3
16 Su	7 36 26	24 32 2	7♊16 25	13 11 37	8 8.2	12 10.5	24 58.9	28 18.5	24 36.1	12 6.4	14 29.1	1 28.2	1 51.2
17 M	7 40 23	25 33 8	19 6 20	25 0 58	8 6.1	13 32.8	26 13.0	28 6.0	24 46.7	12 1.6	14 32.4	1 26.5	1 50.1
18 Tu	7 44 19	26 34 12	0♋55 50	6♋51 15	8 4.2	14 51.3	27 27.0	27 52.8	24 57.4	11 56.9	14 35.8	1 24.8	1 49.0
19 W	7 48 16	27 35 17	12 47 30	18 44 52	8 2.8	16 5.3	28 40.9	27 38.8	25 8.2	11 52.2	14 39.2	1 23.1	1 47.9
20 Th	7 52 13	28 36 20	24 43 35	0♌43 52	8 2.0	17 14.3	29 54.8	27 24.1	25 19.1	11 47.5	14 42.5	1 21.5	1 46.9
21 F	7 56 9	29 37 23	6♌45 57	12 50 2	8D 1.7	18 17.3	1♓ 8.7	27 8.6	25 30.1	11 42.9	14 45.9	1 19.8	1 45.8
22 Sa	8 0 6	0♒38 25	18 56 19	25 5 2	8 1.8	19 13.7	2 22.5	26 52.4	25 41.3	11 38.4	14 49.3	1 18.1	1 44.8
23 Su	8 4 2	1 39 26	1♍16 23	7♍30 35	8 2.3	20 2.4	3 36.3	26 35.5	25 52.5	11 33.9	14 52.7	1 16.4	1 43.7
24 M	8 7 59	2 40 27	13 47 52	20 8 28	8 2.9	20 42.8	4 50.1	26 17.9	26 3.8	11 29.4	14 56.2	1 14.7	1 42.7
25 Tu	8 11 55	3 41 27	26 32 39	3♎ 0 39	8 3.4	21 13.9	6 3.8	25 59.7	26 15.2	11 25.0	14 59.6	1 13.0	1 41.7
26 W	8 15 52	4 42 27	9♎32 42	16 9 4	8 3.8	21 34.9	7 17.4	25 40.9	26 26.8	11 20.6	15 3.0	1 11.3	1 40.7
27 Th	8 19 48	5 43 26	22 49 56	29 35 30	8 4.0	21R45.3	8 31.0	25 21.4	26 38.4	11 16.3	15 6.5	1 9.6	1 39.7
28 F	8 23 45	6 44 25	6♏25 55	13♏21 14	8R 4.1	21 44.6	9 44.5	25 1.4	26 50.1	11 12.1	15 10.0	1 7.9	1 38.7
29 Sa	8 27 42	7 45 23	20 21 28	27 26 32	8D 4.1	21 32.5	10 58.0	24 40.8	27 1.9	11 7.9	15 13.4	1 6.2	1 37.8
30 Su	8 31 38	8 46 20	4♐36 12	11♐50 12	8 4.1	21 9.1	12 11.5	24 19.7	27 13.8	11 3.8	15 16.9	1 4.6	1 36.9
31 M	8 35 35	9 47 17	19 8 2	26 29 11	8 4.2	20 34.7	13 24.9	23 58.1	27 25.8	10 59.8	15 20.4	1 2.9	1 35.9

LONGITUDE FEBRUARY 1916

Day	Sid.Time	☉	0 hr ☽	Noon ☽	True ☊	☿	♀	♂	♃	♄	♅	♆	♇
1 Tu	8 39 31	10♒48 13	3♑52 57	11♑18 31	8♒ 4.5	19♒50.2	14♓38.2	23♌36.1	27♓37.9	10♋55.8	15♒23.9	1♌ 1.2	1♋35.0
2 W	8 43 28	11 49 9	18 45 0	26 11 29	8 4.7	18R56.6	15 51.5	23R13.6	27 50.1	10R51.9	15 27.3	0R59.6	1R34.1
3 Th	8 47 24	12 50 3	3♒36 57	11♒ 0 26	8R 4.9	17 55.4	17 4.8	22 50.9	28 2.3	10 48.1	15 30.8	0 57.9	1 33.3
4 F	8 51 21	13 50 56	18 20 59	25 37 45	8 4.9	16 48.5	18 17.9	22 27.8	28 14.7	10 44.3	15 34.3	0 56.3	1 32.4
5 Sa	8 55 17	14 51 48	2♓49 57	9♓56 56	8 4.4	15 37.6	19 31.1	22 4.4	28 27.1	10 40.7	15 37.8	0 54.6	1 31.6
6 Su	8 59 14	15 52 39	16 58 12	23 53 23	8 3.7	14 25.0	20 44.1	21 40.8	28 39.6	10 37.1	15 41.3	0 53.0	1 30.7
7 M	9 3 11	16 53 28	0♈42 15	7♈24 46	8 2.6	13 12.7	21 57.1	21 17.0	28 52.2	10 33.6	15 44.8	0 51.4	1 29.9
8 Tu	9 7 7	17 54 16	14 0 58	20 31 3	8 1.3	12 2.5	23 10.0	20 53.1	29 4.8	10 30.1	15 48.3	0 49.7	1 29.1
9 W	9 11 4	18 55 2	26 55 19	3♉14 9	8 0.2	10 56.2	24 22.9	20 29.1	29 17.5	10 26.8	15 51.8	0 48.1	1 28.3
10 Th	9 15 0	19 55 47	9♉27 59	15 37 20	7D59.4	9 55.2	25 35.6	20 5.1	29 30.3	10 23.6	15 55.3	0 46.6	1 27.6
11 F	9 18 57	20 56 30	21 42 46	27 44 52	7 59.2	9 0.6	26 48.3	19 41.1	29 43.2	10 20.4	15 58.7	0 45.0	1 26.8
12 Sa	9 22 53	21 57 11	3♊44 13	9♊41 26	7 59.5	8 13.2	28 0.9	19 17.2	29 56.1	10 17.3	16 2.2	0 43.4	1 26.1
13 Su	9 26 50	22 57 52	15 37 7	21 31 51	8 0.5	7 33.4	29 13.5	18 53.4	0♈ 9.1	10 14.3	16 5.7	0 41.9	1 25.4
14 M	9 30 46	23 58 30	27 26 11	3♋20 41	8 1.9	7 1.6	0♈26.0	18 29.7	0 22.2	10 11.5	16 9.2	0 40.3	1 24.7
15 Tu	9 34 43	24 59 7	9♋15 52	15 12 12	8 3.4	6 37.7	1 38.3	18 6.2	0 35.3	10 8.7	16 12.6	0 38.8	1 24.1
16 W	9 38 40	25 59 42	21 10 7	27 10 2	8 4.8	6 21.6	2 50.6	17 43.0	0 48.5	10 6.0	16 16.1	0 37.3	1 23.4
17 Th	9 42 36	27 0 15	3♌12 17	9♌17 11	8R 5.5	6D13.1	4 2.8	17 20.0	1 1.7	10 3.4	16 19.5	0 35.8	1 22.8
18 F	9 46 33	28 0 47	15 24 59	21 35 54	8 5.4	6 11.9	5 15.0	16 57.3	1 15.0	10 0.9	16 23.0	0 34.4	1 22.2
19 Sa	9 50 29	29 1 17	27 50 5	4♍ 7 39	8 4.2	6 17.5	6 27.0	16 35.1	1 28.4	9 58.5	16 26.4	0 32.9	1 21.6
20 Su	9 54 26	0♓ 1 46	10♍28 41	16 53 12	8 2.0	6 29.6	7 38.9	16 13.2	1 41.8	9 56.2	16 29.8	0 31.5	1 21.1
21 M	9 58 22	1 2 13	23 21 12	29 52 40	7 58.8	6 47.7	8 50.8	15 51.7	1 55.3	9 54.0	16 33.2	0 30.0	1 20.5
22 Tu	10 2 19	2 2 38	6♎27 32	13♎ 5 43	7 55.0	7 11.4	10 2.5	15 30.7	2 8.8	9 51.9	16 36.6	0 28.6	1 20.0
23 W	10 6 15	3 3 2	19 47 8	26 31 42	7 51.1	7 40.3	11 14.2	15 10.2	2 22.4	9 49.9	16 40.0	0 27.3	1 19.5
24 Th	10 10 12	4 3 25	3♏19 19	10♏ 9 52	7 47.7	8 14.1	12 25.8	14 50.3	2 36.0	9 48.0	16 43.4	0 25.9	1 19.0
25 F	10 14 9	5 3 46	17 3 16	23 59 25	7 45.3	8 52.4	13 37.2	14 30.9	2 49.7	9 46.2	16 46.8	0 24.6	1 18.6
26 Sa	10 18 5	6 4 6	0♐58 11	7♐59 27	7D44.1	9 34.8	14 48.6	14 12.1	3 3.4	9 44.6	16 50.1	0 23.2	1 18.1
27 Su	10 22 2	7 4 25	15 3 5	22 8 53	7 44.2	10 21.0	15 59.8	13 53.9	3 17.2	9 43.0	16 53.4	0 21.9	1 17.7
28 M	10 25 58	8 4 42	29 16 39	6♑26 8	7 45.3	11 10.8	17 11.0	13 36.3	3 31.0	9 41.5	16 56.8	0 20.7	1 17.3
29 Tu	10 29 55	9 4 58	13♑37 0	20 48 53	7 46.9	12 3.8	18 22.1	13 19.4	3 44.9	9 40.2	17 0.1	0 19.4	1 17.0

Astro Data Dy Hr Mn	Planet Ingress Dy Hr Mn	Last Aspect Dy Hr Mn	☽ Ingress Dy Hr Mn	Last Aspect Dy Hr Mn	☽ Ingress Dy Hr Mn	☽ Phases & Eclipses Dy Hr Mn
☽0N 9 21:57	☿ ♒ 8 1:22	2 7:25 ♂ □	♐ 2 7:43	2 14:51 ♃ ⚹	♒ 2 18:09	5 4:45 ● 13♑32
☽0S 24 14:38	♀ ♓ 20 1:41	4 7:02 ♂ △	♑ 4 7:25	4 6:35 ♂ ☍	♓ 4 19:16	12 3:37 ☽ 20♈37
☿ R 27 10:28	☉ ♒ 21 8:54	6 1:50 ☿ ☌	♒ 6 6:58	6 20:42 ♃ ☌	♈ 6 22:45	20 8:29 ○ 28♋58
		8 7:27 ♂ ☍	♓ 8 8:21	8 12:18 ♂ △	♉ 9 5:50	20 8:39 ☍ P 0.133
☽0N 6 7:56	♃ ♈ 12 7:11	10 1:31 ♃ ☌	♈ 10 13:07	11 16:14 ♃ ⚹	♊ 11 16:30	28 0:35 ☽ 6♏46
♀0N 14 22:37	♀ ♈ 13 15:24	12 19:33 ♂ △	♉ 12 21:43	13 16:18 ☉ △	♋ 14 5:12	
♃△♆ 15 5:45	☉ ♓ 19 23:18	15 6:11 ♂ □	♊ 15 9:18	15 1:46 ♄ ☌	♌ 16 17:38	3 16:05 ● 13♒31
♅⚼♇ 17 19:32		17 17:56 ♂ ⚹	♋ 17 22:07	19 2:28 ☉ ☍	♍ 19 4:08	3 16:00:03 ☌ T 2'36"
☿ D 17 16:11		20 8:29 ☉ ☍	♌ 20 10:33	19 22:59 ♄ ⚹	♎ 21 12:13	10 22:20 ☽ 20♉52
♃□♇ 18 12:22		22 15:08 ♂ ☌	♍ 22 21:32	22 18:24 ♅ △	♏ 23 18:09	19 2:28 ○ 29♌08
♃∠♅ 18 19:10		24 23:27 ♃ ☍	♎ 25 6:26	24 23:31 ♅ □	♐ 25 22:20	26 9:24 ☽ 6♐28
☽0S 20 20:47		27 4:23 ♂ ⚹	♏ 27 12:43	27 3:08 ♅ ⚹	♑ 28 1:13	
♃0N 23 21:33		29 11:28 ♃ △	♐ 29 16:18			
		31 13:43 ♃ □	♑ 31 17:42			

Astro Data

1 JANUARY 1916
Julian Day # 5844
Delta T 18.2 sec
SVP 06♓25'45"
Obliquity 23°27'06"
⚷ Chiron 18♓34.8
☽ Mean ☊ 9♒45.0

1 FEBRUARY 1916
Julian Day # 5875
Delta T 18.3 sec
SVP 06♓25'39"
Obliquity 23°27'06"
⚷ Chiron 19♓49.5
☽ Mean ☊ 8♒06.6

MARCH 1916 — LONGITUDE

Day	Sid.Time	☉	0 hr ☽	Noon ☽	True ☊	☿	♀	♂	♃	♄	♅	♆	♇
1 W	10 33 51	10♓ 5 12	28♑ 1 19	5♒13 50	7♒48.1	12♒60.0	19♈33.0	13♌ 3.2	3♈58.8	9♋38.9	17♒ 3.4	0♌18.2	1♋16.6
2 Th	10 37 48	11 5 24	12♒25 52	19 36 48	7R48.3	13 58.9	20 43.9	12R47.7	4 12.7	9R37.8	17 6.6	0R17.0	1R16.3
3 F	10 41 44	12 5 35	26 46 0	3♓52 51	7 47.0	15 0.5	21 54.6	12 32.9	4 26.7	9 36.8	17 9.9	0 15.8	1 16.0
4 Sa	10 45 41	13 5 44	10♓56 43	17 56 58	7 43.8	16 4.6	23 5.2	12 18.9	4 40.7	9 35.9	17 13.1	0 14.6	1 15.7
5 Su	10 49 38	14 5 52	24 53 7	1♈44 39	7 39.0	17 11.1	24 15.7	12 5.6	4 54.8	9 35.1	17 16.3	0 13.5	1 15.4
6 M	10 53 34	15 5 57	8♈31 14	15 12 36	7 32.8	18 19.7	25 26.1	11 53.1	5 8.9	9 34.4	17 19.5	0 12.4	1 15.2
7 Tu	10 57 31	16 6 0	21 48 34	28 19 8	7 26.2	19 30.4	26 36.4	11 41.4	5 23.0	9 33.8	17 22.7	0 11.3	1 15.0
8 W	11 1 27	17 6 1	4♉44 22	11♉ 4 26	7 19.7	20 43.0	27 46.5	11 30.4	5 37.1	9 33.4	17 25.8	0 10.2	1 14.8
9 Th	11 5 24	18 6 1	17 19 37	23 30 19	7 14.3	21 57.5	28 56.5	11 20.2	5 51.3	9 33.0	17 29.0	0 9.2	1 14.6
10 F	11 9 20	19 5 58	29 36 57	5♊40 3	7 10.4	23 13.8	0♉ 6.3	11 10.9	6 5.5	9 32.8	17 32.1	0 8.2	1 14.5
11 Sa	11 13 17	20 5 53	11♊40 10	17 37 54	7D 8.3	24 31.8	1 16.1	11 2.3	6 19.8	9D 32.7	17 35.2	0 7.2	1 14.4
12 Su	11 17 13	21 5 46	23 33 53	29 28 45	7 7.9	25 51.4	2 25.7	10 54.5	6 34.0	9 32.6	17 38.2	0 6.3	1 14.3
13 M	11 21 10	22 5 36	5♋23 12	11♋17 51	7 8.7	27 12.6	3 35.1	10 47.5	6 48.3	9 32.7	17 41.3	0 5.4	1 14.2
14 Tu	11 25 7	23 5 24	17 13 21	23 10 21	7 10.2	28 35.3	4 44.4	10 41.4	7 2.6	9 33.0	17 44.3	0 4.5	1 14.2
15 W	11 29 3	24 5 11	29 9 25	5♌11 6	7R11.5	29 59.5	5 53.5	10 35.9	7 17.0	9 33.3	17 47.2	0 3.6	1D14.1
16 Th	11 33 0	25 4 54	11♌15 57	17 24 23	7 11.7	1♓25.2	7 2.5	10 31.3	7 31.3	9 33.7	17 50.2	0 2.8	1 14.1
17 F	11 36 56	26 4 36	23 36 49	29 53 32	7 10.2	2 52.3	8 11.3	10 27.5	7 45.7	9 34.3	17 53.1	0 2.0	1 14.1
18 Sa	11 40 53	27 4 15	6♍14 46	12♍40 41	7 6.5	4 20.7	9 19.9	10 24.4	8 0.1	9 34.9	17 56.0	0 1.2	1 14.2
19 Su	11 44 49	28 3 53	19 11 17	25 46 33	7 0.6	5 50.6	10 28.4	10 22.1	8 14.5	9 35.7	17 58.9	0 0.5	1 14.2
20 M	11 48 46	29 3 28	2♎26 20	9♎10 23	6 52.8	7 21.8	11 36.7	10 20.5	8 28.9	9 36.6	18 1.7	29♋59.7	1 14.3
21 Tu	11 52 42	0♈ 3 1	15 58 24	22 50 0	6 43.8	8 54.3	12 44.9	10D19.7	8 43.3	9 37.6	18 4.6	29 59.1	1 14.4
22 W	11 56 39	1 2 33	29 44 44	6♏42 11	6 34.5	10 28.2	13 52.8	10 19.6	8 57.8	9 38.7	18 7.3	29 58.4	1 14.6
23 Th	12 0 35	2 2 2	13♏41 50	20 43 14	6 26.1	12 3.4	15 0.6	10 20.3	9 12.2	9 39.9	18 10.1	29 57.8	1 14.7
24 F	12 4 32	3 1 30	27 45 56	4♐49 32	6 19.4	13 40.0	16 8.2	10 21.6	9 26.7	9 41.2	18 12.8	29 57.2	1 14.9
25 Sa	12 8 29	4 0 56	11♐53 40	18 58 3	6 15.0	15 17.9	17 15.6	10 23.7	9 41.2	9 42.7	18 15.5	29 56.6	1 15.1
26 Su	12 12 25	5 0 20	26 2 24	3♑ 6 32	6D 12.9	16 57.1	18 22.8	10 26.5	9 55.7	9 44.2	18 18.2	29 56.1	1 15.3
27 M	12 16 22	5 59 43	10♑10 17	17 13 32	6 12.6	18 37.6	19 29.8	10 29.9	10 10.2	9 45.9	18 20.8	29 55.6	1 15.6
28 Tu	12 20 18	6 59 4	24 16 7	1♒17 58	6R13.2	20 19.5	20 36.6	10 34.1	10 24.7	9 47.6	18 23.4	29 55.1	1 15.9
29 W	12 24 15	7 58 23	8♒18 55	15 18 50	6 13.6	22 2.8	21 43.3	10 38.9	10 39.2	9 49.5	18 26.0	29 54.7	1 16.2
30 Th	12 28 11	8 57 40	22 17 32	29 14 46	6 12.5	23 47.5	22 49.7	10 44.3	10 53.7	9 51.4	18 28.5	29 54.3	1 16.5
31 F	12 32 8	9 56 55	6♓10 18	13♓ 3 49	6 9.1	25 33.5	23 55.9	10 50.4	11 8.2	9 53.5	18 31.0	29 53.9	1 16.8

APRIL 1916 — LONGITUDE

Day	Sid.Time	☉	0 hr ☽	Noon ☽	True ☊	☿	♀	♂	♃	♄	♅	♆	♇
1 Sa	12 36 4	10♈56 8	19♓54 59	26♓43 27	6♒ 2.9	27♓20.9	25♉ 1.9	10♌57.2	11♈22.8	9♋55.7	18♒33.4	29♋53.6	1♋17.2
2 Su	12 40 1	11 55 20	3♈28 54	10♈10 58	5R54.1	29 9.7	26 7.6	11 4.6	11 37.3	9 58.0	18 35.8	29R53.3	1 17.6
3 M	12 43 58	12 54 29	16 49 21	23 23 49	5 43.3	0♈59.9	27 13.1	11 12.6	11 51.8	10 0.4	18 38.2	29 53.0	1 18.0
4 Tu	12 47 54	13 53 37	29 54 7	6♉20 11	5 31.3	2 51.5	28 18.4	11 21.2	12 6.3	10 2.9	18 40.6	29 52.8	1 18.4
5 W	12 51 51	14 52 42	12♉41 55	18 59 24	5 19.5	4 44.6	29 23.5	11 30.4	12 20.8	10 5.5	18 42.9	29 52.6	1 18.8
6 Th	12 55 47	15 51 45	25 12 45	1♊22 10	5 8.9	6 39.0	0♊28.3	11 40.2	12 35.3	10 8.2	18 45.1	29 52.4	1 19.3
7 F	12 59 44	16 50 46	7♊27 59	13 30 33	5 0.4	8 34.9	1 32.8	11 50.6	12 49.8	10 11.0	18 47.4	29 52.3	1 19.8
8 Sa	13 3 40	17 49 45	19 30 20	25 27 50	4 54.4	10 32.2	2 37.1	12 1.6	13 4.3	10 13.9	18 49.6	29 52.2	1 20.3
9 Su	13 7 37	18 48 42	1♋23 36	7♋18 17	4 50.9	12 30.8	3 41.1	12 13.1	13 18.8	10 16.9	18 51.7	29 52.1	1 20.9
10 M	13 11 33	19 47 36	13 12 29	19 6 55	4D49.5	14 30.8	4 44.8	12 25.1	13 33.2	10 20.0	18 53.8	29D52.1	1 21.4
11 Tu	13 15 30	20 46 28	25 2 13	0♌59 7	4R49.4	16 32.1	5 48.2	12 37.7	13 47.7	10 23.2	18 55.9	29 52.1	1 22.0
12 W	13 19 27	21 45 18	6♌58 17	13 0 23	4 49.5	18 34.6	6 51.3	12 50.7	14 2.1	10 26.5	18 57.9	29 52.1	1 22.6
13 Th	13 23 23	22 44 5	19 6 4	25 15 55	4 48.8	20 38.2	7 54.1	13 4.3	14 16.6	10 29.9	18 59.9	29 52.2	1 23.2
14 F	13 27 20	23 42 50	1♍30 29	7♍50 14	4 46.2	22 42.9	8 56.5	13 18.4	14 31.0	10 33.4	19 1.9	29 52.3	1 23.9
15 Sa	13 31 16	24 41 33	14 15 32	20 46 39	4 41.2	24 48.5	9 58.7	13 33.0	14 45.4	10 37.0	19 3.8	29 52.4	1 24.6
16 Su	13 35 13	25 40 14	27 23 44	4♎ 6 47	4 33.5	26 54.8	11 0.5	13 48.0	14 59.7	10 40.7	19 5.6	29 52.6	1 25.2
17 M	13 39 9	26 38 52	10♎55 39	17 50 4	4 23.4	29 1.7	12 1.9	14 3.5	15 14.1	10 44.4	19 7.4	29 52.8	1 25.9
18 Tu	13 43 6	27 37 29	24 49 49	1♏53 41	4 11.9	1♉ 9.0	13 3.0	14 19.4	15 28.4	10 48.3	19 9.2	29 53.0	1 26.7
19 W	13 47 2	28 36 4	9♏ 1 38	16 12 43	3 60.0	3 16.4	14 3.7	14 35.8	15 42.7	10 52.2	19 10.9	29 53.2	1 27.4
20 Th	13 50 59	29 34 37	23 26 6	0♐40 57	3 48.9	5 23.7	15 4.1	14 52.6	15 57.0	10 56.3	19 12.6	29 53.5	1 28.2
21 F	13 54 56	0♉33 8	7♐56 27	15 11 51	3 39.9	7 30.6	16 4.0	15 9.8	16 11.3	11 0.4	19 14.3	29 53.9	1 29.0
22 Sa	13 58 52	1 31 37	22 26 26	29 39 37	3 33.6	9 36.7	17 3.6	15 27.4	16 25.6	11 4.6	19 15.9	29 54.2	1 29.8
23 Su	14 2 49	2 30 5	6♑50 56	13♑59 59	3 30.0	11 41.9	18 2.7	15 45.5	16 39.8	11 8.9	19 17.4	29 54.6	1 30.6
24 M	14 6 45	3 28 31	21 6 31	28 10 21	3 28.6	13 45.6	19 1.4	16 3.9	16 54.0	11 13.3	19 19.0	29 55.1	1 31.4
25 Tu	14 10 42	4 26 56	5♒11 23	12♒ 9 37	3 28.5	15 47.7	19 59.7	16 22.7	17 8.2	11 17.8	19 20.4	29 55.5	1 32.3
26 W	14 14 38	5 25 19	19 5 2	25 57 41	3 28.2	17 47.9	20 57.5	16 41.9	17 22.3	11 22.3	19 21.8	29 56.0	1 33.2
27 Th	14 18 35	6 23 41	2♓47 37	9♓34 52	3 26.5	19 45.8	21 54.8	17 1.5	17 36.4	11 27.0	19 23.2	29 56.6	1 34.1
28 F	14 22 31	7 22 0	16 19 28	23 1 24	3 22.5	21 41.1	22 51.7	17 21.5	17 50.5	11 31.7	19 24.5	29 57.1	1 35.0
29 Sa	14 26 28	8 20 19	29 40 38	6♈17 8	3 15.5	23 33.6	23 48.1	17 41.8	18 4.5	11 36.5	19 25.8	29 57.7	1 35.9
30 Su	14 30 25	9 18 35	12♈50 48	19 21 34	3 5.8	25 23.2	24 44.0	18 2.4	18 18.6	11 41.4	19 27.1	29 58.3	1 36.9

Astro Data Dy Hr Mn	Planet Ingress Dy Hr Mn	Last Aspect Dy Hr Mn	☽ Ingress Dy Hr Mn	Last Aspect Dy Hr Mn	☽ Ingress Dy Hr Mn	☽ Phases & Eclipses Dy Hr Mn	Astro Data
☽0N 4 18:23	♀ ♉ 9 21:49	29 8:38 ♀ □	♒ 1 3:18	1 17:37 ♆ △	♈ 1 17:48	4 3:57 ● 13♓16	1 MARCH 1916
♄ D 11 13:51	☿ ♓ 15 0:08	2 15:07 ♀ ✶	♓ 3 5:27	3 23:58 ♆ □	♉ 4 0:11	11 18:33 ☽ 20♊52	Julian Day # 5904
♇ D 15 16:59	♆ ♋ 19 15:22	4 3:57 ☉ ☌	♈ 5 8:56	6 9:04 ♆ ✶	♊ 6 9:19	19 17:26 ○ 28♍47	Delta T 18.4 sec
☽0S 19 4:32	☉ ♈ 20 22:47	7 9:42 ♀ ☌	♉ 7 15:08	7 22:38 ♅ △	♋ 8 21:11	26 16:22 ☽ 5♑41	SVP 06♓25'35"
♂ D 21 14:43		9 10:01 ☿ □	♊ 10 0:45	11 9:45 ♆ ☌	♌ 11 10:01		Obliquity 23°27'07"
♃□♄ 25 2:41	☿ ♈ 2 11:00	12 5:14 ☿ △	♋ 12 13:03	13 7:42 ☉ △	♍ 13 21:07	2 16:21 ● 12♈36	⚷ Chiron 21♓26.3
	♀ ♊ 5 13:31	14 12:55 ☉ △	♌ 15 1:41	16 4:27 ♆ ✶	♎ 16 4:40	10 14:35 ☽ 20♋23	☽ Mean ☊ 6♒34.4
☽0N 1 3:00	☿ ♉ 17 11:00	16 12:53 ♅ ☍	♍ 17 12:12	18 8:36 ♆ □	♏ 18 8:48	18 5:07 ○ 27♎50	
☿0N 4 20:01	☉ ♉ 20 10:25	19 19:37 ♆ ✶	♎ 19 19:37	20 10:42 ♆ △	♐ 20 10:52	24 22:38 ☽ 4♒24	1 APRIL 1916
♆ D 10 13:12		22 0:24 ♆ □	♏ 22 0:26	21 18:44 ♅ ✶	♑ 22 12:34		Julian Day # 5935
☽0S 15 13:18		24 3:43 ♆ △	♐ 24 3:48	24 14:59 ♆ ☍	♒ 24 15:07		Delta T 18.4 sec
☽0N 28 8:59		25 10:50 ♅ ✶	♑ 26 6:43	26 3:30 ♀ △	♓ 26 19:05		SVP 06♓25'31"
		28 9:38 ♆ ☍	♒ 28 9:47	29 0:31 ♆ △	♈ 29 0:35		Obliquity 23°27'07"
		30 1:00 ♀ □	♓ 30 13:18				⚷ Chiron 23♓17.8
							☽ Mean ☊ 4♒55.9

LONGITUDE — MAY 1916

Day	Sid.Time	☉	0 hr ☽	Noon ☽	True ☊	☿	♀	♂	♃	♄	♅	♆	♇
1 M	14 34 21	10♉16 50	25♈49 18	2♉13 56	2♒53.9	27♉ 9.5	25♊39.3	18♌23.4	18♈32.5	11♋46.3	19♒28.2	29♋59.0	1♋37.8
2 Tu	14 38 18	11 15 4	8♉35 22	14 53 33	2R 40.8	28 52.4	26 34.1	18 44.8	18 46.5	11 51.4	19 29.4	29 59.7	1 38.8
3 W	14 42 14	12 13 16	21 8 27	27 20 8	2 27.7	0♊31.8	27 28.3	19 6.5	19 0.4	11 56.5	19 30.5	0♌ 0.4	1 39.8
4 Th	14 46 11	13 11 26	3♊28 39	9♊34 8	2 15.7	2 7.5	28 21.9	19 28.5	19 14.2	12 1.7	19 31.5	0 1.2	1 40.8
5 F	14 50 7	14 9 34	15 36 49	21 36 58	2 5.9	3 39.5	29 15.0	19 50.8	19 28.1	12 6.9	19 32.5	0 1.9	1 41.9
6 Sa	14 54 4	15 7 40	27 34 53	3♋31 0	1 58.7	5 7.6	0♋ 7.3	20 13.4	19 41.9	12 12.3	19 33.5	0 2.8	1 42.9
7 Su	14 58 0	16 5 45	9♋25 44	15 19 37	1 54.2	6 31.7	0 59.1	20 36.4	19 55.6	12 17.7	19 34.4	0 3.6	1 44.0
8 M	15 1 57	17 3 48	21 13 11	27 7 2	1D 52.1	7 51.8	1 50.1	20 59.6	20 9.3	12 23.2	19 35.2	0 4.5	1 45.1
9 Tu	15 5 54	18 1 48	3♌ 1 49	8♌58 11	1 51.7	9 7.8	2 40.5	21 23.2	20 22.9	12 28.7	19 36.0	0 5.4	1 46.2
10 W	15 9 50	18 59 47	14 56 49	20 58 24	1R 51.9	10 19.6	3 30.1	21 47.0	20 36.5	12 34.3	19 36.8	0 6.3	1 47.3
11 Th	15 13 47	19 57 44	27 3 36	3♍13 6	1 51.7	11 27.2	4 18.9	22 11.1	20 50.1	12 40.0	19 37.5	0 7.3	1 48.4
12 F	15 17 43	20 55 40	9♍27 31	15 47 27	1 50.2	12 30.5	5 6.9	22 35.4	21 3.6	12 45.8	19 38.1	0 8.3	1 49.5
13 Sa	15 21 40	21 53 33	22 13 23	28 45 44	1 46.6	13 29.5	5 54.1	23 0.1	21 17.1	12 51.6	19 38.7	0 9.3	1 50.7
14 Su	15 25 36	22 51 25	5♎24 49	12♎10 46	1 40.6	14 24.0	6 40.5	23 25.0	21 30.5	12 57.5	19 39.3	0 10.4	1 51.9
15 M	15 29 33	23 49 14	19 3 35	26 3 7	1 32.5	15 14.0	7 25.9	23 50.1	21 43.8	13 3.4	19 39.8	0 11.5	1 53.0
16 Tu	15 33 29	24 47 3	3♏ 8 58	10♏20 38	1 22.9	15 59.5	8 10.5	24 15.5	21 57.1	13 9.4	19 40.3	0 12.6	1 54.2
17 W	15 37 26	25 44 50	17 37 22	24 58 19	1 12.8	16 40.4	8 54.1	24 41.1	22 10.3	13 15.5	19 40.7	0 13.7	1 55.4
18 Th	15 41 23	26 42 35	2♐22 30	9♐48 50	1 3.4	17 16.6	9 36.6	25 7.0	22 23.5	13 21.6	19 41.0	0 14.9	1 56.7
19 F	15 45 19	27 40 19	17 16 13	24 43 35	0 55.8	17 48.0	10 18.2	25 33.1	22 36.6	13 27.8	19 41.3	0 16.1	1 57.9
20 Sa	15 49 16	28 38 2	2♑ 9 53	9♑34 13	0 50.5	18 14.8	10 58.7	25 59.5	22 49.7	13 34.1	19 41.6	0 17.3	1 59.1
21 Su	15 53 12	29 35 44	16 55 46	24 13 53	0D 47.7	18 36.7	11 38.0	26 26.0	23 2.7	13 40.4	19 41.8	0 18.6	2 0.4
22 M	15 57 9	0♊33 24	1♒28 3	8♒37 56	0 47.0	18 53.8	12 16.3	26 52.8	23 15.7	13 46.7	19 42.0	0 19.9	2 1.7
23 Tu	16 1 5	1 31 4	15 43 16	22 43 59	0 47.5	19 6.1	12 53.3	27 19.8	23 28.6	13 53.1	19 42.1	0 21.2	2 3.0
24 W	16 5 2	2 28 42	29 40 4	6♓31 36	0R 48.1	19 13.7	13 29.1	27 47.0	23 41.4	13 59.6	19R 42.2	0 22.5	2 4.2
25 Th	16 8 58	3 26 20	13♓18 41	20 1 31	0 47.7	19R 16.5	14 3.6	28 14.5	23 54.2	14 6.1	19 42.2	0 23.9	2 5.5
26 F	16 12 55	4 23 56	26 40 17	3♈15 11	0 45.5	19 14.7	14 36.8	28 42.1	24 6.8	14 12.7	19 42.2	0 25.3	2 6.9
27 Sa	16 16 52	5 21 32	9♈46 25	16 14 10	0 41.0	19 8.4	15 8.6	29 10.0	24 19.5	14 19.3	19 42.1	0 26.7	2 8.2
28 Su	16 20 48	6 19 7	22 38 36	28 59 53	0 34.3	18 57.8	15 39.0	29 38.0	24 32.0	14 26.0	19 42.0	0 28.1	2 9.5
29 M	16 24 45	7 16 40	5♉18 9	11♉33 31	0 25.9	18 43.1	16 7.9	0♍ 6.3	24 44.5	14 32.7	19 41.8	0 29.6	2 10.8
30 Tu	16 28 41	8 14 13	17 46 7	23 56 2	0 16.5	18 24.6	16 35.2	0 34.7	24 56.9	14 39.5	19 41.5	0 31.1	2 12.2
31 W	16 32 38	9 11 45	0♊ 3 24	6♊ 8 21	0 7.0	18 2.6	17 1.0	1 3.3	25 9.3	14 46.3	19 41.3	0 32.6	2 13.5

LONGITUDE — JUNE 1916

Day	Sid.Time	☉	0 hr ☽	Noon ☽	True ☊	☿	♀	♂	♃	♄	♅	♆	♇
1 Th	16 36 34	10♊ 9 16	12♊11 1	18♊11 34	29♑58.4	17♊37.5	17♋25.1	1♍32.2	25♈21.5	14♋53.1	19♒41.0	0♌34.1	2♋14.9
2 F	16 40 31	11 6 46	24 10 10	0♋ 7 5	29R 51.4	17R 9.7	17 47.5	2 1.2	25 33.7	15 0.1	19R 40.6	0 35.7	2 16.3
3 Sa	16 44 27	12 4 15	6♋ 2 34	11 56 56	29 46.5	16 39.7	18 8.1	2 30.4	25 45.8	15 7.0	19 40.2	0 37.3	2 17.7
4 Su	16 48 24	13 1 43	17 50 31	23 43 43	29 43.7	16 8.0	18 26.9	2 59.8	25 57.8	15 14.0	19 39.7	0 38.9	2 19.1
5 M	16 52 21	13 59 9	29 36 59	5♌30 47	29D 42.8	15 35.1	18 43.8	3 29.3	26 9.8	15 21.0	19 39.2	0 40.5	2 20.5
6 Tu	16 56 17	14 56 35	11♌25 38	17 22 5	29 43.4	15 1.6	18 58.7	3 59.1	26 21.7	15 28.1	19 38.6	0 42.2	2 21.9
7 W	17 0 14	15 53 59	23 20 44	29 22 11	29 44.8	14 28.1	19 11.6	4 29.0	26 33.4	15 35.2	19 38.0	0 43.9	2 23.3
8 Th	17 4 10	16 51 22	5♍27 3	11♍35 57	29 46.1	13 55.2	19 22.5	4 59.1	26 45.1	15 42.3	19 37.4	0 45.6	2 24.7
9 F	17 8 7	17 48 45	17 49 32	24 8 21	29R 46.7	13 23.4	19 31.1	5 29.3	26 56.7	15 49.5	19 36.7	0 47.3	2 26.1
10 Sa	17 12 3	18 46 6	0♎32 59	7♎ 3 54	29 46.0	12 53.2	19 37.6	5 59.7	27 8.2	15 56.7	19 35.9	0 49.0	2 27.5
11 Su	17 16 0	19 43 26	13 41 31	20 26 8	29 43.7	12 25.2	19 41.8	6 30.2	27 19.7	16 4.0	19 35.1	0 50.8	2 29.0
12 M	17 19 56	20 40 45	27 17 54	4♏16 49	29 39.8	11 59.9	19R 43.7	7 0.9	27 31.0	16 11.3	19 34.3	0 52.5	2 30.4
13 Tu	17 23 53	21 38 3	11♏22 44	18 35 17	29 34.8	11 37.6	19 43.3	7 31.8	27 42.2	16 18.6	19 33.4	0 54.3	2 31.8
14 W	17 27 50	22 35 20	25 53 54	3♐17 52	29 29.4	11 18.7	19 40.5	8 2.8	27 53.4	16 25.9	19 32.5	0 56.1	2 33.3
15 Th	17 31 46	23 32 37	10♐46 15	18 18 0	29 24.2	11 3.6	19 35.4	8 34.0	28 4.5	16 33.3	19 31.5	0 58.0	2 34.7
16 F	17 35 43	24 29 53	25 51 57	3♑26 54	29 20.1	10 52.5	19 27.8	9 5.3	28 15.4	16 40.7	19 30.5	0 59.8	2 36.2
17 Sa	17 39 39	25 27 9	11♑ 1 37	18 34 55	29 17.5	10 45.7	19 17.8	9 36.7	28 26.3	16 48.1	19 29.4	1 1.7	2 37.6
18 Su	17 43 36	26 24 24	26 5 43	3♒33 4	29D 16.4	10D 43.2	19 5.3	10 8.3	28 37.0	16 55.6	19 28.3	1 3.6	2 39.1
19 M	17 47 32	27 21 38	10♒56 7	18 14 14	29 16.8	10 45.3	18 50.5	10 40.0	28 47.7	17 3.1	19 27.2	1 5.5	2 40.6
20 Tu	17 51 29	28 18 52	25 26 56	2♓33 54	29 18.0	10 52.0	18 33.4	11 11.9	28 58.3	17 10.6	19 26.0	1 7.4	2 42.0
21 W	17 55 26	29 16 6	9♓34 56	16 30 2	29 19.4	11 3.4	18 13.9	11 43.9	29 8.7	17 18.1	19 24.8	1 9.4	2 43.5
22 Th	17 59 22	0♋13 20	23 19 14	0♈ 2 43	29R 20.4	11 19.5	17 52.2	12 16.0	29 19.1	17 25.7	19 23.5	1 11.3	2 44.9
23 F	18 3 19	1 10 34	6♈40 43	13 13 31	29 20.4	11 40.3	17 28.4	12 48.3	29 29.3	17 33.3	19 22.2	1 13.3	2 46.4
24 Sa	18 7 15	2 7 48	19 41 27	26 4 52	29 19.3	12 5.7	17 2.5	13 20.7	29 39.4	17 40.9	19 20.9	1 15.3	2 47.9
25 Su	18 11 12	3 5 1	2♉24 6	8♉39 32	29 17.0	12 35.8	16 34.6	13 53.2	29 49.5	17 48.5	19 19.5	1 17.3	2 49.3
26 M	18 15 8	4 2 15	14 51 30	21 0 21	29 13.7	13 10.5	16 5.0	14 25.8	29 59.4	17 56.1	19 18.1	1 19.3	2 50.8
27 Tu	18 19 5	4 59 29	27 6 24	3♊ 9 57	29 9.9	13 49.7	15 33.7	14 58.6	0♉ 9.2	18 3.8	19 16.6	1 21.3	2 52.3
28 W	18 23 1	5 56 42	9♊11 18	15 10 44	29 6.0	14 33.5	15 0.9	15 31.6	0 18.8	18 11.4	19 15.1	1 23.3	2 53.7
29 Th	18 26 58	6 53 56	21 8 31	27 4 55	29 2.6	15 21.6	14 26.8	16 4.6	0 28.4	18 19.1	19 13.6	1 25.4	2 55.2
30 F	18 30 55	7 51 9	3♋ 0 10	8♋54 34	28 59.9	16 14.1	13 51.6	16 37.8	0 37.9	18 26.8	19 12.0	1 27.5	2 56.7

Astro Data	Planet Ingress	Last Aspect	☽ Ingress	Last Aspect	☽ Ingress	☽ Phases & Eclipses	Astro Data
Dy Hr Mn	Dy Hr Mn	Dy Hr Mn	Dy Hr Mn	Dy Hr Mn	Dy Hr Mn	Dy Hr Mn	1 MAY 1916
♃⚹♅ 5 8:19	☿ ♊ 2 16:14	1 7:47 ♆ □	♉ 1 7:49	2 2:51 ♃ ⚹	♋ 2 11:46	2 5:29 ● 11♉28	Julian Day # 5965
☽0S 12 21:54	♆ ♌ 2 10:49	2 20:51 ♅ □	♊ 3 17:12	4 16:51 ♃ □	♌ 5 0:47	10 8:47 ☽ 19♌21	Delta T 18.5 sec
♅ R 24 20:13	♀ ♋ 5 20:37	5 8:44 ♂ ⚹	♋ 6 4:53	7 6:31 ♃ △	♍ 7 13:15	17 14:11 ○ 26♏19	SVP 06♓25'28"
☽0N 25 13:35	☉ ♊ 21 10:06	7 21:47 ♃ □	♌ 8 17:51	9 3:16 ♀ ⚹	♎ 9 22:59	24 5:16 ☽ 2♓41	Obliquity 23°27'06"
☿ R 25 2:33	♂ ♍ 28 18:42	10 14:04 ♂ ☌	♍ 11 5:45	12 0:23 ♃ ☍	♏ 12 4:40	31 19:37 ● 9♊59	⚷ Chiron 24♓53.1
	☊ ♑ 31 19:17	12 23:20 ☉ △	♎ 13 14:15	13 13:50 ♀ △	♐ 14 6:40		☽ Mean ☊ 3♒20.6
☽0S 9 5:24		15 8:28 ♂ ⚹	♏ 15 18:42	16 3:50 ♃ △	♑ 16 6:33	8 23:58 ☽ 17♍49	
♀ R 12 7:48	☉ ♋ 21 18:24	17 14:11 ☉ ☍	♐ 17 20:09	18 4:06 ♃ □	♒ 18 6:16	15 21:41 ○ 24♐24	1 JUNE 1916
☿ D 18 1:02	♃ ♉ 26 1:32	19 13:44 ♂ △	♑ 19 20:30	20 6:00 ♃ ⚹	♓ 20 7:39	22 13:16 ☽ 0♈45	Julian Day # 5996
☽0N 21 19:05		21 10:12 ♃ □	♒ 21 21:33	21 14:39 ♀ △	♈ 22 11:55	30 10:43 ● 8♋17	Delta T 18.6 sec
		23 20:37 ♂ ☍	♓ 24 0:35	24 19:02 ♃ ☌	♉ 24 19:26		SVP 06♓25'23"
		25 10:39 ☿ □	♈ 26 6:03	26 8:39 ♅ □	♊ 27 5:43		Obliquity 23°27'05"
		28 13:43 ♂ △	♉ 28 13:54	28 20:09 ♅ △	♋ 29 17:55		⚷ Chiron 25♓59.8
		30 3:44 ♅ □	♊ 30 23:53				☽ Mean ☊ 1♒42.1

JULY 1916 — LONGITUDE

Day	Sid.Time	☉	0 hr ☽	Noon ☽	True ☊	☿	♀	♂	♃	♄	♅	♆	♇
1 Sa	18 34 51	8♋48 23	14♋48 22	20♋41 50	28♑58.2	17♊10.9	13♋15.5	17♍11.1	0♉47.2	18♋34.5	19♒10.4	1♌29.5	2♋58.1
2 Su	18 38 48	9 45 36	26 35 16	2♌28 59	28D 57.5	18 12.0	12R 38.7	17 44.5	0 56.4	18 42.3	19R 8.7	1 31.6	2 59.6
3 M	18 42 44	10 42 49	8♌23 19	14 18 37	28 57.8	19 17.2	12 1.5	18 18.1	1 5.4	18 50.0	19 7.1	1 33.7	3 1.0
4 Tu	18 46 41	11 40 2	20 15 17	26 13 42	28 58.7	20 26.6	11 24.0	18 51.7	1 14.4	18 57.8	19 5.3	1 35.9	3 2.5
5 W	18 50 37	12 37 14	2♍14 19	8♍17 36	29 0.0	21 40.1	10 46.6	19 25.5	1 23.2	19 5.5	19 3.6	1 38.0	3 3.9
6 Th	18 54 34	13 34 27	14 24 0	20 34 2	29 1.4	22 57.6	10 9.4	19 59.4	1 31.9	19 13.3	19 1.8	1 40.1	3 5.4
7 F	18 58 30	14 31 39	26 48 11	3♎ 6 57	29 2.4	24 19.1	9 32.7	20 33.4	1 40.4	19 21.1	18 60.0	1 42.2	3 6.8
8 Sa	19 2 27	15 28 51	9♎30 49	16 0 13	29R 3.0	25 44.4	8 56.7	21 7.5	1 48.8	19 28.8	18 58.2	1 44.4	3 8.3
9 Su	19 6 24	16 26 3	22 35 34	29 17 11	29 3.0	27 13.7	8 21.7	21 41.8	1 57.1	19 36.6	18 56.3	1 46.5	3 9.7
10 M	19 10 20	17 23 15	6♏ 5 21	13♏ 0 11	29 2.5	28 46.7	7 47.8	22 16.1	2 5.3	19 44.4	18 54.4	1 48.7	3 11.1
11 Tu	19 14 17	18 20 27	20 1 41	27 9 45	29 1.5	0♋23.3	7 15.3	22 50.6	2 13.3	19 52.2	18 52.4	1 50.9	3 12.6
12 W	19 18 13	19 17 39	4♐24 3	11♐44 8	29 0.4	2 3.6	6 44.3	23 25.1	2 21.2	19 60.0	18 50.5	1 53.1	3 14.0
13 Th	19 22 10	20 14 51	19 9 20	26 38 51	28 59.4	3 47.3	6 15.0	23 59.8	2 28.9	20 7.8	18 48.5	1 55.2	3 15.4
14 F	19 26 6	21 12 3	4♑11 43	11♑46 50	28 58.6	5 34.4	5 47.5	24 34.5	2 36.5	20 15.6	18 46.5	1 57.4	3 16.8
15 Sa	19 30 3	22 9 15	19 23 3	26 59 9	28D 58.2	7 24.5	5 22.1	25 9.4	2 43.9	20 23.4	18 44.5	1 59.6	3 18.2
16 Su	19 33 59	23 6 28	4♒33 57	12♒ 6 17	28 58.2	9 17.7	4 58.7	25 44.4	2 51.2	20 31.2	18 42.4	2 1.8	3 19.6
17 M	19 37 56	24 3 41	19 35 6	26 59 28	28 58.4	11 13.5	4 37.5	26 19.5	2 58.4	20 38.9	18 40.3	2 4.0	3 21.0
18 Tu	19 41 53	25 0 54	4♓18 36	11♓31 53	28 58.8	13 11.8	4 18.6	26 54.6	3 5.4	20 46.7	18 38.2	2 6.2	3 22.4
19 W	19 45 49	25 58 9	18 38 52	25 39 18	28 59.1	15 12.3	4 2.0	27 29.9	3 12.2	20 54.5	18 36.1	2 8.5	3 23.8
20 Th	19 49 46	26 55 23	2♈33 3	9♈20 8	28 59.3	17 14.7	3 47.8	28 5.3	3 18.9	21 2.3	18 33.9	2 10.7	3 25.1
21 F	19 53 42	27 52 39	16 0 43	22 35 3	28 59.4	19 18.6	3 36.0	28 40.7	3 25.5	21 10.0	18 31.7	2 12.9	3 26.5
22 Sa	19 57 39	28 49 56	29 3 28	5♉26 23	28 59.4	21 23.9	3 26.6	29 16.3	3 31.9	21 17.8	18 29.6	2 15.1	3 27.8
23 Su	20 1 35	29 47 13	11♉44 14	17 57 30	28 59.4	23 30.0	3 19.7	29 52.0	3 38.1	21 25.5	18 27.3	2 17.3	3 29.2
24 M	20 5 32	0♌44 31	24 6 41	0♊12 18	28 59.5	25 36.8	3 15.1	0♎27.8	3 44.2	21 33.2	18 25.1	2 19.6	3 30.5
25 Tu	20 9 28	1 41 51	6♊14 50	12 14 46	28 59.8	27 43.9	3D 12.8	1 3.6	3 50.1	21 41.0	18 22.9	2 21.8	3 31.8
26 W	20 13 25	2 39 11	18 12 34	24 8 43	29 0.1	29 51.0	3 13.0	1 39.6	3 55.8	21 48.7	18 20.6	2 24.0	3 33.1
27 Th	20 17 22	3 36 32	0♋ 3 36	5♋57 38	29 0.6	1♌57.8	3 15.4	2 15.7	4 1.4	21 56.4	18 18.3	2 26.2	3 34.5
28 F	20 21 18	4 33 54	11 51 11	17 44 38	29 1.0	4 4.2	3 20.0	2 51.8	4 6.8	22 4.1	18 16.0	2 28.5	3 35.7
29 Sa	20 25 15	5 31 17	23 38 16	29 32 26	29R 1.3	6 9.9	3 26.9	3 28.1	4 12.0	22 11.7	18 13.7	2 30.7	3 37.0
30 Su	20 29 11	6 28 40	5♌27 25	11♌23 29	29 1.3	8 14.8	3 35.9	4 4.5	4 17.1	22 19.4	18 11.4	2 32.9	3 38.3
31 M	20 33 8	7 26 5	17 20 54	23 19 57	29 0.8	10 18.6	3 47.1	4 40.9	4 22.0	22 27.0	18 9.1	2 35.1	3 39.6

AUGUST 1916 — LONGITUDE

Day	Sid.Time	☉	0 hr ☽	Noon ☽	True ☊	☿	♀	♂	♃	♄	♅	♆	♇
1 Tu	20 37 4	8♌23 30	29♌20 52	5♍23 57	28♑60.0	12♌21.2	4♋ 0.2	5♎17.5	4♉26.7	22♋34.6	18♒ 6.7	2♌37.4	3♋40.8
2 W	20 41 1	9 20 56	11♍29 26	17 37 37	28R 58.7	14 22.6	4 15.4	5 54.1	4 31.3	22 42.2	18R 4.4	2 39.6	3 42.0
3 Th	20 44 57	10 18 22	23 48 46	0♎ 3 10	28 57.2	16 22.6	4 32.4	6 30.9	4 35.6	22 49.8	18 2.0	2 41.8	3 43.3
4 F	20 48 54	11 15 50	6♎21 8	12 42 58	28 55.7	18 21.2	4 51.3	7 7.7	4 39.8	22 57.3	17 59.6	2 44.0	3 44.5
5 Sa	20 52 51	12 13 18	19 8 57	25 39 23	28 54.3	20 18.4	5 12.1	7 44.6	4 43.8	23 4.9	17 57.3	2 46.2	3 45.7
6 Su	20 56 47	13 10 47	2♏14 34	8♏54 45	28D 53.4	22 14.1	5 34.5	8 21.6	4 47.6	23 12.4	17 54.9	2 48.4	3 46.9
7 M	21 0 44	14 8 17	15 40 8	22 30 54	28 53.2	24 8.2	5 58.7	8 58.7	4 51.3	23 19.8	17 52.5	2 50.6	3 48.0
8 Tu	21 4 40	15 5 47	29 27 7	6♐28 49	28 53.6	26 0.9	6 24.5	9 35.9	4 54.8	23 27.3	17 50.1	2 52.8	3 49.2
9 W	21 8 37	16 3 19	13♐35 54	20 48 8	28 54.5	27 52.0	6 51.8	10 13.2	4 58.0	23 34.7	17 47.7	2 55.0	3 50.3
10 Th	21 12 33	17 0 51	28 5 11	5♑26 34	28 55.7	29 41.6	7 20.7	10 50.5	5 1.1	23 42.1	17 45.3	2 57.2	3 51.5
11 F	21 16 30	17 58 24	12♑51 40	20 19 43	28 56.8	1♍29.6	7 51.1	11 28.0	5 4.0	23 49.5	17 42.9	2 59.3	3 52.6
12 Sa	21 20 26	18 55 59	27 49 49	5♒21 0	28R 57.3	3 16.1	8 22.9	12 5.5	5 6.8	23 56.8	17 40.6	3 1.5	3 53.7
13 Su	21 24 23	19 53 34	12♒52 13	20 22 22	28 56.9	5 1.2	8 56.0	12 43.1	5 9.3	24 4.1	17 38.2	3 3.6	3 54.8
14 M	21 28 20	20 51 10	27 50 21	5♓15 10	28 55.4	6 44.7	9 30.5	13 20.8	5 11.6	24 11.4	17 35.8	3 5.8	3 55.8
15 Tu	21 32 16	21 48 47	12♓35 50	19 51 31	28 52.9	8 26.7	10 6.2	13 58.6	5 13.8	24 18.6	17 33.4	3 7.9	3 56.9
16 W	21 36 13	22 46 26	27 1 32	4♈ 5 21	28 49.7	10 7.3	10 43.2	14 36.5	5 15.7	24 25.8	17 31.0	3 10.0	3 57.9
17 Th	21 40 9	23 44 7	11♈ 2 37	17 53 7	28 46.3	11 46.4	11 21.4	15 14.4	5 17.5	24 33.0	17 28.6	3 12.2	3 58.9
18 F	21 44 6	24 41 49	24 36 49	1♉13 50	28 43.2	13 24.1	12 0.7	15 52.5	5 19.1	24 40.1	17 26.3	3 14.3	3 60.0
19 Sa	21 48 2	25 39 32	7♉44 23	14 8 51	28 40.9	15 0.4	12 41.1	16 30.6	5 20.4	24 47.2	17 23.9	3 16.4	4 0.9
20 Su	21 51 59	26 37 17	20 27 38	26 41 15	28D 39.7	16 35.2	13 22.6	17 8.8	5 21.6	24 54.2	17 21.5	3 18.4	4 1.9
21 M	21 55 55	27 35 4	2♊50 15	8♊55 13	28 39.6	18 8.6	14 5.1	17 47.1	5 22.6	25 1.2	17 19.2	3 20.5	4 2.9
22 Tu	21 59 52	28 32 53	14 56 46	20 55 29	28 40.6	19 40.5	14 48.5	18 25.5	5 23.4	25 8.2	17 16.9	3 22.6	4 3.8
23 W	22 3 49	29 30 43	26 52 1	2♋46 56	28 42.2	21 11.0	15 33.0	19 3.9	5 24.0	25 15.1	17 14.5	3 24.6	4 4.7
24 Th	22 7 45	0♍28 36	8♋40 48	14 34 11	28 44.0	22 40.1	16 18.3	19 42.5	5 24.3	25 22.0	17 12.2	3 26.7	4 5.6
25 F	22 11 42	1 26 29	20 27 36	26 21 31	28R 45.2	24 7.8	17 4.5	20 21.1	5R 24.5	25 28.8	17 9.9	3 28.7	4 6.5
26 Sa	22 15 38	2 24 25	2♌16 23	8♌12 36	28 45.5	25 34.0	17 51.6	20 59.8	5 24.5	25 35.6	17 7.6	3 30.7	4 7.4
27 Su	22 19 35	3 22 22	14 10 30	20 10 25	28 44.3	26 58.7	18 39.4	21 38.6	5 24.3	25 42.4	17 5.4	3 32.7	4 8.3
28 M	22 23 31	4 20 21	26 12 37	2♍17 19	28 41.4	28 21.9	19 28.1	22 17.5	5 23.8	25 49.1	17 3.1	3 34.7	4 9.1
29 Tu	22 27 28	5 18 21	8♍24 43	14 34 57	28 36.8	29 43.6	20 17.5	22 56.5	5 23.2	25 55.7	17 0.9	3 36.6	4 9.9
30 W	22 31 24	6 16 23	20 48 10	27 4 26	28 30.9	1♎ 3.7	21 7.6	23 35.5	5 22.4	26 2.3	16 58.6	3 38.6	4 10.7
31 Th	22 35 21	7 14 26	3♎23 50	9♎46 25	28 24.2	2 22.2	21 58.4	24 14.6	5 21.4	26 8.9	16 56.4	3 40.5	4 11.5

Astro Data	Planet Ingress	Last Aspect	☽ Ingress	Last Aspect	☽ Ingress	☽ Phases & Eclipses
Dy Hr Mn	Dy Hr Mn	Dy Hr Mn	Dy Hr Mn	Dy Hr Mn	Dy Hr Mn	Dy Hr Mn
♄⚻♅ 4 19:07	☿ ♋ 10 18:17	1 7:46 ♄ ☌	♌ 2 6:57	31 1:36 ♅ ☍	♍ 1 1:18	8 11:54 ☽ 15♎57
☽0S 6 11:42	☉ ♌ 23 5:21	4 0:25 ☿ ✶	♍ 4 19:32	2 22:05 ♄ ✶	♎ 3 11:54	15 4:40 ○ 22♑20
♃□♆ 7 6:52	♂ ♎ 23 5:23	6 18:38 ☿ □	♎ 7 6:06	5 7:20 ♄ □	♏ 5 19:56	15 4:46 ☍ P 0.794
☽0N 19 2:58	☿ ♌ 26 1:42	9 9:24 ☿ △	♏ 9 13:16	7 17:09 ☿ □	♐ 8 0:56	21 23:33 ☽ 28♈49
♃✶♇ 21 4:47		11 4:57 ♂ ✶	♐ 11 16:43	10 3:00 ☿ △	♑ 10 3:08	30 2:15 ● 6♌34
♅Q♇ 22 11:36	☿ ♍ 10 4:04	13 8:05 ♂ □	♑ 13 17:20	11 17:44 ♄ ☍	♒ 12 3:28	30 2:05:52 ☌ A 6'24"
♂0S 24 18:24	☉ ♍ 23 12:09	15 9:28 ♂ △	♒ 15 16:46	13 12:00 ☉ ☍	♓ 14 3:29	
♀ D 25 10:48	☿ ♎ 29 4:52	16 22:32 ♅ ☌	♓ 17 16:55	15 19:36 ♄ △	♈ 16 5:02	6 21:05 ☽ 14♏01
		19 15:52 ♂ ☍	♈ 19 19:32	18 0:10 ☉ △	♉ 18 9:45	13 12:00 ○ 20♒22
☽0S 2 17:25		21 23:33 ☉ □	♉ 22 1:46	20 12:52 ☉ □	♊ 20 18:27	20 12:52 ☽ 27♉08
☽0N 15 13:00		24 3:34 ♅ ✶	♊ 24 11:36	23 5:50 ☉ ✶	♋ 23 6:21	28 17:24 ● 5♍02
♃ R 25 9:34		26 0:16 ♅ △	♋ 26 23:53	25 10:19 ♄ ☌	♌ 25 19:24	
☿0S 28 0:47		28 21:02 ♄ ☌	♌ 29 12:56	27 15:47 ♂ ✶	♍ 28 7:30	
☽0S 29 23:29				30 10:07 ♄ ✶	♎ 30 17:34	

Astro Data

1 JULY 1916
Julian Day # 6026
Delta T 18.6 sec
SVP 06♓25'17"
Obliquity 23°27'05"
⚷ Chiron 26♓20.8R
☽ Mean ☊ 0♒06.8

1 AUGUST 1916
Julian Day # 6057
Delta T 18.7 sec
SVP 06♓25'12"
Obliquity 23°27'05"
⚷ Chiron 25♓53.6R
☽ Mean ☊ 28♑28.3

LONGITUDE — SEPTEMBER 1916

Day	Sid.Time	☉	0 hr ☽	Noon ☽	True ☊	☿	♀	♂	♃	♄	♅	♆	♇
1 F	22 39 18	8♍12 31	16♎12 16	22♎41 24	28♑17.4	3♎39.1	22♋49.9	24♎53.9	5♉20.1	26♋15.4	16♒54.2	3♌42.4	4♋12.2
2 Sa	22 43 14	9 10 37	29 13 52	5♏49 44	28R 11.4	4 54.2	23 42.1	25 33.1	5R 18.7	26 21.8	16R 52.1	3 44.3	4 12.9
3 Su	22 47 11	10 8 45	12♏29 2	19 11 52	28 6.7	6 7.6	24 34.8	26 12.5	5 17.1	26 28.2	16 49.9	3 46.2	4 13.7
4 M	22 51 7	11 6 55	25 58 16	2♐48 17	28 3.8	7 19.1	25 28.2	26 52.0	5 15.2	26 34.5	16 47.8	3 48.1	4 14.4
5 Tu	22 55 4	12 5 6	9♐42 0	16 39 25	28D 2.7	8 28.6	26 22.2	27 31.5	5 13.2	26 40.8	16 45.7	3 49.9	4 15.0
6 W	22 59 0	13 3 18	23 40 31	0♑45 15	28 3.1	9 36.1	27 16.8	28 11.1	5 11.0	26 47.0	16 43.7	3 51.7	4 15.7
7 Th	23 2 57	14 1 32	7♑53 28	15 4 57	28 4.2	10 41.5	28 11.9	28 50.8	5 8.6	26 53.1	16 41.6	3 53.5	4 16.3
8 F	23 6 53	14 59 48	22 19 24	29 36 23	28R 5.2	11 44.6	29 7.5	29 30.6	5 6.0	26 59.2	16 39.6	3 55.3	4 16.9
9 Sa	23 10 50	15 58 5	6♒55 25	14♒15 49	28 5.0	12 45.3	0♌ 3.7	0♏10.4	5 3.2	27 5.3	16 37.6	3 57.1	4 17.5
10 Su	23 14 47	16 56 23	21 36 54	28 57 49	28 2.9	13 43.5	1 0.4	0 50.3	5 0.2	27 11.2	16 35.6	3 58.8	4 18.1
11 M	23 18 43	17 54 43	6♓17 44	13♓35 43	27 58.6	14 38.9	1 57.5	1 30.3	4 57.0	27 17.1	16 33.7	4 0.6	4 18.6
12 Tu	23 22 40	18 53 5	20 50 54	28 2 26	27 52.2	15 31.4	2 55.2	2 10.4	4 53.6	27 23.0	16 31.8	4 2.3	4 19.2
13 W	23 26 36	19 51 28	5♈ 9 33	12♈11 35	27 44.2	16 20.8	3 53.3	2 50.5	4 50.1	27 28.7	16 29.9	4 3.9	4 19.7
14 Th	23 30 33	20 49 54	19 8 0	25 58 25	27 35.5	17 6.9	4 51.9	3 30.7	4 46.3	27 34.4	16 28.0	4 5.6	4 20.2
15 F	23 34 29	21 48 21	2♉42 36	9♉20 28	27 27.2	17 49.4	5 50.9	4 11.0	4 42.4	27 40.1	16 26.2	4 7.2	4 20.6
16 Sa	23 38 26	22 46 51	15 52 6	22 17 40	27 20.1	18 28.0	6 50.4	4 51.4	4 38.3	27 45.6	16 24.4	4 8.8	4 21.1
17 Su	23 42 22	23 45 23	28 37 30	4♊52 1	27 14.9	19 2.5	7 50.3	5 31.9	4 34.0	27 51.1	16 22.7	4 10.4	4 21.5
18 M	23 46 19	24 43 57	11♊ 1 43	17 7 10	27 11.8	19 32.5	8 50.5	6 12.4	4 29.5	27 56.6	16 21.0	4 12.0	4 21.9
19 Tu	23 50 16	25 42 34	23 8 58	29 7 48	27D 10.7	19 57.7	9 51.2	6 53.0	4 24.8	28 1.9	16 19.3	4 13.5	4 22.3
20 W	23 54 12	26 41 12	5♋ 4 18	10♋59 11	27 10.9	20 17.7	10 52.3	7 33.7	4 20.0	28 7.2	16 17.6	4 15.1	4 22.6
21 Th	23 58 9	27 39 53	16 53 5	22 46 42	27R 11.7	20 32.2	11 53.7	8 14.5	4 15.0	28 12.4	16 16.0	4 16.6	4 23.0
22 F	0 2 5	28 38 36	28 40 40	4♌35 34	27 12.1	20R 40.8	12 55.5	8 55.3	4 9.9	28 17.6	16 14.5	4 18.0	4 23.3
23 Sa	0 6 2	29 37 21	10♌32 0	16 30 28	27 11.1	20 43.1	13 57.6	9 36.2	4 4.5	28 22.6	16 12.9	4 19.5	4 23.6
24 Su	0 9 58	0♎36 9	22 31 28	28 35 23	27 8.0	20 38.8	15 0.0	10 17.2	3 59.0	28 27.6	16 11.4	4 20.9	4 23.8
25 M	0 13 55	1 34 58	4♍42 35	10♍53 19	27 2.3	20 27.4	16 2.8	10 58.3	3 53.4	28 32.5	16 9.9	4 22.3	4 24.1
26 Tu	0 17 51	2 33 50	17 7 48	23 26 9	26 54.1	20 8.8	17 5.9	11 39.4	3 47.6	28 37.3	16 8.5	4 23.7	4 24.3
27 W	0 21 48	3 32 43	29 48 24	6♎14 33	26 43.8	19 42.8	18 9.3	12 20.6	3 41.6	28 42.1	16 7.1	4 25.0	4 24.5
28 Th	0 25 45	4 31 39	12♎44 30	19 18 6	26 32.1	19 9.2	19 13.1	13 1.9	3 35.5	28 46.7	16 5.8	4 26.3	4 24.6
29 F	0 29 41	5 30 36	25 55 10	2♏35 28	26 20.3	18 28.3	20 17.1	13 43.3	3 29.3	28 51.3	16 4.5	4 27.6	4 24.8
30 Sa	0 33 38	6 29 36	9♏18 46	16 4 48	26 9.4	17 40.4	21 21.3	14 24.8	3 22.9	28 55.8	16 3.2	4 28.8	4 24.9

LONGITUDE — OCTOBER 1916

Day	Sid.Time	☉	0 hr ☽	Noon ☽	True ☊	☿	♀	♂	♃	♄	♅	♆	♇
1 Su	0 37 34	7♎28 38	22♏53 19	29♏44 8	26♑ 0.6	16♎45.8	22♌25.9	15♏ 6.3	3♉16.4	29♋ 0.2	16♒ 2.0	4♌30.1	4♋25.0
2 M	0 41 31	8 27 41	6♐37 1	13♐31 50	25R 54.4	15R 45.6	23 30.7	15 47.9	3R 9.7	29 4.5	16R 0.8	4 31.3	4 25.1
3 Tu	0 45 27	9 26 46	20 28 26	27 26 43	25 50.9	14 40.7	24 35.8	16 29.6	3 3.0	29 8.7	15 59.7	4 32.4	4 25.2
4 W	0 49 24	10 25 53	4♑26 37	11♑28 4	25D 49.6	13 32.6	25 41.2	17 11.3	2 56.1	29 12.8	15 58.6	4 33.6	4 25.2
5 Th	0 53 20	11 25 2	18 31 0	25 35 19	25R 49.6	12 22.8	26 46.8	17 53.1	2 49.1	29 16.9	15 57.6	4 34.7	4R 25.2
6 F	0 57 17	12 24 12	2♒40 54	9♒47 35	25 49.5	11 13.1	27 52.6	18 35.0	2 42.0	29 20.9	15 56.6	4 35.8	4 25.2
7 Sa	1 1 14	13 23 25	16 55 8	24 3 15	25 48.2	10 5.5	28 58.7	19 17.0	2 34.7	29 24.7	15 55.6	4 36.8	4 25.2
8 Su	1 5 10	14 22 38	1♓11 33	8♓19 34	25 44.5	9 1.9	0♍ 5.0	19 59.0	2 27.4	29 28.5	15 54.7	4 37.8	4 25.1
9 M	1 9 7	15 21 54	15 26 46	22 32 35	25 37.9	8 4.1	1 11.6	20 41.1	2 20.0	29 32.2	15 53.9	4 38.8	4 25.0
10 Tu	1 13 3	16 21 11	29 36 23	6♈37 32	25 28.6	7 13.7	2 18.3	21 23.2	2 12.5	29 35.8	15 53.0	4 39.8	4 24.9
11 W	1 17 0	17 20 31	13♈35 26	20 29 30	25 17.1	6 32.2	3 25.3	22 5.5	2 4.9	29 39.2	15 52.3	4 40.7	4 24.8
12 Th	1 20 56	18 19 52	27 19 13	4♉ 4 10	25 4.6	6 0.5	4 32.5	22 47.8	1 57.3	29 42.6	15 51.5	4 41.6	4 24.6
13 F	1 24 53	19 19 16	10♉44 2	17 18 38	24 52.2	5 39.4	5 40.0	23 30.2	1 49.5	29 45.9	15 50.9	4 42.5	4 24.5
14 Sa	1 28 49	20 18 42	23 47 52	0♊11 49	24 41.3	5D 29.2	6 47.6	24 12.6	1 41.7	29 49.1	15 50.2	4 43.3	4 24.3
15 Su	1 32 46	21 18 10	6♊30 37	12 44 32	24 32.7	5 30.1	7 55.4	24 55.1	1 33.9	29 52.3	15 49.7	4 44.1	4 24.1
16 M	1 36 42	22 17 40	18 53 58	24 59 20	24 26.7	5 41.9	9 3.5	25 37.7	1 26.0	29 55.3	15 49.1	4 44.9	4 23.8
17 Tu	1 40 39	23 17 13	1♋ 1 11	7♋ 0 6	24 23.3	6 4.0	10 11.7	26 20.4	1 18.0	29 58.2	15 48.7	4 45.7	4 23.6
18 W	1 44 36	24 16 48	12 56 43	18 51 41	24 22.0	6 36.1	11 20.1	27 3.1	1 10.0	0♌ 1.0	15 48.2	4 46.4	4 23.3
19 Th	1 48 32	25 16 25	24 45 42	0♌39 28	24 21.8	7 17.2	12 28.7	27 45.9	1 1.9	0 3.7	15 47.8	4 47.0	4 23.0
20 F	1 52 29	26 16 4	6♌33 41	12 29 3	24 21.6	8 6.6	13 37.5	28 28.7	0 53.9	0 6.3	15 47.5	4 47.7	4 22.6
21 Sa	1 56 25	27 15 46	18 26 14	24 25 53	24 20.3	9 3.6	14 46.5	29 11.7	0 45.7	0 8.8	15 47.2	4 48.3	4 22.3
22 Su	2 0 22	28 15 30	0♍28 35	6♍34 53	24 17.0	10 7.2	15 55.6	29 54.7	0 37.6	0 11.2	15 47.0	4 48.9	4 21.9
23 M	2 4 18	29 15 16	12 45 16	19 0 8	24 11.0	11 16.7	17 5.0	0♐37.8	0 29.5	0 13.4	15 46.8	4 49.4	4 21.5
24 Tu	2 8 15	0♏15 4	25 19 47	1♎44 25	24 2.3	12 31.4	18 14.4	1 20.9	0 21.3	0 15.6	15 46.7	4 49.9	4 21.1
25 W	2 12 11	1 14 54	8♎14 9	14 48 59	23 51.2	13 50.4	19 24.0	2 4.1	0 13.2	0 17.7	15 46.6	4 50.4	4 20.7
26 Th	2 16 8	2 14 47	21 28 45	28 13 14	23 38.6	15 13.2	20 33.8	2 47.4	0 5.0	0 19.7	15D 46.6	4 50.8	4 20.2
27 F	2 20 5	3 14 41	5♏ 2 6	11♏54 55	23 25.7	16 39.1	21 43.7	3 30.8	29♈56.9	0 21.5	15 46.6	4 51.2	4 19.7
28 Sa	2 24 1	4 14 38	18 51 11	25 50 22	23 13.8	18 7.7	22 53.8	4 14.2	29 48.8	0 23.3	15 46.6	4 51.6	4 19.2
29 Su	2 27 58	5 14 36	2♐51 54	9♐55 13	23 4.0	19 38.4	24 4.0	4 57.7	29 40.7	0 24.9	15 46.8	4 52.0	4 18.7
30 M	2 31 54	6 14 36	16 59 47	24 5 8	22 57.0	21 10.9	25 14.4	5 41.3	29 32.7	0 26.4	15 46.9	4 52.3	4 18.1
31 Tu	2 35 51	7 14 38	1♑10 49	8♑16 28	22 53.0	22 44.9	26 24.9	6 24.9	29 24.7	0 27.9	15 47.2	4 52.6	4 17.6

Astro Data

	Dy Hr Mn
☽0N	11 23:31
♃⚹♇	19 12:01
♃□♆	20 18:21
☿ R	22 20:27
☽0S	26 6:31
♆⚺♇	26 13:01
♇ R	5 1:22
☽0N	9 8:29
☿ D	14 10:01
☽0S	23 14:29
♃□♄	24 13:22
♅ D	26 3:18

Planet Ingress

	Dy Hr Mn
♀ ♌	8 22:26
♂ ♏	8 17:44
☉ ♎	23 9:15
♀ ♍	7 22:11
♄ ♌	17 15:35
♂ ♐	22 2:58
☉ ♏	23 17:57
♃ ♈	26 14:53

Last Aspect / ☽ Ingress (September)

Last Aspect Dy Hr Mn		☽ Ingress Dy Hr Mn
1 18:42	♄ □	♏ 2 1:24
4 1:04	♄ △	♐ 4 7:05
6 8:02	♂ ⚹	♑ 6 10:44
8 12:24	♂ □	♒ 8 12:39
9 15:49	♅ ☌	♓ 10 13:42
12 10:58	♄ △	♈ 12 15:17
14 14:56	♄ □	♉ 14 19:09
16 22:31	♄ ⚹	♊ 17 2:38
19 5:35	☉ □	♋ 19 13:45
21 23:55	☉ ⚹	♌ 22 2:41
23 20:18	☿ ⚹	♍ 24 14:47
26 21:55	♄ ⚹	♎ 27 0:22
29 5:19	♄ □	♏ 29 7:21

Last Aspect / ☽ Ingress (October)

Last Aspect Dy Hr Mn		☽ Ingress Dy Hr Mn
1 10:47	♄ △	♐ 1 12:28
3 7:42	♀ △	♑ 3 16:23
5 18:20	♄ ☍	♒ 5 19:28
7 21:59	♀ ☍	♓ 7 22:00
9 23:59	♄ △	♈ 10 0:40
12 4:15	♄ □	♉ 12 4:45
14 11:20	♄ ⚹	♊ 14 11:38
16 7:16	☉ △	♋ 16 21:58
19 6:30	♂ △	♌ 19 10:40
21 22:49	♂ □	♍ 21 23:03
23 9:10	♀ ☌	♎ 24 8:45
26 15:09	♃ ☍	♏ 26 15:09
28 7:35	♀ ⚹	♐ 28 19:07
30 21:02	♃ △	♑ 30 22:00

☽ Phases & Eclipses

Dy Hr Mn	
5 4:26	☽ 12♐16
11 20:30	○ 18♓45
19 5:35	☽ 25♊56
27 7:34	● 3♎51
4 11:00	☽ 10♑53
11 7:01	○ 17♈38
19 1:08	☽ 25♋19
26 20:37	● 3♏06

Astro Data

1 SEPTEMBER 1916
Julian Day # 6088
Delta T 18.8 sec
SVP 06♓25'08"
Obliquity 23°27'05"
⚷ Chiron 24♓46.2R
☽ Mean ☊ 26♑49.8

1 OCTOBER 1916
Julian Day # 6118
Delta T 18.9 sec
SVP 06♓25'05"
Obliquity 23°27'05"
⚷ Chiron 23♓25.2R
☽ Mean ☊ 25♑14.5

NOVEMBER 1916 LONGITUDE

Day	Sid.Time	☉	0 hr ☽	Noon ☽	True ☊	☿	♀	♂	♃	♄	♅	♆	♇
1 W	2 39 47	8♏14 42	15♑21 49	22♑26 36	22♑51.4	24♎20.0	27♍35.5	7♐ 8.6	29♈16.7	0♌29.2	15♒47.4	4♌52.8	4♋17.0
2 Th	2 43 44	9 14 47	29 30 41	6♒33 55	22R 51.3	25 55.9	28 46.2	7 52.3	29R 8.8	0 30.4	15 47.8	4 53.0	4R 16.4
3 F	2 47 40	10 14 53	13♒36 13	20 37 30	22 51.4	27 32.5	29 57.1	8 36.1	29 1.0	0 31.5	15 48.2	4 53.2	4 15.8
4 Sa	2 51 37	11 15 1	27 37 41	4♓36 40	22 50.4	29 9.6	1♎ 8.1	9 20.0	28 53.2	0 32.4	15 48.6	4 53.3	4 15.1
5 Su	2 55 34	12 15 10	11♓34 20	18 30 31	22 47.3	0♏47.0	2 19.2	10 4.0	28 45.5	0 33.3	15 49.1	4 53.4	4 14.5
6 M	2 59 30	13 15 21	25 25 1	2♈17 36	22 41.4	2 24.7	3 30.4	10 47.9	28 37.9	0 34.0	15 49.6	4 53.5	4 13.8
7 Tu	3 3 27	14 15 34	9♈ 7 59	15 55 53	22 32.8	4 2.4	4 41.7	11 32.0	28 30.3	0 34.7	15 50.2	4R 53.5	4 13.1
8 W	3 7 23	15 15 48	22 40 58	29 22 56	22 22.2	5 40.1	5 53.2	12 16.1	28 22.8	0 35.2	15 50.8	4 53.5	4 12.3
9 Th	3 11 20	16 16 4	6♉ 1 29	12♉36 23	22 10.6	7 17.8	7 4.7	13 0.3	28 15.5	0 35.6	15 51.5	4 53.5	4 11.6
10 F	3 15 16	17 16 21	19 7 22	25 34 19	21 59.0	8 55.4	8 16.4	13 44.6	28 8.2	0 35.9	15 52.2	4 53.4	4 10.9
11 Sa	3 19 13	18 16 41	1♊57 8	8♊15 49	21 48.7	10 32.9	9 28.2	14 28.9	28 1.0	0 36.1	15 53.0	4 53.3	4 10.1
12 Su	3 23 9	19 17 2	14 30 25	20 41 6	21 40.4	12 10.1	10 40.1	15 13.2	27 54.0	0R 36.2	15 53.9	4 53.2	4 9.3
13 M	3 27 6	20 17 25	26 48 7	2♋51 45	21 34.8	13 47.2	11 52.1	15 57.7	27 47.0	0 36.2	15 54.7	4 53.0	4 8.5
14 Tu	3 31 3	21 17 49	8♋52 24	14 50 31	21 31.6	15 24.0	13 4.2	16 42.1	27 40.2	0 36.0	15 55.7	4 52.8	4 7.6
15 W	3 34 59	22 18 16	20 46 36	26 41 13	21D 30.7	17 0.7	14 16.4	17 26.7	27 33.5	0 35.8	15 56.7	4 52.6	4 6.8
16 Th	3 38 56	23 18 44	2♌34 58	8♌28 29	21 31.2	18 37.1	15 28.7	18 11.3	27 26.9	0 35.4	15 57.7	4 52.3	4 5.9
17 F	3 42 52	24 19 14	14 22 26	20 17 29	21R 32.2	20 13.2	16 41.1	18 56.0	27 20.5	0 34.9	15 58.8	4 52.0	4 5.1
18 Sa	3 46 49	25 19 46	26 14 20	2♍13 39	21 32.6	21 49.1	17 53.5	19 40.7	27 14.2	0 34.3	15 59.9	4 51.6	4 4.2
19 Su	3 50 45	26 20 19	8♍16 7	14 22 22	21 31.7	23 24.8	19 6.1	20 25.5	27 8.0	0 33.6	16 1.1	4 51.3	4 3.3
20 M	3 54 42	27 20 55	20 33 0	26 48 32	21 28.8	25 0.3	20 18.7	21 10.3	27 2.0	0 32.8	16 2.3	4 50.9	4 2.3
21 Tu	3 58 38	28 21 32	3♎ 9 28	9♎36 9	21 23.7	26 35.6	21 31.5	21 55.2	26 56.1	0 31.8	16 3.6	4 50.4	4 1.4
22 W	4 2 35	29 22 10	16 8 51	22 47 44	21 16.6	28 10.7	22 44.3	22 40.2	26 50.4	0 30.8	16 4.9	4 49.9	4 0.4
23 Th	4 6 32	0♐22 51	29 32 47	6♏23 52	21 8.2	29 45.5	23 57.2	23 25.2	26 44.8	0 29.6	16 6.3	4 49.4	3 59.5
24 F	4 10 28	1 23 33	13♏20 41	20 22 50	20 59.3	1♐20.3	25 10.1	24 10.3	26 39.4	0 28.4	16 7.8	4 48.9	3 58.5
25 Sa	4 14 25	2 24 16	27 29 43	4♐40 40	20 51.1	2 54.8	26 23.2	24 55.5	26 34.2	0 27.0	16 9.2	4 48.3	3 57.5
26 Su	4 18 21	3 25 1	11♐54 54	19 11 36	20 44.3	4 29.3	27 36.3	25 40.7	26 29.2	0 25.5	16 10.8	4 47.7	3 56.5
27 M	4 22 18	4 25 48	26 29 53	3♑48 54	20 39.7	6 3.6	28 49.5	26 25.9	26 24.3	0 23.9	16 12.3	4 47.1	3 55.5
28 Tu	4 26 14	5 26 35	11♑ 7 52	18 26 1	20D 37.5	7 37.8	0♏ 2.7	27 11.2	26 19.6	0 22.2	16 13.9	4 46.4	3 54.4
29 W	4 30 11	6 27 23	25 42 43	2♒57 23	20 37.2	9 11.8	1 16.0	27 56.6	26 15.1	0 20.4	16 15.6	4 45.8	3 53.4
30 Th	4 34 8	7 28 13	10♒ 9 35	17 18 58	20 38.2	10 45.8	2 29.4	28 42.0	26 10.8	0 18.5	16 17.3	4 45.0	3 52.3

DECEMBER 1916 LONGITUDE

Day	Sid.Time	☉	0 hr ☽	Noon ☽	True ☊	☿	♀	♂	♃	♄	♅	♆	♇
1 F	4 38 4	8♐29 3	24♒25 15	1♓28 18	20♑39.5	12♐19.8	3♏42.8	29♐27.5	26♈ 6.6	0♌16.5	16♒19.1	4♌44.3	3♋51.3
2 Sa	4 42 1	9 29 54	8♓27 59	15 24 15	20R 40.2	13 53.7	4 56.2	0♑13.0	26R 2.7	0R 14.3	16 20.9	4R 43.5	3R 50.2
3 Su	4 45 57	10 30 46	22 17 7	29 6 35	20 39.6	15 27.5	6 9.8	0 58.5	25 58.9	0 12.1	16 22.7	4 42.7	3 49.1
4 M	4 49 54	11 31 38	5♈52 42	12♈35 29	20 37.1	17 1.3	7 23.3	1 44.1	25 55.3	0 9.8	16 24.6	4 41.8	3 48.0
5 Tu	4 53 50	12 32 32	19 14 59	25 51 14	20 32.8	18 35.1	8 37.0	2 29.8	25 51.9	0 7.3	16 26.5	4 40.9	3 46.9
6 W	4 57 47	13 33 26	2♉24 14	8♉54 2	20 27.1	20 8.9	9 50.7	3 15.5	25 48.8	0 4.8	16 28.5	4 40.0	3 45.8
7 Th	5 1 43	14 34 21	15 20 37	21 44 1	20 20.7	21 42.7	11 4.4	4 1.3	25 45.8	0 2.2	16 30.5	4 39.1	3 44.6
8 F	5 5 40	15 35 17	28 4 14	4♊21 19	20 14.3	23 16.5	12 18.2	4 47.1	25 43.0	29♋59.5	16 32.6	4 38.1	3 43.5
9 Sa	5 9 37	16 36 14	10♊35 18	16 46 16	20 8.6	24 50.3	13 32.0	5 32.9	25 40.4	29 56.6	16 34.7	4 37.1	3 42.3
10 Su	5 13 33	17 37 11	22 54 19	28 59 36	20 4.2	26 24.1	14 45.9	6 18.8	25 38.0	29 53.7	16 36.8	4 36.1	3 41.2
11 M	5 17 30	18 38 10	5♋ 2 17	11♋ 2 36	20 1.4	27 58.0	15 59.8	7 4.7	25 35.9	29 50.7	16 39.0	4 35.1	3 40.0
12 Tu	5 21 26	19 39 9	17 0 50	22 57 17	20D 0.2	29 31.8	17 13.8	7 50.7	25 33.9	29 47.6	16 41.2	4 34.0	3 38.9
13 W	5 25 23	20 40 10	28 52 18	4♌46 19	20 0.6	1♑ 5.6	18 27.8	8 36.8	25 32.1	29 44.5	16 43.5	4 32.9	3 37.7
14 Th	5 29 19	21 41 11	10♌39 46	16 33 9	20 1.9	2 39.4	19 41.9	9 22.8	25 30.6	29 41.2	16 45.8	4 31.8	3 36.5
15 F	5 33 16	22 42 13	22 26 59	28 21 50	20 3.8	4 13.1	20 56.0	10 9.0	25 29.2	29 37.8	16 48.1	4 30.7	3 35.3
16 Sa	5 37 12	23 43 16	4♍18 17	10♍16 57	20 5.6	5 46.7	22 10.1	10 55.1	25 28.1	29 34.4	16 50.5	4 29.5	3 34.1
17 Su	5 41 9	24 44 20	16 18 26	22 23 23	20R 6.8	7 20.3	23 24.3	11 41.3	25 27.1	29 30.8	16 52.9	4 28.3	3 33.0
18 M	5 45 6	25 45 25	28 32 24	4♎46 4	20 7.1	8 53.6	24 38.5	12 27.6	25 26.4	29 27.2	16 55.4	4 27.1	3 31.8
19 Tu	5 49 2	26 46 30	11♎ 4 57	17 29 34	20 6.3	10 26.7	25 52.8	13 13.9	25 25.9	29 23.5	16 57.9	4 25.8	3 30.6
20 W	5 52 59	27 47 37	24 0 21	0♏37 38	20 4.4	11 59.5	27 7.1	14 0.2	25D 25.6	29 19.8	17 0.4	4 24.5	3 29.3
21 Th	5 56 55	28 48 44	7♏21 39	14 12 30	20 1.7	13 31.9	28 21.4	14 46.6	25 25.5	29 15.9	17 2.9	4 23.3	3 28.1
22 F	6 0 52	29 49 52	21 10 8	28 14 20	19 58.7	15 3.8	29 35.7	15 33.0	25 25.6	29 12.0	17 5.5	4 21.9	3 26.9
23 Sa	6 4 48	0♑51 1	5♐24 44	12♐40 47	19 55.9	16 35.0	0♐50.1	16 19.5	25 25.9	29 8.0	17 8.2	4 20.6	3 25.7
24 Su	6 8 45	1 52 10	20 1 45	27 26 46	19 53.6	18 5.4	2 4.6	17 6.0	25 26.4	29 4.0	17 10.8	4 19.3	3 24.5
25 M	6 12 41	2 53 20	4♑54 53	12♑25 2	19 52.2	19 34.9	3 19.0	17 52.6	25 27.2	28 59.9	17 13.5	4 17.9	3 23.3
26 Tu	6 16 38	3 54 30	19 56 7	27 27 1	19D 51.7	21 3.1	4 33.5	18 39.2	25 28.1	28 55.7	17 16.3	4 16.5	3 22.1
27 W	6 20 35	4 55 40	4♒56 41	12♒24 9	19 52.1	22 29.9	5 48.0	19 25.8	25 29.3	28 51.4	17 19.0	4 15.1	3 20.9
28 Th	6 24 31	5 56 50	19 48 31	27 9 2	19 53.0	23 55.0	7 2.5	20 12.4	25 30.6	28 47.1	17 21.8	4 13.6	3 19.7
29 F	6 28 28	6 58 1	4♓25 7	11♓36 17	19 54.2	25 17.9	8 17.0	20 59.1	25 32.2	28 42.7	17 24.7	4 12.2	3 18.5
30 Sa	6 32 24	7 59 10	18 42 13	25 42 45	19 55.1	26 38.3	9 31.5	21 45.8	25 34.0	28 38.3	17 27.5	4 10.7	3 17.2
31 Su	6 36 21	9 0 20	2♈37 48	9♈27 24	19R 55.6	27 55.8	10 46.1	22 32.6	25 36.0	28 33.8	17 30.4	4 9.2	3 16.0

Astro Data Dy Hr Mn	Planet Ingress Dy Hr Mn	Last Aspect Dy Hr Mn	☽ Ingress Dy Hr Mn	Last Aspect Dy Hr Mn	☽ Ingress Dy Hr Mn	☽ Phases & Eclipses Dy Hr Mn	Astro Data
☽0N 5 14:48	♀ ♎ 3 0:59	1 23:23 ♃ □	♒ 2 0:50	1 9:03 ♂ ✶	♓ 1 9:29	2 17:50 ☽ 9♒59	1 NOVEMBER 1916
♀0S 6 3:16	☿ ♏ 4 12:25	4 2:58 ☿ △	♓ 4 4:04	2 10:35 ☿ □	♈ 3 13:34	9 20:18 ○ 17♉07	Julian Day # 6149
♆ R 7 10:37	☉ ♐ 22 14:58	5 1:16 ☉ △	♈ 6 7:59	5 11:58 ♃ ☌	♉ 5 19:35	17 22:00 ☽ 25♌15	Delta T 18.9 sec
♄ R 12 5:10	☿ ♐ 23 3:40	8 10:06 ♃ ☌	♉ 8 13:07	8 3:39 ♄ ✶	♊ 8 3:40	25 8:50 ● 2♐47	SVP 06♓25'01"
☽0S 19 22:40	♀ ♏ 27 23:07	9 20:18 ☉ ☍	♊ 10 20:19	10 7:54 ☿ ☍	♋ 10 14:00		Obliquity 23°27'04"
		13 1:55 ♃ ✶	♋ 13 6:19	13 1:45 ♄ ☌	♌ 13 2:18	2 1:55 ☽ 9♓35	⚷ Chiron 22♓16.0R
☽0N 2 19:26	♂ ♑ 1 17:10	15 13:39 ♃ □	♌ 15 18:44	15 6:09 ♃ △	♍ 15 15:19	9 12:43 ○ 17♊09	☽ Mean ☊ 23♑36.0
☽0S 17 6:17	♄ ♋ 7 19:21	18 1:59 ♃ △	♍ 18 7:33	18 1:46 ♄ ✶	♎ 18 2:50	17 18:06 ☽ 25♍30	
♃ D 20 23:37	☿ ♑ 12 7:13	20 14:09 ☉ ✶	♎ 20 18:03	20 9:37 ♄ □	♏ 20 10:52	24 20:31 ● 2♑44	1 DECEMBER 1916
☽0N 30 1:11	☉ ♑ 22 3:59	22 19:05 ♃ ☍	♏ 23 0:48	22 13:33 ♄ △	♐ 22 14:58	24 20:45:55 P 0.012	Julian Day # 6179
	♀ ♐ 22 7:50	24 4:46 ♅ □	♐ 25 4:12	24 8:46 ♃ △	♑ 24 16:07	31 12:07 ☽ 9♈31	Delta T 19.0 sec
		27 4:10 ♀ ✶	♑ 27 5:45	26 14:18 ♄ ☍	♒ 26 16:05		SVP 06♓24'57"
		29 0:53 ♃ □	♒ 29 7:06	28 9:20 ♃ ✶	♓ 28 16:41		Obliquity 23°27'03"
				30 16:58 ♄ △	♈ 30 19:25		⚷ Chiron 21♓48.0R
							☽ Mean ☊ 22♑00.7

LONGITUDE JANUARY 1917

Day	Sid.Time	☉	0 hr ☽	Noon ☽	True ☊	☿	♀	♂	♃	♄	♅	♆	♇
1 M	6 40 17	10♑ 1 30	16♈11 41	22♈50 51	19♑55.6	29♑ 9.7	12♐ 0.7	23♑19.4	25♈38.2	28♋29.3	17♒33.3	4♌ 7.7	3♋14.8
2 Tu	6 44 14	11 2 39	29 25 6	5♉54 45	19R 55.1	0♒19.6	13 15.3	24 6.2	25 40.5	28R 24.8	17 36.3	4R 6.2	3R 13.6
3 W	6 48 10	12 3 48	12♉20 4	18 41 22	19 54.3	1 24.7	14 29.9	24 53.0	25 43.1	28 20.1	17 39.2	4 4.7	3 12.4
4 Th	6 52 7	13 4 57	24 58 57	1♊13 8	19 53.4	2 24.4	15 44.5	25 39.9	25 45.9	28 15.5	17 42.2	4 3.1	3 11.2
5 F	6 56 4	14 6 6	7♊24 12	13 32 26	19 52.5	3 17.8	16 59.2	26 26.8	25 48.9	28 10.8	17 45.2	4 1.6	3 10.0
6 Sa	7 0 0	15 7 14	19 38 7	25 41 30	19 51.8	4 4.0	18 13.8	27 13.7	25 52.1	28 6.1	17 48.3	4 0.0	3 8.9
7 Su	7 3 57	16 8 22	1♋42 50	7♋42 22	19 51.4	4 42.1	19 28.5	28 0.7	25 55.5	28 1.3	17 51.4	3 58.4	3 7.7
8 M	7 7 53	17 9 30	13 40 20	19 36 58	19D 51.2	5 11.4	20 43.2	28 47.7	25 59.1	27 56.5	17 54.5	3 56.8	3 6.5
9 Tu	7 11 50	18 10 38	25 32 32	1♌27 16	19 51.2	5 30.7	21 57.9	29 34.7	26 2.8	27 51.7	17 57.6	3 55.2	3 5.3
10 W	7 15 46	19 11 45	7♌21 26	13 15 20	19R 51.3	5R 39.5	23 12.6	0♒21.7	26 6.8	27 46.9	18 0.7	3 53.6	3 4.2
11 Th	7 19 43	20 12 52	19 9 16	25 3 34	19 51.3	5 37.0	24 27.4	1 8.8	26 11.0	27 42.0	18 3.9	3 52.0	3 3.0
12 F	7 23 40	21 13 59	0♍58 35	6♍54 43	19 51.2	5 22.8	25 42.1	1 55.9	26 15.3	27 37.1	18 7.0	3 50.3	3 1.9
13 Sa	7 27 36	22 15 6	12 52 21	18 51 57	19 50.9	4 56.8	26 56.9	2 43.0	26 19.8	27 32.2	18 10.2	3 48.7	3 0.7
14 Su	7 31 33	23 16 13	24 53 58	0♎58 54	19 50.6	4 19.3	28 11.7	3 30.1	26 24.5	27 27.3	18 13.5	3 47.0	2 59.6
15 M	7 35 29	24 17 19	7♎ 7 15	13 19 32	19 50.2	3 30.9	29 26.5	4 17.2	26 29.4	27 22.4	18 16.7	3 45.4	2 58.5
16 Tu	7 39 26	25 18 25	19 36 14	25 57 54	19D 49.9	2 32.7	0♑41.3	5 4.4	26 34.5	27 17.4	18 20.0	3 43.7	2 57.4
17 W	7 43 22	26 19 31	2♏24 59	8♏57 56	19 49.9	1 26.4	1 56.1	5 51.6	26 39.7	27 12.5	18 23.2	3 42.0	2 56.2
18 Th	7 47 19	27 20 36	15 37 8	22 22 52	19 50.3	0 14.0	3 10.9	6 38.8	26 45.2	27 7.6	18 26.5	3 40.4	2 55.2
19 F	7 51 15	28 21 42	29 15 21	6♐14 40	19 50.9	28♑57.7	4 25.7	7 26.1	26 50.8	27 2.6	18 29.9	3 38.7	2 54.1
20 Sa	7 55 12	29 22 47	13♐20 44	20 33 20	19 51.8	27 39.9	5 40.6	8 13.4	26 56.6	26 57.7	18 33.2	3 37.0	2 53.0
21 Su	7 59 9	0♒23 52	27 52 4	5♑16 19	19 52.6	26 23.1	6 55.4	9 0.6	27 2.5	26 52.7	18 36.5	3 35.3	2 51.9
22 M	8 3 5	1 24 56	12♑45 20	20 18 11	19R 53.1	25 9.3	8 10.3	9 47.9	27 8.7	26 47.8	18 39.9	3 33.6	2 50.9
23 Tu	8 7 2	2 25 59	27 53 46	5♒30 53	19 53.1	24 0.5	9 25.2	10 35.3	27 15.0	26 42.9	18 43.3	3 31.9	2 49.8
24 W	8 10 58	3 27 2	13♒ 8 18	20 44 43	19 52.4	22 58.3	10 40.0	11 22.6	27 21.5	26 38.0	18 46.6	3 30.2	2 48.8
25 Th	8 14 55	4 28 4	28 18 54	5♓49 43	19 51.0	22 3.7	11 54.9	12 9.9	27 28.1	26 33.1	18 50.0	3 28.5	2 47.8
26 F	8 18 51	5 29 5	13♓16 6	20 37 12	19 49.0	21 17.6	13 9.8	12 57.3	27 34.9	26 28.3	18 53.4	3 26.9	2 46.8
27 Sa	8 22 48	6 30 5	27 52 21	5♈ 1 1	19 46.8	20 40.4	14 24.6	13 44.7	27 41.9	26 23.4	18 56.9	3 25.2	2 45.8
28 Su	8 26 44	7 31 3	12♈ 2 54	18 57 53	19 44.9	20 12.0	15 39.5	14 32.1	27 49.0	26 18.6	19 0.3	3 23.5	2 44.8
29 M	8 30 41	8 32 0	25 46 0	2♉27 23	19 43.5	19 52.5	16 54.4	15 19.4	27 56.3	26 13.8	19 3.7	3 21.8	2 43.9
30 Tu	8 34 38	9 32 57	9♉ 2 21	15 31 16	19D 43.0	19D 41.6	18 9.2	16 6.8	28 3.7	26 9.1	19 7.1	3 20.1	2 42.9
31 W	8 38 34	10 33 51	21 54 34	28 12 45	19 43.4	19 38.7	19 24.1	16 54.2	28 11.3	26 4.4	19 10.6	3 18.4	2 42.0

LONGITUDE FEBRUARY 1917

Day	Sid.Time	☉	0 hr ☽	Noon ☽	True ☊	☿	♀	♂	♃	♄	♅	♆	♇
1 Th	8 42 31	11♒34 45	4♊26 18	10♊35 47	19♑44.7	19♑43.5	20♑39.0	17♒41.7	28♈19.1	25♋59.7	19♒14.1	3♌16.7	2♋41.1
2 F	8 46 27	12 35 37	16 41 42	22 44 35	19 46.4	19 55.4	21 53.9	18 29.1	28 27.0	25R 55.0	19 17.5	3R 15.1	2R 40.2
3 Sa	8 50 24	13 36 28	28 44 55	4♋43 10	19 48.1	20 13.9	23 8.7	19 16.5	28 35.0	25 50.4	19 21.0	3 13.4	2 39.3
4 Su	8 54 20	14 37 18	10♋39 47	16 35 10	19R 49.3	20 38.5	24 23.6	20 3.9	28 43.2	25 45.9	19 24.5	3 11.8	2 38.4
5 M	8 58 17	15 38 6	22 29 43	28 23 46	19 49.6	21 8.6	25 38.5	20 51.4	28 51.6	25 41.4	19 27.9	3 10.1	2 37.6
6 Tu	9 2 13	16 38 53	4♌17 38	10♌11 35	19 48.7	21 43.9	26 53.3	21 38.8	29 0.0	25 37.0	19 31.4	3 8.5	2 36.7
7 W	9 6 10	17 39 39	16 5 56	22 0 53	19 46.2	22 23.8	28 8.2	22 26.2	29 8.7	25 32.6	19 34.9	3 6.8	2 35.9
8 Th	9 10 7	18 40 23	27 56 41	3♍53 34	19 42.3	23 8.0	29 23.1	23 13.7	29 17.4	25 28.2	19 38.4	3 5.2	2 35.1
9 F	9 14 3	19 41 6	9♍51 45	15 51 26	19 37.3	23 56.2	0♒37.9	24 1.1	29 26.3	25 23.9	19 41.8	3 3.6	2 34.3
10 Sa	9 18 0	20 41 48	21 52 54	27 56 20	19 31.6	24 47.9	1 52.8	24 48.5	29 35.3	25 19.7	19 45.3	3 2.0	2 33.6
11 Su	9 21 56	21 42 28	4♎ 2 3	10♎10 18	19 25.8	25 42.9	3 7.6	25 36.0	29 44.5	25 15.5	19 48.8	3 0.4	2 32.8
12 M	9 25 53	22 43 8	16 21 24	22 35 40	19 20.5	26 40.9	4 22.5	26 23.4	29 53.8	25 11.4	19 52.3	2 58.8	2 32.1
13 Tu	9 29 49	23 43 46	28 53 28	5♏15 8	19 16.4	27 41.6	5 37.4	27 10.9	0♉ 3.2	25 7.4	19 55.7	2 57.3	2 31.4
14 W	9 33 46	24 44 23	11♏41 5	18 11 39	19 13.9	28 45.0	6 52.2	27 58.3	0 12.7	25 3.4	19 59.2	2 55.7	2 30.7
15 Th	9 37 42	25 44 59	24 47 13	1♐28 9	19D 13.0	29 50.7	8 7.1	28 45.8	0 22.4	24 59.5	20 2.7	2 54.2	2 30.0
16 F	9 41 39	26 45 34	8♐14 43	15 7 10	19 13.5	0♒58.6	9 22.0	29 33.2	0 32.1	24 55.7	20 6.2	2 52.6	2 29.4
17 Sa	9 45 36	27 46 8	22 5 39	29 10 13	19 14.8	2 8.5	10 36.8	0♓20.6	0 42.1	24 51.9	20 9.6	2 51.1	2 28.7
18 Su	9 49 32	28 46 40	6♑20 48	13♑37 8	19R 16.2	3 20.4	11 51.7	1 8.1	0 52.1	24 48.3	20 13.1	2 49.6	2 28.1
19 M	9 53 29	29 47 11	20 58 49	28 25 15	19 16.7	4 34.1	13 6.5	1 55.5	1 2.2	24 44.7	20 16.5	2 48.2	2 27.5
20 Tu	9 57 25	0♓47 41	5♒55 40	13♒29 6	19 15.6	5 49.4	14 21.4	2 42.9	1 12.5	24 41.2	20 20.0	2 46.7	2 27.0
21 W	10 1 22	1 48 10	21 4 27	28 40 30	19 12.5	7 6.4	15 36.3	3 30.4	1 22.9	24 37.7	20 23.4	2 45.3	2 26.4
22 Th	10 5 18	2 48 36	6♓15 58	13♓49 32	19 7.4	8 24.9	16 51.1	4 17.8	1 33.3	24 34.4	20 26.8	2 43.8	2 25.9
23 F	10 9 15	3 49 1	21 19 58	28 46 7	19 0.6	9 44.8	18 5.9	5 5.2	1 43.9	24 31.1	20 30.2	2 42.4	2 25.4
24 Sa	10 13 11	4 49 24	6♈ 6 56	13♈21 38	18 53.2	11 6.1	19 20.8	5 52.6	1 54.6	24 27.9	20 33.6	2 41.0	2 24.9
25 Su	10 17 8	5 49 45	20 29 34	27 30 20	18 46.1	12 28.8	20 35.6	6 39.9	2 5.4	24 24.8	20 37.0	2 39.7	2 24.4
26 M	10 21 5	6 50 5	4♉23 43	11♉ 9 42	18 40.2	13 52.7	21 50.4	7 27.3	2 16.4	24 21.9	20 40.4	2 38.3	2 24.0
27 Tu	10 25 1	7 50 22	17 48 27	24 20 15	18 36.1	15 17.9	23 5.2	8 14.7	2 27.4	24 19.0	20 43.8	2 37.0	2 23.6
28 W	10 28 58	8 50 38	0♊45 33	7♊ 4 51	18D 34.0	16 44.3	24 20.0	9 2.0	2 38.5	24 16.1	20 47.2	2 35.7	2 23.2

Astro Data Dy Hr Mn	Planet Ingress Dy Hr Mn	Last Aspect Dy Hr Mn	☽ Ingress Dy Hr Mn	Last Aspect Dy Hr Mn	☽ Ingress Dy Hr Mn	☽ Phases & Eclipses Dy Hr Mn	Astro Data
♅⚼♇ 10 19:18	☿ ♒ 1 17:07	1 22:10 ♄ □	♉ 2 1:04	2 23:40 ♃ ⚹	♋ 3 2:31	8 7:42 ○ 17♋29	1 JANUARY 1917
☿ R 10 6:49	♂ ♒ 9 12:55	4 6:15 ♄ ⚹	♊ 4 9:39	5 13:06 ♃ □	♌ 5 15:16	8 7:44 ☍T 1.364	Julian Day # 6210
☽0S 13 13:02	♀ ♑ 15 10:46	6 12:25 ♃ ⚹	♋ 6 20:35	8 2:45 ♃ △	♍ 8 4:09	16 11:42 ☽ 25♎48	Delta T 19.1 sec
♃□♄ 20 2:25	☿ ♑ 18 4:29	9 8:46 ♂ ☍	♌ 9 9:03	10 6:48 ♄ ⚹	♎ 10 16:04	23 7:40 ● 2♒45	SVP 06♓24'51"
☽0N 26 10:02	☉ ♒ 20 14:37	11 14:22 ♃ △	♍ 11 22:01	12 21:32 ☿ □	♏ 13 2:06	23 7:28:12 P 0.726	Obliquity 23°27'03"
☿ D 30 20:44		14 7:15 ♀ □	♎ 14 10:04	15 7:37 ♂ □	♐ 15 9:23	30 1:01 ☽ 9♉36	⚷ Chiron 22♓10.5
	♀ ♒ 8 11:51	16 14:23 ♄ □	♏ 16 19:32	17 10:22 ☉ ⚹	♑ 17 13:24		☽ Mean ☊ 20♑22.2
☽0S 9 19:19	♃ ♉ 12 15:58	18 23:32 ☿ ⚹	♐ 19 1:17	19 6:04 ♄ ☍	♒ 19 14:32	7 3:28 ○ 17♌48	
☽0N 22 21:11	☿ ♒ 15 3:21	20 22:39 ♃ △	♑ 21 3:28	20 22:55 ♅ ☌	♓ 21 14:06	15 1:53 ☽ 25♏50	1 FEBRUARY 1917
♃⚹♇ 26 16:03	♂ ♓ 16 13:33	22 22:58 ♃ □	♒ 23 3:19	23 5:06 ♄ △	♈ 23 14:00	21 18:09 ● 2♓34	Julian Day # 6241
♃□♆ 27 18:36	☉ ♓ 19 5:05	24 22:39 ♃ ⚹	♓ 25 2:41	25 6:40 ♄ □	♉ 25 16:19	28 16:43 ☽ 9♊33	Delta T 19.2 sec
		26 21:33 ♄ △	♈ 27 3:33	27 11:55 ♄ ⚹	♊ 27 22:34		SVP 06♓24'46"
		29 3:55 ♃ ☌	♉ 29 7:34				Obliquity 23°27'03"
		31 7:52 ♄ ⚹	♊ 31 15:26				⚷ Chiron 23♓20.6
							☽ Mean ☊ 18♑43.8

MARCH 1917 — LONGITUDE

Day	Sid.Time	☉	0 hr ☽	Noon ☽	True ☊	☿	♀	♂	♃	♄	♅	♆	♇
1 Th	10 32 54	9♓50 51	13♊18 43	19♊27 47	18♑33.7	18♒11.9	25♒34.8	9♓49.3	2♉49.7	24♋13.4	20♒50.5	2♌34.4	2♋22.8
2 F	10 36 51	10 51 3	25 32 42	1♋34 8	18 34.6	19 40.7	26 49.5	10 36.6	3 1.0	24R 10.8	20 53.8	2R 33.1	2R 22.4
3 Sa	10 40 47	11 51 12	7♋32 42	13 29 5	18R 35.7	21 10.7	28 4.3	11 23.9	3 12.4	24 8.3	20 57.1	2 31.9	2 22.1
4 Su	10 44 44	12 51 19	19 23 51	25 17 36	18 36.3	22 41.8	29 19.0	12 11.2	3 23.9	24 5.9	21 0.4	2 30.7	2 21.8
5 M	10 48 40	13 51 24	1♌10 52	7♌ 4 7	18 35.3	24 14.0	0♓33.8	12 58.4	3 35.5	24 3.6	21 3.7	2 29.5	2 21.5
6 Tu	10 52 37	14 51 28	12 57 49	18 52 21	18 32.1	25 47.3	1 48.5	13 45.7	3 47.1	24 1.4	21 7.0	2 28.3	2 21.2
7 W	10 56 34	15 51 29	24 48 5	0♍45 18	18 26.4	27 21.8	3 3.2	14 32.9	3 58.9	23 59.2	21 10.2	2 27.2	2 21.0
8 Th	11 0 30	16 51 28	6♍44 15	12 45 9	18 18.2	28 57.4	4 17.9	15 20.1	4 10.7	23 57.2	21 13.5	2 26.1	2 20.8
9 F	11 4 27	17 51 25	18 48 10	24 53 25	18 8.0	0♓34.1	5 32.6	16 7.2	4 22.6	23 55.3	21 16.7	2 25.0	2 20.6
10 Sa	11 8 23	18 51 20	1♎ 1 3	7♎11 8	17 56.5	2 12.0	6 47.3	16 54.4	4 34.6	23 53.5	21 19.8	2 23.9	2 20.4
11 Su	11 12 20	19 51 13	13 23 44	19 38 58	17 44.7	3 51.0	8 2.0	17 41.5	4 46.7	23 51.8	21 23.0	2 22.8	2 20.2
12 M	11 16 16	20 51 5	25 56 53	2♏17 36	17 33.8	5 31.2	9 16.7	18 28.6	4 58.9	23 50.2	21 26.2	2 21.8	2 20.1
13 Tu	11 20 13	21 50 54	8♏41 14	15 7 55	17 24.7	7 12.5	10 31.4	19 15.7	5 11.1	23 48.7	21 29.3	2 20.8	2 20.0
14 W	11 24 9	22 50 42	21 37 49	28 11 8	17 18.1	8 55.1	11 46.0	20 2.8	5 23.4	23 47.3	21 32.4	2 19.9	2 19.9
15 Th	11 28 6	23 50 29	4♐48 3	11♐28 48	17 14.1	10 38.8	13 0.7	20 49.8	5 35.8	23 46.0	21 35.5	2 19.0	2 19.9
16 F	11 32 2	24 50 14	18 13 37	25 2 43	17D 12.5	12 23.7	14 15.3	21 36.8	5 48.3	23 44.9	21 38.5	2 18.1	2D 19.8
17 Sa	11 35 59	25 49 57	1♑56 16	8♑54 25	17 12.4	14 9.8	15 30.0	22 23.8	6 0.8	23 43.8	21 41.6	2 17.2	2 19.8
18 Su	11 39 56	26 49 38	15 57 13	23 4 39	17R 12.7	15 57.2	16 44.6	23 10.8	6 13.4	23 42.9	21 44.6	2 16.3	2 19.8
19 M	11 43 52	27 49 18	0♒16 34	7♒32 41	17 12.1	17 45.8	17 59.2	23 57.8	6 26.1	23 42.0	21 47.6	2 15.5	2 19.9
20 Tu	11 47 49	28 48 56	14 52 33	22 15 34	17 9.6	19 35.6	19 13.8	24 44.7	6 38.8	23 41.3	21 50.5	2 14.7	2 19.9
21 W	11 51 45	29 48 32	29 40 59	7♓ 7 54	17 4.4	21 26.7	20 28.4	25 31.6	6 51.6	23 40.7	21 53.4	2 14.0	2 20.0
22 Th	11 55 42	0♈48 6	14♓35 18	22 2 5	16 56.3	23 19.0	21 43.0	26 18.4	7 4.5	23 40.2	21 56.3	2 13.2	2 20.1
23 F	11 59 38	1 47 38	29 27 7	6♈49 17	16 46.1	25 12.6	22 57.6	27 5.3	7 17.4	23 39.8	21 59.2	2 12.5	2 20.2
24 Sa	12 3 35	2 47 8	14♈ 7 32	21 20 55	16 34.6	27 7.5	24 12.2	27 52.1	7 30.4	23 39.5	22 2.1	2 11.9	2 20.4
25 Su	12 7 31	3 46 36	28 28 41	5♉30 10	16 23.3	29 3.6	25 26.7	28 38.9	7 43.5	23 39.3	22 4.9	2 11.2	2 20.6
26 M	12 11 28	4 46 2	12♉25 0	19 12 54	16 13.3	1♈ 0.8	26 41.2	29 25.6	7 56.6	23D 39.2	22 7.7	2 10.6	2 20.8
27 Tu	12 15 25	5 45 26	25 53 51	2♊27 58	16 5.6	2 59.3	27 55.8	0♈12.3	8 9.7	23 39.3	22 10.4	2 10.0	2 21.0
28 W	12 19 21	6 44 47	8♊55 32	15 16 54	16 0.5	4 58.8	29 10.3	0 59.0	8 22.9	23 39.4	22 13.1	2 9.5	2 21.2
29 Th	12 23 18	7 44 7	21 32 37	27 43 13	15 57.8	6 59.4	0♈24.8	1 45.7	8 36.2	23 39.7	22 15.8	2 9.0	2 21.5
30 F	12 27 14	8 43 24	3♋49 22	9♋51 42	15D 57.0	9 0.9	1 39.3	2 32.3	8 49.5	23 40.1	22 18.5	2 8.5	2 21.8
31 Sa	12 31 11	9 42 38	15 50 56	21 47 46	15R 57.0	11 3.3	2 53.7	3 18.8	9 2.9	23 40.6	22 21.1	2 8.1	2 22.1

APRIL 1917 — LONGITUDE

Day	Sid.Time	☉	0 hr ☽	Noon ☽	True ☊	☿	♀	♂	♃	♄	♅	♆	♇
1 Su	12 35 7	10♈41 51	27♋42 52	3♌36 56	15♑56.6	13♈ 6.4	4♈ 8.2	4♈ 5.4	9♉16.3	23♋41.2	22♒23.7	2♌ 7.7	2♋22.4
2 M	12 39 4	11 41 0	9♌30 37	15 24 30	15R 54.9	15 10.0	5 22.6	4 51.9	9 29.7	23 41.9	22 26.3	2R 7.3	2 22.8
3 Tu	12 43 0	12 40 8	21 19 10	27 15 9	15 50.9	17 14.0	6 37.0	5 38.3	9 43.2	23 42.7	22 28.8	2 6.9	2 23.2
4 W	12 46 57	13 39 13	3♍12 55	9♍12 51	15 44.1	19 18.2	7 51.4	6 24.7	9 56.8	23 43.6	22 31.3	2 6.6	2 23.6
5 Th	12 50 54	14 38 17	15 15 19	21 20 35	15 34.6	21 22.2	9 5.8	7 11.1	10 10.4	23 44.7	22 33.7	2 6.3	2 24.0
6 F	12 54 50	15 37 17	27 28 52	3♎40 18	15 22.8	23 25.9	10 20.2	7 57.5	10 24.0	23 45.8	22 36.2	2 6.1	2 24.4
7 Sa	12 58 47	16 36 16	9♎55 0	16 12 59	15 9.5	25 28.9	11 34.5	8 43.8	10 37.6	23 47.1	22 38.5	2 5.8	2 24.9
8 Su	13 2 43	17 35 13	22 34 13	28 58 39	14 55.9	27 30.9	12 48.9	9 30.0	10 51.3	23 48.4	22 40.9	2 5.7	2 25.4
9 M	13 6 40	18 34 8	5♏26 13	11♏56 46	14 43.1	29 31.5	14 3.2	10 16.3	11 5.1	23 49.9	22 43.2	2 5.5	2 25.9
10 Tu	13 10 36	19 33 1	18 30 14	25 6 28	14 32.3	1♉30.5	15 17.5	11 2.5	11 18.8	23 51.5	22 45.5	2 5.4	2 26.4
11 W	13 14 33	20 31 52	1♐45 25	8♐26 59	14 24.3	3 27.3	16 31.8	11 48.6	11 32.6	23 53.2	22 47.7	2 5.3	2 27.0
12 Th	13 18 29	21 30 41	15 11 9	21 57 53	14 19.2	5 21.8	17 46.1	12 34.7	11 46.5	23 55.0	22 49.9	2 5.2	2 27.6
13 F	13 22 26	22 29 29	28 47 13	5♑39 10	14 16.8	7 13.5	19 0.4	13 20.8	12 0.3	23 56.9	22 52.1	2D 5.2	2 28.2
14 Sa	13 26 23	23 28 15	12♑33 46	19 31 6	14 16.2	9 2.1	20 14.7	14 6.8	12 14.3	23 58.9	22 54.2	2 5.2	2 28.8
15 Su	13 30 19	24 26 59	26 31 9	3♒33 55	14 16.2	10 47.4	21 28.9	14 52.8	12 28.2	24 1.0	22 56.3	2 5.3	2 29.4
16 M	13 34 16	25 25 42	10♒39 19	17 47 12	14 15.6	12 28.9	22 43.2	15 38.8	12 42.1	24 3.2	22 58.3	2 5.4	2 30.1
17 Tu	13 38 12	26 24 23	24 57 20	2♓ 9 23	14 13.1	14 6.6	23 57.4	16 24.7	12 56.1	24 5.5	23 0.3	2 5.5	2 30.8
18 W	13 42 9	27 23 2	9♓22 54	16 37 19	14 8.1	15 40.1	25 11.6	17 10.6	13 10.1	24 7.9	23 2.3	2 5.6	2 31.5
19 Th	13 46 5	28 21 39	23 51 59	1♈ 6 10	14 0.4	17 9.2	26 25.9	17 56.4	13 24.2	24 10.4	23 4.2	2 5.8	2 32.2
20 F	13 50 2	29 20 15	8♈19 4	15 29 54	13 50.4	18 33.8	27 40.1	18 42.2	13 38.2	24 13.0	23 6.0	2 6.0	2 32.9
21 Sa	13 53 58	0♉18 48	22 37 50	29 42 7	13 39.2	19 53.7	28 54.2	19 27.9	13 52.3	24 15.8	23 7.9	2 6.3	2 33.7
22 Su	13 57 55	1 17 21	6♉42 5	13♉37 9	13 28.0	21 8.8	0♉ 8.4	20 13.6	14 6.4	24 18.6	23 9.7	2 6.6	2 34.5
23 M	14 1 51	2 15 51	20 26 53	27 10 56	13 18.0	22 19.0	1 22.6	20 59.3	14 20.5	24 21.5	23 11.4	2 6.9	2 35.3
24 Tu	14 5 48	3 14 19	3♊49 9	10♊21 32	13 10.0	23 24.1	2 36.7	21 44.9	14 34.7	24 24.5	23 13.1	2 7.2	2 36.1
25 W	14 9 45	4 12 45	16 48 9	23 9 15	13 4.6	24 24.1	3 50.9	22 30.5	14 48.8	24 27.6	23 14.8	2 7.6	2 36.9
26 Th	14 13 41	5 11 9	29 25 10	5♋36 20	13 1.7	25 18.9	5 5.0	23 16.0	15 3.0	24 30.9	23 16.4	2 8.0	2 37.8
27 F	14 17 38	6 9 32	11♋43 16	17 46 31	13D 0.9	26 8.3	6 19.1	24 1.4	15 17.2	24 34.2	23 17.9	2 8.5	2 38.7
28 Sa	14 21 34	7 7 52	23 46 43	29 44 31	13 1.2	26 52.4	7 33.2	24 46.8	15 31.4	24 37.6	23 19.5	2 8.9	2 39.6
29 Su	14 25 31	8 6 10	5♌40 35	11♌35 35	13R 1.7	27 31.1	8 47.2	25 32.2	15 45.6	24 41.1	23 20.9	2 9.5	2 40.5
30 M	14 29 27	9 4 25	17 30 11	23 25 4	13 1.3	28 4.4	10 1.3	26 17.5	15 59.8	24 44.7	23 22.4	2 10.0	2 41.4

Astro Data	Dy Hr Mn
☽0S	9 1:41
♆⊻♇	13 22:49
♇ D	16 23:12
☽0N	22 8:06
♄ D	26 1:53
☿0N	27 4:18
♂0N	29 5:43
♀0N	31 7:44
☽0S	5 8:27
♆ D	13 1:02
☽0N	18 16:34

Planet Ingress	Dy Hr Mn
♀ ♓	4 13:09
☿ ♓	8 15:34
☉ ♈	21 4:37
☿ ♈	25 11:35
♂ ♈	26 17:40
♀ ♈	28 16:01
☿ ♉	9 5:43
☉ ♉	20 16:17
♀ ♉	21 21:17

Last Aspect Dy Hr Mn		☽ Ingress Dy Hr Mn
2 2:50	♀ △	♋ 2 8:52
4 9:32	♄ ☌	♌ 4 21:36
7 5:58	☿ ☍	♍ 7 10:29
9 10:04	♄ ⚹	♎ 9 22:01
11 20:00	♄ □	♏ 12 7:40
14 3:57	♄ △	♐ 14 15:18
16 12:33	☉ □	♑ 16 20:38
18 19:37	☉ ⚹	♒ 18 23:33
20 11:22	♅ ☌	♓ 21 0:31
22 19:57	♂ ☌	♈ 23 0:53
24 15:52	♄ □	♉ 25 2:35
27 4:05	♀ ⚹	♊ 27 7:28
29 1:24	♅ △	♋ 29 16:28

Last Aspect Dy Hr Mn		☽ Ingress Dy Hr Mn
31 15:49	♄ ☌	♌ 1 4:39
3 2:22	♅ ☍	♍ 3 17:32
5 16:44	♄ ⚹	♎ 6 4:54
8 11:00	☿ ☍	♏ 8 13:54
10 9:45	♄ △	♐ 10 20:50
12 13:34	♅ ⚹	♑ 13 2:08
14 20:12	☉ □	♒ 15 5:56
17 2:36	☉ ⚹	♓ 17 8:25
19 0:31	♄ △	♈ 19 10:10
21 11:40	♀ ☌	♉ 21 12:30
23 6:58	♄ ⚹	♊ 23 17:04
25 12:12	♅ △	♋ 26 1:07
28 6:36	☿ ⚹	♌ 28 12:31

☽ Phases & Eclipses Dy Hr Mn	
8 21:58	○ 17♍46
16 12:33	☽ 25♐21
23 4:05	● 1♈58
30 10:36	☽ 9♋10
7 13:48	○ 17♎10
14 20:12	☽ 24♑18
21 14:01	● 0♉53
29 5:21	☽ 8♌19

Astro Data

1 MARCH 1917
Julian Day # 6269
Delta T 19.3 sec
SVP 06♓24'42"
Obliquity 23°27'03"
⚷ Chiron 24♓51.1
☽ Mean ☊ 17♑14.8

1 APRIL 1917
Julian Day # 6300
Delta T 19.4 sec
SVP 06♓24'39"
Obliquity 23°27'03"
⚷ Chiron 26♓41.5
☽ Mean ☊ 15♑36.3

LONGITUDE — MAY 1917

Day	Sid.Time	☉	0 hr ☽	Noon ☽	True ☊	☿	♀	♂	♃	♄	♅	♆	♇
1 Tu	14 33 24	10♉ 2 39	29♌20 52	5♍18 12	12♑59.3	28♉32.1	11♉15.3	27♈ 2.8	16♉14.0	24♋48.3	23♒23.7	2♌10.6	2♋42.4
2 W	14 37 21	11 0 51	11♍17 36	17 19 37	12R55.0	28 54.4	12 29.3	27 48.0	16 28.2	24 52.1	23 25.1	2 11.2	2 43.3
3 Th	14 41 17	11 59 1	23 24 43	29 33 16	12 48.5	29 11.2	13 43.3	28 33.1	16 42.5	24 56.0	23 26.4	2 11.8	2 44.3
4 F	14 45 14	12 57 9	5♎45 37	12♎ 2 1	12 40.0	29 22.6	14 57.3	29 18.2	16 56.7	24 59.9	23 27.6	2 12.5	2 45.3
5 Sa	14 49 10	13 55 15	18 22 37	24 47 30	12 30.2	29R28.7	16 11.3	0♉ 3.3	17 10.9	25 3.9	23 28.8	2 13.2	2 46.3
6 Su	14 53 7	14 53 19	1♏16 40	7♏50 2	12 20.0	29 29.5	17 25.2	0 48.3	17 25.2	25 8.1	23 30.0	2 13.9	2 47.3
7 M	14 57 3	15 51 22	14 27 27	21 8 42	12 10.4	29 25.2	18 39.2	1 33.3	17 39.4	25 12.3	23 31.1	2 14.7	2 48.4
8 Tu	15 1 0	16 49 23	27 53 31	4♐41 34	12 2.4	29 16.1	19 53.1	2 18.2	17 53.7	25 16.6	23 32.1	2 15.5	2 49.5
9 W	15 4 56	17 47 22	11♐32 33	18 26 7	11 56.6	29 2.4	21 7.0	3 3.0	18 7.9	25 21.0	23 33.1	2 16.3	2 50.5
10 Th	15 8 53	18 45 20	25 21 57	2♑19 43	11 53.2	28 44.4	22 20.9	3 47.8	18 22.2	25 25.4	23 34.1	2 17.2	2 51.6
11 F	15 12 50	19 43 17	9♑19 8	16 19 57	11D52.0	28 22.5	23 34.8	4 32.6	18 36.4	25 30.0	23 35.0	2 18.1	2 52.7
12 Sa	15 16 46	20 41 12	23 21 56	0♒24 53	11 52.4	27 57.0	24 48.7	5 17.3	18 50.7	25 34.6	23 35.9	2 19.0	2 53.9
13 Su	15 20 43	21 39 6	7♒28 37	14 32 58	11 53.4	27 28.6	26 2.6	6 2.0	19 4.9	25 39.3	23 36.7	2 20.0	2 55.0
14 M	15 24 39	22 36 59	21 37 45	28 42 49	11R54.0	26 57.6	27 16.5	6 46.6	19 19.1	25 44.1	23 37.5	2 21.0	2 56.2
15 Tu	15 28 36	23 34 50	5♓47 57	12♓52 56	11 53.3	26 24.7	28 30.3	7 31.2	19 33.4	25 48.9	23 38.2	2 22.0	2 57.3
16 W	15 32 32	24 32 41	19 57 28	27 1 17	11 50.8	25 50.5	29 44.2	8 15.7	19 47.6	25 53.9	23 38.9	2 23.0	2 58.5
17 Th	15 36 29	25 30 30	4♈ 4 0	11♈ 5 15	11 46.4	25 15.5	0♊58.0	9 0.1	20 1.8	25 58.9	23 39.5	2 24.1	2 59.7
18 F	15 40 25	26 28 18	18 4 37	25 1 40	11 40.3	24 40.4	2 11.9	9 44.5	20 16.0	26 4.0	23 40.1	2 25.2	3 0.9
19 Sa	15 44 22	27 26 4	1♉55 57	8♉47 5	11 33.2	24 5.8	3 25.7	10 28.9	20 30.2	26 9.2	23 40.6	2 26.3	3 2.1
20 Su	15 48 18	28 23 50	15 34 39	22 18 19	11 26.1	23 32.3	4 39.5	11 13.2	20 44.4	26 14.4	23 41.1	2 27.5	3 3.4
21 M	15 52 15	29 21 34	28 57 49	5♊32 56	11 19.7	23 0.4	5 53.3	11 57.4	20 58.5	26 19.7	23 41.5	2 28.6	3 4.6
22 Tu	15 56 12	0♊19 18	12♊ 3 33	18 29 36	11 14.8	22 30.7	7 7.1	12 41.6	21 12.7	26 25.1	23 41.9	2 29.9	3 5.9
23 W	16 0 8	1 16 59	24 51 9	1♋ 8 20	11 11.6	22 3.6	8 20.9	13 25.8	21 26.8	26 30.6	23 42.2	2 31.1	3 7.2
24 Th	16 4 5	2 14 40	7♋21 21	13 30 30	11D10.3	21 39.5	9 34.6	14 9.8	21 40.9	26 36.1	23 42.5	2 32.4	3 8.4
25 F	16 8 1	3 12 19	19 36 8	25 38 42	11 10.5	21 18.9	10 48.4	14 53.9	21 55.0	26 41.7	23 42.7	2 33.7	3 9.7
26 Sa	16 11 58	4 9 56	1♌38 38	7♌36 30	11 11.8	21 2.0	12 2.1	15 37.8	22 9.1	26 47.4	23 42.9	2 35.0	3 11.0
27 Su	16 15 54	5 7 32	13 32 50	19 28 14	11 13.5	20 49.1	13 15.9	16 21.8	22 23.1	26 53.1	23 43.0	2 36.3	3 12.3
28 M	16 19 51	6 5 7	25 23 19	1♍18 41	11R14.9	20 40.4	14 29.6	17 5.6	22 37.2	26 58.9	23 43.1	2 37.7	3 13.7
29 Tu	16 23 48	7 2 40	7♍14 59	13 12 49	11 15.4	20D35.9	15 43.3	17 49.4	22 51.2	27 4.7	23R43.1	2 39.1	3 15.0
30 W	16 27 44	8 0 12	19 12 49	25 15 33	11 14.7	20 35.9	16 57.0	18 33.2	23 5.2	27 10.7	23 43.1	2 40.5	3 16.3
31 Th	16 31 41	8 57 42	1♎21 34	7♎31 23	11 12.7	20 40.3	18 10.7	19 16.8	23 19.1	27 16.6	23 43.0	2 42.0	3 17.7

LONGITUDE — JUNE 1917

Day	Sid.Time	☉	0 hr ☽	Noon ☽	True ☊	☿	♀	♂	♃	♄	♅	♆	♇
1 F	16 35 37	9♊55 11	13♎45 26	20♎ 4 8	11♑ 9.3	20♉49.3	19♊24.3	20♉ 0.5	23♉33.0	27♋22.7	23♒42.9	2♌43.5	3♋19.0
2 Sa	16 39 34	10 52 39	26 27 46	2♏56 33	11R 5.1	21 2.7	20 38.0	20 44.0	23 46.9	27 28.8	23R42.8	2 45.0	3 20.4
3 Su	16 43 30	11 50 6	9♏30 38	16 10 2	11 0.6	21 20.5	21 51.6	21 27.5	24 0.8	27 34.9	23 42.6	2 46.5	3 21.8
4 M	16 47 27	12 47 32	22 54 39	29 44 18	10 56.2	21 42.8	23 5.2	22 11.0	24 14.6	27 41.1	23 42.3	2 48.0	3 23.2
5 Tu	16 51 23	13 44 56	6♐38 43	13♐37 29	10 52.6	22 9.4	24 18.9	22 54.4	24 28.4	27 47.4	23 42.0	2 49.6	3 24.6
6 W	16 55 20	14 42 20	20 40 10	27 46 12	10 50.2	22 40.3	25 32.5	23 37.8	24 42.2	27 53.7	23 41.6	2 51.2	3 26.0
7 Th	16 59 17	15 39 43	4♑55 0	12♑ 5 59	10D49.1	23 15.3	26 46.1	24 21.1	24 56.0	28 0.1	23 41.2	2 52.8	3 27.4
8 F	17 3 13	16 37 5	19 18 30	26 31 57	10 49.2	23 54.5	27 59.7	25 4.3	25 9.7	28 6.6	23 40.8	2 54.5	3 28.8
9 Sa	17 7 10	17 34 27	3♒45 43	10♒59 16	10 50.1	24 37.6	29 13.2	25 47.5	25 23.3	28 13.0	23 40.3	2 56.1	3 30.2
10 Su	17 11 6	18 31 48	18 12 6	25 23 44	10 51.5	25 24.7	0♋26.8	26 30.6	25 37.0	28 19.6	23 39.8	2 57.8	3 31.6
11 M	17 15 3	19 29 8	2♓33 47	9♓41 55	10 52.7	26 15.6	1 40.4	27 13.7	25 50.6	28 26.2	23 39.2	2 59.5	3 33.1
12 Tu	17 18 59	20 26 28	16 47 48	23 51 14	10R53.3	27 10.3	2 53.9	27 56.7	26 4.1	28 32.8	23 38.5	3 1.2	3 34.5
13 W	17 22 56	21 23 47	0♈51 58	7♈49 51	10 53.1	28 8.6	4 7.5	28 39.7	26 17.7	28 39.5	23 37.9	3 3.0	3 35.9
14 Th	17 26 52	22 21 6	14 44 44	21 36 30	10 52.0	29 10.6	5 21.0	29 22.6	26 31.1	28 46.2	23 37.1	3 4.8	3 37.4
15 F	17 30 49	23 18 25	28 25 1	5♉10 14	10 50.3	0♊16.0	6 34.5	0♊ 5.4	26 44.6	28 53.0	23 36.4	3 6.5	3 38.8
16 Sa	17 34 46	24 15 43	11♉52 2	18 30 23	10 48.1	1 25.0	7 48.1	0 48.2	26 58.0	28 59.8	23 35.5	3 8.3	3 40.3
17 Su	17 38 42	25 13 2	25 5 14	1♊36 32	10 45.9	2 37.4	9 1.6	1 31.0	27 11.3	29 6.7	23 34.7	3 10.2	3 41.7
18 M	17 42 39	26 10 19	8♊ 4 17	14 28 30	10 44.0	3 53.2	10 15.1	2 13.7	27 24.6	29 13.6	23 33.8	3 12.0	3 43.2
19 Tu	17 46 35	27 7 37	20 49 12	27 6 29	10 42.6	5 12.3	11 28.6	2 56.3	27 37.9	29 20.5	23 32.8	3 13.9	3 44.7
20 W	17 50 32	28 4 53	3♋20 26	9♋31 12	10D41.9	6 34.8	12 42.1	3 38.9	27 51.1	29 27.5	23 31.8	3 15.8	3 46.1
21 Th	17 54 28	29 2 10	15 38 57	21 43 55	10 41.8	8 0.5	13 55.6	4 21.4	28 4.2	29 34.5	23 30.8	3 17.7	3 47.6
22 F	17 58 25	29 59 26	27 46 20	3♌46 32	10 42.3	9 29.4	15 9.1	5 3.8	28 17.3	29 41.6	23 29.7	3 19.6	3 49.1
23 Sa	18 2 21	0♋56 41	9♌44 51	15 41 39	10 43.1	11 1.5	16 22.5	5 46.2	28 30.4	29 48.7	23 28.6	3 21.5	3 50.5
24 Su	18 6 18	1 53 56	21 37 22	27 32 27	10 44.1	12 36.8	17 36.0	6 28.6	28 43.4	29 55.9	23 27.4	3 23.4	3 52.0
25 M	18 10 15	2 51 10	3♍27 24	9♍22 42	10 44.9	14 15.3	18 49.4	7 10.8	28 56.3	0♌ 3.0	23 26.2	3 25.4	3 53.5
26 Tu	18 14 11	3 48 24	15 18 55	21 16 35	10 45.5	15 56.8	20 2.9	7 53.0	29 9.2	0 10.2	23 24.9	3 27.4	3 55.0
27 W	18 18 8	4 45 37	27 16 18	3♎18 36	10R45.9	17 41.3	21 16.3	8 35.2	29 22.0	0 17.5	23 23.6	3 29.4	3 56.4
28 Th	18 22 4	5 42 49	9♎24 5	15 33 17	10 45.9	19 28.8	22 29.7	9 17.3	29 34.7	0 24.7	23 22.3	3 31.4	3 57.9
29 F	18 26 1	6 40 1	21 46 45	28 4 58	10 45.7	21 19.2	23 43.1	9 59.3	29 47.4	0 32.1	23 20.9	3 33.4	3 59.4
30 Sa	18 29 57	7 37 13	4♏28 23	10♏57 23	10 45.5	23 12.3	24 56.4	10 41.3	0♊ 0.1	0 39.4	23 19.5	3 35.4	4 0.8

Astro Data

	Dy Hr Mn
☽0S	2 15:40
☿ R	5 15:47
♃∠♇	7 16:17
☽0N	15 22:21
☽0S	29 23:10
☿ D	29 12:11
♅ R	29 3:27
♃□♅	1 16:54
☽0N	12 3:12
☽0S	26 6:38

Planet Ingress

	Dy Hr Mn
♂ ♉	4 22:14
♀ ♊	16 5:08
☉ ♊	21 15:59
♀ ♋	9 15:15
☿ ♊	14 18:14
♂ ♊	14 20:58
☉ ♋	22 0:14
♄ ♌	24 13:53
♃ ♊	29 23:51

Last Aspect / ☽ Ingress

Last Aspect Dy Hr Mn		☽ Ingress Dy Hr Mn
30 22:18	☿ □	♍ 1 1:19
3 11:29	☿ △	♎ 3 12:52
5 12:35	♄ □	♏ 5 21:39
8 2:24	☿ ☍	♐ 8 3:44
9 20:53	♅ ⚹	♑ 10 8:00
12 7:34	☿ △	♒ 12 11:18
14 10:28	♀ □	♓ 14 14:11
16 10:09	♄ △	♈ 16 17:04
18 13:53	♄ □	♉ 18 20:38
21 0:46	☉ ☌	♊ 21 1:53
22 21:49	♅ △	♋ 23 9:49
25 14:12	♄ ☌	♌ 25 20:42
27 20:37	♅ ☍	♍ 28 9:21
30 15:55	♄ ⚹	♎ 30 21:20

Last Aspect / ☽ Ingress

Last Aspect Dy Hr Mn		☽ Ingress Dy Hr Mn
2 1:55	♄ □	♏ 2 6:34
4 8:28	♄ △	♐ 4 12:27
6 9:01	♀ ☍	♑ 6 15:45
8 14:44	♄ ☍	♒ 8 17:45
10 14:36	♂ □	♓ 10 19:42
12 20:11	♄ △	♈ 12 22:31
15 0:50	♄ □	♉ 15 2:48
17 7:27	♄ ⚹	♊ 17 9:02
19 13:02	☉ ☌	♋ 19 17:33
22 3:52	♄ ☌	♌ 22 4:27
24 14:40	♃ □	♍ 24 16:59
27 4:15	♃ △	♎ 27 5:26
29 4:06	♀ □	♏ 29 15:37

☽ Phases & Eclipses

Dy Hr Mn	
7 2:43	○ 15♏58
14 1:48	☽ 22♒41
21 0:46	● 29♉23
28 23:33	☽ 7♍02
5 13:06	○ 14♐16
12 6:38	☽ 20♓42
19 13:02	● 27♊39
19 13:15:55	✔ P 0.473
27 16:08	☽ 5♎24

Astro Data

1 MAY 1917
Julian Day # 6330
Delta T 19.5 sec
SVP 06♓24'35"
Obliquity 23°27'03"
⚷ Chiron 28♓18.4
☽ Mean ☊ 14♑00.9

1 JUNE 1917
Julian Day # 6361
Delta T 19.6 sec
SVP 06♓24'31"
Obliquity 23°27'02"
⚷ Chiron 29♓29.3
☽ Mean ☊ 12♑22.5

JULY 1917 — LONGITUDE

Day	Sid.Time	☉	0 hr ☽	Noon ☽	True ☊	☿	♀	♂	♃	♄	♅	♆	♇
1 Su	18 33 54	8♋34 25	17♏32 17	24♏13 17	10♑45.2	25♊ 8.1	26♋ 9.8	11♊23.2	0♊12.6	0♌46.7	23♒18.1	3♌37.5	4♋ 2.3
2 M	18 37 50	9 31 36	1♐ 0 28	7♐53 51	10R45.0	27 6.3	27 23.2	12 5.1	0 25.2	0 54.1	23R16.6	3 39.5	4 3.8
3 Tu	18 41 47	10 28 47	14 53 15	21 58 23	10D45.0	29 6.8	28 36.5	12 46.9	0 37.6	1 1.6	23 15.1	3 41.6	4 5.2
4 W	18 45 44	11 25 58	29 8 48	6♑23 58	10R45.0	1♋ 9.4	29 49.8	13 28.6	0 50.0	1 9.0	23 13.5	3 43.7	4 6.7
5 Th	18 49 40	12 23 8	13♑43 9	21 5 33	10 45.0	3 13.9	1♌ 3.1	14 10.3	1 2.3	1 16.5	23 11.9	3 45.8	4 8.2
6 F	18 53 37	13 20 19	28 30 17	5♒56 25	10 44.9	5 19.9	2 16.4	14 52.0	1 14.5	1 24.0	23 10.3	3 47.9	4 9.6
7 Sa	18 57 33	14 17 30	13♒22 59	20 49 0	10 44.7	7 27.3	3 29.7	15 33.5	1 26.7	1 31.5	23 8.6	3 50.0	4 11.1
8 Su	19 1 30	15 14 41	28 13 36	5♓35 55	10 44.3	9 35.6	4 43.0	16 15.0	1 38.8	1 39.0	23 6.9	3 52.1	4 12.5
9 M	19 5 26	16 11 52	12♓55 12	20 10 51	10 43.8	11 44.7	5 56.2	16 56.5	1 50.8	1 46.6	23 5.2	3 54.2	4 14.0
10 Tu	19 9 23	17 9 4	27 22 20	4♈29 17	10 43.3	13 54.2	7 9.5	17 37.9	2 2.7	1 54.1	23 3.4	3 56.4	4 15.4
11 W	19 13 19	18 6 16	11♈31 26	18 28 37	10D43.0	16 3.8	8 22.7	18 19.3	2 14.6	2 1.7	23 1.6	3 58.5	4 16.9
12 Th	19 17 16	19 3 29	25 20 48	2♉ 8 2	10 43.0	18 13.3	9 35.9	19 0.6	2 26.4	2 9.3	22 59.8	4 0.7	4 18.3
13 F	19 21 13	20 0 42	8♉50 24	15 28 5	10 43.3	20 22.4	10 49.1	19 41.8	2 38.1	2 17.0	22 58.0	4 2.9	4 19.7
14 Sa	19 25 9	20 57 56	22 1 17	28 30 14	10 44.1	22 30.8	12 2.3	20 23.0	2 49.7	2 24.6	22 56.1	4 5.0	4 21.2
15 Su	19 29 6	21 55 11	4♊55 10	11♊16 23	10 45.1	24 38.4	13 15.5	21 4.1	3 1.3	2 32.3	22 54.2	4 7.2	4 22.6
16 M	19 33 2	22 52 26	17 34 6	23 48 37	10 46.0	26 45.0	14 28.7	21 45.2	3 12.7	2 39.9	22 52.2	4 9.4	4 24.0
17 Tu	19 36 59	23 49 41	0♋ 0 9	6♋ 8 58	10R46.8	28 50.4	15 41.9	22 26.2	3 24.1	2 47.6	22 50.2	4 11.6	4 25.4
18 W	19 40 55	24 46 58	12 15 17	18 19 20	10 47.0	0♌54.5	16 55.0	23 7.1	3 35.4	2 55.3	22 48.2	4 13.8	4 26.8
19 Th	19 44 52	25 44 14	24 21 22	0♌21 36	10 46.6	2 57.1	18 8.2	23 48.0	3 46.6	3 3.0	22 46.2	4 16.0	4 28.2
20 F	19 48 49	26 41 31	6♌20 15	12 17 35	10 45.3	4 58.2	19 21.3	24 28.8	3 57.7	3 10.8	22 44.2	4 18.2	4 29.6
21 Sa	19 52 45	27 38 49	18 13 51	24 9 20	10 43.3	6 57.7	20 34.4	25 9.6	4 8.7	3 18.5	22 42.1	4 20.4	4 31.0
22 Su	19 56 42	28 36 7	0♍ 4 18	5♍59 6	10 40.7	8 55.7	21 47.5	25 50.3	4 19.6	3 26.2	22 40.0	4 22.6	4 32.3
23 M	20 0 38	29 33 25	11 54 3	17 49 32	10 37.8	10 51.9	23 0.6	26 31.0	4 30.4	3 33.9	22 37.8	4 24.9	4 33.7
24 Tu	20 4 35	0♌30 44	23 45 58	29 43 46	10 34.9	12 46.4	24 13.7	27 11.5	4 41.2	3 41.7	22 35.7	4 27.1	4 35.0
25 W	20 8 31	1 28 3	5♎43 23	11♎45 20	10 32.4	14 39.3	25 26.7	27 52.1	4 51.8	3 49.4	22 33.5	4 29.3	4 36.4
26 Th	20 12 28	2 25 23	17 50 5	23 58 11	10 30.7	16 30.4	26 39.7	28 32.5	5 2.3	3 57.2	22 31.3	4 31.5	4 37.7
27 F	20 16 24	3 22 43	0♏10 10	6♏26 31	10D29.9	18 19.8	27 52.7	29 12.9	5 12.7	4 4.9	22 29.1	4 33.8	4 39.0
28 Sa	20 20 21	4 20 3	12 47 48	19 14 28	10 30.1	20 7.5	29 5.7	29 53.3	5 23.1	4 12.7	22 26.9	4 36.0	4 40.3
29 Su	20 24 18	5 17 25	25 46 58	2♐25 43	10 31.2	21 53.5	0♍18.7	0♋33.6	5 33.3	4 20.4	22 24.7	4 38.2	4 41.6
30 M	20 28 14	6 14 46	9♐10 58	16 2 58	10 32.6	23 37.8	1 31.6	1 13.8	5 43.4	4 28.2	22 22.4	4 40.4	4 42.9
31 Tu	20 32 11	7 12 9	23 1 45	0♑ 7 16	10 34.0	25 20.4	2 44.5	1 53.9	5 53.4	4 35.9	22 20.1	4 42.7	4 44.2

AUGUST 1917 — LONGITUDE

Day	Sid.Time	☉	0 hr ☽	Noon ☽	True ☊	☿	♀	♂	♃	♄	♅	♆	♇
1 W	20 36 7	8♌ 9 31	7♑19 16	14♑37 19	10♑34.7	27♌ 1.3	3♍57.4	2♋34.0	6♊ 3.3	4♌43.7	22♒17.9	4♌44.9	4♋45.5
2 Th	20 40 4	9 6 55	22 0 51	29 29 2	10R34.4	28 40.6	5 10.3	3 14.1	6 13.1	4 51.4	22R15.6	4 47.1	4 46.7
3 F	20 44 0	10 4 19	7♒ 0 56	14♒35 27	10 32.7	0♍18.1	6 23.1	3 54.1	6 22.7	4 59.1	22 13.2	4 49.3	4 48.0
4 Sa	20 47 57	11 1 45	22 11 22	29 47 25	10 29.6	1 54.0	7 35.9	4 34.0	6 32.3	5 6.9	22 10.9	4 51.5	4 49.2
5 Su	20 51 53	11 59 11	7♓22 21	14♓54 57	10 25.6	3 28.2	8 48.7	5 13.9	6 41.7	5 14.6	22 8.6	4 53.8	4 50.4
6 M	20 55 50	12 56 38	22 24 5	29 48 45	10 21.1	5 0.8	10 1.5	5 53.7	6 51.0	5 22.3	22 6.2	4 56.0	4 51.6
7 Tu	20 59 47	13 54 6	7♈ 8 10	14♈21 42	10 16.9	6 31.7	11 14.3	6 33.4	7 0.2	5 30.0	22 3.9	4 58.2	4 52.8
8 W	21 3 43	14 51 36	21 28 54	28 29 32	10 13.7	8 0.9	12 27.0	7 13.1	7 9.3	5 37.7	22 1.5	5 0.4	4 54.0
9 Th	21 7 40	15 49 8	5♉23 32	12♉10 58	10D11.8	9 28.4	13 39.7	7 52.7	7 18.3	5 45.3	21 59.1	5 2.6	4 55.2
10 F	21 11 36	16 46 40	18 52 3	25 27 4	10 11.3	10 54.3	14 52.4	8 32.3	7 27.1	5 53.0	21 56.8	5 4.8	4 56.3
11 Sa	21 15 33	17 44 14	1♊56 25	8♊20 32	10 12.0	12 18.3	16 5.0	9 11.8	7 35.8	6 0.7	21 54.4	5 7.0	4 57.5
12 Su	21 19 29	18 41 50	14 39 53	20 54 57	10 13.5	13 40.7	17 17.7	9 51.3	7 44.4	6 8.3	21 52.0	5 9.1	4 58.6
13 M	21 23 26	19 39 27	27 6 13	3♋14 10	10 14.9	15 1.2	18 30.3	10 30.7	7 52.9	6 15.9	21 49.6	5 11.3	4 59.7
14 Tu	21 27 22	20 37 5	9♋19 15	15 21 53	10R15.7	16 19.9	19 42.9	11 10.0	8 1.2	6 23.5	21 47.2	5 13.5	5 0.8
15 W	21 31 19	21 34 45	21 22 29	27 21 25	10 15.0	17 36.7	20 55.5	11 49.3	8 9.4	6 31.1	21 44.8	5 15.6	5 1.9
16 Th	21 35 16	22 32 26	3♌19 0	9♌15 32	10 12.4	18 51.6	22 8.1	12 28.5	8 17.4	6 38.7	21 42.4	5 17.8	5 3.0
17 F	21 39 12	23 30 9	15 11 20	21 6 37	10 7.9	20 4.4	23 20.6	13 7.7	8 25.3	6 46.2	21 40.0	5 19.9	5 4.0
18 Sa	21 43 9	24 27 53	27 1 38	2♍56 36	10 1.4	21 15.2	24 33.1	13 46.8	8 33.1	6 53.8	21 37.6	5 22.1	5 5.1
19 Su	21 47 5	25 25 38	8♍51 44	14 47 16	9 53.4	22 23.9	25 45.6	14 25.8	8 40.7	7 1.3	21 35.3	5 24.2	5 6.1
20 M	21 51 2	26 23 25	20 43 25	26 40 25	9 44.6	23 30.3	26 58.0	15 4.8	8 48.2	7 8.8	21 32.9	5 26.3	5 7.1
21 Tu	21 54 58	27 21 12	2♎38 32	8♎38 2	9 35.8	24 34.4	28 10.5	15 43.7	8 55.5	7 16.2	21 30.5	5 28.4	5 8.1
22 W	21 58 55	28 19 1	14 39 14	20 42 30	9 27.8	25 36.0	29 22.8	16 22.5	9 2.7	7 23.6	21 28.1	5 30.5	5 9.0
23 Th	22 2 51	29 16 52	26 48 10	2♏56 40	9 21.5	26 35.0	0♎35.2	17 1.3	9 9.8	7 31.0	21 25.7	5 32.6	5 10.0
24 F	22 6 48	0♍14 43	9♏ 8 26	15 23 56	9 17.1	27 31.3	1 47.5	17 40.0	9 16.7	7 38.4	21 23.4	5 34.6	5 10.9
25 Sa	22 10 44	1 12 36	21 43 37	28 7 59	9D14.8	28 24.7	2 59.8	18 18.6	9 23.4	7 45.8	21 21.0	5 36.7	5 11.8
26 Su	22 14 41	2 10 30	4♐37 31	11♐12 41	9 14.4	29 15.1	4 12.1	18 57.2	9 30.0	7 53.1	21 18.7	5 38.7	5 12.7
27 M	22 18 38	3 8 26	17 53 54	24 41 30	9 15.1	0♎ 2.2	5 24.3	19 35.7	9 36.4	8 0.4	21 16.4	5 40.8	5 13.6
28 Tu	22 22 34	4 6 22	1♑35 46	8♑36 51	9R15.9	0 45.9	6 36.5	20 14.1	9 42.7	8 7.6	21 14.0	5 42.8	5 14.5
29 W	22 26 31	5 4 20	15 44 44	22 59 16	9 16.0	1 26.0	7 48.7	20 52.5	9 48.8	8 14.8	21 11.7	5 44.8	5 15.3
30 Th	22 30 27	6 2 19	0♒20 4	7♒46 33	9 14.3	2 2.2	9 0.8	21 30.8	9 54.8	8 22.0	21 9.5	5 46.8	5 16.1
31 F	22 34 24	7 0 20	15 17 56	22 53 13	9 10.3	2 34.2	10 12.9	22 9.1	10 0.5	8 29.2	21 7.2	5 48.7	5 16.9

Astro Data	Dy Hr Mn
♃⚹♄	8 1:19
☽0N	9 9:24
♃⚹♆	22 8:24
☽0S	23 13:43
♃⚺♇	23 8:15
♄☌♆	1 5:20
♄⚺♇	1 6:45
♆⚺♇	1 14:53
☽0N	5 18:08
☽0S	19 20:16
☿0S	21 23:22
♀0S	24 2:12

Planet Ingress	Dy Hr Mn
☿ ♋	3 10:27
♀ ♌	4 3:20
☿ ♌	17 13:26
☉ ♌	23 11:08
♀ ♍	28 17:52
♂ ♋	28 4:00
☿ ♍	2 19:31
♀ ♎	22 12:19
☉ ♍	23 17:54
☿ ♎	26 22:50

Last Aspect Dy Hr Mn	☽ Ingress Dy Hr Mn
1 16:59 ♀ △	♐ 1 22:14
3 14:07 ♅ ⚹	♑ 4 1:25
4 21:40 ☉ ☍	♒ 6 2:25
7 15:44 ♅ ☌	♓ 8 2:53
9 6:58 ♂ □	♈ 10 4:25
11 19:53 ♅ ⚹	♉ 12 8:13
14 1:41 ♅ □	♊ 14 14:47
16 10:10 ♅ △	♋ 16 24:00
19 3:00 ☉ ☌	♌ 19 11:17
21 14:53 ♂ ⚹	♍ 21 23:51
24 7:19 ♂ □	♎ 24 12:33
26 22:03 ♂ △	♏ 26 23:40
28 17:51 ♅ □	♐ 29 7:38
31 4:28 ☿ △	♑ 31 11:48

Last Aspect Dy Hr Mn	☽ Ingress Dy Hr Mn
31 19:44 ♇ ☍	♒ 2 12:50
3 23:59 ♅ ☌	♓ 4 12:20
5 2:29 ♀ ☍	♈ 6 12:18
8 0:55 ♅ ⚹	♉ 8 14:36
10 5:34 ♅ □	♊ 10 20:24
12 13:48 ♅ △	♋ 13 5:39
14 23:00 ♀ ⚹	♌ 15 17:19
17 18:21 ☉ ☌	♍ 18 6:02
20 14:01 ♀ ☌	♎ 20 18:42
23 5:16 ☉ ⚹	♏ 23 6:16
25 13:24 ☿ ⚹	♐ 25 15:28
27 5:58 ♅ ⚹	♑ 27 21:15
29 8:54 ♂ ☍	♒ 29 23:27
31 9:11 ♅ ☌	♓ 31 23:11

☽ Phases & Eclipses Dy Hr Mn	
4 21:40	○ 12♑18
4 21:39	☍T 1.618
11 12:12	☽ 18♈35
19 3:00	● 25♋51
19 2:42:22	☌P 0.086
27 6:40	☽ 3♏39
3 5:10	○ 10♒17
9 19:56	☽ 16♉37
17 18:21	● 24♌14
25 19:08	☽ 1♐59

Astro Data

1 JULY 1917
Julian Day # 6391
Delta T 19.7 sec
SVP 06♓24'26"
Obliquity 23°27'01"
⚷ Chiron 29♓56.0
☽ Mean ☊ 10♑47.2

1 AUGUST 1917
Julian Day # 6422
Delta T 19.8 sec
SVP 06♓24'20"
Obliquity 23°27'01"
⚷ Chiron 29♓35.0R
☽ Mean ☊ 9♑08.7

LONGITUDE SEPTEMBER 1917

Day	Sid.Time	☉	0 hr ☽	Noon ☽	True ☊	☿	♀	♂	♃	♄	♅	♆	♇
1 Sa	22 38 20	7♍58 22	0♓31 12	8♓10 34	9♑ 4.0	3♎ 1.9	11♎25.0	22♋47.3	10♊ 6.2	8♌36.3	21♒ 4.9	5♌50.7	5♋17.7
2 Su	22 42 17	8 56 26	15 49 55	23 27 49	8R 55.8	3 24.9	12 37.0	23 25.4	10 11.6	8 43.4	21R 2.7	5 52.6	5 18.5
3 M	22 46 13	9 54 31	1♈ 2 54	8♈33 52	8 46.8	3 42.9	13 49.0	24 3.5	10 16.9	8 50.4	21 0.4	5 54.5	5 19.2
4 Tu	22 50 10	10 52 38	15 59 38	23 19 17	8 38.0	3 55.6	15 0.9	24 41.4	10 22.1	8 57.4	20 58.2	5 56.5	5 20.0
5 W	22 54 7	11 50 48	0♉32 8	7♉37 44	8 30.6	4R 2.9	16 12.8	25 19.4	10 27.0	9 4.4	20 56.0	5 58.3	5 20.7
6 Th	22 58 3	12 48 59	14 35 51	21 26 29	8 25.2	4 4.3	17 24.7	25 57.2	10 31.8	9 11.3	20 53.9	6 0.2	5 21.4
7 F	23 2 0	13 47 12	28 9 46	4♊46 2	8 22.0	3 59.6	18 36.5	26 35.0	10 36.4	9 18.1	20 51.7	6 2.1	5 22.0
8 Sa	23 5 56	14 45 27	11♊15 40	17 39 13	8D 20.9	3 48.6	19 48.3	27 12.8	10 40.9	9 25.0	20 49.6	6 3.9	5 22.7
9 Su	23 9 53	15 43 45	23 57 13	0♋10 18	8 21.0	3 31.1	21 0.0	27 50.5	10 45.1	9 31.8	20 47.5	6 5.7	5 23.3
10 M	23 13 49	16 42 4	6♋19 6	12 24 13	8R 21.4	3 7.0	22 11.8	28 28.1	10 49.2	9 38.5	20 45.4	6 7.5	5 23.9
11 Tu	23 17 46	17 40 26	18 26 16	24 25 50	8 21.0	2 36.3	23 23.5	29 5.6	10 53.1	9 45.2	20 43.3	6 9.3	5 24.5
12 W	23 21 42	18 38 49	0♌23 28	6♌19 41	8 18.8	1 59.2	24 35.1	29 43.1	10 56.9	9 51.8	20 41.3	6 11.1	5 25.0
13 Th	23 25 39	19 37 15	12 14 56	18 9 39	8 14.0	1 15.9	25 46.7	0♌20.5	11 0.4	9 58.4	20 39.3	6 12.8	5 25.6
14 F	23 29 36	20 35 42	24 4 12	29 58 55	8 6.5	0 26.9	26 58.3	0 57.8	11 3.7	10 5.0	20 37.3	6 14.5	5 26.1
15 Sa	23 33 32	21 34 12	5♍54 5	11♍49 56	7 56.2	29♍32.8	28 9.8	1 35.0	11 6.9	10 11.5	20 35.4	6 16.2	5 26.6
16 Su	23 37 29	22 32 43	17 46 40	23 44 29	7 43.9	28 34.5	29 21.3	2 12.2	11 9.9	10 17.9	20 33.4	6 17.9	5 27.1
17 M	23 41 25	23 31 17	29 43 33	5♎44 0	7 30.3	27 33.1	0♏32.8	2 49.3	11 12.7	10 24.3	20 31.5	6 19.5	5 27.5
18 Tu	23 45 22	24 29 52	11♎45 58	17 49 37	7 16.6	26 29.8	1 44.2	3 26.4	11 15.3	10 30.6	20 29.7	6 21.1	5 28.0
19 W	23 49 18	25 28 29	23 55 5	0♏ 2 35	7 4.0	25 26.1	2 55.5	4 3.3	11 17.7	10 36.9	20 27.9	6 22.7	5 28.4
20 Th	23 53 15	26 27 8	6♏12 18	12 24 29	6 53.5	24 23.4	4 6.8	4 40.2	11 19.9	10 43.1	20 26.1	6 24.3	5 28.7
21 F	23 57 11	27 25 49	18 39 23	24 57 19	6 45.7	23 23.3	5 18.1	5 17.0	11 21.9	10 49.2	20 24.3	6 25.9	5 29.1
22 Sa	0 1 8	28 24 32	1♐18 38	7♐43 42	6 40.8	22 27.4	6 29.3	5 53.7	11 23.7	10 55.3	20 22.6	6 27.4	5 29.5
23 Su	0 5 5	29 23 16	14 12 54	20 46 38	6 38.4	21 37.2	7 40.5	6 30.4	11 25.3	11 1.4	20 20.9	6 28.9	5 29.8
24 M	0 9 1	0♎22 2	27 25 18	4♑ 9 15	6 37.8	20 53.9	8 51.6	7 7.0	11 26.7	11 7.3	20 19.2	6 30.4	5 30.1
25 Tu	0 12 58	1 20 50	10♑58 50	17 54 17	6 37.8	20 18.8	10 2.7	7 43.5	11 28.0	11 13.2	20 17.6	6 31.9	5 30.3
26 W	0 16 54	2 19 39	24 55 45	2♒ 3 15	6 37.1	19 52.7	11 13.7	8 19.9	11 29.0	11 19.1	20 16.0	6 33.3	5 30.6
27 Th	0 20 51	3 18 30	9♒16 39	16 35 37	6 34.5	19 36.2	12 24.6	8 56.2	11 29.8	11 24.8	20 14.4	6 34.7	5 30.8
28 F	0 24 47	4 17 23	23 59 39	1♓28 0	6 29.4	19D 29.9	13 35.5	9 32.5	11 30.5	11 30.6	20 12.9	6 36.1	5 31.0
29 Sa	0 28 44	5 16 18	8♓59 47	16 33 51	6 21.5	19 33.7	14 46.3	10 8.7	11 30.9	11 36.2	20 11.4	6 37.4	5 31.2
30 Su	0 32 40	6 15 14	24 8 59	1♈43 52	6 11.4	19 47.8	15 57.1	10 44.8	11R 31.1	11 41.8	20 10.0	6 38.7	5 31.4

LONGITUDE OCTOBER 1917

Day	Sid.Time	☉	0 hr ☽	Noon ☽	True ☊	☿	♀	♂	♃	♄	♅	♆	♇
1 M	0 36 37	7♎14 12	9♈17 8	16♈47 28	6♑ 0.0	20♍11.9	17♏ 7.8	11♌20.8	11♊31.2	11♌47.3	20♒ 8.6	6♌40.0	5♋31.5
2 Tu	0 40 34	8 13 13	24 13 39	1♉34 37	5R 48.8	20 45.5	18 18.4	11 56.7	11R 31.0	11 52.7	20R 7.2	6 41.3	5 31.6
3 W	0 44 30	9 12 15	8♉49 31	15 57 40	5 39.0	21 28.1	19 29.0	12 32.6	11 30.6	11 58.0	20 5.9	6 42.5	5 31.7
4 Th	0 48 27	10 11 20	22 58 38	29 52 13	5 31.5	22 19.2	20 39.5	13 8.4	11 30.1	12 3.3	20 4.7	6 43.8	5 31.8
5 F	0 52 23	11 10 27	6♊38 23	13♊17 18	5 26.7	23 18.0	21 50.0	13 44.1	11 29.3	12 8.5	20 3.4	6 44.9	5 31.8
6 Sa	0 56 20	12 9 37	19 49 17	26 14 46	5 24.3	24 23.8	23 0.4	14 19.7	11 28.3	12 13.7	20 2.2	6 46.1	5R 31.8
7 Su	1 0 16	13 8 49	2♋34 17	8♋48 26	5 23.6	25 35.8	24 10.7	14 55.3	11 27.2	12 18.7	20 1.1	6 47.2	5 31.8
8 M	1 4 13	14 8 3	14 57 51	21 3 13	5 23.6	26 53.4	25 21.0	15 30.7	11 25.8	12 23.7	19 60.0	6 48.3	5 31.8
9 Tu	1 8 9	15 7 19	27 5 12	3♌ 4 28	5 23.2	28 15.8	26 31.1	16 6.1	11 24.2	12 28.6	19 58.9	6 49.4	5 31.8
10 W	1 12 6	16 6 38	9♌ 1 40	14 57 25	5 21.1	29 42.3	27 41.3	16 41.3	11 22.5	12 33.4	19 57.9	6 50.4	5 31.7
11 Th	1 16 3	17 5 59	20 52 19	26 46 53	5 16.7	1♎12.3	28 51.3	17 16.5	11 20.5	12 38.2	19 56.9	6 51.5	5 31.6
12 F	1 19 59	18 5 22	2♍41 38	8♍37 0	5 9.5	2 45.2	0♐ 1.3	17 51.6	11 18.3	12 42.8	19 56.0	6 52.4	5 31.5
13 Sa	1 23 56	19 4 47	14 33 22	20 31 4	4 59.6	4 20.6	1 11.2	18 26.6	11 15.9	12 47.4	19 55.1	6 53.4	5 31.3
14 Su	1 27 52	20 4 15	26 30 23	2♎31 32	4 47.5	5 57.9	2 21.0	19 1.5	11 13.3	12 51.9	19 54.3	6 54.3	5 31.2
15 M	1 31 49	21 3 45	8♎34 42	14 40 2	4 34.1	7 36.8	3 30.8	19 36.3	11 10.6	12 56.3	19 53.5	6 55.2	5 31.0
16 Tu	1 35 45	22 3 16	20 47 37	26 57 31	4 20.6	9 16.9	4 40.5	20 11.1	11 7.6	13 0.6	19 52.8	6 56.0	5 30.8
17 W	1 39 42	23 2 50	3♏ 9 49	9♏24 33	4 8.1	10 57.9	5 50.0	20 45.7	11 4.4	13 4.9	19 52.1	6 56.8	5 30.6
18 Th	1 43 38	24 2 26	15 41 46	22 1 30	3 57.6	12 39.5	6 59.6	21 20.2	11 1.1	13 9.0	19 51.4	6 57.6	5 30.3
19 F	1 47 35	25 2 4	28 23 50	4♐48 53	3 49.9	14 21.6	8 9.0	21 54.6	10 57.5	13 13.1	19 50.8	6 58.4	5 30.0
20 Sa	1 51 31	26 1 44	11♐16 45	17 47 36	3 45.1	16 3.9	9 18.3	22 28.9	10 53.8	13 17.0	19 50.3	6 59.1	5 29.7
21 Su	1 55 28	27 1 25	24 21 36	0♑58 59	3D 42.9	17 46.3	10 27.5	23 3.1	10 49.9	13 20.9	19 49.8	6 59.8	5 29.4
22 M	1 59 25	28 1 9	7♑39 57	14 24 44	3 42.6	19 28.7	11 36.7	23 37.2	10 45.7	13 24.7	19 49.3	7 0.5	5 29.1
23 Tu	2 3 21	29 0 54	21 13 32	28 6 32	3R 43.1	21 10.9	12 45.7	24 11.2	10 41.5	13 28.4	19 48.9	7 1.1	5 28.7
24 W	2 7 18	0♏ 0 41	5♒ 3 52	12♒ 5 34	3 43.1	22 52.9	13 54.6	24 45.1	10 37.0	13 32.0	19 48.6	7 1.7	5 28.3
25 Th	2 11 14	1 0 29	19 11 36	26 21 49	3 41.7	24 34.6	15 3.4	25 18.8	10 32.3	13 35.4	19 48.3	7 2.2	5 27.9
26 F	2 15 11	2 0 19	3♓35 54	10♓53 25	3 38.1	26 15.9	16 12.1	25 52.5	10 27.5	13 38.8	19 48.0	7 2.8	5 27.5
27 Sa	2 19 7	3 0 10	18 13 45	25 36 10	3 32.0	27 56.9	17 20.7	26 26.1	10 22.5	13 42.1	19 47.8	7 3.3	5 27.0
28 Su	2 23 4	4 0 4	2♈59 49	10♈23 42	3 23.9	29 37.5	18 29.1	26 59.5	10 17.4	13 45.3	19 47.7	7 3.7	5 26.5
29 M	2 27 0	4 59 59	17 46 48	25 8 5	3 14.6	1♏17.6	19 37.4	27 32.8	10 12.0	13 48.4	19 47.6	7 4.1	5 26.0
30 Tu	2 30 57	5 59 55	2♉26 30	9♉41 7	3 5.3	2 57.3	20 45.6	28 6.0	10 6.5	13 51.5	19D 47.5	7 4.5	5 25.5
31 W	2 34 54	6 59 54	16 51 5	23 55 42	2 57.1	4 36.5	21 53.7	28 39.1	10 0.9	13 54.4	19 47.5	7 4.9	5 25.0

Astro Data Dy Hr Mn	Planet Ingress Dy Hr Mn	Last Aspect Dy Hr Mn	☽ Ingress Dy Hr Mn	Last Aspect Dy Hr Mn	☽ Ingress Dy Hr Mn	☽ Phases & Eclipses Dy Hr Mn	Astro Data
☽0N 2 4:51	♂ ♌ 12 10:52	2 12:27 ♂ △	♈ 2 22:20	1 17:22 ♅ ✶	♉ 2 9:25	1 12:28 ○ 8♓29	1 SEPTEMBER 1917
☿ R 5 17:37	☿ ♍ 14 12:12	4 14:55 ♂ □	♉ 4 23:06	3 22:47 ☿ △	♊ 4 12:14	8 7:05 ☽ 15♊03	Julian Day # 6453
☽0S 16 2:24	♀ ♏ 16 13:00	6 21:01 ♂ ✶	♊ 7 3:19	6 9:23 ☿ □	♋ 6 19:06	16 10:27 ● 22♍58	Delta T 19.9 sec
♅♇♇ 18 18:31	☉ ♎ 23 15:00	8 17:58 ♅ △	♋ 9 11:40	9 2:40 ☿ ✶	♌ 9 5:50	24 5:41 ☽ 0♑36	SVP 06♓24'16"
☿0N 20 11:17		11 22:34 ♂ ☌	♌ 11 23:13	11 17:59 ♀ □	♍ 11 18:32	30 20:31 ○ 7♈06	Obliquity 23°27'02"
♃✶♄ 27 23:38	☿ ♎ 10 4:48	14 6:33 ♀ ✶	♍ 14 12:02	12 17:23 ♃ □	♎ 14 6:58		⚷ Chiron 28♓32.0R
☿ D 28 2:56	♀ ♐ 11 23:33	16 20:00 ☿ ☌	♎ 17 0:33	16 2:41 ☉ ☌	♏ 16 17:53	7 22:14 ☽ 14♋04	☽ Mean ☊ 7♑30.2
☽0N 29 15:41	☉ ♏ 23 23:44	18 17:13 ♅ △	♏ 19 11:55	18 11:12 ♂ □	♐ 19 3:00	16 2:41 ● 22♎10	
♃ R 30 16:05	☿ ♏ 28 5:23	21 18:05 ☉ ✶	♐ 21 21:32	21 5:14 ☉ ✶	♑ 21 10:14	23 14:37 ☽ 29♑37	1 OCTOBER 1917
♇ R 6 12:13		23 12:48 ☿ □	♑ 24 4:37	23 14:37 ☉ □	♒ 23 15:17	30 6:19 ○ 6♉16	Julian Day # 6483
☽0S 13 8:32		25 15:37 ☿ △	♒ 26 8:33	25 10:40 ♂ ☍	♓ 25 18:03		Delta T 20.0 sec
☿0S 13 3:23		27 17:54 ♅ ☌	♓ 28 9:39	26 22:26 ♀ □	♈ 27 19:08		SVP 06♓24'13"
☽0N 27 0:36		29 16:59 ☿ ☍	♈ 30 9:15	29 16:35 ♂ △	♉ 29 19:59		Obliquity 23°27'02"
♅ D 30 10:32				31 20:56 ♂ □	♊ 31 22:26		⚷ Chiron 27♓11.8R
							☽ Mean ☊ 5♑54.8

NOVEMBER 1917 LONGITUDE

Day	Sid.Time	☉	0 hr ☽	Noon ☽	True ☊	☿	♀	♂	♃	♄	♅	♆	♇
1 Th	2 38 50	7♏59 55	0♊54 26	7♊46 55	2♑50.8	6♏15.3	23♐ 1.6	29♌12.1	9♊55.1	13♌57.2	19♒47.6	7♌ 5.2	5♋24.4
2 F	2 42 47	8 59 58	14 32 57	21 12 29	2R 46.9	7 53.7	24 9.4	29 45.0	9R 49.1	13 59.9	19 47.7	7 5.5	5R 23.8
3 Sa	2 46 43	10 0 3	27 45 39	4♋12 42	2D 45.3	9 31.6	25 17.0	0♍17.7	9 43.0	14 2.5	19 47.9	7 5.8	5 23.2
4 Su	2 50 40	11 0 10	10♋34 0	16 49 59	2 45.4	11 9.0	26 24.5	0 50.3	9 36.8	14 5.0	19 48.1	7 6.0	5 22.6
5 M	2 54 36	12 0 19	23 1 12	29 8 13	2 46.5	12 46.1	27 31.8	1 22.8	9 30.4	14 7.4	19 48.3	7 6.2	5 22.0
6 Tu	2 58 33	13 0 30	5♌11 40	11♌12 11	2R 47.7	14 22.7	28 39.0	1 55.2	9 23.9	14 9.7	19 48.6	7 6.3	5 21.3
7 W	3 2 29	14 0 43	17 10 26	23 7 3	2 47.9	15 58.9	29 46.0	2 27.4	9 17.2	14 11.8	19 49.0	7 6.4	5 20.7
8 Th	3 6 26	15 0 58	29 2 42	4♍57 58	2 46.6	17 34.8	0♑52.9	2 59.5	9 10.4	14 13.9	19 49.4	7 6.5	5 20.0
9 F	3 10 23	16 1 15	10♍53 29	16 49 47	2 43.4	19 10.3	1 59.6	3 31.5	9 3.5	14 15.9	19 49.9	7R 6.6	5 19.2
10 Sa	3 14 19	17 1 34	22 47 22	28 46 43	2 38.1	20 45.4	3 6.1	4 3.3	8 56.5	14 17.7	19 50.4	7 6.6	5 18.5
11 Su	3 18 16	18 1 55	4♎48 15	10♎52 17	2 31.1	22 20.2	4 12.4	4 35.0	8 49.4	14 19.5	19 50.9	7 6.6	5 17.7
12 M	3 22 12	19 2 17	16 59 9	23 9 3	2 23.1	23 54.7	5 18.6	5 6.5	8 42.1	14 21.1	19 51.6	7 6.5	5 17.0
13 Tu	3 26 9	20 2 42	29 22 11	5♏38 38	2 14.8	25 28.9	6 24.5	5 37.9	8 34.8	14 22.7	19 52.2	7 6.4	5 16.2
14 W	3 30 5	21 3 9	11♏58 29	18 21 42	2 7.1	27 2.8	7 30.3	6 9.2	8 27.3	14 24.1	19 52.9	7 6.3	5 15.4
15 Th	3 34 2	22 3 37	24 48 17	1♐18 9	2 0.8	28 36.4	8 35.8	6 40.3	8 19.8	14 25.4	19 53.7	7 6.2	5 14.6
16 F	3 37 58	23 4 7	7♐51 11	14 27 18	1 56.3	0♐ 9.8	9 41.1	7 11.2	8 12.1	14 26.6	19 54.5	7 6.0	5 13.7
17 Sa	3 41 55	24 4 38	21 6 21	27 48 15	1D 53.9	1 42.9	10 46.2	7 42.0	8 4.4	14 27.7	19 55.4	7 5.8	5 12.9
18 Su	3 45 52	25 5 11	4♑32 51	11♑20 5	1 53.4	3 15.8	11 51.1	8 12.6	7 56.7	14 28.7	19 56.3	7 5.5	5 12.0
19 M	3 49 48	26 5 45	18 9 52	25 2 5	1 54.3	4 48.5	12 55.7	8 43.0	7 48.8	14 29.5	19 57.3	7 5.2	5 11.1
20 Tu	3 53 45	27 6 20	1♒56 43	8♒53 40	1 55.9	6 21.0	14 0.1	9 13.3	7 40.9	14 30.3	19 58.3	7 4.9	5 10.2
21 W	3 57 41	28 6 57	15 52 53	22 54 14	1R 57.2	7 53.2	15 4.2	9 43.4	7 32.9	14 30.9	19 59.4	7 4.5	5 9.3
22 Th	4 1 38	29 7 34	29 57 38	7♓ 2 53	1 57.8	9 25.2	16 8.1	10 13.4	7 24.9	14 31.5	20 0.5	7 4.1	5 8.3
23 F	4 5 34	0♐ 8 13	14♓ 9 46	21 18 1	1 57.0	10 57.1	17 11.6	10 43.1	7 16.9	14 31.9	20 1.7	7 3.7	5 7.4
24 Sa	4 9 31	1 8 53	28 27 14	5♈37 2	1 54.7	12 28.7	18 14.9	11 12.7	7 8.8	14 32.2	20 2.9	7 3.3	5 6.4
25 Su	4 13 27	2 9 33	12♈46 56	19 56 21	1 51.1	14 0.1	19 17.8	11 42.1	7 0.6	14 32.4	20 4.2	7 2.8	5 5.4
26 M	4 17 24	3 10 15	27 4 45	4♉11 29	1 46.9	15 31.3	20 20.4	12 11.3	6 52.5	14R 32.5	20 5.5	7 2.2	5 4.4
27 Tu	4 21 21	4 10 59	11♉15 58	18 17 36	1 42.5	17 2.3	21 22.7	12 40.4	6 44.3	14 32.4	20 6.8	7 1.7	5 3.4
28 W	4 25 17	5 11 43	25 15 49	2♊10 7	1 38.6	18 33.0	22 24.7	13 9.2	6 36.2	14 32.3	20 8.3	7 1.1	5 2.4
29 Th	4 29 14	6 12 29	9♊ 0 6	15 45 25	1 35.8	20 3.5	23 26.3	13 37.9	6 28.0	14 32.0	20 9.7	7 0.5	5 1.4
30 F	4 33 10	7 13 15	22 25 50	29 1 14	1D 34.3	21 33.7	24 27.5	14 6.4	6 19.8	14 31.6	20 11.2	6 59.8	5 0.3

DECEMBER 1917 LONGITUDE

Day	Sid.Time	☉	0 hr ☽	Noon ☽	True ☊	☿	♀	♂	♃	♄	♅	♆	♇
1 Sa	4 37 7	8♐14 4	5♋31 35	11♋56 56	1♑34.1	23♐ 3.5	25♑28.3	14♍34.6	6♊11.6	14♌31.2	20♒12.8	6♌59.2	4♋59.3
2 Su	4 41 3	9 14 53	18 17 29	24 33 27	1 34.9	24 33.0	26 28.8	15 2.7	6R 3.5	14R 30.6	20 14.4	6R 58.5	4R 58.2
3 M	4 45 0	10 15 44	0♌45 12	6♌53 7	1 36.4	26 2.0	27 28.8	15 30.5	5 55.3	14 29.9	20 16.0	6 57.7	4 57.1
4 Tu	4 48 57	11 16 36	12 57 39	18 59 19	1 38.1	27 30.5	28 28.4	15 58.2	5 47.2	14 29.1	20 17.7	6 56.9	4 56.0
5 W	4 52 53	12 17 29	24 58 39	0♍56 15	1 39.5	28 58.4	29 27.6	16 25.6	5 39.1	14 28.1	20 19.5	6 56.1	4 54.9
6 Th	4 56 50	13 18 24	6♍52 42	12 48 36	1R 40.4	0♑25.6	0♒26.3	16 52.8	5 31.1	14 27.1	20 21.2	6 55.3	4 53.8
7 F	5 0 46	14 19 19	18 44 34	24 41 12	1 40.5	1 52.0	1 24.5	17 19.8	5 23.1	14 25.9	20 23.1	6 54.4	4 52.7
8 Sa	5 4 43	15 20 16	0♎39 5	6♎38 49	1 39.7	3 17.4	2 22.3	17 46.5	5 15.1	14 24.7	20 24.9	6 53.6	4 51.6
9 Su	5 8 39	16 21 15	12 40 55	18 45 54	1 38.3	4 41.8	3 19.6	18 13.0	5 7.2	14 23.3	20 26.8	6 52.6	4 50.4
10 M	5 12 36	17 22 14	24 54 14	1♏ 6 18	1 36.4	6 4.8	4 16.3	18 39.3	4 59.4	14 21.8	20 28.8	6 51.7	4 49.3
11 Tu	5 16 32	18 23 15	7♏22 27	13 42 57	1 34.3	7 26.3	5 12.5	19 5.3	4 51.6	14 20.2	20 30.8	6 50.7	4 48.1
12 W	5 20 29	19 24 16	20 8 1	26 37 45	1 32.4	8 46.0	6 8.1	19 31.0	4 43.9	14 18.5	20 32.8	6 49.7	4 47.0
13 Th	5 24 26	20 25 19	3♐12 10	9♐51 14	1 30.9	10 3.7	7 3.1	19 56.5	4 36.3	14 16.7	20 34.9	6 48.7	4 45.8
14 F	5 28 22	21 26 22	16 34 49	23 22 40	1 30.0	11 18.8	7 57.5	20 21.8	4 28.8	14 14.8	20 37.1	6 47.6	4 44.6
15 Sa	5 32 19	22 27 27	0♑14 31	7♑10 1	1D 29.7	12 31.2	8 51.3	20 46.7	4 21.3	14 12.8	20 39.2	6 46.5	4 43.4
16 Su	5 36 15	23 28 31	14 8 44	21 10 15	1 29.9	13 40.2	9 44.4	21 11.4	4 14.0	14 10.7	20 41.4	6 45.4	4 42.3
17 M	5 40 12	24 29 37	28 14 5	5♒19 44	1 30.4	14 45.3	10 36.9	21 35.8	4 6.8	14 8.5	20 43.7	6 44.3	4 41.1
18 Tu	5 44 8	25 30 43	12♒26 45	19 34 39	1 31.0	15 46.1	11 28.6	21 59.9	3 59.6	14 6.2	20 46.0	6 43.1	4 39.9
19 W	5 48 5	26 31 49	26 42 59	3♓51 20	1 31.6	16 41.6	12 19.5	22 23.7	3 52.6	14 3.7	20 48.3	6 41.9	4 38.7
20 Th	5 52 1	27 32 55	10♓59 19	18 6 36	1 31.9	17 31.4	13 9.6	22 47.2	3 45.7	14 1.2	20 50.7	6 40.7	4 37.5
21 F	5 55 58	28 34 2	25 12 50	2♈17 46	1R 32.1	18 14.4	13 59.0	23 10.4	3 39.0	13 58.6	20 53.1	6 39.5	4 36.3
22 Sa	5 59 55	29 35 9	9♈21 9	16 22 44	1 32.0	18 50.0	14 47.4	23 33.3	3 32.3	13 55.9	20 55.5	6 38.2	4 35.0
23 Su	6 3 51	0♑36 15	23 22 19	0♉19 41	1D 32.0	19 17.0	15 35.0	23 55.9	3 25.9	13 53.1	20 58.0	6 36.9	4 33.8
24 M	6 7 48	1 37 22	7♉14 41	14 7 7	1 31.9	19 34.8	16 21.6	24 18.1	3 19.5	13 50.2	21 0.5	6 35.6	4 32.6
25 Tu	6 11 44	2 38 30	20 56 48	27 43 36	1 32.0	19R 42.3	17 7.3	24 40.0	3 13.3	13 47.2	21 3.1	6 34.3	4 31.4
26 W	6 15 41	3 39 37	4♊27 21	11♊ 7 53	1 32.2	19 38.9	17 51.9	25 1.6	3 7.2	13 44.1	21 5.6	6 33.0	4 30.2
27 Th	6 19 37	4 40 44	17 45 6	24 18 53	1 32.4	19 24.0	18 35.5	25 22.9	3 1.3	13 40.9	21 8.3	6 31.6	4 29.0
28 F	6 23 34	5 41 52	0♋49 9	7♋15 50	1R 32.5	18 57.2	19 18.0	25 43.7	2 55.5	13 37.7	21 10.9	6 30.2	4 27.8
29 Sa	6 27 30	6 43 0	13 38 57	19 58 30	1 32.4	18 18.6	19 59.4	26 4.3	2 49.9	13 34.3	21 13.6	6 28.8	4 26.5
30 Su	6 31 27	7 44 8	26 14 33	2♌27 15	1 31.9	17 28.8	20 39.5	26 24.4	2 44.5	13 30.9	21 16.3	6 27.4	4 25.3
31 M	6 35 24	8 45 16	8♌36 44	14 43 15	1 31.1	16 28.8	21 18.4	26 44.2	2 39.2	13 27.4	21 19.1	6 26.0	4 24.1

Astro Data	Planet Ingress	Last Aspect	☽ Ingress	Last Aspect	☽ Ingress	☽ Phases & Eclipses	Astro Data
Dy Hr Mn	Dy Hr Mn	Dy Hr Mn	Dy Hr Mn	Dy Hr Mn	Dy Hr Mn	Dy Hr Mn	1 NOVEMBER 1917
☽0S 9 15:12	♂ ♍ 2 11:00	2 19:01 ♀ ☍	♋ 3 4:09	2 17:05 ♀ ☍	♌ 2 22:32	6 17:03 ☽ 13♌43	Julian Day # 6514
♆ R 9 22:27	♀ ♑ 7 5:01	4 1:17 ☿ △	♌ 5 13:42	5 9:10 ☿ △	♍ 5 10:07	14 18:28 ● 21♏50	Delta T 20.1 sec
☽0N 23 6:49	☿ ♐ 15 21:29	7 5:20 ♅ ☍	♍ 8 1:56	6 21:02 ♂ ☌	♎ 7 22:42	21 22:28 ☽ 29♒04	SVP 06♓24'10"
♃✱♆ 24 17:21	☉ ♐ 22 20:45	9 19:17 ☿ ✱	♎ 10 14:26	9 15:20 ♅ ✱	♏ 10 9:52	28 18:41 ○ 5♊59	Obliquity 23°27'01"
♅Q♇ 25 13:03		12 5:37 ♅ △	♏ 13 1:13	12 0:46 ♅ ☐	♐ 12 18:10		⚷ Chiron 25♓59.4R
♄ R 26 4:38	☿ ♑ 5 16:57	15 7:59 ☿ ☌	♐ 15 9:36	14 9:17 ☉ ☌	♑ 14 23:35	6 14:13 ☽ 13♍54	☽ Mean ☊ 4♑16.3
	♀ ♒ 5 13:14	16 21:52 ♅ ✱	♑ 17 15:55	16 12:23 ♂ △	♒ 17 2:59	14 9:17 ● 21♐50	
☽0S 6 22:40	☉ ♑ 22 9:46	19 14:56 ☉ ✱	♒ 19 20:38	18 23:40 ☉ ✱	♓ 19 5:31	14 9:26:56 ✔ A 1'16"	1 DECEMBER 1917
♃⊻♇ 11 12:43		21 22:28 ☉ ☐	♓ 22 0:04	21 6:07 ☉ ☐	♈ 21 8:06	21 6:07 ☽ 28♓50	Julian Day # 6544
☽0N 20 11:52		23 5:30 ☉ ✱	♈ 24 2:35	22 19:51 ♅ ✱	♉ 23 11:26	28 9:51 ○ 6♋07	Delta T 20.2 sec
☿ R 25 4:43		25 12:14 ♅ ✱	♉ 26 4:55	25 6:45 ♂ △	♊ 25 16:03	28 9:46 ✔ T 1.006	SVP 06♓24'05"
		27 18:41 ♀ △	♊ 28 8:13	27 14:21 ♂ ☐	♋ 27 22:29		Obliquity 23°27'00"
		29 22:14 ☿ ☍	♋ 30 13:48	30 0:20 ♂ ✱	♌ 30 7:15		⚷ Chiron 25♓25.5R
							☽ Mean ☊ 2♑41.0

LONGITUDE — JANUARY 1918

Day	Sid.Time	☉	0 hr ☽	Noon ☽	True ☊	☿	♀	♂	♃	♄	♅	♆	♇
1 Tu	6 39 20	9♑46 25	20♌47 3	26♌48 27	1♑30.0	15♑20.0	21♒56.1	27♍ 3.6	2♊34.1	13♌23.8	21♒21.8	6♌24.5	4♋22.9
2 W	6 43 17	10 47 33	2♍47 51	8♍45 38	1R 28.7	14R 4.6	22 32.3	27 22.7	2R 29.2	13R 20.1	21 24.6	6R 23.0	4R 21.7
3 Th	6 47 13	11 48 42	14 42 17	20 38 16	1 27.4	12 45.0	23 7.3	27 41.3	2 24.4	13 16.4	21 27.5	6 21.5	4 20.5
4 F	6 51 10	12 49 51	26 34 7	2♎30 24	1 26.3	11 23.8	23 40.7	27 59.5	2 19.8	13 12.5	21 30.4	6 20.0	4 19.3
5 Sa	6 55 6	13 51 0	8♎27 40	14 26 32	1D 25.7	10 3.6	24 12.7	28 17.3	2 15.4	13 8.6	21 33.3	6 18.5	4 18.1
6 Su	6 59 3	14 52 10	20 27 34	26 31 24	1 25.7	8 46.9	24 43.1	28 34.6	2 11.2	13 4.7	21 36.2	6 17.0	4 16.9
7 M	7 2 59	15 53 19	2♏38 34	8♏49 40	1 26.4	7 35.9	25 11.9	28 51.5	2 7.2	13 0.6	21 39.1	6 15.4	4 15.7
8 Tu	7 6 56	16 54 29	15 5 13	21 25 41	1 27.5	6 32.4	25 39.0	29 8.0	2 3.3	12 56.5	21 42.1	6 13.9	4 14.5
9 W	7 10 53	17 55 39	27 51 30	4♐22 59	1 28.9	5 37.5	26 4.4	29 24.0	1 59.7	12 52.4	21 45.1	6 12.3	4 13.3
10 Th	7 14 49	18 56 49	11♐ 0 23	17 43 51	1 30.3	4 52.2	26 28.0	29 39.5	1 56.2	12 48.2	21 48.2	6 10.7	4 12.1
11 F	7 18 46	19 57 59	24 33 23	1♑28 52	1R 31.1	4 16.6	26 49.8	29 54.5	1 52.9	12 43.9	21 51.2	6 9.1	4 11.0
12 Sa	7 22 42	20 59 8	8♑30 1	15 36 27	1 31.1	3 51.0	27 9.6	0♎ 9.1	1 49.9	12 39.5	21 54.3	6 7.5	4 9.8
13 Su	7 26 39	22 0 18	22 47 37	0♒ 2 49	1 30.0	3 35.0	27 27.4	0 23.1	1 47.0	12 35.1	21 57.4	6 5.9	4 8.7
14 M	7 30 35	23 1 26	7♒21 15	14 42 5	1 27.9	3D 28.2	27 43.2	0 36.7	1 44.3	12 30.7	22 0.5	6 4.2	4 7.5
15 Tu	7 34 32	24 2 35	22 4 21	29 27 7	1 24.9	3 30.1	27 56.8	0 49.7	1 41.9	12 26.2	22 3.7	6 2.6	4 6.4
16 W	7 38 29	25 3 42	6♓49 27	14♓10 29	1 21.5	3 40.1	28 8.2	1 2.1	1 39.6	12 21.7	22 6.9	6 0.9	4 5.2
17 Th	7 42 25	26 4 49	21 29 25	28 45 34	1 18.3	3 57.4	28 17.4	1 14.0	1 37.5	12 17.1	22 10.0	5 59.3	4 4.1
18 F	7 46 22	27 5 55	5♈58 22	13♈ 7 21	1 15.8	4 21.6	28 24.2	1 25.4	1 35.7	12 12.4	22 13.3	5 57.6	4 3.0
19 Sa	7 50 18	28 7 0	20 12 14	27 12 48	1D 14.4	4 51.9	28 28.7	1 36.2	1 34.0	12 7.8	22 16.5	5 55.9	4 1.9
20 Su	7 54 15	29 8 5	4♉ 8 58	11♉ 0 45	1 14.2	5 27.8	28R 30.7	1 46.4	1 32.6	12 3.1	22 19.7	5 54.3	4 0.8
21 M	7 58 11	0♒ 9 8	17 48 12	24 31 28	1 15.2	6 8.8	28 30.3	1 56.1	1 31.3	11 58.4	22 23.0	5 52.6	3 59.7
22 Tu	8 2 8	1 10 10	1♊10 42	7♊46 8	1 16.8	6 54.3	28 27.3	2 5.1	1 30.3	11 53.6	22 26.3	5 50.9	3 58.7
23 W	8 6 4	2 11 12	14 17 56	20 46 19	1 18.4	7 44.0	28 21.9	2 13.6	1 29.5	11 48.8	22 29.6	5 49.2	3 57.6
24 Th	8 10 1	3 12 12	27 11 30	3♋33 39	1R 19.4	8 37.4	28 13.9	2 21.4	1 28.8	11 44.0	22 32.9	5 47.5	3 56.6
25 F	8 13 58	4 13 12	9♋52 57	16 9 32	1 19.1	9 34.2	28 3.3	2 28.7	1 28.4	11 39.2	22 36.2	5 45.8	3 55.5
26 Sa	8 17 54	5 14 10	22 23 32	28 35 6	1 17.2	10 34.0	27 50.2	2 35.2	1D 28.2	11 34.3	22 39.6	5 44.2	3 54.5
27 Su	8 21 51	6 15 8	4♌44 21	10♌51 24	1 13.4	11 36.6	27 34.6	2 41.2	1 28.2	11 29.4	22 42.9	5 42.5	3 53.5
28 M	8 25 47	7 16 4	16 56 22	22 59 23	1 7.9	12 41.7	27 16.6	2 46.4	1 28.4	11 24.6	22 46.3	5 40.8	3 52.5
29 Tu	8 29 44	8 17 0	29 0 38	5♍ 0 17	1 1.1	13 49.2	26 56.2	2 51.0	1 28.8	11 19.7	22 49.7	5 39.1	3 51.5
30 W	8 33 40	9 17 55	10♍58 33	16 55 42	0 53.6	14 58.7	26 33.4	2 54.9	1 29.4	11 14.8	22 53.1	5 37.4	3 50.5
31 Th	8 37 37	10 18 49	22 52 0	28 47 48	0 46.1	16 10.2	26 8.5	2 58.2	1 30.2	11 9.9	22 56.5	5 35.7	3 49.6

LONGITUDE — FEBRUARY 1918

Day	Sid.Time	☉	0 hr ☽	Noon ☽	True ☊	☿	♀	♂	♃	♄	♅	♆	♇
1 F	8 41 33	11♒19 42	4♎43 29	10♎39 27	0♑39.5	17♑23.4	25♒41.4	3♎ 0.7	1♊31.2	11♌ 4.9	22♒59.9	5♌34.0	3♋48.6
2 Sa	8 45 30	12 20 34	16 36 10	22 34 10	0R 34.4	18 38.4	25R 12.5	3 2.5	1 32.4	11R 0.0	23 3.3	5R 32.3	3R 47.7
3 Su	8 49 27	13 21 26	28 33 57	4♏36 6	0 31.1	19 54.8	24 41.7	3R 3.6	1 33.9	10 55.1	23 6.7	5 30.7	3 46.8
4 M	8 53 23	14 22 16	10♏41 13	16 49 54	0D 29.7	21 12.8	24 9.4	3 3.9	1 35.5	10 50.2	23 10.2	5 29.0	3 45.9
5 Tu	8 57 20	15 23 6	23 2 47	29 20 26	0 29.9	22 32.0	23 35.7	3 3.5	1 37.3	10 45.3	23 13.6	5 27.3	3 45.0
6 W	9 1 16	16 23 55	5♐43 28	12♐12 23	0 31.1	23 52.6	23 0.8	3 2.3	1 39.3	10 40.5	23 17.1	5 25.7	3 44.2
7 Th	9 5 13	17 24 43	18 47 41	25 29 45	0R 32.4	25 14.3	22 24.9	3 0.4	1 41.5	10 35.6	23 20.5	5 24.0	3 43.3
8 F	9 9 9	18 25 30	2♑18 49	9♑15 1	0 32.9	26 37.3	21 48.4	2 57.7	1 43.9	10 30.7	23 24.0	5 22.4	3 42.5
9 Sa	9 13 6	19 26 15	16 18 20	23 28 30	0 31.7	28 1.3	21 11.4	2 54.2	1 46.5	10 25.9	23 27.5	5 20.7	3 41.7
10 Su	9 17 2	20 27 0	0♒45 6	8♒ 7 28	0 28.4	29 26.4	20 34.1	2 50.0	1 49.3	10 21.1	23 30.9	5 19.1	3 40.9
11 M	9 20 59	21 27 44	15 34 46	23 5 57	0 22.7	0♒52.5	19 56.9	2 44.9	1 52.3	10 16.3	23 34.4	5 17.5	3 40.1
12 Tu	9 24 56	22 28 26	0♓39 49	8♓15 4	0 15.2	2 19.6	19 20.0	2 39.1	1 55.5	10 11.6	23 37.9	5 15.9	3 39.4
13 W	9 28 52	23 29 6	15 50 23	23 24 26	0 6.7	3 47.7	18 43.7	2 32.5	1 58.9	10 6.8	23 41.4	5 14.3	3 38.6
14 Th	9 32 49	24 29 45	0♈55 57	8♈23 51	29♐58.3	5 16.8	18 8.1	2 25.1	2 2.5	10 2.2	23 44.8	5 12.7	3 37.9
15 F	9 36 45	25 30 23	15 47 9	23 5 8	29 51.1	6 46.8	17 33.5	2 16.9	2 6.2	9 57.5	23 48.3	5 11.1	3 37.2
16 Sa	9 40 42	26 30 58	0♉17 14	7♉23 7	29 45.9	8 17.7	17 0.1	2 7.9	2 10.2	9 52.9	23 51.8	5 9.6	3 36.5
17 Su	9 44 38	27 31 32	14 22 38	21 15 48	29 43.1	9 49.6	16 28.2	1 58.1	2 14.3	9 48.3	23 55.2	5 8.0	3 35.9
18 M	9 48 35	28 32 5	28 2 47	4♊43 51	29D 42.2	11 22.4	15 57.9	1 47.6	2 18.6	9 43.8	23 58.7	5 6.5	3 35.2
19 Tu	9 52 31	29 32 35	11♊19 22	17 49 43	29 42.7	12 56.1	15 29.4	1 36.3	2 23.1	9 39.3	24 2.2	5 5.0	3 34.6
20 W	9 56 28	0♓33 3	24 15 22	0♋36 47	29R 43.4	14 30.8	15 2.9	1 24.2	2 27.8	9 34.9	24 5.6	5 3.5	3 34.0
21 Th	10 0 25	1 33 30	6♋54 23	13 8 39	29 43.2	16 6.4	14 38.4	1 11.4	2 32.7	9 30.5	24 9.1	5 2.0	3 33.5
22 F	10 4 21	2 33 55	19 19 57	25 28 41	29 41.3	17 42.9	14 16.1	0 57.9	2 37.7	9 26.2	24 12.5	5 0.5	3 32.9
23 Sa	10 8 18	3 34 18	1♌35 10	7♌39 44	29 36.7	19 20.4	13 56.1	0 43.6	2 42.9	9 22.0	24 16.0	4 59.1	3 32.4
24 Su	10 12 14	4 34 39	13 42 37	19 44 4	29 29.3	20 58.8	13 38.5	0 28.6	2 48.3	9 17.8	24 19.4	4 57.7	3 31.8
25 M	10 16 11	5 34 58	25 44 16	1♍43 23	29 19.3	22 38.2	13 23.3	0 12.9	2 53.8	9 13.6	24 22.8	4 56.2	3 31.3
26 Tu	10 20 7	6 35 16	7♍41 36	13 39 4	29 7.1	24 18.6	13 10.5	29♍56.5	2 59.5	9 9.5	24 26.2	4 54.8	3 30.9
27 W	10 24 4	7 35 31	19 35 56	25 32 21	28 53.8	26 0.0	13 0.3	29 39.5	3 5.4	9 5.5	24 29.6	4 53.5	3 30.4
28 Th	10 28 0	8 35 45	1♎28 30	7♎24 36	28 40.4	27 42.4	12 52.5	29 21.8	3 11.4	9 1.6	24 33.0	4 52.1	3 30.0

Astro Data	Dy Hr Mn
☽0S	3 6:46
☿ D	14 6:34
☽0N	16 18:30
♀ R	20 7:51
♃ D	26 12:48
☽0S	30 14:44
♂ R	3 23:01
☽0N	13 4:02
☽0S	26 21:48

Planet Ingress	Dy Hr Mn
♂ ♎	11 8:55
☉ ♒	20 20:25
☿ ♒	10 9:24
☊ ♐	13 18:58
☉ ♓	19 10:53
♂ ♍	25 19:00

Last Aspect Dy Hr Mn		☽ Ingress Dy Hr Mn
1 2:25	♀ ☍	♍ 1 18:23
4 2:57	♂ ☌	♎ 4 6:56
6 8:48	♀ △	♏ 6 18:50
9 2:55	♂ ✶	♐ 9 3:58
11 4:03	♀ ✶	♑ 11 9:27
12 22:35	☉ ☌	♒ 13 11:55
15 9:41	♀ ☌	♓ 15 12:53
17 8:08	☉ ✶	♈ 17 14:03
19 14:38	☉ □	♉ 19 16:48
21 19:06	♀ □	♊ 21 21:52
24 1:56	♀ △	♋ 24 5:17
24 23:21	☿ ☍	♌ 26 14:45
28 19:59	♀ ☍	♍ 29 1:59
30 8:57	☿ △	♎ 31 14:26

Last Aspect Dy Hr Mn		☽ Ingress Dy Hr Mn
2 16:35	♀ △	♏ 3 2:52
5 1:00	♀ □	♐ 5 13:15
7 8:12	♅ ✶	♑ 7 19:57
9 21:37	☿ ☌	♒ 9 22:46
11 12:48	♅ ☌	♓ 11 22:57
12 4:44	♇ △	♈ 13 22:30
15 17:13	☉ ✶	♉ 15 23:31
18 0:56	☉ □	♊ 18 3:29
19 23:42	♅ △	♋ 20 10:50
20 17:36	♇ ☌	♌ 22 20:53
24 21:16	♅ ☍	♍ 25 8:33
27 19:50	♂ ☌	♎ 27 21:01

☽ Phases & Eclipses Dy Hr Mn		
5 11:49	☽	14♎21
12 22:35	●	21♑57
19 14:38	☽	28♈44
27 3:14	○	6♌23
4 7:51	☽	14♏42
11 10:04	●	21♒53
18 0:56	☽	28♉34
25 21:34	○	6♍29

Astro Data

1 JANUARY 1918
Julian Day # 6575
Delta T 20.3 sec
SVP 06♓23'59"
Obliquity 23°27'00"
⚷ Chiron 25♓41.2
☽ Mean ☊ 1♑02.6

1 FEBRUARY 1918
Julian Day # 6606
Delta T 20.3 sec
SVP 06♓23'54"
Obliquity 23°27'00"
⚷ Chiron 26♓45.5
☽ Mean ☊ 29♐24.1

MARCH 1918 LONGITUDE

Day	Sid.Time	☉	0 hr ☽	Noon ☽	True ☊	☿	♀	♂	♃	♄	♅	♆	♇
1 F	10 31 57	9♓35 58	13♎20 53	19♎17 37	28♐28.1	29♒25.8	12♒47.2	29♍ 3.5	3♊17.6	8♌57.7	24♒36.4	4♌50.8	3♋29.6
2 Sa	10 35 53	10 36 9	25 15 7	1♏13 45	28R 17.8	1♓10.3	12D 44.4	28R 44.6	3 24.0	8R 53.9	24 39.8	4R 49.5	3R 29.2
3 Su	10 39 50	11 36 18	7♏13 56	13 16 6	28 10.1	2 55.8	12 44.1	28 25.2	3 30.5	8 50.1	24 43.2	4 48.2	3 28.8
4 M	10 43 47	12 36 25	19 20 46	25 28 26	28 5.2	4 42.4	12 46.2	28 5.2	3 37.2	8 46.5	24 46.5	4 46.9	3 28.5
5 Tu	10 47 43	13 36 32	1♐39 43	7♐55 10	28 2.9	6 30.1	12 50.6	27 44.6	3 44.0	8 42.9	24 49.8	4 45.6	3 28.2
6 W	10 51 40	14 36 36	14 15 23	20 40 58	28D 2.3	8 18.9	12 57.4	27 23.7	3 51.0	8 39.4	24 53.2	4 44.4	3 27.9
7 Th	10 55 36	15 36 39	27 12 29	3♑50 27	28R 2.5	10 8.7	13 6.4	27 2.2	3 58.2	8 36.0	24 56.5	4 43.2	3 27.6
8 F	10 59 33	16 36 41	10♑35 17	17 27 21	28 2.0	11 59.7	13 17.6	26 40.4	4 5.5	8 32.6	24 59.8	4 42.0	3 27.3
9 Sa	11 3 29	17 36 40	24 26 48	1♒33 41	27 59.8	13 51.7	13 31.0	26 18.1	4 12.9	8 29.4	25 3.1	4 40.9	3 27.1
10 Su	11 7 26	18 36 39	8♒47 47	16 8 44	27 55.2	15 44.8	13 46.4	25 55.6	4 20.5	8 26.2	25 6.3	4 39.8	3 26.9
11 M	11 11 22	19 36 35	23 35 50	1♓ 8 12	27 47.7	17 38.9	14 3.9	25 32.8	4 28.2	8 23.1	25 9.6	4 38.7	3 26.7
12 Tu	11 15 19	20 36 29	8♓44 43	16 24 5	27 37.8	19 34.1	14 23.2	25 9.7	4 36.1	8 20.1	25 12.8	4 37.6	3 26.6
13 W	11 19 16	21 36 22	24 4 50	1♈45 29	27 26.6	21 30.2	14 44.5	24 46.4	4 44.1	8 17.2	25 16.0	4 36.5	3 26.4
14 Th	11 23 12	22 36 13	9♈24 30	17 0 29	27 15.2	23 27.3	15 7.6	24 23.0	4 52.3	8 14.4	25 19.2	4 35.5	3 26.3
15 F	11 27 9	23 36 1	24 32 9	1♉58 25	27 5.1	25 25.2	15 32.4	23 59.4	5 0.5	8 11.7	25 22.3	4 34.5	3 26.2
16 Sa	11 31 5	24 35 48	9♉18 26	16 31 36	26 57.4	27 23.8	15 58.8	23 35.8	5 9.0	8 9.1	25 25.5	4 33.5	3 26.2
17 Su	11 35 2	25 35 32	23 37 32	0♊36 6	26 52.4	29 23.1	16 26.9	23 12.2	5 17.5	8 6.5	25 28.6	4 32.6	3 26.1
18 M	11 38 58	26 35 14	7♊27 21	14 11 30	26 49.9	1♈22.8	16 56.5	22 48.6	5 26.2	8 4.1	25 31.7	4 31.7	3D 26.1
19 Tu	11 42 55	27 34 54	20 48 54	27 20 0	26 49.2	3 22.9	17 27.7	22 25.1	5 35.0	8 1.8	25 34.8	4 30.8	3 26.1
20 W	11 46 51	28 34 32	3♋45 20	10♋ 5 27	26 49.1	5 23.1	18 0.2	22 1.8	5 44.0	7 59.6	25 37.8	4 29.9	3 26.1
21 Th	11 50 48	29 34 7	16 20 56	22 32 22	26 48.5	7 23.1	18 34.2	21 38.6	5 53.0	7 57.4	25 40.9	4 29.1	3 26.2
22 F	11 54 45	0♈33 40	28 40 18	4♌45 18	26 46.1	9 22.8	19 9.4	21 15.6	6 2.2	7 55.4	25 43.9	4 28.3	3 26.3
23 Sa	11 58 41	1 33 11	10♌47 52	16 48 28	26 41.1	11 21.8	19 46.0	20 52.9	6 11.5	7 53.5	25 46.9	4 27.5	3 26.4
24 Su	12 2 38	2 32 39	22 47 31	28 45 24	26 33.2	13 19.8	20 23.8	20 30.5	6 20.9	7 51.6	25 49.8	4 26.8	3 26.5
25 M	12 6 34	3 32 5	4♍42 27	10♍38 57	26 22.5	15 16.4	21 2.8	20 8.4	6 30.5	7 49.9	25 52.7	4 26.1	3 26.6
26 Tu	12 10 31	4 31 29	16 35 10	22 31 17	26 9.6	17 11.2	21 42.9	19 46.7	6 40.1	7 48.3	25 55.6	4 25.4	3 26.8
27 W	12 14 27	5 30 51	28 27 31	4♎24 1	25 55.5	19 3.9	22 24.1	19 25.4	6 49.9	7 46.8	25 58.5	4 24.7	3 27.0
28 Th	12 18 24	6 30 11	10♎20 58	16 18 31	25 41.2	20 54.0	23 6.3	19 4.5	6 59.8	7 45.4	26 1.4	4 24.1	3 27.2
29 F	12 22 20	7 29 29	22 16 49	28 16 3	25 28.0	22 41.1	23 49.6	18 44.1	7 9.8	7 44.1	26 4.2	4 23.5	3 27.4
30 Sa	12 26 17	8 28 45	4♏16 25	10♏18 9	25 16.8	24 24.8	24 33.9	18 24.2	7 19.9	7 42.9	26 7.0	4 23.0	3 27.7
31 Su	12 30 14	9 27 59	16 21 30	22 26 47	25 8.4	26 4.8	25 19.1	18 4.9	7 30.0	7 41.8	26 9.7	4 22.4	3 28.0

APRIL 1918 LONGITUDE

Day	Sid.Time	☉	0 hr ☽	Noon ☽	True ☊	☿	♀	♂	♃	♄	♅	♆	♇
1 M	12 34 10	10♈27 11	28♏34 19	4♐44 30	25♐ 2.9	27♈40.5	26♒ 5.2	17♍46.1	7♊40.3	7♌40.8	26♒12.4	4♌21.9	3♋28.3
2 Tu	12 38 7	11 26 21	10♐57 46	17 14 32	25R 0.1	29 11.7	26 52.2	17R 28.0	7 50.7	7R 39.9	26 15.1	4R 21.5	3 28.6
3 W	12 42 3	12 25 30	23 35 19	0♑ 0 35	24D 59.3	0♉38.1	27 40.0	17 10.4	8 1.3	7 39.2	26 17.8	4 21.0	3 28.9
4 Th	12 46 0	13 24 36	6♑30 50	13 6 32	24R 59.5	1 59.2	28 28.5	16 53.5	8 11.9	7 38.5	26 20.4	4 20.6	3 29.3
5 F	12 49 56	14 23 41	19 48 9	26 36 1	24 59.5	3 15.0	29 17.9	16 37.2	8 22.6	7 38.0	26 23.0	4 20.3	3 29.7
6 Sa	12 53 53	15 22 45	3♒30 25	10♒31 30	24 58.2	4 25.1	0♓ 8.0	16 21.7	8 33.3	7 37.5	26 25.6	4 19.9	3 30.1
7 Su	12 57 49	16 21 46	17 39 15	24 53 30	24 54.7	5 29.3	0 58.8	16 6.8	8 44.2	7 37.2	26 28.1	4 19.6	3 30.6
8 M	13 1 46	17 20 46	2♓13 50	9♓39 38	24 48.8	6 27.5	1 50.3	15 52.7	8 55.2	7 37.0	26 30.6	4 19.4	3 31.0
9 Tu	13 5 42	18 19 44	17 10 5	24 44 8	24 40.7	7 19.5	2 42.4	15 39.3	9 6.3	7D 36.8	26 33.1	4 19.1	3 31.5
10 W	13 9 39	19 18 40	2♈20 34	9♈58 3	24 31.2	8 5.2	3 35.2	15 26.6	9 17.4	7 36.8	26 35.5	4 18.9	3 32.0
11 Th	13 13 36	20 17 34	17 35 13	25 10 38	24 21.4	8 44.5	4 28.5	15 14.7	9 28.7	7 36.9	26 37.9	4 18.8	3 32.5
12 F	13 17 32	21 16 26	2♉42 59	10♉11 4	24 12.6	9 17.3	5 22.4	15 3.6	9 40.0	7 37.1	26 40.2	4 18.6	3 33.1
13 Sa	13 21 29	22 15 16	17 33 51	24 50 31	24 5.8	9 43.6	6 16.9	14 53.3	9 51.4	7 37.5	26 42.6	4 18.5	3 33.7
14 Su	13 25 25	23 14 4	2♊ 0 28	9♊ 3 18	24 1.5	10 3.5	7 11.9	14 43.8	10 2.9	7 37.9	26 44.8	4 18.5	3 34.3
15 M	13 29 22	24 12 50	15 58 52	22 47 11	23D 59.5	10 16.9	8 7.4	14 35.0	10 14.5	7 38.5	26 47.1	4D 18.4	3 34.9
16 Tu	13 33 18	25 11 34	29 28 27	6♋ 2 57	23 59.3	10R 24.0	9 3.4	14 27.1	10 26.2	7 39.1	26 49.3	4 18.4	3 35.5
17 W	13 37 15	26 10 16	12♋31 8	18 53 30	24 0.1	10 24.9	9 59.9	14 20.0	10 37.9	7 39.9	26 51.4	4 18.5	3 36.2
18 Th	13 41 11	27 8 55	25 10 37	1♌23 4	24R 0.7	10 19.8	10 56.8	14 13.6	10 49.7	7 40.7	26 53.6	4 18.5	3 36.9
19 F	13 45 8	28 7 32	7♌31 28	13 36 24	24 0.2	10 8.9	11 54.2	14 8.1	11 1.6	7 41.7	26 55.7	4 18.6	3 37.6
20 Sa	13 49 5	29 6 7	19 38 30	25 38 18	23 57.9	9 52.7	12 52.0	14 3.3	11 13.6	7 42.8	26 57.7	4 18.8	3 38.3
21 Su	13 53 1	0♉ 4 39	1♍36 22	7♍33 11	23 53.3	9 31.5	13 50.2	13 59.3	11 25.6	7 44.0	26 59.7	4 18.9	3 39.0
22 M	13 56 58	1 3 10	13 29 14	19 24 57	23 46.7	9 5.7	14 48.8	13 56.1	11 37.7	7 45.3	27 1.7	4 19.1	3 39.8
23 Tu	14 0 54	2 1 38	25 20 41	1♎16 47	23 38.2	8 35.9	15 47.8	13 53.7	11 49.8	7 46.7	27 3.6	4 19.3	3 40.5
24 W	14 4 51	3 0 4	7♎13 32	13 11 13	23 28.8	8 2.8	16 47.1	13 52.0	12 2.0	7 48.2	27 5.5	4 19.6	3 41.3
25 Th	14 8 47	3 58 29	19 10 3	25 10 13	23 19.2	7 26.9	17 46.9	13D 51.2	12 14.3	7 49.8	27 7.3	4 19.9	3 42.2
26 F	14 12 44	4 56 51	1♏11 55	7♏15 16	23 10.2	6 48.9	18 46.9	13 51.0	12 26.7	7 51.5	27 9.1	4 20.2	3 43.0
27 Sa	14 16 40	5 55 12	13 20 27	19 27 37	23 2.8	6 9.6	19 47.4	13 51.6	12 39.1	7 53.4	27 10.8	4 20.6	3 43.8
28 Su	14 20 37	6 53 31	25 36 54	1♐48 29	22 57.4	5 29.7	20 48.1	13 52.9	12 51.6	7 55.3	27 12.5	4 21.0	3 44.7
29 M	14 24 34	7 51 48	8♐ 2 33	14 19 18	22 54.2	4 49.9	21 49.2	13 55.0	13 4.1	7 57.3	27 14.2	4 21.4	3 45.6
30 Tu	14 28 30	8 50 4	20 38 58	27 1 47	22D 53.0	4 10.9	22 50.6	13 57.7	13 16.7	7 59.4	27 15.8	4 21.9	3 46.5

Astro Data	Dy Hr Mn
♃⚺♇	2 18:06
♀ D	2 15:24
☽0N	12 15:17
♃✶♆	12 3:56
☿0N	18 8:07
♇ D	18 6:19
☽0S	26 3:50
♃✶♄	1 0:58
☽0N	9 1:51
♄ D	9 13:34
♆ D	15 11:59
☿ R	16 15:28
☽0S	22 9:31
♂ D	25 16:44

Planet Ingress	Dy Hr Mn
☿ ♓	1 7:52
☿ ♈	17 7:24
☉ ♈	21 10:26
☿ ♉	2 13:15
♀ ♓	5 20:11
☉ ♉	20 22:05

Last Aspect Dy Hr Mn		☽ Ingress Dy Hr Mn
1 22:49	♅ △	♏ 2 9:32
4 16:37	♂ ✶	♐ 4 20:47
6 23:42	♂ □	♑ 7 5:05
9 3:04	♂ △	♒ 9 9:23
11 2:30	♅ ☌	♓ 11 10:12
13 1:03	♂ ☍	♈ 13 9:15
15 1:21	♅ ✶	♉ 15 8:48
17 3:37	☉ ✶	♊ 17 10:57
19 13:30	☉ □	♋ 19 16:58
21 9:57	♂ ✶	♌ 22 2:37
24 6:08	♅ ☍	♍ 24 14:30
26 6:16	♂ ☌	♎ 27 3:07
29 7:38	♅ △	♏ 29 15:28

Last Aspect Dy Hr Mn		☽ Ingress Dy Hr Mn
31 19:22	♅ □	♐ 1 2:47
3 8:09	♀ ✶	♑ 3 11:59
4 18:26	♂ △	♒ 5 17:56
7 14:38	♅ ☌	♓ 7 20:22
8 21:37	♂ ☍	♈ 9 20:19
11 14:21	♅ ✶	♉ 11 19:40
13 15:09	♅ □	♊ 13 20:37
15 19:12	♅ △	♋ 16 0:57
18 4:07	☉ □	♌ 18 9:19
20 20:39	☉ △	♍ 20 20:46
22 2:55	♀ ☍	♎ 23 9:25
25 15:56	♅ △	♏ 25 21:37
28 3:06	♅ □	♐ 28 8:30
30 12:28	♅ ✶	♑ 30 17:33

☽ Phases & Eclipses Dy Hr Mn	
6 0:43	☽ 14♐38
12 19:52	● 21♓26
19 13:30	☽ 28♊08
27 15:32	○ 6♎09
4 13:33	☽ 13♑58
11 4:34	● 20♈29
18 4:07	☽ 27♋19
26 8:05	○ 5♏17

Astro Data

1 MARCH 1918
Julian Day # 6634
Delta T 20.4 sec
SVP 06♓23'51"
Obliquity 23°27'00"
⚷ Chiron 28♓12.6
☽ Mean ☊ 27♐55.1

1 APRIL 1918
Julian Day # 6665
Delta T 20.4 sec
SVP 06♓23'48"
Obliquity 23°27'00"
⚷ Chiron 0♈01.9
☽ Mean ☊ 26♐16.6

LONGITUDE — MAY 1918

Day	Sid.Time	☉	0 hr ☽	Noon ☽	True ☊	☿	♀	♂	♃	♄	♅	♆	♇
1 W	14 32 27	9♉48 18	3♑28 2	9♑58 0	22♐53.4	3♉33.5	23♓52.2	14♍ 1.2	13♊29.3	8♌ 1.7	27♒17.4	4♌22.4	3♋47.5
2 Th	14 36 23	10 46 30	16 31 59	23 10 15	22 54.7	2R58.1	24 54.2	14 5.4	13 42.0	8 4.0	27 18.9	4 22.9	3 48.4
3 F	14 40 20	11 44 41	29 53 5	6♒40 41	22R56.0	2 25.5	25 56.4	14 10.2	13 54.7	8 6.5	27 20.4	4 23.5	3 49.4
4 Sa	14 44 16	12 42 51	13♒33 16	20 30 54	22 56.6	1 56.0	26 59.0	14 15.7	14 7.5	8 9.0	27 21.9	4 24.1	3 50.3
5 Su	14 48 13	13 40 59	27 33 36	4♓41 15	22 55.7	1 30.0	28 1.7	14 21.9	14 20.4	8 11.6	27 23.3	4 24.7	3 51.3
6 M	14 52 9	14 39 5	11♓53 35	19 10 14	22 53.3	1 8.0	29 4.8	14 28.8	14 33.3	8 14.4	27 24.6	4 25.3	3 52.4
7 Tu	14 56 6	15 37 11	26 30 37	3♈54 3	22 49.3	0 50.2	0♈ 8.0	14 36.3	14 46.2	8 17.2	27 25.9	4 26.0	3 53.4
8 W	15 0 3	16 35 15	11♈19 41	18 46 35	22 44.3	0 36.8	1 11.5	14 44.4	14 59.2	8 20.1	27 27.2	4 26.8	3 54.4
9 Th	15 3 59	17 33 17	26 13 43	3♉40 0	22 39.1	0 28.0	2 15.3	14 53.1	15 12.3	8 23.1	27 28.4	4 27.5	3 55.5
10 F	15 7 56	18 31 18	11♉ 4 22	18 25 49	22 34.4	0D23.7	3 19.2	15 2.5	15 25.3	8 26.3	27 29.6	4 28.3	3 56.6
11 Sa	15 11 52	19 29 18	25 43 24	2♊56 20	22 30.8	0 24.2	4 23.3	15 12.5	15 38.5	8 29.5	27 30.7	4 29.1	3 57.7
12 Su	15 15 49	20 27 16	10♊ 3 55	17 5 40	22D28.7	0 29.3	5 27.7	15 23.1	15 51.6	8 32.8	27 31.7	4 29.9	3 58.8
13 M	15 19 45	21 25 12	24 1 14	0♋50 26	22 28.2	0 39.0	6 32.2	15 34.3	16 4.9	8 36.2	27 32.8	4 30.8	3 59.9
14 Tu	15 23 42	22 23 7	7♋33 15	14 9 47	22 28.9	0 53.3	7 37.0	15 46.0	16 18.1	8 39.7	27 33.7	4 31.7	4 1.0
15 W	15 27 38	23 21 0	20 40 15	27 5 0	22 30.3	1 12.0	8 41.9	15 58.4	16 31.4	8 43.3	27 34.7	4 32.7	4 2.2
16 Th	15 31 35	24 18 51	3♌24 26	9♌39 2	22 31.9	1 35.1	9 47.0	16 11.2	16 44.7	8 47.0	27 35.5	4 33.6	4 3.4
17 F	15 35 32	25 16 41	15 49 20	21 55 53	22R33.1	2 2.5	10 52.3	16 24.7	16 58.0	8 50.7	27 36.4	4 34.6	4 4.6
18 Sa	15 39 28	26 14 29	27 59 15	4♍ 0 2	22 33.5	2 34.0	11 57.7	16 38.6	17 11.4	8 54.6	27 37.2	4 35.7	4 5.8
19 Su	15 43 25	27 12 15	9♍58 49	15 56 9	22 32.7	3 9.5	13 3.3	16 53.1	17 24.8	8 58.5	27 37.9	4 36.7	4 7.0
20 M	15 47 21	28 9 59	21 52 36	27 48 43	22 30.9	3 48.9	14 9.0	17 8.0	17 38.3	9 2.6	27 38.6	4 37.8	4 8.2
21 Tu	15 51 18	29 7 42	3♎44 58	9♎41 49	22 28.1	4 32.1	15 14.9	17 23.5	17 51.7	9 6.7	27 39.2	4 38.9	4 9.4
22 W	15 55 14	0♊ 5 23	15 39 43	21 39 3	22 24.8	5 19.0	16 21.0	17 39.5	18 5.2	9 10.9	27 39.8	4 40.1	4 10.7
23 Th	15 59 11	1 3 3	27 40 10	3♏43 21	22 21.3	6 9.4	17 27.2	17 55.9	18 18.8	9 15.2	27 40.3	4 41.2	4 11.9
24 F	16 3 7	2 0 41	9♏48 54	15 57 1	22 18.0	7 3.2	18 33.6	18 12.8	18 32.3	9 19.5	27 40.8	4 42.4	4 13.2
25 Sa	16 7 4	2 58 19	22 7 54	28 21 42	22 15.4	8 0.3	19 40.1	18 30.2	18 45.9	9 24.0	27 41.3	4 43.7	4 14.5
26 Su	16 11 1	3 55 55	4♐38 32	10♐58 30	22 13.7	9 0.7	20 46.7	18 48.0	18 59.5	9 28.5	27 41.7	4 44.9	4 15.8
27 M	16 14 57	4 53 29	17 21 40	23 48 5	22D12.9	10 4.3	21 53.5	19 6.2	19 13.1	9 33.1	27 42.0	4 46.2	4 17.1
28 Tu	16 18 54	5 51 3	0♑17 47	6♑50 48	22 13.0	11 10.9	23 0.4	19 24.9	19 26.7	9 37.8	27 42.3	4 47.5	4 18.4
29 W	16 22 50	6 48 36	13 27 8	20 6 48	22 13.8	12 20.5	24 7.5	19 44.0	19 40.4	9 42.6	27 42.5	4 48.8	4 19.7
30 Th	16 26 47	7 46 7	26 49 49	3♒36 8	22 14.9	13 33.1	25 14.7	20 3.5	19 54.1	9 47.4	27 42.7	4 50.2	4 21.0
31 F	16 30 43	8 43 38	10♒25 46	17 18 39	22 16.0	14 48.5	26 22.0	20 23.4	20 7.8	9 52.3	27 42.9	4 51.6	4 22.4

LONGITUDE — JUNE 1918

Day	Sid.Time	☉	0 hr ☽	Noon ☽	True ☊	☿	♀	♂	♃	♄	♅	♆	♇
1 Sa	16 34 40	9♊41 8	24♒14 44	1♓13 54	22♐16.8	16♉ 6.8	27♈29.4	20♍43.7	20♊21.5	9♌57.3	27♒43.0	4♌53.0	4♋23.7
2 Su	16 38 36	10 38 37	8♓16 2	15 20 54	22R17.2	17 27.9	28 37.0	21 4.4	20 35.2	10 2.4	27R43.0	4 54.4	4 25.1
3 M	16 42 33	11 36 6	22 28 18	29 37 54	22 17.0	18 51.7	29 44.6	21 25.5	20 48.9	10 7.5	27 43.0	4 55.9	4 26.5
4 Tu	16 46 30	12 33 33	6♈49 20	14♈ 2 8	22 16.4	20 18.3	0♉52.4	21 46.9	21 2.7	10 12.7	27 43.0	4 57.4	4 27.9
5 W	16 50 26	13 31 0	21 15 49	28 29 50	22 15.5	21 47.6	2 0.3	22 8.7	21 16.4	10 18.0	27 42.9	4 58.9	4 29.2
6 Th	16 54 23	14 28 27	5♉43 32	12♉56 19	22 14.6	23 19.6	3 8.3	22 30.9	21 30.2	10 23.4	27 42.8	5 0.4	4 30.6
7 F	16 58 19	15 25 53	20 7 31	27 16 29	22 13.8	24 54.2	4 16.4	22 53.5	21 44.0	10 28.8	27 42.6	5 2.0	4 32.0
8 Sa	17 2 16	16 23 18	4♊22 37	11♊25 20	22 13.3	26 31.6	5 24.6	23 16.4	21 57.8	10 34.3	27 42.3	5 3.6	4 33.4
9 Su	17 6 12	17 20 42	18 24 8	25 18 33	22D13.1	28 11.5	6 32.9	23 39.6	22 11.6	10 39.9	27 42.0	5 5.2	4 34.9
10 M	17 10 9	18 18 6	2♋ 8 17	8♋53 3	22 13.1	29 54.1	7 41.2	24 3.2	22 25.4	10 45.5	27 41.7	5 6.8	4 36.3
11 Tu	17 14 6	19 15 29	15 32 43	22 7 14	22 13.3	1♊39.3	8 49.7	24 27.1	22 39.2	10 51.2	27 41.3	5 8.4	4 37.7
12 W	17 18 2	20 12 51	28 36 38	5♌ 1 5	22 13.6	3 27.0	9 58.3	24 51.4	22 53.0	10 57.0	27 40.9	5 10.1	4 39.2
13 Th	17 21 59	21 10 12	11♌20 47	17 36 2	22 13.8	5 17.3	11 6.9	25 15.9	23 6.9	11 2.8	27 40.4	5 11.8	4 40.6
14 F	17 25 55	22 7 32	23 47 13	29 54 45	22R13.8	7 10.1	12 15.6	25 40.8	23 20.7	11 8.7	27 39.9	5 13.5	4 42.0
15 Sa	17 29 52	23 4 51	5♍59 6	12♍ 0 47	22 13.8	9 5.3	13 24.5	26 6.0	23 34.5	11 14.6	27 39.3	5 15.3	4 43.5
16 Su	17 33 48	24 2 9	18 0 20	23 58 18	22D13.7	11 2.9	14 33.4	26 31.5	23 48.3	11 20.6	27 38.7	5 17.0	4 44.9
17 M	17 37 45	24 59 27	29 55 17	5♎51 49	22 13.7	13 2.7	15 42.3	26 57.2	24 2.1	11 26.7	27 38.0	5 18.8	4 46.4
18 Tu	17 41 41	25 56 43	11♎48 30	17 45 54	22 13.9	15 4.6	16 51.4	27 23.3	24 15.9	11 32.8	27 37.3	5 20.6	4 47.9
19 W	17 45 38	26 53 59	23 44 32	29 44 56	22 14.2	17 8.4	18 0.5	27 49.7	24 29.7	11 39.0	27 36.5	5 22.4	4 49.3
20 Th	17 49 34	27 51 14	5♏47 36	11♏52 58	22 14.8	19 14.1	19 9.7	28 16.3	24 43.5	11 45.2	27 35.7	5 24.2	4 50.8
21 F	17 53 31	28 48 29	18 1 27	24 13 26	22 15.4	21 21.3	20 19.0	28 43.2	24 57.3	11 51.5	27 34.9	5 26.1	4 52.3
22 Sa	17 57 28	29 45 42	0♐29 11	6♐48 58	22 16.0	23 29.8	21 28.4	29 10.3	25 11.1	11 57.8	27 34.0	5 28.0	4 53.7
23 Su	18 1 24	0♋42 56	13 12 58	19 41 17	22R16.5	25 39.4	22 37.8	29 37.7	25 24.8	12 4.2	27 33.1	5 29.8	4 55.2
24 M	18 5 21	1 40 9	26 13 58	2♑50 58	22 16.5	27 49.9	23 47.3	0♎ 5.4	25 38.6	12 10.6	27 32.1	5 31.7	4 56.7
25 Tu	18 9 17	2 37 21	9♑32 13	16 17 31	22 16.1	0♋ 0.9	24 56.9	0 33.3	25 52.4	12 17.1	27 31.1	5 33.7	4 58.2
26 W	18 13 14	3 34 34	23 6 39	29 59 21	22 15.2	2 12.2	26 6.6	1 1.5	26 6.1	12 23.7	27 30.0	5 35.6	4 59.6
27 Th	18 17 10	4 31 46	6♒55 15	13♒54 0	22 13.9	4 23.4	27 16.4	1 29.9	26 19.8	12 30.3	27 28.9	5 37.6	5 1.1
28 F	18 21 7	5 28 58	20 55 12	27 58 27	22 12.3	6 34.4	28 26.2	1 58.6	26 33.5	12 36.9	27 27.7	5 39.5	5 2.6
29 Sa	18 25 4	6 26 10	5♓ 3 20	12♓ 9 26	22 10.8	8 44.8	29 36.1	2 27.4	26 47.2	12 43.6	27 26.6	5 41.5	5 4.1
30 Su	18 29 0	7 23 22	19 16 22	26 23 44	22 9.6	10 54.4	0♊46.0	2 56.5	27 0.9	12 50.3	27 25.3	5 43.5	5 5.6

Astro Data	Dy Hr Mn
☽0N	6 10:04
♀0N	9 18:53
☿ D	10 9:46
☽0S	19 15:53
♃∠♆	29 16:28
☽0N	2 16:04
♅ R	2 12:30
☽0S	15 23:27
♂0S	25 9:25
☽0N	29 21:29

Planet Ingress	Dy Hr Mn
♀ ♈	6 20:58
☉ ♊	21 21:46
♀ ♉	3 5:27
☿ ♊	10 1:22
☉ ♋	22 6:00
♂ ♎	23 19:19
☿ ♋	24 23:50
♀ ♊	29 8:12

Last Aspect Dy Hr Mn		☽ Ingress Dy Hr Mn
2 16:23	♀ ⚹	♒ 3 0:12
4 23:42	♅ ☌	♓ 5 4:07
6 4:53	☉ ⚹	♈ 7 5:41
9 2:01	♅ ⚹	♉ 9 6:05
11 2:58	♅ □	♊ 11 7:06
13 6:11	♅ △	♋ 13 10:31
15 5:24	☉ ⚹	♌ 15 17:31
17 23:16	♅ ☍	♍ 18 4:00
20 13:50	☉ △	♎ 20 16:25
23 0:00	♅ △	♏ 23 4:38
25 10:43	♅ □	♐ 25 15:08
27 19:13	♅ ⚹	♑ 27 23:27
29 20:55	♀ □	♒ 30 5:38

Last Aspect Dy Hr Mn		☽ Ingress Dy Hr Mn
1 6:04	♀ ⚹	♓ 1 9:53
2 22:12	♂ ☍	♈ 3 12:37
5 10:42	♅ ⚹	♉ 5 14:30
7 12:44	♅ □	♊ 7 16:36
9 16:11	♅ △	♋ 9 20:14
11 16:49	♂ ⚹	♌ 12 2:35
14 7:35	♅ ☍	♍ 14 12:10
16 17:47	♂ ☌	♎ 17 0:10
19 7:43	♅ △	♏ 19 12:30
21 21:24	♂ ⚹	♐ 21 23:04
24 3:29	☿ ☍	♑ 24 6:51
26 5:44	♀ △	♒ 26 12:01
28 13:56	♀ □	♓ 28 15:26
30 13:15	♃ □	♈ 30 18:04

☽ Phases & Eclipses Dy Hr Mn	
3 22:26	☽ 12♒39
10 13:01	● 19♉03
17 20:14	☽ 26♌05
25 22:32	○ 3♐52
2 4:20	☽ 10♓49
8 22:02	● 17♊16
8 22:07:21	T 2'23"
16 13:11	☽ 24♍34
24 10:38	○ 2♑05
24 10:28	P 0.130

Astro Data

1 MAY 1918
Julian Day # 6695
Delta T 20.5 sec
SVP 06♓23'45"
Obliquity 23°26'59"
⚷ Chiron 1♈40.4
☽ Mean ☊ 24♐41.3

1 JUNE 1918
Julian Day # 6726
Delta T 20.5 sec
SVP 06♓23'40"
Obliquity 23°26'58"
⚷ Chiron 2♈55.3
☽ Mean ☊ 23♐02.8

JULY 1918 LONGITUDE

Day	Sid.Time	☉	0 hr ☽	Noon ☽	True ☊	☿	♀	♂	♃	♄	♅	♆	♇
1 M	18 32 57	8♋20 34	3♈31 11	10♈38 24	22♐ 8.9	13♋ 3.0	1♊56.1	3♎25.9	27♊14.6	12♌57.1	27♒24.0	5♌45.5	5♋ 7.0
2 Tu	18 36 53	9 17 46	17 45 3	24 50 51	22D 9.0	15 10.5	3 6.2	3 55.5	27 28.2	13 3.9	27R22.7	5 47.5	5 8.5
3 W	18 40 50	10 14 59	1♉55 31	8♉58 47	22 9.8	17 16.6	4 16.4	4 25.2	27 41.8	13 10.7	27 21.4	5 49.6	5 10.0
4 Th	18 44 46	11 12 12	16 0 25	23 0 8	22 11.0	19 21.2	5 26.6	4 55.3	27 55.4	13 17.6	27 20.0	5 51.6	5 11.5
5 F	18 48 43	12 9 25	29 57 43	6♊52 54	22 12.3	21 24.2	6 36.9	5 25.5	28 9.0	13 24.6	27 18.5	5 53.7	5 12.9
6 Sa	18 52 39	13 6 39	13♊45 27	20 35 7	22R13.2	23 25.5	7 47.3	5 55.9	28 22.6	13 31.6	27 17.1	5 55.8	5 14.4
7 Su	18 56 36	14 3 52	27 21 41	4♋ 4 55	22 13.3	25 25.1	8 57.8	6 26.6	28 36.1	13 38.6	27 15.6	5 57.8	5 15.9
8 M	19 0 33	15 1 6	10♋44 39	17 20 42	22 12.3	27 22.8	10 8.3	6 57.5	28 49.6	13 45.6	27 14.0	5 59.9	5 17.3
9 Tu	19 4 29	15 58 20	23 52 57	0♌21 20	22 10.2	29 18.7	11 18.8	7 28.6	29 3.1	13 52.7	27 12.4	6 2.1	5 18.8
10 W	19 8 26	16 55 34	6♌45 48	13 6 24	22 7.0	1♌12.7	12 29.5	7 59.8	29 16.6	13 59.9	27 10.8	6 4.2	5 20.3
11 Th	19 12 22	17 52 48	19 23 12	25 36 22	22 3.0	3 4.8	13 40.1	8 31.3	29 30.0	14 7.0	27 9.2	6 6.3	5 21.7
12 F	19 16 19	18 50 2	1♍46 6	7♍52 40	21 58.8	4 55.0	14 50.9	9 3.0	29 43.4	14 14.2	27 7.5	6 8.4	5 23.2
13 Sa	19 20 15	19 47 17	13 56 24	19 57 40	21 54.8	6 43.3	16 1.7	9 34.9	29 56.7	14 21.4	27 5.8	6 10.6	5 24.6
14 Su	19 24 12	20 44 31	25 56 56	1♎54 39	21 51.5	8 29.6	17 12.5	10 6.9	0♋10.0	14 28.7	27 4.0	6 12.7	5 26.0
15 M	19 28 8	21 41 45	7♎51 20	13 47 32	21 49.2	10 14.0	18 23.5	10 39.2	0 23.3	14 36.0	27 2.2	6 14.9	5 27.5
16 Tu	19 32 5	22 38 59	19 43 51	25 40 51	21D48.3	11 56.5	19 34.4	11 11.6	0 36.6	14 43.3	27 0.4	6 17.1	5 28.9
17 W	19 36 2	23 36 14	1♏39 8	7♏39 19	21 48.6	13 37.1	20 45.4	11 44.2	0 49.8	14 50.6	26 58.5	6 19.2	5 30.3
18 Th	19 39 58	24 33 28	13 42 1	19 47 47	21 49.8	15 15.8	21 56.5	12 17.0	1 3.0	14 58.0	26 56.7	6 21.4	5 31.7
19 F	19 43 55	25 30 43	25 57 12	2♐10 46	21 51.4	16 52.5	23 7.7	12 50.0	1 16.1	15 5.4	26 54.8	6 23.6	5 33.1
20 Sa	19 47 51	26 27 58	8♐28 59	14 52 13	21 52.8	18 27.3	24 18.9	13 23.1	1 29.2	15 12.8	26 52.8	6 25.8	5 34.5
21 Su	19 51 48	27 25 14	21 20 49	27 54 59	21R53.5	20 0.2	25 30.1	13 56.4	1 42.3	15 20.2	26 50.9	6 28.0	5 35.9
22 M	19 55 44	28 22 30	4♑34 53	11♑20 29	21 52.8	21 31.2	26 41.4	14 29.9	1 55.3	15 27.7	26 48.9	6 30.2	5 37.3
23 Tu	19 59 41	29 19 46	18 11 41	25 8 13	21 50.5	23 0.2	27 52.8	15 3.5	2 8.3	15 35.2	26 46.9	6 32.4	5 38.7
24 W	20 3 37	0♌17 3	2♒ 9 42	9♒15 38	21 46.5	24 27.3	29 4.2	15 37.3	2 21.2	15 42.7	26 44.8	6 34.6	5 40.1
25 Th	20 7 34	1 14 20	16 25 22	23 38 11	21 41.2	25 52.3	0♋15.7	16 11.2	2 34.1	15 50.2	26 42.7	6 36.9	5 41.4
26 F	20 11 31	2 11 38	0♓53 20	8♓ 9 57	21 35.2	27 15.4	1 27.3	16 45.4	2 46.9	15 57.7	26 40.7	6 39.1	5 42.8
27 Sa	20 15 27	3 8 57	15 27 15	22 44 25	21 29.2	28 36.4	2 38.9	17 19.6	2 59.7	16 5.3	26 38.5	6 41.3	5 44.1
28 Su	20 19 24	4 6 17	0♈ 0 42	7♈15 28	21 24.2	29 55.3	3 50.5	17 54.0	3 12.4	16 12.8	26 36.4	6 43.5	5 45.5
29 M	20 23 20	5 3 37	14 28 8	21 38 14	21 20.8	1♍12.1	5 2.2	18 28.6	3 25.1	16 20.4	26 34.2	6 45.7	5 46.8
30 Tu	20 27 17	6 0 59	28 45 25	5♉49 27	21D19.1	2 26.7	6 14.0	19 3.3	3 37.7	16 28.0	26 32.1	6 48.0	5 48.1
31 W	20 31 13	6 58 22	12♉50 9	19 47 27	21 19.0	3 39.0	7 25.9	19 38.2	3 50.3	16 35.6	26 29.9	6 50.2	5 49.4

AUGUST 1918 LONGITUDE

Day	Sid.Time	☉	0 hr ☽	Noon ☽	True ☊	☿	♀	♂	♃	♄	♅	♆	♇
1 Th	20 35 10	7♌55 46	26♉41 20	3♊31 50	21♐19.9	4♍49.0	8♋37.8	20♎13.3	4♋ 2.8	16♌43.3	26♒27.7	6♌52.4	5♋50.7
2 F	20 39 6	8 53 12	10♊19 0	17 2 55	21R21.0	5 56.7	9 49.7	20 48.5	4 15.3	16 50.9	26R25.4	6 54.6	5 52.0
3 Sa	20 43 3	9 50 38	23 43 40	0♋21 20	21 21.4	7 1.9	11 1.7	21 23.8	4 27.7	16 58.6	26 23.2	6 56.9	5 53.2
4 Su	20 47 0	10 48 6	6♋55 59	13 27 39	21 20.2	8 4.5	12 13.8	21 59.3	4 40.0	17 6.2	26 20.9	6 59.1	5 54.5
5 M	20 50 56	11 45 35	19 56 23	26 22 13	21 16.9	9 4.4	13 25.9	22 34.9	4 52.3	17 13.9	26 18.6	7 1.3	5 55.7
6 Tu	20 54 53	12 43 5	2♌45 8	9♌ 5 10	21 11.3	10 1.5	14 38.1	23 10.7	5 4.6	17 21.6	26 16.3	7 3.5	5 57.0
7 W	20 58 49	13 40 36	15 22 19	21 36 37	21 3.5	10 55.6	15 50.3	23 46.6	5 16.7	17 29.2	26 14.0	7 5.8	5 58.2
8 Th	21 2 46	14 38 7	27 48 7	3♍56 54	20 54.2	11 46.7	17 2.6	24 22.7	5 28.8	17 36.9	26 11.7	7 8.0	5 59.4
9 F	21 6 42	15 35 40	10♍ 3 5	16 6 49	20 44.1	12 34.6	18 14.9	24 58.9	5 40.9	17 44.6	26 9.4	7 10.2	6 0.6
10 Sa	21 10 39	16 33 14	22 8 19	28 7 49	20 34.2	13 19.0	19 27.3	25 35.2	5 52.8	17 52.3	26 7.0	7 12.4	6 1.8
11 Su	21 14 35	17 30 49	4♎ 5 40	10♎ 2 11	20 25.5	13 59.9	20 39.7	26 11.7	6 4.7	17 60.0	26 4.7	7 14.6	6 2.9
12 M	21 18 32	18 28 24	15 57 49	21 53 1	20 18.5	14 37.0	21 52.2	26 48.3	6 16.5	18 7.7	26 2.3	7 16.8	6 4.1
13 Tu	21 22 29	19 26 1	27 48 17	3♏44 12	20 13.8	15 10.1	23 4.7	27 25.1	6 28.3	18 15.4	25 59.9	7 19.0	6 5.2
14 W	21 26 25	20 23 39	9♏41 19	15 40 17	20D11.4	15 39.1	24 17.3	28 1.9	6 39.9	18 23.0	25 57.5	7 21.2	6 6.3
15 Th	21 30 22	21 21 17	21 41 43	27 46 17	20 10.7	16 3.6	25 29.9	28 39.0	6 51.5	18 30.7	25 55.2	7 23.3	6 7.5
16 F	21 34 18	22 18 57	3♐54 37	10♐ 7 23	20 11.2	16 23.6	26 42.6	29 16.1	7 3.1	18 38.4	25 52.8	7 25.5	6 8.5
17 Sa	21 38 15	23 16 38	16 25 9	22 48 31	20R11.7	16 38.6	27 55.4	29 53.4	7 14.5	18 46.1	25 50.4	7 27.7	6 9.6
18 Su	21 42 11	24 14 19	29 17 57	5♑53 52	20 11.4	16 48.6	29 8.1	0♏30.8	7 25.9	18 53.8	25 48.0	7 29.8	6 10.7
19 M	21 46 8	25 12 2	12♑36 33	19 26 11	20 9.4	16R53.3	0♌21.0	1 8.3	7 37.1	19 1.4	25 45.6	7 32.0	6 11.7
20 Tu	21 50 4	26 9 46	26 22 43	3♒25 59	20 5.0	16 52.5	1 33.8	1 45.9	7 48.3	19 9.1	25 43.2	7 34.1	6 12.8
21 W	21 54 1	27 7 31	10♒35 37	17 51 2	19 58.2	16 46.0	2 46.7	2 23.7	7 59.4	19 16.7	25 40.8	7 36.2	6 13.8
22 Th	21 57 58	28 5 18	25 11 27	2♓35 57	19 49.3	16 33.8	3 59.7	3 1.5	8 10.5	19 24.4	25 38.4	7 38.4	6 14.8
23 F	22 1 54	29 3 6	10♓ 3 28	17 32 49	19 39.3	16 15.7	5 12.7	3 39.5	8 21.4	19 32.0	25 36.0	7 40.5	6 15.8
24 Sa	22 5 51	0♍ 0 55	25 2 49	2♈32 17	19 29.3	15 51.7	6 25.8	4 17.6	8 32.3	19 39.6	25 33.7	7 42.6	6 16.7
25 Su	22 9 47	0 58 46	10♈ 0 4	17 25 10	19 20.5	15 22.0	7 38.9	4 55.8	8 43.0	19 47.2	25 31.3	7 44.6	6 17.7
26 M	22 13 44	1 56 38	24 46 45	2♉ 4 5	19 13.9	14 46.8	8 52.1	5 34.2	8 53.7	19 54.8	25 28.9	7 46.7	6 18.6
27 Tu	22 17 40	2 54 33	9♉16 40	16 24 10	19 9.7	14 6.4	10 5.3	6 12.6	9 4.3	20 2.4	25 26.5	7 48.8	6 19.5
28 W	22 21 37	3 52 29	23 26 25	0♊23 22	19D 7.9	13 21.2	11 18.6	6 51.2	9 14.8	20 9.9	25 24.2	7 50.8	6 20.4
29 Th	22 25 33	4 50 27	7♊15 7	14 1 50	19R 7.6	12 31.8	12 32.0	7 29.9	9 25.2	20 17.5	25 21.8	7 52.9	6 21.3
30 F	22 29 30	5 48 28	20 43 47	27 21 15	19 7.7	11 39.0	13 45.3	8 8.7	9 35.5	20 25.0	25 19.5	7 54.9	6 22.1
31 Sa	22 33 27	6 46 30	3♋54 32	10♋23 59	19 7.0	10 43.8	14 58.8	8 47.6	9 45.7	20 32.5	25 17.1	7 56.9	6 23.0

Astro Data	Planet Ingress	Last Aspect	☽ Ingress	Last Aspect	☽ Ingress	☽ Phases & Eclipses	Astro Data
Dy Hr Mn	Dy Hr Mn	Dy Hr Mn	Dy Hr Mn	Dy Hr Mn	Dy Hr Mn	Dy Hr Mn	1 JULY 1918
♃△♅ 1 15:13	☿ ♌ 9 8:39	2 16:43 ♃ ⚹	♉ 2 20:44	31 23:36 ♅ □	♊ 1 5:48	1 8:43 ☽ 8♈41	Julian Day # 6756
♃∠♄ 7 9:09	♃ ♋ 13 5:54	4 19:26 ♅ □	♊ 5 0:04	3 4:47 ♅ △	♋ 3 11:21	8 8:22 ● 15♋21	Delta T 20.6 sec
☽0S 13 7:52	☉ ♌ 23 16:51	7 2:15 ♃ ☌	♋ 7 4:42	5 5:10 ♂ □	♌ 5 18:49	16 6:24 ☽ 22♎54	SVP 06♓23'35"
☽0N 27 4:14	♀ ♋ 24 18:44	8 8:22 ☉ ☌	♌ 9 11:20	7 20:53 ♅ ☍	♍ 8 4:17	23 20:34 ○ 0♒09	Obliquity 23°26'58"
	☿ ♍ 28 1:27	11 19:56 ♃ ⚹	♍ 11 20:33	9 18:03 ♀ ⚹	♎ 10 15:45	30 13:14 ☽ 6♉33	⚷ Chiron 3♈27.6
☽0S 9 16:07		13 12:40 ☉ ⚹	♎ 14 8:09	12 23:10 ♂ ☌	♏ 13 4:27		☽ Mean ☊ 21♐27.5
♃☌♇ 10 20:03	♂ ♏ 17 4:16	16 14:38 ♅ △	♏ 16 20:41	15 8:21 ♀ △	♐ 15 16:22	6 20:29 ● 13♌32	
♃⚺♆ 18 10:24	♀ ♌ 18 17:06	19 1:51 ♅ □	♐ 19 7:49	17 17:34 ♅ ⚹	♑ 18 1:17	14 23:16 ☽ 21♏20	1 AUGUST 1918
☿ R 19 8:32	☉ ♍ 23 23:37	21 10:02 ♅ ⚹	♑ 21 15:46	19 7:33 ☿ △	♒ 20 6:11	22 5:02 ○ 28♒17	Julian Day # 6787
☽0N 23 13:11		22 18:18 ♂ □	♒ 23 20:19	22 5:02 ☉ ☍	♓ 22 7:48	28 19:27 ☽ 4♊39	Delta T 20.7 sec
		25 17:22 ☿ ☍	♓ 25 22:32	23 9:42 ☿ ☍	♈ 24 7:56		SVP 06♓23'30"
		26 7:58 ♇ △	♈ 27 23:59	26 1:09 ♅ ⚹	♉ 26 8:35		Obliquity 23°26'58"
		29 20:15 ♅ ⚹	♉ 30 2:06	28 3:22 ♅ □	♊ 28 11:19		⚷ Chiron 3♈12.7R
				30 8:17 ♅ △	♋ 30 16:50		☽ Mean ☊ 19♐49.0

LONGITUDE SEPTEMBER 1918

Day	Sid.Time	☉	0 hr ☽	Noon ☽	True ☊	☿	♀	♂	♃	♄	♅	♆	♇
1 Su	22 37 23	7♍44 34	16♋49 53	23♋12 32	19♐ 4.4	9♍47.1	16♌12.2	9♏26.7	9♋55.8	20♌40.0	25♒14.8	7♌58.9	6♋23.8
2 M	22 41 20	8 42 39	29 32 11	5♌49 4	18R 59.1	8R 50.0	17 25.8	10 5.8	10 5.7	20 47.4	25R 12.5	8 0.9	6 24.6
3 Tu	22 45 16	9 40 47	12♌ 3 24	18 15 20	18 50.9	7 53.8	18 39.3	10 45.1	10 15.6	20 54.9	25 10.2	8 2.8	6 25.3
4 W	22 49 13	10 38 56	24 25 2	0♍32 35	18 40.0	6 59.8	19 53.0	11 24.5	10 25.4	21 2.3	25 7.9	8 4.8	6 26.1
5 Th	22 53 9	11 37 7	6♍38 7	12 41 45	18 27.1	6 9.2	21 6.6	12 4.0	10 35.1	21 9.7	25 5.6	8 6.7	6 26.8
6 F	22 57 6	12 35 20	18 43 34	24 43 43	18 13.1	5 23.2	22 20.3	12 43.6	10 44.6	21 17.0	25 3.4	8 8.6	6 27.6
7 Sa	23 1 2	13 33 35	0♎42 20	6♎39 36	17 59.2	4 42.8	23 34.1	13 23.3	10 54.1	21 24.4	25 1.1	8 10.5	6 28.3
8 Su	23 4 59	14 31 51	12 35 43	18 30 58	17 46.7	4 9.2	24 47.8	14 3.1	11 3.4	21 31.7	24 58.9	8 12.4	6 28.9
9 M	23 8 56	15 30 9	24 25 38	0♏20 5	17 36.3	3 43.1	26 1.7	14 43.0	11 12.6	21 39.0	24 56.7	8 14.3	6 29.6
10 Tu	23 12 52	16 28 28	6♏14 43	12 9 59	17 28.7	3 25.1	27 15.5	15 23.1	11 21.7	21 46.2	24 54.5	8 16.1	6 30.2
11 W	23 16 49	17 26 49	18 6 22	24 4 27	17 23.9	3D 15.9	28 29.4	16 3.2	11 30.7	21 53.4	24 52.4	8 17.9	6 30.8
12 Th	23 20 45	18 25 12	0♐ 4 47	6♐ 8 1	17 21.6	3 15.7	29 43.4	16 43.4	11 39.5	22 0.6	24 50.2	8 19.7	6 31.4
13 F	23 24 42	19 23 36	12 14 46	18 25 44	17 20.9	3 24.7	0♍57.4	17 23.8	11 48.2	22 7.7	24 48.1	8 21.5	6 32.0
14 Sa	23 28 38	20 22 2	24 41 31	1♑ 2 48	17 20.9	3 43.0	2 11.4	18 4.2	11 56.9	22 14.9	24 46.0	8 23.3	6 32.5
15 Su	23 32 35	21 20 30	7♑30 11	14 4 10	17 20.3	4 10.4	3 25.5	18 44.8	12 5.3	22 21.9	24 44.0	8 25.0	6 33.1
16 M	23 36 31	22 18 59	20 45 14	27 33 42	17 18.0	4 46.7	4 39.5	19 25.4	12 13.7	22 29.0	24 41.9	8 26.8	6 33.6
17 Tu	23 40 28	23 17 30	4♒29 45	11♒33 22	17 13.4	5 31.6	5 53.7	20 6.2	12 21.9	22 36.0	24 39.9	8 28.5	6 34.1
18 W	23 44 25	24 16 2	18 44 21	26 2 15	17 6.2	6 24.5	7 7.8	20 47.0	12 30.0	22 42.9	24 37.9	8 30.2	6 34.5
19 Th	23 48 21	25 14 36	3♓26 25	10♓55 56	16 56.8	7 25.0	8 22.0	21 27.9	12 37.9	22 49.8	24 36.0	8 31.8	6 35.0
20 F	23 52 18	26 13 12	18 29 41	26 6 25	16 46.0	8 32.6	9 36.3	22 9.0	12 45.8	22 56.7	24 34.0	8 33.4	6 35.4
21 Sa	23 56 14	27 11 50	3♈44 44	11♈23 11	16 35.1	9 46.6	10 50.6	22 50.1	12 53.5	23 3.6	24 32.1	8 35.1	6 35.8
22 Su	0 0 11	28 10 30	19 0 23	26 35 0	16 25.4	11 6.3	12 4.9	23 31.3	13 1.0	23 10.3	24 30.3	8 36.6	6 36.2
23 M	0 4 7	29 9 12	4♉ 5 50	11♉31 55	16 17.9	12 31.2	13 19.2	24 12.6	13 8.4	23 17.1	24 28.4	8 38.2	6 36.5
24 Tu	0 8 4	0♎ 7 56	18 52 28	26 6 54	16 13.1	14 0.7	14 33.6	24 54.0	13 15.7	23 23.8	24 26.6	8 39.8	6 36.8
25 W	0 12 0	1 6 42	3♊14 53	10♊16 17	16D 10.8	15 34.0	15 48.0	25 35.5	13 22.8	23 30.4	24 24.8	8 41.3	6 37.2
26 Th	0 15 57	2 5 31	17 11 6	23 59 31	16 10.3	17 10.6	17 2.5	26 17.1	13 29.8	23 37.1	24 23.1	8 42.8	6 37.4
27 F	0 19 53	3 4 22	0♋41 47	7♋18 18	16R 10.5	18 50.0	18 17.0	26 58.8	13 36.6	23 43.6	24 21.4	8 44.2	6 37.7
28 Sa	0 23 50	4 3 15	13 49 28	20 15 43	16 10.2	20 31.7	19 31.5	27 40.6	13 43.3	23 50.1	24 19.7	8 45.7	6 38.0
29 Su	0 27 47	5 2 10	26 37 33	2♌55 23	16 8.2	22 15.2	20 46.1	28 22.5	13 49.8	23 56.6	24 18.1	8 47.1	6 38.2
30 M	0 31 43	6 1 8	9♌ 9 41	15 20 52	16 3.8	24 0.1	22 0.7	29 4.4	13 56.2	24 3.0	24 16.5	8 48.5	6 38.4

LONGITUDE OCTOBER 1918

Day	Sid.Time	☉	0 hr ☽	Noon ☽	True ☊	☿	♀	♂	♃	♄	♅	♆	♇
1 Tu	0 35 40	7♎ 0 8	21♌29 19	27♌35 21	15♐56.6	25♍46.0	23♍15.3	29♏46.5	14♋ 2.4	24♌ 9.3	24♒14.9	8♌49.9	6♋38.5
2 W	0 39 36	7 59 10	3♍39 19	9♍41 28	15R 46.9	27 32.7	24 29.9	0♐28.6	14 8.5	24 15.6	24R 13.4	8 51.2	6 38.7
3 Th	0 43 33	8 58 15	15 42 4	21 41 18	15 35.3	29 19.8	25 44.6	1 10.9	14 14.4	24 21.8	24 11.9	8 52.5	6 38.8
4 F	0 47 29	9 57 21	27 39 22	3♎36 28	15 22.6	1♎ 7.2	26 59.3	1 53.2	14 20.1	24 28.0	24 10.4	8 53.8	6 38.9
5 Sa	0 51 26	10 56 29	9♎32 45	15 28 24	15 10.0	2 54.6	28 14.1	2 35.6	14 25.7	24 34.1	24 9.0	8 55.1	6 39.0
6 Su	0 55 22	11 55 40	21 23 35	27 18 32	14 58.6	4 41.9	29 28.9	3 18.2	14 31.1	24 40.2	24 7.6	8 56.3	6 39.0
7 M	0 59 19	12 54 53	3♏13 26	9♏ 8 34	14 49.2	6 29.0	0♎43.6	4 0.8	14 36.4	24 46.2	24 6.3	8 57.5	6R 39.1
8 Tu	1 3 16	13 54 7	15 4 12	21 0 41	14 42.4	8 15.7	1 58.5	4 43.5	14 41.4	24 52.1	24 5.0	8 58.7	6 39.1
9 W	1 7 12	14 53 24	26 58 23	2♐57 42	14 38.3	10 2.0	3 13.3	5 26.2	14 46.3	24 58.0	24 3.7	8 59.8	6 39.0
10 Th	1 11 9	15 52 42	8♐59 7	15 3 7	14D 36.5	11 47.7	4 28.2	6 9.1	14 51.1	25 3.8	24 2.5	9 0.9	6 39.0
11 F	1 15 5	16 52 3	21 10 13	27 21 0	14 36.5	13 33.0	5 43.1	6 52.0	14 55.6	25 9.6	24 1.4	9 2.0	6 38.9
12 Sa	1 19 2	17 51 25	3♑36 2	9♑55 54	14 37.4	15 17.6	6 58.0	7 35.1	15 0.0	25 15.2	24 0.3	9 3.0	6 38.9
13 Su	1 22 58	18 50 49	16 21 10	22 52 24	14R 38.1	17 1.5	8 12.9	8 18.2	15 4.2	25 20.8	23 59.2	9 4.1	6 38.8
14 M	1 26 55	19 50 14	29 30 3	6♒14 33	14 37.6	18 44.8	9 27.9	9 1.4	15 8.3	25 26.4	23 58.2	9 5.1	6 38.6
15 Tu	1 30 51	20 49 41	13♒ 6 12	20 5 9	14 35.3	20 27.5	10 42.8	9 44.6	15 12.1	25 31.8	23 57.2	9 6.0	6 38.5
16 W	1 34 48	21 49 10	27 11 23	4♓24 43	14 31.0	22 9.5	11 57.8	10 28.0	15 15.8	25 37.2	23 56.2	9 7.0	6 38.3
17 Th	1 38 45	22 48 41	11♓44 43	19 10 43	14 24.7	23 50.8	13 12.8	11 11.4	15 19.3	25 42.5	23 55.3	9 7.8	6 38.1
18 F	1 42 41	23 48 14	26 41 52	4♈17 6	14 17.2	25 31.5	14 27.8	11 54.9	15 22.6	25 47.8	23 54.5	9 8.7	6 37.9
19 Sa	1 46 38	24 47 48	11♈55 9	19 34 40	14 9.4	27 11.5	15 42.9	12 38.5	15 25.7	25 53.0	23 53.7	9 9.5	6 37.6
20 Su	1 50 34	25 47 24	27 14 13	4♉52 25	14 2.4	28 50.9	16 57.9	13 22.1	15 28.7	25 58.1	23 52.9	9 10.3	6 37.3
21 M	1 54 31	26 47 3	12♉27 55	19 59 30	13 57.1	0♏29.6	18 13.0	14 5.8	15 31.4	26 3.1	23 52.2	9 11.1	6 37.1
22 Tu	1 58 27	27 46 43	27 26 8	4♊46 58	13 53.9	2 7.7	19 28.1	14 49.6	15 34.0	26 8.0	23 51.6	9 11.9	6 36.7
23 W	2 2 24	28 46 26	12♊ 1 24	19 9 1	13D 52.8	3 45.3	20 43.2	15 33.5	15 36.4	26 12.9	23 51.0	9 12.6	6 36.4
24 Th	2 6 20	29 46 11	26 9 36	3♋ 3 7	13 53.3	5 22.2	21 58.3	16 17.4	15 38.6	26 17.7	23 50.4	9 13.2	6 36.1
25 F	2 10 17	0♏45 58	9♋49 44	16 29 40	13 54.6	6 58.6	23 13.5	17 1.5	15 40.5	26 22.4	23 49.9	9 13.9	6 35.7
26 Sa	2 14 14	1 45 48	23 3 18	29 31 4	13R 55.8	8 34.5	24 28.7	17 45.6	15 42.4	26 27.0	23 49.4	9 14.5	6 35.3
27 Su	2 18 10	2 45 39	5♌53 27	12♌10 57	13 56.1	10 9.8	25 43.9	18 29.7	15 44.0	26 31.6	23 49.0	9 15.1	6 34.8
28 M	2 22 7	3 45 33	18 24 8	24 33 30	13 54.9	11 44.6	26 59.1	19 14.0	15 45.4	26 36.0	23 48.6	9 15.6	6 34.4
29 Tu	2 26 3	4 45 29	0♍39 35	6♍42 52	13 51.9	13 18.9	28 14.3	19 58.3	15 46.6	26 40.4	23 48.3	9 16.1	6 33.9
30 W	2 30 0	5 45 27	12 43 51	18 42 57	13 47.1	14 52.8	29 29.5	20 42.7	15 47.6	26 44.7	23 48.1	9 16.6	6 33.4
31 Th	2 33 56	6 45 27	24 40 35	0♎37 7	13 41.0	16 26.1	0♏44.8	21 27.1	15 48.4	26 48.9	23 47.8	9 17.0	6 32.9

Astro Data	Dy Hr Mn
♃□♅	2 13:16
☽0S	5 23:18
♄∠♇	7 14:02
☿ D	11 12:30
☽0N	19 23:45
♄☍♅	1 17:02
☽0S	3 5:12
☿0S	5 14:44
♇ R	7 19:13
♀0S	9 2:56
☽0N	17 10:17
☽0S	30 10:32

Planet Ingress		Dy Hr Mn
♀	♍	12 5:23
☉	♎	23 20:46
♂	♐	1 7:42
☿	♎	3 8:59
♀	♎	6 10:00
☿	♏	20 16:47
☉	♏	24 5:33
♀	♏	30 9:43

Last Aspect Dy Hr Mn		☽ Ingress Dy Hr Mn
31 11:45	☿ ⚹	♌ 2 0:53
4 1:24	♅ ☍	♍ 4 10:56
5 11:22	♂ ⚹	♎ 6 22:35
9 3:38	♀ ⚹	♏ 9 11:19
11 23:13	♀ □	♐ 11 23:50
14 0:09	♅ ⚹	♑ 14 10:02
16 2:59	☉ △	♒ 16 16:15
18 9:41	♅ ☌	♓ 18 18:27
20 13:01	☉ ☍	♈ 20 18:07
22 8:41	♅ ⚹	♉ 22 17:27
24 10:29	♂ ☍	♊ 24 18:31
26 12:40	♅ △	♋ 26 22:45
29 3:31	♂ △	♌ 29 6:25

Last Aspect Dy Hr Mn		☽ Ingress Dy Hr Mn
1 5:24	♅ ☍	♍ 1 16:46
3 22:30	♀ ☌	♎ 4 4:43
6 6:42	♄ ⚹	♏ 6 17:28
8 19:56	♄ □	♐ 9 6:04
11 7:49	♄ △	♑ 11 17:06
13 4:59	☉ □	♒ 14 0:54
15 21:21	♄ ☍	♓ 16 4:42
17 5:49	♃ △	♈ 18 5:14
20 2:50	☿ ☍	♉ 20 4:20
21 21:53	♄ □	♊ 22 4:10
24 0:14	♄ ⚹	♋ 24 6:40
26 2:54	♀ □	♌ 26 12:54
28 18:41	♀ ⚹	♍ 28 22:42
30 17:04	♂ □	♎ 31 10:45

☽ Phases & Eclipses Dy Hr Mn	
5 10:43	● 12♍03
13 15:02	☽ 20♐00
20 13:01	○ 26♓45
27 4:38	☽ 3♋16
5 3:05	● 11♎04
13 4:59	☽ 19♑03
19 21:34	○ 25♈41
26 17:35	☽ 2♌30

Astro Data

1 SEPTEMBER 1918
Julian Day # 6818
Delta T 20.7 sec
SVP 06♓23'26"
Obliquity 23°26'58"
⚷ Chiron 2♈14.2R
☽ Mean ☊ 18♐10.5

1 OCTOBER 1918
Julian Day # 6848
Delta T 20.8 sec
SVP 06♓23'23"
Obliquity 23°26'58"
⚷ Chiron 0♈55.1R
☽ Mean ☊ 16♐35.2

NOVEMBER 1918 LONGITUDE

Day	Sid.Time	☉	0 hr ☽	Noon ☽	True ☊	☿	♀	♂	♃	♄	♅	♆	♇
1 F	2 37 53	7♏45 30	6♎32 54	12♎28 14	13♐34.1	17♏59.0	2♏ 0.0	22♐11.7	15♋49.0	26♌53.0	23♒47.7	9♌17.5	6♋32.4
2 Sa	2 41 49	8 45 34	18 23 23	24 18 37	13R 27.3	19 31.5	3 15.3	22 56.3	15 49.4	26 57.0	23R 47.5	9 17.8	6R 31.8
3 Su	2 45 46	9 45 40	0♏14 9	6♏10 14	13 21.1	21 3.6	4 30.6	23 41.0	15R 49.7	27 0.9	23D 47.5	9 18.2	6 31.3
4 M	2 49 42	10 45 48	12 7 4	18 4 51	13 16.1	22 35.2	5 45.9	24 25.7	15 49.7	27 4.8	23 47.5	9 18.5	6 30.7
5 Tu	2 53 39	11 45 58	24 3 49	0♐ 4 11	13 12.7	24 6.4	7 1.2	25 10.5	15 49.5	27 8.5	23 47.5	9 18.7	6 30.1
6 W	2 57 36	12 46 10	6♐ 6 12	12 10 8	13D 11.1	25 37.2	8 16.5	25 55.4	15 49.1	27 12.2	23 47.6	9 19.0	6 29.4
7 Th	3 1 32	13 46 24	18 16 16	24 24 55	13 10.9	27 7.6	9 31.9	26 40.3	15 48.5	27 15.7	23 47.7	9 19.2	6 28.8
8 F	3 5 29	14 46 39	0♑36 25	6♑51 9	13 12.0	28 37.5	10 47.2	27 25.3	15 47.7	27 19.2	23 47.9	9 19.4	6 28.1
9 Sa	3 9 25	15 46 56	13 9 27	19 31 45	13 13.6	0♐ 7.1	12 2.5	28 10.4	15 46.7	27 22.5	23 48.2	9 19.5	6 27.4
10 Su	3 13 22	16 47 14	25 58 26	2♒29 53	13 15.3	1 36.2	13 17.9	28 55.5	15 45.6	27 25.8	23 48.5	9 19.6	6 26.7
11 M	3 17 18	17 47 34	9♒ 6 28	15 48 31	13R 16.4	3 4.8	14 33.3	29 40.7	15 44.2	27 29.0	23 48.8	9 19.7	6 26.0
12 Tu	3 21 15	18 47 55	22 36 17	29 29 56	13 16.7	4 33.0	15 48.6	0♑26.0	15 42.6	27 32.0	23 49.2	9R 19.7	6 25.2
13 W	3 25 11	19 48 17	6♓29 35	13♓35 9	13 15.7	6 0.7	17 4.0	1 11.3	15 40.8	27 35.0	23 49.7	9 19.7	6 24.4
14 Th	3 29 8	20 48 41	20 46 26	28 3 6	13 13.8	7 27.9	18 19.3	1 56.7	15 38.8	27 37.9	23 50.2	9 19.7	6 23.7
15 F	3 33 5	21 49 6	5♈24 36	12♈50 15	13 11.2	8 54.5	19 34.7	2 42.1	15 36.6	27 40.6	23 50.7	9 19.6	6 22.8
16 Sa	3 37 1	22 49 32	20 19 12	27 50 26	13 8.3	10 20.6	20 50.1	3 27.6	15 34.2	27 43.3	23 51.3	9 19.5	6 22.0
17 Su	3 40 58	23 50 0	5♉22 54	12♉55 25	13 5.7	11 45.9	22 5.5	4 13.1	15 31.7	27 45.9	23 52.0	9 19.3	6 21.2
18 M	3 44 54	24 50 29	20 26 50	27 55 58	13 3.9	13 10.6	23 20.9	4 58.7	15 28.9	27 48.3	23 52.7	9 19.2	6 20.3
19 Tu	3 48 51	25 51 0	5♊21 47	12♊43 19	13D 2.9	14 34.4	24 36.3	5 44.3	15 25.9	27 50.7	23 53.4	9 19.0	6 19.5
20 W	3 52 47	26 51 33	19 59 45	27 10 25	13 2.9	15 57.3	25 51.7	6 30.0	15 22.8	27 52.9	23 54.2	9 18.7	6 18.6
21 Th	3 56 44	27 52 7	4♋14 50	11♋12 43	13 3.6	17 19.3	27 7.1	7 15.8	15 19.4	27 55.1	23 55.1	9 18.4	6 17.7
22 F	4 0 41	28 52 43	18 3 53	24 48 22	13 4.7	18 40.1	28 22.5	8 1.6	15 15.9	27 57.1	23 56.0	9 18.1	6 16.8
23 Sa	4 4 37	29 53 21	1♌26 18	7♌57 57	13 6.0	19 59.6	29 37.9	8 47.4	15 12.2	27 59.0	23 56.9	9 17.8	6 15.8
24 Su	4 8 34	0♐54 0	14 23 39	20 43 51	13 6.9	21 17.6	0♐53.3	9 33.3	15 8.3	28 0.9	23 58.0	9 17.4	6 14.9
25 M	4 12 30	1 54 40	26 59 2	3♍ 9 43	13R 7.4	22 34.0	2 8.8	10 19.3	15 4.2	28 2.6	23 59.0	9 17.0	6 13.9
26 Tu	4 16 27	2 55 23	9♍16 29	15 19 53	13 7.4	23 48.5	3 24.2	11 5.3	14 59.9	28 4.2	24 0.1	9 16.6	6 12.9
27 W	4 20 23	3 56 7	21 20 30	27 18 54	13 6.9	25 0.9	4 39.6	11 51.3	14 55.5	28 5.7	24 1.3	9 16.1	6 11.9
28 Th	4 24 20	4 56 52	3♎15 37	9♎11 12	13 6.0	26 10.7	5 55.1	12 37.4	14 50.9	28 7.1	24 2.5	9 15.6	6 10.9
29 F	4 28 16	5 57 39	15 6 8	21 0 54	13 5.0	27 17.8	7 10.5	13 23.6	14 46.1	28 8.4	24 3.7	9 15.1	6 9.9
30 Sa	4 32 13	6 58 27	26 55 56	2♏51 39	13 4.0	28 21.5	8 26.0	14 9.8	14 41.1	28 9.5	24 5.0	9 14.5	6 8.9

DECEMBER 1918 LONGITUDE

Day	Sid.Time	☉	0 hr ☽	Noon ☽	True ☊	☿	♀	♂	♃	♄	♅	♆	♇
1 Su	4 36 9	7♐59 17	8♏48 24	14♏46 32	13♐ 3.3	29♐21.6	9♐41.4	14♑56.0	14♋36.0	28♌10.6	24♒ 6.4	9♌13.9	6♋ 7.8
2 M	4 40 6	9 0 8	20 46 20	26 48 4	13R 2.7	0♑17.4	10 56.9	15 42.3	14R 30.6	28 11.5	24 7.8	9R 13.2	6R 6.8
3 Tu	4 44 3	10 1 1	2♐51 59	8♐58 16	13D 2.5	1 8.3	12 12.4	16 28.7	14 25.2	28 12.4	24 9.2	9 12.6	6 5.7
4 W	4 47 59	11 1 54	15 7 5	21 18 38	13 2.4	1 53.8	13 27.8	17 15.1	14 19.6	28 13.1	24 10.7	9 11.9	6 4.6
5 Th	4 51 56	12 2 49	27 33 1	3♑50 22	13 2.5	2 32.9	14 43.3	18 1.5	14 13.8	28 13.7	24 12.2	9 11.2	6 3.5
6 F	4 55 52	13 3 45	10♑10 48	16 34 27	13R 2.5	3 5.1	15 58.8	18 48.0	14 7.8	28 14.2	24 13.8	9 10.4	6 2.4
7 Sa	4 59 49	14 4 42	23 1 24	29 31 46	13 2.5	3 29.4	17 14.3	19 34.5	14 1.8	28 14.6	24 15.5	9 9.6	6 1.3
8 Su	5 3 45	15 5 39	6♒ 5 38	12♒43 7	13 2.3	3 44.9	18 29.7	20 21.0	13 55.5	28 14.8	24 17.1	9 8.8	6 0.2
9 M	5 7 42	16 6 37	19 24 18	26 9 15	13 2.0	3R 50.9	19 45.2	21 7.6	13 49.2	28R 15.0	24 18.9	9 7.9	5 59.1
10 Tu	5 11 39	17 7 36	2♓58 2	9♓50 40	13 1.7	3 46.5	21 0.6	21 54.2	13 42.7	28 15.0	24 20.6	9 7.1	5 57.9
11 W	5 15 35	18 8 35	16 47 9	23 47 25	13D 1.6	3 31.1	22 16.1	22 40.9	13 36.1	28 15.0	24 22.4	9 6.2	5 56.8
12 Th	5 19 32	19 9 35	0♈51 21	7♈58 45	13 1.7	3 4.3	23 31.6	23 27.6	13 29.3	28 14.8	24 24.3	9 5.2	5 55.6
13 F	5 23 28	20 10 35	15 9 21	22 22 46	13 2.1	2 26.0	24 47.0	24 14.3	13 22.5	28 14.5	24 26.2	9 4.3	5 54.5
14 Sa	5 27 25	21 11 36	29 38 35	6♉56 14	13 2.8	1 36.4	26 2.5	25 1.1	13 15.5	28 14.1	24 28.1	9 3.3	5 53.3
15 Su	5 31 21	22 12 37	14♉15 6	21 34 30	13 3.6	0 36.5	27 17.9	25 47.9	13 8.4	28 13.6	24 30.1	9 2.2	5 52.1
16 M	5 35 18	23 13 39	28 53 41	6♊11 51	13R 4.2	29♐27.5	28 33.4	26 34.7	13 1.2	28 13.0	24 32.2	9 1.2	5 50.9
17 Tu	5 39 14	24 14 41	13♊28 13	20 41 59	13 4.5	28 11.5	29 48.8	27 21.5	12 53.9	28 12.2	24 34.2	9 0.1	5 49.7
18 W	5 43 11	25 15 44	27 52 25	4♋58 51	13 4.2	26 50.6	1♑ 4.2	28 8.4	12 46.5	28 11.4	24 36.4	8 59.0	5 48.5
19 Th	5 47 8	26 16 48	12♋ 0 42	18 57 27	13 3.1	25 27.8	2 19.7	28 55.3	12 39.0	28 10.4	24 38.5	8 57.9	5 47.4
20 F	5 51 4	27 17 52	25 48 46	2♌34 23	13 1.4	24 5.6	3 35.1	29 42.2	12 31.5	28 9.4	24 40.7	8 56.8	5 46.2
21 Sa	5 55 1	28 18 57	9♌14 11	15 48 11	12 59.3	22 47.0	4 50.5	0♒29.2	12 23.8	28 8.2	24 42.9	8 55.6	5 44.9
22 Su	5 58 57	29 20 3	22 16 29	28 39 19	12 57.0	21 34.2	6 6.0	1 16.2	12 16.1	28 6.9	24 45.2	8 54.4	5 43.7
23 M	6 2 54	0♑21 9	4♍56 59	11♍ 9 55	12 54.9	20 29.3	7 21.4	2 3.2	12 8.4	28 5.5	24 47.5	8 53.2	5 42.5
24 Tu	6 6 50	1 22 16	17 18 33	23 23 25	12 53.3	19 33.7	8 36.8	2 50.2	12 0.5	28 4.0	24 49.9	8 51.9	5 41.3
25 W	6 10 47	2 23 24	29 25 5	5♎24 8	12D 52.6	18 48.3	9 52.2	3 37.3	11 52.6	28 2.4	24 52.3	8 50.7	5 40.1
26 Th	6 14 43	3 24 32	11♎21 10	17 16 50	12 52.8	18 13.6	11 7.7	4 24.3	11 44.7	28 0.7	24 54.7	8 49.4	5 38.9
27 F	6 18 40	4 25 40	23 11 44	29 6 28	12 53.9	17 49.6	12 23.1	5 11.4	11 36.7	27 58.9	24 57.1	8 48.0	5 37.6
28 Sa	6 22 37	5 26 50	5♏ 1 39	10♏57 51	12 55.5	17D 36.0	13 38.5	5 58.6	11 28.6	27 57.0	24 59.6	8 46.7	5 36.4
29 Su	6 26 33	6 27 59	16 55 36	22 55 24	12 57.3	17 32.4	14 53.9	6 45.7	11 20.6	27 54.9	25 2.2	8 45.4	5 35.2
30 M	6 30 30	7 29 10	28 57 43	5♐ 2 57	12 58.8	17 38.0	16 9.3	7 32.9	11 12.5	27 52.8	25 4.8	8 44.0	5 34.0
31 Tu	6 34 26	8 30 20	11♐11 28	17 23 32	12R 59.6	17 52.2	17 24.8	8 20.1	11 4.4	27 50.6	25 7.4	8 42.6	5 32.8

Astro Data Dy Hr Mn	Planet Ingress Dy Hr Mn	Last Aspect Dy Hr Mn	☽ Ingress Dy Hr Mn	Last Aspect Dy Hr Mn	☽ Ingress Dy Hr Mn	☽ Phases & Eclipses Dy Hr Mn
♃ R 3 13:52	☿ ♐ 8 22:06	2 17:27 ♄ ⚹	♏ 2 23:31	2 14:47 ♄ □	♐ 2 18:20	3 21:01 ● 10♏38
♅ D 3 18:27	♂ ♑ 11 10:13	5 6:11 ♄ □	♐ 5 11:52	5 1:18 ♄ △	♑ 5 4:41	11 16:46 ☽ 18♒30
♆ R 12 9:18	☉ ♐ 23 2:38	7 17:37 ♄ △	♑ 7 22:50	6 17:11 ♂ ☌	♒ 7 12:52	18 7:33 ○ 25♉10
☽0N 13 19:04	♀ ♐ 23 7:02	9 5:23 ☉ ⚹	♒ 10 7:25	9 15:42 ♄ ☍	♓ 9 18:47	25 10:25 ☽ 2♍21
☽0S 26 16:47		12 8:38 ♄ ☍	♓ 12 12:52	11 10:42 ♂ ⚹	♈ 11 22:33	
	☿ ♑ 1 16:19	14 0:04 ☉ △	♈ 14 15:11	13 21:41 ♄ △	♉ 14 0:35	3 15:19 ● 10♐40
☿ R 9 2:05	☿ ♐ 15 13:03	16 11:51 ♄ △	♉ 16 15:26	15 22:53 ♄ □	♊ 16 1:49	3 15:21:39 • A 7'06"
♄ R 9 21:31	♀ ♑ 17 3:34	18 11:50 ♄ □	♊ 18 15:20	18 0:32 ♄ ⚹	♋ 18 3:35	11 2:31 ☽ 18♓15
☽0N 11 1:36	♂ ♒ 20 9:05	20 13:14 ♄ ⚹	♋ 20 16:46	20 7:19 ♂ ☍	♌ 20 7:25	17 19:17 ○ 25♊04
♃∠♄ 14 5:00	☉ ♑ 22 15:42	22 20:57 ☉ △	♌ 22 21:23	22 14:27 ☉ △	♍ 22 14:33	17 19:06 • A 0.834
☽0S 24 0:55		25 2:03 ♄ ☌	♍ 25 5:50	24 4:09 ☿ □	♎ 25 1:10	25 6:30 ☽ 2♎40
☿ D 28 21:10		27 8:11 ☿ □	♎ 27 17:25	27 9:41 ♄ ⚹	♏ 27 13:49	
		30 3:10 ☿ ⚹	♏ 30 6:13	29 21:52 ♄ □	♐ 30 2:03	

Astro Data

1 NOVEMBER 1918
Julian Day # 6879
Delta T 20.8 sec
SVP 06♓23'20"
Obliquity 23°26'57"
⚷ Chiron 29♓40.0R
☽ Mean ☊ 14♐56.6

1 DECEMBER 1918
Julian Day # 6909
Delta T 20.9 sec
SVP 06♓23'16"
Obliquity 23°26'56"
⚷ Chiron 29♓00.5R
☽ Mean ☊ 13♐21.3

LONGITUDE — JANUARY 1919

Day	Sid.Time	☉	0 hr ☽	Noon ☽	True ☊	☿	♀	♂	♃	♄	♅	♆	♇
1 W	6 38 23	9♑31 31	23♐39 24	29♐59 14	12♐59.1	18♐14.2	18♑40.2	9♒ 7.3	10♋56.2	27♌48.3	25♒10.0	8♌41.2	5♋31.5
2 Th	6 42 19	10 32 42	6♑23 5	12♑51 1	12R 57.2	18 43.3	19 55.6	9 54.5	10R 48.1	27R 45.8	25 12.7	8R 39.7	5R 30.3
3 F	6 46 16	11 33 53	19 22 57	25 58 48	12 53.9	19 18.7	21 11.0	10 41.8	10 40.0	27 43.3	25 15.4	8 38.3	5 29.1
4 Sa	6 50 12	12 35 4	2♒38 23	9♒21 30	12 49.4	19 59.8	22 26.4	11 29.1	10 31.8	27 40.7	25 18.1	8 36.8	5 27.9
5 Su	6 54 9	13 36 15	16 7 55	22 57 19	12 44.2	20 46.1	23 41.8	12 16.3	10 23.7	27 38.0	25 20.9	8 35.3	5 26.7
6 M	6 58 6	14 37 25	29 49 27	6♓44 0	12 39.1	21 36.9	24 57.1	13 3.6	10 15.6	27 35.1	25 23.7	8 33.8	5 25.5
7 Tu	7 2 2	15 38 35	13♓40 41	20 39 13	12 34.7	22 31.7	26 12.5	13 50.9	10 7.6	27 32.2	25 26.5	8 32.3	5 24.3
8 W	7 5 59	16 39 45	27 39 22	4♈40 52	12 31.6	23 30.1	27 27.8	14 38.2	9 59.5	27 29.2	25 29.4	8 30.8	5 23.1
9 Th	7 9 55	17 40 54	11♈43 31	18 47 6	12D 30.2	24 31.8	28 43.2	15 25.5	9 51.5	27 26.1	25 32.3	8 29.2	5 21.9
10 F	7 13 52	18 42 3	25 51 27	2♉56 22	12 30.2	25 36.4	29 58.5	16 12.9	9 43.6	27 23.0	25 35.2	8 27.7	5 20.7
11 Sa	7 17 48	19 43 11	10♉ 1 39	17 7 6	12 31.4	26 43.5	1♒13.8	17 0.2	9 35.7	27 19.7	25 38.1	8 26.1	5 19.5
12 Su	7 21 45	20 44 19	24 12 29	1♊17 31	12 32.9	27 52.9	2 29.2	17 47.5	9 27.8	27 16.4	25 41.1	8 24.5	5 18.3
13 M	7 25 41	21 45 26	8♊21 54	15 25 18	12R 33.8	29 4.5	3 44.5	18 34.9	9 20.1	27 12.9	25 44.1	8 22.9	5 17.2
14 Tu	7 29 38	22 46 32	22 27 20	29 27 34	12 33.5	0♑17.8	4 59.7	19 22.2	9 12.3	27 9.4	25 47.1	8 21.3	5 16.0
15 W	7 33 35	23 47 38	6♋25 34	13♋20 55	12 31.2	1 32.9	6 15.0	20 9.5	9 4.7	27 5.8	25 50.2	8 19.7	5 14.9
16 Th	7 37 31	24 48 43	20 13 8	27 1 51	12 26.8	2 49.6	7 30.3	20 56.9	8 57.1	27 2.2	25 53.2	8 18.1	5 13.7
17 F	7 41 28	25 49 48	3♌46 40	10♌27 16	12 20.4	4 7.7	8 45.5	21 44.2	8 49.7	26 58.5	25 56.3	8 16.5	5 12.6
18 Sa	7 45 24	26 50 52	17 3 25	23 34 56	12 12.5	5 27.0	10 0.8	22 31.6	8 42.3	26 54.6	25 59.4	8 14.8	5 11.4
19 Su	7 49 21	27 51 56	0♍ 1 46	6♍23 56	12 4.0	6 47.6	11 16.0	23 18.9	8 35.0	26 50.8	26 2.6	8 13.2	5 10.3
20 M	7 53 17	28 52 59	12 41 33	18 54 48	11 55.9	8 9.3	12 31.2	24 6.3	8 27.8	26 46.8	26 5.7	8 11.5	5 9.2
21 Tu	7 57 14	29 54 2	25 4 1	1♎ 9 32	11 48.9	9 32.0	13 46.4	24 53.6	8 20.7	26 42.8	26 8.9	8 9.8	5 8.1
22 W	8 1 10	0♒55 4	7♎11 48	13 11 21	11 43.7	10 55.7	15 1.6	25 41.0	8 13.7	26 38.7	26 12.1	8 8.2	5 7.0
23 Th	8 5 7	1 56 6	19 8 43	25 4 30	11 40.5	12 20.3	16 16.7	26 28.3	8 6.8	26 34.6	26 15.3	8 6.5	5 5.9
24 F	8 9 4	2 57 8	0♏59 21	6♏53 54	11D 39.4	13 45.9	17 31.9	27 15.6	8 0.1	26 30.4	26 18.6	8 4.8	5 4.9
25 Sa	8 13 0	3 58 8	12 48 51	18 44 51	11 39.8	15 12.2	18 47.0	28 3.0	7 53.5	26 26.1	26 21.8	8 3.1	5 3.8
26 Su	8 16 57	4 59 9	24 42 34	0♐42 41	11 40.9	16 39.4	20 2.2	28 50.3	7 47.0	26 21.8	26 25.1	8 1.4	5 2.8
27 M	8 20 53	6 0 9	6♐45 47	12 52 28	11R 41.8	18 7.4	21 17.3	29 37.6	7 40.6	26 17.4	26 28.4	7 59.7	5 1.7
28 Tu	8 24 50	7 1 8	19 3 15	25 18 38	11 41.7	19 36.1	22 32.4	0♓25.0	7 34.4	26 13.0	26 31.7	7 58.1	5 0.7
29 W	8 28 46	8 2 6	1♑38 58	8♑ 4 33	11 39.5	21 5.6	23 47.5	1 12.3	7 28.3	26 8.6	26 35.0	7 56.4	4 59.7
30 Th	8 32 43	9 3 4	14 35 34	21 12 5	11 35.0	22 35.8	25 2.6	1 59.6	7 22.3	26 4.0	26 38.4	7 54.7	4 58.7
31 F	8 36 40	10 4 1	27 54 3	4♒41 16	11 27.9	24 6.8	26 17.6	2 46.9	7 16.5	25 59.5	26 41.7	7 53.0	4 57.8

LONGITUDE — FEBRUARY 1919

Day	Sid.Time	☉	0 hr ☽	Noon ☽	True ☊	☿	♀	♂	♃	♄	♅	♆	♇
1 Sa	8 40 36	11♒ 4 57	11♒33 27	18♒30 7	11♐18.7	25♑38.5	27♒32.7	3♓34.2	7♋10.9	25♌54.9	26♒45.1	7♌51.3	4♋56.8
2 Su	8 44 33	12 5 52	25 30 47	2♓34 47	11R 8.3	27 10.9	28 47.7	4 21.5	7R 5.4	25R 50.3	26 48.4	7R 49.6	4R 55.8
3 M	8 48 29	13 6 45	9♓41 28	16 50 7	10 57.8	28 44.0	0♓ 2.7	5 8.7	7 0.1	25 45.6	26 51.8	7 47.9	4 54.9
4 Tu	8 52 26	14 7 37	24 0 2	1♈10 31	10 48.4	0♒17.9	1 17.7	5 56.0	6 54.9	25 40.9	26 55.2	7 46.2	4 54.0
5 W	8 56 22	15 8 28	8♈20 58	15 30 48	10 41.0	1 52.5	2 32.6	6 43.2	6 50.0	25 36.2	26 58.6	7 44.6	4 53.1
6 Th	9 0 19	16 9 18	22 39 36	29 46 57	10 36.2	3 27.8	3 47.6	7 30.5	6 45.1	25 31.4	27 2.0	7 42.9	4 52.2
7 F	9 4 15	17 10 6	6♉52 36	13♉56 20	10D 34.0	5 3.9	5 2.5	8 17.7	6 40.5	25 26.6	27 5.4	7 41.2	4 51.3
8 Sa	9 8 12	18 10 52	20 58 3	27 57 41	10 33.6	6 40.8	6 17.3	9 4.9	6 36.0	25 21.8	27 8.9	7 39.6	4 50.5
9 Su	9 12 8	19 11 37	4♊55 12	11♊50 36	10R 34.0	8 18.4	7 32.2	9 52.0	6 31.8	25 17.0	27 12.3	7 37.9	4 49.6
10 M	9 16 5	20 12 21	18 43 54	25 35 4	10 33.8	9 56.9	8 47.0	10 39.2	6 27.6	25 12.2	27 15.8	7 36.3	4 48.8
11 Tu	9 20 2	21 13 3	2♋24 6	9♋10 55	10 31.9	11 36.1	10 1.8	11 26.3	6 23.7	25 7.4	27 19.2	7 34.6	4 48.0
12 W	9 23 58	22 13 43	15 55 28	22 37 37	10 27.4	13 16.2	11 16.6	12 13.4	6 20.0	25 2.5	27 22.7	7 33.0	4 47.3
13 Th	9 27 55	23 14 21	29 17 12	5♌54 4	10 20.0	14 57.1	12 31.4	13 0.5	6 16.4	24 57.6	27 26.1	7 31.4	4 46.5
14 F	9 31 51	24 14 58	12♌28 2	18 58 56	10 9.7	16 38.8	13 46.1	13 47.6	6 13.1	24 52.8	27 29.6	7 29.8	4 45.7
15 Sa	9 35 48	25 15 34	25 26 34	1♍50 49	9 57.3	18 21.4	15 0.8	14 34.6	6 9.9	24 47.9	27 33.0	7 28.2	4 45.0
16 Su	9 39 44	26 16 8	8♍11 35	14 28 49	9 43.8	20 4.9	16 15.4	15 21.7	6 6.9	24 43.1	27 36.5	7 26.6	4 44.3
17 M	9 43 41	27 16 40	20 42 32	26 52 49	9 30.5	21 49.3	17 30.0	16 8.7	6 4.1	24 38.2	27 40.0	7 25.0	4 43.6
18 Tu	9 47 37	28 17 12	2♎59 48	9♎ 3 43	9 18.5	23 34.5	18 44.6	16 55.6	6 1.5	24 33.3	27 43.4	7 23.5	4 43.0
19 W	9 51 34	29 17 41	15 4 52	21 3 37	9 8.8	25 20.7	19 59.2	17 42.6	5 59.1	24 28.5	27 46.9	7 21.9	4 42.3
20 Th	9 55 31	0♓18 10	27 0 23	2♏55 40	9 1.9	27 7.8	21 13.7	18 29.5	5 56.9	24 23.7	27 50.3	7 20.4	4 41.7
21 F	9 59 27	1 18 37	8♏50 2	14 44 3	8 57.7	28 55.8	22 28.2	19 16.4	5 54.8	24 18.8	27 53.8	7 18.8	4 41.1
22 Sa	10 3 24	2 19 2	20 38 22	26 33 39	8 55.8	0♓44.8	23 42.7	20 3.3	5 53.0	24 14.0	27 57.3	7 17.3	4 40.5
23 Su	10 7 20	3 19 27	2♐30 34	8♐29 51	8 55.4	2 34.6	24 57.2	20 50.1	5 51.4	24 9.3	28 0.7	7 15.8	4 39.9
24 M	10 11 17	4 19 50	14 32 11	20 38 15	8 55.4	4 25.3	26 11.6	21 36.9	5 50.0	24 4.5	28 4.2	7 14.4	4 39.4
25 Tu	10 15 13	5 20 11	26 48 43	3♑ 4 13	8 54.5	6 16.9	27 26.0	22 23.7	5 48.7	23 59.8	28 7.6	7 12.9	4 38.8
26 W	10 19 10	6 20 32	9♑25 17	15 52 23	8 51.8	8 9.3	28 40.3	23 10.5	5 47.7	23 55.1	28 11.1	7 11.5	4 38.3
27 Th	10 23 6	7 20 50	22 25 54	29 6 4	8 46.6	10 2.4	29 54.7	23 57.3	5 46.9	23 50.4	28 14.5	7 10.1	4 37.9
28 F	10 27 3	8 21 7	5♒52 58	12♒46 31	8 38.5	11 56.3	1♈ 9.0	24 44.0	5 46.2	23 45.7	28 17.9	7 8.7	4 37.4

Astro Data	Planet Ingress	Last Aspect	☽ Ingress	Last Aspect	☽ Ingress	☽ Phases & Eclipses	Astro Data
Dy Hr Mn	Dy Hr Mn	Dy Hr Mn	Dy Hr Mn	Dy Hr Mn	Dy Hr Mn	Dy Hr Mn	1 JANUARY 1919
♃□♅ 5 6:16	♀ ♒ 10 0:28	1 7:51 ♄ △	♑ 1 12:01	2 6:07 ♀ ☌	♓ 2 7:38	2 8:24 ● 10♑54	Julian Day # 6940
☽0N 7 7:20	☿ ♑ 13 18:13	3 3:38 ♀ ☌	♒ 3 19:15	2 19:30 ♃ △	♈ 4 10:02	9 10:55 ☽ 18♈09	Delta T 21.0 sec
☽0S 20 10:28	☉ ♒ 21 2:21	5 20:07 ♄ ☍	♓ 6 0:18	6 7:24 ♅ ⚹	♉ 6 12:22	16 8:44 ○ 25♋11	SVP 06♓23'10"
♃⚻♆ 23 1:38	♂ ♓ 27 11:20	7 23:38 ♀ ⚹	♈ 8 4:00	8 10:39 ♅ □	♊ 8 15:31	24 4:22 ☽ 3♏08	Obliquity 23°26'56"
♄☍♅ 25 13:37		10 2:35 ♄ △	♉ 10 7:01	10 15:01 ♅ △	♋ 10 19:46	31 23:07 ● 11♒03	⚷ Chiron 29♓09.6
	♀ ♓ 2 23:08	12 5:10 ♄ □	♊ 12 9:49	11 17:00 ♂ △	♌ 13 1:17		☽ Mean ☊ 11♐42.9
☽0N 3 14:29	☿ ♒ 3 19:27	14 8:01 ♄ ⚹	♋ 14 12:56	15 3:57 ♅ ☍	♍ 15 8:32	7 18:52 ☽ 17♉58	
☽0S 16 19:41	☉ ♓ 19 16:48	16 8:44 ☉ ☍	♌ 16 17:16	16 17:07 ♀ ☍	♎ 17 18:06	14 23:38 ○ 25♌15	1 FEBRUARY 1919
	☿ ♓ 21 14:10	18 18:05 ♄ ☌	♍ 18 23:57	20 1:42 ♅ △	♏ 20 6:04	23 1:47 ☽ 3♐24	Julian Day # 6971
	♀ ♈ 27 1:43	19 16:00 ♃ ⚹	♎ 21 9:43	22 14:53 ♅ □	♐ 22 18:57		Delta T 21.0 sec
		23 15:53 ♂ △	♏ 23 22:00	25 2:33 ♅ ⚹	♑ 25 6:08		SVP 06♓23'05"
		26 8:51 ♂ □	♐ 26 10:35	27 2:56 ♂ ⚹	♒ 27 13:36		Obliquity 23°26'56"
		28 14:23 ♅ ⚹	♑ 28 20:54				⚷ Chiron 0♈08.1
		30 16:22 ☿ ☌	♒ 31 3:44				☽ Mean ☊ 10♐04.4

MARCH 1919 — LONGITUDE

Day	Sid.Time	☉	0 hr ☽	Noon ☽	True ☊	☿	♀	♂	♃	♄	♅	♆	♇
1 Sa	10 31 0	9♓21 23	19♒46 27	26♒52 22	8♐28.1	13♓50.7	2♈23.2	25♓30.7	5♋45.8	23♌41.1	28♒21.3	7♌ 7.3	4♋36.9
2 Su	10 34 56	10 21 37	4♓ 3 36	11♓19 24	8R 16.1	15 45.7	3 37.4	26 17.3	5D 45.6	23R 36.6	28 24.8	7R 5.9	4R 36.5
3 M	10 38 53	11 21 49	18 38 51	26 0 56	8 3.8	17 41.0	4 51.6	27 3.9	5 45.5	23 32.0	28 28.2	7 4.6	4 36.1
4 Tu	10 42 49	12 21 59	3♈24 35	10♈48 45	7 52.6	19 36.6	6 5.8	27 50.5	5 45.7	23 27.6	28 31.5	7 3.2	4 35.8
5 W	10 46 46	13 22 7	18 12 24	25 34 35	7 43.7	21 32.2	7 19.9	28 37.1	5 46.0	23 23.1	28 34.9	7 1.9	4 35.4
6 Th	10 50 42	14 22 13	2♉54 31	10♉11 31	7 37.6	23 27.6	8 33.9	29 23.6	5 46.6	23 18.7	28 38.3	7 0.6	4 35.1
7 F	10 54 39	15 22 17	17 25 1	24 34 41	7 34.4	25 22.6	9 48.0	0♈10.1	5 47.4	23 14.4	28 41.7	6 59.4	4 34.8
8 Sa	10 58 35	16 22 19	1♊40 17	8♊41 40	7D 33.3	27 16.8	11 2.0	0 56.5	5 48.3	23 10.1	28 45.0	6 58.2	4 34.5
9 Su	11 2 32	17 22 19	15 38 52	22 31 56	7R 33.3	29 10.0	12 15.9	1 42.9	5 49.5	23 5.9	28 48.3	6 56.9	4 34.2
10 M	11 6 29	18 22 17	29 21 2	6♋ 6 18	7 33.0	1♈ 1.7	13 29.8	2 29.3	5 50.8	23 1.7	28 51.7	6 55.8	4 34.0
11 Tu	11 10 25	19 22 12	12♋47 57	19 26 10	7 31.1	2 51.6	14 43.6	3 15.6	5 52.4	22 57.6	28 55.0	6 54.6	4 33.8
12 W	11 14 22	20 22 6	26 1 8	2♌33 0	7 26.7	4 39.2	15 57.5	4 1.9	5 54.1	22 53.6	28 58.3	6 53.5	4 33.6
13 Th	11 18 18	21 21 57	9♌ 1 55	15 27 58	7 19.5	6 24.0	17 11.2	4 48.2	5 56.0	22 49.6	29 1.5	6 52.3	4 33.4
14 F	11 22 15	22 21 45	21 51 14	28 11 47	7 9.5	8 5.7	18 24.9	5 34.4	5 58.1	22 45.7	29 4.8	6 51.3	4 33.3
15 Sa	11 26 11	23 21 32	4♍29 39	10♍44 51	6 57.5	9 43.6	19 38.6	6 20.6	6 0.4	22 41.9	29 8.0	6 50.2	4 33.2
16 Su	11 30 8	24 21 17	16 57 25	23 7 24	6 44.3	11 17.3	20 52.2	7 6.7	6 2.9	22 38.1	29 11.2	6 49.1	4 33.1
17 M	11 34 4	25 20 59	29 14 50	5♎19 49	6 31.3	12 46.2	22 5.7	7 52.8	6 5.6	22 34.4	29 14.4	6 48.1	4 33.0
18 Tu	11 38 1	26 20 40	11♎22 28	17 22 56	6 19.5	14 10.0	23 19.2	8 38.9	6 8.4	22 30.8	29 17.6	6 47.2	4 32.9
19 W	11 41 58	27 20 18	23 21 26	29 18 14	6 9.8	15 28.2	24 32.7	9 24.9	6 11.5	22 27.2	29 20.8	6 46.2	4D 32.9
20 Th	11 45 54	28 19 55	5♏13 38	11♏ 8 0	6 2.7	16 40.3	25 46.1	10 10.8	6 14.7	22 23.7	29 23.9	6 45.3	4 32.9
21 F	11 49 51	29 19 30	17 1 45	22 55 22	5 58.4	17 46.0	26 59.5	10 56.8	6 18.1	22 20.4	29 27.0	6 44.4	4 32.9
22 Sa	11 53 47	0♈19 3	28 49 22	4♐44 19	5D 56.5	18 44.9	28 12.8	11 42.7	6 21.7	22 17.0	29 30.1	6 43.5	4 33.0
23 Su	11 57 44	1 18 35	10♐40 49	16 39 30	5 56.4	19 36.7	29 26.0	12 28.5	6 25.5	22 13.8	29 33.2	6 42.6	4 33.0
24 M	12 1 40	2 18 4	22 41 2	28 46 5	5R 57.0	20 21.3	0♉39.3	13 14.3	6 29.4	22 10.7	29 36.3	6 41.8	4 33.1
25 Tu	12 5 37	3 17 32	4♑55 20	11♑ 9 25	5 57.3	20 58.3	1 52.4	14 0.1	6 33.5	22 7.6	29 39.3	6 41.0	4 33.2
26 W	12 9 33	4 16 58	17 28 59	23 54 36	5 56.4	21 27.8	3 5.5	14 45.8	6 37.8	22 4.6	29 42.3	6 40.3	4 33.4
27 Th	12 13 30	5 16 23	0♒26 46	7♒ 5 52	5 53.5	21 49.6	4 18.6	15 31.5	6 42.3	22 1.7	29 45.3	6 39.6	4 33.5
28 F	12 17 27	6 15 45	13 52 11	20 45 50	5 48.3	22 3.7	5 31.6	16 17.1	6 46.9	21 59.0	29 48.2	6 38.9	4 33.7
29 Sa	12 21 23	7 15 6	27 46 45	4♓54 40	5 41.1	22R 10.2	6 44.5	17 2.7	6 51.7	21 56.2	29 51.2	6 38.2	4 33.9
30 Su	12 25 20	8 14 25	12♓ 9 8	19 29 28	5 32.4	22 9.3	7 57.4	17 48.3	6 56.6	21 53.6	29 54.1	6 37.6	4 34.1
31 M	12 29 16	9 13 42	26 54 47	4♈24 5	5 23.3	22 1.2	9 10.3	18 33.8	7 1.8	21 51.1	29 56.9	6 37.0	4 34.4

APRIL 1919 — LONGITUDE

Day	Sid.Time	☉	0 hr ☽	Noon ☽	True ☊	☿	♀	♂	♃	♄	♅	♆	♇
1 Tu	12 33 13	10♈12 57	11♈56 10	19♈29 47	5♐14.9	21♈46.3	10♉23.1	19♈19.2	7♋ 7.1	21♌48.7	29♒59.8	6♌36.4	4♋34.7
2 W	12 37 9	11 12 10	27 3 42	4♉36 40	5R 8.2	21R 25.0	11 35.8	20 4.7	7 12.5	21R 46.4	0♓ 2.6	6R 35.8	4 35.0
3 Th	12 41 6	12 11 20	12♉ 7 31	19 35 15	5 3.9	20 57.8	12 48.5	20 50.0	7 18.2	21 44.1	0 5.4	6 35.3	4 35.3
4 F	12 45 2	13 10 29	26 59 0	4♊18 5	5D 1.9	20 25.4	14 1.1	21 35.4	7 23.9	21 42.0	0 8.2	6 34.9	4 35.6
5 Sa	12 48 59	14 9 36	11♊31 59	18 40 22	5 1.8	19 48.4	15 13.7	22 20.6	7 29.9	21 40.0	0 10.9	6 34.4	4 36.0
6 Su	12 52 55	15 8 40	25 43 4	2♋40 3	5 2.7	19 7.8	16 26.1	23 5.9	7 36.0	21 38.0	0 13.6	6 34.0	4 36.4
7 M	12 56 52	16 7 42	9♋31 25	16 17 19	5R 3.7	18 24.2	17 38.6	23 51.1	7 42.2	21 36.2	0 16.2	6 33.6	4 36.8
8 Tu	13 0 49	17 6 41	22 58 0	29 33 46	5 3.7	17 38.7	18 50.9	24 36.2	7 48.6	21 34.5	0 18.9	6 33.3	4 37.2
9 W	13 4 45	18 5 38	6♌ 4 56	12♌31 49	5 2.0	16 52.1	20 3.2	25 21.3	7 55.2	21 32.9	0 21.5	6 33.0	4 37.7
10 Th	13 8 42	19 4 33	18 54 46	25 14 6	4 58.3	16 5.4	21 15.4	26 6.3	8 1.9	21 31.4	0 24.0	6 32.7	4 38.2
11 F	13 12 38	20 3 25	1♍30 6	7♍43 5	4 52.7	15 19.4	22 27.6	26 51.3	8 8.7	21 29.9	0 26.6	6 32.4	4 38.7
12 Sa	13 16 35	21 2 16	13 53 18	20 0 59	4 45.6	14 35.0	23 39.7	27 36.2	8 15.7	21 28.6	0 29.1	6 32.2	4 39.2
13 Su	13 20 31	22 1 4	26 6 21	2♎ 9 38	4 37.7	13 52.9	24 51.7	28 21.1	8 22.8	21 27.4	0 31.5	6 32.0	4 39.7
14 M	13 24 28	22 59 50	8♎11 1	14 10 41	4 29.7	13 13.8	26 3.6	29 5.9	8 30.1	21 26.3	0 34.0	6 31.9	4 40.3
15 Tu	13 28 24	23 58 33	20 8 50	26 5 40	4 22.6	12 38.3	27 15.5	29 50.7	8 37.5	21 25.3	0 36.4	6 31.8	4 40.9
16 W	13 32 21	24 57 15	2♏ 1 24	7♏56 16	4 16.9	12 6.8	28 27.2	0♉35.4	8 45.0	21 24.4	0 38.7	6 31.7	4 41.5
17 Th	13 36 18	25 55 56	13 50 31	19 44 27	4 12.9	11 39.8	29 39.0	1 20.1	8 52.7	21 23.6	0 41.0	6 31.6	4 42.1
18 F	13 40 14	26 54 34	25 38 23	1♐32 39	4D 10.9	11 17.5	0♊50.6	2 4.7	9 0.5	21 22.9	0 43.3	6D 31.6	4 42.8
19 Sa	13 44 11	27 53 10	7♐27 40	13 23 50	4 10.5	11 0.1	2 2.2	2 49.3	9 8.4	21 22.4	0 45.6	6 31.6	4 43.5
20 Su	13 48 7	28 51 45	19 21 38	25 21 32	4 11.5	10 47.8	3 13.7	3 33.8	9 16.4	21 21.9	0 47.8	6 31.7	4 44.2
21 M	13 52 4	29 50 18	1♑24 6	7♑29 51	4 13.1	10D 40.5	4 25.1	4 18.3	9 24.6	21 21.5	0 49.9	6 31.7	4 44.9
22 Tu	13 56 0	0♉48 49	13 39 21	19 53 11	4 14.7	10 38.4	5 36.4	5 2.7	9 32.9	21 21.3	0 52.1	6 31.9	4 45.6
23 W	13 59 57	1 47 19	26 11 53	2♒36 1	4R 15.8	10 41.4	6 47.7	5 47.1	9 41.4	21D 21.1	0 54.2	6 32.0	4 46.4
24 Th	14 3 53	2 45 47	9♒ 6 5	15 42 29	4 15.8	10 49.3	7 58.8	6 31.4	9 49.9	21 21.1	0 56.2	6 32.2	4 47.1
25 F	14 7 50	3 44 13	22 25 37	29 15 42	4 14.4	11 2.1	9 9.9	7 15.7	9 58.6	21 21.2	0 58.2	6 32.4	4 47.9
26 Sa	14 11 47	4 42 38	6♓12 51	13♓17 0	4 11.8	11 19.6	10 21.0	7 60.0	10 7.4	21 21.3	1 0.2	6 32.6	4 48.7
27 Su	14 15 43	5 41 1	20 27 58	27 45 17	4 8.3	11 41.6	11 31.9	8 44.2	10 16.3	21 21.6	1 2.1	6 32.9	4 49.6
28 M	14 19 40	6 39 23	5♈ 8 23	12♈36 26	4 4.4	12 8.1	12 42.8	9 28.3	10 25.4	21 22.0	1 4.0	6 33.2	4 50.4
29 Tu	14 23 36	7 37 43	20 8 28	27 43 22	4 0.7	12 38.8	13 53.6	10 12.4	10 34.5	21 22.5	1 5.9	6 33.6	4 51.3
30 W	14 27 33	8 36 1	5♉19 55	12♉56 51	3 57.9	13 13.6	15 4.2	10 56.4	10 43.7	21 23.1	1 7.7	6 34.0	4 52.2

Astro Data	Dy Hr Mn
♀0N	1 1:09
☽0N	2 23:50
♃ D	2 16:35
♂0N	8 18:50
☿0N	9 15:22
☽0S	16 3:08
♇ D	19 17:34
♃⊻♆	26 11:39
♃∠♄	29 14:29
☿ R	29 9:01
☽0N	30 10:19
☽0S	12 8:46
♆ D	18 1:28
☿ D	21 21:57

Planet Ingress	Dy Hr Mn
♂ ♈	6 18:48
☿ ♈	9 10:42
☉ ♈	21 16:19
♀ ♉	23 11:08
♅ ♓	1 1:47
♂ ♉	15 5:00
♀ ♊	17 7:03
☉ ♉	21 3:59
♄ D	23 21:10
☽0N	26 20:13

Last Aspect Dy Hr Mn		☽ Ingress	Dy Hr Mn
1 14:33	♅ ☌	♓	1 17:14
3 14:28	♂ ☌	♈	3 18:28
5 16:59	♅ ⚹	♉	5 19:14
7 19:01	♅ □	♊	7 21:10
9 23:08	♅ △	♋	10 1:09
11 12:51	☉ △	♌	12 7:18
14 13:44	♅ ☍	♍	14 15:26
16 15:41	☉ ☍	♎	17 1:29
19 12:08	♅ △	♏	19 13:24
22 1:23	♅ □	♐	22 2:23
24 13:42	♅ ⚹	♑	24 14:25
26 7:42	☿ □	♒	26 23:11
29 3:31	♅ ☌	♓	29 3:45
29 16:26	♀ ⚹	♈	31 4:57

Last Aspect Dy Hr Mn		☽ Ingress	Dy Hr Mn
1 15:38	♄ △	♉	2 4:40
3 15:26	♄ □	♊	4 4:56
5 19:16	♂ ⚹	♋	6 7:22
8 3:09	♂ □	♌	8 12:48
10 14:32	♂ △	♍	10 21:07
12 21:16	♀ △	♎	13 7:43
15 8:25	☉ ☍	♏	15 19:54
17 15:21	♄ □	♐	18 8:52
20 20:38	☉ △	♑	20 21:14
21 18:09	☿ □	♒	23 7:09
24 22:06	♄ ☍	♓	25 13:17
26 7:41	♀ □	♈	27 15:40
29 1:58	♄ △	♉	29 15:36

☽ Phases & Eclipses Dy Hr Mn	
2 11:11	● 10♓50
9 3:14	☽ 17♊30
16 15:41	○ 25♍00
24 20:34	☽ 3♑09
31 21:04	● 10♈06
7 12:38	☽ 16♋39
15 8:25	○ 24♎19
23 11:21	☽ 2♒15
30 5:30	● 8♉49

Astro Data

1 MARCH 1919
Julian Day # 6999
Delta T 21.0 sec
SVP 06♓23'01"
Obliquity 23°26'56"
⚷ Chiron 1♈31.9
☽ Mean ☊ 8♐35.4

1 APRIL 1919
Julian Day # 7030
Delta T 21.0 sec
SVP 06♓22'59"
Obliquity 23°26'56"
⚷ Chiron 3♈20.1
☽ Mean ☊ 6♐56.9

LONGITUDE — MAY 1919

Day	Sid.Time	☉	0 hr ☽	Noon ☽	True ☊	☿	♀	♂	♃	♄	♅	♆	♇
1 Th	14 31 29	9♉34 18	20♉32 55	28♉ 6 53	3♐56.2	13♈52.2	16♊14.9	11♉40.4	10♋53.1	21♌23.8	1♓ 9.4	6♌34.4	4♋53.1
2 F	14 35 26	10 32 33	5♊37 39	13♊ 4 14	3D 55.7	14 34.7	17 25.4	12 24.3	11 2.6	21 24.6	1 11.1	6 34.8	4 54.0
3 Sa	14 39 22	11 30 46	20 25 49	27 41 46	3 56.3	15 20.7	18 35.8	13 8.2	11 12.2	21 25.6	1 12.8	6 35.3	4 55.0
4 Su	14 43 19	12 28 57	4♋51 36	11♋55 3	3 57.5	16 10.2	19 46.1	13 52.0	11 21.9	21 26.6	1 14.4	6 35.8	4 55.9
5 M	14 47 16	13 27 6	18 52 0	25 42 26	3 58.9	17 2.9	20 56.4	14 35.8	11 31.6	21 27.7	1 16.0	6 36.4	4 56.9
6 Tu	14 51 12	14 25 13	2♌26 31	9♌ 4 28	3 59.9	17 58.9	22 6.5	15 19.5	11 41.5	21 29.0	1 17.6	6 36.9	4 57.9
7 W	14 55 9	15 23 18	15 36 37	22 3 19	4R 0.3	18 57.9	23 16.6	16 3.2	11 51.5	21 30.3	1 19.1	6 37.5	4 58.9
8 Th	14 59 5	16 21 22	28 25 1	4♍42 8	3 59.9	19 59.9	24 26.5	16 46.8	12 1.6	21 31.8	1 20.5	6 38.2	4 59.9
9 F	15 3 2	17 19 23	10♍55 8	17 4 27	3 58.7	21 4.7	25 36.3	17 30.4	12 11.8	21 33.3	1 21.9	6 38.9	5 1.0
10 Sa	15 6 58	18 17 22	23 10 32	29 13 50	3 56.9	22 12.2	26 46.0	18 13.8	12 22.1	21 35.0	1 23.3	6 39.6	5 2.1
11 Su	15 10 55	19 15 20	5♎14 45	11♎13 41	3 54.7	23 22.5	27 55.6	18 57.3	12 32.4	21 36.7	1 24.6	6 40.3	5 3.1
12 M	15 14 51	20 13 15	17 11 0	23 7 3	3 52.6	24 35.3	29 5.1	19 40.7	12 42.9	21 38.6	1 25.9	6 41.1	5 4.2
13 Tu	15 18 48	21 11 10	29 2 10	4♏56 40	3 50.7	25 50.7	0♋14.5	20 24.1	12 53.4	21 40.6	1 27.1	6 41.9	5 5.3
14 W	15 22 45	22 9 2	10♏50 50	16 44 58	3 49.3	27 8.6	1 23.8	21 7.4	13 4.0	21 42.6	1 28.3	6 42.7	5 6.5
15 Th	15 26 41	23 6 53	22 39 20	28 34 13	3D 48.5	28 28.8	2 32.9	21 50.6	13 14.8	21 44.8	1 29.4	6 43.5	5 7.6
16 F	15 30 38	24 4 43	4♐29 52	10♐26 36	3 48.3	29 51.5	3 41.9	22 33.8	13 25.5	21 47.1	1 30.5	6 44.4	5 8.7
17 Sa	15 34 34	25 2 31	16 24 40	22 24 24	3 48.5	1♉16.5	4 50.8	23 16.9	13 36.4	21 49.4	1 31.5	6 45.4	5 9.9
18 Su	15 38 31	26 0 18	28 26 5	4♑30 4	3 49.1	2 43.9	5 59.6	24 0.0	13 47.4	21 51.9	1 32.5	6 46.3	5 11.1
19 M	15 42 27	26 58 3	10♑36 42	16 46 19	3 49.8	4 13.5	7 8.3	24 43.0	13 58.4	21 54.5	1 33.4	6 47.3	5 12.3
20 Tu	15 46 24	27 55 48	22 59 19	29 16 5	3 50.5	5 45.5	8 16.8	25 26.0	14 9.6	21 57.1	1 34.3	6 48.3	5 13.5
21 W	15 50 20	28 53 31	5♒36 59	12♒ 2 25	3 51.0	7 19.7	9 25.2	26 9.0	14 20.7	21 59.9	1 35.2	6 49.3	5 14.7
22 Th	15 54 17	29 51 13	18 32 44	25 8 17	3R 51.3	8 56.1	10 33.5	26 51.9	14 32.0	22 2.7	1 36.0	6 50.4	5 16.0
23 F	15 58 14	0♊48 54	1♓49 22	8♓36 12	3 51.4	10 34.8	11 41.6	27 34.7	14 43.4	22 5.7	1 36.7	6 51.5	5 17.2
24 Sa	16 2 10	1 46 34	15 28 56	22 27 40	3 51.3	12 15.7	12 49.6	28 17.5	14 54.8	22 8.7	1 37.4	6 52.6	5 18.5
25 Su	16 6 7	2 44 13	29 32 18	6♈42 40	3 51.2	13 58.9	13 57.5	29 0.2	15 6.3	22 11.8	1 38.1	6 53.8	5 19.7
26 M	16 10 3	3 41 52	13♈58 25	21 19 6	3D 51.1	15 44.3	15 5.2	29 42.9	15 17.8	22 15.1	1 38.7	6 55.0	5 21.0
27 Tu	16 14 0	4 39 29	28 44 2	6♉12 28	3 51.2	17 32.0	16 12.8	0♊25.5	15 29.5	22 18.4	1 39.2	6 56.2	5 22.3
28 W	16 17 56	5 37 5	13♉43 29	21 16 3	3 51.3	19 21.9	17 20.2	1 8.1	15 41.2	22 21.8	1 39.7	6 57.4	5 23.6
29 Th	16 21 53	6 34 40	28 49 4	6♊21 26	3R 51.4	21 13.9	18 27.5	1 50.6	15 52.9	22 25.3	1 40.2	6 58.7	5 24.9
30 F	16 25 49	7 32 15	13♊52 1	21 19 46	3 51.3	23 8.2	19 34.7	2 33.1	16 4.7	22 28.9	1 40.6	6 60.0	5 26.3
31 Sa	16 29 46	8 29 48	28 43 40	6♋ 2 53	3 51.1	25 4.6	20 41.6	3 15.6	16 16.6	22 32.6	1 41.0	7 1.3	5 27.6

LONGITUDE — JUNE 1919

Day	Sid.Time	☉	0 hr ☽	Noon ☽	True ☊	☿	♀	♂	♃	♄	♅	♆	♇
1 Su	16 33 43	9♊27 20	13♋16 41	20♋24 31	3♐50.6	27♉ 3.1	21♋48.5	3♊57.9	16♋28.6	22♌36.3	1♓41.3	7♌ 2.6	5♋29.0
2 M	16 37 39	10 24 51	27 25 58	4♌20 49	3R 49.9	29 3.6	22 55.1	4 40.3	16 40.6	22 40.2	1 41.5	7 4.0	5 30.3
3 Tu	16 41 36	11 22 20	11♌ 8 58	17 50 30	3 49.2	1♊ 6.0	24 1.6	5 22.6	16 52.7	22 44.1	1 41.8	7 5.4	5 31.7
4 W	16 45 32	12 19 48	24 25 36	0♍54 33	3 48.5	3 10.3	25 7.9	6 4.8	17 4.8	22 48.2	1 41.9	7 6.8	5 33.1
5 Th	16 49 29	13 17 15	7♍17 44	13 35 36	3D 48.1	5 16.2	26 14.0	6 46.9	17 17.0	22 52.3	1 42.0	7 8.3	5 34.4
6 F	16 53 25	14 14 41	19 48 39	25 57 23	3 48.1	7 23.7	27 19.9	7 29.1	17 29.2	22 56.5	1R 42.1	7 9.8	5 35.8
7 Sa	16 57 22	15 12 5	2♎ 2 23	8♎ 4 12	3 48.5	9 32.6	28 25.6	8 11.1	17 41.5	23 0.7	1 42.1	7 11.3	5 37.2
8 Su	17 1 18	16 9 29	14 3 24	20 0 30	3 49.4	11 42.6	29 31.2	8 53.1	17 53.8	23 5.1	1 42.1	7 12.8	5 38.6
9 M	17 5 15	17 6 51	25 56 4	1♏50 35	3 50.6	13 53.4	0♌36.5	9 35.1	18 6.2	23 9.5	1 42.0	7 14.3	5 40.0
10 Tu	17 9 12	18 4 12	7♏44 32	13 38 23	3 51.9	16 5.0	1 41.6	10 17.0	18 18.6	23 14.1	1 41.9	7 15.9	5 41.5
11 W	17 13 8	19 1 33	19 32 33	25 27 25	3 52.9	18 16.9	2 46.5	10 58.9	18 31.1	23 18.7	1 41.7	7 17.5	5 42.9
12 Th	17 17 5	19 58 53	1♐23 21	7♐20 40	3R 53.4	20 29.0	3 51.2	11 40.7	18 43.6	23 23.3	1 41.5	7 19.1	5 44.3
13 F	17 21 1	20 56 11	13 19 41	19 20 39	3 53.1	22 40.9	4 55.6	12 22.4	18 56.2	23 28.1	1 41.2	7 20.7	5 45.8
14 Sa	17 24 58	21 53 30	25 23 48	1♑29 23	3 52.0	24 52.4	5 59.9	13 4.1	19 8.8	23 32.9	1 40.9	7 22.4	5 47.2
15 Su	17 28 54	22 50 47	7♑37 33	13 48 31	3 50.1	27 3.2	7 3.9	13 45.8	19 21.5	23 37.8	1 40.5	7 24.1	5 48.6
16 M	17 32 51	23 48 4	20 2 27	26 19 29	3 47.4	29 13.0	8 7.6	14 27.4	19 34.2	23 42.8	1 40.1	7 25.8	5 50.1
17 Tu	17 36 47	24 45 20	2♒39 47	9♒ 3 29	3 44.3	1♋21.7	9 11.1	15 9.0	19 46.9	23 47.8	1 39.6	7 27.5	5 51.6
18 W	17 40 44	25 42 36	15 30 45	22 1 42	3 41.2	3 29.1	10 14.3	15 50.5	19 59.7	23 52.9	1 39.1	7 29.2	5 53.0
19 Th	17 44 41	26 39 52	28 36 28	5♓15 12	3 38.6	5 34.9	11 17.3	16 32.0	20 12.5	23 58.1	1 38.6	7 31.0	5 54.5
20 F	17 48 37	27 37 8	11♓58 0	18 44 59	3 36.7	7 39.0	12 20.0	17 13.4	20 25.3	24 3.4	1 38.0	7 32.8	5 56.0
21 Sa	17 52 34	28 34 23	25 36 11	2♈31 40	3D 35.9	9 41.4	13 22.5	17 54.8	20 38.2	24 8.7	1 37.3	7 34.6	5 57.4
22 Su	17 56 30	29 31 38	9♈31 24	16 35 19	3 36.2	11 41.9	14 24.6	18 36.1	20 51.1	24 14.1	1 36.6	7 36.4	5 58.9
23 M	18 0 27	0♋28 53	23 43 15	0♉54 57	3 37.2	13 40.4	15 26.5	19 17.4	21 4.1	24 19.6	1 35.9	7 38.3	6 0.4
24 Tu	18 4 23	1 26 8	8♉10 6	15 28 16	3 38.6	15 36.8	16 28.1	19 58.6	21 17.0	24 25.1	1 35.1	7 40.1	6 1.9
25 W	18 8 20	2 23 23	22 48 52	0♊11 16	3R 39.8	17 31.2	17 29.4	20 39.8	21 30.0	24 30.7	1 34.3	7 42.0	6 3.3
26 Th	18 12 16	3 20 37	7♊34 42	14 58 22	3 40.0	19 23.5	18 30.3	21 20.9	21 43.1	24 36.4	1 33.4	7 43.9	6 4.8
27 F	18 16 13	4 17 52	22 21 23	29 42 49	3 39.0	21 13.6	19 31.0	22 2.0	21 56.2	24 42.1	1 32.5	7 45.8	6 6.3
28 Sa	18 20 10	5 15 7	7♋ 1 47	14♋17 25	3 36.4	23 1.6	20 31.3	22 43.1	22 9.3	24 47.9	1 31.5	7 47.7	6 7.8
29 Su	18 24 6	6 12 21	21 28 55	28 35 35	3 32.5	24 47.4	21 31.3	23 24.1	22 22.4	24 53.7	1 30.5	7 49.7	6 9.3
30 M	18 28 3	7 9 35	5♌36 50	12♌32 15	3 27.6	26 31.0	22 30.9	24 5.0	22 35.5	24 59.6	1 29.4	7 51.6	6 10.8

Astro Data	Planet Ingress	Last Aspect	☽ Ingress	Last Aspect	☽ Ingress	☽ Phases & Eclipses	Astro Data
Dy Hr Mn	Dy Hr Mn	Dy Hr Mn	Dy Hr Mn	Dy Hr Mn	Dy Hr Mn	Dy Hr Mn	1 MAY 1919
☽0S 9 14:01	♀ ♋ 12 18:59	1 1:21 ♄ □	♊ 1 15:00	2 3:17 ☿ ✶	♌ 2 4:26	6 23:33 ☽ 15♌22	Julian Day # 7060
☽0N 24 4:25	☿ ♉ 16 2:25	3 1:38 ♄ ✶	♋ 3 15:50	3 21:00 ♄ ☌	♍ 4 10:18	15 1:01 ○ 23♏09	Delta T 21.0 sec
	☉ ♊ 22 3:39	4 20:37 ☿ □	♌ 5 19:38	6 16:09 ♀ ✶	♎ 6 19:58	15 1:14 ☍A 0.910	SVP 06♓22'56"
♃□♅ 2 1:55	♂ ♊ 26 9:38	7 15:44 ♀ ✶	♍ 8 3:01	8 18:20 ♄ ✶	♏ 9 8:15	22 22:04 ☽ 0♓44	Obliquity 23°26'56"
☽0S 5 20:36		10 7:52 ♀ □	♎ 10 13:32	11 7:42 ♄ □	♐ 11 21:12	29 13:12 ● 7♊06	⚷ Chiron 5♈00.0
♅ R 6 19:12	☿ ♊ 2 11:06	12 16:45 ☿ ☍	♏ 13 1:57	13 22:44 ☿ ☍	♑ 14 9:04	29 13:08:33 ☌T 6'51"	☽ Mean ☊ 5♐21.5
☽0N 20 10:59	♀ ♌ 8 10:35	15 1:01 ☉ ☍	♐ 15 14:54	15 23:05 ♃ ☍	♒ 16 18:58		
	☿ ♋ 16 8:44	17 10:52 ♄ △	♑ 18 3:06	18 20:12 ☉ △	♓ 19 2:31	5 12:22 ☽ 13♍47	1 JUNE 1919
	☉ ♋ 22 11:54	20 10:14 ☉ △	♒ 20 13:23	21 5:33 ☉ □	♈ 21 7:38	13 16:28 ○ 21♐36	Julian Day # 7091
		22 15:58 ♂ □	♓ 22 20:45	23 1:01 ♄ △	♉ 23 10:29	21 5:33 ☽ 28♓48	Delta T 21.0 sec
		24 23:03 ♂ ✶	♈ 25 0:47	25 2:47 ♄ □	♊ 25 11:42	27 20:52 ● 5♋08	SVP 06♓22'51"
		26 13:34 ♄ △	♉ 27 2:02	27 3:51 ♄ ✶	♋ 27 12:28		Obliquity 23°26'55"
		28 13:48 ♄ □	♊ 29 1:53	29 6:20 ☿ ☌	♌ 29 14:24		⚷ Chiron 6♈18.8
		30 13:55 ♄ ✶	♋ 31 2:05				☽ Mean ☊ 3♐43.1

JULY 1919 — LONGITUDE

Day	Sid.Time	☉	0 hr ☽	Noon ☽	True ☊	☿	♀	♂	♃	♄	♅	♆	♇
1 Tu	18 31 59	8♋ 6 49	19♌21 32	26♌ 4 32	3♐22.4	28♋12.4	23♌30.1	24♊45.9	22♋48.7	25♌ 5.6	1♓28.3	7♌53.6	6♋12.3
2 W	18 35 56	9 4 2	2♍41 16	9♍11 49	3R 17.6	29 51.7	24 29.0	25 26.8	23 1.9	25 11.6	1R 27.2	7 55.6	6 13.8
3 Th	18 39 52	10 1 15	15 36 29	21 55 35	3 13.8	1♌28.7	25 27.5	26 7.6	23 15.1	25 17.7	1 26.0	7 57.6	6 15.2
4 F	18 43 49	10 58 28	28 9 35	4♎18 57	3 11.3	3 3.6	26 25.5	26 48.4	23 28.3	25 23.8	1 24.8	7 59.6	6 16.7
5 Sa	18 47 45	11 55 40	10♎24 17	16 26 9	3D 10.4	4 36.2	27 23.1	27 29.1	23 41.6	25 30.0	1 23.5	8 1.6	6 18.2
6 Su	18 51 42	12 52 52	22 25 11	28 22 1	3 10.9	6 6.6	28 20.3	28 9.7	23 54.8	25 36.3	1 22.2	8 3.7	6 19.7
7 M	18 55 39	13 50 4	4♏17 17	10♏11 37	3 12.2	7 34.7	29 17.1	28 50.3	24 8.1	25 42.6	1 20.9	8 5.7	6 21.2
8 Tu	18 59 35	14 47 16	16 5 37	21 59 53	3 13.8	9 0.6	0♍13.4	29 30.9	24 21.4	25 48.9	1 19.5	8 7.8	6 22.6
9 W	19 3 32	15 44 28	27 54 57	3♐51 22	3R 14.8	10 24.2	1 9.2	0♋11.4	24 34.7	25 55.3	1 18.1	8 9.9	6 24.1
10 Th	19 7 28	16 41 39	9♐49 36	15 50 3	3 14.7	11 45.4	2 4.5	0 51.9	24 48.0	26 1.8	1 16.6	8 12.0	6 25.6
11 F	19 11 25	17 38 51	21 53 8	27 59 10	3 12.9	13 4.3	2 59.2	1 32.3	25 1.3	26 8.3	1 15.1	8 14.1	6 27.0
12 Sa	19 15 21	18 36 3	4♑ 8 23	10♑21 0	3 9.2	14 20.8	3 53.5	2 12.7	25 14.7	26 14.8	1 13.6	8 16.2	6 28.5
13 Su	19 19 18	19 33 15	16 37 11	22 56 59	3 3.5	15 34.7	4 47.1	2 53.0	25 28.0	26 21.4	1 12.0	8 18.3	6 30.0
14 M	19 23 14	20 30 27	29 20 27	5♒47 33	2 56.2	16 46.2	5 40.3	3 33.3	25 41.4	26 28.0	1 10.4	8 20.4	6 31.4
15 Tu	19 27 11	21 27 40	12♒18 14	18 52 23	2 48.1	17 55.0	6 32.8	4 13.6	25 54.8	26 34.7	1 8.8	8 22.6	6 32.9
16 W	19 31 8	22 24 52	25 29 52	2♓10 34	2 39.9	19 1.2	7 24.7	4 53.8	26 8.1	26 41.4	1 7.1	8 24.7	6 34.3
17 Th	19 35 4	23 22 6	8♓54 17	15 40 54	2 32.6	20 4.6	8 15.9	5 33.9	26 21.5	26 48.2	1 5.4	8 26.9	6 35.7
18 F	19 39 1	24 19 20	22 30 15	29 22 12	2 26.8	21 5.1	9 6.5	6 14.0	26 34.9	26 55.0	1 3.7	8 29.1	6 37.2
19 Sa	19 42 57	25 16 34	6♈16 38	13♈13 26	2 23.2	22 2.7	9 56.5	6 54.1	26 48.2	27 1.8	1 1.9	8 31.2	6 38.6
20 Su	19 46 54	26 13 50	20 12 31	27 13 45	2D 21.6	22 57.2	10 45.7	7 34.2	27 1.6	27 8.7	1 0.1	8 33.4	6 40.0
21 M	19 50 50	27 11 6	4♉17 4	11♉22 18	2 21.6	23 48.5	11 34.2	8 14.1	27 15.0	27 15.6	0 58.3	8 35.6	6 41.4
22 Tu	19 54 47	28 8 23	18 29 19	25 37 54	2R 22.4	24 36.5	12 22.0	8 54.1	27 28.4	27 22.6	0 56.4	8 37.8	6 42.8
23 W	19 58 43	29 5 41	2♊47 47	9♊58 39	2 22.8	25 21.0	13 8.9	9 34.0	27 41.8	27 29.6	0 54.5	8 40.0	6 44.2
24 Th	20 2 40	0♌ 3 0	17 10 6	24 21 38	2 22.0	26 1.9	13 55.1	10 13.9	27 55.1	27 36.7	0 52.6	8 42.2	6 45.6
25 F	20 6 37	1 0 20	1♋32 43	8♋42 45	2 19.0	26 39.0	14 40.5	10 53.7	28 8.5	27 43.7	0 50.6	8 44.4	6 47.0
26 Sa	20 10 33	1 57 41	15 51 6	22 57 6	2 13.5	27 12.2	15 24.9	11 33.5	28 21.9	27 50.8	0 48.6	8 46.6	6 48.4
27 Su	20 14 30	2 55 2	0♌ 0 5	6♌59 27	2 5.6	27 41.3	16 8.5	12 13.2	28 35.3	27 58.0	0 46.6	8 48.8	6 49.7
28 M	20 18 26	3 52 24	13 54 37	20 45 7	1 56.1	28 6.1	16 51.1	12 52.9	28 48.6	28 5.1	0 44.6	8 51.0	6 51.1
29 Tu	20 22 23	4 49 46	27 30 33	4♍10 41	1 45.8	28 26.4	17 32.8	13 32.5	29 2.0	28 12.3	0 42.5	8 53.3	6 52.4
30 W	20 26 19	5 47 10	10♍45 20	17 14 29	1 36.0	28 42.1	18 13.4	14 12.1	29 15.3	28 19.6	0 40.5	8 55.5	6 53.7
31 Th	20 30 16	6 44 33	23 38 15	29 56 51	1 27.4	28 53.0	18 53.0	14 51.7	29 28.6	28 26.8	0 38.3	8 57.7	6 55.1

AUGUST 1919 — LONGITUDE

Day	Sid.Time	☉	0 hr ☽	Noon ☽	True ☊	☿	♀	♂	♃	♄	♅	♆	♇
1 F	20 34 12	7♌41 58	6♎10 34	12♎19 49	1♐21.0	28♌58.9	19♍31.4	15♋31.2	29♋41.9	28♌34.1	0♓36.2	8♌59.9	6♋56.4
2 Sa	20 38 9	8 39 23	18 25 5	24 26 56	1R 16.8	28R 59.7	20 8.7	16 10.7	29 55.2	28 41.4	0R 34.1	9 2.2	6 57.7
3 Su	20 42 6	9 36 49	0♏25 56	6♏22 44	1D 14.8	28 55.4	20 44.9	16 50.1	0♌ 8.5	28 48.7	0 31.9	9 4.4	6 59.0
4 M	20 46 2	10 34 15	12 17 59	18 12 22	1 14.5	28 45.9	21 19.7	17 29.5	0 21.8	28 56.1	0 29.7	9 6.6	7 0.2
5 Tu	20 49 59	11 31 42	24 6 34	0♐ 1 16	1R 14.8	28 31.1	21 53.3	18 8.8	0 35.0	29 3.5	0 27.5	9 8.8	7 1.5
6 W	20 53 55	12 29 10	5♐57 6	11 54 43	1 14.8	28 11.0	22 25.6	18 48.1	0 48.2	29 10.9	0 25.3	9 11.1	7 2.8
7 Th	20 57 52	13 26 39	17 54 43	23 57 39	1 13.6	27 45.9	22 56.4	19 27.4	1 1.4	29 18.3	0 23.0	9 13.3	7 4.0
8 F	21 1 48	14 24 8	0♑ 4 1	6♑14 14	1 10.3	27 15.9	23 25.8	20 6.6	1 14.6	29 25.7	0 20.8	9 15.5	7 5.2
9 Sa	21 5 45	15 21 39	12 28 41	18 47 36	1 4.5	26 41.3	23 53.7	20 45.8	1 27.8	29 33.2	0 18.5	9 17.7	7 6.5
10 Su	21 9 42	16 19 10	25 11 11	1♒39 31	0 56.2	26 2.5	24 20.0	21 24.9	1 40.9	29 40.7	0 16.2	9 19.9	7 7.7
11 M	21 13 38	17 16 42	8♒12 34	14 50 13	0 45.7	25 20.0	24 44.7	22 4.0	1 54.1	29 48.2	0 13.9	9 22.1	7 8.9
12 Tu	21 17 35	18 14 15	21 32 16	28 18 24	0 34.0	24 34.4	25 7.8	22 43.0	2 7.1	29 55.7	0 11.6	9 24.4	7 10.0
13 W	21 21 31	19 11 50	5♓ 8 16	12♓ 1 25	0 22.2	23 46.4	25 29.1	23 22.0	2 20.2	0♍ 3.2	0 9.2	9 26.6	7 11.2
14 Th	21 25 28	20 9 25	18 57 25	25 55 46	0 11.5	22 56.9	25 48.6	24 1.0	2 33.2	0 10.7	0 6.9	9 28.7	7 12.3
15 F	21 29 24	21 7 2	2♈56 2	9♈57 44	0 2.8	22 6.8	26 6.2	24 39.9	2 46.3	0 18.3	0 4.5	9 30.9	7 13.5
16 Sa	21 33 21	22 4 41	17 0 30	24 3 57	29♏56.8	21 16.9	26 22.0	25 18.8	2 59.2	0 25.8	0 2.2	9 33.1	7 14.6
17 Su	21 37 17	23 2 21	1♉ 7 48	8♉11 50	29 53.5	20 28.3	26 35.8	25 57.6	3 12.2	0 33.4	29♒59.8	9 35.3	7 15.7
18 M	21 41 14	24 0 3	15 15 49	22 19 37	29D 52.3	19 41.9	26 47.5	26 36.4	3 25.1	0 41.0	29 57.4	9 37.5	7 16.8
19 Tu	21 45 10	24 57 46	29 23 7	6♊26 13	29R 52.1	18 58.8	26 57.2	27 15.2	3 38.0	0 48.6	29 55.1	9 39.6	7 17.9
20 W	21 49 7	25 55 31	13♊28 49	20 30 46	29 51.8	18 19.9	27 4.8	27 53.9	3 50.8	0 56.2	29 52.7	9 41.8	7 18.9
21 Th	21 53 4	26 53 18	27 31 56	4♋32 7	29 50.1	17 46.0	27 10.2	28 32.6	4 3.7	1 3.8	29 50.3	9 44.0	7 20.0
22 F	21 57 0	27 51 6	11♋31 6	18 28 35	29 45.9	17 17.8	27R 13.4	29 11.3	4 16.4	1 11.4	29 47.9	9 46.1	7 21.0
23 Sa	22 0 57	28 48 56	25 24 15	2♌17 46	29 38.9	16 56.0	27 14.4	29 49.9	4 29.2	1 19.0	29 45.5	9 48.2	7 22.0
24 Su	22 4 53	29 46 48	9♌ 8 42	15 56 43	29 29.1	16 41.3	27 13.0	0♌28.5	4 41.9	1 26.6	29 43.1	9 50.4	7 23.0
25 M	22 8 50	0♍44 41	22 41 24	29 22 25	29 17.3	16D 33.9	27 9.3	1 7.0	4 54.5	1 34.2	29 40.7	9 52.5	7 24.0
26 Tu	22 12 46	1 42 36	5♍59 28	12♍32 18	29 4.6	16 34.3	27 3.3	1 45.5	5 7.2	1 41.8	29 38.3	9 54.6	7 24.9
27 W	22 16 43	2 40 32	19 0 47	25 24 48	28 52.2	16 42.7	26 54.8	2 23.9	5 19.7	1 49.5	29 35.9	9 56.7	7 25.9
28 Th	22 20 39	3 38 30	1♎44 22	7♎59 36	28 41.2	16 59.2	26 44.0	3 2.3	5 32.3	1 57.1	29 33.5	9 58.7	7 26.8
29 F	22 24 36	4 36 29	14 10 42	20 17 56	28 32.4	17 23.8	26 30.8	3 40.7	5 44.7	2 4.7	29 31.1	10 0.8	7 27.7
30 Sa	22 28 33	5 34 29	26 21 41	2♏22 21	28 26.4	17 56.4	26 15.3	4 19.0	5 57.2	2 12.3	29 28.8	10 2.9	7 28.6
31 Su	22 32 29	6 32 31	8♏20 28	14 16 35	28 22.9	18 37.0	25 57.4	4 57.3	6 9.5	2 19.9	29 26.4	10 4.9	7 29.4

Astro Data

	Dy Hr Mn
☽0S	3 5:08
☽0N	17 17:03
♃⚺♄	21 2:25
☽0S	30 14:48
☿ R	1 16:02
♃⚻♅	4 12:20
♀0S	6 18:33
☽0N	13 23:58
♄☍♅	13 14:43
♀ R	22 21:51
☿ D	25 10:48
☽0S	27 0:05

Planet Ingress

	Dy Hr Mn
☿ ♌	2 2:02
♀ ♍	7 18:17
♂ ♋	8 17:14
☉ ♌	23 22:45
♃ ♌	2 8:39
♄ ♍	12 13:52
☊ ♏	15 9:53
♅ ♒	16 22:07
♂ ♌	23 6:17
☉ ♍	24 5:28

Last Aspect / ☽ Ingress

Last Aspect Dy Hr Mn		☽ Ingress Dy Hr Mn
1 10:19	♄ ☌	♍ 1 19:06
3 21:14	♂ □	♎ 4 3:34
6 12:59	♀ ⚹	♏ 6 15:18
8 19:55	♄ □	♐ 9 4:13
11 8:27	♄ △	♑ 11 15:56
13 17:02	♃ ☍	♒ 14 1:14
16 2:10	♄ ☍	♓ 16 8:06
18 7:15	♃ △	♈ 18 13:06
20 11:57	♄ △	♉ 20 16:43
22 17:22	☉ ⚹	♊ 22 19:19
24 17:34	♄ ⚹	♋ 24 21:25
26 21:33	♃ ☌	♌ 26 24:00
29 1:42	☿ ☌	♍ 29 4:28
31 11:18	♃ ⚹	♎ 31 12:06

Last Aspect / ☽ Ingress

Last Aspect Dy Hr Mn		☽ Ingress Dy Hr Mn
2 21:00	☿ ⚹	♏ 2 23:08
5 10:09	♄ □	♐ 5 11:57
7 22:44	♄ △	♑ 7 23:52
9 22:21	♀ △	♒ 10 8:56
12 5:06	☿ ☍	♓ 12 14:59
14 12:03	♀ ☍	♈ 14 18:59
16 14:48	♂ □	♉ 16 22:05
19 0:54	♅ □	♊ 19 1:03
21 3:56	♅ △	♋ 21 4:14
23 3:11	♀ ⚹	♌ 23 8:00
25 12:31	♅ ☍	♍ 25 13:08
27 14:38	♀ ☌	♎ 27 20:41
30 6:12	♅ △	♏ 30 7:15

☽ Phases & Eclipses

Dy Hr Mn	
5 3:17	☽ 12♎03
13 6:02	○ 19♑48
20 11:03	☽ 26♈40
27 5:22	● 3♌08
3 20:11	☽ 10♏25
11 17:39	○ 17♒59
18 15:56	☽ 24♉38
25 15:37	● 1♍22

Astro Data

1 JULY 1919
Julian Day # 7121
Delta T 21.1 sec
SVP 06♓22'46"
Obliquity 23°26'54"
⚷ Chiron 6♈56.6
☽ Mean ☊ 2♐07.8

1 AUGUST 1919
Julian Day # 7152
Delta T 21.1 sec
SVP 06♓22'41"
Obliquity 23°26'55"
⚷ Chiron 6♈47.7R
☽ Mean ☊ 0♐29.3

LONGITUDE — SEPTEMBER 1919

Day	Sid.Time	☉	0 hr ☽	Noon ☽	True ☊	☿	♀	♂	♃	♄	♅	♆	♇
1 M	22 36 26	7♍30 34	20♏11 18	26♏ 5 16	28♏21.6	19♌25.3	25♍37.3	5♌35.5	6♌21.9	2♍27.5	29♒24.0	10♌ 6.9	7♋30.3
2 Tu	22 40 22	8 28 39	1♐59 8	7♐53 36	28R21.4	20 21.0	25R14.9	6 13.7	6 34.1	2 35.1	29R21.7	10 9.0	7 31.1
3 W	22 44 19	9 26 45	13 49 21	19 47 4	28 21.4	21 23.8	24 50.5	6 51.9	6 46.4	2 42.7	29 19.3	10 11.0	7 31.9
4 Th	22 48 15	10 24 52	25 47 27	1♑51 7	28 20.5	22 33.3	24 24.0	7 30.0	6 58.5	2 50.3	29 17.0	10 12.9	7 32.7
5 F	22 52 12	11 23 1	7♑58 43	14 10 46	28 17.7	23 49.1	23 55.5	8 8.0	7 10.6	2 57.9	29 14.6	10 14.9	7 33.5
6 Sa	22 56 8	12 21 12	20 27 46	26 50 7	28 12.7	25 10.7	23 25.4	8 46.1	7 22.7	3 5.4	29 12.3	10 16.9	7 34.2
7 Su	23 0 5	13 19 24	3♒18 7	9♒51 58	28 5.1	26 37.5	22 53.6	9 24.0	7 34.7	3 13.0	29 10.0	10 18.8	7 35.0
8 M	23 4 2	14 17 37	16 31 42	23 17 14	27 55.3	28 9.1	22 20.4	10 2.0	7 46.6	3 20.5	29 7.7	10 20.7	7 35.7
9 Tu	23 7 58	15 15 52	0♓ 8 22	7♓ 4 44	27 44.3	29 44.9	21 46.0	10 39.9	7 58.5	3 28.0	29 5.5	10 22.6	7 36.4
10 W	23 11 55	16 14 9	14 5 50	21 11 5	27 33.0	1♍24.3	21 10.5	11 17.7	8 10.3	3 35.5	29 3.2	10 24.5	7 37.0
11 Th	23 15 51	17 12 28	28 19 46	5♈31 9	27 22.7	3 6.9	20 34.3	11 55.6	8 22.0	3 43.0	29 1.0	10 26.4	7 37.7
12 F	23 19 48	18 10 48	12♈44 28	19 58 55	27 14.5	4 52.1	19 57.5	12 33.3	8 33.7	3 50.5	28 58.7	10 28.3	7 38.3
13 Sa	23 23 44	19 9 10	27 13 45	4♉28 19	27 8.8	6 39.5	19 20.4	13 11.1	8 45.3	3 57.9	28 56.5	10 30.1	7 38.9
14 Su	23 27 41	20 7 35	11♉42 0	18 54 18	27 5.8	8 28.7	18 43.3	13 48.8	8 56.9	4 5.4	28 54.3	10 31.9	7 39.5
15 M	23 31 37	21 6 1	26 4 47	3♊13 9	27D 4.9	10 19.1	18 6.3	14 26.4	9 8.3	4 12.8	28 52.2	10 33.7	7 40.0
16 Tu	23 35 34	22 4 30	10♊19 11	17 22 42	27R 5.2	12 10.5	17 29.7	15 4.1	9 19.7	4 20.2	28 50.0	10 35.5	7 40.6
17 W	23 39 31	23 3 1	24 23 37	1♋21 53	27 5.5	14 2.5	16 53.9	15 41.7	9 31.1	4 27.5	28 47.9	10 37.2	7 41.1
18 Th	23 43 27	24 1 35	8♋17 29	15 10 24	27 4.7	15 54.9	16 18.9	16 19.2	9 42.3	4 34.9	28 45.8	10 39.0	7 41.6
19 F	23 47 24	25 0 10	22 0 36	28 48 5	27 1.7	17 47.4	15 45.0	16 56.7	9 53.5	4 42.2	28 43.7	10 40.7	7 42.1
20 Sa	23 51 20	25 58 48	5♌32 48	12♌14 42	26 56.3	19 39.8	15 12.5	17 34.2	10 4.6	4 49.5	28 41.7	10 42.4	7 42.5
21 Su	23 55 17	26 57 28	18 53 42	25 29 42	26 48.5	21 31.9	14 41.4	18 11.6	10 15.6	4 56.8	28 39.6	10 44.1	7 43.0
22 M	23 59 13	27 56 9	2♍ 2 37	8♍32 20	26 38.9	23 23.6	14 12.1	18 49.0	10 26.6	5 4.0	28 37.6	10 45.7	7 43.4
23 Tu	0 3 10	28 54 53	14 58 46	21 21 50	26 28.5	25 14.7	13 44.5	19 26.3	10 37.4	5 11.2	28 35.7	10 47.3	7 43.8
24 W	0 7 6	29 53 39	27 41 29	3♎57 43	26 18.2	27 5.3	13 18.9	20 3.6	10 48.2	5 18.4	28 33.7	10 48.9	7 44.1
25 Th	0 11 3	0♎52 27	10♎10 33	16 20 5	26 9.2	28 55.1	12 55.4	20 40.9	10 58.9	5 25.6	28 31.8	10 50.5	7 44.5
26 F	0 14 59	1 51 17	22 26 28	28 29 54	26 2.0	0♎44.2	12 34.0	21 18.1	11 9.5	5 32.7	28 29.9	10 52.1	7 44.8
27 Sa	0 18 56	2 50 9	4♏30 37	10♏28 59	25 57.2	2 32.4	12 14.9	21 55.2	11 20.0	5 39.8	28 28.1	10 53.6	7 45.1
28 Su	0 22 53	3 49 3	16 25 20	22 20 9	25D54.7	4 19.9	11 58.1	22 32.3	11 30.4	5 46.8	28 26.2	10 55.1	7 45.3
29 M	0 26 49	4 47 58	28 13 52	4♐ 7 3	25 54.2	6 6.5	11 43.7	23 9.4	11 40.7	5 53.8	28 24.5	10 56.6	7 45.6
30 Tu	0 30 46	5 46 56	10♐ 0 16	15 54 8	25 55.0	7 52.2	11 31.6	23 46.4	11 50.9	6 0.8	28 22.7	10 58.0	7 45.8

LONGITUDE — OCTOBER 1919

Day	Sid.Time	☉	0 hr ☽	Noon ☽	True ☊	☿	♀	♂	♃	♄	♅	♆	♇
1 W	0 34 42	6♎45 55	21♐49 15	27♐46 18	25♏56.3	9♎37.1	11♍22.0	24♌23.4	12♌ 1.0	6♍ 7.8	28♒21.0	10♌59.5	7♋46.0
2 Th	0 38 39	7 44 56	3♑45 57	9♑48 51	25R57.2	11 21.0	11R14.8	25 0.3	12 11.1	6 14.7	28R19.3	11 0.9	7 46.2
3 F	0 42 35	8 43 59	15 55 39	22 6 59	25 57.0	13 4.2	11 10.1	25 37.2	12 21.0	6 21.5	28 17.6	11 2.3	7 46.4
4 Sa	0 46 32	9 43 3	28 23 26	4♒45 31	25 55.1	14 46.4	11D 7.7	26 14.1	12 30.8	6 28.3	28 16.0	11 3.6	7 46.5
5 Su	0 50 28	10 42 10	11♒13 41	17 48 17	25 51.3	16 27.8	11 7.7	26 50.8	12 40.6	6 35.1	28 14.4	11 4.9	7 46.6
6 M	0 54 25	11 41 18	24 29 33	1♓17 33	25 45.9	18 8.4	11 10.1	27 27.6	12 50.2	6 41.8	28 12.9	11 6.2	7 46.7
7 Tu	0 58 22	12 40 27	8♓12 15	15 13 23	25 39.3	19 48.2	11 14.8	28 4.3	12 59.7	6 48.5	28 11.4	11 7.5	7 46.8
8 W	1 2 18	13 39 39	22 20 35	29 33 16	25 32.4	21 27.2	11 21.8	28 40.9	13 9.1	6 55.1	28 9.9	11 8.7	7 46.8
9 Th	1 6 15	14 38 53	6♈50 43	14♈12 4	25 26.1	23 5.4	11 31.0	29 17.5	13 18.4	7 1.7	28 8.5	11 10.0	7R46.8
10 F	1 10 11	15 38 8	21 36 23	29 2 38	25 21.1	24 42.8	11 42.4	29 54.1	13 27.6	7 8.2	28 7.1	11 11.1	7 46.8
11 Sa	1 14 8	16 37 26	6♉29 48	13♉56 51	25 17.9	26 19.5	11 55.9	0♍30.6	13 36.6	7 14.7	28 5.8	11 12.3	7 46.8
12 Su	1 18 4	17 36 46	21 22 49	28 46 51	25D16.6	27 55.4	12 11.6	1 7.1	13 45.6	7 21.2	28 4.5	11 13.4	7 46.7
13 M	1 22 1	18 36 8	6♊ 8 10	13♊26 8	25 16.9	29 30.7	12 29.2	1 43.5	13 54.4	7 27.6	28 3.2	11 14.5	7 46.7
14 Tu	1 25 57	19 35 32	20 40 15	27 50 9	25 18.2	1♏ 5.3	12 48.8	2 19.9	14 3.1	7 33.9	28 2.0	11 15.6	7 46.6
15 W	1 29 54	20 34 59	4♋55 34	11♋56 22	25 19.6	2 39.1	13 10.3	2 56.2	14 11.8	7 40.2	28 0.8	11 16.6	7 46.4
16 Th	1 33 51	21 34 29	18 52 30	25 44 0	25R20.4	4 12.4	13 33.7	3 32.5	14 20.2	7 46.4	27 59.7	11 17.6	7 46.3
17 F	1 37 47	22 34 0	2♌30 57	9♌13 29	25 20.0	5 44.9	13 58.8	4 8.7	14 28.6	7 52.6	27 58.6	11 18.6	7 46.1
18 Sa	1 41 44	23 33 34	15 51 46	22 25 58	25 18.1	7 16.8	14 25.6	4 44.9	14 36.8	7 58.7	27 57.6	11 19.6	7 45.9
19 Su	1 45 40	24 33 10	28 56 16	5♍22 52	25 14.8	8 48.1	14 54.1	5 21.0	14 44.9	8 4.7	27 56.6	11 20.5	7 45.7
20 M	1 49 37	25 32 48	11♍45 57	18 5 40	25 10.4	10 18.8	15 24.2	5 57.1	14 52.9	8 10.7	27 55.6	11 21.4	7 45.5
21 Tu	1 53 33	26 32 28	24 22 14	0♎35 46	25 5.5	11 48.8	15 55.8	6 33.2	15 0.7	8 16.7	27 54.7	11 22.2	7 45.2
22 W	1 57 30	27 32 11	6♎46 27	12 54 26	25 0.6	13 18.2	16 28.8	7 9.1	15 8.4	8 22.5	27 53.8	11 23.0	7 44.9
23 Th	2 1 26	28 31 56	18 59 53	25 2 59	24 56.3	14 47.0	17 3.3	7 45.1	15 16.0	8 28.3	27 53.0	11 23.8	7 44.6
24 F	2 5 23	29 31 42	1♏ 3 54	7♏ 2 51	24 53.1	16 15.1	17 39.2	8 20.9	15 23.4	8 34.1	27 52.2	11 24.6	7 44.3
25 Sa	2 9 20	0♏31 31	13 0 3	18 55 46	24 51.2	17 42.6	18 16.3	8 56.7	15 30.7	8 39.7	27 51.5	11 25.3	7 43.9
26 Su	2 13 16	1 31 22	24 50 17	0♐43 56	24D50.6	19 9.4	18 54.8	9 32.5	15 37.9	8 45.4	27 50.8	11 26.0	7 43.6
27 M	2 17 13	2 31 14	6♐37 3	12 30 2	24 51.1	20 35.6	19 34.4	10 8.2	15 44.9	8 50.9	27 50.2	11 26.6	7 43.2
28 Tu	2 21 9	3 31 8	18 23 18	24 17 21	24 52.4	22 1.0	20 15.2	10 43.8	15 51.7	8 56.4	27 49.6	11 27.3	7 42.8
29 W	2 25 6	4 31 5	0♑12 38	6♑ 9 42	24 54.1	23 25.7	20 57.2	11 19.4	15 58.5	9 1.8	27 49.1	11 27.9	7 42.3
30 Th	2 29 2	5 31 2	12 9 5	18 11 23	24 55.7	24 49.6	21 40.2	11 54.9	16 5.0	9 7.1	27 48.6	11 28.4	7 41.9
31 F	2 32 59	6 31 2	24 17 9	0♒26 59	24 56.9	26 12.6	22 24.3	12 30.4	16 11.4	9 12.3	27 48.2	11 28.9	7 41.4

Astro Data Dy Hr Mn	Planet Ingress Dy Hr Mn
♃⊻♇ 7 0:35	☿ ♍ 9 3:43
☽0N 10 8:29	☉ ♎ 24 2:35
☽0S 23 7:43	☿ ♎ 25 14:16
♃☌♆ 24 1:59	
♀0N 26 1:48	♂ ♍ 10 3:53
☿0S 27 8:38	☿ ♏ 13 7:25
	☉ ♏ 24 11:21
♀ D 4 11:46	
☽0N 7 18:21	
♇ R 9 4:02	
♄✶♇ 15 23:33	
☽0S 20 13:31	

Last Aspect Dy Hr Mn	☽ Ingress Dy Hr Mn	Last Aspect Dy Hr Mn	☽ Ingress Dy Hr Mn
1 18:41 ♅ ☐	♐ 1 19:58	1 13:08 ♅ ✶	♑ 1 16:28
4 6:54 ♅ ✶	♑ 4 8:21	2 17:30 ☿ ☐	♒ 4 3:03
6 5:23 ♀ △	♒ 6 17:54	6 6:35 ♅ ☌	♓ 6 9:44
8 23:14 ♅ ☌	♓ 8 23:45	7 5:16 ♀ ☍	♈ 8 12:44
10 11:30 ♀ ☍	♈ 11 2:48	10 10:30 ♅ ✶	♉ 10 13:32
13 2:50 ♅ ✶	♉ 13 4:35	12 10:50 ♅ ☐	♊ 12 13:59
15 4:40 ♅ ☐	♊ 15 6:35	14 12:19 ♅ △	♋ 14 15:39
17 7:33 ♅ △	♋ 17 9:39	16 5:04 ☉ ☐	♌ 16 19:32
19 5:41 ☉ ✶	♌ 19 14:08	18 22:10 ♅ ☍	♍ 19 1:58
21 17:45 ♅ ☍	♍ 21 20:15	20 7:11 ♀ ☌	♎ 21 10:51
23 22:39 ♀ ☌	♎ 24 4:24	23 20:39 ☉ ☌	♏ 23 21:52
26 11:58 ♅ △	♏ 26 14:59	26 6:07 ♅ ☐	♐ 26 10:30
29 0:22 ♅ ☐	♐ 29 3:36	28 19:10 ♅ ✶	♑ 28 23:34
		31 4:14 ☿ ✶	♒ 31 11:08

☽ Phases & Eclipses Dy Hr Mn	
2 14:22	☽ 9♐03
10 3:54	○ 16♓24
16 21:31	☽ 22♊57
24 4:34	● 0♎05
2 8:37	☽ 8♑06
9 13:38	○ 15♈13
16 5:04	☽ 21♋47
23 20:39	● 29♎23

Astro Data

1 SEPTEMBER 1919
Julian Day # 7183
Delta T 21.1 sec
SVP 06♓22'38"
Obliquity 23°26'55"
⚷ Chiron 5♈53.8R
☽ Mean ☊ 28♏50.8

1 OCTOBER 1919
Julian Day # 7213
Delta T 21.1 sec
SVP 06♓22'35"
Obliquity 23°26'55"
⚷ Chiron 4♈36.2R
☽ Mean ☊ 27♏15.4

NOVEMBER 1919 LONGITUDE

Day	Sid.Time	☉	0 hr ☽	Noon ☽	True ☊	☿	♀	♂	♃	♄	♅	♆	♇
1 Sa	2 36 55	7♏31 3	6♒41 28	13♒ 1 8	24♏57.3	27♏34.8	23♍ 9.4	13♍ 5.8	16♌17.7	9♍17.5	27♒47.8	11♌29.4	7♋40.9
2 Su	2 40 52	8 31 6	19 26 32	25 58 5	24R57.0	28 56.1	23 55.4	13 41.1	16 23.8	9 22.6	27R47.5	11 29.9	7R40.3
3 M	2 44 49	9 31 10	2♓36 11	9♓21 6	24 55.9	0♐16.3	24 42.4	14 16.4	16 29.8	9 27.6	27 47.2	11 30.3	7 39.8
4 Tu	2 48 45	10 31 15	16 13 2	23 11 58	24 54.3	1 35.3	25 30.3	14 51.6	16 35.5	9 32.6	27 47.0	11 30.7	7 39.2
5 W	2 52 42	11 31 23	0♈17 46	7♈30 7	24 52.5	2 53.2	26 19.1	15 26.8	16 41.2	9 37.5	27 46.8	11 31.1	7 38.6
6 Th	2 56 38	12 31 32	14 48 31	22 12 19	24 50.9	4 9.7	27 8.7	16 1.9	16 46.7	9 42.2	27 46.7	11 31.4	7 38.0
7 F	3 0 35	13 31 42	29 40 38	7♉12 30	24 49.7	5 24.7	27 59.1	16 36.9	16 52.0	9 47.0	27 46.6	11 31.7	7 37.4
8 Sa	3 4 31	14 31 55	14♉46 48	22 22 21	24D 49.0	6 38.1	28 50.3	17 11.9	16 57.1	9 51.6	27D 46.6	11 31.9	7 36.7
9 Su	3 8 28	15 32 9	29 57 58	7♊32 25	24 48.9	7 49.6	29 42.3	17 46.8	17 2.1	9 56.1	27 46.6	11 32.1	7 36.1
10 M	3 12 24	16 32 25	15♊ 4 36	22 33 28	24 49.3	8 59.1	0♎35.0	18 21.6	17 6.9	10 0.6	27 46.7	11 32.3	7 35.4
11 Tu	3 16 21	17 32 43	29 58 8	7♋17 51	24 49.9	10 6.3	1 28.5	18 56.4	17 11.6	10 5.0	27 46.8	11 32.5	7 34.7
12 W	3 20 18	18 33 3	14♋32 3	21 40 18	24 50.5	11 10.9	2 22.6	19 31.1	17 16.1	10 9.3	27 47.0	11 32.6	7 34.0
13 Th	3 24 14	19 33 24	28 42 23	5♌38 9	24 51.0	12 12.6	3 17.4	20 5.8	17 20.4	10 13.5	27 47.2	11 32.7	7 33.2
14 F	3 28 11	20 33 48	12♌27 41	19 11 5	24R51.3	13 11.0	4 12.8	20 40.4	17 24.5	10 17.6	27 47.5	11R32.7	7 32.5
15 Sa	3 32 7	21 34 14	25 48 36	2♍20 32	24 51.3	14 5.7	5 8.8	21 14.9	17 28.5	10 21.7	27 47.8	11 32.7	7 31.7
16 Su	3 36 4	22 34 41	8♍47 14	15 9 7	24 51.2	14 56.2	6 5.4	21 49.3	17 32.2	10 25.6	27 48.2	11 32.7	7 30.9
17 M	3 40 0	23 35 11	21 26 34	27 40 0	24 51.1	15 42.1	7 2.6	22 23.7	17 35.8	10 29.4	27 48.6	11 32.7	7 30.1
18 Tu	3 43 57	24 35 42	3♎49 52	9♎56 33	24D 51.0	16 22.6	8 0.3	22 58.0	17 39.3	10 33.2	27 49.1	11 32.6	7 29.2
19 W	3 47 53	25 36 15	16 0 27	22 1 57	24 51.0	16 57.3	8 58.6	23 32.2	17 42.5	10 36.9	27 49.6	11 32.5	7 28.4
20 Th	3 51 50	26 36 49	28 1 23	3♏59 6	24 51.2	17 25.3	9 57.3	24 6.3	17 45.5	10 40.4	27 50.2	11 32.3	7 27.5
21 F	3 55 46	27 37 25	9♏55 25	15 50 38	24 51.4	17 45.9	10 56.6	24 40.4	17 48.4	10 43.9	27 50.9	11 32.1	7 26.6
22 Sa	3 59 43	28 38 3	21 45 2	27 38 53	24R51.5	17R58.4	11 56.3	25 14.4	17 51.1	10 47.3	27 51.5	11 31.9	7 25.7
23 Su	4 3 40	29 38 43	3♐32 27	9♐26 0	24 51.4	18 2.0	12 56.5	25 48.3	17 53.6	10 50.6	27 52.3	11 31.6	7 24.8
24 M	4 7 36	0♐39 24	15 19 48	21 14 8	24 51.1	17 55.9	13 57.1	26 22.1	17 55.9	10 53.8	27 53.1	11 31.3	7 23.8
25 Tu	4 11 33	1 40 6	27 9 17	3♑ 5 32	24 50.4	17 39.6	14 58.2	26 55.8	17 58.0	10 56.9	27 53.9	11 31.0	7 22.9
26 W	4 15 29	2 40 49	9♑ 3 14	15 2 42	24 49.3	17 12.6	15 59.6	27 29.5	17 59.9	10 59.9	27 54.8	11 30.6	7 21.9
27 Th	4 19 26	3 41 34	21 4 19	27 8 27	24 48.1	16 34.8	17 1.5	28 3.0	18 1.7	11 2.8	27 55.8	11 30.3	7 21.0
28 F	4 23 22	4 42 19	3♒15 32	9♒25 59	24 46.8	15 46.2	18 3.7	28 36.5	18 3.2	11 5.6	27 56.7	11 29.8	7 20.0
29 Sa	4 27 19	5 43 6	15 40 14	21 58 45	24 45.7	14 47.5	19 6.3	29 9.9	18 4.6	11 8.2	27 57.8	11 29.4	7 19.0
30 Su	4 31 16	6 43 54	28 21 58	4♓50 18	24D 45.0	13 39.8	20 9.3	29 43.2	18 5.7	11 10.8	27 58.9	11 28.9	7 17.9

DECEMBER 1919 LONGITUDE

Day	Sid.Time	☉	0 hr ☽	Noon ☽	True ☊	☿	♀	♂	♃	♄	♅	♆	♇
1 M	4 35 12	7♐44 42	11♓24 11	18♓ 3 58	24♏44.9	12♐24.9	21♎12.6	0♎16.3	18♌ 6.7	11♍13.3	28♒ 0.0	11♌28.4	7♋16.9
2 Tu	4 39 9	8 45 32	24 49 57	1♈42 21	24 45.4	11R 4.9	22 16.2	0 49.4	18 7.4	11 15.7	28 1.2	11R27.8	7R15.9
3 W	4 43 5	9 46 22	8♈41 17	15 46 43	24 46.4	9 42.3	23 20.2	1 22.4	18 8.0	11 18.0	28 2.4	11 27.2	7 14.8
4 Th	4 47 2	10 47 13	22 58 31	0♉16 20	24 47.6	8 19.9	24 24.5	1 55.4	18 8.4	11 20.1	28 3.7	11 26.6	7 13.7
5 F	4 50 58	11 48 5	7♉39 40	15 7 51	24 48.7	7 0.6	25 29.1	2 28.2	18R 8.5	11 22.2	28 5.1	11 25.9	7 12.7
6 Sa	4 54 55	12 48 58	22 40 1	0♊15 9	24R49.2	5 46.9	26 34.0	3 0.9	18 8.5	11 24.2	28 6.5	11 25.2	7 11.6
7 Su	4 58 51	13 49 52	7♊52 6	15 29 40	24 48.9	4 41.0	27 39.2	3 33.5	18 8.3	11 26.0	28 7.9	11 24.5	7 10.5
8 M	5 2 48	14 50 47	23 6 32	0♋41 27	24 47.5	3 44.5	28 44.7	4 6.0	18 7.9	11 27.8	28 9.4	11 23.8	7 9.4
9 Tu	5 6 45	15 51 43	8♋13 13	15 40 42	24 45.1	2 58.7	29 50.4	4 38.5	18 7.3	11 29.4	28 10.9	11 23.0	7 8.2
10 W	5 10 41	16 52 40	23 2 59	0♌19 15	24 42.1	2 24.1	0♏56.5	5 10.8	18 6.5	11 30.9	28 12.5	11 22.2	7 7.1
11 Th	5 14 38	17 53 38	7♌28 56	14 31 38	24 38.8	2 0.8	2 2.7	5 43.0	18 5.5	11 32.4	28 14.1	11 21.4	7 6.0
12 F	5 18 34	18 54 37	21 27 9	28 15 27	24 36.0	1D 48.6	3 9.3	6 15.1	18 4.3	11 33.7	28 15.8	11 20.5	7 4.8
13 Sa	5 22 31	19 55 37	4♍56 41	11♍31 7	24 33.9	1 47.0	4 16.1	6 47.1	18 2.9	11 34.9	28 17.5	11 19.6	7 3.7
14 Su	5 26 27	20 56 38	17 59 7	24 21 9	24D 33.0	1 55.3	5 23.1	7 19.0	18 1.3	11 36.0	28 19.2	11 18.7	7 2.5
15 M	5 30 24	21 57 40	0♎37 44	6♎49 26	24 33.3	2 12.8	6 30.3	7 50.7	17 59.5	11 37.0	28 21.0	11 17.8	7 1.3
16 Tu	5 34 20	22 58 44	12 56 51	19 0 34	24 34.5	2 38.5	7 37.8	8 22.4	17 57.5	11 37.8	28 22.9	11 16.8	7 0.1
17 W	5 38 17	23 59 48	25 1 11	0♏59 16	24 36.4	3 11.8	8 45.5	8 53.9	17 55.3	11 38.6	28 24.7	11 15.8	6 59.0
18 Th	5 42 14	25 0 53	6♏55 22	12 50 1	24 38.2	3 51.7	9 53.4	9 25.3	17 52.9	11 39.2	28 26.7	11 14.7	6 57.8
19 F	5 46 10	26 1 59	18 43 42	24 36 52	24R39.3	4 37.5	11 1.4	9 56.6	17 50.4	11 39.8	28 28.7	11 13.7	6 56.6
20 Sa	5 50 7	27 3 6	0♐29 56	6♐23 16	24 39.3	5 28.6	12 9.7	10 27.7	17 47.6	11 40.2	28 30.7	11 12.6	6 55.4
21 Su	5 54 3	28 4 13	12 17 13	18 12 4	24 37.7	6 24.4	13 18.2	10 58.7	17 44.7	11 40.5	28 32.7	11 11.5	6 54.2
22 M	5 58 0	29 5 21	24 8 5	0♑ 5 31	24 34.3	7 24.2	14 26.8	11 29.6	17 41.5	11 40.7	28 34.8	11 10.3	6 52.9
23 Tu	6 1 56	0♑ 6 29	6♑ 4 34	12 5 26	24 29.1	8 27.5	15 35.6	12 0.4	17 38.2	11R40.8	28 37.0	11 9.2	6 51.7
24 W	6 5 53	1 7 38	18 8 16	24 13 15	24 22.6	9 34.1	16 44.5	12 31.0	17 34.7	11 40.8	28 39.2	11 8.0	6 50.5
25 Th	6 9 49	2 8 48	0♒20 34	6♒30 21	24 15.3	10 43.4	17 53.7	13 1.4	17 31.0	11 40.7	28 41.4	11 6.8	6 49.3
26 F	6 13 46	3 9 57	12 42 49	18 58 8	24 8.0	11 55.1	19 2.9	13 31.8	17 27.1	11 40.4	28 43.7	11 5.5	6 48.1
27 Sa	6 17 43	4 11 6	25 16 32	1♓38 14	24 1.5	13 9.0	20 12.4	14 1.9	17 23.1	11 40.1	28 46.0	11 4.3	6 46.9
28 Su	6 21 39	5 12 16	8♓ 3 29	14 32 34	23 56.4	14 24.7	21 21.9	14 31.9	17 18.8	11 39.6	28 48.3	11 3.0	6 45.6
29 M	6 25 36	6 13 25	21 5 44	27 43 17	23 53.3	15 42.2	22 31.6	15 1.8	17 14.4	11 39.0	28 50.7	11 1.7	6 44.4
30 Tu	6 29 32	7 14 35	4♈25 29	11♈12 34	23D 52.1	17 1.1	23 41.5	15 31.5	17 9.8	11 38.4	28 53.1	11 0.4	6 43.2
31 W	6 33 29	8 15 44	18 4 45	25 2 10	23 52.4	18 21.4	24 51.4	16 1.1	17 5.1	11 37.6	28 55.5	10 59.0	6 41.9

Astro Data Dy Hr Mn	Planet Ingress Dy Hr Mn	Last Aspect Dy Hr Mn	☽ Ingress Dy Hr Mn	Last Aspect Dy Hr Mn	☽ Ingress Dy Hr Mn	☽ Phases & Eclipses Dy Hr Mn	Astro Data
☽0N 4 4:23	☿ ♐ 2 19:07	2 15:19 ♅ ☌	♓ 2 19:19	1 1:40 ☿ □	♈ 2 9:02	1 1:43 ☽ 7♒35	1 NOVEMBER 1919
♅ D 8 0:35	♀ ♎ 9 8:05	4 16:53 ♀ ☍	♈ 4 23:30	4 8:24 ♅ ⚹	♉ 4 11:33	7 23:35 ○ 14♉31	Julian Day # 7244
♀0S 10 16:04	☉ ♐ 23 8:25	6 20:57 ♅ ⚹	♉ 7 0:31	6 8:38 ♅ □	♊ 6 11:36	7 23:44 ☍ P 0.178	Delta T 21.1 sec
♆ R 14 21:40	♂ ♎ 30 12:10	8 23:34 ♀ △	♊ 9 0:03	8 9:37 ♀ △	♋ 8 10:54	14 15:40 ☽ 21♌13	SVP 06♓22'32"
☽0S 16 18:47		10 20:27 ♅ △	♋ 11 0:03	9 5:15 ♄ ⚹	♌ 10 11:28	22 15:19 ● 29♏17	Obliquity 23°26'54"
☿ R 22 21:12	♀ ♏ 9 3:29	12 8:43 ♂ ⚹	♌ 13 2:14	12 12:02 ♅ ☍	♍ 12 15:06	22 15:13:50 ☌ A 11'36"	⚷ Chiron 3♈18.7R
☽0N 1 13:14	☉ ♑ 22 21:27	15 3:38 ♅ ☍	♍ 15 7:41	14 6:02 ☉ □	♎ 14 22:47	30 16:47 ☽ 7♓26	☽ Mean ☊ 25♏36.9
♃ R 5 9:36		17 4:29 ☉ ⚹	♎ 17 16:32	17 6:50 ♅ △	♏ 17 10:01		
♄⊻♆ 6 10:08		19 23:38 ♅ △	♏ 20 3:58	19 19:56 ♅ □	♐ 19 22:59	7 10:03 ○ 14♊15	1 DECEMBER 1919
♂0S 7 23:27		22 15:19 ☉ ☌	♐ 22 16:47	22 10:55 ☉ ☌	♑ 22 11:49	14 6:02 ☽ 21♍12	Julian Day # 7274
☿ D 12 15:39		25 1:30 ♅ ⚹	♑ 25 5:45	23 20:57 ♀ ⚹	♒ 24 23:20	22 10:55 ● 29♐33	Delta T 21.1 sec
☽0S 14 1:38		27 14:27 ♂ △	♒ 27 17:37	27 6:37 ♅ ☌	♓ 27 8:55	30 5:25 ☽ 7♈28	SVP 06♓22'28"
♄ R 23 8:08		29 23:17 ♅ ☌	♓ 30 3:03	29 2:51 ♀ △	♈ 29 16:06		Obliquity 23°26'53"
☽0N 28 20:24				31 18:42 ♅ ⚹	♉ 31 20:28		⚷ Chiron 2♈34.0R
							☽ Mean ☊ 24♏01.6

LONGITUDE — JANUARY 1920

Day	Sid.Time	☉	0 hr ☽	Noon ☽	True ☊	☿	♀	♂	♃	♄	♅	♆	♇
1 Th	6 37 25	9♑16 53	2♉ 4 53	9♉12 53	23♍53.6	19♐42.8	26♏ 1.5	16♎30.4	17♌ 0.1	11♍36.7	28♒58.0	10♌57.7	6♋40.7
2 F	6 41 22	10 18 2	16 25 59	23 43 53	23R54.7	21 5.4	27 11.8	16 59.7	16R55.1	11R35.6	29 0.6	10R56.3	6R39.5
3 Sa	6 45 18	11 19 11	1♊ 6 6	8♊32 2	23 54.7	22 28.9	28 22.1	17 28.7	16 49.8	11 34.5	29 3.1	10 54.9	6 38.3
4 Su	6 49 15	12 20 19	16 0 51	23 31 38	23 52.8	23 53.3	29 32.6	17 57.6	16 44.4	11 33.3	29 5.7	10 53.4	6 37.1
5 M	6 53 12	13 21 28	1♋ 3 18	8♋34 41	23 48.5	25 18.5	0♐43.1	18 26.3	16 38.9	11 32.0	29 8.3	10 52.0	6 35.8
6 Tu	6 57 8	14 22 36	16 4 37	23 31 52	23 42.0	26 44.4	1 53.8	18 54.9	16 33.2	11 30.5	29 11.0	10 50.5	6 34.6
7 W	7 1 5	15 23 44	0♌55 21	8♌14 2	23 33.8	28 11.1	3 4.6	19 23.3	16 27.4	11 29.0	29 13.7	10 49.1	6 33.4
8 Th	7 5 1	16 24 52	15 27 4	22 33 44	23 24.9	29 38.4	4 15.6	19 51.4	16 21.4	11 27.3	29 16.4	10 47.6	6 32.2
9 F	7 8 58	17 26 0	29 33 34	6♍26 17	23 16.5	1♑ 6.3	5 26.6	20 19.4	16 15.3	11 25.6	29 19.2	10 46.1	6 31.0
10 Sa	7 12 54	18 27 8	13♍11 45	19 50 4	23 9.4	2 34.8	6 37.7	20 47.2	16 9.0	11 23.7	29 22.0	10 44.5	6 29.8
11 Su	7 16 51	19 28 16	26 21 28	2♎46 19	23 4.4	4 3.9	7 48.9	21 14.9	16 2.6	11 21.7	29 24.8	10 43.0	6 28.6
12 M	7 20 47	20 29 24	9♎ 5 5	15 18 20	23 1.6	5 33.6	9 0.2	21 42.3	15 56.1	11 19.7	29 27.6	10 41.5	6 27.4
13 Tu	7 24 44	21 30 32	21 26 41	27 30 48	23D 0.8	7 3.8	10 11.6	22 9.5	15 49.5	11 17.5	29 30.5	10 39.9	6 26.2
14 W	7 28 41	22 31 40	3♏31 21	9♏29 2	23 1.3	8 34.5	11 23.1	22 36.5	15 42.7	11 15.3	29 33.4	10 38.3	6 25.1
15 Th	7 32 37	23 32 47	15 24 33	21 18 33	23R 2.2	10 5.7	12 34.7	23 3.3	15 35.8	11 12.9	29 36.3	10 36.7	6 23.9
16 F	7 36 34	24 33 55	27 11 41	3♐ 4 32	23 2.3	11 37.5	13 46.4	23 29.9	15 28.9	11 10.4	29 39.3	10 35.1	6 22.7
17 Sa	7 40 30	25 35 2	8♐57 42	14 51 42	23 0.8	13 9.8	14 58.1	23 56.2	15 21.8	11 7.9	29 42.3	10 33.5	6 21.6
18 Su	7 44 27	26 36 9	20 46 59	26 43 58	22 56.9	14 42.7	16 9.9	24 22.3	15 14.6	11 5.2	29 45.3	10 31.9	6 20.4
19 M	7 48 23	27 37 16	2♑43 0	8♑44 23	22 50.2	16 16.0	17 21.8	24 48.2	15 7.3	11 2.5	29 48.3	10 30.3	6 19.3
20 Tu	7 52 20	28 38 22	14 48 21	20 55 5	22 40.8	17 49.9	18 33.8	25 13.8	14 59.9	10 59.6	29 51.4	10 28.6	6 18.2
21 W	7 56 16	29 39 27	27 4 42	3♒17 17	22 29.3	19 24.4	19 45.8	25 39.2	14 52.5	10 56.7	29 54.5	10 27.0	6 17.0
22 Th	8 0 13	0♒40 32	9♒32 51	15 51 24	22 16.4	20 59.4	20 57.9	26 4.4	14 45.0	10 53.7	29 57.6	10 25.3	6 15.9
23 F	8 4 10	1 41 36	22 12 54	28 37 20	22 3.4	22 35.0	22 10.0	26 29.2	14 37.4	10 50.6	0♓ 0.7	10 23.6	6 14.8
24 Sa	8 8 6	2 42 39	5♓ 4 38	11♓34 47	21 51.5	24 11.2	23 22.2	26 53.9	14 29.7	10 47.4	0 3.9	10 22.0	6 13.7
25 Su	8 12 3	3 43 41	18 7 44	24 43 30	21 41.6	25 47.9	24 34.5	27 18.2	14 22.0	10 44.1	0 7.0	10 20.3	6 12.7
26 M	8 15 59	4 44 42	1♈22 7	8♈ 3 38	21 34.6	27 25.3	25 46.8	27 42.3	14 14.2	10 40.8	0 10.2	10 18.6	6 11.6
27 Tu	8 19 56	5 45 43	14 48 9	21 35 44	21 30.4	29 3.3	26 59.1	28 6.1	14 6.4	10 37.3	0 13.4	10 16.9	6 10.6
28 W	8 23 52	6 46 42	28 26 31	5♉20 36	21D28.8	0♒41.9	28 11.6	28 29.6	13 58.5	10 33.8	0 16.7	10 15.3	6 9.5
29 Th	8 27 49	7 47 39	12♉18 5	19 19 1	21R28.6	2 21.2	29 24.0	28 52.8	13 50.6	10 30.2	0 19.9	10 13.6	6 8.5
30 F	8 31 45	8 48 36	26 23 23	3♊31 7	21 28.6	4 1.2	0♑36.5	29 15.7	13 42.7	10 26.5	0 23.2	10 11.9	6 7.5
31 Sa	8 35 42	9 49 31	10♊42 1	17 55 46	21 27.5	5 41.8	1 49.1	29 38.3	13 34.8	10 22.8	0 26.5	10 10.2	6 6.5

LONGITUDE — FEBRUARY 1920

Day	Sid.Time	☉	0 hr ☽	Noon ☽	True ☊	☿	♀	♂	♃	♄	♅	♆	♇
1 Su	8 39 39	10♒50 25	25♊11 58	2♋30 3	21♍24.1	7♒23.2	3♑ 1.7	0♏ 0.6	13♌26.8	10♍19.0	0♓29.8	10♌ 8.5	6♋ 5.5
2 M	8 43 35	11 51 18	9♋49 20	17 9 0	21R17.9	9 5.2	4 14.3	0 22.6	13R18.8	10R15.1	0 33.1	10R 6.8	6R 4.5
3 Tu	8 47 32	12 52 10	24 28 12	1♌45 58	21 8.7	10 48.0	5 27.0	0 44.3	13 10.8	10 11.2	0 36.4	10 5.1	6 3.6
4 W	8 51 28	13 53 0	9♌ 1 22	16 13 29	20 57.3	12 31.4	6 39.8	1 5.7	13 2.8	10 7.2	0 39.7	10 3.5	6 2.6
5 Th	8 55 25	14 53 49	23 21 28	0♍24 33	20 44.9	14 15.7	7 52.5	1 26.7	12 54.8	10 3.1	0 43.1	10 1.8	6 1.7
6 F	8 59 21	15 54 37	7♍22 7	14 13 43	20 32.6	16 0.6	9 5.3	1 47.4	12 46.9	9 59.0	0 46.4	10 0.1	6 0.8
7 Sa	9 3 18	16 55 23	20 59 4	27 38 0	20 21.9	17 46.3	10 18.2	2 7.7	12 38.9	9 54.8	0 49.8	9 58.4	5 59.9
8 Su	9 7 14	17 56 9	4♎10 35	10♎36 57	20 13.6	19 32.7	11 31.1	2 27.7	12 31.0	9 50.6	0 53.2	9 56.7	5 59.0
9 M	9 11 11	18 56 54	16 57 27	23 12 28	20 8.0	21 19.7	12 44.0	2 47.3	12 23.1	9 46.3	0 56.6	9 55.1	5 58.2
10 Tu	9 15 8	19 57 37	29 22 31	5♏28 12	20 5.0	23 7.5	13 57.0	3 6.5	12 15.2	9 41.9	0 60.0	9 53.4	5 57.3
11 W	9 19 4	20 58 20	11♏30 7	17 28 59	20 4.0	24 55.9	15 10.0	3 25.4	12 7.4	9 37.5	1 3.4	9 51.7	5 56.5
12 Th	9 23 1	21 59 1	23 25 27	29 20 16	20 3.9	26 44.9	16 23.1	3 43.8	11 59.6	9 33.1	1 6.8	9 50.1	5 55.7
13 F	9 26 57	22 59 42	5♐14 8	11♐ 7 43	20 3.6	28 34.4	17 36.2	4 1.9	11 51.8	9 28.6	1 10.2	9 48.5	5 54.9
14 Sa	9 30 54	24 0 21	17 1 43	22 56 46	20 1.9	0♓24.4	18 49.3	4 19.5	11 44.1	9 24.1	1 13.7	9 46.8	5 54.1
15 Su	9 34 50	25 0 59	28 53 27	4♑52 20	19 57.9	2 14.7	20 2.4	4 36.7	11 36.5	9 19.5	1 17.1	9 45.2	5 53.4
16 M	9 38 47	26 1 36	10♑53 53	16 58 32	19 51.1	4 5.2	21 15.6	4 53.5	11 29.0	9 14.9	1 20.6	9 43.6	5 52.6
17 Tu	9 42 43	27 2 11	23 6 39	29 18 29	19 41.6	5 55.8	22 28.8	5 9.8	11 21.5	9 10.3	1 24.0	9 42.0	5 51.9
18 W	9 46 40	28 2 45	5♒34 14	11♒54 0	19 29.7	7 46.3	23 42.0	5 25.7	11 14.1	9 5.6	1 27.5	9 40.4	5 51.2
19 Th	9 50 37	29 3 18	18 17 48	24 45 35	19 16.3	9 36.5	24 55.3	5 41.1	11 6.8	9 0.9	1 30.9	9 38.8	5 50.5
20 F	9 54 33	0♓ 3 49	1♓17 14	7♓52 32	19 2.7	11 26.2	26 8.5	5 56.1	10 59.5	8 56.2	1 34.4	9 37.2	5 49.9
21 Sa	9 58 30	1 4 19	14 31 17	21 13 11	18 50.2	13 15.0	27 21.8	6 10.5	10 52.4	8 51.5	1 37.8	9 35.7	5 49.2
22 Su	10 2 26	2 4 47	27 57 57	4♈45 18	18 39.7	15 2.7	28 35.1	6 24.5	10 45.4	8 46.7	1 41.3	9 34.1	5 48.6
23 M	10 6 23	3 5 13	11♈34 57	18 26 39	18 32.2	16 48.8	29 48.4	6 37.9	10 38.4	8 42.0	1 44.7	9 32.6	5 48.0
24 Tu	10 10 19	4 5 37	25 20 12	2♉15 24	18 27.6	18 32.9	1♒ 1.8	6 50.8	10 31.6	8 37.2	1 48.2	9 31.1	5 47.4
25 W	10 14 16	5 5 59	9♉12 8	16 10 17	18D25.7	20 14.6	2 15.1	7 3.3	10 24.9	8 32.4	1 51.7	9 29.6	5 46.9
26 Th	10 18 12	6 6 20	23 9 47	0♊10 34	18 25.5	21 53.4	3 28.5	7 15.1	10 18.3	8 27.6	1 55.1	9 28.1	5 46.3
27 F	10 22 9	7 6 38	7♊12 36	14 15 47	18R25.7	23 28.7	4 41.9	7 26.5	10 11.9	8 22.8	1 58.6	9 26.7	5 45.8
28 Sa	10 26 6	8 6 55	21 20 1	28 25 9	18 25.1	24 60.0	5 55.3	7 37.3	10 5.5	8 17.9	2 2.0	9 25.2	5 45.3
29 Su	10 30 2	9 7 9	5♋30 59	12♋37 14	18 22.5	26 26.6	7 8.7	7 47.5	9 59.3	8 13.1	2 5.4	9 23.8	5 44.9

Astro Data Dy Hr Mn	Planet Ingress Dy Hr Mn
☽0S 10 11:06	♀ ♐ 4 9:20
☽0N 25 2:47	☿ ♑ 8 5:55
	☉ ♒ 21 8:04
♄⊻♆ 5 13:18	♅ ♓ 22 18:32
☽0S 6 21:58	☿ ♒ 27 13:49
☽0N 21 9:53	♀ ♑ 29 11:55
☿0N 29 21:20	♂ ♏ 31 23:18
	☿ ♓ 13 18:41
	☉ ♓ 19 22:29
	♀ ♒ 23 3:47

Last Aspect Dy Hr Mn	☽ Ingress Dy Hr Mn	Last Aspect Dy Hr Mn	☽ Ingress Dy Hr Mn
2 20:40 ♅ □	♊ 2 22:13	31 4:45 ♃ ✶	♋ 1 7:54
4 20:56 ♅ △	♋ 4 22:19	2 0:42 ♄ ✶	♌ 3 9:05
6 4:43 ♂ □	♌ 6 22:30	4 8:42 ☉ ☍	♍ 5 11:18
8 23:35 ♅ ☍	♍ 9 0:46	6 4:32 ♄ ☌	♎ 7 16:19
10 10:17 ☉ △	♎ 11 6:47	9 9:47 ☿ △	♏ 10 1:13
13 16:02 ♅ △	♏ 13 16:57	12 7:58 ☿ □	♐ 12 13:21
16 5:02 ♅ □	♐ 16 5:43	14 15:28 ☉ ✶	♑ 15 2:14
18 18:09 ♅ ✶	♑ 18 18:34	16 22:38 ♀ ☌	♒ 17 13:20
21 5:27 ☉ ☌	♒ 21 5:39	19 21:34 ☉ ☌	♓ 19 21:39
23 8:17 ♂ △	♓ 23 14:34	22 1:12 ♀ ✶	♈ 22 3:36
25 15:53 ♀ ✶	♈ 25 21:32	22 22:22 ♃ △	♉ 24 8:06
28 0:05 ♂ ☍	♉ 28 2:43	25 21:32 ☿ ✶	♊ 26 11:42
29 2:37 ♃ □	♊ 30 6:05	28 6:56 ☿ □	♋ 28 14:40

☽ Phases & Eclipses Dy Hr Mn	Astro Data
5 21:05 ○ 14♋15	1 JANUARY 1920
13 0:08 ☽ 21♎31	Julian Day # 7305
21 5:27 ● 29♑53	Delta T 21.2 sec
28 15:38 ☽ 7♉26	SVP 06♓22'23"
	Obliquity 23°26'53"
4 8:42 ○ 14♌15	⚷ Chiron 2♈36.5
11 20:49 ☽ 21♏51	☽ Mean ☊ 22♍23.1
19 21:34 ● 29♒58	
26 23:49 ☽ 7♊06	1 FEBRUARY 1920
	Julian Day # 7336
	Delta T 21.3 sec
	SVP 06♓22'17"
	Obliquity 23°26'53"
	⚷ Chiron 3♈29.4
	☽ Mean ☊ 20♍44.6

MARCH 1920 LONGITUDE

Day	Sid.Time	☉	0 hr ☽	Noon ☽	True ☊	☿	♀	♂	♃	♄	♅	♆	♇
1 M	10 33 59	10♓ 7 21	19♋43 33	26♋49 29	18♏17.3	27♓48.0	8♒22.1	7♏57.1	9♌53.3	8♍ 8.3	2♓ 8.9	9♌22.4	5♋44.4
2 Tu	10 37 55	11 7 32	3♌54 34	10♌58 15	18R 9.5	29 3.6	9 35.6	8 6.2	9R47.4	8R 3.5	2 12.3	9R21.0	5R44.0
3 W	10 41 52	12 7 40	17 59 57	24 59 5	17 59.6	0♈12.7	10 49.0	8 14.7	9 41.6	7 58.7	2 15.7	9 19.6	5 43.6
4 Th	10 45 48	13 7 46	1♍55 5	8♍47 24	17 48.6	1 14.9	12 2.5	8 22.5	9 35.9	7 53.9	2 19.1	9 18.3	5 43.2
5 F	10 49 45	14 7 50	15 35 34	22 19 13	17 37.8	2 9.6	13 16.0	8 29.8	9 30.4	7 49.2	2 22.5	9 16.9	5 42.8
6 Sa	10 53 41	15 7 52	28 58 1	5♎31 48	17 28.2	2 56.4	14 29.5	8 36.4	9 25.1	7 44.4	2 25.9	9 15.6	5 42.5
7 Su	10 57 38	16 7 53	12♎ 0 29	18 24 7	17 20.6	3 34.8	15 43.0	8 42.4	9 19.9	7 39.7	2 29.3	9 14.3	5 42.2
8 M	11 1 35	17 7 52	24 42 51	0♏56 55	17 15.6	4 4.7	16 56.5	8 47.8	9 14.9	7 34.9	2 32.7	9 13.1	5 41.9
9 Tu	11 5 31	18 7 49	7♏ 6 39	13 12 29	17D13.0	4 25.7	18 10.0	8 52.4	9 10.0	7 30.2	2 36.1	9 11.8	5 41.6
10 W	11 9 28	19 7 44	19 14 55	25 14 29	17 12.5	4R37.9	19 23.6	8 56.4	9 5.3	7 25.6	2 39.4	9 10.6	5 41.4
11 Th	11 13 24	20 7 38	1♐11 47	7♐ 7 26	17 13.2	4 41.1	20 37.2	8 59.8	9 0.8	7 20.9	2 42.8	9 9.4	5 41.2
12 F	11 17 21	21 7 30	13 2 7	18 56 29	17R14.2	4 35.7	21 50.7	9 2.4	8 56.4	7 16.3	2 46.1	9 8.2	5 41.0
13 Sa	11 21 17	22 7 20	24 51 13	0♑46 59	17 14.4	4 21.7	23 4.3	9 4.3	8 52.2	7 11.7	2 49.4	9 7.1	5 40.8
14 Su	11 25 14	23 7 9	6♑44 27	12 44 13	17 13.2	3 59.8	24 17.9	9 5.5	8 48.2	7 7.2	2 52.7	9 5.9	5 40.6
15 M	11 29 10	24 6 56	18 46 54	24 53 3	17 10.0	3 30.5	25 31.5	9R 5.9	8 44.3	7 2.7	2 56.0	9 4.8	5 40.5
16 Tu	11 33 7	25 6 41	1♒ 3 8	7♒17 35	17 4.7	2 54.5	26 45.1	9 5.7	8 40.7	6 58.2	2 59.3	9 3.8	5 40.4
17 W	11 37 4	26 6 25	13 36 44	20 0 49	16 57.5	2 12.8	27 58.8	9 4.6	8 37.2	6 53.8	3 2.5	9 2.7	5 40.3
18 Th	11 41 0	27 6 6	26 29 59	3♓ 4 17	16 49.0	1 26.2	29 12.4	9 2.9	8 33.8	6 49.4	3 5.8	9 1.7	5 40.3
19 F	11 44 57	28 5 46	9♓43 38	16 27 51	16 40.2	0 35.9	0♓26.0	9 0.3	8 30.7	6 45.1	3 9.0	9 0.7	5 40.2
20 Sa	11 48 53	29 5 24	23 16 41	0♈ 9 44	16 31.9	29♓43.1	1 39.7	8 57.0	8 27.8	6 40.8	3 12.2	8 59.7	5D40.2
21 Su	11 52 50	0♈ 5 0	7♈ 6 35	14 6 44	16 25.2	28 48.9	2 53.3	8 52.9	8 25.0	6 36.6	3 15.4	8 58.8	5 40.2
22 M	11 56 46	1 4 33	21 9 37	28 14 42	16 20.5	27 54.5	4 6.9	8 48.1	8 22.4	6 32.4	3 18.5	8 57.9	5 40.2
23 Tu	12 0 43	2 4 5	5♉21 25	12♉29 16	16D18.0	27 1.0	5 20.6	8 42.5	8 20.0	6 28.3	3 21.7	8 57.0	5 40.3
24 W	12 4 39	3 3 34	19 37 44	26 46 23	16 17.6	26 9.5	6 34.2	8 36.1	8 17.8	6 24.3	3 24.8	8 56.1	5 40.4
25 Th	12 8 36	4 3 1	3♊54 49	11♊ 2 42	16 18.4	25 20.7	7 47.9	8 28.9	8 15.8	6 20.3	3 27.9	8 55.3	5 40.5
26 F	12 12 32	5 2 26	18 9 46	25 15 45	16 19.8	24 35.7	9 1.5	8 21.0	8 14.0	6 16.4	3 31.0	8 54.5	5 40.6
27 Sa	12 16 29	6 1 49	2♋20 27	9♋23 41	16R20.7	23 54.9	10 15.2	8 12.3	8 12.4	6 12.5	3 34.0	8 53.7	5 40.8
28 Su	12 20 26	7 1 9	16 25 18	23 25 8	16 20.3	23 19.0	11 28.8	8 2.8	8 10.9	6 8.7	3 37.0	8 53.0	5 40.9
29 M	12 24 22	8 0 27	0♌23 1	7♌18 47	16 18.3	22 48.3	12 42.5	7 52.6	8 9.7	6 5.0	3 40.0	8 52.3	5 41.1
30 Tu	12 28 19	8 59 42	14 12 15	21 3 13	16 14.7	22 23.1	13 56.1	7 41.7	8 8.6	6 1.3	3 43.0	8 51.6	5 41.4
31 W	12 32 15	9 58 55	27 51 30	4♍36 53	16 9.6	22 3.5	15 9.7	7 30.0	8 7.8	5 57.8	3 46.0	8 51.0	5 41.6

APRIL 1920 LONGITUDE

Day	Sid.Time	☉	0 hr ☽	Noon ☽	True ☊	☿	♀	♂	♃	♄	♅	♆	♇
1 Th	12 36 12	10♈58 6	11♍19 9	17♍58 8	16♏ 3.8	21♓49.7	16♓23.4	7♏17.5	8♌ 7.1	5♍54.3	3♓48.9	8♌50.4	5♋41.9
2 F	12 40 8	11 57 15	24 33 38	1♎ 5 32	15R58.1	21D41.6	17 37.0	7R 4.4	8R 6.6	5R50.9	3 51.8	8R49.8	5 42.2
3 Sa	12 44 5	12 56 21	7♎33 43	13 58 7	15 53.0	21 39.1	18 50.7	6 50.5	8 6.3	5 47.5	3 54.7	8 49.2	5 42.5
4 Su	12 48 1	13 55 26	20 18 43	26 35 35	15 49.1	21 42.2	20 4.3	6 36.0	8D 6.2	5 44.2	3 57.5	8 48.7	5 42.8
5 M	12 51 58	14 54 28	2♏48 49	8♏58 34	15 46.8	21 50.6	21 17.9	6 20.7	8 6.3	5 41.1	4 0.3	8 48.2	5 43.2
6 Tu	12 55 55	15 53 28	15 5 5	21 8 39	15D46.0	22 4.1	22 31.6	6 4.8	8 6.6	5 38.0	4 3.1	8 47.7	5 43.6
7 W	12 59 51	16 52 27	27 9 36	3♐ 8 19	15 46.6	22 22.6	23 45.2	5 48.3	8 7.0	5 34.9	4 5.9	8 47.3	5 44.0
8 Th	13 3 48	17 51 24	9♐ 5 16	15 0 55	15 48.0	22 45.9	24 58.9	5 31.1	8 7.7	5 32.0	4 8.6	8 46.9	5 44.4
9 F	13 7 44	18 50 19	20 55 48	26 50 28	15 49.8	23 13.7	26 12.5	5 13.3	8 8.5	5 29.2	4 11.3	8 46.5	5 44.9
10 Sa	13 11 41	19 49 12	2♑45 31	8♑41 31	15 51.4	23 45.9	27 26.2	4 55.0	8 9.5	5 26.4	4 14.0	8 46.2	5 45.3
11 Su	13 15 37	20 48 3	14 39 6	20 38 53	15R52.4	24 22.1	28 39.9	4 36.1	8 10.7	5 23.7	4 16.6	8 45.9	5 45.8
12 M	13 19 34	21 46 53	26 41 27	2♒47 26	15 52.5	25 2.2	29 53.5	4 16.7	8 12.1	5 21.2	4 19.2	8 45.6	5 46.3
13 Tu	13 23 30	22 45 41	8♒57 21	15 11 46	15 51.5	25 46.1	1♈ 7.2	3 56.8	8 13.7	5 18.7	4 21.8	8 45.4	5 46.9
14 W	13 27 27	23 44 27	21 31 8	27 55 51	15 49.5	26 33.5	2 20.8	3 36.4	8 15.5	5 16.3	4 24.3	8 45.2	5 47.4
15 Th	13 31 24	24 43 12	4♓26 14	11♓ 2 32	15 46.9	27 24.2	3 34.5	3 15.6	8 17.4	5 14.0	4 26.8	8 45.0	5 48.0
16 F	13 35 20	25 41 54	17 44 50	24 33 8	15 43.9	28 18.1	4 48.1	2 54.5	8 19.5	5 11.8	4 29.3	8 44.9	5 48.6
17 Sa	13 39 17	26 40 35	1♈27 18	8♈27 3	15 41.1	29 15.1	6 1.8	2 33.0	8 21.8	5 9.7	4 31.7	8 44.8	5 49.2
18 Su	13 43 13	27 39 14	15 32 0	22 41 36	15 38.9	0♈15.0	7 15.4	2 11.2	8 24.3	5 7.7	4 34.1	8 44.7	5 49.9
19 M	13 47 10	28 37 51	29 55 13	7♉12 8	15 37.5	1 17.6	8 29.1	1 49.1	8 27.0	5 5.7	4 36.5	8D44.7	5 50.6
20 Tu	13 51 6	29 36 27	14♉31 32	21 52 36	15D37.0	2 23.0	9 42.7	1 26.9	8 29.8	5 3.9	4 38.8	8 44.7	5 51.2
21 W	13 55 3	0♉35 0	29 14 28	6♊36 17	15 37.3	3 30.8	10 56.4	1 4.4	8 32.9	5 2.2	4 41.1	8 44.7	5 52.0
22 Th	13 58 59	1 33 31	13♊57 18	21 16 45	15 38.2	4 41.2	12 10.0	0 41.9	8 36.1	5 0.6	4 43.4	8 44.8	5 52.7
23 F	14 2 56	2 32 1	28 34 1	5♋48 31	15 39.2	5 53.9	13 23.7	0 19.3	8 39.4	4 59.1	4 45.6	8 44.9	5 53.4
24 Sa	14 6 53	3 30 28	12♋59 47	20 7 29	15 40.1	7 8.9	14 37.3	29♎56.7	8 43.0	4 57.7	4 47.8	8 45.0	5 54.2
25 Su	14 10 49	4 28 53	27 11 19	4♌11 6	15R40.7	8 26.1	15 50.9	29 34.1	8 46.7	4 56.4	4 49.9	8 45.2	5 55.0
26 M	14 14 46	5 27 15	11♌ 6 45	17 58 12	15 40.7	9 45.5	17 4.5	29 11.6	8 50.6	4 55.2	4 52.0	8 45.4	5 55.8
27 Tu	14 18 42	6 25 36	24 45 27	1♍28 35	15 40.3	11 7.0	18 18.1	28 49.2	8 54.6	4 54.1	4 54.0	8 45.6	5 56.6
28 W	14 22 39	7 23 54	8♍ 7 40	14 42 48	15 39.5	12 30.6	19 31.7	28 26.9	8 58.9	4 53.1	4 56.1	8 45.9	5 57.5
29 Th	14 26 35	8 22 10	21 14 8	27 41 47	15 38.6	13 56.3	20 45.3	28 4.9	9 3.2	4 52.2	4 58.0	8 46.2	5 58.4
30 F	14 30 32	9 20 25	4♎ 5 54	10♎26 38	15 37.7	15 23.9	21 58.9	27 43.1	9 7.8	4 51.4	4 60.0	8 46.5	5 59.2

Astro Data	Dy Hr Mn	Planet Ingress	Dy Hr Mn
☽0S	5 8:01	☿ ♈	2 19:25
♃☌♆	8 11:58	♀ ♓	18 15:31
☿ R	10 20:51	☿ ♓	19 16:26
♂ R	15 3:04	☉ ♈	20 21:59
☽0N	19 18:22		
♇ D	20 2:47	♀ ♈	12 2:07
☿0S	25 18:47	☿ ♈	17 18:06
☽0S	1 15:42	☉ ♉	20 9:39
☿ D	2 22:39	♂ ♎	23 20:29
♄✱♇	4 9:32		
♃ D	4 1:36	☿0N	23 8:57
♀0N	14 23:35	♃☌♆	24 13:52
☽0N	16 3:48	♄☍♅	27 0:25
♆ D	19 13:37	☽0S	28 21:25

Last Aspect Dy Hr Mn		☽ Ingress Dy Hr Mn
1 15:00	☿ △	♌ 1 17:22
2 10:34	♀ ☍	♍ 3 20:40
4 21:12	☉ ☍	♎ 6 1:53
7 7:41	♀ △	♏ 8 10:10
10 0:19	♀ □	♐ 10 21:35
12 19:58	♀ ✱	♑ 13 10:25
15 11:25	☉ ✱	♒ 15 21:58
18 5:28	♀ ☌	♓ 18 6:25
20 10:55	☉ ☌	♈ 20 11:43
21 3:13	♆ △	♉ 22 14:58
24 10:22	☿ ✱	♊ 24 17:25
26 10:21	☿ □	♋ 26 20:02
28 11:23	☿ △	♌ 28 23:20
29 14:42	♆ ☌	♍ 31 3:48

Last Aspect Dy Hr Mn		☽ Ingress Dy Hr Mn
1 18:48	☿ ☍	♎ 2 9:59
3 10:54	☉ ☍	♏ 4 18:33
6 16:25	♀ △	♐ 7 5:42
9 11:58	♀ □	♑ 9 18:25
11 20:32	☿ ✱	♒ 12 6:32
14 4:31	☉ ✱	♓ 14 15:50
16 19:54	☿ ☌	♈ 16 21:29
18 21:43	☉ ☌	♉ 19 0:08
19 14:32	♆ □	♊ 21 1:14
21 20:49	♀ ✱	♋ 23 2:22
25 3:58	♂ □	♌ 25 4:48
27 7:03	♂ ✱	♍ 27 9:21
27 22:34	☉ △	♎ 29 16:18

☽ Phases & Eclipses Dy Hr Mn	
4 21:12	○ 14♍01
12 17:57	☽ 21♐52
20 10:55	● 29♓33
27 6:45	☽ 6♋18
3 10:54	○ 13♎23
11 13:24	☽ 21♑21
18 21:43	● 28♈32
25 13:27	☽ 5♌02

Astro Data

1 MARCH 1920
Julian Day # 7365
Delta T 21.3 sec
SVP 06♓22'14"
Obliquity 23°26'53"
⚷ Chiron 4♈53.2
☽ Mean ☊ 19♏12.5

1 APRIL 1920
Julian Day # 7396
Delta T 21.4 sec
SVP 06♓22'11"
Obliquity 23°26'53"
⚷ Chiron 6♈40.3
☽ Mean ☊ 17♏34.0

LONGITUDE — MAY 1920

Day	Sid.Time	☉	0 hr ☽	Noon ☽	True ☊	☿	♀	♂	♃	♄	♅	♆	♇
1 Sa	14 34 28	10♉18 37	16♎44 9	22♎58 34	15♏37.0	16♈53.5	23♈12.5	27♎21.6	9♌12.5	4♍50.7	5♓ 1.9	8♌46.9	6♋ 0.1
2 Su	14 38 25	11 16 48	29 10 5	5♏18 52	15R36.6	18 25.1	24 26.1	27R 0.4	9 17.4	4R50.2	5 3.7	8 47.3	6 1.1
3 M	14 42 21	12 14 56	11♏25 6	17 28 58	15D36.4	19 58.6	25 39.7	26 39.6	9 22.4	4 49.7	5 5.5	8 47.7	6 2.0
4 Tu	14 46 18	13 13 4	23 30 42	29 30 31	15 36.5	21 34.1	26 53.2	26 19.2	9 27.6	4 49.3	5 7.3	8 48.1	6 3.0
5 W	14 50 15	14 11 9	5♐28 42	11♐25 32	15 36.6	23 11.5	28 6.8	25 59.2	9 32.9	4 49.1	5 9.0	8 48.6	6 3.9
6 Th	14 54 11	15 9 13	17 21 19	23 16 24	15R36.6	24 50.8	29 20.4	25 39.7	9 38.4	4 48.9	5 10.7	8 49.2	6 4.9
7 F	14 58 8	16 7 15	29 11 10	5♑ 6 1	15 36.6	26 32.0	0♉34.0	25 20.7	9 44.0	4D48.8	5 12.3	8 49.7	6 6.0
8 Sa	15 2 4	17 5 16	11♑ 1 23	16 57 45	15 36.5	28 15.2	1 47.6	25 2.2	9 49.8	4 48.9	5 13.9	8 50.3	6 7.0
9 Su	15 6 1	18 3 16	22 55 35	28 55 24	15 36.3	0♉ 0.3	3 1.1	24 44.3	9 55.7	4 49.1	5 15.5	8 50.9	6 8.0
10 M	15 9 57	19 1 14	4♒57 44	11♒ 3 8	15 36.1	1 47.4	4 14.7	24 27.1	10 1.8	4 49.3	5 17.0	8 51.6	6 9.1
11 Tu	15 13 54	19 59 11	17 12 8	23 25 17	15D36.0	3 36.4	5 28.3	24 10.4	10 8.0	4 49.7	5 18.5	8 52.3	6 10.2
12 W	15 17 50	20 57 6	29 43 5	6♓ 6 3	15 36.0	5 27.3	6 41.9	23 54.4	10 14.4	4 50.2	5 19.9	8 53.0	6 11.3
13 Th	15 21 47	21 55 1	12♓34 36	19 9 9	15 36.3	7 20.1	7 55.5	23 39.0	10 20.9	4 50.7	5 21.3	8 53.7	6 12.4
14 F	15 25 44	22 52 54	25 49 59	2♈37 19	15 36.9	9 14.9	9 9.0	23 24.4	10 27.6	4 51.4	5 22.6	8 54.5	6 13.5
15 Sa	15 29 40	23 50 45	9♈31 14	16 31 42	15 37.6	11 11.6	10 22.6	23 10.4	10 34.3	4 52.2	5 23.9	8 55.3	6 14.6
16 Su	15 33 37	24 48 36	23 38 30	0♉51 17	15 38.3	13 10.2	11 36.2	22 57.2	10 41.3	4 53.1	5 25.1	8 56.2	6 15.8
17 M	15 37 33	25 46 25	8♉ 9 31	15 32 33	15R38.8	15 10.6	12 49.8	22 44.8	10 48.3	4 54.1	5 26.3	8 57.0	6 16.9
18 Tu	15 41 30	26 44 13	22 59 31	0♊29 27	15 38.8	17 12.7	14 3.4	22 33.1	10 55.5	4 55.2	5 27.4	8 58.0	6 18.1
19 W	15 45 26	27 42 0	8♊ 1 19	15 33 59	15 38.2	19 16.6	15 17.0	22 22.2	11 2.9	4 56.4	5 28.5	8 58.9	6 19.3
20 Th	15 49 23	28 39 45	23 6 17	0♋37 8	15 37.0	21 22.0	16 30.5	22 12.2	11 10.3	4 57.7	5 29.6	8 59.9	6 20.5
21 F	15 53 19	29 37 29	8♋ 5 28	15 30 20	15 35.5	23 29.0	17 44.1	22 2.9	11 17.9	4 59.1	5 30.6	9 0.9	6 21.8
22 Sa	15 57 16	0♊35 11	22 50 55	0♌ 6 34	15 33.7	25 37.3	18 57.7	21 54.4	11 25.6	5 0.6	5 31.5	9 1.9	6 23.0
23 Su	16 1 13	1 32 52	7♌16 46	14 21 10	15 32.2	27 46.7	20 11.3	21 46.8	11 33.5	5 2.2	5 32.4	9 2.9	6 24.2
24 M	16 5 9	2 30 31	21 19 36	28 12 0	15D31.2	29 57.1	21 24.8	21 39.9	11 41.4	5 4.0	5 33.3	9 4.0	6 25.5
25 Tu	16 9 6	3 28 9	4♍58 27	11♍39 7	15 30.9	2♊ 8.3	22 38.4	21 33.9	11 49.5	5 5.8	5 34.1	9 5.1	6 26.8
26 W	16 13 2	4 25 45	18 14 16	24 44 13	15 31.4	4 19.9	23 51.9	21 28.7	11 57.7	5 7.7	5 34.9	9 6.3	6 28.1
27 Th	16 16 59	5 23 19	1♎ 9 19	7♎29 58	15 32.5	6 31.8	25 5.5	21 24.4	12 6.0	5 9.7	5 35.6	9 7.4	6 29.4
28 F	16 20 55	6 20 52	13 46 34	19 59 30	15 34.0	8 43.7	26 19.1	21 20.8	12 14.5	5 11.8	5 36.2	9 8.6	6 30.7
29 Sa	16 24 52	7 18 24	26 9 10	2♏15 58	15 35.4	10 55.3	27 32.6	21 18.1	12 23.0	5 14.0	5 36.9	9 9.9	6 32.0
30 Su	16 28 48	8 15 55	8♏20 15	14 22 21	15R36.4	13 6.2	28 46.2	21 16.1	12 31.7	5 16.3	5 37.4	9 11.1	6 33.3
31 M	16 32 45	9 13 24	20 22 36	26 21 18	15 36.5	15 16.4	29 59.7	21D15.0	12 40.5	5 18.8	5 37.9	9 12.4	6 34.6

LONGITUDE — JUNE 1920

Day	Sid.Time	☉	0 hr ☽	Noon ☽	True ☊	☿	♀	♂	♃	♄	♅	♆	♇
1 Tu	16 36 42	10♊10 52	2♐18 45	8♐15 11	15♏35.4	17♊25.4	1♊13.3	21♎14.6	12♌49.3	5♍21.3	5♓38.4	9♌13.7	6♋36.0
2 W	16 40 38	11 8 19	14 10 53	20 6 6	15R33.1	19 33.2	2 26.9	21 15.1	12 58.3	5 23.9	5 38.8	9 15.0	6 37.4
3 Th	16 44 35	12 5 46	26 1 5	1♑56 5	15 29.7	21 39.3	3 40.4	21 16.3	13 7.4	5 26.6	5 39.2	9 16.4	6 38.7
4 F	16 48 31	13 3 11	7♑51 21	13 47 10	15 25.3	23 43.8	4 54.0	21 18.3	13 16.6	5 29.3	5 39.5	9 17.8	6 40.1
5 Sa	16 52 28	14 0 36	19 43 50	25 41 40	15 20.5	25 46.3	6 7.6	21 21.1	13 25.9	5 32.2	5 39.8	9 19.2	6 41.5
6 Su	16 56 24	14 57 59	1♒40 59	7♒42 10	15 15.7	27 46.9	7 21.2	21 24.6	13 35.3	5 35.2	5 40.1	9 20.6	6 42.9
7 M	17 0 21	15 55 22	13 45 36	19 51 42	15 11.5	29 45.2	8 34.7	21 28.8	13 44.8	5 38.3	5 40.2	9 22.1	6 44.3
8 Tu	17 4 17	16 52 45	26 0 54	2♓13 40	15 8.3	1♋41.4	9 48.3	21 33.8	13 54.4	5 41.4	5 40.4	9 23.5	6 45.7
9 W	17 8 14	17 50 7	8♓30 27	14 51 45	15D 6.6	3 35.2	11 1.9	21 39.5	14 4.1	5 44.7	5 40.4	9 25.1	6 47.1
10 Th	17 12 11	18 47 28	21 18 1	27 49 42	15 6.2	5 26.6	12 15.5	21 45.9	14 13.9	5 48.0	5R40.5	9 26.6	6 48.5
11 F	17 16 7	19 44 49	4♈27 12	11♈10 53	15 6.9	7 15.6	13 29.1	21 53.0	14 23.8	5 51.5	5 40.5	9 28.1	6 50.0
12 Sa	17 20 4	20 42 9	18 1 1	24 57 47	15 8.3	9 2.2	14 42.7	22 0.9	14 33.8	5 55.0	5 40.4	9 29.7	6 51.4
13 Su	17 24 0	21 39 29	2♉ 1 12	9♉11 10	15R 9.6	10 46.3	15 56.4	22 9.4	14 43.8	5 58.6	5 40.3	9 31.3	6 52.8
14 M	17 27 57	22 36 49	16 27 26	23 49 30	15 10.1	12 27.9	17 10.0	22 18.6	14 54.0	6 2.3	5 40.1	9 32.9	6 54.3
15 Tu	17 31 53	23 34 8	1♊16 44	8♊48 15	15 9.2	14 7.0	18 23.6	22 28.5	15 4.2	6 6.1	5 39.9	9 34.6	6 55.7
16 W	17 35 50	24 31 27	16 23 4	23 59 58	15 6.5	15 43.6	19 37.3	22 39.0	15 14.6	6 9.9	5 39.7	9 36.3	6 57.2
17 Th	17 39 47	25 28 45	1♋37 43	9♋14 57	15 2.1	17 17.6	20 50.9	22 50.2	15 25.0	6 13.9	5 39.4	9 37.9	6 58.7
18 F	17 43 43	26 26 3	16 50 21	24 22 41	14 56.5	18 49.1	22 4.6	23 2.0	15 35.5	6 17.9	5 39.0	9 39.7	7 0.1
19 Sa	17 47 40	27 23 20	1♌50 46	9♌13 39	14 50.3	20 17.9	23 18.2	23 14.5	15 46.1	6 22.0	5 38.6	9 41.4	7 1.6
20 Su	17 51 36	28 20 36	16 30 31	23 40 47	14 44.5	21 44.2	24 31.9	23 27.6	15 56.7	6 26.2	5 38.2	9 43.1	7 3.1
21 M	17 55 33	29 17 52	0♍44 6	7♍40 16	14 39.9	23 7.8	25 45.6	23 41.3	16 7.5	6 30.5	5 37.7	9 44.9	7 4.6
22 Tu	17 59 29	0♋15 7	14 29 18	21 11 22	14 37.0	24 28.7	26 59.2	23 55.6	16 18.3	6 34.9	5 37.1	9 46.7	7 6.0
23 W	18 3 26	1 12 21	27 46 45	4♎15 52	14D35.8	25 47.0	28 12.9	24 10.5	16 29.2	6 39.3	5 36.5	9 48.5	7 7.5
24 Th	18 7 22	2 9 34	10♎39 10	16 57 13	14 36.0	27 2.4	29 26.6	24 25.9	16 40.2	6 43.8	5 35.9	9 50.4	7 9.0
25 F	18 11 19	3 6 48	23 10 33	29 19 44	14 37.1	28 15.1	0♋40.3	24 41.9	16 51.2	6 48.4	5 35.2	9 52.2	7 10.5
26 Sa	18 15 16	4 4 0	5♏25 22	11♏27 59	14R38.3	29 24.8	1 53.9	24 58.5	17 2.3	6 53.1	5 34.5	9 54.1	7 12.0
27 Su	18 19 12	5 1 12	17 28 8	23 26 20	14 38.6	0♌31.6	3 7.6	25 15.6	17 13.5	6 57.9	5 33.7	9 55.9	7 13.5
28 M	18 23 9	5 58 24	29 23 1	5♐18 39	14 37.3	1 35.4	4 21.3	25 33.2	17 24.7	7 2.7	5 32.9	9 57.8	7 15.0
29 Tu	18 27 5	6 55 35	11♐13 36	17 8 15	14 34.0	2 36.1	5 35.0	25 51.3	17 36.1	7 7.6	5 32.0	9 59.8	7 16.5
30 W	18 31 2	7 52 46	23 2 53	28 57 49	14 28.3	3 33.6	6 48.7	26 10.0	17 47.4	7 12.5	5 31.1	10 1.7	7 18.0

Astro Data (Dy Hr Mn)

♄ D	7 0:04	
☽0N	13 13:13	
☽0S	26 3:02	
♂ D	31 22:25	
♄☍♅	7 15:37	
☽0N	9 21:44	
♅ R	10 4:07	
☽0S	22 10:20	

Planet Ingress (Dy Hr Mn)

♀	♉	6 12:55
☿	♉	8 23:55
☉	♊	21 9:22
☿	♊	24 0:32
♀	♊	31 0:05
☿	♋	7 3:02
☉	♋	21 17:40
♀	♋	24 10:53
☿	♌	26 12:30

Last Aspect / ☽ Ingress (May)

Last Aspect Dy Hr Mn		☽ Ingress Dy Hr Mn
1 19:55	♂ ☌	♏ 2 1:37
3 1:47	☉ ☍	♐ 4 12:59
6 17:43	☿ △	♑ 7 1:39
9 3:33	♂ □	♒ 9 14:09
11 13:09	♂ △	♓ 12 0:32
13 18:19	☉ ✶	♈ 14 7:23
15 22:52	♂ ☍	♉ 16 10:35
18 6:25	☉ ☌	♊ 18 11:13
19 22:35	♂ △	♋ 20 11:01
22 5:22	☿ ✶	♌ 22 11:49
24 0:35	♂ ✶	♍ 24 15:10
26 11:28	♀ △	♎ 26 21:50
28 14:34	♂ ☌	♏ 29 7:32
30 8:26	♃ □	♐ 31 19:20

Last Aspect / ☽ Ingress (June)

Last Aspect Dy Hr Mn		☽ Ingress Dy Hr Mn
2 14:21	♂ ✶	♑ 3 8:05
5 3:17	♂ □	♒ 5 20:38
7 15:16	♂ △	♓ 8 7:43
9 18:58	☉ □	♈ 10 15:57
12 7:00	♂ ☍	♉ 12 20:35
13 21:25	♃ □	♊ 14 21:57
16 13:41	☉ ☌	♋ 16 21:26
18 9:59	♂ □	♌ 18 21:01
20 21:22	☉ ✶	♍ 20 22:44
23 0:53	♀ □	♎ 23 4:05
25 10:56	☿ □	♏ 25 13:19
26 23:30	♃ □	♐ 28 1:15
30 6:30	♂ ✶	♑ 30 14:06

☽ Phases & Eclipses (Dy Hr Mn)

3 1:47	○ 12♏19
3 1:51	☍ T 1.220
11 5:51	☽ 20♒13
18 6:25	● 26♉60
18 6:14:33	☌ P 0.974
24 21:07	☽ 3♍21
1 17:18	○ 10♐52
9 18:58	☽ 18♓35
16 13:41	● 25♊04
23 6:49	☽ 1♎29

Astro Data

1 MAY 1920
Julian Day # 7426
Delta T 21.5 sec
SVP 06♓22'09"
Obliquity 23°26'52"
⚷ Chiron 8♈21.3
☽ Mean ☊ 15♏58.6

1 JUNE 1920
Julian Day # 7457
Delta T 21.6 sec
SVP 06♓22'04"
Obliquity 23°26'52"
⚷ Chiron 9♈42.9
☽ Mean ☊ 14♏20.1

JULY 1920 LONGITUDE

Day	Sid.Time	☉	0 hr ☽	Noon ☽	True ☊	☿	♀	♂	♃	♄	♅	♆	♇
1 Th	18 34 58	8♋49 57	4♑53 16	10♑49 29	14♏20.5	4♌27.8	8♋ 2.5	26♎29.1	17♌58.9	7♍17.6	5♓30.2	10♌ 3.6	7♋19.5
2 F	18 38 55	9 47 8	16 46 40	22 45 0	14R 11.1	5 18.6	9 16.2	26 48.8	18 10.4	7 22.7	5R 29.2	10 5.6	7 20.9
3 Sa	18 42 51	10 44 19	28 44 41	4♒45 53	14 0.7	6 5.9	10 29.9	27 8.9	18 22.0	7 27.9	5 28.2	10 7.6	7 22.4
4 Su	18 46 48	11 41 29	10♒48 49	16 53 40	13 50.3	6 49.5	11 43.7	27 29.4	18 33.6	7 33.1	5 27.1	10 9.6	7 23.9
5 M	18 50 45	12 38 40	23 0 41	29 10 7	13 40.8	7 29.4	12 57.4	27 50.4	18 45.3	7 38.4	5 26.0	10 11.6	7 25.4
6 Tu	18 54 41	13 35 51	5♓22 14	11♓37 20	13 33.1	8 5.4	14 11.2	28 11.9	18 57.0	7 43.8	5 24.8	10 13.6	7 26.9
7 W	18 58 38	14 33 3	17 55 47	24 17 55	13 27.6	8 37.3	15 24.9	28 33.8	19 8.8	7 49.2	5 23.6	10 15.6	7 28.4
8 Th	19 2 34	15 30 14	0♈44 7	7♈14 47	13 24.6	9 5.1	16 38.7	28 56.2	19 20.7	7 54.8	5 22.3	10 17.7	7 29.9
9 F	19 6 31	16 27 26	13 50 18	20 31 1	13D 23.5	9 28.6	17 52.5	29 18.9	19 32.6	8 0.3	5 21.1	10 19.8	7 31.3
10 Sa	19 10 27	17 24 39	27 17 18	4♉ 9 25	13 23.7	9 47.7	19 6.3	29 42.1	19 44.6	8 6.0	5 19.7	10 21.8	7 32.8
11 Su	19 14 24	18 21 52	11♉ 7 32	18 11 46	13R 24.2	10 2.3	20 20.1	0♏ 5.7	19 56.6	8 11.7	5 18.4	10 23.9	7 34.3
12 M	19 18 20	19 19 6	25 22 1	2♊38 5	13 23.7	10 12.2	21 34.0	0 29.7	20 8.6	8 17.4	5 17.0	10 26.0	7 35.8
13 Tu	19 22 17	20 16 20	9♊59 34	17 25 51	13 21.3	10R 17.4	22 47.8	0 54.1	20 20.8	8 23.2	5 15.5	10 28.1	7 37.2
14 W	19 26 14	21 13 35	24 56 9	2♋29 27	13 16.5	10 17.8	24 1.6	1 18.9	20 32.9	8 29.1	5 14.0	10 30.2	7 38.7
15 Th	19 30 10	22 10 50	10♋ 4 39	17 40 26	13 9.2	10 13.4	25 15.5	1 44.1	20 45.1	8 35.1	5 12.5	10 32.4	7 40.2
16 F	19 34 7	23 8 6	25 15 31	2♌48 32	12 59.9	10 4.2	26 29.4	2 9.7	20 57.4	8 41.1	5 11.0	10 34.5	7 41.6
17 Sa	19 38 3	24 5 22	10♌18 13	17 43 25	12 49.8	9 50.2	27 43.2	2 35.6	21 9.7	8 47.1	5 9.4	10 36.6	7 43.1
18 Su	19 42 0	25 2 38	25 3 7	2♍16 31	12 40.0	9 31.7	28 57.1	3 1.9	21 22.1	8 53.2	5 7.7	10 38.8	7 44.5
19 M	19 45 56	25 59 55	9♍23 2	16 22 19	12 31.6	9 8.6	0♌11.0	3 28.6	21 34.4	8 59.4	5 6.1	10 41.0	7 45.9
20 Tu	19 49 53	26 57 11	23 14 11	29 58 42	12 25.4	8 41.3	1 24.9	3 55.6	21 46.9	9 5.6	5 4.4	10 43.1	7 47.4
21 W	19 53 49	27 54 28	6♎36 4	13♎ 6 38	12 21.7	8 10.2	2 38.8	4 22.9	21 59.3	9 11.9	5 2.7	10 45.3	7 48.8
22 Th	19 57 46	28 51 46	19 30 50	25 49 15	12D 20.0	7 35.5	3 52.7	4 50.6	22 11.8	9 18.2	5 0.9	10 47.5	7 50.2
23 F	20 1 43	29 49 4	2♏ 2 28	8♏11 7	12R 19.8	6 57.8	5 6.6	5 18.6	22 24.4	9 24.5	4 59.1	10 49.7	7 51.6
24 Sa	20 5 39	0♌46 22	14 15 53	20 17 24	12 19.9	6 17.7	6 20.5	5 47.0	22 36.9	9 30.9	4 57.3	10 51.9	7 53.0
25 Su	20 9 36	1 43 40	26 16 19	2♐13 15	12 19.2	5 35.7	7 34.4	6 15.7	22 49.6	9 37.4	4 55.4	10 54.1	7 54.4
26 M	20 13 32	2 40 59	8♐ 8 49	14 3 33	12 16.8	4 52.6	8 48.4	6 44.6	23 2.2	9 43.9	4 53.5	10 56.3	7 55.8
27 Tu	20 17 29	3 38 18	19 57 58	25 52 32	12 12.0	4 9.1	10 2.3	7 13.9	23 14.9	9 50.5	4 51.6	10 58.5	7 57.1
28 W	20 21 25	4 35 38	1♑47 39	7♑43 41	12 4.4	3 26.0	11 16.2	7 43.5	23 27.6	9 57.1	4 49.7	11 0.7	7 58.5
29 Th	20 25 22	5 32 59	13 40 57	19 39 43	11 54.3	2 44.1	12 30.2	8 13.4	23 40.3	10 3.7	4 47.7	11 2.9	7 59.8
30 F	20 29 18	6 30 20	25 40 10	1♒42 31	11 42.1	2 4.1	13 44.1	8 43.5	23 53.1	10 10.4	4 45.7	11 5.1	8 1.2
31 Sa	20 33 15	7 27 42	7♒46 53	13 53 23	11 28.7	1 26.8	14 58.1	9 14.0	24 5.8	10 17.1	4 43.7	11 7.3	8 2.5

AUGUST 1920 LONGITUDE

Day	Sid.Time	☉	0 hr ☽	Noon ☽	True ☊	☿	♀	♂	♃	♄	♅	♆	♇
1 Su	20 37 12	8♌25 5	20♒ 2 7	26♒13 9	11♏15.3	0♌53.0	16♌12.1	9♏44.7	24♌18.6	10♍23.9	4♓41.6	11♌ 9.6	8♋ 3.8
2 M	20 41 8	9 22 29	2♓26 35	8♓42 29	11R 2.9	0R 23.3	17 26.0	10 15.7	24 31.5	10 30.7	4R 39.5	11 11.8	8 5.2
3 Tu	20 45 5	10 19 54	15 0 58	21 22 9	10 52.7	29♋58.3	18 40.0	10 46.9	24 44.3	10 37.5	4 37.4	11 14.0	8 6.5
4 W	20 49 1	11 17 20	27 46 10	4♈13 12	10 45.1	29 38.5	19 54.0	11 18.4	24 57.2	10 44.4	4 35.3	11 15.9	8 7.7
5 Th	20 52 58	12 14 47	10♈43 28	17 17 12	10 40.5	29 24.5	21 8.0	11 50.2	25 10.1	10 51.3	4 33.2	11 18.4	8 9.0
6 F	20 56 54	13 12 15	23 54 37	0♉36 0	10 38.3	29D 16.6	22 22.0	12 22.2	25 23.0	10 58.2	4 31.0	11 20.7	8 10.3
7 Sa	21 0 51	14 9 44	7♉21 36	14 11 39	10 37.7	29 15.1	23 36.0	12 54.5	25 36.0	11 5.2	4 28.8	11 22.9	8 11.5
8 Su	21 4 47	15 7 15	21 6 19	28 5 44	10 37.7	29 20.2	24 50.0	13 27.0	25 48.9	11 12.2	4 26.6	11 25.1	8 12.8
9 M	21 8 44	16 4 48	5♊ 9 57	12♊18 52	10 36.8	29 32.1	26 4.0	13 59.8	26 1.9	11 19.3	4 24.4	11 27.3	8 14.0
10 Tu	21 12 41	17 2 22	19 32 17	26 49 48	10 34.2	29 50.9	27 18.0	14 32.8	26 14.9	11 26.4	4 22.2	11 29.6	8 15.2
11 W	21 16 37	17 59 57	4♋10 56	11♋34 56	10 29.0	0♌16.7	28 32.0	15 6.1	26 27.9	11 33.5	4 19.9	11 31.8	8 16.4
12 Th	21 20 34	18 57 34	19 0 59	26 28 6	10 21.1	0 49.5	29 46.1	15 39.6	26 40.9	11 40.6	4 17.6	11 34.0	8 17.6
13 F	21 24 30	19 55 12	3♌55 10	11♌21 6	10 11.2	1 29.1	1♍ 0.1	16 13.3	26 54.0	11 47.8	4 15.3	11 36.2	8 18.8
14 Sa	21 28 27	20 52 51	18 44 44	26 5 0	10 0.2	2 15.6	2 14.2	16 47.3	27 7.0	11 55.0	4 13.0	11 38.4	8 20.0
15 Su	21 32 23	21 50 32	3♍20 55	10♍31 37	9 49.3	3 8.8	3 28.2	17 21.5	27 20.1	12 2.2	4 10.7	11 40.6	8 21.1
16 M	21 36 20	22 48 14	17 36 25	24 34 50	9 39.9	4 8.5	4 42.3	17 55.9	27 33.1	12 9.5	4 8.4	11 42.8	8 22.2
17 Tu	21 40 16	23 45 56	1♎26 33	8♎11 27	9 32.8	5 14.5	5 56.4	18 30.5	27 46.2	12 16.8	4 6.1	11 45.0	8 23.4
18 W	21 44 13	24 43 40	14 49 35	21 21 9	9 28.2	6 26.6	7 10.4	19 5.4	27 59.3	12 24.1	4 3.7	11 47.2	8 24.5
19 Th	21 48 10	25 41 26	27 46 28	4♏ 6 0	9D 26.0	7 44.5	8 24.5	19 40.4	28 12.4	12 31.4	4 1.3	11 49.4	8 25.5
20 F	21 52 6	26 39 12	10♏20 16	16 29 50	9 25.5	9 7.9	9 38.5	20 15.7	28 25.4	12 38.7	3 59.0	11 51.5	8 26.6
21 Sa	21 56 3	27 36 59	22 35 22	28 37 30	9R 25.7	10 36.4	10 52.6	20 51.2	28 38.5	12 46.1	3 56.6	11 53.7	8 27.7
22 Su	21 59 59	28 34 48	4♐36 55	10♐34 16	9 25.7	12 9.6	12 6.7	21 26.9	28 51.6	12 53.5	3 54.2	11 55.9	8 28.7
23 M	22 3 56	29 32 38	16 30 14	22 25 25	9 24.2	13 47.1	13 20.7	22 2.8	29 4.7	13 0.9	3 51.8	11 58.0	8 29.7
24 Tu	22 7 52	0♍30 29	28 20 27	4♑15 52	9 20.7	15 28.5	14 34.8	22 38.8	29 17.8	13 8.3	3 49.5	12 0.1	8 30.7
25 W	22 11 49	1 28 21	10♑12 12	16 9 55	9 14.8	17 13.4	15 48.8	23 15.1	29 30.9	13 15.7	3 47.1	12 2.3	8 31.7
26 Th	22 15 45	2 26 15	22 9 25	28 11 4	9 6.5	19 1.2	17 2.9	23 51.5	29 43.9	13 23.1	3 44.7	12 4.4	8 32.7
27 F	22 19 42	3 24 10	4♒15 10	10♒21 57	8 56.2	20 51.6	18 17.0	24 28.2	29 57.0	13 30.6	3 42.3	12 6.5	8 33.6
28 Sa	22 23 39	4 22 6	16 31 35	22 44 12	8 44.8	22 44.1	19 31.0	25 5.0	0♍10.1	13 38.1	3 39.9	12 8.6	8 34.6
29 Su	22 27 35	5 20 4	28 59 52	5♓18 36	8 33.3	24 38.2	20 45.0	25 42.0	0 23.1	13 45.5	3 37.5	12 10.7	8 35.5
30 M	22 31 32	6 18 3	11♓40 24	18 5 14	8 22.8	26 33.7	21 59.1	26 19.1	0 36.2	13 53.0	3 35.1	12 12.7	8 36.4
31 Tu	22 35 28	7 16 4	24 33 1	1♈ 3 43	8 14.1	28 30.0	23 13.1	26 56.5	0 49.2	14 0.5	3 32.7	12 14.8	8 37.2

Astro Data Dy Hr Mn	Planet Ingress Dy Hr Mn	Last Aspect Dy Hr Mn	☽ Ingress Dy Hr Mn	Last Aspect Dy Hr Mn	☽ Ingress Dy Hr Mn	☽ Phases & Eclipses Dy Hr Mn	Astro Data
♄✶♇ 1 12:27	♂ ♏ 10 18:14	2 20:43 ♂ □	♒ 3 2:30	1 8:27 ♃ ☍	♓ 1 19:18	1 8:40 ○ 9♑11	1 JULY 1920
☽0N 7 5:01	♀ ♌ 18 20:26	5 9:42 ♂ △	♓ 5 13:37	4 3:25 ☿ △	♈ 4 4:10	9 5:05 ☽ 16♈40	Julian Day # 7487
☿ R 13 14:05	☉ ♌ 23 4:35	6 18:43 ♀ △	♈ 7 22:38	6 9:36 ☿ □	♉ 6 10:56	15 20:25 ● 22♋60	Delta T 21.7 sec
☽0S 19 19:45		10 4:22 ♂ ☍	♉ 10 4:45	8 14:18 ☿ ✶	♊ 8 15:15	22 19:20 ☽ 29♎38	SVP 06♓21'59"
♃∠♇ 25 10:17	☿ ♋ 2 22:10	11 17:04 ♀ ✶	♊ 12 7:40	10 13:57 ♀ ✶	♋ 10 17:11	30 23:19 ○ 7♒26	Obliquity 23°26'51"
	☿ ♌ 10 9:13	13 16:54 ♃ ✶	♋ 14 8:03	11 18:22 ♂ △	♌ 12 17:41		⚷ Chiron 10♈24.6
☽0N 3 11:32	♀ ♍ 12 4:31	16 2:07 ♀ ☌	♌ 16 7:32	14 13:54 ♃ ☌	♍ 14 18:27	7 12:50 ☽ 14♉41	☽ Mean ☊ 12♏44.8
☿ D 6 17:37	☉ ♍ 23 11:21	17 17:52 ♃ ☌	♍ 18 8:12	16 0:35 ♂ ✶	♎ 16 21:28	14 3:44 ● 21♌02	
♄⚺♆ 10 15:41	♃ ♍ 27 5:29	20 7:06 ☉ ✶	♎ 20 12:02	19 0:50 ♃ ✶	♏ 19 4:12	21 10:51 ☽ 28♏03	1 AUGUST 1920
☽0S 16 6:18	☿ ♍ 31 18:29	22 19:20 ☉ □	♏ 22 20:03	21 12:15 ♃ □	♐ 21 14:45	29 13:02 ○ 5♓52	Julian Day # 7518
☽0N 30 18:12		24 16:57 ♃ □	♐ 25 7:31	24 1:58 ♃ △	♑ 24 3:22		Delta T 21.8 sec
		27 6:47 ♃ △	♑ 27 20:22	26 3:35 ♂ ✶	♒ 26 15:36		SVP 06♓21'55"
		28 16:38 ♄ △	♒ 30 8:37	28 17:22 ♂ □	♓ 29 1:55		Obliquity 23°26'52"
				31 4:38 ♂ △	♈ 31 10:03		⚷ Chiron 10♈20.2R
							☽ Mean ☊ 11♏06.3

LONGITUDE SEPTEMBER 1920

Day	Sid.Time	☉	0 hr ☽	Noon ☽	True ☊	☿	♀	♂	♃	♄	♅	♆	♇
1 W	22 39 25	8♍14 7	7♈37 16	14♈13 36	8♏ 7.9	0♍26.9	24♍27.2	27♏34.0	1♍ 2.3	14♍ 8.0	3♓30.3	12♌16.9	8♋38.1
2 Th	22 43 21	9 12 12	20 52 42	27 34 32	8R 4.2	2 24.1	25 41.2	28 11.6	1 15.3	14 15.5	3R 27.9	12 18.9	8 38.9
3 F	22 47 18	10 10 18	4♉19 8	11♉ 6 30	8D 2.9	4 21.4	26 55.3	28 49.5	1 28.3	14 23.1	3 25.6	12 20.9	8 39.8
4 Sa	22 51 14	11 8 27	17 56 42	24 49 45	8 3.1	6 18.5	28 9.3	29 27.5	1 41.3	14 30.6	3 23.2	12 22.9	8 40.6
5 Su	22 55 11	12 6 37	1♊45 41	8♊44 31	8R 3.9	8 15.1	29 23.3	0♐ 5.7	1 54.3	14 38.1	3 20.8	12 24.9	8 41.4
6 M	22 59 7	13 4 50	15 46 14	22 50 44	8 4.2	10 11.3	0♎37.4	0 44.0	2 7.2	14 45.7	3 18.5	12 26.9	8 42.1
7 Tu	23 3 4	14 3 4	29 57 52	7♋ 7 22	8 3.1	12 6.8	1 51.4	1 22.5	2 20.2	14 53.2	3 16.1	12 28.9	8 42.9
8 W	23 7 1	15 1 21	14♋18 55	21 32 5	7 60.0	14 1.4	3 5.5	2 1.1	2 33.1	15 0.8	3 13.8	12 30.8	8 43.6
9 Th	23 10 57	15 59 40	28 46 18	6♌ 0 56	7 54.7	15 55.3	4 19.5	2 40.0	2 46.0	15 8.3	3 11.5	12 32.7	8 44.3
10 F	23 14 54	16 58 1	13♌15 18	20 28 37	7 47.7	17 48.2	5 33.5	3 18.9	2 58.9	15 15.8	3 9.2	12 34.7	8 45.0
11 Sa	23 18 50	17 56 23	27 40 8	4♍49 2	7 39.8	19 40.1	6 47.6	3 58.0	3 11.8	15 23.4	3 6.9	12 36.6	8 45.6
12 Su	23 22 47	18 54 48	11♍54 37	18 56 11	7 31.9	21 31.0	8 1.6	4 37.3	3 24.7	15 30.9	3 4.6	12 38.4	8 46.3
13 M	23 26 43	19 53 14	25 53 11	2♎45 8	7 25.0	23 20.9	9 15.7	5 16.8	3 37.5	15 38.4	3 2.3	12 40.3	8 46.9
14 Tu	23 30 40	20 51 43	9♎31 42	16 12 41	7 19.9	25 9.7	10 29.7	5 56.3	3 50.3	15 46.0	3 0.1	12 42.2	8 47.5
15 W	23 34 36	21 50 13	22 48 1	29 17 44	7 16.9	26 57.4	11 43.7	6 36.1	4 3.0	15 53.5	2 57.8	12 44.0	8 48.0
16 Th	23 38 33	22 48 45	5♏42 1	12♏ 1 9	7D 15.8	28 44.1	12 57.7	7 15.9	4 15.8	16 1.0	2 55.6	12 45.8	8 48.6
17 F	23 42 30	23 47 18	18 15 29	24 25 28	7 16.3	0♎29.7	14 11.7	7 55.9	4 28.5	16 8.5	2 53.4	12 47.6	8 49.1
18 Sa	23 46 26	24 45 54	0♐31 37	6♐34 29	7 17.7	2 14.3	15 25.7	8 36.1	4 41.2	16 16.0	2 51.2	12 49.3	8 49.6
19 Su	23 50 23	25 44 31	12 34 39	18 32 45	7 19.1	3 57.8	16 39.7	9 16.4	4 53.8	16 23.5	2 49.1	12 51.1	8 50.1
20 M	23 54 19	26 43 10	24 29 24	0♑25 15	7R 19.9	5 40.3	17 53.7	9 56.8	5 6.4	16 30.9	2 46.9	12 52.8	8 50.6
21 Tu	23 58 16	27 41 50	6♑20 55	12 17 2	7 19.5	7 21.8	19 7.7	10 37.3	5 19.0	16 38.4	2 44.8	12 54.5	8 51.0
22 W	0 2 12	28 40 32	18 14 11	24 12 56	7 17.5	9 2.3	20 21.7	11 18.0	5 31.5	16 45.8	2 42.8	12 56.2	8 51.5
23 Th	0 6 9	29 39 16	0♒13 47	6♒17 15	7 13.8	10 41.8	21 35.6	11 58.8	5 44.0	16 53.3	2 40.7	12 57.9	8 51.9
24 F	0 10 5	0♎38 2	12 23 43	18 33 35	7 8.8	12 20.4	22 49.6	12 39.8	5 56.5	17 0.7	2 38.7	12 59.5	8 52.2
25 Sa	0 14 2	1 36 49	24 47 8	1♓ 4 36	7 2.9	13 58.0	24 3.5	13 20.8	6 8.9	17 8.1	2 36.6	13 1.1	8 52.6
26 Su	0 17 59	2 35 38	7♓26 7	13 51 48	6 56.8	15 34.7	25 17.5	14 2.0	6 21.2	17 15.4	2 34.7	13 2.7	8 52.9
27 M	0 21 55	3 34 29	20 21 39	26 55 35	6 51.2	17 10.5	26 31.4	14 43.3	6 33.6	17 22.8	2 32.7	13 4.3	8 53.2
28 Tu	0 25 52	4 33 22	3♈33 31	10♈15 13	6 46.7	18 45.3	27 45.3	15 24.7	6 45.9	17 30.1	2 30.8	13 5.8	8 53.5
29 W	0 29 48	5 32 17	17 0 30	23 49 5	6 43.7	20 19.3	28 59.2	16 6.2	6 58.1	17 37.4	2 28.9	13 7.3	8 53.8
30 Th	0 33 45	6 31 14	0♉40 41	7♉34 59	6D 42.3	21 52.4	0♏13.1	16 47.8	7 10.3	17 44.7	2 27.0	13 8.8	8 54.0

LONGITUDE OCTOBER 1920

Day	Sid.Time	☉	0 hr ☽	Noon ☽	True ☊	☿	♀	♂	♃	♄	♅	♆	♇
1 F	0 37 41	7♎30 13	14♉31 41	21♉30 28	6♏42.4	23♎24.7	1♏27.0	17♐29.6	7♍22.4	17♍52.0	2♓25.2	13♌10.3	8♋54.2
2 Sa	0 41 38	8 29 15	28 31 2	5♊33 8	6 43.5	24 56.1	2 40.9	18 11.5	7 34.5	17 59.2	2R 23.4	13 11.7	8 54.4
3 Su	0 45 34	9 28 19	12♊36 28	19 40 46	6 45.0	26 26.7	3 54.7	18 53.4	7 46.6	18 6.4	2 21.6	13 13.2	8 54.6
4 M	0 49 31	10 27 25	26 45 50	3♋51 23	6 46.3	27 56.4	5 8.6	19 35.5	7 58.6	18 13.6	2 19.9	13 14.5	8 54.7
5 Tu	0 53 27	11 26 33	10♋57 11	18 3 0	6R 46.8	29 25.3	6 22.5	20 17.7	8 10.5	18 20.8	2 18.2	13 15.9	8 54.8
6 W	0 57 24	12 25 44	25 8 32	2♌13 32	6 46.3	0♏53.3	7 36.3	21 0.0	8 22.4	18 27.9	2 16.5	13 17.3	8 54.9
7 Th	1 1 21	13 24 57	9♌17 40	16 20 38	6 44.7	2 20.4	8 50.2	21 42.4	8 34.2	18 35.0	2 14.9	13 18.6	8 55.0
8 F	1 5 17	14 24 13	23 22 4	0♍21 36	6 42.2	3 46.7	10 4.0	22 25.0	8 46.0	18 42.1	2 13.3	13 19.9	8 55.1
9 Sa	1 9 14	15 23 30	7♍18 54	14 13 33	6 39.1	5 12.1	11 17.8	23 7.6	8 57.7	18 49.1	2 11.8	13 21.1	8R 55.1
10 Su	1 13 10	16 22 50	21 5 15	27 53 37	6 36.1	6 36.6	12 31.7	23 50.3	9 9.3	18 56.1	2 10.2	13 22.3	8 55.1
11 M	1 17 7	17 22 12	4♎38 23	11♎19 17	6 33.5	8 0.1	13 45.5	24 33.1	9 20.9	19 3.1	2 8.8	13 23.5	8 55.1
12 Tu	1 21 3	18 21 37	17 56 8	24 28 47	6 31.7	9 22.7	14 59.3	25 16.1	9 32.4	19 10.0	2 7.3	13 24.7	8 55.0
13 W	1 25 0	19 21 3	0♏57 11	7♏21 18	6D 30.9	10 44.3	16 13.1	25 59.1	9 43.9	19 16.9	2 5.9	13 25.8	8 55.0
14 Th	1 28 56	20 20 31	13 41 15	19 57 8	6 30.9	12 4.8	17 26.9	26 42.3	9 55.3	19 23.7	2 4.6	13 27.0	8 54.9
15 F	1 32 53	21 20 1	26 9 11	2♐17 41	6 31.7	13 24.2	18 40.7	27 25.5	10 6.6	19 30.6	2 3.2	13 28.0	8 54.8
16 Sa	1 36 50	22 19 34	8♐22 58	14 25 26	6 32.9	14 42.4	19 54.4	28 8.8	10 17.8	19 37.3	2 2.0	13 29.1	8 54.6
17 Su	1 40 46	23 19 8	20 25 30	26 23 40	6 34.2	15 59.3	21 8.2	28 52.2	10 29.0	19 44.1	2 0.7	13 30.1	8 54.5
18 M	1 44 43	24 18 43	2♑20 27	8♑16 24	6 35.3	17 14.9	22 21.9	29 35.7	10 40.1	19 50.7	1 59.5	13 31.1	8 54.3
19 Tu	1 48 39	25 18 21	14 12 5	20 8 6	6 36.1	18 29.0	23 35.7	0♑19.3	10 51.1	19 57.4	1 58.4	13 32.1	8 54.1
20 W	1 52 36	26 18 0	26 5 3	2♒ 3 30	6R 36.4	19 41.5	24 49.4	1 3.0	11 2.0	20 4.0	1 57.3	13 33.0	8 53.8
21 Th	1 56 32	27 17 41	8♒ 4 4	14 7 18	6 36.1	20 52.4	26 3.1	1 46.8	11 12.9	20 10.5	1 56.2	13 33.9	8 53.6
22 F	2 0 29	28 17 24	20 13 45	26 23 57	6 35.5	22 1.3	27 16.8	2 30.6	11 23.6	20 17.0	1 55.2	13 34.8	8 53.3
23 Sa	2 4 25	29 17 8	2♓38 19	8♓57 18	6 34.7	23 8.2	28 30.4	3 14.6	11 34.3	20 23.5	1 54.3	13 35.6	8 53.0
24 Su	2 8 22	0♏16 54	15 21 13	21 50 19	6 33.8	24 12.9	29 44.1	3 58.6	11 44.9	20 29.8	1 53.3	13 36.4	8 52.7
25 M	2 12 19	1 16 42	28 24 47	5♈ 4 40	6 33.1	25 15.0	0♐57.7	4 42.7	11 55.4	20 36.2	1 52.5	13 37.2	8 52.3
26 Tu	2 16 15	2 16 32	11♈49 57	18 40 30	6 32.6	26 14.5	2 11.3	5 26.8	12 5.9	20 42.5	1 51.6	13 37.9	8 52.0
27 W	2 20 12	3 16 24	25 36 2	2♉36 12	6D 32.3	27 10.8	3 24.9	6 11.1	12 16.2	20 48.7	1 50.8	13 38.6	8 51.6
28 Th	2 24 8	4 16 17	9♉40 32	16 48 31	6 32.3	28 3.8	4 38.5	6 55.4	12 26.5	20 54.9	1 50.1	13 39.3	8 51.2
29 F	2 28 5	5 16 12	23 59 29	1♊12 49	6 32.3	28 53.0	5 52.1	7 39.8	12 36.6	21 1.0	1 49.4	13 39.9	8 50.7
30 Sa	2 32 1	6 16 10	8♊27 46	15 43 39	6R 32.4	29 38.1	7 5.7	8 24.2	12 46.7	21 7.1	1 48.8	13 40.5	8 50.3
31 Su	2 35 58	7 16 10	22 59 46	0♋15 26	6 32.4	0♐18.5	8 19.2	9 8.7	12 56.7	21 13.1	1 48.2	13 41.1	8 49.8

Astro Data Dy Hr Mn	Planet Ingress Dy Hr Mn	Last Aspect Dy Hr Mn	☽ Ingress Dy Hr Mn	Last Aspect Dy Hr Mn	☽ Ingress Dy Hr Mn	☽ Phases & Eclipses Dy Hr Mn	Astro Data
♀0S 7 14:32	♂ ♐ 4 20:27	1 8:30 ♆ △	♉ 2 16:19	1 5:48 ♄ △	♊ 2 2:32	5 19:05 ☽ 12♊53	1 SEPTEMBER 1920
♃☍♅ 10 16:10	♀ ♎ 5 11:53	4 19:30 ♀ △	♊ 4 20:58	4 2:13 ☿ △	♋ 4 5:29	12 12:51 ● 19♍26	Julian Day # 7549
☽0S 12 16:19	☿ ♎ 16 17:13	5 22:16 ♄ □	♋ 7 0:04	5 12:36 ♄ ✶	♌ 6 8:14	20 4:55 ☽ 26♐55	Delta T 21.9 sec
☿0S 17 23:38	☉ ♎ 23 8:28	8 1:16 ☉ ✶	♌ 9 2:02	7 22:17 ♂ △	♍ 8 11:23	28 1:56 ○ 4♈38	SVP 06♓21'51"
☽0N 27 1:56	♀ ♏ 29 19:45	9 22:52 ♆ ☌	♍ 11 3:54	10 5:06 ♂ □	♎ 10 15:44		Obliquity 23°26'52"
		12 18:56 ☿ ☌	♎ 13 7:10	12 14:14 ♂ ✶	♏ 12 22:14	5 0:53 ☽ 11♋29	⚷ Chiron 9♈30.0R
♃✶♇ 8 18:39	☿ ♏ 5 9:27	14 5:42 ♆ ✶	♏ 15 13:19	14 11:02 ♄ ✶	♐ 15 7:30	12 0:50 ● 18♎24	☽ Mean ☊ 9♏27.8
♇ R 9 14:24	♂ ♑ 18 13:22	17 11:41 ☉ ✶	♐ 17 22:58	17 18:06 ♂ ☌	♑ 17 19:16	20 0:28 ☽ 26♑19	
☽0S 10 0:28	☉ ♏ 23 17:13	20 4:55 ☉ □	♑ 20 11:09	20 0:28 ☉ □	♒ 20 7:52	27 14:09 ○ 3♉52	1 OCTOBER 1920
☽0N 24 10:59	♀ ♐ 24 5:11	22 22:45 ☉ △	♒ 22 23:33	22 17:01 ☉ △	♓ 22 18:57	27 14:11 ☍T 1.398	Julian Day # 7579
	☿ ♐ 30 12:40	24 22:27 ♀ △	♓ 25 9:57	24 17:46 ♄ △	♈ 25 2:52		Delta T 22.0 sec
		26 18:27 ♄ ☍	♈ 27 17:35	26 3:10 ♆ △	♉ 27 7:33		SVP 06♓21'49"
		29 6:36 ☿ ☍	♉ 29 22:49	29 8:36 ☿ ☍	♊ 29 9:59		Obliquity 23°26'52"
				30 21:03 ♄ □	♋ 31 11:34		⚷ Chiron 8♈13.6R
							☽ Mean ☊ 7♏52.5

NOVEMBER 1920 LONGITUDE

Day	Sid.Time	☉	0 hr ☽	Noon ☽	True ☊	☿	♀	♂	♃	♄	♅	♆	♇
1 M	2 39 54	8♏16 11	7♋30 3	14♋43 4	6♏32.2	0♐53.7	9♐32.7	9♑53.3	13♍ 6.6	21♍19.1	1♓47.7	13♌41.6	8♋49.3
2 Tu	2 43 51	9 16 15	21 54 0	29 2 27	6R 32.1	1 23.2	10 46.2	10 38.0	13 16.3	21 25.0	1R 47.2	13 42.2	8R 48.8
3 W	2 47 48	10 16 21	6♌ 8 5	13♌10 39	6D 32.0	1 46.4	11 59.7	11 22.7	13 26.0	21 30.8	1 46.7	13 42.6	8 48.3
4 Th	2 51 44	11 16 29	20 9 58	27 5 55	6 32.0	2 2.6	13 13.2	12 7.5	13 35.6	21 36.6	1 46.3	13 43.1	8 47.7
5 F	2 55 41	12 16 40	3♍58 24	10♍47 24	6 32.3	2R 11.1	14 26.6	12 52.4	13 45.1	21 42.3	1 46.0	13 43.5	8 47.1
6 Sa	2 59 37	13 16 52	17 32 55	24 14 57	6 32.9	2 11.4	15 40.1	13 37.3	13 54.4	21 47.9	1 45.7	13 43.8	8 46.5
7 Su	3 3 34	14 17 6	0♎53 32	7♎28 43	6 33.6	2 2.7	16 53.5	14 22.3	14 3.7	21 53.5	1 45.4	13 44.2	8 45.9
8 M	3 7 30	15 17 22	14 0 32	20 29 3	6 34.3	1 44.6	18 6.9	15 7.4	14 12.8	21 59.0	1 45.2	13 44.5	8 45.2
9 Tu	3 11 27	16 17 41	26 54 20	3♏16 25	6R 34.9	1 16.7	19 20.3	15 52.5	14 21.9	22 4.4	1 45.1	13 44.8	8 44.6
10 W	3 15 23	17 18 1	9♏35 23	15 51 19	6 35.0	0 38.7	20 33.7	16 37.7	14 30.8	22 9.8	1 45.0	13 45.0	8 43.9
11 Th	3 19 20	18 18 22	22 4 18	28 14 29	6 34.6	29♏50.8	21 47.1	17 23.0	14 39.6	22 15.1	1D 45.0	13 45.2	8 43.2
12 F	3 23 17	19 18 46	4♐21 59	10♐26 58	6 33.4	28 53.6	23 0.4	18 8.3	14 48.3	22 20.3	1 45.0	13 45.4	8 42.5
13 Sa	3 27 13	20 19 11	16 29 40	22 30 18	6 31.6	27 47.9	24 13.7	18 53.7	14 56.9	22 25.5	1 45.0	13 45.5	8 41.7
14 Su	3 31 10	21 19 38	28 29 9	4♑26 32	6 29.4	26 35.2	25 27.0	19 39.1	15 5.3	22 30.5	1 45.1	13 45.6	8 41.0
15 M	3 35 6	22 20 6	10♑22 49	16 18 23	6 26.9	25 17.4	26 40.3	20 24.6	15 13.6	22 35.5	1 45.3	13 45.7	8 40.2
16 Tu	3 39 3	23 20 35	22 13 41	28 9 11	6 24.5	23 56.9	27 53.5	21 10.1	15 21.8	22 40.5	1 45.5	13R 45.7	8 39.4
17 W	3 42 59	24 21 6	4♒ 5 23	10♒ 2 49	6 22.5	22 36.1	29 6.7	21 55.7	15 29.9	22 45.3	1 45.8	13 45.7	8 38.6
18 Th	3 46 56	25 21 38	16 2 3	22 3 40	6D 21.3	21 17.9	0♑19.9	22 41.3	15 37.8	22 50.1	1 46.1	13 45.6	8 37.7
19 F	3 50 52	26 22 12	28 8 14	4♓16 20	6 21.0	20 4.7	1 33.1	23 27.0	15 45.7	22 54.7	1 46.5	13 45.6	8 36.9
20 Sa	3 54 49	27 22 46	10♓28 34	16 45 29	6 21.6	18 58.8	2 46.2	24 12.7	15 53.3	22 59.3	1 46.9	13 45.5	8 36.0
21 Su	3 58 46	28 23 22	23 7 36	29 35 23	6 22.9	18 2.1	3 59.3	24 58.5	16 0.9	23 3.9	1 47.4	13 45.3	8 35.1
22 M	4 2 42	29 23 59	6♈ 9 14	12♈49 27	6 24.5	17 16.0	5 12.3	25 44.3	16 8.3	23 8.3	1 47.9	13 45.1	8 34.2
23 Tu	4 6 39	0♐24 37	19 36 15	26 29 42	6 25.9	16 41.2	6 25.3	26 30.1	16 15.6	23 12.6	1 48.5	13 44.9	8 33.3
24 W	4 10 35	1 25 16	3♉29 42	10♉36 2	6R 26.7	16 18.1	7 38.3	27 16.0	16 22.7	23 16.9	1 49.1	13 44.7	8 32.4
25 Th	4 14 32	2 25 57	17 48 16	25 5 51	6 26.3	16D 6.5	8 51.3	28 1.9	16 29.7	23 21.1	1 49.8	13 44.4	8 31.4
26 F	4 18 28	3 26 39	2♊28 0	9♊53 50	6 24.6	16 6.1	10 4.2	28 47.9	16 36.5	23 25.2	1 50.5	13 44.1	8 30.5
27 Sa	4 22 25	4 27 22	17 22 19	24 52 21	6 21.5	16 16.2	11 17.0	29 33.9	16 43.2	23 29.2	1 51.3	13 43.7	8 29.5
28 Su	4 26 21	5 28 7	2♋22 47	9♋52 29	6 17.4	16 36.1	12 29.8	0♒19.9	16 49.8	23 33.1	1 52.1	13 43.4	8 28.5
29 M	4 30 18	6 28 53	17 20 22	24 45 26	6 13.0	17 4.7	13 42.6	1 6.0	16 56.2	23 37.0	1 53.0	13 43.0	8 27.5
30 Tu	4 34 15	7 29 40	2♌ 6 48	9♌23 48	6 8.9	17 41.4	14 55.4	1 52.1	17 2.5	23 40.7	1 53.9	13 42.5	8 26.5

DECEMBER 1920 LONGITUDE

Day	Sid.Time	☉	0 hr ☽	Noon ☽	True ☊	☿	♀	♂	♃	♄	♅	♆	♇
1 W	4 38 11	8♐30 29	16♌35 51	23♌42 35	6♏ 5.7	18♏25.1	16♑ 8.1	2♒38.2	17♍ 8.6	23♍44.3	1♓54.9	13♌42.0	8♋25.5
2 Th	4 42 8	9 31 19	0♍43 47	7♍39 23	6D 4.0	19 15.1	17 20.7	3 24.3	17 14.6	23 47.9	1 55.9	13R 41.5	8R 24.4
3 F	4 46 4	10 32 11	14 29 25	21 14 4	6 3.7	20 10.7	18 33.3	4 10.5	17 20.4	23 51.4	1 57.0	13 41.0	8 23.4
4 Sa	4 50 1	11 33 4	27 53 32	4♎28 9	6 4.6	21 11.0	19 45.9	4 56.8	17 26.0	23 54.7	1 58.1	13 40.4	8 22.3
5 Su	4 53 57	12 33 58	10♎58 13	17 24 6	6 6.3	22 15.6	20 58.4	5 43.0	17 31.5	23 58.0	1 59.3	13 39.8	8 21.2
6 M	4 57 54	13 34 54	23 46 9	0♏ 4 43	6R 7.8	23 23.8	22 10.9	6 29.3	17 36.8	24 1.2	2 0.5	13 39.2	8 20.1
7 Tu	5 1 50	14 35 51	6♏20 8	12 32 43	6 8.4	24 35.1	23 23.3	7 15.6	17 42.0	24 4.2	2 1.8	13 38.5	8 19.0
8 W	5 5 47	15 36 49	18 42 44	24 50 28	6 7.5	25 49.2	24 35.7	8 1.9	17 47.0	24 7.2	2 3.1	13 37.8	8 17.9
9 Th	5 9 44	16 37 49	0♐56 7	6♐59 54	6 4.6	27 5.7	25 48.0	8 48.3	17 51.8	24 10.1	2 4.5	13 37.1	8 16.8
10 F	5 13 40	17 38 49	13 2 1	19 2 38	5 59.6	28 24.1	27 0.3	9 34.7	17 56.5	24 12.9	2 5.9	13 36.3	8 15.7
11 Sa	5 17 37	18 39 50	25 1 55	1♑ 0 3	5 52.6	29 44.4	28 12.5	10 21.1	18 1.0	24 15.5	2 7.4	13 35.5	8 14.5
12 Su	5 21 33	19 40 52	6♑57 11	12 53 33	5 44.1	1♐ 6.2	29 24.7	11 7.6	18 5.3	24 18.1	2 8.9	13 34.7	8 13.4
13 M	5 25 30	20 41 55	18 49 19	24 44 46	5 34.8	2 29.2	0♒36.8	11 54.0	18 9.5	24 20.6	2 10.5	13 33.9	8 12.2
14 Tu	5 29 26	21 42 58	0♒40 9	6♒35 47	5 25.8	3 53.5	1 48.8	12 40.5	18 13.5	24 23.0	2 12.1	13 33.0	8 11.0
15 W	5 33 23	22 44 2	12 32 2	18 29 17	5 17.7	5 18.7	3 0.7	13 27.0	18 17.3	24 25.2	2 13.7	13 32.1	8 9.9
16 Th	5 37 19	23 45 6	24 27 58	0♓28 34	5 11.4	6 44.8	4 12.6	14 13.5	18 20.9	24 27.4	2 15.4	13 31.1	8 8.7
17 F	5 41 16	24 46 11	6♓31 37	12 37 38	5 7.2	8 11.6	5 24.4	15 0.0	18 24.4	24 29.4	2 17.2	13 30.2	8 7.5
18 Sa	5 45 13	25 47 16	18 47 13	25 0 57	5D 5.2	9 39.1	6 36.2	15 46.6	18 27.6	24 31.4	2 19.0	13 29.2	8 6.3
19 Su	5 49 9	26 48 21	1♈19 24	7♈43 12	5 5.0	11 7.2	7 47.8	16 33.1	18 30.7	24 33.2	2 20.8	13 28.1	8 5.1
20 M	5 53 6	27 49 27	14 12 52	20 48 55	5 5.9	12 35.8	8 59.4	17 19.7	18 33.6	24 35.0	2 22.7	13 27.1	8 3.9
21 Tu	5 57 2	28 50 32	27 31 46	4♉21 47	5R 6.9	14 4.9	10 10.9	18 6.3	18 36.4	24 36.6	2 24.6	13 26.0	8 2.7
22 W	6 0 59	29 51 38	11♉19 7	18 23 50	5 7.0	15 34.4	11 22.3	18 52.8	18 38.9	24 38.1	2 26.6	13 24.9	8 1.5
23 Th	6 4 55	0♑52 45	25 35 46	2♊54 33	5 5.1	17 4.3	12 33.6	19 39.4	18 41.3	24 39.5	2 28.6	13 23.8	8 0.2
24 F	6 8 52	1 53 51	10♊19 35	17 50 1	5 0.9	18 34.6	13 44.8	20 26.0	18 43.4	24 40.8	2 30.6	13 22.6	7 59.0
25 Sa	6 12 48	2 54 58	25 24 50	3♋ 2 48	4 54.2	20 5.3	14 55.9	21 12.6	18 45.4	24 42.0	2 32.7	13 21.5	7 57.8
26 Su	6 16 45	3 56 5	10♋42 31	18 22 32	4 45.6	21 36.3	16 6.9	21 59.2	18 47.2	24 43.1	2 34.8	13 20.3	7 56.6
27 M	6 20 42	4 57 13	26 1 24	3♌37 42	4 36.0	23 7.6	17 17.8	22 45.8	18 48.8	24 44.1	2 37.0	13 19.0	7 55.4
28 Tu	6 24 38	5 58 20	11♌10 8	18 37 37	4 26.8	24 39.2	18 28.6	23 32.4	18 50.3	24 45.0	2 39.2	13 17.8	7 54.1
29 W	6 28 35	6 59 28	25 59 13	3♍14 18	4 19.0	26 11.2	19 39.2	24 19.0	18 51.5	24 45.8	2 41.5	13 16.5	7 52.9
30 Th	6 32 31	8 0 37	10♍22 25	17 23 21	4 13.4	27 43.4	20 49.8	25 5.6	18 52.5	24 46.4	2 43.8	13 15.2	7 51.7
31 F	6 36 28	9 1 46	24 17 6	1♎ 3 49	4 10.2	29 16.0	22 0.3	25 52.2	18 53.4	24 47.0	2 46.1	13 13.9	7 50.4

Astro Data Dy Hr Mn	Planet Ingress Dy Hr Mn	Last Aspect Dy Hr Mn	☽ Ingress Dy Hr Mn	Last Aspect Dy Hr Mn	☽ Ingress Dy Hr Mn	☽ Phases & Eclipses Dy Hr Mn
♃⚺♆ 4 19:45	☿ ♏ 10 19:45	1 23:11 ♄ ⚹	♌ 2 13:37	1 3:14 ☿ □	♍ 1 22:45	3 7:35 ☽ 10♌35
☿ R 5 12:47	♀ ♑ 17 17:28	3 12:55 ♆ ☌	♍ 4 17:03	3 16:47 ♄ ☌	♎ 4 3:50	10 16:05 ● 17♏58
☽0S 6 6:40	☉ ♐ 22 14:15	6 7:39 ♄ ☌	♎ 6 22:23	5 20:41 ♀ □	♏ 6 11:51	10 15:51:53 ✓ P 0.742
♅ D 11 7:16	♂ ♒ 27 13:38	8 8:24 ♀ ⚹	♏ 9 5:49	8 15:32 ☿ ☌	♐ 8 22:09	18 20:12 ☽ 26♒13
♆ R 16 8:24		11 14:05 ☿ ☌	♐ 11 15:26	10 22:27 ♄ □	♑ 11 9:59	26 1:42 ○ 3♊31
☽0N 20 20:43	☿ ♐ 11 4:37	13 17:13 ♀ ☌	♑ 14 3:03	13 11:13 ♄ △	♒ 13 22:39	
☿ D 25 12:50	♀ ♒ 12 11:46	16 3:08 ☿ ⚹	♒ 16 15:44	15 22:26 ☉ ⚹	♓ 16 11:03	2 16:29 ☽ 10♍13
	☉ ♑ 22 3:17	18 20:12 ☉ □	♓ 19 3:39	18 14:40 ☉ □	♈ 18 21:30	10 10:04 ● 18♐04
☽0S 3 12:31	☿ ♑ 31 11:22	21 10:37 ☉ △	♈ 21 12:45	21 2:31 ☉ △	♉ 21 4:22	18 14:40 ☽ 26♓25
☽0N 18 5:55		23 12:43 ♂ □	♉ 23 18:02	22 22:27 ♄ △	♊ 23 7:15	25 12:38 ○ 3♋27
☽0S 30 20:12		25 17:43 ♂ △	♊ 25 20:00	24 22:52 ♄ □	♋ 25 7:13	
		27 9:50 ♄ □	♋ 27 20:12	26 21:58 ♄ ⚹	♌ 27 6:16	
		29 10:12 ♄ ⚹	♌ 29 20:32	29 0:22 ☿ △	♍ 29 6:37	
				31 9:56 ☿ □	♎ 31 10:06	

Astro Data

1 NOVEMBER 1920
Julian Day # 7610
Delta T 22.1 sec
SVP 06♓21'46"
Obliquity 23°26'51"
⚷ Chiron 6♈54.4R
☽ Mean ☊ 6♏14.0

1 DECEMBER 1920
Julian Day # 7640
Delta T 22.2 sec
SVP 06♓21'41"
Obliquity 23°26'50"
⚷ Chiron 6♈06.0R
☽ Mean ☊ 4♏38.7

LONGITUDE — JANUARY 1921

Day	Sid.Time	☉	0 hr ☽	Noon ☽	True ☊	☿	♀	♂	♃	♄	♅	♆	♇
1 Sa	6 40 24	10♑ 2 55	7♎43 50	14♎17 31	4♏ 9.2	0♑48.9	23♒10.6	26♒38.7	18♍54.0	24♍47.4	2♓48.5	13♌12.6	7♋49.2
2 Su	6 44 21	11 4 5	20 45 21	27 7 54	4D 9.4	2 22.2	24 20.8	27 25.3	18 54.5	24 47.7	2 50.9	13R 11.2	7R 48.0
3 M	6 48 17	12 5 15	3♏25 41	9♏39 18	4R 9.8	3 55.8	25 30.9	28 11.9	18R 54.8	24 47.9	2 53.3	13 9.8	7 46.7
4 Tu	6 52 14	13 6 25	15 49 15	21 56 6	4 9.1	5 29.7	26 40.9	28 58.5	18 54.9	24R 48.1	2 55.8	13 8.4	7 45.5
5 W	6 56 11	14 7 35	28 0 20	4♐ 2 23	4 6.4	7 4.0	27 50.7	29 45.1	18 54.7	24 48.0	2 58.3	13 7.0	7 44.3
6 Th	7 0 7	15 8 46	10♐ 2 40	16 1 34	4 0.9	8 38.7	29 0.4	0♓31.7	18 54.4	24 47.9	3 0.8	13 5.6	7 43.1
7 F	7 4 4	16 9 56	21 59 23	27 56 23	3 52.4	10 13.7	0♓10.0	1 18.3	18 53.9	24 47.7	3 3.4	13 4.1	7 41.8
8 Sa	7 8 0	17 11 7	3♑52 50	9♑48 55	3 41.0	11 49.2	1 19.4	2 4.9	18 53.2	24 47.4	3 6.0	13 2.7	7 40.6
9 Su	7 11 57	18 12 17	15 44 50	21 40 43	3 27.5	13 25.0	2 28.7	2 51.5	18 52.3	24 46.9	3 8.7	13 1.2	7 39.4
10 M	7 15 53	19 13 27	27 36 44	3♒33 3	3 12.8	15 1.3	3 37.9	3 38.0	18 51.2	24 46.4	3 11.4	12 59.7	7 38.2
11 Tu	7 19 50	20 14 37	9♒29 49	15 27 12	2 58.2	16 38.1	4 46.8	4 24.6	18 50.0	24 45.7	3 14.1	12 58.2	7 37.0
12 W	7 23 46	21 15 46	21 25 26	27 24 44	2 44.8	18 15.3	5 55.6	5 11.2	18 48.5	24 44.9	3 16.8	12 56.6	7 35.8
13 Th	7 27 43	22 16 55	3♓25 23	9♓27 42	2 33.7	19 53.0	7 4.3	5 57.7	18 46.8	24 44.0	3 19.6	12 55.1	7 34.6
14 F	7 31 40	23 18 3	15 32 3	21 38 49	2 25.5	21 31.1	8 12.7	6 44.2	18 44.9	24 43.0	3 22.4	12 53.5	7 33.4
15 Sa	7 35 36	24 19 11	27 48 29	4♈ 1 31	2 20.3	23 9.8	9 21.0	7 30.7	18 42.9	24 41.9	3 25.3	12 52.0	7 32.3
16 Su	7 39 33	25 20 18	10♈18 27	16 39 49	2 17.8	24 48.9	10 29.1	8 17.2	18 40.6	24 40.7	3 28.1	12 50.4	7 31.1
17 M	7 43 29	26 21 24	23 6 10	29 38 2	2 17.1	26 28.6	11 37.0	9 3.7	18 38.2	24 39.4	3 31.0	12 48.8	7 29.9
18 Tu	7 47 26	27 22 29	6♉15 56	13♉ 0 18	2 17.1	28 8.8	12 44.7	9 50.2	18 35.6	24 38.0	3 34.0	12 47.2	7 28.8
19 W	7 51 22	28 23 33	19 51 32	26 49 50	2 16.4	29 49.6	13 52.1	10 36.6	18 32.8	24 36.5	3 36.9	12 45.6	7 27.6
20 Th	7 55 19	29 24 37	3♊55 20	11♊ 7 55	2 13.8	1♒30.9	14 59.4	11 23.0	18 29.8	24 34.9	3 39.9	12 43.9	7 26.5
21 F	7 59 15	0♒25 39	18 27 18	25 52 56	2 8.6	3 12.7	16 6.5	12 9.4	18 26.6	24 33.1	3 42.9	12 42.3	7 25.4
22 Sa	8 3 12	1 26 41	3♋24 3	10♋59 37	2 0.6	4 55.0	17 13.3	12 55.8	18 23.3	24 31.3	3 45.9	12 40.7	7 24.3
23 Su	8 7 9	2 27 42	18 38 25	26 19 4	1 50.2	6 37.9	18 19.8	13 42.2	18 19.8	24 29.4	3 49.0	12 39.0	7 23.2
24 M	8 11 5	3 28 42	4♌ 0 4	11♌39 54	1 38.5	8 21.2	19 26.1	14 28.5	18 16.1	24 27.4	3 52.0	12 37.4	7 22.1
25 Tu	8 15 2	4 29 41	19 17 5	26 50 14	1 27.0	10 5.1	20 32.2	15 14.8	18 12.2	24 25.2	3 55.1	12 35.7	7 21.0
26 W	8 18 58	5 30 39	4♍18 11	11♍39 56	1 16.9	11 49.3	21 38.0	16 1.1	18 8.1	24 23.0	3 58.3	12 34.0	7 19.9
27 Th	8 22 55	6 31 37	18 54 46	26 2 12	1 9.2	13 34.0	22 43.6	16 47.3	18 3.9	24 20.7	4 1.4	12 32.3	7 18.8
28 F	8 26 51	7 32 34	3♎ 2 0	9♎54 7	1 4.3	15 18.9	23 48.8	17 33.6	17 59.5	24 18.3	4 4.5	12 30.7	7 17.8
29 Sa	8 30 48	8 33 30	16 38 43	23 16 7	1 2.0	17 4.2	24 53.8	18 19.8	17 55.0	24 15.8	4 7.7	12 29.0	7 16.8
30 Su	8 34 44	9 34 25	29 46 47	6♏11 12	1 1.5	18 49.6	25 58.5	19 6.0	17 50.2	24 13.1	4 10.9	12 27.3	7 15.7
31 M	8 38 41	10 35 20	12♏30 0	18 43 47	1 1.5	20 35.0	27 2.9	19 52.1	17 45.3	24 10.4	4 14.1	12 25.6	7 14.7

LONGITUDE — FEBRUARY 1921

Day	Sid.Time	☉	0 hr ☽	Noon ☽	True ☊	☿	♀	♂	♃	♄	♅	♆	♇
1 Tu	8 42 38	11♒36 14	24♏53 13	0♐58 56	1♏ 0.9	22♒20.3	28♓ 7.0	20♓38.3	17♍40.3	24♍ 7.7	4♓17.4	12♌23.9	7♋13.7
2 W	8 46 34	12 37 8	7♐ 1 33	13 1 40	0R 58.5	24 5.3	29 10.8	21 24.4	17R 35.1	24R 4.8	4 20.6	12R 22.2	7R 12.8
3 Th	8 50 31	13 38 0	18 59 50	24 56 36	0 53.5	25 49.9	0♈14.3	22 10.5	17 29.7	24 1.8	4 23.9	12 20.5	7 11.8
4 F	8 54 27	14 38 52	0♑52 24	6♑47 41	0 45.5	27 33.7	1 17.4	22 56.6	17 24.2	23 58.8	4 27.2	12 18.9	7 10.8
5 Sa	8 58 24	15 39 42	12 42 49	18 38 7	0 34.8	29 16.6	2 20.2	23 42.6	17 18.6	23 55.6	4 30.5	12 17.2	7 9.9
6 Su	9 2 20	16 40 32	24 33 51	0♒30 16	0 22.0	0♓58.1	3 22.7	24 28.6	17 12.8	23 52.4	4 33.8	12 15.5	7 9.0
7 M	9 6 17	17 41 20	6♒27 34	12 25 54	0 7.9	2 37.9	4 24.7	25 14.6	17 6.9	23 49.1	4 37.1	12 13.8	7 8.1
8 Tu	9 10 13	18 42 7	18 25 25	24 26 15	29♎53.8	4 15.6	5 26.4	26 0.5	17 0.8	23 45.7	4 40.5	12 12.1	7 7.2
9 W	9 14 10	19 42 53	0♓28 32	6♓32 23	29 40.9	5 50.6	6 27.7	26 46.5	16 54.6	23 42.3	4 43.8	12 10.4	7 6.3
10 Th	9 18 7	20 43 37	12 37 56	18 45 23	29 30.1	7 22.6	7 28.6	27 32.3	16 48.3	23 38.7	4 47.2	12 8.8	7 5.5
11 F	9 22 3	21 44 20	24 54 54	1♈ 6 42	29 22.2	8 50.7	8 29.1	28 18.2	16 41.8	23 35.1	4 50.6	12 7.1	7 4.6
12 Sa	9 26 0	22 45 2	7♈21 3	13 38 16	29 17.2	10 14.6	9 29.1	29 4.0	16 35.3	23 31.4	4 54.0	12 5.5	7 3.8
13 Su	9 29 56	23 45 42	19 58 40	26 22 36	29D 14.9	11 33.4	10 28.7	29 49.8	16 28.6	23 27.7	4 57.4	12 3.8	7 3.0
14 M	9 33 53	24 46 20	2♉50 28	9♉22 40	29 14.6	12 46.4	11 27.8	0♈35.6	16 21.8	23 23.8	5 0.8	12 2.2	7 2.2
15 Tu	9 37 49	25 46 56	15 59 36	22 41 37	29R 15.1	13 53.1	12 26.4	1 21.3	16 15.0	23 20.0	5 4.2	12 0.5	7 1.5
16 W	9 41 46	26 47 31	29 29 3	6♊22 11	29 15.3	14 52.5	13 24.5	2 7.0	16 8.0	23 16.0	5 7.6	11 58.9	7 0.7
17 Th	9 45 42	27 48 4	13♊21 9	20 26 1	29 14.2	15 44.1	14 22.1	2 52.6	16 0.9	23 12.0	5 11.0	11 57.3	6 60.0
18 F	9 49 39	28 48 35	27 36 40	4♋52 48	29 10.9	16 27.3	15 19.1	3 38.2	15 53.8	23 7.9	5 14.5	11 55.7	6 59.3
19 Sa	9 53 36	29 49 5	12♋13 58	19 39 29	29 5.3	17 1.4	16 15.6	4 23.8	15 46.5	23 3.8	5 17.9	11 54.1	6 58.6
20 Su	9 57 32	0♓49 32	27 8 30	4♌40 0	28 57.6	17 26.0	17 11.4	5 9.3	15 39.2	22 59.6	5 21.3	11 52.5	6 57.9
21 M	10 1 29	1 49 58	12♌12 48	19 45 41	28 48.7	17R 40.7	18 6.7	5 54.8	15 31.8	22 55.4	5 24.8	11 50.9	6 57.3
22 Tu	10 5 25	2 50 22	27 17 20	4♍46 30	28 39.7	17 45.4	19 1.3	6 40.2	15 24.4	22 51.1	5 28.2	11 49.4	6 56.7
23 W	10 9 22	3 50 44	12♍12 1	19 32 51	28 31.8	17 40.1	19 55.3	7 25.6	15 16.8	22 46.8	5 31.7	11 47.8	6 56.0
24 Th	10 13 18	4 51 5	26 48 7	3♎57 8	28 25.8	17 24.9	20 48.6	8 11.0	15 9.3	22 42.4	5 35.1	11 46.3	6 55.5
25 F	10 17 15	5 51 24	10♎59 26	17 54 44	28 22.1	17 0.3	21 41.3	8 56.3	15 1.6	22 38.0	5 38.6	11 44.8	6 54.9
26 Sa	10 21 11	6 51 41	24 42 58	1♏24 12	28D 20.7	16 26.8	22 33.1	9 41.6	14 54.0	22 33.5	5 42.0	11 43.3	6 54.3
27 Su	10 25 8	7 51 57	7♏58 41	14 26 46	28 20.9	15 45.4	23 24.3	10 26.8	14 46.2	22 29.1	5 45.5	11 41.8	6 53.8
28 M	10 29 5	8 52 11	20 48 55	27 5 40	28 22.1	14 57.1	24 14.7	11 12.0	14 38.5	22 24.5	5 48.9	11 40.3	6 53.3

Astro Data

	Dy Hr Mn
♃ R	3 21:37
♄ R	4 10:52
☽0N	14 13:44
☽0S	27 6:30
♀0N	1 22:32
☽0N	10 20:26
♂0N	14 18:16
☿ R	21 23:12
☽0S	23 17:59

Planet Ingress

	Dy Hr Mn
♂ ♓	5 7:39
♀ ♓	6 20:33
☿ ♒	19 2:28
☉ ♒	20 13:55
♀ ♈	2 18:35
☿ ♓	5 10:14
☊ ♎	7 13:22
♂ ♈	13 5:21
☉ ♓	19 4:20

Last Aspect / ☽ Ingress (January)

Last Aspect Dy Hr Mn		☽ Ingress Dy Hr Mn
2 13:22	♂ △	♏ 2 17:27
5 3:42	♂ □	♐ 5 3:58
7 5:39	♄ □	♑ 7 16:10
9 18:16	♄ △	♒ 10 4:50
11 6:59	♆ ☍	♓ 12 17:10
14 17:58	♄ ☍	♈ 15 4:15
17 7:08	☿ □	♉ 17 12:40
19 15:48	☉ △	♊ 19 17:23
21 9:50	♄ □	♋ 21 18:35
23 9:07	♄ ✶	♌ 23 17:45
24 13:29	♆ ☌	♍ 25 17:04
27 9:06	♄ ☌	♎ 27 18:46
29 0:53	☿ △	♏ 30 0:25

Last Aspect / ☽ Ingress (February)

Last Aspect Dy Hr Mn		☽ Ingress Dy Hr Mn
1 6:57	♀ △	♐ 1 10:04
3 16:09	☿ ✶	♑ 3 22:14
5 23:49	♂ ✶	♒ 6 10:59
8 0:36	☉ ☌	♓ 8 23:03
11 7:00	♂ ☌	♈ 11 9:51
13 7:43	☉ ✶	♉ 13 18:45
15 18:53	☉ □	♊ 16 0:54
18 2:08	☉ △	♋ 18 3:58
19 17:23	♄ ✶	♌ 20 4:34
21 9:59	♀ △	♍ 22 4:20
23 17:15	♄ ☌	♎ 24 5:21
25 19:54	♀ ☍	♏ 26 9:28
28 3:01	♄ ✶	♐ 28 17:36

☽ Phases & Eclipses

Dy Hr Mn	
1 4:34	☽ 10♎15
9 5:26	● 18♑26
17 6:30	☽ 26♈38
23 23:07	○ 3♌26
30 20:02	☽ 10♏25
8 0:36	● 18♒44
15 18:53	☽ 26♉35
22 9:32	○ 3♍14

Astro Data

1 JANUARY 1921
Julian Day # 7671
Delta T 22.3 sec
SVP 06♓21'36"
Obliquity 23°26'50"
⚷ Chiron 6♈03.8
☽ Mean ☊ 3♏00.2

1 FEBRUARY 1921
Julian Day # 7702
Delta T 22.3 sec
SVP 06♓21'32"
Obliquity 23°26'50"
⚷ Chiron 6♈52.6
☽ Mean ☊ 1♏21.7

MARCH 1921 LONGITUDE

Day	Sid.Time	☉	0 hr ☽	Noon ☽	True ☊	☿	♀	♂	♃	♄	♅	♆	♇
1 Tu	10 33 1	9♓52 24	3♐17 35	9♐25 17	28♎23.2	14♓ 3.3	25♈ 4.2	11♈57.2	14♍30.7	22♍20.0	5♓52.4	11♌38.9	6♋52.8
2 W	10 36 58	10 52 36	15 29 25	21 30 36	28R 23.3	13R 5.1	25 53.0	12 42.3	14R 22.9	22R 15.4	5 55.8	11R 37.4	6R 52.4
3 Th	10 40 54	11 52 46	27 29 27	3♑26 36	28 21.8	12 4.3	26 40.9	13 27.4	14 15.1	22 10.7	5 59.2	11 36.0	6 51.9
4 F	10 44 51	12 52 54	9♑22 36	15 18 1	28 18.2	11 2.2	27 27.9	14 12.4	14 7.2	22 6.1	6 2.7	11 34.6	6 51.5
5 Sa	10 48 47	13 53 1	21 13 20	27 9 1	28 12.8	10 0.3	28 13.9	14 57.4	13 59.4	22 1.4	6 6.1	11 33.2	6 51.1
6 Su	10 52 44	14 53 6	3♒ 5 30	9♒ 3 8	28 5.7	8 60.0	28 59.1	15 42.4	13 51.6	21 56.7	6 9.5	11 31.9	6 50.8
7 M	10 56 40	15 53 10	15 2 15	21 3 8	27 57.7	8 2.5	29 43.2	16 27.3	13 43.7	21 52.0	6 13.0	11 30.5	6 50.4
8 Tu	11 0 37	16 53 12	27 5 59	3♓11 0	27 49.5	7 8.9	0♉26.2	17 12.2	13 35.9	21 47.3	6 16.4	11 29.2	6 50.1
9 W	11 4 34	17 53 11	9♓18 21	15 28 9	27 42.0	6 20.2	1 8.2	17 57.0	13 28.1	21 42.6	6 19.8	11 27.9	6 49.8
10 Th	11 8 30	18 53 9	21 40 29	27 55 27	27 35.9	5 36.9	1 49.1	18 41.8	13 20.3	21 37.8	6 23.2	11 26.6	6 49.5
11 F	11 12 27	19 53 5	4♈13 6	10♈33 31	27 31.6	4 59.5	2 28.8	19 26.6	13 12.5	21 33.0	6 26.5	11 25.4	6 49.3
12 Sa	11 16 23	20 52 59	16 56 47	23 22 57	27D 29.2	4 28.4	3 7.3	20 11.3	13 4.7	21 28.3	6 29.9	11 24.1	6 49.0
13 Su	11 20 20	21 52 51	29 52 8	6♉24 26	27 28.7	4 3.8	3 44.6	20 55.9	12 57.0	21 23.5	6 33.3	11 22.9	6 48.8
14 M	11 24 16	22 52 41	12♉59 58	19 38 52	27 29.6	3 45.7	4 20.5	21 40.6	12 49.4	21 18.8	6 36.6	11 21.7	6 48.6
15 Tu	11 28 13	23 52 29	26 21 17	3♊ 7 18	27 31.1	3 34.1	4 55.0	22 25.1	12 41.8	21 14.0	6 40.0	11 20.6	6 48.5
16 W	11 32 9	24 52 14	9♊57 4	16 50 38	27 32.6	3D 28.7	5 28.2	23 9.7	12 34.3	21 9.3	6 43.3	11 19.4	6 48.3
17 Th	11 36 6	25 51 57	23 48 4	0♋49 18	27R 33.3	3 29.5	5 59.8	23 54.1	12 26.8	21 4.5	6 46.6	11 18.3	6 48.2
18 F	11 40 2	26 51 38	7♋54 15	15 2 41	27 32.9	3 36.1	6 30.0	24 38.6	12 19.4	20 59.8	6 49.9	11 17.2	6 48.1
19 Sa	11 43 59	27 51 17	22 14 20	29 28 46	27 31.0	3 48.4	6 58.5	25 22.9	12 12.0	20 55.1	6 53.2	11 16.2	6 48.1
20 Su	11 47 56	28 50 53	6♌45 27	14♌ 3 46	27 28.0	4 6.0	7 25.3	26 7.3	12 4.7	20 50.4	6 56.5	11 15.1	6 48.0
21 M	11 51 52	29 50 27	21 22 58	28 42 16	27 24.2	4 28.6	7 50.5	26 51.6	11 57.6	20 45.7	6 59.7	11 14.1	6D 48.0
22 Tu	11 55 49	0♈49 58	6♍ 0 49	13♍17 46	27 20.2	4 56.1	8 13.8	27 35.8	11 50.5	20 41.1	7 2.9	11 13.2	6 48.0
23 W	11 59 45	1 49 28	20 32 16	27 43 31	27 16.8	5 28.0	8 35.3	28 20.0	11 43.4	20 36.5	7 6.2	11 12.2	6 48.0
24 Th	12 3 42	2 48 55	4♎50 49	11♎53 32	27 14.2	6 4.2	8 54.9	29 4.1	11 36.5	20 31.9	7 9.3	11 11.3	6 48.1
25 F	12 7 38	3 48 20	18 51 10	25 43 21	27D 12.9	6 44.4	9 12.6	29 48.2	11 29.7	20 27.3	7 12.5	11 10.4	6 48.1
26 Sa	12 11 35	4 47 44	2♏29 51	9♏10 33	27 12.8	7 28.4	9 28.2	0♉32.2	11 23.0	20 22.7	7 15.7	11 9.5	6 48.2
27 Su	12 15 31	5 47 5	15 45 28	22 14 46	27 13.6	8 15.9	9 41.7	1 16.2	11 16.4	20 18.2	7 18.8	11 8.7	6 48.4
28 M	12 19 28	6 46 25	28 38 39	4♐57 28	27 15.0	9 6.8	9 53.1	2 0.2	11 9.9	20 13.8	7 21.9	11 7.9	6 48.5
29 Tu	12 23 25	7 45 43	11♐11 36	17 21 32	27 16.6	10 0.8	10 2.3	2 44.1	11 3.5	20 9.3	7 25.0	11 7.1	6 48.7
30 W	12 27 21	8 44 59	23 27 47	29 30 53	27 17.8	10 57.8	10 9.2	3 27.9	10 57.2	20 5.0	7 28.1	11 6.3	6 48.9
31 Th	12 31 18	9 44 13	5♑31 24	11♑29 57	27R 18.5	11 57.7	10 13.9	4 11.7	10 51.1	20 0.6	7 31.2	11 5.6	6 49.1

APRIL 1921 LONGITUDE

Day	Sid.Time	☉	0 hr ☽	Noon ☽	True ☊	☿	♀	♂	♃	♄	♅	♆	♇
1 F	12 35 14	10♈43 25	17♑27 6	23♑23 28	27♎18.4	13♓ 0.2	10♉16.2	4♉55.5	10♍45.1	19♍56.3	7♓34.2	11♌ 4.9	6♋49.3
2 Sa	12 39 11	11 42 36	29 19 36	5♒16 5	27R 17.6	14 5.3	10R 16.1	5 39.2	10R 39.2	19R 52.1	7 37.2	11R 4.2	6 49.6
3 Su	12 43 7	12 41 45	11♒13 26	17 12 9	27 16.1	15 12.8	10 13.7	6 22.9	10 33.5	19 47.9	7 40.2	11 3.6	6 49.9
4 M	12 47 4	13 40 52	23 12 43	29 15 34	27 14.3	16 22.6	10 8.7	7 6.5	10 27.9	19 43.7	7 43.1	11 3.0	6 50.2
5 Tu	12 51 0	14 39 57	5♓21 4	11♓29 32	27 12.3	17 34.7	10 1.4	7 50.1	10 22.4	19 39.6	7 46.1	11 2.4	6 50.5
6 W	12 54 57	15 39 0	17 41 16	23 56 29	27 10.6	18 48.9	9 51.5	8 33.6	10 17.1	19 35.6	7 49.0	11 1.9	6 50.8
7 Th	12 58 54	16 38 2	0♈15 21	6♈37 58	27 9.2	20 5.1	9 39.2	9 17.1	10 11.9	19 31.6	7 51.8	11 1.4	6 51.2
8 F	13 2 50	17 37 1	13 4 24	19 34 39	27 8.4	21 23.4	9 24.5	10 0.5	10 6.9	19 27.7	7 54.7	11 0.9	6 51.6
9 Sa	13 6 47	18 35 58	26 8 41	2♉46 23	27D 8.1	22 43.5	9 7.3	10 43.9	10 2.0	19 23.8	7 57.5	11 0.5	6 52.0
10 Su	13 10 43	19 34 54	9♉27 39	16 12 19	27 8.3	24 5.6	8 47.8	11 27.2	9 57.3	19 20.0	8 0.3	11 0.0	6 52.5
11 M	13 14 40	20 33 47	23 0 13	29 51 7	27 8.7	25 29.5	8 25.9	12 10.5	9 52.8	19 16.3	8 3.1	10 59.7	6 52.9
12 Tu	13 18 36	21 32 38	6♊44 48	13♊41 3	27 9.3	26 55.1	8 1.9	12 53.8	9 48.4	19 12.7	8 5.8	10 59.3	6 53.4
13 W	13 22 33	22 31 27	20 39 37	27 40 16	27 9.8	28 22.6	7 35.7	13 37.0	9 44.2	19 9.1	8 8.5	10 59.0	6 54.0
14 Th	13 26 29	23 30 14	4♋42 45	11♋46 46	27 10.1	29 51.7	7 7.5	14 20.1	9 40.1	19 5.6	8 11.2	10 58.7	6 54.5
15 F	13 30 26	24 28 59	18 52 6	25 58 26	27R 10.3	1♈22.6	6 37.4	15 3.2	9 36.2	19 2.2	8 13.8	10 58.5	6 55.0
16 Sa	13 34 23	25 27 41	3♌ 5 29	10♌12 55	27 10.3	2 55.2	6 5.6	15 46.2	9 32.5	18 58.8	8 16.4	10 58.3	6 55.6
17 Su	13 38 19	26 26 21	17 20 26	24 27 39	27D 10.2	4 29.4	5 32.3	16 29.2	9 29.0	18 55.5	8 19.0	10 58.1	6 56.2
18 M	13 42 16	27 24 58	1♍34 13	8♍39 43	27 10.2	6 5.3	4 57.6	17 12.2	9 25.6	18 52.3	8 21.5	10 57.9	6 56.8
19 Tu	13 46 12	28 23 33	15 43 46	22 45 57	27 10.3	7 42.9	4 21.8	17 55.1	9 22.4	18 49.2	8 24.0	10 57.8	6 57.5
20 W	13 50 9	29 22 7	29 45 51	6♎43 5	27 10.5	9 22.1	3 45.0	18 37.9	9 19.4	18 46.2	8 26.5	10 57.7	6 58.1
21 Th	13 54 5	0♉20 38	13♎37 16	20 28 3	27R 10.6	11 3.0	3 7.7	19 20.7	9 16.6	18 43.2	8 29.0	10 57.7	6 58.8
22 F	13 58 2	1 19 7	27 15 7	3♏58 15	27 10.7	12 45.6	2 29.9	20 3.4	9 13.9	18 40.3	8 31.4	10D 57.6	6 59.5
23 Sa	14 1 58	2 17 34	10♏37 12	17 11 52	27 10.6	14 29.8	1 51.9	20 46.1	9 11.4	18 37.6	8 33.7	10 57.7	7 0.3
24 Su	14 5 55	3 15 59	23 42 10	0♐ 8 6	27 10.2	16 15.8	1 14.1	21 28.8	9 9.1	18 34.9	8 36.1	10 57.7	7 1.0
25 M	14 9 51	4 14 23	6♐29 45	12 47 16	27 9.4	18 3.4	0 36.5	22 11.4	9 7.0	18 32.3	8 38.4	10 57.8	7 1.8
26 Tu	14 13 48	5 12 45	19 0 52	25 10 49	27 8.4	19 52.8	29♈59.6	22 53.9	9 5.1	18 29.7	8 40.6	10 57.9	7 2.6
27 W	14 17 45	6 11 5	1♑17 28	7♑21 12	27 7.3	21 43.8	29 23.6	23 36.4	9 3.3	18 27.3	8 42.8	10 58.1	7 3.4
28 Th	14 21 41	7 9 24	13 22 28	19 21 46	27 6.2	23 36.6	28 48.6	24 18.9	9 1.8	18 25.0	8 45.0	10 58.2	7 4.2
29 F	14 25 38	8 7 41	25 19 35	1♒16 28	27 5.4	25 31.0	28 14.9	25 1.3	9 0.4	18 22.7	8 47.2	10 58.4	7 5.0
30 Sa	14 29 34	9 5 57	7♒13 1	13 9 46	27D 5.1	27 27.2	27 42.6	25 43.7	8 59.1	18 20.6	8 49.3	10 58.7	7 5.9

Astro Data	Planet Ingress	Last Aspect	☽ Ingress	Last Aspect	☽ Ingress	☽ Phases & Eclipses	Astro Data
Dy Hr Mn	Dy Hr Mn	Dy Hr Mn	Dy Hr Mn	Dy Hr Mn	Dy Hr Mn	Dy Hr Mn	1 MARCH 1921
☽0N 10 3:02	♀ ♉ 7 9:18	2 22:15 ♀ △	♑ 3 5:03	1 5:00 ♄ △	♒ 2 1:22	1 14:03 ☽ 10♐28	Julian Day # 7730
☿ D 16 8:55	☉ ♈ 21 3:51	5 15:09 ♀ □	♒ 5 17:46	3 3:14 ☉ ⚹	♓ 4 13:28	9 18:09 ● 18♓39	Delta T 22.3 sec
♅△♇ 17 11:20	♂ ♉ 25 6:26	7 3:01 ♂ ⚹	♓ 8 5:44	6 3:39 ♄ ☍	♈ 6 23:31	17 3:49 ☽ 26♊01	SVP 06♓21'29"
♇ D 21 10:00		9 23:55 ♄ ☍	♈ 10 15:58	8 9:05 ☉ ☌	♉ 9 7:00	23 20:18 ○ 2♎40	Obliquity 23°26'51"
☽0S 23 4:28	☿ ♈ 14 2:12	12 6:26 ♂ ☌	♉ 13 0:14	11 4:52 ☿ ⚹	♊ 11 12:16	31 9:13 ☽ 10♑07	⚷ Chiron 8♈10.6
♃⚺♆ 28 8:39	☉ ♉ 20 15:32	14 19:13 ☉ ⚹	♊ 15 6:29	13 14:45 ☿ □	♋ 13 15:58		☽ Mean ☊ 29♎52.7
	♀ ♈ 25 23:46	17 3:49 ☉ □	♋ 17 10:36	15 10:11 ☉ □	♌ 15 18:47	8 9:05 ● 17♈59	
♀ R 1 11:19		19 10:00 ☉ △	♌ 19 12:52	17 16:28 ☉ △	♍ 17 21:21	8 9:14:37 • A 1'50"	1 APRIL 1921
☽0N 6 10:32		21 9:27 ♂ △	♍ 21 14:07	19 5:15 ♄ ☌	♎ 20 0:24	15 10:11 ☽ 24♋54	Julian Day # 7761
☿0N 17 21:01		23 0:07 ♄ ☌	♎ 23 15:49	20 19:22 ♆ ⚹	♏ 22 4:54	22 7:49 ○ 1♏38	Delta T 22.3 sec
☽0S 19 12:39		24 10:47 ♆ ⚹	♏ 25 19:33	23 19:39 ♂ ☍	♐ 24 11:45	22 7:44 • T 1.068	SVP 06♓21'26"
♆ D 22 2:06		27 8:21 ♄ ⚹	♐ 28 2:34	26 20:26 ♀ △	♑ 26 21:27	30 4:08 ☽ 9♒16	Obliquity 23°26'51"
		29 17:23 ♄ □	♑ 30 12:58	29 5:38 ♀ □	♒ 29 9:26		⚷ Chiron 9♈56.6
							☽ Mean ☊ 28♎14.2

LONGITUDE — MAY 1921

Day	Sid.Time	☉	0 hr ☽	Noon ☽	True ☊	☿	♀	♂	♃	♄	♅	♆	♇
1 Su	14 33 31	10♉ 4 11	19♒ 7 20	25♒ 6 17	27♎ 5.2	29♈25.1	27♈12.0	26♉26.0	8♍58.1	18♍18.5	8♓51.3	10♌59.0	7♋ 6.8
2 M	14 37 27	11 2 24	1♓ 7 11	7♓10 37	27 6.0	1♉24.6	26R43.3	27 8.3	8R57.3	18R16.5	8 53.4	10 59.3	7 7.7
3 Tu	14 41 24	12 0 35	13 17 6	19 27 7	27 7.1	3 25.7	26 16.4	27 50.5	8 56.6	18 14.7	8 55.3	10 59.6	7 8.6
4 W	14 45 20	12 58 44	25 41 7	1♈59 29	27 8.4	5 28.4	25 51.7	28 32.7	8 56.1	18 12.9	8 57.3	11 0.0	7 9.5
5 Th	14 49 17	13 56 52	8♈22 33	14 50 34	27 9.6	7 32.6	25 29.2	29 14.8	8 55.9	18 11.2	8 59.2	11 0.4	7 10.5
6 F	14 53 14	14 54 59	21 23 42	28 1 59	27R10.3	9 38.2	25 8.9	29 56.9	8D55.7	18 9.6	9 1.1	11 0.9	7 11.5
7 Sa	14 57 10	15 53 4	4♉45 25	11♉33 51	27 10.3	11 45.1	24 50.9	0♊39.0	8 55.8	18 8.2	9 2.9	11 1.3	7 12.5
8 Su	15 1 7	16 51 7	18 27 2	25 24 37	27 9.3	13 53.2	24 35.3	1 21.0	8 56.1	18 6.8	9 4.7	11 1.8	7 13.5
9 M	15 5 3	17 49 9	2♊26 11	9♊31 10	27 7.3	16 2.2	24 22.1	2 3.0	8 56.5	18 5.5	9 6.4	11 2.4	7 14.5
10 Tu	15 9 0	18 47 10	16 39 2	23 49 7	27 4.6	18 12.1	24 11.3	2 44.9	8 57.2	18 4.3	9 8.1	11 3.0	7 15.5
11 W	15 12 56	19 45 8	1♋ 0 46	8♋13 20	27 1.5	20 22.5	24 2.9	3 26.7	8 58.0	18 3.3	9 9.7	11 3.6	7 16.6
12 Th	15 16 53	20 43 5	15 26 10	22 38 40	26 58.6	22 33.3	23 56.9	4 8.6	8 59.0	18 2.3	9 11.4	11 4.2	7 17.7
13 F	15 20 49	21 41 0	29 50 17	7♌ 0 33	26 56.3	24 44.2	23 53.3	4 50.3	9 0.2	18 1.4	9 12.9	11 4.9	7 18.8
14 Sa	15 24 46	22 38 53	14♌ 9 3	21 15 26	26D55.1	26 54.9	23D52.1	5 32.1	9 1.5	18 0.7	9 14.4	11 5.6	7 19.9
15 Su	15 28 43	23 36 45	28 19 26	5♍20 51	26 54.9	29 5.1	23 53.2	6 13.8	9 3.1	18 0.0	9 15.9	11 6.3	7 21.0
16 M	15 32 39	24 34 34	12♍19 33	19 15 24	26 55.7	1♊14.6	23 56.6	6 55.4	9 4.8	17 59.5	9 17.3	11 7.1	7 22.1
17 Tu	15 36 36	25 32 22	26 8 21	2♎53 20	26 57.2	3 23.1	24 2.3	7 37.0	9 6.7	17 59.0	9 18.7	11 7.9	7 23.3
18 W	15 40 32	26 30 8	9♎45 21	16 29 21	26 58.6	5 30.2	24 10.2	8 18.5	9 8.7	17 58.7	9 20.1	11 8.7	7 24.5
19 Th	15 44 29	27 27 52	23 10 19	29 48 14	26R59.4	7 35.8	24 20.2	9 0.0	9 11.0	17 58.4	9 21.3	11 9.6	7 25.6
20 F	15 48 25	28 25 35	6♏23 3	12♏54 46	26 59.1	9 39.6	24 32.3	9 41.5	9 13.4	17D58.3	9 22.6	11 10.4	7 26.8
21 Sa	15 52 22	29 23 17	19 23 21	25 48 47	26 57.3	11 41.4	24 46.5	10 22.9	9 16.0	17 58.2	9 23.8	11 11.4	7 28.0
22 Su	15 56 18	0♊20 57	2♐11 3	8♐30 10	26 53.9	13 41.0	25 2.6	11 4.2	9 18.8	17 58.3	9 24.9	11 12.3	7 29.3
23 M	16 0 15	1 18 36	14 46 10	20 59 9	26 49.0	15 38.3	25 20.7	11 45.5	9 21.7	17 58.4	9 26.1	11 13.3	7 30.5
24 Tu	16 4 12	2 16 14	27 9 12	3♑16 28	26 43.1	17 33.1	25 40.6	12 26.8	9 24.8	17 58.7	9 27.1	11 14.3	7 31.7
25 W	16 8 8	3 13 50	9♑21 10	15 23 32	26 36.8	19 25.3	26 2.3	13 8.1	9 28.1	17 59.1	9 28.1	11 15.3	7 33.0
26 Th	16 12 5	4 11 26	21 23 52	27 22 31	26 30.6	21 14.8	26 25.8	13 49.2	9 31.5	17 59.6	9 29.1	11 16.4	7 34.3
27 F	16 16 1	5 9 1	3♒19 52	9♒16 23	26 25.4	23 1.5	26 50.9	14 30.4	9 35.1	18 0.1	9 30.0	11 17.5	7 35.6
28 Sa	16 19 58	6 6 34	15 12 31	21 8 49	26 21.5	24 45.4	27 17.7	15 11.5	9 38.9	18 0.8	9 30.9	11 18.6	7 36.9
29 Su	16 23 54	7 4 7	27 5 48	3♓ 4 6	26D19.3	26 26.5	27 46.0	15 52.6	9 42.8	18 1.6	9 31.7	11 19.8	7 38.2
30 M	16 27 51	8 1 38	9♓ 4 17	15 6 58	26 18.7	28 4.6	28 15.8	16 33.6	9 46.9	18 2.5	9 32.5	11 20.9	7 39.5
31 Tu	16 31 47	8 59 9	21 12 47	27 22 19	26 19.4	29 39.8	28 47.1	17 14.6	9 51.1	18 3.5	9 33.2	11 22.1	7 40.8

LONGITUDE — JUNE 1921

Day	Sid.Time	☉	0 hr ☽	Noon ☽	True ☊	☿	♀	♂	♃	♄	♅	♆	♇
1 W	16 35 44	9♊56 40	3♈36 11	9♈54 54	26♎20.7	1♋12.0	29♈19.7	17♊55.5	9♍55.5	18♍ 4.5	9♓33.9	11♌23.4	7♋42.2
2 Th	16 39 41	10 54 9	16 18 59	22 48 51	26R22.0	2 41.1	29 53.7	18 36.4	10 0.1	18 5.7	9 34.5	11 24.6	7 43.5
3 F	16 43 37	11 51 38	29 24 51	6♉ 7 12	26 22.3	4 7.3	0♉29.0	19 17.3	10 4.8	18 7.0	9 35.1	11 25.9	7 44.9
4 Sa	16 47 34	12 49 6	12♉56 0	19 51 12	26 21.1	5 30.4	1 5.4	19 58.1	10 9.7	18 8.4	9 35.7	11 27.2	7 46.2
5 Su	16 51 30	13 46 33	26 52 36	3♊59 47	26 17.8	6 50.3	1 43.1	20 38.9	10 14.7	18 9.9	9 36.1	11 28.6	7 47.6
6 M	16 55 27	14 43 59	11♊12 15	18 29 15	26 12.6	8 7.1	2 21.9	21 19.7	10 19.9	18 11.5	9 36.6	11 30.0	7 49.0
7 Tu	16 59 23	15 41 25	25 49 57	3♋13 22	26 5.8	9 20.8	3 1.7	22 0.4	10 25.3	18 13.2	9 37.0	11 31.4	7 50.4
8 W	17 3 20	16 38 49	10♋38 30	18 4 14	25 58.2	10 31.1	3 42.6	22 41.0	10 30.7	18 15.0	9 37.3	11 32.8	7 51.8
9 Th	17 7 16	17 36 13	25 29 33	2♌53 26	25 50.8	11 38.2	4 24.5	23 21.7	10 36.4	18 16.9	9 37.6	11 34.2	7 53.2
10 F	17 11 13	18 33 36	10♌14 59	17 33 27	25 44.5	12 41.8	5 7.4	24 2.3	10 42.2	18 18.9	9 37.9	11 35.7	7 54.7
11 Sa	17 15 10	19 30 57	24 48 11	1♍58 44	25 40.0	13 42.0	5 51.2	24 42.8	10 48.1	18 21.0	9 38.0	11 37.2	7 56.1
12 Su	17 19 6	20 28 18	9♍ 4 46	16 6 6	25D37.7	14 38.7	6 35.8	25 23.3	10 54.2	18 23.2	9 38.2	11 38.7	7 57.5
13 M	17 23 3	21 25 38	23 2 40	29 54 32	25 37.1	15 31.7	7 21.4	26 3.8	11 0.4	18 25.5	9 38.3	11 40.3	7 59.0
14 Tu	17 26 59	22 22 56	6♎41 49	13♎24 44	25 37.7	16 21.1	8 7.7	26 44.2	11 6.7	18 27.8	9R38.3	11 41.8	8 0.4
15 W	17 30 56	23 20 14	20 3 28	26 38 19	25R38.4	17 6.6	8 54.8	27 24.6	11 13.2	18 30.3	9 38.3	11 43.4	8 1.9
16 Th	17 34 52	24 17 31	3♏ 9 30	9♏37 17	25 38.3	17 48.2	9 42.7	28 4.9	11 19.8	18 32.9	9 38.3	11 45.0	8 3.3
17 F	17 38 49	25 14 47	16 1 54	22 23 34	25 36.4	18 25.8	10 31.4	28 45.2	11 26.6	18 35.5	9 38.2	11 46.7	8 4.8
18 Sa	17 42 45	26 12 2	28 42 28	4♐58 45	25 32.1	18 59.3	11 20.7	29 25.5	11 33.5	18 38.3	9 38.0	11 48.3	8 6.2
19 Su	17 46 42	27 9 17	11♐12 34	17 24 2	25 25.2	19 28.5	12 10.8	0♋ 5.7	11 40.5	18 41.1	9 37.8	11 50.0	8 7.7
20 M	17 50 39	28 6 31	23 33 16	29 40 22	25 16.0	19 53.5	13 1.5	0 45.9	11 47.6	18 44.1	9 37.6	11 51.7	8 9.2
21 Tu	17 54 35	29 3 45	5♑45 26	11♑48 36	25 5.1	20 14.0	13 52.9	1 26.1	11 54.9	18 47.1	9 37.3	11 53.4	8 10.7
22 W	17 58 32	0♋ 0 58	17 49 59	23 49 45	24 53.4	20 30.1	14 44.8	2 6.2	12 2.3	18 50.2	9 37.0	11 55.1	8 12.2
23 Th	18 2 28	0 58 11	29 48 7	5♒45 17	24 41.8	20 41.7	15 37.4	2 46.3	12 9.8	18 53.4	9 36.6	11 56.9	8 13.6
24 F	18 6 25	1 55 24	11♒41 34	17 37 17	24 31.5	20 48.6	16 30.6	3 26.4	12 17.5	18 56.7	9 36.2	11 58.7	8 15.1
25 Sa	18 10 21	2 52 36	23 32 47	29 28 30	24 23.1	20R51.0	17 24.3	4 6.4	12 25.2	19 0.1	9 35.7	12 0.5	8 16.6
26 Su	18 14 18	3 49 49	5♓24 55	11♓22 31	24 17.1	20 48.8	18 18.5	4 46.3	12 33.1	19 3.6	9 35.2	12 2.3	8 18.1
27 M	18 18 14	4 47 1	17 21 53	23 23 34	24 13.7	20 42.1	19 13.3	5 26.3	12 41.1	19 7.2	9 34.6	12 4.1	8 19.6
28 Tu	18 22 11	5 44 14	29 28 13	5♈36 26	24D12.2	20 30.9	20 8.6	6 6.2	12 49.3	19 10.8	9 34.0	12 6.0	8 21.1
29 W	18 26 8	6 41 26	11♈48 53	18 6 11	24R12.2	20 15.5	21 4.3	6 46.1	12 57.5	19 14.5	9 33.3	12 7.9	8 22.6
30 Th	18 30 4	7 38 39	24 28 57	0♉57 44	24 12.4	19 56.1	22 0.5	7 25.9	13 5.8	19 18.4	9 32.6	12 9.8	8 24.1

Astro Data	Planet Ingress	Last Aspect	☽ Ingress	Last Aspect	☽ Ingress	☽ Phases & Eclipses	Astro Data
Dy Hr Mn	Dy Hr Mn	Dy Hr Mn	Dy Hr Mn	Dy Hr Mn	Dy Hr Mn	Dy Hr Mn	1 MAY 1921
☽0N 3 19:11	☿ ♉ 1 7:03	1 15:34 ♂ □	♓ 1 21:46	2 4:29 ♂ ⚹	♉ 3 1:03	7 21:01 ● 16♉44	Julian Day # 7791
♃☍♅ 3 12:18	♂ ♊ 6 1:45	4 5:47 ♂ ⚹	♈ 4 8:14	4 9:04 ♄ △	♊ 5 5:17	14 15:24 ☽ 23♌16	Delta T 22.3 sec
♃ D 6 1:47	☿ ♊ 15 10:09	6 6:39 ♀ ☌	♉ 6 15:32	6 17:27 ♂ ☌	♋ 7 6:46	21 20:15 ○ 0♐12	SVP 06♓21'23"
♀ D 14 0:27	☉ ♊ 21 15:17	7 23:25 ♄ △	♊ 8 19:51	8 12:19 ♄ ⚹	♌ 9 7:18	29 21:44 ☽ 7♓56	Obliquity 23°26'50"
☽0S 16 19:00	☿ ♋ 31 5:12	10 12:29 ♀ ⚹	♋ 10 22:19	10 23:51 ♂ ⚹	♍ 11 8:41		⚷ Chiron 11♈38.9
♄ D 20 21:36		12 14:06 ♀ □	♌ 13 0:16	13 5:32 ♂ □	♎ 13 12:10	6 6:14 ● 14♊59	☽ Mean ☊ 26♎38.9
♃☍♅ 25 0:45	♀ ♉ 2 4:21	15 1:32 ☿ □	♍ 15 2:51	15 14:08 ♂ △	♏ 15 18:10	12 20:59 ☽ 21♍18	
☽0N 31 4:29	♂ ♋ 18 20:34	16 22:52 ☉ △	♎ 17 6:46	17 4:50 ♄ ⚹	♐ 18 2:28	20 9:41 ○ 28♐30	1 JUNE 1921
	☉ ♋ 21 23:36	19 2:08 ♀ ☍	♏ 19 12:21	20 9:41 ☉ ☍	♑ 20 12:39	28 13:17 ☽ 6♈16	Julian Day # 7822
☽0S 13 1:13		20 21:22 ♄ ⚹	♐ 21 19:53	22 5:26 ☿ ☍	♒ 23 0:24		Delta T 22.3 sec
♅ R 14 10:56		23 21:02 ♀ △	♑ 24 5:34	24 10:33 ♀ □	♓ 25 13:04		SVP 06♓21'19"
♃⊻♆ 20 17:35		26 10:28 ♀ □	♒ 26 17:17	27 6:34 ☿ △	♈ 28 1:02		Obliquity 23°26'49"
☿ R 25 0:26		29 1:24 ♀ ⚹	♓ 29 5:50	29 15:41 ☿ □	♉ 30 10:14		⚷ Chiron 13♈04.4
☽0N 27 13:27		30 17:48 ♄ ☍	♈ 31 17:05				☽ Mean ☊ 25♎00.4

JULY 1921 LONGITUDE

Day	Sid.Time	☉	0 hr ☽	Noon ☽	True ☊	☿	♀	♂	♃	♄	♅	♆	♇
1 F	18 34 1	8♋35 51	7♉33 1	14♉15 12	24♎11.8	19♋32.8	22♉57.2	8♋ 5.7	13♍14.3	19♍22.3	9♓31.8	12♌11.7	8♋25.6
2 Sa	18 37 57	9 33 4	21 4 35	28 1 15	24R 9.4	19R 6.0	23 54.3	8 45.5	13 22.9	19 26.2	9R31.0	12 13.6	8 27.1
3 Su	18 41 54	10 30 18	5♊ 5 10	12♊16 5	24 4.6	18 36.1	24 51.8	9 25.3	13 31.6	19 30.3	9 30.2	12 15.5	8 28.6
4 M	18 45 50	11 27 31	19 33 30	26 56 43	23 57.3	18 3.5	25 49.7	10 5.0	13 40.4	19 34.5	9 29.3	12 17.5	8 30.1
5 Tu	18 49 47	12 24 45	4♋24 51	11♋56 47	23 47.8	17 28.8	26 48.1	10 44.7	13 49.3	19 38.7	9 28.4	12 19.5	8 31.6
6 W	18 53 43	13 21 58	19 31 17	27 7 1	23 37.3	16 52.5	27 46.8	11 24.4	13 58.3	19 43.0	9 27.4	12 21.4	8 33.1
7 Th	18 57 40	14 19 12	4♌42 37	12♌16 44	23 26.8	16 15.1	28 45.8	12 4.0	14 7.4	19 47.4	9 26.4	12 23.4	8 34.6
8 F	19 1 37	15 16 26	19 48 10	27 15 49	23 17.7	15 37.3	29 45.2	12 43.6	14 16.6	19 51.8	9 25.3	12 25.5	8 36.1
9 Sa	19 5 33	16 13 39	4♍38 45	11♍56 18	23 10.8	14 59.8	0♊45.0	13 23.1	14 25.9	19 56.4	9 24.2	12 27.5	8 37.6
10 Su	19 9 30	17 10 52	19 7 58	26 13 28	23 6.5	14 23.2	1 45.0	14 2.6	14 35.4	20 1.0	9 23.1	12 29.5	8 39.1
11 M	19 13 26	18 8 6	3♎12 40	10♎ 5 39	23 4.5	13 48.1	2 45.4	14 42.1	14 44.9	20 5.7	9 21.9	12 31.6	8 40.6
12 Tu	19 17 23	19 5 19	16 52 35	23 33 46	23 4.1	13 15.2	3 46.1	15 21.6	14 54.5	20 10.5	9 20.6	12 33.6	8 42.0
13 W	19 21 19	20 2 32	0♏ 9 32	6♏40 19	23 4.0	12 45.0	4 47.1	16 1.0	15 4.2	20 15.3	9 19.4	12 35.7	8 43.5
14 Th	19 25 16	20 59 45	13 6 32	19 28 37	23 3.1	12 18.2	5 48.4	16 40.4	15 14.0	20 20.2	9 18.0	12 37.8	8 45.0
15 F	19 29 12	21 56 58	25 47 0	2♐ 2 4	23 0.3	11 55.1	6 50.0	17 19.8	15 23.8	20 25.2	9 16.7	12 39.9	8 46.5
16 Sa	19 33 9	22 54 12	8♐14 13	14 23 46	22 55.0	11 36.3	7 51.9	17 59.1	15 33.8	20 30.2	9 15.3	12 42.0	8 47.9
17 Su	19 37 6	23 51 25	20 31 3	26 36 18	22 46.8	11 22.2	8 54.0	18 38.4	15 43.9	20 35.3	9 13.9	12 44.1	8 49.4
18 M	19 41 2	24 48 39	2♑39 48	8♑41 43	22 35.9	11 13.0	9 56.4	19 17.7	15 54.0	20 40.5	9 12.4	12 46.3	8 50.8
19 Tu	19 44 59	25 45 54	14 42 14	20 41 33	22 23.2	11D 9.0	10 59.1	19 56.9	16 4.2	20 45.8	9 10.9	12 48.4	8 52.3
20 W	19 48 55	26 43 8	26 39 47	2♒37 8	22 9.5	11 10.5	12 2.0	20 36.1	16 14.6	20 51.1	9 9.3	12 50.6	8 53.7
21 Th	19 52 52	27 40 23	8♒33 44	14 29 47	21 55.9	11 17.6	13 5.2	21 15.3	16 25.0	20 56.5	9 7.8	12 52.7	8 55.2
22 F	19 56 48	28 37 39	20 25 28	26 21 3	21 43.7	11 30.5	14 8.7	21 54.4	16 35.4	21 1.9	9 6.2	12 54.9	8 56.6
23 Sa	20 0 45	29 34 56	2♓16 47	8♓12 59	21 33.6	11 49.1	15 12.3	22 33.5	16 46.0	21 7.4	9 4.5	12 57.1	8 58.0
24 Su	20 4 42	0♌32 13	14 10 0	20 8 15	21 26.1	12 13.6	16 16.2	23 12.6	16 56.6	21 13.0	9 2.8	12 59.2	8 59.4
25 M	20 8 38	1 29 31	26 8 10	2♈10 15	21 21.4	12 44.0	17 20.3	23 51.7	17 7.3	21 18.6	9 1.1	13 1.4	9 0.8
26 Tu	20 12 35	2 26 49	8♈15 1	14 23 2	21 19.2	13 20.3	18 24.7	24 30.7	17 18.1	21 24.3	8 59.3	13 3.6	9 2.2
27 W	20 16 31	3 24 9	20 34 53	26 51 10	21D 18.6	14 2.4	19 29.3	25 9.8	17 29.0	21 30.1	8 57.6	13 5.8	9 3.6
28 Th	20 20 28	4 21 30	3♉12 30	9♉39 26	21R 18.7	14 50.3	20 34.0	25 48.8	17 39.9	21 35.9	8 55.7	13 8.0	9 5.0
29 F	20 24 24	5 18 52	16 12 33	22 52 17	21 18.4	15 44.0	21 39.0	26 27.7	17 50.9	21 41.8	8 53.9	13 10.2	9 6.4
30 Sa	20 28 21	6 16 15	29 39 3	6♊33 6	21 16.5	16 43.2	22 44.2	27 6.7	18 2.0	21 47.7	8 52.0	13 12.4	9 7.8
31 Su	20 32 17	7 13 39	13♊34 33	20 43 18	21 12.4	17 48.0	23 49.6	27 45.6	18 13.1	21 53.7	8 50.1	13 14.6	9 9.1

AUGUST 1921 LONGITUDE

Day	Sid.Time	☉	0 hr ☽	Noon ☽	True ☊	☿	♀	♂	♃	♄	♅	♆	♇
1 M	20 36 14	8♌11 4	27♊59 5	5♋21 22	21♎ 5.9	18♋58.3	24♊55.2	28♋24.5	18♍24.3	21♍59.7	8♓48.2	13♌16.8	9♋10.5
2 Tu	20 40 10	9 8 30	12♋49 24	20 22 13	20R57.2	20 13.7	26 1.0	29 3.3	18 35.6	22 5.8	8R46.2	13 19.1	9 11.8
3 W	20 44 7	10 5 58	27 58 37	5♌37 18	20 47.4	21 34.3	27 6.9	29 42.2	18 47.0	22 11.9	8 44.2	13 21.3	9 13.1
4 Th	20 48 4	11 3 26	13♌16 50	20 55 46	20 37.5	22 59.8	28 13.0	0♌21.0	18 58.4	22 18.1	8 42.2	13 23.5	9 14.4
5 F	20 52 0	12 0 55	28 32 42	6♍ 6 18	20 28.8	24 30.1	29 19.3	0 59.8	19 9.8	22 24.4	8 40.2	13 25.7	9 15.7
6 Sa	20 55 57	12 58 25	13♍35 28	20 59 13	20 22.2	26 4.7	0♋25.8	1 38.6	19 21.4	22 30.7	8 38.1	13 28.0	9 17.0
7 Su	20 59 53	13 55 56	28 16 50	5♎27 49	20 18.1	27 43.6	1 32.4	2 17.3	19 32.9	22 37.0	8 36.0	13 30.2	9 18.3
8 M	21 3 50	14 53 28	12♎31 54	19 28 59	20D 16.3	29 26.3	2 39.2	2 56.0	19 44.6	22 43.4	8 33.9	13 32.4	9 19.6
9 Tu	21 7 46	15 51 1	26 19 8	3♏ 2 36	20 16.2	1♌12.6	3 46.1	3 34.7	19 56.3	22 49.8	8 31.7	13 34.6	9 20.8
10 W	21 11 43	16 48 34	9♏39 43	16 10 54	20R 16.7	3 2.1	4 53.2	4 13.3	20 8.1	22 56.3	8 29.6	13 36.9	9 22.1
11 Th	21 15 39	17 46 8	22 36 37	28 57 23	20 16.8	4 54.3	6 0.4	4 52.0	20 19.9	23 2.9	8 27.4	13 39.1	9 23.3
12 F	21 19 36	18 43 44	5♐13 43	11♐26 8	20 15.4	6 49.1	7 7.8	5 30.6	20 31.7	23 9.4	8 25.2	13 41.3	9 24.5
13 Sa	21 23 33	19 41 20	17 35 10	23 41 16	20 11.9	8 45.9	8 15.4	6 9.2	20 43.7	23 16.0	8 23.0	13 43.5	9 25.7
14 Su	21 27 29	20 38 57	29 44 54	5♑46 29	20 6.0	10 44.3	9 23.1	6 47.7	20 55.6	23 22.7	8 20.8	13 45.7	9 26.9
15 M	21 31 26	21 36 35	11♑46 24	17 44 59	19 57.9	12 44.1	10 30.9	7 26.2	21 7.6	23 29.4	8 18.5	13 47.9	9 28.1
16 Tu	21 35 22	22 34 14	23 42 34	29 39 23	19 48.1	14 44.7	11 38.9	8 4.8	21 19.7	23 36.1	8 16.2	13 50.2	9 29.2
17 W	21 39 19	23 31 55	5♒35 43	11♒31 46	19 37.5	16 46.0	12 47.0	8 43.2	21 31.8	23 42.9	8 14.0	13 52.4	9 30.4
18 Th	21 43 15	24 29 36	17 27 46	23 23 53	19 27.0	18 47.5	13 55.3	9 21.7	21 44.0	23 49.7	8 11.7	13 54.6	9 31.5
19 F	21 47 12	25 27 19	29 20 19	5♓17 17	19 17.5	20 49.1	15 3.7	10 0.1	21 56.2	23 56.5	8 9.3	13 56.7	9 32.6
20 Sa	21 51 8	26 25 4	11♓14 59	17 13 39	19 9.8	22 50.5	16 12.2	10 38.6	22 8.4	24 3.4	8 7.0	13 58.9	9 33.7
21 Su	21 55 5	27 22 49	23 13 32	29 14 54	19 4.3	24 51.4	17 20.9	11 16.9	22 20.7	24 10.3	8 4.7	14 1.1	9 34.8
22 M	21 59 2	28 20 36	5♈18 6	11♈23 26	19 1.1	26 51.7	18 29.7	11 55.3	22 33.0	24 17.3	8 2.3	14 3.3	9 35.8
23 Tu	22 2 58	29 18 25	17 31 19	23 42 9	19D 0.1	28 51.2	19 38.6	12 33.7	22 45.4	24 24.3	7 60.0	14 5.4	9 36.9
24 W	22 6 55	0♍16 16	29 56 22	6♉14 26	19 0.5	0♍49.8	20 47.7	13 12.0	22 57.8	24 31.3	7 57.6	14 7.6	9 37.9
25 Th	22 10 51	1 14 8	12♉36 50	19 4 2	19 1.7	2 47.5	21 56.9	13 50.3	23 10.2	24 38.3	7 55.2	14 9.7	9 38.9
26 F	22 14 48	2 12 2	25 36 29	2♊14 37	19R 2.7	4 44.1	23 6.2	14 28.6	23 22.7	24 45.4	7 52.9	14 11.9	9 39.9
27 Sa	22 18 44	3 9 58	8♊58 47	15 49 16	19 2.8	6 39.5	24 15.7	15 6.9	23 35.2	24 52.5	7 50.5	14 14.0	9 40.9
28 Su	22 22 41	4 7 56	22 46 14	29 49 43	19 1.2	8 33.8	25 25.2	15 45.1	23 47.7	24 59.6	7 48.1	14 16.2	9 41.9
29 M	22 26 37	5 5 56	6♋59 36	14♋15 34	18 57.9	10 26.8	26 34.9	16 23.4	24 0.3	25 6.7	7 45.7	14 18.3	9 42.8
30 Tu	22 30 34	6 3 57	21 37 7	29 3 33	18 52.9	12 18.6	27 44.7	17 1.6	24 12.9	25 13.9	7 43.3	14 20.4	9 43.8
31 W	22 34 31	7 2 1	6♌33 59	14♌ 7 21	18 47.0	14 9.2	28 54.7	17 39.8	24 25.5	25 21.1	7 40.9	14 22.5	9 44.7

Astro Data	Planet Ingress	Last Aspect	☽ Ingress	Last Aspect	☽ Ingress	☽ Phases & Eclipses	Astro Data
Dy Hr Mn	Dy Hr Mn	Dy Hr Mn	Dy Hr Mn	Dy Hr Mn	Dy Hr Mn	Dy Hr Mn	1 JULY 1921
☽0S 10 8:55	♀ ♊ 8 5:57	2 5:17 ♀ ☌	♊ 2 15:23	31 18:33 ♀ ☌	♋ 1 3:18	5 13:36 ● 12♋57	Julian Day # 7852
☿ D 19 5:33	☉ ♌ 23 10:30	4 0:02 ♄ □	♋ 4 16:55	3 2:50 ♂ ☌	♌ 3 3:11	12 4:15 ☽ 19♎15	Delta T 22.3 sec
☽0N 24 21:18		6 13:57 ♀ ⚹	♌ 6 16:33	5 1:20 ♀ ⚹	♍ 5 2:18	20 0:07 ○ 26♑43	SVP 06♓21'14"
♅△♇ 25 1:56	♂ ♌ 3 11:01	7 12:12 ♆ ☌	♍ 8 16:26	6 22:58 ☿ ⚹	♎ 7 2:51	28 2:20 ☽ 4♉27	Obliquity 23°26'49"
	♀ ♋ 5 14:42	10 1:30 ♄ ☌	♎ 10 18:28	8 4:21 ☉ ⚹	♏ 9 6:33		⚷ Chiron 13♈51.5
☽0S 6 18:34	☿ ♌ 8 7:42	12 4:15 ☉ □	♏ 12 23:43	11 0:50 ♄ ⚹	♐ 11 13:59	3 20:17 ● 10♌55	☽ Mean ☊ 23♎25.1
☽0N 21 3:57	☉ ♍ 23 17:15	14 16:06 ☉ △	♐ 15 8:05	13 11:16 ♄ □	♑ 14 0:30	10 14:13 ☽ 17♏23	
	☿ ♍ 23 13:54	17 0:09 ♄ □	♑ 17 18:43	15 23:47 ♄ △	♒ 16 12:42	18 15:28 ○ 25♒07	1 AUGUST 1921
	☿ ♌ 31 22:24	20 0:07 ☉ ☍	♒ 20 6:43	18 15:28 ☉ ☍	♓ 19 1:20	26 12:51 ☽ 2♊43	Julian Day # 7883
		21 10:03 ♀ △	♓ 22 19:23	21 1:54 ♄ ☍	♈ 21 13:30		Delta T 22.3 sec
		24 19:12 ♂ △	♈ 25 7:42	23 4:33 ♀ □	♉ 24 0:07		SVP 06♓21'09"
		27 9:16 ♂ □	♉ 27 17:58	25 22:26 ♄ △	♊ 26 7:58		Obliquity 23°26'49"
		29 19:18 ♂ ⚹	♊ 30 0:37	28 3:50 ♄ □	♋ 28 12:17		⚷ Chiron 13♈53.3R
				30 10:43 ♀ ☌	♌ 30 13:31		☽ Mean ☊ 21♎46.6

LONGITUDE — SEPTEMBER 1921

Day	Sid.Time	☉	0 hr ☽	Noon ☽	True ☊	☿	♀	♂	♃	♄	♅	♆	♇
1 Th	22 38 27	8♍ 0 6	21♌42 28	29♌18 4	18♎40.9	15♍58.5	0♌ 4.7	18♌18.0	24♍38.2	25♍28.3	7♓38.5	14♌24.5	9♋45.6
2 F	22 42 24	8 58 13	6♍52 50	14♍25 31	18R 35.5	17 46.6	1 14.8	18 56.1	24 50.9	25 35.6	7R 36.1	14 26.6	9 46.4
3 Sa	22 46 20	9 56 21	21 54 57	29 20 2	18 31.5	19 33.5	2 25.1	19 34.3	25 3.6	25 42.9	7 33.7	14 28.7	9 47.3
4 Su	22 50 17	10 54 31	6♎39 55	13♎53 52	18D 29.2	21 19.1	3 35.4	20 12.4	25 16.3	25 50.1	7 31.3	14 30.7	9 48.1
5 M	22 54 13	11 52 43	21 1 24	28 2 12	18 28.7	23 3.5	4 45.9	20 50.5	25 29.1	25 57.5	7 28.9	14 32.7	9 48.9
6 Tu	22 58 10	12 50 57	4♏56 6	11♏43 11	18 29.6	24 46.7	5 56.4	21 28.6	25 41.9	26 4.8	7 26.5	14 34.8	9 49.7
7 W	23 2 6	13 49 11	18 23 35	24 57 36	18 31.0	26 28.7	7 7.1	22 6.6	25 54.7	26 12.1	7 24.2	14 36.8	9 50.5
8 Th	23 6 3	14 47 28	1♐25 37	7♐48 5	18 32.5	28 9.5	8 17.9	22 44.6	26 7.5	26 19.5	7 21.8	14 38.7	9 51.3
9 F	23 10 0	15 45 46	14 5 31	20 18 25	18R 33.2	29 49.2	9 28.7	23 22.7	26 20.4	26 26.8	7 19.4	14 40.7	9 52.0
10 Sa	23 13 56	16 44 5	26 27 23	2♑32 56	18 32.7	1♎27.7	10 39.7	24 0.6	26 33.3	26 34.2	7 17.1	14 42.7	9 52.7
11 Su	23 17 53	17 42 26	8♑35 38	14 36 0	18 30.8	3 5.1	11 50.7	24 38.6	26 46.1	26 41.6	7 14.7	14 44.6	9 53.4
12 M	23 21 49	18 40 49	20 34 33	26 31 45	18 27.6	4 41.4	13 1.9	25 16.6	26 59.0	26 49.0	7 12.4	14 46.5	9 54.1
13 Tu	23 25 46	19 39 13	2♒28 5	8♒23 55	18 23.4	6 16.6	14 13.1	25 54.5	27 11.9	26 56.4	7 10.1	14 48.5	9 54.7
14 W	23 29 42	20 37 39	14 19 40	20 15 40	18 18.7	7 50.7	15 24.4	26 32.4	27 24.9	27 3.9	7 7.7	14 50.3	9 55.3
15 Th	23 33 39	21 36 6	26 12 14	2♓ 9 39	18 13.9	9 23.7	16 35.9	27 10.3	27 37.8	27 11.3	7 5.4	14 52.2	9 56.0
16 F	23 37 35	22 34 35	8♓ 8 11	14 8 2	18 9.7	10 55.6	17 47.4	27 48.1	27 50.7	27 18.7	7 3.1	14 54.1	9 56.5
17 Sa	23 41 32	23 33 6	20 9 27	26 12 37	18 6.3	12 26.5	18 59.0	28 26.0	28 3.7	27 26.2	7 0.9	14 55.9	9 57.1
18 Su	23 45 28	24 31 39	2♈17 44	8♈25 0	18 4.2	13 56.3	20 10.7	29 3.8	28 16.6	27 33.6	6 58.6	14 57.7	9 57.6
19 M	23 49 25	25 30 14	14 34 35	20 46 42	18D 3.3	15 25.0	21 22.5	29 41.6	28 29.6	27 41.1	6 56.4	14 59.5	9 58.2
20 Tu	23 53 22	26 28 51	27 1 32	3♉19 19	18 3.5	16 52.6	22 34.4	0♍19.4	28 42.6	27 48.5	6 54.2	15 1.3	9 58.7
21 W	23 57 18	27 27 30	9♉40 16	16 4 38	18 4.5	18 19.2	23 46.3	0 57.2	28 55.5	27 56.0	6 52.0	15 3.0	9 59.1
22 Th	0 1 15	28 26 12	22 32 39	29 4 33	18 5.9	19 44.6	24 58.4	1 35.0	29 8.5	28 3.4	6 49.8	15 4.8	9 59.6
23 F	0 5 11	29 24 55	5♊40 35	12♊20 57	18 7.3	21 8.9	26 10.5	2 12.7	29 21.5	28 10.9	6 47.6	15 6.5	10 0.0
24 Sa	0 9 8	0♎23 41	19 5 52	25 55 29	18R 8.3	22 32.1	27 22.8	2 50.4	29 34.5	28 18.4	6 45.5	15 8.2	10 0.4
25 Su	0 13 4	1 22 29	2♋49 51	9♋49 1	18 8.6	23 54.1	28 35.1	3 28.2	29 47.5	28 25.8	6 43.4	15 9.9	10 0.8
26 M	0 17 1	2 21 19	16 52 54	24 1 18	18 8.2	25 14.9	29 47.5	4 5.9	0♎ 0.4	28 33.3	6 41.3	15 11.5	10 1.2
27 Tu	0 20 57	3 20 12	1♌13 55	8♌30 20	18 7.0	26 34.4	0♍60.0	4 43.5	0 13.4	28 40.7	6 39.2	15 13.1	10 1.5
28 W	0 24 54	4 19 7	15 49 59	23 12 12	18 5.5	27 52.6	2 12.5	5 21.2	0 26.4	28 48.2	6 37.1	15 14.7	10 1.9
29 Th	0 28 51	5 18 4	0♍36 12	8♍ 1 5	18 3.9	29 9.5	3 25.2	5 58.8	0 39.4	28 55.6	6 35.1	15 16.3	10 2.2
30 F	0 32 47	6 17 3	15 25 57	22 49 50	18 2.4	0♏24.9	4 37.9	6 36.5	0 52.3	29 3.0	6 33.1	15 17.9	10 2.4

LONGITUDE — OCTOBER 1921

Day	Sid.Time	☉	0 hr ☽	Noon ☽	True ☊	☿	♀	♂	♃	♄	♅	♆	♇
1 Sa	0 36 44	7♎16 5	0♎11 47	7♎30 53	18♎ 1.5	1♏38.8	5♍50.7	7♍14.1	1♎ 5.3	29♍10.4	6♓31.2	15♌19.4	10♋ 2.7
2 Su	0 40 40	8 15 8	14 46 17	21 57 16	18D 1.1	2 51.1	7 3.5	7 51.7	1 18.2	29 17.8	6R 29.2	15 20.9	10 2.9
3 M	0 44 37	9 14 14	29 3 12	6♏ 3 37	18 1.2	4 1.8	8 16.5	8 29.2	1 31.2	29 25.2	6 27.3	15 22.4	10 3.1
4 Tu	0 48 33	10 13 21	12♏58 9	19 46 38	18 1.7	5 10.5	9 29.5	9 6.8	1 44.1	29 32.6	6 25.4	15 23.9	10 3.3
5 W	0 52 30	11 12 31	26 28 58	3♐ 5 15	18 2.4	6 17.4	10 42.5	9 44.3	1 57.0	29 40.0	6 23.6	15 25.3	10 3.4
6 Th	0 56 26	12 11 42	9♐35 39	16 0 26	18 3.0	7 22.1	11 55.7	10 21.8	2 9.9	29 47.4	6 21.8	15 26.7	10 3.6
7 F	1 0 23	13 10 55	22 19 59	28 34 42	18 3.5	8 24.5	13 8.9	10 59.3	2 22.8	29 54.7	6 20.0	15 28.1	10 3.7
8 Sa	1 4 20	14 10 10	4♑45 7	10♑51 43	18R 3.8	9 24.4	14 22.1	11 36.8	2 35.7	0♎ 2.0	6 18.3	15 29.4	10 3.8
9 Su	1 8 16	15 9 26	16 55 5	22 55 46	18 3.9	10 21.6	15 35.4	12 14.3	2 48.5	0 9.3	6 16.6	15 30.8	10 3.8
10 M	1 12 13	16 8 45	28 54 21	4♒51 24	18 3.8	11 15.9	16 48.8	12 51.7	3 1.3	0 16.6	6 14.9	15 32.0	10 3.8
11 Tu	1 16 9	17 8 5	10♒47 30	16 43 12	18D 3.7	12 6.9	18 2.2	13 29.1	3 14.2	0 23.9	6 13.3	15 33.3	10R 3.9
12 W	1 20 6	18 7 27	22 39 0	28 35 24	18 3.6	12 54.4	19 15.7	14 6.5	3 26.9	0 31.1	6 11.6	15 34.6	10 3.9
13 Th	1 24 2	19 6 51	4♓32 53	10♓31 52	18 3.7	13 37.9	20 29.3	14 43.9	3 39.7	0 38.3	6 10.1	15 35.8	10 3.8
14 F	1 27 59	20 6 16	16 32 45	22 35 53	18 3.9	14 17.3	21 42.9	15 21.2	3 52.4	0 45.5	6 8.6	15 36.9	10 3.8
15 Sa	1 31 55	21 5 44	28 41 33	4♈50 2	18 4.1	14 51.9	22 56.6	15 58.5	4 5.1	0 52.7	6 7.1	15 38.1	10 3.7
16 Su	1 35 52	22 5 13	11♈ 1 32	17 16 14	18R 4.3	15 21.4	24 10.3	16 35.8	4 17.8	0 59.8	6 5.6	15 39.2	10 3.6
17 M	1 39 48	23 4 44	23 34 16	29 55 43	18 4.3	15 45.3	25 24.1	17 13.1	4 30.5	1 7.0	6 4.2	15 40.3	10 3.4
18 Tu	1 43 45	24 4 18	6♉20 38	12♉49 2	18 4.0	16 3.0	26 37.9	17 50.4	4 43.1	1 14.0	6 2.8	15 41.4	10 3.3
19 W	1 47 42	25 3 53	19 20 56	25 56 15	18 3.4	16 14.0	27 51.8	18 27.7	4 55.7	1 21.1	6 1.5	15 42.4	10 3.1
20 Th	1 51 38	26 3 31	2♊34 57	9♊16 57	18 2.5	16R 17.8	29 5.8	19 4.9	5 8.2	1 28.1	6 0.2	15 43.4	10 2.9
21 F	1 55 35	27 3 11	16 2 10	22 50 29	18 1.4	16 13.9	0♎19.8	19 42.1	5 20.8	1 35.1	5 59.0	15 44.4	10 2.7
22 Sa	1 59 31	28 2 53	29 41 47	6♋35 57	18 0.3	16 1.6	1 33.9	20 19.4	5 33.2	1 42.1	5 57.8	15 45.4	10 2.5
23 Su	2 3 28	29 2 37	13♋32 51	20 32 19	17 59.5	15 40.7	2 48.0	20 56.5	5 45.7	1 49.0	5 56.6	15 46.3	10 2.2
24 M	2 7 24	0♏ 2 24	27 34 11	4♌38 15	17D 59.1	15 10.9	4 2.1	21 33.7	5 58.1	1 55.9	5 55.5	15 47.1	10 1.9
25 Tu	2 11 21	1 2 13	11♌44 17	18 52 2	17 59.3	14 32.0	5 16.4	22 10.9	6 10.5	2 2.8	5 54.4	15 48.0	10 1.6
26 W	2 15 17	2 2 4	26 1 11	3♍11 24	18 0.0	13 44.2	6 30.6	22 48.0	6 22.8	2 9.6	5 53.4	15 48.8	10 1.3
27 Th	2 19 14	3 1 57	10♍22 17	17 33 22	18 1.1	12 48.1	7 44.9	23 25.1	6 35.1	2 16.4	5 52.4	15 49.6	10 0.9
28 F	2 23 11	4 1 52	24 44 12	1♎54 15	18 2.3	11 44.4	8 59.3	24 2.2	6 47.4	2 23.1	5 51.5	15 50.4	10 0.5
29 Sa	2 27 7	5 1 50	9♎ 2 58	16 9 48	18R 3.1	10 34.4	10 13.7	24 39.3	6 59.6	2 29.9	5 50.6	15 51.1	10 0.1
30 Su	2 31 4	6 1 50	23 14 10	0♏15 33	18 3.2	9 19.7	11 28.1	25 16.4	7 11.8	2 36.5	5 49.7	15 51.8	9 59.7
31 M	2 35 0	7 1 51	7♏13 25	14 7 19	18 2.3	8 2.5	12 42.6	25 53.4	7 23.9	2 43.1	5 48.9	15 52.4	9 59.2

Astro Data Dy Hr Mn	Planet Ingress Dy Hr Mn	Last Aspect Dy Hr Mn	☽ Ingress Dy Hr Mn	Last Aspect Dy Hr Mn	☽ Ingress Dy Hr Mn	☽ Phases & Eclipses Dy Hr Mn	Astro Data
☽0S 3 5:25	☿ ♎ 9 2:37	31 18:23 ♂ ☌	♍ 1 13:06	2 0:58 ♆ ⚹	♏ 3 1:37	2 3:33 ● 9♍07	1 SEPTEMBER 1921
☿0S 9 17:50	♂ ♍ 19 11:40	3 6:11 ♄ ☌	♎ 3 13:05	5 5:49 ♄ ⚹	♐ 5 6:22	9 3:29 ☽ 15♐54	Julian Day # 7914
♃☌♄ 10 4:14	☉ ♎ 23 14:20	4 23:41 ♂ ⚹	♏ 5 15:24	7 14:44 ♄ □	♑ 7 14:45	17 7:20 ○ 23♓51	Delta T 22.4 sec
☽0N 17 10:13	♃ ♎ 25 23:10	7 17:01 ☿ ⚹	♐ 7 21:20	8 21:04 ♀ △	♒ 10 2:12	24 21:17 ☽ 1♋16	SVP 06♓21'06"
♃∠♆ 26 23:23	♀ ♍ 26 4:08	10 0:14 ♄ □	♑ 10 6:58	11 14:01 ☉ △	♓ 12 14:51		Obliquity 23°26'50"
☽0S 30 15:59	☿ ♏ 29 16:01	12 13:09 ♃ △	♒ 12 19:01	14 11:24 ♀ ☍	♈ 15 2:34	1 12:26 ● 7♎47	⚷ Chiron 13♈08.1R
♃0S 7 16:30		15 2:04 ♂ ☍	♓ 15 7:39	16 22:59 ☉ ☍	♉ 17 12:08	1 12:35:34 • T 1'52"	☽ Mean ☊ 20♎08.1
♇ R 11 1:05	♄ ♎ 7 17:22	17 15:56 ♃ ☍	♈ 17 19:29	19 17:04 ♀ △	♊ 19 19:21	8 20:11 ☽ 15♑00	
♄∠♆ 12 13:45	♀ ♎ 20 17:35	19 14:33 ♀ △	♉ 20 5:41	21 20:54 ☉ △	♋ 22 0:32	16 22:59 ○ 23♈02	1 OCTOBER 1921
☽0N 14 17:14	☉ ♏ 23 23:02	22 12:19 ♃ △	♊ 22 13:41	23 13:17 ♂ ⚹	♌ 24 4:08	16 22:54 • P 0.931	Julian Day # 7944
☿ R 20 0:00		24 18:39 ♃ □	♋ 24 19:06	25 6:51 ♆ ☌	♍ 26 6:40	24 4:31 ☽ 0♌14	Delta T 22.4 sec
♀0S 23 15:52		26 19:44 ♄ ⚹	♌ 26 21:57	27 22:47 ♂ ☌	♎ 28 8:49	30 23:38 ● 7♏01	SVP 06♓21'04"
♃⚻♅ 23 19:20		28 21:26 ☿ ⚹	♍ 28 23:01	29 11:29 ♆ ⚹	♏ 30 11:33		Obliquity 23°26'50"
☽0S 28 0:54		30 22:19 ♄ ☌	♎ 30 23:41				⚷ Chiron 11♈53.6R
							☽ Mean ☊ 18♎32.7

NOVEMBER 1921 LONGITUDE

Day	Sid.Time	☉	0 hr ☽	Noon ☽	True ☊	☿	♀	♂	♃	♄	♅	♆	♇
1 Tu	2 38 57	8♏ 1 55	20♏56 53	27♏41 46	18♎ 0.4	6♏45.1	13♎57.1	26♍30.4	7♎35.9	2♎49.7	5♓48.2	15♌53.0	9♋58.8
2 W	2 42 53	9 2 0	4♐21 46	10♐56 45	17R57.6	5R29.7	15 11.7	27 7.4	7 47.9	2 56.2	5R47.5	15 53.6	9R58.3
3 Th	2 46 50	10 2 7	17 26 41	23 51 38	17 54.2	4 18.9	16 26.3	27 44.3	7 59.9	3 2.7	5 46.9	15 54.2	9 57.8
4 F	2 50 46	11 2 16	0♑11 45	6♑27 18	17 50.6	3 14.8	17 40.9	28 21.3	8 11.8	3 9.2	5 46.2	15 54.7	9 57.2
5 Sa	2 54 43	12 2 26	12 38 36	18 46 3	17 47.4	2 19.3	18 55.6	28 58.2	8 23.7	3 15.6	5 45.7	15 55.2	9 56.7
6 Su	2 58 40	13 2 38	24 50 6	0♒51 17	17 44.9	1 33.9	20 10.2	29 35.1	8 35.5	3 21.9	5 45.2	15 55.7	9 56.1
7 M	3 2 36	14 2 52	6♒50 7	12 47 14	17D43.5	0 59.5	21 25.0	0♎12.0	8 47.2	3 28.2	5 44.7	15 56.1	9 55.5
8 Tu	3 6 33	15 3 7	18 43 11	24 38 38	17 43.3	0 36.8	22 39.7	0 48.8	8 58.9	3 34.4	5 44.3	15 56.5	9 54.9
9 W	3 10 29	16 3 23	0♓34 11	6♓30 28	17 44.2	0D25.7	23 54.5	1 25.6	9 10.5	3 40.6	5 44.0	15 56.8	9 54.2
10 Th	3 14 26	17 3 41	12 28 4	18 27 36	17 45.8	0 26.0	25 9.3	2 2.4	9 22.0	3 46.7	5 43.7	15 57.1	9 53.6
11 F	3 18 22	18 4 0	24 29 37	0♈34 37	17 47.7	0 37.2	26 24.1	2 39.2	9 33.5	3 52.8	5 43.4	15 57.4	9 52.9
12 Sa	3 22 19	19 4 21	6♈43 5	12 55 25	17R49.1	0 58.6	27 39.0	3 15.9	9 44.9	3 58.8	5 43.2	15 57.7	9 52.2
13 Su	3 26 15	20 4 43	19 12 0	25 33 4	17 49.6	1 29.3	28 53.9	3 52.6	9 56.2	4 4.7	5 43.1	15 57.9	9 51.5
14 M	3 30 12	21 5 7	1♉58 49	8♉29 21	17 48.7	2 8.6	0♏ 8.8	4 29.3	10 7.5	4 10.6	5 42.9	15 58.1	9 50.7
15 Tu	3 34 9	22 5 32	15 4 40	21 44 40	17 46.1	2 55.4	1 23.7	5 6.0	10 18.7	4 16.4	5D42.9	15 58.2	9 50.0
16 W	3 38 5	23 5 59	28 29 12	5♊17 57	17 41.8	3 49.0	2 38.7	5 42.6	10 29.8	4 22.2	5 42.9	15 58.3	9 49.2
17 Th	3 42 2	24 6 28	12♊10 34	19 6 39	17 36.2	4 48.4	3 53.7	6 19.2	10 40.9	4 27.9	5 42.9	15 58.4	9 48.4
18 F	3 45 58	25 6 58	26 5 42	3♋ 7 13	17 30.0	5 53.0	5 8.7	6 55.8	10 51.9	4 33.5	5 43.0	15R58.5	9 47.6
19 Sa	3 49 55	26 7 30	10♋10 41	17 15 33	17 24.0	7 2.0	6 23.8	7 32.4	11 2.8	4 39.1	5 43.2	15 58.5	9 46.8
20 Su	3 53 51	27 8 4	24 21 22	1♌27 39	17 18.9	8 14.9	7 38.8	8 9.0	11 13.6	4 44.6	5 43.4	15 58.4	9 45.9
21 M	3 57 48	28 8 39	8♌33 59	15 40 3	17 15.4	9 31.0	8 53.9	8 45.5	11 24.4	4 50.1	5 43.7	15 58.4	9 45.1
22 Tu	4 1 44	29 9 16	22 45 31	29 50 10	17D13.7	10 49.9	10 9.1	9 22.0	11 35.0	4 55.4	5 44.0	15 58.3	9 44.2
23 W	4 5 41	0♐ 9 55	6♍53 47	13♍56 13	17 13.7	12 11.1	11 24.2	9 58.5	11 45.6	5 0.8	5 44.3	15 58.2	9 43.3
24 Th	4 9 38	1 10 36	20 57 21	27 57 2	17 14.8	13 34.4	12 39.4	10 34.9	11 56.1	5 6.0	5 44.7	15 58.0	9 42.4
25 F	4 13 34	2 11 18	4♎55 11	11♎51 40	17R16.1	14 59.4	13 54.5	11 11.3	12 6.5	5 11.1	5 45.2	15 57.8	9 41.5
26 Sa	4 17 31	3 12 1	18 46 20	25 39 1	17 16.6	16 25.7	15 9.7	11 47.7	12 16.8	5 16.2	5 45.7	15 57.6	9 40.5
27 Su	4 21 27	4 12 47	2♏29 32	9♏17 40	17 15.4	17 53.3	16 25.0	12 24.1	12 27.1	5 21.3	5 46.2	15 57.3	9 39.5
28 M	4 25 24	5 13 33	16 3 11	22 45 50	17 12.1	19 21.8	17 40.2	13 0.4	12 37.2	5 26.2	5 46.9	15 57.0	9 38.6
29 Tu	4 29 20	6 14 22	29 25 24	6♐ 1 38	17 6.3	20 51.2	18 55.5	13 36.7	12 47.2	5 31.1	5 47.5	15 56.7	9 37.6
30 W	4 33 17	7 15 11	12♐34 19	19 3 18	16 58.3	22 21.3	20 10.7	14 13.0	12 57.2	5 35.8	5 48.2	15 56.3	9 36.6

DECEMBER 1921 LONGITUDE

Day	Sid.Time	☉	0 hr ☽	Noon ☽	True ☊	☿	♀	♂	♃	♄	♅	♆	♇
1 Th	4 37 13	8♐16 2	25♐28 27	1♑49 42	16♎48.8	23♏51.9	21♏26.0	14♎49.2	13♎ 7.0	5♎40.5	5♓49.0	15♌55.9	9♋35.6
2 F	4 41 10	9 16 54	8♑ 7 6	14 20 41	16R38.6	25 23.0	22 41.3	15 25.4	13 16.8	5 45.2	5 49.8	15R55.5	9R34.5
3 Sa	4 45 7	10 17 46	20 30 37	26 37 8	16 28.9	26 54.4	23 56.6	16 1.5	13 26.4	5 49.7	5 50.7	15 55.0	9 33.5
4 Su	4 49 3	11 18 40	2♒40 33	8♒41 14	16 20.6	28 26.2	25 11.9	16 37.7	13 36.0	5 54.2	5 51.6	15 54.6	9 32.4
5 M	4 53 0	12 19 34	14 39 37	20 36 12	16 14.2	29 58.2	26 27.2	17 13.7	13 45.4	5 58.6	5 52.6	15 54.0	9 31.4
6 Tu	4 56 56	13 20 30	26 31 32	2♓26 12	16 10.2	1♐30.5	27 42.6	17 49.8	13 54.7	6 2.9	5 53.6	15 53.5	9 30.3
7 W	5 0 53	14 21 25	8♓20 51	14 16 6	16D 8.4	3 2.9	28 57.9	18 25.8	14 3.9	6 7.1	5 54.7	15 52.9	9 29.2
8 Th	5 4 49	15 22 22	20 12 40	26 11 13	16 8.3	4 35.5	0♐13.3	19 1.8	14 13.1	6 11.2	5 55.8	15 52.2	9 28.1
9 F	5 8 46	16 23 19	2♈12 25	8♈16 56	16 9.1	6 8.2	1 28.6	19 37.7	14 22.0	6 15.2	5 56.9	15 51.6	9 27.0
10 Sa	5 12 42	17 24 17	14 25 25	20 38 27	16R 9.7	7 41.0	2 44.0	20 13.6	14 30.9	6 19.2	5 58.2	15 50.9	9 25.8
11 Su	5 16 39	18 25 16	26 56 34	3♉20 14	16 9.1	9 13.9	3 59.3	20 49.5	14 39.7	6 23.0	5 59.4	15 50.2	9 24.7
12 M	5 20 36	19 26 15	9♉49 48	16 25 31	16 6.5	10 47.0	5 14.7	21 25.3	14 48.3	6 26.8	6 0.7	15 49.4	9 23.6
13 Tu	5 24 32	20 27 15	23 7 31	29 55 46	16 1.3	12 20.1	6 30.1	22 1.1	14 56.9	6 30.5	6 2.1	15 48.7	9 22.4
14 W	5 28 29	21 28 16	6♊50 4	13♊50 4	15 53.5	13 53.3	7 45.5	22 36.8	15 5.3	6 34.1	6 3.5	15 47.8	9 21.3
15 Th	5 32 25	22 29 17	20 55 16	28 5 1	15 43.6	15 26.7	9 0.9	23 12.6	15 13.6	6 37.6	6 5.0	15 47.0	9 20.1
16 F	5 36 22	23 30 19	5♋18 32	12♋34 55	15 32.5	17 0.2	10 16.3	23 48.2	15 21.7	6 41.0	6 6.5	15 46.1	9 18.9
17 Sa	5 40 18	24 31 21	19 53 15	27 12 35	15 21.6	18 33.7	11 31.7	24 23.9	15 29.8	6 44.3	6 8.0	15 45.2	9 17.7
18 Su	5 44 15	25 32 25	4♌31 58	11♌50 33	15 11.9	20 7.5	12 47.1	24 59.5	15 37.7	6 47.5	6 9.6	15 44.3	9 16.5
19 M	5 48 11	26 33 29	19 7 34	26 22 20	15 4.6	21 41.3	14 2.5	25 35.0	15 45.4	6 50.6	6 11.3	15 43.4	9 15.3
20 Tu	5 52 8	27 34 34	3♍34 21	10♍43 14	14 59.9	23 15.4	15 18.0	26 10.5	15 53.1	6 53.6	6 13.0	15 42.4	9 14.1
21 W	5 56 5	28 35 39	17 48 43	24 50 40	14D57.8	24 49.6	16 33.4	26 46.0	16 0.6	6 56.6	6 14.7	15 41.4	9 12.9
22 Th	6 0 1	29 36 46	1♎49 1	8♎43 50	14R57.4	26 23.9	17 48.8	27 21.4	16 8.0	6 59.4	6 16.5	15 40.3	9 11.7
23 F	6 3 58	0♑37 53	15 35 11	22 23 13	14 57.6	27 58.5	19 4.3	27 56.8	16 15.2	7 2.1	6 18.3	15 39.3	9 10.5
24 Sa	6 7 54	1 39 1	29 8 5	5♏49 55	14 56.9	29 33.3	20 19.8	28 32.2	16 22.3	7 4.7	6 20.1	15 38.2	9 9.3
25 Su	6 11 51	2 40 10	12♏28 50	19 4 58	14 54.2	1♑ 8.4	21 35.2	29 7.4	16 29.3	7 7.3	6 22.1	15 37.1	9 8.1
26 M	6 15 47	3 41 19	25 38 24	2♐ 9 9	14 48.7	2 43.6	22 50.7	29 42.7	16 36.1	7 9.7	6 24.0	15 35.9	9 6.8
27 Tu	6 19 44	4 42 28	8♐37 14	15 2 39	14 40.0	4 19.2	24 6.1	0♏17.9	16 42.8	7 12.0	6 26.0	15 34.8	9 5.6
28 W	6 23 40	5 43 39	21 25 23	27 45 22	14 28.4	5 55.0	25 21.6	0 53.0	16 49.3	7 14.2	6 28.0	15 33.6	9 4.4
29 Th	6 27 37	6 44 49	4♑ 2 33	10♑16 56	14 14.7	7 31.1	26 37.1	1 28.1	16 55.7	7 16.4	6 30.1	15 32.4	9 3.1
30 F	6 31 34	7 46 0	16 28 30	22 37 17	14 0.1	9 7.5	27 52.6	2 3.1	17 1.9	7 18.4	6 32.3	15 31.1	9 1.9
31 Sa	6 35 30	8 47 10	28 43 20	4♒46 48	13 45.7	10 44.2	29 8.0	2 38.1	17 8.0	7 20.3	6 34.4	15 29.9	9 0.7

Astro Data	Planet Ingress	Last Aspect	☽ Ingress	Last Aspect	☽ Ingress	☽ Phases & Eclipses	Astro Data
Dy Hr Mn	Dy Hr Mn	Dy Hr Mn	Dy Hr Mn	Dy Hr Mn	Dy Hr Mn	Dy Hr Mn	1 NOVEMBER 1921
☿ D 9 11:18	♂ ♎ 6 16:13	1 10:21 ♂ ✱	♐ 1 16:08	30 6:13 ♆ △	♑ 1 8:32	7 15:53 ☽ 14♒43	Julian Day # 7975
☽0N 11 1:46	♀ ♏ 13 21:11	3 20:19 ♂ □	♑ 3 23:38	3 14:23 ☿ ✱	♒ 3 18:41	15 13:39 ○ 22♉40	Delta T 22.4 sec
♂0S 11 15:54	☉ ♐ 22 20:05	6 9:58 ♂ △	♒ 6 10:17	6 2:41 ♀ □	♓ 6 7:03	22 11:41 ☽ 29♌39	SVP 06♓21'01"
♃□♇ 12 14:32		8 8:55 ♀ △	♓ 8 22:51	7 13:19 ☉ □	♈ 8 19:37	29 13:25 ● 6♐48	Obliquity 23°26'49"
♅ D 15 12:50	☿ ♐ 5 0:28	10 10:03 ☉ △	♈ 11 10:52	10 11:46 ♂ ☍	♉ 11 5:46		⚷ Chiron 10♈32.6R
♆ R 18 20:57	♀ ♐ 7 19:47	13 20:14 ♀ ☍	♉ 13 20:19	12 10:54 ♆ □	♊ 13 12:07	7 13:19 ☽ 14♓55	☽ Mean ☊ 16♎54.2
♄0S 23 1:06	☉ ♑ 22 9:07	15 13:39 ☉ ☍	♊ 16 2:41	15 4:01 ♂ △	♋ 15 15:12	15 2:50 ○ 22♊36	
☽0S 24 7:56	☿ ♑ 24 6:45	17 6:35 ♆ ✱	♋ 18 6:41	17 7:42 ♂ □	♌ 17 16:34	21 19:54 ☽ 29♍26	1 DECEMBER 1921
	♂ ♏ 26 11:48	20 5:03 ☉ △	♌ 20 9:32	19 13:15 ☉ △	♍ 19 18:02	29 5:39 ● 6♑59	Julian Day # 8005
♄⊼♅ 3 6:29	♀ ♑ 31 16:31	22 11:41 ☉ □	♍ 22 12:17	21 19:54 ☉ □	♎ 21 20:52		Delta T 22.4 sec
☽0N 8 11:27		23 9:59 ☿ ✱	♎ 24 15:31	24 0:51 ☿ ✱	♏ 24 1:33		SVP 06♓20'57"
♃✱♆ 18 18:17		25 19:07 ☿ ✱	♏ 26 19:37	25 5:41 ♆ □	♐ 26 8:01		Obliquity 23°26'49"
☽0S 21 14:25		28 6:39 ☿ ☌	♐ 29 1:03	28 8:16 ♀ ☌	♑ 28 16:16		⚷ Chiron 9♈39.2R
				30 1:06 ♃ □	♒ 31 2:31		☽ Mean ☊ 15♎18.9

LONGITUDE — JANUARY 1922

Day	Sid.Time	☉	0 hr ☽	Noon ☽	True ☊	☿	♀	♂	♃	♄	♅	♆	♇
1 Su	6 39 27	9♑48 21	10♒47 50	16♒46 42	13♎32.9	12♑21.2	0♑23.5	3♏13.0	17♎13.9	7♎22.1	6♓36.6	15♌28.6	8♋59.4
2 M	6 43 23	10 49 31	22 43 40	28 39 7	13R 22.6	13 58.6	1 39.0	3 47.9	17 19.7	7 23.8	6 38.9	15R 27.3	8R 58.2
3 Tu	6 47 20	11 50 42	4♓33 29	10♓27 12	13 15.1	15 36.3	2 54.5	4 22.7	17 25.3	7 25.4	6 41.1	15 25.9	8 56.9
4 W	6 51 16	12 51 52	16 20 51	22 15 0	13 10.7	17 14.3	4 9.9	4 57.4	17 30.7	7 26.9	6 43.5	15 24.6	8 55.7
5 Th	6 55 13	13 53 1	28 10 16	4♈ 7 19	13 8.6	18 52.6	5 25.4	5 32.1	17 36.0	7 28.2	6 45.8	15 23.2	8 54.5
6 F	6 59 9	14 54 11	10♈ 6 51	16 9 32	13 8.1	20 31.3	6 40.8	6 6.7	17 41.2	7 29.5	6 48.2	15 21.8	8 53.2
7 Sa	7 3 6	15 55 20	22 16 6	28 27 14	13 8.1	22 10.3	7 56.3	6 41.3	17 46.1	7 30.7	6 50.6	15 20.4	8 52.0
8 Su	7 7 3	16 56 29	4♉43 36	11♉ 5 50	13 7.2	23 49.6	9 11.7	7 15.8	17 50.9	7 31.7	6 53.1	15 19.0	8 50.8
9 M	7 10 59	17 57 37	17 34 26	24 9 53	13 4.5	25 29.2	10 27.2	7 50.2	17 55.5	7 32.7	6 55.6	15 17.6	8 49.6
10 Tu	7 14 56	18 58 44	0♊52 31	7♊42 28	12 59.2	27 9.1	11 42.6	8 24.6	18 0.0	7 33.5	6 58.2	15 16.1	8 48.3
11 W	7 18 52	19 59 52	14 39 46	21 44 12	12 51.2	28 49.2	12 58.1	8 58.9	18 4.3	7 34.2	7 0.7	15 14.6	8 47.1
12 Th	7 22 49	21 0 59	28 55 21	6♋12 37	12 40.9	0♒29.4	14 13.5	9 33.1	18 8.4	7 34.9	7 3.3	15 13.1	8 45.9
13 F	7 26 45	22 2 5	13♋35 9	21 1 57	12 29.1	2 9.7	15 28.9	10 7.3	18 12.4	7 35.4	7 6.0	15 11.6	8 44.7
14 Sa	7 30 42	23 3 11	28 31 50	6♌ 3 36	12 17.3	3 50.1	16 44.4	10 41.4	18 16.2	7 35.8	7 8.7	15 10.1	8 43.5
15 Su	7 34 39	24 4 16	13♌35 57	21 7 37	12 6.7	5 30.3	17 59.8	11 15.5	18 19.8	7 36.1	7 11.4	15 8.6	8 42.3
16 M	7 38 35	25 5 21	28 37 27	6♍ 4 23	11 58.5	7 10.4	19 15.2	11 49.4	18 23.2	7 36.3	7 14.1	15 7.0	8 41.2
17 Tu	7 42 32	26 6 26	13♍27 33	20 46 15	11 53.1	8 50.2	20 30.6	12 23.3	18 26.5	7R 36.4	7 16.9	15 5.5	8 40.0
18 W	7 46 28	27 7 30	27 59 59	5♎ 8 25	11 50.5	10 29.4	21 46.0	12 57.2	18 29.6	7 36.3	7 19.7	15 3.9	8 38.8
19 Th	7 50 25	28 8 34	12♎11 23	19 8 53	11D 49.9	12 8.0	23 1.4	13 30.9	18 32.5	7 36.2	7 22.5	15 2.3	8 37.7
20 F	7 54 21	29 9 38	26 1 2	2♏48 0	11R 50.2	13 45.6	24 16.9	14 4.6	18 35.2	7 36.0	7 25.4	15 0.7	8 36.5
21 Sa	7 58 18	0♒10 41	9♏30 5	16 7 34	11 49.9	15 22.0	25 32.3	14 38.2	18 37.7	7 35.6	7 28.2	14 59.1	8 35.4
22 Su	8 2 14	1 11 44	22 40 47	29 10 3	11 47.9	16 56.9	26 47.7	15 11.8	18 40.1	7 35.1	7 31.1	14 57.4	8 34.2
23 M	8 6 11	2 12 47	5♐35 41	11♐58 0	11 43.3	18 29.9	28 3.1	15 45.2	18 42.3	7 34.6	7 34.1	14 55.8	8 33.1
24 Tu	8 10 8	3 13 49	18 17 14	24 33 39	11 35.9	20 0.5	29 18.5	16 18.6	18 44.3	7 33.9	7 37.1	14 54.2	8 32.0
25 W	8 14 4	4 14 51	0♑47 27	6♑58 48	11 25.9	21 28.2	0♒33.9	16 51.8	18 46.1	7 33.1	7 40.1	14 52.5	8 30.9
26 Th	8 18 1	5 15 51	13 7 50	19 14 42	11 13.8	22 52.6	1 49.3	17 25.0	18 47.7	7 32.2	7 43.1	14 50.9	8 29.8
27 F	8 21 57	6 16 52	25 19 31	1♒22 22	11 0.9	24 12.9	3 4.6	17 58.1	18 49.1	7 31.2	7 46.1	14 49.2	8 28.7
28 Sa	8 25 54	7 17 51	7♒23 24	13 22 44	10 48.1	25 28.6	4 20.0	18 31.1	18 50.3	7 30.1	7 49.2	14 47.5	8 27.6
29 Su	8 29 50	8 18 49	19 20 31	25 16 56	10 36.7	26 38.8	5 35.4	19 4.0	18 51.4	7 28.9	7 52.3	14 45.9	8 26.6
30 M	8 33 47	9 19 46	1♓12 11	7♓ 6 33	10 27.4	27 42.9	6 50.7	19 36.8	18 52.2	7 27.6	7 55.4	14 44.2	8 25.5
31 Tu	8 37 43	10 20 42	13 0 18	18 53 49	10 20.8	28 39.9	8 6.1	20 9.5	18 52.9	7 26.2	7 58.5	14 42.5	8 24.5

LONGITUDE — FEBRUARY 1922

Day	Sid.Time	☉	0 hr ☽	Noon ☽	True ☊	☿	♀	♂	♃	♄	♅	♆	♇
1 W	8 41 40	11♒21 37	24♓47 28	0♈41 42	10♎16.9	29♒29.1	9♒21.4	20♏42.1	18♎53.4	7♎24.7	8♓ 1.7	14♌40.8	8♋23.5
2 Th	8 45 37	12 22 31	6♈37 2	12 33 59	10D 15.5	0♓ 9.8	10 36.8	21 14.6	18R 53.6	7R 23.0	8 4.8	14R 39.1	8R 22.5
3 F	8 49 33	13 23 23	18 33 8	24 35 6	10 15.7	0 41.0	11 52.1	21 47.0	18 53.7	7 21.3	8 8.0	14 37.5	8 21.5
4 Sa	8 53 30	14 24 14	0♉40 30	6♉49 59	10 16.7	1 2.2	13 7.4	22 19.3	18 53.6	7 19.5	8 11.2	14 35.8	8 20.5
5 Su	8 57 26	15 25 4	13 4 13	19 23 50	10R 17.4	1R 12.9	14 22.7	22 51.5	18 53.4	7 17.6	8 14.5	14 34.1	8 19.5
6 M	9 1 23	16 25 52	25 49 25	2♊21 32	10 16.9	1 12.7	15 38.0	23 23.6	18 52.9	7 15.5	8 17.7	14 32.4	8 18.6
7 Tu	9 5 19	17 26 39	9♊ 0 37	15 47 1	10 14.6	1 1.5	16 53.2	23 55.6	18 52.2	7 13.4	8 21.0	14 30.7	8 17.7
8 W	9 9 16	18 27 24	22 40 58	29 42 28	10 10.1	0 39.5	18 8.5	24 27.4	18 51.3	7 11.2	8 24.3	14 29.0	8 16.8
9 Th	9 13 12	19 28 8	6♋51 23	14♋ 7 20	10 3.7	0 7.0	19 23.7	24 59.1	18 50.3	7 8.9	8 27.6	14 27.3	8 15.9
10 F	9 17 9	20 28 50	21 29 43	28 57 42	9 56.1	29♒25.0	20 39.0	25 30.8	18 49.1	7 6.5	8 30.9	14 25.7	8 15.0
11 Sa	9 21 6	21 29 31	6♌30 17	14♌ 6 16	9 48.2	28 34.3	21 54.2	26 2.3	18 47.6	7 4.0	8 34.2	14 24.0	8 14.1
12 Su	9 25 2	22 30 10	21 44 19	29 23 5	9 41.1	27 36.5	23 9.4	26 33.7	18 46.0	7 1.4	8 37.5	14 22.3	8 13.3
13 M	9 28 59	23 30 48	7♍ 1 10	14♍37 15	9 35.6	26 33.2	24 24.6	27 4.9	18 44.2	6 58.8	8 40.9	14 20.7	8 12.4
14 Tu	9 32 55	24 31 24	22 10 8	29 38 45	9 32.2	25 26.1	25 39.8	27 36.1	18 42.3	6 56.0	8 44.2	14 19.0	8 11.6
15 W	9 36 52	25 31 59	7♎ 2 17	14♎20 3	9D 31.0	24 17.0	26 54.9	28 7.1	18 40.1	6 53.1	8 47.6	14 17.3	8 10.8
16 Th	9 40 48	26 32 33	21 31 35	28 36 39	9 31.4	23 8.0	28 10.1	28 38.0	18 37.7	6 50.2	8 51.0	14 15.7	8 10.1
17 F	9 44 45	27 33 5	5♏35 9	12♏27 7	9 32.7	22 0.6	29 25.2	29 8.7	18 35.2	6 47.2	8 54.4	14 14.1	8 9.3
18 Sa	9 48 41	28 33 37	19 12 46	25 52 22	9R 34.0	20 56.4	0♓40.4	29 39.3	18 32.5	6 44.1	8 57.7	14 12.4	8 8.6
19 Su	9 52 38	29 34 7	2♐26 15	8♐54 51	9 34.3	19 56.8	1 55.5	0♐ 9.8	18 29.6	6 40.9	9 1.2	14 10.8	8 7.9
20 M	9 56 34	0♓34 36	15 18 33	21 37 50	9 33.2	19 2.9	3 10.6	0 40.2	18 26.5	6 37.6	9 4.6	14 9.2	8 7.2
21 Tu	10 0 31	1 35 3	27 53 7	4♑ 4 50	9 30.2	18 15.4	4 25.7	1 10.3	18 23.2	6 34.3	9 8.0	14 7.6	8 6.5
22 W	10 4 28	2 35 30	10♑13 24	16 19 12	9 25.5	17 34.9	5 40.8	1 40.4	18 19.8	6 30.9	9 11.4	14 6.0	8 5.8
23 Th	10 8 24	3 35 55	22 22 36	28 23 55	9 19.6	17 1.7	6 55.9	2 10.2	18 16.2	6 27.4	9 14.8	14 4.4	8 5.2
24 F	10 12 21	4 36 18	4♒23 27	10♒21 30	9 12.9	16 35.8	8 10.9	2 39.9	18 12.4	6 23.8	9 18.3	14 2.9	8 4.6
25 Sa	10 16 17	5 36 40	16 18 19	22 14 9	9 6.4	16 17.4	9 26.0	3 9.5	18 8.4	6 20.2	9 21.7	14 1.3	8 4.0
26 Su	10 20 14	6 37 0	28 9 14	4♓ 3 46	9 0.5	16 6.1	10 41.0	3 38.9	18 4.3	6 16.4	9 25.2	13 59.8	8 3.4
27 M	10 24 10	7 37 18	9♓58 0	15 52 10	8 55.9	16D 1.9	11 56.0	4 8.1	17 60.0	6 12.7	9 28.6	13 58.2	8 2.8
28 Tu	10 28 7	8 37 35	21 46 30	27 41 17	8 52.9	16 4.3	13 11.0	4 37.1	17 55.5	6 8.8	9 32.1	13 56.7	8 2.3

Astro Data (Dy Hr Mn)	Planet Ingress (Dy Hr Mn)	Last Aspect (Dy Hr Mn)	☽ Ingress (Dy Hr Mn)	Last Aspect (Dy Hr Mn)	☽ Ingress (Dy Hr Mn)	☽ Phases & Eclipses (Dy Hr Mn)
☽0N 4 21:01	☿ ♒ 11 16:58	1 13:01 ♃ △	♓ 2 14:44	31 15:17 ♂ △	♈ 1 10:35	6 10:23 ☽ 15♈21
☽0S 17 22:21	☉ ♒ 20 19:48	4 2:06 ☿ ✱	♈ 5 3:42	3 0:41 ♃ ☍	♉ 3 22:41	13 14:36 ○ 22♋39
♄ R 17 5:56	♀ ♒ 24 13:13	6 23:47 ☿ □	♉ 7 14:58	5 19:17 ♂ ☍	♊ 6 7:42	20 6:00 ☽ 29♎25
♄⊼♅ 23 3:16		9 16:25 ☿ △	♊ 9 22:27	7 17:23 ♃ △	♋ 8 12:30	27 23:48 ● 7♒17
	☿ ♓ 1 17:43	11 5:50 ♃ △	♋ 12 1:47	10 6:43 ♂ △	♌ 10 13:39	
☽0N 1 5:14	☿ ♒ 9 4:25	13 14:36 ☉ ☍	♌ 14 2:21	12 8:38 ☿ ☍	♍ 12 12:58	5 4:52 ☽ 15♉37
♃ R 2 23:30	♀ ♓ 17 11:06	15 7:34 ♃ ✱	♍ 16 2:13	14 9:01 ♂ ✱	♎ 14 12:34	12 1:17 ○ 22♌33
☿ R 5 11:35	♂ ♐ 18 16:15	17 22:26 ☉ △	♎ 18 3:21	16 12:21 ♀ △	♏ 16 14:23	18 18:18 ☽ 29♏20
♅△♇ 6 5:04	☉ ♓ 19 10:16	20 6:00 ☉ □	♏ 20 7:02	18 18:18 ☉ □	♐ 18 19:31	26 18:47 ● 7♓24
☽0S 14 8:35		22 8:25 ♀ ✱	♐ 22 13:33	20 6:39 ☿ ✱	♑ 21 4:05	
☿ D 27 3:12		24 3:43 ☿ ✱	♑ 24 22:28	22 15:54 ♃ □	♒ 23 15:12	
☽0N 28 11:55		26 11:08 ♃ □	♒ 27 9:16	25 3:41 ♃ △	♓ 26 3:45	
		29 16:15 ☿ ☌	♓ 29 21:34	27 4:28 ♀ ☌	♈ 28 16:41	

Astro Data

1 JANUARY 1922
Julian Day # 8036
Delta T 22.4 sec
SVP 06♓20'51"
Obliquity 23°26'48"
⚷ Chiron 9♈30.7
☽ Mean ☊ 13♎40.4

1 FEBRUARY 1922
Julian Day # 8067
Delta T 22.5 sec
SVP 06♓20'47"
Obliquity 23°26'49"
⚷ Chiron 10♈13.9
☽ Mean ☊ 12♎01.9

MARCH 1922 LONGITUDE

Day	Sid.Time	☉	0 hr ☽	Noon ☽	True ☊	☿	♀	♂	♃	♄	♅	♆	♇
1 W	10 32 3	9♓37 49	3♈36 47	9♈33 19	8♎51.5	16♒13.0	14♓26.0	5♐ 5.9	17♎50.9	6♎ 4.9	9♓35.5	13♌55.2	8♋ 1.8
2 Th	10 36 0	10 38 2	15 31 15	21 30 56	8D 51.5	16 27.6	15 41.0	5 34.6	17R 46.1	6R 1.0	9 38.9	13R 53.8	8R 1.3
3 F	10 39 57	11 38 13	27 32 46	3♉37 12	8 52.7	16 47.9	16 55.9	6 3.1	17 41.2	5 56.9	9 42.4	13 52.3	8 0.8
4 Sa	10 43 53	12 38 22	9♉44 41	15 55 43	8 54.4	17 13.4	18 10.9	6 31.4	17 36.1	5 52.9	9 45.8	13 50.9	8 0.4
5 Su	10 47 50	13 38 29	22 10 46	28 30 22	8 56.1	17 43.8	19 25.8	6 59.4	17 30.9	5 48.7	9 49.3	13 49.4	7 60.0
6 M	10 51 46	14 38 34	4♊54 59	11♊25 5	8R 57.3	18 18.7	20 40.6	7 27.3	17 25.5	5 44.5	9 52.7	13 48.0	7 59.6
7 Tu	10 55 43	15 38 37	18 1 6	24 43 23	8 57.6	18 57.9	21 55.5	7 55.0	17 20.0	5 40.3	9 56.1	13 46.6	7 59.2
8 W	10 59 39	16 38 37	1♋32 14	8♋27 48	8 56.8	19 41.0	23 10.4	8 22.5	17 14.3	5 36.0	9 59.6	13 45.3	7 58.8
9 Th	11 3 36	17 38 36	15 30 6	22 39 1	8 55.1	20 27.8	24 25.2	8 49.8	17 8.5	5 31.7	10 3.0	13 43.9	7 58.5
10 F	11 7 32	18 38 32	29 54 16	7♌15 20	8 52.7	21 18.0	25 40.0	9 16.8	17 2.6	5 27.4	10 6.4	13 42.6	7 58.2
11 Sa	11 11 29	19 38 26	14♌41 33	22 12 5	8 50.1	22 11.5	26 54.7	9 43.7	16 56.6	5 23.0	10 9.8	13 41.3	7 57.9
12 Su	11 15 26	20 38 18	29 45 54	7♍21 51	8 47.7	23 7.9	28 9.5	10 10.3	16 50.4	5 18.5	10 13.2	13 40.0	7 57.6
13 M	11 19 22	21 38 8	14♍58 44	22 35 16	8 45.9	24 7.2	29 24.2	10 36.7	16 44.1	5 14.1	10 16.6	13 38.7	7 57.4
14 Tu	11 23 19	22 37 55	0♎10 13	7♎42 23	8D 45.0	25 9.1	0♈38.9	11 2.9	16 37.7	5 9.6	10 20.0	13 37.5	7 57.2
15 W	11 27 15	23 37 41	15 10 42	22 34 13	8 44.9	26 13.5	1 53.6	11 28.8	16 31.2	5 5.0	10 23.4	13 36.3	7 57.0
16 Th	11 31 12	24 37 25	29 52 12	7♏ 4 1	8 45.6	27 20.2	3 8.3	11 54.5	16 24.6	5 0.5	10 26.8	13 35.1	7 56.8
17 F	11 35 8	25 37 7	14♏ 9 18	21 7 47	8 46.6	28 29.2	4 22.9	12 19.9	16 17.8	4 55.9	10 30.1	13 33.9	7 56.7
18 Sa	11 39 5	26 36 48	27 59 26	4♐44 19	8 47.6	29 40.3	5 37.5	12 45.1	16 11.0	4 51.3	10 33.5	13 32.8	7 56.5
19 Su	11 43 1	27 36 27	11♐22 37	17 54 39	8 48.5	0♓53.4	6 52.1	13 10.0	16 4.1	4 46.6	10 36.8	13 31.6	7 56.4
20 M	11 46 58	28 36 4	24 20 47	0♑41 30	8R 48.9	2 8.5	8 6.7	13 34.7	15 57.1	4 42.0	10 40.1	13 30.5	7 56.3
21 Tu	11 50 55	29 35 39	6♑57 15	13 8 34	8 48.9	3 25.4	9 21.3	13 59.0	15 50.0	4 37.3	10 43.4	13 29.5	7 56.3
22 W	11 54 51	0♈35 13	19 15 59	25 20 1	8 48.4	4 44.1	10 35.8	14 23.1	15 42.8	4 32.6	10 46.7	13 28.4	7D 56.3
23 Th	11 58 48	1 34 44	1♒21 11	7♒20 0	8 47.6	6 4.6	11 50.3	14 46.9	15 35.6	4 28.0	10 50.0	13 27.4	7 56.3
24 F	12 2 44	2 34 14	13 16 57	19 12 30	8 46.8	7 26.7	13 4.8	15 10.4	15 28.3	4 23.3	10 53.3	13 26.4	7 56.3
25 Sa	12 6 41	3 33 43	25 7 5	1♓ 1 6	8 45.9	8 50.4	14 19.3	15 33.6	15 20.9	4 18.6	10 56.5	13 25.4	7 56.3
26 Su	12 10 37	4 33 9	6♓54 57	12 48 57	8 45.3	10 15.7	15 33.8	15 56.5	15 13.5	4 13.9	10 59.8	13 24.5	7 56.4
27 M	12 14 34	5 32 33	18 43 27	24 38 45	8 44.9	11 42.5	16 48.2	16 19.0	15 6.0	4 9.2	11 3.0	13 23.6	7 56.5
28 Tu	12 18 30	6 31 55	0♈35 7	6♈32 49	8D 44.7	13 10.9	18 2.6	16 41.2	14 58.4	4 4.5	11 6.2	13 22.7	7 56.6
29 W	12 22 27	7 31 16	12 32 6	18 33 13	8 44.7	14 40.8	19 17.0	17 3.1	14 50.9	3 59.8	11 9.3	13 21.8	7 56.7
30 Th	12 26 23	8 30 34	24 36 23	0♉41 51	8R 44.7	16 12.1	20 31.3	17 24.6	14 43.2	3 55.1	11 12.5	13 21.0	7 56.9
31 F	12 30 20	9 29 50	6♉49 50	13 0 35	8 44.7	17 44.9	21 45.7	17 45.8	14 35.6	3 50.4	11 15.6	13 20.2	7 57.1

APRIL 1922 LONGITUDE

Day	Sid.Time	☉	0 hr ☽	Noon ☽	True ☊	☿	♀	♂	♃	♄	♅	♆	♇
1 Sa	12 34 17	10♈29 4	19♉14 20	25♉31 21	8♎44.6	19♓19.2	22♈60.0	18♐ 6.6	14♎27.9	3♎45.8	11♓18.8	13♌19.4	7♋57.3
2 Su	12 38 13	11 28 16	1♊51 53	8♊16 11	8R 44.3	20 54.9	24 14.2	18 27.0	14R 20.2	3R 41.1	11 21.9	13R 18.7	7 57.5
3 M	12 42 10	12 27 25	14 44 32	21 17 10	8 43.9	22 32.0	25 28.5	18 47.1	14 12.5	3 36.5	11 24.9	13 18.0	7 57.7
4 Tu	12 46 6	13 26 33	27 54 19	4♋36 13	8 43.6	24 10.6	26 42.7	19 6.8	14 4.8	3 31.9	11 28.0	13 17.3	7 58.0
5 W	12 50 3	14 25 38	11♋23 2	18 14 52	8D 43.4	25 50.6	27 56.9	19 26.1	13 57.1	3 27.3	11 31.0	13 16.7	7 58.3
6 Th	12 53 59	15 24 41	25 11 48	2♌13 48	8 43.5	27 32.1	29 11.1	19 45.0	13 49.3	3 22.8	11 34.0	13 16.1	7 58.6
7 F	12 57 56	16 23 41	9♌20 44	16 32 21	8 43.9	29 15.1	0♉25.2	20 3.5	13 41.6	3 18.2	11 37.0	13 15.5	7 59.0
8 Sa	13 1 52	17 22 39	23 48 20	1♍ 8 11	8 44.6	0♈59.5	1 39.3	20 21.5	13 33.9	3 13.8	11 40.0	13 14.9	7 59.4
9 Su	13 5 49	18 21 34	8♍31 16	15 56 54	8 45.3	2 45.4	2 53.4	20 39.2	13 26.3	3 9.3	11 42.9	13 14.4	7 59.8
10 M	13 9 46	19 20 28	23 24 13	0♎52 18	8 46.0	4 32.8	4 7.4	20 56.4	13 18.6	3 4.9	11 45.8	13 13.9	8 0.2
11 Tu	13 13 42	20 19 19	8♎20 10	15 46 51	8R 46.3	6 21.6	5 21.4	21 13.1	13 11.0	3 0.5	11 48.7	13 13.5	8 0.6
12 W	13 17 39	21 18 8	23 11 18	0♏32 37	8 46.0	8 12.0	6 35.4	21 29.5	13 3.4	2 56.2	11 51.5	13 13.0	8 1.1
13 Th	13 21 35	22 16 55	7♏49 54	15 2 24	8 45.0	10 4.0	7 49.4	21 45.3	12 55.8	2 51.9	11 54.3	13 12.6	8 1.6
14 F	13 25 32	23 15 40	22 9 28	29 10 37	8 43.4	11 57.4	9 3.3	22 0.7	12 48.3	2 47.6	11 57.1	13 12.3	8 2.1
15 Sa	13 29 28	24 14 24	6♐ 5 30	12♐53 56	8 41.4	13 52.3	10 17.2	22 15.6	12 40.9	2 43.4	11 59.9	13 11.9	8 2.6
16 Su	13 33 25	25 13 6	19 35 54	26 11 27	8 39.3	15 48.8	11 31.1	22 30.0	12 33.5	2 39.2	12 2.6	13 11.6	8 3.1
17 M	13 37 21	26 11 46	2♑40 50	9♑ 4 20	8 37.5	17 46.8	12 44.9	22 43.8	12 26.1	2 35.1	12 5.3	13 11.4	8 3.7
18 Tu	13 41 18	27 10 24	15 22 23	21 35 26	8 36.2	19 46.2	13 58.7	22 57.2	12 18.8	2 31.1	12 8.0	13 11.1	8 4.3
19 W	13 45 15	28 9 1	27 44 2	3♒48 44	8D 35.7	21 47.1	15 12.5	23 10.0	12 11.6	2 27.1	12 10.7	13 10.9	8 4.9
20 Th	13 49 11	29 7 36	9♒50 7	15 48 48	8 36.1	23 49.3	16 26.3	23 22.3	12 4.5	2 23.1	12 13.3	13 10.8	8 5.6
21 F	13 53 8	0♉ 6 9	21 45 23	27 40 28	8 37.3	25 52.9	17 40.0	23 34.0	11 57.4	2 19.2	12 15.9	13 10.6	8 6.2
22 Sa	13 57 4	1 4 41	3♓34 37	9♓28 25	8 38.9	27 57.7	18 53.7	23 45.1	11 50.4	2 15.4	12 18.4	13 10.5	8 6.9
23 Su	14 1 1	2 3 11	15 22 23	21 17 2	8 40.5	0♉ 3.6	20 7.4	23 55.7	11 43.5	2 11.6	12 20.9	13 10.5	8 7.6
24 M	14 4 57	3 1 39	27 12 49	3♈10 11	8R 41.9	2 10.5	21 21.1	24 5.6	11 36.7	2 7.9	12 23.4	13D 10.4	8 8.3
25 Tu	14 8 54	4 0 6	9♈ 9 29	15 11 5	8 42.3	4 18.2	22 34.7	24 14.9	11 30.0	2 4.3	12 25.8	13 10.4	8 9.0
26 W	14 12 50	4 58 30	21 15 16	27 22 17	8 41.7	6 26.6	23 48.3	24 23.6	11 23.4	2 0.7	12 28.3	13 10.4	8 9.8
27 Th	14 16 47	5 56 53	3♉32 20	9♉45 34	8 39.7	8 35.3	25 1.9	24 31.7	11 16.9	1 57.2	12 30.6	13 10.5	8 10.6
28 F	14 20 43	6 55 15	16 2 7	22 22 4	8 36.4	10 44.3	26 15.4	24 39.2	11 10.5	1 53.8	12 33.0	13 10.6	8 11.4
29 Sa	14 24 40	7 53 34	28 45 26	5♊12 16	8 32.0	12 53.1	27 28.9	24 46.0	11 4.2	1 50.4	12 35.3	13 10.7	8 12.2
30 Su	14 28 37	8 51 52	11♊42 33	18 16 15	8 27.1	15 1.6	28 42.4	24 52.1	10 58.1	1 47.2	12 37.5	13 10.9	8 13.1

Astro Data	Planet Ingress	Last Aspect	☽ Ingress	Last Aspect	☽ Ingress	☽ Phases & Eclipses	Astro Data
Dy Hr Mn	Dy Hr Mn	Dy Hr Mn	Dy Hr Mn	Dy Hr Mn	Dy Hr Mn	Dy Hr Mn	
♄0N 2 8:53	♀ ♈ 13 11:30	2 4:29 ♃ ☍	♉ 3 4:52	1 0:11 ☿ ⚹	♊ 1 20:29	6 19:21 ☽ 15♊27	1 MARCH 1922
☽0S 13 20:00	☿ ♓ 18 6:32	4 18:09 ♀ ⚹	♊ 5 14:49	3 21:38 ♀ ⚹	♋ 4 3:46	13 11:14 ○ 22♍06	Julian Day # 8095
♀0N 15 20:14	☉ ♈ 21 9:49	7 7:44 ♀ □	♋ 7 21:19	6 7:29 ♀ □	♌ 6 8:13	13 11:28 ☍A 0.132	Delta T 22.5 sec
♇ D 22 18:41		9 16:21 ♀ △	♌ 10 0:09	7 18:12 ♂ △	♍ 8 10:09	20 8:43 ☽ 28♐58	SVP 06♓20'44"
☽0N 27 18:03	♀ ♉ 6 15:50	11 12:46 ☿ ☍	♍ 12 0:22	9 19:58 ♂ □	♎ 10 10:36	28 13:03 ● 7♈04	Obliquity 23°26'49"
	☿ ♈ 7 10:22	13 11:14 ☉ ☍	♎ 13 23:44	11 21:12 ♂ ⚹	♏ 12 11:07	28 13:05:03 ☌A 7'50"	⚷ Chiron 11♈28.5
☽0S 10 6:48	☉ ♉ 20 21:29	15 19:28 ☿ △	♏ 16 0:13	13 8:56 ♆ □	♐ 14 13:25		☽ Mean ☊ 10♎32.9
☿0N 10 6:05	☿ ♉ 22 23:19	18 3:16 ☿ □	♐ 18 3:33	16 11:03 ☉ △	♑ 16 19:01	5 5:45 ☽ 14♋40	1 APRIL 1922
♃⚹♆ 10 15:42		20 8:43 ☉ □	♑ 20 10:41	19 0:53 ☉ □	♒ 19 4:28	11 20:43 ○ 21♎10	Julian Day # 8126
♃⚻♅ 19 2:18		21 17:06 ♃ □	♒ 22 21:18	21 10:08 ☿ ⚹	♓ 21 16:44	11 20:32 ☍A 0.781	Delta T 22.6 sec
☽0N 24 0:56		24 4:23 ♃ △	♓ 25 9:56	23 17:36 ♂ □	♈ 24 5:37	19 0:53 ☽ 28♑11	SVP 06♓20'42"
♆ D 24 15:22		26 18:57 ♂ □	♈ 27 22:49	26 6:15 ♂ △	♉ 26 17:08	27 5:03 ● 6♉09	Obliquity 23°26'49"
		29 14:59 ♀ ☌	♉ 30 10:38	28 21:22 ♀ ☌	♊ 29 2:19		⚷ Chiron 13♈13.3
							☽ Mean ☊ 8♎54.4

LONGITUDE — MAY 1922

Day	Sid.Time	☉	0 hr ☽	Noon ☽	True ☊	☿	♀	♂	♃	♄	♅	♆	♇
1 M	14 32 33	9♉50 7	24♊53 21	1♋33 47	8♎22.3	17♉ 9.4	29♉55.8	24♐57.5	10♎52.1	1♎44.0	12♓39.8	13♌11.1	8♋13.9
2 Tu	14 36 30	10 48 21	8♋17 31	15 4 30	8R18.1	19 16.3	1♊ 9.3	25 2.3	10R46.2	1R40.9	12 42.0	13 11.3	8 14.8
3 W	14 40 26	11 46 33	21 54 40	28 47 58	8 15.1	21 21.9	2 22.6	25 6.4	10 40.4	1 37.8	12 44.1	13 11.6	8 15.7
4 Th	14 44 23	12 44 42	5♌44 20	12♌43 41	8D13.6	23 25.9	3 36.0	25 9.8	10 34.8	1 34.9	12 46.2	13 11.9	8 16.6
5 F	14 48 19	13 42 50	19 45 55	26 50 54	8 13.6	25 28.1	4 49.3	25 12.5	10 29.2	1 32.0	12 48.3	13 12.2	8 17.5
6 Sa	14 52 16	14 40 56	3♍58 25	11♍ 8 16	8 14.6	27 28.2	6 2.6	25 14.5	10 23.9	1 29.2	12 50.3	13 12.6	8 18.5
7 Su	14 56 12	15 38 59	18 20 9	25 33 40	8 15.9	29 25.9	7 15.8	25 15.8	10 18.7	1 26.5	12 52.3	13 13.0	8 19.5
8 M	15 0 9	16 37 1	2♎48 24	10♎ 3 49	8R16.9	1♊21.0	8 29.0	25R16.3	10 13.6	1 23.9	12 54.3	13 13.4	8 20.5
9 Tu	15 4 6	17 35 1	17 19 20	24 34 18	8 16.7	3 13.4	9 42.2	25 16.1	10 8.7	1 21.3	12 56.2	13 13.9	8 21.5
10 W	15 8 2	18 32 59	1♏48 1	8♏59 47	8 14.8	5 2.8	10 55.4	25 15.2	10 3.9	1 18.9	12 58.1	13 14.4	8 22.5
11 Th	15 11 59	19 30 55	16 8 52	23 14 36	8 10.9	6 49.2	12 8.5	25 13.6	9 59.2	1 16.6	12 59.9	13 14.9	8 23.5
12 F	15 15 55	20 28 50	0♐16 20	7♐13 31	8 5.3	8 32.3	13 21.5	25 11.2	9 54.8	1 14.3	13 1.7	13 15.4	8 24.6
13 Sa	15 19 52	21 26 44	14 5 41	20 52 30	7 58.5	10 12.1	14 34.6	25 8.0	9 50.5	1 12.1	13 3.4	13 16.0	8 25.7
14 Su	15 23 48	22 24 36	27 33 42	4♑ 9 13	7 51.2	11 48.6	15 47.6	25 4.1	9 46.3	1 10.0	13 5.1	13 16.6	8 26.8
15 M	15 27 45	23 22 27	10♑39 4	17 3 22	7 44.4	13 21.6	17 0.5	24 59.5	9 42.3	1 8.0	13 6.8	13 17.3	8 27.9
16 Tu	15 31 41	24 20 16	23 22 23	29 36 28	7 38.8	14 51.1	18 13.5	24 54.0	9 38.5	1 6.2	13 8.4	13 18.0	8 29.0
17 W	15 35 38	25 18 4	5♒46 1	11♒51 34	7 34.9	16 16.9	19 26.4	24 47.9	9 34.8	1 4.4	13 10.0	13 18.7	8 30.1
18 Th	15 39 35	26 15 51	17 53 39	23 52 52	7D32.8	17 39.2	20 39.2	24 40.9	9 31.3	1 2.7	13 11.5	13 19.4	8 31.3
19 F	15 43 31	27 13 37	29 49 51	5♓45 15	7 32.4	18 57.8	21 52.1	24 33.2	9 28.0	1 1.0	13 13.0	13 20.2	8 32.4
20 Sa	15 47 28	28 11 22	11♓39 43	17 33 56	7 33.1	20 12.6	23 4.9	24 24.8	9 24.8	0 59.5	13 14.5	13 21.0	8 33.6
21 Su	15 51 24	29 9 5	23 28 30	29 24 5	7 34.3	21 23.6	24 17.6	24 15.6	9 21.8	0 58.1	13 15.9	13 21.9	8 34.8
22 M	15 55 21	0♊ 6 48	5♈21 16	11♈20 37	7R35.1	22 30.8	25 30.4	24 5.6	9 19.0	0 56.8	13 17.2	13 22.7	8 36.0
23 Tu	15 59 17	1 4 29	17 22 39	23 27 49	7 34.6	23 34.1	26 43.1	23 55.0	9 16.4	0 55.6	13 18.5	13 23.6	8 37.2
24 W	16 3 14	2 2 10	29 36 33	5♉49 9	7 32.2	24 33.5	27 55.8	23 43.6	9 13.9	0 54.4	13 19.8	13 24.6	8 38.5
25 Th	16 7 10	2 59 49	12♉ 5 54	18 26 57	7 27.5	25 28.8	29 8.4	23 31.5	9 11.6	0 53.4	13 21.0	13 25.5	8 39.7
26 F	16 11 7	3 57 27	24 52 25	1♊22 17	7 20.5	26 20.0	0♋21.0	23 18.7	9 9.5	0 52.5	13 22.2	13 26.5	8 41.0
27 Sa	16 15 4	4 55 4	7♊56 29	14 34 51	7 11.8	27 7.1	1 33.6	23 5.3	9 7.5	0 51.7	13 23.3	13 27.5	8 42.3
28 Su	16 19 0	5 52 40	21 17 9	28 3 5	7 2.0	27 49.8	2 46.1	22 51.3	9 5.8	0 51.0	13 24.4	13 28.6	8 43.6
29 M	16 22 57	6 50 15	4♋52 21	11♋44 33	6 52.3	28 28.3	3 58.6	22 36.6	9 4.2	0 50.4	13 25.4	13 29.7	8 44.9
30 Tu	16 26 53	7 47 48	18 39 19	25 36 17	6 43.6	29 2.4	5 11.0	22 21.4	9 2.8	0 49.9	13 26.4	13 30.8	8 46.2
31 W	16 30 50	8 45 21	2♌35 4	9♌35 21	6 36.8	29 32.0	6 23.4	22 5.6	9 1.6	0 49.4	13 27.3	13 31.9	8 47.5

LONGITUDE — JUNE 1922

Day	Sid.Time	☉	0 hr ☽	Noon ☽	True ☊	☿	♀	♂	♃	♄	♅	♆	♇
1 Th	16 34 46	9♊42 51	16♌36 50	23♌39 16	6♎32.4	29♊57.1	7♋35.8	21♐49.3	9♎ 0.6	0♎49.1	13♓28.2	13♌33.1	8♋48.8
2 F	16 38 43	10 40 21	0♍42 26	7♍46 9	6D30.3	0♋17.5	8 48.1	21R32.5	8R59.7	0R48.9	13 29.0	13 34.3	8 50.2
3 Sa	16 42 39	11 37 49	14 50 15	21 54 36	6 30.0	0 33.4	10 0.4	21 15.2	8 59.0	0D48.8	13 29.8	13 35.5	8 51.5
4 Su	16 46 36	12 35 16	28 59 4	6♎ 3 30	6R30.4	0 44.7	11 12.7	20 57.5	8 58.6	0 48.8	13 30.5	13 36.7	8 52.9
5 M	16 50 33	13 32 41	13♎ 7 42	20 11 29	6 30.4	0R51.3	12 24.9	20 39.5	8 58.3	0 48.9	13 31.2	13 38.0	8 54.3
6 Tu	16 54 29	14 30 6	27 14 34	4♏16 40	6 28.8	0 53.3	13 37.0	20 21.1	8D58.1	0 49.1	13 31.9	13 39.3	8 55.6
7 W	16 58 26	15 27 29	11♏17 26	18 16 28	6 24.9	0 50.8	14 49.1	20 2.4	8 58.2	0 49.4	13 32.5	13 40.7	8 57.0
8 Th	17 2 22	16 24 51	25 13 20	2♐ 7 37	6 18.3	0 43.9	16 1.2	19 43.4	8 58.4	0 49.8	13 33.0	13 42.0	8 58.4
9 F	17 6 19	17 22 13	8♐58 51	15 46 38	6 9.2	0 32.7	17 13.2	19 24.2	8 58.8	0 50.3	13 33.5	13 43.4	8 59.8
10 Sa	17 10 15	18 19 33	22 30 34	29 10 20	5 58.3	0 17.5	18 25.2	19 4.9	8 59.4	0 50.9	13 34.0	13 44.8	9 1.3
11 Su	17 14 12	19 16 53	5♑45 40	12♑16 24	5 46.6	29♊58.5	19 37.1	18 45.4	9 0.2	0 51.6	13 34.4	13 46.2	9 2.7
12 M	17 18 8	20 14 12	18 42 28	25 3 52	5 35.4	29 36.0	20 49.0	18 25.7	9 1.1	0 52.4	13 34.8	13 47.7	9 4.1
13 Tu	17 22 5	21 11 31	1♒20 43	7♒33 14	5 25.5	29 10.3	22 0.8	18 6.1	9 2.3	0 53.3	13 35.1	13 49.2	9 5.6
14 W	17 26 2	22 8 49	13 41 42	19 46 32	5 17.8	28 42.0	23 12.6	17 46.4	9 3.6	0 54.4	13 35.3	13 50.7	9 7.0
15 Th	17 29 58	23 6 6	25 48 9	1♓47 5	5 12.6	28 11.4	24 24.3	17 26.7	9 5.0	0 55.5	13 35.5	13 52.2	9 8.4
16 F	17 33 55	24 3 24	7♓43 55	13 39 14	5 9.8	27 39.1	25 36.0	17 7.1	9 6.7	0 56.7	13 35.7	13 53.7	9 9.9
17 Sa	17 37 51	25 0 40	19 33 42	25 27 59	5D 8.8	27 5.6	26 47.6	16 47.6	9 8.5	0 58.0	13 35.8	13 55.3	9 11.4
18 Su	17 41 48	25 57 57	1♈22 46	7♈18 44	5R 8.7	26 31.4	27 59.2	16 28.3	9 10.5	0 59.4	13R35.9	13 56.9	9 12.8
19 M	17 45 44	26 55 13	13 16 34	19 16 56	5 8.6	25 57.2	29 10.7	16 9.2	9 12.7	1 0.9	13 35.9	13 58.5	9 14.3
20 Tu	17 49 41	27 52 29	25 20 26	1♉27 41	5 7.3	25 23.6	0♌22.2	15 50.4	9 15.0	1 2.5	13 35.9	14 0.2	9 15.8
21 W	17 53 37	28 49 45	7♉39 12	13 55 27	5 4.0	24 51.0	1 33.7	15 31.9	9 17.6	1 4.2	13 35.8	14 1.8	9 17.3
22 Th	17 57 34	29 47 0	20 16 47	26 43 30	4 58.2	24 20.2	2 45.1	15 13.7	9 20.2	1 6.0	13 35.6	14 3.5	9 18.7
23 F	18 1 31	0♋44 16	3♊15 46	9♊53 36	4 49.8	23 51.5	3 56.4	14 55.9	9 23.1	1 7.9	13 35.5	14 5.2	9 20.2
24 Sa	18 5 27	1 41 31	16 36 56	23 25 32	4 39.3	23 25.5	5 7.7	14 38.6	9 26.1	1 9.9	13 35.2	14 7.0	9 21.7
25 Su	18 9 24	2 38 46	0♋19 3	7♋17 2	4 27.5	23 2.7	6 19.0	14 21.7	9 29.3	1 12.0	13 35.0	14 8.7	9 23.2
26 M	18 13 20	3 36 1	14 18 56	21 24 5	4 15.7	22 43.4	7 30.1	14 5.3	9 32.7	1 14.2	13 34.7	14 10.5	9 24.7
27 Tu	18 17 17	4 33 15	28 31 48	5♌41 24	4 5.0	22 28.0	8 41.3	13 49.5	9 36.2	1 16.4	13 34.3	14 12.3	9 26.2
28 W	18 21 13	5 30 29	12♌52 10	20 3 27	3 56.5	22 16.8	9 52.3	13 34.3	9 39.9	1 18.8	13 33.9	14 14.1	9 27.7
29 Th	18 25 10	6 27 43	27 14 39	4♍25 14	3 50.8	22D 9.9	11 3.4	13 19.7	9 43.8	1 21.3	13 33.4	14 15.9	9 29.2
30 F	18 29 7	7 24 56	11♍34 46	18 42 55	3 47.7	22 7.7	12 14.3	13 5.8	9 47.8	1 23.9	13 32.9	14 17.8	9 30.8

Astro Data Dy Hr Mn	Planet Ingress Dy Hr Mn	Last Aspect Dy Hr Mn	☽ Ingress Dy Hr Mn	Last Aspect Dy Hr Mn	☽ Ingress Dy Hr Mn	☽ Phases & Eclipses Dy Hr Mn	Astro Data
☽0S 7 15:44	♀ ♊ 1 1:22	1 0:08 ♂ ☍	♋ 1 9:12	1 8:42 ♂ △	♍ 1 22:48	4 12:55 ☽ 13♌16	1 MAY 1922
♂ R 8 6:09	☿ ♊ 7 7:03	2 22:52 ☿ ⚹	♌ 3 14:05	3 10:40 ♂ □	♎ 4 1:43	11 6:06 ○ 19♏46	Julian Day # 8156
☽0N 21 9:13	☉ ♊ 21 21:10	5 11:16 ☿ □	♍ 5 17:19	5 12:31 ♂ ⚹	♏ 6 4:42	18 18:17 ☽ 26♒60	Delta T 22.6 sec
	♀ ♋ 25 17:04	7 11:31 ♂ □	♎ 7 19:21	7 6:38 ♀ △	♐ 8 8:18	26 18:04 ● 4♊41	SVP 06♓20'39"
☽0S 3 22:53		9 13:09 ♂ ⚹	♏ 9 21:00	9 18:01 ♂ ☌	♑ 10 13:30		Obliquity 23°26'49"
♄ D 3 13:07	☿ ♋ 1 3:08	11 6:06 ☉ ☍	♐ 11 23:32	12 4:23 ♀ ☍	♒ 12 21:25	2 18:10 ☽ 11♍24	⚷ Chiron 14♈57.0
☿ R 5 22:38	☿ ♊ 10 22:13	13 19:32 ♂ ☌	♑ 14 4:25	15 4:35 ☿ △	♓ 15 8:25	9 15:58 ○ 18♐00	☽ Mean ☊ 7♎19.1
♃ D 6 4:49	♀ ♌ 19 16:32	16 2:00 ☉ △	♒ 16 12:46	17 16:21 ♀ △	♈ 17 21:12	17 12:03 ☽ 25♓29	
♃□♇ 7 23:38	☉ ♋ 22 5:27	18 18:17 ☉ □	♓ 19 0:21	20 5:24 ☉ ⚹	♉ 20 9:09	25 4:19 ● 2♋49	1 JUNE 1922
☽0N 17 18:32		21 12:30 ☉ ⚹	♈ 21 13:13	21 12:14 ♆ □	♊ 22 18:02		Julian Day # 8187
♅ R 18 19:50		23 20:22 ♀ ⚹	♉ 24 0:46	24 11:40 ☿ ☌	♋ 24 23:27		Delta T 22.7 sec
♃□♇ 20 17:37		25 2:31 ♆ □	♊ 26 9:29	25 22:45 ♅ △	♌ 27 2:28		SVP 06♓20'34"
☿ D 29 23:28		28 12:12 ☿ ☌	♋ 28 15:26	28 15:34 ☿ ⚹	♍ 29 4:36		Obliquity 23°26'48"
		29 14:56 ♅ △	♌ 30 19:34				⚷ Chiron 16♈26.3
							☽ Mean ☊ 5♎40.6

JULY 1922 LONGITUDE

Day	Sid.Time	☉	0 hr ☽	Noon ☽	True ☊	☿	♀	♂	♃	♄	♅	♆	♇
1 Sa	18 33 3	8♋22 9	25♍49 25	2♎54 5	3♎46.6	22♊10.2	13♌25.2	12♐52.5	9♎52.0	1♎26.5	13♓32.3	14♌19.6	9♋32.3
2 Su	18 37 0	9 19 21	9♎56 46	16 57 25	3R46.6	22 17.5	14 36.0	12R40.0	9 56.3	1 29.3	13R31.7	14 21.5	9 33.8
3 M	18 40 56	10 16 33	23 55 58	0♏52 24	3 46.2	22 29.8	15 46.8	12 28.2	10 0.8	1 32.1	13 31.1	14 23.4	9 35.3
4 Tu	18 44 53	11 13 44	7♏46 39	14 38 41	3 44.3	22 47.1	16 57.5	12 17.1	10 5.5	1 35.0	13 30.4	14 25.3	9 36.8
5 W	18 48 49	12 10 56	21 28 25	28 15 46	3 40.0	23 9.4	18 8.1	12 6.8	10 10.3	1 38.1	13 29.6	14 27.2	9 38.3
6 Th	18 52 46	13 8 7	5♐ 0 36	11♐42 45	3 32.9	23 36.7	19 18.6	11 57.3	10 15.2	1 41.2	13 28.9	14 29.2	9 39.8
7 F	18 56 42	14 5 18	18 22 4	24 58 21	3 23.4	24 9.0	20 29.1	11 48.5	10 20.4	1 44.4	13 28.0	14 31.2	9 41.3
8 Sa	19 0 39	15 2 29	1♑31 27	8♑ 1 11	3 11.9	24 46.2	21 39.5	11 40.6	10 25.6	1 47.7	13 27.2	14 33.1	9 42.8
9 Su	19 4 36	15 59 40	14 27 25	20 50 3	2 59.6	25 28.3	22 49.8	11 33.4	10 31.0	1 51.0	13 26.2	14 35.1	9 44.3
10 M	19 8 32	16 56 51	27 9 3	3♒24 24	2 47.6	26 15.4	24 0.1	11 27.1	10 36.6	1 54.5	13 25.3	14 37.1	9 45.8
11 Tu	19 12 29	17 54 2	9♒36 12	15 44 34	2 37.0	27 7.2	25 10.3	11 21.6	10 42.3	1 58.0	13 24.3	14 39.1	9 47.3
12 W	19 16 25	18 51 14	21 49 42	27 51 55	2 28.6	28 3.8	26 20.4	11 17.0	10 48.1	2 1.7	13 23.2	14 41.2	9 48.8
13 Th	19 20 22	19 48 26	3♓51 32	9♓48 57	2 22.8	29 5.2	27 30.4	11 13.1	10 54.1	2 5.4	13 22.1	14 43.2	9 50.3
14 F	19 24 18	20 45 39	15 44 39	21 39 9	2 19.4	0♋11.1	28 40.3	11 10.1	11 0.2	2 9.2	13 21.0	14 45.3	9 51.8
15 Sa	19 28 15	21 42 52	27 33 1	3♈26 50	2D18.2	1 21.7	29 50.2	11 8.0	11 6.5	2 13.1	13 19.8	14 47.4	9 53.2
16 Su	19 32 11	22 40 5	9♈21 16	15 16 58	2 18.2	2 36.8	0♍60.0	11 6.6	11 12.9	2 17.0	13 18.6	14 49.4	9 54.7
17 M	19 36 8	23 37 19	21 14 37	27 14 52	2R18.6	3 56.3	2 9.7	11D 6.1	11 19.4	2 21.1	13 17.3	14 51.5	9 56.2
18 Tu	19 40 5	24 34 34	3♉18 26	9♉25 56	2 18.3	5 20.1	3 19.3	11 6.5	11 26.1	2 25.2	13 16.0	14 53.6	9 57.7
19 W	19 44 1	25 31 50	15 38 0	21 55 12	2 16.4	6 48.2	4 28.9	11 7.6	11 32.9	2 29.4	13 14.7	14 55.7	9 59.1
20 Th	19 47 58	26 29 6	28 18 2	4♊46 53	2 12.4	8 20.4	5 38.3	11 9.7	11 39.9	2 33.7	13 13.3	14 57.9	10 0.6
21 F	19 51 54	27 26 23	11♊22 4	18 3 46	2 6.1	9 56.6	6 47.7	11 12.5	11 46.9	2 38.0	13 11.9	14 60.0	10 2.0
22 Sa	19 55 51	28 23 41	24 51 59	1♋46 35	1 57.8	11 36.6	7 57.0	11 16.2	11 54.1	2 42.4	13 10.5	15 2.1	10 3.5
23 Su	19 59 47	29 21 0	8♋47 17	15 53 36	1 48.3	13 20.3	9 6.2	11 20.6	12 1.5	2 47.0	13 9.0	15 4.3	10 4.9
24 M	20 3 44	0♌18 19	23 4 56	0♌20 30	1 38.7	15 7.4	10 15.3	11 25.9	12 8.9	2 51.5	13 7.4	15 6.5	10 6.4
25 Tu	20 7 40	1 15 39	7♌39 26	15 0 48	1 29.9	16 57.7	11 24.3	11 32.0	12 16.5	2 56.2	13 5.9	15 8.6	10 7.8
26 W	20 11 37	2 13 0	22 23 38	29 46 57	1 23.0	18 51.0	12 33.2	11 38.9	12 24.2	3 0.9	13 4.3	15 10.8	10 9.2
27 Th	20 15 34	3 10 21	7♍ 9 49	14♍31 25	1 18.5	20 46.9	13 42.1	11 46.6	12 32.1	3 5.7	13 2.6	15 13.0	10 10.6
28 F	20 19 30	4 7 43	21 50 58	29 7 52	1D16.4	22 45.2	14 50.8	11 55.1	12 40.0	3 10.6	13 0.9	15 15.2	10 12.0
29 Sa	20 23 27	5 5 5	6♎21 38	13♎31 52	1 16.1	24 45.4	15 59.4	12 4.4	12 48.1	3 15.6	12 59.2	15 17.4	10 13.4
30 Su	20 27 23	6 2 28	20 38 19	27 40 52	1 16.9	26 47.4	17 7.9	12 14.4	12 56.3	3 20.6	12 57.5	15 19.6	10 14.8
31 M	20 31 20	6 59 51	4♏39 24	11♏33 58	1R17.5	28 50.6	18 16.3	12 25.1	13 4.6	3 25.7	12 55.7	15 21.8	10 16.2

AUGUST 1922 LONGITUDE

Day	Sid.Time	☉	0 hr ☽	Noon ☽	True ☊	☿	♀	♂	♃	♄	♅	♆	♇
1 Tu	20 35 16	7♌57 15	18♏24 35	25♏11 22	1♎17.0	0♌54.8	19♍24.6	12♐36.7	13♎13.0	3♎30.8	12♓53.9	15♌24.0	10♋17.5
2 W	20 39 13	8 54 39	1♐54 24	8♐33 50	1R14.7	2 59.7	20 32.7	12 48.9	13 21.6	3 36.0	12R52.1	15 26.2	10 18.9
3 Th	20 43 9	9 52 4	15 9 44	21 42 14	1 10.2	5 5.0	21 40.8	13 1.8	13 30.2	3 41.3	12 50.2	15 28.4	10 20.2
4 F	20 47 6	10 49 30	28 11 26	4♑37 24	1 3.8	7 10.3	22 48.7	13 15.4	13 39.0	3 46.7	12 48.3	15 30.6	10 21.6
5 Sa	20 51 3	11 46 56	11♑ 0 13	17 19 57	0 55.9	9 15.4	23 56.5	13 29.8	13 47.8	3 52.1	12 46.4	15 32.8	10 22.9
6 Su	20 54 59	12 44 23	23 36 40	29 50 26	0 47.3	11 20.1	25 4.2	13 44.7	13 56.8	3 57.5	12 44.4	15 35.1	10 24.2
7 M	20 58 56	13 41 52	6♒ 1 19	12♒ 9 27	0 38.9	13 24.1	26 11.7	14 0.4	14 5.8	4 3.1	12 42.4	15 37.3	10 25.5
8 Tu	21 2 52	14 39 21	18 14 57	24 17 57	0 31.5	15 27.3	27 19.1	14 16.6	14 15.0	4 8.7	12 40.4	15 39.5	10 26.8
9 W	21 6 49	15 36 51	0♓18 40	6♓17 19	0 25.8	17 29.5	28 26.4	14 33.5	14 24.3	4 14.3	12 38.4	15 41.7	10 28.1
10 Th	21 10 45	16 34 23	12 14 10	18 9 33	0 22.1	19 30.7	29 33.5	14 51.1	14 33.7	4 20.0	12 36.3	15 43.9	10 29.4
11 F	21 14 42	17 31 55	24 3 49	29 57 22	0D20.3	21 30.7	0♎40.5	15 9.2	14 43.1	4 25.8	12 34.3	15 46.2	10 30.6
12 Sa	21 18 38	18 29 29	5♈50 40	11♈44 11	0 20.2	23 29.4	1 47.3	15 27.9	14 52.7	4 31.6	12 32.1	15 48.4	10 31.8
13 Su	21 22 35	19 27 4	17 38 28	23 34 4	0 21.3	25 26.8	2 54.0	15 47.2	15 2.4	4 37.5	12 30.0	15 50.6	10 33.1
14 M	21 26 31	20 24 41	29 31 34	5♉31 35	0 22.9	27 22.8	4 0.5	16 7.1	15 12.1	4 43.4	12 27.9	15 52.8	10 34.3
15 Tu	21 30 28	21 22 19	11♉34 45	17 41 40	0R24.2	29 17.5	5 6.9	16 27.5	15 22.0	4 49.4	12 25.7	15 55.0	10 35.5
16 W	21 34 25	22 19 59	23 52 59	0♊ 9 16	0 24.7	1♍10.7	6 13.2	16 48.5	15 31.9	4 55.5	12 23.5	15 57.3	10 36.7
17 Th	21 38 21	23 17 40	6♊31 5	12 58 56	0 23.8	3 2.5	7 19.3	17 10.0	15 42.0	5 1.6	12 21.3	15 59.5	10 37.8
18 F	21 42 18	24 15 24	19 33 13	26 14 15	0 21.4	4 52.9	8 25.2	17 32.1	15 52.1	5 7.7	12 19.1	16 1.7	10 39.0
19 Sa	21 46 14	25 13 8	3♋ 2 15	9♋57 13	0 17.6	6 41.8	9 30.9	17 54.7	16 2.3	5 13.9	12 16.8	16 3.9	10 40.1
20 Su	21 50 11	26 10 54	16 59 4	24 7 29	0 12.9	8 29.4	10 36.5	18 17.8	16 12.6	5 20.2	12 14.5	16 6.1	10 41.3
21 M	21 54 7	27 8 42	1♌22 0	8♌41 57	0 7.9	10 15.5	11 41.9	18 41.4	16 23.0	5 26.5	12 12.3	16 8.3	10 42.4
22 Tu	21 58 4	28 6 32	16 6 31	23 34 44	0 3.4	12 0.3	12 47.2	19 5.5	16 33.5	5 32.8	12 10.0	16 10.5	10 43.5
23 W	22 2 0	29 4 22	1♍ 5 32	8♍37 46	29♍59.9	13 43.7	13 52.2	19 30.1	16 44.0	5 39.2	12 7.7	16 12.7	10 44.5
24 Th	22 5 57	0♍ 2 15	16 10 18	23 42 0	29D57.9	15 25.7	14 57.1	19 55.1	16 54.7	5 45.6	12 5.3	16 14.8	10 45.6
25 F	22 9 54	1 0 8	1♎11 48	8♎38 45	29 57.3	17 6.3	16 1.8	20 20.7	17 5.4	5 52.1	12 3.0	16 17.0	10 46.7
26 Sa	22 13 50	1 58 3	16 2 2	23 20 58	29 57.9	18 45.6	17 6.2	20 46.7	17 16.2	5 58.6	12 0.7	16 19.2	10 47.7
27 Su	22 17 47	2 55 59	0♏35 1	7♏43 49	29 59.3	20 23.6	18 10.5	21 13.2	17 27.1	6 5.2	11 58.3	16 21.3	10 48.7
28 M	22 21 43	3 53 57	14 47 9	21 44 53	0♎ 0.7	22 0.2	19 14.5	21 40.0	17 38.0	6 11.8	11 55.9	16 23.5	10 49.7
29 Tu	22 25 40	4 51 56	28 37 3	5♐23 44	0R 1.5	23 35.6	20 18.4	22 7.4	17 49.0	6 18.4	11 53.6	16 25.6	10 50.7
30 W	22 29 36	5 49 56	12♐ 5 8	18 41 27	0 1.5	25 9.6	21 22.0	22 35.1	18 0.1	6 25.1	11 51.2	16 27.7	10 51.6
31 Th	22 33 33	6 47 57	25 12 58	1♑39 58	0 0.4	26 42.3	22 25.3	23 3.3	18 11.3	6 31.8	11 48.8	16 29.9	10 52.6

Astro Data	Planet Ingress	Last Aspect	☽ Ingress	Last Aspect	☽ Ingress	☽ Phases & Eclipses	Astro Data
Dy Hr Mn	Dy Hr Mn	Dy Hr Mn	Dy Hr Mn	Dy Hr Mn	Dy Hr Mn	Dy Hr Mn	1 JULY 1922
☽0S 1 5:26	☿ ♋ 13 20:04	30 17:48 ☿ □	♎ 1 7:04	1 1:55 ♀ ⚹	♐ 1 20:35	1 22:51 ☽ 9♎17	Julian Day # 8217
☽0N 15 3:47	♀ ♍ 15 3:22	2 21:29 ☿ △	♏ 3 10:29	3 13:06 ♀ □	♑ 4 3:22	9 3:07 ○ 16♑07	Delta T 22.7 sec
♂ D 17 2:12	☉ ♌ 23 16:20	4 17:34 ♀ □	♐ 5 15:05	6 3:05 ♀ △	♒ 6 12:19	17 5:11 ☽ 23♈50	SVP 06♓20'29"
☽0S 28 12:54	☿ ♌ 31 13:25	7 11:00 ☿ ☍	♑ 7 21:12	7 18:52 ☿ ☍	♓ 8 23:23	24 12:47 ● 0♌49	Obliquity 23°26'48"
♃⊼♅ 30 2:51		9 3:07 ☉ ☍	♒ 10 5:27	10 5:26 ♂ □	♈ 11 12:05	31 4:21 ☽ 7♏10	⚷ Chiron 17♈18.9
	♀ ♎ 10 9:30	12 13:32 ☿ △	♓ 12 16:16	13 18:51 ☿ △	♉ 14 0:57		☽ Mean ☊ 4♎05.3
♀0S 10 16:30	☿ ♍ 15 8:59	14 11:05 ☉ △	♈ 15 4:59	15 20:45 ☉ □	♊ 16 11:42	7 16:18 ○ 14♒21	
☽0N 11 11:55	☊ ♍ 22 23:24	17 5:11 ☉ □	♉ 17 17:28	18 9:07 ☉ ⚹	♋ 18 18:40	15 20:45 ☽ 22♉12	1 AUGUST 1922
♄0S 18 11:19	☉ ♍ 23 23:04	19 20:20 ☉ ⚹	♊ 20 3:10	19 22:40 ♃ □	♌ 20 21:45	22 20:34 ● 28♌56	Julian Day # 8248
♃⚹♆ 19 4:43	☊ ♎ 27 12:16	21 6:33 ♆ ⚹	♋ 22 8:56	22 20:34 ☉ ☌	♍ 22 22:16	29 11:55 ☽ 5♐21	Delta T 22.8 sec
☽0S 24 22:06	☊ ♍ 31 6:07	23 8:47 ☿ ☌	♌ 24 11:26	24 6:09 ♂ □	♎ 24 22:05		SVP 06♓20'25"
		25 12:15 ♆ ☌	♍ 26 12:21	26 8:01 ♂ ⚹	♏ 26 23:02		Obliquity 23°26'48"
		28 1:43 ☿ ⚹	♎ 28 13:26	28 14:04 ☿ ⚹	♐ 29 2:26		⚷ Chiron 17♈27.0R
		30 12:16 ☿ □	♏ 30 15:59	31 3:08 ☿ □	♑ 31 8:53		☽ Mean ☊ 2♎26.8

LONGITUDE SEPTEMBER 1922

Day	Sid.Time	☉	0 hr ☽	Noon ☽	True ☊	☿	♀	♂	♃	♄	♅	♆	♇
1 F	22 37 29	7♍46 0	8♑ 2 46	14♑21 41	29♍58.4	28♍13.7	23♎28.4	23♐31.8	18♎22.5	6♎38.6	11♓46.4	16♌32.0	10♋53.5
2 Sa	22 41 26	8 44 4	20 37 1	26 49 4	29R55.5	29 43.9	24 31.3	24 0.7	18 33.8	6 45.4	11R44.0	16 34.1	10 54.4
3 Su	22 45 23	9 42 10	2♒58 8	9♒ 4 30	29 52.4	1♎12.7	25 33.9	24 30.1	18 45.2	6 52.2	11 41.6	16 36.2	10 55.3
4 M	22 49 19	10 40 17	15 8 25	21 10 10	29 49.3	2 40.2	26 36.2	24 59.7	18 56.6	6 59.1	11 39.2	16 38.2	10 56.1
5 Tu	22 53 16	11 38 26	27 9 59	3♓ 8 7	29 46.6	4 6.4	27 38.3	25 29.8	19 8.1	7 5.9	11 36.8	16 40.3	10 57.0
6 W	22 57 12	12 36 36	9♓ 4 49	15 0 21	29 44.7	5 31.2	28 40.0	26 0.2	19 19.6	7 12.9	11 34.4	16 42.3	10 57.8
7 Th	23 1 9	13 34 49	20 54 58	26 48 56	29D43.7	6 54.7	29 41.5	26 30.9	19 31.3	7 19.8	11 32.0	16 44.4	10 58.6
8 F	23 5 5	14 33 2	2♈42 33	8♈36 8	29 43.5	8 16.8	0♏42.7	27 2.0	19 42.9	7 26.8	11 29.6	16 46.4	10 59.4
9 Sa	23 9 2	15 31 18	14 30 1	20 24 32	29 44.0	9 37.4	1 43.5	27 33.4	19 54.7	7 33.8	11 27.2	16 48.4	11 0.2
10 Su	23 12 58	16 29 36	26 20 7	2♉17 8	29 45.0	10 56.6	2 44.0	28 5.1	20 6.5	7 40.8	11 24.9	16 50.4	11 0.9
11 M	23 16 55	17 27 56	8♉16 3	14 17 20	29 46.1	12 14.3	3 44.3	28 37.1	20 18.3	7 47.9	11 22.5	16 52.4	11 1.6
12 Tu	23 20 52	18 26 17	20 21 27	26 28 55	29 47.3	13 30.4	4 44.1	29 9.5	20 30.2	7 55.0	11 20.1	16 54.3	11 2.3
13 W	23 24 48	19 24 41	2♊40 14	8♊55 55	29 48.1	14 44.8	5 43.7	29 42.1	20 42.2	8 2.1	11 17.7	16 56.3	11 3.0
14 Th	23 28 45	20 23 7	15 16 29	21 42 23	29R48.5	15 57.6	6 42.8	0♑15.1	20 54.2	8 9.2	11 15.4	16 58.2	11 3.7
15 F	23 32 41	21 21 36	28 14 4	4♋51 55	29 48.5	17 8.6	7 41.6	0 48.3	21 6.2	8 16.4	11 13.0	17 0.1	11 4.3
16 Sa	23 36 38	22 20 6	11♋36 13	18 27 12	29 48.1	18 17.7	8 40.0	1 21.9	21 18.4	8 23.6	11 10.7	17 2.0	11 5.0
17 Su	23 40 34	23 18 39	25 24 56	2♌29 22	29 47.5	19 24.9	9 38.0	1 55.7	21 30.5	8 30.8	11 8.3	17 3.9	11 5.6
18 M	23 44 31	24 17 13	9♌40 17	16 57 17	29 46.9	20 29.9	10 35.7	2 29.8	21 42.7	8 38.0	11 6.0	17 5.8	11 6.1
19 Tu	23 48 27	25 15 50	24 19 50	1♍47 10	29 46.3	21 32.7	11 32.9	3 4.1	21 55.0	8 45.3	11 3.7	17 7.6	11 6.7
20 W	23 52 24	26 14 29	9♍18 24	16 52 29	29 46.0	22 33.1	12 29.6	3 38.8	22 7.3	8 52.5	11 1.4	17 9.5	11 7.2
21 Th	23 56 20	27 13 10	24 28 19	2♎ 4 40	29D45.8	23 31.0	13 25.9	4 13.7	22 19.7	8 59.8	10 59.1	17 11.3	11 7.7
22 F	0 0 17	28 11 53	9♎40 20	17 14 6	29 45.8	24 26.1	14 21.7	4 48.8	22 32.0	9 7.1	10 56.9	17 13.1	11 8.2
23 Sa	0 4 14	29 10 38	24 44 53	2♏11 40	29R45.9	25 18.2	15 17.1	5 24.2	22 44.5	9 14.4	10 54.6	17 14.8	11 8.7
24 Su	0 8 10	0♎ 9 24	9♏33 34	16 49 55	29 45.9	26 7.2	16 11.9	5 59.9	22 56.9	9 21.7	10 52.4	17 16.6	11 9.1
25 M	0 12 7	1 8 13	24 0 10	1♐ 3 59	29 45.8	26 52.7	17 6.2	6 35.8	23 9.5	9 29.0	10 50.2	17 18.3	11 9.5
26 Tu	0 16 3	2 7 3	8♐ 1 9	14 51 40	29 45.6	27 34.4	17 60.0	7 12.0	23 22.0	9 36.4	10 48.0	17 20.0	11 9.9
27 W	0 20 0	3 5 55	21 35 36	28 13 12	29D45.4	28 12.1	18 53.2	7 48.3	23 34.6	9 43.7	10 45.8	17 21.7	11 10.3
28 Th	0 23 56	4 4 49	4♑44 45	11♑10 38	29 45.4	28 45.3	19 45.8	8 24.9	23 47.2	9 51.1	10 43.7	17 23.3	11 10.7
29 F	0 27 53	5 3 44	17 31 17	23 47 10	29 45.5	29 13.8	20 37.7	9 1.7	23 59.9	9 58.4	10 41.5	17 25.0	11 11.0
30 Sa	0 31 49	6 2 42	29 58 47	6♒ 6 36	29 45.9	29 37.1	21 29.0	9 38.8	24 12.5	10 5.8	10 39.4	17 26.6	11 11.3

LONGITUDE OCTOBER 1922

Day	Sid.Time	☉	0 hr ☽	Noon ☽	True ☊	☿	♀	♂	♃	♄	♅	♆	♇
1 Su	0 35 46	7♎ 1 40	12♒11 8	18♒12 51	29♍46.6	29♎54.8	22♏19.7	10♑16.0	24♎25.3	10♎13.2	10♓37.4	17♌28.2	11♋11.6
2 M	0 39 43	8 0 41	24 12 14	0♓ 9 42	29 47.4	0♏ 6.4	23 9.6	10 53.4	24 38.0	10 20.6	10R35.3	17 29.8	11 11.9
3 Tu	0 43 39	8 59 44	6♓ 5 42	12 0 36	29 48.3	0R11.6	23 58.8	11 31.0	24 50.8	10 27.9	10 33.3	17 31.3	11 12.1
4 W	0 47 36	9 58 48	17 54 47	23 48 35	29 48.9	0 9.9	24 47.3	12 8.9	25 3.6	10 35.3	10 31.3	17 32.8	11 12.3
5 Th	0 51 32	10 57 54	29 42 20	5♈36 20	29R49.2	0 1.0	25 34.9	12 46.9	25 16.4	10 42.7	10 29.3	17 34.3	11 12.5
6 F	0 55 29	11 57 3	11♈30 51	17 26 10	29 48.9	29♎44.3	26 21.8	13 25.0	25 29.2	10 50.1	10 27.4	17 35.8	11 12.7
7 Sa	0 59 25	12 56 13	23 22 33	29 20 13	29 47.9	29 19.8	27 7.7	14 3.4	25 42.1	10 57.4	10 25.5	17 37.2	11 12.8
8 Su	1 3 22	13 55 26	5♉19 28	11♉20 32	29 46.3	28 47.2	27 52.8	14 41.9	25 55.0	11 4.8	10 23.6	17 38.6	11 12.9
9 M	1 7 18	14 54 40	17 23 42	23 29 13	29 44.1	28 6.6	28 37.0	15 20.6	26 7.9	11 12.2	10 21.7	17 40.0	11 13.0
10 Tu	1 11 15	15 53 57	29 37 23	5♊48 30	29 41.7	27 18.2	29 20.3	15 59.5	26 20.8	11 19.6	10 19.9	17 41.4	11 13.1
11 W	1 15 12	16 53 16	12♊ 2 53	18 20 52	29 39.3	26 22.7	0♐ 2.5	16 38.5	26 33.8	11 26.9	10 18.1	17 42.7	11 13.1
12 Th	1 19 8	17 52 38	24 42 46	1♋ 8 56	29 37.3	25 20.7	0 43.7	17 17.7	26 46.7	11 34.3	10 16.4	17 44.0	11R13.2
13 F	1 23 5	18 52 1	7♋39 42	14 15 23	29D36.0	24 13.6	1 23.9	17 57.0	26 59.7	11 41.6	10 14.6	17 45.3	11 13.2
14 Sa	1 27 1	19 51 28	20 56 15	27 42 35	29 35.6	23 2.7	2 2.9	18 36.5	27 12.7	11 49.0	10 13.0	17 46.6	11 13.1
15 Su	1 30 58	20 50 56	4♌34 32	11♌32 14	29 36.1	21 49.9	2 40.8	19 16.2	27 25.8	11 56.3	10 11.3	17 47.8	11 13.1
16 M	1 34 54	21 50 27	18 35 41	25 44 46	29 37.3	20 37.1	3 17.4	19 56.0	27 38.8	12 3.6	10 9.7	17 49.0	11 13.0
17 Tu	1 38 51	22 50 0	2♍59 16	10♍18 46	29 38.7	19 26.4	3 52.9	20 35.9	27 51.8	12 10.9	10 8.1	17 50.2	11 12.9
18 W	1 42 47	23 49 35	17 42 44	25 10 27	29R39.9	18 20.0	4 27.0	21 16.0	28 4.9	12 18.2	10 6.6	17 51.3	11 12.8
19 Th	1 46 44	24 49 12	2♎41 5	10♎13 38	29 40.2	17 19.7	4 59.7	21 56.2	28 17.9	12 25.5	10 5.1	17 52.4	11 12.7
20 F	1 50 40	25 48 52	17 47 1	25 20 5	29 39.3	16 27.5	5 31.1	22 36.6	28 31.0	12 32.8	10 3.6	17 53.5	11 12.5
21 Sa	1 54 37	26 48 33	2♏51 38	10♏20 32	29 37.0	15 44.6	6 1.0	23 17.1	28 44.1	12 40.0	10 2.2	17 54.6	11 12.3
22 Su	1 58 34	27 48 17	17 45 42	25 6 9	29 33.5	15 12.1	6 29.3	23 57.7	28 57.2	12 47.3	10 0.8	17 55.6	11 12.1
23 M	2 2 30	28 48 3	2♐21 4	9♐29 48	29 29.2	14 50.8	6 56.1	24 38.5	29 10.2	12 54.5	9 59.5	17 56.6	11 11.9
24 Tu	2 6 27	29 47 50	16 31 52	23 27 0	29 24.7	14D40.7	7 21.2	25 19.4	29 23.3	13 1.7	9 58.2	17 57.5	11 11.6
25 W	2 10 23	0♏47 39	0♑15 4	6♑56 9	29 20.8	14 42.0	7 44.6	26 0.4	29 36.4	13 8.8	9 56.9	17 58.5	11 11.3
26 Th	2 14 20	1 47 30	13 30 26	19 58 15	29 17.9	14 54.2	8 6.3	26 41.5	29 49.5	13 16.0	9 55.7	17 59.3	11 11.0
27 F	2 18 16	2 47 23	26 20 2	2♒36 16	29D16.4	15 16.8	8 26.0	27 22.8	0♏ 2.6	13 23.1	9 54.5	18 0.2	11 10.7
28 Sa	2 22 13	3 47 17	8♒47 32	14 54 25	29 16.3	15 49.1	8 43.9	28 4.2	0 15.7	13 30.2	9 53.4	18 1.0	11 10.3
29 Su	2 26 9	4 47 12	20 57 33	26 57 33	29 17.4	16 30.3	8 59.7	28 45.6	0 28.7	13 37.3	9 52.3	18 1.8	11 10.0
30 M	2 30 6	5 47 10	2♓55 3	8♓50 39	29 19.1	17 19.5	9 13.6	29 27.2	0 41.8	13 44.3	9 51.3	18 2.6	11 9.6
31 Tu	2 34 3	6 47 9	14 44 57	20 38 29	29 20.8	18 15.9	9 25.3	0♒ 8.8	0 54.9	13 51.3	9 50.3	18 3.3	11 9.2

Astro Data Dy Hr Mn	Planet Ingress Dy Hr Mn	Last Aspect Dy Hr Mn	☽ Ingress Dy Hr Mn	Last Aspect Dy Hr Mn	☽ Ingress Dy Hr Mn	☽ Phases & Eclipses Dy Hr Mn	Astro Data
☿0S 1 20:57	☿ ♎ 2 4:20	2 8:14 ♀ □	♒ 2 18:12	2 0:53 ♃ △	♓ 2 11:40	6 7:47 ○ 12♓55	1 SEPTEMBER 1922
☽0N 7 18:38	♀ ♏ 7 7:15	5 1:02 ♀ △	♓ 5 5:41	4 15:00 ♀ △	♈ 5 0:36	14 10:20 ☽ 20♊48	Julian Day # 8279
♅△♇ 17 23:02	♂ ♑ 13 13:02	7 11:55 ♂ □	♈ 7 18:29	7 11:30 ☿ ☍	♉ 7 13:20	21 4:38 ● 27♍24	Delta T 22.8 sec
☽0S 21 8:49	☉ ♎ 23 20:10	10 3:42 ♂ △	♉ 10 7:24	9 23:25 ♀ ☍	♊ 10 0:44	21 4:40:08 ☌ T 5'59"	SVP 06♓20'21"
		11 19:53 ☉ △	♊ 12 18:50	12 3:56 ♃ △	♋ 12 9:52	27 22:40 ☽ 4♑02	Obliquity 23°26'49"
♄⚻♅ 3 13:42	☿ ♏ 1 9:14	14 10:41 ♃ △	♋ 15 3:13	14 11:18 ♃ □	♌ 14 16:01		⚷ Chiron 16♈47.0R
☿ R 3 6:17	☿ ♎ 5 1:45	16 20:07 ☉ ⚹	♌ 17 7:48	16 15:24 ♃ ⚹	♍ 16 19:04	6 0:58 ○ 11♈59	☽ Mean ☊ 0♎48.3
☽0N 5 0:42	♀ ♐ 10 22:33	18 20:02 ♃ ⚹	♍ 19 9:08	18 6:00 ♂ △	♎ 18 19:43	6 0:43 ☍ A 0.636	
♃⚼♅ 5 20:59	☉ ♏ 24 4:53	21 4:38 ☉ ☌	♎ 21 8:43	20 17:19 ♃ ☌	♏ 20 19:26	13 21:55 ☽ 19♋46	1 OCTOBER 1922
♄□♇ 9 2:42	♃ ♏ 26 19:16	23 0:57 ☿ ☌	♏ 23 8:27	22 10:37 ♂ ⚹	♐ 22 20:05	20 13:40 ● 26♎23	Julian Day # 8309
♇ R 12 14:08	♂ ♒ 30 18:55	24 12:46 ♆ □	♐ 25 10:11	24 22:50 ♃ ⚹	♑ 24 23:33	27 13:26 ☽ 3♒21	Delta T 22.9 sec
☽0S 18 19:51		27 12:31 ☿ ⚹	♑ 27 15:15	27 2:06 ♂ ☌	♒ 27 7:00		SVP 06♓20'19"
☿ D 24 9:18		29 23:17 ☿ □	♒ 30 0:02	28 18:10 ♆ ☍	♓ 29 18:07		Obliquity 23°26'49"
							⚷ Chiron 15♈34.8R
							☽ Mean ☊ 29♍12.9

NOVEMBER 1922 LONGITUDE

Day	Sid.Time	☉	0 hr ☽	Noon ☽	True ☊	☿	♀	♂	♃	♄	♅	♆	♇
1 W	2 37 59	7♏47 9	26♓31 47	2♈25 20	29♍21.7	19♎18.7	9♐34.8	0♒50.6	1♏ 7.9	13♎58.3	9♓49.3	18♌ 4.0	11♋ 8.7
2 Th	2 41 56	8 47 12	8♈19 35	14 14 54	29R21.3	20 26.9	9 42.1	1 32.5	1 20.9	14 5.3	9R48.4	18 4.7	11R 8.2
3 F	2 45 52	9 47 16	20 11 39	26 10 9	29 19.0	21 40.0	9 47.1	2 14.4	1 34.0	14 12.2	9 47.6	18 5.4	11 7.8
4 Sa	2 49 49	10 47 22	2♉10 39	8♉13 22	29 14.7	22 57.2	9R49.8	2 56.4	1 47.0	14 19.1	9 46.8	18 6.0	11 7.3
5 Su	2 53 45	11 47 30	14 18 29	20 26 8	29 8.6	24 17.8	9 50.2	3 38.6	1 60.0	14 25.9	9 46.0	18 6.5	11 6.7
6 M	2 57 42	12 47 39	26 36 28	2♊49 33	29 0.9	25 41.5	9 48.1	4 20.8	2 13.0	14 32.7	9 45.3	18 7.1	11 6.2
7 Tu	3 1 38	13 47 51	9♊ 5 27	15 24 17	28 52.5	27 7.6	9 43.6	5 3.0	2 25.9	14 39.5	9 44.6	18 7.6	11 5.6
8 W	3 5 35	14 48 4	21 46 4	28 10 55	28 44.1	28 35.7	9 36.7	5 45.4	2 38.9	14 46.3	9 44.0	18 8.0	11 5.0
9 Th	3 9 32	15 48 19	4♋38 53	11♋10 4	28 36.7	0♏ 5.6	9 27.3	6 27.8	2 51.8	14 53.0	9 43.5	18 8.5	11 4.4
10 F	3 13 28	16 48 36	17 44 35	24 22 34	28 31.0	1 36.8	9 15.5	7 10.3	3 4.8	14 59.6	9 42.9	18 8.9	11 3.8
11 Sa	3 17 25	17 48 56	1♌ 4 8	7♌49 25	28 27.5	3 9.1	9 1.2	7 52.9	3 17.7	15 6.3	9 42.5	18 9.3	11 3.1
12 Su	3 21 21	18 49 17	14 38 35	21 31 43	28D26.0	4 42.3	8 44.6	8 35.6	3 30.5	15 12.8	9 42.1	18 9.6	11 2.5
13 M	3 25 18	19 49 40	28 28 56	5♍30 15	28 26.2	6 16.2	8 25.7	9 18.3	3 43.4	15 19.4	9 41.7	18 9.9	11 1.8
14 Tu	3 29 14	20 50 5	12♍35 38	19 44 59	28 27.2	7 50.7	8 4.5	10 1.1	3 56.2	15 25.9	9 41.4	18 10.2	11 1.0
15 W	3 33 11	21 50 32	26 58 3	4♎14 31	28R27.9	9 25.5	7 41.2	10 44.0	4 9.0	15 32.3	9 41.1	18 10.4	11 0.3
16 Th	3 37 7	22 51 1	11♎33 53	18 55 33	28 27.2	11 0.7	7 15.8	11 26.9	4 21.8	15 38.7	9 40.9	18 10.6	10 59.6
17 F	3 41 4	23 51 31	26 18 47	3♏42 44	28 24.2	12 36.0	6 48.4	12 9.9	4 34.5	15 45.1	9 40.7	18 10.7	10 58.8
18 Sa	3 45 1	24 52 4	11♏ 6 27	18 28 57	28 18.7	14 11.4	6 19.3	12 53.0	4 47.2	15 51.4	9 40.6	18 10.9	10 58.0
19 Su	3 48 57	25 52 38	25 49 12	3♐ 6 13	28 10.8	15 46.9	5 48.6	13 36.1	4 59.9	15 57.7	9D40.5	18 11.0	10 57.2
20 M	3 52 54	26 53 14	10♐19 6	17 27 1	28 1.3	17 22.4	5 16.3	14 19.3	5 12.6	16 3.9	9 40.5	18 11.0	10 56.4
21 Tu	3 56 50	27 53 51	24 29 19	1♑25 29	27 51.1	18 57.9	4 42.8	15 2.5	5 25.2	16 10.0	9 40.5	18R11.1	10 55.5
22 W	4 0 47	28 54 29	8♑15 9	14 58 12	27 41.5	20 33.3	4 8.3	15 45.8	5 37.8	16 16.1	9 40.6	18 11.1	10 54.7
23 Th	4 4 43	29 55 9	21 34 35	28 4 29	27 33.5	22 8.6	3 32.9	16 29.2	5 50.3	16 22.2	9 40.8	18 11.0	10 53.8
24 F	4 8 40	0♐55 49	4♒28 10	10♒46 2	27 27.7	23 43.8	2 56.9	17 12.6	6 2.8	16 28.1	9 41.0	18 10.9	10 52.9
25 Sa	4 12 36	1 56 31	16 58 37	23 6 27	27 24.3	25 18.9	2 20.6	17 56.0	6 15.2	16 34.1	9 41.2	18 10.8	10 52.0
26 Su	4 16 33	2 57 14	29 10 11	5♓10 29	27D23.1	26 53.9	1 44.2	18 39.5	6 27.7	16 39.9	9 41.5	18 10.7	10 51.1
27 M	4 20 30	3 57 58	11♓ 8 2	17 3 32	27 23.2	28 28.8	1 7.9	19 23.1	6 40.0	16 45.7	9 41.9	18 10.5	10 50.1
28 Tu	4 24 26	4 58 43	22 57 40	28 51 8	27R23.7	0♐ 3.6	0 32.0	20 6.6	6 52.3	16 51.5	9 42.3	18 10.3	10 49.1
29 W	4 28 23	5 59 29	4♈44 34	10♈38 37	27 23.5	1 38.3	29♏56.8	20 50.3	7 4.6	16 57.2	9 42.7	18 10.0	10 48.2
30 Th	4 32 19	7 0 16	16 33 51	22 30 48	27 21.6	3 12.8	29 22.4	21 33.9	7 16.8	17 2.8	9 43.2	18 9.7	10 47.2

DECEMBER 1922 LONGITUDE

Day	Sid.Time	☉	0 hr ☽	Noon ☽	True ☊	☿	♀	♂	♃	♄	♅	♆	♇
1 F	4 36 16	8♐ 1 4	28♈29 57	4♉31 43	27♍17.3	4♐47.3	28♏49.2	22♒17.6	7♏29.0	17♎ 8.3	9♓43.7	18♌ 9.4	10♋46.2
2 Sa	4 40 12	9 1 53	10♉36 27	16 44 27	27R10.2	6 21.7	28R17.4	23 1.3	7 41.1	17 13.8	9 44.4	18R 9.1	10R45.2
3 Su	4 44 9	10 2 43	22 55 54	29 10 57	27 0.3	7 56.0	27 47.0	23 45.0	7 53.2	17 19.3	9 45.0	18 8.7	10 44.1
4 M	4 48 5	11 3 34	5♊29 40	11♊52 2	26 48.3	9 30.3	27 18.4	24 28.8	8 5.2	17 24.6	9 45.7	18 8.3	10 43.1
5 Tu	4 52 2	12 4 26	18 18 0	24 47 25	26 35.1	11 4.5	26 51.7	25 12.6	8 17.1	17 29.9	9 46.5	18 7.8	10 42.0
6 W	4 55 59	13 5 20	1♋20 9	7♋56 1	26 22.0	12 38.8	26 27.0	25 56.4	8 29.0	17 35.1	9 47.3	18 7.4	10 41.0
7 Th	4 59 55	14 6 14	14 34 47	21 16 17	26 10.1	14 13.0	26 4.5	26 40.3	8 40.9	17 40.3	9 48.1	18 6.8	10 39.9
8 F	5 3 52	15 7 10	28 0 17	4♌46 39	26 0.4	15 47.2	25 44.3	27 24.2	8 52.7	17 45.4	9 49.0	18 6.3	10 38.8
9 Sa	5 7 48	16 8 6	11♌35 14	18 25 56	25 53.7	17 21.5	25 26.4	28 8.0	9 4.4	17 50.4	9 50.0	18 5.7	10 37.7
10 Su	5 11 45	17 9 4	25 18 40	2♍13 24	25 49.9	18 55.8	25 10.9	28 52.0	9 16.0	17 55.3	9 51.0	18 5.1	10 36.6
11 M	5 15 41	18 10 3	9♍10 8	16 8 51	25D48.4	20 30.1	24 57.9	29 35.9	9 27.6	18 0.1	9 52.1	18 4.5	10 35.5
12 Tu	5 19 38	19 11 3	23 9 33	0♎12 12	25R48.3	22 4.6	24 47.4	0♓19.9	9 39.2	18 4.9	9 53.2	18 3.8	10 34.3
13 W	5 23 34	20 12 4	7♎16 45	14 23 3	25 48.0	23 39.1	24 39.4	1 3.8	9 50.6	18 9.6	9 54.3	18 3.1	10 33.2
14 Th	5 27 31	21 13 7	21 30 55	28 40 4	25 46.4	25 13.7	24 34.0	1 47.8	10 2.0	18 14.2	9 55.5	18 2.4	10 32.0
15 F	5 31 28	22 14 10	5♏50 8	13♏ 0 38	25 42.2	26 48.4	24D31.0	2 31.8	10 13.3	18 18.8	9 56.8	18 1.6	10 30.9
16 Sa	5 35 24	23 15 14	20 11 1	27 20 38	25 34.9	28 23.2	24 30.4	3 15.9	10 24.6	18 23.3	9 58.1	18 0.8	10 29.7
17 Su	5 39 21	24 16 20	4♐28 47	11♐34 46	25 24.8	29 58.2	24 32.3	3 59.9	10 35.7	18 27.6	9 59.4	17 60.0	10 28.5
18 M	5 43 17	25 17 26	18 37 52	25 37 23	25 12.5	1♑33.3	24 36.6	4 44.0	10 46.8	18 31.9	10 0.8	17 59.1	10 27.3
19 Tu	5 47 14	26 18 32	2♑32 41	9♑23 15	24 59.4	3 8.5	24 43.3	5 28.1	10 57.8	18 36.1	10 2.3	17 58.2	10 26.1
20 W	5 51 10	27 19 40	16 8 40	22 48 38	24 46.6	4 43.9	24 52.2	6 12.2	11 8.8	18 40.3	10 3.8	17 57.3	10 24.9
21 Th	5 55 7	28 20 47	29 23 0	5♒51 43	24 35.5	6 19.4	25 3.4	6 56.3	11 19.6	18 44.3	10 5.3	17 56.4	10 23.7
22 F	5 59 4	29 21 55	12♒14 54	18 32 48	24 27.0	7 55.0	25 16.7	7 40.4	11 30.4	18 48.3	10 6.9	17 55.4	10 22.5
23 Sa	6 3 0	0♑23 3	24 45 43	0♓54 7	24 21.3	9 30.7	25 32.2	8 24.5	11 41.1	18 52.1	10 8.5	17 54.4	10 21.3
24 Su	6 6 57	1 24 12	6♓58 30	12 59 26	24 18.3	11 6.5	25 49.7	9 8.6	11 51.6	18 55.9	10 10.2	17 53.4	10 20.1
25 M	6 10 53	2 25 20	18 57 34	24 53 32	24D17.3	12 42.3	26 9.2	9 52.7	12 2.1	18 59.6	10 11.9	17 52.3	10 18.8
26 Tu	6 14 50	3 26 28	0♈48 4	6♈41 52	24R17.3	14 18.2	26 30.6	10 36.9	12 12.6	19 3.2	10 13.7	17 51.3	10 17.6
27 W	6 18 46	4 27 37	12 35 37	18 30 2	24 17.1	15 54.0	26 53.9	11 21.0	12 22.9	19 6.7	10 15.5	17 50.2	10 16.4
28 Th	6 22 43	5 28 45	24 25 48	0♉23 33	24 15.5	17 29.8	27 19.0	12 5.1	12 33.1	19 10.1	10 17.4	17 49.0	10 15.1
29 F	6 26 39	6 29 54	6♉23 56	12 27 28	24 11.9	19 5.4	27 45.8	12 49.2	12 43.2	19 13.4	10 19.3	17 47.9	10 13.9
30 Sa	6 30 36	7 31 2	18 34 40	24 45 57	24 5.5	20 40.8	28 14.3	13 33.4	12 53.2	19 16.7	10 21.2	17 46.7	10 12.7
31 Su	6 34 32	8 32 11	1♊ 1 40	7♊22 4	23 56.4	22 15.9	28 44.5	14 17.5	13 3.2	19 19.8	10 23.2	17 45.5	10 11.4

Astro Data Dy Hr Mn	Planet Ingress Dy Hr Mn	Last Aspect Dy Hr Mn	☽ Ingress Dy Hr Mn	Last Aspect Dy Hr Mn	☽ Ingress Dy Hr Mn	☽ Phases & Eclipses Dy Hr Mn	Astro Data
☽0N 1 7:25	☿ ♏ 8 22:32	30 16:41 ♇ △	♈ 1 7:04	30 10:45 ♂ ⚹	♉ 1 3:00	4 18:36 ○ 11♉34	1 NOVEMBER 1922
♀ R 4 15:21	☉ ♐ 23 1:55	3 3:19 ☿ ☍	♉ 3 19:40	3 8:59 ♀ ☍	♊ 3 13:34	12 7:52 ☽ 19♌09	Julian Day # 8340
☽0S 15 5:40	☿ ♐ 27 23:05	5 7:28 ♆ □	♊ 6 6:33	5 13:32 ♂ △	♋ 5 21:34	19 0:06 ● 25♏53	Delta T 22.9 sec
♅ D 19 18:06	♀ ♏ 28 21:47	8 14:27 ☿ △	♋ 8 15:23	7 20:04 ♀ △	♌ 8 3:33	26 8:15 ☽ 3♓18	SVP 06♓20'16"
♆ R 21 6:47		9 22:10 ☉ △	♌ 10 22:05	10 6:31 ♂ ☍	♍ 10 8:09		Obliquity 23°26'48"
☽0N 28 15:42	♂ ♓ 11 13:10	12 7:52 ☉ □	♍ 13 2:36	12 2:45 ♀ ⚹	♎ 12 11:39	4 11:23 ○ 11♊32	⚷ Chiron 14♈12.2R
	☿ ♑ 17 0:27	14 14:51 ☉ ⚹	♎ 15 5:01	14 7:00 ☿ ⚹	♏ 14 14:14	11 16:40 ☽ 18♍52	☽ Mean ☊ 27♍34.4
♄⚹♆ 11 19:03	☉ ♑ 22 14:57	16 10:47 ♆ ⚹	♏ 17 5:59	16 7:15 ♀ ☌	♐ 16 16:28	18 12:20 ● 25♐49	
☽0S 12 13:28		19 0:06 ☉ ☌	♐ 19 6:52	18 12:20 ☉ ☌	♑ 18 19:34	26 5:53 ☽ 3♈41	1 DECEMBER 1922
♃△♅ 13 8:42		20 13:15 ♆ △	♑ 21 9:31	20 15:58 ♀ ⚹	♒ 21 1:08		Julian Day # 8370
♀ D 15 17:08		23 1:11 ☿ ⚹	♒ 23 15:36	23 1:32 ♀ □	♓ 23 10:14		Delta T 23.0 sec
♃△♇ 16 9:57		25 18:49 ☿ □	♓ 26 1:39	25 15:00 ♀ △	♈ 25 22:22		SVP 06♓20'13"
☽0N 26 1:20		26 23:24 ♇ △	♈ 28 14:20	27 13:18 ♄ ☍	♉ 28 11:13		Obliquity 23°26'48"
♅△♇ 27 6:43				30 19:27 ♀ ☍	♊ 30 22:02		⚷ Chiron 13♈14.2R
							☽ Mean ☊ 25♍59.1

LONGITUDE JANUARY 1923

Day	Sid.Time	☉	0 hr ☽	Noon ☽	True ☊	☿	♀	♂	♃	♄	♅	♆	♇
1 M	6 38 29	9♑33 19	13♊47 17	20♊17 22	23♍45.2	23♑50.5	29♏16.2	15♓ 1.6	13♏13.0	19♎22.8	10♓25.2	17♌44.3	10♋10.2
2 Tu	6 42 26	10 34 28	26 52 15	3♋31 46	23R32.6	25 24.6	29 49.4	15 45.7	13 22.7	19 25.8	10 27.3	17R43.0	10R 8.9
3 W	6 46 22	11 35 36	10♋15 39	17 3 34	23 20.0	26 57.9	0♐24.1	16 29.8	13 32.4	19 28.6	10 29.4	17 41.7	10 7.7
4 Th	6 50 19	12 36 45	23 55 4	0♌49 43	23 8.5	28 30.2	1 0.1	17 13.9	13 41.9	19 31.4	10 31.6	17 40.4	10 6.5
5 F	6 54 15	13 37 53	7♌47 1	14 46 27	22 59.2	0♒ 1.3	1 37.5	17 57.9	13 51.3	19 34.0	10 33.8	17 39.1	10 5.2
6 Sa	6 58 12	14 39 1	21 47 34	28 49 54	22 52.7	1 30.9	2 16.2	18 42.0	14 0.6	19 36.6	10 36.0	17 37.8	10 4.0
7 Su	7 2 8	15 40 10	5♍53 4	12♍56 42	22 49.1	2 58.7	2 56.2	19 26.0	14 9.8	19 39.0	10 38.3	17 36.4	10 2.7
8 M	7 6 5	16 41 18	20 0 32	27 4 20	22D48.0	4 24.3	3 37.3	20 10.1	14 18.9	19 41.4	10 40.6	17 35.0	10 1.5
9 Tu	7 10 2	17 42 27	4♎ 7 56	11♎11 12	22 48.2	5 47.3	4 19.6	20 54.1	14 27.9	19 43.6	10 42.9	17 33.6	10 0.3
10 W	7 13 58	18 43 35	18 14 1	25 16 17	22R48.6	7 7.2	5 3.0	21 38.1	14 36.7	19 45.8	10 45.3	17 32.2	9 59.1
11 Th	7 17 55	19 44 44	2♏17 55	9♏18 48	22 47.9	8 23.3	5 47.4	22 22.1	14 45.5	19 47.8	10 47.7	17 30.8	9 57.8
12 F	7 21 51	20 45 53	16 18 46	23 17 39	22 45.2	9 35.2	6 32.8	23 6.1	14 54.1	19 49.7	10 50.2	17 29.3	9 56.6
13 Sa	7 25 48	21 47 2	0♐15 13	7♐11 12	22 39.8	10 42.0	7 19.3	23 50.1	15 2.6	19 51.6	10 52.7	17 27.9	9 55.4
14 Su	7 29 44	22 48 10	14 5 17	20 57 8	22 32.0	11 43.0	8 6.6	24 34.1	15 11.0	19 53.3	10 55.2	17 26.4	9 54.2
15 M	7 33 41	23 49 19	27 46 24	4♑32 43	22 22.3	12 37.4	8 54.9	25 18.1	15 19.2	19 54.9	10 57.8	17 24.9	9 53.0
16 Tu	7 37 37	24 50 27	11♑15 43	17 55 7	22 11.7	13 24.3	9 43.9	26 2.0	15 27.4	19 56.5	11 0.4	17 23.4	9 51.8
17 W	7 41 34	25 51 34	24 30 37	1♒ 2 1	22 1.3	14 2.8	10 33.9	26 45.9	15 35.4	19 57.9	11 3.0	17 21.8	9 50.6
18 Th	7 45 31	26 52 42	7♒29 9	13 52 0	21 52.3	14 32.0	11 24.6	27 29.9	15 43.2	19 59.2	11 5.7	17 20.3	9 49.4
19 F	7 49 27	27 53 48	20 10 33	26 24 55	21 45.3	14 51.2	12 16.0	28 13.8	15 51.0	20 0.4	11 8.4	17 18.7	9 48.2
20 Sa	7 53 24	28 54 54	2♓35 18	8♓41 58	21 40.8	14R59.6	13 8.2	28 57.6	15 58.6	20 1.5	11 11.1	17 17.2	9 47.1
21 Su	7 57 20	29 55 59	14 45 16	20 45 38	21D38.8	14 56.7	14 1.0	29 41.5	16 6.0	20 2.5	11 13.9	17 15.6	9 45.9
22 M	8 1 17	0♒57 3	26 43 32	2♈39 30	21 38.6	14 42.3	14 54.5	0♈25.4	16 13.3	20 3.4	11 16.7	17 14.0	9 44.7
23 Tu	8 5 13	1 58 6	8♈34 7	14 28 0	21 39.7	14 16.2	15 48.7	1 9.2	16 20.5	20 4.2	11 19.5	17 12.4	9 43.6
24 W	8 9 10	2 59 8	20 21 48	26 16 11	21 41.0	13 39.0	16 43.5	1 53.0	16 27.5	20 4.8	11 22.3	17 10.7	9 42.5
25 Th	8 13 6	4 0 9	2♉11 48	8♉ 9 21	21R41.8	12 51.3	17 38.9	2 36.8	16 34.4	20 5.4	11 25.2	17 9.1	9 41.3
26 F	8 17 3	5 1 9	14 9 28	20 12 49	21 41.3	11 54.5	18 34.8	3 20.5	16 41.2	20 5.8	11 28.1	17 7.5	9 40.2
27 Sa	8 21 0	6 2 8	26 20 0	2♊31 33	21 38.9	10 50.0	19 31.3	4 4.2	16 47.8	20 6.2	11 31.1	17 5.8	9 39.1
28 Su	8 24 56	7 3 6	8♊48 0	15 9 44	21 34.6	9 39.8	20 28.3	4 48.0	16 54.3	20 6.4	11 34.0	17 4.2	9 38.0
29 M	8 28 53	8 4 2	21 37 6	28 10 18	21 28.7	8 26.1	21 25.9	5 31.6	17 0.6	20R 6.6	11 37.0	17 2.5	9 37.0
30 Tu	8 32 49	9 4 58	4♋49 26	11♋34 29	21 21.6	7 10.9	22 23.9	6 15.3	17 6.7	20 6.6	11 40.0	17 0.9	9 35.9
31 W	8 36 46	10 5 52	18 25 16	25 21 30	21 14.3	5 56.6	23 22.4	6 58.9	17 12.8	20 6.5	11 43.0	16 59.2	9 34.8

LONGITUDE FEBRUARY 1923

Day	Sid.Time	☉	0 hr ☽	Noon ☽	True ☊	☿	♀	♂	♃	♄	♅	♆	♇
1 Th	8 40 42	11♒ 6 45	2♌22 44	9♌28 26	21♍ 7.5	4♒45.2	24♐21.4	7♈42.5	17♏18.6	20♎ 6.3	11♓46.1	16♌57.5	9♋33.8
2 F	8 44 39	12 7 37	16 37 58	23 50 35	21R 2.2	3R38.3	25 20.9	8 26.1	17 24.3	20R 6.1	11 49.2	16R55.8	9R32.8
3 Sa	8 48 35	13 8 28	1♍ 5 31	8♍22 0	20 58.7	2 37.4	26 20.7	9 9.6	17 29.9	20 5.7	11 52.3	16 54.2	9 31.8
4 Su	8 52 32	14 9 18	15 39 16	22 56 33	20D57.2	1 43.7	27 21.0	9 53.1	17 35.2	20 5.2	11 55.4	16 52.5	9 30.8
5 M	8 56 29	15 10 7	0♎13 11	7♎28 34	20 57.4	0 57.7	28 21.7	10 36.6	17 40.5	20 4.5	11 58.6	16 50.8	9 29.8
6 Tu	9 0 25	16 10 55	14 42 11	21 53 35	20 58.6	0 20.0	29 22.7	11 20.0	17 45.5	20 3.8	12 1.7	16 49.1	9 28.8
7 W	9 4 22	17 11 42	29 2 27	6♏ 8 30	21 0.1	29♑50.7	0♑24.2	12 3.4	17 50.4	20 3.0	12 4.9	16 47.4	9 27.8
8 Th	9 8 18	18 12 28	13♏11 33	20 11 27	21R 1.1	29 29.7	1 26.0	12 46.8	17 55.2	20 2.1	12 8.1	16 45.7	9 26.9
9 F	9 12 15	19 13 14	27 8 9	4♐ 1 34	21 0.9	29 16.9	2 28.2	13 30.2	17 59.7	20 1.1	12 11.3	16 44.0	9 26.0
10 Sa	9 16 11	20 13 58	10♐51 41	17 38 30	20 59.3	29D11.8	3 30.6	14 13.5	18 4.2	19 59.9	12 14.6	16 42.4	9 25.1
11 Su	9 20 8	21 14 41	24 22 0	1♑ 2 12	20 56.3	29 14.1	4 33.4	14 56.8	18 8.4	19 58.7	12 17.8	16 40.7	9 24.2
12 M	9 24 4	22 15 23	7♑39 6	14 12 42	20 52.2	29 23.3	5 36.6	15 40.1	18 12.5	19 57.4	12 21.1	16 39.0	9 23.3
13 Tu	9 28 1	23 16 4	20 42 59	27 9 58	20 47.5	29 38.9	6 40.0	16 23.3	18 16.3	19 55.9	12 24.4	16 37.3	9 22.5
14 W	9 31 58	24 16 44	3♒33 40	9♒54 5	20 42.9	0♒ 0.6	7 43.7	17 6.6	18 20.1	19 54.4	12 27.7	16 35.7	9 21.6
15 Th	9 35 54	25 17 22	16 11 17	22 25 18	20 38.9	0 27.8	8 47.6	17 49.7	18 23.6	19 52.7	12 31.0	16 34.0	9 20.8
16 F	9 39 51	26 17 59	28 36 15	4♓44 15	20 36.0	1 0.2	9 51.9	18 32.9	18 27.0	19 51.0	12 34.3	16 32.3	9 20.0
17 Sa	9 43 47	27 18 34	10♓49 28	16 52 5	20D34.4	1 37.2	10 56.3	19 16.0	18 30.2	19 49.2	12 37.7	16 30.7	9 19.2
18 Su	9 47 44	28 19 8	22 52 21	28 50 35	20 34.0	2 18.5	12 1.1	19 59.1	18 33.2	19 47.2	12 41.0	16 29.0	9 18.4
19 M	9 51 40	29 19 40	4♈47 6	10♈42 16	20 34.7	3 3.9	13 6.0	20 42.2	18 36.0	19 45.2	12 44.4	16 27.4	9 17.7
20 Tu	9 55 37	0♓20 11	16 36 31	22 30 18	20 36.1	3 52.9	14 11.2	21 25.2	18 38.6	19 43.0	12 47.8	16 25.7	9 17.0
21 W	9 59 33	1 20 39	28 24 7	4♉18 30	20 37.8	4 45.3	15 16.6	22 8.2	18 41.1	19 40.8	12 51.1	16 24.1	9 16.2
22 Th	10 3 30	2 21 6	10♉14 0	16 11 13	20 39.3	5 40.9	16 22.2	22 51.2	18 43.4	19 38.5	12 54.5	16 22.5	9 15.6
23 F	10 7 26	3 21 31	22 10 44	28 13 8	20 40.4	6 39.4	17 28.0	23 34.1	18 45.5	19 36.1	12 57.9	16 20.9	9 14.9
24 Sa	10 11 23	4 21 54	4♊19 3	10♊29 4	20R40.8	7 40.5	18 34.1	24 17.0	18 47.4	19 33.6	13 1.3	16 19.3	9 14.2
25 Su	10 15 20	5 22 15	16 43 45	23 3 37	20 40.4	8 44.1	19 40.3	24 59.8	18 49.1	19 31.0	13 4.8	16 17.7	9 13.6
26 M	10 19 16	6 22 34	29 29 8	6♋ 0 44	20 39.4	9 50.1	20 46.7	25 42.7	18 50.7	19 28.3	13 8.2	16 16.1	9 13.0
27 Tu	10 23 13	7 22 51	12♋38 41	19 23 13	20 37.9	10 58.3	21 53.3	26 25.4	18 52.0	19 25.6	13 11.6	16 14.6	9 12.4
28 W	10 27 9	8 23 6	26 14 23	3♌12 8	20 36.2	12 8.5	23 0.0	27 8.2	18 53.2	19 22.7	13 15.0	16 13.1	9 11.9

Astro Data	Planet Ingress	Last Aspect	☽ Ingress	Last Aspect	☽ Ingress	☽ Phases & Eclipses	Astro Data
Dy Hr Mn	Dy Hr Mn	Dy Hr Mn	Dy Hr Mn	Dy Hr Mn	Dy Hr Mn	Dy Hr Mn	1 JANUARY 1923
☽0S 8 20:07	♀ ♐ 2 7:27	1 10:22 ♄ △	♋ 2 5:39	2 15:34 ♀ △	♍ 2 22:12	3 2:33 ○ 11♋42	Julian Day # 8401
☿ R 20 5:59	☿ ♒ 4 23:40	4 8:57 ☿ ☍	♌ 4 10:34	4 20:42 ♀ □	♎ 4 23:38	10 0:54 ☽ 18♎46	Delta T 23.0 sec
☽0N 22 11:02	☉ ♒ 21 1:35	5 20:16 ♄ ⚹	♍ 6 13:59	7 1:19 ☿ □	♏ 7 1:37	17 2:41 ● 25♑58	SVP 06♓20'07"
♂0N 22 12:02	♂ ♈ 21 10:07	8 0:17 ♂ ☍	♎ 8 16:59	9 3:41 ☿ ⚹	♐ 9 4:59	25 3:59 ☽ 4♉10	Obliquity 23°26'48"
♃□♆ 29 5:56		10 2:37 ♄ ☌	♏ 10 20:04	10 17:58 ☉ ⚹	♑ 11 10:08		⚷ Chiron 12♈59.4
♄ R 29 18:45	☿ ♑ 6 15:36	12 12:19 ♂ △	♐ 12 23:34	13 17:07 ☿ ☌	♒ 13 17:18	1 15:53 ○ 11♌47	☽ Mean ☊ 24♍20.6
	♀ ♑ 6 14:34	14 19:24 ♂ □	♑ 15 3:56	15 19:07 ☉ ☌	♓ 16 2:43	8 9:16 ☽ 18♏36	
☽0S 5 3:35	☿ ♒ 13 23:24	17 4:23 ♂ ⚹	♒ 17 10:05	17 15:19 ♃ △	♈ 18 14:20	15 19:07 ● 26♒06	1 FEBRUARY 1923
☿ D 10 4:20	☉ ♓ 19 16:00	18 23:41 ♄ △	♓ 19 18:57	20 10:26 ♂ ☌	♉ 21 3:15	24 0:06 ☽ 4♊22	Julian Day # 8432
☽0N 18 19:25		21 2:43 ♃ △	♈ 22 6:37	22 17:08 ♃ ☍	♊ 23 15:31		Delta T 23.1 sec
		23 23:25 ♄ ☍	♉ 24 19:34	25 16:33 ♂ ⚹	♋ 26 0:57		SVP 06♓20'02"
		26 5:53 ♆ □	♊ 27 7:07	28 1:38 ♂ □	♌ 28 6:30		Obliquity 23°26'48"
		28 23:38 ♀ ☍	♋ 29 15:19				⚷ Chiron 13♈36.8
		31 2:56 ♄ □	♌ 31 19:57				☽ Mean ☊ 22♍42.1

MARCH 1923 — LONGITUDE

Day	Sid.Time	☉	0 hr ☽	Noon ☽	True ☊	☿	♀	♂	♃	♄	♅	♆	♇
1 Th	10 31 6	9♓23 20	10♌16 13	17♌26 17	20♍34.7	13♒20.7	24♑ 7.0	27♈50.9	18♏54.2	19♎19.8	13♓18.5	16♌11.5	9♋11.3
2 F	10 35 2	10 23 31	24 41 46	2♍ 1 59	20R33.5	14 34.7	25 14.1	28 33.6	18 55.0	19R16.8	13 21.9	16R10.0	9R10.8
3 Sa	10 38 59	11 23 40	9♍26 7	16 53 14	20D32.9	15 50.4	26 21.3	29 16.2	18 55.6	19 13.7	13 25.3	16 8.5	9 10.3
4 Su	10 42 55	12 23 48	24 22 18	1♎52 16	20 32.8	17 7.8	27 28.8	29 58.8	18 56.0	19 10.5	13 28.8	16 7.0	9 9.8
5 M	10 46 52	13 23 53	9♎22 5	16 50 44	20 33.0	18 26.8	28 36.3	0♉41.3	18R56.3	19 7.3	13 32.2	16 5.6	9 9.4
6 Tu	10 50 49	14 23 57	24 17 14	1♏40 46	20 33.5	19 47.4	29 44.1	1 23.8	18 56.3	19 3.9	13 35.6	16 4.1	9 8.9
7 W	10 54 45	15 23 59	9♏ 0 34	16 16 2	20 34.1	21 9.4	0♒52.0	2 6.3	18 56.2	19 0.5	13 39.1	16 2.7	9 8.5
8 Th	10 58 42	16 24 0	23 26 43	0♐32 16	20 34.5	22 32.8	1 60.0	2 48.7	18 55.9	18 57.1	13 42.5	16 1.3	9 8.1
9 F	11 2 38	17 24 0	7♐32 31	14 27 21	20R34.7	23 57.6	3 8.2	3 31.2	18 55.4	18 53.5	13 46.0	15 59.9	9 7.8
10 Sa	11 6 35	18 23 57	21 16 49	28 1 1	20 34.8	25 23.8	4 16.5	4 13.5	18 54.7	18 49.9	13 49.4	15 58.5	9 7.4
11 Su	11 10 31	19 23 53	4♑40 7	11♑14 21	20 34.7	26 51.3	5 24.9	4 55.9	18 53.8	18 46.2	13 52.8	15 57.1	9 7.1
12 M	11 14 28	20 23 48	17 43 59	24 9 18	20D34.7	28 20.1	6 33.4	5 38.2	18 52.7	18 42.5	13 56.2	15 55.8	9 6.8
13 Tu	11 18 24	21 23 40	0♒30 36	6♒48 11	20 34.7	29 50.1	7 42.1	6 20.4	18 51.5	18 38.7	13 59.7	15 54.5	9 6.5
14 W	11 22 21	22 23 31	13 2 22	19 13 25	20 34.9	1♓21.5	8 50.9	7 2.6	18 50.0	18 34.8	14 3.1	15 53.2	9 6.3
15 Th	11 26 18	23 23 20	25 21 39	1♓27 19	20 35.1	2 54.1	9 59.8	7 44.8	18 48.4	18 30.9	14 6.5	15 51.9	9 6.0
16 F	11 30 14	24 23 8	7♓30 42	13 32 1	20 35.4	4 27.9	11 8.8	8 27.0	18 46.5	18 26.9	14 9.9	15 50.6	9 5.8
17 Sa	11 34 11	25 22 53	19 31 33	25 29 32	20R35.5	6 3.0	12 17.9	9 9.1	18 44.5	18 22.9	14 13.3	15 49.4	9 5.7
18 Su	11 38 7	26 22 36	1♈26 12	7♈21 49	20 35.4	7 39.3	13 27.1	9 51.2	18 42.3	18 18.8	14 16.7	15 48.2	9 5.5
19 M	11 42 4	27 22 18	13 16 38	19 10 55	20 34.9	9 16.9	14 36.4	10 33.3	18 40.0	18 14.6	14 20.1	15 47.0	9 5.4
20 Tu	11 46 0	28 21 57	25 4 58	0♉59 7	20 34.0	10 55.7	15 45.8	11 15.3	18 37.4	18 10.4	14 23.4	15 45.9	9 5.2
21 W	11 49 57	29 21 34	6♉53 40	12 49 1	20 32.8	12 35.8	16 55.2	11 57.2	18 34.7	18 6.2	14 26.8	15 44.7	9 5.2
22 Th	11 53 53	0♈21 9	18 45 32	24 43 39	20 31.4	14 17.1	18 4.8	12 39.2	18 31.7	18 1.9	14 30.1	15 43.6	9 5.1
23 F	11 57 50	1 20 42	0♊43 48	6♊46 27	20 30.1	15 59.7	19 14.4	13 21.1	18 28.6	17 57.6	14 33.5	15 42.5	9 5.1
24 Sa	12 1 46	2 20 12	12 52 6	19 1 15	20 28.9	17 43.6	20 24.2	14 2.9	18 25.4	17 53.2	14 36.8	15 41.5	9D 5.0
25 Su	12 5 43	3 19 41	25 14 25	1♋32 6	20D28.2	19 28.8	21 34.0	14 44.8	18 21.9	17 48.9	14 40.1	15 40.4	9 5.1
26 M	12 9 40	4 19 7	7♋54 49	14 23 1	20 28.1	21 15.3	22 43.8	15 26.5	18 18.3	17 44.4	14 43.4	15 39.4	9 5.1
27 Tu	12 13 36	5 18 30	20 57 8	27 37 32	20 28.6	23 3.1	23 53.8	16 8.3	18 14.5	17 40.0	14 46.7	15 38.5	9 5.1
28 W	12 17 33	6 17 52	4♌24 30	11♌18 13	20 29.6	24 52.2	25 3.8	16 50.0	18 10.6	17 35.5	14 49.9	15 37.5	9 5.2
29 Th	12 21 29	7 17 10	18 18 43	25 25 57	20 30.8	26 42.7	26 13.9	17 31.6	18 6.5	17 31.0	14 53.2	15 36.6	9 5.3
30 F	12 25 26	8 16 27	2♍39 37	9♍59 18	20 32.0	28 34.5	27 24.1	18 13.3	18 2.2	17 26.4	14 56.4	15 35.7	9 5.5
31 Sa	12 29 22	9 15 41	17 24 23	24 54 3	20R32.5	0♈27.7	28 34.3	18 54.8	17 57.8	17 21.9	14 59.6	15 34.8	9 5.6

APRIL 1923 — LONGITUDE

Day	Sid.Time	☉	0 hr ☽	Noon ☽	True ☊	☿	♀	♂	♃	♄	♅	♆	♇
1 Su	12 33 19	10♈14 54	2♎27 22	10♎ 3 12	20♍32.2	2♈22.2	29♒44.6	19♉36.4	17♏53.2	17♎17.3	15♓ 2.8	15♌34.0	9♋ 5.8
2 M	12 37 15	11 14 4	17 40 21	25 17 33	20R30.9	4 18.1	0♓54.9	20 17.9	17R48.4	17R12.7	15 6.0	15R33.2	9 6.0
3 Tu	12 41 12	12 13 12	2♏53 32	10♏27 4	20 28.6	6 15.2	2 5.4	20 59.3	17 43.5	17 8.1	15 9.1	15 32.4	9 6.2
4 W	12 45 9	13 12 18	17 57 0	25 22 21	20 25.7	8 13.7	3 15.9	21 40.8	17 38.5	17 3.5	15 12.3	15 31.6	9 6.4
5 Th	12 49 5	14 11 22	2♐42 17	9♐56 7	20 22.6	10 13.4	4 26.4	22 22.2	17 33.3	16 58.9	15 15.4	15 30.9	9 6.7
6 F	12 53 2	15 10 25	17 3 26	24 3 57	20 19.8	12 14.3	5 37.1	23 3.5	17 28.0	16 54.2	15 18.5	15 30.2	9 7.0
7 Sa	12 56 58	16 9 26	0♑57 35	7♑44 22	20 17.8	14 16.4	6 47.7	23 44.8	17 22.5	16 49.6	15 21.6	15 29.6	9 7.3
8 Su	13 0 55	17 8 25	14 24 33	20 58 23	20D17.0	16 19.5	7 58.5	24 26.1	17 16.9	16 45.0	15 24.6	15 28.9	9 7.7
9 M	13 4 51	18 7 23	27 26 18	3♒48 45	20 17.3	18 23.6	9 9.3	25 7.3	17 11.1	16 40.3	15 27.7	15 28.3	9 8.0
10 Tu	13 8 48	19 6 18	10♒ 6 12	16 19 12	20 18.5	20 28.4	10 20.1	25 48.5	17 5.3	16 35.7	15 30.7	15 27.8	9 8.4
11 W	13 12 44	20 5 12	22 28 14	28 33 51	20 20.2	22 33.9	11 31.0	26 29.7	16 59.3	16 31.1	15 33.7	15 27.2	9 8.8
12 Th	13 16 41	21 4 4	4♓36 32	10♓36 47	20 21.8	24 39.8	12 42.0	27 10.8	16 53.1	16 26.4	15 36.6	15 26.7	9 9.2
13 F	13 20 38	22 2 54	16 35 1	22 31 42	20R22.8	26 45.9	13 53.0	27 51.9	16 46.9	16 21.8	15 39.6	15 26.2	9 9.7
14 Sa	13 24 34	23 1 43	28 27 11	4♈21 51	20 22.5	28 52.0	15 4.0	28 33.0	16 40.5	16 17.2	15 42.5	15 25.8	9 10.2
15 Su	13 28 31	24 0 29	10♈16 1	16 9 59	20 20.6	0♉57.8	16 15.1	29 14.0	16 34.1	16 12.6	15 45.3	15 25.4	9 10.7
16 M	13 32 27	24 59 14	22 4 1	27 58 23	20 17.1	3 3.0	17 26.2	29 55.0	16 27.5	16 8.1	15 48.2	15 25.0	9 11.2
17 Tu	13 36 24	25 57 56	3♉53 19	9♉49 2	20 11.9	5 7.3	18 37.4	0♊36.0	16 20.8	16 3.5	15 51.0	15 24.7	9 11.7
18 W	13 40 20	26 56 37	15 45 47	21 43 46	20 5.5	7 10.3	19 48.6	1 16.9	16 14.1	15 59.0	15 53.8	15 24.3	9 12.3
19 Th	13 44 17	27 55 16	27 43 15	3♊44 28	19 58.5	9 11.8	20 59.8	1 57.8	16 7.2	15 54.5	15 56.6	15 24.1	9 12.9
20 F	13 48 13	28 53 52	9♊47 41	15 53 11	19 51.5	11 11.3	22 11.1	2 38.7	16 0.2	15 50.0	15 59.3	15 23.8	9 13.5
21 Sa	13 52 10	29 52 27	22 1 19	28 12 22	19 45.3	13 8.7	23 22.4	3 19.5	15 53.2	15 45.6	16 2.1	15 23.6	9 14.1
22 Su	13 56 7	0♉51 0	4♋26 45	10♋44 49	19 40.6	15 3.4	24 33.8	4 0.3	15 46.1	15 41.2	16 4.7	15 23.4	9 14.8
23 M	14 0 3	1 49 30	17 6 58	23 33 38	19 37.7	16 55.4	25 45.2	4 41.0	15 38.9	15 36.8	16 7.4	15 23.3	9 15.5
24 Tu	14 4 0	2 47 58	0♌ 5 12	6♌42 3	19D36.5	18 44.3	26 56.6	5 21.7	15 31.7	15 32.5	16 10.0	15 23.1	9 16.2
25 W	14 7 56	3 46 24	13 24 34	20 13 1	19 36.9	20 29.8	28 8.0	6 2.4	15 24.4	15 28.2	16 12.6	15 23.1	9 16.9
26 Th	14 11 53	4 44 48	27 7 39	4♍ 8 36	19 38.0	22 11.8	29 19.5	6 43.0	15 17.0	15 23.9	16 15.1	15 23.0	9 17.6
27 F	14 15 49	5 43 9	11♍15 50	18 29 15	19R39.1	23 50.0	0♈31.0	7 23.6	15 9.6	15 19.7	16 17.7	15D23.0	9 18.4
28 Sa	14 19 46	6 41 29	25 48 30	3♎13 5	19 39.2	25 24.3	1 42.5	8 4.2	15 2.1	15 15.6	16 20.1	15 23.0	9 19.1
29 Su	14 23 42	7 39 46	10♎42 18	18 15 16	19 37.5	26 54.6	2 54.1	8 44.7	14 54.6	15 11.4	16 22.6	15 23.0	9 19.9
30 M	14 27 39	8 38 2	25 50 55	3♏28 3	19 33.7	28 20.7	4 5.6	9 25.2	14 47.1	15 7.4	16 25.0	15 23.1	9 20.8

Astro Data Dy Hr Mn	Planet Ingress Dy Hr Mn	Last Aspect Dy Hr Mn	☽ Ingress Dy Hr Mn	Last Aspect Dy Hr Mn	☽ Ingress Dy Hr Mn	☽ Phases & Eclipses Dy Hr Mn	Astro Data
☽0S 4 13:05	♂ ♉ 4 0:42	2 6:39 ♂ △	♍ 2 8:41	1 23:17 ♄ ☌	♏ 2 19:26	3 3:23 ○ 11♍32	1 MARCH 1923
♃ R 5 18:50	♀ ♒ 6 5:38	4 5:23 ♀ △	♎ 4 9:00	4 6:18 ♂ ☍	♐ 4 19:33	3 3:32 P 0.370	Julian Day # 8460
♃⊻♄ 8 9:10	☿ ♓ 13 2:36	5 16:01 ☿ △	♏ 6 9:16	5 23:44 ♄ ✶	♑ 6 22:19	9 18:31 ☽ 18♐10	Delta T 23.1 sec
☽0N 18 2:13	☉ ♈ 21 15:29	7 22:20 ☿ □	♐ 8 11:05	8 19:26 ♂ △	♒ 9 4:48	17 12:51 ● 25♓55	SVP 06♓19'59"
♇ D 24 2:06	☿ ♈ 30 18:09	10 8:12 ☿ ✶	♑ 10 15:34	11 8:23 ♂ □	♓ 11 14:51	17 12:44:34 A 7'51"	Obliquity 23°26'49"
☽0S 1 0:07		12 5:23 ☉ ✶	♒ 12 23:02	14 0:13 ♂ ✶	♈ 14 3:08	25 16:41 ☽ 4♋01	⚷ Chiron 14♈48.0
☿0N 1 20:13	♀ ♓ 1 5:16	14 11:13 ♃ □	♓ 15 9:08	16 6:28 ☉ ☌	♉ 16 16:07		☽ Mean ☊ 21♍13.2
♅⊼♆ 9 4:26	☿ ♉ 14 12:58	17 12:51 ☉ ☌	♈ 17 21:06	18 9:03 ♀ ✶	♊ 19 4:33	1 13:10 ○ 10♎47	
☽0N 14 8:18	♂ ♊ 16 2:54	19 10:02 ♄ ☍	♉ 20 10:00	21 2:55 ♀ □	♋ 21 15:28	8 5:22 ☽ 17♑22	1 APRIL 1923
♄⊼♅ 18 17:01	☉ ♉ 21 3:06	21 23:32 ♃ ☍	♊ 22 22:33	23 17:40 ♀ △	♌ 23 23:51	16 6:28 ● 25♈15	Julian Day # 8491
♃△♅ 20 2:13	♀ ♈ 26 13:36	24 16:12 ♀ △	♋ 25 9:05	25 14:16 ☿ □	♍ 26 4:56	24 5:20 ☽ 3♌01	Delta T 23.1 sec
♃⊻♄ 23 17:35	♆ D 27 2:19	27 4:24 ☿ △	♌ 27 16:13	27 23:16 ☿ △	♎ 28 6:48	30 21:30 ○ 9♏30	SVP 06♓19'57"
♃□♆ 25 4:22	☽0S 28 11:08	29 14:31 ♀ ☍	♍ 29 19:36	29 7:27 ♆ ✶	♏ 30 6:32		Obliquity 23°26'49"
♄✶♆ 26 5:17	♀0N 29 15:54	31 2:32 ♂ △	♎ 31 20:06				⚷ Chiron 16♈31.4
							☽ Mean ☊ 19♍34.6

LONGITUDE — MAY 1923

Day	Sid.Time	☉	0 hr ☽	Noon ☽	True ☊	☿	♀	♂	♃	♄	♅	♆	♇
1 Tu	14 31 35	9♉36 15	11♏ 5 21	18♏41 31	19♍27.9	29♉42.5	5♈17.3	10♊ 5.6	14♏39.5	15♎ 3.4	16♓27.4	15♌23.2	9♋21.6
2 W	14 35 32	10 34 27	26 15 11	3♐45 8	19R20.5	1♊ 0.0	6 28.9	10 46.0	14R31.9	14R59.4	16 29.7	15 23.4	9 22.5
3 Th	14 39 29	11 32 38	11♐10 14	18 29 34	19 12.6	2 13.0	7 40.6	11 26.4	14 24.3	14 55.5	16 32.0	15 23.6	9 23.3
4 F	14 43 25	12 30 46	25 42 21	2♑48 7	19 5.2	3 21.5	8 52.3	12 6.8	14 16.7	14 51.7	16 34.3	15 23.8	9 24.2
5 Sa	14 47 22	13 28 54	9♑46 30	16 37 27	18 59.1	4 25.4	10 4.1	12 47.1	14 9.1	14 47.9	16 36.6	15 24.0	9 25.1
6 Su	14 51 18	14 27 0	23 21 0	29 57 25	18 54.9	5 24.6	11 15.8	13 27.4	14 1.4	14 44.2	16 38.8	15 24.3	9 26.1
7 M	14 55 15	15 25 4	6♒27 4	12♒50 24	18D52.8	6 19.1	12 27.6	14 7.6	13 53.8	14 40.5	16 40.9	15 24.6	9 27.0
8 Tu	14 59 11	16 23 7	19 8 0	25 20 27	18 52.4	7 8.8	13 39.5	14 47.8	13 46.1	14 36.9	16 43.0	15 25.0	9 28.0
9 W	15 3 8	17 21 9	1♓28 23	7♓32 26	18 53.0	7 53.6	14 51.3	15 28.0	13 38.5	14 33.4	16 45.1	15 25.3	9 29.0
10 Th	15 7 4	18 19 9	13 33 16	19 31 30	18R53.8	8 33.5	16 3.2	16 8.2	13 30.9	14 29.9	16 47.2	15 25.7	9 30.0
11 F	15 11 1	19 17 8	25 27 43	1♈22 31	18 53.7	9 8.5	17 15.1	16 48.3	13 23.3	14 26.5	16 49.2	15 26.2	9 31.0
12 Sa	15 14 58	20 15 5	7♈16 26	13 9 55	18 51.9	9 38.5	18 27.1	17 28.4	13 15.7	14 23.2	16 51.1	15 26.7	9 32.0
13 Su	15 18 54	21 13 2	19 3 27	24 57 25	18 47.7	10 3.4	19 39.0	18 8.5	13 8.2	14 19.9	16 53.1	15 27.2	9 33.1
14 M	15 22 51	22 10 56	0♉52 10	6♉48 0	18 40.9	10 23.3	20 51.0	18 48.5	13 0.7	14 16.7	16 54.9	15 27.7	9 34.2
15 Tu	15 26 47	23 8 50	12 45 12	18 43 57	18 31.7	10 38.2	22 3.0	19 28.5	12 53.2	14 13.6	16 56.8	15 28.3	9 35.3
16 W	15 30 44	24 6 42	24 44 28	0♊46 53	18 20.6	10 48.1	23 15.0	20 8.5	12 45.8	14 10.6	16 58.6	15 28.9	9 36.4
17 Th	15 34 40	25 4 32	6♊51 22	12 58 1	18 8.5	10R53.0	24 27.1	20 48.4	12 38.4	14 7.7	17 0.3	15 29.5	9 37.5
18 F	15 38 37	26 2 21	19 6 58	25 18 19	17 56.4	10 53.1	25 39.1	21 28.3	12 31.1	14 4.8	17 2.1	15 30.2	9 38.6
19 Sa	15 42 33	27 0 9	1♋32 13	7♋48 48	17 45.4	10 48.5	26 51.2	22 8.2	12 23.9	14 2.1	17 3.7	15 30.9	9 39.8
20 Su	15 46 30	27 57 55	14 8 15	20 30 44	17 36.4	10 39.4	28 3.3	22 48.1	12 16.7	13 59.4	17 5.4	15 31.6	9 40.9
21 M	15 50 27	28 55 40	26 56 30	3♌25 46	17 29.9	10 26.0	29 15.4	23 27.9	12 9.6	13 56.8	17 7.0	15 32.4	9 42.1
22 Tu	15 54 23	29 53 23	9♌58 49	16 35 56	17 26.2	10 8.5	0♉27.5	24 7.7	12 2.6	13 54.2	17 8.5	15 33.2	9 43.3
23 W	15 58 20	0♊51 4	23 17 23	0♍ 3 26	17D24.7	9 47.4	1 39.7	24 47.4	11 55.7	13 51.8	17 10.0	15 34.0	9 44.5
24 Th	16 2 16	1 48 43	6♍54 20	13 50 17	17R24.6	9 22.9	2 51.8	25 27.2	11 48.8	13 49.4	17 11.4	15 34.9	9 45.8
25 F	16 6 13	2 46 21	20 51 22	27 57 37	17 24.7	8 55.5	4 4.0	26 6.9	11 42.1	13 47.2	17 12.9	15 35.7	9 47.0
26 Sa	16 10 9	3 43 58	5♎ 8 55	12♎25 0	17 23.7	8 25.8	5 16.2	26 46.5	11 35.4	13 45.0	17 14.2	15 36.7	9 48.2
27 Su	16 14 6	4 41 33	19 45 27	27 9 42	17 20.8	7 54.2	6 28.4	27 26.2	11 28.9	13 42.9	17 15.5	15 37.6	9 49.5
28 M	16 18 2	5 39 7	4♏36 56	12♏ 6 16	17 15.2	7 21.2	7 40.7	28 5.8	11 22.4	13 40.9	17 16.8	15 38.6	9 50.8
29 Tu	16 21 59	6 36 39	19 36 37	27 6 51	17 7.1	6 47.5	8 52.9	28 45.4	11 16.1	13 39.1	17 18.0	15 39.6	9 52.1
30 W	16 25 56	7 34 10	4♐35 44	12♐ 2 5	16 57.0	6 13.7	10 5.2	29 24.9	11 9.8	13 37.3	17 19.2	15 40.6	9 53.4
31 Th	16 29 52	8 31 40	19 24 46	26 42 47	16 46.0	5 40.3	11 17.5	0♋ 4.4	11 3.7	13 35.5	17 20.3	15 41.7	9 54.7

LONGITUDE — JUNE 1923

Day	Sid.Time	☉	0 hr ☽	Noon ☽	True ☊	☿	♀	♂	♃	♄	♅	♆	♇
1 F	16 33 49	9♊29 9	3♑55 14	11♑ 1 26	16♍35.3	5♊ 7.9	12♉29.8	0♋43.9	10♏57.7	13♎33.9	17♓21.4	15♌42.8	9♋56.0
2 Sa	16 37 45	10 26 38	18 0 54	24 53 21	16R26.2	4R37.0	13 42.1	1 23.4	10R51.9	13R32.4	17 22.5	15 43.9	9 57.3
3 Su	16 41 42	11 24 5	1♒38 40	8♒16 57	16 19.3	4 8.3	14 54.5	2 2.8	10 46.1	13 31.0	17 23.5	15 45.0	9 58.7
4 M	16 45 38	12 21 31	14 48 26	21 13 29	16 15.0	3 42.0	16 6.9	2 42.2	10 40.5	13 29.7	17 24.4	15 46.2	10 0.0
5 Tu	16 49 35	13 18 57	27 32 34	3♓46 16	16 12.9	3 18.8	17 19.3	3 21.6	10 35.0	13 28.4	17 25.3	15 47.4	10 1.4
6 W	16 53 31	14 16 22	9♓55 10	15 59 57	16 12.4	2 58.9	18 31.7	4 1.0	10 29.6	13 27.3	17 26.2	15 48.7	10 2.8
7 Th	16 57 28	15 13 47	22 1 16	27 59 49	16 12.3	2 42.6	19 44.1	4 40.3	10 24.4	13 26.2	17 27.0	15 49.9	10 4.2
8 F	17 1 25	16 11 10	3♈56 17	9♈51 18	16 11.7	2 30.3	20 56.6	5 19.6	10 19.3	13 25.3	17 27.7	15 51.2	10 5.6
9 Sa	17 5 21	17 8 34	15 45 31	21 39 32	16 9.4	2 22.1	22 9.1	5 58.9	10 14.4	13 24.5	17 28.5	15 52.5	10 7.0
10 Su	17 9 18	18 5 56	27 33 53	3♉29 5	16 4.8	2D18.2	23 21.6	6 38.2	10 9.6	13 23.7	17 29.1	15 53.8	10 8.4
11 M	17 13 14	19 3 18	9♉25 36	15 23 49	15 57.5	2 18.7	24 34.1	7 17.4	10 5.0	13 23.1	17 29.7	15 55.2	10 9.8
12 Tu	17 17 11	20 0 40	21 24 4	27 26 39	15 47.5	2 23.8	25 46.7	7 56.7	10 0.5	13 22.5	17 30.3	15 56.6	10 11.2
13 W	17 21 7	20 58 1	3♊31 47	9♊39 38	15 35.5	2 33.3	26 59.2	8 35.9	9 56.2	13 22.1	17 30.8	15 58.0	10 12.7
14 Th	17 25 4	21 55 21	15 50 18	22 3 53	15 22.4	2 47.4	28 11.8	9 15.0	9 52.0	13 21.7	17 31.3	15 59.5	10 14.1
15 F	17 29 0	22 52 41	28 20 23	4♋39 49	15 9.2	3 6.1	29 24.4	9 54.2	9 48.0	13 21.5	17 31.7	16 0.9	10 15.6
16 Sa	17 32 57	23 50 0	11♋ 2 10	17 27 24	14 57.2	3 29.3	0♊37.0	10 33.3	9 44.2	13D21.4	17 32.1	16 2.4	10 17.0
17 Su	17 36 54	24 47 19	23 55 29	0♌26 25	14 47.3	3 56.9	1 49.7	11 12.5	9 40.5	13 21.3	17 32.4	16 3.9	10 18.5
18 M	17 40 50	25 44 36	7♌ 0 11	13 36 48	14 40.2	4 29.0	3 2.3	11 51.5	9 37.0	13 21.4	17 32.7	16 5.5	10 19.9
19 Tu	17 44 47	26 41 53	20 16 20	26 58 50	14 35.8	5 5.4	4 15.0	12 30.6	9 33.7	13 21.5	17 32.9	16 7.0	10 21.4
20 W	17 48 43	27 39 9	3♍44 24	10♍33 8	14D34.0	5 46.1	5 27.7	13 9.6	9 30.5	13 21.8	17 33.1	16 8.6	10 22.9
21 Th	17 52 40	28 36 25	17 25 9	24 20 31	14R33.7	6 30.9	6 40.4	13 48.7	9 27.5	13 22.2	17 33.2	16 10.2	10 24.4
22 F	17 56 36	29 33 39	1♎19 18	8♎21 32	14 33.8	7 20.0	7 53.1	14 27.7	9 24.7	13 22.6	17 33.3	16 11.9	10 25.9
23 Sa	18 0 33	0♋30 53	15 27 7	22 35 56	14 33.1	8 13.1	9 5.9	15 6.6	9 22.0	13 23.2	17R33.3	16 13.5	10 27.4
24 Su	18 4 29	1 28 7	29 47 43	7♏ 2 6	14 30.5	9 10.2	10 18.6	15 45.6	9 19.6	13 23.8	17 33.3	16 15.2	10 28.9
25 M	18 8 26	2 25 19	14♏18 34	21 36 31	14 25.5	10 11.3	11 31.4	16 24.5	9 17.3	13 24.6	17 33.2	16 16.9	10 30.4
26 Tu	18 12 23	3 22 31	28 55 14	6♐13 52	14 18.1	11 16.2	12 44.2	17 3.4	9 15.1	13 25.5	17 33.1	16 18.6	10 31.9
27 W	18 16 19	4 19 43	13♐31 34	20 47 25	14 8.8	12 25.0	13 57.1	17 42.3	9 13.2	13 26.4	17 33.0	16 20.3	10 33.4
28 Th	18 20 16	5 16 54	28 0 31	5♑10 2	13 58.5	13 37.6	15 9.9	18 21.1	9 11.4	13 27.5	17 32.7	16 22.1	10 34.9
29 F	18 24 12	6 14 6	12♑15 12	19 15 22	13 48.5	14 53.9	16 22.8	18 60.0	9 9.8	13 28.6	17 32.5	16 23.9	10 36.4
30 Sa	18 28 9	7 11 17	26 10 2	2♒58 50	13 39.9	16 14.0	17 35.7	19 38.8	9 8.4	13 29.9	17 32.2	16 25.7	10 37.9

Astro Data

	Dy Hr Mn
☽0N	11 14:59
☿ R	17 12:31
☽0S	25 20:43
☽0N	7 23:03
♃△♇	10 4:56
☿ D	10 9:10
♄ D	16 21:42
☽0S	22 4:21
♅ R	23 2:41

Planet Ingress

	Dy Hr Mn
☿ ♊	1 5:18
♀ ♉	21 14:50
☉ ♊	22 2:45
♂ ♋	30 21:19
♀ ♊	15 11:46
☉ ♋	22 11:03

Last Aspect / ☽ Ingress

Last Aspect Dy Hr Mn		☽ Ingress Dy Hr Mn
1 8:29	♅ △	♐ 2 5:59
3 8:48	♅ □	♑ 4 7:14
5 12:00	♅ ✶	♒ 6 12:05
7 18:18	☉ □	♓ 8 21:06
10 10:25	☉ ✶	♈ 11 9:12
13 1:21	♀ ☌	♉ 13 22:14
15 22:38	☉ ☌	♊ 16 10:27
18 14:02	♀ ✶	♋ 18 21:03
21 4:44	♀ □	♌ 21 5:40
23 2:49	♂ ✶	♍ 23 11:54
25 9:20	♂ □	♎ 25 15:25
27 13:01	♂ △	♏ 27 16:35
28 20:18	♅ △	♐ 29 16:37
30 20:37	♅ □	♑ 31 17:27

Last Aspect / ☽ Ingress

Last Aspect Dy Hr Mn		☽ Ingress Dy Hr Mn
1 22:53	♅ ✶	♒ 2 21:04
4 2:41	♀ □	♓ 5 4:43
6 18:55	♀ ✶	♈ 7 16:02
9 3:04	☉ ✶	♉ 10 4:56
12 9:40	♀ ☌	♊ 12 17:03
14 12:42	☉ ☌	♋ 15 3:10
16 12:09	♅ △	♌ 17 11:12
19 12:22	☉ ✶	♍ 19 17:22
21 20:46	☉ □	♎ 21 21:44
23 1:18	♆ ✶	♏ 24 0:20
25 5:20	♅ △	♐ 26 1:46
27 6:38	♅ □	♑ 28 3:20
29 12:07	♂ ☍	♒ 30 6:44

☽ Phases & Eclipses

Dy Hr Mn		
7 18:18	☽	16♒09
15 22:38	●	24♉03
23 14:25	☽	1♍26
30 5:07	○	7♐46
6 9:19	☽	14♓39
14 12:42	●	22♊26
21 20:46	☽	29♍26
28 13:04	○	5♑48

Astro Data

1 MAY 1923
Julian Day # 8521
Delta T 23.2 sec
SVP 06♓19'54"
Obliquity 23°26'48"
⚷ Chiron 18♈16.5
☽ Mean ☊ 17♍59.3

1 JUNE 1923
Julian Day # 8552
Delta T 23.2 sec
SVP 06♓19'50"
Obliquity 23°26'48"
⚷ Chiron 19♈49.6
☽ Mean ☊ 16♍20.8

JULY 1923 LONGITUDE

Day	Sid.Time	☉	0 hr ☽	Noon ☽	True ☊	☿	♀	♂	♃	♄	♅	♆	♇
1 Su	18 32 5	8♋ 8 27	9♒41 34	16♒18 11	13♍33.3	17♊37.7	18♊48.6	20♋17.6	9♏ 7.2	13♎31.3	17♓31.8	16♌27.5	10♋39.4
2 M	18 36 2	9 5 38	22 48 45	29 13 31	13R 29.2	19 5.0	20 1.5	20 56.4	9R 6.2	13 32.7	17R 31.4	16 29.3	10 40.9
3 Tu	18 39 59	10 2 49	5♓32 47	11♓47 0	13D 27.3	20 35.9	21 14.5	21 35.2	9 5.3	13 34.2	17 31.0	16 31.2	10 42.4
4 W	18 43 55	11 0 0	17 56 39	24 2 17	13 27.1	22 10.3	22 27.5	22 13.9	9 4.6	13 35.9	17 30.5	16 33.1	10 43.9
5 Th	18 47 52	11 57 12	0♈ 4 33	6♈ 4 3	13 27.7	23 48.1	23 40.5	22 52.6	9 4.1	13 37.6	17 30.0	16 34.9	10 45.5
6 F	18 51 48	12 54 23	12 1 28	17 57 26	13R 28.2	25 29.3	24 53.5	23 31.4	9 3.7	13 39.5	17 29.4	16 36.8	10 47.0
7 Sa	18 55 45	13 51 35	23 52 38	29 47 42	13 27.6	27 13.8	26 6.6	24 10.1	9D 3.6	13 41.4	17 28.7	16 38.8	10 48.5
8 Su	18 59 41	14 48 47	5♉43 15	11♉39 52	13 25.3	29 1.4	27 19.7	24 48.7	9 3.6	13 43.4	17 28.1	16 40.7	10 50.0
9 M	19 3 38	15 46 0	17 38 7	23 38 29	13 20.8	0♋52.1	28 32.8	25 27.4	9 3.8	13 45.5	17 27.3	16 42.6	10 51.5
10 Tu	19 7 34	16 43 13	29 41 25	5♊47 18	13 14.2	2 45.6	29 46.0	26 6.1	9 4.2	13 47.8	17 26.6	16 44.6	10 53.0
11 W	19 11 31	17 40 26	11♊56 28	18 9 10	13 5.8	4 41.8	0♋59.1	26 44.7	9 4.8	13 50.1	17 25.7	16 46.6	10 54.5
12 Th	19 15 28	18 37 40	24 25 35	0♋45 49	12 56.4	6 40.4	2 12.3	27 23.3	9 5.5	13 52.5	17 24.9	16 48.6	10 56.0
13 F	19 19 24	19 34 54	7♋ 9 54	13 37 50	12 46.9	8 41.3	3 25.6	28 2.0	9 6.5	13 55.0	17 24.0	16 50.6	10 57.5
14 Sa	19 23 21	20 32 8	20 9 31	26 44 49	12 38.2	10 44.2	4 38.8	28 40.6	9 7.6	13 57.6	17 23.0	16 52.6	10 59.0
15 Su	19 27 17	21 29 23	3♌23 33	10♌ 5 32	12 31.2	12 48.7	5 52.1	29 19.1	9 8.9	14 0.3	17 22.0	16 54.7	11 0.5
16 M	19 31 14	22 26 38	16 50 31	23 38 18	12 26.3	14 54.6	7 5.4	29 57.7	9 10.3	14 3.0	17 21.0	16 56.7	11 2.0
17 Tu	19 35 10	23 23 53	0♍28 39	7♍21 23	12D 23.7	17 1.5	8 18.7	0♌36.3	9 12.0	14 5.9	17 19.9	16 58.8	11 3.5
18 W	19 39 7	24 21 9	14 16 16	21 13 9	12 23.1	19 9.2	9 32.0	1 14.8	9 13.8	14 8.9	17 18.8	17 0.9	11 5.0
19 Th	19 43 3	25 18 24	28 11 53	5♎12 19	12 23.8	21 17.4	10 45.4	1 53.3	9 15.8	14 11.9	17 17.6	17 3.0	11 6.5
20 F	19 47 0	26 15 40	12♎14 19	19 17 44	12 25.0	23 25.7	11 58.8	2 31.8	9 18.0	14 15.0	17 16.4	17 5.1	11 8.0
21 Sa	19 50 57	27 12 56	26 22 26	3♏28 11	12R 25.6	25 33.8	13 12.2	3 10.3	9 20.4	14 18.2	17 15.2	17 7.2	11 9.4
22 Su	19 54 53	28 10 12	10♏34 49	17 42 2	12 24.9	27 41.6	14 25.6	3 48.8	9 22.9	14 21.6	17 13.9	17 9.3	11 10.9
23 M	19 58 50	29 7 28	24 49 30	1♐56 53	12 22.5	29 48.8	15 39.1	4 27.3	9 25.6	14 24.9	17 12.6	17 11.4	11 12.3
24 Tu	20 2 46	0♌ 4 45	9♐ 3 43	16 9 32	12 18.4	1♌55.2	16 52.5	5 5.7	9 28.5	14 28.4	17 11.2	17 13.5	11 13.8
25 W	20 6 43	1 2 2	23 13 51	0♑16 7	12 12.8	4 0.5	18 6.0	5 44.2	9 31.5	14 32.0	17 9.8	17 15.7	11 15.2
26 Th	20 10 39	1 59 20	7♑15 50	14 12 27	12 6.6	6 4.8	19 19.5	6 22.6	9 34.7	14 35.6	17 8.4	17 17.9	11 16.7
27 F	20 14 36	2 56 38	21 5 32	27 54 40	12 0.5	8 7.7	20 33.1	7 1.0	9 38.1	14 39.4	17 6.9	17 20.0	11 18.1
28 Sa	20 18 32	3 53 57	4♒39 29	11♒19 43	11 55.3	10 9.3	21 46.7	7 39.4	9 41.6	14 43.2	17 5.4	17 22.2	11 19.5
29 Su	20 22 29	4 51 16	17 55 13	24 25 54	11 51.4	12 9.5	23 0.3	8 17.8	9 45.3	14 47.1	17 3.8	17 24.4	11 20.9
30 M	20 26 26	5 48 37	0♓51 46	7♓12 56	11D 49.3	14 8.2	24 13.9	8 56.2	9 49.2	14 51.0	17 2.2	17 26.5	11 22.3
31 Tu	20 30 22	6 45 58	13 29 36	19 42 3	11 48.7	16 5.4	25 27.5	9 34.5	9 53.2	14 55.1	17 0.6	17 28.7	11 23.7

AUGUST 1923 LONGITUDE

Day	Sid.Time	☉	0 hr ☽	Noon ☽	True ☊	☿	♀	♂	♃	♄	♅	♆	♇
1 W	20 34 19	7♌43 20	25♓50 39	1♈55 47	11♍49.5	18♌ 0.9	26♋41.2	10♌12.9	9♏57.4	14♎59.2	16♓58.9	17♌30.9	11♋25.1
2 Th	20 38 15	8 40 43	7♈57 56	13 57 39	11 51.0	19 54.9	27 54.9	10 51.2	10 1.8	15 3.4	16R 57.2	17 33.1	11 26.5
3 F	20 42 12	9 38 8	19 55 26	25 51 55	11 52.7	21 47.3	29 8.7	11 29.6	10 6.3	15 7.7	16 55.5	17 35.3	11 27.9
4 Sa	20 46 8	10 35 33	1♉47 40	7♉43 19	11R 53.9	23 38.1	0♌22.4	12 7.9	10 11.0	15 12.0	16 53.7	17 37.5	11 29.2
5 Su	20 50 5	11 33 0	13 39 28	19 36 44	11 54.3	25 27.3	1 36.2	12 46.2	10 15.8	15 16.5	16 51.9	17 39.7	11 30.6
6 M	20 54 1	12 30 28	25 35 43	1♊36 58	11 53.4	27 14.8	2 50.0	13 24.5	10 20.8	15 21.0	16 50.1	17 42.0	11 31.9
7 Tu	20 57 58	13 27 57	7♊41 4	13 48 28	11 51.3	29 0.8	4 3.9	14 2.8	10 25.9	15 25.6	16 48.3	17 44.2	11 33.2
8 W	21 1 55	14 25 28	19 59 39	26 14 59	11 48.2	0♍45.3	5 17.7	14 41.2	10 31.2	15 30.2	16 46.4	17 46.4	11 34.5
9 Th	21 5 51	15 23 0	2♋34 48	8♋59 20	11 44.4	2 28.1	6 31.6	15 19.4	10 36.7	15 34.9	16 44.5	17 48.6	11 35.8
10 F	21 9 48	16 20 33	15 28 44	22 3 4	11 40.4	4 9.4	7 45.6	15 57.7	10 42.3	15 39.7	16 42.5	17 50.8	11 37.1
11 Sa	21 13 44	17 18 7	28 42 19	5♌26 21	11 36.7	5 49.1	8 59.5	16 36.0	10 48.0	15 44.6	16 40.5	17 53.1	11 38.4
12 Su	21 17 41	18 15 43	12♌14 59	19 7 53	11 33.8	7 27.3	10 13.5	17 14.3	10 53.9	15 49.6	16 38.5	17 55.3	11 39.7
13 M	21 21 37	19 13 20	26 4 43	3♍ 5 3	11 32.0	9 4.0	11 27.5	17 52.6	10 60.0	15 54.6	16 36.5	17 57.5	11 40.9
14 Tu	21 25 34	20 10 58	10♍ 8 24	17 14 15	11D 31.3	10 39.2	12 41.5	18 30.8	11 6.2	15 59.6	16 34.4	17 59.7	11 42.2
15 W	21 29 30	21 8 37	24 22 5	1♎31 23	11 31.7	12 12.8	13 55.6	19 9.1	11 12.5	16 4.8	16 32.4	18 2.0	11 43.4
16 Th	21 33 27	22 6 17	8♎41 37	15 52 17	11 32.7	13 44.9	15 9.6	19 47.3	11 19.0	16 10.0	16 30.3	18 4.2	11 44.6
17 F	21 37 24	23 3 58	23 2 57	0♏13 10	11 34.0	15 15.4	16 23.7	20 25.6	11 25.6	16 15.3	16 28.1	18 6.4	11 45.8
18 Sa	21 41 20	24 1 40	7♏22 32	14 30 44	11 35.1	16 44.4	17 37.8	21 3.8	11 32.4	16 20.6	16 26.0	18 8.6	11 47.0
19 Su	21 45 17	24 59 23	21 37 26	28 42 21	11R 35.6	18 11.9	18 52.0	21 42.0	11 39.3	16 26.0	16 23.8	18 10.8	11 48.2
20 M	21 49 13	25 57 8	5♐45 15	12♐45 53	11 35.4	19 37.8	20 6.1	22 20.3	11 46.3	16 31.5	16 21.6	18 13.0	11 49.3
21 Tu	21 53 10	26 54 53	19 44 3	26 39 34	11 34.6	21 2.0	21 20.3	22 58.5	11 53.4	16 37.0	16 19.4	18 15.3	11 50.5
22 W	21 57 6	27 52 40	3♑32 15	10♑21 56	11 33.2	22 24.7	22 34.5	23 36.7	12 0.7	16 42.6	16 17.2	18 17.5	11 51.6
23 Th	22 1 3	28 50 28	17 8 28	23 51 44	11 31.5	23 45.7	23 48.7	24 14.9	12 8.2	16 48.2	16 15.0	18 19.7	11 52.7
24 F	22 4 59	29 48 17	0♒31 35	7♒ 7 56	11 29.9	25 5.1	25 2.9	24 53.1	12 15.7	16 53.9	16 12.7	18 21.9	11 53.8
25 Sa	22 8 56	0♍46 7	13 40 43	20 9 51	11 28.7	26 22.7	26 17.2	25 31.3	12 23.4	16 59.7	16 10.4	18 24.0	11 54.8
26 Su	22 12 53	1 43 59	26 35 22	2♓57 15	11 27.8	27 38.5	27 31.4	26 9.4	12 31.2	17 5.5	16 8.1	18 26.2	11 55.9
27 M	22 16 49	2 41 52	9♓15 34	15 30 25	11D 27.5	28 52.4	28 45.7	26 47.6	12 39.2	17 11.3	16 5.8	18 28.4	11 56.9
28 Tu	22 20 46	3 39 47	21 41 57	27 50 22	11 27.6	0♎ 4.5	0♍ 0.0	27 25.8	12 47.2	17 17.2	16 3.5	18 30.6	11 58.0
29 W	22 24 42	4 37 43	3♈55 54	9♈58 49	11 28.1	1 14.5	1 14.4	28 4.0	12 55.4	17 23.2	16 1.2	18 32.7	11 59.0
30 Th	22 28 39	5 35 41	15 59 27	21 58 10	11 28.7	2 22.5	2 28.7	28 42.1	13 3.7	17 29.2	15 58.8	18 34.9	11 60.0
31 F	22 32 35	6 33 41	27 55 24	3♉51 34	11 29.3	3 28.3	3 43.1	29 20.3	13 12.1	17 35.3	15 56.5	18 37.0	12 0.9

Astro Data	Dy Hr Mn
☽0N	5 8:12
♃ D	7 8:21
☽0S	19 10:46
♅⚻♆	23 7:59
☽0N	1 17:28
☽0S	15 17:30
♄⚻♅	18 17:08
♃△♇	20 12:08
☿0S	25 19:32
☽0N	29 1:50

Planet Ingress	Dy Hr Mn
☿ ♋	8 12:47
♀ ♋	10 4:36
♂ ♌	16 1:26
☉ ♌	23 22:01
☿ ♌	23 2:07
♀ ♌	3 16:42
☿ ♍	7 13:33
☉ ♍	24 4:52
☿ ♎	27 22:30
♀ ♍	27 23:59

Last Aspect Dy Hr Mn		☽ Ingress Dy Hr Mn
1 18:19	♀ △	♓ 2 13:28
4 9:52	♀ □	♈ 4 23:51
7 8:00	☿ ⚹	♉ 7 12:25
9 16:29	♂ ⚹	♊ 10 0:37
11 10:36	♅ □	♋ 12 10:34
14 16:17	♂ ☌	♌ 14 17:53
16 0:11	♆ ☌	♍ 16 23:10
18 18:40	☉ ⚹	♎ 19 3:05
21 1:32	☉ □	♏ 21 6:08
23 7:46	☉ △	♐ 23 8:43
24 13:51	♆ △	♑ 25 11:32
26 22:58	♀ ☍	♒ 27 15:42
28 23:03	♆ ☍	♓ 29 22:23

Last Aspect Dy Hr Mn		☽ Ingress Dy Hr Mn
1 1:50	♀ △	♈ 1 8:11
3 4:28	☿ △	♉ 3 20:22
6 3:52	☿ □	♊ 6 8:47
7 19:42	♆ ⚹	♋ 8 19:08
10 2:15	♅ △	♌ 11 2:19
12 11:16	☉ ☌	♍ 13 6:44
14 10:51	♅ ☍	♎ 15 9:27
17 0:02	☉ ⚹	♏ 17 11:38
19 6:07	☉ □	♐ 19 14:12
21 13:23	☉ △	♑ 21 17:49
23 13:07	☿ △	♒ 23 23:03
26 1:57	♀ ☍	♓ 26 6:25
27 13:06	♅ ☌	♈ 28 16:15
31 3:01	♂ △	♉ 31 4:12

☽ Phases & Eclipses Dy Hr Mn	
6 1:56	☽ 12♈59
14 0:45	● 20♋34
21 1:32	☽ 27♎17
27 22:32	○ 3♒50
4 19:22	☽ 11♉22
12 11:16	● 18♌43
19 6:07	☽ 25♏14
26 10:29	○ 2♓09
26 10:39	☍ P 0.163

Astro Data

1 JULY 1923
Julian Day # 8582
Delta T 23.3 sec
SVP 06♓19'45"
Obliquity 23°26'48"
⚷ Chiron 20♈47.7
☽ Mean ☊ 14♍45.5

1 AUGUST 1923
Julian Day # 8613
Delta T 23.3 sec
SVP 06♓19'41"
Obliquity 23°26'48"
⚷ Chiron 21♈02.3R
☽ Mean ☊ 13♍07.0

LONGITUDE SEPTEMBER 1923

Day	Sid.Time	☉	0 hr ☽	Noon ☽	True ☊	☿	♀	♂	♃	♄	♅	♆	♇
1 Sa	22 36 32	7♍31 43	9♉47 9	15♉42 41	11♍29.8	4♎31.8	4♍57.5	29♌58.5	13♏20.6	17♎41.4	15♓54.1	18♌39.1	12♋ 1.9
2 Su	22 40 28	8 29 46	21 38 41	27 35 42	11 30.1	5 32.9	6 11.9	0♍36.7	13 29.3	17 47.6	15R51.8	18 41.3	12 2.8
3 M	22 44 25	9 27 52	3♊34 19	9♊35 6	11R30.2	6 31.5	7 26.3	1 14.8	13 38.0	17 53.8	15 49.4	18 43.4	12 3.7
4 Tu	22 48 21	10 25 59	15 38 38	21 45 27	11 30.2	7 27.4	8 40.8	1 53.0	13 46.9	18 0.1	15 47.0	18 45.5	12 4.6
5 W	22 52 18	11 24 9	27 56 8	4♋11 10	11D30.2	8 20.4	9 55.3	2 31.2	13 55.9	18 6.4	15 44.6	18 47.6	12 5.5
6 Th	22 56 15	12 22 21	10♋31 2	16 56 9	11 30.2	9 10.3	11 9.8	3 9.3	14 5.0	18 12.8	15 42.2	18 49.6	12 6.4
7 F	23 0 11	13 20 34	23 26 50	0♌ 3 21	11 30.4	9 57.0	12 24.3	3 47.5	14 14.2	18 19.2	15 39.8	18 51.7	12 7.2
8 Sa	23 4 8	14 18 50	6♌45 51	13 34 23	11 30.6	10 40.3	13 38.9	4 25.7	14 23.5	18 25.6	15 37.4	18 53.8	12 8.0
9 Su	23 8 4	15 17 7	20 28 52	27 29 4	11 30.9	11 19.7	14 53.4	5 3.8	14 33.0	18 32.1	15 35.0	18 55.8	12 8.8
10 M	23 12 1	16 15 26	4♍34 38	11♍45 5	11R31.1	11 55.2	16 8.0	5 42.0	14 42.5	18 38.6	15 32.6	18 57.8	12 9.6
11 Tu	23 15 57	17 13 47	18 59 49	26 18 5	11 31.1	12 26.4	17 22.6	6 20.2	14 52.1	18 45.2	15 30.2	18 59.9	12 10.4
12 W	23 19 54	18 12 10	3♎39 5	11♎ 1 57	11 30.8	12 53.1	18 37.2	6 58.3	15 1.9	18 51.8	15 27.8	19 1.9	12 11.1
13 Th	23 23 50	19 10 35	18 25 45	25 49 34	11 30.1	13 14.8	19 51.8	7 36.5	15 11.7	18 58.5	15 25.4	19 3.9	12 11.8
14 F	23 27 47	20 9 2	3♏12 31	10♏33 48	11 29.2	13 31.3	21 6.4	8 14.7	15 21.6	19 5.2	15 23.0	19 5.8	12 12.5
15 Sa	23 31 44	21 7 30	17 52 38	25 8 23	11 28.2	13 42.2	22 21.1	8 52.8	15 31.7	19 11.9	15 20.6	19 7.8	12 13.2
16 Su	23 35 40	22 6 0	2♐20 32	9♐28 39	11 27.3	13R47.1	23 35.7	9 31.0	15 41.8	19 18.6	15 18.3	19 9.7	12 13.9
17 M	23 39 37	23 4 31	16 32 26	23 31 43	11D26.8	13 45.8	24 50.4	10 9.1	15 52.0	19 25.4	15 15.9	19 11.6	12 14.5
18 Tu	23 43 33	24 3 4	0♑26 24	7♑16 28	11 26.8	13 37.9	26 5.1	10 47.3	16 2.3	19 32.3	15 13.5	19 13.6	12 15.1
19 W	23 47 30	25 1 39	14 1 59	20 43 5	11 27.3	13 23.2	27 19.8	11 25.5	16 12.7	19 39.1	15 11.2	19 15.4	12 15.7
20 Th	23 51 26	26 0 15	27 19 55	3♒52 41	11 28.4	13 1.5	28 34.5	12 3.6	16 23.2	19 46.0	15 8.8	19 17.3	12 16.3
21 F	23 55 23	26 58 53	10♒21 34	16 46 48	11 29.6	12 32.7	29 49.2	12 41.8	16 33.8	19 52.9	15 6.5	19 19.2	12 16.8
22 Sa	23 59 19	27 57 33	23 8 36	29 27 10	11 30.8	11 56.8	1♎ 3.9	13 19.9	16 44.4	19 59.8	15 4.1	19 21.0	12 17.3
23 Su	0 3 16	28 56 14	5♓42 43	11♓55 26	11R31.5	11 14.1	2 18.6	13 58.1	16 55.2	20 6.8	15 1.8	19 22.8	12 17.8
24 M	0 7 13	29 54 58	18 5 31	24 13 10	11 31.5	10 24.8	3 33.4	14 36.2	17 6.0	20 13.8	14 59.5	19 24.6	12 18.3
25 Tu	0 11 9	0♎53 43	0♈18 33	6♈21 52	11 30.5	9 29.7	4 48.1	15 14.4	17 16.9	20 20.8	14 57.2	19 26.4	12 18.8
26 W	0 15 6	1 52 30	12 23 19	18 23 6	11 28.4	8 29.7	6 2.9	15 52.6	17 27.9	20 27.9	14 55.0	19 28.1	12 19.2
27 Th	0 19 2	2 51 19	24 21 27	0♉18 36	11 25.5	7 25.7	7 17.6	16 30.7	17 39.0	20 34.9	14 52.7	19 29.9	12 19.6
28 F	0 22 59	3 50 11	6♉14 51	12 10 28	11 21.8	6 19.2	8 32.4	17 8.9	17 50.1	20 42.0	14 50.5	19 31.6	12 20.0
29 Sa	0 26 55	4 49 4	18 5 48	24 1 12	11 17.9	5 11.7	9 47.2	17 47.1	18 1.3	20 49.1	14 48.3	19 33.3	12 20.4
30 Su	0 30 52	5 48 0	29 57 5	5♊53 53	11 14.2	4 5.0	11 2.0	18 25.3	18 12.6	20 56.3	14 46.1	19 35.0	12 20.7

LONGITUDE OCTOBER 1923

Day	Sid.Time	☉	0 hr ☽	Noon ☽	True ☊	☿	♀	♂	♃	♄	♅	♆	♇
1 M	0 34 48	6♎46 58	11♊52 3	17♊52 5	11♍11.1	3♎ 0.8	12♎16.8	19♍ 3.4	18♏24.0	21♎ 3.4	14♓43.9	19♌36.6	12♋21.0
2 Tu	0 38 45	7 45 59	23 54 30	29 59 51	11R 9.0	2R 0.8	13 31.6	19 41.6	18 35.5	21 10.6	14R41.7	19 38.2	12 21.3
3 W	0 42 41	8 45 1	6♋ 8 41	12♋21 33	11D 8.1	1 6.7	14 46.4	20 19.8	18 47.0	21 17.8	14 39.6	19 39.8	12 21.6
4 Th	0 46 38	9 44 6	18 39 1	25 1 37	11 8.4	0 20.0	16 1.3	20 58.0	18 58.6	21 25.0	14 37.5	19 41.4	12 21.8
5 F	0 50 35	10 43 14	1♌29 51	8♌ 4 8	11 9.6	29♍41.9	17 16.1	21 36.2	19 10.2	21 32.2	14 35.4	19 43.0	12 22.1
6 Sa	0 54 31	11 42 23	14 44 53	21 32 20	11 11.2	29 13.5	18 31.0	22 14.4	19 21.9	21 39.4	14 33.4	19 44.5	12 22.3
7 Su	0 58 28	12 41 35	28 26 39	5♍27 51	11R12.5	28 55.3	19 45.8	22 52.6	19 33.7	21 46.7	14 31.3	19 46.0	12 22.5
8 M	1 2 24	13 40 49	12♍35 46	19 50 4	11 13.0	28D47.8	21 0.7	23 30.8	19 45.6	21 53.9	14 29.3	19 47.5	12 22.6
9 Tu	1 6 21	14 40 6	27 10 14	4♎35 32	11 12.1	28 51.0	22 15.6	24 9.1	19 57.5	22 1.2	14 27.3	19 49.0	12 22.7
10 W	1 10 17	15 39 24	12♎ 5 3	19 37 45	11 9.6	29 4.8	23 30.5	24 47.3	20 9.5	22 8.5	14 25.4	19 50.4	12 22.8
11 Th	1 14 14	16 38 45	27 12 26	4♏47 50	11 5.4	29 28.8	24 45.4	25 25.5	20 21.5	22 15.8	14 23.4	19 51.8	12 22.9
12 F	1 18 10	17 38 7	12♏22 40	19 55 41	11 0.2	0♎ 2.6	26 0.3	26 3.7	20 33.6	22 23.1	14 21.5	19 53.2	12 23.0
13 Sa	1 22 7	18 37 32	27 25 42	4♐51 43	10 54.6	0 45.3	27 15.2	26 42.0	20 45.8	22 30.4	14 19.7	19 54.5	12 23.0
14 Su	1 26 4	19 36 58	12♐12 50	19 28 22	10 49.5	1 36.4	28 30.1	27 20.2	20 58.0	22 37.7	14 17.9	19 55.8	12R23.0
15 M	1 30 0	20 36 26	26 37 51	3♑40 59	10 45.6	2 35.0	29 45.0	27 58.4	21 10.2	22 45.0	14 16.1	19 57.1	12 23.0
16 Tu	1 33 57	21 35 56	10♑37 39	17 27 53	10D43.4	3 40.4	0♏59.9	28 36.7	21 22.6	22 52.3	14 14.3	19 58.4	12 23.0
17 W	1 37 53	22 35 28	24 11 52	0♒49 53	10 42.8	4 51.7	2 14.8	29 14.9	21 34.9	22 59.6	14 12.6	19 59.6	12 22.9
18 Th	1 41 50	23 35 2	7♒22 18	13 49 31	10 43.6	6 8.2	3 29.7	29 53.2	21 47.4	23 6.9	14 10.9	20 0.9	12 22.8
19 F	1 45 46	24 34 37	20 11 59	26 30 10	10 45.0	7 29.2	4 44.6	0♎31.4	21 59.8	23 14.2	14 9.2	20 2.0	12 22.7
20 Sa	1 49 43	25 34 14	2♓44 33	8♓55 33	10R46.2	8 54.0	5 59.5	1 9.7	22 12.3	23 21.5	14 7.6	20 3.2	12 22.6
21 Su	1 53 39	26 33 52	15 3 38	21 9 11	10 46.4	10 22.0	7 14.5	1 47.9	22 24.9	23 28.8	14 6.0	20 4.3	12 22.4
22 M	1 57 36	27 33 33	27 12 34	3♈14 8	10 44.9	11 52.8	8 29.4	2 26.2	22 37.5	23 36.1	14 4.5	20 5.4	12 22.3
23 Tu	2 1 33	28 33 15	9♈14 10	15 12 58	10 41.1	13 25.7	9 44.3	3 4.4	22 50.1	23 43.4	14 2.9	20 6.5	12 22.1
24 W	2 5 29	29 32 59	21 10 45	27 7 44	10 35.0	15 0.5	10 59.2	3 42.7	23 2.8	23 50.7	14 1.5	20 7.5	12 21.8
25 Th	2 9 26	0♏32 45	3♉ 4 8	9♉ 0 8	10 26.8	16 36.7	12 14.1	4 21.0	23 15.6	23 58.0	14 0.0	20 8.5	12 21.6
26 F	2 13 22	1 32 34	14 55 56	20 51 43	10 17.1	18 14.0	13 29.0	4 59.2	23 28.3	24 5.3	13 58.6	20 9.5	12 21.3
27 Sa	2 17 19	2 32 24	26 47 42	2♊44 5	10 6.6	19 52.1	14 43.9	5 37.5	23 41.1	24 12.5	13 57.3	20 10.4	12 21.0
28 Su	2 21 15	3 32 16	8♊41 8	14 39 8	9 56.4	21 30.9	15 58.9	6 15.8	23 54.0	24 19.8	13 56.0	20 11.3	12 20.7
29 M	2 25 12	4 32 11	20 38 22	26 39 13	9 47.3	23 10.1	17 13.8	6 54.1	24 6.9	24 27.0	13 54.7	20 12.2	12 20.3
30 Tu	2 29 8	5 32 7	2♋42 2	8♋47 17	9 40.1	24 49.6	18 28.7	7 32.4	24 19.8	24 34.3	13 53.5	20 13.1	12 20.0
31 W	2 33 5	6 32 6	14 55 24	21 6 54	9 35.3	26 29.2	19 43.6	8 10.7	24 32.7	24 41.5	13 52.3	20 13.9	12 19.6

Astro Data	Planet Ingress	Last Aspect	☽ Ingress	Last Aspect	☽ Ingress	☽ Phases & Eclipses	Astro Data
Dy Hr Mn	Dy Hr Mn	Dy Hr Mn	Dy Hr Mn	Dy Hr Mn	Dy Hr Mn	Dy Hr Mn	1 SEPTEMBER 1923
☽0S 12 1:56	♂ ♍ 1 0:57	1 18:00 ♆ □	♊ 2 16:50	1 18:32 ♄ △	♋ 2 12:00	3 12:47 ☽ 9♊59	Julian Day # 8644
♃△♅ 14 2:43	♀ ♎ 21 3:29	4 6:09 ♆ ⚹	♋ 5 3:59	4 20:49 ☿ ⚹	♌ 4 21:14	10 20:52 ● 17♍06	Delta T 23.3 sec
♄⚹♆ 14 3:23	☉ ♎ 24 2:04	6 14:29 ♄ □	♌ 7 11:54	6 12:19 ♄ ⚹	♍ 7 2:41	10 20:47:05 • T 3'37"	SVP 06♓19'37"
☿ R 16 7:09		8 21:19 ♆ ☌	♍ 9 16:16	9 2:45 ☿ ☌	♎ 9 4:35	17 12:04 ☽ 23♐34	Obliquity 23°26'49"
♀0S 23 14:08	☿ ♍ 4 11:53	10 21:04 ♀ ☌	♎ 11 18:03	10 19:46 ♀ ☌	♏ 11 4:25	25 1:16 ○ 0♈57	⚷ Chiron 20♈27.8R
☽0N 25 8:55	☿ ♎ 11 22:23	13 1:02 ♆ ⚹	♏ 13 18:47	12 22:47 ♂ ⚹	♐ 13 4:08		☽ Mean ☊ 11♍28.5
☿0N 5 20:49	♀ ♏ 15 4:49	15 8:05 ♀ ⚹	♐ 15 20:05	15 2:23 ♂ □	♑ 15 5:43	3 5:29 ☽ 8♋59	
♃□♆ 8 4:26	♂ ♎ 18 4:18	17 15:41 ♀ □	♑ 17 23:14	17 9:35 ♂ △	♒ 17 10:29	10 6:05 ● 15♎54	1 OCTOBER 1923
☿ D 8 4:47	☉ ♏ 24 10:51	20 2:30 ♀ △	♒ 20 4:53	19 9:02 ☉ △	♓ 19 18:43	16 20:53 ☽ 22♑28	Julian Day # 8674
☽0S 9 12:22		21 18:00 ♄ △	♓ 22 13:03	21 14:45 ♃ △	♈ 22 5:33	24 18:26 ○ 0♉19	Delta T 23.4 sec
♇ R 14 0:00		23 22:02 ♃ △	♈ 24 23:23	24 5:26 ♄ ☍	♉ 24 17:48		SVP 06♓19'35"
☿0S 16 13:38		26 16:20 ♄ ☍	♉ 27 11:22	26 17:36 ♃ ☍	♊ 27 6:29		Obliquity 23°26'49"
☽0N 22 15:15		29 2:58 ♆ □	♊ 30 0:06	29 7:41 ♄ △	♋ 29 18:39		⚷ Chiron 19♈18.4R
♂0S 22 1:37							☽ Mean ☊ 9♍53.1

NOVEMBER 1923 LONGITUDE

Day	Sid.Time	☉	0 hr ☽	Noon ☽	True ☊	☿	♀	♂	♃	♄	♅	♆	♇
1 Th	2 37 1	7♏32 7	27♋22 18	3♌42 8	9♍32.8	28♎ 8.9	20♏58.6	8♎49.0	24♏45.7	24♎48.7	13♓51.2	20♌14.7	12♋19.2
2 F	2 40 58	8 32 10	10♌ 6 56	16 37 14	9D 32.2	29 48.5	22 13.5	9 27.4	24 58.7	24 55.9	13R 50.1	20 15.4	12R 18.8
3 Sa	2 44 55	9 32 15	23 13 31	29 56 15	9 32.7	1♏27.9	23 28.4	10 5.7	25 11.8	25 3.1	13 49.0	20 16.1	12 18.3
4 Su	2 48 51	10 32 22	6♍45 47	13♍42 22	9R 33.3	3 7.2	24 43.4	10 44.0	25 24.9	25 10.2	13 48.0	20 16.8	12 17.8
5 M	2 52 48	11 32 31	20 46 5	27 56 53	9 32.9	4 46.3	25 58.3	11 22.4	25 38.0	25 17.3	13 47.1	20 17.5	12 17.3
6 Tu	2 56 44	12 32 43	5♎14 30	12♎38 26	9 30.3	6 25.0	27 13.3	12 0.7	25 51.1	25 24.5	13 46.1	20 18.1	12 16.8
7 W	3 0 41	13 32 56	20 7 58	27 42 10	9 25.2	8 3.5	28 28.2	12 39.1	26 4.2	25 31.5	13 45.3	20 18.7	12 16.3
8 Th	3 4 37	14 33 11	5♏19 50	12♏59 41	9 17.5	9 41.7	29 43.2	13 17.5	26 17.4	25 38.6	13 44.5	20 19.2	12 15.7
9 F	3 8 34	15 33 29	20 40 16	28 20 4	9 8.0	11 19.5	0♐58.1	13 55.8	26 30.6	25 45.7	13 43.7	20 19.7	12 15.1
10 Sa	3 12 30	16 33 48	5♐57 39	13♐31 38	8 57.6	12 57.0	2 13.1	14 34.2	26 43.8	25 52.7	13 43.0	20 20.2	12 14.5
11 Su	3 16 27	17 34 8	21 0 48	28 24 9	8 47.7	14 34.2	3 28.0	15 12.6	26 57.1	25 59.7	13 42.3	20 20.7	12 13.9
12 M	3 20 24	18 34 31	5♑40 52	12♑50 27	8 39.5	16 11.1	4 43.0	15 51.0	27 10.3	26 6.6	13 41.7	20 21.1	12 13.2
13 Tu	3 24 20	19 34 54	19 52 34	26 47 8	8 33.6	17 47.6	5 57.9	16 29.4	27 23.6	26 13.6	13 41.1	20 21.5	12 12.6
14 W	3 28 17	20 35 19	3♒34 17	10♒14 17	8 30.3	19 23.9	7 12.9	17 7.7	27 36.9	26 20.5	13 40.6	20 21.8	12 11.9
15 Th	3 32 13	21 35 46	16 47 30	23 14 27	8D 29.1	20 59.8	8 27.8	17 46.1	27 50.2	26 27.3	13 40.1	20 22.1	12 11.2
16 F	3 36 10	22 36 13	29 35 41	5♓51 49	8R 29.1	22 35.4	9 42.7	18 24.5	28 3.5	26 34.2	13 39.7	20 22.4	12 10.4
17 Sa	3 40 6	23 36 42	12♓ 3 27	18 11 13	8 29.2	24 10.8	10 57.6	19 2.9	28 16.8	26 41.0	13 39.3	20 22.7	12 9.7
18 Su	3 44 3	24 37 12	24 15 42	0♈17 30	8 28.2	25 45.9	12 12.6	19 41.3	28 30.2	26 47.7	13 38.9	20 22.9	12 8.9
19 M	3 47 59	25 37 44	6♈17 9	12 15 9	8 25.0	27 20.7	13 27.5	20 19.7	28 43.5	26 54.5	13 38.7	20 23.1	12 8.1
20 Tu	3 51 56	26 38 17	18 11 56	24 7 56	8 19.1	28 55.3	14 42.4	20 58.1	28 56.8	27 1.2	13 38.4	20 23.2	12 7.3
21 W	3 55 53	27 38 51	0♉ 3 30	5♉58 56	8 10.1	0♐29.7	15 57.3	21 36.5	29 10.2	27 7.8	13 38.3	20 23.3	12 6.5
22 Th	3 59 49	28 39 26	11 54 30	17 50 26	7 58.3	2 3.9	17 12.2	22 15.0	29 23.5	27 14.4	13 38.1	20 23.4	12 5.7
23 F	4 3 46	29 40 3	23 46 55	29 44 8	7 44.5	3 38.0	18 27.1	22 53.4	29 36.9	27 21.0	13D 38.1	20R 23.4	12 4.8
24 Sa	4 7 42	0♐40 42	5♊42 13	11♊41 19	7 29.7	5 11.8	19 42.0	23 31.8	29 50.2	27 27.6	13 38.0	20 23.4	12 3.9
25 Su	4 11 39	1 41 22	17 41 34	23 43 5	7 15.0	6 45.5	20 56.9	24 10.3	0♐ 3.6	27 34.1	13 38.1	20 23.4	12 3.0
26 M	4 15 35	2 42 3	29 46 4	5♋50 42	7 1.8	8 19.1	22 11.8	24 48.7	0 17.0	27 40.5	13 38.1	20 23.3	12 2.1
27 Tu	4 19 32	3 42 46	11♋57 11	18 5 46	6 50.9	9 52.5	23 26.6	25 27.2	0 30.3	27 46.9	13 38.3	20 23.3	12 1.2
28 W	4 23 28	4 43 30	24 16 46	0♌30 31	6 42.9	11 25.9	24 41.5	26 5.6	0 43.7	27 53.3	13 38.4	20 23.1	12 0.3
29 Th	4 27 25	5 44 15	6♌47 22	13 7 45	6 38.0	12 59.1	25 56.4	26 44.1	0 57.0	27 59.6	13 38.7	20 23.0	11 59.3
30 F	4 31 22	6 45 3	19 32 5	26 0 51	6 35.7	14 32.2	27 11.3	27 22.6	1 10.4	28 5.8	13 39.0	20 22.8	11 58.4

DECEMBER 1923 LONGITUDE

Day	Sid.Time	☉	0 hr ☽	Noon ☽	True ☊	☿	♀	♂	♃	♄	♅	♆	♇
1 Sa	4 35 18	7♐45 51	2♍34 28	9♍13 25	6♍35.2	16♐ 5.3	28♐26.1	28♎ 1.0	1♐23.7	28♎12.1	13♓39.3	20♌22.5	11♋57.4
2 Su	4 39 15	8 46 41	15 58 4	22 48 47	6R 35.1	17 38.3	29 41.0	28 39.5	1 37.0	28 18.2	13 39.7	20R 22.3	11R 56.4
3 M	4 43 11	9 47 33	29 45 48	6♎49 14	6 34.2	19 11.2	0♑55.8	29 18.0	1 50.4	28 24.3	13 40.1	20 22.0	11 55.3
4 Tu	4 47 8	10 48 26	13♎59 5	21 15 7	6 31.3	20 44.0	2 10.7	29 56.5	2 3.7	28 30.4	13 40.6	20 21.6	11 54.3
5 W	4 51 4	11 49 20	28 36 54	6♏ 3 50	6 25.6	22 16.8	3 25.5	0♏35.0	2 17.0	28 36.4	13 41.1	20 21.3	11 53.3
6 Th	4 55 1	12 50 16	13♏35 1	21 9 24	6 17.2	23 49.4	4 40.4	1 13.5	2 30.3	28 42.3	13 41.7	20 20.9	11 52.2
7 F	4 58 57	13 51 13	28 45 46	6♐22 45	6 6.5	25 22.0	5 55.2	1 52.0	2 43.5	28 48.2	13 42.4	20 20.4	11 51.1
8 Sa	5 2 54	14 52 11	13♐58 56	21 32 56	5 54.7	26 54.4	7 10.1	2 30.5	2 56.8	28 54.1	13 43.1	20 20.0	11 50.1
9 Su	5 6 51	15 53 10	29 3 23	6♑29 7	5 43.3	28 26.7	8 24.9	3 9.1	3 10.0	28 59.8	13 43.8	20 19.5	11 49.0
10 M	5 10 47	16 54 10	13♑49 7	21 2 36	5 33.5	29 58.9	9 39.7	3 47.6	3 23.2	29 5.6	13 44.6	20 18.9	11 47.9
11 Tu	5 14 44	17 55 11	28 8 59	5♒ 7 58	5 26.2	1♑30.8	10 54.5	4 26.1	3 36.4	29 11.2	13 45.5	20 18.4	11 46.8
12 W	5 18 40	18 56 12	11♒59 26	18 43 27	5 21.7	3 2.4	12 9.3	5 4.6	3 49.6	29 16.8	13 46.4	20 17.8	11 45.6
13 Th	5 22 37	19 57 14	25 20 17	1♓50 19	5D 19.7	4 33.7	13 24.1	5 43.1	4 2.7	29 22.3	13 47.3	20 17.1	11 44.5
14 F	5 26 33	20 58 16	8♓14 2	14 32 2	5 19.4	6 4.5	14 38.9	6 21.6	4 15.9	29 27.8	13 48.3	20 16.5	11 43.3
15 Sa	5 30 30	21 59 19	20 44 55	26 53 21	5R 19.6	7 34.9	15 53.7	7 0.2	4 28.9	29 33.2	13 49.4	20 15.8	11 42.2
16 Su	5 34 27	23 0 22	2♈58 1	8♈59 33	5 19.2	9 4.7	17 8.4	7 38.7	4 42.0	29 38.5	13 50.4	20 15.1	11 41.0
17 M	5 38 23	24 1 25	14 58 37	20 55 51	5 17.0	10 33.8	18 23.2	8 17.2	4 55.0	29 43.7	13 51.6	20 14.3	11 39.8
18 Tu	5 42 20	25 2 29	26 51 48	2♉47 2	5 12.4	12 1.9	19 37.9	8 55.7	5 8.0	29 48.9	13 52.8	20 13.5	11 38.7
19 W	5 46 16	26 3 34	8♉42 3	14 37 16	5 4.9	13 29.0	20 52.6	9 34.3	5 21.0	29 54.0	13 54.0	20 12.7	11 37.5
20 Th	5 50 13	27 4 38	20 33 7	26 29 54	4 55.0	14 54.9	22 7.3	10 12.8	5 33.9	29 59.1	13 55.3	20 11.9	11 36.3
21 F	5 54 9	28 5 44	2♊27 56	8♊27 26	4 43.0	16 19.2	23 21.9	10 51.3	5 46.8	0♏ 4.1	13 56.7	20 11.0	11 35.1
22 Sa	5 58 6	29 6 49	14 28 37	20 31 37	4 30.0	17 41.7	24 36.6	11 29.9	5 59.7	0 9.0	13 58.1	20 10.1	11 33.9
23 Su	6 2 2	0♑ 7 55	26 36 33	2♋43 32	4 17.2	19 2.1	25 51.2	12 8.4	6 12.5	0 13.8	13 59.5	20 9.2	11 32.7
24 M	6 5 59	1 9 2	8♋52 38	15 3 55	4 5.5	20 19.9	27 5.8	12 47.0	6 25.3	0 18.5	14 1.0	20 8.2	11 31.4
25 Tu	6 9 56	2 10 9	21 17 27	27 33 20	3 56.0	21 34.9	28 20.4	13 25.5	6 38.0	0 23.2	14 2.5	20 7.2	11 30.2
26 W	6 13 52	3 11 16	3♌51 40	10♌12 33	3 49.1	22 46.3	29 35.0	14 4.1	6 50.7	0 27.8	14 4.1	20 6.2	11 29.0
27 Th	6 17 49	4 12 24	16 36 10	23 2 40	3 45.1	23 53.7	0♒49.6	14 42.6	7 3.4	0 32.3	14 5.7	20 5.2	11 27.8
28 F	6 21 45	5 13 32	29 32 18	6♍ 5 17	3D 43.6	24 56.4	2 4.1	15 21.2	7 16.0	0 36.7	14 7.4	20 4.1	11 26.5
29 Sa	6 25 42	6 14 41	12♍41 53	19 22 22	3 43.8	25 53.8	3 18.6	15 59.7	7 28.6	0 41.1	14 9.1	20 3.0	11 25.3
30 Su	6 29 38	7 15 50	26 6 58	2♎55 56	3R 44.6	26 44.9	4 33.1	16 38.3	7 41.1	0 45.4	14 10.9	20 1.9	11 24.0
31 M	6 33 35	8 16 59	9♎49 28	16 47 39	3 45.1	27 29.0	5 47.6	17 16.9	7 53.5	0 49.6	14 12.7	20 0.8	11 22.8

Astro Data	Dy Hr Mn
♃ ⊻ ♄	1 12:16
☽ 0 S	5 23:43
♃ ⊼ ♇	12 4:59
☽ 0 N	18 21:57
♅ D	23 23:29
♆ R	23 16:52
☽ 0 S	3 10:02
♄ ⊼ ♅	5 21:15
☽ 0 N	16 5:58
☽ 0 S	30 18:02

Planet Ingress	Dy Hr Mn
☿ ♏	2 2:47
♀ ♐	8 5:23
☿ ♐	20 16:26
☉ ♐	23 7:54
♃ ♐	24 17:31
♀ ♑	2 6:06
♂ ♏	4 2:11
☿ ♑	10 0:18
♄ ♏	20 4:25
☉ ♑	22 20:53
♀ ♒	26 8:03

Last Aspect Dy Hr Mn		☽ Ingress Dy Hr Mn
1 1:42	☿ □	♌ 1 5:00
3 3:36	♃ □	♍ 3 12:07
5 9:32	♀ ✶	♎ 5 15:24
7 8:38	♄ ☌	♏ 7 15:37
9 9:16	♃ ☌	♐ 9 14:37
11 8:08	♄ ✶	♑ 11 14:37
13 13:17	♃ ✶	♒ 13 17:39
15 21:02	♃ □	♓ 16 0:46
18 8:35	♃ △	♈ 18 11:25
20 18:01	♄ ☍	♉ 20 23:53
23 11:59	♃ ☍	♊ 23 12:32
25 19:49	♄ △	♋ 26 0:28
28 7:01	♄ □	♌ 28 11:01
30 15:57	♄ ✶	♍ 30 19:19

Last Aspect Dy Hr Mn		☽ Ingress Dy Hr Mn
2 3:19	☿ □	♎ 3 0:24
4 23:59	♄ ☌	♏ 5 2:14
6 10:43	♆ □	♐ 7 1:57
8 23:54	♄ ✶	♑ 9 1:31
11 1:47	♄ □	♒ 11 3:10
13 7:29	♄ △	♓ 13 8:35
15 2:38	☉ □	♈ 15 18:08
18 6:01	♄ ☍	♉ 18 6:21
20 3:32	♀ △	♊ 20 19:03
22 11:17	♆ ✶	♋ 23 6:40
25 14:59	♀ ☍	♌ 25 16:40
27 6:30	♆ ☌	♍ 28 0:51
30 1:11	☿ △	♎ 30 6:51

☽ Phases & Eclipses Dy Hr Mn	
1 20:49	☽ 8♌24
8 15:27	● 15♏12
15 9:41	☽ 22♒00
23 12:58	○ 0♊13
1 10:09	☽ 8♍12
8 1:30	● 14♐56
15 2:38	☽ 22♓06
23 7:33	○ 0♋27
30 21:07	☽ 8♎10

Astro Data
1 NOVEMBER 1923
Julian Day # 8705
Delta T 23.4 sec
SVP 06♓19'32"
Obliquity 23°26'49"
⚷ Chiron 17♈54.5R
☽ Mean ☊ 8♍14.6

1 DECEMBER 1923
Julian Day # 8735
Delta T 23.5 sec
SVP 06♓19'28"
Obliquity 23°26'48"
⚷ Chiron 16♈51.9R
☽ Mean ☊ 6♍39.3

LONGITUDE — JANUARY 1924

Day	Sid.Time	☉	0 hr ☽	Noon ☽	True ☊	☿	♀	♂	♃	♄	♅	♆	♇
1 Tu	6 37 31	9♑18 9	23♎50 32	0♏58 2	3♍44.0	28♑ 5.2	7♒ 2.1	17♏55.4	8♐ 6.0	0♏53.7	14♓14.5	19♌59.6	11♋21.5
2 W	6 41 28	10 19 19	8♏ 9 56	15 25 52	3R40.9	28 32.5	8 16.5	18 34.0	8 18.3	0 57.7	14 16.4	19R58.4	11R20.3
3 Th	6 45 25	11 20 30	22 45 17	0♐ 7 33	3 35.5	28 50.1	9 30.9	19 12.6	8 30.6	1 1.6	14 18.3	19 57.2	11 19.0
4 F	6 49 21	12 21 41	7♐31 48	14 57 7	3 28.2	28R57.1	10 45.3	19 51.2	8 42.9	1 5.5	14 20.3	19 55.9	11 17.8
5 Sa	6 53 18	13 22 53	22 22 27	29 46 43	3 20.0	28 53.0	11 59.7	20 29.7	8 55.1	1 9.3	14 22.3	19 54.7	11 16.6
6 Su	6 57 14	14 24 4	7♑ 8 51	14♑27 49	3 11.8	28 37.1	13 14.1	21 8.3	9 7.2	1 12.9	14 24.4	19 53.4	11 15.3
7 M	7 1 11	15 25 15	21 42 41	28 52 37	3 4.7	28 9.3	14 28.4	21 46.9	9 19.3	1 16.5	14 26.5	19 52.1	11 14.1
8 Tu	7 5 7	16 26 26	5♒56 57	12♒55 14	2 59.6	27 29.9	15 42.7	22 25.4	9 31.3	1 20.0	14 28.6	19 50.8	11 12.8
9 W	7 9 4	17 27 37	19 47 7	26 32 27	2D56.6	26 39.5	16 57.0	23 4.0	9 43.3	1 23.4	14 30.8	19 49.4	11 11.6
10 Th	7 13 0	18 28 47	3♓11 17	9♓43 46	2 55.7	25 39.2	18 11.2	23 42.5	9 55.2	1 26.7	14 33.1	19 48.0	11 10.3
11 F	7 16 57	19 29 57	16 10 10	22 30 54	2 56.4	24 30.8	19 25.4	24 21.1	10 7.0	1 29.9	14 35.3	19 46.6	11 9.1
12 Sa	7 20 54	20 31 6	28 46 25	4♈57 17	2 57.9	23 16.3	20 39.6	24 59.6	10 18.7	1 33.1	14 37.6	19 45.2	11 7.9
13 Su	7 24 50	21 32 15	11♈ 4 5	17 7 25	2R59.4	21 58.0	21 53.7	25 38.2	10 30.4	1 36.1	14 40.0	19 43.8	11 6.6
14 M	7 28 47	22 33 23	23 7 56	29 6 17	2 59.9	20 38.5	23 7.8	26 16.7	10 42.0	1 39.0	14 42.3	19 42.3	11 5.4
15 Tu	7 32 43	23 34 30	5♉ 3 5	10♉58 57	2 59.0	19 20.3	24 21.9	26 55.3	10 53.5	1 41.9	14 44.8	19 40.9	11 4.2
16 W	7 36 40	24 35 37	16 54 30	22 50 16	2 56.4	18 5.7	25 35.9	27 33.8	11 5.0	1 44.6	14 47.2	19 39.4	11 3.0
17 Th	7 40 36	25 36 43	28 46 47	4♊44 33	2 52.1	16 56.6	26 49.9	28 12.3	11 16.4	1 47.2	14 49.7	19 37.9	11 1.8
18 F	7 44 33	26 37 48	10♊43 59	16 45 28	2 46.4	15 54.7	28 3.8	28 50.8	11 27.7	1 49.8	14 52.2	19 36.4	11 0.6
19 Sa	7 48 29	27 38 53	22 49 20	28 55 52	2 39.9	15 1.0	29 17.7	29 29.4	11 38.9	1 52.2	14 54.8	19 34.9	10 59.4
20 Su	7 52 26	28 39 56	5♋ 5 17	11♋17 44	2 33.4	14 16.2	0♓31.5	0♐ 7.9	11 50.0	1 54.6	14 57.4	19 33.3	10 58.2
21 M	7 56 23	29 41 0	17 33 21	23 52 11	2 27.4	13 40.8	1 45.3	0 46.4	12 1.1	1 56.8	14 60.0	19 31.8	10 57.0
22 Tu	8 0 19	0♒42 2	0♌14 16	6♌39 36	2 22.7	13 14.8	2 59.1	1 24.9	12 12.1	1 59.0	15 2.7	19 30.2	10 55.9
23 W	8 4 16	1 43 3	13 8 8	19 39 49	2 19.6	12 57.9	4 12.8	2 3.4	12 23.0	2 1.0	15 5.3	19 28.6	10 54.7
24 Th	8 8 12	2 44 4	26 14 35	2♍52 21	2D18.1	12D49.7	5 26.4	2 41.9	12 33.8	2 3.0	15 8.1	19 27.0	10 53.6
25 F	8 12 9	3 45 4	9♍33 2	16 16 35	2 18.1	12 49.9	6 40.0	3 20.4	12 44.5	2 4.8	15 10.8	19 25.4	10 52.4
26 Sa	8 16 5	4 46 4	23 2 56	29 52 2	2 19.2	12 57.8	7 53.5	3 58.9	12 55.1	2 6.6	15 13.6	19 23.8	10 51.3
27 Su	8 20 2	5 47 3	6♎43 48	13♎38 13	2 20.8	13 13.0	9 7.0	4 37.4	13 5.6	2 8.2	15 16.4	19 22.2	10 50.2
28 M	8 23 58	6 48 1	20 35 11	27 34 38	2 22.3	13 34.7	10 20.5	5 15.9	13 16.1	2 9.7	15 19.2	19 20.6	10 49.0
29 Tu	8 27 55	7 48 58	4♏36 26	11♏40 28	2R23.1	14 2.5	11 33.9	5 54.4	13 26.4	2 11.2	15 22.1	19 18.9	10 47.9
30 W	8 31 52	8 49 56	18 46 30	25 54 18	2 22.8	14 35.8	12 47.2	6 32.9	13 36.6	2 12.5	15 25.0	19 17.3	10 46.9
31 Th	8 35 48	9 50 52	3♐ 3 30	10♐13 45	2 21.4	15 14.2	14 0.5	7 11.4	13 46.8	2 13.7	15 27.9	19 15.6	10 45.8

LONGITUDE — FEBRUARY 1924

Day	Sid.Time	☉	0 hr ☽	Noon ☽	True ☊	☿	♀	♂	♃	♄	♅	♆	♇
1 F	8 39 45	10♒51 48	17♐24 34	24♐35 27	2♍19.0	15♑57.1	15♓13.7	7♐49.8	13♐56.8	2♏14.8	15♓30.9	19♌14.0	10♋44.7
2 Sa	8 43 41	11 52 43	1♑45 48	8♑55 3	2R16.2	16 44.2	16 26.9	8 28.3	14 6.8	2 15.8	15 33.9	19R12.3	10R43.7
3 Su	8 47 38	12 53 37	16 2 33	23 7 42	2 13.3	17 35.1	17 40.0	9 6.8	14 16.6	2 16.8	15 36.9	19 10.6	10 42.6
4 M	8 51 34	13 54 30	0♒ 9 53	7♒ 8 35	2 10.9	18 29.4	18 53.1	9 45.2	14 26.4	2 17.6	15 39.9	19 9.0	10 41.6
5 Tu	8 55 31	14 55 22	14 3 17	20 53 36	2 9.2	19 26.8	20 6.1	10 23.6	14 36.0	2 18.3	15 43.0	19 7.3	10 40.6
6 W	8 59 27	15 56 13	27 39 12	4♓19 53	2D 8.4	20 27.2	21 19.0	11 2.1	14 45.5	2 18.9	15 46.0	19 5.6	10 39.6
7 Th	9 3 24	16 57 2	10♓55 30	17 26 3	2 8.5	21 30.1	22 31.9	11 40.5	14 54.9	2 19.3	15 49.1	19 3.9	10 38.6
8 F	9 7 21	17 57 50	23 51 37	0♈12 23	2 9.3	22 35.5	23 44.6	12 18.9	15 4.2	2 19.7	15 52.2	19 2.2	10 37.7
9 Sa	9 11 17	18 58 37	6♈28 36	12 40 36	2 10.5	23 43.1	24 57.4	12 57.2	15 13.3	2 20.0	15 55.4	19 0.5	10 36.7
10 Su	9 15 14	19 59 22	18 48 47	24 53 37	2 11.8	24 52.8	26 10.0	13 35.6	15 22.4	2 20.1	15 58.5	18 58.9	10 35.8
11 M	9 19 10	21 0 6	0♉55 35	6♉55 14	2 12.8	26 4.4	27 22.6	14 14.0	15 31.3	2R20.2	16 1.7	18 57.2	10 34.8
12 Tu	9 23 7	22 0 48	12 53 9	18 49 54	2R13.5	27 17.7	28 35.1	14 52.3	15 40.1	2 20.2	16 4.9	18 55.5	10 33.9
13 W	9 27 3	23 1 28	24 46 5	0♊42 18	2 13.6	28 32.8	29 47.5	15 30.6	15 48.8	2 20.0	16 8.1	18 53.8	10 33.1
14 Th	9 31 0	24 2 7	6♊39 8	12 37 11	2 13.3	29 49.4	0♈59.8	16 8.9	15 57.4	2 19.7	16 11.4	18 52.1	10 32.2
15 F	9 34 56	25 2 44	18 36 59	24 39 5	2 12.7	1♒ 7.5	2 12.0	16 47.2	16 5.8	2 19.4	16 14.6	18 50.4	10 31.3
16 Sa	9 38 53	26 3 20	0♋43 57	6♋52 4	2 12.0	2 26.9	3 24.2	17 25.5	16 14.2	2 18.9	16 17.9	18 48.8	10 30.5
17 Su	9 42 50	27 3 53	13 3 48	19 19 29	2 11.2	3 47.8	4 36.2	18 3.8	16 22.4	2 18.4	16 21.2	18 47.1	10 29.7
18 M	9 46 46	28 4 25	25 39 25	2♌ 3 47	2 10.6	5 9.9	5 48.2	18 42.0	16 30.4	2 17.7	16 24.5	18 45.4	10 28.9
19 Tu	9 50 43	29 4 56	8♌32 43	15 6 14	2 10.2	6 33.2	7 0.1	19 20.3	16 38.3	2 16.9	16 27.8	18 43.8	10 28.1
20 W	9 54 39	0♓ 5 24	21 44 20	28 26 53	2D10.0	7 57.8	8 11.8	19 58.5	16 46.1	2 16.0	16 31.1	18 42.1	10 27.4
21 Th	9 58 36	1 5 51	5♍13 42	12♍ 4 30	2 10.0	9 23.5	9 23.5	20 36.7	16 53.8	2 15.0	16 34.4	18 40.5	10 26.6
22 F	10 2 32	2 6 16	18 58 58	25 56 44	2R10.0	10 50.3	10 35.1	21 14.9	17 1.3	2 14.0	16 37.8	18 38.8	10 25.9
23 Sa	10 6 29	3 6 40	2♎57 21	10♎ 0 23	2 10.0	12 18.2	11 46.6	21 53.1	17 8.7	2 12.8	16 41.1	18 37.2	10 25.2
24 Su	10 10 25	4 7 2	17 5 21	24 11 48	2 9.8	13 47.2	12 57.9	22 31.3	17 15.9	2 11.5	16 44.5	18 35.6	10 24.5
25 M	10 14 22	5 7 23	1♏19 15	8♏27 15	2 9.6	15 17.3	14 9.2	23 9.4	17 23.1	2 10.1	16 47.9	18 34.0	10 23.9
26 Tu	10 18 19	6 7 42	15 35 24	22 43 17	2 9.2	16 48.4	15 20.4	23 47.6	17 30.0	2 8.6	16 51.2	18 32.4	10 23.2
27 W	10 22 15	7 8 0	29 50 34	6♐56 55	2D 9.0	18 20.6	16 31.4	24 25.7	17 36.8	2 7.0	16 54.6	18 30.8	10 22.6
28 Th	10 26 12	8 8 17	14♐ 2 2	21 5 41	2 9.0	19 53.9	17 42.4	25 3.8	17 43.5	2 5.4	16 58.0	18 29.2	10 22.0
29 F	10 30 8	9 8 32	28 7 37	5♑ 7 36	2 9.3	21 28.2	18 53.2	25 41.9	17 50.0	2 3.6	17 1.4	18 27.7	10 21.4

Astro Data Dy Hr Mn	Planet Ingress Dy Hr Mn
☿ R 4 3:14	♀ ♓ 19 13:45
☽0N 12 15:19	♂ ♐ 19 19:06
♃⚻♇ 15 20:12	☉ ♒ 21 7:28
☿ D 24 11:24	
☽0S 27 0:16	♀ ♈ 13 4:10
	☿ ♒ 14 3:18
☽0N 9 0:58	☉ ♓ 19 21:51
♄ R 11 1:16	
♀0N 14 10:42	
♃□♅ 16 18:07	
☽0S 23 6:53	
♃∠♄ 23 11:27	
♄⚼♅ 29 9:45	

Last Aspect Dy Hr Mn	☽ Ingress Dy Hr Mn	Last Aspect Dy Hr Mn	☽ Ingress Dy Hr Mn
1 7:26 ☿ □	♏ 1 10:23	1 3:02 ♆ △	♑ 1 21:03
3 10:01 ☿ ⚹	♐ 3 11:48	3 3:00 ♀ ⚹	♒ 3 23:43
4 20:01 ♆ △	♑ 5 12:22	5 8:52 ♆ ☍	♓ 6 4:12
7 10:21 ☿ ☌	♒ 7 13:54	7 23:46 ♀ ☌	♈ 8 11:36
9 6:06 ♂ □	♓ 9 18:13	10 13:16 ☿ □	♉ 10 22:09
11 16:21 ♂ △	♈ 12 2:22	13 8:33 ☿ △	♊ 13 10:35
13 24:00 ♀ ⚹	♉ 14 13:48	15 13:57 ☉ △	♋ 15 22:34
16 22:47 ♂ ☍	♊ 17 2:28	17 6:21 ♅ △	♌ 18 8:09
18 17:37 ♆ ⚹	♋ 19 14:05	19 20:40 ♂ △	♍ 20 14:45
20 19:06 ♅ △	♌ 21 23:33	22 4:06 ♂ □	♎ 22 18:57
23 11:38 ♆ ☌	♍ 24 6:49	24 9:36 ♂ ⚹	♏ 24 21:47
25 10:05 ♅ ☍	♎ 26 12:14	26 4:57 ♆ □	♐ 27 0:16
27 21:52 ♆ ⚹	♏ 28 16:09	28 19:39 ♂ ☌	♑ 29 3:12
30 0:52 ♆ □	♐ 30 18:52		

☽ Phases & Eclipses Dy Hr Mn	
6 12:48	● 14♑57
13 22:44	☽ 22♈30
22 0:57	○ 0♌44
29 5:53	☽ 8♏04
5 1:38	● 14♒60
12 20:09	☽ 22♉52
20 16:07	○ 0♍46
20 16:09	☍T 1.599
27 13:15	☽ 7♐41

Astro Data

1 JANUARY 1924
Julian Day # 8766
Delta T 23.5 sec
SVP 06♓19'23"
Obliquity 23°26'48"
⚷ Chiron 16♈30.7
☽ Mean ☊ 5♍00.8

1 FEBRUARY 1924
Julian Day # 8797
Delta T 23.5 sec
SVP 06♓19'18"
Obliquity 23°26'49"
⚷ Chiron 17♈02.3
☽ Mean ☊ 3♍22.3

MARCH 1924 LONGITUDE

Day	Sid.Time	☉	0 hr ☽	Noon ☽	True ☊	☿	♀	♂	♃	♄	♅	♆	♇
1 Sa	10 34 5	10♓ 8 46	12♑ 5 28	19♑ 0 59	2♍ 9.9	23♒ 3.5	20♈ 3.9	26♐20.0	17♐56.4	2♏ 1.7	17♓ 4.9	18♌26.1	10♋20.9
2 Su	10 38 1	11 8 58	25 54 1	2♒44 21	2 10.7	24 39.9	21 14.6	26 58.0	18 2.6	1R59.7	17 8.3	18R24.6	10R20.4
3 M	10 41 58	12 9 9	9♒31 50	16 16 18	2 11.6	26 17.3	22 25.1	27 36.0	18 8.7	1 57.7	17 11.7	18 23.1	10 19.9
4 Tu	10 45 54	13 9 18	22 57 36	29 35 35	2R12.1	27 55.8	23 35.4	28 14.0	18 14.6	1 55.5	17 15.1	18 21.6	10 19.4
5 W	10 49 51	14 9 25	6♓10 8	12♓41 9	2 12.2	29 35.4	24 45.7	28 52.0	18 20.4	1 53.3	17 18.6	18 20.1	10 18.9
6 Th	10 53 47	15 9 30	19 8 36	25 32 25	2 11.7	1♓16.1	25 55.8	29 29.9	18 26.0	1 50.9	17 22.0	18 18.6	10 18.4
7 F	10 57 44	16 9 33	1♈52 39	8♈ 9 21	2 10.4	2 57.8	27 5.8	0♑ 7.8	18 31.4	1 48.5	17 25.4	18 17.1	10 18.0
8 Sa	11 1 41	17 9 35	14 22 37	20 32 39	2 8.5	4 40.7	28 15.7	0 45.7	18 36.7	1 46.0	17 28.9	18 15.7	10 17.6
9 Su	11 5 37	18 9 34	26 39 38	2♉43 51	2 6.0	6 24.7	29 25.4	1 23.6	18 41.8	1 43.4	17 32.3	18 14.3	10 17.2
10 M	11 9 34	19 9 31	8♉45 38	14 45 21	2 3.4	8 9.8	0♉35.0	2 1.4	18 46.7	1 40.7	17 35.7	18 12.9	10 16.9
11 Tu	11 13 30	20 9 26	20 43 26	26 40 20	2 0.9	9 56.1	1 44.5	2 39.2	18 51.5	1 37.9	17 39.2	18 11.5	10 16.6
12 W	11 17 27	21 9 19	2♊36 33	8♊32 37	1 59.0	11 43.5	2 53.8	3 16.9	18 56.1	1 35.0	17 42.6	18 10.1	10 16.3
13 Th	11 21 23	22 9 10	14 29 7	20 26 36	1D57.9	13 32.1	4 2.9	3 54.6	19 0.6	1 32.1	17 46.0	18 8.8	10 16.0
14 F	11 25 20	23 8 59	26 25 40	2♋26 56	1 57.7	15 21.8	5 11.9	4 32.3	19 4.9	1 29.1	17 49.5	18 7.4	10 15.7
15 Sa	11 29 16	24 8 45	8♋30 59	14 38 23	1 58.4	17 12.8	6 20.7	5 10.0	19 9.0	1 26.0	17 52.9	18 6.1	10 15.5
16 Su	11 33 13	25 8 29	20 49 44	27 5 30	1 59.8	19 4.9	7 29.4	5 47.6	19 12.9	1 22.8	17 56.3	18 4.8	10 15.3
17 M	11 37 10	26 8 11	3♌26 12	9♌52 12	2 1.5	20 58.2	8 37.9	6 25.2	19 16.7	1 19.5	17 59.7	18 3.6	10 15.1
18 Tu	11 41 6	27 7 51	16 23 52	23 1 24	2 2.9	22 52.7	9 46.2	7 2.7	19 20.3	1 16.2	18 3.1	18 2.3	10 14.9
19 W	11 45 3	28 7 28	29 44 56	6♍34 27	2R 3.6	24 48.3	10 54.4	7 40.3	19 23.7	1 12.8	18 6.5	18 1.1	10 14.8
20 Th	11 48 59	29 7 3	13♍29 49	20 30 46	2 3.2	26 45.0	12 2.3	8 17.7	19 26.9	1 9.3	18 9.9	17 59.9	10 14.6
21 F	11 52 56	0♈ 6 37	27 36 51	4♎47 31	2 1.4	28 42.8	13 10.1	8 55.2	19 30.0	1 5.8	18 13.3	17 58.8	10 14.5
22 Sa	11 56 52	1 6 8	12♎ 2 4	19 19 44	1 58.2	0♈41.6	14 17.7	9 32.6	19 32.9	1 2.2	18 16.7	17 57.6	10 14.5
23 Su	12 0 49	2 5 37	26 39 38	4♏ 0 50	1 54.1	2 41.3	15 25.1	10 10.0	19 35.6	0 58.5	18 20.0	17 56.5	10 14.4
24 M	12 4 45	3 5 4	11♏22 26	18 43 32	1 49.5	4 41.9	16 32.3	10 47.3	19 38.1	0 54.8	18 23.4	17 55.4	10D14.4
25 Tu	12 8 42	4 4 29	26 3 16	3♐20 54	1 45.2	6 43.2	17 39.3	11 24.6	19 40.4	0 51.0	18 26.7	17 54.3	10 14.4
26 W	12 12 39	5 3 53	10♐35 47	17 47 24	1 41.8	8 45.1	18 46.1	12 1.9	19 42.6	0 47.2	18 30.1	17 53.3	10 14.4
27 Th	12 16 35	6 3 15	24 55 20	1♑59 18	1D39.8	10 47.4	19 52.7	12 39.1	19 44.6	0 43.3	18 33.4	17 52.3	10 14.5
28 F	12 20 32	7 2 35	8♑59 10	15 54 50	1 39.3	12 50.0	20 59.1	13 16.3	19 46.4	0 39.3	18 36.7	17 51.3	10 14.5
29 Sa	12 24 28	8 1 53	22 46 20	29 33 45	1 40.1	14 52.5	22 5.2	13 53.4	19 48.0	0 35.3	18 40.0	17 50.3	10 14.6
30 Su	12 28 25	9 1 10	6♒17 12	12♒56 51	1 41.6	16 54.7	23 11.2	14 30.5	19 49.4	0 31.2	18 43.3	17 49.4	10 14.8
31 M	12 32 21	10 0 25	19 32 53	26 5 28	1R43.0	18 56.3	24 16.9	15 7.6	19 50.6	0 27.1	18 46.5	17 48.5	10 14.9

APRIL 1924 LONGITUDE

Day	Sid.Time	☉	0 hr ☽	Noon ☽	True ☊	☿	♀	♂	♃	♄	♅	♆	♇
1 Tu	12 36 18	10♈59 38	2♓34 47	9♓ 1 0	1♍43.5	20♈57.1	25♉22.4	15♑44.5	19♐51.7	0♏23.0	18♓49.8	17♌47.6	10♋15.1
2 W	12 40 14	11 58 49	15 24 14	21 44 39	1R42.6	22 56.6	26 27.6	16 21.5	19 52.5	0R18.8	18 53.0	17R46.7	10 15.3
3 Th	12 44 11	12 57 58	28 2 22	4♈17 27	1 39.6	24 54.5	27 32.6	16 58.3	19 53.2	0 14.5	18 56.2	17 45.9	10 15.5
4 F	12 48 7	13 57 5	10♈30 1	16 40 9	1 34.6	26 50.5	28 37.4	17 35.1	19 53.7	0 10.2	18 59.4	17 45.1	10 15.7
5 Sa	12 52 4	14 56 11	22 47 58	28 53 34	1 27.8	28 44.0	29 41.8	18 11.9	19 54.0	0 5.9	19 2.6	17 44.4	10 16.0
6 Su	12 56 1	15 55 14	4♉57 6	10♉58 42	1 19.6	0♉34.9	0♊46.1	18 48.5	19R54.1	0 1.6	19 5.8	17 43.6	10 16.2
7 M	12 59 57	16 54 15	16 58 34	22 56 57	1 10.8	2 22.6	1 50.0	19 25.2	19 54.0	29♎57.2	19 8.9	17 42.9	10 16.6
8 Tu	13 3 54	17 53 14	28 54 6	4♊50 22	1 2.3	4 6.9	2 53.7	20 1.7	19 53.7	29 52.8	19 12.0	17 42.2	10 16.9
9 W	13 7 50	18 52 10	10♊46 5	16 41 40	0 54.9	5 47.4	3 57.1	20 38.2	19 53.3	29 48.3	19 15.1	17 41.6	10 17.2
10 Th	13 11 47	19 51 5	22 37 35	28 34 20	0 49.2	7 23.8	5 0.1	21 14.6	19 52.6	29 43.9	19 18.2	17 41.0	10 17.6
11 F	13 15 43	20 49 57	4♋32 26	10♋32 29	0 45.6	8 55.8	6 2.9	21 50.9	19 51.8	29 39.4	19 21.3	17 40.4	10 18.0
12 Sa	13 19 40	21 48 47	16 35 3	22 40 45	0D44.0	10 23.2	7 5.3	22 27.2	19 50.8	29 34.8	19 24.3	17 39.8	10 18.4
13 Su	13 23 36	22 47 35	28 50 14	5♌ 4 6	0 44.0	11 45.8	8 7.4	23 3.4	19 49.6	29 30.3	19 27.3	17 39.3	10 18.9
14 M	13 27 33	23 46 20	11♌22 58	17 47 24	0 44.9	13 3.3	9 9.2	23 39.6	19 48.2	29 25.8	19 30.3	17 38.8	10 19.4
15 Tu	13 31 30	24 45 3	24 17 54	0♍54 54	0R45.9	14 15.7	10 10.6	24 15.6	19 46.6	29 21.2	19 33.3	17 38.4	10 19.9
16 W	13 35 26	25 43 44	7♍38 45	14 29 38	0 45.8	15 22.7	11 11.7	24 51.6	19 44.9	29 16.7	19 36.2	17 37.9	10 20.4
17 Th	13 39 23	26 42 23	21 27 38	28 32 35	0 44.0	16 24.2	12 12.3	25 27.5	19 42.9	29 12.1	19 39.1	17 37.5	10 20.9
18 F	13 43 19	27 41 0	5♎44 12	13♎ 1 55	0 39.9	17 20.1	13 12.6	26 3.3	19 40.8	29 7.5	19 42.0	17 37.2	10 21.5
19 Sa	13 47 16	28 39 34	20 25 3	27 52 38	0 33.4	18 10.3	14 12.5	26 39.1	19 38.5	29 2.9	19 44.9	17 36.9	10 22.1
20 Su	13 51 12	29 38 7	5♏23 35	12♏56 42	0 25.2	18 54.7	15 11.9	27 14.7	19 36.0	28 58.3	19 47.7	17 36.6	10 22.7
21 M	13 55 9	0♉36 37	20 30 42	28 4 16	0 16.2	19 33.4	16 11.0	27 50.3	19 33.3	28 53.7	19 50.5	17 36.3	10 23.3
22 Tu	13 59 5	1 35 6	5♐36 9	13♐ 5 11	0 7.4	20 6.2	17 9.6	28 25.8	19 30.5	28 49.2	19 53.3	17 36.1	10 23.9
23 W	14 3 2	2 33 34	20 30 24	27 50 56	29♌60.0	20 33.1	18 7.8	29 1.2	19 27.5	28 44.6	19 56.0	17 35.9	10 24.6
24 Th	14 6 59	3 31 59	5♑ 6 10	12♑15 39	29 54.7	20 54.1	19 5.5	29 36.5	19 24.3	28 40.0	19 58.7	17 35.7	10 25.3
25 F	14 10 55	4 30 23	19 19 9	26 16 35	29 51.7	21 9.3	20 2.7	0♒11.8	19 20.9	28 35.5	20 1.4	17 35.6	10 26.0
26 Sa	14 14 52	5 28 46	3♒ 8 2	9♒53 42	29D50.7	21 18.8	20 59.4	0 46.9	19 17.4	28 30.9	20 4.1	17 35.5	10 26.7
27 Su	14 18 48	6 27 7	16 33 50	23 8 50	29 50.9	21R22.6	21 55.7	1 21.9	19 13.7	28 26.4	20 6.7	17 35.4	10 27.5
28 M	14 22 45	7 25 26	29 39 3	6♓ 4 54	29R51.3	21 20.9	22 51.4	1 56.8	19 9.8	28 21.9	20 9.3	17D35.3	10 28.3
29 Tu	14 26 41	8 23 44	12♓26 48	18 45 10	29 50.6	21 13.9	23 46.6	2 31.6	19 5.7	28 17.4	20 11.9	17 35.3	10 29.1
30 W	14 30 38	9 22 0	25 0 21	1♈12 44	29 47.9	21 1.8	24 41.2	3 6.3	19 1.5	28 12.9	20 14.4	17 35.4	10 29.9

Astro Data Dy Hr Mn	Planet Ingress Dy Hr Mn	Last Aspect Dy Hr Mn	☽ Ingress Dy Hr Mn	Last Aspect Dy Hr Mn	☽ Ingress Dy Hr Mn	☽ Phases & Eclipses Dy Hr Mn	Astro Data
♃△♆ 4 22:57	☿ ♓ 5 5:53	1 15:07 ♀ □	♒ 2 7:11	2 22:58 ♀ ⚹	♈ 3 3:45	5 15:58 ● 14♓49	1 MARCH 1924
☽0N 7 9:43	♂ ♑ 6 19:02	4 10:16 ☿ ☌	♓ 4 12:44	5 13:48 ☿ ☌	♉ 5 14:11	5 15:43:55 ☌ P 0.582	Julian Day # 8826
♅⚻♆ 17 19:56	♀ ♉ 9 11:55	5 22:40 ♃ □	♈ 6 20:26	7 5:10 ♂ △	♊ 8 2:13	13 16:50 ☽ 22♊51	Delta T 23.5 sec
☽0S 21 15:32	☉ ♈ 20 21:20	9 6:02 ♀ ☌	♉ 9 6:35	10 14:15 ♄ △	♋ 10 14:53	21 4:30 ○ 0♎18	SVP 06♓19'15"
☿0N 23 1:49	☿ ♈ 21 15:37	10 22:45 ☉ ⚹	♊ 11 18:43	13 1:17 ♄ □	♌ 13 2:15	27 20:24 ☽ 6♑54	Obliquity 23°26'49"
♇ D 24 12:43		13 16:50 ☉ □	♋ 14 7:08	15 9:08 ♄ ⚹	♍ 15 10:21		⚷ Chiron 18♈12.9
	☿ ♉ 5 16:23	16 8:59 ☉ △	♌ 16 17:31	17 7:06 ♂ △	♎ 17 14:27	4 7:17 ● 14♈15	☽ Mean ☊ 1♍50.2
☽0N 3 17:01	♀ ♊ 5 6:46	18 5:22 ♃ △	♍ 19 0:27	19 14:10 ☉ ☍	♏ 19 15:24	12 11:12 ☽ 22♋16	
♃ R 6 1:27	♄ ♎ 6 8:36	21 2:08 ☿ ☍	♎ 21 4:00	21 12:06 ♂ ⚹	♐ 21 15:04	19 14:10 ○ 29♎14	1 APRIL 1924
♃□♅ 17 18:11	☉ ♉ 20 8:59	22 12:24 ♃ ⚹	♏ 23 5:27	23 13:24 ♄ ⚹	♑ 23 15:33	26 4:28 ☽ 5♒40	Julian Day # 8857
☽0S 18 2:04	☊ ♌ 22 23:55	24 11:30 ♅ △	♐ 25 6:29	25 15:57 ♄ □	♒ 25 18:30		Delta T 23.5 sec
☿ R 27 4:28	♂ ♒ 24 15:58	26 15:15 ♃ ☌	♑ 27 8:37	27 21:38 ♄ △	♓ 28 0:39		SVP 06♓19'12"
♆ D 28 15:25		28 22:41 ♀ △	♒ 29 12:47	29 23:20 ♀ □	♈ 30 9:39		Obliquity 23°26'49"
☽0N 30 23:27		31 9:28 ♀ □	♓ 31 19:13				⚷ Chiron 19♈55.6
							☽ Mean ☊ 0♍11.7

LONGITUDE MAY 1924

Day	Sid.Time	☉	0 hr ☽	Noon ☽	True ☊	☿	♀	♂	♃	♄	♅	♆	♇
1 Th	14 34 34	10♉20 15	7♈22 35	13♈30 13	29♌42.6	20♉45.1	25♊35.3	3♒40.9	18♐57.2	28♎ 8.5	20♓16.9	17♌35.4	10♋30.7
2 F	14 38 31	11 18 28	19 35 51	25 39 43	29R 34.4	20R 23.9	26 28.7	4 15.3	18R 52.6	28R 4.1	20 19.3	17 35.5	10 31.5
3 Sa	14 42 28	12 16 40	1♉41 59	7♉42 50	29 23.7	19 58.9	27 21.6	4 49.6	18 47.9	27 59.7	20 21.8	17 35.7	10 32.4
4 Su	14 46 24	13 14 49	13 42 25	19 40 52	29 11.0	19 30.4	28 13.8	5 23.8	18 43.1	27 55.3	20 24.2	17 35.8	10 33.3
5 M	14 50 21	14 12 57	25 38 21	1♊35 2	28 57.5	18 59.1	29 5.3	5 57.9	18 38.1	27 51.0	20 26.5	17 36.0	10 34.2
6 Tu	14 54 17	15 11 4	7♊31 6	13 26 46	28 44.2	18 25.4	29 56.2	6 31.8	18 33.0	27 46.7	20 28.8	17 36.2	10 35.2
7 W	14 58 14	16 9 9	19 22 16	25 17 54	28 32.2	17 50.0	0♋46.3	7 5.6	18 27.7	27 42.5	20 31.1	17 36.5	10 36.1
8 Th	15 2 10	17 7 12	1♋14 0	7♋10 57	28 22.4	17 13.6	1 35.7	7 39.2	18 22.3	27 38.3	20 33.4	17 36.8	10 37.1
9 F	15 6 7	18 5 13	13 9 10	19 9 7	28 15.4	16 36.8	2 24.4	8 12.7	18 16.7	27 34.2	20 35.6	17 37.1	10 38.1
10 Sa	15 10 3	19 3 12	25 11 19	1♌16 18	28 11.0	16 0.2	3 12.2	8 46.1	18 11.0	27 30.0	20 37.7	17 37.5	10 39.1
11 Su	15 14 0	20 1 9	7♌24 41	13 37 3	28 9.1	15 24.6	3 59.2	9 19.2	18 5.2	27 26.0	20 39.9	17 37.9	10 40.1
12 M	15 17 57	20 59 5	19 54 0	26 16 11	28 8.6	14 50.4	4 45.4	9 52.3	17 59.2	27 22.0	20 42.0	17 38.3	10 41.1
13 Tu	15 21 53	21 56 59	2♍44 9	9♍18 27	28 8.6	14 18.3	5 30.6	10 25.1	17 53.2	27 18.0	20 44.0	17 38.8	10 42.2
14 W	15 25 50	22 54 51	15 59 34	22 47 52	28 7.9	13 48.7	6 14.9	10 57.9	17 47.0	27 14.1	20 46.0	17 39.3	10 43.2
15 Th	15 29 46	23 52 41	29 43 34	6♎46 47	28 5.3	13 22.2	6 58.2	11 30.4	17 40.7	27 10.2	20 48.0	17 39.8	10 44.3
16 F	15 33 43	24 50 29	13♎57 20	21 14 55	28 0.3	12 59.1	7 40.6	12 2.8	17 34.3	27 6.4	20 49.9	17 40.3	10 45.4
17 Sa	15 37 39	25 48 16	28 38 58	6♏ 8 39	27 52.7	12 39.7	8 21.8	12 35.0	17 27.7	27 2.7	20 51.8	17 40.9	10 46.5
18 Su	15 41 36	26 46 1	13♏42 57	21 20 36	27 43.0	12 24.3	9 2.0	13 7.0	17 21.1	26 59.0	20 53.7	17 41.5	10 47.7
19 M	15 45 32	27 43 45	29 0 15	6♐40 26	27 32.2	12 13.2	9 41.1	13 38.9	17 14.4	26 55.4	20 55.5	17 42.2	10 48.8
20 Tu	15 49 29	28 41 28	14♐19 39	21 56 30	27 21.6	12 6.4	10 19.0	14 10.5	17 7.6	26 51.9	20 57.3	17 42.9	10 50.0
21 W	15 53 26	29 39 9	29 29 40	6♑58 3	27 12.4	12D 4.1	10 55.7	14 42.0	17 0.7	26 48.4	20 59.0	17 43.6	10 51.2
22 Th	15 57 22	0♊36 49	14♑20 44	21 37 2	27 5.5	12 6.3	11 31.1	15 13.3	16 53.7	26 45.0	21 0.7	17 44.3	10 52.4
23 F	16 1 19	1 34 28	28 46 30	5♒48 56	27 1.2	12 13.0	12 5.2	15 44.4	16 46.7	26 41.6	21 2.3	17 45.1	10 53.6
24 Sa	16 5 15	2 32 7	12♒44 17	19 32 41	26 59.2	12 24.3	12 38.0	16 15.2	16 39.5	26 38.3	21 3.9	17 45.9	10 54.8
25 Su	16 9 12	3 29 44	26 14 25	2♓49 53	26 58.8	12 40.0	13 9.3	16 45.9	16 32.3	26 35.1	21 5.5	17 46.8	10 56.1
26 M	16 13 8	4 27 20	9♓19 31	15 43 50	26 58.8	13 0.2	13 39.2	17 16.3	16 25.0	26 32.0	21 7.0	17 47.6	10 57.3
27 Tu	16 17 5	5 24 55	22 3 21	28 18 36	26 58.0	13 24.7	14 7.6	17 46.5	16 17.7	26 28.9	21 8.5	17 48.5	10 58.6
28 W	16 21 1	6 22 29	4♈30 7	10♈38 25	26 55.3	13 53.5	14 34.5	18 16.4	16 10.3	26 25.9	21 9.9	17 49.5	10 59.8
29 Th	16 24 58	7 20 2	16 43 57	22 47 11	26 50.1	14 26.4	14 59.7	18 46.1	16 2.9	26 23.0	21 11.3	17 50.4	11 1.1
30 F	16 28 55	8 17 35	28 48 28	4♉48 12	26 42.1	15 3.3	15 23.3	19 15.5	15 55.4	26 20.2	21 12.6	17 51.4	11 2.4
31 Sa	16 32 51	9 15 6	10♉46 41	16 44 11	26 31.5	15 44.2	15 45.1	19 44.7	15 47.9	26 17.5	21 13.9	17 52.4	11 3.7

LONGITUDE JUNE 1924

Day	Sid.Time	☉	0 hr ☽	Noon ☽	True ☊	☿	♀	♂	♃	♄	♅	♆	♇
1 Su	16 36 48	10♊12 37	22♉40 58	28♉37 14	26♌19.1	16♉28.9	16♋ 5.1	20♒13.6	15♐40.3	26♎14.8	21♓15.1	17♌53.5	11♋ 5.1
2 M	16 40 44	11 10 7	4♊33 11	10♊29 0	26R 5.7	17 17.4	16 23.3	20 42.2	15R 32.7	26R 12.2	21 16.3	17 54.5	11 6.4
3 Tu	16 44 41	12 7 36	16 24 52	22 20 57	25 52.5	18 9.5	16 39.6	21 10.6	15 25.1	26 9.7	21 17.5	17 55.6	11 7.8
4 W	16 48 37	13 5 3	28 17 27	4♋14 35	25 40.6	19 5.1	16 53.9	21 38.6	15 17.5	26 7.3	21 18.6	17 56.8	11 9.1
5 Th	16 52 34	14 2 30	10♋12 33	16 11 39	25 30.8	20 4.2	17 6.2	22 6.4	15 9.8	26 5.0	21 19.6	17 57.9	11 10.5
6 F	16 56 30	14 59 56	22 12 10	28 14 27	25 23.7	21 6.7	17 16.4	22 33.8	15 2.2	26 2.7	21 20.6	17 59.1	11 11.9
7 Sa	17 0 27	15 57 21	4♌18 52	10♌25 51	25 19.3	22 12.5	17 24.4	23 0.9	14 54.5	26 0.6	21 21.6	18 0.4	11 13.3
8 Su	17 4 24	16 54 45	16 35 52	22 49 22	25D 17.4	23 21.6	17 30.2	23 27.7	14 46.9	25 58.5	21 22.5	18 1.6	11 14.7
9 M	17 8 20	17 52 7	29 6 54	5♍28 58	25 17.1	24 33.8	17 33.8	23 54.2	14 39.2	25 56.6	21 23.4	18 2.9	11 16.1
10 Tu	17 12 17	18 49 29	11♍56 7	18 28 50	25R 17.6	25 49.2	17R 35.0	24 20.3	14 31.6	25 54.7	21 24.2	18 4.2	11 17.5
11 W	17 16 13	19 46 49	25 7 35	1♎52 46	25 17.6	27 7.7	17 33.9	24 46.1	14 24.0	25 52.9	21 25.0	18 5.5	11 18.9
12 Th	17 20 10	20 44 9	8♎44 41	15 43 32	25 16.2	28 29.3	17 30.4	25 11.6	14 16.4	25 51.2	21 25.7	18 6.8	11 20.3
13 F	17 24 6	21 41 27	22 49 19	0♏ 1 53	25 12.8	29 53.9	17 24.5	25 36.6	14 8.9	25 49.6	21 26.4	18 8.2	11 21.8
14 Sa	17 28 3	22 38 45	7♏20 52	14 45 42	25 7.1	1♊21.5	17 16.2	26 1.4	14 1.4	25 48.1	21 27.0	18 9.6	11 23.2
15 Su	17 31 59	23 36 1	22 15 35	29 49 29	24 59.6	2 52.1	17 5.5	26 25.7	13 53.9	25 46.7	21 27.6	18 11.1	11 24.7
16 M	17 35 56	24 33 17	7♐26 14	15♐ 4 31	24 51.0	4 25.7	16 52.3	26 49.7	13 46.5	25 45.4	21 28.1	18 12.5	11 26.1
17 Tu	17 39 53	25 30 33	22 42 56	0♑20 4	24 42.4	6 2.2	16 36.8	27 13.2	13 39.1	25 44.1	21 28.6	18 14.0	11 27.6
18 W	17 43 49	26 27 47	7♑54 35	15 25 15	24 34.9	7 41.6	16 18.9	27 36.4	13 31.8	25 43.0	21 29.0	18 15.5	11 29.1
19 Th	17 47 46	27 25 2	22 50 59	0♒10 55	24 29.3	9 23.9	15 58.7	27 59.2	13 24.6	25 42.0	21 29.4	18 17.0	11 30.6
20 F	17 51 42	28 22 16	7♒24 24	14 31 0	24 26.0	11 9.1	15 36.3	28 21.5	13 17.4	25 41.1	21 29.8	18 18.6	11 32.0
21 Sa	17 55 39	29 19 29	21 30 27	28 22 44	24D 24.8	12 57.0	15 11.7	28 43.4	13 10.3	25 40.2	21 30.1	18 20.1	11 33.5
22 Su	17 59 35	0♋16 43	5♓ 7 59	11♓46 28	24 25.1	14 47.7	14 45.1	29 4.8	13 3.2	25 39.5	21 30.3	18 21.7	11 35.0
23 M	18 3 32	1 13 56	18 18 32	24 44 38	24 26.0	16 41.0	14 16.6	29 25.8	12 56.3	25 38.8	21 30.5	18 23.4	11 36.5
24 Tu	18 7 28	2 11 9	1♈ 5 19	7♈21 6	24R 26.6	18 36.8	13 46.3	29 46.2	12 49.4	25 38.3	21 30.6	18 25.0	11 38.0
25 W	18 11 25	3 8 22	13 32 34	19 40 17	24 26.0	20 35.1	13 14.5	0♓ 6.2	12 42.6	25 37.8	21 30.7	18 26.7	11 39.5
26 Th	18 15 22	4 5 36	25 44 49	1♉46 42	24 23.6	22 35.7	12 41.2	0 25.7	12 35.9	25 37.5	21R 30.8	18 28.3	11 41.0
27 F	18 19 18	5 2 49	7♉46 28	13 44 34	24 19.2	24 38.3	12 6.6	0 44.7	12 29.3	25 37.2	21 30.8	18 30.0	11 42.5
28 Sa	18 23 15	6 0 2	19 41 28	25 37 35	24 12.8	26 42.9	11 31.1	1 3.1	12 22.8	25 37.1	21 30.7	18 31.8	11 44.1
29 Su	18 27 11	6 57 15	1♊33 16	7♊28 51	24 5.0	28 49.1	10 54.7	1 21.0	12 16.4	25D 37.0	21 30.7	18 33.5	11 45.6
30 M	18 31 8	7 54 28	13 24 39	19 20 54	23 56.4	0♋56.7	10 17.7	1 38.3	12 10.1	25 37.1	21 30.5	18 35.3	11 47.1

Astro Data	Planet Ingress	Last Aspect	☽ Ingress	Last Aspect	☽ Ingress	☽ Phases & Eclipses	Astro Data
Dy Hr Mn	Dy Hr Mn	Dy Hr Mn	Dy Hr Mn	Dy Hr Mn	Dy Hr Mn	Dy Hr Mn	1 MAY 1924
☽0S 15 13:00	♀ ♋ 6 1:49	2 16:40 ♄ ☍	♉ 2 20:37	31 21:06 ♅ ⚹	♊ 1 14:47	3 23:00 ● 13♉12	Julian Day # 8887
♃△♆ 15 3:05	☉ ♊ 21 8:40	4 13:30 ♅ ⚹	♊ 5 8:48	3 19:38 ♄ △	♋ 4 3:27	12 2:13 ☽ 21♌04	Delta T 23.5 sec
☿ D 21 0:21		7 16:47 ♄ △	♋ 7 21:30	6 7:37 ♄ □	♌ 6 15:29	18 21:52 ○ 27♏39	SVP 06♓19'09"
☽0N 28 6:03	☿ ♊ 13 1:42	10 4:33 ♄ □	♌ 10 9:30	8 17:59 ♄ ⚹	♍ 9 1:41	25 14:16 ☽ 4♓04	Obliquity 23°26'49"
	☉ ♋ 21 16:59	12 13:59 ♄ ⚹	♍ 12 18:57	11 3:58 ☿ △	♎ 11 8:41		⚷ Chiron 21♈41.8
♀ R 10 0:50	♂ ♓ 24 16:27	14 13:07 ☉ △	♎ 15 0:28	13 5:01 ♄ ☌	♏ 13 11:57	2 14:34 ● 11♊45	☽ Mean ☊ 28♌36.3
☽0S 11 22:41	☿ ♋ 29 13:22	16 21:25 ♄ ☌	♏ 17 2:10	15 6:48 ♂ □	♐ 15 12:17	10 13:37 ☽ 19♍22	
☽0N 24 13:42		18 21:52 ☉ ☍	♐ 19 1:33	17 7:17 ♂ ⚹	♑ 17 11:28	17 4:41 ○ 25♐42	1 JUNE 1924
♅ R 26 12:03		20 19:44 ♄ ⚹	♑ 21 0:48	19 4:38 ♄ □	♒ 19 11:42	24 2:16 ☽ 2♈17	Julian Day # 8918
♄ D 29 0:43		22 20:30 ♄ □	♒ 23 2:04	21 14:42 ☉ △	♓ 21 14:52		Delta T 23.5 sec
		25 0:37 ♄ △	♓ 25 6:49	23 5:57 ♅ ☌	♈ 23 21:56		SVP 06♓19'05"
		26 22:15 ♅ ☌	♈ 27 15:16	25 23:45 ♄ ☍	♉ 26 8:27		Obliquity 23°26'49"
		29 19:05 ♄ ☍	♉ 30 2:23	28 3:41 ♅ ⚹	♊ 28 20:51		⚷ Chiron 23♈18.0
							☽ Mean ☊ 26♌57.8

JULY 1924 LONGITUDE

Day	Sid.Time	☉	0 hr ☽	Noon☽	True☊	☿	♀	♂	♃	♄	♅	♆	♇
1 Tu	18 35 4	8♋51 42	25♊17 53	1♋15 47	23♌47.9	3♋ 5.4	9♋40.4	1♓55.1	12♐ 4.0	25♎37.2	21♓30.3	18♌37.1	11♋48.6
2 W	18 39 1	9 48 55	7♋14 48	13 15 8	23R40.2	5 15.0	9R 2.9	2 11.3	11R57.9	25 37.5	21R30.1	18 38.9	11 50.1
3 Th	18 42 57	10 46 8	19 16 59	25 20 32	23 34.1	7 25.1	8 25.5	2 26.8	11 52.0	25 37.8	21 29.8	18 40.7	11 51.7
4 F	18 46 54	11 43 21	1♌25 59	7♌33 33	23 29.9	9 35.6	7 48.5	2 41.8	11 46.2	25 38.2	21 29.5	18 42.5	11 53.2
5 Sa	18 50 51	12 40 34	13 43 29	19 56 2	23D27.6	11 46.0	7 12.1	2 56.2	11 40.5	25 38.8	21 29.1	18 44.4	11 54.7
6 Su	18 54 47	13 37 47	26 11 29	2♍30 8	23 27.2	13 56.1	6 36.4	3 9.9	11 35.0	25 39.4	21 28.6	18 46.3	11 56.2
7 M	18 58 44	14 34 59	8♍52 19	15 18 23	23 28.0	16 5.7	6 1.8	3 23.0	11 29.6	25 40.2	21 28.2	18 48.2	11 57.8
8 Tu	19 2 40	15 32 12	21 48 39	28 23 28	23 29.5	18 14.6	5 28.4	3 35.4	11 24.3	25 41.0	21 27.6	18 50.1	11 59.3
9 W	19 6 37	16 29 24	5♎ 3 9	11♎47 57	23R30.8	20 22.5	4 56.4	3 47.2	11 19.2	25 42.0	21 27.1	18 52.0	12 0.8
10 Th	19 10 33	17 26 37	18 38 8	25 33 47	23 31.2	22 29.2	4 26.0	3 58.3	11 14.3	25 43.0	21 26.4	18 54.0	12 2.3
11 F	19 14 30	18 23 49	2♏34 59	9♏41 38	23 30.4	24 34.6	3 57.3	4 8.8	11 9.5	25 44.1	21 25.8	18 55.9	12 3.8
12 Sa	19 18 26	19 21 1	16 53 29	24 10 12	23 28.1	26 38.6	3 30.5	4 18.5	11 4.8	25 45.4	21 25.1	18 57.9	12 5.3
13 Su	19 22 23	20 18 13	1♐31 12	8♐55 48	23 24.6	28 41.1	3 5.7	4 27.6	11 0.3	25 46.7	21 24.3	18 59.9	12 6.9
14 M	19 26 20	21 15 25	16 23 9	23 52 17	23 20.3	0♌42.0	2 43.0	4 35.9	10 56.0	25 48.1	21 23.5	19 1.9	12 8.4
15 Tu	19 30 16	22 12 38	1♑22 8	8♑51 35	23 16.0	2 41.1	2 22.5	4 43.6	10 51.8	25 49.7	21 22.7	19 3.9	12 9.9
16 W	19 34 13	23 9 50	16 19 32	23 44 53	23 12.2	4 38.6	2 4.3	4 50.5	10 47.8	25 51.3	21 21.8	19 5.9	12 11.4
17 Th	19 38 9	24 7 3	1♒ 6 38	8♒23 55	23 9.5	6 34.3	1 48.4	4 56.7	10 43.9	25 53.0	21 20.8	19 8.0	12 12.9
18 F	19 42 6	25 4 17	15 36 0	22 42 19	23D 8.1	8 28.3	1 34.9	5 2.1	10 40.2	25 54.8	21 19.9	19 10.0	12 14.4
19 Sa	19 46 2	26 1 30	29 42 26	6♓36 8	23 8.1	10 20.4	1 23.8	5 6.8	10 36.7	25 56.7	21 18.8	19 12.1	12 15.9
20 Su	19 49 59	26 58 45	13♓23 19	20 4 4	23 9.0	12 10.8	1 15.2	5 10.7	10 33.3	25 58.7	21 17.8	19 14.2	12 17.3
21 M	19 53 55	27 56 0	26 38 32	3♈ 7 2	23 10.5	13 59.3	1 8.9	5 13.8	10 30.1	26 0.8	21 16.7	19 16.3	12 18.8
22 Tu	19 57 52	28 53 16	9♈29 57	15 47 43	23 12.0	15 46.1	1 5.0	5 16.2	10 27.1	26 3.0	21 15.5	19 18.4	12 20.3
23 W	20 1 49	29 50 33	22 0 50	28 9 51	23R13.0	17 31.1	1D 3.5	5 17.8	10 24.3	26 5.3	21 14.3	19 20.5	12 21.8
24 Th	20 5 45	0♌47 51	4♉15 19	10♉17 48	23 13.1	19 14.2	1 4.3	5R18.5	10 21.6	26 7.6	21 13.1	19 22.6	12 23.2
25 F	20 9 42	1 45 9	16 17 52	22 16 4	23 12.4	20 55.7	1 7.4	5 18.5	10 19.1	26 10.1	21 11.8	19 24.7	12 24.7
26 Sa	20 13 38	2 42 29	28 12 58	4♊ 9 3	23 10.7	22 35.3	1 12.8	5 17.7	10 16.8	26 12.6	21 10.5	19 26.9	12 26.1
27 Su	20 17 35	3 39 50	10♊ 4 51	16 0 48	23 8.3	24 13.2	1 20.3	5 16.0	10 14.6	26 15.3	21 9.2	19 29.0	12 27.6
28 M	20 21 31	4 37 11	21 57 21	27 54 52	23 5.5	25 49.3	1 30.0	5 13.6	10 12.7	26 18.0	21 7.8	19 31.2	12 29.0
29 Tu	20 25 28	5 34 34	3♋53 43	9♋54 14	23 2.7	27 23.6	1 41.8	5 10.4	10 10.9	26 20.9	21 6.3	19 33.4	12 30.4
30 W	20 29 24	6 31 57	15 56 41	22 1 20	23 0.2	28 56.2	1 55.6	5 6.4	10 9.3	26 23.8	21 4.9	19 35.5	12 31.8
31 Th	20 33 21	7 29 21	28 8 22	4♌18 0	22 58.3	0♍27.0	2 11.4	5 1.6	10 7.9	26 26.8	21 3.4	19 37.7	12 33.2

AUGUST 1924 LONGITUDE

Day	Sid.Time	☉	0 hr ☽	Noon☽	True☊	☿	♀	♂	♃	♄	♅	♆	♇
1 F	20 37 18	8♌26 47	10♌30 23	16♌45 40	22♌57.2	1♍56.0	2♋29.1	4♓56.0	10♐ 6.7	26♎29.9	21♓ 1.8	19♌39.9	12♋34.6
2 Sa	20 41 14	9 24 13	23 3 57	29 25 22	22D56.8	3 23.2	2 48.7	4R49.7	10R 5.7	26 33.1	21R 0.2	19 42.1	12 36.0
3 Su	20 45 11	10 21 40	5♍49 59	12♍17 55	22 57.1	4 48.6	3 10.0	4 42.6	10 4.8	26 36.3	20 58.6	19 44.3	12 37.4
4 M	20 49 7	11 19 7	18 49 13	25 24 0	22 57.9	6 12.2	3 33.0	4 34.8	10 4.1	26 39.7	20 57.0	19 46.5	12 38.8
5 Tu	20 53 4	12 16 36	2♎ 2 18	8♎44 12	22 58.8	7 33.8	3 57.7	4 26.3	10 3.6	26 43.1	20 55.3	19 48.7	12 40.1
6 W	20 57 0	13 14 5	15 29 44	22 18 56	22 59.7	8 53.5	4 24.0	4 17.2	10 3.4	26 46.6	20 53.6	19 50.9	12 41.5
7 Th	21 0 57	14 11 35	29 11 47	6♏ 8 15	23 0.3	10 11.3	4 51.9	4 7.4	10D 3.2	26 50.2	20 51.8	19 53.1	12 42.8
8 F	21 4 53	15 9 6	13♏ 8 15	20 11 39	23R 0.6	11 27.0	5 21.3	3 56.9	10 3.3	26 53.9	20 50.0	19 55.3	12 44.1
9 Sa	21 8 50	16 6 37	27 18 13	4♐27 41	23 0.5	12 40.6	5 52.1	3 45.9	10 3.6	26 57.7	20 48.2	19 57.5	12 45.5
10 Su	21 12 47	17 4 10	11♐39 42	18 53 49	23 0.1	13 52.1	6 24.3	3 34.2	10 4.0	27 1.5	20 46.3	19 59.8	12 46.8
11 M	21 16 43	18 1 43	26 9 30	3♑26 11	22 59.6	15 1.4	6 57.8	3 22.1	10 4.7	27 5.5	20 44.5	20 2.0	12 48.1
12 Tu	21 20 40	18 59 17	10♑43 13	17 59 54	22 59.1	16 8.4	7 32.6	3 9.4	10 5.5	27 9.5	20 42.6	20 4.2	12 49.3
13 W	21 24 36	19 56 53	25 15 31	2♒29 20	22 58.8	17 13.0	8 8.7	2 56.3	10 6.5	27 13.6	20 40.6	20 6.5	12 50.6
14 Th	21 28 33	20 54 29	9♒40 39	16 48 48	22D58.6	18 15.1	8 46.0	2 42.7	10 7.7	27 17.7	20 38.7	20 8.7	12 51.9
15 F	21 32 29	21 52 6	23 53 10	0♓53 15	22 58.6	19 14.5	9 24.5	2 28.7	10 9.0	27 22.0	20 36.7	20 10.9	12 53.1
16 Sa	21 36 26	22 49 45	7♓48 35	14 38 51	22R58.6	20 11.2	10 4.1	2 14.3	10 10.6	27 26.3	20 34.7	20 13.1	12 54.3
17 Su	21 40 22	23 47 25	21 23 49	28 3 23	22 58.6	21 5.0	10 44.8	1 59.6	10 12.3	27 30.7	20 32.6	20 15.3	12 55.5
18 M	21 44 19	24 45 7	4♈37 31	11♈ 6 19	22 58.4	21 55.8	11 26.5	1 44.5	10 14.2	27 35.1	20 30.5	20 17.5	12 56.7
19 Tu	21 48 16	25 42 50	17 30 0	23 48 48	22 58.1	22 43.4	12 9.3	1 29.2	10 16.3	27 39.7	20 28.4	20 19.8	12 57.9
20 W	21 52 12	26 40 34	0♉ 3 4	6♉13 14	22 57.8	23 27.5	12 53.0	1 13.7	10 18.6	27 44.3	20 26.3	20 22.0	12 59.1
21 Th	21 56 9	27 38 20	12 19 46	18 23 9	22 57.5	24 8.1	13 37.7	0 58.0	10 21.0	27 49.0	20 24.2	20 24.2	13 0.2
22 F	22 0 5	28 36 8	24 23 55	0♊22 40	22D57.2	24 44.9	14 23.2	0 42.2	10 23.6	27 53.7	20 22.0	20 26.4	13 1.4
23 Sa	22 4 2	29 33 58	6♊19 56	12 16 20	22 57.3	25 17.6	15 9.7	0 26.3	10 26.4	27 58.5	20 19.8	20 28.6	13 2.5
24 Su	22 7 58	0♍31 50	18 12 25	24 8 45	22 57.6	25 46.1	15 56.9	0 10.4	10 29.4	28 3.4	20 17.6	20 30.8	13 3.6
25 M	22 11 55	1 29 43	0♋ 5 55	6♋ 4 25	22 58.3	26 10.1	16 45.0	29♒54.5	10 32.6	28 8.4	20 15.4	20 33.0	13 4.7
26 Tu	22 15 51	2 27 38	12 4 45	18 7 24	22 59.2	26 29.3	17 33.8	29 38.6	10 35.9	28 13.4	20 13.2	20 35.2	13 5.7
27 W	22 19 48	3 25 35	24 12 47	0♌21 17	23 0.2	26 43.4	18 23.4	29 22.8	10 39.4	28 18.5	20 10.9	20 37.4	13 6.8
28 Th	22 23 45	4 23 33	6♌33 12	12 48 50	23 1.0	26 52.3	19 13.8	29 7.2	10 43.1	28 23.7	20 8.6	20 39.6	13 7.8
29 F	22 27 41	5 21 33	19 8 21	25 31 56	23R 1.5	26R55.6	20 4.8	28 51.8	10 46.9	28 28.9	20 6.4	20 41.7	13 8.9
30 Sa	22 31 38	6 19 35	1♍59 39	8♍31 30	23 1.3	26 53.1	20 56.5	28 36.7	10 50.9	28 34.2	20 4.0	20 43.9	13 9.9
31 Su	22 35 34	7 17 38	15 7 27	21 47 23	23 0.5	26 44.6	21 48.8	28 21.8	10 55.1	28 39.5	20 1.7	20 46.0	13 10.8

Astro Data	Planet Ingress	Last Aspect	☽ Ingress	Last Aspect	☽ Ingress	☽ Phases & Eclipses	Astro Data
Dy Hr Mn	Dy Hr Mn	Dy Hr Mn	Dy Hr Mn	Dy Hr Mn	Dy Hr Mn	Dy Hr Mn	1 JULY 1924
♃⚻♇ 3 1:02	☿ ♌ 13 15:38	1 0:39 ♄ △	♋ 1 9:28	2 6:37 ♄ ⚹	♍ 2 13:05	2 5:35 ● 10♋02	Julian Day # 8948
☽0S 9 6:12	☉ ♌ 23 3:58	3 12:35 ♄ □	♌ 3 21:11	4 3:53 ♅ ☍	♎ 4 20:20	9 21:46 ☽ 17♎21	Delta T 23.6 sec
♃∠♄ 15 9:01	☿ ♍ 30 16:48	5 22:59 ♄ ⚹	♍ 6 7:15	6 19:53 ♄ ☌	♏ 7 1:24	16 11:49 ○ 23♑38	SVP 06♓19'00"
☽0N 21 22:27		7 23:21 ♅ ☍	♎ 8 14:55	8 13:03 ♅ △	♐ 9 4:32	23 16:36 ☽ 0♉30	Obliquity 23°26'49"
♀ D 23 3:34	☉ ♍ 23 10:48	10 12:17 ♄ ☌	♏ 10 19:36	11 1:33 ♄ ⚹	♑ 11 6:20	31 19:42 ● 8♌16	⚷ Chiron 24♈20.5
♂ R 24 11:01	♂ ♒ 24 15:38	12 18:39 ☿ △	♐ 12 21:32	13 3:17 ♄ □	♒ 13 7:52	31 19:57:58 • P 0.192	☽ Mean ☊ 25♌22.5
		14 15:07 ♄ ⚹	♑ 14 21:49	15 5:59 ♄ △	♓ 15 10:28		
☽0S 5 12:05		16 15:27 ♄ □	♒ 16 22:11	16 23:24 ☿ ☍	♈ 17 15:32	8 3:41 ☽ 15♏18	1 AUGUST 1924
♃ D 7 2:11		18 17:31 ♄ △	♓ 19 0:30	19 19:30 ♄ ☍	♉ 19 23:54	14 20:19 ○ 21♒43	Julian Day # 8979
☽0N 18 7:43		21 2:34 ☉ △	♈ 21 6:12	22 9:10 ☉ □	♊ 22 11:14	14 20:20 • T 1.652	Delta T 23.6 sec
☿0S 20 6:33		23 7:58 ♄ ☍	♉ 23 15:36	24 23:37 ♂ △	♋ 24 23:48	22 9:10 ☽ 28♉58	SVP 06♓18'55"
♅⚻♆ 20 23:57		25 10:49 ☿ □	♊ 26 3:36	27 8:04 ♄ □	♌ 27 11:19	30 8:37 ● 6♍40	Obliquity 23°26'49"
☿ R 29 1:50		28 8:59 ☿ ⚹	♋ 28 16:11	29 17:51 ♂ ☍	♍ 29 20:19	30 8:22:35 • P 0.425	⚷ Chiron 24♈40.2R
		30 20:40 ♄ □	♌ 31 3:38				☽ Mean ☊ 23♌44.0

LONGITUDE SEPTEMBER 1924

Day	Sid.Time	☉	0 hr ☽	Noon ☽	True ☊	☿	♀	♂	♃	♄	♅	♆	♇
1 M	22 39 31	8♍15 43	28♍31 7	5♎18 28	22♌59.0	26♍30.0	22♋41.7	28♒ 7.3	10♐59.5	28♎45.0	19♓59.4	20♌48.2	13♋11.8
2 Tu	22 43 27	9 13 50	12♎ 9 9	19 2 52	22R56.9	26R 9.1	23 35.3	27R53.2	11 4.0	28 50.4	19R57.1	20 50.3	13 12.8
3 W	22 47 24	10 11 58	25 59 19	2♏58 10	22 54.7	25 41.9	24 29.4	27 39.5	11 8.7	28 56.0	19 54.7	20 52.5	13 13.7
4 Th	22 51 20	11 10 7	9♏59 5	17 1 43	22 52.5	25 8.6	25 24.1	27 26.3	11 13.5	29 1.6	19 52.3	20 54.6	13 14.6
5 F	22 55 17	12 8 18	24 5 44	1♐10 50	22 50.9	24 29.4	26 19.4	27 13.7	11 18.5	29 7.2	19 50.0	20 56.7	13 15.5
6 Sa	22 59 14	13 6 31	8♐16 42	15 23 3	22D50.2	23 44.6	27 15.1	27 1.5	11 23.7	29 12.9	19 47.6	20 58.8	13 16.4
7 Su	23 3 10	14 4 45	22 29 34	29 36 0	22 50.3	22 54.7	28 11.4	26 50.0	11 29.0	29 18.7	19 45.2	21 0.9	13 17.2
8 M	23 7 7	15 3 1	6♑42 4	13♑47 29	22 51.2	22 0.6	29 8.2	26 39.0	11 34.5	29 24.5	19 42.8	21 2.9	13 18.1
9 Tu	23 11 3	16 1 18	20 51 58	27 55 13	22 52.6	21 3.0	0♌ 5.5	26 28.7	11 40.2	29 30.4	19 40.4	21 5.0	13 18.9
10 W	23 15 0	16 59 36	4♒56 57	11♒56 49	22 53.9	20 3.1	1 3.2	26 19.1	11 46.0	29 36.3	19 38.0	21 7.1	13 19.7
11 Th	23 18 56	17 57 56	18 54 30	25 49 40	22R54.7	19 2.1	2 1.4	26 10.1	11 52.0	29 42.3	19 35.6	21 9.1	13 20.4
12 F	23 22 53	18 56 18	2♓42 0	9♓31 11	22 54.4	18 1.4	3 0.0	26 1.8	11 58.1	29 48.3	19 33.2	21 11.1	13 21.2
13 Sa	23 26 49	19 54 42	16 16 55	22 58 56	22 52.8	17 2.4	3 59.1	25 54.2	12 4.3	29 54.4	19 30.8	21 13.1	13 21.9
14 Su	23 30 46	20 53 7	29 37 1	6♈11 1	22 49.9	16 6.4	4 58.6	25 47.4	12 10.7	0♏ 0.5	19 28.4	21 15.1	13 22.6
15 M	23 34 42	21 51 34	12♈40 48	19 6 21	22 45.7	15 15.0	5 58.5	25 41.2	12 17.3	0 6.7	19 26.0	21 17.1	13 23.3
16 Tu	23 38 39	22 50 3	25 27 41	1♉44 55	22 40.8	14 29.3	6 58.8	25 35.9	12 24.0	0 12.9	19 23.6	21 19.1	13 24.0
17 W	23 42 36	23 48 35	7♉58 12	14 7 48	22 35.7	13 50.7	7 59.5	25 31.3	12 30.8	0 19.2	19 21.2	21 21.0	13 24.6
18 Th	23 46 32	24 47 8	20 14 2	26 17 17	22 31.0	13 20.0	9 0.6	25 27.4	12 37.8	0 25.5	19 18.8	21 22.9	13 25.3
19 F	23 50 29	25 45 44	2♊17 59	8♊16 36	22 27.3	12 58.1	10 2.0	25 24.4	12 45.0	0 31.8	19 16.5	21 24.8	13 25.9
20 Sa	23 54 25	26 44 22	14 13 41	20 9 47	22 24.9	12D45.5	11 3.8	25 22.1	12 52.2	0 38.2	19 14.1	21 26.7	13 26.4
21 Su	23 58 22	27 43 2	26 5 31	2♋ 1 28	22D24.0	12 42.7	12 6.0	25 20.6	12 59.6	0 44.7	19 11.7	21 28.6	13 27.0
22 M	0 2 18	28 41 44	7♋58 16	13 56 33	22 24.4	12 49.6	13 8.5	25D19.9	13 7.2	0 51.2	19 9.4	21 30.5	13 27.5
23 Tu	0 6 15	29 40 29	19 56 57	26 0 3	22 25.8	13 6.4	14 11.3	25 20.0	13 14.9	0 57.7	19 7.0	21 32.3	13 28.1
24 W	0 10 11	0♎39 16	2♌ 6 26	8♌16 39	22 27.4	13 32.8	15 14.4	25 20.9	13 22.7	1 4.2	19 4.7	21 34.2	13 28.6
25 Th	0 14 8	1 38 5	14 31 10	20 50 27	22R28.7	14 8.5	16 17.9	25 22.5	13 30.6	1 10.8	19 2.3	21 36.0	13 29.0
26 F	0 18 5	2 36 56	27 14 49	3♍44 32	22 28.8	14 53.0	17 21.6	25 25.0	13 38.7	1 17.5	19 0.0	21 37.8	13 29.5
27 Sa	0 22 1	3 35 49	10♍19 46	17 0 33	22 27.4	15 45.8	18 25.6	25 28.3	13 46.9	1 24.1	18 57.7	21 39.5	13 29.9
28 Su	0 25 58	4 34 45	23 46 48	0♎38 19	22 23.9	16 46.2	19 30.0	25 32.4	13 55.3	1 30.8	18 55.4	21 41.3	13 30.3
29 M	0 29 54	5 33 42	7♎34 46	14 35 41	22 18.6	17 53.5	20 34.5	25 37.2	14 3.7	1 37.6	18 53.1	21 43.0	13 30.7
30 Tu	0 33 51	6 32 42	21 40 31	28 48 36	22 11.9	19 7.2	21 39.4	25 42.9	14 12.3	1 44.4	18 50.9	21 44.7	13 31.0

LONGITUDE OCTOBER 1924

Day	Sid.Time	☉	0 hr ☽	Noon ☽	True ☊	☿	♀	♂	♃	♄	♅	♆	♇
1 W	0 37 47	7♎31 43	5♏59 15	13♏11 41	22♌ 4.6	20♍26.4	22♌44.5	25♒49.3	14♐21.1	1♏51.2	18♓48.6	21♌46.4	13♋31.4
2 Th	0 41 44	8 30 47	20 25 11	27 38 59	21R57.6	21 50.4	23 49.9	25 56.5	14 29.9	1 58.0	18R46.4	21 48.0	13 31.7
3 F	0 45 40	9 29 52	4♐52 25	12♐ 4 53	21 51.8	23 18.7	24 55.5	26 4.4	14 38.9	2 4.9	18 44.2	21 49.7	13 31.9
4 Sa	0 49 37	10 28 59	19 15 50	26 24 53	21 47.9	24 50.6	26 1.4	26 13.2	14 48.0	2 11.8	18 42.0	21 51.3	13 32.2
5 Su	0 53 34	11 28 8	3♑31 39	10♑35 56	21D45.9	26 25.6	27 7.5	26 22.6	14 57.2	2 18.7	18 39.8	21 52.9	13 32.4
6 M	0 57 30	12 27 19	17 37 34	24 36 26	21 45.8	28 3.0	28 13.8	26 32.8	15 6.5	2 25.6	18 37.7	21 54.5	13 32.7
7 Tu	1 1 27	13 26 31	1♒32 31	8♒25 49	21 46.6	29 42.4	29 20.3	26 43.7	15 15.9	2 32.6	18 35.6	21 56.0	13 32.8
8 W	1 5 23	14 25 45	15 16 21	22 4 9	21R47.6	1♎23.5	0♍27.1	26 55.3	15 25.4	2 39.6	18 33.5	21 57.5	13 33.0
9 Th	1 9 20	15 25 1	28 49 13	5♓31 35	21 47.5	3 5.7	1 34.1	27 7.6	15 35.1	2 46.6	18 31.4	21 59.0	13 33.2
10 F	1 13 16	16 24 19	12♓11 14	18 48 8	21 45.5	4 48.9	2 41.3	27 20.6	15 44.8	2 53.6	18 29.4	22 0.5	13 33.3
11 Sa	1 17 13	17 23 38	25 22 13	1♈53 28	21 41.2	6 32.8	3 48.7	27 34.2	15 54.7	3 0.7	18 27.4	22 1.9	13 33.4
12 Su	1 21 9	18 23 0	8♈21 46	14 47 3	21 34.2	8 17.0	4 56.3	27 48.5	16 4.7	3 7.8	18 25.4	22 3.3	13 33.4
13 M	1 25 6	19 22 23	21 9 16	27 28 21	21 25.0	10 1.4	6 4.1	28 3.4	16 14.7	3 14.9	18 23.4	22 4.7	13 33.5
14 Tu	1 29 2	20 21 48	3♉44 18	9♉57 8	21 14.3	11 45.9	7 12.1	28 18.9	16 24.9	3 22.0	18 21.5	22 6.1	13R33.5
15 W	1 32 59	21 21 16	16 6 54	22 13 46	21 3.0	13 30.3	8 20.3	28 35.0	16 35.2	3 29.1	18 19.6	22 7.4	13 33.5
16 Th	1 36 56	22 20 46	28 17 52	4♊19 28	20 52.1	15 14.5	9 28.7	28 51.7	16 45.6	3 36.3	18 17.7	22 8.7	13 33.5
17 F	1 40 52	23 20 18	10♊18 51	16 16 23	20 42.7	16 58.5	10 37.3	29 9.0	16 56.0	3 43.4	18 15.9	22 10.0	13 33.4
18 Sa	1 44 49	24 19 52	22 12 30	28 7 39	20 35.5	18 42.0	11 46.1	29 26.9	17 6.6	3 50.6	18 14.1	22 11.3	13 33.4
19 Su	1 48 45	25 19 29	4♋ 2 23	9♋57 15	20 30.7	20 25.1	12 55.0	29 45.3	17 17.3	3 57.8	18 12.3	22 12.5	13 33.3
20 M	1 52 42	26 19 8	15 52 52	21 49 53	20D28.2	22 7.8	14 4.1	0♓ 4.2	17 28.0	4 5.0	18 10.5	22 13.7	13 33.1
21 Tu	1 56 38	27 18 49	27 48 57	3♌50 46	20 27.6	23 50.0	15 13.4	0 23.7	17 38.9	4 12.2	18 8.8	22 14.8	13 33.0
22 W	2 0 35	28 18 32	9♌55 58	16 5 16	20R28.0	25 31.6	16 22.8	0 43.7	17 49.8	4 19.4	18 7.2	22 16.0	13 32.8
23 Th	2 4 31	29 18 18	22 19 16	28 38 35	20 28.2	27 12.7	17 32.4	1 4.3	18 0.9	4 26.6	18 5.5	22 17.1	13 32.6
24 F	2 8 28	0♏18 5	5♍ 3 44	11♍35 11	20 27.3	28 53.3	18 42.2	1 25.3	18 12.0	4 33.9	18 3.9	22 18.2	13 32.4
25 Sa	2 12 25	1 17 55	18 13 16	24 58 10	20 24.3	0♏33.4	19 52.1	1 46.8	18 23.2	4 41.1	18 2.4	22 19.2	13 32.2
26 Su	2 16 21	2 17 47	1♎49 56	8♎48 28	20 18.6	2 12.9	21 2.2	2 8.8	18 34.5	4 48.3	18 0.8	22 20.2	13 31.9
27 M	2 20 18	3 17 42	15 53 25	23 4 19	20 10.3	3 51.9	22 12.4	2 31.3	18 45.9	4 55.6	17 59.4	22 21.2	13 31.6
28 Tu	2 24 14	4 17 38	0♏20 26	7♏40 56	19 59.9	5 30.3	23 22.7	2 54.2	18 57.3	5 2.8	17 57.9	22 22.2	13 31.3
29 W	2 28 11	5 17 36	15 4 47	22 30 54	19 48.5	7 8.2	24 33.2	3 17.6	19 8.9	5 10.1	17 56.5	22 23.1	13 31.0
30 Th	2 32 7	6 17 36	29 58 8	7♐25 20	19 37.4	8 45.7	25 43.8	3 41.5	19 20.5	5 17.3	17 55.1	22 24.0	13 30.6
31 F	2 36 4	7 17 39	14♐51 23	22 15 20	19 27.8	10 22.6	26 54.5	4 5.8	19 32.2	5 24.6	17 53.8	22 24.9	13 30.2

Astro Data	Dy Hr Mn
☽0S	1 18:02
☿0N	9 4:05
☽0N	14 16:36
☿ D	20 19:04
♂ D	22 9:15
♃⊼♇	24 18:51
☽0S	29 1:48
☿0S	9 18:05
☽0N	12 0:30
♄⚼♅	13 22:40
♇ R	14 9:40
♃□♅	23 8:48
☽0S	26 11:53

Planet Ingress	Dy Hr Mn
♀ ♌	8 21:43
♄ ♏	13 21:59
☉ ♎	23 7:58
☿ ♎	7 4:12
♀ ♍	7 14:16
♂ ♓	19 18:42
☉ ♏	23 16:44
☿ ♏	24 15:59

Last Aspect Dy Hr Mn		☽ Ingress Dy Hr Mn
31 20:29	☿ ☌	♎ 1 2:38
3 5:06	♄ ☌	♏ 3 6:54
5 5:14	♂ □	♐ 5 10:00
7 11:36	♄ ⚹	♑ 7 12:41
9 14:48	♄ □	♒ 9 15:33
11 18:54	♄ △	♓ 11 19:16
13 7:00	☉ ☍	♈ 14 0:42
16 0:15	♂ ⚹	♉ 16 8:39
18 10:18	♂ □	♊ 18 19:24
21 3:35	☉ □	♋ 21 7:54
22 22:21	♅ △	♌ 23 19:52
25 20:35	♂ ☍	♍ 26 5:06
27 15:26	♅ ☍	♎ 28 10:53
30 6:51	♂ △	♏ 30 14:00

Last Aspect Dy Hr Mn		☽ Ingress Dy Hr Mn
2 9:15	♂ □	♐ 2 15:54
4 12:17	♀ △	♑ 4 18:02
6 20:23	☿ △	♒ 6 21:19
8 20:56	♂ ☌	♓ 9 2:06
10 11:24	♅ ☌	♈ 11 8:31
13 13:23	♂ ⚹	♉ 13 16:50
16 1:09	♂ □	♊ 16 3:23
18 15:04	♂ △	♋ 18 15:48
20 22:54	☉ □	♌ 21 4:21
23 14:22	☉ ⚹	♍ 23 14:33
25 3:14	♀ ☌	♎ 25 20:49
27 10:49	♆ ⚹	♏ 27 23:26
29 16:36	♀ ⚹	♐ 30 0:03

☽ Phases & Eclipses Dy Hr Mn	
6 8:45	☽ 13♐28
13 7:00	○ 20♓12
21 3:35	☽ 27♊52
28 20:16	● 5♎25
5 14:30	☽ 12♑04
12 20:21	○ 19♈13
20 22:54	☽ 27♋16
28 6:57	● 4♏35

Astro Data

1 SEPTEMBER 1924
Julian Day # 9010
Delta T 23.6 sec
SVP 06♓18'52"
Obliquity 23°26'50"
⚷ Chiron 24♈10.1R
☽ Mean ☊ 22♌05.5

1 OCTOBER 1924
Julian Day # 9040
Delta T 23.6 sec
SVP 06♓18'50"
Obliquity 23°26'50"
⚷ Chiron 23♈02.7R
☽ Mean ☊ 20♌30.2

NOVEMBER 1924 LONGITUDE

Day	Sid.Time	☉	0 hr ☽	Noon ☽	True ☊	☿	♀	♂	♃	♄	♅	♆	♇
1 Sa	2 40 0	8♏17 42	29♐36 17	6♑53 34	19♌20.7	11♏59.1	28♍ 5.4	4♓30.5	19♐44.0	5♏31.8	17♓52.5	22♌25.7	13♋29.8
2 Su	2 43 57	9 17 48	14♑ 6 39	21 15 10	19R16.4	13 35.1	29 16.4	4 55.6	19 55.8	5 39.1	17R51.3	22 26.5	13R29.4
3 M	2 47 54	10 17 55	28 18 55	5♒17 51	19D14.5	15 10.7	0♎27.5	5 21.1	20 7.7	5 46.3	17 50.1	22 27.3	13 29.0
4 Tu	2 51 50	11 18 3	12♒12 0	19 1 31	19R14.1	16 45.8	1 38.7	5 47.0	20 19.7	5 53.5	17 49.0	22 28.0	13 28.5
5 W	2 55 47	12 18 13	25 46 36	2♓27 32	19 14.1	18 20.6	2 50.0	6 13.2	20 31.8	6 0.8	17 47.9	22 28.7	13 28.0
6 Th	2 59 43	13 18 24	9♓ 4 33	15 37 56	19 13.0	19 54.9	4 1.5	6 39.9	20 43.9	6 8.0	17 46.8	22 29.4	13 27.5
7 F	3 3 40	14 18 37	22 7 56	28 34 49	19 9.8	21 28.8	5 13.0	7 6.9	20 56.1	6 15.2	17 45.8	22 30.0	13 27.0
8 Sa	3 7 36	15 18 51	4♈58 46	11♈19 58	19 3.6	23 2.4	6 24.7	7 34.2	21 8.4	6 22.4	17 44.8	22 30.6	13 26.4
9 Su	3 11 33	16 19 7	17 38 33	23 54 39	18 54.4	24 35.7	7 36.4	8 1.9	21 20.7	6 29.6	17 43.9	22 31.2	13 25.8
10 M	3 15 29	17 19 25	0♉ 8 21	6♉19 43	18 42.5	26 8.6	8 48.3	8 29.8	21 33.1	6 36.7	17 43.0	22 31.7	13 25.2
11 Tu	3 19 26	18 19 44	12 28 48	18 35 41	18 28.6	27 41.2	10 0.3	8 58.2	21 45.5	6 43.9	17 42.2	22 32.2	13 24.6
12 W	3 23 23	19 20 5	24 40 25	0♊43 6	18 13.9	29 13.5	11 12.3	9 26.8	21 58.0	6 51.0	17 41.4	22 32.7	13 24.0
13 Th	3 27 19	20 20 28	6♊43 51	12 42 49	17 59.7	0♐45.5	12 24.5	9 55.7	22 10.6	6 58.2	17 40.7	22 33.1	13 23.3
14 F	3 31 16	21 20 52	18 40 12	24 36 14	17 47.1	2 17.2	13 36.8	10 24.9	22 23.2	7 5.3	17 40.0	22 33.5	13 22.6
15 Sa	3 35 12	22 21 18	0♋31 14	6♋25 32	17 36.9	3 48.6	14 49.1	10 54.3	22 35.9	7 12.4	17 39.4	22 33.9	13 21.9
16 Su	3 39 9	23 21 46	12 19 33	18 13 43	17 29.7	5 19.7	16 1.6	11 24.1	22 48.6	7 19.4	17 38.8	22 34.2	13 21.2
17 M	3 43 5	24 22 16	24 8 34	0♌ 4 39	17 25.3	6 50.5	17 14.1	11 54.1	23 1.4	7 26.5	17 38.2	22 34.5	13 20.5
18 Tu	3 47 2	25 22 48	6♌ 2 33	12 2 55	17D23.4	8 21.0	18 26.7	12 24.4	23 14.2	7 33.5	17 37.7	22 34.7	13 19.7
19 W	3 50 58	26 23 21	18 6 25	24 13 44	17R23.0	9 51.2	19 39.5	12 54.9	23 27.1	7 40.5	17 37.3	22 35.0	13 18.9
20 Th	3 54 55	27 23 56	0♍25 32	6♍42 30	17 23.1	11 21.1	20 52.3	13 25.7	23 40.0	7 47.5	17 36.9	22 35.2	13 18.1
21 F	3 58 52	28 24 33	13 5 15	19 34 24	17 22.3	12 50.7	22 5.1	13 56.8	23 53.0	7 54.5	17 36.6	22 35.3	13 17.3
22 Sa	4 2 48	29 25 11	26 10 26	2♎53 45	17 19.7	14 19.9	23 18.1	14 28.0	24 6.0	8 1.4	17 36.3	22 35.5	13 16.5
23 Su	4 6 45	0♐25 51	9♎44 36	16 43 4	17 14.7	15 48.7	24 31.1	14 59.5	24 19.1	8 8.3	17 36.0	22 35.5	13 15.6
24 M	4 10 41	1 26 33	23 49 3	1♏ 2 13	17 6.9	17 17.1	25 44.2	15 31.3	24 32.2	8 15.2	17 35.8	22 35.6	13 14.7
25 Tu	4 14 38	2 27 16	8♏22 0	15 47 37	16 57.0	18 45.0	26 57.4	16 3.2	24 45.4	8 22.0	17 35.7	22R35.6	13 13.8
26 W	4 18 34	3 28 1	23 18 2	0♐52 5	16 45.8	20 12.3	28 10.6	16 35.4	24 58.6	8 28.9	17 35.6	22 35.6	13 12.9
27 Th	4 22 31	4 28 48	8♐28 25	16 5 40	16 34.7	21 39.1	29 23.9	17 7.8	25 11.8	8 35.7	17D35.6	22 35.6	13 12.0
28 F	4 26 27	5 29 35	23 42 26	1♑17 22	16 25.1	23 5.2	0♏37.3	17 40.4	25 25.1	8 42.4	17 35.6	22 35.5	13 11.1
29 Sa	4 30 24	6 30 24	8♑49 14	16 17 1	16 17.8	24 30.5	1 50.7	18 13.2	25 38.4	8 49.1	17 35.7	22 35.4	13 10.1
30 Su	4 34 21	7 31 14	23 39 50	0♒57 3	16 13.3	25 54.8	3 4.2	18 46.2	25 51.8	8 55.8	17 35.8	22 35.2	13 9.2

DECEMBER 1924 LONGITUDE

Day	Sid.Time	☉	0 hr ☽	Noon ☽	True ☊	☿	♀	♂	♃	♄	♅	♆	♇
1 M	4 38 17	8♐32 5	8♒ 8 15	15♒13 10	16♌11.4	27♐18.2	4♏17.8	19♓19.4	26♐ 5.2	9♏ 2.5	17♓36.0	22♌35.0	13♋ 8.2
2 Tu	4 42 14	9 32 57	22 11 46	29 4 8	16D11.3	28 40.3	5 31.4	19 52.8	26 18.6	9 9.1	17 36.2	22R34.8	13R 7.2
3 W	4 46 10	10 33 49	5♓50 29	12♓31 7	16R11.8	0♑ 1.1	6 45.0	20 26.3	26 32.0	9 15.6	17 36.5	22 34.6	13 6.2
4 Th	4 50 7	11 34 42	19 6 23	25 36 43	16 11.6	1 20.2	7 58.7	21 0.1	26 45.5	9 22.2	17 36.8	22 34.3	13 5.1
5 F	4 54 3	12 35 36	2♈ 2 32	8♈24 14	16 9.6	2 37.4	9 12.4	21 34.0	26 59.0	9 28.6	17 37.2	22 33.9	13 4.1
6 Sa	4 58 0	13 36 31	14 42 15	20 56 59	16 5.3	3 52.5	10 26.2	22 8.0	27 12.5	9 35.1	17 37.6	22 33.6	13 3.0
7 Su	5 1 56	14 37 27	27 8 45	3♉17 55	15 58.3	5 5.2	11 40.0	22 42.2	27 26.0	9 41.5	17 38.1	22 33.2	13 2.0
8 M	5 5 53	15 38 23	9♉24 45	15 29 32	15 48.9	6 14.9	12 53.9	23 16.6	27 39.6	9 47.8	17 38.6	22 32.8	13 0.9
9 Tu	5 9 50	16 39 20	21 32 28	27 33 45	15 37.8	7 21.2	14 7.9	23 51.1	27 53.2	9 54.1	17 39.2	22 32.3	12 59.8
10 W	5 13 46	17 40 18	3♊33 35	9♊32 8	15 25.9	8 23.8	15 21.8	24 25.8	28 6.8	10 0.4	17 39.8	22 31.8	12 58.7
11 Th	5 17 43	18 41 17	15 29 33	21 26 0	15 14.4	9 21.9	16 35.8	25 0.6	28 20.5	10 6.6	17 40.5	22 31.3	12 57.6
12 F	5 21 39	19 42 16	27 21 39	3♋16 43	15 4.2	10 14.9	17 49.9	25 35.5	28 34.1	10 12.7	17 41.2	22 30.8	12 56.4
13 Sa	5 25 36	20 43 17	9♋11 24	15 5 58	14 56.0	11 2.2	19 4.0	26 10.5	28 47.8	10 18.9	17 42.0	22 30.2	12 55.3
14 Su	5 29 32	21 44 18	21 0 41	26 55 52	14 50.4	11 42.8	20 18.1	26 45.7	29 1.5	10 24.9	17 42.9	22 29.6	12 54.2
15 M	5 33 29	22 45 20	2♌51 54	8♌49 12	14 47.3	12 16.1	21 32.3	27 21.0	29 15.2	10 30.9	17 43.7	22 28.9	12 53.0
16 Tu	5 37 25	23 46 23	14 48 13	20 49 25	14D46.4	12 41.0	22 46.6	27 56.4	29 28.9	10 36.9	17 44.7	22 28.3	12 51.8
17 W	5 41 22	24 47 27	26 53 22	3♍ 0 36	14 47.0	12 56.8	24 0.8	28 31.9	29 42.6	10 42.8	17 45.7	22 27.6	12 50.7
18 Th	5 45 19	25 48 32	9♍11 44	15 27 19	14 48.3	13R 2.6	25 15.1	29 7.6	29 56.3	10 48.6	17 46.7	22 26.8	12 49.5
19 F	5 49 15	26 49 37	21 47 59	28 14 17	14R49.4	12 57.5	26 29.4	29 43.3	0♑10.1	10 54.4	17 47.8	22 26.0	12 48.3
20 Sa	5 53 12	27 50 43	4♎46 46	11♎25 52	14 49.2	12 41.1	27 43.8	0♈19.2	0 23.8	11 0.1	17 48.9	22 25.2	12 47.1
21 Su	5 57 8	28 51 51	18 11 58	25 5 21	14 47.4	12 12.9	28 58.2	0 55.2	0 37.6	11 5.8	17 50.1	22 24.4	12 45.9
22 M	6 1 5	29 52 58	2♏ 6 4	9♏14 4	14 43.5	11 33.1	0♐12.6	1 31.2	0 51.3	11 11.4	17 51.3	22 23.6	12 44.7
23 Tu	6 5 1	0♑54 7	16 29 4	23 50 34	14 38.0	10 42.0	1 27.1	2 7.4	1 5.1	11 16.9	17 52.6	22 22.7	12 43.4
24 W	6 8 58	1 55 16	1♐17 49	8♐49 55	14 31.4	9 40.8	2 41.6	2 43.7	1 18.9	11 22.4	17 54.0	22 21.8	12 42.2
25 Th	6 12 54	2 56 26	16 25 44	24 3 58	14 24.6	8 30.9	3 56.1	3 20.1	1 32.7	11 27.8	17 55.3	22 20.8	12 41.0
26 F	6 16 51	3 57 37	1♑43 17	9♑22 15	14 18.7	7 14.4	5 10.6	3 56.5	1 46.4	11 33.2	17 56.8	22 19.8	12 39.8
27 Sa	6 20 48	4 58 47	16 59 32	24 33 49	14 14.3	5 53.8	6 25.2	4 33.1	2 0.2	11 38.4	17 58.2	22 18.8	12 38.5
28 Su	6 24 44	5 59 58	2♒ 3 59	9♒29 3	14D11.8	4 31.6	7 39.8	5 9.8	2 14.0	11 43.7	17 59.8	22 17.8	12 37.3
29 M	6 28 41	7 1 9	16 48 16	24 1 4	14 11.3	3 10.8	8 54.4	5 46.5	2 27.7	11 48.8	18 1.3	22 16.8	12 36.0
30 Tu	6 32 37	8 2 20	1♓ 7 7	8♓ 6 15	14 12.2	1 53.7	10 9.0	6 23.3	2 41.5	11 53.9	18 3.0	22 15.7	12 34.8
31 W	6 36 34	9 3 30	14 58 27	21 43 55	14 13.7	0 42.7	11 23.6	7 0.2	2 55.2	11 58.9	18 4.6	22 14.6	12 33.5

Astro Data	Planet Ingress	Last Aspect	☽ Ingress	Last Aspect	☽ Ingress	☽ Phases & Eclipses	Astro Data
Dy Hr Mn	Dy Hr Mn	Dy Hr Mn	Dy Hr Mn	Dy Hr Mn	Dy Hr Mn	Dy Hr Mn	
♀0S 5 16:53	♀ ♎ 2 14:44	31 21:18 ♀ □	♑ 1 0:39	2 12:33 ☿ ✶	♓ 2 13:38	3 22:18 ☽ 11♒14	1 NOVEMBER 1924
☽0N 8 7:23	☿ ♐ 12 12:08	2 6:16 ♅ ✶	♒ 3 2:53	4 14:23 ♃ □	♈ 4 20:10	11 12:31 ○ 18♉51	Julian Day # 9071
♃∠♄ 10 16:40	☉ ♐ 22 13:46	4 18:07 ♆ ☍	♓ 5 7:34	7 0:34 ♃ △	♉ 7 5:33	19 17:38 ☽ 27♌08	Delta T 23.6 sec
♃△♆ 14 20:04	♀ ♏ 27 11:48	6 22:38 ☿ △	♈ 7 14:39	9 4:50 ♂ ✶	♊ 9 16:52	26 17:15 ● 4♐12	SVP 06♓18'47"
☽0S 22 23:04		9 9:20 ♆ △	♉ 9 23:44	12 2:30 ♃ ☍	♋ 12 5:21		Obliquity 23°26'50"
♆ R 25 2:48	☿ ♑ 2 23:41	12 10:21 ☿ ☍	♊ 12 10:34	14 12:16 ♂ △	♌ 14 18:13	3 9:10 ☽ 10♓57	⚷ Chiron 21♈38.0R
♅ D 27 4:02	♃ ♑ 18 6:25	14 7:52 ♆ ✶	♋ 14 22:57	17 5:39 ♃ △	♍ 17 6:07	11 7:03 ○ 18♊59	☽ Mean ☊ 18♌51.7
	♂ ♈ 19 11:09	17 0:30 ☉ △	♌ 17 11:51	19 10:11 ☉ □	♎ 19 15:15	19 10:11 ☽ 27♍16	
☽0N 5 13:59	♀ ♐ 21 19:56	19 17:38 ☉ □	♍ 19 23:11	21 19:56 ☉ ✶	♏ 21 20:26	26 3:46 ● 4♑07	1 DECEMBER 1924
♅ R 18 1:00	☉ ♑ 22 2:45	22 6:18 ☉ ✶	♎ 22 6:51	23 9:37 ♆ □	♐ 23 21:55		Julian Day # 9101
☽0S 20 9:06	☿ ♐ 31 15:52	24 3:30 ♀ ☌	♏ 24 10:17	25 9:18 ♆ △	♑ 25 21:18		Delta T 23.6 sec
♂0N 20 12:22		25 22:52 ♆ □	♐ 26 10:38	27 1:33 ♅ ✶	♒ 27 20:41		SVP 06♓18'42"
		28 2:45 ♃ ☌	♑ 28 9:57	29 9:05 ♆ ☍	♓ 29 22:06		Obliquity 23°26'49"
		29 15:43 ♂ ✶	♒ 30 10:25				⚷ Chiron 20♈31.9R
							☽ Mean ☊ 17♌16.4

LONGITUDE — JANUARY 1925

Day	Sid.Time	☉	0 hr ☽	Noon ☽	True ☊	☿	♀	♂	♃	♄	♅	♆	♇
1 Th	6 40 30	10♑ 4 41	28♓22 53	4♈55 43	14♌15.1	29♐39.6	12♐38.3	7♈37.2	3♑ 9.0	12♏ 3.8	18♓ 6.3	22♌13.4	12♋32.3
2 F	6 44 27	11 5 51	11♈22 52	17 44 47	14R 15.7	28R 45.5	13 52.9	8 14.3	3 22.7	12 8.7	18 8.1	22R 12.3	12R 31.0
3 Sa	6 48 24	12 7 1	24 1 58	0♉14 56	14 14.9	28 1.3	15 7.6	8 51.4	3 36.4	12 13.4	18 9.9	22 11.1	12 29.8
4 Su	6 52 20	13 8 10	6♉24 12	12 30 14	14 12.7	27 27.4	16 22.3	9 28.6	3 50.1	12 18.1	18 11.7	22 9.9	12 28.5
5 M	6 56 17	14 9 20	18 33 32	24 34 32	14 9.0	27 3.7	17 37.0	10 5.8	4 3.8	12 22.8	18 13.6	22 8.6	12 27.3
6 Tu	7 0 13	15 10 28	0♊33 40	6♊31 18	14 4.3	26D 49.9	18 51.7	10 43.2	4 17.5	12 27.3	18 15.5	22 7.4	12 26.0
7 W	7 4 10	16 11 37	12 27 47	18 23 29	13 59.1	26 45.5	20 6.4	11 20.5	4 31.1	12 31.8	18 17.5	22 6.1	12 24.8
8 Th	7 8 6	17 12 46	24 18 39	0♋13 35	13 53.9	26 50.1	21 21.2	11 58.0	4 44.8	12 36.2	18 19.5	22 4.8	12 23.5
9 F	7 12 3	18 13 54	6♋ 8 33	12 3 45	13 49.5	27 2.8	22 35.9	12 35.5	4 58.4	12 40.5	18 21.6	22 3.5	12 22.3
10 Sa	7 15 59	19 15 1	17 59 27	23 55 51	13 46.1	27 23.0	23 50.7	13 13.0	5 12.0	12 44.7	18 23.7	22 2.2	12 21.0
11 Su	7 19 56	20 16 9	29 53 12	5♌51 43	13 44.0	27 50.0	25 5.5	13 50.6	5 25.6	12 48.9	18 25.8	22 0.8	12 19.8
12 M	7 23 53	21 17 16	11♌51 40	17 53 18	13D 43.2	28 23.2	26 20.3	14 28.3	5 39.1	12 53.0	18 28.0	21 59.4	12 18.6
13 Tu	7 27 49	22 18 23	23 56 54	0♍ 2 48	13 43.5	29 2.0	27 35.1	15 5.9	5 52.6	12 56.9	18 30.2	21 58.0	12 17.3
14 W	7 31 46	23 19 30	6♍11 17	12 22 45	13 44.7	29 45.8	28 49.9	15 43.7	6 6.1	13 0.8	18 32.4	21 56.6	12 16.1
15 Th	7 35 42	24 20 36	18 37 33	24 56 4	13 46.3	0♑34.1	0♑ 4.8	16 21.5	6 19.6	13 4.7	18 34.7	21 55.2	12 14.9
16 F	7 39 39	25 21 42	1♎18 42	7♎45 51	13 47.8	1 26.5	1 19.6	16 59.3	6 33.0	13 8.4	18 37.1	21 53.7	12 13.6
17 Sa	7 43 35	26 22 48	14 17 54	20 55 11	13 48.9	2 22.5	2 34.5	17 37.1	6 46.5	13 12.0	18 39.4	21 52.2	12 12.4
18 Su	7 47 32	27 23 53	27 38 1	4♏26 39	13R 49.3	3 21.7	3 49.3	18 15.1	6 59.8	13 15.6	18 41.8	21 50.7	12 11.2
19 M	7 51 28	28 24 58	11♏21 15	18 21 49	13 48.9	4 23.9	5 4.2	18 53.0	7 13.2	13 19.0	18 44.3	21 49.2	12 10.0
20 Tu	7 55 25	29 26 3	25 28 19	2♐40 31	13 47.8	5 28.8	6 19.1	19 31.0	7 26.5	13 22.4	18 46.8	21 47.7	12 8.8
21 W	7 59 22	0♒27 8	9♐58 1	17 20 17	13 46.3	6 36.1	7 34.0	20 9.0	7 39.8	13 25.7	18 49.3	21 46.2	12 7.6
22 Th	8 3 18	1 28 12	24 46 35	2♑16 4	13 44.6	7 45.5	8 48.9	20 47.1	7 53.0	13 28.9	18 51.8	21 44.6	12 6.5
23 F	8 7 15	2 29 16	9♑47 45	17 20 31	13 43.2	8 56.9	10 3.8	21 25.2	8 6.2	13 32.0	18 54.4	21 43.1	12 5.3
24 Sa	8 11 11	3 30 19	24 53 14	2♒24 44	13 42.3	10 10.2	11 18.7	22 3.4	8 19.4	13 35.0	18 57.0	21 41.5	12 4.1
25 Su	8 15 8	4 31 22	9♒53 53	17 19 39	13D 41.9	11 25.1	12 33.6	22 41.6	8 32.5	13 37.9	18 59.7	21 39.9	12 3.0
26 M	8 19 4	5 32 23	24 41 3	1♓57 18	13 42.0	12 41.5	13 48.5	23 19.8	8 45.6	13 40.7	19 2.4	21 38.3	12 1.8
27 Tu	8 23 1	6 33 23	9♓ 7 45	16 11 56	13 42.4	13 59.4	15 3.4	23 58.0	8 58.6	13 43.4	19 5.1	21 36.7	12 0.7
28 W	8 26 57	7 34 23	23 9 33	0♈ 0 26	13 43.1	15 18.6	16 18.3	24 36.3	9 11.6	13 46.0	19 7.8	21 35.1	11 59.6
29 Th	8 30 54	8 35 21	6♈44 37	13 22 14	13 43.6	16 39.0	17 33.3	25 14.6	9 24.5	13 48.6	19 10.6	21 33.5	11 58.5
30 F	8 34 51	9 36 18	19 53 33	26 18 55	13 44.1	18 0.6	18 48.2	25 53.0	9 37.4	13 51.0	19 13.4	21 31.8	11 57.4
31 Sa	8 38 47	10 37 13	2♉38 47	8♉53 36	13R 44.3	19 23.3	20 3.1	26 31.4	9 50.2	13 53.3	19 16.2	21 30.2	11 56.3

LONGITUDE — FEBRUARY 1925

Day	Sid.Time	☉	0 hr ☽	Noon ☽	True ☊	☿	♀	♂	♃	♄	♅	♆	♇
1 Su	8 42 44	11♒38 7	15♉ 3 57	21♉10 21	13♌44.3	20♑47.0	21♑18.0	27♈ 9.7	10♑ 3.0	13♏55.5	19♓19.1	21♌28.5	11♋55.2
2 M	8 46 40	12 39 0	27 13 23	3♊13 37	13R 44.2	22 11.7	22 32.9	27 48.2	10 15.8	13 57.7	19 22.0	21R 26.9	11R 54.2
3 Tu	8 50 37	13 39 52	9♊11 38	15 7 57	13D 44.2	23 37.4	23 47.8	28 26.6	10 28.4	13 59.7	19 24.9	21 25.2	11 53.1
4 W	8 54 33	14 40 42	21 3 7	26 57 38	13 44.3	25 4.0	25 2.7	29 5.0	10 41.0	14 1.6	19 27.9	21 23.5	11 52.1
5 Th	8 58 30	15 41 31	2♋51 58	8♋46 34	13 44.5	26 31.6	26 17.6	29 43.5	10 53.6	14 3.5	19 30.8	21 21.9	11 51.1
6 F	9 2 26	16 42 19	14 41 50	20 38 8	13 44.8	27 60.0	27 32.5	0♉22.0	11 6.1	14 5.2	19 33.8	21 20.2	11 50.1
7 Sa	9 6 23	17 43 5	26 35 49	2♌35 10	13 45.1	29 29.3	28 47.4	1 0.5	11 18.5	14 6.8	19 36.9	21 18.5	11 49.1
8 Su	9 10 20	18 43 50	8♌36 28	14 39 57	13R 45.3	0♒59.4	0♒ 2.3	1 39.0	11 30.9	14 8.3	19 39.9	21 16.8	11 48.1
9 M	9 14 16	19 44 33	20 45 49	26 54 16	13 45.3	2 30.4	1 17.2	2 17.5	11 43.2	14 9.8	19 43.0	21 15.1	11 47.1
10 Tu	9 18 13	20 45 15	3♍ 5 28	9♍19 32	13 44.9	4 2.3	2 32.1	2 56.0	11 55.4	14 11.1	19 46.0	21 13.5	11 46.2
11 W	9 22 9	21 45 56	15 36 38	21 56 52	13 44.1	5 34.9	3 47.0	3 34.6	12 7.6	14 12.3	19 49.2	21 11.8	11 45.3
12 Th	9 26 6	22 46 35	28 20 21	4♎47 12	13 43.0	7 8.5	5 1.9	4 13.1	12 19.7	14 13.4	19 52.3	21 10.1	11 44.4
13 F	9 30 2	23 47 13	11♎17 31	17 51 24	13 41.6	8 42.9	6 16.8	4 51.7	12 31.8	14 14.4	19 55.4	21 8.4	11 43.5
14 Sa	9 33 59	24 47 50	24 28 56	1♏10 14	13 40.3	10 18.1	7 31.6	5 30.3	12 43.7	14 15.3	19 58.6	21 6.7	11 42.6
15 Su	9 37 55	25 48 26	7♏55 21	14 44 21	13 39.2	11 54.2	8 46.5	6 8.9	12 55.6	14 16.1	20 1.8	21 5.0	11 41.7
16 M	9 41 52	26 49 1	21 37 16	28 34 4	13D 38.6	13 31.2	10 1.4	6 47.5	13 7.4	14 16.8	20 5.0	21 3.4	11 40.9
17 Tu	9 45 49	27 49 34	5♐34 44	12♐39 6	13 38.7	15 9.0	11 16.3	7 26.1	13 19.2	14 17.4	20 8.2	21 1.7	11 40.1
18 W	9 49 45	28 50 6	19 47 2	26 58 13	13 39.4	16 47.8	12 31.2	8 4.7	13 30.9	14 17.9	20 11.5	21 0.0	11 39.2
19 Th	9 53 42	29 50 38	4♑12 18	11♑28 52	13 40.5	18 27.5	13 46.1	8 43.3	13 42.4	14 18.3	20 14.7	20 58.3	11 38.5
20 F	9 57 38	0♓51 7	18 47 20	26 7 5	13 41.8	20 8.0	15 0.9	9 22.0	13 54.0	14 18.6	20 18.0	20 56.7	11 37.7
21 Sa	10 1 35	1 51 36	3♒27 26	10♒47 35	13R 42.7	21 49.6	16 15.8	10 0.6	14 5.4	14 18.8	20 21.3	20 55.0	11 36.9
22 Su	10 5 31	2 52 3	18 6 44	25 24 4	13 42.9	23 32.0	17 30.7	10 39.3	14 16.7	14R 18.9	20 24.6	20 53.4	11 36.2
23 M	10 9 28	3 52 28	2♓38 46	9♓50 4	13 42.0	25 15.5	18 45.5	11 17.9	14 28.0	14 18.8	20 27.9	20 51.8	11 35.5
24 Tu	10 13 24	4 52 51	16 57 15	23 59 43	13 40.1	26 59.9	20 0.4	11 56.6	14 39.2	14 18.7	20 31.3	20 50.1	11 34.8
25 W	10 17 21	5 53 13	0♈56 57	7♈48 36	13 37.1	28 45.2	21 15.2	12 35.3	14 50.2	14 18.4	20 34.6	20 48.5	11 34.1
26 Th	10 21 17	6 53 33	14 34 23	21 14 12	13 33.6	0♓31.6	22 30.1	13 14.0	15 1.2	14 18.1	20 38.0	20 46.9	11 33.5
27 F	10 25 14	7 53 51	27 48 4	4♉16 6	13 29.9	2 19.0	23 44.9	13 52.6	15 12.1	14 17.7	20 41.3	20 45.3	11 32.9
28 Sa	10 29 11	8 54 7	10♉38 34	16 55 48	13 26.7	4 7.4	24 59.7	14 31.3	15 22.9	14 17.1	20 44.7	20 43.7	11 32.3

Astro Data	Dy Hr Mn
☽0N	1 21:27
♄△♇	5 18:39
☿ D	6 23:27
☽0S	16 16:31
♃⊼♆	17 9:19
☽0N	29 6:22
♃☍♇	9 7:10
☽0S	12 22:05
♃⚹♄	22 4:32
♄ R	22 4:52
☽0N	25 16:11
♅⊼♆	27 19:09

Planet Ingress	Dy Hr Mn
☿ ♑	14 7:16
♀ ♑	14 22:28
☉ ♒	20 13:20
♂ ♉	5 10:17
☿ ♒	7 8:12
♀ ♒	7 23:16
☉ ♓	19 3:43
☿ ♓	25 16:53

Last Aspect Dy Hr Mn		☽ Ingress Dy Hr Mn
1 2:10	☿ □	♈ 1 2:57
3 7:19	☿ △	♉ 3 11:31
5 7:08	♆ □	♊ 5 22:52
8 5:11	☿ ☍	♋ 8 11:32
10 2:47	☉ ☍	♌ 11 0:14
13 10:38	☿ △	♍ 13 11:55
15 11:50	☉ △	♎ 15 21:33
17 23:33	☉ □	♏ 18 4:11
20 7:07	☉ ⚹	♐ 20 7:34
21 19:08	♆ △	♑ 22 8:22
23 19:18	♂ □	♒ 24 8:09
25 21:41	♂ ⚹	♓ 26 8:46
27 17:01	♅ ☌	♈ 28 11:59
30 11:47	♂ ☌	♉ 30 18:58

Last Aspect Dy Hr Mn		☽ Ingress Dy Hr Mn
1 13:39	♀ △	♊ 2 5:32
4 17:15	♂ ⚹	♋ 4 18:11
7 6:38	☿ ☍	♌ 7 6:50
9 0:57	♆ ☌	♍ 9 18:01
11 8:01	♅ ☍	♎ 12 3:06
14 0:37	☉ △	♏ 14 9:54
16 9:41	☉ □	♐ 16 14:28
18 16:14	☉ ⚹	♑ 18 17:02
20 2:29	♅ ⚹	♒ 20 18:21
22 10:07	☿ ☌	♓ 22 19:36
24 6:05	♅ ☌	♈ 24 22:21
26 15:48	♀ ⚹	♉ 27 4:04

☽ Phases & Eclipses Dy Hr Mn	
1 23:25	☽ 11♈04
10 2:47	○ 19♋22
17 23:33	☽ 27♎23
24 14:45	● 4♒08
24 14:53:40	✔ T 2'32"
31 16:43	☽ 11♉20
8 21:49	○ 19♌39
8 21:42	☍ P 0.730
16 9:41	☽ 27♏13
23 2:12	● 3♓58

Astro Data

1 JANUARY 1925
Julian Day # 9132
Delta T 23.6 sec
SVP 06♓18'37"
Obliquity 23°26'50"
⚷ Chiron 20♈06.0
☽ Mean ☊ 15♌37.9

1 FEBRUARY 1925
Julian Day # 9163
Delta T 23.6 sec
SVP 06♓18'32"
Obliquity 23°26'50"
⚷ Chiron 20♈33.3
☽ Mean ☊ 13♌59.4

MARCH 1925 LONGITUDE

Day	Sid.Time	☉	0 hr ☽	Noon ☽	True ☊	☿	♀	♂	♃	♄	♅	♆	♇
1 Su	10 33 7	9♓54 21	23♉ 8 12	29♉16 17	13♌24.3	5♓56.8	26♒14.5	15♉10.0	15♑33.6	14♏16.5	20♓48.1	20♌42.1	11♋31.7
2 M	10 37 4	10 54 33	5♊20 35	11♊21 40	13D 23.1	7 47.2	27 29.3	15 48.7	15 44.2	14R 15.7	20 51.5	20R 40.5	11R 31.1
3 Tu	10 41 0	11 54 43	17 20 10	23 16 42	13 23.1	9 38.7	28 44.1	16 27.4	15 54.7	14 14.8	20 54.9	20 39.0	11 30.6
4 W	10 44 57	12 54 51	29 11 53	5♋ 6 21	13 24.1	11 31.1	29 58.9	17 6.1	16 5.1	14 13.9	20 58.3	20 37.4	11 30.0
5 Th	10 48 53	13 54 56	11♋ 0 43	16 55 36	13 25.8	13 24.4	1♓13.7	17 44.8	16 15.4	14 12.8	21 1.7	20 35.9	11 29.5
6 F	10 52 50	14 55 0	22 51 32	28 49 4	13 27.7	15 18.7	2 28.4	18 23.5	16 25.6	14 11.7	21 5.1	20 34.4	11 29.1
7 Sa	10 56 46	15 55 2	4♌48 42	10♌50 53	13R 29.0	17 13.8	3 43.1	19 2.1	16 35.7	14 10.4	21 8.5	20 32.9	11 28.6
8 Su	11 0 43	16 55 1	16 56 0	23 4 23	13 29.3	19 9.8	4 57.9	19 40.8	16 45.7	14 9.1	21 11.9	20 31.4	11 28.2
9 M	11 4 40	17 54 58	29 16 20	5♍32 3	13 28.1	21 6.5	6 12.6	20 19.5	16 55.6	14 7.6	21 15.4	20 30.0	11 27.8
10 Tu	11 8 36	18 54 54	11♍51 40	18 15 16	13 25.1	23 3.8	7 27.3	20 58.1	17 5.4	14 6.1	21 18.8	20 28.5	11 27.4
11 W	11 12 33	19 54 47	24 42 52	1♎14 23	13 20.5	25 1.5	8 42.0	21 36.8	17 15.1	14 4.4	21 22.2	20 27.1	11 27.0
12 Th	11 16 29	20 54 39	7♎49 44	14 28 45	13 14.5	26 59.7	9 56.7	22 15.4	17 24.6	14 2.7	21 25.7	20 25.7	11 26.7
13 F	11 20 26	21 54 28	21 11 13	27 56 54	13 8.0	28 57.9	11 11.4	22 54.1	17 34.0	14 0.8	21 29.1	20 24.3	11 26.4
14 Sa	11 24 22	22 54 16	4♏45 32	11♏36 52	13 1.5	0♈56.1	12 26.1	23 32.7	17 43.4	13 58.9	21 32.5	20 22.9	11 26.1
15 Su	11 28 19	23 54 2	18 30 38	25 26 35	12 55.9	2 54.0	13 40.7	24 11.4	17 52.6	13 56.9	21 35.9	20 21.6	11 25.8
16 M	11 32 15	24 53 46	2♐24 28	9♐24 5	12 52.0	4 51.3	14 55.4	24 50.0	18 1.6	13 54.8	21 39.4	20 20.2	11 25.5
17 Tu	11 36 12	25 53 29	16 25 13	23 27 43	12D 49.8	6 47.7	16 10.0	25 28.6	18 10.6	13 52.6	21 42.8	20 18.9	11 25.3
18 W	11 40 9	26 53 10	0♑31 22	7♑36 3	12 49.5	8 42.8	17 24.7	26 7.2	18 19.5	13 50.3	21 46.2	20 17.6	11 25.1
19 Th	11 44 5	27 52 49	14 41 33	21 47 42	12 50.3	10 36.2	18 39.3	26 45.9	18 28.2	13 47.9	21 49.6	20 16.3	11 24.9
20 F	11 48 2	28 52 27	28 54 17	6♒ 1 2	12R 51.6	12 27.6	19 53.9	27 24.5	18 36.8	13 45.4	21 53.1	20 15.1	11 24.8
21 Sa	11 51 58	29 52 3	13♒ 7 39	20 13 46	12 52.2	14 16.5	21 8.5	28 3.1	18 45.2	13 42.9	21 56.5	20 13.9	11 24.7
22 Su	11 55 55	0♈51 37	27 19 0	4♓22 54	12 51.2	16 2.4	22 23.1	28 41.7	18 53.6	13 40.3	21 59.9	20 12.7	11 24.6
23 M	11 59 51	1 51 9	11♓24 58	18 24 44	12 48.2	17 44.9	23 37.7	29 20.3	19 1.8	13 37.5	22 3.3	20 11.5	11 24.5
24 Tu	12 3 48	2 50 39	25 21 40	2♈15 17	12 42.7	19 23.7	24 52.3	29 58.9	19 9.8	13 34.7	22 6.7	20 10.3	11 24.4
25 W	12 7 44	3 50 7	9♈ 5 8	15 50 49	12 35.1	20 58.1	26 6.9	0♊37.5	19 17.8	13 31.8	22 10.1	20 9.2	11D 24.4
26 Th	12 11 41	4 49 33	22 32 0	29 8 26	12 26.1	22 27.8	27 21.4	1 16.0	19 25.6	13 28.9	22 13.4	20 8.1	11 24.4
27 F	12 15 38	5 48 57	5♉39 59	12♉ 6 35	12 16.6	23 52.5	28 36.0	1 54.6	19 33.2	13 25.8	22 16.8	20 7.0	11 24.4
28 Sa	12 19 34	6 48 19	18 28 19	24 45 19	12 7.5	25 11.8	29 50.5	2 33.2	19 40.7	13 22.7	22 20.1	20 5.9	11 24.4
29 Su	12 23 31	7 47 39	0♊57 52	7♊ 6 17	11 59.9	26 25.3	1♈ 5.0	3 11.8	19 48.1	13 19.5	22 23.5	20 4.9	11 24.5
30 M	12 27 27	8 46 56	13 11 0	19 12 30	11 54.3	27 32.7	2 19.5	3 50.3	19 55.3	13 16.2	22 26.8	20 3.9	11 24.6
31 Tu	12 31 24	9 46 11	25 11 20	1♋ 8 6	11 51.0	28 33.9	3 34.0	4 28.9	20 2.4	13 12.9	22 30.1	20 2.9	11 24.7

APRIL 1925 LONGITUDE

Day	Sid.Time	☉	0 hr ☽	Noon ☽	True ☊	☿	♀	♂	♃	♄	♅	♆	♇
1 W	12 35 20	10♈45 24	7♋ 3 25	12♋57 57	11♌49.7	29♈28.6	4♈48.4	5♊ 7.4	20♑ 9.4	13♏ 9.5	22♓33.5	20♌ 2.0	11♋24.8
2 Th	12 39 17	11 44 34	18 52 22	24 47 20	11D 49.8	0♉16.5	6 2.9	5 45.9	20 16.2	13R 6.0	22 36.8	20R 1.1	11 25.0
3 F	12 43 13	12 43 42	0♌43 32	6♌41 38	11R 50.6	0 57.7	7 17.3	6 24.4	20 22.8	13 2.5	22 40.0	20 0.2	11 25.2
4 Sa	12 47 10	13 42 48	12 42 15	18 45 59	11 51.0	1 31.9	8 31.7	7 2.9	20 29.3	12 58.8	22 43.3	19 59.3	11 25.4
5 Su	12 51 6	14 41 52	24 53 24	1♍ 4 58	11 50.1	1 59.1	9 46.1	7 41.4	20 35.6	12 55.2	22 46.5	19 58.5	11 25.6
6 M	12 55 3	15 40 53	7♍21 7	13 42 10	11 47.2	2 19.3	11 0.5	8 19.9	20 41.8	12 51.5	22 49.8	19 57.7	11 25.8
7 Tu	12 59 0	16 39 52	20 8 21	26 39 49	11 41.7	2 32.6	12 14.8	8 58.4	20 47.9	12 47.7	22 53.0	19 56.9	11 26.1
8 W	13 2 56	17 38 48	3♎16 34	9♎58 29	11 33.7	2R 39.0	13 29.2	9 36.8	20 53.7	12 43.8	22 56.2	19 56.1	11 26.4
9 Th	13 6 53	18 37 43	16 45 22	23 36 52	11 23.8	2 38.8	14 43.5	10 15.3	20 59.5	12 39.9	22 59.4	19 55.4	11 26.7
10 F	13 10 49	19 36 36	0♏32 32	7♏31 52	11 12.8	2 32.1	15 57.8	10 53.7	21 5.0	12 36.0	23 2.5	19 54.7	11 27.1
11 Sa	13 14 46	20 35 27	14 34 16	21 39 5	11 1.9	2 19.2	17 12.1	11 32.1	21 10.4	12 32.0	23 5.7	19 54.1	11 27.5
12 Su	13 18 42	21 34 15	28 45 43	5♐53 31	10 52.3	2 0.6	18 26.4	12 10.5	21 15.6	12 27.9	23 8.8	19 53.4	11 27.9
13 M	13 22 39	22 33 3	13♐ 1 55	20 10 22	10 44.8	1 36.7	19 40.7	12 48.9	21 20.7	12 23.9	23 11.9	19 52.8	11 28.3
14 Tu	13 26 35	23 31 48	27 18 26	4♑25 43	10 40.0	1 7.9	20 55.0	13 27.3	21 25.6	12 19.7	23 15.0	19 52.3	11 28.7
15 W	13 30 32	24 30 32	11♑31 56	18 36 52	10 37.6	0 35.1	22 9.3	14 5.7	21 30.4	12 15.5	23 18.0	19 51.7	11 29.2
16 Th	13 34 29	25 29 14	25 40 21	2♒42 16	10D 37.1	29♈58.8	23 23.5	14 44.1	21 35.0	12 11.3	23 21.1	19 51.2	11 29.7
17 F	13 38 25	26 27 54	9♒42 33	16 41 10	10R 37.2	29 19.7	24 37.7	15 22.4	21 39.4	12 7.1	23 24.1	19 50.8	11 30.2
18 Sa	13 42 22	27 26 33	23 38 3	0♓33 9	10 36.8	28 38.6	25 52.0	16 0.8	21 43.6	12 2.8	23 27.1	19 50.3	11 30.7
19 Su	13 46 18	28 25 10	7♓26 23	14 17 37	10 34.5	27 56.4	27 6.2	16 39.1	21 47.7	11 58.5	23 30.1	19 49.9	11 31.3
20 M	13 50 15	29 23 45	21 6 44	27 53 33	10 29.6	27 13.8	28 20.4	17 17.4	21 51.5	11 54.1	23 33.0	19 49.5	11 31.8
21 Tu	13 54 11	0♉22 19	4♈37 51	11♈19 25	10 21.7	26 31.6	29 34.6	17 55.8	21 55.2	11 49.7	23 35.9	19 49.2	11 32.4
22 W	13 58 8	1 20 51	17 58 0	24 33 23	10 11.2	25 50.5	0♉48.7	18 34.1	21 58.8	11 45.3	23 38.8	19 48.9	11 33.0
23 Th	14 2 4	2 19 21	1♉ 5 20	7♉33 40	9 58.8	25 11.3	2 2.9	19 12.4	22 2.1	11 40.9	23 41.7	19 48.6	11 33.7
24 F	14 6 1	3 17 49	13 58 17	20 19 4	9 45.6	24 34.6	3 17.0	19 50.7	22 5.3	11 36.4	23 44.5	19 48.3	11 34.4
25 Sa	14 9 58	4 16 15	26 36 1	2♊49 11	9 32.9	24 0.9	4 31.2	20 29.0	22 8.3	11 31.9	23 47.3	19 48.1	11 35.0
26 Su	14 13 54	5 14 39	8♊58 44	15 4 52	9 21.7	23 30.8	5 45.3	21 7.3	22 11.1	11 27.4	23 50.1	19 47.9	11 35.7
27 M	14 17 51	6 13 2	21 7 52	27 8 6	9 12.8	23 4.5	6 59.4	21 45.5	22 13.7	11 22.9	23 52.9	19 47.8	11 36.5
28 Tu	14 21 47	7 11 22	3♋ 6 0	9♋ 2 4	9 6.7	22 42.6	8 13.5	22 23.8	22 16.2	11 18.4	23 55.6	19 47.7	11 37.2
29 W	14 25 44	8 9 40	14 56 49	20 50 53	9 3.2	22 25.1	9 27.5	23 2.1	22 18.5	11 13.9	23 58.3	19 47.6	11 38.0
30 Th	14 29 40	9 7 56	26 44 52	2♌39 26	9 1.8	22 12.2	10 41.6	23 40.3	22 20.5	11 9.4	24 0.9	19 47.5	11 38.8

Astro Data Dy Hr Mn	Planet Ingress Dy Hr Mn	Last Aspect Dy Hr Mn	☽ Ingress Dy Hr Mn	Last Aspect Dy Hr Mn	☽ Ingress Dy Hr Mn	☽ Phases & Eclipses Dy Hr Mn	Astro Data
☽0S 12 4:02	♀ ♓ 4 0:21	1 6:45 ♀ □	♊ 1 13:26	2 7:37 ♅ △	♌ 2 22:32	2 12:06 ☽ 11♊25	1 MARCH 1925
☿0N 14 5:54	☿ ♈ 13 12:36	3 7:15 ♅ □	♋ 4 1:38	4 14:23 ♆ ☌	♍ 5 9:55	10 14:21 ○ 19♍31	Julian Day # 9191
☽0N 25 1:38	☉ ♈ 21 3:12	5 20:24 ♅ △	♌ 6 14:22	7 5:05 ♅ ☍	♎ 7 18:04	17 17:21 ☽ 26♐37	Delta T 23.7 sec
♇ D 25 23:07	♂ ♊ 24 0:42	8 7:01 ♆ ☌	♍ 9 1:24	9 7:28 ♃ □	♏ 9 23:04	24 14:03 ● 3♈25	SVP 06♓18'29"
♀0N 30 18:37	♀ ♈ 28 3:04	11 0:41 ☿ ☍	♎ 11 9:44	11 14:30 ♅ △	♐ 12 2:05		Obliquity 23°26'51"
♃⊼♆ 31 1:30		12 22:36 ♆ ⚹	♏ 13 15:37	13 17:11 ☉ △	♑ 14 4:32	1 8:12 ☽ 11♋06	⚷ Chiron 21♈38.4
	☿ ♉ 1 15:21	15 10:19 ♂ ☍	♐ 15 19:51	16 7:02 ☿ □	♒ 16 7:23	9 3:33 ○ 18♎46	☽ Mean ☊ 12♌30.4
☽0S 8 12:03	☿ ♈ 15 23:12	17 17:21 ☉ □	♑ 17 23:07	18 8:16 ☿ ⚹	♓ 18 11:02	15 23:40 ☽ 25♑28	
☿ R 8 11:02	☉ ♉ 20 14:51	19 23:57 ☉ ⚹	♒ 20 1:51	20 4:19 ♅ ☌	♈ 20 15:45	23 2:28 ● 2♉25	1 APRIL 1925
☽0N 21 9:45	♀ ♉ 21 8:14	22 2:27 ♂ □	♓ 22 4:33	22 13:40 ☿ ☌	♉ 22 22:00		Julian Day # 9222
♄△♇ 24 9:34		23 23:04 ♀ ☌	♈ 24 8:04	24 18:36 ♅ ⚹	♊ 25 6:33		Delta T 23.7 sec
		25 23:52 ☿ ☌	♉ 26 13:34	27 5:30 ♅ □	♋ 27 17:45		SVP 06♓18'26"
		28 7:24 ♅ ⚹	♊ 28 22:08	29 18:25 ♅ △	♌ 30 6:36		Obliquity 23°26'51"
		31 7:24 ☿ ⚹	♋ 31 9:42				⚷ Chiron 23♈19.6
							☽ Mean ☊ 10♌51.9

LONGITUDE — MAY 1925

Day	Sid.Time	☉	0 hr ☽	Noon ☽	True ☊	☿	♀	♂	♃	♄	♅	♆	♇
1 F	14 33 37	10♉ 6 11	8♌35 16	14♌33 5	9♌ 1.6	22♈ 4.1	11♉55.6	24♊18.5	22♑22.4	11♏ 4.8	24♓ 3.6	19♌47.5	11♋39.6
2 Sa	14 37 33	11 4 23	20 33 32	26 37 20	9R 1.4	22D 0.9	13 9.6	24 56.7	22 24.1	11R 0.3	24 6.2	19D 47.5	11 40.4
3 Su	14 41 30	12 2 33	2♍45 7	8♍57 30	9 0.3	22 2.4	14 23.6	25 34.9	22 25.7	10 55.7	24 8.7	19 47.6	11 41.3
4 M	14 45 27	13 0 41	15 15 3	21 38 14	8 57.2	22 8.8	15 37.6	26 13.1	22 27.0	10 51.2	24 11.3	19 47.6	11 42.1
5 Tu	14 49 23	13 58 47	28 7 26	4♎42 55	8 51.7	22 19.8	16 51.6	26 51.3	22 28.1	10 46.7	24 13.8	19 47.8	11 43.0
6 W	14 53 20	14 56 52	11♎24 50	18 13 8	8 43.6	22 35.5	18 5.6	27 29.5	22 29.1	10 42.2	24 16.2	19 47.9	11 43.9
7 Th	14 57 16	15 54 54	25 7 41	2♏ 8 6	8 33.4	22 55.7	19 19.5	28 7.6	22 29.9	10 37.6	24 18.7	19 48.1	11 44.9
8 F	15 1 13	16 52 55	9♏13 54	16 24 26	8 22.0	23 20.2	20 33.4	28 45.8	22 30.5	10 33.1	24 21.1	19 48.3	11 45.8
9 Sa	15 5 9	17 50 54	23 38 54	0♐56 26	8 10.6	23 49.0	21 47.3	29 23.9	22 30.9	10 28.6	24 23.4	19 48.5	11 46.8
10 Su	15 9 6	18 48 51	8♐16 5	15 36 54	8 0.5	24 22.0	23 1.2	0♋ 2.0	22R31.1	10 24.2	24 25.8	19 48.8	11 47.7
11 M	15 13 2	19 46 48	22 57 56	0♑18 19	7 52.5	24 58.8	24 15.1	0 40.1	22 31.1	10 19.7	24 28.1	19 49.1	11 48.8
12 Tu	15 16 59	20 44 42	7♑37 15	14 54 4	7 47.2	25 39.6	25 29.0	1 18.2	22 31.0	10 15.3	24 30.3	19 49.5	11 49.8
13 W	15 20 56	21 42 36	22 8 14	29 19 18	7 44.6	26 24.0	26 42.9	1 56.3	22 30.6	10 10.9	24 32.5	19 49.8	11 50.8
14 Th	15 24 52	22 40 28	6♒27 1	13♒31 10	7D 43.9	27 12.0	27 56.7	2 34.4	22 30.1	10 6.5	24 34.7	19 50.3	11 51.9
15 F	15 28 49	23 38 19	20 31 40	27 28 32	7R 44.1	28 3.5	29 10.6	3 12.5	22 29.3	10 2.2	24 36.9	19 50.7	11 52.9
16 Sa	15 32 45	24 36 9	4♓21 47	11♓11 32	7 43.8	28 58.2	0♊24.4	3 50.5	22 28.4	9 57.8	24 39.0	19 51.2	11 54.0
17 Su	15 36 42	25 33 58	17 57 52	24 40 53	7 41.9	29 56.2	1 38.2	4 28.6	22 27.3	9 53.5	24 41.0	19 51.7	11 55.1
18 M	15 40 38	26 31 45	1♈20 42	7♈57 24	7 37.7	0♉57.3	2 52.1	5 6.7	22 26.0	9 49.3	24 43.1	19 52.2	11 56.2
19 Tu	15 44 35	27 29 31	14 31 4	21 1 43	7 30.8	2 1.3	4 5.9	5 44.7	22 24.5	9 45.1	24 45.0	19 52.8	11 57.4
20 W	15 48 31	28 27 17	27 29 23	3♉54 5	7 21.5	3 8.4	5 19.7	6 22.7	22 22.8	9 40.9	24 47.0	19 53.4	11 58.5
21 Th	15 52 28	29 25 1	10♉15 49	16 34 34	7 10.4	4 18.2	6 33.5	7 0.8	22 21.0	9 36.7	24 48.9	19 54.0	11 59.7
22 F	15 56 25	0♊22 43	22 50 22	29 3 13	6 58.5	5 30.9	7 47.2	7 38.8	22 18.9	9 32.6	24 50.8	19 54.7	12 0.9
23 Sa	16 0 21	1 20 25	5♊13 11	11♊20 20	6 47.0	6 46.2	9 1.0	8 16.8	22 16.7	9 28.6	24 52.6	19 55.4	12 2.1
24 Su	16 4 18	2 18 5	17 24 48	23 26 45	6 36.9	8 4.2	10 14.8	8 54.8	22 14.3	9 24.6	24 54.4	19 56.1	12 3.3
25 M	16 8 14	3 15 44	29 26 24	5♋24 1	6 28.8	9 24.9	11 28.5	9 32.8	22 11.7	9 20.6	24 56.1	19 56.9	12 4.5
26 Tu	16 12 11	4 13 22	11♋19 57	17 14 33	6 23.3	10 48.1	12 42.2	10 10.8	22 8.9	9 16.7	24 57.8	19 57.7	12 5.7
27 W	16 16 7	5 10 58	23 8 17	29 1 36	6 20.3	12 13.9	13 56.0	10 48.8	22 6.0	9 12.8	24 59.5	19 58.5	12 7.0
28 Th	16 20 4	6 8 33	4♌55 4	10♌49 13	6D 19.3	13 42.2	15 9.7	11 26.8	22 2.8	9 9.0	25 1.1	19 59.3	12 8.3
29 F	16 24 0	7 6 7	16 44 40	22 42 4	6 19.7	15 13.0	16 23.4	12 4.8	21 59.5	9 5.3	25 2.7	20 0.2	12 9.5
30 Sa	16 27 57	8 3 39	28 42 3	4♍45 17	6R 20.5	16 46.3	17 37.0	12 42.7	21 56.0	9 1.6	25 4.2	20 1.1	12 10.8
31 Su	16 31 54	9 1 10	10♍52 26	17 4 10	6 20.8	18 22.0	18 50.7	13 20.7	21 52.4	8 58.0	25 5.7	20 2.1	12 12.1

LONGITUDE — JUNE 1925

Day	Sid.Time	☉	0 hr ☽	Noon ☽	True ☊	☿	♀	♂	♃	♄	♅	♆	♇
1 M	16 35 50	9♊58 39	23♍21 4	29♍43 43	6♌19.8	20♉ 0.3	20♊ 4.4	13♋58.7	21♑48.5	8♏54.4	25♓ 7.1	20♌ 3.1	12♋13.4
2 Tu	16 39 47	10 56 7	6♎12 37	12♎48 9	6R 16.9	21 40.9	21 18.0	14 36.6	21R 44.5	8R 50.9	25 8.5	20 4.1	12 14.8
3 W	16 43 43	11 53 34	19 30 38	26 20 10	6 12.0	23 24.1	22 31.6	15 14.5	21 40.4	8 47.5	25 9.8	20 5.1	12 16.1
4 Th	16 47 40	12 51 0	3♏16 46	10♏20 14	6 5.4	25 9.6	23 45.2	15 52.4	21 36.0	8 44.1	25 11.1	20 6.1	12 17.5
5 F	16 51 36	13 48 24	17 30 10	24 46 0	5 57.6	26 57.6	24 58.8	16 30.4	21 31.6	8 40.8	25 12.4	20 7.2	12 18.8
6 Sa	16 55 33	14 45 48	2♐ 6 59	9♐32 11	5 49.7	28 48.0	26 12.4	17 8.3	21 26.9	8 37.6	25 13.6	20 8.4	12 20.2
7 Su	16 59 29	15 43 10	17 0 34	24 31 1	5 42.6	0♊40.8	27 26.0	17 46.2	21 22.1	8 34.4	25 14.8	20 9.5	12 21.6
8 M	17 3 26	16 40 32	2♑ 2 20	9♑33 24	5 37.2	2 35.9	28 39.6	18 24.1	21 17.2	8 31.4	25 15.9	20 10.7	12 23.0
9 Tu	17 7 23	17 37 53	17 3 7	24 30 29	5 33.8	4 33.2	29 53.1	19 2.0	21 12.1	8 28.4	25 17.0	20 11.9	12 24.4
10 W	17 11 19	18 35 14	1♒54 38	9♒14 51	5D 32.5	6 32.7	1♋ 6.7	19 39.8	21 6.8	8 25.4	25 18.0	20 13.1	12 25.8
11 Th	17 15 16	19 32 34	16 30 36	23 41 28	5 32.8	8 34.3	2 20.2	20 17.7	21 1.5	8 22.6	25 19.0	20 14.4	12 27.2
12 F	17 19 12	20 29 53	0♓47 12	7♓47 41	5 34.0	10 37.8	3 33.8	20 55.6	20 55.9	8 19.8	25 19.9	20 15.7	12 28.6
13 Sa	17 23 9	21 27 12	14 42 54	21 32 56	5R 34.9	12 43.2	4 47.3	21 33.5	20 50.3	8 17.1	25 20.8	20 17.0	12 30.1
14 Su	17 27 5	22 24 31	28 17 56	4♈58 6	5 35.0	14 50.1	6 0.8	22 11.3	20 44.5	8 14.5	25 21.6	20 18.3	12 31.5
15 M	17 31 2	23 21 49	11♈33 42	18 4 57	5 33.4	16 58.5	7 14.3	22 49.2	20 38.5	8 11.9	25 22.4	20 19.7	12 33.0
16 Tu	17 34 58	24 19 7	24 32 9	0♉55 33	5 30.1	19 8.1	8 27.8	23 27.1	20 32.5	8 9.5	25 23.1	20 21.0	12 34.4
17 W	17 38 55	25 16 24	7♉15 24	13 31 57	5 25.1	21 18.6	9 41.3	24 4.9	20 26.3	8 7.1	25 23.8	20 22.5	12 35.9
18 Th	17 42 52	26 13 42	19 45 25	25 56 2	5 18.9	23 29.9	10 54.8	24 42.8	20 20.0	8 4.8	25 24.5	20 23.9	12 37.4
19 F	17 46 48	27 10 58	2♊ 4 0	8♊ 9 30	5 12.1	25 41.5	12 8.2	25 20.6	20 13.5	8 2.6	25 25.1	20 25.4	12 38.8
20 Sa	17 50 45	28 8 15	14 12 44	20 13 54	5 5.5	27 53.2	13 21.7	25 58.5	20 7.0	8 0.5	25 25.6	20 26.9	12 40.3
21 Su	17 54 41	29 5 31	26 13 11	2♋10 49	4 59.8	0♋ 4.8	14 35.2	26 36.4	20 0.4	7 58.5	25 26.1	20 28.4	12 41.8
22 M	17 58 38	0♋ 2 47	8♋ 7 0	14 2 0	4 55.4	2 16.0	15 48.6	27 14.2	19 53.6	7 56.5	25 26.6	20 29.9	12 43.3
23 Tu	18 2 34	1 0 2	19 56 5	25 49 34	4 52.6	4 26.5	17 2.0	27 52.1	19 46.8	7 54.7	25 27.0	20 31.5	12 44.8
24 W	18 6 31	1 57 17	1♌42 46	7♌36 5	4D 51.5	6 36.1	18 15.5	28 29.9	19 39.9	7 52.9	25 27.4	20 33.0	12 46.3
25 Th	18 10 27	2 54 32	13 29 55	19 24 41	4 51.8	8 44.6	19 28.9	29 7.8	19 32.8	7 51.3	25 27.7	20 34.7	12 47.8
26 F	18 14 24	3 51 46	25 20 54	1♍19 3	4 53.0	10 51.8	20 42.3	29 45.6	19 25.7	7 49.7	25 27.9	20 36.3	12 49.3
27 Sa	18 18 21	4 48 59	7♍19 41	13 23 20	4 54.7	12 57.5	21 55.7	0♌23.5	19 18.6	7 48.2	25 28.1	20 37.9	12 50.8
28 Su	18 22 17	5 46 12	19 30 36	25 42 2	4 56.3	15 1.6	23 9.0	1 1.3	19 11.3	7 46.8	25 28.3	20 39.6	12 52.4
29 M	18 26 14	6 43 25	1♎58 12	8♎19 41	4R 57.1	17 4.0	24 22.4	1 39.1	19 4.0	7 45.6	25 28.4	20 41.3	12 53.9
30 Tu	18 30 10	7 40 37	14 46 57	21 20 27	4 57.0	19 4.6	25 35.7	2 17.0	18 56.6	7 44.4	25R 28.5	20 43.0	12 55.4

Astro Data Dy Hr Mn	Planet Ingress Dy Hr Mn	Last Aspect Dy Hr Mn	☽ Ingress Dy Hr Mn	Last Aspect Dy Hr Mn	☽ Ingress Dy Hr Mn	☽ Phases & Eclipses Dy Hr Mn	Astro Data
♆ D 1 1:21	♂ ♋ 9 22:44	2 9:10 ♂ ⚹	♍ 2 18:38	1 3:21 ♅ ☍	♎ 1 12:30	1 3:20 ☽ 10♌14	1 MAY 1925
☿ D 2 4:15	♀ ♊ 15 16:04	4 21:33 ♂ □	♎ 5 3:26	3 5:51 ♀ △	♏ 3 18:21	8 13:42 ○ 17♏26	Julian Day # 9252
☽0S 5 21:57	☿ ♉ 17 1:32	7 5:24 ♂ △	♏ 7 8:22	5 17:49 ☿ ☍	♐ 5 20:33	15 5:46 ☽ 23♒52	Delta T 23.7 sec
♃ R 10 15:30	☉ ♊ 21 14:33	9 1:14 ♅ △	♐ 9 10:27	7 18:08 ♀ ☍	♑ 7 20:45	22 15:48 ● 1♊01	SVP 06♓18'23"
☽0N 18 16:32		11 3:27 ☿ △	♑ 11 11:30	9 13:16 ♅ ⚹	♒ 9 20:54	30 20:04 ☽ 8♍52	Obliquity 23°26'51"
♄□♅ 19 0:01	☿ ♊ 6 15:23	13 8:21 ♀ △	♒ 13 13:08	11 6:13 ♆ ☍	♓ 11 22:40		⚷ Chiron 25♈07.3
	♀ ♋ 9 2:14	15 13:55 ☿ ⚹	♓ 15 16:23	13 18:45 ♅ ☌	♈ 14 3:03	6 21:48 ○ 15♐38	☽ Mean ☊ 9♌16.6
☽0S 2 8:15	☿ ♋ 20 23:07	17 14:39 ☉ ⚹	♈ 17 21:34	15 23:34 ☉ ⚹	♉ 16 10:15	13 12:44 ☽ 21♓58	
☽0N 14 22:51	☉ ♋ 21 22:50	19 14:31 ♃ □	♉ 20 4:41	18 10:59 ♅ ⚹	♊ 18 19:57	21 6:17 ● 29♊21	1 JUNE 1925
♃⚻♆ 17 11:51	♂ ♌ 26 9:08	22 3:52 ♅ ⚹	♊ 22 13:50	21 6:17 ☉ ☌	♋ 21 7:36	29 9:43 ☽ 7♎07	Julian Day # 9283
☽0S 29 17:18		24 14:57 ♅ □	♋ 25 1:07	23 17:05 ♂ ☌	♌ 23 20:30		Delta T 23.7 sec
♅ R 30 19:13		27 3:47 ♅ △	♌ 27 13:59	25 14:24 ♆ ☌	♍ 26 9:21		SVP 06♓18'19"
		29 6:35 ♆ ☌	♍ 30 2:35	28 11:34 ♅ ☍	♎ 28 20:15		Obliquity 23°26'50"
							⚷ Chiron 26♈47.4
							☽ Mean ☊ 7♌38.1

JULY 1925 LONGITUDE

Day	Sid.Time	☉	0 hr ☽	Noon ☽	True ☊	☿	♀	♂	♃	♄	♅	♆	♇
1 W	18 34 7	8♋37 48	28♎ 0 35	4♏47 36	4♌55.8	21♋ 3.4	26♋49.1	2♌54.8	18♑49.2	7♏43.3	25♓28.5	20♌44.7	12♋56.9
2 Th	18 38 3	9 35 0	11♏41 38	18 42 42	4R 53.5	23 0.2	28 2.4	3 32.6	18R 41.7	7R 42.3	25R 28.4	20 46.5	12 58.5
3 F	18 42 0	10 32 11	25 50 36	3♐ 5 0	4 50.5	24 55.1	29 15.7	4 10.5	18 34.1	7 41.3	25 28.4	20 48.3	12 60.0
4 Sa	18 45 56	11 29 21	10♐25 21	17 50 55	4 47.4	26 47.9	0♌29.0	4 48.3	18 26.6	7 40.5	25 28.2	20 50.1	13 1.5
5 Su	18 49 53	12 26 32	25 20 49	2♑54 1	4 44.5	28 38.8	1 42.2	5 26.1	18 19.0	7 39.8	25 28.1	20 51.9	13 3.1
6 M	18 53 50	13 23 43	10♑29 21	18 5 37	4 42.5	0♌27.6	2 55.5	6 3.9	18 11.3	7 39.2	25 27.8	20 53.7	13 4.6
7 Tu	18 57 46	14 20 53	25 41 36	3♒16 4	4D 41.4	2 14.5	4 8.7	6 41.8	18 3.7	7 38.7	25 27.6	20 55.6	13 6.1
8 W	19 1 43	15 18 4	10♒47 56	18 16 10	4 41.3	3 59.3	5 22.0	7 19.6	17 56.0	7 38.3	25 27.3	20 57.4	13 7.6
9 Th	19 5 39	16 15 15	25 39 56	2♓58 30	4 42.0	5 42.0	6 35.2	7 57.4	17 48.3	7 37.9	25 26.9	20 59.3	13 9.2
10 F	19 9 36	17 12 26	10♓11 22	17 18 8	4 43.1	7 22.8	7 48.4	8 35.3	17 40.6	7 37.7	25 26.5	21 1.2	13 10.7
11 Sa	19 13 32	18 9 38	24 18 37	1♈12 45	4 44.3	9 1.5	9 1.6	9 13.1	17 32.8	7D 37.6	25 26.0	21 3.1	13 12.2
12 Su	19 17 29	19 6 50	8♈ 0 35	14 42 18	4R 45.1	10 38.2	10 14.7	9 50.9	17 25.1	7 37.5	25 25.5	21 5.1	13 13.8
13 M	19 21 25	20 4 3	21 18 9	27 48 27	4 45.4	12 12.9	11 27.9	10 28.8	17 17.4	7 37.6	25 24.9	21 7.0	13 15.3
14 Tu	19 25 22	21 1 16	4♉13 34	10♉33 54	4 45.0	13 45.5	12 41.0	11 6.6	17 9.7	7 37.7	25 24.3	21 9.0	13 16.8
15 W	19 29 19	21 58 30	16 49 52	23 1 54	4 44.0	15 16.1	13 54.2	11 44.5	17 2.0	7 38.0	25 23.7	21 11.0	13 18.3
16 Th	19 33 15	22 55 45	29 10 25	5♊15 49	4 42.6	16 44.6	15 7.3	12 22.3	16 54.4	7 38.4	25 23.0	21 13.0	13 19.8
17 F	19 37 12	23 53 0	11♊18 32	17 18 56	4 41.1	18 11.0	16 20.4	13 0.2	16 46.7	7 38.8	25 22.3	21 15.0	13 21.4
18 Sa	19 41 8	24 50 16	23 17 22	29 14 13	4 39.7	19 35.3	17 33.5	13 38.0	16 39.1	7 39.4	25 21.5	21 17.0	13 22.9
19 Su	19 45 5	25 47 32	5♋ 9 46	11♋ 4 23	4 38.5	20 57.5	18 46.6	14 15.9	16 31.6	7 40.0	25 20.7	21 19.0	13 24.4
20 M	19 49 1	26 44 49	16 58 19	22 51 54	4 37.7	22 17.5	19 59.7	14 53.8	16 24.1	7 40.8	25 19.8	21 21.1	13 25.9
21 Tu	19 52 58	27 42 7	28 45 24	4♌39 6	4D 37.3	23 35.3	21 12.7	15 31.7	16 16.6	7 41.6	25 18.9	21 23.2	13 27.4
22 W	19 56 54	28 39 25	10♌33 18	16 28 16	4 37.3	24 50.8	22 25.8	16 9.5	16 9.2	7 42.6	25 17.9	21 25.2	13 28.9
23 Th	20 0 51	29 36 43	22 24 20	28 21 49	4 37.6	26 4.0	23 38.8	16 47.4	16 1.9	7 43.6	25 16.9	21 27.3	13 30.3
24 F	20 4 48	0♌34 2	4♍21 2	10♍22 20	4 38.0	27 14.7	24 51.8	17 25.3	15 54.6	7 44.8	25 15.8	21 29.4	13 31.8
25 Sa	20 8 44	1 31 22	16 26 6	22 32 43	4 38.3	28 23.0	26 4.8	18 3.2	15 47.4	7 46.0	25 14.7	21 31.5	13 33.3
26 Su	20 12 41	2 28 42	28 42 35	4♎56 5	4 38.6	29 28.7	27 17.7	18 41.1	15 40.3	7 47.3	25 13.6	21 33.6	13 34.8
27 M	20 16 37	3 26 2	11♎13 41	17 35 45	4 38.8	0♍31.8	28 30.7	19 19.0	15 33.2	7 48.8	25 12.4	21 35.8	13 36.2
28 Tu	20 20 34	4 23 23	24 2 44	0♏34 58	4 38.8	1 32.2	29 43.6	19 56.9	15 26.3	7 50.3	25 11.2	21 37.9	13 37.7
29 W	20 24 30	5 20 44	7♏12 49	13 56 33	4 38.9	2 29.6	0♍56.5	20 34.9	15 19.4	7 51.9	25 9.9	21 40.0	13 39.1
30 Th	20 28 27	6 18 6	20 46 23	27 42 26	4 38.9	3 24.1	2 9.3	21 12.8	15 12.6	7 53.6	25 8.6	21 42.2	13 40.5
31 F	20 32 23	7 15 28	4♐44 43	11♐53 5	4 39.0	4 15.5	3 22.2	21 50.7	15 6.0	7 55.4	25 7.3	21 44.4	13 42.0

AUGUST 1925 LONGITUDE

Day	Sid.Time	☉	0 hr ☽	Noon ☽	True ☊	☿	♀	♂	♃	♄	♅	♆	♇
1 Sa	20 36 20	8♌12 51	19♐ 7 16	26♐26 51	4♌39.3	5♍ 3.5	4♍35.0	22♌28.7	14♑59.4	7♏57.3	25♓ 5.9	21♌46.5	13♋43.4
2 Su	20 40 17	9 10 15	3♑51 14	11♑19 40	4 39.7	5 48.2	5 47.8	23 6.6	14R 53.0	7 59.4	25R 4.5	21 48.7	13 44.8
3 M	20 44 13	10 7 40	18 51 16	26 25 0	4 40.0	6 29.3	7 0.6	23 44.5	14 46.7	8 1.4	25 3.1	21 50.9	13 46.2
4 Tu	20 48 10	11 5 5	3♒59 48	11♒34 29	4R 40.2	7 6.6	8 13.3	24 22.5	14 40.4	8 3.6	25 1.6	21 53.1	13 47.6
5 W	20 52 6	12 2 31	19 7 53	26 38 52	4 40.0	7 40.0	9 26.1	25 0.4	14 34.3	8 5.9	25 0.0	21 55.3	13 49.0
6 Th	20 56 3	12 59 58	4♓ 6 23	11♓29 28	4 39.5	8 9.2	10 38.8	25 38.4	14 28.4	8 8.3	24 58.5	21 57.5	13 50.4
7 F	20 59 59	13 57 26	18 47 18	25 59 15	4 38.6	8 34.1	11 51.4	26 16.4	14 22.5	8 10.7	24 56.9	21 59.7	13 51.7
8 Sa	21 3 56	14 54 55	3♈ 4 50	10♈ 3 44	4 37.4	8 54.5	13 4.1	26 54.4	14 16.8	8 13.3	24 55.2	22 1.9	13 53.1
9 Su	21 7 52	15 52 26	16 55 49	23 41 6	4 36.2	9 10.1	14 16.7	27 32.4	14 11.3	8 15.9	24 53.5	22 4.1	13 54.4
10 M	21 11 49	16 49 58	0♉19 42	6♉51 55	4 35.3	9 20.8	15 29.3	28 10.4	14 5.8	8 18.7	24 51.8	22 6.3	13 55.7
11 Tu	21 15 46	17 47 31	13 18 4	19 38 36	4D 34.8	9R 26.4	16 41.9	28 48.4	14 0.5	8 21.5	24 50.1	22 8.5	13 57.0
12 W	21 19 42	18 45 6	25 54 0	2♊ 4 48	4 34.8	9 26.7	17 54.4	29 26.4	13 55.4	8 24.4	24 48.3	22 10.7	13 58.3
13 Th	21 23 39	19 42 43	8♊11 32	14 14 46	4 35.5	9 21.6	19 7.0	0♍ 4.4	13 50.4	8 27.4	24 46.5	22 13.0	13 59.6
14 F	21 27 35	20 40 21	20 15 3	26 12 56	4 36.7	9 11.0	20 19.5	0 42.5	13 45.6	8 30.5	24 44.7	22 15.2	14 0.9
15 Sa	21 31 32	21 38 0	2♋ 8 58	8♋ 3 38	4 38.1	8 54.9	21 31.9	1 20.6	13 40.9	8 33.6	24 42.8	22 17.4	14 2.2
16 Su	21 35 28	22 35 41	13 57 26	19 50 48	4 39.5	8 33.1	22 44.4	1 58.6	13 36.4	8 36.9	24 40.9	22 19.6	14 3.4
17 M	21 39 25	23 33 23	25 44 10	1♌37 55	4R 40.4	8 6.0	23 56.8	2 36.7	13 32.0	8 40.2	24 39.0	22 21.8	14 4.7
18 Tu	21 43 21	24 31 7	7♌32 25	13 28 0	4 40.7	7 33.5	25 9.2	3 14.8	13 27.8	8 43.7	24 37.0	22 24.1	14 5.9
19 W	21 47 18	25 28 52	19 24 56	25 23 30	4 39.9	6 56.1	26 21.6	3 52.9	13 23.8	8 47.2	24 35.0	22 26.3	14 7.1
20 Th	21 51 15	26 26 38	1♍23 57	7♍26 31	4 38.1	6 14.2	27 34.0	4 31.1	13 19.9	8 50.8	24 33.0	22 28.5	14 8.3
21 F	21 55 11	27 24 26	13 31 23	19 38 47	4 35.3	5 28.2	28 46.3	5 9.2	13 16.3	8 54.4	24 31.0	22 30.7	14 9.5
22 Sa	21 59 8	28 22 15	25 48 52	2♎ 1 51	4 31.7	4 38.8	29 58.6	5 47.4	13 12.7	8 58.2	24 28.9	22 33.0	14 10.6
23 Su	22 3 4	29 20 6	8♎17 55	14 37 14	4 27.7	3 47.0	1♎10.8	6 25.5	13 9.4	9 2.0	24 26.8	22 35.2	14 11.8
24 M	22 7 1	0♍17 57	21 0 1	27 26 26	4 23.9	2 53.4	2 23.1	7 3.7	13 6.3	9 6.0	24 24.7	22 37.4	14 12.9
25 Tu	22 10 57	1 15 50	3♏56 42	10♏31 1	4 20.8	1 59.3	3 35.3	7 41.9	13 3.3	9 10.0	24 22.5	22 39.6	14 14.0
26 W	22 14 54	2 13 45	17 9 34	23 52 31	4 18.7	1 5.7	4 47.4	8 20.1	13 0.5	9 14.0	24 20.4	22 41.8	14 15.1
27 Th	22 18 50	3 11 40	0♐40 3	7♐32 14	4D 17.8	0 13.6	5 59.6	8 58.3	12 57.9	9 18.2	24 18.2	22 44.0	14 16.2
28 F	22 22 47	4 9 37	14 29 10	21 30 51	4 18.2	29♌24.3	7 11.6	9 36.5	12 55.5	9 22.4	24 16.0	22 46.2	14 17.3
29 Sa	22 26 44	5 7 35	28 37 12	5♑48 1	4 19.3	28 38.8	8 23.7	10 14.7	12 53.2	9 26.7	24 13.8	22 48.4	14 18.4
30 Su	22 30 40	6 5 35	13♑ 3 2	20 21 51	4 20.8	27 58.2	9 35.7	10 53.0	12 51.2	9 31.1	24 11.6	22 50.6	14 19.4
31 M	22 34 37	7 3 36	27 43 54	5♒ 8 32	4R 21.8	27 23.4	10 47.7	11 31.2	12 49.3	9 35.6	24 9.3	22 52.7	14 20.4

Astro Data	Planet Ingress	Last Aspect	☽ Ingress	Last Aspect	☽ Ingress	☽ Phases & Eclipses	Astro Data
Dy Hr Mn	Dy Hr Mn	Dy Hr Mn	Dy Hr Mn	Dy Hr Mn	Dy Hr Mn	Dy Hr Mn	1 JULY 1925
♄ D 11 21:18	♀ ♌ 3 14:31	30 21:39 ♀ □	♏ 1 3:33	1 9:47 ♅ □	♑ 1 17:46	6 4:54 ○ 13♑35	Julian Day # 9313
☽0N 12 5:49	☿ ♌ 5 17:52	3 6:13 ♀ △	♐ 3 6:55	3 9:49 ♅ ✶	♒ 3 17:40	12 21:34 ☽ 19♈58	Delta T 23.7 sec
☽0S 27 0:11	☉ ♌ 23 9:45	5 0:12 ♅ □	♑ 5 7:24	5 9:47 ♂ ☍	♓ 5 17:23	20 21:40 ● 27♋37	SVP 06♓18'14"
	☿ ♍ 26 11:46	6 23:38 ♅ ✶	♒ 7 6:49	7 10:14 ♅ ☌	♈ 7 18:46	20 21:48:19 ✔ A 7'14"	Obliquity 23°26'50"
☽0N 8 14:09	♀ ♍ 28 5:25	8 16:23 ♆ ☍	♓ 9 7:06	9 19:53 ♂ △	♉ 9 23:24	28 20:23 ☽ 5♏12	⚷ Chiron 27♈55.7
♃☍♇ 11 12:59		11 1:56 ♅ ☌	♈ 11 9:53	12 7:14 ♂ □	♊ 12 7:57		☽ Mean ☊ 6♌02.8
☿ R 11 13:27	♂ ♍ 12 21:12	12 23:40 ♆ △	♉ 13 16:05	14 9:01 ♅ □	♋ 14 19:39	4 11:59 ○ 11♒34	
☽0S 23 5:30	♀ ♎ 22 0:28	15 16:35 ♅ ✶	♊ 16 1:37	16 21:48 ♅ △	♌ 17 8:41	4 11:53 ☍ P 0.746	1 AUGUST 1925
♀0S 23 13:52	☉ ♍ 23 16:33	18 4:10 ♅ □	♋ 18 13:33	19 13:15 ☉ ☌	♍ 19 21:13	11 9:11 ☽ 18♉10	Julian Day # 9344
♄⚼♅ 27 0:05	☿ ♌ 27 6:28	20 21:40 ☉ ☌	♌ 21 2:32	21 21:25 ♅ ☍	♎ 22 8:05	19 13:15 ● 26♌01	Delta T 23.8 sec
		23 8:12 ☿ ☌	♍ 23 15:17	24 3:03 ♆ ✶	♏ 24 16:44	27 4:46 ☽ 3♐23	SVP 06♓18'09"
		25 17:15 ♅ ☍	♎ 26 2:30	26 12:47 ♅ △	♐ 26 22:50		Obliquity 23°26'51"
		27 19:31 ♆ ✶	♏ 28 10:56	29 0:03 ☿ △	♑ 29 2:19		⚷ Chiron 28♈22.4
		30 7:34 ♅ △	♐ 30 15:56	30 18:12 ♅ ✶	♒ 31 3:41		☽ Mean ☊ 4♌24.3

LONGITUDE SEPTEMBER 1925

Day	Sid.Time	☉	0 hr ☽	Noon ☽	True ☊	☿	♀	♂	♃	♄	♅	♆	♇
1 Tu	22 38 33	8♍ 1 38	12♒34 58	20♒ 2 19	4♌21.7	26♌55.3	11♎59.6	12♍ 9.5	12♑47.6	9♏40.1	24♓ 7.0	22♌54.9	14♋21.4
2 W	22 42 30	8 59 42	27 29 37	4♓55 51	4R 20.0	26R 34.5	13 11.5	12 47.8	12R 46.2	9 44.7	24R 4.8	22 57.0	14 22.4
3 Th	22 46 26	9 57 47	12♓20 0	19 41 4	4 16.7	26 21.7	14 23.4	13 26.1	12 44.9	9 49.4	24 2.5	22 59.2	14 23.4
4 F	22 50 23	10 55 54	26 58 8	4♈10 23	4 11.9	26D 17.2	15 35.2	14 4.4	12 43.8	9 54.1	24 0.1	23 1.3	14 24.3
5 Sa	22 54 19	11 54 2	11♈17 7	18 17 48	4 6.2	26 21.4	16 46.9	14 42.7	12 42.8	9 58.9	23 57.8	23 3.5	14 25.2
6 Su	22 58 16	12 52 13	25 12 3	1♉59 41	4 0.3	26 34.3	17 58.7	15 21.1	12 42.1	10 3.8	23 55.5	23 5.6	14 26.1
7 M	23 2 13	13 50 25	8♉40 38	15 15 0	3 55.1	26 56.0	19 10.4	15 59.4	12 41.6	10 8.7	23 53.1	23 7.7	14 27.0
8 Tu	23 6 9	14 48 40	21 43 1	28 5 3	3 51.0	27 26.4	20 22.0	16 37.8	12 41.2	10 13.7	23 50.8	23 9.8	14 27.9
9 W	23 10 6	15 46 57	4♊21 31	10♊32 57	3 48.6	28 5.3	21 33.6	17 16.2	12D 41.1	10 18.8	23 48.4	23 11.9	14 28.7
10 Th	23 14 2	16 45 15	16 39 55	22 43 3	3D 47.8	28 52.3	22 45.2	17 54.6	12 41.1	10 23.9	23 46.0	23 14.0	14 29.6
11 F	23 17 59	17 43 36	28 42 57	4♋40 18	3 48.4	29 47.2	23 56.8	18 33.0	12 41.3	10 29.1	23 43.6	23 16.0	14 30.4
12 Sa	23 21 55	18 41 59	10♋35 44	16 29 54	3 49.8	0♍49.5	25 8.2	19 11.5	12 41.8	10 34.4	23 41.2	23 18.1	14 31.2
13 Su	23 25 52	19 40 24	22 23 24	28 16 50	3R 51.2	1 58.7	26 19.7	19 50.0	12 42.4	10 39.8	23 38.9	23 20.2	14 31.9
14 M	23 29 48	20 38 52	4♌10 47	10♌ 5 44	3 51.8	3 14.1	27 31.1	20 28.5	12 43.2	10 45.1	23 36.5	23 22.2	14 32.7
15 Tu	23 33 45	21 37 21	16 2 10	22 0 31	3 50.9	4 35.4	28 42.5	21 7.0	12 44.2	10 50.6	23 34.1	23 24.2	14 33.4
16 W	23 37 42	22 35 52	28 1 10	4♍ 4 24	3 48.0	6 1.7	29 53.8	21 45.5	12 45.4	10 56.1	23 31.6	23 26.2	14 34.1
17 Th	23 41 38	23 34 25	10♍10 30	16 19 39	3 42.8	7 32.7	1♏ 5.1	22 24.1	12 46.7	11 1.7	23 29.2	23 28.2	14 34.8
18 F	23 45 35	24 33 0	22 32 1	28 47 42	3 35.6	9 7.6	2 16.3	23 2.6	12 48.3	11 7.3	23 26.8	23 30.2	14 35.4
19 Sa	23 49 31	25 31 37	5♎ 6 43	11♎29 6	3 26.8	10 46.0	3 27.5	23 41.2	12 50.1	11 13.0	23 24.4	23 32.1	14 36.1
20 Su	23 53 28	26 30 16	17 54 48	24 23 47	3 17.2	12 27.2	4 38.7	24 19.8	12 52.0	11 18.8	23 22.0	23 34.1	14 36.7
21 M	23 57 24	27 28 57	0♏55 57	7♏31 13	3 7.8	14 10.7	5 49.8	24 58.4	12 54.2	11 24.5	23 19.6	23 36.0	14 37.3
22 Tu	0 1 21	28 27 39	14 9 32	20 50 49	2 59.5	15 56.2	7 0.8	25 37.1	12 56.5	11 30.4	23 17.2	23 37.9	14 37.9
23 W	0 5 17	29 26 24	27 35 0	4♐22 2	2 53.3	17 43.1	8 11.8	26 15.7	12 59.0	11 36.3	23 14.8	23 39.8	14 38.4
24 Th	0 9 14	0♎25 10	11♐11 55	18 4 37	2 49.4	19 31.1	9 22.7	26 54.4	13 1.7	11 42.3	23 12.5	23 41.6	14 38.9
25 F	0 13 10	1 23 58	25 0 7	1♑58 26	2D 47.7	21 20.0	10 33.6	27 33.1	13 4.6	11 48.3	23 10.1	23 43.5	14 39.5
26 Sa	0 17 7	2 22 48	8♑59 31	16 3 20	2 47.6	23 9.2	11 44.5	28 11.8	13 7.7	11 54.3	23 7.7	23 45.3	14 39.9
27 Su	0 21 4	3 21 39	23 9 45	0♒18 36	2R 48.3	24 58.8	12 55.2	28 50.5	13 11.0	12 0.4	23 5.4	23 47.2	14 40.4
28 M	0 25 0	4 20 32	7♒29 40	14 42 36	2 48.5	26 48.4	14 5.9	29 29.3	13 14.4	12 6.6	23 3.0	23 49.0	14 40.8
29 Tu	0 28 57	5 19 27	21 56 58	29 12 15	2 47.0	28 37.8	15 16.6	0♎ 8.1	13 18.0	12 12.8	23 0.7	23 50.7	14 41.3
30 W	0 32 53	6 18 23	6♓27 49	13♓42 58	2 43.2	0♎26.9	16 27.1	0 46.8	13 21.8	12 19.0	22 58.3	23 52.5	14 41.6

LONGITUDE OCTOBER 1925

Day	Sid.Time	☉	0 hr ☽	Noon ☽	True ☊	☿	♀	♂	♃	♄	♅	♆	♇
1 Th	0 36 50	7♎17 22	20♓56 58	28♓ 9 0	2♌36.7	2♎15.7	17♏37.6	1♎25.6	13♑25.8	12♏25.3	22♓56.0	23♌54.2	14♋42.0
2 F	0 40 46	8 16 22	5♈18 17	12♈24 4	2R 27.8	4 3.9	18 48.1	2 4.5	13 30.0	12 31.6	22R 53.7	23 55.9	14 42.4
3 Sa	0 44 43	9 15 24	19 25 37	26 22 22	2 17.3	5 51.6	19 58.4	2 43.3	13 34.3	12 38.0	22 51.5	23 57.6	14 42.7
4 Su	0 48 39	10 14 28	3♉13 49	9♉59 35	2 6.2	7 38.6	21 8.7	3 22.2	13 38.8	12 44.4	22 49.2	23 59.3	14 43.0
5 M	0 52 36	11 13 35	16 39 29	23 13 26	1 55.8	9 24.9	22 19.0	4 1.1	13 43.5	12 50.9	22 46.9	24 0.9	14 43.2
6 Tu	0 56 33	12 12 44	29 41 28	6♊ 3 49	1 47.1	11 10.6	23 29.1	4 40.0	13 48.3	12 57.4	22 44.7	24 2.6	14 43.5
7 W	1 0 29	13 11 55	12♊20 46	18 32 44	1 40.7	12 55.5	24 39.2	5 18.9	13 53.3	13 3.9	22 42.5	24 4.2	14 43.7
8 Th	1 4 26	14 11 8	24 40 12	0♋43 45	1 36.7	14 39.7	25 49.2	5 57.9	13 58.5	13 10.5	22 40.3	24 5.7	14 43.9
9 F	1 8 22	15 10 24	6♋43 59	12 41 34	1D 35.0	16 23.1	26 59.2	6 36.9	14 3.9	13 17.1	22 38.1	24 7.3	14 44.1
10 Sa	1 12 19	16 9 42	18 37 10	24 31 29	1 34.7	18 5.8	28 9.0	7 15.9	14 9.4	13 23.7	22 36.0	24 8.8	14 44.3
11 Su	1 16 15	17 9 2	0♌25 13	6♌19 3	1R 34.9	19 47.8	29 18.8	7 54.9	14 15.1	13 30.4	22 33.9	24 10.3	14 44.4
12 M	1 20 12	18 8 25	12 13 39	18 9 41	1 34.5	21 29.0	0♐28.5	8 34.0	14 21.0	13 37.1	22 31.8	24 11.8	14 44.5
13 Tu	1 24 8	19 7 50	24 7 43	0♍ 8 20	1 32.4	23 9.4	1 38.2	9 13.1	14 27.0	13 43.8	22 29.7	24 13.3	14 44.6
14 W	1 28 5	20 7 17	6♍12 0	12 19 11	1 27.9	24 49.2	2 47.7	9 52.2	14 33.1	13 50.6	22 27.6	24 14.7	14 44.6
15 Th	1 32 2	21 6 46	18 30 14	24 45 24	1 20.7	26 28.3	3 57.2	10 31.3	14 39.5	13 57.4	22 25.6	24 16.1	14R 44.7
16 F	1 35 58	22 6 17	1♎ 4 54	7♎28 48	1 10.7	28 6.6	5 6.6	11 10.5	14 46.0	14 4.2	22 23.6	24 17.5	14 44.7
17 Sa	1 39 55	23 5 51	13 57 8	20 29 48	0 58.7	29 44.3	6 15.9	11 49.7	14 52.6	14 11.1	22 21.6	24 18.8	14 44.7
18 Su	1 43 51	24 5 27	27 6 36	3♏47 19	0 45.6	1♏21.4	7 25.1	12 28.9	14 59.4	14 18.0	22 19.7	24 20.1	14 44.6
19 M	1 47 48	25 5 4	10♏31 38	17 19 11	0 32.6	2 57.8	8 34.2	13 8.1	15 6.4	14 24.9	22 17.8	24 21.4	14 44.6
20 Tu	1 51 44	26 4 44	24 9 36	1♐ 2 30	0 21.1	4 33.6	9 43.2	13 47.3	15 13.5	14 31.8	22 15.9	24 22.7	14 44.5
21 W	1 55 41	27 4 26	7♐57 28	14 54 12	0 12.0	6 8.8	10 52.1	14 26.6	15 20.8	14 38.8	22 14.0	24 23.9	14 44.4
22 Th	1 59 37	28 4 9	21 52 20	28 51 39	0 5.9	7 43.4	12 0.9	15 5.9	15 28.2	14 45.8	22 12.2	24 25.2	14 44.2
23 F	2 3 34	29 3 54	5♑51 53	12♑52 54	0 2.6	9 17.4	13 9.6	15 45.2	15 35.8	14 52.8	22 10.4	24 26.3	14 44.1
24 Sa	2 7 31	0♏ 3 41	19 54 34	26 56 46	0 1.5	10 50.9	14 18.2	16 24.6	15 43.5	14 59.8	22 8.7	24 27.5	14 43.9
25 Su	2 11 27	1 3 30	3♒59 26	11♒ 2 28	0 1.4	12 23.9	15 26.7	17 3.9	15 51.3	15 6.8	22 7.0	24 28.6	14 43.7
26 M	2 15 24	2 3 20	18 5 49	25 9 18	0 1.0	13 56.2	16 35.0	17 43.3	15 59.3	15 13.9	22 5.3	24 29.7	14 43.5
27 Tu	2 19 20	3 3 12	2♓12 48	9♓16 3	29♋58.9	15 28.1	17 43.3	18 22.7	16 7.4	15 21.0	22 3.6	24 30.8	14 43.2
28 W	2 23 17	4 3 5	16 18 47	23 20 39	29 54.2	16 59.5	18 51.3	19 2.2	16 15.7	15 28.1	22 2.0	24 31.8	14 42.9
29 Th	2 27 13	5 3 0	0♈21 14	7♈20 5	29 46.5	18 30.3	19 59.3	19 41.6	16 24.1	15 35.2	22 0.5	24 32.8	14 42.6
30 F	2 31 10	6 2 57	14 16 44	21 10 40	29 36.2	20 0.6	21 7.1	20 21.1	16 32.6	15 42.3	21 58.9	24 33.8	14 42.3
31 Sa	2 35 6	7 2 56	28 1 24	4♉48 28	29 24.0	21 30.4	22 14.7	21 0.6	16 41.3	15 49.4	21 57.4	24 34.7	14 41.9

Astro Data Dy Hr Mn	Planet Ingress Dy Hr Mn	Last Aspect Dy Hr Mn	☽ Ingress Dy Hr Mn	Last Aspect Dy Hr Mn	☽ Ingress Dy Hr Mn	☽ Phases & Eclipses Dy Hr Mn	Astro Data
☽0N 4 23:41	☿ ♍ 11 5:09	1 22:33 ☿ ☍	♓ 2 4:02	1 3:18 ♅ ☌	♈ 1 15:06	2 19:53 ○ 9♓48	1 SEPTEMBER 1925
☿ D 4 0:34	♀ ♏ 16 2:05	3 19:07 ♅ ☌	♈ 4 5:02	3 7:50 ♆ △	♉ 3 18:20	10 0:11 ☽ 16♊46	Julian Day # 9375
♃ D 9 7:17	☉ ♎ 23 13:43	6 2:28 ☿ △	♉ 6 8:27	5 13:29 ♆ □	♊ 6 0:35	18 4:12 ● 24♍43	Delta T 23.8 sec
♅⚻♆ 17 5:45	♂ ♎ 28 19:01	8 11:20 ☿ □	♊ 8 15:39	7 22:52 ♆ ⚹	♋ 8 10:33	25 11:51 ☽ 1♑53	SVP 06♓18'05"
☽0S 19 11:02	☿ ♎ 29 18:04	11 2:21 ☿ ⚹	♋ 11 2:35	10 21:30 ♀ △	♌ 10 23:09		Obliquity 23°26'52"
		13 8:56 ♀ □	♌ 13 15:30	13 0:11 ♆ ☌	♍ 13 11:43	2 5:23 ○ 8♈30	⚷ Chiron 27♈58.5R
☿0S 1 18:56	♀ ♐ 11 14:10	15 14:50 ♆ ☌	♍ 16 3:56	15 7:31 ♅ ☍	♎ 15 21:57	9 18:34 ☽ 15♋56	☽ Mean ☊ 2♌45.8
♂0S 1 23:33	☿ ♏ 17 3:52	18 4:12 ☉ ☌	♎ 18 14:18	17 18:58 ♆ ⚹	♏ 18 5:12	17 18:06 ● 23♎51	
☽0N 2 9:31	☉ ♏ 23 22:31	20 10:30 ♆ ⚹	♏ 20 22:18	20 0:23 ♆ □	♐ 20 10:11	24 18:38 ☽ 0♒50	1 OCTOBER 1925
♃☍♇ 15 19:15	☊ ♋ 26 15:23	23 3:33 ☉ ⚹	♐ 23 4:17	22 11:28 ☉ ⚹	♑ 22 13:57	31 17:16 ○ 7♉46	Julian Day # 9405
♇ R 15 20:16		25 4:37 ♂ □	♑ 25 8:37	24 3:48 ♅ ⚹	♒ 24 17:12		Delta T 23.8 sec
☽0S 16 18:26		27 9:59 ♂ △	♒ 27 11:29	26 10:53 ♆ ☍	♓ 26 20:14		SVP 06♓18'03"
♄△♇ 21 18:48		29 3:09 ♆ ☍	♓ 29 13:19	28 9:45 ♅ ☌	♈ 28 23:24		Obliquity 23°26'52"
☽0N 29 18:25				30 17:57 ♆ △	♉ 31 3:29		⚷ Chiron 26♈54.5R
							☽ Mean ☊ 1♌10.4

NOVEMBER 1925 LONGITUDE

Day	Sid.Time	☉	0 hr ☽	Noon ☽	True ☊	☿	♀	♂	♃	♄	♅	♆	♇
1 Su	2 39 3	8♏ 2 56	11♉31 29	18♉10 6	29♋11.1	22♏59.8	23♐22.2	21♎40.1	16♑50.1	15♏56.5	21♓56.0	24♌35.6	14♋41.6
2 M	2 42 59	9 2 59	24 44 5	1♊13 16	28R58.8	24 28.6	24 29.6	22 19.7	16 59.0	16 3.7	21R54.6	24 36.5	14R41.2
3 Tu	2 46 56	10 3 3	7♊37 37	13 57 11	28 48.1	25 56.8	25 36.8	22 59.3	17 8.1	16 10.9	21 53.2	24 37.3	14 40.8
4 W	2 50 53	11 3 9	20 12 9	26 22 46	28 40.0	27 24.6	26 43.8	23 38.9	17 17.3	16 18.0	21 51.9	24 38.1	14 40.3
5 Th	2 54 49	12 3 18	2♋29 22	8♋32 24	28 34.6	28 51.7	27 50.7	24 18.5	17 26.6	16 25.2	21 50.6	24 38.9	14 39.9
6 F	2 58 46	13 3 28	14 32 22	20 29 49	28 31.8	0♐18.3	28 57.4	24 58.2	17 36.0	16 32.4	21 49.3	24 39.7	14 39.4
7 Sa	3 2 42	14 3 41	26 25 22	2♌19 39	28D31.0	1 44.3	0♑ 4.0	25 37.9	17 45.5	16 39.6	21 48.1	24 40.4	14 38.9
8 Su	3 6 39	15 3 55	8♌13 22	14 7 12	28R31.1	3 9.6	1 10.3	26 17.6	17 55.2	16 46.8	21 47.0	24 41.1	14 38.4
9 M	3 10 35	16 4 12	20 1 51	25 58 0	28 31.2	4 34.3	2 16.5	26 57.4	18 5.0	16 54.0	21 45.8	24 41.7	14 37.8
10 Tu	3 14 32	17 4 30	1♍56 21	7♍57 33	28 30.1	5 58.1	3 22.4	27 37.2	18 14.9	17 1.1	21 44.8	24 42.3	14 37.2
11 W	3 18 28	18 4 51	14 2 14	20 10 56	28 27.0	7 21.2	4 28.2	28 17.0	18 24.9	17 8.3	21 43.7	24 42.9	14 36.6
12 Th	3 22 25	19 5 13	26 24 11	2♎42 23	28 21.3	8 43.3	5 33.8	28 56.8	18 35.1	17 15.5	21 42.8	24 43.5	14 36.0
13 F	3 26 22	20 5 37	9♎ 5 53	15 34 53	28 13.1	10 4.5	6 39.2	29 36.7	18 45.3	17 22.7	21 41.8	24 44.0	14 35.4
14 Sa	3 30 18	21 6 3	22 9 30	28 49 42	28 2.9	11 24.5	7 44.3	0♏16.6	18 55.6	17 29.9	21 40.9	24 44.5	14 34.7
15 Su	3 34 15	22 6 31	5♏35 20	12♏26 6	27 51.6	12 43.3	8 49.2	0 56.5	19 6.1	17 37.1	21 40.1	24 44.9	14 34.1
16 M	3 38 11	23 7 1	19 21 37	26 21 21	27 40.2	14 0.8	9 53.9	1 36.4	19 16.7	17 44.3	21 39.3	24 45.3	14 33.4
17 Tu	3 42 8	24 7 32	3♐24 43	10♐31 3	27 30.1	15 16.7	10 58.4	2 16.4	19 27.4	17 51.4	21 38.5	24 45.7	14 32.6
18 W	3 46 4	25 8 5	17 39 39	24 49 51	27 22.2	16 30.8	12 2.6	2 56.4	19 38.1	17 58.6	21 37.9	24 46.1	14 31.9
19 Th	3 50 1	26 8 39	2♑ 0 57	9♑12 20	27 16.9	17 42.9	13 6.5	3 36.4	19 49.0	18 5.8	21 37.2	24 46.4	14 31.2
20 F	3 53 57	27 9 15	16 23 26	23 33 48	27D14.4	18 52.8	14 10.2	4 16.5	20 0.0	18 12.9	21 36.6	24 46.6	14 30.4
21 Sa	3 57 54	28 9 51	0♒43 0	7♒50 44	27 14.0	20 0.2	15 13.6	4 56.6	20 11.1	18 20.0	21 36.1	24 46.9	14 29.6
22 Su	4 1 51	29 10 29	14 56 47	22 0 57	27 14.6	21 4.6	16 16.6	5 36.7	20 22.3	18 27.2	21 35.6	24 47.1	14 28.8
23 M	4 5 47	0♐11 9	29 3 8	6♓ 3 15	27R15.2	22 5.7	17 19.4	6 16.8	20 33.5	18 34.3	21 35.1	24 47.3	14 27.9
24 Tu	4 9 44	1 11 49	13♓ 1 13	19 56 59	27 14.5	23 3.1	18 21.9	6 56.9	20 44.9	18 41.4	21 34.7	24 47.4	14 27.1
25 W	4 13 40	2 12 30	26 50 30	3♈41 42	27 11.8	23 56.1	19 24.0	7 37.1	20 56.4	18 48.4	21 34.4	24 47.5	14 26.2
26 Th	4 17 37	3 13 12	10♈30 29	17 16 44	27 6.7	24 44.4	20 25.7	8 17.3	21 7.9	18 55.5	21 34.1	24 47.6	14 25.3
27 F	4 21 33	4 13 55	24 0 18	0♉41 4	26 59.4	25 27.1	21 27.1	8 57.6	21 19.5	19 2.5	21 33.8	24R47.6	14 24.4
28 Sa	4 25 30	5 14 40	7♉18 50	13 53 27	26 50.5	26 3.7	22 28.2	9 37.8	21 31.2	19 9.5	21 33.6	24 47.6	14 23.5
29 Su	4 29 26	6 15 25	20 24 46	26 52 38	26 41.0	26 33.3	23 28.8	10 18.1	21 43.0	19 16.5	21 33.5	24 47.6	14 22.6
30 M	4 33 23	7 16 12	3♊16 59	9♊37 43	26 31.9	26 55.1	24 29.0	10 58.4	21 54.9	19 23.5	21 33.4	24 47.5	14 21.6

DECEMBER 1925 LONGITUDE

Day	Sid.Time	☉	0 hr ☽	Noon ☽	True ☊	☿	♀	♂	♃	♄	♅	♆	♇
1 Tu	4 37 20	8♐17 0	15♊54 50	22♊ 8 22	26♋24.1	27♐ 8.4	25♑28.9	11♏38.8	22♑ 6.9	19♏30.5	21♓33.3	24♌47.4	14♋20.7
2 W	4 41 16	9 17 49	28 18 27	4♋25 13	26R18.2	27R12.3	26 28.3	12 19.1	22 18.9	19 37.4	21D33.3	24R47.3	14R19.7
3 Th	4 45 13	10 18 40	10♋28 55	16 29 50	26 14.5	27 6.1	27 27.2	12 59.5	22 31.1	19 44.3	21 33.4	24 47.1	14 18.7
4 F	4 49 9	11 19 32	22 28 20	28 24 49	26D13.0	26 49.1	28 25.7	13 40.0	22 43.3	19 51.2	21 33.5	24 46.9	14 17.7
5 Sa	4 53 6	12 20 25	4♌19 46	10♌13 41	26 13.3	26 20.9	29 23.7	14 20.4	22 55.5	19 58.0	21 33.6	24 46.7	14 16.7
6 Su	4 57 2	13 21 19	16 7 7	22 0 40	26 14.6	25 41.5	0♒21.2	15 0.9	23 7.9	20 4.8	21 33.9	24 46.4	14 15.6
7 M	5 0 59	14 22 14	27 54 58	3♍50 39	26 16.3	24 51.1	1 18.1	15 41.4	23 20.3	20 11.6	21 34.1	24 46.1	14 14.6
8 Tu	5 4 56	15 23 11	9♍48 23	15 48 49	26R17.5	23 50.5	2 14.6	16 22.0	23 32.8	20 18.4	21 34.4	24 45.8	14 13.5
9 W	5 8 52	16 24 9	21 52 36	28 0 23	26 17.5	22 41.0	3 10.5	17 2.6	23 45.4	20 25.1	21 34.8	24 45.4	14 12.4
10 Th	5 12 49	17 25 8	4♎12 46	10♎30 17	26 15.9	21 24.6	4 5.8	17 43.2	23 58.0	20 31.8	21 35.2	24 45.0	14 11.3
11 F	5 16 45	18 26 8	16 53 26	23 22 36	26 12.6	20 3.5	5 0.5	18 23.8	24 10.7	20 38.5	21 35.7	24 44.5	14 10.2
12 Sa	5 20 42	19 27 9	29 58 6	6♏40 5	26 7.8	18 40.5	5 54.6	19 4.5	24 23.5	20 45.1	21 36.2	24 44.1	14 9.1
13 Su	5 24 38	20 28 11	13♏28 37	20 23 33	26 2.1	17 18.4	6 48.0	19 45.2	24 36.3	20 51.7	21 36.8	24 43.6	14 8.0
14 M	5 28 35	21 29 15	27 24 39	4♐31 27	25 56.2	15 59.9	7 40.8	20 25.9	24 49.2	20 58.3	21 37.4	24 43.0	14 6.8
15 Tu	5 32 31	22 30 19	11♐43 23	18 59 43	25 50.9	14 47.5	8 32.8	21 6.7	25 2.2	21 4.8	21 38.1	24 42.5	14 5.7
16 W	5 36 28	23 31 24	26 19 37	3♑42 11	25 46.8	13 43.1	9 24.2	21 47.5	25 15.2	21 11.2	21 38.8	24 41.9	14 4.5
17 Th	5 40 25	24 32 30	11♑ 6 27	18 31 26	25 44.4	12 48.3	10 14.7	22 28.3	25 28.2	21 17.7	21 39.6	24 41.2	14 3.4
18 F	5 44 21	25 33 36	25 56 11	3♒19 49	25D43.7	12 4.1	11 4.5	23 9.1	25 41.4	21 24.1	21 40.4	24 40.6	14 2.2
19 Sa	5 48 18	26 34 43	10♒41 32	18 0 39	25 44.3	11 30.7	11 53.5	23 50.0	25 54.6	21 30.4	21 41.3	24 39.9	14 1.0
20 Su	5 52 14	27 35 50	25 16 34	2♓28 50	25 45.7	11 8.4	12 41.6	24 30.9	26 7.8	21 36.7	21 42.2	24 39.2	13 59.8
21 M	5 56 11	28 36 57	9♓37 6	16 41 10	25 47.2	10D56.7	13 28.7	25 11.8	26 21.1	21 43.0	21 43.2	24 38.4	13 58.6
22 Tu	6 0 7	29 38 4	23 40 52	0♈36 10	25R48.2	10 55.2	14 15.0	25 52.8	26 34.4	21 49.2	21 44.2	24 37.6	13 57.4
23 W	6 4 4	0♑39 12	7♈27 4	14 13 40	25 48.1	11 3.1	15 0.2	26 33.7	26 47.8	21 55.3	21 45.3	24 36.8	13 56.2
24 Th	6 8 0	1 40 19	20 56 3	27 34 22	25 46.9	11 19.7	15 44.5	27 14.7	27 1.2	22 1.4	21 46.4	24 35.9	13 55.0
25 F	6 11 57	2 41 27	4♉ 8 45	10♉39 23	25 44.5	11 44.2	16 27.6	27 55.7	27 14.7	22 7.5	21 47.6	24 35.1	13 53.7
26 Sa	6 15 54	3 42 34	17 6 25	23 30 0	25 41.3	12 15.9	17 9.6	28 36.8	27 28.2	22 13.5	21 48.8	24 34.2	13 52.5
27 Su	6 19 50	4 43 42	29 50 17	6♊ 7 26	25 37.8	12 53.9	17 50.5	29 17.9	27 41.8	22 19.4	21 50.1	24 33.2	13 51.3
28 M	6 23 47	5 44 50	12♊21 35	18 32 53	25 34.5	13 37.7	18 30.2	29 59.0	27 55.4	22 25.3	21 51.4	24 32.3	13 50.0
29 Tu	6 27 43	6 45 58	24 41 29	0♋47 33	25 31.7	14 26.6	19 8.6	0♐40.1	28 9.0	22 31.1	21 52.8	24 31.3	13 48.8
30 W	6 31 40	7 47 7	6♋51 14	12 52 43	25 29.8	15 20.0	19 45.7	1 21.3	28 22.7	22 36.9	21 54.2	24 30.3	13 47.5
31 Th	6 35 36	8 48 15	18 52 14	24 50 0	25D28.8	16 17.3	20 21.4	2 2.5	28 36.4	22 42.6	21 55.7	24 29.2	13 46.3

Astro Data	Planet Ingress	Last Aspect	☽ Ingress	Last Aspect	☽ Ingress	☽ Phases & Eclipses	Astro Data
Dy Hr Mn	Dy Hr Mn	Dy Hr Mn	Dy Hr Mn	Dy Hr Mn	Dy Hr Mn	Dy Hr Mn	1 NOVEMBER 1925
☽0S 13 4:00	☿ ♐ 5 18:54	1 23:46 ♆ □	♊ 2 9:44	1 21:51 ☿ ☍	♋ 2 3:19	8 15:13 ☽ 15♌42	Julian Day # 9436
☽0N 26 1:39	♀ ♑ 6 22:34	4 13:57 ♀ ☍	♋ 4 19:06	4 13:06 ♀ ☍	♌ 4 15:13	16 6:58 ● 23♏25	Delta T 23.8 sec
♆ R 27 12:22	♂ ♏ 13 14:02	6 22:18 ♂ □	♌ 7 7:16	6 18:13 ☿ △	♍ 7 4:13	23 2:05 ☽ 0♓16	SVP 06♓18'00"
♃✶♅ 28 4:45	☉ ♐ 22 19:35	9 14:49 ♂ ✶	♍ 9 20:07	9 3:46 ♃ △	♎ 9 15:52	30 8:11 ○ 7♊37	Obliquity 23°26'52"
		11 14:59 ♅ ☍	♎ 12 6:52	11 14:30 ♆ ✶	♏ 12 0:03		⚷ Chiron 25♈29.2R
☿ R 1 21:30	♀ ♒ 5 15:09	14 4:40 ♆ ✶	♏ 14 14:05	13 19:31 ♃ ✶	♐ 14 4:23	8 12:11 ☽ 15♍54	☽ Mean ☊ 29♋31.9
♅ D 1 9:02	☉ ♑ 22 8:37	16 9:16 ♆ □	♐ 16 18:13	15 21:21 ♆ △	♑ 16 5:59	15 19:05 ● 23♐19	
☽0S 10 14:16	♂ ♐ 28 0:36	18 11:54 ♆ △	♑ 18 20:38	17 23:36 ♃ ☌	♒ 18 6:35	22 11:08 ☽ 0♈06	1 DECEMBER 1925
♃⚻♆ 13 13:01		20 19:23 ☉ ✶	♒ 20 22:48	20 4:09 ☉ ✶	♓ 20 7:51	30 2:01 ○ 7♋52	Julian Day # 9466
♄△♅ 21 1:05		22 16:43 ♆ ☍	♓ 23 1:37	22 5:05 ♃ ✶	♈ 22 10:57		Delta T 23.8 sec
☿ D 21 15:44		24 18:36 ☿ □	♈ 25 5:31	24 11:11 ♃ □	♉ 24 16:25		SVP 06♓17'56"
☽0N 23 7:48		27 2:44 ☿ △	♉ 27 10:46	26 22:55 ♂ ☍	♊ 27 0:18		Obliquity 23°26'51"
		29 8:07 ♆ □	♊ 29 17:50	28 23:40 ♆ ✶	♋ 29 10:26		⚷ Chiron 24♈18.7R
				31 20:00 ♃ ☍	♌ 31 22:26		☽ Mean ☊ 27♋56.6

LONGITUDE JANUARY 1926

Day	Sid.Time	☉	0 hr ☽	Noon ☽	True ☊	☿	♀	♂	♃	♄	♅	♆	♇
1 F	6 39 33	9♑49 24	0♌46 17	6♌41 21	25♋28.7	17♐18.3	20♒55.7	2♐43.7	28♑50.2	22♏48.3	21♓57.2	24♌28.1	13♋45.0
2 Sa	6 43 29	10 50 32	12 35 34	18 29 16	25 29.4	18 22.3	21 28.5	3 25.0	29 4.0	22 53.9	21 58.8	24R 27.1	13R 43.8
3 Su	6 47 26	11 51 41	24 22 51	0♍16 44	25 30.6	19 29.2	21 59.8	4 6.3	29 17.8	22 59.5	22 0.4	24 25.9	13 42.5
4 M	6 51 23	12 52 50	6♍11 25	12 7 21	25 31.9	20 38.5	22 29.6	4 47.6	29 31.6	23 4.9	22 2.0	24 24.8	13 41.3
5 Tu	6 55 19	13 53 59	18 5 6	24 5 12	25 33.1	21 50.1	22 57.6	5 28.9	29 45.5	23 10.4	22 3.7	24 23.6	13 40.0
6 W	6 59 16	14 55 9	0♎ 8 12	6♎14 41	25 34.0	23 3.6	23 24.0	6 10.3	29 59.4	23 15.7	22 5.5	24 22.4	13 38.7
7 Th	7 3 12	15 56 18	12 25 14	18 40 24	25R 34.4	24 18.9	23 48.6	6 51.7	0♒13.3	23 21.0	22 7.2	24 21.2	13 37.5
8 F	7 7 9	16 57 27	25 0 44	1♏26 45	25 34.3	25 35.8	24 11.4	7 33.2	0 27.3	23 26.2	22 9.1	24 19.9	13 36.2
9 Sa	7 11 5	17 58 37	7♏58 51	14 37 26	25 33.9	26 54.2	24 32.2	8 14.6	0 41.3	23 31.4	22 10.9	24 18.7	13 35.0
10 Su	7 15 2	18 59 47	21 22 46	28 14 58	25 33.2	28 13.8	24 51.2	8 56.1	0 55.3	23 36.5	22 12.9	24 17.4	13 33.7
11 M	7 18 58	20 0 57	5♐14 4	12♐19 54	25 32.5	29 34.7	25 8.1	9 37.7	1 9.4	23 41.5	22 14.8	24 16.1	13 32.5
12 Tu	7 22 55	21 2 6	19 32 9	26 50 20	25 31.9	0♑56.6	25 22.9	10 19.2	1 23.4	23 46.5	22 16.8	24 14.7	13 31.2
13 W	7 26 52	22 3 16	4♑13 45	11♑41 35	25 31.5	2 19.5	25 35.6	11 0.8	1 37.5	23 51.3	22 18.9	24 13.4	13 30.0
14 Th	7 30 48	23 4 25	19 12 51	26 46 26	25D 31.3	3 43.4	25 46.0	11 42.4	1 51.6	23 56.1	22 21.0	24 12.0	13 28.7
15 F	7 34 45	24 5 34	4♒21 11	11♒55 54	25 31.4	5 8.2	25 54.2	12 24.1	2 5.7	24 0.9	22 23.1	24 10.6	13 27.5
16 Sa	7 38 41	25 6 42	19 29 25	27 0 36	25R 31.4	6 33.7	26 0.1	13 5.7	2 19.8	24 5.5	22 25.3	24 9.2	13 26.3
17 Su	7 42 38	26 7 50	4♓28 26	11♓52 3	25 31.4	8 0.1	26R 3.5	13 47.4	2 34.0	24 10.1	22 27.5	24 7.8	13 25.0
18 M	7 46 34	27 8 57	19 10 42	26 23 50	25 31.3	9 27.1	26 4.6	14 29.1	2 48.1	24 14.6	22 29.7	24 6.3	13 23.8
19 Tu	7 50 31	28 10 2	3♈31 2	10♈32 5	25 31.1	10 54.9	26 3.2	15 10.9	3 2.3	24 19.0	22 32.0	24 4.9	13 22.6
20 W	7 54 27	29 11 7	17 26 53	24 15 29	25D 30.8	12 23.4	25 59.2	15 52.6	3 16.5	24 23.4	22 34.3	24 3.4	13 21.4
21 Th	7 58 24	0♒12 12	0♉58 2	7♉34 47	25 30.8	13 52.6	25 52.7	16 34.4	3 30.6	24 27.6	22 36.7	24 1.9	13 20.2
22 F	8 2 21	1 13 15	14 6 2	20 32 10	25 30.9	15 22.4	25 43.7	17 16.2	3 44.8	24 31.8	22 39.1	24 0.4	13 19.0
23 Sa	8 6 17	2 14 17	26 53 34	3♊10 39	25 31.4	16 52.8	25 32.2	17 58.1	3 59.0	24 35.9	22 41.5	23 58.9	13 17.8
24 Su	8 10 14	3 15 18	9♊23 50	15 33 33	25 32.1	18 23.9	25 18.1	18 39.9	4 13.2	24 39.9	22 44.0	23 57.3	13 16.6
25 M	8 14 10	4 16 18	21 40 11	27 44 9	25 33.0	19 55.6	25 1.5	19 21.8	4 27.4	24 43.9	22 46.5	23 55.8	13 15.4
26 Tu	8 18 7	5 17 17	3♋45 48	9♋45 30	25 33.9	21 28.0	24 42.5	20 3.8	4 41.6	24 47.7	22 49.1	23 54.2	13 14.3
27 W	8 22 3	6 18 16	15 43 33	21 40 16	25R 34.6	23 1.0	24 21.1	20 45.7	4 55.8	24 51.5	22 51.7	23 52.6	13 13.1
28 Th	8 26 0	7 19 13	27 35 58	3♌30 53	25 34.8	24 34.7	23 57.5	21 27.7	5 10.0	24 55.2	22 54.3	23 51.0	13 12.0
29 F	8 29 56	8 20 9	9♌25 18	15 19 28	25 34.3	26 9.0	23 31.7	22 9.7	5 24.2	24 58.8	22 56.9	23 49.4	13 10.9
30 Sa	8 33 53	9 21 4	21 13 38	27 8 4	25 33.1	27 44.0	23 3.8	22 51.7	5 38.3	25 2.3	22 59.6	23 47.8	13 9.8
31 Su	8 37 50	10 21 58	3♍ 3 1	8♍58 47	25 31.2	29 19.6	22 34.0	23 33.8	5 52.5	25 5.7	23 2.3	23 46.2	13 8.7

LONGITUDE FEBRUARY 1926

Day	Sid.Time	☉	0 hr ☽	Noon ☽	True ☊	☿	♀	♂	♃	♄	♅	♆	♇
1 M	8 41 46	11♒22 52	14♍55 39	20♍53 55	25♋28.8	0♒56.0	22♒ 2.6	24♐15.9	6♒ 6.7	25♏ 9.0	23♓ 5.0	23♌44.6	13♋ 7.6
2 Tu	8 45 43	12 23 44	26 53 56	2♎56 4	25R 26.0	2 33.0	21R 29.6	24 58.0	6 20.9	25 12.3	23 7.8	23R 42.9	13R 6.5
3 W	8 49 39	13 24 35	9♎ 0 41	15 8 12	25 23.4	4 10.8	20 55.3	25 40.2	6 35.0	25 15.4	23 10.6	23 41.3	13 5.4
4 Th	8 53 36	14 25 26	21 19 3	27 33 40	25 21.1	5 49.3	20 19.9	26 22.4	6 49.2	25 18.5	23 13.4	23 39.6	13 4.3
5 F	8 57 32	15 26 16	3♏52 30	10♏16 1	25D 19.7	7 28.5	19 43.7	27 4.6	7 3.3	25 21.4	23 16.3	23 38.0	13 3.3
6 Sa	9 1 29	16 27 4	16 44 39	23 18 49	25 19.2	9 8.5	19 6.9	27 46.8	7 17.4	25 24.3	23 19.2	23 36.3	13 2.3
7 Su	9 5 25	17 27 52	29 58 53	6♐45 11	25 19.7	10 49.3	18 29.7	28 29.1	7 31.5	25 27.1	23 22.1	23 34.6	13 1.3
8 M	9 9 22	18 28 39	13♐37 54	20 37 12	25 20.9	12 30.8	17 52.4	29 11.4	7 45.6	25 29.8	23 25.0	23 32.9	13 0.3
9 Tu	9 13 19	19 29 25	27 43 3	4♑55 18	25 22.5	14 13.2	17 15.3	29 53.7	7 59.7	25 32.3	23 28.0	23 31.3	12 59.3
10 W	9 17 15	20 30 10	12♑13 36	19 37 28	25R 23.7	15 56.3	16 38.7	0♑36.0	8 13.8	25 34.8	23 31.0	23 29.6	12 58.3
11 Th	9 21 12	21 30 54	27 6 10	4♒38 51	25 24.2	17 40.3	16 2.7	1 18.4	8 27.8	25 37.2	23 34.0	23 27.9	12 57.3
12 F	9 25 8	22 31 37	12♒14 28	19 51 49	25 23.3	19 25.2	15 27.6	2 0.8	8 41.9	25 39.5	23 37.0	23 26.2	12 56.4
13 Sa	9 29 5	23 32 18	27 29 38	5♓ 6 37	25 21.0	21 10.8	14 53.6	2 43.2	8 55.9	25 41.7	23 40.1	23 24.5	12 55.5
14 Su	9 33 1	24 32 58	12♓41 28	20 12 57	25 17.4	22 57.3	14 20.9	3 25.7	9 9.8	25 43.8	23 43.2	23 22.8	12 54.6
15 M	9 36 58	25 33 36	27 39 58	5♈ 1 32	25 13.0	24 44.6	13 49.8	4 8.1	9 23.8	25 45.8	23 46.3	23 21.2	12 53.7
16 Tu	9 40 54	26 34 12	12♈16 56	19 25 34	25 8.3	26 32.8	13 20.4	4 50.6	9 37.7	25 47.7	23 49.4	23 19.5	12 52.8
17 W	9 44 51	27 34 47	26 27 7	3♉21 23	25 4.2	28 21.7	12 52.9	5 33.1	9 51.6	25 49.5	23 52.5	23 17.8	12 52.0
18 Th	9 48 48	28 35 20	10♉ 8 25	16 48 23	25 1.3	0♓11.5	12 27.3	6 15.7	10 5.5	25 51.2	23 55.7	23 16.1	12 51.1
19 F	9 52 44	29 35 51	23 21 35	29 48 27	24D 59.8	2 2.0	12 3.9	6 58.2	10 19.3	25 52.8	23 58.9	23 14.4	12 50.3
20 Sa	9 56 41	0♓36 20	6♊ 9 27	12♊25 9	24 59.7	3 53.2	11 42.7	7 40.8	10 33.1	25 54.3	24 2.1	23 12.8	12 49.5
21 Su	10 0 37	1 36 48	18 36 8	24 42 58	25 0.9	5 45.0	11 23.8	8 23.4	10 46.9	25 55.7	24 5.3	23 11.1	12 48.7
22 M	10 4 34	2 37 14	0♋46 17	6♋46 40	25 2.6	7 37.4	11 7.4	9 6.0	11 0.6	25 57.0	24 8.6	23 9.4	12 48.0
23 Tu	10 8 30	3 37 37	12 44 40	18 40 49	25 4.2	9 30.3	10 53.3	9 48.7	11 14.3	25 58.2	24 11.8	23 7.8	12 47.2
24 W	10 12 27	4 37 59	24 35 40	0♌29 39	25R 4.9	11 23.5	10 41.7	10 31.3	11 27.9	25 59.3	24 15.1	23 6.1	12 46.5
25 Th	10 16 23	5 38 19	6♌23 12	12 16 44	25 4.1	13 17.0	10 32.6	11 14.0	11 41.6	26 0.3	24 18.4	23 4.5	12 45.8
26 F	10 20 20	6 38 37	18 10 34	24 5 2	25 1.4	15 10.5	10 25.9	11 56.7	11 55.1	26 1.2	24 21.7	23 2.9	12 45.1
27 Sa	10 24 17	7 38 54	0♍ 0 24	5♍56 54	24 56.6	17 3.8	10 21.8	12 39.5	12 8.7	26 2.0	24 25.0	23 1.2	12 44.5
28 Su	10 28 13	8 39 8	11 54 46	17 54 11	24 49.8	18 56.7	10D 20.1	13 22.2	12 22.2	26 2.7	24 28.3	22 59.6	12 43.8

Astro Data Dy Hr Mn	Planet Ingress Dy Hr Mn	Last Aspect Dy Hr Mn	☽ Ingress Dy Hr Mn	Last Aspect Dy Hr Mn	☽ Ingress Dy Hr Mn	☽ Phases & Eclipses Dy Hr Mn	Astro Data
☽0S 6 23:10	♃ ♒ 6 1:01	3 0:06 ♆ ☌	♍ 3 11:26	1 20:36 ♄ ⚹	♎ 2 6:11	7 7:22 ☽ 16♎15	1 JANUARY 1926
♄□♆ 16 14:42	☿ ♑ 11 7:27	5 23:42 ♃ △	♎ 5 23:44	4 10:18 ♂ ⚹	♏ 4 16:39	14 6:35 ● 23♑21	Julian Day # 9497
♀ R 17 22:10	☉ ♒ 20 19:12	8 1:13 ☿ ⚹	♏ 8 9:19	6 15:50 ♄ ☌	♐ 7 0:02	14 6:36:34 ● T 4'11"	Delta T 23.9 sec
☽0N 19 14:33	☿ ♒ 31 10:04	10 6:13 ♀ □	♐ 10 15:02	8 16:56 ♆ △	♑ 9 3:49	20 22:31 ☽ 0♉08	SVP 06♓17'50"
		12 9:46 ♀ ⚹	♑ 12 17:09	10 21:37 ♄ ⚹	♒ 11 4:37	28 21:35 ○ 8♌14	Obliquity 23°26'51"
☽0S 3 5:43	♂ ♑ 9 3:35	14 7:32 ♄ ⚹	♒ 14 17:07	12 21:10 ♄ □	♓ 13 3:57	28 21:20 ● A 0.555	⚷ Chiron 23♈46.3R
♅⊼♆ 9 16:58	☿ ♓ 17 21:30	16 10:26 ♀ ☌	♓ 16 16:48	14 20:55 ♄ △	♈ 15 3:47		☽ Mean ☊ 26♋18.1
♃∠♅ 11 13:24	☉ ♓ 19 9:35	18 14:17 ☉ ⚹	♈ 18 18:03	17 3:48 ☿ ⚹	♉ 17 6:08	5 23:25 ☽ 16♏26	
☽0N 15 23:14		20 14:58 ♀ ⚹	♉ 20 22:16	19 4:41 ♄ ☍	♊ 19 12:22	12 17:20 ● 23♒15	1 FEBRUARY 1926
♀ D 28 4:47		22 21:28 ♀ □	♊ 23 5:55	21 10:49 ♅ □	♋ 21 22:28	19 12:36 ☽ 0♊08	Julian Day # 9528
		25 6:28 ♀ △	♋ 25 16:30	24 2:50 ♄ △	♌ 24 11:00	27 16:51 ○ 8♍21	Delta T 23.9 sec
		27 18:33 ♄ △	♌ 28 4:52	26 15:57 ♄ □	♍ 26 23:59		SVP 06♓17'45"
		30 7:47 ♄ □	♍ 30 17:49				Obliquity 23°26'52"
							⚷ Chiron 24♈07.4
							☽ Mean ☊ 24♋39.7

MARCH 1926

LONGITUDE

Day	Sid.Time	☉	0 hr ☽	Noon ☽	True ☊	☿	♀	♂	♃	♄	♅	♆	♇
1 M	10 32 10	9♓39 21	23♍55 21	29♍58 24	24♋41.6	20♓49.0	10♒20.8	14♑ 5.0	12♒35.6	26♏ 3.3	24♓31.6	22♌58.0	12♋43.2
2 Tu	10 36 6	10 39 32	6♎ 3 30	12♎10 51	24R 32.7	22 40.2	10 23.9	14 47.8	12 49.0	26 3.7	24 35.0	22R 56.4	12R 42.6
3 W	10 40 3	11 39 41	18 20 36	24 32 57	24 23.8	24 30.1	10 29.4	15 30.7	13 2.4	26 4.1	24 38.3	22 54.8	12 42.0
4 Th	10 43 59	12 39 49	0♏48 8	7♏ 6 22	24 16.0	26 18.3	10 37.1	16 13.5	13 15.7	26 4.4	24 41.7	22 53.3	12 41.5
5 F	10 47 56	13 39 55	13 27 54	19 53 3	24 9.9	28 4.2	10 47.1	16 56.4	13 28.9	26 4.6	24 45.1	22 51.7	12 41.0
6 Sa	10 51 52	14 39 59	26 22 4	2♐55 19	24 6.0	29 47.5	10 59.3	17 39.3	13 42.2	26R 4.6	24 48.5	22 50.2	12 40.4
7 Su	10 55 49	15 40 2	9♐33 4	16 15 38	24D 4.2	1♈27.7	11 13.7	18 22.3	13 55.3	26 4.6	24 51.9	22 48.6	12 40.0
8 M	10 59 46	16 40 4	23 3 17	29 56 15	24 4.2	3 4.1	11 30.0	19 5.2	14 8.4	26 4.5	24 55.3	22 47.1	12 39.5
9 Tu	11 3 42	17 40 4	6♑54 41	13♑58 40	24 5.1	4 36.3	11 48.4	19 48.2	14 21.5	26 4.2	24 58.7	22 45.6	12 39.0
10 W	11 7 39	18 40 2	21 8 7	28 22 51	24R 5.8	6 3.8	12 8.7	20 31.2	14 34.5	26 3.9	25 2.1	22 44.1	12 38.6
11 Th	11 11 35	19 39 59	5♒42 30	13♒ 6 34	24 5.3	7 26.0	12 30.8	21 14.2	14 47.4	26 3.5	25 5.5	22 42.7	12 38.2
12 F	11 15 32	20 39 53	20 34 19	28 4 53	24 2.7	8 42.3	12 54.7	21 57.2	15 0.3	26 2.9	25 8.9	22 41.2	12 37.9
13 Sa	11 19 28	21 39 46	5♓37 14	13♓10 12	23 57.5	9 52.4	13 20.4	22 40.3	15 13.1	26 2.3	25 12.4	22 39.8	12 37.5
14 Su	11 23 25	22 39 38	20 42 34	28 13 4	23 50.0	10 55.8	13 47.7	23 23.4	15 25.9	26 1.5	25 15.8	22 38.3	12 37.2
15 M	11 27 21	23 39 27	5♈40 30	13♈ 3 43	23 40.8	11 52.0	14 16.6	24 6.4	15 38.6	26 0.7	25 19.2	22 36.9	12 36.9
16 Tu	11 31 18	24 39 14	20 21 44	27 33 44	23 31.0	12 40.7	14 47.0	24 49.5	15 51.2	25 59.7	25 22.6	22 35.6	12 36.6
17 W	11 35 15	25 38 59	4♉39 4	11♉37 21	23 21.8	13 21.6	15 18.8	25 32.6	16 3.8	25 58.7	25 26.1	22 34.2	12 36.3
18 Th	11 39 11	26 38 41	18 28 20	25 12 2	23 14.2	13 54.6	15 52.1	26 15.8	16 16.3	25 57.5	25 29.5	22 32.8	12 36.1
19 F	11 43 8	27 38 22	1♊48 34	8♊18 16	23 8.9	14 19.3	16 26.8	26 58.9	16 28.7	25 56.3	25 32.9	22 31.5	12 35.9
20 Sa	11 47 4	28 38 0	14 41 32	20 58 55	23 5.9	14 35.9	17 2.7	27 42.1	16 41.0	25 55.0	25 36.4	22 30.2	12 35.7
21 Su	11 51 1	29 37 37	27 10 59	3♋18 23	23D 4.9	14R 44.3	17 39.9	28 25.2	16 53.3	25 53.5	25 39.8	22 28.9	12 35.5
22 M	11 54 57	0♈37 10	9♋21 47	15 21 53	23 5.1	14 44.6	18 18.3	29 8.4	17 5.5	25 52.0	25 43.2	22 27.7	12 35.4
23 Tu	11 58 54	1 36 42	21 19 22	27 14 52	23R 5.5	14 37.1	18 57.8	29 51.6	17 17.6	25 50.4	25 46.6	22 26.4	12 35.3
24 W	12 2 50	2 36 11	3♌ 9 4	9♌ 2 33	23 5.1	14 22.0	19 38.5	0♒34.8	17 29.7	25 48.6	25 50.0	22 25.2	12 35.2
25 Th	12 6 47	3 35 38	14 55 54	20 49 39	23 2.8	13 60.0	20 20.3	1 18.1	17 41.7	25 46.8	25 53.5	22 24.0	12 35.1
26 F	12 10 43	4 35 3	26 44 16	2♍40 11	22 58.0	13 31.4	21 3.0	2 1.3	17 53.6	25 44.9	25 56.9	22 22.9	12 35.1
27 Sa	12 14 40	5 34 25	8♍37 45	14 37 17	22 50.4	12 57.1	21 46.8	2 44.6	18 5.4	25 42.9	26 0.3	22 21.7	12D 35.1
28 Su	12 18 37	6 33 45	20 39 3	26 43 15	22 40.2	12 17.7	22 31.5	3 27.8	18 17.1	25 40.8	26 3.6	22 20.6	12 35.1
29 M	12 22 33	7 33 3	2♎50 1	8♎59 29	22 28.0	11 34.3	23 17.1	4 11.1	18 28.7	25 38.7	26 7.0	22 19.5	12 35.1
30 Tu	12 26 30	8 32 19	15 11 42	21 26 42	22 14.7	10 47.7	24 3.7	4 54.4	18 40.3	25 36.4	26 10.4	22 18.5	12 35.1
31 W	12 30 26	9 31 33	27 44 30	4♏ 5 7	22 1.5	9 59.0	24 51.0	5 37.7	18 51.8	25 34.1	26 13.8	22 17.4	12 35.2

APRIL 1926

LONGITUDE

Day	Sid.Time	☉	0 hr ☽	Noon ☽	True ☊	☿	♀	♂	♃	♄	♅	♆	♇
1 Th	12 34 23	10♈30 45	10♏28 32	16♏54 45	21♋49.6	9♈ 9.2	25♒39.2	6♒21.0	19♒ 3.2	25♏31.6	26♓17.1	22♌16.4	12♋35.3
2 F	12 38 19	11 29 56	23 23 49	29 55 45	21R 39.9	8R 19.2	26 28.2	7 4.4	19 14.4	25R 29.1	26 20.5	22R 15.4	12 35.4
3 Sa	12 42 16	12 29 4	6♐30 38	13♐ 8 34	21 33.0	7 30.1	27 17.9	7 47.7	19 25.7	25 26.5	26 23.8	22 14.5	12 35.6
4 Su	12 46 12	13 28 11	19 49 39	26 34 3	21 29.0	6 42.8	28 8.4	8 31.1	19 36.8	25 23.8	26 27.1	22 13.5	12 35.8
5 M	12 50 9	14 27 15	3♑21 54	10♑13 21	21D 27.3	5 58.0	28 59.5	9 14.5	19 47.8	25 21.0	26 30.4	22 12.6	12 36.0
6 Tu	12 54 6	15 26 19	17 8 32	24 7 33	21R 27.1	5 16.6	29 51.3	9 57.9	19 58.7	25 18.2	26 33.7	22 11.7	12 36.2
7 W	12 58 2	16 25 20	1♒10 26	8♒17 6	21 27.0	4 39.0	0♓43.8	10 41.2	20 9.5	25 15.3	26 37.0	22 10.9	12 36.4
8 Th	13 1 59	17 24 20	15 27 27	22 41 11	21 25.6	4 5.9	1 36.9	11 24.6	20 20.3	25 12.3	26 40.3	22 10.1	12 36.7
9 F	13 5 55	18 23 17	29 57 53	7♓17 2	21 22.1	3 37.5	2 30.6	12 8.1	20 30.9	25 9.2	26 43.5	22 9.3	12 37.0
10 Sa	13 9 52	19 22 13	14♓37 57	21 59 49	21 15.7	3 14.2	3 24.8	12 51.5	20 41.4	25 6.0	26 46.8	22 8.5	12 37.3
11 Su	13 13 48	20 21 8	29 21 43	6♈42 41	21 6.6	2 56.1	4 19.6	13 34.9	20 51.8	25 2.8	26 50.0	22 7.8	12 37.6
12 M	13 17 45	21 20 0	14♈ 1 43	21 17 49	20 55.4	2 43.3	5 14.9	14 18.3	21 2.2	24 59.5	26 53.2	22 7.1	12 38.0
13 Tu	13 21 41	22 18 50	28 30 3	5♉37 37	20 43.5	2D 35.9	6 10.7	15 1.7	21 12.4	24 56.2	26 56.4	22 6.4	12 38.4
14 W	13 25 38	23 17 39	12♉39 47	19 36 3	20 31.9	2 33.8	7 7.0	15 45.1	21 22.5	24 52.7	26 59.5	22 5.7	12 38.8
15 Th	13 29 35	24 16 25	26 26 1	3♊ 9 30	20 22.1	2 36.9	8 3.8	16 28.5	21 32.4	24 49.2	27 2.7	22 5.1	12 39.2
16 F	13 33 31	25 15 9	9♊46 28	16 17 3	20 14.6	2 45.2	9 1.0	17 11.9	21 42.3	24 45.7	27 5.8	22 4.6	12 39.7
17 Sa	13 37 28	26 13 51	22 41 31	29 0 14	20 9.9	2 58.4	9 58.6	17 55.4	21 52.1	24 42.0	27 8.9	22 4.0	12 40.2
18 Su	13 41 24	27 12 31	5♋13 41	11♋22 25	20 7.6	3 16.4	10 56.7	18 38.8	22 1.7	24 38.4	27 12.0	22 3.5	12 40.7
19 M	13 45 21	28 11 9	17 27 4	23 28 16	20 6.9	3 39.0	11 55.2	19 22.2	22 11.2	24 34.6	27 15.1	22 3.0	12 41.2
20 Tu	13 49 17	29 9 44	29 26 43	5♌23 5	20 7.0	4 6.1	12 54.0	20 5.6	22 20.6	24 30.8	27 18.1	22 2.5	12 41.8
21 W	13 53 14	0♉ 8 17	11♌18 4	17 12 22	20 6.5	4 37.4	13 53.2	20 49.0	22 29.9	24 27.0	27 21.1	22 2.1	12 42.3
22 Th	13 57 10	1 6 48	23 6 36	29 1 25	20 4.6	5 12.8	14 52.8	21 32.3	22 39.1	24 23.1	27 24.1	22 1.7	12 42.9
23 F	14 1 7	2 5 17	4♍57 23	10♍55 4	20 0.5	5 52.1	15 52.8	22 15.7	22 48.1	24 19.1	27 27.1	22 1.4	12 43.5
24 Sa	14 5 4	3 3 44	16 54 55	22 57 23	19 53.8	6 35.1	16 53.0	22 59.1	22 57.0	24 15.1	27 30.1	22 1.0	12 44.2
25 Su	14 9 0	4 2 8	29 2 50	5♎11 31	19 44.5	7 21.7	17 53.6	23 42.5	23 5.8	24 11.1	27 33.0	22 0.7	12 44.8
26 M	14 12 57	5 0 31	11♎23 42	17 39 29	19 33.2	8 11.7	18 54.6	24 25.8	23 14.5	24 7.0	27 35.9	22 0.5	12 45.5
27 Tu	14 16 53	5 58 52	23 58 58	0♏22 9	19 20.9	9 4.9	19 55.8	25 9.2	23 23.0	24 2.9	27 38.7	22 0.2	12 46.2
28 W	14 20 50	6 57 11	6♏48 58	13 19 19	19 8.5	10 1.3	20 57.4	25 52.6	23 31.4	23 58.7	27 41.6	22 0.0	12 46.9
29 Th	14 24 46	7 55 28	19 53 3	26 29 58	18 57.4	11 0.7	21 59.2	26 35.9	23 39.7	23 54.5	27 44.4	21 59.9	12 47.7
30 F	14 28 43	8 53 43	3♐ 9 54	9♐52 39	18 48.3	12 2.9	23 1.3	27 19.3	23 47.8	23 50.2	27 47.2	21 59.7	12 48.4

Astro Data	Dy Hr Mn
♃⊼♇	1 13:01
☽0S	2 10:56
☿0N	5 18:47
♄ R	6 4:53
☽0N	15 9:32
☿ R	21 12:55
♄△♅	23 17:30
♇ D	27 8:09
☽0S	29 16:47
☽0N	11 19:50
☿ D	13 21:35
♃☍♆	18 4:12
☽0S	26 0:21
♃□♄	30 4:43

Planet Ingress	Dy Hr Mn
☿ ♈	6 2:57
☉ ♈	21 9:01
♂ ♒	23 4:39
♀ ♓	6 3:59
☉ ♉	20 20:36

Last Aspect Dy Hr Mn		☽ Ingress Dy Hr Mn
1 4:14	♄ ✶	♎ 1 12:03
3 8:50	♆ ✶	♏ 3 22:28
5 23:28	♄ ☌	♐ 6 6:40
8 3:17	♅ □	♑ 8 12:06
10 8:10	♄ ✶	♒ 10 14:40
12 8:45	♄ □	♓ 12 15:03
14 8:29	♄ △	♈ 14 14:52
16 7:49	♂ □	♉ 16 16:06
18 15:47	☉ ✶	♊ 18 20:42
21 5:12	☉ □	♋ 21 5:30
23 9:07	♄ △	♌ 23 17:35
25 22:00	♄ □	♍ 26 6:36
28 10:45	♅ ☍	♎ 28 18:27
30 18:08	♀ △	♏ 31 4:17

Last Aspect Dy Hr Mn		☽ Ingress Dy Hr Mn
2 6:02	♀ □	♐ 2 12:08
4 15:46	♀ ✶	♑ 4 18:04
6 16:13	♅ ✶	♒ 6 22:01
8 16:06	♄ □	♓ 9 0:03
10 19:52	♅ ☌	♈ 11 1:02
12 13:21	♆ △	♉ 13 2:31
15 1:05	♅ ✶	♊ 15 6:20
17 8:29	♅ □	♋ 17 13:55
19 23:23	☉ □	♌ 20 1:07
22 2:34	♄ □	♍ 22 13:59
24 21:03	♅ ☍	♎ 25 1:52
27 2:20	♂ △	♏ 27 11:19
29 14:17	♅ △	♐ 29 18:19

☽ Phases & Eclipses Dy Hr Mn	
7 11:49	☽ 16♐10
14 3:20	● 22♓48
21 5:12	☽ 29♊51
29 10:00	○ 7♎58
5 20:50	☽ 15♑19
12 12:56	● 21♈52
19 23:23	☽ 29♋08
28 0:16	○ 6♏58

Astro Data

1 MARCH 1926
Julian Day # 9556
Delta T 24.0 sec
SVP 06♓17'42"
Obliquity 23°26'53"
⚷ Chiron 25♈08.6
☽ Mean ☊ 23♋10.7

1 APRIL 1926
Julian Day # 9587
Delta T 24.0 sec
SVP 06♓17'39"
Obliquity 23°26'53"
⚷ Chiron 26♈48.3
☽ Mean ☊ 21♋32.2

LONGITUDE — MAY 1926

Day	Sid.Time	☉	0 hr ☽	Noon ☽	True ☊	☿	♀	♂	♃	♄	♅	♆	♇
1 Sa	14 32 39	9♉51 57	16♐37 59	23♐25 46	18♋41.9	13♈ 7.9	24♓ 3.7	28♒ 2.6	23♒55.8	23♏46.0	27♓50.0	21♌59.6	12♋49.2
2 Su	14 36 36	10 50 9	0♑15 51	7♑ 8 4	18R38.3	14 15.6	25 6.4	28 45.9	24 3.7	23R41.7	27 52.7	21R59.6	12 50.0
3 M	14 40 33	11 48 20	14 2 22	20 58 40	18D37.0	15 25.9	26 9.3	29 29.2	24 11.4	23 37.3	27 55.4	21D59.5	12 50.9
4 Tu	14 44 29	12 46 29	27 56 55	4♒57 3	18 37.1	16 38.7	27 12.5	0♓12.5	24 19.0	23 33.0	27 58.1	21 59.5	12 51.7
5 W	14 48 26	13 44 37	11♒59 1	19 2 43	18R37.5	17 53.9	28 15.9	0 55.8	24 26.4	23 28.6	28 0.7	21 59.6	12 52.6
6 Th	14 52 22	14 42 43	26 8 3	3♓14 49	18 37.0	19 11.5	29 19.5	1 39.1	24 33.7	23 24.2	28 3.3	21 59.6	12 53.5
7 F	14 56 19	15 40 48	10♓22 47	17 31 37	18 34.7	20 31.4	0♈23.4	2 22.3	24 40.9	23 19.8	28 5.9	21 59.7	12 54.4
8 Sa	15 0 15	16 38 52	24 40 56	1♈50 14	18 30.0	21 53.5	1 27.5	3 5.6	24 47.9	23 15.3	28 8.4	21 59.8	12 55.3
9 Su	15 4 12	17 36 54	8♈58 59	16 6 35	18 22.9	23 17.9	2 31.8	3 48.8	24 54.7	23 10.8	28 10.9	22 0.0	12 56.2
10 M	15 8 8	18 34 54	23 12 23	0♉15 45	18 14.2	24 44.5	3 36.3	4 31.9	25 1.4	23 6.4	28 13.4	22 0.2	12 57.2
11 Tu	15 12 5	19 32 54	7♉16 3	14 12 41	18 4.6	26 13.2	4 41.0	5 15.1	25 8.0	23 1.9	28 15.9	22 0.4	12 58.2
12 W	15 16 1	20 30 52	21 5 9	27 53 0	17 55.3	27 44.1	5 45.9	5 58.2	25 14.4	22 57.4	28 18.3	22 0.7	12 59.2
13 Th	15 19 58	21 28 48	4♊35 54	11♊13 38	17 47.3	29 17.1	6 50.9	6 41.3	25 20.6	22 52.9	28 20.7	22 1.0	13 0.2
14 F	15 23 55	22 26 43	17 46 6	24 13 19	17 41.3	0♉52.2	7 56.2	7 24.4	25 26.7	22 48.4	28 23.0	22 1.3	13 1.2
15 Sa	15 27 51	23 24 36	0♋35 25	6♋52 37	17 37.7	2 29.4	9 1.6	8 7.4	25 32.6	22 43.9	28 25.3	22 1.7	13 2.3
16 Su	15 31 48	24 22 28	13 5 14	19 13 42	17D36.2	4 8.7	10 7.1	8 50.4	25 38.3	22 39.4	28 27.6	22 2.1	13 3.3
17 M	15 35 44	25 20 18	25 18 28	1♌20 5	17 36.3	5 50.1	11 12.9	9 33.4	25 43.9	22 34.9	28 29.8	22 2.5	13 4.4
18 Tu	15 39 41	26 18 6	7♌19 8	13 16 13	17 37.4	7 33.6	12 18.7	10 16.3	25 49.4	22 30.4	28 32.0	22 3.0	13 5.5
19 W	15 43 37	27 15 52	19 11 58	25 7 3	17R38.4	9 19.2	13 24.8	10 59.2	25 54.6	22 25.9	28 34.1	22 3.4	13 6.6
20 Th	15 47 34	28 13 37	1♍ 2 6	6♍57 47	17 38.7	11 6.8	14 31.0	11 42.1	25 59.7	22 21.5	28 36.3	22 4.0	13 7.8
21 F	15 51 31	29 11 20	12 54 43	18 53 31	17 37.5	12 56.6	15 37.3	12 24.9	26 4.7	22 17.0	28 38.3	22 4.5	13 8.9
22 Sa	15 55 27	0♊ 9 2	24 54 46	0♎58 57	17 34.5	14 48.5	16 43.8	13 7.7	26 9.4	22 12.6	28 40.4	22 5.1	13 10.1
23 Su	15 59 24	1 6 42	7♎ 6 36	13 18 5	17 29.6	16 42.4	17 50.4	13 50.4	26 14.0	22 8.1	28 42.4	22 5.7	13 11.3
24 M	16 3 20	2 4 20	19 33 46	25 53 54	17 23.2	18 38.3	18 57.1	14 33.1	26 18.4	22 3.7	28 44.3	22 6.4	13 12.5
25 Tu	16 7 17	3 1 58	2♏18 41	8♏48 11	17 15.9	20 36.3	20 4.0	15 15.7	26 22.7	21 59.4	28 46.2	22 7.0	13 13.7
26 W	16 11 13	3 59 33	15 22 24	22 1 15	17 8.5	22 36.2	21 11.0	15 58.4	26 26.7	21 55.0	28 48.1	22 7.8	13 14.9
27 Th	16 15 10	4 57 8	28 44 32	5♐32 0	17 1.7	24 38.0	22 18.1	16 40.9	26 30.6	21 50.7	28 50.0	22 8.5	13 16.1
28 F	16 19 6	5 54 41	12♐23 20	19 18 8	16 56.4	26 41.6	23 25.3	17 23.4	26 34.4	21 46.4	28 51.8	22 9.3	13 17.4
29 Sa	16 23 3	6 52 14	26 16 0	3♑16 28	16 52.8	28 46.9	24 32.7	18 5.9	26 37.9	21 42.1	28 53.5	22 10.1	13 18.7
30 Su	16 27 0	7 49 45	10♑19 6	17 23 28	16D51.2	0♊53.8	25 40.2	18 48.4	26 41.3	21 37.9	28 55.2	22 10.9	13 19.9
31 M	16 30 56	8 47 15	24 29 7	1♒35 40	16 51.3	3 2.1	26 47.8	19 30.7	26 44.5	21 33.7	28 56.9	22 11.8	13 21.2

LONGITUDE — JUNE 1926

Day	Sid.Time	☉	0 hr ☽	Noon ☽	True ☊	☿	♀	♂	♃	♄	♅	♆	♇
1 Tu	16 34 53	9♊44 45	8♒42 46	15♒50 4	16♋52.4	5♊11.6	27♈55.6	20♓13.1	26♒47.5	21♏29.5	28♓58.5	22♌12.7	13♋22.5
2 W	16 38 49	10 42 13	22 57 17	0♓ 4 8	16 53.7	7 22.2	29 3.4	20 55.3	26 50.3	21R25.4	29 0.1	22 13.6	13 23.9
3 Th	16 42 46	11 39 41	7♓10 22	14 15 45	16R54.6	9 33.5	0♉11.4	21 37.5	26 52.9	21 21.3	29 1.6	22 14.6	13 25.2
4 F	16 46 42	12 37 9	21 20 4	28 23 4	16 54.4	11 45.3	1 19.4	22 19.7	26 55.4	21 17.3	29 3.1	22 15.6	13 26.5
5 Sa	16 50 39	13 34 35	5♈24 31	12♈24 10	16 52.8	13 57.4	2 27.6	23 1.8	26 57.6	21 13.3	29 4.6	22 16.6	13 27.9
6 Su	16 54 35	14 32 1	19 21 47	26 17 5	16 49.7	16 9.5	3 35.8	23 43.8	26 59.7	21 9.3	29 6.0	22 17.6	13 29.2
7 M	16 58 32	15 29 26	3♉ 9 48	9♉59 40	16 45.6	18 21.3	4 44.2	24 25.8	27 1.6	21 5.4	29 7.4	22 18.7	13 30.6
8 Tu	17 2 29	16 26 51	16 46 24	23 29 47	16 40.9	20 32.5	5 52.6	25 7.6	27 3.3	21 1.5	29 8.7	22 19.8	13 32.0
9 W	17 6 25	17 24 15	0♊ 9 36	6♊45 39	16 36.4	22 42.9	7 1.2	25 49.4	27 4.8	20 57.7	29 10.0	22 20.9	13 33.4
10 Th	17 10 22	18 21 38	13 17 47	19 45 57	16 32.5	24 52.3	8 9.8	26 31.2	27 6.1	20 54.0	29 11.2	22 22.1	13 34.8
11 F	17 14 18	19 19 1	26 10 6	2♋30 16	16 29.8	27 0.4	9 18.5	27 12.8	27 7.3	20 50.3	29 12.4	22 23.3	13 36.2
12 Sa	17 18 15	20 16 23	8♋46 33	14 59 6	16D28.4	29 7.0	10 27.4	27 54.4	27 8.2	20 46.7	29 13.5	22 24.5	13 37.6
13 Su	17 22 11	21 13 44	21 8 8	27 13 57	16 28.3	1♋12.0	11 36.2	28 35.9	27 8.9	20 43.1	29 14.6	22 25.7	13 39.1
14 M	17 26 8	22 11 4	3♌16 52	9♌17 17	16 29.1	3 15.2	12 45.2	29 17.3	27 9.5	20 39.6	29 15.6	22 27.0	13 40.5
15 Tu	17 30 4	23 8 24	15 15 38	21 12 24	16 30.6	5 16.4	13 54.2	29 58.6	27 9.9	20 36.2	29 16.6	22 28.3	13 42.0
16 W	17 34 1	24 5 42	27 8 6	3♍ 3 17	16 32.3	7 15.7	15 3.4	0♈39.8	27R10.0	20 32.8	29 17.6	22 29.6	13 43.4
17 Th	17 37 58	25 3 0	8♍58 30	14 54 21	16 33.7	9 12.8	16 12.6	1 20.9	27 10.0	20 29.5	29 18.5	22 31.0	13 44.9
18 F	17 41 54	26 0 16	20 51 26	26 50 20	16R34.4	11 7.7	17 21.8	2 1.9	27 9.8	20 26.3	29 19.3	22 32.4	13 46.4
19 Sa	17 45 51	26 57 32	2♎51 40	8♎56 0	16 34.4	13 0.5	18 31.2	2 42.8	27 9.4	20 23.1	29 20.1	22 33.8	13 47.8
20 Su	17 49 47	27 54 48	15 3 53	21 15 49	16 33.5	14 51.0	19 40.6	3 23.7	27 8.8	20 20.0	29 20.9	22 35.2	13 49.3
21 M	17 53 44	28 52 2	27 32 18	3♏53 43	16 31.9	16 39.2	20 50.1	4 4.4	27 8.0	20 17.0	29 21.6	22 36.6	13 50.8
22 Tu	17 57 40	29 49 16	10♏20 25	16 52 38	16 29.9	18 25.1	21 59.6	4 45.0	27 7.0	20 14.0	29 22.3	22 38.1	13 52.3
23 W	18 1 37	0♋46 29	23 30 32	0♐14 9	16 27.7	20 8.8	23 9.3	5 25.5	27 5.8	20 11.1	29 22.9	22 39.6	13 53.8
24 Th	18 5 33	1 43 42	7♐ 3 25	13 58 9	16 25.7	21 50.1	24 19.0	6 5.9	27 4.4	20 8.3	29 23.4	22 41.1	13 55.3
25 F	18 9 30	2 40 55	20 58 2	28 2 40	16 24.2	23 29.1	25 28.7	6 46.2	27 2.9	20 5.6	29 24.0	22 42.7	13 56.8
26 Sa	18 13 27	3 38 7	5♑11 31	12♑23 58	16D23.4	25 5.7	26 38.6	7 26.4	27 1.1	20 3.0	29 24.4	22 44.2	13 58.3
27 Su	18 17 23	4 35 19	19 39 18	26 56 49	16 23.2	26 40.0	27 48.5	8 6.5	26 59.2	20 0.4	29 24.8	22 45.8	13 59.9
28 M	18 21 20	5 32 30	4♒15 44	11♒35 17	16 23.6	28 12.0	28 58.5	8 46.5	26 57.1	19 57.9	29 25.2	22 47.5	14 1.4
29 Tu	18 25 16	6 29 42	18 54 42	26 13 16	16 24.3	29 41.6	0♊ 8.5	9 26.4	26 54.8	19 55.5	29 25.5	22 49.1	14 2.9
30 W	18 29 13	7 26 53	3♓30 22	10♓45 23	16 25.1	1♌ 8.8	1 18.7	10 6.1	26 52.3	19 53.2	29 25.8	22 50.8	14 4.4

Astro Data Dy Hr Mn	Planet Ingress Dy Hr Mn	Last Aspect Dy Hr Mn	☽ Ingress Dy Hr Mn	Last Aspect Dy Hr Mn	☽ Ingress Dy Hr Mn	☽ Phases & Eclipses Dy Hr Mn	Astro Data
♆ D 3 13:12	♂ ♓ 3 17:03	1 21:14 ♂ ⚹	♑ 1 23:32	2 11:11 ♀ ⚹	♓ 2 11:53	5 3:13 ☽ 13♒52	1 MAY 1926
☽0N 9 4:37	♀ ♈ 6 15:13	4 0:02 ♅ ⚹	♒ 4 3:31	4 13:10 ♅ ☌	♈ 4 14:45	11 22:55 ● 20♉28	Julian Day # 9617
♀0N 9 13:50	☿ ♉ 13 10:53	5 21:19 ♃ ☌	♓ 6 6:32	6 13:16 ♃ ⚹	♉ 6 18:28	19 17:48 ☽ 27♌59	Delta T 24.1 sec
☽0S 23 9:19	☉ ♊ 21 20:15	8 5:49 ♅ ☌	♈ 8 8:55	8 22:12 ♅ ⚹	♊ 8 23:43	27 11:48 ○ 5♐25	SVP 06♓17'36"
♄□♆ 23 11:31	☿ ♊ 29 13:51	10 3:06 ♃ ⚹	♉ 10 11:33	11 5:45 ♅ □	♋ 11 7:15		Obliquity 23°26'53"
		12 12:47 ♅ ⚹	♊ 12 15:46	13 16:00 ♅ △	♌ 13 17:29	3 8:09 ☽ 11♓59	⚷ Chiron 28♈37.2
☽0N 5 11:26	♀ ♉ 2 19:59	14 19:53 ♅ □	♋ 14 22:53	16 0:04 ♃ ☍	♍ 16 5:48	10 10:08 ● 18♊46	☽ Mean ☊ 19♋56.8
♃ R 16 8:35	☿ ♋ 12 10:08	17 6:21 ♅ △	♌ 17 9:20	18 16:59 ♅ ☍	♎ 18 18:19	18 11:13 ☽ 26♍27	
☽0S 19 18:27	♂ ♈ 15 0:50	19 17:48 ☉ □	♍ 19 21:54	21 2:44 ☉ △	♏ 21 4:40	25 21:13 ○ 3♑31	1 JUNE 1926
♂0N 23 12:37	☉ ♋ 22 4:30	22 7:28 ♅ ☍	♎ 22 10:04	23 10:29 ♅ △	♐ 23 11:35	25 21:25 A 0.675	Julian Day # 9648
	♀ ♊ 28 21:05	24 12:50 ♃ △	♏ 24 19:42	25 14:17 ♅ □	♑ 25 15:18		Delta T 24.1 sec
	☿ ♌ 29 5:01	27 0:10 ♅ △	♐ 27 2:14	27 16:03 ♅ ⚹	♒ 27 17:01		SVP 06♓17'31"
		29 4:31 ♅ □	♑ 29 6:24	29 13:06 ♃ ☌	♓ 29 18:13		Obliquity 23°26'53"
		31 7:33 ♅ ⚹	♒ 31 9:19				⚷ Chiron 0♉21.5
							☽ Mean ☊ 18♋18.3

JULY 1926 — LONGITUDE

Day	Sid.Time	☉	0 hr ☽	Noon ☽	True ☊	☿	♀	♂	♃	♄	♅	♆	♇
1 Th	18 33 9	8♋24 5	17♓57 51	25♓ 7 18	16♋25.7	2♌33.5	2♊28.9	10♈45.7	26♒49.6	19♏51.0	29♓26.1	22♌52.4	14♋ 6.0
2 F	18 37 6	9 21 16	2♈13 27	9♈16 0	16R 26.1	3 55.8	3 39.1	11 25.2	26R 46.7	19R 48.8	29 26.2	22 54.1	14 7.5
3 Sa	18 41 2	10 18 28	16 14 48	23 9 43	16 26.1	5 15.7	4 49.4	12 4.5	26 43.7	19 46.8	29 26.4	22 55.9	14 9.0
4 Su	18 44 59	11 15 41	0♉ 0 42	6♉47 44	16 25.8	6 33.0	5 59.8	12 43.7	26 40.5	19 44.8	29 26.4	22 57.6	14 10.6
5 M	18 48 56	12 12 53	13 30 49	20 10 2	16 25.4	7 47.7	7 10.3	13 22.7	26 37.0	19 42.9	29R 26.5	22 59.4	14 12.1
6 Tu	18 52 52	13 10 6	26 45 26	3♊17 7	16 25.0	8 59.8	8 20.8	14 1.6	26 33.4	19 41.1	29 26.5	23 1.2	14 13.6
7 W	18 56 49	14 7 19	9♊45 10	16 9 43	16 24.7	10 9.2	9 31.4	14 40.4	26 29.7	19 39.4	29 26.4	23 3.0	14 15.2
8 Th	19 0 45	15 4 33	22 30 53	28 48 46	16 24.5	11 15.9	10 42.1	15 19.0	26 25.7	19 37.8	29 26.3	23 4.8	14 16.7
9 F	19 4 42	16 1 46	5♋ 3 32	11♋15 20	16 24.5	12 19.6	11 52.8	15 57.4	26 21.6	19 36.3	29 26.1	23 6.6	14 18.3
10 Sa	19 8 38	16 59 0	17 24 19	23 30 40	16 24.5	13 20.5	13 3.5	16 35.6	26 17.3	19 34.9	29 25.9	23 8.5	14 19.8
11 Su	19 12 35	17 56 14	29 34 36	5♌36 19	16 24.5	14 18.3	14 14.4	17 13.7	26 12.9	19 33.5	29 25.7	23 10.4	14 21.3
12 M	19 16 31	18 53 28	11♌36 6	17 34 13	16 24.3	15 12.9	15 25.2	17 51.6	26 8.3	19 32.3	29 25.4	23 12.3	14 22.9
13 Tu	19 20 28	19 50 42	23 30 58	29 26 42	16 24.0	16 4.3	16 36.2	18 29.4	26 3.5	19 31.1	29 25.0	23 14.2	14 24.4
14 W	19 24 25	20 47 57	5♍21 48	11♍16 40	16 23.5	16 52.3	17 47.2	19 6.9	25 58.5	19 30.1	29 24.6	23 16.1	14 26.0
15 Th	19 28 21	21 45 11	17 11 44	23 7 29	16 22.8	17 36.7	18 58.2	19 44.3	25 53.4	19 29.1	29 24.2	23 18.0	14 27.5
16 F	19 32 18	22 42 26	29 4 23	5♎ 2 59	16 22.2	18 17.5	20 9.3	20 21.5	25 48.2	19 28.3	29 23.7	23 20.0	14 29.0
17 Sa	19 36 14	23 39 40	11♎ 3 47	17 7 21	16 21.7	18 54.5	21 20.4	20 58.4	25 42.8	19 27.5	29 23.1	23 22.0	14 30.5
18 Su	19 40 11	24 36 55	23 14 15	29 25 0	16D 21.5	19 27.5	22 31.6	21 35.2	25 37.2	19 26.8	29 22.5	23 23.9	14 32.1
19 M	19 44 7	25 34 10	5♏40 8	12♏ 0 11	16 21.6	19 56.3	23 42.9	22 11.8	25 31.5	19 26.2	29 21.9	23 25.9	14 33.6
20 Tu	19 48 4	26 31 25	18 25 37	24 56 49	16 22.2	20 20.9	24 54.2	22 48.2	25 25.7	19 25.8	29 21.2	23 28.0	14 35.1
21 W	19 52 0	27 28 41	1♐34 8	8♐17 50	16 23.0	20 41.1	26 5.6	23 24.3	25 19.8	19 25.4	29 20.5	23 30.0	14 36.6
22 Th	19 55 57	28 25 57	15 8 2	22 4 44	16 24.0	20 56.7	27 17.0	24 0.3	25 13.7	19 25.1	29 19.7	23 32.0	14 38.1
23 F	19 59 54	29 23 13	29 7 50	6♑17 2	16 24.9	21 7.5	28 28.5	24 36.0	25 7.4	19 24.9	29 18.9	23 34.1	14 39.6
24 Sa	20 3 50	0♌20 30	13♑31 53	20 51 46	16R 25.3	21R 13.5	29 40.0	25 11.6	25 1.1	19D 24.8	29 18.1	23 36.2	14 41.1
25 Su	20 7 47	1 17 47	28 15 56	5♒43 29	16 25.1	21 14.6	0♋51.6	25 46.9	24 54.6	19 24.8	29 17.2	23 38.2	14 42.6
26 M	20 11 43	2 15 5	13♒13 25	20 44 39	16 24.1	21 10.6	2 3.3	26 21.9	24 48.1	19 24.9	29 16.2	23 40.3	14 44.1
27 Tu	20 15 40	3 12 23	28 16 4	5♓46 34	16 22.5	21 1.6	3 15.0	26 56.8	24 41.4	19 25.1	29 15.2	23 42.4	14 45.6
28 W	20 19 36	4 9 42	13♓15 4	20 40 37	16 20.3	20 47.5	4 26.7	27 31.3	24 34.6	19 25.4	29 14.2	23 44.5	14 47.0
29 Th	20 23 33	5 7 2	28 2 22	5♈19 36	16 18.1	20 28.5	5 38.5	28 5.7	24 27.7	19 25.8	29 13.1	23 46.7	14 48.5
30 F	20 27 29	6 4 24	12♈31 47	19 38 29	16 16.3	20 4.7	6 50.4	28 39.8	24 20.7	19 26.3	29 12.0	23 48.8	14 50.0
31 Sa	20 31 26	7 1 46	26 39 29	3♉34 41	16D 15.1	19 36.3	8 2.3	29 13.6	24 13.6	19 26.9	29 10.8	23 50.9	14 51.4

AUGUST 1926 — LONGITUDE

Day	Sid.Time	☉	0 hr ☽	Noon ☽	True ☊	☿	♀	♂	♃	♄	♅	♆	♇
1 Su	20 35 23	7♌59 9	10♉24 5	17♉ 7 51	16♋14.8	19♌ 3.6	9♋14.3	29♈47.2	24♒ 6.4	19♏27.6	29♓ 9.6	23♌53.1	14♋52.8
2 M	20 39 19	8 56 34	23 46 10	0♊19 19	16 15.4	18R 26.9	10 26.4	0♉20.4	23R 59.1	19 28.4	29R 8.4	23 55.2	14 54.3
3 Tu	20 43 16	9 54 0	6♊47 38	13 11 28	16 16.7	17 46.9	11 38.5	0 53.4	23 51.8	19 29.3	29 7.1	23 57.4	14 55.7
4 W	20 47 12	10 51 27	19 31 12	25 47 10	16 18.3	17 4.0	12 50.6	1 26.1	23 44.4	19 30.2	29 5.8	23 59.6	14 57.1
5 Th	20 51 9	11 48 55	1♋59 46	8♋ 9 21	16 19.6	16 18.9	14 2.8	1 58.5	23 36.9	19 31.3	29 4.4	24 1.8	14 58.5
6 F	20 55 5	12 46 25	14 16 15	20 20 46	16R 20.3	15 32.3	15 15.1	2 30.6	23 29.4	19 32.5	29 3.0	24 3.9	14 59.9
7 Sa	20 59 2	13 43 55	26 23 12	2♌23 50	16 19.9	14 45.1	16 27.4	3 2.4	23 21.7	19 33.8	29 1.5	24 6.1	15 1.3
8 Su	21 2 59	14 41 27	8♌22 56	14 20 44	16 18.1	13 58.2	17 39.8	3 33.8	23 14.1	19 35.1	29 0.1	24 8.3	15 2.7
9 M	21 6 55	15 39 0	20 17 29	26 13 25	16 14.9	13 12.4	18 52.2	4 4.9	23 6.4	19 36.6	28 58.5	24 10.5	15 4.0
10 Tu	21 10 52	16 36 33	2♍ 8 46	8♍ 3 46	16 10.4	12 28.6	20 4.6	4 35.7	22 58.6	19 38.2	28 57.0	24 12.7	15 5.4
11 W	21 14 48	17 34 8	13 58 42	19 53 49	16 5.1	11 47.6	21 17.2	5 6.1	22 50.9	19 39.8	28 55.4	24 15.0	15 6.7
12 Th	21 18 45	18 31 44	25 49 26	1♎45 51	15 59.3	11 10.4	22 29.7	5 36.2	22 43.1	19 41.6	28 53.7	24 17.2	15 8.1
13 F	21 22 41	19 29 21	7♎43 26	13 42 34	15 53.9	10 37.7	23 42.3	6 5.9	22 35.2	19 43.4	28 52.1	24 19.4	15 9.4
14 Sa	21 26 38	20 26 58	19 43 40	25 47 9	15 49.2	10 10.2	24 55.0	6 35.2	22 27.4	19 45.3	28 50.4	24 21.6	15 10.7
15 Su	21 30 34	21 24 37	1♏53 31	8♏ 3 14	15 45.9	9 48.4	26 7.7	7 4.2	22 19.5	19 47.4	28 48.6	24 23.8	15 12.0
16 M	21 34 31	22 22 17	14 16 50	20 34 48	15D 44.1	9 33.1	27 20.5	7 32.8	22 11.7	19 49.5	28 46.9	24 26.0	15 13.2
17 Tu	21 38 27	23 19 58	26 57 40	3♐25 56	15 43.9	9D 24.5	28 33.3	8 1.0	22 3.8	19 51.7	28 45.1	24 28.3	15 14.5
18 W	21 42 24	24 17 40	10♐ 0 2	16 40 25	15 44.8	9 23.0	29 46.1	8 28.8	21 56.0	19 54.0	28 43.2	24 30.5	15 15.8
19 Th	21 46 21	25 15 23	23 27 22	0♑21 8	15 46.2	9 28.9	0♌59.0	8 56.1	21 48.1	19 56.4	28 41.4	24 32.7	15 17.0
20 F	21 50 17	26 13 7	7♑21 50	14 29 24	15R 47.3	9 42.3	2 11.9	9 23.1	21 40.3	19 58.9	28 39.5	24 34.9	15 18.2
21 Sa	21 54 14	27 10 52	21 43 38	29 4 5	15 47.4	10 3.3	3 24.9	9 49.6	21 32.5	20 1.5	28 37.6	24 37.2	15 19.4
22 Su	21 58 10	28 8 39	6♒30 9	14♒ 1 1	15 45.9	10 32.0	4 38.0	10 15.8	21 24.8	20 4.2	28 35.6	24 39.4	15 20.6
23 M	22 2 7	29 6 26	21 35 40	29 12 54	15 42.4	11 8.2	5 51.1	10 41.4	21 17.0	20 6.9	28 33.6	24 41.6	15 21.8
24 Tu	22 6 3	0♍ 4 15	6♓51 27	14♓29 57	15 37.2	11 51.9	7 4.2	11 6.6	21 9.4	20 9.8	28 31.6	24 43.8	15 23.0
25 W	22 10 0	1 2 6	22 7 1	29 41 20	15 30.7	12 42.9	8 17.4	11 31.4	21 1.7	20 12.7	28 29.6	24 46.0	15 24.1
26 Th	22 13 56	1 59 58	7♈11 43	14♈37 6	15 23.9	13 40.9	9 30.6	11 55.7	20 54.1	20 15.7	28 27.5	24 48.2	15 25.3
27 F	22 17 53	2 57 52	21 56 38	29 9 42	15 17.7	14 45.6	10 43.9	12 19.5	20 46.6	20 18.8	28 25.5	24 50.4	15 26.4
28 Sa	22 21 50	3 55 48	6♉15 52	13♉14 54	15 12.9	15 56.9	11 57.2	12 42.8	20 39.1	20 22.0	28 23.3	24 52.7	15 27.5
29 Su	22 25 46	4 53 45	20 6 48	26 51 41	15 9.9	17 14.1	13 10.6	13 5.6	20 31.7	20 25.3	28 21.2	24 54.9	15 28.6
30 M	22 29 43	5 51 44	3♊29 50	10♊ 1 39	15D 8.8	18 37.1	14 24.1	13 27.8	20 24.4	20 28.6	28 19.1	24 57.0	15 29.6
31 Tu	22 33 39	6 49 46	16 27 35	22 48 8	15 9.2	20 5.2	15 37.5	13 49.5	20 17.2	20 32.1	28 16.9	24 59.2	15 30.7

Astro Data

	Dy Hr Mn
☽0N	2 17:10
♅ R	5 5:02
☽0S	17 2:25
☿ R	24 17:05
♄ D	24 9:37
☽0N	29 23:28
♃☍♆	2 9:53
☽0S	13 8:41
☿ D	17 16:54
☽0N	26 7:39
♃□♄	29 14:29

Planet Ingress

	Dy Hr Mn
☉ ♌	23 15:25
♀ ♋	24 6:42
♂ ♉	1 9:14
♀ ♌	18 4:35
☉ ♍	23 22:14

Last Aspect / ☽ Ingress (July)

Last Aspect Dy Hr Mn		☽ Ingress Dy Hr Mn
1 19:17	♅ ☌	♈ 1 20:14
3 18:10	♃ ⚹	♉ 3 23:59
6 4:55	♅ ⚹	♊ 6 5:57
8 13:12	♅ □	♋ 8 14:16
10 23:42	♅ △	♌ 11 0:50
13 5:06	♃ ☍	♍ 13 13:07
16 0:39	♅ ☍	♎ 16 1:52
18 4:37	♃ △	♏ 18 13:08
20 19:59	♅ △	♐ 20 21:10
23 0:19	♅ □	♑ 23 1:28
25 1:39	♅ ⚹	♒ 25 2:48
26 21:48	♂ ⚹	♓ 27 2:46
29 1:56	♅ ☌	♈ 29 3:13
31 4:37	♂ ☌	♉ 31 5:46

Last Aspect / ☽ Ingress (August)

Last Aspect Dy Hr Mn		☽ Ingress Dy Hr Mn
2 9:48	♅ ⚹	♊ 2 11:24
4 18:21	♅ □	♋ 4 20:08
7 5:15	♅ △	♌ 7 7:12
9 7:53	♆ ☌	♍ 9 19:39
12 6:12	♅ ☍	♎ 12 8:26
14 11:25	♀ □	♏ 14 20:18
17 3:20	♅ △	♐ 17 5:39
19 9:06	♅ □	♑ 19 11:24
21 11:15	♅ ⚹	♒ 21 13:31
23 12:38	☉ ☍	♓ 23 13:14
25 10:05	♅ ☌	♈ 25 12:30
27 4:48	♆ △	♉ 27 13:24
29 14:39	♅ ⚹	♊ 29 17:39

☽ Phases & Eclipses

Dy Hr Mn	
2 13:02	☽ 9♈52
9 23:06	● 16♋57
9 23:05:37	A 3'39"
18 2:55	☽ 24♎44
25 5:13	○ 1♒30
25 4:60	A 0.354
31 19:25	☽ 7♉48
8 13:48	● 15♌15
16 16:38	☽ 23♏02
23 12:38	○ 29♒37
30 4:40	☽ 6♊03

Astro Data

1 JULY 1926
Julian Day # 9678
Delta T 24.2 sec
SVP 06♓17'26"
Obliquity 23°26'53"
⚷ Chiron 1♉35.7
☽ Mean ☊ 16♋43.0

1 AUGUST 1926
Julian Day # 9709
Delta T 24.2 sec
SVP 06♓17'21"
Obliquity 23°26'53"
⚷ Chiron 2♉09.7
☽ Mean ☊ 15♋04.6

LONGITUDE SEPTEMBER 1926

Day	Sid.Time	☉	0 hr ☽	Noon ☽	True ☊	☿	♀	♂	♃	♄	♅	♆	♇
1 W	22 37 36	7♍47 49	29♊ 3 53	5♋15 22	15♋10.2	21♌38.0	16♌51.1	14♉10.7	20♒10.0	20♏35.6	28♓14.7	25♌ 1.4	15♋31.7
2 Th	22 41 32	8 45 54	11♋23 9	17 27 46	15R 11.1	23 15.1	18 4.6	14 31.3	20R 2.9	20 39.2	28R 12.5	25 3.6	15 32.7
3 F	22 45 29	9 44 1	23 29 45	29 29 34	15 10.7	24 55.9	19 18.3	14 51.3	19 55.9	20 42.9	28 10.3	25 5.8	15 33.7
4 Sa	22 49 25	10 42 10	5♌27 41	11♌24 30	15 8.5	26 40.0	20 31.9	15 10.7	19 49.1	20 46.7	28 8.0	25 7.9	15 34.7
5 Su	22 53 22	11 40 21	17 20 23	23 15 40	15 3.9	28 26.8	21 45.7	15 29.5	19 42.3	20 50.6	28 5.7	25 10.1	15 35.7
6 M	22 57 19	12 38 34	29 10 38	5♍ 5 33	14 56.8	0♍15.8	22 59.4	15 47.7	19 35.6	20 54.5	28 3.4	25 12.2	15 36.6
7 Tu	23 1 15	13 36 48	11♍ 0 38	16 56 7	14 47.4	2 6.7	24 13.2	16 5.3	19 29.0	20 58.5	28 1.1	25 14.4	15 37.5
8 W	23 5 12	14 35 4	22 52 10	28 48 59	14 36.5	3 59.0	25 27.0	16 22.2	19 22.6	21 2.6	27 58.8	25 16.5	15 38.4
9 Th	23 9 8	15 33 22	4♎46 46	10♎45 40	14 24.7	5 52.3	26 40.9	16 38.4	19 16.3	21 6.8	27 56.5	25 18.6	15 39.3
10 F	23 13 5	16 31 41	16 45 56	22 47 47	14 13.3	7 46.3	27 54.8	16 54.0	19 10.1	21 11.0	27 54.2	25 20.7	15 40.2
11 Sa	23 17 1	17 30 3	28 51 28	4♏57 16	14 3.2	9 40.8	29 8.8	17 8.9	19 4.1	21 15.3	27 51.8	25 22.8	15 41.0
12 Su	23 20 58	18 28 25	11♏ 5 31	17 16 33	13 55.2	11 35.3	0♍22.8	17 23.1	18 58.2	21 19.7	27 49.4	25 24.9	15 41.8
13 M	23 24 54	19 26 50	23 30 48	29 48 39	13 49.7	13 29.8	1 36.8	17 36.6	18 52.4	21 24.2	27 47.1	25 27.0	15 42.6
14 Tu	23 28 51	20 25 16	6♐10 33	12♐36 58	13 46.7	15 24.0	2 50.9	17 49.4	18 46.8	21 28.7	27 44.7	25 29.0	15 43.4
15 W	23 32 48	21 23 44	19 8 22	25 45 10	13D 45.7	17 17.8	4 5.0	18 1.5	18 41.3	21 33.4	27 42.3	25 31.1	15 44.2
16 Th	23 36 44	22 22 13	2♑27 49	9♑16 38	13R 46.0	19 11.0	5 19.1	18 12.8	18 36.0	21 38.1	27 39.9	25 33.1	15 44.9
17 F	23 40 41	23 20 44	16 11 55	23 13 47	13 46.2	21 3.5	6 33.3	18 23.3	18 30.8	21 42.8	27 37.5	25 35.2	15 45.6
18 Sa	23 44 37	24 19 17	0♒22 16	7♒37 12	13 45.2	22 55.3	7 47.5	18 33.1	18 25.8	21 47.6	27 35.1	25 37.2	15 46.3
19 Su	23 48 34	25 17 51	14 58 13	22 24 44	13 42.1	24 46.2	9 1.7	18 42.2	18 20.9	21 52.5	27 32.7	25 39.2	15 47.0
20 M	23 52 30	26 16 27	29 55 57	7♓30 54	13 36.4	26 36.3	10 16.0	18 50.4	18 16.3	21 57.5	27 30.3	25 41.1	15 47.7
21 Tu	23 56 27	27 15 5	15♓ 8 21	22 47 0	13 28.2	28 25.5	11 30.3	18 57.9	18 11.7	22 2.5	27 27.9	25 43.1	15 48.3
22 W	0 0 23	28 13 44	0♈25 25	8♈ 2 11	13 18.1	0♎13.7	12 44.7	19 4.5	18 7.4	22 7.6	27 25.5	25 45.1	15 48.9
23 Th	0 4 20	29 12 26	15 35 54	23 5 20	13 7.4	2 1.0	13 59.0	19 10.3	18 3.2	22 12.7	27 23.1	25 47.0	15 49.5
24 F	0 8 16	0♎11 9	0♉29 21	7♉47 4	12 57.2	3 47.4	15 13.4	19 15.3	17 59.2	22 18.0	27 20.7	25 48.9	15 50.1
25 Sa	0 12 13	1 9 55	14 57 50	22 1 13	12 48.8	5 32.8	16 27.9	19 19.5	17 55.4	22 23.2	27 18.3	25 50.8	15 50.6
26 Su	0 16 10	2 8 43	28 57 1	5♊45 14	12 42.8	7 17.2	17 42.4	19 22.8	17 51.7	22 28.6	27 15.9	25 52.7	15 51.1
27 M	0 20 6	3 7 33	12♊26 4	18 59 50	12 39.4	9 0.8	18 56.9	19 25.2	17 48.3	22 34.0	27 13.5	25 54.5	15 51.6
28 Tu	0 24 3	4 6 26	25 27 0	1♋48 7	12D 38.0	10 43.4	20 11.4	19 26.7	17 45.0	22 39.4	27 11.1	25 56.4	15 52.1
29 W	0 27 59	5 5 20	8♋ 3 45	14 14 35	12R 37.8	12 25.0	21 26.0	19R 27.4	17 41.9	22 45.0	27 8.7	25 58.2	15 52.5
30 Th	0 31 56	6 4 18	20 21 16	26 24 26	12 37.7	14 5.8	22 40.6	19 27.2	17 39.0	22 50.5	27 6.4	26 0.0	15 53.0

LONGITUDE OCTOBER 1926

Day	Sid.Time	☉	0 hr ☽	Noon ☽	True ☊	☿	♀	♂	♃	♄	♅	♆	♇
1 F	0 35 52	7♎ 3 17	2♌24 44	8♌22 48	12♋36.5	15♎45.7	23♍55.3	19♉26.0	17♒36.3	22♏56.2	27♓ 4.0	26♌ 1.8	15♋53.4
2 Sa	0 39 49	8 2 19	14 19 12	20 14 30	12R 33.2	17 24.7	25 10.0	19R 24.0	17R 33.8	23 1.9	27R 1.6	26 3.6	15 53.8
3 Su	0 43 45	9 1 22	26 9 10	2♍ 3 40	12 27.2	19 2.9	26 24.7	19 21.0	17 31.4	23 7.6	26 59.3	26 5.3	15 54.1
4 M	0 47 42	10 0 28	7♍58 23	13 53 40	12 18.3	20 40.3	27 39.4	19 17.2	17 29.3	23 13.4	26 57.0	26 7.0	15 54.5
5 Tu	0 51 39	10 59 37	19 49 49	25 47 4	12 6.6	22 16.8	28 54.2	19 12.4	17 27.3	23 19.3	26 54.6	26 8.8	15 54.8
6 W	0 55 35	11 58 47	1♎45 39	7♎45 42	11 53.1	23 52.6	0♎ 9.0	19 6.8	17 25.6	23 25.2	26 52.3	26 10.4	15 55.1
7 Th	0 59 32	12 57 59	13 47 23	19 50 49	11 38.6	25 27.5	1 23.8	19 0.2	17 24.0	23 31.1	26 50.0	26 12.1	15 55.3
8 F	1 3 28	13 57 14	25 56 6	2♏ 3 20	11 24.4	27 1.7	2 38.6	18 52.7	17 22.7	23 37.2	26 47.8	26 13.7	15 55.6
9 Sa	1 7 25	14 56 30	8♏12 38	14 24 7	11 11.6	28 35.1	3 53.5	18 44.4	17 21.5	23 43.2	26 45.5	26 15.3	15 55.8
10 Su	1 11 21	15 55 49	20 37 54	26 54 12	11 1.3	0♏ 7.8	5 8.4	18 35.2	17 20.6	23 49.3	26 43.3	26 16.9	15 56.0
11 M	1 15 18	16 55 9	3♐13 12	9♐35 8	10 53.9	1 39.8	6 23.3	18 25.2	17 19.8	23 55.5	26 41.0	26 18.5	15 56.1
12 Tu	1 19 14	17 54 31	16 0 17	22 28 57	10 49.6	3 11.0	7 38.2	18 14.3	17 19.3	24 1.7	26 38.8	26 20.0	15 56.3
13 W	1 23 11	18 53 55	29 1 27	5♑38 8	10D 47.7	4 41.5	8 53.2	18 2.6	17 19.0	24 7.9	26 36.7	26 21.6	15 56.4
14 Th	1 27 8	19 53 21	12♑19 20	19 5 21	10R 47.3	6 11.2	10 8.1	17 50.1	17D 18.8	24 14.2	26 34.5	26 23.0	15 56.5
15 F	1 31 4	20 52 49	25 56 27	2♒52 52	10 47.3	7 40.3	11 23.1	17 36.8	17 18.9	24 20.5	26 32.4	26 24.5	15 56.6
16 Sa	1 35 1	21 52 18	9♒54 41	17 1 55	10 46.3	9 8.6	12 38.1	17 22.8	17 19.1	24 26.9	26 30.3	26 26.0	15 56.6
17 Su	1 38 57	22 51 49	24 14 24	1♓31 48	10 43.3	10 36.1	13 53.1	17 8.1	17 19.6	24 33.3	26 28.2	26 27.4	15R 56.6
18 M	1 42 54	23 51 21	8♓53 38	16 19 11	10 37.7	12 3.0	15 8.2	16 52.7	17 20.3	24 39.8	26 26.1	26 28.8	15 56.6
19 Tu	1 46 50	24 50 56	23 47 36	1♈17 52	10 29.5	13 29.0	16 23.2	16 36.6	17 21.1	24 46.3	26 24.1	26 30.1	15 56.6
20 W	1 50 47	25 50 32	8♈48 48	16 19 11	10 19.3	14 54.3	17 38.3	16 19.9	17 22.2	24 52.8	26 22.1	26 31.4	15 56.5
21 Th	1 54 43	26 50 10	23 47 48	1♉13 25	10 8.3	16 18.7	18 53.4	16 2.6	17 23.4	24 59.3	26 20.1	26 32.8	15 56.5
22 F	1 58 40	27 49 50	8♉34 56	15 51 23	9 57.7	17 42.3	20 8.5	15 44.8	17 24.9	25 5.9	26 18.1	26 34.0	15 56.4
23 Sa	2 2 37	28 49 32	23 1 57	0♊ 6 2	9 48.8	19 5.0	21 23.6	15 26.4	17 26.6	25 12.6	26 16.2	26 35.3	15 56.2
24 Su	2 6 33	29 49 17	7♊ 3 14	13 53 23	9 42.3	20 26.8	22 38.7	15 7.5	17 28.4	25 19.2	26 14.3	26 36.5	15 56.1
25 M	2 10 30	0♏49 3	20 36 26	27 12 34	9 38.5	21 47.6	23 53.9	14 48.2	17 30.5	25 25.9	26 12.5	26 37.7	15 55.9
26 Tu	2 14 26	1 48 52	3♋42 5	10♋ 5 23	9D 36.9	23 7.4	25 9.1	14 28.5	17 32.7	25 32.7	26 10.6	26 38.9	15 55.7
27 W	2 18 23	2 48 43	16 23 0	22 35 31	9 36.9	24 26.0	26 24.2	14 8.4	17 35.1	25 39.4	26 8.8	26 40.0	15 55.5
28 Th	2 22 19	3 48 36	28 43 33	4♌47 45	9R 37.4	25 43.4	27 39.5	13 48.1	17 37.8	25 46.2	26 7.1	26 41.1	15 55.3
29 F	2 26 16	4 48 32	10♌48 49	16 47 23	9 37.3	26 59.4	28 54.7	13 27.4	17 40.6	25 53.0	26 5.4	26 42.2	15 55.0
30 Sa	2 30 12	5 48 29	22 44 8	28 39 41	9 35.7	28 14.0	0♏ 9.9	13 6.6	17 43.6	25 59.9	26 3.7	26 43.2	15 54.7
31 Su	2 34 9	6 48 29	4♍34 39	10♍29 34	9 31.8	29 27.1	1 25.2	12 45.6	17 46.8	26 6.7	26 2.0	26 44.2	15 54.4

Astro Data Dy Hr Mn	Planet Ingress Dy Hr Mn
☽0S 9 13:58	☿ ♍ 5 20:33
☽0N 22 17:46	♀ ♍ 11 16:37
☿0S 23 10:34	☿ ♎ 21 20:57
♂ R 29 5:43	☉ ♎ 23 19:27
☽0S 6 19:40	♀ ♎ 5 21:07
♀0S 8 13:53	☿ ♏ 9 21:58
♃ D 14 4:48	☉ ♏ 24 4:18
♅⊼♆ 17 5:36	♀ ♏ 29 20:50
♇ R 17 8:51	☿ ♐ 31 11:01
☽0N 20 4:35	
♄△♅ 30 10:44	

Last Aspect Dy Hr Mn	☽ Ingress Dy Hr Mn	Last Aspect Dy Hr Mn	☽ Ingress Dy Hr Mn
31 22:26 ♅ □	♋ 1 1:48	2 23:52 ♆ ☌	♍ 3 7:49
3 9:19 ♅ △	♌ 3 13:01	5 20:24 ♀ ☌	♎ 5 20:28
5 15:55 ♆ ☌	♍ 6 1:40	8 2:28 ☿ ☌	♏ 8 7:59
8 10:17 ♅ ☍	♎ 8 14:23	10 11:37 ♅ △	♐ 10 17:54
11 0:38 ♀ ⚹	♏ 11 2:15	12 19:36 ♅ □	♑ 13 1:47
13 8:08 ♅ △	♐ 13 12:22	15 1:02 ♅ ⚹	♒ 15 7:02
15 15:28 ♅ □	♑ 15 19:37	17 3:40 ♆ ☍	♓ 17 9:30
17 19:21 ♅ ⚹	♒ 17 23:23	19 4:10 ♅ ☌	♈ 19 9:56
19 17:13 ♆ ☍	♓ 20 0:06	21 5:15 ☉ ☍	♉ 21 10:01
21 20:19 ☉ ☍	♈ 21 23:20	23 6:01 ♆ □	♊ 23 11:50
23 16:23 ♆ △	♉ 23 23:12	25 10:57 ♅ ⚹	♋ 25 17:08
25 21:04 ♆ ⚹	♊ 26 1:50	27 21:40 ♀ □	♌ 28 2:31
28 3:15 ♅ □	♋ 28 8:35	30 12:25 ☿ □	♍ 30 14:43
30 13:21 ♅ △	♌ 30 19:10		

☽ Phases & Eclipses Dy Hr Mn	Astro Data
7 5:45 ● 13♍51	1 SEPTEMBER 1926
15 4:26 ☽ 21♐35	Julian Day # 9740
21 20:19 ○ 28♓05	Delta T 24.3 sec
28 17:48 ☽ 4♋50	SVP 06♓17'18"
	Obliquity 23°26'54"
6 22:13 ● 12♎54	⚷ Chiron 1♉52.5R
14 14:28 ☽ 20♑29	☽ Mean ☊ 13♋26.1
21 5:15 ○ 27♈03	1 OCTOBER 1926
28 10:57 ☽ 4♌16	Julian Day # 9770
	Delta T 24.3 sec
	SVP 06♓17'15"
	Obliquity 23°26'54"
	⚷ Chiron 0♉52.5R
	☽ Mean ☊ 11♋50.7

NOVEMBER 1926 LONGITUDE

Day	Sid.Time	☉	0 hr ☽	Noon ☽	True ☊	☿	♀	♂	♃	♄	♅	♆	♇
1 M	2 38 6	7♏48 30	16♍25 0	22♍21 22	9♋25.4	0♐38.3	2♏40.4	12♉24.4	17♒50.2	26♏13.6	26♓ 0.4	26♌45.2	15♋54.1
2 Tu	2 42 2	8 48 34	28 19 7	4♎18 36	9R 16.7	1 47.6	3 55.7	12R 3.3	17 53.8	26 20.5	25R 58.8	26 46.2	15R 53.7
3 W	2 45 59	9 48 40	10♎20 6	16 23 54	9 6.1	2 54.8	5 11.0	11 42.1	17 57.6	26 27.5	25 57.3	26 47.1	15 53.3
4 Th	2 49 55	10 48 48	22 30 9	28 39 2	8 54.7	3 59.6	6 26.3	11 21.0	18 1.6	26 34.4	25 55.8	26 48.0	15 52.9
5 F	2 53 52	11 48 58	4♏50 36	11♏ 4 56	8 43.5	5 1.7	7 41.6	10 59.9	18 5.7	26 41.4	25 54.3	26 48.9	15 52.5
6 Sa	2 57 48	12 49 9	17 22 4	23 41 58	8 33.4	6 0.8	8 56.9	10 39.1	18 10.1	26 48.4	25 52.9	26 49.7	15 52.0
7 Su	3 1 45	13 49 23	0♐ 4 39	6♐30 7	8 25.3	6 56.5	10 12.2	10 18.4	18 14.6	26 55.4	25 51.5	26 50.5	15 51.6
8 M	3 5 41	14 49 38	12 58 20	19 29 19	8 19.8	7 48.5	11 27.6	9 58.1	18 19.3	27 2.5	25 50.1	26 51.2	15 51.1
9 Tu	3 9 38	15 49 55	26 3 5	2♑39 43	8D 16.8	8 36.3	12 42.9	9 38.0	18 24.2	27 9.5	25 48.8	26 52.0	15 50.5
10 W	3 13 35	16 50 13	9♑19 15	16 1 48	8 16.1	9 19.3	13 58.3	9 18.3	18 29.3	27 16.6	25 47.6	26 52.7	15 50.0
11 Th	3 17 31	17 50 33	22 47 27	29 36 19	8 16.8	9 57.0	15 13.6	8 59.0	18 34.6	27 23.7	25 46.4	26 53.3	15 49.4
12 F	3 21 28	18 50 54	6♒28 31	13♒24 5	8R 17.9	10 28.9	16 29.0	8 40.2	18 40.0	27 30.7	25 45.2	26 54.0	15 48.8
13 Sa	3 25 24	19 51 17	20 23 6	27 25 30	8 18.4	10 54.1	17 44.4	8 21.9	18 45.6	27 37.8	25 44.1	26 54.6	15 48.2
14 Su	3 29 21	20 51 41	4♓31 12	11♓39 59	8 17.5	11 12.1	18 59.7	8 4.0	18 51.4	27 45.0	25 43.0	26 55.1	15 47.6
15 M	3 33 17	21 52 6	18 51 35	26 5 33	8 14.7	11R 22.1	20 15.1	7 46.8	18 57.3	27 52.1	25 41.9	26 55.7	15 47.0
16 Tu	3 37 14	22 52 33	3♈21 22	10♈38 23	8 9.8	11 23.3	21 30.5	7 30.2	19 3.4	27 59.2	25 41.0	26 56.1	15 46.3
17 W	3 41 10	23 53 0	17 55 53	25 13 2	8 3.5	11 15.1	22 45.9	7 14.1	19 9.7	28 6.3	25 40.0	26 56.6	15 45.6
18 Th	3 45 7	24 53 30	2♉29 0	9♉42 56	7 56.4	10 57.0	24 1.2	6 58.8	19 16.2	28 13.5	25 39.1	26 57.0	15 44.9
19 F	3 49 4	25 54 0	16 53 59	24 1 23	7 49.5	10 28.4	25 16.6	6 44.1	19 22.8	28 20.6	25 38.3	26 57.4	15 44.2
20 Sa	3 53 0	26 54 33	1♊ 4 26	8♊ 2 35	7 43.8	9 49.3	26 32.0	6 30.1	19 29.5	28 27.7	25 37.5	26 57.8	15 43.4
21 Su	3 56 57	27 55 6	14 55 22	21 42 29	7 39.7	8 59.9	27 47.4	6 16.8	19 36.5	28 34.9	25 36.7	26 58.1	15 42.6
22 M	4 0 53	28 55 42	28 23 46	4♋59 10	7D 37.5	8 0.7	29 2.8	6 4.3	19 43.6	28 42.0	25 36.0	26 58.4	15 41.9
23 Tu	4 4 50	29 56 19	11♋28 49	17 52 55	7 37.2	6 52.9	0♐18.2	5 52.5	19 50.8	28 49.2	25 35.3	26 58.7	15 41.0
24 W	4 8 46	0♐56 57	24 11 47	0♌25 48	7 38.2	5 38.1	1 33.7	5 41.5	19 58.2	28 56.3	25 34.7	26 58.9	15 40.2
25 Th	4 12 43	1 57 37	6♌35 29	12 41 20	7 39.9	4 18.4	2 49.1	5 31.2	20 5.8	29 3.5	25 34.2	26 59.1	15 39.4
26 F	4 16 39	2 58 19	18 43 56	24 43 53	7 41.6	2 56.3	4 4.5	5 21.8	20 13.5	29 10.6	25 33.7	26 59.2	15 38.5
27 Sa	4 20 36	3 59 2	0♍41 49	6♍38 22	7R 42.5	1 34.6	5 19.9	5 13.1	20 21.4	29 17.8	25 33.2	26 59.4	15 37.6
28 Su	4 24 33	4 59 47	12 34 9	18 29 48	7 42.2	0 16.0	6 35.4	5 5.3	20 29.4	29 24.9	25 32.8	26 59.4	15 36.7
29 M	4 28 29	6 0 34	24 25 55	0♎23 4	7 40.5	29♏ 3.1	7 50.8	4 58.2	20 37.5	29 32.0	25 32.4	26R 59.5	15 35.8
30 Tu	4 32 26	7 1 21	6♎21 47	12 22 34	7 37.4	27 58.1	9 6.2	4 52.0	20 45.8	29 39.1	25 32.1	26 59.5	15 34.9

DECEMBER 1926 LONGITUDE

Day	Sid.Time	☉	0 hr ☽	Noon ☽	True ☊	☿	♀	♂	♃	♄	♅	♆	♇
1 W	4 36 22	8♐ 2 11	18♎25 53	24♎32 7	7♋33.1	27♏ 2.7	10♐21.7	4♉46.6	20♒54.3	29♏46.2	25♓31.8	26♌59.5	15♋33.9
2 Th	4 40 19	9 3 1	0♏41 36	6♏54 37	7R 28.1	26R 17.9	11 37.1	4R 42.0	21 2.9	29 53.3	25R 31.6	26R 59.4	15R 33.0
3 F	4 44 15	10 3 53	13 11 21	19 31 59	7 23.1	25 44.6	12 52.6	4 38.2	21 11.6	0♐ 0.4	25 31.5	26 59.4	15 32.0
4 Sa	4 48 12	11 4 47	25 56 33	2♐25 4	7 18.7	25 22.8	14 8.0	4 35.3	21 20.5	0 7.5	25 31.4	26 59.2	15 31.0
5 Su	4 52 8	12 5 41	8♐57 29	15 33 41	7 15.2	25D 12.2	15 23.5	4 33.2	21 29.5	0 14.6	25D 31.3	26 59.1	15 30.0
6 M	4 56 5	13 6 37	22 13 31	28 56 47	7 13.1	25 12.5	16 39.0	4 31.9	21 38.6	0 21.6	25 31.3	26 58.9	15 29.0
7 Tu	5 0 2	14 7 34	5♑43 14	12♑32 40	7D 12.4	25 22.8	17 54.4	4D 31.4	21 47.9	0 28.6	25 31.3	26 58.7	15 27.9
8 W	5 3 58	15 8 31	19 24 48	26 19 22	7 12.8	25 42.4	19 9.9	4 31.7	21 57.3	0 35.6	25 31.4	26 58.4	15 26.9
9 Th	5 7 55	16 9 30	3♒16 8	10♒14 50	7 14.0	26 10.4	20 25.3	4 32.8	22 6.9	0 42.6	25 31.6	26 58.1	15 25.8
10 F	5 11 51	17 10 29	17 15 15	24 17 7	7 15.4	26 46.0	21 40.8	4 34.7	22 16.5	0 49.6	25 31.8	26 57.8	15 24.7
11 Sa	5 15 48	18 11 28	1♓20 15	8♓24 23	7 16.7	27 28.4	22 56.3	4 37.4	22 26.3	0 56.6	25 32.0	26 57.4	15 23.6
12 Su	5 19 44	19 12 28	15 29 19	22 34 48	7R 17.3	28 16.7	24 11.7	4 40.9	22 36.2	1 3.5	25 32.4	26 57.1	15 22.5
13 M	5 23 41	20 13 29	29 40 34	6♈46 22	7 17.1	29 10.2	25 27.2	4 45.1	22 46.3	1 10.4	25 32.7	26 56.6	15 21.4
14 Tu	5 27 37	21 14 30	13♈51 53	20 56 46	7 16.1	0♐ 8.4	26 42.6	4 50.1	22 56.4	1 17.3	25 33.1	26 56.2	15 20.3
15 W	5 31 34	22 15 31	28 0 42	5♉ 3 17	7 14.5	1 10.7	27 58.0	4 55.8	23 6.7	1 24.1	25 33.6	26 55.7	15 19.1
16 Th	5 35 31	23 16 33	12♉ 4 7	19 2 48	7 12.6	2 16.5	29 13.5	5 2.2	23 17.1	1 30.9	25 34.1	26 55.2	15 18.0
17 F	5 39 27	24 17 36	25 58 57	2♊52 11	7 10.7	3 25.3	0♑28.9	5 9.3	23 27.6	1 37.7	25 34.6	26 54.6	15 16.8
18 Sa	5 43 24	25 18 39	9♊42 7	16 28 26	7 9.3	4 36.9	1 44.3	5 17.1	23 38.2	1 44.5	25 35.3	26 54.0	15 15.7
19 Su	5 47 20	26 19 42	23 10 52	29 49 12	7 8.3	5 50.8	2 59.7	5 25.5	23 48.9	1 51.2	25 35.9	26 53.4	15 14.5
20 M	5 51 17	27 20 47	6♋23 17	12♋53 2	7D 8.0	7 6.8	4 15.2	5 34.7	23 59.7	1 58.0	25 36.7	26 52.7	15 13.3
21 Tu	5 55 13	28 21 51	19 18 26	25 39 34	7 8.2	8 24.7	5 30.6	5 44.4	24 10.7	2 4.6	25 37.4	26 52.1	15 12.1
22 W	5 59 10	29 22 57	1♌56 33	8♌ 9 36	7 8.8	9 44.1	6 46.0	5 54.8	24 21.7	2 11.3	25 38.2	26 51.4	15 10.9
23 Th	6 3 6	0♑24 3	14 19 0	20 25 5	7 9.6	11 4.9	8 1.4	6 5.9	24 32.9	2 17.9	25 39.1	26 50.6	15 9.7
24 F	6 7 3	1 25 9	26 28 15	2♍28 55	7 10.3	12 26.9	9 16.8	6 17.5	24 44.1	2 24.5	25 40.0	26 49.8	15 8.5
25 Sa	6 11 0	2 26 16	8♍27 36	14 24 49	7 10.9	13 50.0	10 32.2	6 29.7	24 55.5	2 31.0	25 41.0	26 49.0	15 7.3
26 Su	6 14 56	3 27 24	20 21 6	26 17 3	7 11.2	15 14.1	11 47.7	6 42.5	25 6.9	2 37.5	25 42.0	26 48.2	15 6.0
27 M	6 18 53	4 28 32	2♎13 15	8♎10 16	7R 11.3	16 39.1	13 3.1	6 55.9	25 18.4	2 43.9	25 43.1	26 47.3	15 4.8
28 Tu	6 22 49	5 29 41	14 8 44	20 9 14	7 11.3	18 4.8	14 18.5	7 9.8	25 30.1	2 50.4	25 44.2	26 46.4	15 3.6
29 W	6 26 46	6 30 50	26 12 19	2♏18 33	7D 11.2	19 31.3	15 33.9	7 24.3	25 41.8	2 56.7	25 45.4	26 45.5	15 2.3
30 Th	6 30 42	7 32 0	8♏28 25	14 42 24	7 11.2	20 58.4	16 49.3	7 39.3	25 53.6	3 3.1	25 46.6	26 44.6	15 1.1
31 F	6 34 39	8 33 10	21 0 54	27 24 14	7 11.3	22 26.2	18 4.7	7 54.9	26 5.5	3 9.3	25 47.8	26 43.6	14 59.8

Astro Data Dy Hr Mn	Planet Ingress Dy Hr Mn	Last Aspect Dy Hr Mn	☽ Ingress Dy Hr Mn	Last Aspect Dy Hr Mn	☽ Ingress Dy Hr Mn	☽ Phases & Eclipses Dy Hr Mn	Astro Data
☽0S 3 2:51	♀ ♐ 22 18:12	1 19:59 ♄ ✶	♎ 2 3:22	1 16:48 ♆ ✶	♏ 1 22:39	5 14:34 ● 12♏26	1 NOVEMBER 1926
♄□♆ 6 4:57	☉ ♐ 23 1:28	4 8:24 ♆ ✶	♏ 4 14:37	4 1:57 ♆ □	♐ 4 7:32	12 23:01 ☽ 19♒49	Julian Day # 9801
☿ R 15 15:18	☿ ♏ 28 5:05	6 18:01 ♄ ☌	♐ 6 23:51	6 8:30 ♆ △	♑ 6 13:52	19 16:21 ○ 26♉35	Delta T 24.4 sec
☽0N 16 14:08		9 1:29 ♆ △	♑ 9 7:11	8 11:17 ☿ ✶	♒ 8 18:22	27 7:15 ☽ 4♍17	SVP 06♓17'11"
♆ R 29 23:02	♄ ♐ 2 22:34	11 8:11 ♄ ✶	♒ 11 12:42	10 17:04 ☿ □	♓ 10 21:44		Obliquity 23°26'54"
☽0S 30 11:26	☿ ♐ 13 20:38	13 12:27 ♄ □	♓ 13 16:22	12 23:05 ☿ △	♈ 13 0:33	5 6:11 ● 12♐21	⚷ Chiron 29♈26.9R
	♀ ♑ 16 14:48	15 15:04 ♄ △	♈ 15 18:28	14 23:55 ♀ △	♉ 15 3:23	12 6:47 ☽ 19♓30	☽ Mean ☊ 10♋12.2
☿ D 5 11:23	☉ ♑ 22 14:33	17 14:51 ♆ △	♉ 17 19:54	17 1:37 ♆ □	♊ 17 6:59	19 6:09 ○ 26♊35	
♅ D 5 13:51		19 19:30 ♄ ☍	♊ 19 22:10	19 6:41 ♆ ✶	♋ 19 12:20	19 6:20 ☍A 1.026	1 DECEMBER 1926
♄⚼♇ 6 21:53		21 21:26 ♆ ✶	♋ 22 2:54	21 11:57 ♅ △	♌ 21 20:17	27 4:59 ☽ 4♎41	Julian Day # 9831
♂ D 7 2:25		24 9:12 ♄ △	♌ 24 11:10	24 0:43 ♆ ☌	♍ 24 7:02		Delta T 24.4 sec
☽0N 13 21:12		26 21:09 ♄ □	♍ 26 22:36	26 10:50 ♅ ☍	♎ 26 19:31		SVP 06♓17'07"
☽0S 27 20:14		29 10:23 ♄ ✶	♎ 29 11:14	29 1:05 ♆ ✶	♏ 29 7:28		Obliquity 23°26'54"
♃⚺♅ 29 8:04				31 10:43 ♆ □	♐ 31 16:50		⚷ Chiron 28♈12.2R
							☽ Mean ☊ 8♋36.9

LONGITUDE — JANUARY 1927

Day	Sid.Time	☉	0 hr ☽	Noon ☽	True ☊	☿	♀	♂	♃	♄	♅	♆	♇
1 Sa	6 38 35	9♑34 20	3♐52 41	10♐26 25	7♋11.6	23♐54.4	19♑20.0	8♉10.9	26♒17.5	3♐15.6	25♓49.2	26♌42.6	14♋58.6
2 Su	6 42 32	10 35 31	17 5 29	23 49 51	7 11.8	25 23.3	20 35.4	8 27.5	26 29.6	3 21.8	25 50.5	26R 41.6	14R 57.3
3 M	6 46 29	11 36 42	0♑39 23	7♑33 50	7R 12.0	26 52.6	21 50.8	8 44.6	26 41.8	3 27.9	25 51.9	26 40.5	14 56.0
4 Tu	6 50 25	12 37 53	14 32 50	21 35 55	7 12.0	28 22.3	23 6.2	9 2.1	26 54.1	3 34.0	25 53.4	26 39.4	14 54.8
5 W	6 54 22	13 39 5	28 42 34	5♒52 10	7 11.7	29 52.6	24 21.6	9 20.1	27 6.4	3 40.1	25 54.9	26 38.3	14 53.5
6 Th	6 58 18	14 40 15	13♒ 4 2	20 17 30	7 11.0	1♑23.3	25 36.9	9 38.6	27 18.8	3 46.1	25 56.5	26 37.2	14 52.3
7 F	7 2 15	15 41 26	27 31 51	4♓46 25	7 10.0	2 54.4	26 52.3	9 57.5	27 31.3	3 52.0	25 58.1	26 36.0	14 51.0
8 Sa	7 6 11	16 42 36	12♓ 0 33	19 13 40	7 8.9	4 25.9	28 7.6	10 16.9	27 43.9	3 57.9	25 59.7	26 34.8	14 49.7
9 Su	7 10 8	17 43 46	26 25 15	3♈34 50	7 7.9	5 57.9	29 23.0	10 36.7	27 56.6	4 3.8	26 1.4	26 33.6	14 48.5
10 M	7 14 5	18 44 55	10♈42 3	17 46 36	7D 7.3	7 30.3	0♒38.3	10 56.9	28 9.3	4 9.5	26 3.1	26 32.4	14 47.2
11 Tu	7 18 1	19 46 4	24 48 16	1♉46 54	7 7.3	9 3.2	1 53.6	11 17.5	28 22.1	4 15.3	26 4.9	26 31.1	14 45.9
12 W	7 21 58	20 47 12	8♉42 22	15 34 37	7 7.8	10 36.5	3 8.9	11 38.5	28 34.9	4 20.9	26 6.7	26 29.8	14 44.7
13 Th	7 25 54	21 48 19	22 23 38	29 9 23	7 8.9	12 10.2	4 24.2	11 59.9	28 47.9	4 26.5	26 8.6	26 28.5	14 43.4
14 F	7 29 51	22 49 26	5♊51 55	12♊31 14	7 10.2	13 44.4	5 39.5	12 21.6	29 0.9	4 32.1	26 10.5	26 27.2	14 42.2
15 Sa	7 33 47	23 50 32	19 7 22	25 40 19	7 11.4	15 19.1	6 54.7	12 43.7	29 13.9	4 37.6	26 12.5	26 25.9	14 40.9
16 Su	7 37 44	24 51 38	2♋10 8	8♋36 51	7R 12.1	16 54.3	8 10.0	13 6.2	29 27.1	4 43.0	26 14.5	26 24.5	14 39.7
17 M	7 41 40	25 52 43	15 0 28	21 21 2	7 12.0	18 30.0	9 25.2	13 29.0	29 40.3	4 48.4	26 16.5	26 23.1	14 38.4
18 Tu	7 45 37	26 53 47	27 38 36	3♌53 13	7 10.8	20 6.2	10 40.4	13 52.1	29 53.5	4 53.7	26 18.6	26 21.7	14 37.2
19 W	7 49 34	27 54 51	10♌ 5 0	16 14 1	7 8.6	21 42.9	11 55.6	14 15.6	0♓ 6.8	4 58.9	26 20.7	26 20.3	14 36.0
20 Th	7 53 30	28 55 54	22 20 28	28 24 29	7 5.3	23 20.1	13 10.8	14 39.3	0 20.2	5 4.1	26 22.9	26 18.9	14 34.8
21 F	7 57 27	29 56 57	4♍26 20	10♍26 15	7 1.4	24 58.0	14 26.0	15 3.4	0 33.6	5 9.2	26 25.1	26 17.4	14 33.5
22 Sa	8 1 23	0♒57 59	16 24 34	22 21 38	6 57.3	26 36.4	15 41.2	15 27.8	0 47.1	5 14.2	26 27.3	26 15.9	14 32.3
23 Su	8 5 20	1 59 1	28 17 50	4♎13 37	6 53.4	28 15.4	16 56.3	15 52.5	1 0.6	5 19.1	26 29.6	26 14.5	14 31.1
24 M	8 9 16	3 0 2	10♎ 9 29	16 5 55	6 50.2	29 55.0	18 11.4	16 17.4	1 14.2	5 24.0	26 31.9	26 12.9	14 29.9
25 Tu	8 13 13	4 1 3	22 3 30	28 2 46	6 48.2	1♒35.2	19 26.6	16 42.6	1 27.8	5 28.9	26 34.2	26 11.4	14 28.7
26 W	8 17 9	5 2 3	4♏ 4 21	10♏ 8 49	6D 47.4	3 16.0	20 41.7	17 8.1	1 41.5	5 33.6	26 36.6	26 9.9	14 27.6
27 Th	8 21 6	6 3 2	16 16 47	22 28 52	6 47.9	4 57.5	21 56.8	17 33.9	1 55.2	5 38.3	26 39.1	26 8.3	14 26.4
28 F	8 25 3	7 4 1	28 45 36	5♐ 7 33	6 49.3	6 39.6	23 11.8	17 59.9	2 9.0	5 42.9	26 41.5	26 6.8	14 25.2
29 Sa	8 28 59	8 5 0	11♐35 10	18 8 52	6 51.0	8 22.4	24 26.9	18 26.2	2 22.8	5 47.4	26 44.0	26 5.2	14 24.1
30 Su	8 32 56	9 5 57	24 48 57	1♑35 38	6R 52.5	10 5.9	25 42.0	18 52.7	2 36.6	5 51.8	26 46.6	26 3.6	14 23.0
31 M	8 36 52	10 6 54	8♑28 57	15 28 49	6 53.0	11 50.0	26 57.0	19 19.5	2 50.5	5 56.2	26 49.1	26 2.0	14 21.8

LONGITUDE — FEBRUARY 1927

Day	Sid.Time	☉	0 hr ☽	Noon ☽	True ☊	☿	♀	♂	♃	♄	♅	♆	♇
1 Tu	8 40 49	11♒ 7 51	22♑34 57	29♑46 56	6♋52.0	13♒34.7	28♒12.0	19♉46.5	3♓ 4.5	6♐ 0.5	26♓51.8	26♌ 0.4	14♋20.7
2 W	8 44 45	12 8 46	7♒ 4 9	14♒25 47	6R 49.2	15 20.0	29 27.0	20 13.8	3 18.5	6 4.7	26 54.4	25R 58.8	14R 19.6
3 Th	8 48 42	13 9 40	21 50 56	29 18 32	6 44.8	17 6.0	0♓42.0	20 41.3	3 32.5	6 8.9	26 57.1	25 57.2	14 18.5
4 F	8 52 38	14 10 33	6♓47 28	14♓16 31	6 39.2	18 52.5	1 56.9	21 9.0	3 46.5	6 12.9	26 59.8	25 55.5	14 17.4
5 Sa	8 56 35	15 11 24	21 44 47	29 10 59	6 33.2	20 39.5	3 11.9	21 36.9	4 0.6	6 16.9	27 2.5	25 53.9	14 16.4
6 Su	9 0 32	16 12 14	6♈34 15	13♈53 45	6 27.6	22 27.0	4 26.8	22 5.0	4 14.7	6 20.7	27 5.3	25 52.2	14 15.3
7 M	9 4 28	17 13 3	21 8 51	28 19 4	6 23.3	24 14.9	5 41.7	22 33.3	4 28.9	6 24.5	27 8.0	25 50.6	14 14.3
8 Tu	9 8 25	18 13 50	5♉24 5	12♉23 45	6 20.7	26 3.1	6 56.5	23 1.8	4 43.1	6 28.3	27 10.9	25 48.9	14 13.2
9 W	9 12 21	19 14 36	19 18 1	26 7 0	6D 19.9	27 51.4	8 11.4	23 30.6	4 57.3	6 31.9	27 13.7	25 47.3	14 12.2
10 Th	9 16 18	20 15 20	2♊50 52	9♊29 53	6 20.5	29 39.8	9 26.2	23 59.5	5 11.5	6 35.4	27 16.6	25 45.6	14 11.2
11 F	9 20 14	21 16 3	16 4 21	22 34 34	6 21.9	1♓28.1	10 41.0	24 28.6	5 25.8	6 38.9	27 19.5	25 43.9	14 10.3
12 Sa	9 24 11	22 16 44	29 0 54	5♋23 41	6R 23.1	3 16.1	11 55.7	24 57.8	5 40.0	6 42.2	27 22.4	25 42.2	14 9.3
13 Su	9 28 7	23 17 23	11♋43 12	17 59 47	6 23.2	5 3.6	13 10.4	25 27.3	5 54.4	6 45.5	27 25.4	25 40.6	14 8.3
14 M	9 32 4	24 18 1	24 13 41	0♌25 8	6 21.4	6 50.2	14 25.1	25 56.9	6 8.7	6 48.7	27 28.4	25 38.9	14 7.4
15 Tu	9 36 1	25 18 37	6♌34 22	12 41 33	6 17.3	8 35.7	15 39.8	26 26.6	6 23.0	6 51.8	27 31.4	25 37.2	14 6.5
16 W	9 39 57	26 19 11	18 46 52	24 50 28	6 10.8	10 19.7	16 54.4	26 56.5	6 37.4	6 54.8	27 34.4	25 35.5	14 5.6
17 Th	9 43 54	27 19 44	0♍52 28	6♍53 2	6 2.2	12 1.8	18 9.0	27 26.6	6 51.8	6 57.7	27 37.5	25 33.8	14 4.7
18 F	9 47 50	28 20 16	12 52 19	18 50 27	5 52.0	13 41.6	19 23.6	27 56.8	7 6.2	7 0.6	27 40.6	25 32.1	14 3.9
19 Sa	9 51 47	29 20 46	24 47 39	0♎44 7	5 41.2	15 18.5	20 38.1	28 27.2	7 20.6	7 3.3	27 43.7	25 30.5	14 3.0
20 Su	9 55 43	0♓21 14	6♎40 6	12 35 53	5 30.7	16 52.0	21 52.6	28 57.7	7 35.0	7 5.9	27 46.8	25 28.8	14 2.2
21 M	9 59 40	1 21 41	18 31 49	24 28 15	5 21.5	18 21.6	23 7.1	29 28.3	7 49.4	7 8.5	27 49.9	25 27.1	14 1.4
22 Tu	10 3 36	2 22 7	0♏25 37	6♏24 23	5 14.2	19 46.5	24 21.5	29 59.1	8 3.9	7 10.9	27 53.1	25 25.4	14 0.6
23 W	10 7 33	3 22 31	12 25 3	18 28 11	5 9.4	21 6.2	25 35.9	0♊30.0	8 18.3	7 13.3	27 56.3	25 23.8	13 59.8
24 Th	10 11 30	4 22 54	24 34 20	0♐44 7	5D 6.9	22 20.0	26 50.3	1 1.0	8 32.8	7 15.5	27 59.4	25 22.1	13 59.1
25 F	10 15 26	5 23 16	6♐58 8	13 17 1	5 6.4	23 27.2	28 4.6	1 32.2	8 47.3	7 17.7	28 2.7	25 20.4	13 58.3
26 Sa	10 19 23	6 23 36	19 41 21	26 11 42	5 6.9	24 27.3	29 18.9	2 3.5	9 1.7	7 19.7	28 5.9	25 18.8	13 57.6
27 Su	10 23 19	7 23 55	2♑48 34	9♑32 22	5R 7.5	25 19.7	0♈33.2	2 34.9	9 16.2	7 21.7	28 9.2	25 17.1	13 56.9
28 M	10 27 16	8 24 12	16 23 24	23 21 49	5 7.0	26 3.8	1 47.5	3 6.4	9 30.7	7 23.6	28 12.4	25 15.5	13 56.2

Astro Data (Dy Hr Mn)

♃☍♆	2 21:39
☽0N	10 2:36
♃⚼♇	16 20:59
♅⚻♆	18 21:22
☽0S	24 3:58
☽0N	6 8:50
♃□♄	17 12:25
☽0S	20 10:18
☿0N	27 9:37
♀0N	28 12:23

Planet Ingress (Dy Hr Mn)

☿	♑	5 1:58
♀	♒	9 11:48
♃	♓	18 11:44
☉	♒	21 1:12
☿	♒	24 1:13
♀	♓	2 10:33
☿	♓	10 4:28
☉	♓	19 15:34
♂	♊	22 0:43
♀	♈	26 13:16

Last Aspect / ☽ Ingress (Dy Hr Mn)

Last Aspect			☽ Ingress	
2 17:02	♆	△	♑	2 22:51
4 19:17	♅	⚹	♒	5 2:10
6 23:59	♃	☌	♓	7 4:05
9 5:26	♀	⚹	♈	9 5:59
11 6:13	♃	⚹	♉	11 8:56
13 11:33	♃	□	♊	13 13:30
15 18:53	♃	△	♋	15 19:59
17 22:27	☉	☍	♌	18 4:31
20 7:50	♆	☌	♍	20 15:10
22 23:54	☿	△	♎	23 3:27
25 8:16	♆	⚹	♏	25 15:54
27 20:03	♅	△	♐	28 2:21
30 3:30	♅	□	♑	30 9:12

Last Aspect / ☽ Ingress (Dy Hr Mn)

Last Aspect			☽ Ingress	
1 7:10	♅	⚹	♒	1 12:22
3 6:36	♆	☍	♓	3 13:07
5 8:34	♅	☌	♈	5 13:19
7 7:50	♆	△	♉	7 14:50
9 17:25	☿	□	♊	9 18:54
11 20:55	♅	□	♋	12 1:51
14 6:18	♅	△	♌	14 11:11
16 16:52	♂	□	♍	16 22:15
19 7:43	♂	△	♎	19 10:31
21 13:57	♆	⚹	♏	21 23:08
24 6:42	♅	△	♐	24 10:35
26 15:32	♅	□	♑	26 18:56
28 20:17	♅	⚹	♒	28 23:14

☽ Phases & Eclipses (Dy Hr Mn)

3 20:28	● 12♑29
3 20:22:27	☽ A 0'02"
10 14:43	☽ 19♈22
17 22:27	○ 26♋50
26 2:05	☽ 5♏07
2 8:54	● 12♒31
8 23:54	☽ 19♉14
16 16:18	○ 27♌00
24 20:42	☽ 5♐15

Astro Data

1 JANUARY 1927
Julian Day # 9862
Delta T 24.5 sec
SVP 06♓17'02"
Obliquity 23°26'54"
⚷ Chiron 27♈33.1R
☽ Mean ☊ 6♋58.4

1 FEBRUARY 1927
Julian Day # 9893
Delta T 24.5 sec
SVP 06♓16'56"
Obliquity 23°26'55"
⚷ Chiron 27♈47.6
☽ Mean ☊ 5♋19.9

MARCH 1927 LONGITUDE

Day	Sid.Time	☉	0 hr ☽	Noon ☽	True ☊	☿	♀	♂	♃	♄	♅	♆	♇
1 Tu	10 31 12	9♓24 28	0♒27 37	7♒40 32	5♋ 4.4	26♓39.3	3♈ 1.7	3♊38.1	9♓45.2	7♐25.4	28♓15.7	25♌13.9	13♋55.6
2 W	10 35 9	10 24 42	15 0 10	22 25 49	4R 59.3	27 5.6	4 15.8	4 9.9	9 59.7	7 27.0	28 19.0	25R 12.3	13R 55.0
3 Th	10 39 5	11 24 55	29 56 35	7♓31 21	4 51.6	27 22.7	5 30.0	4 41.8	10 14.2	7 28.6	28 22.3	25 10.7	13 54.4
4 F	10 43 2	12 25 5	15♓ 8 51	22 47 39	4 42.0	27R 30.4	6 44.1	5 13.7	10 28.7	7 30.1	28 25.6	25 9.1	13 53.8
5 Sa	10 46 59	13 25 14	0♈26 20	8♈ 3 26	4 31.5	27 28.7	7 58.1	5 45.9	10 43.2	7 31.4	28 29.0	25 7.5	13 53.2
6 Su	10 50 55	14 25 21	15 37 38	23 7 42	4 21.4	27 17.8	9 12.2	6 18.1	10 57.7	7 32.7	28 32.3	25 5.9	13 52.7
7 M	10 54 52	15 25 26	0♉32 39	7♉51 40	4 13.0	26 58.0	10 26.1	6 50.4	11 12.1	7 33.9	28 35.7	25 4.3	13 52.1
8 Tu	10 58 48	16 25 29	15 4 12	22 9 55	4 7.0	26 30.0	11 40.1	7 22.8	11 26.6	7 34.9	28 39.0	25 2.8	13 51.6
9 W	11 2 45	17 25 29	29 8 42	6♊ 0 35	4 3.6	25 54.5	12 54.0	7 55.3	11 41.1	7 35.9	28 42.4	25 1.2	13 51.2
10 Th	11 6 41	18 25 28	12♊45 47	19 24 38	4D 2.4	25 12.3	14 7.8	8 27.9	11 55.5	7 36.8	28 45.8	24 59.7	13 50.7
11 F	11 10 38	19 25 24	25 57 33	2♋25 1	4R 2.3	24 24.4	15 21.6	9 0.6	12 10.0	7 37.5	28 49.2	24 58.2	13 50.3
12 Sa	11 14 34	20 25 19	8♋47 32	15 5 38	4 2.4	23 32.2	16 35.4	9 33.4	12 24.4	7 38.2	28 52.6	24 56.7	13 49.9
13 Su	11 18 31	21 25 10	21 19 51	27 30 40	4 1.3	22 36.7	17 49.1	10 6.3	12 38.8	7 38.8	28 56.0	24 55.2	13 49.5
14 M	11 22 28	22 25 0	3♌38 34	9♌43 59	3 57.9	21 39.4	19 2.7	10 39.2	12 53.2	7 39.2	28 59.4	24 53.8	13 49.1
15 Tu	11 26 24	23 24 48	15 47 20	21 48 57	3 51.8	20 41.6	20 16.3	11 12.2	13 7.6	7 39.6	29 2.8	24 52.3	13 48.8
16 W	11 30 21	24 24 33	27 49 9	3♍48 13	3 42.7	19 44.4	21 29.9	11 45.3	13 21.9	7 39.8	29 6.2	24 50.9	13 48.5
17 Th	11 34 17	25 24 16	9♍46 22	15 43 50	3 30.9	18 49.1	22 43.4	12 18.5	13 36.3	7 40.0	29 9.6	24 49.5	13 48.2
18 F	11 38 14	26 23 57	21 40 46	27 37 20	3 17.2	17 56.7	23 56.8	12 51.8	13 50.6	7R 40.0	29 13.1	24 48.1	13 47.9
19 Sa	11 42 10	27 23 36	3♎33 42	9♎30 1	3 2.5	17 8.1	25 10.2	13 25.1	14 4.9	7 40.0	29 16.5	24 46.7	13 47.7
20 Su	11 46 7	28 23 14	15 26 28	21 23 12	2 48.2	16 24.1	26 23.5	13 58.5	14 19.1	7 39.8	29 19.9	24 45.4	13 47.4
21 M	11 50 3	29 22 49	27 20 28	3♏18 29	2 35.3	15 45.2	27 36.8	14 32.0	14 33.4	7 39.6	29 23.3	24 44.1	13 47.2
22 Tu	11 54 0	0♈22 22	9♏17 31	15 17 56	2 24.8	15 11.8	28 50.1	15 5.5	14 47.6	7 39.2	29 26.8	24 42.7	13 47.1
23 W	11 57 56	1 21 53	21 20 3	27 24 19	2 17.1	14 44.3	0♉ 3.2	15 39.1	15 1.8	7 38.8	29 30.2	24 41.5	13 46.9
24 Th	12 1 53	2 21 23	3♐31 10	9♐41 6	2 12.4	14 22.8	1 16.4	16 12.8	15 16.0	7 38.3	29 33.6	24 40.2	13 46.8
25 F	12 5 50	3 20 51	15 54 39	22 12 22	2 10.3	14 7.3	2 29.5	16 46.5	15 30.2	7 37.6	29 37.1	24 38.9	13 46.7
26 Sa	12 9 46	4 20 17	28 34 48	5♑ 2 31	2 9.7	13 57.9	3 42.5	17 20.3	15 44.3	7 36.9	29 40.5	24 37.7	13 46.6
27 Su	12 13 43	5 19 42	11♑36 4	18 15 55	2 9.7	13D 54.4	4 55.5	17 54.2	15 58.4	7 36.0	29 43.9	24 36.5	13 46.6
28 M	12 17 39	6 19 5	25 2 30	1♒56 7	2 8.8	13 56.6	6 8.4	18 28.1	16 12.4	7 35.1	29 47.3	24 35.3	13D 46.5
29 Tu	12 21 36	7 18 25	8♒56 57	16 4 58	2 6.2	14 4.4	7 21.2	19 2.1	16 26.5	7 34.0	29 50.7	24 34.2	13 46.5
30 W	12 25 32	8 17 45	23 20 1	0♓41 38	2 0.9	14 17.5	8 34.0	19 36.1	16 40.5	7 32.9	29 54.1	24 33.1	13 46.6
31 Th	12 29 29	9 17 2	8♓ 9 11	15 41 46	1 53.0	14 35.8	9 46.8	20 10.2	16 54.4	7 31.7	29 57.5	24 32.0	13 46.6

APRIL 1927 LONGITUDE

Day	Sid.Time	☉	0 hr ☽	Noon ☽	True ☊	☿	♀	♂	♃	♄	♅	♆	♇
1 F	12 33 25	10♈16 17	23♓18 15	0♈57 20	1♋43.0	14♓58.9	10♉59.5	20♊44.4	17♓ 8.3	7♐30.3	0♈ 0.9	24♌30.9	13♋46.7
2 Sa	12 37 22	11 15 31	8♈37 36	16 17 33	1R 31.9	15 26.7	12 12.1	21 18.6	17 22.2	7R 28.9	0 4.3	24R 29.8	13 46.7
3 Su	12 41 19	12 14 42	23 55 43	1♉30 41	1 21.0	15 58.8	13 24.7	21 52.9	17 36.1	7 27.4	0 7.7	24 28.8	13 46.9
4 M	12 45 15	13 13 51	9♉ 1 13	16 26 14	1 11.7	16 35.1	14 37.2	22 27.2	17 49.9	7 25.8	0 11.1	24 27.8	13 47.0
5 Tu	12 49 12	14 12 58	23 44 54	0♊56 39	1 4.9	17 15.3	15 49.7	23 1.6	18 3.6	7 24.1	0 14.4	24 26.8	13 47.2
6 W	12 53 8	15 12 3	8♊ 1 7	14 58 9	1 0.7	17 59.2	17 2.1	23 36.1	18 17.3	7 22.2	0 17.8	24 25.9	13 47.4
7 Th	12 57 5	16 11 6	21 47 49	28 30 21	0D 59.0	18 46.7	18 14.4	24 10.6	18 31.0	7 20.4	0 21.1	24 25.0	13 47.6
8 F	13 1 1	17 10 6	5♋ 6 5	11♋35 29	0 58.8	19 37.5	19 26.6	24 45.1	18 44.6	7 18.4	0 24.4	24 24.1	13 47.8
9 Sa	13 4 58	18 9 4	17 59 4	24 17 25	0R 59.0	20 31.4	20 38.8	25 19.7	18 58.2	7 16.3	0 27.7	24 23.2	13 48.1
10 Su	13 8 54	19 8 0	0♌31 8	6♌40 48	0 58.4	21 28.4	21 50.9	25 54.3	19 11.7	7 14.1	0 31.0	24 22.4	13 48.4
11 M	13 12 51	20 6 53	12 47 1	18 50 20	0 56.1	22 28.2	23 3.0	26 29.0	19 25.2	7 11.9	0 34.3	24 21.6	13 48.7
12 Tu	13 16 48	21 5 45	24 51 19	0♍50 28	0 51.3	23 30.7	24 15.0	27 3.7	19 38.6	7 9.6	0 37.6	24 20.8	13 49.0
13 W	13 20 44	22 4 33	6♍48 13	12 44 59	0 43.9	24 35.9	25 26.8	27 38.4	19 51.9	7 7.1	0 40.8	24 20.1	13 49.4
14 Th	13 24 41	23 3 20	18 41 9	24 37 2	0 34.0	25 43.6	26 38.7	28 13.2	20 5.2	7 4.6	0 44.1	24 19.3	13 49.7
15 F	13 28 37	24 2 4	0♎32 55	6♎29 3	0 22.4	26 53.6	27 50.4	28 48.1	20 18.5	7 2.1	0 47.3	24 18.7	13 50.1
16 Sa	13 32 34	25 0 47	12 25 39	18 22 55	0 10.0	28 6.0	29 2.1	29 22.9	20 31.7	6 59.4	0 50.5	24 18.0	13 50.6
17 Su	13 36 30	25 59 27	24 21 0	0♏20 5	29♊57.7	29 20.6	0♊13.6	29 57.8	20 44.8	6 56.6	0 53.7	24 17.4	13 51.0
18 M	13 40 27	26 58 6	6♏20 19	12 21 52	29 46.8	0♈37.4	1 25.2	0♋32.8	20 57.9	6 53.8	0 56.9	24 16.8	13 51.5
19 Tu	13 44 23	27 56 42	18 24 55	24 29 40	29 37.8	1 56.2	2 36.6	1 7.8	21 10.9	6 50.9	1 0.0	24 16.2	13 52.0
20 W	13 48 20	28 55 17	0♐36 20	6♐45 11	29 31.5	3 17.1	3 47.9	1 42.8	21 23.9	6 47.9	1 3.1	24 15.7	13 52.5
21 Th	13 52 16	29 53 50	12 56 30	19 10 37	29 27.7	4 40.0	4 59.2	2 17.8	21 36.8	6 44.9	1 6.3	24 15.2	13 53.0
22 F	13 56 13	0♉52 21	25 27 53	1♑48 40	29D 26.3	6 4.9	6 10.4	2 52.9	21 49.6	6 41.8	1 9.4	24 14.7	13 53.6
23 Sa	14 0 10	1 50 51	8♑13 24	14 42 29	29 26.5	7 31.6	7 21.5	3 28.1	22 2.4	6 38.6	1 12.4	24 14.3	13 54.2
24 Su	14 4 6	2 49 19	21 16 20	27 55 20	29R 27.4	9 0.3	8 32.5	4 3.2	22 15.1	6 35.3	1 15.5	24 13.8	13 54.8
25 M	14 8 3	3 47 45	4♒39 50	11♒30 7	29 27.8	10 30.8	9 43.5	4 38.4	22 27.7	6 32.0	1 18.5	24 13.5	13 55.4
26 Tu	14 11 59	4 46 10	18 26 23	25 28 43	29 26.9	12 3.1	10 54.3	5 13.7	22 40.3	6 28.6	1 21.5	24 13.1	13 56.1
27 W	14 15 56	5 44 34	2♓37 2	9♓51 7	29 24.1	13 37.3	12 5.1	5 48.9	22 52.8	6 25.1	1 24.5	24 12.8	13 56.8
28 Th	14 19 52	6 42 55	17 10 31	24 34 40	29 19.2	15 13.3	13 15.8	6 24.2	23 5.2	6 21.6	1 27.4	24 12.5	13 57.5
29 F	14 23 49	7 41 15	2♈ 2 44	9♈33 46	29 12.6	16 51.1	14 26.4	6 59.6	23 17.5	6 18.0	1 30.4	24 12.3	13 58.2
30 Sa	14 27 45	8 39 34	17 6 38	24 40 6	29 5.0	18 30.7	15 36.9	7 34.9	23 29.8	6 14.4	1 33.3	24 12.1	13 58.9

Astro Data	Dy Hr Mn
☿ R	4 7:34
☽ 0 N	5 17:39
☿ 0 S	13 18:42
♃ △ ♇	17 19:37
♄ R	18 0:48
☽ 0 S	19 16:00
☿ D	27 2:33
♇ D	28 16:02
☽ 0 N	2 4:27
☽ 0 S	15 22:06
☿ 0 N	22 3:11
☽ 0 N	29 15:15

Planet Ingress	Dy Hr Mn
☉ ♈	21 14:59
♀ ♉	22 22:56
♅ ♈	31 17:25
♀ ♊	16 19:25
☊ ♊	16 19:27
☿ ♈	17 12:24
♂ ♋	17 1:29
☉ ♉	21 2:32

Last Aspect Dy Hr Mn		☽ Ingress Dy Hr Mn
2 16:25	♆ ☍	♓ 3 0:05
4 20:55	♅ ☌	♈ 4 23:19
6 15:09	♆ △	♉ 6 23:07
8 23:14	♅ ⚹	♊ 9 1:29
11 5:19	♅ □	♋ 11 7:29
13 14:51	♅ △	♌ 13 16:52
15 18:04	♆ ☌	♍ 16 4:22
18 15:18	♅ ☍	♎ 18 16:48
21 0:37	♀ ☍	♏ 21 5:21
23 16:12	♅ △	♐ 23 17:06
26 2:03	♅ □	♑ 26 2:39
28 8:19	♅ ⚹	♒ 28 8:39
30 2:00	♆ ☍	♓ 30 10:53

Last Aspect Dy Hr Mn		☽ Ingress Dy Hr Mn
31 19:48	♂ □	♈ 1 10:30
3 0:52	♆ △	♉ 3 9:36
5 1:09	♆ □	♊ 5 10:25
7 4:39	♆ ⚹	♋ 7 14:42
9 5:35	♀ ⚹	♌ 9 23:00
12 4:38	♂ ⚹	♍ 12 10:19
14 20:17	♂ □	♎ 14 22:53
17 3:35	☉ ☍	♏ 17 11:20
19 11:33	♆ □	♐ 19 22:49
21 21:41	♆ △	♑ 22 8:35
24 1:48	♃ ⚹	♒ 24 15:43
26 9:52	♆ ☍	♓ 26 19:37
28 9:43	♃ ☌	♈ 28 20:43
30 11:15	♆ △	♉ 30 20:28

☽ Phases & Eclipses Dy Hr Mn	
3 19:24	● 12♓14
10 11:03	☽ 18♊53
18 10:24	○ 26♍50
26 11:35	☽ 4♑49
2 4:24	● 11♈26
9 0:20	☽ 18♋10
17 3:35	○ 26♎08
24 22:21	☽ 3♒44

Astro Data

1 MARCH 1927
Julian Day # 9921
Delta T 24.5 sec
SVP 06♓16'53"
Obliquity 23°26'55"
⚷ Chiron 28♈44.8
☽ Mean ☊ 3♋51.0

1 APRIL 1927
Julian Day # 9952
Delta T 24.5 sec
SVP 06♓16'50"
Obliquity 23°26'56"
⚷ Chiron 0♉22.7
☽ Mean ☊ 2♋12.5

LONGITUDE — MAY 1927

Day	Sid.Time	☉	0 hr ☽	Noon ☽	True ☊	☿	♀	♂	♃	♄	♅	♆	♇
1 Su	14 31 42	9♉37 50	2♉12 56	9♉43 52	28♊57.4	20♈12.1	16♊47.3	8♋10.3	23♓42.0	6♐10.7	1♈36.2	24♌11.9	13♋59.7
2 M	14 35 39	10 36 6	17 11 42	24 35 20	28R 50.9	21 55.4	17 57.7	8 45.8	23 54.1	6R 6.9	1 39.0	24R 11.7	14 0.4
3 Tu	14 39 35	11 34 19	1♊53 52	9♊ 6 33	28 46.2	23 40.4	19 7.9	9 21.2	24 6.1	6 3.1	1 41.8	24 11.6	14 1.2
4 W	14 43 32	12 32 31	16 12 49	23 12 20	28D 43.6	25 27.3	20 18.0	9 56.7	24 18.0	5 59.2	1 44.6	24 11.5	14 2.1
5 Th	14 47 28	13 30 40	0♋ 4 56	6♋50 38	28 43.0	27 16.0	21 28.1	10 32.3	24 29.9	5 55.3	1 47.4	24D 11.5	14 2.9
6 F	14 51 25	14 28 48	13 29 35	20 2 4	28 43.7	29 6.5	22 38.0	11 7.8	24 41.7	5 51.3	1 50.1	24 11.5	14 3.8
7 Sa	14 55 21	15 26 54	26 28 29	2♌49 19	28 45.1	0♉58.9	23 47.9	11 43.4	24 53.4	5 47.3	1 52.9	24 11.5	14 4.7
8 Su	14 59 18	16 24 58	9♌ 5 5	15 16 21	28R 46.2	2 53.0	24 57.6	12 19.0	25 5.0	5 43.3	1 55.5	24 11.5	14 5.6
9 M	15 3 15	17 23 0	21 23 43	27 27 46	28 46.3	4 49.0	26 7.2	12 54.7	25 16.5	5 39.2	1 58.2	24 11.6	14 6.5
10 Tu	15 7 11	18 21 0	3♍29 6	9♍28 17	28 45.0	6 46.8	27 16.7	13 30.4	25 27.9	5 35.0	2 0.8	24 11.7	14 7.4
11 W	15 11 8	19 18 58	15 25 52	21 22 24	28 42.0	8 46.4	28 26.1	14 6.0	25 39.2	5 30.9	2 3.4	24 11.9	14 8.4
12 Th	15 15 4	20 16 54	27 18 21	3♎14 12	28 37.4	10 47.6	29 35.3	14 41.8	25 50.5	5 26.7	2 5.9	24 12.0	14 9.4
13 F	15 19 1	21 14 49	9♎10 19	15 7 7	28 31.5	12 50.6	0♋44.5	15 17.5	26 1.6	5 22.4	2 8.5	24 12.3	14 10.4
14 Sa	15 22 57	22 12 42	21 4 55	27 4 1	28 25.0	14 55.1	1 53.5	15 53.3	26 12.6	5 18.2	2 10.9	24 12.5	14 11.4
15 Su	15 26 54	23 10 33	3♏ 4 40	9♏ 7 6	28 18.5	17 1.1	3 2.4	16 29.1	26 23.6	5 13.9	2 13.4	24 12.8	14 12.4
16 M	15 30 50	24 8 23	15 11 30	21 18 3	28 12.8	19 8.5	4 11.2	17 4.9	26 34.4	5 9.5	2 15.8	24 13.1	14 13.4
17 Tu	15 34 47	25 6 11	27 26 53	3♐38 9	28 8.3	21 17.0	5 19.8	17 40.7	26 45.2	5 5.2	2 18.2	24 13.4	14 14.5
18 W	15 38 43	26 3 58	9♐51 59	16 8 30	28 5.3	23 26.7	6 28.3	18 16.6	26 55.8	5 0.8	2 20.6	24 13.8	14 15.6
19 Th	15 42 40	27 1 43	22 27 50	28 50 8	28D 3.9	25 37.1	7 36.7	18 52.4	27 6.3	4 56.4	2 22.9	24 14.2	14 16.7
20 F	15 46 37	27 59 28	5♑15 32	11♑44 12	28 4.0	27 48.2	8 45.0	19 28.3	27 16.8	4 52.0	2 25.1	24 14.7	14 17.8
21 Sa	15 50 33	28 57 11	18 16 17	24 51 58	28 5.1	29 59.7	9 53.1	20 4.3	27 27.1	4 47.6	2 27.4	24 15.1	14 19.0
22 Su	15 54 30	29 54 53	1♒31 25	8♒14 46	28 6.6	2♊11.3	11 1.1	20 40.2	27 37.3	4 43.2	2 29.6	24 15.6	14 20.1
23 M	15 58 26	0♊52 33	15 2 11	21 53 44	28 8.0	4 22.7	12 8.9	21 16.2	27 47.4	4 38.7	2 31.8	24 16.2	14 21.3
24 Tu	16 2 23	1 50 13	28 49 30	5♓49 26	28R 8.7	6 33.7	13 16.6	21 52.2	27 57.4	4 34.3	2 33.9	24 16.7	14 22.4
25 W	16 6 19	2 47 52	12♓53 28	20 1 24	28 8.4	8 44.0	14 24.1	22 28.2	28 7.3	4 29.8	2 36.0	24 17.3	14 23.6
26 Th	16 10 16	3 45 30	27 12 56	4♈27 41	28 7.0	10 53.3	15 31.5	23 4.3	28 17.1	4 25.3	2 38.0	24 18.0	14 24.9
27 F	16 14 13	4 43 7	11♈45 5	19 4 33	28 4.7	13 1.4	16 38.7	23 40.4	28 26.7	4 20.9	2 40.1	24 18.6	14 26.1
28 Sa	16 18 9	5 40 43	26 25 19	3♉46 36	28 1.8	15 7.9	17 45.8	24 16.5	28 36.3	4 16.4	2 42.0	24 19.3	14 27.3
29 Su	16 22 6	6 38 18	11♉ 7 31	18 27 13	27 58.9	17 12.8	18 52.7	24 52.6	28 45.7	4 11.9	2 44.0	24 20.1	14 28.6
30 M	16 26 2	7 35 52	25 44 48	2♊59 26	27 56.5	19 15.9	19 59.5	25 28.7	28 55.0	4 7.5	2 45.9	24 20.8	14 29.8
31 Tu	16 29 59	8 33 25	10♊10 22	17 16 56	27 54.8	21 16.8	21 6.1	26 4.9	29 4.2	4 3.0	2 47.7	24 21.6	14 31.1

LONGITUDE — JUNE 1927

Day	Sid.Time	☉	0 hr ☽	Noon ☽	True ☊	☿	♀	♂	♃	♄	♅	♆	♇
1 W	16 33 55	9♊30 57	24♊18 34	1♋14 50	27♊54.1	23♊15.6	22♋12.5	26♋41.1	29♓13.2	3♐58.6	2♈49.5	24♌22.4	14♋32.4
2 Th	16 37 52	10 28 28	8♋ 5 28	14 50 17	27D 54.3	25 12.1	23 18.8	27 17.3	29 22.1	3R 54.1	2 51.3	24 23.3	14 33.7
3 F	16 41 48	11 25 58	21 29 15	28 2 28	27 55.2	27 6.1	24 24.9	27 53.6	29 30.9	3 49.7	2 53.0	24 24.2	14 35.0
4 Sa	16 45 45	12 23 27	4♌30 6	10♌52 28	27 56.4	28 57.7	25 30.7	28 29.8	29 39.6	3 45.3	2 54.7	24 25.1	14 36.4
5 Su	16 49 42	13 20 54	17 9 54	23 22 51	27 57.7	0♋46.8	26 36.4	29 6.1	29 48.1	3 40.9	2 56.3	24 26.0	14 37.7
6 M	16 53 38	14 18 20	29 31 49	5♍37 17	27 58.6	2 33.2	27 41.9	29 42.4	29 56.5	3 36.6	2 57.9	24 27.0	14 39.1
7 Tu	16 57 35	15 15 45	11♍39 49	17 39 59	27R 59.1	4 17.0	28 47.2	0♌18.8	0♈ 4.7	3 32.2	2 59.5	24 28.0	14 40.4
8 W	17 1 31	16 13 9	23 38 21	29 35 30	27 59.0	5 58.2	29 52.3	0 55.1	0 12.8	3 27.9	3 1.0	24 29.0	14 41.8
9 Th	17 5 28	17 10 32	5♎32 0	11♎28 23	27 58.4	7 36.7	0♌57.1	1 31.5	0 20.8	3 23.6	3 2.5	24 30.1	14 43.2
10 F	17 9 24	18 7 53	17 25 11	23 22 53	27 57.4	9 12.5	2 1.8	2 7.9	0 28.6	3 19.4	3 3.9	24 31.2	14 44.6
11 Sa	17 13 21	19 5 14	29 21 59	5♏22 53	27 56.2	10 45.5	3 6.2	2 44.3	0 36.3	3 15.2	3 5.3	24 32.3	14 46.0
12 Su	17 17 17	20 2 34	11♏26 0	17 31 41	27 55.1	12 15.8	4 10.3	3 20.7	0 43.9	3 11.0	3 6.6	24 33.4	14 47.4
13 M	17 21 14	20 59 53	23 40 12	29 51 51	27 54.2	13 43.4	5 14.3	3 57.2	0 51.3	3 6.8	3 7.9	24 34.6	14 48.9
14 Tu	17 25 11	21 57 11	6♐ 6 49	12♐25 16	27 53.5	15 8.1	6 18.0	4 33.6	0 58.5	3 2.7	3 9.1	24 35.8	14 50.3
15 W	17 29 7	22 54 28	18 47 18	25 13 1	27D 53.2	16 30.0	7 21.4	5 10.1	1 5.7	2 58.7	3 10.3	24 37.0	14 51.7
16 Th	17 33 4	23 51 45	1♑42 24	8♑15 28	27 53.1	17 49.0	8 24.5	5 46.6	1 12.6	2 54.6	3 11.5	24 38.3	14 53.2
17 F	17 37 0	24 49 1	14 52 9	21 32 22	27 53.3	19 5.1	9 27.4	6 23.2	1 19.4	2 50.6	3 12.6	24 39.6	14 54.7
18 Sa	17 40 57	25 46 17	28 16 0	5♒ 2 56	27 53.5	20 18.3	10 30.1	6 59.7	1 26.1	2 46.7	3 13.6	24 40.9	14 56.1
19 Su	17 44 53	26 43 32	11♒52 58	18 45 58	27 53.6	21 28.4	11 32.4	7 36.3	1 32.6	2 42.8	3 14.7	24 42.2	14 57.6
20 M	17 48 50	27 40 47	25 41 43	2♓40 1	27R 53.7	22 35.4	12 34.5	8 12.9	1 39.0	2 39.0	3 15.6	24 43.6	14 59.1
21 Tu	17 52 46	28 38 2	9♓40 39	16 43 22	27 53.7	23 39.3	13 36.2	8 49.5	1 45.2	2 35.2	3 16.5	24 45.0	15 0.6
22 W	17 56 43	29 35 16	23 47 57	0♈54 5	27D 53.6	24 40.0	14 37.7	9 26.1	1 51.2	2 31.4	3 17.4	24 46.4	15 2.1
23 Th	18 0 40	0♋32 30	8♈ 1 29	15 9 50	27 53.7	25 37.3	15 38.8	10 2.8	1 57.1	2 27.8	3 18.2	24 47.8	15 3.6
24 F	18 4 36	1 29 45	22 18 46	29 27 57	27 53.8	26 31.3	16 39.7	10 39.5	2 2.8	2 24.1	3 19.0	24 49.3	15 5.1
25 Sa	18 8 33	2 26 59	6♉36 56	13♉45 19	27 54.1	27 21.7	17 40.2	11 16.2	2 8.3	2 20.6	3 19.7	24 50.8	15 6.6
26 Su	18 12 29	3 24 13	20 52 38	27 58 27	27 54.6	28 8.6	18 40.3	11 52.9	2 13.7	2 17.1	3 20.4	24 52.3	15 8.1
27 M	18 16 26	4 21 28	5♊ 2 18	12♊ 3 43	27 55.1	28 51.7	19 40.2	12 29.6	2 18.9	2 13.6	3 21.1	24 53.8	15 9.6
28 Tu	18 20 22	5 18 42	19 2 16	25 57 32	27R 55.5	29 30.9	20 39.6	13 6.4	2 24.0	2 10.2	3 21.6	24 55.4	15 11.2
29 W	18 24 19	6 15 56	2♋49 8	9♋36 47	27 55.5	0♌ 6.2	21 38.7	13 43.2	2 28.8	2 6.9	3 22.2	24 57.0	15 12.7
30 Th	18 28 15	7 13 10	16 20 12	22 59 11	27 55.1	0 37.5	22 37.4	14 20.1	2 33.5	2 3.7	3 22.7	24 58.6	15 14.2

Astro Data	Dy Hr Mn
♅0 N	1 22:27
♃⊼♆	3 10:58
♆ D	5 23:55
☽0 S	13 5:07
☽0 N	27 0:08
☽0 S	9 12:53
♄△♅	12 19:19
☽0 N	23 6:34
♃△♄	26 9:14

Planet Ingress		Dy Hr Mn
☿	♉	6 11:28
♀	♋	12 8:33
☿	♊	21 0:03
☉	♊	22 2:08
☿	♋	4 13:38
♂	♌	6 11:36
♃	♈	6 10:14
♀	♌	8 2:51
☉	♋	22 10:22
☿	♌	28 19:33

Last Aspect Dy Hr Mn			☽ Ingress	Dy Hr Mn
2 11:21	♆	□	♊	2 20:52
4 18:18	☿	✶	♋	4 23:51
6 20:59	♃	△	♌	7 6:39
9 10:19	♀	✶	♍	9 17:03
12 5:07	♀	□	♎	12 5:27
14 6:17	♆	✶	♏	14 17:52
16 22:38	♃	△	♐	17 4:58
19 8:52	♃	□	♑	19 14:11
21 20:53	☉	△	♒	21 21:16
23 16:08	♆	☍	♓	24 2:01
26 1:48	♃	☌	♈	26 4:37
27 20:34	♆	△	♉	28 5:50
30 5:18	♃	✶	♊	30 7:02

Last Aspect Dy Hr Mn			☽ Ingress	Dy Hr Mn
1 8:34	♃	□	♋	1 9:50
3 14:53	♃	△	♌	3 15:37
5 14:04	♆	☌	♍	6 0:55
7 7:49	☉	□	♎	8 12:49
10 14:18	♆	✶	♏	11 1:16
13 1:46	♆	□	♐	13 12:16
15 10:54	♆	△	♑	15 20:51
17 8:22	☿	☍	♒	18 3:05
20 3:40	☉	△	♓	20 7:25
22 1:35	☿	△	♈	22 10:29
24 7:31	☿	□	♉	24 12:54
26 12:57	☿	✶	♊	26 15:26
28 10:13	♆	✶	♋	28 19:03

☽ Phases & Eclipses Dy Hr Mn		
1 12:40	●	10♉09
8 15:27	☽	17♌02
16 19:03	○	24♏54
24 5:34	☽	2♓04
30 21:06	●	8♊26
7 7:49	☽	15♍34
15 8:19	○	23♐14
15 8:24	☍ T	1.012
22 10:29	☽	0♈00
29 6:32	●	6♋32
29 6:23:01	☌ T	0'50"

Astro Data

1 MAY 1927
Julian Day # 9982
Delta T 24.4 sec
SVP 06♓16'47"
Obliquity 23°26'56"
⚷ Chiron 2♉12.9
☽ Mean ☊ 0♋37.1

1 JUNE 1927
Julian Day # 10013
Delta T 24.4 sec
SVP 06♓16'42"
Obliquity 23°26'55"
⚷ Chiron 4♉01.3
☽ Mean ☊ 28♊58.6

JULY 1927 LONGITUDE

Day	Sid.Time	☉	0 hr ☽	Noon ☽	True ☊	☿	♀	♂	♃	♄	♅	♆	♇
1 F	18 32 12	8♋10 24	29♋33 38	6♌ 3 30	27♊54.2	1♌ 4.5	23♌35.8	14♌56.9	2♈38.0	2♐ 0.5	3♈23.1	25♌ 0.2	15♋15.8
2 Sa	18 36 9	9 7 37	12♌28 49	18 49 42	27R52.9	1 27.2	24 33.7	15 33.8	2 42.4	1R57.4	3 23.5	25 1.8	15 17.3
3 Su	18 40 5	10 4 50	25 6 21	1♍19 1	27 51.3	1 45.5	25 31.2	16 10.7	2 46.6	1 54.4	3 23.8	25 3.5	15 18.8
4 M	18 44 2	11 2 3	7♍28 1	13 33 45	27 49.7	1 59.2	26 28.2	16 47.6	2 50.5	1 51.4	3 24.1	25 5.2	15 20.4
5 Tu	18 47 58	11 59 16	19 36 38	25 37 10	27 48.2	2 8.4	27 24.8	17 24.5	2 54.3	1 48.5	3 24.4	25 6.9	15 21.9
6 W	18 51 55	12 56 28	1♎35 50	7♎33 13	27 47.2	2R12.8	28 20.9	18 1.5	2 58.0	1 45.7	3 24.6	25 8.6	15 23.5
7 Th	18 55 51	13 53 40	13 29 51	19 26 19	27D46.8	2 12.6	29 16.5	18 38.5	3 1.4	1 43.0	3 24.7	25 10.4	15 25.0
8 F	18 59 48	14 50 52	25 23 13	1♏21 7	27 47.2	2 7.7	0♍11.6	19 15.4	3 4.7	1 40.3	3 24.8	25 12.2	15 26.6
9 Sa	19 3 44	15 48 4	7♏20 37	13 22 15	27 48.1	1 58.1	1 6.2	19 52.5	3 7.7	1 37.7	3R24.9	25 14.0	15 28.1
10 Su	19 7 41	16 45 15	19 26 33	25 34 2	27 49.5	1 43.9	2 0.3	20 29.5	3 10.6	1 35.2	3 24.9	25 15.8	15 29.7
11 M	19 11 38	17 42 27	1♐45 9	8♐ 0 18	27 51.0	1 25.4	2 53.8	21 6.6	3 13.3	1 32.8	3 24.8	25 17.6	15 31.2
12 Tu	19 15 34	18 39 39	14 19 50	20 44 1	27 52.1	1 2.6	3 46.7	21 43.7	3 15.9	1 30.5	3 24.7	25 19.5	15 32.8
13 W	19 19 31	19 36 51	27 13 3	3♑47 2	27R52.6	0 35.9	4 39.0	22 20.8	3 18.2	1 28.2	3 24.6	25 21.3	15 34.3
14 Th	19 23 27	20 34 3	10♑25 59	17 9 48	27 52.2	0 5.6	5 30.7	22 57.9	3 20.3	1 26.1	3 24.4	25 23.2	15 35.9
15 F	19 27 24	21 31 15	23 58 20	0♒51 18	27 50.6	29♋32.1	6 21.7	23 35.0	3 22.3	1 24.0	3 24.2	25 25.1	15 37.4
16 Sa	19 31 20	22 28 27	7♒48 19	14 48 57	27 48.0	28 55.9	7 12.1	24 12.2	3 24.1	1 22.0	3 23.9	25 27.0	15 39.0
17 Su	19 35 17	23 25 40	21 52 41	28 58 58	27 44.6	28 17.5	8 1.7	24 49.4	3 25.6	1 20.1	3 23.5	25 29.0	15 40.5
18 M	19 39 14	24 22 54	6♓ 7 14	13♓16 51	27 40.9	27 37.7	8 50.7	25 26.6	3 27.0	1 18.3	3 23.2	25 30.9	15 42.0
19 Tu	19 43 10	25 20 8	20 27 15	27 37 53	27 37.5	26 57.0	9 38.9	26 3.9	3 28.2	1 16.6	3 22.7	25 32.9	15 43.6
20 W	19 47 7	26 17 23	4♈48 13	11♈57 49	27 35.0	26 16.1	10 26.3	26 41.1	3 29.2	1 14.9	3 22.3	25 34.9	15 45.1
21 Th	19 51 3	27 14 38	19 6 14	26 13 10	27D33.5	25 35.8	11 12.9	27 18.4	3 30.0	1 13.4	3 21.7	25 36.8	15 46.6
22 F	19 55 0	28 11 54	3♉18 20	10♉21 29	27 33.4	24 56.7	11 58.7	27 55.7	3 30.6	1 11.9	3 21.2	25 38.9	15 48.1
23 Sa	19 58 56	29 9 12	17 22 26	24 21 4	27 34.3	24 19.6	12 43.7	28 33.1	3 31.0	1 10.5	3 20.5	25 40.9	15 49.7
24 Su	20 2 53	0♌ 6 30	1♊17 15	8♊10 52	27 35.7	23 45.2	13 27.8	29 10.5	3R31.2	1 9.3	3 19.9	25 42.9	15 51.2
25 M	20 6 49	1 3 49	15 1 52	21 50 7	27R37.0	23 14.2	14 10.9	29 47.9	3 31.2	1 8.1	3 19.2	25 45.0	15 52.7
26 Tu	20 10 46	2 1 9	28 35 33	5♋18 4	27 37.6	22 47.0	14 53.1	0♍25.3	3 31.0	1 7.0	3 18.4	25 47.0	15 54.2
27 W	20 14 43	2 58 30	11♋57 34	18 33 58	27 36.7	22 24.3	15 34.4	1 2.7	3 30.6	1 6.0	3 17.6	25 49.1	15 55.7
28 Th	20 18 39	3 55 51	25 7 8	1♌37 1	27 34.1	22 6.4	16 14.6	1 40.2	3 30.0	1 5.1	3 16.8	25 51.2	15 57.2
29 F	20 22 36	4 53 14	8♌ 3 31	14 26 38	27 29.8	21 53.9	16 53.7	2 17.7	3 29.3	1 4.3	3 15.9	25 53.3	15 58.7
30 Sa	20 26 32	5 50 37	20 46 19	27 2 38	27 23.9	21D47.1	17 31.7	2 55.3	3 28.3	1 3.6	3 15.0	25 55.4	16 0.1
31 Su	20 30 29	6 48 1	3♍15 39	9♍25 29	27 17.1	21 46.2	18 8.5	3 32.8	3 27.1	1 3.0	3 14.0	25 57.5	16 1.6

AUGUST 1927 LONGITUDE

Day	Sid.Time	☉	0 hr ☽	Noon ☽	True ☊	☿	♀	♂	♃	♄	♅	♆	♇
1 M	20 34 25	7♌45 25	15♍32 20	21♍36 26	27♊10.1	21♋51.4	18♍44.2	4♍10.4	3♈25.7	1♐ 2.5	3♈13.0	25♌59.6	16♋ 3.1
2 Tu	20 38 22	8 42 50	27 38 5	3♎37 39	27R 3.5	22 2.9	19 18.5	4 48.0	3R24.1	1R 2.1	3R11.9	26 1.8	16 4.5
3 W	20 42 18	9 40 16	9♎35 31	15 32 10	26 58.1	22 20.8	19 51.6	5 25.6	3 22.4	1 1.7	3 10.8	26 3.9	16 6.0
4 Th	20 46 15	10 37 42	21 28 4	27 23 47	26 54.3	22 45.1	20 23.3	6 3.3	3 20.4	1 1.5	3 9.6	26 6.1	16 7.4
5 F	20 50 11	11 35 10	3♏19 52	9♏16 56	26D52.3	23 16.0	20 53.6	6 41.0	3 18.3	1D 1.4	3 8.4	26 8.2	16 8.8
6 Sa	20 54 8	12 32 37	15 15 37	21 16 30	26 51.9	23 53.3	21 22.5	7 18.7	3 15.9	1 1.4	3 7.2	26 10.4	16 10.2
7 Su	20 58 5	13 30 6	27 20 16	3♐27 30	26 52.7	24 37.0	21 49.8	7 56.4	3 13.4	1 1.4	3 5.9	26 12.6	16 11.6
8 M	21 2 1	14 27 36	9♐38 49	15 54 46	26 54.0	25 27.1	22 15.5	8 34.2	3 10.6	1 1.6	3 4.6	26 14.7	16 13.0
9 Tu	21 5 58	15 25 6	22 15 52	28 42 33	26R54.9	26 23.4	22 39.6	9 12.0	3 7.7	1 1.9	3 3.2	26 16.9	16 14.4
10 W	21 9 54	16 22 37	5♑15 11	11♑54 1	26 54.7	27 25.7	23 2.0	9 49.8	3 4.6	1 2.2	3 1.8	26 19.1	16 15.8
11 Th	21 13 51	17 20 10	18 39 10	25 30 36	26 52.7	28 34.0	23 22.6	10 27.7	3 1.3	1 2.7	3 0.4	26 21.3	16 17.2
12 F	21 17 47	18 17 43	2♒28 9	9♒31 29	26 48.5	29 48.0	23 41.4	11 5.5	2 57.8	1 3.2	2 58.9	26 23.5	16 18.5
13 Sa	21 21 44	19 15 17	16 40 7	23 53 23	26 42.3	1♌ 7.6	23 58.3	11 43.4	2 54.2	1 3.9	2 57.4	26 25.7	16 19.9
14 Su	21 25 41	20 12 52	1♓10 29	8♓30 33	26 34.6	2 32.3	24 13.3	12 21.3	2 50.4	1 4.6	2 55.9	26 28.0	16 21.2
15 M	21 29 37	21 10 29	15 52 35	23 15 35	26 26.3	4 2.0	24 26.3	12 59.3	2 46.3	1 5.5	2 54.3	26 30.2	16 22.5
16 Tu	21 33 34	22 8 7	0♈38 34	8♈ 0 34	26 18.4	5 36.3	24 37.2	13 37.3	2 42.1	1 6.4	2 52.7	26 32.4	16 23.8
17 W	21 37 30	23 5 46	15 20 45	22 38 22	26 11.9	7 14.9	24 46.1	14 15.3	2 37.8	1 7.5	2 51.0	26 34.6	16 25.1
18 Th	21 41 27	24 3 27	29 52 47	7♉ 3 34	26 7.4	8 57.3	24 52.8	14 53.3	2 33.2	1 8.6	2 49.3	26 36.8	16 26.4
19 F	21 45 23	25 1 9	14♉10 21	21 12 58	26D 5.1	10 43.2	24 57.2	15 31.4	2 28.5	1 9.8	2 47.6	26 39.0	16 27.7
20 Sa	21 49 20	25 58 54	28 11 19	5♊ 5 26	26 4.6	12 32.2	24R59.5	16 9.5	2 23.6	1 11.1	2 45.9	26 41.3	16 28.9
21 Su	21 53 16	26 56 40	11♊55 23	18 41 19	26 5.1	14 23.8	24 59.5	16 47.6	2 18.6	1 12.6	2 44.1	26 43.5	16 30.2
22 M	21 57 13	27 54 28	25 23 26	2♋ 1 54	26R 5.6	16 17.6	24 57.1	17 25.8	2 13.4	1 14.1	2 42.2	26 45.7	16 31.4
23 Tu	22 1 10	28 52 17	8♋36 56	15 8 43	26 4.9	18 13.2	24 52.4	18 4.0	2 8.0	1 15.7	2 40.4	26 47.9	16 32.6
24 W	22 5 6	29 50 8	21 37 25	28 3 12	26 2.2	20 10.3	24 45.4	18 42.2	2 2.5	1 17.4	2 38.5	26 50.2	16 33.8
25 Th	22 9 3	0♍48 1	4♌26 9	10♌46 23	25 56.8	22 8.3	24 36.0	19 20.5	1 56.8	1 19.2	2 36.6	26 52.4	16 35.0
26 F	22 12 59	1 45 55	17 3 59	23 19 1	25 48.7	24 7.0	24 24.2	19 58.7	1 51.0	1 21.1	2 34.6	26 54.6	16 36.1
27 Sa	22 16 56	2 43 51	29 31 32	5♍41 35	25 38.3	26 6.1	24 10.1	20 37.1	1 45.1	1 23.1	2 32.7	26 56.8	16 37.3
28 Su	22 20 52	3 41 48	11♍49 14	17 54 35	25 26.3	28 5.3	23 53.6	21 15.4	1 38.9	1 25.2	2 30.7	26 59.0	16 38.4
29 M	22 24 49	4 39 47	23 57 45	29 58 53	25 13.7	0♍ 4.4	23 34.9	21 53.8	1 32.7	1 27.4	2 28.6	27 1.2	16 39.5
30 Tu	22 28 45	5 37 48	5♎58 10	11♎55 51	25 1.7	2 3.1	23 13.9	22 32.2	1 26.3	1 29.6	2 26.6	27 3.5	16 40.6
31 W	22 32 42	6 35 49	17 52 12	23 47 35	24 51.2	4 1.2	22 50.7	23 10.7	1 19.8	1 32.0	2 24.5	27 5.7	16 41.7

Astro Data	Planet Ingress	Last Aspect	☽ Ingress	Last Aspect	☽ Ingress	☽ Phases & Eclipses	Astro Data
Dy Hr Mn	Dy Hr Mn	Dy Hr Mn	Dy Hr Mn	Dy Hr Mn	Dy Hr Mn	Dy Hr Mn	
☽0S 6 20:44	♀ ♍ 7 18:55	29 22:02 ♇ ☌	♌ 1 0:48	1 12:40 ☿ ⚹	♎ 2 4:44	7 0:52 ☽ 13♎56	1 JULY 1927
☿ R 6 10:50	☿ ♋ 14 4:08	3 0:52 ♀ ☌	♍ 3 9:27	4 9:24 ♆ ⚹	♏ 4 17:16	14 19:22 ○ 21♑20	Julian Day # 10043
♃0N 7 11:51	☉ ♌ 23 21:17	4 15:33 ♇ ⚹	♎ 5 20:47	6 21:46 ♆ □	♐ 7 5:14	21 14:43 ☽ 27♈50	Delta T 24.4 sec
♅ R 9 12:31	♂ ♍ 25 7:47	7 23:38 ♆ ⚹	♏ 8 9:17	9 7:31 ♆ △	♑ 9 14:23	28 17:36 ● 4♌38	SVP 06♓16'36"
♃☌♅ 15 21:37		10 11:26 ♆ □	♐ 10 20:37	11 18:57 ☿ ☍	♒ 11 19:46		Obliquity 23°26'55"
☽0N 20 11:41	☿ ♌ 12 3:43	12 20:34 ♆ △	♑ 13 5:06	13 16:14 ♆ ☍	♓ 13 22:04	5 18:05 ☽ 12♏18	⚷ Chiron 5♉21.8
♃ R 24 13:10	☉ ♍ 24 4:05	15 9:18 ☿ ☍	♒ 15 10:31	15 14:06 ♀ ☍	♈ 15 22:57	13 4:37 ○ 19♒26	☽ Mean ☊ 27♊23.3
☿ D 30 15:42	☿ ♍ 28 23:07	17 6:07 ♆ ☍	♓ 17 13:43	17 18:34 ♆ △	♉ 18 0:12	19 19:54 ☽ 25♉49	
♄⚻♇ 31 16:44		19 10:22 ☿ △	♈ 19 15:58	19 21:24 ♆ □	♊ 20 3:08	27 6:45 ● 3♍00	1 AUGUST 1927
☽0S 3 4:03		21 14:43 ☉ □	♉ 21 18:24	22 4:53 ☉ ⚹	♋ 22 8:19		Julian Day # 10074
♃0S 3 9:38	☽0N 16 17:35	23 20:10 ♂ □	♊ 23 21:46	24 5:46 ♀ ⚹	♌ 24 15:39		Delta T 24.4 sec
♄ D 5 18:58	♀ R 20 11:42	25 18:59 ♆ ⚹	♋ 26 2:31	26 19:00 ♆ ☌	♍ 27 0:55		SVP 06♓16'31"
♀0S 7 9:48	♃△♄ 29 14:53	27 18:35 ☿ ☌	♌ 28 9:00	28 23:16 ♀ ☌	♎ 29 12:02		Obliquity 23°26'56"
♃☌♅ 11 11:02	☽0S 30 10:35	30 9:53 ♆ ☌	♍ 30 17:42				⚷ Chiron 6♉03.4
							☽ Mean ☊ 25♊44.9

LONGITUDE SEPTEMBER 1927

Day	Sid.Time	☉	0 hr ☽	Noon ☽	True ☊	☿	♀	♂	♃	♄	♅	♆	♇
1 Th	22 36 38	7♍33 53	29♎42 23	5♏37 4	24♊43.0	5♍58.7	22♍25.5	23♍49.2	1♈13.2	1♐34.4	2♈22.4	27♌ 7.9	16♋42.8
2 F	22 40 35	8 31 57	11♏32 5	17 28 1	24R37.4	7 55.4	21R58.2	24 27.7	1R 6.4	1 37.0	2R20.3	27 10.0	16 43.8
3 Sa	22 44 32	9 30 4	23 25 25	29 24 55	24 34.3	9 51.1	21 29.2	25 6.2	0 59.6	1 39.6	2 18.1	27 12.2	16 44.8
4 Su	22 48 28	10 28 11	5♐27 10	11♐32 49	24D33.2	11 45.9	20 58.4	25 44.8	0 52.6	1 42.3	2 15.9	27 14.4	16 45.9
5 M	22 52 25	11 26 20	17 42 32	23 56 59	24R33.2	13 39.7	20 26.1	26 23.4	0 45.5	1 45.1	2 13.7	27 16.6	16 46.9
6 Tu	22 56 21	12 24 31	0♑16 47	6♑42 31	24 33.2	15 32.4	19 52.5	27 2.0	0 38.3	1 48.0	2 11.5	27 18.8	16 47.8
7 W	23 0 18	13 22 43	13 14 43	19 53 48	24 32.0	17 23.9	19 17.7	27 40.7	0 31.1	1 51.0	2 9.3	27 20.9	16 48.8
8 Th	23 4 14	14 20 57	26 40 4	3♒33 40	24 28.9	19 14.4	18 41.9	28 19.4	0 23.7	1 54.1	2 7.1	27 23.1	16 49.7
9 F	23 8 11	15 19 12	10♒34 35	17 42 35	24 23.1	21 3.7	18 5.5	28 58.1	0 16.3	1 57.3	2 4.8	27 25.2	16 50.6
10 Sa	23 12 7	16 17 29	24 57 13	2♓17 51	24 14.8	22 51.8	17 28.5	29 36.9	0 8.8	2 0.5	2 2.5	27 27.3	16 51.5
11 Su	23 16 4	17 15 47	9♓43 36	17 13 26	24 4.6	24 38.8	16 51.3	0♎15.7	0 1.2	2 3.8	2 0.2	27 29.5	16 52.4
12 M	23 20 1	18 14 7	24 46 7	2♈20 23	23 53.5	26 24.7	16 14.1	0 54.5	29♓53.5	2 7.3	1 57.9	27 31.6	16 53.3
13 Tu	23 23 57	19 12 29	9♈54 53	17 28 19	23 42.7	28 9.4	15 37.2	1 33.3	29 45.8	2 10.7	1 55.6	27 33.7	16 54.1
14 W	23 27 54	20 10 53	24 59 27	2♉27 13	23 33.6	29 53.1	15 0.8	2 12.2	29 38.0	2 14.3	1 53.2	27 35.8	16 54.9
15 Th	23 31 50	21 9 19	9♉50 42	17 9 11	23 26.9	1♎35.6	14 25.2	2 51.2	29 30.2	2 18.0	1 50.9	27 37.8	16 55.7
16 F	23 35 47	22 7 47	24 22 10	1♊29 20	23 22.9	3 17.0	13 50.5	3 30.1	29 22.3	2 21.7	1 48.5	27 39.9	16 56.5
17 Sa	23 39 43	23 6 17	8♊30 33	15 25 49	23 21.3	4 57.4	13 17.0	4 9.1	29 14.4	2 25.5	1 46.2	27 42.0	16 57.3
18 Su	23 43 40	24 4 50	22 15 18	28 59 15	23 21.0	6 36.8	12 44.9	4 48.2	29 6.5	2 29.4	1 43.8	27 44.0	16 58.0
19 M	23 47 36	25 3 25	5♋37 58	12♋11 50	23 20.8	8 15.1	12 14.4	5 27.3	28 58.5	2 33.4	1 41.4	27 46.1	16 58.7
20 Tu	23 51 33	26 2 2	18 41 14	25 6 33	23 19.6	9 52.4	11 45.6	6 6.4	28 50.5	2 37.5	1 39.0	27 48.1	16 59.4
21 W	23 55 30	27 0 41	1♌28 10	7♌46 26	23 16.1	11 28.7	11 18.7	6 45.5	28 42.5	2 41.6	1 36.6	27 50.1	17 0.1
22 Th	23 59 26	27 59 22	14 1 43	20 14 17	23 9.9	13 4.1	10 53.8	7 24.7	28 34.5	2 45.8	1 34.2	27 52.1	17 0.7
23 F	0 3 23	28 58 6	26 24 23	2♍32 17	23 0.7	14 38.4	10 31.1	8 3.9	28 26.4	2 50.1	1 31.8	27 54.0	17 1.3
24 Sa	0 7 19	29 56 52	8♍38 9	14 42 9	22 48.9	16 11.8	10 10.5	8 43.2	28 18.4	2 54.5	1 29.4	27 56.0	17 1.9
25 Su	0 11 16	0♎55 39	20 44 27	26 45 11	22 35.4	17 44.3	9 52.3	9 22.5	28 10.4	2 58.9	1 27.0	27 57.9	17 2.5
26 M	0 15 12	1 54 29	2♎44 29	8♎42 29	22 21.1	19 15.8	9 36.4	10 1.8	28 2.4	3 3.4	1 24.6	27 59.9	17 3.1
27 Tu	0 19 9	2 53 21	14 39 22	20 35 16	22 7.4	20 46.4	9 22.8	10 41.2	27 54.4	3 8.0	1 22.1	28 1.8	17 3.6
28 W	0 23 5	3 52 14	26 30 26	2♏25 6	21 55.4	22 16.0	9 11.7	11 20.6	27 46.5	3 12.7	1 19.7	28 3.7	17 4.1
29 Th	0 27 2	4 51 10	8♏19 32	14 14 4	21 45.7	23 44.7	9 3.0	12 0.1	27 38.5	3 17.4	1 17.3	28 5.5	17 4.6
30 F	0 30 59	5 50 7	20 9 6	26 5 3	21 38.9	25 12.4	8 56.7	12 39.5	27 30.7	3 22.2	1 14.9	28 7.4	17 5.1

LONGITUDE OCTOBER 1927

Day	Sid.Time	☉	0 hr ☽	Noon ☽	True ☊	☿	♀	♂	♃	♄	♅	♆	♇
1 Sa	0 34 55	6♎49 7	2♐ 2 23	8♐ 1 37	21♊34.9	26♎39.1	8♍52.9	13♎19.1	27♓22.8	3♐27.1	1♈12.5	28♌ 9.2	17♋ 5.5
2 Su	0 38 52	7 48 8	14 3 19	20 8 4	21D33.3	28 4.9	8D51.4	13 58.6	27R15.1	3 32.0	1R10.1	28 11.0	17 5.9
3 M	0 42 48	8 47 11	26 16 31	2♑29 17	21 33.1	29 29.7	8 52.3	14 38.2	27 7.4	3 37.0	1 7.7	28 12.8	17 6.3
4 Tu	0 46 45	9 46 16	8♑47 0	15 10 18	21R33.4	0♏53.5	8 55.5	15 17.8	26 59.7	3 42.1	1 5.4	28 14.6	17 6.7
5 W	0 50 41	10 45 22	21 39 46	28 15 55	21 32.9	2 16.2	9 1.1	15 57.5	26 52.1	3 47.2	1 3.0	28 16.4	17 7.1
6 Th	0 54 38	11 44 30	4♒59 11	11♒49 54	21 30.7	3 37.9	9 8.8	16 37.2	26 44.6	3 52.4	1 0.6	28 18.1	17 7.4
7 F	0 58 34	12 43 40	18 48 12	25 54 5	21 26.2	4 58.4	9 18.8	17 16.9	26 37.2	3 57.6	0 58.3	28 19.8	17 7.7
8 Sa	1 2 31	13 42 52	3♓ 7 20	10♓27 28	21 19.3	6 17.7	9 31.0	17 56.7	26 29.9	4 3.0	0 55.9	28 21.5	17 8.0
9 Su	1 6 28	14 42 6	17 53 47	25 25 23	21 10.4	7 35.8	9 45.2	18 36.5	26 22.7	4 8.3	0 53.6	28 23.2	17 8.2
10 M	1 10 24	15 41 21	3♈ 1 6	10♈39 39	21 0.6	8 52.7	10 1.5	19 16.4	26 15.5	4 13.8	0 51.3	28 24.8	17 8.5
11 Tu	1 14 21	16 40 39	18 19 36	25 59 31	20 51.0	10 8.1	10 19.7	19 56.2	26 8.5	4 19.3	0 49.0	28 26.4	17 8.7
12 W	1 18 17	17 39 58	3♉37 56	11♉13 32	20 42.7	11 22.0	10 39.9	20 36.2	26 1.5	4 24.8	0 46.7	28 28.0	17 8.8
13 Th	1 22 14	18 39 20	18 45 6	26 11 37	20 36.7	12 34.4	11 2.0	21 16.1	25 54.7	4 30.4	0 44.5	28 29.6	17 9.0
14 F	1 26 10	19 38 44	3♊32 19	10♊46 37	20 33.3	13 45.1	11 25.9	21 56.1	25 48.0	4 36.1	0 42.2	28 31.2	17 9.1
15 Sa	1 30 7	20 38 10	17 54 10	24 54 49	20D32.1	14 53.9	11 51.5	22 36.2	25 41.5	4 41.8	0 40.0	28 32.7	17 9.2
16 Su	1 34 3	21 37 38	1♋48 35	8♋35 38	20 32.4	16 0.8	12 18.9	23 16.3	25 35.0	4 47.6	0 37.8	28 34.2	17 9.3
17 M	1 38 0	22 37 9	15 16 17	21 50 54	20R33.2	17 5.5	12 47.8	23 56.4	25 28.7	4 53.4	0 35.6	28 35.7	17 9.4
18 Tu	1 41 56	23 36 43	28 19 55	4♌43 49	20 33.3	18 7.8	13 18.4	24 36.6	25 22.5	4 59.3	0 33.4	28 37.1	17R 9.4
19 W	1 45 53	24 36 18	11♌ 3 5	17 18 15	20 31.8	19 7.6	13 50.5	25 16.8	25 16.5	5 5.2	0 31.3	28 38.6	17 9.4
20 Th	1 49 50	25 35 56	23 29 46	29 38 7	20 28.1	20 4.5	14 24.0	25 57.0	25 10.6	5 11.2	0 29.2	28 40.0	17 9.4
21 F	1 53 46	26 35 36	5♍43 43	11♍47 0	20 22.0	20 58.2	14 58.9	26 37.3	25 4.8	5 17.3	0 27.1	28 41.3	17 9.4
22 Sa	1 57 43	27 35 18	17 48 19	23 47 59	20 13.9	21 48.5	15 35.2	27 17.7	24 59.2	5 23.3	0 25.0	28 42.7	17 9.3
23 Su	2 1 39	28 35 2	29 46 19	5♎43 34	20 4.2	22 34.9	16 12.8	27 58.0	24 53.8	5 29.5	0 22.9	28 44.0	17 9.2
24 M	2 5 36	29 34 48	11♎40 0	17 35 48	19 54.0	23 17.1	16 51.6	28 38.5	24 48.5	5 35.6	0 20.9	28 45.3	17 9.1
25 Tu	2 9 32	0♏34 37	23 31 12	29 26 22	19 44.1	23 54.5	17 31.7	29 18.9	24 43.4	5 41.9	0 18.9	28 46.6	17 9.0
26 W	2 13 29	1 34 27	5♏21 32	11♏16 52	19 35.4	24 26.8	18 12.8	29 59.4	24 38.4	5 48.1	0 16.9	28 47.8	17 8.8
27 Th	2 17 25	2 34 20	17 12 37	23 9 0	19 28.6	24 53.3	18 55.2	0♏40.0	24 33.7	5 54.4	0 15.0	28 49.0	17 8.6
28 F	2 21 22	3 34 14	29 6 18	5♐ 4 47	19 24.1	25 13.6	19 38.5	1 20.6	24 29.1	6 0.8	0 13.1	28 50.2	17 8.4
29 Sa	2 25 19	4 34 10	11♐ 4 48	17 6 44	19D21.8	25 26.9	20 22.9	2 1.2	24 24.6	6 7.2	0 11.2	28 51.3	17 8.2
30 Su	2 29 15	5 34 8	23 10 57	29 17 54	19 21.5	25R32.7	21 8.4	2 41.9	24 20.4	6 13.6	0 9.4	28 52.5	17 7.9
31 M	2 33 12	6 34 8	5♑28 3	11♑41 54	19 22.5	25 30.3	21 54.7	3 22.6	24 16.4	6 20.1	0 7.6	28 53.5	17 7.7

Astro Data Dy Hr Mn	Planet Ingress Dy Hr Mn	Last Aspect Dy Hr Mn	☽ Ingress Dy Hr Mn	Last Aspect Dy Hr Mn	☽ Ingress Dy Hr Mn	☽ Phases & Eclipses Dy Hr Mn	Astro Data
♄⚼♇ 5 21:20	♂ ♎ 10 14:19	31 18:45 ♆ ⚹	♏ 1 0:36	3 7:02 ☿ ⚹	♑ 3 7:13	4 10:44 ☽ 10♐54	1 SEPTEMBER 1927
♄△♅ 10 8:35	♃ ♓ 11 3:43	3 7:36 ♆ □	♐ 3 13:10	5 9:23 ♃ ⚹	♒ 5 15:07	11 12:54 ○ 17♓47	Julian Day # 10105
☽0N 13 1:54	☿ ♎ 14 1:37	5 18:23 ♆ △	♑ 5 23:28	7 16:05 ♆ ☍	♓ 7 18:50	18 3:29 ☽ 24♊13	Delta T 24.4 sec
♂0S 13 5:52	☉ ♎ 24 1:17	8 3:03 ♂ △	♒ 8 5:50	9 13:24 ♃ ☌	♈ 9 19:15	25 22:11 ● 1♎50	SVP 06♓16'28"
☿0S 15 2:16		10 4:07 ♆ ☍	♓ 10 8:16	11 15:52 ♆ △	♉ 11 18:17		Obliquity 23°26'57"
♅0S 16 14:02	☿ ♏ 3 8:38	12 8:03 ♃ ☌	♈ 12 8:18	13 15:46 ♆ □	♊ 13 18:12	4 2:01 ☽ 9♑51	⚷ Chiron 5♉53.5R
♀0N 21 2:16	☉ ♏ 24 10:07	14 4:11 ♆ △	♉ 14 8:03	15 18:20 ♆ ⚹	♋ 15 20:50	10 21:14 ○ 16♈34	☽ Mean ☊ 24♊06.4
☽0S 26 16:38	♂ ♏ 26 0:20	16 8:20 ♃ ⚹	♊ 16 9:29	17 18:33 ♃ △	♌ 18 3:07	17 14:32 ☽ 23♋13	
♃⚻♆ 26 6:08		18 12:06 ♃ □	♋ 18 13:49	20 10:07 ♆ ☌	♍ 20 12:43	25 15:37 ● 1♏14	1 OCTOBER 1927
♀ D 2 2:50		20 18:50 ♃ △	♌ 20 21:13	22 14:16 ♃ ☍	♎ 23 0:28		Julian Day # 10135
☽0N 10 12:35		23 2:56 ♆ ☌	♍ 23 7:01	25 12:28 ♂ ☌	♏ 25 13:08		Delta T 24.4 sec
♇ R 18 23:12		25 14:41 ♃ ☍	♎ 25 18:30	27 23:28 ♆ □	♐ 28 1:48		SVP 06♓16'25"
☽0S 23 22:47		28 3:10 ♆ ⚹	♏ 28 7:05	30 11:11 ♆ △	♑ 30 13:22		Obliquity 23°26'57"
☿ R 30 5:19		30 16:09 ♆ □	♐ 30 19:54				⚷ Chiron 4♉57.9R
							☽ Mean ☊ 22♊31.0

NOVEMBER 1927 LONGITUDE

Day	Sid.Time	☉	0 hr ☽	Noon ☽	True ☊	☿	♀	♂	♃	♄	♅	♆	♇
1 Tu	2 37 8	7♏34 9	17♑59 57	24♑22 44	19♊24.0	25♏19.3	22♍42.0	4♏ 3.3	24♓12.5	6♐26.6	0♈ 5.8	28♌54.6	17♋ 7.4
2 W	2 41 5	8 34 12	0♒50 43	7♒24 23	19R 25.2	24R 59.1	23 30.2	4 44.1	24R 8.8	6 33.1	0R 4.1	28 55.6	17R 7.0
3 Th	2 45 1	9 34 17	14 4 11	20 50 26	19 25.4	24 29.3	24 19.2	5 24.9	24 5.3	6 39.7	0 2.4	28 56.6	17 6.7
4 F	2 48 58	10 34 23	27 43 24	4♓43 12	19 24.0	23 50.0	25 9.0	6 5.8	24 2.0	6 46.3	0 0.7	28 57.6	17 6.3
5 Sa	2 52 54	11 34 30	11♓49 47	19 2 57	19 21.0	23 1.2	25 59.7	6 46.7	23 58.9	6 52.9	29♓59.1	28 58.5	17 5.9
6 Su	2 56 51	12 34 39	26 22 18	3♈47 13	19 16.5	22 3.4	26 51.1	7 27.6	23 56.0	6 59.6	29 57.5	28 59.4	17 5.5
7 M	3 0 48	13 34 50	11♈16 52	18 50 15	19 11.2	20 57.7	27 43.2	8 8.6	23 53.3	7 6.3	29 55.9	29 0.3	17 5.0
8 Tu	3 4 44	14 35 2	26 26 14	4♉ 3 32	19 5.9	19 45.4	28 36.1	8 49.6	23 50.8	7 13.0	29 54.4	29 1.1	17 4.6
9 W	3 8 41	15 35 16	11♉40 50	19 16 48	19 1.4	18 28.4	29 29.7	9 30.7	23 48.5	7 19.8	29 52.9	29 2.0	17 4.1
10 Th	3 12 37	16 35 32	26 50 10	4♊19 47	18 58.2	17 8.9	0♎24.0	10 11.8	23 46.4	7 26.6	29 51.5	29 2.7	17 3.6
11 F	3 16 34	17 35 49	11♊44 38	19 3 53	18D 56.7	15 49.4	1 18.9	10 53.0	23 44.5	7 33.4	29 50.1	29 3.5	17 3.0
12 Sa	3 20 30	18 36 9	26 16 54	3♋23 14	18 56.7	14 32.5	2 14.4	11 34.2	23 42.8	7 40.3	29 48.8	29 4.2	17 2.5
13 Su	3 24 27	19 36 30	10♋22 40	17 15 6	18 57.8	13 20.7	3 10.6	12 15.4	23 41.3	7 47.1	29 47.5	29 4.9	17 1.9
14 M	3 28 23	20 36 53	24 0 38	0♌39 29	18 59.4	12 16.3	4 7.3	12 56.7	23 40.0	7 54.0	29 46.2	29 5.5	17 1.3
15 Tu	3 32 20	21 37 18	7♌11 59	13 38 31	19 0.9	11 21.0	5 4.6	13 38.0	23 38.9	8 0.9	29 45.0	29 6.1	17 0.7
16 W	3 36 17	22 37 45	19 59 35	26 15 42	19R 1.7	10 36.3	6 2.5	14 19.4	23 38.0	8 7.9	29 43.8	29 6.7	17 0.1
17 Th	3 40 13	23 38 14	2♍27 22	8♍35 11	19 1.3	10 2.9	7 0.8	15 0.8	23 37.3	8 14.8	29 42.6	29 7.3	16 59.4
18 F	3 44 10	24 38 44	14 39 40	20 41 22	18 59.8	9 41.2	7 59.7	15 42.3	23 36.9	8 21.8	29 41.5	29 7.8	16 58.7
19 Sa	3 48 6	25 39 17	26 40 48	2♎38 27	18 57.2	9D 31.2	8 59.1	16 23.8	23D 36.6	8 28.8	29 40.5	29 8.2	16 58.0
20 Su	3 52 3	26 39 51	8♎34 48	14 30 16	18 53.8	9 32.4	9 59.0	17 5.3	23 36.5	8 35.8	29 39.5	29 8.7	16 57.3
21 M	3 55 59	27 40 26	20 25 16	26 20 8	18 50.1	9 44.3	10 59.3	17 46.9	23 36.7	8 42.8	29 38.5	29 9.1	16 56.5
22 Tu	3 59 56	28 41 4	2♏15 13	8♏10 50	18 46.4	10 6.0	11 60.0	18 28.6	23 37.0	8 49.8	29 37.6	29 9.5	16 55.8
23 W	4 3 52	29 41 43	14 7 15	20 4 42	18 43.3	10 36.7	13 1.2	19 10.3	23 37.6	8 56.9	29 36.7	29 9.8	16 55.0
24 Th	4 7 49	0♐42 24	26 3 26	2♐ 3 40	18 41.1	11 15.4	14 2.7	19 52.0	23 38.4	9 4.0	29 35.9	29 10.1	16 54.2
25 F	4 11 46	1 43 6	8♐ 5 36	14 9 26	18D 39.8	12 1.4	15 4.7	20 33.8	23 39.4	9 11.0	29 35.2	29 10.4	16 53.4
26 Sa	4 15 42	2 43 49	20 15 24	26 23 40	18 39.4	12 53.7	16 7.0	21 15.6	23 40.6	9 18.1	29 34.4	29 10.6	16 52.5
27 Su	4 19 39	3 44 34	2♑34 29	8♑48 4	18 39.9	13 51.5	17 9.8	21 57.4	23 42.0	9 25.2	29 33.8	29 10.8	16 51.7
28 M	4 23 35	4 45 19	15 4 40	21 24 32	18 40.9	14 54.3	18 12.8	22 39.3	23 43.6	9 32.3	29 33.2	29 11.0	16 50.8
29 Tu	4 27 32	5 46 6	27 47 55	4♒15 6	18 42.2	16 1.2	19 16.2	23 21.3	23 45.4	9 39.4	29 32.6	29 11.2	16 49.9
30 W	4 31 28	6 46 54	10♒46 22	17 21 57	18 43.3	17 11.8	20 20.0	24 3.2	23 47.4	9 46.5	29 32.1	29 11.3	16 49.0

DECEMBER 1927 LONGITUDE

Day	Sid.Time	☉	0 hr ☽	Noon ☽	True ☊	☿	♀	♂	♃	♄	♅	♆	♇
1 Th	4 35 25	7♐47 43	24♒ 2 7	0♓47 4	18♊44.1	18♏25.5	21♎24.1	24♏45.3	23♓49.6	9♐53.6	29♓31.6	29♌11.3	16♋48.1
2 F	4 39 21	8 48 33	7♓36 58	14 31 54	18R 44.4	19 41.9	22 28.4	25 27.3	23 52.0	10 0.8	29R 31.2	29R 11.3	16R 47.1
3 Sa	4 43 18	9 49 23	21 31 53	28 36 50	18 44.2	21 0.6	23 33.1	26 9.4	23 54.6	10 7.9	29 30.8	29 11.3	16 46.2
4 Su	4 47 15	10 50 15	5♈46 33	13♈ 0 43	18 43.6	22 21.3	24 38.1	26 51.6	23 57.5	10 15.0	29 30.5	29 11.3	16 45.2
5 M	4 51 11	11 51 7	20 18 52	27 40 26	18 42.9	23 43.7	25 43.3	27 33.8	24 0.5	10 22.1	29 30.2	29 11.2	16 44.2
6 Tu	4 55 8	12 52 0	5♉ 4 40	12♉30 46	18 42.1	25 7.5	26 48.9	28 16.0	24 3.7	10 29.2	29 30.0	29 11.1	16 43.2
7 W	4 59 4	13 52 54	19 57 48	27 24 48	18 41.6	26 32.5	27 54.7	28 58.3	24 7.1	10 36.3	29 29.8	29 11.0	16 42.1
8 Th	5 3 1	14 53 48	4♊50 45	12♊14 40	18D 41.3	27 58.6	29 0.8	29 40.6	24 10.7	10 43.4	29 29.7	29 10.8	16 41.1
9 F	5 6 57	15 54 44	19 35 36	26 52 39	18 41.2	29 25.6	0♏ 7.1	0♐22.9	24 14.5	10 50.5	29D 29.6	29 10.6	16 40.1
10 Sa	5 10 54	16 55 41	4♋ 5 5	11♋12 15	18 41.2	0♐53.4	1 13.7	1 5.3	24 18.5	10 57.6	29 29.6	29 10.4	16 39.0
11 Su	5 14 51	17 56 39	18 13 39	25 8 56	18R 41.3	2 21.8	2 20.5	1 47.8	24 22.7	11 4.7	29 29.6	29 10.1	16 37.9
12 M	5 18 47	18 57 37	1♌57 55	8♌40 32	18 41.4	3 50.8	3 27.6	2 30.3	24 27.1	11 11.8	29 29.7	29 9.8	16 36.8
13 Tu	5 22 44	19 58 37	15 16 52	21 47 6	18 41.3	5 20.3	4 34.9	3 12.8	24 31.6	11 18.9	29 29.9	29 9.4	16 35.7
14 W	5 26 40	20 59 38	28 11 33	4♍30 35	18 41.1	6 50.3	5 42.4	3 55.4	24 36.4	11 25.9	29 30.1	29 9.1	16 34.6
15 Th	5 30 37	22 0 39	10♍44 41	16 54 19	18 40.9	8 20.6	6 50.1	4 38.0	24 41.3	11 33.0	29 30.3	29 8.7	16 33.5
16 F	5 34 33	23 1 42	23 0 5	29 2 31	18D 40.8	9 51.2	7 58.0	5 20.7	24 46.4	11 40.0	29 30.6	29 8.2	16 32.4
17 Sa	5 38 30	24 2 45	5♎ 2 13	10♎59 47	18 40.9	11 22.2	9 6.2	6 3.4	24 51.7	11 47.0	29 30.9	29 7.7	16 31.2
18 Su	5 42 26	25 3 50	16 55 49	22 50 53	18 41.3	12 53.5	10 14.5	6 46.1	24 57.2	11 54.0	29 31.3	29 7.2	16 30.0
19 M	5 46 23	26 4 55	28 45 33	4♏40 19	18 42.0	14 25.0	11 23.0	7 28.9	25 2.8	12 1.0	29 31.8	29 6.7	16 28.9
20 Tu	5 50 20	27 6 1	10♏35 44	16 32 15	18 43.0	15 56.7	12 31.7	8 11.8	25 8.6	12 8.0	29 32.3	29 6.1	16 27.7
21 W	5 54 16	28 7 8	22 30 16	28 30 13	18 43.9	17 28.7	13 40.6	8 54.7	25 14.7	12 15.0	29 32.8	29 5.5	16 26.5
22 Th	5 58 13	29 8 16	4♐32 25	10♐37 11	18 44.7	19 0.9	14 49.6	9 37.6	25 20.8	12 21.9	29 33.4	29 4.9	16 25.3
23 F	6 2 9	0♑ 9 24	16 44 45	22 55 20	18R 45.1	20 33.4	15 58.8	10 20.6	25 27.2	12 28.8	29 34.1	29 4.2	16 24.1
24 Sa	6 6 6	1 10 33	29 9 6	5♑26 10	18 44.8	22 6.0	17 8.1	11 3.6	25 33.7	12 35.7	29 34.8	29 3.5	16 22.9
25 Su	6 10 2	2 11 42	11♑46 37	18 10 29	18 43.9	23 38.9	18 17.6	11 46.6	25 40.4	12 42.6	29 35.6	29 2.8	16 21.7
26 M	6 13 59	3 12 52	24 37 47	1♒ 8 30	18 42.3	25 12.1	19 27.3	12 29.7	25 47.3	12 49.4	29 36.4	29 2.0	16 20.5
27 Tu	6 17 55	4 14 2	7♒42 36	14 20 2	18 40.1	26 45.5	20 37.0	13 12.9	25 54.3	12 56.2	29 37.2	29 1.2	16 19.2
28 W	6 21 52	5 15 11	21 0 44	27 44 37	18 37.7	28 19.1	21 46.9	13 56.1	26 1.5	13 3.0	29 38.1	29 0.4	16 18.0
29 Th	6 25 49	6 16 21	4♓31 37	11♓21 38	18 35.4	29 53.0	22 57.0	14 39.3	26 8.8	13 9.8	29 39.1	28 59.6	16 16.7
30 F	6 29 45	7 17 31	18 14 35	25 10 22	18 33.6	1♑27.1	24 7.1	15 22.5	26 16.3	13 16.5	29 40.1	28 58.7	16 15.5
31 Sa	6 33 42	8 18 40	2♈ 8 53	9♈ 9 59	18D 32.7	3 1.5	25 17.4	16 5.8	26 24.0	13 23.2	29 41.2	28 57.8	16 14.2

Astro Data Dy Hr Mn	Planet Ingress Dy Hr Mn	Last Aspect Dy Hr Mn	☽ Ingress Dy Hr Mn	Last Aspect Dy Hr Mn	☽ Ingress Dy Hr Mn	☽ Phases & Eclipses Dy Hr Mn	Astro Data
☽0N 6 23:51	♅ ♓ 4 10:30	1 13:27 ☿ ⚹	♒ 1 22:26	1 9:11 ♆ ☍	♓ 1 10:37	2 15:16 ☽ 9♒12	1 NOVEMBER 1927
♀0S 11 5:11	♀ ♎ 9 13:26	4 2:08 ♆ ☍	♓ 4 3:56	3 13:30 ♅ ☌	♈ 3 14:20	9 6:36 ○ 15♉52	Julian Day # 10166
☿ D 19 9:17	☉ ♐ 23 7:14	6 5:49 ♅ ☌	♈ 6 5:53	5 14:27 ♆ △	♉ 5 15:47	16 5:28 ☽ 22♌52	Delta T 24.4 sec
♃ D 19 18:48		8 4:04 ♆ △	♉ 8 5:37	7 15:21 ♅ ⚹	♊ 7 16:10	24 10:09 ● 1♐08	SVP 06♓16'21"
☽0S 20 5:27	♀ ♏ 8 21:26	10 4:49 ♅ ⚹	♊ 10 5:03	9 16:20 ♅ □	♋ 9 17:11		Obliquity 23°26'57"
	♂ ♐ 8 11:01	12 5:56 ♅ □	♋ 12 6:15	11 19:38 ♅ △	♌ 11 20:31	2 2:15 ☽ 8♓54	⚷ Chiron 3♉32.7R
♆ R 2 8:53	☿ ♐ 9 9:26	14 10:22 ♅ △	♌ 14 10:48	14 1:49 ♆ ☌	♍ 14 3:25	8 17:32 ○ 15♊38	☽ Mean ☊ 20♊52.5
☽0N 4 9:16	☉ ♑ 22 20:19	16 17:31 ♆ ☌	♍ 16 19:14	16 12:56 ♅ ☍	♎ 16 13:55	8 17:35 T 1.351	
♅ D 9 18:16	☿ ♑ 29 1:48	19 6:01 ♅ ☍	♎ 19 6:41	19 0:43 ♆ ⚹	♏ 19 2:31	16 0:03 ☽ 23♍02	1 DECEMBER 1927
☽0S 17 12:45		21 17:43 ♆ ⚹	♏ 21 19:26	21 14:05 ♅ △	♐ 21 14:59	24 4:13 ● 1♑21	Julian Day # 10196
☽0N 31 15:36		24 7:05 ♅ △	♐ 24 7:53	24 0:49 ♅ □	♑ 24 1:38	24 3:59:14 P 0.549	Delta T 24.4 sec
		26 18:10 ♅ □	♑ 26 19:01	26 9:11 ♅ ⚹	♒ 26 9:54	31 11:22 ☽ 8♈48	SVP 06♓16'16"
		29 3:15 ♅ ⚹	♒ 29 4:06	28 14:43 ☿ ⚹	♓ 28 16:00		Obliquity 23°26'57"
				30 19:46 ♅ ☌	♈ 30 20:19		⚷ Chiron 2♉13.9R
							☽ Mean ☊ 19♊17.2

LONGITUDE JANUARY 1928

Day	Sid.Time	☉	0 hr ☽	Noon ☽	True ☊	☿	♀	♂	♃	♄	♅	♆	♇
1 Su	6 37 38	9♑19 50	16♈13 30	23♈19 17	18♊32.7	4♑36.3	26♏27.8	16♐49.2	26♓31.8	13♐29.8	29♓42.3	28♌56.8	16♋13.0
2 M	6 41 35	10 20 59	0♉27 4	7♉36 36	18 33.6	6 11.3	27 38.3	17 32.6	26 39.7	13 36.5	29 43.4	28R 55.9	16R 11.7
3 Tu	6 45 31	11 22 8	14 47 31	21 59 28	18 35.0	7 46.7	28 49.0	18 16.0	26 47.9	13 43.1	29 44.7	28 54.9	16 10.5
4 W	6 49 28	12 23 16	29 11 57	6♊24 29	18 36.4	9 22.4	29 59.7	18 59.4	26 56.1	13 49.6	29 45.9	28 53.8	16 9.2
5 Th	6 53 24	13 24 25	13♊36 31	20 47 25	18R 37.3	10 58.5	1♐10.6	19 42.9	27 4.5	13 56.1	29 47.2	28 52.8	16 7.9
6 F	6 57 21	14 25 33	27 56 36	5♋ 3 25	18 37.1	12 35.0	2 21.5	20 26.5	27 13.1	14 2.6	29 48.6	28 51.7	16 6.7
7 Sa	7 1 18	15 26 42	12♋ 7 16	19 7 33	18 35.5	14 11.8	3 32.6	21 10.1	27 21.8	14 9.1	29 50.0	28 50.6	16 5.4
8 Su	7 5 14	16 27 50	26 3 46	2♌55 27	18 32.5	15 49.1	4 43.7	21 53.7	27 30.6	14 15.5	29 51.4	28 49.5	16 4.1
9 M	7 9 11	17 28 57	9♌42 15	16 23 54	18 28.2	17 26.7	5 55.0	22 37.3	27 39.6	14 21.8	29 52.9	28 48.4	16 2.9
10 Tu	7 13 7	18 30 5	23 0 16	29 31 16	18 23.2	19 4.8	7 6.4	23 21.0	27 48.7	14 28.2	29 54.5	28 47.2	16 1.6
11 W	7 17 4	19 31 13	5♍57 0	12♍17 38	18 18.0	20 43.3	8 17.8	24 4.8	27 57.9	14 34.4	29 56.1	28 46.0	16 0.3
12 Th	7 21 0	20 32 20	18 33 25	24 44 43	18 13.3	22 22.3	9 29.3	24 48.6	28 7.3	14 40.7	29 57.7	28 44.8	15 59.1
13 F	7 24 57	21 33 27	0♎51 58	6♎55 38	18 9.8	24 1.8	10 41.0	25 32.4	28 16.8	14 46.9	29 59.4	28 43.5	15 57.8
14 Sa	7 28 53	22 34 35	12 56 17	18 54 30	18D 7.7	25 41.6	11 52.7	26 16.3	28 26.5	14 53.0	0♈ 1.1	28 42.3	15 56.5
15 Su	7 32 50	23 35 42	24 50 54	0♏46 7	18 7.1	27 22.0	13 4.4	27 0.2	28 36.2	14 59.1	0 2.9	28 41.0	15 55.3
16 M	7 36 47	24 36 49	6♏40 47	12 35 34	18 7.9	29 2.8	14 16.3	27 44.1	28 46.1	15 5.2	0 4.7	28 39.6	15 54.0
17 Tu	7 40 43	25 37 55	18 31 6	24 28 0	18 9.5	0♒44.0	15 28.2	28 28.1	28 56.1	15 11.2	0 6.5	28 38.3	15 52.8
18 W	7 44 40	26 39 2	0♐26 52	6♐28 16	18 11.2	2 25.7	16 40.3	29 12.2	29 6.2	15 17.1	0 8.4	28 37.0	15 51.5
19 Th	7 48 36	27 40 8	12 32 44	18 40 41	18R 12.5	4 7.7	17 52.3	29 56.2	29 16.5	15 23.0	0 10.4	28 35.6	15 50.3
20 F	7 52 33	28 41 14	24 52 34	1♑ 8 40	18 12.4	5 50.1	19 4.5	0♑40.4	29 26.9	15 28.8	0 12.4	28 34.2	15 49.0
21 Sa	7 56 29	29 42 19	7♑29 16	13 54 31	18 10.5	7 32.8	20 16.7	1 24.5	29 37.4	15 34.6	0 14.4	28 32.8	15 47.8
22 Su	8 0 26	0♒43 24	20 24 28	26 59 7	18 6.5	9 15.8	21 29.0	2 8.7	29 48.0	15 40.4	0 16.5	28 31.4	15 46.6
23 M	8 4 23	1 44 29	3♒38 19	10♒21 53	18 0.5	10 59.0	22 41.3	2 52.9	29 58.7	15 46.0	0 18.6	28 29.9	15 45.4
24 Tu	8 8 19	2 45 32	17 9 29	24 0 46	17 53.1	12 42.2	23 53.7	3 37.2	0♈ 9.5	15 51.6	0 20.8	28 28.4	15 44.2
25 W	8 12 16	3 46 35	0♓55 19	7♓52 39	17 45.0	14 25.4	25 6.1	4 21.5	0 20.5	15 57.2	0 23.0	28 27.0	15 42.9
26 Th	8 16 12	4 47 36	14 52 18	21 53 46	17 37.2	16 8.5	26 18.6	5 5.8	0 31.5	16 2.7	0 25.2	28 25.5	15 41.8
27 F	8 20 9	5 48 37	28 56 36	6♈ 0 22	17 30.6	17 51.3	27 31.1	5 50.2	0 42.7	16 8.1	0 27.5	28 23.9	15 40.6
28 Sa	8 24 5	6 49 36	13♈ 4 40	20 9 10	17 25.9	19 33.6	28 43.7	6 34.6	0 53.9	16 13.5	0 29.8	28 22.4	15 39.4
29 Su	8 28 2	7 50 34	27 13 37	4♉17 45	17D 23.5	21 15.1	29 56.3	7 19.0	1 5.3	16 18.8	0 32.1	28 20.9	15 38.2
30 M	8 31 58	8 51 31	11♉21 24	18 24 25	17 23.0	22 55.6	1♑ 9.0	8 3.5	1 16.7	16 24.0	0 34.5	28 19.3	15 37.1
31 Tu	8 35 55	9 52 27	25 26 41	2♊28 4	17 23.7	24 34.8	2 21.7	8 48.0	1 28.3	16 29.2	0 36.9	28 17.8	15 35.9

LONGITUDE FEBRUARY 1928

Day	Sid.Time	☉	0 hr ☽	Noon ☽	True ☊	☿	♀	♂	♃	♄	♅	♆	♇
1 W	8 39 52	10♒53 21	9♊28 29	16♊27 45	17♊24.7	26♒12.4	3♑34.4	9♒32.6	1♈39.9	16♐34.3	0♈39.4	28♌16.2	15♋34.8
2 Th	8 43 48	11 54 14	23 25 46	0♋22 17	17R 24.7	27 47.8	4 47.2	10 17.1	1 51.6	16 39.4	0 41.9	28R 14.6	15R 33.6
3 F	8 47 45	12 55 6	7♋17 7	14 10 0	17 22.9	29 20.8	6 0.1	11 1.8	2 3.5	16 44.3	0 44.4	28 13.0	15 32.5
4 Sa	8 51 41	13 55 57	21 0 37	27 48 41	17 18.6	0♓50.6	7 12.9	11 46.4	2 15.4	16 49.2	0 47.0	28 11.4	15 31.4
5 Su	8 55 38	14 56 46	4♌33 52	11♌15 51	17 11.6	2 16.8	8 25.8	12 31.1	2 27.4	16 54.1	0 49.6	28 9.8	15 30.4
6 M	8 59 34	15 57 34	17 54 21	24 29 6	17 2.3	3 38.7	9 38.8	13 15.8	2 39.5	16 58.8	0 52.2	28 8.1	15 29.3
7 Tu	9 3 31	16 58 21	0♍59 53	7♍26 35	16 51.4	4 55.6	10 51.8	14 0.5	2 51.6	17 3.5	0 54.9	28 6.5	15 28.2
8 W	9 7 27	17 59 7	13 49 6	20 7 28	16 40.0	6 6.8	12 4.8	14 45.3	3 3.9	17 8.1	0 57.6	28 4.8	15 27.2
9 Th	9 11 24	18 59 51	26 21 45	2♎32 9	16 29.2	7 11.5	13 17.8	15 30.1	3 16.2	17 12.7	1 0.3	28 3.2	15 26.1
10 F	9 15 21	20 0 35	8♎38 56	14 42 25	16 20.0	8 9.0	14 30.9	16 15.0	3 28.6	17 17.2	1 3.0	28 1.5	15 25.1
11 Sa	9 19 17	21 1 17	20 43 1	26 41 13	16 13.0	8 58.6	15 44.0	16 59.9	3 41.1	17 21.5	1 5.8	27 59.9	15 24.1
12 Su	9 23 14	22 1 58	2♏37 34	8♏32 37	16 8.5	9 39.5	16 57.2	17 44.8	3 53.7	17 25.9	1 8.6	27 58.2	15 23.1
13 M	9 27 10	23 2 38	14 27 1	20 21 25	16D 6.4	10 11.1	18 10.4	18 29.7	4 6.4	17 30.1	1 11.5	27 56.5	15 22.1
14 Tu	9 31 7	24 3 17	26 16 30	2♐12 58	16 6.0	10 32.9	19 23.6	19 14.7	4 19.1	17 34.3	1 14.4	27 54.8	15 21.2
15 W	9 35 3	25 3 55	8♐11 29	14 12 44	16R 6.4	10R 44.5	20 36.8	19 59.8	4 31.9	17 38.3	1 17.3	27 53.2	15 20.2
16 Th	9 39 0	26 4 31	20 17 25	26 26 6	16 6.5	10 45.6	21 50.1	20 44.8	4 44.7	17 42.3	1 20.2	27 51.5	15 19.3
17 F	9 42 56	27 5 7	2♑39 24	8♑57 49	16 5.3	10 36.3	23 3.4	21 29.9	4 57.7	17 46.2	1 23.1	27 49.8	15 18.4
18 Sa	9 46 53	28 5 41	15 21 45	21 51 31	16 1.8	10 16.7	24 16.8	22 15.0	5 10.7	17 50.1	1 26.1	27 48.1	15 17.5
19 Su	9 50 50	29 6 14	28 27 21	5♒ 9 16	15 55.6	9 47.4	25 30.1	23 0.2	5 23.7	17 53.8	1 29.1	27 46.4	15 16.6
20 M	9 54 46	0♓ 6 45	11♒57 13	18 50 57	15 46.7	9 8.9	26 43.5	23 45.4	5 36.9	17 57.5	1 32.2	27 44.8	15 15.8
21 Tu	9 58 43	1 7 15	25 50 4	2♓54 2	15 35.7	8 22.5	27 56.9	24 30.6	5 50.1	18 1.1	1 35.2	27 43.1	15 14.9
22 W	10 2 39	2 7 43	10♓ 2 11	17 13 44	15 23.6	7 29.2	29 10.3	25 15.8	6 3.3	18 4.6	1 38.3	27 41.4	15 14.1
23 Th	10 6 36	3 8 10	24 27 52	1♈43 40	15 11.8	6 30.5	0♒23.7	26 1.0	6 16.6	18 8.0	1 41.4	27 39.7	15 13.3
24 F	10 10 32	4 8 35	9♈ 0 16	16 16 51	15 1.5	5 27.9	1 37.1	26 46.3	6 30.0	18 11.3	1 44.5	27 38.0	15 12.5
25 Sa	10 14 29	5 8 58	23 32 38	0♉46 57	14 53.7	4 23.2	2 50.6	27 31.6	6 43.4	18 14.5	1 47.6	27 36.4	15 11.7
26 Su	10 18 25	6 9 19	7♉59 16	15 9 8	14 48.8	3 17.9	4 4.1	28 17.0	6 56.9	18 17.7	1 50.8	27 34.7	15 11.0
27 M	10 22 22	7 9 38	22 16 16	29 20 27	14 46.5	2 13.6	5 17.5	29 2.3	7 10.4	18 20.7	1 54.0	27 33.1	15 10.3
28 Tu	10 26 18	8 9 55	6♊21 34	13♊19 37	14 46.0	1 11.9	6 31.0	29 47.7	7 24.0	18 23.7	1 57.2	27 31.4	15 9.6
29 W	10 30 15	9 10 10	20 14 38	27 6 41	14 45.9	0 13.8	7 44.5	0♒33.1	7 37.6	18 26.5	2 0.4	27 29.8	15 8.9

Astro Data	Dy Hr Mn
☽0S	13 20:25
♃⊼♆	15 10:13
♄⊼♇	22 21:40
♃☌♅	25 6:49
☽0N	27 20:22
♃0N	6 2:31
☽0S	10 4:06
☿ R	15 14:35
♅0N	21 12:04
☽0N	24 2:31

Planet Ingress	Dy Hr Mn
♀ ♐	4 0:06
♅ ♈	13 8:47
☿ ♒	16 13:35
♂ ♑	19 2:02
☉ ♒	21 6:57
♃ ♈	23 2:54
♀ ♑	29 1:13
☿ ♓	3 10:22
☉ ♓	19 21:19
♀ ♒	22 16:15
♂ ♒	28 6:30
☿ ♒	29 6:00

Last Aspect Dy Hr Mn		☽ Ingress Dy Hr Mn
1 21:27	♆ △	♉ 1 23:15
4 0:57	♅ ⚹	♊ 4 1:20
6 3:09	♅ □	♋ 6 3:28
8 6:38	♅ △	♌ 8 6:52
10 10:37	♆ ☌	♍ 10 12:53
12 22:16	♅ ☍	♎ 12 22:18
15 7:45	♆ ⚹	♏ 15 10:26
17 21:16	♃ △	♐ 17 23:06
20 8:53	♃ □	♑ 20 9:49
22 17:19	♃ ⚹	♒ 22 17:27
24 19:43	♆ ☍	♓ 24 22:24
26 21:21	♀ □	♈ 27 1:48
29 1:54	♆ △	♉ 29 4:42
31 4:52	♆ □	♊ 31 7:47

Last Aspect Dy Hr Mn		☽ Ingress Dy Hr Mn
2 8:30	☿ △	♋ 2 11:21
3 14:23	♇ ☌	♌ 4 15:53
6 18:40	♆ ☌	♍ 6 22:09
8 6:20	♄ □	♎ 9 7:03
11 14:37	♆ ⚹	♏ 11 18:41
14 3:19	♆ □	♐ 14 7:32
16 14:43	♆ △	♑ 16 18:54
18 18:06	♀ ☌	♒ 19 2:47
21 3:12	♆ ☍	♓ 21 7:05
23 2:43	♂ ⚹	♈ 23 9:09
25 6:58	♂ □	♉ 25 10:42
27 12:08	♂ △	♊ 27 13:07
29 16:24	☿ △	♋ 29 17:04

☽ Phases & Eclipses Dy Hr Mn	
7 6:08	○ 15♋42
14 21:14	☽ 23♎29
22 20:19	● 1♒35
29 19:25	☽ 8♉40
5 20:11	○ 15♌48
13 19:05	☽ 23♏51
21 9:41	● 1♓32
28 3:21	☽ 8♊18

Astro Data

1 JANUARY 1928
Julian Day # 10227
Delta T 24.3 sec
SVP 06♓16'11"
Obliquity 23°26'57"
⚷ Chiron 1♉27.8R
☽ Mean ☊ 17♊38.7

1 FEBRUARY 1928
Julian Day # 10258
Delta T 24.3 sec
SVP 06♓16'06"
Obliquity 23°26'57"
⚷ Chiron 1♉35.5
☽ Mean ☊ 16♊00.3

MARCH 1928 LONGITUDE

Day	Sid.Time	☉	0 hr ☽	Noon ☽	True ☊	☿	♀	♂	♃	♄	♅	♆	♇
1 Th	10 34 12	10♓10 23	3♋55 50	10♋42 12	14♊45.1	29♒20.5	8♒58.0	1♒18.5	7♈51.3	18♐29.3	2♈ 3.6	27♌28.1	15♋ 8.2
2 F	10 38 8	11 10 34	17 25 52	24 6 52	14R42.1	28R32.8	10 11.6	2 4.0	8 5.0	18 32.0	2 6.9	27R26.5	15R 7.6
3 Sa	10 42 5	12 10 43	0♌45 14	7♌20 58	14 36.4	27 51.3	11 25.1	2 49.5	8 18.8	18 34.6	2 10.1	27 24.9	15 7.0
4 Su	10 46 1	13 10 49	13 54 3	20 24 24	14 27.6	27 16.3	12 38.7	3 35.0	8 32.6	18 37.1	2 13.4	27 23.3	15 6.4
5 M	10 49 58	14 10 54	26 51 57	3♍16 37	14 16.0	26 48.2	13 52.2	4 20.5	8 46.5	18 39.5	2 16.7	27 21.7	15 5.8
6 Tu	10 53 54	15 10 57	9♍38 19	15 56 59	14 2.7	26 27.0	15 5.8	5 6.0	9 0.4	18 41.8	2 20.0	27 20.1	15 5.3
7 W	10 57 51	16 10 58	22 12 35	28 25 6	13 48.6	26 12.6	16 19.4	5 51.6	9 14.3	18 44.0	2 23.3	27 18.5	15 4.7
8 Th	11 1 47	17 10 57	4♎34 35	10♎41 8	13 35.0	26D 4.9	17 33.0	6 37.2	9 28.2	18 46.1	2 26.6	27 16.9	15 4.2
9 F	11 5 44	18 10 54	16 44 54	22 46 6	13 23.1	26 3.6	18 46.6	7 22.8	9 42.3	18 48.1	2 30.0	27 15.4	15 3.7
10 Sa	11 9 41	19 10 49	28 45 1	4♏42 0	13 13.7	26 8.6	20 0.2	8 8.4	9 56.3	18 50.1	2 33.3	27 13.8	15 3.3
11 Su	11 13 37	20 10 43	10♏37 27	16 31 49	13 7.2	26 19.4	21 13.8	8 54.1	10 10.4	18 51.9	2 36.7	27 12.3	15 2.8
12 M	11 17 34	21 10 35	22 25 39	28 19 30	13 3.4	26 35.9	22 27.4	9 39.8	10 24.5	18 53.6	2 40.0	27 10.8	15 2.4
13 Tu	11 21 30	22 10 25	4♐13 59	10♐ 9 45	13D 1.8	26 57.6	23 41.1	10 25.5	10 38.6	18 55.3	2 43.4	27 9.3	15 2.0
14 W	11 25 27	23 10 14	16 7 28	22 7 50	13R 1.6	27 24.3	24 54.8	11 11.2	10 52.8	18 56.8	2 46.8	27 7.8	15 1.6
15 Th	11 29 23	24 10 1	28 11 32	4♑19 16	13 1.6	27 55.6	26 8.4	11 56.9	11 7.0	18 58.2	2 50.2	27 6.3	15 1.3
16 F	11 33 20	25 9 46	10♑31 41	16 49 26	13 0.8	28 31.3	27 22.1	12 42.7	11 21.2	18 59.6	2 53.6	27 4.9	15 0.9
17 Sa	11 37 16	26 9 30	23 13 4	29 43 4	12 58.0	29 11.1	28 35.8	13 28.5	11 35.5	19 0.8	2 57.0	27 3.5	15 0.6
18 Su	11 41 13	27 9 12	6♒19 49	13♒ 3 34	12 52.8	29 54.8	29 49.5	14 14.3	11 49.8	19 2.0	3 0.4	27 2.0	15 0.4
19 M	11 45 10	28 8 52	19 54 23	26 52 11	12 45.0	0♓42.0	1♓ 3.2	15 0.1	12 4.1	19 3.0	3 3.9	27 0.7	15 0.1
20 Tu	11 49 6	29 8 30	3♓56 42	11♓ 7 26	12 35.1	1 32.6	2 16.9	15 45.9	12 18.4	19 3.9	3 7.3	26 59.3	14 59.9
21 W	11 53 3	0♈ 8 6	18 23 45	25 44 46	12 24.0	2 26.4	3 30.6	16 31.7	12 32.7	19 4.8	3 10.7	26 57.9	14 59.7
22 Th	11 56 59	1 7 40	3♈ 9 30	10♈36 51	12 13.0	3 23.2	4 44.3	17 17.6	12 47.1	19 5.5	3 14.1	26 56.6	14 59.5
23 F	12 0 56	2 7 12	18 5 38	25 34 43	12 3.3	4 22.7	5 58.0	18 3.5	13 1.5	19 6.1	3 17.6	26 55.2	14 59.3
24 Sa	12 4 52	3 6 42	3♉ 2 56	10♉29 18	11 55.9	5 25.0	7 11.7	18 49.3	13 15.9	19 6.7	3 21.0	26 53.9	14 59.2
25 Su	12 8 49	4 6 10	17 52 52	25 12 54	11 51.3	6 29.7	8 25.4	19 35.2	13 30.3	19 7.1	3 24.4	26 52.7	14 59.1
26 M	12 12 45	5 5 36	2♊28 49	9♊40 12	11D49.2	7 36.9	9 39.1	20 21.1	13 44.7	19 7.5	3 27.8	26 51.4	14 59.0
27 Tu	12 16 42	6 4 59	16 46 48	23 48 27	11 49.0	8 46.3	10 52.8	21 7.0	13 59.2	19 7.7	3 31.3	26 50.2	14 58.9
28 W	12 20 39	7 4 21	0♋45 11	7♋37 5	11R49.5	9 57.9	12 6.5	21 52.9	14 13.6	19R 7.8	3 34.7	26 49.0	14D58.9
29 Th	12 24 35	8 3 39	14 24 19	21 7 4	11 49.4	11 11.5	13 20.2	22 38.8	14 28.1	19 7.9	3 38.1	26 47.8	14 58.9
30 F	12 28 32	9 2 56	27 45 37	4♌20 10	11 47.8	12 27.2	14 33.9	23 24.8	14 42.6	19 7.8	3 41.5	26 46.6	14 58.9
31 Sa	12 32 28	10 2 10	10♌51 1	17 18 23	11 43.8	13 44.8	15 47.6	24 10.7	14 57.0	19 7.6	3 45.0	26 45.5	14 58.9

APRIL 1928 LONGITUDE

Day	Sid.Time	☉	0 hr ☽	Noon ☽	True ☊	☿	♀	♂	♃	♄	♅	♆	♇
1 Su	12 36 25	11♈ 1 21	23♌42 28	0♍ 3 30	11♊37.3	15♓ 4.2	17♓ 1.3	24♒56.6	15♈11.5	19♐ 7.4	3♈48.4	26♌44.4	14♋59.0
2 M	12 40 21	12 0 31	6♍21 38	12 37 1	11R28.6	16 25.5	18 15.0	25 42.6	15 26.0	19R 7.0	3 51.8	26R43.3	14 59.1
3 Tu	12 44 18	12 59 38	18 49 47	25 0 3	11 18.3	17 48.5	19 28.7	26 28.5	15 40.5	19 6.5	3 55.2	26 42.2	14 59.2
4 W	12 48 14	13 58 43	1♎ 7 56	7♎13 32	11 7.3	19 13.2	20 42.4	27 14.4	15 55.0	19 6.0	3 58.6	26 41.2	14 59.3
5 Th	12 52 11	14 57 46	13 16 58	19 18 23	10 56.7	20 39.7	21 56.1	28 0.4	16 9.5	19 5.3	4 1.9	26 40.2	14 59.5
6 F	12 56 8	15 56 47	25 17 56	1♏15 48	10 47.4	22 7.7	23 9.8	28 46.4	16 24.0	19 4.6	4 5.3	26 39.2	14 59.6
7 Sa	13 0 4	16 55 45	7♏12 13	13 7 26	10 40.2	23 37.5	24 23.5	29 32.3	16 38.5	19 3.7	4 8.7	26 38.2	14 59.8
8 Su	13 4 1	17 54 42	19 1 45	24 55 32	10 35.3	25 8.8	25 37.2	0♓18.3	16 53.0	19 2.8	4 12.0	26 37.3	15 0.1
9 M	13 7 57	18 53 37	0♐49 11	6♐43 7	10D32.8	26 41.7	26 50.9	1 4.3	17 7.5	19 1.7	4 15.4	26 36.4	15 0.3
10 Tu	13 11 54	19 52 31	12 37 49	18 33 51	10 32.2	28 16.2	28 4.6	1 50.3	17 22.0	19 0.6	4 18.7	26 35.5	15 0.6
11 W	13 15 50	20 51 22	24 31 44	0♑32 4	10 33.0	29 52.3	29 18.3	2 36.2	17 36.5	18 59.3	4 22.1	26 34.7	15 0.9
12 Th	13 19 47	21 50 12	6♑35 30	12 42 37	10 34.3	1♈29.9	0♈32.0	3 22.2	17 50.9	18 58.0	4 25.4	26 33.9	15 1.2
13 F	13 23 43	22 49 0	18 54 5	25 10 31	10R35.2	3 9.1	1 45.7	4 8.2	18 5.4	18 56.6	4 28.7	26 33.1	15 1.6
14 Sa	13 27 40	23 47 46	1♒32 30	8♒ 0 34	10 35.0	4 49.9	2 59.4	4 54.2	18 19.9	18 55.1	4 32.0	26 32.3	15 1.9
15 Su	13 31 37	24 46 31	14 35 13	21 16 48	10 33.1	6 32.3	4 13.1	5 40.2	18 34.3	18 53.4	4 35.2	26 31.6	15 2.3
16 M	13 35 33	25 45 14	28 5 34	5♓ 1 38	10 29.3	8 16.3	5 26.8	6 26.2	18 48.8	18 51.7	4 38.5	26 30.9	15 2.8
17 Tu	13 39 30	26 43 55	12♓ 4 55	19 15 10	10 24.0	10 1.8	6 40.5	7 12.1	19 3.2	18 49.9	4 41.8	26 30.2	15 3.2
18 W	13 43 26	27 42 34	26 31 54	3♈54 28	10 17.6	11 49.0	7 54.2	7 58.1	19 17.6	18 48.1	4 45.0	26 29.6	15 3.7
19 Th	13 47 23	28 41 12	11♈22 0	18 53 27	10 11.1	13 37.8	9 7.8	8 44.1	19 32.0	18 46.1	4 48.2	26 29.0	15 4.1
20 F	13 51 19	29 39 48	26 27 39	4♉ 3 22	10 5.4	15 28.2	10 21.5	9 30.0	19 46.4	18 44.0	4 51.4	26 28.4	15 4.7
21 Sa	13 55 16	0♉38 22	11♉39 18	19 14 12	10 1.1	17 20.2	11 35.2	10 16.0	20 0.8	18 41.9	4 54.6	26 27.8	15 5.2
22 Su	13 59 12	1 36 54	26 46 54	4♊16 18	9D58.7	19 13.8	12 48.9	11 1.9	20 15.1	18 39.6	4 57.7	26 27.3	15 5.7
23 M	14 3 9	2 35 24	11♊41 31	19 1 49	9 58.1	21 9.1	14 2.6	11 47.8	20 29.5	18 37.3	5 0.9	26 26.8	15 6.3
24 Tu	14 7 5	3 33 52	26 16 38	3♋25 35	9 58.8	23 5.9	15 16.2	12 33.7	20 43.8	18 34.9	5 4.0	26 26.4	15 6.9
25 W	14 11 2	4 32 17	10♋28 28	17 25 13	10 0.2	25 4.4	16 29.9	13 19.6	20 58.1	18 32.4	5 7.1	26 26.0	15 7.6
26 Th	14 14 59	5 30 41	24 15 53	1♌ 0 38	10R 1.5	27 4.4	17 43.6	14 5.5	21 12.3	18 29.8	5 10.2	26 25.6	15 8.2
27 F	14 18 55	6 29 3	7♌39 44	14 13 29	10 2.0	29 5.9	18 57.2	14 51.3	21 26.6	18 27.2	5 13.2	26 25.2	15 8.9
28 Sa	14 22 52	7 27 22	20 42 13	27 6 20	10 1.2	1♉ 8.9	20 10.9	15 37.2	21 40.8	18 24.4	5 16.2	26 24.9	15 9.6
29 Su	14 26 48	8 25 39	3♍26 11	9♍42 10	9 58.9	3 13.3	21 24.5	16 23.0	21 55.0	18 21.6	5 19.3	26 24.6	15 10.3
30 M	14 30 45	9 23 54	15 54 40	22 4 2	9 55.3	5 19.0	22 38.1	17 8.8	22 9.1	18 18.7	5 22.2	26 24.3	15 11.0

Astro Data	Planet Ingress	Last Aspect	☽ Ingress	Last Aspect	☽ Ingress	☽ Phases & Eclipses		Astro Data
Dy Hr Mn	Dy Hr Mn	Dy Hr Mn	Dy Hr Mn	Dy Hr Mn	Dy Hr Mn	Dy Hr Mn		1 MARCH 1928
☽0S 8 11:23	☿ ♓18 2:45	1 19:53 ♇ ☌	♌ 2 22:38	1 5:43 ♆ ☌	♍ 1 11:53	6 11:27	○ 15♍40	Julian Day # 10287
☿ D 8 16:44	♀ ♓18 3:25	5 0:55 ♆ ☌	♍ 5 5:51	3 1:24 ♀ ☍	♎ 3 21:47	14 15:20	☽ 23♐48	Delta T 24.3 sec
♃⚼♆ 18 18:48	☉ ♈20 20:44	6 17:18 ♄ □	♎ 7 15:04	6 7:28 ♂ △	♏ 6 9:27	21 20:29	● 0♈59	SVP 06♓16'02"
☽0N 22 11:31		9 20:57 ♆ ⚹	♏ 10 2:31	8 15:26 ♆ □	♐ 8 22:20	28 11:54	☽ 7♋34	Obliquity 23°26'58"
♄ R 28 20:37	♂ ♓ 7 14:27	12 9:39 ♆ □	♐ 12 15:24	11 10:38 ♀ □	♑ 11 10:56			⚷ Chiron 2♉30.8
♇ D 28 23:46	☿ ♈11 1:55	14 23:27 ☿ ⚹	♑ 15 3:33	13 8:09 ☉ □	♒ 13 21:07	5 3:38	○ 15♎07	☽ Mean ☊ 14♊28.1
♃□♇ 31 3:07	♀ ♈11 13:35	17 5:54 ☉ ⚹	♒ 17 12:31	15 21:14 ♆ ☍	♓ 16 3:19	13 8:09	☽ 23♑09	
	☉ ♉20 8:17	19 12:13 ♆ ☍	♓ 19 17:20	17 11:17 ♄ □	♈ 18 5:40	20 5:25	● 29♈53	1 APRIL 1928
☽0S 4 18:04	☿ ♉27 10:35	21 1:07 ♄ □	♈ 21 18:54	20 5:25 ☉ ☌	♉ 20 5:36	26 21:42	☽ 6♌23	Julian Day # 10318
☿0N 14 9:58		23 14:08 ♆ △	♉ 23 19:06	21 23:29 ♆ □	♊ 22 5:09			Delta T 24.3 sec
♀0N 14 10:53		25 14:43 ♆ □	♊ 25 19:53	24 0:16 ♆ ⚹	♋ 24 6:14			SVP 06♓15'58"
♃△♄ 16 4:25		27 17:11 ♆ ⚹	♋ 27 22:42	26 5:51 ☿ □	♌ 26 10:11			Obliquity 23°26'58"
☽0N 18 22:24		29 1:01 ♇ ☌	♌ 30 4:04	28 10:42 ♆ ☌	♍ 28 17:28			⚷ Chiron 4♉07.7
								☽ Mean ☊ 12♊49.6

LONGITUDE — MAY 1928

Day	Sid.Time	☉	0 hr ☽	Noon ☽	True ☊	☿	♀	♂	♃	♄	♅	♆	♇
1 Tu	14 34 41	10♉22 7	28♍10 36	4♎14 42	9♊50.7	7♉25.9	23♈51.8	17♓54.6	22♈23.2	18♐15.8	5♈25.2	26♌24.1	15♋11.8
2 W	14 38 38	11 20 19	10♎16 38	16 16 42	9R 45.8	9 33.8	25 5.4	18 40.4	22 37.3	18R 12.7	5 28.1	26R 23.9	15 12.5
3 Th	14 42 34	12 18 28	22 15 8	28 12 14	9 41.0	11 42.6	26 19.0	19 26.2	22 51.4	18 9.6	5 31.0	26 23.7	15 13.3
4 F	14 46 31	13 16 35	4♏ 8 13	10♏ 3 20	9 36.9	13 52.0	27 32.6	20 11.9	23 5.4	18 6.5	5 33.9	26 23.6	15 14.2
5 Sa	14 50 28	14 14 41	15 57 51	21 52 0	9 33.8	16 2.0	28 46.2	20 57.6	23 19.4	18 3.2	5 36.8	26 23.5	15 15.0
6 Su	14 54 24	15 12 46	27 46 4	3♐40 20	9 32.0	18 12.1	29 59.8	21 43.3	23 33.4	17 59.9	5 39.6	26 23.4	15 15.9
7 M	14 58 21	16 10 48	9♐35 6	15 30 42	9D 31.4	20 22.2	1♉13.4	22 29.0	23 47.3	17 56.5	5 42.4	26D 23.4	15 16.7
8 Tu	15 2 17	17 8 49	21 27 28	27 25 49	9 31.9	22 31.9	2 27.0	23 14.7	24 1.2	17 53.1	5 45.2	26 23.4	15 17.6
9 W	15 6 14	18 6 49	3♑26 7	9♑28 50	9 33.2	24 41.1	3 40.7	24 0.3	24 15.0	17 49.6	5 48.0	26 23.4	15 18.5
10 Th	15 10 10	19 4 47	15 34 25	21 43 20	9 34.7	26 49.3	4 54.3	24 45.9	24 28.8	17 46.0	5 50.7	26 23.5	15 19.5
11 F	15 14 7	20 2 44	27 56 5	4♒13 10	9 36.2	28 56.4	6 7.9	25 31.5	24 42.6	17 42.4	5 53.4	26 23.6	15 20.4
12 Sa	15 18 3	21 0 40	10♒35 3	17 2 12	9R 37.2	1♊ 1.9	7 21.5	26 17.1	24 56.3	17 38.7	5 56.0	26 23.7	15 21.4
13 Su	15 22 0	21 58 34	23 35 4	0♓14 0	9 37.5	3 5.8	8 35.1	27 2.7	25 10.0	17 35.0	5 58.7	26 23.9	15 22.4
14 M	15 25 57	22 56 27	6♓59 18	13 51 10	9 37.0	5 7.6	9 48.7	27 48.2	25 23.7	17 31.2	6 1.3	26 24.1	15 23.4
15 Tu	15 29 53	23 54 19	20 49 42	27 54 48	9 35.8	7 7.3	11 2.3	28 33.7	25 37.3	17 27.4	6 3.8	26 24.3	15 24.4
16 W	15 33 50	24 52 9	5♈ 6 17	12♈23 44	9 34.2	9 4.6	12 15.9	29 19.1	25 50.8	17 23.5	6 6.4	26 24.6	15 25.5
17 Th	15 37 46	25 49 59	19 46 34	27 14 4	9 32.5	10 59.3	13 29.5	0♈ 4.6	26 4.3	17 19.5	6 8.9	26 24.9	15 26.6
18 F	15 41 43	26 47 47	4♉45 19	12♉19 16	9 31.0	12 51.4	14 43.1	0 50.0	26 17.8	17 15.5	6 11.3	26 25.2	15 27.6
19 Sa	15 45 39	27 45 34	19 54 46	27 30 38	9 29.9	14 40.6	15 56.7	1 35.3	26 31.2	17 11.5	6 13.8	26 25.5	15 28.7
20 Su	15 49 36	28 43 19	5♊ 5 39	12♊38 38	9D 29.5	16 27.0	17 10.3	2 20.7	26 44.5	17 7.4	6 16.2	26 25.9	15 29.9
21 M	15 53 32	29 41 4	20 8 28	27 34 12	9 29.6	18 10.3	18 23.9	3 6.0	26 57.8	17 3.3	6 18.5	26 26.4	15 31.0
22 Tu	15 57 29	0♊38 47	4♋54 58	12♋10 7	9 30.1	19 50.6	19 37.5	3 51.2	27 11.1	16 59.2	6 20.9	26 26.8	15 32.1
23 W	16 1 26	1 36 28	19 19 7	26 21 40	9 30.8	21 27.8	20 51.1	4 36.4	27 24.2	16 55.0	6 23.1	26 27.3	15 33.3
24 Th	16 5 22	2 34 8	3♌17 34	10♌ 6 49	9 31.4	23 1.8	22 4.7	5 21.6	27 37.4	16 50.8	6 25.4	26 27.8	15 34.5
25 F	16 9 19	3 31 47	16 49 32	23 25 55	9 31.9	24 32.7	23 18.3	6 6.7	27 50.4	16 46.6	6 27.6	26 28.4	15 35.7
26 Sa	16 13 15	4 29 23	29 56 17	6♍21 3	9R 32.1	26 0.2	24 31.9	6 51.8	28 3.4	16 42.3	6 29.8	26 29.0	15 36.9
27 Su	16 17 12	5 26 59	12♍40 37	18 55 28	9 32.1	27 24.5	25 45.5	7 36.8	28 16.4	16 38.0	6 31.9	26 29.6	15 38.1
28 M	16 21 8	6 24 32	25 6 6	1♎13 1	9 31.9	28 45.4	26 59.1	8 21.8	28 29.2	16 33.6	6 34.0	26 30.2	15 39.4
29 Tu	16 25 5	7 22 5	7♎16 43	13 17 42	9 31.7	0♋ 3.0	28 12.7	9 6.8	28 42.1	16 29.3	6 36.1	26 30.9	15 40.6
30 W	16 29 2	8 19 36	19 16 27	25 13 24	9 31.5	1 17.2	29 26.3	9 51.7	28 54.8	16 24.9	6 38.1	26 31.6	15 41.9
31 Th	16 32 58	9 17 6	1♏ 9 0	7♏ 3 41	9D 31.4	2 27.9	0♊39.9	10 36.5	29 7.5	16 20.5	6 40.1	26 32.4	15 43.2

LONGITUDE — JUNE 1928

Day	Sid.Time	☉	0 hr ☽	Noon ☽	True ☊	☿	♀	♂	♃	♄	♅	♆	♇
1 F	16 36 55	10♊14 34	12♏57 48	18♏51 45	9♊31.4	3♋35.0	1♊53.4	11♈21.3	29♈20.1	16♐16.1	6♈42.1	26♌33.2	15♋44.5
2 Sa	16 40 51	11 12 2	24 45 50	0♐40 24	9 31.5	4 38.6	3 7.0	12 6.1	29 32.6	16R 11.7	6 44.0	26 34.0	15 45.8
3 Su	16 44 48	12 9 28	6♐35 44	12 32 7	9R 31.6	5 38.6	4 20.6	12 50.8	29 45.1	16 7.3	6 45.8	26 34.8	15 47.1
4 M	16 48 44	13 6 54	18 29 49	24 29 7	9 31.6	6 34.8	5 34.2	13 35.5	29 57.5	16 2.9	6 47.7	26 35.7	15 48.4
5 Tu	16 52 41	14 4 18	0♑30 15	6♑33 29	9 31.3	7 27.2	6 47.8	14 20.1	0♉ 9.8	15 58.4	6 49.4	26 36.6	15 49.8
6 W	16 56 37	15 1 42	12 39 5	18 47 17	9 30.8	8 15.7	8 1.4	15 4.7	0 22.1	15 54.0	6 51.2	26 37.5	15 51.1
7 Th	17 0 34	15 59 5	24 58 22	1♒12 37	9 30.1	9 0.3	9 15.0	15 49.2	0 34.3	15 49.6	6 52.9	26 38.4	15 52.5
8 F	17 4 31	16 56 28	7♒30 17	13 51 40	9 29.2	9 40.8	10 28.6	16 33.7	0 46.4	15 45.1	6 54.6	26 39.4	15 53.9
9 Sa	17 8 27	17 53 49	20 17 2	26 46 41	9 28.3	10 17.1	11 42.2	17 18.1	0 58.4	15 40.7	6 56.2	26 40.4	15 55.3
10 Su	17 12 24	18 51 10	3♓20 52	9♓59 49	9 27.6	10 49.2	12 55.8	18 2.5	1 10.3	15 36.2	6 57.7	26 41.5	15 56.7
11 M	17 16 20	19 48 31	16 43 45	23 32 50	9D 27.2	11 17.0	14 9.4	18 46.8	1 22.2	15 31.8	6 59.3	26 42.6	15 58.1
12 Tu	17 20 17	20 45 51	0♈27 8	7♈26 43	9 27.4	11 40.4	15 23.1	19 31.1	1 34.0	15 27.4	7 0.8	26 43.7	15 59.5
13 W	17 24 13	21 43 11	14 31 29	21 41 16	9 28.0	11 59.4	16 36.7	20 15.3	1 45.7	15 23.0	7 2.2	26 44.8	16 0.9
14 Th	17 28 10	22 40 30	28 55 45	6♉14 32	9 28.9	12 13.8	17 50.3	20 59.4	1 57.3	15 18.6	7 3.6	26 45.9	16 2.4
15 F	17 32 6	23 37 49	13♉37 2	21 2 34	9 29.9	12 23.7	19 4.0	21 43.5	2 8.8	15 14.2	7 4.9	26 47.1	16 3.8
16 Sa	17 36 3	24 35 8	28 30 20	5♊59 25	9R 30.6	12R 29.0	20 17.6	22 27.5	2 20.2	15 9.8	7 6.2	26 48.3	16 5.3
17 Su	17 40 0	25 32 26	13♊28 50	20 57 34	9 30.8	12 29.8	21 31.3	23 11.4	2 31.6	15 5.5	7 7.5	26 49.6	16 6.8
18 M	17 43 56	26 29 44	28 24 34	5♋48 50	9 30.2	12 26.1	22 45.0	23 55.3	2 42.8	15 1.2	7 8.7	26 50.9	16 8.2
19 Tu	17 47 53	27 27 1	13♋ 9 26	20 25 31	9 28.7	12 18.0	23 58.6	24 39.1	2 54.0	14 56.9	7 9.9	26 52.2	16 9.7
20 W	17 51 49	28 24 18	27 36 22	4♌41 24	9 26.5	12 5.6	25 12.3	25 22.8	3 5.1	14 52.6	7 11.0	26 53.5	16 11.2
21 Th	17 55 46	29 21 34	11♌40 13	18 32 33	9 23.9	11 49.2	26 26.0	26 6.5	3 16.0	14 48.3	7 12.1	26 54.8	16 12.7
22 F	17 59 42	0♋18 50	25 18 18	1♍57 31	9 21.2	11 28.9	27 39.7	26 50.1	3 26.9	14 44.1	7 13.1	26 56.2	16 14.2
23 Sa	18 3 39	1 16 4	8♍30 21	14 57 6	9 19.0	11 5.0	28 53.4	27 33.6	3 37.7	14 40.0	7 14.1	26 57.6	16 15.7
24 Su	18 7 35	2 13 18	21 18 7	27 33 53	9D 17.6	10 37.9	0♋ 7.1	28 17.0	3 48.3	14 35.8	7 15.0	26 59.0	16 17.2
25 M	18 11 32	3 10 32	3♎44 55	9♎51 44	9 17.2	10 8.0	1 20.8	29 0.4	3 58.9	14 31.7	7 15.9	27 0.5	16 18.7
26 Tu	18 15 29	4 7 45	15 54 57	21 55 8	9 17.7	9 35.9	2 34.4	29 43.7	4 9.3	14 27.7	7 16.8	27 1.9	16 20.3
27 W	18 19 25	5 4 57	27 52 55	3♏48 52	9 19.0	9 1.9	3 48.2	0♉26.9	4 19.7	14 23.6	7 17.5	27 3.4	16 21.8
28 Th	18 23 22	6 2 9	9♏43 34	15 37 34	9 20.7	8 26.6	5 1.9	1 10.0	4 29.9	14 19.7	7 18.3	27 5.0	16 23.3
29 F	18 27 18	6 59 21	21 31 25	27 25 36	9 22.3	7 50.7	6 15.6	1 53.1	4 40.0	14 15.7	7 19.0	27 6.5	16 24.9
30 Sa	18 31 15	7 56 32	3♐20 36	9♐16 49	9R 23.3	7 14.8	7 29.3	2 36.0	4 50.0	14 11.8	7 19.6	27 8.1	16 26.4

Astro Data	Planet Ingress	Last Aspect	☽ Ingress	Last Aspect	☽ Ingress	☽ Phases & Eclipses	Astro Data
Dy Hr Mn	Dy Hr Mn	Dy Hr Mn	Dy Hr Mn	Dy Hr Mn	Dy Hr Mn	Dy Hr Mn	1 MAY 1928
☽0S 2 0:18	♀ ♉ 6 0:03	30 4:39 ♄ □	♎ 1 3:36	2 3:40 ♆ □	♐ 2 10:38	4 20:12 ○ 14♏05	Julian Day # 10348
♆ D 7 12:31	☿ ♊ 11 12:07	3 9:08 ♀ ☍	♏ 3 15:38	4 16:14 ♆ △	♑ 4 23:00	12 20:50 ☽ 21♒51	Delta T 24.3 sec
☽0N 16 8:55	♂ ♈ 16 21:35	5 21:12 ♆ ☍	♐ 6 4:32	6 6:17 ♇ ☍	♒ 7 9:41	19 13:14 ● 28♉17	SVP 06♓15'55"
♃△♆ 18 13:38	☉ ♊ 21 7:52	8 9:55 ♆ △	♑ 8 17:09	9 11:49 ♆ ☍	♓ 9 17:54	19 13:23:56 ◑ T non-C	Obliquity 23°26'58"
♂0N 21 14:30	☿ ♋ 28 23:03	11 2:19 ☿ △	♒ 11 3:58	11 5:51 ☉ □	♈ 11 23:13	26 9:11 ☽ 4♍51	⚷ Chiron 5♉59.3
☽0S 29 6:31	♀ ♊ 30 11:00	13 5:06 ♆ ☍	♓ 13 11:35	13 20:25 ♆ △	♉ 14 1:46		☽ Mean ☊ 11♊14.3
		15 13:49 ♂ ☌	♈ 15 15:30	15 21:16 ♆ □	♊ 16 2:24	3 12:13 ○ 12♐39	
♄⚻♇ 6 11:52	♃ ♉ 4 4:51	17 10:41 ♆ △	♉ 17 16:25	17 21:29 ♆ ✶	♋ 18 2:34	3 12:10 ◐ T 1.242	1 JUNE 1928
♃⚼♄ 7 22:11	☉ ♋ 21 16:06	19 13:14 ☉ ☌	♊ 19 15:56	19 20:04 ♂ □	♌ 20 4:02	11 5:51 ☽ 20♓02	Julian Day # 10379
☽0N 12 17:14	♀ ♋ 23 21:42	21 11:11 ♃ ✶	♋ 21 15:57	22 4:39 ♀ ✶	♍ 22 8:27	17 20:42 ● 26♊22	Delta T 24.2 sec
☿ R 16 16:11	♂ ♉ 26 9:04	23 14:01 ♃ □	♌ 23 18:17	23 14:29 ♇ ✶	♎ 24 16:43	17 20:27:01 ◑ P 0.038	SVP 06♓15'51"
☽0S 25 13:10		25 20:27 ♃ △	♍ 26 0:07	26 22:20 ♆ ✶	♏ 27 4:17	24 22:47 ☽ 3♎08	Obliquity 23°26'58"
		28 8:01 ☿ □	♎ 28 9:36	29 11:23 ♆ □	♐ 29 17:13		⚷ Chiron 7♉51.5
		30 19:49 ♃ ☍	♏ 30 21:40				☽ Mean ☊ 9♊35.8

JULY 1928 LONGITUDE

Day	Sid.Time	☉	0 hr ☽	Noon ☽	True ☊	☿	♀	♂	♃	♄	♅	♆	♇
1 Su	18 35 11	8♋53 43	15♐14 40	21♐14 28	9♊23.3	6♋39.4	8♋43.0	3♉18.9	4♉59.9	14♐ 8.0	7♈20.2	27♌ 9.7	16♋28.0
2 M	18 39 8	9 50 54	27 16 32	3♑21 7	9R22.0	6R 5.2	9 56.7	4 1.7	5 9.7	14R 4.2	7 20.8	27 11.3	16 29.5
3 Tu	18 43 4	10 48 5	9♑28 27	15 38 41	9 19.2	5 32.8	11 10.5	4 44.5	5 19.4	14 0.5	7 21.3	27 12.9	16 31.1
4 W	18 47 1	11 45 15	21 52 0	28 8 28	9 15.0	5 2.7	12 24.2	5 27.1	5 29.0	13 56.8	7 21.8	27 14.6	16 32.6
5 Th	18 50 58	12 42 26	4♒28 12	10♒51 14	9 9.8	4 35.5	13 38.0	6 9.7	5 38.4	13 53.2	7 22.2	27 16.3	16 34.2
6 F	18 54 54	13 39 37	17 17 38	23 47 23	9 4.2	4 11.7	14 51.7	6 52.2	5 47.7	13 49.6	7 22.5	27 18.0	16 35.7
7 Sa	18 58 51	14 36 48	0♓20 32	6♓57 6	8 58.8	3 51.6	16 5.5	7 34.6	5 56.9	13 46.1	7 22.8	27 19.7	16 37.3
8 Su	19 2 47	15 33 59	13 37 4	20 20 28	8 54.3	3 35.8	17 19.3	8 16.9	6 6.0	13 42.7	7 23.1	27 21.4	16 38.8
9 M	19 6 44	16 31 10	27 7 19	3♈57 36	8 51.1	3 24.5	18 33.1	8 59.1	6 15.0	13 39.3	7 23.3	27 23.2	16 40.4
10 Tu	19 10 40	17 28 22	10♈51 19	17 48 26	8D49.6	3D17.9	19 46.9	9 41.2	6 23.8	13 36.0	7 23.5	27 25.0	16 41.9
11 W	19 14 37	18 25 35	24 48 56	1♉52 41	8 49.6	3 16.4	21 0.7	10 23.2	6 32.5	13 32.7	7 23.6	27 26.8	16 43.5
12 Th	19 18 33	19 22 48	8♉59 35	16 9 24	8 50.6	3 20.0	22 14.5	11 5.2	6 41.1	13 29.6	7R23.7	27 28.6	16 45.1
13 F	19 22 30	20 20 2	23 21 51	0♊36 36	8 51.8	3 28.9	23 28.3	11 47.0	6 49.5	13 26.4	7 23.7	27 30.4	16 46.6
14 Sa	19 26 27	21 17 16	7♊53 10	15 11 1	8R52.5	3 43.1	24 42.2	12 28.8	6 57.8	13 23.4	7 23.7	27 32.3	16 48.2
15 Su	19 30 23	22 14 31	22 29 30	29 47 56	8 51.8	4 2.9	25 56.0	13 10.4	7 6.0	13 20.4	7 23.6	27 34.2	16 49.7
16 M	19 34 20	23 11 46	7♋ 5 32	14♋21 29	8 49.2	4 28.0	27 9.9	13 51.9	7 14.0	13 17.5	7 23.5	27 36.1	16 51.3
17 Tu	19 38 16	24 9 2	21 35 0	28 45 16	8 44.5	4 58.7	28 23.8	14 33.4	7 21.9	13 14.7	7 23.3	27 38.0	16 52.8
18 W	19 42 13	25 6 19	5♌51 36	12♌53 19	8 38.1	5 34.7	29 37.6	15 14.7	7 29.6	13 12.0	7 23.1	27 39.9	16 54.4
19 Th	19 46 9	26 3 35	19 49 53	26 40 53	8 30.6	6 16.2	0♌51.5	15 55.9	7 37.2	13 9.3	7 22.8	27 41.8	16 55.9
20 F	19 50 6	27 0 52	3♍26 2	10♍ 5 13	8 22.9	7 3.1	2 5.4	16 37.0	7 44.6	13 6.7	7 22.5	27 43.8	16 57.5
21 Sa	19 54 3	27 58 9	16 38 23	23 5 42	8 15.9	7 55.3	3 19.3	17 18.0	7 52.0	13 4.2	7 22.1	27 45.8	16 59.0
22 Su	19 57 59	28 55 27	29 27 23	5♎43 47	8 10.3	8 52.8	4 33.2	17 58.8	7 59.1	13 1.8	7 21.7	27 47.8	17 0.5
23 M	20 1 56	29 52 45	11♎55 20	18 2 34	8 6.6	9 55.4	5 47.1	18 39.6	8 6.1	12 59.4	7 21.2	27 49.8	17 2.1
24 Tu	20 5 52	0♌50 3	24 6 1	0♏ 6 18	8D 4.8	11 3.2	7 1.0	19 20.2	8 13.0	12 57.2	7 20.7	27 51.8	17 3.6
25 W	20 9 49	1 47 21	6♏ 4 4	11 59 58	8 4.7	12 15.9	8 14.9	20 0.7	8 19.6	12 55.0	7 20.2	27 53.8	17 5.1
26 Th	20 13 45	2 44 41	17 54 39	23 48 48	8 5.5	13 33.5	9 28.9	20 41.1	8 26.2	12 52.9	7 19.6	27 55.8	17 6.6
27 F	20 17 42	3 42 0	29 43 2	5♐37 59	8R 6.5	14 55.9	10 42.8	21 21.4	8 32.6	12 50.9	7 18.9	27 57.9	17 8.1
28 Sa	20 21 38	4 39 20	11♐34 15	17 32 22	8 6.7	16 23.0	11 56.7	22 1.5	8 38.8	12 49.0	7 18.2	27 60.0	17 9.6
29 Su	20 25 35	5 36 41	23 32 51	29 36 10	8 5.4	17 54.4	13 10.6	22 41.6	8 44.9	12 47.2	7 17.5	28 2.0	17 11.1
30 M	20 29 32	6 34 2	5♑42 41	11♑52 45	8 1.9	19 30.2	14 24.6	23 21.5	8 50.8	12 45.4	7 16.7	28 4.1	17 12.6
31 Tu	20 33 28	7 31 24	18 6 36	24 24 25	7 56.1	21 9.9	15 38.5	24 1.2	8 56.5	12 43.8	7 15.9	28 6.2	17 14.1

AUGUST 1928 LONGITUDE

Day	Sid.Time	☉	0 hr ☽	Noon ☽	True ☊	☿	♀	♂	♃	♄	♅	♆	♇
1 W	20 37 25	8♌28 47	0♒46 18	7♒12 18	7♊48.1	22♋53.4	16♌52.5	24♉40.9	9♉ 2.1	12♐42.2	7♈15.0	28♌ 8.4	17♋15.6
2 Th	20 41 21	9 26 10	13 42 20	20 16 18	7R38.5	24 40.5	18 6.4	25 20.4	9 7.5	12R40.7	7R14.1	28 10.5	17 17.0
3 F	20 45 18	10 23 34	26 54 1	3♓35 15	7 28.0	26 30.7	19 20.4	25 59.8	9 12.8	12 39.4	7 13.1	28 12.6	17 18.5
4 Sa	20 49 14	11 21 0	10♓19 45	17 7 14	7 17.8	28 23.8	20 34.3	26 39.1	9 17.8	12 38.1	7 12.1	28 14.7	17 20.0
5 Su	20 53 11	12 18 26	23 57 23	0♈49 57	7 9.0	0♌19.4	21 48.3	27 18.2	9 22.7	12 36.9	7 11.1	28 16.9	17 21.4
6 M	20 57 7	13 15 54	7♈44 37	14 41 11	7 2.2	2 17.2	23 2.3	27 57.2	9 27.5	12 35.8	7 10.0	28 19.0	17 22.8
7 Tu	21 1 4	14 13 23	21 39 24	28 39 7	6 57.9	4 16.7	24 16.3	28 36.1	9 32.0	12 34.8	7 8.8	28 21.2	17 24.2
8 W	21 5 1	15 10 53	5♉40 9	12♉42 24	6D56.0	6 17.7	25 30.3	29 14.8	9 36.4	12 33.9	7 7.7	28 23.4	17 25.7
9 Th	21 8 57	16 8 24	19 45 43	26 50 1	6 55.7	8 19.7	26 44.2	29 53.3	9 40.6	12 33.0	7 6.4	28 25.6	17 27.1
10 F	21 12 54	17 5 58	3♊55 9	11♊ 0 57	6R56.0	10 22.4	27 58.2	0♊31.8	9 44.6	12 32.3	7 5.2	28 27.7	17 28.4
11 Sa	21 16 50	18 3 32	18 7 15	25 13 47	6 55.7	12 25.6	29 12.3	1 10.0	9 48.5	12 31.7	7 3.9	28 29.9	17 29.8
12 Su	21 20 47	19 1 8	2♋20 14	9♋26 13	6 53.5	14 28.9	0♍26.3	1 48.1	9 52.1	12 31.1	7 2.5	28 32.1	17 31.2
13 M	21 24 43	19 58 46	16 31 19	23 35 2	6 48.8	16 32.0	1 40.3	2 26.1	9 55.6	12 30.7	7 1.1	28 34.3	17 32.6
14 Tu	21 28 40	20 56 25	0♌36 51	7♌36 13	6 41.4	18 34.8	2 54.3	3 3.9	9 58.9	12 30.4	6 59.7	28 36.5	17 33.9
15 W	21 32 36	21 54 5	14 32 35	21 25 25	6 31.5	20 37.0	4 8.4	3 41.5	10 2.0	12 30.1	6 58.3	28 38.8	17 35.2
16 Th	21 36 33	22 51 47	28 14 16	4♍58 43	6 19.9	22 38.4	5 22.4	4 19.0	10 4.9	12 30.0	6 56.8	28 41.0	17 36.6
17 F	21 40 30	23 49 29	11♍38 26	18 13 13	6 7.9	24 38.9	6 36.4	4 56.3	10 7.6	12D29.9	6 55.2	28 43.2	17 37.9
18 Sa	21 44 26	24 47 13	24 42 56	1♎ 7 35	5 56.6	26 38.5	7 50.5	5 33.4	10 10.2	12 30.0	6 53.6	28 45.4	17 39.2
19 Su	21 48 23	25 44 58	7♎27 17	13 42 14	5 47.1	28 36.9	9 4.5	6 10.4	10 12.5	12 30.1	6 52.0	28 47.6	17 40.4
20 M	21 52 19	26 42 44	19 52 46	25 59 15	5 39.9	0♍34.2	10 18.5	6 47.1	10 14.6	12 30.4	6 50.4	28 49.8	17 41.7
21 Tu	21 56 16	27 40 32	2♏ 2 11	8♏ 2 5	5 35.4	2 30.2	11 32.6	7 23.7	10 16.6	12 30.7	6 48.7	28 52.1	17 43.0
22 W	22 0 12	28 38 20	13 59 34	19 55 14	5 33.1	4 24.9	12 46.6	8 0.1	10 18.3	12 31.1	6 47.0	28 54.3	17 44.2
23 Th	22 4 9	29 36 10	25 49 46	1♐43 51	5 32.5	6 18.4	14 0.6	8 36.4	10 19.9	12 31.7	6 45.2	28 56.5	17 45.4
24 F	22 8 5	0♍34 1	7♐38 10	13 33 25	5 32.5	8 10.5	15 14.7	9 12.4	10 21.3	12 32.3	6 43.4	28 58.7	17 46.6
25 Sa	22 12 2	1 31 54	19 30 15	25 29 21	5 32.0	10 1.3	16 28.7	9 48.2	10 22.4	12 33.1	6 41.6	29 1.0	17 47.8
26 Su	22 15 59	2 29 47	1♑31 20	7♑36 45	5 30.0	11 50.8	17 42.7	10 23.9	10 23.4	12 33.9	6 39.8	29 3.2	17 49.0
27 M	22 19 55	3 27 42	13 46 9	19 59 58	5 25.8	13 39.0	18 56.7	10 59.4	10 24.2	12 34.8	6 37.9	29 5.4	17 50.2
28 Tu	22 23 52	4 25 39	26 18 34	2♒42 13	5 19.0	15 25.8	20 10.8	11 34.6	10 24.8	12 35.8	6 36.0	29 7.6	17 51.3
29 W	22 27 48	5 23 36	9♒11 4	15 45 11	5 9.7	17 11.4	21 24.8	12 9.7	10 25.1	12 37.0	6 34.1	29 9.8	17 52.5
30 Th	22 31 45	6 21 36	22 24 29	29 8 48	4 58.4	18 55.6	22 38.8	12 44.6	10R25.3	12 38.2	6 32.1	29 12.1	17 53.6
31 F	22 35 41	7 19 36	5♓57 49	12♓51 7	4 46.2	20 38.6	23 52.8	13 19.2	10 25.3	12 39.5	6 30.1	29 14.3	17 54.7

Astro Data	Dy Hr Mn
☽0N	9 23:01
☿ D	10 19:21
♅ R	12 22:35
♃⚺♅	17 4:18
☽0S	22 20:29
☽0N	6 3:42
♄ D	17 0:17
☽0S	19 4:17
♃ R	30 9:18

Planet Ingress	Dy Hr Mn
♀ ♌	18 7:16
☉ ♌	23 3:02
☿ ♌	4 20:00
♂ ♊	9 4:10
♀ ♍	11 15:29
☿ ♍	19 16:59
☉ ♍	23 9:53

Last Aspect Dy Hr Mn		☽ Ingress Dy Hr Mn
1 23:50	♆ △	♑ 2 5:23
3 13:43	♇ ☍	♒ 4 15:32
6 18:29	♆ ☍	♓ 6 23:23
8 7:17	♀ △	♈ 9 5:04
11 4:29	♆ △	♉ 11 8:49
13 6:53	♆ □	♊ 13 11:00
15 8:21	♆ ✶	♋ 15 12:20
17 12:28	♀ ☌	♌ 17 14:06
19 13:50	♆ ☌	♍ 19 17:53
21 22:54	☉ ✶	♎ 22 1:02
24 7:32	♆ ✶	♏ 24 11:47
26 20:26	♆ □	♐ 27 0:34
29 8:56	♆ △	♑ 29 12:47
31 11:53	♂ △	♒ 31 22:33

Last Aspect Dy Hr Mn		☽ Ingress Dy Hr Mn
3 2:22	♆ ☍	♓ 3 5:35
5 6:08	♂ ✶	♈ 5 10:33
7 11:31	♆ △	♉ 7 14:18
9 14:44	♆ □	♊ 9 17:22
11 17:34	♆ ✶	♋ 11 20:03
13 1:44	♇ ☌	♌ 13 22:57
16 0:47	♆ ☌	♍ 16 3:07
17 10:56	♇ ✶	♎ 18 9:53
20 17:41	♆ ✶	♏ 20 19:57
23 8:21	☉ □	♐ 23 8:29
25 19:05	♆ △	♑ 25 20:59
27 11:04	♀ △	♒ 28 6:57
30 12:08	♆ ☍	♓ 30 13:31

☽ Phases & Eclipses Dy Hr Mn	
3 2:48	○ 10♑55
10 12:16	☽ 17♈58
17 4:35	● 24♋20
24 14:38	☽ 1♏25
1 15:30	○ 9♒06
8 17:24	☽ 15♉53
15 13:48	● 22♌27
23 8:21	☽ 29♏56
31 2:34	○ 7♓26

Astro Data

1 JULY 1928
Julian Day # 10409
Delta T 24.2 sec
SVP 06♓15'45"
Obliquity 23°26'58"
⚷ Chiron 9♉17.4
☽ Mean ☊ 8♊00.5

1 AUGUST 1928
Julian Day # 10440
Delta T 24.2 sec
SVP 06♓15'40"
Obliquity 23°26'58"
⚷ Chiron 10♉05.6
☽ Mean ☊ 6♊22.0

Day	Sid.Time	☉	0 hr ☽	Noon ☽	True ☊	☿	♀	♂	♃	♄	♅	♆	♇
1 Sa	22 39 38	8♍17 38	19♓48 15	26♓48 38	4♊34.2	22♍20.3	25♍ 6.8	13♊53.7	10♉25.1	12♐40.9	6♈28.1	29♌16.5	17♋55.8
2 Su	22 43 34	9 15 42	3♈51 41	10♈56 46	4R23.6	24 0.7	26 20.8	14 27.9	10R24.6	12 42.4	6R26.0	29 18.7	17 56.8
3 M	22 47 31	10 13 48	18 3 19	25 10 45	4 15.5	25 40.0	27 34.8	15 1.9	10 24.0	12 44.0	6 23.9	29 20.9	17 57.9
4 Tu	22 51 27	11 11 56	2♉18 33	9♉26 16	4 10.1	27 18.0	28 48.8	15 35.7	10 23.2	12 45.7	6 21.8	29 23.0	17 58.9
5 W	22 55 24	12 10 5	16 33 32	23 40 3	4 7.5	28 54.8	0♎ 2.8	16 9.3	10 22.2	12 47.5	6 19.7	29 25.2	17 59.9
6 Th	22 59 21	13 8 17	0♊45 34	7♊49 57	4 6.7	0♎30.4	1 16.8	16 42.7	10 21.0	12 49.3	6 17.6	29 27.4	18 0.9
7 F	23 3 17	14 6 31	14 53 3	21 54 47	4 6.7	2 4.9	2 30.8	17 15.8	10 19.5	12 51.3	6 15.4	29 29.6	18 1.9
8 Sa	23 7 14	15 4 47	28 55 4	5♋53 50	4 6.2	3 38.2	3 44.8	17 48.6	10 17.9	12 53.4	6 13.2	29 31.8	18 2.8
9 Su	23 11 10	16 3 5	12♋50 59	19 46 26	4 4.0	5 10.3	4 58.8	18 21.3	10 16.1	12 55.5	6 11.0	29 33.9	18 3.8
10 M	23 15 7	17 1 25	26 40 0	3♌31 31	3 59.2	6 41.2	6 12.8	18 53.6	10 14.1	12 57.8	6 8.8	29 36.1	18 4.7
11 Tu	23 19 3	17 59 47	10♌20 47	17 7 34	3 51.7	8 11.0	7 26.8	19 25.8	10 11.8	13 0.1	6 6.5	29 38.2	18 5.6
12 W	23 23 0	18 58 11	23 51 36	0♍32 36	3 41.6	9 39.6	8 40.8	19 57.6	10 9.4	13 2.6	6 4.3	29 40.3	18 6.4
13 Th	23 26 57	19 56 38	7♍10 20	13 44 33	3 29.9	11 7.1	9 54.8	20 29.2	10 6.8	13 5.1	6 2.0	29 42.4	18 7.3
14 F	23 30 53	20 55 5	20 15 4	26 41 42	3 17.6	12 33.3	11 8.7	21 0.5	10 4.0	13 7.7	5 59.7	29 44.6	18 8.1
15 Sa	23 34 50	21 53 35	3♎ 4 23	9♎23 4	3 6.0	13 58.4	12 22.7	21 31.5	10 1.0	13 10.4	5 57.4	29 46.7	18 8.9
16 Su	23 38 46	22 52 7	15 37 48	21 48 44	2 56.0	15 22.2	13 36.7	22 2.3	9 57.8	13 13.2	5 55.0	29 48.7	18 9.7
17 M	23 42 43	23 50 40	27 56 2	4♏ 0 1	2 48.4	16 44.8	14 50.6	22 32.7	9 54.4	13 16.1	5 52.7	29 50.8	18 10.5
18 Tu	23 46 39	24 49 16	10♏ 1 1	15 59 27	2 43.4	18 6.1	16 4.6	23 2.9	9 50.8	13 19.1	5 50.3	29 52.9	18 11.2
19 W	23 50 36	25 47 53	21 55 48	27 50 37	2D41.0	19 26.0	17 18.6	23 32.7	9 47.0	13 22.1	5 48.0	29 54.9	18 12.0
20 Th	23 54 32	26 46 31	3♐44 27	9♐37 56	2 40.4	20 44.6	18 32.5	24 2.3	9 43.1	13 25.3	5 45.6	29 57.0	18 12.7
21 F	23 58 29	27 45 12	15 31 44	21 26 30	2 40.8	22 1.8	19 46.4	24 31.5	9 38.9	13 28.5	5 43.2	29 59.0	18 13.4
22 Sa	0 2 25	28 43 54	27 22 55	3♑21 41	2R41.3	23 17.4	21 0.4	25 0.5	9 34.6	13 31.9	5 40.8	0♍ 1.0	18 14.0
23 Su	0 6 22	29 42 38	9♑23 29	15 28 56	2 40.8	24 31.6	22 14.3	25 29.1	9 30.1	13 35.3	5 38.4	0 3.0	18 14.7
24 M	0 10 19	0♎41 24	21 38 41	27 53 18	2 38.5	25 44.0	23 28.2	25 57.4	9 25.4	13 38.8	5 36.0	0 5.0	18 15.3
25 Tu	0 14 15	1 40 11	4♒13 16	10♒39 0	2 34.0	26 54.8	24 42.1	26 25.3	9 20.6	13 42.3	5 33.6	0 6.9	18 15.9
26 W	0 18 12	2 39 1	17 10 49	23 48 54	2 27.4	28 3.7	25 56.0	26 52.9	9 15.6	13 46.0	5 31.2	0 8.9	18 16.5
27 Th	0 22 8	3 37 52	0♓33 18	7♓23 56	2 18.9	29 10.6	27 9.8	27 20.2	9 10.4	13 49.7	5 28.8	0 10.8	18 17.0
28 F	0 26 5	4 36 44	14 20 31	21 22 40	2 9.4	0♏15.4	28 23.7	27 47.1	9 5.1	13 53.5	5 26.4	0 12.7	18 17.5
29 Sa	0 30 1	5 35 39	28 29 50	5♈41 20	2 0.1	1 18.0	29 37.5	28 13.6	8 59.6	13 57.4	5 24.0	0 14.6	18 18.0
30 Su	0 33 58	6 34 35	12♈56 22	20 14 6	1 51.9	2 18.2	0♏51.4	28 39.8	8 53.9	14 1.4	5 21.6	0 16.5	18 18.5

Day	Sid.Time	☉	0 hr ☽	Noon ☽	True ☊	☿	♀	♂	♃	♄	♅	♆	♇
1 M	0 37 54	7♎33 34	27♈33 37	4♉54 2	1♊45.6	3♏15.7	2♏ 5.2	29♊ 5.6	8♉48.1	14♐ 5.4	5♈19.1	0♍18.4	18♋19.0
2 Tu	0 41 51	8 32 35	12♉14 28	19 34 9	1R41.8	4 10.4	3 19.0	29 31.1	8R42.1	14 9.6	5R16.7	0 20.2	18 19.4
3 W	0 45 48	9 31 38	26 52 21	4♊ 8 28	1D40.2	5 2.0	4 32.8	29 56.1	8 36.0	14 13.8	5 14.3	0 22.0	18 19.8
4 Th	0 49 44	10 30 43	11♊22 0	18 32 34	1 40.4	5 50.3	5 46.7	0♋20.7	8 29.8	14 18.1	5 11.9	0 23.8	18 20.2
5 F	0 53 41	11 29 51	25 39 54	2♋43 49	1 41.4	6 34.9	7 0.5	0 45.0	8 23.4	14 22.4	5 9.5	0 25.6	18 20.6
6 Sa	0 57 37	12 29 2	9♋44 11	16 41 0	1R42.2	7 15.5	8 14.2	1 8.8	8 16.9	14 26.8	5 7.1	0 27.4	18 20.9
7 Su	1 1 34	13 28 14	23 34 14	0♌23 56	1 41.8	7 51.8	9 28.0	1 32.2	8 10.2	14 31.3	5 4.7	0 29.2	18 21.3
8 M	1 5 30	14 27 29	7♌10 9	13 52 58	1 39.4	8 23.3	10 41.8	1 55.1	8 3.4	14 35.9	5 2.4	0 30.9	18 21.5
9 Tu	1 9 27	15 26 46	20 32 25	27 8 34	1 35.1	8 49.6	11 55.6	2 17.6	7 56.5	14 40.6	4 60.0	0 32.6	18 21.8
10 W	1 13 23	16 26 5	3♍41 27	10♍11 7	1 28.8	9 10.3	13 9.3	2 39.7	7 49.5	14 45.3	4 57.6	0 34.3	18 22.1
11 Th	1 17 20	17 25 27	16 37 34	23 0 50	1 21.3	9 24.8	14 23.1	3 1.2	7 42.4	14 50.1	4 55.3	0 35.9	18 22.3
12 F	1 21 17	18 24 51	29 20 57	5♎37 56	1 13.3	9R32.7	15 36.8	3 22.3	7 35.1	14 54.9	4 53.0	0 37.6	18 22.5
13 Sa	1 25 13	19 24 17	11♎51 51	18 2 44	1 5.7	9 33.4	16 50.6	3 42.9	7 27.8	14 59.9	4 50.6	0 39.2	18 22.6
14 Su	1 29 10	20 23 45	24 10 43	0♏15 55	0 59.2	9 26.6	18 4.3	4 3.0	7 20.4	15 4.9	4 48.3	0 40.8	18 22.8
15 M	1 33 6	21 23 15	6♏18 31	12 18 43	0 54.5	9 11.7	19 18.0	4 22.6	7 12.8	15 9.9	4 46.0	0 42.3	18 22.9
16 Tu	1 37 3	22 22 47	18 16 47	24 13 1	0 51.7	8 48.4	20 31.7	4 41.6	7 5.2	15 15.0	4 43.7	0 43.9	18 23.0
17 W	1 40 59	23 22 21	0♐ 7 48	6♐ 1 31	0D50.8	8 16.6	21 45.4	5 0.1	6 57.5	15 20.2	4 41.5	0 45.4	18 23.1
18 Th	1 44 56	24 21 57	11 54 36	17 47 34	0 51.4	7 36.2	22 59.1	5 18.1	6 49.8	15 25.5	4 39.2	0 46.9	18 23.1
19 F	1 48 52	25 21 34	23 40 56	29 35 16	0 52.9	6 47.3	24 12.7	5 35.5	6 41.9	15 30.8	4 37.0	0 48.3	18R23.1
20 Sa	1 52 49	26 21 14	5♑31 10	11♑29 14	0 54.7	5 50.6	25 26.4	5 52.4	6 34.1	15 36.2	4 34.8	0 49.8	18 23.1
21 Su	1 56 46	27 20 55	17 30 6	23 34 25	0R56.1	4 47.0	26 40.0	6 8.7	6 26.1	15 41.6	4 32.7	0 51.2	18 23.1
22 M	2 0 42	28 20 38	29 42 48	5♒55 52	0 56.6	3 37.6	27 53.6	6 24.4	6 18.1	15 47.1	4 30.5	0 52.6	18 23.1
23 Tu	2 4 39	29 20 23	12♒14 10	18 38 16	0 55.7	2 24.1	29 7.2	6 39.4	6 10.1	15 52.7	4 28.4	0 53.9	18 23.0
24 W	2 8 35	0♏20 9	25 8 35	1♓45 29	0 53.5	1 8.5	0♐20.8	6 53.9	6 2.0	15 58.3	4 26.3	0 55.3	18 22.9
25 Th	2 12 32	1 19 57	8♓29 13	15 19 54	0 50.1	29♎52.9	1 34.4	7 7.8	5 53.9	16 4.0	4 24.2	0 56.6	18 22.8
26 F	2 16 28	2 19 47	22 17 29	29 21 46	0 45.9	28 39.6	2 47.9	7 21.0	5 45.8	16 9.7	4 22.1	0 57.9	18 22.6
27 Sa	2 20 25	3 19 38	6♈32 21	13♈48 41	0 41.7	27 31.0	4 1.5	7 33.6	5 37.7	16 15.4	4 20.1	0 59.1	18 22.5
28 Su	2 24 21	4 19 32	21 10 3	28 35 33	0 38.0	26 29.0	5 15.0	7 45.6	5 29.5	16 21.3	4 18.1	1 0.3	18 22.3
29 M	2 28 18	5 19 27	6♉ 4 13	13♉34 56	0 35.2	25 35.6	6 28.5	7 56.9	5 21.4	16 27.2	4 16.1	1 1.5	18 22.0
30 Tu	2 32 14	6 19 24	21 6 37	28 38 8	0D33.8	24 52.2	7 41.9	8 7.5	5 13.2	16 33.1	4 14.2	1 2.7	18 21.8
31 W	2 36 11	7 19 23	6♊ 8 24	13♊36 26	0 33.6	24 19.6	8 55.4	8 17.4	5 5.1	16 39.1	4 12.3	1 3.8	18 21.5

Astro Data	Planet Ingress	Last Aspect	☽ Ingress	Last Aspect	☽ Ingress	☽ Phases & Eclipses	Astro Data
Dy Hr Mn	Dy Hr Mn	Dy Hr Mn	Dy Hr Mn	Dy Hr Mn	Dy Hr Mn	Dy Hr Mn	1 SEPTEMBER 1928
☽0N 2 9:36	♀ ♎ 4 23:05	1 9:59 ♀ ☍	♈ 1 17:26	1 2:35 ♂ ⚹	♉ 1 3:59	6 22:35 ☽ 14♊03	Julian Day # 10471
☿0S 5 23:24	☿ ♎ 5 16:20	3 19:04 ♆ △	♉ 3 20:07	2 9:58 ♇ ⚹	♊ 3 5:09	14 1:20 ● 20♍58	Delta T 24.2 sec
♀0S 7 1:29	♆ ♍ 21 12:03	5 21:47 ♆ □	♊ 5 22:43	4 4:55 ♄ ☍	♋ 5 7:21	22 2:58 ☽ 28♐51	SVP 06♓15'36"
☽0S 15 12:04	☉ ♎ 23 7:06	8 1:03 ♆ ⚹	♋ 8 1:51	6 14:54 ♇ ☌	♌ 7 11:18	29 12:42 ○ 6♈07	Obliquity 23°26'59"
☽0N 29 18:08	☿ ♏ 27 18:12	9 9:02 ♇ ☌	♌ 10 5:49	8 14:04 ☉ ⚹	♍ 9 17:13		⚷ Chiron 10♉01.9R
	♀ ♏ 29 7:18	12 10:28 ♆ ☌	♍ 12 11:01	11 3:16 ♇ ⚹	♎ 12 1:14	6 5:06 ☽ 12♋42	☽ Mean ☊ 4♊43.5
☽0S 12 19:14		14 1:28 ♂ □	♎ 14 18:12	13 15:56 ☉ ☌	♏ 14 11:29	13 15:56 ● 20♎04	
☿ R 12 14:32	♂ ♋ 3 3:46	17 3:47 ♆ ⚹	♏ 17 4:05	16 5:04 ♀ ☌	♐ 16 23:44	21 21:06 ☽ 28♑13	1 OCTOBER 1928
♇ R 19 12:07	☉ ♏ 23 15:55	19 16:16 ♆ □	♐ 19 16:23	19 3:44 ☉ ⚹	♑ 19 12:50	28 22:43 ○ 5♉16	Julian Day # 10501
☽0N 27 4:51	♀ ♐ 23 17:12	22 2:58 ☉ □	♑ 22 5:16	21 21:06 ☉ □	♒ 22 0:33		Delta T 24.1 sec
	☿ ♎ 24 21:43	24 8:42 ☿ □	♒ 24 16:01	23 6:54 ♄ ⚹	♓ 24 8:50		SVP 06♓15'33"
		26 21:21 ☿ △	♓ 26 23:01	25 17:16 ♇ △	♈ 26 13:04		Obliquity 23°27'00"
		28 23:32 ♂ □	♈ 29 2:31	28 8:05 ☿ ☍	♉ 28 14:16		⚷ Chiron 9♉10.2R
				29 19:37 ♇ ⚹	♊ 30 14:11		☽ Mean ☊ 3♊08.2

NOVEMBER 1928 LONGITUDE

Day	Sid.Time	☉	0 hr ☽	Noon ☽	True ☊	☿	♀	♂	♃	♄	♅	♆	♇
1 Th	2 40 8	8♏19 24	21♊ 1 21	28♊22 24	0♊34.5	23♎58.6	10♐ 8.8	8♋26.6	4♉57.0	16♐45.1	4♈10.4	1♍ 4.9	18♋21.2
2 F	2 44 4	9 19 28	5♋38 59	12♋50 39	0 35.8	23D 49.1	11 22.3	8 35.1	4R 48.9	16 51.2	4R 8.5	1 6.0	18R 20.9
3 Sa	2 48 1	10 19 33	19 57 5	26 58 6	0 37.2	23 51.0	12 35.7	8 42.8	4 40.8	16 57.3	4 6.7	1 7.0	18 20.6
4 Su	2 51 57	11 19 41	3♌53 38	10♌43 44	0R 38.0	24 3.8	13 49.0	8 49.8	4 32.8	17 3.5	4 4.9	1 8.1	18 20.2
5 M	2 55 54	12 19 50	17 28 31	24 8 11	0 38.1	24 26.9	15 2.4	8 56.1	4 24.7	17 9.7	4 3.2	1 9.0	18 19.8
6 Tu	2 59 50	13 20 2	0♍42 56	7♍13 5	0 37.3	24 59.5	16 15.8	9 1.5	4 16.8	17 16.0	4 1.5	1 10.0	18 19.4
7 W	3 3 47	14 20 16	13 38 52	20 0 38	0 35.7	25 40.6	17 29.1	9 6.2	4 8.9	17 22.3	3 59.8	1 10.9	18 19.0
8 Th	3 7 44	15 20 32	26 18 39	2♎33 13	0 33.7	26 29.4	18 42.4	9 10.1	4 1.0	17 28.6	3 58.1	1 11.8	18 18.5
9 F	3 11 40	16 20 49	8♎44 37	14 53 8	0 31.4	27 25.0	19 55.7	9 13.1	3 53.2	17 35.0	3 56.5	1 12.6	18 18.1
10 Sa	3 15 37	17 21 9	20 59 1	27 2 31	0 29.3	28 26.7	21 9.0	9 15.4	3 45.5	17 41.4	3 55.0	1 13.5	18 17.6
11 Su	3 19 33	18 21 30	3♏ 3 54	9♏ 3 22	0 27.6	29 33.5	22 22.2	9 16.8	3 37.8	17 47.9	3 53.4	1 14.3	18 17.0
12 M	3 23 30	19 21 54	15 1 11	20 57 35	0 26.5	0♏44.8	23 35.5	9R 17.4	3 30.2	17 54.4	3 51.9	1 15.0	18 16.5
13 Tu	3 27 26	20 22 19	26 52 49	2♐47 7	0D 26.1	1 60.0	24 48.7	9 17.1	3 22.8	18 0.9	3 50.5	1 15.7	18 15.9
14 W	3 31 23	21 22 45	8♐40 47	14 34 7	0 26.2	3 18.4	26 1.9	9 16.0	3 15.4	18 7.5	3 49.1	1 16.4	18 15.3
15 Th	3 35 19	22 23 13	20 27 24	26 21 1	0 26.7	4 39.7	27 15.0	9 14.0	3 8.1	18 14.1	3 47.7	1 17.1	18 14.7
16 F	3 39 16	23 23 43	2♑15 18	8♑10 41	0 27.4	6 3.3	28 28.2	9 11.1	3 0.9	18 20.7	3 46.4	1 17.7	18 14.1
17 Sa	3 43 13	24 24 14	14 7 34	20 6 26	0 28.2	7 28.8	29 41.3	9 7.4	2 53.8	18 27.4	3 45.1	1 18.3	18 13.4
18 Su	3 47 9	25 24 47	26 7 45	2♒12 2	0 28.8	8 56.0	0♑54.4	9 2.8	2 46.9	18 34.1	3 43.9	1 18.9	18 12.7
19 M	3 51 6	26 25 20	8♒19 47	14 31 32	0 29.2	10 24.6	2 7.4	8 57.4	2 40.1	18 40.8	3 42.7	1 19.4	18 12.1
20 Tu	3 55 2	27 25 55	20 47 50	27 9 10	0R 29.4	11 54.2	3 20.4	8 51.0	2 33.4	18 47.6	3 41.5	1 19.9	18 11.3
21 W	3 58 59	28 26 31	3♓36 1	10♓ 8 51	0 29.4	13 24.8	4 33.4	8 43.8	2 26.8	18 54.4	3 40.4	1 20.4	18 10.6
22 Th	4 2 55	29 27 9	16 48 3	23 33 52	0 29.4	14 56.1	5 46.3	8 35.8	2 20.3	19 1.2	3 39.4	1 20.8	18 9.8
23 F	4 6 52	0♐27 47	0♈26 32	7♈26 6	0D 29.3	16 28.0	6 59.2	8 26.8	2 14.0	19 8.0	3 38.3	1 21.2	18 9.1
24 Sa	4 10 48	1 28 26	14 32 29	21 45 25	0 29.4	18 0.4	8 12.1	8 17.1	2 7.9	19 14.9	3 37.4	1 21.5	18 8.3
25 Su	4 14 45	2 29 7	29 4 28	6♉29 3	0 29.5	19 33.1	9 24.9	8 6.4	2 1.9	19 21.8	3 36.4	1 21.9	18 7.4
26 M	4 18 42	3 29 49	13♉58 22	21 31 27	0 29.7	21 6.2	10 37.7	7 55.0	1 56.0	19 28.7	3 35.6	1 22.1	18 6.6
27 Tu	4 22 38	4 30 32	29 7 13	6♊44 29	0R 29.8	22 39.4	11 50.4	7 42.7	1 50.3	19 35.6	3 34.7	1 22.4	18 5.8
28 W	4 26 35	5 31 16	14♊22 0	21 58 30	0 29.7	24 12.9	13 3.1	7 29.6	1 44.8	19 42.5	3 34.0	1 22.6	18 4.9
29 Th	4 30 31	6 32 2	29 32 46	7♋ 3 40	0 29.3	25 46.4	14 15.8	7 15.7	1 39.4	19 49.5	3 33.2	1 22.8	18 4.0
30 F	4 34 28	7 32 49	14♋30 12	21 51 31	0 28.6	27 20.1	15 28.4	7 1.0	1 34.2	19 56.5	3 32.6	1 23.0	18 3.1

DECEMBER 1928 LONGITUDE

Day	Sid.Time	☉	0 hr ☽	Noon ☽	True ☊	☿	♀	♂	♃	♄	♅	♆	♇
1 Sa	4 38 24	8♐33 38	29♋ 6 56	6♌15 58	0♊27.7	28♏53.8	16♑40.9	6♋45.5	1♉29.2	20♐ 3.5	3♈31.9	1♍23.1	18♋ 2.2
2 Su	4 42 21	9 34 28	13♌18 18	20 13 48	0R 26.8	0♐27.5	17 53.5	6R 29.3	1R 24.3	20 10.5	3R 31.3	1 23.2	18R 1.2
3 M	4 46 17	10 35 19	27 2 30	3♍44 32	0 26.0	2 1.3	19 5.9	6 12.4	1 19.6	20 17.5	3 30.8	1R 23.2	18 0.3
4 Tu	4 50 14	11 36 11	10♍20 11	16 49 47	0D 25.7	3 35.1	20 18.3	5 54.7	1 15.1	20 24.6	3 30.3	1 23.2	17 59.3
5 W	4 54 11	12 37 5	23 13 46	29 32 35	0 25.9	5 8.9	21 30.7	5 36.4	1 10.8	20 31.6	3 29.9	1 23.2	17 58.3
6 Th	4 58 7	13 38 0	5♎46 45	11♎56 47	0 26.7	6 42.7	22 43.0	5 17.4	1 6.7	20 38.7	3 29.5	1 23.1	17 57.3
7 F	5 2 4	14 38 57	18 3 10	24 6 25	0 27.9	8 16.6	23 55.3	4 57.7	1 2.7	20 45.7	3 29.2	1 23.1	17 56.3
8 Sa	5 6 0	15 39 54	0♏ 7 2	6♏ 5 28	0 29.4	9 50.4	25 7.5	4 37.5	0 58.9	20 52.8	3 28.9	1 22.9	17 55.3
9 Su	5 9 57	16 40 53	12 2 9	17 57 29	0 30.7	11 24.3	26 19.6	4 16.8	0 55.4	20 59.9	3 28.6	1 22.8	17 54.2
10 M	5 13 53	17 41 53	23 51 52	29 45 39	0R 31.5	12 58.3	27 31.7	3 55.5	0 52.0	21 7.0	3 28.5	1 22.6	17 53.1
11 Tu	5 17 50	18 42 54	5♐39 8	11♐32 38	0 31.6	14 32.2	28 43.8	3 33.8	0 48.8	21 14.1	3 28.3	1 22.4	17 52.1
12 W	5 21 46	19 43 56	17 26 25	23 20 44	0 30.6	16 6.3	29 55.7	3 11.7	0 45.8	21 21.2	3D 28.2	1 22.1	17 51.0
13 Th	5 25 43	20 44 59	29 15 51	5♑12 0	0 28.6	17 40.4	1♒ 7.6	2 49.2	0 43.1	21 28.3	3 28.2	1 21.8	17 49.9
14 F	5 29 40	21 46 2	11♑ 9 25	17 8 20	0 25.5	19 14.6	2 19.5	2 26.3	0 40.5	21 35.4	3 28.2	1 21.5	17 48.8
15 Sa	5 33 36	22 47 6	23 9 0	29 11 42	0 21.8	20 48.8	3 31.2	2 3.2	0 38.1	21 42.5	3 28.3	1 21.1	17 47.6
16 Su	5 37 33	23 48 11	5♒16 41	11♒24 16	0 17.7	22 23.2	4 42.9	1 39.9	0 36.0	21 49.6	3 28.5	1 20.7	17 46.5
17 M	5 41 29	24 49 16	17 34 45	23 48 28	0 13.8	23 57.8	5 54.6	1 16.4	0 34.0	21 56.7	3 28.6	1 20.3	17 45.3
18 Tu	5 45 26	25 50 21	0♓ 5 47	6♓27 4	0 10.6	25 32.4	7 6.1	0 52.8	0 32.2	22 3.8	3 28.9	1 19.8	17 44.2
19 W	5 49 22	26 51 27	12 52 40	19 22 59	0 8.4	27 7.2	8 17.5	0 29.0	0 30.7	22 10.9	3 29.2	1 19.3	17 43.0
20 Th	5 53 19	27 52 33	25 58 21	2♈39 7	0D 7.6	28 42.2	9 28.9	0 5.3	0 29.4	22 18.0	3 29.5	1 18.8	17 41.8
21 F	5 57 15	28 53 39	9♈25 33	16 17 54	0 8.0	0♑17.4	10 40.2	29♊41.6	0 28.2	22 25.0	3 29.9	1 18.2	17 40.6
22 Sa	6 1 12	29 54 45	23 16 17	0♉20 45	0 9.3	1 52.8	11 51.3	29 18.0	0 27.3	22 32.1	3 30.3	1 17.6	17 39.4
23 Su	6 5 9	0♑55 52	7♉31 12	14 47 22	0 10.9	3 28.3	13 2.4	28 54.5	0 26.6	22 39.2	3 30.8	1 17.0	17 38.2
24 M	6 9 5	1 56 58	22 8 51	29 35 4	0R 12.0	5 4.2	14 13.4	28 31.2	0 26.1	22 46.2	3 31.3	1 16.4	17 37.0
25 Tu	6 13 2	2 58 5	7♊ 5 14	14♊38 27	0 12.1	6 40.2	15 24.2	28 8.2	0D 25.8	22 53.2	3 31.9	1 15.7	17 35.8
26 W	6 16 58	3 59 12	22 13 37	29 49 33	0 10.5	8 16.5	16 35.0	27 45.3	0 25.8	23 0.3	3 32.6	1 15.0	17 34.6
27 Th	6 20 55	5 0 20	7♋24 59	14♋58 40	0 7.2	9 53.0	17 45.6	27 22.9	0 25.9	23 7.3	3 33.3	1 14.2	17 33.3
28 F	6 24 51	6 1 27	22 29 22	29 55 55	0 2.3	11 29.8	18 56.2	27 0.7	0 26.2	23 14.3	3 34.0	1 13.5	17 32.1
29 Sa	6 28 48	7 2 35	7♌17 20	14♌32 46	29♉56.5	13 6.8	20 6.6	26 39.0	0 26.8	23 21.2	3 34.8	1 12.7	17 30.9
30 Su	6 32 45	8 3 43	21 41 33	28 43 17	29 50.5	14 44.1	21 16.9	26 17.7	0 27.6	23 28.2	3 35.7	1 11.8	17 29.6
31 M	6 36 41	9 4 52	5♍37 42	12♍24 46	29 45.3	16 21.6	22 27.0	25 56.8	0 28.5	23 35.1	3 36.6	1 11.0	17 28.4

Astro Data	Planet Ingress	Last Aspect	☽ Ingress	Last Aspect	☽ Ingress	☽ Phases & Eclipses	Astro Data
Dy Hr Mn	Dy Hr Mn	Dy Hr Mn	Dy Hr Mn	Dy Hr Mn	Dy Hr Mn	Dy Hr Mn	1 NOVEMBER 1928
☿ D 2 7:52	☿ ♏ 11 9:05	1 4:44 ☿ △	♋ 1 14:40	30 23:35 ☿ △	♌ 1 1:28	4 14:06 ☽ 11♌55	Julian Day # 10532
♃ ⊻ ♅ 8 11:05	♀ ♑ 17 6:09	3 6:43 ☿ □	♌ 3 17:14	2 12:00 ♄ △	♍ 3 5:16	12 9:35 ● 19♏46	Delta T 24.1 sec
☽ 0 S 9 1:31	☉ ♐ 22 13:00	5 13:04 ☿ ✶	♍ 5 22:41	4 20:26 ♀ △	♎ 5 12:52	12 9:48:01 ✔ P 0.808	SVP 06♓15'29"
♂ R 12 4:13		7 8:47 ♇ ✶	♎ 8 7:05	7 12:55 ♀ □	♏ 7 23:46	20 13:36 ☽ 28♒00	Obliquity 23°26'59"
♃ ⊡ ♄ 14 13:38	☿ ♐ 1 16:57	10 16:16 ☿ ☌	♏ 10 17:53	10 8:18 ♀ ✶	♐ 10 12:29	27 9:05 ○ 4♊54	⚷ Chiron 7♉45.2R
♄ ⊼ ♇ 15 2:03	♀ ♒ 12 1:25	12 9:35 ☉ ☌	♐ 13 6:20	12 8:02 ♄ ☌	♑ 13 1:29	27 9:01 ♪ T 1.149	☽ Mean ☊ 1♊29.7
☽ 0 N 23 15:36	☿ ♑ 20 19:37	15 15:26 ♀ ☌	♑ 15 19:25	14 13:20 ♇ ☍	♒ 15 13:36		
	♂ ♊ 20 5:23	17 22:27 ☉ ✶	♒ 18 7:40	17 15:10 ☉ ✶	♓ 17 23:49	4 2:31 ☽ 11♍43	1 DECEMBER 1928
♃ △ ♆ 2 5:46	☉ ♑ 22 2:04	20 13:36 ☉ □	♓ 20 17:19	20 7:12 ♂ □	♈ 20 7:15	12 5:06 ● 19♐57	Julian Day # 10562
♆ R 3 20:48	☊ ♉ 28 9:48	22 4:00 ♄ □	♈ 22 23:14	22 9:58 ♂ ✶	♉ 22 11:25	20 3:43 ☽ 28♓02	Delta T 24.1 sec
☽ 0 S 6 7:18		24 7:55 ♄ △	♉ 25 1:30	23 16:38 ♇ ✶	♊ 24 12:40	26 19:55 ○ 4♋50	SVP 06♓15'24"
♅ D 12 23:57		26 12:38 ☿ ☍	♊ 27 1:23	26 8:31 ♂ ☌	♋ 26 12:17		Obliquity 23°26'59"
☽ 0 N 20 23:59		28 8:29 ♄ ☍	♋ 29 0:43	27 16:05 ♇ ☌	♌ 28 12:07		⚷ Chiron 6♉23.0R
♃ D 25 20:33				30 7:39 ♂ ✶	♍ 30 14:12		☽ Mean ☊ 29♉54.4

LONGITUDE JANUARY 1929

Day	Sid.Time	☉	0 hr ☽	Noon ☽	True ☊	☿	♀	♂	♃	♄	♅	♆	♇
1 Tu	6 40 38	10♑ 6 0	19♍ 4 35	25♍37 27	29♉41.4	17♑59.3	23♒37.1	25♊36.5	0♉29.7	23♐42.1	3♈37.5	1♍10.1	17♋27.1
2 W	6 44 34	11 7 9	2♎ 3 43	8♎23 54	29D 39.2	19 37.2	24 47.0	25R 16.7	0 31.0	23 49.0	3 38.5	1R 9.1	17R 25.8
3 Th	6 48 31	12 8 19	14 38 33	20 48 16	29 38.8	21 15.3	25 56.8	24 57.5	0 32.6	23 55.8	3 39.6	1 8.2	17 24.6
4 F	6 52 27	13 9 28	26 53 42	2♏55 30	29 39.7	22 53.6	27 6.4	24 38.9	0 34.4	24 2.7	3 40.7	1 7.2	17 23.3
5 Sa	6 56 24	14 10 38	8♏54 18	14 50 46	29 41.2	24 31.9	28 15.9	24 20.9	0 36.4	24 9.5	3 41.8	1 6.2	17 22.0
6 Su	7 0 20	15 11 48	20 45 28	26 39 2	29R 42.6	26 10.3	29 25.3	24 3.6	0 38.6	24 16.3	3 43.0	1 5.2	17 20.8
7 M	7 4 17	16 12 58	2♐31 59	8♐24 50	29 42.9	27 48.6	0♓34.5	23 46.9	0 41.0	24 23.1	3 44.3	1 4.1	17 19.5
8 Tu	7 8 14	17 14 9	14 18 2	20 12 1	29 41.6	29 26.7	1 43.6	23 31.0	0 43.6	24 29.9	3 45.6	1 3.0	17 18.2
9 W	7 12 10	18 15 19	26 7 8	2♑ 3 43	29 37.9	1♒ 4.6	2 52.5	23 15.9	0 46.4	24 36.6	3 46.9	1 1.9	17 16.9
10 Th	7 16 7	19 16 29	8♑ 2 0	14 2 15	29 31.9	2 42.2	4 1.3	23 1.4	0 49.4	24 43.3	3 48.3	1 0.8	17 15.7
11 F	7 20 3	20 17 39	20 4 38	26 9 19	29 23.7	4 19.2	5 9.9	22 47.8	0 52.6	24 50.0	3 49.8	0 59.6	17 14.4
12 Sa	7 24 0	21 18 48	2♒16 23	8♒25 58	29 13.9	5 55.4	6 18.3	22 34.9	0 56.0	24 56.6	3 51.3	0 58.4	17 13.1
13 Su	7 27 56	22 19 57	14 38 9	20 53 0	29 3.3	7 30.7	7 26.5	22 22.9	0 59.5	25 3.2	3 52.8	0 57.2	17 11.8
14 M	7 31 53	23 21 6	27 10 35	3♓31 0	28 52.9	9 4.7	8 34.5	22 11.6	1 3.3	25 9.7	3 54.4	0 56.0	17 10.6
15 Tu	7 35 49	24 22 13	9♓54 22	16 20 48	28 43.8	10 37.2	9 42.4	22 1.1	1 7.3	25 16.3	3 56.0	0 54.7	17 9.3
16 W	7 39 46	25 23 21	22 50 25	29 23 25	28 36.8	12 7.8	10 50.0	21 51.5	1 11.5	25 22.7	3 57.7	0 53.4	17 8.0
17 Th	7 43 43	26 24 27	5♈59 58	12♈40 17	28 32.3	13 36.0	11 57.5	21 42.7	1 15.8	25 29.2	3 59.4	0 52.1	17 6.8
18 F	7 47 39	27 25 32	19 24 35	26 13 1	28D 30.3	15 1.5	13 4.7	21 34.7	1 20.4	25 35.6	4 1.2	0 50.8	17 5.5
19 Sa	7 51 36	28 26 37	3♉ 5 49	10♉ 3 5	28 30.0	16 23.6	14 11.7	21 27.5	1 25.1	25 42.0	4 3.0	0 49.4	17 4.3
20 Su	7 55 32	29 27 41	17 4 54	24 11 14	28R 30.7	17 41.7	15 18.5	21 21.2	1 30.0	25 48.3	4 4.8	0 48.1	17 3.0
21 M	7 59 29	0♒28 44	1♊22 0	8♊36 56	28 31.0	18 55.3	16 25.0	21 15.7	1 35.1	25 54.6	4 6.7	0 46.7	17 1.8
22 Tu	8 3 25	1 29 46	15 55 38	23 17 34	28 29.8	20 3.5	17 31.3	21 11.0	1 40.4	26 0.8	4 8.7	0 45.3	17 0.6
23 W	8 7 22	2 30 47	0♋42 3	8♋ 8 13	28 26.1	21 5.5	18 37.3	21 7.1	1 45.8	26 7.0	4 10.6	0 43.9	16 59.3
24 Th	8 11 18	3 31 47	15 35 7	23 1 42	28 19.7	22 0.6	19 43.1	21 4.0	1 51.4	26 13.1	4 12.7	0 42.4	16 58.1
25 F	8 15 15	4 32 46	0♌26 51	7♌49 29	28 10.8	22 47.9	20 48.6	21 1.7	1 57.2	26 19.2	4 14.7	0 41.0	16 56.9
26 Sa	8 19 12	5 33 44	15 8 30	22 22 58	28 0.1	23 26.5	21 53.8	21 0.2	2 3.2	26 25.3	4 16.8	0 39.5	16 55.7
27 Su	8 23 8	6 34 42	29 32 3	6♍35 4	27 49.0	23 55.7	22 58.8	20D 59.4	2 9.3	26 31.3	4 19.0	0 38.0	16 54.5
28 M	8 27 5	7 35 38	13♍31 33	20 21 11	27 38.5	24 14.7	24 3.4	20 59.4	2 15.6	26 37.2	4 21.2	0 36.5	16 53.3
29 Tu	8 31 1	8 36 34	27 3 52	3♎39 40	27 29.9	24R 22.9	25 7.8	21 0.1	2 22.1	26 43.1	4 23.4	0 35.0	16 52.1
30 W	8 34 58	9 37 29	10♎ 8 47	16 31 35	27 23.7	24 20.0	26 11.8	21 1.6	2 28.8	26 49.0	4 25.7	0 33.5	16 51.0
31 Th	8 38 54	10 38 23	22 48 31	29 0 8	27 20.0	24 5.8	27 15.5	21 3.9	2 35.6	26 54.8	4 28.0	0 31.9	16 49.8

LONGITUDE FEBRUARY 1929

Day	Sid.Time	☉	0 hr ☽	Noon ☽	True ☊	☿	♀	♂	♃	♄	♅	♆	♇
1 F	8 42 51	11♒39 17	5♏ 7 4	11♏ 9 58	27♉18.6	23♒40.4	28♓18.9	21♊ 6.8	2♉42.5	27♐ 0.5	4♈30.3	0♍30.4	16♋48.7
2 Sa	8 46 47	12 40 10	17 9 31	23 6 27	27R 18.5	23R 4.3	29 21.9	21 10.5	2 49.6	27 6.2	4 32.7	0R 28.8	16R 47.5
3 Su	8 50 44	13 41 2	29 1 27	4♐55 12	27 18.6	22 18.4	0♈24.6	21 14.8	2 56.9	27 11.8	4 35.1	0 27.2	16 46.4
4 M	8 54 41	14 41 53	10♐48 24	16 41 41	27 17.9	21 23.9	1 26.9	21 19.9	3 4.3	27 17.4	4 37.5	0 25.6	16 45.3
5 Tu	8 58 37	15 42 43	22 35 39	28 30 51	27 15.2	20 22.2	2 28.9	21 25.6	3 11.9	27 22.9	4 40.0	0 24.0	16 44.2
6 W	9 2 34	16 43 33	4♑27 47	10♑26 54	27 9.9	19 15.2	3 30.5	21 32.0	3 19.7	27 28.4	4 42.6	0 22.4	16 43.1
7 Th	9 6 30	17 44 21	16 28 34	22 33 6	27 1.7	18 4.7	4 31.7	21 39.1	3 27.6	27 33.7	4 45.1	0 20.8	16 42.0
8 F	9 10 27	18 45 8	28 40 45	4♒51 41	26 50.7	16 52.9	5 32.4	21 46.8	3 35.6	27 39.1	4 47.7	0 19.1	16 41.0
9 Sa	9 14 23	19 45 54	11♒ 6 0	17 23 45	26 37.6	15 41.7	6 32.8	21 55.1	3 43.8	27 44.3	4 50.3	0 17.5	16 39.9
10 Su	9 18 20	20 46 38	23 44 53	0♓ 9 22	26 23.5	14 32.8	7 32.7	22 4.1	3 52.1	27 49.5	4 53.0	0 15.8	16 38.9
11 M	9 22 16	21 47 22	6♓37 4	13 7 53	26 9.6	13 28.0	8 32.2	22 13.6	4 0.6	27 54.7	4 55.7	0 14.2	16 37.9
12 Tu	9 26 13	22 48 3	19 41 37	26 18 10	25 57.2	12 28.6	9 31.2	22 23.8	4 9.2	27 59.7	4 58.4	0 12.5	16 36.9
13 W	9 30 10	23 48 43	2♈57 22	9♈39 7	25 47.3	11 35.5	10 29.7	22 34.5	4 18.0	28 4.7	5 1.1	0 10.9	16 35.9
14 Th	9 34 6	24 49 22	16 23 19	23 9 55	25 40.4	10 49.6	11 27.6	22 45.9	4 26.8	28 9.6	5 3.9	0 9.2	16 34.9
15 F	9 38 3	25 49 59	29 58 54	6♉50 16	25 36.6	10 11.1	12 25.1	22 57.8	4 35.9	28 14.5	5 6.7	0 7.5	16 34.0
16 Sa	9 41 59	26 50 34	13♉44 3	20 40 18	25 35.1	9 40.5	13 22.0	23 10.2	4 45.0	28 19.3	5 9.6	0 5.8	16 33.0
17 Su	9 45 56	27 51 8	27 39 1	4♊40 15	25 34.9	9 17.7	14 18.4	23 23.2	4 54.3	28 24.0	5 12.4	0 4.2	16 32.1
18 M	9 49 52	28 51 39	11♊43 57	18 50 1	25 34.6	9 2.6	15 14.1	23 36.7	5 3.7	28 28.6	5 15.3	0 2.5	16 31.2
19 Tu	9 53 49	29 52 9	25 58 17	3♋ 8 31	25 32.9	8D 54.8	16 9.3	23 50.7	5 13.2	28 33.2	5 18.3	0 0.8	16 30.3
20 W	9 57 45	0♓52 37	10♋20 18	17 33 12	25 28.8	8 54.2	17 3.8	24 5.2	5 22.9	28 37.7	5 21.2	29♌59.1	16 29.4
21 Th	10 1 42	1 53 3	24 46 37	1♌59 54	25 21.7	9 0.3	17 57.6	24 20.2	5 32.7	28 42.1	5 24.2	29 57.4	16 28.6
22 F	10 5 39	2 53 27	9♌12 17	16 23 0	25 11.9	9 12.8	18 50.8	24 35.6	5 42.6	28 46.5	5 27.2	29 55.8	16 27.8
23 Sa	10 9 35	3 53 50	23 31 16	0♍36 17	25 0.3	9 31.1	19 43.3	24 51.5	5 52.6	28 50.7	5 30.2	29 54.1	16 27.0
24 Su	10 13 32	4 54 10	7♍37 20	14 33 49	24 47.8	9 55.0	20 35.0	25 7.9	6 2.7	28 54.9	5 33.3	29 52.4	16 26.2
25 M	10 17 28	5 54 29	21 25 12	28 11 5	24 36.0	10 24.1	21 25.9	25 24.7	6 13.0	28 59.0	5 36.3	29 50.7	16 25.4
26 Tu	10 21 25	6 54 47	4♎51 14	11♎25 33	24 26.0	10 57.9	22 16.1	25 41.9	6 23.3	29 3.1	5 39.4	29 49.1	16 24.6
27 W	10 25 21	7 55 2	17 54 4	24 16 56	24 18.4	11 36.2	23 5.5	25 59.6	6 33.8	29 7.0	5 42.5	29 47.4	16 23.9
28 Th	10 29 18	8 55 16	0♏34 27	6♏47 0	24 13.6	12 18.5	23 54.0	26 17.6	6 44.3	29 10.9	5 45.6	29 45.7	16 23.2

Astro Data	Planet Ingress	Last Aspect	☽ Ingress	Last Aspect	☽ Ingress	☽ Phases & Eclipses	Astro Data
Dy Hr Mn	Dy Hr Mn	Dy Hr Mn	Dy Hr Mn	Dy Hr Mn	Dy Hr Mn	Dy Hr Mn	1 JANUARY 1929
☽0S 2 13:41	♀ ♓ 6 12:01	1 11:40 ♂ □	♎ 1 20:08	2 11:15 ☿ □	♐ 3 1:59	2 18:44 ☽ 11♎55	Julian Day # 10593
♃△♆ 12 12:23	☿ ♒ 8 8:09	4 0:28 ♀ △	♏ 4 6:10	5 9:47 ♄ ☌	♑ 5 15:00	11 0:28 ● 20♑19	Delta T 24.1 sec
☽0N 17 5:25	☉ ♒ 20 12:42	6 12:48 ☿ ⚹	♐ 6 18:50	7 0:27 ♇ ☍	♒ 8 2:34	18 15:15 ☽ 28♈04	SVP 06♓15'18"
♂ D 27 12:02		8 20:55 ♄ ☌	♑ 9 7:51	10 7:42 ♄ ⚹	♓ 10 11:43	25 7:09 ○ 4♌51	Obliquity 23°26'59"
☽0S 29 21:30	♀ ♈ 2 14:34	11 0:28 ☉ ☌	♒ 11 19:33	12 15:09 ♄ □	♈ 12 18:41		⚷ Chiron 5♉31.3R
☿ R 29 5:48	☉ ♓ 19 3:07	13 20:08 ♄ ⚹	♓ 14 5:21	14 20:56 ♄ △	♉ 15 0:02	1 14:10 ☽ 12♏15	☽ Mean ☊ 28♉15.9
	♆ ♌ 19 11:25	16 5:05 ☉ ⚹	♈ 16 13:07	17 0:22 ☉ □	♊ 17 4:01	9 17:55 ● 20♒31	
♀0N 1 14:57		18 15:15 ☉ □	♉ 18 18:37	19 4:21 ♄ ☍	♋ 19 6:45	17 0:22 ☽ 27♉52	1 FEBRUARY 1929
☽0N 13 10:00		20 1:09 ☿ □	♊ 20 21:43	20 11:56 ♀ □	♌ 21 8:41	23 18:59 ○ 4♍42	Julian Day # 10624
♃⚺♅ 19 18:00		22 16:32 ♄ ☍	♋ 22 22:52	23 10:47 ♆ ☌	♍ 23 10:58		Delta T 24.1 sec
☿ D 19 14:07		24 7:11 ♀ △	♌ 24 23:16	25 13:30 ♄ □	♎ 25 15:15		SVP 06♓15'13"
☽0S 26 6:26		26 18:53 ♄ △	♍ 27 0:47	27 22:27 ♆ ⚹	♏ 27 22:54		Obliquity 23°27'00"
		28 23:22 ♄ □	♎ 29 5:19				⚷ Chiron 5♉33.5
		31 8:00 ♄ ⚹	♏ 31 13:57				☽ Mean ☊ 26♉37.4

MARCH 1929 LONGITUDE

Day	Sid.Time	☉	0 hr ☽	Noon ☽	True ☊	☿	♀	♂	♃	♄	♅	♆	♇
1 F	10 33 14	9♓55 29	12♏55 4	18♏59 11	24♉11.3	13♒ 4.7	24♈41.6	26♊36.1	6♉55.0	29♐14.6	5♈48.8	29♌44.1	16♋22.5
2 Sa	10 37 11	10 55 40	24 59 58	0♐58 3	24D10.8	13 54.4	25 28.3	26 54.9	7 5.8	29 18.4	5 52.0	29R42.4	16R21.8
3 Su	10 41 8	11 55 50	6♐54 7	12 48 52	24R11.1	14 47.4	26 14.1	27 14.1	7 16.7	29 22.0	5 55.2	29 40.8	16 21.2
4 M	10 45 4	12 55 58	18 42 59	24 37 10	24 11.0	15 43.4	26 58.9	27 33.7	7 27.7	29 25.5	5 58.4	29 39.2	16 20.5
5 Tu	10 49 1	13 56 5	0♑32 5	6♑28 22	24 9.6	16 42.3	27 42.7	27 53.7	7 38.7	29 29.0	6 1.6	29 37.6	16 19.9
6 W	10 52 57	14 56 10	12 26 40	18 27 31	24 6.0	17 43.8	28 25.4	28 14.0	7 49.9	29 32.3	6 4.8	29 35.9	16 19.3
7 Th	10 56 54	15 56 13	24 31 26	0♒38 53	23 59.9	18 47.9	29 7.1	28 34.6	8 1.2	29 35.6	6 8.1	29 34.3	16 18.8
8 F	11 0 50	16 56 15	6♒50 13	13 5 44	23 51.3	19 54.3	29 47.6	28 55.6	8 12.6	29 38.8	6 11.4	29 32.8	16 18.2
9 Sa	11 4 47	17 56 15	19 25 38	25 50 2	23 40.8	21 2.8	0♉26.9	29 17.0	8 24.1	29 41.9	6 14.7	29 31.2	16 17.7
10 Su	11 8 43	18 56 13	2♓18 56	8♓52 17	23 29.2	22 13.5	1 5.0	29 38.7	8 35.6	29 44.9	6 18.0	29 29.6	16 17.2
11 M	11 12 40	19 56 9	15 29 54	22 11 34	23 17.6	23 26.2	1 41.9	0♋ 0.6	8 47.3	29 47.8	6 21.3	29 28.0	16 16.7
12 Tu	11 16 37	20 56 3	28 56 57	5♈45 43	23 7.3	24 40.7	2 17.4	0 22.9	8 59.0	29 50.6	6 24.6	29 26.5	16 16.3
13 W	11 20 33	21 55 55	12♈37 29	19 31 50	22 59.1	25 57.1	2 51.5	0 45.5	9 10.8	29 53.4	6 27.9	29 25.0	16 15.8
14 Th	11 24 30	22 55 46	26 28 23	3♉26 45	22 53.6	27 15.1	3 24.2	1 8.5	9 22.7	29 56.0	6 31.3	29 23.4	16 15.4
15 F	11 28 26	23 55 34	10♉26 35	17 27 36	22D50.8	28 34.8	3 55.4	1 31.7	9 34.7	29 58.6	6 34.6	29 21.9	16 15.0
16 Sa	11 32 23	24 55 20	24 29 31	1♊32 8	22 50.2	29 56.2	4 25.1	1 55.1	9 46.8	0♑ 1.0	6 38.0	29 20.4	16 14.7
17 Su	11 36 19	25 55 3	8♊35 14	15 38 42	22 50.8	1♓19.1	4 53.1	2 18.9	9 58.9	0 3.4	6 41.4	29 19.0	16 14.3
18 M	11 40 16	26 54 45	22 42 22	29 46 6	22R51.5	2 43.4	5 19.5	2 42.9	10 11.1	0 5.7	6 44.8	29 17.5	16 14.0
19 Tu	11 44 12	27 54 24	6♋49 47	13♋53 15	22 51.2	4 9.3	5 44.1	3 7.2	10 23.4	0 7.8	6 48.2	29 16.1	16 13.7
20 W	11 48 9	28 53 59	20 56 16	27 58 39	22 49.0	5 36.6	6 7.0	3 31.8	10 35.8	0 9.9	6 51.6	29 14.7	16 13.5
21 Th	11 52 6	29 53 36	5♌ 0 4	12♌ 0 15	22 44.7	7 5.3	6 27.9	3 56.6	10 48.2	0 11.9	6 55.0	29 13.3	16 13.2
22 F	11 56 2	0♈53 8	18 58 47	25 55 19	22 38.2	8 35.5	6 47.0	4 21.6	11 0.7	0 13.8	6 58.4	29 11.9	16 13.0
23 Sa	11 59 59	1 52 38	2♍49 25	9♍40 41	22 30.2	10 7.0	7 4.0	4 46.9	11 13.3	0 15.6	7 1.8	29 10.5	16 12.8
24 Su	12 3 55	2 52 6	16 28 43	23 13 9	22 21.5	11 39.9	7 19.0	5 12.4	11 25.9	0 17.3	7 5.2	29 9.2	16 12.6
25 M	12 7 52	3 51 31	29 53 39	6♎30 0	22 13.2	13 14.1	7 31.9	5 38.1	11 38.7	0 18.9	7 8.7	29 7.8	16 12.5
26 Tu	12 11 48	4 50 55	13♎ 2 0	19 29 32	22 6.2	14 49.7	7 42.6	6 4.0	11 51.4	0 20.4	7 12.1	29 6.5	16 12.4
27 W	12 15 45	5 50 16	25 52 36	2♏11 16	22 1.0	16 26.7	7 51.0	6 30.2	12 4.2	0 21.8	7 15.5	29 5.2	16 12.3
28 Th	12 19 41	6 49 36	8♏25 42	14 36 9	21 58.0	18 5.0	7 57.2	6 56.6	12 17.1	0 23.1	7 18.9	29 4.0	16 12.2
29 F	12 23 38	7 48 54	20 42 54	26 46 23	21D56.9	19 44.7	8 1.1	7 23.1	12 30.1	0 24.3	7 22.4	29 2.7	16 12.2
30 Sa	12 27 35	8 48 10	2♐47 1	8♐45 18	21 57.5	21 25.8	8R 2.6	7 49.9	12 43.1	0 25.4	7 25.8	29 1.5	16D12.1
31 Su	12 31 31	9 47 24	14 41 49	20 37 7	21 58.9	23 8.2	8 1.7	8 16.9	12 56.1	0 26.4	7 29.2	29 0.3	16 12.1

APRIL 1929 LONGITUDE

Day	Sid.Time	☉	0 hr ☽	Noon ☽	True ☊	☿	♀	♂	♃	♄	♅	♆	♇
1 M	12 35 28	10♈46 36	26♐31 50	2♑26 35	22♉ 0.5	24♓52.0	7♉58.4	8♋44.0	13♉ 9.3	0♑27.4	7♈32.6	28♌59.2	16♋12.2
2 Tu	12 39 24	11 45 47	8♑22 1	14 18 48	22R 1.4	26 37.3	7R52.6	9 11.4	13 22.4	0 28.2	7 36.1	28R58.0	16 12.2
3 W	12 43 21	12 44 56	20 17 33	26 18 53	22 1.1	28 23.9	7 44.3	9 38.9	13 35.7	0 28.9	7 39.5	28 56.9	16 12.3
4 Th	12 47 17	13 44 3	2♒23 24	8♒31 39	21 59.3	0♈12.0	7 33.6	10 6.6	13 48.9	0 29.5	7 42.9	28 55.8	16 12.4
5 F	12 51 14	14 43 8	14 44 8	21 1 18	21 55.9	2 1.5	7 20.4	10 34.5	14 2.3	0 30.0	7 46.3	28 54.7	16 12.5
6 Sa	12 55 10	15 42 11	27 23 30	3♓50 59	21 51.0	3 52.5	7 4.8	11 2.6	14 15.6	0 30.5	7 49.7	28 53.7	16 12.6
7 Su	12 59 7	16 41 13	10♓23 57	17 2 27	21 45.4	5 44.9	6 46.8	11 30.8	14 29.1	0 30.8	7 53.1	28 52.6	16 12.8
8 M	13 3 4	17 40 12	23 46 26	0♈35 42	21 39.7	7 38.7	6 26.4	11 59.2	14 42.5	0 31.0	7 56.5	28 51.6	16 13.0
9 Tu	13 7 0	18 39 10	7♈30 0	14 28 55	21 34.5	9 34.0	6 3.8	12 27.8	14 56.0	0R31.1	7 59.9	28 50.7	16 13.2
10 W	13 10 57	19 38 6	21 31 58	28 38 34	21 30.5	11 30.7	5 39.0	12 56.5	15 9.6	0 31.1	8 3.3	28 49.7	16 13.5
11 Th	13 14 53	20 36 59	5♉48 6	12♉59 54	21 28.0	13 28.8	5 12.1	13 25.4	15 23.2	0 31.0	8 6.7	28 48.8	16 13.7
12 F	13 18 50	21 35 51	20 13 17	27 27 36	21D27.2	15 28.3	4 43.3	13 54.5	15 36.8	0 30.9	8 10.0	28 47.9	16 14.0
13 Sa	13 22 46	22 34 41	4♊42 11	11♊56 27	21 27.7	17 29.2	4 12.7	14 23.7	15 50.5	0 30.6	8 13.4	28 47.1	16 14.3
14 Su	13 26 43	23 33 28	19 9 53	26 21 59	21 29.0	19 31.3	3 40.4	14 53.1	16 4.2	0 30.2	8 16.7	28 46.2	16 14.7
15 M	13 30 39	24 32 14	3♋32 21	10♋40 39	21 30.4	21 34.7	3 6.6	15 22.6	16 17.9	0 29.7	8 20.1	28 45.4	16 15.0
16 Tu	13 34 36	25 30 57	17 46 36	24 49 59	21R31.4	23 39.1	2 31.6	15 52.2	16 31.7	0 29.2	8 23.4	28 44.7	16 15.4
17 W	13 38 33	26 29 38	1♌50 36	8♌48 20	21 31.5	25 44.6	1 55.5	16 22.0	16 45.5	0 28.5	8 26.7	28 43.9	16 15.9
18 Th	13 42 29	27 28 16	15 43 2	22 34 39	21 30.5	27 50.9	1 18.6	16 51.9	16 59.4	0 27.7	8 30.0	28 43.2	16 16.3
19 F	13 46 26	28 26 52	29 23 4	6♍ 8 15	21 28.4	29 58.0	0 41.1	17 22.0	17 13.2	0 26.9	8 33.3	28 42.5	16 16.7
20 Sa	13 50 22	29 25 26	12♍50 8	19 28 39	21 25.5	2♉ 5.5	0 3.3	17 52.1	17 27.1	0 25.9	8 36.5	28 41.9	16 17.2
21 Su	13 54 19	0♉23 58	26 3 47	2♎35 30	21 22.3	4 13.3	29♈25.4	18 22.4	17 41.0	0 24.8	8 39.8	28 41.3	16 17.7
22 M	13 58 15	1 22 27	9♎ 3 45	15 28 35	21 19.3	6 21.1	28 47.6	18 52.9	17 55.0	0 23.7	8 43.0	28 40.7	16 18.3
23 Tu	14 2 12	2 20 55	21 49 59	28 8 2	21 16.8	8 28.6	28 10.3	19 23.4	18 8.9	0 22.4	8 46.2	28 40.1	16 18.8
24 W	14 6 8	3 19 21	4♏22 47	10♏34 22	21 15.1	10 35.7	27 33.6	19 54.1	18 22.9	0 21.1	8 49.4	28 39.6	16 19.4
25 Th	14 10 5	4 17 45	16 42 56	22 48 39	21D14.4	12 41.8	26 57.8	20 24.8	18 37.0	0 19.7	8 52.6	28 39.1	16 20.0
26 F	14 14 1	5 16 7	28 51 48	4♐52 37	21 14.5	14 46.9	26 23.2	20 55.7	18 51.0	0 18.1	8 55.8	28 38.6	16 20.6
27 Sa	14 17 58	6 14 28	10♐51 26	16 48 36	21 15.2	16 50.4	25 49.9	21 26.7	19 5.0	0 16.5	8 58.9	28 38.2	16 21.2
28 Su	14 21 55	7 12 47	22 44 31	28 39 38	21 16.4	18 52.2	25 18.2	21 57.8	19 19.1	0 14.8	9 2.0	28 37.8	16 21.9
29 M	14 25 51	8 11 4	4♑34 25	10♑29 22	21 17.7	20 51.9	24 48.2	22 29.0	19 33.2	0 13.0	9 5.1	28 37.4	16 22.6
30 Tu	14 29 48	9 9 20	16 25 1	22 21 54	21 18.8	22 49.3	24 20.0	23 0.3	19 47.3	0 11.2	9 8.2	28 37.0	16 23.3

Astro Data	Planet Ingress	Last Aspect	☽ Ingress	Last Aspect	☽ Ingress	☽ Phases & Eclipses	Astro Data
Dy Hr Mn	Dy Hr Mn	Dy Hr Mn	Dy Hr Mn	Dy Hr Mn	Dy Hr Mn	Dy Hr Mn	
♄△♆ 6 17:46	♀ ♉ 8 7:29	2 9:26 ♆ □	♐ 2 10:03	1 4:59 ♆ △	♑ 1 7:03	3 11:09 ☽ 12♐24	1 MARCH 1929
☽0N 12 16:24	♂ ♋ 10 23:18	4 22:10 ♆ △	♑ 4 22:55	3 18:56 ☿ ✶	♒ 3 19:18	11 8:36 ● 20♓18	Julian Day # 10652
☽0S 25 15:11	♄ ♑ 15 13:48	7 9:33 ♀ □	♒ 7 10:44	6 2:48 ♆ ☍	♓ 6 4:52	18 7:41 ☽ 27♊14	Delta T 24.1 sec
♀ R 30 3:03	☿ ♓ 16 1:07	9 19:15 ♄ ✶	♓ 9 19:44	7 10:31 ♇ △	♈ 8 10:58	25 7:46 ○ 4♎11	SVP 06♓15'09"
♇ D 30 11:51	☉ ♈ 21 2:35	12 1:35 ♄ □	♈ 12 1:51	10 12:18 ♆ △	♉ 10 14:17		Obliquity 23°27'00"
		14 5:59 ♄ △	♉ 14 6:05	12 14:12 ♆ □	♊ 12 16:12	2 7:29 ☽ 12♑04	⚷ Chiron 6♉22.8
☿0N 6 9:17	☿ ♈ 3 21:21	16 8:15 ♆ ✶	♊ 16 9:23	14 16:00 ♆ ✶	♋ 14 18:04	9 20:32 ● 19♈30	☽ Mean ☊ 25♉08.5
☽0N 9 1:20	☿ ♉ 19 0:23	18 11:10 ♆ ✶	♋ 18 12:24	16 14:09 ☉ □	♌ 16 20:50	16 14:09 ☽ 26♋06	
♄ R 9 16:01	☉ ♉ 20 14:10	20 14:36 ☉ △	♌ 20 15:27	18 22:48 ♆ ☌	♍ 19 1:05	23 21:47 ○ 3♏14	1 APRIL 1929
♃⚼♄ 11 13:41	♀ ♈ 20 2:05	22 17:39 ♆ ☌	♍ 22 19:05	20 9:27 ♂ ✶	♎ 21 7:13		Julian Day # 10683
♃✶♇ 14 18:49		23 23:32 ♇ ✶	♎ 25 0:11	23 13:01 ♆ ✶	♏ 23 15:34		Delta T 24.1 sec
☽0S 21 22:35		27 6:05 ♆ ✶	♏ 27 7:49	25 23:34 ♆ □	♐ 26 2:16		SVP 06♓15'06"
		29 16:30 ♆ □	♐ 29 18:26	28 11:56 ♆ △	♑ 28 14:43		Obliquity 23°27'00"
							⚷ Chiron 7♉57.5
							☽ Mean ☊ 23♉30.0

LONGITUDE — MAY 1929

Day	Sid.Time	☉	0 hr ☽	Noon ☽	True ☊	☿	♀	♂	♃	♄	♅	♆	♇
1 W	14 33 44	10♉ 7 34	28♑20 37	4♒21 44	21♉19.6	24♉44.0	23♈53.9	23♋31.8	20♉ 1.5	0♑ 9.2	9♈11.3	28♌36.7	16♋24.0
2 Th	14 37 41	11 5 46	10♒25 49	16 33 27	21R 19.9	26 36.0	23R 29.8	24 3.3	20 15.6	0R 7.1	9 14.3	28R 36.5	16 24.8
3 F	14 41 37	12 3 58	22 45 11	29 1 32	21 19.7	28 24.9	23 8.0	24 34.9	20 29.8	0 5.0	9 17.3	28 36.2	16 25.5
4 Sa	14 45 34	13 2 7	5♓23 1	11♓50 0	21 19.1	0♊10.5	22 48.5	25 6.6	20 43.9	0 2.7	9 20.3	28 36.0	16 26.3
5 Su	14 49 30	14 0 15	18 22 52	25 1 52	21 18.3	1 52.8	22 31.4	25 38.5	20 58.1	0 0.4	9 23.3	28 35.8	16 27.1
6 M	14 53 27	14 58 22	1♈47 8	8♈38 42	21 17.5	3 31.7	22 16.7	26 10.4	21 12.3	29♐58.0	9 26.3	28 35.7	16 28.0
7 Tu	14 57 24	15 56 27	15 36 28	22 40 10	21 16.8	5 6.8	22 4.3	26 42.4	21 26.5	29 55.5	9 29.2	28 35.5	16 28.8
8 W	15 1 20	16 54 31	29 49 25	7♉ 3 41	21 16.4	6 38.3	21 54.4	27 14.5	21 40.7	29 53.0	9 32.1	28 35.5	16 29.7
9 Th	15 5 17	17 52 34	14♉22 16	21 44 24	21D 16.2	8 6.0	21 47.0	27 46.8	21 54.9	29 50.3	9 34.9	28D 35.4	16 30.6
10 F	15 9 13	18 50 35	29 9 12	6♊35 42	21 16.2	9 29.9	21 41.9	28 19.1	22 9.1	29 47.6	9 37.8	28 35.4	16 31.5
11 Sa	15 13 10	19 48 34	14♊ 2 55	21 29 53	21 16.3	10 49.8	21D 39.3	28 51.5	22 23.3	29 44.8	9 40.6	28 35.4	16 32.4
12 Su	15 17 6	20 46 31	28 55 40	6♋19 22	21R 16.4	12 5.7	21 39.0	29 24.0	22 37.5	29 41.9	9 43.4	28 35.5	16 33.4
13 M	15 21 3	21 44 27	13♋40 12	20 57 30	21 16.4	13 17.5	21 41.0	29 56.5	22 51.8	29 39.0	9 46.2	28 35.5	16 34.4
14 Tu	15 25 0	22 42 22	28 10 43	5♌19 25	21 16.3	14 25.2	21 45.3	0♌29.2	23 6.0	29 35.9	9 48.9	28 35.7	16 35.4
15 W	15 28 56	23 40 14	12♌23 18	19 22 12	21D 16.2	15 28.7	21 51.8	1 2.0	23 20.2	29 32.9	9 51.6	28 35.8	16 36.4
16 Th	15 32 53	24 38 4	26 16 1	3♍ 4 46	21 16.1	16 28.0	22 0.5	1 34.8	23 34.4	29 29.7	9 54.3	28 36.0	16 37.4
17 F	15 36 49	25 35 53	9♍48 33	16 27 31	21 16.3	17 23.0	22 11.4	2 7.7	23 48.6	29 26.4	9 56.9	28 36.2	16 38.4
18 Sa	15 40 46	26 33 40	23 1 52	29 31 51	21 16.6	18 13.6	22 24.3	2 40.7	24 2.8	29 23.1	9 59.5	28 36.4	16 39.5
19 Su	15 44 42	27 31 25	5♎57 41	12♎19 40	21 17.1	18 59.7	22 39.2	3 13.7	24 17.0	29 19.8	10 2.1	28 36.7	16 40.6
20 M	15 48 39	28 29 9	18 38 3	24 53 7	21 17.8	19 41.4	22 56.0	3 46.9	24 31.2	29 16.3	10 4.6	28 37.0	16 41.7
21 Tu	15 52 35	29 26 51	1♏ 5 8	7♏14 21	21 18.5	20 18.4	23 14.8	4 20.1	24 45.4	29 12.9	10 7.1	28 37.4	16 42.8
22 W	15 56 32	0♊24 32	13 21 1	19 25 23	21R 18.9	20 50.9	23 35.4	4 53.4	24 59.5	29 9.3	10 9.6	28 37.7	16 43.9
23 Th	16 0 28	1 22 11	25 27 41	1♐28 10	21 19.0	21 18.6	23 57.7	5 26.7	25 13.7	29 5.7	10 12.1	28 38.2	16 45.1
24 F	16 4 25	2 19 49	7♐27 3	13 24 36	21 18.5	21 41.6	24 21.8	6 0.2	25 27.8	29 2.0	10 14.5	28 38.6	16 46.2
25 Sa	16 8 22	3 17 26	19 21 5	25 16 44	21 17.5	21 59.9	24 47.5	6 33.7	25 42.0	28 58.3	10 16.8	28 39.1	16 47.4
26 Su	16 12 18	4 15 2	1♑11 51	7♑ 6 46	21 15.9	22 13.5	25 14.8	7 7.2	25 56.1	28 54.5	10 19.2	28 39.6	16 48.6
27 M	16 16 15	5 12 37	13 1 46	18 57 14	21 13.9	22 22.3	25 43.7	7 40.9	26 10.2	28 50.7	10 21.5	28 40.1	16 49.8
28 Tu	16 20 11	6 10 10	24 53 33	0♒51 8	21 11.8	22R 26.4	26 14.0	8 14.6	26 24.3	28 46.9	10 23.8	28 40.7	16 51.1
29 W	16 24 8	7 7 43	6♒50 23	12 51 48	21 9.7	22 25.9	26 45.8	8 48.3	26 38.3	28 42.9	10 26.0	28 41.3	16 52.3
30 Th	16 28 4	8 5 15	18 55 50	25 3 1	21 8.1	22 20.9	27 18.9	9 22.2	26 52.4	28 39.0	10 28.2	28 41.9	16 53.6
31 F	16 32 1	9 2 46	1♓13 50	7♓28 49	21D 7.2	22 11.5	27 53.4	9 56.1	27 6.4	28 35.0	10 30.3	28 42.6	16 54.8

LONGITUDE — JUNE 1929

Day	Sid.Time	☉	0 hr ☽	Noon ☽	True ☊	☿	♀	♂	♃	♄	♅	♆	♇
1 Sa	16 35 58	10♊ 0 16	13♓48 27	20♓13 15	21♉ 7.0	21♊58.0	28♈29.1	10♌30.1	27♉20.5	28♐30.9	10♈32.5	28♌43.3	16♋56.1
2 Su	16 39 54	10 57 45	26 43 38	3♈20 0	21 7.7	21R 40.6	29 6.0	11 4.1	27 34.4	28R 26.8	10 34.6	28 44.0	16 57.4
3 M	16 43 51	11 55 14	10♈ 2 43	16 51 58	21 8.8	21 19.6	29 44.1	11 38.2	27 48.4	28 22.7	10 36.6	28 44.8	16 58.7
4 Tu	16 47 47	12 52 42	23 47 55	0♉50 32	21 10.2	20 55.4	0♉23.4	12 12.4	28 2.4	28 18.5	10 38.6	28 45.5	17 0.0
5 W	16 51 44	13 50 9	7♉59 40	15 14 58	21R 11.4	20 28.4	1 3.6	12 46.6	28 16.3	28 14.3	10 40.6	28 46.4	17 1.4
6 Th	16 55 40	14 47 36	22 35 55	0♊ 1 51	21 11.8	19 59.0	1 45.0	13 20.9	28 30.2	28 10.1	10 42.5	28 47.2	17 2.7
7 F	16 59 37	15 45 2	7♊31 52	15 4 58	21 11.1	19 27.8	2 27.3	13 55.3	28 44.1	28 5.8	10 44.4	28 48.1	17 4.1
8 Sa	17 3 33	16 42 27	22 40 1	0♋15 48	21 9.2	18 55.2	3 10.6	14 29.7	28 57.9	28 1.5	10 46.2	28 49.0	17 5.5
9 Su	17 7 30	17 39 52	7♋51 3	15 24 32	21 6.2	18 21.8	3 54.7	15 4.3	29 11.7	27 57.2	10 48.0	28 50.0	17 6.8
10 M	17 11 27	18 37 15	22 55 7	0♌21 45	21 2.6	17 48.2	4 39.8	15 38.8	29 25.5	27 52.9	10 49.8	28 50.9	17 8.2
11 Tu	17 15 23	19 34 37	7♌43 31	14 59 43	20 58.9	17 15.0	5 25.7	16 13.4	29 39.3	27 48.5	10 51.5	28 51.9	17 9.7
12 W	17 19 20	20 31 59	22 9 49	29 13 28	20 55.7	16 42.7	6 12.4	16 48.1	29 53.0	27 44.2	10 53.2	28 53.0	17 11.1
13 Th	17 23 16	21 29 19	6♍10 29	13♍ 0 54	20 53.5	16 11.9	6 59.8	17 22.9	0♊ 6.6	27 39.8	10 54.8	28 54.0	17 12.5
14 F	17 27 13	22 26 39	19 44 48	26 22 28	20D 52.6	15 43.1	7 48.1	17 57.7	0 20.3	27 35.4	10 56.4	28 55.1	17 13.9
15 Sa	17 31 9	23 23 57	2♎54 14	9♎20 29	20 52.9	15 16.7	8 37.0	18 32.5	0 33.9	27 31.0	10 57.9	28 56.2	17 15.4
16 Su	17 35 6	24 21 14	15 41 42	21 58 20	20 54.2	14 53.3	9 26.7	19 7.4	0 47.4	27 26.5	10 59.4	28 57.4	17 16.8
17 M	17 39 2	25 18 31	28 10 54	4♏19 51	20 55.8	14 33.3	10 17.0	19 42.4	1 1.0	27 22.1	11 0.9	28 58.5	17 18.3
18 Tu	17 42 59	26 15 47	10♏25 42	16 28 54	20R 57.1	14 16.9	11 7.9	20 17.4	1 14.4	27 17.7	11 2.3	28 59.7	17 19.8
19 W	17 46 56	27 13 2	22 29 51	28 28 59	20 57.6	14 4.4	11 59.5	20 52.5	1 27.9	27 13.2	11 3.7	29 1.0	17 21.2
20 Th	17 50 52	28 10 17	4♐26 40	10♐23 13	20 56.6	13 56.2	12 51.7	21 27.6	1 41.3	27 8.8	11 5.0	29 2.2	17 22.7
21 F	17 54 49	29 7 31	16 18 59	22 14 13	20 53.9	13D 52.3	13 44.5	22 2.8	1 54.6	27 4.4	11 6.3	29 3.5	17 24.2
22 Sa	17 58 45	0♋ 4 45	28 9 13	4♑ 4 12	20 49.4	13 53.0	14 37.9	22 38.0	2 8.0	26 60.0	11 7.5	29 4.8	17 25.7
23 Su	18 2 42	1 1 58	9♑59 25	15 55 5	20 43.3	13 58.3	15 31.8	23 13.3	2 21.2	26 55.5	11 8.7	29 6.1	17 27.2
24 M	18 6 38	1 59 11	21 51 26	27 48 42	20 36.1	14 8.4	16 26.2	23 48.7	2 34.4	26 51.1	11 9.8	29 7.5	17 28.7
25 Tu	18 10 35	2 56 23	3♒47 8	9♒47 0	20 28.4	14 23.1	17 21.2	24 24.0	2 47.6	26 46.7	11 10.9	29 8.9	17 30.3
26 W	18 14 31	3 53 36	15 48 33	21 52 7	20 21.0	14 42.7	18 16.6	24 59.5	3 0.7	26 42.3	11 12.0	29 10.3	17 31.8
27 Th	18 18 28	4 50 48	27 58 2	4♓ 6 39	20 14.6	15 7.0	19 12.5	25 35.0	3 13.8	26 38.0	11 13.0	29 11.7	17 33.3
28 F	18 22 25	5 48 1	10♓18 22	16 33 35	20 9.8	15 36.0	20 8.9	26 10.5	3 26.8	26 33.6	11 13.9	29 13.2	17 34.9
29 Sa	18 26 21	6 45 13	22 52 44	29 16 16	20 6.9	16 9.8	21 5.7	26 46.1	3 39.8	26 29.3	11 14.8	29 14.7	17 36.4
30 Su	18 30 18	7 42 25	5♈44 37	12♈18 13	20D 5.8	16 48.2	22 3.0	27 21.8	3 52.7	26 25.0	11 15.7	29 16.2	17 37.9

Astro Data Dy Hr Mn	Planet Ingress Dy Hr Mn	Last Aspect Dy Hr Mn	☽ Ingress Dy Hr Mn	Last Aspect Dy Hr Mn	☽ Ingress Dy Hr Mn	☽ Phases & Eclipses Dy Hr Mn	Astro Data
☽0N 6 11:29	☿ ♊ 3 21:34	30 15:24 ☿ △	♒ 1 3:19	2 3:07 ♄ □	♈ 2 5:58	2 1:25 ☽ 11♒09	1 MAY 1929
♆ D 9 23:42	♄ ♐ 5 4:19	3 12:37 ♆ □	♓ 3 13:51	4 8:29 ♆ △	♉ 4 10:34	9 6:07 ● 18♉07	Julian Day # 10713
♀ D 11 15:01	♂ ♌ 13 2:33	5 20:48 ♄ □	♈ 5 20:51	6 10:01 ♆ □	♊ 6 11:57	9 6:10:10 ● T 5'07"	Delta T 24.1 sec
☽0S 19 4:30	☉ ♊ 21 13:48	8 0:06 ♄ △	♉ 8 0:18	8 9:44 ♆ ⚹	♋ 8 11:35	15 20:56 ☽ 24♌31	SVP 06♓15'02"
♃∠♅ 22 20:41		9 23:05 ♆ □	♊ 10 1:22	10 10:39 ♃ ⚹	♌ 10 11:25	23 12:50 ○ 1♐53	Obliquity 23°27'00"
☿ R 28 9:17	♀ ♉ 3 9:48	12 1:15 ♄ ☍	♋ 12 1:44	12 11:26 ♆ ☌	♍ 12 13:20	23 12:37 ☍ A 0.937	⚷ Chiron 9♉50.3
♄△♆ 29 8:36	♃ ♊ 12 12:20	13 15:24 ♃ ⚹	♌ 14 3:03	14 14:08 ♄ □	♎ 14 18:38	31 16:13 ☽ 9♓42	☽ Mean ☊ 21♉54.6
☽0N 2 20:54	☉ ♋ 21 22:01	16 5:39 ♄ △	♍ 16 6:33	17 1:33 ♆ ⚹	♏ 17 3:32		
♃⊼♄ 4 21:22		18 11:41 ♄ □	♎ 18 12:52	19 13:06 ♆ □	♐ 19 15:03	7 13:56 ● 16♊18	1 JUNE 1929
♃□♆ 7 7:29		20 20:23 ♄ ⚹	♏ 20 21:54	22 1:53 ♆ △	♑ 22 3:45	14 5:14 ☽ 22♍39	Julian Day # 10744
☽0S 15 9:53		23 6:20 ♆ □	♐ 23 9:04	23 15:08 ♇ ☍	♒ 24 16:24	22 4:15 ○ 0♑15	Delta T 24.1 sec
☿ D 21 8:28		25 19:23 ♄ ☌	♑ 25 21:34	27 2:25 ♆ ☍	♓ 27 3:59	30 3:54 ☽ 7♈52	SVP 06♓14'57"
♃∠♇ 23 12:19		28 3:07 ♃ △	♒ 28 10:17	29 6:45 ♄ □	♈ 29 13:22		Obliquity 23°27'00"
☽0N 30 4:09		30 19:07 ♆ ☍	♓ 30 21:37				⚷ Chiron 11♉47.0
							☽ Mean ☊ 20♉16.2

JULY 1929 LONGITUDE

Day	Sid.Time	☉	0 hr ☽	Noon ☽	True ☊	☿	♀	♂	♃	♄	♅	♆	♇
1 M	18 34 14	8♋39 38	18♈57 28	25♈42 44	20♉ 6.2	17♊31.2	23♉ 0.7	27♌57.5	4♊ 5.5	26♐20.7	11♈16.5	29♌17.7	17♋39.5
2 Tu	18 38 11	9 36 50	2♉34 16	9♉32 16	20 7.2	18 18.7	23 58.8	28 33.3	4 18.3	26R16.4	11 17.3	29 19.3	17 41.0
3 W	18 42 7	10 34 3	16 36 48	23 47 46	20R 8.0	19 10.7	24 57.2	29 9.1	4 31.0	26 12.2	11 18.0	29 20.9	17 42.6
4 Th	18 46 4	11 31 17	1♊ 4 54	8♊27 45	20 7.6	20 7.2	25 56.1	29 45.0	4 43.7	26 8.0	11 18.6	29 22.5	17 44.2
5 F	18 50 0	12 28 30	15 55 39	23 27 45	20 5.3	21 8.0	26 55.3	0♍20.9	4 56.3	26 3.8	11 19.3	29 24.1	17 45.7
6 Sa	18 53 57	13 25 44	1♋ 3 1	8♋40 14	20 0.7	22 13.1	27 54.9	0 56.9	5 8.9	25 59.7	11 19.8	29 25.7	17 47.3
7 Su	18 57 54	14 22 58	16 18 6	23 55 16	19 54.1	23 22.5	28 54.8	1 32.9	5 21.4	25 55.6	11 20.4	29 27.4	17 48.9
8 M	19 1 50	15 20 12	1♌30 21	9♌ 2 5	19 46.2	24 36.0	29 55.0	2 9.0	5 33.8	25 51.5	11 20.8	29 29.1	17 50.4
9 Tu	19 5 47	16 17 26	16 29 17	23 50 57	19 37.9	25 53.7	0♊55.5	2 45.1	5 46.1	25 47.5	11 21.3	29 30.8	17 52.0
10 W	19 9 43	17 14 40	1♍ 6 19	8♍14 48	19 30.3	27 15.5	1 56.3	3 21.3	5 58.4	25 43.5	11 21.6	29 32.6	17 53.6
11 Th	19 13 40	18 11 54	15 16 3	22 9 54	19 24.3	28 41.3	2 57.5	3 57.6	6 10.6	25 39.6	11 22.0	29 34.3	17 55.1
12 F	19 17 36	19 9 7	28 56 25	5♎35 48	19 20.4	0♋11.0	3 58.9	4 33.8	6 22.7	25 35.7	11 22.2	29 36.1	17 56.7
13 Sa	19 21 33	20 6 21	12♎ 8 24	18 34 40	19D18.5	1 44.5	5 0.6	5 10.2	6 34.8	25 31.8	11 22.5	29 37.9	17 58.3
14 Su	19 25 30	21 3 35	24 55 7	1♏10 20	19 18.3	3 21.8	6 2.6	5 46.6	6 46.8	25 28.1	11 22.7	29 39.7	17 59.8
15 M	19 29 26	22 0 48	7♏20 55	13 27 31	19R18.9	5 2.7	7 4.8	6 23.0	6 58.7	25 24.3	11 22.8	29 41.5	18 1.4
16 Tu	19 33 23	22 58 2	19 30 44	25 31 10	19 19.3	6 47.1	8 7.3	6 59.5	7 10.5	25 20.7	11 22.9	29 43.4	18 3.0
17 W	19 37 19	23 55 16	1♐29 24	7♐26 0	19 18.5	8 34.8	9 10.1	7 36.0	7 22.3	25 17.0	11R22.9	29 45.2	18 4.5
18 Th	19 41 16	24 52 30	13 21 26	19 16 11	19 15.8	10 25.6	10 13.1	8 12.6	7 34.0	25 13.5	11 22.9	29 47.1	18 6.1
19 F	19 45 12	25 49 45	25 10 41	1♑ 5 16	19 10.6	12 19.4	11 16.4	8 49.2	7 45.6	25 10.0	11 22.8	29 49.0	18 7.6
20 Sa	19 49 9	26 47 0	7♑ 0 18	12 56 4	19 2.8	14 15.8	12 19.9	9 25.9	7 57.1	25 6.5	11 22.7	29 50.9	18 9.2
21 Su	19 53 5	27 44 15	18 52 48	24 50 42	18 52.6	16 14.5	13 23.6	10 2.6	8 8.5	25 3.2	11 22.6	29 52.9	18 10.8
22 M	19 57 2	28 41 31	0♒49 59	6♒50 48	18 40.8	18 15.4	14 27.5	10 39.3	8 19.8	24 59.8	11 22.4	29 54.8	18 12.3
23 Tu	20 0 59	29 38 47	12 53 17	18 57 36	18 28.3	20 18.0	15 31.7	11 16.2	8 31.1	24 56.6	11 22.1	29 56.8	18 13.8
24 W	20 4 55	0♌36 4	25 3 52	1♓12 16	18 16.1	22 22.1	16 36.1	11 53.0	8 42.2	24 53.4	11 21.8	29 58.8	18 15.4
25 Th	20 8 52	1 33 22	7♓22 56	13 36 5	18 5.2	24 27.3	17 40.7	12 29.9	8 53.3	24 50.3	11 21.5	0♍ 0.7	18 16.9
26 F	20 12 48	2 30 40	19 51 56	26 10 42	17 56.6	26 33.3	18 45.5	13 6.9	9 4.3	24 47.2	11 21.1	0 2.8	18 18.5
27 Sa	20 16 45	3 27 59	2♈32 42	8♈58 14	17 50.6	28 39.8	19 50.6	13 43.9	9 15.2	24 44.3	11 20.6	0 4.8	18 20.0
28 Su	20 20 41	4 25 20	15 27 36	22 1 10	17 47.3	0♌46.5	20 55.8	14 20.9	9 26.0	24 41.4	11 20.1	0 6.8	18 21.5
29 M	20 24 38	5 22 41	28 39 16	5♉22 14	17D46.0	2 53.1	22 1.2	14 58.0	9 36.7	24 38.5	11 19.6	0 8.8	18 23.0
30 Tu	20 28 34	6 20 3	12♉10 22	19 3 54	17R46.0	4 59.3	23 6.8	15 35.2	9 47.3	24 35.8	11 19.0	0 10.9	18 24.5
31 W	20 32 31	7 17 27	26 3 1	3♊ 7 47	17 45.9	7 5.0	24 12.6	16 12.4	9 57.8	24 33.1	11 18.4	0 13.0	18 26.0

AUGUST 1929 LONGITUDE

Day	Sid.Time	☉	0 hr ☽	Noon ☽	True ☊	☿	♀	♂	♃	♄	♅	♆	♇
1 Th	20 36 28	8♌14 52	10♊18 6	17♊33 45	17♉44.5	9♌ 9.9	25♊18.6	16♍49.7	10♊ 8.2	24♐30.5	11♈17.7	0♍15.1	18♋27.5
2 F	20 40 24	9 12 18	24 54 20	2♋19 15	17R40.9	11 13.9	26 24.8	17 27.0	10 18.5	24R28.0	11R17.0	0 17.2	18 29.0
3 Sa	20 44 21	10 9 45	9♋47 43	17 18 46	17 34.7	13 16.8	27 31.1	18 4.3	10 28.7	24 25.6	11 16.2	0 19.3	18 30.5
4 Su	20 48 17	11 7 13	24 51 18	2♌24 6	17 26.0	15 18.6	28 37.6	18 41.7	10 38.8	24 23.2	11 15.4	0 21.4	18 32.0
5 M	20 52 14	12 4 42	9♌55 53	17 25 23	17 15.4	17 19.0	29 44.3	19 19.2	10 48.8	24 21.0	11 14.5	0 23.5	18 33.4
6 Tu	20 56 10	13 2 12	24 51 24	2♍12 49	17 4.3	19 18.1	0♋51.1	19 56.7	10 58.6	24 18.8	11 13.6	0 25.7	18 34.9
7 W	21 0 7	13 59 43	9♍28 43	16 38 21	16 53.8	21 15.8	1 58.1	20 34.3	11 8.4	24 16.7	11 12.7	0 27.8	18 36.3
8 Th	21 4 3	14 57 15	23 41 10	0♎36 52	16 45.2	23 12.1	3 5.2	21 11.9	11 18.0	24 14.7	11 11.7	0 30.0	18 37.8
9 F	21 8 0	15 54 48	7♎25 20	14 6 36	16 39.0	25 6.8	4 12.5	21 49.5	11 27.6	24 12.7	11 10.6	0 32.1	18 39.2
10 Sa	21 11 57	16 52 21	20 40 56	27 8 40	16 35.3	27 0.1	5 19.9	22 27.2	11 37.0	24 10.9	11 9.6	0 34.3	18 40.6
11 Su	21 15 53	17 49 56	3♏30 17	9♏46 20	16 33.8	28 51.8	6 27.5	23 5.0	11 46.3	24 9.1	11 8.4	0 36.5	18 42.0
12 M	21 19 50	18 47 31	15 57 27	22 4 15	16 33.5	0♍42.1	7 35.2	23 42.8	11 55.4	24 7.5	11 7.3	0 38.6	18 43.4
13 Tu	21 23 46	19 45 8	28 7 25	4♐ 7 37	16 33.4	2 30.9	8 43.0	24 20.6	12 4.5	24 5.9	11 6.1	0 40.8	18 44.8
14 W	21 27 43	20 42 45	10♐ 5 31	16 1 45	16 32.3	4 18.1	9 51.0	24 58.5	12 13.4	24 4.4	11 4.8	0 43.0	18 46.2
15 Th	21 31 39	21 40 23	21 56 56	27 51 39	16 29.4	6 3.9	10 59.1	25 36.5	12 22.2	24 3.1	11 3.5	0 45.2	18 47.5
16 F	21 35 36	22 38 3	3♑46 24	9♑41 41	16 23.9	7 48.2	12 7.4	26 14.5	12 30.9	24 1.8	11 2.2	0 47.4	18 48.9
17 Sa	21 39 32	23 35 43	15 37 56	21 35 31	16 15.7	9 31.1	13 15.8	26 52.5	12 39.4	24 0.6	11 0.8	0 49.6	18 50.2
18 Su	21 43 29	24 33 25	27 34 45	3♒35 55	16 5.0	11 12.4	14 24.3	27 30.6	12 47.8	23 59.5	10 59.4	0 51.9	18 51.5
19 M	21 47 26	25 31 8	9♒39 12	15 44 47	15 52.6	12 52.4	15 33.0	28 8.7	12 56.1	23 58.5	10 57.9	0 54.1	18 52.8
20 Tu	21 51 22	26 28 52	21 52 48	28 3 19	15 39.4	14 30.9	16 41.8	28 46.9	13 4.2	23 57.5	10 56.5	0 56.3	18 54.1
21 W	21 55 19	27 26 37	4♓16 23	10♓32 3	15 26.4	16 8.1	17 50.7	29 25.1	13 12.3	23 56.7	10 54.9	0 58.5	18 55.4
22 Th	21 59 15	28 24 24	16 50 21	23 11 18	15 14.9	17 43.8	18 59.8	0♎ 3.4	13 20.1	23 56.0	10 53.4	1 0.7	18 56.7
23 F	22 3 12	29 22 12	29 34 55	6♈ 1 17	15 5.7	19 18.1	20 8.9	0 41.7	13 27.9	23 55.4	10 51.8	1 2.9	18 57.9
24 Sa	22 7 8	0♍20 2	12♈30 26	19 2 30	14 59.3	20 51.0	21 18.2	1 20.1	13 35.5	23 54.8	10 50.1	1 5.2	18 59.2
25 Su	22 11 5	1 17 53	25 37 35	2♉15 49	14 55.7	22 22.5	22 27.6	1 58.5	13 42.9	23 54.4	10 48.4	1 7.4	19 0.4
26 M	22 15 1	2 15 47	8♉57 24	15 42 30	14D54.3	23 52.7	23 37.2	2 37.0	13 50.2	23 54.0	10 46.7	1 9.6	19 1.6
27 Tu	22 18 58	3 13 42	22 31 17	29 23 54	14R54.3	25 21.4	24 46.8	3 15.5	13 57.4	23 53.8	10 45.0	1 11.8	19 2.8
28 W	22 22 55	4 11 39	6♊20 28	13♊21 4	14 54.5	26 48.7	25 56.6	3 54.1	14 4.4	23 53.6	10 43.2	1 14.1	19 4.0
29 Th	22 26 51	5 9 38	20 25 39	27 34 7	14 53.7	28 14.6	27 6.5	4 32.8	14 11.3	23D53.6	10 41.4	1 16.3	19 5.2
30 F	22 30 48	6 7 39	4♋46 12	12♋ 1 34	14 50.8	29 39.1	28 16.5	5 11.4	14 18.0	23 53.6	10 39.6	1 18.5	19 6.3
31 Sa	22 34 44	7 5 42	19 19 41	26 39 53	14 45.6	1♎ 2.1	29 26.7	5 50.2	14 24.6	23 53.8	10 37.7	1 20.7	19 7.4

Astro Data	Planet Ingress	Last Aspect	☽ Ingress	Last Aspect	☽ Ingress	☽ Phases & Eclipses	Astro Data
Dy Hr Mn	Dy Hr Mn	Dy Hr Mn	Dy Hr Mn	Dy Hr Mn	Dy Hr Mn	Dy Hr Mn	1 JULY 1929
☽0S 12 16:05	♂ ♍ 4 10:03	1 18:20 ♆ △	♉ 1 19:31	2 2:39 ♀ ☌	♋ 2 8:15	6 20:47 ● 14♋15	Julian Day # 10774
♅ R 17 6:26	♀ ♊ 8 2:00	3 21:43 ♂ □	♊ 3 22:14	3 13:56 ♇ ☌	♌ 4 8:11	13 16:05 ☽ 20♎45	Delta T 24.1 sec
☽0N 27 9:21	☿ ♋ 11 21:07	5 21:26 ♆ ⚹	♋ 5 22:21	5 23:07 ♄ △	♍ 6 8:22	21 19:21 ○ 28♑30	SVP 06♓14'52"
	☉ ♌ 23 8:53	7 21:18 ♀ ⚹	♌ 7 21:37	8 0:57 ♄ □	♎ 8 10:56	29 12:56 ☽ 5♉54	Obliquity 23°27'00"
♃⚹♅ 7 9:39	♆ ♍ 24 15:03	9 21:24 ♆ ☌	♍ 9 22:10	10 13:44 ☿ ⚹	♏ 10 17:22		⚷ Chiron 13♉19.7
☽0S 8 23:55	☿ ♌ 27 15:12	11 18:05 ♄ □	♎ 12 1:54	12 16:05 ♂ ⚹	♐ 13 3:44	5 3:40 ● 12♌13	☽ Mean ☊ 18♉40.9
☽0N 23 14:06		14 9:07 ♆ ⚹	♏ 14 9:44	15 7:51 ♂ □	♑ 15 16:21	12 6:01 ☽ 19♏02	
♂0S 24 1:58	♀ ♋ 5 5:39	16 20:30 ♆ □	♐ 16 21:00	17 23:51 ♂ △	♒ 18 4:50	20 9:42 ○ 26♒52	1 AUGUST 1929
☿0S 29 8:43	☿ ♍ 11 14:48	19 9:27 ♆ △	♑ 19 9:48	20 9:42 ☉ ☍	♓ 20 15:46	27 20:02 ☽ 4♊02	Julian Day # 10805
♄ D 29 0:57	♂ ♎ 21 21:52	21 19:21 ☉ ☍	♒ 21 22:20	22 13:23 ♄ □	♈ 23 0:47		Delta T 24.0 sec
	☉ ♍ 23 15:41	24 9:38 ♆ ☍	♓ 24 9:39	24 20:53 ♄ △	♉ 25 7:55		SVP 06♓14'46"
	☿ ♎ 30 6:01	26 15:15 ☿ △	♈ 26 19:13	27 5:33 ☿ △	♊ 27 13:03		Obliquity 23°27'00"
	♀ ♌ 31 11:24	28 16:47 ♄ △	♉ 29 2:25	29 14:34 ☿ □	♋ 29 16:04		⚷ Chiron 14♉16.7
		30 10:53 ♇ ⚹	♊ 31 6:43	30 23:40 ♇ ☌	♌ 31 17:26		☽ Mean ☊ 17♉02.4

LONGITUDE SEPTEMBER 1929

Day	Sid.Time	☉	0 hr ☽	Noon ☽	True ☊	☿	♀	♂	♃	♄	♅	♆	♇
1 Su	22 38 41	8♍ 3 46	4♌ 1 25	11♌23 23	14♉37.9	2♎23.6	0♌36.9	6♎29.0	14♊31.0	23♐54.0	10♈35.8	1♍22.9	19♋ 8.6
2 M	22 42 37	9 1 53	18 44 50	26 4 46	14R28.5	3 43.5	1 47.2	7 7.8	14 37.2	23 54.3	10R33.9	1 25.2	19 9.7
3 Tu	22 46 34	10 0 1	3♍22 11	10♍36 10	14 18.5	5 1.9	2 57.7	7 46.7	14 43.3	23 54.8	10 31.9	1 27.4	19 10.7
4 W	22 50 30	10 58 11	17 45 51	24 50 31	14 9.0	6 18.6	4 8.2	8 25.7	14 49.2	23 55.3	10 29.9	1 29.6	19 11.8
5 Th	22 54 27	11 56 22	1♎49 35	8♎42 38	14 1.0	7 33.7	5 18.9	9 4.7	14 55.0	23 55.9	10 27.9	1 31.8	19 12.8
6 F	22 58 24	12 54 36	15 29 24	22 9 50	13 55.3	8 47.0	6 29.6	9 43.7	15 0.6	23 56.7	10 25.8	1 34.0	19 13.9
7 Sa	23 2 20	13 52 50	28 43 57	5♏12 0	13 52.1	9 58.5	7 40.4	10 22.8	15 6.0	23 57.5	10 23.8	1 36.2	19 14.9
8 Su	23 6 17	14 51 7	11♏34 16	17 51 10	13D50.9	11 8.0	8 51.4	11 1.9	15 11.2	23 58.4	10 21.7	1 38.3	19 15.9
9 M	23 10 13	15 49 24	24 3 14	0♐11 0	13 51.3	12 15.5	10 2.4	11 41.1	15 16.3	23 59.4	10 19.5	1 40.5	19 16.8
10 Tu	23 14 10	16 47 44	6♐15 6	12 16 9	13R52.2	13 21.0	11 13.5	12 20.4	15 21.3	24 0.6	10 17.4	1 42.7	19 17.8
11 W	23 18 6	17 46 5	18 14 49	24 11 45	13 52.6	14 24.1	12 24.7	12 59.7	15 26.0	24 1.8	10 15.2	1 44.8	19 18.7
12 Th	23 22 3	18 44 28	0♑ 7 36	6♑ 3 0	13 51.8	15 24.9	13 36.0	13 39.0	15 30.6	24 3.1	10 13.0	1 47.0	19 19.6
13 F	23 25 59	19 42 52	11 58 33	17 54 51	13 49.1	16 23.2	14 47.4	14 18.4	15 35.0	24 4.5	10 10.8	1 49.1	19 20.5
14 Sa	23 29 56	20 41 18	23 52 24	29 51 42	13 44.2	17 18.7	15 58.9	14 57.9	15 39.2	24 6.0	10 8.6	1 51.3	19 21.4
15 Su	23 33 53	21 39 45	5♒53 12	11♒57 16	13 37.4	18 11.3	17 10.5	15 37.4	15 43.2	24 7.6	10 6.4	1 53.4	19 22.2
16 M	23 37 49	22 38 14	18 4 12	24 14 16	13 29.0	19 0.8	18 22.2	16 16.9	15 47.1	24 9.3	10 4.1	1 55.5	19 23.1
17 Tu	23 41 46	23 36 45	0♓27 39	6♓44 29	13 19.9	19 46.9	19 33.9	16 56.5	15 50.7	24 11.1	10 1.8	1 57.6	19 23.9
18 W	23 45 42	24 35 18	13 4 50	19 28 41	13 10.9	20 29.5	20 45.7	17 36.2	15 54.2	24 13.0	9 59.5	1 59.7	19 24.7
19 Th	23 49 39	25 33 52	25 56 1	2♈26 43	13 3.0	21 8.1	21 57.7	18 15.9	15 57.5	24 15.0	9 57.2	2 1.8	19 25.4
20 F	23 53 35	26 32 28	9♈ 0 43	15 37 50	12 56.8	21 42.6	23 9.7	18 55.6	16 0.7	24 17.0	9 54.9	2 3.8	19 26.2
21 Sa	23 57 32	27 31 7	22 17 57	29 0 55	12 52.7	22 12.5	24 21.8	19 35.4	16 3.6	24 19.2	9 52.5	2 5.9	19 26.9
22 Su	0 1 28	28 29 47	5♉46 33	12♉34 46	12D50.9	22 37.6	25 33.9	20 15.3	16 6.3	24 21.5	9 50.2	2 7.9	19 27.6
23 M	0 5 25	29 28 30	19 25 25	26 18 25	12 50.8	22 57.4	26 46.2	20 55.2	16 8.9	24 23.8	9 47.8	2 10.0	19 28.3
24 Tu	0 9 21	0♎27 15	3♊13 40	10♊11 5	12 51.9	23 11.6	27 58.6	21 35.1	16 11.3	24 26.2	9 45.4	2 12.0	19 28.9
25 W	0 13 18	1 26 2	17 10 34	24 12 3	12 53.2	23R19.7	29 11.0	22 15.2	16 13.4	24 28.8	9 43.1	2 14.0	19 29.6
26 Th	0 17 15	2 24 51	1♋15 23	8♋20 25	12R53.9	23 21.5	0♍23.5	22 55.2	16 15.4	24 31.4	9 40.7	2 16.0	19 30.2
27 F	0 21 11	3 23 43	15 26 56	22 34 41	12 53.3	23 16.5	1 36.1	23 35.4	16 17.2	24 34.1	9 38.3	2 18.0	19 30.8
28 Sa	0 25 8	4 22 38	29 43 21	6♌52 31	12 51.0	23 4.3	2 48.8	24 15.5	16 18.8	24 36.9	9 35.9	2 19.9	19 31.4
29 Su	0 29 4	5 21 34	14♌ 1 44	21 10 29	12 47.1	22 44.8	4 1.5	24 55.8	16 20.2	24 39.8	9 33.5	2 21.9	19 31.9
30 M	0 33 1	6 20 33	28 18 13	5♍24 20	12 41.9	22 17.6	5 14.3	25 36.1	16 21.4	24 42.8	9 31.0	2 23.8	19 32.4

LONGITUDE OCTOBER 1929

Day	Sid.Time	☉	0 hr ☽	Noon ☽	True ☊	☿	♀	♂	♃	♄	♅	♆	♇
1 Tu	0 36 57	7♎19 33	12♍28 14	19♍29 21	12♉36.3	21♎42.9	6♍27.2	26♎16.4	16♊22.4	24♐45.9	9♈28.6	2♍25.7	19♋32.9
2 W	0 40 54	8 18 36	26 27 6	3♎21 1	12R30.9	21R 0.6	7 40.2	26 56.8	16 23.2	24 49.0	9R26.2	2 27.6	19 33.4
3 Th	0 44 50	9 17 41	10♎10 39	16 55 40	12 26.4	20 11.2	8 53.2	27 37.2	16 23.8	24 52.3	9 23.8	2 29.5	19 33.8
4 F	0 48 47	10 16 48	23 35 50	0♏11 0	12 23.4	19 15.2	10 6.3	28 17.7	16 24.1	24 55.6	9 21.3	2 31.3	19 34.3
5 Sa	0 52 44	11 15 58	6♏41 7	13 6 17	12D22.0	18 13.5	11 19.5	28 58.3	16R24.3	24 59.0	9 18.9	2 33.2	19 34.7
6 Su	0 56 40	12 15 9	19 26 39	25 42 26	12 22.1	17 7.3	12 32.7	29 38.9	16 24.3	25 2.5	9 16.5	2 35.0	19 35.1
7 M	1 0 37	13 14 21	1♐54 1	8♐ 1 45	12 23.2	15 58.0	13 46.0	0♏19.6	16 24.1	25 6.1	9 14.1	2 36.8	19 35.4
8 Tu	1 4 33	14 13 36	14 6 8	20 7 38	12 25.0	14 47.3	14 59.3	1 0.3	16 23.7	25 9.8	9 11.7	2 38.5	19 35.7
9 W	1 8 30	15 12 53	26 6 51	2♑ 4 19	12 26.7	13 37.0	16 12.8	1 41.1	16 23.0	25 13.5	9 9.3	2 40.3	19 36.0
10 Th	1 12 26	16 12 11	8♑ 0 39	13 56 29	12R27.8	12 29.2	17 26.2	2 21.9	16 22.2	25 17.3	9 6.9	2 42.0	19 36.3
11 F	1 16 23	17 11 32	19 52 24	25 49 1	12 28.1	11 25.9	18 39.7	3 2.8	16 21.2	25 21.3	9 4.5	2 43.7	19 36.6
12 Sa	1 20 19	18 10 54	1♒46 56	7♒46 43	12 27.3	10 28.7	19 53.3	3 43.7	16 20.0	25 25.3	9 2.1	2 45.4	19 36.8
13 Su	1 24 16	19 10 17	13 48 56	19 54 5	12 25.3	9 39.4	21 7.0	4 24.7	16 18.5	25 29.3	8 59.7	2 47.1	19 37.0
14 M	1 28 13	20 9 43	26 2 36	2♓14 55	12 22.6	8 59.3	22 20.7	5 5.7	16 16.9	25 33.5	8 57.3	2 48.8	19 37.2
15 Tu	1 32 9	21 9 10	8♓31 22	14 52 12	12 19.3	8 29.4	23 34.4	5 46.8	16 15.1	25 37.7	8 55.0	2 50.4	19 37.4
16 W	1 36 6	22 8 39	21 17 38	27 47 46	12 16.1	8 10.3	24 48.2	6 27.9	16 13.0	25 42.0	8 52.6	2 52.0	19 37.5
17 Th	1 40 2	23 8 10	4♈22 37	11♈ 2 7	12 13.2	8D 2.3	26 2.1	7 9.1	16 10.8	25 46.4	8 50.3	2 53.6	19 37.6
18 F	1 43 59	24 7 43	17 46 9	24 34 27	12 11.1	8 5.4	27 16.0	7 50.3	16 8.4	25 50.8	8 48.0	2 55.1	19 37.7
19 Sa	1 47 55	25 7 18	1♉26 45	8♉22 41	12D 9.9	8 19.3	28 29.9	8 31.6	16 5.8	25 55.3	8 45.7	2 56.6	19 37.8
20 Su	1 51 52	26 6 55	15 21 49	22 23 45	12 9.7	8 43.5	29 44.0	9 13.0	16 3.0	25 59.9	8 43.4	2 58.1	19 37.8
21 M	1 55 48	27 6 34	29 27 59	6♊34 2	12 10.2	9 17.4	0♎58.0	9 54.4	15 59.9	26 4.6	8 41.1	2 59.6	19R37.8
22 Tu	1 59 45	28 6 16	13♊41 26	20 49 44	12 11.2	10 0.3	2 12.1	10 35.8	15 56.7	26 9.3	8 38.9	3 1.1	19 37.8
23 W	2 3 42	29 5 59	27 58 28	5♋ 7 15	12 12.3	10 51.2	3 26.3	11 17.4	15 53.4	26 14.1	8 36.7	3 2.5	19 37.8
24 Th	2 7 38	0♏ 5 45	12♋15 41	19 23 25	12 13.2	11 49.4	4 40.5	11 58.9	15 49.8	26 19.0	8 34.4	3 3.9	19 37.7
25 F	2 11 35	1 5 33	26 30 9	3♌35 34	12R13.7	12 54.1	5 54.8	12 40.5	15 46.0	26 23.9	8 32.3	3 5.3	19 37.6
26 Sa	2 15 31	2 5 24	10♌39 26	17 41 30	12 13.6	14 4.3	7 9.1	13 22.2	15 42.0	26 29.0	8 30.1	3 6.6	19 37.5
27 Su	2 19 28	3 5 16	24 41 33	1♍39 21	12 13.1	15 19.5	8 23.5	14 4.0	15 37.9	26 34.0	8 28.0	3 7.9	19 37.4
28 M	2 23 24	4 5 11	8♍34 42	15 27 26	12 12.2	16 38.8	9 37.9	14 45.8	15 33.6	26 39.2	8 25.8	3 9.2	19 37.2
29 Tu	2 27 21	5 5 8	22 17 20	29 4 15	12 11.3	18 1.8	10 52.3	15 27.6	15 29.0	26 44.4	8 23.7	3 10.5	19 37.0
30 W	2 31 17	6 5 7	5♎48 0	12♎28 26	12 10.4	19 27.7	12 6.8	16 9.5	15 24.4	26 49.6	8 21.7	3 11.7	19 36.8
31 Th	2 35 14	7 5 8	19 5 25	25 38 52	12 9.9	20 56.1	13 21.4	16 51.5	15 19.5	26 55.0	8 19.6	3 12.9	19 36.6

Astro Data Dy Hr Mn	Planet Ingress Dy Hr Mn	Last Aspect Dy Hr Mn	☽ Ingress Dy Hr Mn	Last Aspect Dy Hr Mn	☽ Ingress Dy Hr Mn	☽ Phases & Eclipses Dy Hr Mn	Astro Data
☽0S 5 9:06	☉ ♎ 23 12:52	2 8:26 ♄ △	♍ 2 18:27	1 21:10 ♄ □	♎ 2 6:09	3 11:47 ● 10♍29	1 SEPTEMBER 1929
☽0N 19 20:18	♀ ♍ 25 16:13	4 10:26 ♄ □	♎ 4 20:51	4 9:01 ♂ ☌	♏ 4 11:40	10 22:57 ☽ 17♐44	Julian Day # 10836
☿ R 25 18:24		6 15:15 ♄ ✶	♏ 7 2:20	6 0:16 ♇ △	♐ 6 20:18	18 23:16 ○ 25♓32	Delta T 24.0 sec
	♂ ♏ 6 12:27	8 14:44 ♇ △	♐ 9 11:38	8 22:12 ♄ ☌	♑ 9 7:49	26 2:07 ☽ 2♋30	SVP 06♓14'42"
☽0S 2 18:22	♀ ♎ 20 5:12	11 11:41 ♄ ☌	♑ 11 23:45	10 23:28 ♇ ☍	♒ 11 20:25		Obliquity 23°27'01"
♃ R 5 9:56	☉ ♏ 23 21:41	13 17:01 ☉ △	♒ 14 12:17	13 23:03 ♄ ✶	♓ 14 7:40	2 22:19 ● 9♎14	⚷ Chiron 14♉21.5R
☽0N 17 4:46		16 11:52 ♄ ✶	♓ 16 23:07	16 8:12 ♄ □	♈ 16 16:02	10 18:05 ☽ 16♑57	☽ Mean ☊ 15♉23.9
☿ D 17 5:15		18 23:16 ☉ ☍	♈ 19 7:30	18 14:19 ♄ △	♉ 18 21:29	18 12:06 ○ 24♈38	
♇ R 21 2:06		21 4:04 ♀ △	♉ 21 13:45	20 7:17 ♇ ✶	♊ 21 0:54	25 8:21 ☽ 1♌26	1 OCTOBER 1929
♀0S 23 3:18		23 14:02 ♀ □	♊ 23 18:25	23 2:02 ☉ △	♋ 23 3:24		Julian Day # 10866
☽0S 30 2:13		25 12:31 ♄ ☍	♋ 25 21:52	24 12:24 ♇ ☌	♌ 25 5:55		Delta T 24.0 sec
		27 14:22 ♂ □	♌ 28 0:28	27 3:15 ♄ △	♍ 27 9:08		SVP 06♓14'39"
		29 19:13 ♂ ✶	♍ 30 2:52	29 7:55 ♄ □	♎ 29 13:39		Obliquity 23°27'02"
				31 14:26 ♄ ✶	♏ 31 20:02		⚷ Chiron 13♉35.7R
							☽ Mean ☊ 13♉48.6

NOVEMBER 1929 LONGITUDE

Day	Sid.Time	☉	0 hr ☽	Noon ☽	True ☊	☿	♀	♂	♃	♄	♅	♆	♇
1 F	2 39 11	8♏ 5 11	2♏ 8 41	8♏34 50	12♉ 9.5	22♎26.5	14♎35.9	17♏33.5	15♊14.4	27♐ 0.4	8♈17.6	3♍14.1	19♋36.3
2 Sa	2 43 7	9 5 16	14 57 20	21 16 11	12D 9.5	23 58.7	15 50.5	18 15.5	15R 9.2	27 5.8	8R15.6	3 15.3	19R36.1
3 Su	2 47 4	10 5 23	27 31 31	3♐43 26	12 9.6	25 32.1	17 5.2	18 57.7	15 3.9	27 11.3	8 13.7	3 16.4	19 35.8
4 M	2 51 0	11 5 32	9♐52 10	15 57 55	12 9.7	27 6.7	18 19.8	19 39.8	14 58.3	27 16.9	8 11.7	3 17.5	19 35.4
5 Tu	2 54 57	12 5 42	22 0 59	28 1 43	12R 9.8	28 42.1	19 34.6	20 22.1	14 52.6	27 22.5	8 9.8	3 18.5	19 35.1
6 W	2 58 53	13 5 54	4♑ 0 30	9♑57 45	12 9.7	0♏18.1	20 49.3	21 4.4	14 46.8	27 28.2	8 8.0	3 19.5	19 34.7
7 Th	3 2 50	14 6 8	15 53 56	21 49 34	12 9.6	1 54.6	22 4.1	21 46.7	14 40.8	27 34.0	8 6.1	3 20.5	19 34.3
8 F	3 6 46	15 6 23	27 45 9	3♒41 16	12 9.3	3 31.4	23 18.9	22 29.1	14 34.6	27 39.8	8 4.3	3 21.5	19 33.9
9 Sa	3 10 43	16 6 39	9♒38 29	15 37 23	12D 9.2	5 8.4	24 33.7	23 11.5	14 28.3	27 45.6	8 2.6	3 22.4	19 33.4
10 Su	3 14 40	17 6 58	21 38 33	27 42 34	12 9.1	6 45.5	25 48.5	23 54.0	14 21.9	27 51.5	8 0.9	3 23.3	19 33.0
11 M	3 18 36	18 7 17	3♓50 1	10♓ 1 26	12 9.4	8 22.6	27 3.4	24 36.6	14 15.3	27 57.5	7 59.2	3 24.2	19 32.5
12 Tu	3 22 33	19 7 38	16 17 20	22 38 11	12 9.9	9 59.7	28 18.3	25 19.2	14 8.6	28 3.5	7 57.5	3 25.1	19 32.0
13 W	3 26 29	20 8 0	29 4 22	5♈36 13	12 10.7	11 36.7	29 33.2	26 1.8	14 1.8	28 9.5	7 55.9	3 25.9	19 31.4
14 Th	3 30 26	21 8 24	12♈13 56	18 57 41	12 11.5	13 13.6	0♏48.2	26 44.5	13 54.9	28 15.6	7 54.3	3 26.6	19 30.9
15 F	3 34 22	22 8 49	25 47 25	2♉43 2	12 12.2	14 50.3	2 3.1	27 27.3	13 47.8	28 21.8	7 52.8	3 27.4	19 30.3
16 Sa	3 38 19	23 9 16	9♉44 17	16 50 44	12R12.6	16 26.8	3 18.1	28 10.1	13 40.7	28 28.0	7 51.3	3 28.1	19 29.7
17 Su	3 42 15	24 9 44	24 1 51	1♊16 59	12 12.4	18 3.2	4 33.2	28 52.9	13 33.4	28 34.2	7 49.8	3 28.7	19 29.0
18 M	3 46 12	25 10 14	8♊35 22	15 56 10	12 11.5	19 39.4	5 48.2	29 35.9	13 26.0	28 40.5	7 48.4	3 29.4	19 28.4
19 Tu	3 50 9	26 10 45	23 18 28	0♋41 20	12 10.0	21 15.3	7 3.3	0♐18.8	13 18.6	28 46.8	7 47.0	3 30.0	19 27.7
20 W	3 54 5	27 11 18	8♋ 3 54	15 25 16	12 8.1	22 51.1	8 18.4	1 1.9	13 11.0	28 53.1	7 45.7	3 30.6	19 27.0
21 Th	3 58 2	28 11 53	22 44 40	0♌ 1 25	12 6.2	24 26.6	9 33.5	1 44.9	13 3.4	28 59.5	7 44.4	3 31.1	19 26.3
22 F	4 1 58	29 12 30	7♌14 54	14 24 41	12 4.5	26 2.0	10 48.6	2 28.1	12 55.7	29 6.0	7 43.1	3 31.6	19 25.6
23 Sa	4 5 55	0♐13 8	21 30 24	28 31 51	12D 3.5	27 37.2	12 3.8	3 11.2	12 47.9	29 12.5	7 41.9	3 32.1	19 24.9
24 Su	4 9 51	1 13 48	5♍28 53	12♍21 29	12 3.3	29 12.2	13 19.0	3 54.5	12 40.0	29 19.0	7 40.8	3 32.6	19 24.1
25 M	4 13 48	2 14 30	19 9 42	25 53 37	12 4.0	0♐47.0	14 34.2	4 37.8	12 32.1	29 25.5	7 39.6	3 33.0	19 23.3
26 Tu	4 17 44	3 15 13	2♎33 24	9♎ 9 13	12 5.4	2 21.7	15 49.4	5 21.1	12 24.1	29 32.1	7 38.6	3 33.3	19 22.5
27 W	4 21 41	4 15 57	15 41 16	22 9 45	12 7.0	3 56.2	17 4.7	6 4.5	12 16.1	29 38.7	7 37.5	3 33.7	19 21.7
28 Th	4 25 38	5 16 44	28 34 51	4♏56 46	12 8.3	5 30.7	18 19.9	6 48.0	12 8.0	29 45.4	7 36.5	3 34.0	19 20.8
29 F	4 29 34	6 17 31	11♏15 41	17 31 46	12R 8.9	7 5.0	19 35.2	7 31.5	11 59.9	29 52.1	7 35.6	3 34.2	19 19.9
30 Sa	4 33 31	7 18 21	23 45 9	29 56 0	12 8.4	8 39.3	20 50.5	8 15.1	11 51.8	29 58.8	7 34.7	3 34.5	19 19.1

DECEMBER 1929 LONGITUDE

Day	Sid.Time	☉	0 hr ☽	Noon ☽	True ☊	☿	♀	♂	♃	♄	♅	♆	♇
1 Su	4 37 27	8♐19 11	6♐ 4 28	12♐10 41	12♉ 6.4	10♐13.4	22♏ 5.8	8♐58.7	11♊43.6	0♑ 5.5	7♈33.9	3♍34.7	19♋18.2
2 M	4 41 24	9 20 3	18 14 47	24 16 58	12R 3.0	11 47.5	23 21.1	9 42.3	11R35.4	0 12.3	7R33.1	3 34.9	19R17.2
3 Tu	4 45 20	10 20 55	0♑17 22	6♑16 14	11 58.4	13 21.6	24 36.4	10 26.1	11 27.3	0 19.1	7 32.3	3 35.0	19 16.3
4 W	4 49 17	11 21 49	12 13 46	18 10 15	11 53.0	14 55.6	25 51.8	11 9.8	11 19.1	0 25.9	7 31.7	3 35.1	19 15.4
5 Th	4 53 14	12 22 44	24 5 58	0♒ 1 16	11 47.3	16 29.6	27 7.1	11 53.6	11 10.9	0 32.8	7 31.0	3 35.1	19 14.4
6 F	4 57 10	13 23 39	5♒56 33	11 52 12	11 42.0	18 3.7	28 22.5	12 37.5	11 2.7	0 39.6	7 30.4	3R35.2	19 13.4
7 Sa	5 1 7	14 24 36	17 48 42	23 46 33	11 37.7	19 37.7	29 37.8	13 21.4	10 54.5	0 46.5	7 29.9	3 35.2	19 12.4
8 Su	5 5 3	15 25 33	29 46 16	5♓48 25	11 34.7	21 11.7	0♐53.2	14 5.4	10 46.4	0 53.5	7 29.4	3 35.1	19 11.4
9 M	5 9 0	16 26 30	11♓53 34	18 2 20	11D 33.4	22 45.7	2 8.6	14 49.4	10 38.3	1 0.4	7 28.9	3 35.0	19 10.3
10 Tu	5 12 56	17 27 29	24 15 17	0♈33 1	11 33.5	24 19.8	3 24.0	15 33.5	10 30.2	1 7.3	7 28.5	3 34.9	19 9.3
11 W	5 16 53	18 28 28	6♈56 7	13 25 4	11 34.7	25 54.0	4 39.3	16 17.6	10 22.1	1 14.3	7 28.2	3 34.8	19 8.2
12 Th	5 20 49	19 29 27	20 0 21	26 42 19	11 36.3	27 28.1	5 54.7	17 1.7	10 14.2	1 21.3	7 27.9	3 34.6	19 7.2
13 F	5 24 46	20 30 27	3♉31 15	10♉27 15	11R 37.6	29 2.3	7 10.1	17 45.9	10 6.2	1 28.3	7 27.6	3 34.4	19 6.1
14 Sa	5 28 43	21 31 28	17 30 19	24 40 12	11 37.7	0♑36.5	8 25.5	18 30.2	9 58.3	1 35.3	7 27.4	3 34.2	19 5.0
15 Su	5 32 39	22 32 29	1♊56 31	9♊18 39	11 36.0	2 10.8	9 41.0	19 14.5	9 50.5	1 42.3	7 27.3	3 33.9	19 3.9
16 M	5 36 36	23 33 31	16 45 45	24 16 51	11 32.3	3 45.1	10 56.4	19 58.9	9 42.8	1 49.4	7 27.2	3 33.6	19 2.7
17 Tu	5 40 32	24 34 33	1♋50 47	9♋26 17	11 26.8	5 19.4	12 11.8	20 43.3	9 35.1	1 56.4	7D 27.2	3 33.2	19 1.6
18 W	5 44 29	25 35 37	17 2 1	24 36 41	11 20.0	6 53.6	13 27.2	21 27.7	9 27.5	2 3.5	7 27.2	3 32.8	19 0.4
19 Th	5 48 25	26 36 40	2♌ 9 1	9♌37 53	11 12.9	8 27.8	14 42.7	22 12.2	9 20.1	2 10.6	7 27.3	3 32.4	18 59.3
20 F	5 52 22	27 37 45	17 2 17	24 21 27	11 6.4	10 1.8	15 58.1	22 56.8	9 12.7	2 17.6	7 27.4	3 32.0	18 58.1
21 Sa	5 56 18	28 38 50	1♍34 46	8♍41 52	11 1.5	11 35.7	17 13.5	23 41.3	9 5.3	2 24.7	7 27.6	3 31.5	18 56.9
22 Su	6 0 15	29 39 56	15 42 32	22 36 46	10 58.5	13 9.4	18 29.0	24 26.0	8 58.1	2 31.8	7 27.8	3 31.0	18 55.8
23 M	6 4 12	0♑41 3	29 24 39	6♎ 6 29	10D 57.4	14 42.8	19 44.5	25 10.7	8 51.1	2 38.9	7 28.0	3 30.5	18 54.6
24 Tu	6 8 8	1 42 10	12♎42 34	19 13 18	10 57.9	16 15.8	20 59.9	25 55.4	8 44.1	2 46.0	7 28.4	3 29.9	18 53.3
25 W	6 12 5	2 43 18	25 39 9	2♏ 0 34	10 59.1	17 48.2	22 15.4	26 40.2	8 37.2	2 53.1	7 28.7	3 29.3	18 52.1
26 Th	6 16 1	3 44 27	8♏18 0	14 31 56	10R 59.9	19 20.0	23 30.9	27 25.0	8 30.5	3 0.2	7 29.2	3 28.6	18 50.9
27 F	6 19 58	4 45 37	20 42 46	26 50 55	10 59.4	20 51.0	24 46.3	28 9.9	8 23.9	3 7.3	7 29.6	3 28.0	18 49.7
28 Sa	6 23 54	5 46 46	2♐56 44	9♐ 0 33	10 56.7	22 21.0	26 1.8	28 54.9	8 17.4	3 14.4	7 30.2	3 27.3	18 48.4
29 Su	6 27 51	6 47 56	15 2 40	21 3 19	10 51.5	23 49.7	27 17.3	29 39.8	8 11.1	3 21.5	7 30.8	3 26.5	18 47.2
30 M	6 31 47	7 49 7	27 2 44	3♑ 1 7	10 43.5	25 16.9	28 32.8	0♑24.9	8 4.9	3 28.6	7 31.4	3 25.8	18 45.9
31 Tu	6 35 44	8 50 18	8♑58 38	14 55 27	10 33.2	26 42.2	29 48.3	1 9.9	7 58.8	3 35.6	7 32.1	3 25.0	18 44.7

Astro Data	Dy Hr Mn
☽0N	13 14:37
☽0S	26 8:05
♆ R	6 7:27
☽0N	10 23:51
♅ D	17 4:19
☽0S	23 13:04
♄△♆	29 15:27

Planet Ingress		Dy Hr Mn
☿	♏	5 19:29
♀	♏	13 8:35
♂	♐	18 13:29
☉	♐	22 18:48
☿	♐	24 12:06
♄	♑	30 4:22
♀	♐	7 7:03
☿	♑	13 14:42
☉	♑	22 7:53
♂	♑	29 10:45
♀	♑	31 3:44

Last Aspect Dy Hr Mn			☽ Ingress	Dy Hr Mn
2 8:49	♇	△	♐	3 4:47
5 15:24	☿	✶	♑	5 15:57
7 13:57	♀	□	♒	8 4:33
10 12:24	♄	✶	♓	10 16:30
12 22:18	♄	□	♈	13 1:43
15 4:31	♄	△	♉	15 7:19
17 8:27	♂	☍	♊	17 9:53
19 8:58	♄	☍	♋	19 10:53
21 9:39	☉	△	♌	21 11:58
23 13:16	♄	△	♍	23 14:32
25 18:30	♄	□	♎	25 19:23
28 2:14	♄	✶	♏	28 2:40
29 17:45	♀	☌	♐	30 12:08

Last Aspect Dy Hr Mn			☽ Ingress	Dy Hr Mn
1 10:59	♃	☍	♑	2 23:25
5 6:51	♀	✶	♒	5 11:57
7 4:13	☿	✶	♓	8 0:27
10 0:10	☿	□	♈	10 10:57
12 15:06	☿	△	♉	12 17:50
14 2:39	♇	✶	♊	14 20:49
16 11:38	☉	☍	♋	16 21:05
18 3:07	♇	☌	♌	18 20:34
20 18:44	☉	△	♍	20 21:22
22 16:04	♂	□	♎	23 1:03
25 2:02	♂	✶	♏	25 8:12
27 0:18	☿	✶	♐	27 18:12
30 3:22	♀	☌	♑	30 5:56

☽ Phases & Eclipses Dy Hr Mn		
1 12:01	●	8♏35
1 12:04:46	● A	3'54"
9 14:10	☽	16♒42
17 0:14	○	24♉10
17 0:03	● A	0.846
23 16:04	☽	0♍54
1 4:48	●	8♐31
9 9:42	☽	16♓51
16 11:38	○	24♊03
23 2:27	☽	0♎47
30 23:42	●	8♑50

Astro Data
1 NOVEMBER 1929
Julian Day # 10897
Delta T 24.0 sec
SVP 06♓14'35"
Obliquity 23°27'01"
⚷ Chiron 12♉12.0R
☽ Mean ☊ 12♉10.0
1 DECEMBER 1929
Julian Day # 10927
Delta T 24.0 sec
SVP 06♓14'30"
Obliquity 23°27'01"
⚷ Chiron 10♉46.0R
☽ Mean ☊ 10♉34.7

LONGITUDE — JANUARY 1930

Day	Sid.Time	☉	0 hr ☽	Noon ☽	True ☊	☿	♀	♂	♃	♄	♅	♆	♇
1 W	6 39 41	9♑51 28	20♑51 44	26♑47 39	10♉21.3	28♑ 5.4	1♑ 3.7	1♑55.0	7♊52.9	3♑42.7	7♈32.8	3♍24.1	18♋43.4
2 Th	6 43 37	10 52 39	2♒43 23	8♒39 7	10R 8.8	29 26.0	2 19.2	2 40.2	7R47.2	3 49.8	7 33.6	3R 23.3	18R 42.2
3 F	6 47 34	11 53 50	14 35 5	20 31 34	9 56.7	0♒43.4	3 34.7	3 25.4	7 41.6	3 56.9	7 34.5	3 22.4	18 40.9
4 Sa	6 51 30	12 55 0	26 28 51	2♓27 17	9 46.0	1 57.2	4 50.2	4 10.6	7 36.2	4 3.9	7 35.4	3 21.5	18 39.6
5 Su	6 55 27	13 56 11	8♓27 15	14 29 12	9 37.7	3 6.7	6 5.7	4 55.9	7 31.0	4 10.9	7 36.3	3 20.6	18 38.4
6 M	6 59 23	14 57 20	20 33 35	26 40 56	9 32.1	4 11.3	7 21.1	5 41.2	7 25.9	4 18.0	7 37.3	3 19.6	18 37.1
7 Tu	7 3 20	15 58 30	2♈51 47	9♈ 6 43	9 29.1	5 10.2	8 36.6	6 26.6	7 21.0	4 25.0	7 38.3	3 18.6	18 35.8
8 W	7 7 16	16 59 39	15 26 20	21 51 12	9D 28.2	6 2.4	9 52.1	7 12.0	7 16.3	4 32.0	7 39.4	3 17.6	18 34.5
9 Th	7 11 13	18 0 47	28 21 52	4♉58 54	9R 28.4	6 47.3	11 7.5	7 57.4	7 11.8	4 39.0	7 40.6	3 16.5	18 33.2
10 F	7 15 10	19 1 56	11♉42 42	18 33 40	9 28.7	7 23.9	12 23.0	8 42.9	7 7.4	4 45.9	7 41.7	3 15.4	18 32.0
11 Sa	7 19 6	20 3 3	25 32 1	2♊37 48	9 27.7	7 51.2	13 38.4	9 28.4	7 3.3	4 52.9	7 43.0	3 14.3	18 30.7
12 Su	7 23 3	21 4 10	9♊50 54	17 10 58	9 24.4	8 8.5	14 53.9	10 14.0	6 59.3	4 59.8	7 44.3	3 13.2	18 29.4
13 M	7 26 59	22 5 17	24 37 24	2♋ 9 22	9 18.5	8R15.0	16 9.3	10 59.5	6 55.5	5 6.7	7 45.6	3 12.1	18 28.1
14 Tu	7 30 56	23 6 23	9♋45 49	17 25 27	9 9.9	8 10.0	17 24.7	11 45.2	6 51.9	5 13.6	7 47.0	3 10.9	18 26.8
15 W	7 34 52	24 7 28	25 6 51	2♌48 30	8 59.3	7 53.3	18 40.2	12 30.8	6 48.5	5 20.4	7 48.4	3 9.7	18 25.6
16 Th	7 38 49	25 8 33	10♌28 53	18 6 30	8 48.0	7 24.9	19 55.6	13 16.6	6 45.3	5 27.3	7 49.9	3 8.5	18 24.3
17 F	7 42 46	26 9 38	25 40 1	3♍ 8 17	8 37.4	6 45.1	21 11.0	14 2.3	6 42.2	5 34.1	7 51.4	3 7.2	18 23.0
18 Sa	7 46 42	27 10 42	10♍30 20	17 45 30	8 28.6	5 54.8	22 26.4	14 48.1	6 39.4	5 40.9	7 53.0	3 6.0	18 21.8
19 Su	7 50 39	28 11 45	24 53 19	1♎53 37	8 22.4	4 55.1	23 41.8	15 33.9	6 36.8	5 47.6	7 54.6	3 4.7	18 20.5
20 M	7 54 35	29 12 49	8♎46 22	15 31 46	8 18.9	3 47.8	24 57.3	16 19.8	6 34.3	5 54.3	7 56.3	3 3.4	18 19.2
21 Tu	7 58 32	0♒13 52	22 10 8	28 41 56	8D 17.6	2 35.0	26 12.7	17 5.6	6 32.1	6 1.0	7 58.0	3 2.0	18 18.0
22 W	8 2 28	1 14 54	5♏ 7 41	11♏27 58	8R 17.4	1 18.7	27 28.1	17 51.6	6 30.1	6 7.7	7 59.8	3 0.7	18 16.7
23 Th	8 6 25	2 15 57	17 43 22	23 54 30	8 17.2	0 1.6	28 43.5	18 37.5	6 28.2	6 14.3	8 1.6	2 59.3	18 15.5
24 F	8 10 21	3 16 58	0♐ 1 59	6♐ 6 23	8 15.7	28♑45.8	29 58.9	19 23.6	6 26.6	6 20.9	8 3.4	2 57.9	18 14.3
25 Sa	8 14 18	4 18 0	12 8 15	18 8 6	8 11.9	27 33.4	1♒14.3	20 9.6	6 25.2	6 27.5	8 5.3	2 56.5	18 13.0
26 Su	8 18 15	5 19 0	24 6 22	0♑ 3 28	8 5.2	26 26.3	2 29.7	20 55.7	6 24.0	6 34.1	8 7.2	2 55.1	18 11.8
27 M	8 22 11	6 20 0	5♑59 46	11 55 35	7 55.3	25 25.9	3 45.0	21 41.8	6 23.0	6 40.6	8 9.2	2 53.6	18 10.6
28 Tu	8 26 8	7 20 59	17 51 12	23 46 49	7 42.7	24 33.2	5 0.4	22 27.9	6 22.2	6 47.0	8 11.2	2 52.1	18 9.4
29 W	8 30 4	8 21 58	29 42 40	5♒38 53	7 28.1	23 48.9	6 15.8	23 14.1	6 21.6	6 53.4	8 13.3	2 50.7	18 8.2
30 Th	8 34 1	9 22 55	11♒35 39	17 33 5	7 12.8	23 13.3	7 31.2	24 0.3	6 21.2	6 59.8	8 15.4	2 49.2	18 7.0
31 F	8 37 57	10 23 52	23 31 21	29 30 35	6 57.8	22 46.5	8 46.5	24 46.5	6D 21.0	7 6.2	8 17.5	2 47.7	18 5.8

LONGITUDE — FEBRUARY 1930

Day	Sid.Time	☉	0 hr ☽	Noon ☽	True ☊	☿	♀	♂	♃	♄	♅	♆	♇
1 Sa	8 41 54	11♒24 47	5♓30 58	11♓32 41	6♉44.5	22♑28.4	10♒ 1.8	25♑32.8	6♊21.0	7♑12.5	8♈19.7	2♍46.1	18♋ 4.7
2 Su	8 45 50	12 25 41	17 35 58	23 41 6	6R 33.7	22D 18.6	11 17.2	26 19.1	6 21.3	7 18.7	8 21.9	2R 44.6	18R 3.5
3 M	8 49 47	13 26 34	29 48 21	5♈58 6	6 26.0	22 16.8	12 32.5	27 5.4	6 21.7	7 24.9	8 24.2	2 43.0	18 2.4
4 Tu	8 53 44	14 27 25	12♈10 44	18 26 41	6 21.5	22 22.4	13 47.8	27 51.8	6 22.4	7 31.1	8 26.5	2 41.5	18 1.2
5 W	8 57 40	15 28 15	24 46 25	1♉10 24	6D 19.5	22 35.0	15 3.1	28 38.1	6 23.2	7 37.2	8 28.8	2 39.9	18 0.1
6 Th	9 1 37	16 29 4	7♉39 9	14 13 9	6R 19.1	22 54.0	16 18.4	29 24.5	6 24.2	7 43.3	8 31.2	2 38.3	17 59.0
7 F	9 5 33	17 29 51	20 52 51	27 38 40	6 19.1	23 19.0	17 33.7	0♒10.9	6 25.5	7 49.3	8 33.6	2 36.7	17 57.9
8 Sa	9 9 30	18 30 37	4♊30 55	11♊29 50	6 18.3	23 49.5	18 48.9	0 57.4	6 26.9	7 55.3	8 36.0	2 35.1	17 56.8
9 Su	9 13 26	19 31 21	18 35 29	25 47 46	6 15.5	24 25.0	20 4.2	1 43.9	6 28.6	8 1.2	8 38.5	2 33.5	17 55.7
10 M	9 17 23	20 32 3	3♋ 6 22	10♋30 46	6 10.0	25 5.0	21 19.4	2 30.4	6 30.5	8 7.0	8 41.0	2 31.8	17 54.7
11 Tu	9 21 19	21 32 44	18 0 14	25 33 46	6 2.0	25 49.3	22 34.6	3 16.9	6 32.5	8 12.9	8 43.6	2 30.2	17 53.7
12 W	9 25 16	22 33 24	3♌10 14	10♌48 18	5 52.0	26 37.5	23 49.9	4 3.4	6 34.8	8 18.6	8 46.2	2 28.6	17 52.6
13 Th	9 29 13	23 34 2	18 26 33	26 3 33	5 41.0	27 29.1	25 5.0	4 50.0	6 37.2	8 24.3	8 48.8	2 26.9	17 51.6
14 F	9 33 9	24 34 38	3♍37 54	11♍ 8 16	5 30.5	28 24.1	26 20.2	5 36.6	6 39.8	8 30.0	8 51.4	2 25.3	17 50.6
15 Sa	9 37 6	25 35 13	18 33 34	25 52 49	5 21.7	29 22.0	27 35.4	6 23.2	6 42.7	8 35.6	8 54.1	2 23.6	17 49.6
16 Su	9 41 2	26 35 47	3♎ 5 21	10♎10 40	5 15.3	0♒22.7	28 50.5	7 9.8	6 45.7	8 41.1	8 56.8	2 21.9	17 48.7
17 M	9 44 59	27 36 19	17 8 31	23 58 53	5 11.6	1 26.0	0♓ 5.7	7 56.4	6 48.9	8 46.6	8 59.6	2 20.3	17 47.7
18 Tu	9 48 55	28 36 50	0♏41 54	7♏17 51	5D 10.2	2 31.6	1 20.8	8 43.1	6 52.3	8 52.0	9 2.3	2 18.6	17 46.8
19 W	9 52 52	29 37 20	13 47 10	20 10 20	5 10.3	3 39.4	2 35.9	9 29.8	6 55.9	8 57.3	9 5.2	2 16.9	17 45.9
20 Th	9 56 48	0♓37 48	26 27 58	2♐40 39	5R 10.9	4 49.3	3 51.0	10 16.5	6 59.6	9 2.6	9 8.0	2 15.2	17 45.0
21 F	10 0 45	1 38 15	8♐49 2	14 53 46	5 10.7	6 1.1	5 6.1	11 3.3	7 3.6	9 7.8	9 10.8	2 13.6	17 44.1
22 Sa	10 4 42	2 38 41	20 55 28	26 54 46	5 8.8	7 14.8	6 21.2	11 50.0	7 7.7	9 13.0	9 13.7	2 11.9	17 43.2
23 Su	10 8 38	3 39 6	2♑52 15	8♑48 27	5 4.5	8 30.1	7 36.3	12 36.8	7 12.1	9 18.1	9 16.7	2 10.2	17 42.4
24 M	10 12 35	4 39 29	14 43 53	20 38 59	4 57.8	9 47.1	8 51.3	13 23.6	7 16.6	9 23.1	9 19.6	2 8.5	17 41.6
25 Tu	10 16 31	5 39 51	26 34 11	2♒29 50	4 48.7	11 5.6	10 6.4	14 10.4	7 21.2	9 28.1	9 22.6	2 6.9	17 40.7
26 W	10 20 28	6 40 11	8♒26 15	14 23 43	4 37.9	12 25.6	11 21.4	14 57.2	7 26.1	9 33.0	9 25.6	2 5.2	17 40.0
27 Th	10 24 24	7 40 29	20 22 26	26 22 36	4 26.4	13 47.0	12 36.4	15 44.0	7 31.1	9 37.8	9 28.6	2 3.5	17 39.2
28 F	10 28 21	8 40 46	2♓24 22	8♓27 54	4 15.1	15 9.8	13 51.4	16 30.9	7 36.3	9 42.6	9 31.6	2 1.8	17 38.4

Astro Data Dy Hr Mn	Planet Ingress Dy Hr Mn	Last Aspect Dy Hr Mn	☽ Ingress Dy Hr Mn	Last Aspect Dy Hr Mn	☽ Ingress Dy Hr Mn	☽ Phases & Eclipses Dy Hr Mn	Astro Data
♃⚹♅ 4 3:25	☿ ♒ 2 10:25	1 16:30 ☿ ☌	♒ 1 18:29	2 18:20 ♂ ⚹	♈ 3 0:23	8 3:11 ☽ 17♈08	1 JANUARY 1930
☽0N 7 6:49	☉ ♒ 20 18:33	2 10:10 ♃ △	♓ 4 7:04	5 7:43 ♂ □	♉ 5 9:49	14 22:21 ○ 24♋03	Julian Day # 10958
☿ R 13 1:46	☿ ♑ 23 0:30	5 20:11 ♇ △	♈ 6 18:27	7 4:30 ☿ △	♊ 7 16:08	21 16:07 ☽ 0♏55	Delta T 24.0 sec
☽0S 19 19:29	♀ ♒ 24 0:22	8 5:53 ♇ □	♉ 9 2:59	9 2:43 ♀ △	♋ 9 18:55	29 19:07 ● 9♒11	SVP 06♓14'24"
♃⚻♄ 24 16:59		10 13:50 ☉ △	♊ 11 7:35	11 13:05 ☿ ☍	♌ 11 19:00		Obliquity 23°27'01"
♃ D 31 9:17	♂ ♒ 6 18:21	11 21:08 ☿ △	♋ 13 8:35	13 11:24 ♀ ☍	♍ 13 18:14	6 17:26 ☽ 17♉13	⚷ Chiron 9♉46.9R
	☿ ♒ 15 15:08	14 22:21 ☉ ☍	♌ 15 7:37	14 22:49 ♇ ⚹	♎ 15 18:50	13 8:39 ○ 23♌56	☽ Mean ☊ 8♉56.3
☿ D 2 17:43	♀ ♓ 16 22:11	15 19:51 ♅ △	♍ 17 6:56	17 19:57 ☉ △	♏ 17 22:45	20 8:44 ☽ 0♐60	
☽0N 3 11:52	☉ ♓ 19 9:00	19 6:05 ☉ △	♎ 19 8:44	19 7:27 ♇ △	♐ 20 6:49	28 13:33 ● 9♓15	1 FEBRUARY 1930
☽0S 16 4:29		21 8:12 ♀ □	♏ 21 14:25	21 4:42 ♂ ⚹	♑ 22 18:13		Julian Day # 10989
♄□♅ 22 8:03		23 23:53 ♀ ⚹	♐ 23 23:56	24 6:00 ♇ ☍	♒ 25 6:57		Delta T 24.0 sec
		24 15:55 ♅ △	♑ 26 11:53	26 14:02 ♂ ☌	♓ 27 19:13		SVP 06♓14'18"
		28 12:44 ☿ ☌	♒ 29 0:35				Obliquity 23°27'01"
		29 19:07 ☉ ☌	♓ 31 12:59				⚷ Chiron 9♉41.2
							☽ Mean ☊ 7♉17.8

MARCH 1930 LONGITUDE

Day	Sid.Time	☉	0 hr ☽	Noon ☽	True ☊	☿	♀	♂	♃	♄	♅	♆	♇
1 Sa	10 32 17	9♓41 1	14♓33 17	20♓40 40	4♉ 5.0	16♒33.8	15♓ 6.4	17♒17.7	7♊41.7	9♑47.2	9♈34.7	2♍ 0.2	17♋37.7
2 Su	10 36 14	10 41 14	26 50 8	3♈ 1 50	3R57.1	17 59.2	16 21.3	18 4.6	7 47.3	9 51.8	9 37.8	1R58.5	17R37.0
3 M	10 40 11	11 41 25	9♈15 53	15 32 29	3 51.6	19 25.8	17 36.3	18 51.5	7 53.0	9 56.4	9 40.9	1 56.9	17 36.3
4 Tu	10 44 7	12 41 34	21 51 47	28 14 1	3D48.6	20 53.6	18 51.2	19 38.4	7 58.9	10 0.8	9 44.0	1 55.2	17 35.7
5 W	10 48 4	13 41 42	4♉39 25	11♉ 8 16	3 47.8	22 22.7	20 6.1	20 25.3	8 4.9	10 5.2	9 47.2	1 53.6	17 35.0
6 Th	10 52 0	14 41 47	17 40 50	24 17 25	3 48.5	23 52.9	21 21.0	21 12.2	8 11.1	10 9.5	9 50.3	1 51.9	17 34.4
7 F	10 55 57	15 41 50	0♊58 17	7♊43 44	3 49.7	25 24.3	22 35.8	21 59.1	8 17.5	10 13.7	9 53.5	1 50.3	17 33.8
8 Sa	10 59 53	16 41 52	14 33 57	21 29 6	3R50.5	26 56.8	23 50.7	22 46.0	8 24.0	10 17.9	9 56.7	1 48.7	17 33.2
9 Su	11 3 50	17 41 51	28 29 17	5♋34 27	3 49.9	28 30.5	25 5.5	23 32.9	8 30.7	10 22.0	9 59.9	1 47.1	17 32.7
10 M	11 7 46	18 41 47	12♋44 26	19 58 56	3 47.6	0♓ 5.4	26 20.3	24 19.9	8 37.6	10 26.0	10 3.2	1 45.5	17 32.1
11 Tu	11 11 43	19 41 42	27 17 29	4♌39 29	3 43.3	1 41.4	27 35.0	25 6.8	8 44.6	10 29.9	10 6.4	1 43.9	17 31.6
12 W	11 15 40	20 41 34	12♌ 4 8	19 30 32	3 37.6	3 18.6	28 49.8	25 53.7	8 51.7	10 33.7	10 9.7	1 42.3	17 31.1
13 Th	11 19 36	21 41 24	26 57 41	4♍24 30	3 31.0	4 56.9	0♈ 4.5	26 40.7	8 59.0	10 37.5	10 13.0	1 40.8	17 30.7
14 F	11 23 33	22 41 12	11♍49 52	19 12 45	3 24.7	6 36.4	1 19.2	27 27.6	9 6.4	10 41.1	10 16.3	1 39.2	17 30.2
15 Sa	11 27 29	23 40 58	26 32 7	3♎47 5	3 19.3	8 17.1	2 33.8	28 14.5	9 14.0	10 44.7	10 19.6	1 37.7	17 29.8
16 Su	11 31 26	24 40 42	10♎56 53	18 0 55	3 15.5	9 59.0	3 48.5	29 1.5	9 21.7	10 48.2	10 22.9	1 36.2	17 29.4
17 M	11 35 22	25 40 24	24 58 47	1♏50 13	3D13.6	11 42.1	5 3.1	29 48.4	9 29.6	10 51.6	10 26.3	1 34.7	17 29.0
18 Tu	11 39 19	26 40 4	8♏35 7	15 13 33	3 13.5	13 26.4	6 17.7	0♓35.4	9 37.6	10 55.0	10 29.6	1 33.2	17 28.7
19 W	11 43 15	27 39 43	21 45 42	28 11 54	3 14.5	15 12.0	7 32.3	1 22.3	9 45.7	10 58.2	10 33.0	1 31.7	17 28.3
20 Th	11 47 12	28 39 20	4♐32 32	10♐48 5	3 16.2	16 58.8	8 46.9	2 9.3	9 54.0	11 1.4	10 36.3	1 30.2	17 28.0
21 F	11 51 8	29 38 55	16 59 4	23 6 5	3 17.7	18 46.8	10 1.4	2 56.2	10 2.4	11 4.4	10 39.7	1 28.8	17 27.8
22 Sa	11 55 5	0♈38 28	29 9 42	5♑10 33	3R18.4	20 36.1	11 15.9	3 43.2	10 10.9	11 7.4	10 43.1	1 27.4	17 27.5
23 Su	11 59 2	1 38 0	11♑ 9 14	17 6 22	3 17.9	22 26.7	12 30.4	4 30.2	10 19.6	11 10.3	10 46.5	1 26.0	17 27.3
24 M	12 2 58	2 37 30	23 2 30	28 58 14	3 16.1	24 18.6	13 44.9	5 17.1	10 28.4	11 13.1	10 49.9	1 24.6	17 27.1
25 Tu	12 6 55	3 36 58	4♒54 4	10♒50 30	3 12.8	26 11.8	14 59.4	6 4.1	10 37.3	11 15.8	10 53.3	1 23.2	17 26.9
26 W	12 10 51	4 36 24	16 48 0	22 46 58	3 8.6	28 6.2	16 13.8	6 51.0	10 46.3	11 18.4	10 56.7	1 21.8	17 26.7
27 Th	12 14 48	5 35 48	28 47 46	4♓50 43	3 3.8	0♈ 1.9	17 28.2	7 37.9	10 55.5	11 21.0	11 0.1	1 20.5	17 26.6
28 F	12 18 44	6 35 10	10♓56 6	17 4 8	2 59.0	1 58.9	18 42.6	8 24.9	11 4.8	11 23.4	11 3.5	1 19.2	17 26.5
29 Sa	12 22 41	7 34 31	23 14 59	29 28 48	2 54.8	3 57.0	19 56.9	9 11.8	11 14.2	11 25.7	11 7.0	1 17.9	17 26.4
30 Su	12 26 37	8 33 49	5♈45 42	12♈ 5 44	2 51.6	5 56.3	21 11.3	9 58.7	11 23.7	11 28.0	11 10.4	1 16.6	17 26.3
31 M	12 30 34	9 33 6	18 28 56	24 55 20	2 49.6	7 56.8	22 25.6	10 45.6	11 33.3	11 30.1	11 13.8	1 15.4	17D26.3

APRIL 1930 LONGITUDE

Day	Sid.Time	☉	0 hr ☽	Noon ☽	True ☊	☿	♀	♂	♃	♄	♅	♆	♇
1 Tu	12 34 31	10♈32 20	1♉24 57	7♉57 45	2♉48.9	9♈58.2	23♈39.9	11♓32.5	11♊43.1	11♑32.2	11♈17.3	1♍14.1	17♋26.3
2 W	12 38 27	11 31 32	14 33 44	21 12 54	2D49.3	12 0.6	24 54.1	12 19.4	11 52.9	11 34.1	11 20.7	1R12.9	17 26.3
3 Th	12 42 24	12 30 42	27 55 13	4♊40 39	2 50.4	14 3.8	26 8.4	13 6.2	12 2.9	11 36.0	11 24.1	1 11.7	17 26.3
4 F	12 46 20	13 29 50	11♊29 13	18 20 51	2 51.8	16 7.6	27 22.6	13 53.1	12 13.0	11 37.8	11 27.5	1 10.6	17 26.4
5 Sa	12 50 17	14 28 56	25 15 31	2♋13 9	2 53.1	18 12.0	28 36.7	14 39.9	12 23.2	11 39.5	11 31.0	1 9.5	17 26.5
6 Su	12 54 13	15 27 59	9♋13 38	16 16 50	2R53.8	20 16.6	29 50.9	15 26.7	12 33.4	11 41.0	11 34.4	1 8.4	17 26.6
7 M	12 58 10	16 27 0	23 22 33	0♌30 31	2 53.8	22 21.3	1♉ 5.0	16 13.5	12 43.8	11 42.5	11 37.8	1 7.3	17 26.8
8 Tu	13 2 6	17 25 59	7♌40 25	14 51 51	2 53.0	24 25.8	2 19.1	17 0.3	12 54.3	11 43.9	11 41.2	1 6.2	17 26.9
9 W	13 6 3	18 24 55	22 4 22	29 17 26	2 51.6	26 29.8	3 33.1	17 47.1	13 4.9	11 45.2	11 44.7	1 5.2	17 27.1
10 Th	13 10 0	19 23 49	6♍30 28	13♍42 52	2 50.0	28 33.0	4 47.1	18 33.8	13 15.6	11 46.4	11 48.1	1 4.2	17 27.3
11 F	13 13 56	20 22 41	20 53 59	28 3 9	2 48.3	0♉35.0	6 1.1	19 20.6	13 26.3	11 47.5	11 51.5	1 3.2	17 27.5
12 Sa	13 17 53	21 21 30	5♎ 9 45	12♎13 10	2 47.0	2 35.6	7 15.1	20 7.3	13 37.2	11 48.4	11 54.9	1 2.2	17 27.8
13 Su	13 21 49	22 20 18	19 12 54	26 8 27	2 46.2	4 34.3	8 29.0	20 54.0	13 48.1	11 49.3	11 58.2	1 1.3	17 28.1
14 M	13 25 46	23 19 3	2♏59 26	9♏45 34	2D46.0	6 30.9	9 42.9	21 40.6	13 59.2	11 50.1	12 1.6	1 0.4	17 28.4
15 Tu	13 29 42	24 17 46	16 26 40	23 2 37	2 46.2	8 24.9	10 56.8	22 27.3	14 10.3	11 50.8	12 5.0	0 59.6	17 28.7
16 W	13 33 39	25 16 28	29 33 28	5♐59 17	2 46.7	10 16.1	12 10.6	23 13.9	14 21.5	11 51.4	12 8.4	0 58.7	17 29.1
17 Th	13 37 35	26 15 8	12♐20 18	18 36 46	2 47.4	12 4.2	13 24.4	24 0.5	14 32.8	11 51.9	12 11.7	0 57.9	17 29.5
18 F	13 41 32	27 13 47	24 49 1	0♑57 29	2 48.1	13 48.8	14 38.2	24 47.1	14 44.2	11 52.3	12 15.1	0 57.1	17 29.9
19 Sa	13 45 29	28 12 23	7♑ 2 37	13 4 56	2 48.5	15 29.7	15 52.0	25 33.7	14 55.6	11 52.7	12 18.4	0 56.4	17 30.3
20 Su	13 49 25	29 10 58	19 4 56	25 3 11	2R48.8	17 6.7	17 5.7	26 20.3	15 7.2	11 52.9	12 21.7	0 55.6	17 30.7
21 M	13 53 22	0♉ 9 31	1♒ 0 17	6♒56 48	2 48.9	18 39.5	18 19.4	27 6.8	15 18.8	11R53.0	12 25.0	0 54.9	17 31.2
22 Tu	13 57 18	1 8 3	12 53 18	18 50 22	2 48.8	20 8.1	19 33.1	27 53.3	15 30.5	11 53.0	12 28.3	0 54.3	17 31.7
23 W	14 1 15	2 6 33	24 48 33	0♓48 24	2D48.8	21 32.1	20 46.7	28 39.8	15 42.2	11 52.9	12 31.6	0 53.6	17 32.2
24 Th	14 5 11	3 5 1	6♓50 26	12 55 5	2 48.7	22 51.6	22 0.3	29 26.2	15 54.1	11 52.7	12 34.9	0 53.0	17 32.8
25 F	14 9 8	4 3 27	19 2 49	25 14 1	2 48.8	24 6.4	23 13.9	0♈12.7	16 6.0	11 52.4	12 38.2	0 52.4	17 33.3
26 Sa	14 13 4	5 1 52	1♈28 58	7♈47 58	2 49.0	25 16.3	24 27.5	0 59.1	16 18.0	11 52.0	12 41.4	0 51.9	17 33.9
27 Su	14 17 1	6 0 15	14 11 12	20 38 48	2 49.2	26 21.3	25 41.0	1 45.4	16 30.0	11 51.6	12 44.6	0 51.4	17 34.5
28 M	14 20 58	6 58 37	27 10 50	3♉47 15	2R49.4	27 21.3	26 54.5	2 31.8	16 42.1	11 51.0	12 47.8	0 50.9	17 35.2
29 Tu	14 24 54	7 56 57	10♉27 59	17 12 51	2 49.4	28 16.2	28 8.0	3 18.1	16 54.3	11 50.3	12 51.0	0 50.4	17 35.8
30 W	14 28 51	8 55 15	24 1 39	0♊54 5	2 49.1	29 6.0	29 21.4	4 4.4	17 6.6	11 49.5	12 54.2	0 50.0	17 36.5

Astro Data	Dy Hr Mn
☽0N	2 16:57
☽0S	15 14:58
♀0N	15 7:05
♃✶♅	27 18:58
☿0N	28 18:58
☽0N	29 23:36
♃⚻♄	30 13:47
♇ D	31 23:39
♄□♅	9 5:47
☽0S	12 0:42
♄ R	21 14:31
☽0N	26 7:49
♂0N	28 4:12

Planet Ingress	Dy Hr Mn
☿ ♓	9 22:39
♀ ♈	12 22:34
♂ ♓	17 5:55
☉ ♈	21 8:30
☿ ♈	26 23:36
♀ ♉	6 2:57
☿ ♉	10 17:05
☉ ♉	20 20:06
♂ ♈	24 17:27
♀ ♊	30 12:37

Last Aspect Dy Hr Mn		☽ Ingress Dy Hr Mn
1 6:02	♇ △	♈ 2 6:08
3 21:56	☿ ✶	♉ 4 15:19
6 12:43	☿ □	♊ 6 22:16
9 0:02	☿ △	♋ 9 2:34
11 0:31	♀ △	♌ 11 4:25
12 23:31	♂ ☍	♍ 13 4:54
14 18:58	☉ ☍	♎ 15 5:43
16 11:06	♇ □	♏ 17 8:46
19 11:55	☉ △	♐ 19 15:23
21 4:07	☿ □	♑ 22 1:40
24 3:03	☿ ✶	♒ 24 14:05
25 22:43	♀ ✶	♓ 27 2:24
28 12:43	♇ △	♈ 29 13:00
31 8:09	♀ ☌	♉ 31 21:24

Last Aspect Dy Hr Mn		☽ Ingress Dy Hr Mn
2 5:12	♇ ✶	♊ 3 3:42
5 6:21	♀ ✶	♋ 5 8:11
6 21:59	☿ □	♌ 7 11:09
9 8:35	☿ △	♍ 9 13:11
10 21:15	♂ ☍	♎ 11 15:17
13 5:48	☉ ☍	♏ 13 18:45
15 11:37	♂ △	♐ 16 0:49
18 5:06	☉ △	♑ 18 10:07
20 15:36	♂ ✶	♒ 20 21:58
22 16:34	☿ □	♓ 23 10:23
25 10:52	☿ ✶	♈ 25 21:10
27 6:19	♇ □	♉ 28 5:08
30 10:13	♀ ☌	♊ 30 10:26

☽ Phases & Eclipses Dy Hr Mn	
8 4:00	☽ 16♊52
14 18:58	○ 23♍28
22 3:12	☽ 0♑46
30 5:46	● 8♈48
6 11:25	☽ 15♋56
13 5:48	○ 22♎35
13 5:58	P 0.106
20 22:08	☽ 0♒05
28 19:08	● 7♉45
28 19:03:09	AT 0'02"

Astro Data

1 MARCH 1930
Julian Day # 11017
Delta T 24.0 sec
SVP 06♓14'15"
Obliquity 23°27'02"
⚷ Chiron 10♉25.3
☽ Mean ☊ 5♉48.8

1 APRIL 1930
Julian Day # 11048
Delta T 24.0 sec
SVP 06♓14'12"
Obliquity 23°27'02"
⚷ Chiron 11♉57.3
☽ Mean ☊ 4♉10.3

LONGITUDE — MAY 1930

Day	Sid.Time	☉	0 hr ☽	Noon ☽	True ☊	☿	♀	♂	♃	♄	♅	♆	♇
1 Th	14 32 47	9♉53 31	7♊49 49	14♊48 29	2♉48.5	29♉50.5	0♊34.8	4♈50.6	17♊18.9	11♑48.6	12♈57.3	0♍49.6	17♋37.2
2 F	14 36 44	10 51 45	21 49 39	28 52 56	2R 47.6	0♊29.8	1 48.2	5 36.8	17 31.3	11R 47.7	13 0.5	0R 49.3	17 37.9
3 Sa	14 40 40	11 49 58	5♋57 54	13♋ 4 6	2 46.6	1 3.8	3 1.5	6 23.0	17 43.7	11 46.6	13 3.6	0 49.0	17 38.7
4 Su	14 44 37	12 48 8	20 11 9	27 18 38	2 45.7	1 32.4	4 14.9	7 9.1	17 56.2	11 45.5	13 6.7	0 48.7	17 39.4
5 M	14 48 33	13 46 17	4♌26 11	11♌33 28	2D 45.1	1 55.6	5 28.1	7 55.2	18 8.8	11 44.2	13 9.8	0 48.4	17 40.2
6 Tu	14 52 30	14 44 23	18 40 8	25 45 54	2 45.0	2 13.6	6 41.4	8 41.3	18 21.4	11 42.9	13 12.8	0 48.2	17 41.0
7 W	14 56 27	15 42 28	2♍50 30	9♍53 39	2 45.4	2 26.1	7 54.6	9 27.3	18 34.0	11 41.4	13 15.8	0 48.0	17 41.9
8 Th	15 0 23	16 40 30	16 55 7	23 54 38	2 46.3	2R 33.5	9 7.7	10 13.3	18 46.7	11 39.9	13 18.8	0 47.8	17 42.7
9 F	15 4 20	17 38 30	0♎52 0	7♎46 57	2 47.4	2 35.7	10 20.9	10 59.2	18 59.5	11 38.3	13 21.8	0 47.7	17 43.6
10 Sa	15 8 16	18 36 29	14 39 18	21 28 49	2 48.5	2 32.8	11 34.0	11 45.1	19 12.3	11 36.6	13 24.8	0 47.6	17 44.5
11 Su	15 12 13	19 34 26	28 15 16	4♏58 30	2R 49.1	2 25.2	12 47.0	12 31.0	19 25.1	11 34.8	13 27.7	0 47.5	17 45.4
12 M	15 16 9	20 32 21	11♏38 19	18 14 35	2 48.9	2 12.9	14 0.0	13 16.8	19 38.0	11 32.9	13 30.6	0D 47.5	17 46.3
13 Tu	15 20 6	21 30 15	24 47 10	1♐16 1	2 47.8	1 56.3	15 13.0	14 2.6	19 51.0	11 30.9	13 33.5	0 47.5	17 47.3
14 W	15 24 2	22 28 7	7♐41 4	14 2 22	2 45.8	1 35.8	16 26.0	14 48.3	20 4.0	11 28.9	13 36.3	0 47.5	17 48.2
15 Th	15 27 59	23 25 58	20 19 57	26 33 58	2 43.0	1 11.7	17 38.9	15 34.1	20 17.0	11 26.7	13 39.2	0 47.6	17 49.2
16 F	15 31 56	24 23 48	2♑44 37	8♑52 6	2 39.7	0 44.4	18 51.8	16 19.7	20 30.1	11 24.5	13 42.0	0 47.7	17 50.2
17 Sa	15 35 52	25 21 36	14 56 44	20 58 52	2 36.3	0 14.5	20 4.6	17 5.3	20 43.2	11 22.2	13 44.7	0 47.8	17 51.2
18 Su	15 39 49	26 19 23	26 58 54	2♒57 16	2 33.2	29♉42.6	21 17.4	17 50.9	20 56.3	11 19.8	13 47.5	0 48.0	17 52.3
19 M	15 43 45	27 17 9	8♒54 28	14 51 1	2 30.8	29 9.1	22 30.2	18 36.5	21 9.5	11 17.3	13 50.2	0 48.2	17 53.4
20 Tu	15 47 42	28 14 54	20 47 28	26 44 24	2D 29.5	28 34.7	23 42.9	19 22.0	21 22.8	11 14.8	13 52.9	0 48.4	17 54.4
21 W	15 51 38	29 12 38	2♓42 22	8♓42 1	2 29.3	28 0.0	24 55.6	20 7.4	21 36.0	11 12.1	13 55.5	0 48.7	17 55.5
22 Th	15 55 35	0♊10 20	14 43 54	20 48 38	2 30.1	27 25.6	26 8.3	20 52.8	21 49.3	11 9.4	13 58.1	0 49.0	17 56.6
23 F	15 59 31	1 8 2	26 56 47	3♈ 8 52	2 31.6	26 52.1	27 20.9	21 38.2	22 2.7	11 6.6	14 0.7	0 49.3	17 57.8
24 Sa	16 3 28	2 5 42	9♈25 24	15 46 49	2 33.2	26 20.0	28 33.5	22 23.5	22 16.0	11 3.7	14 3.3	0 49.6	17 58.9
25 Su	16 7 25	3 3 21	22 13 28	28 45 39	2R 34.5	25 50.0	29 46.1	23 8.8	22 29.4	11 0.8	14 5.8	0 50.0	18 0.1
26 M	16 11 21	4 1 0	5♉23 32	12♉ 7 12	2 34.8	25 22.4	0♋58.6	23 54.0	22 42.9	10 57.8	14 8.3	0 50.5	18 1.3
27 Tu	16 15 18	4 58 37	18 56 35	25 51 31	2 33.8	24 57.6	2 11.1	24 39.2	22 56.3	10 54.7	14 10.8	0 50.9	18 2.5
28 W	16 19 14	5 56 13	2♊51 40	9♊56 34	2 31.3	24 36.2	3 23.6	25 24.3	23 9.8	10 51.5	14 13.2	0 51.4	18 3.7
29 Th	16 23 11	6 53 49	17 5 40	24 18 15	2 27.3	24 18.4	4 36.0	26 9.4	23 23.3	10 48.3	14 15.6	0 51.9	18 4.9
30 F	16 27 7	7 51 23	1♋33 35	8♋50 49	2 22.3	24 4.5	5 48.4	26 54.4	23 36.8	10 45.0	14 17.9	0 52.5	18 6.1
31 Sa	16 31 4	8 48 56	16 9 7	23 27 37	2 17.0	23 54.7	7 0.7	27 39.4	23 50.4	10 41.7	14 20.3	0 53.1	18 7.4

LONGITUDE — JUNE 1930

Day	Sid.Time	☉	0 hr ☽	Noon ☽	True ☊	☿	♀	♂	♃	♄	♅	♆	♇
1 Su	16 35 1	9♊46 28	0♌45 33	8♌ 2 9	2♉12.1	23♉49.1	8♋13.0	28♈24.3	24♊ 4.0	10♑38.2	14♈22.6	0♍53.7	18♋ 8.7
2 M	16 38 57	10 43 58	15 16 47	22 28 54	2R 8.3	23D 47.9	9 25.2	29 9.1	24 17.6	10R 34.7	14 24.8	0 54.3	18 10.0
3 Tu	16 42 54	11 41 27	29 38 4	6♍43 57	2D 6.1	23 51.1	10 37.4	29 53.9	24 31.2	10 31.2	14 27.0	0 55.0	18 11.3
4 W	16 46 50	12 38 54	13♍46 21	20 45 8	2 5.5	23 58.8	11 49.6	0♉38.7	24 44.8	10 27.6	14 29.2	0 55.7	18 12.6
5 Th	16 50 47	13 36 21	27 40 15	4♎31 42	2 6.2	24 11.0	13 1.7	1 23.3	24 58.5	10 23.9	14 31.3	0 56.5	18 13.9
6 F	16 54 43	14 33 46	11♎19 34	18 3 55	2 7.5	24 27.6	14 13.8	2 8.0	25 12.1	10 20.2	14 33.4	0 57.2	18 15.2
7 Sa	16 58 40	15 31 10	24 44 53	1♏22 33	2R 8.6	24 48.7	15 25.8	2 52.5	25 25.8	10 16.4	14 35.5	0 58.1	18 16.6
8 Su	17 2 36	16 28 33	7♏57 2	14 28 27	2 8.6	25 14.2	16 37.8	3 37.0	25 39.5	10 12.6	14 37.5	0 58.9	18 17.9
9 M	17 6 33	17 25 55	20 56 52	27 22 22	2 7.0	25 44.0	17 49.7	4 21.5	25 53.2	10 8.8	14 39.5	0 59.8	18 19.3
10 Tu	17 10 30	18 23 16	3♐45 0	10♐ 4 49	2 3.2	26 18.0	19 1.6	5 5.9	26 6.9	10 4.8	14 41.4	1 0.6	18 20.7
11 W	17 14 26	19 20 36	16 21 53	22 36 13	1 57.4	26 56.2	20 13.4	5 50.2	26 20.6	10 0.9	14 43.3	1 1.6	18 22.1
12 Th	17 18 23	20 17 56	28 47 55	4♑57 3	1 49.8	27 38.5	21 25.2	6 34.5	26 34.4	9 56.9	14 45.2	1 2.5	18 23.5
13 F	17 22 19	21 15 15	11♑ 3 44	17 8 6	1 41.0	28 24.7	22 36.9	7 18.7	26 48.1	9 52.8	14 47.0	1 3.5	18 24.9
14 Sa	17 26 16	22 12 33	23 10 20	29 10 40	1 31.8	29 14.9	23 48.6	8 2.9	27 1.9	9 48.8	14 48.8	1 4.5	18 26.4
15 Su	17 30 12	23 9 51	5♒ 9 21	11♒ 6 42	1 23.1	0♊ 8.9	25 0.2	8 47.0	27 15.6	9 44.6	14 50.5	1 5.6	18 27.8
16 M	17 34 9	24 7 8	17 3 7	22 58 59	1 15.8	1 6.7	26 11.8	9 31.1	27 29.4	9 40.5	14 52.2	1 6.6	18 29.2
17 Tu	17 38 5	25 4 25	28 54 47	4♓51 0	1 10.3	2 8.2	27 23.3	10 15.1	27 43.1	9 36.3	14 53.8	1 7.7	18 30.7
18 W	17 42 2	26 1 41	10♓48 12	16 46 56	1 6.9	3 13.3	28 34.8	10 59.0	27 56.9	9 32.1	14 55.4	1 8.9	18 32.2
19 Th	17 45 59	26 58 57	22 47 50	28 51 31	1D 5.6	4 21.9	29 46.2	11 42.9	28 10.7	9 27.8	14 57.0	1 10.0	18 33.6
20 F	17 49 55	27 56 13	4♈58 36	11♈ 9 44	1 5.7	5 34.1	0♌57.5	12 26.7	28 24.4	9 23.5	14 58.5	1 11.2	18 35.1
21 Sa	17 53 52	28 53 29	17 25 31	23 46 32	1 6.5	6 49.8	2 8.9	13 10.4	28 38.2	9 19.2	14 60.0	1 12.4	18 36.6
22 Su	17 57 48	29 50 44	0♉13 19	6♉46 18	1R 7.0	8 8.9	3 20.1	13 54.1	28 52.0	9 14.9	15 1.4	1 13.7	18 38.1
23 M	18 1 45	0♋48 0	13 25 53	20 12 17	1 6.3	9 31.4	4 31.3	14 37.7	29 5.7	9 10.6	15 2.8	1 14.9	18 39.6
24 Tu	18 5 41	1 45 15	27 5 35	4♊ 5 44	1 3.7	10 57.3	5 42.5	15 21.3	29 19.5	9 6.2	15 4.1	1 16.2	18 41.1
25 W	18 9 38	2 42 31	11♊12 29	18 25 21	0 58.7	12 26.5	6 53.6	16 4.8	29 33.2	9 1.8	15 5.4	1 17.5	18 42.7
26 Th	18 13 34	3 39 46	25 43 43	3♋ 6 44	0 51.5	13 59.0	8 4.7	16 48.2	29 47.0	8 57.4	15 6.7	1 18.9	18 44.2
27 F	18 17 31	4 37 1	10♋33 25	18 2 38	0 42.6	15 34.7	9 15.6	17 31.5	0♋ 0.7	8 53.0	15 7.9	1 20.3	18 45.7
28 Sa	18 21 28	5 34 16	25 33 13	3♌ 3 55	0 33.1	17 13.7	10 26.6	18 14.8	0 14.5	8 48.6	15 9.1	1 21.7	18 47.3
29 Su	18 25 24	6 31 30	10♌33 33	18 1 1	0 24.2	18 55.8	11 37.5	18 58.0	0 28.2	8 44.2	15 10.2	1 23.1	18 48.8
30 M	18 29 21	7 28 44	25 25 20	2♍45 40	0 16.8	20 40.9	12 48.3	19 41.2	0 41.9	8 39.7	15 11.2	1 24.5	18 50.4

Astro Data Dy Hr Mn	Planet Ingress Dy Hr Mn	Last Aspect Dy Hr Mn	☽ Ingress Dy Hr Mn	Last Aspect Dy Hr Mn	☽ Ingress Dy Hr Mn	☽ Phases & Eclipses Dy Hr Mn	Astro Data
♃⚺♇ 2 13:40	☿ ♊ 1 5:31	1 16:32 ♃ ☌	♋ 2 13:54	3 0:28 ♂ △	♍ 3 0:37	5 16:53 ☽ 14♌27	1 MAY 1930
☿ R 8 22:19	☿ ♉ 17 11:06	3 19:44 ♇ ☌	♌ 4 16:32	4 19:14 ♃ □	♎ 5 4:04	12 17:29 ○ 21♏15	Julian Day # 11078
☽0S 9 8:10	☉ ♊ 21 19:42	5 23:28 ♃ ⚹	♍ 6 19:11	7 1:15 ♃ △	♏ 7 9:30	20 16:21 ☽ 28♒54	Delta T 24.0 sec
♆ D 12 11:55	♀ ♋ 25 4:36	8 3:14 ♃ □	♎ 8 22:30	9 9:20 ☿ ☍	♐ 9 16:56	28 5:36 ● 6♊10	SVP 06♓14'08"
☽0N 23 16:31		10 8:07 ♃ △	♏ 11 3:06	11 19:36 ♃ ☍	♑ 12 2:20		Obliquity 23°27'02"
	♂ ♉ 3 3:15	12 17:29 ☉ ☍	♐ 13 9:39	14 13:07 ☿ △	♒ 14 13:39	3 21:56 ☽ 12♍34	⚷ Chiron 13♉51.2
☿ D 1 18:38	☿ ♊ 14 20:09	14 23:54 ♃ ☍	♑ 15 18:39	16 21:32 ♃ △	♓ 17 2:12	11 6:12 ○ 19♐35	☽ Mean ☊ 2♉35.0
☽0S 5 13:30	♀ ♌ 19 4:39	18 5:14 ☿ △	♒ 18 6:03	19 10:52 ♃ □	♈ 19 14:15	19 9:00 ☽ 27♓20	
☽0N 20 0:23	☉ ♋ 22 3:53	20 16:21 ☉ □	♓ 20 18:34	21 23:15 ☉ ⚹	♉ 21 23:35	26 13:46 ● 4♋13	1 JUNE 1930
	♃ ♋ 26 22:42	23 0:52 ♀ □	♈ 23 5:56	23 9:18 ♇ ⚹	♊ 24 5:00		Julian Day # 11109
		25 1:48 ♂ ☌	♉ 25 14:15	26 6:42 ♃ ☌	♋ 26 6:57		Delta T 24.0 sec
		27 10:11 ☿ ☌	♊ 27 19:07	27 13:10 ♇ ☌	♌ 28 7:06		SVP 06♓14'02"
		29 15:54 ♂ ⚹	♋ 29 21:26	29 15:16 ☿ ⚹	♍ 30 7:28		Obliquity 23°27'01"
		31 19:55 ♂ □	♌ 31 22:45				⚷ Chiron 15♉52.4
							☽ Mean ☊ 0♉56.5

JULY 1930 — LONGITUDE

Day	Sid.Time	☉	0 hr ☽	Noon ☽	True ☊	☿	♀	♂	♃	♄	♅	♆	♇
1 Tu	18 33 17	8♋25 57	10♍ 1 24	17♍12 3	0♉11.6	22♊29.1	13♌59.0	20♉24.2	0♋55.6	8♑35.3	15♈12.3	1♍26.0	18♋51.9
2 W	18 37 14	9 23 10	24 17 20	1♎17 7	0R 8.9	24 20.1	15 9.7	21 7.2	1 9.3	8R30.9	15 13.2	1 27.5	18 53.5
3 Th	18 41 10	10 20 23	8♎11 26	15 0 24	0D 8.0	26 13.9	16 20.3	21 50.1	1 23.0	8 26.4	15 14.2	1 29.0	18 55.0
4 F	18 45 7	11 17 35	21 44 15	28 23 15	0R 8.2	28 10.3	17 30.8	22 33.0	1 36.6	8 22.0	15 15.0	1 30.6	18 56.6
5 Sa	18 49 3	12 14 47	4♏57 44	11♏28 2	0 8.3	0♋ 9.1	18 41.3	23 15.7	1 50.2	8 17.6	15 15.9	1 32.1	18 58.2
6 Su	18 53 0	13 11 59	17 54 29	24 17 27	0 7.1	2 10.2	19 51.6	23 58.4	2 3.9	8 13.2	15 16.6	1 33.7	18 59.7
7 M	18 56 57	14 9 10	0♐37 12	6♐54 4	0 3.7	4 13.3	21 2.0	24 41.1	2 17.4	8 8.8	15 17.4	1 35.4	19 1.3
8 Tu	19 0 53	15 6 22	13 8 16	19 20 3	29♈57.6	6 18.1	22 12.2	25 23.6	2 31.0	8 4.4	15 18.1	1 37.0	19 2.9
9 W	19 4 50	16 3 33	25 29 36	1♑37 4	29 48.8	8 24.4	23 22.3	26 6.1	2 44.6	8 0.0	15 18.7	1 38.7	19 4.5
10 Th	19 8 46	17 0 45	7♑42 37	13 46 23	29 37.6	10 31.9	24 32.4	26 48.5	2 58.1	7 55.7	15 19.3	1 40.3	19 6.0
11 F	19 12 43	17 57 57	19 48 29	25 49 4	29 24.8	12 40.3	25 42.4	27 30.8	3 11.6	7 51.3	15 19.8	1 42.0	19 7.6
12 Sa	19 16 39	18 55 9	1♒48 16	7♒46 14	29 11.4	14 49.3	26 52.3	28 13.1	3 25.1	7 47.0	15 20.3	1 43.8	19 9.2
13 Su	19 20 36	19 52 21	13 43 10	19 39 18	28 58.6	16 58.6	28 2.2	28 55.3	3 38.5	7 42.7	15 20.8	1 45.5	19 10.8
14 M	19 24 33	20 49 33	25 34 53	1♓30 14	28 47.4	19 7.9	29 11.9	29 37.4	3 52.0	7 38.5	15 21.2	1 47.3	19 12.3
15 Tu	19 28 29	21 46 46	7♓25 42	13 21 40	28 38.5	21 16.9	0♍21.6	0♊19.4	4 5.4	7 34.2	15 21.5	1 49.0	19 13.9
16 W	19 32 26	22 44 0	19 18 36	25 17 0	28 32.3	23 25.4	1 31.1	1 1.4	4 18.7	7 30.0	15 21.8	1 50.8	19 15.5
17 Th	19 36 22	23 41 14	1♈17 23	7♈20 19	28 28.7	25 33.2	2 40.6	1 43.3	4 32.1	7 25.8	15 22.1	1 52.7	19 17.1
18 F	19 40 19	24 38 28	13 26 26	19 36 20	28 27.2	27 40.0	3 50.0	2 25.1	4 45.4	7 21.7	15 22.3	1 54.5	19 18.6
19 Sa	19 44 15	25 35 44	25 50 40	2♉10 3	28 27.0	29 45.8	4 59.3	3 6.8	4 58.7	7 17.6	15 22.4	1 56.3	19 20.2
20 Su	19 48 12	26 33 0	8♉35 6	15 6 22	28 26.8	1♌50.3	6 8.6	3 48.4	5 11.9	7 13.5	15 22.5	1 58.2	19 21.8
21 M	19 52 8	27 30 17	21 44 21	28 29 26	28 25.7	3 53.5	7 17.7	4 30.0	5 25.1	7 9.5	15R22.6	2 0.1	19 23.4
22 Tu	19 56 5	28 27 35	5♊21 52	12♊21 46	28 22.5	5 55.2	8 26.7	5 11.5	5 38.3	7 5.5	15 22.6	2 2.0	19 24.9
23 W	20 0 2	29 24 53	19 29 3	26 43 24	28 16.9	7 55.4	9 35.7	5 52.9	5 51.5	7 1.6	15 22.5	2 3.9	19 26.5
24 Th	20 3 58	0♌22 13	4♋ 4 19	11♋31 0	28 8.7	9 54.0	10 44.6	6 34.2	6 4.6	6 57.7	15 22.5	2 5.9	19 28.0
25 F	20 7 55	1 19 33	19 2 31	26 37 39	27 58.7	11 51.0	11 53.3	7 15.5	6 17.6	6 53.9	15 22.3	2 7.9	19 29.6
26 Sa	20 11 51	2 16 54	4♌15 6	11♌53 27	27 47.8	13 46.4	13 2.0	7 56.6	6 30.6	6 50.1	15 22.1	2 9.8	19 31.2
27 Su	20 15 48	3 14 16	19 31 17	27 7 12	27 37.4	15 40.1	14 10.5	8 37.7	6 43.6	6 46.3	15 21.9	2 11.8	19 32.7
28 M	20 19 44	4 11 38	4♍39 56	12♍ 8 23	27 28.6	17 32.1	15 19.0	9 18.7	6 56.5	6 42.6	15 21.6	2 13.8	19 34.2
29 Tu	20 23 41	5 9 0	19 31 38	26 48 59	27 22.3	19 22.4	16 27.3	9 59.5	7 9.4	6 39.0	15 21.3	2 15.8	19 35.8
30 W	20 27 37	6 6 24	3♎59 58	11♎ 4 21	27 18.7	21 11.0	17 35.5	10 40.3	7 22.3	6 35.4	15 20.9	2 17.9	19 37.3
31 Th	20 31 34	7 3 47	18 2 2	24 53 7	27D 17.2	22 57.9	18 43.6	11 21.0	7 35.0	6 31.9	15 20.5	2 19.9	19 38.8

AUGUST 1930 — LONGITUDE

Day	Sid.Time	☉	0 hr ☽	Noon ☽	True ☊	☿	♀	♂	♃	♄	♅	♆	♇
1 F	20 35 31	8♌ 1 12	1♏37 49	8♏16 30	27♈17.1	24♌43.2	19♍51.6	12♊ 1.6	7♋47.8	6♑28.5	15♈20.0	2♍22.0	19♋40.3
2 Sa	20 39 27	8 58 36	14 49 32	21 17 22	27R17.0	26 26.8	20 59.5	12 42.2	8 0.5	6R25.1	15R19.5	2 24.0	19 41.8
3 Su	20 43 24	9 56 2	27 40 30	3♐59 23	27 15.9	28 8.8	22 7.2	13 22.6	8 13.1	6 21.8	15 18.9	2 26.1	19 43.3
4 M	20 47 20	10 53 28	10♐14 30	16 26 19	27 12.8	29 49.1	23 14.8	14 2.9	8 25.7	6 18.5	15 18.3	2 28.2	19 44.8
5 Tu	20 51 17	11 50 55	22 35 14	28 41 40	27 7.1	1♍27.7	24 22.3	14 43.2	8 38.2	6 15.3	15 17.6	2 30.3	19 46.3
6 W	20 55 13	12 48 23	4♑45 56	10♑48 22	26 58.6	3 4.7	25 29.6	15 23.3	8 50.7	6 12.2	15 16.9	2 32.4	19 47.8
7 Th	20 59 10	13 45 51	16 49 14	22 48 48	26 47.9	4 40.1	26 36.8	16 3.4	9 3.1	6 9.2	15 16.1	2 34.5	19 49.3
8 F	21 3 6	14 43 21	28 47 16	4♒44 50	26 35.6	6 13.9	27 43.9	16 43.4	9 15.4	6 6.2	15 15.3	2 36.7	19 50.7
9 Sa	21 7 3	15 40 51	10♒41 42	16 38 1	26 22.7	7 46.0	28 50.8	17 23.2	9 27.7	6 3.3	15 14.5	2 38.8	19 52.2
10 Su	21 11 0	16 38 23	22 33 58	28 29 45	26 10.4	9 16.5	29 57.5	18 3.0	9 40.0	6 0.5	15 13.6	2 40.9	19 53.6
11 M	21 14 56	17 35 55	4♓25 33	10♓21 37	25 59.5	10 45.3	1♎ 4.1	18 42.7	9 52.1	5 57.7	15 12.7	2 43.1	19 55.0
12 Tu	21 18 53	18 33 29	16 18 12	22 15 35	25 50.9	12 12.5	2 10.6	19 22.3	10 4.2	5 55.0	15 11.7	2 45.3	19 56.5
13 W	21 22 49	19 31 4	28 14 7	4♈14 8	25 44.9	13 38.0	3 16.9	20 1.8	10 16.3	5 52.4	15 10.7	2 47.4	19 57.9
14 Th	21 26 46	20 28 40	10♈16 5	16 20 25	25 41.6	15 1.8	4 23.0	20 41.2	10 28.3	5 49.9	15 9.6	2 49.6	19 59.3
15 F	21 30 42	21 26 18	22 27 36	28 38 11	25D 40.4	16 23.8	5 28.9	21 20.5	10 40.2	5 47.5	15 8.5	2 51.8	20 0.7
16 Sa	21 34 39	22 23 57	4♉52 42	11♉11 42	25 40.6	17 44.1	6 34.7	21 59.7	10 52.0	5 45.1	15 7.3	2 54.0	20 2.0
17 Su	21 38 35	23 21 38	17 35 45	24 5 23	25R41.2	19 2.6	7 40.4	22 38.8	11 3.8	5 42.8	15 6.1	2 56.2	20 3.4
18 M	21 42 32	24 19 21	0♊41 6	7♊23 20	25 41.2	20 19.3	8 45.8	23 17.8	11 15.5	5 40.6	15 4.9	2 58.4	20 4.8
19 Tu	21 46 29	25 17 5	14 12 25	21 8 34	25 39.6	21 34.0	9 51.1	23 56.7	11 27.1	5 38.5	15 3.6	3 0.6	20 6.1
20 W	21 50 25	26 14 51	28 11 51	5♋22 9	25 35.9	22 46.8	10 56.2	24 35.5	11 38.7	5 36.5	15 2.3	3 2.8	20 7.4
21 Th	21 54 22	27 12 38	12♋39 8	20 2 18	25 30.0	23 57.5	12 1.1	25 14.2	11 50.1	5 34.6	15 0.9	3 5.0	20 8.7
22 F	21 58 18	28 10 28	27 30 50	5♌ 3 47	25 22.5	25 6.1	13 5.8	25 52.8	12 1.5	5 32.7	14 59.5	3 7.2	20 10.0
23 Sa	22 2 15	29 8 18	12♌39 59	20 18 9	25 14.1	26 12.5	14 10.4	26 31.3	12 12.9	5 31.0	14 58.1	3 9.5	20 11.3
24 Su	22 6 11	0♍ 6 11	27 56 52	5♍34 44	25 5.9	27 16.6	15 14.7	27 9.6	12 24.1	5 29.3	14 56.6	3 11.7	20 12.6
25 M	22 10 8	1 4 4	13♍10 24	20 42 37	24 59.1	28 18.2	16 18.8	27 47.9	12 35.3	5 27.8	14 55.1	3 13.9	20 13.9
26 Tu	22 14 4	2 1 59	28 10 15	5♎32 24	24 54.3	29 17.3	17 22.7	28 26.0	12 46.3	5 26.3	14 53.5	3 16.1	20 15.1
27 W	22 18 1	2 59 55	12♎48 22	19 57 40	24D 51.7	0♎13.7	18 26.4	29 4.0	12 57.3	5 24.9	14 51.9	3 18.4	20 16.3
28 Th	22 21 58	3 57 53	27 0 1	3♏55 20	24 51.1	1 7.2	19 29.8	29 42.0	13 8.2	5 23.6	14 50.3	3 20.6	20 17.5
29 F	22 25 54	4 55 52	10♏43 42	17 25 20	24 51.8	1 57.7	20 33.0	0♋19.7	13 19.0	5 22.4	14 48.6	3 22.8	20 18.7
30 Sa	22 29 51	5 53 53	24 0 35	0♐29 50	24 52.9	2 44.9	21 36.0	0 57.4	13 29.7	5 21.3	14 46.9	3 25.0	20 19.9
31 Su	22 33 47	6 51 54	6♐53 35	13 12 21	24R53.5	3 28.8	22 38.7	1 34.9	13 40.3	5 20.3	14 45.2	3 27.3	20 21.1

Astro Data Dy Hr Mn	Planet Ingress Dy Hr Mn
☽0S 2 18:24	☿ ♋ 4 22:10
♃✱♆ 3 12:03	☊ ♈ 7 15:55
☽0N 17 6:46	♀ ♍ 14 16:34
♅ R 21 16:09	♂ ♊ 14 12:54
♃☍♄ 27 3:55	☿ ♌ 19 2:44
☽0S 30 0:52	☉ ♌ 23 14:42
♀0S 10 6:16	☿ ♍ 4 2:38
☽0N 13 12:06	♀ ♎ 10 0:54
☿0S 22 22:51	☉ ♍ 23 21:26
☽0S 26 9:47	☿ ♎ 26 18:04
	♂ ♋ 28 11:27

Last Aspect Dy Hr Mn	☽ Ingress Dy Hr Mn	Last Aspect Dy Hr Mn	☽ Ingress Dy Hr Mn
2 0:05 ☿ □	♎ 2 9:47	3 1:02 ☿ □	♐ 3 4:24
4 13:39 ☿ △	♏ 4 14:56	5 3:51 ♀ □	♑ 5 14:35
6 12:05 ♂ ☍	♐ 6 22:49	7 21:39 ♀ △	♒ 8 2:26
8 19:26 ♀ △	♑ 9 8:49	9 14:20 ♂ △	♓ 10 15:03
11 16:21 ♂ △	♒ 11 20:23	12 7:21 ♇ △	♈ 13 3:32
14 8:42 ♂ □	♓ 14 8:57	14 21:50 ☉ △	♉ 15 14:38
16 10:04 ♂ ✱	♈ 16 21:26	17 11:30 ☉ □	♊ 17 22:46
18 23:29 ☉ □	♉ 19 7:54	19 20:28 ☉ ✱	♋ 20 3:02
21 11:02 ☉ ✱	♊ 21 14:39	21 19:50 ☿ ✱	♌ 22 3:58
22 17:06 ♅ ✱	♋ 23 17:22	23 22:43 ♂ ✱	♍ 24 3:13
25 0:43 ♇ ☌	♌ 25 17:19	26 1:56 ☿ ☌	♎ 26 2:58
26 17:28 ♅ △	♍ 27 16:34	28 4:53 ♂ △	♏ 28 5:11
29 0:07 ♇ ✱	♎ 29 17:18	29 17:16 ♇ △	♐ 30 11:04
31 9:54 ☿ ✱	♏ 31 21:05		

☽ Phases & Eclipses Dy Hr Mn	
3 4:03	☽ 10♎30
10 20:01	○ 17♑48
18 23:29	☽ 25♈34
25 20:42	● 2♌09
1 12:26	☽ 8♏31
9 10:58	○ 16♒07
17 11:30	☽ 23♉49
24 3:37	● 0♍15
30 23:57	☽ 6♐52

Astro Data

1 JULY 1930
Julian Day # 11139
Delta T 24.0 sec
SVP 06♓13'57"
Obliquity 23°27'01"
⚷ Chiron 17♉32.4
☽ Mean ☊ 29♈21.2

1 AUGUST 1930
Julian Day # 11170
Delta T 24.0 sec
SVP 06♓13'52"
Obliquity 23°27'02"
⚷ Chiron 18♉38.6
☽ Mean ☊ 27♈42.8

LONGITUDE — SEPTEMBER 1930

Day	Sid.Time	☉	0 hr ☽	Noon ☽	True ☊	☿	♀	♂	♃	♄	♅	♆	♇
1 M	22 37 44	7♍49 58	19♐26 40	25♐37 4	24♈52.7	4♎ 8.9	23♎41.1	2♋12.4	13♋50.8	5♑19.4	14♈43.4	3♍29.5	20♋22.2
2 Tu	22 41 40	8 48 2	1♑44 5	7♑48 14	24R 50.1	4 45.2	24 43.3	2 49.7	14 1.3	5R 18.5	14R 41.6	3 31.7	20 23.4
3 W	22 45 37	9 46 8	13 50 0	19 49 51	24 45.5	5 17.4	25 45.2	3 26.9	14 11.6	5 17.8	14 39.8	3 33.9	20 24.5
4 Th	22 49 33	10 44 15	25 48 11	1♒45 24	24 39.2	5 45.1	26 46.8	4 3.9	14 21.8	5 17.2	14 37.9	3 36.1	20 25.6
5 F	22 53 30	11 42 24	7♒41 51	13 37 52	24 31.7	6 8.1	27 48.0	4 40.9	14 31.9	5 16.7	14 36.0	3 38.3	20 26.7
6 Sa	22 57 27	12 40 35	19 33 42	25 29 39	24 23.8	6 26.1	28 49.0	5 17.7	14 42.0	5 16.2	14 34.1	3 40.6	20 27.7
7 Su	23 1 23	13 38 47	1♓25 56	7♓22 46	24 16.1	6 38.8	29 49.7	5 54.4	14 51.9	5 15.9	14 32.1	3 42.8	20 28.8
8 M	23 5 20	14 37 0	13 20 22	19 18 56	24 9.5	6R 45.8	0♏50.0	6 30.9	15 1.7	5 15.6	14 30.1	3 44.9	20 29.8
9 Tu	23 9 16	15 35 16	25 18 40	1♈19 48	24 4.4	6 47.0	1 50.0	7 7.3	15 11.4	5D 15.5	14 28.1	3 47.1	20 30.8
10 W	23 13 13	16 33 33	7♈22 33	13 27 10	24 1.1	6 41.9	2 49.7	7 43.6	15 21.0	5 15.4	14 26.1	3 49.3	20 31.8
11 Th	23 17 9	17 31 52	19 33 55	25 43 5	23D 59.7	6 30.4	3 49.0	8 19.8	15 30.5	5 15.5	14 24.0	3 51.5	20 32.7
12 F	23 21 6	18 30 13	1♉55 0	8♉ 9 59	23 59.9	6 12.3	4 47.9	8 55.9	15 39.9	5 15.6	14 21.9	3 53.7	20 33.7
13 Sa	23 25 2	19 28 36	14 28 26	20 50 41	24 1.1	5 47.5	5 46.4	9 31.8	15 49.2	5 15.9	14 19.8	3 55.8	20 34.6
14 Su	23 28 59	20 27 2	27 17 9	3♊48 12	24 2.8	5 16.0	6 44.6	10 7.5	15 58.3	5 16.2	14 17.7	3 58.0	20 35.5
15 M	23 32 55	21 25 29	10♊24 12	17 5 28	24R 4.1	4 37.9	7 42.3	10 43.2	16 7.3	5 16.7	14 15.5	4 0.1	20 36.4
16 Tu	23 36 52	22 23 59	23 52 17	0♋44 49	24 4.5	3 53.6	8 39.6	11 18.6	16 16.3	5 17.2	14 13.3	4 2.3	20 37.3
17 W	23 40 49	23 22 31	7♋43 12	14 47 24	24 3.7	3 3.4	9 36.5	11 54.0	16 25.1	5 17.9	14 11.1	4 4.4	20 38.1
18 Th	23 44 45	24 21 5	21 57 14	29 12 24	24 1.6	2 8.1	10 32.9	12 29.2	16 33.7	5 18.6	14 8.9	4 6.5	20 39.0
19 F	23 48 42	25 19 41	6♌32 24	13♌56 35	23 58.4	1 8.6	11 28.9	13 4.2	16 42.3	5 19.4	14 6.6	4 8.6	20 39.8
20 Sa	23 52 38	26 18 20	21 24 7	28 54 4	23 54.6	0 6.0	12 24.4	13 39.1	16 50.7	5 20.4	14 4.4	4 10.7	20 40.5
21 Su	23 56 35	27 17 0	6♍25 21	13♍56 51	23 50.8	29♍ 1.6	13 19.4	14 13.9	16 59.0	5 21.4	14 2.1	4 12.8	20 41.3
22 M	0 0 31	28 15 43	21 27 23	28 55 50	23 47.7	27 57.0	14 13.9	14 48.5	17 7.2	5 22.5	13 59.8	4 14.9	20 42.0
23 Tu	0 4 28	29 14 27	6♎21 6	13♎42 16	23 45.6	26 53.6	15 7.9	15 22.9	17 15.2	5 23.8	13 57.5	4 17.0	20 42.8
24 W	0 8 24	0♎13 14	20 58 28	28 9 3	23D 44.8	25 53.1	16 1.3	15 57.1	17 23.1	5 25.1	13 55.1	4 19.0	20 43.5
25 Th	0 12 21	1 12 2	5♏13 31	12♏11 34	23 45.1	24 57.1	16 54.1	16 31.2	17 30.8	5 26.5	13 52.8	4 21.1	20 44.1
26 F	0 16 18	2 10 52	19 3 2	25 47 54	23 46.2	24 7.1	17 46.3	17 5.1	17 38.4	5 28.0	13 50.4	4 23.1	20 44.8
27 Sa	0 20 14	3 9 44	2♐26 19	8♐58 31	23 47.6	23 24.4	18 37.9	17 38.9	17 45.9	5 29.6	13 48.1	4 25.1	20 45.4
28 Su	0 24 11	4 8 38	15 24 52	21 45 46	23 49.0	22 50.2	19 28.8	18 12.5	17 53.2	5 31.4	13 45.7	4 27.1	20 46.0
29 M	0 28 7	5 7 34	28 1 43	4♑13 13	23R 49.8	22 25.3	20 19.1	18 45.9	18 0.4	5 33.2	13 43.3	4 29.1	20 46.6
30 Tu	0 32 4	6 6 31	10♑20 50	16 25 6	23 49.9	22D 10.3	21 8.6	19 19.1	18 7.5	5 35.1	13 40.9	4 31.0	20 47.2

LONGITUDE — OCTOBER 1930

Day	Sid.Time	☉	0 hr ☽	Noon ☽	True ☊	☿	♀	♂	♃	♄	♅	♆	♇
1 W	0 36 0	7♎ 5 30	22♑26 37	28♑25 55	23♈49.2	22♍ 5.6	21♏57.4	19♋52.2	18♋14.4	5♑37.1	13♈38.5	4♍33.0	20♋47.7
2 Th	0 39 57	8 4 31	4♒23 32	10♒20 0	23R 47.8	22 11.3	22 45.4	20 25.0	18 21.1	5 39.2	13R 36.1	4 34.9	20 48.2
3 F	0 43 53	9 3 33	16 15 49	22 11 26	23 45.9	22 27.2	23 32.6	20 57.7	18 27.7	5 41.4	13 33.7	4 36.8	20 48.7
4 Sa	0 47 50	10 2 37	28 7 17	4♓ 3 46	23 43.7	22 53.2	24 19.0	21 30.2	18 34.2	5 43.7	13 31.2	4 38.7	20 49.2
5 Su	0 51 47	11 1 44	10♓ 1 15	16 0 4	23 41.7	23 28.6	25 4.5	22 2.5	18 40.5	5 46.0	13 28.8	4 40.6	20 49.6
6 M	0 55 43	12 0 52	22 0 30	28 2 48	23 40.0	24 12.9	25 49.1	22 34.6	18 46.6	5 48.5	13 26.4	4 42.5	20 50.0
7 Tu	0 59 40	13 0 1	4♈ 7 13	10♈13 57	23 38.8	25 5.6	26 32.8	23 6.6	18 52.6	5 51.1	13 24.0	4 44.3	20 50.4
8 W	1 3 36	13 59 13	16 23 10	22 35 3	23D 38.2	26 5.7	27 15.5	23 38.3	18 58.4	5 53.7	13 21.5	4 46.1	20 50.8
9 Th	1 7 33	14 58 27	28 49 44	5♉ 7 20	23 38.2	27 12.7	27 57.2	24 9.8	19 4.0	5 56.4	13 19.1	4 48.0	20 51.1
10 F	1 11 29	15 57 43	11♉28 0	17 51 49	23 38.6	28 25.7	28 37.8	24 41.1	19 9.5	5 59.3	13 16.7	4 49.7	20 51.5
11 Sa	1 15 26	16 57 2	24 18 57	0♊49 28	23 39.1	29 44.0	29 17.3	25 12.3	19 14.9	6 2.2	13 14.3	4 51.5	20 51.8
12 Su	1 19 22	17 56 22	7♊23 29	14 1 7	23 39.8	1♎ 6.8	29 55.7	25 43.2	19 20.0	6 5.2	13 11.8	4 53.2	20 52.0
13 M	1 23 19	18 55 45	20 42 26	27 27 33	23 40.3	2 33.6	0♐32.9	26 13.9	19 25.1	6 8.3	13 9.4	4 55.0	20 52.3
14 Tu	1 27 16	19 55 11	4♋16 29	11♋ 9 17	23 40.6	4 3.8	1 8.8	26 44.3	19 29.9	6 11.5	13 7.0	4 56.7	20 52.5
15 W	1 31 12	20 54 38	18 5 54	25 6 17	23R 40.8	5 36.7	1 43.5	27 14.6	19 34.5	6 14.7	13 4.6	4 58.4	20 52.7
16 Th	1 35 9	21 54 8	2♌10 18	9♌17 44	23 40.7	7 11.8	2 16.9	27 44.6	19 39.0	6 18.1	13 2.2	5 0.0	20 52.9
17 F	1 39 5	22 53 40	16 28 18	23 41 36	23D 40.7	8 48.8	2 48.8	28 14.4	19 43.3	6 21.5	12 59.8	5 1.7	20 53.1
18 Sa	1 43 2	23 53 15	0♍57 12	8♍14 31	23 40.6	10 27.3	3 19.3	28 44.0	19 47.5	6 25.1	12 57.5	5 3.3	20 53.2
19 Su	1 46 58	24 52 52	15 32 56	22 51 44	23 40.7	12 6.9	3 48.4	29 13.3	19 51.4	6 28.7	12 55.1	5 4.9	20 53.3
20 M	1 50 55	25 52 30	0♎10 12	7♎27 32	23 40.8	13 47.3	4 15.9	29 42.3	19 55.2	6 32.4	12 52.7	5 6.4	20 53.4
21 Tu	1 54 51	26 52 11	14 42 58	21 55 44	23R 41.0	15 28.3	4 41.7	0♌11.1	19 58.8	6 36.1	12 50.4	5 8.0	20 53.4
22 W	1 58 48	27 51 54	29 5 8	6♏10 31	23 41.0	17 9.7	5 6.0	0 39.6	20 2.2	6 40.0	12 48.1	5 9.5	20R 53.4
23 Th	2 2 45	28 51 40	13♏11 20	20 7 8	23 40.8	18 51.3	5 28.4	1 7.9	20 5.4	6 43.9	12 45.7	5 11.0	20 53.4
24 F	2 6 41	29 51 27	26 57 34	3♐42 26	23 40.3	20 33.0	5 49.1	1 35.9	20 8.5	6 48.0	12 43.5	5 12.4	20 53.4
25 Sa	2 10 38	0♏51 16	10♐21 37	16 55 9	23 39.4	22 14.6	6 7.9	2 3.6	20 11.3	6 52.1	12 41.2	5 13.9	20 53.4
26 Su	2 14 34	1 51 6	23 23 10	29 45 52	23 38.4	23 56.1	6 24.7	2 31.1	20 14.0	6 56.3	12 38.9	5 15.3	20 53.3
27 M	2 18 31	2 50 59	6♑ 3 35	12♑16 42	23 37.4	25 37.4	6 39.6	2 58.2	20 16.4	7 0.5	12 36.7	5 16.7	20 53.2
28 Tu	2 22 27	3 50 53	18 25 41	24 31 1	23 36.5	27 18.4	6 52.4	3 25.1	20 18.7	7 4.8	12 34.5	5 18.0	20 53.1
29 W	2 26 24	4 50 49	0♒33 15	6♒32 58	23D 36.1	28 59.0	7 3.1	3 51.6	20 20.8	7 9.3	12 32.3	5 19.4	20 52.9
30 Th	2 30 20	5 50 46	12 30 44	18 27 10	23 36.1	0♏39.3	7 11.5	4 17.9	20 22.7	7 13.7	12 30.1	5 20.7	20 52.8
31 F	2 34 17	6 50 45	24 22 52	0♓18 24	23 36.8	2 19.3	7 17.7	4 43.9	20 24.4	7 18.3	12 27.9	5 22.0	20 52.6

Astro Data	Planet Ingress	Last Aspect	☽ Ingress	Last Aspect	☽ Ingress	☽ Phases & Eclipses	Astro Data
Dy Hr Mn	Dy Hr Mn	Dy Hr Mn	Dy Hr Mn	Dy Hr Mn	Dy Hr Mn	Dy Hr Mn	1 SEPTEMBER 1930
♃□♅ 5 8:10	♀ ♏ 7 4:05	1 8:59 ♀ ✶	♑ 1 20:35	30 23:18 ☿ △	♒ 1 15:09	8 2:48 ○ 14♓44	Julian Day # 11201
☿ R 8 16:32	☿ ♍ 20 2:16	4 2:09 ♀ □	♒ 4 8:27	3 15:46 ♀ □	♓ 4 3:48	15 21:13 ☽ 22♊17	Delta T 24.0 sec
☽0N 9 17:29	☉ ♎ 23 18:36	6 20:28 ♀ △	♓ 6 21:06	6 8:04 ♀ △	♈ 6 15:52	22 11:42 ● 28♍44	SVP 06♓13'47"
♄ D 9 23:54		8 14:23 ♇ △	♈ 9 9:21	8 14:39 ♂ □	♉ 9 2:14	29 14:58 ☽ 5♑44	Obliquity 23°27'02"
☽0S 22 20:19	☿ ♎ 11 4:45	11 1:55 ♇ □	♉ 11 20:18	11 9:39 ♀ ☍	♊ 11 10:29		⚷ Chiron 18♉52.9R
☿0N 24 16:08	♀ ♐ 12 2:45	13 11:31 ♇ ✶	♊ 14 5:01	12 20:34 ☉ △	♋ 13 16:29	7 18:55 ○ 13♈47	☽ Mean ☊ 26♈04.3
☿ D 30 22:53	♂ ♌ 20 14:43	15 21:13 ☉ □	♋ 16 10:42	15 16:13 ♂ ☌	♌ 15 20:19	7 19:07 ☍P 0.025	
	☉ ♏ 24 3:26	18 4:16 ☉ ✶	♌ 18 13:18	17 11:28 ☉ ✶	♍ 17 22:26	15 5:12 ☽ 21♋08	1 OCTOBER 1930
☽0N 6 23:56	☿ ♏ 29 14:35	19 12:14 ♅ △	♍ 20 13:45	19 23:13 ♂ ✶	♎ 19 23:43	21 21:48 ● 27♎46	Julian Day # 11231
☿0S 14 8:16		22 11:42 ☉ ☌	♎ 22 13:43	21 21:48 ☉ ☌	♏ 22 1:32	21 21:43:29 ☌T 1'55"	Delta T 24.0 sec
☽0S 20 6:28		23 23:35 ♇ □	♏ 24 15:07	23 13:21 ♇ △	♐ 24 5:23	29 9:22 ☽ 5♒14	SVP 06♓13'44"
♇ R 22 13:32		26 8:31 ☿ ✶	♐ 26 19:34	26 1:11 ☿ ✶	♑ 26 12:27		Obliquity 23°27'03"
♃∠♆ 27 6:05		28 13:34 ☿ □	♑ 29 3:48	28 20:22 ☿ □	♒ 28 22:54		⚷ Chiron 18♉14.0R
				29 23:59 ♅ ✶	♓ 31 11:23		☽ Mean ☊ 24♈28.9

NOVEMBER 1930 LONGITUDE

Day	Sid.Time	☉	0 hr ☽	Noon ☽	True ☊	☿	♀	♂	♃	♄	♅	♆	♇
1 Sa	2 38 14	7♏50 46	6♓14 21	12♓11 16	23♈37.9	3♏58.8	7♐21.7	5♌ 9.5	20♋25.9	7♑22.9	12♈25.8	5♍23.2	20♋52.3
2 Su	2 42 10	8 50 48	18 9 41	24 10 5	23 39.3	5 37.9	7R23.2	5 34.9	20 27.2	7 27.6	12R23.7	5 24.4	20R52.1
3 M	2 46 7	9 50 52	0♈12 54	6♈18 33	23 40.6	7 16.6	7 22.4	5 59.9	20 28.3	7 32.4	12 21.6	5 25.6	20 51.8
4 Tu	2 50 3	10 50 58	12 27 22	18 39 40	23R41.7	8 54.8	7 19.2	6 24.5	20 29.2	7 37.2	12 19.5	5 26.8	20 51.5
5 W	2 54 0	11 51 5	24 55 40	1♉15 32	23 42.0	10 32.7	7 13.5	6 48.9	20 29.9	7 42.1	12 17.5	5 27.9	20 51.2
6 Th	2 57 56	12 51 14	7♉39 22	14 7 14	23 41.4	12 10.1	7 5.4	7 12.9	20 30.5	7 47.1	12 15.5	5 29.0	20 50.9
7 F	3 1 53	13 51 25	20 39 5	27 14 52	23 39.8	13 47.1	6 54.8	7 36.5	20 30.8	7 52.2	12 13.6	5 30.1	20 50.5
8 Sa	3 5 49	14 51 37	3♊54 24	10♊37 33	23 37.2	15 23.8	6 41.8	7 59.8	20R30.9	7 57.3	12 11.6	5 31.1	20 50.1
9 Su	3 9 46	15 51 52	17 24 3	24 13 40	23 34.0	17 0.0	6 26.3	8 22.8	20 30.8	8 2.5	12 9.7	5 32.1	20 49.7
10 M	3 13 43	16 52 9	1♋ 6 6	8♋ 1 5	23 30.5	18 35.9	6 8.5	8 45.3	20 30.6	8 7.7	12 7.8	5 33.1	20 49.3
11 Tu	3 17 39	17 52 27	14 58 19	21 57 31	23 27.3	20 11.5	5 48.4	9 7.5	20 30.1	8 13.0	12 6.0	5 34.0	20 48.8
12 W	3 21 36	18 52 47	28 58 23	6♌ 0 40	23 25.0	21 46.7	5 26.1	9 29.3	20 29.4	8 18.4	12 4.2	5 35.0	20 48.3
13 Th	3 25 32	19 53 10	13♌ 4 7	20 8 29	23D23.7	23 21.6	5 1.7	9 50.7	20 28.6	8 23.8	12 2.4	5 35.9	20 47.8
14 F	3 29 29	20 53 34	27 13 33	4♍19 5	23 23.7	24 56.2	4 35.3	10 11.7	20 27.5	8 29.3	12 0.7	5 36.7	20 47.3
15 Sa	3 33 25	21 54 0	11♍24 52	18 30 37	23 24.6	26 30.6	4 7.0	10 32.2	20 26.2	8 34.8	11 59.0	5 37.5	20 46.8
16 Su	3 37 22	22 54 28	25 36 7	2♎41 4	23 26.2	28 4.6	3 37.0	10 52.4	20 24.7	8 40.4	11 57.3	5 38.3	20 46.2
17 M	3 41 18	23 54 58	9♎45 9	16 48 2	23R27.6	29 38.5	3 5.4	11 12.0	20 23.0	8 46.1	11 55.7	5 39.1	20 45.6
18 Tu	3 45 15	24 55 30	23 49 21	0♏48 43	23 28.1	1♐12.1	2 32.5	11 31.3	20 21.2	8 51.8	11 54.1	5 39.8	20 45.0
19 W	3 49 12	25 56 3	7♏45 43	14 39 56	23 27.3	2 45.4	1 58.5	11 50.1	20 19.1	8 57.6	11 52.5	5 40.5	20 44.3
20 Th	3 53 8	26 56 38	21 31 1	28 18 33	23 24.8	4 18.6	1 23.5	12 8.4	20 16.8	9 3.4	11 51.0	5 41.1	20 43.7
21 F	3 57 5	27 57 15	5♐ 2 13	11♐41 45	23 20.5	5 51.5	0 47.8	12 26.2	20 14.3	9 9.3	11 49.5	5 41.8	20 43.0
22 Sa	4 1 1	28 57 53	18 16 56	24 47 38	23 14.7	7 24.3	0 11.7	12 43.6	20 11.7	9 15.3	11 48.1	5 42.4	20 42.3
23 Su	4 4 58	29 58 33	1♑13 47	7♑35 25	23 8.1	8 56.9	29♏35.3	13 0.4	20 8.8	9 21.2	11 46.7	5 42.9	20 41.6
24 M	4 8 54	0♐59 14	13 52 39	20 5 42	23 1.4	10 29.3	28 59.0	13 16.7	20 5.8	9 27.3	11 45.3	5 43.4	20 40.8
25 Tu	4 12 51	1 59 56	26 14 50	2♒20 26	22 55.4	12 1.5	28 23.0	13 32.6	20 2.5	9 33.4	11 44.0	5 43.9	20 40.1
26 W	4 16 47	3 0 39	8♒22 53	14 22 43	22 50.7	13 33.6	27 47.4	13 47.9	19 59.1	9 39.5	11 42.8	5 44.4	20 39.3
27 Th	4 20 44	4 1 23	20 20 26	26 16 38	22 47.7	15 5.5	27 12.7	14 2.6	19 55.5	9 45.7	11 41.6	5 44.8	20 38.5
28 F	4 24 41	5 2 8	2♓11 56	8♓ 6 56	22D46.5	16 37.2	26 38.9	14 16.8	19 51.6	9 51.9	11 40.4	5 45.2	20 37.7
29 Sa	4 28 37	6 2 54	14 2 19	19 58 43	22 46.8	18 8.7	26 6.3	14 30.4	19 47.6	9 58.2	11 39.2	5 45.6	20 36.8
30 Su	4 32 34	7 3 41	25 56 49	1♈57 13	22 48.1	19 40.1	25 35.2	14 43.5	19 43.5	10 4.5	11 38.2	5 45.9	20 35.9

DECEMBER 1930 LONGITUDE

Day	Sid.Time	☉	0 hr ☽	Noon ☽	True ☊	☿	♀	♂	♃	♄	♅	♆	♇
1 M	4 36 30	8♐ 4 29	8♈ 0 32	14♈ 7 22	22♈49.6	21♐11.2	25♏ 5.7	14♌56.0	19♋39.1	10♑10.8	11♈37.1	5♍46.2	20♋35.1
2 Tu	4 40 27	9 5 18	20 18 14	26 33 35	22R50.5	22 42.0	24R38.0	15 7.9	19R34.6	10 17.2	11R36.1	5 46.4	20R34.2
3 W	4 44 23	10 6 8	2♉53 50	9♉19 17	22 50.0	24 12.6	24 12.2	15 19.2	19 29.9	10 23.7	11 35.2	5 46.6	20 33.3
4 Th	4 48 20	11 6 59	15 50 8	22 26 28	22 47.4	25 42.9	23 48.5	15 29.9	19 25.0	10 30.1	11 34.3	5 46.8	20 32.3
5 F	4 52 16	12 7 51	29 8 16	5♊55 22	22 42.6	27 12.8	23 27.0	15 40.0	19 20.0	10 36.6	11 33.4	5 46.9	20 31.4
6 Sa	4 56 13	13 8 44	12♊47 30	19 44 16	22 35.7	28 42.3	23 7.8	15 49.4	19 14.8	10 43.2	11 32.6	5 47.1	20 30.4
7 Su	5 0 10	14 9 38	26 45 8	3♋49 31	22 27.3	0♑11.3	22 50.9	15 58.2	19 9.4	10 49.8	11 31.9	5 47.1	20 29.4
8 M	5 4 6	15 10 33	10♋56 45	18 6 6	22 18.2	1 39.7	22 36.5	16 6.4	19 3.9	10 56.4	11 31.2	5R47.2	20 28.4
9 Tu	5 8 3	16 11 29	25 16 51	2♌28 18	22 9.7	3 7.4	22 24.6	16 13.8	18 58.2	11 3.0	11 30.5	5 47.2	20 27.4
10 W	5 11 59	17 12 26	9♌39 47	16 50 42	22 2.6	4 34.3	22 15.2	16 20.6	18 52.3	11 9.7	11 29.9	5 47.2	20 26.4
11 Th	5 15 56	18 13 25	24 0 33	1♍ 8 54	21 57.7	6 0.2	22 8.3	16 26.7	18 46.4	11 16.4	11 29.3	5 47.1	20 25.3
12 F	5 19 52	19 14 24	8♍15 27	15 19 56	21D55.2	7 25.0	22 3.9	16 32.0	18 40.2	11 23.2	11 28.8	5 47.0	20 24.3
13 Sa	5 23 49	20 15 25	22 22 13	29 22 12	21 54.6	8 48.4	22D 2.0	16 36.7	18 34.0	11 29.9	11 28.4	5 46.9	20 23.2
14 Su	5 27 46	21 16 26	6♎19 50	13♎15 8	21 55.2	10 10.3	22 2.6	16 40.6	18 27.5	11 36.7	11 28.0	5 46.7	20 22.1
15 M	5 31 42	22 17 29	20 8 6	26 58 44	21R55.8	11 30.4	22 5.6	16 43.7	18 21.0	11 43.5	11 27.6	5 46.5	20 21.0
16 Tu	5 35 39	23 18 33	3♏47 3	10♏33 1	21 55.2	12 48.2	22 11.0	16 46.1	18 14.3	11 50.4	11 27.3	5 46.3	20 19.9
17 W	5 39 35	24 19 38	17 16 36	23 57 42	21 52.4	14 3.6	22 18.7	16 47.8	18 7.5	11 57.3	11 27.0	5 46.0	20 18.8
18 Th	5 43 32	25 20 43	0♐36 13	7♐12 2	21 46.7	15 16.0	22 28.7	16R48.6	18 0.6	12 4.2	11 26.8	5 45.7	20 17.6
19 F	5 47 28	26 21 50	13 44 59	20 14 57	21 38.2	16 24.9	22 40.9	16 48.7	17 53.6	12 11.1	11 26.7	5 45.4	20 16.5
20 Sa	5 51 25	27 22 57	26 41 46	3♑ 5 19	21 27.3	17 29.8	22 55.3	16 47.9	17 46.5	12 18.0	11 26.6	5 45.1	20 15.3
21 Su	5 55 21	28 24 4	9♑25 30	15 42 18	21 14.7	18 30.1	23 11.8	16 46.4	17 39.2	12 25.0	11D26.5	5 44.7	20 14.2
22 M	5 59 18	29 25 12	21 55 43	28 5 48	21 1.8	19 25.1	23 30.3	16 44.0	17 31.9	12 32.0	11 26.5	5 44.2	20 13.0
23 Tu	6 3 15	0♑26 21	4♒12 41	10♒16 36	20 49.6	20 13.9	23 50.7	16 40.9	17 24.5	12 39.0	11 26.6	5 43.8	20 11.8
24 W	6 7 11	1 27 29	16 17 48	22 16 38	20 39.1	20 55.9	24 13.1	16 36.9	17 16.9	12 46.0	11 26.7	5 43.3	20 10.6
25 Th	6 11 8	2 28 38	28 13 31	4♓ 8 55	20 31.2	21 30.0	24 37.2	16 32.1	17 9.3	12 53.0	11 26.8	5 42.7	20 9.4
26 F	6 15 4	3 29 47	10♓ 3 20	15 57 23	20 26.0	21 55.4	25 3.2	16 26.4	17 1.7	13 0.0	11 27.1	5 42.2	20 8.2
27 Sa	6 19 1	4 30 55	21 51 39	27 46 49	20 23.4	22R11.2	25 30.8	16 20.0	16 53.9	13 7.1	11 27.3	5 41.6	20 6.9
28 Su	6 22 57	5 32 4	3♈43 32	9♈42 31	20D22.6	22 16.5	26 0.1	16 12.7	16 46.1	13 14.1	11 27.6	5 40.9	20 5.7
29 M	6 26 54	6 33 13	15 44 28	21 50 5	20R22.7	22 10.6	26 31.0	16 4.6	16 38.3	13 21.2	11 28.0	5 40.3	20 4.5
30 Tu	6 30 50	7 34 22	28 0 1	4♉14 55	20 22.6	21 53.1	27 3.4	15 55.6	16 30.3	13 28.3	11 28.4	5 39.6	20 3.2
31 W	6 34 47	8 35 31	10♉35 21	17 1 49	20 21.0	21 23.7	27 37.3	15 45.9	16 22.4	13 35.4	11 28.9	5 38.9	20 2.0

Astro Data	Planet Ingress	Last Aspect	☽ Ingress	Last Aspect	☽ Ingress	☽ Phases & Eclipses	Astro Data
Dy Hr Mn	Dy Hr Mn	Dy Hr Mn	Dy Hr Mn	Dy Hr Mn	Dy Hr Mn	Dy Hr Mn	1 NOVEMBER 1930
♀ R 2 3:50	☿ ♐ 17 5:31	2 5:25 ♇ △	♈ 2 23:34	2 5:15 ☿ △	♉ 2 18:32	6 10:28 ○ 13♉17	Julian Day # 11262
☽0N 3 7:38	♀ ♏ 22 7:44	4 16:13 ♇ □	♉ 5 9:37	4 14:04 ♀ ☍	♊ 5 1:32	13 12:27 ☽ 20♌25	Delta T 24.0 sec
♃∠♆ 7 19:27	☉ ♐ 23 0:34	7 0:21 ♇ ⚹	♊ 7 16:58	6 5:19 ♂ ⚹	♋ 7 5:31	20 10:21 ● 27♏23	SVP 06♓13'40"
♃ R 8 3:21		8 14:45 ♅ ⚹	♋ 9 22:05	8 19:16 ♀ △	♌ 9 7:53	28 6:18 ☽ 5♓18	Obliquity 23°27'02"
☽0S 16 14:16	☿ ♑ 6 20:57	11 10:07 ☿ △	♌ 12 1:45	10 20:53 ♀ □	♍ 11 10:04		⚷ Chiron 16♉52.6R
♆∠♇ 21 22:41	☉ ♑ 22 13:40	13 19:38 ☿ □	♍ 14 4:42	12 23:26 ♀ ⚹	♎ 13 13:05	6 0:40 ○ 13♊10	☽ Mean ☊ 22♈50.4
☽0N 30 15:49		16 4:43 ☿ ⚹	♎ 16 7:27	15 4:05 ☉ ⚹	♏ 15 17:19	12 20:07 ☽ 20♍06	
♆ R 8 20:17		17 18:45 ♇ □	♏ 18 10:36	17 9:08 ♀ ☌	♐ 17 22:54	20 1:24 ● 27♐26	1 DECEMBER 1930
♄□♅ 12 18:48		20 10:21 ☉ ☌	♐ 20 15:00	20 1:24 ☉ ☌	♑ 20 6:11	28 3:59 ☽ 5♈42	Julian Day # 11292
☽0S 13 19:26		21 13:39 ♂ △	♑ 22 21:42	22 3:08 ♀ ⚹	♒ 22 15:43		Delta T 24.0 sec
♀ D 13 6:23		25 4:00 ♀ ⚹	♒ 25 7:23	24 16:28 ♀ □	♓ 25 3:35		SVP 06♓13'35"
♂ R 18 13:45		27 13:15 ♀ □	♓ 27 19:33	27 7:43 ♀ △	♈ 27 16:29		Obliquity 23°27'02"
♅ D 21 10:18		29 23:18 ♀ △	♈ 30 8:06	29 12:25 ☿ □	♉ 30 3:52		⚷ Chiron 15♉23.1R
☽0N 27 23:22	☿ R 27 23:38						☽ Mean ☊ 21♈15.1

LONGITUDE — JANUARY 1931

Day	Sid.Time	☉	0 hr ☽	Noon ☽	True ☊	☿	♀	♂	♃	♄	♅	♆	♇
1 Th	6 38 44	9♑36 39	23♉34 44	0♊14 22	20♈17.2	20♑42.6	28♏12.6	15♌35.3	16♋14.4	13♑42.5	11♈29.4	5♍38.1	20♋ 0.7
2 F	6 42 40	10 37 48	7♊ 0 50	13 54 7	20R 10.6	19R 50.4	28 49.3	15R 24.0	16R 6.4	13 49.6	11 30.0	5R 37.3	19R 59.5
3 Sa	6 46 37	11 38 56	20 54 0	28 0 5	20 1.2	18 48.4	29 27.3	15 11.8	15 58.3	13 56.7	11 30.6	5 36.5	19 58.2
4 Su	6 50 33	12 40 5	5♋11 45	12♋28 15	19 49.9	17 38.2	0♐ 6.6	14 58.9	15 50.2	14 3.8	11 31.3	5 35.7	19 56.9
5 M	6 54 30	13 41 13	19 48 40	27 11 59	19 37.6	16 21.9	0 47.0	14 45.2	15 42.1	14 10.9	11 32.0	5 34.8	19 55.6
6 Tu	6 58 26	14 42 21	4♌37 4	12♌ 2 49	19 25.8	15 2.0	1 28.7	14 30.7	15 34.0	14 18.0	11 32.8	5 33.9	19 54.4
7 W	7 2 23	15 43 29	19 28 8	26 52 2	19 15.7	13 41.2	2 11.5	14 15.5	15 25.9	14 25.1	11 33.6	5 33.0	19 53.1
8 Th	7 6 20	16 44 37	4♍13 35	11♍32 5	19 8.3	12 21.9	2 55.3	13 59.5	15 17.8	14 32.2	11 34.5	5 32.1	19 51.8
9 F	7 10 16	17 45 46	18 46 55	25 57 39	19 3.8	11 6.7	3 40.2	13 42.8	15 9.7	14 39.3	11 35.4	5 31.1	19 50.5
10 Sa	7 14 13	18 46 54	3♎ 4 2	10♎ 5 56	19 1.8	9 57.6	4 26.1	13 25.4	15 1.6	14 46.4	11 36.4	5 30.1	19 49.2
11 Su	7 18 9	19 48 2	17 3 21	23 56 21	19 1.4	8 56.0	5 13.0	13 7.3	14 53.5	14 53.5	11 37.4	5 29.0	19 47.9
12 M	7 22 6	20 49 10	0♏45 6	7♏29 48	19 1.3	8 3.3	6 0.7	12 48.6	14 45.5	15 0.6	11 38.5	5 28.0	19 46.7
13 Tu	7 26 2	21 50 19	14 10 41	20 48 0	19 0.0	7 20.1	6 49.4	12 29.2	14 37.5	15 7.6	11 39.7	5 26.9	19 45.4
14 W	7 29 59	22 51 27	27 21 57	3♐52 45	18 56.5	6 46.5	7 38.9	12 9.3	14 29.5	15 14.7	11 40.8	5 25.8	19 44.1
15 Th	7 33 55	23 52 35	10♐20 36	16 45 38	18 50.0	6 22.7	8 29.2	11 48.8	14 21.6	15 21.8	11 42.1	5 24.6	19 42.8
16 F	7 37 52	24 53 43	23 7 57	29 27 40	18 40.4	6 8.4	9 20.3	11 27.7	14 13.7	15 28.8	11 43.3	5 23.5	19 41.5
17 Sa	7 41 49	25 54 51	5♑44 49	11♑59 26	18 28.1	6D 3.1	10 12.2	11 6.2	14 5.9	15 35.9	11 44.7	5 22.3	19 40.2
18 Su	7 45 45	26 55 58	18 11 35	24 21 16	18 14.0	6 6.2	11 4.7	10 44.2	13 58.2	15 42.9	11 46.1	5 21.1	19 39.0
19 M	7 49 42	27 57 4	0♒28 33	6♒33 28	17 59.4	6 17.2	11 58.0	10 21.8	13 50.5	15 49.9	11 47.5	5 19.8	19 37.7
20 Tu	7 53 38	28 58 10	12 36 9	18 36 42	17 45.4	6 35.4	12 51.8	9 59.0	13 42.9	15 56.9	11 49.0	5 18.6	19 36.4
21 W	7 57 35	29 59 15	24 35 18	0♓32 11	17 33.2	7 0.2	13 46.4	9 35.9	13 35.4	16 3.9	11 50.5	5 17.3	19 35.2
22 Th	8 1 31	1♒ 0 20	6♓27 38	12 21 59	17 23.7	7 31.1	14 41.5	9 12.6	13 27.9	16 10.9	11 52.0	5 16.0	19 33.9
23 F	8 5 28	2 1 23	18 15 37	24 9 0	17 17.1	8 7.4	15 37.2	8 49.0	13 20.6	16 17.8	11 53.6	5 14.7	19 32.6
24 Sa	8 9 24	3 2 26	0♈ 2 37	5♈57 2	17 13.4	8 48.6	16 33.5	8 25.2	13 13.3	16 24.7	11 55.3	5 13.3	19 31.4
25 Su	8 13 21	4 3 27	11 52 49	17 50 38	17D 12.0	9 34.4	17 30.3	8 1.2	13 6.2	16 31.6	11 57.0	5 11.9	19 30.1
26 M	8 17 18	5 4 28	23 51 8	29 55 0	17 12.0	10 24.2	18 27.6	7 37.2	12 59.1	16 38.5	11 58.8	5 10.6	19 28.9
27 Tu	8 21 14	6 5 27	6♉ 2 55	12♉15 34	17R 12.3	11 17.6	19 25.4	7 13.2	12 52.2	16 45.4	12 0.5	5 9.2	19 27.7
28 W	8 25 11	7 6 25	18 33 38	24 57 42	17 11.7	12 14.4	20 23.8	6 49.1	12 45.4	16 52.2	12 2.4	5 7.7	19 26.4
29 Th	8 29 7	8 7 23	1♊28 21	8♊ 6 2	17 9.2	13 14.2	21 22.5	6 25.1	12 38.7	16 59.0	12 4.3	5 6.3	19 25.2
30 F	8 33 4	9 8 18	14 51 3	21 43 38	17 4.4	14 16.7	22 21.8	6 1.2	12 32.2	17 5.8	12 6.2	5 4.8	19 24.0
31 Sa	8 37 0	10 9 13	28 43 45	5♋51 13	16 57.0	15 21.7	23 21.4	5 37.4	12 25.7	17 12.5	12 8.2	5 3.4	19 22.8

LONGITUDE — FEBRUARY 1931

Day	Sid.Time	☉	0 hr ☽	Noon ☽	True ☊	☿	♀	♂	♃	♄	♅	♆	♇
1 Su	8 40 57	11♒10 7	13♋ 5 37	20♋26 19	16♈47.7	16♑29.1	24♐21.5	5♌13.9	12♋19.5	17♑19.3	12♈10.2	5♍ 1.9	19♋21.6
2 M	8 44 53	12 10 59	27 52 26	5♌22 57	16R 37.4	17 38.5	25 22.0	4R 50.5	12R 13.3	17 26.0	12 12.2	5R 0.4	19R 20.5
3 Tu	8 48 50	13 11 50	12♌56 38	20 32 12	16 27.3	18 49.9	26 22.9	4 27.5	12 7.3	17 32.6	12 14.3	4 58.9	19 19.3
4 W	8 52 47	14 12 40	28 8 17	5♍43 33	16 18.6	20 3.0	27 24.2	4 4.8	12 1.4	17 39.2	12 16.4	4 57.3	19 18.1
5 Th	8 56 43	15 13 29	13♍16 46	20 46 49	16 12.2	21 17.9	28 25.8	3 42.4	11 55.7	17 45.8	12 18.6	4 55.8	19 17.0
6 F	9 0 40	16 14 17	28 12 43	5♎33 44	16 8.5	22 34.2	29 27.8	3 20.4	11 50.2	17 52.4	12 20.8	4 54.2	19 15.9
7 Sa	9 4 36	17 15 3	12♎49 17	19 59 1	16D 7.2	23 52.1	0♑30.1	2 58.8	11 44.8	17 58.9	12 23.1	4 52.7	19 14.7
8 Su	9 8 33	18 15 49	27 2 43	4♏ 0 23	16 7.5	25 11.3	1 32.8	2 37.7	11 39.5	18 5.4	12 25.4	4 51.1	19 13.6
9 M	9 12 29	19 16 34	10♏52 6	17 38 5	16R 8.3	26 31.8	2 35.8	2 17.1	11 34.4	18 11.8	12 27.7	4 49.5	19 12.5
10 Tu	9 16 26	20 17 18	24 18 35	0♐53 59	16 8.5	27 53.6	3 39.1	1 57.0	11 29.5	18 18.3	12 30.1	4 47.9	19 11.5
11 W	9 20 22	21 18 1	7♐24 36	13 50 51	16 7.1	29 16.5	4 42.7	1 37.5	11 24.8	18 24.6	12 32.5	4 46.3	19 10.4
12 Th	9 24 19	22 18 43	20 13 5	26 31 41	16 3.4	0♒40.6	5 46.6	1 18.6	11 20.2	18 31.0	12 34.9	4 44.6	19 9.3
13 F	9 28 16	23 19 24	2♑46 59	8♑59 19	15 57.4	2 5.7	6 50.7	1 0.3	11 15.8	18 37.2	12 37.4	4 43.0	19 8.3
14 Sa	9 32 12	24 20 3	15 8 58	21 16 11	15 49.2	3 32.0	7 55.2	0 42.7	11 11.6	18 43.5	12 39.9	4 41.4	19 7.3
15 Su	9 36 9	25 20 42	27 21 12	3♒24 14	15 39.6	4 59.2	8 59.8	0 25.7	11 7.6	18 49.7	12 42.4	4 39.7	19 6.3
16 M	9 40 5	26 21 19	9♒25 28	15 25 5	15 29.6	6 27.5	10 4.7	0 9.5	11 3.7	18 55.8	12 45.0	4 38.1	19 5.3
17 Tu	9 44 2	27 21 54	21 23 16	27 20 10	15 19.9	7 56.7	11 9.9	29♋53.9	11 0.0	19 1.9	12 47.6	4 36.4	19 4.3
18 W	9 47 58	28 22 28	3♓16 0	9♓10 57	15 11.5	9 27.0	12 15.2	29 39.1	10 56.5	19 8.0	12 50.3	4 34.8	19 3.3
19 Th	9 51 55	29 23 0	15 5 15	20 59 8	15 5.1	10 58.1	13 20.8	29 25.0	10 53.2	19 14.0	12 52.9	4 33.1	19 2.4
20 F	9 55 51	0♓23 31	26 52 55	2♈46 53	15 1.0	12 30.3	14 26.6	29 11.7	10 50.1	19 20.0	12 55.7	4 31.4	19 1.4
21 Sa	9 59 48	1 24 0	8♈41 26	14 36 58	14D 59.0	14 3.4	15 32.6	28 59.1	10 47.2	19 25.9	12 58.4	4 29.7	19 0.5
22 Su	10 3 45	2 24 27	20 33 54	26 32 44	14 59.0	15 37.5	16 38.8	28 47.4	10 44.5	19 31.7	13 1.2	4 28.1	18 59.6
23 M	10 7 41	3 24 53	2♉34 0	8♉38 14	15 0.1	17 12.5	17 45.2	28 36.4	10 42.0	19 37.5	13 4.0	4 26.4	18 58.8
24 Tu	10 11 38	4 25 16	14 46 1	20 57 56	15 1.7	18 48.5	18 51.8	28 26.3	10 39.6	19 43.2	13 6.8	4 24.7	18 57.9
25 W	10 15 34	5 25 38	27 14 35	3♊36 32	15R 3.0	20 25.4	19 58.5	28 16.9	10 37.5	19 48.9	13 9.7	4 23.0	18 57.1
26 Th	10 19 31	6 25 57	10♊ 4 20	16 38 28	15 3.3	22 3.4	21 5.4	28 8.3	10 35.5	19 54.6	13 12.5	4 21.4	18 56.2
27 F	10 23 27	7 26 15	23 19 23	0♋ 7 22	15 2.0	23 42.3	22 12.5	28 0.6	10 33.8	20 0.1	13 15.5	4 19.7	18 55.5
28 Sa	10 27 24	8 26 31	7♋ 2 37	14 5 9	14 59.1	25 22.2	23 19.7	27 53.6	10 32.3	20 5.6	13 18.4	4 18.0	18 54.7

Astro Data (Dy Hr Mn)	Planet Ingress (Dy Hr Mn)	Last Aspect (Dy Hr Mn)	☽ Ingress (Dy Hr Mn)	Last Aspect (Dy Hr Mn)	☽ Ingress (Dy Hr Mn)	☽ Phases & Eclipses (Dy Hr Mn)	Astro Data
☽0S 10 0:11	♀ ♐ 3 20:03	1 8:46 ♀ ☍	♊ 1 11:34	1 10:14 ♇ ☌	♌ 2 3:25	4 13:15 ○ 13♋14	1 JANUARY 1931
♃☍♄ 11 0:07	☉ ♒ 21 0:18	2 14:23 ♂ ✱	♋ 3 15:21	3 22:45 ♀ △	♍ 4 2:56	11 5:09 ☽ 20♎01	Julian Day # 11323
☿ D 17 2:52		5 0:11 ♇ ☌	♌ 5 16:32	6 2:11 ♀ □	♎ 6 2:54	18 18:35 ● 27♑43	Delta T 24.0 sec
☽0N 24 5:47	♀ ♑ 6 12:25	6 15:43 ♂ ☌	♍ 7 17:06	7 20:30 ☿ □	♏ 8 5:04	27 0:05 ☽ 6♉06	SVP 06♓13'29"
	☿ ♒ 11 12:27	9 1:46 ♇ ✱	♎ 9 18:48	10 7:16 ☿ ✱	♐ 10 10:21		Obliquity 23°27'02"
♃□♅ 2 3:12	♂ ♋ 16 14:27	11 5:09 ☉ □	♏ 11 22:40	12 4:19 ☉ ✱	♑ 12 18:39	3 0:26 ○ 13♌13	⚷ Chiron 14♉16.3R
☽0S 6 7:22	☉ ♓ 19 14:40	13 15:03 ☉ ✱	♐ 14 4:51	14 7:46 ♇ ☍	♒ 15 5:14	9 16:10 ☽ 19♏57	☽ Mean ☊ 19♈36.7
♄☍♇ 17 8:00		15 2:40 ♂ △	♑ 16 13:02	17 13:11 ☉ ☌	♓ 17 17:23	17 13:11 ● 27♒55	
☽0N 20 11:34		18 18:35 ☉ ☌	♒ 18 23:04	20 4:37 ♂ △	♈ 20 6:21	25 16:42 ☽ 6♊08	1 FEBRUARY 1931
♄⚼♆ 21 12:23		20 0:34 ♀ ✱	♓ 21 10:55	22 16:14 ♂ □	♉ 22 18:54		Julian Day # 11354
		23 2:37 ♇ △	♈ 23 23:55	25 1:57 ♂ ✱	♊ 25 5:13		Delta T 24.0 sec
		25 15:18 ♇ □	♉ 26 12:10	27 0:46 ☿ △	♋ 27 11:47		SVP 06♓13'23"
		28 1:40 ♇ ✱	♊ 28 21:18				Obliquity 23°27'02"
		30 14:06 ♀ ☍	♋ 31 2:09				⚷ Chiron 14♉02.1
							☽ Mean ☊ 17♈58.2

MARCH 1931 LONGITUDE

Day	Sid.Time	☉	0 hr ☽	Noon ☽	True ☊	☿	♀	♂	♃	♄	♅	♆	♇
1 Su	10 31 20	9♓26 45	21♋14 49	28♋31 16	14♈54.9	27♒ 3.2	24♑27.1	27♋47.4	10♋30.9	20♑11.1	13♈21.4	4♍16.3	18♋53.9
2 M	10 35 17	10 26 56	5♌53 57	13♌22 3	14R49.8	28 45.1	25 34.7	27R42.0	10R29.8	20 16.5	13 24.3	4R14.7	18R53.2
3 Tu	10 39 14	11 27 6	20 54 39	28 30 34	14 44.7	0♓28.2	26 42.4	27 37.4	10 28.8	20 21.8	13 27.4	4 13.0	18 52.5
4 W	10 43 10	12 27 14	6♍ 8 34	13♍47 20	14 40.3	2 12.2	27 50.2	27 33.6	10 28.1	20 27.1	13 30.4	4 11.4	18 51.8
5 Th	10 47 7	13 27 19	21 25 30	29 1 46	14 37.1	3 57.4	28 58.2	27 30.5	10 27.5	20 32.3	13 33.5	4 9.7	18 51.1
6 F	10 51 3	14 27 23	6♎34 56	14♎ 3 56	14D35.6	5 43.6	0♒ 6.4	27 28.2	10 27.1	20 37.4	13 36.5	4 8.1	18 50.4
7 Sa	10 55 0	15 27 25	21 27 52	28 46 2	14 35.5	7 30.9	1 14.6	27 26.7	10D27.0	20 42.5	13 39.6	4 6.4	18 49.8
8 Su	10 58 56	16 27 26	5♏57 55	13♏ 3 12	14 36.5	9 19.3	2 23.0	27D25.9	10 27.0	20 47.5	13 42.8	4 4.8	18 49.2
9 M	11 2 53	17 27 25	20 1 43	26 53 30	14 38.1	11 8.8	3 31.6	27 25.9	10 27.2	20 52.5	13 45.9	4 3.2	18 48.6
10 Tu	11 6 49	18 27 22	3♐38 41	10♐17 30	14 39.5	12 59.5	4 40.2	27 26.5	10 27.6	20 57.3	13 49.1	4 1.5	18 48.0
11 W	11 10 46	19 27 18	16 50 19	23 17 31	14R40.2	14 51.3	5 49.0	27 27.9	10 28.2	21 2.1	13 52.3	3 59.9	18 47.5
12 Th	11 14 43	20 27 12	29 39 32	5♑56 50	14 39.9	16 44.1	6 57.9	27 30.0	10 29.1	21 6.9	13 55.5	3 58.3	18 46.9
13 F	11 18 39	21 27 5	12♑ 9 55	18 19 16	14 38.4	18 38.1	8 6.9	27 32.8	10 30.1	21 11.5	13 58.7	3 56.7	18 46.4
14 Sa	11 22 36	22 26 55	24 25 19	0♒28 34	14 36.0	20 33.1	9 16.0	27 36.3	10 31.3	21 16.1	14 1.9	3 55.2	18 46.0
15 Su	11 26 32	23 26 44	6♒29 24	12 28 15	14 32.8	22 29.2	10 25.2	27 40.5	10 32.7	21 20.6	14 5.2	3 53.6	18 45.5
16 M	11 30 29	24 26 32	18 25 30	24 21 30	14 29.4	24 26.2	11 34.5	27 45.4	10 34.2	21 25.1	14 8.4	3 52.0	18 45.1
17 Tu	11 34 25	25 26 17	0♓16 34	6♓11 1	14 26.1	26 24.1	12 44.0	27 50.9	10 36.0	21 29.5	14 11.7	3 50.5	18 44.7
18 W	11 38 22	26 26 0	12 5 8	17 59 12	14 23.3	28 22.9	13 53.5	27 57.1	10 38.0	21 33.7	14 15.0	3 49.0	18 44.3
19 Th	11 42 18	27 25 42	23 53 27	29 48 10	14 21.3	0♈22.4	15 3.0	28 3.9	10 40.1	21 38.0	14 18.3	3 47.5	18 43.9
20 F	11 46 15	28 25 21	5♈43 36	11♈40 0	14D20.2	2 22.4	16 12.7	28 11.3	10 42.5	21 42.1	14 21.6	3 46.0	18 43.6
21 Sa	11 50 12	29 24 58	17 37 38	23 36 47	14 20.0	4 22.9	17 22.5	28 19.4	10 45.0	21 46.1	14 25.0	3 44.5	18 43.3
22 Su	11 54 8	0♈24 34	29 37 45	5♉40 50	14 20.6	6 23.7	18 32.3	28 28.0	10 47.7	21 50.1	14 28.3	3 43.0	18 43.0
23 M	11 58 5	1 24 7	11♉46 23	17 54 45	14 21.6	8 24.5	19 42.2	28 37.3	10 50.6	21 54.0	14 31.7	3 41.5	18 42.7
24 Tu	12 2 1	2 23 38	24 6 18	0♊21 26	14 22.7	10 25.1	20 52.2	28 47.2	10 53.7	21 57.8	14 35.1	3 40.1	18 42.5
25 W	12 5 58	3 23 7	6♊40 32	13 4 0	14 23.8	12 25.2	22 2.3	28 57.6	10 57.0	22 1.6	14 38.4	3 38.7	18 42.2
26 Th	12 9 54	4 22 33	19 32 14	26 5 34	14 24.6	14 24.6	23 12.4	29 8.6	11 0.5	22 5.2	14 41.8	3 37.3	18 42.0
27 F	12 13 51	5 21 58	2♋44 22	9♋28 54	14R24.9	16 22.7	24 22.6	29 20.1	11 4.1	22 8.8	14 45.2	3 35.9	18 41.9
28 Sa	12 17 47	6 21 20	16 19 22	23 15 53	14 24.8	18 19.4	25 32.8	29 32.2	11 7.9	22 12.3	14 48.6	3 34.6	18 41.7
29 Su	12 21 44	7 20 39	0♌18 27	7♌26 56	14 24.3	20 14.2	26 43.2	29 44.8	11 11.9	22 15.7	14 52.0	3 33.2	18 41.6
30 M	12 25 41	8 19 56	14 41 2	22 0 21	14 23.7	22 6.6	27 53.6	29 57.9	11 16.0	22 19.0	14 55.4	3 31.9	18 41.5
31 Tu	12 29 37	9 19 11	29 24 17	6♍52 3	14 23.1	23 56.4	29 4.0	0♌11.5	11 20.4	22 22.2	14 58.9	3 30.6	18 41.4

APRIL 1931 LONGITUDE

Day	Sid.Time	☉	0 hr ☽	Noon ☽	True ☊	☿	♀	♂	♃	♄	♅	♆	♇
1 W	12 33 34	10♈18 24	14♍22 47	21♍55 28	14♈22.6	25♈43.1	0♓14.5	0♌25.6	11♋24.9	22♑25.3	15♈ 2.3	3♍29.3	18♋41.4
2 Th	12 37 30	11 17 34	29 29 0	7♎ 2 15	14R22.3	27 26.2	1 25.1	0 40.1	11 29.5	22 28.4	15 5.7	3R28.1	18D41.4
3 F	12 41 27	12 16 42	14♎34 3	22 3 18	14D22.3	29 5.5	2 35.7	0 55.2	11 34.4	22 31.3	15 9.1	3 26.8	18 41.4
4 Sa	12 45 23	13 15 48	29 28 59	6♏50 10	14 22.3	0♉40.5	3 46.4	1 10.6	11 39.4	22 34.2	15 12.5	3 25.6	18 41.4
5 Su	12 49 20	14 14 53	14♏ 6 5	21 16 6	14R22.3	2 11.0	4 57.2	1 26.6	11 44.5	22 37.0	15 16.0	3 24.4	18 41.5
6 M	12 53 16	15 13 55	28 19 48	5♐16 52	14 22.3	3 36.6	6 8.0	1 42.9	11 49.8	22 39.7	15 19.4	3 23.3	18 41.5
7 Tu	12 57 13	16 12 56	12♐ 7 11	18 50 48	14 22.1	4 57.1	7 18.8	1 59.7	11 55.3	22 42.3	15 22.8	3 22.1	18 41.6
8 W	13 1 9	17 11 55	25 27 50	1♑58 35	14 21.9	6 12.2	8 29.8	2 16.9	12 1.0	22 44.8	15 26.3	3 21.0	18 41.8
9 Th	13 5 6	18 10 52	8♑23 24	14 42 43	14D21.7	7 21.7	9 40.7	2 34.5	12 6.8	22 47.3	15 29.7	3 19.9	18 41.9
10 F	13 9 3	19 9 47	20 57 0	27 6 49	14 21.7	8 25.5	10 51.8	2 52.5	12 12.7	22 49.6	15 33.1	3 18.8	18 42.1
11 Sa	13 12 59	20 8 41	3♒12 42	9♒15 12	14 21.8	9 23.3	12 2.8	3 10.9	12 18.8	22 51.8	15 36.6	3 17.8	18 42.3
12 Su	13 16 56	21 7 33	15 14 55	21 12 22	14 22.3	10 15.1	13 13.9	3 29.7	12 25.1	22 54.0	15 40.0	3 16.8	18 42.5
13 M	13 20 52	22 6 23	27 8 8	3♓ 2 42	14 23.0	11 0.7	14 25.1	3 48.9	12 31.5	22 56.0	15 43.4	3 15.8	18 42.8
14 Tu	13 24 49	23 5 11	8♓56 36	14 50 16	14 23.9	11 40.1	15 36.3	4 8.4	12 38.0	22 58.0	15 46.8	3 14.8	18 43.0
15 W	13 28 45	24 3 57	20 44 10	26 38 41	14 24.8	12 13.2	16 47.6	4 28.3	12 44.7	22 59.8	15 50.2	3 13.9	18 43.3
16 Th	13 32 42	25 2 42	2♈34 11	8♈31 1	14 25.5	12 39.9	17 58.8	4 48.6	12 51.6	23 1.6	15 53.6	3 13.0	18 43.6
17 F	13 36 38	26 1 25	14 29 30	20 29 53	14R25.8	13 0.4	19 10.2	5 9.2	12 58.6	23 3.3	15 57.0	3 12.1	18 44.0
18 Sa	13 40 35	27 0 6	26 32 25	2♉37 21	14 25.4	13 14.5	20 21.5	5 30.1	13 5.7	23 4.8	16 0.4	3 11.2	18 44.4
19 Su	13 44 32	27 58 44	8♉44 50	14 55 5	14 24.4	13R22.5	21 32.9	5 51.4	13 13.0	23 6.3	16 3.8	3 10.4	18 44.8
20 M	13 48 28	28 57 21	21 8 16	27 24 31	14 22.8	13 24.5	22 44.3	6 13.0	13 20.4	23 7.7	16 7.1	3 9.6	18 45.2
21 Tu	13 52 25	29 55 56	3♊43 59	10♊ 6 49	14 20.6	13 20.6	23 55.8	6 34.9	13 27.9	23 9.0	16 10.5	3 8.8	18 45.6
22 W	13 56 21	0♉54 29	16 33 9	23 3 6	14 18.3	13 11.0	25 7.3	6 57.1	13 35.6	23 10.1	16 13.9	3 8.1	18 46.1
23 Th	14 0 18	1 53 0	29 36 48	6♋14 23	14 16.0	12 56.2	26 18.8	7 19.7	13 43.4	23 11.2	16 17.2	3 7.4	18 46.6
24 F	14 4 14	2 51 29	12♋55 57	19 41 36	14 14.3	12 36.4	27 30.4	7 42.5	13 51.4	23 12.2	16 20.5	3 6.7	18 47.1
25 Sa	14 8 11	3 49 56	26 31 23	3♌25 22	14D13.4	12 12.1	28 41.9	8 5.6	13 59.4	23 13.1	16 23.9	3 6.1	18 47.6
26 Su	14 12 7	4 48 20	10♌23 32	17 25 48	14 13.3	11 43.8	29 53.6	8 29.0	14 7.6	23 13.9	16 27.2	3 5.4	18 48.2
27 M	14 16 4	5 46 42	24 32 2	1♍42 2	14 14.1	11 12.1	1♈ 5.2	8 52.7	14 15.9	23 14.6	16 30.4	3 4.9	18 48.8
28 Tu	14 20 1	6 45 2	8♍55 30	16 12 2	14 15.3	10 37.5	2 16.8	9 16.7	14 24.4	23 15.2	16 33.7	3 4.3	18 49.4
29 W	14 23 57	7 43 20	23 31 6	0♎52 8	14 16.6	10 0.8	3 28.5	9 40.9	14 32.9	23 15.7	16 37.0	3 3.8	18 50.0
30 Th	14 27 54	8 41 36	8♎14 26	15 37 12	14R17.5	9 22.6	4 40.2	10 5.4	14 41.6	23 16.1	16 40.2	3 3.3	18 50.6

Astro Data Dy Hr Mn	Planet Ingress Dy Hr Mn	Last Aspect Dy Hr Mn	☽ Ingress Dy Hr Mn	Last Aspect Dy Hr Mn	☽ Ingress Dy Hr Mn	☽ Phases & Eclipses Dy Hr Mn	Astro Data
☽0S 5 17:33	☿ ♓ 2 17:28	1 10:44 ♂ ☌	♌ 1 14:25	1 12:50 ♄ △	♎ 2 0:49	4 10:36 ○ 12♍54	1 MARCH 1931
♃ D 7 8:40	♀ ♒ 5 21:46	2 12:06 ♅ △	♍ 3 14:21	3 12:48 ♄ □	♏ 4 0:50	11 5:15 ☽ 19♐40	Julian Day # 11382
♂ D 8 13:52	☿ ♈ 18 19:31	5 12:52 ♀ △	♎ 5 13:32	5 14:19 ♄ ✶	♐ 6 2:52	19 7:51 ● 27♓45	Delta T 24.0 sec
☽0N 19 17:28	☉ ♈ 21 14:06	7 9:48 ♂ □	♏ 7 14:03	7 7:52 ☉ △	♑ 8 8:20	27 5:04 ☽ 5♋34	SVP 06♓13'19"
☿0N 19 23:02	♂ ♌ 30 3:48	9 12:58 ♂ △	♐ 9 17:30	10 3:39 ♄ ☌	♒ 10 17:40		Obliquity 23°27'03"
♆∠♇ 22 0:47	♀ ♓ 31 19:04	11 5:15 ☉ □	♑ 12 0:39	12 12:54 ☉ ✶	♓ 13 5:49	2 20:05 ○ 12♎07	⚷ Chiron 14♉40.2
		14 6:20 ♂ ☍	♒ 14 11:03	15 4:36 ♄ ✶	♈ 15 18:48	2 20:08 ☍ T 1.502	☽ Mean ☊ 16♈29.2
☽0S 2 4:49	☿ ♉ 3 13:38	15 15:19 ♅ ✶	♓ 16 23:26	18 1:00 ☉ ☌	♉ 18 6:50	9 20:15 ☽ 19♑01	
♇ D 2 11:24	☉ ♉ 21 1:40	19 8:34 ♂ △	♈ 19 12:24	20 3:50 ♄ △	♊ 20 16:56	18 1:00 ● 27♈03	1 APRIL 1931
☽0N 15 23:54	♀ ♈ 26 2:10	21 21:40 ♂ □	♉ 22 0:44	22 17:23 ♀ □	♋ 23 0:42	18 0:45:09 ✓ P 0.511	Julian Day # 11413
☿ R 19 19:51		24 9:07 ♂ ✶	♊ 24 11:19	25 4:09 ♀ △	♌ 25 6:04	25 13:40 ☽ 4♌23	Delta T 24.0 sec
☽0S 29 14:38		26 7:24 ♀ △	♋ 26 19:04	26 10:23 ♅ △	♍ 27 9:10		SVP 06♓13'16"
♀0N 29 4:15		28 23:02 ♂ ☌	♌ 28 23:29	28 23:35 ♄ △	♎ 29 10:35		Obliquity 23°27'03"
		30 23:24 ♀ ☍	♍ 31 0:58				⚷ Chiron 16♉09.2
							☽ Mean ☊ 14♈50.7

LONGITUDE — MAY 1931

Day	Sid.Time	☉	0 hr ☽	Noon ☽	True ☊	☿	♀	♂	♃	♄	♅	♆	♇
1 F	14 31 50	9♉39 50	22♎59 38	0♏20 50	14♈17.4	8♉43.6	5♈52.0	10♌30.1	14♋50.4	23♑16.4	16♈43.5	3♍ 2.8	18♋51.3
2 Sa	14 35 47	10 38 2	7♏39 57	14 56 7	14R 16.0	8R 4.6	7 3.7	10 55.1	14 59.3	23 16.6	16 46.7	3R 2.4	18 52.0
3 Su	14 39 43	11 36 13	22 8 32	29 16 29	14 13.3	7 26.2	8 15.5	11 20.3	15 8.3	23R 16.7	16 49.9	3 2.0	18 52.7
4 M	14 43 40	12 34 21	6♐19 22	13♐16 41	14 9.5	6 49.1	9 27.3	11 45.7	15 17.5	23 16.7	16 53.0	3 1.6	18 53.5
5 Tu	14 47 36	13 32 29	20 8 6	26 53 23	14 5.1	6 14.0	10 39.2	12 11.4	15 26.7	23 16.6	16 56.2	3 1.3	18 54.2
6 W	14 51 33	14 30 34	3♑32 29	10♑ 5 27	14 0.7	5 41.3	11 51.1	12 37.3	15 36.1	23 16.4	16 59.4	3 0.9	18 55.0
7 Th	14 55 30	15 28 39	16 32 28	22 53 50	13 56.9	5 11.7	13 3.0	13 3.4	15 45.5	23 16.1	17 2.5	3 0.7	18 55.8
8 F	14 59 26	16 26 42	29 9 56	5♒21 13	13 54.2	4 45.4	14 14.9	13 29.8	15 55.1	23 15.8	17 5.6	3 0.4	18 56.6
9 Sa	15 3 23	17 24 43	11♒28 14	17 31 31	13D 52.8	4 22.9	15 26.9	13 56.3	16 4.8	23 15.3	17 8.7	3 0.2	18 57.5
10 Su	15 7 19	18 22 43	23 31 42	29 29 24	13 52.7	4 4.5	16 38.9	14 23.1	16 14.5	23 14.7	17 11.7	3 0.0	18 58.3
11 M	15 11 16	19 20 42	5♓25 14	11♓19 51	13 53.7	3 50.4	17 50.9	14 50.1	16 24.4	23 14.0	17 14.8	2 59.9	18 59.2
12 Tu	15 15 12	20 18 39	17 13 52	23 7 53	13 55.4	3 40.7	19 2.9	15 17.2	16 34.4	23 13.3	17 17.8	2 59.8	19 0.1
13 W	15 19 9	21 16 35	29 2 29	4♈58 12	13 57.0	3D 35.6	20 14.9	15 44.6	16 44.4	23 12.4	17 20.8	2 59.7	19 1.1
14 Th	15 23 5	22 14 30	10♈55 34	16 55 2	13R 57.9	3 35.2	21 27.0	16 12.2	16 54.6	23 11.4	17 23.7	2 59.6	19 2.0
15 F	15 27 2	23 12 23	22 57 0	29 1 52	13 57.5	3 39.3	22 39.1	16 40.0	17 4.8	23 10.4	17 26.7	2D 59.6	19 3.0
16 Sa	15 30 59	24 10 15	5♉ 9 55	11♉21 24	13 55.4	3 48.0	23 51.2	17 8.0	17 15.2	23 9.2	17 29.6	2 59.6	19 3.9
17 Su	15 34 55	25 8 6	17 36 30	23 55 20	13 51.4	4 1.3	25 3.3	17 36.1	17 25.6	23 8.0	17 32.5	2 59.7	19 5.0
18 M	15 38 52	26 5 55	0♊17 57	6♊44 22	13 45.6	4 19.1	26 15.5	18 4.5	17 36.1	23 6.6	17 35.3	2 59.8	19 6.0
19 Tu	15 42 48	27 3 43	13 14 32	19 48 20	13 38.7	4 41.3	27 27.7	18 33.0	17 46.8	23 5.2	17 38.2	2 59.9	19 7.0
20 W	15 46 45	28 1 30	26 25 40	3♋ 6 20	13 31.1	5 7.7	28 39.9	19 1.7	17 57.5	23 3.7	17 41.0	3 0.0	19 8.1
21 Th	15 50 41	28 59 15	9♋50 11	16 37 0	13 24.0	5 38.3	29 52.1	19 30.6	18 8.2	23 2.1	17 43.8	3 0.2	19 9.2
22 F	15 54 38	29 56 59	23 26 36	0♌18 49	13 17.9	6 13.0	1♉ 4.3	19 59.7	18 19.1	23 0.4	17 46.5	3 0.4	19 10.3
23 Sa	15 58 35	0♊54 41	7♌13 26	14 10 20	13 13.6	6 51.6	2 16.5	20 28.9	18 30.1	22 58.6	17 49.3	3 0.7	19 11.4
24 Su	16 2 31	1 52 21	21 9 21	28 10 21	13D 11.3	7 34.0	3 28.8	20 58.3	18 41.1	22 56.7	17 52.0	3 1.0	19 12.5
25 M	16 6 28	2 50 0	5♍13 12	12♍17 44	13 10.8	8 20.1	4 41.0	21 27.8	18 52.2	22 54.7	17 54.6	3 1.3	19 13.6
26 Tu	16 10 24	3 47 37	19 23 49	26 31 15	13 11.5	9 9.7	5 53.3	21 57.5	19 3.4	22 52.7	17 57.3	3 1.6	19 14.8
27 W	16 14 21	4 45 12	3♎39 47	10♎49 10	13R 12.5	10 2.9	7 5.6	22 27.4	19 14.6	22 50.5	17 59.9	3 2.0	19 16.0
28 Th	16 18 17	5 42 47	17 59 2	25 9 0	13 12.7	10 59.5	8 17.9	22 57.4	19 25.9	22 48.3	18 2.4	3 2.4	19 17.2
29 F	16 22 14	6 40 19	2♏18 36	9♏27 18	13 11.2	11 59.3	9 30.2	23 27.5	19 37.3	22 46.0	18 5.0	3 2.8	19 18.4
30 Sa	16 26 10	7 37 51	16 34 33	23 39 45	13 7.5	13 2.4	10 42.6	23 57.8	19 48.8	22 43.6	18 7.5	3 3.3	19 19.6
31 Su	16 30 7	8 35 21	0♐42 18	7♐41 38	13 1.4	14 8.6	11 54.9	24 28.3	20 0.3	22 41.1	18 9.9	3 3.8	19 20.9

LONGITUDE — JUNE 1931

Day	Sid.Time	☉	0 hr ☽	Noon ☽	True ☊	☿	♀	♂	♃	♄	♅	♆	♇
1 M	16 34 4	9♊32 51	14♐37 11	21♐28 28	12♈53.3	15♉17.9	13♉ 7.3	24♌58.9	20♋11.9	22♑38.6	18♈12.4	3♍ 4.4	19♋22.1
2 Tu	16 38 0	10 30 19	28 15 4	4♑56 42	12R 44.0	16 30.1	14 19.7	25 29.6	20 23.6	22R 35.9	18 14.8	3 4.9	19 23.4
3 W	16 41 57	11 27 46	11♑33 8	18 4 18	12 34.3	17 45.4	15 32.2	26 0.4	20 35.3	22 33.2	18 17.2	3 5.5	19 24.7
4 Th	16 45 53	12 25 13	24 30 12	0♒50 59	12 25.5	19 3.5	16 44.6	26 31.4	20 47.1	22 30.5	18 19.5	3 6.2	19 26.0
5 F	16 49 50	13 22 39	7♒ 6 53	13 18 13	12 18.2	20 24.5	17 57.1	27 2.6	20 59.0	22 27.6	18 21.8	3 6.8	19 27.3
6 Sa	16 53 46	14 20 4	19 25 25	25 28 59	12 13.0	21 48.3	19 9.5	27 33.8	21 10.9	22 24.7	18 24.1	3 7.5	19 28.6
7 Su	16 57 43	15 17 28	1♓29 26	7♓27 23	12 10.0	23 15.0	20 22.0	28 5.2	21 22.9	22 21.6	18 26.3	3 8.2	19 30.0
8 M	17 1 39	16 14 52	13 23 27	19 18 19	12D 8.9	24 44.4	21 34.6	28 36.7	21 34.9	22 18.6	18 28.5	3 9.0	19 31.3
9 Tu	17 5 36	17 12 15	25 12 38	1♈ 7 5	12 9.1	26 16.6	22 47.1	29 8.4	21 47.0	22 15.4	18 30.6	3 9.8	19 32.7
10 W	17 9 33	18 9 37	7♈ 2 19	12 59 1	12R 9.6	27 51.5	23 59.7	29 40.1	21 59.1	22 12.2	18 32.7	3 10.6	19 34.0
11 Th	17 13 29	19 6 59	18 57 48	24 59 15	12 9.5	29 29.2	25 12.3	0♍12.0	22 11.3	22 8.9	18 34.8	3 11.5	19 35.4
12 F	17 17 26	20 4 21	1♉ 3 55	7♉12 18	12 7.8	1♊ 9.5	26 24.9	0 44.0	22 23.6	22 5.5	18 36.8	3 12.3	19 36.8
13 Sa	17 21 22	21 1 42	13 24 49	19 41 47	12 3.9	2 52.6	27 37.5	1 16.2	22 35.9	22 2.1	18 38.8	3 13.2	19 38.2
14 Su	17 25 19	21 59 2	26 3 29	2♊30 3	11 57.5	4 38.3	28 50.1	1 48.4	22 48.3	21 58.6	18 40.8	3 14.2	19 39.7
15 M	17 29 15	22 56 22	9♊ 1 33	15 37 55	11 48.6	6 26.6	0♊ 2.8	2 20.8	23 0.7	21 55.1	18 42.7	3 15.2	19 41.1
16 Tu	17 33 12	23 53 42	22 19 1	29 4 34	11 38.0	8 17.5	1 15.5	2 53.3	23 13.1	21 51.5	18 44.6	3 16.2	19 42.5
17 W	17 37 8	24 51 1	5♋54 14	12♋47 35	11 26.6	10 11.0	2 28.2	3 26.0	23 25.6	21 47.8	18 46.4	3 17.2	19 44.0
18 Th	17 41 5	25 48 19	19 44 9	26 43 25	11 15.6	12 6.9	3 40.9	3 58.7	23 38.2	21 44.1	18 48.2	3 18.2	19 45.5
19 F	17 45 2	26 45 37	3♌44 52	10♌47 59	11 6.0	14 5.1	4 53.7	4 31.5	23 50.7	21 40.4	18 50.0	3 19.3	19 46.9
20 Sa	17 48 58	27 42 53	17 52 16	24 57 17	10 58.8	16 5.5	6 6.4	5 4.5	24 3.4	21 36.5	18 51.7	3 20.4	19 48.4
21 Su	17 52 55	28 40 10	2♍ 2 39	9♍ 8 2	10 54.3	18 8.0	7 19.2	5 37.6	24 16.0	21 32.7	18 53.4	3 21.6	19 49.9
22 M	17 56 51	29 37 25	16 13 11	23 17 54	10 52.2	20 12.5	8 32.0	6 10.7	24 28.7	21 28.8	18 55.0	3 22.8	19 51.4
23 Tu	18 0 48	0♋34 40	0♎22 0	7♎25 22	10 51.7	22 18.6	9 44.8	6 44.0	24 41.5	21 24.8	18 56.6	3 24.0	19 52.9
24 W	18 4 44	1 31 53	14 27 53	21 29 28	10 51.8	24 26.2	10 57.6	7 17.4	24 54.3	21 20.8	18 58.1	3 25.2	19 54.4
25 Th	18 8 41	2 29 7	28 30 0	5♏29 21	10 51.0	26 35.1	12 10.4	7 50.9	25 7.1	21 16.7	18 59.6	3 26.4	19 55.9
26 F	18 12 37	3 26 19	12♏27 20	19 23 45	10 48.3	28 44.9	13 23.3	8 24.5	25 19.9	21 12.7	19 1.0	3 27.7	19 57.5
27 Sa	18 16 34	4 23 32	26 18 23	3♐10 55	10 43.0	0♋55.5	14 36.2	8 58.2	25 32.8	21 8.5	19 2.4	3 29.0	19 59.0
28 Su	18 20 31	5 20 44	10♐ 1 4	16 48 29	10 34.9	3 6.4	15 49.1	9 32.0	25 45.7	21 4.4	19 3.8	3 30.4	20 0.5
29 M	18 24 27	6 17 55	23 32 52	0♑13 53	10 24.4	5 17.5	17 2.0	10 5.8	25 58.7	21 0.2	19 5.1	3 31.7	20 2.1
30 Tu	18 28 24	7 15 7	6♑51 15	13 24 43	10 12.3	7 28.5	18 14.9	10 39.8	26 11.6	20 56.0	19 6.4	3 33.1	20 3.6

Astro Data Dy Hr Mn	Planet Ingress Dy Hr Mn	Last Aspect Dy Hr Mn	☽ Ingress Dy Hr Mn	Last Aspect Dy Hr Mn	☽ Ingress Dy Hr Mn	☽ Phases & Eclipses Dy Hr Mn	Astro Data
♄ R 3 14:28	♀ ♉ 21 2:38	1 0:27 ♄ □	♏ 1 11:26	1 18:54 ♂ △	♑ 2 3:07	2 5:14 ○ 10♏51	1 MAY 1931
☽0N 13 6:49	☉ ♊ 22 1:15	3 1:54 ♄ ✶	♐ 3 13:14	3 20:16 ♄ ☌	♒ 4 10:23	9 12:48 ☽ 17♒56	Julian Day # 11443
☿ D 13 14:32		4 18:22 ♅ △	♑ 5 17:35	6 16:53 ♂ ☍	♓ 6 21:01	17 15:28 ● 25♉45	Delta T 24.0 sec
♆ D 15 1:10	♂ ♍ 10 14:58	7 12:42 ♄ ☌	♒ 8 1:37	9 2:30 ☿ ✶	♈ 9 9:44	24 19:39 ☽ 2♍40	SVP 06♓13'12"
♃□♅ 17 21:31	☿ ♊ 11 7:27	9 12:48 ☉ □	♓ 10 13:02	11 6:33 ♃ □	♉ 11 21:54	31 14:33 ○ 9♐10	Obliquity 23°27'03"
♃∠♆ 20 5:50	♀ ♊ 14 23:04	12 12:10 ♄ ✶	♈ 13 1:57	14 5:44 ♀ ☌	♊ 14 7:22		⚷ Chiron 18♉03.9
☽0S 26 21:38	☉ ♋ 22 9:28	15 0:26 ♄ □	♉ 15 13:54	16 3:02 ☉ ☌	♋ 16 13:38		☽ Mean ☊ 13♈15.4
♃☌♇ 27 3:13	☿ ♋ 26 13:49	17 15:28 ☉ ☌	♊ 17 23:26	18 6:48 ♃ ☌	♌ 18 17:36	8 6:18 ☽ 16♓30	
♅♇♆ 27 23:39		20 4:26 ♀ ✶	♋ 20 6:26	20 17:53 ☉ ✶	♍ 20 20:32	16 3:02 ● 24♊01	1 JUNE 1931
		21 23:14 ♄ ☍	♌ 22 11:27	22 14:13 ♃ ✶	♎ 22 23:23	23 0:23 ☽ 0♎36	Julian Day # 11474
☽0N 9 13:55		23 23:40 ♂ ☌	♍ 24 15:07	24 20:07 ☿ △	♏ 25 2:34	30 0:47 ○ 7♑17	Delta T 23.9 sec
♃☍♄ 10 20:13		26 5:51 ♄ △	♎ 26 17:51	26 22:39 ♃ △	♐ 27 6:26		SVP 06♓13'07"
☽0S 23 2:29		28 8:38 ♂ ✶	♏ 28 20:08	28 16:02 ♅ △	♑ 29 11:35		Obliquity 23°27'02"
		30 12:59 ♂ □	♐ 30 22:48				⚷ Chiron 20♉09.7
							☽ Mean ☊ 11♈36.9

JULY 1931 LONGITUDE

Day	Sid.Time	☉	0 hr ☽	Noon ☽	True ☊	☿	♀	♂	♃	♄	♅	♆	♇
1 W	18 32 20	8♋12 18	19♑54 7	26♑19 18	9♈59.8	9♋39.0	19♊27.9	11♍13.9	26♋24.6	20♑51.7	19♈ 7.6	3♍34.5	20♋ 5.2
2 Th	18 36 17	9 9 29	2♒40 15	8♒57 2	9R 48.0	11 48.9	20 40.9	11 48.1	26 37.7	20R 47.4	19 8.8	3 36.0	20 6.8
3 F	18 40 13	10 6 40	15 9 45	21 18 37	9 37.9	13 57.9	21 53.9	12 22.3	26 50.7	20 43.1	19 9.9	3 37.4	20 8.3
4 Sa	18 44 10	11 3 51	27 23 57	3♓26 8	9 30.2	16 5.9	23 6.9	12 56.7	27 3.8	20 38.8	19 11.0	3 38.9	20 9.9
5 Su	18 48 7	12 1 2	9♓25 34	15 22 48	9 25.2	18 12.5	24 20.0	13 31.1	27 16.9	20 34.5	19 12.0	3 40.4	20 11.5
6 M	18 52 3	12 58 14	21 18 21	27 12 51	9 22.6	20 17.8	25 33.1	14 5.7	27 30.0	20 30.1	19 13.0	3 41.9	20 13.0
7 Tu	18 56 0	13 55 25	3♈ 6 56	9♈ 1 14	9 21.7	22 21.6	26 46.2	14 40.3	27 43.2	20 25.7	19 14.0	3 43.5	20 14.6
8 W	18 59 56	14 52 37	14 56 29	20 53 19	9 21.7	24 23.7	27 59.3	15 15.0	27 56.3	20 21.3	19 14.9	3 45.1	20 16.2
9 Th	19 3 53	15 49 50	26 52 28	2♉54 34	9 21.4	26 24.2	29 12.5	15 49.8	28 9.5	20 16.9	19 15.7	3 46.7	20 17.8
10 F	19 7 49	16 47 3	9♉ 0 16	15 10 10	9 19.8	28 22.8	0♋25.7	16 24.7	28 22.7	20 12.5	19 16.5	3 48.3	20 19.4
11 Sa	19 11 46	17 44 16	21 24 50	27 44 41	9 16.1	0♌19.7	1 38.9	16 59.7	28 36.0	20 8.0	19 17.3	3 49.9	20 20.9
12 Su	19 15 42	18 41 30	4♊10 9	10♊41 28	9 10.0	2 14.7	2 52.1	17 34.8	28 49.2	20 3.6	19 18.0	3 51.6	20 22.5
13 M	19 19 39	19 38 44	17 18 47	24 2 8	9 1.4	4 7.9	4 5.4	18 10.0	29 2.5	19 59.1	19 18.6	3 53.3	20 24.1
14 Tu	19 23 36	20 35 59	0♋51 21	7♋46 12	8 50.9	5 59.2	5 18.7	18 45.3	29 15.7	19 54.7	19 19.2	3 55.0	20 25.7
15 W	19 27 32	21 33 14	14 46 13	21 50 52	8 39.6	7 48.6	6 32.0	19 20.6	29 29.0	19 50.3	19 19.8	3 56.7	20 27.3
16 Th	19 31 29	22 30 30	28 59 28	6♌11 17	8 28.5	9 36.1	7 45.3	19 56.1	29 42.3	19 45.8	19 20.3	3 58.5	20 28.9
17 F	19 35 25	23 27 45	13♌25 28	20 41 13	8 18.9	11 21.8	8 58.7	20 31.6	29 55.6	19 41.4	19 20.8	4 0.3	20 30.5
18 Sa	19 39 22	24 25 1	27 57 43	5♍14 11	8 11.6	13 5.5	10 12.1	21 7.3	0♌ 9.0	19 37.0	19 21.2	4 2.1	20 32.1
19 Su	19 43 18	25 22 18	12♍29 55	19 44 19	8 7.0	14 47.4	11 25.5	21 43.0	0 22.3	19 32.6	19 21.6	4 3.9	20 33.7
20 M	19 47 15	26 19 34	26 56 52	4♎ 7 12	8D 4.9	16 27.4	12 38.9	22 18.8	0 35.6	19 28.2	19 21.9	4 5.7	20 35.2
21 Tu	19 51 11	27 16 50	11♎15 1	18 20 5	8 4.6	18 5.5	13 52.3	22 54.6	0 48.9	19 23.8	19 22.1	4 7.5	20 36.8
22 W	19 55 8	28 14 7	25 22 19	2♏21 37	8R 4.9	19 41.7	15 5.8	23 30.6	1 2.3	19 19.4	19 22.4	4 9.4	20 38.4
23 Th	19 59 5	29 11 24	9♏17 59	16 11 26	8 4.5	21 16.0	16 19.3	24 6.6	1 15.6	19 15.1	19 22.5	4 11.3	20 40.0
24 F	20 3 1	0♌ 8 42	23 1 57	29 49 35	8 2.5	22 48.5	17 32.8	24 42.7	1 29.0	19 10.7	19 22.7	4 13.2	20 41.5
25 Sa	20 6 58	1 6 0	6♐34 20	13♐16 11	7 58.1	24 19.1	18 46.4	25 18.9	1 42.3	19 6.4	19 22.7	4 15.1	20 43.1
26 Su	20 10 54	2 3 18	19 55 7	26 31 4	7 51.3	25 47.7	19 59.9	25 55.2	1 55.6	19 2.2	19R 22.8	4 17.0	20 44.7
27 M	20 14 51	3 0 37	3♑ 4 1	9♑33 51	7 42.2	27 14.5	21 13.5	26 31.6	2 9.0	18 57.9	19 22.7	4 19.0	20 46.2
28 Tu	20 18 47	3 57 56	16 0 32	22 24 0	7 31.7	28 39.2	22 27.1	27 8.0	2 22.3	18 53.7	19 22.7	4 21.0	20 47.8
29 W	20 22 44	4 55 16	28 44 12	5♒ 1 7	7 20.7	0♍ 2.0	23 40.7	27 44.5	2 35.6	18 49.5	19 22.5	4 22.9	20 49.4
30 Th	20 26 40	5 52 36	11♒14 46	17 25 14	7 10.4	1 22.8	24 54.4	28 21.1	2 49.0	18 45.4	19 22.4	4 24.9	20 50.9
31 F	20 30 37	6 49 58	23 32 37	29 37 5	7 1.6	2 41.5	26 8.1	28 57.8	3 2.3	18 41.3	19 22.2	4 26.9	20 52.4

AUGUST 1931 LONGITUDE

Day	Sid.Time	☉	0 hr ☽	Noon ☽	True ☊	☿	♀	♂	♃	♄	♅	♆	♇
1 Sa	20 34 34	7♌47 20	5♓38 52	11♓38 15	6♈54.9	3♍58.1	27♋21.8	29♍34.5	3♌15.6	18♑37.2	19♈21.9	4♍29.0	20♋54.0
2 Su	20 38 30	8 44 43	17 35 33	23 31 11	6R 50.7	5 12.6	28 35.5	0♎11.3	3 28.9	18R 33.2	19R 21.6	4 31.0	20 55.5
3 M	20 42 27	9 42 7	29 25 35	5♈19 15	6D 48.7	6 24.9	29 49.3	0 48.2	3 42.2	18 29.2	19 21.2	4 33.0	20 57.0
4 Tu	20 46 23	10 39 33	11♈12 44	17 6 36	6 48.5	7 34.8	1♌ 3.1	1 25.2	3 55.5	18 25.2	19 20.8	4 35.1	20 58.5
5 W	20 50 20	11 36 59	23 1 27	28 57 58	6 49.3	8 42.4	2 16.9	2 2.2	4 8.8	18 21.3	19 20.3	4 37.2	21 0.0
6 Th	20 54 16	12 34 27	4♉56 45	10♉58 30	6R 50.3	9 47.6	3 30.7	2 39.3	4 22.0	18 17.4	19 19.8	4 39.3	21 1.5
7 F	20 58 13	13 31 56	17 3 51	23 13 28	6 50.5	10 50.2	4 44.6	3 16.6	4 35.3	18 13.6	19 19.3	4 41.3	21 3.0
8 Sa	21 2 9	14 29 26	29 27 56	5♊47 49	6 49.2	11 50.1	5 58.5	3 53.8	4 48.5	18 9.9	19 18.7	4 43.5	21 4.5
9 Su	21 6 6	15 26 58	12♊13 38	18 45 45	6 46.1	12 47.3	7 12.4	4 31.2	5 1.8	18 6.2	19 18.0	4 45.6	21 6.0
10 M	21 10 3	16 24 31	25 24 29	2♋ 9 59	6 41.0	13 41.6	8 26.3	5 8.6	5 15.0	18 2.5	19 17.3	4 47.7	21 7.5
11 Tu	21 13 59	17 22 6	9♋ 2 17	16 1 12	6 34.4	14 32.8	9 40.3	5 46.1	5 28.2	17 59.0	19 16.6	4 49.8	21 8.9
12 W	21 17 56	18 19 42	23 6 27	0♌17 29	6 26.9	15 20.8	10 54.3	6 23.7	5 41.3	17 55.4	19 15.8	4 52.0	21 10.4
13 Th	21 21 52	19 17 19	7♌33 41	14 54 12	6 19.4	16 5.4	12 8.3	7 1.4	5 54.5	17 52.0	19 15.0	4 54.1	21 11.8
14 F	21 25 49	20 14 57	22 18 7	29 44 24	6 13.0	16 46.5	13 22.4	7 39.2	6 7.6	17 48.6	19 14.1	4 56.3	21 13.2
15 Sa	21 29 45	21 12 37	7♍12 0	14♍39 51	6 8.3	17 23.8	14 36.5	8 17.0	6 20.7	17 45.2	19 13.2	4 58.5	21 14.6
16 Su	21 33 42	22 10 17	22 6 56	29 32 19	6D 5.6	17 57.1	15 50.6	8 54.9	6 33.8	17 42.0	19 12.2	5 0.6	21 16.1
17 M	21 37 38	23 7 59	6♎55 11	14♎14 50	6 4.9	18 26.2	17 4.7	9 32.8	6 46.8	17 38.8	19 11.2	5 2.8	21 17.4
18 Tu	21 41 35	24 5 42	21 30 41	28 42 20	6 5.5	18 51.0	18 18.8	10 10.9	6 59.9	17 35.6	19 10.1	5 5.0	21 18.8
19 W	21 45 32	25 3 25	5♏49 29	12♏51 57	6 6.8	19 11.1	19 32.9	10 49.0	7 12.9	17 32.6	19 9.0	5 7.2	21 20.2
20 Th	21 49 28	26 1 10	19 49 41	26 42 40	6R 7.8	19 26.3	20 47.1	11 27.2	7 25.8	17 29.6	19 7.9	5 9.4	21 21.5
21 F	21 53 25	26 58 56	3♐31 1	10♐14 51	6 7.7	19 36.3	22 1.3	12 5.5	7 38.8	17 26.7	19 6.7	5 11.6	21 22.9
22 Sa	21 57 21	27 56 44	16 54 19	23 29 38	6 6.2	19R 41.1	23 15.5	12 43.8	7 51.7	17 23.8	19 5.5	5 13.8	21 24.2
23 Su	22 1 18	28 54 32	0♑ 0 58	6♑28 32	6 2.9	19 40.3	24 29.7	13 22.2	8 4.5	17 21.1	19 4.2	5 16.0	21 25.5
24 M	22 5 14	29 52 21	12 52 31	19 13 7	5 58.2	19 33.7	25 44.0	14 0.7	8 17.4	17 18.4	19 2.9	5 18.3	21 26.8
25 Tu	22 9 11	0♍50 12	25 30 30	1♒44 51	5 52.6	19 21.3	26 58.3	14 39.2	8 30.2	17 15.8	19 1.5	5 20.5	21 28.1
26 W	22 13 7	1 48 4	7♒56 19	14 5 4	5 46.6	19 2.9	28 12.5	15 17.8	8 42.9	17 13.2	19 0.2	5 22.7	21 29.4
27 Th	22 17 4	2 45 58	20 11 16	26 15 5	5 40.9	18 38.6	29 26.9	15 56.5	8 55.7	17 10.8	18 58.7	5 24.9	21 30.7
28 F	22 21 1	3 43 53	2♓16 43	8♓16 21	5 36.2	18 8.4	0♍41.2	16 35.3	9 8.3	17 8.4	18 57.2	5 27.1	21 31.9
29 Sa	22 24 57	4 41 49	14 14 12	20 10 32	5 32.9	17 32.6	1 55.5	17 14.1	9 21.0	17 6.2	18 55.7	5 29.4	21 33.1
30 Su	22 28 54	5 39 47	26 5 36	1♈59 44	5D 31.0	16 51.4	3 9.9	17 53.0	9 33.6	17 4.0	18 54.2	5 31.6	21 34.3
31 M	22 32 50	6 37 47	7♈53 15	13 46 33	5 30.6	16 5.3	4 24.3	18 32.0	9 46.1	17 1.9	18 52.6	5 33.8	21 35.5

Astro Data	Dy Hr Mn
☽0N	6 20:53
♄☍♇	8 20:27
☽0S	20 7:23
♄□♅	21 8:29
♄⚻♆	23 14:31
♅ R	26 0:36
♅⚻♆	28 19:28
☽0N	3 3:32
♂0S	3 9:52
♃⊻♆	7 13:02
☽0S	16 14:27
☿ R	22 8:33
☽0N	30 9:54

Planet Ingress	Dy Hr Mn
♀ ♋	9 15:35
☿ ♌	10 19:56
♃ ♌	17 7:52
☉ ♌	23 20:21
☿ ♍	28 23:24
♂ ♎	1 16:38
♀ ♌	3 3:29
☉ ♍	24 3:10
♀ ♍	27 10:42

Last Aspect Dy Hr Mn		☽ Ingress Dy Hr Mn
1 12:23	♃ ☍	♒ 1 18:56
3 14:37	♀ △	♓ 4 5:09
6 12:49	♃ △	♈ 6 17:40
9 5:11	♀ ⚹	♉ 9 6:14
11 13:51	♃ ⚹	♊ 11 16:14
13 3:35	♅ ⚹	♋ 13 22:30
16 1:13	♃ ☌	♌ 16 1:41
17 9:48	♅ △	♍ 18 3:22
19 22:53	☉ ⚹	♎ 20 5:06
22 5:16	☉ □	♏ 22 7:56
24 3:06	♂ ⚹	♐ 24 12:18
26 12:01	☿ △	♑ 26 18:22
28 22:01	♂ △	♒ 29 2:24
30 15:49	♅ ⚹	♓ 31 12:45

Last Aspect Dy Hr Mn		☽ Ingress Dy Hr Mn
3 0:54	♀ △	♈ 3 1:10
4 19:53	♇ □	♉ 5 14:05
7 7:48	♇ ⚹	♊ 8 1:01
9 12:58	♅ ⚹	♋ 10 8:11
11 20:44	♇ ☌	♌ 12 11:31
13 20:27	☉ ☌	♍ 14 12:25
15 22:38	♇ ⚹	♎ 16 12:45
18 4:36	☉ ⚹	♏ 18 14:10
20 11:36	☉ □	♐ 20 17:47
22 21:47	☉ △	♑ 22 23:58
24 16:16	♇ ☍	♒ 25 8:38
26 21:37	♅ ⚹	♓ 27 19:27
29 14:49	♇ △	♈ 30 7:56

☽ Phases & Eclipses Dy Hr Mn	
7 23:52	☽ 14♈52
15 12:20	● 22♋03
22 5:16	☽ 28♎27
29 12:47	○ 5♒26
6 16:28	☽ 13♉14
13 20:27	● 20♌06
20 11:36	☽ 26♏29
28 3:09	○ 3♓51

Astro Data

1 JULY 1931
Julian Day # 11504
Delta T 23.9 sec
SVP 06♓13'01"
Obliquity 23°27'02"
⚷ Chiron 21♉57.3
☽ Mean ☊ 10♈01.6

1 AUGUST 1931
Julian Day # 11535
Delta T 23.9 sec
SVP 06♓12'56"
Obliquity 23°27'02"
⚷ Chiron 23♉13.5
☽ Mean ☊ 8♈23.2

LONGITUDE — SEPTEMBER 1931

Day	Sid.Time	☉	0 hr ☽	Noon ☽	True ☊	☿	♀	♂	♃	♄	♅	♆	♇
1 Tu	22 36 47	7♍35 48	19♈40 2	25♈34 10	5♈31.4	15♍15.0	5♍38.7	19♎11.0	9♌58.7	16♑59.8	18♈51.0	5♍36.0	21♋36.7
2 W	22 40 43	8 33 51	1♉29 25	7♉26 18	5 32.9	14R 21.2	6 53.1	19 50.1	10 11.1	16R 57.9	18R 49.3	5 38.3	21 37.9
3 Th	22 44 40	9 31 56	13 25 22	19 27 9	5 34.7	13 24.8	8 7.5	20 29.3	10 23.6	16 56.1	18 47.6	5 40.5	21 39.0
4 F	22 48 36	10 30 3	25 32 16	1♊41 17	5 36.1	12 27.0	9 22.0	21 8.5	10 35.9	16 54.3	18 45.9	5 42.7	21 40.2
5 Sa	22 52 33	11 28 13	7♊54 46	14 13 17	5R 36.9	11 28.9	10 36.5	21 47.9	10 48.3	16 52.6	18 44.1	5 44.9	21 41.3
6 Su	22 56 30	12 26 24	20 37 21	27 7 27	5 36.7	10 31.8	11 51.0	22 27.3	11 0.5	16 51.1	18 42.3	5 47.1	21 42.4
7 M	23 0 26	13 24 37	3♋43 58	10♋27 14	5 35.5	9 37.0	13 5.5	23 6.7	11 12.8	16 49.6	18 40.5	5 49.4	21 43.5
8 Tu	23 4 23	14 22 52	17 17 24	24 14 33	5 33.4	8 45.7	14 20.0	23 46.3	11 24.9	16 48.2	18 38.7	5 51.6	21 44.5
9 W	23 8 19	15 21 10	1♌18 34	8♌29 10	5 30.9	7 59.3	15 34.6	24 25.9	11 37.1	16 46.9	18 36.8	5 53.8	21 45.6
10 Th	23 12 16	16 19 29	15 45 54	23 8 8	5 28.2	7 18.8	16 49.2	25 5.6	11 49.1	16 45.7	18 34.8	5 56.0	21 46.6
11 F	23 16 12	17 17 50	0♍35 2	8♍ 5 39	5 25.9	6 45.2	18 3.8	25 45.3	12 1.1	16 44.6	18 32.9	5 58.2	21 47.6
12 Sa	23 20 9	18 16 13	15 38 55	23 13 39	5 24.4	6 19.5	19 18.4	26 25.2	12 13.1	16 43.6	18 30.9	6 0.4	21 48.6
13 Su	23 24 5	19 14 38	0♎48 41	8♎22 49	5D 23.7	6 2.2	20 33.0	27 5.1	12 24.9	16 42.6	18 28.9	6 2.5	21 49.5
14 M	23 28 2	20 13 4	15 54 56	23 23 59	5 23.8	5D 53.8	21 47.6	27 45.0	12 36.8	16 41.8	18 26.8	6 4.7	21 50.5
15 Tu	23 31 59	21 11 33	0♏49 4	8♏ 9 27	5 24.6	5 54.7	23 2.3	28 25.1	12 48.5	16 41.1	18 24.8	6 6.9	21 51.4
16 W	23 35 55	22 10 3	15 24 30	22 33 49	5 25.6	6 5.0	24 16.9	29 5.2	13 0.2	16 40.5	18 22.7	6 9.0	21 52.3
17 Th	23 39 52	23 8 34	29 37 7	6♐34 15	5 26.6	6 24.6	25 31.6	29 45.4	13 11.8	16 39.9	18 20.6	6 11.2	21 53.2
18 F	23 43 48	24 7 8	13♐25 15	20 10 12	5R 27.2	6 53.5	26 46.3	0♏25.6	13 23.4	16 39.5	18 18.4	6 13.3	21 54.1
19 Sa	23 47 45	25 5 43	26 49 20	3♑22 54	5 27.4	7 31.4	28 1.0	1 6.0	13 34.9	16 39.2	18 16.3	6 15.5	21 54.9
20 Su	23 51 41	26 4 19	9♑51 15	16 14 44	5 27.1	8 17.7	29 15.6	1 46.3	13 46.3	16 39.0	18 14.1	6 17.6	21 55.7
21 M	23 55 38	27 2 58	22 33 44	28 48 40	5 26.4	9 12.1	0♎30.4	2 26.8	13 57.6	16D 38.8	18 11.9	6 19.7	21 56.5
22 Tu	23 59 34	28 1 38	4♒59 56	11♒ 7 56	5 25.5	10 14.1	1 45.1	3 7.3	14 8.9	16 38.8	18 9.6	6 21.8	21 57.3
23 W	0 3 31	29 0 19	17 13 1	23 15 35	5 24.6	11 22.9	2 59.8	3 47.9	14 20.0	16 38.9	18 7.4	6 23.9	21 58.1
24 Th	0 7 28	29 59 3	29 15 59	5♓14 32	5 23.8	12 38.0	4 14.5	4 28.6	14 31.1	16 39.0	18 5.1	6 26.0	21 58.8
25 F	0 11 24	0♎57 48	11♓11 34	17 7 23	5 23.2	13 58.6	5 29.3	5 9.3	14 42.2	16 39.3	18 2.8	6 28.1	21 59.5
26 Sa	0 15 21	1 56 35	23 2 16	28 56 30	5 22.9	15 24.3	6 44.0	5 50.1	14 53.1	16 39.7	18 0.5	6 30.1	22 0.2
27 Su	0 19 17	2 55 24	4♈50 22	10♈44 8	5D 22.8	16 54.2	7 58.7	6 30.9	15 4.0	16 40.1	17 58.2	6 32.2	22 0.9
28 M	0 23 14	3 54 15	16 38 5	22 32 30	5 22.9	18 27.9	9 13.5	7 11.8	15 14.8	16 40.7	17 55.9	6 34.2	22 1.5
29 Tu	0 27 10	4 53 9	28 27 42	4♉23 59	5R 22.9	20 4.7	10 28.3	7 52.8	15 25.4	16 41.3	17 53.5	6 36.2	22 2.1
30 W	0 31 7	5 52 4	10♉21 40	16 21 7	5 22.9	21 44.0	11 43.1	8 33.9	15 36.1	16 42.1	17 51.2	6 38.2	22 2.7

LONGITUDE — OCTOBER 1931

Day	Sid.Time	☉	0 hr ☽	Noon ☽	True ☊	☿	♀	♂	♃	♄	♅	♆	♇
1 Th	0 35 3	6♎51 1	22♉22 41	28♉26 47	5♈22.8	23♍25.5	12♎57.8	9♏15.0	15♌46.6	16♑42.9	17♈48.8	6♍40.2	22♋ 3.3
2 F	0 39 0	7 50 1	4♊33 49	10♊44 12	5R 22.6	25 8.7	14 12.6	9 56.2	15 57.0	16 43.9	17R 46.4	6 42.2	22 3.9
3 Sa	0 42 57	8 49 3	16 58 22	23 16 47	5 22.3	26 53.1	15 27.5	10 37.5	16 7.4	16 45.0	17 44.0	6 44.1	22 4.4
4 Su	0 46 53	9 48 8	29 39 51	6♋ 8 0	5D 22.0	28 38.5	16 42.3	11 18.8	16 17.6	16 46.1	17 41.6	6 46.1	22 4.9
5 M	0 50 50	10 47 14	12♋41 38	19 21 5	5 22.0	0♎24.6	17 57.1	12 0.2	16 27.8	16 47.4	17 39.2	6 48.0	22 5.4
6 Tu	0 54 46	11 46 23	26 6 38	2♌58 29	5 22.1	2 11.0	19 11.9	12 41.7	16 37.8	16 48.7	17 36.8	6 49.9	22 5.9
7 W	0 58 43	12 45 35	9♌56 44	17 1 22	5 22.6	3 57.7	20 26.8	13 23.2	16 47.8	16 50.2	17 34.4	6 51.8	22 6.3
8 Th	1 2 39	13 44 48	24 12 11	1♍28 53	5 23.3	5 44.3	21 41.6	14 4.8	16 57.6	16 51.7	17 32.0	6 53.7	22 6.7
9 F	1 6 36	14 44 4	8♍50 57	16 17 44	5 24.0	7 30.8	22 56.5	14 46.5	17 7.4	16 53.3	17 29.5	6 55.5	22 7.1
10 Sa	1 10 32	15 43 22	23 48 25	1♎21 59	5R 24.6	9 17.1	24 11.4	15 28.3	17 17.0	16 55.1	17 27.1	6 57.4	22 7.5
11 Su	1 14 29	16 42 42	8♎57 23	16 33 25	5 24.7	11 3.0	25 26.2	16 10.1	17 26.6	16 56.9	17 24.7	6 59.2	22 7.8
12 M	1 18 25	17 42 5	24 8 51	1♏42 31	5 24.3	12 48.5	26 41.1	16 52.0	17 36.0	16 58.8	17 22.2	7 1.0	22 8.1
13 Tu	1 22 22	18 41 29	9♏13 13	16 39 55	5 23.2	14 33.5	27 56.0	17 33.9	17 45.3	17 0.9	17 19.8	7 2.8	22 8.4
14 W	1 26 19	19 40 55	24 1 41	1♐17 45	5 21.5	16 17.9	29 10.9	18 16.0	17 54.6	17 3.0	17 17.4	7 4.5	22 8.7
15 Th	1 30 15	20 40 24	8♐27 32	15 30 37	5 19.6	18 1.7	0♏25.8	18 58.0	18 3.7	17 5.2	17 14.9	7 6.3	22 8.9
16 F	1 34 12	21 39 54	22 26 48	29 16 1	5 17.7	19 45.0	1 40.7	19 40.2	18 12.6	17 7.5	17 12.5	7 8.0	22 9.1
17 Sa	1 38 8	22 39 26	5♑58 22	12♑34 4	5 16.2	21 27.6	2 55.6	20 22.4	18 21.5	17 9.9	17 10.1	7 9.7	22 9.3
18 Su	1 42 5	23 38 59	19 3 27	25 26 56	5D 15.5	23 9.6	4 10.4	21 4.7	18 30.3	17 12.4	17 7.7	7 11.3	22 9.5
19 M	1 46 1	24 38 35	1♒45 1	7♒58 12	5 15.6	24 50.9	5 25.3	21 47.1	18 38.9	17 15.0	17 5.2	7 13.0	22 9.6
20 Tu	1 49 58	25 38 12	14 7 4	20 12 9	5 16.5	26 31.6	6 40.2	22 29.5	18 47.4	17 17.7	17 2.8	7 14.6	22 9.8
21 W	1 53 55	26 37 50	26 14 1	2♓13 15	5 18.0	28 11.7	7 55.1	23 11.9	18 55.8	17 20.5	17 0.4	7 16.2	22 9.8
22 Th	1 57 51	27 37 31	8♓10 22	14 5 53	5 19.7	29 51.2	9 10.0	23 54.5	19 4.0	17 23.4	16 58.1	7 17.8	22 9.9
23 F	2 1 48	28 37 13	20 0 17	25 54 1	5 21.2	1♏30.0	10 24.9	24 37.1	19 12.1	17 26.3	16 55.7	7 19.3	22 10.0
24 Sa	2 5 44	29 36 57	1♈47 31	7♈41 9	5R 22.0	3 8.3	11 39.8	25 19.7	19 20.1	17 29.4	16 53.3	7 20.9	22R 10.0
25 Su	2 9 41	0♏36 43	13 35 17	19 30 13	5 21.8	4 46.0	12 54.7	26 2.5	19 28.0	17 32.5	16 51.0	7 22.4	22 10.0
26 M	2 13 37	1 36 31	25 26 15	1♉23 37	5 20.2	6 23.1	14 9.6	26 45.3	19 35.7	17 35.7	16 48.6	7 23.8	22 9.9
27 Tu	2 17 34	2 36 20	7♉22 35	13 23 21	5 17.3	7 59.7	15 24.5	27 28.1	19 43.4	17 39.0	16 46.3	7 25.3	22 9.9
28 W	2 21 30	3 36 12	19 26 7	25 31 4	5 13.1	9 35.7	16 39.4	28 11.0	19 50.8	17 42.4	16 44.0	7 26.7	22 9.8
29 Th	2 25 27	4 36 6	1♊38 24	7♊48 18	5 8.1	11 11.3	17 54.3	28 54.0	19 58.1	17 45.9	16 41.7	7 28.1	22 9.7
30 F	2 29 23	5 36 2	14 0 57	20 16 33	5 2.7	12 46.3	19 9.1	29 37.1	20 5.3	17 49.5	16 39.4	7 29.5	22 9.5
31 Sa	2 33 20	6 36 0	26 35 18	2♋57 27	4 57.7	14 20.9	20 24.0	0♐20.2	20 12.4	17 53.2	16 37.2	7 30.8	22 9.4

Astro Data

	Dy Hr Mn
☽0S	13 0:13
☿ D	14 9:44
♄ D	21 19:54
♀0S	23 0:42
☽0N	26 16:05
☿0S	7 2:13
♃⊼♄	7 6:49
☽0S	10 11:20
♃△♅	10 20:09
♆∠♇	16 18:36
♄□♅	17 0:37
☽0N	23 22:16
♇ R	24 1:48

Planet Ingress

	Dy Hr Mn
♂ ♏	17 8:43
♀ ♎	20 14:15
☉ ♎	24 0:23
☿ ♎	4 18:27
♀ ♏	14 15:45
☿ ♏	22 2:08
☉ ♏	24 9:16
♂ ♐	30 12:46

Last Aspect / ☽ Ingress

Last Aspect Dy Hr Mn		☽ Ingress Dy Hr Mn
1 3:58	♇ □	♉ 1 20:59
3 16:22	♇ ✱	♊ 4 8:43
6 3:35	♂ △	♋ 6 17:15
8 11:45	♂ □	♌ 8 21:47
10 15:52	♂ ✱	♍ 10 23:04
12 9:46	♇ ✱	♎ 12 22:43
14 19:55	♂ ☌	♏ 14 22:40
16 16:21	♀ ✱	♐ 17 0:39
19 2:24	♀ □	♑ 19 5:48
21 9:20	☉ △	♒ 21 14:18
23 1:47	♅ ✱	♓ 24 1:28
25 21:54	♇ △	♈ 26 14:09
28 10:58	♇ □	♉ 29 3:07

Last Aspect / ☽ Ingress

Last Aspect Dy Hr Mn		☽ Ingress Dy Hr Mn
1 2:25	☿ △	♊ 1 15:03
3 21:47	☿ □	♋ 4 0:38
5 16:54	♇ ☌	♌ 6 6:49
7 19:26	♀ ✱	♍ 8 9:34
9 21:19	♇ ✱	♎ 10 9:50
12 4:23	♀ ☌	♏ 12 9:17
13 20:55	♇ △	♐ 14 9:51
15 22:32	☉ ✱	♑ 16 13:18
18 9:20	☉ □	♒ 18 20:39
21 4:33	☿ △	♓ 21 7:32
23 9:59	♂ △	♈ 23 20:21
25 17:23	♇ □	♉ 26 9:12
28 18:18	♂ ☍	♊ 28 20:48
30 11:45	♃ ✱	♋ 31 6:26

☽ Phases & Eclipses

Dy Hr Mn	
5 7:21	☽ 11♊46
12 4:26	● 18♍27
12 4:40:58	P 0.047
18 20:37	☽ 24♐57
26 19:45	○ 2♈45
26 19:48	T 1.321
4 20:15	☽ 10♋38
11 13:06	● 17♎15
11 12:55:15	P 0.901
18 9:20	☽ 24♑02
26 13:34	○ 2♉10

Astro Data

1 SEPTEMBER 1931
Julian Day # 11566
Delta T 23.9 sec
SVP 06♓12'52"
Obliquity 23°27'03"
⚷ Chiron 23♉38.4R
☽ Mean ☊ 6♈44.7

1 OCTOBER 1931
Julian Day # 11596
Delta T 23.9 sec
SVP 06♓12'48"
Obliquity 23°27'03"
⚷ Chiron 23♉07.5R
☽ Mean ☊ 5♈09.3

NOVEMBER 1931 LONGITUDE

Day	Sid.Time	☉	0 hr ☽	Noon ☽	True ☊	☿	♀	♂	♃	♄	♅	♆	♇
1 Su	2 37 17	7♏36 0	9♋23 13	15♋52 51	4♈53.5	15♏55.0	21♏38.9	1♐ 3.3	20♌19.3	17♑56.9	16♈35.0	7♍32.1	22♋ 9.2
2 M	2 41 13	8 36 2	22 26 35	29 4 41	4R50.8	17 28.6	22 53.8	1 46.6	20 26.1	18 0.7	16R32.8	7 33.4	22R 9.0
3 Tu	2 45 10	9 36 6	5♌47 22	12♌34 51	4D49.6	19 1.9	24 8.8	2 29.9	20 32.7	18 4.6	16 30.6	7 34.7	22 8.8
4 W	2 49 6	10 36 13	19 27 17	26 24 48	4 49.8	20 34.7	25 23.7	3 13.3	20 39.1	18 8.6	16 28.4	7 35.9	22 8.5
5 Th	2 53 3	11 36 21	3♍27 25	10♍35 4	4 51.0	22 7.1	26 38.6	3 56.7	20 45.4	18 12.7	16 26.3	7 37.1	22 8.2
6 F	2 56 59	12 36 32	17 47 34	25 4 38	4 52.4	23 39.1	27 53.5	4 40.2	20 51.6	18 16.8	16 24.1	7 38.3	22 7.9
7 Sa	3 0 56	13 36 44	2♎25 46	9♎50 24	4R53.3	25 10.7	29 8.4	5 23.8	20 57.6	18 21.0	16 22.0	7 39.5	22 7.6
8 Su	3 4 52	14 36 59	17 17 45	24 46 56	4 52.7	26 41.9	0♐23.3	6 7.4	21 3.5	18 25.3	16 20.0	7 40.6	22 7.2
9 M	3 8 49	15 37 16	2♏16 57	9♏46 43	4 50.2	28 12.8	1 38.2	6 51.1	21 9.1	18 29.7	16 17.9	7 41.7	22 6.9
10 Tu	3 12 46	16 37 34	17 15 5	24 40 58	4 45.7	29 43.3	2 53.1	7 34.8	21 14.7	18 34.2	16 15.9	7 42.7	22 6.5
11 W	3 16 42	17 37 54	2♐ 3 15	9♐21 0	4 39.4	1♐13.4	4 8.1	8 18.6	21 20.0	18 38.7	16 13.9	7 43.7	22 6.0
12 Th	3 20 39	18 38 16	16 33 22	23 39 40	4 32.2	2 43.1	5 23.0	9 2.5	21 25.2	18 43.3	16 12.0	7 44.7	22 5.6
13 F	3 24 35	19 38 40	0♑39 25	7♑32 17	4 25.0	4 12.4	6 37.9	9 46.4	21 30.3	18 48.0	16 10.1	7 45.7	22 5.1
14 Sa	3 28 32	20 39 5	14 18 9	20 57 4	4 18.6	5 41.3	7 52.8	10 30.4	21 35.1	18 52.7	16 8.2	7 46.6	22 4.6
15 Su	3 32 28	21 39 31	27 29 13	3♒54 56	4 13.8	7 9.7	9 7.7	11 14.5	21 39.8	18 57.5	16 6.3	7 47.5	22 4.1
16 M	3 36 25	22 39 59	10♒14 38	16 28 51	4 10.9	8 37.7	10 22.6	11 58.6	21 44.3	19 2.4	16 4.5	7 48.4	22 3.6
17 Tu	3 40 22	23 40 28	22 38 10	28 43 12	4D10.0	10 5.2	11 37.5	12 42.8	21 48.7	19 7.4	16 2.7	7 49.2	22 3.0
18 W	3 44 18	24 40 58	4♓44 38	10♓43 7	4 10.5	11 32.2	12 52.4	13 27.0	21 52.9	19 12.4	16 0.9	7 50.0	22 2.4
19 Th	3 48 15	25 41 30	16 39 19	22 33 55	4 11.7	12 58.6	14 7.3	14 11.3	21 56.9	19 17.5	15 59.2	7 50.8	22 1.8
20 F	3 52 11	26 42 2	28 27 31	4♈20 45	4R12.8	14 24.3	15 22.2	14 55.6	22 0.7	19 22.7	15 57.5	7 51.5	22 1.2
21 Sa	3 56 8	27 42 36	10♈14 11	16 8 20	4 12.7	15 49.3	16 37.0	15 40.0	22 4.3	19 27.9	15 55.9	7 52.2	22 0.5
22 Su	4 0 4	28 43 12	22 3 41	28 0 40	4 10.8	17 13.6	17 51.9	16 24.4	22 7.8	19 33.2	15 54.3	7 52.9	21 59.8
23 M	4 4 1	29 43 48	3♉59 39	10♉ 0 57	4 6.5	18 36.9	19 6.8	17 9.0	22 11.1	19 38.6	15 52.7	7 53.6	21 59.1
24 Tu	4 7 57	0♐44 26	16 4 51	22 11 31	3 59.6	19 59.3	20 21.6	17 53.5	22 14.2	19 44.0	15 51.2	7 54.2	21 58.4
25 W	4 11 54	1 45 5	28 21 7	4♊33 45	3 50.5	21 20.4	21 36.5	18 38.1	22 17.1	19 49.5	15 49.7	7 54.7	21 57.7
26 Th	4 15 51	2 45 46	10♊49 28	17 8 16	3 39.8	22 40.4	22 51.3	19 22.8	22 19.9	19 55.0	15 48.3	7 55.3	21 56.9
27 F	4 19 47	3 46 28	23 30 9	29 55 3	3 28.3	23 58.8	24 6.2	20 7.5	22 22.4	20 0.6	15 46.9	7 55.8	21 56.2
28 Sa	4 23 44	4 47 12	6♋22 57	12♋53 47	3 17.3	25 15.5	25 21.0	20 52.3	22 24.8	20 6.2	15 45.5	7 56.3	21 55.4
29 Su	4 27 40	5 47 57	19 27 31	26 4 6	3 7.8	26 30.3	26 35.8	21 37.2	22 27.0	20 12.0	15 44.2	7 56.7	21 54.6
30 M	4 31 37	6 48 43	2♌43 33	9♌25 53	3 0.5	27 42.9	27 50.7	22 22.0	22 29.0	20 17.7	15 42.9	7 57.1	21 53.7

DECEMBER 1931 LONGITUDE

Day	Sid.Time	☉	0 hr ☽	Noon ☽	True ☊	☿	♀	♂	♃	♄	♅	♆	♇
1 Tu	4 35 33	7♐49 31	16♌11 8	22♌59 21	2♈55.9	28♐52.9	29♐ 5.5	23♐ 7.0	22♌30.8	20♑23.6	15♈41.7	7♍57.5	21♋52.9
2 W	4 39 30	8 50 20	29 50 37	6♍45 0	2D53.8	29 60.0	0♑20.3	23 52.0	22 32.4	20 29.4	15R40.5	7 57.8	21R52.0
3 Th	4 43 26	9 51 11	13♍42 34	20 43 21	2 53.5	1♑ 3.7	1 35.1	24 37.1	22 33.8	20 35.4	15 39.3	7 58.1	21 51.1
4 F	4 47 23	10 52 3	27 47 19	4♎54 24	2R53.9	2 3.6	2 49.9	25 22.2	22 35.0	20 41.3	15 38.2	7 58.4	21 50.2
5 Sa	4 51 20	11 52 57	12♎ 4 25	19 17 6	2 53.7	2 59.1	4 4.7	26 7.3	22 36.0	20 47.4	15 37.2	7 58.6	21 49.3
6 Su	4 55 16	12 53 51	26 32 3	3♏48 46	2 51.7	3 49.6	5 19.5	26 52.6	22 36.9	20 53.4	15 36.2	7 58.8	21 48.3
7 M	4 59 13	13 54 48	11♏ 6 38	18 24 54	2 46.9	4 34.3	6 34.3	27 37.8	22 37.5	20 59.6	15 35.2	7 59.0	21 47.4
8 Tu	5 3 9	14 55 45	25 42 45	2♐59 19	2 39.3	5 12.6	7 49.1	28 23.2	22 37.9	21 5.8	15 34.3	7 59.1	21 46.4
9 W	5 7 6	15 56 44	10♐13 40	17 24 57	2 29.1	5 43.5	9 3.9	29 8.5	22R38.2	21 12.0	15 33.4	7 59.2	21 45.4
10 Th	5 11 2	16 57 43	24 32 18	1♑34 59	2 17.2	6 6.3	10 18.7	29 54.0	22 38.2	21 18.3	15 32.6	7 59.2	21 44.4
11 F	5 14 59	17 58 44	8♑32 22	15 24 0	2 4.9	6R20.1	11 33.5	0♑39.5	22 38.1	21 24.6	15 31.8	7R59.3	21 43.3
12 Sa	5 18 55	18 59 45	22 9 32	28 48 48	1 53.6	6 24.1	12 48.2	1 25.0	22 37.7	21 30.9	15 31.1	7 59.3	21 42.3
13 Su	5 22 52	20 0 47	5♒21 48	11♒48 40	1 44.2	6 17.4	14 3.0	2 10.6	22 37.2	21 37.3	15 30.4	7 59.2	21 41.2
14 M	5 26 49	21 1 49	18 9 40	24 25 11	1 37.5	5 59.6	15 17.7	2 56.2	22 36.4	21 43.8	15 29.8	7 59.1	21 40.2
15 Tu	5 30 45	22 2 52	0♓35 43	6♓41 49	1 33.5	5 30.2	16 32.4	3 41.9	22 35.5	21 50.3	15 29.3	7 59.0	21 39.1
16 W	5 34 42	23 3 55	12 44 5	18 43 12	1D31.7	4 49.2	17 47.1	4 27.6	22 34.3	21 56.8	15 28.7	7 58.9	21 38.0
17 Th	5 38 38	24 4 59	24 39 51	0♈34 45	1R31.4	3 57.1	19 1.8	5 13.4	22 33.0	22 3.3	15 28.3	7 58.7	21 36.9
18 F	5 42 35	25 6 3	6♈28 37	12 22 8	1 31.4	2 54.9	20 16.5	5 59.2	22 31.5	22 9.9	15 27.8	7 58.5	21 35.8
19 Sa	5 46 31	26 7 7	18 15 59	24 10 50	1 30.5	1 44.1	21 31.2	6 45.0	22 29.7	22 16.5	15 27.5	7 58.2	21 34.6
20 Su	5 50 28	27 8 12	0♉ 7 17	6♉ 5 56	1 27.7	0 26.8	22 45.8	7 30.9	22 27.8	22 23.2	15 27.1	7 57.9	21 33.5
21 M	5 54 24	28 9 17	12 7 15	18 11 44	1 22.3	29♐ 5.3	24 0.4	8 16.8	22 25.7	22 29.9	15 26.9	7 57.6	21 32.3
22 Tu	5 58 21	29 10 23	24 19 43	0♊31 31	1 14.0	27 42.5	25 15.0	9 2.8	22 23.4	22 36.6	15 26.7	7 57.3	21 31.1
23 W	6 2 18	0♑11 28	6♊47 21	13 7 20	1 3.0	26 21.2	26 29.6	9 48.8	22 20.9	22 43.4	15 26.5	7 56.9	21 30.0
24 Th	6 6 14	1 12 35	19 31 31	25 59 50	0 50.0	25 3.9	27 44.2	10 34.9	22 18.2	22 50.2	15 26.4	7 56.5	21 28.8
25 F	6 10 11	2 13 41	2♋32 10	9♋ 8 19	0 36.2	23 52.9	28 58.7	11 21.0	22 15.3	22 57.0	15D26.3	7 56.0	21 27.6
26 Sa	6 14 7	3 14 48	15 48 1	22 30 59	0 22.7	22 50.2	0♒13.3	12 7.2	22 12.2	23 3.8	15 26.3	7 55.5	21 26.4
27 Su	6 18 4	4 15 55	29 16 53	6♌ 5 23	0 10.9	21 56.9	1 27.8	12 53.4	22 9.0	23 10.7	15 26.4	7 55.0	21 25.1
28 M	6 22 0	5 17 3	12♌56 10	19 48 56	0 1.6	21 13.9	2 42.3	13 39.6	22 5.6	23 17.5	15 26.5	7 54.5	21 23.9
29 Tu	6 25 57	6 18 11	26 43 23	3♍39 20	29♓55.5	20 41.5	3 56.7	14 25.9	22 1.9	23 24.5	15 26.6	7 53.9	21 22.7
30 W	6 29 54	7 19 19	10♍36 35	17 35 1	29 52.3	20 19.7	5 11.2	15 12.2	21 58.1	23 31.4	15 26.8	7 53.3	21 21.4
31 Th	6 33 50	8 20 28	24 34 32	1♎35 3	29D51.3	20D 8.0	6 25.6	15 58.5	21 54.2	23 38.3	15 27.1	7 52.7	21 20.2

Astro Data	Dy Hr Mn
☽0S	6 21:25
☽0N	20 4:37
♃⊻♇	20 2:39
☽0S	4 4:34
♃ R	9 17:29
☿ R	11 21:11
♆ R	11 6:19
♄☍♇	13 12:30
☽0N	17 11:21
♃⊼♄	20 12:36
♄⚼♆	24 20:55
♅ D	25 15:29
☽0S	31 9:15
☿ D	31 16:55

Planet Ingress	Dy Hr Mn
♀ ♐	7 16:32
☿ ♐	10 4:27
☉ ♐	23 6:25
♀ ♑	1 17:29
☿ ♑	2 0:00
♂ ♑	10 3:11
☿ ♐	20 7:59
☉ ♑	22 19:30
♀ ♒	25 19:44
☊ ♓	28 5:24

Last Aspect Dy Hr Mn		☽ Ingress Dy Hr Mn
2 0:55	♀ △	♌ 2 13:39
4 11:15	♀ □	♍ 4 18:08
6 18:09	♀ ⚹	♎ 6 20:03
8 7:44	♇ □	♏ 8 20:21
10 7:50	♇ △	♐ 10 20:39
12 8:15	♃ △	♑ 12 22:52
14 14:03	♇ ☍	♒ 15 4:40
17 2:13	☉ □	♓ 17 14:32
19 20:05	☉ △	♈ 20 3:08
22 0:08	♃ △	♉ 22 16:00
24 12:08	♃ □	♊ 25 3:12
27 1:15	♀ ☍	♋ 27 12:09
29 4:27	♇ ☌	♌ 29 19:06

Last Aspect Dy Hr Mn		☽ Ingress Dy Hr Mn
1 12:56	♂ △	♍ 2 0:16
3 19:40	♂ □	♎ 4 3:44
6 0:36	♂ ⚹	♏ 6 5:43
7 18:56	♃ □	♐ 8 7:04
9 20:47	♃ △	♑ 10 9:17
11 23:11	♇ ☍	♒ 12 14:10
14 8:30	♃ ☍	♓ 14 22:50
16 22:43	☉ □	♈ 17 10:49
19 17:25	☉ △	♉ 19 23:45
22 2:00	♀ △	♊ 22 10:59
24 9:24	☿ ☍	♋ 24 19:22
26 13:05	♄ ☍	♌ 27 1:16
28 15:54	♃ ☌	♍ 29 5:41
30 22:23	♄ △	♎ 31 9:17

☽ Phases & Eclipses Dy Hr Mn	
3 7:17	☽ 9♌54
9 22:55	● 16♏35
17 2:13	☽ 23♒46
25 7:10	○ 2♊03
2 16:50	☽ 9♍33
9 10:16	● 16♐23
16 22:43	☽ 24♓02
24 23:23	○ 2♋12

Astro Data

1 NOVEMBER 1931
Julian Day # 11627
Delta T 23.9 sec
SVP 06♓12'44"
Obliquity 23°27'02"
⚷ Chiron 21♉49.4R
☽ Mean ☊ 3♈30.8

1 DECEMBER 1931
Julian Day # 11657
Delta T 23.9 sec
SVP 06♓12'39"
Obliquity 23°27'02"
⚷ Chiron 20♉16.9R
☽ Mean ☊ 1♈55.5

LONGITUDE JANUARY 1932

Day	Sid.Time	☉	0 hr ☽	Noon ☽	True ☊	☿	♀	♂	♃	♄	♅	♆	♇
1 F	6 37 47	9♑21 37	8♎36 32	15♎38 55	29♓51.3	20♐ 6.1	7♒40.0	16♑44.9	21♌50.0	23♑45.3	15♈27.4	7♍52.0	21♋18.9
2 Sa	6 41 43	10 22 47	22 42 8	29 46 5	29R50.9	20 13.2	8 54.4	17 31.3	21R45.7	23 52.3	15 27.7	7R51.3	21R17.7
3 Su	6 45 40	11 23 57	6♏50 35	13♏55 26	29 48.8	20 28.6	10 8.7	18 17.8	21 41.1	23 59.3	15 28.1	7 50.5	21 16.4
4 M	6 49 36	12 25 8	21 0 19	28 4 54	29 44.1	20 51.6	11 23.0	19 4.3	21 36.5	24 6.3	15 28.6	7 49.8	21 15.1
5 Tu	6 53 33	13 26 18	5♐ 8 44	12♐11 18	29 36.4	21 21.5	12 37.4	19 50.9	21 31.6	24 13.4	15 29.1	7 49.0	21 13.8
6 W	6 57 29	14 27 29	19 12 6	26 10 32	29 26.1	21 57.6	13 51.6	20 37.4	21 26.6	24 20.4	15 29.6	7 48.2	21 12.6
7 Th	7 1 26	15 28 40	3♑ 6 3	9♑58 7	29 14.1	22 39.2	15 5.9	21 24.1	21 21.4	24 27.5	15 30.3	7 47.3	21 11.3
8 F	7 5 23	16 29 51	16 46 15	23 30 0	29 1.5	23 25.8	16 20.1	22 10.7	21 16.1	24 34.6	15 30.9	7 46.4	21 10.0
9 Sa	7 9 19	17 31 2	0♒ 9 4	6♒43 13	28 49.7	24 16.8	17 34.3	22 57.4	21 10.6	24 41.7	15 31.6	7 45.5	21 8.7
10 Su	7 13 16	18 32 12	13 12 19	19 36 23	28 39.8	25 11.7	18 48.5	23 44.1	21 5.0	24 48.8	15 32.4	7 44.6	21 7.4
11 M	7 17 12	19 33 22	25 55 31	2♓ 9 55	28 32.4	26 10.2	20 2.6	24 30.9	20 59.2	24 55.9	15 33.2	7 43.6	21 6.1
12 Tu	7 21 9	20 34 32	8♓19 55	14 25 54	28 27.9	27 11.9	21 16.7	25 17.6	20 53.2	25 3.0	15 34.1	7 42.6	21 4.8
13 W	7 25 5	21 35 41	20 28 22	26 27 49	28D25.8	28 16.4	22 30.8	26 4.4	20 47.2	25 10.1	15 35.0	7 41.6	21 3.5
14 Th	7 29 2	22 36 49	2♈24 53	8♈20 12	28 25.6	29 23.4	23 44.8	26 51.3	20 41.0	25 17.3	15 36.0	7 40.5	21 2.2
15 F	7 32 58	23 37 56	14 14 24	20 8 12	28R26.1	0♑32.7	24 58.8	27 38.1	20 34.6	25 24.4	15 37.0	7 39.4	21 1.0
16 Sa	7 36 55	24 39 3	26 2 17	1♉57 21	28 26.4	1 44.0	26 12.7	28 25.0	20 28.2	25 31.5	15 38.1	7 38.3	20 59.7
17 Su	7 40 52	25 40 10	7♉54 4	13 53 7	28 25.5	2 57.3	27 26.6	29 11.9	20 21.6	25 38.6	15 39.2	7 37.2	20 58.4
18 M	7 44 48	26 41 15	19 55 6	26 0 38	28 22.5	4 12.2	28 40.5	29 58.9	20 14.9	25 45.8	15 40.4	7 36.0	20 57.1
19 Tu	7 48 45	27 42 20	2♊10 12	8♊24 17	28 17.2	5 28.7	29 54.3	0♒45.8	20 8.0	25 52.9	15 41.6	7 34.9	20 55.8
20 W	7 52 41	28 43 24	14 43 14	21 7 20	28 9.6	6 46.6	1♓ 8.0	1 32.8	20 1.1	26 0.0	15 42.9	7 33.7	20 54.5
21 Th	7 56 38	29 44 27	27 36 44	4♋11 31	28 0.1	8 5.8	2 21.8	2 19.8	19 54.1	26 7.2	15 44.2	7 32.4	20 53.2
22 F	8 0 34	0♒45 29	10♋51 35	17 36 46	27 49.8	9 26.2	3 35.4	3 6.9	19 47.0	26 14.3	15 45.6	7 31.2	20 52.0
23 Sa	8 4 31	1 46 31	24 26 46	1♌21 12	27 39.6	10 47.8	4 49.0	3 53.9	19 39.8	26 21.4	15 47.0	7 29.9	20 50.7
24 Su	8 8 27	2 47 32	8♌19 32	15 21 15	27 30.6	12 10.4	6 2.6	4 41.0	19 32.5	26 28.5	15 48.5	7 28.6	20 49.4
25 M	8 12 24	3 48 33	22 25 43	29 32 21	27 23.8	13 34.0	7 16.1	5 28.1	19 25.1	26 35.6	15 50.0	7 27.3	20 48.2
26 Tu	8 16 21	4 49 31	6♍40 30	13♍49 35	27 19.5	14 58.6	8 29.5	6 15.2	19 17.6	26 42.7	15 51.5	7 26.0	20 46.9
27 W	8 20 17	5 50 29	20 59 4	28 8 27	27D17.6	16 24.0	9 42.9	7 2.3	19 10.0	26 49.8	15 53.1	7 24.6	20 45.7
28 Th	8 24 14	6 51 27	5♎17 20	12♎25 23	27 17.7	17 50.4	10 56.3	7 49.5	19 2.4	26 56.9	15 54.8	7 23.3	20 44.4
29 F	8 28 10	7 52 24	19 32 17	26 37 49	27 18.7	19 17.6	12 9.5	8 36.7	18 54.8	27 3.9	15 56.5	7 21.9	20 43.2
30 Sa	8 32 7	8 53 21	3♏41 50	10♏44 11	27R19.6	20 45.5	13 22.8	9 23.9	18 47.0	27 11.0	15 58.2	7 20.5	20 42.0
31 Su	8 36 3	9 54 17	17 44 45	24 43 25	27 19.4	22 14.3	14 35.9	10 11.1	18 39.2	27 18.0	15 60.0	7 19.0	20 40.8

LONGITUDE FEBRUARY 1932

Day	Sid.Time	☉	0 hr ☽	Noon ☽	True ☊	☿	♀	♂	♃	♄	♅	♆	♇
1 M	8 40 0	10♒55 12	1♐40 6	8♐34 41	27♓17.4	23♑43.9	15♓49.0	10♒58.3	18♌31.4	27♑25.0	16♈ 1.8	7♍17.6	20♋39.6
2 Tu	8 43 56	11 56 7	15 27 1	22 16 59	27R13.4	25 14.3	17 2.1	11 45.6	18R23.5	27 32.0	16 3.7	7R16.1	20R38.4
3 W	8 47 53	12 57 0	29 4 23	5♑49 2	27 7.4	26 45.4	18 15.1	12 32.9	18 15.6	27 39.0	16 5.6	7 14.6	20 37.2
4 Th	8 51 50	13 57 53	12♑30 47	19 9 24	27 0.0	28 17.3	19 28.0	13 20.2	18 7.7	27 45.9	16 7.6	7 13.1	20 36.0
5 F	8 55 46	14 58 45	25 44 43	2♒16 34	26 52.3	29 49.9	20 40.9	14 7.5	17 59.8	27 52.9	16 9.6	7 11.6	20 34.8
6 Sa	8 59 43	15 59 36	8♒44 49	15 9 23	26 44.9	1♒23.3	21 53.7	14 54.8	17 51.8	27 59.8	16 11.6	7 10.1	20 33.7
7 Su	9 3 39	17 0 26	21 30 13	27 47 19	26 38.8	2 57.5	23 6.4	15 42.1	17 43.8	28 6.7	16 13.7	7 8.6	20 32.5
8 M	9 7 36	18 1 14	4♓ 0 46	10♓10 41	26 34.4	4 32.4	24 19.1	16 29.4	17 35.8	28 13.6	16 15.8	7 7.0	20 31.4
9 Tu	9 11 32	19 2 1	16 17 17	22 20 49	26D32.0	6 8.1	25 31.6	17 16.8	17 27.9	28 20.4	16 18.0	7 5.4	20 30.3
10 W	9 15 29	20 2 47	28 21 37	4♈20 4	26 31.4	7 44.6	26 44.1	18 4.1	17 19.9	28 27.2	16 20.2	7 3.9	20 29.2
11 Th	9 19 26	21 3 31	10♈16 34	16 11 39	26 32.3	9 21.8	27 56.6	18 51.5	17 11.9	28 34.0	16 22.4	7 2.3	20 28.1
12 F	9 23 22	22 4 13	22 5 48	27 59 36	26 34.0	10 59.9	29 8.9	19 38.9	17 4.0	28 40.8	16 24.7	7 0.7	20 27.0
13 Sa	9 27 19	23 4 54	3♉53 40	9♉48 35	26 35.8	12 38.8	0♈21.2	20 26.2	16 56.1	28 47.5	16 27.0	6 59.1	20 25.9
14 Su	9 31 15	24 5 33	15 45 0	21 43 34	26R37.1	14 18.6	1 33.3	21 13.6	16 48.2	28 54.2	16 29.4	6 57.4	20 24.9
15 M	9 35 12	25 6 11	27 44 55	3♊49 40	26 37.4	15 59.2	2 45.4	22 1.0	16 40.4	29 0.9	16 31.8	6 55.8	20 23.8
16 Tu	9 39 8	26 6 47	9♊58 26	16 11 47	26 36.4	17 40.7	3 57.4	22 48.4	16 32.6	29 7.5	16 34.2	6 54.2	20 22.8
17 W	9 43 5	27 7 21	22 30 12	28 54 10	26 34.1	19 23.0	5 9.3	23 35.8	16 24.8	29 14.1	16 36.7	6 52.6	20 21.8
18 Th	9 47 1	28 7 53	5♋24 0	11♋59 58	26 30.6	21 6.2	6 21.1	24 23.2	16 17.2	29 20.7	16 39.2	6 50.9	20 20.8
19 F	9 50 58	29 8 24	18 42 12	25 30 43	26 26.4	22 50.4	7 32.8	25 10.5	16 9.5	29 27.2	16 41.7	6 49.3	20 19.8
20 Sa	9 54 55	0♓ 8 53	2♌25 23	9♌25 55	26 22.2	24 35.5	8 44.4	25 57.9	16 2.0	29 33.7	16 44.3	6 47.6	20 18.9
21 Su	9 58 51	1 9 20	16 31 53	23 42 44	26 18.4	26 21.5	9 55.9	26 45.3	15 54.5	29 40.2	16 46.9	6 45.9	20 17.9
22 M	10 2 48	2 9 46	0♍57 48	8♍16 16	26 15.7	28 8.4	11 7.3	27 32.7	15 47.1	29 46.6	16 49.6	6 44.3	20 17.0
23 Tu	10 6 44	3 10 9	15 37 18	22 59 59	26D14.1	29 56.2	12 18.6	28 20.1	15 39.8	29 52.9	16 52.2	6 42.6	20 16.1
24 W	10 10 41	4 10 31	0♎23 27	7♎46 46	26 13.9	1♓45.1	13 29.8	29 7.5	15 32.5	29 59.3	16 54.9	6 40.9	20 15.2
25 Th	10 14 37	5 10 52	15 9 8	22 29 46	26 14.6	3 34.8	14 40.8	29 54.9	15 25.4	0♒ 5.6	16 57.7	6 39.3	20 14.3
26 F	10 18 34	6 11 11	29 48 0	7♏ 3 16	26 15.9	5 25.4	15 51.8	0♓42.2	15 18.3	0 11.8	17 0.4	6 37.6	20 13.5
27 Sa	10 22 30	7 11 29	14♏15 7	21 23 11	26 17.2	7 17.0	17 2.6	1 29.6	15 11.4	0 18.0	17 3.2	6 35.9	20 12.7
28 Su	10 26 27	8 11 45	28 27 13	5♐27 3	26R18.1	9 9.4	18 13.4	2 17.0	15 4.5	0 24.2	17 6.1	6 34.2	20 11.8
29 M	10 30 23	9 12 0	12♐22 37	19 13 53	26 18.3	11 2.7	19 24.0	3 4.4	14 57.8	0 30.3	17 8.9	6 32.6	20 11.0

Astro Data	Planet Ingress	Last Aspect	☽ Ingress	Last Aspect	☽ Ingress	☽ Phases & Eclipses	Astro Data
Dy Hr Mn	Dy Hr Mn	Dy Hr Mn	Dy Hr Mn	Dy Hr Mn	Dy Hr Mn	Dy Hr Mn	1 JANUARY 1932
♃⊻♇ 9 10:34	☿ ♑ 14 12:47	2 2:00 ♄ □	♏ 2 12:24	2 5:07 ♃ △	♑ 3 1:39	1 1:23 ☽ 9♎25	Julian Day # 11688
☽0N 13 18:35	♂ ♒ 18 0:35	4 5:18 ♄ ✱	♐ 4 15:15	5 3:57 ♄ ☌	♒ 5 7:48	7 23:29 ● 16♑29	Delta T 23.9 sec
☽0S 27 14:20	♀ ♓ 19 1:52	6 4:58 ☿ ☌	♑ 6 18:37	6 16:56 ♃ ☍	♓ 7 16:15	15 20:55 ☽ 24♈31	SVP 06♓12'33"
	☉ ♒ 21 6:07	8 14:03 ♄ ☌	♒ 8 23:44	10 0:11 ♄ ✱	♈ 10 3:17	23 13:44 ○ 2♌21	Obliquity 23°27'02"
☽0N 10 2:05		11 0:31 ☿ ✱	♓ 11 7:49	12 13:32 ♄ □	♉ 12 16:05	30 9:32 ☽ 9♏18	⚷ Chiron 19♉02.1R
♀0N 13 22:49	☿ ♒ 5 2:36	13 17:15 ☿ □	♈ 13 19:07	15 2:32 ♄ △	♊ 15 4:27		☽ Mean ☊ 0♈17.1
♃△♅ 15 20:08	♀ ♈ 12 16:58	16 5:10 ♂ □	♉ 16 8:02	17 9:25 ☉ △	♋ 17 14:02	6 14:45 ● 16♒37	
☽0S 23 22:18	☉ ♓ 19 20:28	18 19:07 ♀ □	♊ 18 19:47	19 19:01 ♄ ☍	♌ 19 19:49	14 18:16 ☽ 24♉52	1 FEBRUARY 1932
	☿ ♓ 23 0:50	20 9:51 ♃ ✱	♋ 21 4:22	21 18:41 ☿ ☍	♍ 21 22:25	22 2:07 ○ 2♍15	Julian Day # 11719
	♄ ♒ 24 2:47	23 3:22 ♄ ☍	♌ 23 9:40	23 23:20 ♄ △	♎ 23 23:22	28 18:03 ☽ 8♐57	Delta T 23.9 sec
	♂ ♓ 25 2:36	24 18:57 ♃ ☌	♍ 25 12:47	25 8:18 ♇ □	♏ 26 0:20		SVP 06♓12'28"
		27 9:53 ♄ △	♎ 27 15:07	27 10:00 ♇ △	♐ 28 2:38		Obliquity 23°27'02"
		29 12:51 ♄ □	♏ 29 17:43				⚷ Chiron 18♉38.6
		31 16:35 ♄ ✱	♐ 31 21:07				☽ Mean ☊ 28♓38.6

MARCH 1932 LONGITUDE

Day	Sid.Time	☉	0 hr ☽	Noon ☽	True ☊	☿	♀	♂	♃	♄	♅	♆	♇
1 Tu	10 34 20	10♓12 14	26♐ 0 54	2♑43 44	26♓17.7	12♓56.7	20♈34.5	3♓51.7	14♌51.2	0♒36.3	17♈11.8	6♍30.9	20♋10.3
2 W	10 38 17	11 12 26	9♑22 30	15 57 20	26R16.4	14 51.4	21 44.9	4 39.1	14R44.7	0 42.3	17 14.7	6R29.2	20R 9.5
3 Th	10 42 13	12 12 36	22 28 21	28 55 43	26 14.6	16 46.7	22 55.1	5 26.5	14 38.3	0 48.3	17 17.6	6 27.6	20 8.8
4 F	10 46 10	13 12 45	5♒19 35	11♒40 6	26 12.6	18 42.5	24 5.2	6 13.8	14 32.1	0 54.2	17 20.6	6 25.9	20 8.1
5 Sa	10 50 6	14 12 52	17 57 24	24 11 39	26 10.8	20 38.7	25 15.2	7 1.2	14 25.9	1 0.1	17 23.6	6 24.2	20 7.4
6 Su	10 54 3	15 12 57	0♓23 0	6♓31 36	26 9.4	22 35.0	26 25.1	7 48.5	14 19.9	1 5.9	17 26.6	6 22.6	20 6.7
7 M	10 57 59	16 13 1	12 37 39	18 41 18	26 8.5	24 31.3	27 34.8	8 35.8	14 14.1	1 11.6	17 29.6	6 20.9	20 6.1
8 Tu	11 1 56	17 13 3	24 42 46	0♈42 16	26D 8.2	26 27.3	28 44.4	9 23.1	14 8.4	1 17.3	17 32.7	6 19.3	20 5.4
9 W	11 5 52	18 13 2	6♈40 3	12 36 24	26 8.4	28 22.7	29 53.9	10 10.4	14 2.8	1 22.9	17 35.8	6 17.6	20 4.8
10 Th	11 9 49	19 13 0	18 31 36	24 26 1	26 8.8	0♈17.4	1♉ 3.2	10 57.7	13 57.4	1 28.5	17 38.9	6 16.0	20 4.2
11 F	11 13 46	20 12 55	0♉19 59	6♉13 56	26 9.5	2 10.8	2 12.3	11 45.0	13 52.2	1 34.0	17 42.0	6 14.4	20 3.7
12 Sa	11 17 42	21 12 49	12 8 18	18 3 32	26 10.1	4 2.7	3 21.3	12 32.2	13 47.1	1 39.5	17 45.1	6 12.8	20 3.1
13 Su	11 21 39	22 12 40	24 0 9	29 58 39	26 10.6	5 52.6	4 30.2	13 19.4	13 42.2	1 44.9	17 48.3	6 11.2	20 2.6
14 M	11 25 35	23 12 30	5♊59 35	12♊ 3 31	26 11.0	7 40.1	5 38.9	14 6.7	13 37.4	1 50.2	17 51.5	6 9.6	20 2.1
15 Tu	11 29 32	24 12 17	18 11 0	24 22 36	26R11.1	9 24.6	6 47.4	14 53.8	13 32.8	1 55.5	17 54.7	6 8.0	20 1.7
16 W	11 33 28	25 12 1	0♋38 52	7♋ 0 18	26D11.1	11 5.9	7 55.7	15 41.0	13 28.4	2 0.7	17 57.9	6 6.4	20 1.2
17 Th	11 37 25	26 11 44	13 27 23	20 0 32	26 11.1	12 43.2	9 3.9	16 28.2	13 24.1	2 5.8	18 1.1	6 4.9	20 0.8
18 F	11 41 21	27 11 24	26 40 5	3♌26 16	26 11.1	14 16.2	10 11.9	17 15.3	13 20.0	2 10.9	18 4.4	6 3.3	20 0.4
19 Sa	11 45 18	28 11 2	10♌19 13	17 18 55	26 11.3	15 44.4	11 19.7	18 2.4	13 16.1	2 15.9	18 7.6	6 1.8	20 0.0
20 Su	11 49 15	29 10 38	24 25 11	1♍37 41	26 11.5	17 7.4	12 27.3	18 49.5	13 12.4	2 20.9	18 10.9	6 0.3	19 59.7
21 M	11 53 11	0♈10 11	8♍55 56	16 19 14	26 11.8	18 24.7	13 34.7	19 36.6	13 8.8	2 25.7	18 14.2	5 58.8	19 59.4
22 Tu	11 57 8	1 9 42	23 46 46	1♎17 34	26R11.9	19 35.9	14 41.9	20 23.6	13 5.4	2 30.5	18 17.5	5 57.3	19 59.0
23 W	12 1 4	2 9 12	8♎50 33	16 24 35	26 11.8	20 40.7	15 48.9	21 10.7	13 2.2	2 35.3	18 20.8	5 55.8	19 58.8
24 Th	12 5 1	3 8 39	23 58 29	1♏31 7	26 11.4	21 38.8	16 55.7	21 57.6	12 59.2	2 39.9	18 24.2	5 54.4	19 58.5
25 F	12 8 57	4 8 4	9♏ 1 22	16 28 15	26 10.6	22 29.9	18 2.2	22 44.6	12 56.4	2 44.5	18 27.5	5 52.9	19 58.3
26 Sa	12 12 54	5 7 28	23 50 54	1♐ 8 36	26 9.6	23 13.8	19 8.6	23 31.6	12 53.7	2 49.0	18 30.9	5 51.5	19 58.1
27 Su	12 16 50	6 6 49	8♐20 48	15 27 8	26 8.6	23 50.4	20 14.7	24 18.5	12 51.2	2 53.5	18 34.2	5 50.1	19 57.9
28 M	12 20 47	7 6 9	22 27 21	29 21 23	26 7.8	24 19.6	21 20.6	25 5.4	12 48.9	2 57.8	18 37.6	5 48.7	19 57.7
29 Tu	12 24 44	8 5 28	6♑ 9 18	12♑51 14	26D 7.5	24 41.3	22 26.3	25 52.3	12 46.8	3 2.1	18 41.0	5 47.3	19 57.6
30 W	12 28 40	9 4 44	19 27 26	25 58 14	26 7.7	24 55.4	23 31.8	26 39.2	12 44.9	3 6.4	18 44.4	5 46.0	19 57.5
31 Th	12 32 37	10 3 59	2♒23 59	8♒45 4	26 8.4	25R 2.2	24 37.0	27 26.0	12 43.2	3 10.5	18 47.8	5 44.7	19 57.4

APRIL 1932 LONGITUDE

Day	Sid.Time	☉	0 hr ☽	Noon ☽	True ☊	☿	♀	♂	♃	♄	♅	♆	♇
1 F	12 36 33	11♈ 3 12	15♒ 1 55	21♒14 56	26♓ 9.6	25♈ 1.8	25♉41.9	28♓12.8	12♌41.7	3♒14.6	18♈51.2	5♍43.4	19♋57.4
2 Sa	12 40 30	12 2 23	27 24 33	3♓31 8	26 11.0	24R54.3	26 46.6	28 59.6	12R40.3	3 18.6	18 54.6	5R42.1	19D57.3
3 Su	12 44 26	13 1 32	9♓35 5	15 36 46	26 12.2	24 40.2	27 51.1	29 46.3	12 39.1	3 22.5	18 58.0	5 40.8	19 57.3
4 M	12 48 23	14 0 39	21 36 31	27 34 38	26R12.9	24 19.8	28 55.3	0♈33.0	12 38.2	3 26.3	19 1.5	5 39.5	19 57.3
5 Tu	12 52 19	14 59 44	3♈31 27	9♈27 13	26 12.8	23 53.8	29 59.2	1 19.7	12 37.4	3 30.0	19 4.9	5 38.3	19 57.4
6 W	12 56 16	15 58 48	15 22 13	21 16 43	26 11.6	23 22.5	1♊ 2.8	2 6.4	12 36.8	3 33.7	19 8.3	5 37.1	19 57.4
7 Th	13 0 13	16 57 49	27 10 57	3♉ 5 11	26 9.5	22 46.9	2 6.1	2 53.0	12 36.4	3 37.2	19 11.7	5 35.9	19 57.5
8 F	13 4 9	17 56 48	8♉59 41	14 54 43	26 6.4	22 7.5	3 9.1	3 39.6	12D36.2	3 40.7	19 15.2	5 34.8	19 57.6
9 Sa	13 8 6	18 55 45	20 50 34	26 47 32	26 2.6	21 25.3	4 11.8	4 26.1	12 36.2	3 44.1	19 18.6	5 33.7	19 57.8
10 Su	13 12 2	19 54 40	2♊45 57	8♊46 10	25 58.6	20 41.1	5 14.2	5 12.6	12 36.4	3 47.5	19 22.0	5 32.6	19 57.9
11 M	13 15 59	20 53 33	14 48 35	20 53 34	25 54.8	19 55.7	6 16.3	5 59.1	12 36.7	3 50.7	19 25.5	5 31.5	19 58.1
12 Tu	13 19 55	21 52 24	27 1 33	3♋13 0	25 51.7	19 10.1	7 18.0	6 45.5	12 37.3	3 53.8	19 28.9	5 30.4	19 58.3
13 W	13 23 52	22 51 12	9♋28 21	15 48 6	25 49.7	18 25.1	8 19.4	7 32.0	12 38.0	3 56.9	19 32.3	5 29.4	19 58.6
14 Th	13 27 48	23 49 58	22 12 41	28 42 33	25D49.0	17 41.5	9 20.4	8 18.3	12 38.9	3 59.9	19 35.8	5 28.4	19 58.8
15 F	13 31 45	24 48 42	5♌18 8	11♌59 47	25 49.4	17 0.1	10 21.0	9 4.6	12 40.1	4 2.7	19 39.2	5 27.4	19 59.1
16 Sa	13 35 42	25 47 24	18 47 49	25 42 26	25 50.6	16 21.4	11 21.2	9 50.9	12 41.4	4 5.5	19 42.6	5 26.5	19 59.4
17 Su	13 39 38	26 46 3	2♍43 43	9♍51 37	25 52.1	15 46.2	12 21.0	10 37.2	12 42.8	4 8.2	19 46.0	5 25.5	19 59.8
18 M	13 43 35	27 44 40	17 5 56	24 26 16	25R53.2	15 14.9	13 20.5	11 23.4	12 44.5	4 10.9	19 49.4	5 24.7	20 0.1
19 Tu	13 47 31	28 43 15	1♎52 2	9♎22 29	25 53.3	14 47.8	14 19.4	12 9.5	12 46.3	4 13.4	19 52.9	5 23.8	20 0.5
20 W	13 51 28	29 41 47	16 56 38	24 33 23	25 52.0	14 25.3	15 18.0	12 55.7	12 48.4	4 15.8	19 56.2	5 22.9	20 0.9
21 Th	13 55 24	0♉40 18	2♏11 31	9♏49 42	25 48.9	14 7.7	16 16.1	13 41.7	12 50.6	4 18.1	19 59.6	5 22.1	20 1.4
22 F	13 59 21	1 38 47	17 26 37	25 0 57	25 44.5	13 55.0	17 13.7	14 27.8	12 53.0	4 20.4	20 3.0	5 21.4	20 1.8
23 Sa	14 3 17	2 37 14	2♐31 30	9♐57 12	25 39.2	13 47.2	18 10.8	15 13.8	12 55.5	4 22.5	20 6.4	5 20.6	20 2.3
24 Su	14 7 14	3 35 40	17 17 11	24 30 43	25 33.8	13D44.6	19 7.4	15 59.7	12 58.3	4 24.6	20 9.8	5 19.9	20 2.8
25 M	14 11 11	4 34 4	1♑37 21	8♑36 48	25 29.1	13 46.9	20 3.5	16 45.7	13 1.2	4 26.6	20 13.1	5 19.2	20 3.3
26 Tu	14 15 7	5 32 26	15 28 58	22 13 58	25 25.7	13 54.2	20 59.1	17 31.5	13 4.3	4 28.4	20 16.5	5 18.5	20 3.9
27 W	14 19 4	6 30 47	28 52 0	5♒23 27	25D23.9	14 6.3	21 54.1	18 17.4	13 7.5	4 30.2	20 19.8	5 17.9	20 4.5
28 Th	14 23 0	7 29 6	11♒48 46	18 8 26	25 23.7	14 23.1	22 48.6	19 3.2	13 11.0	4 31.9	20 23.1	5 17.3	20 5.1
29 F	14 26 57	8 27 24	24 23 2	0♓33 8	25 24.6	14 44.4	23 42.5	19 48.9	13 14.6	4 33.5	20 26.5	5 16.7	20 5.7
30 Sa	14 30 53	9 25 40	6♓39 19	12 42 12	25 26.1	15 10.2	24 35.8	20 34.7	13 18.3	4 35.0	20 29.7	5 16.2	20 6.3

Astro Data

	Dy Hr Mn
☽0N	8 9:14
☿0N	10 5:02
☽0S	22 8:52
☿ R	31 10:27
♇ D	2 22:58
☽0N	4 15:33
♂0N	6 0:25
♃ D	8 14:10
☽0S	18 19:51
♅□♇	21 14:04
☿ D	24 0:45
♅⚼♆	26 12:21

Planet Ingress

	Dy Hr Mn
☿ ♈	9 20:21
♀ ♉	9 2:07
☉ ♈	20 19:54
♂ ♈	3 7:02
♀ ♊	5 0:19
☉ ♉	20 7:28

Last Aspect / ☽ Ingress

Last Aspect Dy Hr Mn		☽ Ingress Dy Hr Mn
29 13:27	♀ △	♑ 1 7:06
3 0:54	♀ □	♒ 3 14:00
5 15:30	♀ ✶	♓ 5 23:15
8 4:09	☿ ☌	♈ 8 10:35
10 3:08	♇ □	♉ 10 23:19
12 20:04	☉ ✶	♊ 13 12:03
15 12:41	☉ □	♋ 15 22:46
18 1:00	☉ △	♌ 18 5:56
19 13:26	♅ △	♍ 20 9:18
21 18:16	♂ ☍	♎ 22 9:56
23 20:04	☿ ☍	♏ 24 9:35
25 23:27	♂ △	♐ 26 10:07
28 4:50	♂ □	♑ 28 13:08
30 14:07	♂ ✶	♒ 30 19:30

Last Aspect / ☽ Ingress

Last Aspect Dy Hr Mn		☽ Ingress Dy Hr Mn
1 22:39	♀ □	♓ 2 5:05
4 16:09	♀ ✶	♈ 4 16:53
6 15:30	☿ ☌	♉ 7 5:44
8 22:13	♇ ✶	♊ 9 18:27
11 13:03	☉ ✶	♋ 12 5:47
14 3:15	☉ □	♌ 14 14:22
16 13:03	☉ △	♍ 16 19:22
18 4:46	♇ ✶	♎ 18 21:00
20 4:51	♇ □	♏ 20 20:33
22 4:06	♇ △	♐ 22 19:57
24 4:46	♅ △	♑ 24 21:15
26 8:32	♅ □	♒ 27 2:04
28 22:36	♀ △	♓ 29 10:55

☽ Phases & Eclipses

Dy Hr Mn	
7 7:44	● 16♓32
7 7:55:25	☌ A 5'19"
15 12:41	☽ 24♊44
22 12:37	○ 1♎41
22 12:32	☍ P 0.966
29 3:43	☽ 8♑15
6 1:21	● 16♈02
14 3:15	☽ 23♋58
20 21:27	○ 0♏34
27 15:14	☽ 7♒08

Astro Data

1 MARCH 1932
Julian Day # 11748
Delta T 23.9 sec
SVP 06♓12'23"
Obliquity 23°27'03"
⚷ Chiron 19♉12.1
☽ Mean ☊ 27♓06.5

1 APRIL 1932
Julian Day # 11779
Delta T 23.9 sec
SVP 06♓12'20"
Obliquity 23°27'03"
⚷ Chiron 20♉38.7
☽ Mean ☊ 25♓28.0

LONGITUDE MAY 1932

Day	Sid.Time	☉	0 hr ☽	Noon ☽	True ☊	☿	♀	♂	♃	♄	♅	♆	♇
1 Su	14 34 50	10♉23 54	18♓42 19	24♓40 13	25♓27.2	15♈40.2	25♊28.5	21♈20.3	13♌22.3	4♒36.4	20♈33.0	5♍15.7	20♋ 7.0
2 M	14 38 46	11 22 7	0♈36 25	6♈31 24	25R 27.3	16 14.3	26 20.5	22 5.9	13 26.4	4 37.7	20 36.3	5R 15.2	20 7.7
3 Tu	14 42 43	12 20 19	12 25 34	18 19 20	25 25.6	16 52.4	27 11.8	22 51.5	13 30.7	4 38.9	20 39.6	5 14.7	20 8.4
4 W	14 46 40	13 18 28	24 13 4	0♉ 7 4	25 21.8	17 34.2	28 2.5	23 37.0	13 35.1	4 40.0	20 42.8	5 14.3	20 9.1
5 Th	14 50 36	14 16 36	6♉ 1 37	11 56 58	25 15.8	18 19.6	28 52.4	24 22.5	13 39.7	4 41.0	20 46.0	5 13.9	20 9.9
6 F	14 54 33	15 14 43	17 53 21	23 50 58	25 7.8	19 8.6	29 41.6	25 8.0	13 44.4	4 41.9	20 49.2	5 13.6	20 10.6
7 Sa	14 58 29	16 12 48	29 50 1	5♊50 40	24 58.5	20 0.8	0♋30.0	25 53.4	13 49.4	4 42.7	20 52.4	5 13.2	20 11.4
8 Su	15 2 26	17 10 51	11♊53 7	17 57 33	24 48.6	20 56.3	1 17.6	26 38.7	13 54.4	4 43.4	20 55.6	5 12.9	20 12.2
9 M	15 6 22	18 8 53	24 4 11	0♋13 12	24 39.1	21 54.9	2 4.4	27 24.0	13 59.7	4 44.0	20 58.7	5 12.7	20 13.1
10 Tu	15 10 19	19 6 53	6♋24 53	12 39 29	24 30.8	22 56.5	2 50.3	28 9.2	14 5.1	4 44.5	21 1.9	5 12.5	20 13.9
11 W	15 14 15	20 4 51	18 57 18	25 18 39	24 24.5	24 1.0	3 35.3	28 54.4	14 10.6	4 44.9	21 5.0	5 12.3	20 14.8
12 Th	15 18 12	21 2 47	1♌43 53	8♌13 20	24 20.4	25 8.3	4 19.4	29 39.5	14 16.3	4 45.2	21 8.1	5 12.1	20 15.7
13 F	15 22 9	22 0 42	14 47 23	21 26 21	24D 18.6	26 18.3	5 2.5	0♉24.6	14 22.1	4 45.4	21 11.2	5 12.0	20 16.7
14 Sa	15 26 5	22 58 34	28 10 36	5♍ 0 24	24 18.5	27 30.9	5 44.6	1 9.7	14 28.1	4R 45.6	21 14.2	5 11.9	20 17.6
15 Su	15 30 2	23 56 25	11♍55 57	18 57 24	24R 19.1	28 46.1	6 25.6	1 54.6	14 34.3	4 45.6	21 17.2	5 11.8	20 18.6
16 M	15 33 58	24 54 14	26 4 45	3♎17 52	24 19.5	0♉ 3.9	7 5.5	2 39.6	14 40.5	4 45.5	21 20.2	5D 11.8	20 19.5
17 Tu	15 37 55	25 52 1	10♎36 26	18 0 0	24 18.5	1 24.1	7 44.3	3 24.4	14 46.9	4 45.3	21 23.2	5 11.8	20 20.5
18 W	15 41 51	26 49 47	25 27 52	2♏59 12	24 15.3	2 46.7	8 21.8	4 9.2	14 53.5	4 45.1	21 26.1	5 11.8	20 21.6
19 Th	15 45 48	27 47 31	10♏32 57	18 7 57	24 9.6	4 11.8	8 58.2	4 54.0	15 0.2	4 44.7	21 29.1	5 11.9	20 22.6
20 F	15 49 44	28 45 13	25 42 56	3♐16 37	24 1.7	5 39.2	9 33.2	5 38.7	15 7.0	4 44.2	21 32.0	5 12.0	20 23.6
21 Sa	15 53 41	29 42 55	10♐47 40	18 14 54	23 52.3	7 9.0	10 7.0	6 23.4	15 14.0	4 43.7	21 34.9	5 12.1	20 24.7
22 Su	15 57 38	0♊40 35	25 37 13	2♑53 43	23 42.6	8 41.1	10 39.3	7 8.0	15 21.1	4 43.0	21 37.7	5 12.3	20 25.8
23 M	16 1 34	1 38 14	10♑ 3 40	17 6 34	23 33.6	10 15.5	11 10.3	7 52.6	15 28.3	4 42.3	21 40.5	5 12.5	20 26.9
24 Tu	16 5 31	2 35 52	24 2 9	0♒50 19	23 26.4	11 52.2	11 39.7	8 37.1	15 35.7	4 41.4	21 43.3	5 12.7	20 28.1
25 W	16 9 27	3 33 29	7♒31 10	14 4 58	23 21.5	13 31.3	12 7.6	9 21.5	15 43.2	4 40.5	21 46.1	5 13.0	20 29.2
26 Th	16 13 24	4 31 5	20 32 6	26 53 3	23 18.8	15 12.6	12 34.0	10 5.9	15 50.8	4 39.4	21 48.8	5 13.3	20 30.4
27 F	16 17 20	5 28 39	3♓ 8 25	9♓18 47	23D 18.0	16 56.2	12 58.7	10 50.3	15 58.5	4 38.3	21 51.6	5 13.6	20 31.5
28 Sa	16 21 17	6 26 13	15 24 50	21 27 14	23R 18.1	18 42.1	13 21.7	11 34.6	16 6.4	4 37.1	21 54.2	5 13.9	20 32.7
29 Su	16 25 13	7 23 47	27 26 39	3♈23 43	23 18.2	20 30.3	13 42.9	12 18.8	16 14.3	4 35.8	21 56.9	5 14.3	20 33.9
30 M	16 29 10	8 21 19	9♈19 5	15 13 21	23 17.1	22 20.8	14 2.3	13 3.0	16 22.4	4 34.3	21 59.5	5 14.8	20 35.2
31 Tu	16 33 7	9 18 50	21 7 5	27 0 46	23 14.0	24 13.5	14 19.9	13 47.1	16 30.7	4 32.8	22 2.1	5 15.2	20 36.4

LONGITUDE JUNE 1932

Day	Sid.Time	☉	0 hr ☽	Noon ☽	True ☊	☿	♀	♂	♃	♄	♅	♆	♇
1 W	16 37 3	10♊16 21	2♉54 54	8♉49 53	23♓ 8.3	26♉ 8.4	14♋35.5	14♉31.2	16♌39.0	4♒31.2	22♈ 4.6	5♍15.7	20♋37.7
2 Th	16 41 0	11 13 50	14 46 6	20 43 50	22R 59.9	28 5.4	14 49.2	15 15.2	16 47.5	4R 29.6	22 7.2	5 16.2	20 38.9
3 F	16 44 56	12 11 19	26 43 21	2♊44 53	22 49.0	0♊ 4.6	15 0.8	15 59.2	16 56.0	4 27.8	22 9.7	5 16.8	20 40.2
4 Sa	16 48 53	13 8 47	8♊48 36	14 54 36	22 36.4	2 5.8	15 10.3	16 43.1	17 4.7	4 25.9	22 12.1	5 17.4	20 41.5
5 Su	16 52 49	14 6 14	21 3 1	27 13 55	22 23.0	4 8.9	15 17.6	17 27.0	17 13.5	4 24.0	22 14.5	5 18.0	20 42.8
6 M	16 56 46	15 3 41	3♋27 22	9♋43 26	22 10.0	6 13.9	15 22.7	18 10.8	17 22.4	4 21.9	22 16.9	5 18.6	20 44.2
7 Tu	17 0 42	16 1 6	16 2 9	22 23 38	21 58.5	8 20.4	15R 25.6	18 54.5	17 31.4	4 19.8	22 19.3	5 19.3	20 45.5
8 W	17 4 39	16 58 30	28 47 56	5♌15 11	21 49.4	10 28.5	15 26.1	19 38.2	17 40.5	4 17.6	22 21.6	5 20.0	20 46.9
9 Th	17 8 36	17 55 53	11♌45 33	18 19 10	21 43.1	12 37.8	15 24.3	20 21.8	17 49.8	4 15.3	22 23.9	5 20.8	20 48.2
10 F	17 12 32	18 53 15	24 56 15	1♍37 0	21 39.6	14 48.2	15 20.1	21 5.4	17 59.1	4 12.9	22 26.1	5 21.5	20 49.6
11 Sa	17 16 29	19 50 36	8♍21 39	15 10 22	21 38.2	16 59.3	15 13.5	21 48.9	18 8.5	4 10.4	22 28.3	5 22.3	20 51.0
12 Su	17 20 25	20 47 56	22 3 23	29 0 47	21 38.1	19 11.0	15 4.5	22 32.3	18 18.0	4 7.9	22 30.5	5 23.2	20 52.4
13 M	17 24 22	21 45 15	6♎ 2 41	13♎ 9 2	21 37.8	21 23.0	14 53.1	23 15.7	18 27.6	4 5.3	22 32.6	5 24.0	20 53.8
14 Tu	17 28 18	22 42 33	20 19 43	27 34 27	21 36.2	23 35.0	14 39.2	23 59.0	18 37.3	4 2.5	22 34.7	5 24.9	20 55.2
15 W	17 32 15	23 39 51	4♏52 49	12♏14 15	21 32.4	25 46.7	14 23.0	24 42.2	18 47.2	3 59.8	22 36.8	5 25.9	20 56.7
16 Th	17 36 11	24 37 7	19 38 2	27 3 17	21 25.9	27 57.8	14 4.3	25 25.4	18 57.1	3 56.9	22 38.8	5 26.8	20 58.1
17 F	17 40 8	25 34 23	4♐29 3	11♐54 15	21 17.0	0♋ 8.1	13 43.5	26 8.6	19 7.0	3 54.0	22 40.7	5 27.8	20 59.6
18 Sa	17 44 5	26 31 38	19 17 48	26 38 37	21 6.4	2 17.4	13 20.3	26 51.6	19 17.1	3 51.0	22 42.7	5 28.8	21 1.0
19 Su	17 48 1	27 28 52	3♑55 42	11♑ 8 8	20 55.2	4 25.5	12 55.1	27 34.7	19 27.3	3 47.9	22 44.6	5 29.9	21 2.5
20 M	17 51 58	28 26 6	18 15 9	25 16 9	20 44.8	6 32.2	12 27.8	28 17.6	19 37.5	3 44.8	22 46.4	5 30.9	21 4.0
21 Tu	17 55 54	29 23 20	2♒10 43	8♒58 35	20 36.1	8 37.2	11 58.7	29 0.5	19 47.9	3 41.6	22 48.2	5 32.0	21 5.5
22 W	17 59 51	0♋20 33	15 39 44	22 14 14	20 29.9	10 40.6	11 27.9	29 43.4	19 58.3	3 38.3	22 50.0	5 33.2	21 7.0
23 Th	18 3 47	1 17 47	28 42 21	5♓ 4 27	20 26.2	12 42.2	10 55.5	0♊26.2	20 8.8	3 34.9	22 51.7	5 34.3	21 8.5
24 F	18 7 44	2 15 0	11♓20 58	17 32 29	20D 24.6	14 41.8	10 21.7	1 8.9	20 19.4	3 31.5	22 53.4	5 35.5	21 10.0
25 Sa	18 11 41	3 12 13	23 39 36	29 42 57	20R 24.4	16 39.5	9 46.7	1 51.6	20 30.0	3 28.0	22 55.1	5 36.7	21 11.6
26 Su	18 15 37	4 9 25	5♈43 12	11♈41 2	20 24.5	18 35.1	9 10.8	2 34.2	20 40.8	3 24.5	22 56.7	5 37.9	21 13.1
27 M	18 19 34	5 6 38	17 37 7	23 32 7	20 23.8	20 28.7	8 34.1	3 16.7	20 51.6	3 20.9	22 58.2	5 39.2	21 14.6
28 Tu	18 23 30	6 3 51	29 26 40	5♉21 22	20 21.5	22 20.2	7 56.9	3 59.2	21 2.5	3 17.3	22 59.7	5 40.5	21 16.2
29 W	18 27 27	7 1 4	11♉16 47	17 13 27	20 16.9	24 9.6	7 19.4	4 41.6	21 13.5	3 13.5	23 1.2	5 41.8	21 17.7
30 Th	18 31 23	7 58 17	23 11 49	29 12 18	20 9.8	25 56.9	6 41.9	5 24.0	21 24.5	3 9.8	23 2.6	5 43.2	21 19.3

Astro Data Dy Hr Mn	Planet Ingress Dy Hr Mn
☽0N 1 21:11	♀ ♋ 6 9:04
♆∠♇ 8 15:08	♂ ♉ 12 10:53
♄ R 14 16:46	☿ ♉ 15 22:49
☽0S 16 4:56	☉ ♊ 21 7:07
♆ D 16 12:31	
☽0N 29 2:52	☿ ♊ 2 23:05
	☿ ♋ 16 22:30
♀ R 7 17:35	☉ ♋ 21 15:23
☽0S 12 11:16	♂ ♊ 22 9:19
☽0N 25 9:21	
♃⊻♇ 29 10:49	

Last Aspect Dy Hr Mn	☽ Ingress Dy Hr Mn	Last Aspect Dy Hr Mn	☽ Ingress Dy Hr Mn
1 14:42 ♀ □	♈ 1 22:46	2 11:51 ♇ ⚹	♊ 3 6:32
4 8:22 ♀ ⚹	♉ 4 11:46	5 2:20 ♅ ⚹	♋ 5 17:21
6 4:37 ♇ ⚹	♊ 7 0:20	7 11:54 ♅ □	♌ 8 2:14
9 6:56 ♂ ⚹	♋ 9 11:34	9 19:28 ♅ △	♍ 10 9:06
11 19:54 ♂ □	♌ 11 20:47	12 0:53 ♂ △	♎ 12 13:42
13 22:43 ☿ △	♍ 14 3:13	14 6:22 ☿ △	♏ 14 16:00
15 21:53 ☉ △	♎ 16 6:32	16 9:50 ♂ ☍	♐ 16 16:45
17 17:31 ♅ ☍	♏ 18 7:15	18 12:38 ☉ ☍	♑ 18 17:31
20 5:09 ☉ ☍	♐ 20 6:48	20 18:10 ♂ △	♒ 20 20:12
21 17:28 ♅ △	♑ 22 7:12	22 13:08 ♅ ⚹	♓ 23 2:25
23 19:57 ♅ □	♒ 24 10:31	24 19:08 ♇ △	♈ 25 12:34
26 2:25 ♅ ⚹	♓ 26 17:57	27 10:53 ♅ ☌	♉ 28 1:08
28 10:12 ♇ △	♈ 29 5:09	30 6:27 ☿ ⚹	♊ 30 13:35
31 1:52 ♅ ☌	♉ 31 18:05		

☽ Phases & Eclipses Dy Hr Mn	
5 18:11	● 15♉01
13 14:02	☽ 22♌35
20 5:09	○ 28♏58
27 4:54	☽ 5♓40
4 9:16	● 13♊31
11 21:39	☽ 20♍42
18 12:38	○ 27♐02
25 20:36	☽ 4♈01

Astro Data

1 MAY 1932
Julian Day # 11809
Delta T 23.9 sec
SVP 06♓12'16"
Obliquity 23°27'02"
⚷ Chiron 22♉34.7
☽ Mean ☊ 23♓52.6

1 JUNE 1932
Julian Day # 11840
Delta T 23.9 sec
SVP 06♓12'11"
Obliquity 23°27'02"
⚷ Chiron 24♉45.2
☽ Mean ☊ 22♓14.2

JULY 1932 LONGITUDE

Day	Sid.Time	☉	0 hr ☽	Noon ☽	True ☊	☿	♀	♂	♃	♄	♅	♆	♇
1 F	18 35 20	8♋55 31	5♊15 16	11♊20 58	20♓ 0.3	27♋42.0	6♋ 4.6	6♊ 6.3	21♌35.6	3♒ 6.0	23♈ 4.0	5♍44.5	21♋20.8
2 Sa	18 39 16	9 52 44	17 29 40	23 41 30	19R49.1	29 25.0	5R27.8	6 48.6	21 46.8	3R 2.1	23 5.4	5 45.9	21 22.4
3 Su	18 43 13	10 49 57	29 56 35	6♋14 57	19 37.1	1♌ 5.8	4 51.6	7 30.8	21 58.1	2 58.2	23 6.6	5 47.3	21 24.0
4 M	18 47 10	11 47 11	12♋36 36	19 1 31	19 25.5	2 44.6	4 16.3	8 12.9	22 9.4	2 54.2	23 7.9	5 48.8	21 25.6
5 Tu	18 51 6	12 44 24	25 29 35	2♌ 0 44	19 15.2	4 21.1	3 42.0	8 54.9	22 20.8	2 50.2	23 9.1	5 50.3	21 27.2
6 W	18 55 3	13 41 38	8♌34 52	15 11 53	19 7.2	5 55.5	3 9.1	9 36.9	22 32.2	2 46.2	23 10.2	5 51.8	21 28.7
7 Th	18 58 59	14 38 51	21 51 41	28 34 12	19 1.7	7 27.8	2 37.7	10 18.9	22 43.7	2 42.1	23 11.3	5 53.3	21 30.3
8 F	19 2 56	15 36 4	5♍19 22	12♍ 7 10	18 58.9	8 57.8	2 7.8	11 0.7	22 55.3	2 37.9	23 12.4	5 54.8	21 31.9
9 Sa	19 6 52	16 33 17	18 57 36	25 50 39	18D58.1	10 25.6	1 39.8	11 42.5	23 6.9	2 33.8	23 13.4	5 56.4	21 33.5
10 Su	19 10 49	17 30 30	2♎46 20	9♎44 39	18 58.5	11 51.3	1 13.7	12 24.3	23 18.6	2 29.6	23 14.4	5 58.0	21 35.1
11 M	19 14 45	18 27 42	16 45 33	23 49 0	18R59.0	13 14.6	0 49.6	13 5.9	23 30.4	2 25.3	23 15.3	5 59.6	21 36.7
12 Tu	19 18 42	19 24 55	0♏54 52	8♏ 2 57	18 58.5	14 35.7	0 27.7	13 47.5	23 42.2	2 21.1	23 16.2	6 1.2	21 38.3
13 W	19 22 39	20 22 8	15 12 59	22 24 36	18 56.1	15 54.4	0 8.0	14 29.1	23 54.0	2 16.8	23 17.0	6 2.9	21 39.9
14 Th	19 26 35	21 19 21	29 37 19	6♐50 37	18 51.5	17 10.8	29♊50.5	15 10.6	24 5.9	2 12.4	23 17.7	6 4.6	21 41.5
15 F	19 30 32	22 16 34	14♐ 3 51	21 16 19	18 44.9	18 24.7	29 35.4	15 52.0	24 17.9	2 8.1	23 18.5	6 6.3	21 43.1
16 Sa	19 34 28	23 13 47	28 27 17	5♑36 0	18 36.8	19 36.2	29 22.7	16 33.3	24 29.9	2 3.7	23 19.2	6 8.0	21 44.7
17 Su	19 38 25	24 11 0	12♑41 46	19 43 53	18 28.2	20 45.0	29 12.3	17 14.6	24 42.0	1 59.4	23 19.8	6 9.7	21 46.3
18 M	19 42 21	25 8 14	26 41 46	3♒34 53	18 20.1	21 51.2	29 4.4	17 55.8	24 54.1	1 55.0	23 20.4	6 11.5	21 47.9
19 Tu	19 46 18	26 5 28	10♒22 53	17 5 28	18 13.4	22 54.7	28 58.8	18 37.0	25 6.2	1 50.6	23 20.9	6 13.3	21 49.5
20 W	19 50 15	27 2 43	23 42 30	0♓14 0	18 8.7	23 55.4	28D55.6	19 18.1	25 18.4	1 46.1	23 21.4	6 15.1	21 51.1
21 Th	19 54 11	27 59 58	6♓40 2	13 0 52	18D 6.1	24 53.1	28 54.8	19 59.1	25 30.7	1 41.7	23 21.8	6 16.9	21 52.7
22 F	19 58 8	28 57 14	19 16 46	25 28 11	18 5.5	25 47.8	28 56.3	20 40.1	25 43.0	1 37.3	23 22.2	6 18.7	21 54.3
23 Sa	20 2 4	29 54 30	1♈35 33	7♈39 25	18 6.2	26 39.3	29 0.1	21 21.0	25 55.3	1 32.8	23 22.5	6 20.6	21 55.8
24 Su	20 6 1	0♌51 48	13 40 21	19 38 58	18 7.5	27 27.6	29 6.2	22 1.8	26 7.7	1 28.3	23 22.8	6 22.5	21 57.4
25 M	20 9 57	1 49 6	25 35 53	1♉31 45	18R 8.5	28 12.3	29 14.4	22 42.6	26 20.1	1 23.9	23 23.1	6 24.3	21 59.0
26 Tu	20 13 54	2 46 26	7♉27 11	13 22 50	18 8.6	28 53.5	29 24.7	23 23.3	26 32.5	1 19.4	23 23.3	6 26.3	22 0.6
27 W	20 17 50	3 43 46	19 19 19	25 17 13	18 7.2	29 31.0	29 37.2	24 4.0	26 45.0	1 15.0	23 23.4	6 28.2	22 2.2
28 Th	20 21 47	4 41 8	1♊17 6	7♊19 27	18 4.0	0♍ 4.5	29 51.6	24 44.6	26 57.5	1 10.5	23 23.5	6 30.1	22 3.7
29 F	20 25 44	5 38 30	13 24 45	19 33 25	17 59.1	0 33.9	0♋ 8.0	25 25.1	27 10.1	1 6.1	23R23.5	6 32.1	22 5.3
30 Sa	20 29 40	6 35 54	25 45 46	2♋ 2 6	17 52.9	0 59.0	0 26.3	26 5.6	27 22.7	1 1.6	23 23.5	6 34.0	22 6.9
31 Su	20 33 37	7 33 18	8♋22 34	14 47 20	17 46.0	1 19.7	0 46.5	26 45.9	27 35.3	0 57.2	23 23.5	6 36.0	22 8.4

AUGUST 1932 LONGITUDE

Day	Sid.Time	☉	0 hr ☽	Noon ☽	True ☊	☿	♀	♂	♃	♄	♅	♆	♇
1 M	20 37 33	8♌30 44	21♋16 25	27♋49 46	17♓39.3	1♍35.7	1♋ 8.4	27♊26.3	27♌48.0	0♒52.8	23♈23.4	6♍38.0	22♋10.0
2 Tu	20 41 30	9 28 10	4♌27 17	11♌ 8 47	17R33.3	1 46.9	1 32.0	28 6.5	28 0.7	0R48.4	23R23.2	6 40.1	22 11.5
3 W	20 45 26	10 25 37	17 54 3	24 42 47	17 28.8	1R53.1	1 57.3	28 46.7	28 13.4	0 44.1	23 23.0	6 42.1	22 13.1
4 Th	20 49 23	11 23 6	1♍34 42	8♍29 26	17 26.1	1 54.2	2 24.1	29 26.8	28 26.2	0 39.7	23 22.8	6 44.1	22 14.6
5 F	20 53 19	12 20 35	15 26 40	22 26 4	17D25.1	1 50.1	2 52.5	0♋ 6.9	28 38.9	0 35.4	23 22.5	6 46.2	22 16.1
6 Sa	20 57 16	13 18 4	29 27 16	6♎30 0	17 25.5	1 40.7	3 22.4	0 46.9	28 51.7	0 31.1	23 22.1	6 48.2	22 17.6
7 Su	21 1 13	14 15 35	13♎33 57	20 38 50	17 26.8	1 26.0	3 53.6	1 26.8	29 4.6	0 26.8	23 21.7	6 50.3	22 19.1
8 M	21 5 9	15 13 7	27 44 24	4♏50 24	17 28.2	1 6.0	4 26.3	2 6.6	29 17.4	0 22.6	23 21.3	6 52.4	22 20.6
9 Tu	21 9 6	16 10 39	11♏56 35	19 2 42	17R29.0	0 40.7	5 0.3	2 46.4	29 30.3	0 18.3	23 20.8	6 54.5	22 22.1
10 W	21 13 2	17 8 12	26 8 30	3♐13 43	17 28.8	0 10.5	5 35.5	3 26.1	29 43.2	0 14.2	23 20.3	6 56.6	22 23.6
11 Th	21 16 59	18 5 46	10♐18 3	17 21 11	17 27.3	29♌35.5	6 12.0	4 5.7	29 56.1	0 10.0	23 19.7	6 58.7	22 25.1
12 F	21 20 55	19 3 21	24 22 48	1♑22 33	17 24.5	28 56.2	6 49.7	4 45.2	0♍ 9.0	0 5.9	23 19.0	7 0.9	22 26.5
13 Sa	21 24 52	20 0 57	8♑20 4	15 15 1	17 20.9	28 13.1	7 28.5	5 24.7	0 22.0	0 1.9	23 18.4	7 3.0	22 28.0
14 Su	21 28 48	20 58 34	22 7 2	28 55 48	17 17.0	27 26.8	8 8.4	6 4.2	0 34.9	29♑57.9	23 17.6	7 5.2	22 29.4
15 M	21 32 45	21 56 12	5♒41 0	12♒22 25	17 13.3	26 37.9	8 49.4	6 43.5	0 47.9	29 53.9	23 16.9	7 7.3	22 30.8
16 Tu	21 36 42	22 53 51	18 59 48	25 33 3	17 10.3	25 47.5	9 31.4	7 22.8	1 0.9	29 50.0	23 16.0	7 9.5	22 32.3
17 W	21 40 38	23 51 31	2♓ 2 3	8♓26 49	17 8.4	24 56.3	10 14.4	8 2.0	1 13.9	29 46.1	23 15.2	7 11.7	22 33.7
18 Th	21 44 35	24 49 12	14 47 23	21 3 55	17D 7.7	24 5.3	10 58.3	8 41.1	1 26.9	29 42.3	23 14.3	7 13.8	22 35.1
19 F	21 48 31	25 46 55	27 16 34	3♈25 39	17 8.0	23 15.7	11 43.2	9 20.2	1 39.9	29 38.5	23 13.3	7 16.0	22 36.5
20 Sa	21 52 28	26 44 40	9♈31 27	15 34 21	17 9.0	22 28.3	12 29.0	9 59.2	1 52.9	29 34.8	23 12.3	7 18.2	22 37.8
21 Su	21 56 24	27 42 26	21 34 48	27 33 15	17 10.5	21 44.2	13 15.6	10 38.1	2 6.0	29 31.1	23 11.3	7 20.4	22 39.2
22 M	22 0 21	28 40 14	3♉30 14	9♉26 16	17 12.0	21 4.4	14 3.1	11 17.0	2 19.0	29 27.5	23 10.2	7 22.6	22 40.5
23 Tu	22 4 17	29 38 3	15 21 55	21 17 47	17 13.2	20 29.7	14 51.4	11 55.7	2 32.1	29 23.9	23 9.1	7 24.8	22 41.9
24 W	22 8 14	0♍35 55	27 14 26	3♊12 29	17R13.8	20 1.0	15 40.4	12 34.5	2 45.1	29 20.5	23 7.9	7 27.0	22 43.2
25 Th	22 12 11	1 33 48	9♊12 30	15 15 5	17 13.7	19 38.9	16 30.2	13 13.1	2 58.2	29 17.0	23 6.7	7 29.2	22 44.5
26 F	22 16 7	2 31 43	21 20 46	27 30 4	17 12.8	19 23.9	17 20.7	13 51.7	3 11.2	29 13.7	23 5.4	7 31.5	22 45.8
27 Sa	22 20 4	3 29 39	3♋43 28	10♋ 1 23	17 11.5	19D16.6	18 11.9	14 30.2	3 24.3	29 10.4	23 4.1	7 33.7	22 47.1
28 Su	22 24 0	4 27 38	16 24 10	22 52 6	17 9.8	19 17.3	19 3.8	15 8.6	3 37.4	29 7.2	23 2.8	7 35.9	22 48.3
29 M	22 27 57	5 25 38	29 25 21	6♌ 4 3	17 8.2	19 26.2	19 56.3	15 46.9	3 50.4	29 4.0	23 1.4	7 38.1	22 49.6
30 Tu	22 31 53	6 23 40	12♌48 9	19 37 33	17 6.8	19 43.3	20 49.4	16 25.2	4 3.5	29 0.9	22 60.0	7 40.4	22 50.8
31 W	22 35 50	7 21 44	26 32 2	3♍31 15	17 5.8	20 8.7	21 43.1	17 3.4	4 16.6	28 57.9	22 58.5	7 42.6	22 52.0

Astro Data	Planet Ingress	Last Aspect	☽ Ingress	Last Aspect	☽ Ingress	☽ Phases & Eclipses	Astro Data
Dy Hr Mn	Dy Hr Mn	Dy Hr Mn	Dy Hr Mn	Dy Hr Mn	Dy Hr Mn	Dy Hr Mn	1 JULY 1932
☽0S 9 15:58	☿ ♌ 2 8:16	2 10:51 ♅ ⚹	♋ 3 0:07	1 3:53 ♅ □	♌ 1 15:57	3 22:20 ● 11♋43	Julian Day # 11870
♃△♅ 9 14:32	♀ ♊ 13 10:33	4 19:40 ♅ □	♌ 5 8:18	3 20:06 ♂ ⚹	♍ 3 21:15	11 3:07 ☽ 18♎35	Delta T 23.9 sec
♀ D 20 20:22	☉ ♌ 23 2:18	7 2:23 ♅ △	♍ 7 14:33	5 11:44 ♇ ⚹	♎ 6 0:56	17 21:06 ○ 25♑01	SVP 06♓12'06"
☽0N 22 16:52	☿ ♍ 27 20:38	9 4:33 ♇ ⚹	♎ 9 19:12	8 2:40 ♃ ⚹	♏ 8 3:49	25 13:41 ☽ 2♉22	Obliquity 23°27'01"
♅ R 29 10:14	♀ ♋ 28 12:36	11 11:38 ♃ ⚹	♏ 11 22:27	10 6:09 ♃ □	♐ 10 6:32		⚷ Chiron 26♉40.1
		13 14:41 ♃ □	♐ 14 0:38	12 7:26 ☿ △	♑ 12 9:38	2 9:42 ● 9♌51	☽ Mean ☊ 20♓38.9
☿ R 3 17:13	♂ ♋ 4 19:52	16 1:32 ♀ ☍	♑ 16 2:35	14 13:46 ♄ ☌	♒ 14 13:54	9 7:40 ☽ 16♏29	
☽0S 5 21:13	☿ ♌ 10 7:32	17 21:06 ☉ ☍	♒ 18 5:44	16 11:41 ☿ ☍	♓ 16 20:13	16 7:41 ○ 23♒12	1 AUGUST 1932
♃⊼♄ 11 19:40	♃ ♍ 11 7:16	20 9:34 ♀ △	♓ 20 11:34	19 4:35 ♄ ⚹	♈ 19 5:18	24 7:21 ☽ 0♊54	Julian Day # 11901
☽0N 19 0:56	♄ ♑ 13 11:14	22 20:24 ☉ △	♈ 22 20:52	21 15:53 ♄ □	♉ 21 16:56	31 19:54 ● 8♍10	Delta T 23.9 sec
☿ D 27 10:02	☉ ♍ 23 9:06	25 7:28 ♀ ⚹	♉ 25 8:54	24 4:13 ♄ △	♊ 24 5:33	31 20:03:16 ☉ T 1'45"	SVP 06♓12'00"
		27 15:12 ♃ □	♊ 27 21:26	26 3:24 ♅ ⚹	♋ 26 16:50		Obliquity 23°27'02"
		30 3:09 ♃ ⚹	♋ 30 8:07	28 23:21 ♄ ☍	♌ 29 1:03		⚷ Chiron 28♉05.8
				30 17:51 ♅ △	♍ 31 5:58		☽ Mean ☊ 19♓00.4

LONGITUDE SEPTEMBER 1932

Day	Sid.Time	☉	0 hr ☽	Noon ☽	True ☊	☿	♀	♂	♃	♄	♅	♆	♇
1 Th	22 39 46	8♍19 49	10♍34 45	17♍42 3	17♓ 5.3	20♌42.3	22♋37.4	17♋41.5	4♍29.6	28♑55.0	22♈57.0	7♍44.8	22♋53.2
2 F	22 43 43	9 17 56	24 52 31	2♎ 5 31	17D 5.4	21 24.0	23 32.3	18 19.6	4 42.7	28R 52.1	22R 55.5	7 47.0	22 54.4
3 Sa	22 47 40	10 16 4	9♎20 23	16 36 22	17 5.7	22 13.5	24 27.6	18 57.5	4 55.7	28 49.3	22 53.9	7 49.3	22 55.6
4 Su	22 51 36	11 14 14	23 52 49	1♏ 9 3	17 6.2	23 10.4	25 23.6	19 35.4	5 8.7	28 46.6	22 52.3	7 51.5	22 56.7
5 M	22 55 33	12 12 26	8♏24 27	15 38 26	17 6.7	24 14.4	26 20.0	20 13.2	5 21.8	28 44.0	22 50.6	7 53.7	22 57.8
6 Tu	22 59 29	13 10 39	22 50 31	0♐ 0 15	17 7.1	25 25.1	27 16.9	20 50.9	5 34.8	28 41.4	22 48.9	7 55.9	22 58.9
7 W	23 3 26	14 8 54	7♐ 7 18	14 11 22	17R 7.2	26 42.0	28 14.2	21 28.5	5 47.8	28 39.0	22 47.2	7 58.2	23 0.0
8 Th	23 7 22	15 7 10	21 12 13	28 9 43	17 7.2	28 4.5	29 12.1	22 6.0	6 0.8	28 36.6	22 45.5	8 0.4	23 1.1
9 F	23 11 19	16 5 28	5♑ 3 43	11♑54 10	17 7.2	29 32.2	0♌10.4	22 43.5	6 13.7	28 34.3	22 43.7	8 2.6	23 2.2
10 Sa	23 15 15	17 3 47	18 41 2	25 24 19	17D 7.1	1♍ 4.6	1 9.1	23 20.9	6 26.7	28 32.1	22 41.8	8 4.8	23 3.2
11 Su	23 19 12	18 2 8	2♒ 4 1	8♒40 9	17 7.2	2 40.9	2 8.2	23 58.2	6 39.6	28 30.0	22 40.0	8 7.0	23 4.2
12 M	23 23 9	19 0 30	15 12 47	21 41 58	17 7.3	4 20.7	3 7.8	24 35.4	6 52.5	28 28.0	22 38.1	8 9.2	23 5.3
13 Tu	23 27 5	19 58 54	28 7 45	4♓30 13	17 7.5	6 3.6	4 7.8	25 12.5	7 5.4	28 26.0	22 36.2	8 11.4	23 6.2
14 W	23 31 2	20 57 19	10♓49 27	17 5 32	17R 7.7	7 48.8	5 8.1	25 49.6	7 18.3	28 24.2	22 34.2	8 13.6	23 7.2
15 Th	23 34 58	21 55 47	23 18 37	29 28 48	17 7.7	9 36.1	6 8.8	26 26.5	7 31.1	28 22.4	22 32.3	8 15.7	23 8.1
16 F	23 38 55	22 54 16	5♈36 17	11♈41 14	17 7.4	11 25.0	7 9.9	27 3.4	7 44.0	28 20.7	22 30.2	8 17.9	23 9.1
17 Sa	23 42 51	23 52 47	17 43 53	23 44 29	17 6.8	13 15.0	8 11.4	27 40.2	7 56.8	28 19.2	22 28.2	8 20.1	23 10.0
18 Su	23 46 48	24 51 21	29 43 19	5♉40 43	17 5.9	15 5.9	9 13.2	28 16.9	8 9.6	28 17.7	22 26.1	8 22.2	23 10.8
19 M	23 50 44	25 49 56	11♉37 2	17 32 40	17 4.7	16 57.3	10 15.4	28 53.5	8 22.3	28 16.3	22 24.1	8 24.4	23 11.7
20 Tu	23 54 41	26 48 34	23 28 3	29 23 38	17 3.4	18 49.0	11 17.9	29 30.0	8 35.0	28 15.0	22 21.9	8 26.5	23 12.5
21 W	23 58 37	27 47 13	5♊19 55	11♊17 26	17 2.3	20 40.7	12 20.8	0♌ 6.5	8 47.7	28 13.8	22 19.8	8 28.7	23 13.4
22 Th	0 2 34	28 45 55	17 16 42	23 18 18	17 1.4	22 32.3	13 23.9	0 42.8	9 0.4	28 12.7	22 17.6	8 30.8	23 14.2
23 F	0 6 31	29 44 40	29 22 46	5♋30 42	17D 1.1	24 23.5	14 27.4	1 19.1	9 13.1	28 11.7	22 15.5	8 32.9	23 14.9
24 Sa	0 10 27	0♎43 26	11♋42 38	17 59 7	17 1.4	26 14.4	15 31.1	1 55.3	9 25.7	28 10.7	22 13.3	8 35.0	23 15.7
25 Su	0 14 24	1 42 15	24 20 40	0♌47 42	17 2.2	28 4.7	16 35.2	2 31.4	9 38.2	28 9.9	22 11.0	8 37.1	23 16.4
26 M	0 18 20	2 41 6	7♌20 38	13 59 46	17 3.4	29 54.3	17 39.5	3 7.3	9 50.8	28 9.2	22 8.8	8 39.2	23 17.1
27 Tu	0 22 17	3 39 59	20 45 18	27 37 19	17 4.7	1♎43.3	18 44.2	3 43.2	10 3.3	28 8.6	22 6.5	8 41.2	23 17.8
28 W	0 26 13	4 38 55	4♍35 46	11♍40 27	17R 5.7	3 31.5	19 49.0	4 19.0	10 15.7	28 8.0	22 4.2	8 43.3	23 18.5
29 Th	0 30 10	5 37 52	18 50 59	26 6 50	17 6.0	5 18.9	20 54.2	4 54.7	10 28.1	28 7.6	22 1.9	8 45.3	23 19.1
30 F	0 34 6	6 36 52	3♎27 21	10♎51 40	17 5.4	7 5.6	21 59.6	5 30.3	10 40.5	28 7.3	21 59.6	8 47.3	23 19.8

LONGITUDE OCTOBER 1932

Day	Sid.Time	☉	0 hr ☽	Noon ☽	True ☊	☿	♀	♂	♃	♄	♅	♆	♇
1 Sa	0 38 3	7♎35 53	18♎18 50	25♎47 49	17♓ 3.8	8♎51.4	23♌ 5.2	6♌ 5.8	10♍52.8	28♑ 7.1	21♈57.3	8♍49.3	23♋20.3
2 Su	0 42 0	8 34 57	3♏17 31	10♏46 51	17R 1.3	10 36.3	24 11.1	6 41.2	11 5.1	28D 6.9	21R 54.9	8 51.3	23 20.9
3 M	0 45 56	9 34 3	18 14 44	25 40 12	16 58.3	12 20.4	25 17.2	7 16.4	11 17.4	28 6.9	21 52.5	8 53.3	23 21.5
4 Tu	0 49 53	10 33 10	3♐ 2 21	10♐20 27	16 55.3	14 3.7	26 23.6	7 51.6	11 29.6	28 7.0	21 50.2	8 55.3	23 22.0
5 W	0 53 49	11 32 20	17 33 54	24 42 16	16 52.8	15 46.2	27 30.1	8 26.7	11 41.7	28 7.2	21 47.8	8 57.2	23 22.5
6 Th	0 57 46	12 31 31	1♑45 17	8♑42 47	16D 51.2	17 27.8	28 36.9	9 1.6	11 53.8	28 7.5	21 45.4	8 59.2	23 23.0
7 F	1 1 42	13 30 44	15 34 47	22 21 21	16 50.9	19 8.6	29 43.9	9 36.5	12 5.9	28 7.8	21 43.0	9 1.1	23 23.4
8 Sa	1 5 39	14 29 58	29 2 41	5♒39 1	16 51.6	20 48.7	0♍51.1	10 11.2	12 17.9	28 8.3	21 40.6	9 3.0	23 23.9
9 Su	1 9 35	15 29 14	12♒10 40	18 37 56	16 53.0	22 27.9	1 58.5	10 45.8	12 29.8	28 8.9	21 38.2	9 4.9	23 24.3
10 M	1 13 32	16 28 32	25 1 10	1♓20 43	16 54.7	24 6.4	3 6.1	11 20.3	12 41.7	28 9.6	21 35.7	9 6.7	23 24.6
11 Tu	1 17 29	17 27 52	7♓36 54	13 50 2	16R 56.0	25 44.1	4 13.9	11 54.7	12 53.5	28 10.4	21 33.3	9 8.6	23 25.0
12 W	1 21 25	18 27 14	20 0 25	26 8 21	16 56.3	27 21.1	5 21.9	12 29.0	13 5.3	28 11.2	21 30.9	9 10.4	23 25.3
13 Th	1 25 22	19 26 37	2♈14 3	8♈17 47	16 55.1	28 57.4	6 30.1	13 3.2	13 17.0	28 12.2	21 28.4	9 12.2	23 25.6
14 F	1 29 18	20 26 3	14 19 46	20 20 12	16 52.3	0♏33.0	7 38.4	13 37.2	13 28.6	28 13.3	21 26.0	9 14.0	23 25.9
15 Sa	1 33 15	21 25 30	26 19 17	2♉17 13	16 47.8	2 8.0	8 47.0	14 11.1	13 40.2	28 14.5	21 23.5	9 15.8	23 26.2
16 Su	1 37 11	22 25 0	8♉14 13	14 10 28	16 41.8	3 42.2	9 55.7	14 44.9	13 51.7	28 15.7	21 21.1	9 17.5	23 26.4
17 M	1 41 8	23 24 32	20 6 13	26 1 43	16 35.0	5 15.9	11 4.6	15 18.6	14 3.1	28 17.1	21 18.6	9 19.2	23 26.6
18 Tu	1 45 4	24 24 6	1♊57 15	7♊53 7	16 27.8	6 48.9	12 13.7	15 52.2	14 14.5	28 18.6	21 16.2	9 20.9	23 26.8
19 W	1 49 1	25 23 42	13 49 41	19 47 19	16 21.2	8 21.2	13 23.0	16 25.7	14 25.8	28 20.2	21 13.8	9 22.6	23 26.9
20 Th	1 52 58	26 23 20	25 46 26	1♋47 29	16 15.6	9 53.0	14 32.4	16 59.0	14 37.1	28 21.8	21 11.3	9 24.3	23 27.1
21 F	1 56 54	27 23 1	7♋50 59	13 57 25	16 11.7	11 24.2	15 42.0	17 32.2	14 48.3	28 23.6	21 8.9	9 25.9	23 27.2
22 Sa	2 0 51	28 22 43	20 7 20	26 21 18	16D 9.7	12 54.7	16 51.7	18 5.2	14 59.4	28 25.5	21 6.5	9 27.5	23 27.3
23 Su	2 4 47	29 22 28	2♌39 52	9♌ 3 35	16 9.3	14 24.7	18 1.6	18 38.1	15 10.4	28 27.5	21 4.1	9 29.1	23 27.3
24 M	2 8 44	0♏22 16	15 32 59	22 8 33	16 10.2	15 54.1	19 11.6	19 10.9	15 21.3	28 29.5	21 1.7	9 30.7	23R 27.4
25 Tu	2 12 40	1 22 5	28 50 41	5♍39 42	16 11.6	17 22.8	20 21.8	19 43.6	15 32.2	28 31.7	20 59.3	9 32.2	23 27.4
26 W	2 16 37	2 21 57	12♍35 49	19 39 4	16R 12.5	18 51.0	21 32.1	20 16.1	15 43.0	28 33.9	20 56.9	9 33.7	23 27.4
27 Th	2 20 33	3 21 51	26 49 20	4♎ 6 17	16 12.0	20 18.6	22 42.6	20 48.4	15 53.7	28 36.3	20 54.5	9 35.2	23 27.3
28 F	2 24 30	4 21 47	11♎29 25	18 57 56	16 9.6	21 45.5	23 53.2	21 20.7	16 4.3	28 38.7	20 52.1	9 36.7	23 27.2
29 Sa	2 28 27	5 21 45	26 30 54	4♏ 7 10	16 4.9	23 11.7	25 3.9	21 52.7	16 14.9	28 41.3	20 49.8	9 38.1	23 27.1
30 Su	2 32 23	6 21 45	11♏45 27	19 24 20	15 58.3	24 37.3	26 14.8	22 24.6	16 25.3	28 43.9	20 47.5	9 39.5	23 27.0
31 M	2 36 20	7 21 47	27 2 25	4♐38 19	15 50.4	26 2.2	27 25.7	22 56.4	16 35.7	28 46.6	20 45.1	9 40.9	23 26.9

Astro Data	Planet Ingress	Last Aspect	☽ Ingress	Last Aspect	☽ Ingress	☽ Phases & Eclipses	Astro Data
Dy Hr Mn	Dy Hr Mn	Dy Hr Mn	Dy Hr Mn	Dy Hr Mn	Dy Hr Mn	Dy Hr Mn	1 SEPTEMBER 1932
☽0S 2 4:46	♀ ♌ 8 19:45	2 6:38 ♄ △	♎ 2 8:32	1 15:43 ♄ □	♏ 1 18:44	7 12:49 ☽ 14♐40	Julian Day # 11932
♅□♇ 2 9:28	☿ ♍ 9 7:20	4 8:03 ♄ □	♏ 4 10:06	3 15:58 ♄ ✶	♐ 3 19:02	14 21:06 ○ 21♓49	Delta T 23.9 sec
♅⚼♆ 4 4:53	♂ ♌ 20 19:43	6 9:46 ♄ ✶	♐ 6 12:00	5 18:11 ♀ △	♑ 5 21:00	14 21:01 ☍P 0.975	SVP 06♓11'55"
♆∠♇ 8 15:45	☉ ♎ 23 6:16	8 13:14 ☿ △	♑ 8 15:11	7 22:22 ♄ ☌	♒ 8 1:44	23 0:47 ☽ 29♊47	Obliquity 23°27'02"
☽0N 15 8:38	☿ ♎ 26 1:15	10 17:35 ♄ ☌	♒ 10 20:16	9 22:01 ☿ △	♓ 10 9:26	30 5:30 ● 6♎50	⚷ Chiron 28♉40.5
♃⚼♅ 15 1:47		12 13:42 ♅ ✶	♓ 13 3:31	12 16:03 ♄ ✶	♈ 12 19:36		☽ Mean ☊ 17♓21.9
♃∠♇ 18 2:35	♀ ♍ 7 5:46	15 9:49 ♄ ✶	♈ 15 13:01	15 3:52 ♄ □	♉ 15 7:24	6 20:05 ☽ 13♑21	
♃☌♆ 19 4:41	☿ ♏ 13 15:41	17 21:08 ♄ □	♉ 18 0:34	17 16:36 ♄ △	♊ 17 20:03	14 13:18 ○ 20♈59	1 OCTOBER 1932
☿0S 27 21:27	☉ ♏ 23 15:04	20 12:53 ♂ ✶	♊ 20 13:14	20 1:20 ☉ △	♋ 20 8:26	22 17:14 ☽ 29♋06	Julian Day # 11962
☽0S 29 14:41		23 0:47 ☉ □	♋ 23 1:13	22 17:14 ☉ □	♌ 22 18:57	29 14:56 ● 5♏59	Delta T 23.9 sec
♄ D 2 17:38		25 8:07 ☿ ✶	♌ 25 10:32	24 9:57 ♅ △	♍ 25 2:03		SVP 06♓11'52"
☽0N 12 15:09		27 2:22 ♅ △	♍ 27 16:07	27 2:58 ♄ △	♎ 27 5:15		Obliquity 23°27'02"
♃⚼♄ 12 13:20		29 15:18 ♄ △	♎ 29 18:22	29 3:27 ♄ □	♏ 29 5:30		⚷ Chiron 28♉17.4R
♇ R 24 17:44	☽0S 27 1:22			31 2:45 ♄ ✶	♐ 31 4:40		☽ Mean ☊ 15♓46.6

NOVEMBER 1932 LONGITUDE

Day	Sid.Time	☉	0 hr ☽	Noon ☽	True ☊	☿	♀	♂	♃	♄	♅	♆	♇
1 Tu	2 40 16	8♏21 51	12♐10 46	19♐38 37	15♓42.2	27♏26.3	28♏36.8	23♌28.0	16♍45.9	28♑49.4	20♈42.8	9♍42.3	23♋26.7
2 W	2 44 13	9 21 56	27 0 56	4♑17 1	15R 34.9	28 49.6	29 48.1	23 59.4	16 56.1	28 52.3	20R 40.6	9 43.6	23R 26.5
3 Th	2 48 9	10 22 3	11♑26 21	18 28 40	15 29.4	0♐12.1	0♎59.4	24 30.7	17 6.2	28 55.4	20 38.3	9 44.9	23 26.3
4 F	2 52 6	11 22 12	25 23 54	2♒12 8	15 26.0	1 33.6	2 10.8	25 1.8	17 16.2	28 58.5	20 36.1	9 46.2	23 26.1
5 Sa	2 56 2	12 22 22	8♒53 36	15 28 42	15D 24.7	2 54.1	3 22.4	25 32.7	17 26.1	29 1.6	20 33.8	9 47.4	23 25.8
6 Su	2 59 59	13 22 34	21 57 50	28 21 33	15 25.0	4 13.5	4 34.0	26 3.5	17 35.9	29 4.9	20 31.6	9 48.7	23 25.5
7 M	3 3 56	14 22 47	4♓40 21	10♓54 47	15R 25.8	5 31.7	5 45.7	26 34.1	17 45.6	29 8.3	20 29.4	9 49.8	23 25.2
8 Tu	3 7 52	15 23 1	17 5 26	23 12 47	15 26.2	6 48.5	6 57.6	27 4.5	17 55.1	29 11.7	20 27.3	9 51.0	23 24.8
9 W	3 11 49	16 23 17	29 17 23	5♈19 40	15 25.1	8 3.8	8 9.5	27 34.7	18 4.6	29 15.2	20 25.2	9 52.1	23 24.5
10 Th	3 15 45	17 23 35	11♈20 5	17 19 0	15 21.7	9 17.5	9 21.6	28 4.8	18 14.0	29 18.9	20 23.1	9 53.2	23 24.1
11 F	3 19 42	18 23 54	23 16 47	29 13 43	15 15.6	10 29.3	10 33.7	28 34.7	18 23.3	29 22.6	20 21.0	9 54.3	23 23.7
12 Sa	3 23 38	19 24 15	5♉10 5	11♉ 6 6	15 6.8	11 39.1	11 46.0	29 4.3	18 32.4	29 26.4	20 18.9	9 55.3	23 23.2
13 Su	3 27 35	20 24 37	17 1 59	22 57 54	14 55.6	12 46.4	12 58.3	29 33.8	18 41.5	29 30.2	20 16.9	9 56.3	23 22.8
14 M	3 31 31	21 25 1	28 54 2	4♊50 33	14 42.8	13 51.2	14 10.7	0♍ 3.1	18 50.4	29 34.2	20 14.9	9 57.3	23 22.3
15 Tu	3 35 28	22 25 27	10♊47 36	16 45 22	14 29.4	14 53.0	15 23.2	0 32.2	18 59.2	29 38.2	20 12.9	9 58.3	23 21.8
16 W	3 39 25	23 25 54	22 44 4	28 43 55	14 16.7	15 51.4	16 35.8	1 1.2	19 7.9	29 42.3	20 11.0	9 59.2	23 21.2
17 Th	3 43 21	24 26 23	4♋45 10	10♋48 7	14 5.5	16 46.0	17 48.5	1 29.9	19 16.5	29 46.5	20 9.1	10 0.1	23 20.7
18 F	3 47 18	25 26 54	16 53 7	23 0 30	13 56.8	17 36.3	19 1.3	1 58.4	19 25.0	29 50.8	20 7.2	10 0.9	23 20.1
19 Sa	3 51 14	26 27 27	29 10 44	5♌24 15	13 50.9	18 21.8	20 14.2	2 26.6	19 33.3	29 55.2	20 5.4	10 1.7	23 19.5
20 Su	3 55 11	27 28 1	11♌41 32	18 3 6	13 47.7	19 1.8	21 27.1	2 54.7	19 41.5	29 59.6	20 3.6	10 2.5	23 18.9
21 M	3 59 7	28 28 37	24 29 28	1♍ 1 9	13D 46.6	19 35.7	22 40.1	3 22.5	19 49.6	0♒ 4.1	20 1.8	10 3.3	23 18.3
22 Tu	4 3 4	29 29 15	7♍38 38	14 22 21	13R 46.7	20 2.7	23 53.2	3 50.2	19 57.6	0 8.7	20 0.1	10 4.0	23 17.6
23 W	4 7 0	0♐29 54	21 12 41	28 9 53	13 46.6	20 22.1	25 6.4	4 17.5	20 5.4	0 13.3	19 58.4	10 4.7	23 16.9
24 Th	4 10 57	1 30 35	5♎14 4	12♎25 11	13 45.1	20R 33.1	26 19.6	4 44.7	20 13.1	0 18.1	19 56.7	10 5.3	23 16.2
25 F	4 14 54	2 31 18	19 42 59	27 7 0	13 41.2	20 34.9	27 32.9	5 11.6	20 20.7	0 22.9	19 55.1	10 5.9	23 15.5
26 Sa	4 18 50	3 32 2	4♏36 32	12♏10 36	13 34.5	20 26.9	28 46.2	5 38.2	20 28.2	0 27.8	19 53.5	10 6.5	23 14.7
27 Su	4 22 47	4 32 48	19 48 5	27 27 39	13 25.2	20 8.4	29 59.7	6 4.6	20 35.5	0 32.7	19 52.0	10 7.1	23 13.9
28 M	4 26 43	5 33 36	5♐ 7 51	12♐47 10	13 14.0	19 39.0	1♏13.2	6 30.8	20 42.6	0 37.7	19 50.5	10 7.6	23 13.1
29 Tu	4 30 40	6 34 24	20 24 9	27 57 24	13 2.2	18 58.6	2 26.7	6 56.6	20 49.6	0 42.8	19 49.0	10 8.1	23 12.3
30 W	4 34 36	7 35 14	5♑25 42	12♑48 1	12 51.4	18 7.5	3 40.3	7 22.2	20 56.5	0 48.0	19 47.6	10 8.6	23 11.5

DECEMBER 1932 LONGITUDE

Day	Sid.Time	☉	0 hr ☽	Noon ☽	True ☊	☿	♀	♂	♃	♄	♅	♆	♇
1 Th	4 38 33	8♐36 5	20♑ 3 35	27♑11 51	12♓42.5	17♐ 6.4	4♏54.0	7♍47.6	21♍ 3.3	0♒53.2	19♈46.2	10♍ 9.0	23♋10.7
2 F	4 42 29	9 36 57	4♒12 31	11♒ 5 31	12R 36.4	15R 56.7	6 7.7	8 12.6	21 9.8	0 58.5	19R 44.9	10 9.4	23R 9.8
3 Sa	4 46 26	10 37 49	17 50 58	24 29 8	12 33.0	14 40.2	7 21.4	8 37.3	21 16.3	1 3.8	19 43.6	10 9.7	23 8.9
4 Su	4 50 23	11 38 43	1♓ 0 28	7♓25 27	12 31.7	13 19.2	8 35.2	9 1.8	21 22.6	1 9.3	19 42.4	10 10.0	23 8.0
5 M	4 54 19	12 39 37	13 44 42	19 58 50	12 31.5	11 56.3	9 49.0	9 25.9	21 28.7	1 14.7	19 41.2	10 10.3	23 7.1
6 Tu	4 58 16	13 40 31	26 8 30	2♈14 21	12 31.3	10 34.4	11 2.9	9 49.8	21 34.7	1 20.3	19 40.0	10 10.5	23 6.1
7 W	5 2 12	14 41 27	8♈17 1	14 17 8	12 29.6	9 16.1	12 16.9	10 13.3	21 40.5	1 25.9	19 38.9	10 10.8	23 5.2
8 Th	5 6 9	15 42 23	20 15 17	26 11 59	12 25.7	8 4.1	13 30.8	10 36.6	21 46.2	1 31.5	19 37.8	10 10.9	23 4.2
9 F	5 10 5	16 43 20	2♉ 7 45	8♉ 3 0	12 18.9	7 0.3	14 44.9	10 59.5	21 51.7	1 37.2	19 36.8	10 11.1	23 3.2
10 Sa	5 14 2	17 44 18	13 58 9	19 53 32	12 9.0	6 6.3	15 58.9	11 22.1	21 57.0	1 43.0	19 35.8	10 11.2	23 2.2
11 Su	5 17 58	18 45 16	25 49 27	1♊46 7	11 56.6	5 23.0	17 13.0	11 44.3	22 2.2	1 48.8	19 34.9	10 11.3	23 1.2
12 M	5 21 55	19 46 16	7♊43 45	13 42 32	11 42.4	4 50.9	18 27.2	12 6.2	22 7.2	1 54.7	19 34.0	10R 11.3	23 0.1
13 Tu	5 25 52	20 47 16	19 42 36	25 44 4	11 27.5	4 30.1	19 41.3	12 27.8	22 12.1	2 0.7	19 33.2	10 11.3	22 59.1
14 W	5 29 48	21 48 16	1♋47 3	7♋51 40	11 13.2	4D 20.1	20 55.5	12 49.0	22 16.8	2 6.6	19 32.4	10 11.3	22 58.0
15 Th	5 33 45	22 49 18	13 58 1	20 6 15	11 0.6	4 20.6	22 9.8	13 9.8	22 21.3	2 12.7	19 31.7	10 11.2	22 56.9
16 F	5 37 41	23 50 20	26 16 31	2♌29 1	10 50.6	4 30.6	23 24.1	13 30.3	22 25.7	2 18.8	19 31.0	10 11.1	22 55.8
17 Sa	5 41 38	24 51 24	8♌43 58	15 1 39	10 43.6	4 49.6	24 38.4	13 50.4	22 29.9	2 24.9	19 30.4	10 11.0	22 54.7
18 Su	5 45 34	25 52 27	21 22 22	27 46 25	10 39.7	5 16.6	25 52.8	14 10.1	22 33.9	2 31.1	19 29.8	10 10.8	22 53.6
19 M	5 49 31	26 53 32	4♍14 13	10♍46 6	10D 38.2	5 50.8	27 7.2	14 29.4	22 37.7	2 37.3	19 29.2	10 10.6	22 52.5
20 Tu	5 53 28	27 54 38	17 22 29	24 3 44	10R 38.1	6 31.4	28 21.6	14 48.3	22 41.4	2 43.6	19 28.8	10 10.4	22 51.3
21 W	5 57 24	28 55 44	0♎50 11	7♎42 8	10 38.3	7 17.8	29 36.1	15 6.8	22 44.9	2 49.9	19 28.3	10 10.1	22 50.2
22 Th	6 1 21	29 56 51	14 39 46	21 43 10	10 37.5	8 9.3	0♐50.6	15 24.8	22 48.2	2 56.3	19 27.9	10 9.8	22 49.0
23 F	6 5 17	0♑57 59	28 52 17	6♏ 6 55	10 34.5	9 5.3	2 5.1	15 42.5	22 51.3	3 2.7	19 27.6	10 9.5	22 47.8
24 Sa	6 9 14	1 59 7	13♏26 38	20 50 50	10 29.0	10 5.2	3 19.6	15 59.6	22 54.3	3 9.2	19 27.3	10 9.1	22 46.6
25 Su	6 13 10	3 0 16	28 18 44	5♐49 20	10 21.0	11 8.6	4 34.2	16 16.3	22 57.1	3 15.7	19 27.1	10 8.7	22 45.4
26 M	6 17 7	4 1 26	13♐21 32	20 54 4	10 11.1	12 15.1	5 48.8	16 32.6	22 59.6	3 22.2	19 26.9	10 8.3	22 44.2
27 Tu	6 21 3	5 2 37	28 25 40	5♑55 2	10 0.5	13 24.3	7 3.4	16 48.4	23 2.0	3 28.8	19 26.8	10 7.8	22 43.0
28 W	6 25 0	6 3 47	13♑20 58	20 42 23	9 50.5	14 35.8	8 18.0	17 3.6	23 4.3	3 35.4	19D 26.7	10 7.3	22 41.7
29 Th	6 28 57	7 4 58	27 58 19	5♒ 8 4	9 42.3	15 49.5	9 32.7	17 18.4	23 6.3	3 42.0	19 26.7	10 6.8	22 40.5
30 F	6 32 53	8 6 9	12♒11 5	19 7 4	9 36.5	17 5.0	10 47.4	17 32.7	23 8.1	3 48.7	19 26.7	10 6.2	22 39.3
31 Sa	6 36 50	9 7 19	25 55 52	2♓37 35	9 33.4	18 22.2	12 2.1	17 46.4	23 9.8	3 55.4	19 26.8	10 5.6	22 38.0

Astro Data Dy Hr Mn	Planet Ingress Dy Hr Mn	Last Aspect Dy Hr Mn	☽ Ingress Dy Hr Mn	Last Aspect Dy Hr Mn	☽ Ingress Dy Hr Mn	☽ Phases & Eclipses Dy Hr Mn	Astro Data
♀0S 5 6:00	☿ ♐ 2 20:28	1 18:53 ♂ △	♑ 2 4:54	1 5:13 ♇ ☍	♒ 1 16:46	5 6:50 ☽ 12♒40	1 NOVEMBER 1932
☽0N 8 20:31	♀ ♎ 2 4:01	4 6:18 ♄ ☌	♒ 4 8:06	3 3:22 ♅ ⚹	♓ 3 22:08	13 7:28 ○ 20♉43	Julian Day # 11993
♃⚻♅ 22 6:14	♂ ♍ 13 21:25	6 7:59 ♂ ☍	♓ 6 15:06	5 18:04 ♇ △	♈ 6 7:35	21 7:58 ☽ 28♌49	Delta T 23.9 sec
☽0S 23 10:28	♄ ♒ 20 2:10	8 23:56 ♄ ⚹	♈ 9 1:24	8 5:40 ♇ □	♉ 8 19:41	28 0:43 ● 5♐35	SVP 06♓11'48"
☿ R 24 16:39	☉ ♐ 22 12:10	11 12:22 ♄ □	♉ 11 13:33	10 18:20 ♇ ⚹	♊ 11 8:26		Obliquity 23°27'02"
	♀ ♏ 27 0:06	14 1:22 ♄ △	♊ 14 2:13	13 5:00 ♃ □	♋ 13 20:28	4 21:45 ☽ 12♓34	⚷ Chiron 27♉02.6R
☽0N 6 1:50		15 18:54 ♅ ⚹	♋ 16 14:32	15 17:48 ♀ △	♌ 16 7:13	13 2:21 ○ 20♊53	☽ Mean ☊ 14♓08.1
♆ R 12 16:30	♀ ♐ 21 7:43	19 1:27 ♄ ☍	♌ 19 1:35	18 9:22 ♀ □	♍ 18 16:09	20 20:22 ☽ 28♍46	
☿ D 14 10:55	☉ ♑ 22 1:14	21 7:58 ☉ □	♍ 21 10:08	20 21:36 ♀ ⚹	♎ 20 22:32	27 11:22 ● 5♑32	1 DECEMBER 1932
☽0S 20 16:47		23 3:35 ♇ ⚹	♎ 23 15:08	22 13:50 ♇ □	♏ 23 1:53		Julian Day # 12023
♃⚹♇ 22 4:15		25 13:50 ♀ ☌	♏ 25 16:38	24 15:22 ♃ ⚹	♐ 25 2:42		Delta T 23.9 sec
♅ D 28 21:01		27 5:22 ♇ △	♐ 27 15:58	26 15:22 ♃ □	♑ 27 2:31		SVP 06♓11'43"
		29 0:41 ♃ □	♑ 29 15:16	28 15:56 ♃ △	♒ 29 3:23		Obliquity 23°27'01"
				30 12:35 ♅ ⚹	♓ 31 7:16		⚷ Chiron 25♉27.7R
							☽ Mean ☊ 12♓32.8

LONGITUDE JANUARY 1933

Day	Sid.Time	☉	0 hr ☽	Noon ☽	True ☊	☿	♀	♂	♃	♄	♅	♆	♇
1 Su	6 40 46	10♑ 8 30	9♓12 25	15♓40 44	9♓32.5	19♐40.9	13♐16.8	17♍59.6	23♍11.2	4♒ 2.2	19♈26.9	10♍ 5.0	22♋36.8
2 M	6 44 43	11 9 40	22 2 59	28 19 42	9D 33.0	21 0.9	14 31.5	18 12.3	23 12.5	4 9.0	19 27.1	10R 4.3	22R 35.5
3 Tu	6 48 39	12 10 50	4♈31 30	10♈39 1	9R 33.9	22 22.1	15 46.2	18 24.4	23 13.5	4 15.8	19 27.4	10 3.6	22 34.2
4 W	6 52 36	13 11 59	16 42 54	22 43 48	9 34.1	23 44.4	17 0.9	18 36.0	23 14.4	4 22.6	19 27.7	10 2.9	22 32.9
5 Th	6 56 32	14 13 9	28 42 22	4♉39 15	9 32.7	25 7.7	18 15.7	18 47.0	23 15.1	4 29.5	19 28.0	10 2.1	22 31.7
6 F	7 0 29	15 14 18	10♉35 3	16 30 19	9 29.1	26 31.8	19 30.5	18 57.4	23 15.6	4 36.3	19 28.4	10 1.4	22 30.4
7 Sa	7 4 26	16 15 26	22 25 34	28 21 19	9 23.3	27 56.8	20 45.2	19 7.3	23 15.9	4 43.3	19 28.9	10 0.5	22 29.1
8 Su	7 8 22	17 16 35	4♊17 58	10♊15 55	9 15.3	29 22.6	22 0.0	19 16.5	23R 16.0	4 50.2	19 29.4	9 59.7	22 27.8
9 M	7 12 19	18 17 43	16 15 28	22 16 55	9 5.8	0♑49.1	23 14.8	19 25.1	23 16.0	4 57.1	19 29.9	9 58.8	22 26.5
10 Tu	7 16 15	19 18 50	28 20 28	4♋26 18	8 55.8	2 16.2	24 29.6	19 33.2	23 15.7	5 4.1	19 30.5	9 57.9	22 25.2
11 W	7 20 12	20 19 57	10♋34 33	16 45 19	8 46.0	3 44.0	25 44.5	19 40.5	23 15.2	5 11.1	19 31.2	9 57.0	22 23.9
12 Th	7 24 8	21 21 4	22 58 40	29 14 38	8 37.4	5 12.5	26 59.3	19 47.3	23 14.6	5 18.2	19 31.9	9 56.1	22 22.6
13 F	7 28 5	22 22 11	5♌33 16	11♌54 36	8 30.8	6 41.5	28 14.2	19 53.4	23 13.7	5 25.2	19 32.6	9 55.1	22 21.3
14 Sa	7 32 2	23 23 17	18 18 39	24 45 27	8 26.5	8 11.1	29 29.0	19 58.8	23 12.7	5 32.2	19 33.5	9 54.1	22 20.0
15 Su	7 35 58	24 24 22	1♍15 6	7♍47 38	8D 24.4	9 41.3	0♑43.9	20 3.5	23 11.4	5 39.3	19 34.3	9 53.0	22 18.7
16 M	7 39 55	25 25 28	14 23 11	21 1 51	8 24.3	11 12.0	1 58.7	20 7.5	23 10.0	5 46.4	19 35.2	9 52.0	22 17.4
17 Tu	7 43 51	26 26 33	27 43 45	4♎29 2	8 25.5	12 43.3	3 13.6	20 10.9	23 8.4	5 53.5	19 36.2	9 50.9	22 16.1
18 W	7 47 48	27 27 38	11♎17 49	18 10 12	8 26.9	14 15.2	4 28.5	20 13.5	23 6.6	6 0.6	19 37.2	9 49.7	22 14.8
19 Th	7 51 44	28 28 42	25 6 16	2♏ 6 2	8R 27.8	15 47.6	5 43.4	20 15.4	23 4.6	6 7.7	19 38.3	9 48.6	22 13.5
20 F	7 55 41	29 29 46	9♏ 9 26	16 16 19	8 27.5	17 20.5	6 58.3	20 16.6	23 2.4	6 14.9	19 39.4	9 47.4	22 12.2
21 Sa	7 59 37	0♒30 50	23 26 27	0♐39 29	8 25.4	18 54.1	8 13.3	20R 17.0	23 0.0	6 22.0	19 40.5	9 46.2	22 10.9
22 Su	8 3 34	1 31 54	7♐54 55	15 12 11	8 21.7	20 28.2	9 28.2	20 16.7	22 57.5	6 29.2	19 41.7	9 45.0	22 9.7
23 M	8 7 31	2 32 57	22 30 34	29 49 18	8 16.6	22 2.9	10 43.1	20 15.6	22 54.7	6 36.3	19 43.0	9 43.8	22 8.4
24 Tu	8 11 27	3 34 0	7♑ 7 32	14♑24 23	8 11.1	23 38.2	11 58.1	20 13.7	22 51.8	6 43.5	19 44.3	9 42.5	22 7.1
25 W	8 15 24	4 35 2	21 39 0	28 50 32	8 5.7	25 14.1	13 13.0	20 11.1	22 48.7	6 50.7	19 45.7	9 41.3	22 5.8
26 Th	8 19 20	5 36 3	5♒58 14	13♒ 1 26	8 1.3	26 50.6	14 28.0	20 7.6	22 45.4	6 57.8	19 47.1	9 40.0	22 4.6
27 F	8 23 17	6 37 4	19 59 35	26 52 16	7 58.4	28 27.7	15 42.9	20 3.4	22 41.9	7 5.0	19 48.5	9 38.6	22 3.3
28 Sa	8 27 13	7 38 3	3♓39 13	10♓20 18	7D 57.2	0♒ 5.5	16 57.9	19 58.4	22 38.2	7 12.2	19 50.0	9 37.3	22 2.1
29 Su	8 31 10	8 39 1	16 55 31	23 24 58	7 57.4	1 44.0	18 12.8	19 52.5	22 34.4	7 19.3	19 51.6	9 35.9	22 0.8
30 M	8 35 6	9 39 58	29 48 55	6♈ 7 42	7 58.7	3 23.1	19 27.8	19 45.9	22 30.4	7 26.5	19 53.2	9 34.5	21 59.6
31 Tu	8 39 3	10 40 54	12♈21 42	18 31 25	8 0.5	5 2.9	20 42.7	19 38.5	22 26.2	7 33.7	19 54.8	9 33.1	21 58.4

LONGITUDE FEBRUARY 1933

Day	Sid.Time	☉	0 hr ☽	Noon ☽	True ☊	☿	♀	♂	♃	♄	♅	♆	♇
1 W	8 43 0	11♒41 48	24♈37 22	0♉40 8	8♓ 2.1	6♒43.4	21♑57.6	19♍30.3	22♍21.8	7♒40.8	19♈56.5	9♍31.7	21♋57.1
2 Th	8 46 56	12 42 42	6♉40 19	12 38 30	8R 3.1	8 24.6	23 12.6	19R 21.3	22R 17.3	7 48.0	19 58.2	9R 30.3	21R 55.9
3 F	8 50 53	13 43 33	18 35 20	24 31 24	8 3.2	10 6.5	24 27.5	19 11.6	22 12.6	7 55.2	20 0.0	9 28.8	21 54.7
4 Sa	8 54 49	14 44 24	0♊27 19	6♊23 38	8 2.1	11 49.2	25 42.4	19 1.0	22 7.8	8 2.3	20 1.8	9 27.3	21 53.5
5 Su	8 58 46	15 45 13	12 20 56	18 19 44	7 60.0	13 32.6	26 57.4	18 49.7	22 2.8	8 9.4	20 3.7	9 25.8	21 52.4
6 M	9 2 42	16 46 1	24 20 29	0♋23 38	7 57.1	15 16.8	28 12.3	18 37.6	21 57.6	8 16.6	20 5.6	9 24.3	21 51.2
7 Tu	9 6 39	17 46 47	6♋29 34	12 38 36	7 53.8	17 1.8	29 27.2	18 24.7	21 52.3	8 23.7	20 7.6	9 22.8	21 50.0
8 W	9 10 35	18 47 32	18 51 1	25 7 0	7 50.5	18 47.4	0♒42.2	18 11.1	21 46.9	8 30.8	20 9.6	9 21.3	21 48.9
9 Th	9 14 32	19 48 15	1♌26 44	7♌50 16	7 47.7	20 33.9	1 57.1	17 56.8	21 41.3	8 37.9	20 11.6	9 19.7	21 47.8
10 F	9 18 29	20 48 57	14 17 39	20 48 50	7 45.6	22 21.1	3 12.0	17 41.7	21 35.5	8 45.0	20 13.7	9 18.2	21 46.6
11 Sa	9 22 25	21 49 38	27 23 47	4♍ 2 21	7D 44.5	24 8.9	4 26.9	17 26.0	21 29.6	8 52.0	20 15.8	9 16.6	21 45.5
12 Su	9 26 22	22 50 17	10♍44 22	17 29 40	7 44.3	25 57.5	5 41.8	17 9.5	21 23.6	8 59.1	20 17.9	9 15.0	21 44.4
13 M	9 30 18	23 50 55	24 18 2	1♎ 9 15	7 44.8	27 46.7	6 56.7	16 52.4	21 17.5	9 6.1	20 20.1	9 13.4	21 43.4
14 Tu	9 34 15	24 51 31	8♎ 3 5	14 59 17	7 45.7	29 36.6	8 11.6	16 34.6	21 11.2	9 13.1	20 22.4	9 11.8	21 42.3
15 W	9 38 11	25 52 7	21 57 37	28 57 51	7 46.8	1♓26.9	9 26.5	16 16.1	21 4.8	9 20.1	20 24.7	9 10.2	21 41.2
16 Th	9 42 8	26 52 41	5♏59 44	13♏ 3 4	7 47.7	3 17.7	10 41.4	15 57.1	20 58.3	9 27.0	20 27.0	9 8.6	21 40.2
17 F	9 46 4	27 53 14	20 7 34	27 12 59	7R 48.2	5 8.8	11 56.3	15 37.5	20 51.7	9 34.0	20 29.3	9 7.0	21 39.2
18 Sa	9 50 1	28 53 46	4♐19 5	11♐25 33	7 48.3	7 0.1	13 11.2	15 17.4	20 45.0	9 40.9	20 31.7	9 5.3	21 38.2
19 Su	9 53 58	29 54 16	18 32 5	25 38 23	7 47.9	8 51.5	14 26.1	14 56.7	20 38.2	9 47.8	20 34.1	9 3.7	21 37.2
20 M	9 57 54	0♓54 46	2♑44 4	9♑48 47	7 47.3	10 42.7	15 41.0	14 35.5	20 31.2	9 54.7	20 36.6	9 2.1	21 36.2
21 Tu	10 1 51	1 55 14	16 52 7	23 53 42	7 46.5	12 33.5	16 55.9	14 13.9	20 24.2	10 1.5	20 39.1	9 0.4	21 35.3
22 W	10 5 47	2 55 40	0♒53 5	7♒49 54	7 45.9	14 23.7	18 10.8	13 51.9	20 17.1	10 8.4	20 41.6	8 58.7	21 34.3
23 Th	10 9 44	3 56 6	14 43 45	21 34 16	7 45.4	16 13.0	19 25.7	13 29.5	20 9.9	10 15.1	20 44.2	8 57.1	21 33.4
24 F	10 13 40	4 56 29	28 21 9	5♓ 4 7	7D 45.2	18 1.0	20 40.6	13 6.7	20 2.6	10 21.9	20 46.8	8 55.4	21 32.5
25 Sa	10 17 37	5 56 51	11♓42 57	18 17 30	7 45.2	19 47.3	21 55.4	12 43.7	19 55.2	10 28.6	20 49.4	8 53.7	21 31.6
26 Su	10 21 33	6 57 11	24 47 43	1♈13 33	7R 45.2	21 31.5	23 10.3	12 20.5	19 47.8	10 35.3	20 52.1	8 52.1	21 30.8
27 M	10 25 30	7 57 29	7♈35 6	13 52 29	7 45.3	23 13.1	24 25.1	11 57.0	19 40.3	10 42.0	20 54.8	8 50.4	21 29.9
28 Tu	10 29 27	8 57 45	20 5 56	26 15 43	7 45.2	24 51.6	25 40.0	11 33.4	19 32.7	10 48.6	20 57.5	8 48.7	21 29.1

Astro Data	Dy Hr Mn
☽0N	2 8:35
♃ R	8 2:22
☽0S	16 21:29
♂ R	21 1:28
☽0N	29 17:14
♃⚼♄	30 8:09
♃⚹♇	7 12:45
☽0S	13 3:15
♄⚻♆	13 20:32
♃⚻♅	19 10:18
☽0N	26 2:31

Planet Ingress	Dy Hr Mn
☿ ♑	8 10:25
♀ ♑	14 9:56
☉ ♒	20 11:53
☿ ♒	27 22:39
♀ ♒	7 10:30
☿ ♓	14 5:06
☉ ♓	19 2:16

Last Aspect Dy Hr Mn		☽ Ingress Dy Hr Mn
2 2:12	♃ ☍	♈ 2 15:13
4 15:51	☿ △	♉ 5 2:36
7 1:42	♃ △	♊ 7 15:19
9 15:31	♀ ☍	♋ 10 3:16
12 0:31	♃ ⚹	♌ 12 13:27
14 2:20	♅ △	♍ 14 21:42
16 21:31	☉ △	♎ 17 4:03
19 6:15	☉ □	♏ 19 8:24
20 23:16	♃ ⚹	♐ 21 10:55
23 0:40	♃ □	♑ 23 12:18
25 6:43	☿ ☌	♒ 25 13:56
26 23:41	♅ ⚹	♓ 27 17:31
29 10:23	♃ ☍	♈ 30 0:21

Last Aspect Dy Hr Mn		☽ Ingress Dy Hr Mn
31 18:44	♇ □	♉ 1 10:40
3 13:16	♀ △	♊ 3 23:05
5 19:17	♃ □	♋ 6 11:13
8 5:41	♇ ☌	♌ 8 21:16
10 17:09	☿ ☍	♍ 11 4:43
12 19:28	♇ ⚹	♎ 13 9:59
15 7:13	☉ △	♏ 15 13:46
17 14:08	☉ □	♐ 17 16:42
19 3:31	♃ □	♑ 19 19:22
21 8:03	♇ ☍	♒ 21 22:29
23 10:34	♅ ⚹	♓ 24 2:56
25 17:56	♇ △	♈ 26 9:42
28 12:04	♀ ⚹	♉ 28 19:20

☽ Phases & Eclipses Dy Hr Mn	
3 16:24	☽ 12♈53
11 20:36	○ 21♋12
19 6:15	☽ 28♎45
25 23:20	● 5♒34
2 13:16	☽ 13♉16
10 13:00	○ 21♌22
10 13:17	☍A 0.018
17 14:08	☽ 28♏29
24 12:44	● 5♓29
24 12:46:15	☾A 1'31"

Astro Data

1 JANUARY 1933
Julian Day # 12054
Delta T 23.9 sec
SVP 06♓11'37"
Obliquity 23°27'01"
⚷ Chiron 24♉05.9R
☽ Mean ☊ 10♓54.3

1 FEBRUARY 1933
Julian Day # 12085
Delta T 23.9 sec
SVP 06♓11'32"
Obliquity 23°27'01"
⚷ Chiron 23♉34.1
☽ Mean ☊ 9♓15.8

MARCH 1933 LONGITUDE

Day	Sid.Time	☉	0 hr ☽	Noon ☽	True ☊	☿	♀	♂	♃	♄	♅	♆	♇
1 W	10 33 23	9♓58 0	2♉22 10	8♉25 41	7♓44.9	26♓26.5	26♒54.8	11♍ 9.6	19♍25.1	10♒55.2	21♈ 0.3	8♍47.0	21♋28.3
2 Th	10 37 20	10 58 12	14 26 42	20 25 43	7R44.6	27 57.1	28 9.6	10R45.9	19R17.5	11 1.8	21 3.1	8R45.4	21R27.5
3 F	10 41 16	11 58 22	26 23 14	2♊19 49	7 44.3	29 23.0	29 24.4	10 22.1	19 9.8	11 8.3	21 5.9	8 43.7	21 26.7
4 Sa	10 45 13	12 58 31	8♊16 2	14 12 29	7D44.1	0♈43.5	0♓39.2	9 58.3	19 2.1	11 14.8	21 8.8	8 42.0	21 26.0
5 Su	10 49 9	13 58 37	20 9 43	26 8 22	7 44.1	1 58.1	1 54.0	9 34.6	18 54.3	11 21.2	21 11.6	8 40.4	21 25.2
6 M	10 53 6	14 58 41	2♋ 8 59	8♋12 9	7 44.4	3 6.1	3 8.8	9 11.1	18 46.5	11 27.6	21 14.5	8 38.7	21 24.5
7 Tu	10 57 2	15 58 43	14 18 23	20 28 13	7 45.1	4 7.2	4 23.6	8 47.7	18 38.7	11 34.0	21 17.5	8 37.0	21 23.9
8 W	11 0 59	16 58 43	26 42 4	3♌ 0 21	7 46.0	5 0.7	5 38.3	8 24.5	18 30.9	11 40.3	21 20.4	8 35.4	21 23.2
9 Th	11 4 56	17 58 41	9♌23 24	15 51 28	7 46.9	5 46.4	6 53.1	8 1.6	18 23.1	11 46.5	21 23.4	8 33.7	21 22.6
10 F	11 8 52	18 58 37	22 24 43	29 3 13	7 47.7	6 23.7	8 7.8	7 38.9	18 15.3	11 52.8	21 26.4	8 32.1	21 21.9
11 Sa	11 12 49	19 58 30	5♍46 57	12♍35 46	7R48.1	6 52.6	9 22.5	7 16.6	18 7.4	11 58.9	21 29.4	8 30.5	21 21.3
12 Su	11 16 45	20 58 22	19 29 27	26 27 37	7 47.9	7 12.8	10 37.2	6 54.7	17 59.6	12 5.1	21 32.5	8 28.8	21 20.8
13 M	11 20 42	21 58 11	3♎29 51	10♎35 37	7 46.9	7R24.3	11 51.9	6 33.2	17 51.8	12 11.1	21 35.6	8 27.2	21 20.2
14 Tu	11 24 38	22 57 59	17 44 19	24 55 18	7 45.3	7 27.1	13 6.6	6 12.1	17 44.1	12 17.2	21 38.7	8 25.6	21 19.7
15 W	11 28 35	23 57 45	2♏ 7 54	9♏21 25	7 43.2	7 21.3	14 21.3	5 51.5	17 36.3	12 23.2	21 41.8	8 24.0	21 19.2
16 Th	11 32 31	24 57 29	16 35 12	23 48 38	7 41.0	7 7.4	15 35.9	5 31.4	17 28.6	12 29.1	21 44.9	8 22.4	21 18.7
17 F	11 36 28	25 57 11	1♐ 1 6	8♐12 8	7 39.1	6 45.6	16 50.6	5 11.8	17 20.9	12 35.0	21 48.1	8 20.8	21 18.2
18 Sa	11 40 25	26 56 52	15 21 16	22 28 9	7D37.9	6 16.7	18 5.2	4 52.8	17 13.3	12 40.8	21 51.3	8 19.2	21 17.8
19 Su	11 44 21	27 56 31	29 32 30	6♑34 5	7 37.5	5 41.4	19 19.9	4 34.4	17 5.7	12 46.6	21 54.5	8 17.7	21 17.4
20 M	11 48 18	28 56 8	13♑32 47	20 28 28	7 38.1	5 0.4	20 34.5	4 16.6	16 58.1	12 52.3	21 57.7	8 16.1	21 17.0
21 Tu	11 52 14	29 55 44	27 21 4	4♒10 34	7 39.3	4 14.8	21 49.1	3 59.5	16 50.6	12 57.9	22 0.9	8 14.6	21 16.6
22 W	11 56 11	0♈55 18	10♒56 57	17 40 13	7 40.8	3 25.6	23 3.8	3 43.0	16 43.2	13 3.6	22 4.2	8 13.1	21 16.3
23 Th	12 0 7	1 54 50	24 20 22	0♓57 25	7 42.1	2 34.0	24 18.4	3 27.2	16 35.9	13 9.1	22 7.4	8 11.6	21 16.0
24 F	12 4 4	2 54 20	7♓31 20	14 2 9	7R42.7	1 40.9	25 33.0	3 12.1	16 28.6	13 14.6	22 10.7	8 10.1	21 15.7
25 Sa	12 8 0	3 53 48	20 29 52	26 54 27	7 42.0	0 47.7	26 47.5	2 57.7	16 21.4	13 20.0	22 14.0	8 8.6	21 15.4
26 Su	12 11 57	4 53 14	3♈15 58	9♈34 24	7 40.0	29♓55.3	28 2.1	2 44.1	16 14.2	13 25.4	22 17.3	8 7.1	21 15.2
27 M	12 15 53	5 52 38	15 49 48	22 2 17	7 36.6	29 4.7	29 16.6	2 31.3	16 7.2	13 30.7	22 20.6	8 5.7	21 14.9
28 Tu	12 19 50	6 52 0	28 11 54	4♉18 50	7 31.9	28 16.9	0♈31.2	2 19.2	16 0.3	13 35.9	22 24.0	8 4.2	21 14.7
29 W	12 23 47	7 51 20	10♉23 16	16 25 25	7 26.6	27 32.7	1 45.7	2 7.8	15 53.4	13 41.1	22 27.3	8 2.8	21 14.6
30 Th	12 27 43	8 50 38	22 25 34	28 24 2	7 21.1	26 52.6	3 0.2	1 57.3	15 46.7	13 46.2	22 30.7	8 1.4	21 14.4
31 F	12 31 40	9 49 54	4♊21 13	10♊17 31	7 16.0	26 17.2	4 14.7	1 47.5	15 40.0	13 51.2	22 34.0	8 0.0	21 14.3

APRIL 1933 LONGITUDE

Day	Sid.Time	☉	0 hr ☽	Noon ☽	True ☊	☿	♀	♂	♃	♄	♅	♆	♇
1 Sa	12 35 36	10♈49 7	16♊13 24	22♊ 9 22	7♓12.0	25♓46.8	5♈29.2	1♍38.6	15♍33.5	13♒56.2	22♈37.4	7♍58.7	21♋14.2
2 Su	12 39 33	11 48 18	28 5 58	4♋ 3 45	7R 9.4	25R21.9	6 43.6	1R30.4	15R27.1	14 1.1	22 40.8	7R57.4	21R14.1
3 M	12 43 29	12 47 27	10♋ 3 18	16 5 15	7D 8.3	25 2.5	7 58.1	1 23.0	15 20.8	14 5.9	22 44.2	7 56.0	21 14.1
4 Tu	12 47 26	13 46 33	22 10 11	28 18 44	7 8.7	24 48.7	9 12.5	1 16.4	15 14.7	14 10.7	22 47.6	7 54.7	21D14.1
5 W	12 51 22	14 45 38	4♌31 28	10♌48 58	7 9.9	24D40.5	10 26.9	1 10.6	15 8.6	14 15.4	22 51.0	7 53.5	21 14.1
6 Th	12 55 19	15 44 39	17 11 46	23 40 17	7 11.5	24 37.8	11 41.3	1 5.6	15 2.7	14 20.0	22 54.4	7 52.2	21 14.1
7 F	12 59 16	16 43 39	0♍14 56	6♍55 58	7R12.7	24 40.6	12 55.7	1 1.4	14 57.0	14 24.5	22 57.8	7 51.0	21 14.2
8 Sa	13 3 12	17 42 36	13 43 32	20 37 40	7 12.7	24 48.7	14 10.0	0 57.9	14 51.3	14 29.0	23 1.3	7 49.8	21 14.2
9 Su	13 7 9	18 41 31	27 38 13	4♎44 51	7 11.0	25 1.9	15 24.4	0 55.2	14 45.8	14 33.4	23 4.7	7 48.6	21 14.3
10 M	13 11 5	19 40 24	11♎57 4	19 14 15	7 7.4	25 20.0	16 38.7	0 53.3	14 40.5	14 37.7	23 8.1	7 47.4	21 14.5
11 Tu	13 15 2	20 39 15	26 35 32	3♏59 59	7 2.0	25 42.9	17 53.0	0 52.1	14 35.3	14 41.9	23 11.5	7 46.3	21 14.6
12 W	13 18 58	21 38 3	11♏26 34	18 54 10	6 55.4	26 10.3	19 7.3	0D51.7	14 30.2	14 46.1	23 15.0	7 45.2	21 14.8
13 Th	13 22 55	22 36 50	26 21 40	3♐48 0	6 48.4	26 42.0	20 21.6	0 52.0	14 25.3	14 50.2	23 18.4	7 44.1	21 15.0
14 F	13 26 51	23 35 36	11♐12 11	18 33 21	6 42.1	27 17.8	21 35.9	0 53.0	14 20.6	14 54.2	23 21.8	7 43.0	21 15.2
15 Sa	13 30 48	24 34 19	25 50 45	3♑ 3 51	6 37.2	27 57.5	22 50.1	0 54.7	14 16.0	14 58.1	23 25.3	7 42.0	21 15.5
16 Su	13 34 45	25 33 1	10♑12 13	17 15 36	6 34.2	28 40.9	24 4.4	0 57.2	14 11.6	15 2.0	23 28.7	7 41.0	21 15.8
17 M	13 38 41	26 31 42	24 13 54	1♒ 7 8	6D33.1	29 27.9	25 18.6	1 0.3	14 7.3	15 5.8	23 32.2	7 40.0	21 16.1
18 Tu	13 42 38	27 30 20	7♒55 24	14 38 54	6 33.4	0♈18.3	26 32.8	1 4.1	14 3.2	15 9.5	23 35.6	7 39.0	21 16.4
19 W	13 46 34	28 28 57	21 17 52	27 52 35	6 34.4	1 11.9	27 47.1	1 8.7	13 59.3	15 13.1	23 39.0	7 38.1	21 16.7
20 Th	13 50 31	29 27 32	4♓23 21	10♓50 28	6R35.2	2 8.6	29 1.3	1 13.8	13 55.5	15 16.6	23 42.5	7 37.2	21 17.1
21 F	13 54 27	0♉26 5	17 14 13	23 34 51	6 34.6	3 8.2	0♉15.4	1 19.7	13 51.9	15 20.0	23 45.9	7 36.3	21 17.5
22 Sa	13 58 24	1 24 37	29 52 38	6♈ 7 46	6 32.0	4 10.6	1 29.6	1 26.2	13 48.5	15 23.4	23 49.3	7 35.4	21 17.9
23 Su	14 2 20	2 23 7	12♈20 26	18 30 49	6 26.9	5 15.7	2 43.8	1 33.3	13 45.2	15 26.6	23 52.7	7 34.6	21 18.4
24 M	14 6 17	3 21 35	24 39 3	0♉45 16	6 19.3	6 23.4	3 57.9	1 41.1	13 42.1	15 29.8	23 56.1	7 33.8	21 18.8
25 Tu	14 10 14	4 20 2	6♉49 35	12 52 8	6 9.6	7 33.6	5 12.1	1 49.5	13 39.2	15 32.9	23 59.5	7 33.0	21 19.3
26 W	14 14 10	5 18 26	18 53 4	24 52 30	5 58.5	8 46.2	6 26.2	1 58.5	13 36.5	15 35.9	24 2.9	7 32.3	21 19.9
27 Th	14 18 7	6 16 49	0♊50 39	6♊47 42	5 47.0	10 1.2	7 40.3	2 8.1	13 33.9	15 38.8	24 6.3	7 31.6	21 20.4
28 F	14 22 3	7 15 10	12 43 55	18 39 34	5 36.1	11 18.4	8 54.4	2 18.4	13 31.6	15 41.7	24 9.7	7 30.9	21 21.0
29 Sa	14 26 0	8 13 28	24 35 0	0♋30 35	5 26.7	12 37.8	10 8.4	2 29.1	13 29.4	15 44.4	24 13.0	7 30.3	21 21.6
30 Su	14 29 56	9 11 45	6♋26 44	12 23 58	5 19.5	13 59.4	11 22.5	2 40.5	13 27.4	15 47.1	24 16.4	7 29.7	21 22.2

Astro Data	Planet Ingress	Last Aspect	☽ Ingress	Last Aspect	☽ Ingress	☽ Phases & Eclipses	Astro Data
Dy Hr Mn	Dy Hr Mn	Dy Hr Mn	Dy Hr Mn	Dy Hr Mn	Dy Hr Mn	Dy Hr Mn	1 MARCH 1933
☿0N 2 4:33	☿ ♈ 3 10:49	3 6:50 ☿ ✶	♊ 3 7:18	1 18:39 ☿ □	♋ 2 3:50	4 10:23 ☽ 13♊25	Julian Day # 12113
♅□♇ 8 18:24	♀ ♓ 3 11:24	5 2:05 ♅ ✶	♋ 5 19:43	4 5:06 ☿ △	♌ 4 15:16	12 2:46 ○ 21♍05	Delta T 23.9 sec
☽0S 12 11:29	☉ ♈ 21 1:43	7 13:47 ♇ ☌	♌ 8 6:18	6 10:38 ♅ △	♍ 6 23:33	12 2:33 ☍A 0.592	SVP 06♓11'28"
☿ R 13 19:43	☿ ♓ 25 21:49	9 22:13 ♅ △	♍ 10 13:42	8 19:29 ☿ ☍	♎ 9 4:00	18 21:04 ☽ 27♐49	Obliquity 23°27'02"
☽0N 25 10:37	♀ ♈ 27 13:58	12 3:12 ♇ ✶	♎ 12 18:03	10 18:27 ♅ ☍	♏ 11 5:32	26 3:20 ● 5♈01	⚷ Chiron 23♉59.8
☿0S 30 21:39		14 6:33 ♅ ☍	♏ 14 20:27	13 0:34 ☿ △	♐ 13 5:52		☽ Mean ☊ 7♓46.9
♀0N 30 5:18	☿ ♈ 17 15:27	16 14:56 ☉ △	♐ 16 22:18	15 3:41 ☿ □	♑ 15 6:53	3 5:56 ☽ 13♋02	
♇ D 4 7:29	☉ ♉ 20 13:18	18 21:04 ☉ □	♑ 19 0:47	17 9:41 ☿ ✶	♒ 17 10:02	10 13:37 ○ 20♎14	1 APRIL 1933
♅⚼♆ 5 12:40	♀ ♉ 20 19:00	20 14:39 ♅ □	♒ 21 4:39	19 14:10 ☉ ✶	♓ 19 15:54	17 4:17 ☽ 26♑42	Julian Day # 12144
☿ D 5 23:35		22 19:59 ♅ ✶	♓ 23 10:16	21 7:40 ♇ △	♈ 22 0:14	24 18:38 ● 4♉07	Delta T 23.9 sec
☽0S 8 21:26		25 13:03 ♀ ☌	♈ 25 17:49	23 22:35 ♅ ☌	♉ 24 10:31		SVP 06♓11'24"
♃⚻♄ 10 7:04		27 12:39 ♅ ☌	♉ 28 3:32	26 4:54 ♇ ✶	♊ 26 22:18		Obliquity 23°27'01"
♂ D 12 2:17		30 8:30 ☿ ✶	♊ 30 15:13	28 23:15 ♅ ✶	♋ 29 10:58		⚷ Chiron 25♉22.0
☽0N 21 16:43	☿0N 23 21:29						☽ Mean ☊ 6♓08.4

LONGITUDE — MAY 1933

Day	Sid.Time	☉	0 hr ☽	Noon ☽	True ☊	☿	♀	♂	♃	♄	♅	♆	♇
1 M	14 33 53	10♉10 0	18♋22 45	24♋23 39	5♓14.8	15♈23.1	12♉36.5	2♍52.4	13♍25.6	15♒49.6	24♈19.7	7♍29.1	21♋22.8
2 Tu	14 37 49	11 8 13	0♌27 16	6♌34 12	5D 12.4	16 48.8	13 50.6	3 4.9	13R 23.9	15 52.1	24 23.1	7R 28.5	21 23.5
3 W	14 41 46	12 6 24	12 45 4	19 0 32	5 11.8	18 16.6	15 4.6	3 17.9	13 22.5	15 54.4	24 26.4	7 28.0	21 24.1
4 Th	14 45 43	13 4 33	25 21 10	1♍47 35	5R 12.2	19 46.4	16 18.6	3 31.4	13 21.2	15 56.7	24 29.7	7 27.5	21 24.9
5 F	14 49 39	14 2 39	8♍20 19	14 59 48	5 12.4	21 18.2	17 32.5	3 45.4	13 20.1	15 58.9	24 33.0	7 27.0	21 25.6
6 Sa	14 53 36	15 0 44	21 46 25	28 40 20	5 11.3	22 52.0	18 46.5	3 59.9	13 19.2	16 1.0	24 36.3	7 26.6	21 26.3
7 Su	14 57 32	15 58 47	5♎41 39	12♎50 11	5 8.1	24 27.8	20 0.4	4 14.9	13 18.5	16 3.0	24 39.5	7 26.2	21 27.1
8 M	15 1 29	16 56 48	20 5 37	27 27 22	5 2.5	26 5.5	21 14.3	4 30.4	13 18.0	16 4.9	24 42.8	7 25.8	21 27.9
9 Tu	15 5 25	17 54 47	4♏54 37	12♏26 21	4 54.4	27 45.2	22 28.2	4 46.4	13 17.6	16 6.7	24 46.0	7 25.5	21 28.7
10 W	15 9 22	18 52 45	20 1 24	27 38 26	4 44.6	29 26.9	23 42.1	5 2.8	13D 17.4	16 8.4	24 49.2	7 25.2	21 29.5
11 Th	15 13 18	19 50 41	5♐16 3	12♐52 50	4 34.1	1♉10.6	24 56.0	5 19.6	13 17.4	16 10.0	24 52.4	7 24.9	21 30.4
12 F	15 17 15	20 48 36	20 27 27	27 58 41	4 24.3	2 56.2	26 9.9	5 36.9	13 17.6	16 11.6	24 55.6	7 24.7	21 31.3
13 Sa	15 21 12	21 46 29	5♑25 27	12♑46 56	4 16.3	4 43.8	27 23.8	5 54.6	13 18.0	16 13.0	24 58.8	7 24.5	21 32.2
14 Su	15 25 8	22 44 21	20 2 28	27 11 38	4 10.7	6 33.4	28 37.6	6 12.8	13 18.6	16 14.3	25 1.9	7 24.3	21 33.1
15 M	15 29 5	23 42 12	4♒14 13	11♒10 12	4 7.6	8 24.9	29 51.4	6 31.3	13 19.3	16 15.6	25 5.0	7 24.1	21 34.0
16 Tu	15 33 1	24 40 2	17 59 43	24 42 59	4D 6.5	10 18.5	1♊ 5.3	6 50.3	13 20.2	16 16.7	25 8.1	7 24.0	21 35.0
17 W	15 36 58	25 37 50	1♓20 23	7♓52 19	4R 6.4	12 13.9	2 19.1	7 9.6	13 21.3	16 17.8	25 11.2	7 23.9	21 35.9
18 Th	15 40 54	26 35 37	14 19 14	20 41 37	4 6.2	14 11.3	3 32.9	7 29.4	13 22.6	16 18.7	25 14.3	7 23.9	21 36.9
19 F	15 44 51	27 33 23	26 59 56	3♈14 38	4 4.6	16 10.6	4 46.7	7 49.5	13 24.0	16 19.5	25 17.3	7D 23.9	21 37.9
20 Sa	15 48 47	28 31 8	9♈26 11	15 34 58	4 0.8	18 11.8	6 0.5	8 10.0	13 25.7	16 20.3	25 20.3	7 23.9	21 39.0
21 Su	15 52 44	29 28 52	21 41 22	27 45 41	3 54.2	20 14.7	7 14.2	8 30.9	13 27.5	16 20.9	25 23.3	7 23.9	21 40.0
22 M	15 56 41	0♊26 35	3♉48 15	9♉49 16	3 44.6	22 19.2	8 28.0	8 52.1	13 29.5	16 21.5	25 26.3	7 24.0	21 41.1
23 Tu	16 0 37	1 24 16	15 49 0	21 47 38	3 32.7	24 25.4	9 41.8	9 13.7	13 31.6	16 21.9	25 29.2	7 24.1	21 42.2
24 W	16 4 34	2 21 56	27 45 21	3♊42 17	3 19.1	26 33.0	10 55.5	9 35.6	13 34.0	16 22.3	25 32.1	7 24.3	21 43.3
25 Th	16 8 30	3 19 36	9♊38 38	15 34 34	3 4.9	28 41.9	12 9.2	9 57.9	13 36.5	16 22.5	25 35.0	7 24.5	21 44.4
26 F	16 12 27	4 17 14	21 30 14	27 25 52	2 51.3	0♊51.9	13 23.0	10 20.6	13 39.2	16 22.7	25 37.9	7 24.7	21 45.6
27 Sa	16 16 23	5 14 50	3♋21 42	9♋18 0	2 39.4	3 2.7	14 36.7	10 43.5	13 42.0	16R 22.8	25 40.7	7 24.9	21 46.7
28 Su	16 20 20	6 12 26	15 15 3	21 13 14	2 30.0	5 14.2	15 50.4	11 6.8	13 45.0	16 22.7	25 43.6	7 25.2	21 47.9
29 M	16 24 17	7 10 0	27 12 56	3♌14 35	2 23.4	7 26.1	17 4.0	11 30.4	13 48.2	16 22.6	25 46.3	7 25.5	21 49.1
30 Tu	16 28 13	8 7 32	9♌18 41	15 25 44	2 19.6	9 38.1	18 17.7	11 54.3	13 51.6	16 22.3	25 49.1	7 25.8	21 50.3
31 W	16 32 10	9 5 4	21 36 18	27 50 58	2D 18.0	11 50.0	19 31.4	12 18.5	13 55.1	16 22.0	25 51.8	7 26.2	21 51.5

LONGITUDE — JUNE 1933

Day	Sid.Time	☉	0 hr ☽	Noon ☽	True ☊	☿	♀	♂	♃	♄	♅	♆	♇
1 Th	16 36 6	10♊ 2 34	4♍10 18	10♍34 54	2♓17.7	14♊ 1.4	20♊45.0	12♍43.0	13♍58.8	16♒21.6	25♈54.5	7♍26.6	21♋52.8
2 F	16 40 3	11 0 2	17 5 20	23 42 5	2R 17.7	16 12.2	21 58.6	13 7.8	14 2.7	16R 21.1	25 57.2	7 27.1	21 54.0
3 Sa	16 43 59	11 57 30	0♎25 37	7♎16 17	2 16.7	18 21.9	23 12.2	13 32.8	14 6.7	16 20.4	25 59.8	7 27.5	21 55.3
4 Su	16 47 56	12 54 56	14 14 15	21 19 36	2 13.8	20 30.5	24 25.8	13 58.2	14 10.9	16 19.7	26 2.4	7 28.0	21 56.6
5 M	16 51 52	13 52 21	28 32 9	5♏51 32	2 8.4	22 37.7	25 39.4	14 23.8	14 15.2	16 18.9	26 5.0	7 28.6	21 57.9
6 Tu	16 55 49	14 49 45	13♏17 8	20 48 8	2 0.7	24 43.3	26 53.0	14 49.7	14 19.7	16 18.0	26 7.5	7 29.1	21 59.2
7 W	16 59 46	15 47 7	28 23 26	6♐ 1 49	1 51.2	26 47.0	28 6.6	15 15.8	14 24.4	16 17.0	26 10.0	7 29.8	22 0.5
8 Th	17 3 42	16 44 29	13♐41 51	21 22 7	1 40.9	28 48.9	29 20.1	15 42.3	14 29.2	16 15.9	26 12.5	7 30.4	22 1.9
9 F	17 7 39	17 41 51	29 1 6	6♑37 26	1 31.2	0♋48.7	0♋33.7	16 8.9	14 34.2	16 14.7	26 14.9	7 31.1	22 3.2
10 Sa	17 11 35	18 39 11	14♑ 9 50	21 37 12	1 23.1	2 46.3	1 47.2	16 35.8	14 39.3	16 13.4	26 17.3	7 31.7	22 4.6
11 Su	17 15 32	19 36 31	28 58 39	6♒13 33	1 17.3	4 41.7	3 0.7	17 2.9	14 44.5	16 12.0	26 19.7	7 32.5	22 6.0
12 M	17 19 28	20 33 50	13♒21 27	20 22 11	1 14.1	6 34.8	4 14.2	17 30.3	14 49.9	16 10.5	26 22.0	7 33.2	22 7.4
13 Tu	17 23 25	21 31 9	27 15 43	4♓ 2 13	1D 13.0	8 25.5	5 27.7	17 57.9	14 55.5	16 9.0	26 24.3	7 34.0	22 8.8
14 W	17 27 21	22 28 27	10♓41 58	17 15 21	1R 13.1	10 13.9	6 41.2	18 25.8	15 1.2	16 7.3	26 26.6	7 34.8	22 10.2
15 Th	17 31 18	23 25 45	23 42 52	0♈ 5 1	1 13.4	11 59.8	7 54.6	18 53.8	15 7.0	16 5.6	26 28.8	7 35.7	22 11.6
16 F	17 35 15	24 23 2	6♈22 21	12 35 25	1 12.7	13 43.3	9 8.1	19 22.1	15 13.0	16 3.7	26 31.0	7 36.6	22 13.1
17 Sa	17 39 11	25 20 19	18 44 46	24 50 56	1 10.2	15 24.3	10 21.6	19 50.6	15 19.2	16 1.8	26 33.2	7 37.5	22 14.5
18 Su	17 43 8	26 17 36	0♉54 26	6♉55 42	1 5.3	17 2.9	11 35.0	20 19.4	15 25.4	15 59.8	26 35.3	7 38.4	22 16.0
19 M	17 47 4	27 14 53	12 55 12	18 53 19	0 58.0	18 39.1	12 48.5	20 48.3	15 31.8	15 57.7	26 37.4	7 39.4	22 17.4
20 Tu	17 51 1	28 12 9	24 50 24	0♊46 45	0 48.5	20 12.7	14 1.9	21 17.5	15 38.4	15 55.5	26 39.4	7 40.4	22 18.9
21 W	17 54 57	29 9 25	6♊42 40	12 38 22	0 37.5	21 43.8	15 15.3	21 46.8	15 45.1	15 53.2	26 41.4	7 41.4	22 20.4
22 Th	17 58 54	0♋ 6 41	18 34 7	24 30 5	0 26.0	23 12.4	16 28.7	22 16.4	15 51.9	15 50.8	26 43.3	7 42.4	22 21.9
23 F	18 2 50	1 3 57	0♋26 29	6♋23 30	0 15.0	24 38.4	17 42.1	22 46.2	15 58.8	15 48.4	26 45.3	7 43.5	22 23.4
24 Sa	18 6 47	2 1 12	12 21 19	18 20 8	0 5.4	26 1.9	18 55.5	23 16.2	16 5.9	15 45.9	26 47.1	7 44.6	22 24.9
25 Su	18 10 44	2 58 27	24 20 11	0♌21 42	29♒57.9	27 22.7	20 8.9	23 46.3	16 13.1	15 43.3	26 49.0	7 45.8	22 26.5
26 M	18 14 40	3 55 41	6♌24 57	12 30 15	29 52.8	28 40.9	21 22.3	24 16.7	16 20.5	15 40.6	26 50.8	7 47.0	22 28.0
27 Tu	18 18 37	4 52 55	18 37 56	24 48 23	29D 50.2	29 56.3	22 35.6	24 47.3	16 27.9	15 37.8	26 52.5	7 48.2	22 29.5
28 W	18 22 33	5 50 8	1♍ 1 59	7♍19 10	29 49.5	1♌ 9.0	23 49.0	25 18.0	16 35.5	15 35.0	26 54.2	7 49.4	22 31.1
29 Th	18 26 30	6 47 21	13 40 24	20 6 7	29 50.2	2 18.9	25 2.3	25 49.0	16 43.2	15 32.1	26 55.9	7 50.6	22 32.6
30 F	18 30 26	7 44 34	26 36 46	3♎12 48	29R 51.2	3 25.9	26 15.6	26 20.1	16 51.1	15 29.1	26 57.5	7 51.9	22 34.2

Astro Data	Planet Ingress
Dy Hr Mn	Dy Hr Mn
☽0S 6 7:09	☿ ♉ 10 7:42
♃ D 10 10:21	♀ ♊ 15 2:47
☽0N 18 21:32	☉ ♊ 21 12:57
♆ D 19 1:36	☿ ♊ 25 14:27
♄ R 27 2:19	
	☿ ♋ 8 14:12
☽0S 2 15:05	♀ ♋ 8 13:01
☽0N 15 2:50	☉ ♋ 21 21:12
♃⊼♄ 21 21:19	☊ ♒ 24 16:35
☽0S 29 20:58	☿ ♌ 27 1:12

Last Aspect	☽ Ingress	Last Aspect	☽ Ingress
Dy Hr Mn	Dy Hr Mn	Dy Hr Mn	Dy Hr Mn
1 11:56 ♅ □	♌ 1 23:06	2 9:48 ♀ □	♎ 2 23:15
3 22:23 ♅ △	♍ 4 8:41	4 19:56 ♅ ☍	♏ 5 2:25
5 23:25 ♇ ⚹	♎ 6 14:17	6 13:54 ♇ △	♐ 7 2:32
8 11:01 ♅ ☍	♏ 8 16:07	8 19:38 ♅ △	♑ 9 1:33
10 6:19 ♀ ☍	♐ 10 15:43	10 19:39 ♅ □	♒ 11 1:41
12 7:09 ♅ △	♑ 12 15:15	12 22:30 ♅ ⚹	♓ 13 4:50
14 15:48 ♀ △	♒ 14 16:46	14 23:25 ☉ □	♈ 15 11:50
16 12:50 ☉ □	♓ 16 21:34	17 15:25 ♅ ☌	♉ 17 22:12
19 1:09 ☉ ⚹	♈ 19 5:45	19 18:54 ♇ ⚹	♊ 20 10:25
21 7:20 ♅ ☌	♉ 21 16:26	22 16:32 ♅ ⚹	♋ 22 23:07
23 21:02 ☿ ☌	♊ 24 4:31	25 6:49 ☿ ☌	♌ 25 11:17
26 8:23 ♅ ⚹	♋ 26 17:12	27 16:02 ♅ △	♍ 27 22:01
28 21:06 ♅ □	♌ 29 5:33	29 23:28 ♂ ☌	♎ 30 6:11
31 8:14 ♅ △	♍ 31 16:06		

☽ Phases & Eclipses	Astro Data
Dy Hr Mn	1 MAY 1933
2 22:39 ☽ 12♌03	Julian Day # 12174
9 22:04 ○ 18♏48	Delta T 23.9 sec
16 12:50 ☽ 25♒11	SVP 06♓11'20"
24 10:07 ● 2♊46	Obliquity 23°27'01"
	⚷ Chiron 27♉18.3
1 11:53 ☽ 10♍31	☽ Mean ☊ 4♓33.0
8 5:05 ○ 16♐57	
14 23:25 ☽ 23♓24	1 JUNE 1933
23 1:22 ● 1♋07	Julian Day # 12205
30 21:40 ☽ 8♎36	Delta T 23.9 sec
	SVP 06♓11'15"
	Obliquity 23°27'00"
	⚷ Chiron 29♉33.6
	☽ Mean ☊ 2♓54.6

JULY 1933 LONGITUDE

Day	Sid.Time	☉	0 hr ☽	Noon ☽	True ☊	☿	♀	♂	♃	♄	♅	♆	♇
1 Sa	18 34 23	8♋41 46	9♎54 36	16♎42 28	29♒51.6	4♌29.9	27♋28.9	26♍51.4	16♍59.0	15♒26.0	26♈59.1	7♍53.2	22♋35.8
2 Su	18 38 19	9 38 58	23 36 39	0♏37 14	29R 50.7	5 30.8	28 42.2	27 22.8	17 7.1	15R 22.9	27 0.6	7 54.5	22 37.3
3 M	18 42 16	10 36 9	7♏44 13	14 57 22	29 47.9	6 28.6	29 55.5	27 54.5	17 15.3	15 19.7	27 2.1	7 55.9	22 38.9
4 Tu	18 46 13	11 33 20	22 16 17	29 40 23	29 43.3	7 23.2	1♌ 8.7	28 26.3	17 23.6	15 16.4	27 3.5	7 57.3	22 40.5
5 W	18 50 9	12 30 31	7♐ 8 54	14♐40 50	29 37.3	8 14.4	2 21.9	28 58.2	17 32.0	15 13.0	27 4.9	7 58.7	22 42.1
6 Th	18 54 6	13 27 42	22 15 4	29 50 23	29 30.6	9 2.1	3 35.2	29 30.4	17 40.5	15 9.6	27 6.3	8 0.1	22 43.7
7 F	18 58 2	14 24 53	7♑25 29	14♑59 5	29 24.1	9 46.2	4 48.4	0♎ 2.6	17 49.1	15 6.2	27 7.6	8 1.6	22 45.3
8 Sa	19 1 59	15 22 4	22 29 56	29 56 55	29 18.7	10 26.5	6 1.5	0 35.1	17 57.9	15 2.7	27 8.9	8 3.1	22 46.9
9 Su	19 5 55	16 19 15	7♒19 3	14♒35 32	29 15.1	11 3.0	7 14.7	1 7.7	18 6.7	14 59.1	27 10.1	8 4.6	22 48.5
10 M	19 9 52	17 16 26	21 45 46	28 49 19	29D 13.4	11 35.5	8 27.9	1 40.4	18 15.7	14 55.4	27 11.3	8 6.1	22 50.1
11 Tu	19 13 49	18 13 37	5♓45 59	12♓35 43	29 13.3	12 3.9	9 41.0	2 13.3	18 24.7	14 51.7	27 12.4	8 7.7	22 51.7
12 W	19 17 45	19 10 49	19 18 38	25 54 58	29 14.3	12 28.0	10 54.1	2 46.4	18 33.9	14 47.9	27 13.5	8 9.2	22 53.3
13 Th	19 21 42	20 8 2	2♈25 5	8♈49 23	29 15.8	12 47.7	12 7.2	3 19.6	18 43.1	14 44.1	27 14.5	8 10.8	22 54.9
14 F	19 25 38	21 5 15	15 8 24	21 22 38	29R 16.8	13 2.8	13 20.3	3 53.0	18 52.5	14 40.3	27 15.5	8 12.5	22 56.5
15 Sa	19 29 35	22 2 28	27 32 39	3♉39 2	29 16.8	13 13.3	14 33.4	4 26.5	19 1.9	14 36.3	27 16.4	8 14.1	22 58.1
16 Su	19 33 31	22 59 42	9♉42 21	15 43 8	29 15.4	13R 19.0	15 46.5	5 0.1	19 11.5	14 32.4	27 17.3	8 15.8	22 59.7
17 M	19 37 28	23 56 57	21 41 56	27 39 15	29 12.4	13 20.0	16 59.5	5 33.9	19 21.1	14 28.4	27 18.1	8 17.5	23 1.3
18 Tu	19 41 24	24 54 13	3♊35 33	9♊31 18	29 8.1	13 16.0	18 12.6	6 7.8	19 30.9	14 24.3	27 18.9	8 19.2	23 2.9
19 W	19 45 21	25 51 29	15 26 54	21 22 42	29 2.8	13 7.3	19 25.6	6 41.9	19 40.7	14 20.2	27 19.7	8 20.9	23 4.5
20 Th	19 49 18	26 48 46	27 19 4	3♋16 17	28 57.0	12 53.6	20 38.6	7 16.2	19 50.6	14 16.1	27 20.4	8 22.7	23 6.1
21 F	19 53 14	27 46 4	9♋14 37	15 14 20	28 51.5	12 35.3	21 51.6	7 50.5	20 0.6	14 11.9	27 21.0	8 24.4	23 7.7
22 Sa	19 57 11	28 43 22	21 15 37	27 18 42	28 46.8	12 12.4	23 4.6	8 25.0	20 10.7	14 7.7	27 21.6	8 26.2	23 9.3
23 Su	20 1 7	29 40 41	3♌23 45	9♌30 57	28 43.2	11 45.2	24 17.5	8 59.7	20 20.9	14 3.4	27 22.2	8 28.0	23 10.9
24 M	20 5 4	0♌38 0	15 40 29	21 52 32	28 41.1	11 14.0	25 30.5	9 34.5	20 31.2	13 59.1	27 22.7	8 29.9	23 12.5
25 Tu	20 9 0	1 35 20	28 7 16	4♍24 54	28D 40.4	10 39.1	26 43.4	10 9.4	20 41.5	13 54.8	27 23.2	8 31.7	23 14.1
26 W	20 12 57	2 32 40	10♍45 39	17 9 42	28 40.9	10 1.0	27 56.3	10 44.4	20 52.0	13 50.5	27 23.6	8 33.6	23 15.7
27 Th	20 16 53	3 30 1	23 37 17	0♎ 8 39	28 42.2	9 20.4	29 9.1	11 19.6	21 2.5	13 46.1	27 23.9	8 35.4	23 17.3
28 F	20 20 50	4 27 22	6♎44 1	13 23 36	28 43.7	8 37.8	0♍22.0	11 54.9	21 13.1	13 41.7	27 24.2	8 37.3	23 18.9
29 Sa	20 24 47	5 24 44	20 7 36	26 56 9	28 45.0	7 53.9	1 34.8	12 30.3	21 23.8	13 37.3	27 24.5	8 39.3	23 20.5
30 Su	20 28 43	6 22 6	3♏49 23	10♏47 18	28R 45.6	7 9.5	2 47.6	13 5.9	21 34.5	13 32.9	27 24.7	8 41.2	23 22.1
31 M	20 32 40	7 19 29	17 49 52	24 56 57	28 45.3	6 25.4	4 0.4	13 41.6	21 45.3	13 28.5	27 24.8	8 43.1	23 23.6

AUGUST 1933 LONGITUDE

Day	Sid.Time	☉	0 hr ☽	Noon ☽	True ☊	☿	♀	♂	♃	♄	♅	♆	♇
1 Tu	20 36 36	8♌16 53	2♐ 8 15	9♐23 23	28♒44.1	5♌42.3	5♍13.2	14♎17.4	21♍56.2	13♒24.0	27♈25.0	8♍45.1	23♋25.2
2 W	20 40 33	9 14 17	16 41 51	24 3 1	28R 42.1	5R 1.2	6 25.9	14 53.3	22 7.2	13R 19.6	27R 25.0	8 47.1	23 26.8
3 Th	20 44 29	10 11 42	1♑26 6	8♑50 18	28 39.8	4 22.7	7 38.6	15 29.3	22 18.2	13 15.1	27 25.0	8 49.1	23 28.3
4 F	20 48 26	11 9 8	16 14 41	23 38 19	28 37.6	3 47.7	8 51.3	16 5.5	22 29.4	13 10.6	27 25.0	8 51.1	23 29.9
5 Sa	20 52 22	12 6 34	1♒ 0 14	8♒19 33	28 35.8	3 16.8	10 4.0	16 41.8	22 40.5	13 6.2	27 24.9	8 53.1	23 31.4
6 Su	20 56 19	13 4 1	15 35 25	22 47 3	28D 34.7	2 50.7	11 16.6	17 18.2	22 51.8	13 1.7	27 24.8	8 55.1	23 33.0
7 M	21 0 16	14 1 29	29 53 51	6♓55 16	28 34.4	2 30.0	12 29.2	17 54.7	23 3.1	12 57.2	27 24.6	8 57.2	23 34.5
8 Tu	21 4 12	14 58 59	13♓50 58	20 40 42	28 34.8	2 15.1	13 41.7	18 31.3	23 14.4	12 52.7	27 24.4	8 59.3	23 36.0
9 W	21 8 9	15 56 29	27 24 23	4♈ 2 3	28 35.7	2D 6.4	14 54.3	19 8.0	23 25.9	12 48.2	27 24.1	9 1.3	23 37.5
10 Th	21 12 5	16 54 1	10♈33 50	17 0 0	28 36.7	2 4.3	16 6.8	19 44.9	23 37.4	12 43.8	27 23.8	9 3.4	23 39.0
11 F	21 16 2	17 51 34	23 20 53	29 36 54	28 37.6	2 9.0	17 19.3	20 21.8	23 48.9	12 39.3	27 23.4	9 5.5	23 40.5
12 Sa	21 19 58	18 49 9	5♉48 30	11♉56 12	28 38.3	2 20.7	18 31.7	20 58.9	24 0.5	12 34.8	27 23.0	9 7.6	23 42.0
13 Su	21 23 55	19 46 45	18 0 32	24 2 4	28R 38.6	2 39.5	19 44.2	21 36.1	24 12.2	12 30.4	27 22.5	9 9.7	23 43.5
14 M	21 27 51	20 44 22	0♊ 1 22	5♊59 1	28 38.5	3 5.4	20 56.6	22 13.4	24 23.9	12 26.0	27 22.0	9 11.8	23 45.0
15 Tu	21 31 48	21 42 2	11 55 33	17 51 32	28 38.0	3 38.4	22 9.0	22 50.8	24 35.7	12 21.6	27 21.4	9 14.0	23 46.4
16 W	21 35 45	22 39 42	23 47 30	29 43 56	28 37.4	4 18.6	23 21.4	23 28.3	24 47.5	12 17.2	27 20.8	9 16.1	23 47.9
17 Th	21 39 41	23 37 25	5♋41 19	11♋40 6	28 36.7	5 5.7	24 33.7	24 5.9	24 59.4	12 12.8	27 20.1	9 18.3	23 49.3
18 F	21 43 38	24 35 8	17 40 40	23 43 23	28 36.1	5 59.6	25 46.0	24 43.7	25 11.4	12 8.5	27 19.4	9 20.4	23 50.7
19 Sa	21 47 34	25 32 53	29 48 34	5♌56 30	28 35.7	7 0.1	26 58.3	25 21.5	25 23.4	12 4.2	27 18.7	9 22.6	23 52.1
20 Su	21 51 31	26 30 40	12♌ 7 25	18 21 30	28 35.5	8 7.0	28 10.5	25 59.5	25 35.4	11 59.9	27 17.9	9 24.8	23 53.5
21 M	21 55 27	27 28 28	24 38 54	0♍59 44	28D 35.4	9 20.0	29 22.7	26 37.5	25 47.5	11 55.7	27 17.0	9 27.0	23 54.9
22 Tu	21 59 24	28 26 18	7♍24 4	13 51 56	28R 35.4	10 38.9	0♎34.9	27 15.7	25 59.6	11 51.4	27 16.1	9 29.2	23 56.3
23 W	22 3 20	29 24 8	20 23 21	26 58 16	28 35.4	12 3.2	1 47.1	27 54.0	26 11.8	11 47.3	27 15.2	9 31.4	23 57.7
24 Th	22 7 17	0♍22 1	3♎36 39	10♎18 26	28 35.2	13 32.6	2 59.2	28 32.4	26 24.0	11 43.1	27 14.2	9 33.6	23 59.0
25 F	22 11 14	1 19 54	17 3 33	23 51 52	28 35.0	15 6.6	4 11.3	29 10.8	26 36.3	11 39.0	27 13.2	9 35.8	24 0.4
26 Sa	22 15 10	2 17 49	0♏43 17	7♏37 39	28 34.6	16 44.8	5 23.4	29 49.4	26 48.6	11 35.0	27 12.1	9 38.0	24 1.7
27 Su	22 19 7	3 15 45	14 34 51	21 34 41	28 34.3	18 26.9	6 35.4	0♏28.1	27 0.9	11 31.0	27 11.0	9 40.2	24 3.0
28 M	22 23 3	4 13 43	28 36 58	5♐41 29	28D 34.1	20 12.2	7 47.4	1 6.9	27 13.3	11 27.0	27 9.8	9 42.4	24 4.3
29 Tu	22 27 0	5 11 41	12♐47 58	19 56 9	28 34.1	22 0.3	8 59.3	1 45.8	27 25.7	11 23.1	27 8.6	9 44.6	24 5.6
30 W	22 30 56	6 9 41	27 5 41	4♑16 12	28 34.4	23 50.8	10 11.2	2 24.8	27 38.2	11 19.2	27 7.4	9 46.8	24 6.8
31 Th	22 34 53	7 7 43	11♑27 17	18 38 29	28 35.1	25 43.3	11 23.1	3 3.9	27 50.7	11 15.4	27 6.1	9 49.1	24 8.1

Astro Data	Planet Ingress	Last Aspect	☽ Ingress	Last Aspect	☽ Ingress	☽ Phases & Eclipses	Astro Data
Dy Hr Mn	Dy Hr Mn	Dy Hr Mn	Dy Hr Mn	Dy Hr Mn	Dy Hr Mn	Dy Hr Mn	1 JULY 1933
♂0S 8 7:33	♀ ♌ 3 1:29	2 9:34 ♀ □	♏ 2 10:57	2 17:29 ♅ △	♑ 2 21:40	7 11:51 ○ 14♑53	Julian Day # 12235
☽0N 12 10:00	♂ ♎ 6 22:03	4 10:23 ♂ ⚹	♐ 4 12:32	4 18:09 ♅ □	♒ 4 22:22	14 12:24 ☽ 21♈35	Delta T 23.9 sec
☿ R 16 16:37	☉ ♌ 23 8:05	6 11:54 ♂ □	♑ 6 12:15	6 19:47 ♅ ⚹	♓ 7 0:10	22 16:03 ● 29♋22	SVP 06♓11'10"
☽0S 27 1:58	♀ ♍ 27 16:45	8 7:29 ♅ □	♒ 8 12:05	8 17:13 ♇ △	♈ 9 4:40	30 4:44 ☽ 6♏33	Obliquity 23°27'00"
		10 9:13 ♅ ⚹	♓ 10 14:01	11 7:43 ♅ ☌	♉ 11 12:45		⚷ Chiron 1♊37.0
♅ R 2 19:44	♀ ♎ 21 12:23	12 6:29 ♇ △	♈ 12 19:31	13 12:32 ♃ △	♊ 13 23:57	5 19:31 ○ 12♒53	☽ Mean ☊ 1♓19.3
☽0N 8 19:03	☉ ♍ 23 14:52	14 23:28 ♅ ☌	♉ 15 4:49	16 7:11 ♅ ⚹	♋ 16 12:32	5 19:46 ◑A 0.232	
☿ D 9 19:32	♂ ♏ 26 6:34	17 4:55 ☉ ⚹	♊ 17 16:44	18 19:05 ♅ □	♌ 19 0:22	13 3:49 ☽ 19♉56	1 AUGUST 1933
♃⚹♇ 10 4:01		20 0:03 ♅ ⚹	♋ 20 5:25	21 5:48 ☉ ☌	♍ 21 10:07	21 5:48 ● 27♌42	Julian Day # 12266
☽0S 23 7:45		22 16:03 ☉ ☌	♌ 22 17:19	23 10:46 ♃ ☌	♎ 23 17:29	21 5:48:47 ◐A 2'03"	Delta T 23.9 sec
♀0S 23 1:17		24 22:35 ♅ △	♍ 25 3:36	25 22:21 ♂ ☌	♏ 25 22:45	28 10:13 ☽ 4♐38	SVP 06♓11'05"
♃⚼♄ 25 4:01		26 23:23 ♇ ⚹	♎ 27 11:44	27 21:36 ♃ ⚹	♐ 28 2:21		Obliquity 23°27'00"
♃⚻♅ 27 17:47		29 12:50 ♅ ☍	♏ 29 17:21	30 0:55 ♃ □	♑ 30 4:52		⚷ Chiron 3♊14.6
		31 9:24 ♇ △	♐ 31 20:27				☽ Mean ☊ 29♒40.8

LONGITUDE SEPTEMBER 1933

Day	Sid.Time	☉	0 hr ☽	Noon ☽	True ☊	☿	♀	♂	♃	♄	♅	♆	♇
1 F	22 38 49	8♍ 5 46	25♑49 19	2♒59 16	28♒35.8	27♌37.2	12♎34.9	3♏43.1	28♍ 3.2	11♒11.7	27♈ 4.7	9♍51.3	24♋ 9.3
2 Sa	22 42 46	9 3 50	10♒ 7 47	17 14 21	28 36.5	29 32.4	13 46.7	4 22.3	28 15.8	11R 8.0	27R 3.4	9 53.5	24 10.5
3 Su	22 46 43	10 1 56	24 18 24	1♓19 27	28R37.0	1♍28.3	14 58.4	5 1.7	28 28.4	11 4.3	27 2.0	9 55.7	24 11.7
4 M	22 50 39	11 0 3	8♓17 0	15 10 39	28 36.8	3 24.6	16 10.1	5 41.2	28 41.0	11 0.7	27 0.5	9 58.0	24 12.9
5 Tu	22 54 36	11 58 12	22 0 2	28 44 51	28 36.0	5 21.2	17 21.7	6 20.7	28 53.6	10 57.2	26 59.0	10 0.2	24 14.1
6 W	22 58 32	12 56 22	5♈24 54	12♈ 0 4	28 34.6	7 17.7	18 33.3	7 0.4	29 6.3	10 53.8	26 57.5	10 2.4	24 15.2
7 Th	23 2 29	13 54 35	18 30 20	24 55 45	28 32.6	9 14.0	19 44.9	7 40.1	29 19.0	10 50.4	26 55.9	10 4.6	24 16.3
8 F	23 6 25	14 52 49	1♉16 28	7♉32 42	28 30.3	11 9.8	20 56.4	8 19.9	29 31.7	10 47.0	26 54.3	10 6.9	24 17.5
9 Sa	23 10 22	15 51 6	13 44 48	19 53 5	28 28.0	13 5.1	22 7.9	8 59.9	29 44.5	10 43.8	26 52.7	10 9.1	24 18.6
10 Su	23 14 18	16 49 24	25 58 1	2♊ 0 4	28 26.1	14 59.6	23 19.3	9 39.9	29 57.2	10 40.6	26 51.0	10 11.3	24 19.6
11 M	23 18 15	17 47 45	7♊59 46	13 57 39	28D24.9	16 53.4	24 30.7	10 20.0	0♎10.0	10 37.5	26 49.3	10 13.5	24 20.7
12 Tu	23 22 12	18 46 8	19 54 19	25 50 20	28 24.6	18 46.3	25 42.0	11 0.2	0 22.9	10 34.4	26 47.5	10 15.7	24 21.7
13 W	23 26 8	19 44 32	1♋46 20	7♋42 54	28 25.1	20 38.3	26 53.3	11 40.5	0 35.7	10 31.5	26 45.8	10 17.9	24 22.8
14 Th	23 30 5	20 42 59	13 40 38	19 40 5	28 26.3	22 29.3	28 4.6	12 20.9	0 48.6	10 28.6	26 43.9	10 20.1	24 23.8
15 F	23 34 1	21 41 29	25 41 50	1♌46 23	28 27.9	24 19.3	29 15.8	13 1.4	1 1.4	10 25.8	26 42.1	10 22.3	24 24.7
16 Sa	23 37 58	22 40 0	7♌54 12	14 5 44	28 29.5	26 8.3	0♏27.0	13 42.0	1 14.3	10 23.0	26 40.2	10 24.5	24 25.7
17 Su	23 41 54	23 38 33	20 21 19	26 41 16	28R30.6	27 56.2	1 38.1	14 22.7	1 27.2	10 20.4	26 38.3	10 26.7	24 26.7
18 M	23 45 51	24 37 8	3♍ 5 48	9♍35 3	28 30.8	29 43.2	2 49.2	15 3.5	1 40.1	10 17.8	26 36.3	10 28.9	24 27.6
19 Tu	23 49 47	25 35 46	16 9 5	22 47 50	28 29.7	1♎29.1	4 0.2	15 44.3	1 53.1	10 15.3	26 34.4	10 31.0	24 28.5
20 W	23 53 44	26 34 25	29 31 10	6♎18 52	28 27.2	3 13.9	5 11.2	16 25.3	2 6.0	10 12.9	26 32.4	10 33.2	24 29.4
21 Th	23 57 40	27 33 6	13♎10 38	20 6 5	28 23.5	4 57.8	6 22.1	17 6.3	2 19.0	10 10.6	26 30.3	10 35.4	24 30.2
22 F	0 1 37	28 31 49	27 4 46	4♏ 6 13	28 19.0	6 40.6	7 32.9	17 47.4	2 31.9	10 8.3	26 28.3	10 37.5	24 31.0
23 Sa	0 5 34	29 30 34	11♏ 9 54	18 15 18	28 14.4	8 22.5	8 43.8	18 28.7	2 44.9	10 6.2	26 26.2	10 39.6	24 31.9
24 Su	0 9 30	0♎29 21	25 21 55	2♐29 16	28 10.2	10 3.4	9 54.5	19 10.0	2 57.9	10 4.1	26 24.1	10 41.8	24 32.7
25 M	0 13 27	1 28 9	9♐36 52	16 44 20	28 7.1	11 43.3	11 5.2	19 51.4	3 10.8	10 2.2	26 21.9	10 43.9	24 33.4
26 Tu	0 17 23	2 27 0	23 51 18	0♑57 28	28D 5.4	13 22.3	12 15.9	20 32.8	3 23.8	10 0.3	26 19.8	10 46.0	24 34.2
27 W	0 21 20	3 25 52	8♑ 2 34	15 6 24	28 5.2	15 0.3	13 26.4	21 14.4	3 36.8	9 58.5	26 17.6	10 48.1	24 34.9
28 Th	0 25 16	4 24 45	22 8 46	29 9 31	28 6.1	16 37.5	14 36.9	21 56.0	3 49.8	9 56.9	26 15.4	10 50.2	24 35.6
29 F	0 29 13	5 23 41	6♒ 8 31	13♒ 5 35	28 7.5	18 13.8	15 47.4	22 37.8	4 2.8	9 55.3	26 13.2	10 52.2	24 36.3
30 Sa	0 33 10	6 22 38	20 0 37	26 53 26	28R 8.7	19 49.1	16 57.8	23 19.6	4 15.8	9 53.8	26 10.9	10 54.3	24 37.0

LONGITUDE OCTOBER 1933

Day	Sid.Time	☉	0 hr ☽	Noon ☽	True ☊	☿	♀	♂	♃	♄	♅	♆	♇
1 Su	0 37 6	7♎21 37	3♓43 52	10♓31 45	28♒ 8.8	21♎23.6	18♏ 8.1	24♏ 1.5	4♎28.7	9♒52.4	26♈ 8.6	10♍56.3	24♋37.6
2 M	0 41 3	8 20 37	17 16 53	23 59 5	28R 7.2	22 57.3	19 18.3	24 43.4	4 41.7	9R51.0	26R 6.3	10 58.4	24 38.2
3 Tu	0 44 59	9 19 40	0♈38 7	7♈13 50	28 3.7	24 30.1	20 28.4	25 25.5	4 54.7	9 49.8	26 4.0	11 0.4	24 38.8
4 W	0 48 56	10 18 44	13 46 4	20 14 41	27 58.1	26 2.1	21 38.5	26 7.6	5 7.6	9 48.7	26 1.7	11 2.4	24 39.4
5 Th	0 52 52	11 17 51	26 39 35	3♉ 0 44	27 51.0	27 33.3	22 48.5	26 49.8	5 20.6	9 47.7	25 59.4	11 4.4	24 39.9
6 F	0 56 49	12 17 0	9♉18 10	15 31 57	27 42.9	29 3.7	23 58.4	27 32.1	5 33.5	9 46.8	25 57.0	11 6.4	24 40.4
7 Sa	1 0 45	13 16 11	21 42 14	27 49 14	27 34.7	0♏33.2	25 8.3	28 14.5	5 46.5	9 46.0	25 54.7	11 8.3	24 40.9
8 Su	1 4 42	14 15 24	3♊53 15	9♊54 36	27 27.3	2 1.9	26 18.1	28 56.9	5 59.4	9 45.2	25 52.3	11 10.3	24 41.4
9 M	1 8 38	15 14 39	15 53 42	21 51 2	27 21.3	3 29.8	27 27.7	29 39.5	6 12.3	9 44.6	25 49.9	11 12.2	24 41.8
10 Tu	1 12 35	16 13 57	27 47 6	3♋42 27	27 17.3	4 56.9	28 37.4	0♐22.1	6 25.2	9 44.1	25 47.5	11 14.1	24 42.3
11 W	1 16 32	17 13 17	9♋37 41	15 33 25	27D15.2	6 23.2	29 46.9	1 4.8	6 38.1	9 43.7	25 45.1	11 16.0	24 42.7
12 Th	1 20 28	18 12 40	21 30 19	27 29 0	27 14.9	7 48.5	0♐56.3	1 47.5	6 51.0	9 43.3	25 42.7	11 17.9	24 43.0
13 F	1 24 25	19 12 4	3♌30 10	9♌34 25	27 15.7	9 13.0	2 5.7	2 30.4	7 3.8	9 43.1	25 40.3	11 19.7	24 43.4
14 Sa	1 28 21	20 11 31	15 42 25	21 54 44	27R16.8	10 36.6	3 15.0	3 13.3	7 16.6	9D43.0	25 37.8	11 21.5	24 43.7
15 Su	1 32 18	21 11 0	28 11 55	4♍34 26	27 17.4	11 59.2	4 24.1	3 56.3	7 29.5	9 43.0	25 35.4	11 23.4	24 44.0
16 M	1 36 14	22 10 32	11♍ 2 41	17 36 56	27 16.4	13 20.9	5 33.2	4 39.4	7 42.3	9 43.0	25 32.9	11 25.2	24 44.3
17 Tu	1 40 11	23 10 5	24 17 21	1♎ 3 58	27 13.2	14 41.5	6 42.2	5 22.6	7 55.0	9 43.2	25 30.5	11 26.9	24 44.5
18 W	1 44 7	24 9 41	7♎56 40	14 55 10	27 7.6	16 1.0	7 51.1	6 5.8	8 7.8	9 43.5	25 28.0	11 28.7	24 44.8
19 Th	1 48 4	25 9 19	21 59 0	29 7 36	26 59.8	17 19.4	8 59.9	6 49.1	8 20.5	9 43.9	25 25.6	11 30.4	24 44.9
20 F	1 52 1	26 8 59	6♏20 15	13♏36 5	26 50.5	18 36.5	10 8.6	7 32.5	8 33.2	9 44.4	25 23.1	11 32.1	24 45.1
21 Sa	1 55 57	27 8 41	20 54 14	28 13 43	26 40.7	19 52.3	11 17.2	8 16.0	8 45.9	9 45.0	25 20.7	11 33.8	24 45.3
22 Su	1 59 54	28 8 25	5♐33 37	12♐53 1	26 31.6	21 6.6	12 25.6	8 59.5	8 58.5	9 45.7	25 18.2	11 35.5	24 45.4
23 M	2 3 50	29 8 11	20 11 7	27 27 12	26 24.3	22 19.4	13 34.0	9 43.2	9 11.1	9 46.5	25 15.8	11 37.1	24 45.5
24 Tu	2 7 47	0♏ 7 58	4♑40 40	11♑51 4	26 19.3	23 30.4	14 42.2	10 26.9	9 23.7	9 47.4	25 13.3	11 38.8	24 45.6
25 W	2 11 43	1 7 47	18 58 5	26 1 30	26D16.7	24 39.6	15 50.3	11 10.6	9 36.2	9 48.4	25 10.9	11 40.4	24 45.6
26 Th	2 15 40	2 7 38	3♒ 1 14	9♒57 16	26 16.1	25 46.8	16 58.3	11 54.5	9 48.7	9 49.5	25 8.5	11 41.9	24R45.6
27 F	2 19 36	3 7 30	16 49 39	23 38 32	26R16.5	26 51.6	18 6.1	12 38.4	10 1.2	9 50.7	25 6.1	11 43.5	24 45.6
28 Sa	2 23 33	4 7 24	0♓24 1	7♓ 6 16	26 16.6	27 53.9	19 13.8	13 22.3	10 13.6	9 52.0	25 3.6	11 45.0	24 45.6
29 Su	2 27 30	5 7 20	13 45 26	20 21 39	26 15.4	28 53.5	20 21.4	14 6.4	10 26.0	9 53.4	25 1.2	11 46.5	24 45.5
30 M	2 31 26	6 7 17	26 55 0	3♈25 35	26 11.7	29 49.9	21 28.8	14 50.5	10 38.3	9 54.9	24 58.8	11 48.0	24 45.5
31 Tu	2 35 23	7 7 16	9♈53 26	16 18 36	26 5.1	0♐42.9	22 36.0	15 34.6	10 50.6	9 56.5	24 56.5	11 49.4	24 45.4

Astro Data	Planet Ingress	Last Aspect	☽ Ingress	Last Aspect	☽ Ingress	☽ Phases & Eclipses	Astro Data
Dy Hr Mn	Dy Hr Mn	Dy Hr Mn	Dy Hr Mn	Dy Hr Mn	Dy Hr Mn	Dy Hr Mn	1 SEPTEMBER 1933
☽0N 5 4:42	☿ ♍ 2 5:44	1 3:47 ♃ △	♒ 1 7:00	2 14:04 ♂ △	♈ 2 22:51	4 5:04 ○ 11♓12	Julian Day # 12297
♄⊼♆ 15 16:42	♃ ♎ 10 5:10	3 4:39 ♅ ⚹	♓ 3 9:44	5 1:55 ☿ ☍	♉ 5 6:18	4 4:52 ☍ A 0.696	Delta T 23.9 sec
☽0S 19 15:21	♀ ♏ 15 14:54	5 12:28 ♃ ☍	♈ 5 14:15	7 13:37 ♂ ☍	♊ 7 16:18	11 21:30 ☽ 18♊40	SVP 06♓11'00"
☿0S 19 12:22	☿ ♎ 18 3:48	7 15:44 ♅ ☌	♉ 7 21:35	9 19:59 ♅ ⚹	♋ 10 4:29	19 18:21 ● 26♍21	Obliquity 23°27'01"
♃0S 22 0:03	☉ ♎ 23 12:01	9 20:45 ♇ ⚹	♊ 10 8:01	12 8:25 ♅ □	♌ 12 17:02	26 15:36 ☽ 3♑05	⚷ Chiron 4♊02.5
		12 13:54 ♅ ⚹	♋ 12 20:25	14 19:03 ♅ △	♍ 15 3:24		☽ Mean ☊ 28♒02.3
☽0N 2 13:13	☿ ♏ 6 15:04	15 7:49 ♀ □	♌ 15 8:31	17 0:48 ♇ ⚹	♎ 17 10:07	3 17:08 ○ 10♈02	
♅⚼♆ 3 20:15	♂ ♐ 9 11:35	17 11:53 ♅ △	♍ 17 18:13	19 5:47 ♅ ☍	♏ 19 13:28	11 16:45 ☽ 17♋55	1 OCTOBER 1933
♄ D 14 17:14	♀ ♐ 11 4:32	19 18:21 ☉ ☌	♎ 20 0:51	21 6:19 ♇ △	♐ 21 14:54	19 5:45 ● 25♎24	Julian Day # 12327
☽0S 17 0:31	☉ ♏ 23 20:48	21 22:58 ♅ ☍	♏ 22 5:00	23 15:53 ☉ ⚹	♑ 23 16:13	25 22:21 ☽ 2♒04	Delta T 23.9 sec
♃△♄ 26 1:37	☿ ♐ 30 4:27	23 22:37 ♇ △	♐ 24 7:49	25 10:32 ♅ □	♒ 25 18:48		SVP 06♓10'57"
♇ R 26 8:09		26 4:10 ♅ △	♑ 26 10:23	27 19:11 ☿ □	♓ 27 23:17		Obliquity 23°27'01"
☽0N 29 19:31		28 7:01 ♅ □	♒ 28 13:27	29 20:02 ♇ △	♈ 30 5:40		⚷ Chiron 3♊50.5R
		30 10:44 ♅ ⚹	♓ 30 17:27				☽ Mean ☊ 26♒27.0

NOVEMBER 1933 LONGITUDE

Day	Sid.Time	☉	0 hr ☽	Noon ☽	True ☊	☿	♀	♂	♃	♄	♅	♆	♇
1 W	2 39 19	8♏ 7 17	22♈41 3	29♈ 0 49	25♒55.7	1♐32.1	23♐43.1	16♐18.9	11♎ 2.9	9♒58.2	24♈54.1	11♍50.9	24♋45.2
2 Th	2 43 16	9 7 19	5♉17 52	11♉32 12	25R43.8	2 16.9	24 50.0	17 3.2	11 15.1	9 60.0	24R51.7	11 52.3	24R45.1
3 F	2 47 12	10 7 23	17 43 49	23 52 46	25 30.5	2 57.0	25 56.7	17 47.5	11 27.3	10 1.9	24 49.4	11 53.6	24 44.9
4 Sa	2 51 9	11 7 30	29 59 6	6♊ 2 57	25 16.9	3 31.8	27 3.3	18 32.0	11 39.4	10 3.9	24 47.1	11 55.0	24 44.7
5 Su	2 55 5	12 7 38	12♊ 4 28	18 3 53	25 4.1	4 0.7	28 9.7	19 16.5	11 51.5	10 6.0	24 44.7	11 56.3	24 44.5
6 M	2 59 2	13 7 48	24 1 29	29 57 34	24 53.2	4 23.1	29 15.9	20 1.0	12 3.5	10 8.2	24 42.4	11 57.6	24 44.2
7 Tu	3 2 59	14 8 0	5♋52 34	11♋46 55	24 44.8	4 38.3	0♑21.9	20 45.7	12 15.5	10 10.5	24 40.2	11 58.8	24 43.9
8 W	3 6 55	15 8 14	17 41 7	23 35 44	24 39.3	4R45.7	1 27.7	21 30.4	12 27.4	10 12.9	24 37.9	12 0.1	24 43.6
9 Th	3 10 52	16 8 31	29 31 21	5♌28 36	24 36.3	4 44.5	2 33.3	22 15.1	12 39.2	10 15.3	24 35.7	12 1.3	24 43.3
10 F	3 14 48	17 8 49	11♌28 10	17 30 44	24D35.3	4 34.1	3 38.7	22 59.9	12 51.0	10 17.9	24 33.5	12 2.4	24 42.9
11 Sa	3 18 45	18 9 9	23 36 58	29 47 34	24R35.3	4 14.1	4 43.9	23 44.8	13 2.8	10 20.6	24 31.3	12 3.6	24 42.6
12 Su	3 22 41	19 9 30	6♍ 3 13	12♍24 31	24 35.0	3 44.0	5 48.8	24 29.8	13 14.5	10 23.4	24 29.1	12 4.7	24 42.2
13 M	3 26 38	20 9 54	18 52 2	25 26 16	24 33.3	3 3.7	6 53.6	25 14.8	13 26.1	10 26.2	24 27.0	12 5.8	24 41.7
14 Tu	3 30 34	21 10 20	2♎ 7 32	8♎56 5	24 29.3	2 13.6	7 58.1	25 59.9	13 37.7	10 29.2	24 24.8	12 6.8	24 41.3
15 W	3 34 31	22 10 48	15 51 57	22 55 0	24 22.5	1 14.1	9 2.3	26 45.0	13 49.2	10 32.2	24 22.7	12 7.9	24 40.8
16 Th	3 38 28	23 11 17	0♏ 4 54	7♏21 3	24 13.1	0 6.3	10 6.3	27 30.2	14 0.6	10 35.3	24 20.7	12 8.8	24 40.3
17 F	3 42 24	24 11 48	14 42 41	22 8 51	24 1.7	28♏51.9	11 10.1	28 15.5	14 12.0	10 38.6	24 18.6	12 9.8	24 39.8
18 Sa	3 46 21	25 12 21	29 38 24	7♐10 6	23 49.6	27 32.9	12 13.5	29 0.8	14 23.3	10 41.9	24 16.6	12 10.7	24 39.2
19 Su	3 50 17	26 12 56	14♐42 40	22 14 49	23 38.2	26 11.7	13 16.7	29 46.2	14 34.5	10 45.3	24 14.6	12 11.6	24 38.7
20 M	3 54 14	27 13 31	29 45 19	7♑13 5	23 28.7	24 51.0	14 19.6	0♑31.6	14 45.7	10 48.8	24 12.7	12 12.5	24 38.1
21 Tu	3 58 10	28 14 9	14♑37 11	21 56 51	23 21.9	23 33.4	15 22.2	1 17.1	14 56.7	10 52.4	24 10.8	12 13.3	24 37.5
22 W	4 2 7	29 14 47	29 11 32	6♒20 51	23 18.0	22 21.6	16 24.5	2 2.7	15 7.7	10 56.1	24 8.9	12 14.1	24 36.8
23 Th	4 6 3	0♐15 26	13♒24 38	20 22 49	23D16.5	21 17.6	17 26.4	2 48.3	15 18.7	10 59.8	24 7.1	12 14.9	24 36.2
24 F	4 10 0	1 16 7	27 15 30	4♓ 2 54	23R16.3	20 23.2	18 27.9	3 33.9	15 29.5	11 3.7	24 5.2	12 15.6	24 35.5
25 Sa	4 13 57	2 16 48	10♓45 17	17 22 57	23 16.1	19 39.6	19 29.2	4 19.6	15 40.3	11 7.6	24 3.5	12 16.3	24 34.8
26 Su	4 17 53	3 17 31	23 56 14	0♈25 31	23 14.7	19 7.5	20 30.0	5 5.4	15 50.9	11 11.6	24 1.7	12 17.0	24 34.1
27 M	4 21 50	4 18 14	6♈51 8	13 13 23	23 10.9	18 47.0	21 30.4	5 51.2	16 1.5	11 15.7	24 0.0	12 17.6	24 33.3
28 Tu	4 25 46	5 18 59	19 32 34	25 48 58	23 4.2	18D38.0	22 30.5	6 37.0	16 12.0	11 19.9	23 58.3	12 18.2	24 32.6
29 W	4 29 43	6 19 45	2♉ 2 47	8♉14 12	22 54.6	18 39.8	23 30.1	7 22.9	16 22.5	11 24.1	23 56.7	12 18.8	24 31.8
30 Th	4 33 39	7 20 32	14 23 24	20 30 31	22 42.5	18 52.0	24 29.2	8 8.9	16 32.8	11 28.5	23 55.1	12 19.3	24 31.0

DECEMBER 1933 LONGITUDE

Day	Sid.Time	☉	0 hr ☽	Noon ☽	True ☊	☿	♀	♂	♃	♄	♅	♆	♇
1 F	4 37 36	8♐21 19	26♉35 39	2♊38 56	22♒28.9	19♏13.6	25♑27.9	8♑54.9	16♎43.0	11♒32.9	23♈53.5	12♍19.8	24♋30.2
2 Sa	4 41 32	9 22 9	8♊40 28	14 40 22	22R14.8	19 43.7	26 26.2	9 40.9	16 53.2	11 37.4	23R52.0	12 20.3	24R29.3
3 Su	4 45 29	10 22 59	20 38 46	26 35 49	22 1.6	20 21.5	27 23.9	10 27.0	17 3.2	11 41.9	23 50.6	12 20.7	24 28.5
4 M	4 49 26	11 23 50	2♋31 44	8♋26 44	21 50.2	21 6.2	28 21.1	11 13.2	17 13.2	11 46.6	23 49.1	12 21.1	24 27.6
5 Tu	4 53 22	12 24 43	14 21 6	20 15 10	21 41.3	21 56.9	29 17.8	11 59.3	17 23.1	11 51.3	23 47.7	12 21.5	24 26.7
6 W	4 57 19	13 25 37	26 9 16	2♌ 3 52	21 35.4	22 53.0	0♒14.0	12 45.6	17 32.8	11 56.1	23 46.4	12 21.8	24 25.8
7 Th	5 1 15	14 26 31	7♌59 25	13 56 27	21 32.2	23 53.6	1 9.6	13 31.8	17 42.5	12 0.9	23 45.1	12 22.1	24 24.8
8 F	5 5 12	15 27 27	19 55 31	25 57 14	21D31.2	24 58.3	2 4.6	14 18.2	17 52.1	12 5.9	23 43.8	12 22.4	24 23.9
9 Sa	5 9 8	16 28 25	2♍ 2 12	8♍11 6	21 31.5	26 6.6	2 58.9	15 4.5	18 1.5	12 10.9	23 42.6	12 22.6	24 22.9
10 Su	5 13 5	17 29 23	14 24 34	20 43 16	21R32.0	27 17.8	3 52.7	15 50.9	18 10.9	12 16.0	23 41.4	12 22.8	24 21.9
11 M	5 17 2	18 30 22	27 7 49	3♎38 46	21 31.7	28 31.8	4 45.7	16 37.4	18 20.1	12 21.1	23 40.3	12 23.0	24 20.9
12 Tu	5 20 58	19 31 23	10♎16 38	17 1 48	21 29.6	29 48.0	5 38.1	17 23.9	18 29.2	12 26.3	23 39.2	12 23.1	24 19.9
13 W	5 24 55	20 32 25	23 54 31	0♏54 52	21 25.2	1♐ 6.2	6 29.8	18 10.4	18 38.3	12 31.6	23 38.2	12 23.2	24 18.8
14 Th	5 28 51	21 33 28	8♏ 2 45	15 17 50	21 18.4	2 26.1	7 20.8	18 57.0	18 47.2	12 36.9	23 37.2	12 23.2	24 17.8
15 F	5 32 48	22 34 31	22 39 33	0♐ 7 7	21 9.9	3 47.6	8 10.9	19 43.6	18 56.0	12 42.4	23 36.2	12R23.3	24 16.7
16 Sa	5 36 44	23 35 36	7♐39 31	15 15 34	21 0.5	5 10.3	9 0.3	20 30.2	19 4.6	12 47.8	23 35.4	12 23.2	24 15.6
17 Su	5 40 41	24 36 42	22 53 55	0♑33 9	20 51.4	6 34.2	9 48.8	21 16.9	19 13.2	12 53.4	23 34.5	12 23.2	24 14.6
18 M	5 44 37	25 37 48	8♑11 50	15 48 37	20 43.8	7 59.0	10 36.5	22 3.7	19 21.6	12 59.0	23 33.7	12 23.1	24 13.4
19 Tu	5 48 34	26 38 55	23 22 12	0♒51 32	20 38.5	9 24.7	11 23.2	22 50.4	19 30.0	13 4.6	23 33.0	12 23.0	24 12.3
20 W	5 52 31	27 40 2	8♒15 40	15 33 57	20D35.7	10 51.2	12 9.0	23 37.3	19 38.1	13 10.4	23 32.3	12 22.9	24 11.2
21 Th	5 56 27	28 41 9	22 45 53	29 51 13	20 35.1	12 18.4	12 53.8	24 24.1	19 46.2	13 16.2	23 31.6	12 22.7	24 10.0
22 F	6 0 24	29 42 17	6♓49 50	13♓41 50	20 35.8	13 46.2	13 37.6	25 10.9	19 54.1	13 22.0	23 31.0	12 22.4	24 8.9
23 Sa	6 4 20	0♑43 24	20 27 25	27 6 53	20R37.0	15 14.5	14 20.3	25 57.8	20 1.9	13 27.9	23 30.5	12 22.2	24 7.7
24 Su	6 8 17	1 44 32	3♈40 35	10♈ 8 59	20 37.4	16 43.3	15 1.8	26 44.8	20 9.6	13 33.8	23 30.0	12 21.9	24 6.5
25 M	6 12 13	2 45 40	16 32 31	22 51 40	20 36.2	18 12.6	15 42.2	27 31.7	20 17.1	13 39.8	23 29.5	12 21.6	24 5.3
26 Tu	6 16 10	3 46 47	29 6 52	5♉18 35	20 33.0	19 42.3	16 21.3	28 18.7	20 24.5	13 45.9	23 29.1	12 21.2	24 4.1
27 W	6 20 6	4 47 55	11♉27 14	17 33 14	20 27.7	21 12.4	16 59.2	29 5.7	20 31.8	13 52.0	23 28.8	12 20.8	24 2.9
28 Th	6 24 3	5 49 3	23 36 55	29 38 37	20 20.6	22 42.8	17 35.7	29 52.7	20 38.9	13 58.1	23 28.5	12 20.4	24 1.7
29 F	6 28 0	6 50 11	5♊38 39	11♊37 17	20 12.2	24 13.7	18 10.9	0♒39.8	20 45.9	14 4.3	23 28.3	12 20.0	24 0.5
30 Sa	6 31 56	7 51 19	17 34 46	23 31 19	20 3.5	25 44.9	18 44.6	1 26.9	20 52.7	14 10.6	23 28.1	12 19.5	23 59.2
31 Su	6 35 53	8 52 28	29 27 8	5♋22 26	19 55.3	27 16.4	19 16.8	2 14.0	20 59.4	14 16.9	23 27.9	12 19.0	23 58.0

Astro Data Dy Hr Mn	Planet Ingress Dy Hr Mn	Last Aspect Dy Hr Mn	☽ Ingress Dy Hr Mn	Last Aspect Dy Hr Mn	☽ Ingress Dy Hr Mn	☽ Phases & Eclipses Dy Hr Mn
♅□♇ 5 3:21	♀ ♑ 6 16:02	1 4:11 ♅ ☌	♉ 1 13:53	30 21:34 ♀ △	♊ 1 6:45	2 7:59 ○ 9♉27
♃⚺♆ 5 10:46	☿ ♏ 16 2:07	3 13:42 ♇ ⚹	♊ 4 0:02	3 6:26 ♅ ⚹	♋ 3 18:53	10 12:18 ☽ 17♌40
☿ R 8 8:47	♂ ♑ 19 7:18	6 11:41 ♀ ☍	♋ 6 12:05	5 20:30 ♇ ☌	♌ 6 7:49	17 16:24 ● 24♏53
☽0S 13 9:48	☉ ♐ 22 17:53	8 14:17 ♇ ☌	♌ 9 0:58	8 11:05 ☿ □	♍ 8 20:00	24 7:38 ☽ 1♓35
☽0N 26 0:10		11 1:46 ♅ △	♍ 11 12:24	11 2:52 ☿ ⚹	♎ 11 5:19	
☿ D 28 7:42	♀ ♒ 5 18:00	13 12:21 ♂ □	♎ 13 20:13	13 0:42 ♇ □	♏ 13 10:27	2 1:31 ○ 9♊26
	☿ ♐ 12 3:43	15 19:28 ♂ ⚹	♏ 15 23:52	15 2:37 ♇ △	♐ 15 11:49	10 6:24 ☽ 17♍46
☽0S 10 17:38	☉ ♑ 22 6:58	17 20:56 ☿ ☌	♐ 18 0:34	17 2:53 ☉ ☌	♑ 17 11:08	17 2:53 ● 24♐44
♄⚻♆ 11 8:53	♂ ♒ 28 3:43	19 15:09 ♅ △	♑ 20 0:24	19 1:20 ♇ ☍	♒ 19 10:37	23 20:09 ☽ 1♈35
♆ R 15 2:59		22 0:06 ☉ ⚹	♒ 22 1:21	21 10:48 ☉ ⚹	♓ 21 12:15	31 20:54 ○ 9♋46
☽0N 23 5:31		23 18:28 ♅ ⚹	♓ 24 4:50	23 10:32 ♂ ⚹	♈ 23 17:15	
		26 1:10 ♇ △	♈ 26 11:13	25 22:21 ♂ □	♉ 26 1:43	
		28 9:33 ♇ □	♉ 28 20:03	28 0:49 ♇ ⚹	♊ 28 12:43	
				30 18:56 ☿ ☍	♋ 31 1:07	

Astro Data

1 NOVEMBER 1933
Julian Day # 12358
Delta T 23.9 sec
SVP 06♓10'53"
Obliquity 23°27'00"
⚷ Chiron 2♊42.0R
☽ Mean ☊ 24♒48.5

1 DECEMBER 1933
Julian Day # 12388
Delta T 23.9 sec
SVP 06♓10'48"
Obliquity 23°26'59"
⚷ Chiron 1♊05.6R
☽ Mean ☊ 23♒13.2

LONGITUDE — JANUARY 1934

Day	Sid.Time	☉	0 hr ☽	Noon ☽	True ☊	☿	♀	♂	♃	♄	♅	♆	♇
1 M	6 39 49	9♑53 36	11♋17 26	17♋12 19	19♒48.4	28♐48.3	19♒47.4	3♒ 1.1	21♎ 6.0	14♒23.2	23♈27.9	12♍18.4	23♋56.7
2 Tu	6 43 46	10 54 44	23 7 19	29 2 40	19R 43.1	0♑20.5	20 16.4	3 48.2	21 12.4	14 29.6	23D 27.8	12R 17.8	23R 55.5
3 W	6 47 42	11 55 52	4♌58 38	10♌55 31	19 39.9	1 53.1	20 43.7	4 35.4	21 18.6	14 36.1	23 27.8	12 17.2	23 54.2
4 Th	6 51 39	12 57 1	16 53 38	22 53 20	19D 38.7	3 26.1	21 9.3	5 22.6	21 24.7	14 42.5	23 27.9	12 16.6	23 52.9
5 F	6 55 36	13 58 9	28 55 1	4♍59 7	19 39.0	4 59.4	21 33.1	6 9.8	21 30.7	14 49.0	23 28.0	12 15.9	23 51.6
6 Sa	6 59 32	14 59 18	11♍ 6 5	17 16 25	19 40.5	6 33.0	21 55.1	6 57.0	21 36.5	14 55.6	23 28.2	12 15.2	23 50.3
7 Su	7 3 29	16 0 26	23 30 36	29 49 10	19 42.3	8 7.1	22 15.1	7 44.3	21 42.1	15 2.2	23 28.4	12 14.4	23 49.1
8 M	7 7 25	17 1 35	6♎12 38	12♎41 28	19R 43.7	9 41.5	22 33.1	8 31.6	21 47.6	15 8.8	23 28.7	12 13.7	23 47.8
9 Tu	7 11 22	18 2 44	19 16 9	25 57 5	19 44.2	11 16.4	22 49.0	9 18.9	21 52.9	15 15.5	23 29.0	12 12.9	23 46.5
10 W	7 15 18	19 3 53	2♏44 34	9♏38 49	19 43.4	12 51.7	23 2.8	10 6.2	21 58.1	15 22.2	23 29.4	12 12.0	23 45.2
11 Th	7 19 15	20 5 2	16 39 55	23 47 47	19 41.2	14 27.4	23 14.5	10 53.5	22 3.1	15 28.9	23 29.9	12 11.2	23 43.9
12 F	7 23 11	21 6 11	1♐ 2 8	8♐22 32	19 37.8	16 3.6	23 23.9	11 40.8	22 7.9	15 35.7	23 30.3	12 10.3	23 42.6
13 Sa	7 27 8	22 7 20	15 48 19	23 18 37	19 33.8	17 40.2	23 31.1	12 28.2	22 12.6	15 42.5	23 30.9	12 9.4	23 41.2
14 Su	7 31 5	23 8 29	0♑52 25	8♑28 34	19 29.8	19 17.3	23 35.9	13 15.6	22 17.1	15 49.3	23 31.5	12 8.4	23 39.9
15 M	7 35 1	24 9 37	16 5 48	23 42 48	19 26.5	20 54.9	23R 38.3	14 3.0	22 21.5	15 56.2	23 32.1	12 7.5	23 38.6
16 Tu	7 38 58	25 10 45	1♒18 16	8♒51 0	19 24.3	22 33.0	23 38.2	14 50.4	22 25.6	16 3.1	23 32.8	12 6.5	23 37.3
17 W	7 42 54	26 11 53	16 19 51	23 43 52	19D 23.4	24 11.6	23 35.7	15 37.8	22 29.6	16 10.0	23 33.6	12 5.4	23 36.0
18 Th	7 46 51	27 13 0	1♓ 2 15	8♓14 24	19 23.7	25 50.8	23 30.7	16 25.2	22 33.4	16 17.0	23 34.4	12 4.4	23 34.7
19 F	7 50 47	28 14 5	15 19 55	22 18 35	19 24.9	27 30.5	23 23.2	17 12.6	22 37.1	16 24.0	23 35.2	12 3.3	23 33.4
20 Sa	7 54 44	29 15 11	29 10 20	5♈55 15	19 26.4	29 10.8	23 13.1	18 0.1	22 40.5	16 31.0	23 36.1	12 2.2	23 32.1
21 Su	7 58 40	0♒16 15	12♈33 34	19 5 37	19 27.7	0♒51.6	23 0.6	18 47.5	22 43.8	16 38.0	23 37.1	12 1.0	23 30.8
22 M	8 2 37	1 17 18	25 31 47	1♉52 32	19R 28.5	2 32.9	22 45.5	19 34.9	22 46.9	16 45.0	23 38.1	11 59.9	23 29.5
23 Tu	8 6 34	2 18 20	8♉ 8 23	14 19 51	19 28.5	4 14.9	22 27.9	20 22.4	22 49.9	16 52.1	23 39.1	11 58.7	23 28.2
24 W	8 10 30	3 19 21	20 27 28	26 31 46	19 27.6	5 57.4	22 7.9	21 9.8	22 52.6	16 59.1	23 40.2	11 57.5	23 26.9
25 Th	8 14 27	4 20 22	2♊33 18	8♊32 32	19 26.1	7 40.4	21 45.6	21 57.3	22 55.2	17 6.2	23 41.4	11 56.3	23 25.6
26 F	8 18 23	5 21 21	14 29 59	20 26 6	19 24.1	9 24.0	21 21.1	22 44.7	22 57.6	17 13.4	23 42.6	11 55.0	23 24.4
27 Sa	8 22 20	6 22 19	26 21 18	2♋15 59	19 21.9	11 8.1	20 54.4	23 32.2	22 59.8	17 20.5	23 43.9	11 53.8	23 23.1
28 Su	8 26 16	7 23 16	8♋10 30	14 5 12	19 19.9	12 52.7	20 25.8	24 19.6	23 1.8	17 27.6	23 45.2	11 52.5	23 21.8
29 M	8 30 13	8 24 12	20 0 24	25 56 22	19 18.3	14 37.8	19 55.3	25 7.1	23 3.6	17 34.8	23 46.5	11 51.2	23 20.6
30 Tu	8 34 9	9 25 7	1♌53 22	7♌51 38	19 17.3	16 23.2	19 23.2	25 54.5	23 5.3	17 41.9	23 47.9	11 49.8	23 19.3
31 W	8 38 6	10 26 1	13 51 25	19 52 55	19D 16.8	18 9.0	18 49.7	26 41.9	23 6.7	17 49.1	23 49.4	11 48.5	23 18.1

LONGITUDE — FEBRUARY 1934

Day	Sid.Time	☉	0 hr ☽	Noon ☽	True ☊	☿	♀	♂	♃	♄	♅	♆	♇
1 Th	8 42 3	11♒26 54	25♌56 22	2♍ 2 0	19♒16.8	19♒55.0	18♒14.9	27♒29.4	23♎ 8.0	17♒56.3	23♈50.8	11♍47.1	23♋16.8
2 F	8 45 59	12 27 45	8♍10 0	14 20 38	19 17.2	21 41.2	17R 39.1	28 16.8	23 9.1	18 3.5	23 52.4	11R 45.7	23R 15.6
3 Sa	8 49 56	13 28 36	20 34 7	26 50 43	19 17.8	23 27.3	17 2.5	29 4.2	23 10.0	18 10.7	23 54.0	11 44.3	23 14.4
4 Su	8 53 52	14 29 26	3♎10 40	9♎34 16	19 18.4	25 13.4	16 25.5	29 51.7	23 10.7	18 17.9	23 55.6	11 42.8	23 13.2
5 M	8 57 49	15 30 15	16 1 45	22 33 25	19 18.8	26 59.1	15 48.2	0♓39.1	23 11.3	18 25.1	23 57.3	11 41.4	23 12.0
6 Tu	9 1 45	16 31 3	29 9 29	5♏50 12	19 19.1	28 44.2	15 10.9	1 26.5	23 11.6	18 32.3	23 59.0	11 39.9	23 10.8
7 W	9 5 42	17 31 50	12♏35 47	19 26 20	19R 19.2	0♓28.6	14 33.9	2 13.9	23R 11.7	18 39.6	24 0.8	11 38.5	23 9.6
8 Th	9 9 38	18 32 36	26 21 58	3♐22 40	19D 19.2	2 11.9	13 57.5	3 1.3	23 11.7	18 46.8	24 2.6	11 37.0	23 8.4
9 F	9 13 35	19 33 22	10♐28 21	17 38 47	19 19.2	3 53.8	13 21.9	3 48.7	23 11.4	18 54.0	24 4.4	11 35.5	23 7.3
10 Sa	9 17 32	20 34 6	24 53 39	2♑12 29	19 19.3	5 33.8	12 47.2	4 36.1	23 11.0	19 1.2	24 6.3	11 33.9	23 6.1
11 Su	9 21 28	21 34 50	9♑34 41	16 59 32	19 19.5	7 11.6	12 13.9	5 23.5	23 10.4	19 8.5	24 8.3	11 32.4	23 5.0
12 M	9 25 25	22 35 32	24 26 13	1♒53 47	19 19.7	8 46.6	11 41.9	6 10.8	23 9.6	19 15.7	24 10.3	11 30.8	23 3.9
13 Tu	9 29 21	23 36 13	9♒21 17	16 47 42	19R 20.0	10 18.2	11 11.6	6 58.2	23 8.6	19 22.9	24 12.3	11 29.3	23 2.8
14 W	9 33 18	24 36 52	24 12 2	1♓33 19	19 20.0	11 46.0	10 43.1	7 45.5	23 7.4	19 30.1	24 14.4	11 27.7	23 1.7
15 Th	9 37 14	25 37 30	8♓50 41	16 3 22	19 19.7	13 9.2	10 16.5	8 32.8	23 6.0	19 37.3	24 16.5	11 26.1	23 0.6
16 F	9 41 11	26 38 7	23 10 42	0♈12 11	19 19.1	14 27.1	9 52.0	9 20.2	23 4.5	19 44.5	24 18.6	11 24.5	22 59.5
17 Sa	9 45 7	27 38 41	7♈ 7 29	13 56 24	19 18.1	15 39.2	9 29.7	10 7.4	23 2.7	19 51.7	24 20.8	11 22.9	22 58.5
18 Su	9 49 4	28 39 14	20 38 52	27 14 59	19 16.9	16 44.6	9 9.6	10 54.7	23 0.7	19 58.9	24 23.0	11 21.3	22 57.4
19 M	9 53 1	29 39 46	3♉44 57	10♉ 9 3	19 15.8	17 42.7	8 51.9	11 42.0	22 58.6	20 6.0	24 25.3	11 19.7	22 56.4
20 Tu	9 56 57	0♓40 15	16 27 43	22 41 23	19 14.9	18 32.9	8 36.6	12 29.2	22 56.3	20 13.2	24 27.6	11 18.0	22 55.4
21 W	10 0 54	1 40 43	28 50 35	4♊55 52	19D 14.5	19 14.5	8 23.7	13 16.4	22 53.8	20 20.3	24 30.0	11 16.4	22 54.4
22 Th	10 4 50	2 41 9	10♊57 50	16 57 5	19 14.6	19 47.1	8 13.3	14 3.6	22 51.1	20 27.5	24 32.4	11 14.7	22 53.5
23 F	10 8 47	3 41 33	22 54 11	28 49 46	19 15.4	20 10.2	8 5.4	14 50.8	22 48.3	20 34.6	24 34.8	11 13.1	22 52.5
24 Sa	10 12 43	4 41 55	4♋44 23	10♋38 37	19 16.6	20R 23.5	7 59.9	15 38.0	22 45.2	20 41.7	24 37.2	11 11.4	22 51.6
25 Su	10 16 40	5 42 15	16 33 0	22 28 0	19 18.1	20 26.9	7D 56.9	16 25.1	22 42.0	20 48.7	24 39.7	11 9.8	22 50.7
26 M	10 20 36	6 42 33	28 24 8	4♌21 48	19 19.6	20 20.5	7 56.3	17 12.2	22 38.6	20 55.8	24 42.3	11 8.1	22 49.8
27 Tu	10 24 33	7 42 50	10♌21 23	16 23 14	19R 20.6	20 4.4	7 58.2	17 59.3	22 35.0	21 2.8	24 44.8	11 6.5	22 48.9
28 W	10 28 30	8 43 4	22 27 40	28 34 54	19 20.8	19 39.2	8 2.4	18 46.3	22 31.3	21 9.8	24 47.4	11 4.8	22 48.0

Astro Data	Dy Hr Mn
♅ D	2 3:05
☽0S	6 23:36
♀ R	15 11:45
♅□♇	18 3:47
☽0N	19 13:35
☽0S	3 4:58
♃□♇	5 10:53
♃ R	7 6:19
☽0N	15 23:59
♃□♇	20 14:10
☿ R	24 20:17
♀ D	25 17:42

Planet Ingress	Dy Hr Mn
☿ ♑	1 18:40
☉ ♒	20 17:37
☿ ♒	20 11:44
♂ ♓	4 4:13
☿ ♓	6 17:24
☉ ♓	19 8:02

Last Aspect Dy Hr Mn		☽ Ingress Dy Hr Mn
2 1:37	♇ ☌	♌ 2 13:56
4 13:09	♅ △	♍ 5 2:09
7 0:35	♇ ✶	♎ 7 12:20
9 8:06	♇ □	♏ 9 19:11
11 11:52	♇ △	♐ 11 22:18
13 12:24	♀ ✶	♑ 13 22:37
15 13:37	☉ ☌	♒ 15 21:56
17 11:44	♅ ✶	♓ 17 22:17
20 0:09	☉ ✶	♈ 20 1:28
21 20:27	♅ ☌	♉ 22 8:26
24 5:53	♇ ✶	♊ 24 18:54
26 18:40	♅ ✶	♋ 27 7:24
29 7:38	♅ □	♌ 29 20:12

Last Aspect Dy Hr Mn		☽ Ingress Dy Hr Mn
1 3:16	♂ ☍	♍ 1 8:00
3 5:07	♇ ✶	♎ 3 18:00
5 23:07	☿ △	♏ 6 1:31
7 18:26	♇ △	♐ 8 6:14
9 22:42	♅ △	♑ 10 8:23
11 23:34	♅ □	♒ 12 8:57
14 0:43	☉ ☌	♓ 14 9:27
15 23:41	♇ △	♈ 16 11:39
18 15:48	☉ ✶	♉ 18 17:03
20 12:26	♇ ✶	♊ 21 2:16
23 3:24	♅ ✶	♋ 23 14:22
25 16:30	♅ □	♌ 26 3:13
28 4:36	♅ △	♍ 28 14:46

☽ Phases & Eclipses Dy Hr Mn	
8 21:36	☽ 17♎57
15 13:37	● 24♑44
22 11:50	☽ 1♉47
30 16:31	○ 10♌07
30 16:42	☍ P 0.112
7 9:21	☽ 17♏56
14 0:43	● 24♒39
14 0:38:17	☌ T 2'52"
21 6:05	☽ 1♊56

Astro Data

1 JANUARY 1934
Julian Day # 12419
Delta T 23.9 sec
SVP 06♓10'42"
Obliquity 23°26'59"
⚷ Chiron 29♉35.4R
☽ Mean ☊ 21♒34.7

1 FEBRUARY 1934
Julian Day # 12450
Delta T 23.9 sec
SVP 06♓10'36"
Obliquity 23°26'59"
⚷ Chiron 28♉52.4R
☽ Mean ☊ 19♒56.2

MARCH 1934 LONGITUDE

Day	Sid.Time	☉	0 hr ☽	Noon ☽	True ☊	☿	♀	♂	♃	♄	♅	♆	♇
1 Th	10 32 26	9♓43 17	4♍45 9	10♍58 35	19♒20.0	19♓ 5.4	8♒ 8.9	19♓33.4	22♎27.4	21♒16.8	24♈50.0	11♍ 3.1	22♋47.2
2 F	10 36 23	10 43 27	17 15 20	23 35 27	19R 18.1	18R 24.0	8 17.6	20 20.4	22R 23.3	21 23.8	24 52.7	11R 1.4	22R 46.4
3 Sa	10 40 19	11 43 36	29 58 59	6♎25 58	19 15.2	17 35.9	8 28.6	21 7.3	22 19.1	21 30.7	24 55.4	10 59.8	22 45.6
4 Su	10 44 16	12 43 44	12♎56 23	19 30 10	19 11.6	16 42.5	8 41.8	21 54.3	22 14.7	21 37.6	24 58.1	10 58.1	22 44.8
5 M	10 48 12	13 43 49	26 7 19	2♏47 45	19 7.8	15 45.2	8 57.0	22 41.2	22 10.1	21 44.5	25 0.9	10 56.4	22 44.0
6 Tu	10 52 9	14 43 53	9♏31 24	16 18 13	19 4.2	14 45.2	9 14.3	23 28.1	22 5.4	21 51.4	25 3.7	10 54.7	22 43.3
7 W	10 56 5	15 43 56	23 8 6	0♐ 1 0	19 1.4	13 44.1	9 33.5	24 15.0	22 0.5	21 58.2	25 6.5	10 53.1	22 42.6
8 Th	11 0 2	16 43 57	6♐56 50	13 55 29	18D 59.8	12 43.4	9 54.7	25 1.8	21 55.5	22 5.0	25 9.3	10 51.4	22 41.9
9 F	11 3 59	17 43 56	20 56 52	28 0 49	18 59.5	11 44.3	10 17.7	25 48.6	21 50.3	22 11.8	25 12.2	10 49.8	22 41.2
10 Sa	11 7 55	18 43 54	5♑ 7 10	12♑15 42	19 0.3	10 48.0	10 42.4	26 35.4	21 45.0	22 18.6	25 15.1	10 48.1	22 40.5
11 Su	11 11 52	19 43 50	19 26 8	26 38 7	19 1.7	9 55.5	11 8.9	27 22.2	21 39.5	22 25.3	25 18.0	10 46.5	22 39.9
12 M	11 15 48	20 43 44	3♒51 16	11♒ 5 4	19 3.1	9 7.7	11 36.9	28 8.9	21 33.9	22 32.0	25 21.0	10 44.8	22 39.3
13 Tu	11 19 45	21 43 37	18 19 1	25 32 30	19R 3.8	8 25.4	12 6.6	28 55.6	21 28.1	22 38.6	25 23.9	10 43.2	22 38.7
14 W	11 23 41	22 43 28	2♓44 53	9♓55 29	19 3.1	7 48.8	12 37.8	29 42.2	21 22.3	22 45.2	25 27.0	10 41.5	22 38.1
15 Th	11 27 38	23 43 17	17 3 38	24 8 40	19 0.7	7 18.4	13 10.4	0♈28.9	21 16.2	22 51.8	25 30.0	10 39.9	22 37.6
16 F	11 31 34	24 43 4	1♈ 9 58	8♈ 6 59	18 56.5	6 54.3	13 44.4	1 15.5	21 10.1	22 58.3	25 33.0	10 38.3	22 37.1
17 Sa	11 35 31	25 42 49	14 59 15	21 46 24	18 50.8	6 36.6	14 19.7	2 2.0	21 3.9	23 4.8	25 36.1	10 36.7	22 36.6
18 Su	11 39 28	26 42 32	28 28 10	5♉ 4 26	18 44.4	6 25.3	14 56.3	2 48.5	20 57.5	23 11.2	25 39.2	10 35.1	22 36.1
19 M	11 43 24	27 42 13	11♉35 9	18 0 26	18 38.0	6D 20.1	15 34.1	3 35.0	20 51.0	23 17.6	25 42.3	10 33.5	22 35.6
20 Tu	11 47 21	28 41 51	24 20 28	0♊35 35	18 32.3	6 21.0	16 13.2	4 21.5	20 44.4	23 24.0	25 45.5	10 31.9	22 35.2
21 W	11 51 17	29 41 28	6♊46 9	12 52 39	18 27.9	6 27.7	16 53.3	5 7.9	20 37.7	23 30.3	25 48.6	10 30.3	22 34.8
22 Th	11 55 14	0♈41 2	18 55 36	24 55 34	18 25.3	6 39.9	17 34.5	5 54.3	20 30.9	23 36.6	25 51.8	10 28.8	22 34.4
23 F	11 59 10	1 40 34	0♋53 11	6♋49 3	18D 24.4	6 57.4	18 16.8	6 40.6	20 24.0	23 42.8	25 55.0	10 27.3	22 34.1
24 Sa	12 3 7	2 40 4	12 43 51	18 38 13	18 25.0	7 20.0	19 0.1	7 26.9	20 17.1	23 49.0	25 58.2	10 25.7	22 33.7
25 Su	12 7 3	3 39 31	24 32 49	0♌28 17	18 26.3	7 47.3	19 44.4	8 13.1	20 10.0	23 55.1	26 1.4	10 24.2	22 33.4
26 M	12 11 0	4 38 56	6♌25 14	12 24 14	18 27.8	8 19.0	20 29.6	8 59.4	20 2.9	24 1.2	26 4.7	10 22.7	22 33.2
27 Tu	12 14 57	5 38 19	18 30 33	24 30 33	18R 28.4	8 55.0	21 15.7	9 45.5	19 55.7	24 7.2	26 8.0	10 21.2	22 32.9
28 W	12 18 53	6 37 39	0♍38 48	6♍50 56	18 27.6	9 35.0	22 2.6	10 31.7	19 48.4	24 13.2	26 11.2	10 19.8	22 32.7
29 Th	12 22 50	7 36 58	13 7 16	19 28 0	18 24.7	10 18.8	22 50.4	11 17.7	19 41.0	24 19.1	26 14.5	10 18.3	22 32.5
30 F	12 26 46	8 36 14	25 53 17	2♎23 7	18 19.6	11 6.1	23 38.9	12 3.8	19 33.6	24 25.0	26 17.8	10 16.9	22 32.3
31 Sa	12 30 43	9 35 28	8♎57 29	15 36 13	18 12.4	11 56.7	24 28.3	12 49.8	19 26.2	24 30.8	26 21.1	10 15.4	22 32.1

APRIL 1934 LONGITUDE

Day	Sid.Time	☉	0 hr ☽	Noon ☽	True ☊	☿	♀	♂	♃	♄	♅	♆	♇
1 Su	12 34 39	10♈34 40	22♎19 6	29♎ 5 50	18♒ 3.8	12♈50.5	25♒18.4	13♈35.7	19♎18.7	24♒36.6	26♈24.5	10♍14.0	22♋32.0
2 M	12 38 36	11 33 49	5♏56 5	12♏49 25	17R 54.7	13 47.4	26 9.2	14 21.6	19R 11.1	24 42.3	26 27.8	10R 12.7	22R 31.9
3 Tu	12 42 32	12 32 58	19 45 25	26 43 40	17 46.0	14 47.1	27 0.7	15 7.5	19 3.5	24 47.9	26 31.2	10 11.3	22 31.8
4 W	12 46 29	13 32 4	3♐43 44	10♐45 13	17 38.7	15 49.4	27 52.8	15 53.3	18 55.9	24 53.5	26 34.5	10 10.0	22 31.7
5 Th	12 50 25	14 31 8	17 47 45	24 51 1	17 33.5	16 54.4	28 45.6	16 39.1	18 48.3	24 59.1	26 37.9	10 8.6	22D 31.7
6 F	12 54 22	15 30 11	1♑54 44	8♑58 41	17 30.6	18 1.8	29 39.0	17 24.9	18 40.6	25 4.5	26 41.3	10 7.3	22 31.7
7 Sa	12 58 19	16 29 12	16 2 41	23 6 34	17D 29.7	19 11.6	0♓33.0	18 10.6	18 32.9	25 10.0	26 44.7	10 6.0	22 31.7
8 Su	13 2 15	17 28 12	0♒10 12	7♒13 28	17 30.2	20 23.6	1 27.5	18 56.3	18 25.2	25 15.3	26 48.1	10 4.8	22 31.7
9 M	13 6 12	18 27 9	14 16 12	21 18 16	17R 30.7	21 37.8	2 22.6	19 41.9	18 17.5	25 20.6	26 51.5	10 3.5	22 31.8
10 Tu	13 10 8	19 26 5	28 19 28	5♓19 35	17 30.3	22 54.1	3 18.2	20 27.4	18 9.8	25 25.8	26 54.9	10 2.3	22 31.9
11 W	13 14 5	20 24 59	12♓18 20	19 15 25	17 27.9	24 12.4	4 14.3	21 13.0	18 2.1	25 31.0	26 58.4	10 1.1	22 32.0
12 Th	13 18 1	21 23 51	26 10 29	3♈ 3 10	17 22.8	25 32.6	5 10.9	21 58.5	17 54.4	25 36.1	27 1.8	9 59.9	22 32.1
13 F	13 21 58	22 22 41	9♈53 5	16 39 50	17 15.1	26 54.8	6 8.0	22 43.9	17 46.7	25 41.1	27 5.2	9 58.8	22 32.3
14 Sa	13 25 54	23 21 30	23 23 5	0♉ 2 30	17 5.0	28 18.8	7 5.4	23 29.3	17 39.0	25 46.0	27 8.7	9 57.7	22 32.5
15 Su	13 29 51	24 20 16	6♉37 49	13 8 50	16 53.6	29 44.7	8 3.4	24 14.6	17 31.4	25 50.9	27 12.1	9 56.6	22 32.7
16 M	13 33 48	25 19 1	19 35 25	25 57 33	16 41.8	1♈12.3	9 1.7	24 59.9	17 23.8	25 55.8	27 15.5	9 55.5	22 33.0
17 Tu	13 37 44	26 17 43	2♊15 18	8♊28 47	16 31.0	2 41.7	10 0.4	25 45.2	17 16.2	26 0.5	27 19.0	9 54.4	22 33.2
18 W	13 41 41	27 16 23	14 38 17	20 44 5	16 21.9	4 12.9	10 59.5	26 30.4	17 8.7	26 5.2	27 22.4	9 53.4	22 33.5
19 Th	13 45 37	28 15 2	26 46 37	2♋46 20	16 15.2	5 45.8	11 59.0	27 15.5	17 1.3	26 9.8	27 25.9	9 52.4	22 33.8
20 F	13 49 34	29 13 38	8♋43 46	14 39 30	16 11.0	7 20.4	12 58.8	28 0.6	16 53.8	26 14.3	27 29.3	9 51.4	22 34.2
21 Sa	13 53 30	0♉12 11	20 34 9	26 28 23	16D 9.1	8 56.6	13 59.0	28 45.7	16 46.5	26 18.8	27 32.7	9 50.5	22 34.5
22 Su	13 57 27	1 10 43	2♌22 52	8♌18 17	16 8.7	10 34.6	14 59.4	29 30.7	16 39.2	26 23.1	27 36.2	9 49.6	22 34.9
23 M	14 1 23	2 9 13	14 15 19	20 14 40	16R 8.9	12 14.3	16 0.3	0♉15.6	16 32.0	26 27.4	27 39.6	9 48.7	22 35.3
24 Tu	14 5 20	3 7 40	26 16 58	2♍22 52	16 8.5	13 55.7	17 1.4	1 0.5	16 24.8	26 31.7	27 43.0	9 47.8	22 35.8
25 W	14 9 17	4 6 5	8♍32 56	14 47 40	16 6.7	15 38.8	18 2.8	1 45.3	16 17.7	26 35.8	27 46.5	9 47.0	22 36.2
26 Th	14 13 13	5 4 28	21 7 32	27 32 51	16 2.5	17 23.6	19 4.5	2 30.1	16 10.8	26 39.9	27 49.9	9 46.2	22 36.7
27 F	14 17 10	6 2 49	4♎ 3 53	10♎40 44	15 55.7	19 10.1	20 6.5	3 14.9	16 3.9	26 43.9	27 53.3	9 45.4	22 37.2
28 Sa	14 21 6	7 1 8	17 23 23	24 11 40	15 46.5	20 58.4	21 8.8	3 59.5	15 57.0	26 47.8	27 56.7	9 44.6	22 37.8
29 Su	14 25 3	7 59 25	1♏ 5 19	8♏ 3 52	15 35.3	22 48.4	22 11.4	4 44.2	15 50.3	26 51.6	28 0.1	9 43.9	22 38.3
30 M	14 28 59	8 57 40	15 6 47	22 13 24	15 23.5	24 40.1	23 14.2	5 28.8	15 43.7	26 55.3	28 3.5	9 43.2	22 38.9

Astro Data	Dy Hr Mn
☽0S	2 11:17
♃△♄	7 4:38
♄⊼♇	13 0:21
☽0N	15 10:27
♂0N	16 13:43
♅⊡♆	17 2:57
☿ D	19 8:25
☽0S	29 19:01
♇ D	5 19:22
☽0N	11 18:44
☿0N	19 3:46
☽0S	26 3:29

Planet Ingress	Dy Hr Mn
♂ ♈	14 9:09
☉ ♈	21 7:28
♀ ♓	6 9:23
☿ ♈	15 4:14
☉ ♉	20 19:00
♂ ♉	22 15:40

Last Aspect Dy Hr Mn		☽ Ingress Dy Hr Mn
2 10:27	♇ ⚹	♎ 3 0:02
4 22:00	♅ ☍	♏ 5 6:59
7 2:04	♂ △	♐ 7 11:58
9 8:45	♂ □	♑ 9 15:22
11 13:58	♂ ⚹	♒ 11 17:36
13 11:48	♅ ⚹	♓ 13 19:25
15 12:08	☉ ☌	♈ 15 22:00
17 18:55	♅ ☌	♉ 18 2:46
20 9:04	☉ ⚹	♊ 20 10:51
22 13:57	♅ ⚹	♋ 22 22:13
25 3:01	♅ □	♌ 25 11:03
27 15:15	♅ △	♍ 27 22:44
29 17:45	♇ ⚹	♎ 30 7:37

Last Aspect Dy Hr Mn		☽ Ingress Dy Hr Mn
1 7:17	♅ ☍	♏ 1 13:35
3 13:19	♀ □	♐ 3 17:37
5 19:54	♀ ⚹	♑ 5 20:45
7 18:15	♅ □	♒ 7 23:43
9 21:35	♅ ⚹	♓ 10 2:52
11 22:47	☿ ☌	♈ 12 6:40
14 6:48	♅ ☌	♉ 14 11:55
16 12:01	♄ □	♊ 16 19:41
19 3:12	☉ ⚹	♋ 19 6:26
21 17:47	♂ □	♌ 21 19:10
24 2:51	♅ △	♍ 24 7:20
26 2:48	♇ ⚹	♎ 26 16:32
28 18:37	♅ ☍	♏ 28 22:07

☽ Phases & Eclipses Dy Hr Mn	
1 10:26	○ 10♍09
8 18:06	☽ 17♐29
15 12:08	● 24♓14
23 1:44	☽ 1♋45
31 1:14	○ 9♎39
7 0:48	☽ 16♑31
13 23:57	● 23♈21
21 21:20	☽ 1♌04
29 12:45	○ 8♏30

Astro Data

1 MARCH 1934
Julian Day # 12478
Delta T 23.9 sec
SVP 06♓10'32"
Obliquity 23°27'00"
⚷ Chiron 29♉09.3
☽ Mean ☊ 18♒27.3

1 APRIL 1934
Julian Day # 12509
Delta T 23.9 sec
SVP 06♓10'30"
Obliquity 23°27'00"
⚷ Chiron 0♊26.0
☽ Mean ☊ 16♒48.7

LONGITUDE — MAY 1934

Day	Sid.Time	☉	0 hr ☽	Noon ☽	True ☊	☿	♀	♂	♃	♄	♅	♆	♇
1 Tu	14 32 56	9♉55 54	29♏23 0	6♐34 47	15♒12.0	26♈33.6	24♓17.2	6♉13.3	15♎37.2	26♒59.0	28♈ 6.9	9♍42.6	22♋39.5
2 W	14 36 52	10 54 6	13♐47 59	21 1 49	15R 2.2	28 28.8	25 20.6	6 57.8	15R 30.8	27 2.6	28 10.3	9R 41.9	22 40.1
3 Th	14 40 49	11 52 17	28 15 36	5♑28 40	14 55.0	0♉25.7	26 24.1	7 42.2	15 24.5	27 6.1	28 13.7	9 41.3	22 40.8
4 F	14 44 46	12 50 26	12♑40 30	19 50 39	14 50.4	2 24.4	27 27.9	8 26.6	15 18.3	27 9.5	28 17.0	9 40.8	22 41.5
5 Sa	14 48 42	13 48 33	26 58 47	4♒ 4 39	14 48.4	4 24.7	28 31.9	9 10.9	15 12.3	27 12.8	28 20.4	9 40.2	22 42.2
6 Su	14 52 39	14 46 39	11♒ 8 6	18 9 2	14 48.0	6 26.6	29 36.1	9 55.2	15 6.3	27 16.1	28 23.7	9 39.7	22 42.9
7 M	14 56 35	15 44 44	25 7 26	2♓ 3 17	14 47.9	8 30.1	0♈40.6	10 39.4	15 0.5	27 19.2	28 27.1	9 39.2	22 43.6
8 Tu	15 0 32	16 42 47	8♓56 36	15 47 25	14 46.8	10 35.1	1 45.2	11 23.6	14 54.9	27 22.3	28 30.4	9 38.8	22 44.4
9 W	15 4 28	17 40 49	22 35 43	29 21 30	14 43.7	12 41.4	2 50.0	12 7.7	14 49.3	27 25.3	28 33.7	9 38.4	22 45.1
10 Th	15 8 25	18 38 50	6♈ 4 42	12♈45 17	14 37.9	14 49.1	3 55.1	12 51.8	14 43.9	27 28.2	28 37.0	9 38.0	22 46.0
11 F	15 12 21	19 36 49	19 23 7	25 58 6	14 29.2	16 57.8	5 0.3	13 35.8	14 38.6	27 31.0	28 40.2	9 37.6	22 46.8
12 Sa	15 16 18	20 34 47	2♉30 6	8♉59 0	14 18.0	19 7.4	6 5.6	14 19.8	14 33.5	27 33.7	28 43.5	9 37.3	22 47.6
13 Su	15 20 15	21 32 43	15 24 40	21 47 0	14 5.3	21 17.7	7 11.2	15 3.7	14 28.5	27 36.3	28 46.7	9 37.0	22 48.5
14 M	15 24 11	22 30 38	28 5 57	4♊21 30	13 52.2	23 28.6	8 16.9	15 47.6	14 23.7	27 38.8	28 50.0	9 36.7	22 49.4
15 Tu	15 28 8	23 28 32	10♊33 40	16 42 33	13 39.9	25 39.7	9 22.8	16 31.4	14 19.0	27 41.3	28 53.2	9 36.5	22 50.3
16 W	15 32 4	24 26 24	22 48 18	28 51 9	13 29.4	27 50.8	10 28.8	17 15.2	14 14.5	27 43.6	28 56.4	9 36.3	22 51.2
17 Th	15 36 1	25 24 14	4♋51 23	10♋49 21	13 21.4	0♊ 1.5	11 34.9	17 58.9	14 10.1	27 45.9	28 59.6	9 36.2	22 52.2
18 F	15 39 57	26 22 3	16 45 28	22 40 13	13 16.1	2 11.7	12 41.3	18 42.6	14 5.9	27 48.0	29 2.7	9 36.0	22 53.2
19 Sa	15 43 54	27 19 50	28 34 7	4♌27 44	13 13.3	4 21.0	13 47.7	19 26.2	14 1.9	27 50.1	29 5.9	9 35.9	22 54.2
20 Su	15 47 50	28 17 35	10♌21 41	16 16 37	13D 12.4	6 29.2	14 54.3	20 9.7	13 58.0	27 52.1	29 9.0	9 35.9	22 55.2
21 M	15 51 47	29 15 19	22 13 12	28 12 7	13R 12.5	8 35.9	16 1.0	20 53.2	13 54.3	27 53.9	29 12.1	9D 35.8	22 56.2
22 Tu	15 55 44	0♊13 1	4♍14 3	10♍19 40	13 12.6	10 41.1	17 7.9	21 36.6	13 50.7	27 55.7	29 15.1	9 35.8	22 57.2
23 W	15 59 40	1 10 42	16 29 39	22 44 35	13 11.5	12 44.3	18 14.8	22 20.0	13 47.4	27 57.4	29 18.2	9 35.9	22 58.3
24 Th	16 3 37	2 8 21	29 5 3	5♎31 31	13 8.6	14 45.5	19 21.9	23 3.3	13 44.2	27 59.0	29 21.2	9 35.9	22 59.4
25 F	16 7 33	3 5 59	12♎ 4 22	18 43 52	13 3.4	16 44.5	20 29.2	23 46.6	13 41.1	28 0.5	29 24.2	9 36.0	23 0.5
26 Sa	16 11 30	4 3 35	25 30 9	2♏23 9	12 55.8	18 41.1	21 36.5	24 29.8	13 38.2	28 1.9	29 27.2	9 36.2	23 1.6
27 Su	16 15 26	5 1 9	9♏22 41	16 28 21	12 46.5	20 35.2	22 43.9	25 13.0	13 35.6	28 3.2	29 30.1	9 36.3	23 2.8
28 M	16 19 23	5 58 43	23 39 36	0♐55 41	12 36.4	22 26.8	23 51.5	25 56.1	13 33.0	28 4.4	29 33.1	9 36.5	23 3.9
29 Tu	16 23 19	6 56 15	8♐15 45	15 38 49	12 26.6	24 15.6	24 59.2	26 39.2	13 30.7	28 5.5	29 36.0	9 36.8	23 5.1
30 W	16 27 16	7 53 47	23 3 51	0♑29 47	12 18.2	26 1.8	26 7.0	27 22.2	13 28.5	28 6.5	29 38.9	9 37.0	23 6.3
31 Th	16 31 13	8 51 17	7♑55 35	15 20 17	12 12.0	27 45.1	27 14.9	28 5.1	13 26.6	28 7.4	29 41.7	9 37.3	23 7.5

LONGITUDE — JUNE 1934

Day	Sid.Time	☉	0 hr ☽	Noon ☽	True ☊	☿	♀	♂	♃	♄	♅	♆	♇
1 F	16 35 9	9♊48 46	22♑43 1	0♒ 3 2	12♒ 8.3	29♊25.6	28♈22.9	28♉48.0	13♎24.7	28♒ 8.2	29♈44.6	9♍37.6	23♋ 8.7
2 Sa	16 39 6	10 46 15	7♒19 44	14 32 39	12D 6.9	1♋ 3.3	29 31.1	29 30.8	13R 23.1	28 8.9	29 47.4	9 38.0	23 10.0
3 Su	16 43 2	11 43 42	21 41 27	28 45 58	12 7.0	2 38.1	0♉39.3	0♊13.6	13 21.7	28 9.5	29 50.1	9 38.4	23 11.2
4 M	16 46 59	12 41 9	5♓46 4	12♓41 47	12R 7.7	4 9.9	1 47.6	0 56.4	13 20.4	28 10.0	29 52.9	9 38.8	23 12.5
5 Tu	16 50 55	13 38 35	19 33 10	26 20 21	12 7.7	5 38.8	2 56.0	1 39.1	13 19.3	28 10.5	29 55.6	9 39.3	23 13.8
6 W	16 54 52	14 36 1	3♈ 3 29	9♈42 43	12 6.1	7 4.8	4 4.6	2 21.7	13 18.4	28 10.8	29 58.3	9 39.8	23 15.1
7 Th	16 58 48	15 33 26	16 18 14	22 50 12	12 2.4	8 27.7	5 13.2	3 4.3	13 17.6	28 11.0	0♉ 0.9	9 40.3	23 16.4
8 F	17 2 45	16 30 51	29 18 47	5♉44 6	11 56.4	9 47.6	6 21.9	3 46.8	13 17.1	28R 11.1	0 3.5	9 40.8	23 17.7
9 Sa	17 6 42	17 28 14	12♉ 6 17	18 25 26	11 48.4	11 4.4	7 30.7	4 29.3	13 16.7	28 11.1	0 6.1	9 41.4	23 19.1
10 Su	17 10 38	18 25 38	24 41 39	0♊55 2	11 39.2	12 18.1	8 39.5	5 11.7	13D 16.5	28 11.1	0 8.7	9 42.0	23 20.4
11 M	17 14 35	19 23 0	7♊ 5 40	13 13 40	11 29.5	13 28.6	9 48.5	5 54.1	13 16.5	28 10.9	0 11.2	9 42.7	23 21.8
12 Tu	17 18 31	20 20 22	19 19 8	25 22 13	11 20.5	14 35.9	10 57.5	6 36.4	13 16.6	28 10.6	0 13.7	9 43.3	23 23.2
13 W	17 22 28	21 17 43	1♋23 5	7♋21 56	11 12.9	15 39.9	12 6.7	7 18.7	13 17.0	28 10.2	0 16.2	9 44.1	23 24.6
14 Th	17 26 24	22 15 4	13 18 59	19 14 33	11 7.2	16 40.4	13 15.9	8 0.9	13 17.5	28 9.8	0 18.6	9 44.8	23 26.0
15 F	17 30 21	23 12 24	25 8 56	1♌ 2 30	11 3.6	17 37.5	14 25.1	8 43.1	13 18.2	28 9.2	0 21.0	9 45.6	23 27.4
16 Sa	17 34 18	24 9 43	6♌55 41	12 48 55	11D 2.2	18 31.1	15 34.5	9 25.2	13 19.1	28 8.5	0 23.3	9 46.4	23 28.8
17 Su	17 38 14	25 7 1	18 42 42	24 37 35	11 2.4	19 21.0	16 43.9	10 7.3	13 20.2	28 7.8	0 25.6	9 47.2	23 30.3
18 M	17 42 11	26 4 18	0♍34 8	6♍32 56	11 3.5	20 7.1	17 53.3	10 49.3	13 21.4	28 6.9	0 27.9	9 48.1	23 31.7
19 Tu	17 46 7	27 1 34	12 34 37	18 39 49	11 4.9	20 49.4	19 2.9	11 31.2	13 22.9	28 5.9	0 30.2	9 49.0	23 33.2
20 W	17 50 4	27 58 50	24 49 9	1♎ 3 14	11R 5.8	21 27.8	20 12.5	12 13.1	13 24.5	28 4.9	0 32.4	9 49.9	23 34.7
21 Th	17 54 0	28 56 5	7♎22 40	13 47 59	11 5.4	22 2.1	21 22.2	12 54.9	13 26.2	28 3.7	0 34.5	9 50.8	23 36.2
22 F	17 57 57	29 53 20	20 19 39	26 58 3	11 3.6	22 32.2	22 31.9	13 36.7	13 28.2	28 2.5	0 36.7	9 51.8	23 37.6
23 Sa	18 1 53	0♋50 33	3♏43 27	10♏35 59	11 0.0	22 58.0	23 41.8	14 18.4	13 30.3	28 1.1	0 38.8	9 52.8	23 39.1
24 Su	18 5 50	1 47 46	17 35 38	24 42 10	10 55.2	23 19.4	24 51.6	15 0.1	13 32.6	27 59.7	0 40.8	9 53.9	23 40.7
25 M	18 9 47	2 44 59	1♐55 12	9♐14 8	10 49.7	23 36.4	26 1.6	15 41.7	13 35.1	27 58.2	0 42.8	9 54.9	23 42.2
26 Tu	18 13 43	3 42 11	16 38 13	24 6 30	10 44.2	23 48.9	27 11.6	16 23.3	13 37.7	27 56.6	0 44.8	9 56.0	23 43.7
27 W	18 17 40	4 39 23	1♑37 56	9♑11 20	10 39.6	23 56.8	28 21.7	17 4.8	13 40.5	27 54.9	0 46.7	9 57.2	23 45.3
28 Th	18 21 36	5 36 35	16 45 32	24 19 18	10 36.3	24R 0.0	29 31.8	17 46.3	13 43.5	27 53.1	0 48.6	9 58.3	23 46.8
29 F	18 25 33	6 33 46	1♒51 31	9♒21 8	10D 34.6	23 58.7	0♊42.1	18 27.7	13 46.6	27 51.2	0 50.5	9 59.5	23 48.4
30 Sa	18 29 29	7 30 57	16 47 13	24 9 1	10 34.5	23 52.7	1 52.3	19 9.1	13 49.9	27 49.2	0 52.3	10 0.7	23 49.9

Astro Data Dy Hr Mn	Planet Ingress Dy Hr Mn
☽0N 9 0:23	☿ ♉ 2 18:45
♀0N 9 8:02	♀ ♈ 6 8:54
♆ D 21 11:52	☿ ♊ 16 23:43
☽0S 23 11:38	☉ ♊ 21 18:35
☽0N 5 4:57	☿ ♋ 1 8:22
♄ R 8 17:06	♀ ♉ 2 10:11
♃ D 10 13:41	♂ ♊ 2 16:21
☽0S 19 18:44	♅ ♉ 6 15:41
☿ R 28 4:57	☉ ♋ 22 2:48
	♀ ♊ 28 9:38

Last Aspect Dy Hr Mn	☽ Ingress Dy Hr Mn	Last Aspect Dy Hr Mn	☽ Ingress Dy Hr Mn
30 19:58 ♄ □	♐ 1 1:02	1 11:32 ♅ □	♒ 1 11:55
2 23:57 ♅ △	♑ 3 2:53	3 13:52 ♅ ✱	♓ 3 14:06
5 2:50 ♀ ✱	♒ 5 5:06	5 6:30 ♇ △	♈ 5 18:31
7 5:46 ♀ ✱	♓ 7 8:26	7 21:54 ♄ ✱	♉ 8 1:17
9 0:17 ♇ △	♈ 9 13:09	10 6:43 ♄ □	♊ 10 10:14
11 17:01 ♅ ☌	♉ 11 19:24	12 17:35 ♄ △	♋ 12 21:14
13 23:08 ♄ □	♊ 14 3:38	14 20:33 ♇ ☌	♌ 15 9:53
16 12:14 ♅ ✱	♋ 16 14:17	17 19:04 ♄ ☍	♍ 17 22:51
19 1:05 ♅ □	♌ 19 2:55	20 6:37 ☉ □	♎ 20 9:59
21 15:20 ☉ □	♍ 21 15:35	22 13:54 ♄ △	♏ 22 17:25
23 12:27 ♇ ✱	♎ 24 1:43	24 17:28 ♄ □	♐ 24 20:49
26 6:56 ♅ ☍	♏ 26 7:52	26 18:05 ♄ ✱	♑ 26 21:24
28 7:19 ♄ □	♐ 28 10:28	28 11:29 ☿ ☍	♒ 28 21:02
30 10:40 ♅ △	♑ 30 11:12	30 17:59 ♄ ☌	♓ 30 21:38

☽ Phases & Eclipses Dy Hr Mn	Astro Data
6 6:41 ☽ 15♒03	1 MAY 1934
13 12:30 ● 22♉03	Julian Day # 12539
21 15:20 ☽ 29♌52	Delta T 23.9 sec
28 21:41 ○ 6♐51	SVP 06♓10'26"
	Obliquity 23°26'59"
	⚷ Chiron 2♊21.9
	☽ Mean ☊ 15♒13.4
4 12:53 ☽ 13♓12	1 JUNE 1934
12 2:11 ● 20♊26	Julian Day # 12570
20 6:37 ☽ 28♍15	Delta T 23.9 sec
27 5:08 ○ 4♑52	SVP 06♓10'20"
	Obliquity 23°26'58"
	⚷ Chiron 4♊42.0
	☽ Mean ☊ 13♒34.9

JULY 1934 — LONGITUDE

Day	Sid.Time	☉	0 hr ☽	Noon ☽	True ☊	☿	♀	♂	♃	♄	♅	♆	♇
1 Su	18 33 26	8♋28 9	1♓25 55	8♓37 29	10♒35.5	23♋42.3	3♊ 2.7	19♊50.4	13♎53.4	27♒47.2	0♉54.1	10♍ 2.0	23♋51.5
2 M	18 37 22	9 25 20	15 43 24	22 43 32	10 36.9	23R27.6	4 13.1	20 31.7	13 57.0	27R45.0	0 55.8	10 3.2	23 53.0
3 Tu	18 41 19	10 22 32	29 37 52	6♈26 28	10R38.1	23 8.6	5 23.6	21 12.9	14 0.8	27 42.8	0 57.5	10 4.5	23 54.6
4 W	18 45 16	11 19 43	13♈ 9 31	19 47 15	10 38.5	22 45.7	6 34.1	21 54.0	14 4.8	27 40.5	0 59.1	10 5.8	23 56.2
5 Th	18 49 12	12 16 55	26 19 56	2♉47 53	10 37.7	22 19.2	7 44.7	22 35.2	14 8.9	27 38.1	1 0.7	10 7.2	23 57.8
6 F	18 53 9	13 14 8	9♉11 26	15 30 55	10 35.6	21 49.5	8 55.4	23 16.2	14 13.2	27 35.6	1 2.3	10 8.5	23 59.4
7 Sa	18 57 5	14 11 21	21 46 40	27 59 1	10 32.5	21 16.9	10 6.1	23 57.2	14 17.6	27 33.0	1 3.8	10 9.9	24 1.0
8 Su	19 1 2	15 8 34	4♊ 8 16	10♊14 44	10 28.7	20 42.0	11 16.9	24 38.2	14 22.2	27 30.3	1 5.3	10 11.3	24 2.6
9 M	19 4 58	16 5 47	16 18 42	22 20 27	10 24.7	20 5.3	12 27.7	25 19.1	14 27.0	27 27.6	1 6.7	10 12.8	24 4.2
10 Tu	19 8 55	17 3 1	28 20 13	4♋18 18	10 20.9	19 27.4	13 38.6	26 0.0	14 31.9	27 24.8	1 8.1	10 14.3	24 5.8
11 W	19 12 51	18 0 15	10♋14 55	16 10 20	10 17.8	18 48.9	14 49.6	26 40.8	14 36.9	27 21.9	1 9.4	10 15.8	24 7.4
12 Th	19 16 48	18 57 29	22 4 49	27 58 38	10 15.6	18 10.5	16 0.6	27 21.6	14 42.1	27 18.9	1 10.7	10 17.3	24 9.0
13 F	19 20 45	19 54 44	3♌52 3	9♌45 23	10D14.6	17 32.9	17 11.7	28 2.3	14 47.5	27 15.9	1 11.9	10 18.8	24 10.6
14 Sa	19 24 41	20 51 58	15 38 57	21 33 6	10 14.5	16 56.7	18 22.8	28 43.0	14 53.0	27 12.8	1 13.1	10 20.4	24 12.3
15 Su	19 28 38	21 49 13	27 28 12	3♍24 39	10 15.3	16 22.6	19 34.0	29 23.6	14 58.7	27 9.6	1 14.3	10 22.0	24 13.9
16 M	19 32 34	22 46 28	9♍22 52	15 23 20	10 16.6	15 51.2	20 45.2	0♋ 4.1	15 4.5	27 6.3	1 15.4	10 23.6	24 15.5
17 Tu	19 36 31	23 43 43	21 26 30	27 32 51	10 18.0	15 23.0	21 56.5	0 44.7	15 10.4	27 3.0	1 16.4	10 25.2	24 17.1
18 W	19 40 27	24 40 58	3♎42 56	9♎57 13	10 19.2	14 58.6	23 7.8	1 25.1	15 16.5	26 59.6	1 17.4	10 26.9	24 18.7
19 Th	19 44 24	25 38 13	16 16 14	22 40 27	10R20.0	14 38.5	24 19.2	2 5.5	15 22.7	26 56.1	1 18.4	10 28.6	24 20.4
20 F	19 48 20	26 35 29	29 10 20	5♏46 17	10 20.2	14 23.0	25 30.6	2 45.9	15 29.1	26 52.6	1 19.3	10 30.2	24 22.0
21 Sa	19 52 17	27 32 45	12♏28 37	19 17 35	10 19.7	14 12.5	26 42.1	3 26.2	15 35.6	26 49.0	1 20.2	10 32.0	24 23.6
22 Su	19 56 14	28 30 1	26 13 18	3♐15 46	10 18.8	14D 7.4	27 53.6	4 6.4	15 42.2	26 45.4	1 21.0	10 33.7	24 25.2
23 M	20 0 10	29 27 18	10♐24 48	17 40 4	10 17.7	14 7.8	29 5.2	4 46.6	15 49.0	26 41.7	1 21.8	10 35.5	24 26.8
24 Tu	20 4 7	0♌24 35	25 1 4	2♑27 7	10 16.5	14 13.9	0♋16.8	5 26.8	15 55.9	26 37.9	1 22.5	10 37.3	24 28.4
25 W	20 8 3	1 21 52	9♑57 22	17 30 48	10 15.5	14 25.9	1 28.5	6 6.9	16 3.0	26 34.1	1 23.1	10 39.1	24 30.1
26 Th	20 12 0	2 19 10	25 6 20	2♒42 46	10 14.9	14 43.8	2 40.3	6 46.9	16 10.1	26 30.2	1 23.8	10 40.9	24 31.7
27 F	20 15 56	3 16 28	10♒18 54	17 53 31	10D14.7	15 7.8	3 52.1	7 26.9	16 17.4	26 26.3	1 24.3	10 42.7	24 33.3
28 Sa	20 19 53	4 13 47	25 25 30	2♓53 48	10 14.9	15 37.7	5 3.9	8 6.9	16 24.8	26 22.4	1 24.9	10 44.6	24 34.9
29 Su	20 23 50	5 11 7	10♓17 31	17 35 54	10 15.2	16 13.7	6 15.8	8 46.8	16 32.4	26 18.3	1 25.3	10 46.4	24 36.5
30 M	20 27 46	6 8 28	24 48 22	1♈54 31	10 15.6	16 55.7	7 27.8	9 26.6	16 40.1	26 14.3	1 25.8	10 48.3	24 38.1
31 Tu	20 31 43	7 5 50	8♈54 6	15 47 1	10 16.0	17 43.7	8 39.8	10 6.4	16 47.9	26 10.2	1 26.2	10 50.2	24 39.7

AUGUST 1934 — LONGITUDE

Day	Sid.Time	☉	0 hr ☽	Noon ☽	True ☊	☿	♀	♂	♃	♄	♅	♆	♇
1 W	20 35 39	8♌ 3 13	22♈33 21	29♈13 14	10♒16.2	18♌37.5	9♋51.9	10♋46.2	16♎55.8	26♒ 6.0	1♉26.5	10♍52.1	24♋41.3
2 Th	20 39 36	9 0 37	5♉46 57	12♉14 51	10R16.2	19 37.0	11 4.0	11 25.9	17 3.8	26R 1.8	1 26.8	10 54.1	24 42.8
3 F	20 43 32	9 58 3	18 37 21	24 54 53	10D16.2	20 42.3	12 16.2	12 5.6	17 11.9	25 57.6	1 27.0	10 56.0	24 44.4
4 Sa	20 47 29	10 55 29	1♊ 7 55	7♊16 58	10 16.2	21 53.0	13 28.5	12 45.2	17 20.2	25 53.3	1 27.2	10 58.0	24 46.0
5 Su	20 51 25	11 52 57	13 22 30	19 25 1	10 16.4	23 9.2	14 40.8	13 24.8	17 28.6	25 49.1	1 27.3	10 60.0	24 47.6
6 M	20 55 22	12 50 26	25 24 59	1♋22 51	10 16.6	24 30.5	15 53.1	14 4.3	17 37.1	25 44.7	1 27.4	11 2.0	24 49.1
7 Tu	20 59 19	13 47 57	7♋19 4	13 14 1	10 17.0	25 56.7	17 5.5	14 43.8	17 45.7	25 40.4	1R27.4	11 4.0	24 50.7
8 W	21 3 15	14 45 28	19 8 7	25 1 42	10 17.3	27 27.7	18 18.0	15 23.2	17 54.4	25 36.0	1 27.4	11 6.0	24 52.2
9 Th	21 7 12	15 43 1	0♌55 7	6♌48 41	10R17.6	29 3.1	19 30.5	16 2.6	18 3.3	25 31.6	1 27.4	11 8.1	24 53.7
10 F	21 11 8	16 40 34	12 42 43	18 37 30	10 17.7	0♍42.7	20 43.0	16 41.9	18 12.2	25 27.2	1 27.2	11 10.1	24 55.3
11 Sa	21 15 5	17 38 9	24 33 17	0♍30 22	10 17.5	2 26.1	21 55.6	17 21.2	18 21.2	25 22.7	1 27.1	11 12.2	24 56.8
12 Su	21 19 1	18 35 45	6♍29 1	12 29 30	10 16.8	4 13.0	23 8.2	18 0.4	18 30.4	25 18.2	1 26.9	11 14.3	24 58.3
13 M	21 22 58	19 33 22	18 32 5	24 37 2	10 15.8	6 3.0	24 20.9	18 39.6	18 39.6	25 13.8	1 26.6	11 16.4	24 59.8
14 Tu	21 26 54	20 31 0	0♎44 41	6♎55 18	10 14.4	7 55.6	25 33.7	19 18.7	18 49.0	25 9.3	1 26.3	11 18.5	25 1.3
15 W	21 30 51	21 28 39	13 9 12	19 26 43	10 13.0	9 50.6	26 46.5	19 57.8	18 58.5	25 4.8	1 25.9	11 20.6	25 2.8
16 Th	21 34 48	22 26 20	25 48 10	2♏13 52	10 11.6	11 47.5	27 59.3	20 36.9	19 8.0	25 0.2	1 25.5	11 22.7	25 4.3
17 F	21 38 44	23 24 1	8♏44 8	15 19 17	10 10.6	13 45.9	29 12.2	21 15.8	19 17.7	24 55.7	1 25.1	11 24.8	25 5.7
18 Sa	21 42 41	24 21 43	21 59 35	28 45 15	10D10.2	15 45.4	0♌25.1	21 54.8	19 27.4	24 51.2	1 24.6	11 27.0	25 7.2
19 Su	21 46 37	25 19 27	5♐36 27	12♐33 18	10 10.4	17 45.8	1 38.1	22 33.7	19 37.3	24 46.7	1 24.0	11 29.1	25 8.6
20 M	21 50 34	26 17 11	19 35 47	26 43 47	10 11.2	19 46.6	2 51.1	23 12.5	19 47.2	24 42.2	1 23.4	11 31.3	25 10.0
21 Tu	21 54 30	27 14 57	3♑57 6	11♑15 19	10 12.3	21 47.6	4 4.1	23 51.3	19 57.2	24 37.6	1 22.8	11 33.5	25 11.5
22 W	21 58 27	28 12 44	18 37 57	26 4 19	10 13.4	23 48.5	5 17.3	24 30.0	20 7.3	24 33.1	1 22.1	11 35.6	25 12.9
23 Th	22 2 23	29 10 32	3♒33 37	11♒ 4 55	10R14.2	25 49.1	6 30.4	25 8.7	20 17.5	24 28.6	1 21.3	11 37.8	25 14.3
24 F	22 6 20	0♍ 8 21	18 37 13	26 9 23	10 14.1	27 49.2	7 43.6	25 47.3	20 27.8	24 24.1	1 20.6	11 40.0	25 15.6
25 Sa	22 10 17	1 6 12	3♓40 20	11♓ 8 57	10 13.0	29 48.6	8 56.9	26 25.9	20 38.2	24 19.7	1 19.7	11 42.2	25 17.0
26 Su	22 14 13	2 4 4	18 34 10	25 55 2	10 10.9	1♍47.2	10 10.1	27 4.4	20 48.6	24 15.2	1 18.8	11 44.4	25 18.4
27 M	22 18 10	3 1 57	3♈10 45	10♈20 37	10 8.1	3 44.9	11 23.5	27 42.9	20 59.2	24 10.8	1 17.9	11 46.6	25 19.7
28 Tu	22 22 6	3 59 53	17 24 7	24 20 57	10 4.8	5 41.6	12 36.9	28 21.4	21 9.8	24 6.3	1 17.0	11 48.8	25 21.0
29 W	22 26 3	4 57 50	1♉10 56	7♉54 3	10 1.7	7 37.2	13 50.3	28 59.7	21 20.5	24 1.9	1 15.9	11 51.0	25 22.3
30 Th	22 29 59	5 55 49	14 30 27	21 0 25	9 59.2	9 31.7	15 3.8	29 38.1	21 31.3	23 57.5	1 14.9	11 53.2	25 23.6
31 F	22 33 56	6 53 50	27 24 16	3♊42 30	9D57.6	11 25.0	16 17.3	0♌16.4	21 42.1	23 53.2	1 13.8	11 55.4	25 24.9

Astro Data Dy Hr Mn	Planet Ingress Dy Hr Mn	Last Aspect Dy Hr Mn	☽ Ingress Dy Hr Mn	Last Aspect Dy Hr Mn	☽ Ingress Dy Hr Mn	☽ Phases & Eclipses Dy Hr Mn	Astro Data
☽0N 2 10:44	♂ ♋ 15 21:33	2 14:02 ♇ △	♈ 3 0:39	1 6:20 ♄ ⚹	♉ 1 13:25	3 20:28 ☽ 11♈11	1 JULY 1934
☽0S 17 0:51	☉ ♌ 23 13:42	5 2:24 ♄ ⚹	♉ 5 6:47	3 13:56 ♄ □	♊ 3 21:48	11 17:06 ● 18♋41	Julian Day # 12600
☿ D 22 10:21	♀ ♋ 23 18:22	7 11:07 ♄ □	♊ 7 15:55	6 0:39 ♄ △	♋ 6 9:13	19 18:53 ☽ 26♎23	Delta T 23.9 sec
☽0N 29 19:03		9 22:09 ♄ △	♋ 10 3:20	8 19:36 ☿ ☌	♌ 8 22:08	26 12:09 ○ 2♒48	SVP 06♓10'15"
	☿ ♌ 9 13:49	12 4:13 ♇ ☌	♌ 12 16:07	11 1:39 ♄ ☍	♍ 11 10:59	26 12:15 ☍ P 0.661	Obliquity 23°26'58"
♅ R 7 5:24	♀ ♌ 17 15:45	15 4:08 ♂ ⚹	♍ 15 5:07	13 12:46 ♇ ⚹	♎ 13 22:33		⚷ Chiron 6♊54.5
☽0S 13 6:35	☉ ♍ 23 20:32	17 5:37 ♇ ⚹	♎ 17 16:47	16 4:31 ♀ □	♏ 16 7:51	2 6:27 ☽ 9♉16	☽ Mean ☊ 11♒59.7
♄⊼♇ 15 7:53	☿ ♍ 25 2:18	19 19:48 ♄ △	♏ 20 1:31	18 5:35 ♇ △	♐ 18 14:12	10 8:46 ● 17♌02	
☽0N 26 5:25	♂ ♌ 30 13:43	22 4:11 ☉ △	♐ 22 6:28	20 12:04 ☉ △	♑ 20 17:27	10 8:37:24 ● A 6'33"	1 AUGUST 1934
		24 2:36 ♄ ⚹	♑ 24 8:03	22 10:38 ♇ ☍	♒ 22 18:18	18 4:33 ☽ 24♏33	Julian Day # 12631
		25 23:05 ♇ ☍	♒ 26 7:43	24 16:53 ☿ ☍	♓ 24 18:08	24 19:37 ○ 0♓56	Delta T 23.9 sec
		28 1:31 ♄ ☌	♓ 28 7:20	26 14:33 ♂ △	♈ 26 18:44	31 19:40 ☽ 7♊41	SVP 06♓10'10"
		29 23:43 ♇ △	♈ 30 8:45	28 19:57 ♂ □	♉ 28 21:55		Obliquity 23°26'58"
				30 20:15 ♇ ⚹	♊ 31 4:55		⚷ Chiron 8♊45.0
							☽ Mean ☊ 10♒21.2

LONGITUDE SEPTEMBER 1934

Day	Sid.Time	☉	0 hr ☽	Noon ☽	True ☊	☿	♀	♂	♃	♄	♅	♆	♇
1 Sa	22 37 52	7♍51 53	9♊55 37	16♊ 4 11	9♒57.3	13♍17.1	17♌30.9	0♌54.7	21♎53.0	23♒48.9	1♉12.6	11♍57.6	25♋26.2
2 Su	22 41 49	8 49 57	22 8 46	28 10 0	9 58.0	15 8.0	18 44.5	1 32.9	22 4.1	23R 44.6	1R 11.4	11 59.9	25 27.4
3 M	22 45 46	9 48 4	4♋ 8 29	10♋ 4 49	9 59.4	16 57.7	19 58.2	2 11.0	22 15.1	23 40.3	1 10.2	12 2.1	25 28.7
4 Tu	22 49 42	10 46 13	15 59 35	21 53 22	10 1.2	18 46.2	21 11.9	2 49.1	22 26.3	23 36.1	1 8.9	12 4.3	25 29.9
5 W	22 53 39	11 44 23	27 46 40	3♌40 0	10 2.7	20 33.5	22 25.7	3 27.2	22 37.5	23 31.9	1 7.6	12 6.6	25 31.1
6 Th	22 57 35	12 42 36	9♌33 50	15 28 35	10R 3.4	22 19.5	23 39.5	4 5.2	22 48.8	23 27.7	1 6.3	12 8.8	25 32.3
7 F	23 1 32	13 40 50	21 24 38	27 22 20	10 2.7	24 4.4	24 53.3	4 43.2	23 0.2	23 23.6	1 4.9	12 11.0	25 33.4
8 Sa	23 5 28	14 39 6	3♍21 58	9♍23 47	10 0.4	25 48.0	26 7.2	5 21.1	23 11.6	23 19.6	1 3.4	12 13.2	25 34.6
9 Su	23 9 25	15 37 24	15 28 2	21 34 52	9 56.4	27 30.5	27 21.1	5 58.9	23 23.1	23 15.5	1 1.9	12 15.5	25 35.7
10 M	23 13 21	16 35 44	27 44 27	3♎56 54	9 50.9	29 11.9	28 35.1	6 36.7	23 34.6	23 11.6	1 0.4	12 17.7	25 36.8
11 Tu	23 17 18	17 34 5	10♎12 20	16 30 50	9 44.5	0♎52.1	29 49.1	7 14.5	23 46.3	23 7.7	0 58.9	12 19.9	25 37.9
12 W	23 21 14	18 32 29	22 52 28	29 17 19	9 37.7	2 31.2	1♍ 3.1	7 52.2	23 57.9	23 3.8	0 57.3	12 22.1	25 39.0
13 Th	23 25 11	19 30 54	5♏45 28	12♏16 58	9 31.3	4 9.2	2 17.2	8 29.8	24 9.7	22 60.0	0 55.6	12 24.3	25 40.1
14 F	23 29 8	20 29 20	18 51 56	25 30 26	9 26.1	5 46.1	3 31.3	9 7.4	24 21.5	22 56.2	0 53.9	12 26.5	25 41.1
15 Sa	23 33 4	21 27 48	2♐12 35	8♐58 27	9 22.6	7 21.9	4 45.5	9 45.0	24 33.3	22 52.5	0 52.2	12 28.8	25 42.1
16 Su	23 37 1	22 26 18	15 48 9	22 41 44	9D 20.9	8 56.7	5 59.7	10 22.4	24 45.3	22 48.9	0 50.5	12 31.0	25 43.1
17 M	23 40 57	23 24 50	29 39 15	6♑40 41	9 20.9	10 30.4	7 13.9	10 59.9	24 57.2	22 45.3	0 48.7	12 33.2	25 44.1
18 Tu	23 44 54	24 23 23	13♑45 59	20 55 0	9 21.9	12 3.0	8 28.1	11 37.3	25 9.2	22 41.8	0 46.9	12 35.4	25 45.1
19 W	23 48 50	25 21 58	28 7 31	5♒23 11	9R 23.0	13 34.6	9 42.4	12 14.6	25 21.3	22 38.4	0 45.1	12 37.5	25 46.0
20 Th	23 52 47	26 20 34	12♒41 34	20 2 5	9 23.4	15 5.2	10 56.7	12 51.8	25 33.4	22 35.0	0 43.2	12 39.7	25 46.9
21 F	23 56 43	27 19 12	27 24 3	4♓46 43	9 22.1	16 34.7	12 11.1	13 29.1	25 45.6	22 31.7	0 41.3	12 41.9	25 47.8
22 Sa	0 0 40	28 17 52	12♓ 9 11	19 30 33	9 18.6	18 3.2	13 25.4	14 6.2	25 57.8	22 28.5	0 39.3	12 44.1	25 48.7
23 Su	0 4 37	29 16 34	26 49 52	4♈ 6 13	9 12.9	19 30.6	14 39.8	14 43.3	26 10.1	22 25.3	0 37.4	12 46.2	25 49.6
24 M	0 8 33	0♎15 17	11♈18 43	18 26 36	9 5.5	20 57.0	15 54.3	15 20.4	26 22.4	22 22.2	0 35.4	12 48.4	25 50.4
25 Tu	0 12 30	1 14 3	25 29 11	2♉25 58	8 57.0	22 22.2	17 8.8	15 57.4	26 34.7	22 19.2	0 33.3	12 50.5	25 51.2
26 W	0 16 26	2 12 51	9♉16 33	16 0 44	8 48.5	23 46.4	18 23.3	16 34.3	26 47.1	22 16.3	0 31.3	12 52.6	25 52.0
27 Th	0 20 23	3 11 41	22 38 28	29 9 50	8 41.0	25 9.5	19 37.8	17 11.2	26 59.5	22 13.4	0 29.2	12 54.7	25 52.8
28 F	0 24 19	4 10 33	5♊35 5	11♊54 33	8 35.1	26 31.4	20 52.4	17 48.1	27 12.0	22 10.7	0 27.1	12 56.9	25 53.5
29 Sa	0 28 16	5 9 28	18 8 40	24 17 59	8 31.4	27 52.2	22 7.0	18 24.9	27 24.5	22 8.0	0 25.0	12 59.0	25 54.3
30 Su	0 32 12	6 8 25	0♋23 3	6♋24 31	8D 29.8	29 11.7	23 21.6	19 1.6	27 37.1	22 5.4	0 22.8	13 1.1	25 55.0

LONGITUDE OCTOBER 1934

Day	Sid.Time	☉	0 hr ☽	Noon ☽	True ☊	☿	♀	♂	♃	♄	♅	♆	♇
1 M	0 36 9	7♎ 7 24	12♋23 2	18♋19 18	8♒29.7	0♏29.9	24♍36.3	19♌38.3	27♎49.7	22♒ 2.8	0♉20.6	13♍ 3.1	25♋55.6
2 Tu	0 40 6	8 6 25	24 13 58	0♌ 7 43	8 30.5	1 46.8	25 51.0	20 14.9	28 2.3	22R 0.4	0R 18.4	13 5.2	25 56.3
3 W	0 44 2	9 5 29	6♌ 1 13	11 55 5	8R 31.1	3 2.3	27 5.7	20 51.5	28 15.0	21 58.0	0 16.2	13 7.2	25 56.9
4 Th	0 47 59	10 4 35	17 49 56	23 46 18	8 30.7	4 16.3	28 20.5	21 28.0	28 27.7	21 55.8	0 14.0	13 9.3	25 57.5
5 F	0 51 55	11 3 43	29 44 41	5♍45 34	8 28.3	5 28.7	29 35.3	22 4.5	28 40.4	21 53.6	0 11.7	13 11.3	25 58.1
6 Sa	0 55 52	12 2 53	11♍49 20	17 56 17	8 23.4	6 39.4	0♎50.1	22 40.8	28 53.2	21 51.5	0 9.4	13 13.3	25 58.7
7 Su	0 59 48	13 2 6	24 6 41	0♎20 43	8 16.0	7 48.3	2 4.9	23 17.2	29 5.9	21 49.5	0 7.1	13 15.3	25 59.2
8 M	1 3 45	14 1 20	6♎38 29	13 0 2	8 6.2	8 55.3	3 19.8	23 53.4	29 18.8	21 47.6	0 4.8	13 17.3	25 59.7
9 Tu	1 7 41	15 0 37	19 25 20	25 54 17	7 54.8	10 0.1	4 34.7	24 29.7	29 31.6	21 45.8	0 2.4	13 19.3	26 0.2
10 W	1 11 38	15 59 56	2♏26 47	9♏ 2 36	7 42.7	11 2.6	5 49.6	25 5.8	29 44.5	21 44.0	0 0.1	13 21.2	26 0.7
11 Th	1 15 35	16 59 17	15 41 35	22 23 30	7 31.3	12 2.7	7 4.5	25 41.9	29 57.4	21 42.4	29♈57.7	13 23.1	26 1.1
12 F	1 19 31	17 58 39	29 8 7	5♐55 15	7 21.6	12 60.0	8 19.5	26 17.9	0♏10.3	21 40.9	29 55.3	13 25.1	26 1.5
13 Sa	1 23 28	18 58 4	12♐44 44	19 36 23	7 14.3	13 54.3	9 34.4	26 53.9	0 23.2	21 39.5	29 52.9	13 27.0	26 1.9
14 Su	1 27 24	19 57 30	26 30 6	3♑25 48	7 9.8	14 45.4	10 49.4	27 29.7	0 36.2	21 38.1	29 50.5	13 28.8	26 2.3
15 M	1 31 21	20 56 59	10♑23 23	17 22 50	7D 7.8	15 32.9	12 4.4	28 5.6	0 49.1	21 36.9	29 48.1	13 30.7	26 2.6
16 Tu	1 35 17	21 56 29	24 24 6	1♒27 7	7R 7.5	16 16.4	13 19.4	28 41.3	1 2.1	21 35.8	29 45.7	13 32.6	26 3.0
17 W	1 39 14	22 56 0	8♒31 48	15 38 2	7 7.6	16 55.6	14 34.5	29 17.0	1 15.1	21 34.7	29 43.2	13 34.4	26 3.2
18 Th	1 43 10	23 55 33	22 45 37	29 54 18	7 6.9	17 30.0	15 49.5	29 52.6	1 28.2	21 33.8	29 40.8	13 36.2	26 3.5
19 F	1 47 7	24 55 8	7♓ 3 44	14♓13 30	7 4.1	17 59.2	17 4.6	0♍28.2	1 41.2	21 32.9	29 38.4	13 38.0	26 3.7
20 Sa	1 51 4	25 54 45	21 23 5	28 31 55	6 58.6	18 22.6	18 19.7	1 3.6	1 54.2	21 32.2	29 35.9	13 39.7	26 4.0
21 Su	1 55 0	26 54 24	5♈39 21	12♈44 44	6 50.2	18 39.7	19 34.8	1 39.1	2 7.3	21 31.6	29 33.5	13 41.5	26 4.1
22 M	1 58 57	27 54 4	19 47 23	26 46 38	6 39.4	18R 49.9	20 49.9	2 14.4	2 20.4	21 31.0	29 31.0	13 43.2	26 4.3
23 Tu	2 2 53	28 53 46	3♉41 53	10♉32 37	6 27.0	18 52.7	22 5.0	2 49.7	2 33.4	21 30.6	29 28.5	13 44.9	26 4.4
24 W	2 6 50	29 53 31	17 18 25	23 58 56	6 14.5	18 47.6	23 20.2	3 24.9	2 46.5	21 30.3	29 26.1	13 46.6	26 4.6
25 Th	2 10 46	0♏53 17	0♊34 1	7♊ 3 35	6 2.9	18 34.0	24 35.3	4 0.0	2 59.6	21 30.0	29 23.6	13 48.2	26 4.7
26 F	2 14 43	1 53 6	13 27 43	19 46 35	5 53.4	18 11.5	25 50.5	4 35.1	3 12.7	21D 29.9	29 21.2	13 49.9	26 4.7
27 Sa	2 18 39	2 52 57	26 0 30	2♋ 9 50	5 46.6	17 39.9	27 5.7	5 10.1	3 25.8	21 29.9	29 18.7	13 51.5	26 4.8
28 Su	2 22 36	3 52 50	8♋15 6	14 16 48	5 42.4	16 59.1	28 20.9	5 45.0	3 38.9	21 30.0	29 16.3	13 53.1	26R 4.8
29 M	2 26 33	4 52 45	20 15 34	26 12 2	5 40.5	16 9.3	29 36.1	6 19.9	3 52.0	21 30.2	29 13.8	13 54.6	26 4.8
30 Tu	2 30 29	5 52 42	2♌ 6 54	8♌ 0 50	5 40.0	15 11.1	0♏51.4	6 54.6	4 5.1	21 30.4	29 11.4	13 56.2	26 4.7
31 W	2 34 26	6 52 42	13 54 34	19 48 47	5 40.0	14 5.5	2 6.6	7 29.3	4 18.2	21 30.8	29 9.0	13 57.7	26 4.7

Astro Data	Dy Hr Mn
♃△♄	8 12:20
☽0S	9 12:43
☿0S	11 5:37
♃□♇	21 4:45
☽0N	22 15:59
♃∠♆	2 6:32
☽0S	6 19:43
♀0S	8 0:31
♃☍♅	11 0:31
☽0N	20 0:40
☿ R	22 20:44
♄ D	26 17:18
♇ R	28 0:33

Planet Ingress	Dy Hr Mn
☿ ♎	10 11:29
♀ ♍	11 3:32
☉ ♎	23 17:45
☿ ♏	30 14:46
♀ ♎	5 7:56
♅ ♈	10 0:36
♃ ♏	11 4:55
♂ ♍	18 4:59
☉ ♏	24 2:36
♀ ♏	29 7:37

Last Aspect Dy Hr Mn		☽ Ingress Dy Hr Mn
2 3:09	♄ △	♋ 2 15:40
4 19:23	♇ ☌	♌ 5 4:32
7 7:49	♀ ☌	♍ 7 17:16
10 3:16	☿ ☌	♎ 10 4:23
12 5:13	♇ □	♏ 12 13:19
14 12:20	♇ △	♐ 14 20:03
16 15:47	♃ ⚹	♑ 17 0:36
18 20:05	♇ ☍	♒ 19 3:06
20 21:17	♃ △	♓ 21 4:14
23 4:19	☉ ☍	♈ 23 5:13
25 1:54	♃ ☍	♉ 25 7:47
27 5:56	♇ ⚹	♊ 27 13:33
29 21:22	☿ △	♋ 29 23:14

Last Aspect Dy Hr Mn		☽ Ingress Dy Hr Mn
2 7:53	♃ □	♌ 2 11:44
4 21:49	♃ ⚹	♍ 5 0:31
7 3:38	♇ ⚹	♎ 7 11:20
9 18:58	♃ ☌	♏ 9 19:31
11 18:44	♂ □	♐ 12 1:32
14 5:47	♅ △	♑ 14 6:04
16 9:06	♅ □	♒ 16 9:32
18 11:35	♅ ⚹	♓ 18 12:10
20 7:51	♇ △	♈ 20 14:28
22 16:41	♅ ☌	♉ 22 17:34
24 15:48	♇ ⚹	♊ 24 22:58
27 6:24	♅ ⚹	♋ 27 7:46
29 18:05	♅ □	♌ 29 19:42

☽ Phases & Eclipses Dy Hr Mn	
9 0:20	● 15♍38
16 12:26	☽ 22♐57
23 4:19	○ 29♓27
30 12:29	☽ 6♋39
8 15:05	● 14♎39
15 19:29	☽ 21♑45
22 15:01	○ 28♈31
30 8:22	☽ 6♌14

Astro Data

1 SEPTEMBER 1934
Julian Day # 12662
Delta T 23.9 sec
SVP 06♓10'06"
Obliquity 23°26'58"
⚷ Chiron 9♊47.7
☽ Mean ☊ 8♒42.7

1 OCTOBER 1934
Julian Day # 12692
Delta T 23.9 sec
SVP 06♓10'02"
Obliquity 23°26'58"
⚷ Chiron 9♊49.1R
☽ Mean ☊ 7♒07.3

NOVEMBER 1934 LONGITUDE

Day	Sid.Time	☉	0 hr ☽	Noon ☽	True ☊	☿	♀	♂	♃	♄	♅	♆	♇
1 Th	2 38 22	7♏52 43	25♌44 10	1♍41 24	5♒39.1	12♏53.8	3♏21.9	8♍ 4.0	4♏31.3	21♒31.3	29♈ 6.5	13♍59.2	26♋ 4.6
2 F	2 42 19	8 52 47	7♍41 6	13 43 51	5R36.5	11R37.9	4 37.2	8 38.5	4 44.4	21 31.9	29R 4.1	14 0.6	26R 4.4
3 Sa	2 46 15	9 52 53	19 50 11	26 0 33	5 31.3	10 19.8	5 52.4	9 13.0	4 57.5	21 32.6	29 1.7	14 2.1	26 4.3
4 Su	2 50 12	10 53 1	2♎15 20	8♎34 48	5 23.4	9 2.0	7 7.7	9 47.3	5 10.6	21 33.4	28 59.3	14 3.5	26 4.1
5 M	2 54 8	11 53 10	14 59 10	21 28 29	5 12.9	7 46.9	8 23.1	10 21.6	5 23.7	21 34.3	28 56.9	14 4.9	26 3.9
6 Tu	2 58 5	12 53 22	28 2 44	4♏41 46	5 0.5	6 37.0	9 38.4	10 55.8	5 36.8	21 35.3	28 54.6	14 6.2	26 3.7
7 W	3 2 2	13 53 36	11♏25 21	18 13 9	4 47.3	5 34.4	10 53.7	11 30.0	5 49.8	21 36.4	28 52.2	14 7.5	26 3.5
8 Th	3 5 58	14 53 51	25 4 44	1♐59 38	4 34.8	4 40.8	12 9.1	12 4.0	6 2.9	21 37.6	28 49.9	14 8.8	26 3.2
9 F	3 9 55	15 54 9	8♐57 20	15 57 18	4 23.9	3 57.7	13 24.4	12 37.9	6 15.9	21 39.0	28 47.5	14 10.1	26 2.9
10 Sa	3 13 51	16 54 28	22 59 2	0♑ 2 3	4 15.8	3 25.9	14 39.8	13 11.8	6 29.0	21 40.4	28 45.2	14 11.4	26 2.6
11 Su	3 17 48	17 54 48	7♑ 5 53	14 10 9	4 10.6	3 5.7	15 55.1	13 45.6	6 42.0	21 41.9	28 42.9	14 12.6	26 2.3
12 M	3 21 44	18 55 10	21 14 33	28 18 50	4D 8.2	2D 57.2	17 10.5	14 19.2	6 54.9	21 43.5	28 40.7	14 13.8	26 1.9
13 Tu	3 25 41	19 55 34	5♒22 47	12♒26 16	4 7.7	2 59.9	18 25.9	14 52.8	7 7.9	21 45.3	28 38.4	14 14.9	26 1.5
14 W	3 29 37	20 55 58	19 29 11	26 31 25	4R 7.9	3 13.4	19 41.2	15 26.3	7 20.9	21 47.1	28 36.2	14 16.0	26 1.1
15 Th	3 33 34	21 56 24	3♓32 54	10♓33 33	4 7.4	3 36.8	20 56.6	15 59.6	7 33.8	21 49.0	28 34.0	14 17.1	26 0.7
16 F	3 37 31	22 56 51	17 33 14	24 31 48	4 5.1	4 9.3	22 12.0	16 32.9	7 46.7	21 51.0	28 31.8	14 18.2	26 0.2
17 Sa	3 41 27	23 57 19	1♈29 4	8♈24 47	4 0.2	4 50.0	23 27.4	17 6.1	7 59.6	21 53.2	28 29.7	14 19.2	25 59.7
18 Su	3 45 24	24 57 49	15 18 41	22 10 27	3 52.6	5 38.0	24 42.8	17 39.1	8 12.4	21 55.4	28 27.5	14 20.2	25 59.2
19 M	3 49 20	25 58 20	28 59 44	5♉46 11	3 42.6	6 32.5	25 58.1	18 12.1	8 25.2	21 57.7	28 25.4	14 21.2	25 58.7
20 Tu	3 53 17	26 58 53	12♉29 28	19 9 14	3 31.1	7 32.6	27 13.5	18 45.0	8 38.0	22 0.1	28 23.3	14 22.1	25 58.1
21 W	3 57 13	27 59 27	25 45 14	2♊17 13	3 19.4	8 37.6	28 28.9	19 17.8	8 50.8	22 2.7	28 21.3	14 23.1	25 57.5
22 Th	4 1 10	29 0 2	8♊45 2	15 8 34	3 8.5	9 46.9	29 44.3	19 50.4	9 3.6	22 5.3	28 19.3	14 23.9	25 56.9
23 F	4 5 6	0♐ 0 39	21 27 50	27 42 54	2 59.4	10 59.8	0♐59.7	20 23.0	9 16.3	22 8.0	28 17.3	14 24.8	25 56.3
24 Sa	4 9 3	1 1 18	3♋53 57	10♋ 1 14	2 52.8	12 15.9	2 15.1	20 55.4	9 28.9	22 10.8	28 15.3	14 25.6	25 55.7
25 Su	4 13 0	2 1 58	16 5 3	22 5 50	2 48.8	13 34.7	3 30.6	21 27.8	9 41.6	22 13.7	28 13.4	14 26.4	25 55.0
26 M	4 16 56	3 2 40	28 4 2	4♌ 0 11	2D47.2	14 55.7	4 46.0	21 60.0	9 54.2	22 16.7	28 11.5	14 27.1	25 54.3
27 Tu	4 20 53	4 3 23	9♌54 50	15 48 38	2 47.3	16 18.6	6 1.4	22 32.1	10 6.7	22 19.7	28 9.6	14 27.8	25 53.6
28 W	4 24 49	5 4 7	21 42 13	27 36 14	2 48.2	17 43.2	7 16.8	23 4.1	10 19.3	22 22.9	28 7.8	14 28.5	25 52.9
29 Th	4 28 46	6 4 53	3♍31 24	9♍28 23	2R48.9	19 9.1	8 32.3	23 36.0	10 31.7	22 26.2	28 6.0	14 29.2	25 52.1
30 F	4 32 42	7 5 41	15 27 51	21 30 29	2 48.5	20 36.2	9 47.7	24 7.7	10 44.2	22 29.5	28 4.2	14 29.8	25 51.3

DECEMBER 1934 LONGITUDE

Day	Sid.Time	☉	0 hr ☽	Noon ☽	True ☊	☿	♀	♂	♃	♄	♅	♆	♇
1 Sa	4 36 39	8♐ 6 30	27♍36 55	3♎47 43	2♒46.3	22♏ 4.3	11♐ 3.1	24♍39.3	10♏56.6	22♒33.0	28♈ 2.5	14♍30.4	25♋50.5
2 Su	4 40 35	9 7 20	10♎ 3 25	16 24 27	2R41.9	23 33.2	12 18.6	25 10.8	11 8.9	22 36.5	28R 0.8	14 30.9	25R49.7
3 M	4 44 32	10 8 12	22 51 11	29 23 51	2 35.4	25 2.8	13 34.0	25 42.2	11 21.3	22 40.2	27 59.2	14 31.4	25 48.9
4 Tu	4 48 29	11 9 6	6♏ 2 35	12♏47 21	2 27.2	26 32.9	14 49.5	26 13.4	11 33.5	22 43.9	27 57.6	14 31.9	25 48.0
5 W	4 52 25	12 10 0	19 38 1	26 34 16	2 18.2	28 3.5	16 4.9	26 44.5	11 45.7	22 47.7	27 56.0	14 32.4	25 47.1
6 Th	4 56 22	13 10 56	3♐35 39	10♐41 38	2 9.5	29 34.6	17 20.4	27 15.5	11 57.9	22 51.6	27 54.5	14 32.8	25 46.2
7 F	5 0 18	14 11 53	17 51 30	25 4 31	2 2.1	1♐ 5.9	18 35.8	27 46.3	12 10.0	22 55.5	27 53.0	14 33.2	25 45.3
8 Sa	5 4 15	15 12 51	2♑19 53	9♑36 46	1 56.6	2 37.5	19 51.3	28 16.9	12 22.0	22 59.6	27 51.5	14 33.5	25 44.4
9 Su	5 8 11	16 13 50	16 54 22	24 11 54	1 53.4	4 9.4	21 6.7	28 47.5	12 34.0	23 3.8	27 50.1	14 33.8	25 43.4
10 M	5 12 8	17 14 49	1♒28 40	8♒44 5	1D52.4	5 41.5	22 22.2	29 17.8	12 46.0	23 8.0	27 48.8	14 34.1	25 42.5
11 Tu	5 16 4	18 15 49	15 57 36	23 8 48	1 53.1	7 13.8	23 37.6	29 48.0	12 57.9	23 12.3	27 47.4	14 34.3	25 41.5
12 W	5 20 1	19 16 50	0♓17 22	7♓23 4	1 54.4	8 46.2	24 53.1	0♎18.1	13 9.7	23 16.7	27 46.2	14 34.6	25 40.5
13 Th	5 23 58	20 17 51	14 25 43	21 25 14	1R55.4	10 18.7	26 8.5	0 48.0	13 21.4	23 21.1	27 44.9	14 34.7	25 39.5
14 F	5 27 54	21 18 52	28 21 34	5♈14 40	1 55.3	11 51.4	27 24.0	1 17.7	13 33.1	23 25.7	27 43.8	14 34.9	25 38.4
15 Sa	5 31 51	22 19 54	12♈ 4 34	18 51 17	1 53.5	13 24.3	28 39.4	1 47.3	13 44.7	23 30.3	27 42.6	14 35.0	25 37.4
16 Su	5 35 47	23 20 57	25 34 48	2♉15 8	1 49.9	14 57.2	29 54.8	2 16.7	13 56.3	23 35.0	27 41.5	14 35.0	25 36.3
17 M	5 39 44	24 22 0	8♉52 17	15 26 16	1 44.7	16 30.3	1♑10.2	2 45.9	14 7.8	23 39.8	27 40.5	14R35.1	25 35.2
18 Tu	5 43 40	25 23 3	21 57 3	28 24 38	1 38.4	18 3.5	2 25.7	3 15.0	14 19.2	23 44.6	27 39.5	14 35.1	25 34.1
19 W	5 47 37	26 24 7	4♊48 59	11♊10 7	1 31.9	19 36.9	3 41.1	3 43.9	14 30.5	23 49.6	27 38.5	14 35.0	25 33.0
20 Th	5 51 33	27 25 11	17 28 3	23 42 49	1 25.9	21 10.5	4 56.5	4 12.6	14 41.8	23 54.6	27 37.6	14 35.0	25 31.9
21 F	5 55 30	28 26 16	29 54 28	6♋ 3 8	1 21.0	22 44.2	6 11.9	4 41.2	14 53.0	23 59.6	27 36.8	14 34.9	25 30.8
22 Sa	5 59 27	29 27 21	12♋ 8 55	18 12 3	1 17.6	24 18.1	7 27.3	5 9.5	15 4.1	24 4.8	27 35.9	14 34.7	25 29.6
23 Su	6 3 23	0♑28 27	24 12 43	0♌11 14	1D15.9	25 52.1	8 42.7	5 37.7	15 15.2	24 10.0	27 35.2	14 34.6	25 28.5
24 M	6 7 20	1 29 33	6♌ 7 54	12 3 5	1 15.7	27 26.4	9 58.1	6 5.7	15 26.1	24 15.2	27 34.5	14 34.3	25 27.3
25 Tu	6 11 16	2 30 40	17 57 14	23 50 48	1 16.8	29 0.9	11 13.5	6 33.5	15 37.0	24 20.6	27 33.8	14 34.1	25 26.1
26 W	6 15 13	3 31 47	29 44 16	5♍38 12	1 18.6	0♑35.6	12 28.9	7 1.0	15 47.8	24 26.0	27 33.2	14 33.8	25 24.9
27 Th	6 19 9	4 32 55	11♍33 9	17 29 42	1 20.5	2 10.6	13 44.3	7 28.4	15 58.6	24 31.5	27 32.6	14 33.5	25 23.7
28 F	6 23 6	5 34 4	23 28 30	29 30 9	1 21.9	3 45.8	14 59.7	7 55.6	16 9.2	24 37.0	27 32.1	14 33.2	25 22.5
29 Sa	6 27 3	6 35 12	5♎35 17	11♎44 30	1R22.6	5 21.3	16 15.1	8 22.5	16 19.7	24 42.6	27 31.7	14 32.8	25 21.3
30 Su	6 30 59	7 36 22	17 58 24	24 17 31	1 22.1	6 57.2	17 30.4	8 49.3	16 30.2	24 48.3	27 31.2	14 32.4	25 20.0
31 M	6 34 56	8 37 31	0♏42 23	7♏13 23	1 20.6	8 33.3	18 45.8	9 15.8	16 40.5	24 54.0	27 30.9	14 32.0	25 18.8

Astro Data

	Dy Hr Mn
♅⚼♆	2 21:48
☽0S	3 3:26
☿ D	12 5:59
☽0N	16 6:35
☽0S	30 11:14
☽0N	13 11:09
♆ R	17 11:49
♃✶♆	19 9:29
♂0S	21 7:17
☽0S	27 18:31

Planet Ingress

	Dy Hr Mn
☉ ♐	22 23:44
♀ ♐	22 4:59
☿ ♐	6 6:42
♂ ♎	11 9:32
♀ ♑	16 1:39
☉ ♑	22 12:49
☿ ♑	25 14:59

Last Aspect / ☽ Ingress

Last Aspect Dy Hr Mn		☽ Ingress Dy Hr Mn
1 6:47	♅ △	♍ 1 8:36
3 12:07	♇ ✶	♎ 3 19:41
6 1:34	♅ ☍	♏ 6 3:32
8 1:42	♇ △	♐ 8 8:33
10 9:48	♅ △	♑ 10 11:57
12 12:35	♅ □	♒ 12 14:52
14 15:31	♅ ✶	♓ 14 17:56
16 14:32	♇ △	♈ 16 21:26
18 23:00	♅ ☌	♉ 19 1:46
21 5:32	♀ ☍	♊ 21 7:47
23 13:04	♅ ✶	♋ 23 16:25
26 0:15	♅ □	♌ 26 3:54
28 13:02	♅ △	♍ 28 16:52

Last Aspect / ☽ Ingress

Last Aspect Dy Hr Mn		☽ Ingress Dy Hr Mn
30 20:32	♇ ✶	♎ 1 4:39
3 9:24	♅ ☍	♏ 3 13:06
5 16:19	☿ ☌	♐ 5 17:53
7 17:04	♂ □	♑ 7 20:09
9 20:16	♂ △	♒ 9 21:34
11 19:46	♅ ✶	♓ 11 23:31
13 22:10	♀ □	♈ 14 2:51
16 3:47	♅ ☌	♉ 16 7:56
18 6:42	♇ ✶	♊ 18 14:58
20 20:53	☉ ☍	♋ 21 0:11
23 6:46	♅ □	♌ 23 11:37
25 19:33	♅ △	♍ 26 0:32
28 3:47	♇ ✶	♎ 28 12:59
30 18:03	♅ ☍	♏ 30 22:41

☽ Phases & Eclipses

Dy Hr Mn		
7 4:44	●	14♏05
14 2:39	☽	21♒03
21 4:26	○	28♉11
29 5:39	☽	6♍19
6 17:25	●	13♐55
13 10:52	☽	20♓45
20 20:53	○	28♊18
29 2:08	☽	6♎41

Astro Data

1 NOVEMBER 1934
Julian Day # 12723
Delta T 23.9 sec
SVP 06♓09'59"
Obliquity 23°26'58"
⚷ Chiron 8♊49.2R
☽ Mean ☊ 5♒28.8

1 DECEMBER 1934
Julian Day # 12753
Delta T 23.9 sec
SVP 06♓09'54"
Obliquity 23°26'57"
⚷ Chiron 7♊12.8R
☽ Mean ☊ 3♒53.5

LONGITUDE — JANUARY 1935

Day	Sid.Time	☉	0 hr ☽	Noon ☽	True ☊	☿	♀	♂	♃	♄	♅	♆	♇
1 Tu	6 38 52	9♑38 41	13♏50 52	20♏35 2	1♒18.1	10♑ 9.7	20♑ 1.2	9♎42.1	16♏50.8	24♒59.8	27♈30.6	14♍31.5	25♋17.5
2 W	6 42 49	10 39 52	27 25 58	4♐23 36	1R 15.1	11 46.5	21 16.6	10 8.1	17 1.0	25 5.6	27R 30.3	14R 31.0	25R 16.3
3 Th	6 46 45	11 41 3	11♐27 42	18 37 53	1 12.1	13 23.6	22 31.9	10 33.9	17 11.1	25 11.5	27 30.1	14 30.4	25 15.0
4 F	6 50 42	12 42 14	25 53 34	3♑14 3	1 9.6	15 1.1	23 47.3	10 59.5	17 21.1	25 17.5	27 30.0	14 29.9	25 13.8
5 Sa	6 54 38	13 43 25	10♑38 27	18 5 49	1 7.8	16 38.9	25 2.7	11 24.8	17 30.9	25 23.5	27 29.9	14 29.3	25 12.5
6 Su	6 58 35	14 44 36	25 35 7	3♒ 5 15	1D 7.0	18 17.2	26 18.0	11 49.8	17 40.7	25 29.5	27D 29.8	14 28.6	25 11.2
7 M	7 2 32	15 45 47	10♒35 9	18 3 48	1 7.1	19 55.7	27 33.3	12 14.6	17 50.4	25 35.7	27 29.8	14 28.0	25 9.9
8 Tu	7 6 28	16 46 57	25 30 14	2♓53 37	1 7.9	21 34.7	28 48.7	12 39.1	17 60.0	25 41.8	27 29.9	14 27.3	25 8.6
9 W	7 10 25	17 48 7	10♓13 13	17 28 29	1 9.0	23 14.0	0♒ 4.0	13 3.4	18 9.4	25 48.0	27 30.0	14 26.6	25 7.3
10 Th	7 14 21	18 49 17	24 38 56	1♈44 18	1 10.0	24 53.6	1 19.3	13 27.3	18 18.8	25 54.3	27 30.2	14 25.8	25 6.0
11 F	7 18 18	19 50 26	8♈44 23	15 39 9	1R 10.7	26 33.6	2 34.6	13 51.0	18 28.0	26 0.6	27 30.4	14 25.0	25 4.7
12 Sa	7 22 14	20 51 34	22 28 37	29 12 54	1 10.9	28 13.9	3 49.9	14 14.4	18 37.1	26 7.0	27 30.7	14 24.2	25 3.4
13 Su	7 26 11	21 52 42	5♉52 11	12♉26 41	1 10.6	29 54.4	5 5.2	14 37.4	18 46.1	26 13.4	27 31.0	14 23.3	25 2.1
14 M	7 30 7	22 53 49	18 56 40	25 22 26	1 9.9	1♒35.2	6 20.4	15 0.2	18 55.0	26 19.9	27 31.4	14 22.5	25 0.8
15 Tu	7 34 4	23 54 55	1♊44 14	8♊ 2 22	1 9.0	3 16.2	7 35.7	15 22.7	19 3.8	26 26.4	27 31.8	14 21.6	24 59.5
16 W	7 38 1	24 56 1	14 17 8	20 28 48	1 8.0	4 57.2	8 50.9	15 44.9	19 12.5	26 32.9	27 32.3	14 20.6	24 58.1
17 Th	7 41 57	25 57 6	26 37 38	2♋43 54	1 7.3	6 38.3	10 6.1	16 6.7	19 21.0	26 39.5	27 32.8	14 19.7	24 56.8
18 F	7 45 54	26 58 11	8♋47 50	14 49 40	1 6.7	8 19.3	11 21.3	16 28.2	19 29.4	26 46.1	27 33.4	14 18.7	24 55.5
19 Sa	7 49 50	27 59 15	20 49 39	26 48 0	1D 6.5	10 0.1	12 36.5	16 49.4	19 37.7	26 52.8	27 34.0	14 17.7	24 54.2
20 Su	7 53 47	29 0 18	2♌44 58	8♌40 47	1 6.4	11 40.6	13 51.7	17 10.3	19 45.9	26 59.5	27 34.7	14 16.6	24 52.9
21 M	7 57 43	0♒ 1 20	14 35 43	20 30 1	1 6.5	13 20.5	15 6.8	17 30.7	19 53.9	27 6.2	27 35.4	14 15.6	24 51.6
22 Tu	8 1 40	1 2 22	26 24 0	2♍17 58	1R 6.5	14 59.6	16 22.0	17 50.9	20 1.8	27 13.0	27 36.2	14 14.5	24 50.3
23 W	8 5 36	2 3 24	8♍12 16	14 7 15	1 6.5	16 37.8	17 37.1	18 10.7	20 9.6	27 19.8	27 37.1	14 13.3	24 49.0
24 Th	8 9 33	3 4 24	20 3 20	26 0 55	1 6.3	18 14.6	18 52.2	18 30.1	20 17.3	27 26.6	27 37.9	14 12.2	24 47.7
25 F	8 13 30	4 5 24	2♎ 0 27	8♎ 2 26	1 5.9	19 49.8	20 7.3	18 49.1	20 24.8	27 33.5	27 38.9	14 11.0	24 46.4
26 Sa	8 17 26	5 6 24	14 7 22	20 15 44	1 5.6	21 23.0	21 22.4	19 7.7	20 32.2	27 40.3	27 39.9	14 9.8	24 45.1
27 Su	8 21 23	6 7 23	26 28 5	2♏44 55	1D 5.3	22 53.7	22 37.4	19 25.9	20 39.4	27 47.3	27 40.9	14 8.6	24 43.8
28 M	8 25 19	7 8 21	9♏ 6 45	15 34 3	1 5.2	24 21.4	23 52.5	19 43.7	20 46.5	27 54.2	27 42.0	14 7.4	24 42.5
29 Tu	8 29 16	8 9 19	22 7 17	28 46 48	1 5.4	25 45.4	25 7.5	20 1.1	20 53.4	28 1.2	27 43.2	14 6.1	24 41.2
30 W	8 33 12	9 10 16	5♐32 55	12♐25 48	1 5.9	27 5.3	26 22.5	20 18.1	21 0.3	28 8.2	27 44.3	14 4.8	24 39.9
31 Th	8 37 9	10 11 12	19 25 31	26 31 59	1 6.7	28 20.3	27 37.5	20 34.6	21 6.9	28 15.3	27 45.6	14 3.5	24 38.7

LONGITUDE — FEBRUARY 1935

Day	Sid.Time	☉	0 hr ☽	Noon ☽	True ☊	☿	♀	♂	♃	♄	♅	♆	♇
1 F	8 41 5	11♒12 8	3♑44 57	11♑ 4 0	1♒ 7.6	29♒29.6	28♒52.5	20♎50.7	21♏13.5	28♒22.3	27♈46.9	14♍ 2.2	24♋37.4
2 Sa	8 45 2	12 13 3	18 28 31	25 57 42	1R 8.3	0♓32.5	0♓ 7.5	21 6.3	21 19.8	28 29.4	27 48.2	14R 0.9	24R 36.2
3 Su	8 48 59	13 13 57	3♒30 37	11♒ 6 9	1 8.5	1 28.2	1 22.4	21 21.4	21 26.0	28 36.5	27 49.6	13 59.5	24 34.9
4 M	8 52 55	14 14 50	18 43 6	26 20 14	1 8.0	2 15.9	2 37.4	21 36.1	21 32.1	28 43.6	27 51.0	13 58.1	24 33.7
5 Tu	8 56 52	15 15 41	3♓56 15	11♓29 57	1 6.8	2 54.7	3 52.3	21 50.3	21 38.0	28 50.8	27 52.5	13 56.7	24 32.5
6 W	9 0 48	16 16 31	19 0 11	26 25 57	1 5.1	3 24.1	5 7.1	22 3.9	21 43.8	28 57.9	27 54.1	13 55.3	24 31.3
7 Th	9 4 45	17 17 20	3♈46 25	11♈ 0 54	1 2.9	3 43.4	6 22.0	22 17.1	21 49.4	29 5.1	27 55.6	13 53.8	24 30.1
8 F	9 8 41	18 18 8	18 8 56	25 10 15	1 0.9	3R 52.2	7 36.8	22 29.7	21 54.8	29 12.3	27 57.3	13 52.4	24 28.9
9 Sa	9 12 38	19 18 53	2♉ 4 43	8♉52 24	0 59.3	3 50.1	8 51.6	22 41.8	22 0.1	29 19.5	27 58.9	13 50.9	24 27.7
10 Su	9 16 34	20 19 38	15 33 27	22 8 10	0D 58.5	3 37.1	10 6.4	22 53.3	22 5.2	29 26.7	28 0.6	13 49.4	24 26.5
11 M	9 20 31	21 20 21	28 36 55	5♊ 0 9	0 58.6	3 13.5	11 21.1	23 4.3	22 10.2	29 34.0	28 2.4	13 47.9	24 25.4
12 Tu	9 24 28	22 21 2	11♊18 21	17 32 1	0 59.6	2 39.8	12 35.9	23 14.8	22 14.9	29 41.2	28 4.2	13 46.4	24 24.2
13 W	9 28 24	23 21 41	23 41 40	29 47 49	1 1.1	1 56.8	13 50.5	23 24.6	22 19.6	29 48.5	28 6.1	13 44.9	24 23.1
14 Th	9 32 21	24 22 19	5♋50 57	11♋51 34	1 2.9	1 5.7	15 5.2	23 33.9	22 24.0	29 55.7	28 8.0	13 43.3	24 22.0
15 F	9 36 17	25 22 55	17 50 7	23 47 2	1 4.3	0 7.7	16 19.8	23 42.6	22 28.3	0♓ 3.0	28 9.9	13 41.8	24 20.9
16 Sa	9 40 14	26 23 30	29 42 43	5♌37 30	1R 5.0	29♒ 4.6	17 34.4	23 50.7	22 32.4	0 10.3	28 11.9	13 40.2	24 19.8
17 Su	9 44 10	27 24 3	11♌31 45	17 25 45	1 4.5	27 58.0	18 49.0	23 58.2	22 36.4	0 17.5	28 13.9	13 38.6	24 18.7
18 M	9 48 7	28 24 34	23 19 48	29 14 9	1 2.6	26 49.9	20 3.5	24 5.1	22 40.2	0 24.8	28 16.0	13 37.0	24 17.6
19 Tu	9 52 3	29 25 4	5♍ 9 4	11♍ 4 44	0 59.2	25 41.9	21 18.0	24 11.3	22 43.8	0 32.1	28 18.1	13 35.4	24 16.6
20 W	9 56 0	0♓25 32	17 1 26	22 59 21	0 54.6	24 35.7	22 32.4	24 16.9	22 47.2	0 39.4	28 20.2	13 33.8	24 15.5
21 Th	9 59 57	1 25 58	28 58 44	4♎59 51	0 49.1	23 32.9	23 46.9	24 21.8	22 50.4	0 46.7	28 22.4	13 32.2	24 14.5
22 F	10 3 53	2 26 23	11♎ 2 55	17 8 14	0 43.3	22 34.7	25 1.3	24 26.1	22 53.5	0 53.9	28 24.6	13 30.5	24 13.5
23 Sa	10 7 50	3 26 47	23 16 6	29 26 50	0 37.8	21 42.1	26 15.6	24 29.6	22 56.4	1 1.2	28 26.9	13 28.9	24 12.5
24 Su	10 11 46	4 27 9	5♏40 47	11♏58 19	0 33.3	20 55.8	27 29.9	24 32.5	22 59.1	1 8.5	28 29.2	13 27.3	24 11.6
25 M	10 15 43	5 27 30	18 19 49	24 45 40	0 30.2	20 16.4	28 44.2	24 34.7	23 1.7	1 15.8	28 31.5	13 25.6	24 10.6
26 Tu	10 19 39	6 27 50	1♐16 16	7♐51 59	0D 28.8	19 44.2	29 58.5	24 36.2	23 4.0	1 23.0	28 33.9	13 24.0	24 9.7
27 W	10 23 36	7 28 8	14 33 11	21 20 9	0 28.9	19 19.2	1♈12.7	24R 36.9	23 6.2	1 30.3	28 36.3	13 22.3	24 8.8
28 Th	10 27 32	8 28 25	28 13 8	5♑12 17	0 30.0	19 1.5	2 26.9	24 36.9	23 8.2	1 37.6	28 38.7	13 20.7	24 7.9

Astro Data Dy Hr Mn	Planet Ingress Dy Hr Mn
♄⊼♇ 3 11:45	♀ ♒ 8 22:44
♅ D 6 8:34	☿ ♒ 13 1:20
☽0N 9 17:19	☉ ♒ 20 23:28
☽0S 24 1:11	
♄✶♅ 25 22:05	☿ ♓ 1 11:16
	♀ ♓ 1 21:36
☽0N 6 2:41	♄ ♓ 14 14:08
☿ R 8 7:25	☿ ♒ 15 3:02
☽0S 20 7:30	☉ ♓ 19 13:52
♅□♆ 23 12:32	♀ ♈ 26 0:30
♀0N 27 23:18	
♂ R 27 12:11	

Last Aspect Dy Hr Mn	☽ Ingress Dy Hr Mn	Last Aspect Dy Hr Mn	☽ Ingress Dy Hr Mn
1 20:14 ♇ △	♐ 2 4:27	2 14:57 ♅ □	♒ 2 18:26
4 2:38 ♅ △	♑ 4 6:44	4 15:54 ♄ ☌	♓ 4 17:47
6 3:04 ♅ □	♒ 6 7:04	6 8:53 ♇ △	♈ 6 17:49
8 3:14 ♅ ✶	♓ 8 7:17	8 19:09 ♄ ✶	♉ 8 20:22
10 0:45 ♇ △	♈ 10 9:03	11 1:48 ♄ □	♊ 11 2:35
12 11:42 ☿ □	♉ 12 13:24	13 12:09 ♄ △	♋ 13 12:24
14 13:55 ♄ □	♊ 14 20:43	15 20:55 ♅ □	♌ 16 0:35
17 1:48 ♅ ✶	♋ 17 6:37	18 11:17 ☉ ☍	♍ 18 13:33
19 15:44 ☉ ☍	♌ 19 18:27	20 14:32 ♇ ✶	♎ 21 2:02
22 2:27 ♅ △	♍ 22 7:19	23 10:06 ♅ ☍	♏ 23 13:04
24 9:32 ♇ ✶	♎ 24 19:59	25 21:22 ♀ △	♐ 25 21:40
27 2:33 ♄ △	♏ 27 6:46	28 0:44 ♅ △	♑ 28 3:05
29 10:44 ♄ □	♐ 29 14:11		
31 16:21 ☿ ✶	♑ 31 17:47		

☽ Phases & Eclipses Dy Hr Mn	Astro Data
5 5:20 ● 13♑57	1 JANUARY 1935
5 5:35:15 • P 0.001	Julian Day # 12784
11 20:55 ☽ 20♈44	Delta T 23.9 sec
19 15:44 ○ 28♋39	SVP 06♓09'48"
19 15:47 • T 1.350	Obliquity 23°26'56"
27 19:59 ☽ 6♏58	⚷ Chiron 5♊34.3R
	☽ Mean ☊ 2♒15.1
3 16:27 ● 13♒56	1 FEBRUARY 1935
3 16:15:56 • P 0.739	Julian Day # 12815
10 9:25 ☽ 20♉43	Delta T 23.9 sec
18 11:17 ○ 28♌53	SVP 06♓09'42"
26 10:14 ☽ 6♐54	Obliquity 23°26'56"
	⚷ Chiron 4♊38.9R
	☽ Mean ☊ 0♒36.6

MARCH 1935 — LONGITUDE

Day	Sid.Time	☉	0 hr ☽	Noon ☽	True ☊	☿	♀	♂	♃	♄	♅	♆	♇
1 F	10 31 29	9♓28 40	12♑17 37	19♑29 2	0♒31.5	18♒50.9	3♈41.0	24♎36.2	23♏10.0	1♓44.8	28♈41.2	13♍19.0	24♋ 7.0
2 Sa	10 35 26	10 28 54	26 46 17	4♒ 8 54	0R 32.4	18D 47.1	4 55.2	24R 34.7	23 11.6	1 52.1	28 43.8	13R 17.3	24R 6.2
3 Su	10 39 22	11 29 6	11♒36 17	19 7 35	0 32.0	18 49.9	6 9.2	24 32.4	23 13.1	1 59.3	28 46.3	13 15.7	24 5.3
4 M	10 43 19	12 29 16	26 41 49	4♓17 52	0 29.7	18 58.9	7 23.3	24 29.4	23 14.3	2 6.5	28 48.9	13 14.0	24 4.5
5 Tu	10 47 15	13 29 25	11♓54 29	19 30 20	0 25.3	19 13.8	8 37.3	24 25.6	23 15.4	2 13.7	28 51.5	13 12.3	24 3.7
6 W	10 51 12	14 29 32	27 4 8	4♈34 37	0 19.1	19 34.2	9 51.2	24 21.0	23 16.2	2 20.9	28 54.2	13 10.6	24 2.9
7 Th	10 55 8	15 29 37	12♈ 0 38	19 21 13	0 12.0	19 59.8	11 5.2	24 15.7	23 16.9	2 28.1	28 56.9	13 9.0	24 2.2
8 F	10 59 5	16 29 39	26 35 32	3♉43 1	0 4.8	20 30.2	12 19.0	24 9.6	23 17.4	2 35.2	28 59.6	13 7.3	24 1.4
9 Sa	11 3 1	17 29 40	10♉43 15	17 36 6	29♑58.5	21 5.1	13 32.9	24 2.7	23 17.7	2 42.4	29 2.3	13 5.6	24 0.7
10 Su	11 6 58	18 29 39	24 21 33	0♊59 47	29 53.8	21 44.3	14 46.6	23 55.0	23R 17.8	2 49.5	29 5.1	13 4.0	24 0.0
11 M	11 10 55	19 29 36	7♊31 8	13 56 2	29 51.1	22 27.3	16 0.4	23 46.5	23 17.7	2 56.6	29 7.9	13 2.3	23 59.4
12 Tu	11 14 51	20 29 30	20 15 0	26 28 37	29D 50.2	23 14.1	17 14.1	23 37.3	23 17.5	3 3.7	29 10.8	13 0.6	23 58.7
13 W	11 18 48	21 29 22	2♋37 31	8♋42 20	29 50.8	24 4.2	18 27.7	23 27.3	23 17.0	3 10.7	29 13.6	12 59.0	23 58.1
14 Th	11 22 44	22 29 12	14 43 44	20 42 20	29 52.0	24 57.6	19 41.3	23 16.6	23 16.4	3 17.8	29 16.5	12 57.3	23 57.5
15 F	11 26 41	23 29 0	26 38 47	2♌33 40	29R 52.8	25 53.9	20 54.8	23 5.1	23 15.6	3 24.8	29 19.5	12 55.7	23 56.9
16 Sa	11 30 37	24 28 45	8♌27 32	14 20 54	29 52.4	26 53.1	22 8.3	22 52.8	23 14.6	3 31.8	29 22.4	12 54.1	23 56.4
17 Su	11 34 34	25 28 29	20 14 15	26 8 0	29 50.1	27 54.9	23 21.7	22 39.9	23 13.4	3 38.7	29 25.4	12 52.4	23 55.8
18 M	11 38 30	26 28 10	2♍ 2 33	7♍58 12	29 45.3	28 59.3	24 35.1	22 26.2	23 12.0	3 45.6	29 28.4	12 50.8	23 55.3
19 Tu	11 42 27	27 27 49	13 55 17	19 53 59	29 38.0	0♓ 6.0	25 48.4	22 11.8	23 10.4	3 52.5	29 31.4	12 49.2	23 54.8
20 W	11 46 24	28 27 25	25 54 33	1♎57 8	29 28.5	1 14.9	27 1.7	21 56.7	23 8.7	3 59.4	29 34.5	12 47.6	23 54.3
21 Th	11 50 20	29 27 0	8♎ 1 52	14 8 52	29 17.4	2 26.0	28 14.9	21 40.9	23 6.7	4 6.2	29 37.5	12 46.0	23 53.9
22 F	11 54 17	0♈26 33	20 18 15	26 30 5	29 5.7	3 39.1	29 28.0	21 24.4	23 4.6	4 13.1	29 40.6	12 44.4	23 53.5
23 Sa	11 58 13	1 26 4	2♏44 30	9♏ 1 35	28 54.5	4 54.2	0♉41.1	21 7.3	23 2.3	4 19.8	29 43.7	12 42.9	23 53.1
24 Su	12 2 10	2 25 33	15 21 29	21 44 19	28 44.8	6 11.2	1 54.2	20 49.6	22 59.8	4 26.6	29 46.9	12 41.3	23 52.7
25 M	12 6 6	3 25 1	28 10 16	4♐39 31	28 37.3	7 30.0	3 7.2	20 31.3	22 57.2	4 33.3	29 50.0	12 39.8	23 52.4
26 Tu	12 10 3	4 24 26	11♐12 18	17 48 51	28 32.5	8 50.5	4 20.1	20 12.4	22 54.3	4 40.0	29 53.2	12 38.2	23 52.0
27 W	12 13 59	5 23 50	24 29 25	1♑14 14	28D 30.1	10 12.8	5 33.0	19 53.0	22 51.3	4 46.6	29 56.4	12 36.7	23 51.7
28 Th	12 17 56	6 23 12	8♑ 3 31	14 57 30	28 29.6	11 36.6	6 45.8	19 33.1	22 48.1	4 53.2	29 59.6	12 35.2	23 51.5
29 F	12 21 53	7 22 33	21 56 17	28 59 55	28R 29.9	13 2.1	7 58.6	19 12.6	22 44.8	4 59.7	0♉ 2.8	12 33.7	23 51.2
30 Sa	12 25 49	8 21 52	6♒ 8 23	13♒21 30	28 29.8	14 29.2	9 11.3	18 51.8	22 41.2	5 6.3	0 6.1	12 32.2	23 51.0
31 Su	12 29 46	9 21 8	20 38 56	28 0 12	28 28.2	15 57.8	10 23.9	18 30.5	22 37.5	5 12.7	0 9.3	12 30.8	23 50.8

APRIL 1935 — LONGITUDE

Day	Sid.Time	☉	0 hr ☽	Noon ☽	True ☊	☿	♀	♂	♃	♄	♅	♆	♇
1 M	12 33 42	10♈20 23	5♓24 41	12♓51 32	28♑24.0	17♓28.0	11♉36.5	18♎ 8.8	22♏33.6	5♓19.2	0♉12.6	12♍29.3	23♋50.6
2 Tu	12 37 39	11 19 36	20 19 50	27 48 29	28R 17.1	18 59.7	12 49.0	17R 46.8	22R 29.6	5 25.6	0 15.9	12R 27.9	23R 50.5
3 W	12 41 35	12 18 47	5♈16 23	12♈42 20	28 7.6	20 32.8	14 1.5	17 24.4	22 25.4	5 31.9	0 19.2	12 26.5	23 50.4
4 Th	12 45 32	13 17 57	20 5 13	27 23 58	27 56.7	22 7.5	15 13.9	17 1.9	22 21.0	5 38.2	0 22.5	12 25.1	23 50.3
5 F	12 49 28	14 17 4	4♉37 40	11♉45 31	27 45.3	23 43.6	16 26.3	16 39.1	22 16.5	5 44.5	0 25.9	12 23.7	23 50.2
6 Sa	12 53 25	15 16 9	18 46 57	25 41 35	27 35.0	25 21.2	17 38.5	16 16.2	22 11.8	5 50.7	0 29.2	12 22.4	23 50.1
7 Su	12 57 22	16 15 12	2♊29 11	9♊ 9 46	27 26.5	27 0.2	18 50.7	15 53.2	22 6.9	5 56.8	0 32.6	12 21.0	23D 50.1
8 M	13 1 18	17 14 12	15 43 28	22 10 36	27 20.6	28 40.8	20 2.9	15 30.1	22 1.9	6 2.9	0 36.0	12 19.7	23 50.1
9 Tu	13 5 15	18 13 11	28 31 35	4♋46 56	27 17.3	0♈22.8	21 15.0	15 7.0	21 56.8	6 9.0	0 39.3	12 18.4	23 50.1
10 W	13 9 11	19 12 7	10♋57 13	17 3 6	27D 16.0	2 6.3	22 27.0	14 43.9	21 51.5	6 15.0	0 42.7	12 17.2	23 50.2
11 Th	13 13 8	20 11 1	23 5 15	29 4 22	27R 15.8	3 51.4	23 38.9	14 20.8	21 46.1	6 20.9	0 46.1	12 15.9	23 50.3
12 F	13 17 4	21 9 52	5♌ 1 7	10♌56 13	27 15.7	5 37.9	24 50.7	13 57.9	21 40.5	6 26.8	0 49.5	12 14.7	23 50.4
13 Sa	13 21 1	22 8 41	16 50 19	22 44 2	27 14.5	7 26.0	26 2.5	13 35.2	21 34.8	6 32.7	0 53.0	12 13.5	23 50.5
14 Su	13 24 57	23 7 28	28 37 59	4♍32 43	27 11.3	9 15.5	27 14.2	13 12.7	21 29.0	6 38.4	0 56.4	12 12.3	23 50.7
15 M	13 28 54	24 6 13	10♍28 43	16 26 27	27 5.5	11 6.7	28 25.8	12 50.4	21 23.1	6 44.2	0 59.8	12 11.1	23 50.8
16 Tu	13 32 50	25 4 55	22 26 17	28 28 34	26 56.9	12 59.3	29 37.3	12 28.4	21 17.0	6 49.8	1 3.2	12 10.0	23 51.0
17 W	13 36 47	26 3 36	4♎33 32	10♎41 24	26 45.8	14 53.5	0♊48.8	12 6.7	21 10.8	6 55.4	1 6.7	12 8.9	23 51.3
18 Th	13 40 44	27 2 14	16 52 18	23 6 19	26 33.0	16 49.3	2 0.1	11 45.4	21 4.5	7 1.0	1 10.1	12 7.8	23 51.5
19 F	13 44 40	28 0 51	29 23 28	5♏43 46	26 19.4	18 46.6	3 11.4	11 24.5	20 58.1	7 6.5	1 13.5	12 6.7	23 51.8
20 Sa	13 48 37	28 59 25	12♏ 7 8	18 33 32	26 6.2	20 45.4	4 22.6	11 4.0	20 51.6	7 11.9	1 17.0	12 5.7	23 52.1
21 Su	13 52 33	29 57 58	25 2 52	1♐35 4	25 54.7	22 45.6	5 33.7	10 44.1	20 45.0	7 17.3	1 20.4	12 4.7	23 52.4
22 M	13 56 30	0♉56 29	8♐10 3	14 47 46	25 45.7	24 47.4	6 44.8	10 24.6	20 38.2	7 22.6	1 23.9	12 3.7	23 52.8
23 Tu	14 0 26	1 54 58	21 28 12	28 11 20	25 39.6	26 50.4	7 55.7	10 5.6	20 31.4	7 27.8	1 27.3	12 2.7	23 53.2
24 W	14 4 23	2 53 26	4♑57 12	11♑45 51	25 36.3	28 54.8	9 6.6	9 47.2	20 24.5	7 33.0	1 30.8	12 1.8	23 53.6
25 Th	14 8 19	3 51 52	18 37 20	25 31 44	25D 35.1	1♉ 0.4	10 17.3	9 29.4	20 17.6	7 38.1	1 34.2	12 0.9	23 54.0
26 F	14 12 16	4 50 16	2♒29 7	9♒29 29	25R 35.1	3 7.1	11 28.0	9 12.2	20 10.5	7 43.2	1 37.7	12 0.0	23 54.5
27 Sa	14 16 13	5 48 39	16 32 50	23 39 4	25 34.8	5 14.6	12 38.6	8 55.7	20 3.4	7 48.1	1 41.1	11 59.2	23 54.9
28 Su	14 20 9	6 47 0	0♓48 2	7♓59 28	25 33.1	7 23.0	13 49.1	8 39.8	19 56.1	7 53.0	1 44.5	11 58.4	23 55.4
29 M	14 24 6	7 45 20	15 12 57	22 28 1	25 29.1	9 31.9	14 59.5	8 24.6	19 48.9	7 57.9	1 48.0	11 57.6	23 56.0
30 Tu	14 28 2	8 43 38	29 44 3	7♈ 0 21	25 22.4	11 41.1	16 9.8	8 10.1	19 41.5	8 2.6	1 51.4	11 56.8	23 56.5

Astro Data (Dy Hr Mn)	Planet Ingress (Dy Hr Mn)
☿ D 2 1:37	☊ ♑ 8 17:39
☽0N 5 14:01	☿ ♓ 18 21:53
♃ R 10 2:47	☉ ♈ 21 13:18
☽0S 19 13:49	♀ ♉ 22 10:29
	♅ ♉ 28 2:58
☽0N 2 0:39	
♇ D 7 7:55	☿ ♈ 8 18:40
☿0N 11 17:38	♀ ♊ 16 7:37
☽0S 15 20:23	☉ ♉ 21 0:50
☽0N 29 8:38	☿ ♉ 24 12:29

Last Aspect (Dy Hr Mn)	☽ Ingress (Dy Hr Mn)	Last Aspect (Dy Hr Mn)	☽ Ingress (Dy Hr Mn)
2 3:12 ♅ □	♒ 2 5:16	2 5:38 ♇ △	♈ 2 15:31
4 3:21 ♅ ✶	♓ 4 5:13	4 6:08 ♇ □	♉ 4 16:18
5 19:12 ♇ △	♈ 6 4:40	6 12:58 ☿ ✶	♊ 6 19:35
8 4:02 ♅ ☌	♉ 8 5:43	8 3:01 ☉ ✶	♋ 9 2:49
9 23:22 ♇ ✶	♊ 10 10:11	11 1:30 ♇ ☌	♌ 11 13:52
12 17:19 ♅ ✶	♋ 12 18:52	13 20:50 ♀ □	♍ 14 2:47
15 5:27 ♅ □	♌ 15 6:48	16 2:49 ♇ ✶	♎ 16 15:01
17 18:46 ♅ △	♍ 17 19:51	18 21:10 ☉ ☍	♏ 19 1:09
20 5:31 ☉ ☍	♎ 20 8:08	20 21:50 ♇ △	♐ 21 9:06
22 18:12 ♅ ☍	♏ 22 18:44	23 11:20 ☿ △	♑ 23 15:13
24 16:00 ♇ △	♐ 25 3:24	25 9:11 ♇ ☍	♒ 25 19:43
27 9:44 ♅ △	♑ 27 9:49	27 5:53 ♃ □	♓ 27 22:40
29 3:16 ♇ ☍	♒ 29 13:41	29 14:26 ♇ △	♈ 30 0:26
31 3:13 ♃ □	♓ 31 15:15		

☽ Phases & Eclipses (Dy Hr Mn)	
5 2:40	● 13♓36
12 0:30	☽ 20♊31
20 5:31	○ 28♍41
27 20:51	☽ 6♑15
3 12:11	● 12♈49
10 17:42	☽ 19♋56
18 21:10	○ 27♎54
26 4:20	☽ 5♒01

Astro Data

1 MARCH 1935
Julian Day # 12843
Delta T 23.9 sec
SVP 06♓09'39"
Obliquity 23°26'57"
⚷ Chiron 4♊45.5
☽ Mean ☊ 29♑07.6

1 APRIL 1935
Julian Day # 12874
Delta T 23.9 sec
SVP 06♓09'35"
Obliquity 23°26'57"
⚷ Chiron 5♊55.3
☽ Mean ☊ 27♑29.1

LONGITUDE — MAY 1935

Day	Sid.Time	☉	0 hr ☽	Noon ☽	True ☊	☿	♀	♂	♃	♄	♅	♆	♇
1 W	14 31 59	9♉41 55	14♈16 7	21♈30 31	25♑13.2	13♉50.4	17♊20.1	7♎56.4	19♏34.1	8♓ 7.3	1♉54.8	11♍56.1	23♋57.1
2 Th	14 35 55	10 40 10	28 42 42	5♉51 50	25R 2.4	15 59.5	18 30.2	7R 43.4	19R 26.7	8 11.9	1 58.2	11R 55.3	23 57.7
3 F	14 39 52	11 38 23	12♉57 8	19 57 55	24 51.2	18 8.1	19 40.2	7 31.2	19 19.2	8 16.5	2 1.7	11 54.7	23 58.3
4 Sa	14 43 48	12 36 35	26 53 36	3♊43 45	24 40.7	20 15.9	20 50.2	7 19.7	19 11.7	8 20.9	2 5.1	11 54.0	23 58.9
5 Su	14 47 45	13 34 44	10♊28 4	17 6 24	24 32.0	22 22.6	21 60.0	7 9.0	19 4.1	8 25.3	2 8.5	11 53.4	23 59.6
6 M	14 51 42	14 32 53	23 38 47	0♋ 5 19	24 25.8	24 28.0	23 9.7	6 59.1	18 56.5	8 29.6	2 11.9	11 52.8	24 0.3
7 Tu	14 55 38	15 30 59	6♋26 16	12 42 0	24 22.2	26 31.7	24 19.3	6 50.0	18 48.9	8 33.9	2 15.2	11 52.3	24 1.0
8 W	14 59 35	16 29 3	18 52 59	24 59 44	24D 20.7	28 33.4	25 28.8	6 41.8	18 41.3	8 38.0	2 18.6	11 51.7	24 1.7
9 Th	15 3 31	17 27 6	1♌ 2 51	7♌ 2 57	24 20.8	0♊33.0	26 38.2	6 34.3	18 33.6	8 42.1	2 22.0	11 51.2	24 2.5
10 F	15 7 28	18 25 6	13 0 41	18 56 43	24R 21.2	2 30.1	27 47.5	6 27.6	18 26.0	8 46.1	2 25.3	11 50.8	24 3.3
11 Sa	15 11 24	19 23 5	24 51 45	0♍46 26	24 21.2	4 24.7	28 56.7	6 21.8	18 18.3	8 50.0	2 28.7	11 50.4	24 4.1
12 Su	15 15 21	20 21 2	6♍41 26	12 37 21	24 19.7	6 16.4	0♋ 5.7	6 16.7	18 10.7	8 53.9	2 32.0	11 49.9	24 4.9
13 M	15 19 17	21 18 57	18 34 48	24 34 20	24 16.2	8 5.2	1 14.6	6 12.5	18 3.1	8 57.6	2 35.3	11 49.6	24 5.7
14 Tu	15 23 14	22 16 50	0♎36 26	6♎41 33	24 10.3	9 51.0	2 23.4	6 9.0	17 55.5	9 1.3	2 38.6	11 49.2	24 6.6
15 W	15 27 11	23 14 41	12 50 3	19 2 14	24 2.3	11 33.5	3 32.0	6 6.4	17 47.9	9 4.9	2 41.9	11 48.9	24 7.5
16 Th	15 31 7	24 12 31	25 18 21	1♏38 31	23 52.7	13 12.9	4 40.5	6 4.5	17 40.3	9 8.4	2 45.2	11 48.7	24 8.4
17 F	15 35 4	25 10 19	8♏ 2 49	14 31 14	23 42.4	14 48.8	5 48.9	6D 3.4	17 32.8	9 11.8	2 48.4	11 48.4	24 9.3
18 Sa	15 39 0	26 8 6	21 3 41	27 40 1	23 32.4	16 21.4	6 57.1	6 3.1	17 25.2	9 15.2	2 51.7	11 48.2	24 10.2
19 Su	15 42 57	27 5 52	4♐20 3	11♐ 3 30	23 23.7	17 50.6	8 5.2	6 3.6	17 17.8	9 18.4	2 54.9	11 48.0	24 11.2
20 M	15 46 53	28 3 36	17 50 7	24 39 35	23 17.0	19 16.2	9 13.1	6 4.8	17 10.4	9 21.6	2 58.1	11 47.9	24 12.2
21 Tu	15 50 50	29 1 19	1♑31 37	8♑25 57	23 12.7	20 38.3	10 20.9	6 6.8	17 3.0	9 24.6	3 1.3	11 47.8	24 13.2
22 W	15 54 46	29 59 0	15 22 17	22 20 23	23D 10.8	21 56.8	11 28.6	6 9.5	16 55.7	9 27.6	3 4.4	11 47.7	24 14.2
23 Th	15 58 43	0♊56 41	29 20 3	6♒21 4	23 10.6	23 11.6	12 36.1	6 12.9	16 48.4	9 30.5	3 7.6	11 47.6	24 15.3
24 F	16 2 40	1 54 20	13♒23 17	20 26 33	23 11.5	24 22.8	13 43.4	6 17.0	16 41.3	9 33.3	3 10.7	11D 47.6	24 16.3
25 Sa	16 6 36	2 51 59	27 30 42	4♓35 34	23R 12.3	25 30.2	14 50.6	6 21.9	16 34.1	9 36.1	3 13.8	11 47.6	24 17.4
26 Su	16 10 33	3 49 36	11♓40 58	18 46 43	23 12.2	26 33.8	15 57.7	6 27.5	16 27.1	9 38.7	3 16.9	11 47.7	24 18.5
27 M	16 14 29	4 47 13	25 52 32	2♈58 7	23 10.3	27 33.5	17 4.5	6 33.7	16 20.1	9 41.2	3 20.0	11 47.8	24 19.6
28 Tu	16 18 26	5 44 48	10♈ 3 9	17 7 13	23 6.5	28 29.3	18 11.3	6 40.7	16 13.2	9 43.7	3 23.0	11 47.9	24 20.8
29 W	16 22 22	6 42 23	24 9 53	1♉10 43	23 0.9	29 21.0	19 17.8	6 48.3	16 6.4	9 46.0	3 26.0	11 48.0	24 21.9
30 Th	16 26 19	7 39 57	8♉ 9 13	15 4 55	22 54.0	0♋ 8.7	20 24.2	6 56.6	15 59.7	9 48.3	3 29.0	11 48.2	24 23.1
31 F	16 30 15	8 37 30	21 57 21	28 46 8	22 46.8	0 52.3	21 30.4	7 5.5	15 53.1	9 50.4	3 32.0	11 48.4	24 24.3

LONGITUDE — JUNE 1935

Day	Sid.Time	☉	0 hr ☽	Noon ☽	True ☊	☿	♀	♂	♃	♄	♅	♆	♇
1 Sa	16 34 12	9♊35 2	5♊30 53	12♊11 19	22♑40.0	1♋31.6	22♋36.4	7♎15.1	15♏46.6	9♓52.5	3♉35.0	11♍48.7	24♋25.5
2 Su	16 38 9	10 32 33	18 47 14	25 18 29	22R 34.4	2 6.5	23 42.2	7 25.4	15R 40.2	9 54.5	3 37.9	11 48.9	24 26.7
3 M	16 42 5	11 30 3	1♋45 3	8♋ 6 59	22 30.6	2 37.1	24 47.8	7 36.2	15 34.0	9 56.3	3 40.8	11 49.3	24 28.0
4 Tu	16 46 2	12 27 32	14 24 26	20 37 39	22D 28.7	3 3.2	25 53.3	7 47.7	15 27.8	9 58.1	3 43.7	11 49.6	24 29.2
5 W	16 49 58	13 25 0	26 46 56	2♌52 39	22 28.5	3 24.8	26 58.5	7 59.8	15 21.7	9 59.8	3 46.5	11 50.0	24 30.5
6 Th	16 53 55	14 22 27	8♌55 16	14 55 15	22 29.5	3 41.9	28 3.5	8 12.5	15 15.8	10 1.4	3 49.3	11 50.4	24 31.8
7 F	16 57 51	15 19 52	20 53 10	26 49 34	22 31.1	3 54.3	29 8.3	8 25.8	15 10.0	10 2.9	3 52.1	11 50.8	24 33.1
8 Sa	17 1 48	16 17 17	2♍45 4	8♍40 17	22 32.6	4 2.1	0♌12.9	8 39.6	15 4.3	10 4.3	3 54.9	11 51.3	24 34.4
9 Su	17 5 45	17 14 40	14 35 49	20 32 19	22R 33.4	4R 5.4	1 17.3	8 54.0	14 58.8	10 5.6	3 57.6	11 51.8	24 35.7
10 M	17 9 41	18 12 2	26 30 23	2♎30 38	22 33.0	4 4.1	2 21.4	9 9.0	14 53.4	10 6.7	4 0.3	11 52.3	24 37.1
11 Tu	17 13 38	19 9 23	8♎33 38	14 39 54	22 31.3	3 58.3	3 25.3	9 24.5	14 48.1	10 7.8	4 3.0	11 52.9	24 38.4
12 W	17 17 34	20 6 43	20 49 57	27 4 12	22 28.2	3 48.3	4 28.9	9 40.5	14 43.0	10 8.8	4 5.6	11 53.5	24 39.8
13 Th	17 21 31	21 4 2	3♏23 1	9♏46 41	22 24.1	3 34.1	5 32.3	9 57.0	14 38.0	10 9.7	4 8.2	11 54.1	24 41.2
14 F	17 25 27	22 1 20	16 15 23	22 49 15	22 19.4	3 16.1	6 35.4	10 14.0	14 33.2	10 10.5	4 10.8	11 54.8	24 42.6
15 Sa	17 29 24	22 58 38	29 28 16	6♐12 20	22 14.8	2 54.4	7 38.2	10 31.6	14 28.5	10 11.2	4 13.3	11 55.5	24 44.0
16 Su	17 33 20	23 55 55	13♐ 1 16	19 54 47	22 10.7	2 29.5	8 40.7	10 49.6	14 24.0	10 11.9	4 15.9	11 56.2	24 45.4
17 M	17 37 17	24 53 11	26 52 29	3♑53 55	22 7.8	2 1.6	9 43.0	11 8.1	14 19.6	10 12.4	4 18.3	11 57.0	24 46.9
18 Tu	17 41 14	25 50 26	10♑58 35	18 5 56	22D 6.2	1 31.4	10 45.0	11 27.0	14 15.4	10 12.8	4 20.8	11 57.7	24 48.3
19 W	17 45 10	26 47 42	25 15 24	2♒26 23	22 5.8	0 59.3	11 46.6	11 46.4	14 11.3	10 13.1	4 23.2	11 58.6	24 49.8
20 Th	17 49 7	27 44 56	9♒38 18	16 50 39	22 6.5	0 25.7	12 48.0	12 6.3	14 7.4	10 13.3	4 25.6	11 59.4	24 51.2
21 F	17 53 3	28 42 11	24 2 52	1♓14 32	22 7.8	29♊51.3	13 49.0	12 26.6	14 3.7	10R 13.4	4 27.9	12 0.3	24 52.7
22 Sa	17 57 0	29 39 25	8♓25 11	15 34 28	22 9.1	29 16.7	14 49.7	12 47.3	14 0.1	10 13.4	4 30.2	12 1.2	24 54.2
23 Su	18 0 56	0♋36 39	22 42 3	29 47 39	22R 10.0	28 42.4	15 50.1	13 8.4	13 56.7	10 13.3	4 32.5	12 2.1	24 55.7
24 M	18 4 53	1 33 53	6♈51 1	13♈51 56	22 10.1	28 9.1	16 50.1	13 30.0	13 53.5	10 13.1	4 34.7	12 3.1	24 57.2
25 Tu	18 8 49	2 31 7	20 50 12	27 45 40	22 9.3	27 37.3	17 49.8	13 51.9	13 50.4	10 12.8	4 36.9	12 4.1	24 58.7
26 W	18 12 46	3 28 21	4♉38 11	11♉27 36	22 7.6	27 7.5	18 49.1	14 14.3	13 47.5	10 12.5	4 39.0	12 5.1	25 0.2
27 Th	18 16 43	4 25 35	18 13 48	24 56 41	22 5.5	26 40.3	19 48.1	14 37.0	13 44.8	10 12.0	4 41.2	12 6.2	25 1.8
28 F	18 20 39	5 22 49	1♊36 8	8♊12 5	22 3.1	26 16.2	20 46.6	15 0.2	13 42.2	10 11.4	4 43.2	12 7.2	25 3.3
29 Sa	18 24 36	6 20 2	14 44 29	21 13 16	22 1.0	25 55.5	21 44.8	15 23.7	13 39.9	10 10.7	4 45.3	12 8.4	25 4.9
30 Su	18 28 32	7 17 16	27 38 27	4♋ 0 4	21 59.3	25 38.7	22 42.5	15 47.6	13 37.7	10 9.9	4 47.3	12 9.5	25 6.4

Astro Data	Planet Ingress	Last Aspect	☽ Ingress	Last Aspect	☽ Ingress	☽ Phases & Eclipses	Astro Data
Dy Hr Mn	Dy Hr Mn	Dy Hr Mn	Dy Hr Mn	Dy Hr Mn	Dy Hr Mn	Dy Hr Mn	1 MAY 1935
☽0S 13 3:18	☿ ♊ 8 17:20	1 16:04 ♇ □	♉ 2 2:09	1 11:19 ♆ □	♋ 2 20:43	2 21:36 ● 11♉33	Julian Day # 12904
♄□♇ 15 23:41	♀ ♋ 11 22:01	3 18:56 ♇ ✶	♊ 4 5:26	5 0:25 ♀ ☌	♌ 5 6:19	10 11:54 ☽ 18♌54	Delta T 23.9 sec
♂ D 17 21:37	☉ ♊ 22 0:25	5 23:01 ♀ ☌	♋ 6 11:50	6 12:35 ♃ □	♍ 7 18:26	18 9:57 ○ 26♏32	SVP 06♓09'32"
♆ D 24 0:16	☿ ♋ 29 19:26	8 10:06 ♇ ☌	♌ 8 21:55	9 20:12 ♇ ✶	♎ 10 7:00	25 9:44 ☽ 3♓15	Obliquity 23°26'56"
☽0N 26 14:05		11 9:11 ♀ ✶	♍ 11 10:26	12 7:24 ♇ □	♏ 12 17:35		⚷ Chiron 7♊50.0
	♀ ♌ 7 19:11	13 11:04 ♇ ✶	♎ 13 22:48	14 15:27 ♇ △	♐ 15 0:57	1 7:52 ● 9♊54	☽ Mean ☊ 25♑53.8
☽0S 9 10:33	☿ ♊ 20 17:58	15 21:46 ♇ □	♏ 16 8:54	16 20:20 ☉ ☍	♑ 17 5:21	9 5:49 ☽ 17♍29	
☿ R 9 5:06	☉ ♋ 22 8:38	18 9:57 ☉ ☍	♐ 18 16:13	18 23:17 ♇ ☍	♒ 19 7:56	16 20:20 ○ 24♐44	1 JUNE 1935
♄ R 21 14:27		20 2:49 ☿ ☍	♑ 20 21:20	21 9:19 ☿ △	♓ 21 9:56	23 14:21 ☽ 1♈11	Julian Day # 12935
☽0N 22 18:56		22 15:17 ♇ ☍	♒ 23 1:08	23 9:46 ☿ □	♈ 23 12:21	30 19:44 ● 8♋04	Delta T 23.8 sec
		24 20:18 ☿ △	♓ 25 4:13	25 11:20 ☿ ✶	♉ 25 15:54	30 19:59:16 • P 0.338	SVP 06♓09'27"
		27 3:03 ☿ □	♈ 27 6:59	27 12:11 ♇ ✶	♊ 27 21:06		Obliquity 23°26'55"
		29 9:25 ☿ ✶	♉ 29 9:59	29 20:20 ☿ ☌	♋ 30 4:26		⚷ Chiron 10♊14.6
		31 4:18 ♇ ✶	♊ 31 14:11				☽ Mean ☊ 24♑15.3

JULY 1935 LONGITUDE

Day	Sid.Time	☉	0 hr ☽	Noon ☽	True ☊	☿	♀	♂	♃	♄	♅	♆	♇
1 M	18 32 29	8♋14 30	10♋18 8	16♋32 47	21♑58.3	25♊26.0	23♌39.8	16♎11.9	13♏35.6	10♓ 9.1	4♉49.2	12♍10.7	25♋ 8.0
2 Tu	18 36 25	9 11 44	22 44 9	28 52 25	21D58.0	25R17.7	24 36.7	16 36.5	13R33.8	10R 8.1	4 51.2	12 11.9	25 9.6
3 W	18 40 22	10 8 57	4♌57 47	11♌ 0 33	21 58.3	25D14.1	25 33.1	17 1.5	13 32.1	10 7.0	4 53.0	12 13.1	25 11.2
4 Th	18 44 18	11 6 10	17 1 1	22 59 32	21 59.1	25 15.2	26 29.1	17 26.9	13 30.7	10 5.8	4 54.9	12 14.3	25 12.7
5 F	18 48 15	12 3 23	28 56 30	4♍52 22	22 0.1	25 21.3	27 24.5	17 52.6	13 29.4	10 4.6	4 56.7	12 15.6	25 14.3
6 Sa	18 52 12	13 0 36	10♍47 35	16 42 40	22 1.0	25 32.3	28 19.4	18 18.6	13 28.2	10 3.2	4 58.4	12 16.9	25 15.9
7 Su	18 56 8	13 57 48	22 38 7	28 34 31	22 1.8	25 48.5	29 13.8	18 44.9	13 27.3	10 1.7	5 0.1	12 18.2	25 17.5
8 M	19 0 5	14 55 1	4♎32 24	10♎32 21	22R 2.2	26 9.7	0♍ 7.7	19 11.6	13 26.5	10 0.2	5 1.8	12 19.6	25 19.1
9 Tu	19 4 1	15 52 13	16 34 56	22 40 44	22 2.4	26 36.1	1 1.0	19 38.6	13 26.0	9 58.6	5 3.4	12 21.0	25 20.7
10 W	19 7 58	16 49 25	28 50 18	5♏ 4 9	22 2.2	27 7.5	1 53.7	20 5.9	13 25.6	9 56.8	5 5.0	12 22.4	25 22.4
11 Th	19 11 54	17 46 37	11♏22 46	17 46 35	22 1.9	27 44.0	2 45.8	20 33.5	13D25.4	9 55.0	5 6.5	12 23.8	25 24.0
12 F	19 15 51	18 43 49	24 15 58	0♐51 11	22 1.5	28 25.6	3 37.3	21 1.4	13 25.3	9 53.1	5 8.0	12 25.3	25 25.6
13 Sa	19 19 47	19 41 1	7♐32 27	14 19 50	22 1.2	29 12.2	4 28.1	21 29.6	13 25.5	9 51.1	5 9.4	12 26.8	25 27.2
14 Su	19 23 44	20 38 13	21 13 16	28 12 36	22 1.0	0♋ 3.7	5 18.2	21 58.1	13 25.8	9 49.0	5 10.8	12 28.3	25 28.8
15 M	19 27 41	21 35 25	5♑17 30	12♑27 31	22D 1.0	1 0.1	6 7.6	22 26.8	13 26.3	9 46.8	5 12.2	12 29.8	25 30.5
16 Tu	19 31 37	22 32 38	19 42 5	27 0 30	22R 1.0	2 1.3	6 56.3	22 55.9	13 27.0	9 44.5	5 13.5	12 31.4	25 32.1
17 W	19 35 34	23 29 51	4♒21 59	11♒45 38	22 1.0	3 7.3	7 44.2	23 25.1	13 27.9	9 42.2	5 14.8	12 32.9	25 33.7
18 Th	19 39 30	24 27 4	19 10 33	26 35 47	22 0.8	4 18.0	8 31.3	23 54.7	13 29.0	9 39.7	5 16.0	12 34.5	25 35.4
19 F	19 43 27	25 24 18	4♓ 0 27	11♓23 40	22 0.6	5 33.4	9 17.6	24 24.5	13 30.2	9 37.2	5 17.2	12 36.2	25 37.0
20 Sa	19 47 23	26 21 32	18 44 38	26 2 39	22 0.2	6 53.2	10 3.1	24 54.6	13 31.6	9 34.6	5 18.3	12 37.8	25 38.6
21 Su	19 51 20	27 18 47	3♈17 7	10♈27 34	21 59.7	8 17.5	10 47.7	25 24.9	13 33.2	9 31.9	5 19.4	12 39.5	25 40.2
22 M	19 55 17	28 16 3	17 33 39	24 35 7	21D59.4	9 46.2	11 31.4	25 55.5	13 34.9	9 29.2	5 20.4	12 41.1	25 41.9
23 Tu	19 59 13	29 13 20	1♉31 49	8♉23 43	21 59.3	11 19.0	12 14.1	26 26.3	13 36.9	9 26.3	5 21.4	12 42.8	25 43.5
24 W	20 3 10	0♌10 38	15 10 50	21 53 17	21 59.5	12 55.8	12 55.9	26 57.4	13 39.0	9 23.4	5 22.3	12 44.6	25 45.1
25 Th	20 7 6	1 7 56	28 31 13	5♊ 4 49	22 0.1	14 36.5	13 36.7	27 28.7	13 41.3	9 20.4	5 23.2	12 46.3	25 46.8
26 F	20 11 3	2 5 16	11♊34 17	17 59 51	22 1.0	16 20.9	14 16.4	28 0.2	13 43.7	9 17.3	5 24.1	12 48.1	25 48.4
27 Sa	20 14 59	3 2 36	24 21 45	0♋40 14	22 1.9	18 8.7	14 55.1	28 32.0	13 46.4	9 14.1	5 24.8	12 49.9	25 50.0
28 Su	20 18 56	3 59 58	6♋55 30	13 7 48	22 2.7	19 59.6	15 32.6	29 4.0	13 49.2	9 10.9	5 25.6	12 51.7	25 51.6
29 M	20 22 52	4 57 20	19 17 22	25 24 24	22R 3.2	21 53.4	16 8.9	29 36.3	13 52.2	9 7.6	5 26.3	12 53.5	25 53.3
30 Tu	20 26 49	5 54 43	1♌29 6	7♌31 43	22 3.0	23 49.7	16 44.1	0♏ 8.8	13 55.3	9 4.2	5 26.9	12 55.4	25 54.9
31 W	20 30 46	6 52 7	13 32 27	19 31 33	22 2.0	25 48.3	17 17.9	0 41.5	13 58.6	9 0.8	5 27.5	12 57.2	25 56.5

AUGUST 1935 LONGITUDE

Day	Sid.Time	☉	0 hr ☽	Noon ☽	True ☊	☿	♀	♂	♃	♄	♅	♆	♇
1 Th	20 34 42	7♌49 31	25♌29 14	1♍25 46	22♑ 0.4	27♋48.8	17♍50.5	1♏14.4	14♏ 2.1	8♓57.3	5♉28.1	12♍59.1	25♋58.1
2 F	20 38 39	8 46 56	7♍21 26	13 16 32	21R58.1	29 50.8	18 21.6	1 47.5	14 5.8	8R53.7	5 28.6	13 1.0	25 59.7
3 Sa	20 42 35	9 44 22	19 11 24	25 6 24	21 55.3	1♌54.0	18 51.3	2 20.8	14 9.6	8 50.1	5 29.0	13 2.9	26 1.3
4 Su	20 46 32	10 41 49	1♎ 1 54	6♎58 20	21 52.5	3 58.1	19 19.6	2 54.4	14 13.6	8 46.4	5 29.4	13 4.9	26 2.9
5 M	20 50 28	11 39 17	12 56 8	18 55 48	21 50.0	6 2.6	19 46.3	3 28.1	14 17.7	8 42.6	5 29.8	13 6.8	26 4.5
6 Tu	20 54 25	12 36 45	24 57 48	1♏ 2 41	21 48.1	8 7.4	20 11.4	4 2.1	14 22.1	8 38.8	5 30.1	13 8.8	26 6.0
7 W	20 58 21	13 34 14	7♏10 58	13 23 10	21D47.1	10 12.2	20 34.9	4 36.3	14 26.5	8 35.0	5 30.3	13 10.7	26 7.6
8 Th	21 2 18	14 31 44	19 39 52	26 1 27	21 47.0	12 16.6	20 56.6	5 10.6	14 31.2	8 31.0	5 30.5	13 12.7	26 9.2
9 F	21 6 15	15 29 14	2♐28 41	9♐ 1 44	21 47.9	14 20.6	21 16.6	5 45.1	14 36.0	8 27.1	5 30.7	13 14.7	26 10.7
10 Sa	21 10 11	16 26 46	15 41 5	22 26 59	21 49.2	16 23.8	21 34.7	6 19.9	14 40.9	8 23.1	5 30.8	13 16.8	26 12.3
11 Su	21 14 8	17 24 18	29 19 38	6♑19 5	21 50.7	18 26.1	21 50.9	6 54.8	14 46.0	8 19.0	5R30.9	13 18.8	26 13.8
12 M	21 18 4	18 21 52	13♑25 12	20 37 44	21R51.7	20 27.5	22 5.1	7 29.9	14 51.3	8 14.9	5 30.9	13 20.8	26 15.4
13 Tu	21 22 1	19 19 26	27 56 14	5♒20 2	21 51.8	22 27.7	22 17.3	8 5.2	14 56.7	8 10.7	5 30.8	13 22.9	26 16.9
14 W	21 25 57	20 17 1	12♒48 21	20 20 11	21 50.6	24 26.7	22 27.5	8 40.6	15 2.3	8 6.5	5 30.7	13 25.0	26 18.4
15 Th	21 29 54	21 14 38	27 54 25	5♓29 50	21 48.1	26 24.5	22 35.4	9 16.2	15 8.0	8 2.3	5 30.6	13 27.1	26 19.9
16 F	21 33 50	22 12 15	13♓ 5 13	20 39 17	21 44.4	28 20.9	22 41.3	9 52.0	15 13.8	7 58.0	5 30.4	13 29.2	26 21.4
17 Sa	21 37 47	23 9 54	28 10 52	5♈38 52	21 40.1	0♍16.0	22 44.8	10 28.0	15 19.9	7 53.7	5 30.2	13 31.3	26 22.9
18 Su	21 41 44	24 7 35	13♈ 2 21	20 20 33	21 35.8	2 9.7	22R46.1	11 4.1	15 26.0	7 49.4	5 29.9	13 33.4	26 24.4
19 M	21 45 40	25 5 17	27 32 53	4♉38 58	21 32.3	4 2.0	22 45.1	11 40.4	15 32.3	7 45.0	5 29.5	13 35.5	26 25.9
20 Tu	21 49 37	26 3 1	11♉38 34	18 31 39	21 30.0	5 52.9	22 41.8	12 16.9	15 38.7	7 40.6	5 29.1	13 37.6	26 27.3
21 W	21 53 33	27 0 46	25 18 19	1♊58 47	21D29.1	7 42.4	22 36.1	12 53.5	15 45.3	7 36.2	5 28.7	13 39.8	26 28.8
22 Th	21 57 30	27 58 33	8♊33 22	15 2 26	21 29.5	9 30.5	22 28.1	13 30.3	15 52.0	7 31.7	5 28.2	13 41.9	26 30.2
23 F	22 1 26	28 56 22	21 26 25	27 45 47	21 30.8	11 17.3	22 17.7	14 7.2	15 58.9	7 27.2	5 27.7	13 44.1	26 31.6
24 Sa	22 5 23	29 54 13	4♋ 1 0	10♋12 31	21 32.4	13 2.6	22 4.9	14 44.3	16 5.9	7 22.8	5 27.1	13 46.3	26 33.0
25 Su	22 9 19	0♍52 5	16 20 49	22 26 18	21R33.4	14 46.6	21 49.8	15 21.6	16 13.0	7 18.2	5 26.5	13 48.4	26 34.4
26 M	22 13 16	1 49 59	28 29 24	4♌30 28	21 33.3	16 29.3	21 32.4	15 59.1	16 20.3	7 13.7	5 25.8	13 50.6	26 35.8
27 Tu	22 17 13	2 47 55	10♌29 52	16 27 54	21 31.4	18 10.6	21 12.7	16 36.6	16 27.7	7 9.2	5 25.1	13 52.8	26 37.2
28 W	22 21 9	3 45 52	22 24 51	28 20 59	21 27.6	19 50.6	20 50.8	17 14.4	16 35.2	7 4.6	5 24.3	13 55.0	26 38.6
29 Th	22 25 6	4 43 51	4♍16 32	10♍11 45	21 21.8	21 29.3	20 26.8	17 52.3	16 42.9	7 0.1	5 23.5	13 57.2	26 39.9
30 F	22 29 2	5 41 51	16 6 50	22 2 0	21 14.3	23 6.8	20 0.8	18 30.3	16 50.7	6 55.5	5 22.6	13 59.4	26 41.2
31 Sa	22 32 59	6 39 53	27 57 27	3♎53 28	21 5.7	24 42.9	19 32.8	19 8.5	16 58.6	6 50.9	5 21.7	14 1.6	26 42.5

Astro Data Dy Hr Mn	Planet Ingress Dy Hr Mn
♄□♇ 1 10:00	♀ ♍ 7 20:33
☿ D 3 6:24	☿ ♋ 13 22:22
☽0S 6 17:54	☉ ♌ 23 19:33
♃ D 11 15:39	♂ ♏ 29 17:32
☽0N 20 1:27	
	☿ ♌ 2 1:48
☽0S 3 0:59	☿ ♍ 16 20:39
♀0S 8 6:21	☉ ♍ 24 2:24
♅ R 11 15:49	
☽0N 16 10:33	
♀ R 18 1:41	
☽0S 30 7:31	

Last Aspect Dy Hr Mn	☽ Ingress Dy Hr Mn	Last Aspect Dy Hr Mn	☽ Ingress Dy Hr Mn
2 4:44 ♇ ☌	♌ 2 14:13	31 0:53 ♃ □	♍ 1 9:07
4 20:39 ♀ ☌	♍ 5 2:08	3 13:53 ♇ ⚹	♎ 3 21:55
7 6:36 ☿ □	♎ 7 14:52	6 2:15 ♇ □	♏ 6 9:57
9 20:31 ☿ △	♏ 10 2:15	8 12:16 ♇ △	♐ 8 19:25
12 2:08 ♇ △	♐ 12 10:27	10 10:41 ♀ □	♑ 11 1:10
14 1:20 ♂ ⚹	♑ 14 15:03	12 21:17 ♇ ☍	♒ 13 3:22
16 9:36 ♇ ☍	♒ 16 16:53	14 21:17 ☿ ☍	♓ 15 3:19
18 7:55 ♂ △	♓ 18 17:30	16 21:07 ♇ △	♈ 17 2:55
20 13:24 ☉ △	♈ 20 18:33	18 22:08 ♇ □	♉ 19 4:07
22 19:42 ☉ □	♉ 22 21:21	21 3:17 ☉ □	♊ 21 8:25
24 19:01 ♇ ⚹	♊ 25 2:42	23 15:26 ☉ ⚹	♋ 23 16:17
27 8:16 ♂ △	♋ 27 10:43	25 20:14 ♇ ☌	♌ 26 3:00
29 12:59 ♇ ☌	♌ 29 21:04	27 12:59 ♂ □	♍ 28 15:20
		30 21:28 ♇ ⚹	♎ 31 4:08

☽ Phases & Eclipses Dy Hr Mn		Astro Data
8 22:28	☽ 15♎49	1 JULY 1935
16 5:00	○ 22♑45	Julian Day # 12965
16 4:60	☍T 1.754	Delta T 23.8 sec
22 19:42	☽ 29♈03	SVP 06♓09'22"
30 9:32	● 6♌18	Obliquity 23°26'55"
30 9:16:04	☌P 0.232	⚷ Chiron 12♊36.5
		☽ Mean ☊ 22♑40.0
7 13:23	☽ 14♏06	1 AUGUST 1935
14 12:43	○ 20♒48	Julian Day # 12996
21 3:17	☽ 27♉09	Delta T 23.8 sec
29 1:00	● 4♍46	SVP 06♓09'16"
		Obliquity 23°26'55"
		⚷ Chiron 14♊41.1
		☽ Mean ☊ 21♑01.5

LONGITUDE — SEPTEMBER 1935

Day	Sid.Time	☉	0 hr ☽	Noon ☽	True ☊	☿	♀	♂	♃	♄	♅	♆	♇
1 Su	22 36 55	7♍37 56	9♎50 15	15♎48 5	20♑56.9	26♍17.7	19♍ 3.1	19♏46.8	17♏ 6.6	6♓46.3	5♉20.8	14♍ 3.8	26♋43.8
2 M	22 40 52	8 36 1	21 47 17	27 48 10	20R48.7	27 51.3	18R31.8	20 25.3	17 14.8	6R41.8	5R19.8	14 6.1	26 45.1
3 Tu	22 44 48	9 34 8	3♏51 6	9♏56 28	20 41.8	29 23.6	17 59.0	21 4.0	17 23.1	6 37.2	5 18.7	14 8.3	26 46.4
4 W	22 48 45	10 32 16	16 4 43	22 16 18	20 36.8	0♎54.7	17 24.9	21 42.7	17 31.5	6 32.7	5 17.6	14 10.5	26 47.6
5 Th	22 52 41	11 30 25	28 31 41	4♐51 23	20 33.9	2 24.5	16 49.7	22 21.6	17 40.0	6 28.1	5 16.5	14 12.7	26 48.9
6 F	22 56 38	12 28 36	11♐15 54	17 45 42	20D32.9	3 53.0	16 13.7	23 0.7	17 48.7	6 23.6	5 15.3	14 14.9	26 50.1
7 Sa	23 0 35	13 26 49	24 21 17	1♑ 3 4	20 33.4	5 20.2	15 37.1	23 39.9	17 57.4	6 19.1	5 14.1	14 17.2	26 51.3
8 Su	23 4 31	14 25 3	7♑51 22	14 46 29	20R34.3	6 46.2	15 0.1	24 19.2	18 6.3	6 14.6	5 12.9	14 19.4	26 52.5
9 M	23 8 28	15 23 18	21 48 30	28 57 25	20 34.8	8 10.8	14 22.9	24 58.6	18 15.3	6 10.1	5 11.5	14 21.6	26 53.7
10 Tu	23 12 24	16 21 35	6♒13 2	13♒34 54	20 33.8	9 34.1	13 45.8	25 38.2	18 24.4	6 5.6	5 10.2	14 23.9	26 54.8
11 W	23 16 21	17 19 53	21 2 26	28 34 46	20 30.7	10 56.0	13 9.0	26 17.9	18 33.6	6 1.2	5 8.8	14 26.1	26 56.0
12 Th	23 20 17	18 18 13	6♓10 51	13♓49 28	20 25.1	12 16.5	12 32.8	26 57.7	18 42.9	5 56.8	5 7.4	14 28.3	26 57.1
13 F	23 24 14	19 16 35	21 29 16	29 8 48	20 17.6	13 35.6	11 57.4	27 37.6	18 52.3	5 52.4	5 5.9	14 30.5	26 58.2
14 Sa	23 28 10	20 14 59	6♈46 39	14♈21 26	20 8.7	14 53.2	11 23.1	28 17.7	19 1.8	5 48.0	5 4.4	14 32.7	26 59.2
15 Su	23 32 7	21 13 24	21 51 54	29 16 59	19 59.8	16 9.2	10 50.0	28 57.9	19 11.4	5 43.7	5 2.9	14 35.0	27 0.3
16 M	23 36 4	22 11 52	6♉35 49	13♉47 45	19 51.8	17 23.7	10 18.4	29 38.2	19 21.2	5 39.4	5 1.3	14 37.2	27 1.3
17 Tu	23 40 0	23 10 22	20 52 24	27 49 34	19 45.7	18 36.4	9 48.4	0♐18.6	19 31.0	5 35.2	4 59.7	14 39.4	27 2.4
18 W	23 43 57	24 8 54	4♊39 16	11♊21 42	19 41.8	19 47.4	9 20.2	0 59.1	19 40.9	5 31.0	4 58.0	14 41.6	27 3.4
19 Th	23 47 53	25 7 29	17 57 11	24 26 10	19D40.1	20 56.6	8 54.0	1 39.8	19 50.9	5 26.8	4 56.3	14 43.8	27 4.3
20 F	23 51 50	26 6 5	0♋49 11	7♋ 6 46	19 40.0	22 3.8	8 29.8	2 20.5	20 1.1	5 22.7	4 54.6	14 46.0	27 5.3
21 Sa	23 55 46	27 4 44	13 19 34	19 28 12	19R40.4	23 8.9	8 7.8	3 1.4	20 11.3	5 18.6	4 52.8	14 48.2	27 6.3
22 Su	23 59 43	28 3 25	25 33 15	1♌35 19	19 40.4	24 11.7	7 48.1	3 42.5	20 21.6	5 14.6	4 51.0	14 50.4	27 7.2
23 M	0 3 39	29 2 8	7♌35 0	13 32 47	19 38.8	25 12.2	7 30.7	4 23.6	20 32.0	5 10.6	4 49.2	14 52.5	27 8.1
24 Tu	0 7 36	0♎ 0 53	19 29 12	25 24 40	19 35.0	26 10.1	7 15.6	5 4.8	20 42.5	5 6.6	4 47.3	14 54.7	27 8.9
25 W	0 11 33	0 59 41	1♍19 35	7♍14 19	19 28.3	27 5.3	7 3.0	5 46.2	20 53.1	5 2.8	4 45.4	14 56.9	27 9.8
26 Th	0 15 29	1 58 30	13 9 9	19 4 22	19 18.8	27 57.5	6 52.8	6 27.7	21 3.7	4 58.9	4 43.5	14 59.0	27 10.6
27 F	0 19 26	2 57 22	25 0 11	0♎56 48	19 7.0	28 46.5	6 45.0	7 9.2	21 14.5	4 55.2	4 41.5	15 1.2	27 11.4
28 Sa	0 23 22	3 56 16	6♎54 25	12 53 9	18 53.6	29 32.0	6 39.6	7 50.9	21 25.3	4 51.5	4 39.5	15 3.3	27 12.2
29 Su	0 27 19	4 55 11	18 53 10	24 54 37	18 39.8	0♏13.7	6D36.6	8 32.7	21 36.2	4 47.8	4 37.5	15 5.4	27 13.0
30 M	0 31 15	5 54 9	0♏57 39	7♏ 2 27	18 26.6	0 51.3	6 36.1	9 14.6	21 47.2	4 44.2	4 35.4	15 7.5	27 13.7

LONGITUDE — OCTOBER 1935

Day	Sid.Time	☉	0 hr ☽	Noon ☽	True ☊	☿	♀	♂	♃	♄	♅	♆	♇
1 Tu	0 35 12	6♎53 9	13♏ 9 14	19♏18 12	18♑15.2	1♏24.4	6♍37.8	9♐56.6	21♏58.3	4♓40.7	4♉33.3	15♍ 9.6	27♋14.5
2 W	0 39 8	7 52 10	25 29 37	1♐43 48	18R 6.4	1 52.7	6 41.9	10 38.8	22 9.5	4R37.3	4R31.2	15 11.7	27 15.2
3 Th	0 43 5	8 51 13	8♐ 1 5	14 21 49	18 0.4	2 15.8	6 48.3	11 21.0	22 20.7	4 33.9	4 29.1	15 13.8	27 15.8
4 F	0 47 2	9 50 19	20 46 26	27 15 18	17 57.2	2 33.1	6 56.9	12 3.3	22 32.1	4 30.6	4 26.9	15 15.9	27 16.5
5 Sa	0 50 58	10 49 26	3♑48 53	10♑27 35	17D56.1	2 44.3	7 7.7	12 45.7	22 43.5	4 27.4	4 24.7	15 18.0	27 17.1
6 Su	0 54 55	11 48 35	17 11 47	24 1 48	17R56.0	2R48.9	7 20.6	13 28.2	22 54.9	4 24.3	4 22.5	15 20.0	27 17.7
7 M	0 58 51	12 47 45	0♒57 54	8♒ 0 12	17 55.7	2 46.5	7 35.5	14 10.9	23 6.5	4 21.2	4 20.3	15 22.0	27 18.3
8 Tu	1 2 48	13 46 57	15 8 44	22 23 19	17 53.9	2 36.6	7 52.5	14 53.6	23 18.1	4 18.2	4 18.1	15 24.1	27 18.9
9 W	1 6 44	14 46 11	29 43 36	7♓ 9 1	17 49.7	2 18.8	8 11.4	15 36.4	23 29.7	4 15.3	4 15.8	15 26.1	27 19.4
10 Th	1 10 41	15 45 27	14♓38 46	22 11 54	17 42.7	1 53.0	8 32.3	16 19.2	23 41.5	4 12.4	4 13.5	15 28.0	27 19.9
11 F	1 14 37	16 44 44	29 47 15	7♈23 32	17 33.2	1 19.0	8 54.9	17 2.2	23 53.3	4 9.7	4 11.2	15 30.0	27 20.4
12 Sa	1 18 34	17 44 4	14♈59 22	22 33 23	17 22.1	0 36.9	9 19.3	17 45.3	24 5.2	4 7.0	4 8.9	15 32.0	27 20.8
13 Su	1 22 31	18 43 26	0♉ 4 15	7♉30 44	17 10.7	29♎46.9	9 45.5	18 28.4	24 17.1	4 4.4	4 6.5	15 33.9	27 21.3
14 M	1 26 27	19 42 49	14 51 48	22 6 36	17 0.2	28 49.7	10 13.4	19 11.7	24 29.1	4 1.9	4 4.2	15 35.8	27 21.7
15 Tu	1 30 24	20 42 15	29 14 29	6♊15 4	16 51.7	27 46.1	10 42.8	19 55.0	24 41.1	3 59.5	4 1.8	15 37.7	27 22.1
16 W	1 34 20	21 41 44	13♊ 8 9	19 53 47	16 45.9	26 37.5	11 13.8	20 38.4	24 53.2	3 57.2	3 59.4	15 39.6	27 22.4
17 Th	1 38 17	22 41 14	26 32 9	3♋ 3 36	16 42.7	25 25.4	11 46.3	21 21.9	25 5.4	3 55.0	3 57.0	15 41.5	27 22.8
18 F	1 42 13	23 40 47	9♋28 34	15 47 38	16D41.6	24 11.6	12 20.3	22 5.5	25 17.7	3 52.8	3 54.6	15 43.4	27 23.1
19 Sa	1 46 10	24 40 22	22 1 23	28 10 29	16R41.5	22 58.2	12 55.6	22 49.2	25 29.9	3 50.8	3 52.2	15 45.2	27 23.3
20 Su	1 50 6	25 40 0	4♌15 36	10♌17 24	16 41.3	21 47.5	13 32.3	23 33.0	25 42.3	3 48.8	3 49.8	15 47.0	27 23.6
21 M	1 54 3	26 39 39	16 16 33	22 13 42	16 39.9	20 41.5	14 10.3	24 16.8	25 54.7	3 47.0	3 47.4	15 48.8	27 23.8
22 Tu	1 58 0	27 39 21	28 9 27	4♍ 4 21	16 36.2	19 42.3	14 49.5	25 0.7	26 7.1	3 45.2	3 44.9	15 50.6	27 24.0
23 W	2 1 56	28 39 5	9♍58 58	15 53 44	16 29.9	18 51.4	15 29.9	25 44.7	26 19.6	3 43.5	3 42.5	15 52.3	27 24.2
24 Th	2 5 53	29 38 51	21 49 5	27 45 24	16 20.7	18 10.4	16 11.5	26 28.8	26 32.2	3 41.9	3 40.0	15 54.1	27 24.4
25 F	2 9 49	0♏38 40	3♎42 58	9♎42 5	16 9.0	17 40.0	16 54.2	27 13.0	26 44.7	3 40.5	3 37.5	15 55.8	27 24.5
26 Sa	2 13 46	1 38 30	15 42 56	21 45 42	15 55.8	17 20.9	17 37.9	27 57.2	26 57.4	3 39.1	3 35.1	15 57.5	27 24.6
27 Su	2 17 42	2 38 23	27 50 30	3♏57 27	15 42.0	17D13.3	18 22.6	28 41.6	27 10.1	3 37.8	3 32.6	15 59.1	27 24.7
28 M	2 21 39	3 38 17	10♏ 6 36	16 18 2	15 28.8	17 16.9	19 8.3	29 26.0	27 22.8	3 36.6	3 30.1	16 0.8	27 24.7
29 Tu	2 25 35	4 38 14	22 31 48	28 47 58	15 17.4	17 31.4	19 55.0	0♑10.4	27 35.6	3 35.5	3 27.7	16 2.4	27R24.8
30 W	2 29 32	5 38 12	5♐ 6 36	11♐27 49	15 8.5	17 56.1	20 42.6	0 55.0	27 48.4	3 34.6	3 25.2	16 4.0	27 24.8
31 Th	2 33 28	6 38 12	17 51 45	24 18 31	15 2.6	18 30.3	21 31.0	1 39.6	28 1.2	3 33.7	3 22.7	16 5.6	27 24.8

Astro Data	Planet Ingress	Last Aspect	☽ Ingress	Last Aspect	☽ Ingress	☽ Phases & Eclipses	Astro Data
Dy Hr Mn	Dy Hr Mn	Dy Hr Mn	Dy Hr Mn	Dy Hr Mn	Dy Hr Mn	Dy Hr Mn	1 SEPTEMBER 1935
☿0S 3 6:47	☿ ♎ 3 9:33	2 9:56 ♇ □	♏ 2 16:22	2 3:24 ♇ △	♐ 2 8:41	6 2:26 ☽ 12♐35	Julian Day # 13027
☽0N 12 21:25	♂ ♐ 16 12:59	4 20:43 ♇ △	♐ 5 2:48	3 13:40 ♆ □	♑ 4 17:02	12 20:18 ○ 19♓08	Delta T 23.8 sec
♀0N 16 1:21	☉ ♎ 23 23:38	6 8:46 ♀ □	♑ 7 10:08	6 17:41 ♇ ☍	♒ 6 22:20	19 14:23 ☽ 25♊43	SVP 06♓09'13"
☽0S 26 13:33	☿ ♏ 28 15:52	9 8:34 ♇ ☍	♒ 9 13:44	8 13:41 ♃ □	♓ 9 0:27	27 17:29 ● 3♎40	Obliquity 23°26'55"
♀ D 29 17:46		11 8:46 ♂ □	♓ 11 14:15	10 20:08 ♇ △	♈ 11 0:20		⚷ Chiron 16♊00.5
	☿ ♎ 12 18:03	13 10:03 ♂ △	♈ 13 13:20	12 23:34 ☿ ☍	♉ 12 23:53	5 13:39 ☽ 11♑23	☽ Mean ☊ 19♑23.0
☿ R 6 3:53	☉ ♏ 24 8:29	15 8:19 ♇ □	♉ 15 13:10	14 20:50 ♇ ⚹	♊ 15 1:17	12 4:39 ○ 17♈56	
♄⚹♅ 8 4:01	♂ ♑ 28 18:22	17 10:39 ♇ ⚹	♊ 17 15:48	16 22:09 ☿ △	♋ 17 6:21	19 5:36 ☽ 24♋54	1 OCTOBER 1935
☽0N 10 8:04		19 14:23 ☉ □	♋ 19 22:27	19 10:28 ♇ ☌	♌ 19 15:35	27 10:15 ● 3♏04	Julian Day # 13057
♄⚹♅ 21 14:43		22 5:24 ☉ ⚹	♌ 22 8:50	21 22:53 ☉ ⚹	♍ 22 3:44		Delta T 23.8 sec
☽0S 23 19:29		24 14:41 ☿ ⚹	♍ 24 21:18	24 11:18 ♇ ⚹	♎ 24 16:31		SVP 06♓09'10"
☿ D 27 4:11		27 4:25 ♇ ⚹	♎ 27 10:05	27 1:47 ♂ ⚹	♏ 27 4:15		Obliquity 23°26'55"
♃△♇ 28 3:41		29 16:36 ♇ □	♏ 29 22:06	29 9:52 ♃ ☌	♐ 29 14:17		⚷ Chiron 16♊17.8R
♇ R 29 14:18				31 7:17 ♀ □	♑ 31 22:31		☽ Mean ☊ 17♑47.7

NOVEMBER 1935 LONGITUDE

Day	Sid.Time	☉	0 hr ☽	Noon ☽	True ☊	☿	♀	♂	♃	♄	♅	♆	♇
1 F	2 37 25	7♏38 14	0♑48 21	7♑21 26	14♑59.5	19♎13.2	22♍20.3	2♑24.3	28♏14.1	3♓32.9	3♉20.3	16♍ 7.1	27♋24.7
2 Sa	2 41 22	8 38 18	13 58 1	20 38 21	14D 58.6	20 3.8	23 10.4	3 9.1	28 27.0	3R 32.3	3R 17.8	16 8.6	27R 24.6
3 Su	2 45 18	9 38 23	27 22 41	4♒11 16	14R 58.9	21 1.4	24 1.3	3 53.9	28 40.0	3 31.7	3 15.4	16 10.1	27 24.5
4 M	2 49 15	10 38 30	11♒ 4 15	18 1 49	14 59.3	22 5.0	24 52.9	4 38.8	28 53.0	3 31.2	3 12.9	16 11.6	27 24.4
5 Tu	2 53 11	11 38 38	25 3 59	2♓10 44	14 58.5	23 13.9	25 45.3	5 23.8	29 6.0	3 30.9	3 10.5	16 13.1	27 24.3
6 W	2 57 8	12 38 48	9♓21 51	16 37 3	14 55.6	24 27.4	26 38.4	6 8.8	29 19.1	3 30.6	3 8.1	16 14.5	27 24.1
7 Th	3 1 4	13 38 59	23 55 49	1♈17 32	14 50.4	25 44.8	27 32.1	6 53.9	29 32.2	3D 30.5	3 5.7	16 15.9	27 23.9
8 F	3 5 1	14 39 11	8♈41 24	16 6 31	14 42.9	27 5.5	28 26.6	7 39.1	29 45.3	3 30.4	3 3.3	16 17.2	27 23.6
9 Sa	3 8 57	15 39 26	23 31 50	0♉56 19	14 33.8	28 29.1	29 21.6	8 24.3	29 58.4	3 30.5	3 0.9	16 18.6	27 23.4
10 Su	3 12 54	16 39 41	8♉18 51	15 38 23	14 24.3	29 54.9	0♎17.3	9 9.6	0♐11.6	3 30.7	2 58.5	16 19.9	27 23.1
11 M	3 16 51	17 39 59	22 53 57	0♊ 4 42	14 15.6	1♏22.8	1 13.6	9 54.9	0 24.7	3 30.9	2 56.1	16 21.2	27 22.8
12 Tu	3 20 47	18 40 19	7♊ 9 56	14 9 7	14 8.5	2 52.2	2 10.4	10 40.3	0 38.0	3 31.3	2 53.8	16 22.4	27 22.5
13 W	3 24 44	19 40 40	21 1 54	27 48 6	14 3.7	4 22.9	3 7.9	11 25.7	0 51.2	3 31.8	2 51.4	16 23.7	27 22.1
14 Th	3 28 40	20 41 3	4♋27 42	11♋ 0 51	14D 1.3	5 54.8	4 5.8	12 11.2	1 4.4	3 32.4	2 49.1	16 24.9	27 21.7
15 F	3 32 37	21 41 28	17 27 50	23 49 0	14 0.9	7 27.4	5 4.3	12 56.8	1 17.7	3 33.1	2 46.8	16 26.0	27 21.3
16 Sa	3 36 33	22 41 55	0♌ 4 51	6♌15 56	14 1.8	9 0.8	6 3.3	13 42.4	1 31.0	3 33.9	2 44.6	16 27.2	27 20.9
17 Su	3 40 30	23 42 23	12 22 49	18 26 9	14 3.0	10 34.6	7 2.8	14 28.0	1 44.3	3 34.8	2 42.3	16 28.3	27 20.5
18 M	3 44 27	24 42 54	24 26 34	0♍24 45	14R 3.6	12 8.9	8 2.7	15 13.7	1 57.6	3 35.8	2 40.1	16 29.4	27 20.0
19 Tu	3 48 23	25 43 26	6♍21 19	12 16 56	14 2.9	13 43.4	9 3.1	15 59.5	2 11.0	3 36.9	2 37.8	16 30.4	27 19.5
20 W	3 52 20	26 44 0	18 12 11	24 7 39	14 0.2	15 18.2	10 4.0	16 45.3	2 24.3	3 38.1	2 35.6	16 31.4	27 19.0
21 Th	3 56 16	27 44 36	0♎ 3 54	6♎ 1 25	13 55.5	16 53.1	11 5.3	17 31.2	2 37.7	3 39.4	2 33.5	16 32.4	27 18.4
22 F	4 0 13	28 45 13	12 0 39	18 1 59	13 48.9	18 28.0	12 6.9	18 17.1	2 51.1	3 40.8	2 31.3	16 33.4	27 17.9
23 Sa	4 4 9	29 45 52	24 5 47	0♏12 17	13 41.0	20 3.0	13 9.0	19 3.1	3 4.5	3 42.4	2 29.2	16 34.3	27 17.3
24 Su	4 8 6	0♐46 33	6♏21 44	12 34 18	13 32.6	21 38.0	14 11.5	19 49.1	3 17.9	3 44.0	2 27.1	16 35.2	27 16.6
25 M	4 12 2	1 47 15	18 50 3	25 9 5	13 24.5	23 12.9	15 14.3	20 35.2	3 31.3	3 45.7	2 25.0	16 36.0	27 16.0
26 Tu	4 15 59	2 47 59	1♐31 22	7♐56 53	13 17.5	24 47.8	16 17.5	21 21.3	3 44.7	3 47.5	2 23.0	16 36.9	27 15.3
27 W	4 19 56	3 48 44	14 25 35	20 57 23	13 12.3	26 22.6	17 21.0	22 7.4	3 58.1	3 49.5	2 21.0	16 37.7	27 14.7
28 Th	4 23 52	4 49 30	27 32 12	4♑ 9 55	13 9.1	27 57.4	18 24.9	22 53.6	4 11.5	3 51.5	2 19.0	16 38.4	27 14.0
29 F	4 27 49	5 50 18	10♑50 29	17 33 47	13D 8.0	29 32.0	19 29.0	23 39.9	4 24.9	3 53.7	2 17.1	16 39.2	27 13.2
30 Sa	4 31 45	6 51 6	24 19 46	1♒ 8 23	13 8.4	1♐ 6.6	20 33.5	24 26.2	4 38.3	3 55.9	2 15.2	16 39.9	27 12.5

DECEMBER 1935 LONGITUDE

Day	Sid.Time	☉	0 hr ☽	Noon ☽	True ☊	☿	♀	♂	♃	♄	♅	♆	♇
1 Su	4 35 42	7♐51 56	7♒59 36	14♒53 23	13♑ 9.8	2♐41.1	21♎38.3	25♑12.5	4♐51.7	3♓58.2	2♉13.3	16♍40.5	27♋11.7
2 M	4 39 38	8 52 47	21 49 40	28 48 25	13 11.4	4 15.6	22 43.3	25 58.9	5 5.1	4 0.7	2R 11.4	16 41.2	27R 10.9
3 Tu	4 43 35	9 53 38	5♓49 32	12♓52 56	13R 12.3	5 49.9	23 48.7	26 45.3	5 18.5	4 3.2	2 9.6	16 41.7	27 10.1
4 W	4 47 31	10 54 30	19 58 25	27 5 46	13 12.0	7 24.2	24 54.3	27 31.7	5 31.9	4 5.8	2 7.9	16 42.3	27 9.3
5 Th	4 51 28	11 55 23	4♈14 41	11♈24 47	13 10.3	8 58.5	26 0.2	28 18.1	5 45.3	4 8.6	2 6.1	16 42.8	27 8.4
6 F	4 55 25	12 56 16	18 35 37	25 46 41	13 7.1	10 32.7	27 6.3	29 4.6	5 58.7	4 11.4	2 4.4	16 43.3	27 7.6
7 Sa	4 59 21	13 57 11	2♉57 24	10♉ 7 8	13 3.0	12 6.9	28 12.7	29 51.2	6 12.1	4 14.3	2 2.8	16 43.8	27 6.7
8 Su	5 3 18	14 58 6	17 15 15	24 21 6	12 58.6	13 41.1	29 19.4	0♒37.7	6 25.4	4 17.3	2 1.1	16 44.2	27 5.8
9 M	5 7 14	15 59 2	1♊24 3	8♊23 31	12 54.5	15 15.4	0♏26.2	1 24.3	6 38.8	4 20.5	1 59.5	16 44.6	27 4.8
10 Tu	5 11 11	16 59 59	15 18 59	22 10 2	12 51.2	16 49.6	1 33.3	2 10.9	6 52.1	4 23.7	1 58.0	16 45.0	27 3.9
11 W	5 15 7	18 0 57	28 56 17	5♋37 31	12 49.2	18 23.9	2 40.7	2 57.5	7 5.4	4 27.0	1 56.5	16 45.3	27 2.9
12 Th	5 19 4	19 1 56	12♋13 37	18 44 33	12D 48.5	19 58.3	3 48.2	3 44.2	7 18.7	4 30.4	1 55.0	16 45.6	27 2.0
13 F	5 23 0	20 2 56	25 10 23	1♌31 18	12 49.0	21 32.7	4 56.0	4 30.9	7 32.0	4 33.8	1 53.6	16 45.8	27 1.0
14 Sa	5 26 57	21 3 56	7♌47 35	13 59 33	12 50.3	23 7.2	6 4.0	5 17.6	7 45.2	4 37.4	1 52.2	16 46.1	26 60.0
15 Su	5 30 54	22 4 58	20 7 38	26 12 18	12 52.0	24 41.8	7 12.2	6 4.3	7 58.5	4 41.1	1 50.9	16 46.3	26 58.9
16 M	5 34 50	23 6 1	2♍14 4	8♍13 29	12 53.6	26 16.5	8 20.5	6 51.1	8 11.7	4 44.8	1 49.6	16 46.4	26 57.9
17 Tu	5 38 47	24 7 4	14 11 9	20 7 38	12R 54.7	27 51.4	9 29.1	7 37.8	8 24.9	4 48.7	1 48.4	16 46.5	26 56.8
18 W	5 42 43	25 8 8	26 3 34	1♎59 33	12 55.1	29 26.4	10 37.8	8 24.6	8 38.1	4 52.6	1 47.2	16 46.6	26 55.7
19 Th	5 46 40	26 9 14	7♎56 11	13 54 4	12 54.6	1♑ 1.6	11 46.7	9 11.5	8 51.2	4 56.6	1 46.0	16R 46.7	26 54.6
20 F	5 50 36	27 10 20	19 53 45	25 55 47	12 53.3	2 36.9	12 55.8	9 58.3	9 4.3	5 0.7	1 44.9	16 46.7	26 53.5
21 Sa	5 54 33	28 11 26	2♏ 0 39	8♏ 8 48	12 51.5	4 12.4	14 5.1	10 45.2	9 17.4	5 4.9	1 43.8	16 46.7	26 52.4
22 Su	5 58 29	29 12 34	14 20 38	20 36 27	12 49.4	5 48.0	15 14.5	11 32.0	9 30.5	5 9.1	1 42.8	16 46.6	26 51.3
23 M	6 2 26	0♑13 43	26 56 32	3♐21 4	12 47.4	7 23.8	16 24.1	12 18.9	9 43.5	5 13.5	1 41.8	16 46.5	26 50.1
24 Tu	6 6 23	1 14 52	9♐50 9	16 23 49	12 45.8	8 59.8	17 33.8	13 5.8	9 56.5	5 17.9	1 40.9	16 46.4	26 49.0
25 W	6 10 19	2 16 1	23 2 0	29 44 34	12 44.6	10 35.9	18 43.6	13 52.8	10 9.4	5 22.4	1 40.0	16 46.2	26 47.8
26 Th	6 14 16	3 17 11	6♑31 19	13♑21 57	12D 44.1	12 12.2	19 53.6	14 39.7	10 22.4	5 27.0	1 39.2	16 46.0	26 46.6
27 F	6 18 12	4 18 21	20 16 10	27 13 33	12 44.1	13 48.5	21 3.7	15 26.7	10 35.3	5 31.7	1 38.5	16 45.8	26 45.4
28 Sa	6 22 9	5 19 32	4♒13 42	11♒16 10	12 44.5	15 25.0	22 13.9	16 13.7	10 48.1	5 36.4	1 37.7	16 45.6	26 44.2
29 Su	6 26 5	6 20 42	18 20 31	25 26 18	12 45.1	17 1.5	23 24.3	17 0.6	11 0.9	5 41.3	1 37.1	16 45.3	26 43.0
30 M	6 30 2	7 21 53	2♓33 3	9♓40 23	12 45.7	18 37.9	24 34.8	17 47.6	11 13.7	5 46.2	1 36.4	16 44.9	26 41.8
31 Tu	6 33 58	8 23 3	16 47 54	23 55 15	12 46.2	20 14.4	25 45.4	18 34.6	11 26.4	5 51.1	1 35.8	16 44.6	26 40.5

Astro Data Dy Hr Mn	Planet Ingress Dy Hr Mn	Last Aspect Dy Hr Mn	☽ Ingress Dy Hr Mn	Last Aspect Dy Hr Mn	☽ Ingress Dy Hr Mn	☽ Phases & Eclipses Dy Hr Mn	Astro Data
☽0N 6 16:30	♀ ♎ 9 16:34	3 2:19 ♃ ⚹	♒ 3 4:38	2 1:40 ♀ △	♓ 2 14:03	3 23:12 ☽ 10♒36	1 NOVEMBER 1935
♄ D 7 21:59	♃ ♐ 9 2:56	5 6:56 ♃ □	♓ 5 8:20	4 13:27 ♂ ⚹	♈ 4 16:53	10 14:42 ○ 17♉17	Julian Day # 13088
♀0S 11 14:07	☿ ♏ 10 1:24	7 9:17 ♃ △	♈ 7 9:54	6 18:31 ♂ □	♉ 6 19:03	18 0:36 ☽ 24♌44	Delta T 23.8 sec
☽0S 20 1:56	☉ ♐ 23 5:35	9 8:52 ☿ ☍	♉ 9 10:29	8 16:39 ♇ ⚹	♊ 8 21:36	26 2:36 ● 2♐55	SVP 06♓09'06"
♃⚻♅ 20 17:27	☿ ♐ 29 7:05	11 7:28 ♇ ⚹	♊ 11 11:52	10 3:10 ☉ ☍	♋ 11 1:54		Obliquity 23°26'54"
♃□♄ 26 5:59		12 15:53 ♆ □	♋ 13 15:56	13 3:28 ♇ ☌	♌ 13 9:07	3 7:28 ☽ 10♓13	⚷ Chiron 15♊29.4R
	♂ ♒ 7 4:34	15 18:45 ♇ ☌	♌ 15 23:51	15 10:22 ☿ △	♍ 15 19:33	10 3:10 ○ 17♊08	☽ Mean ☊ 16♑09.2
☽0N 3 22:17	♀ ♏ 8 14:36	18 0:36 ☉ □	♍ 18 11:10	18 7:54 ☿ □	♎ 18 7:58	17 21:57 ☽ 25♍03	
☽0S 17 9:22	☿ ♑ 18 8:28	20 18:53 ☉ ⚹	♎ 20 23:52	20 15:47 ☉ ⚹	♏ 20 20:03	25 17:49 ● 3♑01	1 DECEMBER 1935
♅⚼♆ 18 10:51	☉ ♑ 22 18:37	23 6:17 ♇ □	♏ 23 11:36	22 23:48 ♇ △	♐ 23 5:45	25 17:59:25 ✔ A 1'30"	Julian Day # 13118
♆ R 19 21:24		25 15:59 ♇ △	♐ 25 21:08	24 12:41 ♆ □	♑ 25 12:27		Delta T 23.7 sec
☽0N 31 3:19		27 5:52 ♀ ⚹	♑ 28 4:28	27 11:11 ♇ ☍	♒ 27 16:46		SVP 06♓09'01"
		30 5:05 ♇ ☍	♒ 30 10:00	29 9:20 ♀ □	♓ 29 19:42		Obliquity 23°26'53"
				31 16:37 ♇ △	♈ 31 22:15		⚷ Chiron 13♊55.3R
							☽ Mean ☊ 14♑33.9

LONGITUDE JANUARY 1936

Day	Sid.Time	☉	0 hr ☽	Noon ☽	True ☊	☿	♀	♂	♃	♄	♅	♆	♇
1 W	6 37 55	9♑24 13	1♈ 2 5	8♈ 8 6	12♑46.4	21♑50.7	26♏56.1	19♒21.6	11♐39.0	5♓56.2	1♉35.3	16♍44.2	26♋39.3
2 Th	6 41 52	10 25 23	15 13 1	22 16 36	12R46.4	23 26.7	28 6.9	20 8.6	11 51.7	6 1.3	1R34.8	16R43.7	26R38.0
3 F	6 45 48	11 26 32	29 18 35	6♉18 45	12 46.3	25 2.5	29 17.8	20 55.6	12 4.2	6 6.5	1 34.4	16 43.3	26 36.8
4 Sa	6 49 45	12 27 42	13♉16 54	20 12 49	12D46.3	26 37.7	0♐28.8	21 42.6	12 16.8	6 11.8	1 34.1	16 42.8	26 35.5
5 Su	6 53 41	13 28 51	27 6 17	3♊57 6	12 46.3	28 12.4	1 39.9	22 29.7	12 29.2	6 17.1	1 33.7	16 42.3	26 34.2
6 M	6 57 38	14 30 0	10♊45 6	17 30 4	12 46.4	29 46.3	2 51.1	23 16.7	12 41.7	6 22.5	1 33.5	16 41.7	26 32.9
7 Tu	7 1 34	15 31 8	24 11 50	0♋50 16	12 46.6	1♒19.1	4 2.4	24 3.7	12 54.0	6 27.9	1 33.3	16 41.1	26 31.7
8 W	7 5 31	16 32 17	7♋25 13	13 56 35	12R46.8	2 50.7	5 13.8	24 50.7	13 6.3	6 33.5	1 33.1	16 40.5	26 30.4
9 Th	7 9 28	17 33 25	20 24 18	26 48 20	12 46.8	4 20.8	6 25.3	25 37.7	13 18.6	6 39.1	1 33.0	16 39.9	26 29.1
10 F	7 13 24	18 34 33	3♌ 8 43	9♌25 31	12 46.5	5 48.9	7 36.9	26 24.7	13 30.8	6 44.7	1D32.9	16 39.2	26 27.8
11 Sa	7 17 21	19 35 40	15 38 51	21 48 53	12 45.8	7 14.7	8 48.6	27 11.7	13 42.9	6 50.4	1 32.9	16 38.5	26 26.5
12 Su	7 21 17	20 36 48	27 55 51	4♍ 0 1	12 44.8	8 37.7	10 0.3	27 58.7	13 55.0	6 56.2	1 33.0	16 37.7	26 25.1
13 M	7 25 14	21 37 55	10♍ 1 43	16 1 21	12 43.5	9 57.5	11 12.1	28 45.6	14 7.0	7 2.1	1 33.1	16 36.9	26 23.8
14 Tu	7 29 10	22 39 2	21 59 19	27 56 6	12 42.2	11 13.4	12 24.0	29 32.6	14 18.9	7 7.9	1 33.2	16 36.1	26 22.5
15 W	7 33 7	23 40 9	3♎52 11	9♎48 8	12 41.1	12 24.7	13 36.0	0♓19.6	14 30.8	7 13.9	1 33.4	16 35.3	26 21.2
16 Th	7 37 3	24 41 15	15 44 28	21 41 48	12D40.3	13 30.8	14 48.1	1 6.6	14 42.6	7 19.9	1 33.7	16 34.4	26 19.9
17 F	7 41 0	25 42 22	27 40 42	3♏41 47	12 40.1	14 30.8	16 0.2	1 53.5	14 54.4	7 26.0	1 34.0	16 33.5	26 18.5
18 Sa	7 44 57	26 43 28	9♏45 39	15 52 51	12 40.5	15 24.0	17 12.4	2 40.5	15 6.1	7 32.1	1 34.3	16 32.6	26 17.2
19 Su	7 48 53	27 44 34	22 3 57	28 19 28	12 41.5	16 9.4	18 24.7	3 27.4	15 17.7	7 38.3	1 34.7	16 31.7	26 15.9
20 M	7 52 50	28 45 40	4♐39 53	11♐ 5 35	12 42.9	16 46.1	19 37.0	4 14.4	15 29.2	7 44.5	1 35.2	16 30.7	26 14.6
21 Tu	7 56 46	29 46 45	17 36 54	24 14 3	12 44.3	17 13.4	20 49.4	5 1.3	15 40.6	7 50.8	1 35.7	16 29.7	26 13.3
22 W	8 0 43	0♒47 50	0♑57 11	7♑46 16	12R45.3	17 30.4	22 1.8	5 48.2	15 52.0	7 57.1	1 36.3	16 28.7	26 11.9
23 Th	8 4 39	1 48 54	14 41 12	21 41 41	12 45.7	17R36.5	23 14.3	6 35.1	16 3.3	8 3.5	1 36.9	16 27.6	26 10.6
24 F	8 8 36	2 49 58	28 47 18	5♒57 32	12 45.0	17 31.3	24 26.9	7 22.0	16 14.5	8 9.9	1 37.6	16 26.5	26 9.3
25 Sa	8 12 32	3 51 1	13♒11 42	20 29 0	12 43.2	17 14.6	25 39.5	8 8.9	16 25.7	8 16.4	1 38.3	16 25.4	26 8.0
26 Su	8 16 29	4 52 3	27 48 37	5♓ 9 38	12 40.5	16 46.4	26 52.1	8 55.8	16 36.7	8 22.9	1 39.1	16 24.3	26 6.7
27 M	8 20 26	5 53 4	12♓31 7	19 52 13	12 37.2	16 7.3	28 4.8	9 42.6	16 47.7	8 29.5	1 39.9	16 23.1	26 5.4
28 Tu	8 24 22	6 54 4	27 12 3	4♈29 54	12 33.9	15 18.1	29 17.5	10 29.4	16 58.6	8 36.1	1 40.8	16 21.9	26 4.1
29 W	8 28 19	7 55 2	11♈45 4	18 57 3	12 31.0	14 20.2	0♑30.3	11 16.2	17 9.3	8 42.7	1 41.7	16 20.7	26 2.8
30 Th	8 32 15	8 56 0	26 5 24	3♉ 9 49	12D29.2	13 15.1	1 43.1	12 3.0	17 20.0	8 49.4	1 42.7	16 19.5	26 1.5
31 F	8 36 12	9 56 56	10♉10 8	17 6 15	12 28.6	12 4.8	2 56.0	12 49.8	17 30.6	8 56.1	1 43.8	16 18.2	26 0.2

LONGITUDE FEBRUARY 1936

Day	Sid.Time	☉	0 hr ☽	Noon ☽	True ☊	☿	♀	♂	♃	♄	♅	♆	♇
1 Sa	8 40 8	10♒57 51	23♉58 10	0♊45 57	12♑29.2	10♒51.3	4♑ 8.9	13♓36.6	17♐41.1	9♓ 2.9	1♉44.8	16♍17.0	25♋58.9
2 Su	8 44 5	11 58 45	7♊29 42	14 9 36	12 30.6	9R37.0	5 21.8	14 23.3	17 51.5	9 9.7	1 46.0	16R15.7	25R57.7
3 M	8 48 1	12 59 37	20 45 48	27 18 29	12 32.3	8 23.9	6 34.8	15 10.0	18 1.9	9 16.5	1 47.2	16 14.4	25 56.4
4 Tu	8 51 58	14 0 28	3♋47 50	10♋14 1	12R33.6	7 13.8	7 47.8	15 56.7	18 12.1	9 23.4	1 48.4	16 13.0	25 55.2
5 W	8 55 55	15 1 18	16 37 13	22 57 32	12 33.8	6 8.5	9 0.8	16 43.3	18 22.2	9 30.3	1 49.7	16 11.7	25 53.9
6 Th	8 59 51	16 2 6	29 15 8	5♌30 7	12 32.5	5 9.3	10 13.9	17 29.9	18 32.2	9 37.2	1 51.0	16 10.3	25 52.7
7 F	9 3 48	17 2 53	11♌42 35	17 52 40	12 29.4	4 17.2	11 27.0	18 16.5	18 42.1	9 44.2	1 52.4	16 8.9	25 51.5
8 Sa	9 7 44	18 3 39	24 0 27	0♍ 6 3	12 24.5	3 32.8	12 40.1	19 3.1	18 51.9	9 51.2	1 53.8	16 7.5	25 50.3
9 Su	9 11 41	19 4 23	6♍ 9 38	12 11 20	12 18.1	2 56.6	13 53.3	19 49.6	19 1.6	9 58.2	1 55.3	16 6.0	25 49.0
10 M	9 15 37	20 5 6	18 11 20	24 9 53	12 10.8	2 28.6	15 6.5	20 36.1	19 11.2	10 5.2	1 56.8	16 4.6	25 47.9
11 Tu	9 19 34	21 5 48	0♎ 7 13	6♎ 3 39	12 3.4	2 8.7	16 19.7	21 22.6	19 20.7	10 12.3	1 58.4	16 3.1	25 46.7
12 W	9 23 30	22 6 29	11 59 32	17 55 15	11 56.5	1 56.8	17 33.0	22 9.1	19 30.0	10 19.4	1 60.0	16 1.6	25 45.5
13 Th	9 27 27	23 7 8	23 51 14	29 47 58	11 50.9	1D52.6	18 46.3	22 55.5	19 39.3	10 26.5	2 1.6	16 0.1	25 44.3
14 F	9 31 24	24 7 47	5♏45 58	11♏45 47	11 47.0	1 55.5	19 59.6	23 41.9	19 48.4	10 33.7	2 3.3	15 58.6	25 43.2
15 Sa	9 35 20	25 8 24	17 47 59	23 53 11	11D45.0	2 5.3	21 12.9	24 28.3	19 57.4	10 40.8	2 5.1	15 57.1	25 42.1
16 Su	9 39 17	26 9 0	0♐ 2 0	6♐15 2	11 44.7	2 21.4	22 26.3	25 14.6	20 6.3	10 48.0	2 6.9	15 55.6	25 40.9
17 M	9 43 13	27 9 35	12 32 54	18 56 10	11 45.6	2 43.4	23 39.7	26 0.9	20 15.1	10 55.2	2 8.7	15 54.0	25 39.8
18 Tu	9 47 10	28 10 9	25 25 21	2♑ 0 55	11 47.0	3 10.8	24 53.1	26 47.2	20 23.8	11 2.5	2 10.6	15 52.5	25 38.7
19 W	9 51 6	29 10 42	8♑43 14	15 32 33	11R47.9	3 43.3	26 6.6	27 33.5	20 32.3	11 9.7	2 12.5	15 50.9	25 37.7
20 Th	9 55 3	0♓11 13	22 28 56	29 32 21	11 47.4	4 20.4	27 20.0	28 19.7	20 40.7	11 17.0	2 14.5	15 49.3	25 36.6
21 F	9 58 59	1 11 43	6♒42 32	13♒59 1	11 44.9	5 1.9	28 33.5	29 5.9	20 49.0	11 24.2	2 16.5	15 47.7	25 35.6
22 Sa	10 2 56	2 12 11	21 21 7	28 47 59	11 40.1	5 47.2	29 47.0	29 52.0	20 57.2	11 31.5	2 18.6	15 46.1	25 34.5
23 Su	10 6 53	3 12 38	6♓18 34	13♓51 41	11 33.2	6 36.3	1♒ 0.5	0♈38.1	21 5.2	11 38.8	2 20.7	15 44.5	25 33.5
24 M	10 10 49	4 13 2	21 26 2	29 0 19	11 25.0	7 28.7	2 14.1	1 24.2	21 13.1	11 46.1	2 22.8	15 42.8	25 32.5
25 Tu	10 14 46	5 13 26	6♈33 15	14♈ 3 36	11 16.5	8 24.2	3 27.6	2 10.3	21 20.8	11 53.5	2 25.0	15 41.2	25 31.5
26 W	10 18 42	6 13 47	21 30 19	28 52 30	11 8.8	9 22.6	4 41.2	2 56.3	21 28.5	12 0.8	2 27.2	15 39.6	25 30.6
27 Th	10 22 39	7 14 6	6♉ 9 25	13♉20 34	11 2.9	10 23.7	5 54.7	3 42.3	21 35.9	12 8.1	2 29.4	15 37.9	25 29.6
28 F	10 26 35	8 14 24	20 25 39	27 24 31	10 59.2	11 27.3	7 8.3	4 28.2	21 43.3	12 15.5	2 31.7	15 36.3	25 28.7
29 Sa	10 30 32	9 14 39	4♊17 14	11♊ 3 56	10D57.7	12 33.2	8 21.9	5 14.1	21 50.5	12 22.8	2 34.1	15 34.6	25 27.8

Astro Data

	Dy Hr Mn
♃⚼♇	1 0:25
♅ D	10 15:20
☽0S	13 17:33
♅⚼♆	16 15:34
☿ R	23 1:05
♃□♆	24 23:30
♃⚼♅	26 5:36
☽0N	27 10:21
☽0S	10 1:34
☿ D	13 1:57
♄⚼♇	15 3:31
☽0N	23 20:12
♂0N	23 21:30

Planet Ingress

	Dy Hr Mn
♀ ♐	3 14:16
☿ ♒	6 3:32
♂ ♓	14 13:59
☉ ♒	21 5:12
♀ ♑	28 14:00
☉ ♓	19 19:33
♀ ♒	22 4:14
♂ ♈	22 4:09

Last Aspect / ☽ Ingress

Last Aspect Dy Hr Mn		☽ Ingress Dy Hr Mn
2 19:24	♇ □	♉ 3 1:11
5 2:10	☿ △	♊ 5 5:04
6 23:44	♂ △	♋ 7 10:29
9 11:23	♇ ☌	♌ 9 18:02
12 0:06	♂ ☍	♍ 12 4:05
14 8:50	♇ ✶	♎ 14 16:10
16 21:16	♇ □	♏ 17 4:38
19 11:51	☉ ✶	♐ 19 15:11
21 6:25	♀ ☌	♑ 21 22:19
23 19:34	♇ ☍	♒ 24 2:02
25 22:19	♀ ✶	♓ 26 3:35
28 3:45	♀ □	♈ 28 4:36
29 23:53	♇ □	♉ 30 6:37

Last Aspect / ☽ Ingress

Last Aspect Dy Hr Mn		☽ Ingress Dy Hr Mn
1 3:32	♇ ✶	♊ 1 10:39
2 18:57	♃ ☍	♋ 3 16:58
5 17:34	♇ ☌	♌ 6 1:26
7 13:48	♃ △	♍ 8 11:48
10 15:16	♇ ✶	♎ 10 23:45
13 3:48	♇ □	♏ 13 12:24
15 15:45	☉ □	♐ 15 23:56
18 5:26	☉ ✶	♑ 18 8:21
20 10:31	♂ ✶	♒ 20 12:47
21 23:21	♃ ✶	♓ 22 13:55
24 6:30	♇ △	♈ 24 13:35
26 6:30	♇ □	♉ 26 13:51
28 8:39	♇ ✶	♊ 28 16:30

☽ Phases & Eclipses

Dy Hr Mn	
1 15:15	☽ 10♈03
8 18:15	○ 17♋19
8 18:10	•T 1.017
16 19:41	☽ 25♎31
24 7:18	● 3♒09
30 23:36	☽ 9♉56
7 11:19	○ 17♌32
15 15:45	☽ 25♏48
22 18:42	● 2♓59
29 9:28	☽ 9♊38

Astro Data

1 JANUARY 1936
Julian Day # 13149
Delta T 23.7 sec
SVP 06♓08'55"
Obliquity 23°26'53"
⚷ Chiron 12♊09.0R
☽ Mean ☊ 12♑55.4

1 FEBRUARY 1936
Julian Day # 13180
Delta T 23.7 sec
SVP 06♓08'50"
Obliquity 23°26'53"
⚷ Chiron 11♊00.0R
☽ Mean ☊ 11♑16.9

MARCH 1936 — LONGITUDE

Day	Sid.Time	☉	0 hr ☽	Noon ☽	True ☊	☿	♀	♂	♃	♄	♅	♆	♇
1 Su	10 34 28	10♓14 52	17♊44 54	24♊20 29	10♑57.8	13♒41.4	9♒35.5	5♈60.0	21♐57.5	12♓30.2	2♉36.5	15♍33.0	25♋26.9
2 M	10 38 25	11 15 4	0♋51 4	7♋17 6	10R 58.6	14 51.6	10 49.1	6 45.8	22 4.4	12 37.5	2 38.9	15R 31.3	25R 26.0
3 Tu	10 42 22	12 15 13	13 39 1	19 57 14	10 58.9	16 3.8	12 2.7	7 31.6	22 11.2	12 44.9	2 41.3	15 29.6	25 25.2
4 W	10 46 18	13 15 20	26 12 10	2♌24 12	10 57.7	17 17.8	13 16.3	8 17.3	22 17.8	12 52.2	2 43.8	15 28.0	25 24.3
5 Th	10 50 15	14 15 25	8♌33 41	14 40 57	10 54.1	18 33.6	14 30.0	9 3.0	22 24.3	12 59.6	2 46.3	15 26.3	25 23.5
6 F	10 54 11	15 15 28	20 46 14	26 49 49	10 47.8	19 51.0	15 43.6	9 48.6	22 30.6	13 7.0	2 48.9	15 24.6	25 22.7
7 Sa	10 58 8	16 15 28	2♍51 54	8♍52 39	10 38.7	21 10.1	16 57.3	10 34.2	22 36.7	13 14.3	2 51.4	15 23.0	25 22.0
8 Su	11 2 4	17 15 27	14 52 15	20 50 51	10 27.3	22 30.7	18 10.9	11 19.8	22 42.8	13 21.6	2 54.1	15 21.3	25 21.2
9 M	11 6 1	18 15 24	26 48 35	2♎45 37	10 14.4	23 52.8	19 24.6	12 5.3	22 48.6	13 29.0	2 56.7	15 19.6	25 20.5
10 Tu	11 9 57	19 15 19	8♎42 7	14 38 16	10 1.1	25 16.4	20 38.3	12 50.8	22 54.3	13 36.3	2 59.4	15 18.0	25 19.8
11 W	11 13 54	20 15 13	20 34 17	26 30 26	9 48.4	26 41.3	21 51.9	13 36.2	22 59.8	13 43.7	3 2.1	15 16.3	25 19.1
12 Th	11 17 50	21 15 4	2♏26 59	8♏24 18	9 37.5	28 7.7	23 5.6	14 21.6	23 5.2	13 51.0	3 4.8	15 14.6	25 18.4
13 F	11 21 47	22 14 54	14 22 44	20 22 44	9 29.0	29 35.4	24 19.3	15 7.0	23 10.4	13 58.3	3 7.6	15 13.0	25 17.8
14 Sa	11 25 44	23 14 42	26 24 45	2♐29 20	9 23.2	1♓ 4.4	25 33.1	15 52.3	23 15.5	14 5.6	3 10.4	15 11.3	25 17.2
15 Su	11 29 40	24 14 28	8♐37 0	14 48 20	9 20.2	2 34.8	26 46.8	16 37.5	23 20.4	14 12.9	3 13.3	15 9.7	25 16.6
16 M	11 33 37	25 14 13	21 3 57	27 24 27	9D 19.1	4 6.4	28 0.5	17 22.8	23 25.1	14 20.2	3 16.1	15 8.0	25 16.0
17 Tu	11 37 33	26 13 56	3♑50 26	10♑22 26	9R 19.2	5 39.4	29 14.3	18 7.9	23 29.7	14 27.4	3 19.0	15 6.4	25 15.4
18 W	11 41 30	27 13 37	17 0 59	23 46 29	9 19.0	7 13.6	0♓28.0	18 53.1	23 34.1	14 34.7	3 21.9	15 4.8	25 14.9
19 Th	11 45 26	28 13 17	0♒39 16	7♒39 30	9 17.6	8 49.1	1 41.8	19 38.2	23 38.3	14 41.9	3 24.9	15 3.1	25 14.4
20 F	11 49 23	29 12 54	14 47 9	22 1 59	9 13.9	10 25.8	2 55.5	20 23.2	23 42.4	14 49.1	3 27.9	15 1.5	25 13.9
21 Sa	11 53 19	0♈12 30	29 23 34	6♓51 12	9 7.5	12 3.9	4 9.3	21 8.2	23 46.2	14 56.3	3 30.8	14 59.9	25 13.5
22 Su	11 57 16	1 12 4	14♓23 57	22 0 39	8 58.5	13 43.2	5 23.0	21 53.2	23 49.9	15 3.5	3 33.9	14 58.3	25 13.0
23 M	12 1 13	2 11 36	29 40 0	7♈20 31	8 47.6	15 23.8	6 36.8	22 38.1	23 53.5	15 10.7	3 36.9	14 56.7	25 12.6
24 Tu	12 5 9	3 11 6	15♈ 0 42	22 39 6	8 36.3	17 5.7	7 50.6	23 23.0	23 56.8	15 17.8	3 40.0	14 55.2	25 12.2
25 W	12 9 6	4 10 34	0♉14 17	7♉45 2	8 25.7	18 48.9	9 4.3	24 7.8	23 60.0	15 24.9	3 43.1	14 53.6	25 11.9
26 Th	12 13 2	5 10 0	15 10 18	22 29 19	8 17.1	20 33.4	10 18.1	24 52.6	24 3.0	15 32.0	3 46.2	14 52.0	25 11.5
27 F	12 16 59	6 9 23	29 41 29	6♊46 29	8 11.2	22 19.2	11 31.8	25 37.3	24 5.8	15 39.1	3 49.3	14 50.5	25 11.2
28 Sa	12 20 55	7 8 45	13♊44 13	20 34 45	8 7.9	24 6.4	12 45.6	26 22.0	24 8.4	15 46.1	3 52.5	14 49.0	25 10.9
29 Su	12 24 52	8 8 4	27 18 19	3♋55 18	8 6.7	25 54.9	13 59.4	27 6.6	24 10.9	15 53.1	3 55.7	14 47.5	25 10.7
30 M	12 28 48	9 7 20	10♋26 7	16 51 19	8 6.6	27 44.8	15 13.1	27 51.2	24 13.2	16 0.1	3 58.9	14 46.0	25 10.4
31 Tu	12 32 45	10 6 34	23 11 26	29 27 3	8 6.3	29 36.0	16 26.8	28 35.7	24 15.2	16 7.1	4 2.1	14 44.5	25 10.2

APRIL 1936 — LONGITUDE

Day	Sid.Time	☉	0 hr ☽	Noon ☽	True ☊	☿	♀	♂	♃	♄	♅	♆	♇
1 W	12 36 42	11♈ 5 46	5♌38 42	11♌46 58	8♑ 4.6	1♈28.6	17♓40.6	29♈20.2	24♐17.1	16♓14.0	4♉ 5.3	14♍43.0	25♋10.0
2 Th	12 40 38	12 4 56	17 52 21	23 55 20	8R 0.6	3 22.6	18 54.3	0♉ 4.6	24 18.9	16 20.9	4 8.5	14R 41.6	25R 9.9
3 F	12 44 35	13 4 3	29 56 22	5♍55 51	7 53.7	5 18.0	20 8.1	0 49.0	24 20.4	16 27.8	4 11.8	14 40.1	25 9.7
4 Sa	12 48 31	14 3 8	11♍54 8	17 51 33	7 44.0	7 14.7	21 21.8	1 33.3	24 21.7	16 34.6	4 15.1	14 38.7	25 9.6
5 Su	12 52 28	15 2 11	23 48 20	29 44 45	7 31.8	9 12.7	22 35.5	2 17.6	24 22.9	16 41.4	4 18.4	14 37.3	25 9.5
6 M	12 56 24	16 1 12	5♎40 59	11♎37 14	7 18.1	11 12.0	23 49.3	3 1.8	24 23.9	16 48.1	4 21.7	14 35.9	25 9.5
7 Tu	13 0 21	17 0 10	17 33 40	23 30 25	7 3.8	13 12.6	25 3.0	3 46.0	24 24.7	16 54.9	4 25.0	14 34.6	25D 9.4
8 W	13 4 17	17 59 7	29 27 41	5♏25 37	6 50.2	15 14.4	26 16.7	4 30.1	24 25.3	17 1.5	4 28.3	14 33.2	25 9.4
9 Th	13 8 14	18 58 1	11♏24 26	17 24 19	6 38.4	17 17.3	27 30.5	5 14.2	24 25.7	17 8.2	4 31.7	14 31.9	25 9.4
10 F	13 12 11	19 56 54	23 25 31	29 28 21	6 29.0	19 21.2	28 44.2	5 58.3	24R 25.9	17 14.8	4 35.0	14 30.6	25 9.5
11 Sa	13 16 7	20 55 45	5♐33 7	11♐40 12	6 22.5	21 26.0	29 57.9	6 42.2	24 26.0	17 21.4	4 38.4	14 29.3	25 9.5
12 Su	13 20 4	21 54 34	17 50 0	24 2 57	6 18.9	23 31.6	1♈11.7	7 26.2	24 25.8	17 27.9	4 41.8	14 28.1	25 9.6
13 M	13 24 0	22 53 22	0♑19 32	6♑40 15	6D 17.5	25 37.7	2 25.4	8 10.1	24 25.5	17 34.4	4 45.2	14 26.8	25 9.7
14 Tu	13 27 57	23 52 7	13 5 37	19 36 8	6R 17.5	27 44.2	3 39.1	8 53.9	24 25.0	17 40.8	4 48.6	14 25.6	25 9.9
15 W	13 31 53	24 50 51	26 12 17	2♒54 29	6 17.7	29 50.8	4 52.8	9 37.7	24 24.3	17 47.2	4 52.0	14 24.4	25 10.1
16 Th	13 35 50	25 49 34	9♒43 7	16 38 26	6 16.9	1♉57.2	6 6.6	10 21.4	24 23.4	17 53.6	4 55.4	14 23.3	25 10.2
17 F	13 39 46	26 48 14	23 40 33	0♓49 27	6 14.3	4 3.3	7 20.3	11 5.1	24 22.3	17 59.9	4 58.8	14 22.1	25 10.5
18 Sa	13 43 43	27 46 53	8♓ 4 53	15 26 25	6 9.2	6 8.6	8 34.0	11 48.8	24 21.0	18 6.1	5 2.3	14 21.0	25 10.7
19 Su	13 47 40	28 45 30	22 53 23	0♈24 54	6 1.9	8 12.9	9 47.7	12 32.4	24 19.6	18 12.3	5 5.7	14 19.9	25 11.0
20 M	13 51 36	29 44 5	7♈59 53	15 37 5	5 52.7	10 15.8	11 1.5	13 15.9	24 17.9	18 18.5	5 9.1	14 18.8	25 11.3
21 Tu	13 55 33	0♉42 39	23 15 9	0♉52 38	5 42.9	12 17.1	12 15.2	13 59.4	24 16.1	18 24.6	5 12.6	14 17.8	25 11.6
22 W	13 59 29	1 41 11	8♉28 10	16 0 26	5 33.7	14 16.3	13 28.9	14 42.9	24 14.1	18 30.6	5 16.0	14 16.7	25 11.9
23 Th	14 3 26	2 39 41	23 28 13	0♊50 34	5 26.2	16 13.2	14 42.6	15 26.3	24 11.9	18 36.6	5 19.5	14 15.7	25 12.3
24 F	14 7 22	3 38 9	8♊ 6 40	15 15 58	5 20.9	18 7.4	15 56.3	16 9.6	24 9.5	18 42.6	5 22.9	14 14.8	25 12.7
25 Sa	14 11 19	4 36 35	22 18 7	29 13 0	5D 18.2	19 58.8	17 10.0	16 52.9	24 6.9	18 48.5	5 26.4	14 13.8	25 13.1
26 Su	14 15 15	5 34 59	6♋ 0 39	12♋41 18	5 17.5	21 47.1	18 23.7	17 36.2	24 4.2	18 54.3	5 29.8	14 12.9	25 13.5
27 M	14 19 12	6 33 20	19 15 17	25 43 2	5 18.0	23 32.0	19 37.4	18 19.4	24 1.3	19 0.1	5 33.3	14 12.0	25 14.0
28 Tu	14 23 9	7 31 40	2♌ 5 4	8♌21 56	5R 18.7	25 13.3	20 51.1	19 2.5	23 58.2	19 5.8	5 36.7	14 11.2	25 14.5
29 W	14 27 5	8 29 58	14 34 14	20 42 34	5 18.7	26 51.0	22 4.7	19 45.6	23 54.9	19 11.4	5 40.2	14 10.3	25 15.0
30 Th	14 31 2	9 28 13	26 47 32	2♍49 41	5 16.9	28 24.8	23 18.4	20 28.6	23 51.5	19 17.0	5 43.6	14 9.5	25 15.6

Astro Data Dy Hr Mn	Planet Ingress Dy Hr Mn
☽0S 8 8:30	☿ ♓ 13 6:40
♄☍♆ 21 9:47	♀ ♓ 17 14:53
☽0N 22 7:20	☉ ♈ 20 18:58
	☿ ♈ 31 5:08
☿0N 2 9:58	
☽0S 4 14:16	♂ ♉ 1 21:30
♇ D 7 23:24	♀ ♈ 11 0:41
♃ R 10 17:49	☿ ♉ 15 1:45
♀0N 13 21:47	☉ ♉ 20 6:31
☽0N 18 17:25	

Last Aspect Dy Hr Mn	☽ Ingress Dy Hr Mn
1 7:43 ♃ ☍	♋ 1 22:25
3 22:28 ♇ ☌	♌ 4 7:20
6 3:28 ♃ △	♍ 6 18:18
8 21:03 ♇ ⚹	♎ 9 6:26
11 14:04 ☿ △	♏ 11 19:03
13 22:06 ☿ □	♐ 14 7:06
16 14:31 ♀ ⚹	♑ 16 16:51
18 19:27 ☉ ⚹	♒ 18 22:52
20 14:48 ♃ ⚹	♓ 21 0:59
22 17:01 ♇ △	♈ 23 0:31
24 16:01 ♇ □	♉ 24 23:37
26 16:29 ♇ ⚹	♊ 27 0:31
28 23:38 ♂ ⚹	♋ 29 4:52
31 11:00 ♂ □	♌ 31 13:04

Last Aspect Dy Hr Mn	☽ Ingress Dy Hr Mn
2 12:48 ♃ △	♍ 3 0:07
5 2:44 ♇ ⚹	♎ 5 12:31
7 15:20 ♇ □	♏ 8 1:05
10 11:44 ♀ △	♐ 10 13:03
12 13:13 ☿ △	♑ 12 23:23
14 22:08 ♇ ☍	♒ 15 6:49
17 5:40 ☉ ⚹	♓ 17 10:38
19 3:40 ♇ △	♈ 19 11:20
21 3:03 ♇ □	♉ 21 10:37
23 2:49 ♇ ⚹	♊ 23 10:37
25 3:07 ♃ ☍	♋ 25 13:22
27 11:06 ♇ ☌	♌ 27 20:03
30 3:41 ☿ □	♍ 30 6:22

☽ Phases & Eclipses Dy Hr Mn	
8 5:14	○ 17♍29
16 8:35	☽ 25♐36
23 4:14	● 2♈22
29 21:22	☽ 9♋01
6 22:46	○ 16♎57
14 21:21	☽ 24♑44
21 12:33	● 1♉13
28 11:16	☽ 7♌59

Astro Data

1 MARCH 1936
Julian Day # 13209
Delta T 23.8 sec
SVP 06♓08'46"
Obliquity 23°26'53"
⚷ Chiron 10♊55.6
☽ Mean ☊ 9♑44.8

1 APRIL 1936
Julian Day # 13240
Delta T 23.8 sec
SVP 06♓08'43"
Obliquity 23°26'53"
⚷ Chiron 11♊58.5
☽ Mean ☊ 8♑06.3

LONGITUDE — MAY 1936

Day	Sid.Time	☉	0 hr ☽	Noon ☽	True ☊	☿	♀	♂	♃	♄	♅	♆	♇
1 F	14 34 58	10♉26 26	8♍49 37	14♍47 49	5♑13.1	29♉54.6	24♈32.0	21♉11.6	23♐47.9	19♓22.6	5♉47.1	14♍ 8.7	25♋16.1
2 Sa	14 38 55	11 24 38	20 44 48	26 40 59	5R 7.1	1♊20.3	25 45.7	21 54.6	23R44.1	19 28.0	5 50.5	14R 8.0	25 16.7
3 Su	14 42 51	12 22 47	2♎36 47	8♎32 34	4 59.1	2 41.8	26 59.3	22 37.5	23 40.1	19 33.5	5 54.0	14 7.3	25 17.3
4 M	14 46 48	13 20 55	14 28 39	20 25 19	4 49.8	3 59.0	28 13.0	23 20.3	23 36.0	19 38.8	5 57.4	14 6.6	25 17.9
5 Tu	14 50 44	14 19 0	26 22 48	2♏21 20	4 40.1	5 11.9	29 26.6	24 3.1	23 31.8	19 44.1	6 0.8	14 5.9	25 18.6
6 W	14 54 41	15 17 4	8♏21 6	14 22 17	4 30.8	6 20.4	0♉40.2	24 45.8	23 27.3	19 49.3	6 4.2	14 5.3	25 19.3
7 Th	14 58 37	16 15 7	20 25 3	26 29 32	4 22.7	7 24.4	1 53.9	25 28.5	23 22.8	19 54.4	6 7.7	14 4.7	25 20.0
8 F	15 2 34	17 13 7	2♐35 56	8♐44 24	4 16.6	8 23.9	3 7.5	26 11.1	23 18.0	19 59.5	6 11.1	14 4.1	25 20.7
9 Sa	15 6 31	18 11 7	14 55 8	21 8 20	4 12.6	9 18.7	4 21.1	26 53.7	23 13.1	20 4.6	6 14.5	14 3.6	25 21.4
10 Su	15 10 27	19 9 5	27 24 15	3♑43 7	4D10.7	10 8.8	5 34.8	27 36.3	23 8.1	20 9.5	6 17.9	14 3.1	25 22.2
11 M	15 14 24	20 7 1	10♑ 5 13	16 30 52	4 10.6	10 54.2	6 48.4	28 18.8	23 2.9	20 14.4	6 21.2	14 2.6	25 23.0
12 Tu	15 18 20	21 4 56	23 0 22	29 34 1	4 11.7	11 34.8	8 2.0	29 1.2	22 57.6	20 19.2	6 24.6	14 2.1	25 23.8
13 W	15 22 17	22 2 50	6♒12 9	12♒55 2	4 13.0	12 10.6	9 15.6	29 43.6	22 52.1	20 23.9	6 28.0	14 1.7	25 24.7
14 Th	15 26 13	23 0 42	19 42 55	26 35 58	4R13.9	12 41.5	10 29.3	0♊26.0	22 46.5	20 28.6	6 31.3	14 1.3	25 25.5
15 F	15 30 10	23 58 33	3♓34 17	10♓37 52	4 13.5	13 7.4	11 42.9	1 8.3	22 40.8	20 33.2	6 34.7	14 1.0	25 26.4
16 Sa	15 34 7	24 56 23	17 46 34	25 0 7	4 11.6	13 28.4	12 56.5	1 50.5	22 34.9	20 37.7	6 38.0	14 0.7	25 27.3
17 Su	15 38 3	25 54 12	2♈18 4	9♈39 51	4 8.1	13 44.5	14 10.1	2 32.7	22 28.9	20 42.1	6 41.3	14 0.4	25 28.2
18 M	15 42 0	26 52 0	17 4 41	24 31 42	4 3.3	13 55.6	15 23.8	3 14.9	22 22.8	20 46.5	6 44.6	14 0.1	25 29.1
19 Tu	15 45 56	27 49 47	1♉59 54	9♉28 13	3 58.0	14R 1.9	16 37.4	3 57.0	22 16.6	20 50.8	6 47.9	13 59.9	25 30.1
20 W	15 49 53	28 47 32	16 55 32	24 20 47	3 53.0	14 3.3	17 51.0	4 39.1	22 10.2	20 55.0	6 51.2	13 59.7	25 31.1
21 Th	15 53 49	29 45 16	1♊42 55	9♊ 1 0	3 48.9	14 0.1	19 4.7	5 21.1	22 3.7	20 59.1	6 54.4	13 59.5	25 32.1
22 F	15 57 46	0♊42 59	16 14 15	23 21 59	3 46.2	13 52.4	20 18.3	6 3.1	21 57.2	21 3.1	6 57.7	13 59.4	25 33.1
23 Sa	16 1 42	1 40 41	0♋23 44	7♋19 11	3D45.2	13 40.3	21 31.9	6 45.0	21 50.5	21 7.1	7 0.9	13 59.3	25 34.2
24 Su	16 5 39	2 38 21	14 8 10	20 50 42	3 45.5	13 24.2	22 45.5	7 26.9	21 43.7	21 11.0	7 4.1	13 59.2	25 35.2
25 M	16 9 36	3 35 59	27 26 55	3♌57 4	3 46.7	13 4.3	23 59.1	8 8.8	21 36.9	21 14.8	7 7.3	13D 59.2	25 36.3
26 Tu	16 13 32	4 33 37	10♌21 29	16 40 38	3 48.3	12 41.0	25 12.8	8 50.5	21 29.9	21 18.5	7 10.4	13 59.2	25 37.4
27 W	16 17 29	5 31 12	22 54 58	29 5 2	3 49.7	12 14.7	26 26.4	9 32.3	21 22.9	21 22.1	7 13.6	13 59.2	25 38.5
28 Th	16 21 25	6 28 46	5♍11 24	11♍14 38	3R50.3	11 45.9	27 40.0	10 14.0	21 15.8	21 25.7	7 16.7	13 59.3	25 39.7
29 F	16 25 22	7 26 19	17 15 20	23 14 3	3 49.9	11 15.0	28 53.6	10 55.6	21 8.6	21 29.1	7 19.8	13 59.4	25 40.8
30 Sa	16 29 18	8 23 50	29 11 21	5♎ 7 47	3 48.3	10 42.6	0♊ 7.2	11 37.2	21 1.4	21 32.5	7 22.9	13 59.5	25 42.0
31 Su	16 33 15	9 21 20	11♎ 3 52	17 0 5	3 45.7	10 9.3	1 20.8	12 18.8	20 54.1	21 35.8	7 25.9	13 59.7	25 43.2

LONGITUDE — JUNE 1936

Day	Sid.Time	☉	0 hr ☽	Noon ☽	True ☊	☿	♀	♂	♃	♄	♅	♆	♇
1 M	16 37 11	10♊18 49	22♎56 53	28♎54 41	3♑42.3	9♊35.6	2♊34.4	13♊ 0.2	20♐46.7	21♓39.0	7♉29.0	13♍59.9	25♋44.4
2 Tu	16 41 8	11 16 17	4♏53 50	10♏54 41	3R38.7	9R 2.1	3 48.0	13 41.7	20R39.3	21 42.1	7 32.0	14 0.1	25 45.6
3 W	16 45 5	12 13 43	16 57 32	23 2 39	3 35.2	8 29.5	5 1.6	14 23.1	20 31.9	21 45.1	7 35.0	14 0.4	25 46.8
4 Th	16 49 1	13 11 9	29 10 13	5♐20 27	3 32.2	7 58.2	6 15.2	15 4.5	20 24.4	21 48.1	7 37.9	14 0.7	25 48.1
5 F	16 52 58	14 8 33	11♐33 29	17 49 27	3 30.1	7 28.8	7 28.8	15 45.8	20 16.8	21 50.9	7 40.9	14 1.0	25 49.4
6 Sa	16 56 54	15 5 57	24 8 27	0♑30 35	3D29.0	7 1.7	8 42.4	16 27.1	20 9.3	21 53.7	7 43.8	14 1.4	25 50.6
7 Su	17 0 51	16 3 20	6♑55 54	13 24 28	3 28.8	6 37.5	9 56.0	17 8.3	20 1.7	21 56.3	7 46.7	14 1.7	25 51.9
8 M	17 4 47	17 0 42	19 56 20	26 31 34	3 29.3	6 16.5	11 9.7	17 49.5	19 54.1	21 58.9	7 49.6	14 2.2	25 53.3
9 Tu	17 8 44	17 58 3	3♒10 10	9♒52 12	3 30.4	5 59.0	12 23.3	18 30.6	19 46.4	22 1.4	7 52.4	14 2.6	25 54.6
10 W	17 12 40	18 55 24	16 37 41	23 26 36	3 31.5	5 45.4	13 36.9	19 11.7	19 38.8	22 3.8	7 55.2	14 3.1	25 55.9
11 Th	17 16 37	19 52 44	0♓18 58	7♓14 43	3 32.5	5 35.9	14 50.5	19 52.7	19 31.1	22 6.1	7 58.0	14 3.6	25 57.3
12 F	17 20 34	20 50 3	14 13 47	21 16 2	3R33.1	5D30.6	16 4.2	20 33.7	19 23.5	22 8.3	8 0.7	14 4.2	25 58.7
13 Sa	17 24 30	21 47 23	28 21 16	5♈29 14	3 33.1	5 29.8	17 17.8	21 14.7	19 15.8	22 10.4	8 3.4	14 4.8	26 0.1
14 Su	17 28 27	22 44 41	12♈39 38	19 52 3	3 32.6	5 33.4	18 31.5	21 55.6	19 8.2	22 12.4	8 6.1	14 5.4	26 1.4
15 M	17 32 23	23 42 0	27 6 1	4♉20 59	3 31.7	5 41.7	19 45.1	22 36.5	19 0.6	22 14.3	8 8.8	14 6.0	26 2.9
16 Tu	17 36 20	24 39 18	11♉36 22	18 51 31	3 30.7	5 54.5	20 58.8	23 17.4	18 53.0	22 16.1	8 11.4	14 6.7	26 4.3
17 W	17 40 16	25 36 36	26 5 44	3♊18 20	3 29.8	6 11.9	22 12.4	23 58.2	18 45.4	22 17.8	8 14.0	14 7.4	26 5.7
18 Th	17 44 13	26 33 54	10♊28 39	17 36 1	3 29.1	6 33.9	23 26.1	24 39.0	18 37.8	22 19.4	8 16.6	14 8.1	26 7.2
19 F	17 48 9	27 31 11	24 39 51	1♋39 37	3D28.7	7 0.4	24 39.8	25 19.7	18 30.3	22 21.0	8 19.1	14 8.9	26 8.6
20 Sa	17 52 6	28 28 28	8♋34 52	15 25 16	3 28.7	7 31.4	25 53.5	26 0.4	18 22.9	22 22.4	8 21.6	14 9.7	26 10.1
21 Su	17 56 3	29 25 44	22 10 33	28 50 36	3 28.9	8 6.8	27 7.2	26 41.0	18 15.5	22 23.7	8 24.1	14 10.5	26 11.6
22 M	17 59 59	0♋23 0	5♌25 22	11♌54 55	3 29.2	8 46.6	28 20.9	27 21.6	18 8.1	22 24.9	8 26.5	14 11.4	26 13.1
23 Tu	18 3 56	1 20 15	18 19 25	24 39 6	3 29.4	9 30.8	29 34.6	28 2.2	18 0.8	22 26.1	8 28.9	14 12.3	26 14.6
24 W	18 7 52	2 17 29	0♍54 17	7♍ 5 22	3 29.6	10 19.1	0♋48.3	28 42.7	17 53.6	22 27.1	8 31.3	14 13.2	26 16.1
25 Th	18 11 49	3 14 43	13 12 46	19 17 0	3R29.7	11 11.6	2 2.0	29 23.1	17 46.4	22 28.0	8 33.6	14 14.2	26 17.6
26 F	18 15 45	4 11 56	25 18 34	1♎18 1	3D29.7	12 8.3	3 15.7	0♋ 3.6	17 39.3	22 28.8	8 35.9	14 15.1	26 19.2
27 Sa	18 19 42	5 9 9	7♎15 54	13 12 49	3 29.7	13 9.0	4 29.4	0 43.9	17 32.3	22 29.6	8 38.1	14 16.1	26 20.7
28 Su	18 23 38	6 6 21	19 9 19	25 5 58	3 29.8	14 13.7	5 43.1	1 24.3	17 25.3	22 30.2	8 40.3	14 17.2	26 22.3
29 M	18 27 35	7 3 33	1♏ 3 20	7♏ 1 57	3 30.0	15 22.3	6 56.9	2 4.6	17 18.5	22 30.7	8 42.5	14 18.3	26 23.8
30 Tu	18 31 32	8 0 45	13 2 19	19 4 54	3 30.4	16 34.8	8 10.6	2 44.8	17 11.7	22 31.1	8 44.7	14 19.4	26 25.4

Astro Data	Planet Ingress	Last Aspect	☽ Ingress	Last Aspect	☽ Ingress	☽ Phases & Eclipses	Astro Data
Dy Hr Mn	Dy Hr Mn	Dy Hr Mn	Dy Hr Mn	Dy Hr Mn	Dy Hr Mn	Dy Hr Mn	1 MAY 1936
☽0S 1 19:44	☿ ♊ 1 1:30	2 9:10 ♇ ⚹	♎ 2 18:43	1 5:38 ♇ □	♏ 1 14:11	6 15:01 ○ 15♏53	Julian Day # 13270
☽0N 16 1:04	♀ ♉ 5 10:53	5 6:52 ♀ ☍	♏ 5 7:16	3 17:24 ♇ △	♐ 4 1:37	14 6:12 ☽ 23♒16	Delta T 23.8 sec
☿ R 19 19:26	♂ ♊ 13 9:17	7 10:37 ♂ ☍	♐ 7 18:54	5 19:44 ♄ □	♑ 6 11:03	20 20:34 ● 29♉37	SVP 06♓08'40"
♃⚼♅ 21 22:50	☉ ♊ 21 6:07	9 15:53 ♃ ☌	♑ 10 4:57	8 10:52 ♇ ☍	♒ 8 18:17	28 2:46 ☽ 6♍35	Obliquity 23°26'53"
♆ D 25 11:08	♀ ♊ 29 21:39	12 11:38 ♂ △	♒ 12 12:47	10 5:17 ♃ ⚹	♓ 10 23:27		⚷ Chiron 13♊52.2
♃□♄ 27 1:45		14 6:12 ☉ □	♓ 14 17:52	12 20:01 ♇ △	♈ 13 2:46	5 5:22 ○ 14♐21	☽ Mean ☊ 6♑31.0
☽0S 29 2:03	☉ ♋ 21 14:22	16 12:46 ♇ △	♈ 16 20:14	14 22:15 ♇ □	♉ 15 4:48	12 12:05 ☽ 21♓19	
	♀ ♋ 23 8:16	18 13:33 ♇ □	♉ 18 20:47	16 24:00 ♇ ⚹	♊ 17 6:29	19 5:14 ● 27♊44	1 JUNE 1936
☽0N 12 6:43	♂ ♋ 25 21:53	20 20:34 ☉ ☌	♊ 20 21:12	19 5:14 ☉ ☌	♋ 19 9:08	19 5:20:06 ● T 2'32"	Julian Day # 13301
☿ D 12 16:35		22 9:32 ♃ ☍	♋ 22 23:19	21 7:14 ♇ ☌	♌ 21 14:06	26 19:23 ☽ 4♎58	Delta T 23.8 sec
☽0S 25 9:44		24 20:38 ♇ ☌	♌ 25 4:41	23 19:32 ♂ ⚹	♍ 23 22:15		SVP 06♓08'35"
		27 7:36 ♀ □	♍ 27 13:48	26 2:01 ♇ ⚹	♎ 26 9:23		Obliquity 23°26'52"
		29 16:57 ♇ ⚹	♎ 30 1:38	28 14:36 ♇ □	♏ 28 21:53		⚷ Chiron 16♊21.4
							☽ Mean ☊ 4♑52.5

JULY 1936 LONGITUDE

Day	Sid.Time	☉	0 hr ☽	Noon ☽	True ☊	☿	♀	♂	♃	♄	♅	♆	♇
1 W	18 35 28	8♋57 56	25♏10 10	1♐18 29	3♑30.9	17♊51.2	9♋24.3	3♋25.1	17♐ 5.1	22♓31.5	8♉46.8	14♍20.5	26♋26.9
2 Th	18 39 25	9 55 7	7♐30 12	13 45 37	3 31.5	19 11.4	10 38.1	4 5.2	16R 58.5	22 31.7	8 48.8	14 21.6	26 28.5
3 F	18 43 21	10 52 18	20 4 58	26 28 24	3 32.0	20 35.3	11 51.8	4 45.4	16 52.1	22R 31.8	8 50.8	14 22.8	26 30.1
4 Sa	18 47 18	11 49 28	2♑56 1	9♑27 53	3R 32.2	22 2.9	13 5.6	5 25.5	16 45.7	22 31.8	8 52.8	14 24.0	26 31.7
5 Su	18 51 14	12 46 39	16 3 57	22 44 7	3 32.0	23 34.2	14 19.3	6 5.5	16 39.5	22 31.8	8 54.8	14 25.3	26 33.3
6 M	18 55 11	13 43 50	29 28 15	6♒16 7	3 31.3	25 9.0	15 33.1	6 45.6	16 33.4	22 31.6	8 56.7	14 26.5	26 34.9
7 Tu	18 59 8	14 41 0	13♒ 7 29	20 2 1	3 30.2	26 47.4	16 46.9	7 25.6	16 27.4	22 31.3	8 58.5	14 27.8	26 36.5
8 W	19 3 4	15 38 11	26 59 24	3♓59 16	3 28.8	28 29.2	18 0.6	8 5.5	16 21.5	22 31.0	9 0.3	14 29.1	26 38.1
9 Th	19 7 1	16 35 22	11♓ 1 16	18 5 1	3 27.3	0♋14.2	19 14.4	8 45.4	16 15.8	22 30.5	9 2.1	14 30.5	26 39.7
10 F	19 10 57	17 32 34	25 10 8	2♈16 16	3 26.0	2 2.5	20 28.2	9 25.3	16 10.2	22 29.9	9 3.9	14 31.8	26 41.4
11 Sa	19 14 54	18 29 46	9♈23 4	16 30 10	3D 25.2	3 53.8	21 42.0	10 5.1	16 4.7	22 29.2	9 5.5	14 33.2	26 43.0
12 Su	19 18 50	19 26 59	23 37 17	0♉44 5	3 25.1	5 47.9	22 55.8	10 44.9	15 59.4	22 28.5	9 7.2	14 34.6	26 44.6
13 M	19 22 47	20 24 12	7♉50 16	14 55 34	3 25.6	7 44.7	24 9.7	11 24.7	15 54.2	22 27.6	9 8.8	14 36.1	26 46.3
14 Tu	19 26 43	21 21 26	21 59 41	29 2 20	3 26.7	9 43.9	25 23.5	12 4.5	15 49.1	22 26.6	9 10.4	14 37.5	26 47.9
15 W	19 30 40	22 18 40	6♊ 3 14	13♊ 2 7	3 27.9	11 45.2	26 37.3	12 44.2	15 44.2	22 25.6	9 11.9	14 39.0	26 49.5
16 Th	19 34 37	23 15 55	19 58 40	26 52 37	3R 29.0	13 48.4	27 51.2	13 23.8	15 39.4	22 24.4	9 13.3	14 40.6	26 51.2
17 F	19 38 33	24 13 11	3♋43 41	10♋31 37	3 29.4	15 53.1	29 5.1	14 3.5	15 34.8	22 23.2	9 14.8	14 42.1	26 52.8
18 Sa	19 42 30	25 10 27	17 16 9	23 57 4	3 28.9	17 59.1	0♌18.9	14 43.1	15 30.4	22 21.8	9 16.2	14 43.7	26 54.5
19 Su	19 46 26	26 7 44	0♌34 12	7♌ 7 25	3 27.2	20 6.0	1 32.8	15 22.6	15 26.1	22 20.3	9 17.5	14 45.3	26 56.1
20 M	19 50 23	27 5 1	13 36 36	20 1 45	3 24.5	22 13.6	2 46.7	16 2.2	15 22.0	22 18.8	9 18.8	14 46.9	26 57.7
21 Tu	19 54 19	28 2 18	26 22 53	2♍40 5	3 20.9	24 21.5	4 0.6	16 41.7	15 18.0	22 17.1	9 20.0	14 48.5	26 59.4
22 W	19 58 16	28 59 36	8♍53 32	15 3 27	3 16.9	26 29.3	5 14.5	17 21.1	15 14.2	22 15.4	9 21.2	14 50.2	27 1.0
23 Th	20 2 12	29 56 54	21 10 7	27 13 54	3 12.9	28 37.0	6 28.4	18 0.5	15 10.6	22 13.6	9 22.4	14 51.8	27 2.7
24 F	20 6 9	0♌54 12	3♎15 10	9♎14 24	3 9.4	0♌44.2	7 42.3	18 39.9	15 7.1	22 11.6	9 23.5	14 53.5	27 4.3
25 Sa	20 10 6	1 51 31	15 12 4	21 8 43	3 7.0	2 50.6	8 56.2	19 19.3	15 3.8	22 9.6	9 24.5	14 55.2	27 5.9
26 Su	20 14 2	2 48 51	27 4 54	3♏ 1 13	3D 5.7	4 56.2	10 10.1	19 58.6	15 0.7	22 7.5	9 25.5	14 57.0	27 7.6
27 M	20 17 59	3 46 11	8♏58 15	14 56 36	3 5.7	7 0.8	11 24.0	20 37.9	14 57.8	22 5.3	9 26.5	14 58.7	27 9.2
28 Tu	20 21 55	4 43 31	20 56 53	26 59 42	3 6.7	9 4.1	12 38.0	21 17.1	14 55.0	22 3.0	9 27.4	15 0.5	27 10.9
29 W	20 25 52	5 40 52	3♐ 5 37	9♐15 10	3 8.3	11 6.2	13 51.9	21 56.3	14 52.4	22 0.7	9 28.3	15 2.3	27 12.5
30 Th	20 29 48	6 38 13	15 28 53	21 47 12	3 9.9	13 6.9	15 5.8	22 35.5	14 50.0	21 58.2	9 29.1	15 4.1	27 14.1
31 F	20 33 45	7 35 36	28 10 30	4♑39 5	3R 10.9	15 6.2	16 19.8	23 14.6	14 47.8	21 55.7	9 29.9	15 6.0	27 15.7

AUGUST 1936 LONGITUDE

Day	Sid.Time	☉	0 hr ☽	Noon ☽	True ☊	☿	♀	♂	♃	♄	♅	♆	♇
1 Sa	20 37 41	8♌32 58	11♑13 10	17♑52 50	3♑10.7	17♌ 3.9	17♌33.7	23♋53.7	14♐45.8	21♓53.1	9♉30.6	15♍ 7.8	27♋17.4
2 Su	20 41 38	9 30 22	24 38 4	1♒28 44	3R 9.0	19 0.1	18 47.6	24 32.8	14R 43.9	21R 50.3	9 31.3	15 9.7	27 19.0
3 M	20 45 35	10 27 46	8♒24 34	15 25 11	3 5.6	20 54.8	20 1.6	25 11.9	14 42.2	21 47.6	9 31.9	15 11.6	27 20.6
4 Tu	20 49 31	11 25 11	22 30 3	29 38 34	3 0.7	22 47.9	21 15.5	25 50.9	14 40.7	21 44.7	9 32.4	15 13.5	27 22.2
5 W	20 53 28	12 22 37	6♓50 2	14♓ 3 42	2 54.9	24 39.4	22 29.5	26 29.8	14 39.4	21 41.7	9 33.0	15 15.4	27 23.8
6 Th	20 57 24	13 20 5	21 18 48	28 34 32	2 49.0	26 29.3	23 43.4	27 8.8	14 38.3	21 38.7	9 33.4	15 17.3	27 25.4
7 F	21 1 21	14 17 33	5♈50 9	13♈ 4 58	2 43.6	28 17.7	24 57.4	27 47.7	14 37.3	21 35.6	9 33.9	15 19.3	27 27.0
8 Sa	21 5 17	15 15 3	20 18 23	27 29 52	2 39.6	0♍ 4.5	26 11.3	28 26.6	14 36.6	21 32.4	9 34.2	15 21.3	27 28.6
9 Su	21 9 14	16 12 34	4♉38 59	11♉45 26	2D 37.4	1 49.7	27 25.3	29 5.5	14 36.0	21 29.2	9 34.6	15 23.3	27 30.1
10 M	21 13 10	17 10 7	18 48 57	25 49 24	2 36.8	3 33.4	28 39.3	29 44.3	14 35.6	21 25.8	9 34.9	15 25.3	27 31.7
11 Tu	21 17 7	18 7 41	2♊46 43	9♊40 52	2 37.5	5 15.6	29 53.3	0♌23.1	14D 35.4	21 22.4	9 35.1	15 27.3	27 33.3
12 W	21 21 4	19 5 16	16 31 51	23 19 43	2 38.7	6 56.2	1♍ 7.3	1 1.9	14 35.3	21 19.0	9 35.3	15 29.3	27 34.8
13 Th	21 25 0	20 2 53	0♋ 4 31	6♋46 17	2R 39.5	8 35.3	2 21.3	1 40.6	14 35.5	21 15.4	9 35.4	15 31.3	27 36.4
14 F	21 28 57	21 0 32	13 25 5	20 0 56	2 38.9	10 12.9	3 35.3	2 19.3	14 35.9	21 11.8	9 35.5	15 33.4	27 37.9
15 Sa	21 32 53	21 58 12	26 33 51	3♌ 3 49	2 36.5	11 49.1	4 49.3	2 58.0	14 36.4	21 8.2	9R 35.5	15 35.5	27 39.4
16 Su	21 36 50	22 55 53	9♌30 51	15 54 54	2 31.7	13 23.7	6 3.3	3 36.7	14 37.1	21 4.4	9 35.5	15 37.5	27 40.9
17 M	21 40 46	23 53 36	22 15 58	28 34 3	2 24.7	14 56.9	7 17.3	4 15.3	14 38.0	21 0.7	9 35.4	15 39.6	27 42.4
18 Tu	21 44 43	24 51 19	4♍49 10	11♍ 1 21	2 15.9	16 28.5	8 31.3	4 53.9	14 39.1	20 56.8	9 35.3	15 41.7	27 43.9
19 W	21 48 39	25 49 5	17 10 41	23 17 17	2 6.1	17 58.7	9 45.3	5 32.5	14 40.4	20 52.9	9 35.1	15 43.8	27 45.4
20 Th	21 52 36	26 46 51	29 21 20	5♎23 2	1 56.2	19 27.3	10 59.3	6 11.0	14 41.8	20 48.9	9 34.9	15 46.0	27 46.9
21 F	21 56 33	27 44 39	11♎22 39	17 20 32	1 47.1	20 54.4	12 13.3	6 49.5	14 43.5	20 44.9	9 34.6	15 48.1	27 48.4
22 Sa	22 0 29	28 42 27	23 17 4	29 12 40	1 39.6	22 20.0	13 27.3	7 28.0	14 45.3	20 40.9	9 34.3	15 50.2	27 49.8
23 Su	22 4 26	29 40 18	5♏ 7 49	11♏ 3 4	1 34.3	23 44.1	14 41.3	8 6.4	14 47.3	20 36.7	9 33.9	15 52.4	27 51.3
24 M	22 8 22	0♍38 9	16 58 58	22 56 8	1 31.2	25 6.5	15 55.3	8 44.8	14 49.5	20 32.6	9 33.5	15 54.5	27 52.7
25 Tu	22 12 19	1 36 2	28 55 12	4♐56 47	1D 30.1	26 27.3	17 9.3	9 23.2	14 51.9	20 28.4	9 33.1	15 56.7	27 54.1
26 W	22 16 15	2 33 56	11♐ 1 35	17 10 13	1 30.3	27 46.5	18 23.3	10 1.6	14 54.5	20 24.1	9 32.6	15 58.9	27 55.5
27 Th	22 20 12	3 31 51	23 23 19	29 41 30	1R 31.0	29 4.0	19 37.3	10 39.9	14 57.2	20 19.8	9 32.0	16 1.1	27 56.9
28 F	22 24 8	4 29 47	6♑ 5 19	12♑35 13	1 31.2	0♎19.7	20 51.3	11 18.2	15 0.1	20 15.5	9 31.4	16 3.2	27 58.3
29 Sa	22 28 5	5 27 45	19 11 35	25 54 42	1 29.8	1 33.6	22 5.3	11 56.4	15 3.2	20 11.2	9 30.7	16 5.4	27 59.6
30 Su	22 32 2	6 25 45	2♒44 40	9♒41 27	1 26.2	2 45.6	23 19.3	12 34.7	15 6.5	20 6.8	9 30.0	16 7.6	28 1.0
31 M	22 35 58	7 23 45	16 44 50	23 54 23	1 20.1	3 55.6	24 33.2	13 12.9	15 9.9	20 2.4	9 29.3	16 9.8	28 2.3

Astro Data Dy Hr Mn	Planet Ingress Dy Hr Mn
♄ R 3 18:52	☿ ♋ 8 20:47
☽0N 9 12:10	♀ ♌ 17 17:51
☽0S 22 18:17	☉ ♌ 23 1:18
♃□♆ 26 19:00	☿ ♌ 23 15:39
☽0N 5 19:09	☿ ♍ 7 22:59
♃ D 11 14:59	♂ ♌ 10 9:43
♅ R 15 2:35	♀ ♍ 11 2:11
☽0S 19 2:35	☉ ♍ 23 8:11
☿0S 26 0:59	☿ ♎ 27 17:43

Last Aspect Dy Hr Mn	☽ Ingress	Last Aspect Dy Hr Mn	☽ Ingress
1 2:31 ♇ △	♐ 1 9:27	2 4:44 ♇ ☍	♒ 2 9:25
3 4:37 ♄ □	♑ 3 18:34	4 0:35 ☿ ☍	♓ 4 12:36
5 18:51 ♇ ☍	♒ 6 0:56	6 10:07 ♇ △	♈ 6 14:21
8 2:56 ☿ △	♓ 8 5:10	8 14:14 ♂ □	♉ 8 16:11
10 2:35 ♇ △	♈ 10 8:10	10 18:31 ♀ □	♊ 10 19:12
12 5:17 ♇ □	♉ 12 10:46	12 8:24 ♄ □	♋ 12 23:52
14 8:12 ♇ ✶	♊ 14 13:38	15 2:01 ♇ ☌	♌ 15 6:20
16 4:13 ♄ □	♋ 16 17:28	17 3:21 ☉ ☌	♍ 17 14:44
18 17:23 ♇ ☌	♌ 18 22:58	19 20:52 ♇ ✶	♎ 20 1:17
20 3:15 ♃ △	♍ 21 6:54	22 11:57 ☉ ✶	♏ 22 13:36
23 11:39 ♇ ✶	♎ 23 17:30	24 21:58 ♇ △	♐ 25 2:09
26 0:05 ♇ □	♏ 26 5:54	27 12:01 ☿ □	♑ 27 12:35
28 12:24 ♇ △	♐ 28 17:56	29 15:42 ♇ ☍	♒ 29 19:12
30 12:18 ♄ □	♑ 31 3:24	30 21:19 ♃ ✶	♓ 31 22:06

☽ Phases & Eclipses Dy Hr Mn	
4 17:34	○ 12♑31
4 17:25	P 0.267
11 16:28	☽ 19♈09
18 15:19	● 25♋47
26 12:36	☽ 3♏19
3 3:47	○ 10♒37
9 20:59	☽ 17♉03
17 3:21	● 24♌02
25 5:49	☽ 1♐50

Astro Data

1 JULY 1936
Julian Day # 13331
Delta T 23.8 sec
SVP 06♓08'30"
Obliquity 23°26'51"
⚷ Chiron 18♊52.8
☽ Mean ☊ 3♑17.2

1 AUGUST 1936
Julian Day # 13362
Delta T 23.8 sec
SVP 06♓08'25"
Obliquity 23°26'51"
⚷ Chiron 21♊11.6
☽ Mean ☊ 1♑38.7

LONGITUDE SEPTEMBER 1936

Day	Sid.Time	☉	0 hr ☽	Noon ☽	True ☊	☿	♀	♂	♃	♄	♅	♆	♇
1 Tu	22 39 55	8♍21 47	1♓ 9 31	8♓29 27	1♑11.9	5♎ 3.6	25♍47.2	13♌51.1	15♐13.5	19♓57.9	9♉28.5	16♍12.0	28♋ 3.6
2 W	22 43 51	9 19 51	15 53 13	23 19 47	1R 2.1	6 9.4	27 1.2	14 29.2	15 17.3	19R53.4	9R27.6	16 14.2	28 4.9
3 Th	22 47 48	10 17 56	0♈47 59	8♈16 39	0 51.9	7 12.9	28 15.1	15 7.3	15 21.2	19 48.9	9 26.7	16 16.5	28 6.2
4 F	22 51 44	11 16 4	15 44 39	23 10 53	0 42.6	8 14.1	29 29.1	15 45.4	15 25.3	19 44.4	9 25.8	16 18.7	28 7.5
5 Sa	22 55 41	12 14 13	0♉34 26	7♉54 28	0 35.1	9 12.7	0♎43.0	16 23.5	15 29.6	19 39.9	9 24.8	16 20.9	28 8.8
6 Su	22 59 37	13 12 24	15 10 21	22 21 37	0 30.0	10 8.6	1 57.0	17 1.5	15 34.1	19 35.3	9 23.8	16 23.1	28 10.0
7 M	23 3 34	14 10 37	29 27 59	6♊29 17	0 27.4	11 1.7	3 11.0	17 39.6	15 38.7	19 30.7	9 22.7	16 25.3	28 11.2
8 Tu	23 7 30	15 8 53	13♊25 31	20 16 47	0D 26.7	11 51.7	4 24.9	18 17.6	15 43.5	19 26.1	9 21.6	16 27.6	28 12.4
9 W	23 11 27	16 7 10	27 3 15	3♋45 11	0R 26.8	12 38.5	5 38.8	18 55.5	15 48.5	19 21.5	9 20.5	16 29.8	28 13.6
10 Th	23 15 24	17 5 30	10♋22 50	16 56 30	0 26.6	13 21.7	6 52.8	19 33.5	15 53.6	19 16.9	9 19.3	16 32.0	28 14.8
11 F	23 19 20	18 3 51	23 26 29	29 53 4	0 24.7	14 1.3	8 6.7	20 11.4	15 58.8	19 12.3	9 18.0	16 34.3	28 16.0
12 Sa	23 23 17	19 2 15	6♌16 30	12♌37 1	0 20.5	14 36.8	9 20.7	20 49.3	16 4.3	19 7.7	9 16.7	16 36.5	28 17.1
13 Su	23 27 13	20 0 41	18 54 48	25 10 2	0 13.2	15 7.9	10 34.6	21 27.1	16 9.9	19 3.1	9 15.4	16 38.7	28 18.2
14 M	23 31 10	20 59 8	1♍22 52	7♍33 23	0 3.2	15 34.5	11 48.5	22 5.0	16 15.6	18 58.4	9 14.0	16 40.9	28 19.3
15 Tu	23 35 6	21 57 38	13 41 42	19 47 54	29♐50.7	15 56.1	13 2.5	22 42.8	16 21.5	18 53.8	9 12.6	16 43.2	28 20.4
16 W	23 39 3	22 56 10	25 52 6	1♎54 22	29 36.9	16 12.4	14 16.4	23 20.6	16 27.6	18 49.2	9 11.1	16 45.4	28 21.4
17 Th	23 42 59	23 54 43	7♎54 52	13 53 43	29 22.8	16 23.0	15 30.3	23 58.3	16 33.8	18 44.6	9 9.6	16 47.6	28 22.5
18 F	23 46 56	24 53 18	19 51 6	25 47 16	29 9.7	16R27.6	16 44.2	24 36.0	16 40.2	18 40.0	9 8.1	16 49.8	28 23.5
19 Sa	23 50 53	25 51 55	1♏42 29	7♏37 3	28 58.5	16 25.9	17 58.1	25 13.7	16 46.7	18 35.5	9 6.5	16 52.0	28 24.5
20 Su	23 54 49	26 50 34	13 31 22	19 25 50	28 49.9	16 17.4	19 12.0	25 51.4	16 53.4	18 30.9	9 4.9	16 54.2	28 25.5
21 M	23 58 46	27 49 15	25 20 56	1♐17 12	28 44.2	16 2.0	20 25.9	26 29.0	17 0.2	18 26.4	9 3.3	16 56.4	28 26.4
22 Tu	0 2 42	28 47 58	7♐15 11	13 15 30	28 41.1	15 39.5	21 39.8	27 6.7	17 7.1	18 21.9	9 1.6	16 58.6	28 27.4
23 W	0 6 39	29 46 42	19 18 47	25 25 41	28 40.0	15 9.7	22 53.6	27 44.2	17 14.3	18 17.4	8 59.8	17 0.8	28 28.3
24 Th	0 10 35	0♎45 28	1♑36 53	7♑53 1	28 39.9	14 32.8	24 7.5	28 21.8	17 21.5	18 12.9	8 58.1	17 3.0	28 29.2
25 F	0 14 32	1 44 16	14 14 46	20 42 41	28 39.6	13 48.8	25 21.3	28 59.3	17 28.9	18 8.5	8 56.3	17 5.1	28 30.1
26 Sa	0 18 28	2 43 5	27 17 19	3♒59 6	28 38.0	12 58.3	26 35.2	29 36.8	17 36.4	18 4.1	8 54.5	17 7.3	28 30.9
27 Su	0 22 25	3 41 56	10♒48 19	17 45 7	28 34.2	12 1.9	27 49.0	0♍14.3	17 44.1	17 59.7	8 52.6	17 9.5	28 31.8
28 M	0 26 22	4 40 49	24 49 28	2♓ 1 7	28 27.8	11 0.5	29 2.8	0 51.7	17 51.9	17 55.4	8 50.7	17 11.6	28 32.6
29 Tu	0 30 18	5 39 44	9♓19 35	16 44 9	28 18.9	9 55.3	0♏16.6	1 29.1	17 59.8	17 51.1	8 48.8	17 13.8	28 33.4
30 W	0 34 15	6 38 40	24 13 53	1♈47 38	28 8.3	8 47.7	1 30.4	2 6.5	18 7.9	17 46.9	8 46.8	17 15.9	28 34.1

LONGITUDE OCTOBER 1936

Day	Sid.Time	☉	0 hr ☽	Noon ☽	True ☊	☿	♀	♂	♃	♄	♅	♆	♇
1 Th	0 38 11	7♎37 39	9♈24 7	17♈ 1 57	27♐57.2	7♎39.3	2♏44.2	2♍43.8	18♐16.1	17♓42.7	8♉44.8	17♍18.0	28♋34.9
2 F	0 42 8	8 36 39	24 39 43	2♉16 2	27R46.8	6R31.9	3 57.9	3 21.2	18 24.4	17R38.5	8R42.8	17 20.1	28 35.6
3 Sa	0 46 4	9 35 42	9♉49 35	17 19 16	27 38.3	5 27.4	5 11.7	3 58.5	18 32.8	17 34.4	8 40.8	17 22.2	28 36.3
4 Su	0 50 1	10 34 47	24 44 8	2♊ 3 26	27 32.4	4 27.5	6 25.4	4 35.8	18 41.4	17 30.3	8 38.7	17 24.3	28 36.9
5 M	0 53 57	11 33 54	9♊16 41	16 23 33	27 29.3	3 33.9	7 39.1	5 13.0	18 50.1	17 26.3	8 36.6	17 26.4	28 37.6
6 Tu	0 57 54	12 33 4	23 23 57	0♋17 54	27D 28.2	2 48.1	8 52.9	5 50.2	18 58.9	17 22.4	8 34.5	17 28.4	28 38.2
7 W	1 1 51	13 32 16	7♋ 5 37	13 47 22	27R 28.3	2 11.2	10 6.6	6 27.4	19 7.9	17 18.5	8 32.3	17 30.5	28 38.8
8 Th	1 5 47	14 31 30	20 23 31	26 54 29	27 28.3	1 44.3	11 20.3	7 4.6	19 16.9	17 14.6	8 30.1	17 32.5	28 39.4
9 F	1 9 44	15 30 47	3♌20 43	9♌42 38	27 26.9	1 28.0	12 34.0	7 41.8	19 26.1	17 10.8	8 27.9	17 34.6	28 39.9
10 Sa	1 13 40	16 30 5	16 0 43	22 15 21	27 23.4	1D 22.4	13 47.7	8 18.9	19 35.4	17 7.1	8 25.7	17 36.6	28 40.5
11 Su	1 17 37	17 29 27	28 26 56	4♍35 50	27 17.1	1 27.7	15 1.4	8 56.0	19 44.8	17 3.4	8 23.5	17 38.6	28 41.0
12 M	1 21 33	18 28 50	10♍42 22	16 46 49	27 8.1	1 43.5	16 15.0	9 33.0	19 54.3	16 59.8	8 21.2	17 40.6	28 41.5
13 Tu	1 25 30	19 28 16	22 49 26	28 50 27	26 56.8	2 9.6	17 28.7	10 10.0	20 4.0	16 56.3	8 18.9	17 42.5	28 41.9
14 W	1 29 26	20 27 43	4♎50 3	10♎48 25	26 44.2	2 45.2	18 42.4	10 47.0	20 13.7	16 52.9	8 16.6	17 44.5	28 42.3
15 Th	1 33 23	21 27 13	16 45 43	22 42 7	26 31.3	3 29.7	19 56.0	11 24.0	20 23.6	16 49.5	8 14.3	17 46.4	28 42.7
16 F	1 37 19	22 26 45	28 37 47	4♏32 55	26 19.3	4 22.3	21 9.6	12 1.0	20 33.6	16 46.2	8 11.9	17 48.3	28 43.1
17 Sa	1 41 16	23 26 19	10♏27 42	16 22 22	26 9.0	5 22.2	22 23.2	12 37.9	20 43.7	16 42.9	8 9.6	17 50.2	28 43.5
18 Su	1 45 13	24 25 55	22 17 12	28 12 29	26 1.2	6 28.7	23 36.9	13 14.7	20 53.8	16 39.8	8 7.2	17 52.1	28 43.8
19 M	1 49 9	25 25 33	4♐ 8 36	10♐ 5 54	25 56.1	7 40.8	24 50.4	13 51.6	21 4.1	16 36.7	8 4.8	17 54.0	28 44.1
20 Tu	1 53 6	26 25 13	16 4 51	22 5 55	25D 53.5	8 58.0	26 4.0	14 28.4	21 14.5	16 33.7	8 2.4	17 55.8	28 44.4
21 W	1 57 2	27 24 54	28 9 37	4♑16 30	25 53.0	10 19.3	27 17.6	15 5.2	21 25.0	16 30.8	7 60.0	17 57.6	28 44.6
22 Th	2 0 59	28 24 38	10♑27 8	16 42 9	25 53.7	11 44.4	28 31.1	15 41.9	21 35.6	16 27.9	7 57.6	17 59.4	28 44.8
23 F	2 4 55	29 24 23	23 2 6	29 27 36	25R 54.5	13 12.5	29 44.7	16 18.6	21 46.3	16 25.2	7 55.1	18 1.2	28 45.0
24 Sa	2 8 52	0♏24 10	5♒59 10	12♒37 18	25 54.5	14 43.1	0♐58.2	16 55.3	21 57.0	16 22.5	7 52.7	18 3.0	28 45.2
25 Su	2 12 48	1 23 58	19 22 25	26 14 47	25 52.9	16 15.8	2 11.7	17 32.0	22 7.9	16 19.9	7 50.2	18 4.7	28 45.4
26 M	2 16 45	2 23 48	3♓14 33	10♓21 40	25 49.2	17 50.2	3 25.2	18 8.6	22 18.9	16 17.5	7 47.8	18 6.4	28 45.5
27 Tu	2 20 42	3 23 40	17 35 55	24 56 49	25 43.4	19 25.9	4 38.6	18 45.1	22 29.9	16 15.1	7 45.3	18 8.1	28 45.6
28 W	2 24 38	4 23 33	2♈23 41	9♈55 38	25 36.1	21 2.7	5 52.0	19 21.7	22 41.0	16 12.8	7 42.9	18 9.8	28 45.7
29 Th	2 28 35	5 23 28	17 31 31	25 10 4	25 28.2	22 40.2	7 5.5	19 58.2	22 52.3	16 10.5	7 40.4	18 11.5	28 45.7
30 F	2 32 31	6 23 25	2♉49 55	10♉29 38	25 20.7	24 18.4	8 18.8	20 34.7	23 3.6	16 8.4	7 37.9	18 13.1	28R45.7
31 Sa	2 36 28	7 23 24	18 7 48	25 43 5	25 14.6	25 56.9	9 32.2	21 11.1	23 15.0	16 6.4	7 35.5	18 14.7	28 45.7

Astro Data	Dy Hr Mn
☽0N	2 4:19
♀0S	6 12:11
☽0S	15 9:38
☿ R	18 5:33
♃□♆	20 4:25
♃□♄	28 6:57
☽0N	29 14:50
♄☍♆	4 23:46
☿0N	10 6:46
☿ D	10 0:17
☽0S	12 15:15
☿0S	15 6:31
☽0N	27 0:59
♃⚼♅	28 3:12

Planet Ingress	Dy Hr Mn
♀ ♎	4 10:02
☊ ♐	14 6:29
☉ ♎	23 5:26
♂ ♍	26 14:51
♀ ♏	28 18:36
☉ ♏	23 14:18
♀ ♐	23 5:00
♇ R	30 5:20

Last Aspect Dy Hr Mn		☽ Ingress Dy Hr Mn
2 19:40	♇ △	♈ 2 22:43
4 20:03	♇ □	♉ 4 23:04
6 21:50	♇ ✱	♊ 7 0:54
8 10:27	♄ □	♋ 9 5:16
11 8:59	♇ ☌	♌ 11 12:13
13 5:07	♂ ☌	♍ 13 21:20
16 4:57	♇ ✱	♎ 16 8:12
18 17:18	♇ □	♏ 18 20:32
21 6:16	♇ △	♐ 21 9:24
23 17:23	♂ △	♑ 23 20:53
26 2:13	♇ ☍	♒ 26 4:53
28 7:43	♀ △	♓ 28 8:39
30 6:54	♇ △	♈ 30 9:10

Last Aspect Dy Hr Mn		☽ Ingress Dy Hr Mn
2 6:12	♇ □	♉ 2 8:25
4 6:21	♇ ✱	♊ 4 8:37
5 16:20	♃ ☍	♋ 6 11:29
8 15:15	♇ ☌	♌ 8 17:45
10 6:57	♃ △	♍ 11 3:01
13 11:43	♇ ✱	♎ 13 14:19
16 0:11	♇ □	♏ 16 2:47
18 13:04	♇ △	♐ 18 15:38
20 22:24	☉ ✱	♑ 21 3:37
23 12:53	☉ □	♒ 23 13:00
25 4:54	♃ ✱	♓ 25 18:28
27 18:10	♇ △	♈ 27 20:09
29 17:38	♇ □	♉ 29 19:34
31 16:51	♇ ✱	♊ 31 18:49

☽ Phases & Eclipses Dy Hr Mn	
1 12:37	○ 8♓52
8 3:14	☽ 15♊17
15 17:41	● 22♍41
23 22:12	☽ 0♑41
30 21:01	○ 7♈30
7 12:28	☽ 14♋03
15 10:20	● 21♎53
23 12:53	☽ 29♑56
30 5:58	○ 6♉38

Astro Data

1 SEPTEMBER 1936
Julian Day # 13393
Delta T 23.9 sec
SVP 06♓08'21"
Obliquity 23°26'52"
⚷ Chiron 22♊48.2
☽ Mean ☊ 0♑00.2

1 OCTOBER 1936
Julian Day # 13423
Delta T 23.9 sec
SVP 06♓08'18"
Obliquity 23°26'52"
⚷ Chiron 23♊22.2
☽ Mean ☊ 28♐24.8

NOVEMBER 1936 LONGITUDE

Day	Sid.Time	☉	0 hr ☽	Noon ☽	True ☊	☿	♀	♂	♃	♄	♅	♆	♇
1 Su	2 40 24	8♏23 25	3♊14 19	10♊40 27	25♐10.6	27♎35.7	10♐45.6	21♍47.5	23♐26.4	16♓ 4.5	7♉33.0	18♍16.3	28♋45.7
2 M	2 44 21	9 23 28	18 0 43	25 14 31	25D 8.7	29 14.7	11 58.9	22 23.9	23 38.0	16R 2.6	7R 30.5	18 17.8	28R 45.6
3 Tu	2 48 17	10 23 33	2♋21 28	9♋21 24	25 8.7	0♏53.6	13 12.2	23 0.3	23 49.6	16 0.9	7 28.0	18 19.4	28 45.5
4 W	2 52 14	11 23 40	16 14 19	23 0 21	25 9.8	2 32.5	14 25.5	23 36.6	24 1.3	15 59.3	7 25.6	18 20.9	28 45.4
5 Th	2 56 11	12 23 50	29 39 48	6♌13 1	25 11.2	4 11.3	15 38.8	24 12.9	24 13.1	15 57.7	7 23.1	18 22.4	28 45.3
6 F	3 0 7	13 24 1	12♌40 28	19 2 36	25R 11.9	5 50.0	16 52.1	24 49.1	24 25.0	15 56.3	7 20.7	18 23.8	28 45.1
7 Sa	3 4 4	14 24 14	25 19 57	1♍33 3	25 11.2	7 28.4	18 5.3	25 25.3	24 36.9	15 54.9	7 18.2	18 25.3	28 44.9
8 Su	3 8 0	15 24 30	7♍42 24	13 48 32	25 8.7	9 6.6	19 18.5	26 1.5	24 48.9	15 53.7	7 15.8	18 26.7	28 44.7
9 M	3 11 57	16 24 47	19 51 55	25 53 0	25 4.5	10 44.5	20 31.7	26 37.6	25 1.0	15 52.6	7 13.3	18 28.1	28 44.5
10 Tu	3 15 53	17 25 6	1♎52 13	7♎49 58	24 58.6	12 22.1	21 44.9	27 13.7	25 13.2	15 51.5	7 10.9	18 29.4	28 44.2
11 W	3 19 50	18 25 28	13 46 35	19 42 25	24 51.9	13 59.4	22 58.0	27 49.8	25 25.4	15 50.6	7 8.5	18 30.7	28 43.9
12 Th	3 23 46	19 25 51	25 37 45	1♏32 50	24 44.8	15 36.5	24 11.2	28 25.8	25 37.7	15 49.8	7 6.1	18 32.0	28 43.6
13 F	3 27 43	20 26 16	7♏27 56	13 23 16	24 38.2	17 13.2	25 24.3	29 1.8	25 50.0	15 49.0	7 3.7	18 33.3	28 43.3
14 Sa	3 31 40	21 26 42	19 19 4	25 15 31	24 32.7	18 49.7	26 37.3	29 37.7	26 2.5	15 48.4	7 1.3	18 34.5	28 42.9
15 Su	3 35 36	22 27 11	1♐12 52	7♐11 19	24 28.7	20 25.8	27 50.4	0♎13.6	26 14.9	15 47.9	6 58.9	18 35.7	28 42.5
16 M	3 39 33	23 27 40	13 11 7	19 12 31	24D 26.4	22 1.7	29 3.4	0 49.5	26 27.5	15 47.5	6 56.6	18 36.9	28 42.1
17 Tu	3 43 29	24 28 12	25 15 48	1♑21 17	24 25.8	23 37.3	0♑16.4	1 25.3	26 40.1	15 47.2	6 54.3	18 38.1	28 41.7
18 W	3 47 26	25 28 45	7♑29 16	13 40 8	24 26.4	25 12.7	1 29.4	2 1.1	26 52.7	15 47.0	6 51.9	18 39.2	28 41.2
19 Th	3 51 22	26 29 19	19 54 16	26 12 3	24 28.0	26 47.9	2 42.3	2 36.8	27 5.5	15D 46.9	6 49.7	18 40.3	28 40.7
20 F	3 55 19	27 29 54	2♒33 55	9♒ 0 16	24 29.7	28 22.8	3 55.2	3 12.5	27 18.2	15 46.9	6 47.4	18 41.4	28 40.2
21 Sa	3 59 15	28 30 31	15 31 30	22 8 1	24 31.1	29 57.4	5 8.1	3 48.1	27 31.1	15 47.1	6 45.1	18 42.4	28 39.7
22 Su	4 3 12	29 31 9	28 50 8	5♓38 8	24R 31.7	1♐31.9	6 20.9	4 23.7	27 43.9	15 47.3	6 42.9	18 43.4	28 39.1
23 M	4 7 9	0♐31 48	12♓32 10	19 32 21	24 31.2	3 6.2	7 33.7	4 59.2	27 56.9	15 47.6	6 40.7	18 44.4	28 38.5
24 Tu	4 11 5	1 32 28	26 38 35	3♈50 41	24 29.6	4 40.4	8 46.5	5 34.7	28 9.8	15 48.1	6 38.5	18 45.3	28 37.9
25 W	4 15 2	2 33 9	11♈ 8 15	18 30 44	24 27.1	6 14.4	9 59.2	6 10.1	28 22.8	15 48.6	6 36.3	18 46.2	28 37.3
26 Th	4 18 58	3 33 51	25 57 25	3♉27 24	24 24.3	7 48.2	11 11.8	6 45.5	28 35.9	15 49.3	6 34.2	18 47.1	28 36.7
27 F	4 22 55	4 34 34	10♉59 40	18 33 6	24 21.5	9 22.0	12 24.4	7 20.9	28 49.0	15 50.1	6 32.1	18 47.9	28 36.0
28 Sa	4 26 51	5 35 19	26 6 30	3♊38 41	24 19.3	10 55.6	13 37.0	7 56.2	29 2.2	15 51.0	6 30.0	18 48.7	28 35.3
29 Su	4 30 48	6 36 5	11♊ 8 29	18 34 49	24D 18.0	12 29.2	14 49.5	8 31.4	29 15.4	15 51.9	6 28.0	18 49.5	28 34.6
30 M	4 34 44	7 36 52	25 56 45	3♋13 26	24 17.6	14 2.6	16 2.0	9 6.6	29 28.6	15 53.0	6 26.0	18 50.2	28 33.8

DECEMBER 1936 LONGITUDE

Day	Sid.Time	☉	0 hr ☽	Noon ☽	True ☊	☿	♀	♂	♃	♄	♅	♆	♇
1 Tu	4 38 41	8♐37 40	10♋24 15	17♋28 43	24♐18.1	15♐36.0	17♑14.4	9♎41.8	29♐41.9	15♓54.2	6♉24.0	18♍51.0	28♋33.1
2 W	4 42 38	9 38 30	24 26 33	1♌17 37	24 19.1	17 9.4	18 26.8	10 16.9	29 55.2	15 55.5	6R 22.0	18 51.6	28R 32.3
3 Th	4 46 34	10 39 21	8♌ 1 57	14 39 41	24 20.4	18 42.7	19 39.1	10 51.9	0♑ 8.5	15 56.9	6 20.1	18 52.3	28 31.5
4 F	4 50 31	11 40 13	21 11 7	27 36 36	24 21.4	20 15.9	20 51.3	11 26.9	0 21.9	15 58.4	6 18.2	18 52.9	28 30.7
5 Sa	4 54 27	12 41 7	3♍56 36	10♍11 35	24R 22.1	21 49.1	22 3.5	12 1.9	0 35.4	16 0.0	6 16.3	18 53.5	28 29.8
6 Su	4 58 24	13 42 2	16 22 6	22 28 43	24 22.3	23 22.3	23 15.7	12 36.8	0 48.8	16 1.7	6 14.5	18 54.0	28 29.0
7 M	5 2 20	14 42 58	28 31 59	4♎32 28	24 21.9	24 55.4	24 27.8	13 11.6	1 2.3	16 3.6	6 12.7	18 54.5	28 28.1
8 Tu	5 6 17	15 43 56	10♎30 45	16 27 22	24 21.1	26 28.4	25 39.8	13 46.4	1 15.8	16 5.5	6 11.0	18 55.0	28 27.2
9 W	5 10 14	16 44 54	22 22 50	28 17 39	24 20.1	28 1.4	26 51.8	14 21.1	1 29.3	16 7.5	6 9.2	18 55.4	28 26.3
10 Th	5 14 10	17 45 54	4♏12 16	10♏ 7 7	24 19.1	29 34.3	28 3.7	14 55.8	1 42.9	16 9.6	6 7.6	18 55.8	28 25.3
11 F	5 18 7	18 46 55	16 2 36	21 59 5	24 18.2	1♑ 7.0	29 15.6	15 30.4	1 56.5	16 11.9	6 5.9	18 56.2	28 24.4
12 Sa	5 22 3	19 47 57	27 56 52	3♐56 15	24 17.6	2 39.6	0♒27.3	16 4.9	2 10.1	16 14.2	6 4.3	18 56.6	28 23.4
13 Su	5 26 0	20 49 0	9♐57 30	16 0 51	24 17.2	4 12.0	1 39.1	16 39.4	2 23.8	16 16.6	6 2.8	18 56.9	28 22.4
14 M	5 29 56	21 50 4	22 6 29	28 14 35	24D 17.1	5 44.2	2 50.7	17 13.8	2 37.5	16 19.2	6 1.2	18 57.1	28 21.4
15 Tu	5 33 53	22 51 8	4♑25 20	10♑38 51	24 17.1	7 16.0	4 2.3	17 48.1	2 51.2	16 21.8	5 59.8	18 57.4	28 20.4
16 W	5 37 49	23 52 13	16 55 18	23 14 48	24R 17.2	8 47.4	5 13.8	18 22.4	3 4.9	16 24.5	5 58.3	18 57.6	28 19.3
17 Th	5 41 46	24 53 19	29 37 30	6♒ 3 30	24 17.2	10 18.4	6 25.2	18 56.6	3 18.6	16 27.4	5 56.9	18 57.7	28 18.3
18 F	5 45 43	25 54 25	12♒32 56	19 5 57	24 17.1	11 48.7	7 36.5	19 30.8	3 32.3	16 30.3	5 55.6	18 57.9	28 17.2
19 Sa	5 49 39	26 55 31	25 42 38	2♓23 7	24 16.8	13 18.4	8 47.7	20 4.8	3 46.1	16 33.3	5 54.3	18 58.0	28 16.1
20 Su	5 53 36	27 56 38	9♓ 7 30	15 55 51	24 16.5	14 47.1	9 58.9	20 38.8	3 59.9	16 36.4	5 53.0	18 58.0	28 15.0
21 M	5 57 32	28 57 45	22 48 14	29 44 38	24D 16.3	16 14.7	11 9.9	21 12.7	4 13.7	16 39.7	5 51.8	18R 58.1	28 13.9
22 Tu	6 1 29	29 58 52	6♈45 0	13♈49 14	24 16.3	17 41.0	12 20.9	21 46.6	4 27.4	16 43.0	5 50.6	18 58.0	28 12.7
23 W	6 5 25	0♑59 59	20 57 7	28 8 23	24 16.6	19 5.7	13 31.7	22 20.3	4 41.2	16 46.4	5 49.5	18 58.0	28 11.6
24 Th	6 9 22	2 1 6	5♉22 39	12♉39 27	24 17.2	20 28.6	14 42.4	22 54.0	4 55.1	16 49.9	5 48.4	18 57.9	28 10.4
25 F	6 13 18	3 2 14	19 58 14	27 18 19	24 18.0	21 49.2	15 53.1	23 27.6	5 8.9	16 53.5	5 47.4	18 57.8	28 9.2
26 Sa	6 17 15	4 3 22	4♊39 0	11♊59 28	24 18.7	23 7.2	17 3.6	24 1.1	5 22.7	16 57.1	5 46.4	18 57.7	28 8.1
27 Su	6 21 12	5 4 29	19 18 56	26 36 33	24R 19.2	24 22.2	18 14.0	24 34.6	5 36.5	17 0.9	5 45.5	18 57.5	28 6.9
28 M	6 25 8	6 5 37	3♋51 30	11♋ 3 1	24 19.1	25 33.5	19 24.2	25 8.0	5 50.3	17 4.8	5 44.6	18 57.3	28 5.7
29 Tu	6 29 5	7 6 46	18 10 25	25 13 5	24 18.3	26 40.6	20 34.4	25 41.3	6 4.2	17 8.7	5 43.8	18 57.0	28 4.5
30 W	6 33 1	8 7 54	2♌10 33	9♌ 2 25	24 16.8	27 42.8	21 44.4	26 14.5	6 18.0	17 12.8	5 43.0	18 56.8	28 3.2
31 Th	6 36 58	9 9 2	15 48 28	22 28 35	24 14.8	28 39.3	22 54.2	26 47.6	6 31.8	17 16.9	5 42.2	18 56.5	28 2.0

Astro Data	Planet Ingress	Last Aspect	☽ Ingress	Last Aspect	☽ Ingress	☽ Phases & Eclipses	Astro Data
Dy Hr Mn	Dy Hr Mn	Dy Hr Mn	Dy Hr Mn	Dy Hr Mn	Dy Hr Mn	Dy Hr Mn	1 NOVEMBER 1936
☽0S 8 20:24	☿ ♏ 2 11:00	2 9:27 ♃ ☍	♋ 2 20:00	2 7:09 ♇ ☌	♌ 2 9:43	6 1:29 ☽ 13♌28	Julian Day # 13454
♄ D 19 7:07	♂ ♎ 14 14:52	4 22:21 ♇ ☌	♌ 5 0:37	3 22:04 ☿ △	♍ 4 16:31	14 4:42 ● 21♏39	Delta T 23.9 sec
♂0S 20 6:32	♀ ♑ 16 18:36	6 22:36 ♃ △	♍ 7 9:00	6 23:52 ♇ ⚹	♎ 7 2:55	22 1:19 ☽ 29♒34	SVP 06♓08'15"
☽0N 23 9:07	☿ ♐ 21 0:39	9 17:43 ♇ ⚹	♎ 9 20:15	9 13:10 ☿ ⚹	♏ 9 15:28	28 16:12 ○ 6♊16	Obliquity 23°26'51"
♃⚻♇ 26 1:18	☉ ♐ 22 11:25	12 6:17 ♇ □	♏ 12 8:52	12 0:53 ♇ △	♐ 12 4:07		⚷ Chiron 22♊47.0R
		14 18:58 ♇ △	♐ 14 21:33	13 23:25 ☉ ☌	♑ 14 15:25	5 18:20 ☽ 13♍28	☽ Mean ☊ 26♐46.3
☽0S 6 2:45	♃ ♑ 2 8:39	17 2:49 ♃ ☌	♑ 17 9:20	16 21:32 ♇ ☍	♒ 17 0:42	13 23:25 ● 21♐49	
☽0N 20 15:11	☿ ♑ 10 6:40	19 16:41 ♇ ☍	♒ 19 19:11	19 2:22 ☉ ⚹	♓ 19 7:43	13 23:27:47 ● A 7'07"	1 DECEMBER 1936
♆ R 21 5:56	♀ ♒ 11 14:51	22 1:19 ☉ □	♓ 22 2:04	21 11:30 ☉ □	♈ 21 12:26	21 11:30 ☽ 29♓27	Julian Day # 13484
♃△♅ 27 14:39	☉ ♑ 22 0:27	24 3:20 ♇ △	♈ 24 5:37	23 12:04 ♇ □	♉ 23 15:06	28 4:00 ○ 6♋16	Delta T 23.9 sec
		26 4:18 ♃ △	♉ 26 6:29	25 13:22 ♇ ⚹	♊ 25 16:24	28 3:49 ○ A 0.845	SVP 06♓08'10"
		28 3:56 ♇ ⚹	♊ 28 6:11	27 9:00 ♂ △	♋ 27 17:36		Obliquity 23°26'50"
		30 5:54 ♃ ☍	♋ 30 6:40	29 16:53 ♇ ☌	♌ 29 20:14		⚷ Chiron 21♊17.0R
							☽ Mean ☊ 25♐11.0

LONGITUDE — JANUARY 1937

Day	Sid.Time	☉	0 hr ☽	Noon ☽	True ☊	☿	♀	♂	♃	♄	♅	♆	♇
1 F	6 40 54	10♑10 11	29♌ 2 46	5♍31 11	24♐12.5	29♑29.4	24♒ 4.0	27♎20.7	6♑45.6	17♓21.1	5♉41.5	18♍56.1	28♋ 0.7
2 Sa	6 44 51	11 11 20	11♍54 3	18 11 42	24R 10.3	0♒12.2	25 13.6	27 53.6	6 59.5	17 25.4	5R 40.9	18R 55.7	27R 59.5
3 Su	6 48 47	12 12 30	24 24 33	0♎33 5	24 8.6	0 46.8	26 23.0	28 26.5	7 13.3	17 29.7	5 40.3	18 55.3	27 58.2
4 M	6 52 44	13 13 39	6♎37 49	12 39 21	24D 7.6	1 12.3	27 32.4	28 59.3	7 27.1	17 34.2	5 39.8	18 54.9	27 56.9
5 Tu	6 56 41	14 14 49	18 38 15	24 35 9	24 7.5	1R 27.7	28 41.5	29 31.9	7 40.9	17 38.7	5 39.3	18 54.4	27 55.7
6 W	7 0 37	15 15 59	0♏30 39	6♏25 24	24 8.3	1 32.4	29 50.5	0♏ 4.5	7 54.7	17 43.3	5 38.8	18 53.9	27 54.4
7 Th	7 4 34	16 17 9	12 20 0	18 15 1	24 9.8	1 25.7	0♓59.4	0 37.0	8 8.5	17 48.0	5 38.4	18 53.3	27 53.1
8 F	7 8 30	17 18 19	24 11 1	0♐ 8 33	24 11.6	1 7.2	2 8.1	1 9.4	8 22.2	17 52.8	5 38.1	18 52.8	27 51.8
9 Sa	7 12 27	18 19 29	6♐ 8 6	12 10 7	24 13.3	0 36.9	3 16.6	1 41.7	8 36.0	17 57.7	5 37.8	18 52.2	27 50.5
10 Su	7 16 23	19 20 40	18 14 59	24 23 4	24R 14.3	29♑55.1	4 25.0	2 13.9	8 49.7	18 2.6	5 37.6	18 51.5	27 49.2
11 M	7 20 20	20 21 50	0♑34 37	6♑49 52	24 14.3	29 2.6	5 33.1	2 46.0	9 3.5	18 7.6	5 37.4	18 50.8	27 47.9
12 Tu	7 24 16	21 23 0	13 8 58	19 32 0	24 12.9	28 0.7	6 41.1	3 17.9	9 17.2	18 12.7	5 37.3	18 50.1	27 46.5
13 W	7 28 13	22 24 9	25 59 0	2♒29 56	24 10.0	26 51.1	7 48.9	3 49.8	9 30.9	18 17.8	5D 37.2	18 49.4	27 45.2
14 Th	7 32 10	23 25 18	9♒ 4 40	15 43 5	24 5.9	25 36.1	8 56.5	4 21.5	9 44.5	18 23.1	5 37.2	18 48.7	27 43.9
15 F	7 36 6	24 26 27	22 24 59	29 10 8	24 0.9	24 17.9	10 3.9	4 53.1	9 58.2	18 28.4	5 37.2	18 47.9	27 42.6
16 Sa	7 40 3	25 27 35	5♓58 17	12♓49 12	23 55.7	22 59.0	11 11.1	5 24.6	10 11.8	18 33.7	5 37.3	18 47.0	27 41.2
17 Su	7 43 59	26 28 42	19 42 36	26 38 14	23 50.9	21 42.0	12 18.1	5 56.0	10 25.4	18 39.2	5 37.5	18 46.2	27 39.9
18 M	7 47 56	27 29 48	3♈35 52	10♈35 15	23 47.3	20 28.9	13 24.8	6 27.2	10 39.0	18 44.7	5 37.6	18 45.3	27 38.6
19 Tu	7 51 52	28 30 54	17 36 11	24 38 29	23D 45.2	19 21.6	14 31.3	6 58.4	10 52.5	18 50.2	5 37.9	18 44.4	27 37.3
20 W	7 55 49	29 31 58	1♉41 58	8♉46 26	23 44.7	18 21.6	15 37.6	7 29.4	11 6.0	18 55.9	5 38.2	18 43.4	27 35.9
21 Th	7 59 45	0♒33 2	15 51 42	22 57 34	23 45.5	17 29.9	16 43.6	8 0.2	11 19.5	19 1.6	5 38.5	18 42.5	27 34.6
22 F	8 3 42	1 34 4	0♊ 3 50	7♊10 13	23 47.0	16 47.1	17 49.3	8 30.9	11 33.0	19 7.3	5 38.9	18 41.5	27 33.3
23 Sa	8 7 39	2 35 6	14 16 25	21 22 7	23R 48.2	16 13.5	18 54.8	9 1.5	11 46.4	19 13.2	5 39.4	18 40.5	27 31.9
24 Su	8 11 35	3 36 7	28 26 56	5♋30 26	23 48.5	15 49.1	19 60.0	9 32.0	11 59.8	19 19.1	5 39.9	18 39.4	27 30.6
25 M	8 15 32	4 37 7	12♋32 9	19 31 38	23 47.0	15 33.7	21 4.9	10 2.3	12 13.1	19 25.0	5 40.5	18 38.4	27 29.3
26 Tu	8 19 28	5 38 6	26 28 24	3♌21 58	23 43.4	15D 26.8	22 9.5	10 32.5	12 26.4	19 31.0	5 41.1	18 37.3	27 28.0
27 W	8 23 25	6 39 3	10♌11 53	16 57 48	23 37.7	15 28.0	23 13.8	11 2.6	12 39.7	19 37.1	5 41.7	18 36.1	27 26.7
28 Th	8 27 21	7 40 0	23 39 21	0♍16 17	23 30.3	15 36.8	24 17.7	11 32.5	12 52.9	19 43.2	5 42.4	18 35.0	27 25.4
29 F	8 31 18	8 40 56	6♍48 28	13 15 49	23 22.1	15 52.7	25 21.4	12 2.2	13 6.1	19 49.3	5 43.2	18 33.8	27 24.1
30 Sa	8 35 15	9 41 51	19 38 21	25 56 14	23 13.8	16 14.9	26 24.7	12 31.8	13 19.3	19 55.6	5 44.0	18 32.6	27 22.8
31 Su	8 39 11	10 42 46	2♎ 9 39	8♎18 57	23 6.4	16 43.1	27 27.6	13 1.3	13 32.4	20 1.8	5 44.9	18 31.4	27 21.5

LONGITUDE — FEBRUARY 1937

Day	Sid.Time	☉	0 hr ☽	Noon ☽	True ☊	☿	♀	♂	♃	♄	♅	♆	♇
1 M	8 43 8	11♒43 39	14♎24 29	20♎26 45	23♐ 0.6	17♑16.8	28♓30.2	13♏30.5	13♑45.5	20♓ 8.2	5♉45.8	18♍30.2	27♋20.2
2 Tu	8 47 4	12 44 32	26 26 14	2♏23 32	22R 56.8	17 55.3	29 32.5	13 59.7	13 58.5	20 14.5	5 46.8	18R 28.9	27R 18.9
3 W	8 51 1	13 45 24	8♏19 16	14 14 3	22D 55.0	18 38.4	0♈34.4	14 28.6	14 11.4	20 21.0	5 47.8	18 27.6	27 17.6
4 Th	8 54 57	14 46 15	20 8 33	26 3 27	22 55.0	19 25.5	1 35.8	14 57.4	14 24.4	20 27.4	5 48.8	18 26.3	27 16.4
5 F	8 58 54	15 47 5	1♐59 25	7♐57 6	22 56.0	20 16.4	2 36.9	15 26.0	14 37.2	20 34.0	5 50.0	18 25.0	27 15.1
6 Sa	9 2 50	16 47 54	13 57 11	20 0 14	22R 57.1	21 10.7	3 37.6	15 54.4	14 50.0	20 40.5	5 51.1	18 23.6	27 13.9
7 Su	9 6 47	17 48 42	26 6 50	2♑17 31	22 57.4	22 8.2	4 37.8	16 22.6	15 2.8	20 47.1	5 52.4	18 22.3	27 12.6
8 M	9 10 44	18 49 29	8♑32 43	14 52 47	22 56.0	23 8.4	5 37.6	16 50.7	15 15.5	20 53.8	5 53.6	18 20.9	27 11.4
9 Tu	9 14 40	19 50 16	21 18 1	27 48 33	22 52.3	24 11.3	6 36.9	17 18.6	15 28.2	21 0.5	5 54.9	18 19.5	27 10.2
10 W	9 18 37	20 51 0	4♒24 28	11♒ 5 41	22 46.1	25 16.7	7 35.8	17 46.2	15 40.7	21 7.2	5 56.3	18 18.0	27 9.0
11 Th	9 22 33	21 51 44	17 52 1	24 43 8	22 37.6	26 24.2	8 34.2	18 13.7	15 53.3	21 14.0	5 57.7	18 16.6	27 7.8
12 F	9 26 30	22 52 26	1♓38 37	8♓37 58	22 27.5	27 33.8	9 32.0	18 40.9	16 5.7	21 20.8	5 59.2	18 15.1	27 6.6
13 Sa	9 30 26	23 53 7	15 40 33	22 45 46	22 16.9	28 45.3	10 29.3	19 7.9	16 18.1	21 27.7	6 0.7	18 13.7	27 5.4
14 Su	9 34 23	24 53 46	29 52 54	7♈ 1 19	22 7.0	29 58.7	11 26.1	19 34.7	16 30.5	21 34.6	6 2.3	18 12.2	27 4.3
15 M	9 38 19	25 54 24	14♈10 22	21 19 29	21 58.8	1♒13.7	12 22.3	20 1.3	16 42.7	21 41.5	6 3.9	18 10.7	27 3.1
16 Tu	9 42 16	26 55 0	28 28 9	5♉35 57	21 53.0	2 30.3	13 18.0	20 27.7	16 54.9	21 48.5	6 5.5	18 9.1	27 2.0
17 W	9 46 12	27 55 34	12♉42 32	19 47 39	21 49.9	3 48.4	14 13.0	20 53.8	17 7.1	21 55.5	6 7.2	18 7.6	27 0.8
18 Th	9 50 9	28 56 6	26 51 8	3♊52 50	21D 49.0	5 7.9	15 7.4	21 19.7	17 19.1	22 2.5	6 9.0	18 6.1	26 59.7
19 F	9 54 6	29 56 36	10♊52 43	17 50 45	21R 49.2	6 28.7	16 1.1	21 45.3	17 31.1	22 9.5	6 10.7	18 4.5	26 58.7
20 Sa	9 58 2	0♓57 5	24 46 53	1♋41 7	21 49.4	7 50.9	16 54.1	22 10.7	17 43.0	22 16.6	6 12.6	18 2.9	26 57.6
21 Su	10 1 59	1 57 32	8♋33 24	15 23 41	21 48.3	9 14.4	17 46.4	22 35.9	17 54.9	22 23.7	6 14.5	18 1.3	26 56.5
22 M	10 5 55	2 57 57	22 11 52	28 57 49	21 44.9	10 39.0	18 37.9	23 0.8	18 6.6	22 30.9	6 16.4	17 59.8	26 55.5
23 Tu	10 9 52	3 58 20	5♌41 24	12♌22 25	21 38.6	12 4.8	19 28.7	23 25.5	18 18.3	22 38.0	6 18.3	17 58.2	26 54.4
24 W	10 13 48	4 58 41	19 0 39	25 35 54	21 29.3	13 31.8	20 18.7	23 49.9	18 29.9	22 45.2	6 20.3	17 56.5	26 53.4
25 Th	10 17 45	5 59 0	2♍ 7 58	8♍36 39	21 17.7	14 59.9	21 7.8	24 14.0	18 41.5	22 52.4	6 22.4	17 54.9	26 52.4
26 F	10 21 41	6 59 17	15 1 49	21 23 21	21 4.7	16 29.2	21 56.1	24 37.8	18 52.9	22 59.7	6 24.5	17 53.3	26 51.5
27 Sa	10 25 38	7 59 33	27 41 13	3♎55 26	20 51.3	17 59.5	22 43.5	25 1.4	19 4.2	23 6.9	6 26.6	17 51.7	26 50.5
28 Su	10 29 35	8 59 47	10♎ 6 5	16 13 21	20 39.0	19 30.9	23 30.0	25 24.7	19 15.5	23 14.2	6 28.8	17 50.0	26 49.6

Astro Data

	Dy Hr Mn
☽0S	2 11:15
☿ R	5 22:03
♅ D	13 21:32
☽0N	16 20:57
♄☍♆	18 2:19
☿ D	26 8:10
☽0S	29 21:05
♀0N	1 7:15
♄∠♅	7 23:16
☽0N	13 4:22
♃△♆	21 11:36
☽0S	26 6:15

Planet Ingress

	Dy Hr Mn
☿ ♒	1 16:41
♂ ♏	5 20:39
♀ ♓	6 3:18
☿ ♑	9 21:28
☉ ♒	20 11:01
♀ ♈	2 10:39
☿ ♒	14 0:26
☉ ♓	19 1:21

Last Aspect / ☽ Ingress

Last Aspect Dy Hr Mn		☽ Ingress Dy Hr Mn
31 20:44	♂ ✶	♍ 1 1:45
3 6:56	♇ ✶	♎ 3 10:55
5 22:30	♀ △	♏ 5 22:58
8 7:24	♇ △	♐ 8 11:43
10 1:12	♆ □	♑ 10 22:53
13 3:16	♇ ☍	♒ 13 7:25
13 17:42	♅ □	♓ 15 13:28
17 13:45	♇ △	♈ 17 17:48
19 20:02	☉ □	♉ 19 21:07
21 19:46	♇ ✶	♊ 21 23:54
23 8:30	♀ □	♋ 24 2:38
26 1:43	♇ ☌	♌ 26 6:08
27 1:33	♂ □	♍ 28 11:30
30 14:45	♇ ✶	♎ 30 19:49

Last Aspect / ☽ Ingress

Last Aspect Dy Hr Mn		☽ Ingress Dy Hr Mn
2 1:46	♇ □	♏ 2 7:10
4 14:26	♇ △	♐ 4 19:59
6 13:27	♄ □	♑ 7 7:34
9 10:49	♇ ☍	♒ 9 16:00
11 7:34	☉ ☌	♓ 11 21:10
14 0:11	☿ ✶	♈ 14 0:12
15 21:35	♇ □	♉ 16 2:34
18 3:50	☉ □	♊ 18 5:22
19 19:37	♄ □	♋ 20 9:04
22 8:22	♇ ☌	♌ 22 13:51
24 9:03	♂ ☍	♍ 24 20:04
26 22:23	♇ ✶	♎ 27 4:26

☽ Phases & Eclipses

Dy Hr Mn		
4 14:22	☽	13♎50
12 16:47	●	22♑06
19 20:02	☽	29♈22
26 17:15	○	6♌22
3 12:04	☽	14♏16
11 7:34	●	22♒11
18 3:50	☽	29♉06
25 7:43	○	6♍18

Astro Data

1 JANUARY 1937
Julian Day # 13515
Delta T 23.9 sec
SVP 06♓08'04"
Obliquity 23°26'49"
⚷ Chiron 19♊24.5R
☽ Mean ☊ 23♐32.6

1 FEBRUARY 1937
Julian Day # 13546
Delta T 23.9 sec
SVP 06♓07'59"
Obliquity 23°26'50"
⚷ Chiron 18♊02.5R
☽ Mean ☊ 21♐54.1

MARCH 1937 LONGITUDE

Day	Sid.Time	☉	0 hr ☽	Noon ☽	True ☊	☿	♀	♂	♃	♄	♅	♆	♇
1 M	10 33 31	10♓ 0 0	22♎17 27	28♎18 42	20♐28.6	21♒ 3.4	24♈15.5	25♏47.7	19♑26.7	23♓21.5	6♉31.0	17♍48.4	26♋48.6
2 Tu	10 37 28	11 0 11	4♏17 31	10♏14 19	20R 20.8	22 36.9	25 0.0	26 10.3	19 37.8	23 28.8	6 33.2	17R 46.7	26R 47.7
3 W	10 41 24	12 0 20	16 9 37	22 4 0	20 15.8	24 11.6	25 43.5	26 32.7	19 48.8	23 36.1	6 35.5	17 45.1	26 46.8
4 Th	10 45 21	13 0 28	27 58 3	3♐52 25	20 13.3	25 47.3	26 25.9	26 54.8	19 59.7	23 43.4	6 37.8	17 43.4	26 46.0
5 F	10 49 17	14 0 34	9♐47 47	15 44 51	20 12.5	27 24.1	27 7.2	27 16.5	20 10.5	23 50.8	6 40.2	17 41.7	26 45.1
6 Sa	10 53 14	15 0 39	21 44 18	27 46 50	20 12.5	29 2.0	27 47.3	27 37.9	20 21.2	23 58.2	6 42.6	17 40.1	26 44.3
7 Su	10 57 10	16 0 42	3♑53 8	10♑ 3 51	20 12.0	0♓41.0	28 26.3	27 58.9	20 31.9	24 5.5	6 45.0	17 38.4	26 43.5
8 M	11 1 7	17 0 43	16 19 35	22 40 52	20 10.1	2 21.1	29 4.0	28 19.6	20 42.4	24 12.9	6 47.5	17 36.7	26 42.7
9 Tu	11 5 4	18 0 43	29 8 8	5♒41 45	20 5.7	4 2.3	29 40.4	28 40.0	20 52.8	24 20.3	6 50.0	17 35.1	26 41.9
10 W	11 9 0	19 0 41	12♒21 55	19 8 40	19 58.6	5 44.6	0♉15.4	28 59.9	21 3.2	24 27.7	6 52.6	17 33.4	26 41.2
11 Th	11 12 57	20 0 38	26 1 55	3♓ 1 24	19 49.0	7 28.1	0 49.1	29 19.5	21 13.4	24 35.2	6 55.1	17 31.7	26 40.5
12 F	11 16 53	21 0 32	10♓ 6 38	17 17 1	19 37.4	9 12.7	1 21.3	29 38.7	21 23.5	24 42.6	6 57.7	17 30.1	26 39.8
13 Sa	11 20 50	22 0 24	24 31 45	1♈49 57	19 25.1	10 58.5	1 52.1	29 57.5	21 33.5	24 50.0	7 0.4	17 28.4	26 39.1
14 Su	11 24 46	23 0 15	9♈10 39	16 32 48	19 13.4	12 45.4	2 21.2	0♐15.9	21 43.4	24 57.4	7 3.1	17 26.7	26 38.4
15 M	11 28 43	24 0 3	23 55 24	1♉17 28	19 3.6	14 33.6	2 48.7	0 33.8	21 53.2	25 4.9	7 5.8	17 25.1	26 37.8
16 Tu	11 32 39	24 59 50	8♉38 8	15 56 38	18 56.5	16 23.0	3 14.6	0 51.4	22 2.9	25 12.3	7 8.5	17 23.4	26 37.2
17 W	11 36 36	25 59 34	23 12 19	0♊24 44	18 52.2	18 13.5	3 38.7	1 8.5	22 12.4	25 19.7	7 11.3	17 21.8	26 36.6
18 Th	11 40 33	26 59 16	7♊33 30	14 38 25	18D 50.5	20 5.3	4 1.0	1 25.2	22 21.9	25 27.2	7 14.1	17 20.1	26 36.0
19 F	11 44 29	27 58 56	21 39 24	28 36 27	18R 50.2	21 58.2	4 21.4	1 41.4	22 31.2	25 34.6	7 16.9	17 18.5	26 35.5
20 Sa	11 48 26	28 58 33	5♋29 36	12♋19 1	18 50.2	23 52.4	4 39.8	1 57.2	22 40.4	25 42.0	7 19.8	17 16.8	26 34.9
21 Su	11 52 22	29 58 8	19 4 49	25 47 11	18 49.0	25 47.7	4 56.3	2 12.5	22 49.5	25 49.5	7 22.7	17 15.2	26 34.5
22 M	11 56 19	0♈57 41	2♌26 16	9♌ 2 13	18 45.7	27 44.2	5 10.7	2 27.3	22 58.5	25 56.9	7 25.6	17 13.6	26 34.0
23 Tu	12 0 15	1 57 11	15 35 10	22 5 12	18 39.5	29 41.8	5 22.9	2 41.7	23 7.3	26 4.3	7 28.5	17 12.0	26 33.5
24 W	12 4 12	2 56 39	28 32 23	4♍56 46	18 30.6	1♈40.5	5 32.9	2 55.5	23 16.0	26 11.7	7 31.5	17 10.4	26 33.1
25 Th	12 8 8	3 56 5	11♍18 23	17 35 15	18 19.2	3 40.2	5 40.7	3 8.9	23 24.6	26 19.1	7 34.5	17 8.8	26 32.7
26 F	12 12 5	4 55 29	23 53 22	0♎ 6 44	18 6.5	5 40.8	5 46.1	3 21.7	23 33.1	26 26.5	7 37.5	17 7.2	26 32.3
27 Sa	12 16 2	5 54 50	6♎17 24	12 25 24	17 53.4	7 42.2	5R 49.2	3 34.0	23 41.4	26 33.8	7 40.5	17 5.7	26 32.0
28 Su	12 19 58	6 54 10	18 30 51	24 33 50	17 41.2	9 44.3	5 50.0	3 45.8	23 49.6	26 41.2	7 43.6	17 4.1	26 31.6
29 M	12 23 55	7 53 27	0♏34 33	6♏33 13	17 30.8	11 47.0	5 48.2	3 57.0	23 57.7	26 48.6	7 46.7	17 2.6	26 31.3
30 Tu	12 27 51	8 52 43	12 30 6	18 25 32	17 22.9	13 49.9	5 44.1	4 7.6	24 5.6	26 55.9	7 49.8	17 1.0	26 31.1
31 W	12 31 48	9 51 57	24 19 55	0♐13 40	17 17.8	15 53.1	5 37.4	4 17.7	24 13.4	27 3.2	7 52.9	16 59.5	26 30.8

APRIL 1937 LONGITUDE

Day	Sid.Time	☉	0 hr ☽	Noon ☽	True ☊	☿	♀	♂	♃	♄	♅	♆	♇
1 Th	12 35 44	10♈51 9	6♐ 7 17	12♐ 1 19	17♐15.2	17♈56.1	5♉28.3	4♐27.2	24♑21.1	27♓10.5	7♉56.1	16♍58.0	26♋30.6
2 F	12 39 41	11 50 19	17 56 21	23 52 58	17D 14.5	19 58.7	5R 16.7	4 36.1	24 28.6	27 17.8	7 59.3	16R 56.5	26R 30.4
3 Sa	12 43 37	12 49 27	29 51 51	5♑53 38	17 15.0	22 0.6	5 2.6	4 44.4	24 36.0	27 25.1	8 2.5	16 55.1	26 30.2
4 Su	12 47 34	13 48 33	11♑59 1	18 8 39	17R 15.5	24 1.5	4 46.2	4 52.1	24 43.3	27 32.3	8 5.7	16 53.6	26 30.0
5 M	12 51 30	14 47 38	24 23 13	0♒43 18	17 15.0	26 1.0	4 27.3	4 59.1	24 50.4	27 39.6	8 8.9	16 52.2	26 29.9
6 Tu	12 55 27	15 46 41	7♒ 9 28	13 42 11	17 12.8	27 58.8	4 6.1	5 5.5	24 57.3	27 46.8	8 12.1	16 50.7	26 29.8
7 W	12 59 24	16 45 42	20 21 51	27 8 40	17 8.4	29 54.5	3 42.7	5 11.2	25 4.1	27 54.0	8 15.4	16 49.3	26 29.7
8 Th	13 3 20	17 44 42	4♓ 2 45	11♓ 3 59	17 1.8	1♉47.7	3 17.1	5 16.3	25 10.8	28 1.1	8 18.7	16 47.9	26 29.7
9 F	13 7 17	18 43 39	18 12 4	25 26 32	16 53.5	3 38.1	2 49.5	5 20.6	25 17.3	28 8.3	8 22.0	16 46.6	26D 29.7
10 Sa	13 11 13	19 42 35	2♈46 39	10♈11 33	16 44.4	5 25.2	2 20.0	5 24.3	25 23.6	28 15.4	8 25.3	16 45.2	26 29.7
11 Su	13 15 10	20 41 28	17 40 12	25 11 26	16 35.6	7 8.9	1 48.8	5 27.3	25 29.8	28 22.5	8 28.6	16 43.9	26 29.7
12 M	13 19 6	21 40 20	2♉44 2	10♉16 46	16 28.2	8 48.7	1 16.0	5 29.5	25 35.9	28 29.5	8 32.0	16 42.6	26 29.7
13 Tu	13 23 3	22 39 10	17 48 26	25 17 57	16 23.0	10 24.5	0 41.8	5 31.1	25 41.7	28 36.6	8 35.3	16 41.3	26 29.8
14 W	13 26 59	23 37 58	2♊44 20	10♊ 6 47	16D 20.1	11 55.8	0 6.5	5R 31.9	25 47.5	28 43.6	8 38.7	16 40.0	26 29.9
15 Th	13 30 56	24 36 43	17 24 38	24 37 27	16 19.4	13 22.6	29♈30.1	5 32.0	25 53.0	28 50.5	8 42.0	16 38.8	26 30.0
16 F	13 34 53	25 35 26	1♋44 54	8♋46 52	16 20.0	14 44.6	28 53.1	5 31.3	25 58.4	28 57.5	8 45.4	16 37.5	26 30.2
17 Sa	13 38 49	26 34 8	15 43 18	22 34 18	16R 21.1	16 1.7	28 15.5	5 29.9	26 3.6	29 4.4	8 48.8	16 36.3	26 30.4
18 Su	13 42 46	27 32 46	29 20 2	6♌ 0 45	16 21.5	17 13.6	27 37.7	5 27.8	26 8.7	29 11.2	8 52.2	16 35.2	26 30.6
19 M	13 46 42	28 31 23	12♌36 42	19 8 12	16 20.4	18 20.3	26 59.8	5 24.9	26 13.6	29 18.1	8 55.6	16 34.0	26 30.8
20 Tu	13 50 39	29 29 57	25 35 33	1♍59 3	16 17.4	19 21.6	26 22.2	5 21.2	26 18.3	29 24.9	8 59.1	16 32.9	26 31.1
21 W	13 54 35	0♉28 29	8♍19 0	14 35 41	16 12.4	20 17.5	25 45.1	5 16.8	26 22.9	29 31.6	9 2.5	16 31.8	26 31.4
22 Th	13 58 32	1 26 59	20 49 21	27 0 14	16 5.7	21 7.8	25 8.8	5 11.7	26 27.3	29 38.3	9 5.9	16 30.7	26 31.7
23 F	14 2 28	2 25 26	3♎ 8 34	9♎14 32	15 58.0	21 52.6	24 33.4	5 5.8	26 31.5	29 45.0	9 9.4	16 29.6	26 32.0
24 Sa	14 6 25	3 23 52	15 18 21	21 20 11	15 50.0	22 31.6	23 59.2	4 59.1	26 35.6	29 51.6	9 12.8	16 28.6	26 32.3
25 Su	14 10 22	4 22 16	27 20 13	3♏18 39	15 42.5	23 4.9	23 26.4	4 51.7	26 39.5	29 58.2	9 16.2	16 27.6	26 32.7
26 M	14 14 18	5 20 38	9♏15 41	15 11 32	15 36.2	23 32.5	22 55.2	4 43.5	26 43.2	0♈ 4.8	9 19.7	16 26.6	26 33.1
27 Tu	14 18 15	6 18 58	21 6 26	27 0 39	15 31.6	23 54.4	22 25.8	4 34.6	26 46.7	0 11.3	9 23.1	16 25.6	26 33.6
28 W	14 22 11	7 17 17	2♐54 30	8♐48 19	15 28.9	24 10.6	21 58.3	4 24.9	26 50.0	0 17.8	9 26.6	16 24.7	26 34.0
29 Th	14 26 8	8 15 33	14 42 27	20 37 19	15D 28.0	24 21.1	21 32.8	4 14.5	26 53.2	0 24.2	9 30.1	16 23.8	26 34.5
30 F	14 30 4	9 13 49	26 33 22	2♑31 5	15 28.6	24R 26.1	21 9.5	4 3.3	26 56.2	0 30.5	9 33.5	16 22.9	26 35.0

Astro Data	Dy Hr Mn
☽0N	12 13:46
☿0N	24 16:34
☽0S	25 13:20
♄△♇	26 18:10
♀ R	27 19:06
☽0N	8 23:56
♇ D	9 13:47
♂ R	14 14:42
☽0S	21 18:37
♃☍♇	23 2:54
☿ R	30 10:03

Planet Ingress	Dy Hr Mn
☿ ♓	6 14:06
♀ ♉	9 13:19
♂ ♐	13 3:16
☉ ♈	21 0:45
☿ ♈	23 3:41
☿ ♉	7 1:09
♀ ♈	14 4:19
☉ ♉	20 12:19
♄ ♈	25 6:29

Last Aspect Dy Hr Mn		☽ Ingress Dy Hr Mn
1 8:59	♇ □	♏ 1 15:23
3 21:47	♂ ☌	♐ 4 4:08
6 12:42	♀ △	♑ 6 16:23
9 1:02	♀ □	♒ 9 1:36
11 5:48	♂ □	♓ 11 6:50
13 3:30	♇ △	♈ 13 9:00
15 4:24	♇ □	♉ 15 9:54
17 5:39	♇ ⚹	♊ 17 11:19
19 11:46	☉ □	♋ 19 14:25
21 14:03	☿ △	♌ 21 19:35
22 9:06	♅ □	♍ 24 2:44
26 5:06	♇ ⚹	♎ 26 11:47
28 15:54	♇ □	♏ 28 22:51
31 5:36	♄ △	♐ 31 11:32

Last Aspect Dy Hr Mn		☽ Ingress Dy Hr Mn
2 19:03	♄ □	♑ 3 0:16
5 6:17	♄ ⚹	♒ 5 10:39
6 17:01	☉ ⚹	♓ 7 16:59
9 16:34	♄ ☌	♈ 9 19:28
11 14:05	♇ □	♉ 11 19:39
13 17:28	♄ ⚹	♊ 13 19:34
15 19:22	♀ ⚹	♋ 15 21:02
17 23:44	♄ △	♌ 18 1:11
20 7:56	☉ △	♍ 20 8:16
22 17:18	♄ ☍	♎ 22 17:51
24 22:38	♃ □	♏ 25 5:21
27 11:35	♃ ⚹	♐ 27 18:05
29 13:25	♀ △	♑ 30 6:56

☽ Phases & Eclipses Dy Hr Mn		
5 9:17	☽	14♐24
12 19:32	●	21♓49
19 11:46	☽	28♊28
26 23:12	○	5♎53
4 3:53	☽	13♑58
11 5:10	●	20♈54
17 20:34	☽	27♋24
25 15:24	○	4♏60

Astro Data

1 MARCH 1937
Julian Day # 13574
Delta T 23.9 sec
SVP 06♓07'56"
Obliquity 23°26'50"
⚷ Chiron 17♊44.9
☽ Mean ☊ 20♐25.1

1 APRIL 1937
Julian Day # 13605
Delta T 23.9 sec
SVP 06♓07'53"
Obliquity 23°26'50"
⚷ Chiron 18♊36.5
☽ Mean ☊ 18♐46.6

LONGITUDE — MAY 1937

Day	Sid.Time	☉	0 hr ☽	Noon ☽	True ☊	☿	♀	♂	♃	♄	♅	♆	♇
1 Sa	14 34 1	10♉12 2	8♑30 58	14♑33 34	15♐30.0	24♉25.7	20♈48.5	3♐51.4	26♑59.0	0♈36.9	9♉37.0	16♍22.1	26♋35.5
2 Su	14 37 57	11 10 14	20 39 26	26 49 9	15 31.7	24R20.0	20R29.7	3R38.8	27 1.7	0 43.1	9 40.4	16R21.2	26 36.1
3 M	14 41 54	12 8 25	3♒ 3 17	9♒22 24	15R33.0	24 9.4	20 13.4	3 25.5	27 4.1	0 49.4	9 43.9	16 20.5	26 36.6
4 Tu	14 45 51	13 6 34	15 47 3	22 17 43	15 33.3	23 54.0	19 59.5	3 11.6	27 6.4	0 55.6	9 47.3	16 19.7	26 37.2
5 W	14 49 47	14 4 42	28 54 50	5♓38 43	15 32.4	23 34.4	19 48.0	2 56.9	27 8.5	1 1.7	9 50.8	16 19.0	26 37.9
6 Th	14 53 44	15 2 48	12♓29 37	19 27 35	15 30.1	23 10.7	19 39.0	2 41.6	27 10.4	1 7.8	9 54.3	16 18.3	26 38.5
7 F	14 57 40	16 0 53	26 32 34	3♈44 17	15 26.8	22 43.6	19 32.4	2 25.6	27 12.1	1 13.8	9 57.7	16 17.6	26 39.2
8 Sa	15 1 37	16 58 56	11♈ 2 17	18 25 56	15 22.8	22 13.5	19 28.2	2 9.1	27 13.6	1 19.7	10 1.1	16 16.9	26 39.9
9 Su	15 5 33	17 56 58	25 54 23	3♉26 38	15 18.9	21 40.9	19D26.4	1 52.0	27 14.9	1 25.6	10 4.6	16 16.3	26 40.6
10 M	15 9 30	18 54 59	11♉ 1 33	18 37 56	15 15.7	21 6.6	19 27.0	1 34.3	27 16.1	1 31.5	10 8.0	16 15.7	26 41.3
11 Tu	15 13 26	19 52 58	26 14 31	3♊50 2	15 13.5	20 31.1	19 29.9	1 16.1	27 17.1	1 37.3	10 11.4	16 15.2	26 42.1
12 W	15 17 23	20 50 55	11♊23 19	18 53 17	15D12.6	19 55.0	19 35.1	0 57.5	27 17.8	1 43.0	10 14.9	16 14.6	26 42.9
13 Th	15 21 20	21 48 51	26 18 59	3♋39 39	15 12.9	19 19.0	19 42.5	0 38.4	27 18.4	1 48.7	10 18.3	16 14.2	26 43.7
14 F	15 25 16	22 46 46	10♋54 40	18 3 37	15 13.9	18 43.6	19 52.0	0 18.9	27 18.8	1 54.3	10 21.7	16 13.7	26 44.5
15 Sa	15 29 13	23 44 38	25 6 14	2♌ 2 25	15 15.3	18 9.6	20 3.7	29♏59.1	27R19.0	1 59.9	10 25.1	16 13.3	26 45.4
16 Su	15 33 9	24 42 29	8♌52 13	15 35 46	15 16.5	17 37.4	20 17.4	29 38.9	27 19.0	2 5.4	10 28.5	16 12.9	26 46.2
17 M	15 37 6	25 40 18	22 13 18	28 45 10	15R17.1	17 7.7	20 33.0	29 18.4	27 18.8	2 10.8	10 31.8	16 12.5	26 47.1
18 Tu	15 41 2	26 38 5	5♍11 42	11♍33 19	15 16.9	16 40.7	20 50.6	28 57.8	27 18.4	2 16.1	10 35.2	16 12.2	26 48.1
19 W	15 44 59	27 35 50	17 50 28	24 3 34	15 15.9	16 17.0	21 10.1	28 36.9	27 17.9	2 21.4	10 38.6	16 11.8	26 49.0
20 Th	15 48 55	28 33 34	0♎13 3	6♎19 21	15 14.2	15 57.0	21 31.3	28 15.9	27 17.1	2 26.7	10 41.9	16 11.6	26 49.9
21 F	15 52 52	29 31 16	12 22 54	18 24 4	15 12.0	15 40.8	21 54.3	27 54.8	27 16.2	2 31.8	10 45.2	16 11.3	26 50.9
22 Sa	15 56 49	0♊28 57	24 23 14	0♏20 46	15 9.7	15 28.7	22 19.0	27 33.6	27 15.1	2 36.9	10 48.5	16 11.1	26 51.9
23 Su	16 0 45	1 26 36	6♏17 1	12 12 15	15 7.6	15 20.9	22 45.3	27 12.4	27 13.8	2 41.9	10 51.8	16 10.9	26 52.9
24 M	16 4 42	2 24 14	18 6 50	24 1 0	15 6.0	15D17.5	23 13.2	26 51.2	27 12.3	2 46.9	10 55.1	16 10.8	26 54.0
25 Tu	16 8 38	3 21 51	29 55 4	5♐49 18	15 4.9	15 18.5	23 42.6	26 30.1	27 10.6	2 51.7	10 58.4	16 10.7	26 55.0
26 W	16 12 35	4 19 26	11♐43 58	17 39 22	15D 4.5	15 24.1	24 13.4	26 9.2	27 8.7	2 56.6	11 1.6	16 10.6	26 56.1
27 Th	16 16 31	5 17 1	23 35 46	29 33 30	15 4.6	15 34.2	24 45.6	25 48.3	27 6.7	3 1.3	11 4.9	16D10.6	26 57.2
28 F	16 20 28	6 14 34	5♑32 50	11♑34 8	15 5.1	15 48.8	25 19.3	25 27.7	27 4.4	3 6.0	11 8.1	16 10.5	26 58.3
29 Sa	16 24 24	7 12 6	17 37 43	23 43 59	15 5.8	16 7.8	25 54.2	25 7.4	27 2.0	3 10.5	11 11.3	16 10.6	26 59.4
30 Su	16 28 21	8 9 38	29 53 18	6♒ 6 2	15 6.6	16 31.2	26 30.3	24 47.3	26 59.4	3 15.1	11 14.5	16 10.6	27 0.6
31 M	16 32 18	9 7 8	12♒22 38	18 43 28	15 7.2	16 58.9	27 7.7	24 27.6	26 56.6	3 19.5	11 17.6	16 10.7	27 1.8

LONGITUDE — JUNE 1937

Day	Sid.Time	☉	0 hr ☽	Noon ☽	True ☊	☿	♀	♂	♃	♄	♅	♆	♇
1 Tu	16 36 14	10♊ 4 38	25♒ 8 57	1♓39 27	15♐ 7.7	17♉30.8	27♈46.2	24♏ 8.2	26♑53.7	3♈23.9	11♉20.8	16♍10.8	27♋ 2.9
2 W	16 40 11	11 2 6	8♓15 19	14 56 51	15R 7.8	18 6.7	28 25.8	23R49.2	26R50.5	3 28.1	11 23.9	16 10.9	27 4.1
3 Th	16 44 7	11 59 34	21 44 17	28 37 46	15 7.8	18 46.7	29 6.5	23 30.7	26 47.2	3 32.3	11 27.0	16 11.1	27 5.4
4 F	16 48 4	12 57 2	5♈37 20	12♈42 56	15 7.6	19 30.6	29 48.2	23 12.6	26 43.7	3 36.5	11 30.0	16 11.3	27 6.6
5 Sa	16 52 0	13 54 28	19 54 20	27 11 11	15 7.5	20 18.3	0♉30.9	22 55.1	26 40.0	3 40.5	11 33.1	16 11.6	27 7.9
6 Su	16 55 57	14 51 54	4♉32 57	11♉58 58	15D 7.4	21 9.6	1 14.5	22 38.2	26 36.2	3 44.5	11 36.1	16 11.8	27 9.1
7 M	16 59 53	15 49 20	19 28 24	27 0 19	15 7.4	22 4.7	1 59.1	22 21.8	26 32.2	3 48.3	11 39.1	16 12.2	27 10.4
8 Tu	17 3 50	16 46 45	4♊33 39	12♊ 7 17	15R 7.5	23 3.2	2 44.5	22 6.1	26 28.0	3 52.1	11 42.1	16 12.5	27 11.7
9 W	17 7 47	17 44 9	19 40 5	27 10 56	15 7.5	24 5.3	3 30.7	21 51.0	26 23.7	3 55.8	11 45.1	16 12.9	27 13.0
10 Th	17 11 43	18 41 32	4♋38 44	12♋ 2 33	15 7.4	25 10.7	4 17.8	21 36.6	26 19.1	3 59.5	11 48.0	16 13.3	27 14.4
11 F	17 15 40	19 38 55	19 21 30	26 34 55	15 7.1	26 19.4	5 5.6	21 22.9	26 14.5	4 3.0	11 51.0	16 13.7	27 15.7
12 Sa	17 19 36	20 36 16	3♌42 15	10♌43 9	15 6.5	27 31.4	5 54.1	21 10.0	26 9.7	4 6.5	11 53.8	16 14.2	27 17.1
13 Su	17 23 33	21 33 37	17 37 23	24 24 55	15 5.9	28 46.7	6 43.4	20 57.8	26 4.7	4 9.8	11 56.7	16 14.7	27 18.5
14 M	17 27 29	22 30 57	1♍ 5 50	7♍40 21	15 5.2	0♊ 5.1	7 33.3	20 46.3	25 59.6	4 13.1	11 59.5	16 15.2	27 19.8
15 Tu	17 31 26	23 28 15	14 8 46	20 31 29	15D 4.8	1 26.7	8 23.9	20 35.7	25 54.3	4 16.3	12 2.3	16 15.8	27 21.2
16 W	17 35 22	24 25 33	26 48 56	3♎ 1 38	15 4.7	2 51.4	9 15.1	20 25.8	25 48.9	4 19.4	12 5.1	16 16.4	27 22.7
17 Th	17 39 19	25 22 50	9♎10 7	15 14 56	15 5.0	4 19.2	10 7.0	20 16.8	25 43.3	4 22.4	12 7.8	16 17.0	27 24.1
18 F	17 43 16	26 20 6	21 16 36	27 15 43	15 5.7	5 50.0	10 59.4	20 8.6	25 37.6	4 25.3	12 10.5	16 17.7	27 25.5
19 Sa	17 47 12	27 17 21	3♏12 46	9♏ 8 18	15 6.8	7 23.9	11 52.4	20 1.2	25 31.8	4 28.1	12 13.2	16 18.4	27 27.0
20 Su	17 51 9	28 14 36	15 2 48	20 56 44	15 8.0	9 0.8	12 46.0	19 54.6	25 25.8	4 30.9	12 15.9	16 19.1	27 28.4
21 M	17 55 5	29 11 50	26 50 33	2♐44 38	15 9.0	10 40.7	13 40.1	19 48.9	25 19.7	4 33.5	12 18.5	16 19.9	27 29.9
22 Tu	17 59 2	0♋ 9 4	8♐39 23	14 35 8	15R 9.7	12 23.5	14 34.7	19 44.0	25 13.5	4 36.0	12 21.1	16 20.6	27 31.4
23 W	18 2 58	1 6 17	20 32 13	26 30 54	15 9.7	14 9.2	15 29.8	19 39.9	25 7.2	4 38.5	12 23.6	16 21.5	27 32.9
24 Th	18 6 55	2 3 29	2♑31 28	8♑34 8	15 9.0	15 57.7	16 25.4	19 36.7	25 0.8	4 40.9	12 26.1	16 22.3	27 34.4
25 F	18 10 51	3 0 42	14 39 8	20 46 41	15 7.4	17 49.0	17 21.5	19 34.3	24 54.2	4 43.1	12 28.6	16 23.2	27 35.9
26 Sa	18 14 48	3 57 54	26 56 57	3♒10 8	15 5.0	19 43.0	18 18.1	19 32.7	24 47.6	4 45.3	12 31.1	16 24.1	27 37.5
27 Su	18 18 45	4 55 6	9♒26 24	15 45 55	15 2.2	21 39.5	19 15.0	19D32.0	24 40.8	4 47.4	12 33.5	16 25.0	27 39.0
28 M	18 22 41	5 52 18	22 8 52	28 35 25	14 59.2	23 38.4	20 12.4	19 32.0	24 34.0	4 49.4	12 35.9	16 26.0	27 40.5
29 Tu	18 26 38	6 49 29	5♓ 5 44	11♓39 58	14 56.4	25 39.5	21 10.3	19 32.9	24 27.0	4 51.2	12 38.2	16 27.0	27 42.1
30 W	18 30 34	7 46 41	18 18 17	25 0 49	14 54.4	27 42.7	22 8.5	19 34.6	24 20.0	4 53.0	12 40.6	16 28.0	27 43.7

Astro Data	Planet Ingress	Last Aspect	☽ Ingress	Last Aspect	☽ Ingress	☽ Phases & Eclipses	Astro Data
Dy Hr Mn	Dy Hr Mn	Dy Hr Mn	Dy Hr Mn	Dy Hr Mn	Dy Hr Mn	Dy Hr Mn	1 MAY 1937
☽0N 6 9:13	♂ ♏ 14 22:52	2 12:27 ♃ ☌	♒ 2 18:08	1 5:06 ♀ ⚹	♓ 1 8:58	3 18:36 ☽ 12♒54	Julian Day # 13635
♀ D 9 5:56	☉ ♊ 21 11:57	4 14:35 ☿ □	♓ 5 1:57	3 9:21 ♇ △	♈ 3 14:22	10 13:18 ● 19♉27	Delta T 23.9 sec
♃ R 15 13:02		7 1:06 ♃ ⚹	♈ 7 5:47	5 11:55 ♇ □	♉ 5 16:36	17 6:49 ☽ 25♌57	SVP 06♓07'50"
☽0S 18 23:49	♀ ♉ 4 6:41	9 2:09 ♃ □	♉ 9 6:32	7 12:17 ♇ ⚹	♊ 7 16:46	25 7:38 ○ 3♐40	Obliquity 23°26'49"
☿ D 24 6:16	☿ ♊ 13 22:28	11 1:39 ♃ △	♊ 11 5:56	8 20:43 ☉ ☌	♋ 9 16:31	25 7:51 ☍A 0.770	⚷ Chiron 20♊26.1
♆ D 27 23:14	☉ ♋ 21 20:12	12 13:13 ♀ ⚹	♋ 13 6:00	11 13:10 ♇ ☌	♌ 11 17:44		☽ Mean ☊ 17♐11.3
♃☍♇ 29 16:30		15 8:14 ♂ △	♌ 15 8:27	13 21:58 ☿ □	♍ 13 22:01	2 5:23 ☽ 11♓15	
		17 12:41 ♂ □	♍ 17 14:19	16 1:05 ♇ ⚹	♎ 16 6:08	8 20:43 ● 17♊36	1 JUNE 1937
☽0N 2 16:50		19 20:29 ☉ △	♎ 19 23:34	18 12:21 ♇ □	♏ 18 17:31	8 20:40:38 ● T 7'04"	Julian Day # 13666
☽0S 15 6:38		22 5:45 ♃ □	♏ 22 11:18	21 1:20 ♇ △	♐ 21 6:25	15 19:03 ☽ 24♍14	Delta T 23.9 sec
♂ D 27 10:08		24 18:26 ♃ ⚹	♐ 25 0:10	22 15:34 ♆ □	♑ 23 18:58	23 22:59 ○ 2♑01	SVP 06♓07'45"
☽0N 29 23:04		27 2:28 ♀ △	♑ 27 12:53	26 1:19 ♇ ☍	♒ 26 5:54		Obliquity 23°26'48"
		29 18:24 ♇ ☍	♒ 30 0:13	28 3:18 ☿ △	♓ 28 14:37		⚷ Chiron 22♊58.6
				30 19:50 ☿ □	♈ 30 20:50		☽ Mean ☊ 15♐32.8

JULY 1937 LONGITUDE

Day	Sid.Time	☉	0 hr ☽	Noon ☽	True ☊	☿	♀	♂	♃	♄	♅	♆	♇
1 Th	18 34 31	8♋43 53	1♈47 42	8♈39 1	14♐53.3	29♊47.7	23♉ 7.1	19♏37.1	24♑12.9	4♈54.7	12♉42.8	16♍29.0	27♋45.2
2 F	18 38 27	9 41 5	15 34 48	22 35 3	14D 53.2	1♋54.2	24 6.1	19 40.4	24R 5.7	4 56.3	12 45.1	16 30.1	27 46.8
3 Sa	18 42 24	10 38 18	29 39 40	6♉48 31	14 54.0	4 2.1	25 5.4	19 44.4	23 58.4	4 57.8	12 47.3	16 31.2	27 48.4
4 Su	18 46 20	11 35 30	14♉ 1 19	21 17 43	14 55.4	6 11.0	26 5.1	19 49.3	23 51.1	4 59.2	12 49.4	16 32.4	27 50.0
5 M	18 50 17	12 32 43	28 37 13	5♊59 14	14 56.7	8 20.6	27 5.1	19 54.9	23 43.7	5 0.5	12 51.6	16 33.5	27 51.6
6 Tu	18 54 14	13 29 57	13♊23 5	20 47 58	14R 57.3	10 30.6	28 5.5	20 1.4	23 36.2	5 1.7	12 53.7	16 34.7	27 53.2
7 W	18 58 10	14 27 10	28 13 0	5♋37 16	14 56.8	12 40.8	29 6.1	20 8.5	23 28.7	5 2.7	12 55.7	16 36.0	27 54.8
8 Th	19 2 7	15 24 24	12♋59 49	20 19 43	14 54.8	14 50.9	0♊ 7.1	20 16.5	23 21.2	5 3.7	12 57.7	16 37.2	27 56.4
9 F	19 6 3	16 21 38	27 36 5	4♌48 7	14 51.5	17 0.6	1 8.4	20 25.2	23 13.6	5 4.6	12 59.7	16 38.5	27 58.0
10 Sa	19 10 0	17 18 52	11♌55 7	18 56 31	14 47.0	19 9.6	2 9.9	20 34.6	23 5.9	5 5.4	13 1.6	16 39.8	27 59.7
11 Su	19 13 56	18 16 6	25 51 55	2♍41 1	14 42.0	21 17.8	3 11.7	20 44.7	22 58.2	5 6.1	13 3.5	16 41.1	28 1.3
12 M	19 17 53	19 13 20	9♍23 44	16 0 4	14 37.2	23 25.0	4 13.8	20 55.6	22 50.6	5 6.7	13 5.3	16 42.5	28 2.9
13 Tu	19 21 50	20 10 34	22 30 12	28 54 23	14 33.1	25 30.9	5 16.2	21 7.2	22 42.8	5 7.1	13 7.1	16 43.8	28 4.6
14 W	19 25 46	21 7 47	5♎13 1	11♎26 33	14 30.4	27 35.5	6 18.8	21 19.4	22 35.1	5 7.5	13 8.9	16 45.3	28 6.2
15 Th	19 29 43	22 5 1	17 35 30	23 40 26	14D 29.1	29 38.7	7 21.6	21 32.4	22 27.4	5 7.8	13 10.6	16 46.7	28 7.9
16 F	19 33 39	23 2 16	29 41 59	5♏40 45	14 29.2	1♌40.3	8 24.7	21 46.0	22 19.6	5 8.0	13 12.3	16 48.1	28 9.5
17 Sa	19 37 36	23 59 30	11♏37 22	17 32 28	14 30.3	3 40.3	9 28.1	22 0.2	22 11.9	5R 8.0	13 13.9	16 49.6	28 11.2
18 Su	19 41 32	24 56 44	23 26 41	29 20 36	14 31.9	5 38.6	10 31.6	22 15.1	22 4.2	5 8.0	13 15.5	16 51.1	28 12.8
19 M	19 45 29	25 53 59	5♐14 48	11♐ 9 50	14R 33.3	7 35.2	11 35.4	22 30.7	21 56.5	5 7.9	13 17.0	16 52.7	28 14.5
20 Tu	19 49 25	26 51 14	17 6 10	23 4 17	14 33.6	9 30.0	12 39.5	22 46.8	21 48.8	5 7.7	13 18.5	16 54.2	28 16.1
21 W	19 53 22	27 48 29	29 4 36	5♑ 7 28	14 32.5	11 23.1	13 43.7	23 3.6	21 41.1	5 7.3	13 20.0	16 55.8	28 17.8
22 Th	19 57 19	28 45 45	11♑13 11	17 21 59	14 29.4	13 14.4	14 48.1	23 20.9	21 33.5	5 6.9	13 21.4	16 57.4	28 19.4
23 F	20 1 15	29 43 1	23 34 6	29 49 38	14 24.4	15 4.0	15 52.8	23 38.8	21 25.9	5 6.4	13 22.8	16 59.0	28 21.1
24 Sa	20 5 12	0♌40 18	6♒ 8 40	12♒31 15	14 17.7	16 51.8	16 57.6	23 57.3	21 18.3	5 5.7	13 24.1	17 0.6	28 22.7
25 Su	20 9 8	1 37 35	18 57 21	25 26 56	14 9.8	18 37.8	18 2.7	24 16.3	21 10.8	5 5.0	13 25.3	17 2.3	28 24.4
26 M	20 13 5	2 34 53	1♓59 55	8♓36 11	14 1.6	20 22.1	19 8.0	24 35.9	21 3.4	5 4.2	13 26.6	17 4.0	28 26.1
27 Tu	20 17 1	3 32 12	15 15 37	21 58 8	13 54.0	22 4.6	20 13.4	24 56.0	20 56.0	5 3.2	13 27.7	17 5.7	28 27.7
28 W	20 20 58	4 29 32	28 43 35	5♈31 52	13 47.7	23 45.4	21 19.1	25 16.6	20 48.6	5 2.2	13 28.9	17 7.4	28 29.3
29 Th	20 24 54	5 26 52	12♈22 53	19 16 34	13 43.3	25 24.4	22 24.9	25 37.8	20 41.3	5 1.1	13 30.0	17 9.2	28 31.0
30 F	20 28 51	6 24 14	26 12 49	3♉11 35	13D 41.1	27 1.7	23 30.9	25 59.4	20 34.1	4 59.8	13 31.0	17 10.9	28 32.6
31 Sa	20 32 48	7 21 37	10♉12 46	17 16 18	13 40.7	28 37.3	24 37.1	26 21.6	20 27.0	4 58.5	13 32.0	17 12.7	28 34.3

AUGUST 1937 LONGITUDE

Day	Sid.Time	☉	0 hr ☽	Noon ☽	True ☊	☿	♀	♂	♃	♄	♅	♆	♇
1 Su	20 36 44	8♌19 1	24♉22 1	1♊29 47	13♐41.3	0♍11.2	25♊43.4	26♏44.2	20♑20.0	4♈57.1	13♉32.9	17♍14.5	28♋35.9
2 M	20 40 41	9 16 27	8♊39 22	15 50 29	13R 42.0	1 43.3	26 50.0	27 7.3	20R 13.0	4R 55.6	13 33.8	17 16.4	28 37.6
3 Tu	20 44 37	10 13 53	23 2 45	0♋15 43	13 41.8	3 13.7	27 56.7	27 30.9	20 6.1	4 53.9	13 34.7	17 18.2	28 39.2
4 W	20 48 34	11 11 21	7♋28 53	14 41 38	13 39.7	4 42.3	29 3.5	27 55.0	19 59.4	4 52.2	13 35.5	17 20.1	28 40.8
5 Th	20 52 30	12 8 50	21 53 19	29 3 14	13 35.1	6 9.2	0♋10.5	28 19.5	19 52.7	4 50.4	13 36.2	17 21.9	28 42.4
6 F	20 56 27	13 6 20	6♌10 41	13♌14 59	13 28.1	7 34.3	1 17.7	28 44.5	19 46.1	4 48.5	13 36.9	17 23.8	28 44.1
7 Sa	21 0 23	14 3 51	20 15 28	27 11 34	13 19.2	8 57.5	2 25.0	29 9.9	19 39.7	4 46.5	13 37.6	17 25.8	28 45.7
8 Su	21 4 20	15 1 23	4♍ 2 48	10♍48 45	13 9.2	10 18.9	3 32.5	29 35.7	19 33.3	4 44.4	13 38.2	17 27.7	28 47.3
9 M	21 8 17	15 58 56	17 29 13	24 4 2	12 59.2	11 38.5	4 40.1	0♐ 2.0	19 27.1	4 42.2	13 38.7	17 29.6	28 48.9
10 Tu	21 12 13	16 56 29	0♎33 13	6♎56 54	12 50.3	12 56.0	5 47.8	0 28.6	19 21.0	4 40.0	13 39.2	17 31.6	28 50.5
11 W	21 16 10	17 54 4	13 15 18	19 28 47	12 43.2	14 11.6	6 55.7	0 55.7	19 15.1	4 37.6	13 39.7	17 33.6	28 52.0
12 Th	21 20 6	18 51 40	25 37 46	1♏42 45	12 38.4	15 25.2	8 3.7	1 23.2	19 9.2	4 35.1	13 40.1	17 35.6	28 53.6
13 F	21 24 3	19 49 16	7♏44 20	13 43 5	12 35.8	16 36.6	9 11.8	1 51.1	19 3.5	4 32.6	13 40.4	17 37.6	28 55.2
14 Sa	21 27 59	20 46 54	19 39 41	25 34 47	12D 35.1	17 45.9	10 20.1	2 19.3	18 58.0	4 30.0	13 40.7	17 39.6	28 56.7
15 Su	21 31 56	21 44 33	1♐29 5	7♐23 14	12R 35.4	18 52.9	11 28.5	2 47.9	18 52.6	4 27.3	13 41.0	17 41.6	28 58.3
16 M	21 35 52	22 42 12	13 17 55	19 13 48	12 35.6	19 57.5	12 37.0	3 16.9	18 47.3	4 24.5	13 41.2	17 43.7	28 59.8
17 Tu	21 39 49	23 39 53	25 11 29	1♑11 33	12 34.9	20 59.6	13 45.7	3 46.3	18 42.2	4 21.6	13 41.3	17 45.7	29 1.4
18 W	21 43 46	24 37 35	7♑14 33	13 20 56	12 32.3	21 59.1	14 54.5	4 16.0	18 37.2	4 18.6	13 41.4	17 47.8	29 2.9
19 Th	21 47 42	25 35 18	19 31 7	25 45 27	12 27.3	22 55.9	16 3.4	4 46.0	18 32.4	4 15.6	13R 41.5	17 49.9	29 4.4
20 F	21 51 39	26 33 2	2♒ 4 9	8♒27 23	12 19.7	23 49.9	17 12.4	5 16.4	18 27.8	4 12.5	13 41.5	17 52.0	29 5.9
21 Sa	21 55 35	27 30 47	14 55 12	21 27 35	12 9.8	24 40.8	18 21.6	5 47.1	18 23.3	4 9.3	13 41.4	17 54.1	29 7.4
22 Su	21 59 32	28 28 33	28 4 24	4♓45 26	11 58.3	25 28.5	19 30.9	6 18.1	18 18.9	4 6.0	13 41.3	17 56.2	29 8.9
23 M	22 3 28	29 26 21	11♓30 24	18 18 55	11 46.3	26 12.8	20 40.3	6 49.4	18 14.8	4 2.7	13 41.2	17 58.3	29 10.4
24 Tu	22 7 25	0♍24 11	25 10 37	2♈ 5 4	11 35.0	26 53.5	21 49.8	7 21.0	18 10.8	3 59.3	13 41.0	18 0.5	29 11.8
25 W	22 11 21	1 22 2	9♈ 1 50	16 0 29	11 25.5	27 30.4	22 59.4	7 52.9	18 7.0	3 55.8	13 40.7	18 2.6	29 13.3
26 Th	22 15 18	2 19 55	23 0 39	0♉ 1 57	11 18.4	28 3.2	24 9.2	8 25.1	18 3.3	3 52.2	13 40.4	18 4.8	29 14.7
27 F	22 19 14	3 17 49	7♉ 4 6	14 6 50	11 14.2	28 31.8	25 19.0	8 57.7	17 59.8	3 48.6	13 40.1	18 6.9	29 16.1
28 Sa	22 23 11	4 15 46	21 9 58	28 13 20	11 12.3	28 55.8	26 29.0	9 30.5	17 56.5	3 44.9	13 39.7	18 9.1	29 17.5
29 Su	22 27 8	5 13 44	5♊16 48	12♊20 15	11 12.0	29 15.1	27 39.1	10 3.5	17 53.4	3 41.2	13 39.3	18 11.3	29 18.9
30 M	22 31 4	6 11 45	19 23 35	26 26 42	11 11.9	29 29.2	28 49.3	10 36.9	17 50.5	3 37.4	13 38.8	18 13.4	29 20.3
31 Tu	22 35 1	7 9 47	3♋29 26	10♋31 37	11 10.8	29 38.0	29 59.6	11 10.5	17 47.7	3 33.5	13 38.3	18 15.6	29 21.7

Astro Data Dy Hr Mn	Planet Ingress Dy Hr Mn	Last Aspect Dy Hr Mn	☽ Ingress Dy Hr Mn	Last Aspect Dy Hr Mn	☽ Ingress Dy Hr Mn	☽ Phases & Eclipses Dy Hr Mn	Astro Data
☽0S 12 15:30	☿ ♋ 1 2:21	2 20:52 ♇ □	♉ 3 0:34	1 7:09 ♇ ✶	♊ 1 9:29	1 13:03 ☽ 9♈15	1 JULY 1937
♄ R 17 5:18	♀ ♊ 7 21:13	4 22:45 ♇ ✶	♊ 5 2:15	3 8:50 ♀ ☌	♋ 3 11:34	8 4:13 ● 15♋34	Julian Day # 13696
☽0N 27 5:06	☿ ♌ 15 4:11	6 5:11 ♆ □	♋ 7 2:53	5 11:26 ♇ ☌	♌ 5 13:35	15 9:36 ☽ 22♎28	Delta T 23.9 sec
	☉ ♌ 23 7:07	9 0:36 ♇ ☌	♌ 9 3:59	7 15:56 ♂ □	♍ 7 16:54	23 12:45 ○ 0♒13	SVP 06♓07'40"
☽0S 9 1:23	☿ ♍ 31 21:07	10 15:00 ♂ □	♍ 11 7:15	9 20:49 ♇ ✶	♎ 9 22:58	30 18:47 ☽ 7♉09	Obliquity 23°26'48"
♅ R 19 13:48		13 10:27 ♇ ✶	♎ 13 14:04	12 6:26 ♇ □	♏ 12 8:37		⚷ Chiron 25♊40.0
☿0S 20 18:27	♀ ♋ 4 20:14	15 20:55 ♇ □	♏ 16 0:36	14 18:53 ♇ △	♐ 14 20:59	6 12:37 ● 13♌37	☽ Mean ☊ 13♐57.5
☽0N 23 12:09	♂ ♐ 8 22:14	18 9:43 ♇ △	♐ 18 13:20	16 20:40 ☉ △	♑ 17 9:37	14 2:28 ☽ 20♏53	
♃△♆ 25 17:55	☉ ♍ 23 13:58	19 23:36 ♆ □	♑ 21 1:50	19 18:22 ♇ ☍	♒ 19 20:05	22 0:47 ○ 28♒30	1 AUGUST 1937
	♀ ♌ 31 0:08	23 9:12 ♇ ☍	♒ 23 12:20	22 0:47 ☉ ☍	♓ 22 3:28	28 23:54 ☽ 5♊14	Julian Day # 13727
		25 10:05 ♂ □	♓ 25 20:21	24 7:00 ♇ △	♈ 24 8:23		Delta T 23.9 sec
		27 23:35 ♇ △	♈ 28 2:15	26 10:40 ♇ □	♉ 26 11:57		SVP 06♓07'35"
		30 4:01 ♇ □	♉ 30 6:31	28 13:51 ♇ ✶	♊ 28 15:01		Obliquity 23°26'48"
				30 17:23 ☿ □	♋ 30 18:03		⚷ Chiron 28♊15.2
							☽ Mean ☊ 12♐19.0

LONGITUDE SEPTEMBER 1937

Day	Sid.Time	☉	0 hr ☽	Noon ☽	True ☊	☿	♀	♂	♃	♄	♅	♆	♇
1 W	22 38 57	8♍ 7 51	17♋33 2	24♋33 23	11♐ 7.5	29♍41.2	1♌10.1	11♐44.4	17♑45.1	3♈29.5	13♉37.7	18♍17.8	29♋23.0
2 Th	22 42 54	9 5 57	1♌32 22	8♌29 35	11R 1.5	29R38.5	2 20.6	12 18.6	17R42.7	3R25.6	13R37.0	18 20.0	29 24.4
3 F	22 46 50	10 4 5	15 24 38	22 17 6	10 52.6	29 29.7	3 31.2	12 53.0	17 40.5	3 21.5	13 36.4	18 22.2	29 25.7
4 Sa	22 50 47	11 2 14	29 6 33	5♍52 33	10 41.4	29 14.7	4 41.9	13 27.7	17 38.5	3 17.4	13 35.6	18 24.5	29 27.0
5 Su	22 54 43	12 0 26	12♍34 45	19 12 50	10 28.8	28 53.3	5 52.8	14 2.6	17 36.7	3 13.3	13 34.8	18 26.7	29 28.3
6 M	22 58 40	12 58 39	25 46 32	2♎15 41	10 16.1	28 25.5	7 3.7	14 37.8	17 35.0	3 9.1	13 34.0	18 28.9	29 29.6
7 Tu	23 2 37	13 56 54	8♎40 13	15 0 11	10 4.5	27 51.5	8 14.7	15 13.2	17 33.6	3 4.8	13 33.1	18 31.1	29 30.9
8 W	23 6 33	14 55 10	21 15 40	27 26 54	9 55.0	27 11.4	9 25.8	15 48.9	17 32.3	3 0.5	13 32.2	18 33.3	29 32.1
9 Th	23 10 30	15 53 28	3♏34 11	9♏37 55	9 48.0	26 25.7	10 37.0	16 24.8	17 31.3	2 56.2	13 31.2	18 35.5	29 33.3
10 F	23 14 26	16 51 48	15 38 32	21 36 35	9 43.8	25 34.8	11 48.3	17 0.9	17 30.4	2 51.8	13 30.2	18 37.8	29 34.5
11 Sa	23 18 23	17 50 9	27 32 38	3♐27 19	9 41.8	24 39.6	12 59.6	17 37.3	17 29.7	2 47.4	13 29.2	18 40.0	29 35.7
12 Su	23 22 19	18 48 32	9♐21 15	15 15 9	9 41.4	23 40.9	14 11.1	18 13.9	17 29.2	2 43.0	13 28.1	18 42.2	29 36.9
13 M	23 26 16	19 46 56	21 9 41	27 5 34	9 41.4	22 40.0	15 22.7	18 50.7	17D 29.0	2 38.5	13 26.9	18 44.5	29 38.1
14 Tu	23 30 12	20 45 22	3♑ 3 28	9♑ 4 3	9 40.9	21 38.0	16 34.3	19 27.7	17 28.9	2 34.0	13 25.7	18 46.7	29 39.2
15 W	23 34 9	21 43 50	15 7 58	21 15 49	9 38.7	20 36.4	17 46.0	20 4.9	17 29.0	2 29.5	13 24.5	18 48.9	29 40.3
16 Th	23 38 6	22 42 19	27 28 7	3♒45 21	9 34.3	19 36.6	18 57.8	20 42.3	17 29.3	2 24.9	13 23.2	18 51.1	29 41.4
17 F	23 42 2	23 40 50	10♒ 7 52	16 35 57	9 27.4	18 40.2	20 9.7	21 19.9	17 29.7	2 20.3	13 21.9	18 53.4	29 42.5
18 Sa	23 45 59	24 39 23	23 9 46	29 49 19	9 18.1	17 48.6	21 21.7	21 57.7	17 30.4	2 15.7	13 20.6	18 55.6	29 43.6
19 Su	23 49 55	25 37 57	6♓34 31	13♓25 8	9 7.2	17 3.0	22 33.7	22 35.6	17 31.3	2 11.1	13 19.2	18 57.8	29 44.6
20 M	23 53 52	26 36 33	20 20 46	27 20 56	8 55.6	16 24.7	23 45.9	23 13.8	17 32.4	2 6.5	13 17.7	19 0.0	29 45.6
21 Tu	23 57 48	27 35 11	4♈25 3	11♈32 26	8 44.7	15 54.7	24 58.1	23 52.1	17 33.6	2 1.9	13 16.2	19 2.2	29 46.6
22 W	0 1 45	28 33 51	18 42 22	25 54 5	8 35.4	15 33.7	26 10.4	24 30.6	17 35.1	1 57.2	13 14.7	19 4.4	29 47.6
23 Th	0 5 41	29 32 33	3♉ 6 54	10♉20 5	8 28.7	15D 22.3	27 22.8	25 9.3	17 36.7	1 52.5	13 13.1	19 6.6	29 48.6
24 F	0 9 38	0♎31 18	17 33 1	24 45 10	8 24.7	15 20.8	28 35.2	25 48.2	17 38.5	1 47.9	13 11.5	19 8.8	29 49.5
25 Sa	0 13 35	1 30 4	1♊56 3	9♊ 5 19	8D 23.1	15 29.3	29 47.8	26 27.2	17 40.5	1 43.2	13 9.9	19 11.0	29 50.4
26 Su	0 17 31	2 28 53	16 12 40	23 17 55	8 23.1	15 47.7	1♍ 0.4	27 6.4	17 42.8	1 38.5	13 8.2	19 13.2	29 51.3
27 M	0 21 28	3 27 44	0♋20 55	7♋21 34	8R 23.5	16 15.8	2 13.1	27 45.8	17 45.1	1 33.9	13 6.5	19 15.4	29 52.2
28 Tu	0 25 24	4 26 38	14 19 51	21 15 41	8 23.2	16 53.2	3 25.9	28 25.3	17 47.7	1 29.2	13 4.8	19 17.5	29 53.0
29 W	0 29 21	5 25 34	28 9 5	4♌59 58	8 21.0	17 39.3	4 38.7	29 5.0	17 50.5	1 24.5	13 3.0	19 19.7	29 53.9
30 Th	0 33 17	6 24 32	11♌48 19	18 34 2	8 16.4	18 33.6	5 51.6	29 44.8	17 53.5	1 19.9	13 1.2	19 21.9	29 54.7

LONGITUDE OCTOBER 1937

Day	Sid.Time	☉	0 hr ☽	Noon ☽	True ☊	☿	♀	♂	♃	♄	♅	♆	♇
1 F	0 37 14	7♎23 32	25♌17 2	1♍57 12	8♐ 9.3	19♍35.3	7♍ 4.6	0♑24.8	17♑56.6	1♈15.2	12♉59.3	19♍24.0	29♋55.5
2 Sa	0 41 10	8 22 35	8♍34 23	15 8 29	8R 0.2	20 43.9	8 17.7	1 4.9	17 59.9	1R 10.6	12R 57.4	19 26.1	29 56.2
3 Su	0 45 7	9 21 39	21 39 21	28 6 51	7 49.8	21 58.5	9 30.8	1 45.2	18 3.4	1 6.0	12 55.5	19 28.3	29 57.0
4 M	0 49 4	10 20 46	4♎30 54	10♎51 25	7 39.2	23 18.5	10 44.0	2 25.7	18 7.1	1 1.4	12 53.5	19 30.4	29 57.7
5 Tu	0 53 0	11 19 55	17 8 25	23 21 54	7 29.5	24 43.2	11 57.3	3 6.3	18 11.0	0 56.8	12 51.6	19 32.5	29 58.4
6 W	0 56 57	12 19 6	29 31 57	5♏38 45	7 21.5	26 11.9	13 10.6	3 47.0	18 15.0	0 52.3	12 49.5	19 34.6	29 59.0
7 Th	1 0 53	13 18 19	11♏42 30	17 43 27	7 15.9	27 44.0	14 24.0	4 27.9	18 19.3	0 47.8	12 47.5	19 36.7	29 59.7
8 F	1 4 50	14 17 34	23 41 58	29 38 26	7 12.6	29 18.9	15 37.4	5 8.9	18 23.7	0 43.3	12 45.4	19 38.7	0♌ 0.3
9 Sa	1 8 46	15 16 50	5♐33 18	11♐27 4	7D 11.5	0♎56.2	16 50.9	5 50.0	18 28.3	0 38.8	12 43.3	19 40.8	0 0.9
10 Su	1 12 43	16 16 9	17 20 18	23 13 35	7 11.9	2 35.4	18 4.5	6 31.3	18 33.0	0 34.4	12 41.2	19 42.8	0 1.5
11 M	1 16 39	17 15 30	29 7 31	5♑ 2 45	7 13.1	4 16.1	19 18.1	7 12.7	18 38.0	0 30.0	12 39.1	19 44.9	0 2.0
12 Tu	1 20 36	18 14 52	10♑59 58	16 59 49	7R 14.3	5 57.8	20 31.8	7 54.3	18 43.1	0 25.7	12 36.9	19 46.9	0 2.5
13 W	1 24 32	19 14 16	23 2 58	29 10 4	7 14.5	7 40.5	21 45.5	8 35.9	18 48.3	0 21.4	12 34.7	19 48.9	0 3.0
14 Th	1 28 29	20 13 42	5♒21 45	11♒38 33	7 13.1	9 23.7	22 59.3	9 17.7	18 53.8	0 17.2	12 32.5	19 50.9	0 3.5
15 F	1 32 26	21 13 9	18 1 1	24 29 33	7 9.8	11 7.2	24 13.1	9 59.5	18 59.4	0 12.9	12 30.2	19 52.9	0 4.0
16 Sa	1 36 22	22 12 38	1♓ 4 29	7♓46 1	7 4.8	12 50.9	25 27.0	10 41.5	19 5.2	0 8.8	12 27.9	19 54.8	0 4.4
17 Su	1 40 19	23 12 9	14 34 13	21 28 59	6 58.3	14 34.7	26 40.9	11 23.6	19 11.1	0 4.7	12 25.7	19 56.7	0 4.8
18 M	1 44 15	24 11 42	28 30 4	5♈37 2	6 51.3	16 18.3	27 54.9	12 5.8	19 17.2	0 0.6	12 23.3	19 58.7	0 5.1
19 Tu	1 48 12	25 11 17	12♈49 19	20 6 10	6 44.5	18 1.7	29 8.9	12 48.1	19 23.5	29♓56.6	12 21.0	20 0.6	0 5.5
20 W	1 52 8	26 10 53	27 26 45	4♉50 7	6 38.8	19 44.9	0♎23.0	13 30.6	19 29.9	29 52.7	12 18.7	20 2.5	0 5.8
21 Th	1 56 5	27 10 32	12♉15 17	19 41 14	6 34.8	21 27.6	1 37.1	14 13.1	19 36.5	29 48.8	12 16.3	20 4.3	0 6.1
22 F	2 0 1	28 10 13	27 6 59	4♊31 37	6D 32.8	23 10.0	2 51.3	14 55.7	19 43.2	29 45.0	12 14.0	20 6.2	0 6.4
23 Sa	2 3 58	29 9 56	11♊54 18	19 14 20	6 32.6	24 52.0	4 5.5	15 38.4	19 50.1	29 41.2	12 11.6	20 8.0	0 6.6
24 Su	2 7 55	0♏ 9 41	26 31 5	3♋44 7	6 33.6	26 33.4	5 19.8	16 21.2	19 57.2	29 37.5	12 9.2	20 9.8	0 6.8
25 M	2 11 51	1 9 29	10♋53 5	17 57 44	6 35.1	28 14.4	6 34.1	17 4.0	20 4.4	29 33.9	12 6.8	20 11.6	0 7.0
26 Tu	2 15 48	2 9 19	24 57 57	1♌53 41	6R 36.2	29 54.9	7 48.5	17 47.0	20 11.7	29 30.3	12 4.3	20 13.4	0 7.2
27 W	2 19 44	3 9 11	8♌44 58	15 31 54	6 36.3	1♏34.8	9 2.9	18 30.1	20 19.2	29 26.8	12 1.9	20 15.1	0 7.3
28 Th	2 23 41	4 9 5	22 14 34	28 53 9	6 34.9	3 14.3	10 17.3	19 13.2	20 26.8	29 23.4	11 59.5	20 16.9	0 7.5
29 F	2 27 37	5 9 1	5♍27 46	11♍58 37	6 32.0	4 53.3	11 31.9	19 56.5	20 34.6	29 20.1	11 57.0	20 18.6	0 7.6
30 Sa	2 31 34	6 9 0	18 25 51	24 49 37	6 27.9	6 31.7	12 46.4	20 39.8	20 42.5	29 16.8	11 54.5	20 20.3	0 7.6
31 Su	2 35 30	7 9 0	1♎10 4	7♎27 21	6 22.9	8 9.7	14 1.0	21 23.2	20 50.6	29 13.6	11 52.1	20 21.9	0R 7.6

Astro Data Dy Hr Mn	Planet Ingress Dy Hr Mn	Last Aspect Dy Hr Mn	☽ Ingress Dy Hr Mn	Last Aspect Dy Hr Mn	☽ Ingress Dy Hr Mn	☽ Phases & Eclipses Dy Hr Mn	Astro Data
☿ R 1 1:08	☉ ♎ 23 11:13	1 20:45 ☿ ⚹	♌ 1 21:21	30 2:09 ♅ □	♍ 1 8:29	4 22:53 ● 11♍58	1 SEPTEMBER 1937
☽0S 5 10:38	♀ ♍ 25 4:03	2 20:52 ♅ □	♍ 4 1:34	3 15:27 ♇ ⚹	♎ 3 15:31	12 20:57 ☽ 19♐40	Julian Day # 13758
☿0N 13 17:02	♂ ♑ 30 9:08	6 6:52 ♇ ⚹	♎ 6 7:48	6 0:53 ♇ □	♏ 6 0:55	20 11:32 ○ 27♓05	Delta T 23.9 sec
♃ D 13 23:18		8 16:06 ♇ □	♏ 8 16:59	7 15:50 ♆ ⚹	♐ 8 12:44	27 5:43 ☽ 3♋42	SVP 06♓07'31"
☽0N 19 20:43	♇ ♌ 7 12:18	11 4:10 ♇ △	♐ 11 4:59	10 4:51 ♆ □	♑ 11 1:47		Obliquity 23°26'48"
☿ D 23 15:38	☿ ♎ 8 10:12	13 2:48 ☿ □	♑ 13 17:52	12 21:10 ♀ △	♒ 13 13:37	4 11:58 ● 10♎50	⚷ Chiron 0♋13.1
☽0S 2 17:58	♄ ♓ 18 3:41	16 4:16 ♇ ☍	♒ 16 4:51	15 6:27 ☉ △	♓ 15 22:03	12 15:47 ☽ 18♑54	☽ Mean ☊ 10♐40.5
☿0S 11 2:55	♀ ♎ 19 16:33	17 21:42 ♂ ⚹	♓ 18 12:19	17 22:54 ♀ ☍	♈ 18 2:32	19 21:47 ○ 26♈05	
♄△♇ 16 23:27	☉ ♏ 23 20:07	20 16:07 ♇ △	♈ 20 16:31	19 21:47 ☉ ☍	♉ 20 4:09	26 13:26 ☽ 2♌43	1 OCTOBER 1937
☽0N 17 6:21	☿ ♏ 26 1:14	22 18:30 ♇ □	♉ 22 18:49	22 4:14 ♄ ⚹	♊ 22 4:40		Julian Day # 13788
♀0S 22 14:29		24 20:30 ♇ ⚹	♊ 24 20:46	24 5:08 ♄ □	♋ 24 5:47		Delta T 23.9 sec
♃△♆ 26 7:09		26 19:23 ♂ ☍	♋ 26 23:24	26 7:49 ♄ △	♌ 26 8:42		SVP 06♓07'29"
☽0S 29 23:23		29 3:03 ♇ ☌	♌ 29 3:14	27 5:46 ♅ □	♍ 28 14:01		Obliquity 23°26'48"
♇ R 31 20:07				30 20:20 ♄ ☍	♎ 30 21:47		⚷ Chiron 1♋09.6
							☽ Mean ☊ 9♐05.1

NOVEMBER 1937 LONGITUDE

Day	Sid.Time	☉	0 hr ☽	Noon ☽	True ☊	☿	♀	♂	♃	♄	♅	♆	♇
1 M	2 39 27	8♏ 9 3	13♎41 37	19♎53 0	6♐17.9	9♏47.2	15♎15.6	22♑ 6.7	20♑58.8	29♓10.5	11♉49.6	20♍23.6	0♌ 7.7
2 Tu	2 43 24	9 9 8	26 1 39	2♏ 7 42	6R 13.3	11 24.2	16 30.2	22 50.3	21 7.2	29R 7.5	11R 47.1	20 25.2	0R 7.6
3 W	2 47 20	10 9 14	8♏11 19	14 12 41	6 9.6	13 0.8	17 44.9	23 34.0	21 15.7	29 4.6	11 44.6	20 26.8	0 7.6
4 Th	2 51 17	11 9 23	20 12 0	26 9 30	6 7.2	14 36.9	18 59.6	24 17.7	21 24.3	29 1.7	11 42.2	20 28.4	0 7.5
5 F	2 55 13	12 9 33	2♐ 5 27	8♐ 0 8	6D 6.2	16 12.6	20 14.4	25 1.5	21 33.0	28 58.9	11 39.7	20 29.9	0 7.4
6 Sa	2 59 10	13 9 45	13 53 52	19 47 2	6 6.3	17 47.9	21 29.2	25 45.4	21 41.9	28 56.3	11 37.2	20 31.4	0 7.3
7 Su	3 3 6	14 9 59	25 40 2	1♑33 19	6 7.4	19 22.8	22 44.0	26 29.4	21 51.0	28 53.7	11 34.7	20 32.9	0 7.2
8 M	3 7 3	15 10 14	7♑27 19	13 22 36	6 9.1	20 57.4	23 58.8	27 13.4	22 0.1	28 51.2	11 32.2	20 34.4	0 7.0
9 Tu	3 10 59	16 10 31	19 19 39	25 19 4	6 10.8	22 31.6	25 13.7	27 57.5	22 9.4	28 48.8	11 29.8	20 35.8	0 6.8
10 W	3 14 56	17 10 50	1♒21 25	7♒27 17	6 12.1	24 5.4	26 28.6	28 41.6	22 18.8	28 46.5	11 27.3	20 37.3	0 6.6
11 Th	3 18 53	18 11 10	13 37 16	19 51 57	6R 12.8	25 38.9	27 43.5	29 25.9	22 28.3	28 44.2	11 24.8	20 38.6	0 6.3
12 F	3 22 49	19 11 31	26 11 53	2♓37 35	6 12.8	27 12.1	28 58.4	0♒10.1	22 38.0	28 42.1	11 22.4	20 40.0	0 6.1
13 Sa	3 26 46	20 11 53	9♓ 9 29	15 47 58	6 11.9	28 45.0	0♏13.4	0 54.5	22 47.7	28 40.1	11 19.9	20 41.3	0 5.8
14 Su	3 30 42	21 12 17	22 33 17	29 25 37	6 10.4	0♐17.6	1 28.4	1 38.8	22 57.6	28 38.2	11 17.5	20 42.7	0 5.4
15 M	3 34 39	22 12 43	6♈24 56	13♈31 5	6 8.6	1 50.0	2 43.4	2 23.3	23 7.6	28 36.3	11 15.1	20 43.9	0 5.1
16 Tu	3 38 35	23 13 9	20 43 43	28 2 19	6 6.8	3 22.0	3 58.4	3 7.8	23 17.7	28 34.6	11 12.7	20 45.2	0 4.7
17 W	3 42 32	24 13 37	5♉26 12	12♉54 30	6 5.4	4 53.8	5 13.5	3 52.3	23 27.9	28 33.0	11 10.3	20 46.4	0 4.3
18 Th	3 46 28	25 14 7	20 26 12	28 0 13	6 4.4	6 25.4	6 28.6	4 36.9	23 38.3	28 31.4	11 7.9	20 47.6	0 3.9
19 F	3 50 25	26 14 38	5♊35 21	13♊10 24	6D 4.1	7 56.6	7 43.6	5 21.5	23 48.7	28 30.0	11 5.5	20 48.8	0 3.4
20 Sa	3 54 22	27 15 11	20 44 13	28 15 40	6 4.4	9 27.6	8 58.8	6 6.2	23 59.2	28 28.7	11 3.1	20 49.9	0 3.0
21 Su	3 58 18	28 15 46	5♋43 45	13♋ 7 37	6 4.9	10 58.4	10 13.9	6 50.9	24 9.9	28 27.5	11 0.8	20 51.0	0 2.5
22 M	4 2 15	29 16 22	20 26 31	27 39 56	6 5.6	12 28.9	11 29.1	7 35.6	24 20.7	28 26.4	10 58.5	20 52.1	0 1.9
23 Tu	4 6 11	0♐16 59	4♌47 28	11♌48 53	6 6.2	13 59.0	12 44.3	8 20.4	24 31.5	28 25.4	10 56.2	20 53.1	0 1.4
24 W	4 10 8	1 17 39	18 44 6	25 33 10	6 6.6	15 28.9	13 59.5	9 5.3	24 42.5	28 24.4	10 53.9	20 54.1	0 0.8
25 Th	4 14 4	2 18 20	2♍16 13	8♍53 29	6R 6.7	16 58.4	15 14.7	9 50.1	24 53.5	28 23.6	10 51.6	20 55.1	0 0.2
26 F	4 18 1	3 19 3	15 25 17	21 51 57	6 6.6	18 27.6	16 29.9	10 35.1	25 4.7	28 22.9	10 49.4	20 56.1	29♋59.6
27 Sa	4 21 57	4 19 47	28 13 54	4♎31 29	6 6.4	19 56.4	17 45.2	11 20.0	25 16.0	28 22.4	10 47.2	20 57.0	29 59.0
28 Su	4 25 54	5 20 33	10♎45 9	16 55 17	6D 6.3	21 24.7	19 0.5	12 5.0	25 27.3	28 21.9	10 45.0	20 57.9	29 58.3
29 M	4 29 51	6 21 20	23 2 17	29 6 32	6 6.3	22 52.5	20 15.8	12 50.0	25 38.8	28 21.5	10 42.8	20 58.7	29 57.6
30 Tu	4 33 47	7 22 9	5♏ 8 22	11♏ 8 10	6 6.4	24 19.7	21 31.1	13 35.1	25 50.3	28 21.2	10 40.6	20 59.6	29 56.9

DECEMBER 1937 LONGITUDE

Day	Sid.Time	☉	0 hr ☽	Noon ☽	True ☊	☿	♀	♂	♃	♄	♅	♆	♇
1 W	4 37 44	8♐22 59	17♏ 6 13	23♏ 2 50	6♐ 6.5	25♐46.2	22♏46.4	14♒20.2	26♑ 1.9	28♓21.1	10♉38.5	21♍ 0.3	29♋56.2
2 Th	4 41 40	9 23 50	28 58 18	4♐52 54	6R 6.7	27 11.9	24 1.7	15 5.3	26 13.6	28D 21.0	10R 36.4	21 1.1	29R 55.4
3 F	4 45 37	10 24 43	10♐46 53	16 40 32	6 6.7	28 36.7	25 17.1	15 50.4	26 25.4	28 21.1	10 34.4	21 1.8	29 54.7
4 Sa	4 49 33	11 25 37	22 34 6	28 27 52	6 6.5	0♑ 0.5	26 32.4	16 35.6	26 37.3	28 21.2	10 32.3	21 2.5	29 53.9
5 Su	4 53 30	12 26 32	4♑22 5	10♑17 4	6 5.9	1 23.1	27 47.8	17 20.8	26 49.3	28 21.5	10 30.3	21 3.2	29 53.1
6 M	4 57 26	13 27 28	16 13 7	22 10 35	6 5.0	2 44.2	29 3.2	18 6.1	27 1.4	28 21.9	10 28.3	21 3.8	29 52.2
7 Tu	5 1 23	14 28 24	28 9 47	4♒11 7	6 3.8	4 3.7	0♐18.6	18 51.3	27 13.5	28 22.4	10 26.4	21 4.4	29 51.4
8 W	5 5 20	15 29 22	10♒14 59	16 21 49	6 2.5	5 21.3	1 33.9	19 36.6	27 25.7	28 23.0	10 24.5	21 5.0	29 50.5
9 Th	5 9 16	16 30 20	22 32 2	28 46 6	6 1.3	6 36.7	2 49.3	20 21.9	27 38.0	28 23.7	10 22.6	21 5.5	29 49.6
10 F	5 13 13	17 31 19	5♓ 4 29	11♓27 39	6 0.5	7 49.5	4 4.7	21 7.2	27 50.4	28 24.5	10 20.8	21 6.0	29 48.7
11 Sa	5 17 9	18 32 18	17 56 1	24 30 1	6D 0.2	8 59.3	5 20.1	21 52.5	28 2.8	28 25.5	10 19.0	21 6.4	29 47.7
12 Su	5 21 6	19 33 18	1♈10 1	7♈56 19	6 0.4	10 5.6	6 35.6	22 37.9	28 15.3	28 26.5	10 17.2	21 6.8	29 46.8
13 M	5 25 2	20 34 19	14 49 7	21 48 32	6 1.3	11 7.9	7 51.0	23 23.2	28 27.9	28 27.6	10 15.5	21 7.2	29 45.8
14 Tu	5 28 59	21 35 20	28 54 32	6♉ 6 57	6 2.5	12 5.7	9 6.4	24 8.6	28 40.5	28 28.9	10 13.8	21 7.6	29 44.8
15 W	5 32 55	22 36 21	13♉25 26	20 49 26	6 3.7	12 58.1	10 21.8	24 54.0	28 53.2	28 30.3	10 12.1	21 7.9	29 43.8
16 Th	5 36 52	23 37 23	28 18 16	5♊51 3	6R 4.5	13 44.6	11 37.2	25 39.4	29 6.0	28 31.7	10 10.5	21 8.2	29 42.8
17 F	5 40 49	24 38 26	13♊26 44	21 4 9	6 4.5	14 24.2	12 52.7	26 24.8	29 18.9	28 33.3	10 8.9	21 8.4	29 41.8
18 Sa	5 44 45	25 39 29	28 42 3	6♋19 8	6 3.5	14 56.1	14 8.1	27 10.2	29 31.8	28 35.0	10 7.4	21 8.6	29 40.7
19 Su	5 48 42	26 40 33	13♋54 8	21 25 51	6 1.4	15 19.4	15 23.6	27 55.6	29 44.7	28 36.8	10 5.9	21 8.8	29 39.6
20 M	5 52 38	27 41 37	28 53 11	6♌15 11	5 58.6	15R 33.2	16 39.0	28 41.0	29 57.8	28 38.6	10 4.5	21 9.0	29 38.6
21 Tu	5 56 35	28 42 42	13♌31 6	20 40 22	5 55.4	15 36.8	17 54.5	29 26.4	0♒10.9	28 40.6	10 3.1	21 9.1	29 37.5
22 W	6 0 31	29 43 48	27 42 37	4♍37 39	5 52.3	15 29.3	19 9.9	0♓11.8	0 24.0	28 42.7	10 1.7	21 9.2	29 36.3
23 Th	6 4 28	0♑44 55	11♍25 30	18 6 17	5 49.9	15 10.2	20 25.4	0 57.2	0 37.2	28 44.9	10 0.4	21R 9.2	29 35.2
24 F	6 8 25	1 46 2	24 40 19	1♎ 7 59	5D 48.6	14 39.4	21 40.8	1 42.6	0 50.4	28 47.2	9 59.1	21 9.2	29 34.1
25 Sa	6 12 21	2 47 10	7♎29 44	13 46 6	5 48.5	13 56.9	22 56.3	2 28.0	1 3.7	28 49.6	9 57.8	21 9.2	29 32.9
26 Su	6 16 18	3 48 18	19 57 39	26 4 59	5 49.5	13 3.4	24 11.8	3 13.5	1 17.1	28 52.1	9 56.7	21 9.1	29 31.7
27 M	6 20 14	4 49 27	2♏ 8 40	8♏ 9 18	5 51.1	12 0.1	25 27.3	3 58.9	1 30.5	28 54.7	9 55.5	21 9.0	29 30.6
28 Tu	6 24 11	5 50 37	14 7 27	20 3 38	5 53.0	10 48.6	26 42.8	4 44.3	1 44.0	28 57.4	9 54.4	21 8.9	29 29.4
29 W	6 28 7	6 51 47	25 58 23	1♐52 9	5R 54.5	9 31.1	27 58.2	5 29.7	1 57.5	29 0.2	9 53.4	21 8.7	29 28.1
30 Th	6 32 4	7 52 57	7♐45 25	13 38 32	5 54.9	8 10.1	29 13.7	6 15.1	2 11.0	29 3.1	9 52.4	21 8.5	29 26.9
31 F	6 36 0	8 54 8	19 31 53	25 25 47	5 53.9	6 48.3	0♑29.2	7 0.6	2 24.6	29 6.1	9 51.4	21 8.3	29 25.7

Astro Data Dy Hr Mn	Planet Ingress Dy Hr Mn	Last Aspect Dy Hr Mn	☽ Ingress Dy Hr Mn	Last Aspect Dy Hr Mn	☽ Ingress Dy Hr Mn	☽ Phases & Eclipses Dy Hr Mn	Astro Data
☽0N 13 15:51	♂ ♒ 11 18:31	1 17:22 ♂ □	♏ 2 7:48	2 1:56 ♇ △	♐ 2 2:05	3 4:16 ● 10♏20	1 NOVEMBER 1937
☽0S 26 4:37	♀ ♏ 12 19:43	4 17:44 ♄ △	♐ 4 19:46	4 11:47 ♄ □	♑ 4 15:07	11 9:33 ☽ 18♒35	Julian Day # 13819
	☿ ♐ 13 19:25	7 6:33 ♄ □	♑ 7 8:50	7 3:23 ♇ ☍	♒ 7 3:40	18 8:09 ○ 25♉35	Delta T 24.0 sec
♄ D 1 23:03	☉ ♐ 22 17:17	9 18:54 ♄ ✶	♒ 9 21:19	8 19:31 ♂ ☌	♓ 9 14:21	18 8:19 • P 0.144	SVP 06♓07'26"
☽0N 11 0:01	♇ ♋ 25 9:03	12 5:46 ♀ △	♓ 12 7:07	11 21:31 ♇ △	♈ 11 21:55	25 0:04 ☽ 2♍19	Obliquity 23°26'47"
♃✶♄ 12 23:29		14 10:36 ♄ ☌	♈ 14 12:59	14 1:24 ♇ □	♉ 14 1:50		⚷ Chiron 0♋54.3R
♃☍♇ 18 15:17	☿ ♑ 3 23:51	16 4:17 ♃ □	♉ 16 15:12	16 2:15 ♇ ✶	♊ 16 2:42	2 23:11 ● 10♐23	☽ Mean ☊ 7♐26.6
☿ R 20 19:54	♀ ♐ 6 18:06	18 12:48 ♄ ✶	♊ 18 15:10	17 23:49 ♄ □	♋ 18 2:03	2 23:05:22 • A 11'13"	
☽0S 23 11:53	♃ ♒ 20 4:05	20 12:20 ♄ □	♋ 20 14:47	20 1:46 ♃ ☍	♌ 20 1:48	11 1:12 ☽ 18♓35	1 DECEMBER 1937
♆ R 23 16:58	♂ ♓ 21 17:46	22 15:49 ☉ △	♌ 22 15:55	22 3:46 ☉ △	♍ 22 3:57	17 18:52 ○ 25♊26	Julian Day # 13849
	☉ ♑ 22 6:22	23 17:39 ☿ △	♍ 24 19:56	24 9:04 ♇ ✶	♎ 24 9:53	24 14:20 ☽ 2♎23	Delta T 24.0 sec
	♀ ♑ 30 14:42	27 3:19 ♇ ✶	♎ 27 3:22	26 18:47 ♇ □	♏ 26 19:45		SVP 06♓07'21"
		29 13:41 ♇ □	♏ 29 13:46	29 7:06 ♇ △	♐ 29 8:12		Obliquity 23°26'46"
				31 19:33 ♄ □	♑ 31 21:17		⚷ Chiron 29♊33.8R
							☽ Mean ☊ 5♐51.3

LONGITUDE JANUARY 1938

Day	Sid.Time	☉	0 hr ☽	Noon ☽	True ☊	☿	♀	♂	♃	♄	♅	♆	♇
1 Sa	6 39 57	9♑55 19	1♑20 32	7♑16 24	5♐51.1	5♑28.4	1♑44.7	7♓46.0	2♒38.2	29♓ 9.3	9♉50.5	21♍ 8.1	29♋24.5
2 Su	6 43 54	10 56 30	13 13 35	19 12 18	5R46.5	4R12.9	3 0.2	8 31.4	2 51.9	29 12.5	9R49.7	21R 7.8	29R23.2
3 M	6 47 50	11 57 41	25 12 45	1♒15 6	5 40.4	3 3.8	4 15.7	9 16.8	3 5.6	29 15.8	9 48.9	21 7.4	29 22.0
4 Tu	6 51 47	12 58 52	7♒19 32	13 26 14	5 33.3	2 2.8	5 31.2	10 2.2	3 19.4	29 19.1	9 48.1	21 7.1	29 20.7
5 W	6 55 43	14 0 3	19 35 23	25 47 10	5 25.9	1 11.0	6 46.7	10 47.6	3 33.2	29 22.6	9 47.4	21 6.7	29 19.4
6 Th	6 59 40	15 1 13	2♓ 1 49	8♓19 33	5 19.0	0 29.1	8 2.2	11 32.9	3 47.0	29 26.2	9 46.7	21 6.2	29 18.1
7 F	7 3 36	16 2 24	14 40 38	21 5 20	5 13.3	29♐57.3	9 17.6	12 18.3	4 0.9	29 29.9	9 46.1	21 5.8	29 16.8
8 Sa	7 7 33	17 3 33	27 33 56	4♈ 6 45	5 9.4	29 35.6	10 33.1	13 3.6	4 14.8	29 33.6	9 45.6	21 5.3	29 15.5
9 Su	7 11 29	18 4 43	10♈44 4	17 26 10	5D 7.5	29D23.6	11 48.6	13 49.0	4 28.7	29 37.5	9 45.1	21 4.7	29 14.2
10 M	7 15 26	19 5 51	24 13 19	1♉ 5 44	5 7.3	29 20.8	13 4.0	14 34.3	4 42.6	29 41.4	9 44.6	21 4.2	29 12.9
11 Tu	7 19 23	20 7 0	8♉ 3 35	15 6 54	5 8.3	29 26.6	14 19.5	15 19.6	4 56.6	29 45.5	9 44.2	21 3.6	29 11.6
12 W	7 23 19	21 8 7	22 15 39	29 29 39	5R 9.6	29 40.4	15 35.0	16 4.9	5 10.6	29 49.6	9 43.9	21 2.9	29 10.3
13 Th	7 27 16	22 9 14	6♊48 34	14♊11 54	5 10.1	0♑ 1.5	16 50.4	16 50.1	5 24.6	29 53.8	9 43.6	21 2.3	29 9.0
14 F	7 31 12	23 10 21	21 39 0	29 9 0	5 9.0	0 29.2	18 5.9	17 35.4	5 38.7	29 58.1	9 43.3	21 1.6	29 7.7
15 Sa	7 35 9	24 11 27	6♋40 56	14♋13 41	5 5.6	1 3.0	19 21.3	18 20.6	5 52.8	0♈ 2.5	9 43.1	21 0.9	29 6.3
16 Su	7 39 5	25 12 32	21 46 3	29 16 49	4 59.9	1 42.2	20 36.7	19 5.8	6 6.9	0 6.9	9 43.0	21 0.1	29 5.0
17 M	7 43 2	26 13 37	6♌44 46	14♌ 8 46	4 52.3	2 26.2	21 52.1	19 51.0	6 21.0	0 11.5	9 42.9	20 59.3	29 3.7
18 Tu	7 46 58	27 14 41	21 27 47	28 40 59	4 43.6	3 14.7	23 7.6	20 36.1	6 35.1	0 16.1	9D42.9	20 58.5	29 2.3
19 W	7 50 55	28 15 45	5♍47 42	12♍47 26	4 34.9	4 7.1	24 23.0	21 21.3	6 49.3	0 20.8	9 42.9	20 57.7	29 1.0
20 Th	7 54 52	29 16 48	19 39 57	26 25 10	4 27.3	5 3.1	25 38.4	22 6.4	7 3.4	0 25.6	9 43.0	20 56.8	28 59.7
21 F	7 58 48	0♒17 51	3♎ 3 11	9♎34 15	4 21.6	6 2.3	26 53.8	22 51.5	7 17.6	0 30.4	9 43.1	20 55.9	28 58.3
22 Sa	8 2 45	1 18 54	15 58 46	22 17 14	4 18.1	7 4.4	28 9.2	23 36.5	7 31.8	0 35.4	9 43.2	20 55.0	28 57.0
23 Su	8 6 41	2 19 56	28 30 12	4♏38 19	4D16.7	8 9.2	29 24.6	24 21.6	7 46.0	0 40.4	9 43.5	20 54.1	28 55.6
24 M	8 10 38	3 20 58	10♏42 15	16 42 40	4 16.9	9 16.3	0♒40.0	25 6.6	8 0.2	0 45.5	9 43.7	20 53.1	28 54.3
25 Tu	8 14 34	4 21 59	22 40 15	28 35 42	4R17.7	10 25.6	1 55.4	25 51.6	8 14.4	0 50.6	9 44.1	20 52.1	28 53.0
26 W	8 18 31	5 23 0	4♐29 41	10♐22 48	4 18.2	11 36.9	3 10.8	26 36.6	8 28.7	0 55.9	9 44.5	20 51.0	28 51.6
27 Th	8 22 27	6 24 0	16 15 39	22 8 49	4 17.3	12 50.0	4 26.2	27 21.5	8 42.9	1 1.2	9 44.9	20 50.0	28 50.3
28 F	8 26 24	7 24 59	28 2 46	3♑57 58	4 14.3	14 4.8	5 41.6	28 6.4	8 57.2	1 6.6	9 45.4	20 48.9	28 49.0
29 Sa	8 30 21	8 25 58	9♑54 48	15 53 37	4 8.6	15 21.1	6 57.0	28 51.3	9 11.4	1 12.0	9 45.9	20 47.8	28 47.7
30 Su	8 34 17	9 26 55	21 54 43	27 58 17	4 0.1	16 38.9	8 12.3	29 36.2	9 25.7	1 17.6	9 46.5	20 46.6	28 46.4
31 M	8 38 14	10 27 52	4♒ 4 30	10♒13 30	3 49.2	17 58.0	9 27.7	0♈21.0	9 39.9	1 23.2	9 47.2	20 45.5	28 45.1

LONGITUDE FEBRUARY 1938

Day	Sid.Time	☉	0 hr ☽	Noon ☽	True ☊	☿	♀	♂	♃	♄	♅	♆	♇
1 Tu	8 42 10	11♒28 48	16♒25 21	22♒40 4	3♐36.7	19♑18.3	10♒43.0	1♈ 5.9	9♒54.2	1♈28.8	9♉47.9	20♍44.3	28♋43.7
2 W	8 46 7	12 29 43	28 57 41	5♓18 11	3R23.6	20 39.9	11 58.4	1 50.6	10 8.5	1 34.5	9 48.6	20R43.1	28R42.5
3 Th	8 50 3	13 30 36	11♓41 32	18 7 44	3 11.1	22 2.5	13 13.7	2 35.4	10 22.7	1 40.3	9 49.4	20 41.8	28 41.2
4 F	8 54 0	14 31 28	24 36 45	1♈ 8 37	3 0.4	23 26.3	14 29.0	3 20.1	10 36.9	1 46.2	9 50.3	20 40.6	28 39.9
5 Sa	8 57 56	15 32 19	7♈43 22	14 21 3	2 52.3	24 51.0	15 44.3	4 4.8	10 51.2	1 52.1	9 51.2	20 39.3	28 38.6
6 Su	9 1 53	16 33 9	21 1 46	27 45 37	2 47.1	26 16.8	16 59.6	4 49.5	11 5.4	1 58.0	9 52.1	20 38.0	28 37.3
7 M	9 5 50	17 33 57	4♉32 45	11♉23 16	2 44.7	27 43.5	18 14.9	5 34.1	11 19.6	2 4.1	9 53.2	20 36.7	28 36.1
8 Tu	9 9 46	18 34 43	18 17 20	25 15 2	2D44.1	29 11.1	19 30.2	6 18.7	11 33.9	2 10.2	9 54.2	20 35.3	28 34.8
9 W	9 13 43	19 35 28	2♊16 26	9♊21 30	2R44.2	0♒39.6	20 45.4	7 3.3	11 48.1	2 16.3	9 55.3	20 34.0	28 33.6
10 Th	9 17 39	20 36 12	16 30 8	23 42 9	2 43.7	2 9.1	22 0.7	7 47.8	12 2.2	2 22.5	9 56.5	20 32.6	28 32.3
11 F	9 21 36	21 36 54	0♋57 12	8♋14 48	2 41.3	3 39.4	23 15.9	8 32.3	12 16.4	2 28.8	9 57.7	20 31.2	28 31.1
12 Sa	9 25 32	22 37 34	15 34 23	22 55 11	2 36.1	5 10.6	24 31.1	9 16.8	12 30.6	2 35.1	9 59.0	20 29.8	28 29.9
13 Su	9 29 29	23 38 12	0♌16 22	7♌37 1	2 28.1	6 42.7	25 46.3	10 1.2	12 44.7	2 41.4	10 0.3	20 28.4	28 28.7
14 M	9 33 25	24 38 49	14 56 8	22 12 44	2 17.5	8 15.7	27 1.5	10 45.5	12 58.8	2 47.9	10 1.6	20 26.9	28 27.5
15 Tu	9 37 22	25 39 25	29 25 54	6♍34 43	2 5.4	9 49.5	28 16.7	11 29.9	13 12.9	2 54.3	10 3.0	20 25.4	28 26.4
16 W	9 41 19	26 39 59	13♍38 29	20 36 32	1 53.1	11 24.2	29 31.8	12 14.2	13 27.0	3 0.8	10 4.5	20 24.0	28 25.2
17 Th	9 45 15	27 40 31	27 28 28	4♎13 59	1 41.8	12 59.8	0♓46.9	12 58.4	13 41.1	3 7.4	10 6.0	20 22.5	28 24.1
18 F	9 49 12	28 41 2	10♎53 0	17 25 32	1 32.7	14 36.3	2 2.1	13 42.7	13 55.1	3 14.0	10 7.5	20 20.9	28 22.9
19 Sa	9 53 8	29 41 32	23 51 49	0♏12 10	1 26.3	16 13.6	3 17.2	14 26.8	14 9.1	3 20.6	10 9.1	20 19.4	28 21.8
20 Su	9 57 5	0♓42 1	6♏27 1	12 36 55	1 22.5	17 51.9	4 32.3	15 11.0	14 23.1	3 27.3	10 10.7	20 17.9	28 20.7
21 M	10 1 1	1 42 28	18 42 26	24 44 14	1 21.0	19 31.2	5 47.4	15 55.1	14 37.1	3 34.1	10 12.4	20 16.3	28 19.6
22 Tu	10 4 58	2 42 54	0♐43 0	6♐39 25	1 20.7	21 11.3	7 2.5	16 39.2	14 51.0	3 40.8	10 14.2	20 14.8	28 18.5
23 W	10 8 54	3 43 18	12 34 13	18 28 4	1 20.6	22 52.5	8 17.5	17 23.2	15 5.0	3 47.7	10 15.9	20 13.2	28 17.5
24 Th	10 12 51	4 43 41	24 21 41	0♑15 44	1 19.4	24 34.6	9 32.6	18 7.2	15 18.8	3 54.5	10 17.7	20 11.6	28 16.4
25 F	10 16 48	5 44 3	6♑10 48	12 7 30	1 16.3	26 17.6	10 47.6	18 51.2	15 32.7	4 1.4	10 19.6	20 10.0	28 15.4
26 Sa	10 20 44	6 44 23	18 6 21	24 7 49	1 10.5	28 1.7	12 2.6	19 35.1	15 46.5	4 8.4	10 21.5	20 8.4	28 14.4
27 Su	10 24 41	7 44 42	0♒12 19	6♒20 10	1 1.9	29 46.8	13 17.6	20 19.0	16 0.3	4 15.3	10 23.5	20 6.8	28 13.4
28 M	10 28 37	8 44 59	12 31 37	18 46 51	0 50.7	1♓32.8	14 32.6	21 2.9	16 14.0	4 22.3	10 25.5	20 5.2	28 12.4

Astro Data Dy Hr Mn	Planet Ingress Dy Hr Mn	Last Aspect Dy Hr Mn	☽ Ingress Dy Hr Mn	Last Aspect Dy Hr Mn	☽ Ingress Dy Hr Mn	☽ Phases & Eclipses Dy Hr Mn	Astro Data
♄△♇ 4 7:52	☿ ♐ 6 21:37	3 8:15 ♇ ☍	♒ 3 9:31	31 13:35 ☉ ☌	♓ 2 1:58	1 18:58 ● 10♑44	1 JANUARY 1938
☽0N 7 6:45	☿ ♑ 12 22:30	4 4:52 ♅ □	♓ 5 20:07	4 7:27 ♇ △	♈ 4 9:54	9 14:13 ☽ 18♈41	Julian Day # 13880
☿ D 9 19:29	♄ ♈ 14 10:31	8 3:41 ♄ ☌	♈ 8 4:29	6 13:31 ♇ □	♉ 6 15:58	16 5:53 ○ 25♋28	Delta T 24.0 sec
♃♀♆ 15 13:06	☉ ♒ 20 16:59	10 9:00 ☿ △	♉ 10 10:06	8 17:41 ♇ ✱	♊ 8 20:08	23 8:09 ☽ 2♏41	SVP 06♓07'16"
♅ D 18 4:53	♀ ♒ 23 11:16	12 12:36 ♄ ✱	♊ 12 12:50	10 10:04 ♀ △	♋ 10 22:26	31 13:35 ● 11♒02	Obliquity 23°26'46"
☽0S 19 21:53	♂ ♈ 30 12:44	13 23:00 ♆ □	♋ 14 13:21	12 21:05 ♇ ☌	♌ 12 23:33		⚷ Chiron 27♊37.1R
♂0N 31 19:03		16 11:40 ♇ ☌	♌ 16 13:09	14 21:53 ♀ ☍	♍ 15 0:57	8 0:32 ☽ 18♉36	☽ Mean ☊ 4♐12.8
♃□♅ 31 12:49	☿ ♒ 8 13:17	17 4:48 ♅ □	♍ 18 14:12	17 1:38 ♇ ✱	♎ 17 4:28	14 17:14 ○ 25♌22	
	♀ ♓ 16 9:00	20 16:36 ♇ ✱	♎ 20 18:27	19 8:29 ♇ □	♏ 19 11:37	22 4:24 ☽ 2♐54	1 FEBRUARY 1938
☽0N 3 13:06	☉ ♓ 19 7:20	23 1:58 ♀ □	♏ 23 2:55	21 19:10 ♇ △	♐ 21 22:33		Julian Day # 13911
☽0S 16 8:58	☿ ♓ 27 3:01	25 12:34 ♇ △	♐ 25 14:51	24 0:31 ☿ ✱	♑ 24 11:28		Delta T 24.0 sec
		28 0:08 ♂ □	♑ 28 3:58	26 20:06 ♇ ☍	♒ 26 23:36		SVP 06♓07'11"
		30 13:33 ♇ ☍	♒ 30 16:00				Obliquity 23°26'46"
							⚷ Chiron 25♊59.4R
							☽ Mean ☊ 2♐34.4

MARCH 1938 — LONGITUDE

Day	Sid.Time	☉	0 hr ☽	Noon ☽	True ☊	☿	♀	♂	♃	♄	♅	♆	♇
1 Tu	10 32 34	9♓45 15	25♒ 5 57	1♓28 57	0♐37.7	3♓20.0	15♓47.6	21♈46.7	16♒27.7	4♈29.4	10♉27.5	20♍ 3.5	28♋11.4
2 W	10 36 30	10 45 28	7♓55 47	14 26 20	0R 24.0	5 8.1	17 2.5	22 30.4	16 41.4	4 36.5	10 29.6	20R 1.9	28R10.5
3 Th	10 40 27	11 45 40	21 0 25	27 37 49	0 11.0	6 57.3	18 17.5	23 14.2	16 55.0	4 43.6	10 31.7	20 0.2	28 9.6
4 F	10 44 23	12 45 50	4♈18 18	11♈ 1 37	29♏59.7	8 47.5	19 32.4	23 57.9	17 8.6	4 50.7	10 33.9	19 58.6	28 8.7
5 Sa	10 48 20	13 45 58	17 47 30	24 35 43	29 51.0	10 38.8	20 47.3	24 41.5	17 22.2	4 57.9	10 36.1	19 56.9	28 7.8
6 Su	10 52 16	14 46 4	1♉26 4	8♉18 23	29 45.4	12 31.1	22 2.2	25 25.1	17 35.7	5 5.1	10 38.3	19 55.3	28 6.9
7 M	10 56 13	15 46 8	15 12 31	22 8 23	29 42.7	14 24.4	23 17.0	26 8.7	17 49.1	5 12.3	10 40.6	19 53.6	28 6.1
8 Tu	11 0 10	16 46 10	29 5 54	6♊ 5 0	29D 41.9	16 18.6	24 31.8	26 52.2	18 2.5	5 19.5	10 42.9	19 51.9	28 5.3
9 W	11 4 6	17 46 10	13♊ 5 40	20 7 51	29R 42.1	18 13.8	25 46.6	27 35.7	18 15.9	5 26.8	10 45.3	19 50.3	28 4.5
10 Th	11 8 3	18 46 8	27 11 27	4♋16 22	29 42.0	20 9.8	27 1.4	28 19.2	18 29.2	5 34.1	10 47.7	19 48.6	28 3.7
11 F	11 11 59	19 46 3	11♋22 26	18 29 24	29 40.2	22 6.7	28 16.2	29 2.6	18 42.4	5 41.4	10 50.1	19 46.9	28 2.9
12 Sa	11 15 56	20 45 56	25 36 57	2♌44 42	29 36.0	24 4.2	29 30.9	29 45.9	18 55.6	5 48.7	10 52.6	19 45.3	28 2.2
13 Su	11 19 52	21 45 47	9♌52 10	16 58 49	29 29.2	26 2.4	0♈45.6	0♉29.2	19 8.8	5 56.1	10 55.1	19 43.6	28 1.5
14 M	11 23 49	22 45 36	24 4 3	1♍ 7 15	29 20.0	28 0.9	2 0.3	1 12.5	19 21.9	6 3.5	10 57.6	19 41.9	28 0.8
15 Tu	11 27 45	23 45 22	8♍ 7 48	15 5 5	29 9.5	29 59.8	3 15.0	1 55.7	19 34.9	6 10.8	11 0.2	19 40.3	28 0.1
16 W	11 31 42	24 45 6	21 58 33	28 47 44	28 58.5	1♈58.7	4 29.6	2 38.9	19 47.9	6 18.2	11 2.8	19 38.6	27 59.4
17 Th	11 35 39	25 44 49	5♎32 12	12♎11 41	28 48.5	3 57.5	5 44.2	3 22.0	20 0.8	6 25.7	11 5.4	19 37.0	27 58.8
18 F	11 39 35	26 44 29	18 45 59	25 15 4	28 40.2	5 55.9	6 58.8	4 5.1	20 13.6	6 33.1	11 8.1	19 35.3	27 58.2
19 Sa	11 43 32	27 44 8	1♏38 59	7♏57 54	28 34.4	7 53.6	8 13.4	4 48.1	20 26.4	6 40.5	11 10.8	19 33.6	27 57.6
20 Su	11 47 28	28 43 45	14 12 5	20 21 53	28 31.1	9 50.2	9 27.9	5 31.1	20 39.1	6 48.0	11 13.5	19 32.0	27 57.1
21 M	11 51 25	29 43 20	26 27 45	2♐30 12	28D 30.0	11 45.5	10 42.5	6 14.1	20 51.8	6 55.5	11 16.3	19 30.4	27 56.5
22 Tu	11 55 21	0♈42 53	8♐29 48	14 27 8	28 30.3	13 38.9	11 57.0	6 57.0	21 4.4	7 2.9	11 19.1	19 28.7	27 56.0
23 W	11 59 18	1 42 24	20 22 51	26 17 37	28 31.3	15 30.1	13 11.4	7 39.9	21 17.0	7 10.4	11 21.9	19 27.1	27 55.5
24 Th	12 3 14	2 41 54	2♑12 7	8♑ 6 59	28R 31.9	17 18.7	14 25.9	8 22.7	21 29.4	7 17.9	11 24.7	19 25.5	27 55.0
25 F	12 7 11	3 41 22	14 2 55	20 0 32	28 31.2	19 4.2	15 40.3	9 5.5	21 41.8	7 25.4	11 27.6	19 23.9	27 54.6
26 Sa	12 11 8	4 40 48	26 0 29	2♒ 3 19	28 28.6	20 46.2	16 54.7	9 48.3	21 54.1	7 32.9	11 30.5	19 22.3	27 54.2
27 Su	12 15 4	5 40 12	8♒ 9 33	14 19 41	28 23.9	22 24.2	18 9.1	10 31.0	22 6.4	7 40.4	11 33.5	19 20.7	27 53.8
28 M	12 19 1	6 39 35	20 34 6	26 53 5	28 17.2	23 57.9	19 23.5	11 13.6	22 18.6	7 47.9	11 36.4	19 19.1	27 53.4
29 Tu	12 22 57	7 38 55	3♓16 54	9♓45 39	28 9.0	25 26.9	20 37.8	11 56.2	22 30.7	7 55.4	11 39.4	19 17.5	27 53.1
30 W	12 26 54	8 38 14	16 19 22	22 57 57	28 0.2	26 50.8	21 52.1	12 38.8	22 42.7	8 3.0	11 42.4	19 16.0	27 52.8
31 Th	12 30 50	9 37 31	29 41 15	6♈28 58	27 51.6	28 9.2	23 6.4	13 21.4	22 54.6	8 10.5	11 45.5	19 14.4	27 52.5

APRIL 1938 — LONGITUDE

Day	Sid.Time	☉	0 hr ☽	Noon ☽	True ☊	☿	♀	♂	♃	♄	♅	♆	♇
1 F	12 34 47	10♈36 45	13♈20 46	20♈16 14	27♏44.2	29♈22.0	24♈20.7	14♉ 3.9	23♒ 6.5	8♈18.0	11♉48.5	19♍12.9	27♋52.2
2 Sa	12 38 43	11 35 58	27 14 52	4♉16 11	27R 38.7	0♉28.8	25 34.9	14 46.3	23 18.3	8 25.5	11 51.6	19R11.3	27R51.9
3 Su	12 42 40	12 35 9	11♉19 41	18 24 50	27 35.4	1 29.3	26 49.1	15 28.7	23 30.0	8 33.0	11 54.7	19 9.8	27 51.7
4 M	12 46 37	13 34 17	25 31 10	2♊38 15	27D 34.3	2 23.5	28 3.3	16 11.1	23 41.6	8 40.5	11 57.9	19 8.3	27 51.5
5 Tu	12 50 33	14 33 23	9♊45 40	16 53 4	27 34.7	3 11.2	29 17.5	16 53.4	23 53.1	8 48.0	12 1.0	19 6.9	27 51.4
6 W	12 54 30	15 32 27	24 0 8	1♋ 6 37	27 36.0	3 52.1	0♉31.6	17 35.7	24 4.5	8 55.5	12 4.2	19 5.4	27 51.2
7 Th	12 58 26	16 31 29	8♋12 18	15 16 57	27R 37.1	4 26.3	1 45.7	18 17.9	24 15.9	9 3.0	12 7.4	19 4.0	27 51.1
8 F	13 2 23	17 30 28	22 20 24	29 22 29	27 37.3	4 53.7	2 59.7	19 0.1	24 27.1	9 10.4	12 10.6	19 2.5	27 51.0
9 Sa	13 6 19	18 29 25	6♌22 59	13♌21 44	27 35.9	5 14.3	4 13.8	19 42.3	24 38.3	9 17.9	12 13.8	19 1.1	27 51.0
10 Su	13 10 16	19 28 19	20 18 33	27 13 10	27 32.8	5 28.1	5 27.8	20 24.4	24 49.3	9 25.3	12 17.1	18 59.7	27 50.9
11 M	13 14 12	20 27 12	4♍ 5 24	10♍54 59	27 28.2	5R 35.2	6 41.7	21 6.4	25 0.3	9 32.8	12 20.4	18 58.3	27D 50.9
12 Tu	13 18 9	21 26 2	17 41 40	24 25 14	27 22.6	5 35.8	7 55.7	21 48.5	25 11.1	9 40.2	12 23.6	18 57.0	27 50.9
13 W	13 22 5	22 24 49	1♎ 5 27	7♎42 8	27 16.7	5 30.1	9 9.6	22 30.4	25 21.9	9 47.6	12 26.9	18 55.6	27 51.0
14 Th	13 26 2	23 23 35	14 15 6	20 44 14	27 11.3	5 18.3	10 23.4	23 12.3	25 32.6	9 55.0	12 30.2	18 54.3	27 51.0
15 F	13 29 59	24 22 19	27 9 29	3♏30 49	27 7.0	5 0.9	11 37.3	23 54.2	25 43.1	10 2.3	12 33.6	18 53.0	27 51.1
16 Sa	13 33 55	25 21 0	9♏48 18	16 2 2	27 4.1	4 38.3	12 51.1	24 36.1	25 53.6	10 9.7	12 36.9	18 51.7	27 51.2
17 Su	13 37 52	26 19 40	22 12 12	28 19 3	27D 2.8	4 10.9	14 4.8	25 17.8	26 3.9	10 17.0	12 40.2	18 50.5	27 51.4
18 M	13 41 48	27 18 18	4♐22 52	10♐24 2	27 2.9	3 39.5	15 18.6	25 59.6	26 14.2	10 24.3	12 43.6	18 49.3	27 51.5
19 Tu	13 45 45	28 16 55	16 22 55	22 20 1	27 4.1	3 4.5	16 32.3	26 41.3	26 24.3	10 31.6	12 47.0	18 48.0	27 51.7
20 W	13 49 41	29 15 29	28 15 49	4♑10 52	27 5.8	2 26.7	17 46.0	27 23.0	26 34.4	10 38.9	12 50.4	18 46.9	27 51.9
21 Th	13 53 38	0♉14 2	10♑ 5 42	16 0 56	27 7.5	1 46.8	18 59.7	28 4.6	26 44.3	10 46.1	12 53.8	18 45.7	27 52.2
22 F	13 57 34	1 12 33	21 57 9	27 54 59	27R 8.8	1 5.7	20 13.3	28 46.2	26 54.1	10 53.4	12 57.2	18 44.5	27 52.4
23 Sa	14 1 31	2 11 3	3♒55 2	9♒57 54	27 9.1	0 24.1	21 26.9	29 27.7	27 3.8	11 0.6	13 0.6	18 43.4	27 52.7
24 Su	14 5 28	3 9 31	16 4 11	22 14 25	27 8.4	29♈42.7	22 40.5	0♊ 9.2	27 13.4	11 7.7	13 4.0	18 42.3	27 53.1
25 M	14 9 24	4 7 57	28 29 8	4♓48 45	27 6.7	29 2.3	23 54.0	0 50.7	27 22.8	11 14.9	13 7.4	18 41.2	27 53.4
26 Tu	14 13 21	5 6 22	11♓13 40	17 44 12	27 4.1	28 23.6	25 7.5	1 32.1	27 32.2	11 22.0	13 10.9	18 40.2	27 53.8
27 W	14 17 17	6 4 45	24 20 31	1♈ 2 43	27 1.2	27 47.2	26 21.0	2 13.5	27 41.4	11 29.1	13 14.3	18 39.2	27 54.2
28 Th	14 21 14	7 3 6	7♈50 47	14 44 33	26 58.2	27 13.7	27 34.4	2 54.9	27 50.5	11 36.1	13 17.8	18 38.2	27 54.6
29 F	14 25 10	8 1 26	21 43 44	28 47 56	26 55.6	26 43.5	28 47.9	3 36.2	27 59.4	11 43.1	13 21.2	18 37.2	27 55.0
30 Sa	14 29 7	8 59 44	5♉56 36	13♉ 9 9	26 53.9	26 17.1	0♊ 1.3	4 17.5	28 8.3	11 50.1	13 24.7	18 36.3	27 55.5

Astro Data Dy Hr Mn	Planet Ingress Dy Hr Mn	Last Aspect Dy Hr Mn	☽ Ingress Dy Hr Mn	Last Aspect Dy Hr Mn	☽ Ingress Dy Hr Mn	☽ Phases & Eclipses Dy Hr Mn	Astro Data
☽0N 2 20:16	☊ ♏ 3 23:16	28 17:19 ♂ ⚹	♓ 1 9:13	2 1:04 ♇ □	♉ 2 4:43	2 5:40 ● 10♓60	1 MARCH 1938
♄0N 5 14:08	♀ ♈ 12 9:20	3 12:56 ♇ △	♈ 3 16:16	4 3:57 ♇ ⚹	♊ 4 7:33	9 8:35 ☽ 18♊08	Julian Day # 13939
♀0N 14 17:40	♂ ♉ 12 7:48	5 18:11 ♇ □	♉ 5 21:29	6 0:07 ♃ △	♋ 6 10:07	16 5:15 ○ 24♍58	Delta T 24.0 sec
☽0S 15 18:44	☿ ♈ 15 0:02	7 22:16 ♇ ⚹	♊ 8 1:33	8 9:24 ♇ ☌	♌ 8 13:04	24 1:06 ☽ 2♑45	SVP 06♓07'07"
☿0N 15 20:28	☉ ♈ 21 6:43	10 2:01 ♂ ⚹	♋ 10 4:46	10 7:56 ♃ ☍	♍ 10 16:51	31 18:52 ● 10♈24	Obliquity 23°26'46"
♃⚻♆ 15 8:50		12 7:21 ♂ □	♌ 12 7:23	12 18:09 ♇ ⚹	♎ 12 22:02		⚷ Chiron 25♊25.0R
☽0N 30 4:38	☿ ♉ 1 13:24	13 15:54 ♃ ☍	♍ 14 10:05	15 1:18 ♇ □	♏ 15 5:21	7 15:10 ☽ 17♋09	☽ Mean ☊ 1♐05.4
	♀ ♉ 5 13:46	16 10:34 ♇ ⚹	♎ 16 14:08	17 11:06 ♇ △	♐ 17 15:19	14 18:21 ○ 24♎08	
♃∠♄ 3 17:44	☉ ♉ 20 18:15	18 17:04 ♇ □	♏ 18 20:53	20 2:12 ☉ △	♑ 20 3:31	22 20:14 ☽ 2♒02	1 APRIL 1938
☿ R 11 14:11	☿ ♈ 23 13:56	21 2:56 ♇ △	♐ 21 7:01	22 14:33 ♂ △	♒ 22 16:11	30 5:28 ● 9♉13	Julian Day # 13970
♇ D 11 1:54	♂ ♊ 23 18:39	23 1:52 ♃ ⚹	♑ 23 19:32	25 1:00 ☿ ⚹	♓ 25 2:53		Delta T 24.0 sec
☽0S 12 1:56	♀ ♊ 29 23:35	26 3:46 ♇ ☍	♒ 26 7:56	27 6:24 ♇ △	♈ 27 10:08		SVP 06♓07'05"
☽0N 26 13:39		28 7:21 ☿ ⚹	♓ 28 17:52	29 10:45 ♃ ⚹	♉ 29 14:02		Obliquity 23°26'46"
♃⚻♇ 28 11:32		30 20:47 ♇ △	♈ 31 0:33				⚷ Chiron 26♊01.9
							☽ Mean ☊ 29♏26.9

LONGITUDE — MAY 1938

Day	Sid.Time	☉	0 hr ☽	Noon ☽	True ☊	☿	♀	♂	♃	♄	♅	♆	♇
1 Su	14 33 3	9♉58 0	20♉24 50	27♉42 55	26♏53.0	25♈54.9	1♊14.6	4♊58.7	28♒17.0	11♈57.1	13♉28.1	18♍35.3	27♋56.0
2 M	14 37 0	10 56 15	5♊ 2 34	12♊22 59	26D53.1	25R36.9	2 27.9	5 39.9	28 25.6	12 4.0	13 31.6	18R34.5	27 56.5
3 Tu	14 40 57	11 54 27	19 43 23	27 3 1	26 53.8	25 23.6	3 41.2	6 21.0	28 34.0	12 10.9	13 35.1	18 33.6	27 57.0
4 W	14 44 53	12 52 38	4♋21 11	11♋37 17	26 54.8	25 14.9	4 54.5	7 2.2	28 42.3	12 17.7	13 38.6	18 32.8	27 57.6
5 Th	14 48 50	13 50 47	18 50 47	26 1 15	26 55.8	25D11.0	6 7.7	7 43.2	28 50.5	12 24.6	13 42.0	18 32.0	27 58.2
6 F	14 52 46	14 48 54	3♌ 8 21	10♌11 48	26R56.5	25 11.8	7 20.9	8 24.3	28 58.6	12 31.3	13 45.5	18 31.2	27 58.8
7 Sa	14 56 43	15 46 59	17 11 25	24 7 6	26 56.7	25 17.3	8 34.1	9 5.2	29 6.5	12 38.1	13 49.0	18 30.4	27 59.5
8 Su	15 0 39	16 45 1	0♍58 46	7♍46 26	26 56.4	25 27.5	9 47.2	9 46.2	29 14.2	12 44.7	13 52.4	18 29.7	28 0.1
9 M	15 4 36	17 43 2	14 30 8	21 9 54	26 55.7	25 42.4	11 0.3	10 27.1	29 21.9	12 51.4	13 55.9	18 29.0	28 0.8
10 Tu	15 8 32	18 41 1	27 45 51	4♎18 3	26 54.8	26 1.7	12 13.3	11 8.0	29 29.3	12 58.0	13 59.3	18 28.4	28 1.5
11 W	15 12 29	19 38 58	10♎46 37	17 11 40	26 53.8	26 25.4	13 26.3	11 48.8	29 36.7	13 4.5	14 2.8	18 27.7	28 2.2
12 Th	15 16 26	20 36 54	23 33 20	29 51 44	26 53.0	26 53.4	14 39.3	12 29.6	29 43.9	13 11.0	14 6.2	18 27.1	28 3.0
13 F	15 20 22	21 34 47	6♏ 7 1	12♏19 20	26 52.4	27 25.5	15 52.2	13 10.3	29 50.9	13 17.5	14 9.7	18 26.6	28 3.8
14 Sa	15 24 19	22 32 40	18 28 50	24 35 43	26D52.1	28 1.6	17 5.1	13 51.0	29 57.8	13 23.9	14 13.1	18 26.0	28 4.6
15 Su	15 28 15	23 30 30	0♐40 8	6♐42 21	26 52.1	28 41.6	18 17.9	14 31.7	0♓ 4.5	13 30.3	14 16.6	18 25.5	28 5.4
16 M	15 32 12	24 28 20	12 42 34	18 41 4	26 52.2	29 25.3	19 30.7	15 12.3	0 11.1	13 36.6	14 20.0	18 25.1	28 6.2
17 Tu	15 36 8	25 26 8	24 38 9	0♑34 8	26 52.3	0♉12.6	20 43.5	15 52.9	0 17.6	13 42.9	14 23.4	18 24.6	28 7.1
18 W	15 40 5	26 23 54	6♑29 23	12 24 16	26R52.4	1 3.4	21 56.3	16 33.5	0 23.9	13 49.1	14 26.8	18 24.2	28 8.0
19 Th	15 44 1	27 21 40	18 19 14	24 14 43	26 52.4	1 57.6	23 9.0	17 14.0	0 30.0	13 55.3	14 30.2	18 23.8	28 8.9
20 F	15 47 58	28 19 24	0♒11 11	6♒ 9 10	26 52.3	2 55.0	24 21.6	17 54.5	0 36.0	14 1.4	14 33.6	18 23.5	28 9.8
21 Sa	15 51 55	29 17 7	12 9 10	18 11 43	26 52.2	3 55.6	25 34.2	18 35.0	0 41.8	14 7.5	14 37.0	18 23.1	28 10.8
22 Su	15 55 51	0♊14 49	24 17 23	0♓26 41	26D52.1	4 59.3	26 46.8	19 15.4	0 47.5	14 13.5	14 40.4	18 22.8	28 11.7
23 M	15 59 48	1 12 30	6♓40 12	12 58 25	26 52.1	6 5.9	27 59.4	19 55.8	0 52.9	14 19.4	14 43.8	18 22.6	28 12.7
24 Tu	16 3 44	2 10 10	19 21 49	25 50 51	26 52.3	7 15.5	29 11.9	20 36.1	0 58.3	14 25.3	14 47.1	18 22.4	28 13.7
25 W	16 7 41	3 7 48	2♈25 53	9♈ 7 12	26 52.7	8 27.8	0♋24.4	21 16.4	1 3.4	14 31.1	14 50.5	18 22.2	28 14.8
26 Th	16 11 37	4 5 26	15 54 59	22 49 18	26 53.3	9 43.0	1 36.8	21 56.7	1 8.4	14 36.9	14 53.8	18 22.0	28 15.8
27 F	16 15 34	5 3 3	29 50 4	6♉57 4	26 54.0	11 0.9	2 49.2	22 37.0	1 13.2	14 42.6	14 57.1	18 21.9	28 16.9
28 Sa	16 19 30	6 0 39	14♉ 9 55	21 28 4	26R54.5	12 21.5	4 1.6	23 17.2	1 17.9	14 48.3	15 0.4	18 21.8	28 18.0
29 Su	16 23 27	6 58 14	28 50 50	6♊17 22	26 54.7	13 44.7	5 13.9	23 57.4	1 22.4	14 53.9	15 3.7	18 21.7	28 19.1
30 M	16 27 24	7 55 48	13♊46 42	21 17 47	26 54.4	15 10.5	6 26.2	24 37.5	1 26.7	14 59.4	15 7.0	18D21.7	28 20.2
31 Tu	16 31 20	8 53 21	28 49 30	6♋20 45	26 53.5	16 39.0	7 38.5	25 17.7	1 30.8	15 4.9	15 10.2	18 21.7	28 21.4

LONGITUDE — JUNE 1938

Day	Sid.Time	☉	0 hr ☽	Noon ☽	True ☊	☿	♀	♂	♃	♄	♅	♆	♇
1 W	16 35 17	9♊50 53	13♋50 27	21♋17 35	26♏52.1	18♉10.0	8♋50.7	25♊57.7	1♓34.7	15♈10.3	15♉13.4	18♍21.7	28♋22.5
2 Th	16 39 13	10 48 23	28 41 14	6♌ 0 38	26R50.5	19 43.5	10 2.8	26 37.8	1 38.5	15 15.6	15 16.7	18 21.8	28 23.7
3 F	16 43 10	11 45 53	13♌15 10	20 24 21	26 49.0	21 19.6	11 14.9	27 17.8	1 42.1	15 20.9	15 19.9	18 21.9	28 24.9
4 Sa	16 47 6	12 43 20	27 27 52	4♍25 34	26 47.8	22 58.2	12 27.0	27 57.8	1 45.5	15 26.1	15 23.0	18 22.0	28 26.2
5 Su	16 51 3	13 40 47	11♍17 24	18 3 27	26D47.3	24 39.3	13 39.0	28 37.8	1 48.7	15 31.2	15 26.2	18 22.2	28 27.4
6 M	16 54 59	14 38 12	24 43 53	1♎18 58	26 47.6	26 22.9	14 51.0	29 17.7	1 51.8	15 36.2	15 29.3	18 22.4	28 28.6
7 Tu	16 58 56	15 35 36	7♎48 59	14 14 18	26 48.5	28 9.0	16 2.9	29 57.6	1 54.6	15 41.2	15 32.5	18 22.6	28 29.9
8 W	17 2 53	16 32 59	20 35 17	26 52 18	26 49.9	29 57.6	17 14.8	0♋37.4	1 57.3	15 46.1	15 35.6	18 22.8	28 31.2
9 Th	17 6 49	17 30 21	3♏ 5 44	9♏15 58	26 51.3	1♊48.6	18 26.6	1 17.2	1 59.8	15 51.0	15 38.6	18 23.1	28 32.5
10 F	17 10 46	18 27 42	15 23 21	21 28 13	26R52.4	3 42.0	19 38.4	1 57.0	2 2.1	15 55.7	15 41.7	18 23.5	28 33.8
11 Sa	17 14 42	19 25 3	27 30 54	3♐31 42	26 52.9	5 37.7	20 50.1	2 36.8	2 4.2	16 0.4	15 44.7	18 23.8	28 35.1
12 Su	17 18 39	20 22 22	9♐30 55	15 28 47	26 52.3	7 35.7	22 1.8	3 16.5	2 6.2	16 5.0	15 47.7	18 24.2	28 36.5
13 M	17 22 35	21 19 40	21 25 36	27 21 36	26 50.5	9 35.9	23 13.4	3 56.2	2 7.9	16 9.6	15 50.7	18 24.6	28 37.9
14 Tu	17 26 32	22 16 58	3♑17 2	9♑12 10	26 47.5	11 38.1	24 24.9	4 35.8	2 9.5	16 14.1	15 53.6	18 25.1	28 39.2
15 W	17 30 28	23 14 16	15 7 13	21 2 30	26 43.5	13 42.3	25 36.4	5 15.5	2 10.9	16 18.4	15 56.6	18 25.6	28 40.6
16 Th	17 34 25	24 11 32	26 58 16	2♒54 50	26 38.9	15 48.2	26 47.9	5 55.1	2 12.1	16 22.7	15 59.5	18 26.1	28 42.0
17 F	17 38 22	25 8 49	8♒52 32	14 51 43	26 34.3	17 55.7	27 59.3	6 34.6	2 13.1	16 27.0	16 2.4	18 26.6	28 43.4
18 Sa	17 42 18	26 6 5	20 52 46	26 56 6	26 30.0	20 4.5	29 10.6	7 14.2	2 13.9	16 31.1	16 5.2	18 27.2	28 44.9
19 Su	17 46 15	27 3 20	3♓ 2 8	9♓11 19	26 26.6	22 14.3	0♌21.9	7 53.7	2 14.5	16 35.2	16 8.0	18 27.8	28 46.3
20 M	17 50 11	28 0 35	15 24 10	21 41 7	26 24.5	24 25.1	1 33.2	8 33.2	2 14.9	16 39.2	16 10.8	18 28.5	28 47.8
21 Tu	17 54 8	28 57 50	28 2 41	4♈29 19	26D23.7	26 36.3	2 44.3	9 12.6	2R15.1	16 43.1	16 13.6	18 29.2	28 49.2
22 W	17 58 4	29 55 5	11♈ 1 29	17 39 36	26 24.2	28 47.9	3 55.4	9 52.1	2 15.1	16 46.9	16 16.3	18 29.9	28 50.7
23 Th	18 2 1	0♋52 20	24 23 58	1♉14 54	26 25.4	0♋59.5	5 6.5	10 31.5	2 15.0	16 50.6	16 19.0	18 30.6	28 52.2
24 F	18 5 57	1 49 35	8♉12 30	15 16 48	26 26.8	3 10.8	6 17.5	11 10.9	2 14.6	16 54.3	16 21.7	18 31.4	28 53.7
25 Sa	18 9 54	2 46 49	22 27 41	29 44 48	26R27.7	5 21.6	7 28.5	11 50.2	2 14.1	16 57.8	16 24.3	18 32.2	28 55.2
26 Su	18 13 51	3 44 4	7♊ 7 40	14♊35 35	26 27.4	7 31.6	8 39.4	12 29.6	2 13.3	17 1.3	16 27.0	18 33.0	28 56.7
27 M	18 17 47	4 41 19	22 7 38	29 42 47	26 25.4	9 40.6	9 50.2	13 8.9	2 12.4	17 4.7	16 29.5	18 33.8	28 58.3
28 Tu	18 21 44	5 38 33	7♋19 50	14♋57 29	26 21.6	11 48.4	11 1.0	13 48.2	2 11.2	17 8.0	16 32.1	18 34.7	28 59.8
29 W	18 25 40	6 35 47	22 34 25	0♌ 9 18	26 16.5	13 54.8	12 11.7	14 27.5	2 9.9	17 11.2	16 34.6	18 35.7	29 1.4
30 Th	18 29 37	7 33 1	7♌40 55	15 8 9	26 10.5	15 59.8	13 22.3	15 6.7	2 8.4	17 14.3	16 37.1	18 36.6	29 2.9

Astro Data	Planet Ingress	Last Aspect	☽ Ingress	Last Aspect	☽ Ingress	☽ Phases & Eclipses	Astro Data
Dy Hr Mn	Dy Hr Mn	Dy Hr Mn	Dy Hr Mn	Dy Hr Mn	Dy Hr Mn	Dy Hr Mn	1 MAY 1938
☿ D 5 7:54	♃ ♓ 14 7:46	1 13:04 ♃ □	♊ 1 15:45	1 23:31 ♇ ☌	♌ 2 2:09	6 21:24 ☽ 15♌41	Julian Day # 14000
☽0S 9 7:19	☿ ♉ 16 17:46	3 14:38 ♃ △	♋ 3 16:50	4 0:54 ♂ ⚹	♍ 4 4:21	14 8:39 ○ 22♏54	Delta T 24.0 sec
☽0N 23 22:29	☉ ♊ 21 17:50	5 15:17 ♇ ☌	♌ 5 18:42	6 8:45 ♂ □	♎ 6 9:35	14 8:44 ☍T 1.097	SVP 06♓07'02"
♆ D 30 10:13	♀ ♋ 24 15:56	7 20:55 ♃ ☍	♍ 7 22:17	8 15:12 ♇ □	♏ 8 18:01	22 12:36 ☽ 0♓45	Obliquity 23°26'46"
		10 0:29 ♇ ⚹	♎ 10 4:06	11 2:08 ♇ △	♐ 11 4:57	29 13:59 ● 7♊32	⚷ Chiron 27♊44.8
♄⊻♅ 2 12:18	♂ ♋ 7 1:28	12 11:52 ♃ △	♏ 12 12:16	12 23:47 ☉ ☍	♑ 13 17:21	29 13:49:55 ☌T 4'04"	☽ Mean ☊ 27♏51.5
☽0S 5 12:59	☿ ♊ 8 0:32	14 18:53 ♇ △	♐ 14 22:40	16 3:30 ♇ ☍	♒ 16 6:07		
☽0N 20 6:28	♀ ♌ 18 16:37	16 15:13 ♀ ☍	♑ 17 10:51	18 11:14 ☉ △	♓ 18 18:02	5 4:32 ☽ 13♍52	1 JUNE 1938
♃ R 21 15:30	☉ ♋ 22 2:04	19 19:55 ♇ ☍	♒ 19 23:37	21 1:52 ☉ □	♈ 21 3:40	12 23:47 ○ 21♐19	Julian Day # 14031
♃∠♄ 28 17:12	☿ ♋ 22 13:09	22 5:24 ♀ △	♓ 22 11:08	23 7:52 ♇ □	♉ 23 9:50	21 1:52 ☽ 29♓02	Delta T 24.0 sec
		24 16:23 ♇ △	♈ 24 19:35	25 10:40 ♇ ⚹	♊ 25 12:25	27 21:10 ● 5♋32	SVP 06♓06'57"
		26 21:21 ♇ □	♉ 27 0:17	26 18:20 ♆ □	♋ 27 12:27		Obliquity 23°26'45"
		28 23:09 ♇ ⚹	♊ 29 1:52	29 10:13 ♇ ☌	♌ 29 11:45		⚷ Chiron 0♋18.9
		30 18:07 ♂ ☌	♋ 31 1:52				☽ Mean ☊ 26♏13.0

JULY 1938 — LONGITUDE

Day	Sid.Time	☉	0 hr ☽	Noon ☽	True ☊	☿	♀	♂	♃	♄	♅	♆	♇
1 F	18 33 33	8♋30 15	22♌30 3	29♌45 52	26♏ 4.7	18♋ 3.1	14♌32.9	15♋45.9	2♓ 6.7	17♈17.3	16♉39.5	18♍37.6	29♋ 4.5
2 Sa	18 37 30	9 27 28	6♍55 5	13♍57 21	25R59.8	20 4.7	15 43.4	16 25.1	2R 4.8	17 20.3	16 41.9	18 38.6	29 6.1
3 Su	18 41 27	10 24 40	20 52 31	27 40 39	25 56.3	22 4.5	16 53.9	17 4.2	2 2.7	17 23.1	16 44.3	18 39.6	29 7.7
4 M	18 45 23	11 21 53	4♎21 55	10♎56 39	25D54.6	24 2.4	18 4.2	17 43.4	2 0.4	17 25.8	16 46.6	18 40.7	29 9.3
5 Tu	18 49 20	12 19 5	17 25 14	23 48 10	25 54.5	25 58.4	19 14.5	18 22.5	1 57.9	17 28.5	16 48.9	18 41.8	29 10.9
6 W	18 53 16	13 16 17	0♏ 5 57	6♏19 10	25 55.5	27 52.4	20 24.7	19 1.6	1 55.3	17 31.0	16 51.2	18 42.9	29 12.5
7 Th	18 57 13	14 13 28	12 28 22	18 34 6	25 56.7	29 44.5	21 34.8	19 40.6	1 52.4	17 33.5	16 53.4	18 44.1	29 14.1
8 F	19 1 9	15 10 40	24 36 54	0♐37 18	25R57.4	1♌34.6	22 44.9	20 19.7	1 49.4	17 35.9	16 55.6	18 45.3	29 15.7
9 Sa	19 5 6	16 7 51	6♐35 47	12 32 47	25 56.8	3 22.7	23 54.8	20 58.7	1 46.2	17 38.1	16 57.8	18 46.5	29 17.3
10 Su	19 9 2	17 5 3	18 28 43	24 23 57	25 54.2	5 8.9	25 4.7	21 37.6	1 42.8	17 40.3	16 59.9	18 47.7	29 19.0
11 M	19 12 59	18 2 15	0♑18 50	6♑13 39	25 49.4	6 53.0	26 14.5	22 16.6	1 39.3	17 42.4	17 2.0	18 49.0	29 20.6
12 Tu	19 16 56	18 59 26	12 8 41	18 4 10	25 42.4	8 35.2	27 24.2	22 55.5	1 35.5	17 44.4	17 4.0	18 50.2	29 22.2
13 W	19 20 52	19 56 38	24 0 19	29 57 20	25 33.5	10 15.4	28 33.8	23 34.5	1 31.6	17 46.3	17 6.0	18 51.6	29 23.9
14 Th	19 24 49	20 53 50	5♒55 25	11♒54 45	25 23.4	11 53.5	29 43.4	24 13.4	1 27.5	17 48.0	17 7.9	18 52.9	29 25.5
15 F	19 28 45	21 51 3	17 55 32	23 57 58	25 13.0	13 29.7	0♍52.8	24 52.2	1 23.3	17 49.7	17 9.9	18 54.3	29 27.2
16 Sa	19 32 42	22 48 16	0♓ 2 18	6♓ 8 47	25 3.2	15 3.9	2 2.2	25 31.1	1 18.9	17 51.3	17 11.7	18 55.7	29 28.8
17 Su	19 36 38	23 45 29	12 17 39	18 29 15	24 55.0	16 36.1	3 11.4	26 9.9	1 14.3	17 52.8	17 13.6	18 57.1	29 30.5
18 M	19 40 35	24 42 43	24 43 54	1♈ 1 58	24 48.8	18 6.3	4 20.6	26 48.7	1 9.5	17 54.2	17 15.3	18 58.5	29 32.2
19 Tu	19 44 31	25 39 58	7♈23 50	13 49 54	24 45.0	19 34.5	5 29.7	27 27.5	1 4.6	17 55.5	17 17.1	18 60.0	29 33.8
20 W	19 48 28	26 37 13	20 20 36	26 56 18	24D43.4	21 0.6	6 38.6	28 6.3	0 59.5	17 56.6	17 18.8	19 1.5	29 35.5
21 Th	19 52 25	27 34 29	3♉37 25	10♉24 17	24 43.3	22 24.6	7 47.5	28 45.1	0 54.3	17 57.7	17 20.5	19 3.0	29 37.1
22 F	19 56 21	28 31 46	17 17 9	24 16 13	24R43.9	23 46.6	8 56.3	29 23.8	0 48.9	17 58.7	17 22.1	19 4.5	29 38.8
23 Sa	20 0 18	29 29 4	1♊21 32	8♊33 1	24 43.9	25 6.3	10 5.0	0♌ 2.5	0 43.4	17 59.6	17 23.6	19 6.1	29 40.5
24 Su	20 4 14	0♌26 23	15 50 25	23 13 15	24 42.3	26 24.0	11 13.5	0 41.2	0 37.7	18 0.4	17 25.2	19 7.7	29 42.2
25 M	20 8 11	1 23 43	0♋40 54	8♋12 30	24 38.4	27 39.3	12 22.0	1 19.9	0 31.9	18 1.0	17 26.7	19 9.3	29 43.8
26 Tu	20 12 7	2 21 4	15 46 59	23 23 12	24 31.9	28 52.4	13 30.4	1 58.6	0 26.0	18 1.6	17 28.1	19 10.9	29 45.5
27 W	20 16 4	3 18 25	0♌59 48	8♌35 26	24 23.3	0♍ 3.2	14 38.7	2 37.3	0 19.9	18 2.1	17 29.5	19 12.6	29 47.2
28 Th	20 20 0	4 15 47	16 8 46	23 38 31	24 13.4	1 11.4	15 46.8	3 15.9	0 13.6	18 2.4	17 30.8	19 14.3	29 48.8
29 F	20 23 57	5 13 9	1♍ 3 32	8♍22 51	24 3.5	2 17.2	16 54.8	3 54.5	0 7.3	18 2.7	17 32.1	19 16.0	29 50.5
30 Sa	20 27 54	6 10 33	15 35 41	22 41 31	23 54.6	3 20.4	18 2.8	4 33.1	0 0.8	18R 2.8	17 33.4	19 17.7	29 52.2
31 Su	20 31 50	7 7 56	29 40 2	6♎31 5	23 47.7	4 20.8	19 10.5	5 11.7	29♒54.2	18 2.9	17 34.6	19 19.4	29 53.8

AUGUST 1938 — LONGITUDE

Day	Sid.Time	☉	0 hr ☽	Noon ☽	True ☊	☿	♀	♂	♃	♄	♅	♆	♇
1 M	20 35 47	8♌ 5 21	13♎14 47	19♎51 22	23♏43.2	5♍18.4	20♍18.2	5♌50.3	29♒47.5	18♈ 2.8	17♉35.7	19♍21.2	29♋55.5
2 Tu	20 39 43	9 2 46	26 21 12	2♏44 46	23R41.0	6 13.0	21 25.7	6 28.8	29R40.7	18R 2.7	17 36.8	19 22.9	29 57.1
3 W	20 43 40	10 0 12	9♏ 2 38	15 15 24	23D40.4	7 4.6	22 33.1	7 7.4	29 33.8	18 2.4	17 37.9	19 24.7	29 58.8
4 Th	20 47 36	10 57 38	21 23 43	27 28 14	23R40.5	7 52.9	23 40.4	7 45.9	29 26.8	18 2.1	17 38.9	19 26.6	0♌ 0.4
5 F	20 51 33	11 55 5	3♐29 37	9♐28 29	23 40.2	8 37.8	24 47.5	8 24.4	29 19.7	18 1.6	17 39.9	19 28.4	0 2.1
6 Sa	20 55 29	12 52 33	15 25 26	21 21 4	23 38.5	9 19.1	25 54.5	9 2.9	29 12.5	18 1.0	17 40.8	19 30.2	0 3.7
7 Su	20 59 26	13 50 1	27 15 54	3♑10 26	23 34.5	9 56.7	27 1.3	9 41.3	29 5.3	18 0.4	17 41.7	19 32.1	0 5.3
8 M	21 3 23	14 47 31	9♑ 5 5	15 0 16	23 27.8	10 30.4	28 8.0	10 19.8	28 57.9	17 59.6	17 42.5	19 34.0	0 7.0
9 Tu	21 7 19	15 45 1	20 56 18	26 53 30	23 18.3	10 59.9	29 14.5	10 58.2	28 50.5	17 58.7	17 43.3	19 35.9	0 8.6
10 W	21 11 16	16 42 32	2♒52 6	8♒52 18	23 6.6	11 25.1	0♎20.9	11 36.6	28 43.0	17 57.7	17 44.0	19 37.8	0 10.2
11 Th	21 15 12	17 40 5	14 54 16	20 58 8	22 53.4	11 45.7	1 27.1	12 15.0	28 35.5	17 56.7	17 44.7	19 39.8	0 11.8
12 F	21 19 9	18 37 38	27 4 1	3♓12 2	22 39.8	12 1.6	2 33.1	12 53.4	28 27.8	17 55.5	17 45.3	19 41.7	0 13.4
13 Sa	21 23 5	19 35 13	9♓22 15	15 34 46	22 26.9	12 12.5	3 39.0	13 31.8	28 20.2	17 54.2	17 45.9	19 43.7	0 15.0
14 Su	21 27 2	20 32 49	21 49 42	28 7 11	22 15.8	12R18.2	4 44.6	14 10.1	28 12.5	17 52.9	17 46.4	19 45.7	0 16.6
15 M	21 30 58	21 30 26	4♈27 22	10♈50 25	22 7.2	12 18.6	5 50.2	14 48.5	28 4.7	17 51.4	17 46.9	19 47.7	0 18.1
16 Tu	21 34 55	22 28 4	17 16 33	23 46 1	22 1.5	12 13.6	6 55.5	15 26.8	27 56.9	17 49.8	17 47.3	19 49.7	0 19.7
17 W	21 38 51	23 25 45	0♉19 5	6♉56 1	21 58.5	12 2.9	8 0.6	16 5.2	27 49.1	17 48.1	17 47.7	19 51.7	0 21.3
18 Th	21 42 48	24 23 27	13 37 6	20 22 37	21 57.5	11 46.6	9 5.6	16 43.5	27 41.3	17 46.4	17 48.0	19 53.7	0 22.8
19 F	21 46 45	25 21 10	27 12 49	4♊ 7 53	21 57.4	11 24.6	10 10.3	17 21.8	27 33.4	17 44.5	17 48.3	19 55.8	0 24.4
20 Sa	21 50 41	26 18 55	11♊ 7 58	18 13 4	21 57.0	10 57.1	11 14.9	18 0.1	27 25.5	17 42.6	17 48.5	19 57.9	0 25.9
21 Su	21 54 38	27 16 42	25 23 5	2♋37 48	21 55.1	10 24.2	12 19.3	18 38.4	27 17.7	17 40.5	17 48.7	19 59.9	0 27.4
22 M	21 58 34	28 14 31	9♋56 47	17 19 27	21 50.8	9 46.2	13 23.4	19 16.7	27 9.8	17 38.4	17 48.9	20 2.0	0 28.9
23 Tu	22 2 31	29 12 21	24 45 4	2♌12 43	21 43.8	9 3.5	14 27.4	19 54.9	27 1.9	17 36.1	17 48.9	20 4.1	0 30.5
24 W	22 6 27	0♍10 13	9♌41 20	17 9 49	21 34.4	8 16.7	15 31.1	20 33.2	26 54.0	17 33.8	17R49.0	20 6.3	0 31.9
25 Th	22 10 24	1 8 6	24 36 59	2♍ 1 39	21 23.6	7 26.5	16 34.6	21 11.4	26 46.2	17 31.4	17 49.0	20 8.4	0 33.4
26 F	22 14 21	2 6 1	9♍22 43	16 39 12	21 12.5	6 33.7	17 37.9	21 49.7	26 38.3	17 28.9	17 48.9	20 10.5	0 34.9
27 Sa	22 18 17	3 3 57	23 50 15	0♎55 13	21 2.4	5 39.2	18 40.9	22 27.9	26 30.5	17 26.3	17 48.8	20 12.6	0 36.3
28 Su	22 22 14	4 1 55	7♎53 36	14 45 9	20 54.4	4 44.0	19 43.7	23 6.1	26 22.8	17 23.6	17 48.6	20 14.8	0 37.8
29 M	22 26 10	4 59 54	21 29 45	28 7 31	20 48.9	3 49.4	20 46.3	23 44.3	26 15.1	17 20.8	17 48.4	20 17.0	0 39.2
30 Tu	22 30 7	5 57 55	4♏38 39	11♏ 3 33	20 46.0	2 56.4	21 48.5	24 22.5	26 7.4	17 17.9	17 48.1	20 19.1	0 40.6
31 W	22 34 3	6 55 57	17 22 39	23 36 31	20D45.0	2 6.2	22 50.5	25 0.7	25 59.8	17 15.0	17 47.8	20 21.3	0 42.0

Astro Data	Planet Ingress	Last Aspect	☽ Ingress	Last Aspect	☽ Ingress	☽ Phases & Eclipses	Astro Data
Dy Hr Mn	Dy Hr Mn	Dy Hr Mn	Dy Hr Mn	Dy Hr Mn	Dy Hr Mn	Dy Hr Mn	1 JULY 1938
☽0S 2 20:38	☿ ♌ 7 3:21	30 15:28 ♄ △	♍ 1 12:24	2 6:45 ♇ □	♏ 2 6:49	4 13:47 ☽ 11♎55	Julian Day # 14061
☽0N 17 13:26	♀ ♍ 14 5:44	3 14:37 ♇ ✱	♎ 3 16:09	4 15:46 ♃ □	♐ 4 17:02	12 15:05 ○ 19♑35	Delta T 24.0 sec
☽0S 30 6:27	♂ ♌ 22 22:26	5 22:17 ♇ □	♏ 5 23:49	7 3:40 ♃ ✱	♑ 7 5:33	20 12:19 ☽ 27♈07	SVP 06♓06'52"
♄ R 30 23:14	☉ ♌ 23 12:57	8 9:18 ♇ △	♐ 8 10:45	8 21:17 ♆ △	♒ 9 18:15	27 3:53 ● 3♌28	Obliquity 23°26'44"
♃⊼♇ 31 1:14	☿ ♍ 26 22:55	10 14:50 ♀ △	♑ 10 23:22	12 2:43 ♃ ☌	♓ 12 5:45		⚷ Chiron 3♋09.7
	♃ ♒ 30 3:02	13 10:54 ♇ ☍	♒ 13 12:05	13 20:02 ♆ ☍	♈ 14 15:34	3 2:00 ☽ 10♏05	☽ Mean ☊ 24♏37.7
♀0S 9 20:08		14 23:48 ♄ ✱	♓ 15 23:55	16 19:29 ♃ ✱	♉ 16 23:25	11 5:57 ○ 17♒54	
☽0N 13 19:51	♇ ♌ 3 17:59	18 9:11 ♇ △	♈ 18 10:02	19 0:36 ♃ □	♊ 19 4:51	18 20:30 ☽ 25♉13	1 AUGUST 1938
☿ R 14 13:51	♀ ♎ 9 16:26	20 16:49 ♇ □	♉ 20 17:31	21 3:22 ☉ ✱	♋ 21 7:39	25 11:17 ● 1♍35	Julian Day # 14092
♄⊻♅ 17 5:07	☉ ♍ 23 19:46	22 21:41 ♂ ✱	♊ 22 21:43	22 16:25 ♆ ✱	♌ 23 8:27		Delta T 24.0 sec
♅ R 24 2:09		24 18:42 ☿ ✱	♋ 24 22:54	25 3:27 ♃ ☍	♍ 25 8:43		SVP 06♓06'48"
☽0S 26 17:11		26 22:05 ♇ ☌	♌ 26 22:26	26 17:54 ♆ ☌	♎ 27 10:26		Obliquity 23°26'45"
		28 3:01 ♄ △	♍ 28 22:17	29 8:30 ♃ △	♏ 29 15:26		⚷ Chiron 6♋02.2
		31 0:24 ♇ ✱	♎ 31 0:35				☽ Mean ☊ 22♏59.3

LONGITUDE — SEPTEMBER 1938

Day	Sid.Time	☉	0 hr ☽	Noon ☽	True ☊	☿	♀	♂	♃	♄	♅	♆	♇
1 Th	22 38 0	7♍54 0	29♏45 45	5♐50 59	20♏45.1	1♍20.1	23♎52.3	25♌38.9	25♒52.2	17♈12.0	17♉47.4	20♍23.5	0♌43.4
2 F	22 41 56	8 52 5	11♐52 53	17 52 8	20R 45.2	0R 39.0	24 53.7	26 17.0	25R 44.7	17R 8.9	17R 47.0	20 25.7	0 44.8
3 Sa	22 45 53	9 50 11	23 49 23	29 45 17	20 44.3	0 3.9	25 54.8	26 55.2	25 37.3	17 5.7	17 46.5	20 27.9	0 46.2
4 Su	22 49 49	10 48 19	5♑40 27	11♑35 29	20 41.4	29♌35.7	26 55.6	27 33.3	25 29.9	17 2.4	17 46.0	20 30.1	0 47.5
5 M	22 53 46	11 46 28	17 30 56	23 27 16	20 36.1	29 15.1	27 56.1	28 11.4	25 22.6	16 59.1	17 45.4	20 32.3	0 48.8
6 Tu	22 57 43	12 44 38	29 24 58	5♒24 24	20 28.3	29D 2.6	28 56.2	28 49.5	25 15.4	16 55.7	17 44.8	20 34.5	0 50.1
7 W	23 1 39	13 42 50	11♒25 55	17 29 47	20 18.4	28 58.7	29 56.0	29 27.7	25 8.3	16 52.2	17 44.2	20 36.7	0 51.4
8 Th	23 5 36	14 41 4	23 36 14	29 45 24	20 7.1	29 3.7	0♏55.5	0♍ 5.8	25 1.3	16 48.6	17 43.4	20 38.9	0 52.7
9 F	23 9 32	15 39 19	5♓57 26	12♓12 22	19 55.3	29 17.6	1 54.5	0 43.8	24 54.4	16 45.0	17 42.7	20 41.1	0 54.0
10 Sa	23 13 29	16 37 36	18 30 14	24 51 2	19 44.1	29 40.4	2 53.2	1 21.9	24 47.6	16 41.3	17 41.9	20 43.3	0 55.2
11 Su	23 17 25	17 35 55	1♈14 44	7♈41 19	19 34.5	0♍12.0	3 51.5	2 0.0	24 40.9	16 37.5	17 41.0	20 45.5	0 56.5
12 M	23 21 22	18 34 16	14 10 43	20 42 56	19 27.2	0 52.2	4 49.4	2 38.1	24 34.4	16 33.7	17 40.1	20 47.8	0 57.7
13 Tu	23 25 18	19 32 38	27 17 55	3♉55 42	19 22.6	1 40.6	5 46.8	3 16.1	24 27.9	16 29.8	17 39.2	20 50.0	0 58.9
14 W	23 29 15	20 31 3	10♉36 17	17 19 43	19D 20.4	2 36.8	6 43.9	3 54.2	24 21.6	16 25.9	17 38.2	20 52.2	1 0.0
15 Th	23 33 12	21 29 30	24 6 5	0♊55 27	19 20.2	3 40.3	7 40.5	4 32.2	24 15.4	16 21.8	17 37.2	20 54.4	1 1.2
16 F	23 37 8	22 27 59	7♊47 53	14 43 26	19 20.9	4 50.7	8 36.6	5 10.3	24 9.3	16 17.8	17 36.1	20 56.7	1 2.3
17 Sa	23 41 5	23 26 30	21 42 8	28 43 59	19R 21.5	6 7.2	9 32.3	5 48.3	24 3.4	16 13.7	17 35.0	20 58.9	1 3.5
18 Su	23 45 1	24 25 4	5♋48 52	12♋56 39	19 20.9	7 29.4	10 27.4	6 26.4	23 57.6	16 9.5	17 33.8	21 1.1	1 4.6
19 M	23 48 58	25 23 39	20 7 3	27 19 42	19 18.5	8 56.5	11 22.1	7 4.4	23 51.9	16 5.3	17 32.6	21 3.4	1 5.7
20 Tu	23 52 54	26 22 17	4♌34 8	11♌49 46	19 13.9	10 28.1	12 16.2	7 42.4	23 46.4	16 1.0	17 31.3	21 5.6	1 6.7
21 W	23 56 51	27 20 57	19 5 54	26 21 49	19 7.3	12 3.4	13 9.8	8 20.5	23 41.0	15 56.7	17 30.0	21 7.8	1 7.8
22 Th	0 0 47	28 19 39	3♍36 40	10♍49 39	18 59.5	13 42.0	14 2.8	8 58.5	23 35.8	15 52.3	17 28.7	21 10.0	1 8.8
23 F	0 4 44	29 18 24	17 59 56	25 6 46	18 51.3	15 23.2	14 55.2	9 36.5	23 30.8	15 47.9	17 27.3	21 12.2	1 9.8
24 Sa	0 8 41	0♎17 10	2♎ 9 27	9♎ 7 23	18 43.9	17 6.7	15 47.1	10 14.5	23 25.9	15 43.5	17 25.8	21 14.4	1 10.8
25 Su	0 12 37	1 15 58	16 0 6	22 47 17	18 38.1	18 51.9	16 38.2	10 52.5	23 21.2	15 39.0	17 24.4	21 16.6	1 11.7
26 M	0 16 34	2 14 48	29 28 44	6♏ 4 23	18 34.2	20 38.5	17 28.8	11 30.5	23 16.6	15 34.5	17 22.9	21 18.8	1 12.7
27 Tu	0 20 30	3 13 40	12♏34 18	18 58 42	18D 32.5	22 26.0	18 18.6	12 8.5	23 12.3	15 29.9	17 21.3	21 21.0	1 13.6
28 W	0 24 27	4 12 34	25 17 52	1♐32 11	18 32.5	24 14.2	19 7.7	12 46.5	23 8.1	15 25.3	17 19.7	21 23.2	1 14.5
29 Th	0 28 23	5 11 30	7♐42 7	13 48 11	18 33.7	26 2.9	19 56.1	13 24.4	23 4.0	15 20.7	17 18.1	21 25.4	1 15.4
30 F	0 32 20	6 10 27	19 50 58	25 51 5	18 35.2	27 51.7	20 43.7	14 2.4	23 0.2	15 16.1	17 16.4	21 27.6	1 16.2

LONGITUDE — OCTOBER 1938

Day	Sid.Time	☉	0 hr ☽	Noon ☽	True ☊	☿	♀	♂	♃	♄	♅	♆	♇
1 Sa	0 36 16	7♎ 9 27	1♑49 8	7♑45 46	18♏36.3	29♍40.5	21♏30.4	14♍40.3	22♒56.6	15♈11.5	17♉14.7	21♍29.7	1♌17.0
2 Su	0 40 13	8 8 28	13 41 36	19 37 18	18R 36.2	1♎29.1	22 16.4	15 18.3	22R 53.1	15R 6.8	17R 13.0	21 31.9	1 17.8
3 M	0 44 9	9 7 30	25 33 26	1♒30 37	18 34.7	3 17.4	23 1.4	15 56.2	22 49.8	15 2.1	17 11.2	21 34.1	1 18.6
4 Tu	0 48 6	10 6 35	7♒29 23	13 30 15	18 31.4	5 5.3	23 45.5	16 34.2	22 46.7	14 57.4	17 9.4	21 36.2	1 19.4
5 W	0 52 3	11 5 41	19 33 41	25 40 4	18 26.6	6 52.7	24 28.7	17 12.1	22 43.8	14 52.7	17 7.5	21 38.3	1 20.1
6 Th	0 55 59	12 4 49	1♓49 46	8♓ 3 4	18 20.7	8 39.6	25 10.8	17 50.0	22 41.1	14 48.0	17 5.7	21 40.4	1 20.8
7 F	0 59 56	13 3 59	14 20 10	20 41 12	18 14.5	10 25.8	25 51.9	18 28.0	22 38.5	14 43.3	17 3.8	21 42.6	1 21.5
8 Sa	1 3 52	14 3 11	27 6 16	3♈35 21	18 8.5	12 11.3	26 32.0	19 5.9	22 36.2	14 38.5	17 1.8	21 44.6	1 22.2
9 Su	1 7 49	15 2 25	10♈ 8 23	16 45 16	18 3.4	13 56.2	27 10.9	19 43.8	22 34.1	14 33.8	16 59.8	21 46.7	1 22.8
10 M	1 11 45	16 1 40	23 25 48	0♉ 9 48	17 59.7	15 40.3	27 48.6	20 21.7	22 32.1	14 29.1	16 57.8	21 48.8	1 23.4
11 Tu	1 15 42	17 0 58	6♉57 1	13 47 10	17D 57.7	17 23.8	28 25.1	20 59.6	22 30.4	14 24.3	16 55.8	21 50.9	1 24.0
12 W	1 19 38	18 0 18	20 40 0	27 35 14	17 57.3	19 6.5	29 0.4	21 37.5	22 28.8	14 19.6	16 53.7	21 52.9	1 24.6
13 Th	1 23 35	18 59 41	4♊32 36	11♊31 51	17 58.1	20 48.5	29 34.3	22 15.4	22 27.5	14 14.9	16 51.6	21 55.0	1 25.2
14 F	1 27 32	19 59 5	18 32 43	25 35 0	17 59.5	22 29.8	0♐ 6.9	22 53.3	22 26.3	14 10.2	16 49.5	21 57.0	1 25.7
15 Sa	1 31 28	20 58 32	2♋38 27	9♋42 51	18 1.0	24 10.4	0 38.1	23 31.2	22 25.4	14 5.5	16 47.4	21 59.0	1 26.2
16 Su	1 35 25	21 58 2	16 47 58	23 53 36	18R 1.9	25 50.3	1 7.8	24 9.1	22 24.6	14 0.9	16 45.2	22 1.0	1 26.6
17 M	1 39 21	22 57 33	0♌59 28	8♌ 5 18	18 1.7	27 29.5	1 35.9	24 47.0	22 24.1	13 56.2	16 43.0	22 3.0	1 27.1
18 Tu	1 43 18	23 57 7	15 10 50	22 15 42	18 0.5	29 8.0	2 2.5	25 24.9	22 23.7	13 51.6	16 40.8	22 4.9	1 27.5
19 W	1 47 14	24 56 43	29 19 35	6♍22 5	17 58.2	0♏45.9	2 27.5	26 2.8	22D 23.6	13 47.0	16 38.5	22 6.9	1 27.9
20 Th	1 51 11	25 56 22	13♍22 49	20 21 23	17 55.2	2 23.2	2 50.7	26 40.7	22 23.6	13 42.4	16 36.3	22 8.8	1 28.3
21 F	1 55 7	26 56 2	27 17 22	4♎10 22	17 52.0	3 59.9	3 12.2	27 18.5	22 23.9	13 37.9	16 34.0	22 10.7	1 28.6
22 Sa	1 59 4	27 55 45	11♎ 0 3	17 46 4	17 49.2	5 35.9	3 31.9	27 56.4	22 24.3	13 33.3	16 31.7	22 12.6	1 28.9
23 Su	2 3 1	28 55 30	24 28 9	1♏ 6 5	17 47.0	7 11.4	3 49.7	28 34.3	22 25.0	13 28.9	16 29.4	22 14.5	1 29.2
24 M	2 6 57	29 55 16	7♏39 43	14 8 58	17D 45.8	8 46.3	4 5.5	29 12.1	22 25.9	13 24.4	16 27.0	22 16.4	1 29.5
25 Tu	2 10 54	0♏55 5	20 33 51	26 54 26	17 45.5	10 20.7	4 19.3	29 50.0	22 26.9	13 20.0	16 24.7	22 18.2	1 29.7
26 W	2 14 50	1 54 56	3♐10 51	9♐23 20	17 46.1	11 54.5	4 31.0	0♎27.9	22 28.2	13 15.6	16 22.3	22 20.0	1 29.9
27 Th	2 18 47	2 54 49	15 32 11	21 37 44	17 47.2	13 27.8	4 40.6	1 5.7	22 29.7	13 11.3	16 19.9	22 21.8	1 30.1
28 F	2 22 43	3 54 43	27 40 23	3♑40 37	17 48.6	15 0.6	4 47.9	1 43.6	22 31.3	13 7.0	16 17.5	22 23.6	1 30.3
29 Sa	2 26 40	4 54 39	9♑38 54	15 35 47	17 49.8	16 32.9	4 53.1	2 21.4	22 33.2	13 2.8	16 15.1	22 25.4	1 30.4
30 Su	2 30 36	5 54 37	21 31 49	27 27 35	17 50.7	18 4.6	4R 55.8	2 59.2	22 35.3	12 58.7	16 12.6	22 27.1	1 30.5
31 M	2 34 33	6 54 36	3♒23 40	9♒20 40	17R 51.2	19 36.0	4 56.3	3 37.1	22 37.6	12 54.5	16 10.2	22 28.8	1 30.6

Astro Data (Dy Hr Mn)	Planet Ingress (Dy Hr Mn)	Last Aspect (Dy Hr Mn)	☽ Ingress (Dy Hr Mn)	Last Aspect (Dy Hr Mn)	☽ Ingress (Dy Hr Mn)	☽ Phases & Eclipses (Dy Hr Mn)
☿ D 6 22:39	☿ ♌ 3 2:58	31 16:28 ♃ □	♐ 1 0:28	2 18:32 ♀ ⚹	♒ 3 8:58	1 17:28 ☽ 8♐36
☽0N 10 2:32	♀ ♏ 7 1:36	3 12:07 ☿ △	♑ 3 12:30	5 10:16 ♀ □	♓ 5 20:27	9 20:08 ○ 16♓28
☽0S 23 3:03	♂ ♍ 7 20:22	5 22:57 ♀ □	♒ 6 1:10	7 22:53 ♀ △	♈ 8 5:22	17 3:12 ☽ 23♊34
	☿ ♍ 10 15:38	8 10:49 ☿ ☍	♓ 8 12:28	9 22:24 ♃ ⚹	♉ 10 11:43	23 20:34 ● 0♎09
☿0S 3 7:02	☉ ♎ 23 17:00	10 4:13 ♆ ☍	♈ 10 21:40	12 15:04 ♀ ☍	♊ 12 16:10	
☽0N 7 10:12		12 18:53 ♃ ⚹	♉ 13 4:54	14 7:45 ♂ □	♋ 14 19:31	1 11:45 ☽ 7♑38
♃ D 19 5:46	☿ ♎ 1 4:19	15 0:16 ♃ □	♊ 15 10:23	16 17:18 ☿ □	♌ 16 22:19	9 9:37 ○ 15♈26
☽0S 20 10:46	♀ ♐ 13 18:49	17 4:00 ♃ △	♋ 17 14:09	18 15:59 ☉ ⚹	♍ 19 1:09	16 9:24 ☽ 22♋21
♂0S 29 12:09	☿ ♏ 18 12:43	19 9:25 ☉ ⚹	♌ 19 16:26	21 0:02 ♂ ☌	♎ 21 4:43	23 8:42 ● 29♎17
♀ R 30 16:22	☉ ♏ 24 1:54	21 7:32 ♃ ☍	♍ 21 18:01	23 8:42 ☉ ☌	♏ 23 10:00	31 7:45 ☽ 7♒14
	♂ ♎ 25 6:20	23 5:24 ♆ ☌	♎ 23 20:19	25 3:33 ♃ □	♐ 25 17:54	
		25 12:56 ♃ △	♏ 26 0:57	27 13:45 ♃ ⚹	♑ 28 4:39	
		27 21:38 ☿ ⚹	♐ 28 9:02	30 1:52 ♆ △	♒ 30 17:08	
		30 18:54 ☿ □	♑ 30 20:20			

Astro Data

1 SEPTEMBER 1938
Julian Day # 14123
Delta T 24.0 sec
SVP 06♓06'44"
Obliquity 23°26'45"
⚷ Chiron 8♋23.7
☽ Mean ☊ 21♏20.7

1 OCTOBER 1938
Julian Day # 14153
Delta T 24.0 sec
SVP 06♓06'41"
Obliquity 23°26'45"
⚷ Chiron 9♋46.6
☽ Mean ☊ 19♏45.4

NOVEMBER 1938 LONGITUDE

Day	Sid.Time	☉	0 hr ☽	Noon ☽	True ☊	☿	♀	♂	♃	♄	♅	♆	♇
1 Tu	2 38 30	7♏54 37	15♒19 11	21♒19 49	17♏51.1	21♏ 6.8	4♐54.3	4♎14.9	22♒40.0	12♈50.5	16♉ 7.7	22♍30.5	1♌30.6
2 W	2 42 26	8 54 39	27 23 7	3♓29 36	17R50.6	22 37.2	4R49.9	4 52.7	22 42.7	12R46.5	16R 5.3	22 32.2	1R30.7
3 Th	2 46 23	9 54 43	9♓39 49	15 54 10	17 49.7	24 7.0	4 43.1	5 30.5	22 45.6	12 42.5	16 2.8	22 33.9	1 30.7
4 F	2 50 19	10 54 49	22 13 5	28 36 51	17 48.8	25 36.4	4 33.8	6 8.3	22 48.6	12 38.7	16 0.4	22 35.5	1 30.7
5 Sa	2 54 16	11 54 56	5♈ 5 45	11♈39 54	17 47.9	27 5.3	4 22.0	6 46.1	22 51.8	12 34.8	15 57.9	22 37.1	1 30.6
6 Su	2 58 12	12 55 5	18 19 22	25 4 7	17 47.3	28 33.8	4 7.8	7 23.9	22 55.3	12 31.1	15 55.4	22 38.7	1 30.5
7 M	3 2 9	13 55 16	1♉53 59	8♉48 43	17 46.9	0♐ 1.7	3 51.2	8 1.7	22 58.9	12 27.4	15 52.9	22 40.2	1 30.4
8 Tu	3 6 5	14 55 28	15 47 57	22 51 14	17D46.8	1 29.0	3 32.3	8 39.5	23 2.7	12 23.8	15 50.4	22 41.8	1 30.3
9 W	3 10 2	15 55 42	29 58 2	7♊ 7 45	17 46.9	2 55.8	3 11.1	9 17.3	23 6.7	12 20.3	15 47.9	22 43.3	1 30.1
10 Th	3 13 59	16 55 58	14♊19 45	21 33 21	17R46.9	4 22.1	2 47.7	9 55.0	23 10.9	12 16.8	15 45.5	22 44.7	1 30.0
11 F	3 17 55	17 56 16	28 47 53	6♋ 2 40	17 47.0	5 47.7	2 22.2	10 32.8	23 15.3	12 13.4	15 43.0	22 46.2	1 29.8
12 Sa	3 21 52	18 56 36	13♋17 6	20 30 35	17 46.9	7 12.6	1 54.8	11 10.6	23 19.8	12 10.1	15 40.5	22 47.6	1 29.5
13 Su	3 25 48	19 56 58	27 42 36	4♌52 41	17 46.8	8 36.7	1 25.6	11 48.4	23 24.6	12 6.9	15 38.0	22 49.0	1 29.3
14 M	3 29 45	20 57 22	12♌ 0 29	19 5 40	17D46.6	10 0.1	0 54.7	12 26.1	23 29.5	12 3.8	15 35.5	22 50.4	1 29.0
15 Tu	3 33 41	21 57 47	26 7 16	3♍ 7 16	17 46.6	11 22.6	0 22.4	13 3.9	23 34.6	12 0.7	15 33.1	22 51.8	1 28.7
16 W	3 37 38	22 58 15	10♍ 3 23	16 56 14	17 46.8	12 44.1	29♏48.9	13 41.7	23 39.9	11 57.7	15 30.6	22 53.1	1 28.3
17 Th	3 41 34	23 58 44	23 45 46	0♎31 58	17 47.3	14 4.5	29 14.3	14 19.4	23 45.3	11 54.8	15 28.1	22 54.4	1 28.0
18 F	3 45 31	24 59 15	7♎14 49	13 54 21	17 47.9	15 23.6	28 38.9	14 57.2	23 50.9	11 52.0	15 25.7	22 55.6	1 27.6
19 Sa	3 49 28	25 59 48	20 30 32	27 3 25	17 48.7	16 41.4	28 2.9	15 34.9	23 56.7	11 49.3	15 23.3	22 56.9	1 27.2
20 Su	3 53 24	27 0 23	3♏33 1	9♏59 23	17 49.3	17 57.6	27 26.6	16 12.7	24 2.7	11 46.7	15 20.8	22 58.1	1 26.7
21 M	3 57 21	28 0 59	16 22 31	22 42 30	17R49.6	19 12.0	26 50.2	16 50.4	24 8.9	11 44.1	15 18.4	22 59.3	1 26.3
22 Tu	4 1 17	29 1 37	28 59 23	5♐13 14	17 49.4	20 24.4	26 14.0	17 28.1	24 15.2	11 41.7	15 16.0	23 0.4	1 25.8
23 W	4 5 14	0♐ 2 16	11♐24 12	17 32 23	17 48.5	21 34.5	25 38.2	18 5.9	24 21.7	11 39.3	15 13.6	23 1.5	1 25.3
24 Th	4 9 10	1 2 57	23 37 58	29 41 9	17 47.0	22 42.0	25 3.1	18 43.6	24 28.3	11 37.1	15 11.3	23 2.6	1 24.8
25 F	4 13 7	2 3 39	5♑42 12	11♑41 22	17 44.8	23 46.5	24 28.8	19 21.3	24 35.1	11 34.9	15 8.9	23 3.7	1 24.2
26 Sa	4 17 3	3 4 22	17 39 0	23 35 27	17 42.4	24 47.6	23 55.6	19 59.0	24 42.1	11 32.9	15 6.6	23 4.7	1 23.6
27 Su	4 21 0	4 5 7	29 31 9	5♒26 32	17 40.0	25 44.9	23 23.8	20 36.7	24 49.3	11 30.9	15 4.2	23 5.7	1 23.0
28 M	4 24 57	5 5 52	11♒22 5	17 18 19	17 37.8	26 37.7	22 53.5	21 14.3	24 56.6	11 29.1	15 1.9	23 6.7	1 22.4
29 Tu	4 28 53	6 6 38	23 15 47	29 15 2	17 36.4	27 25.5	22 24.8	21 52.0	25 4.0	11 27.3	14 59.7	23 7.6	1 21.7
30 W	4 32 50	7 7 26	5♓16 41	11♓21 17	17D35.8	28 7.6	21 58.1	22 29.7	25 11.6	11 25.7	14 57.4	23 8.5	1 21.1

DECEMBER 1938 LONGITUDE

Day	Sid.Time	☉	0 hr ☽	Noon ☽	True ☊	☿	♀	♂	♃	♄	♅	♆	♇
1 Th	4 36 46	8♐ 8 14	17♓29 28	23♓41 47	17♏36.1	28♐43.3	21♏33.3	23♎ 7.3	25♒19.4	11♈24.2	14♉55.2	23♍ 9.4	1♌20.4
2 F	4 40 43	9 9 3	29 58 47	6♈21 1	17 37.2	29 11.9	21R10.6	23 44.9	25 27.3	11R22.7	14R53.0	23 10.2	1R19.6
3 Sa	4 44 39	10 9 53	12♈48 54	19 22 50	17 38.7	29 32.4	20 50.2	24 22.6	25 35.3	11 21.4	14 50.8	23 11.0	1 18.9
4 Su	4 48 36	11 10 44	26 3 8	2♉49 57	17 40.3	29R44.0	20 32.1	25 0.2	25 43.6	11 20.1	14 48.6	23 11.8	1 18.1
5 M	4 52 32	12 11 36	9♉43 21	16 43 14	17R41.4	29 46.0	20 16.4	25 37.8	25 51.9	11 19.0	14 46.5	23 12.5	1 17.3
6 Tu	4 56 29	13 12 29	23 49 21	1♊ 1 16	17 41.4	29 37.6	20 3.1	26 15.4	26 0.4	11 18.0	14 44.4	23 13.2	1 16.5
7 W	5 0 26	14 13 23	8♊18 23	15 39 57	17 40.2	29 18.2	19 52.3	26 53.0	26 9.0	11 17.1	14 42.3	23 13.9	1 15.7
8 Th	5 4 22	15 14 18	23 5 4	0♋32 42	17 37.6	28 47.4	19 44.0	27 30.6	26 17.8	11 16.3	14 40.2	23 14.5	1 14.9
9 F	5 8 19	16 15 14	8♋ 1 46	15 31 9	17 33.8	28 5.4	19 38.2	28 8.2	26 26.7	11 15.6	14 38.2	23 15.1	1 14.0
10 Sa	5 12 15	17 16 11	22 59 44	0♌26 29	17 29.4	27 12.4	19D34.9	28 45.8	26 35.8	11 15.0	14 36.2	23 15.7	1 13.1
11 Su	5 16 12	18 17 9	7♌50 24	15 10 41	17 25.1	26 9.5	19 34.1	29 23.3	26 45.0	11 14.5	14 34.3	23 16.2	1 12.2
12 M	5 20 8	19 18 8	22 26 40	29 37 49	17 21.5	24 58.1	19 35.7	0♏ 0.9	26 54.3	11 14.2	14 32.4	23 16.7	1 11.3
13 Tu	5 24 5	20 19 8	6♍43 47	13♍44 23	17 19.2	23 40.2	19 39.8	0 38.5	27 3.7	11 13.9	14 30.5	23 17.2	1 10.3
14 W	5 28 1	21 20 9	20 39 32	27 29 19	17D18.4	22 18.4	19 46.2	1 16.0	27 13.3	11D13.8	14 28.6	23 17.6	1 9.4
15 Th	5 31 58	22 21 11	4♎13 52	10♎53 26	17 18.9	20 55.4	19 55.0	1 53.5	27 23.0	11 13.7	14 26.8	23 18.0	1 8.4
16 F	5 35 55	23 22 14	17 28 16	23 58 44	17 20.4	19 33.9	20 6.0	2 31.1	27 32.8	11 13.8	14 25.0	23 18.4	1 7.4
17 Sa	5 39 51	24 23 18	0♏25 8	6♏47 48	17 22.0	18 16.7	20 19.2	3 8.6	27 42.8	11 14.0	14 23.2	23 18.7	1 6.4
18 Su	5 43 48	25 24 24	13 7 4	19 23 16	17R23.1	17 6.1	20 34.6	3 46.1	27 52.8	11 14.2	14 21.5	23 19.0	1 5.3
19 M	5 47 44	26 25 30	25 36 38	1♐47 29	17 22.8	16 3.9	20 52.0	4 23.6	28 3.0	11 14.6	14 19.9	23 19.3	1 4.3
20 Tu	5 51 41	27 26 36	7♐56 1	14 2 26	17 20.6	15 11.6	21 11.5	5 1.0	28 13.3	11 15.2	14 18.2	23 19.5	1 3.2
21 W	5 55 37	28 27 44	20 6 57	26 9 44	17 16.3	14 29.8	21 32.8	5 38.5	28 23.8	11 15.8	14 16.6	23 19.7	1 2.1
22 Th	5 59 34	29 28 52	2♑10 56	8♑10 43	17 10.0	13 58.9	21 56.1	6 16.0	28 34.3	11 16.5	14 15.1	23 19.9	1 1.0
23 F	6 3 30	0♑30 0	14 9 15	20 6 42	17 1.9	13 38.9	22 21.1	6 53.4	28 45.0	11 17.3	14 13.6	23 20.0	0 59.9
24 Sa	6 7 27	1 31 9	26 3 16	1♒59 10	16 52.9	13D29.3	22 47.9	7 30.8	28 55.7	11 18.3	14 12.1	23 20.1	0 58.8
25 Su	6 11 24	2 32 18	7♒54 40	13 50 2	16 43.7	13 29.6	23 16.4	8 8.2	29 6.6	11 19.4	14 10.7	23 20.2	0 57.7
26 M	6 15 20	3 33 27	19 45 36	25 41 44	16 35.2	13 39.1	23 46.5	8 45.6	29 17.6	11 20.5	14 9.3	23R20.2	0 56.5
27 Tu	6 19 17	4 34 36	1♓38 51	7♓37 24	16 28.2	13 57.0	24 18.1	9 23.0	29 28.7	11 21.8	14 8.0	23 20.2	0 55.3
28 W	6 23 13	5 35 45	13 37 53	19 40 49	16 23.2	14 22.6	24 51.3	10 0.3	29 39.9	11 23.2	14 6.7	23 20.1	0 54.1
29 Th	6 27 10	6 36 55	25 46 46	1♈56 19	16D20.5	14 55.2	25 25.9	10 37.6	29 51.2	11 24.7	14 5.4	23 20.0	0 53.0
30 F	6 31 6	7 38 4	8♈10 5	14 28 39	16 19.8	15 33.9	26 1.8	11 15.0	0♓ 2.6	11 26.3	14 4.2	23 19.9	0 51.7
31 Sa	6 35 3	8 39 13	20 52 37	27 22 32	16 20.4	16 18.2	26 39.1	11 52.2	0 14.1	11 28.0	14 3.0	23 19.8	0 50.5

Astro Data Dy Hr Mn	Planet Ingress Dy Hr Mn	Last Aspect Dy Hr Mn	☽ Ingress Dy Hr Mn	Last Aspect Dy Hr Mn	☽ Ingress Dy Hr Mn	☽ Phases & Eclipses Dy Hr Mn
♇ R 2 12:20	☿ ♐ 6 23:33	1 14:43 ♃ ☌	♓ 2 5:09	1 22:28 ☿ □	♈ 2 0:02	7 22:23 ○ 14♉51
☽0N 3 18:57	♀ ♏ 15 16:07	4 7:13 ☿ △	♈ 4 14:35	4 6:35 ☿ △	♉ 4 7:01	7 22:26 ☍T 1.352
☽0S 16 16:35	☉ ♐ 22 23:06	6 8:14 ♃ ✱	♉ 6 20:41	6 3:42 ♃ □	♊ 6 10:18	14 16:20 ☽ 21♌38
		8 12:23 ♃ □	♊ 9 0:03	8 8:48 ☿ ☍	♋ 8 11:08	22 0:05 ● 29♏02
☽0N 1 4:10	♂ ♏ 11 23:25	10 14:46 ♃ △	♋ 11 1:59	10 9:42 ♂ □	♌ 10 11:17	22 23:52:02 ☌P 0.778
☿ R 4 16:46	☉ ♑ 22 12:13	12 15:50 ♆ ✱	♌ 13 3:50	12 7:31 ♃ ☍	♍ 12 12:37	30 3:59 ☽ 7♓18
♃∠♄ 7 20:13	♃ ♓ 29 18:34	14 19:36 ♃ ☍	♍ 15 6:38	14 4:37 ♆ ☌	♎ 14 16:27	
♀ D 10 19:52		17 9:18 ♀ ✱	♎ 17 11:03	16 18:53 ♃ △	♏ 16 23:13	7 10:22 ○ 14♊40
☽0S 13 22:29		19 6:20 ♃ △	♏ 19 17:26	19 4:48 ♃ □	♐ 19 8:31	14 1:17 ☽ 21♍23
♄ D 14 21:34		22 0:05 ☉ ☌	♐ 22 1:56	21 18:07 ☉ ☌	♑ 21 19:39	21 18:07 ● 29♐14
☿ D 24 11:10		24 1:40 ♃ ✱	♑ 24 12:37	23 18:30 ♆ △	♒ 24 7:59	29 22:53 ☽ 7♈35
♆ R 26 2:27		26 12:08 ♀ ✱	♒ 27 0:58	26 19:34 ♃ ☌	♓ 26 20:41	
☽0N 28 12:49		29 8:54 ☿ ✱	♓ 29 13:30	28 23:17 ♀ △	♈ 29 8:14	
				30 14:54 ☿ △	♉ 31 16:47	

Astro Data

1 NOVEMBER 1938
Julian Day # 14184
Delta T 24.0 sec
SVP 06♓06'38"
Obliquity 23°26'44"
⚷ Chiron 9♋57.0R
☽ Mean ☊ 18♏06.9

1 DECEMBER 1938
Julian Day # 14214
Delta T 24.0 sec
SVP 06♓06'34"
Obliquity 23°26'43"
⚷ Chiron 8♋52.4R
☽ Mean ☊ 16♏31.6

LONGITUDE — JANUARY 1939

Day	Sid.Time	☉	0 hr ☽	Noon ☽	True ☊	☿	♀	♂	♃	♄	♅	♆	♇
1 Su	6 38 59	9♑40 22	3♉58 54	10♉42 8	16♏21.5	17♐ 7.4	27♏17.7	12♏29.5	0♓25.7	11♈29.8	14♉ 1.9	23♍19.6	0♌49.3
2 M	6 42 56	10 41 31	17 32 33	24 30 20	16R22.0	18 0.9	27 57.6	13 6.8	0 37.4	11 31.7	14R 0.9	23R19.4	0R48.1
3 Tu	6 46 53	11 42 40	1♊35 29	8♊47 49	16 20.9	18 58.4	28 38.6	13 44.0	0 49.1	11 33.8	13 59.9	23 19.1	0 46.8
4 W	6 50 49	12 43 48	16 6 57	23 32 14	16 17.6	19 59.3	29 20.7	14 21.3	1 1.0	11 35.9	13 58.9	23 18.8	0 45.5
5 Th	6 54 46	13 44 56	1♋ 2 49	8♋37 38	16 11.7	21 3.3	0♐ 4.0	14 58.5	1 13.0	11 38.2	13 58.0	23 18.5	0 44.3
6 F	6 58 42	14 46 5	16 15 26	23 54 49	16 3.7	22 10.1	0 48.3	15 35.7	1 25.0	11 40.5	13 57.1	23 18.2	0 43.0
7 Sa	7 2 39	15 47 13	1♌34 21	9♌12 35	15 54.4	23 19.3	1 33.7	16 12.8	1 37.1	11 43.0	13 56.3	23 17.8	0 41.7
8 Su	7 6 35	16 48 21	16 48 8	24 19 43	15 44.9	24 30.6	2 20.0	16 50.0	1 49.3	11 45.5	13 55.5	23 17.4	0 40.4
9 M	7 10 32	17 49 29	1♍46 18	9♍ 7 0	15 36.4	25 44.0	3 7.3	17 27.2	2 1.6	11 48.1	13 54.8	23 16.9	0 39.1
10 Tu	7 14 28	18 50 37	16 21 11	23 28 28	15 29.9	26 59.0	3 55.5	18 4.3	2 14.0	11 50.9	13 54.1	23 16.4	0 37.8
11 W	7 18 25	19 51 45	0♎28 40	7♎21 47	15 25.9	28 15.7	4 44.5	18 41.4	2 26.5	11 53.7	13 53.5	23 15.9	0 36.5
12 Th	7 22 22	20 52 53	14 8 1	20 47 40	15D24.2	29 33.8	5 34.4	19 18.5	2 39.0	11 56.7	13 52.9	23 15.4	0 35.2
13 F	7 26 18	21 54 0	27 21 8	3♏48 54	15 24.1	0♑53.2	6 25.1	19 55.5	2 51.6	11 59.7	13 52.4	23 14.8	0 33.9
14 Sa	7 30 15	22 55 8	10♏11 30	16 29 28	15R24.6	2 13.9	7 16.6	20 32.6	3 4.3	12 2.9	13 51.9	23 14.2	0 32.5
15 Su	7 34 11	23 56 16	22 43 21	28 53 41	15 24.4	3 35.6	8 8.8	21 9.6	3 17.1	12 6.1	13 51.5	23 13.5	0 31.2
16 M	7 38 8	24 57 24	5♐ 0 58	11♐ 5 40	15 22.5	4 58.4	9 1.7	21 46.6	3 29.9	12 9.5	13 51.1	23 12.9	0 29.9
17 Tu	7 42 4	25 58 31	17 8 14	23 9 2	15 18.1	6 22.1	9 55.3	22 23.6	3 42.8	12 12.9	13 50.8	23 12.1	0 28.5
18 W	7 46 1	26 59 38	29 8 26	5♑ 6 42	15 10.6	7 46.7	10 49.5	23 0.5	3 55.8	12 16.5	13 50.5	23 11.4	0 27.2
19 Th	7 49 57	28 0 45	11♑ 4 7	17 0 53	15 0.2	9 12.2	11 44.4	23 37.5	4 8.8	12 20.1	13 50.3	23 10.6	0 25.9
20 F	7 53 54	29 1 51	22 57 13	28 53 17	14 47.3	10 38.5	12 39.9	24 14.4	4 21.9	12 23.8	13 50.2	23 9.8	0 24.5
21 Sa	7 57 51	0♒ 2 56	4♒49 14	10♒45 13	14 32.9	12 5.5	13 35.9	24 51.2	4 35.1	12 27.6	13 50.1	23 9.0	0 23.2
22 Su	8 1 47	1 4 1	16 41 24	22 37 57	14 18.2	13 33.3	14 32.5	25 28.1	4 48.3	12 31.5	13D 50.0	23 8.2	0 21.8
23 M	8 5 44	2 5 5	28 35 3	4♓32 56	14 4.3	15 1.8	15 29.6	26 4.9	5 1.6	12 35.5	13 50.0	23 7.3	0 20.5
24 Tu	8 9 40	3 6 8	10♓31 50	16 32 3	13 52.3	16 31.0	16 27.3	26 41.6	5 14.9	12 39.6	13 50.1	23 6.4	0 19.1
25 W	8 13 37	4 7 10	22 33 56	28 37 52	13 43.1	18 0.8	17 25.4	27 18.4	5 28.3	12 43.8	13 50.2	23 5.4	0 17.8
26 Th	8 17 33	5 8 11	4♈44 16	10♈53 37	13 36.9	19 31.4	18 24.0	27 55.1	5 41.8	12 48.1	13 50.3	23 4.4	0 16.4
27 F	8 21 30	6 9 11	17 6 25	23 23 13	13 33.5	21 2.6	19 23.0	28 31.8	5 55.3	12 52.4	13 50.5	23 3.4	0 15.1
28 Sa	8 25 26	7 10 10	29 44 33	6♉11 0	13D32.3	22 34.5	20 22.5	29 8.4	6 8.9	12 56.8	13 50.8	23 2.4	0 13.8
29 Su	8 29 23	8 11 8	12♉43 6	19 21 23	13R32.2	24 7.1	21 22.5	29 45.0	6 22.5	13 1.4	13 51.1	23 1.4	0 12.4
30 M	8 33 20	9 12 5	26 6 16	2♊58 7	13 31.9	25 40.3	22 22.8	0♐21.6	6 36.2	13 6.0	13 51.5	23 0.3	0 11.1
31 Tu	8 37 16	10 13 0	9♊57 10	17 3 29	13 30.1	27 14.2	23 23.5	0 58.2	6 49.9	13 10.6	13 51.9	22 59.2	0 9.8

LONGITUDE — FEBRUARY 1939

Day	Sid.Time	☉	0 hr ☽	Noon ☽	True ☊	☿	♀	♂	♃	♄	♅	♆	♇
1 W	8 41 13	11♒13 54	24♊16 57	1♋37 14	13♏26.0	28♑48.8	24♐24.6	1♐34.7	7♓ 3.7	13♈15.4	13♉52.4	22♍58.1	0♌ 8.5
2 Th	8 45 9	12 14 47	9♋ 3 45	16 35 41	13R19.0	0♒24.1	25 26.1	2 11.2	7 17.5	13 20.3	13 52.9	22R56.9	0R 7.2
3 F	8 49 6	13 15 38	24 11 58	1♌51 20	13 9.4	2 0.1	26 27.9	2 47.6	7 31.3	13 25.2	13 53.5	22 55.7	0 5.9
4 Sa	8 53 2	14 16 29	9♌32 24	17 13 37	12 58.1	3 36.8	27 30.1	3 24.0	7 45.2	13 30.2	13 54.2	22 54.5	0 4.6
5 Su	8 56 59	15 17 18	24 53 29	2♍30 31	12 46.4	5 14.2	28 32.6	4 0.4	7 59.1	13 35.3	13 54.8	22 53.3	0 3.3
6 M	9 0 56	16 18 5	10♍ 3 21	17 30 51	12 35.6	6 52.4	29 35.5	4 36.8	8 13.1	13 40.4	13 55.6	22 52.1	0 2.0
7 Tu	9 4 52	17 18 52	24 52 4	2♎ 6 18	12 27.1	8 31.4	0♑38.6	5 13.1	8 27.1	13 45.6	13 56.4	22 50.8	0 0.7
8 W	9 8 49	18 19 38	9♎13 7	16 12 17	12 21.2	10 11.1	1 42.1	5 49.4	8 41.1	13 50.9	13 57.2	22 49.5	29♋59.4
9 Th	9 12 45	19 20 23	23 3 49	29 47 54	12 18.1	11 51.6	2 45.9	6 25.6	8 55.2	13 56.3	13 58.1	22 48.2	29 58.1
10 F	9 16 42	20 21 7	6♏24 53	12♏55 12	12D17.0	13 32.9	3 49.9	7 1.8	9 9.3	14 1.7	13 59.0	22 46.9	29 56.9
11 Sa	9 20 38	21 21 49	19 19 23	25 38 2	12R17.0	15 15.0	4 54.2	7 38.0	9 23.5	14 7.3	14 0.0	22 45.5	29 55.7
12 Su	9 24 35	22 22 31	1♐51 47	8♐ 1 15	12 16.7	16 58.0	5 58.8	8 14.1	9 37.6	14 12.8	14 1.1	22 44.2	29 54.4
13 M	9 28 31	23 23 12	14 7 4	20 9 51	12 15.1	18 41.8	7 3.7	8 50.2	9 51.9	14 18.5	14 2.2	22 42.8	29 53.2
14 Tu	9 32 28	24 23 51	26 10 11	2♑ 8 36	12 11.0	20 26.5	8 8.7	9 26.2	10 6.1	14 24.2	14 3.3	22 41.4	29 52.0
15 W	9 36 24	25 24 30	8♑ 5 36	14 1 38	12 4.1	22 12.0	9 14.1	10 2.2	10 20.4	14 30.0	14 4.5	22 39.9	29 50.8
16 Th	9 40 21	26 25 7	19 57 6	25 52 22	11 54.4	23 58.4	10 19.6	10 38.1	10 34.6	14 35.8	14 5.7	22 38.5	29 49.6
17 F	9 44 18	27 25 42	1♒47 44	7♒43 28	11 42.2	25 45.7	11 25.4	11 14.0	10 49.0	14 41.7	14 7.0	22 37.0	29 48.4
18 Sa	9 48 14	28 26 17	13 39 47	19 36 52	11 28.5	27 33.8	12 31.3	11 49.8	11 3.3	14 47.7	14 8.4	22 35.6	29 47.3
19 Su	9 52 11	29 26 49	25 34 53	1♓33 59	11 14.3	29 22.8	13 37.5	12 25.6	11 17.7	14 53.8	14 9.8	22 34.1	29 46.1
20 M	9 56 7	0♓27 21	7♓34 18	13 35 59	11 0.9	1♓12.6	14 43.9	13 1.4	11 32.0	14 59.8	14 11.2	22 32.6	29 45.0
21 Tu	10 0 4	1 27 50	19 39 9	25 43 59	10 49.3	3 3.2	15 50.4	13 37.0	11 46.4	15 6.0	14 12.7	22 31.0	29 43.8
22 W	10 4 0	2 28 18	1♈50 39	7♈59 23	10 40.3	4 54.5	16 57.1	14 12.7	12 0.8	15 12.2	14 14.2	22 29.5	29 42.7
23 Th	10 7 57	3 28 44	14 10 25	20 24 3	10 34.3	6 46.6	18 4.1	14 48.2	12 15.3	15 18.5	14 15.8	22 28.0	29 41.6
24 F	10 11 53	4 29 9	26 40 35	3♉ 0 25	10 31.1	8 39.3	19 11.1	15 23.7	12 29.7	15 24.8	14 17.4	22 26.4	29 40.6
25 Sa	10 15 50	5 29 31	9♉23 54	15 51 28	10D30.2	10 32.6	20 18.4	15 59.2	12 44.2	15 31.2	14 19.1	22 24.8	29 39.5
26 Su	10 19 47	6 29 52	22 23 31	29 0 28	10 30.6	12 26.3	21 25.7	16 34.6	12 58.6	15 37.6	14 20.8	22 23.2	29 38.5
27 M	10 23 43	7 30 10	5♊42 42	12♊30 32	10R31.0	14 20.4	22 33.3	17 9.9	13 13.1	15 44.1	14 22.6	22 21.6	29 37.4
28 Tu	10 27 40	8 30 27	19 24 16	26 24 0	10 30.5	16 14.6	23 41.0	17 45.2	13 27.6	15 50.6	14 24.4	22 20.0	29 36.4

Astro Data

	Dy Hr Mn
♃⚻♇	2 19:44
☽0S	10 6:41
♅ D	22 12:05
☽0N	24 20:17
☽0S	6 17:28
♄⚺♅	9 9:33
☽0N	21 2:51

Planet Ingress

		Dy Hr Mn
♀	♐	4 21:48
☿	♑	12 7:57
☉	♒	20 22:51
♂	♐	29 9:49
☿	♒	1 17:57
♀	♑	6 9:20
♇	♋	7 12:55
☉	♓	19 13:09
☿	♓	19 8:09

Last Aspect / ☽ Ingress

Last Aspect Dy Hr Mn			☽ Ingress	Dy Hr Mn
2 18:47	♀	☍	♊	2 21:19
4 11:38	♆	□	♋	4 22:20
6 11:02	♆	⚹	♌	6 21:32
8 13:23	☿	△	♍	8 21:08
10 19:48	☿	□	♎	10 23:10
12 13:11	☉	□	♏	13 4:54
15 2:34	☉	⚹	♐	15 14:10
17 12:05	♆	□	♑	18 1:44
20 13:27	☉	☌	♒	20 14:15
22 18:41	♂	□	♓	23 2:51
25 9:53	♂	△	♈	25 14:42
27 8:35	☿	□	♉	28 0:29
29 23:08	☿	△	♊	30 6:50

Last Aspect / ☽ Ingress

Last Aspect Dy Hr Mn			☽ Ingress	Dy Hr Mn
1 0:14	♀	☍	♋	1 9:22
2 22:00	♆	⚹	♌	3 9:06
5 6:10	♀	△	♍	5 8:02
6 20:41	♆	☌	♎	7 8:29
9 12:17	♇	□	♏	9 12:22
11 20:13	♇	△	♐	11 20:24
13 20:07	☉	⚹	♑	14 7:41
16 19:59	♇	☍	♒	16 20:22
19 8:28	☉	☌	♓	19 8:52
21 19:50	♇	△	♈	21 20:23
24 5:42	♇	□	♉	24 6:19
26 13:07	♇	⚹	♊	26 13:47
28 5:02	♆	□	♋	28 18:07

☽ Phases & Eclipses

Dy Hr Mn		
5 21:30	○	14♋40
12 13:11	☽	21♎26
20 13:27	●	29♑36
28 15:00	☽	7♉48
4 7:55	○	14♌37
11 4:12	☽	21♏32
19 8:28	●	29♒48
27 3:26	☽	7♊39

Astro Data

1 JANUARY 1939
Julian Day # 14245
Delta T 24.0 sec
SVP 06♓06'29"
Obliquity 23°26'43"
⚷ Chiron 6♋55.9R
☽ Mean ☊ 14♏53.1

1 FEBRUARY 1939
Julian Day # 14276
Delta T 24.0 sec
SVP 06♓06'24"
Obliquity 23°26'43"
⚷ Chiron 5♋02.9R
☽ Mean ☊ 13♏14.6

MARCH 1939 LONGITUDE

Day	Sid.Time	☉	0 hr ☽	Noon ☽	True ☊	☿	♀	♂	♃	♄	♅	♆	♇
1 W	10 31 36	9♓30 41	3♋29 48	10♋41 31	10♏28.1	18♓ 8.9	24♑48.8	18♐20.4	13♓42.1	15♈57.2	14♉26.3	22♍18.4	29♋35.4
2 Th	10 35 33	10 30 54	17 58 49	25 21 13	10R 23.3	20 2.8	25 56.8	18 55.5	13 56.6	16 3.8	14 28.2	22R 16.8	29R 34.5
3 F	10 39 29	11 31 4	2♌47 59	10♌18 14	10 16.4	21 56.3	27 4.9	19 30.6	14 11.1	16 10.5	14 30.1	22 15.2	29 33.5
4 Sa	10 43 26	12 31 12	17 50 53	25 24 44	10 7.8	23 49.1	28 13.2	20 5.6	14 25.6	16 17.2	14 32.1	22 13.6	29 32.6
5 Su	10 47 22	13 31 19	2♍58 30	10♍30 53	9 58.8	25 40.7	29 21.5	20 40.6	14 40.1	16 24.0	14 34.1	22 11.9	29 31.7
6 M	10 51 19	14 31 23	18 0 36	25 26 30	9 50.4	27 30.8	0♒30.0	21 15.4	14 54.6	16 30.8	14 36.2	22 10.3	29 30.8
7 Tu	10 55 16	15 31 25	2♎47 32	10♎ 2 51	9 43.6	29 19.0	1 38.7	21 50.3	15 9.1	16 37.6	14 38.3	22 8.6	29 29.9
8 W	10 59 12	16 31 26	17 11 47	24 13 54	9 39.1	1♈ 4.9	2 47.4	22 25.0	15 23.7	16 44.5	14 40.4	22 7.0	29 29.0
9 Th	11 3 9	17 31 25	1♏ 8 58	7♏56 54	9D 37.0	2 47.9	3 56.3	22 59.7	15 38.2	16 51.4	14 42.6	22 5.3	29 28.2
10 F	11 7 5	18 31 23	14 37 50	21 12 2	9 36.8	4 27.7	5 5.3	23 34.3	15 52.7	16 58.4	14 44.8	22 3.7	29 27.4
11 Sa	11 11 2	19 31 18	27 39 51	4♐ 1 46	9 37.7	6 3.6	6 14.4	24 8.9	16 7.2	17 5.4	14 47.1	22 2.0	29 26.6
12 Su	11 14 58	20 31 13	10♐18 20	16 30 7	9R 38.9	7 35.1	7 23.6	24 43.3	16 21.7	17 12.4	14 49.4	22 0.3	29 25.8
13 M	11 18 55	21 31 5	22 37 44	28 41 49	9 39.4	9 1.7	8 33.0	25 17.7	16 36.2	17 19.5	14 51.8	21 58.7	29 25.0
14 Tu	11 22 51	22 30 56	4♑43 0	10♑41 54	9 38.4	10 23.0	9 42.4	25 52.0	16 50.7	17 26.6	14 54.2	21 57.0	29 24.3
15 W	11 26 48	23 30 45	16 39 6	22 35 9	9 35.6	11 38.4	10 51.9	26 26.2	17 5.1	17 33.7	14 56.6	21 55.3	29 23.6
16 Th	11 30 45	24 30 32	28 30 36	4♒25 56	9 30.7	12 47.5	12 1.5	27 0.4	17 19.6	17 40.9	14 59.0	21 53.7	29 22.9
17 F	11 34 41	25 30 18	10♒21 36	16 17 59	9 24.1	13 49.8	13 11.2	27 34.4	17 34.0	17 48.1	15 1.5	21 52.0	29 22.2
18 Sa	11 38 38	26 30 1	22 15 28	28 14 19	9 16.3	14 45.0	14 21.0	28 8.3	17 48.5	17 55.3	15 4.1	21 50.3	29 21.6
19 Su	11 42 34	27 29 43	4♓14 50	10♓17 13	9 8.0	15 32.8	15 30.9	28 42.2	18 2.9	18 2.6	15 6.6	21 48.7	29 20.9
20 M	11 46 31	28 29 23	16 21 40	22 28 20	9 0.2	16 13.0	16 40.8	29 16.0	18 17.3	18 9.9	15 9.2	21 47.0	29 20.3
21 Tu	11 50 27	29 29 1	28 37 20	4♈48 46	8 53.5	16 45.2	17 50.8	29 49.6	18 31.7	18 17.2	15 11.9	21 45.3	29 19.8
22 W	11 54 24	0♈28 37	11♈ 2 45	17 19 23	8 48.5	17 9.5	19 0.9	0♑23.2	18 46.1	18 24.5	15 14.5	21 43.7	29 19.2
23 Th	11 58 20	1 28 11	23 38 43	0♉ 0 52	8 45.5	17 25.8	20 11.1	0 56.6	19 0.4	18 31.9	15 17.2	21 42.1	29 18.7
24 F	12 2 17	2 27 43	6♉25 58	12 54 6	8D 44.3	17R 34.1	21 21.3	1 30.0	19 14.8	18 39.3	15 19.9	21 40.4	29 18.2
25 Sa	12 6 13	3 27 12	19 25 26	26 0 7	8 44.8	17 34.5	22 31.6	2 3.2	19 29.1	18 46.7	15 22.7	21 38.8	29 17.7
26 Su	12 10 10	4 26 40	2♊38 17	9♊20 7	8 46.1	17 27.3	23 42.0	2 36.3	19 43.4	18 54.1	15 25.5	21 37.2	29 17.2
27 M	12 14 7	5 26 5	16 5 46	22 55 21	8 47.7	17 12.8	24 52.4	3 9.3	19 57.6	19 1.5	15 28.3	21 35.6	29 16.8
28 Tu	12 18 3	6 25 28	29 48 57	6♋46 38	8R 48.8	16 51.4	26 2.9	3 42.2	20 11.9	19 9.0	15 31.2	21 33.9	29 16.4
29 W	12 22 0	7 24 48	13♋48 21	20 54 0	8 48.8	16 23.8	27 13.5	4 15.0	20 26.1	19 16.5	15 34.1	21 32.4	29 16.0
30 Th	12 25 56	8 24 6	28 3 21	5♌16 4	8 47.4	15 50.5	28 24.1	4 47.7	20 40.2	19 24.0	15 37.0	21 30.8	29 15.6
31 F	12 29 53	9 23 22	12♌31 42	19 49 43	8 44.7	15 12.3	29 34.7	5 20.2	20 54.4	19 31.5	15 39.9	21 29.2	29 15.3

APRIL 1939 LONGITUDE

Day	Sid.Time	☉	0 hr ☽	Noon ☽	True ☊	☿	♀	♂	♃	♄	♅	♆	♇
1 Sa	12 33 49	10♈22 35	27♌ 9 25	4♍30 1	8♏41.1	14♈30.1	0♓45.5	5♑52.6	21♓ 8.5	19♈39.0	15♉42.9	21♍27.6	29♋15.0
2 Su	12 37 46	11 21 46	11♍50 43	19 10 37	8R 37.2	13R 44.8	1 56.2	6 24.9	21 22.6	19 46.5	15 45.8	21R 26.1	29R 14.7
3 M	12 41 42	12 20 55	26 28 48	3♎44 26	8 33.4	12 57.3	3 7.1	6 57.1	21 36.6	19 54.1	15 48.9	21 24.5	29 14.5
4 Tu	12 45 39	13 20 1	10♎56 40	18 4 48	8 30.5	12 8.6	4 17.9	7 29.1	21 50.6	20 1.6	15 51.9	21 23.0	29 14.2
5 W	12 49 36	14 19 6	25 8 13	2♏ 6 23	8D 28.7	11 19.8	5 28.9	8 1.0	22 4.6	20 9.2	15 54.9	21 21.5	29 14.0
6 Th	12 53 32	15 18 9	8♏58 58	15 45 45	8 28.2	10 31.7	6 39.9	8 32.8	22 18.6	20 16.7	15 58.0	21 20.0	29 13.8
7 F	12 57 29	16 17 9	22 26 38	29 1 39	8 28.7	9 45.2	7 50.9	9 4.5	22 32.5	20 24.3	16 1.1	21 18.5	29 13.7
8 Sa	13 1 25	17 16 8	5♐30 58	11♐54 50	8 30.0	9 1.2	9 2.0	9 36.0	22 46.3	20 31.9	16 4.3	21 17.0	29 13.5
9 Su	13 5 22	18 15 5	18 13 35	24 27 39	8 31.5	8 20.3	10 13.1	10 7.3	23 0.1	20 39.5	16 7.4	21 15.6	29 13.4
10 M	13 9 18	19 14 1	0♑37 31	6♑43 41	8 32.9	7 43.2	11 24.3	10 38.5	23 13.9	20 47.0	16 10.6	21 14.2	29 13.4
11 Tu	13 13 15	20 12 54	12 46 44	18 47 13	8R 33.8	7 10.3	12 35.6	11 9.6	23 27.7	20 54.6	16 13.8	21 12.7	29 13.3
12 W	13 17 11	21 11 46	24 45 44	0♒42 52	8 34.0	6 42.0	13 46.8	11 40.4	23 41.4	21 2.2	16 17.0	21 11.3	29D 13.3
13 Th	13 21 8	22 10 36	6♒39 13	12 35 20	8 33.3	6 18.7	14 58.2	12 11.2	23 55.0	21 9.8	16 20.2	21 9.9	29 13.3
14 F	13 25 5	23 9 25	18 31 47	24 29 5	8 32.0	6 0.5	16 9.5	12 41.7	24 8.6	21 17.4	16 23.5	21 8.6	29 13.3
15 Sa	13 29 1	24 8 11	0♓27 43	6♓28 8	8 30.1	5 47.5	17 20.9	13 12.1	24 22.2	21 25.0	16 26.7	21 7.2	29 13.3
16 Su	13 32 58	25 6 56	12 30 46	18 35 58	8 28.1	5D 39.8	18 32.4	13 42.3	24 35.7	21 32.6	16 30.0	21 5.9	29 13.4
17 M	13 36 54	26 5 39	24 44 3	0♈55 18	8 26.2	5 37.3	19 43.8	14 12.3	24 49.1	21 40.2	16 33.3	21 4.6	29 13.5
18 Tu	13 40 51	27 4 20	7♈ 9 54	13 28 2	8 24.6	5 40.0	20 55.3	14 42.1	25 2.5	21 47.7	16 36.6	21 3.3	29 13.6
19 W	13 44 47	28 2 59	19 49 48	26 15 17	8 23.6	5 47.7	22 6.9	15 11.7	25 15.9	21 55.3	16 39.9	21 2.0	29 13.8
20 Th	13 48 44	29 1 36	2♉44 28	9♉17 19	8D 23.1	6 0.4	23 18.5	15 41.1	25 29.2	22 2.9	16 43.3	21 0.8	29 14.0
21 F	13 52 40	0♉ 0 12	15 53 48	22 33 47	8 23.1	6 17.9	24 30.1	16 10.3	25 42.4	22 10.4	16 46.6	20 59.6	29 14.2
22 Sa	13 56 37	0 58 45	29 17 9	6♊ 3 44	8 23.5	6 40.0	25 41.7	16 39.3	25 55.6	22 17.9	16 50.0	20 58.4	29 14.4
23 Su	14 0 33	1 57 17	12♊53 23	19 45 55	8 24.1	7 6.6	26 53.4	17 8.1	26 8.7	22 25.5	16 53.4	20 57.2	29 14.7
24 M	14 4 30	2 55 46	26 41 7	3♋38 47	8 24.7	7 37.4	28 5.0	17 36.7	26 21.7	22 33.0	16 56.8	20 56.0	29 14.9
25 Tu	14 8 27	3 54 14	10♋38 42	17 40 38	8 25.1	8 12.3	29 16.8	18 5.0	26 34.7	22 40.5	17 0.2	20 54.9	29 15.2
26 W	14 12 23	4 52 39	24 44 22	1♌49 37	8R 25.4	8 51.1	0♈28.5	18 33.1	26 47.7	22 48.0	17 3.6	20 53.8	29 15.6
27 Th	14 16 20	5 51 2	8♌56 7	16 3 34	8 25.4	9 33.6	1 40.2	19 1.0	27 0.5	22 55.5	17 7.0	20 52.7	29 15.9
28 F	14 20 16	6 49 22	23 11 38	0♍19 59	8 25.3	10 19.7	2 52.0	19 28.7	27 13.3	23 2.9	17 10.4	20 51.7	29 16.3
29 Sa	14 24 13	7 47 41	7♍28 14	14 35 58	8D 25.3	11 9.2	4 3.8	19 56.1	27 26.1	23 10.4	17 13.9	20 50.6	29 16.7
30 Su	14 28 9	8 45 57	21 42 45	28 48 10	8 25.3	12 2.1	5 15.7	20 23.2	27 38.7	23 17.8	17 17.3	20 49.6	29 17.2

Astro Data	Planet Ingress	Last Aspect	☽ Ingress	Last Aspect	☽ Ingress	☽ Phases & Eclipses	Astro Data
Dy Hr Mn	Dy Hr Mn	Dy Hr Mn	Dy Hr Mn	Dy Hr Mn	Dy Hr Mn	Dy Hr Mn	1 MARCH 1939
♃□♇ 4 10:49	♀ ♒ 5 13:29	2 18:48 ♇ ☌	♌ 2 19:30	31 11:36 ♄ △	♍ 1 4:39	5 18:00 ○ 14♍16	Julian Day # 14304
♃✱♅ 4 12:24	☿ ♈ 7 9:14	4 3:42 ♂ △	♍ 4 19:17	3 4:33 ♇ ✱	♎ 3 5:48	12 21:37 ☽ 21♐25	Delta T 24.1 sec
☽0S 6 5:02	☉ ♈ 21 12:28	6 18:37 ♇ ✱	♎ 6 19:25	5 7:02 ♇ □	♏ 5 8:21	21 1:49 ● 29♓34	SVP 06♓06'21"
☿0N 7 6:49	♂ ♑ 21 7:25	8 21:04 ♇ □	♏ 8 22:00	7 12:22 ♇ △	♐ 7 13:47	28 12:16 ☽ 6♋56	Obliquity 23°26'43"
♃⊻♄ 18 22:56	♀ ♓ 31 8:34	11 3:20 ♇ △	♐ 11 4:23	9 9:21 ♃ □	♑ 9 22:47		⚷ Chiron 4♋08.7R
☽0N 20 9:23		13 5:31 ♂ ☌	♑ 13 14:35	12 8:59 ♇ ☍	♒ 12 10:33	4 4:18 ○ 13♎31	☽ Mean ☊ 11♏45.6
☿ R 24 13:17	☉ ♉ 20 23:55	16 1:46 ♇ ☍	♒ 16 3:01	14 10:10 ☉ ✱	♓ 14 23:04	11 16:11 ☽ 20♑53	
☽0S 2 15:06	♀ ♈ 25 14:28	18 12:23 ♂ ✱	♓ 18 15:31	17 8:43 ♇ △	♈ 17 10:13	19 16:35 ● 28♈43	1 APRIL 1939
♃☍♆ 2 5:23		21 2:27 ♂ □	♈ 21 2:41	19 17:31 ♇ □	♉ 19 18:57	19 16:45:27 ✓ A 1'49"	Julian Day # 14335
♇ D 12 15:17		23 10:40 ♇ □	♉ 23 11:58	21 23:55 ♇ ✱	♊ 22 1:16	26 18:25 ☽ 5♌37	Delta T 24.1 sec
♄⊼♆ 13 0:22		25 17:57 ♇ ✱	♊ 25 19:15	24 2:39 ♀ □	♋ 24 5:43		SVP 06♓06'18"
☽0N 16 16:42		27 16:51 ♀ △	♋ 28 0:19	26 7:40 ♇ ☌	♌ 26 8:55		Obliquity 23°26'43"
☿ D 16 23:26		30 2:01 ♇ ☌	♌ 30 3:15	27 23:45 ♄ △	♍ 28 11:26		⚷ Chiron 4♋26.5
♀0N 28 16:24	☽0S 29 22:44			30 12:50 ♇ ✱	♎ 30 14:02		☽ Mean ☊ 10♏07.1

LONGITUDE — MAY 1939

Day	Sid.Time	☉	0 hr ☽	Noon ☽	True ☊	☿	♀	♂	♃	♄	♅	♆	♇
1 M	14 32 6	9♉44 12	5♎51 46	12♎53 6	8♏25.3	12♈58.0	6♈27.5	20♑50.1	27♓51.3	23♈25.2	17♉20.8	20♍48.6	29♋17.6
2 Tu	14 36 2	10 42 24	19 51 44	26 47 14	8 25.5	13 57.0	7 39.4	21 16.8	28 3.8	23 32.6	17 24.2	20R 47.7	29 18.1
3 W	14 39 59	11 40 35	3♏39 16	10♏27 29	8R 25.6	14 59.0	8 51.3	21 43.2	28 16.3	23 39.9	17 27.7	20 46.8	29 18.6
4 Th	14 43 56	12 38 44	17 11 38	23 51 28	8 25.6	16 3.7	10 3.2	22 9.3	28 28.6	23 47.3	17 31.1	20 45.9	29 19.1
5 F	14 47 52	13 36 51	0♐26 53	6♐57 48	8 25.3	17 11.1	11 15.2	22 35.1	28 40.9	23 54.6	17 34.6	20 45.0	29 19.7
6 Sa	14 51 49	14 34 57	13 24 14	19 46 16	8 24.7	18 21.2	12 27.1	23 0.7	28 53.2	24 1.9	17 38.1	20 44.1	29 20.3
7 Su	14 55 45	15 33 1	26 4 4	2♑17 51	8 23.9	19 33.8	13 39.2	23 25.9	29 5.3	24 9.1	17 41.5	20 43.3	29 20.9
8 M	14 59 42	16 31 4	8♑27 56	14 34 39	8 22.9	20 48.8	14 51.2	23 50.9	29 17.4	24 16.4	17 45.0	20 42.5	29 21.5
9 Tu	15 3 38	17 29 5	20 38 26	26 39 42	8 21.9	22 6.3	16 3.2	24 15.5	29 29.4	24 23.6	17 48.5	20 41.8	29 22.1
10 W	15 7 35	18 27 5	2♒38 59	8♒36 48	8 21.0	23 26.2	17 15.3	24 39.9	29 41.3	24 30.7	17 52.0	20 41.0	29 22.8
11 Th	15 11 31	19 25 3	14 33 42	20 30 14	8D 20.6	24 48.3	18 27.4	25 3.9	29 53.1	24 37.9	17 55.4	20 40.3	29 23.5
12 F	15 15 28	20 23 0	26 27 1	2♓24 36	8 20.6	26 12.7	19 39.5	25 27.5	0♈ 4.8	24 45.0	17 58.9	20 39.7	29 24.2
13 Sa	15 19 25	21 20 56	8♓23 36	14 24 32	8 21.2	27 39.4	20 51.7	25 50.8	0 16.5	24 52.1	18 2.4	20 39.0	29 25.0
14 Su	15 23 21	22 18 51	20 28 0	26 34 28	8 22.2	29 8.2	22 3.8	26 13.8	0 28.0	24 59.2	18 5.9	20 38.4	29 25.8
15 M	15 27 18	23 16 44	2♈44 27	8♈58 21	8 23.4	0♉39.3	23 16.0	26 36.3	0 39.5	25 6.2	18 9.3	20 37.8	29 26.5
16 Tu	15 31 14	24 14 36	15 16 34	21 39 24	8 24.7	2 12.5	24 28.2	26 58.6	0 50.9	25 13.2	18 12.8	20 37.3	29 27.4
17 W	15 35 11	25 12 27	28 7 3	4♉39 42	8R 25.5	3 47.9	25 40.4	27 20.4	1 2.2	25 20.1	18 16.3	20 36.7	29 28.2
18 Th	15 39 7	26 10 16	11♉17 24	18 0 5	8 25.8	5 25.5	26 52.7	27 41.8	1 13.3	25 27.0	18 19.7	20 36.2	29 29.0
19 F	15 43 4	27 8 4	24 47 37	1♊39 46	8 25.1	7 5.1	28 4.9	28 2.8	1 24.4	25 33.9	18 23.2	20 35.8	29 29.9
20 Sa	15 47 0	28 5 51	8♊36 12	15 36 28	8 23.5	8 47.0	29 17.2	28 23.4	1 35.4	25 40.7	18 26.6	20 35.4	29 30.8
21 Su	15 50 57	29 3 36	22 40 6	29 46 33	8 21.1	10 31.0	0♉29.5	28 43.5	1 46.3	25 47.5	18 30.0	20 35.0	29 31.8
22 M	15 54 54	0♊ 1 20	6♋55 11	14♋ 5 24	8 18.3	12 17.1	1 41.8	29 3.3	1 57.1	25 54.3	18 33.5	20 34.6	29 32.7
23 Tu	15 58 50	0 59 2	21 16 36	28 28 11	8 15.4	14 5.3	2 54.1	29 22.6	2 7.8	26 1.0	18 36.9	20 34.3	29 33.7
24 W	16 2 47	1 56 43	5♌39 34	12♌50 15	8 12.9	15 55.7	4 6.4	29 41.4	2 18.4	26 7.7	18 40.3	20 33.9	29 34.7
25 Th	16 6 43	2 54 22	19 59 47	27 7 47	8D 11.3	17 48.2	5 18.8	29 59.8	2 28.9	26 14.3	18 43.7	20 33.7	29 35.7
26 F	16 10 40	3 52 0	4♍13 55	11♍17 54	8 10.8	19 42.8	6 31.1	0♒17.7	2 39.3	26 20.9	18 47.1	20 33.4	29 36.7
27 Sa	16 14 36	4 49 36	18 19 34	25 18 44	8 11.3	21 39.5	7 43.5	0 35.1	2 49.5	26 27.4	18 50.5	20 33.2	29 37.7
28 Su	16 18 33	5 47 11	2♎15 16	9♎ 9 5	8 12.6	23 38.1	8 55.9	0 52.0	2 59.7	26 33.9	18 53.8	20 33.0	29 38.8
29 M	16 22 29	6 44 44	16 0 7	22 48 17	8 14.1	25 38.8	10 8.3	1 8.4	3 9.7	26 40.3	18 57.2	20 32.9	29 39.9
30 Tu	16 26 26	7 42 16	29 33 32	6♏15 48	8R 15.2	27 41.3	11 20.7	1 24.4	3 19.7	26 46.7	19 0.5	20 32.8	29 41.0
31 W	16 30 23	8 39 46	12♏55 1	19 31 9	8 15.4	29 45.6	12 33.1	1 39.8	3 29.5	26 53.0	19 3.9	20 32.7	29 42.1

LONGITUDE — JUNE 1939

Day	Sid.Time	☉	0 hr ☽	Noon ☽	True ☊	☿	♀	♂	♃	♄	♅	♆	♇
1 Th	16 34 19	9♊37 15	26♏ 4 8	2♐33 53	8♏14.2	1♊51.6	13♉45.6	1♒54.6	3♈39.2	26♈59.3	19♉ 7.2	20♍32.7	29♋43.3
2 F	16 38 16	10 34 44	9♐ 0 24	15 23 38	8R 11.4	3 59.1	14 58.1	2 9.0	3 48.8	27 5.5	19 10.5	20D 32.6	29 44.4
3 Sa	16 42 12	11 32 11	21 43 37	28 0 21	8 7.1	6 7.9	16 10.5	2 22.7	3 58.2	27 11.7	19 13.8	20 32.7	29 45.6
4 Su	16 46 9	12 29 37	4♑13 55	10♑24 26	8 1.7	8 17.9	17 23.0	2 35.9	4 7.6	27 17.8	19 17.0	20 32.7	29 46.8
5 M	16 50 5	13 27 3	16 32 4	22 37 2	7 55.6	10 28.8	18 35.6	2 48.6	4 16.8	27 23.9	19 20.3	20 32.8	29 48.0
6 Tu	16 54 2	14 24 27	28 39 34	4♒40 0	7 49.5	12 40.4	19 48.1	3 0.6	4 25.9	27 29.9	19 23.5	20 32.9	29 49.3
7 W	16 57 58	15 21 51	10♒38 43	16 36 5	7 44.1	14 52.3	21 0.7	3 12.0	4 34.9	27 35.9	19 26.7	20 33.1	29 50.5
8 Th	17 1 55	16 19 14	22 32 36	28 28 45	7 39.9	17 4.4	22 13.3	3 22.8	4 43.7	27 41.8	19 29.9	20 33.2	29 51.8
9 F	17 5 52	17 16 37	4♓25 3	10♓22 6	7 37.3	19 16.4	23 25.9	3 33.0	4 52.4	27 47.6	19 33.1	20 33.4	29 53.1
10 Sa	17 9 48	18 13 59	16 20 29	22 20 48	7D 36.3	21 28.0	24 38.5	3 42.5	5 1.0	27 53.4	19 36.3	20 33.7	29 54.4
11 Su	17 13 45	19 11 20	28 23 40	4♈29 41	7 36.7	23 38.9	25 51.1	3 51.3	5 9.5	27 59.1	19 39.4	20 34.0	29 55.7
12 M	17 17 41	20 8 41	10♈39 29	16 53 37	7 38.0	25 48.9	27 3.8	3 59.5	5 17.8	28 4.7	19 42.5	20 34.3	29 57.0
13 Tu	17 21 38	21 6 2	23 12 39	29 37 1	7 39.3	27 57.7	28 16.5	4 7.0	5 26.0	28 10.3	19 45.6	20 34.6	29 58.4
14 W	17 25 34	22 3 22	6♉ 7 9	12♉43 22	7R 40.1	0♋ 5.2	29 29.2	4 13.8	5 34.0	28 15.8	19 48.7	20 35.0	29 59.7
15 Th	17 29 31	23 0 41	19 25 51	26 14 40	7 39.5	2 11.1	0♊41.9	4 19.9	5 41.9	28 21.3	19 51.7	20 35.4	0♌ 1.1
16 F	17 33 27	23 58 0	3♊ 9 45	10♊10 52	7 37.0	4 15.3	1 54.6	4 25.3	5 49.7	28 26.7	19 54.8	20 35.8	0 2.5
17 Sa	17 37 24	24 55 19	17 17 36	24 29 24	7 32.5	6 17.7	3 7.4	4 29.9	5 57.3	28 32.0	19 57.8	20 36.3	0 3.9
18 Su	17 41 21	25 52 37	1♋45 32	9♋ 5 11	7 26.2	8 18.2	4 20.2	4 33.9	6 4.8	28 37.3	20 0.8	20 36.8	0 5.3
19 M	17 45 17	26 49 55	16 27 23	23 51 8	7 18.9	10 16.7	5 32.9	4 37.0	6 12.1	28 42.5	20 3.7	20 37.3	0 6.8
20 Tu	17 49 14	27 47 12	1♌15 23	8♌39 10	7 11.4	12 13.0	6 45.8	4 39.5	6 19.3	28 47.6	20 6.6	20 37.9	0 8.2
21 W	17 53 10	28 44 28	16 1 30	23 21 34	7 4.8	14 7.2	7 58.6	4 41.2	6 26.3	28 52.6	20 9.5	20 38.5	0 9.7
22 Th	17 57 7	29 41 44	0♍38 38	7♍52 8	6 59.7	15 59.2	9 11.4	4R 42.1	6 33.2	28 57.6	20 12.4	20 39.1	0 11.1
23 F	18 1 3	0♋38 59	15 1 37	22 6 47	6 56.7	17 49.0	10 24.3	4 42.3	6 39.9	29 2.5	20 15.3	20 39.8	0 12.6
24 Sa	18 5 0	1 36 13	29 7 30	6♎ 3 41	6D 55.6	19 36.6	11 37.1	4 41.8	6 46.5	29 7.3	20 18.1	20 40.5	0 14.1
25 Su	18 8 57	2 33 26	12♎55 25	19 42 49	6 55.9	21 21.9	12 50.0	4 40.5	6 52.9	29 12.1	20 20.9	20 41.2	0 15.6
26 M	18 12 53	3 30 39	26 26 2	3♏ 5 18	6R 56.8	23 4.9	14 2.9	4 38.5	6 59.1	29 16.7	20 23.6	20 42.0	0 17.1
27 Tu	18 16 50	4 27 52	9♏40 50	16 12 51	6 57.1	24 45.7	15 15.9	4 35.7	7 5.2	29 21.3	20 26.3	20 42.7	0 18.7
28 W	18 20 46	5 25 3	22 41 34	29 7 12	6 55.9	26 24.2	16 28.8	4 32.2	7 11.2	29 25.8	20 29.0	20 43.6	0 20.2
29 Th	18 24 43	6 22 15	5♐29 54	11♐49 51	6 52.5	28 0.4	17 41.8	4 27.9	7 16.9	29 30.3	20 31.7	20 44.4	0 21.7
30 F	18 28 39	7 19 26	18 7 10	24 21 58	6 46.6	29 34.3	18 54.8	4 22.9	7 22.5	29 34.6	20 34.4	20 45.3	0 23.3

Astro Data Dy Hr Mn	Planet Ingress Dy Hr Mn	Last Aspect Dy Hr Mn	☽ Ingress Dy Hr Mn	Last Aspect Dy Hr Mn	☽ Ingress Dy Hr Mn	☽ Phases & Eclipses Dy Hr Mn	Astro Data
♃△♇ 8 8:43	♃ ♈ 11 14:08	2 16:23 ♇ □	♏ 2 17:36	1 6:45 ♇ △	♐ 1 7:15	3 15:15 ○ 12♏18	1 MAY 1939
☽0N 14 1:02	☿ ♉ 14 13:43	4 21:57 ♇ △	♐ 4 23:11	3 10:32 ♄ △	♑ 3 15:50	3 15:11 ☍T 1.177	Julian Day # 14365
♃0N 26 0:46	♀ ♉ 20 14:13	7 5:54 ♃ □	♑ 7 7:34	6 2:19 ♇ ☍	♒ 6 2:40	11 10:40 ☽ 19♒51	Delta T 24.1 sec
☽0S 27 4:45	☉ ♊ 21 23:27	9 17:57 ♃ ⚹	♒ 9 18:41	8 10:30 ♄ ⚹	♓ 8 15:04	19 4:25 ● 27♉19	SVP 06♓06'15"
	♂ ♒ 25 0:19	11 23:27 ☿ ⚹	♓ 12 7:09	11 3:02 ♇ △	♈ 11 3:10	25 23:20 ☽ 3♍50	Obliquity 23°26'43"
♆ D 1 22:38	☿ ♊ 31 2:45	14 17:35 ♇ △	♈ 14 18:41	13 12:41 ♇ □	♉ 13 12:43		⚷ Chiron 5♋58.6
♃∠♅ 5 14:17		17 2:30 ♇ □	♉ 17 3:28	15 2:03 ♆ △	♊ 15 18:32	2 3:11 ○ 10♐42	☽ Mean ☊ 8♏31.8
☽0N 10 9:57	☿ ♋ 13 23:01	19 8:14 ♇ ⚹	♊ 19 9:06	17 18:48 ♄ ⚹	♋ 17 21:06	10 4:07 ☽ 18♓24	
♂ R 22 18:34	♀ ♊ 14 10:11	21 5:20 ♄ ⚹	♋ 21 12:23	19 19:59 ♄ □	♌ 19 21:58	17 13:37 ● 25♊28	1 JUNE 1939
☽0S 23 11:03	♇ ♌ 14 4:50	23 13:50 ♇ ☌	♌ 23 14:33	21 22:19 ☉ ⚹	♍ 21 22:56	24 4:35 ☽ 1♎47	Julian Day # 14396
	☉ ♋ 22 7:39	25 10:35 ♄ △	♍ 25 16:51	23 9:33 ♆ ☌	♎ 24 1:30		Delta T 24.1 sec
	☿ ♌ 30 6:41	27 19:29 ♇ ⚹	♎ 27 20:06	26 5:09 ♄ ☍	♏ 26 6:25		SVP 06♓06'11"
		30 0:13 ♇ □	♏ 30 0:47	28 7:55 ☿ △	♐ 28 13:39		Obliquity 23°26'42"
				30 22:12 ♄ △	♑ 30 22:53		⚷ Chiron 8♋31.5
							☽ Mean ☊ 6♏53.3

JULY 1939 LONGITUDE

Day	Sid.Time	☉	0 hr ☽	Noon ☽	True ☊	☿	♀	♂	♃	♄	♅	♆	♇
1 Sa	18 32 36	8♋16 37	0♑34 20	6♑44 22	6♏38.3	1♌ 5.8	20♊ 7.8	4♒17.2	7♈28.0	29♈38.9	20♉37.0	20♍46.2	0♌24.9
2 Su	18 36 32	9 13 48	12 52 9	18 57 48	6R28.0	2 35.1	21 20.8	4R10.8	7 33.3	29 43.1	20 39.5	20 47.1	0 26.5
3 M	18 40 29	10 10 59	25 1 25	1♒ 3 9	6 16.6	4 2.0	22 33.8	4 3.6	7 38.4	29 47.2	20 42.1	20 48.1	0 28.0
4 Tu	18 44 26	11 8 9	7♒ 3 9	13 1 38	6 5.0	5 26.5	23 46.9	3 55.7	7 43.3	29 51.3	20 44.6	20 49.1	0 29.6
5 W	18 48 22	12 5 20	18 58 52	24 55 8	5 54.4	6 48.7	25 0.0	3 47.2	7 48.1	29 55.2	20 47.0	20 50.1	0 31.2
6 Th	18 52 19	13 2 31	0♓50 47	6♓46 13	5 45.4	8 8.4	26 13.1	3 37.9	7 52.7	29 59.1	20 49.5	20 51.1	0 32.8
7 F	18 56 15	13 59 42	12 41 51	18 38 11	5 38.8	9 25.6	27 26.3	3 28.0	7 57.1	0♉ 2.9	20 51.9	20 52.2	0 34.4
8 Sa	19 0 12	14 56 53	24 35 46	0♈35 9	5 34.6	10 40.3	28 39.4	3 17.4	8 1.3	0 6.6	20 54.2	20 53.3	0 36.1
9 Su	19 4 8	15 54 5	6♈36 57	12 41 46	5D32.7	11 52.3	29 52.6	3 6.2	8 5.4	0 10.2	20 56.6	20 54.5	0 37.7
10 M	19 8 5	16 51 17	18 50 16	25 3 6	5 32.3	13 1.8	1♋ 5.9	2 54.4	8 9.3	0 13.7	20 58.9	20 55.6	0 39.3
11 Tu	19 12 1	17 48 29	1♉20 52	7♉44 10	5R32.6	14 8.5	2 19.1	2 42.0	8 13.0	0 17.1	21 1.1	20 56.8	0 41.0
12 W	19 15 58	18 45 42	14 13 35	20 49 33	5 32.4	15 12.3	3 32.4	2 29.1	8 16.5	0 20.5	21 3.3	20 58.0	0 42.6
13 Th	19 19 55	19 42 56	27 32 27	4♊22 32	5 30.7	16 13.3	4 45.7	2 15.6	8 19.9	0 23.7	21 5.5	20 59.3	0 44.3
14 F	19 23 51	20 40 10	11♊19 53	18 24 24	5 26.7	17 11.3	5 59.0	2 1.7	8 23.0	0 26.9	21 7.7	21 0.6	0 45.9
15 Sa	19 27 48	21 37 25	25 35 46	2♋53 29	5 20.2	18 6.2	7 12.3	1 47.2	8 26.0	0 29.9	21 9.8	21 1.9	0 47.6
16 Su	19 31 44	22 34 40	10♋16 48	17 44 48	5 11.4	18 57.8	8 25.7	1 32.4	8 28.8	0 32.9	21 11.8	21 3.2	0 49.2
17 M	19 35 41	23 31 55	25 16 21	2♌50 13	5 1.1	19 46.1	9 39.1	1 17.2	8 31.4	0 35.8	21 13.9	21 4.5	0 50.9
18 Tu	19 39 37	24 29 11	10♌25 5	17 59 35	4 50.5	20 30.9	10 52.5	1 1.6	8 33.8	0 38.6	21 15.8	21 5.9	0 52.6
19 W	19 43 34	25 26 27	25 32 28	3♍ 2 31	4 40.8	21 12.1	12 6.0	0 45.8	8 36.0	0 41.3	21 17.8	21 7.3	0 54.3
20 Th	19 47 30	26 23 44	10♍28 43	17 50 13	4 33.1	21 49.5	13 19.4	0 29.7	8 38.0	0 43.9	21 19.7	21 8.8	0 55.9
21 F	19 51 27	27 21 0	25 6 22	2♎16 43	4 27.9	22 22.9	14 32.9	0 13.4	8 39.8	0 46.4	21 21.5	21 10.2	0 57.6
22 Sa	19 55 24	28 18 17	9♎21 3	16 19 16	4 25.2	22 52.2	15 46.4	29♑56.9	8 41.5	0 48.8	21 23.4	21 11.7	0 59.3
23 Su	19 59 20	29 15 34	23 11 27	29 57 47	4 24.3	23 17.3	16 59.9	29 40.4	8 42.9	0 51.1	21 25.1	21 13.2	1 1.0
24 M	20 3 17	0♌12 52	6♏38 35	13♏14 11	4 24.3	23 37.9	18 13.5	29 23.8	8 44.1	0 53.3	21 26.9	21 14.7	1 2.6
25 Tu	20 7 13	1 10 10	19 44 59	26 11 23	4 23.8	23 53.9	19 27.0	29 7.1	8 45.2	0 55.4	21 28.5	21 16.3	1 4.3
26 W	20 11 10	2 7 28	2♐33 48	8♐52 38	4 21.8	24 5.2	20 40.6	28 50.6	8 46.0	0 57.4	21 30.2	21 17.9	1 6.0
27 Th	20 15 6	3 4 46	15 8 15	21 21 2	4 17.3	24R11.7	21 54.2	28 34.1	8 46.7	0 59.3	21 31.8	21 19.5	1 7.7
28 F	20 19 3	4 2 6	27 31 15	3♑39 11	4 10.0	24 13.1	23 7.9	28 17.7	8 47.2	1 1.1	21 33.3	21 21.1	1 9.4
29 Sa	20 22 59	4 59 25	9♑45 6	15 49 12	3 60.0	24 9.5	24 21.5	28 1.5	8R47.4	1 2.8	21 34.9	21 22.7	1 11.0
30 Su	20 26 56	5 56 46	21 51 39	27 52 39	3 47.8	24 0.8	25 35.2	27 45.4	8 47.5	1 4.4	21 36.3	21 24.4	1 12.7
31 M	20 30 53	6 54 7	3♒52 19	9♒50 50	3 34.2	23 46.9	26 48.9	27 29.7	8 47.4	1 6.0	21 37.7	21 26.1	1 14.4

AUGUST 1939 LONGITUDE

Day	Sid.Time	☉	0 hr ☽	Noon ☽	True ☊	☿	♀	♂	♃	♄	♅	♆	♇
1 Tu	20 34 49	7♌51 29	15♒48 20	21♒44 59	3♏20.5	23♌28.0	28♋ 2.6	27♑14.2	8♈47.1	1♉ 7.4	21♉39.1	21♍27.8	1♌16.1
2 W	20 38 46	8 48 51	27 40 59	3♓36 32	3R 7.6	23R 4.2	29 16.4	26R59.1	8R46.6	1 8.7	21 40.5	21 29.5	1 17.7
3 Th	20 42 42	9 46 15	9♓31 54	15 27 23	2 56.7	22 35.6	0♌30.2	26 44.3	8 45.8	1 9.9	21 41.7	21 31.2	1 19.4
4 F	20 46 39	10 43 40	21 23 17	27 20 0	2 48.3	22 2.6	1 44.0	26 30.0	8 44.9	1 11.0	21 43.0	21 33.0	1 21.1
5 Sa	20 50 35	11 41 5	3♈17 57	9♈17 37	2 42.7	21 25.6	2 57.8	26 16.0	8 43.8	1 12.0	21 44.2	21 34.8	1 22.7
6 Su	20 54 32	12 38 32	15 19 30	21 24 9	2 39.7	20 44.9	4 11.6	26 2.6	8 42.5	1 12.9	21 45.3	21 36.6	1 24.4
7 M	20 58 28	13 36 1	27 32 8	3♉44 6	2D38.7	20 1.3	5 25.5	25 49.7	8 41.0	1 13.6	21 46.4	21 38.4	1 26.0
8 Tu	21 2 25	14 33 30	10♉ 0 37	16 22 18	2R38.7	19 15.4	6 39.4	25 37.3	8 39.3	1 14.3	21 47.4	21 40.3	1 27.7
9 W	21 6 22	15 31 1	22 49 46	29 23 31	2 38.6	18 27.9	7 53.4	25 25.5	8 37.4	1 14.9	21 48.4	21 42.1	1 29.3
10 Th	21 10 18	16 28 33	6♊ 4 3	12♊51 43	2 37.3	17 39.7	9 7.3	25 14.3	8 35.3	1 15.4	21 49.4	21 44.0	1 31.0
11 F	21 14 15	17 26 7	19 46 46	26 49 15	2 33.9	16 51.7	10 21.3	25 3.8	8 33.0	1 15.8	21 50.3	21 45.9	1 32.6
12 Sa	21 18 11	18 23 42	3♋59 4	11♋15 52	2 28.1	16 4.8	11 35.3	24 53.9	8 30.6	1 16.0	21 51.2	21 47.8	1 34.2
13 Su	21 22 8	19 21 19	18 39 6	26 7 57	2 20.0	15 19.9	12 49.4	24 44.7	8 27.9	1 16.2	21 52.0	21 49.8	1 35.9
14 M	21 26 4	20 18 57	3♌41 24	11♌18 14	2 10.3	14 37.9	14 3.4	24 36.3	8 25.0	1R16.3	21 52.7	21 51.7	1 37.5
15 Tu	21 30 1	21 16 36	18 57 7	26 36 35	2 0.2	13 59.6	15 17.5	24 28.6	8 22.0	1 16.2	21 53.4	21 53.7	1 39.1
16 W	21 33 57	22 14 16	4♍15 12	11♍51 35	1 50.8	13 26.0	16 31.6	24 21.6	8 18.7	1 16.1	21 54.1	21 55.7	1 40.7
17 Th	21 37 54	23 11 58	19 24 27	26 52 43	1 43.3	12 57.7	17 45.7	24 15.4	8 15.3	1 15.8	21 54.7	21 57.6	1 42.3
18 F	21 41 51	24 9 40	4♎15 28	11♎32 2	1 38.3	12 35.3	18 59.9	24 10.1	8 11.7	1 15.4	21 55.2	21 59.6	1 43.8
19 Sa	21 45 47	25 7 24	18 41 58	25 45 1	1D35.7	12 19.5	20 14.1	24 5.5	8 7.9	1 15.0	21 55.7	22 1.7	1 45.4
20 Su	21 49 44	26 5 9	2♏41 8	9♏30 26	1 35.1	12D10.6	21 28.2	24 1.8	8 3.9	1 14.4	21 56.2	22 3.7	1 47.0
21 M	21 53 40	27 2 55	16 13 9	22 49 40	1R35.6	12 9.0	22 42.4	23 58.8	7 59.7	1 13.7	21 56.6	22 5.7	1 48.5
22 Tu	21 57 37	28 0 42	29 20 23	5♐45 46	1 35.8	12 15.0	23 56.7	23 56.8	7 55.4	1 12.9	21 57.0	22 7.8	1 50.1
23 W	22 1 33	28 58 31	12♐ 6 20	18 22 36	1 35.0	12 28.7	25 10.9	23D55.5	7 50.9	1 12.0	21 57.3	22 9.9	1 51.6
24 Th	22 5 30	29 56 20	24 35 4	0♑44 13	1 32.1	12 50.2	26 25.2	23 55.1	7 46.2	1 11.0	21 57.5	22 12.0	1 53.1
25 F	22 9 26	0♍54 11	6♑50 31	12 54 24	1 26.9	13 19.4	27 39.4	23 55.5	7 41.4	1 10.0	21 57.7	22 14.1	1 54.6
26 Sa	22 13 23	1 52 3	18 56 15	24 56 26	1 19.3	13 56.4	28 53.7	23 56.8	7 36.4	1 8.8	21 57.9	22 16.2	1 56.1
27 Su	22 17 20	2 49 56	0♒55 17	6♒53 3	1 9.8	14 41.0	0♍ 8.0	23 58.8	7 31.2	1 7.5	21 58.0	22 18.3	1 57.6
28 M	22 21 16	3 47 51	12 50 2	18 46 27	0 59.2	15 32.9	1 22.4	24 1.7	7 25.9	1 6.1	21R58.1	22 20.4	1 59.1
29 Tu	22 25 13	4 45 47	24 42 30	0♓38 24	0 48.3	16 32.0	2 36.7	24 5.4	7 20.4	1 4.6	21 58.1	22 22.5	2 0.5
30 W	22 29 9	5 43 45	6♓34 20	12 30 30	0 38.2	17 37.8	3 51.1	24 9.9	7 14.7	1 3.0	21 58.0	22 24.7	2 2.0
31 Th	22 33 6	6 41 44	18 27 6	24 24 21	0 29.7	18 50.1	5 5.5	24 15.2	7 9.0	1 1.3	21 57.9	22 26.8	2 3.4

Astro Data Dy Hr Mn	Planet Ingress Dy Hr Mn	Last Aspect Dy Hr Mn	☽ Ingress Dy Hr Mn	Last Aspect Dy Hr Mn	☽ Ingress Dy Hr Mn	☽ Phases & Eclipses Dy Hr Mn	Astro Data
☽0N 7 18:34	♄ ♉ 6 5:45	3 9:32 ♄ □	♒ 3 9:54	1 14:59 ☿ ☍	♓ 2 4:41	1 16:16 ○ 8♑55	1 JULY 1939
♅△♆ 7 6:23	♀ ♋ 9 2:25	5 22:15 ♄ ✱	♓ 5 22:17	4 10:07 ♂ ✱	♈ 4 17:22	9 19:49 ☽ 16♈41	Julian Day # 14426
☽0S 20 19:06	♂ ♑ 21 19:31	8 9:04 ♀ □	♈ 8 10:50	6 20:44 ♂ □	♉ 7 4:47	16 21:03 ● 23♋25	Delta T 24.2 sec
☿ R 27 18:54	☉ ♌ 23 18:37	9 19:49 ☉ □	♉ 10 21:27	9 4:42 ♂ △	♊ 9 13:06	23 11:34 ☽ 29♎43	SVP 06♓06'06"
♃ R 29 21:01		12 12:27 ♆ ☌	♊ 13 4:21	11 3:25 ♆ □	♋ 11 17:21	31 6:37 ○ 7♒10	Obliquity 23°26'42"
	♀ ♌ 2 14:11	14 16:23 ♆ □	♋ 15 7:16	13 9:41 ♂ ☍	♌ 13 18:09		⚷ Chiron 11♋30.5
☽0N 4 2:10	☉ ♍ 24 1:31	16 21:03 ☉ ☌	♌ 17 7:30	15 4:36 ♅ □	♍ 15 17:19		☽ Mean ☊ 5♏18.0
♅△♆ 14 19:19	♀ ♍ 26 21:24	18 17:14 ♅ □	♍ 19 7:07	17 7:44 ♂ △	♎ 17 17:03	8 9:18 ☽ 14♉56	
♄ R 14 1:03		21 4:00 ☉ ✱	♎ 21 8:10	19 11:44 ☉ ✱	♏ 19 19:20	15 3:53 ● 21♌26	1 AUGUST 1939
☽0S 17 5:08		23 11:34 ☉ □	♏ 23 12:04	21 21:21 ☉ □	♐ 22 1:14	21 21:21 ☽ 27♏54	Julian Day # 14457
☿ D 20 17:07		25 17:08 ♂ ✱	♐ 25 19:10	24 3:58 ♀ △	♑ 24 10:33	29 22:09 ○ 5♓39	Delta T 24.2 sec
♂ D 23 23:58		27 17:34 ☿ △	♑ 28 4:51	26 10:02 ♂ ☌	♒ 26 22:09		SVP 06♓06'01"
♅ R 28 14:27		30 11:30 ♂ ☌	♒ 30 16:15	28 18:27 ♅ □	♓ 29 10:42		Obliquity 23°26'42"
☽0N 31 8:42				31 11:48 ♂ ✱	♈ 31 23:15		⚷ Chiron 14♋40.4
							☽ Mean ☊ 3♏39.5

LONGITUDE — SEPTEMBER 1939

Day	Sid.Time	☉	0 hr ☽	Noon ☽	True ☊	☿	♀	♂	♃	♄	♅	♆	♇
1 F	22 37 2	7♍39 45	0♈22 30	6♈21 49	0♏23.3	20♌ 8.4	6♍19.9	24♑21.4	7♈ 3.0	0♉59.5	21♉57.8	22♍29.0	2♌ 4.8
2 Sa	22 40 59	8 37 48	12 22 36	18 25 11	0R 19.3	21 32.2	7 34.3	24 28.2	6R 56.9	0R 57.6	21R 57.6	22 31.2	2 6.3
3 Su	22 44 55	9 35 52	24 29 56	0♉37 16	0D 17.6	23 1.2	8 48.7	24 35.9	6 50.7	0 55.6	21 57.3	22 33.3	2 7.7
4 M	22 48 52	10 33 58	6♉47 37	13 1 26	0 17.6	24 34.8	10 3.2	24 44.3	6 44.4	0 53.6	21 57.0	22 35.5	2 9.0
5 Tu	22 52 48	11 32 7	19 19 13	25 41 28	0 18.6	26 12.5	11 17.7	24 53.5	6 37.9	0 51.4	21 56.7	22 37.7	2 10.4
6 W	22 56 45	12 30 17	2♊ 8 39	8♊41 16	0R 19.8	27 53.7	12 32.2	25 3.4	6 31.3	0 49.1	21 56.3	22 39.9	2 11.7
7 Th	23 0 42	13 28 30	15 19 43	22 4 23	0 20.2	29 38.0	13 46.7	25 14.1	6 24.6	0 46.7	21 55.9	22 42.1	2 13.1
8 F	23 4 38	14 26 44	28 55 32	5♋53 20	0 19.2	1♍24.9	15 1.2	25 25.5	6 17.7	0 44.3	21 55.4	22 44.3	2 14.4
9 Sa	23 8 35	15 25 1	12♋57 48	20 8 47	0 16.4	3 14.0	16 15.8	25 37.6	6 10.8	0 41.7	21 54.8	22 46.5	2 15.7
10 Su	23 12 31	16 23 19	27 25 55	4♌48 41	0 11.8	5 4.7	17 30.3	25 50.5	6 3.7	0 39.1	21 54.2	22 48.8	2 17.0
11 M	23 16 28	17 21 40	12♌16 20	19 47 55	0 6.0	6 56.6	18 44.9	26 4.0	5 56.5	0 36.4	21 53.6	22 51.0	2 18.3
12 Tu	23 20 24	18 20 2	27 22 20	4♍58 23	29♎59.7	8 49.5	19 59.5	26 18.2	5 49.3	0 33.5	21 52.9	22 53.2	2 19.5
13 W	23 24 21	19 18 27	12♍34 44	20 10 4	29 53.8	10 43.0	21 14.1	26 33.1	5 41.9	0 30.6	21 52.2	22 55.4	2 20.8
14 Th	23 28 17	20 16 53	27 43 8	5♎12 43	29 49.1	12 36.8	22 28.8	26 48.7	5 34.5	0 27.6	21 51.4	22 57.6	2 22.0
15 F	23 32 14	21 15 22	12♎37 49	19 57 31	29 46.2	14 30.6	23 43.4	27 5.0	5 26.9	0 24.6	21 50.6	22 59.9	2 23.2
16 Sa	23 36 11	22 13 52	27 11 10	4♏18 18	29D 45.1	16 24.3	24 58.1	27 21.9	5 19.3	0 21.4	21 49.7	23 2.1	2 24.4
17 Su	23 40 7	23 12 23	11♏18 36	18 12 0	29 45.5	18 17.7	26 12.7	27 39.4	5 11.7	0 18.2	21 48.8	23 4.3	2 25.5
18 M	23 44 4	24 10 57	24 58 32	1♐38 25	29 46.8	20 10.6	27 27.4	27 57.6	5 3.9	0 14.8	21 47.8	23 6.5	2 26.7
19 Tu	23 48 0	25 9 32	8♐11 57	14 39 31	29 48.4	22 2.9	28 42.1	28 16.3	4 56.1	0 11.4	21 46.8	23 8.8	2 27.8
20 W	23 51 57	26 8 9	21 1 36	27 18 41	29R 49.3	23 54.5	29 56.8	28 35.7	4 48.3	0 8.0	21 45.7	23 11.0	2 28.9
21 Th	23 55 53	27 6 47	3♑31 20	9♑40 6	29 49.3	25 45.4	1♎11.5	28 55.7	4 40.4	0 4.4	21 44.6	23 13.2	2 30.0
22 F	23 59 50	28 5 27	15 45 30	21 48 6	29 47.8	27 35.5	2 26.2	29 16.2	4 32.5	0 0.8	21 43.4	23 15.5	2 31.1
23 Sa	0 3 46	29 4 9	27 48 25	3♒46 55	29 44.9	29 24.7	3 40.9	29 37.3	4 24.5	29♈57.1	21 42.2	23 17.7	2 32.1
24 Su	0 7 43	0♎ 2 53	9♒44 6	15 40 23	29 40.8	1♎13.0	4 55.6	29 58.9	4 16.5	29 53.4	21 41.0	23 19.9	2 33.1
25 M	0 11 40	1 1 38	21 36 11	27 31 50	29 36.0	3 0.4	6 10.3	0♒21.0	4 8.5	29 49.5	21 39.7	23 22.1	2 34.1
26 Tu	0 15 36	2 0 25	3♓27 42	9♓24 3	29 31.0	4 46.9	7 25.1	0 43.7	4 0.5	29 45.6	21 38.4	23 24.3	2 35.1
27 W	0 19 33	2 59 14	15 21 12	21 19 21	29 26.4	6 32.5	8 39.8	1 6.8	3 52.4	29 41.7	21 37.0	23 26.5	2 36.1
28 Th	0 23 29	3 58 5	27 18 46	3♈19 39	29 22.6	8 17.1	9 54.6	1 30.5	3 44.4	29 37.7	21 35.6	23 28.7	2 37.0
29 F	0 27 26	4 56 58	9♈22 12	15 26 37	29 20.0	10 0.9	11 9.3	1 54.6	3 36.4	29 33.6	21 34.1	23 30.9	2 37.9
30 Sa	0 31 22	5 55 52	21 33 6	27 41 51	29D 18.6	11 43.7	12 24.1	2 19.2	3 28.3	29 29.5	21 32.6	23 33.1	2 38.8

LONGITUDE — OCTOBER 1939

Day	Sid.Time	☉	0 hr ☽	Noon ☽	True ☊	☿	♀	♂	♃	♄	♅	♆	♇
1 Su	0 35 19	6♎54 49	3♉53 6	10♉ 7 2	29♎18.4	13♎25.6	13♎38.9	2♒44.2	3♈20.3	29♈25.3	21♉31.1	23♍35.3	2♌39.7
2 M	0 39 15	7 53 49	16 23 55	22 43 59	29 19.2	15 6.7	14 53.6	3 9.7	3R 12.3	29R 21.1	21R 29.5	23 37.5	2 40.5
3 Tu	0 43 12	8 52 50	29 7 31	5♊34 46	29 20.6	16 46.8	16 8.4	3 35.6	3 4.3	29 16.8	21 27.9	23 39.6	2 41.4
4 W	0 47 8	9 51 54	12♊ 6 0	18 41 29	29 22.1	18 26.2	17 23.2	4 2.0	2 56.4	29 12.4	21 26.3	23 41.8	2 42.2
5 Th	0 51 5	10 51 0	25 21 28	2♋ 6 9	29 23.3	20 4.7	18 38.0	4 28.7	2 48.5	29 8.1	21 24.6	23 44.0	2 43.0
6 F	0 55 2	11 50 8	8♋55 43	15 50 14	29R 23.9	21 42.4	19 52.9	4 55.9	2 40.7	29 3.6	21 22.9	23 46.1	2 43.7
7 Sa	0 58 58	12 49 19	22 49 44	29 54 9	29 23.7	23 19.3	21 7.7	5 23.4	2 32.8	28 59.2	21 21.1	23 48.2	2 44.5
8 Su	1 2 55	13 48 32	7♌ 3 17	14♌16 48	29 22.7	24 55.4	22 22.5	5 51.3	2 25.1	28 54.7	21 19.3	23 50.4	2 45.2
9 M	1 6 51	14 47 47	21 34 16	28 55 5	29 21.2	26 30.8	23 37.3	6 19.7	2 17.4	28 50.1	21 17.5	23 52.5	2 45.9
10 Tu	1 10 48	15 47 5	6♍18 34	13♍43 51	29 19.5	28 5.4	24 52.2	6 48.3	2 9.8	28 45.5	21 15.6	23 54.6	2 46.5
11 W	1 14 44	16 46 25	21 10 4	28 36 13	29 17.9	29 39.3	26 7.0	7 17.4	2 2.2	28 40.9	21 13.7	23 56.7	2 47.2
12 Th	1 18 41	17 45 47	6♎ 1 19	13♎24 23	29 16.7	1♏12.4	27 21.9	7 46.8	1 54.8	28 36.3	21 11.7	23 58.8	2 47.8
13 F	1 22 37	18 45 11	20 44 28	28 0 44	29D 16.1	2 44.9	28 36.8	8 16.6	1 47.4	28 31.6	21 9.8	24 0.8	2 48.4
14 Sa	1 26 34	19 44 37	5♏12 25	12♏18 54	29 16.0	4 16.6	29 51.6	8 46.7	1 40.1	28 26.9	21 7.8	24 2.9	2 48.9
15 Su	1 30 31	20 44 5	19 19 43	26 14 32	29 16.4	5 47.7	1♏ 6.5	9 17.1	1 32.9	28 22.2	21 5.7	24 4.9	2 49.5
16 M	1 34 27	21 43 35	3♐ 3 9	9♐45 32	29 17.1	7 18.0	2 21.4	9 47.9	1 25.8	28 17.5	21 3.7	24 7.0	2 50.0
17 Tu	1 38 24	22 43 7	16 21 45	22 52 2	29 17.8	8 47.7	3 36.2	10 18.9	1 18.8	28 12.7	21 1.6	24 9.0	2 50.5
18 W	1 42 20	23 42 41	29 16 39	5♑36 0	29 18.4	10 16.7	4 51.1	10 50.3	1 12.0	28 8.0	20 59.5	24 11.0	2 51.0
19 Th	1 46 17	24 42 17	11♑50 31	18 0 42	29 18.8	11 45.0	6 6.0	11 22.0	1 5.2	28 3.2	20 57.3	24 13.0	2 51.4
20 F	1 50 13	25 41 54	24 7 5	0♒10 14	29R 18.9	13 12.6	7 20.9	11 54.0	0 58.6	27 58.4	20 55.2	24 14.9	2 51.8
21 Sa	1 54 10	26 41 33	6♒10 43	12 9 7	29 18.8	14 39.4	8 35.7	12 26.3	0 52.1	27 53.6	20 53.0	24 16.9	2 52.2
22 Su	1 58 6	27 41 14	18 6 1	24 1 57	29 18.7	16 5.5	9 50.6	12 58.8	0 45.8	27 48.8	20 50.8	24 18.8	2 52.6
23 M	2 2 3	28 40 56	29 57 28	5♓53 6	29D 18.6	17 30.9	11 5.5	13 31.6	0 39.5	27 44.0	20 48.5	24 20.8	2 52.9
24 Tu	2 6 0	29 40 40	11♓49 19	17 46 35	29 18.6	18 55.5	12 20.3	14 4.6	0 33.4	27 39.2	20 46.3	24 22.7	2 53.2
25 W	2 9 56	0♏40 26	23 45 18	29 45 52	29 18.7	20 19.2	13 35.2	14 37.9	0 27.5	27 34.5	20 44.0	24 24.6	2 53.5
26 Th	2 13 53	1 40 14	5♈48 37	11♈53 50	29 18.9	21 42.1	14 50.1	15 11.5	0 21.7	27 29.7	20 41.7	24 26.4	2 53.7
27 F	2 17 49	2 40 3	18 1 46	24 12 39	29R 19.1	23 4.1	16 4.9	15 45.2	0 16.1	27 24.9	20 39.3	24 28.3	2 54.0
28 Sa	2 21 46	3 39 55	0♉26 37	6♉43 50	29 19.2	24 25.1	17 19.8	16 19.2	0 10.6	27 20.2	20 37.0	24 30.1	2 54.2
29 Su	2 25 42	4 39 48	13 4 22	19 28 18	29 19.0	25 45.0	18 34.7	16 53.5	0 5.3	27 15.5	20 34.6	24 31.9	2 54.4
30 M	2 29 39	5 39 43	25 55 38	2♊26 23	29 18.5	27 3.9	19 49.5	17 27.9	0 0.2	27 10.7	20 32.3	24 33.7	2 54.5
31 Tu	2 33 35	6 39 41	9♊ 0 32	15 38 3	29 17.7	28 21.5	21 4.4	18 2.6	29♓55.2	27 6.0	20 29.9	24 35.5	2 54.6

Astro Data	Planet Ingress	Last Aspect	☽ Ingress	Last Aspect	☽ Ingress	☽ Phases & Eclipses	Astro Data
Dy Hr Mn	Dy Hr Mn	Dy Hr Mn	Dy Hr Mn	Dy Hr Mn	Dy Hr Mn	Dy Hr Mn	1 SEPTEMBER 1939
♃∠♅ 1 21:26	☿ ♍ 7 4:58	3 0:12 ♂ □	♉ 3 10:47	2 13:43 ♆ △	♊ 3 1:38	6 20:24 ☽ 13♊20	Julian Day # 14488
☽0S 13 16:09	☊ ♎ 11 22:47	5 14:55 ☿ □	♊ 5 20:02	5 6:42 ♄ ✶	♋ 5 8:16	13 11:22 ● 19♍46	Delta T 24.2 sec
♀0S 22 11:19	♀ ♎ 20 1:02	7 13:09 ♆ □	♋ 8 1:52	7 10:24 ♄ □	♌ 7 12:10	20 10:34 ☽ 26♐34	SVP 06♓05'58"
☿0S 24 23:21	♄ ♈ 22 5:18	9 21:21 ♂ ☍	♌ 10 4:12	9 11:48 ♄ △	♍ 9 13:46	28 14:27 ○ 4♈34	Obliquity 23°26'42"
☽0N 27 14:54	☉ ♎ 23 22:49	11 15:19 ♅ □	♍ 12 4:09	11 4:29 ♆ ☌	♎ 11 14:15		⚷ Chiron 17♋27.5
♃0S 27 19:50	☿ ♎ 23 7:48	13 22:32 ♂ △	♎ 14 3:39	13 14:14 ♀ ☌	♏ 13 15:18	6 5:27 ☽ 12♋04	☽ Mean ☊ 2♏01.0
	♂ ♒ 24 1:13	16 0:18 ♂ □	♏ 16 4:43	15 8:15 ♆ ✶	♐ 15 18:36	12 20:30 ● 18♎37	
♃△♇ 5 15:25		18 5:29 ♂ ✶	♐ 18 9:02	17 21:51 ♄ △	♑ 18 1:22	12 20:39:57 ☌ T 1'33"	1 OCTOBER 1939
☽0S 11 2:29	☿ ♏ 11 5:20	20 10:34 ☉ □	♑ 20 17:11	20 7:35 ♄ □	♒ 20 11:40	20 3:24 ☽ 25♑50	Julian Day # 14518
☽0N 24 21:51	♀ ♏ 14 2:41	23 4:17 ♄ □	♒ 23 4:24	22 21:11 ☉ △	♓ 23 0:05	28 6:42 ○ 3♉57	Delta T 24.3 sec
	☉ ♏ 24 7:46	25 16:33 ♄ ✶	♓ 25 17:00	25 1:19 ♆ ☍	♈ 25 12:28	28 6:36 ☍ P 0.987	SVP 06♓05'56"
	♃ ♓ 30 0:45	27 16:18 ♆ ☍	♈ 28 5:22	27 18:04 ♄ ☌	♉ 27 23:09		Obliquity 23°26'42"
		30 15:24 ♄ ☌	♉ 30 16:29	30 7:28 ♃ ✶	♊ 30 7:31		⚷ Chiron 19♋20.8
							☽ Mean ☊ 0♏25.6

NOVEMBER 1939 LONGITUDE

Day	Sid.Time	☉	0 hr ☽	Noon ☽	True ☊	☿	♀	♂	♃	♄	♅	♆	♇
1 W	2 37 32	7♏39 40	22♊18 53	29♊ 2 58	29♎16.7	29♏37.8	22♏19.3	18♒37.4	29♓50.4	27♈ 1.4	20♉27.5	24♍37.2	2♌54.7
2 Th	2 41 29	8 39 42	5♋50 14	12♋40 35	29R 15.6	0♐52.7	23 34.2	19 12.5	29R 45.7	26R 56.7	20R 25.1	24 39.0	2 54.8
3 F	2 45 25	9 39 46	19 33 56	26 30 10	29 14.7	2 6.0	24 49.0	19 47.7	29 41.3	26 52.1	20 22.6	24 40.7	2 54.9
4 Sa	2 49 22	10 39 52	3♌29 10	10♌30 45	29D 14.1	3 17.5	26 3.9	20 23.1	29 37.0	26 47.5	20 20.2	24 42.3	2R 54.9
5 Su	2 53 18	11 40 0	17 34 47	24 41 0	29 14.1	4 27.0	27 18.8	20 58.7	29 32.9	26 43.0	20 17.7	24 44.0	2 54.9
6 M	2 57 15	12 40 10	1♍49 10	8♍58 57	29 14.6	5 34.4	28 33.7	21 34.5	29 29.0	26 38.5	20 15.3	24 45.6	2 54.9
7 Tu	3 1 11	13 40 22	16 10 1	23 21 55	29 15.6	6 39.3	29 48.5	22 10.5	29 25.2	26 34.0	20 12.8	24 47.3	2 54.8
8 W	3 5 8	14 40 36	0♎34 13	7♎46 22	29 16.8	7 41.5	1♐ 3.4	22 46.7	29 21.7	26 29.5	20 10.3	24 48.9	2 54.7
9 Th	3 9 4	15 40 52	14 57 49	22 8 0	29 17.8	8 40.7	2 18.3	23 23.0	29 18.3	26 25.2	20 7.8	24 50.4	2 54.6
10 F	3 13 1	16 41 10	29 16 17	6♏22 6	29R 18.2	9 36.4	3 33.2	23 59.5	29 15.2	26 20.8	20 5.3	24 52.0	2 54.5
11 Sa	3 16 57	17 41 30	13♏24 51	20 24 0	29 17.7	10 28.3	4 48.1	24 36.1	29 12.2	26 16.5	20 2.8	24 53.5	2 54.3
12 Su	3 20 54	18 41 52	27 19 4	4♐ 9 38	29 16.2	11 15.8	6 2.9	25 13.0	29 9.5	26 12.3	20 0.4	24 55.0	2 54.1
13 M	3 24 51	19 42 16	10♐55 24	17 36 8	29 13.7	11 58.5	7 17.8	25 49.9	29 6.9	26 8.1	19 57.9	24 56.4	2 53.9
14 Tu	3 28 47	20 42 41	24 11 41	0♑42 4	29 10.5	12 35.8	8 32.7	26 27.1	29 4.6	26 3.9	19 55.4	24 57.9	2 53.7
15 W	3 32 44	21 43 7	7♑ 7 19	13 27 39	29 6.9	13 6.9	9 47.6	27 4.4	29 2.4	25 59.9	19 52.9	24 59.3	2 53.4
16 Th	3 36 40	22 43 35	19 43 18	25 54 37	29 3.5	13 31.3	11 2.5	27 41.8	29 0.5	25 55.8	19 50.4	25 0.7	2 53.1
17 F	3 40 37	23 44 4	2♒ 2 1	8♒ 6 0	29 0.8	13 48.1	12 17.3	28 19.3	28 58.7	25 51.9	19 47.9	25 2.0	2 52.8
18 Sa	3 44 33	24 44 35	14 7 3	20 5 46	28D 59.1	13R 56.7	13 32.2	28 57.0	28 57.2	25 48.0	19 45.4	25 3.4	2 52.4
19 Su	3 48 30	25 45 6	26 2 43	1♓58 32	28 58.5	13 56.3	14 47.1	29 34.8	28 55.9	25 44.2	19 42.9	25 4.7	2 52.1
20 M	3 52 26	26 45 39	7♓53 50	13 49 15	28 59.1	13 46.3	16 1.9	0♓12.8	28 54.7	25 40.4	19 40.4	25 6.0	2 51.7
21 Tu	3 56 23	27 46 14	19 45 23	25 42 52	29 0.6	13 26.0	17 16.7	0 50.8	28 53.8	25 36.8	19 38.0	25 7.2	2 51.2
22 W	4 0 20	28 46 49	1♈42 15	7♈44 6	29 2.4	12 55.2	18 31.6	1 29.0	28 53.1	25 33.2	19 35.5	25 8.4	2 50.8
23 Th	4 4 16	29 47 26	13 48 54	19 57 9	29 4.1	12 13.7	19 46.4	2 7.3	28 52.6	25 29.6	19 33.1	25 9.6	2 50.3
24 F	4 8 13	0♐48 4	26 9 12	2♉25 25	29R 5.0	11 21.8	21 1.2	2 45.6	28D 52.3	25 26.2	19 30.6	25 10.8	2 49.8
25 Sa	4 12 9	1 48 43	8♉46 2	15 11 14	29 4.6	10 20.3	22 16.1	3 24.1	28 52.3	25 22.8	19 28.2	25 11.9	2 49.3
26 Su	4 16 6	2 49 24	21 41 7	28 15 40	29 2.5	9 10.4	23 30.9	4 2.7	28 52.4	25 19.5	19 25.8	25 13.0	2 48.8
27 M	4 20 2	3 50 5	4♊54 46	11♊38 16	28 58.8	7 54.0	24 45.7	4 41.4	28 52.7	25 16.3	19 23.4	25 14.1	2 48.2
28 Tu	4 23 59	4 50 49	18 25 53	25 17 15	28 53.6	6 33.2	26 0.5	5 20.1	28 53.3	25 13.2	19 21.0	25 15.1	2 47.6
29 W	4 27 55	5 51 33	2♋12 0	9♋ 9 40	28 47.5	5 10.7	27 15.3	5 59.0	28 54.0	25 10.2	19 18.7	25 16.1	2 47.0
30 Th	4 31 52	6 52 19	16 9 46	23 11 50	28 41.3	3 49.3	28 30.1	6 37.9	28 55.0	25 7.2	19 16.3	25 17.1	2 46.4

DECEMBER 1939 LONGITUDE

Day	Sid.Time	☉	0 hr ☽	Noon ☽	True ☊	☿	♀	♂	♃	♄	♅	♆	♇
1 F	4 35 49	7♐53 6	0♌15 21	7♌19 54	28♎35.7	2♐31.7	29♐44.8	7♓17.0	28♓56.1	25♈ 4.3	19♉14.0	25♍18.0	2♌45.7
2 Sa	4 39 45	8 53 55	14 25 3	21 30 25	28R 31.5	1R 20.3	0♑59.6	7 56.1	28 57.5	25R 1.6	19R 11.7	25 19.0	2R 45.0
3 Su	4 43 42	9 54 45	28 35 42	5♍40 38	28D 29.1	0 17.4	2 14.4	8 35.3	28 59.1	24 58.9	19 9.4	25 19.8	2 44.3
4 M	4 47 38	10 55 37	12♍44 57	19 48 31	28 28.5	29♏24.3	3 29.2	9 14.5	29 0.8	24 56.3	19 7.1	25 20.7	2 43.6
5 Tu	4 51 35	11 56 30	26 51 9	3♎52 43	28 29.3	28 42.2	4 43.9	9 53.9	29 2.8	24 53.8	19 4.8	25 21.5	2 42.8
6 W	4 55 31	12 57 24	10♎53 5	17 52 7	28 30.6	28 11.5	5 58.7	10 33.3	29 5.0	24 51.4	19 2.6	25 22.3	2 42.0
7 Th	4 59 28	13 58 20	24 49 40	1♏45 34	28R 31.6	27 52.2	7 13.4	11 12.8	29 7.4	24 49.1	19 0.4	25 23.0	2 41.2
8 F	5 3 24	14 59 17	8♏39 36	15 31 32	28 31.1	27D 44.0	8 28.2	11 52.4	29 10.0	24 46.9	18 58.2	25 23.8	2 40.4
9 Sa	5 7 21	16 0 15	22 21 8	29 8 7	28 28.6	27 46.4	9 42.9	12 32.0	29 12.8	24 44.8	18 56.1	25 24.5	2 39.6
10 Su	5 11 18	17 1 14	5♐52 12	12♐33 7	28 23.7	27 58.6	10 57.6	13 11.7	29 15.8	24 42.8	18 53.9	25 25.1	2 38.7
11 M	5 15 14	18 2 14	19 10 36	25 44 25	28 16.5	28 19.8	12 12.4	13 51.5	29 19.0	24 40.9	18 51.9	25 25.7	2 37.9
12 Tu	5 19 11	19 3 15	2♑14 24	8♑40 25	28 7.4	28 49.1	13 27.1	14 31.3	29 22.3	24 39.1	18 49.8	25 26.3	2 37.0
13 W	5 23 7	20 4 17	15 2 23	21 20 21	27 57.4	29 25.8	14 41.8	15 11.2	29 25.9	24 37.4	18 47.8	25 26.9	2 36.0
14 Th	5 27 4	21 5 20	27 34 22	3♒44 38	27 47.5	0♐ 9.0	15 56.5	15 51.2	29 29.7	24 35.8	18 45.7	25 27.4	2 35.1
15 F	5 31 0	22 6 23	9♒51 22	15 54 55	27 38.6	0 57.9	17 11.1	16 31.2	29 33.7	24 34.3	18 43.8	25 27.9	2 34.1
16 Sa	5 34 57	23 7 26	21 55 39	27 54 2	27 31.6	1 51.9	18 25.8	17 11.3	29 37.8	24 33.0	18 41.8	25 28.3	2 33.2
17 Su	5 38 54	24 8 30	3♓50 35	9♓45 52	27 26.8	2 50.4	19 40.5	17 51.4	29 42.2	24 31.7	18 39.9	25 28.7	2 32.2
18 M	5 42 50	25 9 35	15 40 29	21 35 4	27D 24.3	3 52.8	20 55.1	18 31.6	29 46.7	24 30.5	18 38.0	25 29.1	2 31.2
19 Tu	5 46 47	26 10 39	27 30 18	3♈26 51	27 23.7	4 58.6	22 9.7	19 11.8	29 51.5	24 29.5	18 36.2	25 29.5	2 30.1
20 W	5 50 43	27 11 44	9♈25 23	15 26 36	27 24.3	6 7.4	23 24.3	19 52.1	29 56.4	24 28.5	18 34.4	25 29.8	2 29.1
21 Th	5 54 40	28 12 50	21 31 10	27 39 40	27R 25.1	7 18.8	24 38.9	20 32.4	0♈ 1.5	24 27.7	18 32.6	25 30.0	2 28.0
22 F	5 58 36	29 13 55	3♉52 44	10♉10 51	27 25.1	8 32.6	25 53.4	21 12.7	0 6.8	24 27.0	18 30.9	25 30.3	2 26.9
23 Sa	6 2 33	0♑15 1	16 34 28	23 3 56	27 23.2	9 48.3	27 8.0	21 53.1	0 12.2	24 26.3	18 29.2	25 30.5	2 25.8
24 Su	6 6 29	1 16 7	29 39 28	6♊21 10	27 18.9	11 5.9	28 22.5	22 33.5	0 17.9	24 25.8	18 27.6	25 30.7	2 24.7
25 M	6 10 26	2 17 14	13♊ 8 58	20 2 42	27 11.9	12 25.0	29 37.0	23 13.9	0 23.7	24 25.5	18 26.0	25 30.8	2 23.6
26 Tu	6 14 23	3 18 21	27 1 58	4♋ 6 16	27 2.6	13 45.5	0♒51.4	23 54.4	0 29.7	24 25.2	18 24.4	25 30.9	2 22.5
27 W	6 18 19	4 19 28	11♋14 58	18 27 15	26 51.8	15 7.2	2 5.9	24 34.9	0 35.9	24 25.0	18 22.9	25 31.0	2 21.3
28 Th	6 22 16	5 20 35	25 42 19	2♌59 13	26 40.6	16 30.0	3 20.3	25 15.5	0 42.2	24D 24.9	18 21.4	25R 31.0	2 20.2
29 F	6 26 12	6 21 43	10♌17 4	17 34 57	26 30.3	17 53.8	4 34.7	25 56.0	0 48.7	24 25.0	18 19.9	25 31.0	2 19.0
30 Sa	6 30 9	7 22 51	24 52 5	2♍ 7 42	26 21.9	19 18.5	5 49.1	26 36.6	0 55.4	24 25.1	18 18.5	25 31.0	2 17.8
31 Su	6 34 5	8 23 59	9♍21 14	16 32 11	26 16.2	20 43.9	7 3.5	27 17.2	1 2.2	24 25.4	18 17.2	25 30.9	2 16.6

Astro Data	Planet Ingress	Last Aspect	☽ Ingress	Last Aspect	☽ Ingress	☽ Phases & Eclipses	Astro Data
Dy Hr Mn	Dy Hr Mn	Dy Hr Mn	Dy Hr Mn	Dy Hr Mn	Dy Hr Mn	Dy Hr Mn	1 NOVEMBER 1939
♇ R 4 8:07	☿ ♐ 1 7:03	1 13:19 ♃ □	♋ 1 13:41	2 17:54 ♄ △	♍ 3 2:23	4 13:12 ☽ 11♌13	Julian Day # 14549
☽0S 7 10:55	♀ ♐ 7 3:41	3 17:24 ♃ △	♌ 3 18:01	5 3:45 ♃ ☍	♎ 5 5:22	11 7:54 ● 18♏01	Delta T 24.3 sec
☿ R 18 11:04	♂ ♓ 19 15:56	5 18:00 ♀ □	♍ 5 20:57	6 23:59 ♄ ☍	♏ 7 8:57	18 23:21 ☽ 25♒43	SVP 06♓05'53"
☽0N 21 6:12	☉ ♐ 23 4:59	7 22:00 ♃ ☍	♎ 7 23:03	9 12:11 ♃ △	♐ 9 13:32	26 21:54 ○ 3♊45	Obliquity 23°26'42"
♃ D 24 21:17		9 19:06 ♄ ☍	♏ 10 1:14	11 18:40 ♃ □	♑ 11 19:51		⚷ Chiron 20♋03.7
♄⚻♆ 27 12:52	♀ ♑ 1 4:52	12 3:12 ♃ △	♐ 12 4:41	14 3:45 ♃ ⚹	♒ 14 4:42	3 20:40 ☽ 10♍47	☽ Mean ☊ 28♎47.1
	☿ ♏ 3 7:22	14 8:58 ♃ □	♑ 14 10:42	16 5:15 ♄ ⚹	♓ 16 16:14	10 21:45 ● 17♐57	
☽0S 4 17:31	☿ ♐ 13 19:16	16 18:01 ♃ ⚹	♒ 16 20:00	19 4:47 ♃ ☌	♈ 19 5:03	18 21:04 ☽ 26♓03	1 DECEMBER 1939
☿ D 8 6:23	♃ ♈ 20 17:03	19 7:33 ♂ ☌	♓ 19 8:00	21 14:15 ☉ △	♉ 21 16:32	26 11:28 ○ 3♋48	Julian Day # 14579
☽0N 18 15:38	☉ ♑ 22 18:06	21 18:22 ♃ ☌	♈ 21 20:36	23 21:26 ♀ △	♊ 24 0:37		Delta T 24.3 sec
♄ D 28 1:11	♀ ♒ 25 7:25	23 22:38 ♄ ☌	♉ 24 7:23	25 21:24 ♆ □	♋ 26 5:03		SVP 06♓05'49"
♆ R 28 14:15		26 13:07 ♃ ⚹	♊ 26 15:09	27 23:41 ♆ ⚹	♌ 28 7:05		Obliquity 23°26'41"
		28 18:17 ♃ □	♋ 28 20:11	29 23:16 ♄ △	♍ 30 8:29		⚷ Chiron 19♋23.3R
		30 21:45 ♃ △	♌ 30 23:34				☽ Mean ☊ 27♎11.8

LONGITUDE JANUARY 1940

Day	Sid.Time	☉	0 hr ☽	Noon ☽	True ☊	☿	♀	♂	♃	♄	♅	♆	♇
1 M	6 38 2	9♑25 8	23♍40 11	0♎45 1	26♎13.2	22♐10.1	8♒17.8	27♓57.8	1♈ 9.2	24♈25.8	18♉15.9	25♍30.8	2♌15.4
2 Tu	6 41 58	10 26 17	7♎46 32	14 44 44	26D 12.3	23 37.0	9 32.1	28 38.5	1 16.4	24 26.3	18R 14.6	25R 30.7	2R 14.1
3 W	6 45 55	11 27 27	21 39 37	28 31 18	26R 12.4	25 4.5	10 46.4	29 19.2	1 23.7	24 26.9	18 13.4	25 30.5	2 12.9
4 Th	6 49 52	12 28 36	5♏19 52	12♏ 5 27	26 12.2	26 32.6	12 0.6	29 59.9	1 31.2	24 27.6	18 12.2	25 30.3	2 11.6
5 F	6 53 48	13 29 47	18 48 11	25 28 8	26 10.4	28 1.3	13 14.9	0♈40.6	1 38.8	24 28.4	18 11.1	25 30.1	2 10.4
6 Sa	6 57 45	14 30 57	2♐ 5 25	8♐40 2	26 6.0	29 30.4	14 29.1	1 21.3	1 46.6	24 29.4	18 10.0	25 29.8	2 9.1
7 Su	7 1 41	15 32 8	15 12 1	21 41 21	25 58.4	1♑ 0.1	15 43.3	2 2.1	1 54.5	24 30.4	18 8.9	25 29.5	2 7.8
8 M	7 5 38	16 33 18	28 7 58	4♑31 50	25 47.9	2 30.3	16 57.4	2 42.9	2 2.6	24 31.6	18 7.9	25 29.2	2 6.5
9 Tu	7 9 34	17 34 29	10♑52 52	17 11 0	25 34.9	4 0.9	18 11.6	3 23.7	2 10.9	24 32.9	18 7.0	25 28.8	2 5.3
10 W	7 13 31	18 35 39	23 26 13	29 38 30	25 20.5	5 32.0	19 25.6	4 4.5	2 19.3	24 34.2	18 6.1	25 28.4	2 4.0
11 Th	7 17 27	19 36 49	5♒47 51	11♒54 23	25 6.0	7 3.6	20 39.7	4 45.3	2 27.8	24 35.7	18 5.3	25 28.0	2 2.6
12 F	7 21 24	20 37 59	17 58 11	23 59 28	24 52.6	8 35.6	21 53.7	5 26.2	2 36.5	24 37.3	18 4.5	25 27.5	2 1.3
13 Sa	7 25 21	21 39 8	29 58 29	5♓55 33	24 41.4	10 8.1	23 7.7	6 7.0	2 45.3	24 39.0	18 3.7	25 27.0	2 0.0
14 Su	7 29 17	22 40 17	11♓51 2	17 45 23	24 33.0	11 41.1	24 21.6	6 47.9	2 54.3	24 40.9	18 3.0	25 26.5	1 58.7
15 M	7 33 14	23 41 25	23 39 6	29 32 44	24 27.6	13 14.5	25 35.5	7 28.8	3 3.4	24 42.8	18 2.4	25 25.9	1 57.3
16 Tu	7 37 10	24 42 32	5♈26 53	11♈22 11	24 24.8	14 48.5	26 49.4	8 9.7	3 12.6	24 44.8	18 1.8	25 25.3	1 56.0
17 W	7 41 7	25 43 39	17 19 17	23 18 55	24 23.9	16 22.9	28 3.2	8 50.6	3 22.0	24 46.9	18 1.3	25 24.6	1 54.7
18 Th	7 45 3	26 44 45	29 21 46	5♉28 32	24 23.8	17 57.8	29 17.0	9 31.5	3 31.5	24 49.2	18 0.8	25 24.0	1 53.3
19 F	7 49 0	27 45 50	11♉39 54	17 56 33	24 23.4	19 33.3	0♓30.7	10 12.4	3 41.1	24 51.5	18 0.3	25 23.3	1 52.0
20 Sa	7 52 56	28 46 54	24 19 4	0♊47 59	24 21.4	21 9.2	1 44.4	10 53.3	3 50.9	24 54.0	17 60.0	25 22.6	1 50.6
21 Su	7 56 53	29 47 57	7♊23 43	14 6 34	24 17.0	22 45.8	2 58.0	11 34.2	4 0.8	24 56.6	17 59.6	25 21.8	1 49.3
22 M	8 0 50	0♒49 0	20 56 41	27 54 2	24 9.9	24 22.9	4 11.6	12 15.1	4 10.8	24 59.2	17 59.4	25 21.0	1 47.9
23 Tu	8 4 46	1 50 2	4♋58 24	12♋ 9 19	24 0.3	26 0.5	5 25.1	12 56.0	4 20.9	25 2.0	17 59.1	25 20.2	1 46.6
24 W	8 8 43	2 51 2	19 26 11	26 48 7	23 48.9	27 38.8	6 38.6	13 36.9	4 31.2	25 4.8	17 59.0	25 19.4	1 45.2
25 Th	8 12 39	3 52 2	4♌14 7	11♌43 3	23 36.9	29 17.6	7 52.0	14 17.8	4 41.5	25 7.8	17 58.8	25 18.5	1 43.9
26 F	8 16 36	4 53 1	19 13 42	26 44 48	23 25.7	0♒57.1	9 5.3	14 58.7	4 52.0	25 10.9	17D 58.8	25 17.6	1 42.5
27 Sa	8 20 32	5 54 0	4♍15 10	11♍43 39	23 16.5	2 37.2	10 18.6	15 39.6	5 2.6	25 14.0	17 58.7	25 16.7	1 41.2
28 Su	8 24 29	6 54 57	19 9 15	26 31 10	23 10.1	4 18.0	11 31.8	16 20.5	5 13.3	25 17.3	17 58.8	25 15.7	1 39.8
29 M	8 28 25	7 55 54	3♎48 43	11♎ 1 26	23 6.5	5 59.4	12 45.0	17 1.4	5 24.1	25 20.6	17 58.9	25 14.7	1 38.5
30 Tu	8 32 22	8 56 50	18 9 2	25 11 22	23D 5.3	7 41.5	13 58.1	17 42.2	5 35.0	25 24.1	17 59.0	25 13.7	1 37.1
31 W	8 36 19	9 57 46	2♏ 8 26	9♏ 0 22	23R 5.4	9 24.3	15 11.1	18 23.1	5 46.0	25 27.6	17 59.2	25 12.7	1 35.8

LONGITUDE FEBRUARY 1940

Day	Sid.Time	☉	0 hr ☽	Noon ☽	True ☊	☿	♀	♂	♃	♄	♅	♆	♇
1 Th	8 40 15	10♒58 41	15♏47 19	22♏29 34	23♎ 5.4	11♒ 7.8	16♓24.1	19♈ 4.0	5♈57.1	25♈31.3	17♉59.4	25♍11.6	1♌34.5
2 F	8 44 12	11 59 35	29 7 24	5♐41 6	23R 4.2	12 51.9	17 37.1	19 44.8	6 8.4	25 35.0	17 59.7	25R 10.5	1R 33.1
3 Sa	8 48 8	13 0 28	12♐11 0	18 37 22	23 0.6	14 36.7	18 49.9	20 25.7	6 19.7	25 38.9	18 0.1	25 9.4	1 31.8
4 Su	8 52 5	14 1 21	25 0 29	1♑20 34	22 54.3	16 22.2	20 2.7	21 6.5	6 31.1	25 42.8	18 0.5	25 8.3	1 30.5
5 M	8 56 1	15 2 13	7♑37 51	13 52 29	22 45.2	18 8.3	21 15.4	21 47.4	6 42.7	25 46.8	18 1.0	25 7.1	1 29.2
6 Tu	8 59 58	16 3 4	20 4 39	26 14 27	22 33.8	19 55.1	22 28.1	22 28.2	6 54.3	25 50.9	18 1.5	25 5.9	1 27.9
7 W	9 3 54	17 3 53	2♒22 0	8♒27 24	22 21.1	21 42.4	23 40.7	23 9.0	7 6.0	25 55.1	18 2.0	25 4.7	1 26.6
8 Th	9 7 51	18 4 42	14 30 46	20 32 12	22 8.3	23 30.3	24 53.2	23 49.8	7 17.8	25 59.4	18 2.7	25 3.5	1 25.3
9 F	9 11 48	19 5 29	26 31 50	2♓29 49	21 56.3	25 18.6	26 5.6	24 30.7	7 29.7	26 3.8	18 3.3	25 2.2	1 24.0
10 Sa	9 15 44	20 6 15	8♓26 21	14 21 39	21 46.3	27 7.3	27 18.0	25 11.5	7 41.7	26 8.2	18 4.0	25 0.9	1 22.7
11 Su	9 19 41	21 6 59	20 15 59	26 9 41	21 38.8	28 56.3	28 30.2	25 52.3	7 53.8	26 12.8	18 4.8	24 59.6	1 21.4
12 M	9 23 37	22 7 42	2♈ 3 5	7♈56 38	21 34.0	0♓45.4	29 42.4	26 33.0	8 6.0	26 17.4	18 5.6	24 58.3	1 20.2
13 Tu	9 27 34	23 8 23	13 50 46	19 46 1	21D 31.8	2 34.6	0♈54.5	27 13.8	8 18.2	26 22.1	18 6.5	24 57.0	1 18.9
14 W	9 31 30	24 9 3	25 42 55	1♉42 5	21 31.6	4 23.6	2 6.6	27 54.6	8 30.5	26 26.9	18 7.4	24 55.6	1 17.7
15 Th	9 35 27	25 9 41	7♉44 6	13 49 39	21 32.4	6 12.3	3 18.5	28 35.3	8 42.9	26 31.8	18 8.4	24 54.2	1 16.5
16 F	9 39 23	26 10 18	19 59 22	26 13 55	21R 33.3	8 0.3	4 30.3	29 16.1	8 55.4	26 36.7	18 9.4	24 52.8	1 15.3
17 Sa	9 43 20	27 10 53	2♊33 54	8♊59 57	21 33.3	9 47.5	5 42.0	29 56.8	9 8.0	26 41.7	18 10.5	24 51.4	1 14.1
18 Su	9 47 17	28 11 26	15 32 34	22 12 13	21 31.7	11 33.4	6 53.7	0♉37.5	9 20.6	26 46.8	18 11.7	24 50.0	1 12.9
19 M	9 51 13	29 11 57	28 59 12	5♋53 43	21 27.9	13 17.7	8 5.2	1 18.2	9 33.3	26 52.0	18 12.8	24 48.5	1 11.7
20 Tu	9 55 10	0♓12 26	12♋55 46	20 5 9	21 22.2	14 59.9	9 16.6	1 58.8	9 46.1	26 57.3	18 14.1	24 47.1	1 10.5
21 W	9 59 6	1 12 54	27 21 27	4♌44 4	21 14.9	16 39.7	10 27.9	2 39.5	9 59.0	27 2.6	18 15.4	24 45.6	1 9.4
22 Th	10 3 3	2 13 20	12♌12 9	19 44 38	21 7.0	18 16.4	11 39.1	3 20.1	10 11.9	27 8.0	18 16.7	24 44.1	1 8.3
23 F	10 6 59	3 13 44	27 20 20	4♍57 57	20 59.4	19 49.5	12 50.2	4 0.7	10 24.9	27 13.5	18 18.1	24 42.6	1 7.1
24 Sa	10 10 56	4 14 6	12♍36 5	20 13 25	20 53.3	21 18.5	14 1.2	4 41.3	10 37.9	27 19.0	18 19.5	24 41.0	1 6.0
25 Su	10 14 52	5 14 27	27 48 38	5♎20 35	20 49.1	22 42.7	15 12.1	5 21.9	10 51.0	27 24.6	18 20.9	24 39.5	1 4.9
26 M	10 18 49	6 14 46	12♎48 16	20 10 50	20D 47.1	24 1.4	16 22.8	6 2.4	11 4.2	27 30.3	18 22.5	24 37.9	1 3.9
27 Tu	10 22 46	7 15 3	27 27 43	4♏38 26	20 47.0	25 14.2	17 33.4	6 43.0	11 17.4	27 36.1	18 24.0	24 36.4	1 2.8
28 W	10 26 42	8 15 20	11♏42 48	18 40 42	20 48.1	26 20.2	18 43.9	7 23.5	11 30.7	27 41.9	18 25.6	24 34.8	1 1.8
29 Th	10 30 39	9 15 34	25 32 14	2♐17 34	20 49.5	27 19.1	19 54.3	8 4.0	11 44.0	27 47.8	18 27.3	24 33.2	1 0.7

Astro Data	Planet Ingress	Last Aspect	☽ Ingress	Last Aspect	☽ Ingress	☽ Phases & Eclipses	Astro Data
Dy Hr Mn	Dy Hr Mn	Dy Hr Mn	Dy Hr Mn	Dy Hr Mn	Dy Hr Mn	Dy Hr Mn	1 JANUARY 1940
☽0S 1 0:04	♂ ♈ 4 0:05	1 7:38 ♂ ☍	♎ 1 10:43	1 16:51 ♆ ⚹	♐ 2 1:36	2 4:56 ☽ 10♎39	Julian Day # 14610
♂0N 4 21:25	☿ ♑ 6 7:56	3 6:40 ☿ ⚹	♏ 3 14:36	4 1:20 ♄ △	♑ 4 9:27	9 13:53 ● 18♑10	Delta T 24.3 sec
♃△♇ 8 9:53	♀ ♓ 18 14:00	5 12:03 ♆ ⚹	♐ 5 20:12	6 11:18 ♄ □	♒ 6 19:21	17 18:21 ☽ 26♈30	SVP 06♓05'43"
♃0N 13 18:35	☉ ♒ 21 4:44	7 19:04 ♆ □	♑ 8 3:30	8 23:03 ♄ ⚹	♓ 9 6:58	24 23:22 ○ 3♌50	Obliquity 23°26'41"
♃∠♅ 14 21:33	☿ ♒ 25 10:14	10 3:56 ♆ △	♒ 10 12:42	11 18:41 ♀ ☌	♈ 11 19:49	31 14:47 ☽ 10♏35	⚷ Chiron 17♋34.4R
☽0N 15 0:56		12 13:18 ♄ ⚹	♓ 13 0:03	14 4:40 ♂ ☌	♉ 14 8:36		☽ Mean ☊ 25♎33.3
♅ D 26 20:26	☿ ♓ 11 14:01	15 3:37 ♆ ☍	♈ 15 12:55	16 12:55 ☉ □	♊ 16 19:10	8 7:45 ● 18♒24	
♄⊼♆ 27 15:06	♀ ♈ 12 5:51	17 23:50 ♀ ⚹	♉ 18 1:15	19 0:24 ☉ △	♋ 19 1:46	16 12:55 ☽ 26♉43	1 FEBRUARY 1940
☽0S 28 8:31	♂ ♉ 17 1:54	20 8:59 ☉ △	♊ 20 10:32	20 23:29 ♄ □	♌ 21 4:19	23 9:55 ○ 3♍39	Julian Day # 14641
	☉ ♓ 19 19:04	22 7:37 ♆ □	♋ 22 15:35	22 23:49 ♄ △	♍ 23 4:11		Delta T 24.4 sec
☽0N 11 8:57		24 15:02 ☿ ☍	♌ 24 17:10	24 19:01 ♆ ☌	♎ 25 3:29		SVP 06♓05'39"
♀0N 13 10:59		26 9:32 ♄ △	♍ 26 17:12	27 0:14 ♄ ☍	♏ 27 4:13		Obliquity 23°26'41"
☽0S 24 19:10		28 9:56 ♆ ☌	♎ 28 17:43	29 3:22 ☿ △	♐ 29 7:54		⚷ Chiron 15♋28.5R
☿0N 28 5:00		30 12:25 ♄ ☍	♏ 30 20:17				☽ Mean ☊ 23♎54.8

MARCH 1940 LONGITUDE

Day	Sid.Time	☉	0 hr ☽	Noon ☽	True ☊	☿	♀	♂	♃	♄	♅	♆	♇
1 F	10 34 35	10♓15 48	8♐57 0	15♐30 51	20♎50.2	28♓10.1	21♈ 4.6	8♉44.4	11♈57.4	27♈53.7	18♉29.0	24♍31.6	0♌59.7
2 Sa	10 38 32	11 16 0	21 59 31	28 23 25	20R49.6	28 52.9	22 14.7	9 24.9	12 10.9	27 59.7	18 30.8	24R30.0	0R58.7
3 Su	10 42 28	12 16 10	4♑42 59	10♑58 36	20 47.3	29 27.0	23 24.7	10 5.3	12 24.4	28 5.8	18 32.6	24 28.4	0 57.8
4 M	10 46 25	13 16 19	17 10 43	23 19 43	20 43.2	29 52.1	24 34.6	10 45.8	12 37.9	28 11.9	18 34.4	24 26.8	0 56.8
5 Tu	10 50 21	14 16 26	29 25 57	5♒29 45	20 37.6	0♈ 8.1	25 44.3	11 26.2	12 51.6	28 18.1	18 36.3	24 25.2	0 55.9
6 W	10 54 18	15 16 31	11♒31 28	17 31 21	20 31.1	0R14.8	26 53.9	12 6.5	13 5.2	28 24.3	18 38.2	24 23.5	0 55.0
7 Th	10 58 15	16 16 35	23 29 42	29 26 44	20 24.5	0 12.4	28 3.4	12 46.9	13 18.9	28 30.6	18 40.2	24 21.9	0 54.1
8 F	11 2 11	17 16 37	5♓22 43	11♓17 52	20 18.3	0 1.0	29 12.7	13 27.3	13 32.7	28 37.0	18 42.2	24 20.2	0 53.2
9 Sa	11 6 8	18 16 37	17 12 24	23 6 33	20 13.2	29♓41.0	0♉21.8	14 7.6	13 46.5	28 43.4	18 44.3	24 18.6	0 52.3
10 Su	11 10 4	19 16 35	29 0 33	4♈54 41	20 9.6	29 13.0	1 30.8	14 47.9	14 0.3	28 49.9	18 46.4	24 16.9	0 51.5
11 M	11 14 1	20 16 31	10♈49 11	16 44 23	20D 7.7	28 37.7	2 39.7	15 28.2	14 14.2	28 56.4	18 48.5	24 15.3	0 50.7
12 Tu	11 17 57	21 16 25	22 40 37	28 38 13	20 7.3	27 56.0	3 48.4	16 8.5	14 28.1	29 3.0	18 50.7	24 13.6	0 49.9
13 W	11 21 54	22 16 17	4♉37 35	10♉39 8	20 8.1	27 8.9	4 56.9	16 48.7	14 42.1	29 9.6	18 52.9	24 11.9	0 49.1
14 Th	11 25 50	23 16 7	16 43 21	22 50 40	20 9.6	26 17.6	6 5.2	17 29.0	14 56.0	29 16.2	18 55.2	24 10.3	0 48.3
15 F	11 29 47	24 15 55	29 1 37	5♊16 41	20 11.4	25 23.2	7 13.4	18 9.2	15 10.1	29 23.0	18 57.5	24 8.6	0 47.6
16 Sa	11 33 43	25 15 41	11♊36 24	18 1 14	20 12.8	24 27.1	8 21.4	18 49.4	15 24.1	29 29.7	18 59.8	24 6.9	0 46.9
17 Su	11 37 40	26 15 24	24 31 41	1♋ 8 10	20R13.5	23 30.4	9 29.2	19 29.5	15 38.2	29 36.5	19 2.2	24 5.3	0 46.2
18 M	11 41 37	27 15 5	7♋51 2	14 40 33	20 13.1	22 34.5	10 36.8	20 9.7	15 52.4	29 43.4	19 4.6	24 3.6	0 45.6
19 Tu	11 45 33	28 14 44	21 36 52	28 39 59	20 11.7	21 40.3	11 44.3	20 49.8	16 6.5	29 50.3	19 7.0	24 1.9	0 44.9
20 W	11 49 30	29 14 20	5♌49 45	13♌ 5 50	20 9.5	20 48.9	12 51.5	21 29.9	16 20.7	29 57.2	19 9.5	24 0.3	0 44.3
21 Th	11 53 26	0♈13 54	20 27 44	27 54 43	20 6.8	20 1.3	13 58.5	22 9.9	16 34.9	0♉ 4.2	19 12.0	23 58.6	0 43.7
22 F	11 57 23	1 13 26	5♍25 55	13♍ 0 16	20 4.2	19 18.0	15 5.3	22 50.0	16 49.1	0 11.2	19 14.6	23 57.0	0 43.1
23 Sa	12 1 19	2 12 56	20 36 39	28 13 47	20 2.2	18 39.8	16 11.9	23 30.0	17 3.4	0 18.2	19 17.2	23 55.3	0 42.6
24 Su	12 5 16	3 12 23	5♎50 25	13♎25 19	20D 0.9	18 6.9	17 18.2	24 10.0	17 17.7	0 25.3	19 19.8	23 53.7	0 42.1
25 M	12 9 12	4 11 49	20 57 18	28 25 19	20 0.5	17 39.8	18 24.4	24 49.9	17 32.0	0 32.4	19 22.5	23 52.0	0 41.6
26 Tu	12 13 9	5 11 13	5♏48 26	13♏ 5 56	20 0.9	17 18.6	19 30.3	25 29.9	17 46.3	0 39.6	19 25.2	23 50.4	0 41.1
27 W	12 17 6	6 10 34	20 17 15	27 21 59	20 1.9	17 3.2	20 35.9	26 9.8	18 0.6	0 46.7	19 27.9	23 48.8	0 40.6
28 Th	12 21 2	7 9 54	4♐19 58	11♐11 7	20 3.0	16 53.8	21 41.4	26 49.7	18 15.0	0 54.0	19 30.6	23 47.2	0 40.2
29 F	12 24 59	8 9 13	17 55 32	24 33 27	20 3.9	16D50.3	22 46.5	27 29.6	18 29.4	1 1.2	19 33.4	23 45.6	0 39.8
30 Sa	12 28 55	9 8 29	1♑ 5 9	7♑31 2	20R 4.5	16 52.4	23 51.5	28 9.4	18 43.8	1 8.5	19 36.2	23 44.0	0 39.4
31 Su	12 32 52	10 7 44	13 51 34	20 7 12	20 4.6	17 0.0	24 56.1	28 49.2	18 58.2	1 15.8	19 39.1	23 42.4	0 39.1

APRIL 1940 LONGITUDE

Day	Sid.Time	☉	0 hr ☽	Noon ☽	True ☊	☿	♀	♂	♃	♄	♅	♆	♇
1 M	12 36 48	11♈ 6 57	26♑18 27	2♒25 51	20♎ 4.2	17♓12.9	26♉ 0.5	29♉29.0	19♈12.6	1♉23.1	19♉41.9	23♍40.8	0♌38.8
2 Tu	12 40 45	12 6 8	8♒29 54	14 31 8	20R 3.5	17 30.9	27 4.7	0♊ 8.8	19 27.0	1 30.5	19 44.9	23R39.2	0R38.5
3 W	12 44 41	13 5 17	20 30 1	26 27 2	20 2.6	17 53.8	28 8.5	0 48.6	19 41.5	1 37.9	19 47.8	23 37.7	0 38.2
4 Th	12 48 38	14 4 25	2♓22 39	8♓17 16	20 1.7	18 21.2	29 12.1	1 28.3	19 55.9	1 45.3	19 50.7	23 36.1	0 37.9
5 F	12 52 35	15 3 30	14 11 17	20 5 4	20 1.0	18 53.0	0♊15.4	2 8.0	20 10.4	1 52.7	19 53.7	23 34.6	0 37.7
6 Sa	12 56 31	16 2 34	25 58 57	1♈53 16	20 0.4	19 29.0	1 18.3	2 47.7	20 24.9	2 0.2	19 56.7	23 33.1	0 37.5
7 Su	13 0 28	17 1 35	7♈48 19	13 44 21	20 0.2	20 8.9	2 21.0	3 27.4	20 39.3	2 7.7	19 59.8	23 31.6	0 37.3
8 M	13 4 24	18 0 35	19 41 40	25 40 30	20D 0.1	20 52.6	3 23.3	4 7.1	20 53.8	2 15.2	20 2.8	23 30.1	0 37.2
9 Tu	13 8 21	18 59 33	1♉41 5	7♉43 41	20 0.1	21 39.8	4 25.3	4 46.7	21 8.3	2 22.7	20 5.9	23 28.6	0 37.1
10 W	13 12 17	19 58 28	13 48 32	19 55 54	20R 0.2	22 30.3	5 27.0	5 26.3	21 22.8	2 30.2	20 9.0	23 27.1	0 37.0
11 Th	13 16 14	20 57 22	26 6 1	2♊19 10	20 0.1	23 24.0	6 28.3	6 5.9	21 37.3	2 37.8	20 12.1	23 25.7	0 36.9
12 F	13 20 10	21 56 13	8♊35 37	14 55 39	19 59.9	24 20.8	7 29.2	6 45.5	21 51.8	2 45.3	20 15.3	23 24.3	0 36.8
13 Sa	13 24 7	22 55 3	21 19 32	27 47 33	19 59.6	25 20.4	8 29.8	7 25.0	22 6.2	2 52.9	20 18.4	23 22.9	0D36.8
14 Su	13 28 3	23 53 50	4♋19 59	10♋57 5	19 59.3	26 22.8	9 30.0	8 4.5	22 20.7	3 0.5	20 21.6	23 21.5	0 36.8
15 M	13 32 0	24 52 34	17 39 5	24 26 9	19D 59.1	27 27.8	10 29.8	8 44.0	22 35.2	3 8.1	20 24.8	23 20.1	0 36.9
16 Tu	13 35 57	25 51 17	1♌18 25	8♌15 56	19 59.1	28 35.3	11 29.1	9 23.5	22 49.7	3 15.7	20 28.1	23 18.7	0 36.9
17 W	13 39 53	26 49 57	15 18 41	22 26 31	19 59.4	29 45.3	12 28.1	10 2.9	23 4.1	3 23.4	20 31.3	23 17.4	0 37.0
18 Th	13 43 50	27 48 35	29 39 10	6♍56 15	19 59.9	0♈57.6	13 26.5	10 42.4	23 18.6	3 31.0	20 34.6	23 16.1	0 37.1
19 F	13 47 46	28 47 11	14♍17 17	21 41 36	20 0.6	2 12.2	14 24.6	11 21.8	23 33.0	3 38.6	20 37.9	23 14.8	0 37.3
20 Sa	13 51 43	29 45 44	29 8 26	6♎36 55	20 1.3	3 28.9	15 22.1	12 1.1	23 47.5	3 46.3	20 41.2	23 13.5	0 37.4
21 Su	13 55 39	0♉44 15	14♎ 6 6	21 34 57	20R 1.8	4 47.8	16 19.1	12 40.5	24 1.9	3 53.9	20 44.5	23 12.3	0 37.6
22 M	13 59 36	1 42 45	29 2 28	6♏27 37	20 1.7	6 8.7	17 15.7	13 19.8	24 16.3	4 1.6	20 47.8	23 11.0	0 37.8
23 Tu	14 3 32	2 41 12	13♏49 27	21 7 5	20 1.0	7 31.7	18 11.7	13 59.1	24 30.7	4 9.2	20 51.1	23 9.8	0 38.1
24 W	14 7 29	3 39 38	28 19 46	5♐26 52	19 59.7	8 56.7	19 7.2	14 38.4	24 45.1	4 16.9	20 54.5	23 8.6	0 38.3
25 Th	14 11 26	4 38 2	12♐27 56	19 22 37	19 57.9	10 23.6	20 2.1	15 17.6	24 59.4	4 24.5	20 57.9	23 7.5	0 38.6
26 F	14 15 22	5 36 25	26 10 47	2♑52 24	19 55.9	11 52.4	20 56.4	15 56.9	25 13.8	4 32.2	21 1.2	23 6.3	0 39.0
27 Sa	14 19 19	6 34 45	9♑27 34	15 56 33	19 54.0	13 23.1	21 50.2	16 36.1	25 28.1	4 39.8	21 4.6	23 5.2	0 39.3
28 Su	14 23 15	7 33 5	22 19 40	28 37 21	19 52.6	14 55.7	22 43.3	17 15.3	25 42.4	4 47.5	21 8.0	23 4.1	0 39.7
29 M	14 27 12	8 31 22	4♒50 4	10♒58 21	19D52.0	16 30.2	23 35.8	17 54.4	25 56.7	4 55.2	21 11.5	23 3.1	0 40.1
30 Tu	14 31 8	9 29 38	17 2 48	23 3 58	19 52.1	18 6.5	24 27.6	18 33.6	26 11.0	5 2.8	21 14.9	23 2.0	0 40.5

Astro Data Dy Hr Mn	Planet Ingress Dy Hr Mn	Last Aspect Dy Hr Mn	☽ Ingress Dy Hr Mn	Last Aspect Dy Hr Mn	☽ Ingress Dy Hr Mn	☽ Phases & Eclipses Dy Hr Mn	Astro Data
☿ R 6 5:32	☿ ♈ 4 10:09	2 13:34 ☿ □	♑ 2 15:02	1 6:34 ♂ △	♒ 1 7:13	1 2:35 ☽ 10♐22	1 MARCH 1940
☽0N 9 15:30	☿ ♓ 8 1:25	4 21:45 ♄ □	♒ 5 1:07	3 16:56 ♀ □	♓ 3 19:11	9 2:23 ● 18♓23	Julian Day # 14670
☿0S 17 20:29	♀ ♉ 8 16:25	7 10:12 ♄ ⚹	♓ 7 13:07	5 19:04 ♆ ☍	♈ 6 8:10	17 3:25 ☽ 26♊24	Delta T 24.4 sec
☽0S 23 6:36	☉ ♈ 20 18:24	10 0:24 ☿ ☌	♈ 10 2:01	8 2:28 ♃ ☌	♉ 8 20:39	23 19:33 ○ 3♎01	SVP 06♓05'36"
♄□♇ 26 4:47	♄ ♉ 20 9:40	12 12:57 ♄ ☌	♉ 12 14:44	10 18:49 ♆ △	♊ 11 7:32	23 19:48 ☍ A 0.079	Obliquity 23°26'41"
☿ D 29 2:57		14 17:26 ☿ ⚹	♊ 15 1:53	13 8:06 ☿ □	♋ 13 16:04	30 16:20 ☽ 9♑49	⚷ Chiron 14♋10.4R
	♂ ♊ 1 18:41	17 9:19 ♄ ⚹	♋ 17 9:57	15 18:51 ☿ △	♌ 15 21:44		☽ Mean ☊ 22♎22.7
♃⚺♅ 3 13:11	♀ ♊ 4 18:10	19 14:05 ♄ □	♌ 19 14:15	17 20:43 ☉ △	♍ 18 0:34	7 20:18 ● 17♈52	
☽0N 5 21:32	☿ ♈ 17 4:56	21 2:53 ♂ □	♍ 21 15:21	19 14:29 ♆ ☌	♎ 20 1:23	7 20:20:56 ☌ A 7'30"	1 APRIL 1940
♇ D 13 3:15	☉ ♉ 20 5:51	23 5:12 ♆ ☌	♎ 23 14:47	21 16:12 ♃ ☍	♏ 22 1:33	15 13:45 ☽ 25♋26	Julian Day # 14701
♃⚻♆ 17 20:13		24 18:27 ♃ ☍	♏ 25 14:33	23 15:22 ♆ ⚹	♐ 24 2:48	22 4:37 ○ 1♏54	Delta T 24.5 sec
☽0S 19 16:58		27 10:26 ♂ ☍	♐ 27 16:31	25 22:17 ♃ △	♑ 26 6:50	22 4:26 ☍ A 0.868	SVP 06♓05'33"
☿0N 22 3:14		29 10:32 ♆ □	♑ 29 21:59	28 6:33 ♃ □	♒ 28 14:39	29 7:49 ☽ 8♒50	Obliquity 23°26'41"
							⚷ Chiron 14♋06.2
							☽ Mean ☊ 20♎44.2

LONGITUDE — MAY 1940

Day	Sid.Time	☉	0 hr ☽	Noon ☽	True ☊	☿	♀	♂	♃	♄	♅	♆	♇
1 W	14 35 5	10♉27 53	29♒ 2 29	4♓58 55	19♎53.0	19♈44.7	25♊18.8	19♊12.7	26♈25.2	5♉10.4	21♉18.3	23♍ 1.0	0♌40.9
2 Th	14 39 1	11 26 6	10♓53 53	16 47 57	19 54.5	21 24.7	26 9.2	19 51.8	26 39.5	5 18.1	21 21.8	23R 0.0	0 41.4
3 F	14 42 58	12 24 17	22 41 39	28 35 31	19 56.2	23 6.6	26 59.0	20 30.9	26 53.7	5 25.7	21 25.2	22 59.0	0 41.9
4 Sa	14 46 55	13 22 27	4♈30 2	10♈25 39	19 57.6	24 50.3	27 47.9	21 10.0	27 7.9	5 33.3	21 28.7	22 58.1	0 42.4
5 Su	14 50 51	14 20 36	16 22 47	22 21 49	19R 58.4	26 35.9	28 36.1	21 49.0	27 22.0	5 40.9	21 32.1	22 57.2	0 42.9
6 M	14 54 48	15 18 43	28 23 3	4♉26 47	19 58.2	28 23.4	29 23.5	22 28.1	27 36.1	5 48.5	21 35.6	22 56.3	0 43.5
7 Tu	14 58 44	16 16 48	10♉33 16	16 42 41	19 56.7	0♉12.7	0♋10.1	23 7.1	27 50.2	5 56.1	21 39.1	22 55.4	0 44.1
8 W	15 2 41	17 14 52	22 55 12	29 10 56	19 53.9	2 3.9	0 55.7	23 46.1	28 4.3	6 3.7	21 42.5	22 54.6	0 44.7
9 Th	15 6 37	18 12 54	5♊29 59	11♊52 25	19 49.9	3 56.9	1 40.5	24 25.0	28 18.3	6 11.3	21 46.0	22 53.8	0 45.4
10 F	15 10 34	19 10 54	18 18 15	24 47 31	19 45.3	5 51.8	2 24.3	25 4.0	28 32.3	6 18.8	21 49.5	22 53.0	0 46.0
11 Sa	15 14 30	20 8 53	1♋20 13	7♋56 20	19 40.5	7 48.6	3 7.1	25 42.9	28 46.3	6 26.3	21 53.0	22 52.3	0 46.7
12 Su	15 18 27	21 6 50	14 35 52	21 18 48	19 36.1	9 47.1	3 48.9	26 21.9	29 0.2	6 33.9	21 56.5	22 51.6	0 47.4
13 M	15 22 24	22 4 45	28 5 7	4♌54 48	19 32.8	11 47.5	4 29.7	27 0.8	29 14.1	6 41.4	21 59.9	22 50.9	0 48.2
14 Tu	15 26 20	23 2 39	11♌47 48	18 44 4	19D 30.8	13 49.5	5 9.3	27 39.6	29 27.9	6 48.8	22 3.4	22 50.2	0 48.9
15 W	15 30 17	24 0 30	25 43 33	2♍46 9	19 30.4	15 53.2	5 47.8	28 18.5	29 41.7	6 56.3	22 6.9	22 49.6	0 49.7
16 Th	15 34 13	24 58 20	9♍51 44	17 0 5	19 31.1	17 58.5	6 25.0	28 57.3	29 55.5	7 3.7	22 10.4	22 49.0	0 50.5
17 F	15 38 10	25 56 8	24 10 59	1♎24 4	19 32.4	20 5.2	7 1.1	29 36.1	0♉ 9.2	7 11.1	22 13.9	22 48.4	0 51.4
18 Sa	15 42 6	26 53 54	8♎38 58	15 55 11	19R 33.6	22 13.3	7 35.8	0♋14.9	0 22.9	7 18.5	22 17.4	22 47.9	0 52.2
19 Su	15 46 3	27 51 39	23 12 9	0♏29 15	19 33.9	24 22.5	8 9.2	0 53.7	0 36.5	7 25.9	22 20.8	22 47.4	0 53.1
20 M	15 49 59	28 49 22	7♏45 45	15 0 56	19 32.7	26 32.6	8 41.2	1 32.5	0 50.1	7 33.2	22 24.3	22 46.9	0 54.0
21 Tu	15 53 56	29 47 4	22 14 3	29 24 21	19 29.6	28 43.5	9 11.7	2 11.2	1 3.6	7 40.5	22 27.8	22 46.5	0 54.9
22 W	15 57 53	0♊44 44	6♐31 7	13♐33 41	19 24.7	0♊54.9	9 40.7	2 49.9	1 17.1	7 47.8	22 31.2	22 46.1	0 55.8
23 Th	16 1 49	1 42 23	20 31 31	27 24 8	19 18.4	3 6.6	10 8.2	3 28.6	1 30.6	7 55.0	22 34.7	22 45.7	0 56.8
24 F	16 5 46	2 40 1	4♑11 13	10♑52 32	19 11.4	5 18.3	10 34.1	4 7.3	1 44.0	8 2.2	22 38.1	22 45.3	0 57.8
25 Sa	16 9 42	3 37 38	17 28 2	23 57 44	19 4.6	7 29.7	10 58.2	4 46.0	1 57.3	8 9.4	22 41.6	22 45.0	0 58.8
26 Su	16 13 39	4 35 14	0♒21 49	6♒40 33	18 58.7	9 40.6	11 20.7	5 24.6	2 10.6	8 16.6	22 45.0	22 44.7	0 59.8
27 M	16 17 35	5 32 48	12 54 19	19 3 33	18 54.4	11 50.6	11 41.4	6 3.2	2 23.8	8 23.7	22 48.4	22 44.5	1 0.8
28 Tu	16 21 32	6 30 22	25 8 47	1♓10 35	18 51.8	13 59.5	12 0.3	6 41.8	2 37.0	8 30.8	22 51.9	22 44.2	1 1.9
29 W	16 25 28	7 27 55	7♓ 9 32	13 6 19	18D 51.0	16 7.1	12 17.2	7 20.4	2 50.1	8 37.9	22 55.3	22 44.0	1 3.0
30 Th	16 29 25	8 25 27	19 1 33	24 55 54	18 51.5	18 13.1	12 32.2	7 59.0	3 3.2	8 44.9	22 58.7	22 43.9	1 4.1
31 F	16 33 22	9 22 58	0♈50 1	6♈44 33	18 52.7	20 17.4	12 45.2	8 37.6	3 16.2	8 51.9	23 2.0	22 43.7	1 5.2

LONGITUDE — JUNE 1940

Day	Sid.Time	☉	0 hr ☽	Noon ☽	True ☊	☿	♀	♂	♃	♄	♅	♆	♇
1 Sa	16 37 18	10♊20 29	12♈40 6	18♈37 15	18♎53.7	22♊19.7	12♋56.1	9♋16.2	3♉29.2	8♉58.8	23♉ 5.4	22♍43.6	1♌ 6.3
2 Su	16 41 15	11 17 58	24 36 33	0♉38 31	18R 53.7	24 20.0	13 4.9	9 54.7	3 42.0	9 5.7	23 8.8	22R 43.6	1 7.5
3 M	16 45 11	12 15 27	6♉43 34	12 52 6	18 52.0	26 18.0	13 11.5	10 33.2	3 54.9	9 12.6	23 12.1	22D 43.6	1 8.7
4 Tu	16 49 8	13 12 55	19 4 24	25 20 45	18 48.1	28 13.8	13 15.9	11 11.7	4 7.6	9 19.4	23 15.4	22 43.6	1 9.9
5 W	16 53 4	14 10 22	1♊41 17	8♊ 6 4	18 41.9	0♋ 7.1	13R 18.1	11 50.2	4 20.3	9 26.2	23 18.8	22 43.6	1 11.1
6 Th	16 57 1	15 7 49	14 35 7	21 8 22	18 33.8	1 58.0	13 17.9	12 28.7	4 32.9	9 33.0	23 22.1	22 43.7	1 12.3
7 F	17 0 57	16 5 14	27 45 37	4♋26 42	18 24.4	3 46.4	13 15.3	13 7.2	4 45.5	9 39.7	23 25.4	22 43.8	1 13.6
8 Sa	17 4 54	17 2 39	11♋11 20	17 59 12	18 14.6	5 32.3	13 10.4	13 45.7	4 58.0	9 46.3	23 28.6	22 43.9	1 14.8
9 Su	17 8 51	18 0 3	24 49 58	1♌43 19	18 5.6	7 15.5	13 3.1	14 24.1	5 10.4	9 52.9	23 31.9	22 44.0	1 16.1
10 M	17 12 47	18 57 25	8♌38 55	15 36 26	17 58.1	8 56.2	12 53.4	15 2.6	5 22.7	9 59.5	23 35.1	22 44.2	1 17.4
11 Tu	17 16 44	19 54 47	22 35 36	29 36 8	17 52.9	10 34.2	12 41.2	15 41.0	5 35.0	10 6.0	23 38.3	22 44.5	1 18.8
12 W	17 20 40	20 52 8	6♍37 51	13♍40 33	17 50.1	12 9.6	12 26.7	16 19.4	5 47.2	10 12.5	23 41.5	22 44.7	1 20.1
13 Th	17 24 37	21 49 27	20 44 4	27 48 16	17D 49.3	13 42.3	12 9.7	16 57.8	5 59.3	10 18.9	23 44.7	22 45.0	1 21.4
14 F	17 28 33	22 46 46	4♎53 0	11♎58 7	17R 49.6	15 12.3	11 50.5	17 36.2	6 11.3	10 25.2	23 47.9	22 45.4	1 22.8
15 Sa	17 32 30	23 44 3	19 3 27	26 8 48	17 49.9	16 39.6	11 28.9	18 14.5	6 23.3	10 31.5	23 51.0	22 45.7	1 24.2
16 Su	17 36 26	24 41 20	3♏13 54	10♏18 29	17 49.1	18 4.2	11 5.2	18 52.9	6 35.1	10 37.8	23 54.1	22 46.1	1 25.6
17 M	17 40 23	25 38 36	17 22 10	24 24 34	17 46.1	19 25.9	10 39.3	19 31.2	6 46.9	10 44.0	23 57.2	22 46.5	1 27.0
18 Tu	17 44 20	26 35 51	1♐25 14	8♐23 41	17 40.5	20 44.9	10 11.5	20 9.6	6 58.6	10 50.1	24 0.3	22 47.0	1 28.4
19 W	17 48 16	27 33 6	15 19 28	22 12 4	17 32.3	22 1.0	9 41.8	20 47.9	7 10.2	10 56.2	24 3.3	22 47.5	1 29.8
20 Th	17 52 13	28 30 20	29 1 4	5♑46 2	17 22.1	23 14.2	9 10.5	21 26.2	7 21.8	11 2.2	24 6.4	22 48.0	1 31.3
21 F	17 56 9	29 27 33	12♑26 39	19 2 39	17 10.8	24 24.5	8 37.6	22 4.5	7 33.2	11 8.2	24 9.4	22 48.5	1 32.7
22 Sa	18 0 6	0♋24 47	25 33 52	2♒ 0 15	16 59.4	25 31.7	8 3.3	22 42.7	7 44.6	11 14.1	24 12.4	22 49.1	1 34.2
23 Su	18 4 2	1 22 0	8♒21 49	14 38 44	16 49.2	26 35.8	7 28.0	23 21.0	7 55.8	11 20.0	24 15.3	22 49.7	1 35.7
24 M	18 7 59	2 19 12	20 51 12	26 59 34	16 40.9	27 36.8	6 51.7	23 59.3	8 7.0	11 25.8	24 18.2	22 50.4	1 37.2
25 Tu	18 11 55	3 16 25	3♓ 4 15	9♓ 5 42	16 35.0	28 34.4	6 14.8	24 37.5	8 18.1	11 31.5	24 21.1	22 51.0	1 38.7
26 W	18 15 52	4 13 37	15 4 28	21 1 8	16 31.5	29 28.8	5 37.4	25 15.8	8 29.1	11 37.2	24 24.0	22 51.7	1 40.2
27 Th	18 19 49	5 10 50	26 56 21	2♈50 45	16D 30.1	0♌19.6	4 59.8	25 54.0	8 39.9	11 42.8	24 26.8	22 52.5	1 41.8
28 F	18 23 45	6 8 2	8♈45 2	14 39 52	16R 29.9	1 6.9	4 22.3	26 32.2	8 50.7	11 48.3	24 29.6	22 53.3	1 43.3
29 Sa	18 27 42	7 5 15	20 35 56	26 33 54	16 29.9	1 50.5	3 45.0	27 10.4	9 1.4	11 53.8	24 32.4	22 54.0	1 44.9
30 Su	18 31 38	8 2 27	2♉34 26	8♉38 9	16 29.1	2 30.4	3 8.3	27 48.6	9 12.0	11 59.2	24 35.2	22 54.9	1 46.4

Astro Data	Planet Ingress	Last Aspect	☽ Ingress	Last Aspect	☽ Ingress	☽ Phases & Eclipses	Astro Data
Dy Hr Mn	Dy Hr Mn	Dy Hr Mn	Dy Hr Mn	Dy Hr Mn	Dy Hr Mn	Dy Hr Mn	1 MAY 1940
☽0N 3 4:20	☿ ♉ 6 21:14	30 18:37 ♃ ✶	♓ 1 1:56	1 23:20 ☿ ✶	♉ 2 10:44	7 12:07 ● 16♉46	Julian Day # 14731
☽0S 17 1:21	♀ ♋ 6 18:47	3 9:23 ♀ □	♈ 3 14:52	4 8:03 ♅ ☌	♊ 4 20:49	14 20:51 ☽ 23♌53	Delta T 24.5 sec
♃□♇ 20 7:23	♃ ♉ 16 7:54	6 2:08 ♀ ✶	♉ 6 3:12	6 14:53 ♆ □	♋ 7 4:02	21 13:33 ○ 0♐20	SVP 06♓05'30"
♄⚻♆ 21 18:37	♂ ♋ 17 14:45	7 23:59 ♆ △	♊ 8 13:34	8 21:43 ♅ ✶	♌ 9 9:00	29 0:40 ☽ 7♓30	Obliquity 23°26'41"
♅△♆ 25 22:05	☉ ♊ 21 5:23	10 19:13 ♃ ✶	♋ 10 21:33	11 1:48 ♅ □	♍ 11 12:41		⚷ Chiron 15♋24.6
☽0N 30 12:34	☿ ♊ 21 13:59	13 2:04 ♃ □	♌ 13 3:22	13 5:08 ♅ △	♎ 13 15:43	6 1:05 ● 15♊10	☽ Mean ☊ 19♎08.8
		15 6:53 ♃ △	♍ 15 7:18	15 8:29 ☉ △	♏ 15 18:31	13 1:59 ☽ 21♍54	
♆ D 3 11:47	☿ ♋ 4 22:29	17 9:26 ♂ □	♎ 17 9:40	17 11:16 ♅ ☍	♐ 17 21:34	19 23:02 ○ 28♐28	1 JUNE 1940
♀ R 5 10:05	☉ ♋ 21 13:36	17 22:11 ♀ □	♏ 19 11:12	19 23:02 ☉ ☍	♑ 20 1:44	27 18:13 ☽ 5♈54	Julian Day # 14762
☽0S 13 8:09	☿ ♌ 26 14:32	21 12:49 ☿ ☍	♐ 21 13:00	21 23:56 ☿ ☍	♒ 22 8:15		Delta T 24.5 sec
♃⚻♆ 22 10:12		23 3:53 ♆ □	♑ 23 16:35	24 6:45 ♅ □	♓ 24 17:55		SVP 06♓05'26"
☽0N 26 21:50		25 9:45 ♆ △	♒ 25 23:19	26 21:46 ♂ △	♈ 27 6:13		Obliquity 23°26'40"
		27 19:28 ♅ □	♓ 28 9:39	29 13:58 ♂ □	♉ 29 18:52		⚷ Chiron 17♋53.6
		30 8:04 ♅ ✶	♈ 30 22:18				☽ Mean ☊ 17♎30.3

JULY 1940 — LONGITUDE

Day	Sid.Time	☉	0 hr ☽	Noon ☽	True ☊	☿	♀	♂	♃	♄	♅	♆	♇
1 M	18 35 35	8♋59 40	14♉45 36	20♉57 17	16♎26.5	3♌ 6.2	2♋32.3	28♋26.9	9♉22.5	12♉ 4.5	24♉37.9	22♍55.7	1♌48.0
2 Tu	18 39 31	9 56 53	27 13 39	3♊35 3	16R 21.5	3 38.1	1R 57.3	29 5.1	9 32.9	12 9.8	24 40.6	22 56.6	1 49.6
3 W	18 43 28	10 54 6	10♊ 1 43	16 33 47	16 13.9	4 5.8	1 23.4	29 43.2	9 43.1	12 15.0	24 43.3	22 57.5	1 51.2
4 Th	18 47 24	11 51 19	23 11 16	29 54 3	16 3.9	4 29.2	0 50.9	0♌21.4	9 53.3	12 20.1	24 45.9	22 58.5	1 52.8
5 F	18 51 21	12 48 33	6♋41 56	13♋34 31	15 52.4	4 48.1	0 20.0	0 59.6	10 3.3	12 25.1	24 48.5	22 59.5	1 54.4
6 Sa	18 55 18	13 45 46	20 31 23	27 31 58	15 40.4	5 2.6	29♊50.8	1 37.8	10 13.3	12 30.1	24 51.1	23 0.5	1 56.0
7 Su	18 59 14	14 42 59	4♌35 39	11♌41 48	15 29.2	5 12.5	29 23.4	2 16.0	10 23.1	12 35.0	24 53.6	23 1.5	1 57.6
8 M	19 3 11	15 40 13	18 49 44	25 58 50	15 19.8	5R 17.6	28 58.0	2 54.1	10 32.8	12 39.9	24 56.1	23 2.6	1 59.2
9 Tu	19 7 7	16 37 26	3♍ 8 28	10♍18 6	15 13.0	5 18.1	28 34.6	3 32.3	10 42.4	12 44.6	24 58.6	23 3.7	2 0.9
10 W	19 11 4	17 34 39	17 27 16	24 35 35	15 9.0	5 13.8	28 13.4	4 10.4	10 51.8	12 49.3	25 1.0	23 4.8	2 2.5
11 Th	19 15 0	18 31 52	1♎42 44	8♎48 30	15 7.3	5 4.8	27 54.5	4 48.6	11 1.2	12 53.9	25 3.4	23 6.0	2 4.2
12 F	19 18 57	19 29 5	15 52 41	22 55 12	15 7.1	4 51.1	27 37.8	5 26.7	11 10.4	12 58.4	25 5.8	23 7.1	2 5.8
13 Sa	19 22 53	20 26 18	29 55 57	6♏54 54	15 6.9	4 33.0	27 23.5	6 4.9	11 19.5	13 2.8	25 8.1	23 8.3	2 7.5
14 Su	19 26 50	21 23 31	13♏51 57	20 47 5	15 5.7	4 10.5	27 11.5	6 43.0	11 28.5	13 7.2	25 10.4	23 9.6	2 9.2
15 M	19 30 47	22 20 44	27 40 6	4♐31 7	15 2.3	3 44.0	27 1.9	7 21.1	11 37.3	13 11.4	25 12.6	23 10.8	2 10.8
16 Tu	19 34 43	23 17 57	11♐19 46	18 5 58	14 56.2	3 13.7	26 54.7	7 59.2	11 46.0	13 15.6	25 14.8	23 12.1	2 12.5
17 W	19 38 40	24 15 10	24 49 31	1♑30 12	14 47.4	2 40.1	26 49.9	8 37.3	11 54.6	13 19.7	25 17.0	23 13.4	2 14.2
18 Th	19 42 36	25 12 24	8♑ 7 47	14 42 5	14 36.5	2 3.6	26D 47.5	9 15.4	12 3.1	13 23.8	25 19.1	23 14.8	2 15.9
19 F	19 46 33	26 9 38	21 12 55	27 40 6	14 24.3	1 24.8	26 47.3	9 53.5	12 11.4	13 27.7	25 21.2	23 16.2	2 17.5
20 Sa	19 50 29	27 6 52	4♒ 3 32	10♒23 11	14 12.1	0 44.4	26 49.5	10 31.6	12 19.6	13 31.5	25 23.3	23 17.5	2 19.2
21 Su	19 54 26	28 4 7	16 39 3	22 51 13	14 1.0	0 2.9	26 54.0	11 9.7	12 27.6	13 35.3	25 25.3	23 19.0	2 20.9
22 M	19 58 22	29 1 22	28 59 51	5♓ 5 9	13 51.8	29♋21.1	27 0.7	11 47.8	12 35.6	13 39.0	25 27.3	23 20.4	2 22.6
23 Tu	20 2 19	29 58 39	11♓ 7 26	17 7 4	13 45.0	28 39.7	27 9.5	12 25.9	12 43.3	13 42.6	25 29.2	23 21.9	2 24.3
24 W	20 6 16	0♌55 55	23 4 28	29 0 8	13 40.9	27 59.5	27 20.5	13 4.0	12 51.0	13 46.1	25 31.1	23 23.4	2 26.0
25 Th	20 10 12	1 53 13	4♈54 36	10♈48 27	13D 39.1	27 21.2	27 33.5	13 42.1	12 58.4	13 49.5	25 32.9	23 24.9	2 27.7
26 F	20 14 9	2 50 32	16 42 19	22 36 50	13 38.8	26 45.5	27 48.5	14 20.1	13 5.8	13 52.8	25 34.7	23 26.4	2 29.4
27 Sa	20 18 5	3 47 51	28 32 41	4♉30 33	13R 39.1	26 13.1	28 5.5	14 58.2	13 13.0	13 56.0	25 36.5	23 28.0	2 31.1
28 Su	20 22 2	4 45 12	10♉31 5	16 34 59	13 39.1	25 44.6	28 24.4	15 36.3	13 20.0	13 59.2	25 38.2	23 29.6	2 32.8
29 M	20 25 58	5 42 34	22 42 53	28 55 24	13 37.7	25 20.7	28 45.1	16 14.4	13 26.9	14 2.2	25 39.9	23 31.2	2 34.5
30 Tu	20 29 55	6 39 57	5♊13 3	11♊36 20	13 34.3	25 1.7	29 7.5	16 52.5	13 33.7	14 5.1	25 41.5	23 32.8	2 36.1
31 W	20 33 51	7 37 20	18 5 36	24 41 9	13 28.6	24 48.1	29 31.6	17 30.6	13 40.2	14 8.0	25 43.1	23 34.4	2 37.8

AUGUST 1940 — LONGITUDE

Day	Sid.Time	☉	0 hr ☽	Noon ☽	True ☊	☿	♀	♂	♃	♄	♅	♆	♇
1 Th	20 37 48	8♌34 45	1♋23 6	8♋11 27	13♎20.8	24♋40.3	29♊57.4	18♌ 8.7	13♉46.7	14♉10.8	25♉44.7	23♍36.1	2♌39.5
2 F	20 41 45	9 32 11	15 6 1	22 6 29	13R 11.4	24D 38.6	0♋24.8	18 46.8	13 52.9	14 13.4	25 46.2	23 37.8	2 41.2
3 Sa	20 45 41	10 29 38	29 12 22	6♌23 2	13 1.5	24 43.2	0 53.6	19 24.9	13 59.1	14 16.0	25 47.6	23 39.5	2 42.9
4 Su	20 49 38	11 27 6	13♌37 42	20 55 33	12 52.1	24 54.2	1 24.0	20 3.0	14 5.0	14 18.5	25 49.0	23 41.3	2 44.6
5 M	20 53 34	12 24 35	28 15 39	5♍37 3	12 44.3	25 11.8	1 55.7	20 41.1	14 10.8	14 20.8	25 50.4	23 43.0	2 46.3
6 Tu	20 57 31	13 22 5	12♍58 49	20 20 6	12 38.8	25 36.0	2 28.8	21 19.2	14 16.4	14 23.1	25 51.7	23 44.8	2 47.9
7 W	21 1 27	14 19 36	27 40 6	4♎58 7	12 35.8	26 6.8	3 3.2	21 57.3	14 21.8	14 25.2	25 53.0	23 46.6	2 49.6
8 Th	21 5 24	15 17 7	12♎13 36	19 26 4	12D 35.0	26 44.3	3 38.8	22 35.4	14 27.1	14 27.3	25 54.2	23 48.4	2 51.3
9 F	21 9 20	16 14 39	26 35 13	3♏40 48	12 35.4	27 28.3	4 15.7	23 13.5	14 32.2	14 29.3	25 55.4	23 50.3	2 52.9
10 Sa	21 13 17	17 12 12	10♏42 41	17 40 49	12R 36.2	28 18.8	4 53.7	23 51.6	14 37.2	14 31.1	25 56.5	23 52.1	2 54.6
11 Su	21 17 14	18 9 46	24 35 12	1♐25 53	12 36.2	29 15.7	5 32.9	24 29.7	14 41.9	14 32.9	25 57.6	23 54.0	2 56.2
12 M	21 21 10	19 7 21	8♐12 56	14 56 26	12 34.5	0♌18.8	6 13.1	25 7.8	14 46.5	14 34.6	25 58.6	23 55.9	2 57.9
13 Tu	21 25 7	20 4 57	21 36 28	28 13 8	12 30.7	1 27.8	6 54.4	25 45.9	14 50.9	14 36.1	25 59.6	23 57.8	2 59.5
14 W	21 29 3	21 2 34	4♑46 28	11♑16 34	12 24.8	2 42.7	7 36.6	26 24.0	14 55.2	14 37.6	26 0.5	23 59.7	3 1.1
15 Th	21 33 0	22 0 11	17 43 29	24 7 14	12 17.1	4 3.1	8 19.9	27 2.1	14 59.2	14 38.9	26 1.4	24 1.7	3 2.8
16 F	21 36 56	22 57 50	0♒27 52	6♒45 25	12 8.5	5 28.7	9 4.1	27 40.3	15 3.1	14 40.2	26 2.2	24 3.6	3 4.4
17 Sa	21 40 53	23 55 30	12 59 58	19 11 33	11 59.8	6 59.2	9 49.2	28 18.4	15 6.8	14 41.3	26 3.0	24 5.6	3 6.0
18 Su	21 44 49	24 53 12	25 20 16	1♓26 15	11 51.9	8 34.3	10 35.2	28 56.5	15 10.3	14 42.3	26 3.7	24 7.6	3 7.6
19 M	21 48 46	25 50 54	7♓29 38	13 30 38	11 45.5	10 13.6	11 22.0	29 34.6	15 13.6	14 43.3	26 4.4	24 9.6	3 9.2
20 Tu	21 52 43	26 48 38	19 29 29	25 26 28	11 41.0	11 56.7	12 9.7	0♍12.8	15 16.8	14 44.1	26 5.1	24 11.6	3 10.7
21 W	21 56 39	27 46 23	1♈21 55	7♈16 12	11D 38.6	13 43.1	12 58.1	0 50.9	15 19.7	14 44.8	26 5.7	24 13.6	3 12.3
22 Th	22 0 36	28 44 10	13 9 45	19 3 1	11 38.0	15 32.4	13 47.3	1 29.1	15 22.5	14 45.4	26 6.2	24 15.6	3 13.9
23 F	22 4 32	29 41 59	24 56 31	0♉50 49	11 38.7	17 24.2	14 37.3	2 7.2	15 25.1	14 45.9	26 6.7	24 17.7	3 15.4
24 Sa	22 8 29	0♍39 49	6♉46 27	12 44 3	11 40.2	19 18.1	15 27.9	2 45.4	15 27.5	14 46.4	26 7.1	24 19.8	3 17.0
25 Su	22 12 25	1 37 42	18 44 14	24 47 38	11 41.7	21 13.6	16 19.3	3 23.5	15 29.6	14 46.7	26 7.5	24 21.8	3 18.5
26 M	22 16 22	2 35 36	0♊54 52	7♊ 6 34	11R 42.5	23 10.4	17 11.3	4 1.7	15 31.6	14 46.8	26 7.8	24 23.9	3 20.0
27 Tu	22 20 18	3 33 31	13 23 18	19 45 39	11 42.0	25 8.0	18 3.9	4 39.9	15 33.5	14R 46.9	26 8.1	24 26.0	3 21.5
28 W	22 24 15	4 31 29	26 14 4	2♋48 57	11 39.9	27 6.3	18 57.2	5 18.1	15 35.1	14 46.9	26 8.4	24 28.1	3 23.0
29 Th	22 28 12	5 29 28	9♋30 36	16 19 11	11 36.5	29 4.8	19 51.0	5 56.3	15 36.5	14 46.8	26 8.6	24 30.3	3 24.5
30 F	22 32 8	6 27 30	23 14 42	0♌17 1	11 31.8	1♍ 3.3	20 45.5	6 34.5	15 37.7	14 46.6	26 8.7	24 32.4	3 26.0
31 Sa	22 36 5	7 25 33	7♌25 47	14 40 30	11 26.7	3 1.6	21 40.4	7 12.7	15 38.7	14 46.2	26 8.8	24 34.5	3 27.4

Astro Data Dy Hr Mn	Planet Ingress Dy Hr Mn	Last Aspect Dy Hr Mn	☽ Ingress Dy Hr Mn	Last Aspect Dy Hr Mn	☽ Ingress Dy Hr Mn	☽ Phases & Eclipses Dy Hr Mn
☿ R 8 14:17	♂ ♌ 3 10:32	2 3:42 ♂ ✱	♊ 2 5:15	2 18:14 ♅ ✱	♌ 3 1:20	5 11:28 ● 13♋16
☽0S 10 14:44	♀ ♊ 5 16:17	3 23:37 ♆ □	♋ 4 12:11	4 20:02 ♅ □	♍ 5 2:50	12 6:35 ☽ 19♎45
♀ D 18 13:13	☿ ♋ 21 1:39	6 7:27 ♅ ✱	♌ 6 16:12	6 21:21 ☿ ✱	♎ 7 3:50	19 9:55 ○ 26♑33
☽0N 24 7:02	☉ ♌ 23 0:34	8 16:33 ♀ ✱	♍ 8 18:44	9 1:35 ☿ □	♏ 9 5:46	27 11:29 ☽ 4♉15
		10 17:43 ♀ □	♎ 10 21:07	11 8:51 ☿ △	♐ 11 9:29	
☿ D 1 18:42	♀ ♋ 1 2:20	12 19:43 ♀ △	♏ 13 0:07	13 7:55 ♂ △	♑ 13 15:15	3 20:09 ● 11♌18
☽0S 6 22:33	☿ ♌ 11 17:06	14 19:42 ♅ ☍	♐ 15 4:05	15 15:36 ♅ △	♒ 15 23:07	10 12:00 ☽ 17♏41
♃☌♄ 8 1:23	♂ ♍ 19 15:58	17 3:35 ♀ ☍	♑ 17 9:17	18 7:28 ♂ ☍	♓ 18 9:10	17 23:02 ○ 24♒51
☽0N 20 15:06	☉ ♍ 23 7:29	19 9:55 ☉ ☍	♒ 19 16:22	20 13:19 ♅ ✱	♈ 20 21:14	26 3:33 ☽ 2♊44
♄ R 27 7:43	☿ ♍ 29 11:11	21 20:04 ♀ △	♓ 22 1:58	22 5:45 ☿ △	♉ 23 10:17	
		24 9:26 ☿ △	♈ 24 14:01	25 14:38 ♅ ☌	♊ 25 22:13	
		26 23:04 ♀ ✱	♉ 27 2:56	28 1:53 ☿ ✱	♋ 28 6:53	
		29 5:44 ♅ ☌	♊ 29 14:04	30 4:58 ♅ ✱	♌ 30 11:31	
		31 21:22 ♀ ☌	♋ 31 21:32			

Astro Data

1 JULY 1940
Julian Day # 14792
Delta T 24.6 sec
SVP 06♓05'21"
Obliquity 23°26'40"
⚷ Chiron 20♋59.0
☽ Mean ☊ 15♎55.0

1 AUGUST 1940
Julian Day # 14823
Delta T 24.6 sec
SVP 06♓05'17"
Obliquity 23°26'40"
⚷ Chiron 24♋25.3
☽ Mean ☊ 14♎16.5

LONGITUDE SEPTEMBER 1940

Day	Sid.Time	☉	0 hr ☽	Noon ☽	True ☊	☿	♀	♂	♃	♄	♅	♆	♇
1 Su	22 40 1	8♍23 38	22♌ 0 29	29♌24 54	11♎21.8	4♍59.5	22♋36.0	7♍51.0	15♉39.5	14♉45.8	26♉ 8.8	24♍36.7	3♌28.9
2 M	22 43 58	9 21 44	6♍52 45	14♍23 0	11R 17.7	6 56.8	23 32.0	8 29.2	15 40.1	14R45.2	26R 8.8	24 38.8	3 30.3
3 Tu	22 47 54	10 19 52	21 54 30	29 26 8	11 15.1	8 53.3	24 28.5	9 7.5	15 40.5	14 44.5	26 8.7	24 41.0	3 31.7
4 W	22 51 51	11 18 2	6♎56 48	14♎25 28	11D 13.9	10 49.1	25 25.5	9 45.7	15R40.8	14 43.8	26 8.6	24 43.2	3 33.1
5 Th	22 55 47	12 16 14	21 51 15	29 13 20	11 14.2	12 43.9	26 23.0	10 24.0	15 40.8	14 42.9	26 8.4	24 45.4	3 34.5
6 F	22 59 44	13 14 27	6♏31 7	13♏44 4	11 15.3	14 37.8	27 21.0	11 2.2	15 40.6	14 41.9	26 8.2	24 47.6	3 35.9
7 Sa	23 3 40	14 12 41	20 51 53	27 54 20	11 16.8	16 30.6	28 19.3	11 40.5	15 40.2	14 40.8	26 8.0	24 49.8	3 37.3
8 Su	23 7 37	15 10 57	4♐51 21	11♐42 57	11R 17.9	18 22.4	29 18.1	12 18.8	15 39.6	14 39.7	26 7.6	24 52.0	3 38.6
9 M	23 11 34	16 9 15	18 29 14	25 10 22	11 18.2	20 13.1	0♌17.4	12 57.1	15 38.8	14 38.4	26 7.3	24 54.2	3 39.9
10 Tu	23 15 30	17 7 34	1♑46 35	8♑18 8	11 17.5	22 2.7	1 17.0	13 35.4	15 37.8	14 37.0	26 6.8	24 56.4	3 41.2
11 W	23 19 27	18 5 55	14 45 17	21 8 21	11 15.6	23 51.1	2 17.0	14 13.7	15 36.6	14 35.5	26 6.4	24 58.6	3 42.5
12 Th	23 23 23	19 4 17	27 27 36	3♒43 21	11 12.9	25 38.4	3 17.4	14 52.1	15 35.2	14 33.9	26 5.9	25 0.8	3 43.8
13 F	23 27 20	20 2 41	9♒55 51	16 5 23	11 9.6	27 24.6	4 18.2	15 30.4	15 33.6	14 32.2	26 5.3	25 3.0	3 45.1
14 Sa	23 31 16	21 1 6	22 12 13	28 16 35	11 6.3	29 9.7	5 19.3	16 8.7	15 31.8	14 30.4	26 4.7	25 5.2	3 46.3
15 Su	23 35 13	21 59 33	4♓18 44	10♓18 56	11 3.4	0♎53.8	6 20.8	16 47.1	15 29.8	14 28.5	26 4.0	25 7.5	3 47.5
16 M	23 39 9	22 58 2	16 17 22	22 14 19	11 1.1	2 36.7	7 22.7	17 25.4	15 27.6	14 26.5	26 3.3	25 9.7	3 48.7
17 Tu	23 43 6	23 56 33	28 10 2	4♈ 4 45	10 59.7	4 18.6	8 24.8	18 3.8	15 25.3	14 24.4	26 2.5	25 11.9	3 49.9
18 W	23 47 3	24 55 6	9♈58 45	15 52 21	10D 59.2	5 59.4	9 27.3	18 42.2	15 22.7	14 22.2	26 1.7	25 14.1	3 51.1
19 Th	23 50 59	25 53 41	21 45 51	27 39 36	10 59.5	7 39.2	10 30.2	19 20.6	15 19.9	14 19.9	26 0.9	25 16.4	3 52.2
20 F	23 54 56	26 52 17	3♉33 58	9♉29 22	11 0.4	9 18.0	11 33.3	19 59.0	15 16.9	14 17.5	25 60.0	25 18.6	3 53.4
21 Sa	23 58 52	27 50 56	15 26 12	21 24 57	11 1.6	10 55.8	12 36.8	20 37.4	15 13.8	14 15.1	25 59.0	25 20.8	3 54.5
22 Su	0 2 49	28 49 38	27 26 4	3♊30 5	11 2.8	12 32.6	13 40.6	21 15.9	15 10.4	14 12.5	25 58.0	25 23.0	3 55.6
23 M	0 6 45	29 48 21	9♊37 29	15 48 50	11 3.8	14 8.5	14 44.6	21 54.3	15 6.9	14 9.8	25 57.0	25 25.3	3 56.6
24 Tu	0 10 42	0♎47 7	22 4 36	28 25 21	11R 4.4	15 43.4	15 49.0	22 32.8	15 3.1	14 7.1	25 55.9	25 27.5	3 57.7
25 W	0 14 38	1 45 55	4♋51 31	11♋23 35	11 4.5	17 17.3	16 53.6	23 11.3	14 59.2	14 4.2	25 54.8	25 29.7	3 58.7
26 Th	0 18 35	2 44 45	18 1 54	24 46 46	11 4.2	18 50.4	17 58.5	23 49.8	14 55.1	14 1.3	25 53.6	25 31.9	3 59.7
27 F	0 22 32	3 43 37	1♌38 23	8♌36 48	11 3.6	20 22.5	19 3.6	24 28.3	14 50.8	13 58.3	25 52.4	25 34.1	4 0.7
28 Sa	0 26 28	4 42 32	15 41 58	22 53 37	11 2.9	21 53.7	20 9.0	25 6.8	14 46.4	13 55.2	25 51.1	25 36.4	4 1.7
29 Su	0 30 25	5 41 29	0♍11 20	7♍34 33	11 2.2	23 24.1	21 14.7	25 45.3	14 41.7	13 52.0	25 49.8	25 38.6	4 2.6
30 M	0 34 21	6 40 28	15 2 28	22 34 11	11 1.8	24 53.5	22 20.6	26 23.9	14 36.9	13 48.7	25 48.4	25 40.8	4 3.5

LONGITUDE OCTOBER 1940

Day	Sid.Time	☉	0 hr ☽	Noon ☽	True ☊	☿	♀	♂	♃	♄	♅	♆	♇
1 Tu	0 38 18	7♎39 29	0♎ 8 38	7♎44 40	11♎ 1.5	26♍22.0	23♌26.7	27♍ 2.5	14♉31.9	13♉45.4	25♉47.0	25♍43.0	4♌ 4.4
2 W	0 42 14	8 38 33	15 21 4	22 56 37	11D 1.5	27 49.6	24 33.0	27 41.1	14R26.7	13R41.9	25R45.6	25 45.1	4 5.3
3 Th	0 46 11	9 37 38	0♏30 7	8♏ 0 29	11 1.5	29 16.2	25 39.6	28 19.7	14 21.4	13 38.4	25 44.1	25 47.3	4 6.1
4 F	0 50 7	10 36 46	15 26 44	22 48 2	11R 1.6	0♏41.9	26 46.4	28 58.3	14 15.9	13 34.8	25 42.6	25 49.5	4 7.0
5 Sa	0 54 4	11 35 55	0♐ 3 41	7♐13 13	11 1.6	2 6.7	27 53.4	29 36.9	14 10.3	13 31.2	25 41.0	25 51.7	4 7.8
6 Su	0 58 0	12 35 6	14 16 18	21 12 46	11 1.5	3 30.4	29 0.6	0♎15.5	14 4.5	13 27.4	25 39.4	25 53.8	4 8.6
7 M	1 1 57	13 34 19	28 2 37	4♑45 57	11 1.4	4 53.2	0♍ 8.0	0 54.2	13 58.5	13 23.6	25 37.8	25 56.0	4 9.3
8 Tu	1 5 54	14 33 34	11♑23 1	17 54 8	11D 1.3	6 14.9	1 15.6	1 32.9	13 52.4	13 19.7	25 36.1	25 58.1	4 10.1
9 W	1 9 50	15 32 50	24 19 40	0♒40 3	11 1.3	7 35.5	2 23.4	2 11.5	13 46.1	13 15.8	25 34.4	26 0.3	4 10.8
10 Th	1 13 47	16 32 8	6♒55 45	13 7 16	11 1.6	8 54.9	3 31.4	2 50.2	13 39.8	13 11.8	25 32.6	26 2.4	4 11.5
11 F	1 17 43	17 31 28	19 15 3	25 19 37	11 2.2	10 13.1	4 39.5	3 28.9	13 33.2	13 7.7	25 30.8	26 4.5	4 12.1
12 Sa	1 21 40	18 30 50	1♓21 25	7♓20 54	11 2.9	11 30.1	5 47.9	4 7.7	13 26.6	13 3.6	25 29.0	26 6.6	4 12.8
13 Su	1 25 36	19 30 13	13 18 30	19 14 38	11 3.8	12 45.6	6 56.4	4 46.4	13 19.8	12 59.4	25 27.2	26 8.7	4 13.4
14 M	1 29 33	20 29 39	25 9 39	1♈ 3 56	11 4.5	13 59.8	8 5.1	5 25.1	13 12.9	12 55.2	25 25.3	26 10.7	4 14.0
15 Tu	1 33 29	21 29 6	6♈57 47	12 51 33	11R 4.9	15 12.3	9 14.0	6 3.9	13 5.9	12 50.9	25 23.3	26 12.8	4 14.5
16 W	1 37 26	22 28 35	18 45 29	24 39 53	11 4.8	16 23.2	10 23.0	6 42.7	12 58.8	12 46.6	25 21.4	26 14.9	4 15.1
17 Th	1 41 23	23 28 6	0♉35 1	6♉31 8	11 4.1	17 32.2	11 32.2	7 21.5	12 51.6	12 42.2	25 19.4	26 16.9	4 15.6
18 F	1 45 19	24 27 40	12 28 29	18 27 21	11 2.7	18 39.2	12 41.6	8 0.3	12 44.3	12 37.7	25 17.4	26 18.9	4 16.1
19 Sa	1 49 16	25 27 15	24 27 58	0♊30 39	11 0.7	19 44.1	13 51.1	8 39.1	12 36.8	12 33.3	25 15.3	26 20.9	4 16.5
20 Su	1 53 12	26 26 53	6♊35 39	12 43 18	10 58.4	20 46.6	15 0.8	9 18.0	12 29.3	12 28.7	25 13.2	26 22.9	4 17.0
21 M	1 57 9	27 26 33	18 53 53	25 7 46	10 56.0	21 46.4	16 10.7	9 56.9	12 21.7	12 24.2	25 11.1	26 24.9	4 17.4
22 Tu	2 1 5	28 26 15	1♋25 18	7♋46 48	10 53.8	22 43.4	17 20.7	10 35.8	12 14.0	12 19.6	25 9.0	26 26.9	4 17.8
23 W	2 5 2	29 25 59	14 12 40	20 43 14	10 52.3	23 37.2	18 30.8	11 14.7	12 6.3	12 14.9	25 6.8	26 28.8	4 18.1
24 Th	2 8 58	0♏25 46	27 18 49	3♌59 45	10D 51.6	24 27.4	19 41.1	11 53.6	11 58.5	12 10.3	25 4.6	26 30.7	4 18.5
25 F	2 12 55	1 25 35	10♌46 17	17 38 35	10 51.8	25 13.7	20 51.6	12 32.6	11 50.6	12 5.6	25 2.4	26 32.7	4 18.8
26 Sa	2 16 52	2 25 26	24 36 48	1♍40 54	10 52.8	25 55.7	22 2.2	13 11.5	11 42.6	12 0.9	25 0.2	26 34.6	4 19.1
27 Su	2 20 48	3 25 19	8♍50 47	16 6 12	10 54.2	26 32.8	23 12.9	13 50.5	11 34.6	11 56.1	24 57.9	26 36.4	4 19.3
28 M	2 24 45	4 25 15	23 26 42	0♎51 44	10 55.5	27 4.7	24 23.7	14 29.5	11 26.6	11 51.3	24 55.6	26 38.3	4 19.5
29 Tu	2 28 41	5 25 12	8♎20 34	15 52 17	10R 56.2	27 30.6	25 34.7	15 8.6	11 18.5	11 46.5	24 53.3	26 40.1	4 19.7
30 W	2 32 38	6 25 12	23 25 52	1♏ 0 11	10 55.8	27 50.1	26 45.7	15 47.6	11 10.4	11 41.7	24 51.0	26 42.0	4 19.9
31 Th	2 36 34	7 25 14	8♏34 3	16 6 17	10 54.0	28 2.5	27 56.9	16 26.7	11 2.3	11 36.9	24 48.7	26 43.8	4 20.1

Astro Data Dy Hr Mn	Planet Ingress Dy Hr Mn	Last Aspect Dy Hr Mn	☽ Ingress Dy Hr Mn	Last Aspect Dy Hr Mn	☽ Ingress Dy Hr Mn	☽ Phases & Eclipses Dy Hr Mn	Astro Data
♅ R 1 4:00	♀ ♌ 8 16:59	1 6:43 ♅ □	♍ 1 12:57	2 21:50 ☿ ☌	♏ 2 23:12	2 4:15 ● 9♍32	1 SEPTEMBER 1940
☽0S 3 8:10	☿ ♎ 14 11:34	3 6:45 ♅ △	♎ 3 12:54	4 23:13 ♂ ✶	♐ 4 23:54	8 19:32 ☽ 15♐58	Julian Day # 14854
♃ R 4 13:00	☉ ♎ 23 4:46	5 7:53 ♀ □	♏ 5 13:16	6 20:16 ♆ □	♑ 7 3:28	16 14:41 ○ 23♓34	Delta T 24.7 sec
☿0S 15 14:38		7 13:40 ♀ △	♐ 7 15:36	9 3:10 ♆ △	♒ 9 10:44	24 17:47 ☽ 1♋31	SVP 06♓05'13"
☽0N 16 21:46	☿ ♏ 3 12:14	9 11:33 ♆ □	♑ 9 20:45	11 12:20 ♅ □	♓ 11 21:18		Obliquity 23°26'41"
☽0S 30 19:05	♂ ♎ 5 14:21	11 21:24 ♅ △	♒ 12 4:51	14 2:04 ♆ ☍	♈ 14 9:50	1 12:41 ● 8♎11	⚷ Chiron 27♋37.9
	♀ ♍ 6 21:10	14 7:38 ♅ □	♓ 14 15:25	16 8:15 ☉ ☍	♉ 16 22:49	1 12:43:41 ✓T 5'36"	☽ Mean ☊ 12♎38.0
♅△♆ 2 2:56	☉ ♏ 23 13:39	16 19:42 ♅ ✶	♈ 17 3:43	19 3:45 ♆ △	♊ 19 10:59	8 6:18 ☽ 14♑49	
♂0S 9 0:50		17 22:50 ♀ △	♉ 19 16:45	21 17:50 ☉ △	♋ 21 21:18	16 8:15 ○ 22♈49	1 OCTOBER 1940
☽0N 14 3:47		22 3:00 ☉ △	♊ 22 5:05	23 22:33 ♆ ✶	♌ 24 4:51	16 8:01 ✓A 0.715	Julian Day # 14884
♃☌♄ 20 4:38		24 6:26 ♆ □	♋ 24 14:57	26 2:21 ♆ □	♍ 26 9:10	24 6:04 ☽ 0♌41	Delta T 24.7 sec
♃□♆ 26 19:40		26 13:56 ♅ ✶	♌ 26 21:09	28 6:05 ☿ ✶	♎ 28 10:37	30 22:03 ● 7♏20	SVP 06♓05'11"
☽0S 28 5:54		28 16:52 ♅ □	♍ 28 23:41	29 11:20 ♂ ☌	♏ 30 10:25		Obliquity 23°26'41"
♄□♆ 29 23:13		30 18:52 ♂ ☌	♎ 30 23:46				⚷ Chiron 0♌03.3
							☽ Mean ☊ 11♎02.7

NOVEMBER 1940 LONGITUDE

Day	Sid.Time	☉	0 hr ☽	Noon ☽	True ☊	☿	♀	♂	♃	♄	♅	♆	♇
1 F	2 40 31	8♏25 18	23♏35 41	1♐ 1 10	10♎50.9	28♏ 7.2	29♍ 8.2	17♎ 5.7	10♉54.1	11♉32.1	24♉46.3	26♍45.5	4♌20.2
2 Sa	2 44 27	9 25 23	8♐21 46	15 36 41	10R46.9	28R 3.5	0♎19.7	17 44.8	10R46.0	11R27.2	24R43.9	26 47.3	4 20.3
3 Su	2 48 24	10 25 30	22 45 16	29 47 4	10 42.4	27 50.9	1 31.2	18 24.0	10 37.8	11 22.4	24 41.5	26 49.0	4 20.3
4 M	2 52 21	11 25 39	6♑41 50	13♑29 28	10 38.3	27 28.9	2 42.8	19 3.1	10 29.6	11 17.6	24 39.1	26 50.8	4 20.4
5 Tu	2 56 17	12 25 50	20 10 5	26 43 53	10 35.0	26 57.2	3 54.6	19 42.2	10 21.5	11 12.7	24 36.7	26 52.5	4R20.4
6 W	3 0 14	13 26 1	3♒11 14	9♒32 35	10D33.1	26 15.7	5 6.4	20 21.4	10 13.3	11 7.9	24 34.3	26 54.1	4 20.4
7 Th	3 4 10	14 26 15	15 48 25	21 59 20	10 32.5	25 24.8	6 18.4	21 0.6	10 5.2	11 3.0	24 31.8	26 55.8	4 20.3
8 F	3 8 7	15 26 30	28 5 55	4♓ 8 48	10 33.3	24 24.9	7 30.4	21 39.8	9 57.1	10 58.2	24 29.4	26 57.4	4 20.3
9 Sa	3 12 3	16 26 46	10♓ 8 37	16 5 59	10 34.9	23 17.2	8 42.5	22 19.0	9 49.0	10 53.4	24 26.9	26 59.0	4 20.2
10 Su	3 16 0	17 27 4	22 1 29	27 55 43	10 36.6	22 3.3	9 54.7	22 58.2	9 41.0	10 48.6	24 24.4	27 0.6	4 20.1
11 M	3 19 56	18 27 23	3♈49 12	9♈42 27	10R37.9	20 45.0	11 7.1	23 37.5	9 33.0	10 43.8	24 21.9	27 2.1	4 19.9
12 Tu	3 23 53	19 27 44	15 35 57	21 30 7	10 38.0	19 24.8	12 19.5	24 16.7	9 25.1	10 39.1	24 19.4	27 3.7	4 19.7
13 W	3 27 50	20 28 6	27 25 19	3♉21 53	10 36.4	18 5.3	13 31.9	24 56.0	9 17.2	10 34.3	24 17.0	27 5.2	4 19.5
14 Th	3 31 46	21 28 30	9♉20 8	15 20 18	10 32.8	16 49.0	14 44.5	25 35.3	9 9.4	10 29.6	24 14.5	27 6.6	4 19.3
15 F	3 35 43	22 28 55	21 22 36	27 27 13	10 27.2	15 38.4	15 57.2	26 14.7	9 1.7	10 24.9	24 12.0	27 8.1	4 19.1
16 Sa	3 39 39	23 29 22	3♊34 16	9♊43 53	10 19.9	14 35.7	17 9.9	26 54.0	8 54.0	10 20.3	24 9.5	27 9.5	4 18.8
17 Su	3 43 36	24 29 51	15 56 11	22 11 15	10 11.6	13 42.6	18 22.8	27 33.4	8 46.4	10 15.6	24 7.0	27 10.9	4 18.5
18 M	3 47 32	25 30 22	28 29 9	4♋49 59	10 3.1	13 0.4	19 35.7	28 12.8	8 38.9	10 11.0	24 4.5	27 12.3	4 18.2
19 Tu	3 51 29	26 30 54	11♋13 51	17 40 52	9 55.2	12 29.6	20 48.7	28 52.2	8 31.5	10 6.5	24 2.0	27 13.6	4 17.8
20 W	3 55 25	27 31 27	24 11 8	0♌44 49	9 48.8	12 10.5	22 1.7	29 31.6	8 24.2	10 2.0	23 59.5	27 15.0	4 17.4
21 Th	3 59 22	28 32 3	7♌22 3	14 3 0	9 44.4	12D 3.0	23 14.9	0♏11.1	8 17.0	9 57.5	23 57.0	27 16.2	4 17.0
22 F	4 3 19	29 32 40	20 47 51	27 36 44	9D42.2	12 6.6	24 28.1	0 50.5	8 9.9	9 53.1	23 54.5	27 17.5	4 16.6
23 Sa	4 7 15	0♐33 19	4♍29 48	11♍27 10	9 41.9	12 20.5	25 41.4	1 30.0	8 3.0	9 48.7	23 52.0	27 18.7	4 16.2
24 Su	4 11 12	1 34 0	18 28 51	25 34 51	9 42.7	12 44.0	26 54.7	2 9.6	7 56.1	9 44.4	23 49.5	27 19.9	4 15.7
25 M	4 15 8	2 34 42	2♎45 0	9♎59 6	9R43.7	13 16.3	28 8.1	2 49.1	7 49.4	9 40.1	23 47.0	27 21.1	4 15.2
26 Tu	4 19 5	3 35 26	17 16 44	24 37 26	9 43.6	13 56.3	29 21.6	3 28.7	7 42.7	9 35.9	23 44.6	27 22.3	4 14.6
27 W	4 23 1	4 36 11	2♏ 0 31	9♏25 13	9 41.6	14 43.3	0♏35.1	4 8.2	7 36.3	9 31.7	23 42.1	27 23.4	4 14.1
28 Th	4 26 58	5 36 58	16 50 38	24 15 46	9 37.0	15 36.4	1 48.7	4 47.8	7 29.9	9 27.6	23 39.7	27 24.4	4 13.5
29 F	4 30 54	6 37 47	1♐39 35	9♐ 1 1	9 30.0	16 34.8	3 2.4	5 27.5	7 23.7	9 23.6	23 37.3	27 25.5	4 12.9
30 Sa	4 34 51	7 38 36	16 19 4	23 32 47	9 20.9	17 37.9	4 16.1	6 7.1	7 17.7	9 19.6	23 34.8	27 26.5	4 12.3

DECEMBER 1940 LONGITUDE

Day	Sid.Time	☉	0 hr ☽	Noon ☽	True ☊	☿	♀	♂	♃	♄	♅	♆	♇
1 Su	4 38 48	8♐39 27	0♑41 22	7♑44 8	9♎10.8	18♏45.1	5♏29.9	6♏46.8	7♉11.8	9♉15.7	23♉32.4	27♍27.5	4♌11.6
2 M	4 42 44	9 40 19	14 40 36	21 30 25	9R 0.9	19 55.7	6 43.7	7 26.5	7R 6.1	9R11.9	23R30.1	27 28.5	4R11.0
3 Tu	4 46 41	10 41 12	28 13 27	4♒49 45	8 52.3	21 9.4	7 57.5	8 6.1	7 0.5	9 8.1	23 27.7	27 29.4	4 10.3
4 W	4 50 37	11 42 6	11♒19 27	17 42 54	8 45.7	22 25.6	9 11.4	8 45.9	6 55.1	9 4.4	23 25.3	27 30.3	4 9.5
5 Th	4 54 34	12 43 0	24 0 31	0♓12 49	8 41.6	23 44.1	10 25.4	9 25.6	6 49.8	9 0.8	23 23.0	27 31.2	4 8.8
6 F	4 58 30	13 43 55	6♓20 23	12 23 53	8D39.7	25 4.5	11 39.4	10 5.3	6 44.8	8 57.3	23 20.7	27 32.0	4 8.0
7 Sa	5 2 27	14 44 51	18 23 57	24 21 19	8 39.4	26 26.5	12 53.4	10 45.1	6 39.9	8 53.8	23 18.4	27 32.8	4 7.2
8 Su	5 6 23	15 45 48	0♈16 40	6♈10 41	8R39.9	27 50.0	14 7.5	11 24.9	6 35.2	8 50.5	23 16.2	27 33.6	4 6.4
9 M	5 10 20	16 46 45	12 4 4	17 57 26	8 40.1	29 14.6	15 21.6	12 4.7	6 30.6	8 47.2	23 13.9	27 34.3	4 5.6
10 Tu	5 14 17	17 47 43	23 51 25	29 46 34	8 38.9	0♐40.3	16 35.7	12 44.5	6 26.3	8 44.0	23 11.7	27 35.0	4 4.8
11 W	5 18 13	18 48 42	5♉43 26	11♉42 26	8 35.4	2 6.9	17 49.9	13 24.4	6 22.1	8 40.9	23 9.5	27 35.7	4 3.9
12 Th	5 22 10	19 49 41	17 44 1	23 48 29	8 29.2	3 34.3	19 4.1	14 4.2	6 18.2	8 37.8	23 7.3	27 36.3	4 3.0
13 F	5 26 6	20 50 41	29 56 7	6♊ 7 5	8 20.2	5 2.3	20 18.4	14 44.1	6 14.4	8 34.9	23 5.2	27 36.9	4 2.1
14 Sa	5 30 3	21 51 42	12♊21 33	18 39 32	8 8.7	6 30.9	21 32.7	15 24.0	6 10.8	8 32.0	23 3.1	27 37.5	4 1.2
15 Su	5 33 59	22 52 43	25 1 3	1♋26 2	7 55.7	8 0.0	22 47.0	16 3.9	6 7.4	8 29.3	23 1.0	27 38.0	4 0.2
16 M	5 37 56	23 53 45	7♋54 22	14 25 54	7 42.3	9 29.6	24 1.4	16 43.9	6 4.2	8 26.6	22 58.9	27 38.5	3 59.2
17 Tu	5 41 52	24 54 48	21 0 29	27 37 55	7 29.7	10 59.6	25 15.7	17 23.9	6 1.2	8 24.0	22 56.9	27 39.0	3 58.3
18 W	5 45 49	25 55 52	4♌18 3	11♌ 0 44	7 19.0	12 29.9	26 30.2	18 3.8	5 58.4	8 21.6	22 54.9	27 39.4	3 57.3
19 Th	5 49 46	26 56 56	17 45 49	24 33 12	7 11.1	14 0.6	27 44.6	18 43.9	5 55.8	8 19.2	22 53.0	27 39.8	3 56.2
20 F	5 53 42	27 58 1	1♍22 51	8♍14 41	7 6.2	15 31.6	28 59.1	19 23.9	5 53.4	8 16.9	22 51.0	27 40.1	3 55.2
21 Sa	5 57 39	28 59 7	15 8 44	22 5 0	7 4.0	17 2.9	0♐13.6	20 4.0	5 51.2	8 14.7	22 49.2	27 40.5	3 54.1
22 Su	6 1 35	0♑ 0 13	29 3 31	6♎ 4 15	7 3.5	18 34.4	1 28.2	20 44.0	5 49.2	8 12.7	22 47.3	27 40.8	3 53.1
23 M	6 5 32	1 1 21	13♎ 7 13	20 12 19	7 3.5	20 6.2	2 42.8	21 24.1	5 47.4	8 10.7	22 45.5	27 41.0	3 52.0
24 Tu	6 9 28	2 2 29	27 19 27	4♏28 21	7 2.5	21 38.3	3 57.4	22 4.3	5 45.8	8 8.8	22 43.7	27 41.2	3 50.9
25 W	6 13 25	3 3 38	11♏38 44	18 50 12	6 59.3	23 10.6	5 12.0	22 44.4	5 44.4	8 7.1	22 41.9	27 41.4	3 49.7
26 Th	6 17 21	4 4 47	26 2 11	3♐14 8	6 53.3	24 43.2	6 26.7	23 24.6	5 43.2	8 5.4	22 40.2	27 41.6	3 48.6
27 F	6 21 18	5 5 57	10♐25 19	17 35 2	6 44.2	26 16.1	7 41.3	24 4.7	5 42.3	8 3.8	22 38.6	27 41.7	3 47.5
28 Sa	6 25 15	6 7 7	24 42 29	1♑46 56	6 32.6	27 49.2	8 56.0	24 45.0	5 41.5	8 2.4	22 36.9	27 41.8	3 46.3
29 Su	6 29 11	7 8 18	8♑47 40	15 44 2	6 19.7	29 22.6	10 10.7	25 25.2	5 41.0	8 1.1	22 35.3	27 41.9	3 45.1
30 M	6 33 8	8 9 29	22 35 30	29 21 38	6 6.7	0♑56.3	11 25.5	26 5.4	5 40.7	7 59.8	22 33.8	27R41.9	3 43.9
31 Tu	6 37 4	9 10 39	6♒ 2 9	12♒36 55	5 54.9	2 30.3	12 40.2	26 45.7	5D40.6	7 58.7	22 32.3	27 41.9	3 42.7

Astro Data Dy Hr Mn	Planet Ingress Dy Hr Mn	Last Aspect Dy Hr Mn	☽ Ingress Dy Hr Mn	Last Aspect Dy Hr Mn	☽ Ingress Dy Hr Mn	☽ Phases & Eclipses Dy Hr Mn	Astro Data
☿ R 1 1:39	♀ ♎ 1 17:24	1 9:44 ♀ ⚹	♐ 1 10:21	2 22:41 ♆ △	♒ 3 3:12	6 21:08 ☽ 14♒19	1 NOVEMBER 1940
♀0S 4 19:16	♂ ♏ 20 17:16	3 6:56 ♆ □	♑ 3 12:22	4 23:25 ☿ □	♓ 5 11:35	15 2:23 ○ 22♉35	Julian Day # 14915
♇ R 5 1:31	☉ ♐ 22 10:49	5 12:17 ♆ △	♒ 5 18:03	7 18:29 ♆ ☍	♈ 7 23:26	22 16:36 ☽ 0♍15	Delta T 24.7 sec
☽0N 10 10:31	♀ ♏ 26 12:32	7 17:19 ☿ □	♓ 8 3:46	9 10:30 ☉ △	♉ 10 12:27	29 8:42 ● 6♐60	SVP 06♓05'08"
☿ D 21 4:05		10 10:09 ♆ ☍	♈ 10 16:13	12 19:28 ♆ △	♊ 13 0:08		Obliquity 23°26'40"
☽0S 24 15:11	☿ ♐ 9 12:45	12 18:40 ♂ ☍	♉ 13 5:13	15 4:54 ♆ □	♋ 15 9:20	6 16:01 ☽ 14♓25	⚷ Chiron 1♌23.0
	♀ ♐ 20 19:36	15 11:24 ♆ △	♊ 15 17:00	17 12:02 ♆ ⚹	♌ 17 16:16	14 19:38 ○ 22♊42	☽ Mean ☊ 9♎24.2
☽0N 7 18:55	☉ ♑ 21 23:55	17 23:27 ♂ △	♋ 18 2:52	19 19:23 ♀ □	♍ 19 21:35	22 1:45 ☽ 0♎05	
☽0S 21 22:32	☿ ♑ 29 9:35	20 10:17 ♂ □	♌ 20 10:38	21 21:38 ♆ ☌	♎ 22 1:37	28 20:56 ● 7♑00	1 DECEMBER 1940
♆ R 30 0:04		22 7:07 ♀ ⚹	♍ 22 16:11	23 13:16 ☿ ⚹	♏ 24 4:30		Julian Day # 14945
♃ D 31 1:20		24 14:58 ♆ ☌	♎ 24 19:25	26 2:46 ♆ ⚹	♐ 26 6:36		Delta T 24.8 sec
		25 2:30 ♇ ⚹	♏ 26 20:44	28 5:55 ☿ ☌	♑ 28 8:58		SVP 06♓05'04"
		28 17:07 ♆ ⚹	♐ 28 21:18	30 9:02 ♆ △	♒ 30 13:09		Obliquity 23°26'39"
		30 18:33 ♆ □	♑ 30 22:50				⚷ Chiron 1♌13.9R
							☽ Mean ☊ 7♎48.8

LONGITUDE JANUARY 1941

Day	Sid.Time	☉	0 hr ☽	Noon ☽	True ☊	☿	♀	♂	♃	♄	♅	♆	♇
1 W	6 41 1	10♑11 50	19♒ 5 55	25♒29 17	5♎45.5	4♑ 4.6	13♐55.0	27♏26.0	5♉40.6	7♉57.7	22♉30.8	27♍41.8	3♌41.5
2 Th	6 44 57	11 13 1	1♓47 15	8♓ 0 12	5R 38.8	5 39.2	15 9.8	28 6.2	5 40.9	7R 56.8	22R 29.4	27R 41.7	3R 40.3
3 F	6 48 54	12 14 11	14 8 35	20 12 55	5 35.0	7 14.1	16 24.5	28 46.6	5 41.5	7 56.0	22 28.0	27 41.6	3 39.0
4 Sa	6 52 50	13 15 21	26 13 48	2♈11 52	5D 33.4	8 49.4	17 39.3	29 26.9	5 42.2	7 55.3	22 26.7	27 41.4	3 37.8
5 Su	6 56 47	14 16 31	8♈ 7 49	14 2 20	5R 33.2	10 25.0	18 54.1	0♐ 7.2	5 43.1	7 54.8	22 25.4	27 41.2	3 36.5
6 M	7 0 44	15 17 40	19 56 8	25 49 54	5 33.2	12 1.0	20 9.0	0 47.6	5 44.2	7 54.3	22 24.1	27 41.0	3 35.2
7 Tu	7 4 40	16 18 49	1♉44 22	7♉40 10	5 32.2	13 37.4	21 23.8	1 28.0	5 45.6	7 54.0	22 23.0	27 40.8	3 34.0
8 W	7 8 37	17 19 58	13 37 59	19 38 22	5 29.3	15 14.3	22 38.6	2 8.4	5 47.1	7 53.8	22 21.8	27 40.5	3 32.7
9 Th	7 12 33	18 21 6	25 41 53	1♊49 1	5 23.8	16 51.5	23 53.5	2 48.8	5 48.9	7D 53.6	22 20.7	27 40.1	3 31.4
10 F	7 16 30	19 22 14	8♊ 0 9	14 15 37	5 15.6	18 29.2	25 8.3	3 29.2	5 50.9	7 53.6	22 19.6	27 39.8	3 30.1
11 Sa	7 20 26	20 23 21	20 35 39	27 0 22	5 5.0	20 7.3	26 23.2	4 9.7	5 53.0	7 53.7	22 18.6	27 39.4	3 28.8
12 Su	7 24 23	21 24 28	3♋29 48	10♋ 3 52	4 52.7	21 45.9	27 38.1	4 50.2	5 55.4	7 54.0	22 17.7	27 39.0	3 27.5
13 M	7 28 19	22 25 34	16 42 25	23 25 11	4 39.9	23 24.9	28 52.9	5 30.7	5 58.0	7 54.3	22 16.8	27 38.5	3 26.1
14 Tu	7 32 16	23 26 40	0♌11 50	7♌ 1 57	4 27.7	25 4.4	0♑ 7.8	6 11.2	6 0.7	7 54.8	22 15.9	27 38.0	3 24.8
15 W	7 36 13	24 27 46	13 55 8	20 50 53	4 17.5	26 44.4	1 22.7	6 51.7	6 3.7	7 55.3	22 15.1	27 37.5	3 23.5
16 Th	7 40 9	25 28 51	27 48 47	4♍48 22	4 9.9	28 24.9	2 37.7	7 32.3	6 6.8	7 56.0	22 14.3	27 37.0	3 22.1
17 F	7 44 6	26 29 56	11♍49 14	18 51 3	4 5.3	0♒ 5.9	3 52.6	8 12.8	6 10.2	7 56.8	22 13.6	27 36.4	3 20.8
18 Sa	7 48 2	27 31 0	25 53 30	2♎56 20	4D 3.3	1 47.3	5 7.5	8 53.4	6 13.7	7 57.7	22 13.0	27 35.7	3 19.4
19 Su	7 51 59	28 32 4	9♎59 21	17 2 25	4 3.1	3 29.2	6 22.4	9 34.1	6 17.5	7 58.7	22 12.3	27 35.1	3 18.1
20 M	7 55 55	29 33 8	24 5 24	1♏ 8 13	4R 3.6	5 11.6	7 37.4	10 14.7	6 21.4	7 59.8	22 11.8	27 34.4	3 16.7
21 Tu	7 59 52	0♒34 11	8♏10 44	15 12 52	4 3.5	6 54.4	8 52.3	10 55.4	6 25.5	8 1.0	22 11.3	27 33.7	3 15.4
22 W	8 3 48	1 35 15	22 14 28	29 15 22	4 1.6	8 37.5	10 7.3	11 36.1	6 29.8	8 2.3	22 10.8	27 33.0	3 14.0
23 Th	8 7 45	2 36 17	6♐15 22	13♐14 11	3 57.3	10 21.0	11 22.3	12 16.8	6 34.3	8 3.8	22 10.4	27 32.2	3 12.6
24 F	8 11 42	3 37 20	20 11 30	27 6 59	3 50.4	12 4.7	12 37.2	12 57.5	6 39.0	8 5.3	22 10.1	27 31.4	3 11.3
25 Sa	8 15 38	4 38 21	4♑ 0 15	10♑50 54	3 41.3	13 48.6	13 52.2	13 38.2	6 43.8	8 7.0	22 9.8	27 30.6	3 9.9
26 Su	8 19 35	5 39 22	17 38 33	24 22 49	3 31.0	15 32.6	15 7.2	14 19.0	6 48.9	8 8.8	22 9.5	27 29.7	3 8.6
27 M	8 23 31	6 40 23	1♒ 3 21	7♒39 53	3 20.5	17 16.6	16 22.2	14 59.8	6 54.1	8 10.7	22 9.3	27 28.8	3 7.2
28 Tu	8 27 28	7 41 22	14 12 10	20 40 5	3 11.0	19 0.4	17 37.1	15 40.6	6 59.5	8 12.7	22 9.2	27 27.9	3 5.9
29 W	8 31 24	8 42 20	27 3 33	3♓22 38	3 3.3	20 43.9	18 52.1	16 21.4	7 5.1	8 14.8	22 9.1	27 27.0	3 4.5
30 Th	8 35 21	9 43 18	9♓37 25	15 48 8	2 57.9	22 26.8	20 7.1	17 2.2	7 10.8	8 17.0	22D 9.0	27 26.0	3 3.1
31 F	8 39 17	10 44 14	21 55 3	27 58 33	2D 55.1	24 8.9	21 22.1	17 43.0	7 16.8	8 19.3	22 9.1	27 25.0	3 1.8

LONGITUDE FEBRUARY 1941

Day	Sid.Time	☉	0 hr ☽	Noon ☽	True ☊	☿	♀	♂	♃	♄	♅	♆	♇
1 Sa	8 43 14	11♒45 9	3♈59 4	9♈57 6	2♎54.3	25♒49.9	22♑37.1	18♐23.9	7♉22.9	8♉21.7	22♉ 9.1	27♍24.0	3♌ 0.5
2 Su	8 47 11	12 46 2	15 53 11	21 47 56	2 55.1	27 29.5	23 52.0	19 4.7	7 29.1	8 24.3	22 9.3	27R 22.9	2R 59.1
3 M	8 51 7	13 46 54	27 41 57	3♉35 53	2 56.4	29 7.4	25 7.0	19 45.6	7 35.6	8 26.9	22 9.4	27 21.8	2 57.8
4 Tu	8 55 4	14 47 45	9♉30 26	15 26 14	2R 57.5	0♓43.0	26 22.0	20 26.5	7 42.2	8 29.6	22 9.7	27 20.7	2 56.4
5 W	8 59 0	15 48 35	21 23 58	27 24 17	2 57.4	2 15.9	27 36.9	21 7.4	7 48.9	8 32.5	22 9.9	27 19.6	2 55.1
6 Th	9 2 57	16 49 23	3♊27 49	9♊35 10	2 55.7	3 45.5	28 51.9	21 48.3	7 55.8	8 35.4	22 10.3	27 18.4	2 53.8
7 F	9 6 53	17 50 10	15 46 52	22 3 24	2 52.0	5 11.3	0♒ 6.8	22 29.3	8 2.9	8 38.4	22 10.7	27 17.3	2 52.5
8 Sa	9 10 50	18 50 55	28 25 9	4♋52 26	2 46.6	6 32.6	1 21.8	23 10.2	8 10.2	8 41.6	22 11.1	27 16.1	2 51.2
9 Su	9 14 46	19 51 39	11♋25 26	18 4 14	2 39.8	7 48.8	2 36.7	23 51.2	8 17.6	8 44.8	22 11.6	27 14.8	2 49.9
10 M	9 18 43	20 52 21	24 48 48	1♌38 56	2 32.4	8 58.9	3 51.7	24 32.2	8 25.1	8 48.2	22 12.2	27 13.6	2 48.6
11 Tu	9 22 40	21 53 1	8♌34 20	15 34 35	2 25.3	10 2.5	5 6.6	25 13.2	8 32.8	8 51.6	22 12.8	27 12.3	2 47.3
12 W	9 26 36	22 53 41	22 39 9	29 47 24	2 19.4	10 58.6	6 21.5	25 54.3	8 40.6	8 55.1	22 13.4	27 11.0	2 46.1
13 Th	9 30 33	23 54 18	6♍58 37	14♍12 7	2 15.2	11 46.6	7 36.5	26 35.3	8 48.6	8 58.8	22 14.1	27 9.7	2 44.8
14 F	9 34 29	24 54 55	21 27 6	28 42 53	2D 12.9	12 25.9	8 51.4	27 16.4	8 56.8	9 2.5	22 14.9	27 8.4	2 43.5
15 Sa	9 38 26	25 55 30	5♎58 45	13♎14 3	2 12.5	12 55.8	10 6.3	27 57.4	9 5.0	9 6.3	22 15.7	27 7.0	2 42.3
16 Su	9 42 22	26 56 4	20 28 15	27 40 51	2 13.5	13 15.8	11 21.2	28 38.5	9 13.5	9 10.2	22 16.5	27 5.7	2 41.1
17 M	9 46 19	27 56 36	4♏51 26	11♏59 41	2 15.0	13R 25.7	12 36.2	29 19.7	9 22.0	9 14.2	22 17.4	27 4.3	2 39.9
18 Tu	9 50 15	28 57 8	19 5 21	26 8 15	2R 16.2	13 25.3	13 51.1	0♑ 0.8	9 30.7	9 18.3	22 18.4	27 2.9	2 38.7
19 W	9 54 12	29 57 38	3♐ 8 14	10♐ 5 12	2 16.5	13 14.5	15 6.0	0 41.9	9 39.5	9 22.4	22 19.4	27 1.4	2 37.5
20 Th	9 58 9	0♓58 7	16 59 6	23 49 52	2 15.5	12 53.8	16 20.9	1 23.1	9 48.5	9 26.7	22 20.5	26 60.0	2 36.3
21 F	10 2 5	1 58 35	0♑37 29	7♑21 54	2 13.0	12 23.5	17 35.8	2 4.3	9 57.6	9 31.1	22 21.6	26 58.5	2 35.1
22 Sa	10 6 2	2 59 1	14 3 6	20 41 2	2 9.2	11 44.5	18 50.7	2 45.5	10 6.8	9 35.5	22 22.7	26 57.1	2 34.0
23 Su	10 9 58	3 59 26	27 15 42	3♒47 4	2 4.7	10 57.8	20 5.6	3 26.7	10 16.2	9 40.0	22 23.9	26 55.6	2 32.8
24 M	10 13 55	4 59 49	10♒15 6	16 39 47	1 60.0	10 4.6	21 20.5	4 7.9	10 25.6	9 44.7	22 25.2	26 54.1	2 31.7
25 Tu	10 17 51	6 0 11	23 1 8	29 19 11	1 55.7	9 6.3	22 35.4	4 49.2	10 35.2	9 49.3	22 26.5	26 52.6	2 30.6
26 W	10 21 48	7 0 31	5♓33 58	11♓45 35	1 52.4	8 4.5	23 50.3	5 30.4	10 45.0	9 54.1	22 27.9	26 51.0	2 29.5
27 Th	10 25 44	8 0 50	17 54 10	23 59 52	1 50.4	7 0.7	25 5.1	6 11.7	10 54.8	9 59.0	22 29.3	26 49.5	2 28.4
28 F	10 29 41	9 1 6	0♈ 2 54	6♈ 3 32	1D 49.6	5 56.5	26 20.0	6 52.9	11 4.8	10 3.9	22 30.7	26 47.9	2 27.4

Astro Data Dy Hr Mn	Planet Ingress Dy Hr Mn	Last Aspect Dy Hr Mn	☽ Ingress Dy Hr Mn	Last Aspect Dy Hr Mn	☽ Ingress Dy Hr Mn	☽ Phases & Eclipses Dy Hr Mn	Astro Data
☽0N 4 4:43	♂ ♐ 4 19:42	1 16:34 ♂ □	♓ 1 20:35	3 3:21 ☿ ✶	♉ 3 4:41	5 13:40 ☽ 14♈51	1 JANUARY 1941
♄ D 9 12:20	♀ ♑ 13 21:29	4 6:51 ♂ △	♈ 4 7:34	5 13:51 ♀ △	♊ 5 17:09	13 11:04 ○ 22♋54	Julian Day # 14976
☽0S 18 5:13	☿ ♒ 16 22:36	6 0:29 ♀ △	♉ 6 20:28	7 21:51 ♆ □	♋ 8 2:57	20 10:01 ☽ 29♎59	Delta T 24.8 sec
♅ D 30 5:02	☉ ♒ 20 10:34	9 3:53 ♆ △	♊ 9 8:27	10 4:15 ♆ ✶	♌ 10 9:07	27 11:03 ● 7♒08	SVP 06♓04'58"
☽0N 31 14:31		11 13:12 ♆ □	♋ 11 17:33	12 5:45 ♂ △	♍ 12 12:21		Obliquity 23°26'39"
	☿ ♓ 3 13:08	13 19:29 ♆ ✶	♌ 13 23:39	14 10:06 ♂ □	♎ 14 14:07	4 11:42 ☽ 15♉17	⚷ Chiron 29♋41.5R
☽0S 14 13:09	♀ ♒ 6 21:49	15 14:25 ♅ □	♍ 16 3:45	16 14:17 ♂ ✶	♏ 16 15:52	12 0:26 ○ 22♌55	☽ Mean ☊ 6♎10.4
♃☌♄ 15 6:36	♂ ♑ 17 23:32	18 2:59 ☉ △	♎ 18 7:00	18 18:07 ☉ □	♐ 18 18:37	18 18:07 ☽ 29♏43	
☿ R 17 10:57	☉ ♓ 19 0:56	20 10:01 ☉ □	♏ 20 10:04	20 17:33 ♆ □	♑ 20 22:54	26 3:02 ● 7♓08	1 FEBRUARY 1941
☽0N 27 22:56		22 9:04 ♆ ✶	♐ 22 13:16	22 23:23 ♆ △	♒ 23 5:02		Julian Day # 15007
		24 12:42 ♆ □	♑ 24 17:01	24 23:06 ♀ ☌	♓ 25 13:18		Delta T 24.9 sec
		26 17:34 ♆ △	♒ 26 22:06	27 17:34 ♆ ☍	♈ 27 23:54		SVP 06♓04'54"
		28 14:46 ♅ □	♓ 29 5:34				Obliquity 23°26'40"
		31 10:52 ♆ ☍	♈ 31 16:02				⚷ Chiron 27♋29.0R
							☽ Mean ☊ 4♎31.9

MARCH 1941 LONGITUDE

Day	Sid.Time	☉	0 hr ☽	Noon ☽	True ☊	☿	♀	♂	♃	♄	♅	♆	♇
1 Sa	10 33 38	10♓ 1 21	12♈ 2 2	17♈58 47	1♎50.0	4♓53.5	27♒34.9	7♑34.2	11♉14.8	10♉ 8.9	22♉32.2	26♍46.3	2♌26.3
2 Su	10 37 34	11 1 34	23 54 9	29 48 34	1 51.2	3R53.0	28 49.7	8 15.5	11 25.0	10 14.0	22 33.8	26R44.8	2R25.3
3 M	10 41 31	12 1 44	5♉42 31	11♉36 30	1 52.8	2 56.2	0♓ 4.5	8 56.8	11 35.3	10 19.2	22 35.4	26 43.2	2 24.3
4 Tu	10 45 27	13 1 53	17 31 3	23 26 44	1 54.4	2 4.1	1 19.3	9 38.1	11 45.8	10 24.5	22 37.0	26 41.6	2 23.3
5 W	10 49 24	14 2 0	29 24 10	5♊23 54	1 55.7	1 17.5	2 34.1	10 19.4	11 56.3	10 29.8	22 38.7	26 40.0	2 22.3
6 Th	10 53 20	15 2 5	11♊26 35	17 32 47	1R56.3	0 37.0	3 48.9	11 0.7	12 6.9	10 35.2	22 40.5	26 38.3	2 21.4
7 F	10 57 17	16 2 7	23 43 6	29 58 6	1 56.2	0 3.0	5 3.7	11 42.1	12 17.6	10 40.7	22 42.3	26 36.7	2 20.5
8 Sa	11 1 13	17 2 8	6♋18 17	12♋44 7	1 55.3	29♒35.6	6 18.5	12 23.4	12 28.5	10 46.2	22 44.1	26 35.1	2 19.5
9 Su	11 5 10	18 2 6	19 15 58	25 54 9	1 53.9	29 15.0	7 33.3	13 4.8	12 39.4	10 51.8	22 46.0	26 33.5	2 18.6
10 M	11 9 7	19 2 2	2♌38 49	9♌30 2	1 52.2	29 1.1	8 48.0	13 46.1	12 50.4	10 57.5	22 47.9	26 31.8	2 17.8
11 Tu	11 13 3	20 1 56	16 27 42	23 31 36	1 50.6	28D53.7	10 2.7	14 27.5	13 1.6	11 3.3	22 49.8	26 30.2	2 16.9
12 W	11 17 0	21 1 48	0♍41 18	7♍56 18	1 49.2	28 52.7	11 17.5	15 8.9	13 12.8	11 9.1	22 51.8	26 28.5	2 16.1
13 Th	11 20 56	22 1 38	15 15 52	22 39 11	1 48.4	28 57.8	12 32.2	15 50.3	13 24.1	11 15.0	22 53.9	26 26.9	2 15.3
14 F	11 24 53	23 1 25	0♎ 5 22	7♎33 23	1D48.1	29 8.7	13 46.9	16 31.7	13 35.5	11 20.9	22 56.0	26 25.2	2 14.5
15 Sa	11 28 49	24 1 11	15 2 13	22 30 52	1 48.2	29 25.2	15 1.5	17 13.1	13 47.0	11 26.9	22 58.1	26 23.5	2 13.7
16 Su	11 32 46	25 0 55	29 58 19	7♏23 39	1 48.7	29 46.8	16 16.2	17 54.5	13 58.6	11 33.0	23 0.3	26 21.9	2 13.0
17 M	11 36 42	26 0 37	14♏46 4	22 4 52	1 49.2	0♓13.4	17 30.9	18 36.0	14 10.3	11 39.1	23 2.5	26 20.2	2 12.2
18 Tu	11 40 39	27 0 18	29 19 27	6♐29 23	1 49.7	0 44.6	18 45.5	19 17.4	14 22.0	11 45.3	23 4.7	26 18.5	2 11.5
19 W	11 44 35	27 59 57	13♐34 21	20 34 10	1 50.0	1 20.2	20 0.2	19 58.9	14 33.8	11 51.6	23 7.0	26 16.9	2 10.9
20 Th	11 48 32	28 59 34	27 28 46	4♑18 9	1R50.1	1 59.8	21 14.8	20 40.4	14 45.8	11 57.9	23 9.3	26 15.2	2 10.2
21 F	11 52 29	29 59 9	11♑ 2 25	17 41 44	1 50.1	2 43.3	22 29.5	21 21.8	14 57.8	12 4.2	23 11.7	26 13.6	2 9.6
22 Sa	11 56 25	0♈58 43	24 16 19	0♒46 25	1D50.0	3 30.4	23 44.1	22 3.3	15 9.8	12 10.6	23 14.1	26 11.9	2 9.0
23 Su	12 0 22	1 58 15	7♒12 17	13 34 12	1 50.0	4 20.9	24 58.7	22 44.8	15 22.0	12 17.1	23 16.5	26 10.2	2 8.4
24 M	12 4 18	2 57 45	19 52 27	26 7 19	1 50.1	5 14.5	26 13.3	23 26.3	15 34.2	12 23.6	23 19.0	26 8.6	2 7.8
25 Tu	12 8 15	3 57 13	2♓19 5	8♓27 59	1 50.3	6 11.1	27 27.9	24 7.8	15 46.5	12 30.2	23 21.5	26 6.9	2 7.3
26 W	12 12 11	4 56 40	14 34 19	20 38 18	1 50.5	7 10.6	28 42.5	24 49.3	15 58.9	12 36.8	23 24.1	26 5.3	2 6.7
27 Th	12 16 8	5 56 4	26 40 10	2♈40 12	1R50.7	8 12.7	29 57.0	25 30.8	16 11.4	12 43.5	23 26.7	26 3.7	2 6.2
28 F	12 20 4	6 55 26	8♈38 36	14 35 37	1 50.6	9 17.4	1♈11.6	26 12.2	16 23.9	12 50.3	23 29.3	26 2.0	2 5.8
29 Sa	12 24 1	7 54 46	20 31 31	26 26 32	1 50.3	10 24.5	2 26.1	26 53.7	16 36.5	12 57.0	23 31.9	26 0.4	2 5.3
30 Su	12 27 58	8 54 5	2♉20 59	8♉15 9	1 49.6	11 33.9	3 40.6	27 35.2	16 49.1	13 3.8	23 34.6	25 58.8	2 4.9
31 M	12 31 54	9 53 21	14 9 21	20 3 57	1 48.6	12 45.4	4 55.1	28 16.7	17 1.8	13 10.7	23 37.3	25 57.2	2 4.5

APRIL 1941 LONGITUDE

Day	Sid.Time	☉	0 hr ☽	Noon ☽	True ☊	☿	♀	♂	♃	♄	♅	♆	♇
1 Tu	12 35 51	10♈52 35	25♉59 18	1♊55 50	1♎47.3	13♓59.1	6♈ 9.6	28♑58.2	17♉14.6	13♉17.6	23♉40.1	25♍55.6	2♌ 4.1
2 W	12 39 47	11 51 46	7♊53 58	13 54 9	1R46.0	15 14.8	7 24.1	29 39.7	17 27.4	13 24.6	23 42.8	25R54.0	2R 3.8
3 Th	12 43 44	12 50 56	19 56 53	26 2 39	1 44.8	16 32.5	8 38.5	0♒21.2	17 40.3	13 31.6	23 45.7	25 52.4	2 3.5
4 F	12 47 40	13 50 3	2♋11 59	8♋25 23	1 44.0	17 52.1	9 53.0	1 2.6	17 53.3	13 38.6	23 48.5	25 50.8	2 3.2
5 Sa	12 51 37	14 49 8	14 43 23	21 6 27	1D43.7	19 13.5	11 7.4	1 44.1	18 6.3	13 45.7	23 51.4	25 49.3	2 2.9
6 Su	12 55 33	15 48 10	27 35 5	4♌ 9 42	1 44.0	20 36.6	12 21.8	2 25.6	18 19.4	13 52.8	23 54.3	25 47.7	2 2.7
7 M	12 59 30	16 47 11	10♌50 38	17 38 10	1 44.8	22 1.5	13 36.2	3 7.0	18 32.5	13 59.9	23 57.2	25 46.2	2 2.5
8 Tu	13 3 27	17 46 9	24 32 27	1♍33 31	1 46.0	23 28.2	14 50.5	3 48.5	18 45.6	14 7.1	24 0.1	25 44.7	2 2.3
9 W	13 7 23	18 45 4	8♍41 16	15 55 24	1 47.2	24 56.5	16 4.9	4 29.9	18 58.9	14 14.3	24 3.1	25 43.2	2 2.1
10 Th	13 11 20	19 43 58	23 15 27	0♎40 47	1R48.0	26 26.4	17 19.2	5 11.4	19 12.1	14 21.5	24 6.1	25 41.7	2 2.0
11 F	13 15 16	20 42 49	8♎10 34	15 43 50	1 48.1	27 58.0	18 33.5	5 52.8	19 25.4	14 28.8	24 9.1	25 40.2	2 1.9
12 Sa	13 19 13	21 41 38	23 19 28	0♏56 14	1 47.1	29 31.3	19 47.8	6 34.2	19 38.8	14 36.1	24 12.2	25 38.7	2 1.8
13 Su	13 23 9	22 40 25	8♏32 54	16 8 12	1 45.2	1♈ 6.1	21 2.1	7 15.7	19 52.2	14 43.4	24 15.3	25 37.3	2 1.7
14 M	13 27 6	23 39 10	23 40 56	1♐ 9 59	1 42.6	2 42.6	22 16.4	7 57.1	20 5.6	14 50.8	24 18.4	25 35.8	2D 1.7
15 Tu	13 31 2	24 37 54	8♐34 23	15 53 21	1 39.6	4 20.6	23 30.7	8 38.5	20 19.1	14 58.2	24 21.5	25 34.4	2 1.7
16 W	13 34 59	25 36 36	23 6 16	0♑12 42	1 36.7	6 0.3	24 44.9	9 19.9	20 32.6	15 5.6	24 24.6	25 33.0	2 1.7
17 Th	13 38 55	26 35 16	7♑12 25	14 5 21	1 34.5	7 41.6	25 59.2	10 1.3	20 46.2	15 13.1	24 27.8	25 31.6	2 1.7
18 F	13 42 52	27 33 54	20 51 33	27 31 16	1D33.3	9 24.5	27 13.4	10 42.7	20 59.8	15 20.5	24 31.0	25 30.3	2 1.8
19 Sa	13 46 49	28 32 31	4♒ 4 48	10♒32 31	1 33.3	11 9.0	28 27.6	11 24.1	21 13.4	15 28.0	24 34.2	25 28.9	2 1.9
20 Su	13 50 45	29 31 6	16 54 54	23 12 24	1 34.2	12 55.1	29 41.8	12 5.5	21 27.1	15 35.5	24 37.4	25 27.6	2 2.0
21 M	13 54 42	0♉29 40	29 25 32	5♓34 48	1 35.8	14 42.9	0♉56.0	12 46.8	21 40.8	15 43.1	24 40.7	25 26.3	2 2.2
22 Tu	13 58 38	1 28 11	11♓40 42	17 43 44	1 37.5	16 32.3	2 10.2	13 28.2	21 54.6	15 50.6	24 43.9	25 25.0	2 2.4
23 W	14 2 35	2 26 42	23 44 21	29 42 59	1R38.7	18 23.4	3 24.3	14 9.5	22 8.3	15 58.2	24 47.2	25 23.8	2 2.6
24 Th	14 6 31	3 25 10	5♈40 2	11♈35 52	1 38.9	20 16.1	4 38.5	14 50.8	22 22.1	16 5.8	24 50.5	25 22.5	2 2.8
25 F	14 10 28	4 23 36	17 30 51	23 25 16	1 37.6	22 10.5	5 52.6	15 32.0	22 36.0	16 13.4	24 53.8	25 21.3	2 3.0
26 Sa	14 14 24	5 22 1	29 19 25	5♉13 34	1 34.7	24 6.5	7 6.7	16 13.3	22 49.8	16 21.0	24 57.2	25 20.1	2 3.3
27 Su	14 18 21	6 20 24	11♉ 7 59	17 2 52	1 30.2	26 4.2	8 20.8	16 54.5	23 3.7	16 28.7	25 0.5	25 18.9	2 3.6
28 M	14 22 18	7 18 46	22 58 29	28 55 3	1 24.3	28 3.4	9 34.9	17 35.7	23 17.7	16 36.3	25 3.9	25 17.8	2 3.9
29 Tu	14 26 14	8 17 5	4♊52 49	10♊52 0	1 17.5	0♉ 4.3	10 49.0	18 16.9	23 31.6	16 44.0	25 7.2	25 16.6	2 4.3
30 W	14 30 11	9 15 23	16 52 54	22 55 48	1 10.6	2 6.7	12 3.0	18 58.0	23 45.6	16 51.6	25 10.6	25 15.5	2 4.7

Astro Data	Planet Ingress	Last Aspect	☽ Ingress	Last Aspect	☽ Ingress	☽ Phases & Eclipses
Dy Hr Mn	Dy Hr Mn	Dy Hr Mn	Dy Hr Mn	Dy Hr Mn	Dy Hr Mn	Dy Hr Mn
♃□♆ 3 15:40	♀ ♓ 2 22:33	2 11:11 ♀ ✶	♉ 2 12:23	1 6:24 ♂ △	♊ 1 8:06	6 7:42 ☽ 15♊21
☿ D 11 15:52	☿ ♒ 7 2:22	4 18:30 ♆ △	♊ 5 1:12	3 11:38 ♆ □	♋ 3 19:44	13 11:47 ○ 22♍31
☽0S 13 23:04	☿ ♓ 16 12:26	7 11:42 ♆ □	♋ 7 12:04	5 20:43 ♅ ✶	♌ 6 4:26	13 11:55 • P 0.323
♄□♆ 14 13:26	☉ ♈ 21 0:20	9 13:09 ♅ ✶	♌ 9 19:19	7 23:04 ♅ □	♍ 8 9:21	20 2:51 ☽ 29♐07
☽0N 27 5:39	♀ ♈ 27 0:58	11 20:59 ☿ ☍	♍ 11 22:51	10 5:45 ☿ ☍	♎ 10 10:54	27 20:14 ● 6♈46
♀0N 29 16:08		13 18:06 ♆ ☌	♎ 13 23:51	11 21:15 ☉ ☍	♏ 12 10:31	27 20:07:43 • A 7'41"
	♂ ♒ 2 11:46	15 23:41 ☿ △	♏ 16 0:03	14 3:03 ♆ ✶	♐ 14 10:07	
☽0S 10 10:07	☿ ♈ 12 7:19	17 19:52 ☉ △	♐ 18 1:08	16 4:31 ☉ △	♑ 16 11:38	5 0:12 ☽ 14♋50
♇ D 14 18:26	☉ ♉ 20 11:50	20 2:51 ☉ □	♑ 20 4:25	18 13:03 ☉ □	♒ 18 16:31	11 21:15 ○ 21♎35
☿0N 15 19:18	♀ ♉ 20 5:53	22 3:32 ♅ △	♒ 22 10:34	20 14:47 ♅ □	♓ 21 1:07	18 13:03 ☽ 28♑06
☽0N 23 11:41	☿ ♉ 28 23:09	24 6:37 ♅ □	♓ 24 19:30	23 3:19 ♆ ☍	♈ 23 12:34	26 13:23 ● 5♉55
		26 22:47 ♆ ☍	♈ 27 6:39	25 11:19 ☿ ☌	♉ 26 1:23	
		29 13:43 ♂ □	♉ 29 19:14	28 4:41 ♆ △	♊ 28 14:11	

Astro Data

1 MARCH 1941
Julian Day # 15035
Delta T 24.9 sec
SVP 06♓04'51"
Obliquity 23°26'40"
⚷ Chiron 25♋51.0R
☽ Mean ☊ 3♎02.9

1 APRIL 1941
Julian Day # 15066
Delta T 24.9 sec
SVP 06♓04'49"
Obliquity 23°26'40"
⚷ Chiron 25♋15.6
☽ Mean ☊ 1♎24.4

LONGITUDE — MAY 1941

Day	Sid.Time	☉	0 hr ☽	Noon ☽	True ☊	☿	♀	♂	♃	♄	♅	♆	♇
1 Th	14 34 7	10♉13 38	29♊ 0 59	5♋ 8 49	1♎ 4.3	4♉10.5	13♉17.1	19♒39.1	23♉59.5	16♉59.3	25♉14.0	25♍14.5	2♌ 5.1
2 F	14 38 4	11 11 52	11♋19 38	17 33 50	0R 59.2	6 15.7	14 31.1	20 20.2	24 13.6	17 7.0	25 17.4	25R 13.4	2 5.5
3 Sa	14 42 0	12 10 3	23 51 49	0♌14 0	0 55.7	8 22.2	15 45.1	21 1.2	24 27.6	17 14.7	25 20.8	25 12.4	2 6.0
4 Su	14 45 57	13 8 13	6♌40 48	13 12 39	0D 54.1	10 29.8	16 59.1	21 42.2	24 41.6	17 22.4	25 24.3	25 11.4	2 6.5
5 M	14 49 53	14 6 21	19 49 56	26 33 1	0 54.0	12 38.3	18 13.1	22 23.2	24 55.7	17 30.1	25 27.7	25 10.4	2 7.0
6 Tu	14 53 50	15 4 26	3♍22 11	10♍17 40	0 55.0	14 47.7	19 27.1	23 4.1	25 9.7	17 37.9	25 31.2	25 9.5	2 7.5
7 W	14 57 47	16 2 30	17 19 34	24 27 51	0R 56.2	16 57.7	20 41.0	23 45.0	25 23.8	17 45.6	25 34.6	25 8.5	2 8.1
8 Th	15 1 43	17 0 32	1♎42 22	9♎ 2 44	0 56.8	19 8.0	21 54.9	24 25.9	25 37.9	17 53.3	25 38.1	25 7.6	2 8.6
9 F	15 5 40	17 58 32	16 28 25	23 58 39	0 55.8	21 18.4	23 8.8	25 6.7	25 52.0	18 1.0	25 41.5	25 6.8	2 9.3
10 Sa	15 9 36	18 56 30	1♏32 32	9♏ 8 56	0 52.9	23 28.7	24 22.7	25 47.5	26 6.1	18 8.7	25 45.0	25 5.9	2 9.9
11 Su	15 13 33	19 54 26	16 46 37	24 24 16	0 47.8	25 38.5	25 36.6	26 28.3	26 20.2	18 16.4	25 48.5	25 5.1	2 10.5
12 M	15 17 29	20 52 21	2♐ 0 33	9♐34 6	0 41.1	27 47.5	26 50.5	27 9.0	26 34.4	18 24.2	25 52.0	25 4.3	2 11.2
13 Tu	15 21 26	21 50 15	17 3 44	24 28 20	0 33.4	29 55.5	28 4.3	27 49.7	26 48.5	18 31.9	25 55.4	25 3.6	2 11.9
14 W	15 25 22	22 48 7	1♑47 1	8♑59 3	0 25.9	2♊ 2.3	29 18.2	28 30.3	27 2.7	18 39.6	25 58.9	25 2.8	2 12.7
15 Th	15 29 19	23 45 58	16 3 58	23 1 31	0 19.4	4 7.4	0♊32.0	29 10.9	27 16.8	18 47.3	26 2.4	25 2.1	2 13.4
16 F	15 33 16	24 43 47	29 51 36	6♒34 22	0 14.7	6 10.8	1 45.8	29 51.4	27 31.0	18 55.0	26 5.9	25 1.5	2 14.2
17 Sa	15 37 12	25 41 36	13♒10 3	19 39 3	0 12.0	8 12.1	2 59.6	0♓31.9	27 45.1	19 2.7	26 9.4	25 0.8	2 15.0
18 Su	15 41 9	26 39 23	26 1 51	2♓19 2	0D 11.2	10 11.1	4 13.4	1 12.4	27 59.3	19 10.4	26 12.9	25 0.2	2 15.8
19 M	15 45 5	27 37 9	8♓31 9	14 38 53	0 11.6	12 7.7	5 27.2	1 52.7	28 13.4	19 18.0	26 16.4	24 59.6	2 16.6
20 Tu	15 49 2	28 34 54	20 42 50	26 43 38	0R 12.5	14 1.8	6 41.0	2 33.1	28 27.6	19 25.7	26 19.9	24 59.1	2 17.5
21 W	15 52 58	29 32 38	2♈41 55	8♈38 15	0 12.8	15 53.2	7 54.7	3 13.3	28 41.7	19 33.3	26 23.4	24 58.6	2 18.4
22 Th	15 56 55	0♊30 21	14 33 11	20 27 15	0 11.6	17 41.8	9 8.5	3 53.5	28 55.9	19 41.0	26 26.9	24 58.1	2 19.3
23 F	16 0 51	1 28 2	26 20 54	2♉14 33	0 8.3	19 27.5	10 22.2	4 33.6	29 10.1	19 48.6	26 30.4	24 57.6	2 20.2
24 Sa	16 4 48	2 25 43	8♉ 8 36	14 3 23	0 2.5	21 10.3	11 35.9	5 13.7	29 24.2	19 56.2	26 33.9	24 57.2	2 21.2
25 Su	16 8 45	3 23 22	19 59 9	25 56 12	29♍54.1	22 50.1	12 49.7	5 53.7	29 38.3	20 3.8	26 37.3	24 56.8	2 22.2
26 M	16 12 41	4 21 0	1♊54 43	7♊54 52	29 43.7	24 26.8	14 3.4	6 33.6	29 52.5	20 11.4	26 40.8	24 56.4	2 23.1
27 Tu	16 16 38	5 18 37	13 56 51	20 0 47	29 31.9	26 0.4	15 17.1	7 13.4	0♊ 6.6	20 19.0	26 44.3	24 56.1	2 24.2
28 W	16 20 34	6 16 13	26 6 49	2♋15 4	29 19.8	27 30.9	16 30.8	7 53.2	0 20.7	20 26.5	26 47.7	24 55.8	2 25.2
29 Th	16 24 31	7 13 48	8♋25 40	14 38 47	29 8.4	28 58.2	17 44.4	8 32.8	0 34.8	20 34.0	26 51.2	24 55.5	2 26.3
30 F	16 28 27	8 11 22	20 54 36	27 13 18	28 58.8	0♋22.3	18 58.1	9 12.4	0 48.9	20 41.5	26 54.7	24 55.3	2 27.3
31 Sa	16 32 24	9 8 54	3♌35 7	10♌ 0 17	28 51.6	1 43.2	20 11.7	9 51.9	1 3.0	20 49.0	26 58.1	24 55.1	2 28.4

LONGITUDE — JUNE 1941

Day	Sid.Time	☉	0 hr ☽	Noon ☽	True ☊	☿	♀	♂	♃	♄	♅	♆	♇
1 Su	16 36 20	10♊ 6 25	16♌29 6	23♌ 1 50	28♍47.0	3♋ 0.8	21♊25.4	10♓31.3	1♊17.0	20♉56.5	27♉ 1.5	24♍54.9	2♌29.6
2 M	16 40 17	11 3 54	29 38 49	6♍20 21	28D 44.8	4 15.0	22 39.0	11 10.6	1 31.1	21 3.9	27 4.9	24R 54.7	2 30.7
3 Tu	16 44 14	12 1 22	13♍ 6 41	19 58 7	28 44.4	5 25.9	23 52.6	11 49.8	1 45.1	21 11.3	27 8.4	24 54.6	2 31.9
4 W	16 48 10	12 58 49	26 54 48	3♎56 50	28R 44.5	6 33.3	25 6.2	12 29.0	1 59.1	21 18.7	27 11.8	24 54.5	2 33.0
5 Th	16 52 7	13 56 15	11♎ 4 15	18 16 52	28 44.1	7 37.2	26 19.7	13 8.0	2 13.1	21 26.1	27 15.1	24D 54.5	2 34.2
6 F	16 56 3	14 53 39	25 34 25	2♏56 25	28 42.0	8 37.5	27 33.3	13 46.9	2 27.0	21 33.4	27 18.5	24 54.5	2 35.4
7 Sa	17 0 0	15 51 2	10♏22 13	17 51 1	28 37.5	9 34.2	28 46.8	14 25.7	2 41.0	21 40.7	27 21.9	24 54.5	2 36.7
8 Su	17 3 56	16 48 25	25 21 48	2♐53 28	28 30.2	10 27.1	0♋ 0.4	15 4.5	2 54.9	21 47.9	27 25.2	24 54.6	2 37.9
9 M	17 7 53	17 45 46	10♐24 49	17 54 37	28 20.8	11 16.3	1 13.9	15 43.1	3 8.8	21 55.2	27 28.6	24 54.6	2 39.2
10 Tu	17 11 49	18 43 7	25 21 38	2♑44 45	28 10.1	12 1.5	2 27.4	16 21.6	3 22.7	22 2.4	27 31.9	24 54.8	2 40.5
11 W	17 15 46	19 40 27	10♑ 2 55	17 15 19	27 59.3	12 42.7	3 40.9	16 60.0	3 36.5	22 9.5	27 35.2	24 54.9	2 41.8
12 Th	17 19 43	20 37 46	24 21 17	1♒20 20	27 49.7	13 19.9	4 54.4	17 38.3	3 50.3	22 16.7	27 38.5	24 55.1	2 43.1
13 F	17 23 39	21 35 5	8♒12 16	14 57 0	27 42.1	13 52.8	6 7.8	18 16.4	4 4.1	22 23.8	27 41.8	24 55.3	2 44.4
14 Sa	17 27 36	22 32 23	21 34 39	28 5 29	27 37.1	14 21.5	7 21.3	18 54.5	4 17.9	22 30.8	27 45.0	24 55.5	2 45.8
15 Su	17 31 32	23 29 41	4♓29 56	10♓48 27	27 34.4	14 45.8	8 34.7	19 32.4	4 31.6	22 37.9	27 48.3	24 55.8	2 47.1
16 M	17 35 29	24 26 58	17 1 39	23 10 9	27 33.5	15 5.7	9 48.2	20 10.2	4 45.3	22 44.9	27 51.5	24 56.1	2 48.5
17 Tu	17 39 25	25 24 15	29 14 35	5♈15 40	27 33.4	15 21.2	11 1.6	20 47.8	4 59.0	22 51.8	27 54.7	24 56.5	2 49.9
18 W	17 43 22	26 21 32	11♈14 3	17 10 25	27 33.0	15 32.0	12 15.0	21 25.3	5 12.6	22 58.7	27 57.9	24 56.8	2 51.3
19 Th	17 47 18	27 18 48	23 5 25	28 59 39	27 31.4	15R 38.3	13 28.4	22 2.6	5 26.2	23 5.6	28 1.0	24 57.2	2 52.7
20 F	17 51 15	28 16 4	4♉53 42	10♉48 6	27 27.5	15 40.1	14 41.8	22 39.8	5 39.7	23 12.4	28 4.2	24 57.7	2 54.2
21 Sa	17 55 12	29 13 20	16 43 20	22 39 51	27 21.0	15 37.3	15 55.2	23 16.9	5 53.3	23 19.2	28 7.3	24 58.1	2 55.6
22 Su	17 59 8	0♋10 36	28 38 0	4♊38 7	27 11.8	15 30.1	17 8.6	23 53.7	6 6.8	23 25.9	28 10.4	24 58.6	2 57.1
23 M	18 3 5	1 7 52	10♊40 27	16 45 14	27 0.3	15 18.6	18 22.0	24 30.4	6 20.2	23 32.6	28 13.5	24 59.2	2 58.6
24 Tu	18 7 1	2 5 7	22 52 36	29 2 40	26 47.4	15 2.9	19 35.3	25 7.0	6 33.6	23 39.3	28 16.5	24 59.7	3 0.0
25 W	18 10 58	3 2 22	5♋15 29	11♋31 7	26 34.1	14 43.2	20 48.7	25 43.3	6 47.0	23 45.9	28 19.5	25 0.3	3 1.5
26 Th	18 14 54	3 59 37	17 49 34	24 10 50	26 21.5	14 19.9	22 2.0	26 19.5	7 0.3	23 52.4	28 22.5	25 1.0	3 3.1
27 F	18 18 51	4 56 51	0♌34 55	7♌ 1 48	26 10.7	13 53.3	23 15.3	26 55.5	7 13.6	23 58.9	28 25.5	25 1.6	3 4.6
28 Sa	18 22 47	5 54 5	13 31 32	20 4 7	26 2.5	13 23.7	24 28.6	27 31.2	7 26.8	24 5.3	28 28.5	25 2.3	3 6.1
29 Su	18 26 44	6 51 19	26 39 38	3♍18 9	25 57.2	12 51.6	25 41.9	28 6.8	7 40.0	24 11.7	28 31.4	25 3.1	3 7.7
30 M	18 30 41	7 48 32	9♍59 48	16 44 42	25 54.6	12 17.6	26 55.2	28 42.2	7 53.1	24 18.1	28 34.3	25 3.8	3 9.2

Astro Data	Dy Hr Mn
♅△♆	1 2:24
♃△♆	5 23:33
☽0S	7 20:46
♃☌♅	8 0:21
☽0N	20 18:27
☽0S	4 5:50
♆ D	5 22:54
♃⚹♇	6 15:52
☽0N	17 2:45
☿ R	19 21:17

Planet Ingress	Dy Hr Mn
☿ ♊	13 0:50
♀ ♊	14 13:36
♂ ♓	16 5:05
☉ ♊	21 11:23
☊ ♍	24 7:48
♃ ♊	26 12:48
☿ ♋	29 17:32
♀ ♋	7 23:53
☉ ♋	21 19:33

Last Aspect Dy Hr Mn		☽ Ingress Dy Hr Mn
30 16:35	♆ □	♋ 1 1:56
3 2:49	♅ ⚹	♌ 3 11:34
5 10:07	♅ □	♍ 5 18:06
7 13:55	♅ △	♎ 7 21:11
9 14:27	♂ △	♏ 9 21:34
11 16:15	☿ ☍	♐ 11 20:49
13 18:20	♂ ⚹	♑ 13 21:03
15 19:47	♃ △	♒ 16 0:15
18 3:47	♃ □	♓ 18 7:33
20 17:06	☉ ⚹	♈ 20 18:34
22 7:31	☿ ⚹	♉ 23 7:26
25 19:50	♃ ☌	♊ 25 20:10
28 3:07	♅ ☌	♋ 28 7:36
30 11:28	♅ ⚹	♌ 30 17:15

Last Aspect Dy Hr Mn		☽ Ingress Dy Hr Mn
1 19:21	♅ □	♍ 2 0:38
4 0:29	♅ △	♎ 4 5:17
6 3:32	♀ △	♏ 6 7:13
8 3:18	♅ ☍	♐ 8 7:24
9 23:17	♆ □	♑ 10 7:31
12 5:39	♅ △	♒ 12 9:41
14 11:25	♅ □	♓ 14 15:33
16 21:21	♅ ⚹	♈ 17 1:30
19 9:20	☉ ⚹	♉ 19 14:03
21 23:04	♅ ☌	♊ 22 2:44
24 4:36	♂ □	♋ 24 13:51
26 19:57	♅ ⚹	♌ 26 22:55
29 3:23	♅ □	♍ 29 6:03

☽ Phases & Eclipses Dy Hr Mn	
4 12:48	☽ 13♌39
11 5:15	○ 20♏07
18 1:17	☽ 26♒34
26 5:18	● 4♊34
2 21:56	☽ 11♍56
9 12:34	○ 18♐16
16 15:45	☽ 25♓05
24 19:22	● 2♋51

Astro Data

1 MAY 1941
Julian Day # 15096
Delta T 25.0 sec
SVP 06♓04'46"
Obliquity 23°26'40"
⚷ Chiron 26♋10.3
☽ Mean ☊ 29♍49.0

1 JUNE 1941
Julian Day # 15127
Delta T 25.0 sec
SVP 06♓04'41"
Obliquity 23°26'39"
⚷ Chiron 28♋27.0
☽ Mean ☊ 28♍10.5

JULY 1941 LONGITUDE

Day	Sid.Time	☉	0 hr ☽	Noon ☽	True ☊	☿	♀	♂	♃	♄	♅	♆	♇
1 Tu	18 34 37	8♋45 45	23♍32 59	0♎24 47	25♍53.8	11♋42.1	28♋ 8.5	29♓17.4	8♊ 6.2	24♉24.4	28♉37.2	25♍ 4.6	3♌10.8
2 W	18 38 34	9 42 57	7♎20 12	14 19 19	25R53.9	11R 5.7	29 21.7	29 52.3	8 19.2	24 30.6	28 40.0	25 5.4	3 12.4
3 Th	18 42 30	10 40 9	21 22 8	28 28 35	25 53.6	10 29.2	0♌34.9	0♈27.1	8 32.2	24 36.8	28 42.8	25 6.2	3 14.0
4 F	18 46 27	11 37 21	5♏38 30	12♏51 35	25 51.8	9 53.0	1 48.2	1 1.6	8 45.1	24 42.9	28 45.6	25 7.1	3 15.6
5 Sa	18 50 23	12 34 32	20 7 27	27 25 31	25 47.6	9 17.8	3 1.3	1 35.9	8 57.9	24 48.9	28 48.3	25 8.0	3 17.2
6 Su	18 54 20	13 31 43	4♐45 9	12♐ 5 32	25 41.0	8 44.3	4 14.5	2 10.0	9 10.7	24 54.9	28 51.1	25 9.0	3 18.8
7 M	18 58 16	14 28 54	19 25 48	26 45 2	25 32.2	8 13.0	5 27.7	2 43.9	9 23.5	25 0.9	28 53.8	25 9.9	3 20.4
8 Tu	19 2 13	15 26 5	4♑ 2 17	11♑16 36	25 22.1	7 44.5	6 40.8	3 17.5	9 36.2	25 6.8	28 56.4	25 10.9	3 22.0
9 W	19 6 10	16 23 16	18 27 7	25 33 5	25 11.9	7 19.4	7 53.9	3 50.8	9 48.8	25 12.6	28 59.0	25 11.9	3 23.7
10 Th	19 10 6	17 20 27	2♒33 50	9♒28 52	25 2.6	6 57.9	9 7.0	4 24.0	10 1.4	25 18.3	29 1.6	25 13.0	3 25.3
11 F	19 14 3	18 17 39	16 17 52	23 0 38	24 55.3	6 40.7	10 20.1	4 56.8	10 13.9	25 24.0	29 4.2	25 14.1	3 27.0
12 Sa	19 17 59	19 14 50	29 37 10	6♓ 7 33	24 50.3	6 27.9	11 33.2	5 29.4	10 26.3	25 29.6	29 6.7	25 15.2	3 28.6
13 Su	19 21 56	20 12 3	12♓32 3	18 51 2	24D47.7	6 20.0	12 46.2	6 1.7	10 38.7	25 35.2	29 9.2	25 16.3	3 30.3
14 M	19 25 52	21 9 15	25 4 57	1♈14 18	24 47.0	6D17.1	13 59.3	6 33.7	10 51.0	25 40.7	29 11.7	25 17.5	3 32.0
15 Tu	19 29 49	22 6 28	7♈19 41	13 21 43	24 47.5	6 19.5	15 12.3	7 5.5	11 3.3	25 46.1	29 14.1	25 18.7	3 33.6
16 W	19 33 45	23 3 42	19 21 3	25 18 20	24R48.1	6 27.3	16 25.3	7 36.9	11 15.4	25 51.5	29 16.5	25 19.9	3 35.3
17 Th	19 37 42	24 0 56	1♉14 14	7♉ 9 25	24 47.8	6 40.5	17 38.3	8 8.1	11 27.5	25 56.7	29 18.9	25 21.1	3 37.0
18 F	19 41 39	24 58 11	13 4 30	19 0 6	24 46.0	6 59.3	18 51.3	8 38.9	11 39.6	26 2.0	29 21.2	25 22.4	3 38.7
19 Sa	19 45 35	25 55 27	24 56 48	0♊55 6	24 42.1	7 23.8	20 4.2	9 9.3	11 51.5	26 7.1	29 23.4	25 23.7	3 40.4
20 Su	19 49 32	26 52 44	6♊55 30	12 58 25	24 36.0	7 53.8	21 17.2	9 39.5	12 3.4	26 12.2	29 25.7	25 25.0	3 42.1
21 M	19 53 28	27 50 1	19 4 13	25 13 13	24 27.9	8 29.4	22 30.1	10 9.3	12 15.2	26 17.2	29 27.9	25 26.4	3 43.8
22 Tu	19 57 25	28 47 19	1♋25 38	7♋41 37	24 18.6	9 10.6	23 43.0	10 38.7	12 26.9	26 22.1	29 30.1	25 27.8	3 45.5
23 W	20 1 21	29 44 38	14 1 18	20 24 41	24 8.8	9 57.3	24 55.9	11 7.8	12 38.6	26 26.9	29 32.2	25 29.2	3 47.2
24 Th	20 5 18	0♌41 57	26 51 44	3♌22 24	23 59.5	10 49.5	26 8.8	11 36.5	12 50.2	26 31.7	29 34.3	25 30.6	3 48.9
25 F	20 9 14	1 39 17	9♌56 32	16 34 0	23 51.7	11 47.0	27 21.6	12 4.8	13 1.6	26 36.4	29 36.3	25 32.1	3 50.6
26 Sa	20 13 11	2 36 37	23 14 35	29 58 8	23 45.9	12 49.9	28 34.4	12 32.7	13 13.0	26 41.0	29 38.3	25 33.6	3 52.3
27 Su	20 17 8	3 33 59	6♍44 27	13♍33 21	23 42.4	13 58.0	29 47.2	13 0.2	13 24.4	26 45.5	29 40.3	25 35.1	3 54.0
28 M	20 21 4	4 31 20	20 24 40	27 18 15	23D41.1	15 11.3	1♍ 0.0	13 27.3	13 35.6	26 50.0	29 42.2	25 36.6	3 55.7
29 Tu	20 25 1	5 28 42	4♎13 59	11♎11 45	23 41.4	16 29.5	2 12.8	13 54.0	13 46.7	26 54.3	29 44.1	25 38.1	3 57.4
30 W	20 28 57	6 26 5	18 11 25	25 12 54	23 42.5	17 52.5	3 25.5	14 20.2	13 57.8	26 58.6	29 45.9	25 39.7	3 59.1
31 Th	20 32 54	7 23 28	2♏16 3	9♏20 45	23R43.4	19 20.3	4 38.2	14 46.0	14 8.7	27 2.8	29 47.7	25 41.3	4 0.8

AUGUST 1941 LONGITUDE

Day	Sid.Time	☉	0 hr ☽	Noon ☽	True ☊	☿	♀	♂	♃	♄	♅	♆	♇
1 F	20 36 50	8♌20 52	16♏26 48	23♏33 58	23♍43.2	20♋52.5	5♍50.9	15♈11.4	14♊19.6	27♉ 6.9	29♉49.5	25♍42.9	4♌ 2.5
2 Sa	20 40 47	9 18 16	0♐41 58	7♐50 27	23R41.4	22 28.9	7 3.6	15 36.3	14 30.3	27 10.9	29 51.2	25 44.6	4 4.3
3 Su	20 44 43	10 15 41	14 59 1	22 7 11	23 37.7	24 9.4	8 16.2	16 0.7	14 41.0	27 14.9	29 52.8	25 46.2	4 6.0
4 M	20 48 40	11 13 7	29 14 26	6♑20 13	23 32.5	25 53.6	9 28.8	16 24.7	14 51.5	27 18.7	29 54.5	25 47.9	4 7.7
5 Tu	20 52 37	12 10 33	13♑23 58	20 25 7	23 26.3	27 41.3	10 41.4	16 48.1	15 2.0	27 22.5	29 56.0	25 49.6	4 9.4
6 W	20 56 33	13 8 0	27 23 7	4♒17 28	23 19.9	29 32.1	11 53.9	17 11.1	15 12.4	27 26.1	29 57.6	25 51.4	4 11.0
7 Th	21 0 30	14 5 28	11♒ 7 43	17 53 31	23 14.2	1♌25.6	13 6.4	17 33.6	15 22.6	27 29.7	29 59.1	25 53.1	4 12.7
8 F	21 4 26	15 2 57	24 34 36	1♓10 47	23 9.7	3 21.5	14 18.9	17 55.5	15 32.8	27 33.2	0♊ 0.5	25 54.9	4 14.4
9 Sa	21 8 23	16 0 28	7♓42 0	14 8 17	23 6.9	5 19.5	15 31.4	18 16.9	15 42.9	27 36.6	0 1.9	25 56.7	4 16.1
10 Su	21 12 19	16 57 59	20 29 45	26 46 37	23D 5.8	7 19.1	16 43.8	18 37.8	15 52.8	27 39.9	0 3.2	25 58.5	4 17.8
11 M	21 16 16	17 55 32	2♈59 11	9♈ 7 50	23 6.2	9 19.9	17 56.2	18 58.1	16 2.6	27 43.2	0 4.5	26 0.3	4 19.4
12 Tu	21 20 12	18 53 5	15 12 59	21 15 8	23 7.5	11 21.7	19 8.5	19 17.8	16 12.4	27 46.3	0 5.8	26 2.1	4 21.1
13 W	21 24 9	19 50 41	27 14 49	3♉12 37	23 9.2	13 24.1	20 20.9	19 36.9	16 22.0	27 49.3	0 7.0	26 4.0	4 22.8
14 Th	21 28 6	20 48 18	9♉ 9 6	15 4 53	23 10.7	15 26.7	21 33.2	19 55.4	16 31.5	27 52.2	0 8.2	26 5.9	4 24.4
15 F	21 32 2	21 45 56	21 0 36	26 56 50	23R11.3	17 29.4	22 45.5	20 13.3	16 40.9	27 55.1	0 9.3	26 7.8	4 26.1
16 Sa	21 35 59	22 43 36	2♊54 13	8♊53 20	23 10.8	19 31.9	23 57.7	20 30.6	16 50.1	27 57.8	0 10.3	26 9.7	4 27.7
17 Su	21 39 55	23 41 17	14 54 44	20 58 58	23 9.0	21 33.8	25 9.9	20 47.2	16 59.3	28 0.5	0 11.4	26 11.6	4 29.4
18 M	21 43 52	24 39 0	27 6 30	3♋17 45	23 6.0	23 35.2	26 22.1	21 3.1	17 8.3	28 3.0	0 12.3	26 13.6	4 31.0
19 Tu	21 47 48	25 36 45	9♋33 7	15 52 52	23 2.1	25 35.7	27 34.3	21 18.4	17 17.2	28 5.5	0 13.2	26 15.5	4 32.6
20 W	21 51 45	26 34 31	22 17 14	28 46 22	22 57.9	27 35.4	28 46.4	21 32.9	17 26.0	28 7.8	0 14.1	26 17.5	4 34.2
21 Th	21 55 41	27 32 19	5♌20 17	11♌58 58	22 53.9	29 34.0	29 58.5	21 46.8	17 34.7	28 10.0	0 14.9	26 19.5	4 35.8
22 F	21 59 38	28 30 8	18 42 18	25 30 2	22 50.6	1♍31.5	1♎10.6	21 59.9	17 43.2	28 12.2	0 15.7	26 21.5	4 37.4
23 Sa	22 3 35	29 27 59	2♍21 55	9♍17 34	22 48.3	3 27.8	2 22.6	22 12.3	17 51.6	28 14.2	0 16.4	26 23.5	4 39.0
24 Su	22 7 31	0♍25 51	16 16 35	23 18 32	22D47.2	5 22.9	3 34.7	22 23.9	17 59.8	28 16.2	0 17.1	26 25.6	4 40.6
25 M	22 11 28	1 23 44	0♎22 56	7♎29 17	22 47.2	7 16.7	4 46.6	22 34.8	18 7.9	28 18.0	0 17.7	26 27.6	4 42.1
26 Tu	22 15 24	2 21 39	14 37 6	21 45 55	22 48.1	9 9.2	5 58.6	22 44.9	18 15.9	28 19.7	0 18.3	26 29.7	4 43.7
27 W	22 19 21	3 19 35	28 55 17	6♏ 4 45	22 49.3	11 0.5	7 10.5	22 54.3	18 23.8	28 21.3	0 18.8	26 31.8	4 45.2
28 Th	22 23 17	4 17 32	13♏13 58	20 22 32	22 50.5	12 50.4	8 22.3	23 2.8	18 31.5	28 22.9	0 19.3	26 33.8	4 46.7
29 F	22 27 14	5 15 31	27 30 9	4♐36 29	22R51.3	14 39.1	9 34.1	23 10.6	18 39.0	28 24.3	0 19.7	26 35.9	4 48.3
30 Sa	22 31 10	6 13 31	11♐41 17	18 44 18	22 51.4	16 26.4	10 45.9	23 17.5	18 46.5	28 25.6	0 20.0	26 38.0	4 49.8
31 Su	22 35 7	7 11 33	25 45 16	2♑43 59	22 50.7	18 12.5	11 57.6	23 23.6	18 53.7	28 26.8	0 20.4	26 40.2	4 51.3

Astro Data	Planet Ingress	Last Aspect	☽ Ingress	Last Aspect	☽ Ingress	☽ Phases & Eclipses	Astro Data
Dy Hr Mn	Dy Hr Mn	Dy Hr Mn	Dy Hr Mn	Dy Hr Mn	Dy Hr Mn	Dy Hr Mn	1 JULY 1941
☽0S 1 13:06	♀ ♌ 2 12:33	1 10:29 ♂ ☍	♎ 1 11:17	1 22:34 ♅ ☍	♐ 1 22:49	2 4:24 ☽ 9♎53	Julian Day # 15157
♄△♆ 8 20:52	♂ ♈ 2 5:17	2 6:12 ☿ □	♏ 3 14:34	3 18:11 ♆ □	♑ 4 1:17	8 20:17 ○ 16♑14	Delta T 25.1 sec
☽0N 14 12:13	☉ ♌ 23 6:26	5 14:18 ♅ ☍	♐ 5 16:13	6 4:28 ♅ △	♒ 6 4:32	16 8:07 ☽ 23♈23	SVP 06♓04'37"
☿ D 14 1:15	♀ ♍ 27 4:12	7 9:25 ♆ □	♑ 7 17:21	8 5:25 ♄ □	♓ 8 9:51	24 7:39 ● 1♌00	Obliquity 23°26'39"
♂0N 17 15:57		9 17:55 ♅ △	♒ 9 19:36	10 13:46 ♄ ⚹	♈ 10 18:13	31 9:19 ☽ 7♏46	⚷ Chiron 1♌33.2
☽0S 28 19:32	☿ ♌ 6 5:57	11 23:04 ♅ □	♓ 12 0:42	12 8:19 ♂ ☌	♉ 13 5:32		☽ Mean ☊ 26♍35.2
	♅ ♊ 7 15:33	14 8:02 ♅ ⚹	♈ 14 9:35	15 14:01 ♄ ☌	♊ 15 18:09	7 5:38 ○ 14♒19	
☽0N 10 21:45	☿ ♍ 21 5:18	16 8:07 ☉ □	♉ 16 21:30	17 22:24 ♀ □	♋ 18 5:37	15 1:40 ☽ 21♉50	1 AUGUST 1941
♀0S 22 12:54	♀ ♎ 21 0:29	19 8:58 ♅ ☌	♊ 19 10:10	20 13:13 ♀ ⚹	♌ 20 14:15	22 18:34 ● 29♌15	Julian Day # 15188
☽0S 25 2:37	☉ ♍ 23 13:17	21 12:27 ♆ □	♋ 21 21:15	22 18:34 ☉ ☌	♍ 22 19:53	29 14:04 ☽ 5♐49	Delta T 25.1 sec
		24 5:01 ♅ ⚹	♌ 24 5:48	24 20:28 ♄ △	♎ 24 23:21		SVP 06♓04'32"
		26 11:26 ♅ □	♍ 26 12:03	26 13:48 ♂ ☍	♏ 27 1:49		Obliquity 23°26'39"
		28 16:12 ♅ △	♎ 28 16:41	29 1:31 ♄ ☍	♐ 29 4:13		⚷ Chiron 5♌13.0
		29 23:24 ☿ □	♏ 30 20:09	31 1:34 ♆ □	♑ 31 7:18		☽ Mean ☊ 24♍56.7

LONGITUDE — SEPTEMBER 1941

Day	Sid.Time	☉	0 hr ☽	Noon ☽	True ☊	☿	♀	♂	♃	♄	♅	♆	♇
1 M	22 39 4	8♍ 9 35	9♑40 13	16♑33 47	22♍49.4	19♍57.3	13♎ 9.3	23♈28.9	19♊ 0.9	28♉27.9	0♊20.6	26♍42.3	4♌52.7
2 Tu	22 43 0	9 7 39	23 24 28	0♒12 5	22R47.7	21 40.8	14 21.0	23 33.4	19 7.9	28 28.9	0 20.8	26 44.4	4 54.2
3 W	22 46 57	10 5 45	6♒56 29	13 37 31	22 45.9	23 23.1	15 32.6	23 37.1	19 14.7	28 29.8	0 21.0	26 46.6	4 55.7
4 Th	22 50 53	11 3 52	20 15 1	26 48 55	22 44.4	25 4.2	16 44.1	23 39.9	19 21.4	28 30.5	0 21.1	26 48.7	4 57.1
5 F	22 54 50	12 2 0	3♓19 8	9♓45 37	22 43.4	26 44.0	17 55.6	23 41.8	19 27.9	28 31.2	0R21.2	26 50.9	4 58.5
6 Sa	22 58 46	13 0 11	16 8 24	22 27 31	22D42.9	28 22.7	19 7.1	23R42.9	19 34.3	28 31.8	0 21.2	26 53.1	4 59.9
7 Su	23 2 43	13 58 23	28 43 4	4♈55 11	22 42.8	0♎ 0.2	20 18.5	23 43.2	19 40.5	28 32.2	0 21.2	26 55.2	5 1.3
8 M	23 6 39	14 56 36	11♈ 4 6	17 10 1	22 43.2	1 36.5	21 29.9	23 42.5	19 46.5	28 32.6	0 21.1	26 57.4	5 2.7
9 Tu	23 10 36	15 54 52	23 13 15	29 14 7	22 43.8	3 11.6	22 41.2	23 41.0	19 52.4	28 32.8	0 20.9	26 59.6	5 4.1
10 W	23 14 32	16 53 10	5♉13 2	11♉10 23	22 44.5	4 45.6	23 52.4	23 38.7	19 58.2	28R32.9	0 20.7	27 1.8	5 5.4
11 Th	23 18 29	17 51 30	17 6 39	23 2 20	22 45.1	6 18.5	25 3.7	23 35.4	20 3.7	28 33.0	0 20.5	27 4.0	5 6.7
12 F	23 22 26	18 49 51	28 57 56	4♊54 1	22 45.5	7 50.2	26 14.9	23 31.3	20 9.2	28 32.9	0 20.2	27 6.2	5 8.1
13 Sa	23 26 22	19 48 15	10♊51 8	16 49 52	22R45.7	9 20.8	27 26.0	23 26.3	20 14.4	28 32.7	0 19.9	27 8.4	5 9.4
14 Su	23 30 19	20 46 41	22 50 48	28 54 29	22 45.8	10 50.3	28 37.1	23 20.5	20 19.5	28 32.4	0 19.5	27 10.7	5 10.6
15 M	23 34 15	21 45 10	5♋ 1 30	11♋12 23	22 45.7	12 18.6	29 48.1	23 13.7	20 24.4	28 32.0	0 19.0	27 12.9	5 11.9
16 Tu	23 38 12	22 43 40	17 27 38	23 47 42	22D45.7	13 45.8	0♏59.1	23 6.2	20 29.1	28 31.5	0 18.6	27 15.1	5 13.2
17 W	23 42 8	23 42 12	0♌13 1	6♌43 51	22 45.8	15 11.9	2 10.0	22 57.8	20 33.6	28 30.9	0 18.0	27 17.3	5 14.4
18 Th	23 46 5	24 40 47	13 20 29	20 3 2	22 45.9	16 36.7	3 20.9	22 48.5	20 38.0	28 30.1	0 17.4	27 19.6	5 15.6
19 F	23 50 1	25 39 24	26 51 30	3♍45 48	22 46.2	18 0.4	4 31.7	22 38.5	20 42.2	28 29.3	0 16.8	27 21.8	5 16.8
20 Sa	23 53 58	26 38 2	10♍45 42	17 50 50	22R46.4	19 22.8	5 42.5	22 27.7	20 46.2	28 28.3	0 16.1	27 24.0	5 18.0
21 Su	23 57 55	27 36 43	25 0 41	2♎14 39	22 46.4	20 44.0	6 53.2	22 16.1	20 50.1	28 27.3	0 15.4	27 26.2	5 19.1
22 M	0 1 51	28 35 26	9♎32 1	16 51 58	22 46.2	22 3.9	8 3.9	22 3.8	20 53.7	28 26.1	0 14.6	27 28.5	5 20.3
23 Tu	0 5 48	29 34 11	24 13 40	1♏36 13	22 45.7	23 22.5	9 14.5	21 50.8	20 57.2	28 24.9	0 13.7	27 30.7	5 21.4
24 W	0 9 44	0♎32 57	8♏58 44	16 20 23	22 44.9	24 39.6	10 25.1	21 37.1	21 0.5	28 23.5	0 12.9	27 32.9	5 22.5
25 Th	0 13 41	1 31 45	23 40 22	0♐57 58	22 44.0	25 55.3	11 35.6	21 22.7	21 3.5	28 22.0	0 11.9	27 35.1	5 23.5
26 F	0 17 37	2 30 36	8♐12 35	15 23 44	22 43.1	27 9.5	12 46.0	21 7.8	21 6.4	28 20.4	0 11.0	27 37.4	5 24.6
27 Sa	0 21 34	3 29 27	22 31 0	29 34 8	22D42.4	28 22.1	13 56.4	20 52.3	21 9.2	28 18.7	0 9.9	27 39.6	5 25.6
28 Su	0 25 30	4 28 21	6♑32 57	13♑27 20	22 42.3	29 32.9	15 6.7	20 36.3	21 11.7	28 17.0	0 8.9	27 41.8	5 26.6
29 M	0 29 27	5 27 16	20 17 19	27 2 57	22 42.7	0♏41.9	16 16.9	20 19.8	21 14.0	28 15.1	0 7.8	27 44.0	5 27.6
30 Tu	0 33 24	6 26 13	3♒44 19	10♒21 35	22 43.5	1 48.9	17 27.1	20 2.8	21 16.2	28 13.1	0 6.6	27 46.2	5 28.6

LONGITUDE — OCTOBER 1941

Day	Sid.Time	☉	0 hr ☽	Noon ☽	True ☊	☿	♀	♂	♃	♄	♅	♆	♇
1 W	0 37 20	7♎25 12	16♒54 54	23♒24 28	22♍44.7	2♏53.9	18♏37.1	19♈45.5	21♊18.1	28♉11.0	0♊ 5.4	27♍48.5	5♌29.5
2 Th	0 41 17	8 24 12	29 50 28	6♓13 5	22 45.9	3 56.6	19 47.1	19R27.8	21 19.8	28R 8.8	0R 4.1	27 50.7	5 30.5
3 F	0 45 13	9 23 15	12♓32 31	18 48 56	22R46.8	4 56.9	20 57.0	19 9.8	21 21.4	28 6.5	0 2.8	27 52.9	5 31.3
4 Sa	0 49 10	10 22 19	25 2 30	1♈13 24	22 47.1	5 54.5	22 6.9	18 51.6	21 22.8	28 4.1	0 1.5	27 55.0	5 32.2
5 Su	0 53 6	11 21 25	7♈21 49	13 27 54	22 46.4	6 49.3	23 16.6	18 33.1	21 23.9	28 1.7	0 0.1	27 57.2	5 33.1
6 M	0 57 3	12 20 33	19 31 51	25 33 49	22 44.8	7 41.0	24 26.3	18 14.4	21 24.9	27 59.1	29♉58.7	27 59.4	5 33.9
7 Tu	1 0 59	13 19 44	1♉34 3	7♉32 45	22 42.2	8 29.3	25 35.9	17 55.6	21 25.6	27 56.4	29 57.2	28 1.6	5 34.7
8 W	1 4 56	14 18 56	13 30 11	19 26 36	22 38.8	9 13.8	26 45.4	17 36.8	21 26.2	27 53.7	29 55.7	28 3.7	5 35.5
9 Th	1 8 52	15 18 11	25 22 20	1♊17 43	22 34.9	9 54.4	27 54.8	17 17.9	21 26.6	27 50.8	29 54.2	28 5.9	5 36.3
10 F	1 12 49	16 17 28	7♊13 8	13 9 0	22 31.2	10 30.5	29 4.1	16 59.1	21R26.7	27 47.9	29 52.6	28 8.0	5 37.0
11 Sa	1 16 46	17 16 47	19 5 44	25 3 51	22 27.9	11 1.7	0♐13.4	16 40.3	21 26.7	27 44.8	29 51.0	28 10.2	5 37.7
12 Su	1 20 42	18 16 8	1♋ 3 51	7♋ 6 15	22 25.4	11 27.7	1 22.5	16 21.6	21 26.5	27 41.7	29 49.3	28 12.3	5 38.4
13 M	1 24 39	19 15 32	13 11 38	19 20 32	22D24.2	11 47.9	2 31.6	16 3.1	21 26.0	27 38.5	29 47.6	28 14.4	5 39.1
14 Tu	1 28 35	20 14 58	25 33 32	1♌51 11	22 24.1	12 1.8	3 40.5	15 44.8	21 25.4	27 35.2	29 45.9	28 16.5	5 39.7
15 W	1 32 32	21 14 26	8♌14 2	14 42 33	22 25.1	12R 8.9	4 49.4	15 26.8	21 24.6	27 31.9	29 44.1	28 18.6	5 40.3
16 Th	1 36 28	22 13 57	21 17 12	27 58 20	22 26.7	12 8.7	5 58.2	15 9.1	21 23.5	27 28.4	29 42.3	28 20.7	5 40.9
17 F	1 40 25	23 13 30	4♍46 12	11♍40 57	22 28.2	12 0.8	7 6.8	14 51.7	21 22.3	27 24.9	29 40.4	28 22.8	5 41.5
18 Sa	1 44 21	24 13 5	18 42 32	25 50 48	22R29.1	11 44.6	8 15.4	14 34.7	21 20.8	27 21.3	29 38.5	28 24.8	5 42.0
19 Su	1 48 18	25 12 42	3♎ 5 22	10♎25 41	22 28.7	11 19.8	9 23.8	14 18.2	21 19.2	27 17.6	29 36.6	28 26.9	5 42.5
20 M	1 52 15	26 12 22	17 51 1	25 20 24	22 26.8	10 46.4	10 32.1	14 2.1	21 17.3	27 13.8	29 34.7	28 28.9	5 43.0
21 Tu	1 56 11	27 12 3	2♏52 48	10♏27 1	22 23.2	10 4.2	11 40.4	13 46.6	21 15.2	27 10.0	29 32.7	28 30.9	5 43.5
22 W	2 0 8	28 11 47	18 1 46	25 35 48	22 18.2	9 13.5	12 48.5	13 31.7	21 13.0	27 6.1	29 30.7	28 32.9	5 43.9
23 Th	2 4 4	29 11 32	3♐ 7 54	10♐36 55	22 12.7	8 15.0	13 56.4	13 17.3	21 10.5	27 2.1	29 28.6	28 34.9	5 44.3
24 F	2 8 1	0♏11 20	18 1 51	25 21 52	22 7.4	7 9.6	15 4.3	13 3.6	21 7.9	26 58.1	29 26.6	28 36.9	5 44.7
25 Sa	2 11 57	1 11 9	2♑36 21	9♑44 50	22 3.0	5 58.7	16 12.0	12 50.5	21 5.0	26 54.0	29 24.4	28 38.8	5 45.0
26 Su	2 15 54	2 11 0	16 47 3	23 42 56	22 0.2	4 44.0	17 19.6	12 38.2	21 2.0	26 49.8	29 22.3	28 40.8	5 45.4
27 M	2 19 50	3 10 52	0♒32 32	7♒16 1	21D59.0	3 27.5	18 27.0	12 26.5	20 58.8	26 45.6	29 20.2	28 42.7	5 45.7
28 Tu	2 23 47	4 10 46	13 53 42	20 25 56	21 59.4	2 11.6	19 34.3	12 15.6	20 55.3	26 41.3	29 18.0	28 44.6	5 46.0
29 W	2 27 44	5 10 42	26 53 7	3♓15 42	22 0.7	0 58.6	20 41.4	12 5.4	20 51.7	26 37.0	29 15.8	28 46.5	5 46.2
30 Th	2 31 40	6 10 39	9♓34 7	15 48 50	22 2.1	29♎50.7	21 48.3	11 56.0	20 47.9	26 32.6	29 13.5	28 48.4	5 46.4
31 F	2 35 37	7 10 38	22 0 17	28 8 52	22R 2.8	28 50.1	22 55.1	11 47.3	20 43.9	26 28.2	29 11.3	28 50.2	5 46.6

Astro Data Dy Hr Mn	Planet Ingress Dy Hr Mn	Last Aspect Dy Hr Mn	☽ Ingress Dy Hr Mn	Last Aspect Dy Hr Mn	☽ Ingress Dy Hr Mn	☽ Phases & Eclipses Dy Hr Mn	Astro Data
♅ R 5 17:36	☿ ♎ 6 23:58	2 8:58 ♄ △	♒ 2 11:39	1 20:50 ♄ □	♓ 2 0:18	5 17:36 ○ 12♓45	1 SEPTEMBER 1941
♂ R 6 18:34	♀ ♏ 15 4:01	4 15:08 ♄ □	♓ 4 17:52	4 5:51 ♄ ⚹	♈ 4 9:37	5 17:47 ☍ P 0.051	Julian Day # 15219
☽0N 7 6:16	☉ ♎ 23 10:33	6 23:39 ♄ ⚹	♈ 7 2:28	6 3:45 ♃ ⚹	♉ 6 20:52	13 19:31 ☽ 20♊36	Delta T 25.1 sec
☿0S 7 10:29	☿ ♏ 28 9:21	9 0:55 ♂ ☌	♉ 9 13:32	9 9:10 ♅ ☌	♊ 9 9:23	21 4:38 ● 27♍48	SVP 06♓04'29"
♄ R 10 17:39		11 23:09 ♄ ☌	♊ 12 2:06	11 18:16 ♆ □	♋ 11 21:53	21 4:33:37 ☌ T 3'22"	Obliquity 23°26'40"
♃∠♇ 11 17:30	♅ ♉ 5 2:07	14 12:40 ♀ △	♋ 14 14:09	14 8:01 ♅ ⚹	♌ 14 8:29	27 20:09 ☽ 4♑19	⚷ Chiron 8♌51.4
☽0S 21 11:31	♀ ♐ 10 19:21	16 20:50 ♄ ⚹	♌ 16 23:36	16 15:03 ♅ □	♍ 16 15:36		☽ Mean ☊ 23♍18.2
☽0N 4 13:23	☉ ♏ 23 19:27	19 2:51 ♄ □	♍ 19 5:29	18 18:16 ♅ △	♎ 18 18:54	5 8:32 ○ 11♈42	
♄△♆ 5 22:23	☿ ♎ 29 20:34	21 5:43 ♄ △	♎ 21 8:17	20 14:20 ☉ ☌	♏ 20 19:25	13 12:52 ☽ 19♋47	1 OCTOBER 1941
♃ R 10 8:00		22 22:29 ☿ ☌	♏ 23 9:24	22 18:11 ♅ ☍	♐ 22 19:00	20 14:20 ● 26♎48	Julian Day # 15249
☿ R 15 11:30		25 7:42 ♄ ☍	♐ 25 10:24	24 17:24 ♆ □	♑ 24 19:40	27 5:04 ☽ 3♒24	Delta T 25.2 sec
☽0S 18 22:11		27 10:52 ☿ ⚹	♑ 27 12:44	26 21:52 ♅ △	♒ 26 23:02		SVP 06♓04'26"
♃∠♇ 30 8:33		29 14:07 ♄ △	♒ 29 17:17	29 4:27 ♅ □	♓ 29 5:51		Obliquity 23°26'40"
☽0N 31 19:43				31 14:00 ♅ ⚹	♈ 31 15:38		⚷ Chiron 11♌52.5
							☽ Mean ☊ 21♍42.9

NOVEMBER 1941 LONGITUDE

Day	Sid.Time	☉	0 hr ☽	Noon ☽	True ☊	☿	♀	♂	♃	♄	♅	♆	♇
1 Sa	2 39 33	8♏10 38	4♈14 58	10♈18 55	22♍ 1.9	27♎58.5	24♐ 1.7	11♈39.4	20♊39.7	26♉23.7	29♉ 9.0	28♍52.0	5♌46.8
2 Su	2 43 30	9 10 40	16 21 3	22 21 38	21R 58.9	27R 17.2	25 8.1	11R 32.4	20R 35.4	26R 19.2	29R 6.7	28 53.8	5 46.9
3 M	2 47 26	10 10 44	28 20 55	4♉19 8	21 53.6	26 47.0	26 14.4	11 26.1	20 30.8	26 14.6	29 4.4	28 55.6	5 47.0
4 Tu	2 51 23	11 10 50	10♉16 30	16 13 11	21 46.1	26 28.4	27 20.4	11 20.6	20 26.1	26 10.0	29 2.0	28 57.4	5 47.1
5 W	2 55 19	12 10 58	22 9 23	28 5 17	21 36.8	26D 21.4	28 26.3	11 15.9	20 21.3	26 5.4	28 59.7	28 59.2	5 47.2
6 Th	2 59 16	13 11 7	4♊ 1 5	9♊56 59	21 26.4	26 25.7	29 31.9	11 12.0	20 16.2	26 0.7	28 57.3	29 0.9	5R 47.2
7 F	3 3 13	14 11 19	15 53 13	21 50 3	21 16.0	26 40.8	0♑37.4	11 8.9	20 11.0	25 56.0	28 54.9	29 2.6	5 47.2
8 Sa	3 7 9	15 11 32	27 47 45	3♋46 41	21 6.4	27 5.9	1 42.6	11 6.7	20 5.6	25 51.3	28 52.5	29 4.3	5 47.2
9 Su	3 11 6	16 11 48	9♋47 11	15 49 41	20 58.5	27 40.2	2 47.6	11 5.2	20 0.1	25 46.5	28 50.1	29 5.9	5 47.2
10 M	3 15 2	17 12 5	21 54 37	28 2 28	20 52.8	28 22.8	3 52.4	11D 4.5	19 54.4	25 41.7	28 47.6	29 7.6	5 47.1
11 Tu	3 18 59	18 12 24	4♌13 46	10♌29 2	20 49.5	29 12.8	4 56.9	11 4.6	19 48.5	25 36.9	28 45.2	29 9.2	5 47.0
12 W	3 22 55	19 12 46	16 48 50	23 13 42	20D 48.3	0♏ 9.4	6 1.2	11 5.5	19 42.5	25 32.0	28 42.7	29 10.8	5 46.9
13 Th	3 26 52	20 13 9	29 44 12	6♍20 49	20 48.6	1 11.8	7 5.3	11 7.2	19 36.3	25 27.2	28 40.2	29 12.3	5 46.7
14 F	3 30 48	21 13 34	13♍ 3 59	19 54 4	20R 49.3	2 19.1	8 9.1	11 9.7	19 30.0	25 22.3	28 37.8	29 13.9	5 46.6
15 Sa	3 34 45	22 14 1	26 51 18	3♎55 46	20 49.4	3 30.7	9 12.6	11 12.9	19 23.6	25 17.5	28 35.3	29 15.4	5 46.4
16 Su	3 38 42	23 14 30	11♎ 7 22	18 25 47	20 47.7	4 46.0	10 15.9	11 16.9	19 17.0	25 12.6	28 32.8	29 16.9	5 46.1
17 M	3 42 38	24 15 0	25 50 31	3♏20 48	20 43.5	6 4.4	11 18.8	11 21.7	19 10.3	25 7.7	28 30.3	29 18.3	5 45.9
18 Tu	3 46 35	25 15 33	10♏55 37	18 33 48	20 36.7	7 25.5	12 21.5	11 27.2	19 3.5	25 2.8	28 27.8	29 19.8	5 45.6
19 W	3 50 31	26 16 7	26 13 59	3♐54 42	20 27.6	8 48.9	13 23.8	11 33.4	18 56.5	24 57.9	28 25.3	29 21.2	5 45.3
20 Th	3 54 28	27 16 42	11♐34 28	19 11 48	20 17.4	10 14.1	14 25.9	11 40.4	18 49.4	24 53.0	28 22.7	29 22.6	5 44.9
21 F	3 58 24	28 17 20	26 45 23	4♑13 59	20 7.1	11 40.9	15 27.6	11 48.1	18 42.2	24 48.1	28 20.2	29 23.9	5 44.6
22 Sa	4 2 21	29 17 58	11♑36 39	18 52 38	19 58.1	13 9.1	16 29.0	11 56.5	18 35.0	24 43.2	28 17.7	29 25.3	5 44.2
23 Su	4 6 17	0♐18 38	26 1 26	3♒ 2 47	19 51.4	14 38.3	17 29.9	12 5.6	18 27.6	24 38.4	28 15.2	29 26.6	5 43.8
24 M	4 10 14	1 19 18	9♒56 38	16 43 7	19 47.2	16 8.3	18 30.6	12 15.4	18 20.1	24 33.5	28 12.7	29 27.9	5 43.3
25 Tu	4 14 11	2 20 0	23 22 31	29 55 15	19D 45.3	17 39.1	19 30.8	12 25.9	18 12.5	24 28.7	28 10.2	29 29.1	5 42.9
26 W	4 18 7	3 20 43	6♓21 50	12♓42 49	19 45.0	19 10.5	20 30.6	12 37.1	18 4.9	24 23.9	28 7.7	29 30.3	5 42.4
27 Th	4 22 4	4 21 27	18 58 49	25 10 24	19R 45.2	20 42.4	21 30.0	12 48.8	17 57.1	24 19.1	28 5.2	29 31.5	5 41.9
28 F	4 26 0	5 22 12	1♈18 14	7♈22 51	19 44.7	22 14.6	22 28.9	13 1.3	17 49.3	24 14.4	28 2.7	29 32.6	5 41.3
29 Sa	4 29 57	6 22 57	13 24 51	19 24 45	19 42.4	23 47.2	23 27.4	13 14.3	17 41.5	24 9.6	28 0.2	29 33.8	5 40.8
30 Su	4 33 53	7 23 44	25 23 1	1♉20 6	19 37.4	25 20.0	24 25.4	13 27.9	17 33.6	24 4.9	27 57.7	29 34.9	5 40.2

DECEMBER 1941 LONGITUDE

Day	Sid.Time	☉	0 hr ☽	Noon ☽	True ☊	☿	♀	♂	♃	♄	♅	♆	♇
1 M	4 37 50	8♐24 32	7♉16 22	13♉12 9	19♍29.4	26♏53.0	25♑22.9	13♈42.1	17♊25.6	24♉ 0.3	27♉55.3	29♍35.9	5♌39.6
2 Tu	4 41 46	9 25 21	19 7 46	25 3 27	19R 18.5	28 26.1	26 19.8	13 56.9	17R 17.6	23R 55.6	27R 52.8	29 37.0	5R 38.9
3 W	4 45 43	10 26 11	0♊59 26	6♊55 52	19 5.2	29 59.3	27 16.3	14 12.3	17 9.5	23 51.1	27 50.4	29 38.0	5 38.3
4 Th	4 49 40	11 27 2	12 52 55	18 50 45	18 50.5	1♐32.6	28 12.1	14 28.1	17 1.4	23 46.5	27 48.0	29 38.9	5 37.6
5 F	4 53 36	12 27 55	24 49 29	0♋49 17	18 35.5	3 6.0	29 7.4	14 44.6	16 53.3	23 42.0	27 45.6	29 39.9	5 36.9
6 Sa	4 57 33	13 28 48	6♋50 17	12 52 40	18 21.6	4 39.4	0♒ 2.1	15 1.5	16 45.1	23 37.6	27 43.2	29 40.8	5 36.1
7 Su	5 1 29	14 29 42	18 56 38	25 2 26	18 9.7	6 12.9	0 56.2	15 19.0	16 37.0	23 33.1	27 40.8	29 41.7	5 35.4
8 M	5 5 26	15 30 38	1♌10 20	7♌20 39	18 0.6	7 46.5	1 49.6	15 36.9	16 28.8	23 28.8	27 38.4	29 42.5	5 34.6
9 Tu	5 9 22	16 31 35	13 33 46	19 50 3	17 54.6	9 20.1	2 42.3	15 55.3	16 20.6	23 24.5	27 36.1	29 43.3	5 33.8
10 W	5 13 19	17 32 33	26 9 57	2♍33 56	17 51.4	10 53.7	3 34.3	16 14.2	16 12.4	23 20.3	27 33.8	29 44.1	5 33.0
11 Th	5 17 15	18 33 32	9♍ 2 28	15 36 1	17 50.4	12 27.4	4 25.6	16 33.6	16 4.3	23 16.1	27 31.5	29 44.9	5 32.2
12 F	5 21 12	19 34 32	22 15 4	29 0 0	17 50.3	14 1.1	5 16.2	16 53.4	15 56.1	23 11.9	27 29.2	29 45.6	5 31.3
13 Sa	5 25 9	20 35 33	5♎51 10	12♎48 49	17 49.8	15 34.9	6 5.9	17 13.6	15 48.0	23 7.9	27 26.9	29 46.3	5 30.4
14 Su	5 29 5	21 36 35	19 53 3	27 3 49	17 47.7	17 8.8	6 54.8	17 34.3	15 39.9	23 3.9	27 24.7	29 46.9	5 29.5
15 M	5 33 2	22 37 38	4♏20 53	11♏43 48	17 43.1	18 42.8	7 42.9	17 55.4	15 31.8	22 60.0	27 22.5	29 47.5	5 28.6
16 Tu	5 36 58	23 38 43	19 11 52	26 44 11	17 35.7	20 16.9	8 30.1	18 17.0	15 23.8	22 56.1	27 20.3	29 48.1	5 27.7
17 W	5 40 55	24 39 48	4♐19 39	11♐56 59	17 25.7	21 51.2	9 16.4	18 38.9	15 15.8	22 52.3	27 18.1	29 48.6	5 26.7
18 Th	5 44 51	25 40 54	19 34 48	27 11 39	17 14.2	23 25.5	10 1.7	19 1.2	15 7.8	22 48.6	27 16.0	29 49.2	5 25.7
19 F	5 48 48	26 42 1	4♑46 7	12♑16 53	17 2.4	25 0.0	10 46.0	19 23.9	14 60.0	22 45.0	27 13.9	29 49.6	5 24.7
20 Sa	5 52 44	27 43 8	19 42 44	27 2 42	16 51.9	26 34.7	11 29.3	19 47.0	14 52.1	22 41.4	27 11.8	29 50.1	5 23.7
21 Su	5 56 41	28 44 16	4♒16 1	11♒22 8	16 43.6	28 9.5	12 11.5	20 10.5	14 44.4	22 37.9	27 9.8	29 50.5	5 22.7
22 M	6 0 38	29 45 23	18 20 47	25 11 52	16 38.1	29 44.6	12 52.5	20 34.3	14 36.7	22 34.6	27 7.7	29 50.9	5 21.6
23 Tu	6 4 34	0♑46 31	1♓55 30	8♓31 57	16 35.4	1♑19.8	13 32.3	20 58.5	14 29.2	22 31.3	27 5.8	29 51.2	5 20.6
24 W	6 8 31	1 47 39	15 1 39	21 25 5	16D 34.6	2 55.2	14 10.9	21 23.0	14 21.7	22 28.0	27 3.8	29 51.5	5 19.5
25 Th	6 12 27	2 48 48	27 42 50	3♈55 33	16R 34.7	4 30.9	14 48.2	21 47.9	14 14.3	22 24.9	27 1.9	29 51.8	5 18.4
26 F	6 16 24	3 49 56	10♈ 3 53	16 8 29	16 34.6	6 6.9	15 24.2	22 13.0	14 7.0	22 21.9	27 0.0	29 52.0	5 17.3
27 Sa	6 20 20	4 51 4	22 10 1	28 9 8	16 33.1	7 43.0	15 58.7	22 38.5	13 59.8	22 18.9	26 58.2	29 52.2	5 16.1
28 Su	6 24 17	5 52 12	4♉ 6 25	10♉ 2 28	16 29.4	9 19.5	16 31.8	23 4.3	13 52.7	22 16.1	26 56.4	29 52.4	5 15.0
29 M	6 28 13	6 53 21	15 57 47	21 52 51	16 22.9	10 56.2	17 3.3	23 30.4	13 45.8	22 13.3	26 54.6	29 52.5	5 13.8
30 Tu	6 32 10	7 54 29	27 48 6	3♊43 55	16 13.7	12 33.2	17 33.3	23 56.7	13 38.9	22 10.6	26 52.9	29 52.6	5 12.6
31 W	6 36 7	8 55 37	9♊40 36	15 38 27	16 2.3	14 10.5	18 1.6	24 23.4	13 32.2	22 8.1	26 51.2	29 52.7	5 11.4

Astro Data (Dy Hr Mn)

	Dy Hr Mn
♅△♆	5 2:57
☿ D	5 2:41
♇ R	6 20:45
♂ D	10 8:33
☽0S	15 9:20
☽0N	28 2:33
☽0S	12 19:08
☽0N	25 10:57

Planet Ingress (Dy Hr Mn)

	Dy Hr Mn
♀ ♑	6 10:17
☿ ♏	11 20:11
☉ ♐	22 16:38
☿ ♐	3 0:11
♀ ♒	5 23:04
☉ ♑	22 5:44
☿ ♑	22 3:54

Last Aspect / ☽ Ingress

Last Aspect Dy Hr Mn	☽ Ingress Dy Hr Mn	Last Aspect Dy Hr Mn	☽ Ingress Dy Hr Mn
2 20:58 ♆ ☍	♉ 3 3:19	2 21:40 ♆ ☍	♊ 2 22:00
5 13:51 ♆ △	♊ 5 15:52	5 9:42 ♆ □	♋ 5 10:22
8 2:34 ♆ □	♋ 8 4:26	7 21:08 ♆ ⚹	♌ 7 21:43
10 14:09 ♆ ⚹	♌ 10 15:49	10 2:37 ♅ □	♍ 10 7:12
12 22:03 ♅ □	♍ 13 0:29	12 13:21 ♆ ☌	♎ 12 13:46
15 4:06 ♆ ☌	♎ 15 5:22	14 3:07 ☉ ⚹	♏ 14 16:51
16 13:17 ♃ △	♏ 17 6:40	16 16:52 ♆ ⚹	♐ 16 17:10
19 4:53 ♆ ⚹	♐ 19 5:53	18 16:10 ♆ □	♑ 18 16:26
21 4:14 ♆ □	♑ 21 5:11	20 16:37 ♆ △	♒ 20 16:53
23 5:50 ♆ △	♒ 23 6:46	22 15:23 ♅ □	♓ 22 20:33
25 8:45 ♅ □	♓ 25 12:09	25 4:08 ♆ ☍	♈ 25 4:24
27 20:32 ♆ ☍	♈ 27 21:26	27 0:59 ♂ ☌	♉ 27 15:43
29 21:54 ♀ □	♉ 30 9:18	30 4:12 ♆ △	♊ 30 4:27

☽ Phases & Eclipses (Dy Hr Mn)

Dy Hr Mn	
4 2:00	○ 11♉16
12 4:53	☽ 19♌25
19 0:04	● 26♏16
25 17:52	☽ 3♓05
3 20:51	○ 11♊19
11 18:48	☽ 19♍21
18 10:18	● 26♐07
25 10:43	☽ 3♈16

Astro Data

1 NOVEMBER 1941
Julian Day # 15280
Delta T 25.2 sec
SVP 06♓04'24"
Obliquity 23°26'40"
⚷ Chiron 13♌57.6
☽ Mean ☊ 20♍04.4

1 DECEMBER 1941
Julian Day # 15310
Delta T 25.3 sec
SVP 06♓04'20"
Obliquity 23°26'39"
⚷ Chiron 14♌33.2R
☽ Mean ☊ 18♍29.1

LONGITUDE — JANUARY 1942

Day	Sid.Time	☉	0 hr ☽	Noon ☽	True ☊	☿	♀	♂	♃	♄	♅	♆	♇
1 Th	6 40 3	9♑56 45	21♊37 40	27♊38 28	15♍49.5	15♑48.0	18♒28.2	24♈50.3	13♊25.6	22♉ 5.6	26♉49.6	29♍52.7	5♌10.2
2 F	6 44 0	10 57 54	3♋40 59	9♋45 19	15R 36.4	17 25.8	18 53.0	25 17.4	13R 19.2	22R 3.2	26R 47.9	29R 52.7	5R 9.0
3 Sa	6 47 56	11 59 2	15 51 36	21 59 53	15 24.1	19 3.9	19 16.0	25 44.9	13 12.9	22 1.0	26 46.4	29 52.7	5 7.8
4 Su	6 51 53	13 0 10	28 10 17	4♌22 52	15 13.7	20 42.3	19 37.1	26 12.5	13 6.7	21 58.8	26 44.9	29 52.6	5 6.6
5 M	6 55 49	14 1 19	10♌37 44	16 55 2	15 5.8	22 20.8	19 56.2	26 40.4	13 0.7	21 56.7	26 43.4	29 52.5	5 5.3
6 Tu	6 59 46	15 2 27	23 14 54	29 37 31	15 0.8	23 59.6	20 13.3	27 8.6	12 54.9	21 54.8	26 41.9	29 52.4	5 4.1
7 W	7 3 42	16 3 35	6♍ 3 6	12♍31 54	14D 58.4	25 38.5	20 28.3	27 36.9	12 49.1	21 52.9	26 40.5	29 52.2	5 2.8
8 Th	7 7 39	17 4 43	19 4 10	25 40 11	14 58.1	27 17.5	20 41.2	28 5.5	12 43.6	21 51.2	26 39.2	29 52.0	5 1.5
9 F	7 11 36	18 5 52	2♎20 15	9♎ 4 39	14 58.8	28 56.5	20 51.8	28 34.3	12 38.2	21 49.5	26 37.9	29 51.8	5 0.2
10 Sa	7 15 32	19 7 0	15 53 36	22 47 19	14R 59.6	0♒35.5	21 0.2	29 3.4	12 33.0	21 48.0	26 36.6	29 51.5	4 58.9
11 Su	7 19 29	20 8 9	29 45 54	6♏49 24	14 59.2	2 14.3	21 6.3	29 32.6	12 27.9	21 46.5	26 35.4	29 51.2	4 57.6
12 M	7 23 25	21 9 17	13♏57 42	21 10 34	14 56.9	3 52.9	21 9.9	0♉ 2.0	12 23.0	21 45.2	26 34.2	29 50.8	4 56.3
13 Tu	7 27 22	22 10 26	28 27 37	5♐48 16	14 52.3	5 31.1	21R 11.2	0 31.7	12 18.3	21 44.0	26 33.1	29 50.5	4 55.0
14 W	7 31 18	23 11 34	13♐11 49	20 37 24	14 45.7	7 8.7	21 10.1	1 1.5	12 13.8	21 42.9	26 32.0	29 50.0	4 53.6
15 Th	7 35 15	24 12 43	28 4 1	5♑30 35	14 37.7	8 45.5	21 6.4	1 31.5	12 9.4	21 41.9	26 31.0	29 49.6	4 52.3
16 F	7 39 11	25 13 51	12♑56 1	20 19 10	14 29.4	10 21.3	21 0.3	2 1.8	12 5.3	21 41.0	26 30.0	29 49.1	4 51.0
17 Sa	7 43 8	26 14 58	27 39 2	4♒54 38	14 21.9	11 55.8	20 51.7	2 32.2	12 1.3	21 40.3	26 29.0	29 48.6	4 49.6
18 Su	7 47 5	27 16 5	12♒ 5 9	19 9 57	14 16.0	13 28.7	20 40.5	3 2.7	11 57.5	21 39.6	26 28.2	29 48.1	4 48.3
19 M	7 51 1	28 17 12	26 8 33	3♓ 0 38	14 12.2	14 59.5	20 26.9	3 33.5	11 53.9	21 39.1	26 27.3	29 47.5	4 46.9
20 Tu	7 54 58	29 18 17	9♓46 6	16 24 58	14D 10.7	16 27.9	20 10.7	4 4.4	11 50.5	21 38.6	26 26.5	29 46.9	4 45.6
21 W	7 58 54	0♒19 22	22 57 27	29 23 49	14 10.9	17 53.3	19 52.2	4 35.5	11 47.3	21 38.3	26 25.8	29 46.3	4 44.2
22 Th	8 2 51	1 20 25	5♈44 30	11♈59 58	14 12.2	19 15.2	19 31.3	5 6.8	11 44.2	21 38.1	26 25.1	29 45.6	4 42.8
23 F	8 6 47	2 21 28	18 10 47	24 17 33	14 13.7	20 33.0	19 8.0	5 38.2	11 41.4	21D 38.0	26 24.5	29 44.9	4 41.5
24 Sa	8 10 44	3 22 30	0♉20 52	6♉21 24	14R 14.6	21 45.9	18 42.6	6 9.7	11 38.8	21 38.0	26 23.9	29 44.2	4 40.1
25 Su	8 14 40	4 23 30	12 19 45	18 16 35	14 14.3	22 53.3	18 15.2	6 41.4	11 36.4	21 38.2	26 23.4	29 43.4	4 38.7
26 M	8 18 37	5 24 30	24 12 28	0♊ 8 1	14 12.2	23 54.3	17 45.8	7 13.3	11 34.2	21 38.4	26 22.9	29 42.6	4 37.4
27 Tu	8 22 34	6 25 28	6♊ 3 46	12 0 15	14 8.4	24 48.0	17 14.7	7 45.2	11 32.2	21 38.8	26 22.5	29 41.8	4 36.0
28 W	8 26 30	7 26 26	17 57 54	23 57 10	14 3.2	25 33.7	16 42.0	8 17.3	11 30.3	21 39.3	26 22.1	29 41.0	4 34.6
29 Th	8 30 27	8 27 22	29 58 24	6♋ 1 56	13 56.9	26 10.6	16 7.9	8 49.6	11 28.7	21 39.9	26 21.8	29 40.1	4 33.3
30 F	8 34 23	9 28 17	12♋ 8 1	18 16 52	13 50.2	26 37.8	15 32.7	9 21.9	11 27.3	21 40.6	26 21.5	29 39.2	4 31.9
31 Sa	8 38 20	10 29 11	24 28 38	0♌43 27	13 44.0	26 54.7	14 56.6	9 54.4	11 26.1	21 41.4	26 21.3	29 38.3	4 30.6

LONGITUDE — FEBRUARY 1942

Day	Sid.Time	☉	0 hr ☽	Noon ☽	True ☊	☿	♀	♂	♃	♄	♅	♆	♇
1 Su	8 42 16	11♒30 4	7♌ 1 23	13♌22 28	13♍38.8	27♒ 0.9	14♒19.8	10♉27.0	11♊25.1	21♉42.3	26♉21.1	29♍37.3	4♌29.2
2 M	8 46 13	12 30 56	19 46 41	26 14 2	13R 35.0	26R 55.9	13R 42.6	10 59.7	11R 24.3	21 43.4	26R 21.0	29R 36.3	4R 27.8
3 Tu	8 50 9	13 31 47	2♍44 29	9♍17 58	13D 32.9	26 39.6	13 5.3	11 32.5	11 23.7	21 44.5	26D 21.0	29 35.3	4 26.5
4 W	8 54 6	14 32 36	15 54 28	22 33 56	13 32.5	26 12.5	12 28.1	12 5.4	11 23.4	21 45.8	26 21.0	29 34.3	4 25.1
5 Th	8 58 3	15 33 25	29 16 19	6♎ 1 35	13 33.2	25 34.9	11 51.3	12 38.5	11D 23.2	21 47.1	26 21.0	29 33.2	4 23.8
6 F	9 1 59	16 34 13	12♎49 44	19 40 43	13 34.7	24 47.8	11 15.2	13 11.6	11 23.2	21 48.6	26 21.1	29 32.1	4 22.5
7 Sa	9 5 56	17 35 0	26 34 31	3♏31 4	13 36.3	23 52.5	10 39.9	13 44.8	11 23.4	21 50.2	26 21.3	29 31.0	4 21.1
8 Su	9 9 52	18 35 45	10♏30 19	17 32 10	13R 37.4	22 50.5	10 5.8	14 18.2	11 23.8	21 51.9	26 21.5	29 29.8	4 19.8
9 M	9 13 49	19 36 30	24 36 27	1♐42 57	13 37.5	21 43.5	9 33.0	14 51.6	11 24.5	21 53.7	26 21.7	29 28.7	4 18.5
10 Tu	9 17 45	20 37 14	8♐51 26	16 1 31	13 36.5	20 33.6	9 1.8	15 25.1	11 25.3	21 55.6	26 22.0	29 27.5	4 17.2
11 W	9 21 42	21 37 57	23 12 48	0♑24 47	13 34.5	19 22.6	8 32.3	15 58.7	11 26.3	21 57.7	26 22.4	29 26.3	4 15.9
12 Th	9 25 38	22 38 39	7♑36 56	14 48 37	13 31.8	18 12.5	8 4.7	16 32.4	11 27.6	21 59.8	26 22.8	29 25.0	4 14.6
13 F	9 29 35	23 39 20	21 59 13	29 8 4	13 28.9	17 5.0	7 39.1	17 6.2	11 29.0	22 2.1	26 23.3	29 23.8	4 13.3
14 Sa	9 33 32	24 39 59	6♒14 31	13♒17 57	13 26.2	16 1.6	7 15.6	17 40.1	11 30.6	22 4.4	26 23.8	29 22.5	4 12.0
15 Su	9 37 28	25 40 37	20 17 48	27 13 33	13 24.3	15 3.7	6 54.4	18 14.1	11 32.5	22 6.9	26 24.4	29 21.2	4 10.8
16 M	9 41 25	26 41 14	4♓ 4 47	10♓51 11	13D 23.2	14 12.1	6 35.5	18 48.2	11 34.5	22 9.4	26 25.0	29 19.9	4 9.5
17 Tu	9 45 21	27 41 49	17 32 33	24 8 44	13 23.0	13 27.5	6 19.0	19 22.3	11 36.7	22 12.1	26 25.7	29 18.5	4 8.3
18 W	9 49 18	28 42 23	0♈39 46	7♈ 5 43	13 23.6	12 50.4	6 4.8	19 56.5	11 39.1	22 14.9	26 26.5	29 17.2	4 7.0
19 Th	9 53 14	29 42 54	13 26 46	19 43 13	13 24.7	12 20.9	5 53.2	20 30.8	11 41.7	22 17.7	26 27.2	29 15.8	4 5.8
20 F	9 57 11	0♓43 24	25 55 23	2♉ 3 43	13 25.9	11 59.1	5 44.0	21 5.2	11 44.6	22 20.7	26 28.1	29 14.4	4 4.6
21 Sa	10 1 7	1 43 52	8♉ 8 39	14 10 42	13 27.1	11 44.8	5 37.3	21 39.6	11 47.6	22 23.8	26 29.0	29 13.0	4 3.4
22 Su	10 5 4	2 44 19	20 10 26	26 8 25	13 27.9	11D 37.8	5 33.0	22 14.2	11 50.8	22 27.0	26 29.9	29 11.5	4 2.2
23 M	10 9 1	3 44 43	2♊ 5 14	8♊ 1 28	13R 28.2	11 37.7	5D 31.2	22 48.7	11 54.1	22 30.2	26 30.9	29 10.1	4 1.1
24 Tu	10 12 57	4 45 6	13 57 43	19 54 35	13 28.0	11 44.3	5 31.8	23 23.4	11 57.7	22 33.6	26 32.0	29 8.6	3 59.9
25 W	10 16 54	5 45 26	25 52 38	1♋52 24	13 27.5	11 57.1	5 34.8	23 58.1	12 1.5	22 37.1	26 33.0	29 7.1	3 58.8
26 Th	10 20 50	6 45 45	7♋54 26	13 59 11	13 26.7	12 15.7	5 40.1	24 32.9	12 5.4	22 40.7	26 34.2	29 5.6	3 57.7
27 F	10 24 47	7 46 2	20 7 5	26 18 32	13 25.9	12 39.8	5 47.7	25 7.7	12 9.5	22 44.3	26 35.4	29 4.1	3 56.6
28 Sa	10 28 43	8 46 17	2♌33 51	8♌53 18	13 25.2	13 8.9	5 57.5	25 42.6	12 13.8	22 48.1	26 36.6	29 2.6	3 55.5

Astro Data	Dy Hr Mn
♆ R	1 10:32
☽ 0 S	9 2:39
♀ R	13 0:41
☽ 0 N	21 20:49
♄ D	23 7:01
☿ R	1 1:16
♅ D	3 14:50
☽ 0 S	5 8:55
♃ D	5 10:02
☽ 0 N	18 6:54
☿ D	22 12:08
♀ D	23 6:02

Planet Ingress	Dy Hr Mn
☿ ♒	9 15:24
♂ ♉	11 22:21
☉ ♒	20 16:24
☉ ♓	19 6:47

Last Aspect Dy Hr Mn		☽ Ingress	Dy Hr Mn
1 16:27	♆ □	♋	1 16:42
4 3:18	♆ ✶	♌	4 3:32
6 7:37	♂ △	♍	6 12:42
8 19:34	♆ ☌	♎	8 19:48
10 23:36	♂ ☍	♏	11 0:24
13 2:16	♆ ✶	♐	13 2:31
15 2:50	♆ □	♑	15 3:07
17 3:33	♆ △	♒	17 3:52
19 0:33	♅ □	♓	19 6:43
21 12:42	♆ ☍	♈	21 13:08
23 5:10	☿ ✶	♉	23 23:18
26 11:08	♆ △	♊	26 11:44
28 23:24	♆ □	♋	29 0:03
31 9:54	♆ ✶	♌	31 10:37

Last Aspect Dy Hr Mn		☽ Ingress	Dy Hr Mn
2 13:04	☿ ☍	♍	2 18:57
5 0:30	♆ ☌	♎	5 1:18
6 19:37	☿ △	♏	7 5:56
9 8:13	♆ ✶	♐	9 9:07
11 10:22	♆ □	♑	11 11:19
13 12:25	♆ △	♒	13 13:27
15 10:35	♅ □	♓	15 16:50
17 21:27	♆ ☍	♈	17 22:46
18 21:59	☿ ✶	♉	20 7:57
22 18:07	♆ △	♊	22 19:47
25 6:29	♆ □	♋	25 8:15
27 17:16	♆ ✶	♌	27 19:06

☽ Phases & Eclipses Dy Hr Mn	
2 15:42	○ 11♋38
10 6:05	☽ 19♎22
16 21:32	● 26♑09
24 6:36	☽ 3♉39
1 9:12	○ 11♌53
8 14:52	☽ 19♏13
15 10:03	● 26♒06
23 3:40	☽ 3♊54

Astro Data

1 JANUARY 1942
Julian Day # 15341
Delta T 25.3 sec
SVP 06♓04'14"
Obliquity 23°26'39"
⚷ Chiron 13♌34.0R
☽ Mean ☊ 16♍50.6

1 FEBRUARY 1942
Julian Day # 15372
Delta T 25.3 sec
SVP 06♓04'09"
Obliquity 23°26'39"
⚷ Chiron 11♌26.7R
☽ Mean ☊ 15♍12.1

MARCH 1942 — LONGITUDE

Day	Sid.Time	☉	0 hr ☽	Noon ☽	True ☊	☿	♀	♂	♃	♄	♅	♆	♇
1 Su	10 32 40	9♓46 30	15♌17 5	21♌45 17	13♍24.8	13♒42.8	6♒ 9.5	26♉17.5	12♊18.3	22♉51.9	26♉37.9	29♍ 1.1	3♌54.4
2 M	10 36 36	10 46 41	28 17 58	4♍55 6	13R 24.5	14 21.0	6 23.6	26 52.5	12 23.0	22 55.9	26 39.3	28R 59.5	3R 53.3
3 Tu	10 40 33	11 46 50	11♍36 34	18 22 12	13D 24.4	15 3.3	6 39.8	27 27.5	12 27.8	22 59.9	26 40.7	28 58.0	3 52.3
4 W	10 44 30	12 46 57	25 11 44	2♎ 4 52	13R 24.4	15 49.4	6 58.0	28 2.6	12 32.8	23 4.0	26 42.1	28 56.4	3 51.3
5 Th	10 48 26	13 47 2	9♎ 1 15	16 0 30	13 24.4	16 39.0	7 18.1	28 37.7	12 38.0	23 8.3	26 43.6	28 54.8	3 50.3
6 F	10 52 23	14 47 6	23 2 11	0♏ 5 53	13 24.3	17 31.9	7 40.1	29 12.9	12 43.3	23 12.6	26 45.1	28 53.2	3 49.3
7 Sa	10 56 19	15 47 8	7♏11 9	14 17 33	13 24.1	18 27.9	8 3.9	29 48.1	12 48.8	23 16.9	26 46.7	28 51.6	3 48.3
8 Su	11 0 16	16 47 9	21 24 41	28 32 8	13 23.8	19 26.7	8 29.4	0♊23.4	12 54.5	23 21.4	26 48.3	28 50.0	3 47.3
9 M	11 4 12	17 47 8	5♐39 32	12♐46 34	13D 23.6	20 28.1	8 56.7	0 58.7	13 0.3	23 26.0	26 50.0	28 48.4	3 46.4
10 Tu	11 8 9	18 47 5	19 52 53	26 58 12	13 23.5	21 32.1	9 25.5	1 34.1	13 6.3	23 30.6	26 51.7	28 46.8	3 45.5
11 W	11 12 5	19 47 1	4♑ 2 16	11♑ 4 49	13 23.7	22 38.4	9 55.9	2 9.5	13 12.5	23 35.4	26 53.5	28 45.1	3 44.6
12 Th	11 16 2	20 46 55	18 5 37	25 4 27	13 24.1	23 47.0	10 27.8	2 45.0	13 18.8	23 40.2	26 55.3	28 43.5	3 43.7
13 F	11 19 59	21 46 48	2♒ 1 5	8♒55 19	13 24.9	24 57.6	11 1.1	3 20.4	13 25.3	23 45.1	26 57.2	28 41.8	3 42.9
14 Sa	11 23 55	22 46 38	15 46 55	22 35 42	13 25.7	26 10.3	11 35.8	3 56.0	13 32.0	23 50.0	26 59.1	28 40.2	3 42.1
15 Su	11 27 52	23 46 27	29 21 29	6♓ 4 3	13 26.4	27 24.9	12 11.8	4 31.6	13 38.8	23 55.1	27 1.0	28 38.5	3 41.2
16 M	11 31 48	24 46 14	12♓43 16	19 18 58	13R 26.7	28 41.3	12 49.1	5 7.2	13 45.7	24 0.2	27 3.0	28 36.9	3 40.5
17 Tu	11 35 45	25 46 0	25 51 4	2♈19 28	13 26.4	29 59.4	13 27.5	5 42.8	13 52.8	24 5.4	27 5.0	28 35.2	3 39.7
18 W	11 39 41	26 45 43	8♈44 9	15 5 7	13 25.4	1♓19.3	14 7.2	6 18.5	14 0.0	24 10.7	27 7.1	28 33.6	3 38.9
19 Th	11 43 38	27 45 24	21 22 27	27 36 15	13 23.7	2 40.7	14 47.9	6 54.3	14 7.4	24 16.1	27 9.2	28 31.9	3 38.2
20 F	11 47 34	28 45 3	3♉46 42	9♉54 2	13 21.5	4 3.8	15 29.7	7 30.0	14 15.0	24 21.5	27 11.4	28 30.2	3 37.5
21 Sa	11 51 31	29 44 40	15 58 32	22 0 31	13 18.9	5 28.4	16 12.6	8 5.8	14 22.6	24 27.0	27 13.6	28 28.6	3 36.8
22 Su	11 55 27	0♈44 14	28 0 24	3♊58 36	13 16.5	6 54.5	16 56.4	8 41.7	14 30.5	24 32.6	27 15.8	28 26.9	3 36.2
23 M	11 59 24	1 43 47	9♊55 36	15 51 55	13 14.4	8 22.0	17 41.2	9 17.6	14 38.4	24 38.2	27 18.1	28 25.2	3 35.6
24 Tu	12 3 21	2 43 17	21 48 5	27 44 40	13 13.1	9 51.0	18 26.9	9 53.5	14 46.5	24 44.0	27 20.4	28 23.6	3 35.0
25 W	12 7 17	3 42 45	3♋42 14	9♋41 25	13D 12.6	11 21.4	19 13.4	10 29.4	14 54.7	24 49.7	27 22.8	28 21.9	3 34.4
26 Th	12 11 14	4 42 11	15 42 48	21 46 57	13 13.1	12 53.3	20 0.8	11 5.3	15 3.1	24 55.6	27 25.2	28 20.3	3 33.8
27 F	12 15 10	5 41 34	27 54 29	4♌ 5 54	13 14.3	14 26.5	20 49.0	11 41.3	15 11.6	25 1.5	27 27.6	28 18.6	3 33.3
28 Sa	12 19 7	6 40 55	10♌21 45	16 42 28	13 15.9	16 1.1	21 38.0	12 17.3	15 20.2	25 7.5	27 30.1	28 17.0	3 32.8
29 Su	12 23 3	7 40 14	23 8 27	29 39 59	13 17.5	17 37.1	22 27.7	12 53.4	15 28.9	25 13.5	27 32.6	28 15.4	3 32.3
30 M	12 27 0	8 39 30	6♍17 18	13♍ 0 31	13R 18.5	19 14.6	23 18.2	13 29.4	15 37.8	25 19.6	27 35.1	28 13.7	3 31.8
31 Tu	12 30 56	9 38 44	19 49 34	26 44 21	13 18.5	20 53.3	24 9.3	14 5.5	15 46.8	25 25.8	27 37.7	28 12.1	3 31.4

APRIL 1942 — LONGITUDE

Day	Sid.Time	☉	0 hr ☽	Noon ☽	True ☊	☿	♀	♂	♃	♄	♅	♆	♇
1 W	12 34 53	10♈37 57	3♎44 32	10♎49 43	13♍17.2	22♓33.5	25♒ 1.2	14♊41.6	15♊55.9	25♉32.0	27♉40.3	28♍10.5	3♌31.0
2 Th	12 38 50	11 37 7	17 59 21	25 12 43	13R 14.6	24 15.1	25 53.6	15 17.7	16 5.1	25 38.3	27 42.9	28R 8.9	3R 30.6
3 F	12 42 46	12 36 15	2♏29 6	9♏47 37	13 10.8	25 58.1	26 46.7	15 53.8	16 14.5	25 44.6	27 45.6	28 7.3	3 30.2
4 Sa	12 46 43	13 35 21	17 7 25	24 27 35	13 6.4	27 42.5	27 40.4	16 30.0	16 23.9	25 51.0	27 48.3	28 5.7	3 29.9
5 Su	12 50 39	14 34 25	1♐47 17	9♐ 5 44	13 2.0	29 28.4	28 34.7	17 6.2	16 33.5	25 57.5	27 51.0	28 4.1	3 29.6
6 M	12 54 36	15 33 28	16 22 11	23 36 3	12 58.3	1♈15.7	29 29.5	17 42.4	16 43.2	26 4.0	27 53.8	28 2.5	3 29.3
7 Tu	12 58 32	16 32 28	0♑46 50	7♑54 9	12 55.9	3 4.4	0♓24.9	18 18.6	16 53.0	26 10.5	27 56.6	28 1.0	3 29.0
8 W	13 2 29	17 31 28	14 57 44	21 57 25	12D 54.9	4 54.7	1 20.8	18 54.8	17 2.9	26 17.1	27 59.4	27 59.4	3 28.8
9 Th	13 6 25	18 30 25	28 53 9	5♒44 56	12 55.2	6 46.4	2 17.2	19 31.1	17 12.9	26 23.8	28 2.3	27 57.9	3 28.6
10 F	13 10 22	19 29 21	12♒32 50	19 16 57	12 56.5	8 39.5	3 14.0	20 7.4	17 23.0	26 30.5	28 5.2	27 56.3	3 28.4
11 Sa	13 14 19	20 28 14	25 57 25	2♓34 23	12 58.0	10 34.1	4 11.3	20 43.7	17 33.2	26 37.3	28 8.1	27 54.8	3 28.3
12 Su	13 18 15	21 27 7	9♓ 8 1	15 38 26	12R 58.9	12 30.2	5 9.1	21 20.0	17 43.5	26 44.1	28 11.0	27 53.3	3 28.1
13 M	13 22 12	22 25 57	22 5 46	28 30 9	12 58.6	14 27.8	6 7.3	21 56.4	17 53.9	26 50.9	28 14.0	27 51.8	3 28.0
14 Tu	13 26 8	23 24 45	4♈51 41	11♈10 27	12 56.5	16 26.8	7 5.9	22 32.7	18 4.4	26 57.8	28 17.0	27 50.4	3 27.9
15 W	13 30 5	24 23 32	17 26 31	23 39 59	12 52.3	18 27.1	8 4.8	23 9.1	18 15.0	27 4.8	28 20.0	27 48.9	3 27.9
16 Th	13 34 1	25 22 16	29 50 55	5♉59 25	12 46.1	20 28.8	9 4.2	23 45.5	18 25.7	27 11.7	28 23.1	27 47.5	3D 27.9
17 F	13 37 58	26 20 59	12♉ 5 36	18 9 35	12 38.5	22 31.8	10 3.9	24 21.9	18 36.5	27 18.8	28 26.1	27 46.0	3 27.9
18 Sa	13 41 54	27 19 40	24 11 33	0♊11 42	12 30.0	24 36.0	11 3.9	24 58.4	18 47.4	27 25.8	28 29.2	27 44.6	3 27.9
19 Su	13 45 51	28 18 18	6♊10 16	12 7 33	12 21.6	26 41.3	12 4.3	25 34.8	18 58.4	27 32.9	28 32.4	27 43.2	3 27.9
20 M	13 49 47	29 16 55	18 3 53	23 59 39	12 13.9	28 47.5	13 5.1	26 11.3	19 9.5	27 40.1	28 35.5	27 41.9	3 28.0
21 Tu	13 53 44	0♉15 29	29 55 16	5♋51 14	12 7.8	0♉54.6	14 6.1	26 47.8	19 20.6	27 47.2	28 38.7	27 40.5	3 28.1
22 W	13 57 41	1 14 2	11♋48 1	17 46 13	12 3.6	3 2.2	15 7.4	27 24.3	19 31.9	27 54.5	28 41.9	27 39.2	3 28.3
23 Th	14 1 37	2 12 32	23 46 23	29 49 8	12D 1.5	5 10.3	16 9.1	28 0.8	19 43.2	28 1.7	28 45.1	27 37.9	3 28.4
24 F	14 5 34	3 11 0	5♌55 5	12♌ 4 51	12 1.1	7 18.5	17 11.0	28 37.3	19 54.6	28 9.0	28 48.3	27 36.6	3 28.6
25 Sa	14 9 30	4 9 26	18 19 5	24 38 21	12 1.9	9 26.7	18 13.2	29 13.9	20 6.0	28 16.3	28 51.5	27 35.3	3 28.8
26 Su	14 13 27	5 7 49	1♍ 3 13	7♍34 10	12R 2.9	11 34.5	19 15.7	29 50.4	20 17.6	28 23.6	28 54.8	27 34.1	3 29.1
27 M	14 17 23	6 6 11	14 11 38	20 55 55	12 3.3	13 41.6	20 18.4	0♋27.0	20 29.2	28 31.0	28 58.1	27 32.9	3 29.3
28 Tu	14 21 20	7 4 30	27 47 11	4♎45 27	12 2.2	15 47.8	21 21.3	1 3.5	20 40.9	28 38.4	29 1.4	27 31.6	3 29.6
29 W	14 25 16	8 2 48	11♎50 35	19 2 12	11 58.9	17 52.7	22 24.6	1 40.1	20 52.7	28 45.8	29 4.7	27 30.5	3 29.9
30 Th	14 29 13	9 1 4	26 19 45	3♏42 30	11 53.4	19 55.9	23 28.0	2 16.7	21 4.5	28 53.3	29 8.0	27 29.3	3 30.3

Astro Data (Dy Hr Mn)	Planet Ingress (Dy Hr Mn)
☽0S 4 15:59	♂ ♊ 7 8:04
☽0N 17 15:47	☿ ♓ 17 0:10
	☉ ♈ 21 6:11
☽0S 1 1:01	
☿0N 7 22:02	☿ ♈ 5 7:06
♅△♆ 7 23:54	♀ ♓ 6 13:14
☽0N 13 23:04	☉ ♉ 20 17:39
♃∠♇ 16 4:44	☿ ♉ 20 13:42
♇ D 16 11:02	♂ ♋ 26 6:18
♄△♆ 20 5:07	
☽0S 28 11:35	

Last Aspect (Dy Hr Mn)	☽ Ingress (Dy Hr Mn)	Last Aspect (Dy Hr Mn)	☽ Ingress (Dy Hr Mn)
1 21:17 ♂ □	♍ 2 3:06	2 13:59 ♀ △	♏ 2 19:54
4 6:31 ♆ ☌	♎ 4 8:23	4 19:41 ♆ △	♐ 4 21:04
5 13:58 ♆ △	♏ 6 11:50	6 19:23 ♆ □	♑ 6 22:41
8 12:29 ♆ ⚹	♐ 8 14:28	8 22:31 ♅ △	♒ 9 1:56
10 15:02 ♆ □	♑ 10 17:08	11 3:57 ♅ □	♓ 11 7:19
12 18:16 ♆ △	♒ 12 20:30	13 11:32 ♅ ⚹	♈ 13 14:49
14 20:11 ♆ ☌	♓ 15 1:09	15 14:33 ☉ ☌	♉ 16 0:18
17 5:03 ♆ ☍	♈ 17 7:41	18 8:37 ♅ ☌	♊ 18 11:37
18 10:44 ♀ ⚹	♉ 19 16:39	20 19:28 ♆ □	♋ 21 0:10
22 0:53 ♆ △	♊ 22 4:00	23 9:56 ♅ ⚹	♌ 23 12:21
24 13:17 ♆ □	♋ 24 16:33	25 21:38 ♂ ⚹	♍ 25 22:02
27 0:47 ♆ ⚹	♌ 27 4:04	28 2:09 ♅ △	♎ 28 3:50
29 8:08 ♅ □	♍ 29 12:37	29 15:15 ♃ △	♏ 30 5:59
31 14:29 ♆ ☌	♎ 31 17:36		

☽ Phases & Eclipses (Dy Hr Mn)	
3 0:20	○ 11♍48
3 0:21	• T 1.561
9 22:00	☽ 18♐42
16 23:50	● 25♓46
16 23:36:41	• P 0.639
25 0:01	☽ 3♋43
1 12:32	○ 11♎09
8 4:43	☽ 17♑43
15 14:33	● 24♈59
23 18:10	☽ 2♌57
30 21:59	○ 9♏54

Astro Data

1 MARCH 1942
Julian Day # 15400
Delta T 25.4 sec
SVP 06♓04'06"
Obliquity 23°26'40"
⚷ Chiron 9♌28.2R
☽ Mean ☊ 13♍43.1

1 APRIL 1942
Julian Day # 15431
Delta T 25.4 sec
SVP 06♓04'04"
Obliquity 23°26'40"
⚷ Chiron 8♌16.1R
☽ Mean ☊ 12♍04.6

LONGITUDE — MAY 1942

Day	Sid.Time	☉	0 hr ☽	Noon ☽	True ☊	☿	♀	♂	♃	♄	♅	♆	♇
1 F	14 33 10	9♉59 17	11♏ 9 30	18♏39 39	11♍45.8	21♉57.4	24♓31.7	2♋53.3	21♊16.4	29♉ 0.8	29♉11.4	27♍28.2	3♌30.6
2 Sa	14 37 6	10 57 29	26 11 46	3♐44 35	11R 37.0	23 56.6	25 35.6	3 29.9	21 28.4	29 8.3	29 14.7	27R 27.1	3 31.0
3 Su	14 41 3	11 55 40	11♐16 50	18 47 18	11 28.2	25 53.4	26 39.8	4 6.5	21 40.5	29 15.8	29 18.1	27 26.0	3 31.5
4 M	14 44 59	12 53 49	26 14 55	3♑38 41	11 20.3	27 47.6	27 44.1	4 43.2	21 52.6	29 23.3	29 21.5	27 24.9	3 31.9
5 Tu	14 48 56	13 51 56	10♑57 52	18 11 51	11 14.3	29 38.9	28 48.7	5 19.8	22 4.7	29 30.9	29 24.9	27 23.9	3 32.4
6 W	14 52 52	14 50 2	25 20 14	2♒22 50	11 10.5	1♊27.2	29 53.4	5 56.5	22 17.0	29 38.5	29 28.3	27 22.9	3 32.9
7 Th	14 56 49	15 48 7	9♒19 34	16 10 31	11D 9.0	3 12.2	0♈58.4	6 33.1	22 29.3	29 46.1	29 31.7	27 21.9	3 33.4
8 F	15 0 45	16 46 10	22 55 54	29 35 59	11 8.9	4 53.9	2 3.6	7 9.8	22 41.6	29 53.7	29 35.2	27 20.9	3 33.9
9 Sa	15 4 42	17 44 12	6♓11 6	12♓41 38	11R 9.4	6 32.2	3 8.9	7 46.5	22 54.0	0♊ 1.4	29 38.6	27 20.0	3 34.5
10 Su	15 8 39	18 42 13	19 7 57	25 30 28	11 9.2	8 6.9	4 14.4	8 23.2	23 6.5	0 9.0	29 42.0	27 19.1	3 35.1
11 M	15 12 35	19 40 12	1♈49 32	8♈ 5 30	11 7.3	9 37.9	5 20.1	8 59.9	23 19.0	0 16.7	29 45.5	27 18.2	3 35.7
12 Tu	15 16 32	20 38 10	14 18 41	20 29 22	11 3.0	11 5.3	6 25.9	9 36.6	23 31.6	0 24.4	29 49.0	27 17.3	3 36.4
13 W	15 20 28	21 36 6	26 37 48	2♉44 13	10 55.9	12 28.9	7 31.9	10 13.3	23 44.3	0 32.1	29 52.4	27 16.5	3 37.0
14 Th	15 24 25	22 34 1	8♉48 48	14 51 42	10 46.1	13 48.6	8 38.0	10 50.1	23 57.0	0 39.8	29 55.9	27 15.7	3 37.7
15 F	15 28 21	23 31 55	20 53 5	26 53 6	10 34.2	15 4.4	9 44.3	11 26.9	24 9.7	0 47.6	29 59.4	27 14.9	3 38.4
16 Sa	15 32 18	24 29 47	2♊51 52	8♊49 35	10 21.0	16 16.3	10 50.8	12 3.6	24 22.5	0 55.3	0♊ 2.9	27 14.2	3 39.2
17 Su	15 36 14	25 27 38	14 46 23	20 42 29	10 7.7	17 24.1	11 57.4	12 40.4	24 35.3	1 3.0	0 6.4	27 13.5	3 39.9
18 M	15 40 11	26 25 27	26 38 6	2♋33 30	9 55.4	18 27.9	13 4.1	13 17.2	24 48.2	1 10.8	0 9.9	27 12.8	3 40.7
19 Tu	15 44 8	27 23 15	8♋28 59	14 24 56	9 45.0	19 27.6	14 10.9	13 54.0	25 1.1	1 18.5	0 13.4	27 12.1	3 41.6
20 W	15 48 4	28 21 1	20 21 43	26 19 48	9 37.1	20 23.0	15 17.9	14 30.8	25 14.1	1 26.3	0 16.9	27 11.5	3 42.4
21 Th	15 52 1	29 18 46	2♌19 40	8♌21 51	9 32.0	21 14.2	16 25.0	15 7.6	25 27.1	1 34.1	0 20.4	27 10.9	3 43.2
22 F	15 55 57	0♊16 29	14 26 54	20 35 27	9 29.4	22 1.0	17 32.2	15 44.5	25 40.2	1 41.8	0 23.9	27 10.3	3 44.1
23 Sa	15 59 54	1 14 10	26 48 6	3♍ 5 28	9 28.6	22 43.4	18 39.5	16 21.3	25 53.2	1 49.6	0 27.4	27 9.8	3 45.0
24 Su	16 3 50	2 11 50	9♍28 10	15 56 47	9 28.5	23 21.4	19 47.0	16 58.2	26 6.4	1 57.4	0 30.9	27 9.3	3 46.0
25 M	16 7 47	3 9 29	22 31 50	29 13 48	9 28.2	23 54.8	20 54.5	17 35.0	26 19.5	2 5.1	0 34.4	27 8.8	3 46.9
26 Tu	16 11 43	4 7 5	6♎ 3 0	12♎59 40	9 26.3	24 23.6	22 2.2	18 11.9	26 32.7	2 12.9	0 37.9	27 8.4	3 47.9
27 W	16 15 40	5 4 41	20 3 48	27 15 16	9 22.2	24 47.7	23 9.9	18 48.7	26 45.9	2 20.7	0 41.4	27 8.0	3 48.9
28 Th	16 19 37	6 2 15	4♏33 40	11♏58 22	9 15.5	25 7.2	24 17.8	19 25.6	26 59.2	2 28.4	0 44.9	27 7.6	3 49.9
29 F	16 23 33	6 59 47	19 28 32	27 3 4	9 6.5	25 22.0	25 25.8	20 2.5	27 12.5	2 36.2	0 48.4	27 7.2	3 50.9
30 Sa	16 27 30	7 57 19	4♐40 44	12♐20 7	8 56.0	25 32.0	26 33.9	20 39.4	27 25.8	2 43.9	0 51.9	27 6.9	3 51.9
31 Su	16 31 26	8 54 49	19 59 45	27 38 13	8 45.2	25R 37.4	27 42.1	21 16.3	27 39.2	2 51.7	0 55.4	27 6.6	3 53.0

LONGITUDE — JUNE 1942

Day	Sid.Time	☉	0 hr ☽	Noon ☽	True ☊	☿	♀	♂	♃	♄	♅	♆	♇
1 M	16 35 23	9♊52 19	5♑14 6	12♑46 9	8♍35.4	25♊38.2	28♈50.4	21♋53.2	27♊52.5	2♊59.4	0♊58.9	27♍ 6.4	3♌54.1
2 Tu	16 39 19	10 49 47	20 13 18	27 34 43	8R 27.7	25R 34.4	29 58.8	22 30.1	28 5.9	3 7.1	1 2.3	27R 6.2	3 55.2
3 W	16 43 16	11 47 15	4♒49 45	11♒58 1	8 22.5	25 26.3	1♉ 7.3	23 7.0	28 19.4	3 14.9	1 5.8	27 6.0	3 56.4
4 Th	16 47 12	12 44 42	18 59 19	25 53 41	8 19.8	25 14.0	2 15.8	23 44.0	28 32.8	3 22.6	1 9.3	27 5.8	3 57.5
5 F	16 51 9	13 42 8	2♓41 15	9♓22 20	8 19.0	24 57.7	3 24.5	24 20.9	28 46.3	3 30.3	1 12.7	27 5.7	3 58.7
6 Sa	16 55 6	14 39 34	15 57 18	22 26 38	8 19.0	24 37.8	4 33.3	24 57.9	28 59.8	3 38.0	1 16.1	27 5.6	3 59.9
7 Su	16 59 2	15 36 59	28 50 47	5♈10 18	8 18.5	24 14.5	5 42.1	25 34.8	29 13.3	3 45.6	1 19.6	27 5.5	4 1.1
8 M	17 2 59	16 34 23	11♈25 42	17 37 28	8 16.5	23 48.2	6 51.1	26 11.8	29 26.9	3 53.3	1 23.0	27D 5.5	4 2.3
9 Tu	17 6 55	17 31 47	23 46 6	29 52 2	8 12.2	23 19.4	8 0.1	26 48.8	29 40.4	4 0.9	1 26.4	27 5.5	4 3.6
10 W	17 10 52	18 29 10	5♉55 42	11♉57 26	8 5.1	22 48.6	9 9.2	27 25.8	29 54.0	4 8.5	1 29.8	27 5.5	4 4.8
11 Th	17 14 48	19 26 33	17 57 36	23 56 28	7 55.3	22 16.2	10 18.4	28 2.8	0♋ 7.6	4 16.1	1 33.2	27 5.6	4 6.1
12 F	17 18 45	20 23 55	29 54 19	5♊51 22	7 43.4	21 42.9	11 27.6	28 39.8	0 21.2	4 23.7	1 36.5	27 5.7	4 7.4
13 Sa	17 22 41	21 21 16	11♊47 48	17 43 50	7 30.2	21 9.2	12 37.0	29 16.9	0 34.8	4 31.3	1 39.9	27 5.8	4 8.7
14 Su	17 26 38	22 18 37	23 39 38	29 35 23	7 16.8	20 35.6	13 46.4	29 53.9	0 48.5	4 38.8	1 43.2	27 6.0	4 10.0
15 M	17 30 35	23 15 57	5♋31 15	11♋27 27	7 4.3	20 2.8	14 55.9	0♌31.0	1 2.1	4 46.4	1 46.6	27 6.2	4 11.4
16 Tu	17 34 31	24 13 17	17 24 13	23 21 46	6 53.8	19 31.3	16 5.4	1 8.1	1 15.8	4 53.9	1 49.9	27 6.4	4 12.8
17 W	17 38 28	25 10 35	29 20 25	5♌20 28	6 45.7	19 1.7	17 15.0	1 45.2	1 29.5	5 1.4	1 53.2	27 6.7	4 14.1
18 Th	17 42 24	26 7 53	11♌22 18	17 26 20	6 40.4	18 34.3	18 24.7	2 22.3	1 43.1	5 8.8	1 56.5	27 7.0	4 15.5
19 F	17 46 21	27 5 11	23 32 59	29 42 45	6 37.7	18 9.8	19 34.4	2 59.4	1 56.8	5 16.2	1 59.7	27 7.3	4 16.9
20 Sa	17 50 17	28 2 27	5♍56 8	12♍13 40	6D 37.0	17 48.5	20 44.3	3 36.5	2 10.5	5 23.6	2 3.0	27 7.7	4 18.4
21 Su	17 54 14	28 59 43	18 35 55	25 3 23	6R 37.3	17 30.8	21 54.1	4 13.6	2 24.2	5 31.0	2 6.2	27 8.1	4 19.8
22 M	17 58 10	29 56 58	1♎36 37	8♎16 3	6 37.5	17 17.0	23 4.1	4 50.7	2 37.9	5 38.3	2 9.4	27 8.5	4 21.3
23 Tu	18 2 7	0♋54 12	15 2 5	21 55 1	6 36.7	17 7.4	24 14.1	5 27.9	2 51.6	5 45.6	2 12.6	27 8.9	4 22.7
24 W	18 6 4	1 51 26	28 54 59	6♏ 2 0	6 33.9	17D 2.1	25 24.1	6 5.0	3 5.3	5 52.9	2 15.7	27 9.4	4 24.2
25 Th	18 10 0	2 48 39	13♏15 51	20 36 8	6 29.0	17 1.3	26 34.2	6 42.2	3 19.0	6 0.1	2 18.9	27 9.9	4 25.7
26 F	18 13 57	3 45 52	28 2 13	5♐33 14	6 21.9	17 5.2	27 44.4	7 19.4	3 32.6	6 7.3	2 22.0	27 10.5	4 27.2
27 Sa	18 17 53	4 43 4	13♐ 8 9	20 45 43	6 13.4	17 13.9	28 54.7	7 56.5	3 46.3	6 14.5	2 25.1	27 11.1	4 28.7
28 Su	18 21 50	5 40 16	28 24 34	6♑ 3 19	6 4.6	17 27.4	0♊ 5.0	8 33.7	4 0.0	6 21.7	2 28.2	27 11.7	4 30.3
29 M	18 25 46	6 37 28	13♑40 32	21 14 54	5 56.6	17 45.7	1 15.3	9 10.9	4 13.7	6 28.8	2 31.2	27 12.3	4 31.8
30 Tu	18 29 43	7 34 39	28 45 11	6♒10 21	5 50.2	18 8.9	2 25.8	9 48.2	4 27.4	6 35.8	2 34.3	27 13.0	4 33.3

Astro Data	Dy Hr Mn
♄☌♅	3 13:20
♀0N	9 2:05
☽0N	11 5:27
☽0S	25 22:13
♃□♆	28 14:47
☿ R	31 16:03
☽0N	7 12:14
♆ D	8 11:44
♂✶♇	9 9:57
♃⚺♅	19 6:42
☽0S	22 7:25
☿ D	24 15:54
♃⚺♇	30 11:46

Planet Ingress	Dy Hr Mn
☿ ♊	5 4:37
♀ ♈	6 2:26
♄ ♊	8 19:39
♅ ♊	15 4:05
☉ ♊	21 17:09
♀ ♉	2 0:26
♃ ♋	10 10:36
♂ ♌	14 3:56
☉ ♋	22 1:16
♀ ♊	27 22:18

Last Aspect Dy Hr Mn		☽ Ingress Dy Hr Mn
2 4:52	♅ ☍	♐ 2 6:03
4 2:35	♀ □	♑ 4 6:04
6 7:23	♄ △	♒ 6 7:56
8 12:39	♄ □	♓ 8 12:44
10 20:03	♅ ✶	♈ 10 20:31
12 18:14	♃ ✶	♉ 13 6:37
15 12:43	♆ △	♊ 15 18:15
18 1:10	♆ □	♋ 18 6:49
20 17:27	☉ ✶	♌ 20 19:21
22 22:13	♃ ✶	♍ 23 6:07
25 8:17	♆ ☌	♎ 25 13:22
27 11:22	♃ △	♏ 27 16:32
29 12:06	♆ ✶	♐ 29 16:39
31 13:05	♀ △	♑ 31 15:43

Last Aspect Dy Hr Mn		☽ Ingress Dy Hr Mn
2 11:13	♆ △	♒ 2 15:59
4 16:57	♃ △	♓ 4 19:14
7 0:43	♃ □	♈ 7 2:11
9 11:50	♃ ✶	♉ 9 12:16
11 21:22	♂ ✶	♊ 12 0:11
14 6:58	♆ □	♋ 14 12:50
16 19:32	♆ ✶	♌ 17 1:19
19 7:29	☉ ✶	♍ 19 12:33
21 20:44	☉ □	♎ 21 21:04
23 3:38	♆ △	♏ 24 1:50
25 23:29	♀ ☍	♐ 26 3:09
27 22:06	♆ □	♑ 28 2:30
29 21:32	♆ △	♒ 30 2:00

☽ Phases & Eclipses Dy Hr Mn		
7 12:13	☽	16♒18
15 5:45	●	23♉46
23 9:11	☽	1♍36
30 5:29	○	8♐10
5 21:26	☽	14♓33
13 21:02	●	22♊12
21 20:44	☽	29♍49
28 12:09	○	6♑09

Astro Data

1 MAY 1942
Julian Day # 15461
Delta T 25.4 sec
SVP 06♓04'02"
Obliquity 23°26'40"
⚷ Chiron 8♌37.3
☽ Mean ☊ 10♍29.2

1 JUNE 1942
Julian Day # 15492
Delta T 25.5 sec
SVP 06♓03'57"
Obliquity 23°26'39"
⚷ Chiron 10♌31.3
☽ Mean ☊ 8♍50.8

JULY 1942 — LONGITUDE

Day	Sid.Time	☉	0 hr ☽	Noon ☽	True ☊	☿	♀	♂	♃	♄	♅	♆	♇
1 W	18 33 40	8♋31 50	13♒29 35	20♒42 16	5♍46.0	18♊36.9	3♊36.3	10♌25.4	4♋41.1	6♊42.9	2♊37.3	27♍13.7	4♌34.9
2 Th	18 37 36	9 29 2	27 47 59	4♓46 34	5D 44.1	19 9.7	4 46.8	11 2.6	4 54.7	6 49.8	2 40.2	27 14.5	4 36.5
3 F	18 41 33	10 26 13	11♓38 1	18 22 28	5 44.0	19 47.2	5 57.4	11 39.9	5 8.4	6 56.8	2 43.2	27 15.2	4 38.1
4 Sa	18 45 29	11 23 25	25 0 13	1♈31 39	5 44.8	20 29.5	7 8.1	12 17.1	5 22.0	7 3.7	2 46.1	27 16.0	4 39.7
5 Su	18 49 26	12 20 37	7♈57 15	14 17 31	5R 45.6	21 16.4	8 18.9	12 54.4	5 35.7	7 10.5	2 49.0	27 16.9	4 41.3
6 M	18 53 22	13 17 49	20 33 1	26 44 17	5 45.4	22 7.9	9 29.7	13 31.7	5 49.3	7 17.4	2 51.9	27 17.7	4 42.9
7 Tu	18 57 19	14 15 2	2♉51 54	8♉56 24	5 43.6	23 4.0	10 40.5	14 9.0	6 2.9	7 24.1	2 54.7	27 18.6	4 44.5
8 W	19 1 15	15 12 15	14 58 20	20 58 10	5 39.6	24 4.5	11 51.4	14 46.3	6 16.5	7 30.9	2 57.5	27 19.5	4 46.1
9 Th	19 5 12	16 9 28	26 56 22	2♊53 22	5 33.7	25 9.5	13 2.4	15 23.7	6 30.1	7 37.5	3 0.3	27 20.5	4 47.8
10 F	19 9 8	17 6 42	8♊49 34	14 45 18	5 26.1	26 18.9	14 13.4	16 1.0	6 43.7	7 44.2	3 3.1	27 21.4	4 49.4
11 Sa	19 13 5	18 3 56	20 40 53	26 36 37	5 17.5	27 32.6	15 24.5	16 38.4	6 57.2	7 50.8	3 5.8	27 22.5	4 51.1
12 Su	19 17 2	19 1 10	2♋32 43	8♋29 27	5 8.7	28 50.5	16 35.7	17 15.8	7 10.8	7 57.3	3 8.5	27 23.5	4 52.7
13 M	19 20 58	19 58 25	14 27 1	20 25 36	5 0.5	0♋12.6	17 46.9	17 53.2	7 24.3	8 3.8	3 11.1	27 24.6	4 54.4
14 Tu	19 24 55	20 55 39	26 25 25	2♌26 40	4 53.7	1 38.8	18 58.1	18 30.6	7 37.8	8 10.2	3 13.8	27 25.7	4 56.1
15 W	19 28 51	21 52 55	8♌29 32	14 34 15	4 48.7	3 9.0	20 9.4	19 8.1	7 51.2	8 16.6	3 16.4	27 26.8	4 57.8
16 Th	19 32 48	22 50 10	20 41 3	26 50 11	4 45.7	4 43.1	21 20.8	19 45.5	8 4.7	8 22.9	3 18.9	27 27.9	4 59.4
17 F	19 36 44	23 47 26	3♍ 1 58	9♍16 41	4D 44.7	6 21.0	22 32.1	20 23.0	8 18.1	8 29.2	3 21.4	27 29.1	5 1.1
18 Sa	19 40 41	24 44 41	15 34 41	21 56 18	4 45.1	8 2.6	23 43.6	21 0.4	8 31.5	8 35.4	3 23.9	27 30.3	5 2.8
19 Su	19 44 38	25 41 57	28 21 55	4♎51 53	4 46.4	9 47.7	24 55.1	21 37.9	8 44.9	8 41.5	3 26.4	27 31.6	5 4.5
20 M	19 48 34	26 39 14	11♎26 34	18 6 18	4 47.8	11 36.1	26 6.6	22 15.4	8 58.2	8 47.6	3 28.8	27 32.8	5 6.2
21 Tu	19 52 31	27 36 30	24 51 22	1♏42 0	4R 48.6	13 27.5	27 18.2	22 53.0	9 11.5	8 53.6	3 31.2	27 34.1	5 7.9
22 W	19 56 27	28 33 47	8♏38 19	15 40 23	4 48.2	15 21.8	28 29.9	23 30.5	9 24.8	8 59.6	3 33.5	27 35.4	5 9.6
23 Th	20 0 24	29 31 4	22 48 3	0♐ 1 6	4 46.4	17 18.7	29 41.6	24 8.1	9 38.0	9 5.5	3 35.8	27 36.8	5 11.4
24 F	20 4 20	0♌28 21	7♐19 7	14 41 30	4 43.1	19 17.9	0♋53.3	24 45.6	9 51.2	9 11.4	3 38.1	27 38.1	5 13.1
25 Sa	20 8 17	1 25 39	22 7 31	29 36 15	4 38.9	21 19.1	2 5.1	25 23.2	10 4.4	9 17.1	3 40.4	27 39.5	5 14.8
26 Su	20 12 13	2 22 57	7♑ 6 43	14♑37 47	4 34.4	23 21.9	3 17.0	26 0.8	10 17.5	9 22.8	3 42.6	27 40.9	5 16.5
27 M	20 16 10	3 20 15	22 8 18	29 37 8	4 30.2	25 26.0	4 28.9	26 38.4	10 30.6	9 28.5	3 44.7	27 42.4	5 18.2
28 Tu	20 20 7	4 17 35	7♒ 3 11	14♒25 27	4 27.0	27 31.1	5 40.8	27 16.0	10 43.7	9 34.1	3 46.8	27 43.9	5 20.0
29 W	20 24 3	5 14 55	21 43 3	28 55 16	4D 25.1	29 36.9	6 52.8	27 53.7	10 56.7	9 39.6	3 48.9	27 45.3	5 21.7
30 Th	20 28 0	6 12 15	6♓ 1 33	13♓ 1 30	4 24.6	1♌43.1	8 4.9	28 31.3	11 9.7	9 45.0	3 51.0	27 46.9	5 23.4
31 F	20 31 56	7 9 37	19 54 56	26 41 46	4 25.2	3 49.3	9 17.0	29 9.0	11 22.6	9 50.4	3 52.9	27 48.4	5 25.1

AUGUST 1942 — LONGITUDE

Day	Sid.Time	☉	0 hr ☽	Noon ☽	True ☊	☿	♀	♂	♃	♄	♅	♆	♇
1 Sa	20 35 53	8♌ 7 0	3♈22 6	9♈56 9	4♍26.6	5♌55.3	10♋29.1	29♌46.7	11♋35.5	9♊55.7	3♊54.9	27♍50.0	5♌26.8
2 Su	20 39 49	9 4 24	16 24 13	22 46 43	4 28.1	8 0.8	11 41.3	0♍24.4	11 48.4	10 1.0	3 56.8	27 51.5	5 28.6
3 M	20 43 46	10 1 49	29 4 6	5♉16 52	4R 29.3	10 5.8	12 53.6	1 2.2	12 1.2	10 6.1	3 58.7	27 53.2	5 30.3
4 Tu	20 47 42	10 59 15	11♉25 35	17 30 47	4 29.8	12 9.8	14 5.9	1 39.9	12 14.0	10 11.2	4 0.5	27 54.8	5 32.0
5 W	20 51 39	11 56 42	23 33 3	29 32 57	4 29.2	14 13.0	15 18.3	2 17.7	12 26.7	10 16.2	4 2.3	27 56.4	5 33.7
6 Th	20 55 35	12 54 11	5♊31 1	11♊27 48	4 27.7	16 15.0	16 30.7	2 55.5	12 39.4	10 21.2	4 4.1	27 58.1	5 35.4
7 F	20 59 32	13 51 41	17 23 48	23 19 30	4 25.3	18 15.8	17 43.2	3 33.3	12 52.0	10 26.0	4 5.8	27 59.8	5 37.1
8 Sa	21 3 29	14 49 12	29 15 20	5♋11 44	4 22.5	20 15.3	18 55.7	4 11.2	13 4.6	10 30.8	4 7.4	28 1.5	5 38.8
9 Su	21 7 25	15 46 44	11♋ 9 3	17 7 40	4 19.5	22 13.4	20 8.3	4 49.1	13 17.1	10 35.5	4 9.0	28 3.3	5 40.5
10 M	21 11 22	16 44 18	23 7 51	29 9 53	4 16.7	24 10.1	21 21.0	5 26.9	13 29.6	10 40.1	4 10.6	28 5.0	5 42.2
11 Tu	21 15 18	17 41 53	5♌14 2	11♌20 28	4 14.5	26 5.4	22 33.6	6 4.8	13 42.0	10 44.7	4 12.1	28 6.8	5 43.9
12 W	21 19 15	18 39 29	17 29 24	23 41 0	4 13.0	27 59.3	23 46.4	6 42.8	13 54.3	10 49.1	4 13.6	28 8.6	5 45.6
13 Th	21 23 11	19 37 6	29 55 24	6♍12 44	4D 12.4	29 51.7	24 59.1	7 20.7	14 6.6	10 53.5	4 15.0	28 10.4	5 47.3
14 F	21 27 8	20 34 44	12♍33 8	18 56 42	4 12.5	1♍42.6	26 11.9	7 58.7	14 18.8	10 57.8	4 16.4	28 12.3	5 49.0
15 Sa	21 31 4	21 32 24	25 23 33	1♎53 48	4 13.1	3 32.0	27 24.8	8 36.7	14 31.0	11 2.0	4 17.7	28 14.1	5 50.7
16 Su	21 35 1	22 30 4	8♎27 33	15 4 54	4 14.1	5 19.9	28 37.7	9 14.7	14 43.1	11 6.1	4 19.0	28 16.0	5 52.3
17 M	21 38 58	23 27 46	21 45 57	28 30 46	4 15.1	7 6.4	29 50.7	9 52.7	14 55.2	11 10.2	4 20.3	28 17.9	5 54.0
18 Tu	21 42 54	24 25 28	5♏19 23	12♏11 52	4 15.8	8 51.4	1♌ 3.7	10 30.8	15 7.1	11 14.1	4 21.4	28 19.8	5 55.6
19 W	21 46 51	25 23 12	19 8 9	26 8 13	4R 16.2	10 35.0	2 16.7	11 8.9	15 19.0	11 18.0	4 22.6	28 21.7	5 57.3
20 Th	21 50 47	26 20 57	3♐11 50	10♐18 54	4 16.2	12 17.2	3 29.8	11 47.0	15 30.9	11 21.7	4 23.7	28 23.7	5 58.9
21 F	21 54 44	27 18 43	17 29 4	24 41 59	4 15.9	13 58.0	4 42.9	12 25.1	15 42.6	11 25.4	4 24.7	28 25.6	6 0.6
22 Sa	21 58 40	28 16 30	1♑57 10	9♑14 6	4 15.4	15 37.3	5 56.1	13 3.2	15 54.3	11 29.0	4 25.7	28 27.6	6 2.2
23 Su	22 2 37	29 14 18	16 32 8	23 50 34	4 14.8	17 15.3	7 9.3	13 41.4	16 6.0	11 32.5	4 26.7	28 29.6	6 3.8
24 M	22 6 33	0♍12 7	1♒ 8 42	8♒25 45	4 14.3	18 51.9	8 22.6	14 19.6	16 17.5	11 35.9	4 27.6	28 31.6	6 5.4
25 Tu	22 10 30	1 9 58	15 40 57	22 53 34	4 14.0	20 27.1	9 35.9	14 57.8	16 29.0	11 39.2	4 28.4	28 33.6	6 7.0
26 W	22 14 27	2 7 50	0♓ 2 54	7♓ 8 19	4D 13.9	22 0.9	10 49.2	15 36.0	16 40.4	11 42.4	4 29.2	28 35.6	6 8.6
27 Th	22 18 23	3 5 43	14 9 17	21 5 21	4 13.9	23 33.4	12 2.6	16 14.2	16 51.7	11 45.5	4 30.0	28 37.7	6 10.1
28 F	22 22 20	4 3 38	27 56 12	4♈41 36	4R 14.0	25 4.5	13 16.1	16 52.5	17 2.9	11 48.6	4 30.7	28 39.7	6 11.7
29 Sa	22 26 16	5 1 35	11♈21 26	17 55 44	4 13.9	26 34.3	14 29.5	17 30.8	17 14.1	11 51.5	4 31.4	28 41.8	6 13.3
30 Su	22 30 13	5 59 33	24 24 35	0♉48 13	4 13.8	28 2.7	15 43.1	18 9.1	17 25.2	11 54.3	4 32.0	28 43.9	6 14.8
31 M	22 34 9	6 57 33	7♉ 6 54	13 21 1	4 13.5	29 29.7	16 56.7	18 47.5	17 36.2	11 57.0	4 32.5	28 46.0	6 16.3

Astro Data	Dy Hr Mn
☽0N	4 20:17
♃⚺♄	18 12:55
☽0S	19 14:36
☽0N	1 5:34
☽0S	15 20:30
☽0N	28 15:20
☿0S	30 17:10

Planet Ingress	Dy Hr Mn
☿ ♋	12 20:24
☉ ♌	23 12:07
♀ ♋	23 6:10
☿ ♌	29 4:24
♂ ♍	1 8:27
☿ ♍	13 1:48
♀ ♌	17 3:04
☉ ♍	23 18:58
☿ ♎	31 8:27

Last Aspect Dy Hr Mn		☽ Ingress Dy Hr Mn
1 8:49	☿ △	♓ 2 3:46
4 4:09	♆ ☍	♈ 4 9:10
6 3:18	☿ ⚹	♉ 6 18:22
9 0:49	♆ △	♊ 9 6:10
11 15:34	☿ ☌	♋ 11 18:51
14 2:00	♆ ⚹	♌ 14 7:08
16 1:26	♀ ⚹	♍ 16 18:08
18 22:26	♆ ☌	♎ 19 3:02
21 5:13	☉ □	♏ 21 9:02
23 11:57	☉ △	♐ 23 11:58
25 8:54	♆ □	♑ 25 12:38
27 8:56	♆ △	♒ 27 12:37
29 10:45	♂ ☍	♓ 29 13:49
31 14:01	♆ ☍	♈ 31 17:55

Last Aspect Dy Hr Mn		☽ Ingress Dy Hr Mn
1 15:19	♃ □	♉ 3 1:47
5 8:48	♆ △	♊ 5 12:54
7 21:30	♆ □	♋ 8 1:30
10 9:53	♆ ⚹	♌ 10 13:39
12 23:52	☿ ☌	♍ 13 0:09
15 5:16	♆ ☌	♎ 15 8:31
17 3:16	☉ ⚹	♏ 17 14:38
19 15:50	♆ ⚹	♐ 19 18:35
21 18:13	♆ □	♑ 21 20:46
23 19:41	♆ △	♒ 23 22:07
24 17:18	♄ △	♓ 25 23:55
28 1:17	♆ ☍	♈ 28 3:39
29 10:53	♃ □	♉ 30 10:29

☽ Phases & Eclipses Dy Hr Mn	
5 8:58	☽ 12♈42
13 12:03	● 20♋27
21 5:13	☽ 27♎49
27 19:14	○ 4♒06
3 23:04	☽ 10♉57
12 2:28	● 18♌45
12 2:44:47	P 0.056
19 11:30	☽ 25♏51
26 3:46	○ 2♓17
26 3:48	T 1.535

Astro Data

1 JULY 1942
Julian Day # 15522
Delta T 25.5 sec
SVP 06♓03'52"
Obliquity 23°26'39"
⚷ Chiron 13♌29.9
☽ Mean ☊ 7♍15.5

1 AUGUST 1942
Julian Day # 15553
Delta T 25.5 sec
SVP 06♓03'48"
Obliquity 23°26'40"
⚷ Chiron 17♌16.6
☽ Mean ☊ 5♍37.0

LONGITUDE — SEPTEMBER 1942

Day	Sid.Time	☉	0 hr ☽	Noon ☽	True ☊	☿	♀	♂	♃	♄	♅	♆	♇
1 Tu	22 38 6	7♍55 36	19♉31 0	25♉37 19	4♍13.2	0♎55.3	18♌10.3	19♍25.8	17♋47.1	11♊59.7	4♊33.0	28♍48.1	6♌17.8
2 W	22 42 2	8 53 40	1♊40 29	7♊41 4	4D13.0	2 19.5	19 24.0	20 4.2	17 57.9	12 2.2	4 33.5	28 50.2	6 19.3
3 Th	22 45 59	9 51 46	13 39 37	19 36 43	4 13.0	3 42.3	20 37.7	20 42.7	18 8.6	12 4.6	4 33.9	28 52.3	6 20.8
4 F	22 49 56	10 49 54	25 32 57	1♋28 53	4 13.2	5 3.5	21 51.4	21 21.1	18 19.3	12 7.0	4 34.2	28 54.4	6 22.3
5 Sa	22 53 52	11 48 4	7♋25 6	13 22 8	4 13.8	6 23.3	23 5.2	21 59.6	18 29.8	12 9.2	4 34.5	28 56.6	6 23.8
6 Su	22 57 49	12 46 15	19 20 30	25 20 42	4 14.6	7 41.6	24 19.1	22 38.1	18 40.3	12 11.3	4 34.8	28 58.7	6 25.2
7 M	23 1 45	13 44 29	1♌23 10	7♌28 19	4 15.5	8 58.2	25 33.0	23 16.7	18 50.6	12 13.3	4 35.0	29 0.9	6 26.7
8 Tu	23 5 42	14 42 45	13 36 31	19 48 5	4 16.4	10 13.2	26 46.9	23 55.2	19 0.9	12 15.2	4 35.1	29 3.1	6 28.1
9 W	23 9 38	15 41 3	26 3 15	2♍22 14	4R17.0	11 26.4	28 0.9	24 33.8	19 11.1	12 17.1	4 35.2	29 5.2	6 29.5
10 Th	23 13 35	16 39 22	8♍45 9	15 12 4	4 17.0	12 37.9	29 14.9	25 12.4	19 21.1	12 18.8	4R35.3	29 7.4	6 30.9
11 F	23 17 31	17 37 43	21 43 2	28 17 58	4 16.5	13 47.4	0♍28.9	25 51.1	19 31.1	12 20.4	4 35.2	29 9.6	6 32.2
12 Sa	23 21 28	18 36 6	4♎56 46	11♎39 19	4 15.2	14 55.0	1 43.0	26 29.8	19 40.9	12 21.8	4 35.2	29 11.8	6 33.6
13 Su	23 25 25	19 34 31	18 25 23	25 14 44	4 13.4	16 0.5	2 57.1	27 8.5	19 50.7	12 23.2	4 35.1	29 14.0	6 34.9
14 M	23 29 21	20 32 58	2♏ 7 8	9♏ 2 17	4 11.2	17 3.7	4 11.3	27 47.2	20 0.3	12 24.5	4 34.9	29 16.2	6 36.3
15 Tu	23 33 18	21 31 26	15 59 53	22 59 39	4 9.1	18 4.5	5 25.4	28 25.9	20 9.8	12 25.7	4 34.7	29 18.4	6 37.6
16 W	23 37 14	22 29 56	0♐ 1 16	7♐ 4 27	4 7.3	19 2.9	6 39.7	29 4.7	20 19.2	12 26.7	4 34.4	29 20.6	6 38.8
17 Th	23 41 11	23 28 28	14 8 54	21 14 21	4D 6.2	19 58.5	7 53.9	29 43.5	20 28.5	12 27.7	4 34.1	29 22.8	6 40.1
18 F	23 45 7	24 27 1	28 20 30	5♑27 5	4 6.0	20 51.2	9 8.2	0♎22.4	20 37.7	12 28.5	4 33.8	29 25.1	6 41.4
19 Sa	23 49 4	25 25 36	12♑33 50	19 40 27	4 6.7	21 40.8	10 22.5	1 1.2	20 46.8	12 29.3	4 33.3	29 27.3	6 42.6
20 Su	23 53 0	26 24 12	26 46 38	3♒52 6	4 8.0	22 27.0	11 36.9	1 40.1	20 55.7	12 29.9	4 32.9	29 29.5	6 43.8
21 M	23 56 57	27 22 50	10♒56 31	17 59 31	4 9.4	23 9.6	12 51.2	2 19.0	21 4.6	12 30.4	4 32.4	29 31.8	6 45.0
22 Tu	0 0 53	28 21 30	25 0 47	1♓59 55	4R10.4	23 48.2	14 5.6	2 58.0	21 13.3	12 30.8	4 31.8	29 34.0	6 46.2
23 W	0 4 50	29 20 11	8♓56 33	15 50 20	4 10.6	24 22.6	15 20.1	3 37.0	21 21.9	12 31.1	4 31.2	29 36.2	6 47.4
24 Th	0 8 47	0♎18 54	22 40 54	29 27 56	4 9.5	24 52.5	16 34.5	4 16.0	21 30.3	12 31.3	4 30.5	29 38.4	6 48.5
25 F	0 12 43	1 17 39	6♈11 9	12♈50 18	4 7.0	25 17.4	17 49.0	4 55.0	21 38.6	12R31.4	4 29.8	29 40.7	6 49.6
26 Sa	0 16 40	2 16 27	19 25 12	25 55 45	4 3.3	25 37.0	19 3.6	5 34.1	21 46.8	12 31.4	4 29.0	29 42.9	6 50.7
27 Su	0 20 36	3 15 16	2♉21 54	8♉43 42	3 58.7	25 50.8	20 18.1	6 13.1	21 54.9	12 31.2	4 28.2	29 45.1	6 51.8
28 M	0 24 33	4 14 7	15 1 16	21 14 46	3 53.7	25R58.5	21 32.7	6 52.3	22 2.9	12 31.0	4 27.4	29 47.3	6 52.8
29 Tu	0 28 29	5 13 1	27 24 29	3♊30 46	3 48.9	25 59.7	22 47.4	7 31.4	22 10.7	12 30.6	4 26.5	29 49.6	6 53.9
30 W	0 32 26	6 11 57	9♊33 59	15 34 35	3 44.9	25 53.9	24 2.0	8 10.6	22 18.3	12 30.2	4 25.5	29 51.8	6 54.9

LONGITUDE — OCTOBER 1942

Day	Sid.Time	☉	0 hr ☽	Noon ☽	True ☊	☿	♀	♂	♃	♄	♅	♆	♇
1 Th	0 36 22	7♎10 55	21♊33 6	27♊30 4	3♍42.1	25♎40.9	25♍16.7	8♎49.8	22♋25.9	12♊29.6	4♊24.5	29♍54.0	6♌55.9
2 F	0 40 19	8 9 56	3♋26 4	9♋21 41	3D40.8	25R20.3	26 31.4	9 29.1	22 33.3	12R28.9	4R23.5	29 56.2	6 56.9
3 Sa	0 44 16	9 8 59	15 17 33	21 14 17	3 40.8	24 52.0	27 46.1	10 8.4	22 40.5	12 28.1	4 22.4	29 58.4	6 57.8
4 Su	0 48 12	10 8 4	27 12 32	3♌12 54	3 42.0	24 15.9	29 0.9	10 47.7	22 47.6	12 27.2	4 21.3	0♎ 0.6	6 58.7
5 M	0 52 9	11 7 11	9♌16 0	15 22 23	3 43.6	23 32.3	0♎15.7	11 27.0	22 54.6	12 26.2	4 20.1	0 2.8	6 59.6
6 Tu	0 56 5	12 6 21	21 32 36	27 47 6	3R45.1	22 41.3	1 30.5	12 6.4	23 1.4	12 25.1	4 18.8	0 5.0	7 0.5
7 W	1 0 2	13 5 32	4♍ 6 19	10♍30 33	3 45.8	21 43.8	2 45.4	12 45.8	23 8.1	12 23.9	4 17.6	0 7.2	7 1.4
8 Th	1 3 58	14 4 47	17 0 4	23 34 59	3 44.9	20 40.6	4 0.3	13 25.3	23 14.6	12 22.5	4 16.2	0 9.4	7 2.2
9 F	1 7 55	15 4 3	0♎15 20	7♎ 1 0	3 42.1	19 33.0	5 15.2	14 4.8	23 21.0	12 21.1	4 14.9	0 11.6	7 3.0
10 Sa	1 11 51	16 3 21	13 51 48	20 47 21	3 37.4	18 22.5	6 30.1	14 44.3	23 27.2	12 19.5	4 13.5	0 13.8	7 3.8
11 Su	1 15 48	17 2 41	27 47 14	4♏50 53	3 31.1	17 11.0	7 45.0	15 23.9	23 33.2	12 17.9	4 12.0	0 15.9	7 4.6
12 M	1 19 45	18 2 4	11♏57 39	19 6 53	3 23.9	16 0.2	8 60.0	16 3.4	23 39.1	12 16.1	4 10.5	0 18.1	7 5.3
13 Tu	1 23 41	19 1 28	26 17 51	3♐29 50	3 16.7	14 52.4	10 15.0	16 43.1	23 44.8	12 14.3	4 9.0	0 20.2	7 6.0
14 W	1 27 38	20 0 54	10♐42 9	17 54 10	3 10.3	13 49.4	11 29.9	17 22.7	23 50.4	12 12.3	4 7.4	0 22.3	7 6.7
15 Th	1 31 34	21 0 22	25 5 20	2♑15 9	3 5.6	12 53.1	12 45.0	18 2.4	23 55.8	12 10.2	4 5.8	0 24.5	7 7.4
16 F	1 35 31	21 59 52	9♑23 14	16 29 16	3D 3.0	12 5.1	13 60.0	18 42.1	24 1.0	12 8.1	4 4.2	0 26.6	7 8.0
17 Sa	1 39 27	22 59 24	23 33 3	0♒34 26	3 2.3	11 26.6	15 15.0	19 21.8	24 6.1	12 5.8	4 2.5	0 28.7	7 8.6
18 Su	1 43 24	23 58 57	7♒33 20	14 29 41	3 2.9	10 58.6	16 30.1	20 1.6	24 11.0	12 3.4	4 0.8	0 30.8	7 9.2
19 M	1 47 20	24 58 32	21 23 29	28 14 44	3R 3.9	10 41.6	17 45.2	20 41.4	24 15.7	12 1.0	3 59.0	0 32.8	7 9.8
20 Tu	1 51 17	25 58 9	5♓ 3 26	11♓49 34	3 4.3	10D35.9	19 0.3	21 21.3	24 20.3	11 58.4	3 57.2	0 34.9	7 10.3
21 W	1 55 14	26 57 47	18 33 7	25 14 2	3 3.2	10 41.2	20 15.4	22 1.1	24 24.6	11 55.7	3 55.3	0 37.0	7 10.8
22 Th	1 59 10	27 57 27	1♈52 15	8♈27 40	2 59.7	10 57.3	21 30.5	22 41.0	24 28.8	11 53.0	3 53.5	0 39.0	7 11.3
23 F	2 3 7	28 57 9	15 0 12	21 29 43	2 53.7	11 23.6	22 45.6	23 21.0	24 32.9	11 50.1	3 51.6	0 41.0	7 11.8
24 Sa	2 7 3	29 56 53	27 56 10	4♉19 25	2 45.2	11 59.4	24 0.8	24 1.0	24 36.7	11 47.2	3 49.6	0 43.0	7 12.2
25 Su	2 11 0	0♏56 39	10♉39 25	16 56 8	2 34.9	12 43.9	25 15.9	24 41.0	24 40.4	11 44.2	3 47.6	0 45.0	7 12.6
26 M	2 14 56	1 56 27	23 9 37	29 19 54	2 23.7	13 36.2	26 31.1	25 21.0	24 43.9	11 41.1	3 45.6	0 47.0	7 13.0
27 Tu	2 18 53	2 56 17	5♊27 8	11♊31 30	2 12.6	14 35.6	27 46.3	26 1.1	24 47.2	11 37.9	3 43.6	0 49.0	7 13.3
28 W	2 22 49	3 56 9	17 33 16	23 32 44	2 2.6	15 41.1	29 1.5	26 41.2	24 50.3	11 34.6	3 41.5	0 50.9	7 13.7
29 Th	2 26 46	4 56 3	29 30 17	5♋26 21	1 54.6	16 52.1	0♏16.7	27 21.4	24 53.3	11 31.2	3 39.4	0 52.8	7 14.0
30 F	2 30 42	5 55 59	11♋21 27	17 16 6	1 49.0	18 7.7	1 31.9	28 1.6	24 56.0	11 27.8	3 37.3	0 54.8	7 14.2
31 Sa	2 34 39	6 55 58	23 10 54	29 6 29	1 45.9	19 27.3	2 47.2	28 41.8	24 58.6	11 24.2	3 35.2	0 56.7	7 14.5

Astro Data	Planet Ingress	Last Aspect	☽ Ingress	Last Aspect	☽ Ingress	☽ Phases & Eclipses	Astro Data
Dy Hr Mn	Dy Hr Mn	Dy Hr Mn	Dy Hr Mn	Dy Hr Mn	Dy Hr Mn	Dy Hr Mn	1 SEPTEMBER 1942
♅ R 10 7:42	♀ ♍ 10 14:38	1 18:21 ♆ △	♊ 1 20:40	1 16:54 ♆ □	♋ 1 17:03	2 15:42 ☽ 9♊32	Julian Day # 15584
♃∠♅ 11 10:05	♂ ♎ 17 10:11	4 6:49 ♆ □	♋ 4 9:00	4 4:02 ♀ ⚹	♌ 4 5:35	10 15:53 ● 17♍18	Delta T 25.6 sec
☽0S 12 2:48	☉ ♎ 23 16:16	6 19:17 ♆ ⚹	♌ 6 21:15	6 2:04 ☿ ⚹	♍ 6 16:13	10 15:39:06 ● P 0.523	SVP 06♓03'44"
♂0S 20 6:38		9 4:09 ♀ ☌	♍ 9 7:31	8 11:29 ♃ ⚹	♎ 8 23:33	17 16:57 ☽ 24♐10	Obliquity 23°26'40"
☽0N 25 0:31	♆ ♎ 3 16:59	11 13:36 ♆ ☌	♎ 11 15:05	10 16:42 ♃ □	♏ 11 3:46	24 14:34 ○ 0♈55	⚷ Chiron 21♌16.4
♄ R 25 5:38	♀ ♎ 4 18:58	13 2:32 ♃ □	♏ 13 20:19	12 19:43 ♃ △	♐ 13 6:10		☽ Mean ☊ 3♍58.5
☿ R 28 16:12	☉ ♏ 24 1:15	15 22:51 ♆ ⚹	♐ 15 23:58	14 16:40 ☉ ⚹	♑ 15 8:13	2 10:27 ☽ 8♋36	
	♀ ♏ 28 18:40	18 1:49 ♆ □	♑ 18 2:48	17 0:57 ♃ ☍	♒ 17 11:01	10 4:06 ● 16♎13	1 OCTOBER 1942
♀0S 7 11:23		20 4:36 ♆ △	♒ 20 5:27	19 6:45 ☉ △	♓ 19 15:05	16 22:58 ☽ 22♑57	Julian Day # 15614
☽0S 9 11:02		21 21:50 ☿ △	♓ 22 8:34	21 10:34 ♃ △	♈ 21 20:37	24 4:05 ○ 0♉07	Delta T 25.6 sec
☿ D 20 0:22		24 12:21 ♆ ☍	♈ 24 12:57	23 17:46 ♃ □	♉ 24 3:52		SVP 06♓03'42"
☽0N 22 8:28		26 11:39 ☿ ☍	♉ 26 19:34	26 3:04 ♃ ⚹	♊ 26 13:18		Obliquity 23°26'41"
		29 4:45 ♆ △	♊ 29 5:05	28 19:25 ♂ △	♋ 29 1:00		⚷ Chiron 24♌51.6
				31 11:50 ♂ □	♌ 31 13:48		☽ Mean ☊ 2♍23.1

NOVEMBER 1942 LONGITUDE

Day	Sid.Time	☉	0 hr ☽	Noon ☽	True ☊	☿	♀	♂	♃	♄	♅	♆	♇
1 Su	2 38 36	7♏55 59	5♌ 3 29	11♌ 2 35	1♍44.7	20♎50.3	4♏ 2.4	29♎22.0	25♋ 1.0	11♊20.6	3♊33.0	0♎58.5	7♌14.7
2 M	2 42 32	8 56 1	17 4 27	23 9 47	1D44.9	22 16.1	5 17.7	0♏ 2.3	25 3.2	11R16.9	3R30.8	1 0.4	7 14.9
3 Tu	2 46 29	9 56 6	29 19 15	5♍33 27	1R45.3	23 44.3	6 33.0	0 42.7	25 5.2	11 13.2	3 28.6	1 2.2	7 15.1
4 W	2 50 25	10 56 13	11♍53 0	18 18 24	1 44.9	25 14.4	7 48.3	1 23.1	25 7.0	11 9.3	3 26.3	1 4.0	7 15.2
5 Th	2 54 22	11 56 22	24 50 4	1♎28 20	1 42.7	26 46.1	9 3.6	2 3.5	25 8.6	11 5.4	3 24.0	1 5.8	7 15.3
6 F	2 58 18	12 56 33	8♎13 21	15 5 10	1 37.9	28 19.1	10 18.9	2 43.9	25 10.0	11 1.4	3 21.7	1 7.6	7 15.4
7 Sa	3 2 15	13 56 46	22 3 36	29 8 20	1 30.4	29 53.2	11 34.2	3 24.4	25 11.2	10 57.4	3 19.4	1 9.4	7 15.4
8 Su	3 6 11	14 57 1	6♏18 49	13♏34 21	1 20.6	1♏28.0	12 49.5	4 5.0	25 12.2	10 53.2	3 17.0	1 11.1	7R15.5
9 M	3 10 8	15 57 18	20 54 3	28 16 56	1 9.3	3 3.4	14 4.9	4 45.5	25 13.0	10 49.1	3 14.7	1 12.8	7 15.5
10 Tu	3 14 5	16 57 37	5♐41 55	13♐ 7 52	0 57.8	4 39.3	15 20.2	5 26.1	25 13.6	10 44.8	3 12.3	1 14.5	7 15.5
11 W	3 18 1	17 57 57	20 33 40	27 58 18	0 47.4	6 15.5	16 35.6	6 6.8	25 14.1	10 40.5	3 9.9	1 16.2	7 15.4
12 Th	3 21 58	18 58 19	5♑20 48	12♑40 22	0 39.3	7 51.8	17 51.0	6 47.4	25R14.3	10 36.2	3 7.5	1 17.9	7 15.3
13 F	3 25 54	19 58 42	19 56 21	27 8 15	0 33.9	9 28.3	19 6.3	7 28.1	25 14.3	10 31.8	3 5.1	1 19.5	7 15.2
14 Sa	3 29 51	20 59 7	4♒15 46	11♒18 44	0 31.1	11 4.9	20 21.7	8 8.9	25 14.1	10 27.3	3 2.6	1 21.1	7 15.1
15 Su	3 33 47	21 59 33	18 17 4	25 10 52	0 30.3	12 41.4	21 37.1	8 49.7	25 13.7	10 22.8	3 0.2	1 22.7	7 14.9
16 M	3 37 44	23 0 0	2♓ 0 15	8♓45 26	0 30.3	14 17.8	22 52.5	9 30.5	25 13.1	10 18.3	2 57.7	1 24.2	7 14.7
17 Tu	3 41 40	24 0 28	15 26 39	22 4 8	0 29.8	15 54.1	24 7.8	10 11.3	25 12.4	10 13.7	2 55.2	1 25.7	7 14.5
18 W	3 45 37	25 0 58	28 38 10	5♈ 8 56	0 27.4	17 30.3	25 23.2	10 52.2	25 11.4	10 9.0	2 52.7	1 27.2	7 14.3
19 Th	3 49 34	26 1 29	11♈36 41	18 1 35	0 22.4	19 6.4	26 38.6	11 33.1	25 10.2	10 4.3	2 50.3	1 28.7	7 14.0
20 F	3 53 30	27 2 1	24 23 45	0♉43 20	0 14.2	20 42.3	27 54.0	12 14.1	25 8.8	9 59.6	2 47.8	1 30.2	7 13.7
21 Sa	3 57 27	28 2 35	7♉ 0 24	13 15 1	0 3.1	22 18.0	29 9.4	12 55.1	25 7.3	9 54.9	2 45.2	1 31.6	7 13.4
22 Su	4 1 23	29 3 10	19 27 14	25 37 5	29♌49.8	23 53.6	0♐24.7	13 36.1	25 5.5	9 50.1	2 42.7	1 33.0	7 13.1
23 M	4 5 20	0♐ 3 46	1♊44 37	7♊49 54	29 35.2	25 28.9	1 40.1	14 17.2	25 3.5	9 45.3	2 40.2	1 34.3	7 12.7
24 Tu	4 9 16	1 4 24	13 53 1	19 54 5	29 20.7	27 4.2	2 55.5	14 58.3	25 1.4	9 40.5	2 37.7	1 35.7	7 12.3
25 W	4 13 13	2 5 4	25 53 16	1♋50 46	29 7.3	28 39.2	4 10.9	15 39.4	24 59.0	9 35.7	2 35.2	1 37.0	7 11.9
26 Th	4 17 9	3 5 45	7♋46 51	13 41 49	28 56.2	0♐14.1	5 26.3	16 20.6	24 56.4	9 30.8	2 32.7	1 38.3	7 11.4
27 F	4 21 6	4 6 27	19 36 2	25 29 56	28 47.9	1 48.9	6 41.8	17 1.8	24 53.7	9 25.9	2 30.1	1 39.5	7 11.0
28 Sa	4 25 3	5 7 11	1♌23 59	7♌18 42	28 42.6	3 23.5	7 57.2	17 43.1	24 50.7	9 21.0	2 27.6	1 40.8	7 10.5
29 Su	4 28 59	6 7 56	13 14 41	19 12 32	28 40.0	4 58.0	9 12.6	18 24.4	24 47.6	9 16.1	2 25.1	1 42.0	7 9.9
30 M	4 32 56	7 8 43	25 12 53	1♍16 26	28D39.2	6 32.5	10 28.0	19 5.7	24 44.3	9 11.2	2 22.6	1 43.1	7 9.4

DECEMBER 1942 LONGITUDE

Day	Sid.Time	☉	0 hr ☽	Noon ☽	True ☊	☿	♀	♂	♃	♄	♅	♆	♇
1 Tu	4 36 52	8♐ 9 31	7♍23 52	13♍35 52	28♌39.2	8♐ 6.8	11♐43.4	19♏47.1	24♋40.8	9♊ 6.3	2♊20.1	1♎44.3	7♌ 8.8
2 W	4 40 49	9 10 21	19 53 6	26 16 12	28R38.8	9 41.1	12 58.8	20 28.5	24R37.1	9R 1.3	2R17.6	1 45.4	7R 8.2
3 Th	4 44 45	10 11 12	2♎45 45	9♎22 13	28 37.0	11 15.3	14 14.3	21 10.0	24 33.2	8 56.4	2 15.1	1 46.5	7 7.6
4 F	4 48 42	11 12 5	16 6 0	22 57 19	28 32.7	12 49.4	15 29.7	21 51.5	24 29.1	8 51.5	2 12.6	1 47.5	7 7.0
5 Sa	4 52 38	12 12 59	29 56 14	7♏ 2 36	28 25.9	14 23.6	16 45.1	22 33.0	24 24.9	8 46.6	2 10.1	1 48.5	7 6.3
6 Su	4 56 35	13 13 54	14♏16 2	21 35 58	28 16.5	15 57.7	18 0.6	23 14.6	24 20.4	8 41.6	2 7.7	1 49.5	7 5.6
7 M	5 0 32	14 14 50	29 1 33	6♐31 47	28 5.5	17 31.9	19 16.0	23 56.2	24 15.8	8 36.7	2 5.2	1 50.5	7 4.9
8 Tu	5 4 28	15 15 48	14♐ 5 27	21 41 14	27 54.2	19 6.0	20 31.5	24 37.9	24 11.0	8 31.9	2 2.8	1 51.4	7 4.1
9 W	5 8 25	16 16 47	29 17 45	6♑53 38	27 43.8	20 40.2	21 46.9	25 19.6	24 6.1	8 27.0	2 0.3	1 52.3	7 3.4
10 Th	5 12 21	17 17 46	14♑27 34	21 58 23	27 35.5	22 14.4	23 2.4	26 1.3	24 1.0	8 22.2	1 57.9	1 53.2	7 2.6
11 F	5 16 18	18 18 46	29 25 5	6♒46 49	27 30.0	23 48.7	24 17.8	26 43.1	23 55.7	8 17.3	1 55.5	1 54.0	7 1.8
12 Sa	5 20 14	19 19 47	14♒ 3 2	21 13 18	27D27.2	25 23.1	25 33.2	27 24.9	23 50.3	8 12.5	1 53.1	1 54.8	7 1.0
13 Su	5 24 11	20 20 48	28 17 25	5♓15 21	27 26.5	26 57.5	26 48.7	28 6.8	23 44.7	8 7.8	1 50.8	1 55.5	7 0.1
14 M	5 28 7	21 21 50	12♓ 7 14	18 53 14	27R26.9	28 31.9	28 4.1	28 48.6	23 38.9	8 3.0	1 48.4	1 56.3	6 59.2
15 Tu	5 32 4	22 22 52	25 33 41	2♈ 8 57	27 27.1	0♑ 6.5	29 19.5	29 30.6	23 33.0	7 58.3	1 46.1	1 57.0	6 58.3
16 W	5 36 1	23 23 55	8♈39 24	15 5 28	27 25.9	1 41.1	0♑34.9	0♐12.5	23 26.9	7 53.7	1 43.8	1 57.6	6 57.4
17 Th	5 39 57	24 24 58	21 27 32	27 46 0	27 22.4	3 15.8	1 50.4	0 54.5	23 20.8	7 49.1	1 41.5	1 58.2	6 56.5
18 F	5 43 54	25 26 1	4♉ 1 15	10♉13 35	27 16.3	4 50.5	3 5.8	1 36.5	23 14.4	7 44.5	1 39.3	1 58.8	6 55.5
19 Sa	5 47 50	26 27 5	16 23 19	22 30 43	27 7.7	6 25.3	4 21.2	2 18.6	23 8.0	7 39.9	1 37.1	1 59.4	6 54.6
20 Su	5 51 47	27 28 9	28 36 2	4♊39 28	26 57.1	8 0.1	5 36.6	3 0.7	23 1.4	7 35.5	1 34.9	1 59.9	6 53.6
21 M	5 55 43	28 29 14	10♊41 12	16 41 24	26 45.3	9 34.8	6 52.0	3 42.8	22 54.7	7 31.0	1 32.7	2 0.4	6 52.6
22 Tu	5 59 40	29 30 19	22 40 14	28 37 51	26 33.6	11 9.6	8 7.4	4 25.0	22 47.9	7 26.6	1 30.5	2 0.9	6 51.6
23 W	6 3 37	0♑31 25	4♋34 24	10♋30 5	26 22.8	12 44.2	9 22.8	5 7.2	22 40.9	7 22.3	1 28.4	2 1.3	6 50.5
24 Th	6 7 33	1 32 31	16 25 5	22 19 39	26 13.9	14 18.7	10 38.2	5 49.5	22 33.9	7 18.0	1 26.3	2 1.7	6 49.4
25 F	6 11 30	2 33 37	28 14 0	4♌ 8 28	26 7.3	15 53.0	11 53.5	6 31.8	22 26.7	7 13.8	1 24.3	2 2.1	6 48.4
26 Sa	6 15 26	3 34 44	10♌ 3 23	15 59 8	26 3.3	17 27.0	13 8.9	7 14.1	22 19.4	7 9.7	1 22.2	2 2.4	6 47.3
27 Su	6 19 23	4 35 52	21 56 8	27 54 52	26D 1.7	19 0.6	14 24.3	7 56.5	22 12.1	7 5.6	1 20.2	2 2.7	6 46.2
28 M	6 23 19	5 37 0	3♍55 51	9♍59 37	26 1.9	20 33.6	15 39.7	8 38.9	22 4.6	7 1.6	1 18.3	2 2.9	6 45.0
29 Tu	6 27 16	6 38 8	16 6 44	22 17 49	26 3.1	22 6.0	16 55.0	9 21.3	21 57.1	6 57.6	1 16.3	2 3.1	6 43.9
30 W	6 31 12	7 39 17	28 33 29	4♎54 18	26R 4.4	23 37.5	18 10.4	10 3.8	21 49.5	6 53.7	1 14.4	2 3.3	6 42.7
31 Th	6 35 9	8 40 26	11♎20 51	17 53 40	26 4.7	25 8.0	19 25.7	10 46.4	21 41.8	6 49.9	1 12.6	2 3.5	6 41.6

Astro Data Dy Hr Mn	Planet Ingress Dy Hr Mn	Last Aspect Dy Hr Mn	☽ Ingress Dy Hr Mn	Last Aspect Dy Hr Mn	☽ Ingress Dy Hr Mn	☽ Phases & Eclipses Dy Hr Mn
☽0S 5 21:20	♂ ♏ 1 22:36	2 11:38 ☿ ⚹	♍ 3 1:19	2 8:52 ♃ ⚹	♎ 2 18:55	1 6:18 ☽ 8♌12
♇ R 8 14:42	☿ ♏ 7 1:44	5 0:34 ♃ ⚹	♎ 5 9:21	4 14:34 ♃ □	♏ 5 0:06	8 15:19 ● 15♏35
♃ R 12 14:25	♀ ♐ 21 16:07	7 5:20 ♃ □	♏ 7 13:27	6 16:22 ♃ △	♐ 7 1:34	15 6:57 ☽ 22♒17
♃∠♄ 17 8:20	☊ ♌ 21 5:55	9 7:02 ♃ △	♐ 9 14:47	8 11:05 ♀ ☌	♑ 9 1:07	22 20:24 ○ 29♉55
☽0N 18 15:17	☉ ♐ 22 22:30	10 8:07 ♄ ☍	♑ 11 15:18	10 19:25 ♂ ⚹	♒ 11 0:57	
	☿ ♐ 25 20:26	13 8:49 ♃ ☍	♒ 13 16:48	12 23:41 ♂ □	♓ 13 2:56	1 1:37 ☽ 8♍14
☽0S 3 8:17		15 6:57 ☉ □	♓ 15 20:28	15 7:35 ♂ △	♈ 15 8:04	8 1:59 ● 15♐21
♅△♆ 11 11:36	☿ ♑ 14 22:21	17 17:42 ♃ △	♈ 18 2:30	17 6:06 ☉ △	♉ 17 16:16	14 17:47 ☽ 22♓07
☽0N 15 22:02	♀ ♑ 15 12:53	20 1:25 ♃ □	♉ 20 10:38	19 13:06 ♃ ⚹	♊ 20 2:46	22 15:03 ○ 0♋09
♃∠♄ 28 20:40	♂ ♐ 15 16:51	22 20:24 ☉ ☍	♊ 22 20:35	20 17:43 ♄ ☌	♋ 22 14:46	30 18:37 ☽ 8♎27
☽0S 30 17:47	☉ ♑ 22 11:40	23 15:42 ♄ ☌	♋ 25 8:17	24 12:21 ♃ ☌	♌ 25 3:35	
		27 10:44 ♃ ☌	♌ 27 21:09	25 18:10 ♄ ⚹	♍ 27 16:10	
		29 11:02 ♂ □	♍ 30 9:29	29 13:15 ☿ △	♎ 30 2:44	

Astro Data

1 NOVEMBER 1942
Julian Day # 15645
Delta T 25.6 sec
SVP 06♓03'39"
Obliquity 23°26'40"
⚷ Chiron 27♌44.6
☽ Mean ☊ 0♍44.6

1 DECEMBER 1942
Julian Day # 15675
Delta T 25.7 sec
SVP 06♓03'35"
Obliquity 23°26'40"
⚷ Chiron 29♌13.6
☽ Mean ☊ 29♌09.3

LONGITUDE JANUARY 1943

Day	Sid.Time	☉	0 hr ☽	Noon ☽	True ☊	☿	♀	♂	♃	♄	♅	♆	♇
1 F	6 39 6	9♑41 35	24♎33 13	1♏19 52	26♌ 3.5	26♑37.1	20♑41.1	11♐28.9	21♋34.1	6♊46.2	1♊10.7	2♎ 3.6	6♌40.4
2 Sa	6 43 2	10 42 45	8♏13 49	15 15 11	26R 0.4	28 4.7	21 56.5	12 11.6	21R26.2	6R42.5	1R 8.9	2 3.7	6R39.2
3 Su	6 46 59	11 43 56	22 23 51	29 39 29	25 55.4	29 30.4	23 11.8	12 54.2	21 18.4	6 39.0	1 7.2	2R 3.7	6 38.0
4 M	6 50 55	12 45 6	7♐ 1 35	14♐29 22	25 49.0	0♒53.7	24 27.2	13 36.9	21 10.5	6 35.5	1 5.5	2 3.7	6 36.7
5 Tu	6 54 52	13 46 17	22 1 53	29 38 0	25 42.2	2 14.4	25 42.5	14 19.6	21 2.5	6 32.1	1 3.8	2 3.7	6 35.5
6 W	6 58 48	14 47 28	7♑16 24	14♑55 43	25 35.8	3 31.8	26 57.8	15 2.4	20 54.5	6 28.7	1 2.2	2 3.7	6 34.2
7 Th	7 2 45	15 48 39	22 34 34	0♒11 34	25 30.8	4 45.3	28 13.2	15 45.2	20 46.4	6 25.5	1 0.6	2 3.6	6 33.0
8 F	7 6 41	16 49 50	7♒45 29	15 15 10	25 27.6	5 54.4	29 28.5	16 28.1	20 38.4	6 22.3	0 59.0	2 3.4	6 31.7
9 Sa	7 10 38	17 51 0	22 39 43	29 58 22	25D 26.4	6 58.3	0♒43.8	17 10.9	20 30.3	6 19.3	0 57.5	2 3.3	6 30.4
10 Su	7 14 35	18 52 10	7♓10 37	14♓16 7	25 26.8	7 56.3	1 59.1	17 53.8	20 22.2	6 16.3	0 56.1	2 3.1	6 29.1
11 M	7 18 31	19 53 19	21 14 46	28 6 33	25 28.2	8 47.4	3 14.4	18 36.8	20 14.1	6 13.4	0 54.6	2 2.9	6 27.8
12 Tu	7 22 28	20 54 28	4♈51 39	11♈30 21	25 29.7	9 30.9	4 29.6	19 19.8	20 6.0	6 10.7	0 53.3	2 2.6	6 26.5
13 W	7 26 24	21 55 36	18 3 1	24 30 3	25R 30.7	10 5.7	5 44.9	20 2.8	19 57.9	6 8.0	0 51.9	2 2.3	6 25.2
14 Th	7 30 21	22 56 44	0♉51 57	7♉ 9 11	25 30.4	10 31.1	7 0.1	20 45.8	19 49.8	6 5.4	0 50.6	2 2.0	6 23.9
15 F	7 34 17	23 57 51	13 22 15	19 31 40	25 28.7	10R46.2	8 15.4	21 28.9	19 41.8	6 2.9	0 49.4	2 1.6	6 22.6
16 Sa	7 38 14	24 58 57	25 37 54	1♊41 24	25 25.4	10 50.4	9 30.6	22 12.0	19 33.7	6 0.5	0 48.2	2 1.2	6 21.2
17 Su	7 42 10	26 0 2	7♊42 36	13 41 55	25 21.0	10 43.0	10 45.8	22 55.2	19 25.7	5 58.2	0 47.1	2 0.8	6 19.9
18 M	7 46 7	27 1 7	19 39 42	25 36 20	25 15.9	10 23.9	12 1.0	23 38.4	19 17.8	5 56.1	0 46.0	2 0.3	6 18.5
19 Tu	7 50 4	28 2 11	1♋32 5	7♋27 16	25 10.7	9 53.2	13 16.1	24 21.6	19 9.8	5 54.0	0 44.9	1 59.8	6 17.2
20 W	7 54 0	29 3 14	13 22 9	19 16 58	25 6.0	9 11.4	14 31.3	25 4.9	19 2.0	5 52.0	0 43.9	1 59.3	6 15.8
21 Th	7 57 57	0♒ 4 17	25 11 59	1♌ 7 24	25 2.2	8 19.3	15 46.4	25 48.2	18 54.1	5 50.2	0 42.9	1 58.7	6 14.5
22 F	8 1 53	1 5 19	7♌ 3 27	13 0 23	24 59.6	7 18.3	17 1.5	26 31.5	18 46.4	5 48.4	0 42.0	1 58.2	6 13.1
23 Sa	8 5 50	2 6 20	18 58 27	24 57 53	24D 58.3	6 10.2	18 16.6	27 14.9	18 38.7	5 46.7	0 41.2	1 57.5	6 11.7
24 Su	8 9 46	3 7 21	0♍58 59	7♍ 2 3	24 58.3	4 57.1	19 31.7	27 58.3	18 31.1	5 45.2	0 40.4	1 56.9	6 10.3
25 M	8 13 43	4 8 21	13 7 23	19 15 22	24 59.3	3 41.1	20 46.8	28 41.8	18 23.5	5 43.8	0 39.6	1 56.2	6 9.0
26 Tu	8 17 39	5 9 20	25 26 21	1♎40 43	25 0.8	2 24.7	22 1.8	29 25.2	18 16.0	5 42.4	0 38.9	1 55.5	6 7.6
27 W	8 21 36	6 10 18	7♎58 53	14 21 16	25 2.3	1 10.1	23 16.9	0♑ 8.8	18 8.7	5 41.2	0 38.2	1 54.7	6 6.2
28 Th	8 25 33	7 11 16	20 48 16	27 20 17	25 3.6	29♑59.1	24 31.9	0 52.3	18 1.4	5 40.1	0 37.6	1 54.0	6 4.8
29 F	8 29 29	8 12 14	3♏57 40	10♏40 44	25R 4.3	28 53.7	25 46.9	1 35.9	17 54.2	5 39.1	0 37.1	1 53.2	6 3.5
30 Sa	8 33 26	9 13 11	17 29 44	24 24 48	25 4.2	27 55.0	27 1.9	2 19.6	17 47.1	5 38.2	0 36.6	1 52.3	6 2.1
31 Su	8 37 22	10 14 7	1♐26 0	8♐33 12	25 3.3	27 4.1	28 16.9	3 3.2	17 40.1	5 37.4	0 36.1	1 51.5	6 0.7

LONGITUDE FEBRUARY 1943

Day	Sid.Time	☉	0 hr ☽	Noon ☽	True ☊	☿	♀	♂	♃	♄	♅	♆	♇
1 M	8 41 19	11♒15 2	15♐46 12	23♐ 4 34	25♌ 1.9	26♑21.5	29♒31.8	3♑47.0	17♋33.2	5♊36.8	0♊35.7	1♎50.6	5♌59.4
2 Tu	8 45 15	12 15 57	0♑27 44	7♑54 56	25R 0.3	25R47.5	0♓46.8	4 30.7	17R26.5	5R36.2	0R35.4	1R49.7	5R58.0
3 W	8 49 12	13 16 51	15 25 18	22 57 49	24 58.7	25 22.2	2 1.7	5 14.5	17 19.8	5 35.8	0 35.1	1 48.7	5 56.6
4 Th	8 53 8	14 17 44	0♒31 20	8♒ 4 42	24 57.6	25 5.3	3 16.6	5 58.3	17 13.3	5 35.5	0 34.9	1 47.7	5 55.3
5 F	8 57 5	15 18 35	15 36 45	23 6 20	24D 57.0	24D 56.7	4 31.4	6 42.1	17 7.0	5 35.3	0 34.7	1 46.7	5 53.9
6 Sa	9 1 2	16 19 26	0♓32 24	7♓53 59	24 56.9	24 55.7	5 46.3	7 26.0	17 0.7	5D 35.2	0 34.5	1 45.7	5 52.6
7 Su	9 4 58	17 20 15	15 10 19	22 20 46	24 57.3	25 2.1	7 1.1	8 9.9	16 54.6	5 35.2	0 34.5	1 44.7	5 51.2
8 M	9 8 55	18 21 3	29 24 52	6♈22 20	24 57.9	25 15.4	8 15.9	8 53.9	16 48.7	5 35.3	0D 34.4	1 43.6	5 49.9
9 Tu	9 12 51	19 21 49	13♈13 2	19 57 1	24 58.5	25 34.9	9 30.7	9 37.8	16 42.9	5 35.6	0 34.5	1 42.5	5 48.5
10 W	9 16 48	20 22 34	26 34 25	3♉ 5 32	24 59.0	26 0.2	10 45.4	10 21.8	16 37.2	5 35.9	0 34.5	1 41.3	5 47.2
11 Th	9 20 44	21 23 17	9♉30 43	15 50 25	24 59.2	26 31.0	12 0.1	11 5.8	16 31.7	5 36.4	0 34.7	1 40.2	5 45.9
12 F	9 24 41	22 23 59	22 5 6	28 15 20	24R 59.3	27 6.7	13 14.8	11 49.9	16 26.4	5 37.0	0 34.9	1 39.0	5 44.6
13 Sa	9 28 37	23 24 39	4♊21 39	10♊24 37	24 59.3	27 46.8	14 29.5	12 34.0	16 21.2	5 37.7	0 35.1	1 37.8	5 43.2
14 Su	9 32 34	24 25 17	16 24 48	22 22 46	24D 59.2	28 31.2	15 44.1	13 18.1	16 16.2	5 38.5	0 35.4	1 36.6	5 42.0
15 M	9 36 31	25 25 54	28 19 3	4♋14 10	24 59.2	29 19.4	16 58.7	14 2.3	16 11.4	5 39.5	0 35.7	1 35.3	5 40.7
16 Tu	9 40 27	26 26 29	10♋ 8 37	16 2 51	24 59.4	0♒11.1	18 13.2	14 46.4	16 6.7	5 40.5	0 36.1	1 34.1	5 39.4
17 W	9 44 24	27 27 2	21 57 18	27 52 22	24 59.6	1 6.0	19 27.8	15 30.7	16 2.2	5 41.7	0 36.6	1 32.8	5 38.1
18 Th	9 48 20	28 27 34	3♌48 24	9♌45 45	24 59.9	2 3.8	20 42.3	16 14.9	15 57.9	5 42.9	0 37.1	1 31.5	5 36.9
19 F	9 52 17	29 28 4	15 44 42	21 45 31	25R 0.2	3 4.5	21 56.7	16 59.2	15 53.8	5 44.3	0 37.6	1 30.1	5 35.6
20 Sa	9 56 13	0♓28 33	27 48 27	3♍53 41	25 0.2	4 7.7	23 11.1	17 43.5	15 49.8	5 45.8	0 38.3	1 28.8	5 34.4
21 Su	10 0 10	1 28 59	10♍ 1 26	16 11 52	24 60.0	5 13.2	24 25.5	18 27.8	15 46.0	5 47.4	0 38.9	1 27.4	5 33.2
22 M	10 4 6	2 29 24	22 25 8	28 41 23	24 59.4	6 21.0	25 39.8	19 12.2	15 42.4	5 49.1	0 39.6	1 26.0	5 32.0
23 Tu	10 8 3	3 29 48	5♎ 0 45	11♎23 23	24 58.4	7 30.8	26 54.2	19 56.6	15 39.0	5 50.9	0 40.4	1 24.6	5 30.8
24 W	10 11 59	4 30 10	17 49 23	24 18 55	24 57.1	8 42.6	28 8.4	20 41.0	15 35.8	5 52.8	0 41.2	1 23.2	5 29.6
25 Th	10 15 56	5 30 31	0♏52 5	7♏29 1	24 55.8	9 56.2	29 22.7	21 25.4	15 32.7	5 54.8	0 42.1	1 21.7	5 28.4
26 F	10 19 53	6 30 50	14 9 49	20 54 35	24 54.6	11 11.5	0♈36.9	22 9.9	15 29.9	5 57.0	0 43.0	1 20.3	5 27.2
27 Sa	10 23 49	7 31 8	27 43 23	4♐36 17	24D 53.8	12 28.5	1 51.0	22 54.4	15 27.2	5 59.2	0 44.0	1 18.8	5 26.1
28 Su	10 27 46	8 31 24	11♐33 15	18 34 16	24 53.7	13 47.1	3 5.2	23 39.0	15 24.7	6 1.6	0 45.0	1 17.3	5 25.0

Astro Data Dy Hr Mn	Planet Ingress Dy Hr Mn	Last Aspect Dy Hr Mn	☽ Ingress Dy Hr Mn	Last Aspect Dy Hr Mn	☽ Ingress Dy Hr Mn	☽ Phases & Eclipses Dy Hr Mn	Astro Data
♄∗♇ 3 10:27	☿ ♒ 3 8:27	1 4:08 ☿ □	♏ 1 9:40	31 15:56 ☉ ∗	♑ 1 23:15	6 12:38 ● 15♑20	1 JANUARY 1943
♆ R 3 21:21	♀ ♒ 8 10:03	3 1:27 ♀ ∗	♐ 3 12:34	3 15:30 ☿ ☌	♒ 3 23:10	13 7:49 ☽ 22♈15	Julian Day # 15706
☽0N 12 6:01	☉ ♒ 20 22:19	4 11:08 ♂ ☌	♑ 5 12:35	4 23:29 ☉ ☌	♓ 5 23:07	21 10:48 ○ 0♌32	Delta T 25.7 sec
☿ R 15 20:46	♂ ♑ 26 19:10	7 9:41 ♀ ☌	♒ 7 11:42	7 16:47 ☿ ∗	♈ 8 1:00	29 8:13 ☽ 8♏33	SVP 06♓03'30"
☽0S 27 0:48	☿ ♑ 27 23:42	8 14:40 ♂ ∗	♓ 9 12:03	9 22:55 ☿ □	♉ 10 6:17		Obliquity 23°26'40"
		10 22:16 ♃ △	♈ 11 15:20	12 10:18 ☿ △	♊ 12 15:25	4 23:29 ● 15♒17	⚷ Chiron 29♌04.0R
☿ D 5 14:50	♀ ♓ 1 9:02	13 7:49 ☉ □	♉ 13 22:22	14 17:37 ☉ △	♋ 15 3:24	4 23:37:45 T 2'35"	☽ Mean ☊ 27♌30.8
♄ D 6 7:52	☿ ♒ 15 19:00	15 22:36 ☉ △	♊ 16 8:39	16 18:21 ♀ △	♌ 17 16:18	12 0:40 ☽ 22♉26	
☽0N 8 15:39	☉ ♓ 19 12:40	18 8:33 ♂ ☍	♋ 18 20:53	18 3:51 ♄ ∗	♍ 20 4:20	20 5:45 ○ 0♍43	1 FEBRUARY 1943
♅ D 8 0:53	♀ ♈ 25 12:04	20 11:22 ♃ ☌	♌ 21 9:44	22 6:54 ♀ ☍	♎ 22 14:30	20 5:38 P 0.761	Julian Day # 15737
♄∗♇ 15 12:34		23 17:37 ♂ △	♍ 23 22:03	24 5:37 ♂ □	♏ 24 22:25	27 18:22 ☽ 8♐17	Delta T 25.7 sec
♃∠♅ 22 15:56		26 8:09 ♂ □	♎ 26 8:47	26 15:02 ♂ ∗	♐ 27 3:59		SVP 06♓03'25"
☽0S 23 6:27		28 15:31 ☿ □	♏ 28 16:51				Obliquity 23°26'40"
♀0N 27 10:34		30 18:06 ♀ □	♐ 30 21:34				⚷ Chiron 27♌21.1R
							☽ Mean ☊ 25♌52.3

MARCH 1943

LONGITUDE

Day	Sid.Time	☉	0 hr ☽	Noon ☽	True ☊	☿	♀	♂	♃	♄	♅	♆	♇
1 M	10 31 42	9♓31 39	25♐39 11	2♑47 50	24♌54.1	15♒ 7.1	4♈19.3	24♑23.6	15♋22.5	6♊ 4.0	0♊46.1	1♎15.8	5♌23.9
2 Tu	10 35 39	10 31 53	9♑59 54	17 15 1	24 55.1	16 28.6	5 33.3	25 8.2	15R20.4	6 6.6	0 47.2	1R14.3	5R22.8
3 W	10 39 35	11 32 5	24 32 43	1♒52 26	24 56.4	17 51.5	6 47.3	25 52.8	15 18.5	6 9.3	0 48.4	1 12.8	5 21.7
4 Th	10 43 32	12 32 15	9♒13 28	16 35 7	24 57.4	19 15.7	8 1.3	26 37.5	15 16.8	6 12.0	0 49.6	1 11.2	5 20.6
5 F	10 47 28	13 32 24	23 56 32	1♓16 55	24R57.9	20 41.3	9 15.3	27 22.1	15 15.3	6 14.9	0 50.9	1 9.7	5 19.6
6 Sa	10 51 25	14 32 31	8♓35 22	15 51 5	24 57.5	22 8.1	10 29.2	28 6.8	15 14.0	6 17.9	0 52.2	1 8.1	5 18.6
7 Su	10 55 22	15 32 36	23 3 16	0♈11 11	24 55.9	23 36.1	11 43.0	28 51.6	15 12.9	6 20.9	0 53.6	1 6.5	5 17.6
8 M	10 59 18	16 32 39	7♈14 14	14 11 55	24 53.4	25 5.4	12 56.8	29 36.3	15 12.0	6 24.1	0 55.0	1 4.9	5 16.6
9 Tu	11 3 15	17 32 40	21 3 52	27 49 50	24 50.1	26 35.9	14 10.6	0♒21.1	15 11.3	6 27.4	0 56.5	1 3.4	5 15.6
10 W	11 7 11	18 32 40	4♉29 43	11♉ 3 34	24 46.5	28 7.6	15 24.3	1 5.9	15 10.7	6 30.8	0 58.0	1 1.7	5 14.7
11 Th	11 11 8	19 32 37	17 31 32	23 53 52	24 43.2	29 40.5	16 38.0	1 50.7	15 10.4	6 34.2	0 59.5	1 0.1	5 13.7
12 F	11 15 4	20 32 32	0♊10 56	6♊23 10	24 40.5	1♓14.6	17 51.6	2 35.5	15D10.3	6 37.8	1 1.2	0 58.5	5 12.8
13 Sa	11 19 1	21 32 24	12 31 4	18 35 11	24D38.9	2 49.9	19 5.2	3 20.4	15 10.4	6 41.5	1 2.8	0 56.9	5 11.9
14 Su	11 22 57	22 32 15	24 36 7	0♋34 28	24 38.6	4 26.3	20 18.7	4 5.3	15 10.7	6 45.2	1 4.5	0 55.2	5 11.1
15 M	11 26 54	23 32 3	6♋30 52	12 25 57	24 39.3	6 4.0	21 32.2	4 50.2	15 11.1	6 49.1	1 6.3	0 53.6	5 10.2
16 Tu	11 30 51	24 31 49	18 20 19	24 14 35	24 40.9	7 42.8	22 45.6	5 35.1	15 11.8	6 53.0	1 8.1	0 52.0	5 9.4
17 W	11 34 47	25 31 33	0♌ 9 22	6♌ 5 10	24 42.7	9 22.8	23 58.9	6 20.0	15 12.7	6 57.1	1 9.9	0 50.3	5 8.6
18 Th	11 38 44	26 31 15	12 2 34	18 2 0	24 44.3	11 4.1	25 12.2	7 5.0	15 13.7	7 1.2	1 11.8	0 48.7	5 7.8
19 F	11 42 40	27 30 54	24 3 55	0♍ 8 42	24R45.0	12 46.5	26 25.5	7 49.9	15 15.0	7 5.4	1 13.7	0 47.0	5 7.0
20 Sa	11 46 37	28 30 32	6♍16 41	12 28 7	24 44.3	14 30.2	27 38.7	8 34.9	15 16.4	7 9.7	1 15.7	0 45.4	5 6.3
21 Su	11 50 33	29 30 7	18 43 12	25 2 6	24 42.0	16 15.2	28 51.8	9 19.9	15 18.0	7 14.1	1 17.7	0 43.7	5 5.6
22 M	11 54 30	0♈29 40	1♎24 51	7♎51 30	24 38.0	18 1.4	0♉ 4.9	10 5.0	15 19.8	7 18.6	1 19.8	0 42.0	5 4.9
23 Tu	11 58 26	1 29 11	14 21 59	20 56 12	24 32.5	19 48.9	1 17.9	10 50.0	15 21.8	7 23.1	1 21.9	0 40.4	5 4.2
24 W	12 2 23	2 28 40	27 34 1	4♏15 15	24 26.1	21 37.7	2 30.8	11 35.1	15 24.0	7 27.8	1 24.0	0 38.7	5 3.5
25 Th	12 6 20	3 28 7	10♏59 41	17 47 7	24 19.6	23 27.7	3 43.7	12 20.2	15 26.4	7 32.5	1 26.2	0 37.1	5 2.9
26 F	12 10 16	4 27 32	24 37 18	1♐30 1	24 13.7	25 19.1	4 56.6	13 5.3	15 29.0	7 37.3	1 28.4	0 35.4	5 2.3
27 Sa	12 14 13	5 26 56	8♐25 3	15 22 11	24 9.2	27 11.8	6 9.3	13 50.4	15 31.7	7 42.2	1 30.7	0 33.7	5 1.7
28 Su	12 18 9	6 26 18	22 21 14	29 22 3	24 6.5	29 5.8	7 22.1	14 35.5	15 34.6	7 47.2	1 33.0	0 32.1	5 1.2
29 M	12 22 6	7 25 38	6♑24 26	13♑28 15	24D 5.5	1♈ 1.0	8 34.7	15 20.7	15 37.7	7 52.2	1 35.3	0 30.4	5 0.7
30 Tu	12 26 2	8 24 56	20 33 19	27 39 29	24 6.0	2 57.6	9 47.3	16 5.9	15 41.0	7 57.3	1 37.7	0 28.8	5 0.2
31 W	12 29 59	9 24 13	4♒46 31	11♒54 11	24 7.2	4 55.4	10 59.9	16 51.1	15 44.5	8 2.5	1 40.1	0 27.2	4 59.7

APRIL 1943

LONGITUDE

Day	Sid.Time	☉	0 hr ☽	Noon ☽	True ☊	☿	♀	♂	♃	♄	♅	♆	♇
1 Th	12 33 55	10♈23 28	19♒ 2 11	26♒10 12	24♌ 8.2	6♈54.5	12♉12.3	17♒36.3	15♋48.1	8♊ 7.8	1♊42.6	0♎25.5	4♌59.2
2 F	12 37 52	11 22 41	3♓17 49	10♓24 36	24R 7.9	8 54.7	13 24.8	18 21.5	15 51.9	8 13.2	1 45.1	0R23.9	4R58.8
3 Sa	12 41 48	12 21 52	17 30 3	24 33 39	24 5.7	10 55.9	14 37.1	19 6.7	15 55.9	8 18.6	1 47.6	0 22.3	4 58.4
4 Su	12 45 45	13 21 1	1♈34 52	8♈33 8	24 1.2	12 58.3	15 49.4	19 51.9	16 0.1	8 24.1	1 50.2	0 20.7	4 58.0
5 M	12 49 42	14 20 9	15 27 57	22 18 51	23 54.5	15 1.5	17 1.6	20 37.2	16 4.4	8 29.7	1 52.7	0 19.1	4 57.6
6 Tu	12 53 38	15 19 14	29 5 24	5♉47 17	23 46.1	17 5.4	18 13.8	21 22.4	16 8.9	8 35.3	1 55.4	0 17.5	4 57.3
7 W	12 57 35	16 18 17	12♉24 15	18 56 11	23 36.8	19 10.0	19 25.9	22 7.6	16 13.6	8 41.0	1 58.0	0 15.9	4 57.0
8 Th	13 1 31	17 17 18	25 23 2	1♊44 54	23 27.7	21 15.0	20 37.9	22 52.9	16 18.4	8 46.8	2 0.7	0 14.3	4 56.7
9 F	13 5 28	18 16 17	8♊ 1 56	14 14 26	23 19.8	23 20.2	21 49.8	23 38.2	16 23.4	8 52.7	2 3.5	0 12.7	4 56.5
10 Sa	13 9 24	19 15 13	20 22 46	26 27 22	23 13.6	25 25.4	23 1.7	24 23.4	16 28.6	8 58.6	2 6.2	0 11.2	4 56.2
11 Su	13 13 21	20 14 8	2♋28 45	8♋27 28	23 9.7	27 30.3	24 13.5	25 8.7	16 33.9	9 4.6	2 9.0	0 9.6	4 56.0
12 M	13 17 17	21 13 0	14 24 8	20 19 22	23D 7.8	29 34.5	25 25.2	25 54.0	16 39.4	9 10.6	2 11.9	0 8.1	4 55.9
13 Tu	13 21 14	22 11 50	26 13 52	2♌ 8 16	23 7.7	1♉37.8	26 36.9	26 39.2	16 45.1	9 16.7	2 14.7	0 6.6	4 55.7
14 W	13 25 11	23 10 38	8♌ 3 16	13 59 31	23 8.4	3 39.9	27 48.4	27 24.5	16 50.9	9 22.9	2 17.6	0 5.1	4 55.6
15 Th	13 29 7	24 9 23	19 57 40	25 58 21	23R 9.0	5 40.4	28 59.9	28 9.8	16 56.8	9 29.1	2 20.5	0 3.6	4 55.5
16 F	13 33 4	25 8 6	2♍ 2 8	8♍ 9 34	23 8.7	7 38.9	0♊11.3	28 55.1	17 3.0	9 35.4	2 23.4	0 2.1	4 55.4
17 Sa	13 37 0	26 6 47	14 21 5	20 37 7	23 6.5	9 35.1	1 22.6	29 40.3	17 9.2	9 41.7	2 26.4	0 0.7	4 55.4
18 Su	13 40 57	27 5 26	26 57 57	3♎23 48	23 1.9	11 28.6	2 33.8	0♓25.6	17 15.6	9 48.1	2 29.4	29♍59.2	4D55.4
19 M	13 44 53	28 4 2	9♎54 47	16 30 53	22 54.8	13 19.3	3 45.0	1 10.9	17 22.2	9 54.5	2 32.4	29 57.8	4 55.4
20 Tu	13 48 50	29 2 37	23 12 1	29 57 55	22 45.6	15 6.8	4 56.0	1 56.2	17 28.9	10 1.0	2 35.5	29 56.4	4 55.4
21 W	13 52 46	0♉ 1 9	6♏48 16	13♏42 39	22 34.9	16 50.7	6 7.0	2 41.4	17 35.7	10 7.6	2 38.5	29 55.0	4 55.5
22 Th	13 56 43	0 59 40	20 40 34	27 41 27	22 23.9	18 31.0	7 17.8	3 26.7	17 42.7	10 14.2	2 41.6	29 53.6	4 55.6
23 F	14 0 40	1 58 9	4♐44 43	11♐49 46	22 13.8	20 7.4	8 28.6	4 12.0	17 49.8	10 20.9	2 44.7	29 52.3	4 55.7
24 Sa	14 4 36	2 56 37	18 56 3	26 3 0	22 5.6	21 39.6	9 39.3	4 57.3	17 57.0	10 27.6	2 47.9	29 50.9	4 55.8
25 Su	14 8 33	3 55 3	3♑10 9	10♑17 6	21 59.8	23 7.6	10 49.9	5 42.5	18 4.4	10 34.3	2 51.0	29 49.6	4 56.0
26 M	14 12 29	4 53 27	17 23 30	24 29 5	21 56.7	24 31.3	12 0.4	6 27.8	18 11.9	10 41.1	2 54.2	29 48.3	4 56.2
27 Tu	14 16 26	5 51 50	1♒33 38	8♒37 2	21D55.6	25 50.4	13 10.8	7 13.1	18 19.6	10 48.0	2 57.4	29 47.0	4 56.4
28 W	14 20 22	6 50 11	15 39 9	22 39 55	21R55.7	27 4.8	14 21.1	7 58.3	18 27.4	10 54.9	3 0.6	29 45.8	4 56.7
29 Th	14 24 19	7 48 30	29 39 16	6♓37 6	21 55.6	28 14.6	15 31.3	8 43.6	18 35.3	11 1.8	3 3.9	29 44.5	4 57.0
30 F	14 28 15	8 46 48	13♓33 21	20 27 53	21 54.1	29 19.6	16 41.4	9 28.8	18 43.3	11 8.8	3 7.1	29 43.3	4 57.3

Astro Data Dy Hr Mn	Planet Ingress Dy Hr Mn	Last Aspect Dy Hr Mn	☽ Ingress Dy Hr Mn	Last Aspect Dy Hr Mn	☽ Ingress Dy Hr Mn	☽ Phases & Eclipses Dy Hr Mn	Astro Data
☽0N 8 1:59	♂ ♒ 8 12:42	28 4:14 ☿ ⚹	♑ 1 7:19	31 21:27 ♂ ☌	♓ 1 18:27	6 10:34 ● 14♓59	1 MARCH 1943
♅△♆ 11 4:21	☿ ♓ 11 4:59	3 2:18 ♂ ☌	♒ 3 8:56	2 21:20 ♃ △	♈ 3 21:17	13 19:30 ☽ 22♊21	Julian Day # 15765
♃ D 12 2:11	☉ ♈ 21 12:03	4 18:07 ☿ ☌	♓ 5 9:54	5 9:33 ♂ ⚹	♉ 6 1:37	21 22:08 ○ 0♎25	Delta T 25.8 sec
☽0S 22 12:50	♀ ♉ 21 22:24	7 10:18 ♂ ⚹	♈ 7 11:41	7 19:02 ♂ □	♊ 8 8:41	29 1:52 ☽ 7♑30	SVP 06♓03'22"
☿0N 30 9:22	☿ ♈ 28 11:19	9 11:03 ☿ ⚹	♉ 9 15:53	10 12:01 ☿ ⚹	♋ 10 19:03		Obliquity 23°26'41"
		11 4:06 ☉ ⚹	♊ 11 23:39	13 0:52 ♀ ⚹	♌ 13 7:39	4 21:53 ● 14♈15	⚷ Chiron 25♌12.9R
☽0N 4 11:35	☿ ♉ 12 4:56	13 19:30 ☉ □	♋ 14 10:51	15 19:58 ♀ □	♍ 15 19:59	12 15:04 ☽ 21♋50	☽ Mean ☊ 24♌23.3
☽0S 18 21:10	♀ ♊ 15 20:12	16 13:44 ☉ △	♌ 16 23:41	18 5:39 ♆ ☌	♎ 18 5:41	20 11:10 ○ 29♎30	
♇ D 18 3:04	♂ ♓ 17 10:25	19 5:11 ♀ △	♍ 19 11:43	20 11:10 ☉ ☍	♏ 20 12:04	27 7:51 ☽ 6♒11	1 APRIL 1943
♃∠♅ 21 17:34	♆ ♍ 17 10:59	20 18:30 ☿ ☍	♎ 21 21:21	22 15:44 ♆ ⚹	♐ 22 15:56		Julian Day # 15796
	☉ ♉ 20 23:32	23 1:50 ♃ □	♏ 24 4:23	24 18:22 ♆ □	♑ 24 18:39		Delta T 25.8 sec
	☿ ♊ 30 15:56	26 1:25 ☿ △	♐ 26 9:23	26 20:59 ♆ △	♒ 26 21:21		SVP 06♓03'19"
		27 9:54 ♂ ⚹	♑ 28 13:05	28 21:22 ☿ □	♓ 29 0:36		Obliquity 23°26'41"
		29 15:43 ♃ ☍	♒ 30 15:57				⚷ Chiron 23♌23.1R
							☽ Mean ☊ 22♌44.8

LONGITUDE — MAY 1943

Day	Sid.Time	☉	0 hr ☽	Noon ☽	True ☊	☿	♀	♂	♃	♄	♅	♆	♇
1 Sa	14 32 12	9♉45 5	27♓20 33	4♈11 9	21♌50.3	0♊19.7	17♊51.5	10♓14.1	18♋51.5	11♊15.8	3♊10.4	29♍42.1	4♌57.6
2 Su	14 36 9	10 43 20	10♈59 28	17 45 15	21R43.6	1 14.8	19 1.4	10 59.3	18 59.8	11 22.9	3 13.7	29R40.9	4 57.9
3 M	14 40 5	11 41 33	24 28 14	1♉ 8 8	21 34.1	2 4.9	20 11.2	11 44.5	19 8.2	11 30.0	3 17.0	29 39.8	4 58.3
4 Tu	14 44 2	12 39 45	7♉44 43	14 17 43	21 22.4	2 49.9	21 20.9	12 29.7	19 16.7	11 37.1	3 20.4	29 38.7	4 58.7
5 W	14 47 58	13 37 55	20 46 58	27 12 19	21 9.5	3 29.8	22 30.5	13 14.8	19 25.4	11 44.3	3 23.7	29 37.6	4 59.2
6 Th	14 51 55	14 36 3	3♊33 41	9♊51 5	20 56.7	4 4.6	23 40.0	13 60.0	19 34.2	11 51.5	3 27.1	29 36.5	4 59.6
7 F	14 55 51	15 34 10	16 4 34	22 14 19	20 45.1	4 34.1	24 49.4	14 45.1	19 43.1	11 58.8	3 30.5	29 35.5	5 0.1
8 Sa	14 59 48	16 32 14	28 20 33	4♋23 36	20 35.6	4 58.3	25 58.7	15 30.2	19 52.1	12 6.1	3 33.9	29 34.4	5 0.6
9 Su	15 3 44	17 30 17	10♋23 50	16 21 42	20 28.7	5 17.4	27 7.8	16 15.3	20 1.2	12 13.4	3 37.3	29 33.4	5 1.1
10 M	15 7 41	18 28 19	22 17 44	28 12 29	20 24.5	5 31.2	28 16.9	17 0.4	20 10.4	12 20.7	3 40.7	29 32.5	5 1.7
11 Tu	15 11 38	19 26 18	4♌ 6 34	10♌ 0 37	20 22.5	5 39.9	29 25.8	17 45.4	20 19.7	12 28.1	3 44.1	29 31.5	5 2.3
12 W	15 15 34	20 24 16	15 55 18	21 51 20	20 22.0	5R43.5	0♋34.5	18 30.5	20 29.1	12 35.5	3 47.5	29 30.6	5 2.9
13 Th	15 19 31	21 22 11	27 49 22	3♍50 6	20 22.0	5 42.1	1 43.2	19 15.5	20 38.7	12 43.0	3 51.0	29 29.7	5 3.5
14 F	15 23 27	22 20 5	9♍54 14	16 2 22	20 21.2	5 35.9	2 51.7	20 0.4	20 48.3	12 50.4	3 54.4	29 28.8	5 4.2
15 Sa	15 27 24	23 17 57	22 15 8	28 33 2	20 18.9	5 25.1	4 0.1	20 45.4	20 58.1	12 57.9	3 57.9	29 28.0	5 4.9
16 Su	15 31 20	24 15 47	4♎56 32	11♎25 58	20 14.2	5 10.0	5 8.3	21 30.3	21 7.9	13 5.4	4 1.4	29 27.2	5 5.6
17 M	15 35 17	25 13 36	18 1 36	24 43 31	20 6.9	4 50.9	6 16.4	22 15.2	21 17.8	13 13.0	4 4.8	29 26.4	5 6.3
18 Tu	15 39 13	26 11 23	1♏31 41	8♏25 52	19 57.3	4 28.1	7 24.3	23 0.0	21 27.9	13 20.5	4 8.3	29 25.6	5 7.1
19 W	15 43 10	27 9 9	15 25 44	22 30 46	19 46.2	4 2.1	8 32.1	23 44.9	21 38.0	13 28.1	4 11.8	29 24.9	5 7.8
20 Th	15 47 6	28 6 53	29 40 18	6♐53 34	19 34.6	3 33.3	9 39.7	24 29.7	21 48.2	13 35.7	4 15.3	29 24.2	5 8.6
21 F	15 51 3	29 4 36	14♐ 9 42	21 27 49	19 23.9	3 2.3	10 47.2	25 14.5	21 58.5	13 43.4	4 18.8	29 23.6	5 9.5
22 Sa	15 55 0	0♊ 2 17	28 46 59	6♑ 6 20	19 15.0	2 29.6	11 54.5	25 59.2	22 8.9	13 51.0	4 22.3	29 22.9	5 10.3
23 Su	15 58 56	0 59 58	13♑25 2	20 42 22	19 8.8	1 55.8	13 1.7	26 44.0	22 19.4	13 58.7	4 25.8	29 22.3	5 11.2
24 M	16 2 53	1 57 37	27 57 42	5♒10 33	19 5.3	1 21.5	14 8.7	27 28.6	22 29.9	14 6.3	4 29.4	29 21.7	5 12.1
25 Tu	16 6 49	2 55 16	12♒20 31	19 27 22	19D 4.0	0 47.3	15 15.5	28 13.3	22 40.6	14 14.0	4 32.9	29 21.2	5 13.0
26 W	16 10 46	3 52 53	26 30 55	3♓31 5	19R 3.9	0 13.7	16 22.2	28 57.9	22 51.3	14 21.7	4 36.4	29 20.7	5 13.9
27 Th	16 14 42	4 50 29	10♓27 53	17 21 19	19 3.9	29♉41.4	17 28.7	29 42.5	23 2.1	14 29.5	4 39.9	29 20.2	5 14.9
28 F	16 18 39	5 48 5	24 11 29	0♈58 27	19 2.7	29 11.0	18 35.0	0♈27.1	23 13.0	14 37.2	4 43.4	29 19.7	5 15.9
29 Sa	16 22 36	6 45 40	7♈42 17	14 23 4	18 59.4	28 42.8	19 41.2	1 11.6	23 24.0	14 44.9	4 46.9	29 19.3	5 16.9
30 Su	16 26 32	7 43 13	21 0 50	27 35 37	18 53.4	28 17.3	20 47.1	1 56.0	23 35.1	14 52.7	4 50.4	29 18.9	5 17.9
31 M	16 30 29	8 40 46	4♉ 7 25	10♉36 14	18 44.9	27 55.0	21 52.9	2 40.4	23 46.2	15 0.5	4 54.0	29 18.5	5 18.9

LONGITUDE — JUNE 1943

Day	Sid.Time	☉	0 hr ☽	Noon ☽	True ☊	☿	♀	♂	♃	♄	♅	♆	♇
1 Tu	16 34 25	9♊38 18	17♉ 2 3	23♉24 49	18♌34.3	27♉36.2	22♋58.4	3♈24.8	23♋57.4	15♊ 8.2	4♊57.5	29♍18.2	5♌20.0
2 W	16 38 22	10 35 49	29 44 31	6♊ 1 9	18R22.6	27R21.2	24 3.8	4 9.1	24 8.7	15 16.0	5 1.0	29R17.9	5 21.1
3 Th	16 42 18	11 33 20	12♊14 43	18 25 16	18 10.9	27 10.2	25 9.0	4 53.4	24 20.0	15 23.8	5 4.5	29 17.6	5 22.2
4 F	16 46 15	12 30 49	24 32 54	0♋37 43	18 0.2	27 3.4	26 14.0	5 37.6	24 31.5	15 31.6	5 8.0	29 17.4	5 23.3
5 Sa	16 50 11	13 28 17	6♋39 55	12 39 44	17 51.4	27D 1.0	27 18.7	6 21.8	24 43.0	15 39.4	5 11.5	29 17.2	5 24.5
6 Su	16 54 8	14 25 44	18 37 27	24 33 26	17 45.1	27 2.9	28 23.3	7 5.9	24 54.5	15 47.2	5 15.0	29 17.0	5 25.7
7 M	16 58 5	15 23 10	0♌28 3	6♌21 47	17 41.2	27 9.3	29 27.6	7 50.0	25 6.1	15 55.0	5 18.4	29 16.9	5 26.8
8 Tu	17 2 1	16 20 35	12 15 8	18 8 38	17D 39.6	27 20.3	0♌31.6	8 34.0	25 17.8	16 2.8	5 21.9	29 16.8	5 28.0
9 W	17 5 58	17 17 59	24 2 52	29 58 29	17 39.7	27 35.7	1 35.4	9 17.9	25 29.6	16 10.6	5 25.4	29 16.7	5 29.3
10 Th	17 9 54	18 15 22	5♍56 6	11♍56 23	17 40.4	27 55.6	2 39.0	10 1.8	25 41.4	16 18.4	5 28.8	29D 16.6	5 30.5
11 F	17 13 51	19 12 44	18 0 0	24 7 37	17R 40.9	28 19.9	3 42.3	10 45.6	25 53.3	16 26.2	5 32.3	29 16.6	5 31.8
12 Sa	17 17 47	20 10 5	0♎19 53	6♎37 23	17 40.4	28 48.6	4 45.4	11 29.4	26 5.2	16 34.0	5 35.7	29 16.6	5 33.1
13 Su	17 21 44	21 7 24	13 0 40	19 30 14	17 38.1	29 21.5	5 48.1	12 13.1	26 17.2	16 41.7	5 39.1	29 16.7	5 34.3
14 M	17 25 40	22 4 43	26 6 26	2♏49 31	17 33.7	29 58.7	6 50.6	12 56.7	26 29.2	16 49.5	5 42.6	29 16.8	5 35.7
15 Tu	17 29 37	23 2 1	9♏39 37	16 36 39	17 27.4	0♊40.1	7 52.8	13 40.3	26 41.3	16 57.3	5 46.0	29 16.9	5 37.0
16 W	17 33 34	23 59 18	23 40 23	0♐50 26	17 19.8	1 25.5	8 54.7	14 23.8	26 53.5	17 5.1	5 49.3	29 17.0	5 38.3
17 Th	17 37 30	24 56 35	8♐ 6 9	15 26 47	17 11.7	2 14.9	9 56.3	15 7.2	27 5.7	17 12.8	5 52.7	29 17.2	5 39.7
18 F	17 41 27	25 53 50	22 51 25	0♑18 59	17 4.1	3 8.3	10 57.6	15 50.6	27 17.9	17 20.6	5 56.1	29 17.4	5 41.1
19 Sa	17 45 23	26 51 6	7♑48 24	15 18 32	16 57.9	4 5.5	11 58.5	16 33.9	27 30.2	17 28.3	5 59.4	29 17.7	5 42.5
20 Su	17 49 20	27 48 20	22 48 15	0♒16 31	16 53.7	5 6.4	12 59.1	17 17.2	27 42.6	17 36.0	6 2.8	29 18.0	5 43.9
21 M	17 53 16	28 45 35	7♒42 24	15 5 5	16D 51.7	6 11.1	13 59.4	18 0.4	27 55.0	17 43.7	6 6.1	29 18.3	5 45.3
22 Tu	17 57 13	29 42 49	22 23 55	29 38 23	16 51.5	7 19.5	14 59.3	18 43.5	28 7.4	17 51.4	6 9.4	29 18.6	5 46.8
23 W	18 1 9	0♋40 3	6♓48 7	13♓52 53	16 52.4	8 31.5	15 58.9	19 26.5	28 19.9	17 59.1	6 12.7	29 19.0	5 48.2
24 Th	18 5 6	1 37 17	20 52 36	27 47 15	16R 53.5	9 47.1	16 58.0	20 9.5	28 32.4	18 6.8	6 15.9	29 19.4	5 49.7
25 F	18 9 3	2 34 30	4♈36 55	11♈21 46	16 53.9	11 6.2	17 56.8	20 52.3	28 45.0	18 14.4	6 19.2	29 19.8	5 51.2
26 Sa	18 12 59	3 31 44	18 1 59	24 37 46	16 52.9	12 28.8	18 55.2	21 35.1	28 57.6	18 22.1	6 22.4	29 20.3	5 52.6
27 Su	18 16 56	4 28 58	1♉ 9 22	7♉37 2	16 50.1	13 54.8	19 53.2	22 17.8	29 10.2	18 29.7	6 25.6	29 20.8	5 54.2
28 M	18 20 52	5 26 12	14 0 59	20 21 28	16 45.5	15 24.3	20 50.8	23 0.5	29 22.9	18 37.3	6 28.8	29 21.3	5 55.7
29 Tu	18 24 49	6 23 26	26 38 40	2♊52 49	16 39.5	16 57.1	21 47.9	23 43.0	29 35.6	18 44.9	6 32.0	29 21.9	5 57.2
30 W	18 28 45	7 20 39	9♊ 4 6	15 12 41	16 32.7	18 33.3	22 44.6	24 25.5	29 48.4	18 52.4	6 35.1	29 22.5	5 58.8

Astro Data Dy Hr Mn	Planet Ingress Dy Hr Mn	Last Aspect Dy Hr Mn	☽ Ingress Dy Hr Mn	Last Aspect Dy Hr Mn	☽ Ingress Dy Hr Mn	☽ Phases & Eclipses Dy Hr Mn	Astro Data
☽0N 1 19:36	♀ ♋ 11 11:56	1 4:07 ♆ ☍	♈ 1 4:39	1 23:09 ♆ △	♊ 2 0:29	4 9:43 ● 13♉03	1 MAY 1943
☿ R 12 5:13	☉ ♊ 21 23:03	2 15:37 ♀ ✶	♉ 3 9:57	4 9:21 ♆ □	♋ 4 10:45	12 9:52 ☽ 20♌48	Julian Day # 15826
☽0S 16 7:04	☿ ♉ 26 10:04	5 16:32 ♀ △	♊ 5 17:16	6 21:45 ♀ ☌	♌ 6 23:03	19 21:13 ○ 28♏00	Delta T 25.9 sec
☽0N 29 2:17	♂ ♈ 27 9:25	8 2:26 ♆ □	♋ 8 3:17	9 7:23 ♆ □	♍ 9 12:03	26 13:34 ☽ 4♓25	SVP 06♓03'16"
		10 14:41 ♆ ✶	♌ 10 15:39	11 21:58 ♆ ☌	♎ 11 23:22		Obliquity 23°26'41"
♂0N 1 23:10	♀ ♌ 7 12:09	12 9:52 ☉ □	♍ 13 4:21	14 0:42 ♃ □	♏ 14 6:59	2 22:33 ● 11♊30	⚷ Chiron 23♌00.6
☿ D 5 1:29	☿ ♊ 14 0:46	15 13:43 ♆ ☌	♎ 15 14:44	16 9:25 ♆ ✶	♐ 16 10:36	11 2:35 ☽ 19♍19	☽ Mean ☊ 21♌09.5
♅✶♇ 10 18:20	☉ ♋ 22 7:12	17 5:57 ♃ □	♏ 17 21:19	18 10:21 ♆ □	♑ 18 11:30	18 5:14 ○ 26♐06	
♆ D 10 22:06	♃ ♌ 30 21:45	19 23:33 ♆ ✶	♐ 20 0:33	20 10:26 ♆ △	♒ 20 11:33	24 20:08 ☽ 2♈25	1 JUNE 1943
☽0S 12 17:05		22 0:59 ♆ □	♑ 22 2:00	21 17:39 ♂ ✶	♓ 22 12:36		Julian Day # 15857
☽0N 25 8:45		24 2:19 ♆ △	♒ 24 3:23	24 14:42 ♆ ☍	♈ 24 15:52		Delta T 25.9 sec
♃✶♆ 27 20:54		25 3:13 ♄ △	♓ 26 5:58	26 20:17 ♃ □	♉ 26 21:52		SVP 06♓03'12"
		28 9:05 ♆ ☍	♈ 28 10:16	29 5:46 ♃ ✶	♊ 29 6:27		Obliquity 23°26'40"
		30 4:45 ♃ □	♉ 30 16:25				⚷ Chiron 24♌18.2
							☽ Mean ☊ 19♌31.0

JULY 1943 LONGITUDE

Day	Sid.Time	☉	0 hr ☽	Noon ☽	True ☊	☿	♀	♂	♃	♄	♅	♆	♇
1 Th	18 32 42	8♋17 53	21♊18 45	27♊22 29	16♌25.8	20♊12.7	23♌40.9	25♈ 7.8	0♌ 1.2	18♊59.9	6♊38.3	29♍23.1	6♌ 0.3
2 F	18 36 38	9 15 7	3♋24 4	9♋23 42	16R 19.6	21 55.4	24 36.6	25 50.1	0 14.0	19 7.5	6 41.4	29 23.8	6 1.9
3 Sa	18 40 35	10 12 21	15 21 35	21 17 56	16 14.6	23 41.1	25 31.9	26 32.3	0 26.9	19 14.9	6 44.4	29 24.5	6 3.5
4 Su	18 44 32	11 9 34	27 13 2	3♌ 7 9	16 11.2	25 29.9	26 26.7	27 14.3	0 39.8	19 22.4	6 47.5	29 25.2	6 5.1
5 M	18 48 28	12 6 48	9♌ 0 36	14 53 45	16D 9.6	27 21.6	27 20.9	27 56.3	0 52.7	19 29.8	6 50.5	29 26.0	6 6.7
6 Tu	18 52 25	13 4 1	20 46 58	26 40 42	16 9.4	29 16.0	28 14.5	28 38.2	1 5.7	19 37.2	6 53.5	29 26.8	6 8.3
7 W	18 56 21	14 1 14	2♍35 24	8♍31 34	16 10.4	1♋13.0	29 7.6	29 19.9	1 18.6	19 44.6	6 56.5	29 27.6	6 9.9
8 Th	19 0 18	14 58 27	14 29 43	20 30 25	16 12.0	3 12.4	0♍ 0.1	0♉ 1.6	1 31.6	19 51.9	6 59.5	29 28.4	6 11.5
9 F	19 4 14	15 55 40	26 34 13	2♎41 42	16 13.7	5 14.0	0 52.0	0 43.1	1 44.7	19 59.2	7 2.4	29 29.3	6 13.2
10 Sa	19 8 11	16 52 53	8♎53 28	15 10 4	16R 14.8	7 17.5	1 43.3	1 24.6	1 57.7	20 6.5	7 5.3	29 30.2	6 14.8
11 Su	19 12 7	17 50 6	21 32 5	27 59 58	16 15.0	9 22.7	2 33.9	2 5.9	2 10.8	20 13.7	7 8.1	29 31.1	6 16.5
12 M	19 16 4	18 47 18	4♏34 12	11♏15 7	16 14.0	11 29.2	3 23.8	2 47.1	2 23.9	20 20.9	7 11.0	29 32.1	6 18.1
13 Tu	19 20 1	19 44 31	18 2 58	24 57 52	16 11.9	13 36.8	4 12.9	3 28.2	2 37.0	20 28.1	7 13.8	29 33.1	6 19.8
14 W	19 23 57	20 41 43	1♐59 47	9♐ 8 29	16 9.0	15 45.1	5 1.4	4 9.2	2 50.1	20 35.2	7 16.6	29 34.1	6 21.5
15 Th	19 27 54	21 38 56	16 23 36	23 44 33	16 5.7	17 53.9	5 49.0	4 50.1	3 3.3	20 42.3	7 19.3	29 35.2	6 23.1
16 F	19 31 50	22 36 9	1♑10 35	8♑40 45	16 2.6	20 2.9	6 35.9	5 30.9	3 16.5	20 49.4	7 22.1	29 36.2	6 24.8
17 Sa	19 35 47	23 33 22	16 14 1	23 49 13	16 0.1	22 11.8	7 21.9	6 11.5	3 29.6	20 56.4	7 24.7	29 37.4	6 26.5
18 Su	19 39 43	24 30 36	1♒25 9	9♒ 0 35	15D 58.6	24 20.2	8 7.1	6 52.0	3 42.8	21 3.4	7 27.4	29 38.5	6 28.2
19 M	19 43 40	25 27 49	16 34 21	24 5 21	15 58.1	26 28.1	8 51.4	7 32.4	3 56.0	21 10.3	7 30.0	29 39.7	6 29.9
20 Tu	19 47 36	26 25 4	1♓32 38	8♓55 23	15 58.6	28 35.2	9 34.7	8 12.7	4 9.3	21 17.2	7 32.6	29 40.9	6 31.6
21 W	19 51 33	27 22 19	16 12 54	23 24 43	15 59.6	0♌41.2	10 17.1	8 52.9	4 22.5	21 24.0	7 35.2	29 42.1	6 33.4
22 Th	19 55 30	28 19 35	0♈30 30	7♈30 4	16 0.9	2 46.2	10 58.5	9 32.9	4 35.7	21 30.8	7 37.7	29 43.3	6 35.1
23 F	19 59 26	29 16 51	14 23 23	21 10 31	16 1.9	4 49.8	11 38.8	10 12.8	4 49.0	21 37.6	7 40.2	29 44.6	6 36.8
24 Sa	20 3 23	0♌14 9	27 51 40	4♉27 3	16R 2.3	6 52.1	12 18.1	10 52.5	5 2.2	21 44.3	7 42.6	29 45.9	6 38.5
25 Su	20 7 19	1 11 27	10♉57 2	17 21 57	16 2.1	8 52.9	12 56.3	11 32.1	5 15.5	21 50.9	7 45.1	29 47.2	6 40.2
26 M	20 11 16	2 8 46	23 42 11	29 58 10	16 1.2	10 52.1	13 33.4	12 11.6	5 28.8	21 57.5	7 47.4	29 48.6	6 42.0
27 Tu	20 15 12	3 6 7	6♊10 17	12♊18 57	15 59.9	12 49.8	14 9.2	12 50.9	5 42.1	22 4.1	7 49.8	29 50.0	6 43.7
28 W	20 19 9	4 3 28	18 24 34	24 27 31	15 58.3	14 45.9	14 43.8	13 30.1	5 55.3	22 10.6	7 52.1	29 51.4	6 45.4
29 Th	20 23 5	5 0 50	0♋28 9	6♋26 50	15 56.6	16 40.3	15 17.1	14 9.1	6 8.6	22 17.1	7 54.4	29 52.8	6 47.2
30 F	20 27 2	5 58 13	12 23 53	18 19 37	15 55.2	18 33.1	15 49.1	14 48.0	6 21.9	22 23.5	7 56.6	29 54.2	6 48.9
31 Sa	20 30 59	6 55 37	24 14 21	0♌ 8 22	15 54.2	20 24.3	16 19.7	15 26.7	6 35.2	22 29.8	7 58.8	29 55.7	6 50.7

AUGUST 1943 LONGITUDE

Day	Sid.Time	☉	0 hr ☽	Noon ☽	True ☊	☿	♀	♂	♃	♄	♅	♆	♇
1 Su	20 34 55	7♌53 2	6♌ 1 58	11♌55 24	15♌53.6	22♌13.8	16♍48.9	16♉ 5.3	6♌48.5	22♊36.1	8♊ 1.0	29♍57.2	6♌52.4
2 M	20 38 52	8 50 27	17 48 59	23 43 0	15D 53.5	24 1.6	17 16.6	16 43.6	7 1.8	22 42.3	8 3.1	29 58.8	6 54.1
3 Tu	20 42 48	9 47 54	29 37 45	5♍33 32	15 53.7	25 47.8	17 42.7	17 21.8	7 15.0	22 48.5	8 5.1	0♎ 0.3	6 55.9
4 W	20 46 45	10 45 21	11♍30 41	17 29 34	15 54.1	27 32.3	18 7.2	17 59.9	7 28.3	22 54.6	8 7.2	0 1.9	6 57.6
5 Th	20 50 41	11 42 49	23 30 32	29 33 59	15 54.6	29 15.3	18 30.0	18 37.7	7 41.6	23 0.7	8 9.2	0 3.5	6 59.3
6 F	20 54 38	12 40 18	5♎40 18	11♎49 55	15 55.0	0♍56.6	18 51.0	19 15.4	7 54.8	23 6.7	8 11.1	0 5.1	7 1.1
7 Sa	20 58 34	13 37 47	18 3 16	24 20 46	15 55.3	2 36.2	19 10.3	19 52.9	8 8.1	23 12.6	8 13.0	0 6.8	7 2.8
8 Su	21 2 31	14 35 18	0♏42 52	7♏ 9 59	15 55.4	4 14.3	19 27.8	20 30.2	8 21.3	23 18.5	8 14.9	0 8.4	7 4.5
9 M	21 6 28	15 32 49	13 42 29	20 20 44	15 55.5	5 50.8	19 43.3	21 7.4	8 34.6	23 24.3	8 16.7	0 10.1	7 6.2
10 Tu	21 10 24	16 30 21	27 5 1	3♐55 31	15 55.5	7 25.7	19 56.8	21 44.3	8 47.8	23 30.0	8 18.5	0 11.8	7 8.0
11 W	21 14 21	17 27 54	10♐52 22	17 55 33	15 55.5	8 59.0	20 8.3	22 21.1	9 1.0	23 35.7	8 20.2	0 13.5	7 9.7
12 Th	21 18 17	18 25 27	25 4 54	2♑20 8	15 55.7	10 30.7	20 17.6	22 57.6	9 14.2	23 41.3	8 21.9	0 15.3	7 11.4
13 F	21 22 14	19 23 2	9♑40 47	17 6 13	15 56.0	12 0.8	20 24.8	23 34.0	9 27.3	23 46.8	8 23.6	0 17.1	7 13.1
14 Sa	21 26 10	20 20 38	24 35 40	2♒ 8 11	15 56.3	13 29.2	20 29.8	24 10.2	9 40.5	23 52.3	8 25.2	0 18.9	7 14.8
15 Su	21 30 7	21 18 14	9♒42 43	17 18 9	15R 56.5	14 56.1	20R 32.6	24 46.1	9 53.6	23 57.7	8 26.7	0 20.7	7 16.5
16 M	21 34 3	22 15 52	24 53 18	2♓26 59	15 56.5	16 21.3	20 33.0	25 21.9	10 6.7	24 3.0	8 28.2	0 22.5	7 18.2
17 Tu	21 38 0	23 13 31	9♓58 4	17 25 28	15 56.1	17 44.8	20 31.1	25 57.4	10 19.8	24 8.2	8 29.7	0 24.3	7 19.9
18 W	21 41 57	24 11 12	24 48 17	2♈ 5 42	15 55.4	19 6.6	20 26.9	26 32.8	10 32.9	24 13.4	8 31.1	0 26.2	7 21.6
19 Th	21 45 53	25 8 53	9♈17 7	16 22 4	15 54.4	20 26.7	20 20.3	27 7.9	10 46.0	24 18.5	8 32.5	0 28.1	7 23.2
20 F	21 49 50	26 6 37	23 20 18	0♉11 40	15 53.3	21 45.0	20 11.3	27 42.8	10 59.0	24 23.5	8 33.8	0 30.0	7 24.9
21 Sa	21 53 46	27 4 22	6♉56 14	13 34 9	15 52.3	23 1.5	19 59.9	28 17.5	11 12.0	24 28.5	8 35.1	0 31.9	7 26.6
22 Su	21 57 43	28 2 9	20 5 43	26 31 18	15D 51.7	24 16.1	19 46.2	28 51.9	11 25.0	24 33.4	8 36.3	0 33.8	7 28.2
23 M	22 1 39	28 59 57	2♊51 19	9♊ 6 18	15 51.6	25 28.8	19 30.1	29 26.1	11 38.0	24 38.1	8 37.5	0 35.8	7 29.8
24 Tu	22 5 36	29 57 47	15 16 44	21 23 12	15 52.1	26 39.4	19 11.8	0♊ 0.1	11 50.9	24 42.9	8 38.6	0 37.7	7 31.5
25 W	22 9 32	0♍55 39	27 26 14	3♋26 22	15 53.1	27 48.0	18 51.2	0 33.8	12 3.8	24 47.5	8 39.7	0 39.7	7 33.1
26 Th	22 13 29	1 53 33	9♋24 11	15 20 9	15 54.4	28 54.3	18 28.4	1 7.2	12 16.7	24 52.1	8 40.7	0 41.7	7 34.7
27 F	22 17 26	2 51 28	21 14 48	27 8 35	15 55.8	29 58.4	18 3.6	1 40.4	12 29.5	24 56.5	8 41.7	0 43.7	7 36.3
28 Sa	22 21 22	3 49 26	3♌ 1 56	8♌55 16	15 57.0	1♎ 0.1	17 36.8	2 13.3	12 42.3	25 0.9	8 42.7	0 45.8	7 37.9
29 Su	22 25 19	4 47 24	14 48 56	20 43 19	15R 57.4	1 59.2	17 8.1	2 46.0	12 55.1	25 5.2	8 43.6	0 47.8	7 39.5
30 M	22 29 15	5 45 25	26 38 42	2♍35 23	15 57.1	2 55.6	16 37.7	3 18.3	13 7.8	25 9.4	8 44.4	0 49.8	7 41.1
31 Tu	22 33 12	6 43 27	8♍33 37	14 33 39	15 55.6	3 49.2	16 5.8	3 50.4	13 20.5	25 13.5	8 45.2	0 51.9	7 42.6

Astro Data Dy Hr Mn	Planet Ingress Dy Hr Mn	Last Aspect Dy Hr Mn	☽ Ingress Dy Hr Mn	Last Aspect Dy Hr Mn	☽ Ingress Dy Hr Mn	☽ Phases & Eclipses Dy Hr Mn
☽0S 10 1:45	☿ ♋ 6 9:05	1 16:01 ♆ □	♋ 1 17:13	2 14:52 ☿ ☌	♍ 3 0:45	2 12:44 ● 9♋45
☽0N 22 16:11	♀ ♍ 7 23:56	4 4:29 ♆ ⚹	♌ 4 5:39	4 23:00 ♄ □	♎ 5 12:51	10 16:29 ☽ 17♎32
♄∠♇ 22 20:19	♂ ♉ 7 23:05	6 16:59 ♂ △	♍ 6 18:45	7 9:55 ♄ △	♏ 7 22:40	17 12:22 ○ 24♑03
	☿ ♌ 20 16:08	9 5:44 ♆ ☌	♎ 9 6:44	9 14:02 ♂ ☍	♐ 10 5:08	24 4:38 ☽ 0♉25
♃☌♇ 1 8:09	☉ ♌ 23 18:05	10 21:32 ♄ △	♏ 11 15:40	11 21:40 ♄ ☍	♑ 12 8:09	
☽0S 6 8:23		13 19:52 ♆ ⚹	♐ 13 20:37	13 23:18 ♂ △	♒ 14 8:36	1 4:06 ● 8♌03
♃⚹♅ 7 10:25	♆ ♎ 2 19:07	15 21:28 ♆ □	♑ 15 22:07	16 0:47 ♂ □	♓ 16 8:06	1 4:15:48 ✔ A 6'58"
♃∠♄ 7 14:42	☿ ♍ 5 10:33	17 21:11 ♆ △	♒ 17 21:46	18 2:58 ♂ ⚹	♈ 18 8:32	9 3:36 ☽ 15♏41
♀0S 9 11:29	♂ ♊ 23 23:58	19 7:23 ♄ △	♓ 19 21:30	20 5:12 ☉ △	♉ 20 11:39	15 19:34 ○ 22♒05
♀ R 15 16:37	☉ ♍ 24 0:55	21 22:40 ♆ ☍	♈ 21 23:08	22 17:12 ♂ ☌	♊ 22 18:34	15 19:28 ☍ P 0.870
☽0N 19 1:07	☿ ♎ 27 0:36	23 12:55 ♄ ⚹	♉ 24 3:53	25 0:48 ☿ □	♋ 25 5:07	22 16:04 ☽ 28♉41
☿0S 24 0:32		26 11:43 ♆ △	♊ 26 12:04	26 17:45 ♀ ⚹	♌ 27 17:49	30 19:59 ● 6♍34
		28 22:49 ♆ □	♋ 28 23:04	29 20:58 ♄ ⚹	♍ 30 6:47	
		31 11:36 ♆ ⚹	♌ 31 11:43			

Astro Data

1 JULY 1943
Julian Day # 15887
Delta T 26.0 sec
SVP 06♓03'07"
Obliquity 23°26'40"
⚷ Chiron 26♌56.6
☽ Mean ☊ 17♌55.7

1 AUGUST 1943
Julian Day # 15918
Delta T 26.0 sec
SVP 06♓03'02"
Obliquity 23°26'41"
⚷ Chiron 0♍39.1
☽ Mean ☊ 16♌17.2

LONGITUDE SEPTEMBER 1943

Day	Sid.Time	☉	0 hr ☽	Noon ☽	True ☊	☿	♀	♂	♃	♄	♅	♆	♇
1 W	22 37 8	7♍41 30	20♍35 44	26♍40 2	15♌53.2	4♎39.8	15♍32.5	4♊22.2	13♌33.2	25♊17.6	8♊45.9	0♎54.0	7♌44.2
2 Th	22 41 5	8 39 35	2♎46 48	8♎56 12	15R49.9	5 27.1	14R58.0	4 53.7	13 45.8	25 21.5	8 46.6	0 56.1	7 45.7
3 F	22 45 1	9 37 42	15 8 28	21 23 47	15 46.1	6 11.1	14 22.6	5 24.9	13 58.4	25 25.4	8 47.2	0 58.2	7 47.3
4 Sa	22 48 58	10 35 50	27 42 22	4♏ 4 26	15 42.3	6 51.4	13 46.3	5 55.8	14 10.9	25 29.2	8 47.8	1 0.3	7 48.8
5 Su	22 52 55	11 34 0	10♏30 13	16 59 55	15 38.9	7 27.7	13 9.6	6 26.3	14 23.4	25 32.8	8 48.4	1 2.4	7 50.3
6 M	22 56 51	12 32 11	23 33 45	0♐11 58	15 36.5	7 59.9	12 32.5	6 56.6	14 35.8	25 36.4	8 48.9	1 4.5	7 51.7
7 Tu	23 0 48	13 30 24	6♐54 45	13 42 16	15D 35.2	8 27.7	11 55.4	7 26.5	14 48.2	25 39.9	8 49.3	1 6.7	7 53.2
8 W	23 4 44	14 28 38	20 34 40	27 32 0	15 35.2	8 50.7	11 18.4	7 56.1	15 0.6	25 43.3	8 49.7	1 8.8	7 54.7
9 Th	23 8 41	15 26 54	4♑34 16	11♑41 24	15 36.1	9 8.7	10 41.8	8 25.3	15 12.9	25 46.6	8 50.0	1 11.0	7 56.1
10 F	23 12 37	16 25 11	18 53 12	26 9 22	15 37.6	9 21.2	10 5.9	8 54.3	15 25.1	25 49.8	8 50.3	1 13.1	7 57.6
11 Sa	23 16 34	17 23 30	3♒29 27	10♒52 52	15R38.8	9R28.1	9 30.9	9 22.8	15 37.3	25 52.9	8 50.5	1 15.3	7 59.0
12 Su	23 20 30	18 21 50	18 18 55	25 46 46	15 39.2	9 29.0	8 57.0	9 51.0	15 49.5	25 55.9	8 50.7	1 17.5	8 0.4
13 M	23 24 27	19 20 12	3♓15 30	10♓44 4	15 38.2	9 23.5	8 24.4	10 18.9	16 1.6	25 58.8	8 50.8	1 19.7	8 1.7
14 Tu	23 28 23	20 18 36	18 11 27	25 36 35	15 35.5	9 11.6	7 53.3	10 46.4	16 13.6	26 1.6	8R50.9	1 21.9	8 3.1
15 W	23 32 20	21 17 1	2♈58 26	10♈16 5	15 31.2	8 52.8	7 23.9	11 13.5	16 25.6	26 4.4	8 50.9	1 24.1	8 4.5
16 Th	23 36 17	22 15 29	17 28 43	24 35 37	15 25.9	8 27.3	6 56.3	11 40.2	16 37.5	26 7.0	8 50.9	1 26.3	8 5.8
17 F	23 40 13	23 13 58	1♉36 18	8♉30 24	15 20.0	7 54.9	6 30.7	12 6.5	16 49.3	26 9.5	8 50.8	1 28.5	8 7.1
18 Sa	23 44 10	24 12 29	15 17 45	21 58 19	15 14.6	7 15.8	6 7.2	12 32.5	17 1.1	26 11.9	8 50.7	1 30.7	8 8.4
19 Su	23 48 6	25 11 3	28 32 13	4♊59 45	15 10.2	6 30.3	5 46.0	12 58.0	17 12.9	26 14.2	8 50.5	1 32.9	8 9.7
20 M	23 52 3	26 9 39	11♊21 16	17 37 15	15 7.3	5 38.9	5 27.0	13 23.1	17 24.5	26 16.4	8 50.3	1 35.1	8 10.9
21 Tu	23 55 59	27 8 17	23 48 13	29 54 45	15D 6.0	4 42.3	5 10.3	13 47.8	17 36.1	26 18.5	8 50.0	1 37.4	8 12.2
22 W	23 59 56	28 6 58	5♋57 30	11♋57 5	15 6.3	3 41.6	4 56.1	14 12.0	17 47.7	26 20.5	8 49.7	1 39.6	8 13.4
23 Th	0 3 52	29 5 40	17 54 10	23 49 24	15 7.5	2 37.8	4 44.2	14 35.7	17 59.2	26 22.4	8 49.3	1 41.8	8 14.6
24 F	0 7 49	0♎ 4 25	29 43 23	5♌36 46	15 9.0	1 32.3	4 34.8	14 59.0	18 10.6	26 24.2	8 48.8	1 44.0	8 15.8
25 Sa	0 11 46	1 3 12	11♌30 7	17 23 58	15R10.0	0 26.8	4 27.9	15 21.9	18 21.9	26 25.9	8 48.4	1 46.3	8 17.0
26 Su	0 15 42	2 2 1	23 18 49	29 15 9	15 9.6	29♍22.7	4 23.4	15 44.2	18 33.1	26 27.4	8 47.8	1 48.5	8 18.1
27 M	0 19 39	3 0 52	5♍13 20	11♍13 46	15 7.4	28 21.9	4D21.2	16 6.0	18 44.3	26 28.9	8 47.2	1 50.7	8 19.2
28 Tu	0 23 35	3 59 46	17 16 42	23 22 25	15 3.0	27 25.9	4 21.5	16 27.4	18 55.4	26 30.2	8 46.6	1 53.0	8 20.3
29 W	0 27 32	4 58 41	29 31 5	5♎42 51	14 56.4	26 36.3	4 24.1	16 48.2	19 6.4	26 31.5	8 45.9	1 55.2	8 21.4
30 Th	0 31 28	5 57 39	11♎57 48	18 16 0	14 48.0	25 54.4	4 29.0	17 8.4	19 17.4	26 32.6	8 45.2	1 57.4	8 22.5

LONGITUDE OCTOBER 1943

Day	Sid.Time	☉	0 hr ☽	Noon ☽	True ☊	☿	♀	♂	♃	♄	♅	♆	♇
1 F	0 35 25	6♎56 38	24♎37 26	1♏ 2 5	14♌38.5	25♍21.2	4♍36.2	17♊28.2	19♌28.2	26♊33.6	8♊44.4	1♎59.6	8♌23.5
2 Sa	0 39 21	7 55 40	7♏29 56	14 0 56	14R28.9	24R57.6	4 45.6	17 47.3	19 39.0	26 34.6	8R43.5	2 1.9	8 24.5
3 Su	0 43 18	8 54 43	20 35 0	27 12 7	14 20.2	24D44.2	4 57.1	18 5.9	19 49.7	26 35.4	8 42.7	2 4.1	8 25.5
4 M	0 47 15	9 53 48	3♐52 15	10♐35 21	14 13.1	24 41.3	5 10.8	18 24.0	20 0.3	26 36.1	8 41.7	2 6.3	8 26.5
5 Tu	0 51 11	10 52 55	17 21 26	24 10 31	14 8.3	24 48.9	5 26.5	18 41.4	20 10.8	26 36.6	8 40.8	2 8.5	8 27.4
6 W	0 55 8	11 52 4	1♑ 2 36	7♑57 43	14D 5.9	25 6.8	5 44.1	18 58.3	20 21.2	26 37.1	8 39.7	2 10.7	8 28.4
7 Th	0 59 4	12 51 15	14 55 53	21 57 4	14 5.4	25 34.6	6 3.7	19 14.5	20 31.6	26 37.5	8 38.7	2 12.9	8 29.3
8 F	1 3 1	13 50 27	29 1 14	6♒ 8 17	14 5.9	26 11.9	6 25.1	19 30.2	20 41.8	26 37.7	8 37.5	2 15.1	8 30.2
9 Sa	1 6 57	14 49 41	13♒18 1	20 30 11	14R 6.4	26 57.9	6 48.4	19 45.2	20 52.0	26R37.9	8 36.4	2 17.3	8 31.0
10 Su	1 10 54	15 48 57	27 44 25	5♓ 0 15	14 5.7	27 52.1	7 13.4	19 59.5	21 2.0	26 37.9	8 35.2	2 19.5	8 31.9
11 M	1 14 50	16 48 15	12♓17 6	19 34 18	14 2.8	28 53.6	7 40.0	20 13.3	21 11.9	26 37.8	8 33.9	2 21.7	8 32.7
12 Tu	1 18 47	17 47 34	26 51 6	4♈ 6 41	13 57.3	0♎ 1.6	8 8.4	20 26.3	21 21.8	26 37.6	8 32.6	2 23.9	8 33.5
13 W	1 22 43	18 46 55	11♈20 13	18 30 52	13 49.2	1 15.5	8 38.3	20 38.7	21 31.5	26 37.3	8 31.3	2 26.0	8 34.2
14 Th	1 26 40	19 46 19	25 37 50	2♉40 24	13 39.2	2 34.4	9 9.7	20 50.4	21 41.2	26 36.9	8 29.9	2 28.2	8 35.0
15 F	1 30 37	20 45 44	9♉37 57	16 30 0	13 28.2	3 57.7	9 42.6	21 1.3	21 50.7	26 36.4	8 28.5	2 30.3	8 35.7
16 Sa	1 34 33	21 45 12	23 16 12	29 56 20	13 17.5	5 24.8	10 17.0	21 11.6	22 0.2	26 35.7	8 27.0	2 32.5	8 36.4
17 Su	1 38 30	22 44 41	6♊30 22	12♊58 23	13 8.1	6 54.9	10 52.7	21 21.1	22 9.5	26 35.0	8 25.5	2 34.6	8 37.0
18 M	1 42 26	23 44 13	19 20 36	25 37 21	13 0.9	8 27.7	11 29.7	21 29.9	22 18.7	26 34.1	8 23.9	2 36.7	8 37.7
19 Tu	1 46 23	24 43 48	1♋49 4	7♋56 17	12 56.1	10 2.6	12 8.1	21 38.0	22 27.8	26 33.2	8 22.3	2 38.8	8 38.3
20 W	1 50 19	25 43 24	13 59 33	19 59 32	12 53.7	11 39.3	12 47.6	21 45.2	22 36.8	26 32.1	8 20.7	2 40.9	8 38.9
21 Th	1 54 16	26 43 3	25 56 53	1♌52 18	12D53.1	13 17.3	13 28.3	21 51.7	22 45.7	26 30.9	8 19.0	2 43.0	8 39.4
22 F	1 58 12	27 42 44	7♌46 28	13 40 6	12R53.3	14 56.3	14 10.2	21 57.4	22 54.4	26 29.6	8 17.3	2 45.1	8 40.0
23 Sa	2 2 9	28 42 28	19 33 52	25 28 26	12 53.2	16 36.1	14 53.2	22 2.2	23 3.1	26 28.2	8 15.6	2 47.1	8 40.5
24 Su	2 6 6	29 42 13	1♍24 26	7♍22 27	12 51.7	18 16.4	15 37.2	22 6.3	23 11.6	26 26.7	8 13.8	2 49.2	8 41.0
25 M	2 10 2	0♏42 1	13 23 1	19 26 38	12 48.1	19 57.1	16 22.2	22 9.4	23 20.0	26 25.1	8 11.9	2 51.2	8 41.4
26 Tu	2 13 59	1 41 51	25 33 41	1♎44 32	12 41.7	21 38.0	17 8.2	22 11.8	23 28.3	26 23.4	8 10.1	2 53.2	8 41.9
27 W	2 17 55	2 41 43	7♎59 24	14 18 29	12 32.5	23 19.0	17 55.2	22 13.3	23 36.4	26 21.6	8 8.2	2 55.2	8 42.3
28 Th	2 21 52	3 41 37	20 41 51	27 9 29	12 20.9	24 59.9	18 43.0	22R13.9	23 44.4	26 19.6	8 6.2	2 57.2	8 42.6
29 F	2 25 48	4 41 33	3♏41 17	10♏17 5	12 7.8	26 40.7	19 31.7	22 13.7	23 52.3	26 17.6	8 4.3	2 59.2	8 43.0
30 Sa	2 29 45	5 41 31	16 56 39	23 39 40	11 54.5	28 21.3	20 21.2	22 12.5	24 0.1	26 15.5	8 2.3	3 1.1	8 43.3
31 Su	2 33 41	6 41 31	0♐25 50	7♐14 46	11 42.2	0♏ 1.6	21 11.6	22 10.5	24 7.7	26 13.2	8 0.2	3 3.1	8 43.6

Astro Data	Planet Ingress	Last Aspect	☽ Ingress	Last Aspect	☽ Ingress	☽ Phases & Eclipses	Astro Data
Dy Hr Mn	Dy Hr Mn	Dy Hr Mn	Dy Hr Mn	Dy Hr Mn	Dy Hr Mn	Dy Hr Mn	1 SEPTEMBER 1943
☽0S 2 13:47	☉ ♎ 23 22:12	1 9:20 ♄ □	♎ 1 18:33	1 3:38 ♄ △	♏ 1 10:04	7 12:33 ☽ 14♐01	Julian Day # 15949
♀0N 10 19:29	☿ ♍ 25 9:56	3 19:46 ♄ △	♏ 4 4:20	3 7:29 ☿ ✶	♐ 3 17:03	14 3:40 ○ 20♓28	Delta T 26.1 sec
☿ R 11 15:23		5 7:19 ♃ □	♐ 6 11:38	5 16:16 ♄ ☍	♑ 5 22:11	21 7:06 ☽ 27♊26	SVP 06♓02'59"
♃∠♆ 14 20:18	☿ ♎ 11 23:27	8 8:55 ♄ ☍	♑ 8 16:13	7 18:59 ☿ △	♒ 8 1:39	29 11:29 ● 5♎27	Obliquity 23°26'42"
♅ R 14 22:36	☉ ♏ 24 7:08	9 19:36 ☉ △	♒ 10 18:18	9 22:10 ♄ △	♓ 10 3:44		⚷ Chiron 4♍51.2
☽0N 15 11:13	☿ ♏ 30 23:37	12 12:17 ♄ △	♓ 12 18:46	11 23:38 ♄ □	♈ 12 5:12	6 20:10 ☽ 12♑42	☽ Mean ☊ 14♌38.7
♀ D 27 9:15		14 12:43 ♄ □	♈ 14 19:08	14 1:40 ♄ ✶	♉ 14 7:26	13 13:23 ○ 19♈20	
☿0N 28 21:38		16 14:38 ♄ ✶	♉ 16 21:14	15 21:43 ♃ □	♊ 16 12:07	21 1:42 ☽ 26♋47	1 OCTOBER 1943
☽0S 29 19:41		18 17:21 ☉ △	♊ 19 2:42	18 13:48 ♄ ☌	♋ 18 20:28	29 1:59 ● 4♏47	Julian Day # 15979
☿ D 3 18:41		21 7:06 ☉ □	♋ 21 12:10	21 1:42 ☉ □	♌ 21 8:12		Delta T 26.1 sec
♄ R 9 18:17		21 22:00 ♀ ✶	♌ 24 0:34	23 20:15 ☉ ✶	♍ 23 21:10		SVP 06♓02'56"
♅✶♇ 11 14:23		26 6:22 ♄ ✶	♍ 26 13:30	26 1:37 ♄ □	♎ 26 8:38		Obliquity 23°26'42"
☽0N 12 21:20	☽0S 27 3:28	28 18:40 ☿ ☌	♎ 29 0:56	28 10:26 ♄ △	♏ 28 17:14		⚷ Chiron 8♍54.0
☿0S 15 10:05	♂ R 28 5:16			30 12:43 ♃ □	♐ 30 23:14		☽ Mean ☊ 13♌03.3

NOVEMBER 1943 LONGITUDE

Day	Sid.Time	☉	0 hr ☽	Noon ☽	True ☊	☿	♀	♂	♃	♄	♅	♆	♇
1 M	2 37 38	7♏41 32	14♐ 6 8	20♐59 35	11♌32.1	1♏41.6	22♍ 2.7	22♊ 7.6	24♌15.2	26♊10.9	7♊58.2	3♎ 5.0	8♌43.9
2 Tu	2 41 35	8 41 36	27 54 50	4♑51 35	11R24.7	3 21.3	22 54.6	22R 3.9	24 22.5	26R 8.4	7R56.1	3 6.9	8 44.1
3 W	2 45 31	9 41 41	11♑49 38	18 48 48	11 20.4	5 0.6	23 47.1	21 59.2	24 29.7	26 5.9	7 54.0	3 8.8	8 44.3
4 Th	2 49 28	10 41 48	25 48 57	2♒49 58	11 18.6	6 39.5	24 40.4	21 53.7	24 36.8	26 3.3	7 51.8	3 10.7	8 44.5
5 F	2 53 24	11 41 56	9♒51 49	16 54 23	11 18.2	8 18.1	25 34.3	21 47.2	24 43.7	26 0.5	7 49.7	3 12.5	8 44.7
6 Sa	2 57 21	12 42 5	23 57 37	1♓ 1 25	11 18.1	9 56.2	26 28.9	21 39.9	24 50.4	25 57.7	7 47.5	3 14.3	8 44.8
7 Su	3 1 17	13 42 17	8♓ 5 38	15 10 5	11 16.7	11 34.0	27 24.1	21 31.7	24 57.1	25 54.8	7 45.2	3 16.2	8 44.9
8 M	3 5 14	14 42 29	22 14 30	29 18 34	11 13.1	13 11.4	28 19.9	21 22.6	25 3.5	25 51.8	7 43.0	3 17.9	8 45.0
9 Tu	3 9 10	15 42 43	6♈21 52	13♈23 59	11 6.5	14 48.4	29 16.3	21 12.7	25 9.8	25 48.7	7 40.7	3 19.7	8 45.1
10 W	3 13 7	16 42 59	20 24 23	27 22 34	10 57.0	16 25.0	0♎13.3	21 2.0	25 16.0	25 45.5	7 38.4	3 21.5	8R45.1
11 Th	3 17 4	17 43 16	4♉17 58	11♉10 5	10 45.4	18 1.3	1 10.8	20 50.3	25 22.0	25 42.2	7 36.1	3 23.2	8 45.1
12 F	3 21 0	18 43 35	17 58 24	24 42 31	10 32.5	19 37.2	2 8.9	20 37.9	25 27.9	25 38.8	7 33.7	3 24.9	8 45.0
13 Sa	3 24 57	19 43 55	1♊22 5	7♊56 51	10 19.8	21 12.9	3 7.4	20 24.6	25 33.6	25 35.4	7 31.4	3 26.6	8 45.0
14 Su	3 28 53	20 44 18	14 26 39	20 51 29	10 8.4	22 48.2	4 6.5	20 10.6	25 39.1	25 31.9	7 29.0	3 28.2	8 44.9
15 M	3 32 50	21 44 42	27 11 25	3♋26 36	9 59.4	24 23.2	5 6.1	19 55.7	25 44.5	25 28.3	7 26.6	3 29.9	8 44.8
16 Tu	3 36 46	22 45 8	9♋37 21	15 44 2	9 53.0	25 57.9	6 6.1	19 40.1	25 49.8	25 24.6	7 24.2	3 31.5	8 44.7
17 W	3 40 43	23 45 36	21 47 5	27 47 1	9 49.4	27 32.3	7 6.6	19 23.8	25 54.8	25 20.8	7 21.8	3 33.1	8 44.5
18 Th	3 44 39	24 46 5	3♌44 27	9♌39 58	9D48.0	29 6.5	8 7.5	19 6.7	25 59.7	25 17.0	7 19.3	3 34.6	8 44.3
19 F	3 48 36	25 46 36	15 34 14	21 27 57	9R48.0	0♐40.5	9 8.9	18 49.0	26 4.4	25 13.1	7 16.9	3 36.2	8 44.1
20 Sa	3 52 33	26 47 10	27 21 49	3♍16 31	9 48.2	2 14.3	10 10.6	18 30.6	26 9.0	25 9.1	7 14.4	3 37.7	8 43.8
21 Su	3 56 29	27 47 44	9♍12 45	15 11 12	9 47.5	3 47.8	11 12.8	18 11.5	26 13.4	25 5.0	7 11.9	3 39.2	8 43.6
22 M	4 0 26	28 48 21	21 12 30	27 17 17	9 45.1	5 21.2	12 15.3	17 51.9	26 17.6	25 0.9	7 9.4	3 40.6	8 43.3
23 Tu	4 4 22	29 48 59	3♎26 4	9♎39 22	9 40.2	6 54.4	13 18.2	17 31.7	26 21.6	24 56.7	7 6.9	3 42.1	8 42.9
24 W	4 8 19	0♐49 39	15 57 33	22 20 57	9 32.8	8 27.4	14 21.5	17 11.0	26 25.5	24 52.5	7 4.4	3 43.5	8 42.6
25 Th	4 12 15	1 50 20	28 49 45	5♏24 1	9 23.1	10 0.3	15 25.1	16 49.9	26 29.2	24 48.2	7 1.9	3 44.8	8 42.2
26 F	4 16 12	2 51 4	12♏ 3 44	18 48 42	9 11.8	11 33.1	16 29.0	16 28.3	26 32.7	24 43.8	6 59.4	3 46.2	8 41.8
27 Sa	4 20 8	3 51 48	25 38 40	2♐33 11	9 0.2	13 5.7	17 33.2	16 6.3	26 36.0	24 39.4	6 56.9	3 47.5	8 41.4
28 Su	4 24 5	4 52 34	9♐31 45	16 33 49	8 49.3	14 38.1	18 37.8	15 44.0	26 39.1	24 34.9	6 54.3	3 48.8	8 40.9
29 M	4 28 2	5 53 21	23 38 44	0♑45 50	8 40.4	16 10.4	19 42.7	15 21.4	26 42.1	24 30.4	6 51.8	3 50.1	8 40.4
30 Tu	4 31 58	6 54 10	7♑54 29	15 4 1	8 34.1	17 42.6	20 47.8	14 58.6	26 44.9	24 25.9	6 49.3	3 51.3	8 39.9

DECEMBER 1943 LONGITUDE

Day	Sid.Time	☉	0 hr ☽	Noon ☽	True ☊	☿	♀	♂	♃	♄	♅	♆	♇
1 W	4 35 55	7♐54 59	22♑13 54	29♑23 36	8♌30.5	19♐14.7	21♎53.2	14♊35.7	26♌47.5	24♊21.2	6♊46.7	3♎52.6	8♌39.4
2 Th	4 39 51	8 55 50	6♒32 40	13♒40 46	8D29.4	20 46.6	22 58.9	14R12.6	26 49.9	24R16.6	6R44.2	3 53.7	8R38.8
3 F	4 43 48	9 56 41	20 47 36	27 52 58	8 29.8	22 18.3	24 4.9	13 49.5	26 52.1	24 11.9	6 41.7	3 54.9	8 38.3
4 Sa	4 47 44	10 57 33	4♓56 42	11♓58 42	8R30.5	23 49.8	25 11.1	13 26.3	26 54.1	24 7.2	6 39.2	3 56.0	8 37.7
5 Su	4 51 41	11 58 26	18 58 52	25 57 7	8 30.4	25 21.1	26 17.5	13 3.2	26 55.9	24 2.4	6 36.6	3 57.1	8 37.0
6 M	4 55 37	12 59 19	2♈53 25	9♈47 39	8 28.5	26 52.1	27 24.2	12 40.2	26 57.5	23 57.6	6 34.1	3 58.2	8 36.4
7 Tu	4 59 34	14 0 14	16 39 44	23 29 32	8 24.3	28 22.9	28 31.1	12 17.3	26 59.0	23 52.8	6 31.6	3 59.2	8 35.7
8 W	5 3 31	15 1 9	0♉16 54	7♉ 1 40	8 17.7	29 53.3	29 38.3	11 54.6	27 0.2	23 48.0	6 29.1	4 0.2	8 35.0
9 Th	5 7 27	16 2 5	13 43 39	20 22 38	8 9.3	1♑23.3	0♏45.7	11 32.2	27 1.3	23 43.1	6 26.6	4 1.2	8 34.3
10 F	5 11 24	17 3 1	26 58 26	3♊30 53	7 59.9	2 52.8	1 53.3	11 10.0	27 2.2	23 38.2	6 24.1	4 2.1	8 33.5
11 Sa	5 15 20	18 3 59	9♊59 48	16 25 6	7 50.6	4 21.7	3 1.1	10 48.2	27 2.8	23 33.3	6 21.7	4 3.0	8 32.7
12 Su	5 19 17	19 4 57	22 46 40	29 4 32	7 42.2	5 49.9	4 9.1	10 26.7	27 3.3	23 28.4	6 19.2	4 3.9	8 31.9
13 M	5 23 13	20 5 56	5♋18 42	11♋29 18	7 35.6	7 17.3	5 17.3	10 5.7	27R 3.6	23 23.5	6 16.8	4 4.7	8 31.1
14 Tu	5 27 10	21 6 56	17 36 29	23 40 31	7 31.1	8 43.7	6 25.7	9 45.1	27 3.7	23 18.5	6 14.4	4 5.5	8 30.3
15 W	5 31 6	22 7 57	29 41 42	5♌40 24	7D28.9	10 9.0	7 34.3	9 24.9	27 3.6	23 13.6	6 11.9	4 6.3	8 29.4
16 Th	5 35 3	23 8 59	11♌37 3	17 32 7	7 28.6	11 32.9	8 43.0	9 5.4	27 3.3	23 8.6	6 9.6	4 7.0	8 28.6
17 F	5 39 0	24 10 2	23 26 8	29 19 40	7 29.7	12 55.1	9 52.0	8 46.3	27 2.8	23 3.7	6 7.2	4 7.8	8 27.7
18 Sa	5 42 56	25 11 6	5♍13 19	11♍ 7 44	7 31.4	14 15.5	11 1.1	8 27.9	27 2.1	22 58.7	6 4.8	4 8.4	8 26.7
19 Su	5 46 53	26 12 10	17 3 33	23 1 26	7R32.8	15 33.6	12 10.4	8 10.1	27 1.2	22 53.8	6 2.5	4 9.1	8 25.8
20 M	5 50 49	27 13 15	29 2 3	5♎ 6 2	7 33.2	16 49.1	13 19.8	7 52.9	27 0.1	22 48.9	6 0.2	4 9.7	8 24.8
21 Tu	5 54 46	28 14 21	11♎14 1	17 26 36	7 32.2	18 1.5	14 29.4	7 36.4	26 58.9	22 43.9	5 57.9	4 10.3	8 23.8
22 W	5 58 42	29 15 28	23 44 19	0♏ 7 38	7 29.4	19 10.2	15 39.2	7 20.6	26 57.4	22 39.0	5 55.6	4 10.8	8 22.8
23 Th	6 2 39	0♑16 36	6♏36 55	13 12 28	7 25.1	20 14.9	16 49.1	7 5.5	26 55.7	22 34.1	5 53.3	4 11.3	8 21.8
24 F	6 6 35	1 17 44	19 54 25	26 42 48	7 19.6	21 14.7	17 59.1	6 51.2	26 53.8	22 29.3	5 51.1	4 11.8	8 20.8
25 Sa	6 10 32	2 18 53	3♐37 28	10♐38 9	7 13.6	22 8.9	19 9.3	6 37.7	26 51.8	22 24.4	5 48.9	4 12.2	8 19.7
26 Su	6 14 29	3 20 2	17 44 23	24 55 36	7 7.9	22 56.8	20 19.5	6 24.9	26 49.5	22 19.6	5 46.7	4 12.6	8 18.7
27 M	6 18 25	4 21 12	2♑11 4	9♑29 58	7 3.3	23 37.5	21 30.0	6 12.9	26 47.1	22 14.8	5 44.6	4 13.0	8 17.6
28 Tu	6 22 22	5 22 23	16 51 24	24 14 27	7 0.2	24 10.2	22 40.5	6 1.7	26 44.4	22 10.0	5 42.5	4 13.3	8 16.5
29 W	6 26 18	6 23 33	1♒38 10	9♒ 1 39	6D58.9	24 33.8	23 51.2	5 51.4	26 41.6	22 5.3	5 40.4	4 13.7	8 15.3
30 Th	6 30 15	7 24 44	16 24 2	23 44 34	6 59.0	24R47.5	25 1.9	5 41.8	26 38.6	22 0.6	5 38.3	4 13.9	8 14.2
31 F	6 34 11	8 25 54	1♓ 2 35	8♓17 32	7 0.2	24 50.5	26 12.8	5 33.1	26 35.4	21 56.0	5 36.3	4 14.2	8 13.0

Astro Data

	Dy Hr Mn
♆0S	1 8:33
☽0N	9 6:10
♇ R	10 9:01
♀0S	11 20:31
♃✶♄	13 4:45
☽0S	23 13:07
☽0N	6 13:13
♄∠♇	11 3:17
♃ R	13 23:25
☽0S	20 23:08
☿ R	30 18:32

Planet Ingress

	Dy Hr Mn
♀ ♎	9 18:25
☿ ♐	18 13:39
☉ ♐	23 4:22
☿ ♑	8 1:47
♀ ♏	8 7:45
☉ ♑	22 17:29

Last Aspect / ☽ Ingress

Last Aspect Dy Hr Mn	☽ Ingress Dy Hr Mn
1 20:56 ♄ ☍	♑ 2 3:37
3 21:55 ♀ △	♒ 4 7:10
6 3:23 ♄ △	♓ 6 10:16
8 11:04 ♀ ☍	♈ 8 13:10
10 9:10 ♄ ✶	♉ 10 16:32
12 13:27 ♃ □	♊ 12 21:31
14 21:13 ♃ ✶	♋ 15 5:22
17 13:15 ☿ △	♌ 17 16:27
19 22:43 ☉ □	♍ 20 5:21
22 16:19 ☉ ✶	♎ 22 17:19
24 19:40 ♃ ✶	♏ 25 2:09
27 1:40 ♃ □	♐ 27 7:35
29 5:11 ♃ △	♑ 29 10:43

Last Aspect / ☽ Ingress

Last Aspect Dy Hr Mn	☽ Ingress Dy Hr Mn
30 23:23 ♀ □	♒ 1 13:01
3 10:18 ♃ ☍	♓ 3 15:36
5 12:18 ☿ □	♈ 5 19:00
7 23:13 ☿ △	♉ 7 23:30
10 0:07 ♃ □	♊ 10 5:32
12 8:09 ♃ ✶	♋ 12 13:46
13 4:20 ☿ ☍	♌ 15 0:37
17 7:21 ♃ ☌	♍ 17 13:22
19 20:03 ☉ □	♎ 20 1:55
22 11:16 ☉ ✶	♏ 22 11:46
24 12:17 ♃ □	♐ 24 17:44
26 15:06 ♃ △	♑ 26 20:24
28 12:14 ☿ ☌	♒ 28 21:21
30 16:42 ♃ ☍	♓ 30 22:17

☽ Phases & Eclipses

Dy Hr Mn	
5 3:22	☽ 11♒50
12 1:27	○ 18♉47
19 22:43	☽ 26♌44
27 15:23	● 4♐31
4 11:03	☽ 11♓26
11 16:24	○ 18♊46
19 20:03	☽ 27♍03
27 3:50	● 4♑31

Astro Data

1 NOVEMBER 1943
Julian Day # 16010
Delta T 26.1 sec
SVP 06♓02'53"
Obliquity 23°26'42"
⚷ Chiron 12♍31.2
☽ Mean ☊ 11♌24.8

1 DECEMBER 1943
Julian Day # 16040
Delta T 26.2 sec
SVP 06♓02'49"
Obliquity 23°26'41"
⚷ Chiron 14♍56.2
☽ Mean ☊ 9♌49.5

LONGITUDE — JANUARY 1944

Day	Sid.Time	☉	0 hr ☽	Noon ☽	True ☊	☿	♀	♂	♃	♄	♅	♆	♇
1 Sa	6 38 8	9♑27 4	15♓28 59	22♓36 37	7♌ 1.8	24♑42.1	27♏23.8	5♊25.2	26♌32.0	21♊51.4	5♊34.3	4♎14.4	8♌11.9
2 Su	6 42 5	10 28 14	29 40 13	6♈39 39	7R 3.0	24R22.0	28 34.8	5R18.2	26R28.4	21R46.8	5R32.4	4 14.5	8R10.7
3 M	6 46 1	11 29 24	13♈34 52	20 25 52	7 3.4	23 50.0	29 46.0	5 12.0	26 24.6	21 42.3	5 30.5	4 14.6	8 9.5
4 Tu	6 49 58	12 30 33	27 12 42	3♉55 29	7 2.6	23 6.4	0♐57.2	5 6.6	26 20.7	21 37.8	5 28.6	4 14.7	8 8.3
5 W	6 53 54	13 31 42	10♉34 20	17 9 21	7 0.6	22 12.1	2 8.6	5 2.1	26 16.6	21 33.4	5 26.7	4 14.8	8 7.0
6 Th	6 57 51	14 32 51	23 40 42	0♊ 8 30	6 57.7	21 8.3	3 20.0	4 58.3	26 12.3	21 29.1	5 24.9	4R14.8	8 5.8
7 F	7 1 47	15 34 0	6♊32 53	12 53 59	6 54.3	19 56.8	4 31.6	4 55.4	26 7.8	21 24.8	5 23.1	4 14.8	8 4.6
8 Sa	7 5 44	16 35 8	19 11 57	25 26 53	6 50.8	18 39.9	5 43.2	4 53.3	26 3.2	21 20.5	5 21.4	4 14.8	8 3.3
9 Su	7 9 40	17 36 16	1♋38 55	7♋48 12	6 47.8	17 20.0	6 54.9	4 52.0	25 58.4	21 16.4	5 19.7	4 14.7	8 2.0
10 M	7 13 37	18 37 24	13 54 53	19 59 7	6 45.5	15 59.7	8 6.7	4D51.4	25 53.5	21 12.2	5 18.1	4 14.6	8 0.8
11 Tu	7 17 34	19 38 31	26 1 5	2♌ 1 0	6D44.2	14 41.6	9 18.5	4 51.7	25 48.4	21 8.2	5 16.4	4 14.4	7 59.5
12 W	7 21 30	20 39 38	7♌59 6	13 55 39	6 43.9	13 27.9	10 30.5	4 52.7	25 43.1	21 4.2	5 14.9	4 14.3	7 58.2
13 Th	7 25 27	21 40 45	19 50 56	25 45 18	6 44.3	12 20.6	11 42.5	4 54.4	25 37.7	21 0.3	5 13.3	4 14.1	7 56.9
14 F	7 29 23	22 41 52	1♍39 6	7♍32 46	6 45.4	11 21.1	12 54.6	4 56.9	25 32.1	20 56.5	5 11.9	4 13.8	7 55.5
15 Sa	7 33 20	23 42 58	13 26 44	19 21 28	6 46.7	10 30.5	14 6.7	5 0.1	25 26.4	20 52.7	5 10.4	4 13.5	7 54.2
16 Su	7 37 16	24 44 4	25 17 28	1♎15 17	6 48.0	9 49.2	15 19.0	5 4.1	25 20.5	20 49.1	5 9.0	4 13.2	7 52.9
17 M	7 41 13	25 45 10	7♎15 28	13 18 35	6 49.0	9 17.6	16 31.3	5 8.8	25 14.5	20 45.5	5 7.6	4 12.9	7 51.5
18 Tu	7 45 9	26 46 16	19 25 12	25 35 56	6R49.6	8 55.5	17 43.6	5 14.1	25 8.3	20 41.9	5 6.3	4 12.5	7 50.2
19 W	7 49 6	27 47 21	1♏51 18	8♏11 53	6 49.6	8D42.7	18 56.1	5 20.1	25 2.0	20 38.5	5 5.1	4 12.1	7 48.8
20 Th	7 53 3	28 48 26	14 38 9	21 10 31	6 49.3	8 38.7	20 8.5	5 26.9	24 55.6	20 35.1	5 3.8	4 11.6	7 47.5
21 F	7 56 59	29 49 31	27 49 23	4♐34 58	6 48.6	8 43.0	21 21.1	5 34.2	24 49.1	20 31.9	5 2.7	4 11.1	7 46.1
22 Sa	8 0 56	0♒50 36	11♐27 24	18 26 41	6 47.9	8 54.9	22 33.7	5 42.3	24 42.4	20 28.7	5 1.5	4 10.6	7 44.7
23 Su	8 4 52	1 51 40	25 32 38	2♑44 55	6 47.2	9 13.9	23 46.4	5 51.0	24 35.7	20 25.6	5 0.5	4 10.1	7 43.4
24 M	8 8 49	2 52 43	10♑ 3 2	17 26 16	6 46.8	9 39.3	24 59.1	6 0.3	24 28.8	20 22.6	4 59.4	4 9.5	7 42.0
25 Tu	8 12 45	3 53 46	24 53 48	2♒24 38	6D46.5	10 10.7	26 11.8	6 10.2	24 21.8	20 19.7	4 58.4	4 8.9	7 40.6
26 W	8 16 42	4 54 48	9♒57 41	17 31 48	6 46.5	10 47.3	27 24.6	6 20.7	24 14.7	20 16.9	4 57.5	4 8.3	7 39.2
27 Th	8 20 38	5 55 49	25 5 48	2♓38 31	6R46.6	11 28.8	28 37.5	6 31.9	24 7.5	20 14.2	4 56.6	4 7.6	7 37.8
28 F	8 24 35	6 56 49	10♓ 8 53	17 35 53	6 46.6	12 14.7	29 50.3	6 43.6	24 0.3	20 11.6	4 55.8	4 6.9	7 36.5
29 Sa	8 28 32	7 57 48	24 58 41	2♈16 33	6 46.5	13 4.6	1♑ 3.2	6 55.9	23 52.9	20 9.1	4 55.0	4 6.2	7 35.1
30 Su	8 32 28	8 58 46	9♈28 59	16 35 34	6 46.3	13 58.1	2 16.2	7 8.7	23 45.5	20 6.7	4 54.3	4 5.4	7 33.7
31 M	8 36 25	9 59 43	23 36 6	0♉30 30	6 46.1	14 54.9	3 29.2	7 22.1	23 38.0	20 4.4	4 53.6	4 4.6	7 32.3

LONGITUDE — FEBRUARY 1944

Day	Sid.Time	☉	0 hr ☽	Noon ☽	True ☊	☿	♀	♂	♃	♄	♅	♆	♇
1 Tu	8 40 21	11♒ 0 38	7♉18 49	14♉ 1 12	6♌46.0	15♑54.6	4♑42.2	7♊36.0	23♌30.4	20♊ 2.2	4♊53.0	4♎ 3.8	7♌30.9
2 W	8 44 18	12 1 32	20 37 55	27 9 14	6D46.0	16 57.1	5 55.3	7 50.4	23R22.7	20R 0.1	4R52.4	4R 2.9	7R29.5
3 Th	8 48 14	13 2 25	3♊35 31	9♊57 10	6 46.4	18 2.0	7 8.4	8 5.4	23 15.0	19 58.1	4 51.9	4 2.1	7 28.2
4 F	8 52 11	14 3 16	16 14 35	22 28 9	6 47.0	19 9.3	8 21.5	8 20.8	23 7.3	19 56.2	4 51.4	4 1.2	7 26.8
5 Sa	8 56 7	15 4 6	28 38 18	4♋45 23	6 47.9	20 18.6	9 34.6	8 36.7	22 59.5	19 54.4	4 51.0	4 0.2	7 25.4
6 Su	9 0 4	16 4 54	10♋49 49	16 51 56	6 48.8	21 29.9	10 47.8	8 53.1	22 51.7	19 52.7	4 50.6	3 59.3	7 24.1
7 M	9 4 1	17 5 42	22 52 3	28 50 31	6 49.5	22 42.9	12 1.0	9 9.9	22 43.8	19 51.2	4 50.3	3 58.3	7 22.7
8 Tu	9 7 57	18 6 28	4♌47 36	10♌43 36	6R49.9	23 57.7	13 14.3	9 27.2	22 35.9	19 49.7	4 50.0	3 57.3	7 21.3
9 W	9 11 54	19 7 12	16 38 46	22 33 22	6 49.7	25 14.0	14 27.6	9 44.9	22 28.0	19 48.4	4 49.8	3 56.2	7 20.0
10 Th	9 15 50	20 7 55	28 27 40	4♍21 54	6 48.7	26 31.8	15 40.9	10 3.0	22 20.1	19 47.1	4 49.7	3 55.2	7 18.6
11 F	9 19 47	21 8 37	10♍16 19	16 11 14	6 47.1	27 51.0	16 54.2	10 21.5	22 12.1	19 46.0	4 49.6	3 54.1	7 17.3
12 Sa	9 23 43	22 9 18	22 6 53	28 3 36	6 44.8	29 11.5	18 7.5	10 40.5	22 4.2	19 45.0	4D49.5	3 52.9	7 16.0
13 Su	9 27 40	23 9 57	4♎ 1 42	10♎ 1 33	6 42.2	0♒33.2	19 20.9	10 59.8	21 56.2	19 44.1	4 49.5	3 51.8	7 14.6
14 M	9 31 36	24 10 35	16 3 30	22 7 57	6 39.5	1 56.2	20 34.3	11 19.5	21 48.3	19 43.3	4 49.6	3 50.6	7 13.3
15 Tu	9 35 33	25 11 12	28 15 19	4♏26 4	6 37.1	3 20.3	21 47.8	11 39.6	21 40.3	19 42.6	4 49.7	3 49.4	7 12.0
16 W	9 39 30	26 11 48	10♏40 39	16 59 31	6 35.4	4 45.5	23 1.2	12 0.0	21 32.4	19 42.0	4 49.8	3 48.2	7 10.7
17 Th	9 43 26	27 12 23	23 23 8	29 51 56	6D34.6	6 11.9	24 14.7	12 20.8	21 24.5	19 41.5	4 50.0	3 47.0	7 9.4
18 F	9 47 23	28 12 56	6♐26 22	13♐ 6 47	6 34.7	7 39.2	25 28.2	12 42.0	21 16.7	19 41.2	4 50.3	3 45.7	7 8.1
19 Sa	9 51 19	29 13 28	19 53 30	26 46 44	6 35.7	9 7.7	26 41.8	13 3.4	21 8.9	19 41.0	4 50.6	3 44.5	7 6.8
20 Su	9 55 16	0♓13 59	3♑46 36	10♑53 3	6 37.2	10 37.1	27 55.3	13 25.3	21 1.1	19D40.8	4 51.0	3 43.2	7 5.6
21 M	9 59 12	1 14 29	18 5 55	25 24 51	6 38.6	12 7.6	29 8.9	13 47.4	20 53.3	19 40.8	4 51.4	3 41.8	7 4.3
22 Tu	10 3 9	2 14 57	2♒49 19	10♒18 33	6R39.4	13 39.0	0♒22.5	14 9.9	20 45.6	19 40.9	4 51.9	3 40.5	7 3.1
23 W	10 7 5	3 15 24	17 51 41	25 27 38	6 39.1	15 11.5	1 36.1	14 32.7	20 38.0	19 41.2	4 52.4	3 39.1	7 1.9
24 Th	10 11 2	4 15 49	3♓ 5 12	10♓43 5	6 37.4	16 44.9	2 49.7	14 55.8	20 30.4	19 41.5	4 53.0	3 37.8	7 0.7
25 F	10 14 59	5 16 12	18 20 0	25 54 38	6 34.3	18 19.3	4 3.3	15 19.2	20 22.9	19 41.9	4 53.7	3 36.4	6 59.5
26 Sa	10 18 55	6 16 34	3♈25 47	10♈52 20	6 30.1	19 54.7	5 17.0	15 42.8	20 15.5	19 42.5	4 54.4	3 34.9	6 58.3
27 Su	10 22 52	7 16 54	18 13 23	25 28 12	6 25.6	21 31.1	6 30.6	16 6.8	20 8.2	19 43.2	4 55.1	3 33.5	6 57.1
28 M	10 26 48	8 17 12	2♉36 14	9♉37 10	6 21.3	23 8.5	7 44.3	16 31.0	20 0.9	19 44.0	4 55.9	3 32.0	6 55.9
29 Tu	10 30 45	9 17 28	16 30 52	23 17 22	6 17.9	24 46.9	8 58.0	16 55.6	19 53.7	19 44.9	4 56.8	3 30.6	6 54.8

Astro Data	Planet Ingress	Last Aspect	☽ Ingress	Last Aspect	☽ Ingress	☽ Phases & Eclipses	Astro Data
Dy Hr Mn	Dy Hr Mn	Dy Hr Mn	Dy Hr Mn	Dy Hr Mn	Dy Hr Mn	Dy Hr Mn	1 JANUARY 1944
☽0N 2 19:27	♀ ♐ 3 4:43	1 21:58 ♀ △	♈ 2 0:34	2 4:59 ♃ □	♊ 2 17:17	2 20:04 ☽ 11♈19	Julian Day # 16071
♆ R 6 6:23	☉ ♒ 21 4:07	3 22:28 ♃ △	♉ 4 4:58	4 13:08 ♃ ✶	♋ 5 2:40	10 10:09 ○ 19♋03	Delta T 26.2 sec
♂ D 10 4:37	♀ ♑ 28 3:11	6 4:39 ♃ □	♊ 6 11:44	6 23:40 ☿ ☍	♌ 7 14:20	18 15:32 ☽ 27♎26	SVP 06♓02'43"
☽0S 17 7:38		8 13:05 ♃ ✶	♋ 8 20:48	9 11:41 ♃ ☌	♍ 10 3:08	25 15:24 ● 4♒33	Obliquity 23°26'42"
☿ D 19 23:21	☿ ♒ 12 14:17	10 10:09 ☉ ☍	♌ 11 7:58	11 19:13 ♄ □	♎ 12 15:54	25 15:26:16 ☌ T 4'09"	⚷ Chiron 15♍48.6R
☽0N 30 2:45	☉ ♓ 19 18:27	13 11:39 ♃ ☌	♍ 13 20:38	14 17:28 ☉ △	♏ 15 3:24		☽ Mean ☊ 8♌11.0
	♀ ♒ 21 16:40	15 22:46 ☉ △	♎ 16 9:29	17 7:42 ☉ □	♐ 17 12:15	1 7:08 ☽ 11♉19	
♅ D 12 12:14		18 15:32 ☉ □	♏ 18 20:27	19 17:29 ☉ ✶	♑ 19 17:33	9 5:29 ○ 19♌21	1 FEBRUARY 1944
☽0S 13 14:02		21 3:52 ☉ ✶	♐ 21 3:53	19 23:54 ♆ □	♒ 21 19:27	9 5:14 ☍ A 0.579	Julian Day # 16102
♄ D 20 13:18		22 22:25 ♃ △	♑ 23 7:27	23 4:21 ♃ ☍	♓ 23 19:09	17 7:42 ☽ 27♏32	Delta T 26.3 sec
☽0N 26 12:09		23 23:20 ☿ ☌	♒ 25 8:09	25 2:10 ♄ □	♈ 25 18:31	24 1:59 ● 4♓21	SVP 06♓02'39"
		27 6:06 ♀ ✶	♓ 27 7:48	27 6:07 ☿ ✶	♉ 27 19:36		Obliquity 23°26'42"
		28 16:10 ♄ □	♈ 29 8:15				⚷ Chiron 14♍52.5R
		31 0:03 ♃ △	♉ 31 11:07				☽ Mean ☊ 6♌32.6

MARCH 1944 — LONGITUDE

Day	Sid.Time	☉	0 hr ☽	Noon ☽	True ☊	☿	♀	♂	♃	♄	♅	♆	♇
1 W	10 34 41	10♓17 41	29♉56 53	6♊29 43	6♌15.9	26♒26.3	10♒11.6	17♊20.3	19♌46.7	19♊45.9	4♊57.7	3♎29.1	6♌53.7
2 Th	10 38 38	11 17 53	12♊56 17	19 17 5	6D 15.4	28 6.8	11 25.3	17 45.4	19R 39.7	19 47.0	4 58.6	3R 27.6	6R 52.6
3 F	10 42 34	12 18 3	25 32 40	1♋43 37	6 16.2	29 48.3	12 39.0	18 10.6	19 32.8	19 48.2	4 59.6	3 26.1	6 51.5
4 Sa	10 46 31	13 18 11	7♋50 30	13 53 55	6 17.8	1♓30.9	13 52.7	18 36.2	19 26.1	19 49.6	5 0.7	3 24.6	6 50.4
5 Su	10 50 27	14 18 16	19 54 27	25 52 38	6 19.5	3 14.5	15 6.4	19 1.9	19 19.5	19 51.1	5 1.8	3 23.0	6 49.3
6 M	10 54 24	15 18 20	1♌49 0	7♌44 3	6R 20.5	4 59.2	16 20.1	19 27.9	19 12.9	19 52.6	5 2.9	3 21.5	6 48.3
7 Tu	10 58 21	16 18 21	13 38 14	19 31 58	6 20.3	6 45.0	17 33.9	19 54.1	19 6.5	19 54.3	5 4.1	3 19.9	6 47.3
8 W	11 2 17	17 18 20	25 25 38	1♍19 32	6 18.3	8 32.0	18 47.6	20 20.5	19 0.3	19 56.1	5 5.4	3 18.4	6 46.3
9 Th	11 6 14	18 18 18	7♍14 1	13 9 19	6 14.3	10 20.0	20 1.3	20 47.2	18 54.1	19 58.0	5 6.7	3 16.8	6 45.3
10 F	11 10 10	19 18 13	19 5 40	25 3 19	6 8.2	12 9.2	21 15.1	21 14.0	18 48.1	19 60.0	5 8.1	3 15.2	6 44.3
11 Sa	11 14 7	20 18 6	1♎ 2 26	7♎ 3 11	6 0.5	13 59.5	22 28.8	21 41.0	18 42.2	20 2.1	5 9.5	3 13.6	6 43.3
12 Su	11 18 3	21 17 58	13 5 47	19 10 23	5 51.9	15 51.0	23 42.6	22 8.3	18 36.5	20 4.3	5 10.9	3 12.0	6 42.4
13 M	11 22 0	22 17 47	25 17 10	1♏26 21	5 43.0	17 43.6	24 56.3	22 35.7	18 30.9	20 6.6	5 12.4	3 10.4	6 41.5
14 Tu	11 25 56	23 17 35	7♏38 7	13 52 44	5 34.8	19 37.3	26 10.1	23 3.3	18 25.5	20 9.0	5 13.9	3 8.7	6 40.6
15 W	11 29 53	24 17 21	20 10 27	26 31 32	5 28.1	21 32.1	27 23.9	23 31.1	18 20.2	20 11.6	5 15.5	3 7.1	6 39.7
16 Th	11 33 50	25 17 6	2♐56 19	9♐25 6	5 23.5	23 28.0	28 37.7	23 59.1	18 15.0	20 14.2	5 17.2	3 5.5	6 38.9
17 F	11 37 46	26 16 48	15 58 14	22 36 1	5D 21.0	25 24.9	29 51.5	24 27.2	18 10.1	20 16.9	5 18.9	3 3.8	6 38.1
18 Sa	11 41 43	27 16 29	29 18 47	6♑ 6 49	5 20.5	27 22.8	1♓ 5.3	24 55.5	18 5.2	20 19.8	5 20.6	3 2.2	6 37.3
19 Su	11 45 39	28 16 9	13♑ 0 20	19 59 30	5 21.2	29 21.6	2 19.1	25 24.0	18 0.6	20 22.7	5 22.4	3 0.6	6 36.5
20 M	11 49 36	29 15 46	27 4 20	4♒14 48	5R 22.1	1♈21.2	3 32.9	25 52.7	17 56.1	20 25.7	5 24.2	2 58.9	6 35.7
21 Tu	11 53 32	0♈15 22	11♒30 39	18 51 30	5 22.2	3 21.5	4 46.7	26 21.5	17 51.8	20 28.9	5 26.1	2 57.2	6 35.0
22 W	11 57 29	1 14 56	26 16 46	3♓45 44	5 20.4	5 22.4	6 0.5	26 50.5	17 47.6	20 32.1	5 28.0	2 55.6	6 34.3
23 Th	12 1 25	2 14 28	11♓17 26	18 50 49	5 16.3	7 23.6	7 14.3	27 19.7	17 43.6	20 35.5	5 29.9	2 53.9	6 33.6
24 F	12 5 22	3 13 58	26 24 41	3♈57 46	5 9.7	9 25.1	8 28.2	27 49.0	17 39.8	20 38.9	5 31.9	2 52.3	6 32.9
25 Sa	12 9 19	4 13 27	11♈28 48	18 56 33	5 1.1	11 26.5	9 42.0	28 18.4	17 36.1	20 42.4	5 34.0	2 50.6	6 32.2
26 Su	12 13 15	5 12 53	26 19 54	3♉37 52	4 51.6	13 27.6	10 55.8	28 48.0	17 32.7	20 46.0	5 36.1	2 48.9	6 31.6
27 M	12 17 12	6 12 17	10♉49 39	17 54 39	4 42.2	15 28.0	12 9.6	29 17.7	17 29.4	20 49.8	5 38.2	2 47.3	6 31.0
28 Tu	12 21 8	7 11 38	24 52 30	1♊43 0	4 34.1	17 27.6	13 23.4	29 47.6	17 26.3	20 53.6	5 40.4	2 45.6	6 30.5
29 W	12 25 5	8 10 58	8♊26 10	15 2 11	4 28.1	19 25.9	14 37.2	0♋17.7	17 23.4	20 57.5	5 42.6	2 44.0	6 29.9
30 Th	12 29 1	9 10 15	21 31 23	27 54 13	4 24.4	21 22.6	15 51.0	0 47.8	17 20.7	21 1.5	5 44.8	2 42.3	6 29.4
31 F	12 32 58	10 9 30	4♋11 12	10♋22 58	4D 22.9	23 17.2	17 4.8	1 18.1	17 18.1	21 5.6	5 47.1	2 40.7	6 28.9

APRIL 1944 — LONGITUDE

Day	Sid.Time	☉	0 hr ☽	Noon ☽	True ☊	☿	♀	♂	♃	♄	♅	♆	♇
1 Sa	12 36 54	11♈ 8 43	16♋30 8	22♋33 23	4♌22.8	25♈ 9.4	18♓18.6	1♋48.5	17♌15.8	21♊ 9.8	5♊49.4	2♎39.1	6♌28.4
2 Su	12 40 51	12 7 53	28 33 23	4♌30 50	4R 23.3	26 58.8	19 32.4	2 19.0	17R 13.6	21 14.0	5 51.8	2R 37.4	6R 28.0
3 M	12 44 48	13 7 1	10♌26 22	16 20 37	4 23.3	28 44.9	20 46.2	2 49.7	17 11.6	21 18.4	5 54.2	2 35.8	6 27.5
4 Tu	12 48 44	14 6 7	22 14 11	28 7 37	4 21.7	0♉27.5	22 0.0	3 20.5	17 9.8	21 22.8	5 56.6	2 34.2	6 27.1
5 W	12 52 41	15 5 10	4♍ 1 26	9♍56 4	4 17.8	2 6.1	23 13.8	3 51.3	17 8.2	21 27.4	5 59.1	2 32.6	6 26.8
6 Th	12 56 37	16 4 11	15 51 57	21 49 25	4 11.2	3 40.5	24 27.6	4 22.3	17 6.8	21 32.0	6 1.6	2 31.0	6 26.4
7 F	13 0 34	17 3 10	27 48 46	3♎50 15	4 1.9	5 10.3	25 41.3	4 53.4	17 5.5	21 36.7	6 4.2	2 29.4	6 26.1
8 Sa	13 4 30	18 2 7	9♎54 3	16 0 19	3 50.4	6 35.2	26 55.1	5 24.6	17 4.5	21 41.4	6 6.8	2 27.8	6 25.8
9 Su	13 8 27	19 1 1	22 9 9	28 20 37	3 37.5	7 55.0	28 8.9	5 55.9	17 3.6	21 46.3	6 9.4	2 26.2	6 25.5
10 M	13 12 23	19 59 54	4♏34 46	10♏51 39	3 24.2	9 9.5	29 22.6	6 27.3	17 2.9	21 51.2	6 12.0	2 24.6	6 25.3
11 Tu	13 16 20	20 58 45	17 11 16	23 33 39	3 11.8	10 18.5	0♈36.4	6 58.9	17 2.4	21 56.2	6 14.7	2 23.1	6 25.0
12 W	13 20 16	21 57 34	29 58 50	6♐26 52	3 1.4	11 21.9	1 50.2	7 30.5	17 2.1	22 1.3	6 17.4	2 21.5	6 24.9
13 Th	13 24 13	22 56 21	12♐57 51	19 31 52	2 53.5	12 19.4	3 3.9	8 2.2	17D 2.0	22 6.5	6 20.2	2 20.0	6 24.7
14 F	13 28 10	23 55 7	26 9 3	2♑49 34	2 48.6	13 11.1	4 17.7	8 34.0	17 2.1	22 11.7	6 23.0	2 18.5	6 24.5
15 Sa	13 32 6	24 53 51	9♑33 35	16 21 16	2 46.2	13 56.7	5 31.5	9 5.9	17 2.4	22 17.0	6 25.8	2 17.0	6 24.4
16 Su	13 36 3	25 52 33	23 12 48	0♒ 8 18	2 45.6	14 36.2	6 45.2	9 37.9	17 2.8	22 22.4	6 28.6	2 15.5	6 24.4
17 M	13 39 59	26 51 13	7♒ 7 52	14 11 32	2 45.6	15 9.6	7 59.0	10 9.9	17 3.5	22 27.9	6 31.5	2 14.0	6 24.3
18 Tu	13 43 56	27 49 52	21 19 15	28 30 48	2 44.8	15 36.8	9 12.8	10 42.1	17 4.3	22 33.4	6 34.4	2 12.5	6D 24.3
19 W	13 47 52	28 48 29	5♓45 55	13♓ 4 9	2 42.2	15 57.9	10 26.5	11 14.4	17 5.3	22 39.0	6 37.3	2 11.1	6 24.2
20 Th	13 51 49	29 47 4	20 24 52	27 47 22	2 36.9	16 12.9	11 40.3	11 46.7	17 6.5	22 44.7	6 40.3	2 9.6	6 24.3
21 F	13 55 45	0♉45 38	5♈10 47	12♈34 9	2 28.8	16 21.9	12 54.0	12 19.1	17 7.8	22 50.4	6 43.3	2 8.2	6 24.3
22 Sa	13 59 42	1 44 10	19 56 26	27 16 37	2 18.4	16R 24.9	14 7.8	12 51.7	17 9.4	22 56.3	6 46.3	2 6.8	6 24.4
23 Su	14 3 39	2 42 40	4♉33 40	11♉46 38	2 6.7	16 22.2	15 21.5	13 24.3	17 11.1	23 2.1	6 49.3	2 5.4	6 24.5
24 M	14 7 35	3 41 8	18 54 43	25 57 12	1 55.1	16 14.0	16 35.2	13 57.0	17 13.1	23 8.1	6 52.4	2 4.1	6 24.6
25 Tu	14 11 32	4 39 34	2♊53 35	9♊43 32	1 44.7	16 0.5	17 49.0	14 29.7	17 15.2	23 14.1	6 55.5	2 2.7	6 24.8
26 W	14 15 28	5 37 59	16 26 52	23 3 36	1 36.5	15 42.2	19 2.7	15 2.6	17 17.5	23 20.1	6 58.6	2 1.4	6 24.9
27 Th	14 19 25	6 36 21	29 33 53	5♋58 1	1 30.9	15 19.4	20 16.4	15 35.5	17 19.9	23 26.3	7 1.7	2 0.1	6 25.2
28 F	14 23 21	7 34 41	12♋16 24	18 29 32	1 27.9	14 52.5	21 30.1	16 8.5	17 22.6	23 32.5	7 4.9	1 58.8	6 25.4
29 Sa	14 27 18	8 33 0	24 37 59	0♌42 24	1D 26.9	14 22.2	22 43.8	16 41.6	17 25.4	23 38.7	7 8.1	1 57.5	6 25.6
30 Su	14 31 14	9 31 16	6♌43 26	12 41 46	1R 26.8	13 49.0	23 57.5	17 14.7	17 28.4	23 45.0	7 11.3	1 56.3	6 25.9

Astro Data Dy Hr Mn	Planet Ingress Dy Hr Mn	Last Aspect Dy Hr Mn	☽ Ingress Dy Hr Mn	Last Aspect Dy Hr Mn	☽ Ingress Dy Hr Mn	☽ Phases & Eclipses Dy Hr Mn	Astro Data
♃∗♄ 1 2:21	☿ ♓ 3 2:45	29 16:45 ☿ □	♊ 1 0:06	1 20:17 ☿ □	♌ 2 2:54	1 20:40 ☽ 11♊10	1 MARCH 1944
♆0N 7 15:06	♀ ♓ 17 2:46	2 12:58 ♄ ☌	♋ 3 8:38	3 22:15 ♄ ∗	♍ 4 15:49	10 0:28 ○ 19♍19	Julian Day # 16131
☽0S 11 19:29	☿ ♈ 19 7:43	4 11:48 ☉ △	♌ 5 20:19	6 19:16 ♀ ☍	♎ 7 4:22	17 20:05 ☽ 27♐07	Delta T 26.3 sec
♃∠♆ 19 0:12	☉ ♈ 20 17:49	7 13:15 ♂ ∗	♍ 8 9:18	8 23:15 ♄ △	♏ 9 15:12	24 11:36 ● 3♈43	SVP 06♓02'36"
☿0N 20 13:59	♂ ♋ 28 9:54	10 4:29 ♂ □	♎ 10 21:55	10 23:43 ♃ □	♐ 12 0:02	31 12:34 ☽ 10♋41	Obliquity 23°26'43"
☽0N 24 22:52		12 23:15 ♀ △	♏ 13 9:12	13 19:39 ☉ △	♑ 14 6:56		⚷ Chiron 12♍50.0R
♄∠♇ 4 21:06	☿ ♉ 3 17:29	15 15:05 ♀ □	♐ 15 18:31	16 4:59 ☉ □	♒ 16 11:46	8 17:22 ○ 18♎45	☽ Mean ☊ 5♌00.4
☽0S 8 1:39	♀ ♈ 10 12:09	17 20:05 ☉ □	♑ 18 1:13	18 11:39 ☉ ∗	♓ 18 14:28	16 4:59 ☽ 26♑05	
♀0N 13 9:05	☉ ♉ 20 5:18	20 3:57 ☉ ∗	♒ 20 4:55	20 3:49 ♄ □	♈ 20 15:35	22 20:43 ● 2♉35	1 APRIL 1944
♃ D 13 2:10		22 0:56 ♂ △	♓ 22 5:59	22 4:56 ♄ ∗	♉ 22 16:28	30 6:06 ☽ 9♌46	Julian Day # 16162
♅∗♇ 14 12:53		24 2:48 ♂ □	♈ 24 5:42	23 21:08 ♃ □	♊ 24 18:59		Delta T 26.4 sec
♇ D 18 19:22		26 4:11 ♂ ∗	♉ 26 6:01	26 12:36 ♄ ☌	♋ 27 0:49		SVP 06♓02'33"
☽0N 21 9:11		27 11:14 ♃ □	♊ 28 8:58	28 19:51 ♀ □	♌ 29 10:36		Obliquity 23°26'43"
♃∠♆ 21 3:05	☿ R 22 0:34	29 23:41 ☿ ∗	♋ 30 15:59				⚷ Chiron 10♍33.3R
							☽ Mean ☊ 3♌21.9

LONGITUDE — MAY 1944

Day	Sid.Time	☉	0 hr ☽	Noon ☽	True ☊	☿	♀	♂	♃	♄	♅	♆	♇
1 M	14 35 11	10♉29 30	18♌38 5	24♌33 4	1♌26.6	13♉13.5	25♈11.2	17♋47.9	17♌31.6	23♊51.4	7♊14.5	1♎55.1	6♌26.2
2 Tu	14 39 8	11 27 42	0♍27 23	6♍21 42	1R 25.3	12R 36.4	26 24.9	18 21.2	17 34.9	23 57.8	7 17.8	1R 53.9	6 26.6
3 W	14 43 4	12 25 52	12 16 36	18 12 39	1 21.9	11 58.4	27 38.6	18 54.6	17 38.4	24 4.3	7 21.0	1 52.7	6 26.9
4 Th	14 47 1	13 24 0	24 10 23	0♎10 15	1 16.0	11 20.2	28 52.3	19 28.0	17 42.1	24 10.8	7 24.3	1 51.5	6 27.3
5 F	14 50 57	14 22 6	6♎12 39	12 17 56	1 7.4	10 42.4	0♉ 5.9	20 1.4	17 45.9	24 17.4	7 27.6	1 50.4	6 27.8
6 Sa	14 54 54	15 20 10	18 26 22	24 38 9	0 56.7	10 5.7	1 19.6	20 35.0	17 49.9	24 24.0	7 30.9	1 49.3	6 28.2
7 Su	14 58 50	16 18 13	0♏53 24	7♏12 12	0 44.6	9 30.8	2 33.3	21 8.6	17 54.1	24 30.7	7 34.2	1 48.2	6 28.7
8 M	15 2 47	17 16 14	13 34 32	20 0 22	0 32.1	8 58.1	3 46.9	21 42.2	17 58.4	24 37.4	7 37.6	1 47.1	6 29.2
9 Tu	15 6 43	18 14 13	26 29 36	3♐ 2 5	0 20.4	8 28.2	5 0.6	22 15.9	18 2.9	24 44.2	7 40.9	1 46.1	6 29.7
10 W	15 10 40	19 12 10	9♐37 41	16 16 13	0 10.5	8 1.6	6 14.2	22 49.7	18 7.6	24 51.0	7 44.3	1 45.1	6 30.2
11 Th	15 14 37	20 10 7	22 57 32	29 41 29	0 3.1	7 38.6	7 27.9	23 23.5	18 12.4	24 57.9	7 47.7	1 44.1	6 30.8
12 F	15 18 33	21 8 2	6♑27 56	13♑16 47	29♋58.5	7 19.6	8 41.5	23 57.4	18 17.4	25 4.8	7 51.1	1 43.2	6 31.4
13 Sa	15 22 30	22 5 55	20 7 56	27 1 21	29D 56.4	7 4.7	9 55.2	24 31.4	18 22.5	25 11.7	7 54.5	1 42.2	6 32.0
14 Su	15 26 26	23 3 48	3♒56 58	10♒54 48	29 56.1	6 54.2	11 8.8	25 5.4	18 27.8	25 18.7	7 58.0	1 41.3	6 32.7
15 M	15 30 23	24 1 39	17 54 46	24 56 52	29R 56.5	6D 48.2	12 22.5	25 39.5	18 33.2	25 25.8	8 1.4	1 40.5	6 33.3
16 Tu	15 34 19	24 59 28	2♓ 0 58	9♓ 6 59	29 56.5	6 46.7	13 36.1	26 13.6	18 38.8	25 32.8	8 4.9	1 39.6	6 34.0
17 W	15 38 16	25 57 17	16 14 40	23 23 47	29 54.8	6 49.8	14 49.7	26 47.8	18 44.5	25 40.0	8 8.3	1 38.8	6 34.7
18 Th	15 42 12	26 55 5	0♈33 57	7♈44 43	29 51.0	6 57.5	16 3.4	27 22.0	18 50.4	25 47.1	8 11.8	1 38.0	6 35.5
19 F	15 46 9	27 52 51	14 55 35	22 5 56	29 44.8	7 9.8	17 17.0	27 56.3	18 56.4	25 54.3	8 15.3	1 37.2	6 36.2
20 Sa	15 50 6	28 50 36	29 15 6	6♉22 26	29 36.5	7 26.6	18 30.7	28 30.6	19 2.5	26 1.5	8 18.7	1 36.5	6 37.0
21 Su	15 54 2	29 48 20	13♉27 13	20 28 48	29 27.1	7 47.7	19 44.3	29 5.0	19 8.9	26 8.8	8 22.2	1 35.8	6 37.8
22 M	15 57 59	0♊46 3	27 26 34	4♊19 59	29 17.6	8 13.2	20 58.0	29 39.5	19 15.3	26 16.1	8 25.7	1 35.1	6 38.7
23 Tu	16 1 55	1 43 45	11♊ 8 36	17 52 6	29 9.1	8 42.8	22 11.6	0♌14.0	19 21.9	26 23.4	8 29.2	1 34.4	6 39.5
24 W	16 5 52	2 41 26	24 30 17	1♋ 3 3	29 2.4	9 16.6	23 25.3	0 48.6	19 28.6	26 30.8	8 32.8	1 33.8	6 40.4
25 Th	16 9 48	3 39 5	7♋30 26	13 52 36	28 58.0	9 54.3	24 38.9	1 23.2	19 35.5	26 38.2	8 36.3	1 33.2	6 41.3
26 F	16 13 45	4 36 42	20 9 48	26 22 23	28D 55.8	10 35.9	25 52.5	1 57.8	19 42.5	26 45.6	8 39.8	1 32.6	6 42.3
27 Sa	16 17 41	5 34 19	2♌30 46	8♌35 28	28 55.4	11 21.2	27 6.2	2 32.6	19 49.6	26 53.0	8 43.3	1 32.1	6 43.2
28 Su	16 21 38	6 31 53	14 37 1	20 36 1	28 56.2	12 10.2	28 19.8	3 7.3	19 56.9	27 0.5	8 46.9	1 31.6	6 44.2
29 M	16 25 35	7 29 27	26 33 6	2♍28 53	28 57.4	13 2.7	29 33.4	3 42.1	20 4.3	27 8.0	8 50.4	1 31.1	6 45.2
30 Tu	16 29 31	8 26 59	8♍24 3	14 19 14	28R 57.9	13 58.6	0♊47.1	4 17.0	20 11.8	27 15.6	8 53.9	1 30.7	6 46.2
31 W	16 33 28	9 24 29	20 15 4	26 12 11	28 57.2	14 58.0	2 0.7	4 51.9	20 19.5	27 23.1	8 57.4	1 30.3	6 47.3

LONGITUDE — JUNE 1944

Day	Sid.Time	☉	0 hr ☽	Noon ☽	True ☊	☿	♀	♂	♃	♄	♅	♆	♇
1 Th	16 37 24	10♊21 59	2♎11 10	8♎12 35	28♋54.6	16♉ 0.5	3♊14.3	5♌26.8	20♌27.2	27♊30.7	9♊ 1.0	1♎29.9	6♌48.3
2 F	16 41 21	11 19 27	14 16 57	20 24 42	28R 50.2	17 6.3	4 27.9	6 1.8	20 35.1	27 38.3	9 4.5	1R 29.6	6 49.4
3 Sa	16 45 17	12 16 54	26 36 13	2♏51 51	28 44.1	18 15.2	5 41.6	6 36.8	20 43.1	27 45.9	9 8.0	1 29.3	6 50.5
4 Su	16 49 14	13 14 19	9♏11 50	15 36 18	28 36.9	19 27.2	6 55.2	7 11.9	20 51.3	27 53.5	9 11.5	1 29.0	6 51.6
5 M	16 53 10	14 11 44	22 5 20	28 38 56	28 29.2	20 42.2	8 8.8	7 47.0	20 59.5	28 1.2	9 15.0	1 28.7	6 52.8
6 Tu	16 57 7	15 9 8	5♐16 58	11♐59 17	28 22.0	22 0.2	9 22.4	8 22.2	21 7.9	28 8.8	9 18.6	1 28.5	6 53.9
7 W	17 1 4	16 6 31	18 45 36	25 35 39	28 16.0	23 21.2	10 36.1	8 57.4	21 16.3	28 16.5	9 22.1	1 28.3	6 55.1
8 Th	17 5 0	17 3 53	2♑29 2	9♑25 23	28 11.7	24 45.0	11 49.7	9 32.7	21 24.9	28 24.2	9 25.6	1 28.2	6 56.3
9 F	17 8 57	18 1 14	16 24 18	23 25 22	28D 9.4	26 11.7	13 3.3	10 7.9	21 33.6	28 31.9	9 29.1	1 28.0	6 57.5
10 Sa	17 12 53	18 58 34	0♒28 12	7♒32 25	28 8.9	27 41.3	14 17.0	10 43.3	21 42.4	28 39.7	9 32.6	1 27.9	6 58.8
11 Su	17 16 50	19 55 54	14 37 40	21 43 37	28 9.6	29 13.7	15 30.6	11 18.6	21 51.3	28 47.4	9 36.1	1 27.9	7 0.0
12 M	17 20 46	20 53 14	28 49 59	5♓56 29	28 11.0	0♊48.9	16 44.2	11 54.1	22 0.3	28 55.2	9 39.6	1D 27.8	7 1.3
13 Tu	17 24 43	21 50 33	13♓ 2 53	20 8 55	28R 12.1	2 26.9	17 57.9	12 29.5	22 9.5	29 2.9	9 43.0	1 27.8	7 2.6
14 W	17 28 39	22 47 52	27 14 23	4♈19 1	28 12.3	4 7.7	19 11.6	13 5.0	22 18.7	29 10.7	9 46.5	1 27.9	7 3.9
15 Th	17 32 36	23 45 10	11♈22 35	18 24 49	28 11.1	5 51.2	20 25.2	13 40.6	22 28.0	29 18.5	9 49.9	1 27.9	7 5.2
16 F	17 36 33	24 42 28	25 25 27	2♉24 10	28 8.5	7 37.4	21 38.9	14 16.1	22 37.4	29 26.3	9 53.4	1 28.0	7 6.6
17 Sa	17 40 29	25 39 46	9♉20 41	16 14 41	28 4.6	9 26.3	22 52.6	14 51.8	22 47.0	29 34.0	9 56.8	1 28.2	7 7.9
18 Su	17 44 26	26 37 3	23 5 51	29 53 54	27 59.9	11 17.9	24 6.2	15 27.4	22 56.6	29 41.8	10 0.2	1 28.3	7 9.3
19 M	17 48 22	27 34 20	6♊38 33	13♊19 33	27 55.2	13 12.0	25 19.9	16 3.2	23 6.3	29 49.7	10 3.7	1 28.5	7 10.7
20 Tu	17 52 19	28 31 37	19 56 41	26 29 49	27 50.9	15 8.5	26 33.6	16 38.9	23 16.1	29 57.5	10 7.1	1 28.8	7 12.1
21 W	17 56 15	29 28 53	2♋58 50	9♋23 44	27 47.7	17 7.4	27 47.3	17 14.7	23 26.0	0♋ 5.3	10 10.4	1 29.0	7 13.5
22 Th	18 0 12	0♋26 9	15 44 31	22 1 18	27D 45.8	19 8.4	29 1.0	17 50.6	23 36.0	0 13.1	10 13.8	1 29.3	7 15.0
23 F	18 4 8	1 23 25	28 14 15	4♌23 36	27 45.3	21 11.6	0♋14.8	18 26.5	23 46.1	0 20.9	10 17.2	1 29.7	7 16.4
24 Sa	18 8 5	2 20 40	10♌29 39	16 32 45	27 45.8	23 16.5	1 28.5	19 2.4	23 56.3	0 28.7	10 20.5	1 30.0	7 17.9
25 Su	18 12 2	3 17 54	22 33 19	28 31 47	27 47.2	25 23.1	2 42.2	19 38.4	24 6.5	0 36.5	10 23.8	1 30.4	7 19.4
26 M	18 15 58	4 15 8	4♍28 40	10♍24 28	27 48.8	27 31.1	3 55.9	20 14.4	24 16.9	0 44.3	10 27.1	1 30.8	7 20.9
27 Tu	18 19 55	5 12 21	16 19 47	22 15 9	27 50.4	29 40.2	5 9.6	20 50.4	24 27.3	0 52.1	10 30.4	1 31.3	7 22.4
28 W	18 23 51	6 9 34	28 11 12	4♎ 8 30	27R 51.3	1♋50.2	6 23.4	21 26.5	24 37.8	0 59.9	10 33.7	1 31.8	7 23.9
29 Th	18 27 48	7 6 47	10♎ 7 40	16 9 17	27 51.5	4 0.8	7 37.1	22 2.6	24 48.4	1 7.7	10 37.0	1 32.3	7 25.5
30 F	18 31 44	8 3 59	22 13 55	28 22 7	27 50.8	6 11.6	8 50.8	22 38.8	24 59.1	1 15.4	10 40.2	1 32.8	7 27.0

Astro Data / Planet Ingress

Astro Data Dy Hr Mn	Planet Ingress Dy Hr Mn
☽0S 5 9:24	♀ ♉ 4 22:04
☿ D 15 19:39	☊ ♋ 11 14:29
☽0N 18 17:44	☉ ♊ 21 4:51
	♂ ♌ 22 14:16
☽0S 1 18:20	♀ ♊ 29 8:39
♆ D 12 10:25	
☽0N 15 0:22	☿ ♊ 11 11:46
☽0S 29 3:16	♄ ♋ 20 7:48
	☉ ♋ 21 13:02
	♀ ♋ 22 19:12
	☿ ♋ 27 3:40

Last Aspect / ☽ Ingress

Last Aspect Dy Hr Mn	☽ Ingress Dy Hr Mn	Last Aspect Dy Hr Mn	☽ Ingress Dy Hr Mn
1 14:50 ♀ △	♍ 1 23:04	3 2:15 ♄ △	♏ 3 6:32
4 0:01 ♄ □	♎ 4 11:40	4 21:57 ♃ □	♐ 5 14:27
6 11:39 ♄ △	♏ 6 22:18	7 16:50 ♄ ☍	♑ 7 19:41
8 15:50 ♂ △	♐ 9 6:27	9 18:42 ♄ △	♒ 9 23:12
11 3:37 ♄ ☍	♑ 11 12:33	12 0:09 ♄ △	♓ 12 1:58
13 7:59 ♂ ☍	♒ 13 17:10	14 3:19 ♄ □	♈ 14 4:41
15 12:56 ♄ △	♓ 15 20:35	16 6:58 ♄ ✶	♉ 16 7:52
17 18:26 ♂ △	♈ 17 23:03	17 23:44 ♃ □	♊ 18 12:11
19 22:42 ♂ □	♉ 20 1:15	20 17:00 ☉ ☌	♋ 20 18:28
22 4:01 ♂ ✶	♊ 22 4:26	20 21:13 ♆ □	♌ 23 3:25
24 3:42 ♄ ☌	♋ 24 10:04	25 6:54 ☿ ✶	♍ 25 14:58
26 12:15 ♀ ✶	♌ 26 19:04	26 12:09 ♅ □	♎ 28 3:40
29 6:47 ♀ □	♍ 29 6:58	30 5:29 ♃ ✶	♏ 30 15:10
31 14:32 ♄ □	♎ 31 19:37		

☽ Phases & Eclipses / Astro Data

☽ Phases & Eclipses Dy Hr Mn	Astro Data
8 7:28 ○ 17♏34	1 MAY 1944
15 11:12 ☽ 24♒29	Julian Day # 16192
22 6:12 ● 1♊01	Delta T 26.4 sec
30 0:06 ☽ 8♍27	SVP 06♓02'29"
	Obliquity 23°26'43"
6 18:58 ○ 15♐54	⚷ Chiron 9♍24.2R
13 15:56 ☽ 22♓29	☽ Mean ☊ 1♌46.6
20 17:00 ● 29♊12	
28 17:27 ☽ 6♎51	1 JUNE 1944
	Julian Day # 16223
	Delta T 26.5 sec
	SVP 06♓02'25"
	Obliquity 23°26'43"
	⚷ Chiron 9♍54.4
	☽ Mean ☊ 0♌08.1

JULY 1944 LONGITUDE

Day	Sid.Time	☉	0 hr ☽	Noon ☽	True ☊	☿	♀	♂	♃	♄	♅	♆	♇
1 Sa	18 35 41	9♋ 1 10	4♏34 22	10♏51 9	27♋49.3	8♋22.5	10♋ 4.6	23♌15.0	25♌ 9.8	1♋23.2	10♊43.4	1♎33.4	7♌28.6
2 Su	18 39 37	9 58 22	17 12 49	23 39 42	27R 47.3	10 33.1	11 18.3	23 51.2	25 20.6	1 31.0	10 46.6	1 34.0	7 30.2
3 M	18 43 34	10 55 33	0♐12 1	6♐49 54	27 45.0	12 43.2	12 32.1	24 27.5	25 31.5	1 38.7	10 49.8	1 34.7	7 31.7
4 Tu	18 47 31	11 52 44	13 33 22	20 22 20	27 42.7	14 52.5	13 45.8	25 3.8	25 42.5	1 46.5	10 52.9	1 35.4	7 33.3
5 W	18 51 27	12 49 55	27 16 36	4♑15 51	27 41.0	17 0.8	14 59.6	25 40.1	25 53.5	1 54.2	10 56.0	1 36.1	7 34.9
6 Th	18 55 24	13 47 5	11♑19 40	18 27 31	27 39.8	19 8.0	16 13.4	26 16.5	26 4.6	2 1.9	10 59.2	1 36.8	7 36.6
7 F	18 59 20	14 44 16	25 38 48	2♒52 52	27D 39.4	21 13.9	17 27.1	26 52.9	26 15.8	2 9.6	11 2.2	1 37.6	7 38.2
8 Sa	19 3 17	15 41 27	10♒ 8 59	17 26 27	27 39.6	23 18.4	18 40.9	27 29.4	26 27.1	2 17.3	11 5.3	1 38.4	7 39.8
9 Su	19 7 13	16 38 38	24 44 30	2♓ 2 28	27 40.2	25 21.3	19 54.7	28 5.9	26 38.4	2 24.9	11 8.3	1 39.2	7 41.5
10 M	19 11 10	17 35 50	9♓19 39	16 35 27	27 41.1	27 22.5	21 8.5	28 42.4	26 49.7	2 32.6	11 11.3	1 40.1	7 43.1
11 Tu	19 15 7	18 33 2	23 49 19	1♈ 0 47	27 41.8	29 22.1	22 22.3	29 19.0	27 1.2	2 40.2	11 14.3	1 41.0	7 44.8
12 W	19 19 3	19 30 14	8♈ 9 28	15 15 2	27R 42.3	1♌19.9	23 36.1	29 55.6	27 12.7	2 47.8	11 17.3	1 41.9	7 46.4
13 Th	19 23 0	20 27 27	22 17 14	29 15 54	27 42.4	3 15.9	24 49.9	0♍32.2	27 24.2	2 55.4	11 20.2	1 42.8	7 48.1
14 F	19 26 56	21 24 41	6♉10 54	13♉ 2 9	27 42.2	5 10.0	26 3.7	1 8.9	27 35.8	3 2.9	11 23.1	1 43.8	7 49.8
15 Sa	19 30 53	22 21 55	19 49 38	26 33 20	27 41.8	7 2.3	27 17.6	1 45.6	27 47.5	3 10.5	11 26.0	1 44.8	7 51.5
16 Su	19 34 49	23 19 10	3♊13 17	9♊49 31	27 41.3	8 52.8	28 31.4	2 22.4	27 59.2	3 18.0	11 28.8	1 45.8	7 53.2
17 M	19 38 46	24 16 25	16 22 6	22 51 6	27 40.9	10 41.5	29 45.3	2 59.2	28 11.0	3 25.5	11 31.6	1 46.9	7 54.9
18 Tu	19 42 42	25 13 41	29 16 36	5♋38 43	27 40.6	12 28.2	0♌59.2	3 36.1	28 22.9	3 32.9	11 34.4	1 48.0	7 56.6
19 W	19 46 39	26 10 58	11♋57 31	18 13 8	27 40.4	14 13.2	2 13.0	4 13.0	28 34.8	3 40.4	11 37.2	1 49.1	7 58.3
20 Th	19 50 36	27 8 15	24 25 43	0♌35 24	27 40.4	15 56.2	3 26.9	4 49.9	28 46.7	3 47.8	11 39.9	1 50.3	8 0.1
21 F	19 54 32	28 5 33	6♌42 23	12 46 50	27 40.4	17 37.5	4 40.8	5 26.9	28 58.7	3 55.2	11 42.6	1 51.5	8 1.8
22 Sa	19 58 29	29 2 51	18 49 1	24 49 9	27 40.3	19 16.9	5 54.7	6 3.9	29 10.8	4 2.5	11 45.3	1 52.7	8 3.5
23 Su	20 2 25	0♌ 0 10	0♍47 33	6♍44 32	27 40.1	20 54.4	7 8.6	6 40.9	29 22.9	4 9.8	11 47.9	1 53.9	8 5.2
24 M	20 6 22	0 57 29	12 40 26	18 35 40	27 39.8	22 30.2	8 22.5	7 18.0	29 35.0	4 17.1	11 50.5	1 55.2	8 7.0
25 Tu	20 10 18	1 54 48	24 30 39	0♎25 49	27 39.3	24 4.0	9 36.4	7 55.1	29 47.2	4 24.4	11 53.0	1 56.5	8 8.7
26 W	20 14 15	2 52 8	6♎21 40	12 18 42	27 38.7	25 36.1	10 50.3	8 32.3	29 59.5	4 31.6	11 55.5	1 57.8	8 10.5
27 Th	20 18 11	3 49 29	18 17 26	24 18 26	27 38.3	27 6.3	12 4.2	9 9.5	0♍11.7	4 38.8	11 58.0	1 59.1	8 12.2
28 F	20 22 8	4 46 50	0♏22 14	6♏29 24	27D 38.0	28 34.6	13 18.1	9 46.7	0 24.1	4 45.9	12 0.5	2 0.5	8 14.0
29 Sa	20 26 5	5 44 11	12 40 29	18 56 1	27 38.0	0♍ 1.0	14 32.1	10 24.0	0 36.4	4 53.0	12 2.9	2 1.9	8 15.7
30 Su	20 30 1	6 41 33	25 16 29	1♐42 22	27 38.4	1 25.5	15 46.0	11 1.3	0 48.8	5 0.1	12 5.3	2 3.3	8 17.5
31 M	20 33 58	7 38 56	8♐14 3	14 51 52	27 39.2	2 48.0	16 59.9	11 38.7	1 1.2	5 7.1	12 7.6	2 4.7	8 19.2

AUGUST 1944 LONGITUDE

Day	Sid.Time	☉	0 hr ☽	Noon ☽	True ☊	☿	♀	♂	♃	♄	♅	♆	♇
1 Tu	20 37 54	8♌36 19	21♐36 1	28♐26 37	27♋40.1	4♍ 8.6	18♌13.8	12♍16.1	1♍13.7	5♋14.1	12♊ 9.9	2♎ 6.2	8♌21.0
2 W	20 41 51	9 33 43	5♑23 40	12♑27 0	27 41.0	5 27.1	19 27.8	12 53.5	1 26.2	5 21.0	12 12.2	2 7.7	8 22.7
3 Th	20 45 47	10 31 8	19 36 19	26 51 7	27R 41.6	6 43.6	20 41.7	13 31.0	1 38.8	5 27.9	12 14.4	2 9.2	8 24.5
4 F	20 49 44	11 28 33	4♒10 48	11♒34 34	27 41.6	7 58.0	21 55.6	14 8.5	1 51.3	5 34.8	12 16.6	2 10.8	8 26.2
5 Sa	20 53 40	12 25 59	19 1 32	26 30 42	27 40.9	9 10.1	23 9.6	14 46.0	2 3.9	5 41.6	12 18.8	2 12.3	8 28.0
6 Su	20 57 37	13 23 27	4♓ 1 0	11♓31 19	27 39.6	10 20.1	24 23.5	15 23.6	2 16.6	5 48.3	12 20.9	2 13.9	8 29.7
7 M	21 1 34	14 20 55	19 0 37	26 27 51	27 37.7	11 27.6	25 37.4	16 1.2	2 29.2	5 55.1	12 22.9	2 15.5	8 31.5
8 Tu	21 5 30	15 18 25	3♈52 5	11♈12 33	27 35.6	12 32.8	26 51.4	16 38.9	2 41.9	6 1.7	12 25.0	2 17.2	8 33.2
9 W	21 9 27	16 15 56	18 28 32	25 39 33	27 33.6	13 35.4	28 5.3	17 16.6	2 54.7	6 8.3	12 27.0	2 18.8	8 34.9
10 Th	21 13 23	17 13 28	2♉45 14	9♉45 21	27 32.2	14 35.4	29 19.3	17 54.3	3 7.4	6 14.9	12 28.9	2 20.5	8 36.7
11 F	21 17 20	18 11 2	16 39 50	23 28 43	27D 31.7	15 32.6	0♍33.2	18 32.1	3 20.2	6 21.4	12 30.8	2 22.2	8 38.4
12 Sa	21 21 16	19 8 37	0♊12 7	6♊50 15	27 32.0	16 27.0	1 47.2	19 9.9	3 33.0	6 27.9	12 32.7	2 23.9	8 40.1
13 Su	21 25 13	20 6 14	13 23 24	19 51 53	27 33.1	17 18.3	3 1.2	19 47.8	3 45.8	6 34.3	12 34.5	2 25.6	8 41.9
14 M	21 29 9	21 3 52	26 16 0	2♋36 8	27 34.6	18 6.4	4 15.1	20 25.7	3 58.6	6 40.6	12 36.3	2 27.4	8 43.6
15 Tu	21 33 6	22 1 32	8♋52 37	15 5 47	27 36.1	18 51.2	5 29.1	21 3.7	4 11.5	6 46.9	12 38.0	2 29.2	8 45.3
16 W	21 37 3	22 59 13	21 15 59	27 23 31	27R 37.1	19 32.4	6 43.1	21 41.7	4 24.4	6 53.2	12 39.7	2 31.0	8 47.0
17 Th	21 40 59	23 56 56	3♌28 40	9♌31 44	27 37.1	20 9.9	7 57.1	22 19.7	4 37.3	6 59.4	12 41.3	2 32.8	8 48.7
18 F	21 44 56	24 54 40	15 32 57	21 32 34	27 35.8	20 43.4	9 11.1	22 57.8	4 50.2	7 5.5	12 42.9	2 34.6	8 50.4
19 Sa	21 48 52	25 52 25	27 30 49	3♍27 57	27 33.1	21 12.7	10 25.0	23 35.9	5 3.1	7 11.6	12 44.5	2 36.5	8 52.1
20 Su	21 52 49	26 50 12	9♍24 10	15 19 43	27 29.1	21 37.6	11 39.0	24 14.1	5 16.1	7 17.6	12 46.0	2 38.4	8 53.8
21 M	21 56 45	27 48 0	21 14 52	27 9 50	27 24.1	21 57.8	12 53.0	24 52.3	5 29.1	7 23.5	12 47.4	2 40.3	8 55.5
22 Tu	22 0 42	28 45 49	3♎ 4 57	9♎ 0 29	27 18.6	22 13.1	14 7.0	25 30.5	5 42.0	7 29.4	12 48.8	2 42.2	8 57.2
23 W	22 4 38	29 43 40	14 56 48	20 54 16	27 13.1	22 23.2	15 21.0	26 8.8	5 55.0	7 35.2	12 50.2	2 44.1	8 58.8
24 Th	22 8 35	0♍41 32	26 53 16	2♏54 14	27 8.2	22R 28.0	16 35.0	26 47.1	6 8.0	7 40.9	12 51.5	2 46.0	9 0.5
25 F	22 12 31	1 39 25	8♏57 39	15 3 58	27 4.5	22 27.1	17 48.9	27 25.5	6 21.0	7 46.6	12 52.8	2 48.0	9 2.1
26 Sa	22 16 28	2 37 20	21 13 43	27 27 25	27D 2.3	22 20.5	19 2.9	28 3.9	6 34.0	7 52.2	12 54.0	2 50.0	9 3.7
27 Su	22 20 25	3 35 15	3♐45 36	10♐ 8 47	27 1.6	22 7.9	20 16.9	28 42.4	6 47.0	7 57.7	12 55.1	2 52.0	9 5.4
28 M	22 24 21	4 33 13	16 37 27	23 12 5	27 2.2	21 49.2	21 30.8	29 20.8	7 0.1	8 3.2	12 56.3	2 54.0	9 7.0
29 Tu	22 28 18	5 31 11	29 53 4	6♑40 44	27 3.6	21 24.5	22 44.8	29 59.4	7 13.1	8 8.6	12 57.3	2 56.0	9 8.6
30 W	22 32 14	6 29 11	13♑35 17	20 36 48	27R 4.9	20 53.8	23 58.7	0♎38.0	7 26.1	8 13.9	12 58.4	2 58.0	9 10.2
31 Th	22 36 11	7 27 12	27 45 13	5♒ 0 15	27 5.5	20 17.3	25 12.7	1 16.6	7 39.1	8 19.1	12 59.3	3 0.1	9 11.8

Astro Data	Planet Ingress	Last Aspect	☽ Ingress	Last Aspect	☽ Ingress	☽ Phases & Eclipses	Astro Data
Dy Hr Mn	Dy Hr Mn	Dy Hr Mn	Dy Hr Mn	Dy Hr Mn	Dy Hr Mn	Dy Hr Mn	1 JULY 1944
♄□♆ 2 10:21	☿ ♌ 11 7:41	2 15:19 ♃ □	♐ 2 23:38	31 17:25 ♀ △	♑ 1 14:42	6 4:27 ○ 13♑58	Julian Day # 16253
☽0N 12 6:13	♂ ♍ 12 2:54	4 21:34 ♃ △	♑ 5 4:42	2 13:20 ♂ △	♒ 3 17:10	6 4:40 ◐ A 0.533	Delta T 26.5 sec
☽0S 26 11:03	♀ ♌ 17 4:47	6 15:23 ☿ ☍	♒ 7 7:14	5 7:14 ♀ ☍	♓ 5 17:35	12 20:39 ☽ 20♈19	SVP 06♓02'20"
	☉ ♌ 22 23:56	9 5:45 ♂ ☍	♓ 9 8:39	6 19:00 ♂ ☍	♈ 7 17:43	20 5:42 ● 27♋22	Obliquity 23°26'43"
♃⊻♆ 5 18:13	♃ ♍ 26 1:03	10 21:22 ♀ △	♈ 11 10:18	9 17:37 ♀ △	♉ 9 19:19	20 5:42:46 ● A 3'42"	⚷ Chiron 11♍59.1
☽0N 8 12:57	☿ ♍ 28 23:44	13 8:55 ♃ △	♉ 13 13:16	11 3:26 ♂ △	♊ 11 23:38	28 9:23 ☽ 5♏09	☽ Mean ☊ 28♋32.8
☿0S 20 16:00		15 14:40 ♀ ⚹	♊ 15 18:11	13 13:27 ☉ ⚹	♋ 14 7:03		
☽0S 22 17:20	♀ ♍ 10 13:13	17 22:18 ♃ ⚹	♋ 18 1:21	16 0:53 ♂ ⚹	♌ 16 17:08	4 12:39 ○ 11♒59	1 AUGUST 1944
☿ R 24 8:25	☉ ♍ 23 6:46	20 5:42 ☉ ☌	♌ 20 10:51	18 20:25 ☉ ☌	♍ 19 5:01	4 12:26 ◐ A 0.478	Julian Day # 16284
☿0N 31 22:32	♂ ♎ 29 0:23	22 21:07 ♃ ☌	♍ 22 22:24	21 7:46 ♂ ☌	♎ 21 17:45	11 2:52 ☽ 18♉18	Delta T 26.5 sec
♂0S 31 9:01		23 22:18 ♅ □	♎ 25 11:08	22 19:44 ♅ △	♏ 24 6:13	18 20:25 ● 25♌44	SVP 06♓02'15"
		27 19:59 ☿ ⚹	♏ 27 23:16	26 13:52 ♂ ⚹	♐ 26 16:52	26 23:39 ☽ 3♐34	Obliquity 23°26'43"
		29 3:58 ♀ □	♐ 30 8:50	29 0:12 ♂ □	♑ 29 0:12		⚷ Chiron 15♍23.4
				30 19:21 ♀ △	♒ 31 3:44		☽ Mean ☊ 26♋54.3

LONGITUDE SEPTEMBER 1944

Day	Sid.Time	☉	0 hr ☽	Noon ☽	True ☊	☿	♀	♂	♃	♄	♅	♆	♇
1 F	22 40 7	8♍25 14	12♒21 28	19♒48 11	27♋ 4.6	19♍35.3	26♍26.6	1♎55.2	7♍52.2	8♋24.3	13♊ 0.3	3♎ 2.1	9♌13.4
2 Sa	22 44 4	9 23 18	27 19 33	4♓54 32	27R 1.9	18R48.3	27 40.6	2 33.9	8 5.2	8 29.4	13 1.1	3 4.2	9 14.9
3 Su	22 48 0	10 21 24	12♓31 54	20 10 21	26 57.2	17 57.0	28 54.5	3 12.7	8 18.2	8 34.4	13 2.0	3 6.3	9 16.5
4 M	22 51 57	11 19 31	27 48 31	5♈25 3	26 51.2	17 2.2	0♎ 8.4	3 51.4	8 31.2	8 39.4	13 2.7	3 8.4	9 18.0
5 Tu	22 55 54	12 17 40	12♈58 38	20 28 7	26 44.4	16 4.7	1 22.3	4 30.3	8 44.3	8 44.2	13 3.5	3 10.5	9 19.5
6 W	22 59 50	13 15 51	27 52 30	5♉10 57	26 38.0	15 5.8	2 36.2	5 9.1	8 57.3	8 49.0	13 4.1	3 12.6	9 21.0
7 Th	23 3 47	14 14 4	12♉22 54	19 27 58	26 32.7	14 6.7	3 50.1	5 48.0	9 10.3	8 53.7	13 4.8	3 14.7	9 22.5
8 F	23 7 43	15 12 19	26 25 57	3♊16 54	26 29.2	13 8.7	5 4.0	6 27.0	9 23.3	8 58.4	13 5.3	3 16.8	9 24.0
9 Sa	23 11 40	16 10 36	10♊ 0 57	16 38 23	26D 27.5	12 13.1	6 17.9	7 6.0	9 36.3	9 2.9	13 5.9	3 19.0	9 25.5
10 Su	23 15 36	17 8 55	23 9 38	29 35 9	26 27.5	11 21.3	7 31.8	7 45.0	9 49.2	9 7.4	13 6.3	3 21.1	9 26.9
11 M	23 19 33	18 7 17	5♋55 26	12♋11 2	26 28.4	10 34.5	8 45.7	8 24.1	10 2.2	9 11.7	13 6.7	3 23.3	9 28.4
12 Tu	23 23 29	19 5 40	18 22 31	24 30 24	26R 29.4	9 54.0	9 59.6	9 3.3	10 15.2	9 16.0	13 7.1	3 25.5	9 29.8
13 W	23 27 26	20 4 6	0♌35 13	6♌37 28	26 29.6	9 20.6	11 13.5	9 42.5	10 28.1	9 20.2	13 7.4	3 27.6	9 31.2
14 Th	23 31 23	21 2 33	12 37 37	18 36 5	26 28.1	8 55.3	12 27.4	10 21.7	10 41.0	9 24.4	13 7.7	3 29.8	9 32.6
15 F	23 35 19	22 1 3	24 33 15	0♍29 28	26 24.4	8 38.7	13 41.3	11 1.0	10 54.0	9 28.4	13 7.9	3 32.0	9 34.0
16 Sa	23 39 16	22 59 34	6♍25 3	12 20 15	26 18.1	8D 31.3	14 55.1	11 40.3	11 6.9	9 32.3	13 8.1	3 34.2	9 35.3
17 Su	23 43 12	23 58 8	18 15 21	24 10 32	26 9.4	8 33.4	16 9.0	12 19.7	11 19.7	9 36.2	13 8.2	3 36.4	9 36.7
18 M	23 47 9	24 56 43	0♎ 6 0	6♎ 1 58	25 58.9	8 45.1	17 22.9	12 59.1	11 32.6	9 39.9	13R 8.2	3 38.6	9 38.0
19 Tu	23 51 5	25 55 21	11 58 36	17 56 6	25 47.3	9 6.2	18 36.7	13 38.6	11 45.4	9 43.6	13 8.2	3 40.8	9 39.3
20 W	23 55 2	26 54 0	23 54 39	29 54 29	25 35.6	9 36.7	19 50.5	14 18.1	11 58.2	9 47.1	13 8.2	3 43.1	9 40.6
21 Th	23 58 58	27 52 41	5♏55 51	11♏59 1	25 24.9	10 16.1	21 4.4	14 57.6	12 11.0	9 50.6	13 8.1	3 45.3	9 41.8
22 F	0 2 55	28 51 24	18 4 18	24 12 2	25 16.1	11 4.0	22 18.2	15 37.2	12 23.8	9 54.0	13 7.9	3 47.5	9 43.1
23 Sa	0 6 52	29 50 8	0♐22 37	6♐36 27	25 9.8	11 59.9	23 32.0	16 16.9	12 36.5	9 57.3	13 7.7	3 49.7	9 44.3
24 Su	0 10 48	0♎48 55	12 54 0	19 15 42	25 6.0	13 3.2	24 45.8	16 56.6	12 49.2	10 0.4	13 7.5	3 52.0	9 45.5
25 M	0 14 45	1 47 43	25 42 4	2♑13 34	25D 4.4	14 13.2	25 59.6	17 36.3	13 1.9	10 3.5	13 7.2	3 54.2	9 46.7
26 Tu	0 18 41	2 46 33	8♑50 38	15 33 43	25 4.4	15 29.4	27 13.4	18 16.1	13 14.6	10 6.5	13 6.8	3 56.4	9 47.9
27 W	0 22 38	3 45 25	22 23 10	29 19 13	25R 4.8	16 50.9	28 27.2	18 55.9	13 27.2	10 9.4	13 6.4	3 58.7	9 49.0
28 Th	0 26 34	4 44 18	6♒22 2	13♒31 35	25 4.4	18 17.2	29 40.9	19 35.8	13 39.7	10 12.2	13 6.0	4 0.9	9 50.2
29 F	0 30 31	5 43 13	20 47 41	28 9 56	25 2.1	19 47.6	0♏54.7	20 15.7	13 52.3	10 14.8	13 5.5	4 3.1	9 51.3
30 Sa	0 34 27	6 42 10	5♓37 41	13♓10 6	24 57.3	21 21.5	2 8.4	20 55.6	14 4.8	10 17.4	13 4.9	4 5.3	9 52.4

LONGITUDE OCTOBER 1944

Day	Sid.Time	☉	0 hr ☽	Noon ☽	True ☊	☿	♀	♂	♃	♄	♅	♆	♇
1 Su	0 38 24	7♎41 8	20♓46 8	28♓24 32	24♋49.9	22♍58.4	3♏22.1	21♎35.6	14♍17.3	10♋19.9	13♊ 4.3	4♎ 7.6	9♌53.4
2 M	0 42 20	8 40 9	6♈ 3 56	13♈42 54	24R 40.3	24 37.7	4 35.8	22 15.7	14 29.7	10 22.3	13R 3.6	4 9.8	9 54.5
3 Tu	0 46 17	9 39 11	21 19 59	28 53 47	24 29.7	26 18.9	5 49.5	22 55.8	14 42.1	10 24.6	13 2.9	4 12.0	9 55.5
4 W	0 50 14	10 38 16	6♉23 4	13♉46 44	24 19.1	28 1.7	7 3.2	23 35.9	14 54.4	10 26.7	13 2.2	4 14.3	9 56.5
5 Th	0 54 10	11 37 23	21 3 56	28 14 4	24 10.0	29 45.7	8 16.9	24 16.1	15 6.8	10 28.8	13 1.4	4 16.5	9 57.5
6 F	0 58 7	12 36 32	5♊16 44	12♊11 46	24 3.1	1♎30.5	9 30.5	24 56.4	15 19.0	10 30.7	13 0.5	4 18.7	9 58.4
7 Sa	1 2 3	13 35 43	18 59 13	25 39 18	23 58.8	3 15.9	10 44.2	25 36.6	15 31.3	10 32.6	12 59.6	4 20.9	9 59.4
8 Su	1 6 0	14 34 57	2♋12 23	8♋38 57	23 56.8	5 1.7	11 57.8	26 17.0	15 43.4	10 34.3	12 58.7	4 23.1	10 0.3
9 M	1 9 56	15 34 13	14 59 32	21 14 46	23 56.4	6 47.6	13 11.4	26 57.4	15 55.6	10 36.0	12 57.7	4 25.3	10 1.2
10 Tu	1 13 53	16 33 32	27 25 17	3♌31 44	23 56.4	8 33.4	14 25.1	27 37.8	16 7.7	10 37.5	12 56.6	4 27.5	10 2.0
11 W	1 17 49	17 32 52	9♌34 46	15 35 2	23 55.7	10 19.2	15 38.7	28 18.3	16 19.7	10 38.9	12 55.5	4 29.7	10 2.9
12 Th	1 21 46	18 32 15	21 33 7	27 29 36	23 53.1	12 4.6	16 52.3	28 58.8	16 31.7	10 40.2	12 54.4	4 31.9	10 3.7
13 F	1 25 43	19 31 40	3♍25 0	9♍19 47	23 48.0	13 49.7	18 5.9	29 39.4	16 43.6	10 41.4	12 53.2	4 34.1	10 4.5
14 Sa	1 29 39	20 31 8	15 14 23	21 9 11	23 39.9	15 34.4	19 19.4	0♏20.1	16 55.5	10 42.5	12 52.0	4 36.2	10 5.2
15 Su	1 33 36	21 30 37	27 4 29	3♎ 0 36	23 29.0	17 18.6	20 33.0	1 0.7	17 7.3	10 43.5	12 50.7	4 38.4	10 6.0
16 M	1 37 32	22 30 9	8♎57 43	14 56 5	23 15.8	19 2.3	21 46.6	1 41.5	17 19.0	10 44.4	12 49.4	4 40.5	10 6.7
17 Tu	1 41 29	23 29 43	20 55 49	26 57 4	23 1.3	20 45.4	23 0.1	2 22.3	17 30.7	10 45.1	12 48.0	4 42.7	10 7.4
18 W	1 45 25	24 29 19	2♏59 57	9♏ 4 35	22 46.7	22 27.9	24 13.6	3 3.1	17 42.4	10 45.8	12 46.6	4 44.8	10 8.1
19 Th	1 49 22	25 28 57	15 11 4	21 19 32	22 33.2	24 9.8	25 27.1	3 44.0	17 53.9	10 46.3	12 45.1	4 46.9	10 8.7
20 F	1 53 18	26 28 36	27 30 7	3♐43 0	22 21.8	25 51.2	26 40.6	4 24.9	18 5.4	10 46.7	12 43.6	4 49.1	10 9.3
21 Sa	1 57 15	27 28 18	9♐58 21	16 16 26	22 13.3	27 31.9	27 54.1	5 5.9	18 16.9	10 47.0	12 42.1	4 51.2	10 9.9
22 Su	2 1 12	28 28 2	22 37 30	29 1 52	22 7.8	29 12.0	29 7.6	5 46.9	18 28.3	10 47.2	12 40.5	4 53.2	10 10.5
23 M	2 5 8	29 27 47	5♑29 52	12♑ 1 50	22 5.1	0♏51.6	0♐21.1	6 28.0	18 39.6	10R 47.3	12 38.9	4 55.3	10 11.0
24 Tu	2 9 5	0♏27 34	18 38 9	25 19 10	22 4.3	2 30.5	1 34.5	7 9.1	18 50.8	10 47.3	12 37.2	4 57.4	10 11.5
25 W	2 13 1	1 27 23	2♒ 5 13	8♒56 35	22 4.4	4 8.9	2 47.9	7 50.3	19 2.0	10 47.1	12 35.5	4 59.4	10 12.0
26 Th	2 16 58	2 27 13	15 53 28	22 56 0	22 3.9	5 46.7	4 1.3	8 31.5	19 13.0	10 46.9	12 33.8	5 1.5	10 12.4
27 F	2 20 54	3 27 5	0♓ 4 8	7♓17 42	22 1.7	7 24.0	5 14.7	9 12.8	19 24.0	10 46.5	12 32.0	5 3.5	10 12.9
28 Sa	2 24 51	4 26 59	14 36 21	21 59 32	21 57.0	9 0.7	6 28.0	9 54.1	19 35.0	10 46.0	12 30.2	5 5.5	10 13.3
29 Su	2 28 47	5 26 54	29 26 31	6♈56 22	21 49.6	10 37.0	7 41.4	10 35.4	19 45.8	10 45.4	12 28.3	5 7.5	10 13.7
30 M	2 32 44	6 26 51	14♈28 1	22 0 16	21 39.9	12 12.7	8 54.7	11 16.8	19 56.6	10 44.7	12 26.5	5 9.5	10 14.0
31 Tu	2 36 41	7 26 49	29 31 50	7♉ 1 27	21 29.0	13 48.0	10 8.0	11 58.3	20 7.3	10 43.9	12 24.5	5 11.4	10 14.3

Astro Data	Planet Ingress	Last Aspect	☽ Ingress	Last Aspect	☽ Ingress	☽ Phases & Eclipses	Astro Data
Dy Hr Mn	Dy Hr Mn	Dy Hr Mn	Dy Hr Mn	Dy Hr Mn	Dy Hr Mn	Dy Hr Mn	1 SEPTEMBER 1944
☽0N 4 21:43	♀ ♎ 3 21:16	1 1:03 ♅ △	♓ 2 4:14	1 3:53 ☿ ☍	♈ 1 14:30	2 20:21 ○ 10♓13	Julian Day # 16315
♆0S 4 14:25	☉ ♎ 23 4:02	3 8:02 ☿ ☍	♈ 4 3:27	3 2:39 ♂ ☍	♉ 3 13:46	9 12:03 ☽ 16♊40	Delta T 26.6 sec
♃✱♄ 4 23:59	♀ ♏ 28 6:12	5 0:08 ♅ ✱	♉ 6 3:28	4 14:03 ♃ △	♊ 5 14:59	17 12:37 ● 24♍29	SVP 06♓02'12"
♀0S 5 23:10		7 3:21 ☉ △	♊ 8 6:13	7 12:34 ♂ △	♋ 7 19:56	25 12:07 ☽ 2♑17	Obliquity 23°26'44"
♃⚺♇ 8 1:32	☿ ♎ 5 3:17	9 12:03 ☉ □	♋ 10 12:47	10 0:26 ♂ □	♌ 10 5:03		⚷ Chiron 19♍34.4
☿ D 16 6:47	♂ ♏ 13 12:09	12 1:31 ☉ ✱	♌ 12 22:50	12 15:55 ♂ ✱	♍ 12 17:04	2 4:22 ○ 8♈51	☽ Mean ☊ 25♋15.8
♄⚺♇ 17 4:50	☿ ♏ 22 11:33	14 1:00 ♅ ✱	♍ 15 11:00	14 9:15 ♀ ✱	♎ 15 5:55	9 1:12 ☽ 15♋37	
☽0S 18 22:50	♀ ♐ 22 17:07	17 12:37 ☉ ☌	♎ 17 23:48	17 5:35 ☉ ☌	♏ 17 18:03	17 5:35 ● 23♎44	1 OCTOBER 1944
♅ R 18 13:31	☉ ♏ 23 12:56	19 14:54 ♀ ☌	♏ 20 12:11	19 22:14 ♀ ☌	♐ 20 4:50	24 22:48 ☽ 1♒24	Julian Day # 16345
♃□♅ 25 9:44		22 22:52 ☉ ✱	♐ 22 23:16	22 11:52 ☉ ✱	♑ 22 13:48	31 13:35 ○ 8♉01	Delta T 26.6 sec
☽0N 2 8:20		25 0:36 ♀ ✱	♑ 25 7:55	24 0:23 ♃ △	♒ 24 20:19		SVP 06♓02'09"
☿0S 7 13:14		27 11:31 ♀ □	♒ 27 13:10	25 18:17 ♅ △	♓ 26 23:53		Obliquity 23°26'44"
☽0S 16 4:50		28 23:05 ♂ △	♓ 29 14:58	28 8:12 ♃ ☍	♈ 29 0:54		⚷ Chiron 23♍52.3
♄ R 23 5:37	☽0N 29 19:16			29 20:47 ♅ ✱	♉ 31 0:45		☽ Mean ☊ 23♋40.4

NOVEMBER 1944 LONGITUDE

Day	Sid.Time	☉	0 hr ☽	Noon ☽	True ☊	☿	♀	♂	♃	♄	♅	♆	♇
1 W	2 40 37	8♏26 50	14♉27 54	21♉50 2	21♋18.0	15♏22.7	11♐21.2	12♏39.8	20♍17.9	10♋43.0	12♊22.6	5♎13.4	10♌14.6
2 Th	2 44 34	9 26 53	29 6 54	6♊17 42	21R 8.4	16 57.1	12 34.5	13 21.4	20 28.4	10R 42.0	12R 20.6	5 15.3	10 14.9
3 F	2 48 30	10 26 57	13♊21 52	20 19 0	21 0.9	18 31.0	13 47.7	14 3.0	20 38.9	10 40.8	12 18.6	5 17.2	10 15.1
4 Sa	2 52 27	11 27 4	27 8 58	3♋51 46	20 56.1	20 4.5	15 0.9	14 44.6	20 49.2	10 39.6	12 16.5	5 19.1	10 15.3
5 Su	2 56 23	12 27 12	10♋27 36	16 56 47	20D 53.8	21 37.7	16 14.1	15 26.3	20 59.5	10 38.2	12 14.5	5 21.0	10 15.5
6 M	3 0 20	13 27 23	23 19 46	29 37 5	20 53.4	23 10.4	17 27.2	16 8.1	21 9.6	10 36.7	12 12.3	5 22.9	10 15.7
7 Tu	3 4 16	14 27 36	5♌49 19	11♌57 6	20R 53.8	24 42.8	18 40.3	16 49.9	21 19.7	10 35.2	12 10.2	5 24.7	10 15.8
8 W	3 8 13	15 27 50	18 1 7	24 2 2	20 54.0	26 14.8	19 53.4	17 31.8	21 29.7	10 33.5	12 8.0	5 26.5	10 15.9
9 Th	3 12 10	16 28 7	0♍ 0 30	5♍57 12	20 53.0	27 46.4	21 6.5	18 13.7	21 39.6	10 31.7	12 5.8	5 28.3	10 16.0
10 F	3 16 6	17 28 26	11 52 43	17 47 40	20 49.8	29 17.7	22 19.6	18 55.7	21 49.4	10 29.8	12 3.6	5 30.1	10 16.0
11 Sa	3 20 3	18 28 46	23 42 35	29 37 58	20 44.2	0♐48.6	23 32.6	19 37.7	21 59.1	10 27.8	12 1.4	5 31.9	10R 16.1
12 Su	3 23 59	19 29 9	5♎34 17	11♎31 55	20 36.0	2 19.2	24 45.6	20 19.7	22 8.7	10 25.7	11 59.1	5 33.6	10 16.1
13 M	3 27 56	20 29 33	17 31 13	23 32 28	20 25.9	3 49.5	25 58.6	21 1.9	22 18.1	10 23.5	11 56.8	5 35.3	10 16.0
14 Tu	3 31 52	21 29 59	29 35 54	5♏41 42	20 14.5	5 19.4	27 11.6	21 44.0	22 27.5	10 21.2	11 54.5	5 37.0	10 16.0
15 W	3 35 49	22 30 27	11♏49 59	18 0 52	20 2.8	6 48.9	28 24.5	22 26.2	22 36.8	10 18.8	11 52.1	5 38.7	10 15.9
16 Th	3 39 45	23 30 56	24 14 22	0♐30 34	19 52.1	8 18.0	29 37.4	23 8.5	22 45.9	10 16.2	11 49.8	5 40.3	10 15.8
17 F	3 43 42	24 31 28	6♐49 26	13 10 59	19 43.1	9 46.8	0♑50.3	23 50.8	22 55.0	10 13.6	11 47.4	5 41.9	10 15.6
18 Sa	3 47 39	25 32 0	19 35 15	26 2 14	19 36.6	11 15.1	2 3.2	24 33.2	23 3.9	10 10.9	11 45.0	5 43.5	10 15.4
19 Su	3 51 35	26 32 35	2♑31 59	9♑ 4 32	19 32.7	12 42.9	3 16.0	25 15.6	23 12.7	10 8.1	11 42.6	5 45.1	10 15.2
20 M	3 55 32	27 33 10	15 40 0	22 18 28	19D 31.2	14 10.2	4 28.8	25 58.1	23 21.4	10 5.2	11 40.1	5 46.7	10 15.0
21 Tu	3 59 28	28 33 47	29 0 3	5♒44 54	19 31.4	15 37.0	5 41.5	26 40.6	23 30.0	10 2.2	11 37.7	5 48.2	10 14.8
22 W	4 3 25	29 34 25	12♒33 9	19 24 55	19 32.5	17 3.1	6 54.2	27 23.2	23 38.5	9 59.1	11 35.2	5 49.7	10 14.5
23 Th	4 7 21	0♐35 4	26 20 18	3♓19 20	19R 33.4	18 28.6	8 6.9	28 5.8	23 46.8	9 56.0	11 32.8	5 51.2	10 14.2
24 F	4 11 18	1 35 44	10♓22 0	17 28 12	19 33.1	19 53.2	9 19.5	28 48.5	23 55.0	9 52.7	11 30.3	5 52.6	10 13.8
25 Sa	4 15 14	2 36 25	24 37 44	1♈50 15	19 31.0	21 17.0	10 32.0	29 31.2	24 3.1	9 49.4	11 27.8	5 54.0	10 13.5
26 Su	4 19 11	3 37 7	9♈ 5 19	16 22 23	19 26.8	22 39.7	11 44.6	0♐13.9	24 11.0	9 45.9	11 25.3	5 55.4	10 13.1
27 M	4 23 8	4 37 50	23 40 45	0♉59 39	19 20.9	24 1.4	12 57.0	0 56.7	24 18.9	9 42.4	11 22.8	5 56.8	10 12.7
28 Tu	4 27 4	5 38 34	8♉18 14	15 35 36	19 14.0	25 21.7	14 9.4	1 39.6	24 26.6	9 38.8	11 20.3	5 58.1	10 12.2
29 W	4 31 1	6 39 20	22 50 52	0♊ 3 9	19 6.9	26 40.5	15 21.8	2 22.5	24 34.1	9 35.1	11 17.7	5 59.4	10 11.8
30 Th	4 34 57	7 40 6	7♊11 40	14 15 43	19 0.6	27 57.6	16 34.1	3 5.4	24 41.6	9 31.4	11 15.2	6 0.7	10 11.3

DECEMBER 1944 LONGITUDE

Day	Sid.Time	☉	0 hr ☽	Noon ☽	True ☊	☿	♀	♂	♃	♄	♅	♆	♇
1 F	4 38 54	8♐40 54	21♊14 43	28♊ 8 12	18♋55.8	29♐12.6	17♑46.4	3♐48.4	24♍48.9	9♋27.6	11♊12.7	6♎ 2.0	10♌10.8
2 Sa	4 42 50	9 41 43	4♋55 53	11♋37 36	18R 53.0	0♑25.5	18 58.6	4 31.5	24 56.0	9R 23.7	11R 10.1	6 3.2	10R 10.2
3 Su	4 46 47	10 42 34	18 13 20	24 43 13	18D 52.1	1 35.6	20 10.7	5 14.6	25 3.0	9 19.7	11 7.6	6 4.4	10 9.7
4 M	4 50 43	11 43 26	1♌ 7 28	7♌26 26	18 52.7	2 42.8	21 22.8	5 57.7	25 9.9	9 15.7	11 5.1	6 5.6	10 9.1
5 Tu	4 54 40	12 44 18	13 40 31	19 50 12	18 54.2	3 46.5	22 34.9	6 40.9	25 16.7	9 11.6	11 2.5	6 6.7	10 8.5
6 W	4 58 37	13 45 13	25 56 4	1♍58 39	18 56.0	4 46.2	23 46.8	7 24.2	25 23.2	9 7.4	10 60.0	6 7.8	10 7.8
7 Th	5 2 33	14 46 8	7♍58 36	13 56 32	18R 57.2	5 41.3	24 58.7	8 7.5	25 29.7	9 3.1	10 57.4	6 8.9	10 7.2
8 F	5 6 30	15 47 5	19 53 4	25 48 51	18 57.4	6 31.2	26 10.6	8 50.8	25 36.0	8 58.8	10 54.9	6 9.9	10 6.5
9 Sa	5 10 26	16 48 2	1♎44 29	7♎40 35	18 56.1	7 15.1	27 22.4	9 34.2	25 42.1	8 54.5	10 52.4	6 10.9	10 5.8
10 Su	5 14 23	17 49 1	13 37 41	19 36 20	18 53.4	7 52.4	28 34.1	10 17.7	25 48.1	8 50.1	10 49.9	6 11.9	10 5.0
11 M	5 18 19	18 50 1	25 37 0	1♏40 8	18 49.4	8 22.0	29 45.7	11 1.2	25 53.9	8 45.6	10 47.3	6 12.9	10 4.3
12 Tu	5 22 16	19 51 3	7♏46 6	13 55 15	18 44.5	8 43.3	0♒57.3	11 44.7	25 59.6	8 41.1	10 44.8	6 13.8	10 3.5
13 W	5 26 12	20 52 5	20 7 50	26 24 2	18 39.4	8R 55.2	2 8.8	12 28.3	26 5.1	8 36.5	10 42.3	6 14.7	10 2.7
14 Th	5 30 9	21 53 8	2♐43 59	9♐ 7 46	18 34.6	8 57.0	3 20.2	13 12.0	26 10.5	8 31.9	10 39.9	6 15.5	10 1.9
15 F	5 34 6	22 54 12	15 35 23	22 6 47	18 30.8	8 48.0	4 31.6	13 55.7	26 15.7	8 27.3	10 37.4	6 16.4	10 1.0
16 Sa	5 38 2	23 55 17	28 41 51	5♑20 27	18 28.1	8 27.6	5 42.8	14 39.4	26 20.7	8 22.6	10 34.9	6 17.2	10 0.1
17 Su	5 41 59	24 56 22	12♑ 2 25	18 47 32	18D 26.9	7 55.5	6 54.0	15 23.2	26 25.6	8 17.8	10 32.5	6 17.9	9 59.3
18 M	5 45 55	25 57 28	25 35 35	2♒26 22	18 26.9	7 11.9	8 5.1	16 7.0	26 30.3	8 13.1	10 30.1	6 18.6	9 58.3
19 Tu	5 49 52	26 58 34	9♒19 38	16 15 10	18 27.8	6 17.4	9 16.1	16 50.9	26 34.8	8 8.3	10 27.6	6 19.3	9 57.4
20 W	5 53 48	27 59 41	23 12 45	0♓12 10	18 29.3	5 13.1	10 27.0	17 34.8	26 39.2	8 3.5	10 25.2	6 20.0	9 56.5
21 Th	5 57 45	29 0 48	7♓13 14	14 15 45	18 30.7	4 0.6	11 37.8	18 18.8	26 43.4	7 58.6	10 22.9	6 20.6	9 55.5
22 F	6 1 41	0♑ 1 55	21 19 29	28 24 13	18R 31.6	2 42.2	12 48.5	19 2.8	26 47.4	7 53.7	10 20.5	6 21.2	9 54.5
23 Sa	6 5 38	1 3 2	5♈29 45	12♈35 47	18 31.7	1 20.3	13 59.1	19 46.9	26 51.2	7 48.8	10 18.2	6 21.8	9 53.5
24 Su	6 9 35	2 4 9	19 42 4	26 48 15	18 31.0	29♐57.8	15 9.5	20 31.0	26 54.9	7 43.9	10 15.9	6 22.3	9 52.4
25 M	6 13 31	3 5 17	3♉54 1	10♉58 57	18 29.6	28 37.4	16 19.9	21 15.1	26 58.4	7 39.0	10 13.6	6 22.8	9 51.4
26 Tu	6 17 28	4 6 24	18 2 40	25 4 44	18 27.7	27 21.6	17 30.1	21 59.3	27 1.7	7 34.1	10 11.3	6 23.2	9 50.3
27 W	6 21 24	5 7 32	2♊ 4 43	9♊ 2 10	18 25.8	26 12.6	18 40.2	22 43.5	27 4.8	7 29.1	10 9.1	6 23.6	9 49.2
28 Th	6 25 21	6 8 39	15 56 42	22 47 54	18 24.2	25 12.0	19 50.2	23 27.8	27 7.8	7 24.2	10 6.8	6 24.0	9 48.1
29 F	6 29 17	7 9 47	29 35 26	6♋19 1	18 23.1	24 21.1	21 0.0	24 12.1	27 10.6	7 19.2	10 4.6	6 24.4	9 47.0
30 Sa	6 33 14	8 10 55	12♋58 24	19 33 25	18D 22.5	23 40.5	22 9.7	24 56.5	27 13.2	7 14.3	10 2.5	6 24.7	9 45.9
31 Su	6 37 11	9 12 3	26 4 0	2♌30 8	18 22.6	23 10.3	23 19.3	25 40.9	27 15.6	7 9.3	10 0.4	6 25.0	9 44.7

Astro Data Dy Hr Mn	Planet Ingress Dy Hr Mn	Last Aspect Dy Hr Mn	☽ Ingress Dy Hr Mn	Last Aspect Dy Hr Mn	☽ Ingress Dy Hr Mn	☽ Phases & Eclipses Dy Hr Mn
♇ R 11 5:11	☿ ♐ 10 11:09	1 9:36 ♃ △	♊ 2 1:28	1 15:15 ☿ ☍	♋ 1 15:16	7 18:29 ☽ 15♌14
☽0S 12 12:13	♀ ♑ 16 7:26	3 12:44 ♃ □	♋ 4 5:04	3 12:44 ♃ ✶	♌ 3 21:53	15 22:29 ● 23♏27
♄⊻♇ 16 4:45	☉ ♐ 22 10:08	5 23:40 ☿ △	♌ 6 12:44	4 22:02 ☉ △	♍ 6 8:04	23 7:53 ☽ 0♓55
☽0N 26 4:34	♂ ♐ 25 16:11	8 18:51 ☿ □	♍ 8 23:59	8 14:10 ♀ △	♎ 8 20:28	30 0:52 ○ 7♊42
		10 23:38 ♀ □	♎ 11 12:45	10 9:12 ☉ ✶	♏ 11 8:42	
♃∠♇ 3 21:18	☿ ♑ 1 15:31	13 18:43 ♀ ✶	♏ 14 0:48	13 11:29 ♃ ✶	♐ 13 18:50	7 14:57 ☽ 15♍24
☽0S 9 20:48	♀ ♒ 11 4:47	15 22:29 ☉ ☌	♐ 16 11:02	15 19:42 ♃ □	♑ 16 2:22	15 14:35 ● 23♐31
☿ R 13 16:11	☉ ♑ 21 23:15	18 6:33 ♃ □	♑ 18 19:20	18 1:37 ♃ △	♒ 18 7:44	22 15:54 ☽ 0♈42
☽0N 23 11:18	☿ ♐ 23 23:21	20 23:09 ☉ ✶	♒ 21 1:47	20 8:52 ☉ ✶	♓ 20 11:39	29 14:38 ○ 7♋47
		23 3:12 ♂ □	♓ 23 6:18	22 9:19 ♃ ☍	♈ 22 14:42	29 14:49 A 1.022
		25 8:34 ♂ △	♈ 25 8:57	24 15:50 ☿ △	♉ 24 17:24	
		27 0:37 ☿ △	♉ 27 10:22	26 15:24 ♃ △	♊ 26 20:26	
		29 2:53 ♃ △	♊ 29 11:55	28 19:42 ♃ □	♋ 29 0:44	
				31 2:13 ♃ ✶	♌ 31 7:19	

Astro Data

1 NOVEMBER 1944
Julian Day # 16376
Delta T 26.7 sec
SVP 06♓02'06"
Obliquity 23°26'44"
⚷ Chiron 28♍01.9
☽ Mean ☊ 22♋01.9

1 DECEMBER 1944
Julian Day # 16406
Delta T 26.7 sec
SVP 06♓02'02"
Obliquity 23°26'44"
⚷ Chiron 1♎14.3
☽ Mean ☊ 20♋26.6

LONGITUDE — JANUARY 1945

Day	Sid.Time	☉	0 hr ☽	Noon ☽	True ☊	☿	♀	♂	♃	♄	♅	♆	♇
1 M	6 41 7	10♑13 11	8♌51 53	15♌ 9 24	18♋23.1	22♐50.6	24♒28.7	26♐25.4	27♍17.8	7♋ 4.4	9♊58.3	6♎25.2	9♌43.6
2 Tu	6 45 4	11 14 20	21 22 54	27 32 39	18 23.8	22D40.8	25 38.0	27 9.9	27 19.8	6R59.4	9R56.2	6 25.4	9R42.4
3 W	6 49 0	12 15 28	3♍39 1	9♍42 24	18 24.5	22 40.5	26 47.1	27 54.4	27 21.7	6 54.5	9 54.1	6 25.6	9 41.2
4 Th	6 52 57	13 16 37	15 43 16	21 42 5	18 25.2	22 49.0	27 56.0	28 39.0	27 23.4	6 49.6	9 52.1	6 25.8	9 40.0
5 F	6 56 53	14 17 46	27 39 25	3♎35 47	18 25.6	23 5.5	29 4.8	29 23.7	27 24.8	6 44.7	9 50.1	6 25.9	9 38.8
6 Sa	7 0 50	15 18 55	9♎31 48	15 28 3	18R25.8	23 29.5	0♓13.4	0♑ 8.4	27 26.1	6 39.8	9 48.2	6 26.0	9 37.5
7 Su	7 4 46	16 20 4	21 25 7	27 23 36	18 25.8	24 0.1	1 21.9	0 53.1	27 27.2	6 34.9	9 46.3	6R26.0	9 36.3
8 M	7 8 43	17 21 14	3♏24 5	9♏27 9	18 25.7	24 36.7	2 30.2	1 37.8	27 28.1	6 30.1	9 44.4	6 26.0	9 35.0
9 Tu	7 12 40	18 22 23	15 33 19	21 43 5	18D25.7	25 18.7	3 38.3	2 22.7	27 28.8	6 25.3	9 42.6	6 26.0	9 33.8
10 W	7 16 36	19 23 33	27 56 54	4♐15 10	18 25.7	26 5.5	4 46.2	3 7.5	27 29.3	6 20.5	9 40.8	6 25.9	9 32.5
11 Th	7 20 33	20 24 42	10♐38 13	17 6 16	18 25.9	26 56.7	5 53.9	3 52.4	27 29.7	6 15.8	9 39.0	6 25.8	9 31.2
12 F	7 24 29	21 25 51	23 39 29	0♑17 57	18 26.2	27 51.8	7 1.4	4 37.4	27R29.8	6 11.1	9 37.3	6 25.7	9 29.9
13 Sa	7 28 26	22 27 1	7♑ 1 35	13 50 16	18R26.4	28 50.3	8 8.8	5 22.4	27 29.8	6 6.4	9 35.6	6 25.5	9 28.6
14 Su	7 32 22	23 28 9	20 43 45	27 41 40	18 26.5	29 51.9	9 15.9	6 7.4	27 29.5	6 1.8	9 34.0	6 25.3	9 27.3
15 M	7 36 19	24 29 18	4♒43 36	11♒48 59	18 26.3	0♑56.3	10 22.8	6 52.4	27 29.1	5 57.2	9 32.4	6 25.1	9 25.9
16 Tu	7 40 15	25 30 26	18 57 16	26 7 49	18 25.7	2 3.2	11 29.5	7 37.6	27 28.4	5 52.7	9 30.8	6 24.8	9 24.6
17 W	7 44 12	26 31 33	3♓19 57	10♓33 1	18 24.9	3 12.4	12 35.9	8 22.7	27 27.6	5 48.2	9 29.3	6 24.5	9 23.2
18 Th	7 48 9	27 32 39	17 46 23	24 59 25	18 23.8	4 23.6	13 42.1	9 7.9	27 26.6	5 43.8	9 27.8	6 24.2	9 21.9
19 F	7 52 5	28 33 45	2♈11 35	9♈22 22	18 22.7	5 36.7	14 48.0	9 53.1	27 25.3	5 39.4	9 26.4	6 23.8	9 20.5
20 Sa	7 56 2	29 34 50	16 31 21	23 38 10	18 21.9	6 51.5	15 53.7	10 38.3	27 23.9	5 35.1	9 25.0	6 23.4	9 19.2
21 Su	7 59 58	0♒35 53	0♉42 31	7♉44 12	18D21.6	8 7.8	16 59.1	11 23.6	27 22.3	5 30.8	9 23.7	6 23.0	9 17.8
22 M	8 3 55	1 36 56	14 43 3	21 38 56	18 22.0	9 25.6	18 4.3	12 8.9	27 20.5	5 26.6	9 22.4	6 22.5	9 16.4
23 Tu	8 7 51	2 37 58	28 31 46	5♊21 32	18 22.8	10 44.6	19 9.1	12 54.3	27 18.5	5 22.5	9 21.1	6 22.0	9 15.0
24 W	8 11 48	3 38 58	12♊ 8 11	18 51 43	18 24.1	12 4.9	20 13.7	13 39.7	27 16.4	5 18.4	9 20.0	6 21.5	9 13.7
25 Th	8 15 44	4 39 58	25 32 6	2♋ 9 22	18 25.4	13 26.4	21 17.9	14 25.1	27 14.0	5 14.5	9 18.8	6 20.9	9 12.3
26 F	8 19 41	5 40 57	8♋43 29	15 14 28	18R26.3	14 48.9	22 21.8	15 10.6	27 11.5	5 10.5	9 17.7	6 20.4	9 10.9
27 Sa	8 23 38	6 41 55	21 42 18	28 7 0	18 26.5	16 12.4	23 25.4	15 56.1	27 8.8	5 6.7	9 16.6	6 19.7	9 9.5
28 Su	8 27 34	7 42 52	4♌28 36	10♌47 7	18 25.7	17 37.0	24 28.7	16 41.6	27 5.8	5 2.9	9 15.6	6 19.1	9 8.1
29 M	8 31 31	8 43 47	17 2 36	23 15 8	18 23.9	19 2.4	25 31.5	17 27.2	27 2.8	4 59.2	9 14.7	6 18.4	9 6.7
30 Tu	8 35 27	9 44 42	29 24 49	5♍31 50	18 21.0	20 28.7	26 34.1	18 12.8	26 59.5	4 55.6	9 13.8	6 17.7	9 5.3
31 W	8 39 24	10 45 36	11♍36 20	17 38 33	18 17.3	21 55.9	27 36.2	18 58.4	26 56.0	4 52.1	9 12.9	6 16.9	9 3.9

LONGITUDE — FEBRUARY 1945

Day	Sid.Time	☉	0 hr ☽	Noon ☽	True ☊	☿	♀	♂	♃	♄	♅	♆	♇
1 Th	8 43 20	11♒46 29	23♍38 47	29♍37 20	18♋13.2	23♑24.0	28♓38.0	19♑44.1	26♍52.4	4♋48.6	9♊12.1	6♎16.1	9♌ 2.5
2 F	8 47 17	12 47 21	5♎34 34	11♎30 54	18R 9.2	24 52.8	29 39.4	20 29.8	26R48.6	4R45.2	9R11.3	6R15.3	9R 1.2
3 Sa	8 51 13	13 48 12	17 26 47	23 22 43	18 5.8	26 22.5	0♈40.3	21 15.6	26 44.6	4 41.9	9 10.6	6 14.5	8 59.8
4 Su	8 55 10	14 49 2	29 19 14	5♏16 51	18 3.4	27 53.0	1 40.9	22 1.3	26 40.5	4 38.8	9 10.0	6 13.6	8 58.4
5 M	8 59 7	15 49 52	11♏16 12	17 17 50	18D 2.2	29 24.3	2 41.0	22 47.1	26 36.2	4 35.6	9 9.4	6 12.7	8 57.0
6 Tu	9 3 3	16 50 40	23 22 23	29 30 27	18 2.3	0♒56.4	3 40.6	23 33.0	26 31.7	4 32.6	9 8.8	6 11.8	8 55.6
7 W	9 7 0	17 51 28	5♐42 38	11♐59 28	18 3.5	2 29.2	4 39.8	24 18.9	26 27.0	4 29.7	9 8.3	6 10.9	8 54.2
8 Th	9 10 56	18 52 15	18 21 30	24 49 12	18 5.1	4 2.9	5 38.5	25 4.8	26 22.2	4 26.9	9 7.9	6 9.9	8 52.9
9 F	9 14 53	19 53 0	1♑22 56	8♑ 3 1	18 6.8	5 37.3	6 36.7	25 50.7	26 17.3	4 24.1	9 7.5	6 8.9	8 51.5
10 Sa	9 18 49	20 53 45	14 49 37	21 42 46	18R 7.7	7 12.6	7 34.4	26 36.7	26 12.1	4 21.5	9 7.1	6 7.9	8 50.1
11 Su	9 22 46	21 54 29	28 42 21	5♒48 6	18 7.3	8 48.6	8 31.6	27 22.7	26 6.9	4 19.0	9 6.8	6 6.8	8 48.8
12 M	9 26 42	22 55 11	12♒59 33	20 16 4	18 5.2	10 25.5	9 28.2	28 8.7	26 1.4	4 16.5	9 6.6	6 5.7	8 47.4
13 Tu	9 30 39	23 55 52	27 36 54	5♓ 1 5	18 1.4	12 3.2	10 24.3	28 54.8	25 55.9	4 14.2	9 6.4	6 4.6	8 46.1
14 W	9 34 36	24 56 31	12♓27 37	19 55 23	17 56.1	13 41.8	11 19.7	29 40.9	25 50.1	4 12.0	9 6.3	6 3.5	8 44.8
15 Th	9 38 32	25 57 9	27 23 17	4♈50 14	17 50.2	15 21.2	12 14.6	0♒27.0	25 44.3	4 9.8	9D 6.2	6 2.3	8 43.4
16 F	9 42 29	26 57 45	12♈15 12	19 37 16	17 44.4	17 1.5	13 8.8	1 13.1	25 38.3	4 7.8	9 6.2	6 1.2	8 42.1
17 Sa	9 46 25	27 58 19	26 55 41	4♉ 9 50	17 39.6	18 42.6	14 2.3	1 59.3	25 32.2	4 5.9	9 6.2	5 60.0	8 40.8
18 Su	9 50 22	28 58 52	11♉19 15	18 23 38	17 36.3	20 24.7	14 55.2	2 45.4	25 25.9	4 4.1	9 6.3	5 58.7	8 39.5
19 M	9 54 18	29 59 22	25 22 52	2♊16 54	17D34.9	22 7.6	15 47.3	3 31.6	25 19.6	4 2.3	9 6.4	5 57.5	8 38.2
20 Tu	9 58 15	0♓59 51	9♊ 5 50	15 49 51	17 35.1	23 51.5	16 38.7	4 17.9	25 13.1	4 0.7	9 6.6	5 56.2	8 36.9
21 W	10 2 11	2 0 18	22 29 12	29 4 8	17 36.3	25 36.4	17 29.3	5 4.1	25 6.5	3 59.3	9 6.9	5 54.9	8 35.7
22 Th	10 6 8	3 0 44	5♋34 59	12♋ 2 3	17R37.6	27 22.1	18 19.1	5 50.4	24 59.8	3 57.9	9 7.2	5 53.6	8 34.4
23 F	10 10 5	4 1 7	18 25 39	24 46 4	17 38.2	29 8.9	19 8.0	6 36.7	24 53.0	3 56.6	9 7.5	5 52.3	8 33.2
24 Sa	10 14 1	5 1 28	1♌ 3 34	7♌18 23	17 37.2	0♓56.6	19 56.1	7 23.0	24 46.1	3 55.4	9 7.9	5 50.9	8 32.0
25 Su	10 17 58	6 1 48	13 30 46	19 40 53	17 34.0	2 45.2	20 43.2	8 9.3	24 39.1	3 54.4	9 8.4	5 49.6	8 30.7
26 M	10 21 54	7 2 6	25 48 54	1♍54 59	17 28.4	4 34.8	21 29.4	8 55.6	24 32.0	3 53.4	9 8.9	5 48.2	8 29.5
27 Tu	10 25 51	8 2 21	7♍59 14	14 1 50	17 20.6	6 25.4	22 14.7	9 42.0	24 24.9	3 52.6	9 9.5	5 46.8	8 28.3
28 W	10 29 47	9 2 36	20 2 52	26 2 31	17 11.0	8 16.9	22 58.9	10 28.4	24 17.6	3 51.9	9 10.1	5 45.3	8 27.2

Astro Data Dy Hr Mn	Planet Ingress Dy Hr Mn	Last Aspect Dy Hr Mn	☽ Ingress Dy Hr Mn	Last Aspect Dy Hr Mn	☽ Ingress Dy Hr Mn	☽ Phases & Eclipses Dy Hr Mn
☿ D 2 12:45	♀ ♓ 5 19:18	2 11:59 ♂ △	♍ 2 16:49	1 10:57 ♀ ☍	♎ 1 12:46	6 12:47 ☽ 15♎52
☽0S 6 5:30	♂ ♑ 5 19:31	5 3:45 ♂ □	♎ 5 4:44	3 20:41 ☿ □	♏ 4 1:22	14 5:07 ● 23♑41
♆ R 7 16:34	☿ ♑ 14 3:04	7 5:27 ☿ ✶	♏ 7 17:13	6 6:09 ♃ ✶	♐ 6 12:57	14 5:01:15 ✔ A 0'15"
♄□♆ 8 20:35	☉ ♒ 20 9:54	9 23:07 ♃ ✶	♐ 10 3:55	8 14:45 ♃ □	♑ 8 21:29	20 23:48 ☽ 0♉35
♃ R 12 4:51		12 8:12 ☿ ☌	♑ 12 11:28	10 21:36 ♂ ☌	♒ 11 2:12	28 6:41 ○ 7♌60
☽0N 19 16:46	♀ ♈ 2 8:07	14 11:39 ♃ △	♒ 14 15:57	12 17:33 ☉ ☌	♓ 13 3:52	
	☿ ♒ 5 9:20	15 8:08 ♅ △	♓ 16 18:27	14 21:22 ♃ ☍	♈ 15 4:12	5 9:55 ☽ 16♏15
♀0N 1 0:24	♂ ♒ 14 9:58	18 17:29 ☉ ✶	♈ 18 20:21	17 1:51 ☉ ✶	♉ 17 5:05	12 17:33 ● 23♒40
☽0S 2 13:12	☉ ♓ 19 0:15	19 13:34 ♂ □	♉ 20 22:48	18 23:54 ♃ △	♊ 19 8:01	19 8:38 ☽ 0♊21
☽0N 15 23:32	☿ ♓ 23 11:25	22 21:52 ♃ △	♊ 23 2:35	21 6:33 ☿ △	♋ 21 13:42	27 0:07 ○ 8♍03
♅ D 15 23:25		25 3:04 ♃ □	♋ 25 8:05	23 12:07 ♃ ✶	♌ 23 21:58	
		27 10:08 ♃ ✶	♌ 27 15:33	25 14:58 ♀ △	♍ 26 8:13	
		28 9:05 ♅ ✶	♍ 30 1:09	28 8:25 ♃ ☌	♎ 28 19:57	

Astro Data

1 JANUARY 1945
Julian Day # 16437
Delta T 26.8 sec
SVP 06♓01'56"
Obliquity 23°26'44"
⚷ Chiron 3♎07.9
☽ Mean ☊ 18♋48.1

1 FEBRUARY 1945
Julian Day # 16468
Delta T 26.8 sec
SVP 06♓01'51"
Obliquity 23°26'45"
⚷ Chiron 3♎11.4R
☽ Mean ☊ 17♋09.6

MARCH 1945 — LONGITUDE

Day	Sid.Time	☉	0 hr ☽	Noon ☽	True ☊	☿	♀	♂	♃	♄	♅	♆	♇
1 Th	10 33 44	10♓ 2 48	2♎ 0 57	7♎58 21	17♋ 0.4	10♓ 9.3	23♈42.1	11♒14.8	24♍10.3	3♋51.3	9♊10.7	5♎43.9	8♌26.0
2 F	10 37 40	11 2 59	13 54 55	19 50 57	16R49.8	12 2.6	24 24.1	12 1.2	24R 2.9	3R50.8	9 11.4	5R42.4	8R24.9
3 Sa	10 41 37	12 3 8	25 46 44	1♏42 37	16 40.2	13 56.7	25 5.1	12 47.7	23 55.4	3 50.4	9 12.2	5 41.0	8 23.7
4 Su	10 45 33	13 3 15	7♏39 0	13 36 18	16 32.3	15 51.6	25 44.9	13 34.1	23 47.9	3 50.1	9 13.0	5 39.5	8 22.6
5 M	10 49 30	14 3 21	19 35 2	25 35 41	16 26.7	17 47.2	26 23.4	14 20.6	23 40.4	3D49.9	9 13.9	5 38.0	8 21.5
6 Tu	10 53 27	15 3 25	1♐38 50	7♐45 4	16 23.5	19 43.3	27 0.7	15 7.1	23 32.7	3 49.9	9 14.8	5 36.5	8 20.4
7 W	10 57 23	16 3 28	13 55 0	20 9 14	16D22.4	21 39.9	27 36.6	15 53.6	23 25.1	3 50.0	9 15.8	5 34.9	8 19.4
8 Th	11 1 20	17 3 29	26 28 25	2♑53 6	16 22.7	23 36.8	28 11.2	16 40.2	23 17.4	3 50.1	9 16.9	5 33.4	8 18.3
9 F	11 5 16	18 3 28	9♑23 53	16 1 13	16R23.4	25 33.8	28 44.4	17 26.7	23 9.6	3 50.4	9 17.9	5 31.8	8 17.3
10 Sa	11 9 13	19 3 26	22 45 31	29 37 4	16 23.4	27 30.8	29 16.1	18 13.3	23 1.9	3 50.8	9 19.1	5 30.3	8 16.3
11 Su	11 13 9	20 3 23	6♒35 59	13♒42 12	16 21.7	29 27.3	29 46.3	18 59.9	22 54.1	3 51.3	9 20.3	5 28.7	8 15.3
12 M	11 17 6	21 3 17	20 55 29	28 15 21	16 17.6	1♈23.3	0♉15.0	19 46.5	22 46.3	3 52.0	9 21.5	5 27.1	8 14.3
13 Tu	11 21 2	22 3 10	5♓41 5	13♓11 46	16 10.8	3 18.2	0 41.9	20 33.1	22 38.5	3 52.7	9 22.8	5 25.5	8 13.4
14 W	11 24 59	23 3 0	20 46 15	28 23 16	16 1.9	5 11.9	1 7.2	21 19.7	22 30.7	3 53.5	9 24.1	5 23.9	8 12.5
15 Th	11 28 56	24 2 49	6♈ 1 24	13♈39 14	15 51.6	7 3.8	1 30.7	22 6.3	22 22.9	3 54.5	9 25.5	5 22.3	8 11.5
16 F	11 32 52	25 2 36	21 15 22	28 48 28	15 41.4	8 53.7	1 52.4	22 52.9	22 15.1	3 55.6	9 26.9	5 20.7	8 10.7
17 Sa	11 36 49	26 2 20	6♉17 24	13♉41 12	15 32.4	10 40.9	2 12.2	23 39.6	22 7.3	3 56.8	9 28.4	5 19.1	8 9.8
18 Su	11 40 45	27 2 3	20 59 6	28 10 37	15 25.5	12 25.1	2 30.0	24 26.2	21 59.5	3 58.1	9 29.9	5 17.4	8 8.9
19 M	11 44 42	28 1 43	5♊15 25	12♊13 25	15 21.3	14 5.8	2 45.8	25 12.8	21 51.8	3 59.5	9 31.5	5 15.8	8 8.1
20 Tu	11 48 38	29 1 21	19 4 41	25 49 27	15D19.4	15 42.6	2 59.5	25 59.5	21 44.1	4 1.0	9 33.1	5 14.2	8 7.3
21 W	11 52 35	0♈ 0 57	2♋28 2	9♋ 0 51	15R19.1	17 14.9	3 11.1	26 46.1	21 36.4	4 2.6	9 34.8	5 12.5	8 6.5
22 Th	11 56 31	1 0 30	15 28 22	21 51 6	15 19.2	18 42.3	3 20.4	27 32.8	21 28.7	4 4.3	9 36.5	5 10.9	8 5.8
23 F	12 0 28	2 0 1	28 9 32	4♌24 12	15 18.6	20 4.4	3 27.5	28 19.4	21 21.2	4 6.2	9 38.3	5 9.2	8 5.0
24 Sa	12 4 25	2 59 30	10♌35 32	16 44 1	15 16.2	21 20.8	3 32.2	29 6.1	21 13.6	4 8.1	9 40.1	5 7.6	8 4.3
25 Su	12 8 21	3 58 56	22 50 4	28 54 2	15 11.2	22 31.2	3R34.6	29 52.8	21 6.2	4 10.2	9 41.9	5 5.9	8 3.6
26 M	12 12 18	4 58 20	4♍56 15	10♍57 2	15 3.2	23 35.2	3 34.5	0♓39.4	20 58.7	4 12.3	9 43.8	5 4.3	8 3.0
27 Tu	12 16 14	5 57 42	16 56 36	22 55 12	14 52.3	24 32.5	3 32.0	1 26.1	20 51.4	4 14.6	9 45.7	5 2.6	8 2.3
28 W	12 20 11	6 57 2	28 53 0	4♎50 11	14 39.3	25 23.0	3 27.0	2 12.7	20 44.1	4 17.0	9 47.7	5 0.9	8 1.7
29 Th	12 24 7	7 56 19	10♎46 55	16 43 20	14 25.0	26 6.4	3 19.5	2 59.4	20 36.9	4 19.4	9 49.8	4 59.3	8 1.1
30 F	12 28 4	8 55 35	22 39 36	28 35 55	14 10.5	26 42.7	3 9.5	3 46.1	20 29.8	4 22.0	9 51.8	4 57.6	8 0.5
31 Sa	12 32 0	9 54 49	4♏32 27	10♏29 26	13 57.2	27 11.6	2 57.1	4 32.7	20 22.8	4 24.7	9 53.9	4 56.0	7 60.0

APRIL 1945 — LONGITUDE

Day	Sid.Time	☉	0 hr ☽	Noon ☽	True ☊	☿	♀	♂	♃	♄	♅	♆	♇
1 Su	12 35 57	10♈54 1	16♏27 8	22♏25 51	13♋45.9	27♈33.2	2♉42.1	5♓19.4	20♍15.8	4♋27.5	9♊56.1	4♎54.3	7♌59.5
2 M	12 39 54	11 53 10	28 25 56	4♐27 45	13R37.4	27 47.6	2R24.8	6 6.1	20R 9.0	4 30.3	9 58.3	4R52.7	7R59.0
3 Tu	12 43 50	12 52 19	10♐31 45	16 38 25	13 31.7	27R54.7	2 5.0	6 52.7	20 2.3	4 33.3	10 0.5	4 51.0	7 58.5
4 W	12 47 47	13 51 25	22 48 14	29 1 48	13 28.8	27 54.8	1 43.0	7 39.4	19 55.6	4 36.4	10 2.8	4 49.4	7 58.0
5 Th	12 51 43	14 50 29	5♑19 38	11♑42 19	13 27.9	27 48.0	1 18.8	8 26.0	19 49.1	4 39.6	10 5.1	4 47.8	7 57.6
6 F	12 55 40	15 49 32	18 10 27	24 44 32	13 27.8	27 34.8	0 52.4	9 12.7	19 42.7	4 42.9	10 7.4	4 46.2	7 57.2
7 Sa	12 59 36	16 48 33	1♒25 3	8♒12 26	13 27.4	27 15.4	0 24.1	9 59.3	19 36.4	4 46.2	10 9.8	4 44.6	7 56.9
8 Su	13 3 33	17 47 33	15 6 57	22 8 45	13 25.4	26 50.5	29♈53.9	10 46.0	19 30.2	4 49.7	10 12.2	4 42.9	7 56.5
9 M	13 7 29	18 46 30	29 17 47	6♓33 50	13 21.1	26 20.5	29 22.1	11 32.6	19 24.1	4 53.2	10 14.7	4 41.3	7 56.2
10 Tu	13 11 26	19 45 26	13♓56 25	21 24 50	13 14.2	25 46.1	28 48.7	12 19.2	19 18.2	4 56.9	10 17.2	4 39.7	7 55.9
11 W	13 15 22	20 44 20	28 58 8	6♈35 9	13 4.9	25 8.0	28 14.1	13 5.8	19 12.4	5 0.7	10 19.7	4 38.2	7 55.6
12 Th	13 19 19	21 43 12	14♈14 34	21 54 56	12 54.0	24 27.1	27 38.4	13 52.4	19 6.7	5 4.5	10 22.3	4 36.6	7 55.4
13 F	13 23 16	22 42 2	29 34 46	7♉12 34	12 43.0	23 44.2	27 1.8	14 39.0	19 1.2	5 8.4	10 24.9	4 35.0	7 55.2
14 Sa	13 27 12	23 40 50	14♉47 0	22 16 49	12 33.2	22 60.0	26 24.5	15 25.6	18 55.8	5 12.4	10 27.6	4 33.5	7 55.0
15 Su	13 31 9	24 39 36	29 41 1	6♊58 48	12 25.4	22 15.5	25 46.9	16 12.1	18 50.6	5 16.6	10 30.2	4 31.9	7 54.8
16 M	13 35 5	25 38 19	14♊ 9 38	21 13 12	12 20.4	21 31.4	25 9.1	16 58.7	18 45.5	5 20.8	10 33.0	4 30.4	7 54.7
17 Tu	13 39 2	26 37 1	28 9 24	4♋58 19	12 17.9	20 48.6	24 31.4	17 45.2	18 40.6	5 25.1	10 35.7	4 28.9	7 54.6
18 W	13 42 58	27 35 41	11♋40 12	18 15 25	12D17.3	20 7.8	23 54.0	18 31.7	18 35.8	5 29.4	10 38.5	4 27.4	7 54.5
19 Th	13 46 55	28 34 18	24 44 25	1♌ 7 44	12R17.4	19 29.7	23 17.2	19 18.2	18 31.2	5 33.9	10 41.3	4 25.9	7 54.5
20 F	13 50 51	29 32 53	7♌25 57	13 39 39	12 17.2	18 54.7	22 41.3	20 4.6	18 26.8	5 38.4	10 44.1	4 24.5	7D54.5
21 Sa	13 54 48	0♉31 26	19 49 23	25 55 46	12 15.6	18 23.5	22 6.3	20 51.1	18 22.5	5 43.1	10 47.0	4 23.0	7 54.5
22 Su	13 58 45	1 29 56	1♍59 20	8♍ 0 35	12 11.7	17 56.5	21 32.7	21 37.5	18 18.3	5 47.8	10 49.9	4 21.6	7 54.5
23 M	14 2 41	2 28 25	14 0 1	19 58 4	12 5.1	17 33.8	21 0.5	22 23.9	18 14.4	5 52.6	10 52.8	4 20.1	7 54.5
24 Tu	14 6 38	3 26 51	25 55 6	1♎51 30	11 56.0	17 15.9	20 29.9	23 10.3	18 10.6	5 57.4	10 55.8	4 18.7	7 54.6
25 W	14 10 34	4 25 15	7♎47 33	13 43 31	11 44.9	17 2.7	20 1.1	23 56.7	18 6.9	6 2.4	10 58.7	4 17.3	7 54.7
26 Th	14 14 31	5 23 37	19 39 40	25 36 10	11 32.6	16 54.5	19 34.3	24 43.0	18 3.5	6 7.4	11 1.7	4 16.0	7 54.9
27 F	14 18 27	6 21 58	1♏33 14	7♏31 1	11 20.2	16D51.3	19 9.6	25 29.3	18 0.2	6 12.5	11 4.8	4 14.6	7 55.0
28 Sa	14 22 24	7 20 16	13 29 42	19 29 26	11 8.7	16 53.0	18 47.1	26 15.6	17 57.1	6 17.7	11 7.8	4 13.3	7 55.2
29 Su	14 26 20	8 18 33	25 30 25	1♐32 51	10 59.0	16 59.5	18 26.8	27 1.9	17 54.1	6 22.9	11 10.9	4 12.0	7 55.4
30 M	14 30 17	9 16 48	7♐36 56	13 42 55	10 51.8	17 10.9	18 8.9	27 48.2	17 51.4	6 28.3	11 14.0	4 10.7	7 55.7

Astro Data (Dy Hr Mn)	Planet Ingress (Dy Hr Mn)
☽0S 1 19:42	☿ ♈ 11 6:45
♄ D 5 22:43	♀ ♉ 11 11:17
♃∠♇ 7 20:34	☉ ♈ 20 23:37
☿0N 11 19:07	♂ ♓ 25 3:43
☽0N 15 8:55	
♀ R 25 11:24	♀ ♈ 7 19:15
☽0S 29 1:39	☉ ♉ 20 11:07
☿ R 3 12:12	
♄□♆ 6 16:00	
☽0N 11 19:57	
♇ D 20 10:21	
☽0S 25 7:55	
☿ D 27 3:46	

Last Aspect (Dy Hr Mn)	☽ Ingress (Dy Hr Mn)	Last Aspect (Dy Hr Mn)	☽ Ingress (Dy Hr Mn)
2 22:31 ♀ ☍	♏ 3 8:32	1 7:35 ♃ ⚹	♐ 2 3:08
5 8:05 ♃ ⚹	♐ 5 20:45	4 9:48 ☿ △	♑ 4 13:51
8 3:22 ♀ △	♑ 8 6:37	6 16:44 ☿ □	♒ 6 21:28
10 11:50 ♀ □	♒ 10 12:40	9 0:07 ♀ ⚹	♓ 9 1:10
11 22:00 ♂ ☌	♓ 12 14:50	10 8:34 ♃ ☍	♈ 11 1:38
14 3:51 ☉ ☌	♈ 14 14:32	12 20:09 ♀ ☌	♉ 13 0:40
16 2:43 ♂ ⚹	♉ 16 13:54	14 6:35 ♃ △	♊ 15 0:31
18 10:50 ☉ ⚹	♊ 18 15:04	16 21:07 ☉ ⚹	♋ 17 3:13
20 19:11 ☉ □	♋ 20 19:31	19 7:46 ☉ □	♌ 19 9:52
22 11:11 ♃ ⚹	♌ 23 3:32	21 4:16 ♀ △	♍ 21 20:03
24 23:19 ☿ △	♍ 25 14:11	23 18:04 ♂ ☍	♎ 24 8:15
27 7:46 ♃ ☌	♎ 28 2:15	25 23:50 ♀ ☍	♏ 26 20:52
30 8:34 ☿ ☍	♏ 30 14:50	29 3:14 ♂ △	♐ 29 8:56

☽ Phases & Eclipses (Dy Hr Mn)		Astro Data
7 4:30	☽ 16♐15	1 MARCH 1945
14 3:51	● 23♓13	Julian Day # 16496
20 19:11	☽ 29♊49	Delta T 26.9 sec
28 17:44	○ 7♎41	SVP 06♓01'48"
		Obliquity 23°26'45"
5 19:18	☽ 15♑38	⚷ Chiron 1♎45.9R
12 12:30	● 22♈14	☽ Mean ☊ 15♋40.7
19 7:46	☽ 28♋53	
27 10:33	○ 6♏48	1 APRIL 1945
		Julian Day # 16527
		Delta T 26.9 sec
		SVP 06♓01'45"
		Obliquity 23°26'45"
		⚷ Chiron 29♍22.9R
		☽ Mean ☊ 14♋02.2

LONGITUDE MAY 1945

Day	Sid.Time	☉	0 hr ☽	Noon ☽	True ☊	☿	♀	♂	♃	♄	♅	♆	♇
1 Tu	14 34 14	10♉15 2	19♐51 6	26♐ 1 48	10♋47.2	17♈27.0	17♈53.4	28♓34.4	17♍48.8	6♋33.7	11♊17.1	4♎ 9.4	7♌55.9
2 W	14 38 10	11 13 14	2♑15 21	8♑32 8	10D 45.0	17 47.6	17R 40.3	29 20.6	17R 46.4	6 39.1	11 20.3	4R 8.1	7 56.2
3 Th	14 42 7	12 11 24	14 52 35	21 17 7	10 44.7	18 12.6	17 29.7	0♈ 6.8	17 44.1	6 44.7	11 23.5	4 6.9	7 56.6
4 F	14 46 3	13 9 33	27 46 9	4♒20 8	10 45.4	18 41.9	17 21.5	0 52.9	17 42.1	6 50.3	11 26.7	4 5.7	7 56.9
5 Sa	14 50 0	14 7 41	10♒59 27	17 44 29	10R 46.1	19 15.3	17 15.8	1 39.1	17 40.2	6 56.0	11 29.9	4 4.5	7 57.3
6 Su	14 53 56	15 5 47	24 35 29	1♓32 38	10 45.7	19 52.7	17D 12.5	2 25.1	17 38.5	7 1.7	11 33.1	4 3.3	7 57.7
7 M	14 57 53	16 3 52	8♓36 1	15 45 31	10 43.6	20 33.8	17 11.6	3 11.2	17 37.0	7 7.5	11 36.4	4 2.2	7 58.1
8 Tu	15 1 49	17 1 55	23 0 52	0♈21 37	10 39.4	21 18.7	17 13.1	3 57.3	17 35.7	7 13.4	11 39.7	4 1.1	7 58.6
9 W	15 5 46	17 59 57	7♈47 5	15 16 27	10 33.2	22 7.0	17 16.9	4 43.3	17 34.5	7 19.3	11 43.0	3 60.0	7 59.0
10 Th	15 9 43	18 57 57	22 48 40	0♉22 35	10 25.8	22 58.8	17 22.9	5 29.2	17 33.6	7 25.3	11 46.3	3 58.9	7 59.5
11 F	15 13 39	19 55 57	7♉56 56	15 30 26	10 18.1	23 53.8	17 31.1	6 15.2	17 32.8	7 31.4	11 49.6	3 57.9	8 0.1
12 Sa	15 17 36	20 53 54	23 1 50	0♊29 54	10 11.1	24 51.9	17 41.5	7 1.1	17 32.2	7 37.5	11 53.0	3 56.8	8 0.6
13 Su	15 21 32	21 51 51	7♊53 35	15 11 59	10 5.7	25 53.1	17 54.0	7 47.0	17 31.8	7 43.7	11 56.3	3 55.8	8 1.2
14 M	15 25 29	22 49 45	22 24 23	29 30 15	10 2.4	26 57.3	18 8.5	8 32.8	17D 31.6	7 50.0	11 59.7	3 54.9	8 1.8
15 Tu	15 29 25	23 47 38	6♋29 17	13♋21 22	10D 1.1	28 4.2	18 25.0	9 18.6	17 31.5	7 56.3	12 3.1	3 53.9	8 2.4
16 W	15 33 22	24 45 30	20 6 31	26 44 57	10 1.4	29 14.0	18 43.3	10 4.3	17 31.7	8 2.6	12 6.5	3 53.0	8 3.1
17 Th	15 37 18	25 43 19	3♌16 57	9♌42 56	10 2.6	0♉26.4	19 3.5	10 50.0	17 32.0	8 9.0	12 9.9	3 52.1	8 3.8
18 F	15 41 15	26 41 7	16 3 24	22 18 53	10R 3.9	1 41.4	19 25.5	11 35.7	17 32.5	8 15.5	12 13.4	3 51.3	8 4.5
19 Sa	15 45 12	27 38 53	28 29 56	4♍37 8	10 4.3	2 59.1	19 49.2	12 21.3	17 33.2	8 22.0	12 16.8	3 50.4	8 5.2
20 Su	15 49 8	28 36 38	10♍41 6	16 42 24	10 3.5	4 19.2	20 14.5	13 6.9	17 34.0	8 28.6	12 20.3	3 49.6	8 6.0
21 M	15 53 5	29 34 21	22 41 36	28 39 14	10 0.9	5 41.9	20 41.4	13 52.4	17 35.1	8 35.2	12 23.7	3 48.8	8 6.8
22 Tu	15 57 1	0♊32 2	4♎35 49	10♎31 49	9 56.7	7 7.0	21 9.9	14 37.9	17 36.3	8 41.9	12 27.2	3 48.1	8 7.6
23 W	16 0 58	1 29 42	16 27 40	22 23 46	9 51.0	8 34.5	21 39.9	15 23.4	17 37.7	8 48.6	12 30.7	3 47.4	8 8.4
24 Th	16 4 54	2 27 20	28 20 29	4♏18 7	9 44.5	10 4.4	22 11.3	16 8.8	17 39.3	8 55.4	12 34.2	3 46.7	8 9.2
25 F	16 8 51	3 24 57	10♏16 58	16 17 17	9 37.9	11 36.7	22 44.0	16 54.1	17 41.0	9 2.2	12 37.7	3 46.0	8 10.1
26 Sa	16 12 47	4 22 33	22 19 15	28 23 6	9 31.7	13 11.3	23 18.1	17 39.5	17 43.0	9 9.0	12 41.2	3 45.4	8 11.0
27 Su	16 16 44	5 20 7	4♐28 59	10♐37 4	9 26.6	14 48.4	23 53.5	18 24.7	17 45.1	9 15.9	12 44.7	3 44.8	8 11.9
28 M	16 20 41	6 17 41	16 47 29	23 0 24	9 23.0	16 27.8	24 30.1	19 10.0	17 47.4	9 22.9	12 48.2	3 44.2	8 12.9
29 Tu	16 24 37	7 15 13	29 15 57	5♑34 18	9D 21.1	18 9.5	25 7.9	19 55.2	17 49.8	9 29.9	12 51.7	3 43.6	8 13.8
30 W	16 28 34	8 12 44	11♑55 36	18 20 2	9 20.7	19 53.6	25 46.8	20 40.3	17 52.4	9 36.9	12 55.3	3 43.1	8 14.8
31 Th	16 32 30	9 10 14	24 47 48	1♒19 4	9 21.4	21 40.0	26 26.8	21 25.4	17 55.2	9 44.0	12 58.8	3 42.6	8 15.8

LONGITUDE JUNE 1945

Day	Sid.Time	☉	0 hr ☽	Noon ☽	True ☊	☿	♀	♂	♃	♄	♅	♆	♇
1 F	16 36 27	10♊ 7 44	7♒54 4	14♒32 58	9♋22.9	23♉28.8	27♈ 7.9	22♈10.4	17♍58.2	9♋51.1	13♊ 2.3	3♎42.2	8♌16.9
2 Sa	16 40 23	11 5 12	21 15 57	28 3 11	9 24.4	25 19.8	27 50.0	22 55.4	18 1.3	9 58.2	13 5.9	3R 41.8	8 17.9
3 Su	16 44 20	12 2 40	4♓54 46	11♓50 47	9R 25.4	27 13.2	28 33.1	23 40.4	18 4.6	10 5.4	13 9.4	3 41.4	8 19.0
4 M	16 48 16	13 0 7	18 51 12	25 55 56	9 25.4	29 8.7	29 17.1	24 25.3	18 8.1	10 12.6	13 13.0	3 41.0	8 20.1
5 Tu	16 52 13	13 57 34	3♈ 4 46	10♈17 23	9 24.4	1♊ 6.5	0♉ 2.0	25 10.1	18 11.7	10 19.8	13 16.5	3 40.7	8 21.2
6 W	16 56 10	14 55 0	17 33 21	24 52 6	9 22.2	3 6.4	0 47.7	25 54.9	18 15.5	10 27.1	13 20.0	3 40.4	8 22.3
7 Th	17 0 6	15 52 25	2♉12 58	9♉35 11	9 19.4	5 8.3	1 34.3	26 39.6	18 19.5	10 34.4	13 23.6	3 40.1	8 23.5
8 F	17 4 3	16 49 50	16 57 53	24 20 10	9 16.4	7 12.0	2 21.7	27 24.3	18 23.6	10 41.8	13 27.1	3 39.9	8 24.7
9 Sa	17 7 59	17 47 14	1♊41 7	8♊59 49	9 13.7	9 17.6	3 9.8	28 8.9	18 27.9	10 49.2	13 30.6	3 39.7	8 25.9
10 Su	17 11 56	18 44 37	16 15 26	23 27 11	9 11.6	11 24.7	3 58.7	28 53.5	18 32.3	10 56.6	13 34.2	3 39.5	8 27.1
11 M	17 15 52	19 42 0	0♋34 22	7♋36 28	9D 10.5	13 33.3	4 48.3	29 38.0	18 36.9	11 4.0	13 37.7	3 39.4	8 28.3
12 Tu	17 19 49	20 39 22	14 33 3	21 23 51	9 10.4	15 43.0	5 38.5	0♉22.5	18 41.6	11 11.5	13 41.2	3 39.2	8 29.6
13 W	17 23 46	21 36 43	28 8 43	4♌47 38	9 11.1	17 53.7	6 29.4	1 6.8	18 46.5	11 19.0	13 44.8	3 39.2	8 30.9
14 Th	17 27 42	22 34 3	11♌20 43	17 48 11	9 12.3	20 5.1	7 20.9	1 51.2	18 51.6	11 26.5	13 48.3	3D 39.1	8 32.2
15 F	17 31 39	23 31 22	24 10 20	0♍27 33	9 13.6	22 16.9	8 13.0	2 35.4	18 56.8	11 34.0	13 51.8	3 39.1	8 33.5
16 Sa	17 35 35	24 28 41	6♍40 17	12 49 2	9 14.7	24 28.9	9 5.7	3 19.6	19 2.2	11 41.6	13 55.3	3 39.1	8 34.8
17 Su	17 39 32	25 25 58	18 54 19	24 56 42	9R 15.3	26 40.7	9 59.0	4 3.7	19 7.7	11 49.2	13 58.8	3 39.2	8 36.1
18 M	17 43 28	26 23 15	0♎56 45	6♎55 2	9 15.4	28 52.1	10 52.8	4 47.8	19 13.3	11 56.8	14 2.3	3 39.3	8 37.5
19 Tu	17 47 25	27 20 31	12 52 7	18 48 33	9 14.8	1♋ 2.8	11 47.1	5 31.8	19 19.1	12 4.4	14 5.7	3 39.4	8 38.9
20 W	17 51 21	28 17 46	24 44 53	0♏41 38	9 13.9	3 12.7	12 41.9	6 15.7	19 25.1	12 12.0	14 9.2	3 39.5	8 40.3
21 Th	17 55 18	29 15 0	6♏39 16	12 38 16	9 12.6	5 21.4	13 37.3	6 59.6	19 31.1	12 19.7	14 12.6	3 39.7	8 41.7
22 F	17 59 15	0♋12 14	18 39 1	24 41 55	9 11.3	7 28.8	14 33.1	7 43.4	19 37.4	12 27.4	14 16.1	3 39.9	8 43.1
23 Sa	18 3 11	1 9 28	0♐47 18	6♐55 26	9 10.2	9 34.7	15 29.3	8 27.1	19 43.7	12 35.0	14 19.5	3 40.2	8 44.5
24 Su	18 7 8	2 6 40	13 6 35	19 20 57	9 9.4	11 39.1	16 26.0	9 10.8	19 50.2	12 42.7	14 22.9	3 40.5	8 46.0
25 M	18 11 4	3 3 53	25 38 41	1♑59 54	9 8.9	13 41.6	17 23.2	9 54.4	19 56.8	12 50.5	14 26.3	3 40.8	8 47.5
26 Tu	18 15 1	4 1 5	8♑24 40	14 53 1	9D 8.7	15 42.4	18 20.7	10 37.9	20 3.6	12 58.2	14 29.7	3 41.1	8 48.9
27 W	18 18 57	4 58 17	21 24 57	28 0 27	9 8.8	17 41.2	19 18.7	11 21.4	20 10.5	13 5.9	14 33.1	3 41.5	8 50.4
28 Th	18 22 54	5 55 29	4♒39 25	11♒21 48	9 9.0	19 38.1	20 17.0	12 4.8	20 17.5	13 13.7	14 36.5	3 41.9	8 52.0
29 F	18 26 50	6 52 40	18 7 30	24 56 22	9 9.3	21 32.9	21 15.8	12 48.1	20 24.7	13 21.4	14 39.8	3 42.3	8 53.5
30 Sa	18 30 47	7 49 52	1♓48 16	8♓43 3	9 9.5	23 25.7	22 14.9	13 31.4	20 32.0	13 29.2	14 43.1	3 42.8	8 55.0

Astro Data	Planet Ingress	Last Aspect	☽ Ingress	Last Aspect	☽ Ingress	☽ Phases & Eclipses	Astro Data
Dy Hr Mn	Dy Hr Mn	Dy Hr Mn	Dy Hr Mn	Dy Hr Mn	Dy Hr Mn	Dy Hr Mn	1 MAY 1945
♂0N 6 16:35	♂ ♈ 2 20:29	1 18:02 ♂ □	♑ 1 19:40	2 12:15 ♀ ⚹	♓ 2 15:25	5 6:02 ☽ 14♒22	Julian Day # 16557
♀ D 6 21:03	☿ ♉ 16 15:21	3 6:30 ☿ □	♒ 4 4:06	3 22:46 ♃ ☍	♈ 4 18:51	11 20:21 ● 20♉45	Delta T 26.9 sec
☽0N 9 6:34	☉ ♊ 21 10:40	5 15:21 ☿ ⚹	♓ 6 9:21	6 14:27 ♂ ☌	♉ 6 20:23	18 22:12 ☽ 27♌35	SVP 06♓01'42"
♃ D 14 17:27		7 15:04 ♃ ☍	♈ 8 11:25	8 2:20 ♃ △	♊ 8 21:15	27 1:49 ○ 5♐24	Obliquity 23°26'45"
♄⊻♇ 16 2:00	☿ ♊ 4 10:30	10 0:17 ☿ ☌	♉ 10 11:24	10 22:19 ♂ ⚹	♋ 10 23:02		⚷ Chiron 27♍29.9R
☽0S 22 15:00	♀ ♉ 4 22:58	11 20:21 ☉ ☌	♊ 12 11:12	12 7:17 ♃ ⚹	♌ 13 3:20	3 13:15 ☽ 12♓34	☽ Mean ☊ 12♋26.8
	♂ ♉ 11 11:52	14 8:19 ☿ ⚹	♋ 14 12:51	14 22:40 ☉ ⚹	♍ 15 11:07	10 4:26 ● 18♊55	
☽0N 5 15:07	☿ ♋ 18 12:27	16 9:02 ☉ ⚹	♌ 16 17:57	17 18:55 ☿ □	♎ 17 22:06	17 14:05 ☽ 25♍60	1 JUNE 1945
♆ D 14 20:49	☉ ♋ 21 18:52	18 22:12 ☉ □	♍ 19 2:56	20 7:47 ☉ △	♏ 20 10:36	25 15:08 ○ 3♑40	Julian Day # 16588
☽0S 18 22:46		20 13:44 ♃ ☌	♎ 21 14:43	22 1:57 ♃ ⚹	♐ 22 22:27	25 15:14 ☍ P 0.859	Delta T 27.0 sec
		23 11:00 ♀ ☍	♏ 24 3:21	24 13:03 ♃ □	♑ 25 8:14		SVP 06♓01'37"
		25 14:49 ♃ ⚹	♐ 26 15:11	26 21:43 ♃ △	♒ 27 15:36		Obliquity 23°26'45"
		28 15:40 ♀ △	♑ 29 1:24	29 5:58 ♀ □	♓ 29 20:51		⚷ Chiron 26♍59.8
		31 3:13 ♀ □	♒ 31 9:35				☽ Mean ☊ 10♋48.3

JULY 1945 LONGITUDE

Day	Sid.Time	☉	0 hr ☽	Noon ☽	True ☊	☿	♀	♂	♃	♄	♅	♆	♇
1 Su	18 34 44	8♋47 4	15♓40 32	22♓40 33	9♋ 9.6	25♋16.4	23♉14.3	14♉14.6	20♍39.4	13♋37.0	14♊46.5	3♎43.3	8♌56.6
2 M	18 38 40	9 44 16	29 42 52	6♈47 15	9D 9.6	27 5.1	24 14.2	14 57.7	20 46.9	13 44.7	14 49.8	3 43.8	8 58.1
3 Tu	18 42 37	10 41 28	13♈53 26	21 1 7	9 9.6	28 51.7	25 14.3	15 40.7	20 54.5	13 52.5	14 53.0	3 44.4	8 59.7
4 W	18 46 33	11 38 40	28 10 0	5♉19 42	9 9.6	0♌36.1	26 14.8	16 23.7	21 2.3	14 0.3	14 56.3	3 45.0	9 1.3
5 Th	18 50 30	12 35 53	12♉29 49	19 39 56	9 9.8	2 18.5	27 15.6	17 6.6	21 10.2	14 8.1	14 59.5	3 45.6	9 2.9
6 F	18 54 26	13 33 6	26 49 35	3♊58 16	9 10.2	3 58.8	28 16.7	17 49.4	21 18.2	14 15.9	15 2.8	3 46.3	9 4.5
7 Sa	18 58 23	14 30 19	11♊ 5 31	18 10 48	9 10.7	5 37.0	29 18.1	18 32.2	21 26.4	14 23.7	15 6.0	3 47.0	9 6.1
8 Su	19 2 19	15 27 33	25 13 39	2♋13 33	9 11.0	7 13.0	0♊19.7	19 14.9	21 34.6	14 31.5	15 9.1	3 47.7	9 7.8
9 M	19 6 16	16 24 47	9♋10 6	16 2 53	9R 11.2	8 47.0	1 21.7	19 57.4	21 43.0	14 39.3	15 12.3	3 48.5	9 9.4
10 Tu	19 10 13	17 22 1	22 51 34	29 35 53	9 11.0	10 18.8	2 23.9	20 39.9	21 51.4	14 47.1	15 15.4	3 49.2	9 11.1
11 W	19 14 9	18 19 15	6♌15 37	12♌50 40	9 10.4	11 48.5	3 26.4	21 22.4	22 0.0	14 54.9	15 18.6	3 50.1	9 12.7
12 Th	19 18 6	19 16 29	19 21 0	25 46 39	9 9.3	13 16.1	4 29.1	22 4.7	22 8.7	15 2.7	15 21.6	3 50.9	9 14.4
13 F	19 22 2	20 13 44	2♍ 7 46	8♍24 32	9 7.9	14 41.4	5 32.0	22 46.9	22 17.5	15 10.5	15 24.7	3 51.8	9 16.1
14 Sa	19 25 59	21 10 58	14 37 14	20 46 14	9 6.3	16 4.6	6 35.3	23 29.1	22 26.4	15 18.2	15 27.7	3 52.7	9 17.8
15 Su	19 29 55	22 8 13	26 51 54	2♎54 43	9 4.9	17 25.5	7 38.7	24 11.2	22 35.5	15 26.0	15 30.8	3 53.6	9 19.5
16 M	19 33 52	23 5 27	8♎55 9	14 53 45	9 3.8	18 44.1	8 42.3	24 53.1	22 44.6	15 33.7	15 33.7	3 54.6	9 21.2
17 Tu	19 37 48	24 2 42	20 51 3	26 47 38	9D 3.3	20 0.3	9 46.2	25 35.0	22 53.8	15 41.5	15 36.7	3 55.6	9 22.9
18 W	19 41 45	24 59 57	2♏44 4	8♏40 57	9 3.5	21 14.2	10 50.3	26 16.8	23 3.1	15 49.2	15 39.6	3 56.6	9 24.6
19 Th	19 45 42	25 57 12	14 38 52	20 38 23	9 4.2	22 25.6	11 54.6	26 58.6	23 12.5	15 57.0	15 42.5	3 57.7	9 26.3
20 F	19 49 38	26 54 27	26 40 3	2♐44 22	9 5.5	23 34.5	12 59.1	27 40.2	23 22.0	16 4.7	15 45.4	3 58.7	9 28.0
21 Sa	19 53 35	27 51 43	8♐51 51	15 2 55	9 7.0	24 40.8	14 3.8	28 21.7	23 31.6	16 12.4	15 48.3	3 59.8	9 29.8
22 Su	19 57 31	28 48 59	21 17 58	27 37 19	9 8.3	25 44.4	15 8.8	29 3.2	23 41.3	16 20.0	15 51.1	4 1.0	9 31.5
23 M	20 1 28	29 46 16	4♑ 1 14	10♑29 52	9R 9.0	26 45.2	16 13.9	29 44.5	23 51.1	16 27.7	15 53.9	4 2.2	9 33.2
24 Tu	20 5 24	0♌43 32	17 3 20	23 41 37	9 8.9	27 43.1	17 19.2	0♊25.8	24 1.0	16 35.4	15 56.6	4 3.4	9 35.0
25 W	20 9 21	1 40 50	0♒24 39	7♒12 13	9 7.8	28 38.0	18 24.7	1 7.0	24 11.0	16 43.0	15 59.3	4 4.6	9 36.7
26 Th	20 13 17	2 38 8	14 4 5	20 59 52	9 5.5	29 29.7	19 30.3	1 48.1	24 21.0	16 50.6	16 2.0	4 5.8	9 38.5
27 F	20 17 14	3 35 27	27 59 10	5♓ 1 29	9 2.5	0♍18.2	20 36.2	2 29.1	24 31.2	16 58.2	16 4.7	4 7.1	9 40.2
28 Sa	20 21 11	4 32 46	12♓ 6 18	19 13 5	8 58.9	1 3.2	21 42.2	3 10.0	24 41.4	17 5.8	16 7.3	4 8.4	9 42.0
29 Su	20 25 7	5 30 7	26 21 16	3♈30 19	8 55.5	1 44.7	22 48.4	3 50.8	24 51.7	17 13.3	16 9.9	4 9.7	9 43.8
30 M	20 29 4	6 27 28	10♈39 42	17 48 58	8 52.7	2 22.4	23 54.8	4 31.5	25 2.1	17 20.8	16 12.5	4 11.1	9 45.5
31 Tu	20 33 0	7 24 51	24 57 41	2♉ 5 28	8D 50.9	2 56.2	25 1.4	5 12.1	25 12.6	17 28.3	16 15.0	4 12.5	9 47.3

AUGUST 1945 LONGITUDE

Day	Sid.Time	☉	0 hr ☽	Noon ☽	True ☊	☿	♀	♂	♃	♄	♅	♆	♇
1 W	20 36 57	8♌22 15	9♉11 59	16♉17 0	8♋50.3	3♍26.0	26♊ 8.1	5♊52.6	25♍23.1	17♋35.8	16♊17.5	4♎13.9	9♌49.0
2 Th	20 40 53	9 19 40	23 20 15	0♊21 34	8 50.9	3 51.4	27 15.0	6 33.0	25 33.8	17 43.3	16 19.9	4 15.3	9 50.8
3 F	20 44 50	10 17 6	7♊20 48	14 17 47	8 52.3	4 12.4	28 22.0	7 13.3	25 44.5	17 50.7	16 22.3	4 16.7	9 52.6
4 Sa	20 48 46	11 14 34	21 12 24	28 4 32	8 53.7	4 28.7	29 29.2	7 53.5	25 55.3	17 58.1	16 24.7	4 18.2	9 54.3
5 Su	20 52 43	12 12 2	4♋54 3	11♋40 49	8R 54.6	4 40.2	0♋36.5	8 33.6	26 6.1	18 5.5	16 27.1	4 19.7	9 56.1
6 M	20 56 40	13 9 32	18 24 42	25 5 33	8 54.3	4R 46.7	1 44.0	9 13.6	26 17.1	18 12.8	16 29.4	4 21.3	9 57.9
7 Tu	21 0 36	14 7 3	1♌43 15	8♌17 41	8 52.4	4 48.0	2 51.7	9 53.5	26 28.1	18 20.1	16 31.6	4 22.8	9 59.7
8 W	21 4 33	15 4 35	14 48 42	21 16 15	8 48.7	4 44.1	3 59.4	10 33.3	26 39.2	18 27.4	16 33.9	4 24.4	10 1.4
9 Th	21 8 29	16 2 9	27 40 16	4♍ 0 44	8 43.4	4 34.8	5 7.3	11 13.0	26 50.3	18 34.6	16 36.1	4 26.0	10 3.2
10 F	21 12 26	16 59 43	10♍17 40	16 31 10	8 37.0	4 20.1	6 15.4	11 52.5	27 1.5	18 41.9	16 38.2	4 27.6	10 4.9
11 Sa	21 16 22	17 57 18	22 41 23	28 48 29	8 30.1	3 60.0	7 23.5	12 31.9	27 12.8	18 49.0	16 40.3	4 29.3	10 6.7
12 Su	21 20 19	18 54 54	4♎52 45	10♎54 30	8 23.5	3 34.6	8 31.8	13 11.2	27 24.2	18 56.2	16 42.4	4 30.9	10 8.4
13 M	21 24 15	19 52 31	16 54 5	22 51 57	8 17.8	3 4.0	9 40.3	13 50.4	27 35.6	19 3.2	16 44.4	4 32.6	10 10.2
14 Tu	21 28 12	20 50 9	28 48 33	4♏44 25	8 13.6	2 28.7	10 48.8	14 29.5	27 47.0	19 10.3	16 46.4	4 34.3	10 11.9
15 W	21 32 9	21 47 48	10♏40 7	16 36 13	8 11.1	1 48.9	11 57.5	15 8.5	27 58.6	19 17.3	16 48.3	4 36.1	10 13.7
16 Th	21 36 5	22 45 28	22 33 20	28 32 5	8D 10.3	1 5.1	13 6.3	15 47.3	28 10.2	19 24.3	16 50.2	4 37.8	10 15.4
17 F	21 40 2	23 43 9	4♐33 7	10♐37 3	8 10.9	0 18.0	14 15.2	16 26.0	28 21.8	19 31.2	16 52.1	4 39.6	10 17.1
18 Sa	21 43 58	24 40 52	16 44 30	22 56 4	8 12.2	29♌28.4	15 24.2	17 4.6	28 33.5	19 38.1	16 53.9	4 41.4	10 18.9
19 Su	21 47 55	25 38 35	29 12 18	5♑33 40	8R 13.4	28 36.9	16 33.4	17 43.1	28 45.3	19 44.9	16 55.7	4 43.2	10 20.6
20 M	21 51 51	26 36 19	12♑ 0 36	18 33 26	8 13.6	27 44.7	17 42.6	18 21.5	28 57.1	19 51.7	16 57.4	4 45.0	10 22.3
21 Tu	21 55 48	27 34 5	25 12 23	1♒57 33	8 12.3	26 52.8	18 52.0	18 59.7	29 9.0	19 58.5	16 59.1	4 46.9	10 24.0
22 W	21 59 44	28 31 52	8♒48 52	15 46 8	8 8.8	26 2.0	20 1.5	19 37.8	29 20.9	20 5.2	17 0.7	4 48.7	10 25.7
23 Th	22 3 41	29 29 40	22 49 1	29 57 0	8 3.3	25 13.6	21 11.1	20 15.7	29 32.9	20 11.8	17 2.3	4 50.6	10 27.4
24 F	22 7 38	0♍27 30	7♓ 9 24	14♓25 27	7 56.1	24 28.6	22 20.9	20 53.6	29 44.9	20 18.4	17 3.8	4 52.5	10 29.1
25 Sa	22 11 34	1 25 21	21 44 16	29 4 54	7 47.9	23 48.0	23 30.7	21 31.3	29 56.9	20 25.0	17 5.3	4 54.4	10 30.8
26 Su	22 15 31	2 23 14	6♈26 24	13♈47 48	7 39.7	23 12.7	24 40.7	22 8.9	0♎ 9.0	20 31.5	17 6.8	4 56.4	10 32.4
27 M	22 19 27	3 21 8	21 8 21	28 26 49	7 32.6	22 43.5	25 50.7	22 46.3	0 21.2	20 37.9	17 8.2	4 58.3	10 34.1
28 Tu	22 23 24	4 19 4	5♉42 57	12♉56 2	7 27.4	22 21.1	27 0.9	23 23.7	0 33.4	20 44.3	17 9.5	5 0.3	10 35.7
29 W	22 27 20	5 17 2	20 5 39	27 11 30	7 24.4	22 6.1	28 11.2	24 0.8	0 45.6	20 50.6	17 10.8	5 2.2	10 37.4
30 Th	22 31 17	6 15 2	4♊13 24	11♊11 17	7D 23.4	21D 58.9	29 21.6	24 37.9	0 57.9	20 56.9	17 12.1	5 4.2	10 39.0
31 F	22 35 13	7 13 4	18 5 10	24 55 9	7 23.7	21 60.0	0♌32.1	25 14.8	1 10.2	21 3.2	17 13.3	5 6.3	10 40.6

Astro Data	Dy Hr Mn
☽0N	2 21:18
♄⊻♅	15 23:58
☽0S	16 6:41
♃∠♇	28 1:39
☽0N	30 2:28
☿ R	6 18:10
☽0S	12 14:08
☽0N	26 8:46
☿ D	30 9:02

Planet Ingress	Dy Hr Mn
☿ ♌	3 15:39
♀ ♊	7 16:20
☉ ♌	23 5:45
♂ ♊	23 8:59
☿ ♍	26 14:48
♀ ♋	4 10:59
☿ ♌	17 8:50
☉ ♍	23 12:35
♃ ♎	25 6:05
♀ ♌	30 13:05

Last Aspect Dy Hr Mn		☽ Ingress Dy Hr Mn
1 18:52	☿ △	♈ 2 0:29
3 1:41	♅ ✶	♉ 4 3:04
6 2:37	♀ ☌	♊ 6 5:20
7 17:43	♃ □	♋ 8 8:10
9 22:12	♃ ✶	♌ 10 12:43
12 5:22	♂ □	♍ 12 19:58
14 18:23	♂ △	♎ 15 6:13
17 7:01	☉ □	♏ 17 18:29
20 2:06	♂ ☍	♐ 20 6:36
22 9:11	☿ △	♑ 22 16:29
24 12:44	♃ △	♒ 24 23:16
26 10:14	♀ △	♓ 27 3:27
28 21:28	♃ ☍	♈ 29 6:07
31 0:07	♀ ✶	♉ 31 8:29

Last Aspect Dy Hr Mn		☽ Ingress Dy Hr Mn
2 3:51	♃ △	♊ 2 11:23
4 8:20	♃ □	♋ 4 15:23
6 14:21	♃ ✶	♌ 6 20:53
8 3:15	♅ ✶	♍ 9 4:24
11 9:00	♃ ☌	♎ 11 14:21
13 6:30	☉ ✶	♏ 14 2:24
16 11:27	♃ ✶	♐ 16 14:56
18 23:08	♃ □	♑ 19 1:31
21 7:08	♃ △	♒ 21 8:32
23 12:03	☉ ☍	♓ 23 12:05
25 3:09	♀ △	♈ 25 13:30
27 8:24	♀ □	♉ 27 14:33
29 14:56	♀ ✶	♊ 29 16:47
31 13:10	♂ ☌	♋ 31 21:00

☽ Phases & Eclipses Dy Hr Mn	
2 18:13	☽ 10♈28
9 13:35	● 16♋57
9 13:27:17	● T 1'16"
17 7:01	☽ 24♎19
25 2:25	○ 1♒47
31 22:30	☽ 8♉19
8 0:32	● 15♌06
16 0:27	☽ 22♏47
23 12:03	○ 29♒59
30 3:44	☽ 6♊24

Astro Data
1 JULY 1945
Julian Day # 16618
Delta T 27.0 sec
SVP 06♓01'32"
Obliquity 23°26'45"
⚷ Chiron 28♍12.0
☽ Mean ☊ 9♋13.0
1 AUGUST 1945
Julian Day # 16649
Delta T 27.1 sec
SVP 06♓01'27"
Obliquity 23°26'46"
⚷ Chiron 0♎58.0
☽ Mean ☊ 7♋34.6

LONGITUDE — SEPTEMBER 1945

Day	Sid.Time	☉	0 hr ☽	Noon ☽	True ☊	☿	♀	♂	♃	♄	♅	♆	♇
1 Sa	22 39 10	8♍11 8	1♋41 22	8♋23 57	7♋24.4	22♌ 9.4	1♌42.7	25♊51.5	1♎22.6	21♋ 9.3	17♊14.5	5♎ 8.3	10♌42.2
2 Su	22 43 7	9 9 14	15 3 6	21 38 58	7R 24.2	22 27.3	2 53.4	26 28.2	1 35.0	21 15.4	17 15.6	5 10.3	10 43.8
3 M	22 47 3	10 7 22	28 11 42	4♌41 27	7 22.3	22 53.6	4 4.2	27 4.6	1 47.5	21 21.5	17 16.6	5 12.4	10 45.4
4 Tu	22 51 0	11 5 31	11♌ 8 19	17 32 23	7 17.9	23 28.3	5 15.1	27 40.9	1 59.9	21 27.5	17 17.6	5 14.4	10 47.0
5 W	22 54 56	12 3 43	23 53 43	0♍12 22	7 10.8	24 11.1	6 26.1	28 17.1	2 12.5	21 33.4	17 18.6	5 16.5	10 48.5
6 Th	22 58 53	13 1 56	6♍28 23	12 41 46	7 1.1	25 1.8	7 37.2	28 53.1	2 25.0	21 39.2	17 19.5	5 18.6	10 50.1
7 F	23 2 49	14 0 11	18 52 35	25 0 54	6 49.5	25 59.9	8 48.4	29 28.9	2 37.6	21 45.0	17 20.4	5 20.7	10 51.6
8 Sa	23 6 46	14 58 27	1♎ 6 47	7♎10 21	6 37.1	27 5.2	9 59.6	0♋ 4.6	2 50.2	21 50.7	17 21.2	5 22.8	10 53.1
9 Su	23 10 42	15 56 46	13 11 47	19 11 15	6 24.8	28 17.0	11 11.0	0 40.1	3 2.8	21 56.4	17 22.0	5 24.9	10 54.6
10 M	23 14 39	16 55 6	25 9 1	1♏ 5 24	6 13.7	29 35.0	12 22.4	1 15.4	3 15.5	22 2.0	17 22.7	5 27.1	10 56.1
11 Tu	23 18 36	17 53 27	7♏ 0 45	12 55 29	6 4.7	0♍58.5	13 33.9	1 50.6	3 28.2	22 7.5	17 23.3	5 29.2	10 57.6
12 W	23 22 32	18 51 51	18 50 4	24 45 2	5 58.3	2 27.1	14 45.6	2 25.5	3 40.9	22 12.9	17 23.9	5 31.4	10 59.1
13 Th	23 26 29	19 50 16	0♐40 54	6♐38 19	5 54.5	4 0.1	15 57.3	3 0.4	3 53.7	22 18.3	17 24.5	5 33.5	11 0.5
14 F	23 30 25	20 48 42	12 37 52	18 40 15	5D 52.9	5 36.9	17 9.0	3 35.0	4 6.4	22 23.6	17 25.0	5 35.7	11 2.0
15 Sa	23 34 22	21 47 11	24 46 6	0♑56 7	5R 52.6	7 17.1	18 20.9	4 9.5	4 19.2	22 28.8	17 25.4	5 37.9	11 3.4
16 Su	23 38 18	22 45 40	7♑10 56	13 31 11	5 52.8	9 0.0	19 32.9	4 43.7	4 32.0	22 34.0	17 25.9	5 40.0	11 4.8
17 M	23 42 15	23 44 12	19 57 26	26 30 12	5 52.1	10 45.3	20 44.9	5 17.8	4 44.9	22 39.0	17 26.2	5 42.2	11 6.2
18 Tu	23 46 11	24 42 45	3♒ 9 52	9♒56 43	5 49.7	12 32.4	21 57.0	5 51.7	4 57.7	22 44.0	17 26.5	5 44.4	11 7.5
19 W	23 50 8	25 41 20	16 50 52	23 52 14	5 44.8	14 20.9	23 9.2	6 25.5	5 10.6	22 48.9	17 26.8	5 46.6	11 8.9
20 Th	23 54 4	26 39 56	1♓ 0 35	8♓15 25	5 37.3	16 10.5	24 21.4	6 59.0	5 23.5	22 53.8	17 26.9	5 48.8	11 10.2
21 F	23 58 1	27 38 35	15 36 3	23 1 36	5 27.5	18 0.8	25 33.8	7 32.3	5 36.3	22 58.5	17 27.1	5 51.1	11 11.5
22 Sa	0 1 58	28 37 15	0♈30 59	8♈ 2 59	5 16.4	19 51.6	26 46.2	8 5.5	5 49.3	23 3.2	17 27.2	5 53.3	11 12.8
23 Su	0 5 54	29 35 57	15 36 21	23 9 45	5 5.3	21 42.5	27 58.7	8 38.4	6 2.2	23 7.8	17R 27.2	5 55.5	11 14.1
24 M	0 9 51	0♎34 41	0♉41 55	8♉11 41	4 55.4	23 33.5	29 11.3	9 11.2	6 15.1	23 12.3	17 27.2	5 57.7	11 15.3
25 Tu	0 13 47	1 33 27	15 38 1	23 0 4	4 47.7	25 24.2	0♍23.9	9 43.7	6 28.0	23 16.7	17 27.1	5 59.9	11 16.6
26 W	0 17 44	2 32 16	0♊17 11	7♊28 52	4 42.7	27 14.6	1 36.6	10 16.1	6 41.0	23 21.0	17 27.0	6 2.2	11 17.8
27 Th	0 21 40	3 31 7	14 34 53	21 35 7	4 40.3	29 4.6	2 49.4	10 48.2	6 54.0	23 25.3	17 26.9	6 4.4	11 19.0
28 F	0 25 37	4 30 0	28 29 36	5♋18 30	4 39.7	0♎54.0	4 2.3	11 20.1	7 6.9	23 29.5	17 26.6	6 6.6	11 20.2
29 Sa	0 29 33	5 28 56	12♋ 2 4	18 40 37	4 39.6	2 42.8	5 15.3	11 51.8	7 19.9	23 33.5	17 26.4	6 8.9	11 21.3
30 Su	0 33 30	6 27 54	25 14 30	1♌44 5	4 38.9	4 30.9	6 28.3	12 23.2	7 32.9	23 37.5	17 26.1	6 11.1	11 22.5

LONGITUDE — OCTOBER 1945

Day	Sid.Time	☉	0 hr ☽	Noon ☽	True ☊	☿	♀	♂	♃	♄	♅	♆	♇
1 M	0 37 27	7♎26 54	8♌ 9 45	14♌31 52	4♋36.3	6♎18.3	7♍41.4	12♋54.5	7♎45.9	23♋41.4	17♊25.7	6♎13.3	11♌23.6
2 Tu	0 41 23	8 25 56	20 50 44	27 6 40	4R 31.0	8 4.9	8 54.5	13 25.4	7 58.8	23 45.2	17R 25.3	6 15.6	11 24.7
3 W	0 45 20	9 25 1	3♍19 56	9♍30 46	4 22.7	9 50.7	10 7.8	13 56.2	8 11.8	23 48.9	17 24.8	6 17.8	11 25.8
4 Th	0 49 16	10 24 8	15 39 22	21 45 54	4 11.6	11 35.7	11 21.1	14 26.7	8 24.8	23 52.6	17 24.3	6 20.0	11 26.8
5 F	0 53 13	11 23 17	27 50 32	3♎53 22	3 58.5	13 19.9	12 34.4	14 56.9	8 37.8	23 56.1	17 23.7	6 22.2	11 27.8
6 Sa	0 57 9	12 22 27	9♎54 33	15 54 12	3 44.2	15 3.3	13 47.8	15 26.9	8 50.8	23 59.5	17 23.0	6 24.5	11 28.8
7 Su	1 1 6	13 21 40	21 52 27	27 49 28	3 30.1	16 45.9	15 1.3	15 56.6	9 3.7	24 2.8	17 22.4	6 26.7	11 29.8
8 M	1 5 2	14 20 56	3♏45 26	9♏40 33	3 17.2	18 27.7	16 14.8	16 26.1	9 16.7	24 6.1	17 21.6	6 28.9	11 30.8
9 Tu	1 8 59	15 20 13	15 35 5	21 29 21	3 6.6	20 8.7	17 28.4	16 55.3	9 29.7	24 9.2	17 20.9	6 31.1	11 31.7
10 W	1 12 56	16 19 32	27 23 40	3♐18 27	2 58.8	21 49.0	18 42.1	17 24.2	9 42.6	24 12.2	17 20.0	6 33.3	11 32.6
11 Th	1 16 52	17 18 52	9♐14 9	15 11 14	2 53.9	23 28.4	19 55.8	17 52.8	9 55.6	24 15.1	17 19.1	6 35.5	11 33.5
12 F	1 20 49	18 18 15	21 10 17	27 11 51	2D 51.5	25 7.2	21 9.5	18 21.1	10 8.5	24 18.0	17 18.2	6 37.7	11 34.4
13 Sa	1 24 45	19 17 40	3♑16 33	9♑25 2	2 50.9	26 45.2	22 23.3	18 49.2	10 21.4	24 20.7	17 17.2	6 39.9	11 35.2
14 Su	1 28 42	20 17 6	15 37 56	21 55 54	2R 51.2	28 22.5	23 37.2	19 16.9	10 34.3	24 23.3	17 16.2	6 42.1	11 36.1
15 M	1 32 38	21 16 34	28 19 34	4♒49 31	2 51.0	29 59.1	24 51.1	19 44.4	10 47.2	24 25.9	17 15.2	6 44.3	11 36.9
16 Tu	1 36 35	22 16 4	11♒26 15	18 10 12	2 49.5	1♏35.1	26 5.0	20 11.5	11 0.1	24 28.3	17 14.0	6 46.5	11 37.6
17 W	1 40 31	23 15 36	25 1 40	2♓ 0 47	2 45.7	3 10.3	27 19.0	20 38.3	11 12.9	24 30.6	17 12.9	6 48.7	11 38.4
18 Th	1 44 28	24 15 9	9♓ 7 29	16 21 30	2 39.5	4 45.0	28 33.1	21 4.8	11 25.8	24 32.8	17 11.7	6 50.8	11 39.1
19 F	1 48 25	25 14 44	23 42 21	1♈ 9 17	2 31.1	6 19.0	29 47.2	21 31.0	11 38.6	24 34.9	17 10.4	6 53.0	11 39.8
20 Sa	1 52 21	26 14 21	8♈41 20	16 17 20	2 21.3	7 52.4	1♎ 1.3	21 56.9	11 51.4	24 36.9	17 9.1	6 55.1	11 40.4
21 Su	1 56 18	27 13 59	23 55 58	1♉35 47	2 11.3	9 25.2	2 15.5	22 22.4	12 4.1	24 38.8	17 7.8	6 57.2	11 41.1
22 M	2 0 14	28 13 40	9♉15 21	16 53 15	2 2.4	10 57.4	3 29.7	22 47.6	12 16.9	24 40.6	17 6.4	6 59.3	11 41.7
23 Tu	2 4 11	29 13 23	24 28 9	1♊58 54	1 55.4	12 29.0	4 44.0	23 12.4	12 29.6	24 42.3	17 4.9	7 1.4	11 42.3
24 W	2 8 7	0♏13 8	9♊24 31	16 44 16	1 51.0	14 0.1	5 58.4	23 36.9	12 42.3	24 43.8	17 3.5	7 3.5	11 42.8
25 Th	2 12 4	1 12 55	23 57 37	1♋ 4 15	1D 49.1	15 30.6	7 12.7	24 1.0	12 55.0	24 45.3	17 1.9	7 5.6	11 43.4
26 F	2 16 0	2 12 45	8♋ 4 3	14 57 4	1 48.9	17 0.5	8 27.2	24 24.7	13 7.6	24 46.6	17 0.4	7 7.7	11 43.9
27 Sa	2 19 57	3 12 36	21 43 29	28 23 37	1R 49.7	18 29.9	9 41.6	24 48.1	13 20.2	24 47.9	16 58.8	7 9.8	11 44.4
28 Su	2 23 54	4 12 30	4♌57 51	11♌26 37	1 50.1	19 58.7	10 56.1	25 11.1	13 32.8	24 49.0	16 57.1	7 11.8	11 44.8
29 M	2 27 50	5 12 26	17 50 23	24 9 39	1 49.2	21 26.9	12 10.7	25 33.6	13 45.3	24 50.0	16 55.5	7 13.8	11 45.3
30 Tu	2 31 47	6 12 24	0♍24 54	6♍36 36	1 46.3	22 54.5	13 25.3	25 55.8	13 57.8	24 51.0	16 53.7	7 15.9	11 45.7
31 W	2 35 43	7 12 25	12 45 11	18 51 4	1 40.9	24 21.6	14 39.9	26 17.5	14 10.3	24 51.7	16 52.0	7 17.9	11 46.0

Astro Data Dy Hr Mn	Planet Ingress Dy Hr Mn	Last Aspect Dy Hr Mn	☽ Ingress Dy Hr Mn	Last Aspect Dy Hr Mn	☽ Ingress Dy Hr Mn	☽ Phases & Eclipses Dy Hr Mn	Astro Data
♃0S 6 16:53	♂ ♋ 7 20:56	2 11:22 ♄ ☌	♌ 3 3:20	1 17:29 ♅ ✶	♍ 2 17:34	6 13:44 ● 13♍35	1 SEPTEMBER 1945
☽0S 8 20:55	☿ ♍ 10 7:21	5 8:45 ♂ ✶	♍ 5 11:36	4 16:14 ♄ ✶	♎ 5 4:17	14 17:38 ☽ 21♐32	Julian Day # 16680
☽0N 22 17:36	☉ ♎ 23 9:50	7 5:39 ♄ ✶	♎ 7 21:48	7 4:24 ♄ □	♏ 7 16:24	21 20:46 ○ 28♓29	Delta T 27.1 sec
♃☌♆ 22 9:00	♀ ♍ 24 16:06	9 17:40 ♄ □	♏ 10 9:48	9 17:29 ♄ △	♐ 10 5:17	28 11:24 ☽ 4♋58	SVP 06♓01'23"
♅ R 23 5:56	☿ ♎ 27 12:08	12 6:55 ♄ △	♐ 12 22:37	12 9:07 ☿ ✶	♑ 12 17:33		Obliquity 23°26'46"
☿0S 29 10:10		14 17:38 ☉ □	♑ 15 10:11	14 16:48 ♀ △	♒ 15 3:07	6 5:22 ● 12♎36	⚷ Chiron 4♎49.4
	☿ ♏ 15 0:13	17 7:31 ☉ △	♒ 17 18:20	16 20:41 ☉ △	♓ 17 8:34	14 9:38 ☽ 20♑41	☽ Mean ☊ 5♋56.1
☽0S 6 3:13	♀ ♎ 19 4:09	19 11:47 ♀ ☍	♓ 19 22:19	19 1:25 ♄ △	♈ 19 10:09	21 5:32 ○ 27♈28	
♃✶♇ 19 2:22	☉ ♏ 23 18:44	21 20:46 ☉ ☍	♈ 21 23:11	21 5:32 ☉ ☍	♉ 21 9:30	27 22:30 ☽ 4♌09	1 OCTOBER 1945
☽0N 20 4:36		23 21:23 ♀ △	♉ 23 22:53	23 0:22 ♄ ✶	♊ 23 8:49		Julian Day # 16710
♀0S 22 1:54		25 18:15 ♀ △	♊ 25 23:32	24 12:30 ♅ ☌	♋ 25 10:11		Delta T 27.2 sec
		27 4:53 ♅ ☌	♋ 28 2:38	27 5:41 ♂ ☌	♌ 27 14:55		SVP 06♓01'20"
		29 21:01 ♄ ☌	♌ 30 8:47	29 7:44 ☿ □	♍ 29 23:12		Obliquity 23°26'47"
							⚷ Chiron 9♎06.0
							☽ Mean ☊ 4♋20.7

NOVEMBER 1945 LONGITUDE

Day	Sid.Time	☉	0 hr ☽	Noon ☽	True ☊	☿	♀	♂	♃	♄	♅	♆	♇
1 Th	2 39 40	8♏12 27	24♍54 39	0♎56 16	1♋33.3	25♏48.0	15♎54.5	26♋38.8	14♎22.7	24♋52.4	16♊50.2	7♎19.8	11♌46.4
2 F	2 43 36	9 12 31	6♎56 14	12 54 50	1R 23.9	27 13.7	17 9.2	26 59.7	14 35.1	24 53.0	16R48.3	7 21.8	11 46.7
3 Sa	2 47 33	10 12 38	18 52 18	24 48 53	1 13.6	28 38.8	18 24.0	27 20.1	14 47.5	24 53.5	16 46.5	7 23.8	11 47.0
4 Su	2 51 29	11 12 46	0♏44 46	6♏40 9	1 3.4	0♐ 3.1	19 38.7	27 40.0	14 59.8	24 53.8	16 44.6	7 25.7	11 47.3
5 M	2 55 26	12 12 56	12 35 14	18 30 13	0 54.1	1 26.7	20 53.5	27 59.5	15 12.1	24 54.0	16 42.6	7 27.6	11 47.5
6 Tu	2 59 22	13 13 9	24 25 18	0♐20 43	0 46.5	2 49.4	22 8.4	28 18.5	15 24.3	24R54.1	16 40.6	7 29.5	11 47.7
7 W	3 3 19	14 13 22	6♐16 42	12 13 33	0 41.1	4 11.2	23 23.2	28 37.0	15 36.5	24 54.1	16 38.6	7 31.4	11 47.9
8 Th	3 7 16	15 13 38	18 11 33	24 11 5	0 38.0	5 32.0	24 38.1	28 55.0	15 48.6	24 54.0	16 36.6	7 33.3	11 48.1
9 F	3 11 12	16 13 55	0♑12 30	6♑16 14	0D 37.1	6 51.7	25 53.0	29 12.5	16 0.7	24 53.8	16 34.5	7 35.1	11 48.2
10 Sa	3 15 9	17 14 14	12 22 45	18 32 32	0 37.7	8 10.2	27 7.9	29 29.5	16 12.7	24 53.5	16 32.4	7 37.0	11 48.3
11 Su	3 19 5	18 14 34	24 46 5	1♒ 3 56	0 39.1	9 27.4	28 22.9	29 46.0	16 24.7	24 53.0	16 30.3	7 38.8	11 48.4
12 M	3 23 2	19 14 56	7♒26 37	13 54 38	0R 40.6	10 43.0	29 37.9	0♌ 1.9	16 36.6	24 52.5	16 28.1	7 40.6	11 48.4
13 Tu	3 26 58	20 15 19	20 28 29	27 8 35	0 41.2	11 57.0	0♏52.9	0 17.3	16 48.5	24 51.8	16 25.9	7 42.3	11R48.4
14 W	3 30 55	21 15 43	3♓55 17	10♓48 50	0 40.4	13 9.1	2 7.9	0 32.1	17 0.3	24 51.0	16 23.7	7 44.1	11 48.4
15 Th	3 34 52	22 16 9	17 49 19	24 56 42	0 37.8	14 19.1	3 22.9	0 46.3	17 12.1	24 50.1	16 21.5	7 45.8	11 48.4
16 F	3 38 48	23 16 36	2♈10 45	9♈31 1	0 33.8	15 26.7	4 38.0	1 0.0	17 23.7	24 49.1	16 19.2	7 47.5	11 48.3
17 Sa	3 42 45	24 17 4	16 56 50	24 27 23	0 28.6	16 31.6	5 53.1	1 13.1	17 35.4	24 48.0	16 16.9	7 49.2	11 48.2
18 Su	3 46 41	25 17 34	2♉ 1 37	9♉38 21	0 23.2	17 33.5	7 8.2	1 25.6	17 46.9	24 46.8	16 14.6	7 50.8	11 48.1
19 M	3 50 38	26 18 5	17 16 16	24 54 3	0 18.2	18 31.8	8 23.3	1 37.4	17 58.4	24 45.4	16 12.2	7 52.5	11 47.9
20 Tu	3 54 34	27 18 37	2♊30 22	10♊ 3 55	0 14.5	19 26.3	9 38.5	1 48.7	18 9.9	24 44.0	16 9.9	7 54.1	11 47.8
21 W	3 58 31	28 19 12	17 33 35	24 58 21	0D 12.3	20 16.4	10 53.6	1 59.3	18 21.2	24 42.5	16 7.5	7 55.7	11 47.6
22 Th	4 2 27	29 19 47	2♋17 25	9♋30 10	0 11.8	21 1.4	12 8.8	2 9.3	18 32.5	24 40.8	16 5.1	7 57.2	11 47.3
23 F	4 6 24	0♐20 25	16 36 11	23 35 14	0 12.6	21 40.8	13 24.0	2 18.6	18 43.8	24 39.0	16 2.7	7 58.8	11 47.1
24 Sa	4 10 21	1 21 4	0♌27 18	7♌12 28	0 14.1	22 13.9	14 39.2	2 27.2	18 54.9	24 37.2	16 0.3	8 0.3	11 46.8
25 Su	4 14 17	2 21 44	13 50 58	20 23 8	0 15.7	22 39.8	15 54.5	2 35.1	19 6.0	24 35.2	15 57.8	8 1.8	11 46.5
26 M	4 18 14	3 22 26	26 49 24	3♍10 15	0R 16.7	22 57.9	17 9.7	2 42.4	19 17.0	24 33.1	15 55.4	8 3.2	11 46.1
27 Tu	4 22 10	4 23 10	9♍26 11	15 37 44	0 16.8	23R 7.3	18 25.0	2 48.9	19 28.0	24 30.9	15 52.9	8 4.6	11 45.8
28 W	4 26 7	5 23 55	21 45 28	27 49 54	0 15.7	23 7.3	19 40.3	2 54.7	19 38.8	24 28.6	15 50.4	8 6.1	11 45.4
29 Th	4 30 3	6 24 42	3♎51 35	9♎51 0	0 13.4	22 57.1	20 55.6	2 59.7	19 49.6	24 26.3	15 47.9	8 7.4	11 45.0
30 F	4 34 0	7 25 30	15 48 40	21 45 0	0 10.2	22 36.3	22 10.9	3 4.0	20 0.3	24 23.8	15 45.4	8 8.8	11 44.5

DECEMBER 1945 LONGITUDE

Day	Sid.Time	☉	0 hr ☽	Noon ☽	True ☊	☿	♀	♂	♃	♄	♅	♆	♇
1 Sa	4 37 56	8♐26 20	27♎40 26	3♏35 22	0♋ 6.4	22♐ 4.3	23♏26.3	3♌ 7.5	20♎10.9	24♋21.2	15♊42.9	8♎10.1	11♌44.0
2 Su	4 41 53	9 27 11	9♏30 8	15 25 4	0R 2.7	21R21.4	24 41.6	3 10.3	20 21.4	24R18.5	15R40.4	8 11.4	11R43.5
3 M	4 45 50	10 28 3	21 20 27	27 16 34	29♊59.3	20 27.7	25 57.0	3 12.2	20 31.8	24 15.7	15 37.8	8 12.7	11 43.0
4 Tu	4 49 46	11 28 57	3♐13 40	9♐11 57	29 56.7	19 24.4	27 12.4	3R13.4	20 42.2	24 12.8	15 35.3	8 13.9	11 42.5
5 W	4 53 43	12 29 52	15 11 40	21 13 1	29 55.0	18 12.7	28 27.7	3 13.8	20 52.4	24 9.9	15 32.7	8 15.1	11 41.9
6 Th	4 57 39	13 30 47	27 16 12	3♑21 27	29D 54.3	16 54.8	29 43.1	3 13.3	21 2.6	24 6.8	15 30.2	8 16.3	11 41.3
7 F	5 1 36	14 31 44	9♑28 59	15 39 1	29 54.6	15 32.9	0♐58.5	3 12.1	21 12.7	24 3.6	15 27.6	8 17.4	11 40.7
8 Sa	5 5 32	15 32 42	21 51 49	28 7 38	29 55.4	14 10.0	2 13.9	3 10.0	21 22.7	24 0.4	15 25.1	8 18.6	11 40.0
9 Su	5 9 29	16 33 40	4♒26 45	10♒49 27	29 56.7	12 48.7	3 29.4	3 7.0	21 32.5	23 57.1	15 22.5	8 19.7	11 39.3
10 M	5 13 25	17 34 39	17 16 1	23 46 44	29 57.9	11 31.7	4 44.8	3 3.3	21 42.3	23 53.7	15 20.0	8 20.7	11 38.7
11 Tu	5 17 22	18 35 39	0♓21 55	7♓ 1 48	29 58.7	10 21.5	6 0.2	2 58.7	21 52.0	23 50.1	15 17.4	8 21.7	11 37.9
12 W	5 21 19	19 36 39	13 46 37	20 36 31	29R 59.3	9 20.0	7 15.6	2 53.3	22 1.5	23 46.6	15 14.9	8 22.7	11 37.2
13 Th	5 25 15	20 37 39	27 31 38	4♈31 58	29 59.3	8 28.5	8 31.0	2 47.0	22 11.0	23 42.9	15 12.4	8 23.7	11 36.4
14 F	5 29 12	21 38 41	11♈37 26	18 47 50	29 58.9	7 47.8	9 46.5	2 39.9	22 20.3	23 39.2	15 9.8	8 24.6	11 35.6
15 Sa	5 33 8	22 39 42	26 2 49	3♉21 54	29 58.1	7 18.2	11 1.9	2 31.9	22 29.6	23 35.3	15 7.3	8 25.5	11 34.8
16 Su	5 37 5	23 40 44	10♉44 29	18 9 49	29 57.4	6 59.7	12 17.4	2 23.1	22 38.7	23 31.5	15 4.8	8 26.4	11 34.0
17 M	5 41 1	24 41 46	25 37 3	3♊ 5 12	29 56.7	6D 52.0	13 32.8	2 13.5	22 47.7	23 27.5	15 2.3	8 27.2	11 33.1
18 Tu	5 44 58	25 42 49	10♊33 18	18 0 18	29 56.3	6 54.4	14 48.2	2 3.1	22 56.7	23 23.5	14 59.8	8 28.0	11 32.2
19 W	5 48 54	26 43 53	25 25 10	2♋46 56	29D 56.1	7 6.1	16 3.7	1 51.8	23 5.5	23 19.4	14 57.3	8 28.8	11 31.3
20 Th	5 52 51	27 44 57	10♋ 4 43	17 17 46	29 56.2	7 26.4	17 19.1	1 39.8	23 14.1	23 15.2	14 54.8	8 29.5	11 30.4
21 F	5 56 48	28 46 2	24 25 24	1♌27 10	29 56.3	7 54.5	18 34.6	1 26.9	23 22.7	23 11.0	14 52.4	8 30.2	11 29.5
22 Sa	6 0 44	29 47 7	8♌22 42	15 11 50	29R 56.3	8 29.6	19 50.1	1 13.2	23 31.1	23 6.7	14 49.9	8 30.9	11 28.5
23 Su	6 4 41	0♑48 13	21 54 30	28 30 50	29 56.3	9 11.0	21 5.5	0 58.8	23 39.5	23 2.4	14 47.5	8 31.6	11 27.5
24 M	6 8 37	1 49 20	5♍ 1 1	11♍25 21	29 56.1	9 57.9	22 21.0	0 43.6	23 47.7	22 58.0	14 45.1	8 32.2	11 26.5
25 Tu	6 12 34	2 50 27	17 44 16	23 58 13	29 55.9	10 49.7	23 36.5	0 27.6	23 55.7	22 53.5	14 42.7	8 32.7	11 25.5
26 W	6 16 30	3 51 34	0♎ 7 43	6♎13 19	29D 55.8	11 45.9	24 52.0	0 10.9	24 3.7	22 49.0	14 40.3	8 33.3	11 24.5
27 Th	6 20 27	4 52 42	12 15 36	18 15 10	29 55.8	12 45.9	26 7.4	29♋53.4	24 11.5	22 44.5	14 38.0	8 33.8	11 23.4
28 F	6 24 23	5 53 51	24 12 36	0♏ 8 30	29 56.1	13 49.3	27 22.9	29 35.3	24 19.2	22 39.9	14 35.6	8 34.2	11 22.3
29 Sa	6 28 20	6 55 0	6♏ 3 25	11 57 55	29 56.8	14 55.7	28 38.4	29 16.6	24 26.7	22 35.3	14 33.3	8 34.7	11 21.2
30 Su	6 32 17	7 56 10	17 52 32	23 47 44	29 57.6	16 4.7	29 53.9	28 57.1	24 34.1	22 30.6	14 31.0	8 35.1	11 20.1
31 M	6 36 13	8 57 20	29 44 0	5♐41 44	29 58.6	17 16.1	1♑ 9.4	28 37.1	24 41.4	22 25.9	14 28.7	8 35.4	11 19.0

Astro Data	Dy Hr Mn
☽0S	2 9:30
♄ R	6 13:02
♃△♅	11 9:29
♇ R	13 1:54
☽0N	16 15:46
☿ R	27 12:00
☽0S	29 16:13
♂ R	4 22:49
☽0N	14 0:42
☿ D	17 6:11
♃□♄	20 2:04
☽0S	26 23:36

Planet Ingress	Dy Hr Mn
☿ ♐	3 23:06
♂ ♌	11 21:05
♀ ♏	12 7:05
☉ ♐	22 15:55
☊ ♊	2 18:34
♀ ♐	6 5:22
☉ ♑	22 5:04
♂ ♋	26 15:04
♀ ♑	30 1:56

Last Aspect Dy Hr Mn	☽ Ingress Dy Hr Mn
1 3:33 ♂ ✶	♎ 1 10:08
3 17:35 ♂ □	♏ 3 22:29
6 8:05 ♂ △	♐ 6 11:18
8 14:24 ♀ ✶	♑ 8 23:35
11 9:45 ♂ ☍	♒ 11 9:59
12 23:34 ☉ □	♓ 13 17:05
15 11:48 ♄ △	♈ 15 20:24
17 12:32 ♄ □	♉ 17 20:48
19 15:13 ☉ ☍	♊ 19 20:02
21 4:37 ♂ ☍	♋ 21 20:14
23 13:49 ♄ ☌	♌ 23 23:12
25 16:39 ☿ △	♍ 26 5:59
28 5:21 ♄ ✶	♎ 28 16:18

Last Aspect Dy Hr Mn	☽ Ingress Dy Hr Mn
30 17:18 ♄ □	♏ 1 4:43
3 10:25 ♀ ☌	♐ 3 17:30
5 11:29 ♃ ✶	♑ 6 5:23
8 4:06 ♄ ☍	♒ 8 15:34
10 8:18 ♃ △	♓ 10 23:20
12 17:26 ♄ △	♈ 13 4:15
14 19:58 ♄ □	♉ 15 6:30
16 20:33 ♄ ✶	♊ 17 7:03
19 2:17 ☉ ☍	♋ 19 7:27
20 22:13 ♃ □	♌ 21 9:30
23 3:12 ♃ ✶	♍ 23 14:44
25 12:35 ♀ □	♎ 25 23:45
28 10:36 ♂ □	♏ 28 11:43
30 21:49 ♂ △	♐ 31 0:32

☽ Phases & Eclipses Dy Hr Mn	
4 23:11	● 12♏11
12 23:34	☽ 20♒14
19 15:13	○ 26♉56
26 13:28	☽ 3♍57
4 18:07	● 12♐15
12 11:05	☽ 20♓05
19 2:17	○ 26♊50
19 2:20	T 1.343
26 8:00	☽ 4♎12

Astro Data

1 NOVEMBER 1945
Julian Day # 16741
Delta T 27.2 sec
SVP 06♓01'17"
Obliquity 23°26'47"
⚷ Chiron 13♋33.2
☽ Mean ☊ 2♋42.2

1 DECEMBER 1945
Julian Day # 16771
Delta T 27.2 sec
SVP 06♓01'12"
Obliquity 23°26'46"
⚷ Chiron 17♋21.3
☽ Mean ☊ 1♋06.9

LONGITUDE — JANUARY 1946

Day	Sid.Time	☉	0 hr ☽	Noon ☽	True ☊	☿	♀	♂	♃	♄	♅	♆	♇
1 Tu	6 40 10	9♑58 31	11♐41 20	17♐43 7	29♊59.4	18♐29.6	2♑24.9	28♋16.6	24♎48.5	22♋21.1	14♊26.5	8♎35.8	11♌17.8
2 W	6 44 6	10 59 41	23 47 22	29 54 22	29R 60.0	19 44.9	3 40.4	27R 55.5	24 55.5	22R 16.3	14R 24.3	8 36.1	11R 16.7
3 Th	6 48 3	12 0 52	6♑ 4 17	12♑17 18	29 60.0	21 1.8	4 55.9	27 33.9	25 2.4	22 11.5	14 22.1	8 36.3	11 15.5
4 F	6 51 59	13 2 3	18 33 32	24 53 4	29 59.3	22 20.3	6 11.4	27 11.8	25 9.1	22 6.7	14 20.0	8 36.6	11 14.3
5 Sa	6 55 56	14 3 14	1♒15 57	7♒42 13	29 57.9	23 40.0	7 26.9	26 49.4	25 15.7	22 1.8	14 17.8	8 36.8	11 13.1
6 Su	6 59 53	15 4 24	14 11 52	20 44 53	29 55.9	25 1.0	8 42.4	26 26.6	25 22.1	21 56.9	14 15.7	8 36.9	11 11.9
7 M	7 3 49	16 5 34	27 21 14	4♓ 0 53	29 53.5	26 23.1	9 57.8	26 3.4	25 28.4	21 52.0	14 13.7	8 37.1	11 10.7
8 Tu	7 7 46	17 6 44	10♓43 47	17 29 53	29 51.1	27 46.1	11 13.3	25 40.0	25 34.5	21 47.1	14 11.6	8 37.1	11 9.4
9 W	7 11 42	18 7 54	24 19 8	1♈11 27	29 49.1	29 10.1	12 28.8	25 16.4	25 40.4	21 42.2	14 9.6	8 37.2	11 8.1
10 Th	7 15 39	19 9 2	8♈ 6 46	15 5 0	29D 47.8	0♑34.9	13 44.3	24 52.6	25 46.2	21 37.2	14 7.7	8R 37.2	11 6.9
11 F	7 19 35	20 10 11	22 6 1	29 9 41	29 47.5	2 0.5	14 59.7	24 28.6	25 51.9	21 32.3	14 5.7	8 37.2	11 5.6
12 Sa	7 23 32	21 11 18	6♉15 48	13♉24 9	29 48.1	3 26.8	16 15.2	24 4.6	25 57.4	21 27.3	14 3.8	8 37.2	11 4.3
13 Su	7 27 28	22 12 25	20 34 27	27 46 19	29 49.3	4 53.9	17 30.6	23 40.6	26 2.7	21 22.4	14 2.0	8 37.1	11 3.0
14 M	7 31 25	23 13 32	4♊59 22	12♊13 5	29 50.8	6 21.6	18 46.1	23 16.6	26 7.9	21 17.4	14 0.2	8 37.0	11 1.7
15 Tu	7 35 22	24 14 38	19 26 57	26 40 22	29R 52.0	7 49.9	20 1.5	22 52.6	26 12.9	21 12.5	13 58.4	8 36.8	11 0.4
16 W	7 39 18	25 15 43	3♋52 42	11♋ 3 17	29 52.2	9 18.9	21 17.0	22 28.8	26 17.7	21 7.6	13 56.6	8 36.6	10 59.0
17 Th	7 43 15	26 16 47	18 11 27	25 16 33	29 51.2	10 48.5	22 32.4	22 5.1	26 22.4	21 2.6	13 54.9	8 36.4	10 57.7
18 F	7 47 11	27 17 51	2♌18 0	9♌15 15	29 48.7	12 18.7	23 47.8	21 41.7	26 26.9	20 57.7	13 53.3	8 36.2	10 56.3
19 Sa	7 51 8	28 18 55	16 7 50	22 55 23	29 44.8	13 49.5	25 3.2	21 18.4	26 31.3	20 52.8	13 51.6	8 35.9	10 55.0
20 Su	7 55 4	29 19 57	29 37 39	6♍14 28	29 40.0	15 20.8	26 18.6	20 55.5	26 35.5	20 48.0	13 50.1	8 35.6	10 53.6
21 M	7 59 1	0♒21 0	12♍45 49	19 11 47	29 34.9	16 52.8	27 34.0	20 32.9	26 39.5	20 43.1	13 48.5	8 35.2	10 52.3
22 Tu	8 2 57	1 22 2	25 32 33	1♎48 24	29 30.0	18 25.3	28 49.4	20 10.6	26 43.3	20 38.3	13 47.0	8 34.8	10 50.9
23 W	8 6 54	2 23 3	7♎59 42	14 6 53	29 26.1	19 58.5	0♒ 4.8	19 48.8	26 47.0	20 33.5	13 45.6	8 34.4	10 49.5
24 Th	8 10 51	3 24 4	20 10 29	26 11 2	29 23.5	21 32.2	1 20.2	19 27.4	26 50.4	20 28.7	13 44.1	8 34.0	10 48.1
25 F	8 14 47	4 25 4	2♏ 9 8	8♏ 5 25	29D 22.5	23 6.5	2 35.6	19 6.5	26 53.8	20 24.0	13 42.8	8 33.5	10 46.7
26 Sa	8 18 44	5 26 4	14 0 31	19 55 5	29 22.8	24 41.5	3 51.0	18 46.1	26 56.9	20 19.3	13 41.5	8 33.0	10 45.3
27 Su	8 22 40	6 27 3	25 49 45	1♐45 10	29 24.2	26 17.0	5 6.4	18 26.3	26 59.8	20 14.6	13 40.2	8 32.4	10 43.9
28 M	8 26 37	7 28 1	7♐41 57	13 40 41	29 26.0	27 53.3	6 21.8	18 7.0	27 2.6	20 10.0	13 39.0	8 31.8	10 42.6
29 Tu	8 30 33	8 28 59	19 41 55	25 46 9	29R 27.5	29 30.1	7 37.1	17 48.4	27 5.2	20 5.4	13 37.8	8 31.2	10 41.2
30 W	8 34 30	9 29 57	1♑53 50	8♑ 5 22	29 27.9	1♒ 7.7	8 52.5	17 30.4	27 7.6	20 0.9	13 36.6	8 30.6	10 39.8
31 Th	8 38 26	10 30 53	14 21 3	20 41 6	29 26.7	2 45.9	10 7.8	17 13.1	27 9.9	19 56.4	13 35.6	8 29.9	10 38.4

LONGITUDE — FEBRUARY 1946

Day	Sid.Time	☉	0 hr ☽	Noon ☽	True ☊	☿	♀	♂	♃	♄	♅	♆	♇
1 F	8 42 23	11♒31 49	27♑ 5 42	3♒34 54	29♊23.4	4♒24.8	11♒23.2	16♋56.5	27♎11.9	19♋52.0	13♊34.5	8♎29.2	10♌37.0
2 Sa	8 46 20	12 32 43	10♒ 8 39	16 46 50	29R 18.1	6 4.4	12 38.5	16R 40.6	27 13.8	19R 47.6	13R 33.5	8R 28.5	10R 35.6
3 Su	8 50 16	13 33 36	23 29 16	0♓15 38	29 11.2	7 44.7	13 53.9	16 25.4	27 15.4	19 43.3	13 32.6	8 27.7	10 34.2
4 M	8 54 13	14 34 29	7♓ 5 37	13 58 47	29 3.2	9 25.8	15 9.2	16 11.0	27 16.9	19 39.0	13 31.7	8 26.9	10 32.7
5 Tu	8 58 9	15 35 20	20 54 44	27 53 0	28 55.2	11 7.6	16 24.5	15 57.3	27 18.2	19 34.8	13 30.9	8 26.1	10 31.4
6 W	9 2 6	16 36 9	4♈53 8	11♈54 44	28 48.0	12 50.2	17 39.8	15 44.4	27 19.3	19 30.7	13 30.1	8 25.2	10 30.0
7 Th	9 6 2	17 36 57	18 57 23	26 0 45	28 42.6	14 33.5	18 55.1	15 32.3	27 20.2	19 26.6	13 29.4	8 24.4	10 28.6
8 F	9 9 59	18 37 44	3♉ 4 31	10♉ 8 27	28 39.3	16 17.6	20 10.3	15 21.0	27 20.9	19 22.6	13 28.7	8 23.4	10 27.2
9 Sa	9 13 55	19 38 29	17 12 18	24 15 56	28D 38.2	18 2.5	21 25.6	15 10.5	27 21.5	19 18.7	13 28.0	8 22.5	10 25.8
10 Su	9 17 52	20 39 12	1♊19 11	8♊21 56	28 38.5	19 48.2	22 40.8	15 0.8	27 21.8	19 14.8	13 27.5	8 21.5	10 24.4
11 M	9 21 49	21 39 54	15 24 3	22 25 23	28R 39.6	21 34.7	23 56.0	14 51.9	27R 22.0	19 11.0	13 26.9	8 20.5	10 23.0
12 Tu	9 25 45	22 40 34	29 25 48	6♋25 4	28 40.1	23 21.9	25 11.3	14 43.9	27 22.0	19 7.3	13 26.5	8 19.5	10 21.7
13 W	9 29 42	23 41 13	13♋23 0	20 19 18	28 39.1	25 9.9	26 26.5	14 36.6	27 21.7	19 3.7	13 26.0	8 18.5	10 20.3
14 Th	9 33 38	24 41 50	27 13 41	4♌ 5 48	28 35.8	26 58.6	27 41.6	14 30.1	27 21.3	19 0.2	13 25.7	8 17.4	10 19.0
15 F	9 37 35	25 42 25	10♌55 20	17 41 53	28 29.8	28 48.0	28 56.8	14 24.4	27 20.7	18 56.7	13 25.4	8 16.3	10 17.6
16 Sa	9 41 31	26 42 59	24 25 9	1♍ 4 48	28 21.3	0♓38.1	0♓11.9	14 19.5	27 19.9	18 53.3	13 25.1	8 15.2	10 16.3
17 Su	9 45 28	27 43 31	7♍40 34	14 12 13	28 11.0	2 28.8	1 27.1	14 15.4	27 19.0	18 50.0	13 24.9	8 14.1	10 14.9
18 M	9 49 24	28 44 2	20 39 37	27 2 42	27 59.9	4 19.9	2 42.2	14 12.1	27 17.8	18 46.8	13 24.7	8 12.9	10 13.6
19 Tu	9 53 21	29 44 31	3♎21 30	9♎36 6	27 48.9	6 11.5	3 57.3	14 9.6	27 16.5	18 43.7	13 24.6	8 11.7	10 12.3
20 W	9 57 18	0♓44 59	15 46 43	21 53 37	27 39.2	8 3.5	5 12.4	14 7.8	27 14.9	18 40.7	13D 24.6	8 10.5	10 11.0
21 Th	10 1 14	1 45 26	27 57 10	3♏57 47	27 31.5	9 55.5	6 27.5	14D 6.7	27 13.2	18 37.7	13 24.6	8 9.3	10 9.7
22 F	10 5 11	2 45 51	9♏55 58	15 52 18	27 26.3	11 47.6	7 42.5	14 6.4	27 11.3	18 34.9	13 24.6	8 8.0	10 8.4
23 Sa	10 9 7	3 46 15	21 47 20	27 41 44	27 23.5	13 39.5	8 57.6	14 6.9	27 9.2	18 32.1	13 24.7	8 6.7	10 7.1
24 Su	10 13 4	4 46 37	3♐36 9	9♐31 16	27D 22.7	15 30.9	10 12.6	14 8.1	27 6.9	18 29.5	13 24.9	8 5.4	10 5.9
25 M	10 17 0	5 46 58	15 27 47	21 26 22	27 23.0	17 21.6	11 27.6	14 10.0	27 4.4	18 26.9	13 25.1	8 4.1	10 4.6
26 Tu	10 20 57	6 47 18	27 27 44	3♑32 29	27R 23.3	19 11.2	12 42.6	14 12.6	27 1.8	18 24.4	13 25.4	8 2.8	10 3.4
27 W	10 24 53	7 47 36	9♑41 16	15 54 38	27 22.6	20 59.5	13 57.6	14 15.9	26 59.0	18 22.1	13 25.7	8 1.4	10 2.2
28 Th	10 28 50	8 47 53	22 13 2	28 36 54	27 19.9	22 45.9	15 12.6	14 20.0	26 56.0	18 19.8	13 26.1	8 0.0	10 1.0

Astro Data Dy Hr Mn	Planet Ingress Dy Hr Mn	Last Aspect Dy Hr Mn	☽ Ingress Dy Hr Mn	Last Aspect Dy Hr Mn	☽ Ingress Dy Hr Mn	☽ Phases & Eclipses Dy Hr Mn
☽0N 10 6:39	☿ ♑ 9 14:09	2 2:15 ♃ ⚹	♑ 2 12:11	1 0:12 ♃ □	♒ 1 5:23	3 12:30 ● 12♑33
♆ R 10 1:15	☉ ♒ 20 15:45	4 15:54 ♂ ☍	♒ 4 21:38	3 6:42 ♃ △	♓ 3 11:32	3 12:15:41 ☌ P 0.553
☽0S 23 7:32	♀ ♒ 22 22:28	6 22:03 ☿ ⚹	♓ 7 4:47	4 21:43 ♄ △	♈ 5 15:38	10 20:27 ☽ 20♈01
	☿ ♒ 29 7:22	9 9:27 ☿ □	♈ 9 9:56	7 14:16 ♃ ☍	♉ 7 18:47	17 14:47 ○ 26♋54
☽0N 6 11:32		11 6:27 ♃ ☍	♉ 11 13:25	9 7:52 ♀ □	♊ 9 21:45	25 5:00 ☽ 4♏38
♃ R 11 8:26	☿ ♓ 15 15:43	13 5:02 ♂ ⚹	♊ 13 15:42	11 20:28 ♃ △	♋ 12 0:59	
☽0S 19 15:35	♀ ♓ 15 20:11	15 11:18 ♃ △	♋ 15 17:32	14 0:13 ♃ □	♌ 14 4:50	2 4:43 ● 12♒45
♅ D 20 12:13	☉ ♓ 19 6:09	17 14:47 ☉ ☍	♌ 17 20:03	16 5:14 ♃ ⚹	♍ 16 10:03	9 4:28 ☽ 19♉50
♂ D 21 21:12		19 18:31 ♃ ⚹	♍ 20 0:40	17 20:30 ♄ ⚹	♎ 18 17:36	16 4:28 ○ 26♌54
		22 6:58 ♀ △	♎ 22 8:31	20 22:33 ♃ ☌	♏ 21 4:05	24 2:36 ☽ 4♐53
		24 13:23 ♃ ☌	♏ 24 19:40	22 17:25 ♄ △	♐ 23 16:41	
		27 1:04 ☿ ⚹	♐ 27 8:27	25 23:09 ♃ ⚹	♑ 26 5:01	
		29 14:38 ♃ ⚹	♑ 29 20:18	28 8:49 ♃ □	♒ 28 14:34	

Astro Data

1 JANUARY 1946
Julian Day # 16802
Delta T 27.3 sec
SVP 06♓01'07"
Obliquity 23°26'46"
⚷ Chiron 20♎10.0
☽ Mean ☊ 29♊28.4

1 FEBRUARY 1946
Julian Day # 16833
Delta T 27.3 sec
SVP 06♓01'01"
Obliquity 23°26'47"
⚷ Chiron 21♎19.1
☽ Mean ☊ 27♊49.9

MARCH 1946 LONGITUDE

Day	Sid.Time	☉	0 hr ☽	Noon ☽	True ☊	☿	♀	♂	♃	♄	♅	♆	♇
1 F	10 32 47	9♓48 8	5♒ 6 31	11♒42 3	27♊14.7	24♓30.1	16♓27.6	14♋24.6	26♎52.8	18♋17.7	13♊26.5	7♎58.6	9♌59.8
2 Sa	10 36 43	10 48 21	18 23 33	25 10 55	27R 6.7	26 11.5	17 42.5	14 30.0	26R 49.4	18R 15.6	13 27.0	7R 57.2	9R 58.6
3 Su	10 40 40	11 48 33	2♓ 3 53	9♓ 2 4	26 56.4	27 49.7	18 57.4	14 36.0	26 45.9	18 13.7	13 27.5	7 55.8	9 57.4
4 M	10 44 36	12 48 43	16 4 55	23 11 48	26 44.6	29 24.1	20 12.3	14 42.7	26 42.2	18 11.8	13 28.1	7 54.3	9 56.3
5 Tu	10 48 33	13 48 51	0♈21 57	7♈34 33	26 32.6	0♈54.1	21 27.2	14 50.0	26 38.3	18 10.1	13 28.7	7 52.9	9 55.2
6 W	10 52 29	14 48 57	14 48 47	22 3 48	26 21.7	2 19.1	22 42.1	14 58.0	26 34.2	18 8.4	13 29.4	7 51.4	9 54.0
7 Th	10 56 26	15 49 2	29 18 50	6♉33 9	26 12.9	3 38.7	23 56.9	15 6.5	26 30.0	18 6.9	13 30.2	7 49.9	9 52.9
8 F	11 0 22	16 49 4	13♉46 8	20 57 18	26 7.0	4 52.2	25 11.8	15 15.7	26 25.6	18 5.5	13 31.0	7 48.4	9 51.9
9 Sa	11 4 19	17 49 4	28 6 15	5♊12 41	26 3.8	5 59.2	26 26.6	15 25.5	26 21.1	18 4.2	13 31.8	7 46.8	9 50.8
10 Su	11 8 15	18 49 2	12♊16 25	19 17 23	26 2.8	6 59.1	27 41.3	15 35.8	26 16.4	18 3.0	13 32.7	7 45.3	9 49.7
11 M	11 12 12	19 48 57	26 15 32	3♋10 54	26 2.7	7 51.5	28 56.1	15 46.7	26 11.5	18 1.9	13 33.7	7 43.8	9 48.7
12 Tu	11 16 9	20 48 51	10♋ 3 32	16 53 29	26 2.3	8 36.1	0♈10.8	15 58.2	26 6.5	18 0.9	13 34.7	7 42.2	9 47.7
13 W	11 20 5	21 48 42	23 40 50	0♌25 37	26 0.2	9 12.4	1 25.5	16 10.1	26 1.4	18 0.0	13 35.8	7 40.6	9 46.7
14 Th	11 24 2	22 48 31	7♌ 7 51	13 47 32	25 55.6	9 40.5	2 40.2	16 22.7	25 56.1	17 59.3	13 36.9	7 39.1	9 45.8
15 F	11 27 58	23 48 18	20 24 36	26 59 0	25 48.0	9 59.9	3 54.8	16 35.7	25 50.6	17 58.6	13 38.0	7 37.5	9 44.8
16 Sa	11 31 55	24 48 2	3♍30 38	9♍59 24	25 37.5	10R 10.9	5 9.5	16 49.2	25 45.0	17 58.1	13 39.3	7 35.9	9 43.9
17 Su	11 35 51	25 47 45	16 25 11	22 47 53	25 24.8	10 13.3	6 24.1	17 3.2	25 39.3	17 57.6	13 40.5	7 34.3	9 43.0
18 M	11 39 48	26 47 25	29 7 26	5♎23 46	25 11.0	10 7.4	7 38.6	17 17.7	25 33.5	17 57.3	13 41.8	7 32.7	9 42.1
19 Tu	11 43 44	27 47 3	11♎36 54	17 46 52	24 57.3	9 53.5	8 53.2	17 32.7	25 27.5	17 57.1	13 43.2	7 31.0	9 41.2
20 W	11 47 41	28 46 40	23 53 47	29 57 48	24 44.9	9 32.1	10 7.7	17 48.1	25 21.4	17D 57.0	13 44.6	7 29.4	9 40.3
21 Th	11 51 38	29 46 14	5♏59 11	11♏58 13	24 34.8	9 3.7	11 22.2	18 4.0	25 15.2	17 57.0	13 46.0	7 27.8	9 39.5
22 F	11 55 34	0♈45 47	17 55 15	23 50 44	24 27.4	8 29.1	12 36.7	18 20.3	25 8.8	17 57.1	13 47.5	7 26.1	9 38.7
23 Sa	11 59 31	1 45 18	29 45 8	5♐38 59	24 22.8	7 49.0	13 51.2	18 37.0	25 2.4	17 57.4	13 49.1	7 24.5	9 37.9
24 Su	12 3 27	2 44 47	11♐32 54	17 27 29	24 20.6	7 4.4	15 5.6	18 54.2	24 55.8	17 57.7	13 50.7	7 22.9	9 37.2
25 M	12 7 24	3 44 15	23 23 23	29 21 18	24 20.1	6 16.3	16 20.0	19 11.7	24 49.2	17 58.2	13 52.3	7 21.2	9 36.4
26 Tu	12 11 20	4 43 41	5♑21 54	11♑25 55	24 20.1	5 25.8	17 34.4	19 29.7	24 42.4	17 58.7	13 54.0	7 19.6	9 35.7
27 W	12 15 17	5 43 5	17 33 59	23 46 48	24 19.7	4 33.9	18 48.7	19 48.1	24 35.6	17 59.4	13 55.8	7 17.9	9 35.0
28 Th	12 19 13	6 42 27	0♒ 4 58	6♒29 1	24 17.6	3 41.8	20 3.1	20 6.8	24 28.6	18 0.2	13 57.5	7 16.3	9 34.4
29 F	12 23 10	7 41 47	12 59 24	19 36 29	24 13.2	2 50.5	21 17.4	20 25.9	24 21.6	18 1.1	13 59.4	7 14.6	9 33.7
30 Sa	12 27 7	8 41 6	26 20 29	3♓11 25	24 6.3	2 0.9	22 31.7	20 45.4	24 14.5	18 2.1	14 1.3	7 12.9	9 33.1
31 Su	12 31 3	9 40 22	10♓ 9 12	17 13 31	23 57.0	1 14.0	23 45.9	21 5.2	24 7.3	18 3.2	14 3.2	7 11.3	9 32.5

APRIL 1946 LONGITUDE

Day	Sid.Time	☉	0 hr ☽	Noon ☽	True ☊	☿	♀	♂	♃	♄	♅	♆	♇
1 M	12 35 0	10♈39 37	24♓23 52	1♈39 34	23♊46.2	0♈30.5	25♈ 0.2	21♋25.4	24♎ 0.0	18♋ 4.5	14♊ 5.1	7♎ 9.6	9♌32.0
2 Tu	12 38 56	11 38 50	8♈59 45	16 23 27	23R 35.0	29♓51.0	26 14.4	21 46.0	23R 52.7	18 5.8	14 7.1	7R 8.0	9R 31.4
3 W	12 42 53	12 38 0	23 49 34	1♉17 0	23 24.7	29R 16.1	27 28.6	22 6.9	23 45.3	18 7.2	14 9.2	7 6.3	9 30.9
4 Th	12 46 49	13 37 9	8♉44 36	16 11 18	23 16.5	28 46.1	28 42.7	22 28.1	23 37.8	18 8.8	14 11.3	7 4.7	9 30.4
5 F	12 50 46	14 36 16	23 36 7	0♊58 13	23 10.9	28 21.3	29 56.9	22 49.7	23 30.4	18 10.5	14 13.4	7 3.0	9 29.9
6 Sa	12 54 42	15 35 20	8♊16 54	15 31 36	23 7.9	28 2.0	1♉11.0	23 11.5	23 22.8	18 12.2	14 15.6	7 1.4	9 29.5
7 Su	12 58 39	16 34 22	22 41 58	29 47 45	23D 7.1	27 48.2	2 25.0	23 33.7	23 15.2	18 14.1	14 17.8	6 59.8	9 29.1
8 M	13 2 36	17 33 22	6♋48 49	13♋45 13	23R 7.5	27 39.9	3 39.1	23 56.2	23 7.6	18 16.1	14 20.1	6 58.2	9 28.7
9 Tu	13 6 32	18 32 19	20 37 0	27 24 19	23 7.7	27D 37.0	4 53.1	24 19.0	23 0.0	18 18.2	14 22.4	6 56.5	9 28.3
10 W	13 10 29	19 31 15	4♌ 7 24	10♌46 25	23 6.7	27 39.6	6 7.0	24 42.0	22 52.3	18 20.4	14 24.7	6 54.9	9 28.0
11 Th	13 14 25	20 30 7	17 21 38	23 53 14	23 3.7	27 47.3	7 21.0	25 5.4	22 44.7	18 22.7	14 27.1	6 53.3	9 27.7
12 F	13 18 22	21 28 58	0♍21 27	6♍46 28	22 58.1	28 0.1	8 34.9	25 29.0	22 37.0	18 25.1	14 29.5	6 51.7	9 27.4
13 Sa	13 22 18	22 27 46	13 8 26	19 27 30	22 50.1	28 17.9	9 48.8	25 52.8	22 29.3	18 27.6	14 31.9	6 50.2	9 27.1
14 Su	13 26 15	23 26 32	25 43 47	1♎57 24	22 40.2	28 40.3	11 2.6	26 17.0	22 21.6	18 30.2	14 34.4	6 48.6	9 26.9
15 M	13 30 11	24 25 16	8♎ 8 27	14 17 0	22 29.4	29 7.3	12 16.4	26 41.4	22 13.9	18 32.9	14 36.9	6 47.0	9 26.7
16 Tu	13 34 8	25 23 58	20 23 12	26 27 7	22 18.7	29 38.5	13 30.2	27 6.0	22 6.2	18 35.7	14 39.5	6 45.5	9 26.5
17 W	13 38 5	26 22 38	2♏28 55	8♏28 45	22 8.9	0♈13.9	14 43.9	27 30.9	21 58.6	18 38.6	14 42.1	6 43.9	9 26.4
18 Th	13 42 1	27 21 16	14 26 48	20 23 19	22 1.0	0 53.2	15 57.6	27 56.0	21 50.9	18 41.6	14 44.7	6 42.4	9 26.2
19 F	13 45 58	28 19 52	26 18 35	2♐12 54	21 55.3	1 36.2	17 11.3	28 21.3	21 43.3	18 44.7	14 47.4	6 40.9	9 26.1
20 Sa	13 49 54	29 18 26	8♐ 6 40	14 0 15	21 52.0	2 22.8	18 25.0	28 46.9	21 35.7	18 47.9	14 50.1	6 39.4	9 26.1
21 Su	13 53 51	0♉16 59	19 54 9	25 48 51	21D 50.9	3 12.8	19 38.6	29 12.7	21 28.2	18 51.2	14 52.8	6 37.9	9 26.0
22 M	13 57 47	1 15 30	1♑44 54	7♑42 53	21 51.3	4 6.0	20 52.2	29 38.7	21 20.7	18 54.6	14 55.6	6 36.4	9D 26.0
23 Tu	14 1 44	2 13 59	13 43 23	19 47 3	21 52.5	5 2.4	22 5.7	0♌ 4.9	21 13.2	18 58.1	14 58.4	6 34.9	9 26.0
24 W	14 5 40	3 12 27	25 54 31	2♒ 6 24	21R 53.6	6 1.7	23 19.2	0 31.3	21 5.8	19 1.6	15 1.2	6 33.5	9 26.0
25 Th	14 9 37	4 10 53	8♒23 20	14 45 53	21 53.7	7 3.8	24 32.7	0 58.0	20 58.4	19 5.3	15 4.0	6 32.1	9 26.1
26 F	14 13 34	5 9 18	21 14 36	27 49 56	21 52.4	8 8.7	25 46.2	1 24.8	20 51.1	19 9.1	15 6.9	6 30.7	9 26.2
27 Sa	14 17 30	6 7 41	4♓32 14	11♓21 42	21 49.1	9 16.2	26 59.6	1 51.9	20 43.9	19 12.9	15 9.8	6 29.3	9 26.3
28 Su	14 21 27	7 6 2	18 18 26	25 22 18	21 44.2	10 26.3	28 13.0	2 19.1	20 36.7	19 16.8	15 12.8	6 27.9	9 26.4
29 M	14 25 23	8 4 21	2♈33 1	9♈50 5	21 38.0	11 38.8	29 26.4	2 46.6	20 29.6	19 20.9	15 15.8	6 26.5	9 26.6
30 Tu	14 29 20	9 2 40	17 12 48	24 40 16	21 31.4	12 53.6	0♊39.8	3 14.2	20 22.6	19 25.0	15 18.8	6 25.2	9 26.8

Astro Data	Planet Ingress	Last Aspect	☽ Ingress	Last Aspect	☽ Ingress	☽ Phases & Eclipses
Dy Hr Mn	Dy Hr Mn	Dy Hr Mn	Dy Hr Mn	Dy Hr Mn	Dy Hr Mn	Dy Hr Mn
☿0N 3 13:46	☿ ♈ 4 9:26	2 14:49 ♃ △	♓ 2 20:25	31 18:55 ♂ △	♈ 1 9:16	3 18:01 ● 12♓34
☽0N 5 18:09	♀ ♈ 11 20:32	4 7:38 ♀ ☌	♈ 4 23:23	3 6:24 ♀ ☌	♉ 3 9:56	10 12:03 ☽ 19♊19
♀0N 14 4:37	☉ ♈ 21 5:33	6 19:22 ♃ ☍	♉ 7 1:08	5 7:33 ☿ ⚹	♊ 5 10:25	17 19:11 ○ 26♍35
☿ R 16 18:55		8 20:56 ♀ ⚹	♊ 9 3:12	7 8:31 ☿ □	♋ 7 12:21	25 22:37 ☽ 4♑40
☽0S 18 23:08	☿ ♓ 1 18:16	11 5:05 ♀ □	♋ 11 6:29	9 12:24 ☿ △	♌ 9 16:37	
♄ D 20 9:29	♀ ♉ 5 1:01	13 4:08 ♃ □	♌ 13 11:14	11 9:48 ♃ ⚹	♍ 11 23:20	2 4:37 ● 11♈50
	☿ ♈ 16 14:54	15 9:51 ♃ ⚹	♍ 15 17:32	14 5:51 ☿ ☍	♎ 14 8:13	8 20:04 ☽ 18♋23
☽0N 2 3:31	☉ ♉ 20 17:02	17 19:11 ☉ ☍	♎ 18 1:40	16 13:45 ♂ △	♏ 16 19:03	16 10:47 ○ 25♎50
☿0S 5 8:44	♂ ♌ 22 19:31	20 2:51 ♃ ☌	♏ 20 12:04	19 4:19 ♂ △	♐ 19 7:30	24 15:18 ☽ 3♒50
☿ D 9 0:38	♀ ♊ 29 10:59	22 0:52 ♂ △	♐ 23 0:30	21 3:09 ♃ ⚹	♑ 21 20:28	
☽0S 15 5:55		25 2:51 ♃ ⚹	♑ 25 13:18	23 18:23 ♀ △	♒ 24 7:56	
♇ D 22 3:51		27 13:26 ♃ □	♒ 27 23:51	26 9:06 ♀ □	♓ 26 15:54	
☿0N 24 0:16		29 20:19 ♃ △	♓ 30 6:26	28 18:20 ♀ ⚹	♈ 28 19:45	
☽0N 29 14:23				30 5:04 ♃ ☍	♉ 30 20:31	

Astro Data

1 MARCH 1946
Julian Day # 16861
Delta T 27.4 sec
SVP 06♓00'58"
Obliquity 23°26'48"
⚷ Chiron 20♎45.1R
☽ Mean ☊ 26♊21.0

1 APRIL 1946
Julian Day # 16892
Delta T 27.4 sec
SVP 06♓00'55"
Obliquity 23°26'48"
⚷ Chiron 18♎45.1R
☽ Mean ☊ 24♊42.5

LONGITUDE — MAY 1946

Day	Sid.Time	☉	0 hr ☽	Noon ☽	True ☊	☿	♀	♂	♃	♄	♅	♆	♇
1 W	14 33 16	10♉ 0 56	2♉11 26	9♉45 9	21♊25.3	14♈10.8	1♊53.1	3♌42.0	20♎15.7	19♋29.2	15♊21.8	6♎23.8	9♌27.0
2 Th	14 37 13	10 59 11	17 20 11	24 55 15	21R 20.4	15 30.2	3 6.4	4 10.0	20R 8.9	19 33.5	15 24.8	6R 22.5	9 27.3
3 F	14 41 9	11 57 24	2♊29 8	10♊ 0 42	21 17.2	16 51.9	4 19.6	4 38.2	20 2.2	19 37.9	15 27.9	6 21.3	9 27.6
4 Sa	14 45 6	12 55 35	17 28 56	24 52 57	21D 16.0	18 15.6	5 32.8	5 6.5	19 55.5	19 42.3	15 31.0	6 20.0	9 27.9
5 Su	14 49 2	13 53 45	2♋12 6	9♋25 50	21 16.3	19 41.5	6 46.0	5 35.1	19 49.0	19 46.9	15 34.1	6 18.8	9 28.2
6 M	14 52 59	14 51 52	16 33 48	23 35 51	21 17.6	21 9.5	7 59.1	6 3.7	19 42.6	19 51.5	15 37.3	6 17.5	9 28.6
7 Tu	14 56 56	15 49 58	0♌31 54	7♌22 2	21 18.9	22 39.5	9 12.2	6 32.6	19 36.3	19 56.2	15 40.5	6 16.3	9 28.9
8 W	15 0 52	16 48 1	14 6 26	20 45 19	21R 19.7	24 11.5	10 25.3	7 1.6	19 30.1	20 1.0	15 43.7	6 15.2	9 29.4
9 Th	15 4 49	17 46 3	27 19 1	3♍47 50	21 19.3	25 45.6	11 38.3	7 30.8	19 24.0	20 5.9	15 46.9	6 14.0	9 29.8
10 F	15 8 45	18 44 2	10♍12 8	16 32 17	21 17.5	27 21.7	12 51.3	8 0.1	19 18.1	20 10.8	15 50.1	6 12.9	9 30.3
11 Sa	15 12 42	19 42 0	22 48 39	29 1 35	21 14.2	28 59.8	14 4.3	8 29.6	19 12.2	20 15.8	15 53.4	6 11.8	9 30.7
12 Su	15 16 38	20 39 56	5♎11 24	11♎18 27	21 9.9	0♉39.9	15 17.2	8 59.2	19 6.5	20 20.9	15 56.6	6 10.7	9 31.3
13 M	15 20 35	21 37 50	17 23 1	23 25 23	21 4.9	2 22.1	16 30.0	9 29.0	19 1.0	20 26.1	15 59.9	6 9.6	9 31.8
14 Tu	15 24 31	22 35 43	29 25 49	5♏24 36	20 59.9	4 6.2	17 42.9	9 58.9	18 55.6	20 31.3	16 3.3	6 8.6	9 32.4
15 W	15 28 28	23 33 34	11♏21 56	17 18 6	20 55.4	5 52.4	18 55.6	10 28.9	18 50.3	20 36.6	16 6.6	6 7.6	9 33.0
16 Th	15 32 25	24 31 23	23 13 20	29 7 53	20 51.9	7 40.6	20 8.4	10 59.1	18 45.1	20 42.0	16 9.9	6 6.6	9 33.6
17 F	15 36 21	25 29 11	5♐ 1 59	10♐55 57	20 49.6	9 30.7	21 21.1	11 29.4	18 40.1	20 47.5	16 13.3	6 5.7	9 34.2
18 Sa	15 40 18	26 26 58	16 50 3	22 44 37	20D 48.6	11 22.9	22 33.8	11 59.9	18 35.3	20 53.0	16 16.7	6 4.7	9 34.9
19 Su	15 44 14	27 24 43	28 39 59	4♑36 31	20 48.8	13 17.1	23 46.4	12 30.5	18 30.6	20 58.6	16 20.1	6 3.8	9 35.6
20 M	15 48 11	28 22 27	10♑34 38	16 34 45	20 49.8	15 13.3	24 59.0	13 1.2	18 26.0	21 4.3	16 23.5	6 3.0	9 36.3
21 Tu	15 52 7	29 20 10	22 37 18	28 42 48	20 51.4	17 11.4	26 11.5	13 32.0	18 21.7	21 10.0	16 26.9	6 2.1	9 37.0
22 W	15 56 4	0♊17 52	4♒51 42	11♒ 4 32	20 52.9	19 11.5	27 24.1	14 2.9	18 17.4	21 15.8	16 30.3	6 1.3	9 37.8
23 Th	16 0 1	1 15 33	17 21 48	23 43 59	20 54.1	21 13.3	28 36.5	14 34.0	18 13.3	21 21.6	16 33.8	6 0.5	9 38.6
24 F	16 3 57	2 13 13	0♓11 33	6♓44 57	20R 54.6	23 17.0	29 49.0	15 5.2	18 9.4	21 27.6	16 37.2	5 59.7	9 39.4
25 Sa	16 7 54	3 10 51	13 24 32	20 10 35	20 54.4	25 22.3	1♋ 1.4	15 36.5	18 5.7	21 33.5	16 40.7	5 59.0	9 40.3
26 Su	16 11 50	4 8 29	27 3 19	4♈ 2 44	20 53.3	27 29.1	2 13.7	16 8.0	18 2.1	21 39.6	16 44.2	5 58.3	9 41.1
27 M	16 15 47	5 6 6	11♈ 8 48	18 21 13	20 51.8	29 37.3	3 26.0	16 39.5	17 58.7	21 45.7	16 47.7	5 57.6	9 42.0
28 Tu	16 19 43	6 3 42	25 39 35	3♉ 3 17	20 49.9	1♊46.8	4 38.3	17 11.2	17 55.4	21 51.8	16 51.2	5 57.0	9 42.9
29 W	16 23 40	7 1 17	10♉31 31	18 3 22	20 48.2	3 57.2	5 50.5	17 43.0	17 52.3	21 58.1	16 54.7	5 56.3	9 43.8
30 Th	16 27 36	7 58 51	25 37 46	3♊13 32	20 46.9	6 8.4	7 2.7	18 14.9	17 49.4	22 4.3	16 58.2	5 55.7	9 44.8
31 F	16 31 33	8 56 24	10♊49 28	18 24 22	20D 46.2	8 20.2	8 14.9	18 46.9	17 46.7	22 10.7	17 1.7	5 55.2	9 45.8

LONGITUDE — JUNE 1946

Day	Sid.Time	☉	0 hr ☽	Noon ☽	True ☊	☿	♀	♂	♃	♄	♅	♆	♇
1 Sa	16 35 30	9♊53 56	25♊57 4	3♋26 28	20♊46.1	10♊32.3	9♋27.0	19♌19.0	17♎44.1	22♋17.1	17♊ 5.3	5♎54.6	9♌46.8
2 Su	16 39 26	10 51 27	10♋51 37	18 11 42	20 46.5	12 44.3	10 39.1	19 51.2	17R 41.8	22 23.5	17 8.8	5R 54.2	9 47.8
3 M	16 43 23	11 48 57	25 26 6	2♌34 20	20 47.2	14 56.1	11 51.1	20 23.6	17 39.6	22 30.0	17 12.3	5 53.7	9 48.9
4 Tu	16 47 19	12 46 25	9♌36 6	16 31 15	20 48.0	17 7.4	13 3.1	20 56.0	17 37.5	22 36.6	17 15.9	5 53.2	9 49.9
5 W	16 51 16	13 43 53	23 19 49	0♍ 1 53	20 48.6	19 17.8	14 15.0	21 28.6	17 35.7	22 43.2	17 19.4	5 52.8	9 51.0
6 Th	16 55 12	14 41 19	6♍37 44	13 7 39	20R 48.9	21 27.2	15 26.9	22 1.2	17 34.0	22 49.8	17 23.0	5 52.5	9 52.1
7 F	16 59 9	15 38 43	19 32 3	25 51 21	20 49.0	23 35.2	16 38.7	22 34.0	17 32.5	22 56.5	17 26.5	5 52.1	9 53.3
8 Sa	17 3 5	16 36 7	2♎ 6 2	8♎16 34	20 48.8	25 41.8	17 50.5	23 6.8	17 31.2	23 3.2	17 30.1	5 51.8	9 54.4
9 Su	17 7 2	17 33 29	14 23 27	20 27 11	20 48.5	27 46.7	19 2.2	23 39.7	17 30.1	23 10.0	17 33.6	5 51.5	9 55.6
10 M	17 10 59	18 30 51	26 28 14	2♏27 4	20 48.2	29 49.8	20 13.9	24 12.8	17 29.2	23 16.8	17 37.2	5 51.3	9 56.8
11 Tu	17 14 55	19 28 11	8♏24 8	14 19 50	20 47.9	1♋50.9	21 25.5	24 45.9	17 28.4	23 23.7	17 40.7	5 51.0	9 58.0
12 W	17 18 52	20 25 31	20 14 35	26 8 45	20D 47.9	3 50.0	22 37.0	25 19.1	17 27.8	23 30.6	17 44.3	5 50.9	9 59.2
13 Th	17 22 48	21 22 50	2♐ 2 40	7♐56 42	20 47.9	5 46.9	23 48.5	25 52.4	17 27.4	23 37.6	17 47.8	5 50.7	10 0.5
14 F	17 26 45	22 20 8	13 51 8	19 46 16	20R 47.9	7 41.5	24 60.0	26 25.8	17D 27.2	23 44.6	17 51.4	5 50.6	10 1.7
15 Sa	17 30 41	23 17 25	25 42 23	1♑39 45	20 47.9	9 33.9	26 11.3	26 59.3	17 27.1	23 51.6	17 54.9	5 50.5	10 3.0
16 Su	17 34 38	24 14 42	7♑38 38	13 39 19	20 47.8	11 23.9	27 22.7	27 32.8	17 27.3	23 58.7	17 58.5	5 50.4	10 4.3
17 M	17 38 34	25 11 58	19 42 3	25 47 6	20 47.4	13 11.6	28 33.9	28 6.5	17 27.6	24 5.8	18 2.0	5D 50.4	10 5.6
18 Tu	17 42 31	26 9 14	1♒54 45	8♒ 5 18	20 46.9	14 56.9	29 45.2	28 40.2	17 28.1	24 12.9	18 5.5	5 50.4	10 7.0
19 W	17 46 28	27 6 30	14 19 1	20 36 13	20 46.1	16 39.8	0♌56.3	29 14.0	17 28.7	24 20.1	18 9.1	5 50.4	10 8.3
20 Th	17 50 24	28 3 45	26 57 12	3♓22 16	20 45.3	18 20.4	2 7.4	29 47.9	17 29.6	24 27.3	18 12.6	5 50.5	10 9.7
21 F	17 54 21	29 1 0	9♓51 43	16 25 50	20 44.6	19 58.5	3 18.4	0♍21.9	17 30.6	24 34.6	18 16.1	5 50.6	10 11.1
22 Sa	17 58 17	29 58 14	23 4 53	29 49 4	20D 44.2	21 34.1	4 29.4	0 56.0	17 31.8	24 41.9	18 19.6	5 50.7	10 12.5
23 Su	18 2 14	0♋55 29	6♈38 33	13♈33 28	20 44.2	23 7.3	5 40.3	1 30.2	17 33.2	24 49.2	18 23.1	5 50.9	10 13.9
24 M	18 6 10	1 52 43	20 33 47	27 39 28	20 44.6	24 38.1	6 51.2	2 4.4	17 34.7	24 56.5	18 26.6	5 51.1	10 15.4
25 Tu	18 10 7	2 49 58	4♉50 17	12♉ 5 55	20 45.4	26 6.4	8 2.0	2 38.7	17 36.5	25 3.9	18 30.0	5 51.3	10 16.8
26 W	18 14 3	3 47 12	19 25 55	26 49 41	20 46.4	27 32.2	9 12.7	3 13.1	17 38.4	25 11.3	18 33.5	5 51.6	10 18.3
27 Th	18 18 0	4 44 26	4♊16 29	11♊45 27	20 47.2	28 55.5	10 23.4	3 47.6	17 40.4	25 18.7	18 37.0	5 51.9	10 19.8
28 F	18 21 57	5 41 41	19 15 40	26 46 5	20R 47.6	0♌16.2	11 34.0	4 22.2	17 42.7	25 26.2	18 40.4	5 52.2	10 21.3
29 Sa	18 25 53	6 38 55	4♋15 39	11♋43 19	20 47.3	1 34.3	12 44.5	4 56.8	17 45.1	25 33.7	18 43.8	5 52.6	10 22.8
30 Su	18 29 50	7 36 9	19 8 4	26 28 57	20 46.2	2 49.7	13 55.0	5 31.6	17 47.7	25 41.2	18 47.2	5 53.0	10 24.3

Astro Data Dy Hr Mn	Planet Ingress Dy Hr Mn	Last Aspect Dy Hr Mn	☽ Ingress Dy Hr Mn	Last Aspect Dy Hr Mn	☽ Ingress Dy Hr Mn	☽ Phases & Eclipses Dy Hr Mn	Astro Data
♃□♄ 5 4:36	☿ ♉ 11 14:29	2 3:32 ♄ ✶	♊ 2 20:03	31 13:03 ♂ ✶	♋ 1 6:28	1 13:16 ● 10♉33	1 MAY 1946
☽0S 12 12:08	☉ ♊ 21 16:34	4 3:55 ♃ △	♋ 4 20:23	2 19:05 ♄ ☌	♌ 3 7:39	8 5:13 ☽ 17♌01	Julian Day # 16922
☽0N 27 0:34	♀ ♋ 24 3:39	6 8:45 ☿ □	♌ 6 23:04	4 20:35 ♂ ☌	♍ 5 11:57	16 2:52 ○ 24♏38	Delta T 27.4 sec
	☿ ♊ 27 4:13	8 20:45 ☿ △	♍ 9 4:57	7 9:14 ☿ □	♎ 7 19:57	24 4:02 ☽ 2♓23	SVP 06♓00'52"
☽0S 8 18:22		10 19:05 ♄ ✶	♎ 11 13:53	9 19:16 ♂ ✶	♏ 10 7:04	30 20:49 ● 8♊49	Obliquity 23°26'48"
♃△♅ 8 5:47	☿ ♋ 10 2:00	13 6:06 ♄ □	♏ 14 1:08	12 10:50 ♂ □	♐ 12 19:50	30 20:59:57 ☌ P 0.887	⚷ Chiron 16♎29.0R
♃ D 14 18:05	♀ ♌ 18 5:00	16 2:52 ☉ ☍	♐ 16 13:46	15 2:43 ♂ △	♑ 15 8:39		☽ Mean ☊ 23♊07.1
♆ D 17 8:19	♂ ♍ 20 8:31	18 12:58 ♀ ☍	♑ 19 2:42	17 19:20 ♀ ☍	♒ 17 20:16	6 16:07 ☽ 15♍20	
☽0N 23 8:27	☉ ♋ 22 0:44	21 14:21 ☉ △	♒ 21 14:31	20 5:35 ♂ ☍	♓ 20 5:43	14 18:42 ○ 23♐05	1 JUNE 1946
	☿ ♌ 27 19:07	23 23:14 ♀ △	♓ 23 23:39	22 2:55 ♄ △	♈ 22 12:19	14 18:39 ☍ T 1.398	Julian Day # 16953
		26 0:53 ☿ ✶	♈ 26 5:05	24 7:43 ☿ □	♉ 24 15:56	22 13:12 ☽ 0♈30	Delta T 27.5 sec
		27 17:44 ♄ □	♉ 28 7:04	26 14:30 ☿ ✶	♊ 26 17:07	29 4:06 ● 6♋49	SVP 06♓00'47"
		29 18:20 ♄ ✶	♊ 30 6:54	27 23:03 ♅ ☌	♋ 28 17:10	29 3:51:28 ☌ P 0.180	Obliquity 23°26'47"
				30 10:47 ♄ ☌	♌ 30 17:47		⚷ Chiron 15♎02.4R
							☽ Mean ☊ 21♊28.6

JULY 1946 LONGITUDE

Day	Sid.Time	☉	0 hr ☽	Noon ☽	True ☊	☿	♀	♂	♃	♄	♅	♆	♇
1 M	18 33 46	8♋33 23	3♌45 7	10♌55 52	20♊44.3	4♌ 2.5	15♌ 5.4	6♍ 6.4	17♎50.5	25♋48.7	18♊50.7	5♎53.4	10♌25.9
2 Tu	18 37 43	9 30 37	18 0 40	24 59 8	20R41.9	5 12.4	16 15.8	6 41.3	17 53.4	25 56.3	18 54.0	5 53.8	10 27.5
3 W	18 41 39	10 27 50	1♍51 1	8♍36 14	20 39.4	6 19.6	17 26.0	7 16.3	17 56.5	26 3.8	18 57.4	5 54.3	10 29.0
4 Th	18 45 36	11 25 3	15 14 53	21 47 9	20 37.2	7 23.8	18 36.2	7 51.3	17 59.8	26 11.4	19 0.8	5 54.9	10 30.6
5 F	18 49 32	12 22 16	28 13 20	4♎33 51	20 35.6	8 24.9	19 46.3	8 26.4	18 3.3	26 19.0	19 4.1	5 55.4	10 32.2
6 Sa	18 53 29	13 19 28	10♎49 9	16 59 45	20D34.9	9 23.0	20 56.3	9 1.6	18 6.9	26 26.6	19 7.4	5 56.0	10 33.8
7 Su	18 57 26	14 16 40	23 6 13	29 9 8	20 35.1	10 17.9	22 6.3	9 36.9	18 10.6	26 34.3	19 10.7	5 56.6	10 35.4
8 M	19 1 22	15 13 52	5♏ 9 6	11♏ 6 42	20 36.2	11 9.5	23 16.1	10 12.2	18 14.6	26 41.9	19 14.0	5 57.2	10 37.0
9 Tu	19 5 19	16 11 4	17 2 32	22 57 8	20 37.8	11 57.6	24 25.9	10 47.6	18 18.7	26 49.6	19 17.3	5 57.9	10 38.7
10 W	19 9 15	17 8 16	28 51 5	4♐44 52	20 39.5	12 42.1	25 35.6	11 23.1	18 22.9	26 57.3	19 20.5	5 58.6	10 40.3
11 Th	19 13 12	18 5 28	10♐38 59	16 33 53	20R40.8	13 23.0	26 45.2	11 58.6	18 27.3	27 5.0	19 23.8	5 59.4	10 42.0
12 F	19 17 8	19 2 40	22 29 59	28 27 38	20 41.2	14 0.0	27 54.7	12 34.3	18 31.9	27 12.7	19 27.0	6 0.1	10 43.6
13 Sa	19 21 5	19 59 52	4♑27 11	10♑28 54	20 40.3	14 33.0	29 4.1	13 9.9	18 36.6	27 20.4	19 30.2	6 0.9	10 45.3
14 Su	19 25 2	20 57 4	16 33 3	22 39 51	20 38.1	15 2.0	0♍13.4	13 45.7	18 41.5	27 28.1	19 33.3	6 1.8	10 47.0
15 M	19 28 58	21 54 16	28 49 28	5♒ 2 3	20 34.4	15 26.6	1 22.6	14 21.5	18 46.5	27 35.9	19 36.5	6 2.6	10 48.7
16 Tu	19 32 55	22 51 29	11♒17 43	17 36 34	20 29.6	15 46.9	2 31.7	14 57.4	18 51.7	27 43.6	19 39.6	6 3.5	10 50.4
17 W	19 36 51	23 48 43	23 58 39	0♓24 4	20 24.2	16 2.6	3 40.7	15 33.4	18 57.0	27 51.3	19 42.7	6 4.4	10 52.1
18 Th	19 40 48	24 45 56	6♓52 50	13 25 1	20 18.8	16 13.6	4 49.6	16 9.4	19 2.5	27 59.1	19 45.7	6 5.4	10 53.8
19 F	19 44 44	25 43 11	20 0 39	26 39 48	20 14.0	16R19.9	5 58.5	16 45.5	19 8.1	28 6.8	19 48.8	6 6.4	10 55.6
20 Sa	19 48 41	26 40 26	3♈22 29	10♈ 8 46	20 10.4	16 21.3	7 7.2	17 21.7	19 13.9	28 14.6	19 51.8	6 7.4	10 57.3
21 Su	19 52 37	27 37 41	16 58 40	23 52 12	20D 8.4	16 17.8	8 15.8	17 57.9	19 19.8	28 22.4	19 54.8	6 8.4	10 59.0
22 M	19 56 34	28 34 58	0♉49 22	7♉50 9	20 7.9	16 9.3	9 24.3	18 34.2	19 25.8	28 30.1	19 57.8	6 9.5	11 0.8
23 Tu	20 0 31	29 32 16	14 54 26	22 2 5	20 8.7	15 56.0	10 32.7	19 10.6	19 32.0	28 37.9	20 0.7	6 10.6	11 2.5
24 W	20 4 27	0♌29 34	29 12 53	6♊26 32	20 10.0	15 37.9	11 41.0	19 47.0	19 38.4	28 45.6	20 3.6	6 11.7	11 4.3
25 Th	20 8 24	1 26 54	13♊42 37	21 0 40	20R11.0	15 15.1	12 49.1	20 23.5	19 44.9	28 53.4	20 6.5	6 12.8	11 6.0
26 F	20 12 20	2 24 14	28 20 4	5♋40 9	20 10.9	14 47.9	13 57.2	21 0.1	19 51.5	29 1.2	20 9.3	6 14.0	11 7.8
27 Sa	20 16 17	3 21 35	13♋ 0 8	20 19 13	20 9.0	14 16.5	15 5.2	21 36.8	19 58.2	29 8.9	20 12.2	6 15.2	11 9.5
28 Su	20 20 13	4 18 57	27 36 33	4♌51 17	20 5.1	13 41.4	16 13.0	22 13.5	20 5.1	29 16.7	20 15.0	6 16.5	11 11.3
29 M	20 24 10	5 16 20	12♌ 2 36	19 9 45	19 59.4	13 3.0	17 20.7	22 50.3	20 12.1	29 24.4	20 17.7	6 17.7	11 13.1
30 Tu	20 28 6	6 13 44	26 12 5	3♍ 9 4	19 52.3	12 21.8	18 28.3	23 27.1	20 19.3	29 32.1	20 20.4	6 19.0	11 14.9
31 W	20 32 3	7 11 8	10♍ 0 17	16 45 30	19 44.8	11 38.5	19 35.8	24 4.0	20 26.6	29 39.9	20 23.1	6 20.3	11 16.6

AUGUST 1946 LONGITUDE

Day	Sid.Time	☉	0 hr ☽	Noon ☽	True ☊	☿	♀	♂	♃	♄	♅	♆	♇
1 Th	20 36 0	8♌ 8 32	23♍24 34	29♍57 31	19♊37.6	10♌53.8	20♍43.1	24♍41.0	20♎34.0	29♋47.6	20♊25.8	6♎21.7	11♌18.4
2 F	20 39 56	9 5 58	6♎24 32	12♎45 51	19R31.6	10R 8.5	21 50.3	25 18.1	20 41.5	29 55.3	20 28.4	6 23.0	11 20.2
3 Sa	20 43 53	10 3 24	19 1 52	25 13 1	19 27.4	9 23.3	22 57.3	25 55.2	20 49.2	0♌ 3.0	20 31.0	6 24.4	11 22.0
4 Su	20 47 49	11 0 51	1♏19 51	7♏22 57	19D25.1	8 39.2	24 4.2	26 32.4	20 56.9	0 10.7	20 33.6	6 25.9	11 23.8
5 M	20 51 46	11 58 18	13 22 56	19 20 27	19 24.6	7 56.9	25 11.0	27 9.6	21 4.8	0 18.3	20 36.1	6 27.3	11 25.5
6 Tu	20 55 42	12 55 46	25 16 8	1♐10 41	19 25.3	7 17.3	26 17.6	27 46.9	21 12.9	0 26.0	20 38.6	6 28.8	11 27.3
7 W	20 59 39	13 53 15	7♐ 4 44	12 58 54	19 26.3	6 41.1	27 24.0	28 24.3	21 21.0	0 33.6	20 41.0	6 30.3	11 29.1
8 Th	21 3 35	14 50 45	18 53 50	24 50 4	19R26.9	6 9.1	28 30.3	29 1.7	21 29.3	0 41.2	20 43.5	6 31.8	11 30.9
9 F	21 7 32	15 48 16	0♑48 10	6♑48 37	19 26.2	5 42.0	29 36.4	29 39.2	21 37.6	0 48.8	20 45.8	6 33.3	11 32.7
10 Sa	21 11 29	16 45 47	12 51 50	18 58 11	19 23.5	5 20.4	0♎42.4	0♎16.8	21 46.1	0 56.4	20 48.2	6 34.9	11 34.4
11 Su	21 15 25	17 43 20	25 8 0	1♒21 30	19 18.5	5 4.7	1 48.1	0 54.4	21 54.7	1 4.0	20 50.5	6 36.5	11 36.2
12 M	21 19 22	18 40 53	7♒38 50	14 0 6	19 11.2	4D55.4	2 53.7	1 32.1	22 3.4	1 11.5	20 52.8	6 38.1	11 38.0
13 Tu	21 23 18	19 38 28	20 25 20	26 54 27	19 1.9	4 52.8	3 59.1	2 9.8	22 12.3	1 19.0	20 55.0	6 39.7	11 39.8
14 W	21 27 15	20 36 4	3♓27 22	10♓ 3 53	18 51.6	4 57.1	5 4.4	2 47.6	22 21.2	1 26.5	20 57.2	6 41.4	11 41.5
15 Th	21 31 11	21 33 41	16 43 50	23 26 57	18 41.2	5 8.7	6 9.4	3 25.5	22 30.2	1 34.0	20 59.3	6 43.1	11 43.3
16 F	21 35 8	22 31 19	0♈13 1	7♈ 1 44	18 31.8	5 27.5	7 14.2	4 3.4	22 39.3	1 41.4	21 1.4	6 44.7	11 45.1
17 Sa	21 39 4	23 28 59	13 52 54	20 46 15	18 24.3	5 53.6	8 18.9	4 41.4	22 48.6	1 48.8	21 3.5	6 46.5	11 46.8
18 Su	21 43 1	24 26 40	27 41 37	4♉38 49	18 19.1	6 27.0	9 23.3	5 19.5	22 57.9	1 56.2	21 5.5	6 48.2	11 48.6
19 M	21 46 58	25 24 23	11♉37 43	18 38 11	18 16.5	7 7.7	10 27.5	5 57.6	23 7.4	2 3.6	21 7.5	6 50.0	11 50.3
20 Tu	21 50 54	26 22 8	25 40 7	2♊43 25	18D15.7	7 55.5	11 31.5	6 35.8	23 16.9	2 10.9	21 9.4	6 51.7	11 52.0
21 W	21 54 51	27 19 55	9♊47 58	16 53 39	18R16.0	8 50.2	12 35.3	7 14.0	23 26.6	2 18.2	21 11.3	6 53.5	11 53.8
22 Th	21 58 47	28 17 43	24 0 17	1♋ 7 38	18 16.0	9 51.6	13 38.9	7 52.4	23 36.3	2 25.5	21 13.2	6 55.4	11 55.5
23 F	22 2 44	29 15 33	8♋15 26	15 23 19	18 14.6	10 59.4	14 42.2	8 30.7	23 46.1	2 32.7	21 15.0	6 57.2	11 57.2
24 Sa	22 6 40	0♍13 24	22 30 53	29 37 37	18 10.9	12 13.5	15 45.3	9 9.2	23 56.1	2 39.9	21 16.8	6 59.1	11 58.9
25 Su	22 10 37	1 11 18	6♌42 59	13♌46 25	18 4.5	13 33.3	16 48.2	9 47.7	24 6.1	2 47.1	21 18.5	7 0.9	12 0.7
26 M	22 14 33	2 9 13	20 47 19	27 45 5	17 55.4	14 58.5	17 50.8	10 26.3	24 16.2	2 54.3	21 20.1	7 2.8	12 2.4
27 Tu	22 18 30	3 7 9	4♍39 12	11♍29 7	17 44.3	16 28.8	18 53.2	11 4.9	24 26.4	3 1.3	21 21.8	7 4.7	12 4.0
28 W	22 22 27	4 5 7	18 14 28	24 54 53	17 32.4	18 3.6	19 55.3	11 43.6	24 36.7	3 8.4	21 23.4	7 6.7	12 5.7
29 Th	22 26 23	5 3 6	1♎30 10	8♎ 0 14	17 20.8	19 42.5	20 57.1	12 22.4	24 47.1	3 15.4	21 24.9	7 8.6	12 7.4
30 F	22 30 20	6 1 7	14 25 5	20 44 51	17 10.6	21 25.0	21 58.6	13 1.2	24 57.5	3 22.4	21 26.4	7 10.6	12 9.1
31 Sa	22 34 16	6 59 9	26 59 47	3♏10 12	17 2.7	23 10.7	22 59.9	13 40.1	25 8.1	3 29.3	21 27.8	7 12.5	12 10.7

Astro Data Dy Hr Mn	Planet Ingress Dy Hr Mn	Last Aspect Dy Hr Mn	☽ Ingress Dy Hr Mn	Last Aspect Dy Hr Mn	☽ Ingress Dy Hr Mn	☽ Phases & Eclipses Dy Hr Mn	Astro Data
☽0S 6 1:12	♀ ♍ 13 19:22	2 1:32 ♅ ✱	♍ 2 20:45	1 11:49 ♄ ✱	♎ 1 12:05	6 5:15 ☽ 13♎32	1 JULY 1946
☿ R 19 18:55	☉ ♌ 23 11:37	4 20:24 ♄ ✱	♎ 5 3:21	3 3:29 ♃ ☌	♏ 3 21:23	14 9:23 ○ 21♑19	Julian Day # 16983
☽0N 20 13:58		7 6:56 ♄ □	♏ 7 13:41	6 5:23 ♂ ✱	♐ 6 9:36	21 19:52 ☽ 28♈25	Delta T 27.5 sec
♃△♅ 30 6:13	♄ ♌ 2 14:42	9 20:06 ♄ △	♐ 10 2:20	8 21:34 ♂ □	♑ 8 22:23	28 11:54 ● 4♌47	SVP 06♓00'41"
	♀ ♎ 9 8:34	12 12:04 ♀ △	♑ 12 15:05	10 17:40 ♃ □	♒ 11 9:24		Obliquity 23°26'48"
☽0S 2 8:52	♂ ♎ 9 13:17	14 21:36 ♄ ☍	♒ 15 2:17	13 3:21 ♃ △	♓ 13 17:41	4 20:55 ☽ 11♏51	⚷ Chiron 15♎12.7
♀0S 9 10:25	☉ ♍ 23 18:26	16 15:56 ♅ △	♓ 17 11:15	15 7:38 ♅ □	♈ 15 23:37	12 22:26 ○ 19♒35	☽ Mean ☊ 19♊53.4
♂0S 11 10:53		19 14:45 ♄ △	♈ 19 17:59	17 17:57 ☉ △	♉ 18 3:59	20 1:17 ☽ 26♉25	
☿ D 12 21:03		21 19:58 ♄ □	♉ 21 22:35	20 1:17 ☉ □	♊ 20 7:22	26 21:07 ● 3♍00	1 AUGUST 1946
☽0N 16 18:45		23 23:14 ♄ ✱	♊ 24 1:18	22 7:45 ☉ ✱	♋ 22 10:06		Julian Day # 17014
☽0S 29 17:04		25 11:28 ♂ □	♋ 26 2:44	24 2:25 ♃ □	♌ 24 12:38		Delta T 27.6 sec
		28 2:47 ♄ ☌	♌ 28 3:57	26 6:04 ♃ ✱	♍ 26 15:54		SVP 06♓00'36"
		29 13:58 ♅ ✱	♍ 30 6:32	28 5:39 ♅ □	♎ 28 21:15		Obliquity 23°26'48"
				30 20:21 ♃ ☌	♏ 31 5:49		⚷ Chiron 17♎04.1
							☽ Mean ☊ 18♊14.9

LONGITUDE — SEPTEMBER 1946

Day	Sid.Time	☉	0 hr ☽	Noon ☽	True ☊	☿	♀	♂	♃	♄	♅	♆	♇
1 Su	22 38 13	7♍57 13	9♏16 33	15♏19 18	16♊57.3	24♌59.0	24♎ 0.8	14♎19.1	25♎18.7	3♌36.2	21♊29.2	7♎14.5	12♌12.3
2 M	22 42 9	8 55 18	21 19 2	27 16 21	16R 54.4	26 49.6	25 1.4	14 58.1	25 29.4	3 43.1	21 30.6	7 16.5	12 14.0
3 Tu	22 46 6	9 53 25	3♐11 54	9♐ 6 21	16D 53.4	28 42.0	26 1.7	15 37.2	25 40.2	3 49.9	21 31.9	7 18.6	12 15.6
4 W	22 50 2	10 51 33	15 0 23	20 54 43	16R 53.3	0♍35.7	27 1.7	16 16.3	25 51.1	3 56.6	21 33.1	7 20.6	12 17.2
5 Th	22 53 59	11 49 42	26 50 1	2♑46 57	16 53.1	2 30.5	28 1.3	16 55.5	26 2.0	4 3.3	21 34.3	7 22.6	12 18.8
6 F	22 57 55	12 47 53	8♑46 11	14 48 18	16 51.7	4 25.9	29 0.5	17 34.8	26 13.0	4 10.0	21 35.5	7 24.7	12 20.4
7 Sa	23 1 52	13 46 6	20 53 53	27 3 24	16 48.2	6 21.6	29 59.4	18 14.1	26 24.1	4 16.6	21 36.6	7 26.8	12 22.0
8 Su	23 5 49	14 44 20	3♒17 17	9♒35 52	16 42.2	8 17.5	0♏57.8	18 53.5	26 35.3	4 23.2	21 37.6	7 28.9	12 23.5
9 M	23 9 45	15 42 35	15 59 24	22 28 1	16 33.5	10 13.3	1 55.9	19 32.9	26 46.5	4 29.7	21 38.6	7 31.0	12 25.1
10 Tu	23 13 42	16 40 52	29 1 44	5♓40 29	16 22.6	12 8.7	2 53.6	20 12.4	26 57.8	4 36.1	21 39.6	7 33.1	12 26.6
11 W	23 17 38	17 39 11	12♓24 2	19 12 6	16 10.4	14 3.7	3 50.8	20 52.0	27 9.2	4 42.5	21 40.5	7 35.2	12 28.1
12 Th	23 21 35	18 37 32	26 4 17	3♈ 0 7	15 58.0	15 58.0	4 47.6	21 31.6	27 20.6	4 48.9	21 41.3	7 37.3	12 29.6
13 F	23 25 31	19 35 54	9♈59 2	17 0 31	15 46.7	17 51.7	5 43.9	22 11.3	27 32.1	4 55.2	21 42.1	7 39.4	12 31.1
14 Sa	23 29 28	20 34 19	24 3 58	1♉ 8 51	15 37.5	19 44.5	6 39.7	22 51.1	27 43.7	5 1.4	21 42.9	7 41.6	12 32.6
15 Su	23 33 24	21 32 45	8♉14 37	15 20 51	15 31.0	21 36.5	7 35.1	23 30.9	27 55.3	5 7.6	21 43.6	7 43.7	12 34.0
16 M	23 37 21	22 31 14	22 27 8	29 33 8	15 27.4	23 27.5	8 29.9	24 10.7	28 7.0	5 13.7	21 44.2	7 45.9	12 35.5
17 Tu	23 41 18	23 29 45	6♊38 35	13♊43 18	15D 26.0	25 17.6	9 24.2	24 50.7	28 18.7	5 19.7	21 44.8	7 48.1	12 36.9
18 W	23 45 14	24 28 18	20 47 9	27 49 59	15R 25.9	27 6.8	10 18.0	25 30.7	28 30.5	5 25.7	21 45.4	7 50.3	12 38.3
19 Th	23 49 11	25 26 53	4♋51 44	11♋52 20	15 25.7	28 54.9	11 11.2	26 10.8	28 42.4	5 31.7	21 45.9	7 52.4	12 39.7
20 F	23 53 7	26 25 31	18 51 39	25 49 37	15 24.2	0♎42.0	12 3.9	26 50.9	28 54.3	5 37.5	21 46.3	7 54.6	12 41.1
21 Sa	23 57 4	27 24 11	2♌46 3	9♌40 47	15 20.4	2 28.1	12 55.9	27 31.1	29 6.3	5 43.3	21 46.7	7 56.8	12 42.4
22 Su	0 1 0	28 22 53	16 33 37	23 24 15	15 13.8	4 13.3	13 47.4	28 11.4	29 18.3	5 49.1	21 47.0	7 59.0	12 43.8
23 M	0 4 57	29 21 37	0♍12 26	6♍57 52	15 4.4	5 57.4	14 38.1	28 51.7	29 30.4	5 54.7	21 47.3	8 1.3	12 45.1
24 Tu	0 8 53	0♎20 23	13 40 14	20 19 14	14 53.1	7 40.5	15 28.2	29 32.1	29 42.6	6 0.3	21 47.6	8 3.5	12 46.4
25 W	0 12 50	1 19 11	26 54 37	3♎26 10	14 40.8	9 22.7	16 17.7	0♏12.5	29 54.7	6 5.9	21 47.7	8 5.7	12 47.7
26 Th	0 16 47	2 18 1	9♎53 42	16 17 7	14 28.7	11 3.9	17 6.3	0 53.0	0♏ 7.0	6 11.3	21 47.9	8 7.9	12 49.0
27 F	0 20 43	3 16 54	22 36 25	28 51 38	14 18.0	12 44.2	17 54.2	1 33.6	0 19.3	6 16.7	21R 47.9	8 10.1	12 50.2
28 Sa	0 24 40	4 15 48	5♏ 2 54	11♏10 28	14 9.5	14 23.6	18 41.4	2 14.2	0 31.6	6 22.0	21 48.0	8 12.4	12 51.4
29 Su	0 28 36	5 14 44	17 14 36	23 15 41	14 3.6	16 2.0	19 27.7	2 55.0	0 44.0	6 27.3	21 47.9	8 14.6	12 52.6
30 M	0 32 33	6 13 42	29 14 9	5♐10 31	14 0.3	17 39.6	20 13.1	3 35.7	0 56.4	6 32.4	21 47.8	8 16.8	12 53.8

LONGITUDE — OCTOBER 1946

Day	Sid.Time	☉	0 hr ☽	Noon ☽	True ☊	☿	♀	♂	♃	♄	♅	♆	♇
1 Tu	0 36 29	7♎12 41	11♐ 5 20	16♐59 11	13♊59.2	19♎16.3	20♏57.7	4♏16.5	1♏ 8.9	6♌37.5	21♊47.7	8♎19.1	12♌55.0
2 W	0 40 26	8 11 43	22 52 43	28 46 34	13D 59.4	20 52.2	21 41.3	4 57.4	1 21.4	6 42.5	21R 47.5	8 21.3	12 56.1
3 Th	0 44 22	9 10 46	4♑41 27	10♑38 2	13R 60.0	22 27.2	22 24.0	5 38.4	1 33.9	6 47.5	21 47.3	8 23.5	12 57.3
4 F	0 48 19	10 9 51	16 37 0	22 39 2	13 59.8	24 1.4	23 5.6	6 19.4	1 46.5	6 52.3	21 47.0	8 25.8	12 58.4
5 Sa	0 52 16	11 8 58	28 44 46	4♒54 50	13 58.1	25 34.7	23 46.2	7 0.5	1 59.1	6 57.1	21 46.7	8 28.0	12 59.4
6 Su	0 56 12	12 8 7	11♒ 9 45	17 30 0	13 54.3	27 7.3	24 25.6	7 41.6	2 11.8	7 1.8	21 46.3	8 30.2	13 0.5
7 M	1 0 9	13 7 17	23 55 59	0♓27 59	13 48.2	28 39.0	25 4.0	8 22.8	2 24.4	7 6.4	21 45.8	8 32.5	13 1.5
8 Tu	1 4 5	14 6 30	7♓ 6 10	13 50 31	13 40.0	0♏10.0	25 41.1	9 4.0	2 37.2	7 10.9	21 45.3	8 34.7	13 2.5
9 W	1 8 2	15 5 44	20 40 58	27 37 11	13 30.6	1 40.2	26 17.0	9 45.3	2 49.9	7 15.3	21 44.8	8 36.9	13 3.5
10 Th	1 11 58	16 4 59	4♈38 48	11♈45 13	13 20.8	3 9.6	26 51.6	10 26.7	3 2.7	7 19.7	21 44.2	8 39.1	13 4.5
11 F	1 15 55	17 4 17	18 55 46	26 9 41	13 11.9	4 38.2	27 24.8	11 8.1	3 15.5	7 24.0	21 43.5	8 41.3	13 5.4
12 Sa	1 19 51	18 3 37	3♉26 8	10♉44 14	13 4.8	6 6.0	27 56.7	11 49.6	3 28.3	7 28.1	21 42.8	8 43.6	13 6.4
13 Su	1 23 48	19 2 59	18 3 9	25 22 3	12 59.9	7 33.0	28 27.1	12 31.2	3 41.2	7 32.2	21 42.1	8 45.8	13 7.2
14 M	1 27 44	20 2 24	2♊40 12	9♊56 55	12D 57.6	8 59.2	28 56.0	13 12.8	3 54.1	7 36.2	21 41.3	8 48.0	13 8.1
15 Tu	1 31 41	21 1 51	17 11 39	24 23 48	12 57.2	10 24.6	29 23.3	13 54.5	4 7.0	7 40.1	21 40.4	8 50.2	13 9.0
16 W	1 35 38	22 1 20	1♋33 28	8♋39 57	12 58.0	11 49.1	29 49.0	14 36.2	4 19.9	7 44.0	21 39.5	8 52.4	13 9.8
17 Th	1 39 34	23 0 51	15 43 13	22 43 11	12R 59.0	13 12.8	0♐13.1	15 18.0	4 32.9	7 47.7	21 38.6	8 54.5	13 10.6
18 F	1 43 31	24 0 25	29 39 49	6♌33 6	12 59.0	14 35.5	0 35.4	15 59.9	4 45.9	7 51.3	21 37.6	8 56.7	13 11.4
19 Sa	1 47 27	25 0 1	13♌23 4	20 9 44	12 57.4	15 57.2	0 55.9	16 41.8	4 58.9	7 54.9	21 36.6	8 58.9	13 12.1
20 Su	1 51 24	25 59 39	26 53 10	3♍33 22	12 53.7	17 18.0	1 14.6	17 23.8	5 11.9	7 58.3	21 35.5	9 1.1	13 12.8
21 M	1 55 20	26 59 19	10♍10 22	16 44 11	12 48.0	18 37.7	1 31.3	18 5.8	5 24.9	8 1.7	21 34.3	9 3.2	13 13.5
22 Tu	1 59 17	27 59 2	23 14 49	29 42 15	12 40.7	19 56.2	1 46.1	18 48.0	5 38.0	8 4.9	21 33.2	9 5.4	13 14.2
23 W	2 3 13	28 58 47	6♎ 6 30	12♎27 33	12 32.7	21 13.5	1 58.8	19 30.1	5 51.0	8 8.1	21 31.9	9 7.5	13 14.8
24 Th	2 7 10	29 58 33	18 45 24	25 0 6	12 24.7	22 29.5	2 9.4	20 12.4	6 4.1	8 11.1	21 30.6	9 9.6	13 15.5
25 F	2 11 7	0♏58 22	1♏11 42	7♏20 17	12 17.7	23 44.0	2 17.9	20 54.7	6 17.2	8 14.1	21 29.3	9 11.7	13 16.0
26 Sa	2 15 3	1 58 13	13 26 0	19 29 1	12 12.3	24 57.0	2 24.1	21 37.1	6 30.3	8 16.9	21 27.9	9 13.8	13 16.6
27 Su	2 19 0	2 58 6	25 29 33	1♐27 52	12 8.8	26 8.3	2 28.1	22 19.5	6 43.4	8 19.6	21 26.5	9 15.9	13 17.1
28 M	2 22 56	3 58 1	7♐24 18	13 19 12	12D 7.3	27 17.7	2R 29.8	23 2.0	6 56.6	8 22.3	21 25.1	9 18.0	13 17.7
29 Tu	2 26 53	4 57 57	19 13 0	25 6 9	12 7.4	28 25.0	2 29.1	23 44.5	7 9.7	8 24.8	21 23.6	9 20.1	13 18.1
30 W	2 30 49	5 57 55	0♑59 10	6♑52 35	12 8.7	29 30.0	2 26.0	24 27.1	7 22.8	8 27.3	21 22.0	9 22.1	13 18.6
31 Th	2 34 46	6 57 55	12 46 58	18 42 57	12 10.5	0♐32.5	2 20.4	25 9.8	7 36.0	8 29.6	21 20.5	9 24.2	13 19.0

Astro Data (Dy Hr Mn)

☽0N	13 1:01
☿0S	21 1:13
☽0S	26 1:09
♅ R	27 22:01
♄∠♅	2 23:09
☽0N	10 9:55
☽0S	23 8:24
♃⊡♅	25 20:04
♀ R	28 4:52

Planet Ingress (Dy Hr Mn)

☿ ♍	3 16:29
♀ ♏	7 0:16
☿ ♎	19 14:34
☉ ♎	23 15:41
♂ ♏	24 16:35
♃ ♏	25 10:19
☿ ♏	7 21:21
♀ ♐	16 10:45
☉ ♏	24 0:35
☿ ♐	30 11:23

Last Aspect / ☽ Ingress (Dy Hr Mn)

Last Aspect		☽ Ingress
2 13:10	☿ □	♐ 2 17:31
5 2:37	♀ ⚹	♑ 5 6:24
7 10:54	♃ □	♒ 7 17:41
9 20:11	♃ △	♓ 10 1:46
11 16:21	♅ □	♈ 12 6:49
14 6:18	♃ ☍	♉ 14 10:03
16 1:57	☿ △	♊ 16 12:45
18 13:20	♃ △	♋ 18 15:42
20 17:34	♃ □	♌ 20 19:13
22 22:45	♃ ⚹	♍ 22 23:38
24 14:40	♅ □	♎ 25 5:40
26 22:28	♅ △	♏ 27 14:12
29 4:43	♀ ☌	♐ 30 1:32

Last Aspect / ☽ Ingress (Dy Hr Mn)

Last Aspect		☽ Ingress
1 21:47	♅ ☍	♑ 2 14:29
4 16:52	☿ □	♒ 5 2:27
7 9:49	☿ △	♓ 7 11:09
9 10:07	♀ △	♈ 9 16:05
11 4:39	♅ ⚹	♉ 11 18:20
13 17:39	♀ ☍	♊ 13 19:37
15 7:27	♅ ☌	♋ 15 21:23
17 13:28	☉ □	♌ 18 0:35
19 22:16	☉ ⚹	♍ 20 5:35
21 20:52	♅ □	♎ 22 12:33
24 5:16	♅ △	♏ 24 21:41
27 1:26	☿ ☌	♐ 27 9:03
29 4:26	♅ ☍	♑ 29 21:59

☽ Phases & Eclipses (Dy Hr Mn)

3 14:49	☽ 10♐29
11 9:59	○ 18♓03
18 6:44	☽ 24♊45
25 8:45	● 1♎41
3 9:53	☽ 9♑35
10 20:40	○ 16♈56
17 13:28	☽ 23♋34
24 23:32	● 0♏57

Astro Data

1 SEPTEMBER 1946
Julian Day # 17045
Delta T 27.6 sec
SVP 06♓00'32"
Obliquity 23°26'49"
⚷ Chiron 20♎17.7
☽ Mean ☊ 16♊36.4

1 OCTOBER 1946
Julian Day # 17075
Delta T 27.7 sec
SVP 06♓00'29"
Obliquity 23°26'49"
⚷ Chiron 24♎15.2
☽ Mean ☊ 15♊01.0

NOVEMBER 1946 LONGITUDE

Day	Sid.Time	☉	0 hr ☽	Noon ☽	True ☊	☿	♀	♂	♃	♄	♅	♆	♇
1 F	2 38 42	7♏57 57	24♑41 8	0♒42 10	12♊12.1	1♐32.2	2♐12.5	25♏52.5	7♏49.1	8♌31.8	21♊18.8	9♎26.2	13♌19.4
2 Sa	2 42 39	8 58 0	6♒46 41	12 55 18	12R 12.9	2 28.7	2R 2.0	26 35.3	8 2.2	8 33.9	21R 17.2	9 28.2	13 19.8
3 Su	2 46 36	9 58 5	19 8 39	25 27 18	12 12.5	3 21.7	1 49.2	27 18.2	8 15.4	8 36.0	21 15.5	9 30.2	13 20.2
4 M	2 50 32	10 58 11	1♓51 44	8♓22 25	12 10.6	4 10.8	1 33.9	28 1.1	8 28.5	8 37.9	21 13.7	9 32.2	13 20.5
5 Tu	2 54 29	11 58 19	14 59 40	21 43 44	12 7.5	4 55.4	1 16.2	28 44.0	8 41.6	8 39.6	21 11.9	9 34.1	13 20.8
6 W	2 58 25	12 58 28	28 34 41	5♈32 29	12 3.5	5 35.2	0 56.2	29 27.0	8 54.8	8 41.3	21 10.1	9 36.1	13 21.0
7 Th	3 2 22	13 58 39	12♈36 51	19 47 25	11 59.1	6 9.5	0 34.0	0♐10.1	9 7.9	8 42.9	21 8.2	9 38.0	13 21.3
8 F	3 6 18	14 58 52	27 3 36	4♉24 39	11 55.0	6 37.8	0 9.6	0 53.2	9 21.0	8 44.4	21 6.4	9 39.9	13 21.5
9 Sa	3 10 15	15 59 6	11♉49 41	19 17 43	11 51.8	6 59.3	29♏43.2	1 36.4	9 34.1	8 45.7	21 4.4	9 41.8	13 21.7
10 Su	3 14 11	16 59 22	26 47 41	4♊18 28	11 49.8	7 13.4	29 14.9	2 19.7	9 47.2	8 47.0	21 2.5	9 43.7	13 21.8
11 M	3 18 8	17 59 40	11♊49 0	19 18 13	11D 49.2	7R 19.5	28 44.8	3 3.0	10 0.3	8 48.1	21 0.5	9 45.5	13 21.9
12 Tu	3 22 5	19 0 0	26 45 10	4♋ 9 0	11 49.7	7 16.7	28 13.2	3 46.3	10 13.4	8 49.2	20 58.4	9 47.4	13 22.0
13 W	3 26 1	20 0 21	11♋29 1	18 44 38	11 51.0	7 4.5	27 40.2	4 29.8	10 26.5	8 50.1	20 56.4	9 49.2	13 22.1
14 Th	3 29 58	21 0 45	25 55 25	3♌ 1 6	11 52.4	6 42.5	27 6.0	5 13.2	10 39.5	8 50.9	20 54.3	9 51.0	13 22.2
15 F	3 33 54	22 1 10	10♌ 1 30	16 56 33	11R 53.5	6 10.2	26 30.9	5 56.8	10 52.6	8 51.6	20 52.2	9 52.8	13R 22.2
16 Sa	3 37 51	23 1 37	23 46 20	0♍30 57	11 53.9	5 27.6	25 55.2	6 40.4	11 5.6	8 52.2	20 50.0	9 54.5	13 22.2
17 Su	3 41 47	24 2 7	7♍10 34	13 45 26	11 53.4	4 35.1	25 18.9	7 24.1	11 18.6	8 52.7	20 47.8	9 56.3	13 22.1
18 M	3 45 44	25 2 37	20 15 47	26 41 54	11 52.0	3 33.3	24 42.5	8 7.8	11 31.6	8 53.0	20 45.6	9 58.0	13 22.0
19 Tu	3 49 41	26 3 10	3♎ 4 4	9♎22 33	11 50.1	2 23.5	24 6.1	8 51.5	11 44.5	8 53.3	20 43.4	9 59.7	13 21.9
20 W	3 53 37	27 3 45	15 37 38	21 49 35	11 47.8	1 7.5	23 30.0	9 35.4	11 57.5	8R 53.4	20 41.1	10 1.3	13 21.8
21 Th	3 57 34	28 4 21	27 58 38	4♏ 5 4	11 45.5	29♏47.3	22 54.5	10 19.3	12 10.4	8 53.4	20 38.8	10 3.0	13 21.7
22 F	4 1 30	29 4 59	10♏ 9 5	16 10 57	11 43.7	28 25.7	22 19.7	11 3.2	12 23.3	8 53.3	20 36.5	10 4.6	13 21.5
23 Sa	4 5 27	0♐ 5 38	22 10 51	28 9 2	11 42.3	27 5.2	21 45.9	11 47.2	12 36.2	8 53.1	20 34.2	10 6.2	13 21.3
24 Su	4 9 23	1 6 19	4♐ 5 45	10♐ 1 13	11D 41.6	25 48.5	21 13.4	12 31.3	12 49.0	8 52.8	20 31.8	10 7.8	13 21.0
25 M	4 13 20	2 7 1	15 55 42	21 49 29	11 41.6	24 38.2	20 42.3	13 15.4	13 1.8	8 52.3	20 29.5	10 9.3	13 20.8
26 Tu	4 17 16	3 7 45	27 42 51	3♑36 9	11 42.0	23 36.3	20 12.8	13 59.6	13 14.6	8 51.8	20 27.1	10 10.8	13 20.5
27 W	4 21 13	4 8 29	9♑29 42	15 23 55	11 42.7	22 44.3	19 45.0	14 43.8	13 27.3	8 51.1	20 24.6	10 12.3	13 20.2
28 Th	4 25 10	5 9 15	21 19 12	27 15 58	11 43.4	22 3.3	19 19.2	15 28.1	13 40.0	8 50.3	20 22.2	10 13.8	13 19.8
29 F	4 29 6	6 10 2	3♒14 44	9♒15 57	11 44.2	21 33.9	18 55.5	16 12.5	13 52.7	8 49.5	20 19.8	10 15.2	13 19.4
30 Sa	4 33 3	7 10 50	15 20 10	21 27 53	11 44.7	21 16.0	18 33.9	16 56.9	14 5.4	8 48.5	20 17.3	10 16.7	13 19.0

DECEMBER 1946 LONGITUDE

Day	Sid.Time	☉	0 hr ☽	Noon ☽	True ☊	☿	♀	♂	♃	♄	♅	♆	♇
1 Su	4 36 59	8♐11 39	27♒39 39	3♓56 1	11♊45.0	21♏ 9.4	18♏14.6	17♐41.3	14♏18.0	8♌47.4	20♊14.8	10♎18.0	13♌18.6
2 M	4 40 56	9 12 29	10♓17 28	16 44 32	11R 45.0	21D 13.5	17R 57.6	18 25.8	14 30.5	8R 46.1	20R 12.3	10 19.4	13R 18.2
3 Tu	4 44 52	10 13 20	23 17 37	29 57 7	11 45.0	21 27.6	17 43.0	19 10.4	14 43.0	8 44.8	20 9.8	10 20.7	13 17.7
4 W	4 48 49	11 14 11	6♈43 19	13♈36 23	11D 44.9	21 50.9	17 30.9	19 55.0	14 55.5	8 43.4	20 7.3	10 22.0	13 17.2
5 Th	4 52 45	12 15 3	20 36 23	27 43 12	11 44.9	22 22.4	17 21.2	20 39.6	15 8.0	8 41.8	20 4.8	10 23.3	13 16.6
6 F	4 56 42	13 15 57	4♉56 35	12♉16 3	11 45.0	23 1.3	17 14.0	21 24.3	15 20.3	8 40.2	20 2.3	10 24.6	13 16.1
7 Sa	5 0 39	14 16 51	19 40 59	27 10 35	11 45.2	23 46.9	17 9.3	22 9.1	15 32.7	8 38.4	19 59.7	10 25.8	13 15.5
8 Su	5 4 35	15 17 45	4♊43 51	12♊19 42	11R 45.4	24 38.2	17D 7.1	22 53.9	15 45.0	8 36.6	19 57.2	10 27.0	13 14.9
9 M	5 8 32	16 18 41	19 56 56	27 34 18	11 45.3	25 34.7	17 7.4	23 38.7	15 57.2	8 34.6	19 54.6	10 28.1	13 14.3
10 Tu	5 12 28	17 19 38	5♋10 31	12♋44 25	11 45.1	26 35.6	17 10.1	24 23.6	16 9.4	8 32.5	19 52.1	10 29.3	13 13.6
11 W	5 16 25	18 20 36	20 14 51	27 40 51	11 44.5	27 40.5	17 15.1	25 8.6	16 21.6	8 30.4	19 49.5	10 30.4	13 12.9
12 Th	5 20 21	19 21 35	5♌ 1 35	12♌16 25	11 43.6	28 48.7	17 22.6	25 53.6	16 33.6	8 28.1	19 47.0	10 31.5	13 12.2
13 F	5 24 18	20 22 35	19 24 51	26 26 37	11 42.7	29 59.9	17 32.3	26 38.6	16 45.7	8 25.7	19 44.4	10 32.5	13 11.5
14 Sa	5 28 14	21 23 36	3♍21 35	10♍ 9 49	11 41.9	1♐13.6	17 44.3	27 23.8	16 57.6	8 23.2	19 41.9	10 33.5	13 10.7
15 Su	5 32 11	22 24 37	16 51 27	23 26 46	11D 41.4	2 29.6	17 58.4	28 8.9	17 9.6	8 20.7	19 39.3	10 34.5	13 10.0
16 M	5 36 8	23 25 40	29 56 8	6♎19 58	11 41.4	3 47.5	18 14.7	28 54.1	17 21.4	8 18.0	19 36.7	10 35.4	13 9.2
17 Tu	5 40 4	24 26 44	12♎38 43	18 52 54	11 42.0	5 7.1	18 33.0	29 39.4	17 33.2	8 15.2	19 34.2	10 36.3	13 8.3
18 W	5 44 1	25 27 49	25 2 59	1♏ 9 30	11 43.1	6 28.2	18 53.3	0♑24.7	17 44.9	8 12.4	19 31.6	10 37.2	13 7.5
19 Th	5 47 57	26 28 54	7♏12 56	13 13 45	11 44.5	7 50.6	19 15.6	1 10.0	17 56.6	8 9.4	19 29.1	10 38.1	13 6.6
20 F	5 51 54	27 30 1	19 12 24	25 9 19	11 45.8	9 14.1	19 39.7	1 55.5	18 8.2	8 6.3	19 26.6	10 38.9	13 5.7
21 Sa	5 55 50	28 31 8	1♐ 4 53	6♐59 27	11R 46.9	10 38.6	20 5.5	2 40.9	18 19.7	8 3.2	19 24.0	10 39.7	13 4.8
22 Su	5 59 47	29 32 16	12 53 23	18 46 59	11 47.2	12 4.0	20 33.1	3 26.4	18 31.2	7 60.0	19 21.5	10 40.4	13 3.9
23 M	6 3 43	0♑33 24	24 40 33	0♑34 19	11 46.6	13 30.2	21 2.4	4 12.0	18 42.6	7 56.7	19 19.0	10 41.2	13 2.9
24 Tu	6 7 40	1 34 33	6♑28 34	12 23 33	11 45.0	14 57.0	21 33.2	4 57.6	18 53.9	7 53.3	19 16.5	10 41.8	13 2.0
25 W	6 11 37	2 35 42	18 19 30	24 16 38	11 42.3	16 24.5	22 5.6	5 43.2	19 5.2	7 49.8	19 14.1	10 42.5	13 1.0
26 Th	6 15 33	3 36 52	0♒15 14	6♒15 32	11 38.7	17 52.6	22 39.5	6 28.9	19 16.3	7 46.2	19 11.6	10 43.1	12 60.0
27 F	6 19 30	4 38 1	12 17 49	18 22 22	11 34.7	19 21.1	23 14.7	7 14.6	19 27.4	7 42.5	19 9.2	10 43.7	12 58.9
28 Sa	6 23 26	5 39 11	24 29 30	0♓39 33	11 30.7	20 50.2	23 51.4	8 0.4	19 38.4	7 38.8	19 6.7	10 44.3	12 57.9
29 Su	6 27 23	6 40 21	6♓52 52	13 9 49	11 27.1	22 19.7	24 29.3	8 46.2	19 49.3	7 35.0	19 4.3	10 44.8	12 56.8
30 M	6 31 19	7 41 30	19 30 47	25 56 10	11 24.6	23 49.6	25 8.5	9 32.0	20 0.2	7 31.1	19 1.9	10 45.2	12 55.7
31 Tu	6 35 16	8 42 40	2♈26 21	9♈ 1 42	11D 23.3	25 19.9	25 48.9	10 17.9	20 10.9	7 27.2	18 59.5	10 45.7	12 54.6

Astro Data

	Dy Hr Mn
♃□♄	4 19:48
☽0N	6 20:43
♃⚺♆	9 16:26
☿ R	11 4:43
♇ R	15 0:41
☽0S	19 14:36
♄ R	20 15:21
♃□♇	26 10:49
☿ D	1 2:32
☽0N	4 7:06
♀ D	8 9:32
☽0S	16 20:24
♃⚻♅	25 15:40
☽0N	31 14:53

Planet Ingress

	Dy Hr Mn
♂ ♐	6 18:22
♀ ♏	8 8:56
☿ ♏	20 20:16
☉ ♐	22 21:46
☿ ♐	13 0:03
♂ ♑	17 10:56
☉ ♑	22 10:53

Last Aspect / ☽ Ingress

Last Aspect Dy Hr Mn		☽ Ingress Dy Hr Mn
1 2:32	♂ ⚹	♒ 1 10:36
3 16:24	♂ □	♓ 3 20:32
6 1:36	♂ △	♈ 6 2:28
7 14:12	♅ ⚹	♉ 8 4:49
10 3:48	♀ ☍	♊ 10 5:07
11 14:42	♅ ☌	♋ 12 5:15
14 1:54	♀ △	♌ 14 6:53
16 3:39	♀ □	♍ 16 11:05
18 9:40	☉ ⚹	♎ 18 18:12
20 9:45	♅ △	♏ 21 3:58
23 8:53	☿ ☌	♐ 23 15:44
25 9:15	♅ ☍	♑ 26 4:40
28 1:25	☿ ⚹	♒ 28 17:30

Last Aspect / ☽ Ingress

Last Aspect Dy Hr Mn		☽ Ingress Dy Hr Mn
30 11:28	☿ □	♓ 1 4:30
2 20:35	☿ △	♈ 3 12:05
5 0:06	♂ △	♉ 5 15:48
7 6:57	☿ ☍	♊ 7 16:30
9 6:07	♂ ☍	♋ 9 15:50
11 12:59	☿ △	♌ 11 15:46
13 13:03	♂ △	♍ 13 18:09
15 21:57	♂ □	♎ 16 0:07
18 0:53	☉ ⚹	♏ 18 9:43
20 0:57	♀ ☌	♐ 20 21:48
22 13:08	♅ ☍	♑ 23 10:50
25 7:59	♀ ⚹	♒ 25 23:29
27 22:41	♀ □	♓ 28 10:43
30 11:06	♀ △	♈ 30 19:31

☽ Phases & Eclipses

Dy Hr Mn	
2 4:40	☽ 9♒10
9 7:10	○ 16♉17
15 22:35	☽ 22♌58
23 17:24	● 0♐50
23 17:36:46	• P 0.776
1 21:48	☽ 9♓07
8 17:52	○ 16♊03
8 17:48	☍ T 1.164
15 10:57	☽ 22♍52
23 13:06	● 1♑07
31 12:23	☽ 9♈14

Astro Data

1 NOVEMBER 1946
Julian Day # 17106
Delta T 27.7 sec
SVP 06♓00'26"
Obliquity 23°26'49"
⚷ Chiron 28♎41.1
☽ Mean ☊ 13♊22.5

1 DECEMBER 1946
Julian Day # 17136
Delta T 27.7 sec
SVP 06♓00'21"
Obliquity 23°26'49"
⚷ Chiron 2♏46.5
☽ Mean ☊ 11♊47.2

LONGITUDE — JANUARY 1947

Day	Sid.Time	☉	0 hr ☽	Noon ☽	True ☊	☿	♀	♂	♃	♄	♅	♆	♇
1 W	6 39 12	9♑43 49	15♈42 33	22♈29 14	11♊23.2	26♐50.6	26♏30.4	11♑ 3.9	20♏21.6	7♌23.2	18♊57.2	10♎46.1	12♌53.5
2 Th	6 43 9	10 44 58	29 21 56	6♉20 48	11 24.3	28 21.8	27 13.1	11 49.8	20 32.2	7R19.1	18R54.9	10 46.5	12R52.3
3 F	6 47 6	11 46 7	13♉25 52	20 37 1	11 25.8	29 53.2	27 56.9	12 35.8	20 42.7	7 15.0	18 52.5	10 46.8	12 51.2
4 Sa	6 51 2	12 47 16	27 53 59	5♊16 20	11R27.2	1♑25.1	28 41.7	13 21.9	20 53.1	7 10.8	18 50.3	10 47.1	12 50.0
5 Su	6 54 59	13 48 24	12♊43 26	20 14 30	11 27.8	2 57.3	29 27.5	14 8.0	21 3.4	7 6.5	18 48.0	10 47.4	12 48.8
6 M	6 58 55	14 49 32	27 48 34	5♋24 32	11 26.8	4 29.9	0♐14.2	14 54.1	21 13.6	7 2.2	18 45.8	10 47.7	12 47.6
7 Tu	7 2 52	15 50 40	13♋ 1 9	20 37 10	11 24.2	6 2.9	1 1.9	15 40.2	21 23.7	6 57.8	18 43.6	10 47.9	12 46.4
8 W	7 6 48	16 51 48	28 11 16	5♌42 15	11 19.8	7 36.3	1 50.5	16 26.4	21 33.7	6 53.4	18 41.4	10 48.1	12 45.2
9 Th	7 10 45	17 52 56	13♌ 8 56	20 30 20	11 14.3	9 10.1	2 39.9	17 12.7	21 43.6	6 48.9	18 39.2	10 48.2	12 43.9
10 F	7 14 42	18 54 4	27 45 38	4♍54 11	11 8.3	10 44.3	3 30.1	17 58.9	21 53.5	6 44.4	18 37.1	10 48.3	12 42.7
11 Sa	7 18 38	19 55 11	11♍55 36	18 49 39	11 2.8	12 19.0	4 21.2	18 45.2	22 3.2	6 39.8	18 35.0	10 48.4	12 41.4
12 Su	7 22 35	20 56 19	25 36 19	2♎15 45	10 58.4	13 54.0	5 13.0	19 31.6	22 12.8	6 35.2	18 33.0	10R48.4	12 40.1
13 M	7 26 31	21 57 26	8♎48 13	15 14 8	10 55.6	15 29.6	6 5.5	20 18.0	22 22.3	6 30.5	18 31.0	10 48.4	12 38.8
14 Tu	7 30 28	22 58 33	21 34 1	27 48 25	10D54.6	17 5.6	6 58.7	21 4.4	22 31.7	6 25.8	18 29.0	10 48.4	12 37.5
15 W	7 34 24	23 59 40	3♏57 56	10♏ 3 14	10 55.1	18 42.0	7 52.6	21 50.8	22 41.0	6 21.1	18 27.0	10 48.3	12 36.2
16 Th	7 38 21	25 0 47	16 4 56	22 3 42	10 56.5	20 19.0	8 47.2	22 37.3	22 50.1	6 16.3	18 25.1	10 48.2	12 34.9
17 F	7 42 17	26 1 54	28 0 9	3♐54 53	10 58.0	21 56.5	9 42.4	23 23.8	22 59.2	6 11.5	18 23.2	10 48.1	12 33.6
18 Sa	7 46 14	27 3 1	9♐48 29	15 41 29	10R58.8	23 34.5	10 38.1	24 10.4	23 8.2	6 6.7	18 21.3	10 47.9	12 32.2
19 Su	7 50 11	28 4 7	21 34 21	27 27 34	10 58.1	25 13.1	11 34.5	24 57.0	23 17.0	6 1.9	18 19.5	10 47.7	12 30.9
20 M	7 54 7	29 5 13	3♑21 30	9♑16 31	10 55.3	26 52.2	12 31.4	25 43.6	23 25.7	5 57.0	18 17.8	10 47.5	12 29.5
21 Tu	7 58 4	0♒ 6 18	15 12 55	21 10 58	10 50.1	28 31.9	13 28.8	26 30.2	23 34.3	5 52.1	18 16.0	10 47.2	12 28.1
22 W	8 2 0	1 7 22	27 10 52	3♒12 50	10 42.5	0♒12.2	14 26.7	27 16.9	23 42.7	5 47.2	18 14.3	10 46.9	12 26.8
23 Th	8 5 57	2 8 26	9♒16 58	15 23 26	10 33.2	1 53.0	15 25.1	28 3.6	23 51.1	5 42.3	18 12.7	10 46.6	12 25.4
24 F	8 9 53	3 9 30	21 32 20	27 43 44	10 22.7	3 34.4	16 24.0	28 50.4	23 59.3	5 37.4	18 11.1	10 46.2	12 24.0
25 Sa	8 13 50	4 10 32	3♓57 45	10♓14 29	10 12.2	5 16.5	17 23.3	29 37.1	24 7.4	5 32.5	18 9.5	10 45.8	12 22.6
26 Su	8 17 46	5 11 33	16 34 2	22 56 32	10 2.5	6 59.1	18 23.1	0♒23.9	24 15.3	5 27.5	18 8.0	10 45.3	12 21.2
27 M	8 21 43	6 12 33	29 22 7	5♈51 0	9 54.7	8 42.3	19 23.2	1 10.7	24 23.2	5 22.6	18 6.5	10 44.9	12 19.8
28 Tu	8 25 40	7 13 32	12♈23 20	18 59 21	9 49.3	10 26.1	20 23.8	1 57.5	24 30.8	5 17.7	18 5.1	10 44.4	12 18.4
29 W	8 29 36	8 14 30	25 39 16	2♉23 20	9 46.4	12 10.4	21 24.8	2 44.4	24 38.4	5 12.8	18 3.7	10 43.8	12 17.0
30 Th	8 33 33	9 15 27	9♉11 45	16 4 43	9D45.6	13 55.3	22 26.1	3 31.3	24 45.8	5 7.8	18 2.3	10 43.3	12 15.6
31 F	8 37 29	10 16 22	23 2 21	0♊ 4 45	9 46.0	15 40.7	23 27.8	4 18.2	24 53.1	5 2.9	18 1.0	10 42.7	12 14.2

LONGITUDE — FEBRUARY 1947

Day	Sid.Time	☉	0 hr ☽	Noon ☽	True ☊	☿	♀	♂	♃	♄	♅	♆	♇
1 Sa	8 41 26	11♒17 17	7♊11 52	14♊23 36	9♊46.6	17♒26.6	24♐29.8	5♒ 5.1	25♏ 0.2	4♌58.1	17♊59.8	10♎42.0	12♌12.8
2 Su	8 45 22	12 18 10	21 39 39	28 59 36	9R46.1	19 12.8	25 32.2	5 52.0	25 7.2	4R53.2	17R58.6	10R41.4	12R11.4
3 M	8 49 19	13 19 1	6♋22 52	13♋48 43	9 43.4	20 59.4	26 34.9	6 39.0	25 14.1	4 48.3	17 57.4	10 40.7	12 10.0
4 Tu	8 53 15	14 19 52	21 16 15	28 44 28	9 38.1	22 46.3	27 37.9	7 26.0	25 20.8	4 43.5	17 56.3	10 40.0	12 8.6
5 W	8 57 12	15 20 41	6♌12 16	13♌38 30	9 30.1	24 33.2	28 41.3	8 13.0	25 27.4	4 38.7	17 55.2	10 39.2	12 7.2
6 Th	9 1 9	16 21 28	21 2 3	28 21 50	9 20.1	26 20.1	29 44.9	8 60.0	25 33.8	4 33.9	17 54.2	10 38.4	12 5.7
7 F	9 5 5	17 22 15	5♍36 52	12♍46 20	9 9.1	28 6.9	0♑48.8	9 47.0	25 40.0	4 29.2	17 53.3	10 37.6	12 4.3
8 Sa	9 9 2	18 23 0	19 49 34	26 46 7	8 58.3	29 53.3	1 53.0	10 34.1	25 46.1	4 24.5	17 52.3	10 36.8	12 2.9
9 Su	9 12 58	19 23 44	3♎35 42	10♎18 15	8 49.0	1♓39.0	2 57.5	11 21.1	25 52.1	4 19.8	17 51.5	10 35.9	12 1.5
10 M	9 16 55	20 24 27	16 53 50	23 22 42	8 42.0	3 23.9	4 2.2	12 8.2	25 57.9	4 15.2	17 50.7	10 35.0	12 0.1
11 Tu	9 20 51	21 25 9	29 45 13	6♏ 1 54	8 37.6	5 7.7	5 7.2	12 55.3	26 3.6	4 10.6	17 49.9	10 34.1	11 58.7
12 W	9 24 48	22 25 50	12♏13 17	18 20 0	8D35.5	6 49.8	6 12.4	13 42.5	26 9.1	4 6.0	17 49.2	10 33.2	11 57.4
13 Th	9 28 44	23 26 30	24 22 43	0♐22 9	8 35.1	8 30.0	7 17.9	14 29.6	26 14.4	4 1.5	17 48.5	10 32.2	11 56.0
14 F	9 32 41	24 27 9	6♐18 59	12 13 56	8R35.2	10 7.8	8 23.6	15 16.8	26 19.6	3 57.0	17 47.9	10 31.2	11 54.6
15 Sa	9 36 38	25 27 47	18 7 41	24 0 53	8 34.9	11 42.6	9 29.5	16 3.9	26 24.6	3 52.6	17 47.3	10 30.1	11 53.2
16 Su	9 40 34	26 28 23	29 54 10	5♑48 7	8 33.0	13 14.0	10 35.6	16 51.1	26 29.4	3 48.2	17 46.8	10 29.1	11 51.9
17 M	9 44 31	27 28 58	11♑43 17	17 40 9	8 28.7	14 41.2	11 41.9	17 38.3	26 34.1	3 43.9	17 46.4	10 28.0	11 50.5
18 Tu	9 48 27	28 29 32	23 39 7	29 40 35	8 21.4	16 3.7	12 48.4	18 25.5	26 38.6	3 39.7	17 46.0	10 26.9	11 49.2
19 W	9 52 24	29 30 5	5♒44 48	11♒52 2	8 11.3	17 20.7	13 55.1	19 12.7	26 43.0	3 35.5	17 45.6	10 25.8	11 47.8
20 Th	9 56 20	0♓30 36	18 2 25	24 16 3	7 58.9	18 31.7	15 2.0	19 60.0	26 47.2	3 31.4	17 45.3	10 24.6	11 46.5
21 F	10 0 17	1 31 5	0♓32 59	6♓53 12	7 45.0	19 35.9	16 9.1	20 47.2	26 51.2	3 27.3	17 45.1	10 23.4	11 45.2
22 Sa	10 4 13	2 31 33	13 16 38	19 43 11	7 30.9	20 32.7	17 16.3	21 34.4	26 55.0	3 23.3	17 44.9	10 22.2	11 43.9
23 Su	10 8 10	3 31 59	26 12 45	2♈45 14	7 17.9	21 21.4	18 23.7	22 21.7	26 58.6	3 19.4	17 44.8	10 21.0	11 42.6
24 M	10 12 7	4 32 23	9♈20 29	15 58 24	7 7.0	22 1.6	19 31.2	23 8.9	27 2.1	3 15.5	17 44.7	10 19.7	11 41.3
25 Tu	10 16 3	5 32 46	22 38 56	29 22 1	6 59.0	22 32.6	20 38.9	23 56.2	27 5.4	3 11.8	17D44.7	10 18.5	11 40.0
26 W	10 20 0	6 33 6	6♉ 7 38	12♉55 48	6 54.1	22 54.3	21 46.7	24 43.4	27 8.5	3 8.1	17 44.7	10 17.2	11 38.7
27 Th	10 23 56	7 33 25	19 46 33	26 39 57	6 51.9	23R 6.3	22 54.7	25 30.7	27 11.5	3 4.4	17 44.8	10 15.9	11 37.5
28 F	10 27 53	8 33 42	3♊36 3	10♊34 53	6 51.4	23 8.6	24 2.8	26 17.9	27 14.3	3 0.9	17 44.9	10 14.5	11 36.2

Astro Data Dy Hr Mn	Planet Ingress Dy Hr Mn
♆ R 12 12:25	☿ ♑ 3 1:46
☽0S 13 3:08	♀ ♐ 5 16:45
☽0N 27 20:02	☉ ♒ 20 21:32
	☿ ♒ 21 21:06
♃∠♆ 6 15:50	♂ ♒ 25 11:44
☽0S 9 11:31	
☽0N 24 0:49	♀ ♑ 6 5:41
♅ D 25 0:30	☿ ♓ 8 1:31
☿ R 27 17:35	☉ ♓ 19 11:52
☿0N 28 10:07	

Last Aspect Dy Hr Mn	☽ Ingress Dy Hr Mn	Last Aspect Dy Hr Mn	☽ Ingress Dy Hr Mn
1 22:03 ☿ △	♉ 2 1:06	2 6:50 ♀ ☍	♋ 2 13:38
4 1:22 ♀ ☍	♊ 4 3:26	4 6:36 ♃ △	♌ 4 14:01
5 9:41 ♅ ☌	♋ 6 3:28	6 9:52 ☿ ☍	♍ 6 14:42
7 13:22 ♃ △	♌ 8 2:53	8 10:20 ♃ ✱	♎ 8 17:39
9 14:10 ♃ □	♍ 10 3:45	10 7:01 ☉ △	♏ 11 0:28
11 17:54 ♃ ✱	♎ 12 7:54	13 3:45 ♃ ☌	♐ 13 11:15
14 2:56 ☉ □	♏ 14 16:15	15 16:21 ☉ ✱	♑ 16 0:12
16 19:38 ☉ ✱	♐ 17 4:03	18 6:00 ♃ ✱	♒ 18 12:39
18 17:24 ♅ ☍	♑ 19 17:10	20 16:55 ♃ □	♓ 20 22:57
22 0:13 ♂ ☌	♒ 22 5:37	23 1:25 ♃ △	♈ 23 6:58
24 4:49 ♃ □	♓ 24 16:23	25 2:27 ♂ ✱	♉ 25 13:08
26 14:37 ♃ △	♈ 27 1:10	27 12:57 ♃ ☍	♊ 27 17:47
28 15:45 ♀ △	♉ 29 7:45		
31 3:11 ♃ ☍	♊ 31 11:52		

☽ Phases & Eclipses Dy Hr Mn	
7 4:47	○ 16♋03
14 2:56	☽ 23♎06
22 8:34	● 1♒29
30 0:07	☽ 9♉16
5 15:50	○ 16♌01
12 21:58	☽ 23♏21
21 2:00	● 1♓36
28 9:12	☽ 8♊57

Astro Data

1 JANUARY 1947
Julian Day # 17167
Delta T 27.8 sec
SVP 06♓00'15"
Obliquity 23°26'49"
⚷ Chiron 6♏13.0
☽ Mean ☊ 10♊08.7

1 FEBRUARY 1947
Julian Day # 17198
Delta T 27.8 sec
SVP 06♓00'10"
Obliquity 23°26'49"
⚷ Chiron 8♏16.9
☽ Mean ☊ 8♊30.3

MARCH 1947

LONGITUDE

Day	Sid.Time	☉	0 hr ☽	Noon☽	True☊	☿	♀	♂	♃	♄	♅	♆	♇
1 Sa	10 31 49	9♓33 56	17♊36 30	24♊40 49	6♊51.3	23♓ 1.2	25♑11.0	27♒ 5.2	27♏16.8	2♌57.4	17♊45.1	10♎13.2	11♌35.0
2 Su	10 35 46	10 34 9	1♋47 46	8♋57 8	6R50.3	22R44.4	26 19.4	27 52.5	27 19.3	2R54.1	17 45.3	10R11.8	11R33.8
3 M	10 39 42	11 34 20	16 8 38	23 21 52	6 47.2	22 18.7	27 27.9	28 39.7	27 21.5	2 50.8	17 45.6	10 10.4	11 32.6
4 Tu	10 43 39	12 34 28	0♌36 18	7♌51 18	6 41.3	21 44.8	28 36.5	29 27.0	27 23.5	2 47.6	17 46.0	10 9.0	11 31.4
5 W	10 47 36	13 34 35	15 6 9	22 20 5	6 32.5	21 3.4	29 45.2	0♓14.2	27 25.4	2 44.4	17 46.4	10 7.6	11 30.3
6 Th	10 51 32	14 34 39	29 32 15	6♍41 50	6 21.5	20 15.8	0♒54.1	1 1.5	27 27.1	2 41.4	17 46.9	10 6.2	11 29.1
7 F	10 55 29	15 34 41	13♍48 2	20 50 5	6 9.4	19 23.0	2 3.1	1 48.7	27 28.5	2 38.5	17 47.4	10 4.7	11 28.0
8 Sa	10 59 25	16 34 42	27 47 23	4♎39 24	5 57.4	18 26.5	3 12.1	2 36.0	27 29.8	2 35.6	17 47.9	10 3.2	11 26.8
9 Su	11 3 22	17 34 40	11♎25 46	18 6 14	5 46.7	17 27.5	4 21.3	3 23.2	27 31.0	2 32.8	17 48.5	10 1.7	11 25.7
10 M	11 7 18	18 34 37	24 40 45	1♏ 9 21	5 38.3	16 27.5	5 30.6	4 10.4	27 31.9	2 30.2	17 49.2	10 0.2	11 24.7
11 Tu	11 11 15	19 34 32	7♏32 14	13 49 42	5 32.7	15 27.9	6 40.0	4 57.7	27 32.6	2 27.6	17 49.9	9 58.7	11 23.6
12 W	11 15 11	20 34 25	20 2 11	26 10 9	5 29.6	14 30.0	7 49.5	5 44.9	27 33.2	2 25.1	17 50.7	9 57.2	11 22.5
13 Th	11 19 8	21 34 17	2♐14 11	8♐14 54	5D28.6	13 34.8	8 59.1	6 32.1	27 33.6	2 22.8	17 51.5	9 55.7	11 21.5
14 F	11 23 5	22 34 7	14 12 57	20 9 1	5R28.8	12 43.4	10 8.8	7 19.3	27R33.8	2 20.5	17 52.4	9 54.1	11 20.5
15 Sa	11 27 1	23 33 56	26 3 48	1♑57 58	5 28.9	11 56.6	11 18.6	8 6.6	27 33.8	2 18.3	17 53.3	9 52.5	11 19.5
16 Su	11 30 58	24 33 42	7♑52 14	13 47 14	5 28.0	11 15.0	12 28.5	8 53.8	27 33.6	2 16.2	17 54.3	9 51.0	11 18.5
17 M	11 34 54	25 33 27	19 43 37	25 41 59	5 25.2	10 39.2	13 38.5	9 41.0	27 33.2	2 14.3	17 55.3	9 49.4	11 17.6
18 Tu	11 38 51	26 33 11	1♒42 53	7♒46 48	5 19.9	10 9.4	14 48.5	10 28.1	27 32.6	2 12.4	17 56.4	9 47.8	11 16.7
19 W	11 42 47	27 32 52	13 54 9	20 5 18	5 12.1	9 45.8	15 58.6	11 15.3	27 31.9	2 10.6	17 57.5	9 46.2	11 15.7
20 Th	11 46 44	28 32 32	26 20 30	2♓39 58	5 2.1	9 28.4	17 8.8	12 2.5	27 30.9	2 8.9	17 58.7	9 44.6	11 14.8
21 F	11 50 40	29 32 9	9♓ 3 46	15 31 56	4 50.7	9 17.3	18 19.1	12 49.6	27 29.8	2 7.4	17 60.0	9 43.0	11 14.0
22 Sa	11 54 37	0♈31 45	22 4 21	28 40 54	4 39.0	9D12.3	19 29.4	13 36.8	27 28.4	2 5.9	18 1.2	9 41.3	11 13.1
23 Su	11 58 33	1 31 19	5♈21 20	12♈ 5 22	4 28.2	9 13.3	20 39.8	14 23.9	27 26.9	2 4.6	18 2.6	9 39.7	11 12.3
24 M	12 2 30	2 30 51	18 52 40	25 42 54	4 19.1	9 19.9	21 50.3	15 11.0	27 25.2	2 3.4	18 4.0	9 38.1	11 11.5
25 Tu	12 6 27	3 30 20	2♉35 41	9♉30 42	4 12.6	9 32.1	23 0.8	15 58.1	27 23.3	2 2.2	18 5.4	9 36.4	11 10.7
26 W	12 10 23	4 29 48	16 27 35	23 26 4	4 8.9	9 49.5	24 11.4	16 45.1	27 21.3	2 1.2	18 6.9	9 34.8	11 10.0
27 Th	12 14 20	5 29 13	0♊25 51	7♊26 45	4D 7.5	10 11.9	25 22.1	17 32.2	27 19.0	2 0.3	18 8.4	9 33.2	11 9.2
28 F	12 18 16	6 28 36	14 28 32	21 31 5	4 7.7	10 39.0	26 32.8	18 19.2	27 16.6	1 59.5	18 10.0	9 31.5	11 8.5
29 Sa	12 22 13	7 27 57	28 34 15	5♋37 54	4R 8.5	11 10.6	27 43.5	19 6.2	27 14.0	1 58.8	18 11.6	9 29.9	11 7.8
30 Su	12 26 9	8 27 15	12♋41 54	19 46 7	4 8.7	11 46.4	28 54.3	19 53.2	27 11.2	1 58.2	18 13.3	9 28.2	11 7.2
31 M	12 30 6	9 26 31	26 50 20	3♌54 20	4 7.3	12 26.1	0♓ 5.2	20 40.2	27 8.2	1 57.8	18 15.0	9 26.6	11 6.5

APRIL 1947

LONGITUDE

Day	Sid.Time	☉	0 hr ☽	Noon☽	True☊	☿	♀	♂	♃	♄	♅	♆	♇
1 Tu	12 34 2	10♈25 45	10♌57 52	18♌ 0 37	4♊ 3.8	13♓ 9.7	1♓16.1	21♓27.1	27♏ 5.1	1♌57.4	18♊16.8	9♎24.9	11♌ 5.9
2 W	12 37 59	11 24 56	25 2 11	2♍ 2 12	3R58.0	13 56.7	2 27.1	22 14.0	27R 1.8	1R57.1	18 18.6	9R23.2	11R 5.3
3 Th	12 41 56	12 24 5	9♍ 0 13	15 55 46	3 50.5	14 47.2	3 38.1	23 0.9	26 58.3	1D57.0	18 20.4	9 21.6	11 4.8
4 F	12 45 52	13 23 12	22 48 25	29 37 45	3 42.0	15 40.8	4 49.1	23 47.8	26 54.6	1 57.0	18 22.3	9 19.9	11 4.2
5 Sa	12 49 49	14 22 16	6♎23 22	13♎ 4 55	3 33.5	16 37.4	6 0.2	24 34.6	26 50.8	1 57.0	18 24.3	9 18.3	11 3.7
6 Su	12 53 45	15 21 19	19 42 10	26 14 56	3 26.0	17 36.9	7 11.4	25 21.5	26 46.8	1 57.2	18 26.2	9 16.7	11 3.2
7 M	12 57 42	16 20 19	2♏43 5	9♏ 6 39	3 20.2	18 39.2	8 22.6	26 8.3	26 42.7	1 57.5	18 28.3	9 15.0	11 2.7
8 Tu	13 1 38	17 19 18	15 25 43	21 40 26	3 16.5	19 44.0	9 33.8	26 55.0	26 38.4	1 57.9	18 30.3	9 13.4	11 2.3
9 W	13 5 35	18 18 14	27 51 5	3♐58 0	3D14.8	20 51.3	10 45.1	27 41.8	26 33.9	1 58.4	18 32.5	9 11.7	11 1.9
10 Th	13 9 31	19 17 9	10♐ 1 35	16 2 19	3 14.8	22 1.0	11 56.5	28 28.5	26 29.3	1 59.1	18 34.6	9 10.1	11 1.5
11 F	13 13 28	20 16 2	22 0 42	27 57 18	3 16.0	23 12.9	13 7.8	29 15.2	26 24.5	1 59.8	18 36.8	9 8.5	11 1.1
12 Sa	13 17 25	21 14 54	3♑52 43	9♑47 34	3 17.6	24 27.1	14 19.3	0♈ 1.9	26 19.6	2 0.6	18 39.1	9 6.9	11 0.8
13 Su	13 21 21	22 13 43	15 42 29	21 38 7	3R18.8	25 43.4	15 30.7	0 48.5	26 14.5	2 1.6	18 41.3	9 5.3	11 0.5
14 M	13 25 18	23 12 31	27 35 6	3♒34 5	3 18.9	27 1.7	16 42.2	1 35.1	26 9.2	2 2.6	18 43.6	9 3.7	11 0.2
15 Tu	13 29 14	24 11 17	9♒35 39	15 40 24	3 17.6	28 22.1	17 53.8	2 21.7	26 3.9	2 3.8	18 46.0	9 2.1	10 60.0
16 W	13 33 11	25 10 2	21 48 52	28 1 31	3 14.5	29 44.3	19 5.3	3 8.3	25 58.4	2 5.1	18 48.4	9 0.5	10 59.7
17 Th	13 37 7	26 8 44	4♓18 46	10♓40 58	3 10.1	1♈ 8.5	20 17.0	3 54.8	25 52.7	2 6.4	18 50.8	8 59.0	10 59.5
18 F	13 41 4	27 7 25	17 8 22	23 41 5	3 4.6	2 34.5	21 28.6	4 41.3	25 46.9	2 7.9	18 53.3	8 57.4	10 59.4
19 Sa	13 45 0	28 6 4	0♈19 12	7♈ 2 37	2 58.7	4 2.4	22 40.3	5 27.7	25 41.0	2 9.5	18 55.8	8 55.9	10 59.2
20 Su	13 48 57	29 4 41	13 51 9	20 44 32	2 53.1	5 32.0	23 52.0	6 14.1	25 35.0	2 11.2	18 58.4	8 54.3	10 59.1
21 M	13 52 54	0♉ 3 17	27 42 22	4♉44 11	2 48.6	7 3.4	25 3.7	7 0.5	25 28.8	2 13.0	19 0.9	8 52.8	10 59.0
22 Tu	13 56 50	1 1 50	11♉49 25	18 57 29	2 45.6	8 36.6	26 15.5	7 46.9	25 22.6	2 14.9	19 3.5	8 51.3	10 58.9
23 W	14 0 47	2 0 22	26 7 45	3♊19 35	2D44.1	10 11.6	27 27.2	8 33.2	25 16.2	2 16.9	19 6.2	8 49.8	10D58.9
24 Th	14 4 43	2 58 52	10♊32 22	17 45 30	2 44.2	11 48.2	28 39.1	9 19.5	25 9.7	2 19.1	19 8.9	8 48.3	10 58.9
25 F	14 8 40	3 57 19	24 58 27	2♋10 42	2 45.2	13 26.7	29 50.9	10 5.7	25 3.1	2 21.3	19 11.6	8 46.8	10 58.9
26 Sa	14 12 36	4 55 45	9♋21 49	16 31 25	2 46.7	15 6.8	1♈ 2.7	10 51.9	24 56.4	2 23.6	19 14.4	8 45.4	10 58.9
27 Su	14 16 33	5 54 8	23 39 11	0♌44 51	2R47.9	16 48.7	2 14.6	11 38.1	24 49.6	2 26.0	19 17.1	8 44.0	10 59.0
28 M	14 20 29	6 52 30	7♌48 11	14 48 59	2 48.3	18 32.3	3 26.5	12 24.2	24 42.7	2 28.6	19 20.0	8 42.5	10 59.1
29 Tu	14 24 26	7 50 49	21 47 7	28 42 26	2 47.7	20 17.7	4 38.4	13 10.3	24 35.8	2 31.2	19 22.8	8 41.1	10 59.2
30 W	14 28 23	8 49 6	5♍34 49	12♍24 10	2 45.9	22 4.8	5 50.4	13 56.3	24 28.7	2 33.9	19 25.7	8 39.7	10 59.4

Astro Data	Dy Hr Mn
☿0S	3 17:49
♄∠♅	4 10:35
☽0S	8 20:53
♃ R	14 11:36
☿ D	22 8:06
☽0N	23 7:35
♄ D	3 19:38
☽0S	5 5:45
♂0N	14 22:30
☽0N	19 16:37
☿0N	20 9:15
♇ D	23 20:47
♀0N	28 4:46

Planet Ingress	Dy Hr Mn
♂ ♓	4 16:46
♀ ♒	5 5:09
☉ ♈	21 11:13
♀ ♓	30 22:14
♂ ♈	11 23:03
☿ ♈	16 4:31
☉ ♉	20 22:39
♀ ♈	25 3:03

Last Aspect Dy Hr Mn		☽ Ingress Dy Hr Mn
1 17:00	♂ △	♋ 1 20:59
3 20:25	♀ ☍	♌ 3 23:00
5 20:31	♃ □	♍ 6 0:46
7 23:30	♃ ⚹	♎ 8 3:51
9 11:29	♅ △	♏ 10 9:51
12 14:44	♃ ☌	♐ 12 19:34
14 18:28	☉ □	♑ 15 8:00
17 15:42	♃ ⚹	♒ 17 20:35
20 2:14	♃ □	♓ 20 6:57
22 9:48	♃ △	♈ 22 14:23
24 5:42	♀ ⚹	♉ 24 19:29
26 18:41	♃ ☍	♊ 26 23:16
28 22:26	♀ △	♋ 29 2:26
31 0:30	♃ △	♌ 31 5:22

Last Aspect Dy Hr Mn		☽ Ingress Dy Hr Mn
2 3:24	♃ □	♍ 2 8:30
4 7:10	♃ ⚹	♎ 4 12:39
5 21:41	♅ △	♏ 6 18:56
8 23:41	♂ △	♐ 9 4:12
11 15:39	♂ □	♑ 11 16:08
13 22:44	☿ ⚹	♒ 14 4:51
16 7:59	♃ □	♓ 16 15:47
18 15:42	♃ △	♈ 18 23:26
20 8:57	♅ ⚹	♉ 21 3:56
23 2:25	♀ ⚹	♊ 23 6:27
24 14:21	♅ ☌	♋ 25 8:22
27 1:58	♃ △	♌ 27 10:44
29 4:49	♃ □	♍ 29 14:15

☽ Phases & Eclipses Dy Hr Mn	
7 3:15	○ 15♍43
14 18:28	☽ 23♐20
22 16:34	● 1♈13
29 16:15	☽ 8♋08
5 15:28	○ 15♎00
13 14:23	☽ 22♑49
21 4:19	● 0♉14
27 22:18	☽ 6♌48

Astro Data

1 MARCH 1947
Julian Day # 17226
Delta T 27.9 sec
SVP 06♓00'06"
Obliquity 23°26'50"
⚷ Chiron 8♏37.4R
☽ Mean ☊ 7♊01.3

1 APRIL 1947
Julian Day # 17257
Delta T 27.9 sec
SVP 06♓00'03"
Obliquity 23°26'51"
⚷ Chiron 7♏21.7R
☽ Mean ☊ 5♊22.8

Day	Sid.Time	☉	0 hr ☽	Noon ☽	True ☊	☿	♀	♂	♃	♄	♅	♆	♇
1 Th	14 32 19	9♉47 20	19♍10 22	25♍53 20	2♊43.2	23♈53.7	7♈ 2.3	14♈42.3	24♏21.6	2♌36.7	19♊28.6	8♎38.4	10♌59.6
2 F	14 36 16	10 45 33	2♎33 0	9♎ 9 17	2R 40.0	25 44.4	8 14.3	15 28.3	24R 14.4	2 39.7	19 31.5	8R 37.0	10 59.8
3 Sa	14 40 12	11 43 44	15 42 6	22 11 27	2 36.9	27 36.8	9 26.3	16 14.2	24 7.2	2 42.7	19 34.5	8 35.7	10 60.0
4 Su	14 44 9	12 41 53	28 37 17	4♏59 38	2 34.1	29 31.0	10 38.4	17 0.1	23 59.9	2 45.8	19 37.5	8 34.4	11 0.3
5 M	14 48 5	13 40 0	11♏18 31	17 34 1	2 32.1	1♉26.9	11 50.4	17 45.9	23 52.5	2 49.0	19 40.5	8 33.1	11 0.5
6 Tu	14 52 2	14 38 6	23 46 14	29 55 21	2D 31.0	3 24.6	13 2.5	18 31.7	23 45.1	2 52.3	19 43.5	8 31.8	11 0.9
7 W	14 55 58	15 36 10	6♐ 1 32	12♐ 5 3	2 30.8	5 24.0	14 14.6	19 17.4	23 37.6	2 55.7	19 46.6	8 30.6	11 1.2
8 Th	14 59 55	16 34 13	18 6 10	24 5 13	2 31.3	7 25.1	15 26.7	20 3.1	23 30.1	2 59.2	19 49.7	8 29.3	11 1.6
9 F	15 3 52	17 32 14	0♑ 2 35	5♑58 41	2 32.4	9 27.8	16 38.8	20 48.8	23 22.6	3 2.8	19 52.8	8 28.1	11 2.0
10 Sa	15 7 48	18 30 13	11 53 58	17 48 54	2 33.8	11 32.1	17 51.0	21 34.4	23 15.0	3 6.4	19 56.0	8 27.0	11 2.4
11 Su	15 11 45	19 28 11	23 44 0	29 39 49	2 35.0	13 37.8	19 3.2	22 20.0	23 7.4	3 10.2	19 59.1	8 25.8	11 2.8
12 M	15 15 41	20 26 8	5♒36 56	11♒35 53	2 35.9	15 44.9	20 15.4	23 5.5	22 59.8	3 14.0	20 2.3	8 24.7	11 3.3
13 Tu	15 19 38	21 24 4	17 37 16	23 41 39	2R 36.3	17 53.2	21 27.6	23 51.0	22 52.2	3 18.0	20 5.5	8 23.5	11 3.8
14 W	15 23 34	22 21 58	29 49 38	6♓ 1 44	2 36.3	20 2.5	22 39.8	24 36.4	22 44.5	3 22.0	20 8.8	8 22.4	11 4.3
15 Th	15 27 31	23 19 51	12♓18 28	18 40 18	2 35.8	22 12.6	23 52.1	25 21.8	22 36.9	3 26.1	20 12.0	8 21.4	11 4.9
16 F	15 31 27	24 17 43	25 7 39	1♈40 50	2 34.9	24 23.4	25 4.4	26 7.1	22 29.3	3 30.3	20 15.3	8 20.3	11 5.5
17 Sa	15 35 24	25 15 33	8♈20 4	15 5 30	2 34.0	26 34.6	26 16.7	26 52.4	22 21.6	3 34.6	20 18.6	8 19.3	11 6.1
18 Su	15 39 21	26 13 22	21 57 7	28 54 48	2 33.2	28 45.9	27 29.0	27 37.7	22 14.0	3 39.0	20 21.9	8 18.3	11 6.7
19 M	15 43 17	27 11 10	5♉58 17	13♉ 7 8	2 32.6	0♊57.0	28 41.3	28 22.9	22 6.4	3 43.4	20 25.2	8 17.3	11 7.3
20 Tu	15 47 14	28 8 57	20 20 49	27 38 39	2D 32.3	3 7.8	29 53.7	29 8.0	21 58.8	3 47.9	20 28.6	8 16.4	11 8.0
21 W	15 51 10	29 6 43	4♊59 53	12♊23 37	2 32.2	5 17.8	1♉ 6.1	29 53.1	21 51.2	3 52.5	20 31.9	8 15.5	11 8.7
22 Th	15 55 7	0♊ 4 27	19 48 55	27 14 52	2 32.3	7 26.9	2 18.4	0♉38.2	21 43.7	3 57.2	20 35.3	8 14.6	11 9.5
23 F	15 59 3	1 2 10	4♋40 31	12♋ 4 57	2 32.5	9 34.7	3 30.8	1 23.2	21 36.2	4 2.0	20 38.7	8 13.7	11 10.2
24 Sa	16 3 0	1 59 51	19 27 21	26 46 57	2R 32.6	11 41.0	4 43.3	2 8.1	21 28.8	4 6.9	20 42.1	8 12.9	11 11.0
25 Su	16 6 56	2 57 31	4♌ 3 8	11♌15 22	2 32.6	13 45.6	5 55.7	2 53.0	21 21.4	4 11.8	20 45.6	8 12.1	11 11.8
26 M	16 10 53	3 55 9	18 23 15	25 26 30	2 32.5	15 48.3	7 8.1	3 37.8	21 14.1	4 16.8	20 49.0	8 11.3	11 12.6
27 Tu	16 14 50	4 52 46	2♍24 56	9♍18 30	2D 32.5	17 48.8	8 20.6	4 22.6	21 6.8	4 21.9	20 52.4	8 10.6	11 13.5
28 W	16 18 46	5 50 21	16 7 11	22 51 4	2 32.5	19 47.1	9 33.0	5 7.3	20 59.6	4 27.0	20 55.9	8 9.9	11 14.4
29 Th	16 22 43	6 47 55	29 30 18	6♎ 5 4	2 32.7	21 43.1	10 45.5	5 52.0	20 52.4	4 32.3	20 59.4	8 9.2	11 15.3
30 F	16 26 39	7 45 27	12♎35 34	19 2 3	2 33.2	23 36.5	11 58.0	6 36.6	20 45.4	4 37.5	21 2.9	8 8.5	11 16.2
31 Sa	16 30 36	8 42 58	25 24 43	1♏43 51	2 33.7	25 27.4	13 10.5	7 21.1	20 38.4	4 42.9	21 6.4	8 7.9	11 17.1

LONGITUDE JUNE 1947

Day	Sid.Time	☉	0 hr ☽	Noon ☽	True ☊	☿	♀	♂	♃	♄	♅	♆	♇
1 Su	16 34 32	9♊40 27	7♏59 42	14♏12 29	2♊34.4	27♊15.6	14♉23.0	8♉ 5.6	20♏31.5	4♌48.3	21♊ 9.9	8♎ 7.3	11♌18.1
2 M	16 38 29	10 37 56	20 22 27	26 29 49	2 34.9	29 1.1	15 35.5	8 50.1	20R 24.7	4 53.8	21 13.4	8R 6.7	11 19.1
3 Tu	16 42 25	11 35 23	2♐34 51	8♐37 45	2R 35.1	0♋43.9	16 48.1	9 34.5	20 17.9	4 59.4	21 16.9	8 6.1	11 20.1
4 W	16 46 22	12 32 50	14 38 45	20 38 5	2 34.8	2 23.9	18 0.6	10 18.8	20 11.3	5 5.0	21 20.4	8 5.6	11 21.1
5 Th	16 50 19	13 30 15	26 36 0	2♑32 45	2 34.1	4 1.1	19 13.2	11 3.1	20 4.8	5 10.7	21 24.0	8 5.1	11 22.2
6 F	16 54 15	14 27 40	8♑28 38	14 23 54	2 32.7	5 35.5	20 25.8	11 47.3	19 58.4	5 16.5	21 27.5	8 4.7	11 23.3
7 Sa	16 58 12	15 25 4	20 18 54	26 13 58	2 31.0	7 7.1	21 38.5	12 31.5	19 52.1	5 22.3	21 31.1	8 4.3	11 24.4
8 Su	17 2 8	16 22 27	2♒ 9 28	8♒ 5 49	2 29.0	8 35.7	22 51.1	13 15.6	19 45.9	5 28.2	21 34.6	8 3.9	11 25.5
9 M	17 6 5	17 19 49	14 3 24	20 2 42	2 27.0	10 1.4	24 3.8	13 59.6	19 39.8	5 34.2	21 38.2	8 3.5	11 26.6
10 Tu	17 10 1	18 17 11	26 4 11	2♓ 8 21	2 25.4	11 24.2	25 16.4	14 43.6	19 33.8	5 40.2	21 41.7	8 3.2	11 27.8
11 W	17 13 58	19 14 32	8♓15 42	14 26 45	2D 24.3	12 44.1	26 29.1	15 27.6	19 28.0	5 46.2	21 45.3	8 2.9	11 29.0
12 Th	17 17 54	20 11 53	20 42 3	27 2 4	2 23.9	14 0.9	27 41.8	16 11.5	19 22.2	5 52.4	21 48.8	8 2.6	11 30.2
13 F	17 21 51	21 9 13	3♈27 19	9♈58 14	2 24.3	15 14.6	28 54.6	16 55.3	19 16.7	5 58.6	21 52.4	8 2.4	11 31.4
14 Sa	17 25 48	22 6 32	16 35 12	23 18 31	2 25.3	16 25.2	0♊ 7.3	17 39.1	19 11.2	6 4.8	21 55.9	8 2.2	11 32.7
15 Su	17 29 44	23 3 52	0♉ 8 26	7♉ 5 2	2 26.7	17 32.7	1 20.1	18 22.8	19 5.9	6 11.1	21 59.5	8 2.0	11 33.9
16 M	17 33 41	24 1 11	14 8 16	21 17 56	2 27.9	18 36.9	2 32.9	19 6.4	19 0.7	6 17.4	22 3.1	8 1.8	11 35.2
17 Tu	17 37 37	24 58 30	28 33 41	5♊54 58	2R 28.6	19 37.8	3 45.7	19 50.0	18 55.7	6 23.8	22 6.7	8 1.7	11 36.5
18 W	17 41 34	25 55 48	13♊21 4	20 51 5	2 28.4	20 35.3	4 58.5	20 33.6	18 50.8	6 30.3	22 10.2	8 1.7	11 37.8
19 Th	17 45 30	26 53 6	28 23 59	5♋58 38	2 27.0	21 29.3	6 11.4	21 17.0	18 46.1	6 36.8	22 13.8	8D 1.6	11 39.2
20 F	17 49 27	27 50 23	13♋33 49	21 8 17	2 24.5	22 19.7	7 24.3	22 0.4	18 41.5	6 43.4	22 17.4	8 1.6	11 40.5
21 Sa	17 53 24	28 47 40	28 40 51	6♌10 24	2 21.1	23 6.5	8 37.1	22 43.8	18 37.0	6 50.0	22 20.9	8 1.6	11 41.9
22 Su	17 57 20	29 44 56	13♌35 54	20 56 31	2 17.5	23 49.4	9 50.0	23 27.1	18 32.8	6 56.6	22 24.5	8 1.7	11 43.3
23 M	18 1 17	0♋42 12	28 11 34	5♍20 34	2 14.2	24 28.4	11 3.0	24 10.3	18 28.7	7 3.3	22 28.0	8 1.8	11 44.7
24 Tu	18 5 13	1 39 26	12♍23 12	19 19 20	2 11.8	25 3.4	12 15.9	24 53.4	18 24.7	7 10.1	22 31.5	8 1.9	11 46.1
25 W	18 9 10	2 36 40	26 8 58	2♎52 15	2D 10.5	25 34.3	13 28.8	25 36.5	18 20.9	7 16.9	22 35.1	8 2.0	11 47.6
26 Th	18 13 6	3 33 54	9♎29 28	16 0 55	2 10.5	26 0.9	14 41.8	26 19.5	18 17.3	7 23.7	22 38.6	8 2.2	11 49.0
27 F	18 17 3	4 31 7	22 27 1	28 48 13	2 11.5	26 23.2	15 54.8	27 2.5	18 13.9	7 30.6	22 42.1	8 2.4	11 50.5
28 Sa	18 20 59	5 28 19	5♏ 4 58	11♏17 45	2 13.0	26 41.1	17 7.8	27 45.4	18 10.6	7 37.5	22 45.6	8 2.7	11 52.0
29 Su	18 24 56	6 25 31	17 27 1	23 33 15	2 14.5	26 54.4	18 20.8	28 28.2	18 7.5	7 44.4	22 49.1	8 3.0	11 53.5
30 M	18 28 53	7 22 42	29 36 52	5♐38 17	2R 15.4	27 3.1	19 33.8	29 11.0	18 4.5	7 51.4	22 52.6	8 3.3	11 55.0

Astro Data

	Dy Hr Mn
☽0S	2 13:01
♃∠♆	8 3:00
☽0N	17 2:34
♃⚻♅	28 8:17
☽0S	29 18:48
☽0N	13 11:33
♆ D	19 18:47
☽0S	26 0:16
♄∠♅	30 7:48

Planet Ingress

	Dy Hr Mn
☿ ♉	4 6:03
☿ ♊	18 13:33
♀ ♉	20 2:06
☉ ♊	21 22:09
♂ ♉	21 3:40
☿ ♋	2 13:40
♀ ♊	13 21:35
☉ ♋	22 6:19

Last Aspect / ☽ Ingress

Last Aspect Dy Hr Mn		☽ Ingress Dy Hr Mn
1 9:11	♃ ⚹	♎ 1 19:24
4 1:58	☿ ☍	♏ 4 2:35
5 23:58	♃ ☌	♐ 6 12:09
8 4:10	♂ △	♑ 8 23:55
10 22:47	♃ ⚹	♒ 11 12:41
13 13:07	♂ ⚹	♓ 14 0:20
15 22:22	☿ ⚹	♈ 16 8:56
18 10:27	♀ ☌	♉ 18 13:51
20 13:44	☉ ☌	♊ 20 15:51
22 1:15	♅ ☌	♋ 22 16:27
24 3:17	♃ △	♌ 24 17:18
26 4:47	♃ □	♍ 26 19:50
28 8:36	♅ □	♎ 29 0:54
31 0:06	☿ △	♏ 31 8:42

Last Aspect / ☽ Ingress

Last Aspect Dy Hr Mn		☽ Ingress Dy Hr Mn
2 0:04	♃ ☌	♐ 2 18:54
4 13:29	♅ ☍	♑ 5 6:51
7 3:00	♀ △	♒ 7 19:38
9 22:15	♀ □	♓ 10 7:47
12 14:38	♀ ⚹	♈ 12 17:34
14 10:37	☉ ⚹	♉ 14 23:45
16 8:47	♂ ☌	♊ 17 2:22
18 21:26	☉ ☌	♋ 19 2:32
20 14:39	☿ ☌	♌ 21 2:06
22 16:59	♂ □	♍ 23 3:01
24 22:59	♂ △	♎ 25 6:51
27 7:37	☿ □	♏ 27 14:17
29 23:05	♂ ☍	♐ 30 0:46

☽ Phases & Eclipses

Dy Hr Mn	
5 4:53	○ 13♏52
13 8:08	☽ 21♒44
20 13:44	● 28♉42
20 13:47:19	● T 5'14"
27 4:36	☽ 5♍04
3 19:27	○ 12♐22
3 19:15	● P 0.020
11 22:58	☽ 20♓09
18 21:26	● 26♊47
25 12:25	☽ 3♎06

Astro Data

1 MAY 1947
Julian Day # 17287
Delta T 27.9 sec
SVP 05♓59'59"
Obliquity 23°26'50"
⚷ Chiron 5♏10.4R
☽ Mean ☊ 3♊47.5

1 JUNE 1947
Julian Day # 17318
Delta T 28.0 sec
SVP 05♓59'55"
Obliquity 23°26'50"
⚷ Chiron 3♏06.6R
☽ Mean ☊ 2♊09.0

JULY 1947 — LONGITUDE

Day	Sid.Time	☉	0 hr ☽	Noon ☽	True ☊	☿	♀	♂	♃	♄	♅	♆	♇
1 Tu	18 32 49	8♋19 54	11♐37 53	17♐36 0	2♊15.0	27♋ 7.3	20♊46.9	29♉53.6	18♏ 1.8	7♌58.5	22♊56.1	8♎ 3.6	11♌56.5
2 W	18 36 46	9 17 5	23 32 57	29 29 4	2R 12.9	27R 6.7	21 59.9	0♊36.3	17R 59.2	8 5.5	22 59.5	8 4.0	11 58.1
3 Th	18 40 42	10 14 15	5♑24 36	11♑19 48	2 9.1	27 1.6	23 13.0	1 18.8	17 56.7	8 12.6	23 3.0	8 4.4	11 59.6
4 F	18 44 39	11 11 26	17 14 55	23 10 10	2 3.6	26 51.8	24 26.1	2 1.4	17 54.5	8 19.8	23 6.4	8 4.8	12 1.2
5 Sa	18 48 35	12 8 37	29 5 48	5♒ 2 2	1 56.8	26 37.7	25 39.3	2 43.8	17 52.4	8 26.9	23 9.8	8 5.3	12 2.8
6 Su	18 52 32	13 5 48	10♒59 7	16 57 19	1 49.3	26 19.2	26 52.4	3 26.2	17 50.6	8 34.1	23 13.2	8 5.8	12 4.4
7 M	18 56 28	14 2 59	22 56 53	28 58 8	1 41.9	25 56.7	28 5.6	4 8.5	17 48.8	8 41.4	23 16.6	8 6.3	12 6.0
8 Tu	19 0 25	15 0 10	5♓ 1 23	11♓ 7 0	1 35.3	25 30.5	29 18.8	4 50.7	17 47.3	8 48.6	23 20.0	8 6.9	12 7.6
9 W	19 4 22	15 57 21	17 15 22	23 26 54	1 30.1	25 0.8	0♋32.1	5 32.9	17 46.0	8 55.9	23 23.4	8 7.5	12 9.2
10 Th	19 8 18	16 54 33	29 42 0	6♈ 1 10	1 26.6	24 28.1	1 45.3	6 15.0	17 44.8	9 3.3	23 26.7	8 8.1	12 10.9
11 F	19 12 15	17 51 45	12♈24 49	18 53 25	1D 25.1	23 53.0	2 58.6	6 57.1	17 43.8	9 10.6	23 30.1	8 8.8	12 12.5
12 Sa	19 16 11	18 48 58	25 27 26	2♉ 7 14	1 25.1	23 15.9	4 11.9	7 39.0	17 43.0	9 18.0	23 33.4	8 9.5	12 14.2
13 Su	19 20 8	19 46 11	8♉53 11	15 45 34	1 26.1	22 37.4	5 25.2	8 21.0	17 42.3	9 25.4	23 36.7	8 10.2	12 15.9
14 M	19 24 4	20 43 25	22 44 31	29 50 6	1R 27.1	21 58.2	6 38.6	9 2.8	17 41.9	9 32.8	23 40.0	8 11.0	12 17.6
15 Tu	19 28 1	21 40 39	7♊ 2 10	14♊20 26	1 27.2	21 19.0	7 52.0	9 44.6	17D 41.6	9 40.3	23 43.2	8 11.7	12 19.2
16 W	19 31 57	22 37 54	21 44 24	29 13 20	1 25.6	20 40.4	9 5.4	10 26.3	17 41.5	9 47.8	23 46.5	8 12.6	12 21.0
17 Th	19 35 54	23 35 10	6♋46 21	14♋22 21	1 21.9	20 3.1	10 18.8	11 8.0	17 41.6	9 55.3	23 49.7	8 13.4	12 22.7
18 F	19 39 51	24 32 26	22 0 7	29 38 18	1 16.1	19 27.7	11 32.3	11 49.5	17 41.9	10 2.8	23 52.9	8 14.3	12 24.4
19 Sa	19 43 47	25 29 42	7♌15 32	14♌50 26	1 8.6	18 55.0	12 45.7	12 31.0	17 42.4	10 10.3	23 56.0	8 15.2	12 26.1
20 Su	19 47 44	26 26 59	22 21 46	29 48 21	1 0.4	18 25.5	13 59.2	13 12.5	17 43.0	10 17.9	23 59.2	8 16.1	12 27.8
21 M	19 51 40	27 24 16	7♍ 9 16	14♍23 45	0 52.6	17 59.8	15 12.7	13 53.8	17 43.9	10 25.5	24 2.3	8 17.1	12 29.6
22 Tu	19 55 37	28 21 33	21 31 17	28 31 32	0 46.1	17 38.4	16 26.3	14 35.1	17 44.9	10 33.1	24 5.4	8 18.1	12 31.3
23 W	19 59 33	29 18 51	5♎24 26	12♎10 2	0 41.5	17 21.6	17 39.8	15 16.3	17 46.0	10 40.7	24 8.5	8 19.1	12 33.1
24 Th	20 3 30	0♌16 9	18 48 35	25 20 27	0D 39.1	17 10.0	18 53.4	15 57.4	17 47.4	10 48.3	24 11.5	8 20.2	12 34.8
25 F	20 7 26	1 13 27	1♏46 6	8♏ 6 3	0 38.5	17D 3.7	20 7.0	16 38.5	17 49.0	10 55.9	24 14.6	8 21.2	12 36.6
26 Sa	20 11 23	2 10 46	14 20 55	20 31 16	0 38.9	17 3.1	21 20.6	17 19.5	17 50.7	11 3.6	24 17.6	8 22.3	12 38.4
27 Su	20 15 20	3 8 5	26 37 44	2♐40 56	0R 39.6	17 8.3	22 34.3	18 0.4	17 52.6	11 11.2	24 20.5	8 23.5	12 40.1
28 M	20 19 16	4 5 24	8♐41 26	14 39 48	0 39.3	17 19.5	23 47.9	18 41.2	17 54.7	11 18.9	24 23.5	8 24.7	12 41.9
29 Tu	20 23 13	5 2 44	20 36 34	26 32 12	0 37.3	17 36.9	25 1.6	19 22.0	17 56.9	11 26.6	24 26.4	8 25.8	12 43.7
30 W	20 27 9	6 0 5	2♑27 9	8♑21 50	0 33.0	18 0.3	26 15.3	20 2.7	17 59.4	11 34.3	24 29.3	8 27.1	12 45.5
31 Th	20 31 6	6 57 26	14 16 35	20 11 42	0 26.0	18 30.0	27 29.1	20 43.3	18 2.0	11 42.0	24 32.1	8 28.3	12 47.3

AUGUST 1947 — LONGITUDE

Day	Sid.Time	☉	0 hr ☽	Noon ☽	True ☊	☿	♀	♂	♃	♄	♅	♆	♇
1 F	20 35 2	7♌54 48	26♑ 7 28	2♒ 4 7	0♊16.6	19♋ 5.8	28♋42.8	21♊23.9	18♏ 4.8	11♌49.7	24♊35.0	8♎29.6	12♌49.1
2 Sa	20 38 59	8 52 11	8♒ 1 51	14 0 51	0R 5.3	19 47.8	29 56.6	22 4.4	18 7.7	11 57.4	24 37.8	8 30.9	12 50.9
3 Su	20 42 55	9 49 35	20 1 16	26 3 16	29♉52.9	20 35.8	1♌10.4	22 44.8	18 10.8	12 5.1	24 40.5	8 32.2	12 52.7
4 M	20 46 52	10 46 59	2♓ 7 0	8♓12 37	29 40.5	21 29.9	2 24.2	23 25.1	18 14.1	12 12.8	24 43.3	8 33.6	12 54.5
5 Tu	20 50 49	11 44 25	14 20 18	20 30 13	29 29.1	22 29.9	3 38.1	24 5.3	18 17.6	12 20.5	24 45.9	8 35.0	12 56.3
6 W	20 54 45	12 41 51	26 42 36	2♈57 43	29 19.7	23 35.6	4 52.0	24 45.5	18 21.2	12 28.2	24 48.6	8 36.4	12 58.0
7 Th	20 58 42	13 39 19	9♈15 48	15 37 12	29 12.8	24 47.0	6 5.9	25 25.6	18 25.0	12 35.9	24 51.2	8 37.8	12 59.8
8 F	21 2 38	14 36 48	22 2 13	28 31 14	29 8.6	26 3.8	7 19.8	26 5.6	18 28.9	12 43.6	24 53.8	8 39.2	13 1.6
9 Sa	21 6 35	15 34 19	5♉ 4 37	11♉42 43	29D 6.8	27 25.8	8 33.7	26 45.6	18 33.0	12 51.3	24 56.4	8 40.7	13 3.4
10 Su	21 10 31	16 31 50	18 25 54	25 14 27	29R 6.4	28 52.9	9 47.7	27 25.5	18 37.3	12 59.0	24 58.9	8 42.2	13 5.2
11 M	21 14 28	17 29 24	2♊ 8 39	9♊ 8 38	29 6.5	0♌24.7	11 1.7	28 5.3	18 41.8	13 6.7	25 1.4	8 43.8	13 7.0
12 Tu	21 18 24	18 26 59	16 14 27	23 26 1	29 5.7	2 0.9	12 15.7	28 45.0	18 46.4	13 14.4	25 3.9	8 45.3	13 8.8
13 W	21 22 21	19 24 35	0♋43 2	8♋ 5 6	29 3.0	3 41.2	13 29.8	29 24.7	18 51.1	13 22.1	25 6.3	8 46.9	13 10.6
14 Th	21 26 18	20 22 13	15 31 31	23 1 28	28 57.7	5 25.2	14 43.9	0♋ 4.2	18 56.1	13 29.8	25 8.7	8 48.5	13 12.4
15 F	21 30 14	21 19 52	0♌33 57	8♌ 7 46	28 49.8	7 12.7	15 58.0	0 43.7	19 1.1	13 37.4	25 11.0	8 50.1	13 14.2
16 Sa	21 34 11	22 17 32	15 41 40	23 14 21	28 39.8	9 3.1	17 12.1	1 23.1	19 6.4	13 45.1	25 13.3	8 51.8	13 16.0
17 Su	21 38 7	23 15 14	0♍44 30	8♍10 54	28 28.7	10 56.0	18 26.2	2 2.5	19 11.8	13 52.8	25 15.6	8 53.4	13 17.8
18 M	21 42 4	24 12 57	15 32 29	22 48 18	28 17.9	12 51.2	19 40.4	2 41.7	19 17.3	14 0.4	25 17.8	8 55.1	13 19.5
19 Tu	21 46 0	25 10 41	29 57 40	7♎ 0 5	28 8.5	14 48.1	20 54.6	3 20.8	19 23.0	14 8.0	25 20.0	8 56.8	13 21.3
20 W	21 49 57	26 8 26	13♎55 15	20 43 6	28 1.4	16 46.3	22 8.8	3 59.9	19 28.9	14 15.6	25 22.2	8 58.6	13 23.1
21 Th	21 53 53	27 6 12	27 23 44	3♏57 24	27 57.0	18 45.6	23 23.0	4 38.9	19 34.9	14 23.2	25 24.3	9 0.3	13 24.8
22 F	21 57 50	28 4 0	10♏24 31	16 45 34	27 54.8	20 45.5	24 37.2	5 17.8	19 41.0	14 30.8	25 26.3	9 2.1	13 26.6
23 Sa	22 1 47	29 1 48	23 1 7	29 11 48	27 54.3	22 45.8	25 51.5	5 56.6	19 47.3	14 38.4	25 28.4	9 3.9	13 28.3
24 Su	22 5 43	29 59 38	5♐18 16	11♐21 10	27 54.2	24 46.2	27 5.7	6 35.3	19 53.7	14 45.9	25 30.3	9 5.7	13 30.1
25 M	22 9 40	0♍57 29	17 21 13	23 19 1	27 53.5	26 46.4	28 20.0	7 14.0	20 0.3	14 53.5	25 32.3	9 7.5	13 31.8
26 Tu	22 13 36	1 55 22	29 15 13	5♑10 25	27 51.2	28 46.2	29 34.3	7 52.5	20 7.0	15 1.0	25 34.2	9 9.4	13 33.5
27 W	22 17 33	2 53 16	11♑ 5 10	16 59 59	27 46.5	0♍45.5	0♍48.7	8 31.0	20 13.9	15 8.4	25 36.0	9 11.2	13 35.3
28 Th	22 21 29	3 51 11	22 55 18	28 51 33	27 39.1	2 44.0	2 3.0	9 9.3	20 20.9	15 15.9	25 37.8	9 13.1	13 37.0
29 F	22 25 26	4 49 7	4♒49 5	10♒48 11	27 29.1	4 41.7	3 17.4	9 47.6	20 28.0	15 23.3	25 39.6	9 15.0	13 38.7
30 Sa	22 29 22	5 47 5	16 49 7	22 52 5	27 16.9	6 38.5	4 31.7	10 25.8	20 35.3	15 30.7	25 41.3	9 16.9	13 40.4
31 Su	22 33 19	6 45 4	28 57 13	5♓ 4 39	27 3.6	8 34.2	5 46.1	11 3.9	20 42.7	15 38.1	25 43.0	9 18.9	13 42.1

Astro Data	Dy Hr Mn
♄✶♆	1 18:29
☿ R	1 9:13
☽0N	10 18:24
♃ D	15 22:53
☽0S	23 6:49
☿ D	25 14:37
☽0N	6 23:28
♄☌♇	11 1:20
☽0S	19 15:09

Planet Ingress	Dy Hr Mn
♂ ♊	1 3:34
♀ ♋	8 13:30
☉ ♌	23 17:14
♀ ♌	2 1:06
☊ ♉	2 10:22
☿ ♌	10 17:40
♂ ♋	13 21:26
☉ ♍	24 0:09
☿ ♍	26 14:50
♀ ♍	26 8:17

Last Aspect Dy Hr Mn		☽ Ingress Dy Hr Mn
1 22:52	♅ ☍	♑ 2 13:03
4 19:07	☿ ☍	♒ 5 1:50
7 11:25	♀ △	♓ 7 14:03
9 14:24	☿ △	♈ 10 0:34
11 20:32	♅ ✶	♉ 12 8:12
13 22:44	☿ ✶	♊ 14 12:17
16 3:17	♅ ☌	♋ 16 13:14
18 4:15	☉ ☌	♌ 18 12:34
20 2:37	♅ ✶	♍ 20 12:19
22 12:35	☉ ✶	♎ 22 14:33
24 9:55	♅ △	♏ 24 20:41
26 15:07	♀ △	♐ 27 6:40
29 7:47	♅ ☍	♑ 29 19:01

Last Aspect Dy Hr Mn		☽ Ingress Dy Hr Mn
1 5:50	♀ ☍	♒ 1 7:50
3 9:18	♅ △	♓ 3 19:49
5 20:19	♅ □	♈ 6 6:20
8 8:20	☿ □	♉ 8 14:43
10 0:20	♃ ☍	♊ 10 20:17
12 21:45	♂ ☌	♋ 12 22:49
14 5:30	♃ △	♌ 14 23:06
16 15:12	♅ ✶	♍ 16 22:49
18 16:12	♅ □	♎ 19 0:04
20 23:26	☉ ✶	♏ 21 4:44
23 12:40	☉ □	♐ 23 13:34
26 0:43	♀ △	♑ 26 1:31
27 18:44	♃ ✶	♒ 28 14:18
30 17:37	♅ △	♓ 31 2:03

☽ Phases & Eclipses Dy Hr Mn	
3 10:39	○ 10♑40
11 10:54	☽ 18♈18
18 4:15	● 24♋43
24 22:54	☽ 1♏11
2 1:50	○ 8♒57
9 20:22	☽ 16♉23
16 11:12	● 22♌44
23 12:40	☽ 29♏32
31 16:34	○ 7♓25

Astro Data

1 JULY 1947
Julian Day # 17348
Delta T 28.0 sec
SVP 05♓59'49"
Obliquity 23°26'50"
⚷ Chiron 2♏18.0R
☽ Mean ☊ 0♊33.7

1 AUGUST 1947
Julian Day # 17379
Delta T 28.1 sec
SVP 05♓59'44"
Obliquity 23°26'51"
⚷ Chiron 3♏07.2
☽ Mean ☊ 28♉55.2

LONGITUDE SEPTEMBER 1947

Day	Sid.Time	☉	0 hr ☽	Noon ☽	True ☊	☿	♀	♂	♃	♄	♅	♆	♇
1 M	22 37 16	7♍43 5	11♓14 27	17♓26 42	26♉50.3	10♍28.9	7♍ 0.5	11♋42.0	20♏50.2	15♌45.5	25♊44.6	9♎20.8	13♌43.7
2 Tu	22 41 12	8 41 7	23 41 26	29 58 41	26R38.0	12 22.4	8 14.9	12 19.9	20 57.8	15 52.8	25 46.2	9 22.8	13 45.4
3 W	22 45 9	9 39 11	6♈18 31	12♈40 59	26 27.8	14 14.8	9 29.4	12 57.7	21 5.6	16 0.1	25 47.7	9 24.8	13 47.0
4 Th	22 49 5	10 37 17	19 6 9	25 34 9	26 20.3	16 6.0	10 43.8	13 35.5	21 13.5	16 7.4	25 49.2	9 26.8	13 48.7
5 F	22 53 2	11 35 25	2♉ 5 6	8♉39 10	26 15.7	17 56.0	11 58.3	14 13.2	21 21.6	16 14.6	25 50.6	9 28.8	13 50.3
6 Sa	22 56 58	12 33 35	15 16 31	21 57 23	26D13.6	19 44.8	13 12.8	14 50.7	21 29.7	16 21.8	25 52.0	9 30.8	13 51.9
7 Su	23 0 55	13 31 47	28 41 57	5♊30 25	26 13.2	21 32.4	14 27.3	15 28.2	21 38.0	16 29.0	25 53.3	9 32.8	13 53.5
8 M	23 4 51	14 30 1	12♊22 58	19 19 43	26R13.4	23 18.9	15 41.8	16 5.6	21 46.4	16 36.1	25 54.6	9 34.9	13 55.1
9 Tu	23 8 48	15 28 17	26 20 46	3♋26 3	26 13.0	25 4.2	16 56.4	16 42.9	21 54.9	16 43.3	25 55.9	9 37.0	13 56.7
10 W	23 12 45	16 26 35	10♋35 27	17 48 43	26 11.0	26 48.3	18 10.9	17 20.1	22 3.6	16 50.3	25 57.1	9 39.0	13 58.3
11 Th	23 16 41	17 24 56	25 5 25	2♌25 0	26 6.5	28 31.2	19 25.5	17 57.2	22 12.4	16 57.4	25 58.2	9 41.1	13 59.9
12 F	23 20 38	18 23 18	9♌46 47	17 9 54	25 59.6	0♎13.1	20 40.1	18 34.2	22 21.2	17 4.4	25 59.3	9 43.2	14 1.4
13 Sa	23 24 34	19 21 42	24 33 27	1♍56 24	25 50.6	1 53.8	21 54.7	19 11.1	22 30.2	17 11.3	26 0.4	9 45.4	14 2.9
14 Su	23 28 31	20 20 9	9♍17 43	16 36 22	25 40.5	3 33.4	23 9.4	19 47.9	22 39.3	17 18.2	26 1.4	9 47.5	14 4.5
15 M	23 32 27	21 18 37	23 51 23	1♎ 1 55	25 30.6	5 11.9	24 24.0	20 24.6	22 48.5	17 25.1	26 2.3	9 49.6	14 6.0
16 Tu	23 36 24	22 17 7	8♎ 7 14	15 6 45	25 21.9	6 49.4	25 38.6	21 1.1	22 57.9	17 31.9	26 3.2	9 51.8	14 7.4
17 W	23 40 20	23 15 39	22 0 4	28 46 58	25 15.3	8 25.8	26 53.3	21 37.6	23 7.3	17 38.7	26 4.0	9 53.9	14 8.9
18 Th	23 44 17	24 14 12	5♏27 23	12♏ 1 24	25 11.2	10 1.2	28 8.0	22 14.0	23 16.8	17 45.4	26 4.8	9 56.1	14 10.4
19 F	23 48 14	25 12 48	18 29 16	24 51 18	25D 9.4	11 35.5	29 22.6	22 50.2	23 26.5	17 52.1	26 5.6	9 58.2	14 11.8
20 Sa	23 52 10	26 11 25	1♐ 7 58	7♐19 48	25 9.3	13 8.9	0♏37.3	23 26.4	23 36.2	17 58.8	26 6.3	10 0.4	14 13.2
21 Su	23 56 7	27 10 4	13 27 20	19 31 14	25 10.1	14 41.2	1 52.0	24 2.4	23 46.1	18 5.3	26 6.9	10 2.6	14 14.6
22 M	0 0 3	28 8 44	25 32 8	1♑30 40	25R10.8	16 12.5	3 6.7	24 38.3	23 56.0	18 11.9	26 7.5	10 4.8	14 16.0
23 Tu	0 4 0	29 7 27	7♑27 31	13 23 20	25 10.4	17 42.8	4 21.4	25 14.1	24 6.1	18 18.4	26 8.0	10 7.0	14 17.4
24 W	0 7 56	0♎ 6 11	19 18 43	25 14 17	25 8.2	19 12.0	5 36.1	25 49.8	24 16.2	18 24.8	26 8.5	10 9.2	14 18.7
25 Th	0 11 53	1 4 56	1♒10 35	7♒ 8 8	25 3.9	20 40.3	6 50.9	26 25.4	24 26.5	18 31.2	26 8.9	10 11.4	14 20.1
26 F	0 15 49	2 3 44	13 7 25	19 8 50	24 57.5	22 7.6	8 5.6	27 0.8	24 36.8	18 37.5	26 9.3	10 13.6	14 21.4
27 Sa	0 19 46	3 2 33	25 12 45	1♓19 27	24 49.4	23 33.8	9 20.3	27 36.2	24 47.2	18 43.8	26 9.6	10 15.8	14 22.7
28 Su	0 23 43	4 1 24	7♓29 11	13 42 7	24 40.2	24 59.0	10 35.1	28 11.4	24 57.7	18 50.0	26 9.9	10 18.1	14 23.9
29 M	0 27 39	5 0 17	19 58 22	26 17 59	24 30.8	26 23.1	11 49.8	28 46.5	25 8.4	18 56.1	26 10.1	10 20.3	14 25.2
30 Tu	0 31 36	5 59 11	2♈40 58	9♈ 7 17	24 22.2	27 46.1	13 4.5	29 21.5	25 19.0	19 2.2	26 10.3	10 22.5	14 26.4

LONGITUDE OCTOBER 1947

Day	Sid.Time	☉	0 hr ☽	Noon ☽	True ☊	☿	♀	♂	♃	♄	♅	♆	♇
1 W	0 35 32	6♎58 8	15♈36 52	22♈ 9 37	24♉15.2	29♎ 8.0	14♎19.3	29♋56.4	25♏29.8	19♌ 8.3	26♊10.4	10♎24.7	14♌27.6
2 Th	0 39 29	7 57 7	28 45 24	5♉24 8	24R10.3	0♏28.7	15 34.1	0♌31.1	25 40.7	19 14.2	26R10.5	10 27.0	14 28.8
3 F	0 43 25	8 56 8	12♉ 5 39	18 49 53	24D 7.6	1 48.2	16 48.8	1 5.7	25 51.6	19 20.1	26 10.5	10 29.2	14 30.0
4 Sa	0 47 22	9 55 11	25 36 43	2♊26 5	24 6.9	3 6.5	18 3.6	1 40.2	26 2.6	19 26.0	26 10.4	10 31.4	14 31.2
5 Su	0 51 18	10 54 17	9♊17 55	16 12 9	24 7.7	4 23.4	19 18.4	2 14.6	26 13.8	19 31.8	26 10.3	10 33.7	14 32.3
6 M	0 55 15	11 53 25	23 8 44	0♋ 7 38	24 9.0	5 39.0	20 33.2	2 48.8	26 25.0	19 37.5	26 10.2	10 35.9	14 33.4
7 Tu	0 59 12	12 52 35	7♋ 8 44	14 11 57	24R10.0	6 53.1	21 48.0	3 22.9	26 36.2	19 43.1	26 10.0	10 38.1	14 34.5
8 W	1 3 8	13 51 48	21 17 8	28 24 3	24 9.9	8 5.6	23 2.8	3 56.9	26 47.6	19 48.7	26 9.7	10 40.4	14 35.6
9 Th	1 7 5	14 51 3	5♌32 26	12♌41 58	24 8.2	9 16.4	24 17.6	4 30.7	26 59.0	19 54.2	26 9.4	10 42.6	14 36.6
10 F	1 11 1	15 50 21	19 52 11	27 2 37	24 4.8	10 25.4	25 32.4	5 4.4	27 10.5	19 59.7	26 9.1	10 44.8	14 37.6
11 Sa	1 14 58	16 49 40	4♍12 42	11♍21 50	23 59.9	11 32.5	26 47.3	5 38.0	27 22.1	20 5.1	26 8.7	10 47.1	14 38.6
12 Su	1 18 54	17 49 2	18 29 24	25 34 45	23 54.2	12 37.5	28 2.1	6 11.4	27 33.7	20 10.4	26 8.2	10 49.3	14 39.6
13 M	1 22 51	18 48 26	2♎37 15	9♎36 20	23 48.6	13 40.1	29 16.9	6 44.7	27 45.4	20 15.6	26 7.7	10 51.5	14 40.5
14 Tu	1 26 47	19 47 52	16 31 27	23 22 11	23 43.6	14 40.3	0♏31.8	7 17.8	27 57.2	20 20.7	26 7.1	10 53.7	14 41.5
15 W	1 30 44	20 47 20	0♏ 8 9	6♏49 8	23 40.0	15 37.7	1 46.6	7 50.7	28 9.0	20 25.8	26 6.5	10 55.9	14 42.4
16 Th	1 34 40	21 46 50	13 24 59	19 55 40	23D38.0	16 32.1	3 1.5	8 23.5	28 20.9	20 30.8	26 5.8	10 58.1	14 43.2
17 F	1 38 37	22 46 23	26 21 16	2♐41 57	23 37.6	17 23.2	4 16.3	8 56.2	28 32.9	20 35.7	26 5.1	11 0.3	14 44.1
18 Sa	1 42 34	23 45 57	8♐57 59	15 9 44	23 38.5	18 10.7	5 31.2	9 28.6	28 45.0	20 40.5	26 4.3	11 2.5	14 44.9
19 Su	1 46 30	24 45 33	21 17 35	27 22 2	23 40.1	18 54.1	6 46.0	10 1.0	28 57.1	20 45.3	26 3.5	11 4.7	14 45.7
20 M	1 50 27	25 45 11	3♑23 35	9♑22 49	23 41.9	19 33.2	8 0.9	10 33.1	29 9.2	20 50.0	26 2.7	11 6.9	14 46.5
21 Tu	1 54 23	26 44 50	15 20 19	21 16 41	23 43.3	20 7.3	9 15.7	11 5.1	29 21.5	20 54.5	26 1.7	11 9.1	14 47.2
22 W	1 58 20	27 44 31	27 12 33	3♒ 8 30	23R43.8	20 36.1	10 30.6	11 36.9	29 33.7	20 59.0	26 0.8	11 11.3	14 48.0
23 Th	2 2 16	28 44 14	9♒ 5 9	15 3 7	23 43.3	20 59.0	11 45.5	12 8.5	29 46.1	21 3.5	25 59.8	11 13.4	14 48.7
24 F	2 6 13	29 43 59	21 2 57	27 5 11	23 41.7	21 15.4	13 0.3	12 40.0	29 58.5	21 7.8	25 58.7	11 15.6	14 49.3
25 Sa	2 10 9	0♏43 46	3♓10 18	9♓18 46	23 39.0	21R24.8	14 15.2	13 11.3	0♐10.9	21 12.0	25 57.6	11 17.7	14 50.0
26 Su	2 14 6	1 43 34	15 30 58	21 47 13	23 35.8	21 26.6	15 30.0	13 42.4	0 23.4	21 16.2	25 56.4	11 19.8	14 50.6
27 M	2 18 3	2 43 23	28 7 46	4♈32 48	23 32.4	21 20.2	16 44.9	14 13.3	0 35.9	21 20.3	25 55.2	11 21.9	14 51.2
28 Tu	2 21 59	3 43 15	11♈ 2 25	17 36 37	23 29.2	21 5.1	17 59.7	14 44.1	0 48.5	21 24.2	25 54.0	11 24.0	14 51.8
29 W	2 25 56	4 43 8	24 15 21	0♉58 27	23 26.8	20 40.9	19 14.5	15 14.6	1 1.1	21 28.1	25 52.7	11 26.1	14 52.3
30 Th	2 29 52	5 43 4	7♉45 42	14 36 50	23 25.2	20 7.4	20 29.4	15 45.0	1 13.8	21 31.9	25 51.3	11 28.2	14 52.8
31 F	2 33 49	6 43 1	21 31 29	28 29 16	23D24.6	19 24.7	21 44.2	16 15.2	1 26.5	21 35.6	25 49.9	11 30.3	14 53.3

Astro Data	Dy Hr Mn
☽0N	3 4:23
☿0S	12 17:46
☽0S	16 0:45
♀0S	21 22:05
☽0N	30 10:52
♃∠♆	30 9:45
♅ R	2 16:05
♃⊼♅	4 16:40
☽0S	13 10:10
☿ R	25 17:25
☽0N	27 19:29

Planet Ingress		Dy Hr Mn
☿	♎	11 20:54
♀	♎	19 12:01
☉	♎	23 21:29
☿	♏	1 15:26
♂	♌	1 2:31
♀	♏	13 13:49
☉	♏	24 6:26
♃	♐	24 3:00

Last Aspect Dy Hr Mn		☽ Ingress Dy Hr Mn
2 3:59	♅ □	♈ 2 12:03
4 12:29	♅ ⚹	♉ 4 20:10
6 11:17	♃ ☍	♊ 7 2:18
8 23:18	♅ ☌	♋ 9 6:12
11 6:22	☿ ⚹	♌ 11 8:03
13 2:21	♅ ⚹	♍ 13 8:51
15 3:38	♅ □	♎ 15 10:16
17 7:11	♅ △	♏ 17 14:10
19 13:45	☉ ⚹	♐ 19 21:49
22 5:42	☉ □	♑ 22 8:58
24 13:54	♂ ☍	♒ 24 21:38
27 1:52	♅ △	♓ 27 9:24
29 17:28	♂ △	♈ 29 18:58

Last Aspect Dy Hr Mn		☽ Ingress Dy Hr Mn
1 19:19	♅ ⚹	♉ 2 2:15
4 0:46	♃ ☍	♊ 4 7:44
6 5:12	♅ ☌	♋ 6 11:47
8 9:25	♃ △	♌ 8 14:41
10 12:23	♃ □	♍ 10 16:57
12 15:35	♃ ⚹	♎ 12 19:31
14 16:51	♅ △	♏ 14 23:45
17 4:12	♃ ☌	♐ 17 6:53
19 9:24	♅ ☍	♑ 19 17:14
22 4:51	♃ ⚹	♒ 22 5:39
24 9:47	♅ △	♓ 24 17:46
26 19:51	♅ □	♈ 27 3:31
29 2:54	♅ ⚹	♉ 29 10:16
31 0:24	♀ ☍	♊ 31 14:36

☽ Phases & Eclipses Dy Hr Mn	
8 3:57	☽ 14♊40
14 19:28	● 21♍08
22 5:42	☽ 28♐23
30 6:41	○ 6♈16
7 10:29	☽ 13♋18
14 6:10	● 20♎03
22 1:11	☽ 27♑47
29 20:07	○ 5♉33

Astro Data

1 SEPTEMBER 1947
Julian Day # 17410
Delta T 28.1 sec
SVP 05♓59'39"
Obliquity 23°26'51"
⚷ Chiron 5♏29.7
☽ Mean ☊ 27♉16.7

1 OCTOBER 1947
Julian Day # 17440
Delta T 28.1 sec
SVP 05♓59'37"
Obliquity 23°26'52"
⚷ Chiron 8♏53.3
☽ Mean ☊ 25♉41.4

NOVEMBER 1947 — LONGITUDE

Day	Sid.Time	☉	0 hr ☽	Noon ☽	True ☊	☿	♀	♂	♃	♄	♅	♆	♇
1 Sa	2 37 45	7♏43 1	5♊29 47	12♊32 35	23♉24.9	18♏32.8	22♏59.1	16♌45.2	1♐39.3	21♌39.2	25♊48.5	11♎32.3	14♌53.8
2 Su	2 41 42	8 43 2	19 37 13	26 43 15	23 25.8	17R32.6	24 13.9	17 14.9	1 52.1	21 42.8	25R47.0	11 34.4	14 54.2
3 M	2 45 38	9 43 6	3♋50 16	10♋57 51	23 26.9	16 25.1	25 28.7	17 44.5	2 5.0	21 46.2	25 45.5	11 36.4	14 54.6
4 Tu	2 49 35	10 43 11	18 5 37	25 13 14	23 27.9	15 11.8	26 43.6	18 13.9	2 17.9	21 49.5	25 44.0	11 38.4	14 55.0
5 W	2 53 32	11 43 19	2♌20 21	9♌26 40	23R28.6	13 54.6	27 58.4	18 43.1	2 30.8	21 52.7	25 42.4	11 40.5	14 55.3
6 Th	2 57 28	12 43 29	16 31 56	23 35 51	23 28.7	12 35.8	29 13.3	19 12.0	2 43.8	21 55.9	25 40.7	11 42.4	14 55.6
7 F	3 1 25	13 43 41	0♍38 11	7♍38 43	23 28.3	11 17.9	0♐28.1	19 40.7	2 56.8	21 58.9	25 39.0	11 44.4	14 55.9
8 Sa	3 5 21	14 43 55	14 37 11	21 33 23	23 27.5	10 3.3	1 43.0	20 9.2	3 9.8	22 1.8	25 37.3	11 46.4	14 56.2
9 Su	3 9 18	15 44 11	28 27 5	5♎18 5	23 26.6	8 54.4	2 57.8	20 37.5	3 22.9	22 4.6	25 35.5	11 48.3	14 56.4
10 M	3 13 14	16 44 29	12♎ 6 9	18 51 6	23 25.6	7 53.4	4 12.7	21 5.5	3 36.0	22 7.4	25 33.7	11 50.2	14 56.6
11 Tu	3 17 11	17 44 49	25 32 46	2♏10 58	23 24.9	7 2.0	5 27.5	21 33.2	3 49.1	22 10.0	25 31.9	11 52.1	14 56.8
12 W	3 21 7	18 45 10	8♏45 35	15 16 30	23 24.5	6 21.2	6 42.4	22 0.8	4 2.3	22 12.5	25 30.0	11 54.0	14 57.0
13 Th	3 25 4	19 45 34	21 43 41	28 7 7	23D24.4	5 52.0	7 57.2	22 28.0	4 15.5	22 14.9	25 28.1	11 55.9	14 57.1
14 F	3 29 1	20 45 59	4♐26 49	10♐42 53	23 24.4	5 34.4	9 12.1	22 55.0	4 28.7	22 17.2	25 26.1	11 57.7	14 57.2
15 Sa	3 32 57	21 46 26	16 55 27	23 4 43	23 24.6	5D28.4	10 26.9	23 21.8	4 42.0	22 19.4	25 24.2	11 59.5	14 57.3
16 Su	3 36 54	22 46 54	29 10 55	5♑14 21	23R24.7	5 33.6	11 41.8	23 48.3	4 55.2	22 21.5	25 22.1	12 1.4	14R57.3
17 M	3 40 50	23 47 24	11♑15 22	17 14 22	23 24.7	5 49.2	12 56.6	24 14.5	5 8.5	22 23.5	25 20.1	12 3.1	14 57.3
18 Tu	3 44 47	24 47 55	23 11 47	29 8 6	23 24.6	6 14.6	14 11.5	24 40.4	5 21.9	22 25.4	25 18.0	12 4.9	14 57.3
19 W	3 48 43	25 48 28	5♒ 3 49	10♒59 30	23 24.4	6 48.7	15 26.3	25 6.0	5 35.2	22 27.2	25 15.9	12 6.7	14 57.2
20 Th	3 52 40	26 49 2	16 55 40	22 52 57	23D24.2	7 30.8	16 41.1	25 31.4	5 48.5	22 28.9	25 13.7	12 8.4	14 57.2
21 F	3 56 36	27 49 37	28 51 54	4♓53 7	23 24.1	8 19.9	17 56.0	25 56.4	6 1.9	22 30.4	25 11.6	12 10.1	14 57.1
22 Sa	4 0 33	28 50 13	10♓57 12	17 4 42	23 24.3	9 15.2	19 10.8	26 21.2	6 15.3	22 31.9	25 9.4	12 11.7	14 56.9
23 Su	4 4 30	29 50 50	23 16 10	29 32 6	23 24.7	10 15.9	20 25.6	26 45.6	6 28.7	22 33.2	25 7.1	12 13.4	14 56.8
24 M	4 8 26	0♐51 29	5♈52 56	12♈19 5	23 25.4	11 21.3	21 40.4	27 9.8	6 42.1	22 34.4	25 4.9	12 15.0	14 56.6
25 Tu	4 12 23	1 52 8	18 50 51	25 28 25	23 26.2	12 30.8	22 55.2	27 33.6	6 55.5	22 35.5	25 2.6	12 16.6	14 56.4
26 W	4 16 19	2 52 49	2♉11 55	9♉ 1 19	23 27.0	13 43.8	24 9.9	27 57.1	7 9.0	22 36.5	25 0.3	12 18.2	14 56.1
27 Th	4 20 16	3 53 31	15 56 30	22 57 10	23R27.5	14 59.8	25 24.7	28 20.2	7 22.4	22 37.4	24 58.0	12 19.8	14 55.9
28 F	4 24 12	4 54 14	0♊ 2 55	7♊13 13	23 27.5	16 18.4	26 39.5	28 43.1	7 35.8	22 38.2	24 55.6	12 21.3	14 55.6
29 Sa	4 28 9	5 54 59	14 27 24	21 44 44	23 26.9	17 39.1	27 54.2	29 5.6	7 49.3	22 38.9	24 53.2	12 22.8	14 55.2
30 Su	4 32 5	6 55 45	29 4 23	6♋25 28	23 25.6	19 1.7	29 9.0	29 27.7	8 2.8	22 39.4	24 50.9	12 24.3	14 54.9

DECEMBER 1947 — LONGITUDE

Day	Sid.Time	☉	0 hr ☽	Noon ☽	True ☊	☿	♀	♂	♃	♄	♅	♆	♇
1 M	4 36 2	7♐56 32	13♋47 5	21♋ 8 23	23♉23.9	20♏25.9	0♑23.7	29♌49.5	8♐16.2	22♌39.9	24♊48.5	12♎25.8	14♌54.5
2 Tu	4 39 59	8 57 21	28 28 32	5♌46 46	23R21.9	21 51.5	1 38.5	0♍10.9	8 29.7	22 40.2	24R46.0	12 27.2	14R54.1
3 W	4 43 55	9 58 11	13♌ 2 27	20 15 1	23 20.1	23 18.1	2 53.2	0 31.9	8 43.2	22 40.5	24 43.6	12 28.6	14 53.7
4 Th	4 47 52	10 59 3	27 24 1	4♍29 8	23 18.8	24 45.8	4 7.9	0 52.6	8 56.6	22R40.6	24 41.1	12 30.0	14 53.2
5 F	4 51 48	11 59 56	11♍30 10	18 26 59	23D18.3	26 14.2	5 22.7	1 12.9	9 10.1	22 40.6	24 38.6	12 31.3	14 52.7
6 Sa	4 55 45	13 0 50	25 19 33	2♎ 7 56	23 18.7	27 43.3	6 37.4	1 32.7	9 23.6	22 40.5	24 36.1	12 32.6	14 52.2
7 Su	4 59 41	14 1 45	8♎52 11	15 32 28	23 19.9	29 13.0	7 52.1	1 52.2	9 37.0	22 40.2	24 33.6	12 33.9	14 51.7
8 M	5 3 38	15 2 42	22 8 55	28 41 43	23 21.4	0♐43.2	9 6.8	2 11.2	9 50.5	22 39.9	24 31.1	12 35.2	14 51.1
9 Tu	5 7 35	16 3 40	5♏11 3	11♏37 4	23 22.9	2 13.7	10 21.5	2 29.8	10 3.9	22 39.4	24 28.6	12 36.4	14 50.5
10 W	5 11 31	17 4 39	17 59 56	24 19 50	23R23.8	3 44.7	11 36.2	2 47.9	10 17.4	22 38.9	24 26.1	12 37.6	14 49.9
11 Th	5 15 28	18 5 39	0♐36 52	6♐51 12	23 23.7	5 15.9	12 50.8	3 5.6	10 30.8	22 38.2	24 23.5	12 38.8	14 49.3
12 F	5 19 24	19 6 41	13 2 57	19 12 14	23 22.3	6 47.5	14 5.5	3 22.9	10 44.2	22 37.4	24 21.0	12 39.9	14 48.6
13 Sa	5 23 21	20 7 43	25 19 12	1♑23 59	23 19.4	8 19.2	15 20.2	3 39.6	10 57.7	22 36.5	24 18.4	12 41.1	14 47.9
14 Su	5 27 17	21 8 46	7♑26 43	13 27 37	23 15.2	9 51.2	16 34.8	3 55.9	11 11.1	22 35.5	24 15.8	12 42.1	14 47.2
15 M	5 31 14	22 9 49	19 26 51	25 24 41	23 10.0	11 23.3	17 49.5	4 11.7	11 24.4	22 34.4	24 13.3	12 43.2	14 46.5
16 Tu	5 35 10	23 10 53	1♒21 23	7♒17 15	23 4.3	12 55.7	19 4.1	4 27.0	11 37.8	22 33.1	24 10.7	12 44.2	14 45.7
17 W	5 39 7	24 11 58	13 12 38	19 7 56	22 58.9	14 28.2	20 18.7	4 41.8	11 51.2	22 31.8	24 8.1	12 45.2	14 44.9
18 Th	5 43 4	25 13 3	25 3 36	1♓ 0 4	22 54.1	16 0.8	21 33.3	4 56.0	12 4.5	22 30.3	24 5.6	12 46.2	14 44.1
19 F	5 47 0	26 14 9	6♓57 53	12 57 35	22 50.7	17 33.6	22 47.9	5 9.7	12 17.8	22 28.8	24 3.0	12 47.1	14 43.3
20 Sa	5 50 57	27 15 15	18 59 43	25 4 53	22D48.8	19 6.6	24 2.4	5 22.9	12 31.1	22 27.1	24 0.4	12 48.0	14 42.4
21 Su	5 54 53	28 16 21	1♈13 41	7♈26 43	22 48.4	20 39.8	25 16.9	5 35.6	12 44.3	22 25.3	23 57.9	12 48.9	14 41.5
22 M	5 58 50	29 17 27	13 44 34	20 7 49	22 49.4	22 13.1	26 31.4	5 47.6	12 57.6	22 23.5	23 55.3	12 49.7	14 40.6
23 Tu	6 2 46	0♑18 33	26 36 57	3♉12 26	22 50.9	23 46.6	27 45.9	5 59.1	13 10.8	22 21.5	23 52.8	12 50.5	14 39.7
24 W	6 6 43	1 19 40	9♉54 38	16 43 46	22R52.4	25 20.4	29 0.4	6 10.1	13 24.0	22 19.4	23 50.2	12 51.2	14 38.8
25 Th	6 10 39	2 20 47	23 39 57	0♊43 9	22 53.0	26 54.3	0♒14.9	6 20.4	13 37.1	22 17.2	23 47.7	12 52.0	14 37.8
26 F	6 14 36	3 21 54	7♊53 6	15 9 23	22 52.1	28 28.4	1 29.3	6 30.1	13 50.2	22 14.9	23 45.2	12 52.7	14 36.8
27 Sa	6 18 33	4 23 1	22 31 21	29 58 11	22 49.1	0♑ 2.8	2 43.7	6 39.3	14 3.3	22 12.6	23 42.7	12 53.3	14 35.8
28 Su	6 22 29	5 24 9	7♋28 51	15♋ 2 12	22 44.2	1 37.4	3 58.0	6 47.8	14 16.4	22 10.1	23 40.2	12 54.0	14 34.8
29 M	6 26 26	6 25 17	22 36 58	0♌11 52	22 37.8	3 12.4	5 12.4	6 55.6	14 29.4	22 7.5	23 37.7	12 54.6	14 33.8
30 Tu	6 30 22	7 26 25	7♌45 36	15 16 55	22 30.7	4 47.5	6 26.7	7 2.8	14 42.4	22 4.8	23 35.2	12 55.1	14 32.7
31 W	6 34 19	8 27 33	22 44 44	0♍ 8 6	22 23.8	6 23.0	7 41.0	7 9.4	14 55.3	22 2.1	23 32.7	12 55.7	14 31.6

Astro Data

	Dy Hr Mn
☽0S	9 17:52
☿ D	15 0:40
♇ R	16 21:42
☽0N	24 5:09
♄ R	4 11:34
☽0S	6 23:30
☽0N	21 13:53
♃⚹♆	21 8:43
♃△♇	29 7:26

Planet Ingress

	Dy Hr Mn
♀ ♐	6 14:59
☉ ♐	23 3:38
♀ ♑	30 16:23
♂ ♍	1 11:44
☿ ♐	7 12:32
☉ ♑	22 16:43
♀ ♒	24 19:13
☿ ♑	26 23:17

Last Aspect / ☽ Ingress (November)

Last Aspect Dy Hr Mn		☽ Ingress Dy Hr Mn
2 10:24	♅ ☌	♋ 2 17:32
4 15:56	♀ △	♌ 4 20:03
6 15:31	♅ ⚹	♍ 6 22:55
8 19:02	♅ □	♎ 9 2:42
10 23:58	♅ △	♏ 11 8:02
13 1:26	♂ □	♐ 13 15:33
15 16:31	♅ ☍	♑ 16 1:37
18 3:32	☉ ⚹	♒ 18 13:45
20 21:44	☉ □	♓ 21 2:16
23 3:33	♅ □	♈ 23 12:53
25 16:13	♂ △	♉ 25 20:06
27 21:42	♂ □	♊ 27 23:55
30 0:39	♂ ⚹	♋ 30 1:31

Last Aspect / ☽ Ingress (December)

Last Aspect Dy Hr Mn		☽ Ingress Dy Hr Mn
1 12:00	☿ △	♌ 2 2:30
3 19:27	♅ ⚹	♍ 4 4:23
6 4:44	☿ ⚹	♎ 6 8:14
8 4:19	♅ △	♏ 8 14:24
10 8:48	♄ □	♐ 10 22:49
12 22:01	♅ ☍	♑ 13 9:14
14 20:22	♀ ☌	♒ 15 21:16
18 0:21	☉ ⚹	♓ 18 9:59
20 17:44	☉ □	♈ 20 21:37
23 2:20	♀ □	♉ 23 6:11
24 21:38	♄ □	♊ 25 10:47
27 1:55	♅ ☌	♋ 27 12:03
28 8:37	♆ □	♌ 29 11:41
31 1:17	♅ ⚹	♍ 31 11:47

☽ Phases & Eclipses

Dy Hr Mn	
5 17:04	☽ 12♌26
12 20:01	● 19♏36
12 20:05:09	◐ A 3'59"
20 21:44	☽ 27♒44
28 8:45	○ 5♊16
28 8:34	◑ A 0.868
5 0:55	☽ 12♍02
12 12:53	● 19♐39
20 17:44	☽ 28♓00
27 20:27	○ 5♋15

Astro Data

1 NOVEMBER 1947
Julian Day # 17471
Delta T 28.2 sec
SVP 05♓59'33"
Obliquity 23°26'51"
⚷ Chiron 13♏01.4
☽ Mean ☊ 24♉02.9

1 DECEMBER 1947
Julian Day # 17501
Delta T 28.2 sec
SVP 05♓59'28"
Obliquity 23°26'51"
⚷ Chiron 17♏07.0
☽ Mean ☊ 22♉27.6

LONGITUDE — JANUARY 1948

Day	Sid.Time	☉	0 hr ☽	Noon ☽	True ☊	☿	♀	♂	♃	♄	♅	♆	♇
1 Th	6 38 15	9♑28 42	7♍26 16	14♍38 40	22♉18.2	7♑58.8	8♒55.3	7♍15.3	15♐ 8.3	21♌59.2	23♊30.3	12♎56.2	14♌30.5
2 F	6 42 12	10 29 51	21 44 57	28 44 57	22R14.4	9 34.9	10 9.5	7 20.4	15 21.1	21R56.2	23R27.8	12 56.6	14R29.4
3 Sa	6 46 9	11 31 0	5♎38 38	12♎26 10	22D12.7	11 11.4	11 23.7	7 24.9	15 34.0	21 53.2	23 25.4	12 57.1	14 28.3
4 Su	6 50 5	12 32 10	19 7 47	25 43 48	22 12.7	12 48.2	12 37.9	7 28.7	15 46.7	21 50.0	23 23.0	12 57.5	14 27.1
5 M	6 54 2	13 33 20	2♏14 39	8♏40 45	22 13.8	14 25.4	13 52.1	7 31.8	15 59.5	21 46.8	23 20.7	12 57.8	14 26.0
6 Tu	6 57 58	14 34 30	15 2 31	21 20 27	22R14.8	16 2.9	15 6.2	7 34.1	16 12.2	21 43.5	23 18.3	12 58.2	14 24.8
7 W	7 1 55	15 35 40	27 34 56	3♐46 24	22 14.9	17 40.9	16 20.3	7 35.7	16 24.8	21 40.1	23 16.0	12 58.4	14 23.6
8 Th	7 5 51	16 36 51	9♐55 12	16 1 43	22 13.1	19 19.2	17 34.4	7R36.5	16 37.4	21 36.6	23 13.7	12 58.7	14 22.4
9 F	7 9 48	17 38 1	22 6 13	28 8 59	22 8.8	20 58.0	18 48.5	7 36.5	16 50.0	21 33.1	23 11.4	12 58.9	14 21.1
10 Sa	7 13 44	18 39 12	4♑10 15	10♑10 13	22 1.8	22 37.1	20 2.5	7 35.8	17 2.5	21 29.4	23 9.1	12 59.1	14 19.9
11 Su	7 17 41	19 40 22	16 9 4	22 6 58	21 52.2	24 16.6	21 16.4	7 34.3	17 14.9	21 25.7	23 6.9	12 59.3	14 18.6
12 M	7 21 38	20 41 32	28 4 5	4♒ 0 35	21 40.8	25 56.6	22 30.4	7 32.0	17 27.3	21 21.9	23 4.7	12 59.4	14 17.4
13 Tu	7 25 34	21 42 42	9♒56 36	15 52 21	21 28.4	27 36.9	23 44.3	7 29.0	17 39.7	21 18.1	23 2.5	12 59.5	14 16.1
14 W	7 29 31	22 43 51	21 48 1	27 43 52	21 16.0	29 17.5	24 58.2	7 25.1	17 51.9	21 14.1	23 0.4	12R59.5	14 14.8
15 Th	7 33 27	23 44 59	3♓40 10	9♓37 13	21 4.8	0♒58.5	26 12.0	7 20.4	18 4.2	21 10.1	22 58.3	12 59.5	14 13.5
16 F	7 37 24	24 46 7	15 35 24	21 35 7	20 55.6	2 39.8	27 25.7	7 15.0	18 16.3	21 6.1	22 56.2	12 59.5	14 12.2
17 Sa	7 41 20	25 47 14	27 36 50	3♈41 1	20 49.1	4 21.3	28 39.5	7 8.7	18 28.4	21 1.9	22 54.1	12 59.5	14 10.9
18 Su	7 45 17	26 48 21	9♈48 12	15 58 59	20 45.2	6 3.0	29 53.2	7 1.6	18 40.4	20 57.7	22 52.1	12 59.4	14 9.5
19 M	7 49 13	27 49 26	22 13 55	28 33 37	20D43.6	7 44.9	1♓ 6.8	6 53.7	18 52.4	20 53.5	22 50.1	12 59.3	14 8.2
20 Tu	7 53 10	28 50 31	4♉58 39	11♉29 37	20 43.6	9 26.7	2 20.4	6 45.0	19 4.3	20 49.2	22 48.2	12 59.1	14 6.8
21 W	7 57 7	29 51 35	18 7 2	24 51 19	20R44.0	11 8.5	3 33.9	6 35.5	19 16.1	20 44.8	22 46.3	12 58.9	14 5.5
22 Th	8 1 3	0♒52 38	1♊42 50	8♊41 48	20 43.6	12 50.0	4 47.4	6 25.3	19 27.8	20 40.4	22 44.4	12 58.7	14 4.1
23 F	8 5 0	1 53 40	15 48 14	23 1 59	20 41.3	14 31.1	6 0.8	6 14.2	19 39.5	20 35.9	22 42.6	12 58.4	14 2.7
24 Sa	8 8 56	2 54 42	0♋22 40	7♋49 39	20 36.3	16 11.7	7 14.2	6 2.4	19 51.1	20 31.4	22 40.8	12 58.1	14 1.3
25 Su	8 12 53	3 55 42	15 22 4	22 58 48	20 28.7	17 51.4	8 27.5	5 49.8	20 2.6	20 26.9	22 39.0	12 57.8	13 59.9
26 M	8 16 49	4 56 41	0♌38 35	8♌19 58	20 18.7	19 30.1	9 40.7	5 36.4	20 14.1	20 22.3	22 37.3	12 57.5	13 58.6
27 Tu	8 20 46	5 57 39	16 1 25	23 41 25	20 7.6	21 7.4	10 53.9	5 22.3	20 25.4	20 17.7	22 35.6	12 57.1	13 57.2
28 W	8 24 42	6 58 37	1♍18 30	8♍51 22	19 56.6	22 42.9	12 7.0	5 7.4	20 36.7	20 13.0	22 34.0	12 56.7	13 55.8
29 Th	8 28 39	7 59 34	16 18 52	23 40 8	19 47.1	24 16.2	13 20.0	4 51.8	20 47.9	20 8.3	22 32.4	12 56.2	13 54.3
30 F	8 32 36	9 0 30	0♎54 29	8♎ 1 32	19 39.9	25 46.9	14 33.0	4 35.5	20 59.1	20 3.6	22 30.8	12 55.7	13 52.9
31 Sa	8 36 32	10 1 25	15 1 7	21 53 14	19 35.5	27 14.5	15 46.0	4 18.5	21 10.1	19 58.8	22 29.3	12 55.2	13 51.5

LONGITUDE — FEBRUARY 1948

Day	Sid.Time	☉	0 hr ☽	Noon ☽	True ☊	☿	♀	♂	♃	♄	♅	♆	♇
1 Su	8 40 29	11♒ 2 19	28♎38 6	5♏16 4	19♉33.4	28♒38.2	16♓58.8	4♍ 0.8	21♐21.1	19♌54.0	22♊27.9	12♎54.6	13♌50.1
2 M	8 44 25	12 3 13	11♏47 36	18 13 11	19R33.0	29 57.6	18 11.6	3R42.5	21 31.9	19R49.2	22R26.4	12R54.1	13R48.7
3 Tu	8 48 22	13 4 6	24 33 25	0♐48 54	19 33.0	1♓11.8	19 24.3	3 23.6	21 42.7	19 44.4	22 25.1	12 53.4	13 47.3
4 W	8 52 18	14 4 58	7♐ 0 13	13 7 57	19 32.1	2 20.1	20 37.0	3 4.0	21 53.4	19 39.5	22 23.7	12 52.8	13 45.8
5 Th	8 56 15	15 5 50	19 12 40	25 14 54	19 29.2	3 21.8	21 49.6	2 43.9	22 4.0	19 34.7	22 22.5	12 52.1	13 44.4
6 F	9 0 11	16 6 40	1♑15 7	7♑13 46	19 23.6	4 16.1	23 2.1	2 23.3	22 14.5	19 29.8	22 21.2	12 51.4	13 43.0
7 Sa	9 4 8	17 7 30	13 11 15	19 7 53	19 14.8	5 2.1	24 14.5	2 2.1	22 24.9	19 24.9	22 20.0	12 50.7	13 41.6
8 Su	9 8 5	18 8 18	25 3 59	0♒59 47	19 3.1	5 39.3	25 26.9	1 40.5	22 35.2	19 20.0	22 18.9	12 49.9	13 40.2
9 M	9 12 1	19 9 5	6♒55 32	12 51 24	18 49.1	6 6.8	26 39.1	1 18.5	22 45.4	19 15.1	22 17.8	12 49.1	13 38.8
10 Tu	9 15 58	20 9 51	18 47 33	24 44 8	18 34.0	6 24.2	27 51.3	0 56.0	22 55.5	19 10.2	22 16.7	12 48.3	13 37.3
11 W	9 19 54	21 10 36	0♓41 18	6♓39 12	18 18.8	6R31.1	29 3.4	0 33.2	23 5.5	19 5.4	22 15.7	12 47.4	13 35.9
12 Th	9 23 51	22 11 19	12 38 0	18 37 53	18 4.8	6 27.2	0♈15.5	0 10.1	23 15.4	19 0.5	22 14.8	12 46.5	13 34.5
13 F	9 27 47	23 12 1	24 39 3	0♈41 46	17 53.1	6 12.7	1 27.4	29♌46.8	23 25.2	18 55.6	22 13.9	12 45.6	13 33.1
14 Sa	9 31 44	24 12 41	6♈46 18	12 53 1	17 44.4	5 47.7	2 39.2	29 23.2	23 34.9	18 50.7	22 13.1	12 44.7	13 31.7
15 Su	9 35 40	25 13 19	19 2 15	25 14 27	17 38.8	5 12.9	3 51.0	28 59.5	23 44.5	18 45.9	22 12.3	12 43.7	13 30.3
16 M	9 39 37	26 13 56	1♉30 3	7♉49 32	17 35.9	4 29.2	5 2.6	28 35.7	23 53.9	18 41.0	22 11.5	12 42.7	13 28.9
17 Tu	9 43 34	27 14 31	14 13 25	20 42 13	17D35.1	3 37.7	6 14.2	28 11.8	24 3.3	18 36.2	22 10.8	12 41.7	13 27.6
18 W	9 47 30	28 15 5	27 16 24	3♊56 28	17R35.2	2 39.7	7 25.6	27 47.8	24 12.5	18 31.4	22 10.2	12 40.7	13 26.2
19 Th	9 51 27	29 15 36	10♊42 49	17 35 45	17 34.8	1 37.0	8 37.0	27 23.9	24 21.6	18 26.7	22 9.6	12 39.6	13 24.8
20 F	9 55 23	0♓16 6	24 35 29	1♋42 5	17 32.8	0 31.1	9 48.2	27 0.1	24 30.6	18 21.9	22 9.1	12 38.5	13 23.5
21 Sa	9 59 20	1 16 34	8♋55 23	16 15 4	17 28.4	29♒23.9	10 59.3	26 36.3	24 39.5	18 17.2	22 8.6	12 37.4	13 22.1
22 Su	10 3 16	2 17 0	23 40 33	1♌11 4	17 21.3	28 17.0	12 10.3	26 12.7	24 48.2	18 12.5	22 8.2	12 36.2	13 20.8
23 M	10 7 13	3 17 24	8♌45 35	16 22 53	17 11.9	27 12.2	13 21.2	25 49.4	24 56.9	18 7.9	22 7.8	12 35.1	13 19.5
24 Tu	10 11 9	4 17 47	24 1 39	1♍40 25	17 1.2	26 10.7	14 32.0	25 26.2	25 5.4	18 3.3	22 7.5	12 33.9	13 18.2
25 W	10 15 6	5 18 7	9♍17 44	16 52 13	16 50.5	25 13.8	15 42.6	25 3.3	25 13.7	17 58.7	22 7.2	12 32.6	13 16.9
26 Th	10 19 3	6 18 26	24 22 33	1♎47 38	16 41.0	24 22.4	16 53.1	24 40.8	25 22.0	17 54.2	22 7.0	12 31.4	13 15.6
27 F	10 22 59	7 18 43	9♎ 6 34	16 18 41	16 33.7	23 37.3	18 3.5	24 18.6	25 30.1	17 49.7	22 6.8	12 30.1	13 14.3
28 Sa	10 26 56	8 18 59	23 23 31	0♏20 53	16 29.1	22 59.0	19 13.8	23 56.8	25 38.1	17 45.3	22 6.7	12 28.9	13 13.0
29 Su	10 30 52	9 19 13	7♏10 46	13 53 19	16D27.0	22 27.7	20 23.9	23 35.5	25 45.9	17 40.9	22D 6.6	12 27.6	13 11.7

Astro Data (Dy Hr Mn)

☽0S	3 4:37
♂ R	8 13:49
♆ R	14 22:02
☽0N	17 20:26
♃△♄	26 12:20
☽0S	30 11:35
♃☍♅	6 13:49
☿ R	11 3:24
♀0N	12 23:14
☽0N	14 1:27
☽0S	26 21:09
♅ D	29 14:23

Planet Ingress (Dy Hr Mn)

☿ ♒	14 10:06
♀ ♓	18 2:14
☉ ♒	21 3:18
☿ ♓	2 0:46
♀ ♈	11 18:51
♂ ♌	12 10:28
☉ ♓	19 17:37
☿ ♒	20 11:08

Last Aspect / ☽ Ingress (Dy Hr Mn)

Last Aspect	☽ Ingress
2 2:55 ♅ □	♎ 2 14:10
4 7:42 ♅ △	♏ 4 19:51
6 12:41 ♄ □	♐ 7 4:41
9 2:09 ♅ ☍	♑ 9 15:41
11 19:01 ☿ ☌	♒ 12 3:54
14 7:09 ♀ ☌	♓ 14 16:35
16 20:02 ☉ ✶	♈ 17 4:44
19 11:32 ☉ □	♉ 19 14:42
21 4:41 ♄ □	♊ 21 21:01
23 11:26 ♅ ☌	♋ 23 23:23
24 20:11 ♆ □	♌ 25 23:00
27 10:16 ♅ ✶	♍ 27 21:56
29 10:08 ♅ □	♎ 29 22:29

Last Aspect / ☽ Ingress (Dy Hr Mn)

Last Aspect	☽ Ingress
1 0:00 ☿ △	♏ 1 2:27
2 14:55 ♄ □	♐ 3 10:26
5 6:16 ♅ ☍	♑ 5 21:30
8 0:52 ♀ ✶	♒ 8 9:59
10 8:28 ♃ ✶	♓ 10 22:37
12 21:31 ♃ □	♈ 13 10:37
15 18:37 ♂ △	♉ 15 21:08
18 1:55 ☉ □	♊ 18 4:56
20 3:59 ♂ ✶	♋ 20 9:09
21 6:04 ♆ □	♌ 22 10:07
24 3:10 ☿ ☍	♍ 24 9:22
26 1:37 ♃ □	♎ 26 9:05
28 3:53 ♃ ✶	♏ 28 11:24

☽ Phases & Eclipses (Dy Hr Mn)

3 11:13	☽ 11♎60
11 7:45	● 20♑00
19 11:32	☽ 28♈19
26 7:11	○ 5♌15
2 0:31	☽ 12♏05
10 3:02	● 20♒18
18 1:55	☽ 28♉20
24 17:16	○ 5♍01

Astro Data

1 JANUARY 1948
Julian Day # 17532
Delta T 28.3 sec
SVP 05♓59'22"
Obliquity 23°26'51"
⚷ Chiron 20♏52.3
☽ Mean ☊ 20♉49.1

1 FEBRUARY 1948
Julian Day # 17563
Delta T 28.3 sec
SVP 05♓59'17"
Obliquity 23°26'52"
⚷ Chiron 23♏34.0
☽ Mean ☊ 19♉10.6

MARCH 1948 LONGITUDE

Day	Sid.Time	☉	0 hr ☽	Noon ☽	True ☊	☿	♀	♂	♃	♄	♅	♆	♇
1 M	10 34 49	10♓19 26	20♏28 52	26♏57 50	16♉26.7	22♒ 3.5	21♈33.9	23♌14.6	25♐53.7	17♌36.6	22♊ 6.6	12♎26.2	13♌10.5
2 Tu	10 38 45	11 19 37	3♐20 45	9♐38 12	16R 27.2	21R 46.5	22 43.7	22R 54.2	26 1.2	17R 32.3	22 6.7	12R 24.9	13R 9.3
3 W	10 42 42	12 19 47	15 50 47	21 59 8	16 27.4	21 36.4	23 53.5	22 34.3	26 8.7	17 28.1	22 6.8	12 23.5	13 8.1
4 Th	10 46 38	13 19 55	28 3 54	4♑ 5 41	16 26.1	21D 33.0	25 3.1	22 15.0	26 16.0	17 24.0	22 6.9	12 22.2	13 6.9
5 F	10 50 35	14 20 2	10♑ 5 7	16 2 44	16 22.7	21 36.1	26 12.5	21 56.3	26 23.2	17 19.9	22 7.1	12 20.8	13 5.7
6 Sa	10 54 32	15 20 7	21 59 4	27 54 38	16 16.8	21 45.4	27 21.8	21 38.2	26 30.2	17 15.8	22 7.4	12 19.4	13 4.5
7 Su	10 58 28	16 20 10	3♒49 50	9♒45 4	16 8.5	22 0.4	28 30.9	21 20.7	26 37.1	17 11.9	22 7.7	12 17.9	13 3.3
8 M	11 2 25	17 20 12	15 40 42	21 37 1	15 58.2	22 20.9	29 39.9	21 4.0	26 43.8	17 8.0	22 8.1	12 16.5	13 2.2
9 Tu	11 6 21	18 20 11	27 34 16	3♓32 41	15 46.8	22 46.5	0♉48.8	20 47.9	26 50.4	17 4.1	22 8.5	12 15.0	13 1.1
10 W	11 10 18	19 20 9	9♓32 26	15 33 42	15 35.3	23 16.9	1 57.5	20 32.5	26 56.8	17 0.4	22 9.0	12 13.5	12 60.0
11 Th	11 14 14	20 20 5	21 36 36	27 41 17	15 24.8	23 51.8	3 6.0	20 17.8	27 3.1	16 56.7	22 9.5	12 12.0	12 58.9
12 F	11 18 11	21 19 59	3♈47 52	9♈56 29	15 16.0	24 30.8	4 14.3	20 3.9	27 9.2	16 53.1	22 10.1	12 10.5	12 57.8
13 Sa	11 22 7	22 19 51	16 7 16	22 20 24	15 9.6	25 13.8	5 22.5	19 50.7	27 15.2	16 49.6	22 10.7	12 9.0	12 56.7
14 Su	11 26 4	23 19 41	28 36 4	4♉54 29	15 5.8	26 0.4	6 30.5	19 38.3	27 21.0	16 46.1	22 11.4	12 7.5	12 55.7
15 M	11 30 1	24 19 29	11♉15 54	17 40 35	15D 4.3	26 50.5	7 38.3	19 26.7	27 26.6	16 42.8	22 12.2	12 5.9	12 54.7
16 Tu	11 33 57	25 19 15	24 8 49	0♊40 55	15 4.6	27 43.8	8 45.9	19 15.9	27 32.1	16 39.5	22 13.0	12 4.4	12 53.7
17 W	11 37 54	26 18 59	7♊17 13	13 57 59	15 5.7	28 40.0	9 53.3	19 5.8	27 37.4	16 36.3	22 13.8	12 2.8	12 52.7
18 Th	11 41 50	27 18 40	20 43 31	27 34 2	15R 6.7	29 39.1	11 0.6	18 56.5	27 42.6	16 33.2	22 14.7	12 1.2	12 51.8
19 F	11 45 47	28 18 19	4♋29 43	11♋30 36	15 6.7	0♓40.9	12 7.6	18 48.1	27 47.6	16 30.2	22 15.7	11 59.6	12 50.8
20 Sa	11 49 43	29 17 56	18 36 40	25 47 42	15 5.0	1 45.2	13 14.4	18 40.4	27 52.4	16 27.2	22 16.7	11 58.0	12 49.9
21 Su	11 53 40	0♈17 30	3♌ 3 24	10♌23 15	15 1.4	2 51.8	14 21.0	18 33.5	27 57.1	16 24.4	22 17.7	11 56.4	12 49.0
22 M	11 57 36	1 17 2	17 46 35	25 12 35	14 56.2	4 0.7	15 27.3	18 27.4	28 1.6	16 21.6	22 18.9	11 54.8	12 48.2
23 Tu	12 1 33	2 16 32	2♍40 18	10♍ 8 41	14 49.8	5 11.8	16 33.5	18 22.1	28 6.0	16 19.0	22 20.0	11 53.2	12 47.3
24 W	12 5 30	3 15 59	17 36 37	25 2 59	14 43.3	6 25.0	17 39.4	18 17.6	28 10.1	16 16.4	22 21.2	11 51.6	12 46.5
25 Th	12 9 26	4 15 25	2♎26 40	9♎46 41	14 37.5	7 40.1	18 45.0	18 13.8	28 14.1	16 13.9	22 22.5	11 49.9	12 45.7
26 F	12 13 23	5 14 48	17 2 8	24 12 15	14 33.1	8 57.1	19 50.4	18 10.8	28 17.9	16 11.6	22 23.8	11 48.3	12 44.9
27 Sa	12 17 19	6 14 9	1♏16 29	8♏14 24	14D 30.6	10 16.0	20 55.6	18 8.6	28 21.6	16 9.3	22 25.1	11 46.7	12 44.2
28 Su	12 21 16	7 13 29	15 5 47	21 50 34	14 29.8	11 36.6	22 0.4	18 7.1	28 25.1	16 7.1	22 26.5	11 45.0	12 43.4
29 M	12 25 12	8 12 46	28 28 51	5♐ 0 49	14 30.5	12 59.0	23 5.1	18D 6.3	28 28.4	16 5.0	22 28.0	11 43.4	12 42.7
30 Tu	12 29 9	9 12 2	11♐26 49	17 47 16	14 32.0	14 23.0	24 9.4	18 6.3	28 31.5	16 3.1	22 29.5	11 41.7	12 42.0
31 W	12 33 5	10 11 16	24 2 39	0♑13 30	14 33.6	15 48.7	25 13.5	18 7.0	28 34.4	16 1.2	22 31.0	11 40.1	12 41.4

APRIL 1948 LONGITUDE

Day	Sid.Time	☉	0 hr ☽	Noon ☽	True ☊	☿	♀	♂	♃	♄	♅	♆	♇
1 Th	12 37 2	11♈10 29	6♑20 25	12♑23 58	14♉34.7	17♓16.0	26♉17.3	18♌ 8.4	28♐37.2	15♌59.4	22♊32.6	11♎38.4	12♌40.7
2 F	12 40 58	12 9 39	18 24 47	24 23 27	14R 34.6	18 44.8	27 20.8	18 10.6	28 39.8	15R 57.7	22 34.3	11R 36.8	12R 40.1
3 Sa	12 44 55	13 8 48	0♒20 35	6♒16 44	14 33.1	20 15.3	28 24.0	18 13.4	28 42.2	15 56.2	22 36.0	11 35.1	12 39.5
4 Su	12 48 52	14 7 55	12 12 27	18 8 16	14 30.2	21 47.2	29 26.9	18 16.9	28 44.4	15 54.7	22 37.7	11 33.5	12 39.0
5 M	12 52 48	15 7 0	24 4 38	0♓ 2 1	14 26.2	23 20.7	0♊29.5	18 21.1	28 46.4	15 53.3	22 39.5	11 31.8	12 38.4
6 Tu	12 56 45	16 6 3	6♓ 0 48	12 1 20	14 21.5	24 55.7	1 31.8	18 26.0	28 48.3	15 52.1	22 41.3	11 30.2	12 37.9
7 W	13 0 41	17 5 4	18 3 56	24 8 51	14 16.6	26 32.3	2 33.7	18 31.6	28 49.9	15 50.9	22 43.2	11 28.5	12 37.4
8 Th	13 4 38	18 4 4	0♈16 18	6♈26 28	14 12.1	28 10.3	3 35.3	18 37.8	28 51.4	15 49.9	22 45.1	11 26.9	12 36.9
9 F	13 8 34	19 3 1	12 39 30	18 55 29	14 8.4	29 49.8	4 36.5	18 44.6	28 52.7	15 48.9	22 47.1	11 25.3	12 36.5
10 Sa	13 12 31	20 1 57	25 14 30	1♉36 38	14 6.0	1♈30.9	5 37.4	18 52.1	28 53.8	15 48.1	22 49.1	11 23.6	12 36.1
11 Su	13 16 27	21 0 50	8♉ 1 53	14 30 18	14D 4.8	3 13.5	6 37.9	19 0.2	28 54.7	15 47.4	22 51.1	11 22.0	12 35.7
12 M	13 20 24	21 59 41	21 1 55	27 36 44	14 4.8	4 57.6	7 38.0	19 8.9	28 55.4	15 46.8	22 53.2	11 20.4	12 35.4
13 Tu	13 24 21	22 58 31	4♊14 46	10♊56 2	14 5.7	6 43.2	8 37.7	19 18.2	28 56.0	15 46.3	22 55.4	11 18.8	12 35.0
14 W	13 28 17	23 57 18	17 40 34	24 28 21	14 7.1	8 30.4	9 37.0	19 28.1	28 56.3	15 45.9	22 57.6	11 17.2	12 34.7
15 Th	13 32 14	24 56 3	1♋19 24	8♋13 40	14 8.5	10 19.1	10 35.8	19 38.6	28R 56.5	15 45.6	22 59.8	11 15.6	12 34.4
16 F	13 36 10	25 54 46	15 11 7	22 11 39	14R 9.4	12 9.4	11 34.2	19 49.6	28 56.4	15 45.4	23 2.0	11 14.0	12 34.2
17 Sa	13 40 7	26 53 26	29 15 8	6♌21 21	14 9.7	14 1.3	12 32.2	20 1.2	28 56.2	15D 45.3	23 4.3	11 12.4	12 34.0
18 Su	13 44 3	27 52 4	13♌30 3	20 40 52	14 9.1	15 54.7	13 29.6	20 13.3	28 55.8	15 45.4	23 6.7	11 10.8	12 33.8
19 M	13 48 0	28 50 40	27 53 25	5♍ 7 10	14 7.9	17 49.7	14 26.6	20 26.0	28 55.2	15 45.5	23 9.1	11 9.3	12 33.6
20 Tu	13 51 56	29 49 14	12♍21 35	19 36 2	14 6.3	19 46.2	15 23.0	20 39.1	28 54.5	15 45.8	23 11.5	11 7.7	12 33.5
21 W	13 55 53	0♉47 45	26 49 51	4♎ 2 23	14 4.5	21 44.3	16 18.9	20 52.8	28 53.5	15 46.1	23 13.9	11 6.2	12 33.4
22 Th	13 59 50	1 46 15	11♎12 55	18 20 48	14 3.1	23 44.0	17 14.3	21 7.0	28 52.3	15 46.6	23 16.4	11 4.6	12 33.3
23 F	14 3 46	2 44 42	25 25 25	2♏26 11	14 2.0	25 45.1	18 9.1	21 21.6	28 51.0	15 47.2	23 18.9	11 3.1	12 33.2
24 Sa	14 7 43	3 43 7	9♏22 39	16 14 24	14D 1.6	27 47.6	19 3.3	21 36.7	28 49.5	15 47.9	23 21.5	11 1.6	12D 33.2
25 Su	14 11 39	4 41 31	23 1 10	29 42 45	14 1.6	29 51.5	19 56.9	21 52.3	28 47.8	15 48.7	23 24.1	11 0.1	12 33.2
26 M	14 15 36	5 39 53	6♐19 5	12♐50 12	14 2.1	1♉56.7	20 49.9	22 8.3	28 45.9	15 49.6	23 26.7	10 58.7	12 33.2
27 Tu	14 19 32	6 38 13	19 16 12	25 37 18	14 2.8	4 3.0	21 42.2	22 24.8	28 43.8	15 50.6	23 29.4	10 57.2	12 33.2
28 W	14 23 29	7 36 32	1♑53 48	8♑ 6 3	14 3.5	6 10.4	22 33.9	22 41.7	28 41.6	15 51.7	23 32.1	10 55.8	12 33.3
29 Th	14 27 25	8 34 49	14 14 30	20 19 35	14 4.1	8 18.6	23 24.8	22 59.0	28 39.1	15 52.9	23 34.9	10 54.3	12 33.4
30 F	14 31 22	9 33 5	26 21 50	2♒21 48	14 4.5	10 27.5	24 15.1	23 16.7	28 36.5	15 54.2	23 37.6	10 52.9	12 33.5

Astro Data	Planet Ingress	Last Aspect	☽ Ingress	Last Aspect	☽ Ingress	☽ Phases & Eclipses	Astro Data
Dy Hr Mn	Dy Hr Mn	Dy Hr Mn	Dy Hr Mn	Dy Hr Mn	Dy Hr Mn	Dy Hr Mn	1 MARCH 1948
☿ D 4 0:19	♀ ♉ 8 6:59	1 4:57 ♂ □	♐ 1 17:41	2 19:42 ♀ △	♒ 2 23:18	2 16:35 ☽ 12♐01	Julian Day # 17592
☽0N 12 6:46	☿ ♓ 18 8:14	3 20:24 ♃ ☌	♑ 4 3:50	5 9:29 ♃ ⚹	♓ 5 11:56	10 21:15 ● 20♓13	Delta T 28.3 sec
♃□♇ 19 13:24	☉ ♈ 20 16:57	6 12:04 ♀ □	♒ 6 16:14	7 21:14 ♃ □	♈ 7 23:28	18 12:27 ☽ 27♊50	SVP 05♓59'13"
☽0S 25 7:51		8 22:31 ♃ ⚹	♓ 9 4:53	10 6:54 ♃ △	♉ 10 8:58	25 3:10 ○ 4♎23	Obliquity 23°26'52"
♂ D 29 12:33	♀ ♊ 4 12:40	11 10:50 ♃ □	♈ 11 16:33	11 20:30 ♂ □	♊ 12 16:20		⚷ Chiron 24♏41.2
	☿ ♈ 9 2:26	13 21:35 ♃ △	♉ 14 2:40	14 19:50 ♃ ☍	♋ 14 21:41	1 10:25 ☽ 11♑36	☽ Mean ☊ 17♉38.5
☽0N 8 13:35	☉ ♉ 20 4:25	16 7:06 ☿ □	♊ 16 10:45	16 19:42 ☉ □	♌ 17 1:16	9 13:17 ● 19♈36	
☿0N 12 4:47	☿ ♉ 25 1:38	18 12:27 ☉ □	♋ 18 16:14	19 1:43 ♃ △	♍ 19 3:30	16 19:42 ☽ 26♋43	1 APRIL 1948
♃ R 15 8:34		19 14:10 ♀ ⚹	♌ 20 18:58	21 3:25 ♃ □	♎ 21 5:16	23 13:28 ○ 3♏17	Julian Day # 17623
♄ D 17 3:19		22 16:37 ♃ △	♍ 22 19:42	23 5:50 ♃ ⚹	♏ 23 7:49	23 13:39 ☍ P 0.023	Delta T 28.4 sec
☽0S 21 17:27		24 17:08 ♃ □	♎ 24 20:01	24 21:55 ♂ □	♐ 25 12:31		SVP 05♓59'09"
♇ D 24 16:58		26 19:01 ♃ ⚹	♏ 26 21:49	27 17:52 ♃ ☌	♑ 27 20:21		Obliquity 23°26'52"
		28 13:23 ♀ ☍	♐ 29 2:46	28 17:29 ♆ □	♒ 30 7:16		⚷ Chiron 24♏12.2R
		31 8:49 ♃ ☌	♑ 31 11:34				☽ Mean ☊ 16♉00.0

LONGITUDE — MAY 1948

Day	Sid.Time	☉	0 hr ☽	Noon ☽	True ☊	☿	♀	♂	♃	♄	♅	♆	♇
1 Sa	14 35 19	10♉31 19	8♒20 2	14♒17 6	14♉ 4.6	12♉36.9	25♊ 4.6	23♌34.9	28♐33.7	15♌55.6	23♊40.4	10♎51.5	12♌33.7
2 Su	14 39 15	11 29 31	20 13 36	26 10 5	14R 4.6	14 46.5	25 53.3	23 53.4	28R 30.7	15 57.2	23 43.3	10R 50.2	12 33.9
3 M	14 43 12	12 27 42	2♓ 7 8	8♓ 5 18	14 4.4	16 56.0	26 41.3	24 12.4	28 27.6	15 58.8	23 46.1	10 48.8	12 34.1
4 Tu	14 47 8	13 25 52	14 5 7	20 7 3	14D 4.3	19 5.3	27 28.4	24 31.7	28 24.3	16 0.5	23 49.0	10 47.5	12 34.3
5 W	14 51 5	14 23 59	26 11 35	2♈19 8	14 4.3	21 13.9	28 14.7	24 51.4	28 20.8	16 2.4	23 51.9	10 46.1	12 34.6
6 Th	14 55 1	15 22 6	8♈30 3	14 44 38	14 4.4	23 21.6	29 0.1	25 11.5	28 17.1	16 4.3	23 54.9	10 44.8	12 34.9
7 F	14 58 58	16 20 11	21 3 10	27 25 49	14 4.6	25 28.1	29 44.6	25 31.9	28 13.3	16 6.4	23 57.9	10 43.6	12 35.2
8 Sa	15 2 54	17 18 14	3♉52 42	10♉23 53	14R 4.8	27 33.1	0♋28.1	25 52.7	28 9.2	16 8.5	24 0.9	10 42.3	12 35.6
9 Su	15 6 51	18 16 16	16 59 20	23 38 59	14 4.8	29 36.4	1 10.6	26 13.9	28 5.1	16 10.7	24 3.9	10 41.1	12 35.9
10 M	15 10 48	19 14 17	0♊22 40	7♊10 12	14 4.6	1♊37.7	1 52.1	26 35.4	28 0.7	16 13.1	24 7.0	10 39.8	12 36.3
11 Tu	15 14 44	20 12 16	14 1 18	20 55 40	14 4.2	3 36.7	2 32.5	26 57.2	27 56.2	16 15.6	24 10.1	10 38.6	12 36.8
12 W	15 18 41	21 10 13	27 52 58	4♋52 49	14 3.4	5 33.2	3 11.8	27 19.4	27 51.6	16 18.1	24 13.2	10 37.5	12 37.2
13 Th	15 22 37	22 8 8	11♋54 51	18 58 41	14 2.6	7 27.1	3 50.0	27 41.9	27 46.8	16 20.8	24 16.3	10 36.3	12 37.7
14 F	15 26 34	23 6 2	26 3 54	3♌10 9	14 1.7	9 18.3	4 26.9	28 4.7	27 41.8	16 23.5	24 19.5	10 35.2	12 38.2
15 Sa	15 30 30	24 3 54	10♌17 3	17 24 15	14 1.0	11 6.4	5 2.6	28 27.8	27 36.7	16 26.3	24 22.7	10 34.1	12 38.8
16 Su	15 34 27	25 1 44	24 31 24	1♍38 12	14D 0.7	12 51.6	5 37.0	28 51.2	27 31.5	16 29.3	24 25.9	10 33.0	12 39.3
17 M	15 38 23	25 59 33	8♍44 21	15 49 32	14 1.0	14 33.6	6 10.0	29 14.9	27 26.1	16 32.3	24 29.1	10 32.0	12 39.9
18 Tu	15 42 20	26 57 19	22 53 30	29 55 56	14 1.7	16 12.4	6 41.6	29 38.9	27 20.6	16 35.4	24 32.3	10 30.9	12 40.5
19 W	15 46 17	27 55 4	6♎56 37	13♎55 14	14 2.7	17 48.0	7 11.7	0♍ 3.2	27 14.9	16 38.7	24 35.6	10 29.9	12 41.2
20 Th	15 50 13	28 52 47	20 51 32	27 45 16	14 3.8	19 20.2	7 40.3	0 27.7	27 9.1	16 42.0	24 38.9	10 28.9	12 41.8
21 F	15 54 10	29 50 29	4♏36 10	11♏24 0	14R 4.6	20 49.0	8 7.4	0 52.5	27 3.2	16 45.4	24 42.2	10 28.0	12 42.5
22 Sa	15 58 6	0♊48 9	18 8 33	24 49 36	14 4.7	22 14.4	8 32.8	1 17.6	26 57.1	16 48.9	24 45.5	10 27.1	12 43.2
23 Su	16 2 3	1 45 48	1♐26 59	8♐ 0 34	14 4.0	23 36.4	8 56.5	1 42.9	26 51.0	16 52.5	24 48.9	10 26.2	12 44.0
24 M	16 5 59	2 43 26	14 30 17	20 56 5	14 2.4	24 54.8	9 18.4	2 8.5	26 44.7	16 56.1	24 52.3	10 25.3	12 44.8
25 Tu	16 9 56	3 41 3	27 17 59	3♑36 4	13 59.9	26 9.7	9 38.5	2 34.3	26 38.3	16 59.9	24 55.6	10 24.4	12 45.5
26 W	16 13 52	4 38 38	9♑50 27	16 1 22	13 56.9	27 20.9	9 56.8	3 0.4	26 31.8	17 3.8	24 59.0	10 23.6	12 46.4
27 Th	16 17 49	5 36 13	22 9 2	28 13 47	13 53.6	28 28.5	10 13.2	3 26.7	26 25.2	17 7.7	25 2.4	10 22.8	12 47.2
28 F	16 21 46	6 33 46	4♒15 58	10♒16 2	13 50.6	29 32.4	10 27.5	3 53.3	26 18.5	17 11.7	25 5.9	10 22.1	12 48.1
29 Sa	16 25 42	7 31 19	16 14 24	22 11 36	13 48.1	0♋32.5	10 39.8	4 20.0	26 11.7	17 15.8	25 9.3	10 21.3	12 49.0
30 Su	16 29 39	8 28 50	28 8 10	4♓ 4 38	13D 46.5	1 28.7	10 50.1	4 47.0	26 4.8	17 20.0	25 12.8	10 20.6	12 49.9
31 M	16 33 35	9 26 21	10♓ 1 35	15 59 38	13 46.1	2 21.0	10 58.1	5 14.3	25 57.8	17 24.3	25 16.2	10 19.9	12 50.8

LONGITUDE — JUNE 1948

Day	Sid.Time	☉	0 hr ☽	Noon ☽	True ☊	☿	♀	♂	♃	♄	♅	♆	♇
1 Tu	16 37 32	10♊23 51	21♓59 22	28♓ 1 22	13♉46.6	3♋ 9.3	11♋ 4.0	5♍41.7	25♐50.8	17♌28.6	25♊19.7	10♎19.3	12♌51.8
2 W	16 41 28	11 21 20	4♈ 6 13	10♈14 30	13 47.9	3 53.6	11 7.7	6 9.4	25R 43.7	17 33.1	25 23.2	10R 18.7	12 52.7
3 Th	16 45 25	12 18 48	16 26 42	22 43 20	13 49.6	4 33.6	11R 9.0	6 37.3	25 36.4	17 37.6	25 26.7	10 18.1	12 53.7
4 F	16 49 21	13 16 16	29 4 48	5♉31 26	13 51.0	5 9.4	11 8.0	7 5.4	25 29.2	17 42.2	25 30.2	10 17.5	12 54.8
5 Sa	16 53 18	14 13 43	12♉ 3 31	18 41 11	13R 51.7	5 40.9	11 4.7	7 33.7	25 21.8	17 46.9	25 33.7	10 17.0	12 55.8
6 Su	16 57 15	15 11 9	25 24 31	2♊13 25	13 51.2	6 8.0	10 59.0	8 2.2	25 14.4	17 51.6	25 37.2	10 16.5	12 56.9
7 M	17 1 11	16 8 35	9♊ 7 41	16 7 1	13 49.3	6 30.7	10 50.9	8 30.9	25 7.0	17 56.5	25 40.8	10 16.0	12 58.0
8 Tu	17 5 8	17 5 59	23 10 56	0♋18 53	13 45.8	6 48.8	10 40.4	8 59.8	24 59.5	18 1.4	25 44.3	10 15.6	12 59.1
9 W	17 9 4	18 3 23	7♋30 11	14 44 7	13 41.2	7 2.4	10 27.5	9 28.9	24 52.0	18 6.4	25 47.9	10 15.2	13 0.2
10 Th	17 13 1	19 0 46	21 59 53	29 16 40	13 36.1	7 11.3	10 12.2	9 58.2	24 44.4	18 11.4	25 51.5	10 14.8	13 1.4
11 F	17 16 57	19 58 8	6♌33 41	13♌50 10	13 31.1	7R 15.7	9 54.6	10 27.7	24 36.8	18 16.5	25 55.0	10 14.5	13 2.6
12 Sa	17 20 54	20 55 30	21 5 26	28 18 53	13 27.0	7 15.6	9 34.7	10 57.3	24 29.2	18 21.8	25 58.6	10 14.1	13 3.8
13 Su	17 24 51	21 52 49	5♍30 0	12♍38 24	13 24.3	7 11.0	9 12.5	11 27.2	24 21.5	18 27.0	26 2.2	10 13.9	13 5.0
14 M	17 28 47	22 50 8	19 43 45	26 45 52	13D 23.2	7 2.0	8 48.1	11 57.2	24 13.9	18 32.4	26 5.7	10 13.6	13 6.2
15 Tu	17 32 44	23 47 26	3♎44 36	10♎39 55	13 23.5	6 48.9	8 21.7	12 27.4	24 6.2	18 37.8	26 9.3	10 13.4	13 7.5
16 W	17 36 40	24 44 43	17 31 49	24 20 19	13 24.7	6 31.7	7 53.3	12 57.8	23 58.6	18 43.2	26 12.9	10 13.2	13 8.8
17 Th	17 40 37	25 42 0	1♏ 5 29	7♏47 25	13R 25.9	6 10.8	7 23.1	13 28.3	23 50.9	18 48.8	26 16.5	10 13.0	13 10.1
18 F	17 44 33	26 39 15	14 26 10	21 1 50	13 26.5	5 46.6	6 51.2	13 59.0	23 43.2	18 54.4	26 20.0	10 12.9	13 11.4
19 Sa	17 48 30	27 36 30	27 34 27	4♐ 4 6	13 25.5	5 19.3	6 17.9	14 29.9	23 35.6	19 0.1	26 23.6	10 12.8	13 12.7
20 Su	17 52 26	28 33 44	10♐30 47	16 54 34	13 22.6	4 49.4	5 43.3	15 0.9	23 28.0	19 5.8	26 27.2	10 12.8	13 14.1
21 M	17 56 23	29 30 58	23 15 27	29 33 28	13 17.6	4 17.4	5 7.6	15 32.1	23 20.4	19 11.6	26 30.8	10D 12.7	13 15.4
22 Tu	18 0 20	0♋28 11	5♑48 40	12♑ 1 5	13 10.7	3 43.8	4 31.1	16 3.4	23 12.8	19 17.4	26 34.3	10 12.8	13 16.8
23 W	18 4 16	1 25 24	18 10 50	24 17 59	13 2.4	3 9.2	3 53.9	16 34.9	23 5.3	19 23.4	26 37.9	10 12.8	13 18.2
24 Th	18 8 13	2 22 37	0♒22 42	6♒25 12	12 53.4	2 34.2	3 16.4	17 6.5	22 57.8	19 29.3	26 41.5	10 12.9	13 19.7
25 F	18 12 9	3 19 49	12 25 41	18 24 27	12 44.7	1 59.3	2 38.8	17 38.3	22 50.4	19 35.4	26 45.0	10 13.0	13 21.1
26 Sa	18 16 6	4 17 1	24 21 50	0♓18 15	12 37.1	1 25.1	2 1.2	18 10.2	22 43.0	19 41.5	26 48.6	10 13.1	13 22.5
27 Su	18 20 2	5 14 14	6♓14 5	12 9 52	12 31.1	0 52.4	1 24.0	18 42.3	22 35.6	19 47.6	26 52.2	10 13.3	13 24.0
28 M	18 23 59	6 11 26	18 6 5	24 3 19	12 27.2	0 21.5	0 47.4	19 14.5	22 28.4	19 53.8	26 55.7	10 13.5	13 25.5
29 Tu	18 27 55	7 8 38	0♈ 2 8	6♈ 3 11	12D 25.4	29♊53.1	0 11.7	19 46.9	22 21.1	20 0.1	26 59.2	10 13.7	13 27.0
30 W	18 31 52	8 5 50	12 7 4	18 14 26	12 25.1	29 27.6	29♊36.9	20 19.4	22 14.0	20 6.4	27 2.8	10 13.9	13 28.5

Astro Data	Planet Ingress	Last Aspect	☽ Ingress	Last Aspect	☽ Ingress	☽ Phases & Eclipses	Astro Data
Dy Hr Mn	Dy Hr Mn	Dy Hr Mn	Dy Hr Mn	Dy Hr Mn	Dy Hr Mn	Dy Hr Mn	1 MAY 1948
☽0N 5 21:43	♀ ♋ 7 8:27	2 16:39 ♃ ⚹	♓ 2 19:44	1 7:36 ♃ □	♈ 1 15:55	1 4:48 ☽ 10♒43	Julian Day # 17653
♃⚻♇ 14 15:21	☿ ♊ 9 4:38	5 4:18 ♀ □	♈ 5 7:28	3 17:18 ♃ △	♉ 4 1:43	9 2:30 ● 18♉22	Delta T 28.4 sec
☽0S 19 0:37	♂ ♍ 18 20:54	7 13:25 ♃ △	♉ 7 16:48	5 10:26 ♄ □	♊ 6 8:06	9 2:25:34 ☌ AT 0'00"	SVP 05♓59'05"
	☉ ♊ 21 3:58	9 17:04 ♂ □	♊ 9 23:20	8 4:20 ♅ ☌	♋ 8 11:28	16 0:55 ☽ 25♌04	Obliquity 23°26'52"
☽0N 2 6:07	☿ ♋ 28 10:50	11 23:58 ♃ ☍	♋ 12 3:38	9 4:50 ♀ ☌	♌ 10 13:11	23 0:37 ○ 1♐47	⚷ Chiron 22♏25.1R
♃☍♅ 3 21:42		13 18:37 ☉ ⚹	♌ 14 6:39	12 8:09 ♅ ⚹	♍ 12 14:49	30 22:43 ☽ 9♓23	☽ Mean ☊ 14♉24.7
♀ R 3 2:01	☉ ♋ 21 12:11	16 7:31 ♂ ☌	♍ 16 9:14	14 10:54 ♅ □	♎ 14 17:33		
☿ R 11 11:15	☿ ♊ 28 17:57	18 7:32 ♃ □	♎ 18 12:07	16 15:24 ♅ △	♏ 16 22:03	7 12:55 ● 16♊39	1 JUNE 1948
☽0S 15 5:49	♀ ♊ 29 7:58	20 10:52 ♃ ⚹	♏ 20 15:56	18 8:11 ♄ □	♐ 19 4:28	14 5:40 ☽ 23♍04	Julian Day # 17684
♆ D 21 7:28		21 21:37 ♄ □	♐ 22 21:22	21 6:13 ♅ ☍	♑ 21 12:51	21 12:54 ○ 0♑02	Delta T 28.4 sec
☽0N 29 13:39		24 22:45 ♃ ☌	♑ 25 5:08	22 20:44 ♂ △	♒ 23 23:15	29 15:23 ☽ 7♈45	SVP 05♓59'01"
		26 1:04 ♆ □	♒ 27 15:31	26 4:58 ♅ △	♓ 26 11:23		Obliquity 23°26'52"
		29 19:53 ♃ ⚹	♓ 30 3:46	28 23:43 ☿ □	♈ 28 23:56		⚷ Chiron 20♏09.9R
							☽ Mean ☊ 12♉46.2

JULY 1948 LONGITUDE

Day	Sid.Time	☉	0 hr ☽	Noon ☽	True ☊	☿	♀	♂	♃	♄	♅	♆	♇
1 Th	18 35 49	9♋ 3 2	24♈25 54	0♉42 6	12♉25.9	29♊ 5.6	29♊ 3.4	20♍52.0	22♐ 6.9	20♌12.7	27♊ 6.3	10♎14.2	13♌30.0
2 F	18 39 45	10 0 15	7♉ 3 34	13 30 50	12R26.6	28R47.3	28R31.4	21 24.8	21R59.9	20 19.1	27 9.8	10 14.6	13 31.6
3 Sa	18 43 42	10 57 27	20 4 19	26 44 22	12 26.5	28 33.2	28 1.0	21 57.7	21 53.0	20 25.6	27 13.3	10 14.9	13 33.2
4 Su	18 47 38	11 54 40	3♊31 11	10♊24 49	12 24.6	28 23.4	27 32.3	22 30.7	21 46.2	20 32.1	27 16.8	10 15.3	13 34.7
5 M	18 51 35	12 51 54	17 25 11	24 31 58	12 20.4	28D18.4	27 5.6	23 3.9	21 39.4	20 38.7	27 20.3	10 15.7	13 36.3
6 Tu	18 55 31	13 49 7	1♋44 42	9♋ 2 43	12 14.0	28 18.2	26 40.8	23 37.3	21 32.8	20 45.3	27 23.8	10 16.2	13 37.9
7 W	18 59 28	14 46 21	16 25 10	23 51 2	12 5.6	28 23.0	26 18.2	24 10.7	21 26.3	20 52.0	27 27.3	10 16.7	13 39.5
8 Th	19 3 24	15 43 34	1♌19 14	8♌48 35	11 56.3	28 32.8	25 57.8	24 44.3	21 19.8	20 58.7	27 30.7	10 17.2	13 41.2
9 F	19 7 21	16 40 48	16 17 55	23 46 4	11 47.1	28 47.9	25 39.7	25 18.0	21 13.5	21 5.4	27 34.2	10 17.7	13 42.8
10 Sa	19 11 18	17 38 2	1♍11 59	8♍34 46	11 39.1	29 8.1	25 23.8	25 51.9	21 7.3	21 12.2	27 37.6	10 18.3	13 44.5
11 Su	19 15 14	18 35 15	15 53 37	23 7 58	11 33.2	29 33.5	25 10.3	26 25.8	21 1.3	21 19.0	27 41.0	10 18.9	13 46.1
12 M	19 19 11	19 32 29	0♎17 24	7♎21 39	11 29.7	0♋ 4.2	24 59.2	26 59.9	20 55.3	21 25.9	27 44.4	10 19.6	13 47.8
13 Tu	19 23 7	20 29 42	14 20 37	21 14 21	11D28.3	0 40.1	24 50.4	27 34.1	20 49.5	21 32.8	27 47.8	10 20.3	13 49.5
14 W	19 27 4	21 26 55	28 2 58	4♏46 41	11 28.3	1 21.1	24 44.0	28 8.5	20 43.8	21 39.7	27 51.1	10 21.0	13 51.1
15 Th	19 31 0	22 24 9	11♏25 46	18 0 32	11R28.6	2 7.3	24 40.0	28 42.9	20 38.2	21 46.7	27 54.4	10 21.7	13 52.8
16 F	19 34 57	23 21 22	24 31 18	0♐58 22	11 27.9	2 58.6	24D38.3	29 17.5	20 32.8	21 53.7	27 57.8	10 22.5	13 54.6
17 Sa	19 38 54	24 18 36	7♐22 4	13 42 38	11 25.4	3 54.8	24 38.9	29 52.1	20 27.5	22 0.8	28 1.1	10 23.3	13 56.3
18 Su	19 42 50	25 15 50	20 0 22	26 15 28	11 20.3	4 56.1	24 41.8	0♎26.9	20 22.4	22 7.9	28 4.4	10 24.1	13 58.0
19 M	19 46 47	26 13 4	2♑28 7	8♑38 30	11 12.5	6 2.2	24 47.0	1 1.8	20 17.4	22 15.0	28 7.6	10 25.0	13 59.7
20 Tu	19 50 43	27 10 19	14 46 45	20 53 0	11 2.0	7 13.2	24 54.3	1 36.9	20 12.6	22 22.2	28 10.9	10 25.9	14 1.5
21 W	19 54 40	28 7 34	26 57 22	2♒59 57	10 49.7	8 28.8	25 3.8	2 12.0	20 7.9	22 29.3	28 14.1	10 26.8	14 3.2
22 Th	19 58 36	29 4 49	9♒ 0 55	15 0 22	10 36.5	9 49.1	25 15.4	2 47.2	20 3.4	22 36.6	28 17.3	10 27.7	14 5.0
23 F	20 2 33	0♌ 2 5	20 58 29	26 55 29	10 23.4	11 14.0	25 29.1	3 22.6	19 59.0	22 43.8	28 20.5	10 28.7	14 6.7
24 Sa	20 6 29	0 59 22	2♓51 35	8♓47 5	10 11.7	12 43.2	25 44.7	3 58.0	19 54.8	22 51.1	28 23.6	10 29.7	14 8.5
25 Su	20 10 26	1 56 39	14 42 17	20 37 34	10 2.0	14 16.6	26 2.2	4 33.6	19 50.7	22 58.4	28 26.8	10 30.8	14 10.3
26 M	20 14 23	2 53 58	26 33 23	2♈30 9	9 54.9	15 54.1	26 21.7	5 9.2	19 46.8	23 5.7	28 29.9	10 31.8	14 12.1
27 Tu	20 18 19	3 51 17	8♈28 26	14 28 46	9 50.6	17 35.5	26 42.9	5 45.0	19 43.1	23 13.1	28 33.0	10 32.9	14 13.8
28 W	20 22 16	4 48 37	20 31 45	26 37 59	9 48.5	19 20.5	27 5.8	6 20.8	19 39.5	23 20.4	28 36.0	10 34.0	14 15.6
29 Th	20 26 12	5 45 58	2♉48 8	9♉ 2 49	9 48.0	21 8.9	27 30.5	6 56.8	19 36.2	23 27.8	28 39.1	10 35.2	14 17.4
30 F	20 30 9	6 43 21	15 22 40	21 48 18	9 48.0	23 0.4	27 56.7	7 32.9	19 32.9	23 35.2	28 42.1	10 36.4	14 19.2
31 Sa	20 34 5	7 40 44	28 20 16	4♊59 2	9 47.3	24 54.7	28 24.6	8 9.1	19 29.9	23 42.7	28 45.0	10 37.6	14 21.0

AUGUST 1948 LONGITUDE

Day	Sid.Time	☉	0 hr ☽	Noon ☽	True ☊	☿	♀	♂	♃	♄	♅	♆	♇
1 Su	20 38 2	8♌38 9	11♊44 58	18♊38 17	9♉44.9	26♋51.5	28♊53.9	8♎45.4	19♐27.0	23♌50.2	28♊48.0	10♎38.8	14♌22.8
2 M	20 41 58	9 35 35	25 39 5	2♋47 12	9R40.0	28 50.3	29 24.7	9 21.8	19R24.4	23 57.6	28 50.9	10 40.1	14 24.6
3 Tu	20 45 55	10 33 2	10♋ 2 19	17 23 50	9 32.6	0♌50.9	29 56.9	9 58.3	19 21.9	24 5.1	28 53.8	10 41.4	14 26.5
4 W	20 49 52	11 30 30	24 50 57	2♌22 40	9 23.0	2 53.0	0♋30.4	10 34.9	19 19.5	24 12.7	28 56.7	10 42.7	14 28.3
5 Th	20 53 48	12 27 59	9♌57 46	17 34 55	9 12.2	4 56.0	1 5.3	11 11.6	19 17.4	24 20.2	28 59.5	10 44.0	14 30.1
6 F	20 57 45	13 25 29	25 12 43	2♍49 45	9 1.4	6 59.8	1 41.3	11 48.4	19 15.4	24 27.8	29 2.3	10 45.4	14 31.9
7 Sa	21 1 41	14 23 0	10♍24 40	17 56 15	8 51.9	9 4.0	2 18.6	12 25.4	19 13.6	24 35.3	29 5.1	10 46.8	14 33.7
8 Su	21 5 38	15 20 31	25 23 26	2♎45 23	8 44.7	11 8.3	2 57.0	13 2.4	19 12.0	24 42.9	29 7.8	10 48.2	14 35.5
9 M	21 9 34	16 18 4	10♎ 1 26	17 11 10	8 40.1	13 12.5	3 36.5	13 39.5	19 10.6	24 50.5	29 10.5	10 49.6	14 37.3
10 Tu	21 13 31	17 15 37	24 14 23	1♏11 3	8 37.9	15 16.2	4 17.1	14 16.7	19 9.4	24 58.1	29 13.2	10 51.1	14 39.2
11 W	21 17 27	18 13 12	8♏ 1 16	14 45 18	8 37.5	17 19.4	4 58.7	14 54.0	19 8.4	25 5.7	29 15.8	10 52.6	14 41.0
12 Th	21 21 24	19 10 47	21 23 27	27 56 10	8 37.5	19 21.8	5 41.3	15 31.4	19 7.5	25 13.3	29 18.4	10 54.1	14 42.8
13 F	21 25 21	20 8 23	4♐23 50	10♐46 58	8 36.8	21 23.2	6 24.8	16 8.9	19 6.9	25 20.9	29 21.0	10 55.7	14 44.6
14 Sa	21 29 17	21 6 0	17 6 0	23 21 23	8 34.4	23 23.7	7 9.3	16 46.5	19 6.4	25 28.6	29 23.5	10 57.2	14 46.4
15 Su	21 33 14	22 3 38	29 33 33	5♑42 54	8 29.5	25 22.9	7 54.7	17 24.1	19 6.1	25 36.2	29 26.0	10 58.8	14 48.2
16 M	21 37 10	23 1 18	11♑49 47	17 54 32	8 21.9	27 21.0	8 40.9	18 1.9	19D 6.0	25 43.8	29 28.5	11 0.4	14 50.0
17 Tu	21 41 7	23 58 58	23 57 26	29 58 45	8 11.8	29 17.8	9 27.9	18 39.8	19 6.1	25 51.5	29 30.9	11 2.1	14 51.8
18 W	21 45 3	24 56 39	5♒58 42	11♒57 28	7 59.7	1♍13.3	10 15.8	19 17.7	19 6.4	25 59.1	29 33.3	11 3.7	14 53.6
19 Th	21 49 0	25 54 22	17 55 16	23 52 16	7 46.8	3 7.5	11 4.4	19 55.8	19 6.8	26 6.8	29 35.6	11 5.4	14 55.4
20 F	21 52 56	26 52 6	29 48 37	5♓44 30	7 34.0	5 0.3	11 53.8	20 33.9	19 7.5	26 14.4	29 38.0	11 7.1	14 57.2
21 Sa	21 56 53	27 49 51	11♓40 8	17 35 42	7 22.4	6 51.7	12 43.9	21 12.1	19 8.3	26 22.0	29 40.2	11 8.8	14 58.9
22 Su	22 0 50	28 47 38	23 31 26	29 27 39	7 12.9	8 41.7	13 34.7	21 50.4	19 9.3	26 29.7	29 42.4	11 10.6	15 0.7
23 M	22 4 46	29 45 26	5♈24 37	11♈22 42	7 6.0	10 30.4	14 26.2	22 28.8	19 10.5	26 37.3	29 44.6	11 12.3	15 2.5
24 Tu	22 8 43	0♍43 16	17 22 18	23 23 52	7 1.7	12 17.7	15 18.4	23 7.3	19 11.9	26 45.0	29 46.8	11 14.1	15 4.3
25 W	22 12 39	1 41 8	29 27 51	5♉34 46	6D59.8	14 3.6	16 11.1	23 45.9	19 13.5	26 52.6	29 48.9	11 15.9	15 6.0
26 Th	22 16 36	2 39 1	11♉45 11	17 59 39	6 59.7	15 48.2	17 4.5	24 24.5	19 15.2	27 0.2	29 50.9	11 17.7	15 7.8
27 F	22 20 32	3 36 57	24 18 44	0♊43 2	7R 0.2	17 31.5	17 58.5	25 3.3	19 17.1	27 7.8	29 53.0	11 19.6	15 9.5
28 Sa	22 24 29	4 34 54	7♊13 3	13 49 19	7 0.5	19 13.5	18 53.0	25 42.1	19 19.3	27 15.4	29 55.0	11 21.4	15 11.2
29 Su	22 28 25	5 32 53	20 32 15	27 22 11	6 59.4	20 54.2	19 48.2	26 21.0	19 21.6	27 23.0	29 56.9	11 23.3	15 13.0
30 M	22 32 22	6 30 54	4♋19 18	11♋23 39	6 56.4	22 33.6	20 43.8	27 0.1	19 24.0	27 30.6	29 58.8	11 25.2	15 14.7
31 Tu	22 36 19	7 28 57	18 35 4	25 53 12	6 51.1	24 11.7	21 40.0	27 39.2	19 26.7	27 38.2	0♋ 0.6	11 27.1	15 16.4

Astro Data	Planet Ingress	Last Aspect	☽ Ingress	Last Aspect	☽ Ingress	☽ Phases & Eclipses	Astro Data
Dy Hr Mn	Dy Hr Mn	Dy Hr Mn	Dy Hr Mn	Dy Hr Mn	Dy Hr Mn	Dy Hr Mn	1 JULY 1948
☿ D 5 13:04	☿ ♋ 11 20:56	1 8:43 ☿ ⚹	♉ 1 10:40	2 6:35 ♀ ☌	♋ 2 7:20	6 21:09 ● 14♋40	Julian Day # 17714
♃△♄ 9 15:00	♂ ♎ 17 5:25	3 3:34 ♂ △	♊ 3 17:48	3 1:04 ♆ □	♌ 4 8:13	13 11:30 ☽ 20♎57	Delta T 28.5 sec
☽0S 12 10:52	☉ ♌ 22 23:08	5 18:17 ☿ ☌	♋ 5 21:07	6 6:03 ♅ ⚹	♍ 6 7:32	21 2:31 ○ 28♑14	SVP 05♓58'55"
♀ D 16 5:25		7 13:01 ♂ ⚹	♌ 7 21:53	8 6:06 ♅ □	♎ 8 7:30	29 6:11 ☽ 6♉01	Obliquity 23°26'52"
♂0S 18 17:07	☿ ♌ 2 13:54	9 20:34 ☿ ⚹	♍ 9 22:03	10 8:37 ♅ △	♏ 10 9:56		⚷ Chiron 18♏40.1R
☽0N 26 19:53	♀ ♋ 3 2:15	11 19:41 ♅ □	♎ 11 23:31	12 7:04 ♄ □	♐ 12 15:49	5 4:13 ● 12♌38	☽ Mean ☊ 11♉10.9
	☿ ♍ 17 8:44	13 23:39 ♅ △	♏ 14 3:28	14 23:45 ♅ ☍	♑ 15 0:51	11 19:40 ☽ 19♏00	
☽0S 8 17:45	☉ ♍ 23 6:03	16 9:17 ♂ ⚹	♐ 16 10:11	16 12:55 ♂ □	♒ 17 12:03	19 17:32 ○ 26♒37	1 AUGUST 1948
♃ D 16 0:40	♅ ♋ 30 15:40	18 15:34 ♅ ☍	♑ 18 19:13	19 23:38 ♅ △	♓ 20 0:23	27 18:46 ☽ 4♊22	Julian Day # 17745
♄∠♆ 18 18:32		21 2:31 ☉ ☍	♒ 21 6:02	22 12:32 ♅ □	♈ 22 13:05		Delta T 28.5 sec
☽0N 23 1:16		23 14:56 ♅ △	♓ 23 18:13	25 0:42 ♅ ⚹	♉ 25 1:03		SVP 05♓58'50"
		26 3:56 ♅ □	♈ 26 6:57	27 5:21 ♄ □	♊ 27 10:40		Obliquity 23°26'52"
		28 15:54 ♅ ⚹	♉ 28 18:34	29 16:31 ♅ ☌	♋ 29 16:34		⚷ Chiron 18♏33.6
		30 16:39 ☿ ⚹	♊ 31 3:01	31 15:34 ♂ □	♌ 31 18:41		☽ Mean ☊ 9♉32.4

LONGITUDE SEPTEMBER 1948

Day	Sid.Time	☉	0 hr ☽	Noon ☽	True ☊	☿	♀	♂	♃	♄	♅	♆	♇
1 W	22 40 15	8♍27 1	3♌17 28	10♌47 2	6♉44.0	25♍48.6	22♋36.6	28♎18.4	19♐29.5	27♌45.8	0♋ 2.4	11♎29.0	15♌18.1
2 Th	22 44 12	9 25 8	18 20 53	25 57 49	6R35.6	27 24.2	23 33.8	28 57.7	19 32.6	27 53.4	0 4.2	11 31.0	15 19.8
3 F	22 48 8	10 23 16	3♍36 30	11♍15 31	6 27.0	28 58.6	24 31.4	29 37.0	19 35.8	28 0.9	0 5.9	11 32.9	15 21.5
4 Sa	22 52 5	11 21 26	18 53 28	26 29 0	6 19.5	0♎31.8	25 29.4	0♏16.5	19 39.1	28 8.4	0 7.6	11 34.9	15 23.1
5 Su	22 56 1	12 19 38	4♎ 0 51	11♎27 58	6 13.8	2 3.7	26 27.9	0 56.1	19 42.7	28 15.9	0 9.2	11 36.9	15 24.8
6 M	22 59 58	13 17 51	18 49 28	26 4 41	6 10.4	3 34.4	27 26.8	1 35.7	19 46.4	28 23.4	0 10.8	11 38.9	15 26.4
7 Tu	23 3 54	14 16 6	3♏13 11	10♏14 44	6D 9.2	5 3.8	28 26.1	2 15.4	19 50.3	28 30.9	0 12.3	11 40.9	15 28.1
8 W	23 7 51	15 14 22	17 9 15	23 56 53	6 9.5	6 32.1	29 25.8	2 55.2	19 54.4	28 38.3	0 13.8	11 43.0	15 29.7
9 Th	23 11 48	16 12 40	0♐37 51	7♐12 30	6 10.6	7 59.1	0♌25.9	3 35.1	19 58.6	28 45.8	0 15.2	11 45.0	15 31.3
10 F	23 15 44	17 10 59	13 41 16	20 4 39	6R11.4	9 24.8	1 26.4	4 15.1	20 3.1	28 53.2	0 16.6	11 47.1	15 32.9
11 Sa	23 19 41	18 9 20	26 23 8	2♑37 16	6 11.0	10 49.2	2 27.2	4 55.2	20 7.6	29 0.6	0 17.9	11 49.2	15 34.5
12 Su	23 23 37	19 7 43	8♑47 35	14 54 35	6 9.0	12 12.3	3 28.4	5 35.3	20 12.4	29 7.9	0 19.2	11 51.2	15 36.1
13 M	23 27 34	20 6 7	20 58 46	27 0 37	6 4.9	13 34.1	4 30.0	6 15.5	20 17.3	29 15.3	0 20.5	11 53.3	15 37.6
14 Tu	23 31 30	21 4 33	3♒ 0 34	8♒59 1	5 59.0	14 54.5	5 31.8	6 55.8	20 22.4	29 22.6	0 21.6	11 55.4	15 39.2
15 W	23 35 27	22 3 0	14 56 20	20 52 52	5 51.6	16 13.6	6 34.1	7 36.2	20 27.6	29 29.8	0 22.8	11 57.6	15 40.7
16 Th	23 39 23	23 1 30	26 48 53	2♓44 41	5 43.5	17 31.1	7 36.6	8 16.6	20 33.0	29 37.1	0 23.9	11 59.7	15 42.2
17 F	23 43 20	24 0 0	8♓40 31	14 36 36	5 35.5	18 47.1	8 39.5	8 57.2	20 38.6	29 44.3	0 24.9	12 1.8	15 43.7
18 Sa	23 47 16	24 58 33	20 33 9	26 30 23	5 28.2	20 1.6	9 42.6	9 37.8	20 44.3	29 51.5	0 25.9	12 4.0	15 45.2
19 Su	23 51 13	25 57 8	2♈28 29	8♈27 41	5 22.5	21 14.4	10 46.1	10 18.5	20 50.2	29 58.6	0 26.8	12 6.1	15 46.6
20 M	23 55 10	26 55 44	14 28 13	20 30 17	5 18.5	22 25.4	11 49.9	10 59.3	20 56.2	0♍ 5.8	0 27.7	12 8.3	15 48.1
21 Tu	23 59 6	27 54 23	26 34 12	2♉40 12	5D16.4	23 34.6	12 53.9	11 40.1	21 2.4	0 12.8	0 28.6	12 10.5	15 49.5
22 W	0 3 3	28 53 3	8♉48 39	14 59 51	5 16.1	24 41.8	13 58.2	12 21.0	21 8.7	0 19.9	0 29.3	12 12.6	15 50.9
23 Th	0 6 59	29 51 46	21 14 11	27 32 2	5 17.0	25 47.0	15 2.9	13 2.0	21 15.2	0 26.9	0 30.1	12 14.8	15 52.3
24 F	0 10 56	0♎50 31	3♊53 47	10♊19 53	5 18.6	26 49.9	16 7.7	13 43.1	21 21.8	0 33.9	0 30.7	12 17.0	15 53.7
25 Sa	0 14 52	1 49 19	16 50 42	23 26 37	5 20.1	27 50.5	17 12.9	14 24.3	21 28.6	0 40.8	0 31.4	12 19.2	15 55.1
26 Su	0 18 49	2 48 9	0♋ 7 58	6♋55 3	5R20.9	28 48.5	18 18.3	15 5.6	21 35.6	0 47.7	0 32.0	12 21.4	15 56.4
27 M	0 22 45	3 47 1	13 48 3	20 47 4	5 20.5	29 43.7	19 23.9	15 46.9	21 42.6	0 54.6	0 32.5	12 23.7	15 57.7
28 Tu	0 26 42	4 45 55	27 52 4	5♌ 2 51	5 18.8	0♏36.0	20 29.8	16 28.3	21 49.9	1 1.4	0 33.0	12 25.9	15 59.1
29 W	0 30 39	5 44 52	12♌19 6	19 40 16	5 15.8	1 25.0	21 36.0	17 9.8	21 57.2	1 8.2	0 33.4	12 28.1	16 0.3
30 Th	0 34 35	6 43 51	27 5 40	4♍34 27	5 12.0	2 10.5	22 42.3	17 51.4	22 4.7	1 14.9	0 33.7	12 30.3	16 1.6

LONGITUDE OCTOBER 1948

Day	Sid.Time	☉	0 hr ☽	Noon ☽	True ☊	☿	♀	♂	♃	♄	♅	♆	♇
1 F	0 38 32	7♎42 52	12♍ 5 36	19♍38 1	5♉ 8.1	2♏52.2	23♌48.9	18♏33.0	22♐12.4	1♍21.6	0♋34.1	12♎32.5	16♌ 2.8
2 Sa	0 42 28	8 41 55	27 10 33	4♎41 59	5R 4.5	3 29.8	24 55.7	19 14.8	22 20.2	1 28.2	0 34.3	12 34.8	16 4.1
3 Su	0 46 25	9 41 0	12♎11 10	19 37 1	5 2.0	4 2.8	26 2.7	19 56.6	22 28.1	1 34.8	0 34.5	12 37.0	16 5.3
4 M	0 50 21	10 40 7	26 58 35	4♏15 1	5D 0.7	4 30.9	27 9.9	20 38.5	22 36.1	1 41.4	0 34.7	12 39.2	16 6.5
5 Tu	0 54 18	11 39 17	11♏25 42	18 30 9	5 0.6	4 53.6	28 17.3	21 20.4	22 44.3	1 47.9	0 34.8	12 41.5	16 7.6
6 W	0 58 14	12 38 28	25 28 4	2♐19 18	5 1.5	5 10.5	29 24.9	22 2.5	22 52.6	1 54.3	0R34.8	12 43.7	16 8.8
7 Th	1 2 11	13 37 41	9♐ 3 53	15 41 59	5 2.9	5 21.2	0♍32.7	22 44.6	23 1.1	2 0.7	0 34.8	12 45.9	16 9.9
8 F	1 6 8	14 36 56	22 13 52	28 39 52	5 4.4	5R25.2	1 40.7	23 26.8	23 9.7	2 7.0	0 34.8	12 48.2	16 11.0
9 Sa	1 10 4	15 36 13	5♑ 0 27	11♑16 6	5R 5.4	5 21.9	2 48.9	24 9.1	23 18.4	2 13.3	0 34.6	12 50.4	16 12.0
10 Su	1 14 1	16 35 32	17 27 21	23 34 43	5 5.8	5 11.0	3 57.2	24 51.4	23 27.2	2 19.5	0 34.5	12 52.7	16 13.1
11 M	1 17 57	17 34 52	29 38 48	5♒40 9	5 5.3	4 52.1	5 5.7	25 33.8	23 36.2	2 25.7	0 34.3	12 54.9	16 14.1
12 Tu	1 21 54	18 34 14	11♒39 18	17 36 48	5 4.0	4 25.0	6 14.4	26 16.3	23 45.2	2 31.8	0 34.0	12 57.1	16 15.1
13 W	1 25 50	19 33 38	23 33 9	29 28 50	5 2.1	3 49.5	7 23.3	26 58.9	23 54.4	2 37.8	0 33.7	12 59.3	16 16.1
14 Th	1 29 47	20 33 3	5♓24 19	11♓20 1	4 59.9	3 5.8	8 32.3	27 41.5	24 3.7	2 43.8	0 33.3	13 1.6	16 17.1
15 F	1 33 43	21 32 31	17 16 18	23 13 31	4 57.7	2 14.2	9 41.5	28 24.2	24 13.2	2 49.7	0 32.9	13 3.8	16 18.0
16 Sa	1 37 40	22 32 0	29 12 1	5♈12 3	4 55.8	1 15.3	10 50.9	29 6.9	24 22.7	2 55.6	0 32.4	13 6.0	16 18.9
17 Su	1 41 37	23 31 31	11♈13 53	17 17 44	4 54.4	0 10.1	12 0.4	29 49.8	24 32.3	3 1.3	0 31.9	13 8.2	16 19.8
18 M	1 45 33	24 31 5	23 23 49	29 32 18	4D 53.5	29♎ 0.0	13 10.0	0♐32.7	24 42.1	3 7.1	0 31.3	13 10.4	16 20.6
19 Tu	1 49 30	25 30 40	5♉43 22	11♉57 9	4 53.3	27 46.7	14 19.8	1 15.7	24 52.0	3 12.7	0 30.6	13 12.6	16 21.4
20 W	1 53 26	26 30 17	18 13 48	24 33 28	4 53.6	26 32.1	15 29.8	1 58.7	25 1.9	3 18.3	0 30.0	13 14.8	16 22.3
21 Th	1 57 23	27 29 57	0♊56 17	7♊22 23	4 54.1	25 18.3	16 39.9	2 41.8	25 12.0	3 23.8	0 29.2	13 17.0	16 23.0
22 F	2 1 19	28 29 38	13 51 53	20 24 57	4 54.8	24 7.7	17 50.2	3 25.0	25 22.2	3 29.3	0 28.4	13 19.2	16 23.8
23 Sa	2 5 16	29 29 22	27 1 42	3♋42 15	4 55.4	23 2.3	19 0.6	4 8.3	25 32.5	3 34.7	0 27.6	13 21.3	16 24.5
24 Su	2 9 12	0♏29 9	10♋26 42	17 15 8	4 55.8	22 4.2	20 11.1	4 51.6	25 42.9	3 40.0	0 26.7	13 23.5	16 25.2
25 M	2 13 9	1 28 57	24 7 36	1♌ 4 5	4R56.1	21 14.9	21 21.8	5 35.0	25 53.4	3 45.2	0 25.8	13 25.6	16 25.9
26 Tu	2 17 6	2 28 48	8♌ 4 32	15 8 49	4 56.1	20 35.8	22 32.6	6 18.5	26 4.0	3 50.4	0 24.8	13 27.8	16 26.6
27 W	2 21 2	3 28 41	22 16 44	29 27 59	4 56.0	20 7.6	23 43.5	7 2.1	26 14.7	3 55.5	0 23.8	13 29.9	16 27.2
28 Th	2 24 59	4 28 36	6♍42 10	13♍58 48	4D 55.9	19D 50.9	24 54.6	7 45.7	26 25.5	4 0.5	0 22.7	13 32.1	16 27.8
29 F	2 28 55	5 28 33	21 17 18	28 36 59	4 55.9	19 45.6	26 5.8	8 29.4	26 36.4	4 5.5	0 21.6	13 34.2	16 28.3
30 Sa	2 32 52	6 28 32	5♎57 9	13♎17 0	4 56.0	19 51.6	27 17.1	9 13.1	26 47.4	4 10.3	0 20.4	13 36.3	16 28.9
31 Su	2 36 48	7 28 34	20 35 42	27 52 28	4R56.2	20 8.3	28 28.5	9 56.9	26 58.5	4 15.1	0 19.2	13 38.4	16 29.4

Astro Data Dy Hr Mn	Planet Ingress Dy Hr Mn	Last Aspect Dy Hr Mn	☽ Ingress Dy Hr Mn	Last Aspect Dy Hr Mn	☽ Ingress Dy Hr Mn	☽ Phases & Eclipses Dy Hr Mn	Astro Data
☿0S 3 17:12	☿ ♎ 3 15:47	2 17:27 ♂ ⚹	♍ 2 18:20	1 16:14 ♃ □	♎ 2 4:30	3 11:21 ● 10♍51	1 SEPTEMBER 1948
☽0S 5 3:07	♂ ♏ 3 13:58	4 11:09 ♀ ⚹	♎ 4 17:35	4 0:20 ♀ ⚹	♏ 4 4:58	10 7:05 ☽ 17♐28	Julian Day # 17776
☽0N 19 6:50	♀ ♌ 8 13:40	6 16:00 ♄ ⚹	♏ 6 18:34	6 7:31 ♀ □	♐ 6 7:55	18 9:43 ○ 25♓22	Delta T 28.6 sec
♄⚹♅ 23 12:03	♄ ♍ 19 4:36	8 20:36 ♄ □	♐ 8 22:52	8 1:45 ♃ ☌	♑ 8 14:31	26 5:07 ☽ 3♋01	SVP 05♓58'45"
	☉ ♎ 23 3:22	11 5:05 ♄ △	♑ 11 6:56	10 15:25 ♂ ⚹	♒ 11 0:42		Obliquity 23°26'53"
☽0S 2 13:55	☿ ♏ 27 7:19	12 22:06 ☉ △	♒ 13 17:58	13 7:23 ♂ □	♓ 13 13:03	2 19:42 ● 9♎30	⚷ Chiron 20♏03.3
♅ R 6 9:51		16 5:44 ♄ ☍	♓ 16 6:27	15 23:49 ♂ △	♈ 16 1:36	9 22:10 ☽ 16♑31	☽ Mean ☊ 7♉53.9
☿ R 8 1:22	♀ ♍ 6 12:25	18 9:43 ☉ ☍	♈ 18 19:02	18 9:58 ☿ ☍	♉ 18 12:54	18 2:23 ○ 24♈37	
☽0N 16 13:26	☿ ♎ 17 3:33	20 17:28 ☿ ☍	♉ 21 6:45	19 20:27 ♇ □	♊ 20 22:15	18 2:35 ☍A 1.014	1 OCTOBER 1948
☿ D 28 23:06	♂ ♐ 17 5:43	22 13:40 ♇ □	♊ 23 16:40	23 4:48 ☉ △	♋ 23 5:21	25 13:41 ☽ 2♌03	Julian Day # 17806
☽0S 29 23:58	☉ ♏ 23 12:18	25 21:27 ☿ △	♋ 25 23:46	24 19:15 ☿ □	♌ 25 10:10		Delta T 28.6 sec
		27 3:36 ♂ △	♌ 28 3:35	27 6:43 ♃ △	♍ 27 12:53		SVP 05♓58'42"
		29 16:21 ♀ ☌	♍ 30 4:40	29 8:49 ♃ □	♎ 29 14:16		Obliquity 23°26'53"
				31 10:39 ♃ ⚹	♏ 31 15:31		⚷ Chiron 22♏46.3
							☽ Mean ☊ 6♉18.6

NOVEMBER 1948 LONGITUDE

Day	Sid.Time	☉	0 hr ☽	Noon ☽	True ☊	☿	♀	♂	♃	♄	♅	♆	♇
1 M	2 40 45	8♏28 37	5♏ 6 29	12♏17 1	4♉56.2	20♎35.1	29♍40.0	10♐40.8	27♐ 9.6	4♍19.8	0♋17.9	13♎40.4	16♌29.9
2 Tu	2 44 41	9 28 43	19 23 25	26 25 6	4R56.1	21 11.1	0♎51.7	11 24.8	27 20.9	4 24.4	0R16.6	13 42.5	16 30.4
3 W	2 48 38	10 28 50	3♐21 37	10♐12 38	4 55.7	21 55.5	2 3.4	12 8.8	27 32.2	4 28.9	0 15.2	13 44.6	16 30.8
4 Th	2 52 35	11 28 59	16 57 56	23 37 26	4 55.0	22 47.5	3 15.2	12 52.9	27 43.7	4 33.4	0 13.8	13 46.6	16 31.2
5 F	2 56 31	12 29 10	0♑11 9	6♑39 15	4 54.1	23 46.1	4 27.2	13 37.1	27 55.2	4 37.8	0 12.4	13 48.6	16 31.6
6 Sa	3 0 28	13 29 22	13 1 58	19 19 37	4 53.1	24 50.5	5 39.2	14 21.3	28 6.8	4 42.0	0 10.9	13 50.6	16 31.9
7 Su	3 4 24	14 29 36	25 32 38	1♒41 28	4 52.2	25 60.0	6 51.3	15 5.6	28 18.4	4 46.2	0 9.3	13 52.6	16 32.2
8 M	3 8 21	15 29 51	7♒46 38	13 48 41	4D51.6	27 13.8	8 3.5	15 49.9	28 30.2	4 50.3	0 7.7	13 54.6	16 32.5
9 Tu	3 12 17	16 30 8	19 48 13	25 45 49	4 51.5	28 31.4	9 15.8	16 34.4	28 42.0	4 54.3	0 6.1	13 56.6	16 32.8
10 W	3 16 14	17 30 26	1♓42 4	7♓37 35	4 51.9	29 52.1	10 28.2	17 18.8	28 53.9	4 58.2	0 4.5	13 58.5	16 33.0
11 Th	3 20 10	18 30 46	13 32 57	19 28 43	4 52.9	1♏15.5	11 40.7	18 3.4	29 5.9	5 2.1	0 2.7	14 0.4	16 33.2
12 F	3 24 7	19 31 7	25 25 28	1♈23 40	4 54.2	2 41.1	12 53.3	18 48.0	29 18.0	5 5.8	0 1.0	14 2.3	16 33.4
13 Sa	3 28 4	20 31 30	7♈23 49	13 26 22	4 55.6	4 8.6	14 5.9	19 32.6	29 30.1	5 9.4	29♊59.2	14 4.2	16 33.6
14 Su	3 32 0	21 31 54	19 31 41	25 40 6	4 56.8	5 37.6	15 18.6	20 17.3	29 42.3	5 13.0	29 57.4	14 6.1	16 33.7
15 M	3 35 57	22 32 19	1♉51 54	8♉ 7 19	4R57.4	7 7.9	16 31.4	21 2.1	29 54.5	5 16.4	29 55.5	14 8.0	16 33.8
16 Tu	3 39 53	23 32 46	14 26 31	20 49 35	4 57.2	8 39.2	17 44.3	21 46.9	0♑ 6.9	5 19.8	29 53.6	14 9.8	16 33.8
17 W	3 43 50	24 33 15	27 16 34	3♊47 26	4 55.9	10 11.3	18 57.3	22 31.8	0 19.3	5 23.1	29 51.7	14 11.6	16R33.9
18 Th	3 47 46	25 33 45	10♊22 7	17 0 30	4 53.7	11 44.1	20 10.3	23 16.7	0 31.7	5 26.2	29 49.7	14 13.4	16 33.9
19 F	3 51 43	26 34 17	23 42 24	0♋27 38	4 50.6	13 17.4	21 23.4	24 1.7	0 44.3	5 29.3	29 47.7	14 15.2	16 33.9
20 Sa	3 55 39	27 34 51	7♋15 58	14 7 7	4 47.2	14 51.0	22 36.6	24 46.8	0 56.8	5 32.3	29 45.7	14 16.9	16 33.8
21 Su	3 59 36	28 35 26	21 0 53	27 56 58	4 43.8	16 25.0	23 49.9	25 31.9	1 9.5	5 35.1	29 43.6	14 18.7	16 33.7
22 M	4 3 33	29 36 3	4♌55 7	11♌55 6	4 41.1	17 59.2	25 3.2	26 17.1	1 22.2	5 37.9	29 41.5	14 20.4	16 33.6
23 Tu	4 7 29	0♐36 41	18 56 41	25 59 38	4D39.4	19 33.6	26 16.6	27 2.3	1 34.9	5 40.6	29 39.4	14 22.1	16 33.5
24 W	4 11 26	1 37 22	3♍ 3 44	10♍ 8 45	4 38.9	21 8.0	27 30.1	27 47.6	1 47.8	5 43.1	29 37.2	14 23.7	16 33.3
25 Th	4 15 22	2 38 4	17 14 29	24 20 42	4 39.5	22 42.5	28 43.6	28 33.0	2 0.6	5 45.6	29 35.0	14 25.4	16 33.2
26 F	4 19 19	3 38 47	1♎27 8	8♎33 32	4 40.9	24 17.0	29 57.2	29 18.4	2 13.5	5 47.9	29 32.8	14 27.0	16 32.9
27 Sa	4 23 15	4 39 32	15 39 33	22 44 52	4 42.5	25 51.5	1♏10.9	0♑ 3.8	2 26.5	5 50.2	29 30.6	14 28.6	16 32.7
28 Su	4 27 12	5 40 19	29 49 7	6♏51 52	4R43.5	27 26.0	2 24.6	0 49.3	2 39.6	5 52.3	29 28.3	14 30.1	16 32.4
29 M	4 31 8	6 41 7	13♏52 42	20 51 12	4 43.2	29 0.4	3 38.3	1 34.9	2 52.6	5 54.4	29 26.0	14 31.7	16 32.1
30 Tu	4 35 5	7 41 57	27 46 53	4♐39 20	4 41.3	0♐34.8	4 52.1	2 20.5	3 5.8	5 56.3	29 23.7	14 33.2	16 31.8

DECEMBER 1948 LONGITUDE

Day	Sid.Time	☉	0 hr ☽	Noon ☽	True ☊	☿	♀	♂	♃	♄	♅	♆	♇
1 W	4 39 2	8♐42 48	11♐28 10	18♐13 1	4♉37.6	2♐ 9.2	6♏ 6.0	3♑ 6.2	3♑18.9	5♍58.1	29♊21.3	14♎34.7	16♌31.4
2 Th	4 42 58	9 43 40	24 53 35	1♑29 39	4R32.4	3 43.5	7 19.9	3 52.0	3 32.1	5 59.8	29R19.0	14 36.2	16R31.0
3 F	4 46 55	10 44 33	8♑ 1 5	14 27 49	4 26.0	5 17.7	8 33.9	4 37.7	3 45.4	6 1.4	29 16.6	14 37.6	16 30.6
4 Sa	4 50 51	11 45 27	20 49 54	27 7 28	4 19.3	6 52.0	9 47.9	5 23.6	3 58.7	6 2.9	29 14.2	14 39.0	16 30.2
5 Su	4 54 48	12 46 22	3♒20 44	9♒30 0	4 13.0	8 26.2	11 1.9	6 9.5	4 12.1	6 4.3	29 11.7	14 40.4	16 29.7
6 M	4 58 44	13 47 18	15 35 38	21 38 5	4 7.8	10 0.3	12 16.0	6 55.4	4 25.4	6 5.6	29 9.3	14 41.8	16 29.2
7 Tu	5 2 41	14 48 15	27 37 51	3♓35 30	4 4.2	11 34.5	13 30.1	7 41.4	4 38.8	6 6.8	29 6.8	14 43.1	16 28.7
8 W	5 6 38	15 49 12	9♓31 36	15 26 47	4D 2.4	13 8.6	14 44.3	8 27.4	4 52.3	6 7.8	29 4.4	14 44.4	16 28.2
9 Th	5 10 34	16 50 10	21 21 42	27 16 59	4 2.3	14 42.8	15 58.5	9 13.4	5 5.8	6 8.8	29 1.9	14 45.7	16 27.6
10 F	5 14 31	17 51 8	3♈13 18	9♈11 19	4 3.4	16 17.0	17 12.7	9 59.5	5 19.3	6 9.6	28 59.4	14 46.9	16 27.0
11 Sa	5 18 27	18 52 8	15 11 38	21 14 53	4 4.9	17 51.3	18 26.9	10 45.7	5 32.8	6 10.3	28 56.8	14 48.1	16 26.4
12 Su	5 22 24	19 53 7	27 21 37	3♉32 21	4R 6.2	19 25.6	19 41.2	11 31.9	5 46.4	6 10.9	28 54.3	14 49.3	16 25.7
13 M	5 26 20	20 54 8	9♉47 32	16 7 33	4 6.2	20 59.9	20 55.6	12 18.1	6 0.0	6 11.4	28 51.8	14 50.5	16 25.1
14 Tu	5 30 17	21 55 9	22 32 40	29 3 6	4 4.4	22 34.4	22 9.9	13 4.4	6 13.7	6 11.8	28 49.2	14 51.6	16 24.4
15 W	5 34 13	22 56 10	5♊38 55	12♊20 3	4 0.3	24 9.0	23 24.3	13 50.7	6 27.3	6 12.1	28 46.7	14 52.7	16 23.6
16 Th	5 38 10	23 57 13	19 6 22	25 57 33	3 54.1	25 43.7	24 38.8	14 37.1	6 41.0	6 12.3	28 44.1	14 53.8	16 22.9
17 F	5 42 7	24 58 16	2♋53 14	9♋52 54	3 46.0	27 18.5	25 53.2	15 23.5	6 54.7	6R12.3	28 41.6	14 54.8	16 22.1
18 Sa	5 46 3	25 59 19	16 55 58	24 1 47	3 37.0	28 53.5	27 7.7	16 9.9	7 8.5	6 12.3	28 39.0	14 55.8	16 21.3
19 Su	5 50 0	27 0 24	1♌ 9 41	8♌18 58	3 28.1	0♑28.7	28 22.2	16 56.4	7 22.2	6 12.1	28 36.4	14 56.8	16 20.5
20 M	5 53 56	28 1 29	15 28 58	22 39 5	3 20.4	2 4.0	29 36.8	17 42.9	7 36.0	6 11.8	28 33.8	14 57.7	16 19.7
21 Tu	5 57 53	29 2 34	29 48 45	6♍57 30	3 14.6	3 39.5	0♐51.4	18 29.5	7 49.8	6 11.4	28 31.3	14 58.6	16 18.8
22 W	6 1 49	0♑ 3 41	14♍ 4 57	21 10 48	3 11.1	5 15.2	2 6.0	19 16.1	8 3.6	6 10.9	28 28.7	14 59.5	16 17.9
23 Th	6 5 46	1 4 48	28 14 50	5♎16 55	3D 9.9	6 51.1	3 20.6	20 2.7	8 17.4	6 10.3	28 26.1	15 0.4	16 17.0
24 F	6 9 42	2 5 56	12♎16 56	19 14 53	3 10.2	8 27.1	4 35.3	20 49.4	8 31.2	6 9.6	28 23.5	15 1.2	16 16.1
25 Sa	6 13 39	3 7 4	26 10 42	3♏ 4 25	3R10.9	10 3.4	5 50.0	21 36.1	8 45.1	6 8.7	28 21.0	15 1.9	16 15.1
26 Su	6 17 36	4 8 14	9♏56 0	16 45 25	3 10.9	11 39.9	7 4.7	22 22.8	8 59.0	6 7.8	28 18.4	15 2.7	16 14.2
27 M	6 21 32	5 9 23	23 32 37	0♐17 31	3 9.0	13 16.5	8 19.4	23 9.6	9 12.8	6 6.7	28 15.9	15 3.4	16 13.2
28 Tu	6 25 29	6 10 34	7♐ 0 0	13 39 54	3 4.4	14 53.3	9 34.1	23 56.4	9 26.7	6 5.6	28 13.3	15 4.1	16 12.2
29 W	6 29 25	7 11 44	20 17 5	26 51 21	2 57.0	16 30.3	10 48.9	24 43.3	9 40.6	6 4.3	28 10.8	15 4.7	16 11.1
30 Th	6 33 22	8 12 55	3♑22 32	9♑50 28	2 46.9	18 7.3	12 3.7	25 30.2	9 54.5	6 2.9	28 8.2	15 5.4	16 10.1
31 F	6 37 18	9 14 7	16 15 1	22 36 5	2 34.8	19 44.4	13 18.5	26 17.1	10 8.4	6 1.4	28 5.7	15 5.9	16 9.0

Astro Data	Planet Ingress	Last Aspect	☽ Ingress	Last Aspect	☽ Ingress	☽ Phases & Eclipses	Astro Data
Dy Hr Mn	Dy Hr Mn	Dy Hr Mn	Dy Hr Mn	Dy Hr Mn	Dy Hr Mn	Dy Hr Mn	1 NOVEMBER 1948
♀0S 4 8:24	♀ ♎ 1 6:42	1 19:07 ♇ □	♐ 2 18:10	2 8:00 ♅ ☍	♑ 2 9:16	1 6:03 ● 8♏44	Julian Day # 17837
☽0N 12 21:03	☿ ♏ 10 2:19	4 19:46 ♃ ☌	♑ 4 23:39	3 12:20 ♆ □	♒ 4 17:32	1 5:58:49 ✓T 1'56"	Delta T 28.6 sec
♃☍♅ 15 1:39	♅ ♊ 12 13:26	7 0:59 ☿ □	♒ 7 8:41	7 2:58 ♅ △	♓ 7 4:46	8 16:46 ☽ 16♒12	SVP 05♓58'39"
♇ R 17 20:18	♃ ♑ 15 10:38	9 19:49 ☿ △	♓ 9 20:34	9 15:29 ♅ □	♈ 9 17:30	16 18:31 ○ 24♉19	Obliquity 23°26'53"
♃⚻♇ 22 21:21	☉ ♐ 22 9:29	12 7:56 ♃ □	♈ 12 9:12	12 3:00 ♅ ⚹	♉ 12 5:09	23 21:22 ☽ 1♍31	⚷ Chiron 26♏26.2
☽0S 26 7:25	♀ ♏ 26 0:55	14 20:16 ♅ ⚹	♉ 14 20:24	13 23:13 ♀ ☍	♊ 14 13:44	30 18:44 ● 8♐29	☽ Mean ☊ 4♉40.1
	♂ ♑ 26 21:59	16 18:31 ☉ ☍	♊ 17 5:02	16 16:46 ♅ ☌	♋ 16 19:01		
☽0N 10 4:58	☿ ♐ 29 15:09	19 10:48 ♅ ☌	♋ 19 11:11	18 18:52 ♀ △	♌ 18 22:03	8 13:57 ☽ 16♓25	1 DECEMBER 1948
♃△♄ 13 20:39		21 14:08 ☉ △	♌ 21 15:32	20 22:37 ☉ △	♍ 21 0:19	16 9:11 ○ 24♊21	Julian Day # 17867
♄ R 17 0:20	☿ ♑ 18 16:46	23 18:11 ♅ ⚹	♍ 23 18:48	23 0:19 ♅ □	♎ 23 2:59	23 5:12 ☽ 1♎18	Delta T 28.7 sec
☽0S 23 12:21	♀ ♐ 20 7:28	25 20:47 ♅ □	♎ 25 21:33	25 3:46 ♅ △	♏ 25 6:39	30 9:45 ● 8♑38	SVP 05♓58'33"
	☉ ♑ 21 22:33	27 23:25 ♅ △	♏ 28 0:19	26 23:17 ♂ ⚹	♐ 27 11:29		Obliquity 23°26'53"
		29 4:34 ♇ □	♐ 30 3:52	29 14:23 ♅ ☍	♑ 29 17:47		⚷ Chiron 0♐19.0
							☽ Mean ☊ 3♉04.8

LONGITUDE — JANUARY 1949

Day	Sid.Time	☉	0 hr ☽	Noon ☽	True ☊	☿	♀	♂	♃	♄	♅	♆	♇
1 Sa	6 41 15	10♑15 18	28♑53 36	5♒ 7 36	2♉21.9	21♑21.6	14♐33.3	27♑ 4.0	10♑22.4	5♍59.8	28♊ 3.2	15♎ 6.5	16♌ 7.9
2 Su	6 45 11	11 16 29	11♒18 9	17 25 24	2R 9.4	22 58.7	15 48.1	27 51.0	10 36.2	5R58.1	28R 0.7	15 7.0	16R 6.8
3 M	6 49 8	12 17 40	23 29 33	29 30 55	1 58.3	24 35.6	17 3.0	28 38.0	10 50.1	5 56.3	27 58.2	15 7.5	16 5.7
4 Tu	6 53 5	13 18 51	5♓29 51	11♓26 45	1 49.5	26 12.4	18 17.8	29 25.0	11 4.1	5 54.4	27 55.8	15 7.9	16 4.5
5 W	6 57 1	14 20 1	17 22 9	23 16 34	1 43.4	27 48.8	19 32.7	0♒12.1	11 18.0	5 52.4	27 53.3	15 8.3	16 3.4
6 Th	7 0 58	15 21 11	29 10 35	5♈ 4 51	1 40.0	29 24.7	20 47.6	0 59.2	11 31.9	5 50.3	27 50.9	15 8.7	16 2.2
7 F	7 4 54	16 22 21	11♈ 0 1	16 56 47	1D 38.7	0♒60.0	22 2.4	1 46.3	11 45.8	5 48.1	27 48.5	15 9.0	16 1.0
8 Sa	7 8 51	17 23 30	22 55 51	28 57 53	1R 38.6	2 34.4	23 17.3	2 33.4	11 59.6	5 45.8	27 46.1	15 9.3	15 59.8
9 Su	7 12 47	18 24 39	5♉ 3 37	11♉13 42	1 38.7	4 7.8	24 32.2	3 20.6	12 13.5	5 43.3	27 43.7	15 9.6	15 58.6
10 M	7 16 44	19 25 47	17 28 45	23 49 20	1 37.8	5 39.9	25 47.1	4 7.7	12 27.4	5 40.8	27 41.4	15 9.8	15 57.3
11 Tu	7 20 40	20 26 55	0♊15 55	6♊48 54	1 34.8	7 10.3	27 2.0	4 54.9	12 41.3	5 38.2	27 39.0	15 10.0	15 56.1
12 W	7 24 37	21 28 3	13 28 31	20 14 52	1 29.1	8 38.7	28 16.9	5 42.1	12 55.1	5 35.5	27 36.7	15 10.2	15 54.8
13 Th	7 28 34	22 29 10	27 7 55	4♋ 7 24	1 20.7	10 4.7	29 31.9	6 29.4	13 8.9	5 32.7	27 34.5	15 10.3	15 53.5
14 F	7 32 30	23 30 16	11♋12 55	18 23 52	1 9.9	11 27.8	0♑46.8	7 16.6	13 22.8	5 29.8	27 32.2	15 10.4	15 52.2
15 Sa	7 36 27	24 31 22	25 39 28	2♌58 48	0 57.8	12 47.4	2 1.7	8 3.9	13 36.6	5 26.9	27 30.0	15 10.5	15 50.9
16 Su	7 40 23	25 32 27	10♌20 52	17 44 37	0 45.6	14 2.9	3 16.7	8 51.1	13 50.4	5 23.8	27 27.8	15R 10.5	15 49.6
17 M	7 44 20	26 33 32	25 8 56	2♍32 48	0 34.7	15 13.7	4 31.6	9 38.4	14 4.1	5 20.7	27 25.6	15 10.5	15 48.3
18 Tu	7 48 16	27 34 37	9♍55 14	17 15 25	0 26.2	16 19.0	5 46.6	10 25.8	14 17.9	5 17.4	27 23.5	15 10.5	15 47.0
19 W	7 52 13	28 35 41	24 32 39	1♎46 21	0 20.6	17 18.0	7 1.6	11 13.1	14 31.6	5 14.1	27 21.4	15 10.4	15 45.6
20 Th	7 56 10	29 36 44	8♎56 10	16 1 49	0 17.7	18 9.8	8 16.5	12 0.4	14 45.3	5 10.7	27 19.3	15 10.3	15 44.3
21 F	8 0 6	0♒37 48	23 3 13	0♏ 0 22	0 16.9	18 53.6	9 31.5	12 47.8	14 59.0	5 7.2	27 17.3	15 10.2	15 42.9
22 Sa	8 4 3	1 38 51	6♏53 20	13 42 16	0 16.8	19 28.6	10 46.5	13 35.2	15 12.7	5 3.7	27 15.3	15 10.0	15 41.5
23 Su	8 7 59	2 39 53	20 27 22	27 8 50	0 16.2	19 53.8	12 1.5	14 22.6	15 26.3	5 0.0	27 13.3	15 9.8	15 40.2
24 M	8 11 56	3 40 56	3♐46 53	10♐21 43	0 13.6	20R 8.7	13 16.5	15 10.0	15 39.9	4 56.3	27 11.3	15 9.6	15 38.8
25 Tu	8 15 52	4 41 57	16 53 30	23 22 24	0 8.3	20 12.6	14 31.5	15 57.4	15 53.5	4 52.5	27 9.4	15 9.3	15 37.4
26 W	8 19 49	5 42 58	29 48 30	6♑11 54	29♈59.8	20 5.1	15 46.5	16 44.8	16 7.0	4 48.7	27 7.6	15 9.0	15 36.0
27 Th	8 23 45	6 43 59	12♑32 39	18 50 48	29 48.5	19 46.1	17 1.6	17 32.2	16 20.5	4 44.7	27 5.8	15 8.6	15 34.6
28 F	8 27 42	7 44 58	25 6 22	1♒19 20	29 35.0	19 16.0	18 16.6	18 19.7	16 34.0	4 40.7	27 4.0	15 8.3	15 33.2
29 Sa	8 31 39	8 45 57	7♒29 45	13 37 39	29 20.5	18 35.1	19 31.6	19 7.2	16 47.5	4 36.7	27 2.2	15 7.9	15 31.7
30 Su	8 35 35	9 46 55	19 43 5	25 46 9	29 6.3	17 44.6	20 46.6	19 54.6	17 0.9	4 32.6	27 0.5	15 7.4	15 30.3
31 M	8 39 32	10 47 51	1♓46 59	7♓45 48	28 53.4	16 45.7	22 1.6	20 42.1	17 14.3	4 28.4	26 58.8	15 6.9	15 28.9

LONGITUDE — FEBRUARY 1949

Day	Sid.Time	☉	0 hr ☽	Noon ☽	True ☊	☿	♀	♂	♃	♄	♅	♆	♇
1 Tu	8 43 28	11♒48 47	13♓42 48	19♓38 18	28♈43.0	15♒40.2	23♑16.6	21♒29.5	17♑27.6	4♍24.1	26♊57.2	15♎ 6.4	15♌27.5
2 W	8 47 25	12 49 41	25 32 39	1♈26 16	28R 35.5	14R 30.0	24 31.6	22 17.0	17 40.9	4R 19.9	26R 55.6	15R 5.9	15R 26.0
3 Th	8 51 21	13 50 34	7♈19 37	13 13 13	28 30.9	13 17.1	25 46.6	23 4.5	17 54.1	4 15.5	26 54.1	15 5.3	15 24.6
4 F	8 55 18	14 51 26	19 7 37	25 3 26	28D 28.8	12 3.6	27 1.6	23 52.0	18 7.3	4 11.1	26 52.6	15 4.7	15 23.2
5 Sa	8 59 14	15 52 16	1♉ 1 20	7♉ 1 58	28 28.5	10 51.7	28 16.6	24 39.4	18 20.5	4 6.7	26 51.1	15 4.1	15 21.8
6 Su	9 3 11	16 53 5	13 6 1	19 14 11	28R 28.8	9 43.1	29 31.6	25 26.9	18 33.6	4 2.2	26 49.7	15 3.4	15 20.3
7 M	9 7 8	17 53 52	25 27 10	1♊45 35	28 28.5	8 39.4	0♒46.6	26 14.4	18 46.7	3 57.7	26 48.4	15 2.7	15 18.9
8 Tu	9 11 4	18 54 38	8♊10 5	14 41 9	28 26.8	7 41.8	2 1.6	27 1.9	18 59.7	3 53.1	26 47.1	15 2.0	15 17.5
9 W	9 15 1	19 55 22	21 19 16	28 4 43	28 22.8	6 51.3	3 16.5	27 49.3	19 12.7	3 48.5	26 45.8	15 1.2	15 16.0
10 Th	9 18 57	20 56 5	4♋57 39	11♋58 3	28 16.3	6 8.4	4 31.5	28 36.8	19 25.6	3 43.9	26 44.6	15 0.5	15 14.6
11 F	9 22 54	21 56 46	19 5 41	26 20 6	28 7.6	5 33.5	5 46.5	29 24.2	19 38.4	3 39.2	26 43.4	14 59.6	15 13.2
12 Sa	9 26 50	22 57 26	3♌40 39	11♌ 6 26	27 57.5	5 6.7	7 1.4	0♓11.7	19 51.2	3 34.5	26 42.3	14 58.8	15 11.8
13 Su	9 30 47	23 58 4	18 36 26	26 9 24	27 47.2	4 47.9	8 16.4	0 59.1	20 4.0	3 29.8	26 41.2	14 57.9	15 10.4
14 M	9 34 43	24 58 40	3♍44 5	11♍19 9	27 37.9	4D 36.9	9 31.3	1 46.6	20 16.7	3 25.0	26 40.2	14 57.0	15 9.0
15 Tu	9 38 40	25 59 16	18 53 18	26 25 20	27 30.6	4 33.4	10 46.3	2 34.0	20 29.3	3 20.2	26 39.2	14 56.1	15 7.6
16 W	9 42 37	26 59 49	3♎54 10	11♎18 54	27 25.9	4 37.0	12 1.2	3 21.4	20 41.9	3 15.5	26 38.3	14 55.1	15 6.2
17 Th	9 46 33	28 0 22	18 38 48	25 53 22	27D 23.7	4 47.2	13 16.2	4 8.8	20 54.4	3 10.7	26 37.4	14 54.2	15 4.8
18 F	9 50 30	29 0 53	3♏ 2 15	10♏ 5 17	27 23.5	5 3.6	14 31.1	4 56.2	21 6.8	3 5.8	26 36.6	14 53.2	15 3.4
19 Sa	9 54 26	0♓ 1 23	17 2 26	23 53 50	27 24.3	5 25.9	15 46.0	5 43.6	21 19.2	3 1.0	26 35.8	14 52.1	15 2.0
20 Su	9 58 23	1 1 52	0♐39 40	7♐20 12	27R 24.8	5 53.5	17 1.0	6 31.0	21 31.5	2 56.2	26 35.1	14 51.1	15 0.6
21 M	10 2 19	2 2 19	13 55 46	20 26 42	27 24.1	6 26.1	18 15.9	7 18.4	21 43.8	2 51.3	26 34.4	14 50.0	14 59.3
22 Tu	10 6 16	3 2 45	26 53 23	3♑16 9	27 21.2	7 3.3	19 30.8	8 5.7	21 55.9	2 46.5	26 33.8	14 48.9	14 57.9
23 W	10 10 12	4 3 10	9♑35 21	15 51 19	27 16.1	7 44.7	20 45.7	8 53.1	22 8.1	2 41.6	26 33.2	14 47.7	14 56.6
24 Th	10 14 9	5 3 34	22 4 18	28 14 37	27 8.6	8 30.1	22 0.6	9 40.4	22 20.1	2 36.8	26 32.7	14 46.6	14 55.2
25 F	10 18 6	6 3 55	4♒22 28	10♒28 4	26 59.5	9 19.1	23 15.6	10 27.8	22 32.1	2 32.0	26 32.2	14 45.4	14 53.9
26 Sa	10 22 2	7 4 16	16 31 38	22 33 19	26 49.6	10 11.4	24 30.5	11 15.1	22 43.9	2 27.1	26 31.8	14 44.2	14 52.6
27 Su	10 25 59	8 4 34	28 33 19	4♓31 46	26 39.7	11 6.9	25 45.3	12 2.4	22 55.7	2 22.3	26 31.5	14 43.0	14 51.3
28 M	10 29 55	9 4 51	10♓28 53	16 24 49	26 30.9	12 5.3	27 0.2	12 49.7	23 7.5	2 17.5	26 31.2	14 41.7	14 50.0

Astro Data

	Dy Hr Mn
☽ 0 N	6 12:16
♆ R	16 9:35
☽ 0 S	19 17:22
♃ □ ♆	21 19:25
♃ ⚻ ♇	23 22:11
☿ R	24 20:17
☽ 0 N	2 18:41
♃ ⚼ ♄	7 14:59
☿ D	14 23:45
☽ 0 S	16 1:05

Planet Ingress

	Dy Hr Mn
♂ ♒	4 17:50
☿ ♒	6 8:53
♀ ♑	13 9:01
☉ ♒	20 9:09
☊ ♈	25 23:35
♀ ♒	6 9:05
♂ ♓	11 18:05
☉ ♓	18 23:27

Last Aspect / ☽ Ingress (January)

Last Aspect Dy Hr Mn		☽ Ingress Dy Hr Mn
31 20:16	♂ ☌	♒ 1 2:07
3 8:53	♅ △	♓ 3 12:58
6 0:33	☿ ⚹	♈ 6 1:40
8 9:36	♅ ⚹	♉ 8 14:03
10 4:02	☉ △	♊ 10 23:31
13 4:33	♀ ☍	♋ 13 4:57
14 21:59	☉ ☍	♌ 15 7:08
17 3:41	♅ ⚹	♍ 17 7:52
19 7:13	☉ △	♎ 19 9:03
21 7:17	♅ △	♏ 21 11:59
22 22:59	☿ □	♐ 23 17:09
25 19:00	♅ ☍	♑ 26 0:22
27 9:28	♀ ☌	♒ 28 9:26
30 14:26	♅ △	♓ 30 20:26

Last Aspect / ☽ Ingress (February)

Last Aspect Dy Hr Mn		☽ Ingress Dy Hr Mn
2 2:48	♅ □	♈ 2 9:04
4 17:51	♀ □	♉ 4 21:57
7 1:37	♂ □	♊ 7 8:40
9 12:15	♂ △	♋ 9 15:22
11 0:55	♃ ☍	♌ 11 18:01
13 12:50	♅ ⚹	♍ 13 18:05
15 12:22	♅ □	♎ 15 17:44
17 16:43	☉ △	♏ 17 18:53
19 7:35	♃ ⚹	♐ 19 22:49
21 23:23	♅ ☍	♑ 22 5:50
24 0:31	♃ ☌	♒ 24 15:26
26 19:56	♅ △	♓ 27 2:54

☽ Phases & Eclipses

Dy Hr Mn	
7 11:52	☽ 16♈53
14 21:59	○ 24♋26
21 14:07	☽ 1♏14
29 2:42	● 8♒53
6 8:05	☽ 17♉14
13 9:08	○ 24♌21
20 0:43	☽ 1♐04
27 20:55	● 8♓57

Astro Data

1 JANUARY 1949
Julian Day # 17898
Delta T 28.7 sec
SVP 05♓58'27"
Obliquity 23°26'53"
⚷ Chiron 4♐07.0
☽ Mean ☊ 1♉26.3

1 FEBRUARY 1949
Julian Day # 17929
Delta T 28.7 sec
SVP 05♓58'21"
Obliquity 23°26'53"
⚷ Chiron 7♐07.9
☽ Mean ☊ 29♈47.8

MARCH 1949 — LONGITUDE

Day	Sid.Time	☉	0 hr ☽	Noon ☽	True ☊	☿	♀	♂	♃	♄	♅	♆	♇
1 Tu	10 33 52	10♓ 5 6	22♓19 48	28♓14 3	26♈23.8	13♒ 6.3	28♒15.1	13♓36.9	23♑19.1	2♍12.7	26♊30.9	14♎40.4	14♌48.7
2 W	10 37 48	11 5 19	4♈ 7 50	10♈ 1 28	26R 18.9	14 9.9	29 30.0	14 24.2	23 30.7	2R 8.0	26R 30.7	14R 39.1	14R 47.5
3 Th	10 41 45	12 5 30	15 55 16	21 49 38	26D 16.2	15 15.8	0♓44.8	15 11.4	23 42.2	2 3.2	26 30.6	14 37.8	14 46.2
4 F	10 45 41	13 5 40	27 44 58	3♉41 45	26 15.5	16 23.9	1 59.6	15 58.6	23 53.6	1 58.5	26 30.5	14 36.5	14 45.0
5 Sa	10 49 38	14 5 47	9♉40 29	15 41 41	26 16.3	17 34.1	3 14.5	16 45.8	24 4.9	1 53.8	26D 30.4	14 35.1	14 43.8
6 Su	10 53 35	15 5 52	21 45 56	27 53 49	26 17.9	18 46.3	4 29.3	17 32.9	24 16.1	1 49.1	26 30.4	14 33.8	14 42.5
7 M	10 57 31	16 5 55	4♊ 5 55	10♊22 51	26 19.4	20 0.3	5 44.1	18 20.1	24 27.2	1 44.5	26 30.5	14 32.4	14 41.4
8 Tu	11 1 28	17 5 56	16 45 10	23 13 26	26R 20.0	21 16.1	6 58.9	19 7.2	24 38.3	1 39.9	26 30.6	14 31.0	14 40.2
9 W	11 5 24	18 5 55	29 48 8	6♋29 40	26 19.3	22 33.6	8 13.7	19 54.3	24 49.2	1 35.4	26 30.8	14 29.5	14 39.0
10 Th	11 9 21	19 5 52	13♋18 20	20 14 18	26 17.0	23 52.8	9 28.4	20 41.3	25 0.0	1 30.9	26 31.1	14 28.1	14 37.9
11 F	11 13 17	20 5 46	27 17 33	4♌27 54	26 13.1	25 13.5	10 43.2	21 28.4	25 10.8	1 26.4	26 31.4	14 26.6	14 36.8
12 Sa	11 17 14	21 5 39	11♌44 58	19 8 10	26 8.3	26 35.8	11 57.9	22 15.4	25 21.5	1 22.0	26 31.7	14 25.2	14 35.6
13 Su	11 21 10	22 5 29	26 36 41	4♍ 9 31	26 3.0	27 59.5	13 12.6	23 2.3	25 32.0	1 17.6	26 32.1	14 23.7	14 34.6
14 M	11 25 7	23 5 17	11♍45 32	19 23 27	25 58.3	29 24.6	14 27.3	23 49.3	25 42.5	1 13.3	26 32.5	14 22.2	14 33.5
15 Tu	11 29 4	24 5 2	27 1 57	4♎39 42	25 54.6	0♓51.2	15 42.0	24 36.2	25 52.8	1 9.0	26 33.0	14 20.7	14 32.4
16 W	11 33 0	25 4 46	12♎15 25	19 47 56	25D 52.4	2 19.1	16 56.7	25 23.1	26 3.1	1 4.8	26 33.6	14 19.1	14 31.4
17 Th	11 36 57	26 4 28	27 16 13	4♏39 24	25 51.9	3 48.4	18 11.4	26 9.9	26 13.2	1 0.6	26 34.2	14 17.6	14 30.4
18 F	11 40 53	27 4 8	11♏56 48	19 7 57	25 52.5	5 19.0	19 26.1	26 56.8	26 23.3	0 56.5	26 34.9	14 16.1	14 29.4
19 Sa	11 44 50	28 3 47	26 12 32	3♐10 28	25 54.0	6 51.0	20 40.7	27 43.6	26 33.2	0 52.5	26 35.6	14 14.5	14 28.4
20 Su	11 48 46	29 3 24	10♐ 1 44	16 46 30	25 55.5	8 24.2	21 55.4	28 30.4	26 43.0	0 48.5	26 36.3	14 12.9	14 27.4
21 M	11 52 43	0♈ 2 59	23 25 1	29 57 38	25R 56.5	9 58.8	23 10.0	29 17.1	26 52.7	0 44.6	26 37.1	14 11.3	14 26.5
22 Tu	11 56 39	1 2 32	6♑24 43	12♑46 44	25 56.5	11 34.7	24 24.6	0♈ 3.8	27 2.3	0 40.7	26 38.0	14 9.8	14 25.6
23 W	12 0 36	2 2 4	19 4 7	25 17 21	25 55.4	13 11.9	25 39.3	0 50.5	27 11.8	0 37.0	26 38.9	14 8.2	14 24.7
24 Th	12 4 33	3 1 33	1♒26 53	7♒33 11	25 53.3	14 50.4	26 53.9	1 37.2	27 21.2	0 33.2	26 39.9	14 6.6	14 23.8
25 F	12 8 29	4 1 1	13 36 40	19 37 45	25 50.3	16 30.2	28 8.5	2 23.8	27 30.4	0 29.6	26 40.9	14 4.9	14 23.0
26 Sa	12 12 26	5 0 27	25 36 51	1♓34 18	25 46.8	18 11.3	29 23.0	3 10.4	27 39.6	0 26.0	26 42.0	14 3.3	14 22.1
27 Su	12 16 22	5 59 51	7♓30 27	13 25 38	25 43.4	19 53.7	0♈37.6	3 56.9	27 48.6	0 22.6	26 43.1	14 1.7	14 21.3
28 M	12 20 19	6 59 14	19 20 7	25 14 13	25 40.3	21 37.5	1 52.2	4 43.4	27 57.4	0 19.2	26 44.3	14 0.1	14 20.6
29 Tu	12 24 15	7 58 34	1♈ 8 11	7♈ 2 16	25 38.0	23 22.7	3 6.7	5 29.9	28 6.2	0 15.8	26 45.5	13 58.4	14 19.8
30 W	12 28 12	8 57 52	12 56 45	18 51 53	25 36.6	25 9.2	4 21.2	6 16.4	28 14.8	0 12.6	26 46.8	13 56.8	14 19.1
31 Th	12 32 8	9 57 8	24 47 55	0♉45 9	25D 36.1	26 57.0	5 35.7	7 2.8	28 23.3	0 9.4	26 48.2	13 55.1	14 18.3

APRIL 1949 — LONGITUDE

Day	Sid.Time	☉	0 hr ☽	Noon ☽	True ☊	☿	♀	♂	♃	♄	♅	♆	♇
1 F	12 36 5	10♈56 22	6♉43 53	12♉44 24	25♈36.4	28♓46.3	6♈50.2	7♈49.2	28♑31.7	0♍ 6.3	26♊49.5	13♎53.5	14♌17.7
2 Sa	12 40 1	11 55 34	18 47 3	24 52 11	25 37.3	0♈36.9	8 4.7	8 35.5	28 39.9	0R 3.3	26 51.0	13R 51.8	14R 17.0
3 Su	12 43 58	12 54 44	1♊ 0 11	7♊11 26	25 38.5	2 28.9	9 19.2	9 21.8	28 48.0	0 0.4	26 52.4	13 50.2	14 16.4
4 M	12 47 55	13 53 51	13 26 19	19 45 17	25 39.7	4 22.3	10 33.6	10 8.0	28 56.0	29♌57.6	26 54.0	13 48.5	14 15.7
5 Tu	12 51 51	14 52 57	26 8 43	2♋37 2	25 40.6	6 17.1	11 48.0	10 54.2	29 3.8	29 54.9	26 55.5	13 46.9	14 15.2
6 W	12 55 48	15 52 0	9♋10 36	15 49 46	25R 41.1	8 13.3	13 2.5	11 40.4	29 11.5	29 52.3	26 57.2	13 45.2	14 14.6
7 Th	12 59 44	16 51 0	22 34 48	29 25 54	25 41.1	10 10.9	14 16.9	12 26.5	29 19.0	29 49.7	26 58.8	13 43.6	14 14.1
8 F	13 3 41	17 49 59	6♌23 10	13♌26 35	25 40.7	12 9.8	15 31.2	13 12.6	29 26.5	29 47.3	27 0.5	13 41.9	14 13.5
9 Sa	13 7 37	18 48 55	20 36 0	27 51 6	25 40.1	14 10.0	16 45.6	13 58.7	29 33.7	29 44.9	27 2.3	13 40.3	14 13.1
10 Su	13 11 34	19 47 48	5♍11 27	12♍36 23	25 39.4	16 11.5	17 59.9	14 44.7	29 40.8	29 42.7	27 4.1	13 38.6	14 12.6
11 M	13 15 30	20 46 39	20 5 7	27 36 45	25 38.8	18 14.1	19 14.2	15 30.6	29 47.8	29 40.5	27 6.0	13 37.0	14 12.2
12 Tu	13 19 27	21 45 29	5♎10 13	12♎44 25	25 38.4	20 17.9	20 28.6	16 16.5	29 54.6	29 38.5	27 7.9	13 35.4	14 11.8
13 W	13 23 24	22 44 16	20 18 10	27 50 19	25D 38.3	22 22.6	21 42.8	17 2.4	0♒ 1.3	29 36.5	27 9.8	13 33.7	14 11.4
14 Th	13 27 20	23 43 1	5♏19 46	12♏45 29	25 38.3	24 28.1	22 57.1	17 48.2	0 7.8	29 34.6	27 11.8	13 32.1	14 11.0
15 F	13 31 17	24 41 44	20 6 33	27 22 15	25 38.4	26 34.3	24 11.4	18 34.0	0 14.2	29 32.9	27 13.8	13 30.5	14 10.7
16 Sa	13 35 13	25 40 25	4♐31 57	11♐35 15	25R 38.4	28 41.1	25 25.6	19 19.7	0 20.4	29 31.2	27 15.9	13 28.9	14 10.4
17 Su	13 39 10	26 39 5	18 31 52	25 21 44	25 38.3	0♉48.0	26 39.9	20 5.4	0 26.5	29 29.7	27 18.0	13 27.3	14 10.1
18 M	13 43 6	27 37 43	2♑ 4 52	8♑41 28	25 38.2	2 55.1	27 54.1	20 51.0	0 32.4	29 28.2	27 20.1	13 25.7	14 9.9
19 Tu	13 47 3	28 36 19	15 11 48	21 36 15	25 38.0	5 1.8	29 8.3	21 36.6	0 38.1	29 26.8	27 22.3	13 24.1	14 9.7
20 W	13 50 59	29 34 54	27 55 14	4♒ 9 16	25D 37.9	7 8.1	0♉22.5	22 22.2	0 43.7	29 25.6	27 24.6	13 22.6	14 9.5
21 Th	13 54 56	0♉33 27	10♒18 52	16 24 35	25 38.0	9 13.5	1 36.7	23 7.7	0 49.2	29 24.4	27 26.9	13 21.0	14 9.3
22 F	13 58 53	1 31 58	22 26 59	28 26 37	25 38.3	11 17.7	2 50.8	23 53.2	0 54.4	29 23.4	27 29.2	13 19.4	14 9.2
23 Sa	14 2 49	2 30 28	4♓24 2	10♓19 45	25 38.9	13 20.4	4 5.0	24 38.6	0 59.5	29 22.4	27 31.5	13 17.9	14 9.1
24 Su	14 6 46	3 28 56	16 14 18	22 8 9	25 39.7	15 21.4	5 19.1	25 24.0	1 4.5	29 21.6	27 33.9	13 16.4	14 9.0
25 M	14 10 42	4 27 22	28 1 45	3♈55 32	25 40.6	17 20.2	6 33.2	26 9.3	1 9.2	29 20.9	27 36.4	13 14.8	14 8.9
26 Tu	14 14 39	5 25 46	9♈49 54	15 45 11	25 41.3	19 16.6	7 47.4	26 54.6	1 13.8	29 20.2	27 38.8	13 13.3	14D 8.9
27 W	14 18 35	6 24 9	21 41 45	27 39 52	25R 41.7	21 10.3	9 1.5	27 39.8	1 18.2	29 19.7	27 41.3	13 11.8	14 8.9
28 Th	14 22 32	7 22 30	3♉39 49	9♉41 50	25 41.6	23 1.1	10 15.5	28 25.0	1 22.5	29 19.3	27 43.9	13 10.3	14 8.9
29 F	14 26 28	8 20 49	15 46 10	21 53 1	25 40.9	24 48.7	11 29.6	29 10.1	1 26.6	29 19.0	27 46.5	13 8.9	14 9.0
30 Sa	14 30 25	9 19 7	28 2 33	4♊14 59	25 39.5	26 33.0	12 43.7	29 55.2	1 30.5	29 18.8	27 49.1	13 7.4	14 9.0

Astro Data Dy Hr Mn	Planet Ingress Dy Hr Mn
☽0N 2 0:38	♀ ♓ 2 9:38
♅ D 5 4:09	☿ ♓ 14 9:52
☽0S 15 11:37	☉ ♈ 20 22:48
♃⊼♅ 19 6:15	♂ ♈ 21 22:02
♂0N 24 7:24	♀ ♈ 26 11:54
☽0N 29 6:39	
♀0N 29 2:53	☿ ♈ 1 16:02
	♄ ♌ 3 3:39
☿0N 3 23:38	♃ ♒ 12 19:18
♃⊼♄ 10 4:50	☿ ♉ 16 14:55
☽0S 11 22:50	♀ ♉ 19 16:44
☽0N 25 13:02	☉ ♉ 20 10:17
♇ D 26 14:00	♂ ♉ 30 2:33

Last Aspect Dy Hr Mn	☽ Ingress Dy Hr Mn	Last Aspect Dy Hr Mn	☽ Ingress Dy Hr Mn
1 8:30 ♅ □	♈ 1 15:36	2 19:39 ♃ △	♊ 2 22:03
3 21:29 ♅ ✶	♉ 4 4:33	5 6:59 ♄ ✶	♋ 5 7:10
6 4:59 ♃ △	♊ 6 16:05	7 11:54 ♃ ☍	♌ 7 12:59
8 18:01 ♅ ☌	♋ 9 0:21	9 15:04 ♄ ☌	♍ 9 15:32
10 20:23 ♃ ☍	♌ 11 4:33	11 15:35 ♃ △	♎ 11 15:48
13 2:26 ☿ ☍	♍ 13 5:24	13 14:48 ♄ ✶	♏ 13 15:27
14 23:15 ♅ □	♎ 15 4:40	15 15:36 ♄ □	♐ 15 16:23
16 22:52 ♅ △	♏ 17 4:25	17 19:19 ♄ △	♑ 17 20:16
19 3:25 ☉ △	♐ 19 6:30	20 3:27 ☉ □	♒ 20 3:59
21 11:26 ♂ □	♑ 21 12:04	22 13:53 ♄ ☍	♓ 22 15:08
23 15:54 ♃ ☌	♒ 23 21:10	24 23:08 ♅ □	♈ 25 4:01
26 2:11 ♅ △	♓ 26 8:50	27 15:20 ♄ △	♉ 27 16:41
28 17:45 ♃ ✶	♈ 28 21:41	30 2:28 ♄ □	♊ 30 3:48
31 7:20 ♃ □	♉ 31 10:29		

☽ Phases & Eclipses Dy Hr Mn	Astro Data
8 0:42 ☽ 17♊08	1 MARCH 1949
14 19:03 ○ 23♍53	Julian Day # 17957
21 13:10 ☽ 0♑36	Delta T 28.8 sec
29 15:11 ● 8♈36	SVP 05♓58'18"
	Obliquity 23°26'54"
6 13:01 ☽ 16♋24	⚷ Chiron 8♐44.7
13 4:08 ○ 22♎54	☽ Mean ☊ 28♈18.9
13 4:11 ☍T 1.425	
20 3:27 ☽ 29♑43	1 APRIL 1949
28 8:02 ● 7♉42	Julian Day # 17988
28 7:48:23 ☌P 0.609	Delta T 28.8 sec
	SVP 05♓58'15"
	Obliquity 23°26'54"
	⚷ Chiron 8♐59.7R
	☽ Mean ☊ 26♈40.4

LONGITUDE MAY 1949

Day	Sid.Time	☉	0 hr ☽	Noon ☽	True ☊	☿	♀	♂	♃	♄	♅	♆	♇
1 Su	14 34 22	10♉17 22	10♊30 27	16♊49 8	25♈37.6	28♉13.7	13♉57.7	0♉40.3	1♒34.2	29♌18.7	27♊51.7	13♎ 6.0	14♌ 9.2
2 M	14 38 18	11 15 36	23 11 12	29 36 48	25R35.4	29 50.8	15 11.7	1 25.2	1 37.7	29D18.7	27 54.4	13R 4.6	14 9.3
3 Tu	14 42 15	12 13 48	6♋ 6 6	12♋39 14	25 33.2	1♊24.1	16 25.7	2 10.2	1 41.1	29 18.9	27 57.2	13 3.2	14 9.5
4 W	14 46 11	13 11 58	19 16 23	25 57 39	25 31.4	2 53.5	17 39.7	2 55.1	1 44.3	29 19.1	27 59.9	13 1.8	14 9.7
5 Th	14 50 8	14 10 6	2♌43 10	9♌33 0	25D30.2	4 18.8	18 53.7	3 39.9	1 47.3	29 19.4	28 2.7	13 0.4	14 9.9
6 F	14 54 4	15 8 12	16 27 14	23 25 50	25 29.8	5 40.1	20 7.7	4 24.7	1 50.1	29 19.9	28 5.5	12 59.1	14 10.1
7 Sa	14 58 1	16 6 16	0♍28 44	7♍35 49	25 30.3	6 57.2	21 21.6	5 9.4	1 52.8	29 20.4	28 8.4	12 57.8	14 10.4
8 Su	15 1 57	17 4 18	14 46 49	22 1 27	25 31.4	8 10.0	22 35.5	5 54.1	1 55.2	29 21.1	28 11.3	12 56.5	14 10.7
9 M	15 5 54	18 2 18	29 19 15	6♎39 41	25 32.8	9 18.5	23 49.4	6 38.7	1 57.5	29 21.8	28 14.2	12 55.2	14 11.0
10 Tu	15 9 51	19 0 16	14♎ 2 8	21 25 50	25R33.8	10 22.7	25 3.3	7 23.2	1 59.6	29 22.7	28 17.1	12 53.9	14 11.4
11 W	15 13 47	19 58 13	28 49 59	6♏13 41	25 34.1	11 22.4	26 17.2	8 7.7	2 1.5	29 23.6	28 20.1	12 52.6	14 11.8
12 Th	15 17 44	20 56 7	13♏36 4	20 56 11	25 33.3	12 17.6	27 31.0	8 52.2	2 3.2	29 24.7	28 23.1	12 51.4	14 12.2
13 F	15 21 40	21 54 1	28 13 12	5♐26 17	25 31.1	13 8.2	28 44.9	9 36.6	2 4.8	29 25.9	28 26.1	12 50.2	14 12.6
14 Sa	15 25 37	22 51 52	12♐34 42	19 37 52	25 27.8	13 54.2	29 58.7	10 20.9	2 6.1	29 27.2	28 29.1	12 49.0	14 13.1
15 Su	15 29 33	23 49 43	26 35 19	3♑26 42	25 23.7	14 35.6	1♊12.5	11 5.3	2 7.3	29 28.5	28 32.2	12 47.9	14 13.6
16 M	15 33 30	24 47 32	10♑11 50	16 50 40	25 19.4	15 12.1	2 26.3	11 49.5	2 8.3	29 30.0	28 35.3	12 46.7	14 14.1
17 Tu	15 37 26	25 45 20	23 23 19	29 49 58	25 15.5	15 43.9	3 40.1	12 33.7	2 9.1	29 31.6	28 38.5	12 45.6	14 14.6
18 W	15 41 23	26 43 7	6♒10 56	12♒26 38	25 12.5	16 10.9	4 53.9	13 17.8	2 9.7	29 33.3	28 41.6	12 44.5	14 15.2
19 Th	15 45 20	27 40 52	18 37 33	24 44 13	25D10.8	16 33.0	6 7.6	14 1.9	2 10.1	29 35.1	28 44.8	12 43.5	14 15.8
20 F	15 49 16	28 38 36	0♓47 12	6♓47 7	25 10.4	16 50.2	7 21.4	14 46.0	2R10.3	29 37.0	28 48.0	12 42.4	14 16.4
21 Sa	15 53 13	29 36 20	12 44 35	18 40 15	25 11.1	17 2.6	8 35.1	15 30.0	2 10.3	29 39.0	28 51.2	12 41.4	14 17.1
22 Su	15 57 9	0♊34 2	24 34 44	0♈28 38	25 12.7	17 10.2	9 48.9	16 13.9	2 10.2	29 41.1	28 54.5	12 40.4	14 17.8
23 M	16 1 6	1 31 43	6♈22 34	12 17 4	25 14.4	17R12.9	11 2.6	16 57.8	2 9.8	29 43.3	28 57.7	12 39.4	14 18.5
24 Tu	16 5 2	2 29 23	18 12 42	24 9 56	25R15.6	17 11.1	12 16.3	17 41.6	2 9.3	29 45.5	29 1.0	12 38.5	14 19.2
25 W	16 8 59	3 27 2	0♉ 9 14	6♉10 59	25 15.7	17 4.7	13 30.0	18 25.4	2 8.5	29 47.9	29 4.3	12 37.6	14 19.9
26 Th	16 12 55	4 24 40	12 15 32	18 23 12	25 14.2	16 54.0	14 43.7	19 9.1	2 7.6	29 50.4	29 7.6	12 36.7	14 20.7
27 F	16 16 52	5 22 17	24 34 10	0♊48 39	25 10.9	16 39.1	15 57.4	19 52.8	2 6.5	29 53.0	29 11.0	12 35.8	14 21.5
28 Sa	16 20 49	6 19 52	7♊ 6 45	13 28 31	25 5.8	16 20.5	17 11.0	20 36.4	2 5.2	29 55.7	29 14.3	12 35.0	14 22.3
29 Su	16 24 45	7 17 27	19 53 59	26 23 5	24 59.3	15 58.3	18 24.7	21 20.0	2 3.7	29 58.5	29 17.7	12 34.2	14 23.2
30 M	16 28 42	8 15 1	2♋55 46	9♋31 54	24 52.0	15 33.0	19 38.3	22 3.5	2 2.0	0♍ 1.3	29 21.1	12 33.4	14 24.1
31 Tu	16 32 38	9 12 33	16 11 22	22 54 0	24 44.8	15 5.1	20 52.0	22 46.9	2 0.1	0 4.3	29 24.5	12 32.7	14 25.0

LONGITUDE JUNE 1949

Day	Sid.Time	☉	0 hr ☽	Noon ☽	True ☊	☿	♀	♂	♃	♄	♅	♆	♇
1 W	16 36 35	10♊10 4	29♋39 40	6♌28 13	24♈38.4	14♊34.9	22♊ 5.6	23♉30.3	1♒58.1	0♍ 7.4	29♊28.0	12♎32.0	14♌25.9
2 Th	16 40 31	11 7 34	13♌19 29	20 13 20	24R33.5	14R 3.1	23 19.2	24 13.7	1R55.8	0 10.5	29 31.4	12R31.3	14 26.8
3 F	16 44 28	12 5 2	27 9 39	4♍ 8 19	24 30.6	13 30.2	24 32.8	24 57.0	1 53.4	0 13.8	29 34.9	12 30.6	14 27.8
4 Sa	16 48 25	13 2 30	11♍ 9 12	18 12 12	24D29.6	12 56.7	25 46.3	25 40.2	1 50.8	0 17.1	29 38.3	12 30.0	14 28.8
5 Su	16 52 21	13 59 55	25 17 9	2♎23 55	24 30.0	12 23.2	26 59.9	26 23.3	1 48.0	0 20.5	29 41.8	12 29.4	14 29.8
6 M	16 56 18	14 57 20	9♎32 16	16 41 57	24 31.0	11 50.2	28 13.4	27 6.4	1 45.1	0 24.0	29 45.3	12 28.8	14 30.9
7 Tu	17 0 14	15 54 44	23 52 40	1♏ 4 2	24R31.6	11 18.5	29 27.0	27 49.5	1 41.9	0 27.6	29 48.8	12 28.2	14 31.9
8 W	17 4 11	16 52 6	8♏15 35	15 26 49	24 30.8	10 48.4	0♋40.5	28 32.5	1 38.6	0 31.3	29 52.3	12 27.7	14 33.0
9 Th	17 8 7	17 49 27	22 37 10	29 46 1	24 28.0	10 20.6	1 54.0	29 15.4	1 35.1	0 35.1	29 55.9	12 27.2	14 34.1
10 F	17 12 4	18 46 48	6♐52 44	13♐56 40	24 22.9	9 55.4	3 7.4	29 58.3	1 31.4	0 39.0	29 59.4	12 26.8	14 35.2
11 Sa	17 16 0	19 44 8	20 57 12	27 53 46	24 15.6	9 33.3	4 20.9	0♊41.1	1 27.6	0 42.9	0♋ 2.9	12 26.4	14 36.4
12 Su	17 19 57	20 41 27	4♑45 53	11♑33 8	24 6.8	9 14.6	5 34.4	1 23.9	1 23.6	0 47.0	0 6.5	12 26.0	14 37.6
13 M	17 23 54	21 38 45	18 15 12	24 51 54	23 57.3	8 59.7	6 47.8	2 6.6	1 19.4	0 51.1	0 10.0	12 25.6	14 38.8
14 Tu	17 27 50	22 36 3	1♒23 10	7♒49 3	23 48.3	8 48.9	8 1.2	2 49.3	1 15.1	0 55.3	0 13.6	12 25.3	14 40.0
15 W	17 31 47	23 33 20	14 9 43	20 25 24	23 40.6	8 42.2	9 14.7	3 31.9	1 10.6	0 59.5	0 17.2	12 25.0	14 41.2
16 Th	17 35 43	24 30 37	26 36 30	2♓43 26	23 34.9	8D39.9	10 28.1	4 14.5	1 5.9	1 3.9	0 20.8	12 24.7	14 42.5
17 F	17 39 40	25 27 54	8♓46 43	14 46 55	23 31.4	8 42.2	11 41.5	4 57.0	1 1.1	1 8.3	0 24.3	12 24.5	14 43.7
18 Sa	17 43 36	26 25 10	20 44 39	26 40 33	23D29.8	8 49.0	12 54.8	5 39.4	0 56.1	1 12.9	0 27.9	12 24.3	14 45.0
19 Su	17 47 33	27 22 26	2♈35 17	8♈29 31	23 29.8	9 0.5	14 8.2	6 21.8	0 51.0	1 17.4	0 31.5	12 24.1	14 46.3
20 M	17 51 29	28 19 41	14 23 56	20 19 12	23R30.3	9 16.6	15 21.6	7 4.1	0 45.7	1 22.1	0 35.1	12 24.0	14 47.7
21 Tu	17 55 26	29 16 57	26 15 57	2♉14 48	23 30.5	9 37.3	16 34.9	7 46.4	0 40.3	1 26.9	0 38.7	12 23.9	14 49.0
22 W	17 59 23	0♋14 12	8♉16 19	14 21 2	23 29.5	10 2.7	17 48.3	8 28.7	0 34.7	1 31.7	0 42.3	12 23.8	14 50.4
23 Th	18 3 19	1 11 27	20 29 25	26 41 52	23 26.4	10 32.6	19 1.6	9 10.8	0 29.0	1 36.6	0 45.9	12D23.7	14 51.8
24 F	18 7 16	2 8 42	2♊58 41	9♊20 7	23 20.8	11 7.1	20 14.9	9 53.0	0 23.2	1 41.5	0 49.5	12 23.7	14 53.2
25 Sa	18 11 12	3 5 57	15 46 17	22 17 13	23 12.7	11 46.0	21 28.2	10 35.0	0 17.2	1 46.6	0 53.1	12 23.7	14 54.6
26 Su	18 15 9	4 3 12	28 52 51	5♋33 2	23 2.6	12 29.4	22 41.5	11 17.0	0 11.1	1 51.7	0 56.6	12 23.8	14 56.0
27 M	18 19 5	5 0 26	12♋17 31	19 5 56	22 51.4	13 17.1	23 54.8	11 59.0	0 4.9	1 56.9	1 0.2	12 23.9	14 57.5
28 Tu	18 23 2	5 57 41	25 57 55	2♌53 0	22 40.1	14 9.1	25 8.1	12 40.9	29♑58.5	2 2.2	1 3.8	12 24.0	14 59.0
29 W	18 26 58	6 54 55	9♌50 43	16 50 35	22 30.0	15 5.2	26 21.3	13 22.7	29 52.1	2 7.5	1 7.4	12 24.2	15 0.4
30 Th	18 30 55	7 52 8	23 52 9	0♍54 57	22 21.9	16 5.6	27 34.6	14 4.5	29 45.5	2 12.9	1 11.0	12 24.3	15 1.9

Astro Data Dy Hr Mn	Planet Ingress Dy Hr Mn	Last Aspect Dy Hr Mn	☽ Ingress Dy Hr Mn	Last Aspect Dy Hr Mn	☽ Ingress Dy Hr Mn	☽ Phases & Eclipses Dy Hr Mn	Astro Data
♄ D 1 8:34	☿ ♊ 2 2:19	2 11:26 ♄ ⚹	♋ 2 12:43	31 12:28 ♂ ⚹	♌ 1 0:36	5 21:33 ☽ 15♌02	1 MAY 1949
☽0S 9 8:18	♀ ♊ 14 0:25	3 20:48 ♀ ⚹	♌ 4 19:11	3 4:11 ♅ ⚹	♍ 3 4:53	12 12:51 ○ 21♏27	Julian Day # 18018
♃ R 20 15:34	☉ ♊ 21 9:51	6 22:04 ♄ ☌	♍ 6 23:11	5 7:29 ♅ □	♎ 5 7:58	19 19:22 ☽ 28♒27	Delta T 28.9 sec
☽0N 22 19:48	♄ ♍ 29 12:58	8 22:13 ♅ □	♎ 9 1:07	7 10:10 ♀ △	♏ 7 10:13	27 22:24 ● 6♊16	SVP 05♓58'11"
☿ R 23 2:16		11 0:55 ♄ ⚹	♏ 11 1:54	9 11:44 ♂ ☍	♐ 9 12:24		Obliquity 23°26'53"
♅∠♇ 31 4:07	♀ ♋ 7 10:47	13 2:01 ♄ □	♐ 13 2:57	10 21:45 ☉ ☍	♑ 11 15:40	4 3:27 ☽ 13♍11	⚷ Chiron 7♐46.7R
	♂ ♊ 10 0:57	15 5:02 ♄ △	♑ 15 5:57	12 13:34 ♆ □	♒ 13 21:26	10 21:45 ○ 19♐39	☽ Mean ☊ 25♈05.0
☽0S 5 14:56	♅ ♋ 10 4:08	17 4:44 ☉ △	♒ 17 12:19	15 19:34 ☉ △	♓ 16 6:38	18 12:29 ☽ 26♓55	
♃⚻♄ 16 5:15	☉ ♋ 21 18:03	19 21:40 ♄ ☍	♓ 19 22:26	18 12:29 ☉ □	♈ 18 18:45	26 10:02 ● 4♋27	1 JUNE 1949
☿ D 16 0:08	♃ ♑ 27 18:30	22 8:51 ♅ □	♈ 22 11:02	21 6:35 ☉ ⚹	♉ 21 7:30		Julian Day # 18049
☽0N 19 2:46		24 23:17 ♄ △	♉ 24 23:42	22 20:50 ♀ ⚹	♊ 23 18:20		Delta T 28.9 sec
♃⚻♅ 21 4:12		27 10:16 ♄ □	♊ 27 10:27	24 22:24 ♇ ⚹	♋ 26 2:01		SVP 05♓58'05"
♆ D 23 20:46		29 17:26 ♅ ☌	♋ 29 18:39	28 6:55 ♃ ☍	♌ 28 7:01		Obliquity 23°26'53"
				29 9:40 ☿ ⚹	♍ 30 10:27		⚷ Chiron 5♐39.4R
							☽ Mean ☊ 23♈26.6

JULY 1949 LONGITUDE

Day	Sid.Time	☉	0 hr ☽	Noon ☽	True ☊	☿	♀	♂	♃	♄	♅	♆	♇
1 F	18 34 52	8♋49 21	7♍58 38	15♍ 2 49	22♈16.5	17♊10.0	28♋47.8	14♊46.2	29♑38.8	2♍18.3	1♋14.6	12♎24.6	15♌ 3.5
2 Sa	18 38 48	9 46 34	22 7 15	29 11 41	22R 13.6	18 18.6	0♌ 1.0	15 27.9	29R 32.0	2 23.8	1 18.1	12 24.8	15 5.0
3 Su	18 42 45	10 43 46	6♎15 58	13♎19 55	22D 12.7	19 31.1	1 14.2	16 9.5	29 25.2	2 29.4	1 21.7	12 25.1	15 6.5
4 M	18 46 41	11 40 58	20 23 26	27 26 24	22R 12.7	20 47.5	2 27.3	16 51.1	29 18.2	2 35.1	1 25.2	12 25.4	15 8.1
5 Tu	18 50 38	12 38 9	4♏28 42	11♏30 11	22 12.4	22 7.8	3 40.5	17 32.6	29 11.2	2 40.8	1 28.8	12 25.7	15 9.7
6 W	18 54 34	13 35 21	18 30 41	25 30 1	22 10.5	23 32.0	4 53.6	18 14.0	29 4.0	2 46.6	1 32.3	12 26.1	15 11.3
7 Th	18 58 31	14 32 32	2♐27 54	9♐24 3	22 6.2	25 0.0	6 6.7	18 55.4	28 56.8	2 52.4	1 35.9	12 26.5	15 12.9
8 F	19 2 27	15 29 43	16 18 9	23 9 50	21 59.1	26 31.7	7 19.8	19 36.7	28 49.5	2 58.3	1 39.4	12 27.0	15 14.5
9 Sa	19 6 24	16 26 54	29 58 45	6♑44 30	21 49.4	28 7.1	8 32.9	20 18.0	28 42.2	3 4.2	1 42.9	12 27.4	15 16.1
10 Su	19 10 21	17 24 6	13♑26 45	20 5 12	21 37.8	29 46.0	9 46.0	20 59.2	28 34.8	3 10.2	1 46.4	12 27.9	15 17.8
11 M	19 14 17	18 21 17	26 39 35	3♒ 9 43	21 25.4	1♋28.4	10 59.0	21 40.4	28 27.3	3 16.3	1 49.9	12 28.5	15 19.4
12 Tu	19 18 14	19 18 29	9♒35 28	15 56 50	21 13.3	3 14.1	12 12.0	22 21.5	28 19.8	3 22.4	1 53.4	12 29.0	15 21.1
13 W	19 22 10	20 15 40	22 13 53	28 26 45	21 2.7	5 3.0	13 25.0	23 2.5	28 12.2	3 28.6	1 56.8	12 29.6	15 22.7
14 Th	19 26 7	21 12 53	4♓35 40	10♓40 59	20 54.2	6 54.9	14 38.0	23 43.5	28 4.6	3 34.8	2 0.3	12 30.3	15 24.4
15 F	19 30 3	22 10 5	16 43 4	22 42 25	20 48.4	8 49.7	15 51.0	24 24.4	27 56.9	3 41.1	2 3.7	12 30.9	15 26.1
16 Sa	19 34 0	23 7 19	28 39 33	4♈35 1	20 45.1	10 47.0	17 3.9	25 5.3	27 49.3	3 47.4	2 7.1	12 31.6	15 27.8
17 Su	19 37 57	24 4 33	10♈29 28	16 23 32	20D 43.8	12 46.6	18 16.8	25 46.2	27 41.6	3 53.8	2 10.5	12 32.3	15 29.5
18 M	19 41 53	25 1 47	22 17 54	28 13 15	20R 43.6	14 48.3	19 29.7	26 26.9	27 33.8	4 0.2	2 13.9	12 33.1	15 31.3
19 Tu	19 45 50	25 59 2	4♉10 16	10♉ 9 38	20 43.5	16 51.8	20 42.6	27 7.7	27 26.1	4 6.7	2 17.3	12 33.9	15 33.0
20 W	19 49 46	26 56 18	16 12 0	22 18 1	20 42.4	18 56.7	21 55.5	27 48.3	27 18.3	4 13.2	2 20.6	12 34.7	15 34.7
21 Th	19 53 43	27 53 35	28 28 15	4♊43 13	20 39.4	21 2.7	23 8.3	28 29.0	27 10.6	4 19.8	2 24.0	12 35.5	15 36.5
22 F	19 57 39	28 50 53	11♊ 3 22	17 29 3	20 34.0	23 9.5	24 21.2	29 9.5	27 2.8	4 26.4	2 27.3	12 36.4	15 38.3
23 Sa	20 1 36	29 48 11	24 0 29	0♋37 48	20 26.0	25 16.8	25 34.0	29 50.0	26 55.1	4 33.0	2 30.6	12 37.3	15 40.0
24 Su	20 5 32	0♌45 31	7♋21 0	14 9 53	20 15.9	27 24.3	26 46.8	0♋30.5	26 47.3	4 39.7	2 33.9	12 38.2	15 41.8
25 M	20 9 29	1 42 51	21 4 11	28 3 26	20 4.6	29 31.7	27 59.6	1 10.9	26 39.6	4 46.5	2 37.1	12 39.2	15 43.6
26 Tu	20 13 26	2 40 11	5♌ 7 7	12♌14 32	19 53.1	1♌38.8	29 12.3	1 51.3	26 31.9	4 53.3	2 40.4	12 40.2	15 45.4
27 W	20 17 22	3 37 33	19 24 59	26 37 39	19 42.8	3 45.3	0♍25.1	2 31.5	26 24.3	5 0.1	2 43.6	12 41.2	15 47.2
28 Th	20 21 19	4 34 55	3♍51 47	11♍ 6 36	19 34.5	5 51.1	1 37.8	3 11.8	26 16.6	5 7.0	2 46.8	12 42.3	15 49.0
29 F	20 25 15	5 32 17	18 21 23	25 35 29	19 28.9	7 55.8	2 50.5	3 51.9	26 9.0	5 13.9	2 49.9	12 43.3	15 50.8
30 Sa	20 29 12	6 29 40	2♎48 22	9♎59 35	19 26.0	9 59.5	4 3.1	4 32.1	26 1.5	5 20.8	2 53.1	12 44.5	15 52.6
31 Su	20 33 8	7 27 3	17 8 46	24 15 39	19D 25.1	12 2.0	5 15.8	5 12.1	25 54.0	5 27.8	2 56.2	12 45.6	15 54.4

AUGUST 1949 LONGITUDE

Day	Sid.Time	☉	0 hr ☽	Noon ☽	True ☊	☿	♀	♂	♃	♄	♅	♆	♇
1 M	20 37 5	8♌24 27	1♏20 4	8♏21 54	19♈25.3	14♌ 3.2	6♍28.4	5♋52.1	25♑46.6	5♍34.8	2♋59.3	12♎46.8	15♌56.2
2 Tu	20 41 1	9 21 52	15 21 5	22 17 35	19R 25.2	16 2.9	7 41.0	6 32.0	25R 39.2	5 41.8	3 2.3	12 47.9	15 58.0
3 W	20 44 58	10 19 17	29 11 25	6♐ 2 33	19 23.9	18 1.3	8 53.5	7 11.9	25 32.0	5 48.9	3 5.4	12 49.2	15 59.8
4 Th	20 48 55	11 16 43	12♐50 59	19 36 41	19 20.3	19 58.1	10 6.0	7 51.8	25 24.7	5 56.0	3 8.4	12 50.4	16 1.7
5 F	20 52 51	12 14 10	26 19 37	2♑59 41	19 14.2	21 53.4	11 18.5	8 31.5	25 17.6	6 3.1	3 11.4	12 51.7	16 3.5
6 Sa	20 56 48	13 11 38	9♑36 51	16 10 58	19 5.8	23 47.2	12 31.0	9 11.2	25 10.6	6 10.3	3 14.4	12 53.0	16 5.3
7 Su	21 0 44	14 9 6	22 41 58	29 9 45	18 55.5	25 39.4	13 43.4	9 50.9	25 3.6	6 17.5	3 17.3	12 54.3	16 7.1
8 M	21 4 41	15 6 35	5♒34 12	11♒55 17	18 44.5	27 30.1	14 55.8	10 30.5	24 56.7	6 24.7	3 20.2	12 55.7	16 9.0
9 Tu	21 8 37	16 4 5	18 12 58	24 27 16	18 33.8	29 19.2	16 8.2	11 10.1	24 50.0	6 32.0	3 23.1	12 57.1	16 10.8
10 W	21 12 34	17 1 37	0♓38 15	6♓46 2	18 24.3	1♍ 6.7	17 20.5	11 49.5	24 43.3	6 39.2	3 25.9	12 58.5	16 12.6
11 Th	21 16 30	17 59 9	12 50 47	18 52 46	18 16.8	2 52.8	18 32.8	12 29.0	24 36.7	6 46.5	3 28.7	12 59.9	16 14.5
12 F	21 20 27	18 56 43	24 52 15	0♈49 37	18 11.7	4 37.3	19 45.1	13 8.4	24 30.3	6 53.9	3 31.5	13 1.4	16 16.3
13 Sa	21 24 24	19 54 18	6♈45 15	12 39 39	18D 9.0	6 20.2	20 57.3	13 47.7	24 23.9	7 1.2	3 34.2	13 2.8	16 18.1
14 Su	21 28 20	20 51 54	18 33 19	24 26 49	18 8.3	8 1.7	22 9.5	14 27.0	24 17.7	7 8.6	3 36.9	13 4.3	16 19.9
15 M	21 32 17	21 49 32	0♉20 43	6♉15 41	18 8.8	9 41.7	23 21.7	15 6.2	24 11.6	7 15.9	3 39.6	13 5.9	16 21.8
16 Tu	21 36 13	22 47 11	12 12 20	18 11 21	18R 9.8	11 20.3	24 33.8	15 45.3	24 5.7	7 23.3	3 42.2	13 7.4	16 23.6
17 W	21 40 10	23 44 52	24 13 23	0♊19 6	18 10.3	12 57.3	25 45.9	16 24.5	23 59.8	7 30.8	3 44.9	13 9.0	16 25.4
18 Th	21 44 6	24 42 35	6♊29 8	12 44 5	18 9.5	14 32.9	26 58.0	17 3.5	23 54.1	7 38.2	3 47.4	13 10.6	16 27.2
19 F	21 48 3	25 40 19	19 4 30	25 30 50	18 6.8	16 7.0	28 10.1	17 42.5	23 48.6	7 45.7	3 50.0	13 12.2	16 29.0
20 Sa	21 51 59	26 38 5	2♋ 3 29	8♋42 42	18 2.2	17 39.7	29 22.1	18 21.5	23 43.2	7 53.1	3 52.5	13 13.9	16 30.9
21 Su	21 55 56	27 35 53	15 28 38	22 21 15	17 55.9	19 11.0	0♎34.1	19 0.4	23 37.9	8 0.6	3 54.9	13 15.5	16 32.7
22 M	21 59 53	28 33 42	29 20 22	6♌25 37	17 48.3	20 40.7	1 46.0	19 39.2	23 32.8	8 8.1	3 57.4	13 17.2	16 34.5
23 Tu	22 3 49	29 31 32	13♌36 30	20 52 18	17 40.6	22 9.0	2 57.9	20 18.0	23 27.8	8 15.6	3 59.8	13 18.9	16 36.3
24 W	22 7 46	0♍29 25	28 12 14	5♍35 20	17 33.5	23 35.8	4 9.8	20 56.7	23 23.0	8 23.2	4 2.1	13 20.7	16 38.1
25 Th	22 11 42	1 27 18	13♍ 0 37	20 27 2	17 28.0	25 1.1	5 21.7	21 35.3	23 18.3	8 30.7	4 4.4	13 22.4	16 39.8
26 F	22 15 39	2 25 13	27 53 34	5♎19 16	17 24.5	26 24.9	6 33.5	22 13.9	23 13.9	8 38.2	4 6.7	13 24.2	16 41.6
27 Sa	22 19 35	3 23 9	12♎43 13	20 4 40	17D 23.0	27 47.2	7 45.2	22 52.5	23 9.5	8 45.8	4 8.9	13 26.0	16 43.4
28 Su	22 23 32	4 21 7	27 22 56	4♏37 32	17 23.2	29 7.8	8 57.0	23 30.9	23 5.4	8 53.3	4 11.1	13 27.8	16 45.2
29 M	22 27 28	5 19 6	11♏48 3	18 54 14	17 24.4	0♎26.8	10 8.7	24 9.3	23 1.4	9 0.9	4 13.3	13 29.6	16 46.9
30 Tu	22 31 25	6 17 7	25 55 56	2♐53 5	17R 25.6	1 44.2	11 20.3	24 47.7	22 57.6	9 8.5	4 15.4	13 31.5	16 48.7
31 W	22 35 22	7 15 8	9♐45 43	16 33 53	17 25.9	2 59.8	12 31.9	25 26.0	22 54.0	9 16.0	4 17.4	13 33.4	16 50.4

Astro Data Dy Hr Mn	Planet Ingress Dy Hr Mn	Last Aspect Dy Hr Mn	☽ Ingress Dy Hr Mn	Last Aspect Dy Hr Mn	☽ Ingress Dy Hr Mn	☽ Phases & Eclipses Dy Hr Mn	Astro Data
☽0S 2 19:39	♀ ♌ 1 23:40	2 12:29 ♃ △	♎ 2 13:22	2 17:41 ♃ ✶	♐ 3 1:25	3 8:08 ☽ 11♎03	1 JULY 1949
☽0N 16 9:44	☿ ♋ 10 3:19	4 15:03 ♃ □	♏ 4 16:22	4 14:45 ☿ △	♑ 5 6:36	10 7:41 ○ 17♑42	Julian Day # 18079
☽0S 30 0:45	☉ ♌ 23 4:57	6 17:59 ♃ ✶	♐ 6 19:45	7 4:20 ♃ ☌	♒ 7 13:34	18 6:02 ☽ 25♈16	Delta T 28.9 sec
	♂ ♋ 23 5:54	8 20:16 ☿ ☍	♑ 9 0:02	8 20:06 ♇ ☍	♓ 9 22:45	25 19:33 ● 2♌30	SVP 05♓58'00"
☽0N 12 16:33	☿ ♌ 25 5:20	11 3:16 ♃ ☌	♒ 11 6:09	11 23:16 ♃ ✶	♈ 12 10:20		Obliquity 23°26'53"
♀0S 22 0:32	♀ ♍ 26 15:43	13 1:39 ♂ △	♓ 13 15:01	14 11:35 ♃ □	♉ 14 23:18	1 12:57 ☽ 8♏55	⚷ Chiron 3♐45.3R
♃⚼♄ 23 23:39		15 22:19 ♃ ✶	♈ 16 2:43	17 3:23 ♀ △	♊ 17 11:23	8 19:33 ○ 15♒53	☽ Mean ☊ 21♈51.3
☽0S 26 8:12	☿ ♍ 9 9:04	18 10:33 ♃ □	♉ 18 15:36	19 18:36 ♀ □	♋ 19 20:15	16 22:59 ☽ 23♉42	1 AUGUST 1949
☿0S 27 7:37	♀ ♎ 20 12:39	20 22:47 ☉ ✶	♊ 21 2:57	21 14:07 ♃ ☍	♌ 22 1:08	24 3:59 ● 0♍39	Julian Day # 18110
	☉ ♍ 23 11:48	23 3:08 ♀ ✶	♋ 23 10:52	23 4:58 ♇ ☌	♍ 24 2:56	30 19:16 ☽ 7♐04	Delta T 29.0 sec
	☿ ♎ 28 15:48	25 9:31 ♃ ☍	♌ 25 15:19	25 21:22 ☿ ☌	♎ 26 3:24		SVP 05♓57'55"
		26 17:55 ♇ ☌	♍ 27 17:36	27 17:21 ♂ □	♏ 28 4:19		Obliquity 23°26'54"
		29 12:49 ♃ △	♎ 29 19:20	29 21:57 ♂ △	♐ 30 7:00		⚷ Chiron 2♐52.0R
		31 14:39 ♃ □	♏ 31 21:44				☽ Mean ☊ 20♈12.8

LONGITUDE SEPTEMBER 1949

Day	Sid.Time	☉	0 hr ☽	Noon ☽	True ☊	☿	♀	♂	♃	♄	♅	♆	♇
1 Th	22 39 18	8♍13 11	23♐17 44	29♐57 24	17♈24.8	4♎13.6	13♎43.5	26♋ 4.2	22♑50.5	9♍23.6	4♋19.5	13♎35.2	16♌52.2
2 F	22 43 15	9 11 16	6♑33 3	13♑ 4 52	17R 22.1	5 25.6	14 55.0	26 42.4	22R 47.2	9 31.2	4 21.4	13 37.2	16 53.9
3 Sa	22 47 11	10 9 22	19 33 0	25 57 38	17 17.7	6 35.6	16 6.5	27 20.5	22 44.2	9 38.8	4 23.4	13 39.1	16 55.6
4 Su	22 51 8	11 7 29	2♒18 56	8♒37 1	17 12.2	7 43.6	17 17.9	27 58.6	22 41.2	9 46.3	4 25.3	13 41.0	16 57.3
5 M	22 55 4	12 5 38	14 52 4	21 4 13	17 6.0	8 49.5	18 29.2	28 36.5	22 38.5	9 53.9	4 27.1	13 43.0	16 59.0
6 Tu	22 59 1	13 3 48	27 13 36	3♓20 23	17 0.1	9 53.1	19 40.5	29 14.5	22 36.0	10 1.5	4 28.9	13 44.9	17 0.7
7 W	23 2 57	14 2 0	9♓24 42	15 26 45	16 54.9	10 54.3	20 51.8	29 52.3	22 33.6	10 9.0	4 30.7	13 46.9	17 2.3
8 Th	23 6 54	15 0 14	21 26 43	27 24 49	16 50.9	11 53.0	22 3.0	0♌30.2	22 31.4	10 16.6	4 32.4	13 48.9	17 4.0
9 F	23 10 51	15 58 30	3♈21 19	9♈16 30	16 48.5	12 49.0	23 14.2	1 7.9	22 29.5	10 24.1	4 34.1	13 50.9	17 5.7
10 Sa	23 14 47	16 56 47	15 10 40	21 4 11	16D 47.6	13 42.1	24 25.3	1 45.6	22 27.7	10 31.7	4 35.7	13 52.9	17 7.3
11 Su	23 18 44	17 55 6	26 57 26	2♉50 52	16 48.0	14 32.2	25 36.3	2 23.2	22 26.1	10 39.2	4 37.2	13 55.0	17 8.9
12 M	23 22 40	18 53 28	8♉44 55	14 40 7	16 49.4	15 19.1	26 47.4	3 0.8	22 24.7	10 46.7	4 38.8	13 57.0	17 10.5
13 Tu	23 26 37	19 51 51	20 36 58	26 36 2	16 51.1	16 2.4	27 58.3	3 38.3	22 23.4	10 54.3	4 40.3	13 59.1	17 12.1
14 W	23 30 33	20 50 17	2♊37 54	8♊43 8	16 52.8	16 41.9	29 9.2	4 15.7	22 22.4	11 1.8	4 41.7	14 1.2	17 13.7
15 Th	23 34 30	21 48 44	14 52 21	21 6 7	16R 53.8	17 17.4	0♏20.1	4 53.1	22 21.6	11 9.3	4 43.1	14 3.3	17 15.3
16 F	23 38 26	22 47 14	27 24 59	3♋49 30	16 53.9	17 48.6	1 30.9	5 30.5	22 20.9	11 16.7	4 44.4	14 5.4	17 16.8
17 Sa	23 42 23	23 45 46	10♋20 6	16 57 12	16 53.0	18 15.1	2 41.6	6 7.7	22 20.5	11 24.2	4 45.7	14 7.5	17 18.4
18 Su	23 46 20	24 44 21	23 41 4	0♌31 53	16 51.1	18 36.5	3 52.3	6 44.9	22D 20.3	11 31.7	4 46.9	14 9.6	17 19.9
19 M	23 50 16	25 42 57	7♌29 40	14 34 17	16 48.5	18 52.6	5 2.9	7 22.1	22 20.2	11 39.1	4 48.1	14 11.8	17 21.4
20 Tu	23 54 13	26 41 36	21 45 26	29 2 37	16 45.7	19 2.9	6 13.5	7 59.1	22 20.3	11 46.5	4 49.3	14 13.9	17 22.9
21 W	23 58 9	27 40 16	6♍25 10	13♍52 15	16 43.1	19R 7.1	7 24.1	8 36.1	22 20.7	11 53.9	4 50.3	14 16.1	17 24.4
22 Th	0 2 6	28 38 59	21 22 53	28 55 59	16 41.2	19 4.9	8 34.5	9 13.1	22 21.2	12 1.3	4 51.4	14 18.2	17 25.8
23 F	0 6 2	29 37 43	6♎30 24	14♎ 4 56	16D 40.1	18 55.8	9 44.9	9 49.9	22 21.9	12 8.7	4 52.3	14 20.4	17 27.3
24 Sa	0 9 59	0♎36 30	21 38 26	29 9 46	16 40.0	18 39.7	10 55.3	10 26.7	22 22.8	12 16.0	4 53.3	14 22.6	17 28.7
25 Su	0 13 55	1 35 19	6♏37 57	14♏ 2 7	16 40.6	18 16.3	12 5.6	11 3.5	22 24.0	12 23.3	4 54.2	14 24.8	17 30.1
26 M	0 17 52	2 34 9	21 21 33	28 35 40	16 41.6	17 45.5	13 15.8	11 40.1	22 25.3	12 30.6	4 55.0	14 27.0	17 31.5
27 Tu	0 21 48	3 33 1	5♐44 4	12♐46 32	16 42.6	17 7.4	14 25.9	12 16.7	22 26.8	12 37.9	4 55.8	14 29.2	17 32.9
28 W	0 25 45	4 31 55	19 42 55	26 33 17	16 43.4	16 22.2	15 36.0	12 53.2	22 28.5	12 45.1	4 56.5	14 31.4	17 34.2
29 Th	0 29 42	5 30 51	3♑17 42	9♑56 26	16R 43.8	15 30.3	16 46.0	13 29.7	22 30.4	12 52.3	4 57.2	14 33.6	17 35.6
30 F	0 33 38	6 29 48	16 29 43	22 57 53	16 43.6	14 32.6	17 55.9	14 6.0	22 32.5	12 59.5	4 57.8	14 35.8	17 36.9

LONGITUDE OCTOBER 1949

Day	Sid.Time	☉	0 hr ☽	Noon ☽	True ☊	☿	♀	♂	♃	♄	♅	♆	♇
1 Sa	0 37 35	7♎28 47	29♑21 19	5♒40 22	16♈43.0	13♎29.8	19♏ 5.7	14♌42.3	22♑34.7	13♍ 6.6	4♋58.3	14♎38.0	17♌38.2
2 Su	0 41 31	8 27 48	11♒55 25	18 6 53	16R 42.1	12R 23.4	20 15.5	15 18.6	22 37.2	13 13.7	4 58.9	14 40.2	17 39.5
3 M	0 45 28	9 26 50	24 15 7	0♓20 29	16 41.1	11 14.7	21 25.2	15 54.7	22 39.9	13 20.8	4 59.3	14 42.5	17 40.7
4 Tu	0 49 24	10 25 55	6♓23 21	12 24 3	16 40.2	10 5.5	22 34.8	16 30.8	22 42.7	13 27.9	4 59.7	14 44.7	17 42.0
5 W	0 53 21	11 25 1	18 22 53	24 20 10	16 39.4	8 57.6	23 44.3	17 6.8	22 45.7	13 34.9	5 0.1	14 46.9	17 43.2
6 Th	0 57 17	12 24 9	0♈16 11	6♈11 14	16 39.0	7 52.9	24 53.7	17 42.7	22 48.9	13 41.8	5 0.4	14 49.1	17 44.4
7 F	1 1 14	13 23 19	12 5 34	17 59 28	16D 38.8	6 53.2	26 3.0	18 18.6	22 52.3	13 48.8	5 0.6	14 51.4	17 45.5
8 Sa	1 5 11	14 22 31	23 53 13	29 47 4	16 38.8	6 0.3	27 12.2	18 54.3	22 55.9	13 55.7	5 0.8	14 53.6	17 46.7
9 Su	1 9 7	15 21 46	5♉41 20	11♉36 19	16 38.9	5 15.5	28 21.4	19 30.0	22 59.7	14 2.5	5 1.0	14 55.8	17 47.8
10 M	1 13 4	16 21 2	17 32 21	23 29 45	16R 39.0	4 40.0	29 30.4	20 5.7	23 3.6	14 9.4	5 1.1	14 58.1	17 48.9
11 Tu	1 17 0	17 20 21	29 28 53	5♊30 8	16 39.0	4 14.8	0♐39.3	20 41.2	23 7.7	14 16.1	5R 1.1	15 0.3	17 50.0
12 W	1 20 57	18 19 42	11♊33 56	17 40 40	16 38.8	4D 0.3	1 48.2	21 16.7	23 12.0	14 22.9	5 1.1	15 2.6	17 51.0
13 Th	1 24 53	19 19 5	23 50 49	0♋ 4 48	16 38.6	3 56.8	2 56.9	21 52.1	23 16.5	14 29.6	5 1.0	15 4.8	17 52.1
14 F	1 28 50	20 18 31	6♋23 5	12 46 8	16 38.3	4 4.1	4 5.5	22 27.4	23 21.2	14 36.2	5 0.9	15 7.0	17 53.1
15 Sa	1 32 46	21 17 59	19 14 22	25 48 10	16D 38.2	4 22.0	5 14.1	23 2.6	23 26.0	14 42.8	5 0.7	15 9.2	17 54.1
16 Su	1 36 43	22 17 29	2♌27 55	9♌13 53	16 38.3	4 50.1	6 22.5	23 37.8	23 31.0	14 49.4	5 0.5	15 11.5	17 55.0
17 M	1 40 40	23 17 1	16 6 16	23 5 9	16 38.6	5 27.5	7 30.8	24 12.9	23 36.2	14 55.9	5 0.2	15 13.7	17 56.0
18 Tu	1 44 36	24 16 36	0♍10 29	7♍22 6	16 39.3	6 13.7	8 39.0	24 47.9	23 41.5	15 2.4	4 59.9	15 15.9	17 56.9
19 W	1 48 33	25 16 13	14 39 38	22 2 33	16 40.0	7 7.7	9 47.1	25 22.8	23 47.1	15 8.8	4 59.5	15 18.1	17 57.8
20 Th	1 52 29	26 15 52	29 30 10	7♎ 1 38	16 40.6	8 8.9	10 55.0	25 57.6	23 52.7	15 15.1	4 59.0	15 20.3	17 58.6
21 F	1 56 26	27 15 33	14♎35 55	22 11 55	16R 40.9	9 16.3	12 2.8	26 32.3	23 58.6	15 21.4	4 58.6	15 22.5	17 59.5
22 Sa	2 0 22	28 15 17	29 48 25	7♏24 11	16 40.7	10 29.2	13 10.5	27 6.9	24 4.6	15 27.7	4 58.0	15 24.7	18 0.3
23 Su	2 4 19	29 15 2	14♏58 0	22 28 43	16 39.9	11 46.8	14 18.1	27 41.4	24 10.8	15 33.9	4 57.4	15 26.9	18 1.1
24 M	2 8 15	0♏14 50	29 55 16	7♐16 45	16 38.4	13 8.6	15 25.5	28 15.9	24 17.1	15 40.0	4 56.8	15 29.1	18 1.8
25 Tu	2 12 12	1 14 39	14♐32 25	21 41 43	16 36.6	14 33.7	16 32.8	28 50.2	24 23.7	15 46.1	4 56.1	15 31.3	18 2.6
26 W	2 16 9	2 14 30	28 44 16	5♑39 52	16 34.7	16 1.8	17 40.0	29 24.5	24 30.3	15 52.1	4 55.3	15 33.5	18 3.3
27 Th	2 20 5	3 14 23	12♑28 30	19 10 17	16 33.1	17 32.2	18 47.0	29 58.6	24 37.2	15 58.1	4 54.5	15 35.6	18 4.0
28 F	2 24 2	4 14 17	25 45 27	2♒14 21	16D 32.1	19 4.6	19 53.8	0♍32.7	24 44.1	16 4.0	4 53.7	15 37.8	18 4.6
29 Sa	2 27 58	5 14 13	8♒37 25	14 55 9	16 31.9	20 38.6	21 0.4	1 6.6	24 51.3	16 9.8	4 52.8	15 39.9	18 5.3
30 Su	2 31 55	6 14 11	21 8 3	27 16 42	16 32.6	22 13.9	22 6.9	1 40.5	24 58.6	16 15.6	4 51.8	15 42.0	18 5.9
31 M	2 35 51	7 14 10	3♓21 38	9♓23 26	16 33.9	23 50.1	23 13.2	2 14.2	25 6.0	16 21.3	4 50.8	15 44.2	18 6.4

Astro Data	Planet Ingress	Last Aspect	☽ Ingress	Last Aspect	☽ Ingress	☽ Phases & Eclipses	Astro Data
Dy Hr Mn	Dy Hr Mn	Dy Hr Mn	Dy Hr Mn	Dy Hr Mn	Dy Hr Mn	Dy Hr Mn	1 SEPTEMBER 1949
☽0N 8 23:05	♂ ♌ 7 4:51	31 12:31 ♇ △	♑ 1 12:05	30 11:15 ♃ ☌	♒ 1 1:13	7 9:59 ○ 14♓26	Julian Day # 18141
♃ D 18 18:47	♀ ♏ 14 17:12	3 15:22 ♂ ☍	♒ 3 19:37	2 17:52 ♀ □	♓ 3 11:19	15 14:29 ☽ 22♊24	Delta T 29.0 sec
☿ R 21 3:49	☉ ♎ 23 9:06	5 7:44 ♀ △	♓ 6 5:26	5 11:57 ♀ △	♈ 5 23:27	22 12:21 ● 29♍09	SVP 05♓57'50"
☽0S 22 18:17		8 2:10 ♃ ⚹	♈ 8 17:13	7 22:03 ♃ □	♉ 8 12:26	29 4:18 ☽ 5♑41	Obliquity 23°26'54"
	♀ ♐ 10 10:18	10 20:56 ♀ ☍	♉ 11 6:12	10 11:11 ♃ △	♊ 11 1:02		⚷ Chiron 3♐29.4
☽0N 6 5:21	☉ ♏ 23 18:03	13 3:34 ♃ △	♊ 13 18:47	12 19:58 ♂ ⚹	♋ 13 11:51	7 2:53 ○ 13♈30	☽ Mean ☊ 18♈34.3
♅ R 11 5:14	♂ ♍ 27 0:58	15 14:29 ☉ □	♋ 16 4:52	15 7:44 ♃ ☍	♌ 15 19:35	7 2:56 • T 1.224	
☿ D 12 19:45		18 2:00 ☉ ⚹	♌ 18 11:05	17 14:31 ♂ ☌	♍ 17 23:42	15 4:06 ☽ 21♋28	1 OCTOBER 1949
☽0S 20 5:27		19 19:27 ☿ ⚹	♍ 20 13:34	19 14:54 ♃ △	♎ 20 0:48	21 21:23 ● 28♎09	Julian Day # 18171
♄⚺♆ 21 6:30		22 12:21 ☉ ☌	♎ 22 13:42	21 21:23 ☉ ☌	♏ 22 0:18	21 21:12:30 • P 0.964	Delta T 29.0 sec
		24 1:11 ♃ □	♏ 24 13:20	23 21:13 ♂ □	♐ 24 0:08	28 17:04 ☽ 4♒57	SVP 05♓57'46"
		26 1:45 ♃ ⚹	♐ 26 14:21	26 1:12 ♂ △	♑ 26 2:10		Obliquity 23°26'54"
		27 20:16 ♇ △	♑ 28 18:07	27 22:07 ♃ ☌	♒ 28 7:50		⚷ Chiron 5♐27.6
				30 2:27 ☿ △	♓ 30 17:21		☽ Mean ☊ 16♈59.0

NOVEMBER 1949 LONGITUDE

Day	Sid.Time	☉	0 hr ☽	Noon ☽	True ☊	☿	♀	♂	♃	♄	♅	♆	♇
1 Tu	2 39 48	8♏14 10	15♓22 37	21♓19 44	16♈35.6	25♎27.1	24♐19.3	2♍47.8	25♑13.6	16♍26.9	4♋49.8	15♎46.3	18♌ 7.0
2 W	2 43 44	9 14 13	27 15 17	3♈ 9 43	16 37.2	27 4.6	25 25.2	3 21.4	25 21.3	16 32.5	4R48.7	15 48.3	18 7.5
3 Th	2 47 41	10 14 17	9♈ 3 29	14 57 0	16R38.3	28 42.5	26 30.9	3 54.8	25 29.2	16 38.0	4 47.5	15 50.4	18 8.0
4 F	2 51 38	11 14 23	20 50 37	26 44 41	16 38.4	0♏20.6	27 36.4	4 28.1	25 37.2	16 43.4	4 46.3	15 52.5	18 8.4
5 Sa	2 55 34	12 14 30	2♉39 30	8♉35 20	16 37.4	1 58.9	28 41.7	5 1.3	25 45.4	16 48.8	4 45.1	15 54.6	18 8.9
6 Su	2 59 31	13 14 40	14 32 27	20 31 5	16 34.9	3 37.2	29 46.8	5 34.4	25 53.7	16 54.1	4 43.8	15 56.6	18 9.3
7 M	3 3 27	14 14 51	26 31 26	2♊33 42	16 31.1	5 15.4	0♑51.6	6 7.4	26 2.1	16 59.3	4 42.4	15 58.6	18 9.7
8 Tu	3 7 24	15 15 4	8♊38 6	14 44 49	16 26.3	6 53.6	1 56.2	6 40.3	26 10.7	17 4.5	4 41.1	16 0.6	18 10.0
9 W	3 11 20	16 15 19	20 54 2	27 5 58	16 21.0	8 31.6	3 0.6	7 13.1	26 19.4	17 9.5	4 39.6	16 2.6	18 10.3
10 Th	3 15 17	17 15 36	3♋20 51	9♋38 54	16 15.8	10 9.4	4 4.7	7 45.7	26 28.2	17 14.5	4 38.2	16 4.6	18 10.6
11 F	3 19 13	18 15 55	16 0 21	22 25 30	16 11.3	11 47.0	5 8.6	8 18.3	26 37.2	17 19.5	4 36.7	16 6.6	18 10.9
12 Sa	3 23 10	19 16 15	28 54 34	5♌27 52	16 8.0	13 24.3	6 12.2	8 50.7	26 46.3	17 24.3	4 35.1	16 8.6	18 11.1
13 Su	3 27 7	20 16 38	12♌ 5 39	18 48 9	16D 6.2	15 1.4	7 15.5	9 23.0	26 55.6	17 29.1	4 33.5	16 10.5	18 11.3
14 M	3 31 3	21 17 3	25 35 38	2♍28 15	16 6.0	16 38.3	8 18.5	9 55.2	27 4.9	17 33.8	4 31.9	16 12.4	18 11.5
15 Tu	3 35 0	22 17 29	9♍26 7	16 29 17	16 6.9	18 14.9	9 21.2	10 27.2	27 14.4	17 38.4	4 30.2	16 14.3	18 11.7
16 W	3 38 56	23 17 57	23 37 40	0♎51 4	16 8.4	19 51.2	10 23.7	10 59.1	27 24.0	17 42.9	4 28.5	16 16.2	18 11.8
17 Th	3 42 53	24 18 28	8♎ 9 10	15 31 28	16R 9.5	21 27.2	11 25.8	11 30.9	27 33.7	17 47.3	4 26.7	16 18.1	18 11.9
18 F	3 46 49	25 19 0	22 57 20	0♏25 57	16 9.6	23 3.1	12 27.6	12 2.5	27 43.6	17 51.7	4 24.9	16 19.9	18 11.9
19 Sa	3 50 46	26 19 33	7♏56 24	15 27 38	16 7.8	24 38.6	13 29.1	12 34.0	27 53.6	17 55.9	4 23.1	16 21.7	18R12.0
20 Su	3 54 42	27 20 9	22 58 31	0♐27 54	16 4.0	26 14.0	14 30.2	13 5.4	28 3.6	18 0.1	4 21.2	16 23.5	18 12.0
21 M	3 58 39	28 20 46	7♐54 36	15 17 34	15 58.4	27 49.1	15 31.0	13 36.6	28 13.8	18 4.2	4 19.3	16 25.3	18 12.0
22 Tu	4 2 36	29 21 25	22 35 47	29 48 27	15 51.5	29 24.0	16 31.3	14 7.7	28 24.2	18 8.2	4 17.3	16 27.1	18 11.9
23 W	4 6 32	0♐22 4	6♑54 53	13♑54 36	15 44.1	0♐58.8	17 31.3	14 38.6	28 34.6	18 12.1	4 15.3	16 28.8	18 11.8
24 Th	4 10 29	1 22 46	20 47 20	27 32 58	15 37.4	2 33.3	18 30.9	15 9.4	28 45.1	18 16.0	4 13.3	16 30.5	18 11.7
25 F	4 14 25	2 23 28	4♒11 34	10♒43 22	15 32.0	4 7.7	19 30.0	15 40.0	28 55.8	18 19.7	4 11.2	16 32.2	18 11.6
26 Sa	4 18 22	3 24 11	17 8 41	23 28 1	15 28.5	5 42.0	20 28.7	16 10.4	29 6.5	18 23.3	4 9.2	16 33.9	18 11.4
27 Su	4 22 18	4 24 55	29 41 52	5♓50 52	15D 26.9	7 16.1	21 27.0	16 40.7	29 17.4	18 26.9	4 7.0	16 35.6	18 11.2
28 M	4 26 15	5 25 40	11♓55 37	17 56 48	15 27.0	8 50.1	22 24.7	17 10.8	29 28.4	18 30.3	4 4.9	16 37.2	18 11.0
29 Tu	4 30 12	6 26 27	23 55 5	29 51 9	15 28.1	10 24.0	23 22.0	17 40.8	29 39.4	18 33.7	4 2.7	16 38.8	18 10.8
30 W	4 34 8	7 27 14	5♈45 37	11♈39 8	15R29.3	11 57.8	24 18.7	18 10.6	29 50.6	18 36.9	4 0.5	16 40.4	18 10.5

DECEMBER 1949 LONGITUDE

Day	Sid.Time	☉	0 hr ☽	Noon ☽	True ☊	☿	♀	♂	♃	♄	♅	♆	♇
1 Th	4 38 5	8♐28 2	17♈32 18	23♈25 39	15♈29.7	13♐31.5	25♑14.8	18♍40.2	0♒ 1.8	18♍40.1	3♋58.3	16♎41.9	18♌10.2
2 F	4 42 1	9 28 51	29 19 44	5♉14 58	15R28.5	15 5.2	26 10.4	19 9.7	0 13.2	18 43.1	3R56.0	16 43.5	18R 9.8
3 Sa	4 45 58	10 29 41	11♉11 49	17 10 35	15 25.0	16 38.8	27 5.4	19 38.9	0 24.6	18 46.1	3 53.7	16 45.0	18 9.5
4 Su	4 49 54	11 30 32	23 11 37	29 15 8	15 19.0	18 12.4	27 59.8	20 8.0	0 36.1	18 49.0	3 51.4	16 46.4	18 9.1
5 M	4 53 51	12 31 24	5♊21 21	11♊30 22	15 10.5	19 46.0	28 53.6	20 36.9	0 47.8	18 51.7	3 49.1	16 47.9	18 8.7
6 Tu	4 57 47	13 32 18	17 42 19	23 57 14	15 0.2	21 19.5	29 46.6	21 5.7	0 59.5	18 54.4	3 46.7	16 49.3	18 8.2
7 W	5 1 44	14 33 12	0♋15 9	6♋36 2	14 48.8	22 53.1	0♒39.0	21 34.2	1 11.3	18 56.9	3 44.3	16 50.7	18 7.8
8 Th	5 5 41	15 34 8	12 59 53	19 26 39	14 37.4	24 26.6	1 30.7	22 2.6	1 23.2	18 59.4	3 41.9	16 52.1	18 7.3
9 F	5 9 37	16 35 4	25 56 21	2♌28 55	14 27.2	26 0.1	2 21.6	22 30.7	1 35.2	19 1.8	3 39.5	16 53.4	18 6.7
10 Sa	5 13 34	17 36 2	9♌ 4 24	15 42 48	14 18.9	27 33.5	3 11.8	22 58.7	1 47.2	19 4.0	3 37.1	16 54.7	18 6.2
11 Su	5 17 30	18 37 0	22 24 11	29 8 37	14 13.3	29 7.0	4 1.1	23 26.5	1 59.3	19 6.2	3 34.6	16 56.0	18 5.6
12 M	5 21 27	19 38 0	5♍56 12	12♍47 1	14 10.3	0♑40.4	4 49.6	23 54.0	2 11.6	19 8.2	3 32.1	16 57.3	18 5.0
13 Tu	5 25 23	20 39 1	19 41 10	26 38 44	14D 9.4	2 13.7	5 37.2	24 21.3	2 23.9	19 10.1	3 29.7	16 58.5	18 4.4
14 W	5 29 20	21 40 2	3♎39 46	10♎44 14	14R 9.7	3 46.9	6 24.0	24 48.4	2 36.2	19 12.0	3 27.1	16 59.7	18 3.7
15 Th	5 33 16	22 41 5	17 52 3	25 3 1	14 9.9	5 20.0	7 9.7	25 15.3	2 48.7	19 13.7	3 24.6	17 0.9	18 3.0
16 F	5 37 13	23 42 9	2♏16 51	9♏33 8	14 8.7	6 53.0	7 54.5	25 42.0	3 1.2	19 15.3	3 22.1	17 2.0	18 2.3
17 Sa	5 41 10	24 43 14	16 51 18	24 10 40	14 5.0	8 25.7	8 38.3	26 8.4	3 13.8	19 16.8	3 19.6	17 3.1	18 1.6
18 Su	5 45 6	25 44 20	1♐30 29	8♐49 52	13 58.5	9 58.0	9 21.1	26 34.6	3 26.5	19 18.2	3 17.0	17 4.2	18 0.9
19 M	5 49 3	26 45 27	16 7 52	23 23 34	13 49.1	11 30.1	10 2.7	27 0.5	3 39.2	19 19.5	3 14.5	17 5.3	18 0.1
20 Tu	5 52 59	27 46 34	0♑36 3	7♑44 26	13 37.7	13 1.6	10 43.2	27 26.2	3 52.0	19 20.7	3 11.9	17 6.3	17 59.3
21 W	5 56 56	28 47 42	14 47 58	21 46 2	13 25.5	14 32.5	11 22.4	27 51.6	4 4.9	19 21.8	3 9.3	17 7.3	17 58.5
22 Th	6 0 52	29 48 50	28 38 9	5♒24 1	13 13.7	16 2.6	12 0.5	28 16.8	4 17.8	19 22.7	3 6.7	17 8.2	17 57.6
23 F	6 4 49	0♑49 59	12♒ 3 29	18 36 33	13 3.6	17 31.9	12 37.2	28 41.6	4 30.8	19 23.6	3 4.2	17 9.1	17 56.7
24 Sa	6 8 45	1 51 7	25 3 24	1♓24 18	12 56.0	19 0.0	13 12.5	29 6.3	4 43.9	19 24.3	3 1.6	17 10.0	17 55.8
25 Su	6 12 42	2 52 16	7♓39 42	13 50 4	12 51.1	20 26.8	13 46.4	29 30.6	4 57.0	19 25.0	2 59.0	17 10.9	17 54.9
26 M	6 16 39	3 53 25	19 55 59	25 58 6	12 48.7	21 51.9	14 18.9	29 54.6	5 10.2	19 25.5	2 56.4	17 11.7	17 54.0
27 Tu	6 20 35	4 54 34	1♈57 5	7♈53 37	12 48.0	23 15.1	14 49.7	0♎18.4	5 23.4	19 25.9	2 53.8	17 12.5	17 53.0
28 W	6 24 32	5 55 42	13 48 26	19 42 14	12 48.0	24 36.0	15 19.0	0 41.9	5 36.7	19 26.2	2 51.2	17 13.3	17 52.0
29 Th	6 28 28	6 56 51	25 35 43	1♉29 33	12 47.5	25 54.1	15 46.6	1 5.0	5 50.0	19 26.4	2 48.7	17 14.0	17 51.0
30 F	6 32 25	7 58 0	7♉24 22	13 20 48	12 45.4	27 9.0	16 12.5	1 27.9	6 3.4	19R26.4	2 46.1	17 14.7	17 50.0
31 Sa	6 36 21	8 59 9	19 19 23	25 20 37	12 40.9	28 20.1	16 36.6	1 50.4	6 16.8	19 26.4	2 43.5	17 15.3	17 49.0

Astro Data Dy Hr Mn	Planet Ingress Dy Hr Mn	Last Aspect Dy Hr Mn	☽ Ingress Dy Hr Mn	Last Aspect Dy Hr Mn	☽ Ingress Dy Hr Mn	☽ Phases & Eclipses Dy Hr Mn	Astro Data
☽0N 2 11:27	☿ ♏ 3 18:58	1 20:06 ♃ ⚹	♈ 2 5:34	1 17:03 ♀ □	♉ 2 1:22	5 21:09 ○ 13♉08	1 NOVEMBER 1949
☽0S 16 15:11	♀ ♑ 6 4:53	4 15:09 ♀ △	♉ 4 18:37	4 10:17 ♀ △	♊ 4 13:28	13 15:48 ☽ 20♌56	Julian Day # 18202
♇ R 19 18:23	☉ ♐ 22 15:16	6 23:01 ♃ △	♊ 7 6:55	6 7:57 ☿ ☍	♋ 6 23:31	20 7:29 ● 27♏39	Delta T 29.1 sec
♄⚺♇ 22 22:15	☿ ♐ 22 9:06	8 18:41 ♇ ⚹	♋ 9 17:35	8 17:27 ♂ ⚹	♌ 9 7:27	27 10:01 ☽ 4♓50	SVP 05♓57'43"
☽0N 29 17:40	♃ ♒ 30 20:08	11 20:01 ♃ ☍	♌ 12 2:00	11 13:30 ☿ △	♍ 11 13:31		Obliquity 23°26'54"
		13 15:48 ☉ □	♍ 14 7:42	13 8:20 ♂ ☌	♎ 13 17:45	5 15:13 ○ 13♊10	⚷ Chiron 8♐32.8
☽0S 13 21:50	♀ ♒ 6 6:06	16 6:21 ♃ △	♎ 16 10:36	15 8:40 ☉ ⚹	♏ 15 20:13	13 1:48 ☽ 20♍44	☽ Mean ☊ 15♈20.5
♃⚻♅ 17 9:07	☿ ♑ 11 13:37	18 7:45 ♃ □	♏ 18 11:18	17 15:41 ♂ ⚹	♐ 17 21:32	19 18:56 ● 27♐34	
♃⚼♄ 22 9:47	☉ ♑ 22 4:23	20 8:14 ♃ ⚹	♐ 20 11:15	19 18:56 ☉ ☌	♑ 19 23:00	27 6:31 ☽ 5♈11	1 DECEMBER 1949
☽0N 27 0:25	♂ ♎ 26 5:23	21 16:46 ♇ △	♑ 22 12:19	21 23:21 ♂ △	♒ 22 2:24		Julian Day # 18232
♅∠♇ 27 12:01		24 14:21 ♃ ☌	♒ 24 16:24	23 10:46 ♇ ☍	♓ 24 9:20		Delta T 29.1 sec
♄ R 30 4:04		26 1:58 ♇ ☍	♓ 27 0:35	26 4:20 ☿ ⚹	♈ 26 20:05		SVP 05♓57'38"
		29 11:47 ♃ ⚹	♈ 29 12:18	29 0:42 ☿ □	♉ 29 8:58		Obliquity 23°26'53"
				31 19:45 ☿ △	♊ 31 21:13		⚷ Chiron 12♐05.1
							☽ Mean ☊ 13♈45.2

LONGITUDE — JANUARY 1950

Day	Sid.Time	☉	0 hr ☽	Noon ☽	True ☊	☿	♀	♂	♃	♄	♅	♆	♇
1 Su	6 40 18	10♑ 0 17	1♊24 56	7♊32 40	12♈33.6	29♑26.8	16♒58.8	2♎12.7	6♒30.3	19♍26.2	2♋41.0	17♎16.0	17♌47.9
2 M	6 44 14	11 1 26	13 44 8	19 59 30	12R 23.4	0♒28.4	17 19.0	2 34.6	6 43.9	19R 26.0	2R 38.4	17 16.6	17R 46.8
3 Tu	6 48 11	12 2 35	26 18 54	2♋42 20	12 10.9	1 24.2	17 37.3	2 56.2	6 57.4	19 25.6	2 35.9	17 17.1	17 45.7
4 W	6 52 8	13 3 43	9♋ 9 47	15 41 6	11 57.1	2 13.2	17 53.5	3 17.4	7 11.1	19 25.2	2 33.3	17 17.6	17 44.6
5 Th	6 56 4	14 4 51	22 16 6	28 54 32	11 43.3	2 54.6	18 7.6	3 38.3	7 24.7	19 24.6	2 30.8	17 18.1	17 43.5
6 F	7 0 1	15 6 0	5♌36 8	12♌20 36	11 30.6	3 27.5	18 19.5	3 58.8	7 38.4	19 23.9	2 28.3	17 18.6	17 42.3
7 Sa	7 3 57	16 7 8	19 7 38	25 56 58	11 20.3	3 51.0	18 29.1	4 19.0	7 52.2	19 23.1	2 25.8	17 19.0	17 41.2
8 Su	7 7 54	17 8 16	2♍48 18	9♍41 27	11 13.0	4R 4.3	18 36.4	4 38.8	8 6.0	19 22.2	2 23.3	17 19.4	17 40.0
9 M	7 11 50	18 9 25	16 36 13	23 32 27	11 8.7	4 6.6	18 41.4	4 58.2	8 19.8	19 21.1	2 20.9	17 19.8	17 38.8
10 Tu	7 15 47	19 10 33	0♎30 4	7♎29 0	11D 7.0	3 57.3	18R 44.0	5 17.3	8 33.7	19 20.0	2 18.4	17 20.1	17 37.5
11 W	7 19 44	20 11 41	14 29 11	21 30 36	11R 6.8	3 36.3	18 44.2	5 35.9	8 47.6	19 18.8	2 16.0	17 20.4	17 36.3
12 Th	7 23 40	21 12 49	28 33 11	5♏36 51	11 6.7	3 3.5	18 41.9	5 54.2	9 1.5	19 17.4	2 13.6	17 20.6	17 35.1
13 F	7 27 37	22 13 58	12♏41 31	19 46 57	11 5.3	2 19.4	18 37.1	6 12.0	9 15.4	19 16.0	2 11.2	17 20.8	17 33.8
14 Sa	7 31 33	23 15 6	26 52 56	3♐59 8	11 1.7	1 25.0	18 29.8	6 29.4	9 29.4	19 14.4	2 8.8	17 21.0	17 32.5
15 Su	7 35 30	24 16 14	11♐ 5 8	18 10 27	10 55.2	0 21.6	18 20.0	6 46.3	9 43.5	19 12.8	2 6.5	17 21.2	17 31.2
16 M	7 39 26	25 17 22	25 14 33	2♑16 51	10 45.9	29♑11.1	18 7.7	7 2.8	9 57.5	19 11.0	2 4.1	17 21.3	17 29.9
17 Tu	7 43 23	26 18 30	9♑16 45	16 13 38	10 34.4	27 55.7	17 53.0	7 18.9	10 11.6	19 9.1	2 1.8	17 21.4	17 28.6
18 W	7 47 19	27 19 37	23 6 57	29 56 11	10 22.0	26 37.7	17 35.8	7 34.4	10 25.7	19 7.2	1 59.6	17R 21.4	17 27.3
19 Th	7 51 16	28 20 44	6♒40 54	13♒20 47	10 9.8	25 19.7	17 16.2	7 49.5	10 39.9	19 5.1	1 57.3	17 21.4	17 26.0
20 F	7 55 13	29 21 50	19 55 35	26 25 13	9 59.2	24 3.9	16 54.3	8 4.1	10 54.0	19 2.9	1 55.1	17 21.4	17 24.6
21 Sa	7 59 9	0♒22 55	2♓49 40	9♓ 9 5	9 51.0	22 52.4	16 30.2	8 18.3	11 8.2	19 0.7	1 52.9	17 21.3	17 23.3
22 Su	8 3 6	1 24 0	15 23 42	21 33 50	9 45.5	21 46.9	16 3.9	8 31.9	11 22.4	18 58.3	1 50.8	17 21.2	17 21.9
23 M	8 7 2	2 25 3	27 39 54	3♈42 25	9 42.6	20 48.8	15 35.7	8 45.0	11 36.6	18 55.8	1 48.6	17 21.1	17 20.5
24 Tu	8 10 59	3 26 5	9♈41 56	15 39 2	9D 41.9	19 59.0	15 5.6	8 57.5	11 50.8	18 53.3	1 46.5	17 20.9	17 19.1
25 W	8 14 55	4 27 7	21 34 24	27 28 40	9 42.3	19 18.1	14 33.9	9 9.5	12 5.0	18 50.6	1 44.5	17 20.7	17 17.8
26 Th	8 18 52	5 28 7	3♉22 33	9♉16 44	9R 42.8	18 46.2	14 0.6	9 21.0	12 19.3	18 47.9	1 42.4	17 20.5	17 16.4
27 F	8 22 48	6 29 6	15 11 55	21 8 46	9 42.4	18 23.4	13 26.1	9 31.9	12 33.6	18 45.0	1 40.4	17 20.3	17 14.9
28 Sa	8 26 45	7 30 4	27 7 56	3♊10 1	9 40.1	18 9.3	12 50.6	9 42.3	12 47.8	18 42.1	1 38.5	17 20.0	17 13.5
29 Su	8 30 42	8 31 1	9♊15 37	15 25 13	9 35.6	18D 3.6	12 14.3	9 52.1	13 2.1	18 39.1	1 36.5	17 19.6	17 12.1
30 M	8 34 38	9 31 57	21 39 14	27 58 2	9 28.7	18 5.8	11 37.4	10 1.3	13 16.4	18 36.0	1 34.6	17 19.3	17 10.7
31 Tu	8 38 35	10 32 52	4♋21 52	10♋50 53	9 19.7	18 15.4	11 0.2	10 9.9	13 30.7	18 32.8	1 32.8	17 18.9	17 9.3

LONGITUDE — FEBRUARY 1950

Day	Sid.Time	☉	0 hr ☽	Noon ☽	True ☊	☿	♀	♂	♃	♄	♅	♆	♇
1 W	8 42 31	11♒33 45	17♋25 6	24♋ 4 28	9♈ 9.5	18♑31.9	10♒22.9	10♎17.9	13♒45.0	18♍29.6	1♋31.0	17♎18.4	17♌ 7.9
2 Th	8 46 28	12 34 38	0♌48 47	7♌37 45	8R 59.1	18 54.7	9R 45.9	10 25.2	13 59.3	18R 26.2	1R 29.2	17R 18.0	17R 6.4
3 F	8 50 24	13 35 29	14 30 58	21 27 59	8 49.6	19 23.3	9 9.4	10 32.0	14 13.7	18 22.8	1 27.5	17 17.5	17 5.0
4 Sa	8 54 21	14 36 19	28 28 15	5♍31 12	8 41.9	19 57.1	8 33.6	10 38.1	14 28.0	18 19.3	1 25.8	17 17.0	17 3.6
5 Su	8 58 17	15 37 8	12♍36 16	19 42 52	8 36.6	20 35.9	7 58.8	10 43.5	14 42.3	18 15.7	1 24.1	17 16.4	17 2.1
6 M	9 2 14	16 37 55	26 50 27	3♎58 32	8D 33.8	21 19.0	7 25.2	10 48.3	14 56.6	18 12.1	1 22.5	17 15.8	17 0.7
7 Tu	9 6 11	17 38 42	11♎ 6 39	18 14 27	8 33.2	22 6.2	6 53.1	10 52.4	15 10.9	18 8.3	1 20.9	17 15.2	16 59.2
8 W	9 10 7	18 39 28	25 21 37	2♏27 52	8 34.0	22 57.1	6 22.6	10 55.8	15 25.2	18 4.6	1 19.4	17 14.6	16 57.8
9 Th	9 14 4	19 40 13	9♏33 0	16 36 52	8R 35.1	23 51.4	5 53.9	10 58.6	15 39.5	18 0.7	1 17.9	17 13.9	16 56.4
10 F	9 18 0	20 40 57	23 39 19	0♐40 13	8 35.5	24 48.8	5 27.1	11 0.6	15 53.8	17 56.8	1 16.5	17 13.2	16 54.9
11 Sa	9 21 57	21 41 40	7♐39 27	14 36 54	8 34.2	25 49.0	5 2.5	11 1.8	16 8.1	17 52.8	1 15.1	17 12.4	16 53.5
12 Su	9 25 53	22 42 22	21 32 25	28 25 49	8 30.9	26 51.8	4 40.0	11R 2.4	16 22.4	17 48.7	1 13.7	17 11.7	16 52.1
13 M	9 29 50	23 43 3	5♑16 57	12♑ 5 35	8 25.6	27 57.0	4 19.9	11 2.2	16 36.7	17 44.6	1 12.4	17 10.9	16 50.6
14 Tu	9 33 46	24 43 42	18 51 31	25 34 32	8 18.7	29 4.5	4 2.1	11 1.3	16 51.0	17 40.4	1 11.2	17 10.0	16 49.2
15 W	9 37 43	25 44 21	2♒14 23	8♒50 52	8 11.1	0♒14.1	3 46.8	10 59.5	17 5.2	17 36.2	1 10.0	17 9.2	16 47.8
16 Th	9 41 40	26 44 58	15 23 48	21 53 3	8 3.5	1 25.5	3 33.9	10 57.1	17 19.5	17 31.9	1 8.8	17 8.3	16 46.4
17 F	9 45 36	27 45 33	28 18 30	4♓40 6	7 56.9	2 38.8	3 23.4	10 53.8	17 33.7	17 27.6	1 7.7	17 7.4	16 45.0
18 Sa	9 49 33	28 46 7	10♓57 53	17 11 53	7 51.9	3 53.8	3 15.5	10 49.8	17 47.9	17 23.2	1 6.7	17 6.4	16 43.5
19 Su	9 53 29	29 46 39	23 22 16	29 29 15	7 48.9	5 10.4	3 10.0	10 45.0	18 2.1	17 18.8	1 5.6	17 5.4	16 42.1
20 M	9 57 26	0♓47 10	5♈33 6	11♈34 9	7D 47.7	6 28.5	3D 6.9	10 39.4	18 16.2	17 14.3	1 4.7	17 4.4	16 40.7
21 Tu	10 1 22	1 47 39	17 32 48	23 29 29	7 48.1	7 48.1	3 6.3	10 33.1	18 30.4	17 9.8	1 3.8	17 3.4	16 39.4
22 W	10 5 19	2 48 6	29 24 44	5♉19 3	7 49.6	9 9.0	3 8.1	10 25.9	18 44.5	17 5.3	1 2.9	17 2.4	16 38.0
23 Th	10 9 15	3 48 31	11♉13 1	17 7 16	7 51.4	10 31.3	3 12.2	10 18.0	18 58.6	17 0.7	1 2.1	17 1.3	16 36.6
24 F	10 13 12	4 48 54	23 2 23	28 59 1	7 53.0	11 54.8	3 18.7	10 9.3	19 12.7	16 56.1	1 1.3	17 0.2	16 35.2
25 Sa	10 17 9	5 49 16	4♊57 50	10♊59 26	7R 53.7	13 19.6	3 27.4	9 59.8	19 26.8	16 51.5	1 0.6	16 59.1	16 33.9
26 Su	10 21 5	6 49 36	17 4 27	23 13 29	7 53.1	14 45.6	3 38.3	9 49.6	19 40.8	16 46.8	0 60.0	16 57.9	16 32.6
27 M	10 25 2	7 49 53	29 27 4	5♋45 43	7 51.1	16 12.8	3 51.3	9 38.6	19 54.8	16 42.1	0 59.4	16 56.7	16 31.2
28 Tu	10 28 58	8 50 9	12♋ 9 49	18 39 44	7 47.9	17 41.1	4 6.4	9 26.8	20 8.8	16 37.4	0 58.8	16 55.6	16 29.9

Astro Data	Planet Ingress	Last Aspect	☽ Ingress	Last Aspect	☽ Ingress	☽ Phases & Eclipses	Astro Data
Dy Hr Mn	Dy Hr Mn	Dy Hr Mn	Dy Hr Mn	Dy Hr Mn	Dy Hr Mn	Dy Hr Mn	1 JANUARY 1950
☿ R 8 16:54	☿ ♒ 1 12:39	2 10:56 ♄ □	♋ 3 6:56	1 2:04 ☿ ☍	♌ 1 22:34	4 7:48 ○ 13♋24	Julian Day # 18263
☽0S 10 2:21	☿ ♑ 15 7:35	4 18:48 ♄ ⚹	♌ 5 13:58	3 4:48 ♆ ⚹	♍ 4 2:37	11 10:31 ☽ 20♎38	Delta T 29.2 sec
♀ R 10 13:35	☉ ♒ 20 15:00	6 22:51 ♀ ☍	♍ 7 19:06	5 14:12 ☿ △	♎ 6 5:19	18 8:00 ● 27♑40	SVP 05♓57'32"
♂0S 13 12:16		9 4:45 ♄ ☌	♎ 9 23:08	7 19:40 ☿ □	♏ 8 7:50	26 4:39 ☽ 5♉40	Obliquity 23°26'53"
♆ R 18 19:19	☿ ♒ 14 19:12	11 10:31 ☉ □	♏ 12 2:28	10 2:08 ☿ ⚹	♐ 10 10:51		⚷ Chiron 15♐46.6
♆⚹♇ 22 12:43	☉ ♓ 19 5:18	13 17:23 ☉ ⚹	♐ 14 5:16	12 2:11 ☉ ⚹	♑ 12 14:45	2 22:16 ○ 13♌31	☽ Mean ☊ 12♈06.7
☽0N 23 7:54		15 13:44 ♄ □	♑ 16 8:06	13 21:54 ♄ △	♒ 14 19:57	9 18:32 ☽ 20♏27	
☿ D 29 5:03		18 8:00 ☉ ☌	♒ 18 12:07	16 22:53 ☉ ☌	♓ 17 3:11	16 22:53 ● 27♒43	1 FEBRUARY 1950
☽0S 6 7:47		19 19:24 ♇ ☍	♓ 20 18:41	18 12:18 ♄ ☍	♈ 19 13:01	25 1:52 ☽ 5♊54	Julian Day # 18294
♃⚼♅ 11 10:42		22 11:29 ☿ ⚹	♈ 23 4:37	21 1:58 ♃ ⚹	♉ 22 1:12		Delta T 29.2 sec
♂ R 12 5:48		24 19:37 ☿ □	♉ 25 17:08	23 16:05 ♃ □	♊ 24 14:03		SVP 05♓57'26"
♃☍♇ 13 21:20	☽0N 19 15:40	27 7:09 ♄ △	♊ 28 5:43	26 5:12 ♃ △	♋ 27 1:03		Obliquity 23°26'54"
♃△♆ 15 6:17	♀ D 20 18:04	29 18:10 ♄ □	♋ 30 15:50				⚷ Chiron 18♐56.7
♃⚻♄ 16 16:09	♄⚺♆ 22 20:01						☽ Mean ☊ 10♈28.2

MARCH 1950 LONGITUDE

Day	Sid.Time	☉	0 hr ☽	Noon ☽	True ☊	☿	♀	♂	♃	♄	♅	♆	♇
1 W	10 32 55	9♓50 22	25♋15 42	1♌57 49	7♈43.9	19♒10.5	4♒23.6	9♎14.3	20♒22.7	16♍32.7	0♋58.3	16♎54.3	16♌28.6
2 Th	10 36 51	10 50 34	8♌46 4	15 40 19	7R 39.6	20 41.1	4 42.7	9R 1.0	20 36.6	16R 27.9	0R 57.9	16R 53.1	16R 27.3
3 F	10 40 48	11 50 44	22 40 16	29 45 30	7 35.6	22 12.8	5 3.7	8 47.0	20 50.5	16 23.2	0 57.5	16 51.8	16 26.0
4 Sa	10 44 44	12 50 51	6♍55 27	14♍ 9 27	7 32.4	23 45.6	5 26.5	8 32.3	21 4.3	16 18.4	0 57.2	16 50.6	16 24.8
5 Su	10 48 41	13 50 57	21 26 45	28 46 30	7 30.4	25 19.5	5 51.1	8 16.9	21 18.1	16 13.6	0 56.9	16 49.2	16 23.5
6 M	10 52 38	14 51 1	6♎ 7 50	13♎29 55	7D 29.7	26 54.5	6 17.5	8 0.9	21 31.8	16 8.8	0 56.7	16 47.9	16 22.2
7 Tu	10 56 34	15 51 3	20 51 52	28 12 55	7 30.1	28 30.6	6 45.4	7 44.1	21 45.6	16 4.0	0 56.5	16 46.6	16 21.0
8 W	11 0 31	16 51 4	5♏32 20	12♏49 29	7 31.2	0♓ 7.8	7 15.0	7 26.7	21 59.2	15 59.3	0 56.3	16 45.2	16 19.8
9 Th	11 4 27	17 51 2	20 3 49	27 14 55	7 32.6	1 46.2	7 46.1	7 8.7	22 12.9	15 54.5	0D 56.3	16 43.8	16 18.6
10 F	11 8 24	18 51 0	4♐22 26	11♐26 7	7 33.7	3 25.7	8 18.7	6 50.0	22 26.5	15 49.7	0 56.3	16 42.4	16 17.4
11 Sa	11 12 20	19 50 56	18 25 48	25 21 25	7R 34.2	5 6.3	8 52.7	6 30.8	22 40.0	15 44.9	0 56.3	16 41.0	16 16.3
12 Su	11 16 17	20 50 50	2♑12 55	9♑ 0 20	7 33.9	6 48.0	9 28.0	6 11.1	22 53.6	15 40.1	0 56.4	16 39.6	16 15.1
13 M	11 20 13	21 50 43	15 43 43	22 23 9	7 32.8	8 31.0	10 4.7	5 50.8	23 7.0	15 35.4	0 56.5	16 38.1	16 14.0
14 Tu	11 24 10	22 50 33	28 58 44	5♒30 35	7 31.1	10 15.1	10 42.6	5 30.0	23 20.4	15 30.7	0 56.7	16 36.7	16 12.9
15 W	11 28 7	23 50 22	11♒58 50	18 23 36	7 29.1	12 0.3	11 21.6	5 8.8	23 33.8	15 25.9	0 57.0	16 35.2	16 11.8
16 Th	11 32 3	24 50 10	24 45 0	1♓ 3 11	7 27.2	13 46.8	12 1.9	4 47.2	23 47.1	15 21.2	0 57.3	16 33.7	16 10.7
17 F	11 36 0	25 49 55	7♓18 15	13 30 23	7 25.6	15 34.5	12 43.2	4 25.2	24 0.4	15 16.5	0 57.6	16 32.2	16 9.6
18 Sa	11 39 56	26 49 38	19 39 42	25 46 22	7 24.5	17 23.4	13 25.6	4 2.8	24 13.6	15 11.9	0 58.1	16 30.7	16 8.6
19 Su	11 43 53	27 49 20	1♈50 34	7♈52 31	7D 24.0	19 13.5	14 9.0	3 40.2	24 26.8	15 7.3	0 58.5	16 29.1	16 7.6
20 M	11 47 49	28 48 59	13 52 25	19 50 32	7 24.0	21 4.9	14 53.3	3 17.3	24 39.9	15 2.7	0 59.0	16 27.6	16 6.6
21 Tu	11 51 46	29 48 37	25 47 9	1♉42 34	7 24.4	22 57.5	15 38.6	2 54.2	24 52.9	14 58.1	0 59.6	16 26.0	16 5.6
22 W	11 55 42	0♈48 12	7♉37 9	13 31 17	7 25.0	24 51.3	16 24.8	2 30.9	25 5.9	14 53.6	1 0.2	16 24.5	16 4.6
23 Th	11 59 39	1 47 45	19 25 21	25 19 50	7 25.7	26 46.3	17 11.9	2 7.6	25 18.8	14 49.1	1 0.9	16 22.9	16 3.7
24 F	12 3 36	2 47 16	1♊15 12	7♊11 57	7 26.3	28 42.5	17 59.7	1 44.1	25 31.6	14 44.6	1 1.7	16 21.3	16 2.8
25 Sa	12 7 32	3 46 45	13 10 37	19 11 46	7 26.7	0♈39.9	18 48.4	1 20.7	25 44.4	14 40.2	1 2.4	16 19.7	16 1.9
26 Su	12 11 29	4 46 11	25 15 56	1♋23 42	7R 26.9	2 38.4	19 37.8	0 57.3	25 57.2	14 35.9	1 3.3	16 18.1	16 1.0
27 M	12 15 25	5 45 35	7♋35 37	13 52 14	7 27.0	4 38.0	20 27.9	0 33.9	26 9.8	14 31.6	1 4.2	16 16.5	16 0.1
28 Tu	12 19 22	6 44 57	20 14 3	26 41 32	7D 26.9	6 38.6	21 18.8	0 10.7	26 22.4	14 27.3	1 5.1	16 14.9	15 59.3
29 W	12 23 18	7 44 16	3♌15 6	9♌55 3	7 26.9	8 40.1	22 10.3	29♍47.6	26 34.9	14 23.1	1 6.1	16 13.3	15 58.5
30 Th	12 27 15	8 43 34	16 41 37	23 34 53	7 27.0	10 42.3	23 2.5	29 24.7	26 47.4	14 19.0	1 7.2	16 11.6	15 57.7
31 F	12 31 11	9 42 48	0♍34 49	7♍41 14	7 27.2	12 45.2	23 55.3	29 2.1	26 59.8	14 14.9	1 8.3	16 10.0	15 57.0

APRIL 1950 LONGITUDE

Day	Sid.Time	☉	0 hr ☽	Noon ☽	True ☊	☿	♀	♂	♃	♄	♅	♆	♇
1 Sa	12 35 8	10♈42 1	14♍53 46	22♍11 53	7♈27.4	14♈48.5	24♒48.7	28♍39.7	27♒12.1	14♍10.8	1♋ 9.4	16♎ 8.4	15♌56.2
2 Su	12 39 5	11 41 11	29 34 56	7♎ 2 3	7R 27.6	16 52.2	25 42.7	28R 17.7	27 24.3	14R 6.9	1 10.6	16R 6.7	15R 55.5
3 M	12 43 1	12 40 19	14♎32 17	22 4 33	7 27.6	18 55.8	26 37.2	27 56.1	27 36.4	14 2.9	1 11.9	16 5.1	15 54.8
4 Tu	12 46 58	13 39 25	29 37 44	7♏10 42	7 27.3	20 59.3	27 32.3	27 34.8	27 48.5	13 59.1	1 13.2	16 3.4	15 54.2
5 W	12 50 54	14 38 30	14♏42 18	22 11 28	7 26.7	23 2.2	28 28.0	27 14.0	28 0.5	13 55.3	1 14.5	16 1.8	15 53.5
6 Th	12 54 51	15 37 32	29 37 17	6♐58 53	7 25.8	25 4.4	29 24.1	26 53.6	28 12.4	13 51.6	1 15.9	16 0.1	15 52.9
7 F	12 58 47	16 36 33	14♐15 36	21 26 56	7 24.9	27 5.3	0♓20.8	26 33.7	28 24.3	13 48.0	1 17.3	15 58.5	15 52.3
8 Sa	13 2 44	17 35 32	28 32 29	5♑32 4	7 24.0	29 4.8	1 17.9	26 14.4	28 36.0	13 44.4	1 18.8	15 56.8	15 51.8
9 Su	13 6 40	18 34 29	12♑25 37	19 13 11	7D 23.5	1♉ 2.4	2 15.5	25 55.6	28 47.7	13 40.9	1 20.4	15 55.2	15 51.2
10 M	13 10 37	19 33 24	25 54 55	2♒31 5	7 23.5	2 57.8	3 13.5	25 37.4	28 59.3	13 37.5	1 22.0	15 53.5	15 50.7
11 Tu	13 14 34	20 32 18	9♒ 1 57	15 27 55	7 24.1	4 50.6	4 11.9	25 19.9	29 10.8	13 34.1	1 23.6	15 51.9	15 50.2
12 W	13 18 30	21 31 10	21 49 19	28 6 34	7 25.1	6 40.5	5 10.7	25 2.9	29 22.2	13 30.9	1 25.3	15 50.3	15 49.8
13 Th	13 22 27	22 30 0	4♓20 3	10♓30 10	7 26.4	8 27.1	6 9.9	24 46.6	29 33.5	13 27.7	1 27.0	15 48.6	15 49.4
14 F	13 26 23	23 28 48	16 37 18	22 41 48	7 27.7	10 10.1	7 9.5	24 31.1	29 44.7	13 24.6	1 28.8	15 47.0	15 48.9
15 Sa	13 30 20	24 27 35	28 44 1	4♈44 16	7R 28.5	11 49.3	8 9.5	24 16.2	29 55.9	13 21.5	1 30.6	15 45.3	15 48.6
16 Su	13 34 16	25 26 19	10♈42 52	16 40 5	7 28.7	13 24.4	9 9.8	24 2.0	0♓ 6.9	13 18.6	1 32.5	15 43.7	15 48.2
17 M	13 38 13	26 25 2	22 36 13	28 31 31	7 28.0	14 55.1	10 10.4	23 48.6	0 17.8	13 15.7	1 34.4	15 42.1	15 47.9
18 Tu	13 42 9	27 23 43	4♉26 13	10♉20 36	7 26.2	16 21.3	11 11.3	23 35.9	0 28.7	13 13.0	1 36.4	15 40.5	15 47.6
19 W	13 46 6	28 22 22	16 14 55	22 9 26	7 23.5	17 42.8	12 12.6	23 24.0	0 39.4	13 10.3	1 38.4	15 38.9	15 47.3
20 Th	13 50 2	29 20 59	28 4 26	4♊ 0 12	7 20.0	18 59.4	13 14.1	23 12.9	0 50.0	13 7.7	1 40.4	15 37.3	15 47.1
21 F	13 53 59	0♉19 33	9♊57 4	15 55 22	7 16.2	20 11.0	14 16.0	23 2.6	1 0.6	13 5.2	1 42.5	15 35.7	15 46.9
22 Sa	13 57 56	1 18 6	21 55 28	27 57 47	7 12.4	21 17.5	15 18.1	22 53.1	1 11.0	13 2.8	1 44.7	15 34.1	15 46.7
23 Su	14 1 52	2 16 37	4♋ 2 42	10♋10 41	7 9.2	22 18.8	16 20.5	22 44.3	1 21.3	13 0.5	1 46.8	15 32.5	15 46.5
24 M	14 5 49	3 15 6	16 22 11	22 37 40	7 6.9	23 14.7	17 23.1	22 36.4	1 31.5	12 58.3	1 49.0	15 31.0	15 46.4
25 Tu	14 9 45	4 13 32	28 57 38	5♌22 32	7D 5.8	24 5.3	18 26.0	22 29.2	1 41.6	12 56.2	1 51.3	15 29.4	15 46.3
26 W	14 13 42	5 11 56	11♌52 50	18 28 56	7 5.8	24 50.3	19 29.2	22 22.9	1 51.6	12 54.1	1 53.6	15 27.9	15 46.2
27 Th	14 17 38	6 10 18	25 11 13	1♍59 56	7 6.8	25 29.9	20 32.6	22 17.3	2 1.5	12 52.2	1 55.9	15 26.4	15 46.1
28 F	14 21 35	7 8 38	8♍55 19	15 57 24	7 8.3	26 3.8	21 36.2	22 12.6	2 11.2	12 50.4	1 58.3	15 24.9	15D 46.1
29 Sa	14 25 31	8 6 56	23 6 8	0♎21 15	7R 9.7	26 32.2	22 40.0	22 8.6	2 20.8	12 48.7	2 0.7	15 23.4	15 46.1
30 Su	14 29 28	9 5 12	7♎42 21	15 8 47	7 10.2	26 55.0	23 44.1	22 5.4	2 30.4	12 47.0	2 3.2	15 21.9	15 46.2

Astro Data	Planet Ingress	Last Aspect	☽ Ingress	Last Aspect	☽ Ingress	☽ Phases & Eclipses	Astro Data
Dy Hr Mn	Dy Hr Mn	Dy Hr Mn	Dy Hr Mn	Dy Hr Mn	Dy Hr Mn	Dy Hr Mn	1 MARCH 1950
♄⊻♇ 2 4:20	☿ ♓ 7 22:04	28 8:48 ♆ □	♌ 1 8:30	1 21:58 ♂ ☌	♎ 2 0:41	4 10:34 ○ 13♍17	Julian Day # 18322
♂0N 4 22:13	☉ ♈ 21 4:35	2 23:07 ☿ ☍	♍ 3 12:24	3 21:04 ♃ △	♏ 4 0:35	11 2:38 ☽ 19♐58	Delta T 29.2 sec
☽0S 5 16:08	☿ ♈ 24 15:52	4 15:28 ♄ ☌	♎ 5 14:00	5 23:37 ♀ □	♐ 6 0:37	18 15:20 ● 27♓28	SVP 05♓57'22"
♅ D 9 19:24	♂ ♍ 28 11:05	7 14:02 ☿ △	♏ 7 14:55	8 1:04 ☿ △	♑ 8 2:29	18 15:31:31 • A non-C	Obliquity 23°26'54"
☽0N 18 22:55		9 3:38 ♃ □	♐ 9 16:37	9 23:29 ♂ △	♒ 10 7:24	26 20:10 ☽ 5♋36	⚷ Chiron 20♐54.8
♅∠♇ 24 15:49	♀ ♓ 6 15:13	11 7:27 ♃ ⚹	♑ 11 20:07	12 14:39 ♃ ☌	♓ 12 15:38		☽ Mean ☊ 8♈59.3
☿0N 26 7:21	☿ ♉ 8 11:13	13 11:55 ☉ ⚹	♒ 14 1:52	14 15:18 ♂ ☍	♈ 15 2:32	2 20:49 ○ 12♎32	
☽0S 2 2:47	♃ ♓ 15 8:58	15 22:08 ♃ ☌	♓ 16 9:59	17 8:25 ☉ ☌	♉ 17 15:00	2 20:44 • T 1.033	1 APRIL 1950
♆⚹♇ 12 9:20	☉ ♉ 20 15:59	18 15:20 ☉ ☌	♈ 18 20:21	19 14:18 ♂ △	♊ 20 3:54	9 11:42 ☽ 19♑03	Julian Day # 18353
☽0N 15 5:08		20 22:08 ♃ ⚹	♉ 21 8:32	22 1:53 ♂ □	♋ 22 16:02	17 8:25 ● 26♈46	Delta T 29.3 sec
♃⚼♆ 18 22:59		23 17:50 ☿ ⚹	♊ 23 21:28	24 14:09 ☿ ⚹	♌ 25 1:57	25 10:40 ☽ 4♌39	SVP 05♓57'19"
♃△♅ 26 6:23		26 1:23 ♃ △	♋ 26 9:17	27 0:35 ☿ □	♍ 27 8:30		Obliquity 23°26'54"
♇ D 28 8:39		28 17:53 ♂ ⚹	♌ 28 18:05	29 5:52 ☿ △	♎ 29 11:25		⚷ Chiron 21♐44.2
☽0S 29 13:27		30 17:47 ♃ ☍	♍ 30 23:01				☽ Mean ☊ 7♈20.8

LONGITUDE — MAY 1950

Day	Sid.Time	☉	0 hr ☽	Noon ☽	True ☊	☿	♀	♂	♃	♄	♅	♆	♇
1 M	14 33 25	10♉ 3 26	22♎39 47	0♏14 20	7♈ 9.4	27♉12.2	24♓48.4	22♍ 3.0	2♓39.8	12♍45.5	2♋ 5.7	15♎20.4	15♌46.2
2 Tu	14 37 21	11 1 38	7♏51 19	15 29 28	7R 7.1	27 23.9	25 52.8	22R 1.4	2 49.0	12R44.1	2 8.2	15R19.0	15 46.3
3 W	14 41 18	11 59 48	23 7 28	0♐44 1	7 3.2	27R30.1	26 57.5	22D 0.5	2 58.2	12 42.7	2 10.8	15 17.5	15 46.4
4 Th	14 45 14	12 57 57	8♐17 48	15 47 39	6 58.2	27 31.0	28 2.4	22 0.4	3 7.2	12 41.5	2 13.4	15 16.1	15 46.6
5 F	14 49 11	13 56 4	23 12 33	0♑31 37	6 52.9	27 26.8	29 7.5	22 1.0	3 16.2	12 40.4	2 16.0	15 14.7	15 46.7
6 Sa	14 53 7	14 54 10	7♑44 14	14 49 55	6 48.1	27 17.6	0♈12.7	22 2.4	3 24.9	12 39.4	2 18.7	15 13.3	15 46.9
7 Su	14 57 4	15 52 14	21 48 28	28 39 49	6 44.3	27 3.7	1 18.2	22 4.5	3 33.6	12 38.4	2 21.4	15 11.9	15 47.2
8 M	15 1 1	16 50 17	5♒24 4	12♒ 1 28	6D 42.0	26 45.4	2 23.8	22 7.3	3 42.1	12 37.6	2 24.1	15 10.6	15 47.4
9 Tu	15 4 57	17 48 18	18 32 25	24 57 19	6 41.4	26 23.2	3 29.6	22 10.8	3 50.5	12 36.9	2 26.9	15 9.2	15 47.7
10 W	15 8 54	18 46 19	1♓16 44	7♓31 11	6 42.0	25 57.4	4 35.6	22 15.0	3 58.8	12 36.3	2 29.7	15 7.9	15 48.0
11 Th	15 12 50	19 44 17	13 41 14	19 47 30	6 43.4	25 28.6	5 41.7	22 19.9	4 6.9	12 35.8	2 32.5	15 6.6	15 48.4
12 F	15 16 47	20 42 15	25 50 31	1♈50 50	6R 44.8	24 57.2	6 47.9	22 25.5	4 14.9	12 35.4	2 35.4	15 5.3	15 48.7
13 Sa	15 20 43	21 40 11	7♈48 59	13 45 27	6 45.3	24 23.9	7 54.3	22 31.8	4 22.7	12 35.1	2 38.3	15 4.1	15 49.1
14 Su	15 24 40	22 38 5	19 40 42	25 35 7	6 44.3	23 49.2	9 0.9	22 38.8	4 30.5	12 34.9	2 41.2	15 2.8	15 49.5
15 M	15 28 36	23 35 59	1♉29 7	7♉23 1	6 41.3	23 13.8	10 7.6	22 46.4	4 38.0	12D 34.8	2 44.2	15 1.6	15 50.0
16 Tu	15 32 33	24 33 51	13 17 7	19 11 42	6 36.1	22 38.2	11 14.4	22 54.6	4 45.4	12 34.8	2 47.1	15 0.4	15 50.4
17 W	15 36 29	25 31 41	25 7 1	1♊ 3 16	6 28.9	22 3.2	12 21.4	23 3.5	4 52.7	12 34.9	2 50.2	14 59.3	15 50.9
18 Th	15 40 26	26 29 31	7♊ 0 39	12 59 24	6 20.0	21 29.3	13 28.5	23 13.0	4 59.8	12 35.1	2 53.2	14 58.1	15 51.5
19 F	15 44 23	27 27 19	18 59 40	25 1 40	6 10.4	20 57.1	14 35.7	23 23.2	5 6.8	12 35.5	2 56.3	14 57.0	15 52.0
20 Sa	15 48 19	28 25 5	1♋ 5 37	7♋11 43	6 0.8	20 27.0	15 43.0	23 33.9	5 13.6	12 35.9	2 59.4	14 55.9	15 52.6
21 Su	15 52 16	29 22 50	13 20 14	19 31 25	5 52.2	19 59.7	16 50.4	23 45.3	5 20.3	12 36.4	3 2.5	14 54.8	15 53.2
22 M	15 56 12	0♊20 33	25 45 33	2♌ 2 59	5 45.3	19 35.4	17 58.0	23 57.2	5 26.8	12 37.1	3 5.6	14 53.8	15 53.9
23 Tu	16 0 9	1 18 15	8♌24 3	14 49 7	5 40.6	19 14.6	19 5.6	24 9.7	5 33.2	12 37.8	3 8.8	14 52.7	15 54.5
24 W	16 4 5	2 15 55	21 18 33	27 52 44	5D 38.1	18 57.6	20 13.4	24 22.8	5 39.4	12 38.7	3 12.0	14 51.7	15 55.2
25 Th	16 8 2	3 13 34	4♍32 2	11♍16 47	5 37.6	18 44.5	21 21.3	24 36.4	5 45.4	12 39.6	3 15.2	14 50.7	15 55.9
26 F	16 11 59	4 11 11	18 7 16	25 3 42	5 38.1	18 35.7	22 29.2	24 50.5	5 51.3	12 40.7	3 18.5	14 49.8	15 56.6
27 Sa	16 15 55	5 8 46	2♎ 6 11	9♎14 42	5R 38.7	18D 31.1	23 37.3	25 5.2	5 57.0	12 41.8	3 21.7	14 48.9	15 57.4
28 Su	16 19 52	6 6 20	16 29 5	23 49 1	5 38.3	18 31.1	24 45.5	25 20.4	6 2.6	12 43.1	3 25.0	14 48.0	15 58.2
29 M	16 23 48	7 3 53	1♏13 56	8♏43 9	5 36.0	18 35.5	25 53.7	25 36.1	6 8.0	12 44.4	3 28.3	14 47.1	15 59.0
30 Tu	16 27 45	8 1 24	16 15 43	23 50 34	5 31.3	18 44.3	27 2.1	25 52.3	6 13.2	12 45.9	3 31.6	14 46.2	15 59.8
31 W	16 31 41	8 58 55	1♐26 30	9♐ 2 12	5 24.2	18 57.7	28 10.5	26 8.9	6 18.3	12 47.5	3 35.0	14 45.4	16 0.7

LONGITUDE — JUNE 1950

Day	Sid.Time	☉	0 hr ☽	Noon ☽	True ☊	☿	♀	♂	♃	♄	♅	♆	♇
1 Th	16 35 38	9♊56 24	16♐36 20	24♐ 7 37	5♈15.4	19♉15.6	29♈19.1	26♍26.1	6♓23.2	12♍49.1	3♋38.3	14♎44.6	16♌ 1.6
2 F	16 39 34	10 53 52	1♑34 49	8♑56 54	5R 5.8	19 37.8	0♉27.7	26 43.7	6 27.9	12 50.9	3 41.7	14R43.9	16 2.5
3 Sa	16 43 31	11 51 20	16 12 57	23 22 19	4 56.6	20 4.3	1 36.4	27 1.7	6 32.5	12 52.8	3 45.1	14 43.2	16 3.4
4 Su	16 47 28	12 48 46	0♒24 31	7♒19 20	4 48.9	20 35.1	2 45.3	27 20.2	6 36.9	12 54.7	3 48.5	14 42.4	16 4.4
5 M	16 51 24	13 46 12	14 6 42	20 46 46	4 43.3	21 10.1	3 54.2	27 39.1	6 41.1	12 56.8	3 51.9	14 41.8	16 5.4
6 Tu	16 55 21	14 43 37	27 19 50	3♓46 17	4 40.0	21 49.1	5 3.2	27 58.5	6 45.1	12 58.9	3 55.4	14 41.1	16 6.4
7 W	16 59 17	15 41 1	10♓ 6 39	16 21 31	4D 38.7	22 32.1	6 12.2	28 18.3	6 49.0	13 1.2	3 58.8	14 40.5	16 7.4
8 Th	17 3 14	16 38 25	22 31 30	28 37 16	4 38.7	23 19.0	7 21.4	28 38.5	6 52.6	13 3.5	4 2.3	14 39.9	16 8.5
9 F	17 7 10	17 35 48	4♈39 28	10♈38 46	4R 38.9	24 9.6	8 30.6	28 59.1	6 56.1	13 6.0	4 5.8	14 39.3	16 9.5
10 Sa	17 11 7	18 33 10	16 35 48	22 31 12	4 38.3	25 4.0	9 39.9	29 20.1	6 59.5	13 8.5	4 9.3	14 38.8	16 10.6
11 Su	17 15 3	19 30 32	28 25 33	4♉19 21	4 36.0	26 1.9	10 49.3	29 41.5	7 2.6	13 11.2	4 12.8	14 38.3	16 11.8
12 M	17 19 0	20 27 54	10♉13 9	16 7 21	4 31.2	27 3.5	11 58.8	0♎ 3.3	7 5.5	13 13.9	4 16.3	14 37.8	16 12.9
13 Tu	17 22 57	21 25 15	22 2 22	27 58 32	4 23.7	28 8.5	13 8.3	0 25.4	7 8.3	13 16.7	4 19.8	14 37.4	16 14.1
14 W	17 26 53	22 22 35	3♊56 9	9♊55 28	4 13.6	29 16.9	14 17.9	0 47.9	7 10.9	13 19.6	4 23.4	14 37.0	16 15.2
15 Th	17 30 50	23 19 55	15 56 40	21 59 57	4 1.4	0♊28.7	15 27.6	1 10.8	7 13.3	13 22.7	4 26.9	14 36.6	16 16.4
16 F	17 34 46	24 17 15	28 5 24	4♋13 10	3 48.2	1 43.8	16 37.3	1 34.1	7 15.5	13 25.8	4 30.5	14 36.3	16 17.7
17 Sa	17 38 43	25 14 34	10♋23 18	16 35 54	3 35.0	3 2.2	17 47.1	1 57.7	7 17.5	13 29.0	4 34.1	14 36.0	16 18.9
18 Su	17 42 39	26 11 52	22 51 2	29 8 47	3 22.9	4 23.8	18 57.0	2 21.7	7 19.3	13 32.3	4 37.6	14 35.7	16 20.2
19 M	17 46 36	27 9 9	5♌29 16	11♌52 37	3 13.0	5 48.6	20 6.9	2 46.0	7 21.0	13 35.6	4 41.2	14 35.4	16 21.5
20 Tu	17 50 32	28 6 26	18 18 58	24 48 30	3 5.7	7 16.6	21 16.9	3 10.6	7 22.4	13 39.1	4 44.8	14 35.2	16 22.8
21 W	17 54 29	29 3 42	1♍21 26	7♍57 59	3 1.3	8 47.7	22 27.0	3 35.6	7 23.7	13 42.6	4 48.4	14 35.0	16 24.1
22 Th	17 58 26	0♋ 0 57	14 38 24	21 22 54	2 59.3	10 21.9	23 37.1	4 0.8	7 24.7	13 46.3	4 52.0	14 34.9	16 25.5
23 F	18 2 22	0 58 12	28 11 44	5♎ 5 5	2 58.9	11 59.2	24 47.2	4 26.4	7 25.6	13 50.0	4 55.6	14 34.7	16 26.8
24 Sa	18 6 19	1 55 25	12♎ 3 7	19 5 51	2 58.8	13 39.6	25 57.4	4 52.3	7 26.3	13 53.8	4 59.2	14 34.7	16 28.2
25 Su	18 10 15	2 52 39	26 13 17	3♏25 15	2 57.8	15 22.9	27 7.7	5 18.5	7 26.7	13 57.7	5 2.8	14 34.6	16 29.6
26 M	18 14 12	3 49 51	10♏41 27	18 1 24	2 54.9	17 9.2	28 18.1	5 45.0	7 27.0	14 1.7	5 6.4	14D 34.6	16 31.0
27 Tu	18 18 8	4 47 4	25 24 29	2♐49 55	2 49.3	18 58.3	29 28.5	6 11.7	7R 27.1	14 5.7	5 10.0	14 34.6	16 32.5
28 W	18 22 5	5 44 15	10♐16 47	17 44 3	2 41.2	20 50.3	0♊38.9	6 38.8	7 27.0	14 9.9	5 13.6	14 34.6	16 33.9
29 Th	18 26 2	6 41 27	25 10 35	2♑35 17	2 31.1	22 44.9	1 49.4	7 6.1	7 26.7	14 14.1	5 17.2	14 34.7	16 35.4
30 F	18 29 58	7 38 38	9♑57 2	17 14 49	2 20.0	24 42.0	2 60.0	7 33.7	7 26.3	14 18.4	5 20.8	14 34.8	16 36.9

Astro Data

	Dy Hr Mn
☿ R	3 16:06
♂ D	3 15:51
♀0N	8 19:22
☽0N	12 10:38
♄ D	15 9:22
☽0S	26 22:04
☿ D	27 12:29
☽0N	8 16:18
♂0S	14 8:14
☽0S	23 4:02
♆ D	26 8:04
♃ R	27 0:14

Planet Ingress

	Dy Hr Mn
♀ ♈	5 19:19
☉ ♊	21 15:27
♀ ♉	1 14:19
♂ ♎	11 20:27
☿ ♊	14 14:33
☉ ♋	21 23:36
♀ ♊	27 10:45

Last Aspect / ☽ Ingress

Last Aspect Dy Hr Mn	☽ Ingress Dy Hr Mn
30 13:00 ♇ ⚹	♏ 1 11:37
3 6:55 ☿ ☍	♐ 3 10:50
5 10:28 ♀ □	♑ 5 11:08
7 9:00 ☿ △	♒ 7 14:22
9 14:14 ☿ □	♓ 9 21:34
11 22:18 ☿ ⚹	♈ 12 8:18
13 16:11 ♇ △	♉ 14 20:59
17 0:54 ☉ ☌	♊ 17 9:52
19 8:52 ♂ □	♋ 19 21:50
21 20:29 ♂ ⚹	♌ 22 8:06
23 21:49 ♀ △	♍ 24 15:51
26 11:50 ♂ ☌	♎ 26 20:26
28 14:39 ♀ ☍	♏ 28 22:01
30 15:29 ♂ ⚹	♐ 30 21:43

Last Aspect / ☽ Ingress

Last Aspect Dy Hr Mn	☽ Ingress Dy Hr Mn
1 16:01 ♂ □	♑ 1 21:27
3 18:37 ♂ △	♒ 3 23:18
5 13:21 ☿ □	♓ 6 4:57
8 12:23 ♂ ☍	♈ 8 14:44
10 4:18 ☉ ⚹	♉ 11 3:12
13 13:38 ☿ ☌	♊ 13 16:05
15 15:53 ☉ ☌	♋ 16 3:45
17 15:45 ♀ ⚹	♌ 18 13:37
20 19:29 ☉ ⚹	♍ 20 21:31
22 17:27 ♀ △	♎ 23 3:09
24 7:33 ♇ ⚹	♏ 25 6:19
27 7:09 ♀ ☍	♐ 27 7:26
28 19:30 ☿ ☍	♑ 29 7:48

☽ Phases & Eclipses

Dy Hr Mn	
2 5:19	○ 11♏15
8 22:32	☽ 17♒45
17 0:54	● 25♉34
24 21:28	☽ 3♍07
31 12:43	○ 9♐29
7 11:35	☽ 16♓09
15 15:53	● 23♊58
23 5:13	☽ 1♎11
29 19:58	○ 7♑29

Astro Data

1 MAY 1950
Julian Day # 18383
Delta T 29.3 sec
SVP 05♓57'15"
Obliquity 23°26'54"
⚷ Chiron 21♐04.9R
☽ Mean ☊ 5♈45.4

1 JUNE 1950
Julian Day # 18414
Delta T 29.3 sec
SVP 05♓57'10"
Obliquity 23°26'53"
⚷ Chiron 19♐17.1R
☽ Mean ☊ 4♈07.0

JULY 1950 LONGITUDE

Day	Sid.Time	☉	0 hr ☽	Noon ☽	True ☊	☿	♀	♂	♃	♄	♅	♆	♇
1 Sa	18 33 55	8♋35 49	24♑27 41	1♒34 56	2♈ 9.3	26♊41.5	4♊10.6	8♎ 1.6	7♓25.6	14♍22.8	5♋24.4	14♎34.9	16♌38.4
2 Su	18 37 51	9 33 0	8♒35 57	15 30 21	1R 60.0	28 43.2	5 21.3	8 29.7	7R 24.7	14 27.2	5 28.0	14 35.1	16 39.9
3 M	18 41 48	10 30 11	22 17 56	28 58 41	1 52.9	0♋46.8	6 32.1	8 58.1	7 23.7	14 31.8	5 31.6	14 35.3	16 41.4
4 Tu	18 45 44	11 27 22	5♓32 44	12♓ 0 21	1 48.4	2 52.2	7 42.9	9 26.7	7 22.4	14 36.4	5 35.2	14 35.5	16 43.0
5 W	18 49 41	12 24 34	18 21 57	24 38 1	1 46.2	4 59.1	8 53.7	9 55.6	7 21.0	14 41.0	5 38.8	14 35.8	16 44.5
6 Th	18 53 37	13 21 45	0♈49 6	6♈55 51	1D 45.7	7 7.1	10 4.7	10 24.7	7 19.3	14 45.8	5 42.4	14 36.1	16 46.1
7 F	18 57 34	14 18 57	12 58 54	18 58 55	1R 45.8	9 16.0	11 15.6	10 54.1	7 17.5	14 50.6	5 46.0	14 36.4	16 47.7
8 Sa	19 1 31	15 16 9	24 56 36	0♉52 35	1 45.4	11 25.6	12 26.7	11 23.7	7 15.5	14 55.5	5 49.6	14 36.7	16 49.3
9 Su	19 5 27	16 13 22	6♉47 33	12 42 6	1 43.7	13 35.4	13 37.8	11 53.5	7 13.3	15 0.5	5 53.1	14 37.1	16 50.9
10 M	19 9 24	17 10 35	18 36 50	24 32 18	1 39.8	15 45.3	14 48.9	12 23.6	7 10.9	15 5.6	5 56.7	14 37.6	16 52.5
11 Tu	19 13 20	18 7 48	0♊28 59	6♊27 21	1 33.3	17 55.0	16 0.1	12 53.9	7 8.3	15 10.7	6 0.2	14 38.0	16 54.2
12 W	19 17 17	19 5 2	12 27 46	18 30 35	1 24.4	20 4.1	17 11.4	13 24.4	7 5.5	15 15.9	6 3.8	14 38.5	16 55.8
13 Th	19 21 13	20 2 17	24 36 3	0♋44 23	1 13.5	22 12.5	18 22.7	13 55.2	7 2.5	15 21.1	6 7.3	14 39.0	16 57.5
14 F	19 25 10	20 59 31	6♋55 44	13 10 11	1 1.5	24 20.0	19 34.0	14 26.2	6 59.4	15 26.4	6 10.8	14 39.6	16 59.2
15 Sa	19 29 6	21 56 46	19 27 47	25 48 31	0 49.5	26 26.4	20 45.4	14 57.4	6 56.0	15 31.8	6 14.4	14 40.1	17 0.9
16 Su	19 33 3	22 54 2	2♌12 22	8♌39 17	0 38.5	28 31.5	21 56.9	15 28.8	6 52.5	15 37.3	6 17.9	14 40.8	17 2.6
17 M	19 37 0	23 51 17	15 9 11	21 42 0	0 29.5	0♌35.2	23 8.4	16 0.4	6 48.8	15 42.8	6 21.4	14 41.4	17 4.3
18 Tu	19 40 56	24 48 33	28 17 40	4♍56 8	0 23.0	2 37.5	24 20.0	16 32.3	6 45.0	15 48.4	6 24.8	14 42.1	17 6.0
19 W	19 44 53	25 45 49	11♍37 21	18 21 20	0 19.2	4 38.2	25 31.6	17 4.3	6 40.9	15 54.0	6 28.3	14 42.8	17 7.8
20 Th	19 48 49	26 43 6	25 8 5	1♎57 37	0D 17.8	6 37.3	26 43.2	17 36.5	6 36.7	15 59.7	6 31.7	14 43.5	17 9.5
21 F	19 52 46	27 40 22	8♎50 0	15 45 14	0 17.9	8 34.7	27 54.9	18 9.0	6 32.3	16 5.5	6 35.2	14 44.3	17 11.3
22 Sa	19 56 42	28 37 39	22 43 22	29 44 22	0R 18.4	10 30.4	29 6.7	18 41.6	6 27.8	16 11.3	6 38.6	14 45.1	17 13.0
23 Su	20 0 39	29 34 56	6♏48 10	13♏54 40	0 18.3	12 24.4	0♋18.5	19 14.4	6 23.0	16 17.2	6 42.0	14 45.9	17 14.8
24 M	20 4 35	0♌32 14	21 3 38	28 14 47	0 16.6	14 16.7	1 30.3	19 47.4	6 18.2	16 23.1	6 45.4	14 46.8	17 16.6
25 Tu	20 8 32	1 29 32	5♐27 42	12♐41 53	0 12.8	16 7.2	2 42.2	20 20.6	6 13.1	16 29.1	6 48.7	14 47.7	17 18.3
26 W	20 12 29	2 26 50	19 56 44	27 11 34	0 6.7	17 56.0	3 54.1	20 54.0	6 7.9	16 35.1	6 52.1	14 48.6	17 20.1
27 Th	20 16 25	3 24 9	4♑25 38	11♑38 9	29♓58.9	19 43.0	5 6.1	21 27.6	6 2.6	16 41.2	6 55.4	14 49.5	17 21.9
28 F	20 20 22	4 21 28	18 48 19	25 55 24	29 50.3	21 28.3	6 18.2	22 1.3	5 57.1	16 47.4	6 58.7	14 50.5	17 23.7
29 Sa	20 24 18	5 18 48	2♒58 40	9♒57 31	29 41.8	23 11.9	7 30.3	22 35.2	5 51.5	16 53.6	7 2.0	14 51.5	17 25.5
30 Su	20 28 15	6 16 8	16 51 26	23 40 1	29 34.5	24 53.7	8 42.4	23 9.3	5 45.7	16 59.9	7 5.3	14 52.6	17 27.4
31 M	20 32 11	7 13 30	0♓23 2	7♓ 0 22	29 29.0	26 33.9	9 54.6	23 43.5	5 39.8	17 6.2	7 8.5	14 53.6	17 29.2

AUGUST 1950 LONGITUDE

Day	Sid.Time	☉	0 hr ☽	Noon ☽	True ☊	☿	♀	♂	♃	♄	♅	♆	♇
1 Tu	20 36 8	8♌10 52	13♓32 0	19♓58 5	29♓25.7	28♌12.4	11♋ 6.8	24♎17.9	5♓33.7	17♍12.5	7♋11.7	14♎54.7	17♌31.0
2 W	20 40 4	9 8 15	26 18 52	2♈34 41	29D 24.5	29 49.1	12 19.1	24 52.5	5R 27.5	17 18.9	7 14.9	14 55.9	17 32.8
3 Th	20 44 1	10 5 40	8♈45 57	14 53 10	29 24.8	1♍24.2	13 31.5	25 27.2	5 21.2	17 25.3	7 18.1	14 57.0	17 34.7
4 F	20 47 58	11 3 5	20 56 54	26 57 42	29 25.9	2 57.5	14 43.9	26 2.1	5 14.8	17 31.8	7 21.3	14 58.2	17 36.5
5 Sa	20 51 54	12 0 32	2♉56 13	8♉53 5	29R 27.1	4 29.2	15 56.3	26 37.1	5 8.2	17 38.4	7 24.4	14 59.4	17 38.3
6 Su	20 55 51	12 58 0	14 48 55	20 44 22	29 27.5	5 59.2	17 8.8	27 12.4	5 1.5	17 45.0	7 27.5	15 0.6	17 40.2
7 M	20 59 47	13 55 29	26 40 5	2♊36 38	29 26.5	7 27.4	18 21.4	27 47.7	4 54.7	17 51.6	7 30.6	15 1.9	17 42.0
8 Tu	21 3 44	14 53 0	8♊34 37	14 34 35	29 23.7	8 53.9	19 34.0	28 23.3	4 47.8	17 58.2	7 33.6	15 3.2	17 43.9
9 W	21 7 40	15 50 32	20 37 0	26 42 21	29 19.2	10 18.7	20 46.6	28 59.0	4 40.8	18 5.0	7 36.7	15 4.5	17 45.7
10 Th	21 11 37	16 48 5	2♋50 58	9♋ 3 13	29 13.1	11 41.7	21 59.3	29 34.8	4 33.7	18 11.7	7 39.7	15 5.8	17 47.6
11 F	21 15 33	17 45 40	15 19 20	21 39 28	29 6.2	13 2.9	23 12.1	0♏10.8	4 26.5	18 18.5	7 42.6	15 7.2	17 49.4
12 Sa	21 19 30	18 43 16	28 3 46	4♌32 13	28 59.1	14 22.2	24 24.9	0 47.0	4 19.3	18 25.3	7 45.6	15 8.6	17 51.3
13 Su	21 23 27	19 40 53	11♌ 4 47	17 41 22	28 52.6	15 39.6	25 37.7	1 23.3	4 11.9	18 32.2	7 48.5	15 10.0	17 53.1
14 M	21 27 23	20 38 31	24 21 47	1♍ 5 50	28 47.4	16 55.0	26 50.6	1 59.7	4 4.5	18 39.1	7 51.4	15 11.5	17 55.0
15 Tu	21 31 20	21 36 11	7♍53 14	14 43 42	28 43.9	18 8.5	28 3.5	2 36.3	3 57.0	18 46.0	7 54.2	15 12.9	17 56.8
16 W	21 35 16	22 33 51	21 36 58	28 32 42	28D 42.2	19 19.9	29 16.5	3 13.1	3 49.4	18 53.0	7 57.0	15 14.4	17 58.6
17 Th	21 39 13	23 31 33	5♎30 36	12♎30 25	28 42.2	20 29.1	0♌29.5	3 50.0	3 41.8	18 60.0	7 59.8	15 15.9	18 0.5
18 F	21 43 9	24 29 16	19 31 51	26 34 39	28 43.3	21 36.0	1 42.6	4 27.0	3 34.1	19 7.0	8 2.6	15 17.5	18 2.3
19 Sa	21 47 6	25 27 0	3♏38 35	10♏43 24	28 44.7	22 40.7	2 55.7	5 4.2	3 26.4	19 14.1	8 5.3	15 19.1	18 4.2
20 Su	21 51 2	26 24 45	17 48 54	24 54 50	28R 45.8	23 42.8	4 8.9	5 41.5	3 18.6	19 21.2	8 8.0	15 20.6	18 6.0
21 M	21 54 59	27 22 31	2♐ 0 57	9♐ 7 1	28 46.0	24 42.4	5 22.1	6 18.9	3 10.8	19 28.3	8 10.6	15 22.3	18 7.8
22 Tu	21 58 56	28 20 18	16 12 43	23 17 46	28 44.8	25 39.3	6 35.3	6 56.5	3 3.0	19 35.4	8 13.2	15 23.9	18 9.7
23 W	22 2 52	29 18 7	0♑21 49	7♑24 30	28 42.4	26 33.4	7 48.6	7 34.2	2 55.1	19 42.6	8 15.8	15 25.6	18 11.5
24 Th	22 6 49	0♍15 56	14 25 27	21 24 15	28 38.9	27 24.4	9 1.9	8 12.1	2 47.2	19 49.8	8 18.3	15 27.2	18 13.3
25 F	22 10 45	1 13 47	28 20 32	5♒13 53	28 34.9	28 12.2	10 15.3	8 50.0	2 39.3	19 57.0	8 20.9	15 28.9	18 15.1
26 Sa	22 14 42	2 11 39	12♒ 3 57	18 50 24	28 31.0	28 56.7	11 28.7	9 28.1	2 31.4	20 4.3	8 23.3	15 30.7	18 16.9
27 Su	22 18 38	3 9 33	25 32 58	2♓11 25	28 27.6	29 37.5	12 42.1	10 6.4	2 23.5	20 11.6	8 25.8	15 32.4	18 18.7
28 M	22 22 35	4 7 27	8♓45 36	15 15 25	28 25.2	0♎14.5	13 55.6	10 44.7	2 15.6	20 18.8	8 28.1	15 34.2	18 20.5
29 Tu	22 26 31	5 5 24	21 40 53	28 2 1	28D 24.0	0 47.5	15 9.2	11 23.2	2 7.7	20 26.1	8 30.5	15 36.0	18 22.3
30 W	22 30 28	6 3 22	4♈19 0	10♈32 2	28 24.0	1 16.2	16 22.7	12 1.7	1 59.9	20 33.5	8 32.8	15 37.8	18 24.1
31 Th	22 34 25	7 1 22	16 41 22	22 47 22	28 24.9	1 40.3	17 36.4	12 40.4	1 52.0	20 40.8	8 35.1	15 39.6	18 25.9

Astro Data Dy Hr Mn	Planet Ingress Dy Hr Mn	Last Aspect Dy Hr Mn	☽ Ingress Dy Hr Mn	Last Aspect Dy Hr Mn	☽ Ingress Dy Hr Mn	☽ Phases & Eclipses Dy Hr Mn	Astro Data
♄⊻♆ 3 19:20	☿ ♋ 2 14:57	30 7:36 ♆ □	♒ 1 9:19	1 6:53 ♄ ☍	♈ 2 7:03	7 2:53 ☽ 14♈26	1 JULY 1950
☽0N 5 22:59	☿ ♌ 16 17:08	2 14:04 ♇ ☍	♓ 3 13:51	4 10:40 ♂ ☍	♉ 4 18:06	15 5:05 ● 22♋09	Julian Day # 18444
☽0S 20 8:39	♀ ♋ 22 17:50	4 16:59 ♄ ☍	♈ 5 22:24	6 6:00 ♄ △	♊ 7 6:44	22 10:50 ☽ 29♎04	Delta T 29.4 sec
♃△♅ 20 15:19	☉ ♌ 23 10:30	7 7:38 ♇ △	♉ 8 10:13	9 17:18 ♂ △	♋ 9 18:27	29 4:18 ○ 5♒29	SVP 05♓57'04"
	☊ ♓ 26 20:56	9 20:50 ☉ ⚹	♊ 10 23:02	11 16:28 ♀ ☌	♌ 12 3:36		Obliquity 23°26'53"
		12 10:24 ♀ ☌	♋ 13 10:34	13 16:48 ☉ ☌	♍ 14 10:03		⚷ Chiron 17♐16.0R
☽0N 2 6:51		15 15:46 ☿ ☌	♌ 15 19:52	15 19:39 ☿ ☌	♎ 16 14:31	5 19:56 ☽ 12♉48	☽ Mean ☊ 2♈31.7
♄⊻♇ 4 23:46	☿ ♍ 2 2:44	17 16:05 ♀ ⚹	♍ 18 3:05	18 9:04 ☉ ⚹	♏ 18 17:49	13 16:48 ● 20♌21	
☽0S 16 14:07	♂ ♏ 10 16:48	20 3:04 ♀ □	♎ 20 8:34	20 15:35 ☉ □	♐ 20 20:36	20 15:35 ☽ 27♏02	1 AUGUST 1950
☿0S 21 12:24	♀ ♌ 16 14:18	22 11:57 ♀ △	♏ 22 12:27	22 22:04 ☉ △	♑ 22 23:23	27 14:51 ○ 3♓45	Julian Day # 18475
☽0N 29 15:13	☉ ♍ 23 17:23	23 17:39 ♇ □	♐ 24 14:55	24 23:45 ☿ △	♒ 25 2:53		Delta T 29.4 sec
	☿ ♎ 27 14:17	26 1:39 ♂ ⚹	♑ 26 16:39	26 11:02 ♇ ☍	♓ 27 8:02		SVP 05♓56'58"
		28 5:38 ♂ □	♒ 28 18:55	28 21:38 ♄ ☍	♈ 29 15:44		Obliquity 23°26'54"
		30 16:12 ☿ ☍	♓ 30 23:19				⚷ Chiron 15♐51.0R
							☽ Mean ☊ 0♈53.2

LONGITUDE — SEPTEMBER 1950

Day	Sid.Time	☉	0 hr ☽	Noon ☽	True ☊	☿	♀	♂	♃	♄	♅	♆	♇
1 F	22 38 21	7♍59 23	28♈50 25	4♉50 57	28♓26.3	1♎59.5	18♌50.0	13♏19.3	1♓44.2	20♍48.2	8♋37.3	15♎41.4	18♌27.6
2 Sa	22 42 18	8 57 27	10♉49 29	16 46 31	28 27.9	2 13.6	20 3.7	13 58.2	1R36.4	20 55.6	8 39.5	15 43.3	18 29.4
3 Su	22 46 14	9 55 33	22 42 37	28* 38 20	28 29.2	2 22.3	21 17.5	14 37.3	1 28.7	21 2.9	8 41.7	15 45.1	18 31.1
4 M	22 50 11	10 53 40	4♊34 17	10♊31 2	28R30.0	2R25.3	22 31.3	15 16.5	1 20.9	21 10.4	8 43.8	15 47.0	18 32.9
5 Tu	22 54 7	11 51 49	16 29 13	22 29 23	28 30.1	2 22.3	23 45.2	15 55.8	1 13.3	21 17.8	8 45.9	15 49.0	18 34.6
6 W	22 58 4	12 50 1	28 32 7	4♋37 57	28 29.4	2 13.2	24 59.0	16 35.2	1 5.7	21 25.2	8 47.9	15 50.9	18 36.3
7 Th	23 2 0	13 48 14	10♋47 25	17 0 57	28 28.1	1 57.7	26 13.0	17 14.8	0 58.1	21 32.7	8 49.9	15 52.8	18 38.0
8 F	23 5 57	14 46 30	23 18 58	29 41 48	28 26.4	1 35.7	27 26.9	17 54.4	0 50.7	21 40.1	8 51.8	15 54.8	18 39.7
9 Sa	23 9 54	15 44 47	6♌ 9 42	12♌42 50	28 24.6	1 7.3	28 41.0	18 34.2	0 43.3	21 47.6	8 53.7	15 56.8	18 41.4
10 Su	23 13 50	16 43 6	19 21 17	26 5 2	28 23.0	0 32.4	29 55.0	19 14.1	0 35.9	21 55.1	8 55.6	15 58.8	18 43.1
11 M	23 17 47	17 41 28	2♍53 56	9♍47 45	28 21.7	29♍51.4	1♍ 9.1	19 54.1	0 28.7	22 2.5	8 57.4	16 0.8	18 44.8
12 Tu	23 21 43	18 39 51	16 46 8	23 48 41	28D21.0	29 4.7	2 23.2	20 34.3	0 21.5	22 10.0	8 59.1	16 2.8	18 46.4
13 W	23 25 40	19 38 15	0♎54 52	8♎ 4 7	28 20.9	28 12.7	3 37.4	21 14.5	0 14.5	22 17.5	9 0.8	16 4.8	18 48.1
14 Th	23 29 36	20 36 42	15 15 48	22 29 16	28 21.1	27 16.4	4 51.6	21 54.9	0 7.5	22 25.0	9 2.5	16 6.9	18 49.7
15 F	23 33 33	21 35 11	29 43 51	6♏58 54	28 21.7	26 16.6	6 5.8	22 35.3	0 0.7	22 32.5	9 4.1	16 8.9	18 51.3
16 Sa	23 37 29	22 33 41	14♏13 47	21 27 55	28 22.2	25 14.6	7 20.0	23 15.9	29♒53.9	22 40.0	9 5.7	16 11.0	18 52.9
17 Su	23 41 26	23 32 13	28 40 46	5♐51 52	28 22.7	24 11.6	8 34.3	23 56.6	29 47.3	22 47.5	9 7.2	16 13.1	18 54.5
18 M	23 45 23	24 30 46	13♐ 0 49	20 7 17	28R22.9	23 9.2	9 48.7	24 37.4	29 40.8	22 55.0	9 8.7	16 15.2	18 56.1
19 Tu	23 49 19	25 29 21	27 10 58	4♑11 40	28 23.0	22 8.8	11 3.0	25 18.2	29 34.4	23 2.5	9 10.1	16 17.3	18 57.6
20 W	23 53 16	26 27 58	11♑ 9 12	18 3 28	28 23.0	21 12.0	12 17.4	25 59.2	29 28.2	23 10.0	9 11.5	16 19.4	18 59.2
21 Th	23 57 12	27 26 37	24 54 22	1♒41 51	28 22.9	20 20.3	13 31.8	26 40.3	29 22.1	23 17.5	9 12.8	16 21.6	19 0.7
22 F	0 1 9	28 25 17	8♒25 52	15 6 25	28D22.8	19 34.9	14 46.2	27 21.5	29 16.1	23 24.9	9 14.1	16 23.7	19 2.2
23 Sa	0 5 5	29 23 58	21 43 31	28 17 9	28 22.9	18 57.2	16 0.7	28 2.8	29 10.3	23 32.4	9 15.4	16 25.9	19 3.7
24 Su	0 9 2	0♎22 42	4♓47 21	11♓14 10	28 23.0	18 28.0	17 15.2	28 44.2	29 4.6	23 39.9	9 16.5	16 28.0	19 5.1
25 M	0 12 58	1 21 27	17 37 38	23 57 49	28R23.2	18 8.1	18 29.7	29 25.7	28 59.0	23 47.3	9 17.7	16 30.2	19 6.6
26 Tu	0 16 55	2 20 14	0♈14 48	6♈28 41	28 23.2	17D58.0	19 44.3	0♐ 7.3	28 53.6	23 54.8	9 18.7	16 32.4	19 8.0
27 W	0 20 52	3 19 3	12 39 37	18 47 44	28 23.1	17 58.1	20 58.9	0 48.9	28 48.4	24 2.2	9 19.8	16 34.5	19 9.5
28 Th	0 24 48	4 17 54	24 53 14	0♉56 19	28 22.6	18 8.2	22 13.5	1 30.7	28 43.3	24 9.6	9 20.7	16 36.7	19 10.9
29 F	0 28 45	5 16 48	6♉57 17	12 56 24	28 21.8	18 28.3	23 28.1	2 12.6	28 38.4	24 17.0	9 21.7	16 38.9	19 12.2
30 Sa	0 32 41	6 15 43	18 54 0	24 50 28	28 20.8	18 58.2	24 42.8	2 54.5	28 33.7	24 24.4	9 22.5	16 41.1	19 13.6

LONGITUDE — OCTOBER 1950

Day	Sid.Time	☉	0 hr ☽	Noon ☽	True ☊	☿	♀	♂	♃	♄	♅	♆	♇
1 Su	0 36 38	7♎14 41	0♊46 12	6♊41 39	28♓19.6	19♍37.2	25♍57.5	3♐36.6	28♒29.1	24♍31.8	9♋23.4	16♎43.3	19♌15.0
2 M	0 40 34	8 13 41	12 37 17	18 33 37	28R18.5	20 25.0	27 12.2	4 18.8	28R24.7	24 39.2	9 24.1	16 45.6	19 16.3
3 Tu	0 44 31	9 12 43	24 31 10	0♋30 30	28 17.6	21 20.7	28 27.0	5 1.0	28 20.4	24 46.5	9 24.9	16 47.8	19 17.6
4 W	0 48 27	10 11 48	6♋32 11	12 36 46	28D17.1	22 23.8	29 41.8	5 43.3	28 16.4	24 53.9	9 25.5	16 50.0	19 18.9
5 Th	0 52 24	11 10 55	18 44 51	24 56 58	28 17.2	23 33.5	0♎56.6	6 25.8	28 12.5	25 1.2	9 26.1	16 52.2	19 20.1
6 F	0 56 21	12 10 4	1♌13 40	7♌35 26	28 17.9	24 49.1	2 11.4	7 8.3	28 8.8	25 8.5	9 26.7	16 54.5	19 21.4
7 Sa	1 0 17	13 9 15	14 2 44	20 35 55	28 19.0	26 9.8	3 26.3	7 50.9	28 5.3	25 15.7	9 27.2	16 56.7	19 22.6
8 Su	1 4 14	14 8 29	27 15 18	4♍ 1 3	28 20.2	27 35.0	4 41.2	8 33.6	28 1.9	25 23.0	9 27.7	16 58.9	19 23.8
9 M	1 8 10	15 7 45	10♍53 13	17 51 45	28 21.3	29 4.0	5 56.1	9 16.4	27 58.8	25 30.2	9 28.1	17 1.2	19 25.0
10 Tu	1 12 7	16 7 3	24 56 25	2♎ 6 48	28R21.9	0♎36.2	7 11.0	9 59.3	27 55.8	25 37.4	9 28.4	17 3.4	19 26.2
11 W	1 16 3	17 6 23	9♎22 23	16 42 27	28 21.7	2 11.1	8 26.0	10 42.3	27 53.1	25 44.6	9 28.7	17 5.6	19 27.3
12 Th	1 20 0	18 5 46	24 6 11	1♏32 36	28 20.4	3 48.2	9 41.0	11 25.4	27 50.5	25 51.7	9 29.0	17 7.9	19 28.4
13 F	1 23 56	19 5 10	9♏ 0 42	16 29 23	28 18.2	5 27.0	10 55.9	12 8.5	27 48.1	25 58.8	9 29.1	17 10.1	19 29.5
14 Sa	1 27 53	20 4 37	23 57 36	1♐24 18	28 15.4	7 7.3	12 11.0	12 51.8	27 46.0	26 5.9	9 29.3	17 12.3	19 30.6
15 Su	1 31 50	21 4 5	8♐48 33	16 9 30	28 12.4	8 48.5	13 26.0	13 35.1	27 44.0	26 13.0	9 29.3	17 14.6	19 31.6
16 M	1 35 46	22 3 35	23 26 28	0♑38 51	28 9.7	10 30.6	14 41.0	14 18.5	27 42.2	26 20.0	9R29.4	17 16.8	19 32.6
17 Tu	1 39 43	23 3 7	7♑46 17	14 48 30	28 7.8	12 13.1	15 56.1	15 2.0	27 40.7	26 27.0	9 29.4	17 19.0	19 33.6
18 W	1 43 39	24 2 41	21 45 22	28 36 54	28D 7.0	13 56.0	17 11.2	15 45.6	27 39.3	26 34.0	9 29.3	17 21.3	19 34.6
19 Th	1 47 36	25 2 16	5♒23 11	12♒ 4 25	28 7.4	15 39.0	18 26.3	16 29.2	27 38.1	26 40.9	9 29.1	17 23.5	19 35.5
20 F	1 51 32	26 1 53	18 40 49	25 12 41	28 8.6	17 22.0	19 41.4	17 13.0	27 37.2	26 47.8	9 28.9	17 25.7	19 36.5
21 Sa	1 55 29	27 1 32	1♓40 18	8♓ 4 1	28 10.3	19 4.8	20 56.5	17 56.8	27 36.4	26 54.6	9 28.7	17 27.9	19 37.4
22 Su	1 59 25	28 1 12	14 24 9	20 40 59	28 11.8	20 47.5	22 11.6	18 40.6	27 35.8	27 1.4	9 28.4	17 30.1	19 38.2
23 M	2 3 22	29 0 54	26 54 50	3♈ 5 57	28R12.5	22 29.9	23 26.7	19 24.6	27 35.5	27 8.2	9 28.1	17 32.3	19 39.1
24 Tu	2 7 19	0♏ 0 38	9♈14 37	15 21 3	28 11.9	24 11.9	24 41.9	20 8.6	27D35.3	27 14.9	9 27.7	17 34.5	19 39.9
25 W	2 11 15	1 0 24	21 25 28	27 28 4	28 9.7	25 53.6	25 57.0	20 52.7	27 35.4	27 21.6	9 27.2	17 36.7	19 40.7
26 Th	2 15 12	2 0 12	3♉29 4	9♉28 38	28 5.7	27 34.8	27 12.2	21 36.9	27 35.6	27 28.2	9 26.7	17 38.9	19 41.4
27 F	2 19 8	3 0 1	15 26 57	21 24 14	28 0.3	29 15.6	28 27.4	22 21.1	27 36.1	27 34.8	9 26.1	17 41.1	19 42.2
28 Sa	2 23 5	3 59 53	27 20 42	3♊16 35	27 53.7	0♏55.9	29 42.6	23 5.5	27 36.7	27 41.3	9 25.5	17 43.3	19 42.9
29 Su	2 27 1	4 59 47	9♊12 7	15 7 37	27 46.6	2 35.8	0♏57.8	23 49.8	27 37.6	27 47.8	9 24.9	17 45.4	19 43.6
30 M	2 30 58	5 59 43	21 3 25	26 59 51	27 39.7	4 15.1	2 13.1	24 34.3	27 38.6	27 54.3	9 24.2	17 47.6	19 44.2
31 Tu	2 34 54	6 59 41	2♋57 19	8♋56 16	27 33.7	5 54.0	3 28.3	25 18.8	27 39.9	28 0.7	9 23.4	17 49.7	19 44.9

Astro Data	Planet Ingress	Last Aspect	☽ Ingress	Last Aspect	☽ Ingress	☽ Phases & Eclipses	Astro Data
Dy Hr Mn	Dy Hr Mn	Dy Hr Mn	Dy Hr Mn	Dy Hr Mn	Dy Hr Mn	Dy Hr Mn	1 SEPTEMBER 1950
☿ R 4 0:14	☿ ♍ 10 19:16	31 3:25 ♇ △	♉ 1 2:19	3 8:48 ♀ □	♋ 3 10:59	4 13:53 ☽ 11♊27	Julian Day # 18506
♃□♆ 7 13:29	♀ ♍ 10 1:37	2 20:48 ♀ □	♊ 3 14:45	5 12:15 ♄ ⚹	♌ 5 21:40	12 3:29 ● 18♍48	Delta T 29.4 sec
☽0S 12 21:58	♃ ♒ 15 2:23	5 16:10 ♀ ⚹	♋ 6 2:54	8 1:23 ♃ ☍	♍ 8 4:54	12 3:38:16 ◐T 1'14"	SVP 05♓56'54"
☿0N 18 0:58	☉ ♎ 23 14:44	7 20:51 ♄ ⚹	♌ 8 12:34	10 1:10 ♄ ☌	♎ 10 8:29	18 20:54 ☽ 25♐22	Obliquity 23°26'54"
☽0N 25 22:59	♂ ♐ 25 19:48	9 23:46 ♂ □	♍ 10 18:55	12 6:01 ♃ △	♏ 12 9:31	26 4:21 ○ 2♈31	⚷ Chiron 15♐44.6
☿ D 26 11:59		12 19:43 ☿ ☌	♎ 12 22:28	14 6:07 ♃ □	♐ 14 9:44	26 4:17 ◑T 1.079	☽ Mean ☊ 29♓14.7
	♀ ♎ 4 5:51	14 5:56 ♇ ⚹	♏ 15 0:27	16 7:04 ♃ ⚹	♑ 16 10:55		
♀0S 6 22:05	☿ ♎ 9 14:40	17 1:50 ♃ □	♐ 17 2:12	18 8:28 ♄ △	♒ 18 14:27	4 7:53 ☽ 10♋31	1 OCTOBER 1950
☽0S 10 8:00	☉ ♏ 23 23:45	19 4:03 ♃ ⚹	♑ 19 4:49	20 16:26 ♃ ☌	♓ 20 20:53	11 13:33 ● 17♎40	Julian Day # 18536
☿0S 12 10:43	☿ ♏ 27 10:36	21 4:49 ☉ △	♒ 21 8:59	23 0:26 ♄ ☍	♈ 23 5:59	18 4:18 ☽ 24♑13	Delta T 29.5 sec
♅ R 16 0:17	♀ ♏ 28 5:33	23 13:32 ♃ ☌	♓ 23 15:09	25 12:15 ♃ ⚹	♉ 25 17:03	25 20:46 ○ 1♉52	SVP 05♓56'51"
☽0N 23 5:22		25 11:47 ♄ ☍	♈ 25 23:32	28 0:42 ♄ △	♊ 28 5:22		Obliquity 23°26'54"
♃ D 24 6:34		28 7:33 ♃ ⚹	♉ 28 10:08	30 13:57 ♄ □	♋ 30 18:03		⚷ Chiron 17♐00.7
♃⊼♄ 27 5:05		30 19:24 ♃ □	♊ 30 22:26				☽ Mean ☊ 27♓39.4

NOVEMBER 1950 LONGITUDE

Day	Sid.Time	☉	0 hr ☽	Noon ☽	True ☊	☿	♀	♂	♃	♄	♅	♆	♇
1 W	2 38 51	7♏59 41	14♋57 11	21♋ 0 32	27♓29.3	7♏32.5	4♏43.6	26♐ 3.4	27♒41.4	28♍ 7.1	9♋22.6	17♎51.9	19♌45.5
2 Th	2 42 48	8 59 43	27 6 53	3♌16 46	27R26.6	9 10.4	5 58.8	26 48.1	27 43.0	28 13.4	9R21.7	17 54.0	19 46.1
3 F	2 46 44	9 59 48	9♌30 45	15 49 26	27D25.7	10 47.9	7 14.1	27 32.9	27 44.9	28 19.6	9 20.8	17 56.1	19 46.6
4 Sa	2 50 41	10 59 54	22 13 21	28 43 1	27 26.3	12 25.0	8 29.4	28 17.7	27 46.9	28 25.8	9 19.8	17 58.2	19 47.1
5 Su	2 54 37	12 0 3	5♍18 56	12♍ 1 30	27 27.6	14 1.6	9 44.7	29 2.5	27 49.2	28 31.9	9 18.8	18 0.3	19 47.6
6 M	2 58 34	13 0 13	18 51 2	25 47 42	27R28.8	15 37.8	10 60.0	29 47.5	27 51.6	28 38.0	9 17.8	18 2.4	19 48.1
7 Tu	3 2 30	14 0 26	2♎51 31	10♎ 2 21	27 28.9	17 13.7	12 15.3	0♑32.5	27 54.3	28 44.1	9 16.6	18 4.4	19 48.5
8 W	3 6 27	15 0 41	17 19 51	24 43 25	27 27.3	18 49.1	13 30.6	1 17.6	27 57.2	28 50.0	9 15.5	18 6.5	19 48.9
9 Th	3 10 23	16 0 57	2♏12 18	9♏45 29	27 23.4	20 24.2	14 46.0	2 2.7	28 0.2	28 55.9	9 14.3	18 8.5	19 49.3
10 F	3 14 20	17 1 16	17 21 47	24 59 56	27 17.4	21 58.9	16 1.3	2 47.9	28 3.4	29 1.8	9 13.0	18 10.5	19 49.7
11 Sa	3 18 16	18 1 36	2♐38 30	10♐16 6	27 9.8	23 33.2	17 16.7	3 33.2	28 6.9	29 7.6	9 11.7	18 12.5	19 50.0
12 Su	3 22 13	19 1 58	17 51 21	25 23 0	27 1.6	25 7.3	18 32.0	4 18.6	28 10.5	29 13.3	9 10.3	18 14.5	19 50.3
13 M	3 26 10	20 2 22	2♑49 59	10♑11 22	26 53.8	26 41.1	19 47.4	5 4.0	28 14.3	29 18.9	9 9.0	18 16.5	19 50.6
14 Tu	3 30 6	21 2 47	17 26 30	24 34 54	26 47.6	28 14.5	21 2.8	5 49.4	28 18.4	29 24.5	9 7.5	18 18.5	19 50.8
15 W	3 34 3	22 3 13	1♒36 21	8♒30 47	26 43.4	29 47.7	22 18.2	6 34.9	28 22.6	29 30.1	9 6.0	18 20.4	19 51.0
16 Th	3 37 59	23 3 40	15 18 21	21 59 16	26D41.4	1♐20.6	23 33.5	7 20.5	28 26.9	29 35.5	9 4.5	18 22.3	19 51.2
17 F	3 41 56	24 4 9	28 33 57	5♓ 2 49	26 41.2	2 53.3	24 48.9	8 6.1	28 31.5	29 40.9	9 2.9	18 24.3	19 51.4
18 Sa	3 45 52	25 4 39	11♓26 23	17 45 11	26 42.0	4 25.7	26 4.3	8 51.8	28 36.3	29 46.2	9 1.3	18 26.1	19 51.5
19 Su	3 49 49	26 5 10	23 59 44	0♈10 35	26R42.7	5 57.8	27 19.7	9 37.6	28 41.2	29 51.5	8 59.6	18 28.0	19 51.6
20 M	3 53 46	27 5 43	6♈18 15	12 23 13	26 42.2	7 29.8	28 35.0	10 23.3	28 46.3	29 56.6	8 57.9	18 29.9	19 51.6
21 Tu	3 57 42	28 6 17	18 25 55	24 26 45	26 39.7	9 1.5	29 50.4	11 9.2	28 51.6	0♎ 1.7	8 56.2	18 31.7	19R51.7
22 W	4 1 39	29 6 52	0♉26 7	6♉24 19	26 34.6	10 33.0	1♐ 5.8	11 55.0	28 57.1	0 6.7	8 54.4	18 33.5	19 51.7
23 Th	4 5 35	0♐ 7 28	12 21 38	18 18 20	26 26.6	12 4.2	2 21.2	12 41.0	29 2.8	0 11.7	8 52.6	18 35.3	19 51.6
24 F	4 9 32	1 8 6	24 14 36	0♊10 39	26 16.1	13 35.2	3 36.6	13 26.9	29 8.6	0 16.6	8 50.7	18 37.1	19 51.6
25 Sa	4 13 28	2 8 45	6♊ 6 39	12 2 46	26 3.7	15 6.0	4 52.0	14 13.0	29 14.6	0 21.4	8 48.9	18 38.8	19 51.5
26 Su	4 17 25	3 9 26	17 59 10	23 56 1	25 50.3	16 36.5	6 7.4	14 59.0	29 20.7	0 26.1	8 46.9	18 40.5	19 51.4
27 M	4 21 21	4 10 8	29 53 30	5♋51 51	25 37.2	18 6.7	7 22.8	15 45.2	29 27.1	0 30.7	8 45.0	18 42.3	19 51.3
28 Tu	4 25 18	5 10 52	11♋51 16	17 52 3	25 25.3	19 36.6	8 38.2	16 31.3	29 33.6	0 35.3	8 43.0	18 43.9	19 51.1
29 W	4 29 15	6 11 37	23 54 31	29 59 1	25 15.6	21 6.1	9 53.6	17 17.5	29 40.2	0 39.7	8 40.9	18 45.6	19 50.9
30 Th	4 33 11	7 12 23	6♌ 5 58	12♌15 46	25 8.7	22 35.3	11 9.0	18 3.8	29 47.1	0 44.1	8 38.9	18 47.2	19 50.7

DECEMBER 1950 LONGITUDE

Day	Sid.Time	☉	0 hr ☽	Noon ☽	True ☊	☿	♀	♂	♃	♄	♅	♆	♇
1 F	4 37 8	8♐13 11	18♌28 56	24♌45 57	25♓ 4.5	24♐ 4.0	12♐24.4	18♑50.1	29♒54.1	0♎48.4	8♋36.8	18♎48.9	19♌50.4
2 Sa	4 41 4	9 14 0	1♍ 7 22	7♍33 42	25D 2.8	25 32.2	13 39.8	19 36.4	0♓ 1.2	0 52.7	8R34.6	18 50.4	19R50.2
3 Su	4 45 1	10 14 50	14 5 29	20 43 13	25R 2.6	26 59.9	14 55.2	20 22.8	0 8.5	0 56.8	8 32.5	18 52.0	19 49.8
4 M	4 48 57	11 15 42	27 27 20	4♎18 13	25 2.7	28 26.8	16 10.6	21 9.2	0 16.0	1 0.8	8 30.3	18 53.5	19 49.5
5 Tu	4 52 54	12 16 36	11♎16 6	18 21 5	25 1.9	29 53.0	17 26.0	21 55.7	0 23.6	1 4.8	8 28.0	18 55.1	19 49.1
6 W	4 56 50	13 17 31	25 33 5	2♏51 51	24 58.9	1♑18.3	18 41.5	22 42.2	0 31.4	1 8.7	8 25.8	18 56.5	19 48.7
7 Th	5 0 47	14 18 27	10♏16 50	17 47 17	24 53.3	2 42.5	19 56.9	23 28.8	0 39.3	1 12.5	8 23.5	18 58.0	19 48.3
8 F	5 4 44	15 19 24	25 22 15	3♐ 0 30	24 44.8	4 5.5	21 12.3	24 15.4	0 47.4	1 16.1	8 21.2	18 59.4	19 47.9
9 Sa	5 8 40	16 20 23	10♐40 41	18 21 20	24 34.1	5 27.1	22 27.8	25 2.0	0 55.6	1 19.7	8 18.9	19 0.9	19 47.4
10 Su	5 12 37	17 21 22	26 0 55	3♑37 58	24 22.4	6 46.9	23 43.2	25 48.7	1 4.0	1 23.2	8 16.5	19 2.2	19 46.9
11 M	5 16 33	18 22 23	11♑11 6	18 39 7	24 11.0	8 4.8	24 58.6	26 35.4	1 12.5	1 26.7	8 14.2	19 3.6	19 46.4
12 Tu	5 20 30	19 23 24	26 1 2	3♒16 5	24 1.3	9 20.4	26 14.1	27 22.1	1 21.2	1 30.0	8 11.8	19 4.9	19 45.8
13 W	5 24 26	20 24 25	10♒23 47	17 23 51	23 54.1	10 33.4	27 29.5	28 8.9	1 30.0	1 33.2	8 9.4	19 6.2	19 45.2
14 Th	5 28 23	21 25 27	24 16 15	1♓ 1 8	23 49.8	11 43.2	28 44.9	28 55.7	1 39.0	1 36.3	8 6.9	19 7.5	19 44.6
15 F	5 32 20	22 26 30	7♓38 48	14 9 42	23 47.8	12 49.4	0♑ 0.3	29 42.5	1 48.1	1 39.3	8 4.5	19 8.7	19 44.0
16 Sa	5 36 16	23 27 33	20 34 21	26 53 21	23 47.4	13 51.5	1 15.7	0♒29.3	1 57.3	1 42.3	8 2.0	19 9.9	19 43.3
17 Su	5 40 13	24 28 36	3♈ 7 19	9♈16 54	23 47.3	14 48.8	2 31.1	1 16.2	2 6.6	1 45.1	7 59.5	19 11.1	19 42.6
18 M	5 44 9	25 29 40	15 22 46	21 25 30	23 46.3	15 40.6	3 46.5	2 3.1	2 16.1	1 47.8	7 57.0	19 12.3	19 41.9
19 Tu	5 48 6	26 30 44	27 25 45	3♉24 3	23 43.2	16 26.2	5 1.9	2 50.0	2 25.7	1 50.4	7 54.5	19 13.4	19 41.2
20 W	5 52 2	27 31 49	9♉20 56	15 16 53	23 37.4	17 4.6	6 17.3	3 37.0	2 35.4	1 52.9	7 52.0	19 14.5	19 40.4
21 Th	5 55 59	28 32 53	21 12 18	27 7 35	23 28.5	17 35.1	7 32.7	4 24.0	2 45.3	1 55.4	7 49.4	19 15.5	19 39.6
22 F	5 59 55	29 33 59	3♊ 3 2	8♊58 56	23 16.9	17 56.7	8 48.1	5 11.0	2 55.3	1 57.7	7 46.9	19 16.6	19 38.8
23 Sa	6 3 52	0♑35 4	14 55 32	20 53 0	23 3.1	18R 8.5	10 3.5	5 58.0	3 5.4	1 59.9	7 44.3	19 17.6	19 38.0
24 Su	6 7 49	1 36 10	26 51 30	2♋51 11	22 48.2	18 9.8	11 18.8	6 45.0	3 15.6	2 2.0	7 41.7	19 18.5	19 37.1
25 M	6 11 45	2 37 17	8♋52 10	14 54 34	22 33.5	17 59.8	12 34.2	7 32.1	3 26.0	2 4.0	7 39.2	19 19.5	19 36.3
26 Tu	6 15 42	3 38 24	20 58 30	27 4 7	22 20.1	17 38.1	13 49.6	8 19.1	3 36.4	2 5.9	7 36.6	19 20.4	19 35.4
27 W	6 19 38	4 39 31	3♌11 33	9♌20 59	22 9.1	17 4.6	15 4.9	9 6.2	3 47.0	2 7.7	7 34.0	19 21.3	19 34.4
28 Th	6 23 35	5 40 38	15 32 39	21 46 47	22 1.0	16 19.5	16 20.3	9 53.3	3 57.7	2 9.4	7 31.4	19 22.1	19 33.5
29 F	6 27 31	6 41 46	28 3 41	4♍23 40	21 56.0	15 23.7	17 35.6	10 40.5	4 8.5	2 11.0	7 28.8	19 22.9	19 32.5
30 Sa	6 31 28	7 42 54	10♍47 7	17 14 24	21D53.7	14 18.3	18 51.0	11 27.6	4 19.4	2 12.5	7 26.3	19 23.7	19 31.5
31 Su	6 35 24	8 44 3	23 45 57	0♎22 9	21 53.2	13 5.4	20 6.3	12 14.8	4 30.4	2 13.9	7 23.7	19 24.4	19 30.5

Astro Data	Planet Ingress	Last Aspect	☽ Ingress	Last Aspect	☽ Ingress	☽ Phases & Eclipses	Astro Data
Dy Hr Mn	Dy Hr Mn	Dy Hr Mn	Dy Hr Mn	Dy Hr Mn	Dy Hr Mn	Dy Hr Mn	1 NOVEMBER 1950
☽0S 6 18:26	♂ ♑ 6 6:40	2 2:11 ♄ ⚹	♌ 2 5:38	1 12:05 ☿ △	♍ 1 21:53	3 1:00 ☽ 10♌02	Julian Day # 18567
☽0N 19 10:34	☿ ♐ 15 3:10	4 11:54 ♂ △	♍ 4 14:21	4 1:57 ☿ □	♎ 4 4:29	9 23:25 ● 16♏60	Delta T 29.5 sec
♇ R 21 15:56	♄ ♎ 20 15:50	6 16:58 ♄ ☌	♎ 6 19:10	5 19:00 ♂ □	♏ 6 7:19	16 15:06 ☽ 23♒42	SVP 05♓56'47"
	♀ ♐ 21 3:03	8 17:15 ♃ △	♏ 8 20:29	7 22:09 ♂ ⚹	♐ 8 7:17	24 15:14 ○ 1♊47	Obliquity 23°26'54"
☽0S 4 3:00	☉ ♐ 22 21:03	10 18:27 ♄ ⚹	♐ 10 19:51	9 20:05 ♀ ☌	♑ 10 6:16		⚷ Chiron 19♐29.8
♃⚻♄ 13 13:10		12 18:17 ♄ □	♑ 12 19:25	12 2:21 ♂ ☌	♒ 12 6:34	2 16:22 ☽ 9♍55	☽ Mean ☊ 26♓00.9
☽0N 16 15:58	♃ ♓ 1 19:57	14 20:30 ☿ ⚹	♒ 14 21:14	14 8:45 ♀ ⚹	♓ 14 10:10	9 9:29 ● 16♐44	
☿ R 23 14:48	☿ ♑ 5 1:57	16 23:56 ♃ ☌	♓ 17 2:38	16 5:56 ☉ □	♈ 16 17:58	16 5:56 ☽ 23♓43	1 DECEMBER 1950
♃⚼♆ 30 10:04	♀ ♑ 14 23:54	19 11:28 ♄ ☍	♈ 19 11:39	18 22:00 ☉ △	♉ 19 5:10	24 10:23 ○ 2♋03	Julian Day # 18597
☽0S 31 8:51	♂ ♒ 15 8:59	21 21:00 ♃ ⚹	♉ 21 23:08	20 20:52 ♇ □	♊ 21 17:49		Delta T 29.5 sec
	☉ ♑ 22 10:13	24 9:59 ♃ □	♊ 24 11:38	23 9:28 ♇ ⚹	♋ 24 6:18		SVP 05♓56'42"
		26 23:06 ♃ △	♋ 27 0:13	25 20:46 ♆ □	♌ 26 17:45		Obliquity 23°26'53"
		28 13:45 ♆ □	♌ 29 12:02	28 7:44 ♇ ☌	♍ 29 3:41		⚷ Chiron 22♐37.8
				30 16:34 ♀ △	♎ 31 11:20		☽ Mean ☊ 24♓25.6

LONGITUDE JANUARY 1951

Day	Sid.Time	☉	0 hr ☽	Noon ☽	True ☊	☿	♀	♂	♃	♄	♅	♆	♇
1 M	6 39 21	9♑45 12	7♎ 3 23	13♎50 1	21♓53.5	11♑47.1	21♑21.7	13♒ 1.9	4♓41.5	2♎15.2	7♋21.1	19♎25.1	19♌29.5
2 Tu	6 43 18	10 46 22	20 42 21	27 40 33	21R53.1	10R25.9	22 37.0	13 49.1	4 52.7	2 16.3	7R18.5	19 25.8	19R28.4
3 W	6 47 14	11 47 32	4♏44 42	11♏54 45	21 51.1	9 4.6	23 52.3	14 36.3	5 4.0	2 17.4	7 15.9	19 26.4	19 27.4
4 Th	6 51 11	12 48 42	19 10 25	26 31 17	21 46.5	7 45.9	25 7.6	15 23.5	5 15.5	2 18.3	7 13.3	19 27.0	19 26.3
5 F	6 55 7	13 49 53	3♐56 43	11♐25 51	21 39.4	6 31.9	26 23.0	16 10.7	5 27.0	2 19.1	7 10.7	19 27.6	19 25.2
6 Sa	6 59 4	14 51 4	18 57 40	26 30 59	21 30.1	5 24.8	27 38.3	16 58.0	5 38.6	2 19.9	7 8.2	19 28.2	19 24.1
7 Su	7 3 0	15 52 14	4♑ 4 33	11♑37 3	21 19.6	4 26.0	28 53.6	17 45.2	5 50.3	2 20.5	7 5.6	19 28.7	19 22.9
8 M	7 6 57	16 53 25	19 7 9	26 33 39	21 9.3	3 36.4	0♒ 8.9	18 32.5	6 2.1	2 21.0	7 3.1	19 29.1	19 21.7
9 Tu	7 10 53	17 54 36	3♒55 26	11♒11 37	21 0.3	2 56.7	1 24.2	19 19.8	6 14.0	2 21.4	7 0.5	19 29.6	19 20.6
10 W	7 14 50	18 55 46	18 21 28	25 24 28	20 53.7	2 27.0	2 39.5	20 7.0	6 26.0	2 21.7	6 58.0	19 30.0	19 19.4
11 Th	7 18 47	19 56 56	2♓20 20	9♓ 8 59	20 49.6	2 7.2	3 54.7	20 54.3	6 38.1	2 21.8	6 55.5	19 30.3	19 18.2
12 F	7 22 43	20 58 5	15 50 29	22 25 6	20D48.0	1D56.9	5 10.0	21 41.6	6 50.3	2R21.9	6 53.0	19 30.7	19 16.9
13 Sa	7 26 40	21 59 14	28 53 12	5♈15 16	20 48.1	1 55.6	6 25.2	22 28.9	7 2.5	2 21.8	6 50.5	19 31.0	19 15.7
14 Su	7 30 36	23 0 22	11♈31 50	17 43 30	20 49.0	2 2.7	7 40.5	23 16.1	7 14.9	2 21.7	6 48.1	19 31.2	19 14.4
15 M	7 34 33	24 1 29	23 50 56	29 54 46	20R49.5	2 17.5	8 55.7	24 3.4	7 27.3	2 21.4	6 45.6	19 31.5	19 13.2
16 Tu	7 38 29	25 2 36	5♉55 40	11♉54 16	20 48.7	2 39.4	10 10.9	24 50.7	7 39.8	2 21.0	6 43.2	19 31.7	19 11.9
17 W	7 42 26	26 3 42	17 51 11	23 47 1	20 45.9	3 7.8	11 26.0	25 38.0	7 52.3	2 20.6	6 40.8	19 31.8	19 10.6
18 Th	7 46 22	27 4 47	29 42 19	5♊37 35	20 40.8	3 42.1	12 41.2	26 25.2	8 5.0	2 20.0	6 38.4	19 31.9	19 9.3
19 F	7 50 19	28 5 51	11♊33 18	17 29 52	20 33.5	4 21.6	13 56.4	27 12.5	8 17.7	2 19.3	6 36.0	19 32.0	19 7.9
20 Sa	7 54 16	29 6 55	23 27 40	29 26 59	20 24.4	5 5.9	15 11.5	27 59.7	8 30.5	2 18.5	6 33.7	19 32.1	19 6.6
21 Su	7 58 12	0♒ 7 58	5♋28 5	11♋31 11	20 14.4	5 54.5	16 26.6	28 47.0	8 43.4	2 17.6	6 31.4	19R32.1	19 5.3
22 M	8 2 9	1 9 0	17 36 28	23 44 3	20 4.4	6 47.0	17 41.7	29 34.2	8 56.3	2 16.5	6 29.1	19 32.1	19 3.9
23 Tu	8 6 5	2 10 2	29 54 2	6♌ 6 30	19 55.3	7 43.0	18 56.8	0♓21.5	9 9.3	2 15.4	6 26.8	19 32.1	19 2.5
24 W	8 10 2	3 11 2	12♌21 30	18 39 5	19 47.9	8 42.2	20 11.9	1 8.7	9 22.4	2 14.2	6 24.6	19 32.0	19 1.2
25 Th	8 13 58	4 12 2	24 59 18	1♍22 13	19 42.8	9 44.2	21 26.9	1 55.9	9 35.5	2 12.9	6 22.3	19 31.9	18 59.8
26 F	8 17 55	5 13 1	7♍47 53	14 16 24	19D39.9	10 48.9	22 41.9	2 43.1	9 48.7	2 11.4	6 20.2	19 31.7	18 58.4
27 Sa	8 21 52	6 14 0	20 47 53	27 22 27	19 39.2	11 55.9	23 57.0	3 30.3	10 1.9	2 9.9	6 18.0	19 31.5	18 57.0
28 Su	8 25 48	7 14 57	4♎ 0 15	10♎41 26	19 39.9	13 5.0	25 11.9	4 17.5	10 15.2	2 8.2	6 15.9	19 31.3	18 55.6
29 M	8 29 45	8 15 54	17 26 10	24 14 36	19 41.4	14 16.2	26 26.9	5 4.7	10 28.6	2 6.5	6 13.8	19 31.1	18 54.2
30 Tu	8 33 41	9 16 51	1♏ 6 50	8♏ 2 58	19R42.6	15 29.2	27 41.9	5 51.8	10 42.0	2 4.6	6 11.7	19 30.8	18 52.7
31 W	8 37 38	10 17 47	15 3 0	22 6 54	19 42.8	16 43.8	28 56.8	6 39.0	10 55.5	2 2.7	6 9.7	19 30.5	18 51.3

LONGITUDE FEBRUARY 1951

Day	Sid.Time	☉	0 hr ☽	Noon ☽	True ☊	☿	♀	♂	♃	♄	♅	♆	♇
1 Th	8 41 34	11♒18 42	29♏14 29	6♐25 31	19♓41.4	18♑ 0.0	0♓11.7	7♓26.1	11♓ 9.1	2♎ 0.6	6♋ 7.7	19♎30.1	18♌49.9
2 F	8 45 31	12 19 36	13♐39 35	20 56 13	19R38.2	19 17.7	1 26.6	8 13.3	11 22.6	1R58.5	6R 5.8	19R29.8	18R48.5
3 Sa	8 49 27	13 20 30	28 14 45	5♑34 28	19 33.7	20 36.7	2 41.5	9 0.4	11 36.3	1 56.2	6 3.8	19 29.3	18 47.0
4 Su	8 53 24	14 21 23	12♑54 32	20 14 6	19 28.2	21 57.0	3 56.4	9 47.5	11 50.0	1 53.9	6 2.0	19 28.9	18 45.6
5 M	8 57 21	15 22 15	27 32 13	4♒48 0	19 22.7	23 18.5	5 11.2	10 34.6	12 3.7	1 51.5	6 0.1	19 28.4	18 44.1
6 Tu	9 1 17	16 23 6	12♒ 0 37	19 9 15	19 17.9	24 41.2	6 26.0	11 21.7	12 17.5	1 48.9	5 58.3	19 27.9	18 42.7
7 W	9 5 14	17 23 56	26 13 15	3♓12 4	19 14.5	26 5.0	7 40.8	12 8.7	12 31.4	1 46.3	5 56.5	19 27.4	18 41.2
8 Th	9 9 10	18 24 44	10♓ 5 18	16 52 40	19D12.6	27 29.8	8 55.6	12 55.7	12 45.3	1 43.6	5 54.8	19 26.8	18 39.8
9 F	9 13 7	19 25 31	23 34 4	0♈ 9 31	19 12.4	28 55.6	10 10.3	13 42.8	12 59.2	1 40.8	5 53.1	19 26.2	18 38.3
10 Sa	9 17 3	20 26 16	6♈39 8	13 3 12	19 13.3	0♒22.4	11 25.1	14 29.7	13 13.1	1 37.9	5 51.5	19 25.5	18 36.9
11 Su	9 21 0	21 27 0	19 22 2	25 36 5	19 15.0	1 50.1	12 39.7	15 16.7	13 27.1	1 34.9	5 49.9	19 24.9	18 35.4
12 M	9 24 56	22 27 42	1♉45 50	7♉51 49	19 16.7	3 18.8	13 54.4	16 3.7	13 41.2	1 31.9	5 48.3	19 24.2	18 34.0
13 Tu	9 28 53	23 28 23	13 54 36	19 54 48	19R18.0	4 48.4	15 9.0	16 50.6	13 55.2	1 28.7	5 46.8	19 23.4	18 32.6
14 W	9 32 50	24 29 2	25 53 2	1♊49 53	19 18.4	6 19.0	16 23.6	17 37.5	14 9.4	1 25.5	5 45.3	19 22.7	18 31.1
15 Th	9 36 46	25 29 39	7♊45 59	13 41 54	19 17.7	7 50.4	17 38.2	18 24.3	14 23.5	1 22.2	5 43.9	19 21.9	18 29.7
16 F	9 40 43	26 30 15	19 38 14	25 35 29	19 15.9	9 22.8	18 52.7	19 11.2	14 37.7	1 18.8	5 42.5	19 21.1	18 28.2
17 Sa	9 44 39	27 30 49	1♋34 12	7♋34 48	19 13.2	10 56.0	20 7.2	19 58.0	14 51.9	1 15.3	5 41.2	19 20.2	18 26.8
18 Su	9 48 36	28 31 22	13 37 44	19 43 22	19 9.9	12 30.2	21 21.6	20 44.8	15 6.1	1 11.8	5 39.9	19 19.4	18 25.4
19 M	9 52 32	29 31 52	25 52 0	2♌ 3 54	19 6.6	14 5.2	22 36.0	21 31.5	15 20.4	1 8.2	5 38.7	19 18.5	18 24.0
20 Tu	9 56 29	0♓32 21	8♌19 17	14 38 15	19 3.5	15 41.2	23 50.4	22 18.3	15 34.7	1 4.5	5 37.5	19 17.5	18 22.6
21 W	10 0 25	1 32 48	21 0 56	27 27 20	19 1.2	17 18.1	25 4.8	23 4.9	15 49.0	1 0.8	5 36.3	19 16.6	18 21.1
22 Th	10 4 22	2 33 14	3♍57 27	10♍31 13	18 59.7	18 55.9	26 19.1	23 51.6	16 3.3	0 57.0	5 35.3	19 15.6	18 19.7
23 F	10 8 19	3 33 37	17 8 31	23 49 15	18D59.1	20 34.7	27 33.3	24 38.2	16 17.7	0 53.1	5 34.2	19 14.6	18 18.3
24 Sa	10 12 15	4 33 59	0♎33 13	7♎20 17	18 59.4	22 14.4	28 47.5	25 24.8	16 32.0	0 49.1	5 33.2	19 13.5	18 17.0
25 Su	10 16 12	5 34 20	14 10 13	21 2 50	19 0.2	23 55.1	0♈ 1.7	26 11.4	16 46.4	0 45.1	5 32.3	19 12.5	18 15.6
26 M	10 20 8	6 34 39	27 57 56	4♏55 18	19 1.3	25 36.7	1 15.9	26 57.9	17 0.8	0 41.1	5 31.4	19 11.4	18 14.2
27 Tu	10 24 5	7 34 57	11♏54 45	18 56 2	19 2.3	27 19.4	2 30.0	27 44.4	17 15.3	0 37.0	5 30.5	19 10.3	18 12.8
28 W	10 28 1	8 35 13	25 58 58	3♐ 3 17	19R 3.0	29 3.1	3 44.1	28 30.9	17 29.7	0 32.8	5 29.7	19 9.1	18 11.5

Astro Data (Dy Hr Mn)	Planet Ingress (Dy Hr Mn)
♆⚹♇ 3 13:23	♀ ♒ 7 21:10
☽0N 12 23:09	☉ ♒ 20 20:52
♃△♅ 12 4:27	♂ ♓ 22 13:05
☿ D 12 15:34	♀ ♓ 31 20:14
♄ R 12 1:18	
♆ R 21 5:28	☿ ♒ 9 17:50
☽0S 27 13:32	☉ ♓ 19 11:10
	♀ ♈ 24 23:26
☽0N 9 8:17	☿ ♓ 28 13:04
☽0S 23 19:36	
♀0N 26 21:37	

Last Aspect (Dy Hr Mn)	☽ Ingress (Dy Hr Mn)
2 3:38 ♀ □	♏ 2 15:58
4 10:38 ♀ ⚹	♐ 4 17:38
6 0:49 ♆ ⚹	♑ 6 17:32
8 0:35 ♆ □	♒ 8 17:35
10 3:09 ♂ ☌	♓ 10 19:56
12 10:08 ☉ ⚹	♈ 13 2:05
15 0:26 ♂ ⚹	♉ 15 12:10
17 18:11 ☉ △	♊ 18 0:36
20 9:44 ♂ △	♋ 20 13:06
22 3:47 ♆ □	♌ 23 0:12
24 16:34 ♀ ☍	♍ 25 9:26
26 6:07 ☿ △	♎ 27 16:46
29 17:27 ♀ △	♏ 29 22:04

Last Aspect (Dy Hr Mn)	☽ Ingress (Dy Hr Mn)
31 6:28 ♇ □	♐ 1 1:16
2 9:37 ♆ ⚹	♑ 3 2:52
4 16:20 ☿ ☌	♒ 5 4:04
6 12:31 ♆ △	♓ 7 6:29
9 10:57 ☿ ⚹	♈ 9 11:43
11 4:21 ☉ ⚹	♉ 11 20:33
13 20:55 ☉ □	♊ 14 8:18
16 15:07 ☉ △	♋ 16 20:51
18 16:55 ♀ △	♌ 19 8:01
20 20:45 ♆ ⚹	♍ 21 16:43
23 20:33 ♀ ☍	♎ 23 23:01
25 19:21 ☿ △	♏ 26 3:31
28 5:57 ☿ □	♐ 28 6:49

☽ Phases & Eclipses (Dy Hr Mn)	
1 5:11	☽ 9♎58
7 20:10	● 16♑44
15 0:23	☽ 24♈02
23 4:47	○ 2♌22
30 15:14	☽ 9♏56
6 7:54	● 16♒43
13 20:55	☽ 24♉21
21 21:12	○ 2♍26
28 22:59	☽ 9♐33

Astro Data

1 JANUARY 1951
Julian Day # 18628
Delta T 29.6 sec
SVP 05♓56'36"
Obliquity 23°26'53"
⚷ Chiron 26♐06.5
☽ Mean ☊ 22♓47.1

1 FEBRUARY 1951
Julian Day # 18659
Delta T 29.6 sec
SVP 05♓56'30"
Obliquity 23°26'53"
⚷ Chiron 29♐17.2
☽ Mean ☊ 21♓08.6

MARCH 1951 LONGITUDE

Day	Sid.Time	☉	0 hr ☽	Noon ☽	True ☊	☿	♀	♂	♃	♄	♅	♆	♇
1 Th	10 31 58	9♓35 28	10♐ 8 46	17♐15 8	19♓ 3.2	0♓47.8	4♈58.1	29♓17.4	17♓44.2	0♎28.6	5♋29.0	19♎ 8.0	18♌10.2
2 F	10 35 54	10 35 42	24 22 7	1♑29 22	19R 3.0	2 33.6	6 12.1	0♈ 3.8	17 58.7	0R 24.3	5R 28.3	19R 6.8	18R 8.8
3 Sa	10 39 51	11 35 54	8♑36 32	15 43 16	19 2.4	4 20.4	7 26.1	0 50.1	18 13.2	0 20.0	5 27.7	19 5.6	18 7.5
4 Su	10 43 48	12 36 5	22 49 9	29 53 46	19 1.7	6 8.2	8 40.0	1 36.5	18 27.7	0 15.6	5 27.1	19 4.3	18 6.2
5 M	10 47 44	13 36 14	6♒56 40	13♒57 24	19 0.9	7 57.2	9 53.9	2 22.8	18 42.2	0 11.2	5 26.5	19 3.1	18 4.9
6 Tu	10 51 41	14 36 21	20 55 34	27 50 43	19 0.4	9 47.2	11 7.7	3 9.1	18 56.7	0 6.8	5 26.1	19 1.8	18 3.7
7 W	10 55 37	15 36 26	4♓42 28	11♓30 30	19 0.1	11 38.2	12 21.5	3 55.3	19 11.2	0 2.3	5 25.6	19 0.5	18 2.4
8 Th	10 59 34	16 36 30	18 14 31	24 54 18	18D 60.0	13 30.3	13 35.2	4 41.5	19 25.8	29♍57.8	5 25.2	18 59.2	18 1.1
9 F	11 3 30	17 36 31	1♈29 41	8♈ 0 36	19 0.0	15 23.5	14 48.9	5 27.7	19 40.3	29 53.2	5 24.9	18 57.9	17 59.9
10 Sa	11 7 27	18 36 31	14 27 3	20 49 6	19R 0.1	17 17.7	16 2.6	6 13.8	19 54.9	29 48.6	5 24.7	18 56.5	17 58.7
11 Su	11 11 23	19 36 29	27 6 53	3♉20 40	19 0.1	19 12.8	17 16.2	6 59.9	20 9.4	29 44.0	5 24.4	18 55.1	17 57.5
12 M	11 15 20	20 36 25	9♉30 41	15 37 20	18 59.9	21 8.9	18 29.8	7 45.9	20 23.9	29 39.4	5 24.3	18 53.7	17 56.3
13 Tu	11 19 16	21 36 18	21 41 0	27 42 8	18 59.7	23 5.8	19 43.3	8 32.0	20 38.5	29 34.7	5 24.2	18 52.3	17 55.1
14 W	11 23 13	22 36 9	3♊41 15	9♊38 51	18 59.4	25 3.6	20 56.7	9 17.9	20 53.0	29 30.1	5D 24.1	18 50.9	17 54.0
15 Th	11 27 10	23 35 59	15 35 31	21 31 48	18D 59.1	27 2.0	22 10.1	10 3.8	21 7.6	29 25.4	5 24.1	18 49.5	17 52.8
16 F	11 31 6	24 35 46	27 28 18	3♋25 37	18 59.1	29 0.9	23 23.5	10 49.7	21 22.1	29 20.7	5 24.2	18 48.0	17 51.7
17 Sa	11 35 3	25 35 30	9♋24 18	15 24 58	18 59.3	1♈ 0.3	24 36.7	11 35.6	21 36.6	29 16.0	5 24.3	18 46.5	17 50.6
18 Su	11 38 59	26 35 13	21 28 9	27 34 22	18 59.8	2 59.9	25 50.0	12 21.4	21 51.1	29 11.3	5 24.5	18 45.1	17 49.5
19 M	11 42 56	27 34 53	3♌44 7	9♌57 51	19 0.6	4 59.5	27 3.1	13 7.1	22 5.6	29 6.5	5 24.7	18 43.6	17 48.5
20 Tu	11 46 52	28 34 31	16 15 56	22 38 41	19 1.6	6 58.8	28 16.3	13 52.8	22 20.1	29 1.8	5 24.9	18 42.0	17 47.4
21 W	11 50 49	29 34 7	29 6 21	5♍39 6	19 2.4	8 57.7	29 29.3	14 38.5	22 34.6	28 57.1	5 25.3	18 40.5	17 46.4
22 Th	11 54 45	0♈33 40	12♍16 58	18 59 56	19R 2.9	10 55.7	0♉42.3	15 24.1	22 49.1	28 52.3	5 25.6	18 39.0	17 45.4
23 F	11 58 42	1 33 12	25 47 51	2♎40 29	19 2.9	12 52.5	1 55.2	16 9.6	23 3.5	28 47.6	5 26.1	18 37.4	17 44.4
24 Sa	12 2 39	2 32 41	9♎37 31	16 38 29	19 2.3	14 47.8	3 8.1	16 55.1	23 18.0	28 42.9	5 26.6	18 35.9	17 43.4
25 Su	12 6 35	3 32 8	23 42 55	0♏50 14	19 0.9	16 41.2	4 20.9	17 40.6	23 32.4	28 38.2	5 27.1	18 34.3	17 42.5
26 M	12 10 32	4 31 34	7♏59 49	15 11 2	18 59.0	18 32.2	5 33.6	18 26.1	23 46.8	28 33.5	5 27.7	18 32.7	17 41.6
27 Tu	12 14 28	5 30 58	22 23 14	29 35 47	18 56.9	20 20.4	6 46.3	19 11.4	24 1.2	28 28.8	5 28.3	18 31.1	17 40.7
28 W	12 18 25	6 30 19	6♐48 7	13♐59 40	18 54.9	22 5.4	7 58.9	19 56.8	24 15.6	28 24.1	5 29.0	18 29.5	17 39.8
29 Th	12 22 21	7 29 40	21 9 58	28 18 35	18 53.4	23 46.8	9 11.5	20 42.1	24 30.0	28 19.5	5 29.8	18 27.9	17 39.0
30 F	12 26 18	8 28 58	5♑25 10	12♑29 27	18D 52.8	25 24.2	10 24.0	21 27.3	24 44.3	28 14.9	5 30.6	18 26.3	17 38.1
31 Sa	12 30 14	9 28 15	19 31 13	26 30 18	18 53.0	26 57.2	11 36.4	22 12.6	24 58.6	28 10.3	5 31.4	18 24.7	17 37.3

APRIL 1951 LONGITUDE

Day	Sid.Time	☉	0 hr ☽	Noon ☽	True ☊	☿	♀	♂	♃	♄	♅	♆	♇
1 Su	12 34 11	10♈27 30	3♒26 35	10♒19 58	18♓54.0	28♈25.4	12♉48.8	22♈57.7	25♓12.9	28♍ 5.7	5♋32.4	18♎23.1	17♌36.5
2 M	12 38 8	11 26 43	17 10 24	23 57 51	18 55.4	29 48.5	14 1.1	23 42.8	25 27.2	28R 1.1	5 33.3	18R 21.4	17R 35.8
3 Tu	12 42 4	12 25 54	0♓42 16	7♓23 38	18 56.9	1♉ 6.2	15 13.3	24 27.9	25 41.4	27 56.6	5 34.3	18 19.8	17 35.0
4 W	12 46 1	13 25 4	14 1 55	20 37 6	18R 57.7	2 18.2	16 25.5	25 12.9	25 55.6	27 52.1	5 35.4	18 18.2	17 34.3
5 Th	12 49 57	14 24 11	27 9 8	3♈38 0	18 57.5	3 24.4	17 37.6	25 57.9	26 9.8	27 47.7	5 36.5	18 16.5	17 33.6
6 F	12 53 54	15 23 17	10♈ 3 42	16 26 12	18 56.1	4 24.4	18 49.7	26 42.8	26 23.9	27 43.3	5 37.7	18 14.9	17 33.0
7 Sa	12 57 50	16 22 20	22 45 32	29 1 43	18 53.2	5 18.2	20 1.6	27 27.7	26 38.1	27 38.9	5 38.9	18 13.2	17 32.3
8 Su	13 1 47	17 21 22	5♉14 52	11♉25 3	18 49.0	6 5.6	21 13.5	28 12.6	26 52.1	27 34.6	5 40.1	18 11.6	17 31.7
9 M	13 5 43	18 20 21	17 32 27	23 37 14	18 44.0	6 46.5	22 25.3	28 57.4	27 6.2	27 30.3	5 41.5	18 9.9	17 31.1
10 Tu	13 9 40	19 19 18	29 39 39	5♊40 0	18 38.6	7 20.7	23 37.1	29 42.1	27 20.2	27 26.1	5 42.8	18 8.3	17 30.6
11 W	13 13 37	20 18 13	11♊38 38	17 35 55	18 33.6	7 48.4	24 48.7	0♉26.8	27 34.2	27 21.9	5 44.3	18 6.6	17 30.0
12 Th	13 17 33	21 17 6	23 32 19	29 28 16	18 29.3	8 9.4	26 0.3	1 11.4	27 48.1	27 17.8	5 45.7	18 5.0	17 29.5
13 F	13 21 30	22 15 57	5♋24 19	11♋21 0	18 26.3	8 23.8	27 11.8	1 56.0	28 2.0	27 13.7	5 47.2	18 3.3	17 29.0
14 Sa	13 25 26	23 14 45	17 18 53	23 18 35	18D 24.8	8R 31.7	28 23.3	2 40.5	28 15.9	27 9.7	5 48.8	18 1.7	17 28.6
15 Su	13 29 23	24 13 32	29 20 41	5♌25 49	18 24.8	8 33.2	29 34.6	3 25.0	28 29.7	27 5.7	5 50.4	18 0.1	17 28.1
16 M	13 33 19	25 12 16	11♌34 35	17 47 34	18 25.8	8 28.5	0♊45.8	4 9.5	28 43.5	27 1.8	5 52.1	17 58.4	17 27.7
17 Tu	13 37 16	26 10 57	24 5 20	0♍28 21	18 27.4	8 18.0	1 57.0	4 53.8	28 57.2	26 58.0	5 53.8	17 56.8	17 27.4
18 W	13 41 12	27 9 37	6♍57 6	13 31 54	18R 28.8	8 1.9	3 8.1	5 38.2	29 10.9	26 54.2	5 55.5	17 55.2	17 27.0
19 Th	13 45 9	28 8 14	20 13 2	27 0 37	18 29.3	7 40.6	4 19.1	6 22.4	29 24.5	26 50.5	5 57.3	17 53.5	17 26.7
20 F	13 49 6	29 6 49	3♎54 37	10♎54 53	18 28.2	7 14.7	5 29.9	7 6.7	29 38.1	26 46.9	5 59.2	17 51.9	17 26.4
21 Sa	13 53 2	0♉ 5 22	18 1 5	25 12 43	18 25.3	6 44.6	6 40.7	7 50.8	29 51.6	26 43.3	6 1.0	17 50.3	17 26.1
22 Su	13 56 59	1 3 53	2♏29 6	9♏49 25	18 20.6	6 11.0	7 51.4	8 34.9	0♈ 5.1	26 39.9	6 3.0	17 48.7	17 25.9
23 M	14 0 55	2 2 22	17 12 44	24 38 2	18 14.5	5 34.5	9 2.0	9 19.0	0 18.5	26 36.4	6 4.9	17 47.1	17 25.7
24 Tu	14 4 52	3 0 49	2♐ 4 15	9♐30 19	18 7.7	4 55.9	10 12.5	10 3.0	0 31.9	26 33.1	6 7.0	17 45.5	17 25.5
25 W	14 8 48	3 59 15	16 55 12	24 17 57	18 1.1	4 15.9	11 23.0	10 47.0	0 45.2	26 29.8	6 9.0	17 44.0	17 25.3
26 Th	14 12 45	4 57 39	1♑37 46	8♑53 57	17 55.7	3 35.2	12 33.3	11 30.9	0 58.5	26 26.6	6 11.1	17 42.4	17 25.2
27 F	14 16 41	5 56 2	16 5 59	23 13 29	17 52.1	2 54.7	13 43.5	12 14.8	1 11.7	26 23.5	6 13.3	17 40.9	17 25.1
28 Sa	14 20 38	6 54 23	0♒16 14	7♒14 6	17D 50.4	2 14.9	14 53.6	12 58.6	1 24.9	26 20.5	6 15.5	17 39.3	17 25.0
29 Su	14 24 35	7 52 43	14 7 8	20 55 26	17 50.3	1 36.7	16 3.6	13 42.4	1 38.0	26 17.6	6 17.7	17 37.8	17 25.0
30 M	14 28 31	8 51 0	27 39 10	4♓18 34	17 51.3	1 0.5	17 13.5	14 26.1	1 51.0	26 14.7	6 20.0	17 36.3	17D 25.0

Astro Data	Planet Ingress	Last Aspect	☽ Ingress	Last Aspect	☽ Ingress	☽ Phases & Eclipses	Astro Data
Dy Hr Mn	Dy Hr Mn	Dy Hr Mn	Dy Hr Mn	Dy Hr Mn	Dy Hr Mn	Dy Hr Mn	1 MARCH 1951
♃⊼♇ 2 15:26	♂ ♈ 1 22:03	1 15:09 ♆ ⚹	♑ 2 9:29	2 12:14 ♂ ⚹	♓ 2 22:44	7 20:51 ● 16♓29	Julian Day # 18687
♂0N 3 19:47	♄ ♍ 7 12:14	3 17:40 ♆ □	♒ 4 12:11	5 1:11 ♄ ☍	♈ 5 5:16	7 20:53:10 ✔ A 0'59"	Delta T 29.6 sec
♃⊼♆ 6 7:45	☿ ♈ 16 11:53	5 20:44 ♆ △	♓ 6 15:45	7 9:34 ♂ ☌	♉ 7 13:52	15 17:40 ☽ 24♊20	SVP 05♓56'26"
☽0N 8 17:45	☉ ♈ 21 10:26	8 21:05 ♄ ☍	♈ 8 21:16	9 19:36 ♄ △	♊ 10 0:41	23 10:50 ○ 2♎00	Obliquity 23°26'54"
♅ D 14 10:41	♀ ♉ 21 10:05	10 8:26 ♆ ☍	♉ 11 5:33	12 8:48 ♃ □	♋ 12 13:04	23 10:37 ✔ A 0.642	⚷ Chiron 1♑27.8
☿0N 17 11:16		13 15:39 ♄ △	♊ 13 16:36	15 0:31 ♀ ⚹	♌ 15 1:18	30 5:35 ☾ 8♑43	☽ Mean ☊ 19♓39.7
☽0S 23 4:00	☿ ♉ 2 3:27	16 3:45 ♄ □	♋ 16 5:06	17 4:17 ☉ △	♍ 17 11:07		
	♂ ♉ 10 9:37	18 15:04 ♄ ⚹	♌ 18 16:44	19 16:28 ♃ ☍	♎ 19 17:13	6 10:52 ● 15♈50	1 APRIL 1951
☽0N 5 1:43	♀ ♊ 15 8:33	21 0:47 ♀ △	♍ 21 1:39	20 23:42 ♆ ☌	♏ 21 19:55	14 12:56 ☽ 23♋46	Julian Day # 18718
♃☍♄ 10 7:44	☉ ♉ 20 21:48	23 5:13 ♄ ☌	♎ 23 7:21	23 15:08 ♄ ⚹	♐ 23 20:40	21 21:30 ○ 0♏58	Delta T 29.7 sec
☿ R 14 17:50	♃ ♈ 21 14:57	24 15:18 ♆ ☌	♏ 25 10:36	25 15:32 ♄ □	♑ 25 21:19	28 12:18 ☾ 7♒24	SVP 05♓56'23"
☽0S 19 13:46		27 10:05 ♄ ⚹	♐ 27 12:40	27 17:19 ♄ △	♒ 27 23:32		Obliquity 23°26'54"
♇ D 30 5:20		29 11:58 ♄ □	♑ 29 14:51	29 6:10 ♆ △	♓ 30 4:13		⚷ Chiron 2♑42.0
		31 14:48 ♄ △	♒ 31 18:02				☽ Mean ☊ 18♓01.2

LONGITUDE — MAY 1951

Day	Sid.Time	☉	0 hr ☽	Noon ☽	True ☊	☿	♀	♂	♃	♄	♅	♆	♇
1 Tu	14 32 28	9♉49 17	10♓53 54	17♓25 25	17♓52.2	0♉27.1	18♊23.3	15♉ 9.8	2♈ 4.0	26♍11.9	6♋22.3	17♎34.8	17♌25.0
2 W	14 36 24	10 47 32	23 53 23	0♈18 4	17R52.2	29♈56.9	19 33.0	15 53.4	2 16.9	26R 9.2	6 24.6	17R33.3	17 25.0
3 Th	14 40 21	11 45 45	6♈39 42	12 58 30	17 50.4	29R30.3	20 42.6	16 37.0	2 29.7	26 6.6	6 27.0	17 31.8	17 25.1
4 F	14 44 17	12 43 56	19 14 38	25 28 16	17 46.3	29 7.7	21 52.1	17 20.5	2 42.5	26 4.1	6 29.5	17 30.3	17 25.2
5 Sa	14 48 14	13 42 7	1♉39 33	7♉48 37	17 39.7	28 49.3	23 1.5	18 4.0	2 55.2	26 1.7	6 31.9	17 28.9	17 25.3
6 Su	14 52 10	14 40 15	13 55 34	20 0 31	17 30.8	28 35.4	24 10.7	18 47.4	3 7.8	25 59.3	6 34.4	17 27.5	17 25.4
7 M	14 56 7	15 38 22	26 3 35	2♊ 4 55	17 20.3	28 26.0	25 19.8	19 30.8	3 20.4	25 57.1	6 37.0	17 26.0	17 25.6
8 Tu	15 0 4	16 36 27	8♊ 4 40	14 3 2	17 9.1	28D21.4	26 28.9	20 14.1	3 32.9	25 54.9	6 39.6	17 24.6	17 25.8
9 W	15 4 0	17 34 31	20 0 12	25 56 28	16 58.1	28 21.4	27 37.8	20 57.3	3 45.3	25 52.9	6 42.2	17 23.3	17 26.1
10 Th	15 7 57	18 32 32	1♋52 7	7♋47 31	16 48.3	28 26.1	28 46.5	21 40.6	3 57.7	25 50.9	6 44.8	17 21.9	17 26.3
11 F	15 11 53	19 30 32	13 43 4	19 39 11	16 40.5	28 35.5	29 55.2	22 23.7	4 10.0	25 49.0	6 47.5	17 20.6	17 26.6
12 Sa	15 15 50	20 28 30	25 36 24	1♌35 13	16 35.1	28 49.5	1♋ 3.7	23 6.8	4 22.2	25 47.3	6 50.3	17 19.2	17 26.9
13 Su	15 19 46	21 26 27	7♌36 13	13 40 0	16 32.1	29 8.0	2 12.0	23 49.9	4 34.3	25 45.6	6 53.0	17 17.9	17 27.3
14 M	15 23 43	22 24 21	19 47 11	25 58 24	16D31.1	29 30.8	3 20.3	24 32.9	4 46.3	25 44.0	6 55.8	17 16.6	17 27.6
15 Tu	15 27 39	23 22 14	2♍14 17	8♍35 26	16 31.3	29 58.0	4 28.3	25 15.8	4 58.2	25 42.5	6 58.6	17 15.4	17 28.0
16 W	15 31 36	24 20 5	15 2 26	21 35 49	16R31.6	0♉29.2	5 36.3	25 58.7	5 10.1	25 41.2	7 1.5	17 14.1	17 28.5
17 Th	15 35 33	25 17 54	28 16 0	5♎ 3 18	16 31.1	1 4.5	6 44.1	26 41.6	5 21.9	25 39.9	7 4.3	17 12.9	17 28.9
18 F	15 39 29	26 15 41	11♎57 55	18 59 51	16 28.8	1 43.7	7 51.7	27 24.4	5 33.6	25 38.7	7 7.3	17 11.7	17 29.4
19 Sa	15 43 26	27 13 27	26 8 55	3♏24 43	16 24.0	2 26.7	8 59.2	28 7.1	5 45.2	25 37.6	7 10.2	17 10.5	17 29.9
20 Su	15 47 22	28 11 11	10♏46 40	18 13 55	16 16.8	3 13.3	10 6.5	28 49.8	5 56.7	25 36.6	7 13.2	17 9.4	17 30.4
21 M	15 51 19	29 8 54	25 45 25	3♐19 59	16 7.5	4 3.4	11 13.6	29 32.4	6 8.1	25 35.8	7 16.2	17 8.2	17 31.0
22 Tu	15 55 15	0♊ 6 36	10♐56 17	18 32 56	15 57.3	4 57.0	12 20.6	0♊15.0	6 19.5	25 35.0	7 19.2	17 7.1	17 31.6
23 W	15 59 12	1 4 16	26 8 35	3♑41 55	15 47.2	5 53.8	13 27.4	0 57.5	6 30.7	25 34.3	7 22.3	17 6.0	17 32.2
24 Th	16 3 8	2 1 55	11♑11 46	18 37 8	15 38.6	6 53.9	14 34.0	1 40.0	6 41.9	25 33.7	7 25.3	17 5.0	17 32.9
25 F	16 7 5	2 59 33	25 57 13	3♒11 26	15 32.1	7 57.1	15 40.4	2 22.5	6 52.9	25 33.3	7 28.5	17 3.9	17 33.5
26 Sa	16 11 2	3 57 10	10♒19 24	17 20 56	15 28.3	9 3.3	16 46.7	3 4.9	7 3.9	25 32.9	7 31.6	17 2.9	17 34.2
27 Su	16 14 58	4 54 46	24 16 3	1♓ 4 53	15D26.6	10 12.6	17 52.8	3 47.2	7 14.7	25 32.6	7 34.8	17 1.9	17 34.9
28 M	16 18 55	5 52 22	7♓47 41	14 24 48	15R26.3	11 24.7	18 58.7	4 29.5	7 25.5	25 32.5	7 37.9	17 1.0	17 35.7
29 Tu	16 22 51	6 49 56	20 56 39	27 23 40	15 26.3	12 39.6	20 4.4	5 11.7	7 36.1	25D32.4	7 41.1	17 0.0	17 36.5
30 W	16 26 48	7 47 29	3♈46 18	10♈ 5 0	15 25.3	13 57.4	21 9.9	5 53.9	7 46.7	25 32.4	7 44.4	16 59.1	17 37.3
31 Th	16 30 44	8 45 2	16 20 13	22 32 20	15 22.4	15 17.9	22 15.2	6 36.1	7 57.1	25 32.6	7 47.6	16 58.2	17 38.1

LONGITUDE — JUNE 1951

Day	Sid.Time	☉	0 hr ☽	Noon ☽	True ☊	☿	♀	♂	♃	♄	♅	♆	♇
1 F	16 34 41	9♊42 33	28♈41 45	4♉48 48	15♓16.7	16♉41.1	23♋20.3	7♊18.2	8♈ 7.5	25♍32.8	7♋50.9	16♎57.3	17♌38.9
2 Sa	16 38 37	10 40 4	10♉53 46	16 56 57	15R 8.2	18 7.0	24 25.2	8 0.2	8 17.7	25 33.2	7 54.2	16R56.5	17 39.8
3 Su	16 42 34	11 37 34	22 58 32	28 58 46	14 57.1	19 35.5	25 29.9	8 42.2	8 27.8	25 33.6	7 57.5	16 55.7	17 40.7
4 M	16 46 31	12 35 3	4♊57 49	10♊55 50	14 44.0	21 6.7	26 34.3	9 24.2	8 37.8	25 34.2	8 0.9	16 54.9	17 41.6
5 Tu	16 50 27	13 32 31	16 52 59	22 49 27	14 29.9	22 40.5	27 38.6	10 6.1	8 47.7	25 34.8	8 4.2	16 54.2	17 42.6
6 W	16 54 24	14 29 59	28 45 22	4♋40 58	14 16.1	24 16.9	28 42.6	10 48.0	8 57.5	25 35.6	8 7.6	16 53.5	17 43.5
7 Th	16 58 20	15 27 25	10♋36 26	16 32 3	14 3.7	25 55.8	29 46.3	11 29.8	9 7.1	25 36.4	8 11.0	16 52.8	17 44.5
8 F	17 2 17	16 24 50	22 28 5	28 24 51	13 53.4	27 37.4	0♌49.8	12 11.5	9 16.6	25 37.4	8 14.4	16 52.1	17 45.6
9 Sa	17 6 13	17 22 15	4♌22 45	10♌22 12	13 46.0	29 21.5	1 53.1	12 53.2	9 26.1	25 38.5	8 17.8	16 51.5	17 46.6
10 Su	17 10 10	18 19 38	16 23 39	22 27 37	13 41.3	1♊ 8.2	2 56.0	13 34.9	9 35.3	25 39.6	8 21.3	16 50.9	17 47.7
11 M	17 14 7	19 17 0	28 34 38	4♍45 17	13 39.1	2 57.4	3 58.7	14 16.5	9 44.5	25 40.9	8 24.7	16 50.3	17 48.7
12 Tu	17 18 3	20 14 21	11♍ 0 9	17 19 50	13 38.5	4 49.0	5 1.2	14 58.1	9 53.5	25 42.3	8 28.2	16 49.8	17 49.9
13 W	17 22 0	21 11 41	23 44 56	0♎16 0	13 38.5	6 43.1	6 3.3	15 39.6	10 2.5	25 43.7	8 31.7	16 49.3	17 51.0
14 Th	17 25 56	22 9 0	6♎53 33	13 38 0	13 37.9	8 39.5	7 5.1	16 21.0	10 11.2	25 45.3	8 35.2	16 48.8	17 52.1
15 F	17 29 53	23 6 18	20 29 40	27 28 45	13 35.7	10 38.2	8 6.6	17 2.4	10 19.9	25 47.0	8 38.7	16 48.3	17 53.3
16 Sa	17 33 49	24 3 35	4♏35 13	11♏48 54	13 31.2	12 39.0	9 7.8	17 43.8	10 28.4	25 48.7	8 42.2	16 47.9	17 54.5
17 Su	17 37 46	25 0 52	19 9 21	26 35 56	13 24.2	14 41.9	10 8.7	18 25.1	10 36.8	25 50.6	8 45.7	16 47.5	17 55.7
18 M	17 41 42	25 58 8	4♐ 7 43	11♐43 37	13 15.1	16 46.6	11 9.2	19 6.4	10 45.0	25 52.5	8 49.3	16 47.1	17 57.0
19 Tu	17 45 39	26 55 23	19 22 21	27 2 29	13 5.0	18 53.1	12 9.3	19 47.6	10 53.2	25 54.6	8 52.8	16 46.8	17 58.2
20 W	17 49 36	27 52 37	4♑42 34	12♑21 8	12 54.9	21 1.0	13 9.1	20 28.8	11 1.1	25 56.7	8 56.4	16 46.5	17 59.5
21 Th	17 53 32	28 49 52	19 56 49	27 28 22	12 46.1	23 10.1	14 8.6	21 9.9	11 9.0	25 59.0	8 60.0	16 46.3	18 0.8
22 F	17 57 29	29 47 5	4♒54 44	12♒15 7	12 39.4	25 20.2	15 7.6	21 51.0	11 16.7	26 1.3	9 3.6	16 46.0	18 2.1
23 Sa	18 1 25	0♋44 19	19 28 53	26 35 42	12 35.3	27 31.1	16 6.3	22 32.0	11 24.2	26 3.8	9 7.2	16 45.8	18 3.5
24 Su	18 5 22	1 41 32	3♓35 22	10♓27 56	12D33.6	29 42.4	17 4.5	23 13.0	11 31.7	26 6.3	9 10.7	16 45.6	18 4.8
25 M	18 9 18	2 38 45	17 13 34	23 52 36	12 33.4	1♋53.8	18 2.3	23 53.9	11 38.9	26 8.9	9 14.3	16 45.5	18 6.2
26 Tu	18 13 15	3 35 58	0♈25 25	6♈52 29	12R33.7	4 5.1	18 59.7	24 34.8	11 46.0	26 11.6	9 17.9	16 45.4	18 7.6
27 W	18 17 11	4 33 11	13 14 21	19 31 31	12 33.4	6 16.1	19 56.7	25 15.7	11 53.0	26 14.4	9 21.6	16 45.3	18 9.0
28 Th	18 21 8	5 30 25	25 44 33	1♉53 59	12 31.5	8 26.4	20 53.2	25 56.5	11 59.8	26 17.3	9 25.2	16D45.3	18 10.4
29 F	18 25 5	6 27 38	8♉ 0 19	14 4 1	12 27.4	10 35.8	21 49.3	26 37.3	12 6.5	26 20.3	9 28.8	16 45.3	18 11.9
30 Sa	18 29 1	7 24 51	20 5 33	26 5 20	12 20.7	12 44.1	22 44.8	27 18.0	12 13.0	26 23.4	9 32.4	16 45.3	18 13.4

Astro Data

	Dy Hr Mn
☽0N	2 7:33
♃∥♇	2 15:15
♃0N	3 4:37
♆✶♇	7 6:29
☿ D	8 11:50
☽0S	16 23:02
☽0N	29 12:18
♃□♅	29 16:24
♄ D	29 3:37
☽0S	13 6:29
☽0N	25 17:50
♆ D	28 21:51

Planet Ingress

	Dy Hr Mn
☿ ♈	1 21:25
♀ ♋	11 1:41
☿ ♉	15 1:40
☉ ♊	21 21:15
♂ ♊	21 15:32
♀ ♌	7 5:10
☿ ♊	9 8:43
☉ ♋	22 5:25
☿ ♋	24 3:13

Last Aspect / ☽ Ingress

Last Aspect Dy Hr Mn		☽ Ingress Dy Hr Mn
2 4:13	♄ ☍	♈ 2 11:26
4 18:37	☿ ☌	♉ 4 20:47
6 23:47	♄ △	♊ 7 7:51
9 17:04	♀ ☌	♋ 9 20:13
12 6:37	☿ □	♌ 12 8:49
14 19:30	☿ △	♍ 14 19:44
16 21:02	♂ △	♎ 17 3:05
18 9:27	♇ ✶	♏ 19 6:23
21 6:18	♂ ☍	♐ 21 6:44
22 23:06	♄ □	♑ 23 6:07
24 23:21	♄ △	♒ 25 6:41
26 12:24	♇ ☍	♓ 27 10:05
29 8:32	♄ ☍	♈ 29 16:53

Last Aspect / ☽ Ingress

Last Aspect Dy Hr Mn		☽ Ingress Dy Hr Mn
31 12:33	♀ □	♉ 1 2:33
3 5:32	♀ ✶	♊ 3 14:03
5 17:36	♄ □	♋ 6 2:31
8 12:10	☿ ✶	♌ 8 15:12
10 4:10	☉ ✶	♍ 11 2:47
13 3:40	♄ ☌	♎ 13 11:31
15 4:50	☉ △	♏ 15 16:17
17 10:49	♄ ✶	♐ 17 17:26
19 12:36	☉ ☍	♑ 19 16:38
21 9:39	♄ △	♒ 21 16:04
23 16:05	☿ △	♓ 23 17:49
25 16:12	♄ ☍	♈ 25 23:13
28 0:25	♂ ✶	♉ 28 8:17
30 12:40	♄ △	♊ 30 19:51

☽ Phases & Eclipses

Dy Hr Mn	
6 1:36	● 14♉44
14 5:32	☽ 22♌38
21 5:45	○ 29♏23
27 20:17	☽ 5♓43
4 16:40	● 13♊15
12 18:52	☽ 20♍59
19 12:36	○ 27♐25
26 6:21	☽ 3♈51

Astro Data

1 MAY 1951
Julian Day # 18748
Delta T 29.7 sec
SVP 05♓56'19"
Obliquity 23°26'53"
⚷ Chiron 2♑31.8R
☽ Mean ☊ 16♓25.9

1 JUNE 1951
Julian Day # 18779
Delta T 29.7 sec
SVP 05♓56'14"
Obliquity 23°26'53"
⚷ Chiron 1♑07.3R
☽ Mean ☊ 14♓47.4

JULY 1951 LONGITUDE

Day	Sid.Time	☉	0 hr ☽	Noon ☽	True ☊	☿	♀	♂	♃	♄	♅	♆	♇
1 Su	18 32 58	8♋22 4	2♊ 3 42	8♊ 1 1	12♓11.8	14♋51.2	23♌39.9	27♊58.7	12♈19.3	26♍26.6	9♋36.0	16♎45.3	18♌14.8
2 M	18 36 54	9 19 18	13 57 34	19 53 36	12R 1.1	16 56.9	24 34.4	28 39.4	12 25.5	26 29.8	9 39.7	16 45.4	18 16.3
3 Tu	18 40 51	10 16 31	25 49 22	1♋45 4	11 49.5	19 1.0	25 28.4	29 20.0	12 31.5	26 33.2	9 43.3	16 45.5	18 17.9
4 W	18 44 47	11 13 45	7♋40 54	13 37 4	11 38.1	21 3.5	26 21.9	0♋ 0.5	12 37.4	26 36.6	9 46.9	16 45.7	18 19.4
5 Th	18 48 44	12 10 58	19 33 44	25 31 8	11 27.9	23 4.2	27 14.7	0 41.0	12 43.1	26 40.1	9 50.5	16 45.9	18 21.0
6 F	18 52 40	13 8 11	1♌29 28	7♌28 58	11 19.5	25 3.1	28 7.0	1 21.5	12 48.6	26 43.8	9 54.1	16 46.1	18 22.5
7 Sa	18 56 37	14 5 24	13 29 54	19 32 33	11 13.5	27 0.2	28 58.7	2 1.9	12 54.0	26 47.4	9 57.7	16 46.3	18 24.1
8 Su	19 0 34	15 2 38	25 37 16	1♍44 23	11 10.0	28 55.4	29 49.7	2 42.3	12 59.2	26 51.2	10 1.4	16 46.6	18 25.7
9 M	19 4 30	15 59 51	7♍54 20	14 7 31	11D 8.7	0♌48.6	0♍40.0	3 22.6	13 4.2	26 55.1	10 5.0	16 46.9	18 27.3
10 Tu	19 8 27	16 57 3	20 24 25	26 45 29	11 9.0	2 39.9	1 29.7	4 2.9	13 9.0	26 59.0	10 8.6	16 47.3	18 28.9
11 W	19 12 23	17 54 16	3♎11 11	9♎42 1	11 10.0	4 29.3	2 18.6	4 43.2	13 13.7	27 3.1	10 12.2	16 47.6	18 30.6
12 Th	19 16 20	18 51 29	16 18 24	23 0 44	11R10.6	6 16.7	3 6.8	5 23.4	13 18.2	27 7.2	10 15.8	16 48.0	18 32.2
13 F	19 20 16	19 48 42	29 49 20	6♏44 25	11 10.2	8 2.1	3 54.1	6 3.5	13 22.5	27 11.3	10 19.4	16 48.5	18 33.9
14 Sa	19 24 13	20 45 54	13♏46 5	20 54 15	11 8.0	9 45.6	4 40.7	6 43.6	13 26.7	27 15.6	10 22.9	16 48.9	18 35.5
15 Su	19 28 9	21 43 7	28 8 41	5♐28 58	11 3.9	11 27.2	5 26.5	7 23.7	13 30.7	27 19.9	10 26.5	16 49.4	18 37.2
16 M	19 32 6	22 40 20	12♐54 25	20 24 14	10 58.2	13 6.8	6 11.3	8 3.7	13 34.4	27 24.4	10 30.1	16 50.0	18 38.9
17 Tu	19 36 3	23 37 33	27 57 23	5♑32 41	10 51.5	14 44.4	6 55.3	8 43.7	13 38.1	27 28.9	10 33.6	16 50.6	18 40.6
18 W	19 39 59	24 34 46	13♑ 8 53	20 44 40	10 44.7	16 20.1	7 38.3	9 23.6	13 41.5	27 33.4	10 37.2	16 51.2	18 42.3
19 Th	19 43 56	25 32 0	28 18 43	5♒49 48	10 38.8	17 53.9	8 20.3	10 3.5	13 44.7	27 38.1	10 40.7	16 51.8	18 44.1
20 F	19 47 52	26 29 14	13♒16 47	20 38 44	10 34.4	19 25.6	9 1.3	10 43.4	13 47.8	27 42.8	10 44.2	16 52.4	18 45.8
21 Sa	19 51 49	27 26 29	27 54 52	5♓ 4 37	10D 32.0	20 55.4	9 41.3	11 23.2	13 50.7	27 47.6	10 47.8	16 53.1	18 47.6
22 Su	19 55 45	28 23 44	12♓ 7 36	19 3 38	10 31.3	22 23.2	10 20.1	12 3.0	13 53.4	27 52.4	10 51.3	16 53.9	18 49.3
23 M	19 59 42	29 21 0	25 52 42	2♈34 58	10 32.1	23 49.0	10 57.9	12 42.7	13 55.9	27 57.4	10 54.7	16 54.6	18 51.1
24 Tu	20 3 39	0♌18 16	9♈10 41	15 40 14	10 33.4	25 12.8	11 34.4	13 22.4	13 58.2	28 2.4	10 58.2	16 55.4	18 52.9
25 W	20 7 35	1 15 34	22 4 2	28 22 37	10R34.7	26 34.5	12 9.8	14 2.1	14 0.3	28 7.4	11 1.7	16 56.2	18 54.6
26 Th	20 11 32	2 12 52	4♉36 31	10♉46 16	10 35.0	27 54.0	12 43.8	14 41.7	14 2.2	28 12.6	11 5.1	16 57.0	18 56.4
27 F	20 15 28	3 10 12	16 52 27	22 55 37	10 34.0	29 11.5	13 16.6	15 21.3	14 3.9	28 17.8	11 8.5	16 57.9	18 58.2
28 Sa	20 19 25	4 7 32	28 56 20	4♊55 5	10 31.4	0♍26.7	13 48.0	16 0.9	14 5.5	28 23.1	11 12.0	16 58.8	19 0.0
29 Su	20 23 21	5 4 54	10♊52 23	16 48 41	10 27.3	1 39.7	14 18.0	16 40.4	14 6.8	28 28.4	11 15.4	16 59.8	19 1.9
30 M	20 27 18	6 2 16	22 44 24	28 39 57	10 22.0	2 50.3	14 46.6	17 19.8	14 8.0	28 33.8	11 18.7	17 0.7	19 3.7
31 Tu	20 31 14	6 59 40	4♋35 40	10♋31 52	10 16.2	3 58.6	15 13.6	17 59.3	14 8.9	28 39.3	11 22.1	17 1.7	19 5.5

AUGUST 1951 LONGITUDE

Day	Sid.Time	☉	0 hr ☽	Noon ☽	True ☊	☿	♀	♂	♃	♄	♅	♆	♇
1 W	20 35 11	7♌57 4	16♋28 51	22♋26 53	10♓10.3	5♍ 4.4	15♍39.1	18♋38.7	14♈ 9.7	28♍44.8	11♋25.4	17♎ 2.7	19♌ 7.3
2 Th	20 39 8	8 54 30	28 26 11	4♌26 59	10R 5.1	6 7.5	16 2.9	19 18.0	14 10.2	28 50.4	11 28.8	17 3.8	19 9.2
3 F	20 43 4	9 51 56	10♌29 29	16 33 51	10 1.0	7 8.0	16 25.0	19 57.4	14 10.6	28 56.0	11 32.1	17 4.9	19 11.0
4 Sa	20 47 1	10 49 23	22 40 18	28 49 1	9 58.3	8 5.7	16 45.4	20 36.6	14R10.8	29 1.7	11 35.3	17 6.0	19 12.9
5 Su	20 50 57	11 46 51	5♍ 0 11	11♍14 2	9D 57.1	9 0.5	17 4.0	21 15.9	14 10.7	29 7.5	11 38.6	17 7.1	19 14.7
6 M	20 54 54	12 44 20	17 30 45	23 50 36	9 57.2	9 52.2	17 20.7	21 55.1	14 10.5	29 13.3	11 41.8	17 8.3	19 16.6
7 Tu	20 58 50	13 41 49	0♎13 48	6♎40 37	9 58.2	10 40.7	17 35.4	22 34.2	14 10.0	29 19.2	11 45.0	17 9.5	19 18.4
8 W	21 2 47	14 39 20	13 11 19	19 46 9	9 59.8	11 25.8	17 48.2	23 13.3	14 9.4	29 25.2	11 48.2	17 10.7	19 20.3
9 Th	21 6 43	15 36 51	26 25 21	3♏ 9 8	10 1.2	12 7.4	17 58.9	23 52.4	14 8.6	29 31.1	11 51.4	17 12.0	19 22.1
10 F	21 10 40	16 34 23	9♏57 41	16 51 6	10R 2.1	12 45.2	18 7.5	24 31.5	14 7.5	29 37.2	11 54.5	17 13.2	19 24.0
11 Sa	21 14 37	17 31 56	23 49 26	0♐52 37	10 2.1	13 19.1	18 13.9	25 10.5	14 6.3	29 43.3	11 57.7	17 14.5	19 25.9
12 Su	21 18 33	18 29 30	8♐ 0 31	15 12 49	10 1.1	13 48.9	18 18.1	25 49.4	14 4.9	29 49.4	12 0.7	17 15.9	19 27.7
13 M	21 22 30	19 27 5	22 29 7	29 48 52	9 59.3	14 14.3	18R20.0	26 28.3	14 3.2	29 55.6	12 3.8	17 17.2	19 29.6
14 Tu	21 26 26	20 24 41	7♑11 23	14♑35 54	9 57.0	14 35.2	18 19.6	27 7.2	14 1.4	0♎ 1.9	12 6.8	17 18.6	19 31.5
15 W	21 30 23	21 22 17	22 1 30	29 27 14	9 54.6	14 51.2	18 16.8	27 46.1	13 59.4	0 8.2	12 9.9	17 20.0	19 33.3
16 Th	21 34 19	22 19 55	6♒52 8	14♒15 13	9 52.5	15 2.3	18 11.7	28 24.9	13 57.2	0 14.5	12 12.8	17 21.5	19 35.2
17 F	21 38 16	23 17 34	21 35 33	28 52 15	9 51.0	15R 8.2	18 4.1	29 3.7	13 54.8	0 20.9	12 15.8	17 22.9	19 37.1
18 Sa	21 42 12	24 15 14	6♓ 4 34	13♓11 51	9D 50.4	15 8.6	17 54.2	29 42.4	13 52.2	0 27.4	12 18.7	17 24.4	19 38.9
19 Su	21 46 9	25 12 55	20 13 37	27 9 30	9 50.6	15 3.5	17 41.9	0♌21.1	13 49.4	0 33.8	12 21.6	17 25.9	19 40.8
20 M	21 50 6	26 10 38	3♈59 17	10♈42 54	9 51.3	14 52.8	17 27.2	0 59.8	13 46.4	0 40.4	12 24.4	17 27.4	19 42.6
21 Tu	21 54 2	27 8 22	17 20 24	23 51 58	9 52.4	14 36.3	17 10.2	1 38.4	13 43.3	0 46.9	12 27.3	17 29.0	19 44.5
22 W	21 57 59	28 6 8	0♉17 52	6♉38 28	9 53.4	14 14.0	16 50.9	2 17.0	13 39.9	0 53.5	12 30.1	17 30.6	19 46.3
23 Th	22 1 55	29 3 56	12 54 10	19 5 28	9 54.3	13 46.0	16 29.4	2 55.5	13 36.4	1 0.2	12 32.8	17 32.2	19 48.2
24 F	22 5 52	0♍ 1 46	25 12 54	1♊16 59	9R 54.7	13 12.6	16 5.8	3 34.1	13 32.7	1 6.9	12 35.5	17 33.8	19 50.0
25 Sa	22 9 48	0 59 37	7♊18 17	13 17 23	9 54.7	12 34.0	15 40.1	4 12.5	13 28.8	1 13.6	12 38.2	17 35.4	19 51.9
26 Su	22 13 45	1 57 30	19 14 51	25 11 15	9 54.2	11 50.5	15 12.5	4 51.0	13 24.7	1 20.4	12 40.9	17 37.1	19 53.7
27 M	22 17 41	2 55 25	1♋ 7 5	7♋ 2 55	9 53.6	11 2.9	14 43.1	5 29.4	13 20.4	1 27.2	12 43.5	17 38.8	19 55.6
28 Tu	22 21 38	3 53 22	12 59 13	18 56 26	9 52.8	10 11.7	14 12.0	6 7.8	13 16.0	1 34.0	12 46.1	17 40.5	19 57.4
29 W	22 25 35	4 51 20	24 55 1	0♌55 20	9 52.0	9 17.8	13 39.5	6 46.2	13 11.3	1 40.9	12 48.7	17 42.2	19 59.2
30 Th	22 29 31	5 49 20	6♌57 44	13 2 32	9 51.5	8 22.3	13 5.7	7 24.5	13 6.6	1 47.8	12 51.2	17 44.0	20 1.0
31 F	22 33 28	6 47 22	19 10 0	25 20 21	9 51.1	7 26.1	12 30.8	8 2.8	13 1.6	1 54.7	12 53.7	17 45.8	20 2.8

Astro Data (Dy Hr Mn)

☽0S	10 12:05
☽0N	23 1:25
♃ R	4 6:53
☽0S	6 17:05
♀0S	11 7:24
♀ R	13 7:51
☿ R	17 14:04
☽0N	19 10:52

Planet Ingress (Dy Hr Mn)

♂	♋	3 23:42
☿	♌	8 13:39
♀	♍	8 4:54
☉	♌	23 16:21
☿	♍	27 15:24
♄	♎	13 16:44
♂	♌	18 10:55
☉	♍	23 23:16

Last Aspect / ☽ Ingress (July)

Last Aspect Dy Hr Mn		☽ Ingress Dy Hr Mn
3 7:32	♂ ☌	♋ 3 8:27
5 14:23	♄ ⚹	♌ 5 21:00
7 9:46	♇ ☌	♍ 8 8:36
10 12:29	♄ ☌	♎ 10 18:04
12 4:56	☉ □	♏ 13 0:19
14 22:39	♄ ⚹	♐ 15 3:03
16 23:15	♄ □	♑ 17 3:14
18 22:55	♄ △	♒ 19 2:41
20 11:09	☿ ☍	♓ 21 3:29
23 6:40	☉ △	♈ 23 7:21
25 9:34	☿ △	♉ 25 15:07
27 22:53	♄ △	♊ 28 2:08
30 11:53	♄ □	♋ 30 14:42

Last Aspect / ☽ Ingress (August)

Last Aspect Dy Hr Mn		☽ Ingress Dy Hr Mn
2 0:49	♄ ⚹	♌ 2 3:08
3 17:12	♇ ☌	♍ 4 14:18
6 22:17	♄ ☌	♎ 6 23:34
8 19:11	♂ □	♏ 9 6:24
11 10:07	♄ ⚹	♐ 11 10:31
13 12:16	♄ □	♑ 13 12:18
15 9:42	♂ ☍	♒ 15 12:53
17 2:59	☉ ☍	♓ 17 13:52
18 19:44	♀ ☍	♈ 19 16:58
21 19:33	☉ △	♉ 21 23:26
23 13:25	♇ □	♊ 24 9:27
26 1:19	♇ ⚹	♋ 26 21:44
28 9:29	♆ □	♌ 29 10:10
31 1:43	♇ ☌	♍ 31 21:00

☽ Phases & Eclipses (Dy Hr Mn)

4 7:48	● 11♋32
12 4:56	☽ 19♎03
18 19:17	○ 25♑21
25 18:59	☽ 2♉01
2 22:39	● 9♌49
10 12:22	☽ 17♏04
17 2:59	○ 23♒25
17 3:14	☍ A 0.119
24 10:20	☽ 0♊27

Astro Data

1 JULY 1951
Julian Day # 18809
Delta T 29.8 sec
SVP 05♓56'08"
Obliquity 23°26'52"
⚷ Chiron 29♐10.5R
☽ Mean ☊ 13♓12.1

1 AUGUST 1951
Julian Day # 18840
Delta T 29.8 sec
SVP 05♓56'03"
Obliquity 23°26'53"
⚷ Chiron 27♐27.6R
☽ Mean ☊ 11♓33.6

LONGITUDE — SEPTEMBER 1951

Day	Sid.Time	☉	0 hr ☽	Noon ☽	True ☊	☿	♀	♂	♃	♄	♅	♆	♇
1 Sa	22 37 24	7♍45 25	1♍33 46	7♍50 24	9♓51.0	6♍30.4	11♍55.0	8♌41.0	12♈56.5	2♎ 1.7	12♋56.1	17♎47.6	20♌ 4.6
2 Su	22 41 21	8 43 30	14 10 22	20 33 44	9D 50.9	5R 36.6	11R 18.5	9 19.2	12R 51.2	2 8.7	12 58.5	17 49.4	20 6.4
3 M	22 45 17	9 41 37	27 0 33	3♎30 50	9R 51.0	4 45.6	10 41.7	9 57.4	12 45.7	2 15.7	13 0.9	17 51.2	20 8.2
4 Tu	22 49 14	10 39 45	10♎ 4 35	16 41 48	9 50.9	3 58.9	10 4.6	10 35.5	12 40.1	2 22.8	13 3.2	17 53.1	20 10.0
5 W	22 53 10	11 37 55	23 22 24	0♏ 6 22	9 50.8	3 17.4	9 27.5	11 13.6	12 34.4	2 29.8	13 5.5	17 54.9	20 11.7
6 Th	22 57 7	12 36 6	6♏53 36	13 44 3	9 50.5	2 42.1	8 50.7	11 51.7	12 28.5	2 37.0	13 7.7	17 56.8	20 13.5
7 F	23 1 3	13 34 19	20 37 35	27 34 6	9 50.2	2 14.0	8 14.4	12 29.7	12 22.4	2 44.1	13 9.9	17 58.7	20 15.2
8 Sa	23 5 0	14 32 34	4♐33 27	11♐35 27	9D 50.0	1 53.7	7 38.9	13 7.7	12 16.2	2 51.2	13 12.1	18 0.6	20 17.0
9 Su	23 8 57	15 30 50	18 39 55	25 46 36	9 49.9	1D 41.8	7 4.3	13 45.6	12 9.9	2 58.4	13 14.2	18 2.6	20 18.7
10 M	23 12 53	16 29 7	2♑55 12	10♑ 5 22	9 50.1	1 38.7	6 30.9	14 23.5	12 3.5	3 5.6	13 16.3	18 4.5	20 20.4
11 Tu	23 16 50	17 27 26	17 16 45	24 28 53	9 50.6	1 44.6	5 58.8	15 1.4	11 56.9	3 12.9	13 18.3	18 6.5	20 22.1
12 W	23 20 46	18 25 47	1♒41 18	8♒53 28	9 51.3	1 59.6	5 28.4	15 39.2	11 50.2	3 20.1	13 20.3	18 8.5	20 23.8
13 Th	23 24 43	19 24 9	16 4 50	23 14 49	9 52.1	2 23.7	4 59.6	16 17.0	11 43.4	3 27.4	13 22.2	18 10.5	20 25.5
14 F	23 28 39	20 22 32	0♓22 50	7♓28 19	9R 52.6	2 56.7	4 32.7	16 54.8	11 36.5	3 34.6	13 24.1	18 12.5	20 27.2
15 Sa	23 32 36	21 20 58	14 30 44	21 29 32	9 52.7	3 38.2	4 7.8	17 32.5	11 29.4	3 41.9	13 26.0	18 14.5	20 28.8
16 Su	23 36 33	22 19 25	28 24 19	5♈14 41	9 52.1	4 28.1	3 45.0	18 10.2	11 22.3	3 49.2	13 27.8	18 16.6	20 30.5
17 M	23 40 29	23 17 54	12♈ 0 20	18 41 4	9 51.0	5 25.6	3 24.5	18 47.8	11 15.0	3 56.6	13 29.5	18 18.6	20 32.1
18 Tu	23 44 26	24 16 25	25 16 45	1♉47 24	9 49.2	6 30.5	3 6.3	19 25.5	11 7.7	4 3.9	13 31.2	18 20.7	20 33.7
19 W	23 48 22	25 14 58	8♉13 4	14 33 56	9 47.0	7 42.0	2 50.4	20 3.0	11 0.3	4 11.2	13 32.9	18 22.8	20 35.3
20 Th	23 52 19	26 13 34	20 50 13	27 2 16	9 44.8	8 59.6	2 37.0	20 40.6	10 52.8	4 18.6	13 34.5	18 24.9	20 36.9
21 F	23 56 15	27 12 11	3♊10 29	9♊15 17	9 42.9	10 22.6	2 25.9	21 18.1	10 45.2	4 26.0	13 36.1	18 27.0	20 38.4
22 Sa	0 0 12	28 10 51	15 17 10	21 16 42	9 41.5	11 50.5	2 17.4	21 55.6	10 37.5	4 33.4	13 37.6	18 29.1	20 40.0
23 Su	0 4 8	29 9 33	27 14 25	3♋10 56	9D 40.9	13 22.6	2 11.2	22 33.0	10 29.8	4 40.7	13 39.1	18 31.2	20 41.5
24 M	0 8 5	0♎ 8 17	9♋ 6 49	15 2 42	9 41.2	14 58.2	2 7.5	23 10.4	10 22.0	4 48.1	13 40.6	18 33.4	20 43.1
25 Tu	0 12 1	1 7 4	20 59 9	26 56 47	9 42.2	16 36.9	2D 6.2	23 47.8	10 14.2	4 55.5	13 41.9	18 35.5	20 44.6
26 W	0 15 58	2 5 53	2♌56 9	8♌57 48	9 43.8	18 18.2	2 7.3	24 25.2	10 6.3	5 3.0	13 43.3	18 37.7	20 46.1
27 Th	0 19 55	3 4 43	15 2 15	21 9 56	9 45.4	20 1.5	2 10.7	25 2.5	9 58.3	5 10.4	13 44.6	18 39.8	20 47.5
28 F	0 23 51	4 3 37	27 21 16	3♍36 36	9R 46.8	21 46.4	2 16.5	25 39.7	9 50.3	5 17.8	13 45.8	18 42.0	20 49.0
29 Sa	0 27 48	5 2 32	9♍56 14	16 20 20	9 47.3	23 32.5	2 24.4	26 17.0	9 42.3	5 25.2	13 47.0	18 44.2	20 50.4
30 Su	0 31 44	6 1 29	22 49 3	29 22 24	9 46.6	25 19.5	2 34.6	26 54.1	9 34.3	5 32.6	13 48.1	18 46.4	20 51.8

LONGITUDE — OCTOBER 1951

Day	Sid.Time	☉	0 hr ☽	Noon ☽	True ☊	☿	♀	♂	♃	♄	♅	♆	♇
1 M	0 35 41	7♎ 0 29	6♎ 0 21	12♎42 46	9♓44.6	27♍ 7.1	2♍46.9	27♌31.3	9♈26.2	5♎40.0	13♋49.2	18♎48.6	20♌53.2
2 Tu	0 39 37	7 59 30	19 29 25	26 20 0	9R 41.4	28 55.1	3 1.3	28 8.4	9R 18.2	5 47.4	13 50.2	18 50.8	20 54.6
3 W	0 43 34	8 58 33	3♏14 10	10♏11 29	9 37.1	0♎43.1	3 17.7	28 45.5	9 10.1	5 54.9	13 51.2	18 53.0	20 56.0
4 Th	0 47 30	9 57 39	17 11 31	24 13 46	9 32.5	2 31.2	3 36.0	29 22.5	9 2.0	6 2.3	13 52.1	18 55.2	20 57.3
5 F	0 51 27	10 56 46	1♐17 47	8♐23 4	9 28.0	4 19.0	3 56.3	29 59.5	8 54.0	6 9.7	13 53.0	18 57.4	20 58.6
6 Sa	0 55 24	11 55 56	15 29 10	22 35 42	9 24.5	6 6.5	4 18.4	0♍36.4	8 45.9	6 17.1	13 53.8	18 59.6	20 59.9
7 Su	0 59 20	12 55 7	29 42 16	6♑48 33	9 22.3	7 53.6	4 42.2	1 13.3	8 37.9	6 24.5	13 54.5	19 1.9	21 1.2
8 M	1 3 17	13 54 19	13♑54 17	20 59 11	9D 21.6	9 40.2	5 7.8	1 50.2	8 29.9	6 31.8	13 55.3	19 4.1	21 2.5
9 Tu	1 7 13	14 53 34	28 3 5	5♒ 5 46	9 22.2	11 26.2	5 35.1	2 27.0	8 21.9	6 39.2	13 55.9	19 6.3	21 3.7
10 W	1 11 10	15 52 50	12♒ 7 5	19 6 51	9 23.6	13 11.6	6 3.9	3 3.8	8 14.0	6 46.6	13 56.5	19 8.6	21 4.9
11 Th	1 15 6	16 52 8	26 4 54	3♓ 1 5	9R 24.9	14 56.4	6 34.3	3 40.6	8 6.1	6 53.9	13 57.1	19 10.8	21 6.1
12 F	1 19 3	17 51 27	9♓55 10	16 46 59	9 25.5	16 40.5	7 6.2	4 17.3	7 58.2	7 1.3	13 57.6	19 13.0	21 7.3
13 Sa	1 22 59	18 50 49	23 36 17	0♈22 51	9 24.6	18 23.9	7 39.5	4 53.9	7 50.4	7 8.6	13 58.0	19 15.3	21 8.4
14 Su	1 26 56	19 50 12	7♈ 6 27	13 46 50	9 21.8	20 6.6	8 14.3	5 30.5	7 42.7	7 15.9	13 58.4	19 17.5	21 9.5
15 M	1 30 53	20 49 37	20 23 48	26 57 11	9 16.9	21 48.7	8 50.4	6 7.1	7 35.1	7 23.2	13 58.8	19 19.7	21 10.6
16 Tu	1 34 49	21 49 5	3♉26 48	9♉52 34	9 10.3	23 30.0	9 27.8	6 43.6	7 27.5	7 30.4	13 59.0	19 22.0	21 11.7
17 W	1 38 46	22 48 34	16 14 27	22 32 27	9 2.5	25 10.7	10 6.5	7 20.1	7 20.0	7 37.7	13 59.3	19 24.2	21 12.8
18 Th	1 42 42	23 48 6	28 46 40	4♊57 16	8 54.4	26 50.7	10 46.3	7 56.6	7 12.6	7 44.9	13 59.5	19 26.4	21 13.8
19 F	1 46 39	24 47 40	11♊ 4 28	17 8 35	8 46.6	28 30.0	11 27.4	8 33.0	7 5.2	7 52.2	13 59.6	19 28.7	21 14.8
20 Sa	1 50 35	25 47 16	23 9 58	29 9 3	8 40.2	0♏ 8.7	12 9.6	9 9.4	6 58.0	7 59.3	13R 59.7	19 30.9	21 15.8
21 Su	1 54 32	26 46 54	5♋ 6 19	11♋ 2 18	8 35.5	1 46.8	12 52.8	9 45.7	6 50.9	8 6.5	13 59.7	19 33.1	21 16.7
22 M	1 58 28	27 46 35	16 57 34	22 52 43	8 32.9	3 24.2	13 37.1	10 22.0	6 43.8	8 13.7	13 59.6	19 35.4	21 17.7
23 Tu	2 2 25	28 46 18	28 48 24	4♌45 15	8D 32.1	5 1.1	14 22.4	10 58.3	6 36.9	8 20.8	13 59.6	19 37.6	21 18.6
24 W	2 6 22	29 46 3	10♌43 57	16 45 8	8 32.6	6 37.4	15 8.7	11 34.5	6 30.1	8 27.9	13 59.4	19 39.8	21 19.5
25 Th	2 10 18	0♏45 50	22 49 27	28 57 32	8 33.8	8 13.1	15 55.9	12 10.6	6 23.4	8 35.0	13 59.2	19 42.0	21 20.3
26 F	2 14 15	1 45 40	5♍ 9 57	11♍27 13	8R 34.6	9 48.3	16 44.0	12 46.7	6 16.9	8 42.0	13 59.0	19 44.2	21 21.1
27 Sa	2 18 11	2 45 31	17 49 49	24 18 5	8 34.2	11 22.9	17 32.9	13 22.8	6 10.4	8 49.0	13 58.7	19 46.4	21 21.9
28 Su	2 22 8	3 45 25	0♎52 18	7♎32 35	8 31.9	12 57.0	18 22.7	13 58.8	6 4.1	8 56.0	13 58.3	19 48.6	21 22.7
29 M	2 26 4	4 45 21	14 18 58	21 11 16	8 27.1	14 30.7	19 13.2	14 34.8	5 58.0	9 2.9	13 57.9	19 50.8	21 23.5
30 Tu	2 30 1	5 45 19	28 9 13	5♏12 21	8 20.0	16 3.8	20 4.6	15 10.7	5 52.0	9 9.9	13 57.4	19 52.9	21 24.2
31 W	2 33 57	6 45 19	12♏20 3	19 31 38	8 11.0	17 36.5	20 56.7	15 46.6	5 46.1	9 16.7	13 56.9	19 55.1	21 24.9

Astro Data Dy Hr Mn	Planet Ingress Dy Hr Mn	Last Aspect Dy Hr Mn	☽ Ingress Dy Hr Mn	Last Aspect Dy Hr Mn	☽ Ingress Dy Hr Mn	☽ Phases & Eclipses Dy Hr Mn
♃□♅ 1 1:09	☉ ♎ 23 20:37	1 21:44 ♅ ⚹	♎ 3 5:32	2 15:52 ♂ ⚹	♏ 2 18:23	1 12:50 ● 8♍16
☽0S 2 23:03		4 18:17 ♇ ⚹	♏ 5 11:49	4 21:41 ♂ □	♐ 4 21:48	1 12:51:21 ☌ A 2'36"
♀0N 5 0:05	☿ ♎ 2 14:25	6 23:21 ♇ □	♐ 7 16:11	6 9:19 ♇ △	♑ 7 0:30	8 18:16 ☽ 15♐17
☿ D 9 20:22	♂ ♍ 5 0:20	9 2:47 ♇ △	♑ 9 19:06	8 8:46 ♆ □	♒ 9 3:19	15 12:38 ○ 21♓52
☽0N 15 20:42	☿ ♏ 19 21:52	11 1:23 ♆ □	♒ 11 21:11	10 15:24 ♇ ☍	♓ 11 6:46	15 12:27 ☍ A 0.804
♄0S 25 4:58	☉ ♏ 24 5:36	13 7:17 ♇ ☍	♓ 13 23:21	12 7:04 ♅ △	♈ 13 11:19	23 4:13 ☽ 29♊20
♀ D 25 0:58		15 12:38 ☉ ☍	♈ 16 2:47	15 2:58 ☿ ☍	♉ 15 17:37	
☽0S 30 6:47		17 15:23 ♇ △	♉ 18 8:41	17 9:28 ♇ □	♊ 18 2:22	1 1:57 ● 7♎05
♄∠♇ 3 4:25		20 11:19 ☉ △	♊ 20 17:47	20 5:43 ☉ △	♋ 20 13:42	8 0:00 ☽ 13♑54
☿0S 4 19:01		23 4:13 ☉ □	♋ 23 5:34	22 23:55 ☉ □	♌ 23 2:25	15 0:51 ○ 20♈52
☽0N 13 5:06		24 19:09 ♆ □	♌ 25 18:08	24 21:04 ♇ ☌	♍ 25 14:01	22 23:55 ☽ 28♋46
♃☍♄ 15 19:12		27 20:34 ♂ ☌	♍ 28 5:05	26 23:26 ♀ ☌	♎ 27 22:25	30 13:54 ● 6♏20
♅ R 20 20:55		30 5:20 ☿ ☌	♎ 30 13:08	29 12:22 ♇ ⚹	♏ 30 3:09	
♃⚼♇ 25 10:02	☽0S 27 15:49					

Astro Data

1 SEPTEMBER 1951
Julian Day # 18871
Delta T 29.8 sec
SVP 05♓55'58"
Obliquity 23°26'53"
⚷ Chiron 26♐47.7
☽ Mean ☊ 9♓55.1

1 OCTOBER 1951
Julian Day # 18901
Delta T 29.9 sec
SVP 05♓55'55"
Obliquity 23°26'53"
⚷ Chiron 27♐27.1
☽ Mean ☊ 8♓19.8

NOVEMBER 1951 LONGITUDE

Day	Sid.Time	☉	0 hr ☽	Noon ☽	True ☊	☿	♀	♂	♃	♄	♅	♆	♇
1 Th	2 37 54	7♏45 21	26♏46 16	4♐ 3 3	8♓ 1.2	19♏ 8.7	21♍49.5	16♍22.4	5♈40.4	9♎23.6	13♋56.3	19♎57.3	21♌25.5
2 F	2 41 51	8 45 25	11♐21 6	18 39 29	7R51.6	20 40.4	22 42.9	16 58.2	5R34.9	9 30.4	13R55.7	19 59.4	21 26.2
3 Sa	2 45 47	9 45 30	25 57 23	3♑14 1	7 43.5	22 11.7	23 37.1	17 33.9	5 29.5	9 37.2	13 55.0	20 1.6	21 26.8
4 Su	2 49 44	10 45 37	10♑28 43	17 40 57	7 37.5	23 42.6	24 31.8	18 9.6	5 24.3	9 43.9	13 54.3	20 3.7	21 27.4
5 M	2 53 40	11 45 46	24 50 17	1♒56 25	7 34.1	25 13.0	25 27.2	18 45.2	5 19.2	9 50.6	13 53.5	20 5.8	21 27.9
6 Tu	2 57 37	12 45 56	8♒59 12	15 58 32	7D32.9	26 43.0	26 23.2	19 20.8	5 14.4	9 57.3	13 52.7	20 7.9	21 28.5
7 W	3 1 33	13 46 7	22 54 25	29 46 54	7 33.0	28 12.5	27 19.7	19 56.3	5 9.7	10 3.9	13 51.8	20 10.0	21 29.0
8 Th	3 5 30	14 46 20	6♓36 6	13♓22 8	7R33.4	29 41.6	28 16.8	20 31.7	5 5.1	10 10.4	13 50.9	20 12.1	21 29.4
9 F	3 9 26	15 46 35	20 5 7	26 45 10	7 32.8	1♐10.2	29 14.5	21 7.1	5 0.8	10 16.9	13 49.9	20 14.2	21 29.9
10 Sa	3 13 23	16 46 50	3♈22 24	9♈56 52	7 30.0	2 38.3	0♎12.7	21 42.4	4 56.6	10 23.4	13 48.9	20 16.2	21 30.3
11 Su	3 17 20	17 47 8	16 28 37	22 57 40	7 24.5	4 5.9	1 11.3	22 17.7	4 52.7	10 29.8	13 47.8	20 18.3	21 30.7
12 M	3 21 16	18 47 27	29 24 0	5♉47 36	7 16.1	5 33.0	2 10.5	22 52.9	4 48.9	10 36.2	13 46.7	20 20.3	21 31.0
13 Tu	3 25 13	19 47 47	12♉ 8 26	18 26 28	7 5.0	6 59.5	3 10.1	23 28.1	4 45.3	10 42.5	13 45.5	20 22.3	21 31.3
14 W	3 29 9	20 48 10	24 41 39	0♊54 1	6 52.0	8 25.3	4 10.3	24 3.2	4 41.9	10 48.8	13 44.3	20 24.3	21 31.6
15 Th	3 33 6	21 48 34	7♊ 3 35	13 10 25	6 38.4	9 50.6	5 10.8	24 38.3	4 38.7	10 55.0	13 43.0	20 26.3	21 31.9
16 F	3 37 2	22 48 59	19 14 38	25 16 26	6 25.1	11 15.1	6 11.8	25 13.3	4 35.7	11 1.2	13 41.7	20 28.3	21 32.2
17 Sa	3 40 59	23 49 27	1♋16 0	7♋13 40	6 13.5	12 38.8	7 13.2	25 48.2	4 32.9	11 7.3	13 40.3	20 30.2	21 32.4
18 Su	3 44 55	24 49 56	13 9 47	19 4 44	6 4.2	14 1.6	8 15.1	26 23.1	4 30.2	11 13.4	13 38.9	20 32.1	21 32.6
19 M	3 48 52	25 50 27	24 59 1	0♌53 9	5 57.7	15 23.5	9 17.3	26 57.9	4 27.8	11 19.4	13 37.5	20 34.1	21 32.7
20 Tu	3 52 49	26 51 0	6♌47 41	12 43 15	5 53.9	16 44.3	10 19.9	27 32.7	4 25.6	11 25.4	13 36.0	20 36.0	21 32.8
21 W	3 56 45	27 51 34	18 40 30	24 40 6	5D52.4	18 3.8	11 22.8	28 7.4	4 23.6	11 31.3	13 34.4	20 37.8	21 32.9
22 Th	4 0 42	28 52 10	0♍42 45	6♍49 8	5R52.1	19 21.9	12 26.2	28 42.0	4 21.8	11 37.1	13 32.8	20 39.7	21 33.0
23 F	4 4 38	29 52 48	12 59 56	19 15 50	5 52.0	20 38.4	13 29.8	29 16.6	4 20.2	11 42.9	13 31.2	20 41.5	21R33.0
24 Sa	4 8 35	0♐53 27	25 37 26	2♎ 5 17	5 50.9	21 53.1	14 33.8	29 51.1	4 18.8	11 48.6	13 29.5	20 43.4	21 33.0
25 Su	4 12 31	1 54 8	8♎39 51	15 21 27	5 47.8	23 5.8	15 38.2	0♎25.6	4 17.6	11 54.2	13 27.8	20 45.2	21 33.0
26 M	4 16 28	2 54 51	22 10 17	29 6 22	5 41.9	24 16.1	16 42.8	0 59.9	4 16.6	11 59.8	13 26.0	20 46.9	21 33.0
27 Tu	4 20 24	3 55 35	6♏ 9 31	13♏19 23	5 33.3	25 23.7	17 47.7	1 34.2	4 15.8	12 5.3	13 24.3	20 48.7	21 32.9
28 W	4 24 21	4 56 21	20 35 21	27 56 37	5 22.4	26 28.3	18 53.0	2 8.4	4 15.3	12 10.8	13 22.4	20 50.4	21 32.8
29 Th	4 28 18	5 57 8	5♐22 13	12♐51 1	5 10.3	27 29.4	19 58.5	2 42.6	4 14.9	12 16.1	13 20.5	20 52.2	21 32.6
30 F	4 32 14	6 57 57	20 21 47	27 53 16	4 58.3	28 26.4	21 4.2	3 16.7	4D14.8	12 21.5	13 18.6	20 53.9	21 32.5

DECEMBER 1951 LONGITUDE

Day	Sid.Time	☉	0 hr ☽	Noon ☽	True ☊	☿	♀	♂	♃	♄	♅	♆	♇
1 Sa	4 36 11	7♐58 47	5♑24 12	12♑53 25	4♓47.9	29♐18.9	22♎10.3	3♎50.7	4♈14.8	12♎26.7	13♋16.7	20♎55.5	21♌32.3
2 Su	4 40 7	8 59 37	20 19 52	27 42 41	4R40.0	0♑ 6.2	23 16.6	4 24.6	4 15.1	12 31.9	13R14.7	20 57.2	21R32.0
3 M	4 44 4	10 0 29	5♒ 1 7	12♒14 41	4 35.0	0 47.6	24 23.1	4 58.4	4 15.6	12 37.0	13 12.7	20 58.8	21 31.8
4 Tu	4 48 0	11 1 22	19 23 2	26 26 0	4 32.7	1 22.4	25 29.9	5 32.2	4 16.3	12 42.0	13 10.6	21 0.4	21 31.5
5 W	4 51 57	12 2 15	3♓23 34	10♓15 50	4 32.1	1 49.7	26 36.8	6 5.9	4 17.2	12 46.9	13 8.6	21 2.0	21 31.2
6 Th	4 55 54	13 3 9	17 3 1	23 45 22	4 32.1	2 8.8	27 44.1	6 39.5	4 18.3	12 51.8	13 6.4	21 3.5	21 30.9
7 F	4 59 50	14 4 3	0♈23 12	6♈56 49	4 31.3	2R18.7	28 51.5	7 13.0	4 19.6	12 56.6	13 4.3	21 5.0	21 30.5
8 Sa	5 3 47	15 4 59	13 26 34	19 52 47	4 28.4	2 18.6	29 59.1	7 46.4	4 21.2	13 1.3	13 2.1	21 6.5	21 30.1
9 Su	5 7 43	16 5 55	26 15 43	2♉35 40	4 22.8	2 7.9	1♏ 7.0	8 19.7	4 22.9	13 5.9	12 59.9	21 8.0	21 29.7
10 M	5 11 40	17 6 52	8♉52 51	15 7 28	4 14.2	1 46.0	2 15.0	8 53.0	4 24.8	13 10.5	12 57.7	21 9.5	21 29.2
11 Tu	5 15 36	18 7 49	21 19 41	27 29 39	4 2.9	1 12.7	3 23.3	9 26.2	4 27.0	13 15.0	12 55.4	21 10.9	21 28.7
12 W	5 19 33	19 8 48	3♊37 27	9♊43 13	3 49.6	0 28.0	4 31.7	9 59.2	4 29.3	13 19.4	12 53.1	21 12.3	21 28.2
13 Th	5 23 29	20 9 47	15 47 1	21 48 59	3 35.6	29♐32.5	5 40.3	10 32.2	4 31.9	13 23.7	12 50.8	21 13.6	21 27.7
14 F	5 27 26	21 10 47	27 49 13	3♋47 51	3 21.9	28 27.3	6 49.1	11 5.1	4 34.6	13 27.9	12 48.5	21 15.0	21 27.1
15 Sa	5 31 23	22 11 48	9♋45 2	15 41 0	3 9.7	27 14.2	7 58.1	11 37.9	4 37.6	13 32.1	12 46.1	21 16.3	21 26.5
16 Su	5 35 19	23 12 49	21 35 59	27 30 15	2 59.9	25 55.1	9 7.3	12 10.6	4 40.7	13 36.1	12 43.7	21 17.6	21 25.9
17 M	5 39 16	24 13 52	3♌24 10	9♌18 7	2 52.9	24 32.7	10 16.6	12 43.3	4 44.0	13 40.1	12 41.3	21 18.8	21 25.3
18 Tu	5 43 12	25 14 55	15 12 32	21 7 55	2 48.8	23 9.9	11 26.0	13 15.8	4 47.6	13 44.0	12 38.9	21 20.0	21 24.6
19 W	5 47 9	26 15 59	27 4 48	3♍ 3 45	2D47.1	21 49.2	12 35.7	13 48.2	4 51.3	13 47.8	12 36.4	21 21.2	21 23.9
20 Th	5 51 5	27 17 3	9♍ 5 24	15 10 23	2 47.1	20 33.5	13 45.5	14 20.5	4 55.2	13 51.5	12 34.0	21 22.4	21 23.2
21 F	5 55 2	28 18 9	21 19 22	27 33 1	2R47.7	19 24.8	14 55.4	14 52.7	4 59.3	13 55.1	12 31.5	21 23.5	21 22.5
22 Sa	5 58 58	29 19 15	3♎51 58	10♎16 50	2 47.8	18 24.9	16 5.5	15 24.8	5 3.6	13 58.6	12 29.0	21 24.6	21 21.7
23 Su	6 2 55	0♑20 22	16 48 12	23 26 32	2 46.4	17 35.0	17 15.7	15 56.8	5 8.1	14 2.0	12 26.5	21 25.7	21 20.9
24 M	6 6 52	1 21 30	0♏12 13	7♏ 5 29	2 42.8	16 55.7	18 26.0	16 28.7	5 12.8	14 5.4	12 24.0	21 26.8	21 20.1
25 Tu	6 10 48	2 22 39	14 6 23	21 14 46	2 36.8	16 27.2	19 36.5	17 0.5	5 17.7	14 8.6	12 21.4	21 27.8	21 19.3
26 W	6 14 45	3 23 48	28 30 17	5♐52 21	2 28.7	16 9.3	20 47.1	17 32.2	5 22.7	14 11.8	12 18.9	21 28.7	21 18.4
27 Th	6 18 41	4 24 58	13♐20 8	20 52 37	2 19.5	16D 1.8	21 57.8	18 3.7	5 27.9	14 14.8	12 16.3	21 29.7	21 17.5
28 F	6 22 38	5 26 8	28 28 33	6♑ 6 38	2 10.1	16 3.8	23 8.6	18 35.1	5 33.4	14 17.8	12 13.7	21 30.6	21 16.6
29 Sa	6 26 34	6 27 18	13♑45 26	21 23 32	2 1.8	16 14.9	24 19.6	19 6.4	5 39.0	14 20.6	12 11.2	21 31.5	21 15.7
30 Su	6 30 31	7 28 29	28 59 36	6♒32 24	1 55.6	16 34.1	25 30.6	19 37.6	5 44.7	14 23.4	12 8.6	21 32.4	21 14.7
31 M	6 34 27	8 29 40	14♒ 0 53	21 24 10	1 51.9	17 0.7	26 41.7	20 8.6	5 50.7	14 26.1	12 6.0	21 33.2	21 13.8

Astro Data	Planet Ingress	Last Aspect	☽ Ingress	Last Aspect	☽ Ingress	☽ Phases & Eclipses	Astro Data
Dy Hr Mn	Dy Hr Mn	Dy Hr Mn	Dy Hr Mn	Dy Hr Mn	Dy Hr Mn	Dy Hr Mn	1 NOVEMBER 1951
☽0N 9 11:05	☿ ♐ 8 4:59	31 15:17 ♀ ⚹	♐ 1 5:20	2 5:10 ♀ □	♒ 2 15:45	6 6:59 ☽ 13♒03	Julian Day # 18932
♀0S 12 0:32	♀ ♎ 9 18:48	2 19:54 ♀ □	♑ 3 6:40	4 11:18 ♀ △	♓ 4 18:08	13 15:52 ○ 20♉28	Delta T 29.9 sec
♇ R 23 16:28	☉ ♐ 23 2:51	5 1:07 ♀ △	♒ 5 8:43	5 17:02 ♅ △	♈ 6 23:18	21 20:01 ☽ 28♌42	SVP 05♓55'52"
☽0S 24 0:41	♂ ♎ 24 6:11	7 10:22 ☿ □	♓ 7 12:23	8 15:02 ♇ △	♉ 9 7:04	29 1:00 ● 5♐60	Obliquity 23°26'52"
♂0S 30 20:59		9 17:48 ♀ ☍	♈ 9 17:53	11 0:18 ♇ □	♊ 11 16:54		⚷ Chiron 29♐22.1
♃ D 30 4:08	☿ ♑ 1 20:41	11 9:19 ♇ △	♉ 12 1:07	14 1:10 ☿ ☍	♋ 14 4:22	5 16:20 ☽ 12♓44	☽ Mean ☊ 6♓41.3
	♀ ♏ 8 0:19	13 22:42 ♂ △	♊ 14 10:15	15 23:23 ♆ □	♌ 16 17:05	13 9:30 ○ 20♊34	
☽0N 6 15:39	☿ ♐ 12 12:39	16 12:30 ♂ □	♋ 16 21:27	18 22:13 ☉ △	♍ 19 5:52	21 14:37 ☽ 28♍55	1 DECEMBER 1951
☿ R 7 11:56	☉ ♑ 22 16:00	19 4:14 ♂ ⚹	♌ 19 10:12	21 14:37 ☉ □	♎ 21 16:41	28 11:43 ● 5♑56	Julian Day # 18962
♄□♅ 8 2:47		21 20:01 ☉ □	♍ 21 22:35	23 8:24 ♆ ☌	♏ 23 23:38		Delta T 29.9 sec
♆⚹♇ 20 10:31		23 16:13 ☿ □	♎ 24 8:09	25 12:07 ♇ □	♐ 26 2:27		SVP 05♓55'46"
☽0S 21 7:59		26 3:59 ☿ ⚹	♏ 26 13:32	27 12:59 ♆ ⚹	♑ 28 2:24		Obliquity 23°26'52"
☿ D 27 6:38		28 1:34 ♇ □	♐ 28 15:20	29 18:02 ♀ ⚹	♒ 30 1:36		⚷ Chiron 2♑04.8
		30 13:42 ☿ ☌	♑ 30 15:22				☽ Mean ☊ 5♓06.0

LONGITUDE JANUARY 1952

Day	Sid.Time	☉	0 hr ☽	Noon ☽	True ☊	☿	♀	♂	♃	♄	♅	♆	♇
1 Tu	6 38 24	9♑30 50	28♒41 37	5♓52 46	1♓50.5	17♐34.1	27♏52.9	20♎39.5	5♈56.8	14♎28.6	12♋ 3.4	21♎34.0	21♌12.8
2 W	6 42 21	10 32 1	12♓57 24	19 55 27	1D 50.8	18 13.4	29 4.3	21 10.3	6 3.1	14 31.1	12R 0.8	21 34.7	21R 11.7
3 Th	6 46 17	11 33 11	26 46 58	3♈32 12	1 51.9	18 58.1	0♐15.7	21 40.9	6 9.6	14 33.4	11 58.2	21 35.4	21 10.7
4 F	6 50 14	12 34 21	10♈11 27	16 45 4	1R 52.7	19 47.6	1 27.2	22 11.4	6 16.2	14 35.7	11 55.6	21 36.1	21 9.6
5 Sa	6 54 10	13 35 30	23 13 29	29 37 9	1 52.2	20 41.4	2 38.8	22 41.7	6 23.0	14 37.8	11 53.0	21 36.8	21 8.6
6 Su	6 58 7	14 36 39	5♉56 30	12♉12 0	1 49.8	21 38.9	3 50.4	23 11.9	6 30.0	14 39.9	11 50.4	21 37.4	21 7.5
7 M	7 2 3	15 37 48	18 24 4	24 33 6	1 45.2	22 39.9	5 2.2	23 42.0	6 37.1	14 41.8	11 47.8	21 38.0	21 6.3
8 Tu	7 6 0	16 38 57	0♊39 29	6♊43 34	1 38.6	23 43.8	6 14.0	24 11.9	6 44.4	14 43.7	11 45.3	21 38.5	21 5.2
9 W	7 9 56	17 40 5	12 45 39	18 46 2	1 30.6	24 50.5	7 25.9	24 41.7	6 51.9	14 45.4	11 42.7	21 39.0	21 4.0
10 Th	7 13 53	18 41 13	24 44 57	0♋42 39	1 22.0	25 59.5	8 37.9	25 11.3	6 59.5	14 47.0	11 40.1	21 39.5	21 2.9
11 F	7 17 50	19 42 20	6♋39 21	12 35 14	1 13.5	27 10.7	9 50.0	25 40.7	7 7.2	14 48.6	11 37.5	21 40.0	21 1.7
12 Sa	7 21 46	20 43 27	18 30 32	24 25 27	1 6.0	28 23.8	11 2.1	26 10.0	7 15.1	14 50.0	11 35.0	21 40.4	21 0.5
13 Su	7 25 43	21 44 34	0♌20 10	6♌14 56	1 0.1	29 38.7	12 14.3	26 39.1	7 23.2	14 51.3	11 32.4	21 40.8	20 59.3
14 M	7 29 39	22 45 41	12 10 0	18 5 38	0 56.2	0♑55.1	13 26.6	27 8.1	7 31.4	14 52.5	11 29.9	21 41.1	20 58.0
15 Tu	7 33 36	23 46 47	24 2 9	29 59 52	0D 54.3	2 13.0	14 38.9	27 36.9	7 39.8	14 53.6	11 27.4	21 41.4	20 56.8
16 W	7 37 32	24 47 53	5♍59 11	12♍ 0 30	0 54.2	3 32.3	15 51.3	28 5.5	7 48.2	14 54.6	11 24.9	21 41.7	20 55.5
17 Th	7 41 29	25 48 58	18 4 16	24 10 57	0 55.3	4 52.7	17 3.8	28 34.0	7 56.9	14 55.5	11 22.4	21 42.0	20 54.2
18 F	7 45 26	26 50 3	0♎21 4	6♎35 7	0 57.0	6 14.3	18 16.3	29 2.2	8 5.7	14 56.3	11 19.9	21 42.2	20 52.9
19 Sa	7 49 22	27 51 8	12 53 38	19 17 9	0 58.7	7 36.9	19 28.9	29 30.3	8 14.6	14 56.9	11 17.4	21 42.3	20 51.6
20 Su	7 53 19	28 52 13	25 46 9	2♏21 7	0R 59.6	9 0.5	20 41.5	29 58.2	8 23.6	14 57.5	11 15.0	21 42.5	20 50.3
21 M	7 57 15	29 53 17	9♏ 2 26	15 50 24	0 59.3	10 25.0	21 54.2	0♏25.9	8 32.8	14 58.0	11 12.5	21 42.6	20 49.0
22 Tu	8 1 12	0♒54 21	22 45 15	29 47 0	0 57.5	11 50.3	23 7.0	0 53.4	8 42.2	14 58.3	11 10.1	21 42.7	20 47.6
23 W	8 5 8	1 55 25	6♐55 34	14♐10 40	0 54.5	13 16.5	24 19.8	1 20.7	8 51.6	14 58.6	11 7.7	21R 42.7	20 46.3
24 Th	8 9 5	2 56 28	21 31 49	28 58 18	0 50.7	14 43.5	25 32.6	1 47.8	9 1.2	14R 58.7	11 5.4	21 42.7	20 44.9
25 F	8 13 1	3 57 31	6♑29 16	14♑ 3 38	0 46.6	16 11.3	26 45.5	2 14.7	9 10.9	14 58.7	11 3.0	21 42.7	20 43.5
26 Sa	8 16 58	4 58 33	21 40 15	29 17 49	0 43.0	17 39.8	27 58.5	2 41.3	9 20.8	14 58.6	11 0.7	21 42.6	20 42.2
27 Su	8 20 55	5 59 34	6♒55 2	14♒30 35	0 40.3	19 9.1	29 11.4	3 7.8	9 30.7	14 58.4	10 58.4	21 42.5	20 40.8
28 M	8 24 51	7 0 34	22 3 16	29 31 59	0D 39.0	20 39.1	0♑24.5	3 34.0	9 40.8	14 58.1	10 56.2	21 42.4	20 39.4
29 Tu	8 28 48	8 1 34	6♓55 46	14♓13 51	0 38.9	22 9.7	1 37.5	3 59.9	9 51.0	14 57.7	10 53.9	21 42.2	20 38.0
30 W	8 32 44	9 2 32	21 25 40	28 30 50	0 39.8	23 41.1	2 50.6	4 25.7	10 1.4	14 57.2	10 51.7	21 42.0	20 36.5
31 Th	8 36 41	10 3 29	5♈29 8	12♈20 32	0 41.2	25 13.2	4 3.7	4 51.1	10 11.8	14 56.6	10 49.5	21 41.8	20 35.1

LONGITUDE FEBRUARY 1952

Day	Sid.Time	☉	0 hr ☽	Noon ☽	True ☊	☿	♀	♂	♃	♄	♅	♆	♇
1 F	8 40 37	11♒ 4 24	19♈ 5 9	25♈43 13	0♓42.6	26♑45.9	5♑16.9	5♏16.4	10♈22.4	14♎55.9	10♋47.4	21♎41.5	20♌33.7
2 Sa	8 44 34	12 5 19	2♉15 3	8♉41 3	0R 43.6	28 19.4	6 30.1	5 41.4	10 33.0	14R 55.0	10R 45.3	21R 41.2	20R 32.2
3 Su	8 48 30	13 6 12	15 1 42	21 17 30	0 43.9	29 53.6	7 43.3	6 6.1	10 43.8	14 54.1	10 43.2	21 40.9	20 30.8
4 M	8 52 27	14 7 4	27 28 57	3♊36 36	0 43.3	1♒28.5	8 56.5	6 30.5	10 54.7	14 53.0	10 41.1	21 40.5	20 29.4
5 Tu	8 56 24	15 7 54	9♊40 58	15 42 33	0 42.0	3 4.1	10 9.8	6 54.7	11 5.7	14 51.9	10 39.1	21 40.1	20 27.9
6 W	9 0 20	16 8 43	21 41 53	27 39 24	0 40.1	4 40.5	11 23.1	7 18.7	11 16.8	14 50.6	10 37.1	21 39.7	20 26.5
7 Th	9 4 17	17 9 31	3♋35 34	9♋30 46	0 37.9	6 17.6	12 36.4	7 42.3	11 28.0	14 49.3	10 35.2	21 39.2	20 25.0
8 F	9 8 13	18 10 17	15 25 26	21 19 52	0 35.9	7 55.4	13 49.8	8 5.7	11 39.3	14 47.8	10 33.3	21 38.7	20 23.6
9 Sa	9 12 10	19 11 2	27 14 26	3♌ 9 26	0 34.1	9 34.1	15 3.1	8 28.7	11 50.7	14 46.3	10 31.4	21 38.2	20 22.1
10 Su	9 16 6	20 11 45	9♌ 5 7	15 1 46	0 32.8	11 13.5	16 16.5	8 51.5	12 2.2	14 44.6	10 29.6	21 37.6	20 20.6
11 M	9 20 3	21 12 27	20 59 37	26 58 54	0D 32.1	12 53.7	17 30.0	9 14.0	12 13.8	14 42.8	10 27.8	21 37.0	20 19.2
12 Tu	9 23 59	22 13 8	2♍59 52	9♍ 2 43	0 32.0	14 34.8	18 43.4	9 36.2	12 25.5	14 41.0	10 26.0	21 36.4	20 17.7
13 W	9 27 56	23 13 47	15 7 42	21 15 3	0 32.3	16 16.7	19 56.9	9 58.0	12 37.2	14 39.0	10 24.3	21 35.7	20 16.3
14 Th	9 31 53	24 14 25	27 25 0	3♎37 49	0 32.8	17 59.4	21 10.4	10 19.5	12 49.1	14 37.0	10 22.6	21 35.1	20 14.8
15 F	9 35 49	25 15 2	9♎53 47	16 13 9	0 33.4	19 43.0	22 23.9	10 40.7	13 1.0	14 34.8	10 21.0	21 34.3	20 13.4
16 Sa	9 39 46	26 15 37	22 36 14	29 3 17	0 33.9	21 27.5	23 37.5	11 1.6	13 13.1	14 32.6	10 19.4	21 33.6	20 11.9
17 Su	9 43 42	27 16 11	5♏34 37	12♏10 29	0 34.3	23 12.8	24 51.0	11 22.1	13 25.2	14 30.2	10 17.8	21 32.8	20 10.5
18 M	9 47 39	28 16 44	18 51 9	25 36 48	0R 34.5	24 59.1	26 4.6	11 42.2	13 37.4	14 27.8	10 16.3	21 32.0	20 9.0
19 Tu	9 51 35	29 17 16	2♐27 36	9♐23 37	0 34.5	26 46.2	27 18.3	12 2.0	13 49.7	14 25.3	10 14.9	21 31.2	20 7.6
20 W	9 55 32	0♓17 47	16 24 52	23 31 13	0D 34.5	28 34.3	28 31.9	12 21.4	14 2.0	14 22.7	10 13.5	21 30.3	20 6.1
21 Th	9 59 28	1 18 17	0♑42 28	7♑58 15	0 34.5	0♓23.2	29 45.5	12 40.4	14 14.5	14 20.0	10 12.1	21 29.4	20 4.7
22 F	10 3 25	2 18 45	15 18 6	22 41 21	0 34.7	2 13.0	0♒59.2	12 59.1	14 27.0	14 17.2	10 10.8	21 28.5	20 3.3
23 Sa	10 7 22	3 19 11	0♒ 7 17	7♒35 2	0 34.9	4 3.6	2 12.9	13 17.3	14 39.6	14 14.3	10 9.5	21 27.6	20 1.9
24 Su	10 11 18	4 19 37	15 3 39	22 32 7	0 35.1	5 55.1	3 26.6	13 35.1	14 52.3	14 11.3	10 8.3	21 26.6	20 0.5
25 M	10 15 15	5 20 0	29 59 24	7♓24 29	0R 35.2	7 47.3	4 40.3	13 52.5	15 5.0	14 8.3	10 7.1	21 25.6	19 59.1
26 Tu	10 19 11	6 20 22	14♓46 24	22 4 16	0 35.1	9 40.3	5 54.0	14 9.4	15 17.8	14 5.2	10 6.0	21 24.6	19 57.7
27 W	10 23 8	7 20 42	29 17 18	6♈24 53	0 34.6	11 33.8	7 7.8	14 25.9	15 30.7	14 2.0	10 4.9	21 23.5	19 56.3
28 Th	10 27 4	8 21 1	13♈26 30	20 21 50	0 33.8	13 28.0	8 21.5	14 41.9	15 43.7	13 58.7	10 3.8	21 22.4	19 54.9
29 F	10 31 1	9 21 17	27 10 42	3♉53 3	0 32.7	15 22.5	9 35.3	14 57.5	15 56.7	13 55.3	10 2.9	21 21.3	19 53.5

Astro Data

	Dy Hr Mn
☽ 0 N	2 21:21
♃ ⚼ ♇	3 3:31
☽ 0 S	17 13:43
♆ R	23 16:28
♄ R	24 17:55
☽ 0 N	30 6:00
♃ □ ♅	2 22:46
☽ 0 S	13 19:11
♃ ☍ ♄	21 8:37
☽ 0 N	26 16:46

Planet Ingress

		Dy Hr Mn
♀	♐	2 18:44
☿	♑	13 6:44
♂	♏	20 1:33
☉	♒	21 2:38
♀	♑	27 15:58
☿	♒	3 1:38
☉	♓	19 16:57
☿	♓	20 18:55
♀	♒	21 4:42

Last Aspect / ☽ Ingress

Last Aspect Dy Hr Mn		☽ Ingress Dy Hr Mn
31 22:32	♀ □	♓ 1 2:10
2 9:33	☿ □	♈ 3 5:42
4 22:58	♂ ☍	♉ 5 12:43
7 5:15	♇ □	♊ 7 22:42
10 2:46	☿ ☍	♋ 10 10:34
12 16:12	♂ □	♌ 12 23:19
15 7:31	♂ ⚹	♍ 15 12:00
17 16:34	☉ △	♎ 17 23:19
20 6:09	☉ □	♏ 20 7:44
21 20:37	♇ □	♐ 22 12:22
24 7:04	♀ ☌	♑ 24 13:39
26 0:04	♆ □	♒ 26 13:06
27 23:27	♆ △	♓ 28 12:45
30 4:16	☿ ⚹	♈ 30 14:32

Last Aspect / ☽ Ingress

Last Aspect Dy Hr Mn		☽ Ingress Dy Hr Mn
1 15:47	☿ □	♉ 1 19:51
3 10:29	♇ □	♊ 4 4:55
5 23:56	♆ △	♋ 6 16:44
8 12:38	♆ □	♌ 9 5:36
11 1:15	♆ ⚹	♍ 11 18:02
13 10:30	♀ △	♎ 14 5:00
16 7:24	☉ △	♏ 16 13:45
18 18:01	☉ □	♐ 18 19:42
20 8:36	♆ ⚹	♑ 20 22:49
22 10:01	♆ □	♒ 22 23:48
24 10:14	♆ △	♓ 25 0:01
25 22:58	♂ △	♈ 27 1:11
28 13:45	♆ ☍	♉ 29 5:02

☽ Phases & Eclipses

Dy Hr Mn	
4 4:42	☽ 12♈46
12 4:55	○ 20♋56
20 6:09	☽ 29♎08
26 22:26	● 5♒56
2 20:01	☽ 12♉56
11 0:28	○ 21♌14
11 0:39	☍ P 0.083
18 18:01	☽ 29♏02
25 9:16	● 5♓43
25 9:11:05	☌ T 3'09"

Astro Data

1 JANUARY 1952
Julian Day # 18993
Delta T 30.0 sec
SVP 05♓55'40"
Obliquity 23°26'52"
⚷ Chiron 5♑17.5
☽ Mean ☊ 3♓27.5

1 FEBRUARY 1952
Julian Day # 19024
Delta T 30.0 sec
SVP 05♓55'35"
Obliquity 23°26'52"
⚷ Chiron 8♑23.8
☽ Mean ☊ 1♓49.0

MARCH 1952 — LONGITUDE

Day	Sid.Time	☉	0 hr ☽	Noon ☽	True ☊	☿	♀	♂	♃	♄	♅	♆	♇
1 Sa	10 34 57	10♓21 31	10♉29 0	16♉58 47	0♓31.5	17♓17.4	10♒49.0	15♏12.7	16♈ 9.8	13♎51.9	10♋ 1.9	21♎20.2	19♌52.2
2 Su	10 38 54	11 21 44	23 22 42	29 41 9	0R 30.6	19 12.4	12 2.8	15 27.3	16 22.9	13R 48.4	10R 1.0	21R 19.0	19R 50.8
3 M	10 42 51	12 21 54	5♊54 38	12♊ 3 40	0D 30.0	21 7.3	13 16.5	15 41.5	16 36.1	13 44.8	10 0.2	21 17.9	19 49.5
4 Tu	10 46 47	13 22 3	18 8 48	24 10 38	0 30.0	23 1.9	14 30.3	15 55.1	16 49.4	13 41.1	9 59.4	21 16.7	19 48.2
5 W	10 50 44	14 22 9	0♋ 9 46	6♋ 6 47	0 30.5	24 55.9	15 44.1	16 8.3	17 2.7	13 37.4	9 58.7	21 15.5	19 46.9
6 Th	10 54 40	15 22 13	12 2 16	17 56 48	0 31.6	26 49.1	16 57.9	16 20.9	17 16.0	13 33.6	9 58.0	21 14.2	19 45.6
7 F	10 58 37	16 22 15	23 50 56	29 45 11	0 33.1	28 41.0	18 11.7	16 33.0	17 29.5	13 29.8	9 57.4	21 13.0	19 44.3
8 Sa	11 2 33	17 22 15	5♌40 3	11♌35 58	0 34.5	0♈31.2	19 25.5	16 44.6	17 42.9	13 25.9	9 56.9	21 11.7	19 43.0
9 Su	11 6 30	18 22 13	17 33 23	23 32 40	0 35.7	2 19.5	20 39.3	16 55.6	17 56.5	13 21.9	9 56.3	21 10.4	19 41.8
10 M	11 10 26	19 22 8	29 34 7	5♍38 4	0R 36.2	4 5.2	21 53.1	17 6.1	18 10.0	13 17.9	9 55.9	21 9.0	19 40.5
11 Tu	11 14 23	20 22 2	11♍44 44	17 54 21	0 35.7	5 47.9	23 6.9	17 16.0	18 23.6	13 13.8	9 55.5	21 7.7	19 39.3
12 W	11 18 20	21 21 54	24 7 3	0♎22 58	0 34.3	7 27.2	24 20.7	17 25.3	18 37.3	13 9.7	9 55.1	21 6.3	19 38.1
13 Th	11 22 16	22 21 43	6♎42 11	13 4 46	0 31.8	9 2.5	25 34.5	17 34.1	18 51.0	13 5.5	9 54.8	21 4.9	19 36.9
14 F	11 26 13	23 21 31	19 30 45	26 0 8	0 28.4	10 33.3	26 48.3	17 42.2	19 4.8	13 1.3	9 54.5	21 3.5	19 35.7
15 Sa	11 30 9	24 21 17	2♏32 55	9♏ 9 4	0 24.7	11 59.1	28 2.2	17 49.7	19 18.6	12 57.0	9 54.3	21 2.1	19 34.5
16 Su	11 34 6	25 21 1	15 48 34	22 31 22	0 21.0	13 19.4	29 16.0	17 56.6	19 32.4	12 52.7	9 54.2	21 0.7	19 33.4
17 M	11 38 2	26 20 44	29 17 27	6♐ 6 45	0 17.9	14 33.8	0♓29.8	18 2.9	19 46.3	12 48.4	9 54.1	20 59.3	19 32.3
18 Tu	11 41 59	27 20 25	12♐59 14	19 54 50	0 15.9	15 41.9	1 43.7	18 8.5	20 0.2	12 44.0	9D 54.1	20 57.8	19 31.2
19 W	11 45 55	28 20 4	26 53 28	3♑55 2	0D 15.1	16 43.2	2 57.6	18 13.4	20 14.1	12 39.6	9 54.1	20 56.3	19 30.1
20 Th	11 49 52	29 19 42	10♑59 24	18 6 23	0 15.6	17 37.5	4 11.4	18 17.7	20 28.1	12 35.1	9 54.1	20 54.8	19 29.0
21 F	11 53 49	0♈19 18	25 15 45	2♒27 12	0 16.8	18 24.5	5 25.3	18 21.3	20 42.2	12 30.6	9 54.3	20 53.3	19 28.0
22 Sa	11 57 45	1 18 52	9♒40 22	16 54 49	0 18.3	19 3.9	6 39.2	18 24.1	20 56.2	12 26.1	9 54.4	20 51.8	19 26.9
23 Su	12 1 42	2 18 24	24 10 2	1♓25 26	0R 19.3	19 35.6	7 53.0	18 26.3	21 10.3	12 21.5	9 54.7	20 50.3	19 25.9
24 M	12 5 38	3 17 54	8♓40 22	15 54 10	0 19.2	19 59.4	9 6.9	18 27.7	21 24.4	12 17.0	9 55.0	20 48.7	19 25.0
25 Tu	12 9 35	4 17 23	23 6 7	0♈15 30	0 17.5	20 15.5	10 20.8	18R 28.4	21 38.6	12 12.4	9 55.3	20 47.2	19 24.0
26 W	12 13 31	5 16 49	7♈21 39	14 23 55	0 14.0	20R 23.7	11 34.6	18 28.4	21 52.7	12 7.8	9 55.7	20 45.6	19 23.0
27 Th	12 17 28	6 16 13	21 21 44	28 14 38	0 8.9	20 24.4	12 48.5	18 27.6	22 6.9	12 3.1	9 56.1	20 44.0	19 22.1
28 F	12 21 24	7 15 36	5♉ 2 15	11♉44 20	0 2.9	20 17.5	14 2.4	18 26.1	22 21.2	11 58.5	9 56.6	20 42.4	19 21.2
29 Sa	12 25 21	8 14 56	18 20 47	24 51 34	29♒56.5	20 3.6	15 16.2	18 23.8	22 35.4	11 53.8	9 57.2	20 40.8	19 20.3
30 Su	12 29 17	9 14 14	1♊16 50	7♊36 47	29 50.6	19 43.1	16 30.1	18 20.8	22 49.7	11 49.2	9 57.8	20 39.2	19 19.5
31 M	12 33 14	10 13 29	13 51 46	20 2 10	29 45.9	19 16.4	17 43.9	18 17.0	23 4.0	11 44.5	9 58.5	20 37.6	19 18.6

APRIL 1952 — LONGITUDE

Day	Sid.Time	☉	0 hr ☽	Noon ☽	True ☊	☿	♀	♂	♃	♄	♅	♆	♇
1 Tu	12 37 11	11♈12 43	26♊ 8 29	2♋11 16	29♒42.8	18♈44.1	18♓57.8	18♏12.5	23♈18.3	11♎39.8	9♋59.2	20♎36.0	19♌17.8
2 W	12 41 7	12 11 54	8♋11 4	14 8 32	29D 41.5	18R 7.1	20 11.6	18R 7.2	23 32.6	11R 35.1	9 60.0	20R 34.4	19R 17.0
3 Th	12 45 4	13 11 3	20 4 18	25 59 0	29 41.7	17 26.2	21 25.5	18 1.1	23 47.0	11 30.5	10 0.8	20 32.8	19 16.3
4 F	12 49 0	14 10 9	1♌53 19	7♌47 52	29 42.9	16 42.1	22 39.3	17 54.3	24 1.3	11 25.8	10 1.7	20 31.1	19 15.5
5 Sa	12 52 57	15 9 13	13 43 17	19 40 11	29 44.3	15 55.9	23 53.1	17 46.7	24 15.7	11 21.1	10 2.6	20 29.5	19 14.8
6 Su	12 56 53	16 8 15	25 39 8	1♍40 39	29R 45.3	15 8.5	25 6.9	17 38.3	24 30.1	11 16.5	10 3.6	20 27.9	19 14.1
7 M	13 0 50	17 7 15	7♍45 12	13 53 14	29 45.1	14 20.7	26 20.8	17 29.2	24 44.5	11 11.8	10 4.6	20 26.2	19 13.5
8 Tu	13 4 46	18 6 12	20 5 4	26 21 0	29 42.9	13 33.6	27 34.6	17 19.3	24 58.9	11 7.2	10 5.7	20 24.6	19 12.8
9 W	13 8 43	19 5 7	2♎41 13	9♎ 5 50	29 38.6	12 48.0	28 48.4	17 8.7	25 13.3	11 2.6	10 6.8	20 22.9	19 12.2
10 Th	13 12 40	20 4 0	15 34 53	22 8 19	29 32.2	12 4.7	0♈ 2.2	16 57.3	25 27.7	10 58.0	10 8.0	20 21.3	19 11.6
11 F	13 16 36	21 2 51	28 46 0	5♏27 42	29 24.1	11 24.4	1 16.0	16 45.2	25 42.2	10 53.4	10 9.2	20 19.6	19 11.1
12 Sa	13 20 33	22 1 41	12♏13 10	19 2 2	29 15.2	10 47.7	2 29.8	16 32.4	25 56.6	10 48.9	10 10.5	20 18.0	19 10.5
13 Su	13 24 29	23 0 28	25 53 58	2♐48 34	29 6.3	10 15.0	3 43.6	16 18.9	26 11.1	10 44.4	10 11.8	20 16.3	19 10.0
14 M	13 28 26	23 59 13	9♐45 27	16 44 13	28 58.5	9 46.8	4 57.4	16 4.6	26 25.5	10 39.9	10 13.2	20 14.7	19 9.5
15 Tu	13 32 22	24 57 57	23 44 32	0♑46 4	28 52.6	9 23.5	6 11.2	15 49.7	26 40.0	10 35.4	10 14.6	20 13.0	19 9.1
16 W	13 36 19	25 56 39	7♑48 32	14 51 41	28 48.9	9 5.1	7 25.0	15 34.1	26 54.4	10 31.0	10 16.1	20 11.4	19 8.7
17 Th	13 40 15	26 55 20	21 55 19	28 59 16	28D 47.5	8 51.8	8 38.8	15 17.9	27 8.9	10 26.6	10 17.6	20 9.8	19 8.3
18 F	13 44 12	27 53 59	6♒ 3 23	13♒ 7 30	28 47.6	8 43.7	9 52.6	15 1.1	27 23.3	10 22.3	10 19.2	20 8.1	19 7.9
19 Sa	13 48 9	28 52 36	20 11 30	27 15 14	28R 48.2	8D 40.8	11 6.4	14 43.6	27 37.8	10 17.9	10 20.8	20 6.5	19 7.5
20 Su	13 52 5	29 51 11	4♓18 28	11♓21 1	28 48.3	8 43.1	12 20.1	14 25.6	27 52.2	10 13.7	10 22.5	20 4.9	19 7.2
21 M	13 56 2	0♉49 45	18 22 36	25 22 54	28 46.7	8 50.3	13 33.9	14 7.0	28 6.7	10 9.4	10 24.2	20 3.3	19 6.9
22 Tu	13 59 58	1 48 17	2♈21 33	9♈18 11	28 42.7	9 2.5	14 47.7	13 47.8	28 21.1	10 5.2	10 26.0	20 1.7	19 6.6
23 W	14 3 55	2 46 47	16 12 22	23 3 42	28 36.1	9 19.4	16 1.5	13 28.2	28 35.5	10 1.1	10 27.8	20 0.1	19 6.4
24 Th	14 7 51	3 45 16	29 51 44	6♉36 8	28 26.9	9 40.9	17 15.3	13 8.2	28 49.9	9 57.0	10 29.7	19 58.5	19 6.2
25 F	14 11 48	4 43 42	13♉16 31	19 52 37	28 16.1	10 6.9	18 29.0	12 47.8	29 4.4	9 53.0	10 31.6	19 56.9	19 6.0
26 Sa	14 15 44	5 42 7	26 24 16	2♊51 19	28 4.5	10 37.1	19 42.8	12 26.9	29 18.8	9 49.0	10 33.5	19 55.3	19 5.9
27 Su	14 19 41	6 40 30	9♊13 47	15 31 43	27 53.5	11 11.5	20 56.5	12 5.8	29 33.2	9 45.1	10 35.5	19 53.7	19 5.7
28 M	14 23 38	7 38 51	21 45 19	27 54 49	27 43.9	11 49.7	22 10.3	11 44.4	29 47.5	9 41.2	10 37.5	19 52.2	19 5.6
29 Tu	14 27 34	8 37 10	4♋ 0 35	10♋ 3 2	27 36.6	12 31.7	23 24.0	11 22.7	0♉ 1.9	9 37.4	10 39.6	19 50.6	19 5.6
30 W	14 31 31	9 35 27	16 2 40	22 0 1	27 31.8	13 17.4	24 37.8	11 0.8	0 16.2	9 33.7	10 41.8	19 49.1	19D 5.5

Astro Data	Planet Ingress	Last Aspect	☽ Ingress	Last Aspect	☽ Ingress	☽ Phases & Eclipses	Astro Data
Dy Hr Mn	Dy Hr Mn	Dy Hr Mn	Dy Hr Mn	Dy Hr Mn	Dy Hr Mn	Dy Hr Mn	1 MARCH 1952
☿0N 7 19:38	☿ ♈ 7 17:10	1 17:22 ♇ □	♊ 2 12:36	31 18:18 ♃ ⚹	♋ 1 7:39	3 13:43 ☽ 12♊56	Julian Day # 19053
☽0S 12 1:39	♀ ♓ 16 14:18	4 11:32 ☿ □	♋ 4 23:40	3 7:41 ♃ □	♌ 3 20:10	11 18:14 ○ 21♍08	Delta T 30.0 sec
♃△♇ 16 1:38	☉ ♈ 20 16:14	7 11:39 ☿ △	♌ 7 12:30	5 21:39 ♃ △	♍ 6 8:40	19 2:40 ☽ 28♐27	SVP 05♓55'31"
♅ D 18 4:12	☊ ♒ 28 10:44	9 7:14 ♆ ⚹	♍ 10 0:51	8 15:53 ♀ ☍	♎ 8 18:56	25 20:13 ● 5♈07	Obliquity 23°26'52"
♃☍♆ 21 17:13		11 18:14 ☉ ☍	♎ 12 11:16	10 18:22 ♃ ☍	♏ 11 2:13		⚷ Chiron 10♑44.4
☽0N 25 3:08	♀ ♈ 9 23:17	14 14:53 ♀ △	♏ 14 19:20	12 12:14 ♇ □	♐ 13 7:08	2 8:48 ☽ 12♋34	☽ Mean ☊ 0♓16.9
♂ R 25 11:07	☉ ♉ 20 3:37	16 18:23 ☉ △	♐ 17 1:15	15 5:05 ♃ △	♑ 15 10:41	10 8:53 ○ 20♎26	
☿ R 26 13:54	♃ ♉ 28 20:50	19 2:40 ☉ □	♑ 19 5:19	17 9:07 ☉ □	♒ 17 13:43	17 9:07 ☽ 27♑18	1 APRIL 1952
☽0S 8 9:18		20 16:41 ♆ □	♒ 21 7:55	19 15:51 ☉ ⚹	♓ 19 16:40	24 7:27 ● 4♉03	Julian Day # 19084
♀0N 12 20:02		22 18:58 ♃ ⚹	♓ 23 9:39	20 16:53 ♂ △	♈ 21 19:56		Delta T 30.1 sec
♄□♅ 18 12:14		24 16:16 ♂ △	♈ 25 11:34	23 22:09 ♃ ☌	♉ 24 0:15		SVP 05♓55'27"
☿ D 19 1:32		27 1:20 ♃ ☌	♉ 27 15:05	25 10:35 ♇ □	♊ 26 6:40		Obliquity 23°26'52"
☽0N 21 11:04		29 1:49 ♇ □	♊ 29 21:36	28 16:00 ♃ ⚹	♋ 28 16:06		⚷ Chiron 12♑13.5
♇ D 30 23:21							☽ Mean ☊ 28♒38.4

LONGITUDE — MAY 1952

Day	Sid.Time	☉	0 hr ☽	Noon ☽	True ☊	☿	♀	♂	♃	♄	♅	♆	♇
1 Th	14 35 27	10♉33 42	27♋55 42	3♌50 20	27♒29.3	14♈ 6.4	25♈51.5	10♏38.8	0♉30.6	9♎30.0	10♋43.9	19♎47.6	19♌ 5.5
2 F	14 39 24	11 31 55	9♌44 34	15 39 7	27D 28.5	14 58.8	27 5.2	10R 16.7	0 44.9	9R 26.4	10 46.1	19R 46.1	19 5.5
3 Sa	14 43 20	12 30 6	21 34 38	27 31 49	27R 28.7	15 54.4	28 18.9	9 54.5	0 59.2	9 22.9	10 48.4	19 44.6	19 5.6
4 Su	14 47 17	13 28 14	3♍31 21	9♍33 51	27 28.6	16 53.0	29 32.6	9 32.3	1 13.4	9 19.4	10 50.7	19 43.1	19 5.6
5 M	14 51 13	14 26 21	15 39 57	21 50 11	27 27.3	17 54.6	0♉46.3	9 10.1	1 27.7	9 16.0	10 53.0	19 41.6	19 5.7
6 Tu	14 55 10	15 24 26	28 5 5	4♎25 1	27 24.0	18 59.0	2 0.0	8 48.0	1 41.9	9 12.7	10 55.4	19 40.2	19 5.9
7 W	14 59 7	16 22 29	10♎50 19	17 21 13	27 18.1	20 6.2	3 13.7	8 26.0	1 56.1	9 9.5	10 57.8	19 38.7	19 6.0
8 Th	15 3 3	17 20 30	23 57 47	0♏39 58	27 9.7	21 16.0	4 27.4	8 4.2	2 10.3	9 6.3	11 0.2	19 37.3	19 6.2
9 F	15 7 0	18 18 30	7♏27 37	14 20 26	26 59.1	22 28.4	5 41.1	7 42.6	2 24.4	9 3.2	11 2.7	19 35.9	19 6.4
10 Sa	15 10 56	19 16 28	21 17 57	28 19 38	26 47.4	23 43.3	6 54.7	7 21.2	2 38.5	9 0.2	11 5.2	19 34.5	19 6.6
11 Su	15 14 53	20 14 24	5♐24 52	12♐32 56	26 35.7	25 0.7	8 8.4	7 0.2	2 52.6	8 57.3	11 7.8	19 33.2	19 6.9
12 M	15 18 49	21 12 19	19 43 6	26 54 38	26 25.3	26 20.5	9 22.1	6 39.4	3 6.7	8 54.4	11 10.4	19 31.8	19 7.2
13 Tu	15 22 46	22 10 13	4♑ 6 49	11♑19 1	26 17.1	27 42.6	10 35.8	6 19.0	3 20.7	8 51.6	11 13.0	19 30.5	19 7.5
14 W	15 26 42	23 8 5	18 30 37	25 41 8	26 11.6	29 7.1	11 49.4	5 59.1	3 34.8	8 49.0	11 15.7	19 29.2	19 7.9
15 Th	15 30 39	24 5 56	2♒50 12	9♒57 28	26 8.8	0♉33.8	13 3.1	5 39.5	3 48.7	8 46.4	11 18.4	19 27.9	19 8.3
16 F	15 34 36	25 3 46	17 2 45	24 5 53	26 7.9	2 2.8	14 16.8	5 20.4	4 2.7	8 43.8	11 21.1	19 26.6	19 8.7
17 Sa	15 38 32	26 1 35	1♓ 6 48	8♓ 5 27	26 7.8	3 34.0	15 30.4	5 1.9	4 16.6	8 41.4	11 23.9	19 25.3	19 9.1
18 Su	15 42 29	26 59 22	15 1 49	21 55 54	26 7.3	5 7.5	16 44.1	4 43.9	4 30.4	8 39.1	11 26.7	19 24.1	19 9.6
19 M	15 46 25	27 57 8	28 47 40	5♈37 5	26 5.0	6 43.2	17 57.8	4 26.4	4 44.3	8 36.8	11 29.5	19 22.9	19 10.1
20 Tu	15 50 22	28 54 54	12♈24 7	19 8 39	26 0.3	8 21.0	19 11.4	4 9.6	4 58.1	8 34.7	11 32.4	19 21.7	19 10.6
21 W	15 54 18	29 52 38	25 50 35	2♉29 47	25 52.6	10 1.1	20 25.1	3 53.4	5 11.8	8 32.6	11 35.3	19 20.5	19 11.1
22 Th	15 58 15	0♊50 21	9♉ 6 6	15 39 21	25 42.3	11 43.4	21 38.8	3 37.8	5 25.5	8 30.6	11 38.2	19 19.4	19 11.7
23 F	16 2 11	1 48 3	22 9 23	28 36 4	25 30.1	13 27.8	22 52.4	3 23.0	5 39.2	8 28.7	11 41.1	19 18.2	19 12.3
24 Sa	16 6 8	2 45 43	4♊59 18	11♊18 59	25 17.1	15 14.5	24 6.1	3 8.9	5 52.8	8 27.0	11 44.1	19 17.1	19 12.9
25 Su	16 10 5	3 43 23	17 35 8	23 47 45	25 4.5	17 3.3	25 19.8	2 55.5	6 6.4	8 25.3	11 47.1	19 16.1	19 13.6
26 M	16 14 1	4 41 1	29 56 58	6♋ 2 57	24 53.4	18 54.3	26 33.4	2 42.9	6 19.9	8 23.7	11 50.2	19 15.0	19 14.2
27 Tu	16 17 58	5 38 37	12♋ 5 56	18 6 15	24 44.6	20 47.5	27 47.1	2 31.0	6 33.4	8 22.2	11 53.3	19 14.0	19 14.9
28 W	16 21 54	6 36 13	24 4 14	0♌ 0 22	24 38.5	22 42.8	29 0.7	2 19.9	6 46.9	8 20.8	11 56.4	19 13.0	19 15.7
29 Th	16 25 51	7 33 47	5♌55 7	11 49 2	24 35.0	24 40.2	0♊14.4	2 9.6	7 0.2	8 19.5	11 59.5	19 12.0	19 16.4
30 F	16 29 47	8 31 20	17 42 42	23 36 46	24D 33.6	26 39.6	1 28.0	2 0.1	7 13.6	8 18.3	12 2.6	19 11.1	19 17.2
31 Sa	16 33 44	9 28 51	29 31 51	5♍28 40	24R 33.5	28 41.0	2 41.7	1 51.5	7 26.9	8 17.1	12 5.8	19 10.1	19 18.0

LONGITUDE — JUNE 1952

Day	Sid.Time	☉	0 hr ☽	Noon ☽	True ☊	☿	♀	♂	♃	♄	♅	♆	♇
1 Su	16 37 41	10♊26 21	11♍27 53	17♍30 11	24♒33.7	0♊44.2	3♊55.3	1♏43.6	7♉40.1	8♎16.1	12♋ 9.0	19♎ 9.2	19♌18.9
2 M	16 41 37	11 23 50	23 36 14	29 46 41	24R 33.1	2 49.2	5 9.0	1R 36.6	7 53.3	8R 15.2	12 12.2	19R 8.4	19 19.7
3 Tu	16 45 34	12 21 17	6♎ 2 8	12♎23 7	24 30.7	4 55.8	6 22.6	1 30.4	8 6.4	8 14.4	12 15.5	19 7.5	19 20.6
4 W	16 49 30	13 18 43	18 50 5	25 23 23	24 26.2	7 3.9	7 36.2	1 25.0	8 19.4	8 13.7	12 18.7	19 6.7	19 21.5
5 Th	16 53 27	14 16 8	2♏ 3 16	8♏49 47	24 19.3	9 13.3	8 49.9	1 20.4	8 32.4	8 13.1	12 22.0	19 5.9	19 22.4
6 F	16 57 23	15 13 32	15 42 54	22 42 21	24 10.4	11 23.6	10 3.5	1 16.7	8 45.4	8 12.6	12 25.3	19 5.2	19 23.4
7 Sa	17 1 20	16 10 55	29 47 44	6♐58 27	24 0.3	13 34.9	11 17.2	1 13.8	8 58.2	8 12.2	12 28.7	19 4.4	19 24.4
8 Su	17 5 16	17 8 17	14♐13 47	21 32 52	23 50.2	15 46.6	12 30.8	1 11.7	9 11.0	8 11.9	12 32.0	19 3.7	19 25.4
9 M	17 9 13	18 5 39	28 54 44	6♑18 23	23 41.1	17 58.7	13 44.5	1 10.4	9 23.8	8 11.7	12 35.4	19 3.1	19 26.4
10 Tu	17 13 10	19 2 59	13♑42 48	21 7 0	23 34.0	20 10.7	14 58.1	1D 9.9	9 36.5	8D 11.6	12 38.8	19 2.4	19 27.5
11 W	17 17 6	20 0 19	28 30 4	5♒51 11	23 29.4	22 22.5	16 11.8	1 10.2	9 49.1	8 11.6	12 42.2	19 1.8	19 28.5
12 Th	17 21 3	20 57 38	13♒ 9 41	20 24 59	23D 27.2	24 33.8	17 25.4	1 11.3	10 1.7	8 11.7	12 45.6	19 1.2	19 29.6
13 F	17 24 59	21 54 57	27 36 41	4♓44 29	23 26.9	26 44.3	18 39.1	1 13.2	10 14.1	8 11.8	12 49.1	19 0.6	19 30.8
14 Sa	17 28 56	22 52 15	11♓48 12	18 47 46	23R 27.4	28 53.8	19 52.7	1 15.8	10 26.6	8 12.1	12 52.5	19 0.1	19 31.9
15 Su	17 32 52	23 49 33	25 43 11	2♈34 31	23 27.8	1♋ 2.0	21 6.4	1 19.3	10 38.9	8 12.5	12 56.0	18 59.6	19 33.1
16 M	17 36 49	24 46 51	9♈21 52	16 5 21	23 26.8	3 8.8	22 20.1	1 23.4	10 51.2	8 13.0	12 59.5	18 59.1	19 34.3
17 Tu	17 40 45	25 44 8	22 45 8	29 21 21	23 23.8	5 14.0	23 33.8	1 28.4	11 3.4	8 13.6	13 3.0	18 58.7	19 35.5
18 W	17 44 42	26 41 25	5♉54 7	12♉23 35	23 18.5	7 17.5	24 47.5	1 34.0	11 15.5	8 14.3	13 6.5	18 58.3	19 36.7
19 Th	17 48 39	27 38 42	18 49 49	25 12 56	23 11.0	9 19.1	26 1.2	1 40.5	11 27.5	8 15.1	13 10.0	18 57.9	19 37.9
20 F	17 52 35	28 35 59	1♊33 0	7♊50 5	23 2.0	11 18.8	27 14.9	1 47.6	11 39.5	8 16.0	13 13.5	18 57.6	19 39.2
21 Sa	17 56 32	29 33 15	14 4 16	20 15 38	22 52.4	13 16.5	28 28.6	1 55.5	11 51.4	8 17.0	13 17.1	18 57.3	19 40.5
22 Su	18 0 28	0♋30 31	26 24 15	2♋30 15	22 43.0	15 12.0	29 42.3	2 4.1	12 3.2	8 18.1	13 20.7	18 57.0	19 41.8
23 M	18 4 25	1 27 47	8♋33 45	14 34 56	22 34.7	17 5.4	0♋56.0	2 13.4	12 14.9	8 19.3	13 24.2	18 56.7	19 43.2
24 Tu	18 8 21	2 25 2	20 34 0	26 31 13	22 28.3	18 56.7	2 9.7	2 23.3	12 26.5	8 20.6	13 27.8	18 56.5	19 44.5
25 W	18 12 18	3 22 17	2♌26 51	8♌21 16	22 24.0	20 45.8	3 23.5	2 34.0	12 38.1	8 22.0	13 31.4	18 56.3	19 45.9
26 Th	18 16 14	4 19 31	14 14 50	20 7 59	22D 21.8	22 32.7	4 37.2	2 45.3	12 49.5	8 23.5	13 35.0	18 56.2	19 47.3
27 F	18 20 11	5 16 45	26 1 13	1♍55 1	22 21.5	24 17.4	5 50.9	2 57.3	13 0.9	8 25.1	13 38.6	18 56.1	19 48.7
28 Sa	18 24 8	6 13 58	7♍49 57	13 46 37	22 22.5	25 59.8	7 4.7	3 10.0	13 12.1	8 26.8	13 42.2	18 56.0	19 50.1
29 Su	18 28 4	7 11 11	19 45 37	25 47 34	22 23.8	27 40.0	8 18.4	3 23.2	13 23.3	8 28.6	13 45.8	18 55.9	19 51.6
30 M	18 32 1	8 8 23	1♎53 7	8♎ 2 54	22R 24.9	29 18.0	9 32.1	3 37.1	13 34.4	8 30.5	13 49.4	18D 55.9	19 53.0

Astro Data	Planet Ingress	Last Aspect	☽ Ingress	Last Aspect	☽ Ingress	☽ Phases & Eclipses
Dy Hr Mn	Dy Hr Mn	Dy Hr Mn	Dy Hr Mn	Dy Hr Mn	Dy Hr Mn	Dy Hr Mn
☽0S 5 17:26	♀ ♉ 4 8:55	30 19:19 ♀ □	♌ 1 4:12	1 1:22 ♅ ✶	♎ 2 12:26	2 3:58 ☽ 11♌42
☽0N 18 16:25	☿ ♉ 14 14:43	3 15:08 ♀ △	♍ 3 16:57	4 0:58 ♇ ✶	♏ 4 20:19	9 20:16 ○ 19♏07
♆✶♇ 26 10:52	☉ ♊ 21 3:04	4 21:23 ☉ △	♎ 6 3:39	6 6:20 ♇ □	♐ 7 0:21	16 14:39 ☽ 25♒39
	♀ ♊ 28 19:19	7 18:39 ☿ ☍	♏ 8 10:49	8 8:32 ♇ △	♑ 9 1:46	23 19:28 ● 2♊35
☽0S 2 1:09	☿ ♊ 31 15:26	9 20:16 ☉ ☍	♐ 10 14:50	10 8:38 ♆ □	♒ 11 2:26	31 21:46 ☽ 10♍21
♃⊼♄ 3 14:00		12 12:12 ☿ △	♑ 12 17:09	12 22:17 ☿ △	♓ 13 4:00	
♂ D 10 2:45	☿ ♋ 14 12:22	14 8:17 ☉ △	♒ 14 19:14	14 20:28 ☉ □	♈ 15 7:29	8 5:07 ○ 17♐21
♄ D 10 13:19	☉ ♋ 21 11:13	16 14:39 ☉ □	♓ 16 22:05	17 5:50 ☉ ✶	♉ 17 13:11	14 20:28 ☽ 23♓41
☽0N 14 21:00	♀ ♋ 22 5:46	18 22:25 ☉ ✶	♈ 19 2:07	19 1:30 ♇ □	♊ 19 21:03	22 8:45 ● 0♋51
☽0S 29 7:58	☿ ♌ 30 10:27	20 12:22 ♆ ☍	♉ 21 7:29	21 10:53 ♇ ✶	♋ 22 7:04	30 13:11 ☽ 8♎40
♆ D 30 9:24		23 1:28 ♀ ☌	♊ 23 14:37	23 20:44 ♆ □	♌ 24 19:02	
		25 3:14 ♆ △	♋ 26 0:06	26 11:19 ♇ ☌	♍ 27 8:06	
		28 11:09 ♀ ✶	♌ 28 11:59	29 18:09 ☿ ✶	♎ 29 20:18	
		30 21:56 ☿ □	♍ 31 0:57			

Astro Data

1 MAY 1952
Julian Day # 19114
Delta T 30.1 sec
SVP 05♓55'23"
Obliquity 23°26'51"
⚷ Chiron 12♑24.3R
☽ Mean ☊ 27♒03.1

1 JUNE 1952
Julian Day # 19145
Delta T 30.1 sec
SVP 05♓55'18"
Obliquity 23°26'51"
⚷ Chiron 11♑20.5R
☽ Mean ☊ 25♒24.6

JULY 1952 LONGITUDE

Day	Sid.Time	☉	0 hr ☽	Noon ☽	True ☊	☿	♀	♂	♃	♄	♅	♆	♇
1 Tu	18 35 57	9♋ 5 35	14♎17 32	20♎37 35	22♒24.9	0♌53.8	10♋45.9	3♏51.6	13♉45.4	8♎32.4	13♋53.0	18♎55.9	19♌54.5
2 W	18 39 54	10 2 47	27 3 34	3♏35 58	22R 23.5	2 27.3	11 59.6	4 6.7	13 56.3	8 34.5	13 56.7	18 55.9	19 56.0
3 Th	18 43 50	10 59 58	10♏15 8	17 1 18	22 20.4	3 58.5	13 13.4	4 22.4	14 7.1	8 36.7	14 0.3	18 56.0	19 57.5
4 F	18 47 47	11 57 9	23 54 34	0♐54 51	22 15.8	5 27.5	14 27.1	4 38.7	14 17.8	8 39.0	14 3.9	18 56.1	19 59.1
5 Sa	18 51 43	12 54 20	8♐ 1 55	15 15 20	22 10.3	6 54.1	15 40.9	4 55.5	14 28.4	8 41.3	14 7.6	18 56.2	20 0.6
6 Su	18 55 40	13 51 31	22 34 29	29 58 34	22 4.5	8 18.4	16 54.7	5 12.9	14 38.8	8 43.8	14 11.2	18 56.4	20 2.2
7 M	18 59 37	14 48 42	7♑26 38	14♑57 36	21 59.4	9 40.4	18 8.4	5 30.8	14 49.2	8 46.3	14 14.8	18 56.6	20 3.8
8 Tu	19 3 33	15 45 53	22 30 21	0♒ 3 40	21 55.4	10 59.9	19 22.2	5 49.3	14 59.5	8 49.0	14 18.5	18 56.8	20 5.3
9 W	19 7 30	16 43 3	7♒36 24	15 7 27	21D 53.1	12 17.0	20 36.0	6 8.2	15 9.7	8 51.7	14 22.1	18 57.1	20 7.0
10 Th	19 11 26	17 40 15	22 35 48	0♓ 0 36	21 52.5	13 31.6	21 49.8	6 27.7	15 19.7	8 54.5	14 25.7	18 57.4	20 8.6
11 F	19 15 23	18 37 26	7♓21 8	14 36 48	21 53.1	14 43.7	23 3.6	6 47.6	15 29.7	8 57.4	14 29.4	18 57.7	20 10.2
12 Sa	19 19 19	19 34 38	21 47 13	28 52 7	21 54.4	15 53.1	24 17.4	7 8.1	15 39.5	9 0.4	14 33.0	18 58.1	20 11.9
13 Su	19 23 16	20 31 50	5♈51 23	12♈45 0	21 55.8	16 59.9	25 31.2	7 29.0	15 49.3	9 3.5	14 36.6	18 58.4	20 13.5
14 M	19 27 13	21 29 3	19 33 4	26 15 45	21R 56.4	18 3.8	26 45.0	7 50.4	15 58.9	9 6.7	14 40.2	18 58.9	20 15.2
15 Tu	19 31 9	22 26 17	2♉53 16	9♉25 54	21 56.0	19 5.0	27 58.8	8 12.3	16 8.4	9 9.9	14 43.9	18 59.3	20 16.9
16 W	19 35 6	23 23 31	15 53 56	22 17 40	21 54.3	20 3.1	29 12.7	8 34.6	16 17.7	9 13.3	14 47.5	18 59.8	20 18.6
17 Th	19 39 2	24 20 46	28 37 27	4♊53 34	21 51.4	20 58.2	0♌26.5	8 57.4	16 27.0	9 16.7	14 51.1	19 0.3	20 20.3
18 F	19 42 59	25 18 1	11♊ 6 20	17 16 3	21 47.6	21 50.1	1 40.4	9 20.6	16 36.1	9 20.3	14 54.7	19 0.9	20 22.0
19 Sa	19 46 55	26 15 18	23 22 58	29 27 23	21 43.4	22 38.6	2 54.2	9 44.2	16 45.1	9 23.9	14 58.3	19 1.5	20 23.8
20 Su	19 50 52	27 12 35	5♋29 32	11♋29 40	21 39.4	23 23.7	4 8.1	10 8.3	16 54.0	9 27.6	15 1.8	19 2.1	20 25.5
21 M	19 54 48	28 9 52	17 28 3	23 24 55	21 35.9	24 5.2	5 22.0	10 32.8	17 2.8	9 31.3	15 5.4	19 2.7	20 27.3
22 Tu	19 58 45	29 7 10	29 20 31	5♌15 6	21 33.3	24 43.0	6 35.9	10 57.7	17 11.4	9 35.2	15 9.0	19 3.4	20 29.0
23 W	20 2 42	0♌ 4 29	11♌ 8 57	17 2 20	21D 31.8	25 16.8	7 49.8	11 23.0	17 19.9	9 39.1	15 12.5	19 4.1	20 30.8
24 Th	20 6 38	1 1 48	22 55 35	28 49 1	21 31.4	25 46.5	9 3.6	11 48.7	17 28.2	9 43.1	15 16.1	19 4.8	20 32.6
25 F	20 10 35	1 59 7	4♍43 0	10♍37 55	21 32.0	26 12.0	10 17.5	12 14.8	17 36.4	9 47.2	15 19.6	19 5.6	20 34.4
26 Sa	20 14 31	2 56 27	16 34 11	22 32 15	21 33.1	26 33.0	11 31.4	12 41.3	17 44.5	9 51.4	15 23.1	19 6.4	20 36.2
27 Su	20 18 28	3 53 48	28 32 35	4♎35 41	21 34.6	26 49.5	12 45.3	13 8.2	17 52.5	9 55.7	15 26.6	19 7.2	20 38.0
28 M	20 22 24	4 51 9	10♎42 3	16 52 12	21 35.9	27 1.2	13 59.2	13 35.4	18 0.3	10 0.0	15 30.1	19 8.1	20 39.8
29 Tu	20 26 21	5 48 31	23 6 40	29 25 57	21 36.9	27R 8.0	15 13.1	14 3.0	18 7.9	10 4.4	15 33.6	19 9.0	20 41.7
30 W	20 30 17	6 45 53	5♏50 34	12♏20 58	21R 37.3	27 9.8	16 27.0	14 30.9	18 15.4	10 8.9	15 37.0	19 9.9	20 43.5
31 Th	20 34 14	7 43 15	18 57 32	25 40 36	21 37.0	27 6.5	17 41.0	14 59.2	18 22.8	10 13.5	15 40.5	19 10.9	20 45.3

AUGUST 1952 LONGITUDE

Day	Sid.Time	☉	0 hr ☽	Noon ☽	True ☊	☿	♀	♂	♃	♄	♅	♆	♇
1 F	20 38 11	8♌40 39	2♐30 22	9♐26 58	21♒36.2	26♌58.0	18♌54.9	15♏27.8	18♉30.0	10♎18.1	15♋43.9	19♎11.8	20♌47.2
2 Sa	20 42 7	9 38 3	16 30 21	23 40 18	21R 35.0	26R 44.4	20 8.8	15 56.7	18 37.1	10 22.8	15 47.3	19 12.9	20 49.0
3 Su	20 46 4	10 35 27	0♑56 29	8♑18 20	21 33.6	26 25.5	21 22.7	16 26.0	18 44.0	10 27.6	15 50.7	19 13.9	20 50.9
4 M	20 50 0	11 32 53	15 45 8	23 16 0	21 32.5	26 1.6	22 36.6	16 55.6	18 50.8	10 32.4	15 54.1	19 15.0	20 52.7
5 Tu	20 53 57	12 30 19	0♒49 55	8♒25 44	21 31.7	25 32.9	23 50.5	17 25.5	18 57.4	10 37.3	15 57.4	19 16.1	20 54.6
6 W	20 57 53	13 27 46	16 2 16	23 38 18	21D 31.3	24 59.6	25 4.4	17 55.7	19 3.9	10 42.3	16 0.7	19 17.2	20 56.5
7 Th	21 1 50	14 25 14	1♓12 38	8♓44 9	21 31.3	24 22.1	26 18.4	18 26.1	19 10.2	10 47.4	16 4.1	19 18.3	20 58.3
8 F	21 5 46	15 22 43	16 11 51	23 34 51	21 31.7	23 41.0	27 32.3	18 56.9	19 16.3	10 52.5	16 7.3	19 19.5	21 0.2
9 Sa	21 9 43	16 20 13	0♈52 26	8♈ 4 2	21 32.1	22 56.6	28 46.2	19 28.0	19 22.3	10 57.7	16 10.6	19 20.7	21 2.1
10 Su	21 13 40	17 17 45	15 9 19	22 8 2	21 32.6	22 9.9	0♍ 0.1	19 59.3	19 28.1	11 2.9	16 13.9	19 22.0	21 4.0
11 M	21 17 36	18 15 18	29 0 9	5♉45 43	21 32.9	21 21.5	1 14.0	20 30.9	19 33.8	11 8.2	16 17.1	19 23.2	21 5.8
12 Tu	21 21 33	19 12 52	12♉24 56	18 58 5	21R 33.0	20 32.3	2 28.0	21 2.8	19 39.3	11 13.6	16 20.3	19 24.5	21 7.7
13 W	21 25 29	20 10 28	25 25 30	1♊47 37	21 33.0	19 43.2	3 41.9	21 35.0	19 44.6	11 19.0	16 23.5	19 25.8	21 9.6
14 Th	21 29 26	21 8 6	8♊ 4 52	14 17 44	21D 33.0	18 55.1	4 55.9	22 7.5	19 49.7	11 24.6	16 26.6	19 27.2	21 11.5
15 F	21 33 22	22 5 45	20 26 41	26 32 11	21 33.0	18 9.1	6 9.8	22 40.2	19 54.7	11 30.1	16 29.8	19 28.5	21 13.4
16 Sa	21 37 19	23 3 26	2♋34 44	8♋34 46	21 33.1	17 26.0	7 23.7	23 13.1	19 59.5	11 35.7	16 32.9	19 29.9	21 15.3
17 Su	21 41 15	24 1 8	14 32 44	20 29 3	21 33.4	16 46.8	8 37.7	23 46.4	20 4.2	11 41.4	16 35.9	19 31.4	21 17.1
18 M	21 45 12	24 58 51	26 24 6	2♌18 16	21 33.7	16 12.3	9 51.6	24 19.8	20 8.6	11 47.2	16 39.0	19 32.8	21 19.0
19 Tu	21 49 9	25 56 36	8♌11 54	14 5 19	21 34.0	15 43.3	11 5.6	24 53.6	20 12.9	11 53.0	16 42.0	19 34.3	21 20.9
20 W	21 53 5	26 54 23	19 58 50	25 52 44	21R 34.1	15 20.4	12 19.5	25 27.5	20 17.0	11 58.8	16 45.0	19 35.8	21 22.8
21 Th	21 57 2	27 52 10	1♍47 19	7♍42 51	21 34.0	15 4.2	13 33.5	26 1.7	20 20.9	12 4.7	16 47.9	19 37.3	21 24.7
22 F	22 0 58	28 50 0	13 39 37	19 37 53	21 33.5	14D 55.1	14 47.4	26 36.2	20 24.7	12 10.7	16 50.9	19 38.8	21 26.5
23 Sa	22 4 55	29 47 50	25 37 56	1♎40 2	21 32.7	14 53.6	16 1.4	27 10.9	20 28.2	12 16.7	16 53.8	19 40.4	21 28.4
24 Su	22 8 51	0♍45 42	7♎44 30	13 51 39	21 31.5	14 59.8	17 15.3	27 45.8	20 31.6	12 22.8	16 56.6	19 42.0	21 30.3
25 M	22 12 48	1 43 35	20 1 46	26 15 13	21 30.2	15 13.9	18 29.3	28 20.9	20 34.8	12 28.9	16 59.5	19 43.6	21 32.1
26 Tu	22 16 44	2 41 29	2♏32 19	8♏53 26	21 28.8	15 35.9	19 43.2	28 56.3	20 37.8	12 35.0	17 2.3	19 45.2	21 34.0
27 W	22 20 41	3 39 25	15 18 54	21 49 4	21 27.8	16 6.0	20 57.1	29 31.9	20 40.6	12 41.3	17 5.1	19 46.9	21 35.8
28 Th	22 24 38	4 37 22	28 24 14	5♐ 4 41	21D 27.2	16 43.8	22 11.1	0♐ 7.6	20 43.2	12 47.5	17 7.8	19 48.6	21 37.7
29 F	22 28 34	5 35 21	11♐50 41	18 42 22	21 27.2	17 29.4	23 25.0	0 43.6	20 45.6	12 53.8	17 10.5	19 50.3	21 39.5
30 Sa	22 32 31	6 33 21	25 39 52	2♑43 9	21 27.8	18 22.4	24 38.9	1 19.9	20 47.8	13 0.2	17 13.2	19 52.0	21 41.4
31 Su	22 36 27	7 31 22	9♑52 6	17 6 28	21 28.8	19 22.6	25 52.8	1 56.3	20 49.9	13 6.6	17 15.8	19 53.8	21 43.2

Astro Data

	Dy Hr Mn
♃✶♅	2 1:19
☽0N	12 3:07
☽0S	26 13:59
☿ R	29 20:31
☽0N	8 11:53
♃⊼♆	8 16:02
☽0S	22 19:46
☿ D	22 16:54

Planet Ingress

	Dy Hr Mn
♀ ♌	16 15:23
☉ ♌	22 22:07
♀ ♍	9 23:58
☉ ♍	23 5:03
♂ ♐	27 18:53

Last Aspect / ☽ Ingress

Last Aspect Dy Hr Mn		☽ Ingress Dy Hr Mn
1 10:40	♇ ✶	♏ 2 5:25
3 17:10	♇ □	♐ 4 10:27
5 19:51	♇ △	♑ 6 12:02
7 18:35	♀ ☍	♒ 8 11:54
9 20:03	♇ ☍	♓ 10 11:59
12 4:37	♀ △	♈ 12 13:56
14 14:11	♀ □	♉ 14 18:45
16 15:13	☉ ✶	♊ 17 2:37
18 22:27	☿ ✶	♋ 19 13:05
21 23:31	☉ ☌	♌ 22 1:20
24 6:02	☿ ☌	♍ 24 14:24
26 2:23	♃ △	♎ 27 2:54
29 7:41	☿ ✶	♏ 29 13:04
31 14:24	☿ □	♐ 31 19:37

Last Aspect / ☽ Ingress

Last Aspect Dy Hr Mn		☽ Ingress Dy Hr Mn
2 16:44	☿ △	♑ 2 22:27
4 5:36	♆ □	♒ 4 22:41
6 15:32	♀ ☍	♓ 6 22:05
8 5:01	♃ ✶	♈ 8 22:33
10 11:24	☿ △	♉ 11 1:46
12 16:32	♂ ☍	♊ 13 8:36
15 3:31	☉ ✶	♋ 15 18:52
17 19:35	♂ △	♌ 18 7:19
20 15:20	☉ ☌	♍ 20 20:22
23 3:15	♂ ✶	♎ 23 8:42
25 2:55	♇ ✶	♏ 25 19:10
27 11:37	♇ □	♐ 28 2:53
29 22:05	♀ □	♑ 30 7:24

☽ Phases & Eclipses

Dy Hr Mn	
7 12:33	○ 15♑19
14 3:42	☽ 21♈38
21 23:31	● 29♋06
30 1:51	☽ 6♏50
5 19:40	○ 13♒17
5 19:47	P 0.532
12 13:27	☽ 19♉45
20 15:20	● 27♌31
20 15:13:05	A 6'40"
28 12:03	☽ 5♐06

Astro Data

1 JULY 1952
Julian Day # 19175
Delta T 30.2 sec
SVP 05♓55'13"
Obliquity 23°26'51"
⚷ Chiron 9♑33.5R
☽ Mean ☊ 23♒49.3

1 AUGUST 1952
Julian Day # 19206
Delta T 30.2 sec
SVP 05♓55'08"
Obliquity 23°26'51"
⚷ Chiron 7♑43.7R
☽ Mean ☊ 22♒10.8

LONGITUDE — SEPTEMBER 1952

Day	Sid.Time	☉	0 hr ☽	Noon ☽	True ☊	☿	♀	♂	♃	♄	♅	♆	♇
1 M	22 40 24	8♍29 25	24♑25 51	1♒49 41	21♒30.0	20♌29.6	27♍ 6.7	2♐32.9	20♉51.7	13♎13.0	17♋18.4	19♎55.5	21♌45.0
2 Tu	22 44 20	9 27 28	9♒17 16	16 47 46	21R30.9	21 42.9	28 20.6	3 9.7	20 53.3	13 19.5	17 21.0	19 57.3	21 46.8
3 W	22 48 17	10 25 34	24 20 12	1♓53 30	21 31.1	23 2.3	29 34.5	3 46.6	20 54.8	13 26.1	17 23.5	19 59.1	21 48.7
4 Th	22 52 13	11 23 41	9♓26 33	16 58 12	21 30.5	24 27.1	0♎48.4	4 23.8	20 56.1	13 32.6	17 26.0	20 0.9	21 50.5
5 F	22 56 10	12 21 49	24 27 18	1♈52 50	21 28.8	25 56.9	2 2.2	5 1.1	20 57.1	13 39.2	17 28.4	20 2.8	21 52.2
6 Sa	23 0 7	13 20 0	9♈13 50	16 29 28	21 26.2	27 31.2	3 16.1	5 38.7	20 58.0	13 45.9	17 30.8	20 4.6	21 54.0
7 Su	23 4 3	14 18 12	23 39 6	0♉42 14	21 23.1	29 9.4	4 30.0	6 16.4	20 58.6	13 52.6	17 33.2	20 6.5	21 55.8
8 M	23 8 0	15 16 26	7♉38 35	14 28 1	21 20.0	0♍51.1	5 43.8	6 54.2	20 59.1	13 59.3	17 35.5	20 8.4	21 57.6
9 Tu	23 11 56	16 14 42	21 10 32	27 46 19	21 17.3	2 35.6	6 57.7	7 32.3	20R59.4	14 6.0	17 37.8	20 10.3	21 59.3
10 W	23 15 53	17 13 1	4♊15 39	10♊38 56	21 15.5	4 22.6	8 11.5	8 10.5	20 59.4	14 12.8	17 40.1	20 12.3	22 1.1
11 Th	23 19 49	18 11 21	16 56 38	23 9 16	21D14.8	6 11.5	9 25.4	8 48.9	20 59.3	14 19.6	17 42.3	20 14.2	22 2.8
12 F	23 23 46	19 9 44	29 17 25	5♋21 39	21 15.2	8 1.9	10 39.2	9 27.5	20 58.9	14 26.5	17 44.4	20 16.2	22 4.5
13 Sa	23 27 42	20 8 9	11♋22 36	17 20 52	21 16.5	9 53.5	11 53.0	10 6.2	20 58.4	14 33.4	17 46.6	20 18.2	22 6.2
14 Su	23 31 39	21 6 36	23 17 3	29 11 42	21 18.3	11 45.9	13 6.9	10 45.1	20 57.7	14 40.3	17 48.6	20 20.2	22 7.9
15 M	23 35 36	22 5 5	5♌ 5 23	10♌58 37	21 19.9	13 38.7	14 20.7	11 24.2	20 56.7	14 47.3	17 50.7	20 22.2	22 9.6
16 Tu	23 39 32	23 3 36	16 51 53	22 45 39	21R20.9	15 31.8	15 34.5	12 3.4	20 55.6	14 54.2	17 52.7	20 24.2	22 11.3
17 W	23 43 29	24 2 9	28 40 17	4♍36 11	21 20.7	17 24.9	16 48.3	12 42.7	20 54.2	15 1.2	17 54.6	20 26.2	22 12.9
18 Th	23 47 25	25 0 44	10♍33 39	16 33 0	21 19.0	19 17.8	18 2.1	13 22.3	20 52.7	15 8.3	17 56.5	20 28.3	22 14.6
19 F	23 51 22	25 59 21	22 34 26	28 38 13	21 15.6	21 10.3	19 15.9	14 2.0	20 50.9	15 15.3	17 58.4	20 30.3	22 16.2
20 Sa	23 55 18	26 58 0	4♎44 29	10♎53 25	21 10.6	23 2.4	20 29.7	14 41.8	20 48.9	15 22.4	18 0.2	20 32.4	22 17.8
21 Su	23 59 15	27 56 41	17 5 7	23 19 44	21 4.4	24 53.8	21 43.5	15 21.8	20 46.8	15 29.5	18 1.9	20 34.5	22 19.4
22 M	0 3 11	28 55 24	29 37 20	5♏58 2	20 57.7	26 44.6	22 57.2	16 1.9	20 44.4	15 36.6	18 3.7	20 36.6	22 21.0
23 Tu	0 7 8	29 54 8	12♏21 56	18 49 7	20 51.1	28 34.6	24 11.0	16 42.2	20 41.9	15 43.8	18 5.3	20 38.7	22 22.6
24 W	0 11 4	0♎52 55	25 19 43	1♐53 50	20 45.5	0♎23.8	25 24.8	17 22.6	20 39.1	15 51.0	18 7.0	20 40.8	22 24.1
25 Th	0 15 1	1 51 43	8♐31 35	15 13 6	20 41.4	2 12.2	26 38.5	18 3.2	20 36.2	15 58.1	18 8.5	20 43.0	22 25.7
26 F	0 18 58	2 50 33	21 58 31	28 47 57	20D39.1	3 59.7	27 52.2	18 43.9	20 33.1	16 5.3	18 10.1	20 45.1	22 27.2
27 Sa	0 22 54	3 49 25	5♑41 28	12♑39 9	20 38.6	5 46.3	29 6.0	19 24.7	20 29.7	16 12.6	18 11.5	20 47.3	22 28.7
28 Su	0 26 51	4 48 18	19 40 59	26 46 54	20 39.3	7 32.0	0♏19.7	20 5.7	20 26.2	16 19.8	18 13.0	20 49.4	22 30.2
29 M	0 30 47	5 47 14	3♒56 47	11♒10 21	20 40.5	9 16.8	1 33.3	20 46.8	20 22.5	16 27.1	18 14.4	20 51.6	22 31.7
30 Tu	0 34 44	6 46 10	18 27 16	25 47 2	20R41.3	11 0.7	2 47.0	21 28.0	20 18.6	16 34.3	18 15.7	20 53.8	22 33.1

LONGITUDE — OCTOBER 1952

Day	Sid.Time	☉	0 hr ☽	Noon ☽	True ☊	☿	♀	♂	♃	♄	♅	♆	♇
1 W	0 38 40	7♎45 9	3♓ 9 3	10♓32 34	20♒40.7	12♎43.7	4♏ 0.7	22♐ 9.3	20♉14.5	16♎41.6	18♋17.0	20♎56.0	22♌34.5
2 Th	0 42 37	8 44 9	17 56 46	25 20 44	20R38.1	14 25.9	5 14.3	22 50.8	20R10.3	16 48.9	18 18.2	20 58.2	22 35.9
3 F	0 46 33	9 43 12	2♈43 30	10♈ 4 3	20 33.2	16 7.2	6 28.0	23 32.4	20 5.9	16 56.2	18 19.4	21 0.4	22 37.3
4 Sa	0 50 30	10 42 16	17 21 31	24 34 55	20 26.3	17 47.6	7 41.6	24 14.0	20 1.2	17 3.5	18 20.5	21 2.6	22 38.7
5 Su	0 54 27	11 41 22	1♉43 29	8♉46 33	20 18.1	19 27.2	8 55.2	24 55.8	19 56.5	17 10.8	18 21.6	21 4.8	22 40.1
6 M	0 58 23	12 40 31	15 43 36	22 34 17	20 9.6	21 6.0	10 8.8	25 37.8	19 51.5	17 18.1	18 22.6	21 7.0	22 41.4
7 Tu	1 2 20	13 39 42	29 18 25	5♊55 58	20 1.7	22 44.1	11 22.3	26 19.8	19 46.4	17 25.4	18 23.6	21 9.2	22 42.7
8 W	1 6 16	14 38 55	12♊27 4	18 51 59	19 55.3	24 21.3	12 35.9	27 1.9	19 41.1	17 32.8	18 24.5	21 11.4	22 44.0
9 Th	1 10 13	15 38 11	25 11 3	1♋24 47	19 50.9	25 57.8	13 49.5	27 44.2	19 35.6	17 40.1	18 25.4	21 13.7	22 45.3
10 F	1 14 9	16 37 28	7♋33 41	13 38 23	19D48.7	27 33.5	15 3.0	28 26.5	19 30.0	17 47.4	18 26.2	21 15.9	22 46.5
11 Sa	1 18 6	17 36 48	19 39 31	25 37 45	19 48.2	29 8.5	16 16.5	29 9.0	19 24.3	17 54.8	18 27.0	21 18.1	22 47.7
12 Su	1 22 2	18 36 11	1♌33 46	7♌28 14	19 48.8	0♏42.8	17 30.1	29 51.6	19 18.3	18 2.1	18 27.7	21 20.4	22 48.9
13 M	1 25 59	19 35 35	13 21 51	19 15 14	19R49.6	2 16.4	18 43.6	0♑34.2	19 12.3	18 9.5	18 28.3	21 22.6	22 50.1
14 Tu	1 29 56	20 35 2	25 9 1	1♍ 3 47	19 49.6	3 49.3	19 57.1	1 17.0	19 6.0	18 16.8	18 28.9	21 24.8	22 51.3
15 W	1 33 52	21 34 32	7♍ 0 5	12 58 23	19 48.0	5 21.6	21 10.6	1 59.9	18 59.7	18 24.1	18 29.5	21 27.1	22 52.4
16 Th	1 37 49	22 34 3	18 59 8	25 2 42	19 44.0	6 53.1	22 24.0	2 42.9	18 53.2	18 31.5	18 30.0	21 29.3	22 53.5
17 F	1 41 45	23 33 36	1♎ 9 22	7♎19 24	19 37.3	8 24.0	23 37.5	3 26.0	18 46.5	18 38.8	18 30.4	21 31.5	22 54.6
18 Sa	1 45 42	24 33 12	13 32 56	19 50 6	19 28.1	9 54.3	24 51.0	4 9.1	18 39.8	18 46.1	18 30.8	21 33.8	22 55.7
19 Su	1 49 38	25 32 50	26 10 54	2♏35 19	19 17.1	11 23.9	26 4.4	4 52.4	18 32.9	18 53.4	18 31.1	21 36.0	22 56.7
20 M	1 53 35	26 32 30	9♏ 3 16	15 34 37	19 5.0	12 52.8	27 17.8	5 35.8	18 25.9	19 0.7	18 31.4	21 38.3	22 57.7
21 Tu	1 57 31	27 32 11	22 9 14	28 46 52	18 53.1	14 21.1	28 31.2	6 19.3	18 18.8	19 8.0	18 31.7	21 40.5	22 58.7
22 W	2 1 28	28 31 55	5♐27 25	12♐10 39	18 42.6	15 48.7	29 44.6	7 2.8	18 11.5	19 15.3	18 31.8	21 42.7	22 59.7
23 Th	2 5 25	29 31 41	18 56 27	25 44 38	18 34.3	17 15.6	0♐58.0	7 46.5	18 4.2	19 22.6	18 31.9	21 44.9	23 0.6
24 F	2 9 21	0♏31 28	2♑35 8	9♑27 50	18 28.7	18 41.8	2 11.3	8 30.2	17 56.8	19 29.8	18R32.0	21 47.2	23 1.6
25 Sa	2 13 18	1 31 17	16 22 41	23 19 40	18 25.9	20 7.3	3 24.7	9 14.0	17 49.3	19 37.1	18 32.0	21 49.4	23 2.4
26 Su	2 17 14	2 31 8	0♒18 45	7♒19 55	18D25.0	21 32.0	4 38.0	9 57.9	17 41.7	19 44.3	18 32.0	21 51.6	23 3.3
27 M	2 21 11	3 31 0	14 23 6	21 28 14	18R25.2	22 56.0	5 51.3	10 41.9	17 34.0	19 51.5	18 31.9	21 53.8	23 4.1
28 Tu	2 25 7	4 30 54	28 35 11	5♓43 44	18 24.9	24 19.1	7 4.6	11 25.9	17 26.3	19 58.7	18 31.7	21 56.0	23 5.0
29 W	2 29 4	5 30 49	12♓53 36	20 4 24	18 23.0	25 41.3	8 17.8	12 10.1	17 18.4	20 5.9	18 31.5	21 58.2	23 5.7
30 Th	2 33 0	6 30 46	27 15 40	4♈26 51	18 18.6	27 2.5	9 31.0	12 54.3	17 10.6	20 13.1	18 31.3	22 0.4	23 6.5
31 F	2 36 57	7 30 45	11♈37 18	18 46 22	18 11.2	28 22.7	10 44.2	13 38.5	17 2.6	20 20.2	18 30.9	22 2.6	23 7.2

Astro Data	Planet Ingress	Last Aspect	☽ Ingress	Last Aspect	☽ Ingress	☽ Phases & Eclipses	Astro Data
Dy Hr Mn	Dy Hr Mn	Dy Hr Mn	Dy Hr Mn	Dy Hr Mn	Dy Hr Mn	Dy Hr Mn	1 SEPTEMBER 1952
☽0N 4 22:31	♀ ♎ 3 8:17	1 4:45 ♀ △	♒ 1 9:03	2 8:20 ♂ □	♈ 2 19:34	4 3:19 ○ 11♓32	Julian Day # 19237
♀0S 5 9:55	☿ ♍ 7 12:02	2 21:44 ☿ ☍	♓ 3 9:00	4 12:00 ♂ △	♉ 4 21:05	11 2:36 ☽ 18♊18	Delta T 30.2 sec
♃ R 9 19:40	☉ ♎ 23 2:24	4 18:22 ♃ ⚹	♈ 5 8:57	6 12:14 ♇ □	♊ 7 1:15	19 7:22 ● 26♍17	SVP 05♓55'03"
☽0S 19 1:58	☿ ♎ 23 18:45	7 10:38 ☿ △	♉ 7 10:48	9 5:11 ♂ ☍	♋ 9 9:16	26 20:31 ☽ 3♑41	Obliquity 23°26'51"
♃⚻♆ 23 15:41	♀ ♏ 27 17:36	9 1:28 ♇ □	♊ 9 16:06	11 3:18 ♆ □	♌ 11 20:50		⚷ Chiron 6♑42.1R
☿0S 25 12:10		11 9:52 ♇ ⚹	♋ 12 1:24	13 19:19 ♇ ☌	♍ 14 9:51	3 12:15 ○ 10♈13	☽ Mean ☊ 20♒32.3
	☿ ♏ 11 13:05	13 19:18 ♃ ⚹	♌ 14 13:38	16 7:32 ♀ ⚹	♎ 16 21:44	10 19:33 ☽ 17♋26	
☽0N 2 9:04	♂ ♑ 12 4:45	16 10:52 ♇ ☌	♍ 17 2:42	18 22:42 ☉ ☌	♏ 19 7:10	18 22:42 ● 25♎30	1 OCTOBER 1952
♄□♅ 15 18:51	♀ ♐ 22 5:02	19 7:22 ☉ ☌	♎ 19 14:41	21 12:42 ♀ ☌	♐ 21 14:12	26 4:04 ☽ 2♒41	Julian Day # 19267
☽0S 16 8:53	☉ ♏ 23 11:22	21 10:06 ♇ ⚹	♏ 22 0:43	23 7:12 ♇ △	♑ 23 19:28		Delta T 30.3 sec
♃⚻♄ 17 13:14		23 18:36 ♇ □	♐ 24 8:33	25 9:26 ♆ □	♒ 25 23:28		SVP 05♓55'00"
♃⚹♅ 19 5:44		26 11:24 ♀ ⚹	♑ 26 14:06	27 16:02 ☿ □	♓ 28 2:23		Obliquity 23°26'51"
♅ R 24 16:47		28 1:56 ♆ □	♒ 28 17:24	29 23:36 ☿ △	♈ 30 4:34		⚷ Chiron 6♑53.7
☽0N 29 17:25		30 6:44 ♇ ☍	♓ 30 18:52				☽ Mean ☊ 18♒57.0

NOVEMBER 1952 LONGITUDE

Day	Sid.Time	☉	0 hr ☽	Noon ☽	True ☊	☿	♀	♂	♃	♄	♅	♆	♇
1 Sa	2 40 54	8♏30 46	25♈53 18	2♉57 23	18♒ 1.1	29♏41.8	11♐57.4	14♑22.9	16♉54.6	20♎27.3	18♋30.6	22♎ 4.7	23♌ 7.9
2 Su	2 44 50	9 30 48	9♉57 57	16 54 21	17R49.1	0♐59.7	13 10.6	15 7.3	16R46.6	20 34.4	18R30.1	22 6.9	23 8.6
3 M	2 48 47	10 30 52	23 46 4	0♊32 38	17 36.5	2 16.3	14 23.7	15 51.8	16 38.5	20 41.5	18 29.7	22 9.0	23 9.2
4 Tu	2 52 43	11 30 59	7♊13 47	13 49 17	17 24.5	3 31.4	15 36.8	16 36.3	16 30.4	20 48.5	18 29.1	22 11.2	23 9.8
5 W	2 56 40	12 31 7	20 19 9	26 43 26	17 14.2	4 45.0	16 49.9	17 20.9	16 22.3	20 55.5	18 28.6	22 13.3	23 10.4
6 Th	3 0 36	13 31 17	3♋ 2 21	9♋16 13	17 6.3	5 56.7	18 2.9	18 5.6	16 14.2	21 2.5	18 27.9	22 15.5	23 11.0
7 F	3 4 33	14 31 29	15 25 28	21 30 35	17 1.3	7 6.5	19 15.9	18 50.3	16 6.0	21 9.5	18 27.3	22 17.6	23 11.5
8 Sa	3 8 29	15 31 44	27 32 9	3♌30 46	16 58.7	8 14.1	20 28.9	19 35.1	15 57.8	21 16.4	18 26.5	22 19.7	23 12.0
9 Su	3 12 26	16 32 0	9♌27 7	15 21 52	16 57.9	9 19.2	21 41.9	20 20.0	15 49.7	21 23.3	18 25.7	22 21.8	23 12.5
10 M	3 16 23	17 32 18	21 15 44	27 9 25	16 57.8	10 21.5	22 54.9	21 4.9	15 41.5	21 30.2	18 24.9	22 23.8	23 13.0
11 Tu	3 20 19	18 32 38	3♍ 3 37	8♍59 1	16 57.4	11 20.7	24 7.8	21 49.9	15 33.3	21 37.0	18 24.0	22 25.9	23 13.4
12 W	3 24 16	19 33 0	14 56 17	20 56 1	16 55.4	12 16.4	25 20.7	22 34.9	15 25.2	21 43.8	18 23.1	22 27.9	23 13.8
13 Th	3 28 12	20 33 24	26 58 48	3♎ 5 7	16 51.1	13 8.1	26 33.6	23 20.0	15 17.1	21 50.6	18 22.1	22 30.0	23 14.1
14 F	3 32 9	21 33 50	9♎15 25	15 30 4	16 43.9	13 55.4	27 46.4	24 5.1	15 9.0	21 57.3	18 21.0	22 32.0	23 14.5
15 Sa	3 36 5	22 34 18	21 49 18	28 13 19	16 34.1	14 37.6	28 59.2	24 50.3	15 0.9	22 4.0	18 19.9	22 34.0	23 14.8
16 Su	3 40 2	23 34 47	4♏42 8	11♏15 45	16 22.1	15 14.3	0♑12.0	25 35.6	14 52.9	22 10.6	18 18.8	22 36.0	23 15.0
17 M	3 43 58	24 35 18	17 53 58	24 36 35	16 8.9	15 44.7	1 24.7	26 20.9	14 45.0	22 17.2	18 17.6	22 38.0	23 15.3
18 Tu	3 47 55	25 35 51	1♐23 15	8♐13 33	15 55.8	16 8.0	2 37.5	27 6.3	14 37.1	22 23.8	18 16.4	22 39.9	23 15.5
19 W	3 51 52	26 36 25	15 7 3	22 3 15	15 44.0	16 23.7	3 50.2	27 51.7	14 29.2	22 30.3	18 15.1	22 41.9	23 15.7
20 Th	3 55 48	27 37 1	29 1 40	6♑ 1 49	15 34.7	16R30.8	5 2.8	28 37.2	14 21.4	22 36.8	18 13.8	22 43.8	23 15.9
21 F	3 59 45	28 37 38	13♑ 3 17	20 5 39	15 28.3	16 28.7	6 15.4	29 22.7	14 13.8	22 43.2	18 12.4	22 45.7	23 16.0
22 Sa	4 3 41	29 38 17	27 8 35	4♒11 48	15 24.9	16 16.6	7 28.0	0♒ 8.2	14 6.1	22 49.6	18 11.0	22 47.6	23 16.1
23 Su	4 7 38	0♐38 56	11♒15 6	18 18 18	15D23.8	15 54.2	8 40.5	0 53.8	13 58.6	22 55.9	18 9.5	22 49.5	23 16.1
24 M	4 11 34	1 39 37	25 21 18	2♓23 58	15R23.9	15 21.0	9 53.0	1 39.5	13 51.2	23 2.2	18 8.0	22 51.3	23R16.2
25 Tu	4 15 31	2 40 18	9♓26 14	16 28 2	15 23.8	14 37.0	11 5.4	2 25.1	13 43.9	23 8.5	18 6.4	22 53.2	23 16.2
26 W	4 19 27	3 41 1	23 29 13	0♈29 41	15 22.3	13 42.7	12 17.8	3 10.9	13 36.6	23 14.7	18 4.8	22 55.0	23 16.2
27 Th	4 23 24	4 41 44	7♈29 14	14 27 39	15 18.4	12 38.9	13 30.1	3 56.6	13 29.5	23 20.8	18 3.2	22 56.8	23 16.1
28 F	4 27 21	5 42 29	21 24 39	28 19 55	15 11.8	11 27.1	14 42.4	4 42.4	13 22.5	23 26.9	18 1.5	22 58.5	23 16.0
29 Sa	4 31 17	6 43 15	5♉13 5	12♉ 3 47	15 2.5	10 9.2	15 54.6	5 28.2	13 15.6	23 32.9	17 59.7	23 0.3	23 15.9
30 Su	4 35 14	7 44 1	18 51 36	25 36 12	14 51.5	8 47.5	17 6.8	6 14.0	13 8.9	23 38.9	17 58.0	23 2.0	23 15.8

DECEMBER 1952 LONGITUDE

Day	Sid.Time	☉	0 hr ☽	Noon ☽	True ☊	☿	♀	♂	♃	♄	♅	♆	♇
1 M	4 39 10	8♐44 49	2♊17 12	8♊54 17	14♒39.6	7♐24.8	18♑18.9	6♒59.9	13♉ 2.2	23♎44.8	17♋56.2	23♎ 3.7	23♌15.6
2 Tu	4 43 7	9 45 38	15 27 15	21 55 53	14R28.3	6R 3.9	19 30.9	7 45.8	12R55.7	23 50.6	17R54.3	23 5.4	23R15.4
3 W	4 47 3	10 46 29	28 20 7	4♋39 58	14 18.5	4 47.5	20 42.9	8 31.7	12 49.4	23 56.4	17 52.4	23 7.0	23 15.2
4 Th	4 51 0	11 47 20	10♋55 29	17 6 52	14 11.0	3 37.9	21 54.8	9 17.6	12 43.2	24 2.2	17 50.5	23 8.7	23 14.9
5 F	4 54 57	12 48 13	23 14 24	29 18 24	14 6.1	2 37.1	23 6.7	10 3.6	12 37.1	24 7.8	17 48.6	23 10.3	23 14.7
6 Sa	4 58 53	13 49 7	5♌19 18	11♌17 35	14D 3.7	1 46.6	24 18.5	10 49.6	12 31.2	24 13.5	17 46.6	23 11.9	23 14.3
7 Su	5 2 50	14 50 2	17 13 48	23 8 31	14 3.4	1 7.0	25 30.2	11 35.6	12 25.4	24 19.0	17 44.5	23 13.4	23 14.0
8 M	5 6 46	15 50 58	29 2 22	4♍56 1	14 4.1	0 38.9	26 41.8	12 21.7	12 19.8	24 24.5	17 42.5	23 15.0	23 13.6
9 Tu	5 10 43	16 51 55	10♍50 8	16 45 24	14R 5.0	0 22.1	27 53.4	13 7.7	12 14.3	24 29.9	17 40.4	23 16.5	23 13.2
10 W	5 14 39	17 52 54	22 42 31	28 42 8	14 5.1	0D16.2	29 4.9	13 53.8	12 9.1	24 35.3	17 38.2	23 18.0	23 12.8
11 Th	5 18 36	18 53 54	4♎44 56	10♎51 31	14 3.5	0 20.6	0♒16.3	14 39.9	12 4.0	24 40.5	17 36.1	23 19.4	23 12.4
12 F	5 22 32	19 54 54	17 2 28	23 18 16	13 59.7	0 34.5	1 27.7	15 26.0	11 59.0	24 45.7	17 33.9	23 20.8	23 11.9
13 Sa	5 26 29	20 55 56	29 39 22	6♏ 6 5	13 53.8	0 57.2	2 39.0	16 12.2	11 54.2	24 50.9	17 31.7	23 22.2	23 11.4
14 Su	5 30 26	21 56 59	12♏38 39	19 17 9	13 46.0	1 27.8	3 50.2	16 58.4	11 49.7	24 56.0	17 29.4	23 23.6	23 10.8
15 M	5 34 22	22 58 3	26 1 34	2♐51 42	13 37.2	2 5.5	5 1.3	17 44.5	11 45.3	25 1.0	17 27.1	23 25.0	23 10.3
16 Tu	5 38 19	23 59 8	9♐47 16	16 47 49	13 28.2	2 49.4	6 12.3	18 30.7	11 41.0	25 5.9	17 24.8	23 26.3	23 9.7
17 W	5 42 15	25 0 14	23 52 47	1♑ 1 29	13 20.0	3 38.9	7 23.3	19 17.0	11 37.0	25 10.7	17 22.5	23 27.6	23 9.1
18 Th	5 46 12	26 1 20	8♑13 14	15 27 12	13 13.7	4 33.3	8 34.1	20 3.2	11 33.2	25 15.5	17 20.2	23 28.9	23 8.4
19 F	5 50 8	27 2 27	22 42 39	29 58 47	13 9.6	5 32.0	9 44.9	20 49.4	11 29.5	25 20.2	17 17.8	23 30.1	23 7.7
20 Sa	5 54 5	28 3 34	7♒14 53	14♒30 18	13D 7.9	6 34.5	10 55.5	21 35.7	11 26.1	25 24.8	17 15.4	23 31.3	23 7.1
21 Su	5 58 1	29 4 41	21 44 27	28 56 51	13 8.0	7 40.3	12 6.0	22 21.9	11 22.8	25 29.4	17 13.0	23 32.5	23 6.3
22 M	6 1 58	0♑ 5 49	6♓ 7 8	13♓14 58	13 9.2	8 49.1	13 16.5	23 8.2	11 19.8	25 33.8	17 10.5	23 33.6	23 5.6
23 Tu	6 5 55	1 6 56	20 20 8	27 22 30	13R10.4	10 0.4	14 26.8	23 54.5	11 16.9	25 38.2	17 8.1	23 34.7	23 4.8
24 W	6 9 51	2 8 4	4♈21 56	11♈18 24	13 10.8	11 13.9	15 37.0	24 40.7	11 14.3	25 42.5	17 5.6	23 35.8	23 4.0
25 Th	6 13 48	3 9 12	18 11 51	25 2 16	13 9.7	12 29.5	16 47.0	25 27.0	11 11.8	25 46.7	17 3.1	23 36.9	23 3.2
26 F	6 17 44	4 10 19	1♉49 39	8♉33 58	13 6.8	13 46.7	17 57.0	26 13.3	11 9.6	25 50.8	17 0.6	23 37.9	23 2.3
27 Sa	6 21 41	5 11 27	15 15 13	21 53 22	13 2.1	15 5.6	19 6.8	26 59.6	11 7.6	25 54.9	16 58.1	23 38.9	23 1.5
28 Su	6 25 37	6 12 35	28 28 22	5♊ 0 11	12 56.1	16 25.8	20 16.4	27 45.9	11 5.7	25 58.8	16 55.5	23 39.9	23 0.6
29 M	6 29 34	7 13 43	11♊28 47	17 54 8	12 49.6	17 47.2	21 26.0	28 32.1	11 4.1	26 2.7	16 53.0	23 40.8	22 59.7
30 Tu	6 33 30	8 14 51	24 16 12	0♋35 0	12 43.3	19 9.7	22 35.3	29 18.4	11 2.7	26 6.5	16 50.4	23 41.7	22 58.7
31 W	6 37 27	9 16 0	6♋50 32	13 2 54	12 38.0	20 33.2	23 44.6	0♓ 4.7	11 1.5	26 10.2	16 47.9	23 42.5	22 57.8

Astro Data	Dy Hr Mn
☽0S	12 16:19
☿ R	20 6:43
♄☌♆	21 13:17
♇ R	24 17:04
☽0N	25 22:56
♄✶♇	26 5:51
♆✶♇	7 7:17
☽0S	9 23:47
☿ D	10 1:28
☽0N	23 3:31

Planet Ingress		Dy Hr Mn
☿	♐	1 5:34
♀	♑	15 20:03
♂	♒	21 19:39
☉	♐	22 8:36
♀	♒	10 18:30
☉	♑	21 21:43
♂	♓	30 21:35

Last Aspect Dy Hr Mn			☽ Ingress	Dy Hr Mn
31 19:20	♇	△	♉	1 6:58
2 22:55	♇	□	♊	3 11:02
5 5:20	♇	✶	♋	5 18:12
7 13:36	♆	□	♌	8 4:56
10 3:59	♇	☌	♍	10 17:47
12 23:05	♀	□	♎	13 5:57
15 14:49	♀	✶	♏	15 15:18
17 15:59	♂	✶	♐	17 21:33
19 14:05	♇	△	♑	20 1:40
22 4:34	☉	✶	♒	22 4:52
23 20:27	♇	☍	♓	24 7:55
25 14:46	♅	△	♈	26 11:09
28 3:33	♄	☍	♉	28 14:54
30 7:49	♇	□	♊	30 19:53

Last Aspect Dy Hr Mn			☽ Ingress	Dy Hr Mn
2 15:41	♄	△	♋	3 3:09
5 1:46	♄	□	♌	5 13:23
7 14:30	♄	✶	♍	8 1:57
10 14:09	♀	△	♎	10 14:35
12 14:52	♄	☌	♏	13 0:39
14 18:56	♇	□	♐	15 7:00
17 2:12	♄	✶	♑	17 10:17
19 4:22	♄	□	♒	19 12:02
21 13:09	☉	✶	♓	21 13:45
22 18:35	♅	△	♈	23 16:30
25 13:29	♂	✶	♉	25 20:46
27 22:37	♂	□	♊	28 2:48
30 10:11	♂	△	♋	30 10:53

☽ Phases & Eclipses Dy Hr Mn		
1 23:10	○	9♉29
9 15:43	☽	17♌11
17 12:56	●	25♏08
24 11:34	☽	2♓09
1 12:41	○	9♊17
9 13:22	☽	17♍26
17 2:02	●	25♐05
23 19:52	☽	1♈58
31 5:06	○	9♋29

Astro Data

1 NOVEMBER 1952
Julian Day # 19298
Delta T 30.3 sec
SVP 05♓54'56"
Obliquity 23°26'50"
⚷ Chiron 8♑20.1
☽ Mean ☊ 17♒18.5

1 DECEMBER 1952
Julian Day # 19328
Delta T 30.3 sec
SVP 05♓54'51"
Obliquity 23°26'50"
⚷ Chiron 10♑39.9
☽ Mean ☊ 15♒43.2

LONGITUDE JANUARY 1953

Day	Sid.Time	☉	0 hr ☽	Noon ☽	True ☊	☿	♀	♂	♃	♄	♅	♆	♇
1 Th	6 41 24	10♑17 8	19♋12 10	25♋18 28	12♒34.0	21♐57.6	24♒53.6	0♓50.9	11♉ 0.5	26♎13.8	16♋45.3	23♎43.4	22♌56.8
2 F	6 45 20	11 18 16	1♌22 2	7♌23 4	12D31.8	23 22.8	26 2.5	1 37.2	10R59.7	26 17.3	16R42.7	23 44.2	22R55.8
3 Sa	6 49 17	12 19 25	13 21 51	19 18 45	12 31.1	24 48.8	27 11.3	2 23.4	10 59.1	26 20.7	16 40.1	23 44.9	22 54.8
4 Su	6 53 13	13 20 33	25 14 8	1♍ 8 25	12 31.8	26 15.4	28 19.8	3 9.6	10 58.7	26 24.1	16 37.5	23 45.7	22 53.7
5 M	6 57 10	14 21 42	7♍ 2 6	12 55 42	12 33.4	27 42.8	29 28.2	3 55.9	10D58.6	26 27.3	16 35.0	23 46.4	22 52.6
6 Tu	7 1 6	15 22 50	18 49 44	24 44 48	12 35.3	29 10.7	0♓36.4	4 42.1	10 58.6	26 30.4	16 32.4	23 47.0	22 51.6
7 W	7 5 3	16 23 59	0♎41 30	6♎40 27	12 37.0	0♑39.2	1 44.5	5 28.3	10 58.9	26 33.5	16 29.7	23 47.7	22 50.5
8 Th	7 8 59	17 25 8	12 42 17	18 47 36	12R37.9	2 8.2	2 52.3	6 14.5	10 59.3	26 36.4	16 27.1	23 48.3	22 49.3
9 F	7 12 56	18 26 17	24 57 3	1♏11 10	12 37.9	3 37.8	3 60.0	7 0.7	10 60.0	26 39.3	16 24.5	23 48.8	22 48.2
10 Sa	7 16 53	19 27 26	7♏30 32	13 55 37	12 36.7	5 7.9	5 7.4	7 46.9	11 0.8	26 42.1	16 21.9	23 49.4	22 47.0
11 Su	7 20 49	20 28 35	20 26 50	27 4 28	12 34.5	6 38.5	6 14.7	8 33.1	11 1.9	26 44.7	16 19.3	23 49.9	22 45.8
12 M	7 24 46	21 29 44	3♐48 44	10♐39 42	12 31.6	8 9.6	7 21.7	9 19.2	11 3.2	26 47.3	16 16.8	23 50.3	22 44.6
13 Tu	7 28 42	22 30 53	17 37 15	24 41 10	12 28.5	9 41.2	8 28.5	10 5.4	11 4.7	26 49.8	16 14.2	23 50.8	22 43.4
14 W	7 32 39	23 32 2	1♑51 2	9♑ 6 16	12 25.8	11 13.3	9 35.1	10 51.5	11 6.4	26 52.1	16 11.6	23 51.2	22 42.2
15 Th	7 36 35	24 33 11	16 26 9	23 49 49	12 23.7	12 45.9	10 41.5	11 37.7	11 8.3	26 54.4	16 9.0	23 51.5	22 41.0
16 F	7 40 32	25 34 19	1♒16 21	8♒44 41	12D22.5	14 19.0	11 47.6	12 23.8	11 10.4	26 56.6	16 6.5	23 51.9	22 39.7
17 Sa	7 44 29	26 35 26	16 13 48	23 42 38	12 22.3	15 52.7	12 53.5	13 9.9	11 12.7	26 58.6	16 3.9	23 52.2	22 38.4
18 Su	7 48 25	27 36 33	1♓10 12	8♓35 34	12 22.8	17 26.8	13 59.1	13 56.0	11 15.2	27 0.6	16 1.4	23 52.4	22 37.1
19 M	7 52 22	28 37 39	15 57 57	23 16 38	12 23.8	19 1.5	15 4.5	14 42.0	11 17.9	27 2.4	15 58.8	23 52.6	22 35.8
20 Tu	7 56 18	29 38 44	0♈31 4	7♈40 50	12 24.9	20 36.7	16 9.6	15 28.1	11 20.8	27 4.2	15 56.3	23 52.8	22 34.5
21 W	8 0 15	0♒39 48	14 45 40	21 45 22	12 25.8	22 12.4	17 14.4	16 14.1	11 23.9	27 5.8	15 53.8	23 53.0	22 33.2
22 Th	8 4 11	1 40 51	28 39 53	5♉29 16	12R26.2	23 48.7	18 18.8	17 0.1	11 27.2	27 7.4	15 51.3	23 53.1	22 31.8
23 F	8 8 8	2 41 54	12♉13 37	18 53 6	12 26.0	25 25.6	19 23.0	17 46.1	11 30.7	27 8.8	15 48.9	23 53.2	22 30.5
24 Sa	8 12 4	3 42 55	25 27 55	1♊58 20	12 25.5	27 3.1	20 26.9	18 32.0	11 34.4	27 10.1	15 46.4	23 53.2	22 29.1
25 Su	8 16 1	4 43 55	8♊24 35	14 46 57	12 24.6	28 41.2	21 30.4	19 17.9	11 38.2	27 11.4	15 44.0	23R53.3	22 27.8
26 M	8 19 58	5 44 54	21 5 42	27 21 7	12 23.6	0♒19.9	22 33.6	20 3.8	11 42.3	27 12.5	15 41.6	23 53.2	22 26.4
27 Tu	8 23 54	6 45 52	3♋33 26	9♋42 54	12 22.8	1 59.3	23 36.4	20 49.7	11 46.6	27 13.5	15 39.2	23 53.2	22 25.0
28 W	8 27 51	7 46 49	15 49 47	21 54 17	12 22.2	3 39.3	24 38.9	21 35.6	11 51.0	27 14.4	15 36.9	23 53.1	22 23.6
29 Th	8 31 47	8 47 45	27 56 39	3♌57 6	12 21.8	5 19.9	25 40.9	22 21.4	11 55.6	27 15.2	15 34.5	23 53.0	22 22.2
30 F	8 35 44	9 48 40	9♌55 52	15 53 11	12D21.7	7 1.3	26 42.6	23 7.2	12 0.4	27 15.9	15 32.2	23 52.8	22 20.7
31 Sa	8 39 40	10 49 34	21 49 17	27 44 25	12 21.7	8 43.3	27 43.9	23 52.9	12 5.4	27 16.5	15 29.9	23 52.7	22 19.3

LONGITUDE FEBRUARY 1953

Day	Sid.Time	☉	0 hr ☽	Noon ☽	True ☊	☿	♀	♂	♃	♄	♅	♆	♇
1 Su	8 43 37	11♒50 27	3♍38 53	9♍32 58	12♒21.8	10♒26.1	28♓44.8	24♓38.6	12♉10.6	27♎17.0	15♋27.7	23♎52.4	22♌17.9
2 M	8 47 33	12 51 19	15 27 0	21 21 19	12R21.8	12 9.5	29 45.2	25 24.3	12 15.9	27 17.4	15R25.4	23R52.2	22R16.5
3 Tu	8 51 30	13 52 10	27 16 18	3♎12 21	12 21.6	13 53.7	0♈45.2	26 10.0	12 21.4	27 17.7	15 23.2	23 51.9	22 15.0
4 W	8 55 27	14 52 59	9♎ 9 55	15 9 27	12 21.4	15 38.5	1 44.7	26 55.6	12 27.1	27 17.8	15 21.0	23 51.6	22 13.6
5 Th	8 59 23	15 53 48	21 11 26	27 16 23	12 21.0	17 24.1	2 43.8	27 41.2	12 32.9	27R17.9	15 18.9	23 51.2	22 12.1
6 F	9 3 20	16 54 37	3♏24 50	9♏37 18	12 20.7	19 10.3	3 42.4	28 26.8	12 39.0	27 17.9	15 16.8	23 50.8	22 10.6
7 Sa	9 7 16	17 55 24	15 54 18	22 16 21	12D20.5	20 57.2	4 40.4	29 12.4	12 45.2	27 17.7	15 14.7	23 50.4	22 9.2
8 Su	9 11 13	18 56 10	28 43 55	5♐17 28	12 20.6	22 44.8	5 38.0	29 57.9	12 51.5	27 17.5	15 12.6	23 50.0	22 7.7
9 M	9 15 9	19 56 55	11♐57 20	18 43 49	12 21.0	24 32.9	6 35.0	0♈43.4	12 58.1	27 17.1	15 10.6	23 49.5	22 6.3
10 Tu	9 19 6	20 57 40	25 37 6	2♑37 12	12 21.7	26 21.6	7 31.4	1 28.8	13 4.7	27 16.6	15 8.7	23 49.0	22 4.8
11 W	9 23 2	21 58 23	9♑44 2	16 57 21	12 22.6	28 10.7	8 27.3	2 14.3	13 11.6	27 16.1	15 6.7	23 48.4	22 3.3
12 Th	9 26 59	22 59 5	24 16 39	1♒41 21	12 23.4	0♓ 0.2	9 22.6	2 59.6	13 18.6	27 15.4	15 4.8	23 47.8	22 1.9
13 F	9 30 56	23 59 46	9♒10 37	16 43 30	12R23.8	1 50.0	10 17.2	3 45.0	13 25.8	27 14.6	15 2.9	23 47.2	22 0.4
14 Sa	9 34 52	25 0 26	24 18 52	1♓55 32	12 23.6	3 40.0	11 11.2	4 30.3	13 33.1	27 13.7	15 1.1	23 46.6	21 58.9
15 Su	9 38 49	26 1 4	9♓32 16	17 7 46	12 22.7	5 29.9	12 4.6	5 15.6	13 40.6	27 12.7	14 59.3	23 45.9	21 57.5
16 M	9 42 45	27 1 40	24 40 52	2♈10 26	12 21.1	7 19.6	12 57.2	6 0.9	13 48.2	27 11.7	14 57.6	23 45.2	21 56.0
17 Tu	9 46 42	28 2 15	9♈35 30	16 55 14	12 19.1	9 8.9	13 49.2	6 46.1	13 56.0	27 10.5	14 55.9	23 44.5	21 54.5
18 W	9 50 38	29 2 48	24 9 1	1♉16 24	12 17.0	10 57.5	14 40.3	7 31.3	14 3.9	27 9.2	14 54.2	23 43.7	21 53.1
19 Th	9 54 35	0♓ 3 19	8♉17 7	15 11 3	12 15.3	12 45.1	15 30.7	8 16.4	14 12.0	27 7.8	14 52.6	23 42.9	21 51.6
20 F	9 58 31	1 3 48	21 58 18	28 39 1	12D14.2	14 31.3	16 20.3	9 1.5	14 20.2	27 6.3	14 51.0	23 42.1	21 50.2
21 Sa	10 2 28	2 4 16	5♊13 31	11♊42 9	12 14.0	16 15.8	17 9.0	9 46.6	14 28.6	27 4.7	14 49.5	23 41.2	21 48.7
22 Su	10 6 25	3 4 42	18 5 22	24 23 38	12 14.6	17 58.2	17 56.9	10 31.6	14 37.1	27 3.0	14 48.0	23 40.4	21 47.3
23 M	10 10 21	4 5 5	0♋37 27	6♋47 19	12 16.0	19 37.8	18 43.8	11 16.6	14 45.7	27 1.2	14 46.5	23 39.5	21 45.9
24 Tu	10 14 18	5 5 27	12 53 44	18 57 12	12 17.7	21 14.3	19 29.8	12 1.6	14 54.5	26 59.3	14 45.1	23 38.5	21 44.4
25 W	10 18 14	6 5 47	24 58 9	0♌57 3	12 19.3	22 47.0	20 14.7	12 46.5	15 3.4	26 57.3	14 43.8	23 37.6	21 43.0
26 Th	10 22 11	7 6 5	6♌54 18	12 50 17	12R20.3	24 15.3	20 58.7	13 31.3	15 12.4	26 55.2	14 42.4	23 36.6	21 41.6
27 F	10 26 7	8 6 21	18 45 21	24 39 49	12 20.2	25 38.7	21 41.6	14 16.1	15 21.5	26 53.0	14 41.2	23 35.6	21 40.2
28 Sa	10 30 4	9 6 36	0♍34 0	6♍28 10	12 18.8	26 56.5	22 23.3	15 0.9	15 30.8	26 50.8	14 40.0	23 34.5	21 38.8

Astro Data	Dy Hr Mn
♃ D	5 7:52
☽ 0 S	6 6:54
☽ 0 N	19 10:10
♆ R	25 0:57
♀ 0 N	31 17:35
☽ 0 S	2 13:36
♄ R	5 2:31
♂ 0 N	9 11:53
☽ 0 N	15 20:00
♃ ⚹ ♅	23 1:57
☿ 0 N	28 6:51

Planet Ingress	Dy Hr Mn
♀ ♓	5 11:10
☿ ♑	6 13:24
☉ ♒	20 8:21
☿ ♒	25 19:10
♀ ♈	2 5:54
♂ ♈	8 1:07
☿ ♓	11 23:57
☉ ♓	18 22:41

Last Aspect Dy Hr Mn		☽ Ingress	Dy Hr Mn
1 13:53	♄ □	♌	1 21:17
4 6:58	♀ ☍	♍	4 9:41
5 19:22	♅ ⚹	♎	6 22:36
9 3:18	♄ ☌	♏	9 9:44
11 4:13	♇ □	♐	11 17:14
13 15:39	♄ ⚹	♑	13 20:55
15 17:01	♄ □	♒	15 21:57
17 17:17	♄ △	♓	17 22:07
19 22:26	☉ ⚹	♈	19 23:08
21 21:18	♄ ☍	♉	22 2:20
24 3:20	☿ △	♊	24 8:21
26 11:44	♄ △	♋	26 17:07
28 22:37	♄ □	♌	29 4:06
31 11:04	♄ ⚹	♍	31 16:35

Last Aspect Dy Hr Mn		☽ Ingress	Dy Hr Mn
2 21:36	♂ ☍	♎	3 5:31
5 12:03	♄ ☌	♏	5 17:21
7 11:45	♇ □	♐	8 2:20
10 2:52	♄ ⚹	♑	10 7:32
12 4:50	♄ □	♒	12 9:17
14 4:36	♄ △	♓	14 8:58
15 8:36	♅ △	♈	16 8:30
18 8:52	☉ ⚹	♉	18 9:50
19 23:46	♇ □	♊	20 14:27
22 17:03	♄ △	♋	22 22:48
25 3:58	♄ □	♌	25 10:05
27 16:28	♄ ⚹	♍	27 22:51

☽ Phases & Eclipses Dy Hr Mn		
8 10:09	☽	17♎51
15 14:08	●	25♑09
22 5:43	☽	1♉55
29 23:44	○	9♌48
29 23:47	☍ T	1.331
7 4:09	☽	18♏06
14 1:10	●	25♒03
14 0:58:59	☌ P	0.760
20 17:44	☽	1♊49
28 18:59	○	9♍54

Astro Data

1 JANUARY 1953
Julian Day # 19359
Delta T 30.4 sec
SVP 05♓54'45"
Obliquity 23°26'49"
⚷ Chiron 13♑36.1
☽ Mean ☊ 14♒04.7

1 FEBRUARY 1953
Julian Day # 19390
Delta T 30.4 sec
SVP 05♓54'40"
Obliquity 23°26'50"
⚷ Chiron 16♑34.4
☽ Mean ☊ 12♒26.3

MARCH 1953 LONGITUDE

Day	Sid.Time	☉	0 hr ☽	Noon ☽	True ☊	☿	♀	♂	♃	♄	♅	♆	♇
1 Su	10 34 0	10♓ 6 48	12♍22 33	18♍17 25	12♒16.0	28♓ 8.1	23♈ 4.0	15♈45.6	15♉40.2	26♎48.4	14♋38.8	23♎33.5	21♌37.4
2 M	10 37 57	11 6 59	24 13 0	0♎ 9 31	12R 11.8	29 13.0	23 43.4	16 30.3	15 49.7	26R 46.0	14R 37.7	23R 32.4	21R 36.1
3 Tu	10 41 54	12 7 8	6♎ 7 13	12 6 19	12 6.6	0♈10.6	24 21.5	17 14.9	15 59.4	26 43.4	14 36.6	23 31.2	21 34.7
4 W	10 45 50	13 7 15	18 7 7	24 9 51	12 0.9	1 0.3	24 58.4	17 59.5	16 9.2	26 40.8	14 35.6	23 30.1	21 33.3
5 Th	10 49 47	14 7 20	0♏14 49	6♏22 21	11 55.4	1 41.8	25 33.9	18 44.1	16 19.0	26 38.1	14 34.6	23 28.9	21 32.0
6 F	10 53 43	15 7 24	12 32 47	18 46 29	11 50.5	2 14.7	26 8.1	19 28.6	16 29.0	26 35.3	14 33.7	23 27.8	21 30.7
7 Sa	10 57 40	16 7 27	25 3 49	1♐25 12	11 47.0	2 38.7	26 40.8	20 13.1	16 39.1	26 32.4	14 32.8	23 26.5	21 29.3
8 Su	11 1 36	17 7 27	7♐51 3	14 21 45	11D 45.0	2 53.6	27 12.0	20 57.5	16 49.4	26 29.5	14 32.0	23 25.3	21 28.0
9 M	11 5 33	18 7 27	20 57 41	27 39 13	11 44.6	2R 59.5	27 41.7	21 41.9	16 59.7	26 26.4	14 31.2	23 24.1	21 26.7
10 Tu	11 9 29	19 7 24	4♑26 40	11♑20 14	11 45.4	2 56.5	28 9.7	22 26.3	17 10.1	26 23.3	14 30.5	23 22.8	21 25.5
11 W	11 13 26	20 7 20	18 20 5	25 26 14	11 46.9	2 44.7	28 36.1	23 10.6	17 20.7	26 20.1	14 29.9	23 21.5	21 24.2
12 Th	11 17 23	21 7 14	2♒38 31	9♒56 41	11R 48.1	2 24.6	29 0.8	23 54.8	17 31.3	26 16.8	14 29.3	23 20.2	21 23.0
13 F	11 21 19	22 7 7	17 20 14	24 48 30	11 48.3	1 56.8	29 23.7	24 39.1	17 42.1	26 13.5	14 28.7	23 18.9	21 21.7
14 Sa	11 25 16	23 6 58	2♓20 38	9♓55 37	11 46.7	1 21.9	29 44.7	25 23.2	17 53.0	26 10.0	14 28.2	23 17.5	21 20.5
15 Su	11 29 12	24 6 47	17 32 15	25 9 18	11 43.1	0 40.8	0♉ 3.9	26 7.4	18 3.9	26 6.5	14 27.7	23 16.1	21 19.3
16 M	11 33 9	25 6 34	2♈45 26	10♈19 19	11 37.6	29♓54.5	0 21.0	26 51.5	18 15.0	26 3.0	14 27.3	23 14.7	21 18.1
17 Tu	11 37 5	26 6 18	17 49 43	25 15 29	11 30.9	29 4.1	0 36.1	27 35.5	18 26.1	25 59.3	14 27.0	23 13.3	21 17.0
18 W	11 41 2	27 6 1	2♉35 41	9♉49 31	11 23.7	28 10.9	0 49.2	28 19.5	18 37.4	25 55.6	14 26.7	23 11.9	21 15.8
19 Th	11 44 58	28 5 42	16 56 26	23 56 5	11 17.1	27 15.9	1 0.0	29 3.5	18 48.7	25 51.9	14 26.4	23 10.5	21 14.7
20 F	11 48 55	29 5 20	0♊48 19	7♊33 11	11 11.9	26 20.4	1 8.6	29 47.4	19 0.1	25 48.1	14 26.3	23 9.0	21 13.6
21 Sa	11 52 51	0♈ 4 57	14 10 52	20 41 44	11 8.6	25 25.6	1 15.0	0♉31.3	19 11.7	25 44.2	14 26.1	23 7.5	21 12.5
22 Su	11 56 48	1 4 31	27 6 14	3♋24 52	11D 7.2	24 32.5	1 19.0	1 15.1	19 23.3	25 40.2	14D 26.1	23 6.0	21 11.4
23 M	12 0 45	2 4 2	9♋38 15	15 47 0	11 7.4	23 42.2	1R 20.6	1 58.8	19 34.9	25 36.3	14 26.0	23 4.5	21 10.4
24 Tu	12 4 41	3 3 32	21 51 45	27 53 8	11 8.5	22 55.5	1 19.7	2 42.6	19 46.7	25 32.2	14 26.1	23 3.0	21 9.3
25 W	12 8 38	4 2 59	3♌51 49	9♌48 21	11R 9.6	22 13.0	1 16.4	3 26.2	19 58.6	25 28.1	14 26.2	23 1.5	21 8.3
26 Th	12 12 34	5 2 23	15 43 22	21 37 22	11 9.7	21 35.4	1 10.7	4 9.9	20 10.5	25 24.0	14 26.3	22 60.0	21 7.3
27 F	12 16 31	6 1 46	27 30 53	3♍24 21	11 8.1	21 3.0	1 2.4	4 53.4	20 22.5	25 19.8	14 26.5	22 58.4	21 6.3
28 Sa	12 20 27	7 1 6	9♍18 11	15 12 44	11 4.2	20 36.3	0 51.6	5 37.0	20 34.6	25 15.6	14 26.7	22 56.9	21 5.4
29 Su	12 24 24	8 0 24	21 8 21	27 5 17	10 57.8	20 15.2	0 38.3	6 20.4	20 46.7	25 11.3	14 27.0	22 55.3	21 4.5
30 M	12 28 20	8 59 40	3♎ 3 46	9♎ 4 1	10 49.0	20 0.0	0 22.5	7 3.9	20 58.9	25 7.0	14 27.4	22 53.7	21 3.6
31 Tu	12 32 17	9 58 53	15 6 10	21 10 23	10 38.5	19 50.6	0 4.3	7 47.3	21 11.2	25 2.6	14 27.8	22 52.1	21 2.7

APRIL 1953 LONGITUDE

Day	Sid.Time	☉	0 hr ☽	Noon ☽	True ☊	☿	♀	♂	♃	♄	♅	♆	♇
1 W	12 36 14	10♈58 5	27♎16 47	3♏25 29	10♒27.1	19♓46.9	29♈43.8	8♉30.6	21♉23.6	24♎58.2	14♋28.3	22♎50.5	21♌ 1.8
2 Th	12 40 10	11 57 15	9♏36 35	15 50 14	10R 15.7	19D 48.9	29R 20.9	9 13.9	21 36.0	24R 53.8	14 28.8	22R 48.9	21R 1.0
3 F	12 44 7	12 56 23	22 6 31	28 25 38	10 5.5	19 56.3	28 55.9	9 57.1	21 48.5	24 49.4	14 29.3	22 47.3	21 0.2
4 Sa	12 48 3	13 55 29	4♐47 44	11♐13 1	9 57.3	20 8.9	28 28.8	10 40.3	22 1.1	24 44.9	14 30.0	22 45.7	20 59.4
5 Su	12 52 0	14 54 34	17 41 43	24 14 4	9 51.6	20 26.6	27 59.7	11 23.5	22 13.7	24 40.4	14 30.6	22 44.1	20 58.6
6 M	12 55 56	15 53 36	0♑50 20	7♑30 47	9 48.4	20 49.1	27 28.9	12 6.6	22 26.4	24 35.9	14 31.4	22 42.4	20 57.9
7 Tu	12 59 53	16 52 37	14 15 41	21 5 17	9D 47.4	21 16.2	26 56.4	12 49.6	22 39.2	24 31.4	14 32.1	22 40.8	20 57.2
8 W	13 3 49	17 51 36	27 59 46	4♒59 16	9R 47.6	21 47.7	26 22.5	13 32.7	22 52.0	24 26.8	14 33.0	22 39.2	20 56.5
9 Th	13 7 46	18 50 34	12♒ 3 51	19 13 24	9 47.8	22 23.3	25 47.4	14 15.6	23 4.9	24 22.2	14 33.9	22 37.5	20 55.8
10 F	13 11 43	19 49 29	26 27 46	3♓46 34	9 46.9	23 2.9	25 11.3	14 58.6	23 17.8	24 17.6	14 34.8	22 35.9	20 55.2
11 Sa	13 15 39	20 48 23	11♓ 9 16	18 35 11	9 43.7	23 46.2	24 34.4	15 41.4	23 30.8	24 13.0	14 35.8	22 34.2	20 54.5
12 Su	13 19 36	21 47 15	26 3 27	3♈33 4	9 37.9	24 33.1	23 57.0	16 24.3	23 43.8	24 8.4	14 36.8	22 32.6	20 54.0
13 M	13 23 32	22 46 5	11♈ 2 55	18 31 49	9 29.4	25 23.3	23 19.3	17 7.1	23 56.9	24 3.8	14 37.9	22 31.0	20 53.4
14 Tu	13 27 29	23 44 53	25 58 35	3♉22 4	9 19.0	26 16.8	22 41.5	17 49.8	24 10.0	23 59.2	14 39.1	22 29.3	20 52.8
15 W	13 31 25	24 43 40	10♉41 12	17 55 4	9 7.8	27 13.3	22 4.0	18 32.5	24 23.2	23 54.6	14 40.3	22 27.7	20 52.3
16 Th	13 35 22	25 42 24	25 2 54	2♊ 4 9	8 57.2	28 12.7	21 26.8	19 15.2	24 36.5	23 49.9	14 41.5	22 26.0	20 51.9
17 F	13 39 18	26 41 6	8♊58 28	15 45 41	8 48.2	29 14.9	20 50.4	19 57.8	24 49.8	23 45.3	14 42.8	22 24.4	20 51.4
18 Sa	13 43 15	27 39 47	22 25 48	28 59 2	8 41.5	0♈19.7	20 14.8	20 40.3	25 3.1	23 40.7	14 44.2	22 22.7	20 51.0
19 Su	13 47 12	28 38 24	5♋25 42	11♋46 14	8 37.4	1 27.1	19 40.4	21 22.9	25 16.5	23 36.1	14 45.6	22 21.1	20 50.6
20 M	13 51 8	29 37 0	18 1 11	24 11 8	8 35.6	2 37.0	19 7.3	22 5.3	25 29.9	23 31.6	14 47.0	22 19.5	20 50.2
21 Tu	13 55 5	0♉35 34	0♌16 45	6♌18 43	8 35.2	3 49.2	18 35.7	22 47.7	25 43.3	23 27.0	14 48.5	22 17.8	20 49.8
22 W	13 59 1	1 34 5	12 17 42	18 14 24	8 35.2	5 3.8	18 5.9	23 30.1	25 56.8	23 22.4	14 50.0	22 16.2	20 49.5
23 Th	14 2 58	2 32 34	24 9 30	0♍ 3 38	8 34.5	6 20.5	17 37.8	24 12.4	26 10.4	23 17.9	14 51.6	22 14.6	20 49.2
24 F	14 6 54	3 31 1	5♍57 25	11 51 26	8 32.0	7 39.4	17 11.8	24 54.7	26 23.9	23 13.4	14 53.3	22 13.0	20 49.0
25 Sa	14 10 51	4 29 26	17 46 13	23 42 15	8 27.1	9 0.4	16 47.9	25 36.9	26 37.5	23 8.9	14 55.0	22 11.4	20 48.7
26 Su	14 14 47	5 27 49	29 39 57	5♎39 41	8 19.5	10 23.4	16 26.2	26 19.1	26 51.2	23 4.4	14 56.7	22 9.8	20 48.5
27 M	14 18 44	6 26 9	11♎41 46	17 46 26	8 9.2	11 48.5	16 6.7	27 1.2	27 4.8	23 0.0	14 58.5	22 8.2	20 48.3
28 Tu	14 22 41	7 24 28	23 53 52	0♏ 4 13	7 56.8	13 15.5	15 49.7	27 43.3	27 18.5	22 55.6	15 0.3	22 6.6	20 48.2
29 W	14 26 37	8 22 45	6♏17 32	12 33 52	7 43.4	14 44.5	15 35.0	28 25.4	27 32.3	22 51.2	15 2.2	22 5.1	20 48.1
30 Th	14 30 34	9 21 1	18 53 12	25 15 32	7 30.0	16 15.5	15 22.8	29 7.3	27 46.0	22 46.9	15 4.1	22 3.5	20 48.0

Astro Data Dy Hr Mn	Planet Ingress Dy Hr Mn	Last Aspect Dy Hr Mn	☽ Ingress Dy Hr Mn	Last Aspect Dy Hr Mn	☽ Ingress Dy Hr Mn	☽ Phases & Eclipses Dy Hr Mn	Astro Data
☽0S 1 19:58	☿ ♈ 2 19:21	2 11:01 ☿ ☍	♎ 2 11:41	1 4:39 ♀ ☍	♏ 1 5:19	8 18:26 ☽ 17♐54	1 MARCH 1953
☿ R 9 3:44	♀ ♉ 14 18:58	4 16:55 ♄ ☌	♏ 4 23:31	2 23:25 ♃ ☍	♐ 3 14:58	15 11:05 ● 24♓34	Julian Day # 19418
☽0N 15 7:23	☿ ♓ 15 21:16	6 17:12 ♇ □	♐ 7 9:20	5 18:09 ♀ △	♑ 5 22:29	22 8:11 ☽ 1♋25	Delta T 30.4 sec
☿0S 22 19:23	☉ ♈ 20 22:01	9 12:31 ♀ △	♑ 9 16:10	7 21:19 ♀ □	♒ 8 3:27	30 12:55 ○ 9♎32	SVP 05♓54'36"
♅ D 22 21:22	♂ ♉ 20 6:54	11 17:48 ♀ □	♒ 11 19:37	9 21:59 ♀ ✱	♓ 10 5:49		Obliquity 23°26'50"
♀ R 23 3:53	♀ ♈ 31 5:17	13 19:47 ♀ ✱	♓ 13 20:17	11 21:27 ☿ ☌	♈ 12 6:19	7 4:58 ☽ 17♑05	⚷ Chiron 18♑51.8
☽0S 29 2:11		15 11:05 ☉ ☌	♈ 15 19:39	13 20:48 ♄ ☍	♉ 14 6:31	13 20:09 ● 23♈35	☽ Mean ☊ 10♒57.3
♃□♇ 30 8:25	☿ ♈ 17 16:48	17 16:38 ♂ ☌	♉ 17 19:44	16 5:48 ☿ ✱	♊ 16 8:27	21 0:41 ☽ 0♌37	
☿ D 1 3:36	☉ ♉ 20 9:25	19 20:45 ☉ ✱	♊ 19 22:35	18 10:20 ☉ ✱	♋ 18 13:53	29 4:20 ○ 8♏33	1 APRIL 1953
♃⚻♆ 7 2:43		21 21:19 ♄ △	♋ 22 5:29	20 14:51 ♃ ✱	♌ 20 23:27		Julian Day # 19449
☽0N 11 17:40		24 7:16 ♄ □	♌ 24 16:14	23 4:10 ♃ □	♍ 23 11:53		Delta T 30.4 sec
♃⚻♄ 13 9:20		26 19:35 ♄ ✱	♍ 27 5:04	25 18:14 ♃ △	♎ 26 0:40		SVP 05♓54'33"
☿0N 23 0:09		28 23:16 ♃ △	♎ 29 17:51	27 22:07 ♄ ☌	♏ 28 11:52		Obliquity 23°26'50"
☽0S 25 8:30				30 20:20 ♂ ☍	♐ 30 20:52		⚷ Chiron 20♑32.8
							☽ Mean ☊ 9♒18.8

LONGITUDE — MAY 1953

Day	Sid.Time	☉	0 hr ☽	Noon ☽	True ☊	☿	♀	♂	♃	♄	♅	♆	♇
1 F	14 34 30	10♉19 14	1♐40 47	8♐ 8 55	7♒17.9	17♈48.3	15♈13.0	29♉49.3	27♉59.8	22♎42.6	15♋ 6.0	22♎ 1.9	20♌47.9
2 Sa	14 38 27	11 17 26	14 39 53	21 13 39	7R 7.9	19 23.1	15R 5.7	0♊31.2	28 13.6	22R38.3	15 8.0	22R 0.4	20D47.9
3 Su	14 42 23	12 15 37	27 50 12	4♑29 33	7 0.8	20 59.7	15 0.8	1 13.1	28 27.5	22 34.1	15 10.1	21 58.9	20 47.8
4 M	14 46 20	13 13 46	11♑11 43	17 56 48	6 56.6	22 38.3	14D58.4	1 54.9	28 41.3	22 30.0	15 12.2	21 57.4	20 47.9
5 Tu	14 50 16	14 11 53	24 44 51	1♒35 59	6D54.8	24 18.7	14 58.3	2 36.6	28 55.2	22 25.8	15 14.3	21 55.9	20 47.9
6 W	14 54 13	15 9 59	8♒30 17	15 27 48	6R54.5	26 1.0	15 0.6	3 18.4	29 9.1	22 21.8	15 16.5	21 54.4	20 48.0
7 Th	14 58 10	16 8 4	22 28 35	29 32 37	6 54.4	27 45.3	15 5.2	4 0.1	29 23.0	22 17.7	15 18.7	21 52.9	20 48.1
8 F	15 2 6	17 6 7	6♓39 48	13♓49 55	6 53.4	29 31.4	15 12.1	4 41.7	29 37.0	22 13.7	15 21.0	21 51.5	20 48.2
9 Sa	15 6 3	18 4 9	21 2 41	28 17 41	6 50.2	1♉19.4	15 21.1	5 23.3	29 50.9	22 9.8	15 23.3	21 50.0	20 48.4
10 Su	15 9 59	19 2 10	5♈34 21	12♈52 1	6 44.5	3 9.4	15 32.4	6 4.9	0♊ 4.9	22 5.9	15 25.6	21 48.6	20 48.6
11 M	15 13 56	20 0 9	20 9 56	27 27 16	6 36.2	5 1.2	15 45.6	6 46.4	0 18.9	22 2.1	15 28.0	21 47.2	20 48.8
12 Tu	15 17 52	20 58 7	4♉43 8	11♉56 37	6 25.9	6 55.0	16 0.9	7 27.9	0 32.9	21 58.4	15 30.4	21 45.8	20 49.0
13 W	15 21 49	21 56 3	19 6 52	26 13 6	6 14.8	8 50.6	16 18.2	8 9.3	0 47.0	21 54.7	15 32.9	21 44.4	20 49.3
14 Th	15 25 45	22 53 58	3♊14 36	10♊10 48	6 4.0	10 48.1	16 37.3	8 50.7	1 1.0	21 51.1	15 35.4	21 43.0	20 49.6
15 F	15 29 42	23 51 52	17 1 17	23 45 46	5 54.7	12 47.4	16 58.2	9 32.1	1 15.1	21 47.5	15 37.9	21 41.7	20 49.9
16 Sa	15 33 39	24 49 44	0♋24 8	6♋56 26	5 47.7	14 48.5	17 20.9	10 13.4	1 29.1	21 44.0	15 40.5	21 40.4	20 50.3
17 Su	15 37 35	25 47 34	13 22 48	19 43 33	5 43.2	16 51.3	17 45.3	10 54.6	1 43.2	21 40.6	15 43.1	21 39.1	20 50.7
18 M	15 41 32	26 45 23	25 59 4	2♌ 9 49	5D41.2	18 55.8	18 11.3	11 35.9	1 57.3	21 37.2	15 45.7	21 37.8	20 51.1
19 Tu	15 45 28	27 43 10	8♌16 22	14 19 18	5 40.8	21 1.8	18 38.8	12 17.0	2 11.4	21 33.9	15 48.4	21 36.5	20 51.5
20 W	15 49 25	28 40 55	20 19 16	26 16 56	5R41.2	23 9.2	19 7.9	12 58.2	2 25.4	21 30.7	15 51.1	21 35.3	20 52.0
21 Th	15 53 21	29 38 39	2♍12 57	8♍ 8 1	5 41.4	25 17.9	19 38.5	13 39.3	2 39.5	21 27.6	15 53.9	21 34.1	20 52.5
22 F	15 57 18	0♊36 21	14 2 46	19 57 52	5 40.4	27 27.7	20 10.4	14 20.3	2 53.6	21 24.5	15 56.6	21 32.9	20 53.0
23 Sa	16 1 14	1 34 1	25 53 55	1♎51 29	5 37.5	29 38.3	20 43.7	15 1.3	3 7.7	21 21.6	15 59.5	21 31.7	20 53.6
24 Su	16 5 11	2 31 40	7♎51 7	13 53 16	5 32.3	1♊49.6	21 18.3	15 42.3	3 21.8	21 18.7	16 2.3	21 30.5	20 54.1
25 M	16 9 8	3 29 18	19 58 23	26 6 48	5 24.8	4 1.3	21 54.2	16 23.2	3 35.9	21 15.8	16 5.2	21 29.4	20 54.7
26 Tu	16 13 4	4 26 54	2♏18 48	8♏34 34	5 15.5	6 13.1	22 31.2	17 4.1	3 50.0	21 13.1	16 8.1	21 28.3	20 55.4
27 W	16 17 1	5 24 29	14 54 16	21 17 57	5 5.3	8 24.8	23 9.4	17 44.9	4 4.0	21 10.4	16 11.0	21 27.2	20 56.0
28 Th	16 20 57	6 22 2	27 45 34	4♐17 4	4 54.9	10 36.2	23 48.8	18 25.7	4 18.1	21 7.9	16 14.0	21 26.1	20 56.7
29 F	16 24 54	7 19 35	10♐52 18	17 31 4	4 45.6	12 46.8	24 29.2	19 6.5	4 32.2	21 5.4	16 17.0	21 25.1	20 57.4
30 Sa	16 28 50	8 17 6	24 13 9	0♑58 19	4 38.0	14 56.5	25 10.7	19 47.2	4 46.3	21 3.0	16 20.0	21 24.1	20 58.2
31 Su	16 32 47	9 14 36	7♑46 17	14 36 49	4 32.8	17 5.0	25 53.1	20 27.9	5 0.3	21 0.7	16 23.1	21 23.1	20 58.9

LONGITUDE — JUNE 1953

Day	Sid.Time	☉	0 hr ☽	Noon ☽	True ☊	☿	♀	♂	♃	♄	♅	♆	♇
1 M	16 36 43	10♊12 6	21♑29 40	28♑24 37	4♒30.0	19♊12.0	26♈36.5	21♊ 8.5	5♊14.4	20♎58.4	16♋26.2	21♎22.1	20♌59.7
2 Tu	16 40 40	11 9 34	5♒21 28	12♒20 2	4D29.3	21 17.4	27 20.9	21 49.2	5 28.4	20R56.3	16 29.3	21R21.2	21 0.6
3 W	16 44 37	12 7 2	19 20 11	26 21 45	4 29.9	23 21.1	28 6.1	22 29.7	5 42.4	20 54.2	16 32.4	21 20.3	21 1.4
4 Th	16 48 33	13 4 29	3♓24 37	10♓28 39	4R30.8	25 22.7	28 52.2	23 10.3	5 56.5	20 52.3	16 35.6	21 19.4	21 2.3
5 F	16 52 30	14 1 56	17 33 41	24 39 32	4 31.1	27 22.2	29 39.1	23 50.7	6 10.5	20 50.4	16 38.8	21 18.5	21 3.1
6 Sa	16 56 26	14 59 21	1♈45 58	8♈52 42	4 29.9	29 19.6	0♉26.8	24 31.2	6 24.5	20 48.6	16 42.0	21 17.7	21 4.1
7 Su	17 0 23	15 56 47	15 59 25	23 5 43	4 26.7	1♋14.6	1 15.2	25 11.6	6 38.4	20 46.9	16 45.2	21 16.9	21 5.0
8 M	17 4 19	16 54 11	0♉11 11	7♉15 19	4 21.6	3 7.2	2 4.4	25 52.0	6 52.4	20 45.3	16 48.5	21 16.1	21 6.0
9 Tu	17 8 16	17 51 35	14 17 38	21 17 36	4 15.0	4 57.4	2 54.3	26 32.4	7 6.4	20 43.8	16 51.7	21 15.4	21 7.0
10 W	17 12 12	18 48 59	28 14 42	5♊ 8 27	4 7.7	6 45.2	3 44.8	27 12.7	7 20.3	20 42.4	16 55.0	21 14.7	21 8.0
11 Th	17 16 9	19 46 22	11♊58 25	18 44 12	4 0.6	8 30.4	4 36.0	27 53.0	7 34.2	20 41.1	16 58.4	21 14.0	21 9.0
12 F	17 20 6	20 43 44	25 25 32	2♋ 2 11	3 54.5	10 13.1	5 27.8	28 33.2	7 48.1	20 39.9	17 1.7	21 13.3	21 10.1
13 Sa	17 24 2	21 41 5	8♋34 1	15 1 3	3 50.0	11 53.2	6 20.2	29 13.4	8 2.0	20 38.8	17 5.1	21 12.7	21 11.2
14 Su	17 27 59	22 38 26	21 23 19	27 41 0	3 47.5	13 30.8	7 13.2	29 53.6	8 15.8	20 37.8	17 8.5	21 12.1	21 12.3
15 M	17 31 55	23 35 46	3♌54 22	10♌ 3 44	3D46.7	15 5.8	8 6.7	0♋33.8	8 29.6	20 36.9	17 11.9	21 11.5	21 13.4
16 Tu	17 35 52	24 33 5	16 9 31	22 12 9	3 47.3	16 38.2	9 0.8	1 13.9	8 43.4	20 36.1	17 15.3	21 11.0	21 14.6
17 W	17 39 48	25 30 23	28 12 10	4♍10 7	3 48.8	18 7.9	9 55.3	1 53.9	8 57.2	20 35.4	17 18.7	21 10.5	21 15.8
18 Th	17 43 45	26 27 40	10♍ 6 34	16 2 9	3 50.4	19 35.0	10 50.4	2 34.0	9 10.9	20 34.7	17 22.2	21 10.0	21 17.0
19 F	17 47 42	27 24 57	21 57 29	27 53 11	3R51.4	20 59.4	11 45.9	3 14.0	9 24.6	20 34.2	17 25.7	21 9.5	21 18.2
20 Sa	17 51 38	28 22 12	3♎49 52	9♎48 10	3 51.4	22 21.1	12 41.9	3 53.9	9 38.3	20 33.8	17 29.1	21 9.1	21 19.4
21 Su	17 55 35	29 19 27	15 48 39	21 51 53	3 50.0	23 40.0	13 38.4	4 33.8	9 51.9	20 33.5	17 32.6	21 8.7	21 20.7
22 M	17 59 31	0♋16 42	27 58 24	4♏ 8 39	3 47.2	24 56.1	14 35.2	5 13.7	10 5.5	20 33.2	17 36.2	21 8.4	21 22.0
23 Tu	18 3 28	1 13 56	10♏23 3	16 41 56	3 43.2	26 9.4	15 32.5	5 53.6	10 19.1	20D33.1	17 39.7	21 8.0	21 23.3
24 W	18 7 24	2 11 9	23 5 34	29 34 58	3 38.5	27 19.8	16 30.3	6 33.4	10 32.6	20 33.1	17 43.2	21 7.7	21 24.6
25 Th	18 11 21	3 8 22	6♐ 7 42	12♐46 17	3 33.6	28 27.2	17 28.4	7 13.2	10 46.1	20 33.2	17 46.8	21 7.5	21 26.0
26 F	18 15 17	4 5 34	19 29 44	26 17 52	3 29.1	29 31.5	18 26.9	7 52.9	10 59.6	20 33.4	17 50.3	21 7.2	21 27.3
27 Sa	18 19 14	5 2 46	3♑10 24	10♑ 6 58	3 25.7	0♌32.7	19 25.7	8 32.7	11 13.0	20 33.6	17 53.9	21 7.0	21 28.7
28 Su	18 23 11	5 59 58	17 7 8	24 10 24	3 23.5	1 30.7	20 25.0	9 12.4	11 26.4	20 34.0	17 57.5	21 6.9	21 30.1
29 M	18 27 7	6 57 9	1♒16 16	8♒24 11	3D22.7	2 25.4	21 24.6	9 52.0	11 39.7	20 34.5	18 1.1	21 6.7	21 31.5
30 Tu	18 31 4	7 54 21	15 33 37	22 44 3	3 23.0	3 16.7	22 24.5	10 31.6	11 53.1	20 35.1	18 4.7	21 6.6	21 33.0

Astro Data (Dy Hr Mn)	Planet Ingress (Dy Hr Mn)	Last Aspect (Dy Hr Mn)	☽ Ingress (Dy Hr Mn)	Last Aspect (Dy Hr Mn)	☽ Ingress (Dy Hr Mn)	☽ Phases & Eclipses (Dy Hr Mn)	Astro Data
♇ D 2 20:21	♂ ♊ 1 6:08	2 14:30 ♄ ✶	♑ 3 3:55	1 9:23 ♀ □	♒ 1 14:45	6 12:21 ☽ 15♒40	1 MAY 1953
♀ D 4 12:33	☿ ♉ 8 6:24	5 7:27 ♃ △	♒ 5 9:12	3 15:50 ♀ ✶	♓ 3 18:12	13 5:06 ● 22♉08	Julian Day # 19479
☽0N 9 1:11	♃ ♊ 9 15:33	7 11:55 ♃ □	♓ 7 12:46	5 19:14 ☿ □	♈ 5 21:01	20 18:20 ☽ 29♌25	Delta T 30.5 sec
♃∠♅ 11 18:44	☉ ♊ 21 8:53	9 14:48 ♃ ✶	♈ 9 14:49	7 16:19 ♂ ✶	♉ 7 23:41	28 17:03 ○ 7♐03	SVP 05♓54'29"
♄☌♆ 17 17:29	☿ ♊ 23 3:58	11 3:04 ♄ ☍	♉ 11 16:12	9 11:43 ♇ □	♊ 10 3:03		Obliquity 23°26'49"
☽0S 22 15:11		13 5:06 ☉ ☌	♊ 13 18:27	12 5:58 ♂ ☌	♋ 12 8:17	4 17:35 ☽ 13♓47	⚷ Chiron 21♑02.1R
♄✶♇ 31 13:33	♀ ♉ 5 10:34	15 8:26 ♄ △	♋ 15 23:16	13 23:39 ♆ □	♌ 14 16:27	11 14:55 ● 20♊22	☽ Mean ☊ 7♒43.5
	☿ ♋ 6 8:23	18 1:37 ☉ ✶	♌ 18 7:47	16 18:08 ☉ ✶	♍ 17 3:37	19 12:01 ☽ 27♍54	
♃⚼♄ 3 17:41	♂ ♋ 14 3:49	20 18:20 ☉ □	♍ 20 19:31	19 12:01 ☉ □	♎ 19 16:16	27 3:29 ○ 5♑11	1 JUNE 1953
☽0N 5 6:21	☉ ♋ 21 17:00	22 3:52 ♅ ✶	♎ 23 8:16	21 17:22 ☿ □	♏ 22 3:57		Julian Day # 19510
♃⚼♆ 5 13:03	☿ ♌ 26 11:01	25 3:59 ♀ ☍	♏ 25 19:32	24 8:37 ☿ △	♐ 24 12:48		Delta T 30.5 sec
♆✶♇ 13 21:10		27 11:20 ♇ □	♐ 28 4:08	26 3:29 ♇ △	♑ 26 18:29		SVP 05♓54'24"
☽0S 18 22:19		30 1:48 ♀ △	♑ 30 10:17	28 6:48 ♆ □	♒ 28 21:51		Obliquity 23°26'48"
♄ D 23 17:25							⚷ Chiron 20♑19.0R
							☽ Mean ☊ 6♒05.0

JULY 1953 — LONGITUDE

Day	Sid.Time	☉	0 hr ☽	Noon ☽	True ☊	☿	♀	♂	♃	♄	♅	♆	♇
1 W	18 35 0	8♋51 32	29♒54 58	7♓ 5 55	3♒24.2	4♌ 4.5	23♉24.8	11♋11.2	12♊ 6.3	20♎35.7	18♋ 8.3	21♎ 6.5	21♌34.4
2 Th	18 38 57	9 48 44	14♓16 27	21 26 11	3 25.5	4 48.6	24 25.3	11 50.8	12 19.5	20 36.5	18 11.9	21D 6.5	21 35.9
3 F	18 42 53	10 45 56	28 34 46	5♈41 53	3R26.6	5 28.9	25 26.2	12 30.3	12 32.7	20 37.4	18 15.5	21 6.5	21 37.4
4 Sa	18 46 50	11 43 8	12♈47 16	19 50 39	3 27.0	6 5.4	26 27.4	13 9.8	12 45.8	20 38.3	18 19.1	21 6.5	21 38.9
5 Su	18 50 46	12 40 20	26 51 49	3♉50 34	3 26.4	6 37.8	27 28.9	13 49.3	12 58.9	20 39.4	18 22.8	21 6.6	21 40.5
6 M	18 54 43	13 37 33	10♉46 42	17 40 2	3 25.0	7 6.1	28 30.7	14 28.8	13 11.9	20 40.5	18 26.4	21 6.6	21 42.0
7 Tu	18 58 40	14 34 46	24 30 25	1♊17 40	3 22.9	7 30.1	29 32.8	15 8.2	13 24.9	20 41.8	18 30.1	21 6.8	21 43.6
8 W	19 2 36	15 32 0	8♊ 1 40	14 42 16	3 20.4	7 49.8	0♊35.1	15 47.6	13 37.8	20 43.2	18 33.7	21 6.9	21 45.1
9 Th	19 6 33	16 29 13	21 19 21	27 52 51	3 18.1	8 4.9	1 37.7	16 27.0	13 50.7	20 44.6	18 37.4	21 7.1	21 46.7
10 F	19 10 29	17 26 27	4♋22 42	10♋48 51	3 16.1	8 15.4	2 40.5	17 6.3	14 3.5	20 46.2	18 41.0	21 7.3	21 48.4
11 Sa	19 14 26	18 23 42	17 11 21	23 30 13	3 14.8	8R21.3	3 43.6	17 45.6	14 16.3	20 47.8	18 44.7	21 7.6	21 50.0
12 Su	19 18 22	19 20 56	29 45 33	5♌57 30	3D14.2	8 22.3	4 46.9	18 24.9	14 29.0	20 49.6	18 48.3	21 7.8	21 51.6
13 M	19 22 19	20 18 11	12♌ 6 15	18 12 1	3 14.4	8 18.6	5 50.4	19 4.2	14 41.7	20 51.4	18 52.0	21 8.1	21 53.3
14 Tu	19 26 15	21 15 25	24 15 6	0♍15 49	3 15.0	8 10.2	6 54.2	19 43.4	14 54.2	20 53.4	18 55.6	21 8.5	21 54.9
15 W	19 30 12	22 12 40	6♍14 32	12 11 41	3 16.0	7 57.0	7 58.2	20 22.6	15 6.8	20 55.4	18 59.3	21 8.9	21 56.6
16 Th	19 34 9	23 9 55	18 7 41	24 3 2	3 17.1	7 39.2	9 2.4	21 1.8	15 19.2	20 57.5	19 2.9	21 9.3	21 58.3
17 F	19 38 5	24 7 10	29 58 14	5♎53 51	3 18.0	7 17.0	10 6.7	21 40.9	15 31.6	20 59.8	19 6.5	21 9.7	22 0.0
18 Sa	19 42 2	25 4 26	11♎50 25	17 48 30	3 18.6	6 50.6	11 11.3	22 20.1	15 44.0	21 2.1	19 10.2	21 10.2	22 1.7
19 Su	19 45 58	26 1 41	23 48 42	29 51 34	3R18.8	6 20.4	12 16.1	22 59.1	15 56.2	21 4.5	19 13.8	21 10.7	22 3.5
20 M	19 49 55	26 58 57	5♏57 41	12♏ 7 35	3 18.7	5 46.6	13 21.1	23 38.2	16 8.4	21 7.0	19 17.4	21 11.2	22 5.2
21 Tu	19 53 51	27 56 13	18 21 47	24 40 46	3 18.4	5 9.9	14 26.3	24 17.2	16 20.5	21 9.6	19 21.1	21 11.8	22 7.0
22 W	19 57 48	28 53 29	1♐ 4 57	7♐34 39	3 17.9	4 30.7	15 31.6	24 56.3	16 32.6	21 12.3	19 24.7	21 12.4	22 8.7
23 Th	20 1 44	29 50 46	14 10 10	20 51 38	3 17.5	3 49.6	16 37.2	25 35.2	16 44.6	21 15.0	19 28.3	21 13.0	22 10.5
24 F	20 5 41	0♌48 3	27 39 6	4♑32 31	3 17.2	3 7.4	17 42.9	26 14.2	16 56.5	21 17.9	19 31.9	21 13.7	22 12.3
25 Sa	20 9 38	1 45 20	11♑31 40	18 36 15	3 17.0	2 24.7	18 48.8	26 53.1	17 8.3	21 20.9	19 35.5	21 14.4	22 14.1
26 Su	20 13 34	2 42 39	25 45 46	2♒59 39	3 17.0	1 42.3	19 54.8	27 32.0	17 20.1	21 23.9	19 39.1	21 15.1	22 15.9
27 M	20 17 31	3 39 57	10♒17 13	17 37 40	3 16.9	1 0.9	21 1.1	28 10.9	17 31.7	21 27.0	19 42.6	21 15.9	22 17.7
28 Tu	20 21 27	4 37 17	25 0 9	2♓23 48	3 16.9	0 21.4	22 7.5	28 49.8	17 43.3	21 30.2	19 46.2	21 16.6	22 19.5
29 W	20 25 24	5 34 37	9♓47 41	17 10 57	3 16.8	29♋44.5	23 14.0	29 28.6	17 54.9	21 33.5	19 49.8	21 17.5	22 21.3
30 Th	20 29 20	6 31 58	24 32 47	1♈52 24	3 16.5	29 10.8	24 20.8	0♌ 7.4	18 6.3	21 36.9	19 53.3	21 18.3	22 23.2
31 F	20 33 17	7 29 20	9♈ 9 9	16 22 29	3 16.1	28 41.1	25 27.7	0 46.2	18 17.7	21 40.4	19 56.8	21 19.2	22 25.0

AUGUST 1953 — LONGITUDE

Day	Sid.Time	☉	0 hr ☽	Noon ☽	True ☊	☿	♀	♂	♃	♄	♅	♆	♇
1 Sa	20 37 13	8♌26 43	23♈31 58	0♉37 14	3♒15.8	28♋15.9	26♊34.7	1♌25.0	18♊28.9	21♎43.9	20♋ 0.3	21♎20.1	22♌26.9
2 Su	20 41 10	9 24 8	7♉38 5	14 34 22	3D15.6	27R55.8	27 41.9	2 3.7	18 40.1	21 47.6	20 3.8	21 21.0	22 28.7
3 M	20 45 7	10 21 33	21 26 3	28 13 9	3 15.7	27 41.2	28 49.3	2 42.4	18 51.2	21 51.3	20 7.3	21 22.0	22 30.6
4 Tu	20 49 3	11 19 0	4♊55 46	11♊34 1	3 16.2	27D32.5	29 56.8	3 21.1	19 2.2	21 55.1	20 10.8	21 23.0	22 32.4
5 W	20 53 0	12 16 28	18 8 5	24 38 9	3 16.9	27 30.1	1♋ 4.4	3 59.8	19 13.1	21 59.0	20 14.3	21 24.0	22 34.3
6 Th	20 56 56	13 13 58	1♋ 4 24	7♋27 4	3 17.8	27 34.0	2 12.2	4 38.5	19 24.0	22 2.9	20 17.7	21 25.0	22 36.2
7 F	21 0 53	14 11 29	13 46 20	20 2 25	3 18.6	27 44.6	3 20.2	5 17.2	19 34.7	22 7.0	20 21.1	21 26.1	22 38.1
8 Sa	21 4 49	15 9 0	26 15 32	2♌25 52	3R19.2	28 1.9	4 28.2	5 55.8	19 45.3	22 11.1	20 24.5	21 27.2	22 40.0
9 Su	21 8 46	16 6 33	8♌33 38	14 39 1	3 19.2	28 26.1	5 36.4	6 34.4	19 55.9	22 15.3	20 27.9	21 28.4	22 41.9
10 M	21 12 43	17 4 7	20 42 13	26 43 29	3 18.6	28 57.0	6 44.7	7 13.0	20 6.3	22 19.6	20 31.3	21 29.6	22 43.8
11 Tu	21 16 39	18 1 42	2♍43 0	8♍41 3	3 17.2	29 34.8	7 53.2	7 51.5	20 16.6	22 23.9	20 34.6	21 30.7	22 45.6
12 W	21 20 36	18 59 18	14 37 51	20 33 43	3 15.2	0♌19.2	9 1.7	8 30.1	20 26.9	22 28.4	20 38.0	21 32.0	22 47.5
13 Th	21 24 32	19 56 55	26 28 58	2♎23 55	3 12.7	1 10.3	10 10.4	9 8.6	20 37.0	22 32.9	20 41.3	21 33.2	22 49.4
14 F	21 28 29	20 54 33	8♎18 57	14 14 29	3 10.0	2 7.8	11 19.2	9 47.1	20 47.0	22 37.4	20 44.5	21 34.5	22 51.3
15 Sa	21 32 25	21 52 13	20 10 55	26 8 45	3 7.5	3 11.6	12 28.2	10 25.6	20 56.9	22 42.1	20 47.8	21 35.8	22 53.2
16 Su	21 36 22	22 49 53	2♏ 8 27	8♏10 32	3 5.5	4 21.5	13 37.2	11 4.0	21 6.7	22 46.8	20 51.0	21 37.1	22 55.1
17 M	21 40 18	23 47 34	14 15 33	20 24 0	3D 4.2	5 37.3	14 46.3	11 42.5	21 16.4	22 51.6	20 54.3	21 38.5	22 57.0
18 Tu	21 44 15	24 45 17	26 36 29	2♐53 29	3 3.9	6 58.6	15 55.6	12 20.9	21 26.0	22 56.5	20 57.4	21 39.9	22 58.9
19 W	21 48 11	25 43 0	9♐15 33	15 43 10	3 4.5	8 25.1	17 5.0	12 59.3	21 35.4	23 1.4	21 0.6	21 41.3	23 0.8
20 Th	21 52 8	26 40 45	22 16 45	28 56 39	3 5.7	9 56.5	18 14.5	13 37.6	21 44.8	23 6.4	21 3.8	21 42.7	23 2.8
21 F	21 56 5	27 38 31	5♑43 10	12♑36 25	3 7.2	11 32.4	19 24.1	14 16.0	21 54.0	23 11.4	21 6.9	21 44.2	23 4.7
22 Sa	22 0 1	28 36 18	19 36 26	26 43 5	3R 8.5	13 12.4	20 33.8	14 54.3	22 3.1	23 16.6	21 10.0	21 45.7	23 6.6
23 Su	22 3 58	29 34 6	3♒56 4	11♒14 53	3 8.9	14 56.0	21 43.6	15 32.7	22 12.1	23 21.8	21 13.0	21 47.2	23 8.4
24 M	22 7 54	0♍31 55	18 38 52	26 7 10	3 8.2	16 42.8	22 53.6	16 10.9	22 20.9	23 27.0	21 16.0	21 48.7	23 10.3
25 Tu	22 11 51	1 29 46	3♓38 48	11♓12 38	3 6.2	18 32.5	24 3.6	16 49.2	22 29.7	23 32.4	21 19.0	21 50.3	23 12.2
26 W	22 15 47	2 27 38	18 47 28	26 22 4	3 2.9	20 24.4	25 13.7	17 27.5	22 38.3	23 37.7	21 22.0	21 51.8	23 14.1
27 Th	22 19 44	3 25 32	3♈55 11	11♈25 41	2 58.9	22 18.3	26 24.0	18 5.7	22 46.8	23 43.2	21 24.9	21 53.4	23 16.0
28 F	22 23 40	4 23 27	18 52 31	26 14 47	2 54.6	24 13.6	27 34.3	18 44.0	22 55.1	23 48.7	21 27.9	21 55.1	23 17.9
29 Sa	22 27 37	5 21 24	3♉31 46	10♉42 55	2 50.8	26 10.1	28 44.8	19 22.2	23 3.3	23 54.2	21 30.7	21 56.7	23 19.7
30 Su	22 31 34	6 19 24	17 47 54	24 46 31	2 48.1	28 7.3	29 55.4	20 0.4	23 11.4	23 59.9	21 33.6	21 58.4	23 21.6
31 M	22 35 30	7 17 25	1♊38 45	8♊24 43	2D46.8	0♍ 5.0	1♌ 6.0	20 38.6	23 19.4	24 5.5	21 36.4	22 0.1	23 23.5

Astro Data (Dy Hr Mn)	Planet Ingress (Dy Hr Mn)	Last Aspect (Dy Hr Mn)	☽ Ingress (Dy Hr Mn)	Last Aspect (Dy Hr Mn)	☽ Ingress (Dy Hr Mn)	☽ Phases & Eclipses (Dy Hr Mn)	Astro Data
☽0N 2 11:17	♀ ♊ 7 10:30	30 12:19 ♀ □	♓ 1 0:08	1 7:48 ☿ □	♉ 1 10:57	3 22:03 ☽ 11♈38	1 JULY 1953
♆ D 2 22:13	☉ ♌ 23 3:52	2 18:19 ♀ ✶	♈ 3 2:23	3 10:55 ☿ ✶	♊ 3 15:10	11 2:28 ● 18♋30	Julian Day # 19540
☿ R 11 17:25	☿ ♋ 28 13:40	4 15:06 ♇ △	♉ 5 5:23	5 8:12 ♇ ✶	♋ 5 21:59	11 2:43:38 ✔ P 0.202	Delta T 30.5 sec
☽0S 16 5:41	♂ ♌ 29 19:25	7 9:38 ♀ ☌	♊ 7 9:42	8 3:32 ☿ ☌	♌ 8 7:16	19 4:47 ☽ 26♎13	SVP 05♓54'18"
♄☌♆ 22 1:21		9 0:50 ♇ ✶	♋ 9 15:54	10 4:02 ♇ ☌	♍ 10 18:33	26 12:21 ○ 3♒12	Obliquity 23°26'48"
☽0N 29 18:06	♀ ♋ 4 1:08	11 7:28 ♆ □	♌ 12 0:28	12 12:12 ♅ ✶	♎ 13 7:08	26 12:21 ✔ T 1.863	⚷ Chiron 18♑44.8R
	☿ ♌ 11 14:04	13 19:21 ♇ ☌	♍ 14 11:28	15 5:28 ♇ ✶	♏ 15 19:43		☽ Mean ☊ 4♒29.7
☿ D 4 21:21	☉ ♍ 23 10:45	16 11:06 ☉ ✶	♎ 17 0:04	17 20:08 ☉ □	♐ 18 6:30	2 3:16 ☽ 9♉32	1 AUGUST 1953
☽0S 12 12:50	☿ ♍ 30 22:59	19 4:47 ☉ □	♏ 19 12:17	20 8:34 ☉ △	♑ 20 13:53	9 16:10 ● 16♌45	Julian Day # 19571
♃⚺♅ 13 15:15	♀ ♌ 30 1:35	21 19:35 ☉ △	♐ 21 21:59	22 6:15 ♄ □	♒ 22 17:29	9 15:54:32 ✔ P 0.373	Delta T 30.6 sec
♄✶♇ 18 19:48		23 14:22 ♇ △	♑ 24 4:07	24 7:46 ♄ △	♓ 24 18:12	17 20:08 ☽ 24♏36	SVP 05♓54'13"
♃△♆ 19 17:47		26 3:05 ♂ ☍	♒ 26 7:03	26 11:03 ♀ △	♈ 26 17:46	24 20:21 ○ 1♓21	Obliquity 23°26'48"
☽0N 26 3:31		27 19:38 ♇ ☍	♓ 28 8:07	28 15:25 ♀ □	♉ 28 18:10	31 10:46 ☽ 7♊43	⚷ Chiron 16♑53.7R
♃✶♇ 31 16:24		30 7:19 ☿ △	♈ 30 8:56	30 20:48 ☿ □	♊ 30 21:07		☽ Mean ☊ 2♒51.2

LONGITUDE — SEPTEMBER 1953

Day	Sid.Time	☉	0 hr ☽	Noon ☽	True ☊	☿	♀	♂	♃	♄	♅	♆	♇
1 Tu	22 39 27	8♍15 28	15♊ 4 38	21♊38 51	2♒46.8	2♍ 2.9	2♌16.8	21♌16.7	23♊27.2	24♎11.3	21♋39.2	22♎ 1.8	23♌25.3
2 W	22 43 23	9 13 33	28 7 43	4♋31 39	2 47.9	4 0.6	3 27.7	21 54.9	23 34.9	24 17.1	21 41.9	22 3.5	23 27.2
3 Th	22 47 20	10 11 40	10♋51 6	17 6 32	2 49.5	5 58.1	4 38.6	22 33.0	23 42.4	24 22.9	21 44.7	22 5.3	23 29.0
4 F	22 51 16	11 9 49	23 18 23	29 27 5	2R 50.8	7 55.2	5 49.7	23 11.2	23 49.8	24 28.8	21 47.3	22 7.1	23 30.9
5 Sa	22 55 13	12 8 0	5♌33 2	11♌36 38	2 51.2	9 51.6	7 0.8	23 49.3	23 57.1	24 34.8	21 50.0	22 8.9	23 32.7
6 Su	22 59 9	13 6 13	17 38 13	23 38 7	2 50.0	11 47.3	8 12.1	24 27.4	24 4.2	24 40.8	21 52.6	22 10.7	23 34.5
7 M	23 3 6	14 4 27	29 36 37	5♍34 0	2 46.8	13 42.1	9 23.4	25 5.4	24 11.1	24 46.8	21 55.2	22 12.5	23 36.3
8 Tu	23 7 3	15 2 43	11♍30 30	17 26 21	2 41.7	15 36.0	10 34.8	25 43.5	24 17.9	24 52.9	21 57.7	22 14.4	23 38.1
9 W	23 10 59	16 1 1	23 21 47	29 16 59	2 34.8	17 29.0	11 46.3	26 21.6	24 24.6	24 59.1	22 0.2	22 16.2	23 39.9
10 Th	23 14 56	16 59 21	5♎12 10	11♎ 7 35	2 26.5	19 20.9	12 57.9	26 59.6	24 31.1	25 5.3	22 2.6	22 18.1	23 41.7
11 F	23 18 52	17 57 43	17 3 27	23 0 3	2 17.8	21 11.8	14 9.6	27 37.6	24 37.4	25 11.6	22 5.1	22 20.0	23 43.4
12 Sa	23 22 49	18 56 6	28 57 38	4♏56 33	2 9.3	23 1.6	15 21.4	28 15.6	24 43.6	25 17.9	22 7.4	22 22.0	23 45.2
13 Su	23 26 45	19 54 31	10♏57 8	16 59 46	2 2.0	24 50.3	16 33.2	28 53.6	24 49.6	25 24.2	22 9.8	22 23.9	23 47.0
14 M	23 30 42	20 52 57	23 4 52	29 12 54	1 56.3	26 37.9	17 45.1	29 31.6	24 55.4	25 30.6	22 12.1	22 25.9	23 48.7
15 Tu	23 34 38	21 51 26	5♐24 19	11♐39 39	1 52.8	28 24.4	18 57.1	0♍ 9.5	25 1.1	25 37.0	22 14.3	22 27.8	23 50.4
16 W	23 38 35	22 49 56	17 59 23	24 24 3	1D 51.3	0♎ 9.9	20 9.2	0 47.5	25 6.7	25 43.5	22 16.5	22 29.8	23 52.1
17 Th	23 42 32	23 48 27	0♑54 9	7♑30 10	1 51.4	1 54.3	21 21.3	1 25.4	25 12.0	25 50.0	22 18.7	22 31.8	23 53.8
18 F	23 46 28	24 47 0	14 12 31	21 1 31	1 52.3	3 37.6	22 33.6	2 3.3	25 17.2	25 56.5	22 20.8	22 33.9	23 55.5
19 Sa	23 50 25	25 45 35	27 57 27	5♒ 0 23	1R 53.1	5 19.9	23 45.9	2 41.2	25 22.3	26 3.1	22 22.9	22 35.9	23 57.2
20 Su	23 54 21	26 44 12	12♒10 17	19 26 54	1 52.7	7 1.1	24 58.3	3 19.0	25 27.1	26 9.8	22 25.0	22 37.9	23 58.9
21 M	23 58 18	27 42 50	26 49 47	4♓18 15	1 50.4	8 41.3	26 10.7	3 56.9	25 31.8	26 16.4	22 27.0	22 40.0	24 0.5
22 Tu	0 2 14	28 41 30	11♓51 25	19 28 12	1 45.7	10 20.6	27 23.2	4 34.7	25 36.3	26 23.1	22 28.9	22 42.1	24 2.1
23 W	0 6 11	29 40 11	27 7 19	4♈47 23	1 38.8	11 58.8	28 35.8	5 12.6	25 40.6	26 29.8	22 30.8	22 44.2	24 3.8
24 Th	0 10 7	0♎38 55	12♈26 59	20 4 39	1 30.3	13 36.1	29 48.5	5 50.4	25 44.8	26 36.6	22 32.7	22 46.2	24 5.4
25 F	0 14 4	1 37 41	27 39 3	5♉ 8 56	1 21.3	15 12.5	1♍ 1.3	6 28.2	25 48.8	26 43.4	22 34.5	22 48.4	24 6.9
26 Sa	0 18 1	2 36 28	12♉33 16	19 51 14	1 12.8	16 47.9	2 14.1	7 6.0	25 52.6	26 50.2	22 36.3	22 50.5	24 8.5
27 Su	0 21 57	3 35 19	27 2 15	4♊ 5 56	1 6.0	18 22.4	3 27.0	7 43.8	25 56.2	26 57.1	22 38.0	22 52.6	24 10.1
28 M	0 25 54	4 34 11	11♊ 2 9	17 50 58	1 1.4	19 56.0	4 39.9	8 21.5	25 59.6	27 4.0	22 39.7	22 54.7	24 11.6
29 Tu	0 29 50	5 33 6	24 32 34	1♋ 7 20	0D 59.0	21 28.7	5 53.0	8 59.3	26 2.9	27 10.9	22 41.3	22 56.9	24 13.1
30 W	0 33 47	6 32 3	7♋35 43	13 58 15	0 58.5	23 0.6	7 6.1	9 37.0	26 6.0	27 17.8	22 42.9	22 59.1	24 14.6

LONGITUDE — OCTOBER 1953

Day	Sid.Time	☉	0 hr ☽	Noon ☽	True ☊	☿	♀	♂	♃	♄	♅	♆	♇
1 Th	0 37 43	7♎31 2	20♋15 30	26♋28 4	0♒58.9	24♎31.5	8♍19.3	10♍14.8	26♊ 8.8	27♎24.8	22♋44.4	23♎ 1.2	24♌16.1
2 F	0 41 40	8 30 4	2♌36 35	8♌41 37	0R 59.1	26 1.6	9 32.5	10 52.5	26 11.5	27 31.8	22 45.9	23 3.4	24 17.6
3 Sa	0 45 36	9 29 8	14 43 47	20 43 37	0 58.2	27 30.8	10 45.8	11 30.2	26 14.0	27 38.8	22 47.3	23 5.6	24 19.0
4 Su	0 49 33	10 28 14	26 41 36	2♍38 15	0 55.2	28 59.2	11 59.2	12 7.9	26 16.3	27 45.9	22 48.7	23 7.8	24 20.5
5 M	0 53 30	11 27 22	8♍33 57	14 29 6	0 49.4	0♏26.6	13 12.6	12 45.6	26 18.4	27 52.9	22 50.1	23 10.0	24 21.9
6 Tu	0 57 26	12 26 32	20 24 1	26 18 59	0 40.8	1 53.2	14 26.1	13 23.3	26 20.4	28 0.0	22 51.3	23 12.2	24 23.3
7 W	1 1 23	13 25 45	2♎14 16	8♎10 4	0 29.6	3 18.8	15 39.7	14 0.9	26 22.1	28 7.1	22 52.6	23 14.4	24 24.6
8 Th	1 5 19	14 25 0	14 6 35	20 3 58	0 16.5	4 43.5	16 53.3	14 38.6	26 23.6	28 14.2	22 53.7	23 16.6	24 26.0
9 F	1 9 16	15 24 16	26 2 24	2♏ 2 0	0 2.6	6 7.3	18 7.0	15 16.2	26 24.9	28 21.4	22 54.9	23 18.8	24 27.3
10 Sa	1 13 12	16 23 35	8♏ 2 56	14 5 24	29♑49.0	7 30.0	19 20.7	15 53.8	26 26.0	28 28.5	22 55.9	23 21.0	24 28.6
11 Su	1 17 9	17 22 56	20 9 33	26 15 38	29 36.8	8 51.8	20 34.5	16 31.4	26 27.0	28 35.7	22 57.0	23 23.3	24 29.9
12 M	1 21 5	18 22 19	2♐23 53	8♐34 36	29 26.9	10 12.5	21 48.3	17 9.0	26 27.7	28 42.9	22 57.9	23 25.5	24 31.1
13 Tu	1 25 2	19 21 43	14 48 7	21 4 47	29 19.9	11 32.0	23 2.2	17 46.6	26 28.2	28 50.1	22 58.9	23 27.7	24 32.4
14 W	1 28 58	20 21 10	27 25 1	3♑49 13	29 15.8	12 50.4	24 16.1	18 24.1	26 28.5	28 57.3	22 59.7	23 30.0	24 33.6
15 Th	1 32 55	21 20 38	10♑17 50	16 51 19	29D 14.0	14 7.5	25 30.1	19 1.7	26R 28.7	29 4.5	23 0.6	23 32.2	24 34.8
16 F	1 36 52	22 20 8	23 30 6	0♒14 34	29R 13.7	15 23.2	26 44.1	19 39.2	26 28.6	29 11.8	23 1.3	23 34.4	24 36.0
17 Sa	1 40 48	23 19 39	7♒ 5 4	14 1 50	29 13.6	16 37.5	27 58.2	20 16.7	26 28.3	29 19.0	23 2.0	23 36.7	24 37.1
18 Su	1 44 45	24 19 13	21 5 1	28 14 34	29 12.5	17 50.3	29 12.3	20 54.2	26 27.8	29 26.2	23 2.7	23 38.9	24 38.2
19 M	1 48 41	25 18 48	5♓30 19	12♓51 52	29 9.2	19 1.3	0♎26.4	21 31.7	26 27.1	29 33.5	23 3.3	23 41.2	24 39.3
20 Tu	1 52 38	26 18 24	20 18 36	27 49 41	29 3.2	20 10.6	1 40.6	22 9.1	26 26.3	29 40.8	23 3.8	23 43.4	24 40.4
21 W	1 56 34	27 18 3	5♈24 6	13♈ 0 37	28 54.5	21 17.8	2 54.9	22 46.6	26 25.2	29 48.0	23 4.3	23 45.6	24 41.5
22 Th	2 0 31	28 17 43	20 37 56	28 14 37	28 43.7	22 22.8	4 9.2	23 24.0	26 23.9	29 55.3	23 4.7	23 47.9	24 42.5
23 F	2 4 27	29 17 26	5♉49 16	13♉20 33	28 32.1	23 25.5	5 23.5	24 1.5	26 22.4	0♏ 2.5	23 5.1	23 50.1	24 43.5
24 Sa	2 8 24	0♏17 10	20 47 14	28 8 18	28 21.1	24 25.4	6 37.9	24 38.9	26 20.7	0 9.8	23 5.5	23 52.3	24 44.5
25 Su	2 12 21	1 16 57	5♊22 55	12♊30 29	28 11.8	25 22.5	7 52.3	25 16.3	26 18.9	0 17.1	23 5.7	23 54.6	24 45.4
26 M	2 16 17	2 16 46	19 30 37	26 23 13	28 5.0	26 16.3	9 6.8	25 53.7	26 16.8	0 24.4	23 6.0	23 56.8	24 46.3
27 Tu	2 20 14	3 16 36	3♋ 8 18	9♋46 7	28 1.0	27 6.5	10 21.3	26 31.1	26 14.5	0 31.6	23 6.1	23 59.0	24 47.2
28 W	2 24 10	4 16 30	16 17 2	22 41 32	27D 59.2	27 52.7	11 35.8	27 8.4	26 12.0	0 38.9	23 6.3	24 1.2	24 48.1
29 Th	2 28 7	5 16 25	29 0 9	5♌13 33	27R 58.9	28 34.4	12 50.4	27 45.8	26 9.4	0 46.1	23R 6.3	24 3.4	24 49.0
30 F	2 32 3	6 16 22	11♌22 22	17 27 17	27 58.9	29 11.2	14 5.0	28 23.1	26 6.5	0 53.4	23 6.3	24 5.6	24 49.8
31 Sa	2 36 0	7 16 22	23 28 57	29 28 1	27 57.9	29 42.6	15 19.7	29 0.4	26 3.4	1 0.7	23 6.3	24 7.8	24 50.6

Astro Data (Dy Hr Mn)	Planet Ingress (Dy Hr Mn)
☽0S 8 19:22	♂ ♍ 14 17:59
☿0S 17 3:07	☿ ♎ 15 21:45
☽0N 22 14:29	☉ ♎ 23 8:06
	♀ ♍ 24 3:48
☽0S 6 1:15	
♃ R 15 2:56	☿ ♏ 4 16:40
☽0N 20 0:52	☊ ♑ 9 4:29
♀0S 21 13:01	♀ ♎ 18 15:27
♅ R 29 14:19	♄ ♏ 22 15:35
	☉ ♏ 23 17:06
	☿ ♐ 31 15:49

Last Aspect (Dy Hr Mn)	☽ Ingress (Dy Hr Mn)	Last Aspect (Dy Hr Mn)	☽ Ingress (Dy Hr Mn)
1 16:49 ♄ △	♋ 2 3:30	1 13:58 ♄ □	♌ 1 18:53
4 2:18 ♄ □	♌ 4 13:05	4 5:16 ☿ ✶	♍ 4 6:40
6 14:25 ♂ ☌	♍ 7 0:47	6 12:05 ♃ □	♎ 6 19:28
9 2:08 ♃ □	♎ 9 13:27	9 4:41 ♄ ☌	♏ 9 7:56
11 22:31 ♂ ✶	♏ 12 2:05	11 8:33 ♇ □	♐ 11 19:19
14 13:17 ♂ □	♐ 14 13:32	14 2:55 ♄ ✶	♑ 14 4:51
16 14:35 ♄ ✶	♑ 16 22:21	16 10:14 ♄ □	♒ 16 11:34
18 20:42 ♄ □	♒ 19 3:30	18 14:06 ♄ △	♓ 18 14:55
20 23:06 ♄ △	♓ 21 5:06	20 9:47 ♃ △	♈ 20 15:27
23 4:16 ☉ ☍	♈ 23 4:30	22 14:46 ♄ ☍	♉ 22 14:47
24 22:31 ♄ ☍	♉ 25 3:45	24 6:34 ♂ △	♊ 24 15:04
26 19:10 ♇ □	♊ 27 5:01	26 11:47 ♃ ☌	♋ 26 18:24
29 4:50 ♄ △	♋ 29 9:56	28 23:08 ☿ △	♌ 29 1:55
		31 12:58 ☿ □	♍ 31 13:04

☽ Phases & Eclipses (Dy Hr Mn)	
8 7:48	● 15♍22
16 9:49	☽ 23♐14
23 4:16	○ 29♓51
29 21:51	☽ 6♋27
8 0:40	● 14♎27
15 21:44	☽ 22♑15
22 12:56	○ 28♈50
29 13:09	☽ 5♌49

Astro Data

1 SEPTEMBER 1953
Julian Day # 19602
Delta T 30.6 sec
SVP 05♓54'09"
Obliquity 23°26'48"
⚷ Chiron 15♑35.9R
☽ Mean ☊ 1♒12.7

1 OCTOBER 1953
Julian Day # 19632
Delta T 30.6 sec
SVP 05♓54'06"
Obliquity 23°26'48"
⚷ Chiron 15♑23.1
☽ Mean ☊ 29♑37.4

NOVEMBER 1953 LONGITUDE

Day	Sid.Time	☉	0 hr ☽	Noon ☽	True ☊	☿	♀	♂	♃	♄	♅	♆	♇
1 Su	2 39 56	8♏16 24	5♍25 9	11♍20 55	27♑55.1	0♐ 7.9	16♎34.4	29♍37.8	26♊ 0.2	1♏ 7.9	23♋ 6.2	24♎10.0	24♌51.3
2 M	2 43 53	9 16 28	17 15 52	23 10 30	27R49.5	0 26.6	17 49.1	0♎15.1	25R56.7	1 15.1	23R 6.0	24 12.2	24 52.1
3 Tu	2 47 50	10 16 33	29 5 18	5♎ 0 39	27 41.1	0R37.9	19 3.9	0 52.3	25 53.1	1 22.3	23 5.8	24 14.4	24 52.8
4 W	2 51 46	11 16 41	10♎56 54	16 54 21	27 30.1	0 41.4	20 18.7	1 29.6	25 49.2	1 29.5	23 5.5	24 16.5	24 53.5
5 Th	2 55 43	12 16 51	22 53 15	28 53 48	27 17.1	0 36.2	21 33.5	2 6.9	25 45.2	1 36.7	23 5.2	24 18.7	24 54.1
6 F	2 59 39	13 17 3	4♏56 8	11♏ 0 24	27 3.2	0 21.9	22 48.4	2 44.1	25 41.0	1 43.9	23 4.8	24 20.9	24 54.7
7 Sa	3 3 36	14 17 17	17 6 42	23 15 6	26 49.5	29♏58.0	24 3.3	3 21.3	25 36.6	1 51.1	23 4.4	24 23.0	24 55.3
8 Su	3 7 32	15 17 32	29 25 40	5♐38 29	26 37.2	29 24.2	25 18.2	3 58.5	25 32.1	1 58.3	23 3.9	24 25.1	24 55.9
9 M	3 11 29	16 17 49	11♐53 38	18 11 13	26 27.2	28 40.6	26 33.2	4 35.7	25 27.3	2 5.4	23 3.4	24 27.2	24 56.5
10 Tu	3 15 25	17 18 8	24 31 21	0♑54 12	26 20.1	27 47.5	27 48.1	5 12.9	25 22.4	2 12.5	23 2.8	24 29.4	24 57.0
11 W	3 19 22	18 18 29	7♑19 57	13 48 49	26 16.0	26 45.5	29 3.1	5 50.0	25 17.3	2 19.6	23 2.1	24 31.5	24 57.5
12 Th	3 23 19	19 18 51	20 21 3	26 56 55	26D14.4	25 35.9	0♏18.1	6 27.2	25 12.1	2 26.7	23 1.4	24 33.5	24 57.9
13 F	3 27 15	20 19 14	3♒36 42	10♒20 41	26 14.4	24 20.4	1 33.2	7 4.3	25 6.7	2 33.7	23 0.7	24 35.6	24 58.3
14 Sa	3 31 12	21 19 39	17 9 5	24 2 9	26R14.9	23 1.1	2 48.2	7 41.4	25 1.1	2 40.8	22 59.9	24 37.7	24 58.7
15 Su	3 35 8	22 20 4	1♓ 0 1	8♓ 2 43	26 14.6	21 40.4	4 3.3	8 18.4	24 55.4	2 47.8	22 59.0	24 39.7	24 59.1
16 M	3 39 5	23 20 32	15 10 12	22 22 16	26 12.6	20 21.0	5 18.4	8 55.5	24 49.5	2 54.8	22 58.1	24 41.7	24 59.4
17 Tu	3 43 1	24 21 0	29 38 35	6♈58 38	26 8.2	19 5.5	6 33.5	9 32.5	24 43.5	3 1.7	22 57.2	24 43.7	24 59.7
18 W	3 46 58	25 21 30	14♈21 42	21 47 0	26 1.4	17 56.3	7 48.6	10 9.5	24 37.3	3 8.6	22 56.2	24 45.7	25 0.0
19 Th	3 50 54	26 22 1	29 13 32	6♉40 15	25 52.8	16 55.6	9 3.8	10 46.5	24 31.0	3 15.5	22 55.1	24 47.7	25 0.3
20 F	3 54 51	27 22 33	14♉ 6 1	21 29 44	25 43.2	16 4.8	10 18.9	11 23.5	24 24.5	3 22.4	22 54.0	24 49.7	25 0.5
21 Sa	3 58 48	28 23 7	28 50 18	6♊ 6 44	25 34.0	15 25.0	11 34.1	12 0.5	24 17.9	3 29.3	22 52.9	24 51.6	25 0.7
22 Su	4 2 44	29 23 43	13♊18 11	20 23 57	25 26.2	14 56.9	12 49.3	12 37.4	24 11.2	3 36.1	22 51.7	24 53.6	25 0.8
23 M	4 6 41	0♐24 20	27 23 31	4♋16 32	25 20.6	14D40.4	14 4.6	13 14.4	24 4.4	3 42.8	22 50.4	24 55.5	25 1.0
24 Tu	4 10 37	1 24 58	11♋ 2 51	17 42 29	25 17.3	14 35.4	15 19.8	13 51.3	23 57.4	3 49.6	22 49.1	24 57.4	25 1.1
25 W	4 14 34	2 25 39	24 15 35	0♌42 28	25D16.3	14 41.2	16 35.1	14 28.2	23 50.4	3 56.3	22 47.8	24 59.3	25 1.1
26 Th	4 18 30	3 26 20	7♌ 3 31	13 19 14	25 16.8	14 57.1	17 50.3	15 5.0	23 43.2	4 3.0	22 46.4	25 1.1	25R 1.2
27 F	4 22 27	4 27 3	19 30 11	25 36 57	25 18.0	15 22.4	19 5.6	15 41.9	23 35.9	4 9.6	22 45.0	25 3.0	25 1.2
28 Sa	4 26 24	5 27 48	1♍40 11	7♍40 31	25R19.0	15 56.1	20 20.9	16 18.7	23 28.5	4 16.2	22 43.5	25 4.8	25 1.2
29 Su	4 30 20	6 28 34	13 38 38	19 35 10	25 18.7	16 37.3	21 36.3	16 55.6	23 21.0	4 22.7	22 42.0	25 6.6	25 1.1
30 M	4 34 17	7 29 22	25 30 45	1♎25 59	25 16.7	17 25.2	22 51.6	17 32.3	23 13.4	4 29.2	22 40.4	25 8.4	25 1.0

DECEMBER 1953 LONGITUDE

Day	Sid.Time	☉	0 hr ☽	Noon ☽	True ☊	☿	♀	♂	♃	♄	♅	♆	♇
1 Tu	4 38 13	8♐30 11	7♎21 26	13♎17 38	25♑12.6	18♏18.9	24♏ 6.9	18♎ 9.1	23♊ 5.8	4♏35.7	22♋38.8	25♎10.1	25♌ 0.9
2 W	4 42 10	9 31 2	19 15 3	25 14 9	25R 6.5	19 17.8	25 22.3	18 45.9	22R58.1	4 42.1	22R37.1	25 11.8	25R 0.8
3 Th	4 46 6	10 31 54	1♏15 17	7♏18 47	24 58.9	20 21.2	26 37.7	19 22.6	22 50.3	4 48.5	22 35.4	25 13.6	25 0.6
4 F	4 50 3	11 32 47	13 24 54	19 33 52	24 50.4	21 28.5	27 53.1	19 59.3	22 42.4	4 54.8	22 33.7	25 15.3	25 0.4
5 Sa	4 53 59	12 33 42	25 45 49	2♐ 0 51	24 42.0	22 39.2	29 8.5	20 36.0	22 34.5	5 1.1	22 31.9	25 16.9	25 0.2
6 Su	4 57 56	13 34 38	8♐19 2	14 40 21	24 34.5	23 52.8	0♐23.9	21 12.6	22 26.5	5 7.4	22 30.1	25 18.6	24 59.9
7 M	5 1 53	14 35 34	21 4 48	27 32 21	24 28.5	25 8.8	1 39.3	21 49.3	22 18.4	5 13.6	22 28.2	25 20.2	24 59.7
8 Tu	5 5 49	15 36 32	4♑ 2 54	10♑36 26	24 24.5	26 27.1	2 54.7	22 25.9	22 10.4	5 19.7	22 26.3	25 21.8	24 59.4
9 W	5 9 46	16 37 31	17 12 50	23 52 6	24D22.7	27 47.2	4 10.2	23 2.5	22 2.3	5 25.8	22 24.4	25 23.4	24 59.0
10 Th	5 13 42	17 38 30	0♒34 8	7♒18 57	24 22.6	29 8.9	5 25.6	23 39.0	21 54.1	5 31.8	22 22.4	25 24.9	24 58.6
11 F	5 17 39	18 39 30	14 6 29	20 56 46	24 23.7	0♐32.0	6 41.0	24 15.5	21 46.0	5 37.8	22 20.4	25 26.4	24 58.2
12 Sa	5 21 35	19 40 31	27 49 46	4♓45 28	24 25.3	1 56.3	7 56.5	24 52.0	21 37.8	5 43.7	22 18.4	25 27.9	24 57.8
13 Su	5 25 32	20 41 32	11♓43 51	18 44 50	24R26.6	3 21.6	9 11.9	25 28.5	21 29.7	5 49.6	22 16.3	25 29.4	24 57.4
14 M	5 29 28	21 42 33	25 48 19	2♈54 7	24 26.8	4 47.8	10 27.4	26 4.9	21 21.5	5 55.4	22 14.2	25 30.8	24 56.9
15 Tu	5 33 25	22 43 35	10♈ 2 0	17 11 40	24 25.6	6 14.7	11 42.8	26 41.3	21 13.3	6 1.1	22 12.0	25 32.2	24 56.4
16 W	5 37 22	23 44 38	24 22 42	1♉34 38	24 22.9	7 42.4	12 58.3	27 17.6	21 5.1	6 6.8	22 9.9	25 33.6	24 55.8
17 Th	5 41 18	24 45 40	8♉46 55	15 58 56	24 19.1	9 10.6	14 13.7	27 54.0	20 57.0	6 12.4	22 7.7	25 35.0	24 55.2
18 F	5 45 15	25 46 44	23 10 2	0♊19 31	24 14.7	10 39.4	15 29.2	28 30.3	20 48.9	6 18.0	22 5.4	25 36.3	24 54.7
19 Sa	5 49 11	26 47 47	7♊26 42	14 30 57	24 10.4	12 8.6	16 44.7	29 6.6	20 40.8	6 23.5	22 3.2	25 37.6	24 54.0
20 Su	5 53 8	27 48 52	21 31 38	28 28 13	24 6.8	13 38.3	18 0.1	29 42.8	20 32.8	6 28.9	22 0.9	25 38.9	24 53.4
21 M	5 57 4	28 49 56	5♋20 15	12♋ 7 24	24 4.3	15 8.4	19 15.6	0♏19.1	20 24.7	6 34.3	21 58.6	25 40.2	24 52.7
22 Tu	6 1 1	29 51 2	18 49 24	25 26 9	24D 3.2	16 38.8	20 31.1	0 55.2	20 16.8	6 39.6	21 56.2	25 41.4	24 52.0
23 W	6 4 57	0♑52 7	1♌57 37	8♌23 53	24 3.3	18 9.5	21 46.5	1 31.4	20 8.9	6 44.9	21 53.9	25 42.6	24 51.3
24 Th	6 8 54	1 53 14	14 45 9	21 1 42	24 4.4	19 40.6	23 2.0	2 7.5	20 1.0	6 50.0	21 51.5	25 43.7	24 50.6
25 F	6 12 51	2 54 21	27 13 53	3♍22 8	24 6.0	21 12.0	24 17.5	2 43.6	19 53.2	6 55.1	21 49.1	25 44.9	24 49.8
26 Sa	6 16 47	3 55 28	9♍26 55	15 28 46	24 7.7	22 43.6	25 33.0	3 19.7	19 45.5	7 0.2	21 46.7	25 46.0	24 49.0
27 Su	6 20 44	4 56 36	21 28 16	27 25 58	24 9.0	24 15.6	26 48.5	3 55.7	19 37.9	7 5.1	21 44.2	25 47.0	24 48.1
28 M	6 24 40	5 57 44	3♎22 30	9♎18 28	24R 9.6	25 47.8	28 4.0	4 31.7	19 30.3	7 10.0	21 41.7	25 48.1	24 47.3
29 Tu	6 28 37	6 58 53	15 14 28	21 11 7	24 9.4	27 20.3	29 19.5	5 7.7	19 22.8	7 14.8	21 39.3	25 49.1	24 46.4
30 W	6 32 33	8 0 2	27 8 58	3♏ 8 37	24 8.3	28 53.2	0♑34.9	5 43.6	19 15.5	7 19.5	21 36.8	25 50.0	24 45.5
31 Th	6 36 30	9 1 12	9♏10 34	15 15 17	24 6.7	0♑26.3	1 50.4	6 19.5	19 8.2	7 24.2	21 34.2	25 51.0	24 44.6

Astro Data Dy Hr Mn	Planet Ingress Dy Hr Mn	Last Aspect Dy Hr Mn	☽ Ingress Dy Hr Mn	Last Aspect Dy Hr Mn	☽ Ingress Dy Hr Mn	☽ Phases & Eclipses Dy Hr Mn
☽0S 2 6:58	♂ ♎ 1 14:19	2 17:32 ♃ □	♎ 3 1:51	2 11:57 ♆ ☌	♏ 2 21:30	6 17:58 ● 14♏02
☿ R 3 21:50	☿ ♏ 6 22:19	5 5:42 ♃ △	♏ 5 14:12	5 7:13 ♀ ☌	♐ 5 8:09	14 7:52 ☽ 21♒39
♂0S 6 6:32	♀ ♏ 11 18:12	7 23:57 ☿ ☌	♐ 8 1:06	7 7:56 ♆ ✶	♑ 7 16:33	20 23:12 ○ 28♉21
♃✶♇ 14 9:26	☉ ♐ 22 14:22	10 6:51 ♀ ✶	♑ 10 10:18	9 21:10 ☿ ✶	♒ 9 22:59	28 8:16 ☽ 5♍49
☽0N 16 8:47		12 8:44 ☿ ✶	♒ 12 17:31	11 19:53 ☿ ✶	♓ 12 3:46	
♃△♆ 16 23:10	♀ ♐ 5 16:24	14 13:38 ♇ ☍	♓ 14 22:17	13 17:57 ♅ △	♈ 14 7:06	6 10:48 ● 14♐02
☿ D 23 22:55	☿ ♐ 10 14:48	16 15:57 ♃ □	♈ 17 0:35	16 5:05 ♂ ☍	♉ 16 9:22	13 16:30 ☽ 21♓23
♆✶♇ 26 0:44	♂ ♏ 20 11:22	18 17:12 ♇ △	♉ 19 1:15	18 2:55 ♇ □	♊ 18 11:27	20 11:44 ○ 28♊19
♇ R 26 20:44	☉ ♑ 22 3:31	20 23:12 ☉ ☍	♊ 21 1:54	20 11:44 ☉ ☍	♋ 20 14:40	28 5:43 ☽ 6♎12
☽0S 29 13:18	♀ ♑ 29 12:53	22 19:54 ♇ ✶	♋ 23 4:31	22 12:29 ♆ □	♌ 22 20:23	
♃⚺♅ 5 9:58	☿ ♑ 30 17:14	25 1:21 ♆ □	♌ 25 10:40	24 21:07 ♆ ✶	♍ 25 5:24	
☽0N 13 14:10		27 10:55 ♆ ✶	♍ 27 20:41	27 12:01 ♀ □	♎ 27 17:11	
♃⚼♄ 15 21:06		29 19:25 ♃ □	♎ 30 9:06	30 4:00 ☿ ✶	♏ 30 5:43	
☽0S 26 20:50						

Astro Data

1 NOVEMBER 1953
Julian Day # 19663
Delta T 30.7 sec
SVP 05♓54'02"
Obliquity 23°26'48"
⚷ Chiron 16♑22.8
☽ Mean ☊ 27♑58.9

1 DECEMBER 1953
Julian Day # 19693
Delta T 30.7 sec
SVP 05♓53'58"
Obliquity 23°26'47"
⚷ Chiron 18♑20.0
☽ Mean ☊ 26♑23.6

LONGITUDE JANUARY 1954

Day	Sid.Time	☉	0 hr ☽	Noon ☽	True ☊	☿	♀	♂	♃	♄	♅	♆	♇
1 F	6 40 26	10♑ 2 22	21♏23 14	27♏34 46	24♑ 4.6	1♑59.7	3♑ 5.9	6♏55.4	19♊ 1.0	7♏28.8	21♋31.7	25♎51.9	24♌43.7
2 Sa	6 44 23	11 3 33	3♐50 14	10♐ 9 51	24R 2.5	3 33.5	4 21.4	7 31.2	18R 54.0	7 33.3	21R 29.2	25 52.8	24R 42.7
3 Su	6 48 20	12 4 44	16 33 48	23 2 11	24 0.7	5 7.6	5 36.9	8 6.9	18 47.0	7 37.7	21 26.6	25 53.6	24 41.7
4 M	6 52 16	13 5 54	29 35 2	6♑12 17	23 59.3	6 42.0	6 52.5	8 42.7	18 40.2	7 42.1	21 24.0	25 54.4	24 40.7
5 Tu	6 56 13	14 7 5	12♑53 48	19 39 23	23D 58.6	8 16.8	8 8.0	9 18.3	18 33.5	7 46.3	21 21.5	25 55.2	24 39.7
6 W	7 0 9	15 8 16	26 28 48	3♒21 42	23 58.4	9 52.0	9 23.5	9 54.0	18 26.9	7 50.5	21 18.9	25 56.0	24 38.6
7 Th	7 4 6	16 9 27	10♒17 44	17 16 31	23 58.7	11 27.5	10 38.9	10 29.6	18 20.5	7 54.6	21 16.3	25 56.7	24 37.5
8 F	7 8 2	17 10 37	24 17 39	1♓20 42	23 59.3	13 3.5	11 54.4	11 5.1	18 14.2	7 58.6	21 13.7	25 57.4	24 36.4
9 Sa	7 11 59	18 11 47	8♓25 16	15 30 57	23 59.9	14 39.8	13 9.9	11 40.6	18 8.0	8 2.5	21 11.1	25 58.0	24 35.3
10 Su	7 15 56	19 12 56	22 37 21	29 44 6	24 0.4	16 16.6	14 25.4	12 16.1	18 2.0	8 6.4	21 8.5	25 58.6	24 34.2
11 M	7 19 52	20 14 5	6♈50 53	13♈57 21	24 0.7	17 53.8	15 40.9	12 51.5	17 56.2	8 10.1	21 5.9	25 59.2	24 33.0
12 Tu	7 23 49	21 15 13	21 3 13	28 8 13	24R 0.8	19 31.4	16 56.3	13 26.8	17 50.5	8 13.8	21 3.3	25 59.7	24 31.9
13 W	7 27 45	22 16 21	5♉12 6	12♉14 35	24 0.7	21 9.5	18 11.8	14 2.1	17 45.0	8 17.3	21 0.7	26 0.2	24 30.7
14 Th	7 31 42	23 17 28	19 15 26	26 14 26	24D 0.7	22 48.1	19 27.3	14 37.3	17 39.6	8 20.8	20 58.1	26 0.7	24 29.5
15 F	7 35 38	24 18 34	3♊11 20	10♊ 5 54	24 0.7	24 27.2	20 42.7	15 12.5	17 34.4	8 24.2	20 55.5	26 1.2	24 28.3
16 Sa	7 39 35	25 19 40	16 57 54	23 47 7	24 0.8	26 6.8	21 58.1	15 47.7	17 29.4	8 27.5	20 52.9	26 1.6	24 27.0
17 Su	7 43 31	26 20 45	0♋33 20	7♋16 22	24 0.9	27 46.9	23 13.6	16 22.8	17 24.5	8 30.7	20 50.3	26 2.0	24 25.8
18 M	7 47 28	27 21 49	13 56 0	20 32 7	24R 1.1	29 27.5	24 29.0	16 57.8	17 19.8	8 33.8	20 47.7	26 2.3	24 24.5
19 Tu	7 51 25	28 22 52	27 4 34	3♌33 18	24 1.2	1♒ 8.7	25 44.4	17 32.8	17 15.3	8 36.9	20 45.1	26 2.6	24 23.2
20 W	7 55 21	29 23 55	9♌58 15	16 19 27	24 1.0	2 50.3	26 59.8	18 7.8	17 11.0	8 39.8	20 42.5	26 2.9	24 21.9
21 Th	7 59 18	0♒24 58	22 36 57	28 50 54	24 0.4	4 32.4	28 15.3	18 42.6	17 6.8	8 42.6	20 40.0	26 3.1	24 20.6
22 F	8 3 14	1 25 59	5♍ 1 26	11♍ 8 50	23 59.5	6 15.0	29 30.7	19 17.5	17 2.9	8 45.4	20 37.4	26 3.3	24 19.3
23 Sa	8 7 11	2 27 1	17 13 21	23 15 20	23 58.4	7 58.1	0♒46.1	19 52.2	16 59.1	8 48.0	20 34.9	26 3.5	24 18.0
24 Su	8 11 7	3 28 1	29 15 11	5♎13 19	23 57.1	9 41.6	2 1.4	20 26.9	16 55.5	8 50.6	20 32.3	26 3.6	24 16.6
25 M	8 15 4	4 29 1	11♎10 14	17 6 26	23 55.9	11 25.5	3 16.8	21 1.6	16 52.1	8 53.0	20 29.8	26 3.7	24 15.2
26 Tu	8 19 0	5 30 0	23 2 27	28 58 52	23 55.0	13 9.7	4 32.2	21 36.2	16 48.9	8 55.4	20 27.3	26 3.8	24 13.9
27 W	8 22 57	6 30 59	4♏56 16	10♏55 14	23D 54.6	14 54.2	5 47.6	22 10.7	16 45.9	8 57.6	20 24.8	26R 3.8	24 12.5
28 Th	8 26 54	7 31 58	16 56 21	23 0 15	23 54.8	16 38.9	7 3.0	22 45.2	16 43.1	8 59.8	20 22.4	26 3.8	24 11.1
29 F	8 30 50	8 32 55	29 7 28	5♐18 34	23 55.6	18 23.6	8 18.3	23 19.6	16 40.5	9 1.8	20 19.9	26 3.8	24 9.7
30 Sa	8 34 47	9 33 52	11♐34 4	17 54 24	23 56.9	20 8.4	9 33.7	23 53.9	16 38.0	9 3.8	20 17.5	26 3.7	24 8.3
31 Su	8 38 43	10 34 49	24 19 58	0♑51 5	23 58.3	21 52.9	10 49.1	24 28.2	16 35.8	9 5.6	20 15.1	26 3.6	24 6.9

LONGITUDE FEBRUARY 1954

Day	Sid.Time	☉	0 hr ☽	Noon ☽	True ☊	☿	♀	♂	♃	♄	♅	♆	♇
1 M	8 42 40	11♒35 44	7♑27 57	14♑10 41	23♑59.5	23♒37.0	12♒ 4.4	25♏ 2.4	16♊33.8	9♏ 7.4	20♋12.7	26♎ 3.5	24♌ 5.4
2 Tu	8 46 36	12 36 39	20 59 17	27 53 35	24R 0.1	25 20.5	13 19.7	25 36.5	16R 32.0	9 9.0	20R 10.4	26R 3.3	24R 4.0
3 W	8 50 33	13 37 32	4♒53 19	11♒58 4	23 59.9	27 3.2	14 35.1	26 10.6	16 30.4	9 10.5	20 8.0	26 3.1	24 2.6
4 Th	8 54 29	14 38 25	19 7 18	26 20 21	23 58.5	28 44.7	15 50.4	26 44.5	16 29.0	9 12.0	20 5.7	26 2.9	24 1.1
5 F	8 58 26	15 39 16	3♓36 27	10♓54 48	23 56.1	0♓24.6	17 5.7	27 18.4	16 27.8	9 13.3	20 3.4	26 2.6	23 59.6
6 Sa	9 2 23	16 40 6	18 14 30	25 34 41	23 53.0	2 2.7	18 21.0	27 52.2	16 26.8	9 14.5	20 1.2	26 2.3	23 58.2
7 Su	9 6 19	17 40 55	2♈54 30	10♈13 9	23 49.6	3 38.4	19 36.3	28 25.9	16 26.0	9 15.7	19 58.9	26 1.9	23 56.7
8 M	9 10 16	18 41 42	17 29 54	24 44 8	23 46.5	5 11.2	20 51.5	28 59.5	16 25.4	9 16.7	19 56.7	26 1.6	23 55.3
9 Tu	9 14 12	19 42 27	1♉55 19	9♉ 3 5	23 44.3	6 40.6	22 6.8	29 33.1	16 25.0	9 17.6	19 54.5	26 1.2	23 53.8
10 W	9 18 9	20 43 11	16 7 7	23 7 15	23D 43.2	8 6.0	23 22.0	0♐ 6.6	16D 24.8	9 18.4	19 52.4	26 0.7	23 52.3
11 Th	9 22 5	21 43 54	0♊ 3 23	6♊55 31	23 43.4	9 26.6	24 37.3	0 39.9	16 24.8	9 19.1	19 50.3	26 0.3	23 50.8
12 F	9 26 2	22 44 34	13 43 43	20 28 3	23 44.6	10 41.9	25 52.5	1 13.2	16 25.0	9 19.7	19 48.2	25 59.7	23 49.4
13 Sa	9 29 58	23 45 14	27 8 40	3♋45 43	23 46.2	11 51.0	27 7.7	1 46.4	16 25.5	9 20.2	19 46.2	25 59.2	23 47.9
14 Su	9 33 55	24 45 51	10♋19 22	16 49 44	23 47.7	12 53.3	28 22.9	2 19.5	16 26.1	9 20.6	19 44.2	25 58.7	23 46.4
15 M	9 37 52	25 46 27	23 16 59	29 41 15	23R 48.4	13 48.1	29 38.0	2 52.5	16 26.9	9 20.9	19 42.2	25 58.1	23 44.9
16 Tu	9 41 48	26 47 1	6♌ 2 39	12♌21 17	23 47.7	14 34.6	0♓53.2	3 25.5	16 28.0	9 21.1	19 40.3	25 57.4	23 43.5
17 W	9 45 45	27 47 34	18 37 15	24 50 38	23 45.2	15 12.2	2 8.3	3 58.3	16 29.2	9R 21.2	19 38.4	25 56.8	23 42.0
18 Th	9 49 41	28 48 4	1♍ 1 32	7♍10 4	23 41.0	15 40.4	3 23.4	4 31.0	16 30.6	9 21.1	19 36.5	25 56.1	23 40.5
19 F	9 53 38	29 48 34	13 16 19	19 20 25	23 35.2	15 58.8	4 38.5	5 3.6	16 32.2	9 21.0	19 34.7	25 55.4	23 39.0
20 Sa	9 57 34	0♓49 2	25 22 34	1♎22 55	23 28.2	16R 7.1	5 53.6	5 36.2	16 34.1	9 20.8	19 32.9	25 54.6	23 37.6
21 Su	10 1 31	1 49 28	7♎21 44	13 19 15	23 20.8	16 5.2	7 8.7	6 8.6	16 36.1	9 20.4	19 31.2	25 53.8	23 36.1
22 M	10 5 27	2 49 53	19 15 49	25 11 47	23 13.8	15 53.3	8 23.7	6 40.9	16 38.3	9 20.0	19 29.5	25 53.0	23 34.7
23 Tu	10 9 24	3 50 16	1♏ 7 33	7♏ 3 35	23 7.7	15 31.5	9 38.8	7 13.1	16 40.7	9 19.5	19 27.8	25 52.2	23 33.2
24 W	10 13 21	4 50 38	13 0 20	18 58 23	23 3.3	15 0.5	10 53.8	7 45.2	16 43.3	9 18.8	19 26.2	25 51.3	23 31.8
25 Th	10 17 17	5 50 59	24 58 15	1♐ 0 32	23 0.7	14 21.1	12 8.8	8 17.2	16 46.0	9 18.1	19 24.6	25 50.4	23 30.3
26 F	10 21 14	6 51 19	7♐ 5 52	13 14 50	22D 59.9	13 34.3	13 23.8	8 49.1	16 49.0	9 17.2	19 23.1	25 49.5	23 28.9
27 Sa	10 25 10	7 51 36	19 28 4	25 46 10	23 0.6	12 41.3	14 38.8	9 20.9	16 52.2	9 16.3	19 21.6	25 48.6	23 27.5
28 Su	10 29 7	8 51 53	2♑ 9 42	8♑39 10	23 1.9	11 43.5	15 53.7	9 52.5	16 55.5	9 15.2	19 20.2	25 47.6	23 26.0

Astro Data	Planet Ingress	Last Aspect	☽ Ingress	Last Aspect	☽ Ingress	☽ Phases & Eclipses	Astro Data
Dy Hr Mn	Dy Hr Mn	Dy Hr Mn	Dy Hr Mn	Dy Hr Mn	Dy Hr Mn	Dy Hr Mn	1 JANUARY 1954
☽0N 9 19:18	☿ ♒ 18 7:43	1 6:29 ♇ □	♐ 1 16:39	2 8:49 ♆ □	♒ 2 15:38	5 2:21 ● 14♑13	Julian Day # 19724
☽0S 23 5:13	☉ ♒ 20 14:11	3 17:16 ♆ ✶	♑ 4 0:45	4 13:11 ♂ □	♓ 4 18:03	5 2:31:27 ☾ A 1'42"	Delta T 30.7 sec
♆ R 27 10:50	♀ ♒ 22 9:20	5 23:02 ♆ □	♒ 6 6:09	6 16:23 ♂ △	♈ 6 19:14	12 0:22 ☽ 21♈16	SVP 05♓53'52"
		8 2:50 ♆ △	♓ 8 9:43	8 14:09 ♆ ☍	♉ 8 20:47	19 2:37 ○ 28♋30	Obliquity 23°26'46"
☽0N 6 2:44	☿ ♓ 4 18:03	9 21:31 ♅ △	♈ 10 12:27	10 13:39 ♀ □	♊ 10 23:54	19 2:32 ☍T 1.032	⚷ Chiron 20♑59.5
♃ D 10 9:27	♂ ♐ 9 19:18	12 8:22 ♆ ☍	♉ 12 15:10	12 23:58 ♀ △	♋ 13 5:10	27 3:28 ☽ 6♏40	☽ Mean ☊ 24♑45.1
♄ R 17 6:16	♀ ♓ 15 7:01	14 8:59 ♇ □	♊ 14 18:29	15 5:01 ♆ □	♌ 15 12:35		
☽0S 19 13:18	☉ ♓ 19 4:32	16 15:58 ♆ △	♋ 16 23:01	17 19:17 ☉ ☍	♍ 17 22:00	3 15:55 ● 14♒18	1 FEBRUARY 1954
☿ R 20 7:33		19 2:37 ☉ ☍	♌ 19 5:24	19 12:26 ♅ ✶	♎ 20 9:14	10 8:29 ☽ 21♉05	Julian Day # 19755
		21 6:36 ♆ ✶	♍ 21 14:14	22 13:23 ♆ ☌	♏ 22 21:43	17 19:17 ○ 28♌36	Delta T 30.8 sec
		23 6:39 ♅ ✶	♎ 24 1:30	24 21:05 ♇ □	♐ 25 10:00	25 23:29 ☽ 6♐50	SVP 05♓53'46"
		26 6:07 ♆ ☌	♏ 26 14:03	27 12:04 ♆ ✶	♑ 27 19:58		Obliquity 23°26'46"
		28 14:18 ♇ □	♐ 29 1:42				⚷ Chiron 23♑49.0
		31 3:12 ♆ ✶	♑ 31 10:27				☽ Mean ☊ 23♑06.6

MARCH 1954 LONGITUDE

Day	Sid.Time	☉	0 hr ☽	Noon ☽	True ☊	☿	♀	♂	♃	♄	♅	♆	♇
1 M	10 33 3	9♓52 8	15♑15 1	21♑57 35	23♑ 3.1	10♓42.5	17♓ 8.7	10♐24.0	16♊59.1	9♏14.1	19♋18.8	25♎46.6	23♌24.6
2 Tu	10 37 0	10 52 21	28 47 7	5♒43 40	23R 3.2	9R39.6	18 23.6	10 55.4	17 2.8	9R12.8	19R17.4	25R45.6	23R23.2
3 W	10 40 56	11 52 33	12♒47 9	19 57 16	23 1.5	8 36.6	19 38.5	11 26.6	17 6.7	9 11.4	19 16.1	25 44.5	23 21.8
4 Th	10 44 53	12 52 43	27 13 33	4♓35 18	22 57.5	7 34.8	20 53.4	11 57.7	17 10.8	9 10.0	19 14.9	25 43.4	23 20.4
5 F	10 48 50	13 52 51	12♓ 1 39	19 31 31	22 51.3	6 35.5	22 8.3	12 28.7	17 15.0	9 8.4	19 13.6	25 42.3	23 19.1
6 Sa	10 52 46	14 52 58	27 3 46	4♈37 6	22 43.6	5 40.0	23 23.1	12 59.5	17 19.5	9 6.8	19 12.5	25 41.2	23 17.7
7 Su	10 56 43	15 53 2	12♈10 16	19 41 58	22 35.1	4 49.0	24 38.0	13 30.2	17 24.1	9 5.0	19 11.4	25 40.0	23 16.4
8 M	11 0 39	16 53 5	27 11 5	4♉36 34	22 27.1	4 3.5	25 52.8	14 0.7	17 28.9	9 3.2	19 10.3	25 38.9	23 15.0
9 Tu	11 4 36	17 53 5	11♉57 33	19 13 23	22 20.5	3 24.0	27 7.6	14 31.0	17 33.9	9 1.2	19 9.3	25 37.7	23 13.7
10 W	11 8 32	18 53 4	26 23 34	3♊27 51	22 16.1	2 50.8	28 22.3	15 1.2	17 39.0	8 59.2	19 8.3	25 36.4	23 12.4
11 Th	11 12 29	19 53 0	10♊26 6	17 18 22	22D 13.9	2 24.1	29 37.1	15 31.3	17 44.3	8 57.1	19 7.4	25 35.2	23 11.1
12 F	11 16 25	20 52 54	24 4 50	0♋45 45	22 13.5	2 4.0	0♈51.8	16 1.2	17 49.8	8 54.9	19 6.6	25 33.9	23 9.8
13 Sa	11 20 22	21 52 46	7♋21 28	13 52 21	22 14.2	1 50.6	2 6.5	16 30.9	17 55.5	8 52.6	19 5.8	25 32.7	23 8.5
14 Su	11 24 19	22 52 35	20 18 50	26 41 18	22R 14.8	1D 43.5	3 21.2	17 0.5	18 1.3	8 50.2	19 5.0	25 31.3	23 7.3
15 M	11 28 15	23 52 23	3♌ 0 11	9♌15 52	22 14.2	1 42.7	4 35.8	17 29.8	18 7.3	8 47.7	19 4.3	25 30.0	23 6.0
16 Tu	11 32 12	24 52 8	15 28 41	21 38 59	22 11.6	1 47.9	5 50.4	17 59.1	18 13.4	8 45.1	19 3.7	25 28.7	23 4.8
17 W	11 36 8	25 51 50	27 47 2	3♍53 7	22 6.3	1 58.9	7 5.0	18 28.1	18 19.7	8 42.5	19 3.1	25 27.3	23 3.6
18 Th	11 40 5	26 51 31	9♍57 25	16 0 9	21 58.3	2 15.3	8 19.6	18 57.0	18 26.1	8 39.7	19 2.5	25 25.9	23 2.4
19 F	11 44 1	27 51 10	22 1 29	28 1 33	21 47.7	2 36.9	9 34.1	19 25.6	18 32.7	8 36.9	19 2.0	25 24.5	23 1.2
20 Sa	11 47 58	28 50 46	4♎ 0 32	9♎58 32	21 35.4	3 3.3	10 48.6	19 54.1	18 39.5	8 34.0	19 1.6	25 23.1	23 0.1
21 Su	11 51 54	29 50 21	15 55 45	21 52 20	21 22.3	3 34.4	12 3.1	20 22.4	18 46.3	8 31.0	19 1.2	25 21.7	22 59.0
22 M	11 55 51	0♈49 53	27 48 30	3♏44 27	21 9.4	4 9.8	13 17.5	20 50.5	18 53.4	8 28.0	19 0.8	25 20.2	22 57.8
23 Tu	11 59 47	1 49 24	9♏40 28	15 36 53	20 58.0	4 49.2	14 32.0	21 18.4	19 0.6	8 24.8	19 0.6	25 18.8	22 56.7
24 W	12 3 44	2 48 53	21 34 1	27 32 18	20 48.7	5 32.5	15 46.4	21 46.1	19 7.9	8 21.6	19 0.3	25 17.3	22 55.7
25 Th	12 7 41	3 48 20	3♐32 9	9♐34 5	20 42.2	6 19.4	17 0.8	22 13.6	19 15.4	8 18.3	19 0.2	25 15.8	22 54.6
26 F	12 11 37	4 47 46	15 38 37	21 46 20	20 38.3	7 9.7	18 15.1	22 40.9	19 23.0	8 15.0	19 0.0	25 14.3	22 53.6
27 Sa	12 15 34	5 47 9	27 57 49	4♑13 40	20D 36.7	8 3.2	19 29.4	23 7.9	19 30.8	8 11.6	18D 60.0	25 12.8	22 52.5
28 Su	12 19 30	6 46 31	10♑34 31	17 0 56	20R 36.5	8 59.6	20 43.8	23 34.7	19 38.7	8 8.1	18 60.0	25 11.3	22 51.5
29 M	12 23 27	7 45 51	23 33 30	0♒12 41	20 36.6	9 59.0	21 58.0	24 1.3	19 46.7	8 4.5	19 0.0	25 9.7	22 50.6
30 Tu	12 27 23	8 45 10	6♒58 55	13 52 28	20 35.8	11 1.0	23 12.3	24 27.6	19 54.9	8 0.9	19 0.1	25 8.2	22 49.6
31 W	12 31 20	9 44 26	20 53 28	28 1 53	20 33.0	12 5.6	24 26.5	24 53.7	20 3.2	7 57.2	19 0.2	25 6.6	22 48.7

APRIL 1954 LONGITUDE

Day	Sid.Time	☉	0 hr ☽	Noon ☽	True ☊	☿	♀	♂	♃	♄	♅	♆	♇
1 Th	12 35 16	10♈43 41	5♓17 26	12♓39 37	20♑27.5	13♓12.6	25♈40.7	25♐19.5	20♊11.6	7♏53.4	19♋ 0.4	25♎ 5.0	22♌47.8
2 F	12 39 13	11 42 54	20 7 43	27 40 45	20R 19.4	14 21.9	26 54.9	25 45.1	20 20.1	7R 49.6	19 0.7	25R 3.4	22R 46.9
3 Sa	12 43 10	12 42 4	5♈17 32	12♈56 44	20 9.2	15 33.5	28 9.1	26 10.4	20 28.8	7 45.8	19 1.0	25 1.8	22 46.0
4 Su	12 47 6	13 41 13	20 36 53	28 16 29	19 58.0	16 47.2	29 23.2	26 35.4	20 37.6	7 41.8	19 1.4	25 0.2	22 45.2
5 M	12 51 3	14 40 20	5♉54 6	13♉28 22	19 47.1	18 3.0	0♉37.3	27 0.1	20 46.6	7 37.9	19 1.8	24 58.6	22 44.4
6 Tu	12 54 59	15 39 25	20 58 4	28 22 16	19 37.8	19 20.7	1 51.4	27 24.5	20 55.6	7 33.8	19 2.3	24 57.0	22 43.6
7 W	12 58 56	16 38 28	5♊40 10	12♊51 17	19 31.0	20 40.4	3 5.4	27 48.7	21 4.8	7 29.8	19 2.8	24 55.4	22 42.8
8 Th	13 2 52	17 37 28	19 55 18	26 52 10	19 26.8	22 1.9	4 19.4	28 12.5	21 14.1	7 25.6	19 3.4	24 53.8	22 42.1
9 F	13 6 49	18 36 26	3♋41 57	10♋24 57	19 25.0	23 25.2	5 33.4	28 36.0	21 23.5	7 21.5	19 4.0	24 52.2	22 41.3
10 Sa	13 10 45	19 35 22	17 1 30	23 32 4	19 24.7	24 50.3	6 47.3	28 59.2	21 33.0	7 17.3	19 4.7	24 50.5	22 40.6
11 Su	13 14 42	20 34 15	29 57 9	6♌17 18	19 24.6	26 17.1	8 1.3	29 22.1	21 42.6	7 13.0	19 5.4	24 48.9	22 40.0
12 M	13 18 39	21 33 6	12♌33 4	18 44 59	19 23.5	27 45.7	9 15.1	29 44.7	21 52.4	7 8.7	19 6.2	24 47.3	22 39.3
13 Tu	13 22 35	22 31 55	24 53 36	0♍59 24	19 20.4	29 15.9	10 29.0	0♑ 6.9	22 2.2	7 4.4	19 7.1	24 45.6	22 38.7
14 W	13 26 32	23 30 41	7♍ 2 51	13 4 22	19 14.5	0♈47.8	11 42.8	0 28.8	22 12.1	7 0.1	19 8.0	24 44.0	22 38.1
15 Th	13 30 28	24 29 26	19 4 18	25 3 1	19 5.8	2 21.4	12 56.6	0 50.4	22 22.2	6 55.7	19 8.9	24 42.3	22 37.6
16 F	13 34 25	25 28 8	1♎ 0 48	6♎57 54	18 54.5	3 56.6	14 10.3	1 11.6	22 32.3	6 51.3	19 9.9	24 40.7	22 37.0
17 Sa	13 38 21	26 26 48	12 54 32	18 50 54	18 41.2	5 33.4	15 24.0	1 32.4	22 42.6	6 46.9	19 11.0	24 39.0	22 36.5
18 Su	13 42 18	27 25 26	24 47 11	0♏43 32	18 27.1	7 11.9	16 37.7	1 52.9	22 52.9	6 42.4	19 12.1	24 37.4	22 36.0
19 M	13 46 14	28 24 2	6♏40 7	12 37 7	18 13.3	8 52.0	17 51.3	2 13.0	23 3.4	6 37.9	19 13.2	24 35.7	22 35.6
20 Tu	13 50 11	29 22 37	18 34 43	24 33 6	18 0.8	10 33.7	19 4.9	2 32.6	23 13.9	6 33.4	19 14.4	24 34.1	22 35.1
21 W	13 54 8	0♉21 9	0♐32 32	6♐33 16	17 50.6	12 17.1	20 18.5	2 51.9	23 24.5	6 28.9	19 15.7	24 32.5	22 34.7
22 Th	13 58 4	1 19 40	12 35 37	18 39 56	17 43.2	14 2.2	21 32.0	3 10.8	23 35.3	6 24.4	19 17.0	24 30.8	22 34.4
23 F	14 2 1	2 18 9	24 46 36	0♑56 4	17 38.6	15 48.9	22 45.5	3 29.3	23 46.1	6 19.8	19 18.4	24 29.2	22 34.0
24 Sa	14 5 57	3 16 37	7♑ 8 47	13 25 16	17D 36.5	17 37.3	23 59.0	3 47.3	23 57.0	6 15.3	19 19.8	24 27.6	22 33.7
25 Su	14 9 54	4 15 3	19 46 1	26 11 34	17 36.2	19 27.4	25 12.5	4 4.9	24 8.0	6 10.7	19 21.2	24 26.0	22 33.4
26 M	14 13 50	5 13 27	2♒42 25	9♒19 5	17R 36.4	21 19.2	26 25.9	4 22.0	24 19.0	6 6.2	19 22.7	24 24.4	22 33.1
27 Tu	14 17 47	6 11 50	16 1 58	22 51 27	17 36.1	23 12.6	27 39.3	4 38.6	24 30.2	6 1.6	19 24.3	24 22.8	22 32.9
28 W	14 21 43	7 10 11	29 47 45	6♓50 58	17 34.2	25 7.8	28 52.6	4 54.8	24 41.4	5 57.1	19 25.9	24 21.2	22 32.7
29 Th	14 25 40	8 8 30	14♓ 1 2	21 17 40	17 30.0	27 4.6	0♊ 5.9	5 10.5	24 52.7	5 52.5	19 27.5	24 19.6	22 32.5
30 F	14 29 37	9 6 48	28 40 24	6♈ 8 31	17 23.4	29 3.0	1 19.2	5 25.7	25 4.1	5 47.9	19 29.2	24 18.0	22 32.3

Astro Data Dy Hr Mn	Planet Ingress Dy Hr Mn	Last Aspect Dy Hr Mn	☽ Ingress Dy Hr Mn	Last Aspect Dy Hr Mn	☽ Ingress Dy Hr Mn	☽ Phases & Eclipses Dy Hr Mn	Astro Data
☽0N 5 12:48	♀ ♈ 11 7:22	1 18:43 ♆ □	♒ 2 2:07	2 9:12 ♂ □	♈ 2 15:40	5 3:11 ● 14♓01	1 MARCH 1954
♀0N 13 15:15	☉ ♈ 21 3:53	3 21:32 ♆ △	♓ 4 4:32	4 9:37 ♂ △	♉ 4 14:43	11 17:52 ☽ 20♊38	Julian Day # 19783
☿ D 14 15:06		5 17:37 ♀ ☌	♈ 6 4:40	6 2:50 ♇ □	♊ 6 14:40	19 12:42 ○ 28♍23	Delta T 30.8 sec
☽0S 18 20:04	♀ ♉ 4 11:55	7 21:32 ♆ ☍	♉ 8 4:32	8 14:46 ♂ ☍	♋ 8 17:29	27 16:14 ☽ 6♑27	SVP 05♓53'43"
♃⚺♅ 22 23:57	♂ ♑ 12 16:28	10 3:40 ♀ ⚹	♊ 10 6:06	10 16:15 ☿ △	♌ 11 0:05		Obliquity 23°26'47"
♅ D 27 17:31	☿ ♈ 13 11:34	12 2:39 ♆ △	♋ 12 10:37	12 23:44 ♆ ⚹	♍ 13 10:03	3 12:25 ● 13♈13	⚷ Chiron 26♑06.1
	☉ ♉ 20 15:20	14 9:47 ♆ □	♌ 14 18:17	15 6:43 ♃ □	♎ 15 21:58	10 5:05 ☽ 19♋48	☽ Mean ☊ 21♑37.7
☽0N 1 23:43	♀ ♊ 28 22:03	16 19:27 ♆ ⚹	♍ 17 4:21	18 5:48 ☉ ☍	♏ 18 10:32	18 5:48 ○ 27♎40	
♃⚼♄ 13 3:46	☿ ♉ 30 11:26	19 12:42 ☉ ☍	♎ 19 15:57	20 8:03 ♇ □	♐ 20 22:55	26 4:57 ☽ 5♒26	1 APRIL 1954
☽0S 15 1:34		21 19:01 ♆ ☌	♏ 22 4:26	22 23:26 ♆ ⚹	♑ 23 10:11		Julian Day # 19814
♃⚹♇ 16 10:29		24 2:44 ♇ □	♐ 24 16:56	25 11:14 ♀ △	♒ 25 19:02		Delta T 30.8 sec
☿0N 17 3:43		26 18:42 ♆ ⚹	♑ 27 3:55	27 22:16 ♀ □	♓ 28 0:21		SVP 05♓53'39"
♃△♆ 26 10:03		29 2:54 ♆ □	♒ 29 11:37	29 18:05 ♃ □	♈ 30 2:08		Obliquity 23°26'47"
☽0N 29 9:15		31 7:06 ♆ △	♓ 31 15:16				⚷ Chiron 27♑54.9
							☽ Mean ☊ 19♑59.1

LONGITUDE — MAY 1954

Day	Sid.Time	☉	0 hr ☽	Noon ☽	True ☊	☿	♀	♂	♃	♄	♅	♆	♇
1 Sa	14 33 33	10♉ 5 5	13♈41 3	21♈16 55	17♑14.8	1♉ 3.1	2♊32.5	5♑40.3	25♊15.6	5♏43.4	19♋31.0	24♎16.4	22♌32.2
2 Su	14 37 30	11 3 19	28 54 47	6♉33 18	17R 5.1	3 4.7	3 45.7	5 54.5	25 27.2	5R38.8	19 32.8	24R14.8	22R32.1
3 M	14 41 26	12 1 33	14♉11 0	21 46 32	16 55.5	5 7.9	4 58.9	6 8.0	25 38.8	5 34.3	19 34.6	24 13.3	22 32.1
4 Tu	14 45 23	12 59 44	29 18 33	6♊45 56	16 47.3	7 12.5	6 12.1	6 21.1	25 50.5	5 29.8	19 36.5	24 11.7	22D32.0
5 W	14 49 19	13 57 54	14♊ 7 42	21 23 7	16 41.3	9 18.5	7 25.2	6 33.6	26 2.3	5 25.3	19 38.4	24 10.2	22 32.0
6 Th	14 53 16	14 56 2	28 31 40	5♋33 3	16 37.7	11 25.7	8 38.3	6 45.5	26 14.1	5 20.8	19 40.4	24 8.7	22 32.0
7 F	14 57 12	15 54 8	12♋27 10	19 14 7	16D36.3	13 34.0	9 51.3	6 56.8	26 26.0	5 16.4	19 42.4	24 7.2	22 32.1
8 Sa	15 1 9	16 52 13	25 54 7	2♌27 32	16 36.5	15 43.2	11 4.3	7 7.6	26 38.0	5 12.0	19 44.5	24 5.7	22 32.2
9 Su	15 5 6	17 50 15	8♌54 50	15 16 30	16R37.3	17 53.2	12 17.3	7 17.8	26 50.1	5 7.5	19 46.6	24 4.2	22 32.3
10 M	15 9 2	18 48 15	21 33 8	27 45 17	16 37.5	20 3.5	13 30.3	7 27.3	27 2.2	5 3.2	19 48.7	24 2.8	22 32.4
11 Tu	15 12 59	19 46 13	3♍53 34	9♍58 33	16 36.4	22 14.2	14 43.1	7 36.2	27 14.3	4 58.8	19 50.9	24 1.3	22 32.6
12 W	15 16 55	20 44 10	16 0 48	22 0 51	16 33.2	24 24.8	15 56.0	7 44.6	27 26.6	4 54.5	19 53.1	23 59.9	22 32.8
13 Th	15 20 52	21 42 5	27 59 13	3♎56 21	16 27.8	26 35.2	17 8.8	7 52.2	27 38.8	4 50.2	19 55.4	23 58.5	22 33.0
14 F	15 24 48	22 39 58	9♎52 41	15 48 36	16 20.3	28 44.9	18 21.6	7 59.3	27 51.2	4 46.0	19 57.7	23 57.1	22 33.2
15 Sa	15 28 45	23 37 49	21 44 26	27 40 30	16 11.3	0♊53.9	19 34.3	8 5.6	28 3.6	4 41.8	20 0.1	23 55.7	22 33.5
16 Su	15 32 41	24 35 39	3♏37 4	9♏34 22	16 1.5	3 1.6	20 47.0	8 11.3	28 16.0	4 37.6	20 2.5	23 54.3	22 33.8
17 M	15 36 38	25 33 27	15 32 37	21 31 59	15 51.9	5 8.0	21 59.6	8 16.4	28 28.5	4 33.5	20 4.9	23 53.0	22 34.1
18 Tu	15 40 35	26 31 14	27 32 40	3♐34 50	15 43.3	7 12.7	23 12.2	8 20.7	28 41.1	4 29.5	20 7.3	23 51.6	22 34.5
19 W	15 44 31	27 28 59	9♐38 39	15 44 18	15 36.4	9 15.5	24 24.8	8 24.4	28 53.7	4 25.5	20 9.9	23 50.3	22 34.9
20 Th	15 48 28	28 26 44	21 51 59	28 1 54	15 31.6	11 16.2	25 37.3	8 27.3	29 6.4	4 21.5	20 12.4	23 49.0	22 35.3
21 F	15 52 24	29 24 27	4♑14 17	10♑29 24	15D29.0	13 14.6	26 49.8	8 29.5	29 19.1	4 17.6	20 15.0	23 47.8	22 35.8
22 Sa	15 56 21	0♊22 8	16 47 32	23 9 0	15 28.3	15 10.6	28 2.2	8 31.0	29 31.8	4 13.7	20 17.6	23 46.5	22 36.2
23 Su	16 0 17	1 19 49	29 34 7	6♒ 3 12	15 29.0	17 4.0	29 14.6	8R31.8	29 44.6	4 9.9	20 20.3	23 45.3	22 36.7
24 M	16 4 14	2 17 28	12♒36 38	19 14 43	15 30.4	18 54.7	0♋26.9	8 31.8	29 57.5	4 6.1	20 22.9	23 44.1	22 37.3
25 Tu	16 8 10	3 15 7	25 57 45	2♓45 59	15R31.5	20 42.6	1 39.3	8 31.1	0♋10.4	4 2.4	20 25.7	23 42.9	22 37.8
26 W	16 12 7	4 12 44	9♓39 36	16 38 41	15 31.6	22 27.8	2 51.5	8 29.6	0 23.3	3 58.8	20 28.4	23 41.7	22 38.4
27 Th	16 16 4	5 10 21	23 43 13	0♈53 3	15 30.1	24 10.0	4 3.7	8 27.4	0 36.3	3 55.2	20 31.2	23 40.6	22 39.0
28 F	16 20 0	6 7 57	8♈ 7 51	15 27 9	15 27.1	25 49.2	5 15.9	8 24.4	0 49.3	3 51.7	20 34.0	23 39.4	22 39.7
29 Sa	16 23 57	7 5 32	22 50 19	0♉16 33	15 22.6	27 25.5	6 28.1	8 20.6	1 2.3	3 48.3	20 36.9	23 38.3	22 40.3
30 Su	16 27 53	8 3 6	7♉44 55	15 14 23	15 17.3	28 58.7	7 40.2	8 16.0	1 15.4	3 44.9	20 39.8	23 37.3	22 41.0
31 M	16 31 50	9 0 39	22 43 50	0♊12 7	15 12.0	0♋28.9	8 52.2	8 10.7	1 28.5	3 41.6	20 42.7	23 36.2	22 41.7

LONGITUDE — JUNE 1954

Day	Sid.Time	☉	0 hr ☽	Noon ☽	True ☊	☿	♀	♂	♃	♄	♅	♆	♇
1 Tu	16 35 46	9♊58 11	7♊38 9	15♊ 0 52	15♑ 7.5	1♋56.0	10♋ 4.3	8♑ 4.7	1♋41.7	3♏38.4	20♋45.7	23♎35.2	22♌42.5
2 W	16 39 43	10 55 43	22 19 21	29 32 48	15R 4.2	3 20.0	11 16.2	7R57.8	1 54.9	3R35.2	20 48.6	23R34.2	22 43.3
3 Th	16 43 39	11 53 13	6♋40 34	13♋42 13	15D 2.6	4 40.8	12 28.2	7 50.3	2 8.1	3 32.1	20 51.7	23 33.2	22 44.1
4 F	16 47 36	12 50 42	20 37 27	27 26 9	15 2.4	5 58.4	13 40.0	7 42.0	2 21.3	3 29.1	20 54.7	23 32.3	22 44.9
5 Sa	16 51 33	13 48 10	4♌ 8 20	10♌44 10	15 3.4	7 12.7	14 51.9	7 32.9	2 34.6	3 26.2	20 57.8	23 31.4	22 45.7
6 Su	16 55 29	14 45 36	17 13 56	23 37 59	15 5.0	8 23.7	16 3.6	7 23.2	2 47.9	3 23.3	21 0.9	23 30.5	22 46.6
7 M	16 59 26	15 43 2	29 56 47	6♍10 50	15 6.4	9 31.4	17 15.4	7 12.8	3 1.3	3 20.5	21 4.0	23 29.6	22 47.5
8 Tu	17 3 22	16 40 26	12♍20 39	18 26 49	15R 7.3	10 35.6	18 27.0	7 1.7	3 14.6	3 17.8	21 7.1	23 28.8	22 48.4
9 W	17 7 19	17 37 49	24 29 55	0♎30 30	15 7.2	11 36.3	19 38.6	6 49.9	3 28.0	3 15.2	21 10.3	23 27.9	22 49.4
10 Th	17 11 15	18 35 12	6♎29 9	12 26 26	15 5.8	12 33.4	20 50.2	6 37.5	3 41.4	3 12.7	21 13.5	23 27.2	22 50.4
11 F	17 15 12	19 32 33	18 22 50	24 18 54	15 3.4	13 26.9	22 1.7	6 24.5	3 54.8	3 10.2	21 16.7	23 26.4	22 51.4
12 Sa	17 19 8	20 29 53	0♏15 5	6♏11 48	15 0.1	14 16.7	23 13.1	6 10.9	4 8.3	3 7.9	21 20.0	23 25.7	22 52.4
13 Su	17 23 5	21 27 12	12 9 28	18 8 26	14 56.4	15 2.5	24 24.5	5 56.7	4 21.8	3 5.6	21 23.3	23 25.0	22 53.4
14 M	17 27 2	22 24 31	24 9 2	0♐11 31	14 52.7	15 44.5	25 35.8	5 42.0	4 35.2	3 3.4	21 26.5	23 24.3	22 54.5
15 Tu	17 30 58	23 21 48	6♐16 10	12 23 11	14 49.4	16 22.4	26 47.1	5 26.8	4 48.7	3 1.3	21 29.9	23 23.6	22 55.6
16 W	17 34 55	24 19 5	18 32 45	24 45 0	14 46.8	16 56.2	27 58.3	5 11.0	5 2.3	2 59.3	21 33.2	23 23.0	22 56.7
17 Th	17 38 51	25 16 22	1♑ 0 6	7♑18 9	14 45.3	17 25.8	29 9.4	4 54.9	5 15.8	2 57.4	21 36.6	23 22.4	22 57.9
18 F	17 42 48	26 13 38	13 39 15	20 3 29	14D44.7	17 51.0	0♌20.5	4 38.3	5 29.3	2 55.5	21 39.9	23 21.9	22 59.1
19 Sa	17 46 44	27 10 53	26 30 57	3♒ 1 43	14 45.1	18 11.8	1 31.5	4 21.3	5 42.9	2 53.8	21 43.3	23 21.4	23 0.2
20 Su	17 50 41	28 8 8	9♒35 52	16 13 29	14 46.0	18 28.2	2 42.5	4 4.0	5 56.5	2 52.1	21 46.7	23 20.9	23 1.5
21 M	17 54 37	29 5 23	22 54 36	29 39 17	14 47.2	18 40.0	3 53.4	3 46.3	6 10.0	2 50.6	21 50.2	23 20.4	23 2.7
22 Tu	17 58 34	0♋ 2 37	6♓27 35	13♓19 30	14 48.3	18 47.3	5 4.2	3 28.4	6 23.6	2 49.1	21 53.6	23 20.0	23 3.9
23 W	18 2 31	0 59 52	20 15 0	27 14 3	14R49.1	18R50.0	6 15.0	3 10.2	6 37.2	2 47.7	21 57.1	23 19.6	23 5.2
24 Th	18 6 27	1 57 6	4♈16 30	11♈22 10	14 49.3	18 48.1	7 25.7	2 51.8	6 50.8	2 46.4	22 0.6	23 19.2	23 6.5
25 F	18 10 24	2 54 20	18 30 48	25 42 4	14 48.9	18 41.8	8 36.3	2 33.3	7 4.4	2 45.3	22 4.1	23 18.8	23 7.8
26 Sa	18 14 20	3 51 34	2♉55 32	10♉10 42	14 48.1	18 31.0	9 46.9	2 14.7	7 18.1	2 44.2	22 7.6	23 18.5	23 9.2
27 Su	18 18 17	4 48 49	17 27 0	24 43 47	14 47.0	18 16.0	10 57.4	1 56.0	7 31.7	2 43.2	22 11.1	23 18.2	23 10.5
28 M	18 22 13	5 46 3	2♊ 0 22	9♊16 1	14 45.9	17 57.0	12 7.8	1 37.3	7 45.3	2 42.3	22 14.6	23 18.0	23 11.9
29 Tu	18 26 10	6 43 17	16 30 1	23 41 38	14 45.0	17 34.2	13 18.2	1 18.7	7 59.0	2 41.5	22 18.2	23 17.8	23 13.3
30 W	18 30 7	7 40 32	0♋50 12	7♋55 5	14D44.5	17 8.0	14 28.5	1 0.1	8 12.6	2 40.8	22 21.8	23 17.6	23 14.7

Astro Data

	Dy Hr Mn
♇ D	4 17:45
☽0S	12 6:52
♂ R	23 12:47
☽0N	26 16:23
☽0S	8 13:15
♃△♄	8 4:48
☽0N	22 21:47
☿ R	23 2:09
♃∠♇	30 4:13

Planet Ingress

	Dy Hr Mn
☿ ♊	14 13:57
☉ ♊	21 14:47
♀ ♋	23 15:04
♃ ♋	24 4:43
☿ ♋	30 16:13
♀ ♌	17 17:04
☉ ♋	21 22:54

Last Aspect / ☽ Ingress (May)

Last Aspect Dy Hr Mn		☽ Ingress Dy Hr Mn
1 18:30	♃ ⚹	♉ 2 1:42
3 13:12	♇ □	♊ 4 1:06
5 20:04	♃ ☌	♋ 6 2:30
7 20:44	♆ □	♌ 8 7:29
10 10:47	♃ ⚹	♍ 10 16:23
12 23:18	♃ □	♎ 13 4:03
15 13:00	♃ △	♏ 15 16:42
17 21:47	☉ ☍	♐ 18 4:53
20 14:20	♃ ☍	♑ 20 15:49
22 13:09	♆ □	♒ 23 0:48
24 20:00	♆ △	♓ 25 7:08
27 0:51	☿ □	♈ 27 10:32
29 8:17	☿ ⚹	♉ 29 11:33
30 23:57	♇ □	♊ 31 11:40

Last Aspect / ☽ Ingress (June)

Last Aspect Dy Hr Mn		☽ Ingress Dy Hr Mn
2 2:04	♆ △	♋ 2 12:46
4 5:06	♆ □	♌ 4 16:34
6 11:45	♆ ⚹	♍ 7 0:06
8 17:22	♅ ⚹	♎ 9 10:59
11 10:13	♆ ☌	♏ 11 23:30
14 3:12	♀ △	♐ 14 11:37
16 12:06	☉ ☍	♑ 16 22:05
18 18:09	♆ □	♒ 19 6:26
21 11:50	☉ △	♓ 21 12:37
23 2:57	♅ △	♈ 23 16:44
25 8:01	♆ ☍	♉ 25 19:09
27 9:27	♇ □	♊ 27 20:41
29 11:20	♆ △	♋ 29 22:35

☽ Phases & Eclipses

Dy Hr Mn	
2 20:22	● 11♉53
9 18:17	☽ 18♌34
17 21:47	○ 26♏26
25 13:49	☽ 3♓48
1 4:03	● 10♊08
8 9:14	☽ 17♍03
16 12:06	○ 24♐48
23 19:46	☽ 1♈47
30 12:26	● 8♋10
30 12:32:05	✔T 2'35"

Astro Data

1 MAY 1954
Julian Day # 19844
Delta T 30.8 sec
SVP 05♓53'36"
Obliquity 23°26'46"
⚷ Chiron 28♑38.8
☽ Mean ☊ 18♑23.8

1 JUNE 1954
Julian Day # 19875
Delta T 30.9 sec
SVP 05♓53'31"
Obliquity 23°26'45"
⚷ Chiron 28♑13.6R
☽ Mean ☊ 16♑45.3

JULY 1954 — LONGITUDE

Day	Sid.Time	☉	0 hr ☽	Noon ☽	True ☊	☿	♀	♂	♃	♄	♅	♆	♇
1 Th	18 34 3	8♋37 46	14♋55 46	21♋51 46	14♑44.3	16♋38.6	15♌38.7	0♑41.7	8♋26.2	2♏40.2	22♋25.3	23♎17.4	23♌16.2
2 F	18 38 0	9 35 0	28 42 45	5♌28 30	14 44.5	16R 6.6	16 48.8	0R 23.5	8 39.8	2R 39.7	22 28.9	23R 17.3	23 17.6
3 Sa	18 41 56	10 32 13	12♌ 8 51	18 43 48	14 44.8	15 32.5	17 58.9	0 5.5	8 53.5	2 39.2	22 32.5	23 17.2	23 19.1
4 Su	18 45 53	11 29 27	25 13 26	1♍37 55	14 45.2	14 56.7	19 8.9	29♐47.8	9 7.1	2 38.9	22 36.1	23 17.2	23 20.6
5 M	18 49 49	12 26 40	7♍57 32	14 12 37	14 45.5	14 19.9	20 18.8	29 30.4	9 20.7	2 38.7	22 39.7	23D 17.1	23 22.1
6 Tu	18 53 46	13 23 53	20 23 33	26 30 48	14 45.6	13 42.7	21 28.7	29 13.4	9 34.3	2D 38.6	22 43.4	23 17.2	23 23.6
7 W	18 57 42	14 21 6	2♎34 53	8♎36 18	14 45.7	13 5.8	22 38.4	28 56.8	9 47.9	2 38.6	22 47.0	23 17.2	23 25.2
8 Th	19 1 39	15 18 18	14 35 37	20 33 25	14 45.7	12 29.7	23 48.0	28 40.7	10 1.5	2 38.7	22 50.6	23 17.3	23 26.7
9 F	19 5 36	16 15 31	26 30 15	2♏26 41	14 45.7	11 55.1	24 57.6	28 25.1	10 15.1	2 38.9	22 54.3	23 17.4	23 28.3
10 Sa	19 9 32	17 12 43	8♏23 18	14 20 37	14 45.9	11 22.6	26 7.1	28 10.0	10 28.6	2 39.1	22 57.9	23 17.5	23 29.9
11 Su	19 13 29	18 9 55	20 19 11	26 19 29	14 46.2	10 52.9	27 16.5	27 55.4	10 42.2	2 39.5	23 1.6	23 17.7	23 31.5
12 M	19 17 25	19 7 8	2♐21 59	8♐27 6	14 46.6	10 26.3	28 25.7	27 41.5	10 55.7	2 40.0	23 5.2	23 17.9	23 33.2
13 Tu	19 21 22	20 4 20	14 35 13	20 46 39	14 47.1	10 3.5	29 34.9	27 28.2	11 9.2	2 40.6	23 8.9	23 18.1	23 34.8
14 W	19 25 18	21 1 33	27 1 41	3♑20 33	14 47.6	9 44.8	0♍44.0	27 15.5	11 22.8	2 41.3	23 12.5	23 18.4	23 36.4
15 Th	19 29 15	21 58 45	9♑43 22	16 10 17	14R 47.8	9 30.7	1 53.0	27 3.5	11 36.3	2 42.0	23 16.2	23 18.7	23 38.1
16 F	19 33 11	22 55 58	22 41 17	29 16 22	14 47.8	9 21.4	3 1.9	26 52.2	11 49.7	2 42.9	23 19.9	23 19.0	23 39.8
17 Sa	19 37 8	23 53 12	5♒55 27	12♒38 23	14 47.3	9D 17.3	4 10.6	26 41.6	12 3.2	2 43.9	23 23.5	23 19.3	23 41.5
18 Su	19 41 5	24 50 25	19 24 59	26 15 1	14 46.4	9 18.5	5 19.3	26 31.7	12 16.6	2 44.9	23 27.2	23 19.7	23 43.2
19 M	19 45 1	25 47 40	3♓ 8 12	10♓ 4 15	14 45.2	9 25.1	6 27.8	26 22.6	12 30.0	2 46.1	23 30.8	23 20.2	23 44.9
20 Tu	19 48 58	26 44 54	17 2 50	24 3 38	14 43.8	9 37.4	7 36.3	26 14.3	12 43.4	2 47.3	23 34.5	23 20.6	23 46.7
21 W	19 52 54	27 42 10	1♈ 6 18	8♈10 30	14 42.5	9 55.3	8 44.6	26 6.7	12 56.8	2 48.7	23 38.2	23 21.1	23 48.4
22 Th	19 56 51	28 39 26	15 15 55	22 22 12	14 41.6	10 19.0	9 52.8	25 60.0	13 10.1	2 50.1	23 41.8	23 21.6	23 50.2
23 F	20 0 47	29 36 43	29 29 2	6♉36 8	14D 41.2	10 48.5	11 0.9	25 54.0	13 23.5	2 51.7	23 45.5	23 22.2	23 51.9
24 Sa	20 4 44	0♌34 2	13♉43 9	20 49 49	14 41.5	11 23.7	12 8.9	25 48.8	13 36.8	2 53.3	23 49.1	23 22.7	23 53.7
25 Su	20 8 40	1 31 21	27 55 49	5♊ 0 51	14 42.4	12 4.6	13 16.8	25 44.5	13 50.0	2 55.1	23 52.8	23 23.4	23 55.5
26 M	20 12 37	2 28 41	12♊ 4 35	19 6 43	14 43.6	12 51.2	14 24.5	25 41.0	14 3.3	2 56.9	23 56.4	23 24.0	23 57.3
27 Tu	20 16 34	3 26 2	26 6 56	3♋ 4 53	14 44.8	13 43.4	15 32.1	25 38.3	14 16.5	2 58.8	24 0.0	23 24.7	23 59.1
28 W	20 20 30	4 23 24	10♋ 0 16	16 52 45	14R 45.5	14 41.1	16 39.7	25 36.5	14 29.7	3 0.9	24 3.7	23 25.4	24 0.9
29 Th	20 24 27	5 20 47	23 42 2	0♌27 51	14 45.3	15 44.3	17 47.0	25D 35.5	14 42.8	3 3.0	24 7.3	23 26.1	24 2.8
30 F	20 28 23	6 18 10	7♌ 9 57	13 48 9	14 44.1	16 52.9	18 54.3	25 35.4	14 55.9	3 5.2	24 10.9	23 26.9	24 4.6
31 Sa	20 32 20	7 15 34	20 22 16	26 52 13	14 41.8	18 6.6	20 1.4	25 36.2	15 9.0	3 7.5	24 14.5	23 27.7	24 6.5

AUGUST 1954 — LONGITUDE

Day	Sid.Time	☉	0 hr ☽	Noon ☽	True ☊	☿	♀	♂	♃	♄	♅	♆	♇
1 Su	20 36 16	8♌12 59	3♍18 0	9♍39 37	14♑38.6	19♋25.4	21♍ 8.3	25♐37.7	15♋22.0	3♏ 9.9	24♋18.1	23♎28.5	24♌ 8.3
2 M	20 40 13	9 10 25	15 57 11	22 10 53	14R 34.8	20 49.2	22 15.2	25 40.2	15 35.0	3 12.4	24 21.7	23 29.4	24 10.2
3 Tu	20 44 9	10 7 52	28 20 57	4♎27 41	14 30.9	22 17.6	23 21.8	25 43.4	15 48.0	3 15.0	24 25.2	23 30.3	24 12.0
4 W	20 48 6	11 5 19	10♎31 28	16 32 43	14 27.4	23 50.6	24 28.3	25 47.6	16 0.9	3 17.6	24 28.8	23 31.2	24 13.9
5 Th	20 52 3	12 2 46	22 31 53	28 29 30	14 24.7	25 27.8	25 34.7	25 52.5	16 13.8	3 20.4	24 32.3	23 32.2	24 15.8
6 F	20 55 59	13 0 15	4♏26 6	10♏22 15	14D 23.2	27 9.0	26 40.9	25 58.3	16 26.6	3 23.2	24 35.8	23 33.1	24 17.7
7 Sa	20 59 56	13 57 44	16 18 32	22 15 35	14 22.8	28 53.9	27 46.9	26 4.8	16 39.4	3 26.2	24 39.4	23 34.2	24 19.6
8 Su	21 3 52	14 55 15	28 13 59	4♐14 21	14 23.6	0♌42.2	28 52.8	26 12.2	16 52.2	3 29.2	24 42.9	23 35.2	24 21.5
9 M	21 7 49	15 52 46	10♐17 15	16 23 17	14 25.1	2 33.5	29 58.5	26 20.4	17 4.9	3 32.3	24 46.3	23 36.3	24 23.4
10 Tu	21 11 45	16 50 17	22 32 57	28 46 46	14 26.7	4 27.4	1♎ 4.0	26 29.3	17 17.5	3 35.5	24 49.8	23 37.4	24 25.3
11 W	21 15 42	17 47 50	5♑ 5 8	11♑28 26	14R 28.0	6 23.6	2 9.3	26 39.0	17 30.1	3 38.8	24 53.3	23 38.5	24 27.2
12 Th	21 19 38	18 45 24	17 56 57	24 30 50	14 28.3	8 21.6	3 14.4	26 49.5	17 42.7	3 42.1	24 56.7	23 39.7	24 29.1
13 F	21 23 35	19 42 59	1♒10 12	7♒55 0	14 27.2	10 21.2	4 19.3	27 0.7	17 55.1	3 45.6	25 0.1	23 40.8	24 31.0
14 Sa	21 27 32	20 40 34	14 45 4	21 40 7	14 24.4	12 21.8	5 24.0	27 12.7	18 7.6	3 49.1	25 3.5	23 42.0	24 32.9
15 Su	21 31 28	21 38 11	28 39 47	5♓43 32	14 20.0	14 23.3	6 28.6	27 25.3	18 20.0	3 52.7	25 6.9	23 43.3	24 34.8
16 M	21 35 25	22 35 49	12♓50 47	20 0 51	14 14.5	16 25.2	7 32.9	27 38.7	18 32.3	3 56.4	25 10.3	23 44.5	24 36.7
17 Tu	21 39 21	23 33 29	27 13 2	4♈26 35	14 8.6	18 27.4	8 36.9	27 52.7	18 44.6	4 0.2	25 13.6	23 45.8	24 38.7
18 W	21 43 18	24 31 10	11♈40 46	18 54 52	14 3.0	20 29.4	9 40.8	28 7.4	18 56.8	4 4.1	25 16.9	23 47.2	24 40.6
19 Th	21 47 14	25 28 52	26 8 16	3♉20 24	13 58.6	22 31.1	10 44.4	28 22.8	19 9.0	4 8.0	25 20.2	23 48.5	24 42.5
20 F	21 51 11	26 26 36	10♉30 46	17 38 59	13 55.7	24 32.3	11 47.9	28 38.9	19 21.1	4 12.0	25 23.5	23 49.9	24 44.4
21 Sa	21 55 7	27 24 22	24 44 45	1♊47 52	13D 54.6	26 32.7	12 51.0	28 55.6	19 33.1	4 16.1	25 26.7	23 51.3	24 46.3
22 Su	21 59 4	28 22 10	8♊48 10	15 45 35	13 55.0	28 32.4	13 54.0	29 12.9	19 45.1	4 20.3	25 30.0	23 52.7	24 48.3
23 M	22 3 1	29 19 59	22 40 5	29 31 39	13 56.1	0♍31.1	14 56.7	29 30.8	19 57.0	4 24.5	25 33.2	23 54.1	24 50.2
24 Tu	22 6 57	0♍17 51	6♋20 18	13♋ 6 3	13R 57.2	2 28.7	15 59.1	29 49.4	20 8.8	4 28.9	25 36.4	23 55.6	24 52.1
25 W	22 10 54	1 15 44	19 48 55	26 28 55	13 57.2	4 25.3	17 1.3	0♑ 8.6	20 20.6	4 33.3	25 39.5	23 57.1	24 54.0
26 Th	22 14 50	2 13 38	3♌ 6 1	9♌40 12	13 55.5	6 20.6	18 3.2	0 28.3	20 32.3	4 37.7	25 42.6	23 58.6	24 55.9
27 F	22 18 47	3 11 34	16 11 26	22 39 40	13 51.6	8 14.8	19 4.8	0 48.7	20 43.9	4 42.3	25 45.7	24 0.2	24 57.8
28 Sa	22 22 43	4 9 32	29 4 51	5♍26 58	13 45.4	10 7.7	20 6.1	1 9.6	20 55.5	4 46.9	25 48.8	24 1.8	24 59.7
29 Su	22 26 40	5 7 31	11♍45 59	18 1 53	13 37.2	11 59.3	21 7.1	1 31.1	21 7.0	4 51.6	25 51.9	24 3.3	25 1.6
30 M	22 30 36	6 5 32	24 14 44	0♎24 36	13 27.8	13 49.7	22 7.9	1 53.1	21 18.4	4 56.4	25 54.9	24 5.0	25 3.5
31 Tu	22 34 33	7 3 34	6♎31 37	12 35 57	13 17.9	15 38.8	23 8.3	2 15.7	21 29.7	5 1.2	25 57.9	24 6.6	25 5.4

Astro Data Dy Hr Mn	Planet Ingress Dy Hr Mn	Last Aspect Dy Hr Mn	☽ Ingress Dy Hr Mn	Last Aspect Dy Hr Mn	☽ Ingress Dy Hr Mn	☽ Phases & Eclipses Dy Hr Mn	Astro Data
♆⚹♇ 1 19:16	♂ ♐ 3 7:23	1 14:29 ♆ □	♌ 2 2:16	2 18:51 ♂ □	♎ 3 3:14	8 1:33 ☽ 15♎22	1 JULY 1954
☽0S 5 21:10	♀ ♍ 13 8:43	4 8:21 ♂ △	♍ 4 8:56	5 6:51 ☿ □	♏ 5 15:03	16 0:29 ○ 22♑57	Julian Day # 19905
♆ D 5 8:33	☉ ♌ 23 9:45	6 16:58 ♂ □	♎ 6 18:53	8 1:26 ♀ ⚹	♐ 8 3:32	16 0:20 ☍P 0.405	Delta T 30.9 sec
♄ D 6 15:53		9 3:47 ♂ ⚹	♏ 9 7:04	10 7:42 ♂ ☌	♑ 10 14:20	23 0:14 ☽ 29♈37	SVP 05♓53'26"
♅□♆ 15 17:37	☿ ♌ 7 14:44	11 15:22 ♀ □	♐ 11 19:19	12 12:50 ♅ ☍	♒ 12 21:54	29 22:20 ● 6♌14	Obliquity 23°26'45"
☿ D 17 6:50	♀ ♎ 9 0:34	14 0:26 ♂ ☌	♑ 14 5:40	14 21:51 ♂ ⚹	♓ 15 2:17		⚷ Chiron 26♑52.9R
☽0N 20 3:18	☿ ♍ 22 17:42	16 1:11 ♅ ☍	♒ 16 13:19	17 1:07 ♂ □	♈ 17 4:37	6 18:51 ☽ 13♏45	☽ Mean ☊ 15♑10.0
♅⚺♇ 26 11:54	☉ ♍ 23 16:36	18 12:21 ♂ ⚹	♓ 18 18:33	19 3:48 ♂ △	♉ 19 6:26	14 11:03 ○ 21♒07	
♂ D 29 15:20	♂ ♑ 24 13:22	20 17:47 ☉ △	♈ 20 22:07	21 4:51 ☉ □	♊ 21 8:56	21 4:51 ☽ 27♉36	1 AUGUST 1954
		23 0:14 ☉ □	♉ 23 0:52	23 12:33 ☉ ⚹	♋ 23 12:50	28 10:21 ● 4♍35	Julian Day # 19936
☽0S 2 5:56		24 17:13 ♇ □	♊ 25 3:30	25 10:33 ♅ ☌	♌ 25 18:22		Delta T 30.9 sec
♀0S 9 0:31		26 23:11 ♂ ☍	♋ 27 6:41	27 16:20 ♇ ☌	♍ 28 1:44		SVP 05♓53'20"
☽0N 16 10:31		29 0:45 ♅ ☌	♌ 29 11:10	30 3:15 ♅ ⚹	♎ 30 11:12		Obliquity 23°26'45"
☽0S 29 14:16		31 9:40 ♂ △	♍ 31 17:49				⚷ Chiron 25♑05.0R
							☽ Mean ☊ 13♑31.6

LONGITUDE SEPTEMBER 1954

Day	Sid.Time	☉	0 hr ☽	Noon ☽	True ☊	☿	♀	♂	♃	♄	♅	♆	♇
1 W	22 38 30	8♍ 1 38	18♎37 50	24♎37 33	13♑ 8.5	17♍26.6	24♎ 8.4	2♑38.8	21♋41.0	5♏ 6.1	26♋ 0.8	24♎ 8.3	25♌ 7.3
2 Th	22 42 26	8 59 43	0♏35 28	6♏31 59	13R 0.6	19 13.2	25 8.1	3 2.4	21 52.1	5 11.1	26 3.7	24 9.9	25 9.2
3 F	22 46 23	9 57 50	12 27 33	18 22 40	12 54.6	20 58.5	26 7.5	3 26.5	22 3.2	5 16.1	26 6.6	24 11.6	25 11.1
4 Sa	22 50 19	10 55 58	24 17 53	0♐13 47	12 50.9	22 42.6	27 6.5	3 51.2	22 14.2	5 21.2	26 9.5	24 13.4	25 12.9
5 Su	22 54 16	11 54 8	6♐10 59	12 10 8	12D49.3	24 25.4	28 5.2	4 16.3	22 25.1	5 26.4	26 12.3	24 15.1	25 14.8
6 M	22 58 12	12 52 19	18 11 53	24 16 53	12 49.2	26 7.1	29 3.4	4 41.8	22 36.0	5 31.6	26 15.1	24 16.9	25 16.6
7 Tu	23 2 9	13 50 31	0♑25 47	6♑39 13	12R49.9	27 47.5	0♏ 1.3	5 7.9	22 46.7	5 36.9	26 17.9	24 18.7	25 18.5
8 W	23 6 5	14 48 46	12 57 46	19 21 58	12 50.4	29 26.8	0 58.7	5 34.4	22 57.4	5 42.3	26 20.6	24 20.5	25 20.3
9 Th	23 10 2	15 47 1	25 52 17	2♒29 2	12 49.6	1♎ 4.9	1 55.7	6 1.3	23 7.9	5 47.7	26 23.3	24 22.3	25 22.2
10 F	23 13 59	16 45 18	9♒12 29	16 2 43	12 46.8	2 41.9	2 52.2	6 28.7	23 18.4	5 53.1	26 25.9	24 24.2	25 24.0
11 Sa	23 17 55	17 43 37	22 59 38	0♓ 2 59	12 41.5	4 17.7	3 48.2	6 56.4	23 28.8	5 58.7	26 28.5	24 26.0	25 25.8
12 Su	23 21 52	18 41 57	7♓12 21	14 27 5	12 33.9	5 52.4	4 43.8	7 24.6	23 39.0	6 4.3	26 31.1	24 27.9	25 27.6
13 M	23 25 48	19 40 19	21 46 24	29 9 20	12 24.5	7 26.0	5 38.9	7 53.2	23 49.2	6 9.9	26 33.7	24 29.8	25 29.4
14 Tu	23 29 45	20 38 43	6♈34 51	14♈ 1 49	12 14.3	8 58.5	6 33.4	8 22.1	23 59.3	6 15.6	26 36.2	24 31.7	25 31.2
15 W	23 33 41	21 37 9	21 29 6	28 55 36	12 4.4	10 29.9	7 27.4	8 51.4	24 9.3	6 21.4	26 38.6	24 33.7	25 32.9
16 Th	23 37 38	22 35 37	6♉20 18	13♉42 17	11 56.2	12 0.2	8 20.8	9 21.1	24 19.1	6 27.2	26 41.0	24 35.6	25 34.7
17 F	23 41 34	23 34 7	21 0 49	28 15 19	11 50.2	13 29.4	9 13.7	9 51.1	24 28.9	6 33.1	26 43.4	24 37.6	25 36.4
18 Sa	23 45 31	24 32 40	5♊25 20	12♊30 38	11 46.8	14 57.4	10 6.0	10 21.5	24 38.6	6 39.0	26 45.8	24 39.6	25 38.2
19 Su	23 49 28	25 31 14	19 31 6	26 26 42	11D45.5	16 24.4	10 57.6	10 52.3	24 48.1	6 45.0	26 48.1	24 41.6	25 39.9
20 M	23 53 24	26 29 51	3♋17 35	10♋ 3 54	11R45.5	17 50.2	11 48.6	11 23.4	24 57.6	6 51.0	26 50.4	24 43.6	25 41.6
21 Tu	23 57 21	27 28 30	16 45 54	23 23 50	11 45.5	19 14.9	12 39.0	11 54.8	25 6.9	6 57.1	26 52.6	24 45.6	25 43.3
22 W	0 1 17	28 27 12	29 57 59	6♌28 36	11 44.3	20 38.5	13 28.6	12 26.5	25 16.2	7 3.2	26 54.8	24 47.6	25 45.0
23 Th	0 5 14	29 25 55	12♌55 56	19 20 13	11 41.0	22 0.8	14 17.6	12 58.6	25 25.3	7 9.3	26 56.9	24 49.7	25 46.6
24 F	0 9 10	0♎24 41	25 41 39	2♍ 0 23	11 34.8	23 22.0	15 5.8	13 31.0	25 34.3	7 15.6	26 59.0	24 51.8	25 48.3
25 Sa	0 13 7	1 23 28	8♍16 34	14 30 17	11 25.6	24 41.8	15 53.2	14 3.6	25 43.1	7 21.8	27 1.0	24 53.8	25 49.9
26 Su	0 17 3	2 22 18	20 41 40	26 50 45	11 13.9	26 0.3	16 39.9	14 36.6	25 51.9	7 28.1	27 3.1	24 55.9	25 51.5
27 M	0 21 0	3 21 10	2♎57 39	9♎ 2 25	11 0.4	27 17.5	17 25.7	15 9.9	26 0.5	7 34.5	27 5.0	24 58.0	25 53.1
28 Tu	0 24 56	4 20 4	15 5 9	21 5 59	10 46.2	28 33.2	18 10.6	15 43.5	26 9.0	7 40.9	27 6.9	25 0.2	25 54.7
29 W	0 28 53	5 19 0	27 5 4	3♏ 2 36	10 32.5	29 47.5	18 54.6	16 17.3	26 17.4	7 47.3	27 8.8	25 2.3	25 56.3
30 Th	0 32 50	6 17 57	8♏58 48	14 53 59	10 20.5	1♏ 0.1	19 37.7	16 51.5	26 25.6	7 53.8	27 10.6	25 4.4	25 57.8

LONGITUDE OCTOBER 1954

Day	Sid.Time	☉	0 hr ☽	Noon ☽	True ☊	☿	♀	♂	♃	♄	♅	♆	♇
1 F	0 36 46	7♎16 57	20♏48 28	26♏42 39	10♑11.0	2♏11.0	20♏19.8	17♑25.9	26♋33.8	8♏ 0.3	27♋12.4	25♎ 6.6	25♌59.4
2 Sa	0 40 43	8 15 58	2♐36 59	8♐31 57	10R 4.3	3 20.1	21 0.9	18 0.5	26 41.7	8 6.8	27 14.1	25 8.7	26 0.9
3 Su	0 44 39	9 15 2	14 28 6	20 26 1	10 0.4	4 27.3	21 40.9	18 35.5	26 49.6	8 13.4	27 15.8	25 10.9	26 2.4
4 M	0 48 36	10 14 7	26 26 19	2♑29 40	9 58.8	5 32.4	22 19.7	19 10.6	26 57.3	8 20.0	27 17.4	25 13.1	26 3.9
5 Tu	0 52 32	11 13 14	8♑36 43	14 48 10	9 58.5	6 35.2	22 57.5	19 46.1	27 4.9	8 26.7	27 19.0	25 15.2	26 5.3
6 W	0 56 29	12 12 23	21 4 39	27 26 50	9 58.4	7 35.7	23 34.0	20 21.7	27 12.3	8 33.4	27 20.5	25 17.4	26 6.8
7 Th	1 0 25	13 11 33	3♒55 17	10♒30 31	9 57.3	8 33.4	24 9.2	20 57.6	27 19.6	8 40.1	27 22.0	25 19.6	26 8.2
8 F	1 4 22	14 10 45	17 12 57	24 2 51	9 54.2	9 28.3	24 43.1	21 33.7	27 26.8	8 46.9	27 23.5	25 21.8	26 9.6
9 Sa	1 8 19	15 9 59	1♓ 0 20	8♓ 5 19	9 48.6	10 20.1	25 15.7	22 10.0	27 33.8	8 53.7	27 24.9	25 24.0	26 11.0
10 Su	1 12 15	16 9 15	15 17 31	22 36 24	9 40.5	11 8.4	25 46.8	22 46.5	27 40.7	9 0.5	27 26.2	25 26.2	26 12.3
11 M	1 16 12	17 8 32	0♈ 1 14	7♈31 1	9 30.2	11 52.9	26 16.4	23 23.2	27 47.4	9 7.3	27 27.5	25 28.5	26 13.7
12 Tu	1 20 8	18 7 52	15 4 38	22 40 45	9 18.9	12 33.4	26 44.5	24 0.2	27 53.9	9 14.2	27 28.7	25 30.7	26 15.0
13 W	1 24 5	19 7 13	0♉17 59	7♉54 57	9 8.0	13 9.3	27 11.0	24 37.3	28 0.4	9 21.1	27 29.9	25 32.9	26 16.3
14 Th	1 28 1	20 6 37	15 30 17	23 2 44	8 58.6	13 40.3	27 35.8	25 14.6	28 6.6	9 28.0	27 31.0	25 35.1	26 17.6
15 F	1 31 58	21 6 3	0♊31 13	7♊54 51	8 51.7	14 5.9	27 59.0	25 52.1	28 12.7	9 35.0	27 32.1	25 37.4	26 18.8
16 Sa	1 35 54	22 5 31	15 12 56	22 25 2	8 47.5	14 25.6	28 20.3	26 29.7	28 18.7	9 41.9	27 33.1	25 39.6	26 20.1
17 Su	1 39 51	23 5 2	29 30 51	6♋30 18	8D45.8	14 38.8	28 39.9	27 7.6	28 24.5	9 48.9	27 34.1	25 41.8	26 21.3
18 M	1 43 48	24 4 34	13♋23 29	20 10 35	8R45.6	14R45.2	28 57.5	27 45.6	28 30.1	9 56.0	27 35.0	25 44.1	26 22.5
19 Tu	1 47 44	25 4 10	26 51 54	3♌27 47	8 45.7	14 44.0	29 13.2	28 23.8	28 35.6	10 3.0	27 35.9	25 46.3	26 23.6
20 W	1 51 41	26 3 47	9♌58 39	16 24 55	8 45.0	14 34.8	29 26.9	29 2.1	28 40.9	10 10.0	27 36.7	25 48.6	26 24.8
21 Th	1 55 37	27 3 27	22 47 3	29 5 25	8 42.2	14 17.3	29 38.5	29 40.6	28 46.1	10 17.1	27 37.5	25 50.8	26 25.9
22 F	1 59 34	28 3 8	5♍20 27	11♍32 30	8 36.8	13 51.0	29 48.0	0♒19.3	28 51.1	10 24.2	27 38.2	25 53.0	26 27.0
23 Sa	2 3 30	29 2 52	17 41 55	23 48 59	8 28.6	13 15.8	29 55.3	0 58.1	28 55.9	10 31.3	27 38.8	25 55.3	26 28.0
24 Su	2 7 27	0♏ 2 39	29 53 58	5♎57 5	8 17.9	12 31.7	0♐ 0.3	1 37.1	29 0.5	10 38.4	27 39.4	25 57.5	26 29.1
25 M	2 11 23	1 2 27	11♎58 33	17 58 32	8 5.6	11 39.2	0R 3.1	2 16.2	29 4.9	10 45.6	27 40.0	25 59.8	26 30.1
26 Tu	2 15 20	2 2 17	23 57 13	29 54 44	7 52.5	10 38.8	0 3.5	2 55.5	29 9.2	10 52.7	27 40.5	26 2.0	26 31.1
27 W	2 19 17	3 2 10	5♏51 16	11♏46 58	7 39.9	9 31.7	0 1.6	3 34.9	29 13.3	10 59.9	27 40.9	26 4.2	26 32.0
28 Th	2 23 13	4 2 4	17 42 2	23 36 41	7 28.8	8 19.2	29♏57.3	4 14.5	29 17.3	11 7.0	27 41.3	26 6.4	26 33.0
29 F	2 27 10	5 2 0	29 31 8	5♐25 42	7 20.0	7 3.4	29 50.6	4 54.2	29 21.0	11 14.2	27 41.6	26 8.7	26 33.9
30 Sa	2 31 6	6 1 58	11♐20 40	17 16 26	7 13.9	5 46.2	29 41.4	5 34.0	29 24.6	11 21.4	27 41.9	26 10.9	26 34.8
31 Su	2 35 3	7 1 58	23 13 23	29 12 0	7 10.5	4 30.2	29 29.8	6 14.0	29 28.0	11 28.6	27 42.1	26 13.1	26 35.6

Astro Data	Planet Ingress	Last Aspect	☽ Ingress	Last Aspect	☽ Ingress	☽ Phases & Eclipses
Dy Hr Mn	Dy Hr Mn	Dy Hr Mn	Dy Hr Mn	Dy Hr Mn	Dy Hr Mn	Dy Hr Mn
☿0S 8 21:51	♀ ♏ 6 23:29	1 14:51 ♅ □	♏ 1 22:49	1 13:02 ♅ △	♐ 1 18:41	5 12:28 ☽ 12♐24
☽0N 12 19:50	☿ ♎ 8 8:05	4 3:47 ♅ △	♐ 4 11:32	3 23:15 ♇ △	♑ 4 7:04	12 20:19 ○ 19♓31
♃□♆ 18 3:04	☉ ♎ 23 13:55	6 23:08 ♀ ⚹	♑ 6 23:10	6 11:50 ♅ ☍	♒ 6 16:45	19 11:11 ☽ 25♊59
☽0S 25 21:08	☿ ♏ 29 4:06	9 0:57 ♅ ☍	♒ 9 7:31	8 15:41 ♇ ☍	♓ 8 22:17	27 0:50 ● 3♎23
♃⊻♇ 25 22:45		11 4:10 ♇ ☍	♓ 11 11:55	10 20:23 ♃ △	♈ 10 23:58	
	♂ ♒ 21 12:03	13 7:49 ♅ △	♈ 13 13:22	12 20:22 ♃ □	♉ 12 23:32	5 5:31 ☽ 11♑27
♃☌♅ 7 10:01	☉ ♏ 23 22:56	15 8:20 ♅ □	♉ 15 13:44	14 20:15 ♃ ⚹	♊ 14 23:10	12 5:10 ○ 18♈21
☽0N 10 6:14	♀ ♐ 23 22:07	17 9:29 ♅ ⚹	♊ 17 14:55	16 18:38 ♇ ⚹	♋ 17 0:50	18 20:30 ☽ 24♋55
☿ R 18 8:25	♀ ♏ 27 10:42	19 11:11 ☉ □	♋ 19 18:13	19 4:21 ♀ △	♌ 19 5:41	26 17:47 ● 2♏47
☽0S 23 2:28		21 21:00 ☉ ⚹	♌ 22 0:04	21 13:14 ♀ □	♍ 21 13:44	
♀ R 25 16:36		24 0:13 ♇ ☌	♍ 24 8:11	23 22:14 ♃ ⚹	♎ 24 0:12	
		26 12:26 ♅ ⚹	♎ 26 18:11	26 10:32 ♃ □	♏ 26 12:11	
		29 0:07 ♅ □	♏ 29 5:52	29 0:39 ♀ ☌	♐ 29 0:59	
				31 6:47 ♇ △	♑ 31 13:36	

Astro Data

1 SEPTEMBER 1954
Julian Day # 19967
Delta T 31.0 sec
SVP 05♓53'17"
Obliquity 23°26'45"
⚷ Chiron 23♑37.0R
☽ Mean ☊ 11♑53.1

1 OCTOBER 1954
Julian Day # 19997
Delta T 31.0 sec
SVP 05♓53'14"
Obliquity 23°26'45"
⚷ Chiron 23♑05.2
☽ Mean ☊ 10♑17.7

NOVEMBER 1954 LONGITUDE

Day	Sid.Time	☉	0 hr ☽	Noon ☽	True ☊	☿	♀	♂	♃	♄	♅	♆	♇
1 M	2 38 59	8♏ 2 0	5♑12 45	11♑16 12	7♑ 9.4	3♏17.5	29♏15.8	6♒54.1	29♋31.2	11♏35.8	27♋42.3	26♎15.3	26♌36.4
2 Tu	2 42 56	9 2 3	17 22 54	23 33 27	7D 9.7	2R10.7	28R59.4	7 34.3	29 34.2	11 43.0	27 42.4	26 17.5	26 37.3
3 W	2 46 52	10 2 8	29 48 28	6♒ 8 33	7R10.6	1 11.6	28 40.7	8 14.6	29 37.0	11 50.2	27R42.4	26 19.7	26 38.0
4 Th	2 50 49	11 2 14	12♒34 17	19 6 13	7 11.0	0 21.9	28 19.7	8 55.1	29 39.7	11 57.4	27 42.4	26 21.9	26 38.8
5 F	2 54 46	12 2 22	25 44 51	2♓30 33	7 10.0	29♎42.8	27 56.4	9 35.6	29 42.1	12 4.6	27 42.4	26 24.1	26 39.5
6 Sa	2 58 42	13 2 31	9♓23 37	16 24 9	7 7.0	29 15.1	27 31.1	10 16.3	29 44.4	12 11.8	27 42.3	26 26.3	26 40.2
7 Su	3 2 39	14 2 42	23 32 6	0♈47 10	7 1.8	28D59.0	27 3.8	10 57.0	29 46.5	12 19.1	27 42.1	26 28.4	26 40.8
8 M	3 6 35	15 2 54	8♈ 8 53	15 36 31	6 54.9	28 54.5	26 34.6	11 37.9	29 48.4	12 26.3	27 41.9	26 30.6	26 41.5
9 Tu	3 10 32	16 3 8	23 9 7	0♉45 32	6 46.9	29 1.2	26 3.8	12 18.8	29 50.0	12 33.5	27 41.6	26 32.7	26 42.1
10 W	3 14 28	17 3 24	8♉24 28	16 4 31	6 39.1	29 18.4	25 31.5	12 59.8	29 51.5	12 40.7	27 41.3	26 34.8	26 42.7
11 Th	3 18 25	18 3 41	23 44 15	1♊22 16	6 32.3	29 45.4	24 57.9	13 41.0	29 52.9	12 47.8	27 40.9	26 37.0	26 43.2
12 F	3 22 21	19 4 0	8♊57 15	16 28 2	6 27.4	0♏21.4	24 23.2	14 22.2	29 54.0	12 55.0	27 40.4	26 39.1	26 43.7
13 Sa	3 26 18	20 4 21	23 53 38	1♋13 17	6D 24.7	1 5.4	23 47.7	15 3.5	29 54.9	13 2.2	27 40.0	26 41.2	26 44.2
14 Su	3 30 15	21 4 44	8♋26 26	15 32 44	6 24.1	1 56.5	23 11.6	15 44.8	29 55.6	13 9.4	27 39.4	26 43.3	26 44.7
15 M	3 34 11	22 5 9	22 32 2	29 24 21	6 24.9	2 54.0	22 35.2	16 26.3	29 56.1	13 16.5	27 38.8	26 45.4	26 45.1
16 Tu	3 38 8	23 5 35	6♌ 9 53	12♌48 53	6 26.3	3 56.9	21 58.6	17 7.8	29 56.5	13 23.7	27 38.2	26 47.4	26 45.5
17 W	3 42 4	24 6 3	19 21 45	25 48 55	6R27.3	5 4.7	21 22.3	17 49.4	29R56.6	13 30.8	27 37.5	26 49.5	26 45.9
18 Th	3 46 1	25 6 34	2♍10 53	8♍28 9	6 27.1	6 16.5	20 46.3	18 31.0	29 56.5	13 38.0	27 36.7	26 51.5	26 46.2
19 F	3 49 57	26 7 6	14 41 14	20 50 38	6 25.3	7 31.9	20 11.0	19 12.8	29 56.2	13 45.1	27 35.9	26 53.5	26 46.6
20 Sa	3 53 54	27 7 39	26 56 51	3♎ 0 22	6 21.6	8 50.2	19 36.6	19 54.6	29 55.8	13 52.2	27 35.0	26 55.5	26 46.8
21 Su	3 57 50	28 8 15	9♎ 1 36	15 0 58	6 16.2	10 11.1	19 3.4	20 36.5	29 55.1	13 59.2	27 34.1	26 57.5	26 47.1
22 M	4 1 47	29 8 52	20 58 52	26 55 36	6 9.5	11 34.2	18 31.5	21 18.4	29 54.2	14 6.3	27 33.2	26 59.5	26 47.3
23 Tu	4 5 44	0♐ 9 31	2♏51 30	8♏46 51	6 2.4	12 59.1	18 1.1	22 0.4	29 53.1	14 13.3	27 32.2	27 1.4	26 47.5
24 W	4 9 40	1 10 11	14 41 53	20 36 52	5 55.5	14 25.5	17 32.4	22 42.5	29 51.9	14 20.4	27 31.1	27 3.4	26 47.7
25 Th	4 13 37	2 10 53	26 32 0	2♐27 31	5 49.5	15 53.2	17 5.5	23 24.7	29 50.4	14 27.4	27 30.0	27 5.3	26 47.8
26 F	4 17 33	3 11 36	8♐23 37	14 20 33	5 44.9	17 21.9	16 40.7	24 6.9	29 48.7	14 34.3	27 28.8	27 7.2	26 47.9
27 Sa	4 21 30	4 12 21	20 18 30	26 17 45	5 42.0	18 51.5	16 18.0	24 49.1	29 46.8	14 41.3	27 27.6	27 9.1	26 48.0
28 Su	4 25 26	5 13 7	2♑18 34	8♑21 15	5D 40.8	20 21.8	15 57.5	25 31.4	29 44.8	14 48.2	27 26.4	27 11.0	26R48.0
29 M	4 29 23	6 13 54	14 26 6	20 33 29	5 41.0	21 52.7	15 39.3	26 13.8	29 42.5	14 55.1	27 25.0	27 12.8	26 48.0
30 Tu	4 33 19	7 14 42	26 43 46	2♒57 22	5 42.3	23 24.1	15 23.5	26 56.2	29 40.0	15 2.0	27 23.7	27 14.7	26 48.0

DECEMBER 1954 LONGITUDE

Day	Sid.Time	☉	0 hr ☽	Noon ☽	True ☊	☿	♀	♂	♃	♄	♅	♆	♇
1 W	4 37 16	8♐15 31	9♒14 42	15♒36 11	5♑44.1	24♏55.9	15♏10.1	27♒38.7	29♋37.4	15♏ 8.8	27♋22.3	27♎16.5	26♌48.0
2 Th	4 41 13	9 16 21	22 2 16	28 33 22	5 45.7	26 27.9	14R59.1	28 21.2	29R34.5	15 15.6	27R20.8	27 18.2	26R47.9
3 F	4 45 9	10 17 12	5♓ 9 52	11♓52 7	5R46.7	28 0.3	14 50.7	29 3.8	29 31.5	15 22.4	27 19.3	27 20.0	26 47.8
4 Sa	4 49 6	11 18 4	18 40 23	25 34 50	5 46.5	29 32.8	14 44.7	29 46.4	29 28.2	15 29.2	27 17.8	27 21.8	26 47.7
5 Su	4 53 2	12 18 56	2♈35 34	9♈42 30	5 45.3	1♐ 5.5	14D41.1	0♓29.0	29 24.8	15 35.9	27 16.2	27 23.5	26 47.5
6 M	4 56 59	13 19 49	16 55 23	24 13 51	5 43.1	2 38.4	14 40.0	1 11.6	29 21.2	15 42.6	27 14.6	27 25.2	26 47.3
7 Tu	5 0 55	14 20 43	1♉37 16	9♉ 4 55	5 40.3	4 11.3	14 41.4	1 54.3	29 17.4	15 49.2	27 12.9	27 26.9	26 47.1
8 W	5 4 52	15 21 38	16 35 53	24 9 5	5 37.4	5 44.4	14 45.1	2 37.1	29 13.5	15 55.8	27 11.2	27 28.5	26 46.8
9 Th	5 8 48	16 22 34	1♊43 23	9♊17 34	5 34.9	7 17.5	14 51.2	3 19.8	29 9.3	16 2.4	27 9.5	27 30.1	26 46.5
10 F	5 12 45	17 23 31	16 50 25	24 20 47	5 33.2	8 50.7	14 59.7	4 2.6	29 5.0	16 8.9	27 7.7	27 31.7	26 46.2
11 Sa	5 16 42	18 24 28	1♋47 33	9♋ 9 46	5D 32.5	10 24.0	15 10.4	4 45.4	29 0.5	16 15.4	27 5.8	27 33.3	26 45.9
12 Su	5 20 38	19 25 27	16 26 39	23 37 32	5 32.7	11 57.4	15 23.3	5 28.3	28 55.8	16 21.9	27 4.0	27 34.9	26 45.5
13 M	5 24 35	20 26 26	0♌42 0	7♌39 44	5 33.6	13 30.9	15 38.4	6 11.1	28 51.0	16 28.3	27 2.1	27 36.4	26 45.1
14 Tu	5 28 31	21 27 26	14 30 40	21 14 49	5 34.8	15 4.4	15 55.5	6 54.0	28 46.0	16 34.6	27 0.1	27 37.9	26 44.7
15 W	5 32 28	22 28 28	27 52 21	4♍23 35	5 36.0	16 38.0	16 14.7	7 36.9	28 40.8	16 41.0	26 58.1	27 39.4	26 44.2
16 Th	5 36 24	23 29 30	10♍48 52	17 8 40	5 36.8	18 11.8	16 35.9	8 19.8	28 35.4	16 47.2	26 56.1	27 40.9	26 43.8
17 F	5 40 21	24 30 33	23 23 29	29 33 51	5R37.1	19 45.6	16 58.9	9 2.7	28 29.9	16 53.5	26 54.1	27 42.3	26 43.2
18 Sa	5 44 17	25 31 37	5♎40 20	11♎43 30	5 36.9	21 19.6	17 23.8	9 45.7	28 24.3	16 59.6	26 52.0	27 43.7	26 42.7
19 Su	5 48 14	26 32 42	17 43 54	23 42 6	5 36.3	22 53.7	17 50.5	10 28.7	28 18.5	17 5.8	26 49.9	27 45.1	26 42.1
20 M	5 52 11	27 33 48	29 38 38	5♏34 1	5 35.3	24 28.0	18 18.8	11 11.7	28 12.5	17 11.9	26 47.7	27 46.4	26 41.5
21 Tu	5 56 7	28 34 55	11♏28 43	17 23 12	5 34.2	26 2.4	18 48.8	11 54.7	28 6.4	17 17.9	26 45.5	27 47.7	26 40.9
22 W	6 0 4	29 36 2	23 17 53	29 13 9	5 33.3	27 37.0	19 20.4	12 37.7	28 0.2	17 23.9	26 43.3	27 49.0	26 40.3
23 Th	6 4 0	0♑37 11	5♐ 9 20	11♐ 6 47	5 32.5	29 11.9	19 53.5	13 20.8	27 53.8	17 29.8	26 41.1	27 50.3	26 39.6
24 F	6 7 57	1 38 19	17 5 45	23 6 31	5 32.1	0♑46.9	20 28.0	14 3.8	27 47.3	17 35.7	26 38.8	27 51.5	26 38.9
25 Sa	6 11 53	2 39 28	29 9 17	5♑14 16	5D 31.9	2 22.2	21 4.0	14 46.9	27 40.6	17 41.5	26 36.5	27 52.7	26 38.2
26 Su	6 15 50	3 40 38	11♑21 39	17 31 37	5 31.9	3 57.7	21 41.2	15 30.0	27 33.9	17 47.2	26 34.2	27 53.9	26 37.4
27 M	6 19 47	4 41 48	23 44 18	29 59 52	5R31.9	5 33.4	22 19.8	16 13.1	27 27.0	17 52.9	26 31.8	27 55.0	26 36.6
28 Tu	6 23 43	5 42 58	6♒18 28	12♒40 15	5 32.0	7 9.5	22 59.6	16 56.2	27 20.0	17 58.5	26 29.5	27 56.1	26 35.8
29 W	6 27 40	6 44 8	19 5 21	25 33 56	5 31.9	8 45.8	23 40.6	17 39.3	27 12.9	18 4.1	26 27.1	27 57.2	26 35.0
30 Th	6 31 36	7 45 18	2♓ 6 8	8♓42 6	5 31.7	10 22.3	24 22.7	18 22.4	27 5.7	18 9.6	26 24.6	27 58.3	26 34.1
31 F	6 35 33	8 46 28	15 21 58	22 5 51	5 31.4	11 59.2	25 5.9	19 5.5	26 58.4	18 15.1	26 22.2	27 59.3	26 33.3

Astro Data	Planet Ingress	Last Aspect	☽ Ingress	Last Aspect	☽ Ingress	☽ Phases & Eclipses	Astro Data
Dy Hr Mn	Dy Hr Mn	Dy Hr Mn	Dy Hr Mn	Dy Hr Mn	Dy Hr Mn	Dy Hr Mn	1 NOVEMBER 1954
♅ R 3 10:58	☿ ♎ 4 12:37	2 23:38 ♃ ☍	♒ 3 0:22	2 12:18 ♂ ☌	♓ 2 14:38	3 20:55 ☽ 10♒55	Julian Day # 20028
☽0N 6 15:53	☿ ♏ 11 10:25	5 6:48 ☿ △	♓ 5 7:34	4 18:36 ♃ △	♈ 4 19:35	10 14:29 ○ 17♉40	Delta T 31.0 sec
☿ D 7 21:30	☉ ♐ 22 20:14	7 10:21 ♃ △	♈ 7 10:42	6 20:15 ♃ □	♉ 6 21:23	17 9:33 ☽ 24♌30	SVP 05♓53'10"
♆⚹♇ 14 20:41		9 10:34 ♃ □	♉ 9 10:48	8 19:57 ♃ ⚹	♊ 8 21:16	25 12:30 ● 2♐43	Obliquity 23°26'44"
♃ R 17 3:02	☿ ♐ 4 7:02	11 9:40 ♃ ⚹	♊ 11 9:50	10 17:09 ♆ △	♋ 10 21:06		⚷ Chiron 23♑41.9
☽0S 19 7:30	♂ ♓ 4 7:41	13 4:38 ♇ ⚹	♋ 13 9:59	12 20:52 ♃ ☌	♌ 12 22:48	3 9:56 ☽ 10♓42	☽ Mean ☊ 8♑39.2
♇ R 28 23:44	☉ ♑ 22 9:24	15 12:56 ♃ ☌	♌ 15 13:03	14 23:36 ♆ ⚹	♍ 15 3:54	10 0:57 ○ 17♊26	
♅□♆ 2 19:05	☿ ♑ 23 12:10	17 13:56 ♆ ⚹	♍ 17 19:52	17 9:51 ♃ ⚹	♎ 17 12:51	17 2:21 ☽ 24♍37	1 DECEMBER 1954
☽0N 3 23:25		20 5:53 ♃ ⚹	♎ 20 6:02	19 21:07 ♃ □	♏ 20 0:43	25 7:33 ● 2♑59	Julian Day # 20058
♀ D 5 22:39		22 18:00 ♃ □	♏ 22 18:13	22 9:27 ♃ △	♐ 22 13:35	25 7:36:11 ● A 7'39"	Delta T 31.0 sec
☽0S 16 14:08		25 6:41 ♃ △	♐ 25 7:01	24 21:28 ♆ ⚹	♑ 25 1:40		SVP 05♓53'05"
♃□♆ 23 10:57		27 13:45 ♆ ⚹	♑ 27 19:24	27 8:02 ♆ □	♒ 27 12:00		Obliquity 23°26'43"
♅⚺♇ 23 22:46		30 5:39 ♃ ☍	♒ 30 6:19	29 16:25 ♆ △	♓ 29 20:09		⚷ Chiron 25♑18.7
☽0N 31 5:07							☽ Mean ☊ 7♑03.9

LONGITUDE JANUARY 1955

Day	Sid.Time	☉	0 hr ☽	Noon ☽	True ☊	☿	♀	♂	♃	♄	♅	♆	♇
1 Sa	6 39 29	9♑47 37	28♓53 52	5♈46 4	5♑31.2	13♑36.4	25♏50.2	19♓48.7	26♋51.0	18♏20.4	26♋19.7	28♎ 0.3	26♌32.3
2 Su	6 43 26	10 48 47	12♈42 28	19 43 1	5D 31.1	15 13.9	26 35.5	20 31.8	26R43.6	18 25.8	26R17.3	28 1.2	26R31.4
3 M	6 47 22	11 49 56	26 47 37	3♉56 3	5 31.3	16 51.7	27 21.7	21 14.9	26 36.0	18 31.0	26 14.8	28 2.1	26 30.5
4 Tu	6 51 19	12 51 5	11♉ 8 3	18 23 12	5 31.8	18 29.8	28 8.9	21 58.0	26 28.4	18 36.2	26 12.3	28 3.0	26 29.5
5 W	6 55 16	13 52 14	25 41 2	3♊ 0 56	5 32.5	20 8.2	28 57.0	22 41.2	26 20.7	18 41.3	26 9.7	28 3.9	26 28.5
6 Th	6 59 12	14 53 23	10♊22 15	17 44 11	5 33.3	21 46.9	29 46.0	23 24.3	26 12.9	18 46.3	26 7.2	28 4.7	26 27.5
7 F	7 3 9	15 54 31	25 5 56	2♋26 38	5R 33.8	23 25.9	0♐35.8	24 7.4	26 5.1	18 51.3	26 4.7	28 5.5	26 26.5
8 Sa	7 7 5	16 55 39	9♋45 26	17 1 30	5 33.9	25 5.1	1 26.4	24 50.5	25 57.2	18 56.2	26 2.1	28 6.3	26 25.4
9 Su	7 11 2	17 56 47	24 14 1	1♌22 18	5 33.4	26 44.5	2 17.8	25 33.5	25 49.3	19 1.1	25 59.5	28 7.0	26 24.3
10 M	7 14 58	18 57 55	8♌25 43	15 23 48	5 32.2	28 24.1	3 9.9	26 16.6	25 41.4	19 5.8	25 57.0	28 7.7	26 23.2
11 Tu	7 18 55	19 59 2	22 16 9	29 2 33	5 30.4	0♒ 3.8	4 2.7	26 59.7	25 33.4	19 10.5	25 54.4	28 8.4	26 22.1
12 W	7 22 51	21 0 9	5♍42 55	12♍17 15	5 28.2	1 43.6	4 56.3	27 42.7	25 25.4	19 15.1	25 51.8	28 9.0	26 21.0
13 Th	7 26 48	22 1 16	18 45 44	25 8 35	5 25.9	3 23.3	5 50.5	28 25.8	25 17.3	19 19.6	25 49.2	28 9.6	26 19.8
14 F	7 30 45	23 2 23	1♎26 11	7♎38 57	5 24.0	5 2.8	6 45.3	29 8.8	25 9.3	19 24.1	25 46.6	28 10.1	26 18.6
15 Sa	7 34 41	24 3 30	13 47 21	19 51 58	5D 22.8	6 42.1	7 40.8	29 51.8	25 1.2	19 28.4	25 43.9	28 10.7	26 17.4
16 Su	7 38 38	25 4 37	25 53 21	1♏52 7	5 22.4	8 20.9	8 36.9	0♈34.8	24 53.1	19 32.7	25 41.3	28 11.2	26 16.2
17 M	7 42 34	26 5 43	7♏48 52	13 44 15	5 22.9	9 59.1	9 33.5	1 17.8	24 45.0	19 37.0	25 38.7	28 11.6	26 15.0
18 Tu	7 46 31	27 6 49	19 38 51	25 33 17	5 24.2	11 36.5	10 30.6	2 0.8	24 37.0	19 41.1	25 36.1	28 12.0	26 13.7
19 W	7 50 27	28 7 55	1♐28 9	7♐23 58	5 25.9	13 12.8	11 28.3	2 43.8	24 28.9	19 45.1	25 33.5	28 12.4	26 12.5
20 Th	7 54 24	29 9 1	13 21 18	19 20 35	5 27.7	14 47.7	12 26.5	3 26.8	24 20.9	19 49.1	25 30.9	28 12.8	26 11.2
21 F	7 58 20	0♒10 6	25 22 17	1♑26 47	5R 29.0	16 20.9	13 25.2	4 9.7	24 12.9	19 53.0	25 28.3	28 13.1	26 9.9
22 Sa	8 2 17	1 11 11	7♑34 23	13 45 24	5 29.4	17 52.0	14 24.4	4 52.7	24 4.9	19 56.8	25 25.7	28 13.4	26 8.6
23 Su	8 6 14	2 12 15	20 0 1	26 18 23	5 28.5	19 20.5	15 23.9	5 35.6	23 56.9	20 0.5	25 23.1	28 13.7	26 7.3
24 M	8 10 10	3 13 18	2♒40 35	9♒ 6 38	5 26.1	20 45.8	16 24.0	6 18.5	23 49.0	20 4.1	25 20.5	28 13.9	26 6.0
25 Tu	8 14 7	4 14 21	15 36 32	22 10 10	5 22.4	22 7.5	17 24.4	7 1.4	23 41.2	20 7.6	25 17.9	28 14.1	26 4.6
26 W	8 18 3	5 15 23	28 47 24	5♓28 4	5 17.7	23 24.8	18 25.2	7 44.3	23 33.4	20 11.1	25 15.4	28 14.2	26 3.3
27 Th	8 22 0	6 16 23	12♓12 0	18 58 56	5 12.4	24 37.0	19 26.4	8 27.2	23 25.7	20 14.4	25 12.8	28 14.3	26 1.9
28 F	8 25 56	7 17 23	25 48 40	2♈40 59	5 7.4	25 43.5	20 28.0	9 10.0	23 18.0	20 17.7	25 10.3	28 14.4	26 0.5
29 Sa	8 29 53	8 18 21	9♈35 38	16 32 25	5 3.3	26 43.3	21 29.9	9 52.9	23 10.4	20 20.9	25 7.7	28R 14.5	25 59.1
30 Su	8 33 49	9 19 19	23 31 8	0♉31 37	5 0.6	27 35.7	22 32.1	10 35.7	23 2.9	20 23.9	25 5.2	28 14.5	25 57.7
31 M	8 37 46	10 20 15	7♉33 40	14 37 7	4D 59.5	28 19.8	23 34.7	11 18.5	22 55.5	20 26.9	25 2.7	28 14.4	25 56.3

LONGITUDE FEBRUARY 1955

Day	Sid.Time	☉	0 hr ☽	Noon ☽	True ☊	☿	♀	♂	♃	♄	♅	♆	♇
1 Tu	8 41 43	11♒21 10	21♉41 48	28♉47 31	4♑59.9	28♒54.9	24♐37.6	12♈ 1.2	22♋48.2	20♏29.8	25♋ 0.2	28♎14.4	25♌54.9
2 W	8 45 39	12 22 3	5♊54 5	13♊ 1 13	5 1.2	29 20.2	25 40.9	12 44.0	22R41.0	20 32.6	24R57.8	28R14.3	25R53.4
3 Th	8 49 36	13 22 55	20 8 41	27 16 8	5 2.7	29R35.1	26 44.4	13 26.7	22 33.8	20 35.3	24 55.3	28 14.2	25 52.0
4 F	8 53 32	14 23 46	4♋23 12	11♋29 27	5R 3.4	29 39.2	27 48.2	14 9.4	22 26.8	20 37.9	24 52.9	28 14.0	25 50.6
5 Sa	8 57 29	15 24 36	18 34 27	25 37 40	5 2.6	29 32.2	28 52.3	14 52.1	22 19.9	20 40.4	24 50.5	28 13.8	25 49.1
6 Su	9 1 25	16 25 24	2♌38 37	9♌36 46	4 59.8	29 14.2	29 56.6	15 34.7	22 13.1	20 42.8	24 48.1	28 13.6	25 47.6
7 M	9 5 22	17 26 11	16 31 37	23 22 43	4 54.9	28 45.4	1♑ 1.2	16 17.3	22 6.4	20 45.2	24 45.7	28 13.3	25 46.2
8 Tu	9 9 18	18 26 56	0♍ 9 39	6♍52 5	4 48.1	28 6.5	2 6.1	16 59.9	21 59.9	20 47.4	24 43.4	28 13.1	25 44.7
9 W	9 13 15	19 27 40	13 29 45	20 2 30	4 40.2	27 18.5	3 11.3	17 42.4	21 53.5	20 49.5	24 41.1	28 12.7	25 43.2
10 Th	9 17 12	20 28 23	26 30 17	2♎53 9	4 31.9	26 22.6	4 16.6	18 25.0	21 47.2	20 51.5	24 38.8	28 12.4	25 41.8
11 F	9 21 8	21 29 5	9♎11 14	15 24 46	4 24.2	25 20.4	5 22.2	19 7.5	21 41.0	20 53.4	24 36.5	28 12.0	25 40.3
12 Sa	9 25 5	22 29 46	21 34 6	27 39 38	4 17.9	24 13.7	6 28.1	19 49.9	21 35.0	20 55.3	24 34.3	28 11.5	25 38.8
13 Su	9 29 1	23 30 26	3♏41 51	9♏41 17	4 13.5	23 4.3	7 34.1	20 32.4	21 29.1	20 57.0	24 32.1	28 11.1	25 37.3
14 M	9 32 58	24 31 4	15 38 30	21 34 9	4D 11.1	21 54.2	8 40.4	21 14.8	21 23.4	20 58.6	24 29.9	28 10.6	25 35.8
15 Tu	9 36 54	25 31 42	27 28 52	3♐23 19	4 10.6	20 45.3	9 46.8	21 57.2	21 17.8	21 0.1	24 27.8	28 10.1	25 34.3
16 W	9 40 51	26 32 18	9♐18 11	15 14 7	4 11.4	19 39.1	10 53.5	22 39.6	21 12.4	21 1.5	24 25.7	28 9.5	25 32.9
17 Th	9 44 47	27 32 53	21 11 47	27 11 50	4 12.6	18 37.2	12 0.3	23 21.9	21 7.1	21 2.9	24 23.6	28 9.0	25 31.4
18 F	9 48 44	28 33 27	3♑14 50	9♑21 22	4R 13.2	17 40.6	13 7.4	24 4.2	21 2.0	21 4.1	24 21.6	28 8.3	25 29.9
19 Sa	9 52 41	29 33 59	15 31 54	21 46 54	4 12.5	16 50.4	14 14.6	24 46.5	20 57.0	21 5.2	24 19.6	28 7.7	25 28.4
20 Su	9 56 37	0♓34 31	28 6 41	4♒31 32	4 9.7	16 7.2	15 21.9	25 28.8	20 52.3	21 6.2	24 17.6	28 7.0	25 26.9
21 M	10 0 34	1 35 0	11♒ 1 33	17 36 49	4 4.3	15 31.2	16 29.5	26 11.0	20 47.7	21 7.1	24 15.7	28 6.3	25 25.4
22 Tu	10 4 30	2 35 28	24 17 14	1♓ 2 37	3 56.6	15 2.8	17 37.1	26 53.3	20 43.2	21 7.9	24 13.8	28 5.6	25 24.0
23 W	10 8 27	3 35 55	7♓52 38	14 46 53	3 47.0	14 41.9	18 45.0	27 35.4	20 39.0	21 8.6	24 11.9	28 4.8	25 22.5
24 Th	10 12 23	4 36 20	21 44 52	28 46 1	3 36.5	14 28.4	19 53.0	28 17.6	20 34.9	21 9.2	24 10.1	28 4.0	25 21.0
25 F	10 16 20	5 36 43	5♈49 44	12♈55 21	3 26.2	14D 22.0	21 1.1	28 59.7	20 31.0	21 9.7	24 8.3	28 3.2	25 19.6
26 Sa	10 20 16	6 37 4	20 2 17	27 9 56	3 17.3	14 22.5	22 9.3	29 41.8	20 27.3	21 10.1	24 6.6	28 2.3	25 18.1
27 Su	10 24 13	7 37 23	4♉17 45	11♉25 17	3 10.7	14 29.5	23 17.7	0♉23.9	20 23.7	21 10.4	24 4.9	28 1.5	25 16.7
28 M	10 28 10	8 37 40	18 32 9	25 38 3	3 6.6	14 42.5	24 26.2	1 5.9	20 20.4	21 10.6	24 3.2	28 0.5	25 15.2

Astro Data Dy Hr Mn	Planet Ingress Dy Hr Mn
♃⊻♇ 3 19:58	♀ ♐ 6 6:48
♃☌♅ 7 2:01	☿ ♒ 10 23:05
☽0S 12 23:06	♂ ♈ 15 4:33
♂0N 16 4:42	☉ ♒ 20 20:02
☽0N 27 10:59	
♆ R 29 19:19	♀ ♑ 6 1:15
	☉ ♓ 19 10:19
☿ R 3 20:55	♂ ♉ 26 10:22
☽0S 9 9:11	
♃△♄ 17 15:54	
☽0N 23 18:37	
☿ D 25 10:17	

Last Aspect Dy Hr Mn	☽ Ingress Dy Hr Mn
31 20:26 ♃ △	♈ 1 1:56
3 2:06 ♆ ☍	♉ 3 5:24
5 5:40 ♀ ☍	♊ 5 7:04
7 4:53 ♆ △	♋ 7 8:00
9 6:31 ♆ □	♌ 9 9:41
11 10:24 ♆ ⚹	♍ 11 13:43
13 19:21 ♂ ☍	♎ 13 21:15
16 4:36 ♆ ☌	♏ 16 8:15
18 16:36 ☉ ⚹	♐ 18 21:01
21 5:38 ♆ ⚹	♑ 21 9:09
23 15:38 ♆ □	♒ 23 18:58
25 23:00 ♆ △	♓ 26 2:11
27 22:53 ♅ △	♈ 28 7:19
30 8:05 ♆ ☍	♉ 30 11:06

Last Aspect Dy Hr Mn	☽ Ingress Dy Hr Mn
1 12:37 ☿ □	♊ 1 14:02
3 16:01 ☿ △	♋ 3 16:36
5 16:26 ♆ □	♌ 5 19:28
7 20:33 ♆ ⚹	♍ 7 23:43
9 20:33 ♅ ⚹	♎ 10 6:33
12 13:03 ♆ ☌	♏ 12 16:38
14 20:08 ♇ □	♐ 15 5:07
17 13:53 ♆ ⚹	♑ 17 17:34
20 0:01 ♆ □	♒ 20 3:33
22 6:46 ♆ △	♓ 22 10:09
24 4:08 ♅ △	♈ 24 14:06
26 13:27 ♅ ☍	♉ 26 16:46
28 11:20 ♇ □	♊ 28 19:24

☽ Phases & Eclipses Dy Hr Mn	
1 20:29	☽ 10♈40
8 12:44	○ 17♋28
8 12:33	☍A 0.856
15 22:14	☽ 25♎00
24 1:07	● 3♒16
31 5:05	☽ 10♉33
7 1:43	○ 17♌31
14 19:40	☽ 25♏21
22 15:54	● 3♓16

Astro Data

1 JANUARY 1955
Julian Day # 20089
Delta T 31.1 sec
SVP 05♓53'00"
Obliquity 23°26'43"
⚷ Chiron 27♑42.0
☽ Mean ☊ 5♑25.4

1 FEBRUARY 1955
Julian Day # 20120
Delta T 31.1 sec
SVP 05♓52'55"
Obliquity 23°26'43"
⚷ Chiron 0♒22.2
☽ Mean ☊ 3♑47.0

MARCH 1955 LONGITUDE

Day	Sid.Time	☉	0 hr ☽	Noon ☽	True ☊	☿	♀	♂	♃	♄	♅	♆	♇
1 Tu	10 32 6	9♓37 56	2♊42 43	9♊46 0	3♑ 4.9	15♒ 1.4	25♑34.8	1♉47.9	20♋17.2	21♏10.6	24♋ 1.6	27♎59.6	25♌13.8
2 W	10 36 3	10 38 9	16 47 48	23 48 2	3D 4.9	15 25.6	26 43.6	2 29.9	20R 14.3	21R 10.6	24R 0.1	27R 58.6	25R 12.3
3 Th	10 39 59	11 38 20	0♋46 39	7♋43 37	3R 5.2	15 54.8	27 52.4	3 11.8	20 11.5	21 10.5	23 58.5	27 57.7	25 10.9
4 F	10 43 56	12 38 29	14 38 53	21 32 22	3 4.8	16 28.7	29 1.4	3 53.8	20 8.9	21 10.2	23 57.1	27 56.6	25 9.5
5 Sa	10 47 52	13 38 36	28 23 58	5♌13 34	3 2.3	17 6.9	0♒10.5	4 35.6	20 6.5	21 9.9	23 55.6	27 55.6	25 8.1
6 Su	10 51 49	14 38 41	12♌ 0 59	18 46 2	2 57.2	17 49.2	1 19.7	5 17.5	20 4.3	21 9.5	23 54.3	27 54.5	25 6.7
7 M	10 55 45	15 38 44	25 28 29	2♍ 8 5	2 49.1	18 35.2	2 29.0	5 59.3	20 2.3	21 8.9	23 52.9	27 53.4	25 5.3
8 Tu	10 59 42	16 38 45	8♍44 37	15 17 50	2 38.4	19 24.7	3 38.4	6 41.0	20 0.5	21 8.3	23 51.6	27 52.3	25 4.0
9 W	11 3 39	17 38 44	21 47 33	28 13 35	2 25.9	20 17.5	4 47.9	7 22.8	19 58.9	21 7.6	23 50.4	27 51.2	25 2.6
10 Th	11 7 35	18 38 41	4♎35 52	10♎54 19	2 12.7	21 13.3	5 57.5	8 4.4	19 57.4	21 6.7	23 49.2	27 50.0	25 1.3
11 F	11 11 32	19 38 36	17 8 59	23 19 58	2 0.1	22 12.0	7 7.1	8 46.1	19 56.2	21 5.8	23 48.0	27 48.8	24 59.9
12 Sa	11 15 28	20 38 29	29 27 27	5♏31 42	1 49.1	23 13.4	8 16.9	9 27.7	19 55.1	21 4.7	23 46.9	27 47.6	24 58.6
13 Su	11 19 25	21 38 21	11♏33 2	17 31 53	1 40.6	24 17.3	9 26.8	10 9.3	19 54.3	21 3.6	23 45.9	27 46.4	24 57.3
14 M	11 23 21	22 38 10	23 28 42	29 24 1	1 34.7	25 23.6	10 36.8	10 50.9	19 53.6	21 2.4	23 44.9	27 45.1	24 56.0
15 Tu	11 27 18	23 37 59	5♐18 24	11♐12 29	1 31.5	26 32.1	11 46.8	11 32.4	19 53.2	21 1.0	23 43.9	27 43.9	24 54.7
16 W	11 31 14	24 37 45	17 6 56	23 2 24	1D 30.3	27 42.7	12 57.0	12 13.9	19D 52.9	20 59.6	23 43.0	27 42.6	24 53.5
17 Th	11 35 11	25 37 30	28 59 37	4♑59 15	1R 30.2	28 55.4	14 7.2	12 55.4	19 52.8	20 58.1	23 42.1	27 41.3	24 52.2
18 F	11 39 8	26 37 13	11♑ 2 0	17 8 32	1 30.0	0♓10.0	15 17.5	13 36.8	19 53.0	20 56.5	23 41.3	27 39.9	24 51.0
19 Sa	11 43 4	27 36 54	23 19 30	29 35 29	1 28.6	1 26.5	16 27.8	14 18.2	19 53.3	20 54.8	23 40.6	27 38.6	24 49.8
20 Su	11 47 1	28 36 34	5♒56 58	12♒24 24	1 25.2	2 44.7	17 38.3	14 59.6	19 53.8	20 52.9	23 39.9	27 37.2	24 48.6
21 M	11 50 57	29 36 12	18 58 5	25 38 12	1 19.0	4 4.6	18 48.8	15 41.0	19 54.5	20 51.0	23 39.3	27 35.8	24 47.4
22 Tu	11 54 54	0♈35 48	2♓24 46	9♓17 40	1 10.2	5 26.2	19 59.3	16 22.3	19 55.4	20 49.0	23 38.7	27 34.4	24 46.2
23 W	11 58 50	1 35 21	16 16 36	23 21 6	0 59.2	6 49.4	21 10.0	17 3.5	19 56.5	20 46.9	23 38.1	27 33.0	24 45.1
24 Th	12 2 47	2 34 53	0♈30 32	7♈44 8	0 47.1	8 14.2	22 20.7	17 44.8	19 57.8	20 44.8	23 37.6	27 31.5	24 44.0
25 F	12 6 43	3 34 23	15 1 1	22 20 15	0 35.1	9 40.5	23 31.4	18 26.0	19 59.2	20 42.5	23 37.2	27 30.1	24 42.9
26 Sa	12 10 40	4 33 51	29 40 51	7♉ 1 51	0 24.5	11 8.3	24 42.2	19 7.2	20 0.9	20 40.1	23 36.8	27 28.6	24 41.8
27 Su	12 14 36	5 33 17	14♉22 19	21 41 26	0 16.4	12 37.6	25 53.1	19 48.3	20 2.7	20 37.7	23 36.5	27 27.1	24 40.7
28 M	12 18 33	6 32 41	28 58 29	6♊12 53	0 11.1	14 8.3	27 4.0	20 29.5	20 4.8	20 35.1	23 36.2	27 25.6	24 39.7
29 Tu	12 22 30	7 32 2	13♊24 12	20 32 7	0 8.6	15 40.5	28 14.9	21 10.5	20 7.0	20 32.5	23 36.0	27 24.1	24 38.6
30 W	12 26 26	8 31 21	27 36 26	4♋37 4	0 7.9	17 14.1	29 26.0	21 51.6	20 9.4	20 29.8	23 35.8	27 22.6	24 37.6
31 Th	12 30 23	9 30 38	11♋34 1	18 27 20	0 7.9	18 49.1	0♓37.0	22 32.6	20 12.0	20 27.1	23 35.7	27 21.1	24 36.7

APRIL 1955 LONGITUDE

Day	Sid.Time	☉	0 hr ☽	Noon ☽	True ☊	☿	♀	♂	♃	♄	♅	♆	♇
1 F	12 34 19	10♈29 52	25♋17 9	2♌ 3 33	0♑ 7.3	20♓25.6	1♓48.1	23♉13.6	20♋14.8	20♏24.2	23♋35.7	27♎19.5	24♌35.7
2 Sa	12 38 16	11 29 4	8♌46 42	15 26 44	0R 4.8	22 3.4	2 59.3	23 54.5	20 17.8	20R 21.3	23D 35.7	27R 18.0	24R 34.8
3 Su	12 42 12	12 28 13	22 3 44	28 37 48	29♐59.8	23 42.7	4 10.4	24 35.4	20 20.9	20 18.2	23 35.7	27 16.4	24 33.8
4 M	12 46 9	13 27 20	5♍ 9 0	11♍37 22	29 51.8	25 23.4	5 21.7	25 16.3	20 24.2	20 15.2	23 35.8	27 14.8	24 33.0
5 Tu	12 50 5	14 26 25	18 2 54	24 25 37	29 41.4	27 5.5	6 32.9	25 57.2	20 27.7	20 12.0	23 36.0	27 13.2	24 32.1
6 W	12 54 2	15 25 28	0♎45 29	7♎ 2 30	29 29.1	28 49.1	7 44.3	26 38.0	20 31.4	20 8.8	23 36.2	27 11.6	24 31.2
7 Th	12 57 59	16 24 29	13 16 40	19 28 1	29 16.2	0♈34.1	8 55.6	27 18.7	20 35.2	20 5.4	23 36.5	27 10.0	24 30.4
8 F	13 1 55	17 23 27	25 36 35	1♏42 27	29 3.6	2 20.6	10 7.0	27 59.5	20 39.2	20 2.1	23 36.8	27 8.4	24 29.6
9 Sa	13 5 52	18 22 24	7♏45 46	13 46 43	28 52.7	4 8.5	11 18.5	28 40.2	20 43.4	19 58.6	23 37.2	27 6.8	24 28.8
10 Su	13 9 48	19 21 19	19 45 32	25 42 30	28 44.0	5 58.0	12 29.9	29 20.8	20 47.8	19 55.1	23 37.6	27 5.2	24 28.1
11 M	13 13 45	20 20 12	1♐37 59	7♐32 22	28 38.0	7 48.9	13 41.5	0♊ 1.4	20 52.3	19 51.6	23 38.1	27 3.6	24 27.4
12 Tu	13 17 41	21 19 3	13 26 8	19 19 47	28 34.6	9 41.3	14 53.0	0 42.0	20 57.0	19 47.9	23 38.6	27 1.9	24 26.7
13 W	13 21 38	22 17 52	25 13 52	1♑ 8 59	28D 33.4	11 35.3	16 4.6	1 22.6	21 1.8	19 44.2	23 39.2	27 0.3	24 26.0
14 Th	13 25 34	23 16 40	7♑ 5 46	13 4 51	28 33.6	13 30.7	17 16.3	2 3.2	21 6.8	19 40.5	23 39.8	26 58.7	24 25.4
15 F	13 29 31	24 15 26	19 6 56	25 12 41	28R 34.2	15 27.6	18 27.9	2 43.7	21 12.0	19 36.7	23 40.5	26 57.0	24 24.7
16 Sa	13 33 28	25 14 10	1♒22 45	7♒37 48	28 34.1	17 26.0	19 39.7	3 24.1	21 17.4	19 32.8	23 41.3	26 55.4	24 24.1
17 Su	13 37 24	26 12 52	13 58 25	20 25 9	28 32.5	19 25.8	20 51.4	4 4.6	21 22.8	19 28.9	23 42.1	26 53.8	24 23.6
18 M	13 41 21	27 11 33	26 58 27	3♓38 39	28 28.8	21 27.0	22 3.2	4 45.0	21 28.5	19 24.9	23 42.9	26 52.1	24 23.0
19 Tu	13 45 17	28 10 12	10♓25 58	17 20 26	28 22.8	23 29.6	23 15.0	5 25.4	21 34.3	19 20.9	23 43.8	26 50.5	24 22.5
20 W	13 49 14	29 8 49	24 21 56	1♈30 8	28 15.0	25 33.4	24 26.8	6 5.7	21 40.2	19 16.8	23 44.8	26 48.8	24 22.0
21 Th	13 53 10	0♉ 7 25	8♈44 31	16 4 20	28 6.0	27 38.4	25 38.7	6 46.0	21 46.3	19 12.7	23 45.8	26 47.2	24 21.6
22 F	13 57 7	1 5 58	23 28 44	0♉56 38	27 56.9	29 44.4	26 50.5	7 26.3	21 52.6	19 8.6	23 46.9	26 45.5	24 21.1
23 Sa	14 1 3	2 4 30	8♉26 55	15 58 24	27 48.9	1♉51.4	28 2.4	8 6.6	21 59.0	19 4.4	23 48.0	26 43.9	24 20.7
24 Su	14 5 0	3 3 0	23 29 51	1♊ 0 9	27 42.8	3 59.1	29 14.4	8 46.8	22 5.5	19 0.2	23 49.1	26 42.3	24 20.3
25 M	14 8 57	4 1 28	8♊28 15	15 53 14	27 39.1	6 7.3	0♈26.3	9 27.0	22 12.2	18 55.9	23 50.4	26 40.6	24 20.0
26 Tu	14 12 53	4 59 54	23 14 20	0♋30 57	27D 37.7	8 15.9	1 38.3	10 7.2	22 19.1	18 51.6	23 51.6	26 39.0	24 19.7
27 W	14 16 50	5 58 18	7♋42 40	14 49 12	27 37.9	10 24.5	2 50.3	10 47.4	22 26.1	18 47.3	23 52.9	26 37.4	24 19.4
28 Th	14 20 46	6 56 40	21 50 26	28 46 21	27 38.9	12 32.9	4 2.3	11 27.5	22 33.2	18 42.9	23 54.3	26 35.8	24 19.1
29 F	14 24 43	7 55 0	5♌37 2	12♌22 39	27R 39.6	14 40.9	5 14.4	12 7.6	22 40.4	18 38.6	23 55.7	26 34.2	24 18.9
30 Sa	14 28 39	8 53 17	19 3 25	25 39 37	27 39.1	16 48.0	6 26.4	12 47.6	22 47.8	18 34.1	23 57.2	26 32.6	24 18.7

Astro Data Dy Hr Mn	Planet Ingress Dy Hr Mn	Last Aspect Dy Hr Mn	☽ Ingress Dy Hr Mn	Last Aspect Dy Hr Mn	☽ Ingress Dy Hr Mn	☽ Phases & Eclipses Dy Hr Mn	Astro Data
♄ R 1 6:19	♀ ♒ 4 20:22	2 19:09 ♆ △	♋ 2 22:40	1 3:36 ♆ □	♌ 1 8:20	1 12:40 ☽ 10♊10	1 MARCH 1955
☽0S 8 18:13	☿ ♓ 17 20:49	4 23:10 ♆ □	♌ 5 2:48	3 9:30 ♆ ✶	♍ 3 14:31	8 15:41 ○ 17♍18	Julian Day # 20148
♃ D 16 20:38	☉ ♈ 21 9:35	7 4:20 ♆ ✶	♍ 7 8:09	5 19:44 ☿ ☍	♎ 5 22:34	16 16:36 ☽ 25♐19	Delta T 31.1 sec
☽0N 23 3:59	♀ ♓ 30 11:30	9 3:48 ♅ ✶	♎ 9 15:20	8 3:00 ♆ ☌	♏ 8 8:38	24 3:42 ● 2♈44	SVP 05♓52'51"
		11 20:44 ♆ ☌	♏ 12 1:04	10 20:32 ♂ ☍	♐ 10 20:41	30 20:10 ☽ 9♋21	Obliquity 23°26'43"
♅ D 1 12:50	☊ ♐ 2 23:07	14 4:17 ☿ □	♐ 14 13:13	13 3:36 ♆ ✶	♑ 13 9:40		⚷ Chiron 2♒37.2
♃△♄ 2 13:42	☿ ♈ 6 16:14	16 23:51 ☿ ✶	♑ 17 2:01	15 15:22 ♆ □	♒ 15 21:20	7 6:35 ○ 16♎41	☽ Mean ☊ 2♑18.0
☽0S 5 0:55	♂ ♊ 10 23:09	19 8:56 ☉ ✶	♒ 19 12:47	18 0:26 ☉ ✶	♓ 18 5:28	15 11:01 ☽ 24♑42	
☿0N 9 10:17	☉ ♉ 20 20:58	21 15:28 ♆ △	♓ 21 19:45	20 0:09 ♀ ☌	♈ 20 9:29	22 13:06 ● 1♉38	1 APRIL 1955
☽0N 19 13:43	☿ ♉ 22 2:57	23 12:28 ♅ △	♈ 23 23:09	22 5:16 ♆ ☍	♉ 22 10:29	29 4:23 ☽ 8♌06	Julian Day # 20179
♀0N 27 16:45	♀ ♈ 24 15:13	25 20:24 ♆ ☍	♉ 26 0:31	24 9:59 ♀ ✶	♊ 24 10:24		Delta T 31.1 sec
		27 20:34 ♀ □	♊ 28 1:42	26 5:36 ♆ △	♋ 26 11:09		SVP 05♓52'48"
		30 3:24 ♀ △	♋ 30 4:05	28 8:12 ♆ □	♌ 28 14:08		Obliquity 23°26'43"
				30 13:35 ♆ ✶	♍ 30 19:58		⚷ Chiron 4♒31.1
							☽ Mean ☊ 0♑39.5

LONGITUDE — MAY 1955

Day	Sid.Time	☉	0 hr ☽	Noon ☽	True ☊	☿	♀	♂	♃	♄	♅	♆	♇
1 Su	14 32 36	9♉51 33	2♍11 30	8♍39 21	27♐36.8	18♉54.1	7♈38.5	13♊27.6	22♋55.3	18♏29.7	23♋58.7	26♎31.0	24♌18.5
2 M	14 36 32	10 49 46	15 3 27	21 24 5	27R 32.4	20 58.8	8 50.6	14 7.6	23 3.0	18R 25.3	24 0.3	26R 29.4	24R 18.3
3 Tu	14 40 29	11 47 57	27 41 28	3♎55 51	27 26.2	23 1.7	10 2.7	14 47.6	23 10.8	18 20.8	24 1.9	26 27.8	24 18.2
4 W	14 44 26	12 46 7	10♎ 7 27	16 16 27	27 18.7	25 2.7	11 14.8	15 27.5	23 18.7	18 16.3	24 3.5	26 26.3	24 18.1
5 Th	14 48 22	13 44 14	22 23 2	28 27 23	27 10.6	27 1.5	12 26.9	16 7.4	23 26.7	18 11.8	24 5.2	26 24.7	24 18.1
6 F	14 52 19	14 42 20	4♏29 41	10♏30 7	27 2.8	28 57.7	13 39.1	16 47.2	23 34.8	18 7.3	24 7.0	26 23.2	24D 18.0
7 Sa	14 56 15	15 40 24	16 28 50	22 26 4	26 56.0	0♊51.3	14 51.3	17 27.0	23 43.1	18 2.8	24 8.8	26 21.6	24 18.0
8 Su	15 0 12	16 38 27	28 22 2	4♐16 59	26 50.8	2 42.0	16 3.5	18 6.8	23 51.5	17 58.3	24 10.6	26 20.1	24 18.0
9 M	15 4 8	17 36 28	10♐11 11	16 4 58	26 47.5	4 29.6	17 15.7	18 46.6	24 0.0	17 53.8	24 12.5	26 18.6	24 18.1
10 Tu	15 8 5	18 34 27	21 58 41	27 52 42	26D 46.0	6 14.1	18 27.9	19 26.3	24 8.7	17 49.3	24 14.5	26 17.1	24 18.2
11 W	15 12 1	19 32 25	3♑47 28	9♑43 26	26 46.1	7 55.2	19 40.2	20 6.1	24 17.4	17 44.8	24 16.4	26 15.6	24 18.3
12 Th	15 15 58	20 30 22	15 41 6	21 41 0	26 47.3	9 32.9	20 52.5	20 45.7	24 26.3	17 40.3	24 18.5	26 14.2	24 18.4
13 F	15 19 55	21 28 17	27 43 40	3♒49 42	26 49.0	11 7.1	22 4.8	21 25.4	24 35.2	17 35.8	24 20.5	26 12.7	24 18.6
14 Sa	15 23 51	22 26 11	9♒59 41	16 14 11	26 50.5	12 37.8	23 17.1	22 5.0	24 44.3	17 31.3	24 22.7	26 11.3	24 18.8
15 Su	15 27 48	23 24 3	22 33 46	28 58 59	26R 51.1	14 4.8	24 29.5	22 44.6	24 53.5	17 26.8	24 24.8	26 9.8	24 19.0
16 M	15 31 44	24 21 55	5♓30 18	12♓ 8 8	26 50.6	15 28.1	25 41.8	23 24.2	25 2.8	17 22.3	24 27.0	26 8.4	24 19.2
17 Tu	15 35 41	25 19 45	18 52 49	25 44 32	26 48.7	16 47.7	26 54.2	24 3.8	25 12.2	17 17.9	24 29.2	26 7.0	24 19.5
18 W	15 39 37	26 17 34	2♈43 20	9♈49 6	26 45.5	18 3.5	28 6.6	24 43.3	25 21.7	17 13.4	24 31.5	26 5.7	24 19.8
19 Th	15 43 34	27 15 22	17 1 33	24 20 10	26 41.6	19 15.4	29 19.0	25 22.8	25 31.3	17 9.0	24 33.8	26 4.3	24 20.2
20 F	15 47 30	28 13 9	1♉44 18	9♉13 3	26 37.6	20 23.4	0♉31.4	26 2.3	25 41.0	17 4.6	24 36.2	26 3.0	24 20.5
21 Sa	15 51 27	29 10 54	16 45 26	24 20 17	26 33.9	21 27.4	1 43.9	26 41.7	25 50.8	17 0.2	24 38.6	26 1.6	24 20.9
22 Su	15 55 24	0♊ 8 39	1♊56 23	9♊32 29	26 31.3	22 27.4	2 56.3	27 21.2	26 0.7	16 55.9	24 41.0	26 0.3	24 21.3
23 M	15 59 20	1 6 22	17 7 22	24 39 51	26D 29.9	23 23.3	4 8.8	28 0.6	26 10.7	16 51.6	24 43.5	25 59.1	24 21.8
24 Tu	16 3 17	2 4 4	2♋ 8 55	9♋33 39	26 29.7	24 15.1	5 21.3	28 39.9	26 20.8	16 47.3	24 46.0	25 57.8	24 22.3
25 W	16 7 13	3 1 44	16 53 19	24 7 21	26 30.5	25 2.6	6 33.8	29 19.3	26 31.0	16 43.0	24 48.6	25 56.6	24 22.8
26 Th	16 11 10	3 59 23	1♌15 22	8♌17 7	26 31.9	25 45.8	7 46.3	29 58.6	26 41.3	16 38.8	24 51.2	25 55.3	24 23.3
27 F	16 15 6	4 57 0	15 12 33	22 1 42	26 33.2	26 24.6	8 58.8	0♋37.9	26 51.7	16 34.6	24 53.8	25 54.1	24 23.9
28 Sa	16 19 3	5 54 35	28 44 43	5♍21 51	26R 34.0	26 58.9	10 11.4	1 17.2	27 2.1	16 30.5	24 56.5	25 53.0	24 24.5
29 Su	16 22 59	6 52 10	11♍53 27	18 19 50	26 34.1	27 28.7	11 23.9	1 56.5	27 12.7	16 26.4	24 59.2	25 51.8	24 25.1
30 M	16 26 56	7 49 42	24 41 25	0♎58 37	26 33.3	27 54.0	12 36.5	2 35.7	27 23.3	16 22.4	25 1.9	25 50.7	24 25.8
31 Tu	16 30 53	8 47 14	7♎11 51	13 21 32	26 31.7	28 14.6	13 49.0	3 14.9	27 34.0	16 18.4	25 4.7	25 49.6	24 26.4

LONGITUDE — JUNE 1955

Day	Sid.Time	☉	0 hr ☽	Noon ☽	True ☊	☿	♀	♂	♃	♄	♅	♆	♇
1 W	16 34 49	9♊44 44	19♎28 5	25♎31 53	26♐29.5	28♊30.6	15♉ 1.6	3♋54.1	27♋44.8	16♏14.4	25♋ 7.5	25♎48.5	24♌27.1
2 Th	16 38 46	10 42 13	1♏33 20	7♏32 47	26R 27.1	28 41.9	16 14.2	4 33.2	27 55.6	16R 10.5	25 10.3	25R 47.4	24 27.8
3 F	16 42 42	11 39 41	13 30 33	19 26 59	26 24.9	28R 48.5	17 26.8	5 12.4	28 6.6	16 6.6	25 13.2	25 46.4	24 28.6
4 Sa	16 46 39	12 37 7	25 22 23	1♐17 2	26 22.9	28 50.6	18 39.4	5 51.5	28 17.6	16 2.8	25 16.1	25 45.4	24 29.4
5 Su	16 50 35	13 34 33	7♐11 14	13 5 15	26 21.6	28 48.1	19 52.1	6 30.5	28 28.7	15 59.1	25 19.0	25 44.4	24 30.2
6 M	16 54 32	14 31 58	18 59 21	24 53 51	26D 20.9	28 41.2	21 4.7	7 9.6	28 39.9	15 55.4	25 22.0	25 43.5	24 31.0
7 Tu	16 58 28	15 29 21	0♑49 0	6♑45 7	26 20.8	28 30.1	22 17.4	7 48.6	28 51.1	15 51.8	25 25.0	25 42.5	24 31.9
8 W	17 2 25	16 26 44	12 42 30	18 41 30	26 21.3	28 14.9	23 30.1	8 27.6	29 2.4	15 48.2	25 28.0	25 41.6	24 32.8
9 Th	17 6 22	17 24 7	24 42 26	0♒45 41	26 22.0	27 55.9	24 42.8	9 6.6	29 13.8	15 44.7	25 31.0	25 40.7	24 33.7
10 F	17 10 18	18 21 28	6♒51 37	13 0 40	26 22.8	27 33.5	25 55.5	9 45.6	29 25.2	15 41.3	25 34.1	25 39.9	24 34.6
11 Sa	17 14 15	19 18 49	19 13 13	25 29 42	26 23.6	27 7.9	27 8.3	10 24.6	29 36.7	15 37.9	25 37.2	25 39.1	24 35.6
12 Su	17 18 11	20 16 9	1♓50 31	8♓16 7	26 24.1	26 39.7	28 21.0	11 3.5	29 48.3	15 34.6	25 40.4	25 38.3	24 36.6
13 M	17 22 8	21 13 29	14 46 51	21 23 6	26R 24.4	26 9.3	29 33.8	11 42.4	29 59.9	15 31.3	25 43.5	25 37.5	24 37.6
14 Tu	17 26 4	22 10 49	28 5 9	4♈53 14	26 24.4	25 37.1	0♊46.6	12 21.3	0♌11.6	15 28.1	25 46.7	25 36.7	24 38.6
15 W	17 30 1	23 8 8	11♈47 30	18 47 58	26 24.2	25 3.8	1 59.5	13 0.2	0 23.4	15 25.0	25 49.9	25 36.0	24 39.7
16 Th	17 33 57	24 5 27	25 54 32	3♉ 6 59	26 24.0	24 29.9	3 12.3	13 39.0	0 35.2	15 22.0	25 53.1	25 35.3	24 40.7
17 F	17 37 54	25 2 45	10♉24 54	17 47 44	26 23.9	23 56.0	4 25.2	14 17.9	0 47.1	15 19.0	25 56.4	25 34.7	24 41.9
18 Sa	17 41 51	26 0 3	25 14 46	2♊45 9	26D 23.8	23 22.7	5 38.0	14 56.7	0 59.1	15 16.2	25 59.7	25 34.0	24 43.0
19 Su	17 45 47	26 57 21	10♊17 53	17 51 54	26 23.8	22 50.5	6 50.9	15 35.5	1 11.1	15 13.4	26 3.0	25 33.4	24 44.1
20 M	17 49 44	27 54 39	25 26 3	2♋59 11	26R 23.8	22 19.9	8 3.9	16 14.3	1 23.1	15 10.6	26 6.3	25 32.9	24 45.3
21 Tu	17 53 40	28 51 56	10♋30 10	17 57 56	26 23.8	21 51.6	9 16.8	16 53.1	1 35.2	15 8.0	26 9.7	25 32.3	24 46.5
22 W	17 57 37	29 49 12	25 21 32	2♌40 8	26 23.6	21 25.9	10 29.7	17 31.8	1 47.4	15 5.4	26 13.0	25 31.8	24 47.8
23 Th	18 1 33	0♋46 28	9♌53 4	16 59 50	26 23.2	21 3.4	11 42.7	18 10.6	1 59.6	15 3.0	26 16.4	25 31.3	24 49.0
24 F	18 5 30	1 43 44	24 0 6	0♍53 40	26 22.7	20 44.4	12 55.7	18 49.3	2 11.9	15 0.6	26 19.8	25 30.9	24 50.3
25 Sa	18 9 26	2 40 58	7♍40 32	14 20 49	26 22.1	20 29.2	14 8.7	19 28.0	2 24.2	14 58.3	26 23.3	25 30.5	24 51.6
26 Su	18 13 23	3 38 12	20 54 43	27 22 36	26 21.6	20 18.1	15 21.7	20 6.7	2 36.5	14 56.0	26 26.7	25 30.1	24 52.9
27 M	18 17 20	4 35 26	3♎44 50	10♎ 1 53	26D 21.4	20D 11.4	16 34.7	20 45.4	2 48.9	14 53.9	26 30.2	25 29.7	24 54.2
28 Tu	18 21 16	5 32 38	16 14 16	22 22 30	26 21.6	20 9.2	17 47.8	21 24.0	3 1.4	14 51.8	26 33.6	25 29.4	24 55.5
29 W	18 25 13	6 29 51	28 27 7	4♏28 41	26 22.2	20 11.7	19 0.8	22 2.6	3 13.9	14 49.9	26 37.1	25 29.1	24 56.9
30 Th	18 29 9	7 27 3	10♏27 43	16 24 45	26 23.1	20 19.1	20 13.9	22 41.2	3 26.4	14 48.0	26 40.6	25 28.8	24 58.3

Astro Data Dy Hr Mn	Planet Ingress Dy Hr Mn	Last Aspect Dy Hr Mn	☽ Ingress Dy Hr Mn	Last Aspect Dy Hr Mn	☽ Ingress Dy Hr Mn	☽ Phases & Eclipses Dy Hr Mn	Astro Data
☽0S 2 5:55	☿ ♊ 6 13:05	2 16:59 ♅ ⚹	♎ 3 4:26	1 18:13 ☿ △	♏ 1 20:54	6 22:14 ○ 15♏36	1 MAY 1955
♇ D 6 18:29	♀ ♉ 19 13:35	5 7:56 ♆ ☌	♏ 5 15:04	4 6:01 ♃ △	♐ 4 9:24	15 1:42 ☽ 23♒28	Julian Day # 20209
♃☌♅ 10 20:38	☉ ♊ 21 20:24	7 15:46 ♇ □	♐ 8 3:19	6 19:24 ☿ ☍	♑ 6 22:21	21 20:59 ● 0♊01	Delta T 31.2 sec
♃⚺♇ 11 2:25	♂ ♋ 26 0:50	10 8:45 ♆ ⚹	♑ 10 16:19	9 9:07 ♃ ☍	♒ 9 10:30	28 14:01 ☽ 6♍28	SVP 05♓52'45"
♅⚺♇ 11 23:15		12 21:00 ♆ □	♒ 13 4:29	11 16:43 ♀ □	♓ 11 20:32		Obliquity 23°26'42"
☽0N 16 22:25	♀ ♊ 13 8:38	15 6:44 ♆ △	♓ 15 13:53	13 19:52 ♅ △	♈ 14 3:24	5 14:08 ○ 14♐08	⚷ Chiron 5♒26.2
♃□♆ 21 23:11	♃ ♌ 13 0:06	17 12:08 ☉ ⚹	♈ 17 19:21	15 23:58 ♅ □	♉ 16 6:50	5 14:23 ☍A 0.622	☽ Mean ☊ 29♐04.1
☽0S 29 11:09	☉ ♋ 22 4:31	19 14:48 ♆ ☍	♉ 19 21:12	18 1:12 ♅ ⚹	♊ 18 7:37	13 12:37 ☽ 21♓44	
		21 14:32 ♃ ⚹	♊ 21 20:56	20 4:12 ☉ ☌	♋ 20 7:15	20 4:12 ● 28♊05	1 JUNE 1955
☿ R 3 22:46		23 18:09 ♂ ☌	♋ 23 20:33	22 1:24 ♅ ☌	♌ 22 7:36	20 4:10:11 ☌T 7'08"	Julian Day # 20240
♅□♆ 11 11:09		25 16:12 ♃ ☌	♌ 25 21:52	24 2:37 ♆ ⚹	♍ 24 10:26	27 1:44 ☽ 4♎40	Delta T 31.2 sec
☽0N 13 5:30		27 20:42 ☿ ⚹	♍ 28 2:16	26 10:18 ♅ ⚹	♎ 26 16:55		SVP 05♓52'40"
☽0S 25 18:18		30 6:18 ☿ □	♎ 30 10:08	28 20:21 ♅ □	♏ 29 3:04		Obliquity 23°26'42"
☿ D 27 23:11							⚷ Chiron 5♒16.4R
							☽ Mean ☊ 27♐25.7

JULY 1955 LONGITUDE

Day	Sid.Time	☉	0 hr ☽	Noon ☽	True ☊	☿	♀	♂	♃	♄	♅	♆	♇
1 F	18 33 6	8♋24 15	22♏20 16	28♏14 46	26♐24.2	20♊31.3	21♊27.0	23♋19.8	3♌38.9	14♏46.2	26♋44.2	25♎28.6	24♌59.7
2 Sa	18 37 2	9 21 26	4♐ 8 42	10♐ 2 29	26 25.3	20 48.4	22 40.1	23 58.4	3 51.5	14R 44.5	26 47.7	25R 28.4	25 1.2
3 Su	18 40 59	10 18 37	15 56 31	21 51 9	26R 26.1	21 10.4	23 53.2	24 37.0	4 4.2	14 42.9	26 51.3	25 28.2	25 2.6
4 M	18 44 55	11 15 48	27 46 43	3♑43 33	26 26.3	21 37.4	25 6.4	25 15.5	4 16.9	14 41.4	26 54.8	25 28.1	25 4.1
5 Tu	18 48 52	12 12 59	9♑41 55	15 42 5	26 25.9	22 9.2	26 19.6	25 54.1	4 29.6	14 40.0	26 58.4	25 28.0	25 5.6
6 W	18 52 49	13 10 10	21 44 16	27 48 43	26 24.6	22 45.9	27 32.8	26 32.6	4 42.3	14 38.7	27 2.0	25 27.9	25 7.1
7 Th	18 56 45	14 7 21	3♒55 39	10♒ 5 15	26 22.6	23 27.5	28 46.0	27 11.1	4 55.1	14 37.4	27 5.6	25D 27.9	25 8.6
8 F	19 0 42	15 4 32	16 17 43	22 33 14	26 20.0	24 13.8	29 59.2	27 49.6	5 7.9	14 36.3	27 9.2	25 27.9	25 10.1
9 Sa	19 4 38	16 1 43	28 52 2	5♓14 16	26 17.1	25 4.8	1♋12.5	28 28.1	5 20.7	14 35.2	27 12.8	25 27.9	25 11.7
10 Su	19 8 35	16 58 55	11♓40 9	18 9 53	26 14.4	26 0.6	2 25.8	29 6.5	5 33.6	14 34.3	27 16.4	25 28.0	25 13.3
11 M	19 12 31	17 56 6	24 43 39	1♈21 37	26 12.2	27 0.9	3 39.1	29 45.0	5 46.5	14 33.4	27 20.1	25 28.0	25 14.9
12 Tu	19 16 28	18 53 19	8♈ 3 58	14 50 51	26D 10.8	28 5.8	4 52.4	0♌23.4	5 59.4	14 32.7	27 23.7	25 28.2	25 16.5
13 W	19 20 24	19 50 32	21 42 20	28 38 29	26 10.4	29 15.2	6 5.8	1 1.9	6 12.4	14 32.0	27 27.3	25 28.3	25 18.1
14 Th	19 24 21	20 47 45	5♉39 19	12♉44 43	26 11.0	0♋29.0	7 19.2	1 40.3	6 25.4	14 31.4	27 31.0	25 28.5	25 19.7
15 F	19 28 18	21 44 59	19 54 31	27 8 27	26 12.2	1 47.2	8 32.6	2 18.7	6 38.4	14 31.0	27 34.7	25 28.7	25 21.4
16 Sa	19 32 14	22 42 14	4♊26 6	11♊46 58	26 13.6	3 9.6	9 46.0	2 57.1	6 51.4	14 30.6	27 38.3	25 28.9	25 23.1
17 Su	19 36 11	23 39 30	19 10 25	26 35 41	26R 14.5	4 36.3	10 59.5	3 35.5	7 4.4	14 30.3	27 42.0	25 29.2	25 24.7
18 M	19 40 7	24 36 46	4♋ 1 57	11♋28 18	26 14.5	6 7.1	12 13.0	4 13.9	7 17.5	14 30.1	27 45.7	25 29.5	25 26.4
19 Tu	19 44 4	25 34 2	18 53 45	26 17 19	26 13.1	7 41.8	13 26.5	4 52.3	7 30.6	14D 30.1	27 49.3	25 29.9	25 28.2
20 W	19 48 0	26 31 19	3♌38 3	10♌55 4	26 10.3	9 20.3	14 40.0	5 30.7	7 43.7	14 30.1	27 53.0	25 30.3	25 29.9
21 Th	19 51 57	27 28 37	18 7 32	25 14 46	26 6.3	11 2.6	15 53.6	6 9.0	7 56.8	14 30.2	27 56.7	25 30.7	25 31.6
22 F	19 55 54	28 25 54	2♍16 13	9♍11 29	26 1.5	12 48.3	17 7.1	6 47.4	8 10.0	14 30.4	28 0.4	25 31.1	25 33.4
23 Sa	19 59 50	29 23 12	16 0 21	22 42 42	25 56.7	14 37.3	18 20.7	7 25.7	8 23.1	14 30.7	28 4.0	25 31.6	25 35.1
24 Su	20 3 47	0♌20 31	29 18 36	5♎48 15	25 52.5	16 29.4	19 34.3	8 4.1	8 36.3	14 31.1	28 7.7	25 32.1	25 36.9
25 M	20 7 43	1 17 50	12♎11 56	18 30 4	25 49.4	18 24.3	20 48.0	8 42.4	8 49.4	14 31.6	28 11.4	25 32.6	25 38.7
26 Tu	20 11 40	2 15 9	24 43 7	0♏51 39	25D 47.8	20 21.6	22 1.6	9 20.7	9 2.6	14 32.2	28 15.1	25 33.2	25 40.5
27 W	20 15 36	3 12 28	6♏56 12	12 57 25	25 47.6	22 21.2	23 15.3	9 59.0	9 15.8	14 32.9	28 18.7	25 33.8	25 42.3
28 Th	20 19 33	4 9 48	18 55 55	24 52 20	25 48.5	24 22.6	24 29.0	10 37.3	9 29.0	14 33.7	28 22.4	25 34.4	25 44.1
29 F	20 23 29	5 7 9	0♐47 17	6♐41 23	25 50.0	26 25.5	25 42.7	11 15.6	9 42.2	14 34.6	28 26.1	25 35.1	25 45.9
30 Sa	20 27 26	6 4 30	12 35 14	18 29 22	25 51.6	28 29.6	26 56.5	11 53.8	9 55.4	14 35.6	28 29.7	25 35.8	25 47.8
31 Su	20 31 23	7 1 52	24 24 19	0♑20 35	25R 52.3	0♌34.6	28 10.2	12 32.1	10 8.7	14 36.7	28 33.4	25 36.5	25 49.6

AUGUST 1955 LONGITUDE

Day	Sid.Time	☉	0 hr ☽	Noon ☽	True ☊	☿	♀	♂	♃	♄	♅	♆	♇
1 M	20 35 19	7♌59 14	6♑18 35	12♑18 44	25♐51.7	2♌40.1	29♋24.0	13♌10.4	10♌21.9	14♏37.9	28♋37.0	25♎37.3	25♌51.5
2 Tu	20 39 16	8 56 37	18 21 21	24 26 44	25R 49.3	4 45.8	0♌37.8	13 48.6	10 35.1	14 39.2	28 40.7	25 38.1	25 53.3
3 W	20 43 12	9 54 1	0♒35 7	6♒46 41	25 45.0	6 51.5	1 51.6	14 26.9	10 48.3	14 40.6	28 44.3	25 38.9	25 55.2
4 Th	20 47 9	10 51 25	13 1 34	19 19 49	25 38.8	8 56.8	3 5.5	15 5.1	11 1.6	14 42.1	28 47.9	25 39.7	25 57.1
5 F	20 51 5	11 48 51	25 41 30	2♓ 6 36	25 31.3	11 1.7	4 19.3	15 43.3	11 14.8	14 43.6	28 51.5	25 40.6	25 59.0
6 Sa	20 55 2	12 46 17	8♓35 6	15 6 55	25 23.2	13 5.8	5 33.2	16 21.5	11 28.0	14 45.3	28 55.1	25 41.5	26 0.9
7 Su	20 58 58	13 43 45	21 41 59	28 20 13	25 15.4	15 9.0	6 47.1	16 59.8	11 41.2	14 47.1	28 58.7	25 42.4	26 2.8
8 M	21 2 55	14 41 14	5♈ 1 33	11♈45 53	25 8.6	17 11.2	8 1.1	17 38.0	11 54.5	14 48.9	29 2.3	25 43.4	26 4.7
9 Tu	21 6 52	15 38 44	18 33 10	25 23 20	25 3.6	19 12.3	9 15.0	18 16.2	12 7.7	14 50.9	29 5.9	25 44.4	26 6.6
10 W	21 10 48	16 36 15	2♉16 21	9♉12 9	25 0.7	21 12.1	10 29.0	18 54.4	12 20.9	14 52.9	29 9.4	25 45.4	26 8.5
11 Th	21 14 45	17 33 48	16 10 41	23 11 55	24D 59.7	23 10.7	11 43.1	19 32.6	12 34.1	14 55.0	29 13.0	25 46.5	26 10.4
12 F	21 18 41	18 31 23	0♊15 44	7♊22 2	25 0.1	25 7.9	12 57.1	20 10.8	12 47.3	14 57.3	29 16.5	25 47.6	26 12.3
13 Sa	21 22 38	19 28 59	14 30 37	21 41 16	25R 1.0	27 3.7	14 11.2	20 49.0	13 0.5	14 59.6	29 20.0	25 48.7	26 14.3
14 Su	21 26 34	20 26 36	28 53 39	6♋ 7 21	25 1.3	28 58.0	15 25.2	21 27.3	13 13.6	15 2.0	29 23.5	25 49.8	26 16.2
15 M	21 30 31	21 24 15	13♋21 53	20 36 41	24 59.9	0♍51.0	16 39.4	22 5.5	13 26.8	15 4.5	29 27.0	25 51.0	26 18.1
16 Tu	21 34 27	22 21 55	27 51 5	5♌ 4 23	24 56.3	2 42.4	17 53.5	22 43.7	13 40.0	15 7.1	29 30.5	25 52.2	26 20.1
17 W	21 38 24	23 19 37	12♌15 51	19 24 43	24 50.2	4 32.5	19 7.7	23 21.9	13 53.1	15 9.8	29 33.9	25 53.4	26 22.0
18 Th	21 42 21	24 17 20	26 30 15	3♍31 48	24 41.9	6 21.1	20 21.8	24 0.1	14 6.2	15 12.5	29 37.3	25 54.7	26 23.9
19 F	21 46 17	25 15 4	10♍28 45	17 20 37	24 32.3	8 8.2	21 36.0	24 38.3	14 19.3	15 15.4	29 40.8	25 55.9	26 25.9
20 Sa	21 50 14	26 12 50	24 7 2	0♎47 46	24 22.3	9 53.9	22 50.2	25 16.4	14 32.4	15 18.3	29 44.2	25 57.2	26 27.8
21 Su	21 54 10	27 10 36	7♎22 41	13 51 50	24 13.0	11 38.3	24 4.5	25 54.6	14 45.5	15 21.4	29 47.5	25 58.6	26 29.7
22 M	21 58 7	28 8 24	20 15 22	26 33 34	24 5.4	13 21.2	25 18.7	26 32.8	14 58.5	15 24.5	29 50.9	25 59.9	26 31.7
23 Tu	22 2 3	29 6 13	2♏46 46	8♏55 27	23 59.9	15 2.7	26 33.0	27 11.0	15 11.6	15 27.7	29 54.2	26 1.3	26 33.6
24 W	22 6 0	0♍ 4 4	15 0 9	21 1 27	23 56.8	16 42.8	27 47.3	27 49.2	15 24.6	15 31.0	29 57.5	26 2.7	26 35.6
25 Th	22 9 56	1 1 55	26 59 57	2♐56 21	23D 55.6	18 21.6	29 1.6	28 27.4	15 37.5	15 34.4	0♌ 0.8	26 4.2	26 37.5
26 F	22 13 53	1 59 48	8♐51 18	14 45 29	23 55.7	19 59.0	0♍15.9	29 5.6	15 50.5	15 37.8	0 4.1	26 5.6	26 39.4
27 Sa	22 17 50	2 57 42	20 39 35	26 34 16	23R 56.1	21 35.1	1 30.2	29 43.7	16 3.4	15 41.4	0 7.3	26 7.1	26 41.4
28 Su	22 21 46	3 55 38	2♑30 10	8♑27 53	23 55.8	23 9.8	2 44.6	0♍21.9	16 16.3	15 45.0	0 10.5	26 8.6	26 43.3
29 M	22 25 43	4 53 34	14 28 0	20 31 1	23 53.9	24 43.2	3 58.9	1 0.1	16 29.2	15 48.7	0 13.7	26 10.2	26 45.2
30 Tu	22 29 39	5 51 32	26 37 24	2♒47 30	23 49.7	26 15.3	5 13.3	1 38.3	16 42.0	15 52.5	0 16.9	26 11.7	26 47.2
31 W	22 33 36	6 49 32	9♒ 1 40	15 20 5	23 42.8	27 46.0	6 27.7	2 16.5	16 54.8	15 56.4	0 20.0	26 13.3	26 49.1

Astro Data	Dy Hr Mn
♆ D	7 19:39
☽ 0 N	10 11:30
♄ D	19 7:30
♆⚹♇	20 6:51
☽ 0 S	23 3:32
☽ 0 N	6 17:33
☽ 0 S	19 13:37
♃□♄	24 16:03

Planet Ingress	Dy Hr Mn
♀ ♋	8 0:15
♂ ♌	11 9:22
☿ ♋	13 14:44
☉ ♌	23 15:25
☿ ♌	30 17:22
♀ ♌	1 11:43
☿ ♍	14 13:08
☉ ♍	23 22:19
♅ ♌	24 18:03
♀ ♍	25 18:52
♂ ♍	27 10:13

Last Aspect Dy Hr Mn		☽ Ingress Dy Hr Mn
1 8:58	♅ △	♐ 1 15:34
3 19:20	♆ ⚹	♑ 4 4:29
6 10:31	♅ ☍	♒ 6 16:18
8 17:33	♆ △	♓ 9 2:09
11 4:45	♅ △	♈ 11 9:33
13 14:18	☿ ⚹	♉ 13 14:20
15 12:46	♅ ⚹	♊ 15 16:43
17 10:13	♆ △	♋ 17 17:30
19 14:34	♅ ☌	♌ 19 18:03
21 12:30	♇ ☌	♍ 21 20:06
23 21:50	♅ ⚹	♎ 24 1:16
26 6:55	♅ □	♏ 26 10:19
28 19:12	♅ △	♐ 28 22:24
31 2:53	♇ △	♑ 31 11:18

Last Aspect Dy Hr Mn		☽ Ingress Dy Hr Mn
2 20:23	♅ ☍	♒ 2 22:52
5 0:33	♇ ☍	♓ 5 8:04
7 13:13	♅ △	♈ 7 15:00
9 18:33	♅ □	♉ 9 20:03
11 22:19	♅ ⚹	♊ 11 23:33
14 0:08	☿ ⚹	♋ 14 1:50
16 2:46	♅ ☌	♌ 16 3:34
17 23:49	♇ ☌	♍ 18 5:57
20 10:08	♅ ⚹	♎ 20 10:34
22 18:25	♅ □	♏ 22 18:37
25 4:34	♀ □	♐ 25 6:03
27 12:16	♇ △	♑ 27 18:57
29 23:11	☿ △	♒ 30 6:35

☽ Phases & Eclipses Dy Hr Mn	
5 5:29	○ 12♑26
12 20:31	☽ 19♈42
19 11:35	● 26♋02
26 16:00	☽ 2♏53
3 19:30	○ 10♒41
11 2:33	☽ 17♉40
17 19:58	● 24♌08
25 8:52	☽ 1♐23

Astro Data

1 JULY 1955
Julian Day # 20270
Delta T 31.2 sec
SVP 05♓52'35"
Obliquity 23°26'41"
⚷ Chiron 4♒08.8R
☽ Mean ☊ 25♐50.4

1 AUGUST 1955
Julian Day # 20301
Delta T 31.2 sec
SVP 05♓52'30"
Obliquity 23°26'41"
⚷ Chiron 2♒26.7R
☽ Mean ☊ 24♐11.9

LONGITUDE SEPTEMBER 1955

Day	Sid.Time	☉	0 hr ☽	Noon ☽	True ☊	☿	♀	♂	♃	♄	♅	♆	♇
1 Th	22 37 32	7♍47 33	21♒42 54	28♒10 10	23♐33.6	29♍15.4	7♍42.1	2♍54.6	17♌ 7.6	16♏ 0.3	0♌23.1	26♎14.9	26♌51.0
2 F	22 41 29	8 45 35	4♓41 50	11♓17 45	23R22.4	0♎43.5	8 56.5	3 32.8	17 20.3	16 4.3	0 26.2	26 16.6	26 52.9
3 Sa	22 45 25	9 43 39	17 57 43	24 41 27	23 10.3	2 10.2	10 11.0	4 11.0	17 33.0	16 8.4	0 29.3	26 18.2	26 54.8
4 Su	22 49 22	10 41 45	1♈28 37	8♈18 51	22 58.5	3 35.6	11 25.4	4 49.2	17 45.7	16 12.6	0 32.3	26 19.9	26 56.7
5 M	22 53 18	11 39 52	15 11 45	22 6 56	22 48.2	4 59.5	12 39.9	5 27.3	17 58.3	16 16.9	0 35.3	26 21.6	26 58.6
6 Tu	22 57 15	12 38 2	29 4 2	6♉ 2 41	22 40.1	6 22.1	13 54.4	6 5.5	18 10.9	16 21.2	0 38.3	26 23.3	27 0.5
7 W	23 1 12	13 36 13	13♉ 2 36	20 3 31	22 34.9	7 43.2	15 8.9	6 43.7	18 23.5	16 25.6	0 41.2	26 25.0	27 2.4
8 Th	23 5 8	14 34 27	27 5 14	4♊ 7 34	22 32.2	9 2.8	16 23.4	7 21.9	18 36.0	16 30.1	0 44.1	26 26.8	27 4.2
9 F	23 9 5	15 32 42	11♊10 24	18 13 37	22 31.4	10 21.0	17 37.9	8 0.1	18 48.5	16 34.6	0 47.0	26 28.6	27 6.1
10 Sa	23 13 1	16 31 0	25 17 7	2♋20 47	22 31.4	11 37.5	18 52.5	8 38.3	19 0.9	16 39.3	0 49.8	26 30.4	27 8.0
11 Su	23 16 58	17 29 20	9♋24 31	16 28 7	22 30.8	12 52.4	20 7.1	9 16.5	19 13.3	16 43.9	0 52.6	26 32.2	27 9.8
12 M	23 20 54	18 27 42	23 31 24	0♌34 6	22 28.4	14 5.6	21 21.7	9 54.7	19 25.6	16 48.7	0 55.4	26 34.0	27 11.6
13 Tu	23 24 51	19 26 6	7♌35 53	14 36 23	22 23.4	15 17.1	22 36.3	10 33.0	19 37.9	16 53.5	0 58.1	26 35.9	27 13.5
14 W	23 28 47	20 24 32	21 35 10	28 31 47	22 15.5	16 26.6	23 50.9	11 11.2	19 50.1	16 58.4	1 0.8	26 37.8	27 15.3
15 Th	23 32 44	21 23 0	5♍25 46	12♍16 38	22 5.0	17 34.2	25 5.5	11 49.4	20 2.3	17 3.4	1 3.5	26 39.6	27 17.1
16 F	23 36 41	22 21 29	19 3 57	25 47 18	21 52.7	18 39.7	26 20.1	12 27.6	20 14.5	17 8.4	1 6.1	26 41.6	27 18.9
17 Sa	23 40 37	23 20 1	2♎26 22	9♎ 0 52	21 39.9	19 43.0	27 34.8	13 5.9	20 26.5	17 13.5	1 8.7	26 43.5	27 20.7
18 Su	23 44 34	24 18 35	15 30 41	21 55 42	21 27.8	20 44.0	28 49.4	13 44.1	20 38.6	17 18.7	1 11.3	26 45.4	27 22.5
19 M	23 48 30	25 17 10	28 16 0	4♏31 42	21 17.4	21 42.4	0♎ 4.1	14 22.4	20 50.5	17 23.9	1 13.8	26 47.4	27 24.2
20 Tu	23 52 27	26 15 48	10♏43 3	16 50 22	21 9.6	22 38.1	1 18.8	15 0.6	21 2.4	17 29.2	1 16.2	26 49.4	27 26.0
21 W	23 56 23	27 14 27	22 54 3	28 54 37	21 4.4	23 30.9	2 33.5	15 38.9	21 14.3	17 34.6	1 18.7	26 51.4	27 27.7
22 Th	0 0 20	28 13 7	4♐52 36	10♐48 35	21 1.8	24 20.5	3 48.2	16 17.1	21 26.1	17 40.0	1 21.1	26 53.4	27 29.4
23 F	0 4 16	29 11 50	16 43 12	22 37 7	21D 1.0	25 6.8	5 2.9	16 55.4	21 37.8	17 45.5	1 23.4	26 55.4	27 31.1
24 Sa	0 8 13	0♎10 34	28 31 2	4♑25 39	21R 1.0	25 49.4	6 17.6	17 33.6	21 49.4	17 51.0	1 25.8	26 57.4	27 32.8
25 Su	0 12 10	1 9 20	10♑21 38	16 19 42	21 0.7	26 28.1	7 32.3	18 11.9	22 1.0	17 56.6	1 28.0	26 59.5	27 34.5
26 M	0 16 6	2 8 8	22 20 28	28 24 36	20 59.1	27 2.5	8 47.0	18 50.2	22 12.6	18 2.2	1 30.3	27 1.5	27 36.2
27 Tu	0 20 3	3 6 57	4♒32 40	10♒45 10	20 55.4	27 32.2	10 1.7	19 28.5	22 24.0	18 7.9	1 32.4	27 3.6	27 37.8
28 W	0 23 59	4 5 48	17 2 34	23 25 10	20 49.2	27 57.0	11 16.4	20 6.7	22 35.4	18 13.7	1 34.6	27 5.7	27 39.5
29 Th	0 27 56	5 4 41	29 53 16	6♓26 57	20 40.5	28 16.3	12 31.2	20 45.0	22 46.7	18 19.5	1 36.7	27 7.8	27 41.1
30 F	0 31 52	6 3 36	13♓ 6 14	19 51 0	20 29.8	28 29.8	13 45.9	21 23.3	22 58.0	18 25.4	1 38.7	27 9.9	27 42.7

LONGITUDE OCTOBER 1955

Day	Sid.Time	☉	0 hr ☽	Noon ☽	True ☊	☿	♀	♂	♃	♄	♅	♆	♇
1 Sa	0 35 49	7♎ 2 33	26♓40 59	3♈35 47	20♐18.1	28♎37.0	15♎ 0.6	22♍ 1.6	23♌ 9.1	18♏31.3	1♌40.7	27♎12.0	27♌44.3
2 Su	0 39 45	8 1 31	10♈34 57	17 37 51	20R 6.6	28R37.5	16 15.4	22 39.9	23 20.2	18 37.2	1 42.7	27 14.2	27 45.9
3 M	0 43 42	9 0 32	24 43 52	1♉52 18	19 56.4	28 31.0	17 30.1	23 18.2	23 31.2	18 43.3	1 44.6	27 16.3	27 47.4
4 Tu	0 47 38	9 59 35	9♉ 2 26	16 13 35	19 48.6	28 17.1	18 44.9	23 56.6	23 42.2	18 49.3	1 46.5	27 18.5	27 48.9
5 W	0 51 35	10 58 40	23 25 8	0♊36 29	19 43.5	27 55.4	19 59.7	24 34.9	23 53.0	18 55.4	1 48.3	27 20.6	27 50.5
6 Th	0 55 32	11 57 47	7♊47 8	14 56 41	19D 41.1	27 25.8	21 14.4	25 13.2	24 3.8	19 1.6	1 50.1	27 22.8	27 52.0
7 F	0 59 28	12 56 57	22 4 48	29 11 14	19 40.6	26 48.4	22 29.2	25 51.6	24 14.5	19 7.8	1 51.9	27 25.0	27 53.4
8 Sa	1 3 25	13 56 9	6♋15 48	13♋18 22	19R 41.0	26 3.2	23 44.0	26 29.9	24 25.1	19 14.0	1 53.5	27 27.2	27 54.9
9 Su	1 7 21	14 55 23	20 18 52	27 17 15	19 41.1	25 10.7	24 58.8	27 8.3	24 35.6	19 20.3	1 55.2	27 29.3	27 56.3
10 M	1 11 18	15 54 40	4♌13 26	11♌ 7 24	19 39.6	24 11.6	26 13.6	27 46.7	24 46.1	19 26.7	1 56.8	27 31.5	27 57.8
11 Tu	1 15 14	16 53 59	17 59 4	24 48 21	19 35.9	23 6.9	27 28.4	28 25.1	24 56.4	19 33.0	1 58.3	27 33.8	27 59.2
12 W	1 19 11	17 53 20	1♍35 8	8♍19 18	19 29.6	21 57.9	28 43.2	29 3.5	25 6.6	19 39.5	1 59.8	27 36.0	28 0.5
13 Th	1 23 7	18 52 43	15 0 40	21 39 6	19 21.0	20 46.3	29 58.0	29 41.9	25 16.8	19 45.9	2 1.2	27 38.2	28 1.9
14 F	1 27 4	19 52 9	28 14 24	4♎46 25	19 10.8	19 33.9	1♏12.8	0♎20.3	25 26.9	19 52.4	2 2.6	27 40.4	28 3.2
15 Sa	1 31 1	20 51 37	11♎14 59	17 40 1	19 0.0	18 22.8	2 27.6	0 58.7	25 36.8	19 58.9	2 4.0	27 42.6	28 4.5
16 Su	1 34 57	21 51 7	24 1 25	0♏19 10	18 49.8	17 15.0	3 42.4	1 37.1	25 46.7	20 5.5	2 5.3	27 44.9	28 5.8
17 M	1 38 54	22 50 39	6♏33 17	12 43 52	18 41.1	16 12.6	4 57.3	2 15.6	25 56.4	20 12.1	2 6.5	27 47.1	28 7.1
18 Tu	1 42 50	23 50 13	18 51 4	24 55 7	18 34.6	15 17.3	6 12.1	2 54.0	26 6.1	20 18.8	2 7.7	27 49.3	28 8.4
19 W	1 46 47	24 49 48	0♐56 18	6♐54 58	18 30.5	14 30.7	7 26.9	3 32.5	26 15.6	20 25.4	2 8.8	27 51.6	28 9.6
20 Th	1 50 43	25 49 26	12 51 32	18 46 29	18D 28.7	13 54.0	8 41.8	4 11.0	26 25.1	20 32.1	2 9.9	27 53.8	28 10.8
21 F	1 54 40	26 49 6	24 40 19	0♑33 36	18 28.7	13 28.1	9 56.6	4 49.4	26 34.4	20 38.9	2 10.9	27 56.1	28 12.0
22 Sa	1 58 36	27 48 47	6♑26 56	12 20 57	18 29.7	13D 13.3	11 11.4	5 27.9	26 43.6	20 45.7	2 11.9	27 58.3	28 13.1
23 Su	2 2 33	28 48 30	18 16 19	24 13 42	18R 31.0	13 9.9	12 26.3	6 6.4	26 52.8	20 52.4	2 12.8	28 0.5	28 14.2
24 M	2 6 30	29 48 15	0♒13 45	6♒17 8	18 31.5	13 17.5	13 41.1	6 44.9	27 1.8	20 59.3	2 13.7	28 2.8	28 15.3
25 Tu	2 10 26	0♏48 2	12 24 31	18 36 30	18 30.7	13 35.8	14 55.9	7 23.4	27 10.6	21 6.1	2 14.5	28 5.0	28 16.4
26 W	2 14 23	1 47 50	24 53 38	1♓16 26	18 28.0	14 4.2	16 10.7	8 1.9	27 19.4	21 13.0	2 15.3	28 7.3	28 17.5
27 Th	2 18 19	2 47 40	7♓45 16	14 20 27	18 23.4	14 41.8	17 25.5	8 40.4	27 28.1	21 19.9	2 16.0	28 9.5	28 18.5
28 F	2 22 16	3 47 31	21 2 11	27 50 28	18 17.2	15 27.9	18 40.4	9 18.9	27 36.6	21 26.8	2 16.6	28 11.7	28 19.5
29 Sa	2 26 12	4 47 24	4♈45 12	11♈46 6	18 10.1	16 21.5	19 55.2	9 57.5	27 45.0	21 33.8	2 17.2	28 14.0	28 20.5
30 Su	2 30 9	5 47 19	18 52 43	26 4 28	18 2.9	17 22.0	21 10.0	10 36.0	27 53.3	21 40.7	2 17.8	28 16.2	28 21.4
31 M	2 34 5	6 47 16	3♉20 38	10♉40 20	17 56.6	18 28.3	22 24.8	11 14.6	28 1.4	21 47.7	2 18.2	28 18.4	28 22.3

Astro Data	Planet Ingress	Last Aspect	☽ Ingress	Last Aspect	☽ Ingress	☽ Phases & Eclipses	Astro Data
Dy Hr Mn	Dy Hr Mn	Dy Hr Mn	Dy Hr Mn	Dy Hr Mn	Dy Hr Mn	Dy Hr Mn	1 SEPTEMBER 1955
☿0S 1 2:14	☿ ♎ 1 12:06	1 9:35 ♇ ☍	♓ 1 15:23	30 15:26 ♂ ☍	♈ 1 5:46	2 7:59 ○ 9♓05	Julian Day # 20332
☽0N 3 0:42	♀ ♎ 18 22:41	2 20:43 ♄ △	♈ 3 21:24	3 6:17 ☿ ☍	♉ 3 8:52	9 7:59 ☽ 15♊52	Delta T 31.3 sec
☽0S 15 22:46	☉ ♎ 23 19:41	5 20:27 ♇ △	♉ 6 1:36	5 7:24 ♇ □	♊ 5 10:59	16 6:19 ● 22♍37	SVP 05♓52'26"
♀0S 21 8:34		7 23:58 ♇ □	♊ 8 4:58	7 9:49 ♇ ✶	♋ 7 13:23	24 3:41 ☽ 0♑20	Obliquity 23°26'42"
☽0N 30 9:15	♀ ♏ 13 0:39	10 3:09 ♇ ✶	♋ 10 8:01	9 12:23 ♆ □	♌ 9 16:41		⚷ Chiron 0♒53.0R
	♂ ♎ 13 11:20	12 5:12 ♆ □	♌ 12 11:02	11 18:24 ♀ ✶	♍ 11 21:11	1 19:17 ○ 7♈50	☽ Mean ☊ 22♐33.4
☿ R 1 13:58	☉ ♏ 24 4:43	14 9:49 ♇ ☌	♍ 14 14:33	13 8:39 ♄ ✶	♎ 14 3:13	8 14:04 ☽ 14♋31	
☽0S 13 5:44		16 14:19 ♀ ☌	♎ 16 19:35	16 7:46 ♇ ✶	♏ 16 11:23	15 19:32 ● 21♎40	1 OCTOBER 1955
♂0S 17 4:26		18 22:21 ♇ ✶	♏ 19 3:18	18 18:26 ♇ □	♐ 18 22:07	23 23:05 ☽ 29♑46	Julian Day # 20362
☿ D 22 19:22		21 9:26 ☉ ✶	♐ 21 14:11	21 7:12 ♇ △	♑ 21 10:52	31 6:04 ○ 7♉02	Delta T 31.3 sec
☽0N 27 18:34		23 22:01 ♇ △	♑ 24 3:01	23 23:05 ☉ □	♒ 23 23:33		SVP 05♓52'23"
		26 9:43 ☿ □	♒ 26 15:07	26 6:25 ♇ ☍	♓ 26 9:37		Obliquity 23°26'41"
		28 20:57 ☿ △	♓ 29 0:12	28 0:44 ♄ △	♈ 28 15:46		⚷ Chiron 0♒06.7R
				30 15:48 ♇ △	♉ 30 18:30		☽ Mean ☊ 20♐58.0

NOVEMBER 1955 LONGITUDE

Day	Sid.Time	☉	0 hr ☽	Noon ☽	True ☊	☿	♀	♂	♃	♄	♅	♆	♇
1 Tu	2 38 2	7♏47 15	18♉ 2 40	25♉26 40	17♐51.9	19♎39.9	23♏39.6	11♎53.1	28♌ 9.4	21♏54.7	2♌18.7	28♎20.6	28♌23.2
2 W	2 41 59	8 47 16	2♊51 21	10♊15 46	17R49.1	20 55.9	24 54.4	12 31.7	28 17.3	22 1.7	2 19.1	28 22.9	28 24.1
3 Th	2 45 55	9 47 19	17 39 3	25 0 25	17D48.3	22 15.6	26 9.2	13 10.3	28 25.1	22 8.8	2 19.4	28 25.1	28 24.9
4 F	2 49 52	10 47 24	2♋19 10	9♋34 46	17 48.9	23 38.6	27 24.0	13 48.9	28 32.8	22 15.8	2 19.7	28 27.3	28 25.8
5 Sa	2 53 48	11 47 31	16 46 46	23 54 51	17 50.3	25 4.3	28 38.8	14 27.5	28 40.3	22 22.9	2 19.9	28 29.5	28 26.5
6 Su	2 57 45	12 47 40	0♌58 49	7♌58 32	17R51.6	26 32.2	29 53.7	15 6.2	28 47.6	22 30.0	2 20.0	28 31.7	28 27.3
7 M	3 1 41	13 47 51	14 53 58	21 45 8	17 52.2	28 2.0	1♐ 8.5	15 44.8	28 54.9	22 37.1	2 20.1	28 33.8	28 28.0
8 Tu	3 5 38	14 48 4	28 32 8	5♍15 2	17 51.3	29 33.3	2 23.3	16 23.5	29 1.9	22 44.2	2R20.2	28 36.0	28 28.7
9 W	3 9 34	15 48 19	11♍54 0	18 29 8	17 48.9	1♏ 5.8	3 38.1	17 2.1	29 8.9	22 51.3	2 20.2	28 38.2	28 29.4
10 Th	3 13 31	16 48 37	25 0 35	1♎28 31	17 45.1	2 39.3	4 52.9	17 40.8	29 15.7	22 58.4	2 20.1	28 40.4	28 30.1
11 F	3 17 28	17 48 56	7♎53 1	14 14 15	17 40.3	4 13.6	6 7.7	18 19.5	29 22.3	23 5.6	2 20.0	28 42.5	28 30.7
12 Sa	3 21 24	18 49 17	20 32 19	26 47 21	17 35.2	5 48.4	7 22.5	18 58.2	29 28.8	23 12.7	2 19.8	28 44.6	28 31.3
13 Su	3 25 21	19 49 40	2♏59 28	9♏ 8 47	17 30.3	7 23.7	8 37.3	19 36.9	29 35.2	23 19.9	2 19.6	28 46.8	28 31.8
14 M	3 29 17	20 50 4	15 15 26	21 19 36	17 26.2	8 59.3	9 52.2	20 15.6	29 41.4	23 27.0	2 19.3	28 48.9	28 32.3
15 Tu	3 33 14	21 50 31	27 21 26	3♐21 9	17 23.3	10 35.0	11 7.0	20 54.3	29 47.4	23 34.2	2 19.0	28 51.0	28 32.8
16 W	3 37 10	22 50 59	9♐18 58	15 15 9	17D21.8	12 11.0	12 21.8	21 33.1	29 53.3	23 41.3	2 18.6	28 53.1	28 33.3
17 Th	3 41 7	23 51 29	21 10 0	27 3 51	17 21.6	13 46.9	13 36.6	22 11.8	29 59.1	23 48.5	2 18.2	28 55.2	28 33.8
18 F	3 45 3	24 52 0	2♑57 6	8♑50 8	17 22.4	15 22.9	14 51.4	22 50.6	0♍ 4.6	23 55.7	2 17.7	28 57.2	28 34.2
19 Sa	3 49 0	25 52 32	14 43 25	20 37 26	17 23.9	16 58.8	16 6.2	23 29.3	0 10.1	24 2.8	2 17.1	28 59.3	28 34.6
20 Su	3 52 57	26 53 6	26 32 43	2♒29 48	17 25.7	18 34.6	17 21.0	24 8.1	0 15.3	24 10.0	2 16.5	29 1.3	28 34.9
21 M	3 56 53	27 53 41	8♒29 15	14 31 41	17 27.2	20 10.4	18 35.8	24 46.9	0 20.4	24 17.1	2 15.9	29 3.4	28 35.2
22 Tu	4 0 50	28 54 17	20 37 40	26 47 49	17R28.2	21 46.0	19 50.5	25 25.7	0 25.3	24 24.3	2 15.1	29 5.4	28 35.5
23 W	4 4 46	29 54 55	3♓ 2 43	9♓22 54	17 28.4	23 21.4	21 5.3	26 4.5	0 30.1	24 31.4	2 14.4	29 7.4	28 35.8
24 Th	4 8 43	0♐55 33	15 48 53	22 21 7	17 27.7	24 56.8	22 20.1	26 43.3	0 34.6	24 38.6	2 13.6	29 9.4	28 36.0
25 F	4 12 39	1 56 13	28 59 56	5♈45 37	17 26.4	26 32.0	23 34.8	27 22.1	0 39.0	24 45.7	2 12.7	29 11.3	28 36.2
26 Sa	4 16 36	2 56 53	12♈38 17	19 37 55	17 24.6	28 7.0	24 49.6	28 0.9	0 43.3	24 52.8	2 11.8	29 13.3	28 36.4
27 Su	4 20 32	3 57 35	26 44 19	3♉57 8	17 22.8	29 41.9	26 4.3	28 39.8	0 47.3	24 59.9	2 10.8	29 15.2	28 36.5
28 M	4 24 29	4 58 18	11♉15 50	18 39 41	17 21.1	1♐16.7	27 19.0	29 18.6	0 51.2	25 7.0	2 9.8	29 17.1	28 36.6
29 Tu	4 28 26	5 59 2	26 7 50	3♊39 16	17 20.0	2 51.4	28 33.8	29 57.5	0 55.0	25 14.1	2 8.7	29 19.0	28 36.7
30 W	4 32 22	6 59 48	11♊12 52	18 47 28	17D19.4	4 25.9	29 48.5	0♏36.4	0 58.5	25 21.2	2 7.6	29 20.9	28 36.7

DECEMBER 1955 LONGITUDE

Day	Sid.Time	☉	0 hr ☽	Noon ☽	True ☊	☿	♀	♂	♃	♄	♅	♆	♇
1 Th	4 36 19	8♐ 0 35	26♊21 54	3♋54 59	17♐19.5	6♐ 0.4	1♑ 3.2	1♏15.2	1♍ 1.9	25♏28.2	2♌ 6.4	29♎22.7	28♌36.8
2 F	4 40 15	9 1 23	11♋25 39	18 52 55	17 20.0	7 34.8	2 17.9	1 54.1	1 5.0	25 35.3	2R 5.2	29 24.6	28R36.8
3 Sa	4 44 12	10 2 12	26 15 57	3♌34 3	17 20.6	9 9.1	3 32.6	2 33.0	1 8.1	25 42.3	2 3.9	29 26.4	28 36.7
4 Su	4 48 8	11 3 3	10♌46 42	17 53 32	17 21.3	10 43.4	4 47.3	3 12.0	1 10.9	25 49.3	2 2.6	29 28.2	28 36.6
5 M	4 52 5	12 3 55	24 54 20	1♍49 3	17 21.7	12 17.6	6 1.9	3 50.9	1 13.5	25 56.3	2 1.3	29 30.0	28 36.5
6 Tu	4 56 1	13 4 48	8♍37 42	15 20 28	17R21.9	13 51.8	7 16.6	4 29.8	1 15.9	26 3.2	1 59.8	29 31.7	28 36.4
7 W	4 59 58	14 5 43	21 57 34	28 29 18	17 21.9	15 26.0	8 31.2	5 8.8	1 18.2	26 10.2	1 58.4	29 33.5	28 36.2
8 Th	5 3 55	15 6 39	4♎56 1	11♎18 5	17 21.8	17 0.2	9 45.9	5 47.8	1 20.3	26 17.1	1 56.9	29 35.2	28 36.1
9 F	5 7 51	16 7 36	17 35 54	23 49 51	17 21.6	18 34.4	11 0.5	6 26.8	1 22.2	26 24.0	1 55.3	29 36.9	28 35.8
10 Sa	5 11 48	17 8 35	0♏ 0 19	6♏ 7 41	17D21.5	20 8.7	12 15.2	7 5.7	1 23.8	26 30.9	1 53.7	29 38.5	28 35.6
11 Su	5 15 44	18 9 34	12 12 19	18 14 33	17 21.6	21 43.0	13 29.8	7 44.7	1 25.3	26 37.7	1 52.1	29 40.2	28 35.3
12 M	5 19 41	19 10 35	24 14 43	0♐13 8	17 21.7	23 17.4	14 44.4	8 23.8	1 26.6	26 44.5	1 50.4	29 41.8	28 35.0
13 Tu	5 23 37	20 11 37	6♐10 4	12 5 49	17R21.9	24 51.9	15 59.0	9 2.8	1 27.8	26 51.3	1 48.7	29 43.4	28 34.6
14 W	5 27 34	21 12 39	18 0 38	23 54 48	17 22.0	26 26.5	17 13.6	9 41.8	1 28.7	26 58.1	1 47.0	29 45.0	28 34.3
15 Th	5 31 31	22 13 43	29 48 33	5♑42 9	17 21.8	28 1.1	18 28.2	10 20.9	1 29.4	27 4.8	1 45.1	29 46.5	28 33.9
16 F	5 35 27	23 14 47	11♑35 54	17 30 2	17 21.4	29 35.9	19 42.8	10 59.9	1 29.9	27 11.5	1 43.3	29 48.0	28 33.4
17 Sa	5 39 24	24 15 51	23 24 53	29 20 46	17 20.6	1♑10.7	20 57.3	11 39.0	1 30.3	27 18.2	1 41.4	29 49.5	28 33.0
18 Su	5 43 20	25 16 56	5♒18 1	11♒16 59	17 19.5	2 45.7	22 11.9	12 18.0	1R30.4	27 24.8	1 39.5	29 51.0	28 32.5
19 M	5 47 17	26 18 2	17 18 5	23 21 43	17 18.2	4 20.7	23 26.4	12 57.1	1 30.3	27 31.4	1 37.5	29 52.4	28 32.0
20 Tu	5 51 13	27 19 8	29 28 20	5♓38 22	17 17.0	5 55.9	24 40.9	13 36.2	1 30.1	27 38.0	1 35.6	29 53.8	28 31.4
21 W	5 55 10	28 20 14	11♓52 19	18 10 37	17 16.0	7 31.1	25 55.4	14 15.3	1 29.6	27 44.5	1 33.5	29 55.2	28 30.9
22 Th	5 59 6	29 21 21	24 33 46	1♈ 2 13	17D15.5	9 6.4	27 9.8	14 54.4	1 29.0	27 50.9	1 31.5	29 56.6	28 30.3
23 F	6 3 3	0♑22 27	7♈36 23	14 16 37	17 15.5	10 41.8	28 24.3	15 33.4	1 28.1	27 57.4	1 29.4	29 57.9	28 29.7
24 Sa	6 7 0	1 23 34	21 3 14	27 56 27	17 16.2	12 17.1	29 38.7	16 12.6	1 27.1	28 3.8	1 27.2	29 59.2	28 29.0
25 Su	6 10 56	2 24 41	4♉56 21	12♉ 2 54	17 17.3	13 52.5	0♒53.1	16 51.7	1 25.9	28 10.1	1 25.1	0♏ 0.5	28 28.3
26 M	6 14 53	3 25 48	19 15 54	26 34 59	17 18.5	15 27.7	2 7.4	17 30.8	1 24.4	28 16.4	1 22.9	0 1.7	28 27.6
27 Tu	6 18 49	4 26 55	3♊59 36	11♊29 0	17R19.5	17 2.8	3 21.8	18 9.9	1 22.8	28 22.7	1 20.6	0 2.9	28 26.9
28 W	6 22 46	5 28 3	19 2 18	26 38 25	17 19.9	18 37.7	4 36.1	18 49.1	1 21.0	28 28.9	1 18.4	0 4.1	28 26.1
29 Th	6 26 42	6 29 10	4♋16 11	11♋54 18	17 19.2	20 12.3	5 50.4	19 28.2	1 19.0	28 35.1	1 16.1	0 5.3	28 25.3
30 F	6 30 39	7 30 18	19 31 30	27 6 29	17 17.6	21 46.5	7 4.6	20 7.4	1 16.8	28 41.2	1 13.8	0 6.4	28 24.5
31 Sa	6 34 35	8 31 26	4♌38 3	12♌ 5 7	17 15.0	23 20.2	8 18.9	20 46.6	1 14.4	28 47.3	1 11.5	0 7.5	28 23.7

Astro Data Dy Hr Mn	Planet Ingress Dy Hr Mn	Last Aspect Dy Hr Mn	☽ Ingress Dy Hr Mn	Last Aspect Dy Hr Mn	☽ Ingress Dy Hr Mn	☽ Phases & Eclipses Dy Hr Mn	Astro Data
♆✶♇ 2 21:54	♀ ♐ 6 2:02	1 16:47 ♇ □	♊ 1 19:23	1 4:48 ♆ △	♋ 1 5:46	6 21:56 ☽ 13♌43	1 NOVEMBER 1955
♃☌♇ 2 23:24	☿ ♏ 8 6:57	3 17:45 ♃ ✶	♋ 3 20:11	3 5:13 ♆ □	♌ 3 6:07	14 12:02 ● 21♏20	Julian Day # 20393
♃✶♆ 2 23:47	♃ ♍ 17 3:59	5 21:58 ♀ △	♌ 5 22:20	5 7:58 ♆ ✶	♍ 5 8:50	22 17:29 ☽ 29♒38	Delta T 31.3 sec
♅ R 8 9:29	☉ ♐ 23 2:01	8 2:03 ☿ ✶	♍ 8 2:36	7 7:47 ♄ ✶	♎ 7 14:48	29 16:50 ○ 6♊42	SVP 05♓52'20"
☽0S 9 10:51	☿ ♐ 27 4:34	9 20:13 ♄ ✶	♎ 10 9:15	9 23:17 ♆ ☌	♏ 9 23:59	29 16:59 ☍ P 0.119	Obliquity 23°26'41"
☽0N 24 3:28	♂ ♏ 29 1:33	12 17:21 ♃ ✶	♏ 12 18:12	12 8:42 ♇ □	♐ 12 11:34		⚷ Chiron 0♒24.0
	♀ ♑ 30 3:42	15 4:54 ♃ □	♐ 15 5:17	14 23:56 ♆ ✶	♑ 15 0:23	6 8:35 ☽ 13♍27	☽ Mean ☊ 19♐19.5
♇ R 1 4:47		17 15:50 ♆ ✶	♑ 17 17:59	17 13:00 ♆ □	♒ 17 13:19	14 7:07 ● 21♐31	1 DECEMBER 1955
☽0S 6 16:10	☿ ♑ 16 6:06	20 5:01 ♆ □	♒ 20 6:58	20 0:50 ♆ △	♓ 20 1:02	14 7:01:54 ● A 12'09"	Julian Day # 20423
♃ R 18 4:30	☉ ♑ 22 15:11	22 17:29 ☉ □	♓ 22 18:10	22 9:39 ☉ □	♈ 22 10:05	22 9:39 ☽ 29♓46	Delta T 31.3 sec
☽0N 21 11:03	♀ ♒ 24 6:52	24 18:58 ♆ △	♈ 25 1:47	24 15:33 ♆ ☍	♉ 24 15:33	29 3:44 ○ 6♋39	SVP 05♓52'16"
♃⊻♅ 24 3:18	♆ ♏ 24 15:19	27 4:13 ♅ ☍	♉ 27 5:27	26 15:02 ♇ □	♊ 26 17:33		Obliquity 23°26'40"
♄□♇ 27 14:27		29 3:58 ♇ □	♊ 29 6:11	28 14:49 ♇ ✶	♋ 28 17:17		⚷ Chiron 1♒42.4
				30 14:36 ♄ △	♌ 30 16:36		☽ Mean ☊ 17♐44.2

LONGITUDE JANUARY 1956

Day	Sid.Time	☉	0 hr ☽	Noon ☽	True ☊	☿	♀	♂	♃	♄	♅	♆	♇
1 Su	6 38 32	9♑32 34	19♌26 47	26♌42 16	17♐11.9	24♑53.2	9♒33.1	21♏25.8	1♍11.8	28♏53.3	1♌ 9.1	0♏ 8.5	28♌22.9
2 M	6 42 29	10 33 43	3♍51 4	10♍52 50	17R 8.7	26 25.2	10 47.3	22 4.9	1R 9.1	28 59.2	1R 6.8	0 9.6	28R22.0
3 Tu	6 46 25	11 34 51	17 47 23	24 34 46	17 6.1	27 56.2	12 1.4	22 44.1	1 6.1	29 5.2	1 4.3	0 10.6	28 21.1
4 W	6 50 22	12 36 1	1♎15 8	7♎48 48	17D 4.4	29 25.8	13 15.5	23 23.4	1 3.0	29 11.0	1 1.9	0 11.5	28 20.1
5 Th	6 54 18	13 37 10	14 16 8	20 37 39	17 3.8	0♒53.8	14 29.6	24 2.6	0 59.6	29 16.8	0 59.5	0 12.5	28 19.2
6 F	6 58 15	14 38 19	26 53 51	3♏ 5 19	17 4.4	2 19.7	15 43.7	24 41.8	0 56.1	29 22.6	0 57.0	0 13.4	28 18.2
7 Sa	7 2 11	15 39 29	9♏12 36	15 16 19	17 5.9	3 43.3	16 57.7	25 21.1	0 52.4	29 28.3	0 54.5	0 14.2	28 17.2
8 Su	7 6 8	16 40 39	21 17 0	27 15 15	17 7.8	5 3.9	18 11.7	26 0.3	0 48.6	29 33.9	0 52.0	0 15.1	28 16.2
9 M	7 10 4	17 41 49	3♐11 34	9♐ 6 27	17 9.5	6 21.2	19 25.6	26 39.6	0 44.5	29 39.5	0 49.5	0 15.9	28 15.1
10 Tu	7 14 1	18 42 59	15 0 21	20 53 43	17R10.3	7 34.4	20 39.6	27 18.8	0 40.3	29 45.0	0 47.0	0 16.7	28 14.1
11 W	7 17 58	19 44 9	26 46 55	2♑40 18	17 9.8	8 43.0	21 53.5	27 58.1	0 35.9	29 50.4	0 44.4	0 17.4	28 13.0
12 Th	7 21 54	20 45 19	8♑34 11	14 28 51	17 7.6	9 46.2	23 7.3	28 37.4	0 31.3	29 55.8	0 41.9	0 18.1	28 11.9
13 F	7 25 51	21 46 29	20 24 33	26 21 30	17 3.6	10 43.1	24 21.1	29 16.7	0 26.6	0♐ 1.2	0 39.3	0 18.8	28 10.8
14 Sa	7 29 47	22 47 38	2♒19 54	8♒19 58	16 58.0	11 33.0	25 34.9	29 56.0	0 21.7	0 6.4	0 36.7	0 19.5	28 9.6
15 Su	7 33 44	23 48 47	14 21 51	20 25 46	16 51.2	12 15.0	26 48.6	0♐35.3	0 16.6	0 11.6	0 34.1	0 20.1	28 8.4
16 M	7 37 40	24 49 55	26 31 54	2♓40 26	16 43.8	12 48.1	28 2.3	1 14.6	0 11.4	0 16.7	0 31.5	0 20.6	28 7.3
17 Tu	7 41 37	25 51 2	8♓51 36	15 5 37	16 36.6	13 11.5	29 15.9	1 53.9	0 6.0	0 21.8	0 28.9	0 21.2	28 6.1
18 W	7 45 33	26 52 9	21 22 46	27 43 17	16 30.4	13R24.4	0♓29.5	2 33.2	0 0.5	0 26.8	0 26.3	0 21.7	28 4.8
19 Th	7 49 30	27 53 15	4♈ 7 30	10♈35 43	16 25.8	13 26.2	1 43.1	3 12.5	29♌54.8	0 31.7	0 23.7	0 22.1	28 3.6
20 F	7 53 27	28 54 20	17 8 14	23 45 24	16D23.2	13 16.5	2 56.6	3 51.8	29 49.0	0 36.5	0 21.1	0 22.6	28 2.3
21 Sa	7 57 23	29 55 24	0♉27 30	7♉14 48	16 22.5	12 55.1	4 10.0	4 31.1	29 43.0	0 41.3	0 18.5	0 23.0	28 1.1
22 Su	8 1 20	0♒56 28	14 7 33	21 5 52	16 23.1	12 22.2	5 23.4	5 10.4	29 36.9	0 46.0	0 15.8	0 23.4	27 59.8
23 M	8 5 16	1 57 30	28 9 50	5♊19 22	16 24.4	11 38.5	6 36.7	5 49.7	29 30.7	0 50.6	0 13.2	0 23.7	27 58.5
24 Tu	8 9 13	2 58 32	12♊34 18	19 54 15	16R25.3	10 44.8	7 49.9	6 29.1	29 24.3	0 55.2	0 10.6	0 24.0	27 57.2
25 W	8 13 9	3 59 32	27 18 42	4♋46 55	16 24.9	9 42.8	9 3.1	7 8.4	29 17.9	0 59.6	0 8.0	0 24.3	27 55.9
26 Th	8 17 6	5 0 32	12♋18 4	19 51 5	16 22.4	8 34.1	10 16.3	7 47.7	29 11.3	1 4.0	0 5.4	0 24.5	27 54.5
27 F	8 21 2	6 1 30	27 24 49	4♌58 4	16 17.6	7 20.9	11 29.3	8 27.1	29 4.6	1 8.3	0 2.8	0 24.7	27 53.2
28 Sa	8 24 59	7 2 28	12♌29 34	19 58 4	16 10.6	6 5.4	12 42.3	9 6.4	28 57.7	1 12.6	0 0.2	0 24.9	27 51.8
29 Su	8 28 56	8 3 24	27 22 27	4♍41 42	16 2.3	4 49.8	13 55.3	9 45.8	28 50.8	1 16.7	29♋57.6	0 25.0	27 50.4
30 M	8 32 52	9 4 20	11♍54 58	19 1 36	15 53.6	3 36.4	15 8.1	10 25.1	28 43.8	1 20.8	29 55.0	0 25.1	27 49.0
31 Tu	8 36 49	10 5 15	26 1 10	2♎53 25	15 45.6	2 27.0	16 20.9	11 4.5	28 36.7	1 24.8	29 52.5	0 25.2	27 47.6

LONGITUDE FEBRUARY 1956

Day	Sid.Time	☉	0 hr ☽	Noon ☽	True ☊	☿	♀	♂	♃	♄	♅	♆	♇
1 W	8 40 45	11♒ 6 9	9♎38 18	16♎15 57	15♐39.2	1♒23.2	17♓33.6	11♐43.9	28♌29.4	1♐28.7	29♋49.9	0♏25.2	27♌46.2
2 Th	8 44 42	12 7 3	22 46 40	29 10 51	15R34.9	0R26.2	18 46.3	12 23.2	28R22.1	1 32.5	29R47.4	0R25.2	27R44.8
3 F	8 48 38	13 7 55	5♏28 59	11♏41 42	15D32.9	29♑37.0	19 58.9	13 2.6	28 14.7	1 36.3	29 44.8	0 25.1	27 43.4
4 Sa	8 52 35	14 8 47	17 49 35	23 53 20	15 32.6	28 56.0	21 11.4	13 42.0	28 7.3	1 39.9	29 42.3	0 25.1	27 41.9
5 Su	8 56 31	15 9 38	29 53 38	5♐51 9	15 33.3	28 23.5	22 23.8	14 21.4	27 59.8	1 43.5	29 39.8	0 24.9	27 40.5
6 M	9 0 28	16 10 28	11♐46 34	17 40 32	15R34.1	27 59.5	23 36.2	15 0.8	27 52.2	1 47.0	29 37.3	0 24.8	27 39.0
7 Tu	9 4 25	17 11 18	23 33 40	29 26 33	15 33.8	27 43.8	24 48.4	15 40.2	27 44.5	1 50.4	29 34.9	0 24.6	27 37.6
8 W	9 8 21	18 12 6	5♑19 43	11♑13 38	15 31.5	27D36.1	26 0.6	16 19.6	27 36.8	1 53.7	29 32.4	0 24.4	27 36.1
9 Th	9 12 18	19 12 53	17 8 46	23 5 28	15 26.8	27 36.1	27 12.7	16 59.0	27 29.0	1 56.9	29 30.0	0 24.2	27 34.6
10 F	9 16 14	20 13 39	29 4 5	5♒ 4 52	15 19.2	27 43.1	28 24.8	17 38.4	27 21.2	2 0.0	29 27.6	0 23.9	27 33.1
11 Sa	9 20 11	21 14 24	11♒ 8 2	17 13 45	15 9.1	27 56.9	29 36.7	18 17.8	27 13.4	2 3.1	29 25.2	0 23.6	27 31.7
12 Su	9 24 7	22 15 7	23 22 8	29 33 15	14 57.1	28 16.9	0♈48.6	18 57.2	27 5.5	2 6.0	29 22.8	0 23.2	27 30.2
13 M	9 28 4	23 15 49	5♓47 8	12♓ 3 50	14 44.0	28 42.6	2 0.3	19 36.6	26 57.6	2 8.8	29 20.5	0 22.9	27 28.7
14 Tu	9 32 0	24 16 29	18 23 20	24 45 39	14 31.3	29 13.6	3 12.0	20 16.0	26 49.7	2 11.6	29 18.2	0 22.5	27 27.2
15 W	9 35 57	25 17 8	1♈10 46	7♈38 44	14 19.9	29 49.4	4 23.6	20 55.4	26 41.8	2 14.2	29 15.9	0 22.0	27 25.7
16 Th	9 39 54	26 17 46	14 9 34	20 43 21	14 10.8	0♒29.7	5 35.0	21 34.7	26 33.8	2 16.8	29 13.6	0 21.5	27 24.2
17 F	9 43 50	27 18 22	27 20 11	4♉ 0 11	14 4.6	1 14.1	6 46.4	22 14.1	26 25.9	2 19.3	29 11.4	0 21.0	27 22.7
18 Sa	9 47 47	28 18 56	10♉43 29	17 30 15	14 1.2	2 2.3	7 57.6	22 53.5	26 18.0	2 21.6	29 9.2	0 20.5	27 21.2
19 Su	9 51 43	29 19 28	24 20 38	1♊14 47	13D60.0	2 54.0	9 8.8	23 32.9	26 10.0	2 23.9	29 7.0	0 19.9	27 19.7
20 M	9 55 40	0♓19 58	8♊12 48	15 14 45	14R 0.0	3 48.8	10 19.8	24 12.2	26 2.2	2 26.1	29 4.9	0 19.3	27 18.2
21 Tu	9 59 36	1 20 27	22 20 36	29 30 15	13 59.9	4 46.7	11 30.7	24 51.6	25 54.3	2 28.2	29 2.8	0 18.7	27 16.7
22 W	10 3 33	2 20 53	6♋43 26	13♋59 49	13 58.3	5 47.3	12 41.5	25 31.0	25 46.4	2 30.2	29 0.7	0 18.0	27 15.2
23 Th	10 7 29	3 21 18	21 18 53	28 39 57	13 54.3	6 50.4	13 52.2	26 10.3	25 38.6	2 32.1	28 58.7	0 17.3	27 13.7
24 F	10 11 26	4 21 41	6♌ 2 17	13♌24 57	13 47.4	7 55.9	15 2.7	26 49.7	25 30.9	2 33.8	28 56.7	0 16.6	27 12.3
25 Sa	10 15 23	5 22 2	20 47 0	28 7 23	13 37.8	9 3.6	16 13.1	27 29.0	25 23.1	2 35.5	28 54.7	0 15.9	27 10.8
26 Su	10 19 19	6 22 21	5♍25 7	12♍39 12	13 26.2	10 13.4	17 23.4	28 8.4	25 15.4	2 37.1	28 52.8	0 15.1	27 9.3
27 M	10 23 16	7 22 38	19 48 47	26 53 6	13 14.0	11 25.1	18 33.5	28 47.7	25 7.8	2 38.6	28 50.9	0 14.3	27 7.8
28 Tu	10 27 12	8 22 54	3♎51 32	10♎43 41	13 2.4	12 38.7	19 43.5	29 27.1	25 0.3	2 40.0	28 49.1	0 13.4	27 6.4
29 W	10 31 9	9 23 8	17 29 18	24 8 16	12 52.5	13 54.0	20 53.4	0♑ 6.4	24 52.8	2 41.3	28 47.2	0 12.6	27 4.9

Astro Data	Dy Hr Mn
☽0S	2 23:57
♃⊻♅	5 3:59
♃✶♆	14 9:30
♃□♄	15 11:38
♄⊻♆	16 20:43
☽0N	17 17:30
♄△♅	17 22:34
☿ R	18 15:51
♅□♆	19 12:11
☽0S	30 10:27
♆ R	1 6:32
♃☌♇	8 2:40
☿ D	8 12:10
♀0N	12 11:24

Planet Ingress	Dy Hr Mn
☿ ♒	4 9:16
♄ ♐	12 18:45
♂ ♐	14 2:28
♀ ♓	17 14:22
♃ ♌	18 2:04
☉ ♒	21 1:48
♅ ♋	28 1:58
☿ ♑	2 12:18
♀ ♈	11 7:46
☿ ♒	15 6:34
☉ ♓	19 16:05
♂ ♑	28 20:05
☽0N	13 23:51

Last Aspect Dy Hr Mn	☽ Ingress Dy Hr Mn
1 15:45 ♄ □	♍ 1 17:31
3 20:17 ☿ △	♎ 3 21:44
6 2:43 ♇ ✶	♏ 6 6:00
8 16:48 ♄ ☌	♐ 8 17:32
11 2:55 ♇ △	♑ 11 6:33
13 18:54 ♂ ✶	♒ 13 19:19
16 3:17 ♀ ☌	♓ 16 6:47
18 11:18 ☉ ✶	♈ 18 16:17
20 22:58 ☉ □	♉ 20 23:11
23 2:15 ♃ □	♊ 23 3:06
25 3:11 ♃ ✶	♋ 25 4:20
25 20:29 ♀ △	♌ 27 4:06
29 2:23 ♃ ☌	♍ 29 4:17
31 6:41 ♅ ✶	♎ 31 6:56

Last Aspect Dy Hr Mn	☽ Ingress Dy Hr Mn
2 13:28 ☿ □	♏ 2 13:33
4 23:32 ♅ △	♐ 5 0:13
7 8:26 ♃ △	♑ 7 13:08
10 0:47 ♅ ☍	♒ 10 1:52
12 8:01 ♇ ☍	♓ 12 12:52
14 21:20 ☿ ✶	♈ 14 21:48
17 3:20 ♅ □	♉ 17 4:48
19 9:21 ☉ □	♊ 19 9:50
21 8:16 ♇ ✶	♋ 21 12:50
23 12:29 ♅ ☌	♌ 23 14:10
25 11:28 ♂ △	♍ 25 15:05
27 16:01 ♂ □	♎ 27 17:20
29 20:28 ♅ □	♏ 29 22:45

☽ Phases & Eclipses Dy Hr Mn	
4 22:41	☽ 13♎34
13 3:01	● 21♑54
20 22:58	☽ 29♈53
27 14:40	○ 6♌39
3 16:08	☽ 13♏49
11 21:38	● 22♒09
19 9:21	☽ 29♉43
26 1:42	○ 6♍27

Astro Data

1 JANUARY 1956
Julian Day # 20454
Delta T 31.4 sec
SVP 05♓52'10"
Obliquity 23°26'39"
⚷ Chiron 3♒50.5
☽ Mean ☊ 16♐05.7

1 FEBRUARY 1956
Julian Day # 20485
Delta T 31.4 sec
SVP 05♓52'05"
Obliquity 23°26'40"
⚷ Chiron 6♒21.1
☽ Mean ☊ 14♐27.3

MARCH 1956 LONGITUDE

Day	Sid.Time	☉	0 hr ☽	Noon ☽	True ☊	☿	♀	♂	♃	♄	♅	♆	♇
1 Th	10 35 5	10♓23 21	0♍40 42	7♍ 6 49	12♐45.2	15♒11.0	22♈ 3.1	0♑45.8	24♌45.3	2♐42.5	28♋45.5	0♏11.7	27♌ 3.4
2 F	10 39 2	11 23 32	13 26 58	19 41 36	12R 40.7	16 29.6	23 12.7	1 25.1	24R 38.0	2 43.6	28R 43.7	0R 10.7	27R 2.0
3 Sa	10 42 58	12 23 41	25 51 18	1♐56 39	12 38.5	17 49.7	24 22.2	2 4.4	24 30.7	2 44.5	28 42.0	0 9.8	27 0.6
4 Su	10 46 55	13 23 49	7♐58 19	13 56 59	12 37.9	19 11.3	25 31.5	2 43.8	24 23.6	2 45.4	28 40.4	0 8.8	26 59.1
5 M	10 50 52	14 23 56	19 53 20	25 48 7	12 37.9	20 34.3	26 40.6	3 23.1	24 16.5	2 46.2	28 38.8	0 7.8	26 57.7
6 Tu	10 54 48	15 24 1	1♑41 59	7♑35 38	12 37.2	21 58.7	27 49.6	4 2.4	24 9.5	2 46.9	28 37.2	0 6.8	26 56.3
7 W	10 58 45	16 24 4	13 29 43	19 24 50	12 34.8	23 24.4	28 58.4	4 41.7	24 2.6	2 47.5	28 35.7	0 5.7	26 54.9
8 Th	11 2 41	17 24 5	25 21 32	1♒20 22	12 29.9	24 51.4	0♉ 7.1	5 21.0	23 55.8	2 48.0	28 34.2	0 4.7	26 53.5
9 F	11 6 38	18 24 5	7♒21 44	13 26 3	12 22.3	26 19.7	1 15.6	6 0.3	23 49.1	2 48.3	28 32.8	0 3.6	26 52.1
10 Sa	11 10 34	19 24 3	19 33 37	25 44 40	12 11.9	27 49.3	2 23.9	6 39.6	23 42.6	2 48.6	28 31.4	0 2.4	26 50.8
11 Su	11 14 31	20 23 59	1♓59 22	8♓17 47	11 59.4	29 20.1	3 32.1	7 18.9	23 36.1	2 48.8	28 30.1	0 1.3	26 49.4
12 M	11 18 27	21 23 54	14 39 58	21 5 49	11 45.9	0♓52.1	4 40.1	7 58.1	23 29.8	2R 48.8	28 28.8	0 0.1	26 48.0
13 Tu	11 22 24	22 23 46	27 35 15	4♈ 8 6	11 32.5	2 25.3	5 47.9	8 37.4	23 23.6	2 48.8	28 27.5	29♎58.9	26 46.7
14 W	11 26 21	23 23 37	10♈44 11	17 23 16	11 20.5	3 59.8	6 55.5	9 16.6	23 17.6	2 48.7	28 26.3	29 57.7	26 45.4
15 Th	11 30 17	24 23 25	24 5 8	0♉49 35	11 10.8	5 35.5	8 2.9	9 55.8	23 11.7	2 48.4	28 25.2	29 56.4	26 44.1
16 F	11 34 14	25 23 12	7♉36 26	14 25 29	11 4.1	7 12.4	9 10.1	10 35.0	23 5.9	2 48.1	28 24.1	29 55.2	26 42.8
17 Sa	11 38 10	26 22 56	21 16 39	28 9 48	11 0.4	8 50.5	10 17.1	11 14.1	23 0.2	2 47.6	28 23.1	29 53.9	26 41.5
18 Su	11 42 7	27 22 38	5♊ 4 52	12♊ 1 50	10D 59.0	10 29.8	11 23.9	11 53.3	22 54.8	2 47.1	28 22.1	29 52.6	26 40.3
19 M	11 46 3	28 22 17	19 0 39	26 1 18	10R 59.0	12 10.4	12 30.5	12 32.4	22 49.4	2 46.5	28 21.1	29 51.3	26 39.0
20 Tu	11 50 0	29 21 55	3♋ 3 44	10♋ 7 51	10 59.1	13 52.2	13 36.9	13 11.5	22 44.2	2 45.7	28 20.2	29 49.9	26 37.8
21 W	11 53 56	0♈21 30	17 13 33	24 20 38	10 58.0	15 35.3	14 43.0	13 50.6	22 39.2	2 44.9	28 19.4	29 48.5	26 36.6
22 Th	11 57 53	1 21 3	1♌28 49	8♌37 45	10 54.8	17 19.6	15 48.9	14 29.7	22 34.3	2 43.9	28 18.6	29 47.2	26 35.4
23 F	12 1 49	2 20 33	15 46 59	22 56 0	10 49.0	19 5.2	16 54.6	15 8.8	22 29.6	2 42.9	28 17.9	29 45.8	26 34.3
24 Sa	12 5 46	3 20 1	0♍ 4 14	7♍11 2	10 40.7	20 52.1	17 60.0	15 47.8	22 25.1	2 41.8	28 17.2	29 44.4	26 33.1
25 Su	12 9 43	4 19 27	14 15 43	21 17 39	10 30.6	22 40.3	19 5.1	16 26.8	22 20.7	2 40.5	28 16.5	29 42.9	26 32.0
26 M	12 13 39	5 18 50	28 16 11	5♎10 45	10 19.8	24 29.8	20 10.0	17 5.9	22 16.5	2 39.2	28 15.9	29 41.5	26 30.9
27 Tu	12 17 36	6 18 12	12♎ 0 50	18 46 4	10 9.4	26 20.6	21 14.6	17 44.8	22 12.5	2 37.8	28 15.4	29 40.0	26 29.8
28 W	12 21 32	7 17 32	25 26 9	2♏ 0 54	10 0.6	28 12.8	22 18.9	18 23.8	22 8.6	2 36.3	28 14.9	29 38.5	26 28.7
29 Th	12 25 29	8 16 49	8♏30 18	14 54 26	9 53.9	0♈ 6.3	23 23.0	19 2.8	22 4.9	2 34.7	28 14.5	29 37.1	26 27.6
30 F	12 29 25	9 16 5	21 13 28	27 27 42	9 49.8	2 1.1	24 26.8	19 41.7	22 1.4	2 33.0	28 14.1	29 35.5	26 26.6
31 Sa	12 33 22	10 15 19	3♐37 31	9♐43 23	9D 48.1	3 57.2	25 30.2	20 20.6	21 58.0	2 31.2	28 13.8	29 34.0	26 25.6

APRIL 1956 LONGITUDE

Day	Sid.Time	☉	0 hr ☽	Noon ☽	True ☊	☿	♀	♂	♃	♄	♅	♆	♇
1 Su	12 37 18	11♈14 31	15♐45 50	21♐45 25	9♐48.0	5♈54.6	26♉33.4	20♑59.5	21♌54.8	2♐29.3	28♋13.5	29♎32.5	26♌24.6
2 M	12 41 15	12 13 41	27 42 47	3♑38 33	9 48.8	7 53.3	27 36.2	21 38.4	21R 51.9	2R 27.3	28R 13.3	29R 31.0	26R 23.6
3 Tu	12 45 12	13 12 50	9♑33 24	15 27 59	9R 49.6	9 53.2	28 38.7	22 17.2	21 49.0	2 25.2	28 13.2	29 29.4	26 22.7
4 W	12 49 8	14 11 57	21 23 0	27 19 5	9 49.4	11 54.3	29 40.9	22 56.0	21 46.4	2 23.1	28 13.1	29 27.9	26 21.8
5 Th	12 53 5	15 11 2	3♒16 53	9♒16 58	9 47.4	13 56.4	0♊42.8	23 34.8	21 44.0	2 20.8	28D 13.0	29 26.3	26 20.9
6 F	12 57 1	16 10 5	15 19 56	21 26 16	9 43.4	15 59.5	1 44.3	24 13.5	21 41.7	2 18.5	28 13.0	29 24.7	26 20.0
7 Sa	13 0 58	17 9 6	27 36 25	3♓50 46	9 37.3	18 3.5	2 45.5	24 52.2	21 39.6	2 16.1	28 13.1	29 23.1	26 19.2
8 Su	13 4 54	18 8 5	10♓ 9 35	16 33 5	9 29.4	20 8.3	3 46.3	25 30.9	21 37.7	2 13.6	28 13.2	29 21.5	26 18.3
9 M	13 8 51	19 7 3	23 1 22	29 34 27	9 20.6	22 13.5	4 46.7	26 9.6	21 36.0	2 11.0	28 13.3	29 19.9	26 17.5
10 Tu	13 12 47	20 5 59	6♈12 14	12♈54 34	9 11.8	24 19.1	5 46.7	26 48.2	21 34.5	2 8.3	28 13.5	29 18.3	26 16.7
11 W	13 16 44	21 4 52	19 41 9	26 31 40	9 3.8	26 24.9	6 46.3	27 26.7	21 33.2	2 5.6	28 13.8	29 16.7	26 16.0
12 Th	13 20 41	22 3 44	3♉25 42	10♉22 50	8 57.5	28 30.5	7 45.5	28 5.2	21 32.0	2 2.8	28 14.1	29 15.1	26 15.3
13 F	13 24 37	23 2 34	17 22 35	24 24 29	8 53.4	0♉35.6	8 44.2	28 43.7	21 31.1	1 59.8	28 14.5	29 13.4	26 14.6
14 Sa	13 28 34	24 1 22	1♊28 5	8♊32 57	8D 51.5	2 40.1	9 42.6	29 22.2	21 30.3	1 56.9	28 15.0	29 11.8	26 13.9
15 Su	13 32 30	25 0 7	15 38 41	22 44 55	8 51.5	4 43.4	10 40.4	0♒ 0.5	21 29.7	1 53.8	28 15.5	29 10.2	26 13.2
16 M	13 36 27	25 58 51	29 51 20	6♋57 40	8 52.5	6 45.4	11 37.8	0 38.9	21 29.4	1 50.7	28 16.0	29 8.5	26 12.6
17 Tu	13 40 23	26 57 32	14♋ 3 39	21 9 6	8R 53.8	8 45.7	12 34.7	1 17.2	21D 29.2	1 47.5	28 16.6	29 6.9	26 12.0
18 W	13 44 20	27 56 10	28 13 47	5♌17 32	8 54.3	10 43.9	13 31.0	1 55.4	21 29.2	1 44.2	28 17.3	29 5.3	26 11.4
19 Th	13 48 16	28 54 47	12♌20 9	19 21 24	8 53.5	12 39.7	14 26.8	2 33.6	21 29.3	1 40.9	28 18.0	29 3.6	26 10.9
20 F	13 52 13	29 53 21	26 21 7	3♍19 1	8 51.0	14 32.8	15 22.1	3 11.8	21 29.7	1 37.5	28 18.7	29 2.0	26 10.4
21 Sa	13 56 10	0♉51 53	10♍14 52	17 8 23	8 46.9	16 22.9	16 16.8	3 49.8	21 30.3	1 34.0	28 19.5	29 0.3	26 9.9
22 Su	14 0 6	1 50 23	23 59 18	0♎47 20	8 41.5	18 9.7	17 10.9	4 27.9	21 31.0	1 30.5	28 20.4	28 58.7	26 9.4
23 M	14 4 3	2 48 51	7♎32 13	14 13 41	8 35.6	19 53.1	18 4.4	5 5.9	21 31.9	1 26.9	28 21.3	28 57.1	26 9.0
24 Tu	14 7 59	3 47 16	20 51 30	27 25 31	8 30.0	21 32.8	18 57.2	5 43.8	21 33.0	1 23.2	28 22.3	28 55.4	26 8.6
25 W	14 11 56	4 45 40	3♏55 36	10♏21 39	8 25.2	23 8.5	19 49.4	6 21.7	21 34.3	1 19.5	28 23.3	28 53.8	26 8.2
26 Th	14 15 52	5 44 2	16 43 41	23 1 44	8 21.8	24 40.2	20 40.9	6 59.5	21 35.8	1 15.7	28 24.3	28 52.2	26 7.8
27 F	14 19 49	6 42 23	29 15 56	5♐26 29	8D 20.0	26 7.7	21 31.7	7 37.3	21 37.4	1 11.9	28 25.5	28 50.5	26 7.5
28 Sa	14 23 45	7 40 41	11♐33 37	17 37 40	8 19.7	27 30.9	22 21.8	8 15.0	21 39.2	1 8.0	28 26.6	28 48.9	26 7.2
29 Su	14 27 42	8 38 58	23 39 0	29 38 3	8 20.5	28 49.7	23 11.1	8 52.7	21 41.2	1 4.1	28 27.9	28 47.3	26 7.0
30 M	14 31 39	9 37 13	5♑35 17	11♑31 13	8 22.1	0♊ 3.9	23 59.6	9 30.3	21 43.4	1 0.2	28 29.1	28 45.7	26 6.7

Astro Data	Planet Ingress	Last Aspect	☽ Ingress	Last Aspect	☽ Ingress	☽ Phases & Eclipses	Astro Data
Dy Hr Mn	Dy Hr Mn	Dy Hr Mn	Dy Hr Mn	Dy Hr Mn	Dy Hr Mn	Dy Hr Mn	1 MARCH 1956
☽0N 12 7:02	♀ ♉ 7 21:31	3 5:35 ♅ △	♐ 3 8:09	2 3:38 ♆ ⚹	♑ 2 4:37	4 11:53 ☽ 13♐54	Julian Day # 20514
♄ R 12 3:29	☿ ♓ 11 10:27	5 15:16 ♀ △	♑ 5 20:32	4 16:17 ♆ □	♒ 4 17:24	12 13:37 ● 21♓58	Delta T 31.4 sec
☽0S 25 7:00	♆ ♎ 12 1:57	8 6:26 ♅ ☍	♒ 8 9:19	7 3:26 ♆ △	♓ 7 4:37	19 17:14 ☽ 29♊05	SVP 05♓52'01"
☿0N 30 23:26	☉ ♈ 20 15:20	10 18:12 ☿ ☌	♓ 10 20:11	9 9:32 ♅ △	♈ 9 12:47	26 13:11 ○ 5♎51	Obliquity 23°26'40"
	☿ ♈ 28 22:41	13 1:36 ♅ △	♈ 13 4:26	11 16:46 ♆ ☍	♉ 11 18:03		⚷ Chiron 8♒37.4
♅ D 5 11:22		15 10:25 ♆ ☍	♉ 15 10:32	13 20:16 ♂ △	♊ 13 21:30	3 8:06 ☽ 13♑33	☽ Mean ☊ 12♐55.1
☽0N 8 15:09	♀ ♊ 4 7:23	17 12:22 ♅ ⚹	♊ 17 15:11	15 22:48 ♆ △	♋ 16 0:15	11 2:39 ● 21♈11	
♃ D 17 12:59	☿ ♉ 12 17:10	19 18:31 ♆ △	♋ 19 18:47	18 1:27 ♆ □	♌ 18 3:00	17 23:28 ☽ 27♋55	1 APRIL 1956
☽0S 21 13:42	♂ ♒ 14 23:40	21 21:09 ♆ □	♌ 21 21:31	20 4:36 ♆ ⚹	♍ 20 6:17	25 1:41 ○ 4♏50	Julian Day # 20545
	☉ ♉ 20 2:43	23 23:27 ♆ ⚹	♍ 23 23:53	22 7:41 ♅ ⚹	♎ 22 10:36		Delta T 31.4 sec
	☿ ♊ 29 22:41	25 24:00 ♅ ⚹	♎ 26 3:00	24 14:43 ♆ ☌	♏ 24 16:44		SVP 05♓51'59"
		28 7:38 ♆ ☌	♏ 28 8:18	26 22:22 ♅ △	♐ 27 1:25		Obliquity 23°26'39"
		30 13:30 ♅ △	♐ 30 16:56	29 10:17 ♆ ⚹	♑ 29 12:44		⚷ Chiron 10♒33.0
							☽ Mean ☊ 11♐16.6

LONGITUDE — MAY 1956

Day	Sid.Time	☉	0 hr ☽	Noon ☽	True ☊	☿	♀	♂	♃	♄	♅	♆	♇
1 Tu	14 35 35	10♉35 27	17♑26 24	23♑21 24	8♐23.9	1♊13.6	24♊47.3	10♒ 7.8	21♌45.8	0♐56.1	28♋30.5	28♎44.1	26♌ 6.5
2 W	14 39 32	11 33 39	29 16 49	5♒13 15	8 25.3	2 18.5	25 34.2	10 45.3	21 48.3	0R 52.1	28 31.8	28R 42.5	26R 6.3
3 Th	14 43 28	12 31 50	11♒11 20	17 11 40	8R 25.9	3 18.7	26 20.2	11 22.6	21 51.0	0 48.0	28 33.2	28 40.9	26 6.2
4 F	14 47 25	13 29 59	23 14 50	29 21 25	8 25.5	4 14.1	27 5.3	11 59.9	21 53.9	0 43.8	28 34.7	28 39.4	26 6.1
5 Sa	14 51 21	14 28 7	5♓31 57	11♓46 56	8 24.0	5 4.6	27 49.5	12 37.2	21 57.0	0 39.7	28 36.2	28 37.8	26 6.0
6 Su	14 55 18	15 26 13	18 6 47	24 31 53	8 21.6	5 50.1	28 32.8	13 14.3	22 0.2	0 35.4	28 37.8	28 36.2	26 5.9
7 M	14 59 14	16 24 18	1♈ 2 30	7♈38 48	8 18.6	6 30.6	29 15.0	13 51.4	22 3.6	0 31.2	28 39.4	28 34.7	26D 5.8
8 Tu	15 3 11	17 22 22	14 20 52	21 8 38	8 15.5	7 6.1	29 56.1	14 28.3	22 7.2	0 26.9	28 41.1	28 33.1	26 5.8
9 W	15 7 7	18 20 24	28 1 56	5♉ 0 29	8 12.7	7 36.5	0♋36.2	15 5.2	22 10.9	0 22.6	28 42.8	28 31.6	26 5.9
10 Th	15 11 4	19 18 24	12♉ 3 52	19 11 34	8 10.6	8 1.8	1 15.2	15 42.0	22 14.8	0 18.3	28 44.6	28 30.1	26 5.9
11 F	15 15 1	20 16 23	26 22 58	3♊37 23	8D 9.3	8 21.9	1 53.0	16 18.7	22 18.9	0 13.9	28 46.4	28 28.6	26 6.0
12 Sa	15 18 57	21 14 21	10♊54 5	18 12 18	8 9.1	8 37.0	2 29.6	16 55.3	22 23.1	0 9.5	28 48.2	28 27.1	26 6.1
13 Su	15 22 54	22 12 17	25 31 15	2♋50 12	8 9.6	8 47.0	3 4.9	17 31.7	22 27.5	0 5.1	28 50.1	28 25.6	26 6.2
14 M	15 26 50	23 10 11	10♋ 8 27	17 25 21	8 10.5	8R 51.9	3 38.9	18 8.1	22 32.1	0 0.7	28 52.1	28 24.2	26 6.4
15 Tu	15 30 47	24 8 4	24 40 19	1♌52 51	8 11.6	8 52.0	4 11.6	18 44.4	22 36.8	29♏56.3	28 54.1	28 22.7	26 6.6
16 W	15 34 43	25 5 54	9♌ 2 34	16 9 7	8 12.5	8 47.2	4 42.8	19 20.5	22 41.7	29 51.8	28 56.1	28 21.3	26 6.8
17 Th	15 38 40	26 3 43	23 12 14	0♍11 44	8R 12.9	8 37.9	5 12.5	19 56.5	22 46.7	29 47.4	28 58.2	28 19.9	26 7.1
18 F	15 42 37	27 1 30	7♍ 7 31	13 59 29	8 12.7	8 24.3	5 40.7	20 32.5	22 51.9	29 42.9	29 0.3	28 18.5	26 7.4
19 Sa	15 46 33	27 59 16	20 47 38	27 31 57	8 12.1	8 6.5	6 7.3	21 8.3	22 57.2	29 38.4	29 2.4	28 17.1	26 7.7
20 Su	15 50 30	28 56 59	4♎12 29	10♎49 16	8 11.1	7 45.1	6 32.2	21 43.9	23 2.7	29 33.9	29 4.6	28 15.7	26 8.0
21 M	15 54 26	29 54 41	17 22 22	23 51 54	8 10.1	7 20.3	6 55.4	22 19.5	23 8.3	29 29.5	29 6.9	28 14.4	26 8.4
22 Tu	15 58 23	0♊52 22	0♏17 55	6♏40 32	8 9.1	6 52.6	7 16.9	22 54.9	23 14.1	29 25.0	29 9.2	28 13.1	26 8.8
23 W	16 2 19	1 50 1	12 59 52	19 16 1	8 8.4	6 22.6	7 36.5	23 30.2	23 20.1	29 20.5	29 11.5	28 11.7	26 9.2
24 Th	16 6 16	2 47 39	25 29 8	1♐39 22	8 7.9	5 50.7	7 54.2	24 5.4	23 26.1	29 16.0	29 13.9	28 10.5	26 9.7
25 F	16 10 12	3 45 16	7♐46 52	13 51 51	8D 7.8	5 17.5	8 10.0	24 40.5	23 32.3	29 11.6	29 16.3	28 9.2	26 10.2
26 Sa	16 14 9	4 42 51	19 54 31	25 55 8	8 7.9	4 43.6	8 23.7	25 15.4	23 38.7	29 7.1	29 18.7	28 7.9	26 10.7
27 Su	16 18 6	5 40 25	1♑53 57	7♑51 16	8 8.1	4 9.5	8 35.4	25 50.1	23 45.2	29 2.7	29 21.2	28 6.7	26 11.2
28 M	16 22 2	6 37 59	13 47 27	19 42 51	8 8.3	3 36.0	8 45.0	26 24.8	23 51.8	28 58.3	29 23.7	28 5.5	26 11.8
29 Tu	16 25 59	7 35 31	25 37 52	1♒32 56	8R 8.4	3 3.5	8 52.4	26 59.2	23 58.6	28 53.9	29 26.3	28 4.3	26 12.4
30 W	16 29 55	8 33 2	7♒28 32	13 25 8	8 8.4	2 32.6	8 57.5	27 33.5	24 5.5	28 49.5	29 28.9	28 3.2	26 13.0
31 Th	16 33 52	9 30 33	19 23 16	25 23 27	8 8.4	2 3.8	9R 0.4	28 7.7	24 12.5	28 45.1	29 31.5	28 2.0	26 13.6

LONGITUDE — JUNE 1956

Day	Sid.Time	☉	0 hr ☽	Noon ☽	True ☊	☿	♀	♂	♃	♄	♅	♆	♇
1 F	16 37 48	10♊28 2	1♓26 14	7♓32 11	8♐ 8.2	1♊37.5	9♋ 1.0	28♒41.6	24♌19.7	28♏40.8	29♋34.2	28♎ 0.9	26♌14.3
2 Sa	16 41 45	11 25 31	13 41 50	19 55 42	8D 8.2	1R 14.3	8R 59.3	29 15.4	24 27.0	28R 36.5	29 36.9	27R 59.8	26 15.0
3 Su	16 45 41	12 22 59	26 14 21	2♈38 12	8 8.3	0 54.5	8 55.1	29 49.0	24 34.4	28 32.2	29 39.6	27 58.7	26 15.8
4 M	16 49 38	13 20 27	9♈ 7 43	15 43 13	8 8.7	0 38.3	8 48.6	0♓22.5	24 41.9	28 27.9	29 42.4	27 57.7	26 16.5
5 Tu	16 53 35	14 17 53	22 24 59	29 13 11	8 9.2	0 26.1	8 39.7	0 55.7	24 49.6	28 23.7	29 45.2	27 56.7	26 17.3
6 W	16 57 31	15 15 19	6♉ 7 51	13♉ 8 52	8 9.8	0 18.1	8 28.4	1 28.7	24 57.4	28 19.5	29 48.1	27 55.7	26 18.1
7 Th	17 1 28	16 12 45	20 16 0	27 28 51	8 10.4	0D 14.3	8 14.7	2 1.5	25 5.3	28 15.3	29 51.0	27 54.7	26 19.0
8 F	17 5 24	17 10 9	4♊46 50	12♊ 9 15	8R 10.7	0 14.9	7 58.7	2 34.1	25 13.4	28 11.2	29 53.9	27 53.8	26 19.8
9 Sa	17 9 21	18 7 33	19 35 15	27 3 53	8 10.5	0 20.1	7 40.3	3 6.5	25 21.5	28 7.1	29 56.8	27 52.8	26 20.7
10 Su	17 13 17	19 4 57	4♋34 5	12♋ 4 47	8 9.9	0 29.7	7 19.7	3 38.7	25 29.8	28 3.1	29 59.8	27 51.9	26 21.6
11 M	17 17 14	20 2 19	19 34 54	27 3 23	8 8.8	0 43.8	6 56.8	4 10.6	25 38.2	27 59.1	0♌ 2.8	27 51.1	26 22.6
12 Tu	17 21 10	20 59 41	4♌29 16	11♌51 40	8 7.3	1 2.5	6 31.8	4 42.3	25 46.7	27 55.2	0 5.8	27 50.2	26 23.6
13 W	17 25 7	21 57 1	19 9 52	26 23 17	8 5.8	1 25.6	6 4.8	5 13.8	25 55.3	27 51.3	0 8.9	27 49.4	26 24.5
14 Th	17 29 4	22 54 20	3♍31 28	10♍34 8	8 4.6	1 53.2	5 35.9	5 45.0	26 4.0	27 47.4	0 12.0	27 48.6	26 25.6
15 F	17 33 0	23 51 39	17 31 7	24 22 25	8D 3.9	2 25.1	5 5.2	6 15.9	26 12.9	27 43.6	0 15.1	27 47.9	26 26.6
16 Sa	17 36 57	24 48 57	1♎ 8 7	7♎48 22	8 3.9	3 1.3	4 32.9	6 46.6	26 21.8	27 39.9	0 18.2	27 47.2	26 27.7
17 Su	17 40 53	25 46 13	14 23 26	20 53 36	8 4.6	3 41.8	3 59.2	7 17.0	26 30.9	27 36.2	0 21.4	27 46.5	26 28.8
18 M	17 44 50	26 43 29	27 19 11	3♏40 33	8 5.8	4 26.3	3 24.3	7 47.2	26 40.0	27 32.6	0 24.6	27 45.8	26 29.9
19 Tu	17 48 46	27 40 44	9♏58 3	16 12 2	8 7.3	5 15.0	2 48.4	8 17.1	26 49.3	27 29.0	0 27.8	27 45.1	26 31.0
20 W	17 52 43	28 37 59	22 22 51	28 30 51	8 8.5	6 7.7	2 11.6	8 46.7	26 58.6	27 25.5	0 31.0	27 44.5	26 32.2
21 Th	17 56 39	29 35 13	4♐36 21	10♐39 38	8R 9.2	7 4.3	1 34.3	9 16.0	27 8.0	27 22.1	0 34.3	27 43.9	26 33.4
22 F	18 0 36	0♋32 26	16 41 0	22 40 44	8 9.0	8 4.8	0 56.7	9 45.0	27 17.6	27 18.7	0 37.6	27 43.4	26 34.6
23 Sa	18 4 33	1 29 39	28 39 4	4♑36 16	8 7.7	9 9.2	0 19.0	10 13.7	27 27.2	27 15.4	0 40.9	27 42.9	26 35.8
24 Su	18 8 29	2 26 52	10♑32 34	16 28 14	8 5.2	10 17.3	29♊41.5	10 42.1	27 37.0	27 12.1	0 44.2	27 42.4	26 37.1
25 M	18 12 26	3 24 4	22 23 30	28 18 38	8 1.6	11 29.1	29 4.5	11 10.2	27 46.8	27 9.0	0 47.6	27 41.9	26 38.4
26 Tu	18 16 22	4 21 16	4♒13 54	10♒ 9 38	7 57.4	12 44.6	28 28.0	11 37.9	27 56.7	27 5.9	0 51.0	27 41.5	26 39.7
27 W	18 20 19	5 18 28	16 6 7	22 3 42	7 52.8	14 3.7	27 52.5	12 5.3	28 6.7	27 2.8	0 54.4	27 41.1	26 41.0
28 Th	18 24 15	6 15 40	28 2 46	4♓ 3 43	7 48.5	15 26.4	27 18.1	12 32.4	28 16.8	26 59.9	0 57.8	27 40.7	26 42.3
29 F	18 28 12	7 12 52	10♓ 6 58	16 12 58	7 45.0	16 52.7	26 45.0	12 59.1	28 27.0	26 57.0	1 1.2	27 40.4	26 43.7
30 Sa	18 32 8	8 10 3	22 22 12	28 35 9	7 42.5	18 22.4	26 13.3	13 25.4	28 37.2	26 54.2	1 4.7	27 40.0	26 45.1

Astro Data Dy Hr Mn	Planet Ingress Dy Hr Mn	Last Aspect Dy Hr Mn	☽ Ingress Dy Hr Mn	Last Aspect Dy Hr Mn	☽ Ingress Dy Hr Mn	☽ Phases & Eclipses Dy Hr Mn	Astro Data
☽0N 5 23:42	♀ ♋ 8 2:17	1 22:51 ♆ □	♒ 2 1:27	3 6:28 ♅ △	♈ 3 7:04	3 2:55 ☽ 12♒39	1 MAY 1956
♅□♆ 5 11:53	♄ ♏ 14 3:47	4 10:36 ♆ △	♓ 4 13:15	5 12:59 ♅ □	♉ 5 13:22	10 13:04 ● 19♉50	Julian Day # 20575
♇ D 7 19:59	☉ ♊ 21 2:13	6 20:32 ♀ □	♈ 6 22:05	7 15:58 ♅ ✶	♊ 7 16:09	17 5:15 ☽ 26♌16	Delta T 31.5 sec
☿ R 14 12:12		9 1:11 ♅ □	♉ 9 3:24	9 13:18 ♅ △	♋ 9 16:42	24 15:26 ○ 3♐25	SVP 05♓51'55"
☽0S 18 18:50	♂ ♓ 3 7:51	11 3:59 ♅ ✶	♊ 11 6:00	11 13:26 ♄ △	♌ 11 16:45	24 15:31 • P 0.965	Obliquity 23°26'39"
♄△♅ 24 7:38	♅ ♌ 10 1:48	13 4:46 ♆ △	♋ 13 7:21	13 14:23 ♆ ✶	♍ 13 18:03		⚷ Chiron 11♒35.2
♀ R 31 18:04	☉ ♋ 21 10:24	15 8:43 ♄ △	♌ 15 8:52	15 17:51 ♄ ✶	♎ 15 21:58		☽ Mean ☊ 9♐41.3
☽0N 2 8:01	♀ ♊ 23 12:10	17 11:14 ♄ □	♍ 17 11:40	18 0:50 ♆ ☌	♏ 18 5:03	1 19:13 ☽ 11♓14	
♅ D 7 8:34		19 15:41 ♄ ✶	♎ 19 16:25	20 9:49 ♄ ☌	♐ 20 14:55	8 21:29 ● 18♊02	1 JUNE 1956
♄⊻♆ 13 14:23		21 21:51 ♅ □	♏ 21 23:26	22 22:07 ♆ ✶	♑ 23 2:43	8 21:20:08 ● T 4'44"	Julian Day # 20606
☽0S 15 0:39		24 7:18 ♄ ☌	♐ 24 8:46	25 10:45 ♆ □	♒ 25 15:25	15 11:56 ☽ 24♍20	Delta T 31.5 sec
♃☌♇ 16 17:44		26 16:24 ♆ ✶	♑ 26 20:11	28 0:28 ♃ ☍	♓ 28 3:54	23 6:14 ○ 1♑44	SVP 05♓51'51"
♃□♅ 22 2:03		29 7:45 ♅ ☍	♒ 29 8:52	30 8:44 ♄ △	♈ 30 14:43		Obliquity 23°26'38"
♃✶♆ 24 12:39	☽0N 29 15:35	31 18:34 ♄ □	♓ 31 21:09				⚷ Chiron 11♒36.3R
							☽ Mean ☊ 8♐02.8

JULY 1956 — LONGITUDE

Day	Sid.Time	☉	0 hr ☽	Noon ☽	True ☊	☿	♀	♂	♃	♄	♅	♆	♇
1 Su	18 36 5	9♋ 7 15	4♈52 18	11♈14 11	7♐41.4	19♊55.6	25♊43.4	13♓51.3	28♌47.6	26♏51.4	1♌ 8.1	27♎39.8	26♌46.5
2 M	18 40 2	10 4 27	17 41 14	24 13 55	7D41.5	21 32.2	25R15.3	14 16.8	28 58.0	26R48.8	1 11.6	27R39.5	26 47.9
3 Tu	18 43 58	11 1 40	0♉52 39	7♉37 44	7 42.6	23 12.2	24 49.1	14 42.0	29 8.5	26 46.2	1 15.1	27 39.3	26 49.3
4 W	18 47 55	11 58 52	14 29 27	21 27 54	7 44.1	24 55.4	24 25.0	15 6.6	29 19.1	26 43.7	1 18.7	27 39.1	26 50.8
5 Th	18 51 51	12 56 5	28 33 5	5♊44 48	7R45.2	26 41.7	24 3.1	15 30.9	29 29.8	26 41.3	1 22.2	27 39.0	26 52.3
6 F	18 55 48	13 53 19	13♊ 2 44	20 26 19	7 45.4	28 31.1	23 43.4	15 54.7	29 40.5	26 38.9	1 25.7	27 38.8	26 53.8
7 Sa	18 59 44	14 50 32	27 54 49	5♋27 19	7 44.1	0♋23.5	23 26.0	16 18.1	29 51.4	26 36.7	1 29.3	27 38.8	26 55.3
8 Su	19 3 41	15 47 46	13♋ 2 42	20 39 46	7 41.0	2 18.5	23 10.9	16 41.0	0♍ 2.3	26 34.5	1 32.9	27 38.7	26 56.8
9 M	19 7 37	16 45 0	28 17 12	5♌53 42	7 36.4	4 16.2	22 58.3	17 3.4	0 13.2	26 32.5	1 36.5	27D38.7	26 58.4
10 Tu	19 11 34	17 42 14	13♌27 57	20 58 45	7 30.7	6 16.1	22 47.9	17 25.3	0 24.3	26 30.5	1 40.1	27 38.7	26 60.0
11 W	19 15 31	18 39 28	28 25 2	5♍45 54	7 24.9	8 18.2	22 40.0	17 46.7	0 35.4	26 28.6	1 43.7	27 38.7	27 1.6
12 Th	19 19 27	19 36 42	13♍ 0 37	20 8 44	7 19.7	10 22.0	22 34.4	18 7.6	0 46.6	26 26.7	1 47.3	27 38.8	27 3.2
13 F	19 23 24	20 33 55	27 9 56	4♎ 4 7	7 15.8	12 27.5	22D31.2	18 28.0	0 57.8	26 25.0	1 50.9	27 38.9	27 4.8
14 Sa	19 27 20	21 31 9	10♎51 22	17 31 52	7D13.7	14 34.1	22 30.3	18 47.9	1 9.1	26 23.4	1 54.6	27 39.0	27 6.4
15 Su	19 31 17	22 28 23	24 5 58	0♏34 4	7 13.1	16 41.7	22 31.7	19 7.2	1 20.5	26 21.8	1 58.2	27 39.2	27 8.1
16 M	19 35 13	23 25 37	6♏56 39	13 14 15	7 13.8	18 49.9	22 35.3	19 26.0	1 32.0	26 20.4	2 1.9	27 39.4	27 9.8
17 Tu	19 39 10	24 22 51	19 27 24	25 36 38	7 15.1	20 58.5	22 41.2	19 44.2	1 43.5	26 19.0	2 5.5	27 39.6	27 11.4
18 W	19 43 6	25 20 5	1♐42 31	7♐45 33	7R16.1	23 7.1	22 49.3	20 1.8	1 55.0	26 17.8	2 9.2	27 39.9	27 13.1
19 Th	19 47 3	26 17 20	13 46 14	19 45 2	7 16.0	25 15.5	22 59.4	20 18.9	2 6.7	26 16.6	2 12.9	27 40.2	27 14.9
20 F	19 51 0	27 14 35	25 42 22	1♑38 38	7 14.2	27 23.3	23 11.7	20 35.3	2 18.3	26 15.5	2 16.6	27 40.5	27 16.6
21 Sa	19 54 56	28 11 50	7♑34 10	13 29 18	7 10.2	29 30.5	23 25.9	20 51.1	2 30.1	26 14.5	2 20.2	27 40.9	27 18.3
22 Su	19 58 53	29 9 6	19 24 19	25 19 28	7 3.9	1♌36.8	23 42.1	21 6.4	2 41.8	26 13.7	2 23.9	27 41.3	27 20.1
23 M	20 2 49	0♌ 6 22	1♒14 58	7♒11 3	6 55.6	3 42.1	24 0.2	21 20.9	2 53.7	26 12.9	2 27.6	27 41.7	27 21.9
24 Tu	20 6 46	1 3 39	13 7 54	19 5 44	6 46.0	5 46.1	24 20.2	21 34.9	3 5.6	26 12.2	2 31.3	27 42.2	27 23.6
25 W	20 10 42	2 0 56	25 4 44	1♓ 5 7	6 35.7	7 48.9	24 41.9	21 48.1	3 17.5	26 11.6	2 35.0	27 42.7	27 25.4
26 Th	20 14 39	2 58 14	7♓ 7 6	13 10 56	6 25.7	9 50.2	25 5.4	22 0.7	3 29.5	26 11.1	2 38.7	27 43.2	27 27.2
27 F	20 18 35	3 55 33	19 16 53	25 25 15	6 17.0	11 50.1	25 30.5	22 12.6	3 41.6	26 10.6	2 42.3	27 43.7	27 29.0
28 Sa	20 22 32	4 52 53	1♈36 23	7♈50 37	6 10.1	13 48.4	25 57.2	22 23.8	3 53.6	26 10.3	2 46.0	27 44.3	27 30.9
29 Su	20 26 29	5 50 14	14 8 22	20 30 2	6 5.6	15 45.2	26 25.5	22 34.2	4 5.8	26 10.1	2 49.7	27 44.9	27 32.7
30 M	20 30 25	6 47 36	26 56 2	3♉26 48	6D 3.4	17 40.3	26 55.3	22 44.0	4 18.0	26D10.0	2 53.4	27 45.6	27 34.5
31 Tu	20 34 22	7 44 59	10♉ 2 47	16 44 20	6 3.0	19 33.8	27 26.5	22 52.9	4 30.2	26 9.9	2 57.1	27 46.2	27 36.4

AUGUST 1956 — LONGITUDE

Day	Sid.Time	☉	0 hr ☽	Noon ☽	True ☊	☿	♀	♂	♃	♄	♅	♆	♇
1 W	20 38 18	8♌42 23	23♉31 49	0♊25 29	6♐ 3.5	21♌25.8	27♊59.1	23♓ 1.1	4♍42.5	26♏10.0	3♌ 0.8	27♎46.9	27♌38.2
2 Th	20 42 15	9 39 49	7♊25 32	14 31 58	6R 3.8	23 16.1	28 33.1	23 8.6	4 54.8	26 10.2	3 4.4	27 47.7	27 40.1
3 F	20 46 11	10 37 16	21 44 41	29 3 24	6 2.9	25 4.7	29 8.3	23 15.2	5 7.1	26 10.5	3 8.1	27 48.5	27 42.0
4 Sa	20 50 8	11 34 43	6♋27 35	13♋56 32	5 59.9	26 51.8	29 44.7	23 21.1	5 19.5	26 10.8	3 11.8	27 49.3	27 43.9
5 Su	20 54 4	12 32 12	21 29 21	29 4 56	5 54.3	28 37.2	0♋22.4	23 26.2	5 31.9	26 11.3	3 15.4	27 50.1	27 45.8
6 M	20 58 1	13 29 43	6♌42 3	14♌19 20	5 46.4	0♍21.1	1 1.2	23 30.4	5 44.4	26 11.8	3 19.1	27 51.0	27 47.7
7 Tu	21 1 58	14 27 14	21 55 25	29 28 56	5 36.9	2 3.3	1 41.1	23 33.8	5 56.9	26 12.5	3 22.7	27 51.9	27 49.6
8 W	21 5 54	15 24 46	6♍58 37	14♍23 21	5 26.9	3 44.0	2 22.0	23 36.4	6 9.5	26 13.3	3 26.4	27 52.8	27 51.5
9 Th	21 9 51	16 22 19	21 42 10	28 54 22	5 17.6	5 23.1	3 3.9	23 38.2	6 22.0	26 14.1	3 30.0	27 53.7	27 53.4
10 F	21 13 47	17 19 53	5♎59 27	12♎57 8	5 10.0	7 0.6	3 46.8	23R39.2	6 34.6	26 15.1	3 33.6	27 54.7	27 55.4
11 Sa	21 17 44	18 17 27	19 47 20	26 30 12	5 4.8	8 36.5	4 30.7	23 39.3	6 47.3	26 16.1	3 37.2	27 55.7	27 57.3
12 Su	21 21 40	19 15 3	3♏ 5 59	9♏35 6	5 1.9	10 10.9	5 15.4	23 38.7	6 59.9	26 17.2	3 40.8	27 56.8	27 59.2
13 M	21 25 37	20 12 40	15 58 2	22 15 23	5D 0.9	11 43.8	6 1.1	23 37.2	7 12.6	26 18.5	3 44.4	27 57.8	28 1.2
14 Tu	21 29 33	21 10 18	28 27 44	4♐35 45	5R 0.9	13 15.0	6 47.5	23 34.9	7 25.3	26 19.8	3 48.0	27 58.9	28 3.1
15 W	21 33 30	22 7 56	10♐40 4	16 41 20	5 0.9	14 44.7	7 34.8	23 31.8	7 38.1	26 21.2	3 51.5	28 0.1	28 5.1
16 Th	21 37 27	23 5 36	22 40 11	28 37 11	4 59.7	16 12.9	8 22.9	23 27.9	7 50.8	26 22.8	3 55.1	28 1.2	28 7.0
17 F	21 41 23	24 3 17	4♑32 54	10♑27 51	4 56.5	17 39.4	9 11.7	23 23.2	8 3.6	26 24.4	3 58.6	28 2.4	28 9.0
18 Sa	21 45 20	25 0 58	16 22 29	22 17 15	4 50.7	19 4.3	10 1.3	23 17.8	8 16.4	26 26.1	4 2.1	28 3.6	28 10.9
19 Su	21 49 16	25 58 41	28 12 29	4♒ 8 32	4 42.0	20 27.6	10 51.6	23 11.5	8 29.2	26 27.9	4 5.6	28 4.9	28 12.9
20 M	21 53 13	26 56 26	10♒ 5 39	16 4 4	4 30.9	21 49.2	11 42.5	23 4.5	8 42.1	26 29.8	4 9.1	28 6.1	28 14.8
21 Tu	21 57 9	27 54 11	22 4 0	28 5 34	4 18.0	23 9.1	12 34.2	22 56.8	8 54.9	26 31.8	4 12.6	28 7.4	28 16.8
22 W	22 1 6	28 51 58	4♓ 8 56	10♓14 13	4 4.3	24 27.2	13 26.5	22 48.3	9 7.8	26 33.9	4 16.0	28 8.7	28 18.8
23 Th	22 5 2	29 49 46	16 21 29	22 30 53	3 50.9	25 43.6	14 19.4	22 39.1	9 20.7	26 36.1	4 19.4	28 10.1	28 20.7
24 F	22 8 59	0♍47 36	28 42 31	4♈56 31	3 39.0	26 58.1	15 12.9	22 29.2	9 33.6	26 38.4	4 22.8	28 11.5	28 22.7
25 Sa	22 12 56	1 45 27	11♈13 2	17 32 16	3 29.5	28 10.6	16 7.0	22 18.7	9 46.6	26 40.7	4 26.2	28 12.9	28 24.6
26 Su	22 16 52	2 43 20	23 54 24	0♉19 42	3 22.7	29 21.2	17 1.6	22 7.5	9 59.5	26 43.2	4 29.6	28 14.3	28 26.6
27 M	22 20 49	3 41 15	6♉48 26	13 20 54	3 18.8	0♎29.7	17 56.8	21 55.6	10 12.5	26 45.7	4 32.9	28 15.7	28 28.5
28 Tu	22 24 45	4 39 12	19 57 25	26 38 16	3 17.2	1 36.1	18 52.6	21 43.2	10 25.4	26 48.3	4 36.3	28 17.2	28 30.5
29 W	22 28 42	5 37 11	3♊23 47	10♊14 13	3 16.9	2 40.2	19 48.8	21 30.2	10 38.4	26 51.1	4 39.6	28 18.7	28 32.4
30 Th	22 32 38	6 35 11	17 9 46	24 10 33	3 16.8	3 41.8	20 45.6	21 16.6	10 51.4	26 53.9	4 42.8	28 20.2	28 34.4
31 F	22 36 35	7 33 14	1♋16 36	8♋27 47	3 15.5	4 41.0	21 42.8	21 2.6	11 4.4	26 56.8	4 46.1	28 21.8	28 36.3

Astro Data	Planet Ingress	Last Aspect	☽ Ingress	Last Aspect	☽ Ingress	☽ Phases & Eclipses	Astro Data
Dy Hr Mn	Dy Hr Mn	Dy Hr Mn	Dy Hr Mn	Dy Hr Mn	Dy Hr Mn	Dy Hr Mn	1 JULY 1956
♄□♇ 2 5:11	☿ ♋ 6 19:02	2 20:51 ♃ △	♉ 2 22:26	1 7:11 ♇ □	♊ 1 11:16	1 8:41 ☽ 9♈28	Julian Day # 20636
♆ D 9 6:09	♃ ♍ 7 19:01	5 1:36 ♃ □	♊ 5 2:26	3 12:39 ♀ ☌	♋ 3 13:32	8 4:38 ● 15♋59	Delta T 31.5 sec
☽0S 12 8:42	☿ ♌ 21 5:35	7 3:08 ♃ ⚹	♋ 7 3:20	5 10:02 ♆ □	♌ 5 13:27	14 20:47 ☽ 22♎21	SVP 05♓51'46"
♀ D 13 21:20	☉ ♌ 22 21:20	8 22:59 ♆ □	♌ 9 2:42	7 9:26 ♆ ⚹	♍ 7 12:50	22 21:29 ○ 0♒00	Obliquity 23°26'38"
♃⊻♅ 19 18:41		10 22:45 ♆ ⚹	♍ 11 2:34	9 7:32 ♄ ⚹	♎ 9 13:50	30 19:31 ☽ 7♉34	⚷ Chiron 10♒39.6R
☽0N 26 22:20	♀ ♋ 4 9:49	12 22:43 ♄ ⚹	♎ 13 4:54	11 14:40 ♇ ⚹	♏ 11 18:20		☽ Mean ☊ 6♐27.5
♄ D 30 18:36	☿ ♍ 5 19:06	15 6:34 ♆ ☌	♏ 15 10:56	13 23:12 ♇ □	♐ 14 3:00	6 11:25 ● 13♌57	
	☉ ♍ 23 4:15	17 15:08 ♇ □	♐ 17 20:38	16 11:01 ♇ △	♑ 16 14:47	13 8:45 ☽ 20♏34	1 AUGUST 1956
☽0S 8 18:51	☿ ♎ 26 13:30	20 3:59 ♆ ⚹	♑ 20 8:40	18 23:45 ♆ □	♒ 19 3:38	21 12:38 ○ 28♒25	Julian Day # 20667
♆⚹♇ 9 7:22		22 16:48 ♆ □	♒ 22 21:28	21 12:38 ☉ ☍	♓ 21 15:47	29 4:13 ☽ 5♊47	Delta T 31.5 sec
♂ R 10 16:18		25 5:16 ♆ △	♓ 25 9:50	23 20:16 ☿ ☍	♈ 24 2:30		SVP 05♓51'41"
☽0N 23 4:41		27 13:28 ♄ △	♈ 27 20:54	26 8:31 ♇ △	♉ 26 11:23		Obliquity 23°26'38"
☿0S 24 3:52		30 1:32 ♆ ☍	♉ 30 5:40	28 15:22 ♇ □	♊ 28 17:59		⚷ Chiron 9♒03.8R
				30 19:30 ♇ ⚹	♋ 30 21:51		☽ Mean ☊ 4♐49.0

LONGITUDE SEPTEMBER 1956

Day	Sid.Time	☉	0 hr ☽	Noon ☽	True ☊	☿	♀	♂	♃	♄	♅	♆	♇
1 Sa	22 40 31	8♍31 18	15♋43 50	23♋ 4 17	3♐12.0	5♎37.5	22♋40.5	20♓48.0	11♍17.4	26♏59.8	4♌49.3	28♎23.4	28♌38.3
2 Su	22 44 28	9 29 25	0♌28 30	7♌55 41	3R 5.9	6 31.2	23 38.7	20R33.1	11 30.4	27 2.8	4 52.5	28 25.0	28 40.2
3 M	22 48 25	10 27 33	15 24 53	22 54 58	2 57.3	7 21.8	24 37.3	20 17.8	11 43.4	27 6.0	4 55.7	28 26.6	28 42.1
4 Tu	22 52 21	11 25 43	0♍24 47	7♍53 5	2 46.7	8 9.2	25 36.3	20 2.1	11 56.4	27 9.2	4 58.9	28 28.2	28 44.1
5 W	22 56 18	12 23 55	15 18 41	22 40 28	2 35.5	8 53.3	26 35.7	19 46.2	12 9.4	27 12.6	5 2.0	28 29.9	28 46.0
6 Th	23 0 14	13 22 8	29 57 26	7♎ 8 45	2 24.9	9 33.6	27 35.5	19 30.0	12 22.4	27 16.0	5 5.1	28 31.6	28 47.9
7 F	23 4 11	14 20 23	14♎13 46	21 12 3	2 16.0	10 10.1	28 35.7	19 13.6	12 35.4	27 19.5	5 8.2	28 33.3	28 49.8
8 Sa	23 8 7	15 18 40	28 3 21	4♏47 37	2 9.7	10 42.3	29 36.2	18 57.1	12 48.4	27 23.1	5 11.2	28 35.0	28 51.7
9 Su	23 12 4	16 16 58	11♏24 58	17 55 40	2 5.9	11 10.1	0♌37.1	18 40.5	13 1.4	27 26.7	5 14.2	28 36.8	28 53.6
10 M	23 16 0	17 15 18	24 20 6	0♐38 46	2D 4.3	11 33.1	1 38.4	18 23.9	13 14.4	27 30.5	5 17.2	28 38.5	28 55.5
11 Tu	23 19 57	18 13 39	6♐52 14	13 1 7	2 4.2	11 51.0	2 40.0	18 7.3	13 27.4	27 34.3	5 20.1	28 40.3	28 57.4
12 W	23 23 54	19 12 2	19 6 4	25 7 45	2R 4.4	12 3.4	3 41.9	17 50.8	13 40.4	27 38.2	5 23.0	28 42.1	28 59.2
13 Th	23 27 50	20 10 27	1♑ 6 50	7♑ 3 59	2 3.8	12R10.0	4 44.2	17 34.4	13 53.4	27 42.2	5 25.9	28 44.0	29 1.1
14 F	23 31 47	21 8 53	12 59 50	18 55 0	2 1.6	12 10.6	5 46.8	17 18.1	14 6.3	27 46.3	5 28.8	28 45.8	29 2.9
15 Sa	23 35 43	22 7 21	24 50 3	0♒45 30	1 57.0	12 4.7	6 49.7	17 2.1	14 19.3	27 50.4	5 31.6	28 47.7	29 4.8
16 Su	23 39 40	23 5 51	6♒41 50	12 39 30	1 49.9	11 52.2	7 52.8	16 46.3	14 32.2	27 54.6	5 34.4	28 49.6	29 6.6
17 M	23 43 36	24 4 22	18 38 50	24 40 11	1 40.4	11 32.8	8 56.3	16 30.8	14 45.2	27 58.9	5 37.1	28 51.5	29 8.4
18 Tu	23 47 33	25 2 55	0♓43 48	6♓49 52	1 29.1	11 6.4	10 0.1	16 15.6	14 58.1	28 3.3	5 39.8	28 53.4	29 10.2
19 W	23 51 29	26 1 29	12 58 33	19 9 56	1 17.1	10 33.1	11 4.2	16 0.9	15 11.0	28 7.7	5 42.5	28 55.3	29 12.0
20 Th	23 55 26	27 0 6	25 24 7	1♈41 5	1 5.4	9 52.9	12 8.5	15 46.5	15 23.8	28 12.2	5 45.1	28 57.3	29 13.8
21 F	23 59 22	27 58 44	8♈ 0 53	14 23 28	0 55.0	9 6.2	13 13.1	15 32.6	15 36.7	28 16.8	5 47.7	28 59.2	29 15.6
22 Sa	0 3 19	28 57 25	20 48 49	27 16 57	0 46.7	8 13.6	14 18.0	15 19.1	15 49.5	28 21.4	5 50.3	29 1.2	29 17.3
23 Su	0 7 16	29 56 7	3♉47 51	10♉21 32	0 41.0	7 15.7	15 23.1	15 6.2	16 2.3	28 26.2	5 52.8	29 3.2	29 19.1
24 M	0 11 12	0♎54 52	16 58 2	23 37 26	0 38.0	6 13.7	16 28.5	14 53.8	16 15.1	28 31.0	5 55.3	29 5.2	29 20.8
25 Tu	0 15 9	1 53 39	0♊19 48	7♊ 5 14	0D 37.1	5 8.7	17 34.2	14 42.0	16 27.9	28 35.8	5 57.8	29 7.3	29 22.5
26 W	0 19 5	2 52 28	13 53 50	20 45 44	0 37.6	4 2.2	18 40.0	14 30.8	16 40.7	28 40.7	6 0.2	29 9.3	29 24.2
27 Th	0 23 2	3 51 20	27 40 59	4♋39 38	0R 38.3	2 55.8	19 46.2	14 20.3	16 53.4	28 45.7	6 2.5	29 11.4	29 25.9
28 F	0 26 58	4 50 14	11♋41 41	18 47 3	0 38.3	1 51.2	20 52.5	14 10.4	17 6.1	28 50.8	6 4.9	29 13.4	29 27.6
29 Sa	0 30 55	5 49 10	25 55 32	3♌ 6 53	0 36.5	0 50.1	21 59.1	14 1.1	17 18.8	28 55.9	6 7.1	29 15.5	29 29.2
30 Su	0 34 51	6 48 9	10♌20 41	17 36 26	0 32.6	29♍54.3	23 5.9	13 52.6	17 31.4	29 1.1	6 9.4	29 17.6	29 30.9

LONGITUDE OCTOBER 1956

Day	Sid.Time	☉	0 hr ☽	Noon ☽	True ☊	☿	♀	♂	♃	♄	♅	♆	♇
1 M	0 38 48	7♎47 10	24♌53 30	2♍11 10	0♐26.6	29♍ 5.2	24♌12.9	13♓44.7	17♍44.0	29♏ 6.4	6♌11.6	29♎19.7	29♌32.5
2 Tu	0 42 45	8 46 12	9♍28 36	16 44 58	0R 19.0	28R 24.1	25 20.1	13R 37.7	17 56.6	29 11.7	6 13.7	29 21.9	29 34.1
3 W	0 46 41	9 45 18	23 59 24	1♎11 2	0 10.7	27 52.1	26 27.5	13 31.3	18 9.1	29 17.1	6 15.8	29 24.0	29 35.7
4 Th	0 50 38	10 44 25	8♎19 4	15 22 48	0 2.8	27 30.1	27 35.1	13 25.8	18 21.7	29 22.5	6 17.9	29 26.1	29 37.3
5 F	0 54 34	11 43 34	22 21 37	29 15 3	29♏56.3	27D 18.4	28 42.9	13 21.0	18 34.1	29 28.0	6 19.9	29 28.3	29 38.8
6 Sa	0 58 31	12 42 45	6♏ 2 48	12♏44 39	29 51.6	27 17.4	29 50.9	13 17.0	18 46.6	29 33.5	6 21.9	29 30.4	29 40.3
7 Su	1 2 27	13 41 59	19 20 34	25 50 40	29D 49.2	27 26.9	0♍59.1	13 13.8	18 59.0	29 39.1	6 23.8	29 32.6	29 41.9
8 M	1 6 24	14 41 14	2♐15 8	8♐34 18	29 48.7	27 46.8	2 7.4	13 11.5	19 11.3	29 44.8	6 25.7	29 34.8	29 43.4
9 Tu	1 10 20	15 40 31	14 48 34	20 58 26	29 49.5	28 16.6	3 15.9	13 9.9	19 23.6	29 50.5	6 27.5	29 37.0	29 44.8
10 W	1 14 17	16 39 50	27 4 26	3♑ 7 9	29 51.0	28 55.7	4 24.6	13D 9.2	19 35.9	29 56.3	6 29.3	29 39.2	29 46.3
11 Th	1 18 14	17 39 11	9♑ 7 11	15 5 11	29R 52.3	29 43.4	5 33.5	13 9.2	19 48.1	0♐ 2.2	6 31.1	29 41.4	29 47.7
12 F	1 22 10	18 38 33	21 1 47	26 57 37	29 52.6	0♎39.1	6 42.5	13 10.1	20 0.3	0 8.0	6 32.8	29 43.6	29 49.1
13 Sa	1 26 7	19 37 57	2♒53 18	8♒49 27	29 51.5	1 41.8	7 51.7	13 11.8	20 12.4	0 14.0	6 34.4	29 45.8	29 50.5
14 Su	1 30 3	20 37 23	14 46 39	20 45 25	29 48.7	2 50.9	9 1.0	13 14.2	20 24.5	0 19.9	6 36.0	29 48.0	29 51.9
15 M	1 34 0	21 36 51	26 46 15	2♓49 36	29 44.2	4 5.6	10 10.5	13 17.5	20 36.5	0 26.0	6 37.5	29 50.2	29 53.3
16 Tu	1 37 56	22 36 20	8♓55 51	15 5 20	29 38.5	5 25.1	11 20.1	13 21.5	20 48.5	0 32.1	6 39.0	29 52.4	29 54.6
17 W	1 41 53	23 35 52	21 18 20	27 35 0	29 32.1	6 48.8	12 29.9	13 26.3	21 0.4	0 38.2	6 40.5	29 54.7	29 55.9
18 Th	1 45 49	24 35 25	3♈55 30	10♈19 54	29 25.7	8 16.1	13 39.8	13 31.9	21 12.3	0 44.3	6 41.9	29 56.9	29 57.2
19 F	1 49 46	25 35 0	16 48 10	23 20 15	29 20.1	9 46.2	14 49.9	13 38.2	21 24.1	0 50.6	6 43.2	29 59.1	29 58.4
20 Sa	1 53 42	26 34 37	29 56 2	6♉35 23	29 15.8	11 18.9	16 0.1	13 45.3	21 35.8	0 56.8	6 44.5	0♏ 1.4	29 59.7
21 Su	1 57 39	27 34 16	13♉18 4	20 3 54	29 13.2	12 53.5	17 10.5	13 53.1	21 47.5	1 3.1	6 45.7	0 3.6	0♍ 0.9
22 M	2 1 36	28 33 57	26 52 37	3♊44 0	29D 12.2	14 29.7	18 21.0	14 1.6	21 59.2	1 9.5	6 46.9	0 5.8	0 2.1
23 Tu	2 5 32	29 33 41	10♊37 49	17 33 49	29 12.6	16 7.2	19 31.6	14 10.8	22 10.7	1 15.8	6 48.1	0 8.1	0 3.3
24 W	2 9 29	0♏33 26	24 31 47	1♋31 31	29 13.9	17 45.7	20 42.4	14 20.7	22 22.2	1 22.3	6 49.2	0 10.3	0 4.4
25 Th	2 13 25	1 33 14	8♋32 49	15 35 29	29 15.4	19 24.9	21 53.3	14 31.3	22 33.7	1 28.7	6 50.2	0 12.6	0 5.5
26 F	2 17 22	2 33 4	22 39 19	29 44 6	29R 16.6	21 4.6	23 4.3	14 42.6	22 45.1	1 35.2	6 51.2	0 14.8	0 6.6
27 Sa	2 21 18	3 32 57	6♌49 37	13♌55 38	29 16.9	22 44.6	24 15.5	14 54.5	22 56.4	1 41.8	6 52.1	0 17.1	0 7.7
28 Su	2 25 15	4 32 51	21 1 51	28 7 59	29 16.0	24 24.8	25 26.8	15 7.1	23 7.6	1 48.3	6 53.0	0 19.3	0 8.7
29 M	2 29 12	5 32 48	5♍13 40	12♍18 31	29 14.0	26 5.0	26 38.1	15 20.3	23 18.8	1 54.9	6 53.8	0 21.5	0 9.7
30 Tu	2 33 8	6 32 47	19 22 9	26 24 7	29 11.2	27 45.3	27 49.6	15 34.2	23 29.9	2 1.6	6 54.5	0 23.8	0 10.7
31 W	2 37 5	7 32 48	3♎23 58	10♎21 17	29 7.9	29 25.3	29 1.3	15 48.6	23 40.9	2 8.3	6 55.2	0 26.0	0 11.7

Astro Data Dy Hr Mn	Planet Ingress Dy Hr Mn	Last Aspect Dy Hr Mn	☽ Ingress Dy Hr Mn	Last Aspect Dy Hr Mn	☽ Ingress Dy Hr Mn	☽ Phases & Eclipses Dy Hr Mn	Astro Data
☽0S 5 5:41	♀ ♌ 8 9:23	1 20:40 ♆ □	♌ 1 23:14	1 7:40 ♇ ☌	♍ 1 8:24	4 18:57 ● 12♍12	1 SEPTEMBER 1956
♃∠♆ 12 3:42	☉ ♎ 23 1:35	3 21:18 ♇ ☌	♍ 3 23:20	3 8:53 ♄ ✱	♎ 3 10:01	12 0:13 ☽ 19♐13	Julian Day # 20698
☿ R 13 14:08	☿ ♍ 29 21:25	5 19:48 ♀ ✱	♎ 6 0:04	5 12:43 ♇ ✱	♏ 5 13:19	20 3:19 ○ 27♓08	Delta T 31.6 sec
☽0N 19 11:19		8 2:58 ♀ □	♏ 8 3:26	7 19:15 ♄ ☌	♐ 7 19:46	27 11:25 ☽ 4♋19	SVP 05♓51'37"
☽0S 2 15:17	☊ ♏ 4 9:37	10 8:44 ♇ □	♐ 10 10:46	10 5:21 ♇ △	♑ 10 5:48		Obliquity 23°26'38"
☿0N 2 6:28	♀ ♍ 6 3:12	12 19:47 ♇ △	♑ 12 21:46	12 17:39 ♆ □	♒ 12 18:09	4 4:25 ● 10♎55	⚷ Chiron 7♒28.2R
♄⊻♆ 5 2:03	♄ ♐ 10 15:10	15 8:03 ♆ □	♒ 15 10:28	15 6:12 ♇ ☍	♓ 15 6:25	11 18:44 ☽ 18♑26	☽ Mean ☊ 3♐10.5
☿ D 5 14:21	☿ ♎ 11 7:30	17 20:55 ♇ ☍	♓ 17 22:34	16 23:25 ♃ ☍	♈ 17 16:35	19 17:25 ○ 26♈18	1 OCTOBER 1956
♄□♇ 7 15:39	♆ ♏ 19 9:26	20 5:24 ♄ △	♈ 20 8:47	20 0:07 ♇ △	♉ 20 0:07	26 18:02 ☽ 3♌18	Julian Day # 20728
♂ D 10 10:06	♇ ♍ 20 6:17	22 15:44 ♇ △	♉ 22 17:01	21 15:16 ♃ △	♊ 22 5:29		Delta T 31.6 sec
☿0S 15 6:34	☉ ♏ 23 10:34	24 22:18 ♇ □	♊ 24 23:25	23 20:14 ♃ □	♋ 24 9:23		SVP 05♓51'34"
☽0N 16 18:49	☿ ♏ 31 8:19	27 3:01 ♇ ✱	♋ 27 4:00	26 0:46 ♀ ✱	♌ 26 12:27		Obliquity 23°26'38"
♆✱♇ 18 7:20	♀ ♎ 31 19:40	29 5:35 ♆ □	♌ 29 6:49	28 6:29 ☿ ✱	♍ 28 15:09		⚷ Chiron 6♒32.5R
♃∠♅ 20 19:55	☽0S 29 22:30			30 15:47 ♀ ☌	♎ 30 18:10		☽ Mean ☊ 1♐35.1

NOVEMBER 1956 LONGITUDE

Day	Sid.Time	☉	0 hr ☽	Noon ☽	True ☊	☿	♀	♂	♃	♄	♅	♆	♇
1 Th	2 41 1	8♏32 51	17♎15 38	24♎ 6 37	29♏ 4.9	1♏ 5.2	0♎13.0	16♓ 3.7	23♍51.8	2♐15.0	6♌55.9	0♏28.2	0♍12.6
2 F	2 44 58	9 32 56	0♏53 53	7♏37 8	29R 2.4	2 44.9	1 24.8	16 19.4	24 2.7	2 21.7	6 56.5	0 30.5	0 13.5
3 Sa	2 48 54	10 33 3	14 16 8	20 50 43	29 0.8	4 24.3	2 36.7	16 35.7	24 13.5	2 28.5	6 57.0	0 32.7	0 14.4
4 Su	2 52 51	11 33 12	27 20 49	3♐46 26	29D 0.2	6 3.3	3 48.7	16 52.5	24 24.2	2 35.3	6 57.5	0 34.9	0 15.3
5 M	2 56 47	12 33 22	10♐ 7 37	16 24 33	29 0.5	7 42.1	5 0.9	17 10.0	24 34.8	2 42.1	6 58.0	0 37.1	0 16.1
6 Tu	3 0 44	13 33 35	22 37 27	28 46 37	29 1.5	9 20.4	6 13.1	17 27.9	24 45.3	2 48.9	6 58.3	0 39.3	0 16.9
7 W	3 4 40	14 33 49	4♑52 25	10♑55 17	29 2.8	10 58.5	7 25.4	17 46.5	24 55.8	2 55.8	6 58.7	0 41.5	0 17.7
8 Th	3 8 37	15 34 4	16 55 39	22 54 3	29 4.1	12 36.1	8 37.7	18 5.5	25 6.1	3 2.7	6 58.9	0 43.7	0 18.4
9 F	3 12 34	16 34 21	28 51 1	4♒47 7	29 5.2	14 13.5	9 50.2	18 25.1	25 16.4	3 9.6	6 59.1	0 45.9	0 19.1
10 Sa	3 16 30	17 34 39	10♒42 57	16 39 5	29R 5.8	15 50.4	11 2.8	18 45.1	25 26.6	3 16.5	6 59.3	0 48.0	0 19.8
11 Su	3 20 27	18 34 59	22 36 9	28 34 43	29 5.9	17 27.0	12 15.4	19 5.7	25 36.7	3 23.5	6 59.4	0 50.2	0 20.5
12 M	3 24 23	19 35 21	4♓35 22	10♓38 42	29 5.5	19 3.3	13 28.1	19 26.7	25 46.6	3 30.5	6R59.4	0 52.4	0 21.1
13 Tu	3 28 20	20 35 43	16 45 12	22 55 22	29 4.7	20 39.3	14 40.9	19 48.2	25 56.5	3 37.4	6 59.4	0 54.5	0 21.7
14 W	3 32 16	21 36 7	29 9 40	5♈28 26	29 3.7	22 14.9	15 53.8	20 10.1	26 6.3	3 44.5	6 59.4	0 56.6	0 22.2
15 Th	3 36 13	22 36 33	11♈52 1	18 20 37	29 2.8	23 50.3	17 6.7	20 32.5	26 16.0	3 51.5	6 59.2	0 58.8	0 22.8
16 F	3 40 9	23 37 0	24 54 23	1♉33 21	29 2.0	25 25.3	18 19.7	20 55.3	26 25.6	3 58.5	6 59.1	1 0.9	0 23.3
17 Sa	3 44 6	24 37 28	8♉17 29	15 6 36	29 1.5	27 0.1	19 32.8	21 18.5	26 35.1	4 5.6	6 58.8	1 3.0	0 23.8
18 Su	3 48 3	25 37 58	22 0 28	28 58 42	29D 1.3	28 34.7	20 46.0	21 42.2	26 44.5	4 12.6	6 58.5	1 5.1	0 24.2
19 M	3 51 59	26 38 29	6♊ 0 52	13♊ 6 27	29 1.3	0♐ 9.0	21 59.2	22 6.2	26 53.7	4 19.7	6 58.2	1 7.1	0 24.6
20 Tu	3 55 56	27 39 2	20 14 54	27 25 33	29 1.4	1 43.1	23 12.5	22 30.6	27 2.9	4 26.8	6 57.8	1 9.2	0 25.0
21 W	3 59 52	28 39 37	4♋37 48	11♋51 0	29R 1.5	3 17.0	24 25.9	22 55.3	27 11.9	4 33.9	6 57.4	1 11.3	0 25.4
22 Th	4 3 49	29 40 13	19 4 30	26 17 44	29 1.5	4 50.8	25 39.3	23 20.5	27 20.9	4 41.0	6 56.9	1 13.3	0 25.7
23 F	4 7 45	0♐40 51	3♌30 8	10♌41 13	29 1.4	6 24.4	26 52.8	23 45.9	27 29.7	4 48.1	6 56.3	1 15.3	0 26.0
24 Sa	4 11 42	1 41 31	17 50 33	24 57 46	29 1.2	7 57.8	28 6.4	24 11.7	27 38.4	4 55.2	6 55.7	1 17.3	0 26.3
25 Su	4 15 38	2 42 12	2♍ 2 35	9♍ 4 45	29D 1.2	9 31.0	29 20.0	24 37.9	27 47.0	5 2.3	6 55.0	1 19.3	0 26.5
26 M	4 19 35	3 42 55	16 4 5	23 0 27	29 1.3	11 4.2	0♏33.7	25 4.4	27 55.5	5 9.4	6 54.3	1 21.3	0 26.7
27 Tu	4 23 32	4 43 39	29 53 45	6♎43 54	29 1.6	12 37.2	1 47.5	25 31.2	28 3.9	5 16.5	6 53.6	1 23.2	0 26.9
28 W	4 27 28	5 44 25	13♎30 53	20 14 37	29 2.2	14 10.1	3 1.3	25 58.3	28 12.1	5 23.7	6 52.7	1 25.2	0 27.1
29 Th	4 31 25	6 45 12	26 55 8	3♏32 23	29 2.9	15 42.9	4 15.1	26 25.8	28 20.2	5 30.8	6 51.9	1 27.1	0 27.2
30 F	4 35 21	7 46 1	10♏ 6 22	16 37 5	29 3.7	17 15.6	5 29.0	26 53.5	28 28.2	5 37.9	6 50.9	1 29.0	0 27.3

DECEMBER 1956 LONGITUDE

Day	Sid.Time	☉	0 hr ☽	Noon ☽	True ☊	☿	♀	♂	♃	♄	♅	♆	♇
1 Sa	4 39 18	8♐46 52	23♏ 4 33	29♏28 46	29♏ 4.1	18♐48.2	6♏43.0	27♓21.5	28♍36.0	5♐45.0	6♌49.9	1♏30.9	0♍27.3
2 Su	4 43 14	9 47 43	5♐49 45	12♐ 7 35	29R 4.1	20 20.7	7 57.0	27 49.9	28 43.7	5 52.1	6R48.9	1 32.7	0R27.3
3 M	4 47 11	10 48 36	18 22 19	24 34 3	29 3.4	21 53.1	9 11.0	28 18.5	28 51.3	5 59.3	6 47.8	1 34.6	0 27.3
4 Tu	4 51 8	11 49 30	0♑42 55	6♑49 5	29 2.1	23 25.3	10 25.1	28 47.4	28 58.8	6 6.4	6 46.7	1 36.4	0 27.3
5 W	4 55 4	12 50 25	12 52 46	18 54 13	29 0.2	24 57.4	11 39.3	29 16.5	29 6.1	6 13.5	6 45.5	1 38.2	0 27.2
6 Th	4 59 1	13 51 21	24 53 42	0♒51 34	28 57.8	26 29.4	12 53.4	29 45.9	29 13.3	6 20.6	6 44.3	1 40.0	0 27.1
7 F	5 2 57	14 52 17	6♒48 13	12 44 2	28 55.4	28 1.1	14 7.6	0♈15.6	29 20.3	6 27.6	6 43.0	1 41.8	0 27.0
8 Sa	5 6 54	15 53 15	18 39 30	24 35 7	28 53.1	29 32.7	15 21.9	0 45.5	29 27.2	6 34.7	6 41.7	1 43.5	0 26.8
9 Su	5 10 50	16 54 13	0♓31 23	6♓28 53	28 51.4	1♑ 3.9	16 36.1	1 15.7	29 33.9	6 41.8	6 40.3	1 45.2	0 26.6
10 M	5 14 47	17 55 11	12 28 10	18 29 51	28D 50.5	2 34.8	17 50.5	1 46.1	29 40.5	6 48.8	6 38.9	1 46.9	0 26.4
11 Tu	5 18 43	18 56 11	24 34 30	0♈42 44	28 50.5	4 5.3	19 4.8	2 16.7	29 47.0	6 55.8	6 37.4	1 48.6	0 26.2
12 W	5 22 40	19 57 10	6♈55 7	13 12 12	28 51.4	5 35.4	20 19.2	2 47.5	29 53.3	7 2.8	6 35.9	1 50.3	0 25.9
13 Th	5 26 37	20 58 11	19 34 29	26 2 26	28 52.8	7 4.8	21 33.6	3 18.5	29 59.4	7 9.8	6 34.4	1 51.9	0 25.6
14 F	5 30 33	21 59 11	2♉36 25	9♉16 43	28 54.5	8 33.6	22 48.0	3 49.8	0♎ 5.4	7 16.8	6 32.8	1 53.5	0 25.2
15 Sa	5 34 30	23 0 13	16 3 29	22 56 46	28R 55.8	10 1.5	24 2.5	4 21.2	0 11.3	7 23.8	6 31.1	1 55.1	0 24.9
16 Su	5 38 26	24 1 15	29 56 27	7♊ 2 16	28 56.3	11 28.4	25 16.9	4 52.8	0 17.0	7 30.7	6 29.4	1 56.6	0 24.5
17 M	5 42 23	25 2 17	14♊13 45	21 30 19	28 55.5	12 54.2	26 31.5	5 24.6	0 22.5	7 37.6	6 27.7	1 58.2	0 24.0
18 Tu	5 46 19	26 3 21	28 51 11	6♋15 29	28 53.4	14 18.5	27 46.0	5 56.6	0 27.9	7 44.5	6 25.9	1 59.7	0 23.6
19 W	5 50 16	27 4 24	13♋42 11	21 10 14	28 50.0	15 41.1	29 0.6	6 28.8	0 33.1	7 51.4	6 24.1	2 1.1	0 23.1
20 Th	5 54 12	28 5 29	28 38 31	6♌ 5 57	28 45.8	17 1.8	0♐15.2	7 1.1	0 38.1	7 58.2	6 22.3	2 2.6	0 22.6
21 F	5 58 9	29 6 34	13♌31 32	20 54 19	28 41.3	18 20.1	1 29.8	7 33.6	0 43.0	8 5.1	6 20.4	2 4.0	0 22.1
22 Sa	6 2 6	0♑ 7 40	28 13 33	5♍28 33	28 37.4	19 35.7	2 44.5	8 6.3	0 47.8	8 11.9	6 18.5	2 5.4	0 21.5
23 Su	6 6 2	1 8 46	12♍38 51	19 44 8	28 34.5	20 48.1	3 59.2	8 39.1	0 52.3	8 18.6	6 16.5	2 6.8	0 20.9
24 M	6 9 59	2 9 53	26 44 11	3♎38 59	28D 33.2	21 56.7	5 13.9	9 12.1	0 56.7	8 25.4	6 14.5	2 8.1	0 20.3
25 Tu	6 13 55	3 11 1	10♎28 35	17 13 8	28 33.2	23 0.9	6 28.6	9 45.2	1 0.9	8 32.1	6 12.5	2 9.4	0 19.6
26 W	6 17 52	4 12 9	23 52 52	0♏28 2	28 34.4	24 0.1	7 43.4	10 18.5	1 5.0	8 38.7	6 10.4	2 10.7	0 18.9
27 Th	6 21 48	5 13 18	6♏58 58	13 25 57	28 36.1	24 53.6	8 58.1	10 51.9	1 8.9	8 45.4	6 8.3	2 12.0	0 18.2
28 F	6 25 45	6 14 28	19 49 19	26 9 22	28R 37.4	25 40.4	10 12.9	11 25.4	1 12.6	8 52.0	6 6.1	2 13.2	0 17.5
29 Sa	6 29 41	7 15 38	2♐26 22	8♐40 36	28 37.7	26 19.8	11 27.7	11 59.1	1 16.1	8 58.6	6 4.0	2 14.4	0 16.7
30 Su	6 33 38	8 16 48	14 52 18	21 1 40	28 36.3	26 50.8	12 42.6	12 33.0	1 19.4	9 5.1	6 1.8	2 15.6	0 15.9
31 M	6 37 35	9 17 59	27 8 53	3♑14 9	28 32.7	27 12.5	13 57.4	13 6.9	1 22.6	9 11.6	5 59.5	2 16.7	0 15.1

Astro Data

	Dy Hr Mn
♀0S	3 21:14
♅ R	12 6:51
☽0N	13 3:12
☽0S	26 4:00
♇ R	2 7:16
♂0N	8 8:45
♄△♅	8 19:55
☽0N	10 11:57
♃⊻♇	17 6:19
☽0S	23 10:06

Planet Ingress

	Dy Hr Mn
☿ ♐	18 21:42
☉ ♐	22 7:50
♀ ♏	25 13:01
♂ ♈	6 11:24
☿ ♑	8 7:11
♃ ♎	13 2:17
♀ ♐	19 19:07
☉ ♑	21 20:59

Last Aspect / ☽ Ingress

Last Aspect Dy Hr Mn		☽ Ingress Dy Hr Mn
31 6:04	♅ ✶	♏ 1 22:24
3 18:28	♃ ✶	♐ 4 4:56
6 4:12	♃ □	♑ 6 14:24
8 16:41	♃ △	♒ 9 2:19
10 15:09	☉ □	♓ 11 14:51
13 18:04	♃ ☍	♈ 14 1:36
15 10:44	♀ ☍	♉ 16 9:12
18 12:45	☿ ☍	♊ 18 13:45
20 11:29	♃ □	♋ 20 16:18
22 13:54	♃ ✶	♌ 22 18:10
24 18:58	♀ ✶	♍ 24 20:32
26 20:46	♃ ☌	♎ 27 0:11
28 1:19	☿ ✶	♏ 29 5:34

Last Aspect / ☽ Ingress

Last Aspect Dy Hr Mn		☽ Ingress Dy Hr Mn
1 10:27	♃ ✶	♐ 1 12:59
3 20:34	♃ □	♑ 3 22:36
6 10:13	♂ ✶	♒ 6 10:16
7 17:52	☉ ✶	♓ 8 22:57
11 10:17	♃ ☍	♈ 11 10:37
13 2:50	☉ △	♉ 13 19:15
15 15:15	♀ ☍	♊ 16 0:06
17 19:06	☉ ☍	♋ 18 1:52
19 3:30	☿ ☍	♌ 20 2:11
20 15:08	♄ △	♍ 22 2:56
23 15:03	☿ △	♎ 24 5:39
26 0:14	☿ □	♏ 26 11:09
28 11:43	☿ ✶	♐ 28 19:20
29 19:20	♀ ☌	♑ 31 5:37

☽ Phases & Eclipses

Dy Hr Mn	
2 16:44	● 10♏15
10 15:09	☽ 18♒13
18 6:45	○ 25♉55
18 6:48	• T 1.317
25 1:13	☽ 2♍45
2 8:13	● 10♐09
2 8:00:04	• P 0.805
10 11:51	☽ 18♓25
17 19:06	○ 25♊51
24 10:10	☽ 2♎36

Astro Data

1 NOVEMBER 1956
Julian Day # 20759
Delta T 31.6 sec
SVP 05♓51'32"
Obliquity 23°26'37"
⚷ Chiron 6♒35.6
☽ Mean ☊ 29♏56.6

1 DECEMBER 1956
Julian Day # 20789
Delta T 31.7 sec
SVP 05♓51'27"
Obliquity 23°26'36"
⚷ Chiron 7♒39.5
☽ Mean ☊ 28♏21.3

LONGITUDE JANUARY 1957

Day	Sid.Time	☉	0 hr ☽	Noon ☽	True ☊	☿	♀	♂	♃	♄	♅	♆	♇
1 Tu	6 41 31	10♑19 10	9♑17 36	15♑19 24	28♏27.1	27♑24.0	15♐12.3	13♈41.0	1♎25.6	9♐18.1	5♌57.3	2♏17.8	0♍14.3
2 W	6 45 28	11 20 20	21 19 41	27 18 37	28R19.5	27R24.6	16 27.1	14 15.3	1 28.4	9 24.5	5R55.0	2 18.9	0R13.4
3 Th	6 49 24	12 21 31	3♒16 23	9♒13 11	28 10.8	27 13.8	17 42.0	14 49.6	1 31.0	9 30.9	5 52.7	2 19.9	0 12.6
4 F	6 53 21	13 22 42	15 9 14	21 4 47	28 1.5	26 51.0	18 56.9	15 24.1	1 33.4	9 37.2	5 50.3	2 20.9	0 11.6
5 Sa	6 57 17	14 23 52	27 0 10	2♓55 41	27 52.7	26 16.5	20 11.8	15 58.7	1 35.7	9 43.5	5 48.0	2 21.9	0 10.7
6 Su	7 1 14	15 25 3	8♓51 44	14 48 45	27 45.1	25 30.5	21 26.7	16 33.3	1 37.7	9 49.8	5 45.6	2 22.9	0 9.7
7 M	7 5 10	16 26 12	20 47 11	26 47 34	27 39.5	24 34.1	22 41.6	17 8.1	1 39.6	9 56.0	5 43.1	2 23.8	0 8.8
8 Tu	7 9 7	17 27 22	2♈50 25	8♈56 20	27 36.0	23 28.7	23 56.6	17 43.0	1 41.3	10 2.2	5 40.7	2 24.7	0 7.8
9 W	7 13 4	18 28 31	15 5 55	21 19 45	27D34.6	22 16.2	25 11.5	18 18.0	1 42.8	10 8.3	5 38.3	2 25.5	0 6.7
10 Th	7 17 0	19 29 39	27 38 27	4♉ 2 37	27 34.9	20 58.8	26 26.4	18 53.1	1 44.1	10 14.3	5 35.8	2 26.3	0 5.7
11 F	7 20 57	20 30 47	10♉32 48	17 9 28	27 35.9	19 39.1	27 41.4	19 28.3	1 45.2	10 20.3	5 33.3	2 27.1	0 4.6
12 Sa	7 24 53	21 31 55	23 53 4	0♊43 53	27R36.8	18 19.6	28 56.3	20 3.6	1 46.1	10 26.3	5 30.8	2 27.9	0 3.5
13 Su	7 28 50	22 33 1	7♊42 4	14 47 36	27 36.4	17 2.7	0♑11.3	20 39.0	1 46.9	10 32.2	5 28.3	2 28.6	0 2.4
14 M	7 32 46	23 34 8	22 0 16	29 19 39	27 33.9	15 50.7	1 26.3	21 14.5	1 47.4	10 38.1	5 25.7	2 29.3	0 1.3
15 Tu	7 36 43	24 35 13	6♋45 6	14♋15 42	27 29.0	14 45.3	2 41.2	21 50.0	1 47.8	10 43.9	5 23.2	2 30.0	0 0.1
16 W	7 40 39	25 36 18	21 50 24	29 27 54	27 21.7	13 47.8	3 56.2	22 25.6	1R48.0	10 49.6	5 20.6	2 30.6	29♌59.0
17 Th	7 44 36	26 37 23	7♌ 6 50	14♌45 46	27 12.7	12 59.2	5 11.2	23 1.3	1 47.9	10 55.3	5 18.0	2 31.2	29 57.8
18 F	7 48 33	27 38 27	22 23 16	29 57 57	27 3.1	12 19.9	6 26.2	23 37.0	1 47.7	11 0.9	5 15.5	2 31.7	29 56.6
19 Sa	7 52 29	28 39 30	7♍28 37	14♍54 14	26 54.1	11 50.1	7 41.2	24 12.9	1 47.3	11 6.5	5 12.9	2 32.2	29 55.3
20 Su	7 56 26	29 40 33	22 13 59	29 27 16	26 46.9	11 29.7	8 56.2	24 48.8	1 46.7	11 12.0	5 10.3	2 32.7	29 54.1
21 M	8 0 22	0♒41 36	6♎33 44	13♎33 13	26 42.0	11D18.4	10 11.2	25 24.7	1 45.9	11 17.5	5 7.6	2 33.2	29 52.8
22 Tu	8 4 19	1 42 38	20 25 45	27 11 32	26D39.5	11 15.6	11 26.2	26 0.7	1 45.0	11 22.9	5 5.0	2 33.6	29 51.6
23 W	8 8 15	2 43 40	3♏50 53	10♏24 12	26 38.9	11 20.9	12 41.2	26 36.8	1 43.8	11 28.2	5 2.4	2 34.0	29 50.3
24 Th	8 12 12	3 44 42	16 51 57	23 14 41	26R39.3	11 33.7	13 56.2	27 13.0	1 42.4	11 33.5	4 59.8	2 34.3	29 49.0
25 F	8 16 8	4 45 43	29 32 53	5♐47 7	26 39.5	11 53.4	15 11.3	27 49.2	1 40.9	11 38.7	4 57.2	2 34.7	29 47.6
26 Sa	8 20 5	5 46 43	11♐57 53	18 5 40	26 38.3	12 19.4	16 26.3	28 25.5	1 39.1	11 43.8	4 54.6	2 34.9	29 46.3
27 Su	8 24 2	6 47 43	24 10 55	0♑14 2	26 34.9	12 51.1	17 41.3	29 1.9	1 37.2	11 48.9	4 51.9	2 35.2	29 45.0
28 M	8 27 58	7 48 42	6♑15 24	12 15 19	26 28.5	13 28.1	18 56.4	29 38.3	1 35.1	11 53.9	4 49.3	2 35.4	29 43.6
29 Tu	8 31 55	8 49 41	18 14 4	24 11 54	26 19.1	14 9.8	20 11.4	0♉14.7	1 32.7	11 58.8	4 46.7	2 35.6	29 42.2
30 W	8 35 51	9 50 38	0♒ 9 2	6♒ 5 37	26 7.1	14 55.8	21 26.5	0 51.2	1 30.2	12 3.7	4 44.1	2 35.7	29 40.8
31 Th	8 39 48	10 51 35	12 1 51	17 57 53	25 53.2	15 45.8	22 41.5	1 27.8	1 27.5	12 8.4	4 41.5	2 35.8	29 39.4

LONGITUDE FEBRUARY 1957

Day	Sid.Time	☉	0 hr ☽	Noon ☽	True ☊	☿	♀	♂	♃	♄	♅	♆	♇
1 F	8 43 44	11♒52 30	23♒53 50	29♒49 54	25♏38.5	16♑39.3	23♑56.5	2♉ 4.4	1♎24.7	12♐13.2	4♌38.9	2♏35.9	29♌38.0
2 Sa	8 47 41	12 53 24	5♓46 15	11♓43 5	25R24.2	17 36.1	25 11.6	2 41.1	1R21.6	12 17.8	4R36.3	2R36.0	29R36.6
3 Su	8 51 37	13 54 17	17 40 38	23 39 11	25 11.5	18 35.8	26 26.6	3 17.9	1 18.4	12 22.4	4 33.7	2 36.0	29 35.2
4 M	8 55 34	14 55 9	29 39 1	5♈40 32	25 1.3	19 38.2	27 41.6	3 54.6	1 15.0	12 26.9	4 31.1	2 35.9	29 33.7
5 Tu	8 59 31	15 56 0	11♈44 6	17 50 12	24 54.0	20 43.1	28 56.6	4 31.4	1 11.4	12 31.3	4 28.6	2 35.9	29 32.3
6 W	9 3 27	16 56 49	23 59 18	0♉11 56	24 49.8	21 50.2	0♒11.7	5 8.3	1 7.6	12 35.6	4 26.0	2 35.8	29 30.8
7 Th	9 7 24	17 57 36	6♉28 40	12 50 4	24 47.9	22 59.5	1 26.7	5 45.2	1 3.6	12 39.9	4 23.5	2 35.6	29 29.3
8 F	9 11 20	18 58 23	19 16 42	25 49 7	24 47.6	24 10.7	2 41.7	6 22.2	0 59.5	12 44.0	4 20.9	2 35.5	29 27.9
9 Sa	9 15 17	19 59 7	2♊27 49	9♊13 16	24 47.5	25 23.7	3 56.7	6 59.1	0 55.3	12 48.1	4 18.4	2 35.3	29 26.4
10 Su	9 19 13	20 59 50	16 5 48	23 5 37	24 46.4	26 38.3	5 11.7	7 36.1	0 50.8	12 52.1	4 16.0	2 35.1	29 24.9
11 M	9 23 10	22 0 32	0♋12 47	7♋27 8	24 43.2	27 54.6	6 26.7	8 13.2	0 46.2	12 56.1	4 13.5	2 34.8	29 23.4
12 Tu	9 27 6	23 1 12	14 48 17	22 15 37	24 37.3	29 12.4	7 41.6	8 50.3	0 41.4	12 59.9	4 11.0	2 34.5	29 21.9
13 W	9 31 3	24 1 50	29 48 17	7♌25 11	24 28.6	0♒31.5	8 56.6	9 27.4	0 36.5	13 3.7	4 8.6	2 34.2	29 20.4
14 Th	9 35 0	25 2 26	15♌ 5 1	22 46 21	24 17.8	1 52.0	10 11.6	10 4.5	0 31.4	13 7.4	4 6.2	2 33.8	29 19.0
15 F	9 38 56	26 3 1	0♍27 39	8♍ 7 25	24 6.2	3 13.8	11 26.5	10 41.7	0 26.2	13 11.0	4 3.8	2 33.4	29 17.4
16 Sa	9 42 53	27 3 35	15 44 9	23 16 33	23 55.0	4 36.8	12 41.5	11 18.9	0 20.8	13 14.5	4 1.5	2 33.0	29 15.9
17 Su	9 46 49	28 4 7	0♎43 29	8♎ 4 3	23 45.6	6 1.0	13 56.5	11 56.1	0 15.3	13 17.9	3 59.1	2 32.5	29 14.4
18 M	9 50 46	29 4 38	15 17 35	22 23 42	23 38.8	7 26.3	15 11.4	12 33.3	0 9.7	13 21.3	3 56.8	2 32.0	29 12.9
19 Tu	9 54 42	0♓ 5 7	29 22 12	6♏13 8	23 34.8	8 52.7	16 26.3	13 10.6	0 3.8	13 24.5	3 54.5	2 31.5	29 11.4
20 W	9 58 39	1 5 36	12♏56 42	19 33 14	23D33.1	10 20.3	17 41.3	13 47.9	29♍57.9	13 27.7	3 52.3	2 31.0	29 9.9
21 Th	10 2 35	2 6 3	26 3 13	2♐27 11	23R32.9	11 48.8	18 56.2	14 25.2	29 51.8	13 30.8	3 50.1	2 30.4	29 8.4
22 F	10 6 32	3 6 28	8♐45 44	14 59 27	23 32.8	13 18.5	20 11.2	15 2.5	29 45.7	13 33.7	3 47.9	2 29.8	29 6.9
23 Sa	10 10 29	4 6 53	21 9 0	27 14 58	23 31.8	14 49.2	21 26.1	15 39.9	29 39.3	13 36.6	3 45.7	2 29.1	29 5.4
24 Su	10 14 25	5 7 16	3♑17 58	9♑18 32	23 28.6	16 20.9	22 41.0	16 17.3	29 32.9	13 39.4	3 43.6	2 28.4	29 3.9
25 M	10 18 22	6 7 37	15 17 13	21 14 30	23 22.8	17 53.6	23 56.0	16 54.7	29 26.4	13 42.1	3 41.5	2 27.7	29 2.4
26 Tu	10 22 18	7 7 57	27 10 47	3♒ 6 28	23 14.0	19 27.4	25 10.9	17 32.1	29 19.7	13 44.8	3 39.4	2 27.0	29 0.9
27 W	10 26 15	8 8 16	9♒ 1 53	14 57 20	23 2.6	21 2.2	26 25.8	18 9.5	29 12.9	13 47.3	3 37.4	2 26.2	28 59.4
28 Th	10 30 11	9 8 33	20 53 4	26 49 17	22 49.3	22 37.9	27 40.7	18 47.0	29 6.1	13 49.7	3 35.4	2 25.4	28 57.9

Astro Data Dy Hr Mn	Planet Ingress Dy Hr Mn	Last Aspect Dy Hr Mn	☽ Ingress Dy Hr Mn	Last Aspect Dy Hr Mn	☽ Ingress Dy Hr Mn	☽ Phases & Eclipses Dy Hr Mn	Astro Data
☿ R 1 13:22	♀ ♑ 12 20:23	2 12:04 ☿ ☌	♒ 2 17:25	1 11:35 ♇ ☍	♓ 1 12:20	1 2:14 ● 10♑25	1 JANUARY 1957
☽0N 6 20:11	♇ ♌ 15 2:39	4 8:35 ♀ ⚹	♓ 5 6:04	3 19:38 ♀ ⚹	♈ 4 0:42	9 7:06 ☽ 18♈47	Julian Day # 20820
♃ R 16 9:22	☉ ♒ 20 7:39	7 6:58 ☿ ⚹	♈ 7 18:23	6 10:40 ♇ △	♉ 6 11:37	16 6:21 ○ 25♋52	Delta T 31.7 sec
☽0S 19 18:50	♂ ♉ 28 14:19	9 21:29 ♀ △	♉ 10 4:27	8 18:34 ♇ □	♊ 8 19:34	22 21:48 ☽ 2♏38	SVP 05♓51'22"
☿ D 21 19:56		11 19:29 ☉ △	♊ 12 10:44	10 22:38 ♇ ⚹	♋ 10 23:39	30 21:25 ● 10♒45	Obliquity 23°26'36"
	♀ ♒ 5 20:16	13 22:41 ♂ ⚹	♋ 14 13:06	11 13:51 ♂ ⚹	♌ 13 0:19		⚷ Chiron 9♒34.7
♆ R 2 15:51	☿ ♒ 12 14:30	16 6:21 ☉ ☍	♌ 16 12:50	14 22:10 ♇ ☌	♍ 14 23:17	7 23:23 ☽ 18♉57	☽ Mean ☊ 26♏42.8
☽0N 3 3:26	☉ ♓ 18 21:58	18 11:57 ♇ ☌	♍ 18 12:03	15 20:03 ♄ □	♎ 16 22:50	14 16:38 ○ 25♌44	
☽0S 16 5:59	♃ ♍ 19 15:38	19 6:51 ☿ △	♎ 20 12:55	18 23:41 ♇ ⚹	♏ 19 1:06	21 12:19 ☽ 2♐37	1 FEBRUARY 1957
		22 16:46 ♇ ⚹	♏ 22 17:02	21 7:04 ♃ ⚹	♐ 21 7:23		Julian Day # 20851
		25 0:28 ♇ □	♐ 25 0:52	23 16:37 ♃ □	♑ 23 17:27		Delta T 31.7 sec
		27 11:01 ♇ △	♑ 27 11:32	26 4:18 ♃ △	♒ 26 5:42		SVP 05♓51'17"
		29 4:24 ♀ ☌	♒ 29 23:42	28 16:18 ♇ ☍	♓ 28 18:25		Obliquity 23°26'36"
							⚷ Chiron 11♒56.3
							☽ Mean ☊ 25♏04.4

MARCH 1957 LONGITUDE

Day	Sid.Time	☉	0 hr ☽	Noon ☽	True ☊	☿	♀	♂	♃	♄	♅	♆	♇
1 F	10 34 8	10♓ 8 48	2♓46 10	8♓43 53	22♏35.2	24♒14.8	28♒55.6	19♉24.5	28♍59.1	13♐52.0	3♌33.4	2♏24.6	28♌56.5
2 Sa	10 38 4	11 9 1	14 42 35	20 42 25	22R21.5	25 52.6	0♓10.4	20 2.0	28R52.0	13 54.3	3R31.5	2R23.7	28R55.0
3 Su	10 42 1	12 9 12	26 43 30	2♈46 2	22 9.2	27 31.5	1 25.3	20 39.5	28 44.9	13 56.4	3 29.6	2 22.9	28 53.5
4 M	10 45 58	13 9 22	8♈50 9	14 56 6	21 59.3	29 11.5	2 40.2	21 17.1	28 37.7	13 58.4	3 27.7	2 21.9	28 52.1
5 Tu	10 49 54	14 9 30	21 4 6	27 14 26	21 52.3	0♓52.5	3 55.0	21 54.6	28 30.4	14 0.4	3 25.9	2 21.0	28 50.6
6 W	10 53 51	15 9 35	3♉27 24	9♉43 22	21 48.2	2 34.6	5 9.8	22 32.2	28 23.0	14 2.2	3 24.1	2 20.0	28 49.2
7 Th	10 57 47	16 9 39	16 2 42	22 25 50	21D46.6	4 17.7	6 24.7	23 9.8	28 15.6	14 4.0	3 22.4	2 19.0	28 47.7
8 F	11 1 44	17 9 41	28 53 11	5♊25 11	21 46.6	6 2.0	7 39.5	23 47.4	28 8.1	14 5.6	3 20.7	2 18.0	28 46.3
9 Sa	11 5 40	18 9 40	12♊ 2 16	18 44 49	21R47.1	7 47.4	8 54.3	24 25.0	28 0.5	14 7.2	3 19.1	2 17.0	28 44.9
10 Su	11 9 37	19 9 37	25 33 10	2♋27 35	21 47.1	9 33.9	10 9.1	25 2.6	27 52.9	14 8.6	3 17.5	2 15.9	28 43.5
11 M	11 13 33	20 9 32	9♋28 11	16 34 59	21 45.4	11 21.6	11 23.8	25 40.3	27 45.3	14 10.0	3 15.9	2 14.8	28 42.1
12 Tu	11 17 30	21 9 25	23 47 49	1♌ 6 20	21 41.5	13 10.4	12 38.6	26 17.9	27 37.6	14 11.2	3 14.4	2 13.7	28 40.8
13 W	11 21 27	22 9 16	8♌29 59	15 58 0	21 35.3	15 0.4	13 53.3	26 55.5	27 29.9	14 12.4	3 12.9	2 12.6	28 39.4
14 Th	11 25 23	23 9 4	23 29 26	1♍ 3 10	21 27.3	16 51.5	15 8.0	27 33.2	27 22.2	14 13.5	3 11.5	2 11.4	28 38.0
15 F	11 29 20	24 8 50	8♍37 59	16 12 33	21 18.4	18 43.8	16 22.8	28 10.8	27 14.4	14 14.4	3 10.1	2 10.2	28 36.7
16 Sa	11 33 16	25 8 34	23 45 32	1♎15 41	21 9.7	20 37.2	17 37.5	28 48.5	27 6.7	14 15.3	3 8.8	2 9.0	28 35.4
17 Su	11 37 13	26 8 16	8♎41 49	16 2 55	21 2.3	22 31.8	18 52.1	29 26.2	26 58.9	14 16.0	3 7.5	2 7.8	28 34.1
18 M	11 41 9	27 7 56	23 18 9	0♏26 53	20 57.0	24 27.5	20 6.8	0♊ 3.8	26 51.1	14 16.7	3 6.3	2 6.5	28 32.8
19 Tu	11 45 6	28 7 34	7♏28 43	14 23 26	20D54.0	26 24.3	21 21.5	0 41.5	26 43.3	14 17.2	3 5.1	2 5.3	28 31.5
20 W	11 49 2	29 7 11	21 11 0	27 51 34	20 53.2	28 22.1	22 36.1	1 19.2	26 35.5	14 17.7	3 3.9	2 4.0	28 30.2
21 Th	11 52 59	0♈ 6 46	4♐25 24	10♐52 54	20 53.8	0♈20.9	23 50.8	1 56.8	26 27.8	14 18.0	3 2.8	2 2.6	28 29.0
22 F	11 56 55	1 6 19	17 14 34	23 30 55	20 55.0	2 20.5	25 5.4	2 34.5	26 20.0	14 18.3	3 1.8	2 1.3	28 27.7
23 Sa	12 0 52	2 5 50	29 42 33	5♑50 5	20R55.8	4 21.0	26 20.0	3 12.2	26 12.3	14 18.4	3 0.8	1 60.0	28 26.5
24 Su	12 4 49	3 5 20	11♑54 8	17 55 19	20 55.4	6 22.1	27 34.6	3 49.9	26 4.6	14R18.5	2 59.9	1 58.6	28 25.3
25 M	12 8 45	4 4 48	23 54 15	29 51 31	20 53.1	8 23.7	28 49.2	4 27.6	25 56.9	14 18.4	2 59.0	1 57.2	28 24.1
26 Tu	12 12 42	5 4 14	5♒47 38	11♒43 8	20 48.9	10 25.6	0♈ 3.8	5 5.3	25 49.3	14 18.3	2 58.1	1 55.8	28 23.0
27 W	12 16 38	6 3 38	17 38 30	23 34 8	20 42.7	12 27.7	1 18.4	5 43.0	25 41.7	14 18.1	2 57.3	1 54.4	28 21.8
28 Th	12 20 35	7 3 0	29 30 26	5♓27 44	20 35.2	14 29.6	2 33.0	6 20.8	25 34.2	14 17.7	2 56.6	1 52.9	28 20.7
29 F	12 24 31	8 2 20	11♓26 21	17 26 30	20 27.0	16 31.1	3 47.5	6 58.5	25 26.7	14 17.3	2 55.9	1 51.5	28 19.6
30 Sa	12 28 28	9 1 39	23 28 25	29 32 18	20 18.9	18 31.9	5 2.1	7 36.2	25 19.3	14 16.7	2 55.3	1 50.0	28 18.5
31 Su	12 32 24	10 0 55	5♈38 16	11♈46 29	20 11.7	20 31.6	6 16.6	8 13.9	25 11.9	14 16.1	2 54.7	1 48.5	28 17.5

APRIL 1957 LONGITUDE

Day	Sid.Time	☉	0 hr ☽	Noon ☽	True ☊	☿	♀	♂	♃	♄	♅	♆	♇
1 M	12 36 21	11♈ 0 9	17♈57 3	24♈10 5	20♏ 6.1	22♈29.9	7♈31.1	8♊51.6	25♍ 4.6	14♐15.3	2♌54.2	1♏47.0	28♌16.4
2 Tu	12 40 18	11 59 22	0♉25 42	6♉43 59	20R 2.3	24 26.5	8 45.6	9 29.4	24R57.4	14R14.5	2R53.7	1R45.5	28R15.4
3 W	12 44 14	12 58 32	13 5 6	19 29 9	20D 0.6	26 20.9	10 0.0	10 7.1	24 50.3	14 13.5	2 53.3	1 44.0	28 14.4
4 Th	12 48 11	13 57 40	25 56 19	2♊26 45	20 0.5	28 12.8	11 14.5	10 44.9	24 43.2	14 12.5	2 52.9	1 42.5	28 13.4
5 F	12 52 7	14 56 46	9♊ 0 39	15 38 11	20 1.6	0♉ 1.7	12 28.9	11 22.6	24 36.3	14 11.3	2 52.6	1 40.9	28 12.5
6 Sa	12 56 4	15 55 50	22 19 33	29 4 55	20 3.1	1 47.3	13 43.4	12 0.3	24 29.4	14 10.1	2 52.3	1 39.4	28 11.6
7 Su	13 0 0	16 54 51	5♋54 25	12♋48 11	20R 4.4	3 29.3	14 57.8	12 38.1	24 22.7	14 8.8	2 52.1	1 37.8	28 10.7
8 M	13 3 57	17 53 50	19 46 14	26 48 32	20 4.9	5 7.2	16 12.2	13 15.8	24 16.0	14 7.4	2 52.0	1 36.2	28 9.8
9 Tu	13 7 53	18 52 47	3♌54 58	11♌ 5 18	20 4.0	6 40.9	17 26.5	13 53.5	24 9.5	14 5.8	2 51.9	1 34.7	28 8.9
10 W	13 11 50	19 51 41	18 19 10	25 36 5	20 1.8	8 10.0	18 40.9	14 31.3	24 3.1	14 4.2	2D51.8	1 33.1	28 8.1
11 Th	13 15 47	20 50 33	2♍55 28	10♍16 34	19 58.4	9 34.3	19 55.2	15 9.0	23 56.8	14 2.5	2 51.8	1 31.5	28 7.3
12 F	13 19 43	21 49 22	17 38 36	25 0 40	19 54.4	10 53.5	21 9.5	15 46.7	23 50.6	14 0.7	2 51.9	1 29.9	28 6.5
13 Sa	13 23 40	22 48 10	2♎21 52	9♎41 15	19 50.5	12 7.5	22 23.8	16 24.4	23 44.5	13 58.9	2 52.0	1 28.2	28 5.7
14 Su	13 27 36	23 46 55	16 57 56	24 11 5	19 47.2	13 16.0	23 38.1	17 2.1	23 38.5	13 56.9	2 52.2	1 26.6	28 5.0
15 M	13 31 33	24 45 39	1♏19 57	8♏23 57	19 45.0	14 19.0	24 52.4	17 39.8	23 32.7	13 54.8	2 52.4	1 25.0	28 4.3
16 Tu	13 35 29	25 44 20	15 22 34	22 15 27	19D44.0	15 16.4	26 6.6	18 17.6	23 27.0	13 52.7	2 52.7	1 23.4	28 3.6
17 W	13 39 26	26 43 0	29 2 24	5♐43 22	19 44.2	16 7.9	27 20.8	18 55.3	23 21.5	13 50.5	2 53.0	1 21.8	28 2.9
18 Th	13 43 22	27 41 38	12♐18 23	18 47 38	19 45.3	16 53.6	28 35.1	19 33.0	23 16.1	13 48.1	2 53.4	1 20.1	28 2.3
19 F	13 47 19	28 40 14	25 11 24	1♑30 2	19 46.8	17 33.4	29 49.3	20 10.6	23 10.8	13 45.7	2 53.8	1 18.5	28 1.7
20 Sa	13 51 16	29 38 48	7♑43 59	13 53 43	19 48.3	18 7.2	1♉ 3.4	20 48.3	23 5.7	13 43.3	2 54.3	1 16.9	28 1.1
21 Su	13 55 12	0♉37 21	19 59 47	26 2 44	19R49.3	18 34.9	2 17.6	21 26.0	23 0.8	13 40.7	2 54.9	1 15.2	28 0.6
22 M	13 59 9	1 35 52	2♒ 3 9	8♒ 1 38	19 49.7	18 56.7	3 31.8	22 3.7	22 56.0	13 38.0	2 55.5	1 13.6	28 0.1
23 Tu	14 3 5	2 34 22	13 58 44	19 55 3	19 49.3	19 12.5	4 45.9	22 41.4	22 51.3	13 35.3	2 56.1	1 11.9	27 59.6
24 W	14 7 2	3 32 49	25 51 9	1♓47 34	19 48.1	19 22.5	6 0.1	23 19.1	22 46.8	13 32.5	2 56.8	1 10.3	27 59.1
25 Th	14 10 58	4 31 16	7♓44 48	13 43 20	19 46.3	19R26.6	7 14.2	23 56.8	22 42.4	13 29.6	2 57.6	1 8.7	27 58.7
26 F	14 14 55	5 29 40	19 43 36	25 46 0	19 44.2	19 25.1	8 28.3	24 34.5	22 38.3	13 26.7	2 58.4	1 7.0	27 58.2
27 Sa	14 18 51	6 28 3	1♈50 54	7♈58 35	19 42.2	19 18.2	9 42.4	25 12.1	22 34.2	13 23.6	2 59.3	1 5.4	27 57.9
28 Su	14 22 48	7 26 24	14 9 19	20 23 18	19 40.4	19 6.1	10 56.5	25 49.8	22 30.4	13 20.5	3 0.2	1 3.8	27 57.5
29 M	14 26 44	8 24 44	26 40 42	3♉ 1 37	19 39.1	18 49.2	12 10.5	26 27.5	22 26.7	13 17.4	3 1.1	1 2.1	27 57.2
30 Tu	14 30 41	9 23 1	9♉26 7	15 54 14	19D38.4	18 27.8	13 24.6	27 5.2	22 23.2	13 14.1	3 2.2	1 0.5	27 56.9

Astro Data	Planet Ingress	Last Aspect	☽ Ingress	Last Aspect	☽ Ingress	☽ Phases & Eclipses	Astro Data
Dy Hr Mn	Dy Hr Mn	Dy Hr Mn	Dy Hr Mn	Dy Hr Mn	Dy Hr Mn	Dy Hr Mn	1 MARCH 1957
♃⊻♇ 1 11:18	♀ ♓ 1 20:39	3 3:59 ♃ ☍	♈ 3 6:31	1 19:51 ♇ △	♉ 1 23:11	1 16:12 ● 10♓49	Julian Day # 20879
☽0N 2 9:52	☿ ♓ 4 11:34	5 15:04 ♇ △	♉ 5 17:20	4 4:13 ♇ □	♊ 4 7:30	9 11:50 ☽ 18♊39	Delta T 31.8 sec
☽0S 15 17:24	♂ ♊ 17 21:34	7 23:47 ♇ □	♊ 8 2:03	6 10:25 ♇ ✱	♋ 6 13:37	16 2:22 ○ 25♍14	SVP 05♓51'13"
☿0N 22 4:46	☉ ♈ 20 21:16	10 5:31 ♇ ✱	♋ 10 7:45	8 7:37 ♃ ✱	♌ 8 17:24	23 5:04 ☽ 2♑18	Obliquity 23°26'37"
♄ R 24 0:45	☿ ♈ 20 19:48	12 6:15 ♃ ✱	♌ 12 10:12	10 16:09 ♇ ☌	♍ 10 19:13	31 9:19 ● 10♈24	⚷ Chiron 14♒04.3
♀0N 28 13:34	♀ ♈ 25 22:46	14 8:09 ♇ ☌	♍ 14 10:20	12 10:02 ♃ ☌	♎ 12 20:08		☽ Mean ☊ 23♏35.4
☽0N 29 16:14		16 8:25 ♂ △	♎ 16 9:59	14 18:31 ♇ ✱	♏ 14 21:45	7 20:33 ☽ 17♋45	
	☿ ♉ 4 23:37	18 8:47 ♇ ✱	♏ 18 11:15	16 22:14 ♇ □	♐ 17 1:43	14 12:09 ○ 24♎17	1 APRIL 1957
♅ D 10 8:20	♀ ♉ 19 3:28	20 15:27 ☉ △	♐ 20 15:53	19 7:09 ☉ △	♑ 19 9:08	21 23:01 ☽ 1♒33	Julian Day # 20910
☽0S 12 2:57	☉ ♉ 20 8:41	22 21:32 ♇ △	♑ 23 0:34	21 5:56 ♃ △	♒ 21 19:53	29 23:54 ● 9♉23	Delta T 31.8 sec
☽0N 25 23:17		25 11:04 ♀ ✱	♒ 25 12:17	24 4:18 ♇ ☍	♓ 24 8:23	29 0:04:54 ☌ A non-C	SVP 05♓51'11"
☿ R 25 5:31		27 21:39 ♇ ☍	♓ 28 1:00	26 10:10 ♂ □	♈ 26 20:22		Obliquity 23°26'36"
		30 3:38 ♃ ☍	♈ 30 12:55	29 2:25 ♇ △	♉ 29 6:18		⚷ Chiron 16♒01.8
							☽ Mean ☊ 21♏56.9

LONGITUDE MAY 1957

Day	Sid.Time	☉	0 hr ☽	Noon ☽	True ☊	☿	♀	♂	♃	♄	♅	♆	♇
1 W	14 34 38	10♉21 17	22♉25 56	29♉ 1 11	19♏38.2	18♉ 2.4	14♉38.6	27♊42.9	22♍19.8	13♐10.8	3♌ 3.2	0♏58.9	27♌56.6
2 Th	14 38 34	11 19 32	5♊39 54	12♊22 0	19 38.5	17R 33.5	15 52.7	28 20.5	22R 16.7	13R 7.4	3 4.4	0R 57.3	27R 56.4
3 F	14 42 31	12 17 44	19 7 20	25 55 47	19 39.1	17 1.6	17 6.7	28 58.2	22 13.7	13 4.0	3 5.5	0 55.7	27 56.2
4 Sa	14 46 27	13 15 55	2♋47 11	9♋41 24	19 39.7	16 27.4	18 20.7	29 35.9	22 10.9	13 0.5	3 6.8	0 54.1	27 56.0
5 Su	14 50 24	14 14 3	16 38 14	23 37 30	19 40.3	15 51.4	19 34.6	0♋13.6	22 8.2	12 56.9	3 8.1	0 52.5	27 55.8
6 M	14 54 20	15 12 10	0♌39 0	7♌42 31	19 40.6	15 14.4	20 48.6	0 51.2	22 5.8	12 53.3	3 9.4	0 50.9	27 55.7
7 Tu	14 58 17	16 10 15	14 47 48	21 54 33	19R 40.8	14 37.0	22 2.5	1 28.9	22 3.5	12 49.6	3 10.8	0 49.3	27 55.6
8 W	15 2 13	17 8 17	29 2 30	6♍11 17	19 40.7	13 59.8	23 16.4	2 6.5	22 1.4	12 45.9	3 12.2	0 47.8	27 55.5
9 Th	15 6 10	18 6 18	13♍20 33	20 29 53	19 40.6	13 23.5	24 30.3	2 44.2	21 59.5	12 42.1	3 13.7	0 46.2	27D 55.5
10 F	15 10 7	19 4 17	27 38 51	4♎47 0	19D 40.5	12 48.7	25 44.2	3 21.8	21 57.7	12 38.2	3 15.2	0 44.7	27 55.5
11 Sa	15 14 3	20 2 14	11♎53 49	18 58 51	19 40.5	12 16.1	26 58.1	3 59.5	21 56.2	12 34.3	3 16.8	0 43.2	27 55.5
12 Su	15 18 0	21 0 9	26 1 37	3♏ 1 37	19 40.5	11 46.0	28 11.9	4 37.1	21 54.8	12 30.4	3 18.4	0 41.6	27 55.6
13 M	15 21 56	21 58 2	9♏58 27	16 51 41	19R 40.6	11 19.1	29 25.8	5 14.7	21 53.6	12 26.4	3 20.1	0 40.1	27 55.6
14 Tu	15 25 53	22 55 54	23 40 59	0♐26 5	19 40.7	10 55.6	0♊39.6	5 52.3	21 52.6	12 22.4	3 21.8	0 38.6	27 55.7
15 W	15 29 49	23 53 45	7♐ 6 45	13 42 50	19 40.5	10 35.9	1 53.4	6 30.0	21 51.8	12 18.3	3 23.5	0 37.2	27 55.9
16 Th	15 33 46	24 51 34	20 14 18	26 41 9	19 40.1	10 20.2	3 7.2	7 7.6	21 51.1	12 14.2	3 25.4	0 35.7	27 56.1
17 F	15 37 42	25 49 22	3♑ 3 30	9♑21 30	19 39.5	10 8.8	4 21.0	7 45.2	21 50.6	12 10.1	3 27.2	0 34.2	27 56.2
18 Sa	15 41 39	26 47 8	15 35 25	21 45 33	19 38.6	10 1.9	5 34.7	8 22.8	21 50.3	12 5.9	3 29.1	0 32.8	27 56.5
19 Su	15 45 36	27 44 54	27 52 18	3♒56 3	19 37.7	9D 59.4	6 48.5	9 0.4	21D 50.2	12 1.7	3 31.1	0 31.4	27 56.7
20 M	15 49 32	28 42 38	9♒57 18	15 56 33	19 36.9	10 1.5	8 2.2	9 38.0	21 50.3	11 57.4	3 33.1	0 30.0	27 57.0
21 Tu	15 53 29	29 40 21	21 54 20	27 51 12	19D 36.3	10 8.1	9 15.9	10 15.6	21 50.6	11 53.2	3 35.1	0 28.6	27 57.3
22 W	15 57 25	0♊38 3	3♓47 44	9♓44 31	19 36.2	10 19.3	10 29.6	10 53.2	21 51.0	11 48.9	3 37.2	0 27.2	27 57.7
23 Th	16 1 22	1 35 44	15 42 8	21 41 9	19 36.6	10 34.9	11 43.3	11 30.8	21 51.6	11 44.5	3 39.3	0 25.9	27 58.0
24 F	16 5 18	2 33 23	27 42 7	3♈45 35	19 37.5	10 55.0	12 57.0	12 8.4	21 52.4	11 40.2	3 41.5	0 24.5	27 58.4
25 Sa	16 9 15	3 31 2	9♈52 3	16 1 58	19 38.6	11 19.4	14 10.7	12 46.0	21 53.4	11 35.8	3 43.7	0 23.2	27 58.9
26 Su	16 13 11	4 28 40	22 15 46	28 33 48	19 39.9	11 48.1	15 24.4	13 23.6	21 54.5	11 31.4	3 45.9	0 21.9	27 59.3
27 M	16 17 8	5 26 17	4♉56 21	11♉23 38	19 40.9	12 20.9	16 38.0	14 1.2	21 55.9	11 27.0	3 48.2	0 20.6	27 59.8
28 Tu	16 21 5	6 23 53	17 55 46	24 32 49	19R 41.4	12 57.7	17 51.7	14 38.8	21 57.4	11 22.6	3 50.5	0 19.4	28 0.3
29 W	16 25 1	7 21 28	1♊14 43	8♊ 1 20	19 41.0	13 38.5	19 5.3	15 16.4	21 59.1	11 18.2	3 52.9	0 18.1	28 0.9
30 Th	16 28 58	8 19 1	14 52 25	21 47 39	19 39.8	14 23.0	20 18.9	15 54.0	22 0.9	11 13.7	3 55.3	0 16.9	28 1.4
31 F	16 32 54	9 16 34	28 46 37	5♋48 53	19 37.8	15 11.2	21 32.6	16 31.6	22 3.0	11 9.3	3 57.8	0 15.7	28 2.0

LONGITUDE JUNE 1957

Day	Sid.Time	☉	0 hr ☽	Noon ☽	True ☊	☿	♀	♂	♃	♄	♅	♆	♇
1 Sa	16 36 51	10♊14 6	12♋53 53	20♋ 1 5	19♏35.1	16♉ 3.1	22♊46.2	17♋ 9.1	22♍ 5.2	11♐ 4.8	4♌ 0.3	0♏14.6	28♌ 2.7
2 Su	16 40 47	11 11 36	27 9 54	4♌19 45	19R 32.3	16 58.5	23 59.7	17 46.7	22 7.6	11R 0.4	4 2.8	0R 13.4	28 3.3
3 M	16 44 44	12 9 5	11♌30 7	18 40 26	19 29.8	17 57.2	25 13.3	18 24.3	22 10.1	10 55.9	4 5.4	0 12.3	28 4.0
4 Tu	16 48 40	13 6 33	25 50 14	2♍59 7	19 27.9	18 59.4	26 26.9	19 1.9	22 12.9	10 51.5	4 8.0	0 11.2	28 4.7
5 W	16 52 37	14 3 59	10♍ 6 41	17 12 38	19D 27.1	20 4.7	27 40.4	19 39.5	22 15.8	10 47.1	4 10.6	0 10.1	28 5.5
6 Th	16 56 34	15 1 24	24 16 42	1♎18 41	19 27.3	21 13.3	28 53.9	20 17.1	22 18.9	10 42.6	4 13.3	0 9.0	28 6.2
7 F	17 0 30	15 58 48	8♎18 24	15 15 42	19 28.3	22 25.1	0♋ 7.4	20 54.7	22 22.1	10 38.2	4 16.0	0 8.0	28 7.0
8 Sa	17 4 27	16 56 11	22 10 28	29 2 35	19 29.8	23 39.9	1 20.9	21 32.3	22 25.5	10 33.8	4 18.8	0 7.0	28 7.8
9 Su	17 8 23	17 53 33	5♏51 58	12♏38 31	19 31.1	24 57.7	2 34.4	22 9.8	22 29.1	10 29.4	4 21.6	0 6.0	28 8.7
10 M	17 12 20	18 50 54	19 22 7	26 2 41	19R 31.6	26 18.6	3 47.8	22 47.4	22 32.8	10 25.0	4 24.4	0 5.1	28 9.6
11 Tu	17 16 16	19 48 14	2♐40 7	9♐14 21	19 31.0	27 42.5	5 1.3	23 25.0	22 36.7	10 20.7	4 27.2	0 4.1	28 10.5
12 W	17 20 13	20 45 33	15 45 17	22 12 51	19 28.8	29 9.3	6 14.7	24 2.6	22 40.8	10 16.3	4 30.1	0 3.2	28 11.4
13 Th	17 24 9	21 42 51	28 37 2	4♑57 49	19 25.2	0♊39.0	7 28.1	24 40.1	22 45.0	10 12.0	4 33.0	0 2.3	28 12.3
14 F	17 28 6	22 40 9	11♑15 14	17 29 21	19 20.2	2 11.7	8 41.5	25 17.7	22 49.4	10 7.7	4 36.0	0 1.5	28 13.3
15 Sa	17 32 3	23 37 26	23 40 18	29 48 15	19 14.5	3 47.2	9 54.9	25 55.3	22 53.9	10 3.4	4 38.9	0 0.7	28 14.3
16 Su	17 35 59	24 34 43	5♒53 25	11♒56 6	19 8.6	5 25.6	11 8.3	26 32.9	22 58.6	9 59.2	4 42.0	29♎59.9	28 15.3
17 M	17 39 56	25 31 59	17 56 36	23 55 20	19 3.1	7 6.8	12 21.6	27 10.4	23 3.4	9 55.0	4 45.0	29 59.1	28 16.4
18 Tu	17 43 52	26 29 15	29 52 43	5♓49 13	18 58.7	8 50.8	13 35.0	27 48.0	23 8.4	9 50.8	4 48.1	29 58.4	28 17.5
19 W	17 47 49	27 26 31	11♓45 22	17 41 41	18 55.7	10 37.6	14 48.3	28 25.6	23 13.5	9 46.7	4 51.1	29 57.6	28 18.6
20 Th	17 51 45	28 23 46	23 38 47	29 37 15	18D 54.3	12 27.1	16 1.6	29 3.2	23 18.8	9 42.6	4 54.3	29 57.0	28 19.7
21 F	17 55 42	29 21 1	5♈37 42	11♈40 45	18 54.4	14 19.3	17 14.9	29 40.7	23 24.3	9 38.5	4 57.4	29 56.3	28 20.8
22 Sa	17 59 38	0♋18 16	17 47 0	23 57 3	18 55.4	16 14.0	18 28.2	0♌18.3	23 29.8	9 34.5	5 0.6	29 55.7	28 22.0
23 Su	18 3 35	1 15 31	0♉11 28	6♉30 46	18 56.9	18 11.2	19 41.5	0 55.9	23 35.6	9 30.5	5 3.8	29 55.1	28 23.2
24 M	18 7 32	2 12 46	12 55 25	19 25 47	18R 58.0	20 10.7	20 54.8	1 33.5	23 41.5	9 26.6	5 7.0	29 54.5	28 24.4
25 Tu	18 11 28	3 10 0	26 2 10	2♊44 44	18 57.9	22 12.4	22 8.1	2 11.1	23 47.5	9 22.7	5 10.3	29 54.0	28 25.7
26 W	18 15 25	4 7 15	9♊33 31	16 28 25	18 56.1	24 16.1	23 21.3	2 48.7	23 53.6	9 18.9	5 13.5	29 53.5	28 26.9
27 Th	18 19 21	5 4 29	23 29 10	0♋35 22	18 52.3	26 21.5	24 34.6	3 26.3	23 59.9	9 15.1	5 16.8	29 53.0	28 28.2
28 F	18 23 18	6 1 44	7♋46 25	15 1 38	18 46.7	28 28.5	25 47.8	4 4.0	24 6.4	9 11.3	5 20.2	29 52.5	28 29.5
29 Sa	18 27 14	6 58 58	22 20 9	29 41 3	18 39.8	0♋36.8	27 1.0	4 41.6	24 13.0	9 7.7	5 23.5	29 52.1	28 30.9
30 Su	18 31 11	7 56 11	7♌ 3 22	14♌26 6	18 32.3	2 46.2	28 14.2	5 19.2	24 19.7	9 4.0	5 26.9	29 51.7	28 32.2

Astro Data	Planet Ingress	Last Aspect	☽ Ingress	Last Aspect	☽ Ingress	☽ Phases & Eclipses	Astro Data
Dy Hr Mn	Dy Hr Mn	Dy Hr Mn	Dy Hr Mn	Dy Hr Mn	Dy Hr Mn	Dy Hr Mn	1 MAY 1957
☽0S 9 10:01	♂ ♋ 4 15:22	1 10:03 ♇ □	♊ 1 13:47	1 15:31 ♃ ⚹	♌ 2 4:45	7 2:29 ☽ 16♌16	Julian Day # 20940
♇ D 9 19:50	♀ ♊ 13 11:08	3 18:10 ♂ ☌	♋ 3 19:08	4 3:46 ♇ ☌	♍ 4 6:59	13 22:34 ○ 22♏52	Delta T 31.8 sec
☿ D 19 1:04	☉ ♊ 21 8:10	5 9:25 ♃ ⚹	♌ 5 22:54	6 8:38 ♀ □	♎ 6 9:45	13 22:31 ☊T 1.299	SVP 05♓51'08"
♃ D 19 2:20		7 22:07 ♇ ☌	♍ 8 1:37	8 10:25 ♇ ⚹	♏ 8 13:41	21 17:03 ☽ 0♓21	Obliquity 23°26'36"
☽0N 23 7:19	♀ ♋ 6 21:35	9 20:29 ♀ △	♎ 10 3:57	10 15:50 ♇ □	♐ 10 19:09	29 11:39 ● 7♊49	⚷ Chiron 17♒11.2
	☿ ♊ 12 13:40	12 3:15 ♇ ⚹	♏ 12 6:48	12 23:13 ♇ △	♑ 13 2:36		☽ Mean ☊ 20♏21.5
☽0S 5 15:48	♆ ♎ 15 20:12	14 7:32 ♇ □	♐ 14 11:13	15 4:38 ♂ ☍	♒ 15 12:23	5 7:10 ☽ 14♍21	
☽0N 19 15:57	☉ ♋ 21 16:21	16 14:21 ♇ △	♑ 16 18:13	18 0:11 ♆ △	♓ 18 0:15	12 10:02 ○ 21♐10	1 JUNE 1957
	♂ ♌ 21 12:18	18 23:44 ☉ △	♒ 19 4:12	20 11:28 ♂ △	♈ 20 12:46	20 10:22 ☽ 28♓49	Julian Day # 20971
	☿ ♋ 28 17:08	21 12:13 ♇ ☍	♓ 21 16:20	22 23:29 ♆ ☍	♉ 22 23:38	27 20:53 ● 5♋54	Delta T 31.9 sec
		23 12:22 ♃ ☍	♈ 24 4:34	25 4:18 ♇ □	♊ 25 7:07		SVP 05♓51'04"
		26 10:55 ♇ △	♉ 26 14:43	27 10:48 ♆ △	♋ 27 11:01		Obliquity 23°26'35"
		28 18:13 ♇ □	♊ 28 21:47	29 12:18 ♆ □	♌ 29 12:31		⚷ Chiron 17♒23.6R
		30 22:44 ♇ ⚹	♋ 31 2:05				☽ Mean ☊ 18♏43.0

JULY 1957 LONGITUDE

Day	Sid.Time	☉	0 hr ☽	Noon ☽	True ☊	☿	♀	♂	♃	♄	♅	♆	♇
1 M	18 35 8	8♋53 25	21♌48 19	29♌ 9 6	18♏25.4	4♋56.2	29♋27.4	5♌56.8	24♍26.5	9♐ 0.5	5♌30.3	29♎51.4	28♌33.6
2 Tu	18 39 4	9 50 38	6♍27 41	13♍43 23	18R 19.8	7 6.7	0♌40.5	6 34.5	24 33.5	8R 57.0	5 33.7	29R 51.0	28 35.0
3 W	18 43 1	10 47 51	20 55 39	28 4 7	18 16.1	9 17.4	1 53.7	7 12.1	24 40.6	8 53.5	5 37.1	29 50.7	28 36.4
4 Th	18 46 57	11 45 3	5♎ 8 29	12♎ 8 39	18D 14.5	11 27.9	3 6.8	7 49.7	24 47.8	8 50.2	5 40.6	29 50.5	28 37.8
5 F	18 50 54	12 42 15	19 4 32	25 56 13	18 14.5	13 38.1	4 19.9	8 27.4	24 55.2	8 46.8	5 44.0	29 50.3	28 39.3
6 Sa	18 54 50	13 39 27	2♏43 47	9♏27 24	18 15.3	15 47.7	5 33.0	9 5.0	25 2.7	8 43.6	5 47.5	29 50.1	28 40.8
7 Su	18 58 47	14 36 38	16 7 15	22 43 32	18R 15.9	17 56.4	6 46.1	9 42.7	25 10.3	8 40.4	5 51.0	29 49.9	28 42.3
8 M	19 2 43	15 33 50	29 16 27	5♐46 10	18 15.4	20 4.0	7 59.1	10 20.3	25 18.0	8 37.3	5 54.5	29 49.7	28 43.8
9 Tu	19 6 40	16 31 1	12♐12 51	18 36 38	18 12.8	22 10.4	9 12.1	10 58.0	25 25.9	8 34.3	5 58.0	29 49.6	28 45.3
10 W	19 10 37	17 28 13	24 57 40	1♑16 2	18 7.9	24 15.5	10 25.1	11 35.6	25 33.8	8 31.3	6 1.6	29 49.6	28 46.9
11 Th	19 14 33	18 25 24	7♑31 48	13 45 5	18 0.4	26 19.1	11 38.1	12 13.3	25 41.9	8 28.4	6 5.1	29D 49.5	28 48.4
12 F	19 18 30	19 22 36	19 55 55	26 4 23	17 50.9	28 21.1	12 51.1	12 50.9	25 50.1	8 25.6	6 8.7	29 49.5	28 50.0
13 Sa	19 22 26	20 19 47	2♒10 36	8♒14 39	17 39.9	0♌21.5	14 4.0	13 28.6	25 58.4	8 22.9	6 12.3	29 49.6	28 51.6
14 Su	19 26 23	21 17 0	14 16 42	20 16 55	17 28.4	2 20.2	15 16.9	14 6.3	26 6.9	8 20.2	6 15.9	29 49.6	28 53.2
15 M	19 30 19	22 14 12	26 15 32	2♓12 48	17 17.5	4 17.1	16 29.8	14 44.0	26 15.4	8 17.6	6 19.5	29 49.7	28 54.9
16 Tu	19 34 16	23 11 25	8♓ 9 3	14 4 38	17 8.1	6 12.2	17 42.7	15 21.7	26 24.0	8 15.1	6 23.1	29 49.8	28 56.5
17 W	19 38 12	24 8 39	19 59 59	25 55 32	17 0.8	8 5.5	18 55.6	15 59.4	26 32.8	8 12.7	6 26.8	29 50.0	28 58.2
18 Th	19 42 9	25 5 53	1♈51 50	7♈49 24	16 55.9	9 57.0	20 8.4	16 37.1	26 41.6	8 10.4	6 30.4	29 50.1	28 59.9
19 F	19 46 6	26 3 7	13 48 50	19 50 45	16 53.4	11 46.6	21 21.2	17 14.8	26 50.6	8 8.1	6 34.0	29 50.4	29 1.6
20 Sa	19 50 2	27 0 23	25 55 47	2♉ 4 35	16D 52.7	13 34.5	22 34.0	17 52.5	26 59.7	8 5.9	6 37.7	29 50.6	29 3.3
21 Su	19 53 59	27 57 39	8♉17 47	14 36 2	16R 52.9	15 20.5	23 46.8	18 30.3	27 8.8	8 3.8	6 41.4	29 50.9	29 5.0
22 M	19 57 55	28 54 57	20 59 55	27 29 57	16 53.0	17 4.7	24 59.6	19 8.0	27 18.1	8 1.8	6 45.0	29 51.2	29 6.8
23 Tu	20 1 52	29 52 15	4♊ 6 35	10♊50 11	16 51.9	18 47.2	26 12.3	19 45.8	27 27.5	7 59.9	6 48.7	29 51.5	29 8.5
24 W	20 5 48	0♌49 34	17 40 56	24 38 54	16 48.7	20 27.8	27 25.0	20 23.6	27 37.0	7 58.1	6 52.4	29 51.9	29 10.3
25 Th	20 9 45	1 46 53	1♋43 56	8♋55 41	16 43.1	22 6.6	28 37.7	21 1.3	27 46.5	7 56.3	6 56.1	29 52.3	29 12.1
26 F	20 13 41	2 44 14	16 13 36	23 36 55	16 35.0	23 43.6	29 50.4	21 39.1	27 56.2	7 54.7	6 59.8	29 52.8	29 13.9
27 Sa	20 17 38	3 41 35	1♌ 4 40	8♌35 43	16 25.1	25 18.8	1♍ 3.1	22 16.9	28 5.9	7 53.1	7 3.5	29 53.2	29 15.7
28 Su	20 21 35	4 38 58	16 8 50	23 42 42	16 14.4	26 52.2	2 15.7	22 54.8	28 15.8	7 51.7	7 7.2	29 53.8	29 17.5
29 M	20 25 31	5 36 20	1♍16 2	8♍47 34	16 4.2	28 23.8	3 28.3	23 32.6	28 25.7	7 50.3	7 10.9	29 54.3	29 19.3
30 Tu	20 29 28	6 33 43	16 16 11	23 40 54	15 55.7	29 53.6	4 40.9	24 10.4	28 35.8	7 49.0	7 14.6	29 54.9	29 21.2
31 W	20 33 24	7 31 7	1♎ 0 55	8♎15 40	15 49.6	1♍21.5	5 53.5	24 48.3	28 45.9	7 47.8	7 18.3	29 55.5	29 23.0

AUGUST 1957 LONGITUDE

Day	Sid.Time	☉	0 hr ☽	Noon ☽	True ☊	☿	♀	♂	♃	♄	♅	♆	♇
1 Th	20 37 21	8♌28 32	15♎24 45	22♎27 56	15♏46.1	2♍47.6	7♍ 6.0	25♌26.1	28♍56.1	7♐46.7	7♌22.0	29♎56.1	29♌24.9
2 F	20 41 17	9 25 57	29 25 12	6♏16 38	15D 44.8	4 11.9	8 18.5	26 4.0	29 6.4	7R 45.7	7 25.7	29 56.8	29 26.8
3 Sa	20 45 14	10 23 23	13♏ 2 27	19 42 55	15R 44.6	5 34.2	9 30.9	26 41.9	29 16.7	7 44.8	7 29.4	29 57.4	29 28.6
4 Su	20 49 10	11 20 49	26 18 24	2♐49 16	15 44.4	6 54.5	10 43.4	27 19.7	29 27.2	7 44.0	7 33.1	29 58.2	29 30.5
5 M	20 53 7	12 18 16	9♐15 55	15 38 44	15 43.0	8 12.9	11 55.8	27 57.6	29 37.7	7 43.3	7 36.8	29 58.9	29 32.4
6 Tu	20 57 4	13 15 44	21 58 5	28 14 20	15 39.4	9 29.2	13 8.2	28 35.5	29 48.3	7 42.6	7 40.5	29 59.7	29 34.3
7 W	21 1 0	14 13 12	4♑27 46	10♑38 41	15 33.1	10 43.5	14 20.5	29 13.5	29 59.0	7 42.1	7 44.2	0♏ 0.5	29 36.2
8 Th	21 4 57	15 10 42	16 47 20	22 53 55	15 23.9	11 55.6	15 32.8	29 51.4	0♎ 9.8	7 41.7	7 47.9	0 1.4	29 38.2
9 F	21 8 53	16 8 12	28 58 39	5♒ 1 40	15 12.2	13 5.4	16 45.1	0♍29.3	0 20.6	7 41.4	7 51.5	0 2.3	29 40.1
10 Sa	21 12 50	17 5 44	11♒ 3 7	17 3 10	14 58.9	14 13.0	17 57.3	1 7.3	0 31.5	7 41.1	7 55.2	0 3.2	29 42.0
11 Su	21 16 46	18 3 16	23 1 56	28 59 35	14 45.1	15 18.1	19 9.5	1 45.2	0 42.5	7D 41.0	7 58.9	0 4.1	29 44.0
12 M	21 20 43	19 0 50	4♓56 18	10♓52 15	14 31.8	16 20.8	20 21.7	2 23.2	0 53.6	7 40.9	8 2.5	0 5.1	29 45.9
13 Tu	21 24 39	19 58 24	16 47 41	22 42 52	14 20.1	17 20.8	21 33.8	3 1.2	1 4.7	7 41.0	8 6.2	0 6.1	29 47.9
14 W	21 28 36	20 56 0	28 38 5	4♈33 43	14 10.8	18 18.2	22 45.9	3 39.2	1 15.9	7 41.1	8 9.8	0 7.1	29 49.8
15 Th	21 32 33	21 53 38	10♈30 10	16 27 51	14 4.3	19 12.6	23 58.0	4 17.2	1 27.1	7 41.4	8 13.4	0 8.2	29 51.8
16 F	21 36 29	22 51 17	22 27 17	28 29 0	14 0.5	20 4.0	25 10.0	4 55.3	1 38.4	7 41.7	8 17.0	0 9.2	29 53.7
17 Sa	21 40 26	23 48 57	4♉33 34	10♉41 36	13D 58.9	20 52.3	26 22.0	5 33.3	1 49.8	7 42.1	8 20.7	0 10.4	29 55.7
18 Su	21 44 22	24 46 40	16 53 41	23 10 29	13R 58.6	21 37.1	27 34.0	6 11.4	2 1.3	7 42.7	8 24.3	0 11.5	29 57.7
19 M	21 48 19	25 44 23	29 32 35	6♊ 0 35	13 58.7	22 18.5	28 45.9	6 49.5	2 12.8	7 43.3	8 27.8	0 12.7	29 59.6
20 Tu	21 52 15	26 42 9	12♊35 1	19 16 21	13 57.8	22 56.1	29 57.8	7 27.6	2 24.3	7 44.0	8 31.4	0 13.9	0♍ 1.6
21 W	21 56 12	27 39 56	26 4 55	3♋ 0 56	13 55.2	23 29.7	1♎ 9.7	8 5.7	2 36.0	7 44.8	8 35.0	0 15.1	0 3.6
22 Th	22 0 8	28 37 45	10♋ 4 26	17 15 16	13 50.1	23 59.2	2 21.5	8 43.8	2 47.7	7 45.8	8 38.5	0 16.3	0 5.6
23 F	22 4 5	29 35 35	24 33 2	1♌57 7	13 42.6	24 24.2	3 33.3	9 22.0	2 59.4	7 46.8	8 42.0	0 17.6	0 7.5
24 Sa	22 8 2	0♍33 27	9♌26 41	17 0 39	13 33.2	24 44.5	4 45.1	10 0.2	3 11.2	7 47.9	8 45.6	0 18.9	0 9.5
25 Su	22 11 58	1 31 21	24 37 48	2♍16 43	13 23.0	24 59.8	5 56.8	10 38.3	3 23.1	7 49.1	8 49.1	0 20.3	0 11.5
26 M	22 15 55	2 29 16	9♍56 0	17 34 11	13 13.1	25 10.0	7 8.5	11 16.6	3 35.0	7 50.4	8 52.5	0 21.6	0 13.5
27 Tu	22 19 51	3 27 13	25 9 55	2♎41 58	13 4.7	25R 14.7	8 20.1	11 54.8	3 46.9	7 51.8	8 56.0	0 23.0	0 15.5
28 W	22 23 48	4 25 11	10♎ 9 15	17 30 57	12 58.7	25 13.8	9 31.7	12 33.0	3 58.9	7 53.3	8 59.4	0 24.4	0 17.4
29 Th	22 27 44	5 23 10	24 46 25	1♏55 16	12 55.3	25 6.9	10 43.3	13 11.3	4 11.0	7 54.9	9 2.9	0 25.9	0 19.4
30 F	22 31 41	6 21 11	8♏57 17	15 52 27	12D 54.0	24 54.1	11 54.8	13 49.6	4 23.1	7 56.6	9 6.3	0 27.3	0 21.4
31 Sa	22 35 37	7 19 13	22 40 54	29 22 55	12 54.2	24 35.0	13 6.2	14 27.8	4 35.3	7 58.4	9 9.6	0 28.8	0 23.4

Astro Data	Planet Ingress	Last Aspect	☽ Ingress	Last Aspect	☽ Ingress	☽ Phases & Eclipses	Astro Data
Dy Hr Mn	Dy Hr Mn	Dy Hr Mn	Dy Hr Mn	Dy Hr Mn	Dy Hr Mn	Dy Hr Mn	1 JULY 1957
☽0S 2 22:14	♀ ♌ 1 10:42	1 13:09 ♆ ⚹	♍ 1 13:23	2 0:55 ♆ ☌	♏ 2 1:01	4 12:09 ☽ 12♎14	Julian Day # 21001
♆ D 11 17:50	☿ ♌ 12 19:41	3 6:20 ♃ ☌	♎ 3 15:16	4 5:54 ♇ □	♐ 4 6:47	11 22:50 ○ 19♑20	Delta T 31.9 sec
☽0N 17 0:20	☉ ♌ 23 3:15	5 18:52 ♆ ☌	♏ 5 19:10	6 15:14 ♃ □	♑ 6 15:23	20 2:17 ☽ 27♈06	SVP 05♓50'58"
☽0S 30 6:39	♀ ♍ 26 3:10	7 23:00 ♇ □	♐ 8 1:20	7 21:18 ♀ △	♒ 9 2:01	27 4:28 ● 3♌52	Obliquity 23°26'35"
♃⚺♇ 4 9:17	☿ ♍ 30 1:44	10 9:15 ♆ ⚹	♑ 10 9:35	11 13:32 ♇ ☍	♓ 11 14:02		⚷ Chiron 16♒38.2R
♄△♅ 6 12:15		12 19:22 ♆ □	♒ 12 19:43	13 10:46 ♀ ☍	♈ 14 2:46	2 18:55 ☽ 10♏11	☽ Mean ☊ 17♏07.7
♃⚺♆ 7 3:40	♆ ♏ 6 8:19	15 7:11 ♆ △	♓ 15 7:32	16 14:50 ♇ △	♉ 16 15:00	10 13:08 ○ 17♒37	
♄ D 11 23:57	♃ ♎ 7 2:11	17 13:25 ♃ ☍	♈ 17 20:14	19 0:51 ♇ □	♊ 19 0:51	18 16:16 ☽ 25♉26	1 AUGUST 1957
☽0N 13 7:46	♂ ♍ 8 5:27	20 7:40 ♆ ☍	♉ 20 7:58	21 2:58 ☉ ⚹	♋ 21 6:48	25 11:33 ● 1♍59	Julian Day # 21032
☿0S 20 5:31	♇ ♍ 19 4:26	22 15:44 ☉ ⚹	♊ 22 16:34	22 23:45 ☿ ⚹	♌ 23 8:51		Delta T 32.0 sec
♀0S 21 12:06	♀ ♎ 20 0:44	24 20:52 ♆ △	♋ 24 21:05	23 22:54 ♅ ☌	♍ 25 8:26		SVP 05♓50'54"
♃0S 21 3:34	☉ ♍ 23 10:08	26 22:05 ♆ □	♌ 26 22:16	27 0:08 ☿ ☌	♎ 27 7:41		Obliquity 23°26'35"
☽0S 26 16:58		28 21:50 ♆ ⚹	♍ 28 21:59	27 22:54 ♀ ☌	♏ 29 8:45		⚷ Chiron 15♒09.9R
☿ R 27 8:04		30 20:16 ♃ ☌	♎ 30 22:20	31 3:18 ☿ ⚹	♐ 31 13:07		☽ Mean ☊ 15♏29.2

LONGITUDE SEPTEMBER 1957

Day	Sid.Time	☉	0 hr ☽	Noon ☽	True ☊	☿	♀	♂	♃	♄	♅	♆	♇
1 Su	22 39 34	8♍17 17	5♐58 52	12♐29 9	12♏54.6	24♍ 9.8	14♎17.7	15♍ 6.2	4♎47.5	8♐ 0.3	9♌13.0	0♏30.3	0♍25.3
2 M	22 43 30	9 15 21	18 54 16	25 14 42	12R 54.2	23R 38.5	15 29.0	15 44.5	4 59.7	8 2.3	9 16.3	0 31.9	0 27.3
3 Tu	22 47 27	10 13 28	1♑30 56	7♑43 29	12 52.0	23 1.3	16 40.4	16 22.8	5 12.0	8 4.3	9 19.7	0 33.4	0 29.2
4 W	22 51 24	11 11 36	13 52 48	19 59 21	12 47.5	22 18.5	17 51.6	17 1.2	5 24.3	8 6.5	9 22.9	0 35.0	0 31.2
5 Th	22 55 20	12 9 45	26 3 30	2♒ 5 39	12 40.5	21 30.7	19 2.8	17 39.6	5 36.7	8 8.7	9 26.2	0 36.6	0 33.2
6 F	22 59 17	13 7 55	8♒ 6 8	14 5 14	12 31.4	20 38.3	20 14.0	18 18.0	5 49.0	8 11.1	9 29.5	0 38.3	0 35.1
7 Sa	23 3 13	14 6 8	20 3 15	26 0 24	12 20.9	19 42.4	21 25.1	18 56.4	6 1.5	8 13.5	9 32.7	0 39.9	0 37.0
8 Su	23 7 10	15 4 22	1♓56 54	7♓52 57	12 9.8	18 43.9	22 36.2	19 34.8	6 14.0	8 16.0	9 35.9	0 41.6	0 39.0
9 M	23 11 6	16 2 37	13 48 46	19 44 31	11 59.1	17 44.0	23 47.2	20 13.3	6 26.5	8 18.6	9 39.0	0 43.3	0 40.9
10 Tu	23 15 3	17 0 54	25 40 25	1♈36 40	11 49.8	16 43.9	24 58.1	20 51.7	6 39.0	8 21.3	9 42.2	0 45.0	0 42.8
11 W	23 18 59	17 59 14	7♈33 29	13 31 9	11 42.6	15 45.0	26 9.0	21 30.2	6 51.6	8 24.1	9 45.3	0 46.8	0 44.7
12 Th	23 22 56	18 57 35	19 29 56	25 30 10	11 37.7	14 48.7	27 19.9	22 8.7	7 4.2	8 27.0	9 48.3	0 48.5	0 46.6
13 F	23 26 53	19 55 58	1♉32 11	7♉36 23	11D 35.2	13 56.4	28 30.6	22 47.3	7 16.8	8 30.0	9 51.4	0 50.3	0 48.5
14 Sa	23 30 49	20 54 23	13 43 13	19 53 8	11 34.6	13 9.4	29 41.4	23 25.8	7 29.4	8 33.0	9 54.4	0 52.1	0 50.4
15 Su	23 34 46	21 52 50	26 6 37	2♊24 10	11 35.4	12 28.8	0♏52.0	24 4.4	7 42.1	8 36.2	9 57.4	0 53.9	0 52.3
16 M	23 38 42	22 51 20	8♊46 18	15 13 33	11 36.6	11 55.8	2 2.6	24 43.0	7 54.9	8 39.4	10 0.4	0 55.8	0 54.1
17 Tu	23 42 39	23 49 52	21 46 21	28 25 11	11R 37.3	11 31.1	3 13.2	25 21.6	8 7.6	8 42.7	10 3.3	0 57.6	0 56.0
18 W	23 46 35	24 48 26	5♋10 23	12♋ 2 14	11 36.8	11 15.4	4 23.7	26 0.3	8 20.4	8 46.1	10 6.2	0 59.5	0 57.9
19 Th	23 50 32	25 47 2	19 0 53	26 6 19	11 34.6	11D 9.1	5 34.1	26 39.0	8 33.2	8 49.6	10 9.1	1 1.4	0 59.7
20 F	23 54 28	26 45 40	3♌18 22	10♌36 39	11 30.5	11 12.5	6 44.5	27 17.7	8 46.0	8 53.1	10 11.9	1 3.3	1 1.5
21 Sa	23 58 25	27 44 20	18 0 35	25 29 22	11 24.9	11 25.7	7 54.8	27 56.4	8 58.8	8 56.8	10 14.7	1 5.2	1 3.3
22 Su	0 2 22	28 43 3	3♍ 2 2	10♍37 25	11 18.5	11 48.4	9 5.1	28 35.1	9 11.7	9 0.5	10 17.4	1 7.2	1 5.1
23 M	0 6 18	29 41 48	18 14 17	25 51 17	11 12.2	12 20.5	10 15.3	29 13.9	9 24.5	9 4.3	10 20.2	1 9.2	1 6.9
24 Tu	0 10 15	0♎40 34	3♎27 5	11♎ 0 24	11 6.9	13 1.5	11 25.4	29 52.7	9 37.4	9 8.2	10 22.9	1 11.1	1 8.7
25 W	0 14 11	1 39 23	18 30 5	25 55 4	11 3.3	13 51.0	12 35.4	0♎31.5	9 50.3	9 12.2	10 25.5	1 13.1	1 10.5
26 Th	0 18 8	2 38 14	3♏14 32	10♏27 49	11D 1.5	14 48.4	13 45.4	1 10.4	10 3.2	9 16.2	10 28.1	1 15.1	1 12.2
27 F	0 22 4	3 37 6	17 34 29	24 34 17	11 1.4	15 53.0	14 55.3	1 49.2	10 16.2	9 20.3	10 30.7	1 17.2	1 14.0
28 Sa	0 26 1	4 36 1	1♐27 8	8♐13 7	11 2.5	17 4.3	16 5.2	2 28.1	10 29.1	9 24.5	10 33.2	1 19.2	1 15.7
29 Su	0 29 57	5 34 57	14 52 29	21 25 31	11 4.0	18 21.4	17 14.9	3 7.0	10 42.1	9 28.8	10 35.7	1 21.3	1 17.4
30 M	0 33 54	6 33 54	27 52 39	4♑14 22	11R 5.3	19 43.8	18 24.6	3 45.9	10 55.0	9 33.2	10 38.2	1 23.3	1 19.1

LONGITUDE OCTOBER 1957

Day	Sid.Time	☉	0 hr ☽	Noon ☽	True ☊	☿	♀	♂	♃	♄	♅	♆	♇
1 Tu	0 37 51	7♎32 54	10♑31 10	16♑43 34	11♏ 5.6	21♍10.7	19♏34.2	4♎24.9	11♎ 8.0	9♐37.6	10♌40.6	1♏25.4	1♍20.8
2 W	0 41 47	8 31 55	22 52 9	28 57 27	11R 4.5	22 41.5	20 43.7	5 3.9	11 21.0	9 42.1	10 43.0	1 27.5	1 22.4
3 Th	0 45 44	9 30 58	4♒59 58	11♒ 0 14	11 2.0	24 15.6	21 53.1	5 42.9	11 34.0	9 46.6	10 45.3	1 29.6	1 24.1
4 F	0 49 40	10 30 3	16 58 43	22 55 53	10 58.1	25 52.5	23 2.5	6 21.9	11 47.0	9 51.3	10 47.6	1 31.7	1 25.7
5 Sa	0 53 37	11 29 10	28 52 9	4♓47 53	10 53.4	27 31.6	24 11.7	7 1.0	11 59.9	9 56.0	10 49.8	1 33.8	1 27.3
6 Su	0 57 33	12 28 18	10♓43 27	16 39 11	10 48.2	29 12.6	25 20.8	7 40.0	12 12.9	10 0.8	10 52.0	1 36.0	1 28.9
7 M	1 1 30	13 27 29	22 35 20	28 32 11	10 43.3	0♎55.0	26 29.9	8 19.1	12 25.9	10 5.6	10 54.2	1 38.1	1 30.4
8 Tu	1 5 26	14 26 41	4♈30 0	10♈28 58	10 39.0	2 38.5	27 38.8	8 58.2	12 38.9	10 10.5	10 56.3	1 40.3	1 32.0
9 W	1 9 23	15 25 55	16 29 19	22 31 16	10 35.9	4 22.7	28 47.7	9 37.4	12 51.9	10 15.5	10 58.4	1 42.4	1 33.5
10 Th	1 13 19	16 25 12	28 35 0	4♉40 44	10D 34.0	6 7.4	29 56.4	10 16.6	13 4.9	10 20.6	11 0.4	1 44.6	1 35.0
11 F	1 17 16	17 24 30	10♉48 41	16 59 4	10 33.4	7 52.5	1♐ 5.0	10 55.8	13 17.8	10 25.7	11 2.4	1 46.8	1 36.5
12 Sa	1 21 13	18 23 51	23 12 9	29 28 11	10 34.0	9 37.6	2 13.5	11 35.0	13 30.8	10 30.8	11 4.3	1 49.0	1 38.0
13 Su	1 25 9	19 23 14	5♊47 26	12♊10 11	10 35.2	11 22.7	3 21.9	12 14.2	13 43.8	10 36.1	11 6.2	1 51.2	1 39.5
14 M	1 29 6	20 22 39	18 36 43	25 7 21	10 36.7	13 7.6	4 30.2	12 53.5	13 56.8	10 41.4	11 8.1	1 53.4	1 40.9
15 Tu	1 33 2	21 22 6	1♋42 22	8♋22 1	10 38.1	14 52.3	5 38.4	13 32.8	14 9.7	10 46.7	11 9.9	1 55.6	1 42.3
16 W	1 36 59	22 21 36	15 6 31	21 56 5	10R 38.9	16 36.6	6 46.5	14 12.2	14 22.7	10 52.2	11 11.6	1 57.8	1 43.7
17 Th	1 40 55	23 21 8	28 50 47	5♌50 41	10 39.0	18 20.5	7 54.4	14 51.6	14 35.6	10 57.6	11 13.3	2 0.0	1 45.1
18 F	1 44 52	24 20 43	12♌55 40	20 5 32	10 38.3	20 3.9	9 2.2	15 31.0	14 48.5	11 3.2	11 15.0	2 2.2	1 46.4
19 Sa	1 48 48	25 20 19	27 19 58	4♍38 29	10 36.9	21 46.8	10 9.9	16 10.4	15 1.4	11 8.8	11 16.6	2 4.5	1 47.8
20 Su	1 52 45	26 19 58	12♍ 0 27	19 25 10	10 35.2	23 29.2	11 17.4	16 49.8	15 14.3	11 14.4	11 18.1	2 6.7	1 49.1
21 M	1 56 42	27 19 39	26 51 43	4♎19 12	10 33.4	25 11.0	12 24.9	17 29.3	15 27.2	11 20.1	11 19.6	2 8.9	1 50.3
22 Tu	2 0 38	28 19 23	11♎46 34	19 12 49	10 32.0	26 52.3	13 32.1	18 8.9	15 40.0	11 25.9	11 21.1	2 11.2	1 51.6
23 W	2 4 35	29 19 8	26 36 56	3♏57 56	10D 31.1	28 33.0	14 39.3	18 48.4	15 52.9	11 31.7	11 22.5	2 13.4	1 52.8
24 Th	2 8 31	0♏18 56	11♏14 59	18 27 18	10 30.9	0♏13.1	15 46.3	19 28.0	16 5.7	11 37.6	11 23.8	2 15.7	1 54.0
25 F	2 12 28	1 18 45	25 34 16	2♐35 26	10 31.1	1 52.7	16 53.1	20 7.6	16 18.5	11 43.5	11 25.1	2 17.9	1 55.2
26 Sa	2 16 24	2 18 36	9♐30 27	16 19 10	10 31.7	3 31.7	17 59.8	20 47.2	16 31.2	11 49.5	11 26.3	2 20.2	1 56.4
27 Su	2 20 21	3 18 29	23 1 33	29 37 42	10 32.5	5 10.2	19 6.3	21 26.9	16 44.0	11 55.5	11 27.5	2 22.4	1 57.5
28 M	2 24 17	4 18 24	6♑ 7 50	12♑32 17	10 33.2	6 48.1	20 12.6	22 6.5	16 56.7	12 1.6	11 28.7	2 24.6	1 58.6
29 Tu	2 28 14	5 18 21	18 51 25	25 5 43	10 33.6	8 25.5	21 18.8	22 46.3	17 9.4	12 7.7	11 29.8	2 26.9	1 59.7
30 W	2 32 11	6 18 19	1♒15 40	7♒21 51	10R 33.9	10 2.4	22 24.8	23 26.0	17 22.0	12 13.9	11 30.8	2 29.1	2 0.7
31 Th	2 36 7	7 18 18	13 24 47	19 25 5	10 33.9	11 38.8	23 30.5	24 5.8	17 34.7	12 20.1	11 31.8	2 31.4	2 1.8

Astro Data Dy Hr Mn	Planet Ingress Dy Hr Mn	Last Aspect Dy Hr Mn	☽ Ingress Dy Hr Mn	Last Aspect Dy Hr Mn	☽ Ingress Dy Hr Mn	☽ Phases & Eclipses Dy Hr Mn
☿0N 6 9:01	♀ ♏ 14 6:20	2 8:33 ☿ □	♑ 2 21:05	1 23:36 ☿ △	♒ 2 14:04	1 4:35 ☽ 8♐28
☽0N 9 14:10	☉ ♎ 23 7:26	4 15:34 ☿ △	♒ 5 7:50	4 13:32 ♀ □	♓ 5 2:17	9 4:55 ○ 16♓15
☿ D 19 3:37	♂ ♎ 24 4:31	7 3:03 ☿ △	♓ 7 20:04	7 8:44 ♀ △	♈ 7 14:57	17 4:02 ☽ 23♊60
♃✶♄ 20 18:41		9 13:43 ♂ ☍	♈ 10 8:45	8 21:42 ☉ ☍	♉ 10 2:48	23 19:18 ● 0♎29
☽0S 23 3:59	☿ ♎ 6 11:09	12 17:20 ♀ ☍	♉ 12 20:57	11 0:27 ♅ □	♊ 12 13:01	30 17:49 ☽ 7♑18
♂0S 27 6:08	♀ ♐ 10 1:16	14 19:52 ♂ △	♊ 15 7:26	14 3:32 ☉ △	♋ 14 20:54	
♃✶♅ 28 9:25	☉ ♏ 23 16:24	17 6:50 ♂ □	♋ 17 14:50	16 13:44 ☉ □	♌ 17 1:59	8 21:42 ○ 15♈20
	☿ ♏ 23 20:50	19 13:31 ♂ ✶	♌ 19 18:31	18 20:28 ☉ ✶	♍ 19 4:23	16 13:44 ☽ 22♋56
☽0N 6 20:13		20 11:22 ♅ ☌	♍ 21 19:11	19 22:45 ♄ □	♎ 21 5:03	23 4:43 ● 29♎31
☿0S 8 23:27		23 18:06 ♂ ☌	♎ 23 18:33	23 4:43 ☉ ☌	♏ 23 5:31	23 4:53:28 ● T non-C
☽0S 20 13:57		24 11:02 ♅ ✶	♏ 25 18:40	24 0:15 ♅ □	♐ 25 7:33	30 10:48 ☽ 6♒45
♄△♅ 20 20:59		26 20:53 ☿ ✶	♐ 27 21:27	26 21:01 ♂ ✶	♑ 27 12:41	
♃∠♇ 28 3:57		29 7:05 ☿ □	♑ 30 3:59	29 7:56 ♂ □	♒ 29 21:32	

Astro Data

1 SEPTEMBER 1957
Julian Day # 21063
Delta T 32.0 sec
SVP 05♓50'50"
Obliquity 23°26'35"
⚷ Chiron 13♒33.8R
☽ Mean ☊ 13♏50.7

1 OCTOBER 1957
Julian Day # 21093
Delta T 32.1 sec
SVP 05♓50'48"
Obliquity 23°26'35"
⚷ Chiron 12♒29.6R
☽ Mean ☊ 12♏15.4

NOVEMBER 1957 LONGITUDE

Day	Sid.Time	☉	0 hr ☽	Noon ☽	True ☊	☿	♀	♂	♃	♄	♅	♆	♇
1 F	2 40 4	8♏18 20	25♒23 19	1♓20 2	10♏33.7	13♏14.7	24♐36.1	24♎45.5	17♎47.3	12♐26.3	11♌32.7	2♏33.6	2♍ 2.8
2 Sa	2 44 0	9 18 22	7♓15 48	13 11 10	10R33.6	14 50.2	25 41.5	25 25.4	17 59.8	12 32.6	11 33.6	2 35.8	2 3.8
3 Su	2 47 57	10 18 27	19 6 37	25 2 38	10D33.5	16 25.2	26 46.6	26 5.2	18 12.3	12 38.9	11 34.4	2 38.1	2 4.7
4 M	2 51 53	11 18 33	0♈59 40	6♈58 7	10 33.5	17 59.8	27 51.5	26 45.1	18 24.8	12 45.3	11 35.1	2 40.3	2 5.6
5 Tu	2 55 50	12 18 41	12 58 21	19 0 42	10 33.7	19 33.9	28 56.2	27 25.0	18 37.3	12 51.7	11 35.8	2 42.5	2 6.5
6 W	2 59 46	13 18 50	25 5 27	1♉12 50	10 33.8	21 7.7	0♑ 0.6	28 4.9	18 49.7	12 58.2	11 36.5	2 44.7	2 7.4
7 Th	3 3 43	14 19 1	7♉23 3	13 36 18	10R34.0	22 41.1	1 4.8	28 44.9	19 2.1	13 4.7	11 37.1	2 46.9	2 8.2
8 F	3 7 40	15 19 14	19 52 41	26 12 19	10 33.9	24 14.2	2 8.8	29 24.9	19 14.4	13 11.2	11 37.6	2 49.2	2 9.0
9 Sa	3 11 36	16 19 29	2♊35 15	9♊ 1 31	10 33.6	25 46.8	3 12.4	0♏ 4.9	19 26.7	13 17.7	11 38.1	2 51.4	2 9.8
10 Su	3 15 33	17 19 45	15 31 10	22 4 12	10 32.9	27 19.2	4 15.8	0 45.0	19 38.9	13 24.3	11 38.5	2 53.5	2 10.6
11 M	3 19 29	18 20 4	28 40 34	5♋20 17	10 32.0	28 51.2	5 19.0	1 25.0	19 51.1	13 31.0	11 38.9	2 55.7	2 11.3
12 Tu	3 23 26	19 20 24	12♋ 3 18	18 49 34	10 30.9	0♐22.9	6 21.8	2 5.2	20 3.3	13 37.6	11 39.2	2 57.9	2 12.0
13 W	3 27 22	20 20 47	25 39 2	2♌31 38	10 29.9	1 54.3	7 24.3	2 45.3	20 15.4	13 44.3	11 39.5	3 0.1	2 12.7
14 Th	3 31 19	21 21 11	9♌27 17	16 25 53	10D29.2	3 25.3	8 26.5	3 25.5	20 27.4	13 51.0	11 39.7	3 2.2	2 13.3
15 F	3 35 15	22 21 37	23 27 17	0♍31 20	10 28.9	4 56.0	9 28.4	4 5.7	20 39.4	13 57.8	11 39.9	3 4.4	2 13.9
16 Sa	3 39 12	23 22 5	7♍37 48	14 46 25	10 29.3	6 26.5	10 30.0	4 46.0	20 51.4	14 4.5	11 40.0	3 6.5	2 14.5
17 Su	3 43 9	24 22 34	21 56 54	29 8 50	10 30.1	7 56.5	11 31.2	5 26.3	21 3.3	14 11.3	11R40.0	3 8.7	2 15.0
18 M	3 47 5	25 23 6	6♎21 48	13♎35 18	10 31.3	9 26.3	12 32.1	6 6.6	21 15.1	14 18.2	11 40.0	3 10.8	2 15.6
19 Tu	3 51 2	26 23 39	20 48 47	28 1 38	10 32.4	10 55.7	13 32.6	6 46.9	21 26.9	14 25.0	11 39.9	3 12.9	2 16.0
20 W	3 54 58	27 24 15	5♏13 15	12♏22 59	10R33.0	12 24.7	14 32.7	7 27.3	21 38.6	14 31.9	11 39.8	3 15.0	2 16.5
21 Th	3 58 55	28 24 51	19 30 12	26 34 16	10 32.9	13 53.3	15 32.4	8 7.7	21 50.3	14 38.8	11 39.6	3 17.1	2 16.9
22 F	4 2 51	29 25 30	3♐34 39	10♐30 50	10 31.8	15 21.5	16 31.7	8 48.2	22 1.9	14 45.7	11 39.4	3 19.1	2 17.3
23 Sa	4 6 48	0♐26 10	17 22 22	24 8 58	10 29.6	16 49.2	17 30.6	9 28.6	22 13.4	14 52.7	11 39.1	3 21.2	2 17.7
24 Su	4 10 44	1 26 51	0♑50 22	7♑26 27	10 26.6	18 16.4	18 29.0	10 9.1	22 24.9	14 59.6	11 38.8	3 23.2	2 18.0
25 M	4 14 41	2 27 33	13 57 13	20 22 46	10 23.2	19 42.9	19 27.0	10 49.7	22 36.3	15 6.6	11 38.4	3 25.3	2 18.4
26 Tu	4 18 38	3 28 17	26 43 15	2♒58 58	10 19.7	21 8.8	20 24.5	11 30.2	22 47.6	15 13.6	11 37.9	3 27.3	2 18.6
27 W	4 22 34	4 29 1	9♒10 18	15 17 39	10 16.7	22 33.9	21 21.4	12 10.8	22 58.8	15 20.6	11 37.4	3 29.3	2 18.9
28 Th	4 26 31	5 29 47	21 21 32	27 22 28	10 14.7	23 58.1	22 17.9	12 51.5	23 10.0	15 27.6	11 36.9	3 31.3	2 19.1
29 F	4 30 27	6 30 33	3♓21 2	9♓17 51	10D13.7	25 21.3	23 13.7	13 32.1	23 21.1	15 34.6	11 36.2	3 33.2	2 19.3
30 Sa	4 34 24	7 31 21	15 13 31	21 8 40	10 14.0	26 43.3	24 9.1	14 12.8	23 32.2	15 41.7	11 35.6	3 35.2	2 19.4

DECEMBER 1957 LONGITUDE

Day	Sid.Time	☉	0 hr ☽	Noon ☽	True ☊	☿	♀	♂	♃	♄	♅	♆	♇
1 Su	4 38 20	8♐32 9	27♓ 3 56	2♈59 56	10♏15.2	28♐ 4.1	25♑ 3.8	14♏53.5	23♎43.1	15♐48.7	11♌34.8	3♏37.1	2♍19.5
2 M	4 42 17	9 32 59	8♈57 15	14 56 29	10 17.0	29 23.3	25 57.8	15 34.2	23 54.0	15 55.8	11R34.1	3 39.0	2 19.6
3 Tu	4 46 13	10 33 49	20 58 8	27 2 44	10 18.8	0♑40.7	26 51.3	16 15.0	24 4.8	16 2.9	11 33.2	3 40.9	2 19.7
4 W	4 50 10	11 34 40	3♉10 42	9♉22 26	10R20.0	1 56.1	27 44.0	16 55.8	24 15.5	16 9.9	11 32.3	3 42.8	2R19.7
5 Th	4 54 7	12 35 32	15 38 15	21 58 23	10 20.1	3 9.1	28 36.1	17 36.7	24 26.1	16 17.0	11 31.4	3 44.6	2 19.7
6 F	4 58 3	13 36 26	28 23 0	4♊52 10	10 18.7	4 19.4	29 27.4	18 17.5	24 36.7	16 24.1	11 30.4	3 46.5	2 19.7
7 Sa	5 2 0	14 37 20	11♊25 54	18 4 4	10 15.5	5 26.6	0♒18.0	18 58.4	24 47.1	16 31.2	11 29.4	3 48.3	2 19.6
8 Su	5 5 56	15 38 15	24 46 31	1♋32 57	10 10.7	6 30.2	1 7.7	19 39.4	24 57.5	16 38.3	11 28.3	3 50.1	2 19.5
9 M	5 9 53	16 39 11	8♋23 5	15 16 30	10 4.8	7 29.7	1 56.7	20 20.3	25 7.8	16 45.4	11 27.2	3 51.8	2 19.4
10 Tu	5 13 49	17 40 8	22 12 48	29 11 31	9 58.5	8 24.4	2 44.7	21 1.3	25 18.0	16 52.5	11 26.0	3 53.6	2 19.3
11 W	5 17 46	18 41 6	6♌12 13	13♌14 27	9 52.5	9 13.6	3 31.9	21 42.4	25 28.1	16 59.6	11 24.8	3 55.3	2 19.1
12 Th	5 21 42	19 42 5	20 17 48	27 21 53	9 47.8	9 56.7	4 18.2	22 23.4	25 38.1	17 6.7	11 23.5	3 57.0	2 18.9
13 F	5 25 39	20 43 5	4♍26 23	11♍30 59	9 44.6	10 32.8	5 3.5	23 4.5	25 48.0	17 13.8	11 22.1	3 58.7	2 18.6
14 Sa	5 29 36	21 44 7	18 35 27	25 39 33	9D43.4	11 1.1	5 47.8	23 45.7	25 57.8	17 20.9	11 20.8	4 0.4	2 18.3
15 Su	5 33 32	22 45 9	2♎43 9	9♎46 3	9 43.7	11 20.7	6 31.0	24 26.8	26 7.5	17 27.9	11 19.3	4 2.0	2 18.0
16 M	5 37 29	23 46 12	16 48 9	23 49 16	9 45.0	11R30.6	7 13.2	25 8.1	26 17.1	17 35.0	11 17.9	4 3.6	2 17.7
17 Tu	5 41 25	24 47 17	0♏49 15	7♏47 56	9R46.2	11 30.2	7 54.2	25 49.3	26 26.6	17 42.1	11 16.3	4 5.2	2 17.3
18 W	5 45 22	25 48 22	14 45 6	21 40 30	9 46.3	11 18.7	8 34.1	26 30.6	26 35.9	17 49.1	11 14.8	4 6.8	2 16.9
19 Th	5 49 18	26 49 28	28 33 53	5♐24 57	9 44.7	10 55.6	9 12.8	27 11.9	26 45.2	17 56.2	11 13.2	4 8.3	2 16.5
20 F	5 53 15	27 50 35	12♐13 24	18 58 53	9 40.7	10 20.8	9 50.2	27 53.2	26 54.4	18 3.2	11 11.5	4 9.8	2 16.1
21 Sa	5 57 11	28 51 42	25 41 8	2♑19 51	9 34.2	9 34.6	10 26.2	28 34.6	27 3.5	18 10.3	11 9.8	4 11.3	2 15.6
22 Su	6 1 8	29 52 50	8♑54 46	15 25 43	9 25.8	8 37.7	11 0.9	29 16.0	27 12.4	18 17.3	11 8.1	4 12.8	2 15.1
23 M	6 5 5	0♑53 59	21 52 33	28 15 12	9 16.1	7 31.3	11 34.2	29 57.4	27 21.2	18 24.3	11 6.3	4 14.2	2 14.5
24 Tu	6 9 1	1 55 7	4♒33 42	10♒48 8	9 6.0	6 17.3	12 5.9	0♐38.9	27 30.0	18 31.3	11 4.5	4 15.6	2 13.9
25 W	6 12 58	2 56 16	16 58 41	23 5 37	8 56.7	4 58.0	12 36.1	1 20.4	27 38.5	18 38.2	11 2.6	4 17.0	2 13.3
26 Th	6 16 54	3 57 25	29 9 16	5♓10 3	8 49.0	3 36.0	13 4.6	2 1.9	27 47.0	18 45.2	11 0.7	4 18.4	2 12.7
27 F	6 20 51	4 58 34	11♓ 8 26	17 4 57	8 43.5	2 14.0	13 31.5	2 43.5	27 55.4	18 52.1	10 58.8	4 19.7	2 12.1
28 Sa	6 24 47	5 59 43	23 0 11	28 54 45	8 40.3	0 54.7	13 56.6	3 25.1	28 3.6	18 59.0	10 56.8	4 21.0	2 11.4
29 Su	6 28 44	7 0 52	4♈49 17	10♈44 29	8D39.1	29♐40.6	14 19.9	4 6.7	28 11.7	19 5.9	10 54.8	4 22.3	2 10.7
30 M	6 32 40	8 2 1	16 41 0	22 39 33	8 39.4	28 33.6	14 41.3	4 48.3	28 19.6	19 12.7	10 52.7	4 23.5	2 9.9
31 Tu	6 36 37	9 3 10	28 40 47	4♉45 21	8R40.3	27 35.3	15 0.7	5 30.0	28 27.5	19 19.6	10 50.7	4 24.7	2 9.2

Astro Data Dy Hr Mn	Planet Ingress Dy Hr Mn	Last Aspect Dy Hr Mn	☽ Ingress Dy Hr Mn	Last Aspect Dy Hr Mn	☽ Ingress Dy Hr Mn	☽ Phases & Eclipses Dy Hr Mn	Astro Data
☽0N 3 2:59	♀ ♑ 5 23:46	31 22:39 ♂ △	♓ 1 9:18	1 2:17 ☿ □	♈ 1 5:56	7 14:32 ○ 14♉55	1 NOVEMBER 1957
☽0S 16 21:47	♂ ♏ 8 21:04	3 17:03 ♀ □	♈ 3 22:00	3 12:32 ♀ □	♉ 3 17:48	7 14:27 T 1.030	Julian Day # 21124
♅ R 17 6:27	☿ ♐ 11 18:00	6 6:13 ♂ ☍	♉ 6 9:38	6 2:08 ♀ △	♊ 6 3:00	14 21:59 ☽ 22♌17	Delta T 32.1 sec
☽0N 30 11:11	☉ ♐ 22 13:39	8 9:26 ☿ ☍	♊ 8 19:09	8 0:20 ♃ △	♋ 8 9:16	21 16:19 ● 29♏06	SVP 05♓50'45"
		10 7:42 ♃ △	♋ 11 2:24	10 5:23 ♃ □	♌ 10 13:23	29 6:58 ☽ 6♓48	Obliquity 23°26'34"
♇ R 4 10:31	☿ ♑ 2 11:19	12 14:23 ♃ □	♌ 13 7:36	12 9:10 ♃ ✶	♍ 12 16:28		⚷ Chiron 12♒18.8
☽0S 14 4:02	♀ ♒ 6 15:26	14 21:59 ☉ □	♍ 15 11:07	14 9:13 ♂ ✶	♎ 14 19:23	7 6:16 ○ 14♊53	☽ Mean ☊ 10♏36.9
☿ R 16 11:05	☉ ♑ 22 2:49	17 4:21 ☉ ✶	♎ 17 13:25	16 16:24 ♃ ☌	♏ 16 22:35	14 5:45 ☽ 21♍59	
☽0N 27 20:29	♂ ♐ 23 1:29	19 1:04 ♃ ☌	♏ 19 15:17	18 21:29 ♂ ☌	♐ 19 2:30	21 6:12 ● 29♐07	1 DECEMBER 1957
♄∠♆ 31 21:52	☿ ♐ 28 17:30	21 16:19 ☉ ☌	♐ 21 17:52	21 6:12 ☉ ☌	♑ 21 7:47	29 4:52 ☽ 7♈13	Julian Day # 21154
		23 8:42 ♃ ✶	♑ 23 22:29	23 10:25 ♃ □	♒ 23 15:19		Delta T 32.1 sec
		25 16:26 ♃ □	♒ 26 6:16	25 21:15 ♃ △	♓ 26 1:41		SVP 05♓50'41"
		28 5:52 ☿ ✶	♓ 28 17:16	27 15:46 ♄ □	♈ 28 14:13		Obliquity 23°26'34"
				30 23:33 ♃ ☍	♉ 31 2:37		⚷ Chiron 13♒08.2
							☽ Mean ☊ 9♏01.6

LONGITUDE — JANUARY 1958

Day	Sid.Time	☉	0 hr ☽	Noon ☽	True ☊	☿	♀	♂	♃	♄	♅	♆	♇
1 W	6 40 34	10♑ 4 19	10♉53 53	17♉ 6 56	8♏40.6	26♐46.8	15♒18.1	6♐11.7	28♎35.2	19♐26.4	10♌48.5	4♏25.9	2♍ 8.4
2 Th	6 44 30	11 5 27	23 25 1	29 48 33	8R 39.5	26R 8.4	15 33.4	6 53.5	28 42.8	19 33.2	10R 46.4	4 27.0	2R 7.6
3 F	6 48 27	12 6 36	6♊17 51	12♊53 8	8 36.0	25 40.5	15 46.6	7 35.2	28 50.2	19 39.9	10 44.2	4 28.1	2 6.7
4 Sa	6 52 23	13 7 44	19 34 27	26 21 45	8 30.0	25 22.7	15 57.5	8 17.0	28 57.5	19 46.6	10 42.0	4 29.2	2 5.9
5 Su	6 56 20	14 8 52	3♋14 49	10♋13 17	8 21.4	25D 14.7	16 6.2	8 58.9	29 4.7	19 53.3	10 39.8	4 30.3	2 5.0
6 M	7 0 16	15 10 0	17 16 36	24 24 10	8 10.9	25 16.0	16 12.5	9 40.7	29 11.7	20 0.0	10 37.5	4 31.3	2 4.1
7 Tu	7 4 13	16 11 8	1♌35 12	8♌48 52	7 59.7	25 25.7	16 16.4	10 22.6	29 18.6	20 6.6	10 35.2	4 32.3	2 3.1
8 W	7 8 9	17 12 16	16 4 19	23 20 40	7 48.8	25 43.4	16R 18.0	11 4.6	29 25.3	20 13.2	10 32.9	4 33.3	2 2.2
9 Th	7 12 6	18 13 23	0♍37 4	7♍52 46	7 39.6	26 8.2	16 17.0	11 46.6	29 31.9	20 19.8	10 30.6	4 34.2	2 1.2
10 F	7 16 3	19 14 31	15 7 4	22 19 24	7 32.8	26 39.4	16 13.6	12 28.6	29 38.4	20 26.3	10 28.2	4 35.1	2 0.2
11 Sa	7 19 59	20 15 39	29 29 21	6♎36 33	7 28.8	27 16.6	16 7.6	13 10.6	29 44.7	20 32.8	10 25.8	4 36.0	1 59.2
12 Su	7 23 56	21 16 46	13♎40 49	20 42 2	7D 27.2	27 58.9	15 59.2	13 52.7	29 50.8	20 39.3	10 23.4	4 36.8	1 58.1
13 M	7 27 52	22 17 54	27 40 9	4♏35 13	7R 27.1	28 46.0	15 48.2	14 34.8	29 56.8	20 45.7	10 20.9	4 37.6	1 57.0
14 Tu	7 31 49	23 19 2	11♏27 18	18 16 30	7 27.2	29 37.4	15 34.8	15 16.9	0♏ 2.7	20 52.1	10 18.5	4 38.4	1 55.9
15 W	7 35 45	24 20 9	25 2 54	1♐46 36	7 26.1	0♑32.5	15 18.9	15 59.1	0 8.4	20 58.4	10 16.0	4 39.1	1 54.8
16 Th	7 39 42	25 21 16	8♐27 39	15 6 7	7 22.8	1 31.0	15 0.6	16 41.3	0 13.9	21 4.7	10 13.5	4 39.8	1 53.7
17 F	7 43 38	26 22 23	21 42 0	28 15 15	7 16.4	2 32.6	14 39.9	17 23.6	0 19.3	21 11.0	10 11.0	4 40.5	1 52.5
18 Sa	7 47 35	27 23 30	4♑45 50	11♑13 40	7 7.0	3 36.9	14 17.0	18 5.8	0 24.5	21 17.2	10 8.4	4 41.1	1 51.3
19 Su	7 51 32	28 24 36	17 38 40	24 0 45	6 54.8	4 43.7	13 51.9	18 48.1	0 29.6	21 23.3	10 5.9	4 41.7	1 50.2
20 M	7 55 28	29 25 42	0♒19 49	6♒35 51	6 40.9	5 52.8	13 24.8	19 30.5	0 34.5	21 29.5	10 3.3	4 42.3	1 48.9
21 Tu	7 59 25	0♒26 47	12 48 49	18 58 44	6 26.4	7 3.9	12 55.8	20 12.8	0 39.2	21 35.5	10 0.8	4 42.9	1 47.7
22 W	8 3 21	1 27 51	25 5 42	1♓ 9 50	6 12.6	8 16.8	12 25.0	20 55.2	0 43.7	21 41.5	9 58.2	4 43.4	1 46.5
23 Th	8 7 18	2 28 55	7♓11 21	13 10 31	6 0.6	9 31.4	11 52.7	21 37.7	0 48.1	21 47.5	9 55.6	4 43.8	1 45.2
24 F	8 11 14	3 29 57	19 7 40	25 3 12	5 51.2	10 47.6	11 18.9	22 20.1	0 52.3	21 53.4	9 53.0	4 44.3	1 43.9
25 Sa	8 15 11	4 30 59	0♈57 34	6♈51 17	5 44.9	12 5.2	10 44.1	23 2.6	0 56.4	21 59.3	9 50.4	4 44.6	1 42.6
26 Su	8 19 7	5 31 59	12 44 55	18 39 5	5 41.3	13 24.2	10 8.2	23 45.1	1 0.2	22 5.1	9 47.8	4 45.0	1 41.3
27 M	8 23 4	6 32 59	24 34 25	0♉31 38	5 39.9	14 44.4	9 31.7	24 27.6	1 3.9	22 10.8	9 45.1	4 45.3	1 40.0
28 Tu	8 27 1	7 33 57	6♉31 23	12 34 25	5 39.7	16 5.8	8 54.8	25 10.2	1 7.5	22 16.5	9 42.5	4 45.6	1 38.6
29 W	8 30 57	8 34 54	18 41 24	24 53 2	5 39.5	17 28.2	8 17.6	25 52.8	1 10.8	22 22.2	9 39.9	4 45.9	1 37.3
30 Th	8 34 54	9 35 50	1♊ 9 58	7♊32 46	5 38.1	18 51.7	7 40.6	26 35.4	1 14.0	22 27.7	9 37.3	4 46.1	1 35.9
31 F	8 38 50	10 36 45	14 1 58	20 37 57	5 34.7	20 16.2	7 3.8	27 18.1	1 17.0	22 33.3	9 34.6	4 46.3	1 34.5

LONGITUDE — FEBRUARY 1958

Day	Sid.Time	☉	0 hr ☽	Noon ☽	True ☊	☿	♀	♂	♃	♄	♅	♆	♇
1 Sa	8 42 47	11♒37 38	27♊21 0	4♋11 13	5♏28.5	21♑41.6	6♒27.7	28♐ 0.8	1♏19.8	22♐38.7	9♌32.0	4♏46.5	1♍33.1
2 Su	8 46 43	12 38 30	11♋ 8 33	18 12 45	5R 19.7	23 8.0	5R 52.4	28 43.5	1 22.4	22 44.1	9R 29.4	4 46.6	1R 31.7
3 M	8 50 40	13 39 21	25 23 21	2♌39 41	5 8.8	24 35.3	5 18.1	29 26.2	1 24.9	22 49.5	9 26.8	4 46.7	1 30.3
4 Tu	8 54 37	14 40 11	10♌ 0 55	17 26 2	4 56.9	26 3.4	4 45.2	0♑ 9.0	1 27.1	22 54.7	9 24.2	4 46.8	1 28.9
5 W	8 58 33	15 40 59	24 53 54	2♍23 21	4 45.3	27 32.3	4 13.7	0 51.8	1 29.2	22 59.9	9 21.6	4R 46.8	1 27.4
6 Th	9 2 30	16 41 47	9♍53 8	17 22 7	4 35.2	29 2.1	3 44.0	1 34.7	1 31.1	23 5.1	9 19.0	4 46.8	1 26.0
7 F	9 6 26	17 42 33	24 49 12	2♎13 28	4 27.7	0♒32.8	3 16.1	2 17.5	1 32.8	23 10.2	9 16.4	4 46.7	1 24.5
8 Sa	9 10 23	18 43 18	9♎34 6	16 50 31	4 23.1	2 4.2	2 50.3	3 0.4	1 34.4	23 15.2	9 13.8	4 46.6	1 23.0
9 Su	9 14 19	19 44 2	24 2 16	1♏ 9 4	4D 21.1	3 36.5	2 26.6	3 43.4	1 35.7	23 20.1	9 11.2	4 46.5	1 21.6
10 M	9 18 16	20 44 46	8♏10 49	15 7 32	4R 20.8	5 9.6	2 5.1	4 26.3	1 36.9	23 25.0	9 8.6	4 46.4	1 20.1
11 Tu	9 22 12	21 45 28	21 59 17	28 46 18	4 21.0	6 43.5	1 46.0	5 9.3	1 37.9	23 29.8	9 6.1	4 46.2	1 18.6
12 W	9 26 9	22 46 9	5♐28 48	12♐ 7 3	4 20.4	8 18.3	1 29.3	5 52.4	1 38.6	23 34.5	9 3.5	4 46.0	1 17.1
13 Th	9 30 5	23 46 49	18 41 20	25 11 56	4 17.8	9 53.9	1 15.1	6 35.4	1 39.2	23 39.2	9 1.0	4 45.7	1 15.6
14 F	9 34 2	24 47 28	1♑39 6	8♑ 3 4	4 12.5	11 30.3	1 3.3	7 18.5	1 39.6	23 43.8	8 58.5	4 45.5	1 14.1
15 Sa	9 37 59	25 48 6	14 24 3	20 42 14	4 4.5	13 7.6	0 54.1	8 1.6	1R 39.9	23 48.3	8 56.0	4 45.1	1 12.6
16 Su	9 41 55	26 48 43	26 57 45	3♒10 45	3 53.9	14 45.8	0 47.3	8 44.8	1 39.9	23 52.7	8 53.6	4 44.8	1 11.1
17 M	9 45 52	27 49 18	9♒21 20	15 29 34	3 41.6	16 24.8	0 43.0	9 28.0	1 39.7	23 57.1	8 51.1	4 44.4	1 9.6
18 Tu	9 49 48	28 49 52	21 35 35	27 39 27	3 28.8	18 4.7	0D 41.1	10 11.2	1 39.4	24 1.4	8 48.7	4 44.0	1 8.1
19 W	9 53 45	29 50 24	3♓41 18	9♓41 14	3 16.5	19 45.5	0 41.7	10 54.4	1 38.8	24 5.6	8 46.3	4 43.6	1 6.6
20 Th	9 57 41	0♓50 54	15 39 26	21 36 5	3 5.8	21 27.3	0 44.6	11 37.6	1 38.1	24 9.7	8 43.9	4 43.1	1 5.0
21 F	10 1 38	1 51 23	27 31 26	3♈25 45	2 57.5	23 9.9	0 49.9	12 20.9	1 37.1	24 13.8	8 41.5	4 42.6	1 3.5
22 Sa	10 5 34	2 51 51	9♈19 24	15 12 44	2 51.8	24 53.5	0 57.5	13 4.2	1 36.0	24 17.7	8 39.2	4 42.0	1 2.0
23 Su	10 9 31	3 52 16	21 6 12	27 0 16	2 48.8	26 38.1	1 7.3	13 47.5	1 34.7	24 21.6	8 36.9	4 41.4	1 0.5
24 M	10 13 28	4 52 40	2♉55 29	8♉52 23	2D 48.0	28 23.6	1 19.3	14 30.9	1 33.2	24 25.4	8 34.6	4 40.8	0 59.0
25 Tu	10 17 24	5 53 1	14 51 36	20 53 45	2 48.6	0♓10.1	1 33.4	15 14.3	1 31.5	24 29.1	8 32.3	4 40.2	0 57.4
26 W	10 21 21	6 53 21	26 59 30	3♊ 9 30	2R 49.5	1 57.6	1 49.5	15 57.7	1 29.7	24 32.8	8 30.1	4 39.5	0 55.9
27 Th	10 25 17	7 53 39	9♊24 24	15 44 50	2 49.9	3 46.1	2 7.6	16 41.1	1 27.6	24 36.3	8 27.9	4 38.8	0 54.4
28 F	10 29 14	8 53 55	22 11 22	28 44 32	2 48.9	5 35.6	2 27.6	17 24.5	1 25.4	24 39.8	8 25.7	4 38.1	0 52.9

Astro Data	Planet Ingress	Last Aspect	☽ Ingress	Last Aspect	☽ Ingress	☽ Phases & Eclipses	Astro Data
Dy Hr Mn	Dy Hr Mn	Dy Hr Mn	Dy Hr Mn	Dy Hr Mn	Dy Hr Mn	Dy Hr Mn	1 JANUARY 1958
☿ D 5 8:39	♃ ♏ 13 12:52	1 8:42 ♀ □	♊ 2 12:21	1 1:14 ♂ ☍	♋ 1 4:41	5 20:09 ○ 15♋00	Julian Day # 21185
♀ R 8 2:47	☿ ♑ 14 10:03	4 16:41 ♃ △	♋ 4 18:22	2 22:31 ☿ ☍	♌ 3 7:38	12 14:01 ☽ 21♎52	Delta T 32.2 sec
☽0S 10 10:46	☉ ♒ 20 13:28	6 20:11 ♃ □	♌ 6 21:21	4 20:56 ♄ △	♍ 5 8:11	19 22:08 ● 29♑21	SVP 05♓50'36"
☽0N 24 5:39		8 22:12 ♃ ⚹	♍ 8 22:59	6 21:19 ♄ □	♎ 7 8:23	28 2:16 ☽ 7♉40	Obliquity 23°26'33"
	♂ ♑ 3 18:57	10 20:06 ☿ □	♎ 11 0:52	8 22:49 ♄ ⚹	♏ 9 10:03		⚷ Chiron 14♒50.5
♃⚹♇ 4 11:29	☿ ♒ 6 15:21	13 3:58 ♃ ☌	♏ 13 4:02	10 23:34 ☉ □	♐ 11 14:11	4 8:05 ○ 15♌01	☽ Mean ☊ 7♏23.1
♆ R 5 3:15	☉ ♓ 19 3:48	14 22:38 ☉ ⚹	♐ 15 8:49	13 10:10 ☉ ⚹	♑ 13 20:55	10 23:34 ☽ 21♏44	
☽0S 6 19:41	☿ ♓ 24 21:44	16 23:03 ♄ ☌	♑ 17 15:13	14 11:14 ♂ ☌	♒ 16 5:51	18 15:38 ● 29♒29	1 FEBRUARY 1958
♃ R 15 14:58		19 22:08 ☉ ☌	♒ 19 23:22	18 15:38 ☉ ☌	♓ 18 16:39	26 20:52 ☽ 7♊46	Julian Day # 21216
♄⚼♅ 16 2:53		21 17:15 ♄ ⚹	♓ 22 9:41	20 17:17 ♄ □	♈ 21 5:02		Delta T 32.2 sec
♀ D 18 6:17		24 6:54 ♂ □	♈ 24 22:03	23 13:13 ☿ ⚹	♉ 23 18:05		SVP 05♓50'31"
☽0N 20 13:29		26 23:45 ♂ △	♉ 27 10:56	25 0:48 ♂ △	♊ 26 5:52		Obliquity 23°26'33"
		28 21:19 ☿ △	♊ 29 21:47	28 4:34 ♄ ☍	♋ 28 14:17		⚷ Chiron 17♒03.1
							☽ Mean ☊ 5♏44.6

MARCH 1958 LONGITUDE

Day	Sid.Time	☉	0 hr ☽	Noon ☽	True ☊	☿	♀	♂	♃	♄	♅	♆	♇
1 Sa	10 33 10	9♓54 9	5♋24 46	12♋12 20	2♏45.9	7♓26.0	2♒49.5	18♑ 8.0	1♏23.0	24♐43.2	8♌23.6	4♏37.4	0♍51.4
2 Su	10 37 7	10 54 21	19 7 25	26 9 58	2R40.8	9 17.5	3 13.2	18 51.5	1R20.4	24 46.4	8R21.5	4R36.6	0R49.9
3 M	10 41 3	11 54 30	3♌19 47	10♌36 24	2 34.0	11 9.8	3 38.7	19 35.0	1 17.6	24 49.7	8 19.4	4 35.8	0 48.5
4 Tu	10 45 0	12 54 38	17 59 11	25 27 14	2 26.2	13 3.1	4 5.8	20 18.5	1 14.6	24 52.8	8 17.4	4 34.9	0 47.0
5 W	10 48 57	13 54 44	2♍59 31	10♍34 50	2 18.4	14 57.3	4 34.5	21 2.1	1 11.5	24 55.8	8 15.4	4 34.1	0 45.5
6 Th	10 52 53	14 54 47	18 11 52	25 49 17	2 11.6	16 52.3	5 4.8	21 45.7	1 8.2	24 58.7	8 13.5	4 33.2	0 44.0
7 F	10 56 50	15 54 49	3♎25 44	10♎59 59	2 6.7	18 48.1	5 36.5	22 29.3	1 4.7	25 1.6	8 11.5	4 32.2	0 42.6
8 Sa	11 0 46	16 54 50	18 30 55	25 57 33	2D 3.9	20 44.5	6 9.8	23 13.0	1 1.0	25 4.3	8 9.6	4 31.3	0 41.1
9 Su	11 4 43	17 54 48	3♏19 8	10♏35 3	2 3.2	22 41.5	6 44.4	23 56.6	0 57.2	25 7.0	8 7.8	4 30.3	0 39.7
10 M	11 8 39	18 54 45	17 44 57	24 48 35	2 3.9	24 38.8	7 20.4	24 40.3	0 53.2	25 9.6	8 6.0	4 29.3	0 38.2
11 Tu	11 12 36	19 54 40	1♐45 54	8♐36 59	2 5.2	26 36.5	7 57.6	25 24.1	0 49.1	25 12.0	8 4.2	4 28.3	0 36.8
12 W	11 16 32	20 54 34	15 22 2	22 1 19	2R 6.3	28 34.2	8 36.1	26 7.8	0 44.7	25 14.4	8 2.5	4 27.2	0 35.4
13 Th	11 20 29	21 54 26	28 35 10	5♑ 3 58	2 6.2	0♈31.7	9 15.7	26 51.6	0 40.2	25 16.7	8 0.8	4 26.1	0 34.0
14 F	11 24 26	22 54 16	11♑28 6	17 47 58	2 4.5	2 28.8	9 56.5	27 35.4	0 35.6	25 18.9	7 59.2	4 25.0	0 32.6
15 Sa	11 28 22	23 54 5	24 3 59	0♒16 32	2 1.0	4 25.1	10 38.4	28 19.2	0 30.8	25 21.0	7 57.6	4 23.9	0 31.2
16 Su	11 32 19	24 53 52	6♒25 59	12 32 41	1 55.9	6 20.3	11 21.3	29 3.0	0 25.8	25 23.0	7 56.0	4 22.8	0 29.9
17 M	11 36 15	25 53 37	18 36 57	24 39 5	1 49.6	8 14.1	12 5.2	29 46.9	0 20.7	25 24.9	7 54.5	4 21.6	0 28.5
18 Tu	11 40 12	26 53 20	0♓39 21	6♓38 0	1 42.9	10 6.1	12 50.1	0♒30.8	0 15.5	25 26.7	7 53.0	4 20.4	0 27.2
19 W	11 44 8	27 53 2	12 35 17	18 31 26	1 36.5	11 55.8	13 35.9	1 14.6	0 10.1	25 28.5	7 51.6	4 19.2	0 25.9
20 Th	11 48 5	28 52 41	24 26 40	0♈21 12	1 31.0	13 42.7	14 22.6	1 58.6	0 4.5	25 30.1	7 50.2	4 17.9	0 24.6
21 F	11 52 1	29 52 19	6♈15 17	12 9 10	1 26.9	15 26.5	15 10.1	2 42.5	29♎58.9	25 31.6	7 48.9	4 16.6	0 23.3
22 Sa	11 55 58	0♈51 54	18 3 6	23 57 22	1 24.4	17 6.7	15 58.4	3 26.4	29 53.0	25 33.0	7 47.6	4 15.4	0 22.0
23 Su	11 59 54	1 51 27	29 52 19	5♉48 15	1D 23.5	18 42.8	16 47.5	4 10.4	29 47.1	25 34.3	7 46.4	4 14.1	0 20.7
24 M	12 3 51	2 50 58	11♉45 34	17 44 41	1 23.9	20 14.3	17 37.3	4 54.3	29 41.0	25 35.5	7 45.2	4 12.7	0 19.5
25 Tu	12 7 48	3 50 27	23 46 1	29 50 3	1 25.3	21 40.9	18 27.9	5 38.3	29 34.9	25 36.7	7 44.0	4 11.4	0 18.3
26 W	12 11 44	4 49 54	5♊57 17	12♊ 8 14	1 27.0	23 2.2	19 19.1	6 22.3	29 28.6	25 37.7	7 42.9	4 10.0	0 17.1
27 Th	12 15 41	5 49 19	18 23 23	24 43 18	1 28.6	24 17.8	20 11.0	7 6.3	29 22.1	25 38.6	7 41.9	4 8.6	0 15.9
28 F	12 19 37	6 48 41	1♋ 8 27	7♋39 20	1R 29.6	25 27.3	21 3.5	7 50.4	29 15.6	25 39.5	7 40.9	4 7.3	0 14.7
29 Sa	12 23 34	7 48 1	14 16 21	20 59 51	1 29.5	26 30.6	21 56.7	8 34.4	29 9.0	25 40.2	7 40.0	4 5.8	0 13.6
30 Su	12 27 30	8 47 19	27 50 6	4♌47 12	1 28.4	27 27.3	22 50.4	9 18.4	29 2.3	25 40.8	7 39.1	4 4.4	0 12.4
31 M	12 31 27	9 46 34	11♌51 10	19 1 48	1 26.4	28 17.2	23 44.7	10 2.5	28 55.4	25 41.3	7 38.3	4 3.0	0 11.3

APRIL 1958 LONGITUDE

Day	Sid.Time	☉	0 hr ☽	Noon ☽	True ☊	☿	♀	♂	♃	♄	♅	♆	♇
1 Tu	12 35 23	10♈45 47	26♌18 44	3♍41 26	1♏23.8	29♈ 0.3	24♒39.6	10♒46.6	28♎48.5	25♐41.8	7♌37.5	4♏ 1.5	0♍10.2
2 W	12 39 20	11 44 57	11♍ 9 8	18 40 56	1R21.1	29 36.2	25 35.0	11 30.7	28R41.5	25 42.1	7R36.7	4R 0.0	0R 9.2
3 Th	12 43 17	12 44 6	26 15 46	3♎52 28	1 18.8	0♉ 5.1	26 30.9	12 14.8	28 34.5	25 42.3	7 36.0	3 58.5	0 8.1
4 F	12 47 13	13 43 12	11♎29 45	19 6 22	1 17.2	0 26.8	27 27.3	12 58.9	28 27.3	25R42.4	7 35.4	3 57.0	0 7.1
5 Sa	12 51 10	14 42 16	26 41 6	4♏12 46	1D 16.5	0 41.4	28 24.2	13 43.0	28 20.1	25 42.5	7 34.8	3 55.5	0 6.1
6 Su	12 55 6	15 41 18	11♏40 21	19 2 57	1 16.7	0R49.0	29 21.5	14 27.1	28 12.8	25 42.4	7 34.3	3 54.0	0 5.1
7 M	12 59 3	16 40 19	26 19 52	3♐30 34	1 17.4	0 49.6	0♓19.3	15 11.3	28 5.4	25 42.2	7 33.8	3 52.5	0 4.1
8 Tu	13 2 59	17 39 18	10♐34 42	17 32 5	1 18.5	0 43.7	1 17.6	15 55.5	27 58.0	25 42.0	7 33.4	3 50.9	0 3.2
9 W	13 6 56	18 38 14	24 22 40	1♑ 6 36	1 19.6	0 31.4	2 16.2	16 39.6	27 50.6	25 41.6	7 33.1	3 49.4	0 2.3
10 Th	13 10 52	19 37 10	7♑44 5	14 15 27	1 20.3	0 13.1	3 15.3	17 23.8	27 43.1	25 41.2	7 32.7	3 47.8	0 1.4
11 F	13 14 49	20 36 3	20 41 4	27 1 24	1R20.6	29♈49.3	4 14.7	18 8.0	27 35.5	25 40.6	7 32.5	3 46.2	0 0.5
12 Sa	13 18 46	21 34 55	3♒16 55	9♒28 8	1 20.3	29 20.6	5 14.5	18 52.2	27 27.9	25 39.9	7 32.3	3 44.6	29♌59.7
13 Su	13 22 42	22 33 45	15 35 32	21 39 38	1 19.7	28 47.5	6 14.7	19 36.4	27 20.3	25 39.2	7 32.1	3 43.0	29 58.9
14 M	13 26 39	23 32 33	27 40 56	3♓39 55	1 18.8	28 10.8	7 15.2	20 20.7	27 12.7	25 38.3	7 32.0	3 41.4	29 58.1
15 Tu	13 30 35	24 31 19	9♓37 2	15 32 43	1 17.8	27 31.2	8 16.0	21 4.9	27 5.0	25 37.4	7D 32.0	3 39.8	29 57.3
16 W	13 34 32	25 30 4	21 27 23	27 21 25	1 16.9	26 49.4	9 17.2	21 49.1	26 57.3	25 36.3	7 32.0	3 38.2	29 56.6
17 Th	13 38 28	26 28 46	3♈15 10	9♈ 8 57	1 16.2	26 6.4	10 18.7	22 33.3	26 49.6	25 35.2	7 32.0	3 36.6	29 55.8
18 F	13 42 25	27 27 27	15 3 7	20 57 55	1 15.8	25 23.0	11 20.4	23 17.5	26 41.9	25 34.0	7 32.2	3 35.0	29 55.2
19 Sa	13 46 21	28 26 6	26 53 40	2♉50 36	1D 15.7	24 39.8	12 22.5	24 1.8	26 34.2	25 32.6	7 32.3	3 33.3	29 54.5
20 Su	13 50 18	29 24 43	8♉48 59	14 49 5	1 15.7	23 57.8	13 24.8	24 46.0	26 26.6	25 31.2	7 32.6	3 31.7	29 53.8
21 M	13 54 14	0♉23 19	20 51 9	26 55 27	1R 15.8	23 17.6	14 27.4	25 30.2	26 18.9	25 29.7	7 32.8	3 30.1	29 53.2
22 Tu	13 58 11	1 21 52	3♊ 2 14	9♊11 47	1 15.8	22 39.9	15 30.2	26 14.4	26 11.3	25 28.1	7 33.2	3 28.4	29 52.7
23 W	14 2 8	2 20 23	15 24 23	21 40 19	1 15.7	22 5.3	16 33.3	26 58.6	26 3.6	25 26.4	7 33.6	3 26.8	29 52.1
24 Th	14 6 4	3 18 52	27 59 55	4♋23 27	1 15.5	21 34.2	17 36.7	27 42.8	25 56.0	25 24.6	7 34.0	3 25.2	29 51.6
25 F	14 10 1	4 17 19	10♋51 15	17 23 34	1 15.3	21 7.1	18 40.2	28 27.0	25 48.5	25 22.7	7 34.5	3 23.5	29 51.1
26 Sa	14 13 57	5 15 44	24 0 42	0♌42 53	1D 15.1	20 44.3	19 44.0	29 11.2	25 41.0	25 20.7	7 35.1	3 21.9	29 50.6
27 Su	14 17 54	6 14 7	7♌30 18	14 23 5	1 15.0	20 26.0	20 48.0	29 55.4	25 33.5	25 18.7	7 35.7	3 20.3	29 50.2
28 M	14 21 50	7 12 27	21 21 17	28 24 52	1 15.2	20 12.5	21 52.2	0♓39.5	25 26.1	25 16.5	7 36.3	3 18.6	29 49.7
29 Tu	14 25 47	8 10 46	5♍33 39	12♍47 22	1 15.6	20 3.8	22 56.6	1 23.7	25 18.7	25 14.3	7 37.0	3 17.0	29 49.4
30 W	14 29 43	9 9 2	20 5 37	27 27 51	1 16.2	19D 59.9	24 1.3	2 7.9	25 11.4	25 12.0	7 37.8	3 15.4	29 49.0

Astro Data

	Dy Hr Mn
☽0S	6 6:34
☿0N	13 9:18
♃✶♇	14 20:56
☽0N	19 19:50
☽0S	2 17:45
♄ R	4 19:38
☿ R	6 14:24
♅ D	15 8:27
☽0N	16 1:40
♃✶♄	29 21:05
☽0S	30 3:33
☿ D	30 6:57

Planet Ingress

	Dy Hr Mn
☿ ♈	12 17:31
♂ ♒	17 7:11
♃ ♎	20 19:14
☉ ♈	21 3:06
☿ ♉	2 19:17
♀ ♓	6 16:00
☿ ♈	10 13:51
♇ ♌	11 14:52
☉ ♉	20 14:27
♂ ♓	27 2:31

Last Aspect / ☽ Ingress (March)

Last Aspect Dy Hr Mn	☽ Ingress Dy Hr Mn
1 23:31 ♂ ☍	♌ 2 18:27
4 11:07 ♄ △	♍ 4 19:15
6 10:42 ♄ □	♎ 6 18:35
8 10:36 ♄ ✶	♏ 8 18:34
10 13:38 ☿ △	♐ 10 20:56
12 17:55 ♄ ☌	♑ 13 2:36
15 8:43 ♂ ☌	♒ 15 11:28
17 13:33 ♄ ✶	♓ 17 22:41
20 9:50 ☉ ☌	♈ 20 11:17
22 23:50 ♃ ☍	♉ 23 0:16
24 12:38 ♀ □	♊ 25 12:20
27 20:32 ♃ △	♋ 27 21:53
30 2:04 ♃ □	♌ 30 3:46

Last Aspect / ☽ Ingress (April)

Last Aspect Dy Hr Mn	☽ Ingress Dy Hr Mn
1 4:36 ☿ △	♍ 1 6:01
2 23:07 ♄ □	♎ 3 5:54
5 2:55 ♀ △	♏ 5 5:16
6 4:45 ♂ □	♐ 7 6:07
9 6:06 ♃ ✶	♑ 9 10:00
11 16:43 ☿ □	♒ 11 17:41
14 4:34 ♇ ☍	♓ 14 4:38
16 8:25 ♄ □	♈ 16 17:23
19 6:05 ♇ △	♉ 19 6:16
21 17:49 ♇ □	♊ 21 18:03
24 3:30 ♇ ✶	♋ 24 3:46
26 2:59 ♃ □	♌ 26 10:44
28 14:23 ♇ ☌	♍ 28 14:40
30 8:18 ♄ □	♎ 30 16:06

☽ Phases & Eclipses

Dy Hr Mn	
5 18:28	○ 14♍41
12 10:48	☽ 21♐21
20 9:50	● 29♓17
28 11:18	☽ 7♋17
4 3:45	○ 13♎52
4 3:60	☍ A 0.013
10 23:50	☽ 20♑36
19 3:23	● 28♈34
19 3:26:44	☌ A 7'07"
26 21:36	☽ 6♌08

Astro Data

1 MARCH 1958
Julian Day # 21244
Delta T 32.3 sec
SVP 05♓50'28"
Obliquity 23°26'34"
⚷ Chiron 19♒07.3
☽ Mean ☊ 4♏15.6

1 APRIL 1958
Julian Day # 21275
Delta T 32.3 sec
SVP 05♓50'25"
Obliquity 23°26'34"
⚷ Chiron 21♒05.7
☽ Mean ☊ 2♏37.1

LONGITUDE — MAY 1958

Day	Sid.Time	☉	0 hr ☽	Noon ☽	True ☊	☿	♀	♂	♃	♄	♅	♆	♇
1 Th	14 33 40	10♉ 7 16	4♎53 23	12♎21 25	1♏16.9	20♈ 0.9	25♓ 6.1	2♓52.0	25♎ 4.2	25♐ 9.6	7♌38.6	3♏13.7	29♌48.7
2 F	14 37 37	11 5 29	19 51 1	27 21 13	1R17.4	20 6.8	26 11.1	3 36.1	24R57.0	25R 7.1	7 39.5	3R12.1	29R48.4
3 Sa	14 41 33	12 3 39	4♏50 59	12♏19 14	1 17.5	20 17.4	27 16.3	4 20.3	24 49.9	25 4.6	7 40.4	3 10.5	29 48.1
4 Su	14 45 30	13 1 48	19 44 57	27 7 11	1 17.1	20 32.7	28 21.6	5 4.4	24 42.9	25 1.9	7 41.4	3 8.9	29 47.8
5 M	14 49 26	13 59 55	4♐25 3	11♐37 47	1 16.1	20 52.5	29 27.2	5 48.5	24 36.0	24 59.2	7 42.4	3 7.3	29 47.6
6 Tu	14 53 23	14 58 1	18 44 49	25 45 40	1 14.5	21 16.8	0♈32.9	6 32.6	24 29.1	24 56.4	7 43.5	3 5.7	29 47.4
7 W	14 57 19	15 56 5	2♑40 2	9♑27 49	1 12.7	21 45.3	1 38.8	7 16.7	24 22.4	24 53.6	7 44.6	3 4.1	29 47.3
8 Th	15 1 16	16 54 8	16 9 0	22 43 44	1 10.9	22 18.0	2 44.9	8 0.7	24 15.7	24 50.6	7 45.8	3 2.5	29 47.2
9 F	15 5 12	17 52 9	29 12 15	5♒34 56	1 9.4	22 54.6	3 51.1	8 44.8	24 9.2	24 47.6	7 47.0	3 0.9	29 47.1
10 Sa	15 9 9	18 50 9	11♒52 12	18 4 33	1D 8.5	23 35.1	4 57.5	9 28.8	24 2.7	24 44.5	7 48.3	2 59.4	29 47.0
11 Su	15 13 6	19 48 7	24 12 32	0♓16 42	1 8.4	24 19.3	6 4.0	10 12.9	23 56.4	24 41.4	7 49.6	2 57.8	29D47.0
12 M	15 17 2	20 46 5	6♓17 39	12 16 0	1 9.1	25 7.0	7 10.7	10 56.9	23 50.2	24 38.1	7 51.0	2 56.3	29 46.9
13 Tu	15 20 59	21 44 1	18 12 18	24 7 10	1 10.4	25 58.2	8 17.5	11 40.8	23 44.1	24 34.8	7 52.4	2 54.7	29 47.0
14 W	15 24 55	22 41 55	0♈ 1 8	5♈54 45	1 12.0	26 52.7	9 24.4	12 24.8	23 38.1	24 31.5	7 53.9	2 53.2	29 47.0
15 Th	15 28 52	23 39 49	11 48 31	17 42 55	1 13.6	27 50.4	10 31.5	13 8.7	23 32.2	24 28.1	7 55.4	2 51.7	29 47.1
16 F	15 32 48	24 37 41	23 38 23	29 35 18	1R14.6	28 51.1	11 38.7	13 52.6	23 26.5	24 24.6	7 57.0	2 50.2	29 47.2
17 Sa	15 36 45	25 35 31	5♉34 3	11♉34 56	1 14.7	29 54.9	12 46.0	14 36.5	23 20.9	24 21.0	7 58.6	2 48.7	29 47.3
18 Su	15 40 41	26 33 21	17 38 14	23 44 10	1 13.7	1♉ 1.5	13 53.4	15 20.3	23 15.4	24 17.4	8 0.3	2 47.2	29 47.5
19 M	15 44 38	27 31 9	29 52 58	6♊ 4 46	1 11.4	2 11.0	15 1.0	16 4.1	23 10.1	24 13.8	8 2.0	2 45.8	29 47.7
20 Tu	15 48 35	28 28 55	12♊19 43	18 37 54	1 7.9	3 23.2	16 8.6	16 47.9	23 4.9	24 10.0	8 3.8	2 44.3	29 47.9
21 W	15 52 31	29 26 41	24 59 24	1♋24 16	1 3.6	4 38.1	17 16.4	17 31.6	22 59.8	24 6.3	8 5.6	2 42.9	29 48.2
22 Th	15 56 28	0♊24 25	7♋52 34	14 24 18	0 58.9	5 55.6	18 24.3	18 15.3	22 54.9	24 2.4	8 7.5	2 41.5	29 48.5
23 F	16 0 24	1 22 7	20 59 31	27 38 14	0 54.5	7 15.7	19 32.3	18 59.0	22 50.2	23 58.6	8 9.4	2 40.1	29 48.8
24 Sa	16 4 21	2 19 48	4♌20 27	11♌ 6 11	0 50.9	8 38.4	20 40.3	19 42.6	22 45.6	23 54.6	8 11.3	2 38.7	29 49.1
25 Su	16 8 17	3 17 27	17 55 27	24 48 15	0 48.5	10 3.5	21 48.5	20 26.2	22 41.2	23 50.7	8 13.3	2 37.4	29 49.5
26 M	16 12 14	4 15 5	1♍44 31	8♍44 14	0D47.6	11 31.1	22 56.8	21 9.7	22 36.9	23 46.7	8 15.4	2 36.0	29 49.9
27 Tu	16 16 10	5 12 41	15 47 18	22 53 44	0 47.9	13 1.2	24 5.1	21 53.2	22 32.8	23 42.6	8 17.5	2 34.7	29 50.3
28 W	16 20 7	6 10 16	0♎ 2 51	7♎14 51	0 49.1	14 33.7	25 13.5	22 36.7	22 28.8	23 38.5	8 19.6	2 33.4	29 50.8
29 Th	16 24 4	7 7 49	14 29 14	21 45 33	0 50.5	16 8.6	26 22.1	23 20.1	22 25.0	23 34.4	8 21.8	2 32.1	29 51.3
30 F	16 28 0	8 5 21	29 3 17	6♏21 49	0R51.2	17 46.0	27 30.7	24 3.5	22 21.4	23 30.3	8 24.0	2 30.8	29 51.8
31 Sa	16 31 57	9 2 51	13♏40 28	20 58 29	0 50.6	19 25.8	28 39.4	24 46.8	22 17.9	23 26.1	8 26.2	2 29.6	29 52.3

LONGITUDE — JUNE 1958

Day	Sid.Time	☉	0 hr ☽	Noon ☽	True ☊	☿	♀	♂	♃	♄	♅	♆	♇
1 Su	16 35 53	10♊ 0 21	28♏15 5	5♐29 29	0♏48.3	21♉ 7.9	29♈48.2	25♓30.0	22♎14.7	23♐21.8	8♌28.5	2♏28.4	29♌52.9
2 M	16 39 50	10 57 49	12♐40 54	19 48 36	0R44.1	22 52.5	0♉57.1	26 13.3	22R11.5	23R17.6	8 30.9	2R27.2	29 53.5
3 Tu	16 43 46	11 55 16	26 51 54	3♑50 16	0 38.4	24 39.5	2 6.0	26 56.4	22 8.6	23 13.3	8 33.3	2 26.0	29 54.1
4 W	16 47 43	12 52 43	10♑43 13	17 30 28	0 31.8	26 28.8	3 15.1	27 39.6	22 5.8	23 9.0	8 35.7	2 24.8	29 54.8
5 Th	16 51 39	13 50 8	24 11 48	0♒47 10	0 25.0	28 20.5	4 24.2	28 22.7	22 3.2	23 4.7	8 38.1	2 23.7	29 55.5
6 F	16 55 36	14 47 33	7♒16 38	13 40 26	0 19.0	0♊14.5	5 33.4	29 5.7	22 0.8	23 0.3	8 40.6	2 22.6	29 56.2
7 Sa	16 59 33	15 44 57	19 58 49	26 12 13	0 14.2	2 10.7	6 42.7	29 48.6	21 58.5	22 56.0	8 43.2	2 21.5	29 56.9
8 Su	17 3 29	16 42 21	2♓21 5	8♓25 59	0 11.2	4 9.1	7 52.1	0♈31.6	21 56.4	22 51.6	8 45.7	2 20.4	29 57.7
9 M	17 7 26	17 39 44	14 27 27	20 26 9	0D10.0	6 9.7	9 1.5	1 14.4	21 54.5	22 47.2	8 48.3	2 19.4	29 58.5
10 Tu	17 11 22	18 37 6	26 22 42	2♈17 46	0 10.2	8 12.2	10 11.0	1 57.2	21 52.8	22 42.8	8 51.0	2 18.3	29 59.3
11 W	17 15 19	19 34 28	8♈11 59	14 6 2	0 11.3	10 16.7	11 20.6	2 39.9	21 51.2	22 38.4	8 53.7	2 17.3	0♍ 0.2
12 Th	17 19 15	20 31 49	20 0 30	25 56 1	0R12.5	12 22.8	12 30.3	3 22.6	21 49.9	22 34.0	8 56.4	2 16.4	0 1.1
13 F	17 23 12	21 29 10	1♉53 8	7♉52 23	0 13.0	14 30.5	13 40.0	4 5.1	21 48.7	22 29.5	8 59.1	2 15.4	0 2.0
14 Sa	17 27 8	22 26 30	13 54 16	19 59 11	0 11.9	16 39.5	14 49.8	4 47.7	21 47.7	22 25.1	9 1.9	2 14.5	0 2.9
15 Su	17 31 5	23 23 50	26 7 29	2♊19 30	0 8.8	18 49.6	15 59.6	5 30.1	21 46.8	22 20.7	9 4.7	2 13.6	0 3.8
16 M	17 35 2	24 21 9	8♊35 24	14 55 23	0 3.4	21 0.5	17 9.6	6 12.4	21 46.2	22 16.2	9 7.6	2 12.7	0 4.8
17 Tu	17 38 58	25 18 28	21 19 29	27 47 42	29♎56.0	23 12.0	18 19.5	6 54.7	21 45.7	22 11.8	9 10.5	2 11.9	0 5.8
18 W	17 42 55	26 15 46	4♋19 57	10♋56 6	29 47.0	25 23.8	19 29.6	7 36.9	21 45.4	22 7.4	9 13.4	2 11.1	0 6.9
19 Th	17 46 51	27 13 4	17 35 57	24 19 16	29 37.3	27 35.7	20 39.7	8 19.0	21D45.3	22 3.0	9 16.4	2 10.3	0 7.9
20 F	17 50 48	28 10 21	1♌ 5 45	7♌55 8	29 28.0	29 47.2	21 49.9	9 1.0	21 45.4	21 58.6	9 19.4	2 9.6	0 9.0
21 Sa	17 54 44	29 7 38	14 47 6	21 41 23	29 20.0	1♋58.3	23 0.1	9 43.0	21 45.7	21 54.2	9 22.4	2 8.8	0 10.1
22 Su	17 58 41	0♋ 4 54	28 37 42	5♍35 49	29 14.0	4 8.6	24 10.4	10 24.8	21 46.1	21 49.8	9 25.4	2 8.1	0 11.3
23 M	18 2 37	1 2 9	12♍35 30	19 36 36	29 10.5	6 17.9	25 20.7	11 6.5	21 46.7	21 45.5	9 28.5	2 7.5	0 12.4
24 Tu	18 6 34	1 59 23	26 38 56	3♎42 21	29D 9.1	8 26.0	26 31.1	11 48.2	21 47.5	21 41.2	9 31.6	2 6.8	0 13.6
25 W	18 10 31	2 56 37	10♎46 44	17 51 56	29 9.1	10 32.7	27 41.5	12 29.7	21 48.5	21 36.9	9 34.7	2 6.2	0 14.8
26 Th	18 14 27	3 53 50	24 57 48	2♏ 4 8	29R 9.6	12 37.9	28 52.0	13 11.2	21 49.6	21 32.6	9 37.9	2 5.6	0 16.0
27 F	18 18 24	4 51 2	9♏10 42	16 17 12	29 9.3	14 41.4	0♊ 2.5	13 52.5	21 51.0	21 28.3	9 41.1	2 5.1	0 17.3
28 Sa	18 22 20	5 48 15	23 23 18	0♐28 37	29 7.2	16 43.2	1 13.1	14 33.8	21 52.5	21 24.1	9 44.3	2 4.5	0 18.6
29 Su	18 26 17	6 45 26	7♐32 40	14 34 58	29 2.7	18 43.1	2 23.8	15 14.9	21 54.2	21 19.9	9 47.5	2 4.1	0 19.9
30 M	18 30 13	7 42 38	21 35 0	28 32 14	28 55.5	20 41.1	3 34.5	15 56.0	21 56.0	21 15.8	9 50.8	2 3.6	0 21.2

Astro Data Dy Hr Mn	Planet Ingress Dy Hr Mn	Last Aspect Dy Hr Mn	☽ Ingress Dy Hr Mn	Last Aspect Dy Hr Mn	☽ Ingress Dy Hr Mn	☽ Phases & Eclipses Dy Hr Mn	Astro Data
♀0N 8 12:22	♀ ♈ 5 11:59	2 15:55 ♇ ⚹	♏ 2 16:14	1 2:42 ♇ □	♐ 1 2:54	3 12:23 ○ 12♏34	1 MAY 1958
♇ D 11 22:01	☿ ♉ 17 1:53	4 16:23 ♇ □	♐ 4 16:43	3 5:13 ♇ △	♑ 3 5:23	3 12:13 ☍ P 0.009	Julian Day # 21305
☽0N 13 8:22	☉ ♊ 21 13:51	6 18:59 ♇ △	♑ 6 19:21	5 8:47 ☿ △	♒ 5 10:34	10 14:38 ☽ 19♒25	Delta T 32.3 sec
☽0S 27 11:21		8 14:42 ♃ □	♒ 9 1:29	7 19:19 ♇ ☍	♓ 7 19:24	18 19:00 ● 27♉19	SVP 05♓50'22"
♄□♅ 30 23:21	♀ ♉ 1 4:07	11 11:01 ♇ ☍	♓ 11 11:27	9 16:38 ♄ □	♈ 10 7:20	26 4:38 ☽ 4♍26	Obliquity 23°26'33"
	☿ ♊ 5 20:59	13 12:53 ♄ □	♈ 13 23:58	12 5:09 ♄ △	♉ 12 20:12		⚷ Chiron 22♒20.8
☽0N 9 16:37	♂ ♈ 7 6:21	16 12:24 ♇ △	♉ 16 12:50	14 2:02 ♀ ☌	♊ 15 7:31	1 20:55 ○ 10♐50	☽ Mean ☊ 1♏01.8
♂0N 14 7:12	♇ ♍ 10 18:56	18 23:50 ♇ □	♊ 19 0:14	17 7:59 ☉ ☌	♋ 17 16:04	9 6:59 ☽ 17♓56	
♃ D 19 1:44	☊ ♎ 16 11:42	21 9:01 ♇ ⚹	♋ 21 9:23	19 7:26 ♃ □	♌ 19 22:04	17 7:59 ● 25♊38	1 JUNE 1958
♃⚹♄ 22 18:10	☿ ♋ 20 2:20	23 3:19 ♃ □	♌ 23 16:14	21 15:35 ♀ □	♍ 22 2:22	24 9:45 ☽ 2♎23	Julian Day # 21336
☽0S 23 17:51	☉ ♋ 21 21:57	25 20:42 ♇ ☌	♍ 25 21:00	23 23:45 ♀ △	♎ 24 5:42		Delta T 32.4 sec
	♀ ♊ 26 23:08	27 13:19 ♄ □	♎ 27 23:55	25 18:42 ♃ ☌	♏ 26 8:30		SVP 05♓50'18"
		30 1:20 ♇ ⚹	♏ 30 1:33	27 10:52 ☿ △	♐ 28 11:12		Obliquity 23°26'32"
				30 0:36 ♃ ⚹	♑ 30 14:32		⚷ Chiron 22♒42.9R
							☽ Mean ☊ 29♎23.3

JULY 1958 LONGITUDE

Day	Sid.Time	☉	0 hr ☽	Noon ☽	True ☊	☿	♀	♂	♃	♄	♅	♆	♇
1 Tu	18 34 10	8♋39 49	5♑26 10	12♑16 18	28♎46.0	22♋37.1	4♊45.3	16♈36.9	21♎58.1	21♐11.6	9♌54.0	2♏ 3.2	0♍22.5
2 W	18 38 7	9 37 0	19 2 15	25 43 38	28R 35.0	24 31.1	5 56.1	17 17.8	22 0.3	21R 7.5	9 57.4	2R 2.8	0 23.9
3 Th	18 42 3	10 34 11	2♒20 13	8♒51 50	28 23.7	26 23.2	7 7.0	17 58.5	22 2.7	21 3.5	10 0.7	2 2.4	0 25.3
4 F	18 46 0	11 31 22	15 18 28	21 40 8	28 13.2	28 13.1	8 17.9	18 39.1	22 5.2	20 59.5	10 4.0	2 2.1	0 26.7
5 Sa	18 49 56	12 28 33	27 57 2	4♓ 9 25	28 4.3	0♌ 1.0	9 28.9	19 19.6	22 7.9	20 55.5	10 7.4	2 1.7	0 28.1
6 Su	18 53 53	13 25 44	10♓17 37	16 22 6	27 57.8	1 46.9	10 39.9	19 60.0	22 10.8	20 51.6	10 10.8	2 1.5	0 29.6
7 M	18 57 49	14 22 55	22 23 21	28 21 56	27 53.6	3 30.7	11 51.0	20 40.2	22 13.9	20 47.7	10 14.2	2 1.2	0 31.0
8 Tu	19 1 46	15 20 7	4♈18 27	10♈13 33	27 51.7	5 12.5	13 2.2	21 20.4	22 17.1	20 43.9	10 17.6	2 1.0	0 32.5
9 W	19 5 42	16 17 19	16 7 53	22 2 9	27 51.3	6 52.2	14 13.4	22 0.4	22 20.5	20 40.1	10 21.1	2 0.8	0 34.0
10 Th	19 9 39	17 14 32	27 57 1	3♉53 10	27 51.3	8 29.8	15 24.6	22 40.2	22 24.0	20 36.4	10 24.6	2 0.7	0 35.5
11 F	19 13 36	18 11 45	9♉51 17	15 52 0	27 50.9	10 5.4	16 36.0	23 20.0	22 27.7	20 32.7	10 28.1	2 0.5	0 37.1
12 Sa	19 17 32	19 8 58	21 55 53	28 3 30	27 48.9	11 38.9	17 47.3	23 59.5	22 31.6	20 29.1	10 31.6	2 0.4	0 38.6
13 Su	19 21 29	20 6 12	4♊15 20	10♊31 48	27 44.7	13 10.3	18 58.8	24 39.0	22 35.6	20 25.5	10 35.1	2 0.4	0 40.2
14 M	19 25 25	21 3 27	16 53 11	23 19 44	27 37.9	14 39.6	20 10.2	25 18.3	22 39.9	20 22.0	10 38.6	2D 0.4	0 41.8
15 Tu	19 29 22	22 0 42	29 51 33	6♋28 37	27 28.6	16 6.9	21 21.7	25 57.4	22 44.2	20 18.6	10 42.2	2 0.4	0 43.4
16 W	19 33 18	22 57 57	13♋10 49	19 57 53	27 17.4	17 31.9	22 33.3	26 36.4	22 48.7	20 15.2	10 45.8	2 0.4	0 45.1
17 Th	19 37 15	23 55 13	26 49 29	3♌45 10	27 5.4	18 54.8	23 44.9	27 15.2	22 53.4	20 11.9	10 49.3	2 0.5	0 46.7
18 F	19 41 11	24 52 29	10♌44 24	17 46 36	26 53.7	20 15.5	24 56.6	27 53.9	22 58.3	20 8.6	10 52.9	2 0.6	0 48.4
19 Sa	19 45 8	25 49 45	24 51 9	1♍57 26	26 43.5	21 34.0	26 8.3	28 32.4	23 3.2	20 5.5	10 56.5	2 0.7	0 50.1
20 Su	19 49 5	26 47 2	9♍ 4 52	16 12 53	26 35.7	22 50.1	27 20.1	29 10.7	23 8.4	20 2.4	11 0.2	2 0.9	0 51.8
21 M	19 53 1	27 44 19	23 21 1	0♎28 49	26 30.7	24 3.9	28 31.9	29 48.8	23 13.7	19 59.3	11 3.8	2 1.1	0 53.5
22 Tu	19 56 58	28 41 36	7♎35 59	14 42 13	26 28.3	25 15.3	29 43.7	0♉26.8	23 19.1	19 56.4	11 7.4	2 1.3	0 55.2
23 W	20 0 54	29 38 54	21 47 19	28 51 8	26 27.7	26 24.2	0♋55.6	1 4.6	23 24.7	19 53.5	11 11.1	2 1.6	0 57.0
24 Th	20 4 51	0♌36 11	5♏53 34	12♏54 31	26 27.6	27 30.6	2 7.6	1 42.2	23 30.4	19 50.6	11 14.7	2 1.9	0 58.7
25 F	20 8 47	1 33 29	19 53 56	26 51 43	26 26.9	28 34.2	3 19.6	2 19.6	23 36.3	19 47.9	11 18.4	2 2.2	1 0.5
26 Sa	20 12 44	2 30 48	3♐47 47	10♐42 0	26 24.3	29 35.1	4 31.6	2 56.8	23 42.4	19 45.2	11 22.1	2 2.6	1 2.3
27 Su	20 16 40	3 28 7	17 34 13	24 24 14	26 19.2	0♍33.2	5 43.7	3 33.8	23 48.5	19 42.7	11 25.8	2 3.0	1 4.1
28 M	20 20 37	4 25 26	1♑11 51	7♑56 48	26 11.3	1 28.2	6 55.8	4 10.7	23 54.8	19 40.2	11 29.5	2 3.4	1 5.9
29 Tu	20 24 34	5 22 46	14 38 51	21 17 45	26 1.0	2 20.2	8 8.0	4 47.3	24 1.3	19 37.7	11 33.2	2 3.9	1 7.7
30 W	20 28 30	6 20 7	27 53 14	4♒25 8	25 49.1	3 8.9	9 20.2	5 23.8	24 7.9	19 35.4	11 36.9	2 4.4	1 9.6
31 Th	20 32 27	7 17 28	10♒53 14	17 17 27	25 36.7	3 54.2	10 32.5	5 60.0	24 14.6	19 33.1	11 40.6	2 4.9	1 11.4

AUGUST 1958 LONGITUDE

Day	Sid.Time	☉	0 hr ☽	Noon ☽	True ☊	☿	♀	♂	♃	♄	♅	♆	♇
1 F	20 36 23	8♌14 50	23♒37 43	29♒54 4	25♎25.1	4♍35.9	11♋44.8	6♉36.0	24♎21.4	19♐30.9	11♌44.3	2♏ 5.4	1♍13.3
2 Sa	20 40 20	9 12 13	6♓ 6 34	12♓15 25	25R 15.2	5 13.9	12 57.2	7 11.8	24 28.4	19R 28.9	11 48.0	2 6.0	1 15.1
3 Su	20 44 16	10 9 37	18 20 51	24 23 11	25 7.6	5 48.0	14 9.6	7 47.4	24 35.5	19 26.8	11 51.7	2 6.6	1 17.0
4 M	20 48 13	11 7 3	0♈22 48	6♈20 10	25 2.7	6 18.0	15 22.0	8 22.7	24 42.8	19 24.9	11 55.4	2 7.3	1 18.9
5 Tu	20 52 9	12 4 29	12 15 48	18 10 14	25 0.1	6 43.7	16 34.6	8 57.9	24 50.2	19 23.1	11 59.1	2 8.0	1 20.8
6 W	20 56 6	13 1 56	24 4 5	29 58 0	24D 59.4	7 5.0	17 47.1	9 32.8	24 57.7	19 21.3	12 2.8	2 8.7	1 22.7
7 Th	21 0 3	13 59 25	5♉52 36	11♉48 36	24R 59.7	7 21.5	18 59.8	10 7.4	25 5.3	19 19.7	12 6.5	2 9.4	1 24.6
8 F	21 3 59	14 56 55	17 46 41	23 47 30	24 59.8	7 33.3	20 12.4	10 41.8	25 13.0	19 18.1	12 10.2	2 10.2	1 26.5
9 Sa	21 7 56	15 54 26	29 51 44	6♊ 0 1	24 58.9	7R 40.0	21 25.2	11 15.9	25 20.9	19 16.6	12 14.0	2 11.0	1 28.5
10 Su	21 11 52	16 51 59	12♊12 56	18 31 1	24 56.1	7 41.4	22 37.9	11 49.8	25 28.9	19 15.2	12 17.7	2 11.8	1 30.4
11 M	21 15 49	17 49 33	24 54 42	1♋24 20	24 51.0	7 37.6	23 50.7	12 23.4	25 37.0	19 14.0	12 21.4	2 12.7	1 32.3
12 Tu	21 19 45	18 47 9	8♋ 0 10	14 42 18	24 43.6	7 28.3	25 3.6	12 56.7	25 45.3	19 12.8	12 25.1	2 13.6	1 34.3
13 W	21 23 42	19 44 46	21 30 41	28 25 7	24 34.5	7 13.6	26 16.5	13 29.8	25 53.6	19 11.6	12 28.8	2 14.5	1 36.2
14 Th	21 27 38	20 42 24	5♌25 16	12♌30 36	24 24.4	6 53.3	27 29.5	14 2.5	26 2.1	19 10.6	12 32.5	2 15.4	1 38.2
15 F	21 31 35	21 40 3	19 40 30	26 54 13	24 14.5	6 27.7	28 42.5	14 35.0	26 10.7	19 9.7	12 36.2	2 16.4	1 40.2
16 Sa	21 35 32	22 37 44	4♍10 53	11♍29 37	24 5.9	5 56.8	29 55.5	15 7.1	26 19.4	19 8.9	12 39.8	2 17.4	1 42.2
17 Su	21 39 28	23 35 26	18 49 32	26 9 45	23 59.5	5 21.0	1♌ 8.6	15 38.9	26 28.2	19 8.2	12 43.5	2 18.5	1 44.1
18 M	21 43 25	24 33 9	3♎29 25	10♎47 50	23 55.5	4 40.6	2 21.7	16 10.5	26 37.1	19 7.5	12 47.2	2 19.6	1 46.1
19 Tu	21 47 21	25 30 53	18 4 21	25 18 26	23D 53.9	3 56.2	3 34.9	16 41.6	26 46.1	19 7.0	12 50.8	2 20.7	1 48.1
20 W	21 51 18	26 28 38	2♏29 41	9♏37 48	23 54.0	3 8.3	4 48.1	17 12.5	26 55.2	19 6.5	12 54.5	2 21.8	1 50.1
21 Th	21 55 14	27 26 25	16 42 34	23 43 53	23R 54.7	2 17.7	6 1.4	17 43.0	27 4.5	19 6.2	12 58.1	2 22.9	1 52.1
22 F	21 59 11	28 24 12	0♐41 42	7♐36 0	23 55.1	1 25.4	7 14.7	18 13.2	27 13.8	19 6.0	13 1.7	2 24.1	1 54.1
23 Sa	22 3 7	29 22 1	14 26 49	21 14 13	23 54.0	0 32.2	8 28.0	18 43.0	27 23.3	19 5.8	13 5.3	2 25.3	1 56.1
24 Su	22 7 4	0♍19 51	27 58 15	4♑38 58	23 50.9	29♌39.1	9 41.4	19 12.5	27 32.8	19D 5.8	13 8.9	2 26.6	1 58.1
25 M	22 11 0	1 17 42	11♑16 26	17 50 41	23 45.5	28 47.4	10 54.8	19 41.6	27 42.4	19 5.8	13 12.5	2 27.9	2 0.1
26 Tu	22 14 57	2 15 34	24 21 44	0♒49 36	23 38.3	27 58.1	12 8.3	20 10.4	27 52.2	19 5.9	13 16.1	2 29.2	2 2.1
27 W	22 18 54	3 13 28	7♒14 19	13 35 52	23 29.8	27 12.3	13 21.8	20 38.8	28 2.0	19 6.2	13 19.6	2 30.5	2 4.1
28 Th	22 22 50	4 11 23	19 54 18	26 9 37	23 20.9	26 30.9	14 35.3	21 6.8	28 11.9	19 6.5	13 23.2	2 31.8	2 6.1
29 F	22 26 47	5 9 19	2♓21 54	8♓31 13	23 12.5	25 55.0	15 48.9	21 34.4	28 21.9	19 7.0	13 26.7	2 33.2	2 8.1
30 Sa	22 30 43	6 7 17	14 37 41	20 41 28	23 5.4	25 25.5	17 2.5	22 1.6	28 32.0	19 7.5	13 30.2	2 34.6	2 10.1
31 Su	22 34 40	7 5 16	26 42 45	2♈41 48	23 0.1	25 2.9	18 16.2	22 28.4	28 42.2	19 8.1	13 33.7	2 36.0	2 12.0

Astro Data Dy Hr Mn	Planet Ingress Dy Hr Mn	Last Aspect Dy Hr Mn	☽ Ingress Dy Hr Mn	Last Aspect Dy Hr Mn	☽ Ingress Dy Hr Mn	☽ Phases & Eclipses Dy Hr Mn	Astro Data
☽0N 7 1:56	☿ ♌ 4 23:46	2 11:26 ☿ ☍	♒ 2 19:44	1 1:24 ♃ △	♓ 1 12:11	1 6:05 ○ 8♑54	1 JULY 1958
♆ D 14 5:52	♂ ♉ 21 7:03	4 12:50 ♃ △	♓ 5 3:57	3 2:10 ♄ □	♈ 3 23:14	9 0:21 ☽ 16♈18	Julian Day # 21366
☽0S 21 0:33	♀ ♋ 22 5:26	6 20:50 ♄ □	♈ 7 15:18	6 1:50 ♃ ☍	♉ 6 12:04	16 18:33 ● 23♋42	Delta T 32.4 sec
	☉ ♌ 23 8:50	9 12:41 ♃ ☍	♉ 10 4:09	8 5:24 ♀ ⚹	♊ 9 0:16	23 14:20 ☽ 0♏13	SVP 05♓50'13"
☽0N 3 11:08	☿ ♍ 26 10:08	11 18:02 ☉ ⚹	♊ 12 15:46	11 1:20 ♃ △	♋ 11 9:25	30 16:47 ○ 7♒00	Obliquity 23°26'32"
☿ R 9 18:47		14 16:28 ♃ ⚹	♋ 15 0:15	13 9:05 ♀ ☌	♌ 13 14:43		⚷ Chiron 22♒08.0R
☽0S 17 8:41	♀ ♌ 16 1:28	17 0:47 ♂ □	♌ 17 5:31	15 10:54 ♃ ⚹	♍ 15 17:07	7 17:49 ☽ 14♉42	☽ Mean ☊ 27♎48.0
♄ D 24 0:31	☉ ♍ 23 15:46	19 6:32 ♂ △	♍ 19 8:42	17 0:30 ♄ □	♎ 17 18:17	15 3:33 ● 21♌49	
☽0N 30 19:07	☿ ♌ 23 14:31	21 9:31 ♀ □	♎ 21 11:11	19 14:35 ♃ ☌	♏ 19 19:50	21 19:45 ☽ 28♏14	1 AUGUST 1958
		23 8:31 ☿ ⚹	♏ 23 13:57	21 19:45 ☉ □	♐ 21 22:48	29 5:53 ○ 5♓24	Julian Day # 21397
		25 16:08 ☿ △	♐ 25 17:25	24 2:50 ☿ △	♑ 24 3:38		Delta T 32.5 sec
		27 11:02 ♃ ⚹	♑ 27 21:53	26 6:35 ♃ □	♒ 26 10:28		SVP 05♓50'08"
		29 17:05 ♃ □	♒ 30 3:52	28 16:09 ♃ △	♓ 28 19:25		Obliquity 23°26'32"
				30 15:13 ♂ ⚹	♈ 31 6:35		⚷ Chiron 20♒47.4R
							☽ Mean ☊ 26♎09.5

LONGITUDE SEPTEMBER 1958

Day	Sid.Time	☉	0 hr ☽	Noon ☽	True ☊	☿	♀	♂	♃	♄	♅	♆	♇
1 M	22 38 36	8♍ 3 18	8♈38 55	14♈34 25	22♎56.9	24♌48.0	19♌29.9	22♉54.8	28♎52.5	19♐ 8.8	13♌37.2	2♏37.5	2♍14.0
2 Tu	22 42 33	9 1 21	20 28 44	26 22 17	22D 55.7	24D 41.1	20 43.7	23 20.7	29 2.9	19 9.6	13 40.6	2 39.0	2 16.0
3 W	22 46 29	9 59 26	2♉15 32	8♉ 9 3	22 56.1	24 42.7	21 57.5	23 46.2	29 13.3	19 10.6	13 44.1	2 40.5	2 18.0
4 Th	22 50 26	10 57 33	14 3 22	19 59 4	22 57.4	24 52.8	23 11.3	24 11.3	29 23.9	19 11.6	13 47.5	2 42.0	2 20.0
5 F	22 54 23	11 55 41	25 56 47	1♊57 8	22 59.0	25 11.5	24 25.2	24 35.9	29 34.5	19 12.7	13 50.9	2 43.5	2 22.0
6 Sa	22 58 19	12 53 52	8♊ 0 46	14 8 19	23R 0.0	25 38.9	25 39.1	24 60.0	29 45.2	19 13.9	13 54.2	2 45.1	2 23.9
7 Su	23 2 16	13 52 5	20 20 24	26 37 36	22 59.9	26 14.7	26 53.1	25 23.6	29 56.0	19 15.2	13 57.6	2 46.7	2 25.9
8 M	23 6 12	14 50 20	3♋ 0 26	9♋29 24	22 58.3	26 58.8	28 7.1	25 46.7	0♏ 6.9	19 16.6	14 0.9	2 48.3	2 27.9
9 Tu	23 10 9	15 48 37	16 4 51	22 47 4	22 55.2	27 50.7	29 21.1	26 9.4	0 17.8	19 18.1	14 4.2	2 50.0	2 29.8
10 W	23 14 5	16 46 56	29 36 10	6♌32 9	22 50.7	28 50.1	0♍35.2	26 31.5	0 28.8	19 19.7	14 7.5	2 51.6	2 31.8
11 Th	23 18 2	17 45 17	13♌34 50	20 43 51	22 45.5	29 56.6	1 49.4	26 53.0	0 39.9	19 21.4	14 10.8	2 53.3	2 33.7
12 F	23 21 58	18 43 40	27 58 39	5♍18 33	22 40.2	1♍ 9.7	3 3.5	27 14.1	0 51.1	19 23.1	14 14.0	2 55.0	2 35.7
13 Sa	23 25 55	19 42 5	12♍42 41	20 10 5	22 35.7	2 28.7	4 17.7	27 34.5	1 2.3	19 25.0	14 17.2	2 56.8	2 37.6
14 Su	23 29 52	20 40 31	27 39 40	5♎10 20	22 32.4	3 53.1	5 31.9	27 54.4	1 13.6	19 27.0	14 20.4	2 58.5	2 39.5
15 M	23 33 48	21 39 0	12♎40 59	20 10 33	22D 30.6	5 22.5	6 46.2	28 13.7	1 25.0	19 29.0	14 23.5	3 0.3	2 41.5
16 Tu	23 37 45	22 37 30	27 38 4	5♏ 2 38	22 30.4	6 56.0	8 0.5	28 32.4	1 36.5	19 31.2	14 26.6	3 2.1	2 43.4
17 W	23 41 41	23 36 2	12♏23 32	19 40 9	22 31.3	8 33.3	9 14.8	28 50.5	1 48.0	19 33.4	14 29.7	3 3.9	2 45.3
18 Th	23 45 38	24 34 36	26 52 3	3♐58 55	22 32.7	10 13.7	10 29.2	29 7.9	1 59.6	19 35.8	14 32.8	3 5.7	2 47.2
19 F	23 49 34	25 33 12	11♐ 0 33	17 56 54	22 34.1	11 56.7	11 43.5	29 24.8	2 11.2	19 38.2	14 35.8	3 7.6	2 49.0
20 Sa	23 53 31	26 31 49	24 48 0	1♑33 56	22R 34.7	13 41.9	12 58.0	29 41.0	2 22.9	19 40.8	14 38.8	3 9.5	2 50.9
21 Su	23 57 27	27 30 27	8♑14 53	14 51 4	22 34.3	15 28.8	14 12.4	29 56.6	2 34.7	19 43.4	14 41.8	3 11.4	2 52.8
22 M	0 1 24	28 29 8	21 22 43	27 50 5	22 32.7	17 16.9	15 26.9	0♊11.5	2 46.5	19 46.1	14 44.8	3 13.3	2 54.6
23 Tu	0 5 21	29 27 50	4♒13 28	10♒33 8	22 30.1	19 6.0	16 41.4	0 25.7	2 58.4	19 48.9	14 47.7	3 15.2	2 56.4
24 W	0 9 17	0♎26 34	16 49 20	23 2 19	22 26.9	20 55.7	17 55.9	0 39.2	3 10.4	19 51.8	14 50.5	3 17.1	2 58.3
25 Th	0 13 14	1 25 19	29 12 22	5♓19 42	22 23.5	22 45.8	19 10.5	0 52.1	3 22.3	19 54.7	14 53.4	3 19.1	3 0.1
26 F	0 17 10	2 24 6	11♓24 33	17 27 9	22 20.3	24 36.0	20 25.0	1 4.2	3 34.4	19 57.8	14 56.2	3 21.1	3 1.9
27 Sa	0 21 7	3 22 56	23 27 43	29 26 30	22 17.6	26 26.2	21 39.6	1 15.6	3 46.5	20 0.9	14 58.9	3 23.0	3 3.7
28 Su	0 25 3	4 21 47	5♈23 43	11♈19 37	22 15.9	28 16.1	22 54.3	1 26.3	3 58.6	20 4.1	15 1.7	3 25.0	3 5.4
29 M	0 29 0	5 20 40	17 14 27	23 8 31	22D 15.0	0♎ 5.7	24 8.9	1 36.2	4 10.8	20 7.5	15 4.4	3 27.1	3 7.2
30 Tu	0 32 56	6 19 35	29 2 6	4♉55 33	22 15.1	1 54.8	25 23.6	1 45.4	4 23.1	20 10.9	15 7.0	3 29.1	3 8.9

LONGITUDE OCTOBER 1958

Day	Sid.Time	☉	0 hr ☽	Noon ☽	True ☊	☿	♀	♂	♃	♄	♅	♆	♇
1 W	0 36 53	7♎18 33	10♉49 12	16♉43 26	22♎15.8	3♎43.3	26♍38.3	1♊53.8	4♏35.4	20♐14.3	15♌ 9.6	3♏31.1	3♍10.6
2 Th	0 40 49	8 17 32	22 38 40	28 35 21	22 17.0	5 31.2	27 53.1	2 1.3	4 47.7	20 17.9	15 12.2	3 33.2	3 12.4
3 F	0 44 46	9 16 34	4♊33 57	10♊34 58	22 18.3	7 18.4	29 7.9	2 8.1	5 0.1	20 21.5	15 14.8	3 35.3	3 14.0
4 Sa	0 48 43	10 15 38	16 38 54	22 46 17	22 19.4	9 5.0	0♎22.7	2 14.1	5 12.6	20 25.3	15 17.3	3 37.4	3 15.7
5 Su	0 52 39	11 14 45	28 57 39	5♋13 33	22 20.2	10 50.7	1 37.5	2 19.2	5 25.1	20 29.1	15 19.8	3 39.5	3 17.4
6 M	0 56 36	12 13 53	11♋34 30	18 0 58	22R 20.5	12 35.8	2 52.3	2 23.5	5 37.6	20 33.0	15 22.2	3 41.6	3 19.0
7 Tu	1 0 32	13 13 5	24 33 24	1♌12 10	22 20.3	14 20.0	4 7.2	2 27.0	5 50.1	20 36.9	15 24.6	3 43.7	3 20.7
8 W	1 4 29	14 12 18	7♌57 34	14 49 47	22 19.7	16 3.5	5 22.1	2 29.6	6 2.7	20 41.0	15 26.9	3 45.8	3 22.3
9 Th	1 8 25	15 11 34	21 48 51	28 54 40	22 19.0	17 46.2	6 37.0	2 31.2	6 15.4	20 45.1	15 29.2	3 48.0	3 23.9
10 F	1 12 22	16 10 51	6♍ 6 59	13♍25 21	22 18.2	19 28.1	7 52.0	2R 32.1	6 28.1	20 49.3	15 31.5	3 50.1	3 25.4
11 Sa	1 16 18	17 10 12	20 49 7	28 17 32	22 17.6	21 9.3	9 6.9	2 32.0	6 40.8	20 53.6	15 33.7	3 52.3	3 27.0
12 Su	1 20 15	18 9 34	5♎49 37	13♎24 19	22 17.2	22 49.7	10 21.9	2 31.0	6 53.5	20 57.9	15 35.9	3 54.5	3 28.5
13 M	1 24 12	19 8 58	21 0 26	28 36 46	22D 17.1	24 29.4	11 36.9	2 29.1	7 6.3	21 2.4	15 38.0	3 56.6	3 30.0
14 Tu	1 28 8	20 8 25	6♏12 6	13♏45 16	22 17.1	26 8.3	12 51.9	2 26.3	7 19.1	21 6.9	15 40.1	3 58.8	3 31.5
15 W	1 32 5	21 7 54	21 15 9	28 40 49	22 17.2	27 46.6	14 7.0	2 22.6	7 32.0	21 11.5	15 42.1	4 1.0	3 33.0
16 Th	1 36 1	22 7 24	6♐ 1 27	13♐16 24	22R 17.3	29 24.1	15 22.0	2 18.0	7 44.8	21 16.1	15 44.1	4 3.2	3 34.5
17 F	1 39 58	23 6 56	20 25 12	27 27 34	22 17.3	1♏ 1.0	16 37.1	2 12.6	7 57.7	21 20.8	15 46.0	4 5.4	3 35.9
18 Sa	1 43 54	24 6 30	4♑23 21	11♑12 33	22 17.2	2 37.3	17 52.2	2 6.2	8 10.7	21 25.6	15 47.9	4 7.6	3 37.3
19 Su	1 47 51	25 6 6	17 55 20	24 31 55	22D 17.1	4 12.9	19 7.3	1 58.9	8 23.6	21 30.5	15 49.8	4 9.9	3 38.7
20 M	1 51 47	26 5 44	1♒ 2 38	7♒27 52	22 17.1	5 47.9	20 22.4	1 50.8	8 36.6	21 35.4	15 51.6	4 12.1	3 40.1
21 Tu	1 55 44	27 5 23	13 48 3	20 3 38	22 17.3	7 22.2	21 37.5	1 41.7	8 49.6	21 40.4	15 53.3	4 14.3	3 41.4
22 W	1 59 41	28 5 4	26 15 5	2♓22 54	22 17.7	8 56.0	22 52.7	1 31.9	9 2.6	21 45.4	15 55.0	4 16.5	3 42.7
23 Th	2 3 37	29 4 46	8♓27 33	14 29 28	22 18.4	10 29.2	24 7.8	1 21.2	9 15.6	21 50.6	15 56.7	4 18.8	3 44.0
24 F	2 7 34	0♏ 4 30	20 29 6	26 26 52	22 19.2	12 1.8	25 23.0	1 9.6	9 28.7	21 55.8	15 58.3	4 21.0	3 45.3
25 Sa	2 11 30	1 4 17	2♈23 9	8♈18 19	22 19.9	13 33.9	26 38.1	0 57.2	9 41.7	22 1.0	15 59.8	4 23.3	3 46.5
26 Su	2 15 27	2 4 5	14 12 43	20 6 39	22R 20.5	15 5.4	27 53.3	0 44.1	9 54.8	22 6.3	16 1.3	4 25.5	3 47.7
27 M	2 19 23	3 3 54	26 0 26	1♉54 20	22 20.6	16 36.4	29 8.5	0 30.1	10 7.9	22 11.7	16 2.8	4 27.7	3 48.9
28 Tu	2 23 20	4 3 46	7♉48 38	13 43 36	22 20.1	18 6.9	0♏23.7	0 15.4	10 21.0	22 17.1	16 4.2	4 30.0	3 50.1
29 W	2 27 16	5 3 40	19 39 29	25 36 32	22 18.9	19 36.8	1 38.9	0 0.0	10 34.2	22 22.6	16 5.5	4 32.2	3 51.3
30 Th	2 31 13	6 3 36	1♊35 2	7♊35 15	22 17.2	21 6.2	2 54.2	29♉43.9	10 47.3	22 28.1	16 6.8	4 34.5	3 52.4
31 F	2 35 9	7 3 34	13 37 29	19 42 0	22 15.0	22 35.0	4 9.4	29 27.1	11 0.4	22 33.8	16 8.1	4 36.7	3 53.5

Astro Data	Planet Ingress	Last Aspect	☽ Ingress	Last Aspect	☽ Ingress	☽ Phases & Eclipses	Astro Data
Dy Hr Mn	Dy Hr Mn	Dy Hr Mn	Dy Hr Mn	Dy Hr Mn	Dy Hr Mn	Dy Hr Mn	1 SEPTEMBER 1958
☿ D 2 7:42	♃ ♏ 7 8:52	2 17:43 ♃ ☍	♉ 2 19:24	2 11:49 ♀ △	♊ 2 14:50	6 10:24 ☽ 13♊19	Julian Day # 21428
☽0S 13 18:35	♀ ♍ 9 12:35	4 22:26 ☿ □	♊ 5 8:07	4 7:27 ♄ ☍	♋ 5 2:00	13 12:02 ● 20♍11	Delta T 32.5 sec
♃✶♇ 22 19:19	☿ ♍ 11 1:10	7 13:50 ♀ ✶	♋ 7 18:22	6 2:13 ☿ □	♌ 7 9:51	20 3:18 ☽ 26♐40	SVP 05♓50'05"
♃☌♆ 24 16:12	♂ ♊ 21 5:26	9 18:27 ♂ ✶	♌ 10 0:42	8 22:11 ♄ △	♍ 9 13:49	27 21:44 ○ 4♈16	Obliquity 23°26'33"
☽0N 27 1:37	☉ ♎ 23 13:09	11 22:45 ♂ □	♍ 12 3:19	11 0:07 ♄ □	♎ 11 14:44		⚷ Chiron 19♒12.4R
☿0S 30 22:37	☿ ♎ 28 22:45	14 0:24 ♂ △	♎ 14 3:44	13 6:10 ☿ ☌	♏ 13 14:11	6 1:20 ☽ 12♋17	☽ Mean ☊ 24♎31.0
		15 10:55 ♄ ✶	♏ 16 3:49	14 15:05 ♅ □	♐ 15 14:09	12 20:52 ● 19♎01	
♃∠♄ 5 11:10	♀ ♎ 3 16:44	18 3:53 ♂ ☍	♐ 18 5:16	17 4:55 ☉ ✶	♑ 17 16:23	12 20:54:55 T 5'11"	1 OCTOBER 1958
♀0S 6 8:49	☿ ♏ 16 8:52	20 3:18 ☉ □	♑ 20 9:13	19 14:07 ☉ □	♒ 19 22:04	19 14:07 ☽ 25♑41	Julian Day # 21458
♂ R 10 9:46	☉ ♏ 23 22:11	22 14:18 ☉ △	♒ 22 16:03	22 3:53 ☉ △	♓ 22 7:19	27 15:41 ○ 3♉43	Delta T 32.6 sec
☽0S 11 5:29	♀ ♏ 27 16:26	24 5:53 ♄ ✶	♓ 25 1:33	24 2:55 ♄ □	♈ 24 19:10	27 15:27 A 0.782	SVP 05♓50'03"
☽0N 24 7:30	♂ ♉ 29 0:01	27 7:03 ☿ ☍	♈ 27 13:07	27 7:08 ♀ ☍	♉ 27 8:07		Obliquity 23°26'33"
		29 5:53 ♄ △	♉ 30 1:58	29 20:22 ♂ ☌	♊ 29 20:49		⚷ Chiron 18♒02.0R
							☽ Mean ☊ 22♎55.6

NOVEMBER 1958 LONGITUDE

Day	Sid.Time	☉	0 hr ☽	Noon ☽	True ☊	☿	♀	♂	♃	♄	♅	♆	♇
1 Sa	2 39 6	8♏ 3 34	25♊49 10	1♋59 17	22♎12.6	24♏ 3.3	5♏24.6	29♉ 9.6	11♏13.6	22♐39.4	16♌ 9.3	4♏39.0	3♍54.6
2 Su	2 43 3	9 3 36	8♋12 43	14 29 50	22R 10.3	25 31.1	6 39.9	28R 51.5	11 26.8	22 45.1	16 10.4	4 41.2	3 55.6
3 M	2 46 59	10 3 40	20 51 0	27 16 36	22 8.6	26 58.2	7 55.2	28 32.8	11 39.9	22 50.9	16 11.5	4 43.4	3 56.6
4 Tu	2 50 56	11 3 46	3♌47 0	10♌22 33	22D 7.6	28 24.8	9 10.5	28 13.6	11 53.1	22 56.7	16 12.6	4 45.7	3 57.6
5 W	2 54 52	12 3 54	17 3 35	23 50 20	22 7.5	29 50.8	10 25.8	27 53.9	12 6.3	23 2.6	16 13.5	4 47.9	3 58.6
6 Th	2 58 49	13 4 4	0♍43 1	7♍41 44	22 8.2	1♐16.0	11 41.1	27 33.8	12 19.5	23 8.5	16 14.5	4 50.1	3 59.5
7 F	3 2 45	14 4 17	14 46 30	21 57 10	22 9.5	2 40.6	12 56.4	27 13.2	12 32.6	23 14.5	16 15.3	4 52.4	4 0.4
8 Sa	3 6 42	15 4 31	29 13 27	6♎34 55	22 11.0	4 4.4	14 11.7	26 52.2	12 45.8	23 20.5	16 16.2	4 54.6	4 1.3
9 Su	3 10 38	16 4 48	14♎ 0 58	21 30 49	22R 11.9	5 27.4	15 27.0	26 30.9	12 59.0	23 26.6	16 16.9	4 56.8	4 2.2
10 M	3 14 35	17 5 6	29 3 31	6♏38 2	22 12.0	6 49.5	16 42.4	26 9.4	13 12.2	23 32.7	16 17.6	4 59.0	4 3.0
11 Tu	3 18 32	18 5 27	14♏13 12	21 47 47	22 10.7	8 10.6	17 57.7	25 47.6	13 25.3	23 38.9	16 18.3	5 1.2	4 3.8
12 W	3 22 28	19 5 49	29 20 34	6♐50 22	22 8.1	9 30.7	19 13.1	25 25.7	13 38.5	23 45.1	16 18.9	5 3.4	4 4.6
13 Th	3 26 25	20 6 12	14♐16 5	21 36 45	22 4.4	10 49.5	20 28.5	25 3.6	13 51.7	23 51.4	16 19.4	5 5.6	4 5.3
14 F	3 30 21	21 6 38	28 51 35	5♑59 58	22 0.0	12 7.0	21 43.8	24 41.6	14 4.8	23 57.7	16 19.9	5 7.8	4 6.0
15 Sa	3 34 18	22 7 4	13♑ 1 27	19 55 49	21 55.7	13 23.0	22 59.2	24 19.5	14 18.0	24 4.0	16 20.3	5 10.0	4 6.7
16 Su	3 38 14	23 7 33	26 43 2	3♒23 11	21 52.1	14 37.3	24 14.6	23 57.5	14 31.1	24 10.4	16 20.7	5 12.1	4 7.3
17 M	3 42 11	24 8 2	9♒56 31	16 23 25	21 49.7	15 49.7	25 29.9	23 35.6	14 44.2	24 16.8	16 21.0	5 14.3	4 8.0
18 Tu	3 46 7	25 8 33	22 44 20	28 59 48	21D 48.7	16 59.9	26 45.3	23 13.8	14 57.3	24 23.3	16 21.3	5 16.4	4 8.6
19 W	3 50 4	26 9 4	5♓10 24	11♓16 44	21 49.1	18 7.7	28 0.7	22 52.3	15 10.4	24 29.8	16 21.5	5 18.6	4 9.1
20 Th	3 54 1	27 9 37	17 19 25	23 19 5	21 50.4	19 12.7	29 16.1	22 31.0	15 23.4	24 36.3	16 21.7	5 20.7	4 9.6
21 F	3 57 57	28 10 12	29 16 21	5♈11 47	21 52.2	20 14.6	0♐31.5	22 10.1	15 36.5	24 42.9	16 21.8	5 22.8	4 10.1
22 Sa	4 1 54	29 10 47	11♈ 5 58	16 59 26	21R 53.8	21 13.0	1 46.8	21 49.5	15 49.5	24 49.5	16R 21.8	5 24.9	4 10.6
23 Su	4 5 50	0♐11 24	22 52 40	28 46 7	21 54.3	22 7.3	3 2.2	21 29.2	16 2.5	24 56.1	16 21.8	5 27.0	4 11.1
24 M	4 9 47	1 12 2	4♉40 12	10♉35 17	21 53.4	22 57.0	4 17.6	21 9.5	16 15.5	25 2.8	16 21.7	5 29.1	4 11.5
25 Tu	4 13 43	2 12 42	16 31 41	22 29 42	21 50.4	23 41.6	5 33.0	20 50.2	16 28.5	25 9.5	16 21.6	5 31.1	4 11.8
26 W	4 17 40	3 13 22	28 29 32	4♊31 26	21 45.5	24 20.3	6 48.4	20 31.4	16 41.4	25 16.2	16 21.4	5 33.2	4 12.2
27 Th	4 21 36	4 14 4	10♊35 32	16 41 59	21 38.7	24 52.5	8 3.8	20 13.2	16 54.3	25 22.9	16 21.2	5 35.2	4 12.5
28 F	4 25 33	5 14 48	22 50 56	29 2 28	21 30.6	25 17.3	9 19.1	19 55.5	17 7.2	25 29.7	16 20.9	5 37.2	4 12.8
29 Sa	4 29 30	6 15 33	5♋16 41	11♋33 43	21 22.0	25 34.0	10 34.5	19 38.5	17 20.0	25 36.5	16 20.5	5 39.2	4 13.0
30 Su	4 33 26	7 16 19	17 53 39	24 16 36	21 13.7	25R 41.7	11 49.9	19 22.1	17 32.9	25 43.4	16 20.1	5 41.2	4 13.3

DECEMBER 1958 LONGITUDE

Day	Sid.Time	☉	0 hr ☽	Noon ☽	True ☊	☿	♀	♂	♃	♄	♅	♆	♇
1 M	4 37 23	8♐17 6	0♌42 43	7♌12 8	21♎ 6.7	25♐39.7	13♐ 5.3	19♉ 6.4	17♏45.7	25♐50.2	16♌19.7	5♏43.2	4♍13.5
2 Tu	4 41 19	9 17 55	13 45 2	20 21 36	21R 1.5	25R 27.3	14 20.7	18R 51.3	17 58.4	25 57.1	16R 19.2	5 45.1	4 13.6
3 W	4 45 16	10 18 46	27 2 1	3♍46 29	20 58.5	25 3.9	15 36.1	18 37.0	18 11.1	26 4.0	16 18.6	5 47.1	4 13.8
4 Th	4 49 12	11 19 37	10♍35 10	17 28 15	20D 57.5	24 29.4	16 51.5	18 23.4	18 23.8	26 10.9	16 18.0	5 49.0	4 13.9
5 F	4 53 9	12 20 30	24 25 49	1♎27 57	20 58.0	23 43.8	18 7.0	18 10.5	18 36.5	26 17.8	16 17.3	5 50.9	4 13.9
6 Sa	4 57 5	13 21 25	8♎34 35	15 45 35	20R 59.1	22 47.6	19 22.4	17 58.4	18 49.1	26 24.8	16 16.6	5 52.8	4R 14.0
7 Su	5 1 2	14 22 21	23 0 43	0♏19 33	20 59.5	21 42.0	20 37.8	17 47.1	19 1.7	26 31.8	16 15.8	5 54.6	4 14.0
8 M	5 4 59	15 23 18	7♏41 33	15 6 2	20 58.3	20 28.5	21 53.2	17 36.6	19 14.2	26 38.7	16 14.9	5 56.5	4 13.9
9 Tu	5 8 55	16 24 16	22 32 9	29 58 58	20 54.7	19 9.3	23 8.6	17 26.8	19 26.7	26 45.7	16 14.1	5 58.3	4 13.9
10 W	5 12 52	17 25 16	7♐25 26	14♐50 29	20 48.6	17 46.8	24 24.0	17 18.0	19 39.1	26 52.8	16 13.1	6 0.1	4 13.8
11 Th	5 16 48	18 26 16	22 13 1	29 32 0	20 40.2	16 24.0	25 39.5	17 9.9	19 51.5	26 59.8	16 12.1	6 1.9	4 13.7
12 F	5 20 45	19 27 17	6♑46 28	13♑55 36	20 30.4	15 3.5	26 54.9	17 2.7	20 3.9	27 6.8	16 11.1	6 3.7	4 13.5
13 Sa	5 24 41	20 28 19	20 58 45	27 55 26	20 20.3	13 48.1	28 10.3	16 56.3	20 16.2	27 13.9	16 10.0	6 5.4	4 13.3
14 Su	5 28 38	21 29 22	4♒45 19	11♒28 19	20 11.1	12 39.9	29 25.7	16 50.7	20 28.4	27 20.9	16 8.9	6 7.1	4 13.1
15 M	5 32 35	22 30 25	18 4 27	24 33 58	20 3.8	11 40.7	0♑41.1	16 46.0	20 40.6	27 28.0	16 7.7	6 8.8	4 12.9
16 Tu	5 36 31	23 31 28	0♓57 9	7♓14 30	19 58.8	10 51.7	1 56.5	16 42.1	20 52.8	27 35.1	16 6.4	6 10.5	4 12.6
17 W	5 40 28	24 32 32	13 26 31	19 33 50	19 56.2	10 13.5	3 11.9	16 39.0	21 4.8	27 42.2	16 5.1	6 12.1	4 12.3
18 Th	5 44 24	25 33 37	25 37 5	1♈36 58	19D 55.5	9 46.5	4 27.3	16 36.8	21 16.9	27 49.2	16 3.8	6 13.8	4 12.0
19 F	5 48 21	26 34 41	7♈34 10	13 29 23	19 55.9	9 30.4	5 42.7	16 35.3	21 28.8	27 56.3	16 2.4	6 15.4	4 11.6
20 Sa	5 52 17	27 35 46	19 23 19	25 16 37	19R 56.3	9D 24.7	6 58.1	16D 34.7	21 40.7	28 3.4	16 1.0	6 16.9	4 11.2
21 Su	5 56 14	28 36 51	1♉ 9 56	7♉ 3 51	19 55.6	9 29.0	8 13.5	16 34.9	21 52.6	28 10.5	15 59.5	6 18.5	4 10.8
22 M	6 0 10	29 37 57	12 58 57	18 55 42	19 53.0	9 42.3	9 28.8	16 35.8	22 4.4	28 17.6	15 58.0	6 20.0	4 10.3
23 Tu	6 4 7	0♑39 3	24 54 34	0♊55 56	19 47.7	10 3.9	10 44.2	16 37.6	22 16.1	28 24.7	15 56.4	6 21.5	4 9.9
24 W	6 8 4	1 40 9	7♊ 0 7	13 7 21	19 39.5	10 33.1	11 59.6	16 40.1	22 27.7	28 31.7	15 54.8	6 23.0	4 9.4
25 Th	6 12 0	2 41 15	19 17 50	25 31 41	19 28.8	11 9.1	13 14.9	16 43.3	22 39.3	28 38.8	15 53.1	6 24.4	4 8.8
26 F	6 15 57	3 42 22	1♋48 56	8♋ 9 35	19 16.1	11 51.0	14 30.3	16 47.3	22 50.8	28 45.9	15 51.4	6 25.9	4 8.2
27 Sa	6 19 53	4 43 29	14 33 34	21 0 48	19 2.6	12 38.4	15 45.6	16 52.0	23 2.3	28 53.0	15 49.7	6 27.2	4 7.7
28 Su	6 23 50	5 44 37	27 31 9	4♌ 4 28	18 49.5	13 30.5	17 1.0	16 57.5	23 13.6	29 0.0	15 47.9	6 28.6	4 7.0
29 M	6 27 46	6 45 44	10♌40 36	17 19 26	18 37.9	14 26.8	18 16.3	17 3.6	23 24.9	29 7.1	15 46.1	6 29.9	4 6.4
30 Tu	6 31 43	7 46 52	24 0 49	0♍44 42	18 28.9	15 26.9	19 31.6	17 10.4	23 36.1	29 14.1	15 44.2	6 31.3	4 5.7
31 W	6 35 39	8 48 1	7♍30 58	14 19 38	18 22.9	16 30.3	20 46.9	17 17.9	23 47.3	29 21.1	15 42.3	6 32.5	4 5.0

Astro Data Dy Hr Mn	Planet Ingress Dy Hr Mn	Last Aspect Dy Hr Mn	☽ Ingress Dy Hr Mn	Last Aspect Dy Hr Mn	☽ Ingress Dy Hr Mn	☽ Phases & Eclipses Dy Hr Mn
☽0S 7 15:53	☿ ♐ 5 2:36	31 17:46 ♄ ☍	♋ 1 8:09	2 22:15 ♄ △	♍ 3 5:18	4 14:19 ☽ 11♌40
☽0N 20 14:14	♀ ♐ 20 13:59	3 14:01 ♂ ⚹	♌ 3 17:02	5 3:13 ♄ □	♎ 5 9:31	11 6:34 ● 18♏22
♅ R 22 4:49	☉ ♐ 22 19:29	5 18:39 ♂ □	♍ 5 22:45	7 5:50 ♄ ⚹	♏ 7 11:28	18 4:59 ☽ 25♒21
♃□♅ 24 11:23		7 20:13 ♂ △	♎ 8 1:16	8 18:57 ♃ ☌	♐ 9 12:02	26 10:17 ○ 3♊39
☿ R 30 7:16	♀ ♑ 14 10:55	9 15:11 ♄ ⚹	♏ 10 1:30	11 7:53 ♄ ☌	♑ 11 12:46	
	☉ ♑ 22 8:40	11 17:55 ♂ ☍	♐ 12 1:03	12 22:46 ♃ ⚹	♒ 13 15:38	4 1:24 ☽ 11♍23
☽0S 5 0:32		13 15:49 ♄ ☌	♑ 14 1:54	15 17:35 ♄ ⚹	♓ 15 22:12	10 17:23 ● 18♐09
♇ R 6 15:43		15 19:14 ♂ △	♒ 16 5:53	18 4:26 ♄ □	♈ 18 8:45	17 23:52 ☽ 25♓33
☽0N 17 22:50		18 8:33 ♀ □	♓ 18 13:56	20 18:19 ☉ △	♉ 20 21:38	26 3:54 ○ 3♋52
☿ D 20 1:27		20 21:34 ☉ △	♈ 21 1:28	22 18:37 ♃ ☍	♊ 23 10:09	
♂ D 20 6:45		23 4:14 ♄ △	♉ 23 14:30	25 18:08 ♄ ☍	♋ 25 20:33	
		25 8:27 ♂ ☌	♊ 26 3:00	27 15:59 ♃ △	♌ 28 4:33	
		28 5:11 ♄ ☍	♋ 28 13:51	30 9:24 ♄ △	♍ 30 10:41	
		30 2:43 ♂ ⚹	♌ 30 22:41			

Astro Data

1 NOVEMBER 1958
Julian Day # 21489
Delta T 32.6 sec
SVP 05♓50'00"
Obliquity 23°26'32"
⚷ Chiron 17♒39.5
☽ Mean ☊ 21♎17.1

1 DECEMBER 1958
Julian Day # 21519
Delta T 32.6 sec
SVP 05♓49'56"
Obliquity 23°26'31"
⚷ Chiron 18♒15.9
☽ Mean ☊ 19♎41.8

LONGITUDE JANUARY 1959

Day	Sid.Time	☉	0 hr ☽	Noon ☽	True ☊	☿	♀	♂	♃	♄	♅	♆	♇
1 Th	6 39 36	9♑49 9	21♍10 41	28♍ 4 8	18♎19.7	17♐36.6	22♑ 2.2	17♉26.1	23♏58.3	29♐28.2	15♌40.3	6♏33.8	4♍ 4.3
2 F	6 43 33	10 50 18	5♎ 0 3	11♎58 26	18R 18.7	18 45.5	23 17.6	17 34.9	24 9.3	29 35.2	15R 38.4	6 35.0	4R 3.5
3 Sa	6 47 29	11 51 28	18 59 19	26 2 40	18 18.6	19 56.7	24 32.9	17 44.4	24 20.2	29 42.1	15 36.3	6 36.2	4 2.7
4 Su	6 51 26	12 52 38	3♏ 8 26	10♏16 26	18 18.2	21 10.0	25 48.2	17 54.5	24 31.0	29 49.1	15 34.3	6 37.4	4 1.9
5 M	6 55 22	13 53 48	17 26 27	24 38 7	18 16.0	22 25.1	27 3.5	18 5.2	24 41.8	29 56.1	15 32.2	6 38.5	4 1.0
6 Tu	6 59 19	14 54 58	1♐50 59	9♐ 4 30	18 11.1	23 41.8	28 18.8	18 16.5	24 52.4	0♑ 3.0	15 30.1	6 39.6	4 0.2
7 W	7 3 15	15 56 9	16 18 0	23 30 45	18 3.1	24 60.0	29 34.0	18 28.4	25 3.0	0 9.9	15 27.9	6 40.7	3 59.3
8 Th	7 7 12	16 57 19	0♑41 58	7♑50 51	17 52.4	26 19.5	0♒49.3	18 40.9	25 13.4	0 16.9	15 25.7	6 41.7	3 58.4
9 F	7 11 8	17 58 30	14 56 35	21 58 28	17 39.9	27 40.3	2 4.6	18 53.9	25 23.8	0 23.7	15 23.5	6 42.7	3 57.4
10 Sa	7 15 5	18 59 40	28 55 49	5♒48 5	17 26.8	29 2.1	3 19.9	19 7.6	25 34.1	0 30.6	15 21.3	6 43.7	3 56.5
11 Su	7 19 2	20 0 50	12♒34 52	19 15 52	17 14.6	0♑25.0	4 35.1	19 21.7	25 44.3	0 37.4	15 19.0	6 44.6	3 55.5
12 M	7 22 58	21 2 0	25 50 58	2♓20 12	17 4.3	1 48.8	5 50.3	19 36.4	25 54.4	0 44.2	15 16.7	6 45.5	3 54.5
13 Tu	7 26 55	22 3 9	8♓43 41	15 1 42	16 56.7	3 13.4	7 5.6	19 51.7	26 4.3	0 51.0	15 14.4	6 46.4	3 53.4
14 W	7 30 51	23 4 17	21 14 38	27 22 58	16 52.0	4 38.9	8 20.8	20 7.4	26 14.2	0 57.8	15 12.0	6 47.3	3 52.4
15 Th	7 34 48	24 5 25	3♈27 15	9♈28 4	16 49.7	6 5.1	9 36.0	20 23.7	26 24.0	1 4.5	15 9.6	6 48.1	3 51.3
16 F	7 38 44	25 6 32	15 26 6	21 22 1	16 49.2	7 32.1	10 51.1	20 40.4	26 33.6	1 11.2	15 7.2	6 48.9	3 50.2
17 Sa	7 42 41	26 7 38	27 16 31	3♉10 20	16 49.2	8 59.7	12 6.3	20 57.6	26 43.2	1 17.9	15 4.8	6 49.6	3 49.1
18 Su	7 46 37	27 8 43	9♉ 4 8	14 58 39	16 48.7	10 28.1	13 21.5	21 15.3	26 52.7	1 24.5	15 2.3	6 50.3	3 47.9
19 M	7 50 34	28 9 48	20 54 30	26 52 21	16 46.5	11 57.0	14 36.6	21 33.4	27 2.0	1 31.1	14 59.9	6 51.0	3 46.8
20 Tu	7 54 31	29 10 52	2♊52 45	8♊56 14	16 41.9	13 26.7	15 51.7	21 51.9	27 11.2	1 37.7	14 57.4	6 51.7	3 45.6
21 W	7 58 27	0♒11 55	15 3 16	21 14 13	16 34.6	14 56.9	17 6.8	22 10.9	27 20.4	1 44.2	14 54.9	6 52.3	3 44.4
22 Th	8 2 24	1 12 57	27 29 24	3♋49 1	16 24.7	16 27.7	18 21.9	22 30.3	27 29.4	1 50.7	14 52.4	6 52.9	3 43.2
23 F	8 6 20	2 13 59	10♋13 12	16 41 56	16 12.8	17 59.2	19 36.9	22 50.1	27 38.2	1 57.2	14 49.8	6 53.4	3 41.9
24 Sa	8 10 17	3 14 59	23 15 10	29 52 42	15 60.0	19 31.3	20 52.0	23 10.3	27 47.0	2 3.6	14 47.3	6 53.9	3 40.7
25 Su	8 14 13	4 15 59	6♌34 18	13♌19 39	15 47.4	21 4.0	22 7.0	23 30.9	27 55.7	2 10.0	14 44.7	6 54.4	3 39.4
26 M	8 18 10	5 16 58	20 8 23	27 0 4	15 36.3	22 37.3	23 22.0	23 51.8	28 4.2	2 16.3	14 42.2	6 54.9	3 38.1
27 Tu	8 22 6	6 17 56	3♍54 17	10♍50 38	15 27.7	24 11.3	24 37.0	24 13.1	28 12.6	2 22.6	14 39.6	6 55.3	3 36.8
28 W	8 26 3	7 18 53	17 48 43	24 48 11	15 21.9	25 45.8	25 51.9	24 34.8	28 20.9	2 28.9	14 37.0	6 55.7	3 35.5
29 Th	8 30 0	8 19 50	1♎48 42	8♎50 2	15D 19.0	27 21.1	27 6.9	24 56.8	28 29.0	2 35.1	14 34.4	6 56.0	3 34.2
30 F	8 33 56	9 20 46	15 51 56	22 54 16	15 18.3	28 57.0	28 21.8	25 19.1	28 37.1	2 41.3	14 31.8	6 56.3	3 32.8
31 Sa	8 37 53	10 21 41	29 56 54	6♏59 42	15R 18.7	0♒33.5	29 36.7	25 41.8	28 45.0	2 47.4	14 29.1	6 56.6	3 31.4

LONGITUDE FEBRUARY 1959

Day	Sid.Time	☉	0 hr ☽	Noon ☽	True ☊	☿	♀	♂	♃	♄	♅	♆	♇
1 Su	8 41 49	11♒22 35	14♏ 2 35	21♏ 5 27	15♎19.0	2♒10.8	0♓51.6	26♉ 4.7	28♏52.7	2♑53.4	14♌26.5	6♏56.8	3♍30.1
2 M	8 45 46	12 23 29	28 8 10	5♐10 36	15R 17.8	3 48.7	2 6.4	26 28.0	29 0.4	2 59.5	14R 23.9	6 57.0	3R 28.7
3 Tu	8 49 42	13 24 23	12♐12 31	19 13 41	15 14.5	5 27.4	3 21.3	26 51.7	29 7.8	3 5.5	14 21.3	6 57.2	3 27.3
4 W	8 53 39	14 25 15	26 13 48	3♑12 30	15 8.6	7 6.8	4 36.1	27 15.6	29 15.2	3 11.4	14 18.6	6 57.4	3 25.8
5 Th	8 57 35	15 26 6	10♑ 9 25	17 4 7	15 0.3	8 46.9	5 50.9	27 39.8	29 22.4	3 17.3	14 16.0	6 57.5	3 24.4
6 F	9 1 32	16 26 57	23 56 10	0♒45 8	14 50.4	10 27.8	7 5.7	28 4.3	29 29.5	3 23.1	14 13.4	6 57.5	3 23.0
7 Sa	9 5 29	17 27 46	7♒30 37	14 12 16	14 39.9	12 9.4	8 20.4	28 29.0	29 36.4	3 28.9	14 10.8	6R 57.6	3 21.5
8 Su	9 9 25	18 28 34	20 49 47	27 22 55	14 30.0	13 51.8	9 35.2	28 54.1	29 43.2	3 34.6	14 8.1	6 57.6	3 20.1
9 M	9 13 22	19 29 21	3♓51 33	10♓15 37	14 21.7	15 35.1	10 49.9	29 19.4	29 49.9	3 40.2	14 5.5	6 57.5	3 18.6
10 Tu	9 17 18	20 30 7	16 35 10	22 50 20	14 15.5	17 19.1	12 4.5	29 45.0	29 56.3	3 45.8	14 2.9	6 57.5	3 17.1
11 W	9 21 15	21 30 51	29 1 20	5♈ 8 29	14 11.9	19 3.9	13 19.2	0♊10.8	0♐ 2.7	3 51.4	14 0.3	6 57.4	3 15.6
12 Th	9 25 11	22 31 33	11♈12 10	17 12 49	14D 10.5	20 49.6	14 33.8	0 36.9	0 8.9	3 56.8	13 57.7	6 57.2	3 14.2
13 F	9 29 8	23 32 14	23 10 58	29 7 11	14 10.8	22 36.0	15 48.4	1 3.3	0 14.9	4 2.3	13 55.1	6 57.1	3 12.7
14 Sa	9 33 4	24 32 53	5♉ 2 2	10♉56 11	14 12.1	24 23.3	17 2.9	1 29.8	0 20.8	4 7.6	13 52.5	6 56.9	3 11.2
15 Su	9 37 1	25 33 31	16 50 17	22 44 59	14R 13.3	26 11.3	18 17.4	1 56.6	0 26.5	4 12.9	13 49.9	6 56.6	3 9.6
16 M	9 40 58	26 34 7	28 40 58	4♊38 54	14 13.7	28 0.1	19 31.9	2 23.6	0 32.1	4 18.1	13 47.4	6 56.4	3 8.1
17 Tu	9 44 54	27 34 41	10♊39 26	16 43 10	14 12.5	29 49.7	20 46.4	2 50.9	0 37.5	4 23.3	13 44.9	6 56.1	3 6.6
18 W	9 48 51	28 35 14	22 50 41	29 2 31	14 9.5	1♓40.0	22 0.8	3 18.3	0 42.7	4 28.4	13 42.3	6 55.7	3 5.1
19 Th	9 52 47	29 35 44	5♋19 7	11♋40 51	14 4.6	3 30.9	23 15.1	3 46.0	0 47.8	4 33.4	13 39.8	6 55.4	3 3.6
20 F	9 56 44	0♓36 13	18 8 1	24 40 46	13 58.1	5 22.5	24 29.5	4 13.8	0 52.7	4 38.4	13 37.3	6 55.0	3 2.1
21 Sa	10 0 40	1 36 40	1♌19 11	8♌ 3 12	13 50.8	7 14.5	25 43.8	4 41.9	0 57.5	4 43.3	13 34.9	6 54.5	3 0.5
22 Su	10 4 37	2 37 6	14 52 37	21 47 9	13 43.5	9 7.0	26 58.0	5 10.1	1 2.1	4 48.1	13 32.4	6 54.1	2 59.0
23 M	10 8 33	3 37 29	28 46 21	5♍49 43	13 37.1	10 59.7	28 12.2	5 38.5	1 6.5	4 52.9	13 30.0	6 53.6	2 57.5
24 Tu	10 12 30	4 37 51	12♍56 37	20 6 25	13 32.2	12 52.5	29 26.4	6 7.1	1 10.8	4 57.6	13 27.6	6 53.1	2 55.9
25 W	10 16 27	5 38 11	27 18 25	4♎31 54	13 29.2	14 45.3	0♈40.5	6 35.8	1 14.9	5 2.2	13 25.2	6 52.5	2 54.4
26 Th	10 20 23	6 38 30	11♎46 11	19 0 37	13D 28.1	16 37.8	1 54.6	7 4.8	1 18.8	5 6.7	13 22.8	6 51.9	2 52.9
27 F	10 24 20	7 38 47	26 14 37	3♏27 39	13 28.6	18 29.8	3 8.7	7 33.9	1 22.5	5 11.2	13 20.5	6 51.3	2 51.4
28 Sa	10 28 16	8 39 3	10♏39 16	17 49 5	13 30.0	20 21.0	4 22.7	8 3.1	1 26.1	5 15.6	13 18.2	6 50.6	2 49.8

Astro Data

	Dy Hr Mn
☽0S	1 7:28
♄□♅	8 23:26
☽0N	14 8:55
☽0S	28 14:18
♄△♇	5 23:40
♆ R	7 13:35
☽0N	10 18:50
☽0S	24 22:38
♀0N	26 8:44

Planet Ingress

	Dy Hr Mn
♄ ♑	5 13:32
♀ ♒	7 8:16
☿ ♑	10 16:47
☉ ♒	20 19:19
☿ ♒	30 15:41
♀ ♓	31 7:28
♂ ♊	10 13:57
♃ ♐	10 13:45
☿ ♓	17 2:15
☉ ♓	19 9:38
♀ ♈	24 10:53

Last Aspect / ☽ Ingress

Last Aspect Dy Hr Mn		☽ Ingress Dy Hr Mn
1 14:33	♄ □	♎ 1 15:21
3 18:21	♄ ✶	♏ 3 18:42
5 17:34	♀ ✶	♐ 5 20:56
7 15:57	☿ ☌	♑ 7 22:50
9 18:07	♃ ✶	♒ 10 1:52
12 0:06	♃ □	♓ 12 7:39
14 9:53	♃ △	♈ 14 17:09
16 21:27	☉ □	♉ 17 5:33
19 15:56	☉ △	♊ 19 18:16
21 4:28	♀ △	♋ 22 4:47
24 8:19	♃ △	♌ 24 12:13
26 14:00	♃ □	♍ 26 17:13
28 18:15	♃ ✶	♎ 28 20:54
30 23:22	♀ △	♏ 31 0:05

Last Aspect / ☽ Ingress

Last Aspect Dy Hr Mn		☽ Ingress Dy Hr Mn
2 1:30	♃ ☌	♐ 2 3:11
3 3:39	♅ △	♑ 4 6:29
6 9:51	♃ ✶	♒ 6 10:40
8 16:27	♃ □	♓ 8 16:50
9 14:30	♀ ☌	♈ 11 1:55
13 0:47	☉ ✶	♉ 13 13:47
15 22:23	☿ □	♊ 16 2:39
18 12:06	☉ △	♋ 18 13:51
20 12:52	♀ △	♌ 20 21:38
21 21:40	♅ ☌	♍ 23 2:06
23 23:52	☿ ☍	♎ 25 4:29
26 2:40	♅ ✶	♏ 27 6:14

☽ Phases & Eclipses

Dy Hr Mn	
2 10:50	☽ 11♎18
9 5:34	● 18♑13
16 21:27	☽ 26♈01
24 19:32	○ 4♌05
31 19:06	☽ 11♏10
7 19:22	● 18♒17
15 19:20	☽ 26♉22
23 8:54	○ 3♍60

Astro Data

1 JANUARY 1959
Julian Day # 21550
Delta T 32.7 sec
SVP 05♓49'50"
Obliquity 23°26'31"
⚷ Chiron 19♒46.1
☽ Mean ☊ 18♎03.3

1 FEBRUARY 1959
Julian Day # 21581
Delta T 32.7 sec
SVP 05♓49'46"
Obliquity 23°26'32"
⚷ Chiron 21♒50.2
☽ Mean ☊ 16♎24.8

MARCH 1959 — LONGITUDE

Day	Sid.Time	☉	0 hr ☽	Noon ☽	True ☊	☿	♀	♂	♃	♄	♅	♆	♇
1 Su	10 32 13	9♓39 17	24♏56 47	2♐ 2 8	13♎31.4	22♓10.9	5♈36.6	8♊32.5	1♐29.5	5♑19.9	13♌15.9	6♏50.0	2♍48.3
2 M	10 36 9	10 39 30	9♐ 4 57	16 5 5	13R32.1	23 59.4	6 50.6	9 2.1	1 32.7	5 24.2	13R13.7	6R49.2	2R46.8
3 Tu	10 40 6	11 39 41	23 2 24	29 56 51	13 31.6	25 45.9	8 4.5	9 31.8	1 35.7	5 28.3	13 11.4	6 48.5	2 45.3
4 W	10 44 2	12 39 51	6♑48 20	13♑36 48	13 29.6	27 30.0	9 18.3	10 1.7	1 38.6	5 32.4	13 9.2	6 47.7	2 43.8
5 Th	10 47 59	13 40 0	20 22 12	27 4 26	13 26.3	29 11.2	10 32.1	10 31.7	1 41.3	5 36.4	13 7.1	6 46.9	2 42.3
6 F	10 51 55	14 40 7	3♒43 29	10♒19 15	13 22.0	0♈49.0	11 45.9	11 1.9	1 43.8	5 40.4	13 4.9	6 46.1	2 40.8
7 Sa	10 55 52	15 40 12	16 51 42	23 20 48	13 17.3	2 22.8	12 59.6	11 32.2	1 46.1	5 44.2	13 2.8	6 45.3	2 39.3
8 Su	10 59 49	16 40 15	29 46 29	6♓ 8 46	13 12.8	3 52.1	14 13.3	12 2.6	1 48.2	5 48.0	13 0.8	6 44.4	2 37.8
9 M	11 3 45	17 40 16	12♓27 40	18 43 13	13 9.2	5 16.3	15 26.9	12 33.2	1 50.2	5 51.7	12 58.7	6 43.5	2 36.4
10 Tu	11 7 42	18 40 16	24 55 30	1♈ 4 39	13 6.7	6 34.9	16 40.5	13 3.9	1 51.9	5 55.3	12 56.7	6 42.5	2 34.9
11 W	11 11 38	19 40 13	7♈10 50	13 14 16	13D 5.5	7 47.4	17 54.0	13 34.7	1 53.5	5 58.8	12 54.8	6 41.5	2 33.5
12 Th	11 15 35	20 40 9	19 15 13	25 14 0	13 5.5	8 53.2	19 7.5	14 5.7	1 54.9	6 2.2	12 52.8	6 40.6	2 32.0
13 F	11 19 31	21 40 3	1♉10 59	7♉ 6 32	13 6.4	9 52.1	20 20.9	14 36.8	1 56.1	6 5.5	12 50.9	6 39.5	2 30.6
14 Sa	11 23 28	22 39 54	13 1 8	18 55 15	13 7.9	10 43.4	21 34.3	15 8.0	1 57.1	6 8.8	12 49.1	6 38.5	2 29.2
15 Su	11 27 24	23 39 44	24 49 24	0♊44 9	13 9.6	11 27.0	22 47.6	15 39.3	1 58.0	6 11.9	12 47.3	6 37.4	2 27.7
16 M	11 31 21	24 39 31	6♊40 3	12 37 42	13 11.0	12 2.5	24 0.9	16 10.8	1 58.6	6 15.0	12 45.5	6 36.3	2 26.3
17 Tu	11 35 18	25 39 16	18 37 42	24 40 39	13R11.9	12 29.7	25 14.1	16 42.3	1 59.1	6 18.0	12 43.8	6 35.2	2 25.0
18 W	11 39 14	26 38 59	0♋47 10	6♋57 49	13 12.0	12 48.7	26 27.2	17 14.0	1R59.3	6 20.9	12 42.1	6 34.1	2 23.6
19 Th	11 43 11	27 38 39	13 13 8	19 33 39	13 11.3	12R59.2	27 40.3	17 45.8	1 59.4	6 23.7	12 40.5	6 32.9	2 22.2
20 F	11 47 7	28 38 17	25 59 47	2♌31 54	13 10.1	13 1.4	28 53.3	18 17.6	1 59.3	6 26.4	12 38.9	6 31.7	2 20.9
21 Sa	11 51 4	29 37 53	9♌10 16	15 55 3	13 8.4	12 55.6	0♉ 6.3	18 49.6	1 59.0	6 29.1	12 37.3	6 30.5	2 19.5
22 Su	11 55 0	0♈37 27	22 46 16	29 43 50	13 6.6	12 42.0	1 19.2	19 21.6	1 58.5	6 31.6	12 35.8	6 29.3	2 18.2
23 M	11 58 57	1 36 58	6♍47 27	13♍56 45	13 5.1	12 21.0	2 32.1	19 53.8	1 57.8	6 34.0	12 34.3	6 28.0	2 16.9
24 Tu	12 2 53	2 36 27	21 11 10	28 30 0	13 4.1	11 53.3	3 44.8	20 26.0	1 57.0	6 36.4	12 32.9	6 26.7	2 15.6
25 W	12 6 50	3 35 55	5♎52 27	13♎17 36	13D 3.5	11 19.4	4 57.5	20 58.3	1 55.9	6 38.6	12 31.5	6 25.4	2 14.4
26 Th	12 10 47	4 35 20	20 44 30	28 12 8	13 3.5	10 40.3	6 10.2	21 30.7	1 54.7	6 40.8	12 30.2	6 24.1	2 13.1
27 F	12 14 43	5 34 43	5♏39 32	13♏ 5 45	13 3.9	9 56.8	7 22.7	22 3.2	1 53.3	6 42.9	12 28.9	6 22.8	2 11.9
28 Sa	12 18 40	6 34 4	20 29 53	27 51 10	13 4.5	9 9.8	8 35.3	22 35.8	1 51.7	6 44.8	12 27.7	6 21.4	2 10.7
29 Su	12 22 36	7 33 24	5♐ 8 56	12♐22 37	13 5.0	8 20.5	9 47.7	23 8.5	1 49.9	6 46.7	12 26.5	6 20.1	2 9.5
30 M	12 26 33	8 32 42	19 31 49	26 36 13	13 5.4	7 29.8	11 0.1	23 41.2	1 48.0	6 48.5	12 25.4	6 18.7	2 8.3
31 Tu	12 30 29	9 31 58	3♑35 39	10♑30 2	13R 5.6	6 38.8	12 12.4	24 14.0	1 45.8	6 50.2	12 24.3	6 17.3	2 7.1

APRIL 1959 — LONGITUDE

Day	Sid.Time	☉	0 hr ☽	Noon ☽	True ☊	☿	♀	♂	♃	♄	♅	♆	♇
1 W	12 34 26	10♈31 12	17♑19 23	24♑ 3 46	13♎ 5.6	5♈48.5	13♉24.7	24♊46.9	1♐43.5	6♑51.8	12♌23.3	6♏15.9	2♍ 6.0
2 Th	12 38 22	11 30 25	0♒43 22	7♒18 21	13R 5.5	4R59.9	14 36.8	25 19.9	1R41.0	6 53.3	12R22.3	6R14.4	2R 4.9
3 F	12 42 19	12 29 36	13 48 57	20 15 25	13D 5.4	4 13.8	15 48.9	25 52.9	1 38.3	6 54.7	12 21.3	6 13.0	2 3.8
4 Sa	12 46 15	13 28 45	26 38 0	2♓56 58	13 5.4	3 31.0	17 1.0	26 26.1	1 35.4	6 56.0	12 20.4	6 11.5	2 2.7
5 Su	12 50 12	14 27 52	9♓12 34	15 25 3	13 5.5	2 52.0	18 13.0	26 59.3	1 32.3	6 57.2	12 19.6	6 10.0	2 1.6
6 M	12 54 9	15 26 57	21 34 41	27 41 41	13 5.7	2 17.5	19 24.9	27 32.5	1 29.1	6 58.3	12 18.8	6 8.5	2 0.6
7 Tu	12 58 5	16 26 0	3♈46 17	9♈48 45	13R 5.9	1 47.8	20 36.7	28 5.9	1 25.7	6 59.3	12 18.1	6 7.0	1 59.6
8 W	13 2 2	17 25 2	15 49 16	21 48 6	13 5.9	1 23.2	21 48.5	28 39.3	1 22.1	7 0.2	12 17.4	6 5.5	1 58.6
9 Th	13 5 58	18 24 1	27 45 29	3♉41 40	13 5.7	1 3.9	23 0.1	29 12.8	1 18.4	7 1.0	12 16.8	6 4.0	1 57.6
10 F	13 9 55	19 22 58	9♉36 56	15 31 32	13 5.2	0 50.0	24 11.7	29 46.3	1 14.5	7 1.7	12 16.2	6 2.4	1 56.7
11 Sa	13 13 51	20 21 54	21 25 49	27 20 6	13 4.4	0 41.6	25 23.3	0♋19.9	1 10.4	7 2.3	12 15.7	6 0.9	1 55.7
12 Su	13 17 48	21 20 47	3♊14 45	9♊10 8	13 3.3	0D38.5	26 34.7	0 53.6	1 6.1	7 2.8	12 15.2	5 59.3	1 54.8
13 M	13 21 44	22 19 38	15 6 42	21 4 53	13 2.0	0 40.7	27 46.1	1 27.4	1 1.7	7 3.2	12 14.8	5 57.7	1 54.0
14 Tu	13 25 41	23 18 26	27 5 9	3♋ 8 0	13 0.8	0 48.1	28 57.3	2 1.2	0 57.2	7 3.5	12 14.4	5 56.2	1 53.1
15 W	13 29 38	24 17 13	9♋13 56	15 23 29	12 59.9	1 0.5	0♊ 8.5	2 35.0	0 52.5	7 3.7	12 14.1	5 54.6	1 52.3
16 Th	13 33 34	25 15 57	21 37 10	27 55 31	12D59.5	1 17.8	1 19.6	3 8.9	0 47.6	7R 3.8	12 13.8	5 53.0	1 51.5
17 F	13 37 31	26 14 39	4♌19 0	10♌48 6	12 59.6	1 39.8	2 30.6	3 42.9	0 42.6	7 3.9	12 13.6	5 51.4	1 50.7
18 Sa	13 41 27	27 13 19	17 23 13	24 4 42	13 0.3	2 6.3	3 41.5	4 16.9	0 37.4	7 3.8	12 13.5	5 49.8	1 50.0
19 Su	13 45 24	28 11 57	0♍52 49	7♍47 40	13 1.3	2 37.1	4 52.3	4 51.0	0 32.1	7 3.6	12 13.4	5 48.1	1 49.2
20 M	13 49 20	29 10 32	14 49 18	21 57 32	13 2.5	3 12.0	6 3.1	5 25.1	0 26.7	7 3.3	12D13.4	5 46.5	1 48.5
21 Tu	13 53 17	0♉ 9 5	29 12 5	6♎32 27	13R 3.5	3 50.8	7 13.7	5 59.3	0 21.1	7 2.9	12 13.4	5 44.9	1 47.9
22 W	13 57 13	1 7 36	13♎57 57	21 27 46	13 3.8	4 33.4	8 24.2	6 33.5	0 15.4	7 2.5	12 13.4	5 43.3	1 47.2
23 Th	14 1 10	2 6 5	29 0 53	6♏36 11	13 3.3	5 19.5	9 34.6	7 7.8	0 9.5	7 1.9	12 13.5	5 41.6	1 46.6
24 F	14 5 7	3 4 33	14♏12 28	21 48 28	13 1.8	6 9.1	10 44.9	7 42.1	0 3.6	7 1.2	12 13.7	5 40.0	1 46.0
25 Sa	14 9 3	4 2 58	29 22 59	6♐54 49	12 59.5	7 1.9	11 55.2	8 16.5	29♏57.5	7 0.5	12 13.9	5 38.4	1 45.5
26 Su	14 13 0	5 1 22	14♐22 53	21 46 17	12 56.6	7 57.9	13 5.3	8 50.9	29 51.3	6 59.6	12 14.2	5 36.7	1 44.9
27 M	14 16 56	5 59 44	29 4 14	6♑16 10	12 53.8	8 56.9	14 15.3	9 25.4	29 45.0	6 58.7	12 14.6	5 35.1	1 44.4
28 Tu	14 20 53	6 58 5	13♑21 41	20 20 35	12 51.4	9 58.8	15 25.2	9 59.9	29 38.6	6 57.6	12 15.0	5 33.5	1 43.9
29 W	14 24 49	7 56 24	27 12 48	3♒58 27	12D49.9	11 3.4	16 35.0	10 34.4	29 32.0	6 56.5	12 15.4	5 31.8	1 43.5
30 Th	14 28 46	8 54 41	10♒37 44	17 10 57	12 49.5	12 10.7	17 44.7	11 9.0	29 25.4	6 55.2	12 15.9	5 30.2	1 43.1

Astro Data Dy Hr Mn	Planet Ingress Dy Hr Mn	Last Aspect Dy Hr Mn	☽ Ingress Dy Hr Mn	Last Aspect Dy Hr Mn	☽ Ingress Dy Hr Mn	☽ Phases & Eclipses Dy Hr Mn	Astro Data
☿0N 5 0:12	☿ ♈ 5 11:52	28 18:39 ☿ △	♐ 1 8:33	31 16:26 ♀ △	♒ 1 22:41	2 2:54 ☽ 10♐47	1 MARCH 1959
☽0N 10 3:09	♀ ♉ 20 21:55	3 5:25 ☿ □	♑ 3 12:05	3 23:36 ♂ △	♓ 4 6:23	9 10:51 ● 18♓07	Julian Day # 21609
♃ R 18 22:10	☉ ♈ 21 8:55	4 11:09 ☉ ✶	♒ 5 17:16	6 12:15 ♂ □	♈ 6 16:33	17 15:10 ☽ 26♊17	Delta T 32.8 sec
☿ R 19 18:34		6 17:00 ♅ ☍	♓ 8 0:25	9 3:05 ♂ ✶	♉ 9 4:32	24 20:02 ○ 3♎26	SVP 05♓49'43"
♄✶♆ 21 9:10	♂ ♋ 10 9:46	9 10:51 ☉ ☌	♈ 10 9:53	11 8:57 ♀ ☌	♊ 11 17:25	24 20:11 ☍ P 0.264	Obliquity 23°26'32"
☽0S 24 8:45	♀ ♊ 14 21:08	11 23:43 ♀ ☌	♉ 12 21:37	13 15:47 ☉ ✶	♋ 14 5:48	31 11:06 ☽ 9♑59	⚷ Chiron 23♒50.4
	☉ ♉ 20 20:17	14 21:25 ☉ ✶	♊ 15 10:31	16 7:33 ☉ □	♌ 16 15:55		☽ Mean ☊ 14♎55.8
☽0N 6 9:39	♃ ♏ 24 14:11	17 15:10 ☉ □	♋ 17 22:28	18 18:56 ☉ △	♍ 18 22:27	8 3:29 ● 17♈34	1 APRIL 1959
☿0S 11 18:47		20 5:53 ♀ □	♌ 20 7:22	19 10:44 ♄ △	♎ 21 1:19	8 3:23:35 ✔ A 7'25"	Julian Day # 21640
☿ D 12 1:53		21 17:49 ♂ ✶	♍ 22 12:28	21 21:12 ♅ ✶	♏ 23 1:34	16 7:33 ☽ 25♋34	Delta T 32.8 sec
♄ R 16 15:32		23 22:43 ♂ □	♎ 24 14:27	25 0:54 ♃ ☌	♐ 25 0:59	23 5:13 ○ 2♏19	SVP 05♓49'40"
☽0S 20 19:35		26 1:17 ♂ △	♏ 26 14:53	25 21:44 ♀ ☍	♑ 27 1:32	29 20:38 ☽ 8♒47	Obliquity 23°26'32"
♅ D 20 6:57		27 11:00 ♅ □	♐ 28 15:31	29 4:04 ♃ ✶	♒ 29 4:55		⚷ Chiron 25♒49.1
☿0N 23 2:59		30 7:19 ♂ ☍	♑ 30 17:49				☽ Mean ☊ 13♎17.3

LONGITUDE — MAY 1959

Day	Sid.Time	☉	0 hr ☽	Noon ☽	True ☊	☿	♀	♂	♃	♄	♅	♆	♇
1 F	14 32 42	9♉52 57	23♒38 31	0♓ 0 52	12♎50.2	13♈20.5	18♊54.2	11♋43.6	29♏18.6	6♑53.9	12♌16.4	5♏28.6	1♍42.7
2 Sa	14 36 39	10 51 12	6♓18 27	12 31 46	12 51.6	14 32.9	20 3.7	12 18.3	29R 11.8	6R 52.5	12 17.1	5R 26.9	1R 42.3
3 Su	14 40 36	11 49 25	18 41 18	24 47 33	12 53.3	15 47.7	21 13.0	12 53.1	29 4.9	6 51.0	12 17.7	5 25.3	1 42.0
4 M	14 44 32	12 47 36	0♈50 58	6♈51 59	12 54.7	17 4.8	22 22.3	13 27.8	28 57.9	6 49.3	12 18.4	5 23.7	1 41.7
5 Tu	14 48 29	13 45 46	12 51 2	18 48 29	12R 55.3	18 24.2	23 31.4	14 2.6	28 50.8	6 47.6	12 19.2	5 22.1	1 41.4
6 W	14 52 25	14 43 54	24 44 42	0♉40 1	12 54.6	19 45.8	24 40.4	14 37.5	28 43.7	6 45.9	12 20.0	5 20.5	1 41.1
7 Th	14 56 22	15 42 1	6♉34 42	12 29 4	12 52.3	21 9.6	25 49.3	15 12.4	28 36.4	6 44.0	12 20.9	5 18.8	1 40.9
8 F	15 0 18	16 40 6	18 23 22	24 17 50	12 48.4	22 35.6	26 58.0	15 47.3	28 29.1	6 42.0	12 21.8	5 17.2	1 40.7
9 Sa	15 4 15	17 38 10	0♊12 42	6♊ 8 14	12 43.0	24 3.7	28 6.6	16 22.3	28 21.8	6 40.0	12 22.8	5 15.6	1 40.6
10 Su	15 8 11	18 36 12	12 4 38	18 2 11	12 36.7	25 33.9	29 15.1	16 57.3	28 14.4	6 37.8	12 23.8	5 14.1	1 40.4
11 M	15 12 8	19 34 12	24 1 7	0♋ 1 44	12 29.9	27 6.2	0♋23.5	17 32.4	28 6.9	6 35.6	12 24.9	5 12.5	1 40.3
12 Tu	15 16 4	20 32 11	6♋ 4 20	12 9 15	12 23.5	28 40.6	1 31.7	18 7.5	27 59.4	6 33.3	12 26.0	5 10.9	1 40.3
13 W	15 20 1	21 30 7	18 16 50	24 27 28	12 18.1	0♉17.0	2 39.8	18 42.6	27 51.9	6 30.9	12 27.2	5 9.4	1D 40.2
14 Th	15 23 58	22 28 2	0♌41 34	6♌59 31	12 14.2	1 55.5	3 47.7	19 17.8	27 44.4	6 28.4	12 28.4	5 7.8	1 40.2
15 F	15 27 54	23 25 56	13 21 48	19 48 49	12D 12.0	3 36.1	4 55.5	19 53.0	27 36.8	6 25.9	12 29.7	5 6.3	1 40.2
16 Sa	15 31 51	24 23 47	26 21 1	2♍58 48	12 11.5	5 18.7	6 3.1	20 28.3	27 29.2	6 23.2	12 31.0	5 4.7	1 40.3
17 Su	15 35 47	25 21 37	9♍42 30	16 32 26	12 12.2	7 3.3	7 10.6	21 3.5	27 21.5	6 20.5	12 32.4	5 3.2	1 40.3
18 M	15 39 44	26 19 24	23 28 48	0♎31 41	12 13.5	8 50.0	8 17.9	21 38.8	27 13.9	6 17.7	12 33.8	5 1.7	1 40.4
19 Tu	15 43 40	27 17 11	7♎41 2	14 56 38	12R 14.4	10 38.8	9 25.0	22 14.2	27 6.3	6 14.9	12 35.3	5 0.2	1 40.6
20 W	15 47 37	28 14 55	22 18 6	29 44 50	12 14.1	12 29.6	10 31.9	22 49.5	26 58.6	6 11.9	12 36.9	4 58.7	1 40.7
21 Th	15 51 33	29 12 38	7♏16 1	14♏50 43	12 11.9	14 22.4	11 38.7	23 24.9	26 51.0	6 8.9	12 38.4	4 57.3	1 40.9
22 F	15 55 30	0♊10 20	22 27 45	0♐ 5 53	12 7.7	16 17.3	12 45.3	24 0.4	26 43.4	6 5.8	12 40.1	4 55.8	1 41.2
23 Sa	15 59 27	1 8 0	7♐43 45	15 20 0	12 1.6	18 14.2	13 51.7	24 35.8	26 35.8	6 2.7	12 41.7	4 54.4	1 41.4
24 Su	16 3 23	2 5 39	22 53 19	0♑22 30	11 54.3	20 13.0	14 58.0	25 11.3	26 28.2	5 59.5	12 43.5	4 53.0	1 41.7
25 M	16 7 20	3 3 17	7♑46 29	15 4 24	11 46.8	22 13.8	16 4.0	25 46.9	26 20.6	5 56.2	12 45.2	4 51.6	1 42.0
26 Tu	16 11 16	4 0 54	22 15 35	29 19 36	11 40.1	24 16.4	17 9.9	26 22.4	26 13.1	5 52.9	12 47.0	4 50.2	1 42.4
27 W	16 15 13	4 58 30	6♒16 14	13♒ 5 26	11 34.9	26 20.7	18 15.5	26 58.0	26 5.6	5 49.4	12 48.9	4 48.8	1 42.7
28 Th	16 19 9	5 56 5	19 47 22	26 22 18	11 31.6	28 26.7	19 21.0	27 33.6	25 58.1	5 46.0	12 50.8	4 47.5	1 43.1
29 F	16 23 6	6 53 39	2♓50 40	9♓12 57	11D 30.3	0♊34.2	20 26.2	28 9.3	25 50.7	5 42.4	12 52.8	4 46.2	1 43.6
30 Sa	16 27 3	7 51 12	15 29 42	21 41 33	11 30.4	2 43.0	21 31.3	28 44.9	25 43.4	5 38.8	12 54.8	4 44.8	1 44.0
31 Su	16 30 59	8 48 44	27 49 5	3♈52 58	11 31.3	4 52.9	22 36.1	29 20.6	25 36.0	5 35.2	12 56.8	4 43.5	1 44.5

LONGITUDE — JUNE 1959

Day	Sid.Time	☉	0 hr ☽	Noon ☽	True ☊	☿	♀	♂	♃	♄	♅	♆	♇
1 M	16 34 56	9♊46 15	9♈53 47	15♈52 8	11♎31.9	7♊ 3.8	23♋40.7	29♋56.4	25♏28.8	5♑31.5	12♌58.9	4♏42.3	1♍45.0
2 Tu	16 38 52	10 43 46	21 48 36	27 43 43	11R 31.3	9 15.3	24 45.1	0♌32.2	25R 21.6	5R 27.7	13 1.0	4R 41.0	1 45.6
3 W	16 42 49	11 41 16	3♉37 57	9♉31 47	11 28.8	11 27.3	25 49.2	1 8.0	25 14.5	5 23.9	13 3.2	4 39.8	1 46.2
4 Th	16 46 45	12 38 45	15 25 35	21 19 43	11 23.9	13 39.4	26 53.1	1 43.8	25 7.5	5 20.1	13 5.4	4 38.5	1 46.8
5 F	16 50 42	13 36 13	27 14 31	3♊10 15	11 16.4	15 51.4	27 56.8	2 19.7	25 0.5	5 16.1	13 7.7	4 37.4	1 47.4
6 Sa	16 54 38	14 33 40	9♊ 7 9	15 5 26	11 6.7	18 3.0	29 0.2	2 55.6	24 53.7	5 12.2	13 10.0	4 36.2	1 48.1
7 Su	16 58 35	15 31 6	21 5 16	27 6 48	10 55.3	20 14.0	0♌ 3.4	3 31.5	24 46.9	5 8.2	13 12.3	4 35.0	1 48.7
8 M	17 2 32	16 28 32	3♋10 13	9♋15 38	10 43.4	22 24.0	1 6.3	4 7.5	24 40.2	5 4.2	13 14.7	4 33.9	1 49.5
9 Tu	17 6 28	17 25 57	15 23 12	21 33 6	10 31.8	24 32.9	2 8.9	4 43.5	24 33.6	5 0.1	13 17.1	4 32.8	1 50.2
10 W	17 10 25	18 23 20	27 45 29	4♌ 0 34	10 21.6	26 40.4	3 11.3	5 19.5	24 27.1	4 56.0	13 19.6	4 31.7	1 51.0
11 Th	17 14 21	19 20 43	10♌18 35	16 39 47	10 13.6	28 46.4	4 13.3	5 55.5	24 20.8	4 51.8	13 22.1	4 30.7	1 51.8
12 F	17 18 18	20 18 5	23 4 27	29 32 53	10 8.2	0♋50.6	5 15.0	6 31.6	24 14.5	4 47.6	13 24.6	4 29.6	1 52.6
13 Sa	17 22 14	21 15 25	6♍ 5 24	12♍42 21	10 5.3	2 53.0	6 16.5	7 7.7	24 8.4	4 43.4	13 27.2	4 28.6	1 53.5
14 Su	17 26 11	22 12 45	19 24 2	26 10 45	10D 4.4	4 53.4	7 17.6	7 43.9	24 2.3	4 39.2	13 29.8	4 27.7	1 54.4
15 M	17 30 7	23 10 4	3♎ 2 46	10♎ 0 16	10R 4.5	6 51.7	8 18.4	8 20.0	23 56.4	4 34.9	13 32.5	4 26.7	1 55.3
16 Tu	17 34 4	24 7 21	17 3 20	24 11 57	10 4.5	8 47.8	9 18.8	8 56.2	23 50.7	4 30.6	13 35.1	4 25.8	1 56.2
17 W	17 38 1	25 4 38	1♏25 56	8♏44 58	10 3.1	10 41.7	10 18.9	9 32.4	23 45.0	4 26.3	13 37.9	4 24.9	1 57.2
18 Th	17 41 57	26 1 54	16 8 30	23 35 51	9 59.5	12 33.3	11 18.6	10 8.6	23 39.5	4 22.0	13 40.6	4 24.0	1 58.2
19 F	17 45 54	26 59 9	1♐ 6 9	8♐38 19	9 53.2	14 22.7	12 17.9	10 44.9	23 34.1	4 17.6	13 43.4	4 23.1	1 59.2
20 Sa	17 49 50	27 56 24	16 11 13	23 43 35	9 44.6	16 9.7	13 16.8	11 21.2	23 28.9	4 13.2	13 46.2	4 22.3	2 0.2
21 Su	17 53 47	28 53 38	1♑14 10	8♑41 44	9 34.3	17 54.4	14 15.4	11 57.5	23 23.8	4 8.9	13 49.1	4 21.5	2 1.3
22 M	17 57 43	29 50 52	16 5 7	23 23 20	9 23.5	19 36.8	15 13.5	12 33.9	23 18.9	4 4.5	13 52.0	4 20.7	2 2.4
23 Tu	18 1 40	0♋48 5	0♒35 33	7♒41 9	9 13.5	21 16.7	16 11.2	13 10.2	23 14.1	4 0.1	13 54.9	4 20.0	2 3.5
24 W	18 5 36	1 45 19	14 39 43	21 31 2	9 5.3	22 54.4	17 8.4	13 46.6	23 9.4	3 55.7	13 57.9	4 19.3	2 4.6
25 Th	18 9 33	2 42 32	28 15 6	4♓52 4	8 59.4	24 29.6	18 5.3	14 23.0	23 4.9	3 51.2	14 0.9	4 18.6	2 5.8
26 F	18 13 30	3 39 44	11♓22 14	17 46 2	8 56.1	26 2.4	19 1.6	14 59.5	23 0.6	3 46.8	14 3.9	4 18.0	2 7.0
27 Sa	18 17 26	4 36 57	24 4 0	0♈16 42	8 54.7	27 32.8	19 57.4	15 36.0	22 56.4	3 42.4	14 6.9	4 17.3	2 8.2
28 Su	18 21 23	5 34 10	6♈24 46	12 28 54	8 54.5	29 0.8	20 52.8	16 12.5	22 52.4	3 38.0	14 10.0	4 16.7	2 9.4
29 M	18 25 19	6 31 23	18 29 45	24 27 59	8 54.3	0♌26.4	21 47.7	16 49.0	22 48.5	3 33.6	14 13.1	4 16.2	2 10.7
30 Tu	18 29 16	7 28 35	0♉24 16	6♉19 15	8 53.2	1 49.5	22 42.0	17 25.6	22 44.8	3 29.2	14 16.2	4 15.6	2 12.0

Astro Data Dy Hr Mn	Planet Ingress Dy Hr Mn	Last Aspect Dy Hr Mn	☽ Ingress Dy Hr Mn	Last Aspect Dy Hr Mn	☽ Ingress Dy Hr Mn	☽ Phases & Eclipses Dy Hr Mn	Astro Data
☽0N 3 15:34	♀ ♋ 10 15:45	1 10:34 ♃ □	♓ 1 11:58	2 6:33 ♀ □	♉ 2 16:37	7 20:11 ● 16♉31	1 MAY 1959
♇ D 13 21:51	☿ ♉ 12 19:48	3 20:18 ♃ △	♈ 3 22:19	5 1:34 ♀ ⚹	♊ 5 5:35	15 20:09 ☽ 24♌14	Julian Day # 21670
☽0S 18 5:42	☉ ♊ 21 19:42	5 23:50 ♀ ⚹	♉ 6 10:39	6 21:55 ☿ ☌	♋ 7 17:44	22 12:56 ○ 0♐41	Delta T 32.8 sec
☽0N 30 22:28	☿ ♊ 28 17:35	8 20:17 ♃ ☍	♊ 8 23:34	9 17:40 ♃ △	♌ 10 4:19	29 8:14 ☽ 7♓13	SVP 05♓49'37"
		11 7:05 ☿ ⚹	♋ 11 11:57	12 2:09 ♃ □	♍ 12 12:50		Obliquity 23°26'32"
☽0S 14 14:12	♂ ♌ 1 2:26	13 18:23 ♃ △	♌ 13 22:40	14 8:10 ♃ ⚹	♎ 14 18:42	6 11:53 ● 15♊02	⚷ Chiron 27♒08.8
♄⚹♆ 17 10:02	♀ ♌ 6 22:42	16 2:03 ♃ □	♍ 16 6:38	16 12:43 ☉ △	♏ 16 21:38	14 5:22 ☽ 22♍26	☽ Mean ☊ 11♎42.0
☽0N 27 7:04	☿ ♋ 11 14:11	18 6:21 ♃ ⚹	♎ 18 11:06	18 12:01 ♃ ☌	♐ 18 22:14	20 20:00 ○ 28♐44	
	☉ ♋ 22 3:50	20 0:53 ♂ □	♏ 20 12:24	20 20:00 ☉ ☍	♑ 20 22:01	27 22:12 ☽ 5♈30	1 JUNE 1959
	☿ ♌ 28 16:31	22 6:38 ♃ ☌	♐ 22 11:51	22 11:49 ♃ ⚹	♒ 22 23:00		Julian Day # 21701
		23 7:51 ♅ △	♑ 24 11:24	24 14:49 ♃ □	♓ 25 3:09		Delta T 32.9 sec
		26 7:16 ♂ ☍	♒ 26 13:09	27 7:37 ☿ △	♈ 27 11:28		SVP 05♓49'33"
		28 11:09 ♃ □	♓ 28 18:42	29 7:10 ♀ △	♉ 29 23:11		Obliquity 23°26'31"
		31 3:10 ♂ △	♈ 31 4:18				⚷ Chiron 27♒39.4
							☽ Mean ☊ 10♎03.5

JULY 1959 LONGITUDE

Day	Sid.Time	☉	0 hr ☽	Noon ☽	True ☊	☿	♀	♂	♃	♄	♅	♆	♇
1 W	18 33 12	8♋25 48	12♉13 31	18♉ 7 37	8♎50.1	3♌10.0	23♌35.8	18♌ 2.2	22♏41.3	3♑24.8	14♌19.4	4♏15.1	2♍13.3
2 Th	18 37 9	9 23 2	24 2 4	29 57 20	8R44.4	4 28.0	24 29.0	18 38.8	22R37.9	3R20.4	14 22.6	4R14.6	2 14.6
3 F	18 41 5	10 20 15	5♊53 50	11♊51 55	8 36.0	5 43.4	25 21.6	19 15.4	22 34.7	3 16.0	14 25.8	4 14.2	2 16.0
4 Sa	18 45 2	11 17 28	17 51 52	23 53 57	8 25.1	6 56.2	26 13.7	19 52.1	22 31.7	3 11.6	14 29.0	4 13.8	2 17.3
5 Su	18 48 59	12 14 41	29 58 22	6♋ 5 14	8 12.5	8 6.2	27 5.1	20 28.8	22 28.8	3 7.3	14 32.3	4 13.4	2 18.7
6 M	18 52 55	13 11 55	12♋14 40	18 26 45	7 59.0	9 13.4	27 55.8	21 5.6	22 26.1	3 3.0	14 35.6	4 13.0	2 20.1
7 Tu	18 56 52	14 9 8	24 41 30	0♌58 58	7 46.0	10 17.7	28 45.9	21 42.4	22 23.6	2 58.7	14 38.9	4 12.7	2 21.6
8 W	19 0 48	15 6 22	7♌19 10	13 42 7	7 34.5	11 19.1	29 35.3	22 19.2	22 21.3	2 54.4	14 42.3	4 12.4	2 23.0
9 Th	19 4 45	16 3 35	20 7 51	26 36 24	7 25.3	12 17.5	0♍24.0	22 56.0	22 19.2	2 50.1	14 45.6	4 12.1	2 24.5
10 F	19 8 41	17 0 48	3♍ 7 52	9♍42 21	7 19.0	13 12.6	1 11.9	23 32.8	22 17.2	2 45.9	14 49.0	4 11.9	2 26.0
11 Sa	19 12 38	17 58 2	16 19 57	23 0 50	7 15.4	14 4.5	1 59.0	24 9.7	22 15.4	2 41.7	14 52.4	4 11.7	2 27.5
12 Su	19 16 34	18 55 15	29 45 10	6♎33 5	7D 14.1	14 53.0	2 45.3	24 46.6	22 13.8	2 37.6	14 55.8	4 11.5	2 29.1
13 M	19 20 31	19 52 28	13♎24 46	20 20 20	7R14.0	15 38.0	3 30.7	25 23.6	22 12.4	2 33.4	14 59.3	4 11.4	2 30.6
14 Tu	19 24 28	20 49 41	27 19 52	4♏23 22	7 14.0	16 19.3	4 15.3	26 0.5	22 11.1	2 29.3	15 2.7	4 11.3	2 32.2
15 W	19 28 24	21 46 54	11♏30 45	18 41 49	7 12.7	16 56.8	4 58.9	26 37.5	22 10.1	2 25.3	15 6.2	4 11.2	2 33.8
16 Th	19 32 21	22 44 7	25 56 17	3♐13 39	7 9.4	17 30.3	5 41.6	27 14.5	22 9.2	2 21.3	15 9.7	4D 11.2	2 35.4
17 F	19 36 17	23 41 21	10♐33 21	17 54 38	7 3.6	17 59.8	6 23.3	27 51.6	22 8.5	2 17.3	15 13.2	4 11.2	2 37.0
18 Sa	19 40 14	24 38 34	25 16 41	2♑38 33	6 55.5	18 24.9	7 4.0	28 28.7	22 8.0	2 13.4	15 16.8	4 11.2	2 38.7
19 Su	19 44 10	25 35 48	9♑59 16	17 17 50	6 45.7	18 45.7	7 43.5	29 5.8	22 7.6	2 9.5	15 20.3	4 11.3	2 40.3
20 M	19 48 7	26 33 2	24 33 16	1♒44 42	6 35.3	19 1.9	8 22.0	29 42.9	22D 7.5	2 5.7	15 23.9	4 11.3	2 42.0
21 Tu	19 52 3	27 30 16	8♒51 22	15 52 36	6 25.5	19 13.5	8 59.3	0♍20.0	22 7.5	2 1.9	15 27.4	4 11.5	2 43.7
22 W	19 56 0	28 27 31	22 47 55	29 37 2	6 17.5	19R20.2	9 35.4	0 57.2	22 7.7	1 58.2	15 31.0	4 11.6	2 45.4
23 Th	19 59 57	29 24 47	6♓19 46	12♓56 7	6 11.7	19 22.1	10 10.3	1 34.4	22 8.1	1 54.5	15 34.6	4 11.8	2 47.2
24 F	20 3 53	0♌22 3	19 26 16	25 50 28	6 8.3	19 19.0	10 43.9	2 11.7	22 8.7	1 50.9	15 38.2	4 12.0	2 48.9
25 Sa	20 7 50	1 19 21	2♈ 9 8	8♈22 42	6D 7.0	19 10.9	11 16.1	2 48.9	22 9.5	1 47.4	15 41.9	4 12.3	2 50.7
26 Su	20 11 46	2 16 39	14 31 45	20 36 51	6 7.2	18 57.9	11 47.0	3 26.2	22 10.4	1 43.9	15 45.5	4 12.5	2 52.4
27 M	20 15 43	3 13 58	26 38 39	2♉37 48	6R 7.8	18 39.9	12 16.4	4 3.6	22 11.5	1 40.4	15 49.2	4 12.9	2 54.2
28 Tu	20 19 39	4 11 18	8♉34 58	14 30 49	6 7.9	18 17.2	12 44.3	4 40.9	22 12.8	1 37.0	15 52.8	4 13.2	2 56.0
29 W	20 23 36	5 8 39	20 25 58	26 21 4	6 6.5	17 49.9	13 10.7	5 18.3	22 14.3	1 33.7	15 56.5	4 13.6	2 57.8
30 Th	20 27 32	6 6 1	2♊16 43	8♊13 27	6 3.2	17 18.3	13 35.5	5 55.8	22 15.9	1 30.5	16 0.2	4 14.0	2 59.7
31 F	20 31 29	7 3 24	14 11 47	20 12 12	5 57.6	16 42.9	13 58.6	6 33.2	22 17.7	1 27.3	16 3.9	4 14.4	3 1.5

AUGUST 1959 LONGITUDE

Day	Sid.Time	☉	0 hr ☽	Noon ☽	True ☊	☿	♀	♂	♃	♄	♅	♆	♇
1 Sa	20 35 26	8♌ 0 48	26♊15 4	2♋20 45	5♎49.9	16♌ 4.0	14♍20.1	7♍10.7	22♏19.8	1♑24.2	16♌ 7.5	4♏14.9	3♍ 3.3
2 Su	20 39 22	8 58 13	8♋29 32	14 41 37	5R40.7	15R22.2	14 39.7	7 48.2	22 21.9	1R21.1	16 11.3	4 15.4	3 5.2
3 M	20 43 19	9 55 39	20 57 9	27 16 13	5 30.7	14 38.2	14 57.6	8 25.8	22 24.3	1 18.2	16 15.0	4 15.9	3 7.1
4 Tu	20 47 15	10 53 6	3♌38 51	10♌ 5 0	5 20.9	13 52.7	15 13.5	9 3.4	22 26.8	1 15.3	16 18.7	4 16.5	3 9.0
5 W	20 51 12	11 50 34	16 34 37	23 7 34	5 12.3	13 6.4	15 27.5	9 41.0	22 29.6	1 12.4	16 22.4	4 17.1	3 10.9
6 Th	20 55 8	12 48 3	29 43 44	6♍22 57	5 5.6	12 20.3	15 39.5	10 18.7	22 32.4	1 9.7	16 26.1	4 17.8	3 12.8
7 F	20 59 5	13 45 33	13♍ 5 4	19 49 56	5 1.3	11 35.0	15 49.4	10 56.3	22 35.5	1 7.0	16 29.8	4 18.4	3 14.7
8 Sa	21 3 1	14 43 4	26 37 25	3♎27 23	4D 59.2	10 51.6	15 57.2	11 34.1	22 38.7	1 4.4	16 33.6	4 19.1	3 16.6
9 Su	21 6 58	15 40 35	10♎19 45	17 14 24	4 59.0	10 10.9	16 2.8	12 11.8	22 42.1	1 1.9	16 37.3	4 19.8	3 18.5
10 M	21 10 55	16 38 7	24 11 15	1♏10 15	4 59.9	9 33.6	16R 6.2	12 49.6	22 45.7	0 59.5	16 41.0	4 20.6	3 20.5
11 Tu	21 14 51	17 35 41	8♏11 18	15 14 18	5R 0.9	9 0.6	16 7.3	13 27.4	22 49.5	0 57.1	16 44.7	4 21.4	3 22.4
12 W	21 18 48	18 33 15	22 19 6	29 25 31	5 1.2	8 32.5	16 6.0	14 5.2	22 53.4	0 54.9	16 48.4	4 22.2	3 24.4
13 Th	21 22 44	19 30 50	6♐33 19	13♐42 11	4 59.9	8 10.1	16 2.4	14 43.1	22 57.4	0 52.7	16 52.2	4 23.0	3 26.3
14 F	21 26 41	20 28 26	20 51 45	28 1 33	4 56.8	7 53.7	15 56.4	15 21.0	23 1.7	0 50.6	16 55.9	4 23.9	3 28.3
15 Sa	21 30 37	21 26 2	5♑11 5	12♑19 47	4 52.0	7D 43.8	15 48.1	15 58.9	23 6.1	0 48.6	16 59.6	4 24.8	3 30.3
16 Su	21 34 34	22 23 40	19 27 4	26 32 18	4 45.9	7 40.8	15 37.3	16 36.9	23 10.7	0 46.7	17 3.3	4 25.8	3 32.3
17 M	21 38 30	23 21 19	3♒34 53	10♒34 13	4 39.3	7 45.0	15 24.1	17 14.9	23 15.4	0 44.8	17 7.0	4 26.8	3 34.3
18 Tu	21 42 27	24 18 59	17 29 48	24 21 9	4 33.2	7 56.5	15 8.5	17 52.9	23 20.3	0 43.1	17 10.8	4 27.8	3 36.3
19 W	21 46 24	25 16 40	1♓ 7 53	7♓49 45	4 28.1	8 15.5	14 50.7	18 31.0	23 25.3	0 41.4	17 14.5	4 28.8	3 38.2
20 Th	21 50 20	26 14 23	14 26 35	20 58 17	4 24.7	8 42.0	14 30.5	19 9.0	23 30.5	0 39.9	17 18.2	4 29.8	3 40.2
21 F	21 54 17	27 12 7	27 24 56	3♈46 39	4D 23.0	9 15.9	14 8.1	19 47.2	23 35.9	0 38.4	17 21.8	4 30.9	3 42.2
22 Sa	21 58 13	28 9 53	10♈ 3 40	16 16 19	4 22.9	9 57.2	13 43.6	20 25.3	23 41.4	0 37.0	17 25.5	4 32.0	3 44.3
23 Su	22 2 10	29 7 40	22 25 0	28 30 9	4 24.0	10 45.7	13 17.2	21 3.5	23 47.0	0 35.7	17 29.2	4 33.2	3 46.3
24 M	22 6 6	0♍ 5 29	4♉32 17	10♉31 57	4 25.6	11 41.3	12 48.8	21 41.7	23 52.8	0 34.5	17 32.9	4 34.4	3 48.3
25 Tu	22 10 3	1 3 19	16 29 43	22 26 12	4 27.2	12 43.6	12 18.7	22 20.0	23 58.8	0 33.4	17 36.5	4 35.5	3 50.3
26 W	22 13 59	2 1 12	28 22 1	4♊17 46	4R28.1	13 52.5	11 47.0	22 58.3	24 4.9	0 32.4	17 40.2	4 36.8	3 52.3
27 Th	22 17 56	2 59 6	10♊14 5	16 11 34	4 27.9	15 7.5	11 13.8	23 36.6	24 11.1	0 31.5	17 43.8	4 38.0	3 54.3
28 F	22 21 52	3 57 2	22 10 48	28 12 19	4 26.4	16 28.2	10 39.5	24 15.0	24 17.5	0 30.6	17 47.4	4 39.3	3 56.3
29 Sa	22 25 49	4 55 0	4♋16 39	10♋24 15	4 23.6	17 54.4	10 4.2	24 53.4	24 24.1	0 29.9	17 51.0	4 40.6	3 58.4
30 Su	22 29 46	5 52 59	16 35 33	22 50 52	4 19.8	19 25.5	9 28.1	25 31.8	24 30.7	0 29.3	17 54.6	4 42.0	4 0.4
31 M	22 33 42	6 51 1	29 10 30	5♌34 39	4 15.5	21 1.0	8 51.4	26 10.3	24 37.6	0 28.7	17 58.2	4 43.3	4 2.4

Astro Data Dy Hr Mn	Planet Ingress Dy Hr Mn	Last Aspect Dy Hr Mn	☽ Ingress Dy Hr Mn	Last Aspect Dy Hr Mn	☽ Ingress Dy Hr Mn	☽ Phases & Eclipses Dy Hr Mn	Astro Data
☽0S 11 21:10	♀ ♍ 8 12:08	2 0:59 ♀ □	♊ 2 12:05	31 4:47 ☿ ⚹	♋ 1 7:24	6 2:00 ● 13♋17	1 JULY 1959
♄△♇ 13 11:51	♂ ♍ 20 11:03	4 17:52 ♀ ⚹	♋ 5 0:03	3 2:47 ♃ △	♌ 3 17:09	13 12:01 ☽ 20♎21	Julian Day # 21731
♆ D 16 16:51	☉ ♌ 23 14:45	6 19:37 ♃ △	♌ 7 10:08	5 10:53 ♃ □	♍ 6 0:29	20 3:33 ○ 26♑42	Delta T 32.9 sec
♃ D 20 7:59		9 5:28 ♂ ☌	♍ 9 18:15	7 16:57 ♃ ⚹	♎ 8 5:56	27 14:22 ☽ 3♉48	SVP 05♓49'29"
☿ R 22 21:02	☉ ♍ 23 21:44	11 10:37 ♃ ⚹	♎ 12 0:26	9 10:59 ♅ ⚹	♏ 10 10:00		Obliquity 23°26'31"
☽0N 24 16:54		13 21:38 ♂ ⚹	♏ 14 4:33	12 0:58 ♃ ☌	♐ 12 12:58	4 14:34 ● 11♌28	⚷ Chiron 27♒14.0R
		16 2:15 ♂ □	♐ 16 6:42	13 23:18 ☉ △	♑ 14 15:18	11 17:10 ☽ 18♏17	☽ Mean ☊ 8♎28.2
♄□♅ 3 11:36		18 5:26 ♂ △	♑ 18 7:42	16 6:20 ♃ ⚹	♒ 16 17:53	18 12:51 ○ 24♒50	
☽0S 8 3:39		20 3:33 ☉ ☍	♒ 20 9:05	18 12:51 ☉ ☍	♓ 18 21:59	26 8:03 ☽ 2♊21	1 AUGUST 1959
♀ R 10 23:16		21 22:50 ♃ □	♓ 22 12:41	20 16:49 ♃ △	♈ 21 4:51		Julian Day # 21762
♀0S 14 15:47		24 5:03 ♃ △	♈ 24 19:53	23 14:23 ☉ △	♉ 23 14:58		Delta T 33.0 sec
☿ D 15 22:05		26 8:33 ☿ △	♉ 27 6:43	25 15:15 ♃ ☍	♊ 26 3:18		SVP 05♓49'24"
☽0N 21 2:41		29 3:40 ♃ ☍	♊ 29 19:23	28 4:22 ♂ □	♋ 28 15:33		Obliquity 23°26'31"
♀0N 28 18:02				30 18:01 ♂ ⚹	♌ 31 1:33		⚷ Chiron 26♒01.2R
							☽ Mean ☊ 6♎49.7

LONGITUDE — SEPTEMBER 1959

Day	Sid.Time	☉	0 hr ☽	Noon ☽	True ☊	☿	♀	♂	♃	♄	♅	♆	♇
1 Tu	22 37 39	7♍49 4	12♌ 3 26	18♌36 52	4♎11.2	22♌40.5	8♍14.4	26♍48.8	24♏44.5	0♑28.3	18♌ 1.8	4♏44.7	4♍ 4.4
2 W	22 41 35	8 47 9	25 14 55	1♍57 27	4R 7.4	24 23.5	7R37.2	27 27.4	24 51.6	0R27.9	18 5.3	4 46.1	4 6.4
3 Th	22 45 32	9 45 15	8♍44 14	15 35 1	4 4.6	26 9.5	7 0.3	28 6.0	24 58.9	0 27.7	18 8.9	4 47.6	4 8.4
4 F	22 49 28	10 43 24	22 29 27	29 27 8	4D 3.0	27 58.0	6 23.6	28 44.6	25 6.2	0 27.5	18 12.4	4 49.0	4 10.5
5 Sa	22 53 25	11 41 34	6♎27 40	13♎30 35	4 2.6	29 48.5	5 47.6	29 23.3	25 13.7	0D 27.5	18 15.9	4 50.5	4 12.5
6 Su	22 57 21	12 39 45	20 35 28	27 41 50	4 3.3	1♍40.7	5 12.5	0♎ 2.0	25 21.4	0 27.5	18 19.4	4 52.0	4 14.5
7 M	23 1 18	13 37 58	4♏49 17	11♏57 23	4 4.5	3 34.2	4 38.3	0 40.7	25 29.2	0 27.7	18 22.9	4 53.6	4 16.5
8 Tu	23 5 15	14 36 13	19 5 45	26 14 1	4 5.8	5 28.5	4 5.4	1 19.5	25 37.1	0 27.9	18 26.3	4 55.2	4 18.5
9 W	23 9 11	15 34 29	3♐21 52	10♐28 58	4R 6.8	7 23.3	3 34.0	1 58.3	25 45.1	0 28.3	18 29.7	4 56.7	4 20.4
10 Th	23 13 8	16 32 47	17 35 2	24 39 48	4 7.1	9 18.5	3 4.1	2 37.2	25 53.3	0 28.7	18 33.1	4 58.4	4 22.4
11 F	23 17 4	17 31 6	1♑43 1	8♑44 24	4 6.6	11 13.6	2 36.0	3 16.0	26 1.5	0 29.2	18 36.5	4 60.0	4 24.4
12 Sa	23 21 1	18 29 26	15 43 44	22 40 46	4 5.5	13 8.6	2 9.9	3 54.9	26 9.9	0 29.9	18 39.9	5 1.6	4 26.4
13 Su	23 24 57	19 27 49	29 35 17	6♒27 1	4 3.8	15 3.2	1 45.8	4 33.9	26 18.5	0 30.6	18 43.2	5 3.3	4 28.4
14 M	23 28 54	20 26 12	13♒15 47	20 1 22	4 1.9	16 57.3	1 23.8	5 12.9	26 27.1	0 31.4	18 46.5	5 5.0	4 30.3
15 Tu	23 32 50	21 24 38	26 43 34	3♓22 15	4 0.2	18 50.7	1 4.0	5 51.9	26 35.9	0 32.4	18 49.8	5 6.8	4 32.3
16 W	23 36 47	22 23 5	9♓57 17	16 28 34	3 58.9	20 43.5	0 46.6	6 31.0	26 44.7	0 33.4	18 53.1	5 8.5	4 34.2
17 Th	23 40 44	23 21 34	22 56 3	29 19 43	3D 58.2	22 35.4	0 31.5	7 10.1	26 53.7	0 34.5	18 56.3	5 10.3	4 36.2
18 F	23 44 40	24 20 5	5♈39 37	11♈55 51	3 58.0	24 26.4	0 18.8	7 49.2	27 2.8	0 35.7	18 59.6	5 12.0	4 38.1
19 Sa	23 48 37	25 18 38	18 8 33	24 17 55	3 58.2	26 16.6	0 8.6	8 28.4	27 12.0	0 37.0	19 2.7	5 13.8	4 40.0
20 Su	23 52 33	26 17 12	0♉24 14	6♉27 45	3 58.8	28 5.8	0 0.8	9 7.6	27 21.3	0 38.5	19 5.9	5 15.7	4 41.9
21 M	23 56 30	27 15 49	12 28 52	18 27 57	3 59.6	29 54.0	29♌55.5	9 46.8	27 30.8	0 40.0	19 9.0	5 17.5	4 43.8
22 Tu	0 0 26	28 14 29	24 25 26	0♊21 48	4 0.3	1♎41.3	29D 52.5	10 26.1	27 40.3	0 41.6	19 12.1	5 19.4	4 45.7
23 W	0 4 23	29 13 10	6♊17 34	12 13 14	4 0.8	3 27.6	29 52.0	11 5.5	27 49.9	0 43.3	19 15.2	5 21.2	4 47.6
24 Th	0 8 19	0♎11 54	18 9 24	24 6 36	4 1.1	5 13.0	29 53.9	11 44.8	27 59.7	0 45.0	19 18.3	5 23.1	4 49.4
25 F	0 12 16	1 10 39	0♋ 5 26	6♋ 6 29	4R 1.2	6 57.3	29 58.0	12 24.3	28 9.5	0 46.9	19 21.3	5 25.1	4 51.3
26 Sa	0 16 13	2 9 28	12 10 19	18 17 30	4 1.2	8 40.7	0♍ 4.5	13 3.7	28 19.5	0 48.9	19 24.3	5 27.0	4 53.1
27 Su	0 20 9	3 8 18	24 28 33	0♌43 58	4D 1.1	10 23.2	0 13.2	13 43.2	28 29.5	0 51.0	19 27.2	5 28.9	4 55.0
28 M	0 24 6	4 7 11	7♌ 4 13	13 29 39	4 1.1	12 4.7	0 24.1	14 22.8	28 39.7	0 53.2	19 30.1	5 30.9	4 56.8
29 Tu	0 28 2	5 6 5	20 0 36	26 37 15	4 1.1	13 45.3	0 37.1	15 2.4	28 49.9	0 55.4	19 33.0	5 32.9	4 58.6
30 W	0 31 59	6 5 3	3♍19 45	10♍ 8 5	4 1.3	15 25.0	0 52.2	15 42.0	29 0.3	0 57.8	19 35.9	5 34.9	5 0.4

LONGITUDE — OCTOBER 1959

Day	Sid.Time	☉	0 hr ☽	Noon ☽	True ☊	☿	♀	♂	♃	♄	♅	♆	♇
1 Th	0 35 55	7♎ 4 2	17♍ 2 7	24♍ 1 37	4♎ 1.5	17♎ 3.8	1♍ 9.3	16♎21.7	29♏10.7	1♑ 0.2	19♌38.7	5♏36.9	5♍ 2.2
2 F	0 39 52	8 3 3	1♎ 6 12	8♎15 21	4R 1.6	18 41.8	1 28.3	17 1.4	29 21.2	1 2.8	19 41.5	5 38.9	5 3.9
3 Sa	0 43 48	9 2 6	15 28 29	22 44 52	4 1.5	20 18.9	1 49.2	17 41.1	29 31.8	1 5.4	19 44.2	5 41.0	5 5.7
4 Su	0 47 45	10 1 12	0♏ 3 43	7♏24 12	4 1.2	21 55.2	2 11.9	18 20.9	29 42.6	1 8.1	19 46.9	5 43.0	5 7.4
5 M	0 51 41	11 0 19	14 45 29	22 6 41	4 0.5	23 30.7	2 36.4	19 0.7	29 53.4	1 10.9	19 49.6	5 45.1	5 9.1
6 Tu	0 55 38	11 59 29	29 27 1	6♐45 44	3 59.7	25 5.3	3 2.5	19 40.6	0♐ 4.2	1 13.8	19 52.2	5 47.2	5 10.8
7 W	0 59 35	12 58 40	14♐ 2 8	21 15 41	3 58.7	26 39.2	3 30.3	20 20.5	0 15.2	1 16.8	19 54.8	5 49.3	5 12.5
8 Th	1 3 31	13 57 53	28 25 53	5♑32 24	3 58.0	28 12.3	3 59.7	21 0.5	0 26.3	1 19.9	19 57.4	5 51.4	5 14.2
9 F	1 7 28	14 57 8	12♑34 56	19 33 21	3D 57.7	29 44.6	4 30.6	21 40.5	0 37.4	1 23.1	19 59.9	5 53.5	5 15.8
10 Sa	1 11 24	15 56 24	26 27 33	3♒17 32	3 57.9	1♏16.1	5 3.0	22 20.5	0 48.6	1 26.3	20 2.4	5 55.6	5 17.5
11 Su	1 15 21	16 55 42	10♒ 3 21	16 45 5	3 58.6	2 46.9	5 36.8	23 0.6	0 59.9	1 29.6	20 4.8	5 57.8	5 19.1
12 M	1 19 17	17 55 2	23 22 51	29 56 49	3 59.7	4 17.0	6 11.9	23 40.7	1 11.3	1 33.1	20 7.2	5 59.9	5 20.7
13 Tu	1 23 14	18 54 24	6♓27 7	12♓53 57	4 0.9	5 46.2	6 48.4	24 20.9	1 22.7	1 36.6	20 9.6	6 2.1	5 22.2
14 W	1 27 10	19 53 47	19 17 26	25 37 46	4 1.9	7 14.8	7 26.2	25 1.1	1 34.3	1 40.2	20 11.9	6 4.3	5 23.8
15 Th	1 31 7	20 53 13	1♈55 5	8♈ 9 32	4R 2.4	8 42.5	8 5.2	25 41.3	1 45.9	1 43.8	20 14.1	6 6.4	5 25.3
16 F	1 35 4	21 52 40	14 21 17	20 30 29	4 2.1	10 9.5	8 45.4	26 21.6	1 57.5	1 47.6	20 16.3	6 8.6	5 26.8
17 Sa	1 39 0	22 52 9	26 37 17	2♉41 51	4 0.9	11 35.7	9 26.7	27 1.9	2 9.3	1 51.4	20 18.5	6 10.8	5 28.3
18 Su	1 42 57	23 51 41	8♉44 22	14 45 3	3 58.6	13 1.1	10 9.2	27 42.3	2 21.1	1 55.3	20 20.7	6 13.0	5 29.8
19 M	1 46 53	24 51 14	20 44 7	26 41 48	3 55.5	14 25.7	10 52.7	28 22.7	2 32.9	1 59.3	20 22.7	6 15.2	5 31.2
20 Tu	1 50 50	25 50 50	2♊38 25	8♊34 17	3 51.8	15 49.4	11 37.2	29 3.2	2 44.9	2 3.4	20 24.8	6 17.4	5 32.7
21 W	1 54 46	26 50 28	14 29 43	20 25 9	3 48.0	17 12.3	12 22.8	29 43.7	2 56.9	2 7.5	20 26.8	6 19.6	5 34.1
22 Th	1 58 43	27 50 8	26 21 0	2♋17 43	3 44.5	18 34.1	13 9.3	0♏24.2	3 8.9	2 11.8	20 28.7	6 21.9	5 35.5
23 F	2 2 39	28 49 50	8♋15 47	14 15 45	3 41.8	19 55.0	13 56.7	1 4.8	3 21.1	2 16.1	20 30.6	6 24.1	5 36.8
24 Sa	2 6 36	29 49 35	20 18 9	26 23 33	3D 40.2	21 14.9	14 45.0	1 45.4	3 33.3	2 20.5	20 32.5	6 26.3	5 38.2
25 Su	2 10 33	0♏49 22	2♌32 32	8♌45 39	3 39.8	22 33.6	15 34.1	2 26.1	3 45.5	2 24.9	20 34.3	6 28.5	5 39.5
26 M	2 14 29	1 49 11	15 3 29	21 26 33	3 40.5	23 51.1	16 24.1	3 6.9	3 57.8	2 29.4	20 36.1	6 30.8	5 40.8
27 Tu	2 18 26	2 49 2	27 55 21	4♍30 19	3 41.9	25 7.3	17 14.9	3 47.6	4 10.2	2 34.0	20 37.8	6 33.0	5 42.0
28 W	2 22 22	3 48 56	11♍11 48	18 0 1	3 43.5	26 22.0	18 6.4	4 28.4	4 22.6	2 38.7	20 39.4	6 35.3	5 43.3
29 Th	2 26 19	4 48 51	24 55 6	1♎57 0	3R 44.7	27 35.3	18 58.7	5 9.3	4 35.1	2 43.4	20 41.0	6 37.5	5 44.5
30 F	2 30 15	5 48 49	9♎ 5 31	16 20 14	3 44.9	28 46.8	19 51.7	5 50.2	4 47.6	2 48.3	20 42.6	6 39.8	5 45.7
31 Sa	2 34 12	6 48 49	23 40 36	1♏ 5 50	3 43.5	29 56.4	20 45.4	6 31.2	5 0.2	2 53.1	20 44.1	6 42.0	5 46.8

Astro Data	Planet Ingress	Last Aspect	☽ Ingress	Last Aspect	☽ Ingress	☽ Phases & Eclipses	Astro Data
Dy Hr Mn	Dy Hr Mn	Dy Hr Mn	Dy Hr Mn	Dy Hr Mn	Dy Hr Mn	Dy Hr Mn	1 SEPTEMBER 1959
☽0S 4 11:04	☿ ♍ 5 2:28	1 23:18 ♃ □	♍ 2 8:31	1 21:00 ♃ ✶	♎ 1 22:08	3 1:56 ● 9♍50	Julian Day # 21793
♄ D 5 1:01	♂ ♎ 5 22:46	4 11:18 ♂ ☌	♎ 4 12:56	3 8:59 ☿ ☌	♏ 3 23:54	9 22:07 ☽ 16♐28	Delta T 33.0 sec
♂0S 8 11:59	♀ ♌ 20 3:01	5 20:09 ♅ ✶	♏ 6 15:53	5 8:18 ♅ □	♐ 6 0:54	17 0:52 ○ 23♓24	SVP 05♓49'20"
☽0N 17 11:15	☿ ♎ 21 1:20	8 11:04 ♃ ☌	♐ 8 18:20	7 23:34 ☿ ✶	♑ 8 2:38	17 1:03 • A 0.987	Obliquity 23°26'31"
☿0S 22 14:00	☉ ♎ 23 19:08	10 1:39 ♅ △	♑ 10 21:04	9 16:28 ♂ □	♒ 10 6:12	25 2:22 ☽ 1♋16	⚷ Chiron 24♒28.3R
♀ D 22 17:15	♀ ♍ 25 8:14	12 18:14 ♃ ✶	♒ 13 0:43	12 0:34 ♂ △	♓ 12 12:06		☽ Mean ☊ 5♎11.2
		14 23:46 ♃ □	♓ 15 5:54	13 0:41 ♀ ☍	♈ 14 20:20	2 12:31 ● 8♎34	
☽0S 1 20:17	♃ ♐ 5 14:39	17 7:31 ♃ △	♈ 17 13:16	17 0:51 ♂ ☍	♉ 17 6:40	2 12:26:27 ● T 3'02"	1 OCTOBER 1959
☽0N 14 18:15	☿ ♏ 9 4:02	19 1:46 ♅ △	♉ 19 23:12	18 23:17 ♅ □	♊ 19 18:40	9 4:22 ☽ 15♑08	Julian Day # 21823
♃⚺♄ 14 17:51	♂ ♏ 21 9:40	22 11:00 ♀ □	♊ 22 11:16	22 3:17 ☉ △	♋ 22 7:22	16 15:59 ○ 22♈32	Delta T 33.0 sec
☽0S 29 6:59	☉ ♏ 24 4:11	24 23:45 ♀ ✶	♋ 24 23:49	24 2:06 ☿ △	♌ 24 19:03	24 20:22 ☽ 0♌40	SVP 05♓49'18"
	☿ ♐ 31 1:16	27 7:49 ♃ △	♌ 27 10:36	26 18:17 ☿ □	♍ 27 3:48	31 22:41 ● 7♏46	Obliquity 23°26'32"
		29 16:11 ♃ □	♍ 29 18:04	29 5:00 ☿ ✶	♎ 29 8:41		⚷ Chiron 23♒13.3R
				30 19:12 ♅ ✶	♏ 31 10:14		☽ Mean ☊ 3♎35.8

NOVEMBER 1959 LONGITUDE

Day	Sid.Time	☉	0 hr ☽	Noon ☽	True ☊	☿	♀	♂	♃	♄	♅	♆	♇
1 Su	2 38 8	7♏48 51	8♏34 59	16♏ 6 58	3♎40.5	1♐ 3.9	21♍39.7	7♏12.2	5♐12.8	2♑58.1	20♌45.6	6♏44.2	5♍48.0
2 M	2 42 5	8 48 54	23 40 36	1♐14 37	3R 36.0	2 9.1	22 34.6	7 53.2	5 25.5	3 3.1	20 47.0	6 46.5	5 49.1
3 Tu	2 46 1	9 49 0	8♐47 48	16 18 55	3 30.6	3 11.8	23 30.2	8 34.3	5 38.2	3 8.2	20 48.3	6 48.7	5 50.2
4 W	2 49 58	10 49 7	23 46 52	1♑10 43	3 25.1	4 11.5	24 26.3	9 15.4	5 51.0	3 13.4	20 49.6	6 51.0	5 51.3
5 Th	2 53 55	11 49 16	8♑29 40	15 43 6	3 20.3	5 8.1	25 23.0	9 56.6	6 3.8	3 18.6	20 50.9	6 53.2	5 52.3
6 F	2 57 51	12 49 27	22 50 38	29 52 0	3 16.8	6 1.1	26 20.3	10 37.8	6 16.7	3 23.9	20 52.1	6 55.5	5 53.3
7 Sa	3 1 48	13 49 39	6♒47 9	13♒36 10	3D 15.1	6 50.0	27 18.1	11 19.1	6 29.6	3 29.2	20 53.2	6 57.7	5 54.3
8 Su	3 5 44	14 49 52	20 19 15	26 56 40	3 15.0	7 34.5	28 16.4	12 0.4	6 42.5	3 34.6	20 54.3	6 59.9	5 55.2
9 M	3 9 41	15 50 7	3♓28 48	9♓56 2	3 16.1	8 13.9	29 15.2	12 41.8	6 55.5	3 40.1	20 55.4	7 2.2	5 56.2
10 Tu	3 13 37	16 50 24	16 18 49	22 37 33	3 17.6	8 47.7	0♎14.4	13 23.2	7 8.5	3 45.6	20 56.3	7 4.4	5 57.1
11 W	3 17 34	17 50 41	28 52 41	5♈ 4 38	3R 18.6	9 15.2	1 14.2	14 4.6	7 21.6	3 51.2	20 57.3	7 6.6	5 57.9
12 Th	3 21 30	18 51 1	11♈13 46	17 20 28	3 18.4	9 35.8	2 14.4	14 46.1	7 34.7	3 56.8	20 58.1	7 8.8	5 58.8
13 F	3 25 27	19 51 21	23 25 2	29 27 46	3 16.2	9 48.8	3 15.0	15 27.6	7 47.8	4 2.5	20 59.0	7 11.0	5 59.6
14 Sa	3 29 24	20 51 44	5♉28 55	11♉28 44	3 11.6	9R 53.5	4 16.1	16 9.2	8 1.0	4 8.2	20 59.7	7 13.2	6 0.4
15 Su	3 33 20	21 52 8	17 27 25	23 25 10	3 4.8	9 49.1	5 17.5	16 50.8	8 14.1	4 14.0	21 0.4	7 15.4	6 1.1
16 M	3 37 17	22 52 34	29 22 10	5♊18 34	2 56.0	9 35.0	6 19.4	17 32.5	8 27.3	4 19.9	21 1.1	7 17.6	6 1.8
17 Tu	3 41 13	23 53 1	11♊14 36	17 10 25	2 45.9	9 10.8	7 21.7	18 14.2	8 40.6	4 25.8	21 1.7	7 19.8	6 2.5
18 W	3 45 10	24 53 30	23 6 15	29 2 21	2 35.4	8 36.3	8 24.4	18 55.9	8 53.9	4 31.7	21 2.2	7 22.0	6 3.2
19 Th	3 49 6	25 54 1	4♋58 59	10♋56 26	2 25.4	7 51.3	9 27.4	19 37.7	9 7.2	4 37.7	21 2.7	7 24.1	6 3.8
20 F	3 53 3	26 54 33	16 55 4	22 55 17	2 16.8	6 56.4	10 30.8	20 19.6	9 20.5	4 43.8	21 3.2	7 26.3	6 4.4
21 Sa	3 56 59	27 55 7	28 57 28	5♌ 2 8	2 10.2	5 52.4	11 34.5	21 1.5	9 33.8	4 49.9	21 3.5	7 28.4	6 5.0
22 Su	4 0 56	28 55 43	11♌ 9 46	17 20 53	2 6.1	4 40.7	12 38.5	21 43.4	9 47.2	4 56.0	21 3.9	7 30.5	6 5.5
23 M	4 4 53	29 56 20	23 36 3	29 55 51	2D 4.3	3 23.1	13 42.9	22 25.4	10 0.6	5 2.2	21 4.1	7 32.7	6 6.1
24 Tu	4 8 49	0♐56 59	6♍20 50	12♍51 33	2 4.2	2 2.0	14 47.6	23 7.4	10 14.0	5 8.5	21 4.3	7 34.8	6 6.5
25 W	4 12 46	1 57 40	19 28 29	26 12 6	2R 4.9	0 40.0	15 52.6	23 49.5	10 27.4	5 14.8	21 4.5	7 36.9	6 7.0
26 Th	4 16 42	2 58 23	3♎ 2 44	10♎ 0 35	2 5.3	29♏19.9	16 57.9	24 31.6	10 40.8	5 21.1	21 4.6	7 38.9	6 7.4
27 F	4 20 39	3 59 7	17 5 45	24 18 4	2 4.3	28 4.4	18 3.5	25 13.8	10 54.3	5 27.4	21R 4.6	7 41.0	6 7.8
28 Sa	4 24 35	4 59 53	1♏37 14	9♏ 2 40	2 1.1	26 55.8	19 9.3	25 56.0	11 7.8	5 33.8	21 4.6	7 43.1	6 8.2
29 Su	4 28 32	6 0 40	16 33 34	24 8 55	1 55.2	25 56.0	20 15.4	26 38.3	11 21.2	5 40.3	21 4.5	7 45.1	6 8.5
30 M	4 32 28	7 1 28	1♐47 28	9♐27 51	1 46.8	25 6.5	21 21.8	27 20.6	11 34.7	5 46.8	21 4.4	7 47.1	6 8.8

DECEMBER 1959 LONGITUDE

Day	Sid.Time	☉	0 hr ☽	Noon ☽	True ☊	☿	♀	♂	♃	♄	♅	♆	♇
1 Tu	4 36 25	8♐ 2 18	17♐ 8 35	24♐48 11	1♎36.8	24♏28.2	22♎28.4	28♏ 3.0	11♐48.2	5♑53.3	21♌ 4.2	7♏49.1	6♍ 9.1
2 W	4 40 22	9 3 10	2♑25 10	9♑58 14	1R 26.4	24R 1.4	23 35.2	28 45.4	12 1.8	5 59.9	21R 4.0	7 51.1	6 9.3
3 Th	4 44 18	10 4 2	17 26 13	24 48 10	1 16.8	23D 46.0	24 42.3	29 27.9	12 15.3	6 6.4	21 3.7	7 53.1	6 9.5
4 F	4 48 15	11 4 55	2♒ 3 22	9♒11 23	1 9.1	23 41.8	25 49.6	0♐10.4	12 28.8	6 13.1	21 3.3	7 55.1	6 9.7
5 Sa	4 52 11	12 5 49	16 11 58	23 5 6	1 4.0	23 48.1	26 57.0	0 52.9	12 42.3	6 19.7	21 2.9	7 57.0	6 9.8
6 Su	4 56 8	13 6 43	29 50 57	6♓29 49	1 1.4	24 4.0	28 4.8	1 35.5	12 55.9	6 26.4	21 2.5	7 59.0	6 9.9
7 M	5 0 4	14 7 39	13♓ 2 8	19 28 25	1D 0.6	24 28.9	29 12.7	2 18.1	13 9.4	6 33.1	21 1.9	8 0.9	6 10.0
8 Tu	5 4 1	15 8 35	25 49 12	2♈ 5 7	1R 0.8	25 1.7	0♏20.8	3 0.8	13 22.9	6 39.9	21 1.4	8 2.8	6R 10.0
9 W	5 7 58	16 9 31	8♈16 44	14 24 41	1 0.7	25 41.7	1 29.1	3 43.5	13 36.5	6 46.6	21 0.7	8 4.6	6 10.0
10 Th	5 11 54	17 10 29	20 29 30	26 31 46	0 59.1	26 28.0	2 37.5	4 26.3	13 50.0	6 53.4	21 0.1	8 6.5	6 10.0
11 F	5 15 51	18 11 27	2♉31 57	8♉30 32	0 55.1	27 19.9	3 46.2	5 9.1	14 3.5	7 0.3	20 59.3	8 8.3	6 10.0
12 Sa	5 19 47	19 12 26	14 27 56	20 24 29	0 48.1	28 16.8	4 55.0	5 51.9	14 17.0	7 7.1	20 58.5	8 10.1	6 9.9
13 Su	5 23 44	20 13 25	26 20 33	2♊16 22	0 38.1	29 17.9	6 4.1	6 34.8	14 30.5	7 14.0	20 57.7	8 11.9	6 9.8
14 M	5 27 40	21 14 25	8♊12 11	14 8 12	0 25.5	0♐22.9	7 13.2	7 17.7	14 44.0	7 20.9	20 56.8	8 13.7	6 9.6
15 Tu	5 31 37	22 15 26	20 4 35	26 1 30	0 11.1	1 31.1	8 22.6	8 0.7	14 57.5	7 27.8	20 55.9	8 15.4	6 9.5
16 W	5 35 33	23 16 28	1♋59 5	7♋57 29	29♍56.0	2 42.2	9 32.1	8 43.8	15 11.0	7 34.7	20 54.9	8 17.2	6 9.2
17 Th	5 39 30	24 17 30	13 56 51	19 57 20	29 41.5	3 55.7	10 41.8	9 26.8	15 24.5	7 41.7	20 53.8	8 18.9	6 9.0
18 F	5 43 27	25 18 34	25 59 9	2♌ 2 30	29 28.7	5 11.5	11 51.6	10 9.9	15 38.0	7 48.6	20 52.7	8 20.5	6 8.7
19 Sa	5 47 23	26 19 37	8♌ 7 40	14 14 55	29 18.5	6 29.1	13 1.5	10 53.1	15 51.4	7 55.6	20 51.6	8 22.2	6 8.5
20 Su	5 51 20	27 20 42	20 24 38	26 37 10	29 11.4	7 48.4	14 11.6	11 36.3	16 4.8	8 2.6	20 50.4	8 23.8	6 8.1
21 M	5 55 16	28 21 48	2♍52 57	9♍12 27	29 7.2	9 9.2	15 21.9	12 19.6	16 18.3	8 9.6	20 49.1	8 25.5	6 7.8
22 Tu	5 59 13	29 22 54	15 36 9	22 4 31	29 5.5	10 31.2	16 32.2	13 2.9	16 31.6	8 16.7	20 47.8	8 27.0	6 7.4
23 W	6 3 9	0♑24 1	28 38 5	5♎17 17	29 5.3	11 54.4	17 42.8	13 46.2	16 45.0	8 23.7	20 46.5	8 28.6	6 7.0
24 Th	6 7 6	1 25 8	12♎ 2 33	18 54 13	29 5.1	13 18.5	18 53.4	14 29.6	16 58.4	8 30.7	20 45.1	8 30.1	6 6.5
25 F	6 11 2	2 26 16	25 52 31	2♏57 33	29 3.7	14 43.6	20 4.1	15 13.1	17 11.7	8 37.8	20 43.7	8 31.6	6 6.0
26 Sa	6 14 59	3 27 25	10♏ 9 16	17 27 21	29 0.1	16 9.4	21 15.0	15 56.5	17 25.0	8 44.9	20 42.2	8 33.1	6 5.5
27 Su	6 18 56	4 28 35	24 51 20	2♐20 29	28 53.7	17 36.0	22 26.0	16 40.1	17 38.3	8 51.9	20 40.6	8 34.6	6 5.0
28 M	6 22 52	5 29 45	9♐53 52	17 30 18	28 44.5	19 3.2	23 37.1	17 23.7	17 51.6	8 59.0	20 39.1	8 36.0	6 4.4
29 Tu	6 26 49	6 30 56	25 8 30	2♑47 2	28 33.4	20 31.0	24 48.3	18 7.3	18 4.8	9 6.1	20 37.5	8 37.4	6 3.8
30 W	6 30 45	7 32 7	10♑24 26	17 59 15	28 21.6	21 59.4	25 59.6	18 50.9	18 18.0	9 13.2	20 35.8	8 38.8	6 3.2
31 Th	6 34 42	8 33 18	25 30 11	2♒56 4	28 10.5	23 28.2	27 11.0	19 34.7	18 31.2	9 20.3	20 34.1	8 40.1	6 2.6

Astro Data	Dy Hr Mn
♃□♇	4 0:30
♃⊻♆	9 14:47
☽0N	11 0:29
♀0S	12 2:51
☿ R	14 0:36
☽0S	25 17:44
♅ R	27 4:47
♄⚻♅	2 14:23
♄△♇	3 11:21
☿ D	3 21:25
☽0N	8 7:30
♇ R	8 20:26
☽0S	23 2:54
♄✶♆	23 21:22

Planet Ingress		Dy Hr Mn
♀	♎	9 18:11
☉	♐	23 1:27
☿	♏	25 11:53
♂	♐	3 18:09
♀	♏	7 16:41
☿	♐	13 15:42
☊	♍	15 17:36
☉	♑	22 14:34

Last Aspect Dy Hr Mn			☽ Ingress	Dy Hr Mn
1 22:09	♀	✶	♐	2 10:02
4 1:08	♀	□	♑	4 10:05
6 6:23	♀	△	♒	6 12:14
8 1:03	♅	☍	♓	8 17:35
10 1:05	☉	△	♈	11 2:10
12 19:11	♅	△	♉	13 13:04
15 9:42	☉	☍	♊	16 1:16
17 19:49	♅	✶	♋	18 13:56
20 21:45	☉	△	♌	21 2:04
22 21:37	♂	□	♍	23 12:08
25 18:05	☿	✶	♎	25 18:41
27 6:39	♅	✶	♏	27 21:21
29 16:41	♂	☌	♐	29 21:12

Last Aspect Dy Hr Mn			☽ Ingress	Dy Hr Mn
1 9:00	♀	✶	♑	1 20:11
3 12:49	♀	□	♒	3 20:35
5 20:33	♀	△	♓	6 0:16
7 22:25	☿	△	♈	8 7:59
10 1:00	♅	△	♉	10 18:56
13 6:34	☿	☍	♊	13 7:24
15 4:49	☉	☍	♋	15 20:00
16 16:47	♀	△	♌	18 7:58
20 14:35	☉	△	♍	20 18:29
22 1:55	♀	✶	♎	23 2:29
24 15:10	♅	✶	♏	25 7:01
26 19:45	♀	☌	♐	27 8:16
28 16:55	♅	△	♑	29 7:38
31 2:56	♀	✶	♒	31 7:15

☽ Phases & Eclipses Dy Hr Mn		
7 13:24	☽	14♒23
15 9:42	○	22♉17
23 13:03	☽	0♍29
30 8:46	●	7♐24
7 2:12	☽	14♓13
15 4:49	○	22♊28
23 3:28	☽	0♎33
29 19:09	●	7♑20

Astro Data

1 NOVEMBER 1959
Julian Day # 21854
Delta T 33.1 sec
SVP 05♓49'16"
Obliquity 23°26'31"
⚷ Chiron 22♒40.9R
☽ Mean ☊ 1♎57.3

1 DECEMBER 1959
Julian Day # 21884
Delta T 33.1 sec
SVP 05♓49'11"
Obliquity 23°26'30"
⚷ Chiron 23♒05.8
☽ Mean ☊ 0♎22.0

LONGITUDE — JANUARY 1960

Day	Sid.Time	☉	0 hr ☽	Noon ☽	True ☊	☿	♀	♂	♃	♄	♅	♆	♇
1 F	6 38 38	9♑34 29	10♒15 54	17♒28 57	28♍ 1.3	24♐57.5	28♏22.4	20♐18.4	18♐44.3	9♑27.4	20♌32.3	8♏41.5	6♍ 1.9
2 Sa	6 42 35	10 35 40	24 34 45	1♓33 0	27R 54.8	26 27.3	29 34.0	21 2.2	18 57.4	9 34.5	20R 30.5	8 42.8	6R 1.2
3 Su	6 46 31	11 36 51	8♓23 41	15 6 54	27 51.1	27 57.5	0♐45.6	21 46.0	19 10.5	9 41.6	20 28.7	8 44.0	6 0.4
4 M	6 50 28	12 38 1	21 42 59	28 12 21	27D 49.8	29 28.2	1 57.4	22 29.9	19 23.5	9 48.6	20 26.8	8 45.3	5 59.7
5 Tu	6 54 25	13 39 12	4♈35 30	10♈53 3	27R 49.7	0♑59.2	3 9.2	23 13.8	19 36.5	9 55.7	20 24.9	8 46.5	5 58.9
6 W	6 58 21	14 40 21	17 5 38	23 13 53	27 49.9	2 30.7	4 21.1	23 57.7	19 49.4	10 2.8	20 23.0	8 47.6	5 58.1
7 Th	7 2 18	15 41 31	29 18 28	5♉20 2	27 49.0	4 2.5	5 33.0	24 41.7	20 2.3	10 9.9	20 21.0	8 48.8	5 57.2
8 F	7 6 14	16 42 40	11♉19 13	17 16 37	27 46.0	5 34.8	6 45.1	25 25.8	20 15.2	10 16.9	20 18.9	8 49.9	5 56.3
9 Sa	7 10 11	17 43 49	23 12 46	29 8 11	27 40.5	7 7.5	7 57.2	26 9.8	20 28.0	10 24.0	20 16.9	8 51.0	5 55.5
10 Su	7 14 7	18 44 57	5♊ 3 20	10♊58 37	27 32.1	8 40.6	9 9.3	26 53.9	20 40.8	10 31.1	20 14.8	8 52.0	5 54.5
11 M	7 18 4	19 46 5	16 54 24	22 51 0	27 21.4	10 14.1	10 21.6	27 38.1	20 53.5	10 38.1	20 12.7	8 53.0	5 53.6
12 Tu	7 22 0	20 47 12	28 48 40	4♋47 37	27 8.9	11 48.0	11 33.9	28 22.3	21 6.2	10 45.1	20 10.5	8 54.0	5 52.6
13 W	7 25 57	21 48 20	10♋48 2	16 50 3	26 55.8	13 22.4	12 46.3	29 6.5	21 18.8	10 52.1	20 8.3	8 55.0	5 51.6
14 Th	7 29 54	22 49 26	22 53 48	28 59 22	26 43.0	14 57.3	13 58.7	29 50.8	21 31.4	10 59.1	20 6.1	8 55.9	5 50.6
15 F	7 33 50	23 50 32	5♌ 6 53	11♌16 24	26 31.9	16 32.6	15 11.2	0♑35.1	21 43.9	11 6.1	20 3.8	8 56.8	5 49.6
16 Sa	7 37 47	24 51 38	17 28 3	23 41 58	26 23.0	18 8.4	16 23.8	1 19.5	21 56.4	11 13.1	20 1.6	8 57.7	5 48.5
17 Su	7 41 43	25 52 44	29 58 17	6♍17 11	26 16.9	19 44.7	17 36.4	2 3.9	22 8.8	11 20.0	19 59.3	8 58.5	5 47.5
18 M	7 45 40	26 53 49	12♍38 52	19 3 36	26 13.6	21 21.5	18 49.1	2 48.3	22 21.1	11 27.0	19 56.9	8 59.3	5 46.3
19 Tu	7 49 36	27 54 53	25 31 38	2♎ 3 16	26D 12.7	22 58.9	20 1.8	3 32.8	22 33.4	11 33.9	19 54.6	9 0.1	5 45.2
20 W	7 53 33	28 55 58	8♎38 48	15 18 33	26 13.1	24 36.8	21 14.6	4 17.3	22 45.7	11 40.8	19 52.2	9 0.8	5 44.1
21 Th	7 57 29	29 57 2	22 2 49	28 51 50	26R 14.0	26 15.2	22 27.4	5 1.9	22 57.8	11 47.6	19 49.8	9 1.5	5 42.9
22 F	8 1 26	0♒58 5	5♏45 50	12♏44 54	26 14.1	27 54.3	23 40.3	5 46.5	23 9.9	11 54.5	19 47.3	9 2.1	5 41.7
23 Sa	8 5 23	1 59 9	19 49 5	26 58 15	26 12.6	29 33.9	24 53.3	6 31.1	23 22.0	12 1.3	19 44.9	9 2.8	5 40.5
24 Su	8 9 19	3 0 12	4♐12 8	11♐30 19	26 8.9	1♒14.1	26 6.3	7 15.8	23 34.0	12 8.1	19 42.4	9 3.4	5 39.3
25 M	8 13 16	4 1 14	18 52 13	26 17 2	26 3.0	2 54.9	27 19.3	8 0.5	23 45.9	12 14.9	19 39.9	9 3.9	5 38.0
26 Tu	8 17 12	5 2 16	3♑43 54	11♑11 46	25 55.5	4 36.4	28 32.4	8 45.3	23 57.7	12 21.6	19 37.4	9 4.5	5 36.8
27 W	8 21 9	6 3 18	18 39 31	26 6 1	25 47.2	6 18.5	29 45.5	9 30.1	24 9.5	12 28.3	19 34.9	9 5.0	5 35.5
28 Th	8 25 5	7 4 18	3♒30 7	10♒50 46	25 39.3	8 1.2	0♑58.7	10 14.9	24 21.2	12 35.0	19 32.4	9 5.4	5 34.2
29 F	8 29 2	8 5 18	18 7 0	25 18 1	25 32.8	9 44.5	2 11.8	10 59.8	24 32.8	12 41.7	19 29.8	9 5.9	5 32.9
30 Sa	8 32 58	9 6 16	2♓23 10	9♓22 0	25 28.3	11 28.4	3 25.1	11 44.7	24 44.4	12 48.3	19 27.2	9 6.3	5 31.6
31 Su	8 36 55	10 7 14	16 14 13	22 59 44	25D 26.0	13 13.0	4 38.3	12 29.6	24 55.8	12 54.9	19 24.7	9 6.6	5 30.2

LONGITUDE — FEBRUARY 1960

Day	Sid.Time	☉	0 hr ☽	Noon ☽	True ☊	☿	♀	♂	♃	♄	♅	♆	♇
1 M	8 40 52	11♒ 8 10	29♓38 35	6♈11 1	25♍25.6	14♒58.1	5♑51.6	13♑14.6	25♐ 7.2	13♑ 1.4	19♌22.1	9♏ 6.9	5♍28.9
2 Tu	8 44 48	12 9 5	12♈37 19	18 57 55	25 26.6	16 43.8	7 4.9	13 59.6	25 18.5	13 8.0	19R 19.5	9 7.2	5R 27.5
3 W	8 48 45	13 9 59	25 13 19	1♉24 5	25 28.2	18 30.0	8 18.2	14 44.6	25 29.7	13 14.4	19 16.8	9 7.5	5 26.1
4 Th	8 52 41	14 10 51	7♉30 49	13 34 7	25R 29.4	20 16.7	9 31.6	15 29.7	25 40.9	13 20.9	19 14.2	9 7.7	5 24.7
5 F	8 56 38	15 11 42	19 34 39	25 33 2	25 29.5	22 3.8	10 44.9	16 14.8	25 51.9	13 27.3	19 11.6	9 7.9	5 23.3
6 Sa	9 0 34	16 12 31	1♊29 53	7♊25 48	25 28.0	23 51.2	11 58.4	16 59.9	26 2.9	13 33.6	19 9.0	9 8.0	5 21.9
7 Su	9 4 31	17 13 19	13 21 22	19 17 6	25 24.8	25 38.8	13 11.8	17 45.1	26 13.7	13 40.0	19 6.4	9 8.2	5 20.4
8 M	9 8 27	18 14 6	25 13 32	1♋11 4	25 20.0	27 26.5	14 25.2	18 30.3	26 24.5	13 46.2	19 3.7	9 8.2	5 19.0
9 Tu	9 12 24	19 14 51	7♋10 10	13 11 8	25 13.9	29 14.2	15 38.7	19 15.5	26 35.2	13 52.5	19 1.1	9 8.3	5 17.5
10 W	9 16 21	20 15 35	19 14 18	25 19 56	25 7.3	1♓ 1.7	16 52.2	20 0.8	26 45.8	13 58.7	18 58.5	9R 8.3	5 16.1
11 Th	9 20 17	21 16 17	1♌28 12	7♌39 18	25 0.8	2 48.7	18 5.8	20 46.1	26 56.3	14 4.8	18 55.8	9 8.3	5 14.6
12 F	9 24 14	22 16 58	13 53 19	20 10 19	24 55.2	4 35.1	19 19.3	21 31.4	27 6.7	14 10.9	18 53.2	9 8.2	5 13.1
13 Sa	9 28 10	23 17 37	26 30 23	2♍53 30	24 50.8	6 20.5	20 32.9	22 16.7	27 17.0	14 16.9	18 50.6	9 8.2	5 11.6
14 Su	9 32 7	24 18 15	9♍19 41	15 48 55	24 48.2	8 4.6	21 46.5	23 2.1	27 27.2	14 22.9	18 48.0	9 8.0	5 10.1
15 M	9 36 3	25 18 51	22 21 10	28 56 27	24D 47.1	9 47.0	23 0.1	23 47.6	27 37.3	14 28.9	18 45.3	9 7.9	5 8.6
16 Tu	9 40 0	26 19 27	5♎34 43	12♎16 0	24 47.5	11 27.3	24 13.7	24 33.0	27 47.3	14 34.8	18 42.7	9 7.7	5 7.1
17 W	9 43 56	27 20 1	19 0 16	25 47 33	24 48.8	13 5.1	25 27.4	25 18.5	27 57.2	14 40.6	18 40.1	9 7.5	5 5.6
18 Th	9 47 53	28 20 33	2♏37 49	9♏31 6	24 50.4	14 39.7	26 41.0	26 4.0	28 7.0	14 46.4	18 37.5	9 7.2	5 4.1
19 F	9 51 50	29 21 5	16 27 20	23 26 29	24 51.8	16 10.6	27 54.7	26 49.5	28 16.7	14 52.2	18 35.0	9 6.9	5 2.5
20 Sa	9 55 46	0♓21 35	0♐28 26	7♐33 4	24R 52.3	17 37.2	29 8.4	27 35.1	28 26.2	14 57.9	18 32.4	9 6.6	5 1.0
21 Su	9 59 43	1 22 4	14 40 8	21 49 22	24 51.7	18 58.9	0♒22.2	28 20.7	28 35.7	15 3.5	18 29.9	9 6.3	4 59.5
22 M	10 3 39	2 22 32	29 0 24	6♑12 46	24 50.1	20 15.1	1 35.9	29 6.4	28 45.0	15 9.1	18 27.3	9 5.9	4 57.9
23 Tu	10 7 36	3 22 58	13♑25 58	20 39 25	24 47.6	21 24.9	2 49.7	29 52.0	28 54.3	15 14.6	18 24.8	9 5.5	4 56.4
24 W	10 11 32	4 23 23	27 52 27	5♒ 4 24	24 44.7	22 27.9	4 3.4	0♒37.7	29 3.4	15 20.0	18 22.3	9 5.0	4 54.9
25 Th	10 15 29	5 23 47	12♒14 35	19 22 19	24 41.9	23 23.3	5 17.2	1 23.4	29 12.4	15 25.4	18 19.8	9 4.5	4 53.3
26 F	10 19 25	6 24 8	26 26 57	3♓27 53	24 39.6	24 10.6	6 31.0	2 9.2	29 21.2	15 30.8	18 17.3	9 4.0	4 51.8
27 Sa	10 23 22	7 24 29	10♓24 36	17 16 42	24 38.2	24 49.4	7 44.8	2 54.9	29 30.0	15 36.0	18 14.9	9 3.5	4 50.2
28 Su	10 27 19	8 24 47	24 3 51	0♈45 49	24D 37.7	25 19.0	8 58.7	3 40.7	29 38.6	15 41.2	18 12.4	9 2.9	4 48.7
29 M	10 31 15	9 25 4	7♈22 31	13 53 56	24 38.0	25 39.4	10 12.5	4 26.5	29 47.1	15 46.4	18 10.0	9 2.3	4 47.2

Astro Data

	Dy Hr Mn
☽0N	4 16:24
♃△♅	8 6:03
☽0S	19 10:02
♃∠♆	26 14:23
☽0N	1 2:51
♆ R	10 0:07
☽0S	15 16:26
☿0N	27 6:41
☽0N	28 13:14

Planet Ingress

		Dy Hr Mn
♀	♐	2 8:43
☿	♑	4 8:24
♂	♑	14 4:59
☉	♒	21 1:10
☿	♒	23 6:16
♀	♑	27 4:46
☿	♓	9 10:13
☉	♓	19 15:26
♀	♒	20 16:47
♂	♒	23 4:11

Last Aspect / ☽ Ingress (January)

Last Aspect Dy Hr Mn			☽ Ingress Dy Hr Mn
2 3:36	☿	⚹	♓ 2 9:19
4 1:31	♂	□	♈ 4 15:21
6 14:18	♂	△	♉ 7 1:22
8 18:05	♅	□	♊ 9 13:45
11 23:03	♂	☍	♋ 12 2:23
13 23:51	☉	☍	♌ 14 13:59
16 8:46	♃	△	♍ 17 0:03
19 4:47	☉	△	♎ 19 8:14
21 8:26	☿	□	♏ 21 13:59
22 23:53	♅	□	♐ 23 17:03
25 14:54	♀	☌	♑ 25 18:00
26 13:59	♄	☌	♒ 27 18:19
29 10:53	♃	⚹	♓ 29 19:56

Last Aspect / ☽ Ingress (February)

Last Aspect Dy Hr Mn			☽ Ingress Dy Hr Mn
31 15:42	♃	□	♈ 1 0:39
3 0:32	♃	△	♉ 3 9:16
5 5:52	☿	□	♊ 5 20:58
8 5:16	☿	△	♋ 8 9:37
10 1:38	♂	☍	♌ 10 21:08
13 1:29	♃	△	♍ 13 6:35
15 9:44	♃	□	♎ 15 13:55
17 16:00	♃	⚹	♏ 17 19:24
19 21:31	♀	⚹	♐ 19 23:12
21 23:34	♃	☌	♑ 22 1:39
23 14:19	☿	⚹	♒ 24 3:32
26 5:00	♃	⚹	♓ 26 6:04
28 10:05	♃	□	♈ 28 10:37

☽ Phases & Eclipses

Dy Hr Mn		
5 18:53	☽	14♈27
13 23:51	○	22♋49
21 15:01	☽	0♏35
28 6:15	●	7♒20
4 14:26	☽	14♉47
12 17:24	○	23♌01
19 23:47	☽	0♐21
26 18:24	●	7♓10

Astro Data

1 JANUARY 1960
Julian Day # 21915
Delta T 33.2 sec
SVP 05♓49'06"
Obliquity 23°26'30"
⚷ Chiron 24♒24.9
☽ Mean ☊ 28♍43.5

1 FEBRUARY 1960
Julian Day # 21946
Delta T 33.2 sec
SVP 05♓49'01"
Obliquity 23°26'31"
⚷ Chiron 26♒20.8
☽ Mean ☊ 27♍05.0

MARCH 1960 LONGITUDE

Day	Sid.Time	☉	0 hr ☽	Noon ☽	True ☊	☿	♀	♂	♃	♄	♅	♆	♇
1 Tu	10 35 12	10♓25 18	20♈20 12	26♈41 30	24♍39.0	25♓50.2	11♒26.3	5♒12.4	29♐55.5	15♑51.5	18♌ 7.6	9♏ 1.7	4♍45.6
2 W	10 39 8	11 25 31	2♉58 8	9♉10 26	24 40.2	25R51.5	12 40.1	5 58.2	0♑ 3.7	15 56.5	18R 5.3	9R 1.0	4R44.1
3 Th	10 43 5	12 25 42	15 18 52	21 23 53	24 41.4	25 43.3	13 54.0	6 44.1	0 11.8	16 1.4	18 2.9	9 0.3	4 42.6
4 F	10 47 1	13 25 50	27 26 0	3♊25 48	24 42.4	25 26.0	15 7.8	7 30.0	0 19.8	16 6.3	18 0.6	8 59.6	4 41.1
5 Sa	10 50 58	14 25 57	9♊23 49	15 20 41	24R42.8	25 0.0	16 21.7	8 15.9	0 27.6	16 11.1	17 58.3	8 58.8	4 39.5
6 Su	10 54 54	15 26 1	21 16 58	27 13 15	24 42.8	24 26.1	17 35.5	9 1.8	0 35.3	16 15.8	17 56.1	8 58.0	4 38.0
7 M	10 58 51	16 26 4	3♋10 8	9♋ 8 11	24 42.4	23 45.0	18 49.4	9 47.8	0 42.9	16 20.5	17 53.9	8 57.2	4 36.5
8 Tu	11 2 47	17 26 4	15 7 55	21 9 51	24 41.7	22 57.9	20 3.2	10 33.7	0 50.3	16 25.1	17 51.7	8 56.4	4 35.0
9 W	11 6 44	18 26 2	27 14 27	3♌22 8	24 40.8	22 5.9	21 17.1	11 19.7	0 57.6	16 29.6	17 49.5	8 55.5	4 33.5
10 Th	11 10 41	19 25 58	9♌33 18	15 48 13	24 40.0	21 10.3	22 30.9	12 5.7	1 4.7	16 34.0	17 47.4	8 54.6	4 32.1
11 F	11 14 37	20 25 52	22 7 9	28 30 18	24 39.4	20 12.3	23 44.8	12 51.7	1 11.7	16 38.4	17 45.3	8 53.7	4 30.6
12 Sa	11 18 34	21 25 43	4♍57 46	11♍29 35	24 39.1	19 13.5	24 58.7	13 37.8	1 18.6	16 42.7	17 43.2	8 52.7	4 29.1
13 Su	11 22 30	22 25 33	18 5 44	24 46 6	24D38.9	18 15.1	26 12.5	14 23.8	1 25.3	16 46.9	17 41.2	8 51.7	4 27.7
14 M	11 26 27	23 25 21	1♎30 31	8♎18 47	24 38.9	17 18.2	27 26.4	15 9.9	1 31.8	16 51.0	17 39.2	8 50.7	4 26.2
15 Tu	11 30 23	24 25 6	15 10 35	22 5 37	24R38.9	16 24.1	28 40.3	15 56.0	1 38.2	16 55.1	17 37.2	8 49.7	4 24.8
16 W	11 34 20	25 24 50	29 3 30	6♏ 3 52	24 38.9	15 33.7	29 54.2	16 42.1	1 44.5	16 59.1	17 35.3	8 48.6	4 23.4
17 Th	11 38 16	26 24 32	13♏ 6 20	20 10 28	24 38.8	14 47.8	1♓ 8.1	17 28.2	1 50.6	17 2.9	17 33.4	8 47.5	4 22.0
18 F	11 42 13	27 24 13	27 15 52	4♐22 11	24 38.5	14 7.0	2 22.0	18 14.3	1 56.5	17 6.8	17 31.6	8 46.4	4 20.6
19 Sa	11 46 10	28 23 51	11♐29 1	18 36 1	24 38.3	13 31.8	3 35.9	19 0.5	2 2.3	17 10.5	17 29.7	8 45.3	4 19.2
20 Su	11 50 6	29 23 28	25 42 52	2♑49 14	24D38.1	13 2.5	4 49.8	19 46.7	2 8.0	17 14.2	17 28.0	8 44.2	4 17.8
21 M	11 54 3	0♈23 4	9♑54 51	16 59 24	24 38.2	12 39.2	6 3.7	20 32.8	2 13.4	17 17.7	17 26.3	8 43.0	4 16.4
22 Tu	11 57 59	1 22 37	24 2 40	1♒ 4 21	24 38.5	12 22.2	7 17.6	21 19.0	2 18.8	17 21.2	17 24.6	8 41.8	4 15.1
23 W	12 1 56	2 22 9	8♒ 4 12	15 1 59	24 39.2	12 11.2	8 31.5	22 5.2	2 23.9	17 24.6	17 22.9	8 40.6	4 13.8
24 Th	12 5 52	3 21 39	21 57 28	28 50 22	24 39.9	12D 6.3	9 45.4	22 51.5	2 28.9	17 27.9	17 21.3	8 39.3	4 12.5
25 F	12 9 49	4 21 7	5♓40 29	12♓27 34	24 40.7	12 7.2	10 59.3	23 37.7	2 33.7	17 31.2	17 19.8	8 38.1	4 11.2
26 Sa	12 13 45	5 20 33	19 11 25	25 51 51	24R41.1	12 13.8	12 13.3	24 23.9	2 38.4	17 34.3	17 18.3	8 36.8	4 9.9
27 Su	12 17 42	6 19 57	2♈28 41	9♈ 1 49	24 41.0	12 25.9	13 27.2	25 10.2	2 42.8	17 37.4	17 16.8	8 35.5	4 8.6
28 M	12 21 39	7 19 19	15 31 9	21 56 39	24 40.3	12 43.1	14 41.1	25 56.4	2 47.2	17 40.3	17 15.4	8 34.1	4 7.4
29 Tu	12 25 35	8 18 40	28 18 19	4♉36 14	24 38.9	13 5.3	15 55.0	26 42.6	2 51.3	17 43.2	17 14.0	8 32.8	4 6.1
30 W	12 29 32	9 17 58	10♉50 31	17 1 21	24 37.0	13 32.2	17 8.9	27 28.9	2 55.3	17 46.0	17 12.7	8 31.4	4 4.9
31 Th	12 33 28	10 17 13	23 8 59	29 13 43	24 34.6	14 3.5	18 22.8	28 15.1	2 59.0	17 48.7	17 11.4	8 30.1	4 3.7

APRIL 1960 LONGITUDE

Day	Sid.Time	☉	0 hr ☽	Noon ☽	True ☊	☿	♀	♂	♃	♄	♅	♆	♇
1 F	12 37 25	11♈16 27	5♊15 53	11♊15 54	24♍32.2	14♓39.1	19♓36.7	29♒ 1.4	3♑ 2.7	17♑51.3	17♌10.1	8♏28.7	4♍ 2.6
2 Sa	12 41 21	12 15 38	17 14 13	23 11 18	24R30.1	15 18.6	20 50.5	29 47.7	3 6.1	17 53.8	17R 9.0	8R27.2	4R 1.4
3 Su	12 45 18	13 14 47	29 7 41	5♋ 3 56	24 28.5	16 1.9	22 4.4	0♓33.9	3 9.4	17 56.2	17 7.8	8 25.8	4 0.3
4 M	12 49 14	14 13 54	11♋ 0 36	16 58 16	24D27.8	16 48.7	23 18.3	1 20.2	3 12.4	17 58.6	17 6.7	8 24.4	3 59.2
5 Tu	12 53 11	15 12 59	22 57 33	28 59 2	24 28.0	17 38.9	24 32.2	2 6.4	3 15.4	18 0.8	17 5.7	8 22.9	3 58.1
6 W	12 57 7	16 12 1	5♌ 3 19	11♌10 56	24 29.0	18 32.3	25 46.0	2 52.7	3 18.1	18 2.9	17 4.7	8 21.4	3 57.0
7 Th	13 1 4	17 11 1	17 22 27	23 38 21	24 30.5	19 28.8	26 59.9	3 38.9	3 20.6	18 5.0	17 3.8	8 20.0	3 56.0
8 F	13 5 1	18 9 58	29 59 4	6♍24 58	24 32.1	20 28.1	28 13.7	4 25.2	3 23.0	18 6.9	17 2.9	8 18.5	3 54.9
9 Sa	13 8 57	19 8 53	12♍56 22	19 33 26	24R33.4	21 30.1	29 27.6	5 11.4	3 25.2	18 8.8	17 2.1	8 16.9	3 53.9
10 Su	13 12 54	20 7 47	26 16 16	3♎ 4 50	24 33.8	22 34.8	0♈41.4	5 57.7	3 27.2	18 10.6	17 1.3	8 15.4	3 53.0
11 M	13 16 50	21 6 37	9♎58 57	16 58 20	24 33.0	23 42.0	1 55.3	6 43.9	3 29.0	18 12.2	17 0.5	8 13.9	3 52.0
12 Tu	13 20 47	22 5 26	24 2 34	1♏11 5	24 30.8	24 51.6	3 9.1	7 30.2	3 30.6	18 13.8	16 59.8	8 12.3	3 51.1
13 W	13 24 43	23 4 13	8♏23 14	15 38 17	24 27.5	26 3.4	4 22.9	8 16.4	3 32.0	18 15.3	16 59.2	8 10.8	3 50.2
14 Th	13 28 40	24 2 58	22 55 24	0♐13 45	24 23.4	27 17.6	5 36.7	9 2.7	3 33.3	18 16.7	16 58.6	8 9.2	3 49.3
15 F	13 32 36	25 1 42	7♐32 30	14 50 50	24 19.0	28 33.8	6 50.6	9 48.9	3 34.4	18 17.9	16 58.1	8 7.6	3 48.4
16 Sa	13 36 33	26 0 23	22 7 59	29 23 18	24 15.1	29 52.2	8 4.4	10 35.1	3 35.3	18 19.1	16 57.7	8 6.0	3 47.6
17 Su	13 40 30	26 59 3	6♑36 11	13♑46 12	24 12.2	1♈12.5	9 18.2	11 21.3	3 36.0	18 20.2	16 57.2	8 4.5	3 46.8
18 M	13 44 26	27 57 41	20 52 57	27 56 12	24D10.7	2 34.9	10 32.0	12 7.6	3 36.5	18 21.2	16 56.9	8 2.9	3 46.0
19 Tu	13 48 23	28 56 18	4♒55 48	11♒51 41	24 10.7	3 59.2	11 45.8	12 53.8	3 36.8	18 22.1	16 56.6	8 1.3	3 45.2
20 W	13 52 19	29 54 53	18 43 49	25 32 16	24 11.7	5 25.4	12 59.6	13 40.0	3R36.9	18 22.9	16 56.3	7 59.6	3 44.5
21 Th	13 56 16	0♉53 26	2♓17 7	8♓58 28	24 13.2	6 53.4	14 13.5	14 26.2	3 36.9	18 23.6	16 56.1	7 58.0	3 43.8
22 F	14 0 12	1 51 58	15 36 27	22 11 10	24R14.4	8 23.3	15 27.3	15 12.3	3 36.6	18 24.2	16 55.9	7 56.4	3 43.1
23 Sa	14 4 9	2 50 27	28 42 43	5♈11 14	24 14.6	9 55.0	16 41.1	15 58.5	3 36.2	18 24.7	16 55.8	7 54.8	3 42.5
24 Su	14 8 5	3 48 56	11♈36 46	17 59 25	24 13.2	11 28.4	17 54.9	16 44.7	3 35.6	18 25.1	16D55.8	7 53.1	3 41.8
25 M	14 12 2	4 47 22	24 19 14	0♉36 18	24 9.8	13 3.7	19 8.7	17 30.8	3 34.8	18 25.4	16 55.8	7 51.5	3 41.2
26 Tu	14 15 59	5 45 46	6♉50 39	13 2 22	24 4.4	14 40.8	20 22.4	18 16.9	3 33.8	18 25.6	16 55.9	7 49.9	3 40.7
27 W	14 19 55	6 44 9	19 11 32	25 18 16	23 57.4	16 19.6	21 36.2	19 3.0	3 32.6	18R25.7	16 56.0	7 48.2	3 40.1
28 Th	14 23 52	7 42 30	1♊22 42	7♊25 0	23 49.4	18 0.2	22 50.0	19 49.1	3 31.2	18 25.7	16 56.2	7 46.6	3 39.6
29 F	14 27 48	8 40 49	13 25 24	19 24 9	23 41.0	19 42.5	24 3.8	20 35.2	3 29.6	18 25.6	16 56.4	7 45.0	3 39.1
30 Sa	14 31 45	9 39 6	25 21 32	1♋17 56	23 33.3	21 26.7	25 17.5	21 21.2	3 27.9	18 25.5	16 56.7	7 43.3	3 38.7

Astro Data

	Dy Hr Mn
☿ R	1 15:10
☿0S	9 14:11
☽0S	13 23:53
♄⚻♅	22 15:49
♃□♅	22 20:27
☿ D	24 8:05
☽0N	26 22:06
☽0S	10 9:08
♀0N	12 7:07
☿0N	20 12:58
♃ R	20 4:55
☽0N	23 5:11
♅ D	24 7:46
♄ R	27 14:06

Planet Ingress

	Dy Hr Mn
♃ ♑	1 13:10
♀ ♓	16 1:53
☉ ♈	20 14:43
♂ ♓	2 6:24
♀ ♈	9 10:32
☿ ♈	16 2:22
☉ ♉	20 2:06

Last Aspect / ☽ Ingress (March)

Last Aspect Dy Hr Mn		☽ Ingress Dy Hr Mn
29 19:53	♅ △	♉ 1 18:18
3 20:08	☿ ⚹	♊ 4 5:08
6 6:03	☿ □	♋ 6 17:37
8 14:33	☿ △	♌ 9 5:25
11 3:24	♀ ☍	♍ 11 14:47
13 8:26	☉ ☍	♎ 13 21:19
16 1:35	♀ △	♏ 16 1:37
18 0:15	☉ △	♐ 18 4:37
20 6:40	☉ □	♑ 20 7:14
21 12:34	♄ ☌	♒ 22 10:10
24 1:39	♂ ☌	♓ 24 14:02
25 21:06	♄ ⚹	♈ 26 19:29
28 20:47	♂ ⚹	♉ 29 3:13
31 10:45	♂ □	♊ 31 13:32

Last Aspect / ☽ Ingress (April)

Last Aspect Dy Hr Mn		☽ Ingress Dy Hr Mn
2 8:06	♀ □	♋ 3 1:46
5 3:30	♀ △	♌ 5 14:01
6 23:36	☉ △	♍ 8 0:02
9 16:50	☿ ☍	♎ 10 6:36
11 20:27	☉ ☍	♏ 12 10:01
14 7:51	☿ △	♐ 14 11:37
16 6:52	☉ △	♑ 16 13:01
18 12:57	☉ □	♒ 18 15:32
19 20:52	♅ ☍	♓ 20 19:55
22 5:06	♄ ⚹	♈ 23 2:23
24 13:08	♀ ☌	♉ 25 10:50
26 23:42	♂ ⚹	♊ 27 21:16
29 23:51	♀ ⚹	♋ 30 9:22

☽ Phases & Eclipses

Dy Hr Mn	
5 11:06	☽ 14♊54
13 8:26	○ 22♍47
13 8:28	☊ T 1.514
20 6:40	☽ 29♐40
27 7:37	● 6♈39
27 7:24:34	☋ P 0.706
4 7:05	☽ 14♋31
11 20:27	○ 21♎57
18 12:57	☽ 28♑29
25 21:44	● 5♉40

Astro Data

1 MARCH 1960
Julian Day # 21975
Delta T 33.2 sec
SVP 05♓48'58"
Obliquity 23°26'31"
⚷ Chiron 28♒21.1
☽ Mean ☊ 25♍32.9

1 APRIL 1960
Julian Day # 22006
Delta T 33.3 sec
SVP 05♓48'56"
Obliquity 23°26'31"
⚷ Chiron 0♓18.7
☽ Mean ☊ 23♍54.3

LONGITUDE — MAY 1960

Day	Sid.Time	☉	0 hr ☽	Noon ☽	True ☊	☿	♀	♂	♃	♄	♅	♆	♇
1 Su	14 35 41	10♉37 22	7♋13 45	13♋ 9 24	23♍26.8	23♈12.6	26♈31.3	22♓ 7.2	3♑25.9	18♑25.2	16♌57.0	7♏41.7	3♍38.2
2 M	14 39 38	11 35 35	19 5 24	25 2 16	23R22.1	25 0.4	27 45.0	22 53.2	3R23.8	18R24.8	16 57.4	7R40.1	3R37.8
3 Tu	14 43 34	12 33 46	1♌ 0 33	7♌ 0 52	23 19.4	26 49.9	28 58.8	23 39.2	3 21.5	18 24.3	16 57.8	7 38.4	3 37.5
4 W	14 47 31	13 31 55	13 3 49	19 10 1	23D18.6	28 41.2	0♉12.5	24 25.1	3 19.0	18 23.7	16 58.3	7 36.8	3 37.1
5 Th	14 51 28	14 30 2	25 20 7	1♍34 42	23 19.1	0♉34.4	1 26.2	25 11.1	3 16.4	18 23.1	16 58.9	7 35.2	3 36.8
6 F	14 55 24	15 28 8	7♍54 23	14 19 41	23 20.2	2 29.3	2 40.0	25 57.0	3 13.5	18 22.3	16 59.5	7 33.6	3 36.5
7 Sa	14 59 21	16 26 11	20 51 6	27 29 1	23R20.9	4 26.0	3 53.7	26 42.8	3 10.5	18 21.4	17 0.2	7 32.0	3 36.3
8 Su	15 3 17	17 24 12	4♎13 41	11♎ 5 17	23 20.4	6 24.4	5 7.4	27 28.7	3 7.3	18 20.5	17 0.9	7 30.3	3 36.1
9 M	15 7 14	18 22 12	18 3 47	25 9 0	23 17.9	8 24.6	6 21.1	28 14.5	3 4.0	18 19.4	17 1.6	7 28.7	3 35.9
10 Tu	15 11 10	19 20 10	2♏20 33	9♏37 51	23 13.2	10 26.5	7 34.8	29 0.3	3 0.4	18 18.3	17 2.5	7 27.1	3 35.7
11 W	15 15 7	20 18 6	17 0 7	24 26 25	23 6.4	12 30.0	8 48.5	29 46.1	2 56.7	18 17.0	17 3.3	7 25.6	3 35.6
12 Th	15 19 3	21 16 1	1♐55 40	9♐26 41	22 58.1	14 35.0	10 2.1	0♈31.8	2 52.9	18 15.7	17 4.2	7 24.0	3 35.4
13 F	15 23 0	22 13 54	16 58 14	24 29 6	22 49.2	16 41.4	11 15.8	1 17.5	2 48.8	18 14.3	17 5.2	7 22.4	3 35.4
14 Sa	15 26 57	23 11 46	1♑58 8	9♑24 15	22 41.0	18 49.2	12 29.5	2 3.2	2 44.6	18 12.8	17 6.2	7 20.8	3 35.3
15 Su	15 30 53	24 9 36	16 46 35	24 4 24	22 34.4	20 58.1	13 43.2	2 48.9	2 40.3	18 11.2	17 7.3	7 19.3	3D35.3
16 M	15 34 50	25 7 26	1♒17 9	8♒24 29	22 29.9	23 7.9	14 56.9	3 34.5	2 35.8	18 9.5	17 8.5	7 17.8	3 35.3
17 Tu	15 38 46	26 5 14	15 26 12	22 22 17	22D27.7	25 18.5	16 10.6	4 20.1	2 31.1	18 7.7	17 9.6	7 16.2	3 35.4
18 W	15 42 43	27 3 1	29 12 48	5♓57 59	22 27.3	27 29.7	17 24.2	5 5.6	2 26.2	18 5.8	17 10.9	7 14.7	3 35.4
19 Th	15 46 39	28 0 47	12♓38 4	19 13 23	22R27.7	29 41.1	18 37.9	5 51.2	2 21.3	18 3.9	17 12.1	7 13.2	3 35.5
20 F	15 50 36	28 58 31	25 44 18	2♈11 9	22 27.9	1♊52.6	19 51.6	6 36.7	2 16.1	18 1.8	17 13.5	7 11.7	3 35.7
21 Sa	15 54 32	29 56 15	8♈34 19	14 54 9	22 26.7	4 3.7	21 5.3	7 22.1	2 10.8	17 59.7	17 14.8	7 10.2	3 35.8
22 Su	15 58 29	0♊53 58	21 10 56	27 24 58	22 23.4	6 14.4	22 19.0	8 7.5	2 5.4	17 57.5	17 16.3	7 8.7	3 36.0
23 M	16 2 26	1 51 39	3♉36 31	9♉45 48	22 17.3	8 24.2	23 32.6	8 52.9	1 59.9	17 55.1	17 17.8	7 7.3	3 36.2
24 Tu	16 6 22	2 49 19	15 53 0	21 58 18	22 8.5	10 32.9	24 46.3	9 38.2	1 54.2	17 52.8	17 19.3	7 5.8	3 36.5
25 W	16 10 19	3 46 59	28 1 50	4♊ 3 45	21 57.4	12 40.3	25 60.0	10 23.5	1 48.3	17 50.3	17 20.9	7 4.4	3 36.8
26 Th	16 14 15	4 44 37	10♊ 4 12	16 3 18	21 44.7	14 46.1	27 13.7	11 8.8	1 42.4	17 47.7	17 22.5	7 3.0	3 37.1
27 F	16 18 12	5 42 13	22 1 13	27 58 8	21 31.5	16 50.1	28 27.3	11 54.0	1 36.3	17 45.1	17 24.2	7 1.6	3 37.4
28 Sa	16 22 8	6 39 49	3♋54 16	9♋49 50	21 18.9	18 52.1	29 41.0	12 39.2	1 30.1	17 42.4	17 25.9	7 0.2	3 37.8
29 Su	16 26 5	7 37 23	15 45 9	21 40 31	21 7.9	20 52.0	0♊54.7	13 24.3	1 23.8	17 39.6	17 27.7	6 58.9	3 38.2
30 M	16 30 1	8 34 56	27 36 19	3♌32 58	20 59.3	22 49.6	2 8.4	14 9.3	1 17.3	17 36.8	17 29.5	6 57.5	3 38.6
31 Tu	16 33 58	9 32 28	9♌30 57	15 30 46	20 53.4	24 44.9	3 22.0	14 54.3	1 10.8	17 33.8	17 31.3	6 56.2	3 39.1

LONGITUDE — JUNE 1960

Day	Sid.Time	☉	0 hr ☽	Noon ☽	True ☊	☿	♀	♂	♃	♄	♅	♆	♇
1 W	16 37 55	10♊29 59	21♌32 59	27♌38 9	20♍50.1	26♊37.6	4♊35.7	15♈39.3	1♑ 4.2	17♑30.8	17♌33.3	6♏54.9	3♍39.6
2 Th	16 41 51	11 27 28	3♍46 55	9♍59 54	20D48.8	28 27.9	5 49.4	16 24.2	0R57.4	17R27.7	17 35.2	6R53.6	3 40.1
3 F	16 45 48	12 24 56	16 17 43	22 40 59	20R48.7	0♋15.5	7 3.0	17 9.1	0 50.6	17 24.6	17 37.2	6 52.3	3 40.7
4 Sa	16 49 44	13 22 22	29 10 16	5♎46 7	20 48.6	2 0.4	8 16.7	17 53.9	0 43.7	17 21.4	17 39.3	6 51.1	3 41.2
5 Su	16 53 41	14 19 48	12♎28 56	19 19 4	20 47.3	3 42.7	9 30.3	18 38.6	0 36.7	17 18.1	17 41.3	6 49.9	3 41.8
6 M	16 57 37	15 17 12	26 16 39	3♏21 42	20 44.1	5 22.2	10 44.0	19 23.4	0 29.6	17 14.8	17 43.5	6 48.7	3 42.5
7 Tu	17 1 34	16 14 35	10♏34 1	17 53 8	20 38.2	6 59.0	11 57.6	20 8.0	0 22.4	17 11.4	17 45.6	6 47.5	3 43.1
8 W	17 5 30	17 11 57	25 18 24	2♐48 56	20 30.0	8 33.0	13 11.3	20 52.6	0 15.2	17 7.9	17 47.9	6 46.3	3 43.8
9 Th	17 9 27	18 9 18	10♐23 35	18 1 6	20 19.9	10 4.2	14 24.9	21 37.2	0 7.9	17 4.4	17 50.1	6 45.2	3 44.6
10 F	17 13 24	19 6 38	25 40 5	3♑19 4	20 9.1	11 32.6	15 38.6	22 21.6	0 0.6	17 0.8	17 52.4	6 44.1	3 45.3
11 Sa	17 17 20	20 3 58	10♑56 39	18 31 27	19 58.8	12 58.1	16 52.3	23 6.1	29♐53.2	16 57.1	17 54.8	6 43.0	3 46.1
12 Su	17 21 17	21 1 17	26 2 17	3♒28 9	19 50.4	14 20.8	18 5.9	23 50.5	29 45.7	16 53.4	17 57.1	6 41.9	3 46.9
13 M	17 25 13	21 58 36	10♒48 14	18 1 58	19 44.3	15 40.6	19 19.6	24 34.8	29 38.2	16 49.7	17 59.6	6 40.9	3 47.7
14 Tu	17 29 10	22 55 54	25 9 0	2♓ 9 12	19 40.8	16 57.4	20 33.3	25 19.1	29 30.7	16 45.9	18 2.0	6 39.9	3 48.6
15 W	17 33 6	23 53 11	9♓ 2 35	15 49 22	19D39.5	18 11.1	21 46.9	26 3.3	29 23.1	16 42.0	18 4.5	6 38.9	3 49.5
16 Th	17 37 3	24 50 28	22 29 49	29 4 21	19R39.3	19 21.9	23 0.6	26 47.4	29 15.5	16 38.1	18 7.1	6 37.9	3 50.4
17 F	17 40 59	25 47 45	5♈33 25	11♈57 29	19 39.1	20 29.5	24 14.3	27 31.5	29 7.9	16 34.2	18 9.6	6 37.0	3 51.3
18 Sa	17 44 56	26 45 2	18 17 3	24 32 38	19 37.8	21 34.0	25 28.0	28 15.6	29 0.2	16 30.2	18 12.3	6 36.0	3 52.3
19 Su	17 48 53	27 42 18	0♉44 42	6♉53 43	19 34.3	22 35.2	26 41.7	28 59.5	28 52.5	16 26.2	18 14.9	6 35.1	3 53.3
20 M	17 52 49	28 39 35	13 0 6	19 4 13	19 28.1	23 33.0	27 55.4	29 43.4	28 44.9	16 22.1	18 17.6	6 34.3	3 54.3
21 Tu	17 56 46	29 36 51	25 6 26	1♊ 7 3	19 19.1	24 27.4	29 9.1	0♉27.2	28 37.2	16 18.0	18 20.3	6 33.4	3 55.3
22 W	18 0 42	0♋34 6	7♊ 6 21	13 4 32	19 7.7	25 18.3	0♋22.8	1 11.0	28 29.5	16 13.8	18 23.1	6 32.6	3 56.4
23 Th	18 4 39	1 31 22	19 1 51	24 58 29	18 54.8	26 5.6	1 36.6	1 54.7	28 21.9	16 9.7	18 25.9	6 31.8	3 57.5
24 F	18 8 35	2 28 37	0♋54 35	6♋50 22	18 41.3	26 49.1	2 50.3	2 38.3	28 14.2	16 5.4	18 28.7	6 31.1	3 58.6
25 Sa	18 12 32	3 25 52	12 46 0	18 41 40	18 28.4	27 28.8	4 4.0	3 21.9	28 6.6	16 1.2	18 31.6	6 30.4	3 59.8
26 Su	18 16 28	4 23 6	24 37 35	0♌33 59	18 17.1	28 4.5	5 17.8	4 5.3	27 59.0	15 56.9	18 34.5	6 29.7	4 0.9
27 M	18 20 25	5 20 20	6♌31 9	12 29 22	18 8.2	28 36.1	6 31.5	4 48.7	27 51.4	15 52.6	18 37.4	6 29.0	4 2.1
28 Tu	18 24 22	6 17 34	18 29 1	24 30 27	18 2.0	29 3.5	7 45.3	5 32.1	27 43.9	15 48.3	18 40.4	6 28.4	4 3.4
29 W	18 28 18	7 14 47	0♍34 7	6♍40 30	17 58.5	29 26.6	8 59.0	6 15.3	27 36.4	15 44.0	18 43.4	6 27.7	4 4.6
30 Th	18 32 15	8 12 0	12 50 5	19 3 25	17D57.1	29 45.2	10 12.8	6 58.5	27 28.9	15 39.6	18 46.4	6 27.2	4 5.9

Astro Data

	Dy Hr Mn
☽ 0 S	7 19:34
♂ 0 N	15 15:29
♇ D	15 0:49
☽ 0 N	20 11:31
♃ ⚼ ♅	20 9:39
♄ ⚻ ♅	31 12:13
☽ 0 S	4 5:46
☽ 0 N	16 18:32

Planet Ingress

	Dy Hr Mn
♀ ♉	3 19:56
☿ ♉	4 16:45
♂ ♈	11 7:19
☿ ♊	19 3:27
☉ ♊	21 1:34
♀ ♊	28 6:11
☿ ♋	2 20:31
♃ ♐	10 1:53
♂ ♉	20 9:05
☉ ♋	21 9:42
♀ ♋	21 16:34

Last Aspect / ☽ Ingress

Last Aspect Dy Hr Mn		☽ Ingress Dy Hr Mn
2 19:28	♀ □	♌ 2 21:59
4 7:42	♅ ☌	♍ 5 8:59
7 11:16	♂ ☍	♎ 7 16:30
9 0:27	♄ □	♏ 9 20:07
11 5:42	☉ ☍	♐ 11 20:55
13 0:11	♅ △	♑ 13 20:50
15 13:01	☉ △	♒ 15 21:51
17 20:24	☿ □	♓ 18 1:23
20 6:30	☉ ⚹	♈ 20 7:55
21 17:51	♄ □	♉ 22 17:00
24 19:31	♀ ☌	♊ 25 3:55
26 14:41	♅ ⚹	♋ 27 16:06
29 3:51	♄ ☍	♌ 30 4:50

Last Aspect / ☽ Ingress

Last Aspect Dy Hr Mn		☽ Ingress Dy Hr Mn
1 11:48	☿ ⚹	♍ 1 16:38
3 2:06	♄ △	♎ 4 1:31
5 11:27	♂ ☍	♏ 6 6:20
7 11:49	♅ □	♐ 8 7:31
10 6:45	♃ ☌	♑ 10 6:48
11 20:18	♂ □	♒ 12 6:23
14 7:23	♃ ⚹	♓ 14 8:17
16 12:13	♃ □	♈ 16 13:42
18 20:25	♃ △	♉ 18 22:33
20 22:36	☿ ⚹	♊ 21 9:46
23 18:39	♃ ☍	♋ 23 22:10
26 7:18	☿ ☌	♌ 26 10:51
28 18:12	♃ △	♍ 28 22:53

☽ Phases & Eclipses

Dy Hr Mn	
4 1:00	☽ 13♌34
11 5:42	○ 20♏32
17 19:54	☽ 26♒53
25 12:26	● 4♊17
2 16:01	☽ 12♍06
9 13:02	○ 18♐40
16 4:35	☽ 25♓01
24 3:27	● 2♋37

Astro Data

1 MAY 1960
Julian Day # 22036
Delta T 33.3 sec
SVP 05♓48'53"
Obliquity 23°26'31"
⚷ Chiron 1♓41.1
☽ Mean ☊ 22♍19.0

1 JUNE 1960
Julian Day # 22067
Delta T 33.3 sec
SVP 05♓48'49"
Obliquity 23°26'30"
⚷ Chiron 2♓17.3
☽ Mean ☊ 20♍40.5

JULY 1960 — LONGITUDE

Day	Sid.Time	☉	0 hr ☽	Noon ☽	True ☊	☿	♀	♂	♃	♄	♅	♆	♇
1 F	18 36 11	9♋ 9 13	25♍21 3	1♎43 32	17♍57.2	29♋59.4	11♋26.5	7♉41.5	27♐21.5	15♑35.3	18♌49.4	6♏26.6	4♍ 7.2
2 Sa	18 40 8	10 6 25	8♎11 25	14 45 13	17R 57.5	0♌ 9.0	12 40.3	8 24.5	27R 14.2	15R 30.9	18 52.5	6R 26.1	4 8.5
3 Su	18 44 4	11 3 36	21 25 23	28 12 20	17 57.1	0R 13.9	13 54.0	9 7.4	27 6.9	15 26.5	18 55.6	6 25.6	4 9.8
4 M	18 48 1	12 0 48	5♏ 6 18	12♏ 7 26	17 55.0	0 14.1	15 7.8	9 50.3	26 59.7	15 22.1	18 58.8	6 25.1	4 11.2
5 Tu	18 51 57	12 57 59	19 15 41	26 30 48	17 50.7	0 9.7	16 21.6	10 33.0	26 52.5	15 17.7	19 1.9	6 24.7	4 12.6
6 W	18 55 54	13 55 10	3♐52 20	11♐19 37	17 44.2	0 0.7	17 35.3	11 15.7	26 45.5	15 13.2	19 5.1	6 24.3	4 14.0
7 Th	18 59 51	14 52 21	18 51 42	26 27 31	17 36.1	29♋47.1	18 49.1	11 58.3	26 38.5	15 8.8	19 8.3	6 23.9	4 15.4
8 F	19 3 47	15 49 32	4♑ 5 46	11♑45 4	17 27.1	29 29.1	20 2.9	12 40.8	26 31.6	15 4.4	19 11.6	6 23.6	4 16.8
9 Sa	19 7 44	16 46 43	19 24 1	27 1 11	17 18.6	29 7.0	21 16.7	13 23.2	26 24.8	14 60.0	19 14.9	6 23.3	4 18.3
10 Su	19 11 40	17 43 54	4♒35 15	12♒ 5 2	17 11.5	28 41.0	22 30.4	14 5.6	26 18.1	14 55.6	19 18.2	6 23.0	4 19.8
11 M	19 15 37	18 41 5	19 29 32	26 47 58	17 6.5	28 11.4	23 44.2	14 47.8	26 11.5	14 51.2	19 21.5	6 22.8	4 21.3
12 Tu	19 19 33	19 38 17	3♓59 45	11♓ 4 34	17D 3.8	27 38.7	24 58.0	15 30.0	26 5.0	14 46.8	19 24.8	6 22.5	4 22.8
13 W	19 23 30	20 35 29	18 2 14	24 52 47	17 3.1	27 3.3	26 11.8	16 12.1	25 58.6	14 42.4	19 28.2	6 22.4	4 24.4
14 Th	19 27 26	21 32 41	1♈36 26	8♈13 28	17 3.7	26 25.8	27 25.6	16 54.0	25 52.3	14 38.0	19 31.6	6 22.2	4 26.0
15 F	19 31 23	22 29 54	14 44 18	21 9 24	17R 4.6	25 46.7	28 39.5	17 35.9	25 46.1	14 33.6	19 35.0	6 22.1	4 27.5
16 Sa	19 35 20	23 27 8	27 29 17	3♉44 30	17 4.7	25 6.8	29 53.3	18 17.8	25 40.1	14 29.3	19 38.4	6 22.0	4 29.1
17 Su	19 39 16	24 24 22	9♉55 37	16 3 9	17 3.4	24 26.7	1♌ 7.1	18 59.5	25 34.2	14 24.9	19 41.8	6 21.9	4 30.8
18 M	19 43 13	25 21 38	22 7 40	28 9 39	17 0.0	23 47.0	2 21.0	19 41.1	25 28.4	14 20.6	19 45.3	6D 21.9	4 32.4
19 Tu	19 47 9	26 18 53	4♊ 9 35	10♊ 7 55	16 54.6	23 8.6	3 34.8	20 22.6	25 22.7	14 16.4	19 48.8	6 21.9	4 34.1
20 W	19 51 6	27 16 10	16 5 2	22 1 20	16 47.3	22 32.0	4 48.7	21 4.0	25 17.2	14 12.1	19 52.3	6 21.9	4 35.7
21 Th	19 55 2	28 13 27	27 57 7	3♋52 43	16 38.8	21 58.0	6 2.5	21 45.3	25 11.8	14 7.9	19 55.8	6 22.0	4 37.4
22 F	19 58 59	29 10 45	9♋48 22	15 44 19	16 29.7	21 27.2	7 16.4	22 26.5	25 6.5	14 3.7	19 59.4	6 22.1	4 39.1
23 Sa	20 2 55	0♌ 8 4	21 40 49	27 38 2	16 21.1	21 0.2	8 30.3	23 7.6	25 1.4	13 59.5	20 2.9	6 22.3	4 40.9
24 Su	20 6 52	1 5 23	3♌36 12	9♌35 30	16 13.6	20 37.5	9 44.1	23 48.6	24 56.4	13 55.4	20 6.5	6 22.4	4 42.6
25 M	20 10 49	2 2 43	15 36 8	21 38 21	16 7.8	20 19.5	10 58.0	24 29.5	24 51.6	13 51.3	20 10.1	6 22.6	4 44.4
26 Tu	20 14 45	3 0 3	27 42 21	3♍48 25	16 4.0	20 6.7	12 11.9	25 10.3	24 47.0	13 47.2	20 13.7	6 22.9	4 46.1
27 W	20 18 42	3 57 24	9♍56 49	16 7 52	16D 2.3	19D 59.4	13 25.8	25 50.9	24 42.5	13 43.2	20 17.3	6 23.1	4 47.9
28 Th	20 22 38	4 54 45	22 21 55	28 39 19	16 2.3	19 57.8	14 39.7	26 31.5	24 38.1	13 39.2	20 20.9	6 23.4	4 49.7
29 F	20 26 35	5 52 7	5♎ 0 26	11♎25 40	16 3.4	20 2.2	15 53.6	27 11.9	24 34.0	13 35.3	20 24.6	6 23.7	4 51.5
30 Sa	20 30 31	6 49 30	17 55 25	24 30 3	16 4.9	20 12.8	17 7.5	27 52.2	24 30.0	13 31.4	20 28.2	6 24.1	4 53.4
31 Su	20 34 28	7 46 53	1♏ 9 56	7♏55 20	16R 5.9	20 29.5	18 21.4	28 32.4	24 26.1	13 27.5	20 31.9	6 24.5	4 55.2

AUGUST 1960 — LONGITUDE

Day	Sid.Time	☉	0 hr ☽	Noon ☽	True ☊	☿	♀	♂	♃	♄	♅	♆	♇
1 M	20 38 24	8♌44 16	14♏46 30	21♏43 33	16♍ 5.9	20♋52.6	19♌35.3	29♉12.5	24♐22.4	13♑23.8	20♌35.5	6♏24.9	4♍57.1
2 Tu	20 42 21	9 41 41	28 46 31	5♐55 17	16R 4.5	21 22.0	20 49.2	29 52.5	24R 18.9	13R 20.0	20 39.2	6 25.4	4 58.9
3 W	20 46 18	10 39 5	13♐ 9 33	20 28 53	16 1.6	21 57.8	22 3.1	0♊32.3	24 15.6	13 16.3	20 42.9	6 25.9	5 0.8
4 Th	20 50 14	11 36 31	27 52 38	5♑20 2	15 57.6	22 39.9	23 17.0	1 12.0	24 12.5	13 12.7	20 46.6	6 26.4	5 2.7
5 F	20 54 11	12 33 57	12♑50 8	20 21 51	15 52.9	23 28.2	24 30.9	1 51.6	24 9.5	13 9.2	20 50.3	6 27.0	5 4.6
6 Sa	20 58 7	13 31 24	27 54 3	5♒25 34	15 48.4	24 22.6	25 44.8	2 31.1	24 6.7	13 5.7	20 54.0	6 27.5	5 6.5
7 Su	21 2 4	14 28 52	12♒55 11	20 21 50	15 44.7	25 23.1	26 58.7	3 10.5	24 4.1	13 2.2	20 57.7	6 28.2	5 8.4
8 M	21 6 0	15 26 21	27 44 30	5♓ 2 18	15 42.2	26 29.4	28 12.6	3 49.7	24 1.6	12 58.8	21 1.4	6 28.8	5 10.4
9 Tu	21 9 57	16 23 51	12♓14 33	19 20 43	15D 41.2	27 41.4	29 26.5	4 28.8	23 59.4	12 55.5	21 5.2	6 29.5	5 12.3
10 W	21 13 53	17 21 23	26 20 26	3♈13 30	15 41.5	28 59.0	0♍40.4	5 7.8	23 57.3	12 52.3	21 8.9	6 30.2	5 14.2
11 Th	21 17 50	18 18 55	9♈59 56	16 39 49	15 42.7	0♌21.8	1 54.3	5 46.6	23 55.4	12 49.1	21 12.6	6 30.9	5 16.2
12 F	21 21 47	19 16 29	23 13 24	29 41 1	15 44.2	1 49.7	3 8.2	6 25.3	23 53.7	12 45.9	21 16.3	6 31.7	5 18.2
13 Sa	21 25 43	20 14 5	6♉ 3 5	12♉20 3	15 45.6	3 22.2	4 22.1	7 3.9	23 52.1	12 42.9	21 20.1	6 32.5	5 20.1
14 Su	21 29 40	21 11 42	18 32 29	24 40 53	15R 46.3	4 59.2	5 36.0	7 42.3	23 50.8	12 39.9	21 23.8	6 33.3	5 22.1
15 M	21 33 36	22 9 20	0♊45 50	6♊47 54	15 46.0	6 40.2	6 49.9	8 20.6	23 49.6	12 37.0	21 27.5	6 34.2	5 24.1
16 Tu	21 37 33	23 7 0	12 47 39	18 45 35	15 44.7	8 24.8	8 3.8	8 58.8	23 48.6	12 34.2	21 31.3	6 35.1	5 26.1
17 W	21 41 29	24 4 42	24 42 16	0♋38 10	15 42.5	10 12.8	9 17.7	9 36.8	23 47.9	12 31.4	21 35.0	6 36.0	5 28.1
18 Th	21 45 26	25 2 25	6♋33 46	12 29 29	15 39.6	12 3.5	10 31.6	10 14.6	23 47.3	12 28.7	21 38.8	6 37.0	5 30.1
19 F	21 49 22	26 0 10	18 25 43	24 22 51	15 36.4	13 56.7	11 45.5	10 52.3	23 46.8	12 26.1	21 42.5	6 38.0	5 32.1
20 Sa	21 53 19	26 57 56	0♌21 11	6♌21 2	15 33.3	15 51.9	12 59.4	11 29.9	23D 46.6	12 23.6	21 46.2	6 39.0	5 34.1
21 Su	21 57 16	27 55 44	12 22 39	18 26 16	15 30.8	17 48.8	14 13.4	12 7.3	23 46.6	12 21.2	21 49.9	6 40.0	5 36.2
22 M	22 1 12	28 53 33	24 32 6	0♍40 20	15 28.9	19 46.8	15 27.3	12 44.5	23 46.7	12 18.8	21 53.7	6 41.1	5 38.2
23 Tu	22 5 9	29 51 23	6♍51 7	13 4 39	15D 28.0	21 45.8	16 41.2	13 21.6	23 47.1	12 16.6	21 57.4	6 42.2	5 40.2
24 W	22 9 5	0♍49 15	19 21 2	25 40 25	15 27.8	23 45.3	17 55.1	13 58.5	23 47.6	12 14.4	22 1.1	6 43.3	5 42.2
25 Th	22 13 2	1 47 8	2♎ 2 58	8♎28 47	15 28.3	25 45.0	19 9.0	14 35.3	23 48.3	12 12.3	22 4.8	6 44.5	5 44.3
26 F	22 16 58	2 45 3	14 58 1	21 30 48	15 29.3	27 44.7	20 22.9	15 11.8	23 49.2	12 10.3	22 8.5	6 45.7	5 46.3
27 Sa	22 20 55	3 42 59	28 7 15	4♏47 31	15 30.3	29 44.2	21 36.8	15 48.2	23 50.3	12 8.3	22 12.2	6 46.9	5 48.3
28 Su	22 24 51	4 40 56	11♏31 40	18 19 49	15 31.2	1♍43.2	22 50.7	16 24.4	23 51.6	12 6.5	22 15.8	6 48.1	5 50.4
29 M	22 28 48	5 38 55	25 11 59	2♐ 8 10	15R 31.8	3 41.6	24 4.6	17 0.5	23 53.1	12 4.7	22 19.5	6 49.4	5 52.4
30 Tu	22 32 44	6 36 55	9♐ 8 19	16 12 18	15 31.9	5 39.2	25 18.4	17 36.4	23 54.7	12 3.1	22 23.2	6 50.7	5 54.5
31 W	22 36 41	7 34 57	23 19 55	0♑30 51	15 31.7	7 36.0	26 32.3	18 12.1	23 56.6	12 1.5	22 26.8	6 52.0	5 56.5

Astro Data	Dy Hr Mn
☽0S	1 14:29
☿ R	3 13:15
☽0N	14 3:05
♆ D	18 6:55
☿ D	27 18:24
☽0S	28 21:24
☽0N	10 12:56
♃ D	20 16:40
☽0S	25 3:22

Planet Ingress	Dy Hr Mn
☿ ♌	1 1:13
☿ ♋	6 1:23
♀ ♌	16 2:11
☉ ♌	22 20:37
♂ ♊	2 4:32
♀ ♍	9 10:54
☿ ♌	10 17:49
☉ ♍	23 3:34
☿ ♍	27 3:11

Last Aspect Dy Hr Mn		☽ Ingress Dy Hr Mn
1 3:46	♃ □	♎ 1 8:46
3 10:00	♃ ✶	♏ 3 15:08
4 23:37	♅ □	♐ 5 17:42
7 12:12	♃ ☌	♑ 7 17:34
9 14:54	☿ ☍	♒ 9 16:43
11 10:55	♃ ✶	♓ 11 17:19
13 15:46	♀ △	♈ 13 21:07
15 20:34	♃ △	♉ 16 4:48
18 6:58	☉ ✶	♊ 18 15:40
20 18:28	♃ ☍	♋ 21 4:09
23 3:06	♂ ✶	♌ 23 16:46
25 18:42	♂ □	♍ 26 4:31
28 8:24	♂ △	♎ 28 14:33
30 11:56	♃ ✶	♏ 30 21:55

Last Aspect Dy Hr Mn		☽ Ingress Dy Hr Mn
2 1:57	♂ ☍	♐ 2 2:04
3 18:05	♃ ☌	♑ 4 3:25
5 18:01	☿ ☍	♒ 6 3:21
8 0:50	♀ ☍	♓ 8 3:42
10 5:05	☿ △	♈ 10 6:21
12 1:14	♃ △	♉ 12 12:36
14 5:37	☉ □	♊ 14 22:29
16 22:37	☉ ✶	♋ 17 10:43
18 11:56	♄ ☍	♌ 19 23:18
22 9:15	☉ ☌	♍ 22 10:41
24 8:27	♃ □	♎ 24 20:09
26 16:13	♃ ✶	♏ 27 3:24
28 21:51	♀ ✶	♐ 29 8:19
31 5:52	♀ □	♑ 31 11:09

☽ Phases & Eclipses Dy Hr Mn	
2 3:48	☽ 10♎15
8 19:37	○ 16♑36
15 15:43	☽ 23♈07
23 18:31	● 0♌52
31 12:38	☽ 8♏17
7 2:41	○ 14♒35
14 5:37	☽ 21♉25
22 9:15	● 29♌16
29 19:22	☽ 6♐26

Astro Data

1 JULY 1960
Julian Day # 22097
Delta T 33.4 sec
SVP 05♓48'44"
Obliquity 23°26'30"
⚷ Chiron 1♓58.8R
☽ Mean ☊ 19♍05.2

1 AUGUST 1960
Julian Day # 22128
Delta T 33.4 sec
SVP 05♓48'40"
Obliquity 23°26'31"
⚷ Chiron 0♓52.4R
☽ Mean ☊ 17♍26.7

LONGITUDE — SEPTEMBER 1960

Day	Sid.Time	☉	0 hr ☽	Noon ☽	True ☊	☿	♀	♂	♃	♄	♅	♆	♇
1 Th	22 40 38	8♍32 59	7♑44 44	15♑ 1 3	15♍31.1	9♍31.9	27♍46.2	18♊47.6	23♐58.6	12♑ 0.0	22♌30.5	6♏53.4	5♍58.5
2 F	22 44 34	9 31 3	22 19 14	29 38 38	15R 30.5	11 26.7	29 0.0	19 22.9	24 0.8	11R 58.7	22 34.1	6 54.8	6 0.6
3 Sa	22 48 31	10 29 9	6♒58 30	14♒18 3	15 29.9	13 20.4	0♎13.9	19 58.0	24 3.2	11 57.4	22 37.7	6 56.2	6 2.6
4 Su	22 52 27	11 27 16	21 36 31	28 53 4	15 29.4	15 13.0	1 27.7	20 33.0	24 5.8	11 56.2	22 41.3	6 57.6	6 4.6
5 M	22 56 24	12 25 24	6♓ 6 56	13♓17 23	15D 29.2	17 4.5	2 41.5	21 7.7	24 8.5	11 55.1	22 44.9	6 59.1	6 6.7
6 Tu	23 0 20	13 23 34	20 23 48	27 25 35	15 29.2	18 54.8	3 55.4	21 42.3	24 11.4	11 54.1	22 48.4	7 0.5	6 8.7
7 W	23 4 17	14 21 46	4♈22 20	11♈13 40	15 29.3	20 43.9	5 9.2	22 16.7	24 14.6	11 53.1	22 52.0	7 2.0	6 10.7
8 Th	23 8 13	15 20 0	17 59 25	24 39 29	15R 29.3	22 31.9	6 23.0	22 50.8	24 17.8	11 52.3	22 55.5	7 3.6	6 12.7
9 F	23 12 10	16 18 16	1♉13 52	7♉42 44	15 29.3	24 18.7	7 36.8	23 24.8	24 21.3	11 51.6	22 59.0	7 5.1	6 14.8
10 Sa	23 16 7	17 16 34	14 6 16	20 24 49	15 29.1	26 4.3	8 50.6	23 58.5	24 24.9	11 51.0	23 2.5	7 6.7	6 16.8
11 Su	23 20 3	18 14 54	26 38 45	2♊48 31	15 28.9	27 48.9	10 4.4	24 32.1	24 28.7	11 50.4	23 6.0	7 8.3	6 18.8
12 M	23 24 0	19 13 16	8♊54 36	14 57 33	15D 28.7	29 32.2	11 18.1	25 5.4	24 32.7	11 50.0	23 9.5	7 9.9	6 20.8
13 Tu	23 27 56	20 11 40	20 57 54	26 56 15	15 28.6	1♎14.5	12 31.9	25 38.5	24 36.9	11 49.7	23 12.9	7 11.6	6 22.8
14 W	23 31 53	21 10 6	2♋53 10	8♋49 14	15 28.8	2 55.7	13 45.7	26 11.4	24 41.2	11 49.4	23 16.3	7 13.2	6 24.8
15 Th	23 35 49	22 8 34	14 45 1	20 41 6	15 29.2	4 35.8	14 59.4	26 44.0	24 45.7	11D 49.3	23 19.7	7 14.9	6 26.7
16 F	23 39 46	23 7 5	26 37 59	2♌36 12	15 29.9	6 14.8	16 13.2	27 16.4	24 50.4	11 49.2	23 23.1	7 16.6	6 28.7
17 Sa	23 43 42	24 5 38	8♌36 13	14 38 29	15 30.8	7 52.8	17 27.0	27 48.6	24 55.2	11 49.3	23 26.5	7 18.4	6 30.7
18 Su	23 47 39	25 4 12	20 43 23	26 51 16	15 31.6	9 29.8	18 40.7	28 20.5	25 0.2	11 49.4	23 29.8	7 20.1	6 32.6
19 M	23 51 36	26 2 49	3♍ 2 25	9♍17 6	15 32.3	11 5.7	19 54.4	28 52.2	25 5.4	11 49.7	23 33.1	7 21.9	6 34.6
20 Tu	23 55 32	27 1 28	15 35 29	21 57 42	15R 32.6	12 40.7	21 8.2	29 23.6	25 10.7	11 50.0	23 36.4	7 23.7	6 36.5
21 W	23 59 29	28 0 9	28 23 48	4♎53 50	15 32.3	14 14.6	22 21.9	29 54.7	25 16.2	11 50.5	23 39.6	7 25.5	6 38.5
22 Th	0 3 25	28 58 51	11♎27 44	18 5 25	15 31.3	15 47.6	23 35.6	0♋25.6	25 21.9	11 51.0	23 42.9	7 27.3	6 40.4
23 F	0 7 22	29 57 36	24 46 44	1♏31 32	15 29.7	17 19.6	24 49.3	0 56.2	25 27.7	11 51.7	23 46.1	7 29.2	6 42.3
24 Sa	0 11 18	0♎56 22	8♏19 35	15 10 41	15 27.6	18 50.6	26 3.0	1 26.5	25 33.6	11 52.4	23 49.2	7 31.1	6 44.2
25 Su	0 15 15	1 55 11	22 4 34	29 0 59	15 25.5	20 20.7	27 16.7	1 56.6	25 39.8	11 53.3	23 52.4	7 33.0	6 46.1
26 M	0 19 11	2 54 1	5♐59 39	13♐ 0 20	15 23.6	21 49.7	28 30.3	2 26.3	25 46.1	11 54.2	23 55.5	7 34.9	6 48.0
27 Tu	0 23 8	3 52 53	20 2 44	27 6 37	15 22.3	23 17.8	29 44.0	2 55.8	25 52.5	11 55.3	23 58.6	7 36.8	6 49.8
28 W	0 27 5	4 51 47	4♑11 43	11♑17 46	15D 21.8	24 44.9	0♏57.6	3 25.0	25 59.1	11 56.4	24 1.6	7 38.7	6 51.7
29 Th	0 31 1	5 50 42	18 24 30	25 31 38	15 22.2	26 11.0	2 11.3	3 53.8	26 5.8	11 57.6	24 4.7	7 40.7	6 53.5
30 F	0 34 58	6 49 39	2♒38 52	9♒45 55	15 23.3	27 36.1	3 24.9	4 22.4	26 12.7	11 59.0	24 7.7	7 42.7	6 55.4

LONGITUDE — OCTOBER 1960

Day	Sid.Time	☉	0 hr ☽	Noon ☽	True ☊	☿	♀	♂	♃	♄	♅	♆	♇
1 Sa	0 38 54	7♎48 38	16♒52 25	23♒58 2	15♍24.7	29♎ 0.2	4♏38.5	4♋50.6	26♐19.8	12♑ 0.4	24♌10.6	7♏44.7	6♍57.2
2 Su	0 42 51	8 47 38	1♓ 2 23	8♓ 5 4	15 25.9	0♏23.1	5 52.1	5 18.6	26 27.0	12 1.9	24 13.6	7 46.7	6 59.0
3 M	0 46 47	9 46 40	15 5 40	22 3 47	15R 26.4	1 45.0	7 5.6	5 46.2	26 34.3	12 3.6	24 16.4	7 48.7	7 0.7
4 Tu	0 50 44	10 45 45	28 59 1	5♈50 58	15 25.8	3 5.8	8 19.2	6 13.5	26 41.7	12 5.3	24 19.3	7 50.7	7 2.5
5 W	0 54 40	11 44 51	12♈39 16	19 23 39	15 23.9	4 25.3	9 32.7	6 40.4	26 49.3	12 7.1	24 22.1	7 52.8	7 4.3
6 Th	0 58 37	12 43 59	26 3 49	2♉39 35	15 20.7	5 43.7	10 46.2	7 7.1	26 57.1	12 9.0	24 24.9	7 54.9	7 6.0
7 F	1 2 33	13 43 9	9♉10 52	15 37 35	15 16.4	7 0.7	11 59.7	7 33.3	27 5.0	12 11.0	24 27.7	7 56.9	7 7.7
8 Sa	1 6 30	14 42 22	21 59 49	28 17 40	15 11.5	8 16.3	13 13.2	7 59.2	27 13.0	12 13.1	24 30.4	7 59.0	7 9.4
9 Su	1 10 27	15 41 37	4♊31 21	10♊41 9	15 6.6	9 30.5	14 26.7	8 24.8	27 21.1	12 15.3	24 33.1	8 1.1	7 11.1
10 M	1 14 23	16 40 54	16 47 26	22 50 36	15 2.4	10 43.2	15 40.2	8 50.0	27 29.4	12 17.6	24 35.7	8 3.2	7 12.8
11 Tu	1 18 20	17 40 13	28 51 7	4♋49 31	14 59.2	11 54.1	16 53.6	9 14.8	27 37.8	12 20.0	24 38.3	8 5.4	7 14.4
12 W	1 22 16	18 39 35	10♋46 21	16 42 13	14D 57.5	13 3.3	18 7.1	9 39.2	27 46.4	12 22.5	24 40.9	8 7.5	7 16.1
13 Th	1 26 13	19 38 59	22 37 43	28 33 29	14 57.2	14 10.5	19 20.5	10 3.2	27 55.0	12 25.0	24 43.4	8 9.6	7 17.7
14 F	1 30 9	20 38 25	4♌30 8	10♌28 20	14 58.0	15 15.6	20 33.9	10 26.8	28 3.8	12 27.7	24 45.9	8 11.8	7 19.3
15 Sa	1 34 6	21 37 54	16 28 40	22 31 44	14 59.6	16 18.4	21 47.3	10 50.0	28 12.8	12 30.4	24 48.3	8 14.0	7 20.8
16 Su	1 38 2	22 37 25	28 38 5	4♍48 15	15 1.3	17 18.7	23 0.7	11 12.7	28 21.8	12 33.3	24 50.8	8 16.1	7 22.4
17 M	1 41 59	23 36 58	11♍ 2 41	17 21 46	15R 2.3	18 16.2	24 14.1	11 35.1	28 31.0	12 36.2	24 53.1	8 18.3	7 23.9
18 Tu	1 45 56	24 36 33	23 45 50	0♎15 4	15 2.0	19 10.7	25 27.5	11 56.9	28 40.3	12 39.2	24 55.4	8 20.5	7 25.4
19 W	1 49 52	25 36 10	6♎49 36	13 29 27	14 59.9	20 1.8	26 40.8	12 18.3	28 49.7	12 42.3	24 57.7	8 22.7	7 26.9
20 Th	1 53 49	26 35 50	20 14 29	27 4 28	14 55.8	20 49.2	27 54.1	12 39.3	28 59.2	12 45.5	24 59.9	8 24.9	7 28.4
21 F	1 57 45	27 35 32	3♏59 5	10♏57 52	14 50.0	21 32.5	29 7.5	12 59.7	29 8.8	12 48.8	25 2.1	8 27.1	7 29.9
22 Sa	2 1 42	28 35 15	18 0 16	25 5 42	14 43.0	22 11.4	0♐20.8	13 19.7	29 18.6	12 52.2	25 4.3	8 29.3	7 31.3
23 Su	2 5 38	29 35 1	2♐13 30	9♐22 58	14 35.6	22 45.2	1 34.1	13 39.2	29 28.4	12 55.6	25 6.4	8 31.5	7 32.7
24 M	2 9 35	0♏34 48	16 33 28	23 44 20	14 28.8	23 13.6	2 47.3	13 58.2	29 38.4	12 59.2	25 8.4	8 33.8	7 34.1
25 Tu	2 13 31	1 34 37	0♑54 59	8♑ 4 54	14 23.4	23 35.9	4 0.6	14 16.6	29 48.5	13 2.8	25 10.4	8 36.0	7 35.4
26 W	2 17 28	2 34 28	15 13 39	22 20 51	14 20.0	23 51.6	5 13.8	14 34.6	29 58.7	13 6.5	25 12.4	8 38.2	7 36.8
27 Th	2 21 25	3 34 21	29 26 15	6♒29 38	14D 18.6	24R 0.1	6 27.0	14 52.0	0♑ 9.0	13 10.3	25 14.3	8 40.5	7 38.1
28 F	2 25 21	4 34 15	13♒30 52	20 29 51	14 18.9	24 0.8	7 40.2	15 8.8	0 19.4	13 14.2	25 16.1	8 42.7	7 39.4
29 Sa	2 29 18	5 34 11	27 26 34	4♓20 57	14 19.9	23 53.1	8 53.4	15 25.1	0 29.9	13 18.2	25 18.0	8 45.0	7 40.6
30 Su	2 33 14	6 34 8	11♓13 0	18 2 41	14R 20.7	23 36.4	10 6.5	15 40.8	0 40.5	13 22.2	25 19.7	8 47.2	7 41.9
31 M	2 37 11	7 34 7	24 49 57	1♈34 44	14 20.2	23 10.6	11 19.6	15 56.0	0 51.2	13 26.3	25 21.4	8 49.5	7 43.1

Astro Data Dy Hr Mn	Planet Ingress Dy Hr Mn	Last Aspect Dy Hr Mn	☽ Ingress Dy Hr Mn	Last Aspect Dy Hr Mn	☽ Ingress Dy Hr Mn	☽ Phases & Eclipses Dy Hr Mn
♀0S 4 20:52	♀ ♎ 2 19:29	2 11:57 ♀ △	♒ 2 12:35	1 16:08 ♃ ⚹	♓ 1 22:14	5 11:19 ○ 12♓53
☽0N 6 23:06	☿ ♎ 12 6:29	4 4:07 ♃ ⚹	♓ 4 13:51	3 19:59 ♃ □	♈ 4 1:46	5 11:21 ☍T 1.424
☿0S 13 5:57	♂ ♋ 21 4:06	6 6:29 ♃ □	♈ 6 16:26	6 1:37 ♃ △	♉ 6 7:09	12 22:19 ☽ 20♊08
♄ D 15 22:48	☉ ♎ 23 0:59	8 11:24 ♃ △	♉ 8 21:44	8 4:47 ♅ □	♊ 8 15:16	20 23:12 ● 27♍58
☽0S 21 10:02	♀ ♏ 27 5:13	11 2:38 ☿ △	♊ 11 6:31	10 21:32 ♃ ☍	♋ 11 2:18	20 22:59:22 ☌ P 0.614
		13 9:51 ♂ ☌	♋ 13 18:10	12 17:25 ☉ □	♌ 13 14:55	28 1:13 ☽ 4♑55
☽0N 4 8:27	☿ ♏ 1 17:17	15 16:17 ☉ ⚹	♌ 16 6:46	15 23:28 ♃ △	♍ 16 2:40	
☽0S 18 18:37	♀ ♐ 21 17:12	18 15:34 ♂ ⚹	♍ 18 18:07	18 9:12 ♃ □	♎ 18 11:32	4 22:16 ○ 11♈41
☿ R 27 14:02	☉ ♏ 23 10:02	21 2:55 ♂ □	♎ 21 2:58	20 15:31 ♃ ⚹	♏ 20 17:06	12 17:25 ☽ 19♋23
☽0N 31 16:17	♃ ♑ 26 3:01	23 1:14 ♃ ⚹	♏ 23 9:18	22 11:59 ♅ □	♐ 22 20:16	20 12:02 ● 27♎06
		25 3:08 ♅ □	♐ 25 13:42	24 22:07 ♃ ☌	♑ 24 22:28	27 7:34 ☽ 3♒53
		27 9:59 ♃ ☌	♑ 27 16:54	26 14:44 ☿ ⚹	♒ 27 0:57	
		29 14:34 ☿ □	♒ 29 19:32	28 20:17 ♅ ☍	♓ 29 4:26	
				30 21:10 ☿ △	♈ 31 9:11	

Astro Data

1 SEPTEMBER 1960
Julian Day # 22159
Delta T 33.4 sec
SVP 05♓48'36"
Obliquity 23°26'31"
⚷ Chiron 29♒22.2R
☽ Mean ☊ 15♍48.2

1 OCTOBER 1960
Julian Day # 22189
Delta T 33.5 sec
SVP 05♓48'33"
Obliquity 23°26'31"
⚷ Chiron 28♒04.9R
☽ Mean ☊ 14♍12.9

NOVEMBER 1960 LONGITUDE

Day	Sid.Time	☉	0 hr ☽	Noon ☽	True ☊	☿	♀	♂	♃	♄	♅	♆	♇
1 Tu	2 41 7	8♏34 7	8♈16 58	14♈56 32	14♍17.6	22♏35.2	12♐32.7	16♋10.6	1♑ 2.0	13♑30.5	25♌23.1	8♏51.7	7♍44.2
2 W	2 45 4	9 34 10	21 33 18	28 7 8	14R 12.5	21R 50.4	13 45.7	16 24.5	1 12.9	13 34.8	25 24.7	8 53.9	7 45.4
3 Th	2 49 0	10 34 14	4♉37 55	11♉ 5 29	14 4.9	20 56.5	14 58.8	16 37.9	1 23.9	13 39.1	25 26.3	8 56.2	7 46.5
4 F	2 52 57	11 34 20	17 29 46	23 50 40	13 55.1	19 54.3	16 11.8	16 50.6	1 35.0	13 43.5	25 27.8	8 58.4	7 47.6
5 Sa	2 56 54	12 34 28	0♊ 8 10	6♊22 16	13 44.1	18 44.9	17 24.7	17 2.7	1 46.2	13 48.0	25 29.3	9 0.7	7 48.7
6 Su	3 0 50	13 34 38	12 33 3	18 40 38	13 32.9	17 30.1	18 37.7	17 14.2	1 57.4	13 52.6	25 30.7	9 2.9	7 49.8
7 M	3 4 47	14 34 49	24 45 15	0♋47 10	13 22.5	16 11.8	19 50.6	17 25.0	2 8.8	13 57.2	25 32.0	9 5.2	7 50.8
8 Tu	3 8 43	15 35 3	6♋46 42	12 44 15	13 13.7	14 52.4	21 3.5	17 35.1	2 20.2	14 2.0	25 33.3	9 7.4	7 51.8
9 W	3 12 40	16 35 19	18 40 17	24 35 19	13 7.3	13 34.5	22 16.3	17 44.5	2 31.7	14 6.7	25 34.6	9 9.6	7 52.8
10 Th	3 16 36	17 35 36	0♌29 54	6♌24 38	13 3.4	12 20.5	23 29.2	17 53.3	2 43.3	14 11.6	25 35.8	9 11.9	7 53.7
11 F	3 20 33	18 35 56	12 20 10	18 17 9	13D 1.7	11 12.9	24 42.0	18 1.3	2 55.0	14 16.5	25 36.9	9 14.1	7 54.6
12 Sa	3 24 29	19 36 17	24 16 17	0♍18 13	13 1.5	10 13.7	25 54.8	18 8.6	3 6.8	14 21.5	25 38.0	9 16.3	7 55.5
13 Su	3 28 26	20 36 41	6♍23 40	12 33 16	13R 2.0	9 24.4	27 7.5	18 15.1	3 18.6	14 26.6	25 39.1	9 18.5	7 56.4
14 M	3 32 23	21 37 6	18 47 39	25 7 23	13 2.0	8 46.1	28 20.2	18 20.9	3 30.5	14 31.7	25 40.1	9 20.8	7 57.2
15 Tu	3 36 19	22 37 33	1♎32 59	8♎ 4 49	13 0.5	8 19.4	29 32.9	18 25.9	3 42.5	14 36.9	25 41.0	9 23.0	7 58.0
16 W	3 40 16	23 38 2	14 43 12	21 28 17	12 56.6	8D 4.4	0♑45.5	18 30.1	3 54.6	14 42.1	25 41.9	9 25.2	7 58.8
17 Th	3 44 12	24 38 33	28 20 2	5♏18 17	12 49.9	8 0.9	1 58.2	18 33.6	4 6.8	14 47.5	25 42.7	9 27.3	7 59.5
18 F	3 48 9	25 39 6	12♏22 40	19 32 38	12 40.8	8 8.4	3 10.7	18 36.2	4 19.0	14 52.8	25 43.5	9 29.5	8 0.2
19 Sa	3 52 5	26 39 40	26 47 28	4♐ 6 18	12 29.8	8 26.1	4 23.3	18 38.0	4 31.3	14 58.3	25 44.2	9 31.7	8 0.9
20 Su	3 56 2	27 40 16	11♐28 7	18 51 53	12 18.1	8 53.3	5 35.8	18R 39.0	4 43.6	15 3.8	25 44.8	9 33.9	8 1.5
21 M	3 59 58	28 40 53	26 16 30	3♑40 54	12 7.0	9 29.0	6 48.3	18 39.2	4 56.1	15 9.4	25 45.4	9 36.0	8 2.2
22 Tu	4 3 55	29 41 32	11♑ 4 5	18 25 8	11 57.9	10 12.3	8 0.7	18 38.5	5 8.6	15 15.0	25 46.0	9 38.2	8 2.8
23 W	4 7 52	0♐42 12	25 43 20	2♒58 3	11 51.4	11 2.4	9 13.1	18 37.0	5 21.1	15 20.7	25 46.5	9 40.3	8 3.3
24 Th	4 11 48	1 42 53	10♒ 8 51	17 15 27	11 47.7	11 58.5	10 25.4	18 34.7	5 33.7	15 26.4	25 46.9	9 42.4	8 3.8
25 F	4 15 45	2 43 35	24 17 41	1♓15 32	11D 46.3	12 59.7	11 37.7	18 31.5	5 46.4	15 32.2	25 47.3	9 44.5	8 4.3
26 Sa	4 19 41	3 44 18	8♓ 9 4	14 58 25	11R 46.2	14 5.4	12 49.9	18 27.4	5 59.2	15 38.0	25 47.6	9 46.6	8 4.8
27 Su	4 23 38	4 45 2	21 43 47	28 25 22	11 46.0	15 15.1	14 2.1	18 22.5	6 12.0	15 43.9	25 47.9	9 48.7	8 5.2
28 M	4 27 34	5 45 47	5♈ 3 26	11♈38 10	11 44.4	16 28.1	15 14.2	18 16.8	6 24.8	15 49.9	25 48.1	9 50.8	8 5.6
29 Tu	4 31 31	6 46 33	18 9 47	24 38 28	11 40.4	17 44.0	16 26.3	18 10.2	6 37.7	15 55.9	25 48.2	9 52.9	8 6.0
30 W	4 35 27	7 47 20	1♉ 4 21	7♉27 34	11 33.3	19 2.4	17 38.3	18 2.7	6 50.7	16 1.9	25 48.3	9 54.9	8 6.3

DECEMBER 1960 LONGITUDE

Day	Sid.Time	☉	0 hr ☽	Noon ☽	True ☊	☿	♀	♂	♃	♄	♅	♆	♇
1 Th	4 39 24	8♐48 8	13♉48 10	20♉ 6 14	11♍23.2	20♏22.8	18♑50.2	17♋54.4	7♑ 3.7	16♑ 8.0	25♌48.3	9♏56.9	8♍ 6.6
2 F	4 43 21	9 48 57	26 21 47	2♊34 52	11R 10.5	21 45.1	20 2.1	17R 45.2	7 16.7	16 14.2	25R 48.3	9 59.0	8 6.9
3 Sa	4 47 17	10 49 47	8♊45 29	14 53 41	10 56.2	23 8.9	21 13.9	17 35.2	7 29.9	16 20.4	25 48.3	10 1.0	8 7.2
4 Su	4 51 14	11 50 38	20 59 30	27 3 4	10 41.5	24 34.1	22 25.6	17 24.4	7 43.0	16 26.6	25 48.1	10 2.9	8 7.4
5 M	4 55 10	12 51 31	3♋ 4 27	9♋ 3 51	10 27.6	26 0.3	23 37.3	17 12.7	7 56.2	16 32.9	25 47.9	10 4.9	8 7.6
6 Tu	4 59 7	13 52 25	15 1 29	20 57 36	10 15.6	27 27.4	24 48.9	17 0.2	8 9.5	16 39.2	25 47.7	10 6.9	8 7.7
7 W	5 3 3	14 53 19	26 52 33	2♌46 42	10 6.3	28 55.4	26 0.4	16 46.8	8 22.8	16 45.6	25 47.4	10 8.8	8 7.8
8 Th	5 7 0	15 54 15	8♌40 30	14 34 27	10 0.0	0♐24.1	27 11.9	16 32.7	8 36.1	16 52.0	25 47.1	10 10.7	8 7.9
9 F	5 10 56	16 55 13	20 29 4	26 24 59	9 56.5	1 53.3	28 23.3	16 17.8	8 49.5	16 58.4	25 46.6	10 12.6	8 8.0
10 Sa	5 14 53	17 56 11	2♍22 47	8♍23 10	9D 55.2	3 23.1	29 34.6	16 2.1	9 2.9	17 4.9	25 46.2	10 14.5	8R 8.0
11 Su	5 18 50	18 57 10	14 26 48	20 34 22	9R 55.0	4 53.3	0♒45.8	15 45.7	9 16.4	17 11.4	25 45.7	10 16.4	8 8.0
12 M	5 22 46	19 58 11	26 46 35	3♎ 4 5	9 54.9	6 23.8	1 56.9	15 28.5	9 29.9	17 18.0	25 45.1	10 18.2	8 7.9
13 Tu	5 26 43	20 59 12	9♎27 31	15 57 27	9 53.7	7 54.7	3 8.0	15 10.6	9 43.4	17 24.6	25 44.5	10 20.0	8 7.9
14 W	5 30 39	22 0 15	22 34 21	29 18 33	9 50.3	9 25.9	4 18.9	14 52.1	9 57.0	17 31.2	25 43.8	10 21.8	8 7.8
15 Th	5 34 36	23 1 18	6♏10 17	13♏ 9 33	9 44.3	10 57.3	5 29.8	14 32.9	10 10.6	17 37.8	25 43.0	10 23.6	8 7.6
16 F	5 38 32	24 2 23	20 16 12	27 29 48	9 35.7	12 29.0	6 40.6	14 13.1	10 24.2	17 44.5	25 42.3	10 25.4	8 7.5
17 Sa	5 42 29	25 3 28	4♐49 46	12♐15 13	9 25.1	14 0.9	7 51.2	13 52.7	10 37.9	17 51.3	25 41.4	10 27.1	8 7.3
18 Su	5 46 25	26 4 35	19 45 8	27 18 19	9 13.7	15 33.0	9 1.8	13 31.8	10 51.5	17 58.0	25 40.5	10 28.8	8 7.0
19 M	5 50 22	27 5 42	4♑53 25	12♑29 6	9 2.7	17 5.3	10 12.3	13 10.4	11 5.3	18 4.8	25 39.6	10 30.5	8 6.8
20 Tu	5 54 19	28 6 49	20 4 1	27 36 53	8 53.5	18 37.8	11 22.7	12 48.5	11 19.0	18 11.6	25 38.6	10 32.2	8 6.5
21 W	5 58 15	29 7 57	5♒ 6 35	12♒32 9	8 46.9	20 10.6	12 33.0	12 26.2	11 32.8	18 18.4	25 37.5	10 33.8	8 6.2
22 Th	6 2 12	0♑ 9 5	19 52 49	27 8 1	8 43.1	21 43.5	13 43.1	12 3.5	11 46.6	18 25.3	25 36.4	10 35.5	8 5.8
23 F	6 6 8	1 10 14	4♓17 24	11♓20 46	8D 41.7	23 16.6	14 53.1	11 40.5	12 0.4	18 32.2	25 35.3	10 37.1	8 5.4
24 Sa	6 10 5	2 11 22	18 18 6	25 9 32	8 41.9	24 49.9	16 3.0	11 17.3	12 14.2	18 39.1	25 34.1	10 38.6	8 5.0
25 Su	6 14 1	3 12 30	1♈55 17	8♈35 38	8R 42.3	26 23.4	17 12.8	10 53.8	12 28.1	18 46.0	25 32.8	10 40.2	8 4.6
26 M	6 17 58	4 13 39	15 10 57	21 41 36	8 41.7	27 57.2	18 22.4	10 30.2	12 41.9	18 52.9	25 31.5	10 41.7	8 4.1
27 Tu	6 21 54	5 14 47	28 7 59	4♉30 30	8 39.1	29 31.2	19 31.9	10 6.4	12 55.8	18 59.9	25 30.2	10 43.2	8 3.6
28 W	6 25 51	6 15 56	10♉49 29	17 5 17	8 34.0	1♑ 5.4	20 41.3	9 42.6	13 9.7	19 6.9	25 28.8	10 44.6	8 3.0
29 Th	6 29 48	7 17 4	23 18 13	29 28 35	8 26.2	2 39.9	21 50.4	9 18.7	13 23.6	19 13.9	25 27.3	10 46.1	8 2.5
30 F	6 33 44	8 18 13	5♊36 36	11♊42 29	8 16.2	4 14.8	22 59.5	8 54.8	13 37.6	19 20.9	25 25.8	10 47.5	8 1.9
31 Sa	6 37 41	9 19 21	17 46 27	23 48 39	8 4.7	5 49.9	24 8.3	8 31.1	13 51.5	19 27.9	25 24.3	10 48.9	8 1.3

Astro Data	Planet Ingress	Last Aspect	☽ Ingress	Last Aspect	☽ Ingress	☽ Phases & Eclipses	Astro Data
Dy Hr Mn	Dy Hr Mn	Dy Hr Mn	Dy Hr Mn	Dy Hr Mn	Dy Hr Mn	Dy Hr Mn	1 NOVEMBER 1960
☽0S 15 4:58	♀ ♑ 15 8:57	2 7:03 ♅ △	♉ 2 15:27	1 22:56 ♅ □	♊ 2 7:01	3 11:58 ○ 11♉04	Julian Day # 22220
☿ D 16 19:27	☉ ♐ 22 7:18	4 15:06 ♅ □	♊ 4 23:44	4 9:31 ♅ ✶	♋ 4 17:52	11 13:47 ☽ 19♌11	Delta T 33.5 sec
♂ R 20 17:04		7 1:33 ♅ ✶	♋ 7 10:26	7 4:45 ☿ △	♌ 7 6:21	18 23:46 ● 26♏39	SVP 05♓48'31"
☽0N 27 23:00	☿ ♐ 7 17:30	8 22:06 ♂ ☌	♌ 9 22:59	9 10:42 ♅ ☌	♍ 9 19:13	25 15:42 ☽ 3♓23	Obliquity 23°26'31"
	♀ ♒ 10 8:34	12 3:39 ♀ △	♍ 12 11:24	11 9:38 ☉ □	♎ 12 6:10		⚷ Chiron 27♒25.8R
♅ R 1 4:21	☉ ♑ 21 20:26	14 19:54 ♀ □	♎ 14 21:07	14 5:39 ♅ ✶	♏ 14 13:13	3 4:24 ○ 11♊01	☽ Mean ☊ 12♍34.3
♃△♇ 5 20:46	☿ ♑ 27 7:21	16 19:26 ♅ ✶	♏ 17 2:53	16 9:02 ♅ □	♐ 16 16:07	11 9:38 ☽ 19♍22	
♇ R 10 4:38		18 23:46 ☉ ☌	♐ 19 5:17	18 10:47 ☉ ☌	♑ 18 16:16	18 10:47 ● 26♐32	1 DECEMBER 1960
☽0S 12 15:33		20 23:10 ♅ △	♑ 21 6:02	19 21:01 ♄ ☌	♒ 20 15:49	25 2:30 ☽ 3♈19	Julian Day # 22250
♃✶♆ 16 2:23		22 12:21 ♂ ☍	♒ 23 7:04	22 9:27 ♅ ☍	♓ 22 16:47		Delta T 33.6 sec
♃⚼♅ 17 5:53		25 2:34 ♅ ☍	♓ 25 9:49	24 12:54 ☿ □	♈ 24 20:34		SVP 05♓48'27"
☽0N 25 5:59		26 18:04 ♂ △	♈ 27 14:51	27 2:58 ☿ △	♉ 27 3:30		Obliquity 23°26'31"
		29 14:10 ♅ △	♉ 29 22:00	29 4:10 ♅ □	♊ 29 13:01		⚷ Chiron 27♒42.0
							☽ Mean ☊ 10♍59.0

LONGITUDE — JANUARY 1961

Day	Sid.Time	☉	0 hr ☽	Noon ☽	True ☊	☿	♀	♂	♃	♄	♅	♆	♇
1 Su	6 41 37	10♑20 30	29♊49 14	5♋48 22	7♍52.9	7♑25.3	25♒17.0	8♋ 7.4	14♑ 5.4	19♑35.0	25♌22.7	10♏50.2	8♍ 0.6
2 M	6 45 34	11 21 38	11♋46 11	17 42 52	7R41.6	9 1.0	26 25.6	7R43.9	14 19.4	19 42.0	25R21.1	10 51.6	7R59.9
3 Tu	6 49 30	12 22 47	23 38 35	29 33 32	7 32.0	10 37.1	27 33.9	7 20.6	14 33.3	19 49.1	25 19.4	10 52.9	7 59.2
4 W	6 53 27	13 23 55	5♌27 58	11♌22 10	7 24.6	12 13.6	28 42.1	6 57.6	14 47.3	19 56.1	25 17.7	10 54.2	7 58.5
5 Th	6 57 23	14 25 4	17 16 25	23 11 5	7 19.7	13 50.4	29 50.1	6 34.8	15 1.3	20 3.2	25 15.9	10 55.4	7 57.7
6 F	7 1 20	15 26 13	29 6 35	5♍ 3 20	7D17.3	15 27.6	0♓57.9	6 12.4	15 15.2	20 10.3	25 14.2	10 56.6	7 57.0
7 Sa	7 5 17	16 27 22	11♍ 1 51	17 2 38	7 17.0	17 5.2	2 5.4	5 50.4	15 29.2	20 17.4	25 12.3	10 57.8	7 56.1
8 Su	7 9 13	17 28 30	23 6 16	29 13 20	7 18.0	18 43.2	3 12.8	5 28.8	15 43.2	20 24.5	25 10.4	10 59.0	7 55.3
9 M	7 13 10	18 29 39	5♎24 26	11♎40 12	7 19.3	20 21.6	4 20.0	5 7.7	15 57.1	20 31.6	25 8.5	11 0.1	7 54.4
10 Tu	7 17 6	19 30 48	18 1 13	24 28 4	7R20.0	22 0.5	5 27.0	4 47.1	16 11.1	20 38.7	25 6.6	11 1.2	7 53.5
11 W	7 21 3	20 31 57	1♏ 1 17	7♏41 18	7 19.4	23 39.8	6 33.7	4 27.0	16 25.1	20 45.8	25 4.6	11 2.2	7 52.6
12 Th	7 24 59	21 33 6	14 28 28	21 23 1	7 17.0	25 19.5	7 40.2	4 7.4	16 39.0	20 52.9	25 2.5	11 3.3	7 51.7
13 F	7 28 56	22 34 15	28 25 0	5♐34 17	7 12.6	26 59.6	8 46.5	3 48.5	16 53.0	21 0.0	25 0.5	11 4.3	7 50.7
14 Sa	7 32 52	23 35 23	12♐50 30	20 13 8	7 6.6	28 40.2	9 52.6	3 30.2	17 6.9	21 7.1	24 58.4	11 5.2	7 49.7
15 Su	7 36 49	24 36 32	27 41 21	5♑14 12	6 59.9	0♒21.2	10 58.4	3 12.6	17 20.9	21 14.3	24 56.3	11 6.2	7 48.7
16 M	7 40 46	25 37 40	12♑50 29	20 28 56	6 53.2	2 2.5	12 3.9	2 55.6	17 34.8	21 21.4	24 54.1	11 7.1	7 47.7
17 Tu	7 44 42	26 38 48	28 8 9	5♒46 44	6 47.6	3 44.2	13 9.2	2 39.3	17 48.7	21 28.5	24 51.9	11 8.0	7 46.6
18 W	7 48 39	27 39 56	13♒23 22	20 56 48	6 43.7	5 26.2	14 14.2	2 23.8	18 2.6	21 35.5	24 49.7	11 8.8	7 45.5
19 Th	7 52 35	28 41 2	28 25 56	5♓49 52	6D41.7	7 8.5	15 18.9	2 9.1	18 16.5	21 42.6	24 47.4	11 9.6	7 44.4
20 F	7 56 32	29 42 8	13♓ 7 55	20 19 34	6 41.6	8 51.0	16 23.3	1 55.0	18 30.4	21 49.7	24 45.1	11 10.4	7 43.3
21 Sa	8 0 28	0♒43 13	27 24 31	4♈22 39	6 42.7	10 33.6	17 27.5	1 41.8	18 44.2	21 56.8	24 42.8	11 11.1	7 42.1
22 Su	8 4 25	1 44 17	11♈14 1	17 58 48	6 44.3	12 16.2	18 31.2	1 29.4	18 58.1	22 3.8	24 40.5	11 11.9	7 41.0
23 M	8 8 21	2 45 20	24 37 15	1♉ 9 45	6R45.5	13 58.7	19 34.7	1 17.8	19 11.9	22 10.8	24 38.1	11 12.5	7 39.8
24 Tu	8 12 18	3 46 22	7♉36 44	13 58 39	6 45.8	15 40.9	20 37.8	1 6.9	19 25.7	22 17.9	24 35.7	11 13.2	7 38.6
25 W	8 16 15	4 47 22	20 15 58	26 29 12	6 44.5	17 22.7	21 40.6	0 56.9	19 39.4	22 24.9	24 33.3	11 13.8	7 37.3
26 Th	8 20 11	5 48 22	2♊38 48	8♊45 15	6 41.8	19 3.9	22 43.0	0 47.7	19 53.2	22 31.9	24 30.9	11 14.4	7 36.1
27 F	8 24 8	6 49 21	14 49 0	20 50 26	6 37.8	20 44.2	23 45.0	0 39.3	20 6.9	22 38.8	24 28.4	11 14.9	7 34.8
28 Sa	8 28 4	7 50 18	26 49 58	2♋47 57	6 32.8	22 23.4	24 46.6	0 31.8	20 20.6	22 45.8	24 25.9	11 15.4	7 33.5
29 Su	8 32 1	8 51 15	8♋44 43	14 40 35	6 27.6	24 1.1	25 47.8	0 25.0	20 34.2	22 52.7	24 23.5	11 15.9	7 32.2
30 M	8 35 57	9 52 10	20 35 47	26 30 38	6 22.6	25 36.9	26 48.6	0 19.1	20 47.9	22 59.7	24 20.9	11 16.3	7 30.9
31 Tu	8 39 54	10 53 5	2♌25 20	8♌20 10	6 18.5	27 10.4	27 48.9	0 13.9	21 1.5	23 6.6	24 18.4	11 16.7	7 29.6

LONGITUDE — FEBRUARY 1961

Day	Sid.Time	☉	0 hr ☽	Noon ☽	True ☊	☿	♀	♂	♃	♄	♅	♆	♇
1 W	8 43 50	11♒53 58	14♌15 19	20♌11 3	6♍15.5	28♒41.0	28♓48.8	0♋ 9.6	21♑15.0	23♑13.4	24♌15.9	11♏17.1	7♍28.2
2 Th	8 47 47	12 54 50	26 7 36	2♍ 5 13	6D13.8	0♓ 8.4	29 48.3	0R 6.0	21 28.5	23 20.3	24R13.3	11 17.5	7R26.9
3 F	8 51 44	13 55 41	8♍ 4 11	14 4 48	6 13.3	1 31.7	0♈47.2	0 3.2	21 42.0	23 27.1	24 10.8	11 17.8	7 25.5
4 Sa	8 55 40	14 56 31	20 7 21	26 12 12	6 14.0	2 50.5	1 45.6	0 1.2	21 55.5	23 33.9	24 8.2	11 18.0	7 24.1
5 Su	8 59 37	15 57 20	2♎19 43	8♎30 17	6 15.3	4 3.8	2 43.6	0 0.0	22 8.9	23 40.7	24 5.6	11 18.3	7 22.7
6 M	9 3 33	16 58 8	14 44 18	21 2 12	6 17.0	5 11.1	3 41.0	29♊59.5	22 22.3	23 47.4	24 3.0	11 18.5	7 21.3
7 Tu	9 7 30	17 58 55	27 24 24	3♏51 19	6 18.4	6 11.6	4 37.8	29D59.8	22 35.6	23 54.1	24 0.4	11 18.6	7 19.8
8 W	9 11 26	18 59 41	10♏23 23	17 0 56	6R19.3	7 4.4	5 34.1	0♋ 0.9	22 48.9	24 0.8	23 57.7	11 18.8	7 18.4
9 Th	9 15 23	20 0 26	23 44 18	0♐33 43	6 19.5	7 48.8	6 29.8	0 2.6	23 2.2	24 7.5	23 55.1	11 18.9	7 16.9
10 F	9 19 19	21 1 11	7♐29 19	14 31 10	6 18.9	8 24.2	7 24.9	0 5.1	23 15.4	24 14.1	23 52.5	11 18.9	7 15.5
11 Sa	9 23 16	22 1 54	21 39 7	28 52 56	6 17.6	8 49.9	8 19.3	0 8.3	23 28.6	24 20.7	23 49.9	11R19.0	7 14.0
12 Su	9 27 13	23 2 36	6♑12 9	13♑36 11	6 16.0	9R 5.5	9 13.2	0 12.2	23 41.7	24 27.2	23 47.2	11 19.0	7 12.5
13 M	9 31 9	24 3 17	21 4 16	28 35 28	6 14.4	9 10.6	10 6.3	0 16.8	23 54.7	24 33.8	23 44.6	11 18.9	7 11.0
14 Tu	9 35 6	25 3 57	6♒ 8 43	13♒42 55	6 13.1	9 5.1	10 58.7	0 22.1	24 7.8	24 40.2	23 42.0	11 18.9	7 9.5
15 W	9 39 2	26 4 35	21 16 51	28 49 20	6 12.2	8 49.1	11 50.4	0 28.0	24 20.7	24 46.7	23 39.3	11 18.8	7 8.0
16 Th	9 42 59	27 5 12	6♓19 14	13♓45 29	6D12.0	8 22.9	12 41.4	0 34.7	24 33.6	24 53.1	23 36.7	11 18.6	7 6.5
17 F	9 46 55	28 5 47	21 7 9	28 23 28	6 12.2	7 47.2	13 31.5	0 41.9	24 46.5	24 59.4	23 34.1	11 18.4	7 5.0
18 Sa	9 50 52	29 6 20	5♈33 49	12♈37 45	6 12.7	7 2.9	14 20.9	0 49.8	24 59.3	25 5.8	23 31.4	11 18.2	7 3.5
19 Su	9 54 48	0♓ 6 52	19 35 0	26 25 28	6 13.4	6 11.2	15 9.4	0 58.4	25 12.0	25 12.0	23 28.8	11 18.0	7 1.9
20 M	9 58 45	1 7 22	3♉ 9 12	9♉46 22	6 13.9	5 13.4	15 57.0	1 7.5	25 24.7	25 18.3	23 26.2	11 17.7	7 0.4
21 Tu	10 2 42	2 7 51	16 17 15	22 42 14	6 14.3	4 11.1	16 43.7	1 17.3	25 37.3	25 24.5	23 23.6	11 17.4	6 58.8
22 W	10 6 38	3 8 17	29 1 45	5♊16 18	6R14.4	3 6.0	17 29.4	1 27.6	25 49.9	25 30.6	23 21.0	11 17.1	6 57.3
23 Th	10 10 35	4 8 41	11♊26 26	17 32 40	6 14.4	1 59.8	18 14.1	1 38.5	26 2.4	25 36.7	23 18.4	11 16.7	6 55.8
24 F	10 14 31	5 9 4	23 35 36	29 35 45	6 14.4	0 54.2	18 57.8	1 50.0	26 14.8	25 42.7	23 15.9	11 16.3	6 54.2
25 Sa	10 18 28	6 9 24	5♋33 42	11♋29 57	6D14.3	29♒50.6	19 40.4	2 2.0	26 27.1	25 48.7	23 13.3	11 15.9	6 52.7
26 Su	10 22 24	7 9 43	17 25 2	23 19 26	6 14.4	28 50.4	20 21.9	2 14.5	26 39.4	25 54.7	23 10.8	11 15.4	6 51.1
27 M	10 26 21	8 10 0	29 13 34	5♌ 7 53	6 14.6	27 54.8	21 2.1	2 27.6	26 51.6	26 0.6	23 8.3	11 14.9	6 49.6
28 Tu	10 30 17	9 10 14	11♌ 2 46	16 58 33	6 14.8	27 4.7	21 41.2	2 41.2	27 3.8	26 6.4	23 5.8	11 14.4	6 48.0

Astro Data	Planet Ingress	Last Aspect	☽ Ingress	Last Aspect	☽ Ingress	☽ Phases & Eclipses	Astro Data
Dy Hr Mn	Dy Hr Mn	Dy Hr Mn	Dy Hr Mn	Dy Hr Mn	Dy Hr Mn	Dy Hr Mn	1 JANUARY 1961
☽0S 9 0:31	♀ ♓ 5 3:31	31 15:09 ♅ ⚹	♋ 1 0:22	1 20:10 ♅ ☌	♍ 2 7:48	1 23:06 ○ 11♋19	Julian Day # 22281
☽0N 21 14:37	☿ ♒ 14 18:58	2 16:11 ♄ ☍	♌ 3 12:54	4 6:52 ♄ △	♎ 4 19:27	10 3:02 ☽ 19♎39	Delta T 33.6 sec
♄⚼♇ 26 12:15	☉ ♒ 20 7:01	5 16:11 ♅ ☌	♍ 6 1:48	7 4:51 ♂ △	♏ 7 4:51	16 21:30 ● 26♑32	SVP 05♓48'21"
♀0N 31 11:18		7 18:37 ♄ △	♎ 8 13:31	9 0:41 ♄ ⚹	♐ 9 11:01	23 16:13 ☽ 3♉27	Obliquity 23°26'30"
	☿ ♓ 1 21:39	10 13:09 ♅ ⚹	♏ 10 22:09	11 3:37 ♅ △	♑ 11 13:50	31 18:47 ○ 11♌41	⚷ Chiron 28♒52.4
☽0S 5 7:17	♀ ♈ 2 4:46	12 21:16 ☿ ⚹	♐ 13 2:40	13 5:37 ♄ ☌	♒ 13 14:14		☽ Mean ☊ 9♍20.6
♃⚼♇ 5 22:21	♂ ♊ 5 0:22	14 19:36 ♅ △	♑ 15 3:41	15 8:10 ☉ ☌	♓ 15 13:53	8 16:49 ☽ 19♏42	
♂ D 6 2:51	♂ ♋ 7 5:25	16 21:30 ☉ ☌	♒ 17 2:55	17 6:25 ♄ ⚹	♈ 17 14:41	15 8:10 ● 26♒25	1 FEBRUARY 1961
♄⚻♅ 7 16:04	☉ ♓ 18 21:16	18 18:10 ♅ ☍	♓ 19 2:32	19 10:00 ♃ □	♉ 19 18:21	15 8:19:15 ● T 2'45"	Julian Day # 22312
♆ R 11 11:32	☿ ♒ 24 20:22	20 14:39 ♄ ⚹	♈ 21 4:26	21 17:49 ♃ △	♊ 22 1:51	22 8:34 ☽ 3♊30	Delta T 33.6 sec
♃⚻♅ 12 8:29		23 0:02 ♅ △	♉ 23 9:51	23 23:21 ♅ ⚹	♋ 24 12:49		SVP 05♓48'16"
☿ R 12 23:32		25 8:14 ♅ □	♊ 25 18:50	26 19:06 ♃ ☍	♌ 27 1:34		Obliquity 23°26'31"
☽0N 18 0:56		27 19:29 ♀ □	♋ 28 6:22				⚷ Chiron 0♓41.4
♃☌♄ 19 0:02		30 13:47 ♀ △	♌ 30 19:05				☽ Mean ☊ 7♍42.1

MARCH 1961 — LONGITUDE

Day	Sid.Time	☉	0 hr ☽	Noon ☽	True ☊	☿	♀	♂	♃	♄	♅	♆	♇
1 W	10 34 14	10♓10 27	22♌55 35	28♌54 9	6♍15.1	26♒20.7	22♈19.0	2♋55.3	27♑15.8	26♑12.2	23♌ 3.3	11♏13.8	6♍46.5
2 Th	10 38 11	11 10 38	4♍54 30	10♍56 52	6R 15.2	25R 43.4	22 55.5	3 9.8	27 27.8	26 17.9	23R 0.8	11R 13.2	6R 44.9
3 F	10 42 7	12 10 47	17 1 30	23 8 34	6 15.1	25 12.9	23 30.7	3 24.8	27 39.8	26 23.6	22 58.3	11 12.6	6 43.4
4 Sa	10 46 4	13 10 55	29 18 16	5♎30 45	6 14.6	24 49.5	24 4.4	3 40.3	27 51.6	26 29.2	22 55.9	11 11.9	6 41.8
5 Su	10 50 0	14 11 0	11♎46 11	18 4 44	6 13.8	24 33.0	24 36.6	3 56.3	28 3.4	26 34.8	22 53.5	11 11.2	6 40.3
6 M	10 53 57	15 11 4	24 26 33	0♏51 48	6 12.7	24D 23.3	25 7.3	4 12.7	28 15.1	26 40.3	22 51.1	11 10.5	6 38.8
7 Tu	10 57 53	16 11 6	7♏20 36	13 53 8	6 11.3	24 20.3	25 36.5	4 29.5	28 26.7	26 45.7	22 48.8	11 9.8	6 37.2
8 W	11 1 50	17 11 6	20 29 32	27 9 55	6 10.1	24 23.6	26 4.0	4 46.7	28 38.2	26 51.1	22 46.4	11 9.0	6 35.7
9 Th	11 5 46	18 11 5	3♐54 25	10♐43 7	6 9.2	24 33.0	26 29.8	5 4.4	28 49.6	26 56.4	22 44.1	11 8.2	6 34.2
10 F	11 9 43	19 11 3	17 36 5	24 33 19	6D 8.8	24 48.1	26 53.9	5 22.4	29 1.0	27 1.7	22 41.8	11 7.4	6 32.7
11 Sa	11 13 39	20 10 58	1♑34 46	8♑40 18	6 9.1	25 8.6	27 16.1	5 40.9	29 12.2	27 6.9	22 39.6	11 6.5	6 31.2
12 Su	11 17 36	21 10 53	15 49 44	23 2 44	6 9.9	25 34.2	27 36.5	5 59.7	29 23.4	27 12.0	22 37.3	11 5.6	6 29.7
13 M	11 21 33	22 10 45	0♒18 56	7♒37 49	6 11.0	26 4.6	27 55.0	6 18.9	29 34.5	27 17.1	22 35.1	11 4.7	6 28.2
14 Tu	11 25 29	23 10 36	14 58 46	22 21 5	6 12.2	26 39.4	28 11.4	6 38.5	29 45.5	27 22.1	22 33.0	11 3.8	6 26.7
15 W	11 29 26	24 10 25	29 44 0	7♓ 6 39	6R 12.9	27 18.3	28 25.8	6 58.5	29 56.4	27 27.0	22 30.8	11 2.8	6 25.3
16 Th	11 33 22	25 10 12	14♓28 11	21 47 42	6 12.8	28 1.2	28 38.1	7 18.8	0♒ 7.2	27 31.9	22 28.7	11 1.8	6 23.8
17 F	11 37 19	26 9 57	29 4 21	6♈17 18	6 11.7	28 47.7	28 48.2	7 39.5	0 17.9	27 36.7	22 26.7	11 0.8	6 22.4
18 Sa	11 41 15	27 9 40	13♈25 52	20 29 24	6 9.6	29 37.7	28 56.1	8 0.4	0 28.5	27 41.4	22 24.6	10 59.8	6 20.9
19 Su	11 45 12	28 9 21	27 27 25	4♉19 34	6 6.6	0♓30.8	29 1.7	8 21.8	0 39.0	27 46.1	22 22.6	10 58.7	6 19.5
20 M	11 49 8	29 9 0	11♉ 5 37	17 45 30	6 3.2	1 27.0	29R 4.9	8 43.4	0 49.4	27 50.7	22 20.7	10 57.6	6 18.1
21 Tu	11 53 5	0♈ 8 36	24 19 15	0♊47 4	5 59.8	2 26.0	29 5.7	9 5.4	0 59.7	27 55.2	22 18.8	10 56.5	6 16.7
22 W	11 57 2	1 8 11	7♊ 9 13	13 26 5	5 57.0	3 27.7	29 4.1	9 27.7	1 9.8	27 59.6	22 16.9	10 55.3	6 15.3
23 Th	12 0 58	2 7 43	19 38 6	25 45 48	5 55.1	4 31.9	29 0.0	9 50.3	1 19.9	28 4.0	22 15.0	10 54.2	6 13.9
24 F	12 4 55	3 7 13	1♋49 44	7♋50 29	5D 54.4	5 38.5	28 53.5	10 13.2	1 29.9	28 8.2	22 13.2	10 53.0	6 12.6
25 Sa	12 8 51	4 6 40	13 48 42	19 44 58	5 54.8	6 47.4	28 44.4	10 36.3	1 39.7	28 12.5	22 11.5	10 51.8	6 11.3
26 Su	12 12 48	5 6 5	25 39 56	1♌34 13	5 56.1	7 58.5	28 32.8	10 59.8	1 49.5	28 16.6	22 9.7	10 50.5	6 9.9
27 M	12 16 44	6 5 28	7♌28 24	13 23 4	5 57.9	9 11.6	28 18.7	11 23.5	1 59.1	28 20.6	22 8.0	10 49.3	6 8.6
28 Tu	12 20 41	7 4 49	19 18 46	25 16 0	5 59.6	10 26.8	28 2.2	11 47.5	2 8.6	28 24.6	22 6.4	10 48.0	6 7.3
29 W	12 24 37	8 4 7	1♍15 14	7♍16 53	6R 0.7	11 43.8	27 43.2	12 11.7	2 18.0	28 28.5	22 4.8	10 46.7	6 6.1
30 Th	12 28 34	9 3 23	13 21 20	19 28 53	6 0.5	13 2.8	27 21.9	12 36.2	2 27.3	28 32.3	22 3.2	10 45.4	6 4.8
31 F	12 32 31	10 2 37	25 39 48	1♎54 16	5 58.8	14 23.5	26 58.3	13 0.9	2 36.5	28 36.0	22 1.7	10 44.0	6 3.6

APRIL 1961 — LONGITUDE

Day	Sid.Time	☉	0 hr ☽	Noon ☽	True ☊	☿	♀	♂	♃	♄	♅	♆	♇
1 Sa	12 36 27	11♈ 1 49	8♎12 25	14♎34 20	5♍55.4	15♓46.0	26♈32.5	13♋25.9	2♒45.5	28♑39.7	22♌ 0.3	10♏42.7	6♍ 2.3
2 Su	12 40 24	12 0 59	21 0 2	27 29 29	5R 50.4	17 10.2	26R 4.7	13 51.1	2 54.4	28 43.2	21R 58.8	10R 41.3	6R 1.1
3 M	12 44 20	13 0 6	4♏ 2 35	10♏39 14	5 44.4	18 36.0	25 35.0	14 16.5	3 3.2	28 46.7	21 57.5	10 39.9	5 59.9
4 Tu	12 48 17	13 59 12	17 19 16	24 2 30	5 38.0	20 3.5	25 3.5	14 42.2	3 11.9	28 50.1	21 56.1	10 38.5	5 58.8
5 W	12 52 13	14 58 16	0♐48 46	7♐37 52	5 31.9	21 32.6	24 30.5	15 8.1	3 20.4	28 53.4	21 54.9	10 37.1	5 57.6
6 Th	12 56 10	15 57 19	14 29 35	21 23 46	5 26.9	23 3.3	23 56.1	15 34.1	3 28.8	28 56.7	21 53.6	10 35.7	5 56.5
7 F	13 0 6	16 56 19	28 20 14	5♑18 50	5 23.5	24 35.6	23 20.5	16 0.4	3 37.1	28 59.8	21 52.4	10 34.2	5 55.4
8 Sa	13 4 3	17 55 18	12♑19 24	19 21 47	5D 22.0	26 9.4	22 44.0	16 26.9	3 45.2	29 2.8	21 51.3	10 32.8	5 54.3
9 Su	13 8 0	18 54 15	26 25 51	3♒31 26	5 22.1	27 44.8	22 6.8	16 53.7	3 53.2	29 5.8	21 50.2	10 31.3	5 53.3
10 M	13 11 56	19 53 10	10♒38 19	17 46 19	5 23.1	29 21.7	21 29.2	17 20.6	4 1.1	29 8.7	21 49.2	10 29.8	5 52.2
11 Tu	13 15 53	20 52 4	24 55 8	2♓ 4 27	5R 24.3	1♈ 0.2	20 51.4	17 47.7	4 8.8	29 11.5	21 48.2	10 28.3	5 51.2
12 W	13 19 49	21 50 55	9♓13 55	16 23 3	5 24.6	2 40.2	20 13.7	18 15.0	4 16.4	29 14.2	21 47.2	10 26.8	5 50.2
13 Th	13 23 46	22 49 45	23 31 24	0♈38 24	5 23.2	4 21.8	19 36.2	18 42.4	4 23.9	29 16.8	21 46.4	10 25.2	5 49.3
14 F	13 27 42	23 48 33	7♈43 30	14 46 7	5 19.6	6 4.9	18 59.3	19 10.1	4 31.2	29 19.3	21 45.5	10 23.7	5 48.3
15 Sa	13 31 39	24 47 19	21 45 41	28 41 38	5 13.7	7 49.6	18 23.2	19 38.0	4 38.3	29 21.7	21 44.7	10 22.1	5 47.4
16 Su	13 35 35	25 46 4	5♉33 29	12♉20 50	5 6.0	9 35.8	17 48.0	20 6.0	4 45.4	29 24.0	21 44.0	10 20.6	5 46.5
17 M	13 39 32	26 44 46	19 3 20	25 40 45	4 57.2	11 23.6	17 14.1	20 34.2	4 52.2	29 26.3	21 43.3	10 19.0	5 45.6
18 Tu	13 43 28	27 43 26	2♊12 59	8♊40 0	4 48.1	13 13.1	16 41.6	21 2.6	4 58.9	29 28.4	21 42.7	10 17.4	5 44.8
19 W	13 47 25	28 42 4	15 1 54	21 18 55	4 39.9	15 4.1	16 10.7	21 31.1	5 5.5	29 30.5	21 42.1	10 15.8	5 44.0
20 Th	13 51 22	29 40 40	27 31 20	3♋39 32	4 33.3	16 56.6	15 41.5	21 59.8	5 11.9	29 32.4	21 41.6	10 14.2	5 43.2
21 F	13 55 18	0♉39 14	9♋43 58	15 45 12	4 28.8	18 50.8	15 14.3	22 28.7	5 18.2	29 34.3	21 41.1	10 12.6	5 42.4
22 Sa	13 59 15	1 37 46	21 43 46	27 40 19	4D 26.4	20 46.6	14 49.1	22 57.7	5 24.2	29 36.1	21 40.7	10 11.0	5 41.7
23 Su	14 3 11	2 36 16	3♌35 29	9♌29 55	4 25.8	22 44.0	14 26.0	23 26.9	5 30.2	29 37.7	21 40.3	10 9.4	5 41.0
24 M	14 7 8	3 34 43	15 24 19	21 19 20	4 26.4	24 42.9	14 5.1	23 56.2	5 36.0	29 39.3	21 40.0	10 7.8	5 40.3
25 Tu	14 11 4	4 33 8	27 15 38	3♍13 51	4R 27.2	26 43.4	13 46.6	24 25.7	5 41.6	29 40.8	21 39.8	10 6.2	5 39.6
26 W	14 15 1	5 31 31	9♍14 35	15 18 25	4 27.3	28 45.3	13 30.4	24 55.3	5 47.0	29 42.2	21 39.6	10 4.5	5 39.0
27 Th	14 18 57	6 29 52	21 25 50	27 37 18	4 25.8	0♉48.7	13 16.6	25 25.0	5 52.3	29 43.4	21 39.4	10 2.9	5 38.4
28 F	14 22 54	7 28 11	3♎53 11	10♎13 45	4 22.0	2 53.4	13 5.3	25 54.9	5 57.5	29 44.6	21 39.3	10 1.3	5 37.8
29 Sa	14 26 51	8 26 28	16 39 14	23 9 42	4 15.8	4 59.3	12 56.4	26 24.9	6 2.4	29 45.7	21D 39.3	9 59.6	5 37.2
30 Su	14 30 47	9 24 44	29 45 7	6♏25 24	4 7.3	7 6.4	12 49.9	26 55.0	6 7.2	29 46.7	21 39.3	9 58.0	5 36.7

Astro Data (Dy Hr Mn)

☽0S	4 13:08
☿ D	6 23:16
☽0N	17 11:39
♀ R	20 20:12
☽0S	31 19:53
☽0N	13 21:13
☿0N	13 15:18
♃⊼♇	24 16:24
☽0S	28 4:24
♅ D	29 7:50

Planet Ingress (Dy Hr Mn)

♃	♒	15 8:01
☿	♓	18 10:16
☉	♈	20 20:32
☿	♈	10 9:22
☉	♉	20 7:55
☿	♉	26 14:34

Last Aspect / ☽ Ingress (Dy Hr Mn)

Last Aspect	☽ Ingress
1 6:31 ☿ ☍	♍ 1 14:12
3 21:09 ♃ △	♎ 4 1:21
6 7:14 ♃ □	♏ 6 10:24
8 14:50 ♃ ⚹	♐ 8 17:04
10 16:27 ♀ △	♑ 10 21:19
12 22:46 ♃ ☌	♒ 12 23:29
14 21:51 ♀ ⚹	♓ 15 0:26
16 21:34 ♄ ⚹	♈ 17 1:32
19 2:45 ♀ ☌	♉ 19 4:25
21 6:42 ♄ △	♊ 21 10:32
23 18:14 ♀ ⚹	♋ 23 20:22
26 5:45 ♀ □	♌ 26 8:48
28 17:07 ♀ △	♍ 28 21:30
31 5:41 ♄ △	♎ 31 8:21

Last Aspect / ☽ Ingress (Dy Hr Mn)

Last Aspect	☽ Ingress
2 14:19 ♄ □	♏ 2 16:36
4 20:35 ♄ ⚹	♐ 4 22:34
6 16:43 ☿ □	♑ 7 2:52
9 4:32 ♄ ☌	♒ 9 6:03
10 18:47 ♅ ☍	♓ 11 8:31
13 9:44 ♄ ⚹	♈ 13 10:55
15 13:12 ♄ □	♉ 15 14:16
17 18:56 ♄ △	♊ 17 19:55
20 4:34 ☉ ⚹	♋ 20 4:50
22 15:57 ♄ ☍	♌ 22 16:43
24 22:42 ☿ △	♍ 25 5:31
27 16:04 ♄ △	♎ 27 16:34
30 0:03 ♄ □	♏ 30 0:27

☽ Phases & Eclipses (Dy Hr Mn)

2 13:35	○ 11♍45
2 13:28	☍P 0.800
10 2:57	☽ 19♐18
16 18:51	● 25♓57
24 2:48	☽ 3♋14
1 5:47	○ 11♎16
8 10:16	☽ 18♑21
15 5:37	● 25♈01
22 21:49	☽ 2♌31
30 18:40	○ 10♏10

Astro Data

1 MARCH 1961
Julian Day # 22340
Delta T 33.7 sec
SVP 05♓48'13"
Obliquity 23°26'32"
⚷ Chiron 2♓33.7
☽ Mean ☊ 6♍13.1

1 APRIL 1961
Julian Day # 22371
Delta T 33.7 sec
SVP 05♓48'11"
Obliquity 23°26'32"
⚷ Chiron 4♓30.9
☽ Mean ☊ 4♍34.6

LONGITUDE — MAY 1961

Day	Sid.Time	☉	0 hr ☽	Noon ☽	True ☊	☿	♀	♂	♃	♄	♅	♆	♇
1 M	14 34 44	10♉22 57	13♏10 17	19♏59 28	3♍57.1	9♉14.4	12♈45.9	27♋25.3	6♒11.8	29♑47.6	21♌39.3	9♏56.4	5♍36.2
2 Tu	14 38 40	11 21 9	26 52 32	3♐49 1	3R 46.2	11 23.3	12D 44.3	27 55.7	6 16.3	29 48.4	21 39.5	9R 54.7	5R 35.8
3 W	14 42 37	12 19 19	10♐48 23	17 50 5	3 35.8	13 32.7	12 45.1	28 26.2	6 20.6	29 49.1	21 39.6	9 53.1	5 35.3
4 Th	14 46 33	13 17 27	24 53 36	1♑58 23	3 26.9	15 42.5	12 48.2	28 56.8	6 24.7	29 49.7	21 39.8	9 51.5	5 34.9
5 F	14 50 30	14 15 34	9♑ 3 56	16 9 52	3 20.3	17 52.4	12 53.6	29 27.6	6 28.7	29 50.2	21 40.1	9 49.9	5 34.5
6 Sa	14 54 26	15 13 40	23 15 46	0♒21 21	3 16.3	20 2.1	13 1.2	29 58.4	6 32.4	29 50.6	21 40.5	9 48.2	5 34.2
7 Su	14 58 23	16 11 44	7♒26 23	14 30 40	3D 14.6	22 11.4	13 11.0	0♌29.4	6 36.0	29 51.0	21 40.9	9 46.6	5 33.9
8 M	15 2 20	17 9 47	21 34 5	28 36 30	3R 14.4	24 20.0	13 23.0	1 0.5	6 39.4	29 51.2	21 41.3	9 45.0	5 33.6
9 Tu	15 6 16	18 7 48	5♓37 50	12♓37 59	3 14.5	26 27.5	13 37.0	1 31.7	6 42.7	29R 51.3	21 41.8	9 43.4	5 33.3
10 W	15 10 13	19 5 48	19 36 52	26 34 20	3 13.7	28 33.8	13 53.0	2 3.0	6 45.7	29 51.3	21 42.3	9 41.8	5 33.1
11 Th	15 14 9	20 3 47	3♈30 14	10♈24 22	3 10.9	0♊38.4	14 11.0	2 34.5	6 48.6	29 51.2	21 42.9	9 40.1	5 32.9
12 F	15 18 6	21 1 44	17 16 29	24 6 20	3 5.3	2 41.2	14 30.8	3 6.0	6 51.3	29 51.0	21 43.6	9 38.5	5 32.7
13 Sa	15 22 2	21 59 41	0♉53 36	7♉37 59	2 56.8	4 41.9	14 52.5	3 37.7	6 53.8	29 50.8	21 44.3	9 37.0	5 32.6
14 Su	15 25 59	22 57 35	14 19 12	20 56 56	2 46.0	6 40.4	15 15.8	4 9.4	6 56.1	29 50.4	21 45.1	9 35.4	5 32.4
15 M	15 29 55	23 55 29	27 30 57	4♊ 1 3	2 33.6	8 36.3	15 40.9	4 41.3	6 58.2	29 49.9	21 45.9	9 33.8	5 32.4
16 Tu	15 33 52	24 53 20	10♊27 5	16 48 59	2 20.8	10 29.6	16 7.5	5 13.2	7 0.2	29 49.4	21 46.7	9 32.2	5 32.3
17 W	15 37 49	25 51 11	23 6 46	29 20 31	2 8.9	12 20.0	16 35.7	5 45.3	7 1.9	29 48.7	21 47.7	9 30.7	5D 32.3
18 Th	15 41 45	26 49 0	5♋30 24	11♋36 43	1 58.7	14 7.6	17 5.4	6 17.5	7 3.5	29 47.9	21 48.6	9 29.1	5 32.3
19 F	15 45 42	27 46 47	17 39 46	23 39 58	1 51.1	15 52.2	17 36.6	6 49.7	7 4.9	29 47.1	21 49.7	9 27.6	5 32.3
20 Sa	15 49 38	28 44 32	29 37 47	5♌33 47	1 46.2	17 33.7	18 9.1	7 22.1	7 6.1	29 46.1	21 50.7	9 26.1	5 32.4
21 Su	15 53 35	29 42 16	11♌28 31	17 22 37	1 43.6	19 12.0	18 42.9	7 54.5	7 7.1	29 45.1	21 51.9	9 24.5	5 32.5
22 M	15 57 31	0♊39 59	23 16 44	29 11 33	1 42.8	20 47.1	19 18.0	8 27.0	7 7.9	29 43.9	21 53.0	9 23.0	5 32.6
23 Tu	16 1 28	1 37 40	5♍ 7 45	11♍ 6 1	1 42.7	22 19.0	19 54.4	8 59.7	7 8.5	29 42.7	21 54.3	9 21.5	5 32.8
24 W	16 5 24	2 35 19	17 7 3	23 11 30	1 42.3	23 47.6	20 31.9	9 32.4	7 8.9	29 41.4	21 55.6	9 20.1	5 33.0
25 Th	16 9 21	3 32 57	29 20 0	5♎33 6	1 40.6	25 12.8	21 10.6	10 5.2	7R 9.2	29 40.0	21 56.9	9 18.6	5 33.2
26 F	16 13 18	4 30 33	11♎51 20	18 15 7	1 36.6	26 34.6	21 50.3	10 38.1	7 9.2	29 38.5	21 58.3	9 17.2	5 33.5
27 Sa	16 17 14	5 28 8	24 44 46	1♏20 29	1 30.2	27 53.0	22 31.2	11 11.0	7 9.1	29 36.9	21 59.7	9 15.7	5 33.7
28 Su	16 21 11	6 25 41	8♏ 2 21	14 50 16	1 21.2	29 7.9	23 13.0	11 44.1	7 8.8	29 35.2	22 1.2	9 14.3	5 34.0
29 M	16 25 7	7 23 13	21 44 2	28 43 16	1 10.5	0♋19.3	23 55.8	12 17.2	7 8.2	29 33.4	22 2.7	9 12.9	5 34.4
30 Tu	16 29 4	8 20 45	5♐47 26	12♐55 53	0 58.9	1 27.2	24 39.6	12 50.4	7 7.5	29 31.5	22 4.3	9 11.5	5 34.8
31 W	16 33 0	9 18 15	20 7 52	27 22 34	0 47.7	2 31.3	25 24.2	13 23.7	7 6.7	29 29.6	22 5.9	9 10.2	5 35.2

LONGITUDE — JUNE 1961

Day	Sid.Time	☉	0 hr ☽	Noon ☽	True ☊	☿	♀	♂	♃	♄	♅	♆	♇
1 Th	16 36 57	10♊15 44	4♑39 5	11♑56 35	0♍38.1	3♋31.8	26♈ 9.8	13♌57.0	7♒ 5.6	29♑27.5	22♌ 7.6	9♏ 8.8	5♍35.6
2 F	16 40 53	11 13 12	19 14 14	26 31 16	0R 30.9	4 28.5	26 56.2	14 30.5	7R 4.3	29R 25.4	22 9.3	9R 7.5	5 36.1
3 Sa	16 44 50	12 10 39	3♒47 1	11♒ 0 54	0 26.4	5 21.4	27 43.4	15 4.0	7 2.8	29 23.2	22 11.1	9 6.2	5 36.5
4 Su	16 48 47	13 8 6	18 12 29	25 21 25	0D 24.4	6 10.3	28 31.3	15 37.6	7 1.2	29 20.9	22 12.9	9 4.9	5 37.1
5 M	16 52 43	14 5 32	2♓27 29	9♓30 30	0R 24.1	6 55.2	29 20.1	16 11.2	6 59.4	29 18.5	22 14.7	9 3.6	5 37.6
6 Tu	16 56 40	15 2 57	16 30 26	23 27 14	0 24.2	7 36.0	0♉ 9.5	16 45.0	6 57.3	29 16.1	22 16.6	9 2.3	5 38.2
7 W	17 0 36	16 0 22	0♈20 58	7♈11 38	0 23.5	8 12.7	0 59.6	17 18.8	6 55.1	29 13.5	22 18.6	9 1.1	5 38.8
8 Th	17 4 33	16 57 46	13 59 19	20 44 2	0 21.0	8 45.1	1 50.5	17 52.7	6 52.7	29 10.9	22 20.6	8 59.9	5 39.4
9 F	17 8 29	17 55 9	27 25 50	4♉ 4 43	0 15.9	9 13.1	2 41.9	18 26.6	6 50.2	29 8.2	22 22.6	8 58.7	5 40.1
10 Sa	17 12 26	18 52 32	10♉40 40	17 13 40	0 8.2	9 36.8	3 34.0	19 0.7	6 47.4	29 5.5	22 24.7	8 57.5	5 40.8
11 Su	17 16 22	19 49 54	23 43 39	0♊10 35	29♌58.3	9 55.9	4 26.6	19 34.8	6 44.4	29 2.6	22 26.8	8 56.4	5 41.5
12 M	17 20 19	20 47 16	6♊34 23	12 55 2	29 46.8	10 10.6	5 19.8	20 9.0	6 41.3	28 59.7	22 29.0	8 55.2	5 42.2
13 Tu	17 24 16	21 44 37	19 12 29	25 26 45	29 35.0	10 20.6	6 13.6	20 43.2	6 38.0	28 56.7	22 31.2	8 54.1	5 43.0
14 W	17 28 12	22 41 58	1♋37 53	7♋45 57	29 23.9	10R 26.1	7 7.9	21 17.6	6 34.5	28 53.6	22 33.5	8 53.1	5 43.8
15 Th	17 32 9	23 39 18	13 51 6	19 53 33	29 14.4	10 27.1	8 2.7	21 51.9	6 30.9	28 50.5	22 35.8	8 52.0	5 44.7
16 F	17 36 5	24 36 37	25 53 30	1♌51 19	29 7.2	10 23.6	8 58.0	22 26.4	6 27.0	28 47.3	22 38.1	8 51.0	5 45.5
17 Sa	17 40 2	25 33 55	7♌47 19	13 41 58	29 2.6	10 15.7	9 53.7	23 1.0	6 23.0	28 44.0	22 40.5	8 50.0	5 46.4
18 Su	17 43 58	26 31 13	19 35 42	25 29 5	29D 0.3	10 3.5	10 49.9	23 35.6	6 18.9	28 40.6	22 42.9	8 49.0	5 47.3
19 M	17 47 55	27 28 30	1♍22 38	7♍16 59	28 59.9	9 47.2	11 46.6	24 10.2	6 14.5	28 37.2	22 45.4	8 48.0	5 48.3
20 Tu	17 51 51	28 25 46	13 12 46	19 10 37	29 0.5	9 27.1	12 43.7	24 45.0	6 10.0	28 33.8	22 47.9	8 47.1	5 49.3
21 W	17 55 48	29 23 1	25 11 14	1♎15 15	29R 1.1	9 3.5	13 41.1	25 19.7	6 5.4	28 30.2	22 50.5	8 46.2	5 50.3
22 Th	17 59 45	0♋20 16	7♎23 21	13 36 9	29 0.9	8 36.8	14 39.0	25 54.6	6 0.6	28 26.6	22 53.0	8 45.3	5 51.3
23 F	18 3 41	1 17 30	19 54 15	26 18 11	28 59.1	8 7.3	15 37.3	26 29.5	5 55.6	28 23.0	22 55.6	8 44.5	5 52.3
24 Sa	18 7 38	2 14 43	2♏48 23	9♏25 12	28 55.3	7 35.4	16 35.9	27 4.5	5 50.5	28 19.3	22 58.3	8 43.6	5 53.4
25 Su	18 11 34	3 11 56	16 8 52	22 59 26	28 49.5	7 1.8	17 34.9	27 39.5	5 45.2	28 15.5	23 1.0	8 42.8	5 54.5
26 M	18 15 31	4 9 9	29 56 50	7♐ 0 46	28 42.1	6 27.0	18 34.3	28 14.6	5 39.8	28 11.7	23 3.7	8 42.1	5 55.6
27 Tu	18 19 27	5 6 21	14♐10 48	21 26 18	28 33.9	5 51.6	19 34.0	28 49.8	5 34.2	28 7.9	23 6.5	8 41.3	5 56.8
28 W	18 23 24	6 3 32	28 46 29	6♑10 25	28 25.9	5 16.1	20 34.1	29 25.0	5 28.5	28 4.0	23 9.3	8 40.6	5 58.0
29 Th	18 27 20	7 0 44	13♑37 4	21 5 22	28 19.0	4 41.2	21 34.4	0♍ 0.3	5 22.7	28 0.0	23 12.1	8 39.9	5 59.2
30 F	18 31 17	7 57 55	28 34 12	6♒ 2 30	28 14.0	4 7.4	22 35.1	0 35.7	5 16.8	27 56.1	23 15.0	8 39.3	6 0.4

Astro Data Dy Hr Mn	Planet Ingress Dy Hr Mn	Last Aspect Dy Hr Mn	☽ Ingress Dy Hr Mn	Last Aspect Dy Hr Mn	☽ Ingress Dy Hr Mn	☽ Phases & Eclipses Dy Hr Mn	Astro Data
♀ D 2 4:15	♂ ♌ 6 1:13	2 5:05 ♄ ⚹	♐ 2 5:25	2 16:45 ♄ ☌	♒ 2 17:45	7 15:57 ☽ 16♒50	1 MAY 1961
♄ R 9 16:21	☿ ♊ 10 16:34	3 18:31 ♅ △	♑ 4 8:40	4 18:23 ♀ ⚹	♓ 4 19:50	14 16:54 ● 23♉38	Julian Day # 22401
☽0N 11 5:02	☉ ♊ 21 7:22	6 11:08 ♄ ☌	♒ 6 11:24	6 22:03 ♄ ⚹	♈ 6 23:23	22 16:18 ☽ 1♍19	Delta T 33.7 sec
♇ D 17 4:24	☿ ♋ 28 17:23	8 5:33 ☿ □	♓ 8 14:23	9 3:04 ♄ □	♉ 9 4:38	30 4:37 ○ 8♐32	SVP 05♓48'09"
☽0S 25 14:13		10 17:41 ♄ ⚹	♈ 10 17:56	11 9:51 ♄ △	♊ 11 11:40		Obliquity 23°26'31"
♃ R 25 18:35	♀ ♉ 5 19:25	12 22:09 ♄ □	♉ 12 22:25	13 6:23 ♅ ⚹	♋ 13 20:50	5 21:19 ☽ 14♓57	⚷ Chiron 5♓56.5
	☊ ♌ 10 20:06	15 4:16 ♄ △	♊ 15 4:34	16 5:48 ♄ ☍	♌ 16 8:16	13 5:16 ● 21♊57	☽ Mean ☊ 2♍59.2
☽0N 7 11:38	☉ ♋ 21 15:30	16 21:28 ♅ ⚹	♋ 17 13:17	18 15:21 ☉ ⚹	♍ 18 21:12	21 9:01 ☽ 29♍45	
☿ R 14 17:06	♂ ♍ 28 23:47	20 0:17 ♄ ☍	♌ 20 0:45	21 9:01 ☉ □	♎ 21 9:32	28 12:37 ○ 6♑34	1 JUNE 1961
☽0S 21 23:57		21 21:10 ♅ ☌	♍ 22 13:38	23 15:47 ♄ □	♏ 23 18:51		Julian Day # 22432
♃⊼♇ 23 12:42		25 0:39 ♄ △	♎ 25 1:18	25 21:01 ♄ ⚹	♐ 26 0:05		Delta T 33.8 sec
		27 8:51 ♄ □	♏ 27 9:34	28 1:05 ♂ △	♑ 28 2:00		SVP 05♓48'04"
		29 13:24 ♄ ⚹	♐ 29 14:11	29 22:59 ♄ ☌	♒ 30 2:18		Obliquity 23°26'31"
		31 9:13 ♀ △	♑ 31 16:20				⚷ Chiron 6♓39.4
							☽ Mean ☊ 1♍20.7

JULY 1961 LONGITUDE

Day	Sid.Time	☉	0 hr ☽	Noon ☽	True ☊	☿	♀	♂	♃	♄	♅	♆	♇
1 Sa	18 35 14	8♋55 6	13♒29 17	20♒53 40	28♌11.2	3♋35.5	23♉36.1	1♍11.0	5♒10.7	27♑52.0	23♌17.9	8♏38.7	6♍ 1.7
2 Su	18 39 10	9 52 17	28 14 52	5♓32 19	28D 10.3	3R 5.8	24 37.4	1 46.5	5R 4.5	27R47.9	23 20.8	8R 38.1	6 2.9
3 M	18 43 7	10 49 29	12♓45 31	19 54 8	28 10.9	2 39.0	25 39.0	2 22.0	4 58.1	27 43.8	23 23.8	8 37.5	6 4.2
4 Tu	18 47 3	11 46 40	26 57 59	3♈56 59	28 12.0	2 15.6	26 40.9	2 57.6	4 51.7	27 39.7	23 26.8	8 37.0	6 5.5
5 W	18 51 0	12 43 52	10♈51 8	17 40 32	28R 12.7	1 55.9	27 43.0	3 33.2	4 45.1	27 35.5	23 29.8	8 36.5	6 6.9
6 Th	18 54 56	13 41 4	24 25 17	1♉ 5 36	28 12.2	1 40.3	28 45.5	4 8.9	4 38.4	27 31.3	23 32.8	8 36.0	6 8.3
7 F	18 58 53	14 38 17	7♉41 39	14 13 40	28 9.9	1 29.1	29 48.1	4 44.7	4 31.7	27 27.0	23 35.9	8 35.5	6 9.6
8 Sa	19 2 49	15 35 30	20 41 52	27 6 26	28 5.8	1D 22.6	0♊51.0	5 20.5	4 24.8	27 22.8	23 39.0	8 35.1	6 11.1
9 Su	19 6 46	16 32 43	3♊27 35	9♊45 29	28 0.1	1 21.0	1 54.2	5 56.4	4 17.8	27 18.5	23 42.2	8 34.7	6 12.5
10 M	19 10 43	17 29 57	16 0 21	22 12 18	27 53.4	1 24.5	2 57.6	6 32.3	4 10.7	27 14.1	23 45.3	8 34.4	6 13.9
11 Tu	19 14 39	18 27 11	28 21 32	4♋28 11	27 46.3	1 33.2	4 1.2	7 8.3	4 3.6	27 9.8	23 48.5	8 34.0	6 15.4
12 W	19 18 36	19 24 25	10♋32 26	16 34 27	27 39.7	1 47.1	5 5.1	7 44.3	3 56.4	27 5.4	23 51.8	8 33.7	6 16.9
13 Th	19 22 32	20 21 40	22 34 25	28 32 33	27 34.1	2 6.4	6 9.2	8 20.5	3 49.1	27 1.0	23 55.0	8 33.5	6 18.4
14 F	19 26 29	21 18 54	4♌29 5	10♌24 17	27 30.1	2 31.0	7 13.4	8 56.6	3 41.7	26 56.6	23 58.3	8 33.2	6 20.0
15 Sa	19 30 25	22 16 9	16 18 26	22 11 53	27D 27.8	3 0.9	8 17.9	9 32.9	3 34.3	26 52.2	24 1.6	8 33.0	6 21.5
16 Su	19 34 22	23 13 25	28 4 58	3♍58 8	27 27.1	3 36.2	9 22.6	10 9.1	3 26.8	26 47.8	24 4.9	8 32.9	6 23.1
17 M	19 38 18	24 10 40	9♍51 48	15 46 27	27 27.8	4 16.8	10 27.4	10 45.5	3 19.2	26 43.4	24 8.3	8 32.7	6 24.7
18 Tu	19 42 15	25 7 56	21 42 36	27 40 47	27 29.3	5 2.6	11 32.5	11 21.9	3 11.6	26 39.0	24 11.6	8 32.6	6 26.3
19 W	19 46 12	26 5 11	3♎41 34	9♎45 33	27 31.0	5 53.7	12 37.7	11 58.3	3 4.0	26 34.5	24 15.0	8 32.6	6 28.0
20 Th	19 50 8	27 2 28	15 53 18	22 5 26	27R 32.3	6 49.9	13 43.1	12 34.8	2 56.3	26 30.1	24 18.4	8D 32.5	6 29.6
21 F	19 54 5	27 59 44	28 22 30	4♏45 4	27 32.8	7 51.2	14 48.7	13 11.4	2 48.6	26 25.6	24 21.9	8 32.5	6 31.3
22 Sa	19 58 1	28 57 0	11♏13 37	17 48 34	27 32.2	8 57.5	15 54.5	13 48.0	2 40.9	26 21.2	24 25.3	8 32.5	6 33.0
23 Su	20 1 58	29 54 17	24 30 16	1♐18 56	27 30.4	10 8.8	17 0.4	14 24.7	2 33.2	26 16.8	24 28.8	8 32.6	6 34.7
24 M	20 5 54	0♌51 34	8♐14 40	15 17 22	27 27.5	11 24.9	18 6.5	15 1.4	2 25.4	26 12.4	24 32.3	8 32.7	6 36.4
25 Tu	20 9 51	1 48 52	22 26 49	29 42 35	27 24.2	12 45.7	19 12.8	15 38.2	2 17.6	26 8.0	24 35.8	8 32.8	6 38.2
26 W	20 13 47	2 46 10	7♑ 4 3	14♑30 25	27 20.8	14 11.1	20 19.2	16 15.0	2 9.9	26 3.6	24 39.3	8 33.0	6 39.9
27 Th	20 17 44	3 43 29	22 0 44	29 33 57	27 17.9	15 40.9	21 25.8	16 51.9	2 2.1	25 59.2	24 42.9	8 33.1	6 41.7
28 F	20 21 41	4 40 48	7♒ 8 54	14♒44 22	27 15.9	17 15.0	22 32.6	17 28.8	1 54.3	25 54.8	24 46.4	8 33.4	6 43.5
29 Sa	20 25 37	5 38 8	22 19 9	29 52 6	27D 15.0	18 53.3	23 39.5	18 5.8	1 46.6	25 50.5	24 50.0	8 33.6	6 45.3
30 Su	20 29 34	6 35 29	7♓22 11	14♓48 26	27 15.2	20 35.3	24 46.6	18 42.8	1 38.9	25 46.2	24 53.6	8 33.9	6 47.1
31 M	20 33 30	7 32 51	22 10 6	29 26 33	27 16.1	22 21.0	25 53.8	19 19.9	1 31.2	25 41.9	24 57.2	8 34.2	6 48.9

AUGUST 1961 LONGITUDE

Day	Sid.Time	☉	0 hr ☽	Noon ☽	True ☊	☿	♀	♂	♃	♄	♅	♆	♇
1 Tu	20 37 27	8♌30 14	6♈37 19	13♈42 6	27♌17.3	24♋10.0	27♊ 1.2	19♍57.1	1♒23.5	25♑37.6	25♌ 0.8	8♏34.5	6♍50.7
2 W	20 41 23	9 27 37	20 40 46	27 33 17	27 18.5	26 2.0	28 8.7	20 34.3	1R 15.9	25R 33.3	25 4.5	8 34.9	6 52.6
3 Th	20 45 20	10 25 3	4♉19 45	11♉ 0 21	27R 19.1	27 56.8	29 16.3	21 11.5	1 8.3	25 29.1	25 8.1	8 35.3	6 54.5
4 F	20 49 16	11 22 29	17 35 21	24 5 3	27 19.1	29 53.8	0♋24.1	21 48.8	1 0.7	25 24.9	25 11.8	8 35.8	6 56.3
5 Sa	20 53 13	12 19 57	0♊29 49	6♊50 1	27 18.4	1♌52.9	1 32.1	22 26.2	0 53.2	25 20.8	25 15.4	8 36.2	6 58.2
6 Su	20 57 10	13 17 25	13 6 3	19 18 19	27 17.1	3 53.6	2 40.1	23 3.6	0 45.8	25 16.7	25 19.1	8 36.8	7 0.1
7 M	21 1 6	14 14 56	25 27 11	1♋33 2	27 15.4	5 55.5	3 48.3	23 41.1	0 38.4	25 12.6	25 22.8	8 37.3	7 2.1
8 Tu	21 5 3	15 12 27	7♋36 15	13 37 10	27 13.6	7 58.4	4 56.7	24 18.6	0 31.1	25 8.5	25 26.5	8 37.9	7 4.0
9 W	21 8 59	16 10 0	19 36 6	25 33 24	27 12.0	10 1.8	6 5.1	24 56.2	0 23.8	25 4.5	25 30.2	8 38.5	7 5.9
10 Th	21 12 56	17 7 33	1♌29 20	7♌24 13	27 10.7	12 5.5	7 13.7	25 33.9	0 16.6	25 0.6	25 33.9	8 39.1	7 7.9
11 F	21 16 52	18 5 8	13 18 19	19 11 56	27 9.9	14 9.3	8 22.4	26 11.6	0 9.6	24 56.7	25 37.6	8 39.8	7 9.8
12 Sa	21 20 49	19 2 45	25 5 20	0♍58 49	27D 9.6	16 12.8	9 31.2	26 49.3	0 2.6	24 52.8	25 41.3	8 40.5	7 11.8
13 Su	21 24 45	20 0 22	6♍52 40	12 47 11	27 9.8	18 15.8	10 40.2	27 27.1	29♑55.7	24 49.0	25 45.1	8 41.2	7 13.8
14 M	21 28 42	20 58 0	18 42 43	24 39 35	27 10.2	20 18.1	11 49.2	28 5.0	29 48.9	24 45.3	25 48.8	8 41.9	7 15.8
15 Tu	21 32 39	21 55 39	0♎38 10	6♎38 50	27 10.7	22 19.7	12 58.4	28 42.9	29 42.2	24 41.6	25 52.5	8 42.7	7 17.8
16 W	21 36 35	22 53 20	12 41 59	18 48 3	27 11.2	24 20.2	14 7.7	29 20.9	29 35.6	24 37.9	25 56.3	8 43.5	7 19.7
17 Th	21 40 32	23 51 2	24 57 28	1♏10 42	27 11.6	26 19.8	15 17.1	29 58.9	29 29.1	24 34.3	26 0.0	8 44.4	7 21.8
18 F	21 44 28	24 48 44	7♏28 10	13 50 20	27 11.9	28 18.1	16 26.6	0♎37.0	29 22.8	24 30.8	26 3.8	8 45.3	7 23.8
19 Sa	21 48 25	25 46 28	20 17 38	26 50 27	27R 12.0	0♍15.2	17 36.2	1 15.1	29 16.5	24 27.3	26 7.5	8 46.2	7 25.8
20 Su	21 52 21	26 44 13	3♐29 8	10♐13 59	27D 12.0	2 11.1	18 45.9	1 53.3	29 10.4	24 23.9	26 11.3	8 47.1	7 27.8
21 M	21 56 18	27 41 59	17 5 11	24 2 51	27 12.0	4 5.7	19 55.7	2 31.5	29 4.4	24 20.6	26 15.0	8 48.1	7 29.8
22 Tu	22 0 14	28 39 46	1♑ 6 55	8♑17 15	27 12.1	5 58.9	21 5.6	3 9.8	28 58.6	24 17.3	26 18.8	8 49.1	7 31.9
23 W	22 4 11	29 37 34	15 33 30	22 55 10	27 12.3	7 50.8	22 15.6	3 48.2	28 52.9	24 14.1	26 22.5	8 50.1	7 33.9
24 Th	22 8 8	0♍35 24	0♒21 36	7♒51 59	27 12.5	9 41.4	23 25.7	4 26.6	28 47.3	24 11.0	26 26.2	8 51.2	7 36.0
25 F	22 12 4	1 33 15	15 25 19	23 0 33	27R 12.8	11 30.5	24 36.0	5 5.0	28 41.9	24 7.9	26 30.0	8 52.3	7 38.0
26 Sa	22 16 1	2 31 7	0♓36 31	8♓12 2	27 12.8	13 18.4	25 46.3	5 43.5	28 36.6	24 4.9	26 33.7	8 53.4	7 40.1
27 Su	22 19 57	3 29 0	15 45 52	23 16 56	27 12.6	15 4.9	26 56.7	6 22.1	28 31.5	24 2.0	26 37.4	8 54.5	7 42.1
28 M	22 23 54	4 26 56	0♈44 8	8♈ 6 35	27 12.0	16 50.1	28 7.2	7 0.7	28 26.6	23 59.2	26 41.2	8 55.7	7 44.2
29 Tu	22 27 50	5 24 52	15 23 31	22 34 20	27 11.2	18 34.0	29 17.9	7 39.3	28 21.7	23 56.4	26 44.9	8 56.9	7 46.2
30 W	22 31 47	6 22 51	29 38 37	6♉36 7	27 10.2	20 16.5	0♌28.6	8 18.0	28 17.1	23 53.7	26 48.6	8 58.1	7 48.3
31 Th	22 35 43	7 20 52	13♉26 46	20 10 37	27 9.2	21 57.8	1 39.4	8 56.8	28 12.6	23 51.1	26 52.3	8 59.4	7 50.3

Astro Data Dy Hr Mn	Planet Ingress Dy Hr Mn	Last Aspect Dy Hr Mn	☽ Ingress Dy Hr Mn	Last Aspect Dy Hr Mn	☽ Ingress Dy Hr Mn	☽ Phases & Eclipses Dy Hr Mn	Astro Data
☽0N 4 18:20	♀ ♊ 7 4:32	1 17:38 ♀ □	♓ 2 2:52	2 14:13 ♀ ⚹	♉ 2 16:19	5 3:32 ☽ 12♈52	1 JULY 1961
☿ D 8 19:36	☉ ♌ 23 2:24	4 1:11 ♄ ⚹	♈ 4 5:12	4 14:24 ♄ △	♊ 4 23:04	12 19:11 ● 20♋10	Julian Day # 22462
☽0S 19 8:16		6 5:32 ♄ □	♉ 6 10:01	6 23:51 ♅ ⚹	♋ 7 8:56	20 23:13 ☽ 27♎58	Delta T 33.8 sec
♆ D 20 18:48	♀ ♋ 3 15:28	8 12:27 ♄ △	♊ 8 17:27	9 11:21 ♂ ⚹	♌ 9 20:59	27 19:50 ○ 4♒31	SVP 05♓47'59"
	☿ ♌ 4 1:15	10 15:05 ♅ ⚹	♋ 11 3:13	12 1:14 ♅ ☌	♍ 12 10:00		Obliquity 23°26'31"
☽0N 1 2:17	♃ ♑ 12 8:54	13 8:52 ♄ ☍	♌ 13 14:56	14 22:09 ♃ △	♎ 14 22:44	3 11:47 ☽ 10♉53	⚷ Chiron 6♓29.0R
♄⚻♅ 5 16:28	♂ ♎ 17 0:41	15 15:48 ♅ ☌	♍ 16 3:55	17 8:40 ♃ □	♏ 17 9:44	11 10:36 ● 18♌31	☽ Mean ☊ 29♌45.4
☽0S 15 14:47	☿ ♍ 18 20:52	18 9:52 ♄ △	♎ 18 16:39	19 16:17 ♃ ⚹	♐ 19 17:44	11 10:46:14 • A 6'35"	
♂0S 19 2:44	☉ ♍ 23 9:19	20 23:13 ☉ □	♏ 21 3:05	21 19:33 ☉ △	♑ 21 22:07	19 10:51 ☽ 26♏13	1 AUGUST 1961
☽0N 28 11:53	♀ ♌ 29 14:18	23 3:08 ♄ ⚹	♐ 23 9:42	23 21:29 ♃ ☌	♒ 23 23:25	26 3:13 ○ 2♓39	Julian Day # 22493
		25 3:35 ♅ △	♑ 25 12:29	25 17:35 ♅ ☍	♓ 25 23:02	26 3:08 • P 0.986	Delta T 33.8 sec
		27 6:17 ♄ ☌	♒ 27 12:41	27 20:19 ♃ ⚹	♈ 27 22:49		SVP 05♓47'55"
		29 4:00 ♅ ☍	♓ 29 12:13	29 21:42 ♃ □	♉ 30 0:37		Obliquity 23°26'32"
		31 6:39 ♀ □	♈ 31 12:56				⚷ Chiron 5♓29.9R
							☽ Mean ☊ 28♌06.9

LONGITUDE — SEPTEMBER 1961

Day	Sid.Time	☉	0 hr ☽	Noon ☽	True ☊	☿	♀	♂	♃	♄	♅	♆	♇
1 F	22 39 40	8♍18 54	26♉47 51	3♊18 48	27♌ 8.5	23♍37.9	2♌50.4	9♎35.6	28♑ 8.3	23♑48.6	26♌56.0	9♏ 0.7	7♍52.4
2 Sa	22 43 37	9 16 59	9♊43 49	16 3 21	27D 8.3	25 16.7	4 1.4	10 14.5	28R 4.1	23R 46.1	26 59.7	9 2.0	7 54.4
3 Su	22 47 33	10 15 5	22 17 56	28 28 4	27 8.6	26 54.3	5 12.5	10 53.4	28 0.1	23 43.8	27 3.4	9 3.3	7 56.5
4 M	22 51 30	11 13 13	4♋34 17	10♋37 9	27 9.4	28 30.6	6 23.7	11 32.4	27 56.3	23 41.5	27 7.0	9 4.7	7 58.6
5 Tu	22 55 26	12 11 24	16 37 11	22 34 56	27 10.7	0♎ 5.7	7 35.0	12 11.5	27 52.7	23 39.3	27 10.7	9 6.1	8 0.6
6 W	22 59 23	13 9 36	28 30 54	4♌25 32	27 12.1	1 39.7	8 46.4	12 50.6	27 49.2	23 37.2	27 14.3	9 7.5	8 2.7
7 Th	23 3 19	14 7 50	10♌19 20	16 12 40	27 13.3	3 12.4	9 57.9	13 29.7	27 45.9	23 35.1	27 18.0	9 9.0	8 4.7
8 F	23 7 16	15 6 6	22 5 58	27 59 35	27R 14.0	4 44.0	11 9.5	14 9.0	27 42.8	23 33.2	27 21.6	9 10.4	8 6.8
9 Sa	23 11 12	16 4 24	3♍53 50	9♍49 3	27 13.9	6 14.3	12 21.1	14 48.2	27 39.9	23 31.4	27 25.2	9 11.9	8 8.8
10 Su	23 15 9	17 2 44	15 45 28	21 43 23	27 12.9	7 43.5	13 32.8	15 27.6	27 37.2	23 29.6	27 28.8	9 13.4	8 10.9
11 M	23 19 6	18 1 5	27 43 1	3♎44 37	27 10.8	9 11.4	14 44.7	16 7.0	27 34.6	23 27.9	27 32.4	9 15.0	8 12.9
12 Tu	23 23 2	18 59 28	9♎48 22	15 54 31	27 7.8	10 38.2	15 56.6	16 46.4	27 32.3	23 26.4	27 35.9	9 16.5	8 14.9
13 W	23 26 59	19 57 53	22 3 16	28 14 51	27 4.2	12 3.7	17 8.5	17 25.9	27 30.1	23 24.9	27 39.5	9 18.1	8 17.0
14 Th	23 30 55	20 56 20	4♏29 27	10♏47 21	27 0.4	13 27.9	18 20.6	18 5.4	27 28.1	23 23.5	27 43.0	9 19.7	8 19.0
15 F	23 34 52	21 54 48	17 8 45	23 33 55	26 56.9	14 50.9	19 32.7	18 45.1	27 26.3	23 22.2	27 46.5	9 21.4	8 21.0
16 Sa	23 38 48	22 53 19	0♐ 3 6	6♐36 33	26 54.2	16 12.6	20 44.9	19 24.7	27 24.8	23 21.0	27 50.0	9 23.0	8 23.0
17 Su	23 42 45	23 51 50	13 14 30	19 57 10	26D 52.6	17 32.9	21 57.2	20 4.4	27 23.4	23 19.9	27 53.5	9 24.7	8 25.0
18 M	23 46 41	24 50 24	26 44 45	3♑37 23	26 52.2	18 51.9	23 9.5	20 44.2	27 22.2	23 18.9	27 56.9	9 26.4	8 27.0
19 Tu	23 50 38	25 48 59	10♑35 9	17 38 4	26 52.8	20 9.4	24 22.0	21 24.0	27 21.2	23 18.0	28 0.4	9 28.2	8 29.0
20 W	23 54 34	26 47 36	24 46 2	1♒58 50	26 54.2	21 25.4	25 34.5	22 3.9	27 20.4	23 17.2	28 3.8	9 29.9	8 31.0
21 Th	23 58 31	27 46 14	9♒16 9	16 37 29	26 55.6	22 39.9	26 47.0	22 43.8	27 19.7	23 16.4	28 7.2	9 31.7	8 33.0
22 F	0 2 28	28 44 54	24 2 15	1♓29 41	26R 56.4	23 52.7	27 59.7	23 23.8	27 19.3	23 15.8	28 10.5	9 33.5	8 34.9
23 Sa	0 6 24	29 43 35	8♓58 55	16 28 56	26 55.9	25 3.8	29 12.4	24 3.9	27D 19.1	23 15.3	28 13.9	9 35.3	8 36.9
24 Su	0 10 21	0♎42 19	23 58 43	1♈27 10	26 53.9	26 13.1	0♍25.1	24 43.9	27 19.1	23 14.9	28 17.2	9 37.1	8 38.8
25 M	0 14 17	1 41 4	8♈53 11	16 15 44	26 50.2	27 20.4	1 38.0	25 24.1	27 19.2	23 14.6	28 20.5	9 38.9	8 40.7
26 Tu	0 18 14	2 39 52	23 33 53	0♉46 47	26 45.2	28 25.7	2 50.9	26 4.3	27 19.6	23 14.3	28 23.7	9 40.8	8 42.7
27 W	0 22 10	3 38 41	7♉53 48	14 54 24	26 39.5	29 28.7	4 3.9	26 44.6	27 20.2	23D 14.2	28 27.0	9 42.7	8 44.6
28 Th	0 26 7	4 37 33	21 48 17	28 35 17	26 33.9	0♏29.4	5 17.0	27 24.9	27 20.9	23 14.2	28 30.2	9 44.6	8 46.5
29 F	0 30 3	5 36 27	5♊15 26	11♊48 52	26 29.2	1 27.4	6 30.1	28 5.2	27 21.9	23 14.2	28 33.4	9 46.5	8 48.4
30 Sa	0 34 0	6 35 24	18 15 53	24 36 53	26 25.8	2 22.8	7 43.3	28 45.7	27 23.0	23 14.4	28 36.5	9 48.4	8 50.2

LONGITUDE — OCTOBER 1961

Day	Sid.Time	☉	0 hr ☽	Noon ☽	True ☊	☿	♀	♂	♃	♄	♅	♆	♇
1 Su	0 37 57	7♎34 22	0♋52 22	7♋ 2 52	26♌24.1	3♏15.1	8♍56.5	29♎26.2	27♑24.3	23♑14.7	28♌39.7	9♏50.4	8♍52.1
2 M	0 41 53	8 33 23	13 9 0	19 11 23	26D 23.9	4 4.1	10 9.9	0♏ 6.7	27 25.9	23 15.0	28 42.8	9 52.4	8 54.0
3 Tu	0 45 50	9 32 26	25 10 40	1♌ 7 30	26 24.9	4 49.7	11 23.3	0 47.3	27 27.6	23 15.5	28 45.8	9 54.4	8 55.8
4 W	0 49 46	10 31 32	7♌ 2 32	12 56 23	26 26.5	5 31.3	12 36.7	1 28.0	27 29.5	23 16.1	28 48.9	9 56.4	8 57.6
5 Th	0 53 43	11 30 40	18 49 39	24 42 54	26R 27.7	6 8.7	13 50.2	2 8.7	27 31.6	23 16.7	28 51.9	9 58.4	8 59.4
6 F	0 57 39	12 29 50	0♍36 40	6♍31 25	26 27.9	6 41.6	15 3.8	2 49.5	27 33.9	23 17.5	28 54.9	10 0.4	9 1.2
7 Sa	1 1 36	13 29 2	12 27 37	18 25 39	26 26.4	7 9.4	16 17.5	3 30.3	27 36.4	23 18.4	28 57.8	10 2.4	9 3.0
8 Su	1 5 32	14 28 16	24 25 50	0♎28 28	26 22.7	7 31.8	17 31.1	4 11.2	27 39.1	23 19.3	29 0.7	10 4.5	9 4.7
9 M	1 9 29	15 27 33	6♎33 46	12 41 56	26 16.8	7 48.3	18 44.9	4 52.1	27 42.0	23 20.4	29 3.6	10 6.6	9 6.5
10 Tu	1 13 26	16 26 51	18 53 5	25 7 19	26 8.9	7R 58.4	19 58.7	5 33.1	27 45.0	23 21.5	29 6.4	10 8.7	9 8.2
11 W	1 17 22	17 26 12	1♏24 39	7♏45 9	25 59.6	8 1.6	21 12.5	6 14.2	27 48.3	23 22.8	29 9.2	10 10.8	9 9.9
12 Th	1 21 19	18 25 34	14 8 46	20 35 31	25 49.9	7 57.4	22 26.4	6 55.3	27 51.7	23 24.2	29 12.0	10 12.9	9 11.6
13 F	1 25 15	19 24 59	27 5 22	3♐38 16	25 40.7	7 45.5	23 40.4	7 36.5	27 55.3	23 25.6	29 14.7	10 15.0	9 13.3
14 Sa	1 29 12	20 24 25	10♐14 15	16 53 16	25 32.9	7 25.4	24 54.4	8 17.7	27 59.1	23 27.2	29 17.4	10 17.1	9 14.9
15 Su	1 33 8	21 23 54	23 35 22	0♑20 34	25 27.3	6 56.9	26 8.4	8 59.0	28 3.1	23 28.8	29 20.1	10 19.3	9 16.6
16 M	1 37 5	22 23 24	7♑ 8 56	14 0 29	25 24.0	6 19.9	27 22.5	9 40.4	28 7.3	23 30.6	29 22.7	10 21.4	9 18.2
17 Tu	1 41 1	23 22 56	20 55 17	27 53 22	25D 22.9	5 34.5	28 36.6	10 21.8	28 11.7	23 32.5	29 25.2	10 23.6	9 19.8
18 W	1 44 58	24 22 29	4♒54 44	11♒59 21	25 23.2	4 41.1	29 50.8	11 3.2	28 16.2	23 34.4	29 27.8	10 25.7	9 21.4
19 Th	1 48 54	25 22 4	19 7 5	26 17 45	25R 23.9	3 40.5	1♎ 5.0	11 44.8	28 20.9	23 36.4	29 30.3	10 27.9	9 22.9
20 F	1 52 51	26 21 41	3♓31 4	10♓46 38	25 23.7	2 33.8	2 19.3	12 26.3	28 25.8	23 38.6	29 32.7	10 30.1	9 24.4
21 Sa	1 56 48	27 21 20	18 3 56	25 22 22	25 21.7	1 22.3	3 33.6	13 7.9	28 30.9	23 40.8	29 35.1	10 32.3	9 26.0
22 Su	2 0 44	28 21 0	2♈41 11	9♈59 35	25 17.2	0 7.8	4 47.9	13 49.6	28 36.1	23 43.1	29 37.5	10 34.5	9 27.4
23 M	2 4 41	29 20 42	17 16 43	24 31 42	25 10.0	28♎52.5	6 2.3	14 31.3	28 41.5	23 45.6	29 39.8	10 36.7	9 28.9
24 Tu	2 8 37	0♏20 26	1♉43 39	8♉51 44	25 0.5	27 38.5	7 16.8	15 13.1	28 47.1	23 48.1	29 42.1	10 38.9	9 30.4
25 W	2 12 34	1 20 12	15 55 14	22 53 32	24 49.8	26 28.2	8 31.2	15 55.0	28 52.8	23 50.7	29 44.3	10 41.1	9 31.8
26 Th	2 16 30	2 20 1	29 46 7	6♊32 40	24 38.8	25 23.6	9 45.7	16 36.9	28 58.7	23 53.4	29 46.5	10 43.4	9 33.2
27 F	2 20 27	3 19 51	13♊12 59	19 47 4	24 28.9	24 26.8	11 0.3	17 18.8	29 4.8	23 56.2	29 48.7	10 45.6	9 34.6
28 Sa	2 24 23	4 19 43	26 15 0	2♋37 3	24 20.9	23 39.2	12 14.9	18 0.8	29 11.0	23 59.1	29 50.8	10 47.8	9 35.9
29 Su	2 28 20	5 19 38	8♋53 35	15 5 3	24 15.4	23 2.1	13 29.5	18 42.9	29 17.4	24 2.0	29 52.9	10 50.1	9 37.3
30 M	2 32 17	6 19 35	21 11 59	27 14 59	24 12.3	22 36.2	14 44.2	19 25.0	29 24.0	24 5.1	29 54.9	10 52.3	9 38.6
31 Tu	2 36 13	7 19 34	3♌14 43	9♌11 51	24D 11.1	22D 21.9	15 58.9	20 7.2	29 30.7	24 8.3	29 56.8	10 54.6	9 39.8

Astro Data Dy Hr Mn	Planet Ingress Dy Hr Mn	Last Aspect Dy Hr Mn	☽ Ingress Dy Hr Mn	Last Aspect Dy Hr Mn	☽ Ingress Dy Hr Mn	☽ Phases & Eclipses Dy Hr Mn	Astro Data
☿0S 5 3:51	☿ ♎ 4 22:32	1 2:26 ♃ △	♊ 1 5:52	3 4:36 ♃ ☍	♌ 3 9:43	1 23:05 ☽ 9♊15	1 SEPTEMBER 1961
☽0S 11 20:21	☉ ♎ 23 6:42	3 10:18 ☿ □	♋ 3 15:00	5 20:32 ♅ ☌	♍ 5 22:45	10 2:50 ● 17♍10	Julian Day # 22524
♃⊼♅ 11 8:59	♀ ♍ 23 15:43	5 22:36 ♃ ☍	♌ 6 3:01	8 6:26 ♃ △	♎ 8 11:04	17 20:23 ☽ 24♐42	Delta T 33.9 sec
♄⚼♇ 15 8:50	☿ ♏ 27 12:16	8 10:46 ♅ ☌	♍ 8 16:05	10 19:41 ♅ ✶	♏ 10 21:19	24 11:33 ○ 1♈11	SVP 05♓47'51"
♃ D 23 15:27		10 23:43 ♃ △	♎ 11 4:33	13 3:58 ♅ □	♐ 13 5:21		Obliquity 23°26'32"
☽0N 24 22:27	♂ ♏ 1 20:02	13 10:55 ♅ ✶	♏ 13 15:23	15 10:15 ♅ △	♑ 15 11:24	1 14:10 ☽ 8♋09	⚷ Chiron 4♓02.9R
♄ D 27 19:32	♀ ♎ 18 2:58	15 19:54 ♅ □	♐ 15 23:54	17 14:31 ♀ △	♒ 17 15:37	9 18:52 ● 16♎14	☽ Mean ☊ 26♌28.4
	☿ ♎ 22 2:29	18 2:07 ♅ △	♑ 18 5:42	19 17:23 ♅ ☍	♓ 19 18:10	17 4:34 ☽ 23♑34	
☽0S 9 2:37	☉ ♏ 23 15:47	20 4:17 ♃ ☌	♒ 20 8:43	21 17:15 ♃ ✶	♈ 21 19:36	23 21:30 ○ 0♉14	1 OCTOBER 1961
☿ R 10 22:42		22 6:56 ♀ ☍	♓ 22 9:36	23 20:36 ♅ △	♉ 23 21:07	31 8:58 ☽ 7♌42	Julian Day # 22554
♀0S 21 0:21		24 5:21 ♃ ✶	♈ 24 9:40	26 0:01 ♅ □	♊ 26 0:24		Delta T 33.9 sec
☽0N 22 8:42		26 8:43 ☿ ☍	♉ 26 10:42	28 6:47 ♅ ✶	♋ 28 7:03		SVP 05♓47'49"
☿ D 31 18:01		28 11:54 ♅ △	♊ 28 14:31	30 16:27 ♃ ☍	♌ 30 17:30		Obliquity 23°26'32"
		30 21:04 ♂ △	♋ 30 22:19				⚷ Chiron 2♓43.3R
							☽ Mean ☊ 24♌53.1

NOVEMBER 1961 LONGITUDE

Day	Sid.Time	☉	0 hr ☽	Noon ☽	True ☊	☿	♀	♂	♃	♄	♅	♆	♇
1 W	2 40 10	8♏19 35	15♌ 7 5	21♌ 1 7	24♌11.2	22♎19.0	17♎13.6	20♏49.5	29♑37.6	24♑11.5	29♌58.7	10♏56.8	9♍41.1
2 Th	2 44 6	9 19 38	26 54 38	2♍48 19	24R 11.3	22 27.3	18 28.4	21 31.8	29 44.6	24 14.8	0♍ 0.6	10 59.0	9 42.3
3 F	2 48 3	10 19 43	8♍42 50	14 38 48	24 10.4	22 46.2	19 43.2	22 14.1	29 51.8	24 18.2	0 2.4	11 1.3	9 43.5
4 Sa	2 51 59	11 19 51	20 36 47	26 37 18	24 7.5	23 14.9	20 58.0	22 56.6	29 59.1	24 21.7	0 4.2	11 3.5	9 44.7
5 Su	2 55 56	12 20 0	2♎40 48	8♎47 42	24 2.0	23 52.7	22 12.9	23 39.0	0♒ 6.6	24 25.3	0 5.9	11 5.8	9 45.9
6 M	2 59 52	13 20 11	14 58 18	21 12 50	23 53.6	24 38.5	23 27.8	24 21.6	0 14.3	24 29.0	0 7.6	11 8.0	9 47.0
7 Tu	3 3 49	14 20 25	27 31 27	3♏54 13	23 42.6	25 31.7	24 42.7	25 4.2	0 22.0	24 32.7	0 9.2	11 10.3	9 48.1
8 W	3 7 46	15 20 40	10♏21 6	16 52 0	23 29.8	26 31.2	25 57.7	25 46.8	0 30.0	24 36.6	0 10.8	11 12.5	9 49.2
9 Th	3 11 42	16 20 57	23 26 46	0♐ 5 9	23 16.3	27 36.3	27 12.6	26 29.5	0 38.1	24 40.5	0 12.3	11 14.8	9 50.2
10 F	3 15 39	17 21 16	6♐46 52	13 31 37	23 3.3	28 46.2	28 27.6	27 12.3	0 46.3	24 44.5	0 13.8	11 17.0	9 51.2
11 Sa	3 19 35	18 21 36	20 19 5	27 8 57	22 52.1	0♏ 0.4	29 42.7	27 55.1	0 54.7	24 48.6	0 15.2	11 19.2	9 52.2
12 Su	3 23 32	19 21 58	4♑ 0 56	10♑54 45	22 43.6	1 18.0	0♏57.7	28 38.0	1 3.2	24 52.8	0 16.6	11 21.5	9 53.2
13 M	3 27 28	20 22 21	17 50 11	24 47 4	22 38.1	2 38.7	2 12.8	29 20.9	1 11.8	24 57.0	0 17.9	11 23.7	9 54.1
14 Tu	3 31 25	21 22 46	1♒45 14	8♒44 36	22 35.4	4 1.9	3 27.9	0♐ 3.9	1 20.6	25 1.3	0 19.1	11 25.9	9 55.0
15 W	3 35 21	22 23 12	15 45 6	22 46 40	22 34.7	5 27.3	4 43.0	0 46.9	1 29.5	25 5.7	0 20.3	11 28.2	9 55.9
16 Th	3 39 18	23 23 40	29 49 14	6♓52 45	22 34.6	6 54.4	5 58.1	1 30.0	1 38.6	25 10.2	0 21.5	11 30.4	9 56.7
17 F	3 43 15	24 24 8	13♓57 6	21 2 8	22 33.9	8 23.0	7 13.2	2 13.1	1 47.7	25 14.8	0 22.6	11 32.6	9 57.5
18 Sa	3 47 11	25 24 38	28 7 36	5♈13 14	22 31.1	9 52.8	8 28.4	2 56.3	1 57.0	25 19.4	0 23.6	11 34.8	9 58.3
19 Su	3 51 8	26 25 9	12♈18 40	19 23 28	22 25.7	11 23.6	9 43.6	3 39.6	2 6.5	25 24.1	0 24.6	11 37.0	9 59.1
20 M	3 55 4	27 25 42	26 27 7	3♉29 5	22 17.2	12 55.2	10 58.8	4 22.9	2 16.0	25 28.9	0 25.5	11 39.2	9 59.8
21 Tu	3 59 1	28 26 16	10♉28 47	17 25 38	22 6.2	14 27.4	12 14.0	5 6.2	2 25.7	25 33.7	0 26.4	11 41.3	10 0.5
22 W	4 2 57	29 26 51	24 19 5	1♊ 8 38	21 53.6	16 0.1	13 29.2	5 49.6	2 35.5	25 38.6	0 27.2	11 43.5	10 1.2
23 Th	4 6 54	0♐27 28	7♊53 48	14 34 16	21 40.7	17 33.2	14 44.4	6 33.1	2 45.4	25 43.6	0 28.0	11 45.7	10 1.8
24 F	4 10 50	1 28 6	21 9 46	27 40 10	21 28.7	19 6.7	15 59.7	7 16.6	2 55.4	25 48.6	0 28.7	11 47.8	10 2.4
25 Sa	4 14 47	2 28 45	4♋ 5 26	10♋25 40	21 18.8	20 40.3	17 15.0	8 0.2	3 5.6	25 53.8	0 29.4	11 50.0	10 3.0
26 Su	4 18 44	3 29 27	16 41 4	22 51 56	21 11.5	22 14.1	18 30.2	8 43.8	3 15.8	25 58.9	0 30.0	11 52.1	10 3.5
27 M	4 22 40	4 30 9	28 58 39	5♌ 1 42	21 7.0	23 48.1	19 45.5	9 27.5	3 26.2	26 4.2	0 30.5	11 54.2	10 4.0
28 Tu	4 26 37	5 30 53	11♌ 1 38	16 59 1	21D 4.9	25 22.1	21 0.9	10 11.2	3 36.7	26 9.5	0 31.0	11 56.3	10 4.5
29 W	4 30 33	6 31 39	22 54 30	28 48 46	21 4.5	26 56.1	22 16.2	10 55.0	3 47.3	26 14.9	0 31.5	11 58.4	10 4.9
30 Th	4 34 30	7 32 26	4♍42 29	10♍36 22	21R 4.7	28 30.2	23 31.5	11 38.9	3 58.0	26 20.3	0 31.8	12 0.5	10 5.4

DECEMBER 1961 LONGITUDE

Day	Sid.Time	☉	0 hr ☽	Noon ☽	True ☊	☿	♀	♂	♃	♄	♅	♆	♇
1 F	4 38 26	8♐33 15	16♍31 7	22♍27 26	21♌ 4.5	0♐ 4.3	24♏46.9	12♐22.8	4♒ 8.8	26♑25.8	0♍32.2	12♏ 2.6	10♍ 5.7
2 Sa	4 42 23	9 34 5	28 25 58	4♎27 22	21R 2.7	1 38.4	26 2.3	13 6.7	4 19.7	26 31.4	0 32.4	12 4.6	10 6.1
3 Su	4 46 19	10 34 56	10♎32 13	16 41 4	20 58.6	3 12.4	27 17.7	13 50.7	4 30.7	26 37.0	0 32.6	12 6.6	10 6.4
4 M	4 50 16	11 35 49	22 54 21	29 12 29	20 52.0	4 46.5	28 33.1	14 34.8	4 41.9	26 42.7	0 32.8	12 8.7	10 6.7
5 Tu	4 54 13	12 36 43	5♏35 43	12♏ 4 14	20 42.8	6 20.5	29 48.5	15 18.9	4 53.1	26 48.4	0 32.9	12 10.7	10 7.0
6 W	4 58 9	13 37 38	18 38 5	25 17 14	20 31.9	7 54.6	1♐ 3.9	16 3.1	5 4.4	26 54.2	0R 32.9	12 12.7	10 7.2
7 Th	5 2 6	14 38 35	2♐ 1 29	8♐50 32	20 20.1	9 28.6	2 19.3	16 47.3	5 15.8	27 0.0	0 32.9	12 14.7	10 7.4
8 F	5 6 2	15 39 33	15 44 0	22 41 22	20 8.7	11 2.6	3 34.8	17 31.5	5 27.3	27 5.9	0 32.8	12 16.6	10 7.5
9 Sa	5 9 59	16 40 31	29 42 5	6♑45 32	19 58.9	12 36.7	4 50.2	18 15.9	5 38.9	27 11.9	0 32.7	12 18.6	10 7.7
10 Su	5 13 55	17 41 31	13♑51 7	20 58 12	19 51.4	14 10.7	6 5.7	19 0.3	5 50.6	27 17.9	0 32.5	12 20.5	10 7.8
11 M	5 17 52	18 42 31	28 6 12	5♒14 37	19 46.8	15 44.8	7 21.1	19 44.7	6 2.4	27 24.0	0 32.3	12 22.4	10 7.8
12 Tu	5 21 48	19 43 32	12♒22 56	19 30 48	19D 44.9	17 19.0	8 36.6	20 29.2	6 14.3	27 30.1	0 32.0	12 24.3	10R 7.9
13 W	5 25 45	20 44 34	26 37 51	3♓43 52	19 44.8	18 53.2	9 52.0	21 13.7	6 26.3	27 36.2	0 31.6	12 26.2	10 7.9
14 Th	5 29 42	21 45 35	10♓48 39	17 52 3	19R 45.5	20 27.5	11 7.5	21 58.2	6 38.3	27 42.4	0 31.2	12 28.0	10 7.8
15 F	5 33 38	22 46 38	24 53 57	1♈54 16	19 45.9	22 1.9	12 23.0	22 42.9	6 50.4	27 48.7	0 30.7	12 29.8	10 7.8
16 Sa	5 37 35	23 47 40	8♈52 56	15 49 50	19 44.7	23 36.4	13 38.4	23 27.5	7 2.6	27 54.9	0 30.2	12 31.6	10 7.7
17 Su	5 41 31	24 48 43	22 44 52	29 37 54	19 41.4	25 11.0	14 53.9	24 12.2	7 14.9	28 1.3	0 29.6	12 33.4	10 7.5
18 M	5 45 28	25 49 47	6♉28 47	13♉17 20	19 35.7	26 45.8	16 9.4	24 57.0	7 27.3	28 7.7	0 29.0	12 35.2	10 7.4
19 Tu	5 49 24	26 50 51	20 3 20	26 46 34	19 27.9	28 20.7	17 24.8	25 41.8	7 39.7	28 14.1	0 28.3	12 36.9	10 7.2
20 W	5 53 21	27 51 55	3♊26 47	10♊ 3 47	19 18.7	29 55.8	18 40.3	26 26.6	7 52.2	28 20.5	0 27.6	12 38.7	10 7.0
21 Th	5 57 17	28 53 0	16 37 21	23 7 19	19 9.3	1♑31.0	19 55.8	27 11.5	8 4.8	28 27.0	0 26.8	12 40.4	10 6.7
22 F	6 1 14	29 54 5	29 33 33	5♋55 57	19 0.4	3 6.5	21 11.2	27 56.5	8 17.5	28 33.6	0 26.0	12 42.0	10 6.4
23 Sa	6 5 11	0♑55 11	12♋14 32	18 29 18	18 53.1	4 42.2	22 26.7	28 41.5	8 30.2	28 40.1	0 25.1	12 43.7	10 6.1
24 Su	6 9 7	1 56 17	24 40 24	0♌48 0	18 47.9	6 18.0	23 42.2	29 26.5	8 43.0	28 46.7	0 24.1	12 45.3	10 5.8
25 M	6 13 4	2 57 23	6♌52 22	12 53 48	18 45.0	7 54.1	24 57.7	0♑11.6	8 55.8	28 53.4	0 23.1	12 46.9	10 5.4
26 Tu	6 17 0	3 58 30	18 52 42	24 49 29	18D 44.1	9 30.4	26 13.2	0 56.7	9 8.8	29 0.1	0 22.1	12 48.5	10 5.0
27 W	6 20 57	4 59 38	0♍44 41	6♍38 49	18 44.8	11 7.0	27 28.7	1 41.9	9 21.8	29 6.8	0 21.0	12 50.1	10 4.6
28 Th	6 24 53	6 0 46	12 32 28	18 26 14	18 46.3	12 43.7	28 44.2	2 27.1	9 34.8	29 13.5	0 19.8	12 51.6	10 4.1
29 F	6 28 50	7 1 54	24 20 47	0♎16 45	18 47.9	14 20.7	29 59.7	3 12.4	9 47.9	29 20.3	0 18.6	12 53.1	10 3.6
30 Sa	6 32 47	8 3 3	6♎14 48	12 15 35	18R 48.7	15 57.9	1♑15.2	3 57.7	10 1.1	29 27.1	0 17.3	12 54.6	10 3.1
31 Su	6 36 43	9 4 13	18 19 46	24 27 57	18 48.2	17 35.3	2 30.6	4 43.1	10 14.3	29 33.9	0 16.0	12 56.0	10 2.5

Astro Data Dy Hr Mn	Planet Ingress Dy Hr Mn	Last Aspect Dy Hr Mn	☽ Ingress Dy Hr Mn	Last Aspect Dy Hr Mn	☽ Ingress Dy Hr Mn	☽ Phases & Eclipses Dy Hr Mn	Astro Data
♃⚻♅ 4 21:11	♅ ♍ 1 15:59	1 14:46 ☿ ⚹	♍ 2 6:17	1 20:09 ♄ △	♎ 2 3:08	8 9:58 ● 15♏46	1 NOVEMBER 1961
☽0S 5 10:42	♃ ♒ 4 2:49	4 7:32 ♄ △	♎ 4 18:42	4 7:19 ♄ □	♏ 4 13:30	15 12:12 ☽ 22♒54	Julian Day # 22585
♄⚼♇ 12 2:55	☿ ♏ 10 23:53	6 19:55 ☿ ☌	♏ 7 4:40	6 15:00 ♄ ⚹	♐ 6 20:25	22 9:44 ○ 29♉51	Delta T 33.9 sec
☽0N 18 17:20	♀ ♏ 11 5:33	9 5:50 ♂ ☌	♐ 9 11:51	8 3:17 ♂ ☌	♑ 9 0:31	30 6:18 ☽ 7♍48	SVP 05♓47'46"
	♂ ♐ 13 21:50	10 5:29 ♇ □	♑ 11 16:59	10 22:48 ♄ ☌	♒ 11 3:11		Obliquity 23°26'32"
☽0S 2 20:22	☉ ♐ 22 13:08	13 20:56 ♂ ⚹	♒ 13 20:59	12 14:23 ♂ ⚹	♓ 13 5:41	7 23:52 ● 15♐39	⚷ Chiron 1♓56.9R
♅ R 6 4:27	☿ ♐ 30 22:54	15 12:12 ☉ □	♓ 16 0:18	15 5:01 ♄ ⚹	♈ 15 8:44	14 20:05 ☽ 22♓37	☽ Mean ☊ 23♌14.6
♇ R 12 11:54		17 19:14 ♄ ⚹	♈ 18 3:10	17 9:16 ♄ □	♉ 17 12:39	22 0:42 ○ 29♊56	
☽0N 16 0:11	♀ ♐ 5 3:40	19 22:20 ♄ □	♉ 20 6:03	19 14:44 ♄ △	♊ 19 17:47	30 3:57 ☽ 8♎13	1 DECEMBER 1961
☽0S 30 6:07	☿ ♑ 20 1:04	22 9:44 ☉ ☍	♊ 22 9:59	22 0:42 ☉ ☍	♋ 22 0:50		Julian Day # 22615
♃⚻♇ 30 3:26	☉ ♑ 22 2:19	23 3:49 ♇ □	♋ 24 16:20	24 8:06 ♄ ☍	♌ 24 10:26		Delta T 34.0 sec
	♂ ♑ 24 17:50	26 18:14 ♄ ☍	♌ 27 2:01	26 16:35 ♀ △	♍ 26 22:29		SVP 05♓47'41"
	♀ ♑ 29 0:07	29 9:26 ☿ □	♍ 29 14:25	29 10:12 ♄ △	♎ 29 11:26		Obliquity 23°26'32"
				31 22:04 ♄ □	♏ 31 22:42		⚷ Chiron 2♓03.7
							☽ Mean ☊ 21♌39.3

LONGITUDE JANUARY 1962

Day	Sid.Time	☉	0 hr ☽	Noon ☽	True ☊	☿	♀	♂	♃	♄	♅	♆	♇
1 M	6 40 40	10♑ 5 22	0♏40 44	6♏58 37	18♌46.0	19♑12.8	3♑46.1	5♑28.5	10♒27.6	29♑40.7	0♍14.7	12♏57.5	10♍ 1.9
2 Tu	6 44 36	11 6 33	13 22 4	19 51 26	18R42.2	20 50.5	5 1.7	6 13.9	10 40.9	29 47.6	0R13.3	12 58.9	10R 1.3
3 W	6 48 33	12 7 43	26 26 59	3♐ 8 50	18 36.9	22 28.2	6 17.2	6 59.4	10 54.3	29 54.5	0 11.8	13 0.2	10 0.6
4 Th	6 52 29	13 8 54	9♐57 0	16 51 19	18 31.0	24 6.0	7 32.7	7 45.0	11 7.8	0♒ 1.4	0 10.3	13 1.6	9 60.0
5 F	6 56 26	14 10 5	23 51 30	0♑57 4	18 25.1	25 43.7	8 48.2	8 30.6	11 21.3	0 8.4	0 8.8	13 2.9	9 59.3
6 Sa	7 0 22	15 11 16	8♑ 7 28	15 21 59	18 20.0	27 21.4	10 3.7	9 16.2	11 34.8	0 15.4	0 7.2	13 4.2	9 58.5
7 Su	7 4 19	16 12 27	22 39 48	0♒ 0 3	18 16.3	28 58.8	11 19.2	10 1.9	11 48.4	0 22.4	0 5.6	13 5.4	9 57.8
8 M	7 8 16	17 13 37	7♒21 50	14 44 14	18D 14.3	0♒35.8	12 34.7	10 47.6	12 2.1	0 29.4	0 3.9	13 6.7	9 57.0
9 Tu	7 12 12	18 14 48	22 6 24	29 27 31	18 13.9	2 12.4	13 50.2	11 33.3	12 15.8	0 36.4	0 2.2	13 7.9	9 56.2
10 W	7 16 9	19 15 58	6♓46 52	14♓ 3 48	18 14.8	3 48.3	15 5.6	12 19.1	12 29.5	0 43.4	0 0.4	13 9.0	9 55.3
11 Th	7 20 5	20 17 7	21 17 50	28 28 31	18 16.3	5 23.3	16 21.1	13 4.9	12 43.3	0 50.5	29♌58.6	13 10.2	9 54.5
12 F	7 24 2	21 18 16	5♈35 34	12♈38 47	18 17.7	6 57.3	17 36.6	13 50.8	12 57.1	0 57.6	29 56.8	13 11.3	9 53.6
13 Sa	7 27 58	22 19 24	19 38 0	26 33 12	18R18.5	8 29.8	18 52.1	14 36.7	13 10.9	1 4.6	29 54.9	13 12.3	9 52.7
14 Su	7 31 55	23 20 31	3♉24 22	10♉11 33	18 18.1	10 0.6	20 7.5	15 22.6	13 24.8	1 11.7	29 53.0	13 13.4	9 51.7
15 M	7 35 51	24 21 38	16 54 48	23 34 15	18 16.6	11 29.2	21 23.0	16 8.6	13 38.7	1 18.8	29 51.0	13 14.4	9 50.7
16 Tu	7 39 48	25 22 44	0♊ 9 58	6♊42 5	18 14.0	12 55.3	22 38.4	16 54.6	13 52.7	1 25.9	29 49.0	13 15.4	9 49.8
17 W	7 43 45	26 23 49	13 10 42	19 35 57	18 10.7	14 18.3	23 53.9	17 40.6	14 6.7	1 33.1	29 47.0	13 16.3	9 48.7
18 Th	7 47 41	27 24 54	25 57 55	2♋16 43	18 7.2	15 37.7	25 9.3	18 26.7	14 20.7	1 40.2	29 44.9	13 17.3	9 47.7
19 F	7 51 38	28 25 58	8♋32 27	14 45 15	18 4.0	16 52.9	26 24.7	19 12.8	14 34.7	1 47.3	29 42.8	13 18.1	9 46.6
20 Sa	7 55 34	29 27 1	20 55 14	27 2 32	18 1.4	18 3.0	27 40.1	19 58.9	14 48.8	1 54.5	29 40.7	13 19.0	9 45.6
21 Su	7 59 31	0♒28 4	3♌ 7 20	9♌ 9 47	17 59.8	19 7.4	28 55.6	20 45.1	15 2.9	2 1.6	29 38.5	13 19.8	9 44.4
22 M	8 3 27	1 29 6	15 10 7	21 8 33	17D 59.1	20 5.2	0♒11.0	21 31.3	15 17.0	2 8.7	29 36.4	13 20.6	9 43.3
23 Tu	8 7 24	2 30 7	27 5 21	3♍ 0 51	17 59.3	20 55.7	1 26.4	22 17.6	15 31.2	2 15.9	29 34.1	13 21.4	9 42.2
24 W	8 11 20	3 31 8	8♍55 23	14 49 20	18 0.2	21 37.9	2 41.8	23 3.8	15 45.4	2 23.0	29 31.9	13 22.1	9 41.0
25 Th	8 15 17	4 32 8	20 43 6	26 37 9	18 1.4	22 11.0	3 57.1	23 50.1	15 59.5	2 30.1	29 29.6	13 22.8	9 39.8
26 F	8 19 14	5 33 7	2♎31 58	8♎28 3	18 2.8	22 34.2	5 12.5	24 36.5	16 13.8	2 37.3	29 27.3	13 23.4	9 38.6
27 Sa	8 23 10	6 34 5	14 25 58	20 26 16	18 3.9	22R46.9	6 27.9	25 22.8	16 28.0	2 44.4	29 24.9	13 24.1	9 37.4
28 Su	8 27 7	7 35 4	26 29 32	2♏36 20	18 4.6	22 48.5	7 43.3	26 9.2	16 42.3	2 51.5	29 22.6	13 24.7	9 36.1
29 M	8 31 3	8 36 1	8♏47 16	15 2 52	18R 4.9	22 38.8	8 58.6	26 55.7	16 56.5	2 58.7	29 20.2	13 25.2	9 34.8
30 Tu	8 35 0	9 36 58	21 23 42	27 50 14	18 4.7	22 17.8	10 14.0	27 42.2	17 10.8	3 5.8	29 17.8	13 25.7	9 33.5
31 W	8 38 56	10 37 54	4♐22 54	11♐ 2 2	18 4.1	21 45.7	11 29.3	28 28.6	17 25.1	3 12.9	29 15.3	13 26.2	9 32.2

LONGITUDE FEBRUARY 1962

Day	Sid.Time	☉	0 hr ☽	Noon ☽	True ☊	☿	♀	♂	♃	♄	♅	♆	♇
1 Th	8 42 53	11♒38 49	17♐47 51	24♐40 30	18♌ 3.4	21♒ 3.3	12♒44.7	29♑15.2	17♒39.4	3♒20.0	29♌12.9	13♏26.7	9♍30.9
2 F	8 46 49	12 39 44	1♑39 55	8♑45 56	18R 2.6	20R11.6	14 0.0	0♒ 1.7	17 53.8	3 27.1	29R10.4	13 27.1	9R29.6
3 Sa	8 50 46	13 40 38	15 58 11	23 16 9	18 2.1	19 11.9	15 15.4	0 48.3	18 8.1	3 34.2	29 7.9	13 27.5	9 28.2
4 Su	8 54 43	14 41 31	0♒39 8	8♒ 6 16	18 1.8	18 6.1	16 30.7	1 34.9	18 22.4	3 41.2	29 5.4	13 27.9	9 26.9
5 M	8 58 39	15 42 22	15 36 35	23 9 1	18D 1.7	16 56.1	17 46.0	2 21.6	18 36.8	3 48.3	29 2.9	13 28.2	9 25.5
6 Tu	9 2 36	16 43 13	0♓42 23	8♓15 34	18 1.7	15 43.8	19 1.3	3 8.2	18 51.2	3 55.3	29 0.3	13 28.5	9 24.1
7 W	9 6 32	17 44 2	15 47 25	23 16 53	18R 1.7	14 31.3	20 16.6	3 54.9	19 5.5	4 2.4	28 57.7	13 28.7	9 22.7
8 Th	9 10 29	18 44 50	0♈42 59	8♈ 4 55	18 1.7	13 20.7	21 31.8	4 41.6	19 19.9	4 9.4	28 55.2	13 28.9	9 21.2
9 F	9 14 25	19 45 36	15 21 59	22 33 41	18 1.6	12 13.5	22 47.1	5 28.3	19 34.2	4 16.3	28 52.6	13 29.1	9 19.8
10 Sa	9 18 22	20 46 21	29 39 40	6♉39 41	18 1.4	11 11.4	24 2.4	6 15.1	19 48.6	4 23.3	28 50.0	13 29.3	9 18.3
11 Su	9 22 18	21 47 4	13♉33 43	20 21 47	18D 1.2	10 15.4	25 17.6	7 1.9	20 3.0	4 30.3	28 47.4	13 29.4	9 16.9
12 M	9 26 15	22 47 46	27 4 3	3♊40 45	18 1.2	9 26.4	26 32.8	7 48.6	20 17.3	4 37.2	28 44.8	13 29.4	9 15.4
13 Tu	9 30 12	23 48 25	10♊12 11	16 38 42	18 1.4	8 45.0	27 48.0	8 35.4	20 31.7	4 44.1	28 42.2	13R29.5	9 13.9
14 W	9 34 8	24 49 4	23 0 39	29 18 26	18 1.9	8 11.4	29 3.2	9 22.3	20 46.0	4 50.9	28 39.5	13 29.5	9 12.4
15 Th	9 38 5	25 49 40	5♋32 27	11♋43 4	18 2.7	7 45.8	0♓18.3	10 9.1	21 0.4	4 57.8	28 36.9	13 29.5	9 10.9
16 F	9 42 1	26 50 15	17 50 39	23 55 35	18 3.6	7 28.0	1 33.5	10 56.0	21 14.7	5 4.6	28 34.3	13 29.4	9 9.4
17 Sa	9 45 58	27 50 48	29 58 11	5♌58 47	18 4.4	7D 17.8	2 48.6	11 42.8	21 29.1	5 11.4	28 31.6	13 29.3	9 7.9
18 Su	9 49 54	28 51 20	11♌57 41	17 55 10	18R 4.9	7 15.0	4 3.7	12 29.7	21 43.4	5 18.2	28 29.0	13 29.2	9 6.4
19 M	9 53 51	29 51 50	23 51 29	29 46 56	18 4.9	7 19.1	5 18.8	13 16.6	21 57.7	5 24.9	28 26.4	13 29.1	9 4.9
20 Tu	9 57 47	0♓52 18	5♍41 44	11♍36 10	18 4.3	7 29.8	6 33.9	14 3.5	22 12.0	5 31.6	28 23.7	13 28.9	9 3.3
21 W	10 1 44	1 52 45	17 30 28	23 24 55	18 2.9	7 46.5	7 49.0	14 50.5	22 26.2	5 38.3	28 21.1	13 28.6	9 1.8
22 Th	10 5 41	2 53 10	29 19 47	5♎15 22	18 0.8	8 9.0	9 4.0	15 37.4	22 40.5	5 44.9	28 18.5	13 28.4	9 0.2
23 F	10 9 37	3 53 33	11♎11 58	17 9 56	17 58.3	8 36.7	10 19.0	16 24.4	22 54.7	5 51.5	28 15.9	13 28.1	8 58.7
24 Sa	10 13 34	4 53 55	23 9 38	29 11 26	17 55.7	9 9.4	11 34.1	17 11.4	23 9.0	5 58.1	28 13.2	13 27.8	8 57.1
25 Su	10 17 30	5 54 16	5♏15 46	11♏23 4	17 53.2	9 46.6	12 49.1	17 58.4	23 23.2	6 4.6	28 10.6	13 27.4	8 55.6
26 M	10 21 27	6 54 35	17 33 46	23 48 21	17 51.2	10 28.1	14 4.0	18 45.4	23 37.4	6 11.1	28 8.0	13 27.0	8 54.0
27 Tu	10 25 23	7 54 53	0♐ 7 18	6♐31 5	17D 50.1	11 13.4	15 19.0	19 32.4	23 51.5	6 17.6	28 5.5	13 26.6	8 52.5
28 W	10 29 20	8 55 9	13 0 8	19 34 53	17 50.0	12 2.4	16 34.0	20 19.4	24 5.7	6 24.0	28 2.9	13 26.1	8 50.9

Astro Data Dy Hr Mn	Planet Ingress Dy Hr Mn	Last Aspect Dy Hr Mn	☽ Ingress Dy Hr Mn	Last Aspect Dy Hr Mn	☽ Ingress Dy Hr Mn	☽ Phases & Eclipses Dy Hr Mn	Astro Data
♄⚻♅ 5 1:09	♄ ♒ 3 19:01	3 6:16 ♄ ⚹	♐ 3 6:23	1 19:45 ♅ △	♑ 1 21:10	6 12:35 ● 15♑43	1 JANUARY 1962
☽0N 12 6:38	☿ ♒ 7 15:08	4 2:06 ♃ ⚹	♑ 5 10:24	2 19:50 ♆ ⚹	♒ 3 22:57	13 5:01 ☽ 22♈32	Julian Day # 22646
♃□♆ 13 2:40	♅ ♌ 10 5:55	7 11:37 ☿ ☌	♒ 7 12:00	5 21:18 ♅ ☍	♓ 5 22:53	20 18:16 ○ 0♌13	Delta T 34.0 sec
☽0S 26 14:22	☉ ♒ 20 12:58	8 9:22 ♆ □	♓ 9 12:53	6 20:19 ♆ △	♈ 7 22:50	28 23:36 ☽ 8♏35	SVP 05♓47'36"
☿ R 27 15:30	♀ ♒ 21 20:31	10 22:11 ☉ ⚹	♈ 11 14:34	9 22:36 ♅ △	♉ 10 0:35		Obliquity 23°26'32"
		13 17:50 ♅ △	♉ 13 18:01	12 3:01 ♅ □	♊ 12 5:18	5 0:10 ● 15♒43	⚷ Chiron 3♓04.6
☽0N 8 14:35	♂ ♒ 1 23:06	15 23:22 ♅ □	♊ 15 23:42	14 12:48 ♀ △	♋ 14 13:20	5 0:12:04 ☍T 4'08"	☽ Mean ☊ 20♌00.8
♆ R 13 20:07	♀ ♓ 14 18:09	18 7:10 ♅ ⚹	♋ 18 7:39	15 15:28 ♆ △	♌ 17 0:04	11 15:43 ☽ 22♉27	
☿ D 17 21:35	☉ ♓ 19 3:15	20 14:45 ♀ ☍	♌ 20 17:50	19 9:15 ♅ ☌	♍ 19 12:27	19 13:18 ○ 0♍25	1 FEBRUARY 1962
☽0S 22 20:46		23 5:00 ♅ ☌	♍ 23 5:53	20 15:49 ♆ ⚹	♎ 22 1:22	19 13:03 ☍A 0.612	Julian Day # 22677
		25 6:47 ♂ △	♎ 25 18:52	24 10:02 ♅ ⚹	♏ 24 13:36	27 15:50 ☽ 8♐35	Delta T 34.0 sec
		28 5:39 ♅ ⚹	♏ 28 6:54	26 20:10 ♅ □	♐ 26 23:46		SVP 05♓47'32"
		30 14:39 ♅ □	♐ 30 15:59				Obliquity 23°26'32"
							⚷ Chiron 4♓46.2
							☽ Mean ☊ 18♌22.3

MARCH 1962 LONGITUDE

Day	Sid.Time	☉	0 hr ☽	Noon ☽	True ☊	☿	♀	♂	♃	♄	♅	♆	♇
1 Th	10 33 16	9♓55 24	26♐15 42	3♑ 2 54	17♌50.7	12♒54.7	17♓48.9	21♒ 6.5	24♒19.8	6♒30.4	28♌ 0.3	13♏25.7	8♍49.3
2 F	10 37 13	10 55 38	9♑56 40	16 57 7	17 52.0	13 50.1	19 3.8	21 53.5	24 33.9	6 36.7	27R 57.8	13R 25.1	8R 47.8
3 Sa	10 41 9	11 55 50	24 4 12	1♒17 41	17 53.5	14 48.3	20 18.7	22 40.6	24 48.0	6 43.0	27 55.2	13 24.6	8 46.2
4 Su	10 45 6	12 56 0	8♒37 13	16 2 13	17R 54.6	15 49.3	21 33.6	23 27.7	25 2.0	6 49.3	27 52.7	13 24.0	8 44.7
5 M	10 49 3	13 56 9	23 31 57	1♓ 5 27	17 54.8	16 52.9	22 48.5	24 14.7	25 16.0	6 55.5	27 50.2	13 23.4	8 43.1
6 Tu	10 52 59	14 56 16	8♓41 38	16 19 18	17 53.6	17 58.7	24 3.3	25 1.8	25 30.0	7 1.6	27 47.7	13 22.8	8 41.6
7 W	10 56 56	15 56 21	23 57 9	1♈33 52	17 51.0	19 6.8	25 18.1	25 48.9	25 44.0	7 7.7	27 45.2	13 22.1	8 40.0
8 Th	11 0 52	16 56 24	9♈ 8 10	16 38 51	17 47.2	20 17.0	26 32.9	26 36.0	25 57.9	7 13.8	27 42.8	13 21.4	8 38.5
9 F	11 4 49	17 56 25	24 4 51	1♉25 17	17 42.8	21 29.2	27 47.7	27 23.1	26 11.8	7 19.8	27 40.3	13 20.6	8 36.9
10 Sa	11 8 45	18 56 24	8♉39 25	15 46 47	17 38.4	22 43.3	29 2.5	28 10.2	26 25.6	7 25.8	27 37.9	13 19.9	8 35.4
11 Su	11 12 42	19 56 21	22 47 3	29 40 8	17 34.8	23 59.2	0♈17.2	28 57.3	26 39.4	7 31.7	27 35.5	13 19.1	8 33.9
12 M	11 16 38	20 56 16	6♊26 5	13♊ 5 8	17 32.3	25 16.8	1 31.9	29 44.4	26 53.2	7 37.5	27 33.2	13 18.3	8 32.3
13 Tu	11 20 35	21 56 8	19 37 35	26 3 52	17D 31.3	26 36.0	2 46.6	0♓31.4	27 6.9	7 43.3	27 30.8	13 17.4	8 30.8
14 W	11 24 32	22 55 59	2♋24 29	8♋39 59	17 31.7	27 56.9	4 1.3	1 18.5	27 20.6	7 49.1	27 28.5	13 16.6	8 29.3
15 Th	11 28 28	23 55 47	14 50 55	20 57 53	17 33.1	29 19.3	5 15.9	2 5.6	27 34.2	7 54.8	27 26.2	13 15.6	8 27.8
16 F	11 32 25	24 55 33	27 1 26	3♌ 2 9	17 34.8	0♓43.1	6 30.5	2 52.7	27 47.8	8 0.4	27 24.0	13 14.7	8 26.4
17 Sa	11 36 21	25 55 16	9♌ 0 34	14 57 11	17R 36.2	2 8.5	7 45.1	3 39.8	28 1.4	8 6.0	27 21.8	13 13.8	8 24.9
18 Su	11 40 18	26 54 58	20 52 29	26 46 53	17 36.5	3 35.3	8 59.6	4 26.8	28 14.9	8 11.5	27 19.6	13 12.8	8 23.4
19 M	11 44 14	27 54 37	2♍40 49	8♍34 38	17 35.2	5 3.4	10 14.1	5 13.9	28 28.3	8 17.0	27 17.4	13 11.8	8 21.9
20 Tu	11 48 11	28 54 14	14 28 38	20 23 8	17 31.9	6 33.0	11 28.6	6 1.0	28 41.7	8 22.4	27 15.3	13 10.7	8 20.5
21 W	11 52 7	29 53 49	26 18 23	2♎14 37	17 26.5	8 3.9	12 43.1	6 48.0	28 55.1	8 27.7	27 13.2	13 9.7	8 19.1
22 Th	11 56 4	0♈53 22	8♎12 3	14 10 52	17 19.4	9 36.2	13 57.5	7 35.1	29 8.4	8 33.0	27 11.1	13 8.6	8 17.6
23 F	12 0 1	1 52 53	20 11 16	26 13 25	17 11.1	11 9.8	15 11.9	8 22.1	29 21.6	8 38.2	27 9.1	13 7.5	8 16.2
24 Sa	12 3 57	2 52 22	2♏17 32	8♏23 48	17 2.3	12 44.7	16 26.3	9 9.2	29 34.8	8 43.3	27 7.1	13 6.3	8 14.8
25 Su	12 7 54	3 51 49	14 32 26	20 43 41	16 54.0	14 21.0	17 40.7	9 56.2	29 47.9	8 48.4	27 5.1	13 5.2	8 13.4
26 M	12 11 50	4 51 14	26 57 47	3♐15 3	16 46.8	15 58.6	18 55.0	10 43.2	0♓ 1.0	8 53.4	27 3.2	13 4.0	8 12.1
27 Tu	12 15 47	5 50 38	9♐35 46	16 0 15	16 41.5	17 37.6	20 9.3	11 30.2	0 14.0	8 58.4	27 1.3	13 2.8	8 10.7
28 W	12 19 43	6 49 59	22 28 53	29 1 59	16 38.3	19 17.9	21 23.6	12 17.2	0 27.0	9 3.3	26 59.5	13 1.6	8 9.4
29 Th	12 23 40	7 49 19	5♑39 54	12♑22 58	16D 37.2	20 59.6	22 37.9	13 4.2	0 39.9	9 8.1	26 57.7	13 0.4	8 8.1
30 F	12 27 36	8 48 38	19 11 27	26 5 36	16 37.6	22 42.6	23 52.1	13 51.2	0 52.7	9 12.8	26 55.9	12 59.1	8 6.8
31 Sa	12 31 33	9 47 54	3♒ 5 33	10♒11 20	16R 38.6	24 27.0	25 6.3	14 38.2	1 5.5	9 17.5	26 54.2	12 57.8	8 5.5

APRIL 1962 LONGITUDE

Day	Sid.Time	☉	0 hr ☽	Noon ☽	True ☊	☿	♀	♂	♃	♄	♅	♆	♇
1 Su	12 35 30	10♈47 9	17♒22 51	24♒39 50	16♌39.1	26♓12.7	26♈20.5	15♓25.2	1♓18.2	9♒22.1	26♌52.5	12♏56.5	8♍ 4.2
2 M	12 39 26	11 46 22	2♓ 1 53	9♓28 23	16R 38.1	27 59.9	27 34.6	16 12.1	1 30.9	9 26.6	26R 50.8	12R 55.2	8R 3.0
3 Tu	12 43 23	12 45 33	16 58 30	24 31 18	16 34.9	29 48.5	28 48.8	16 59.0	1 43.4	9 31.1	26 49.2	12 53.8	8 1.7
4 W	12 47 19	13 44 42	2♈ 5 39	9♈40 18	16 29.3	1♈38.4	0♉ 2.8	17 46.0	1 55.9	9 35.5	26 47.7	12 52.5	8 0.5
5 Th	12 51 16	14 43 49	17 14 0	24 45 26	16 21.5	3 29.8	1 16.9	18 32.8	2 8.4	9 39.8	26 46.2	12 51.1	7 59.3
6 F	12 55 12	15 42 54	2♉13 24	9♉36 44	16 12.3	5 22.7	2 31.0	19 19.7	2 20.7	9 44.0	26 44.7	12 49.7	7 58.1
7 Sa	12 59 9	16 41 57	16 54 31	24 5 58	16 3.0	7 16.9	3 45.0	20 6.6	2 33.0	9 48.1	26 43.3	12 48.3	7 57.0
8 Su	13 3 5	17 40 58	1♊10 31	8♊ 7 49	15 54.5	9 12.5	4 58.9	20 53.4	2 45.2	9 52.2	26 41.9	12 46.8	7 55.8
9 M	13 7 2	18 39 57	14 57 45	21 40 19	15 47.9	11 9.6	6 12.9	21 40.3	2 57.3	9 56.2	26 40.6	12 45.4	7 54.7
10 Tu	13 10 58	19 38 53	28 15 46	4♋44 26	15 43.5	13 8.0	7 26.8	22 27.0	3 9.4	10 0.1	26 39.3	12 43.9	7 53.6
11 W	13 14 55	20 37 47	11♋ 6 48	17 23 23	15D 41.4	15 7.8	8 40.7	23 13.8	3 21.4	10 3.9	26 38.0	12 42.5	7 52.6
12 Th	13 18 52	21 36 39	23 34 50	29 41 46	15 40.9	17 8.9	9 54.5	24 0.6	3 33.2	10 7.7	26 36.9	12 41.0	7 51.5
13 F	13 22 48	22 35 29	5♌44 51	11♌44 47	15R 41.4	19 11.3	11 8.3	24 47.3	3 45.0	10 11.3	26 35.7	12 39.5	7 50.5
14 Sa	13 26 45	23 34 16	17 42 13	23 37 47	15 41.6	21 14.7	12 22.1	25 34.0	3 56.8	10 14.9	26 34.6	12 38.0	7 49.5
15 Su	13 30 41	24 33 1	29 32 7	5♍25 47	15 40.7	23 19.3	13 35.9	26 20.7	4 8.4	10 18.4	26 33.6	12 36.4	7 48.5
16 M	13 34 38	25 31 44	11♍19 18	17 13 12	15 37.6	25 24.8	14 49.6	27 7.3	4 19.9	10 21.8	26 32.6	12 34.9	7 47.6
17 Tu	13 38 34	26 30 24	23 7 52	29 3 44	15 32.0	27 31.1	16 3.2	27 53.9	4 31.4	10 25.2	26 31.7	12 33.4	7 46.6
18 W	13 42 31	27 29 3	5♎ 1 6	11♎ 0 16	15 23.6	29 37.9	17 16.9	28 40.5	4 42.7	10 28.4	26 30.8	12 31.8	7 45.7
19 Th	13 46 27	28 27 39	17 1 28	23 4 52	15 12.9	1♉45.2	18 30.5	29 27.1	4 54.0	10 31.6	26 29.9	12 30.2	7 44.9
20 F	13 50 24	29 26 13	29 10 37	5♏18 49	15 0.4	3 52.7	19 44.0	0♈13.6	5 5.2	10 34.6	26 29.1	12 28.7	7 44.0
21 Sa	13 54 21	0♉24 46	11♏29 33	17 42 53	14 47.3	6 0.1	20 57.6	1 0.1	5 16.2	10 37.6	26 28.4	12 27.1	7 43.2
22 Su	13 58 17	1 23 17	23 58 51	0♐17 30	14 34.6	8 7.1	22 11.1	1 46.6	5 27.2	10 40.5	26 27.7	12 25.5	7 42.4
23 M	14 2 14	2 21 46	6♐38 53	13 3 4	14 23.4	10 13.5	23 24.5	2 33.1	5 38.1	10 43.3	26 27.1	12 23.9	7 41.6
24 Tu	14 6 10	3 20 13	19 30 9	26 0 14	14 14.7	12 18.9	24 38.0	3 19.5	5 48.9	10 46.0	26 26.5	12 22.3	7 40.8
25 W	14 10 7	4 18 39	2♑33 28	9♑10 0	14 8.8	14 23.0	25 51.4	4 5.9	5 59.6	10 48.7	26 26.0	12 20.7	7 40.1
26 Th	14 14 3	5 17 3	15 50 2	22 33 46	14 5.6	16 25.5	27 4.7	4 52.3	6 10.2	10 51.2	26 25.5	12 19.1	7 39.4
27 F	14 18 0	6 15 25	29 21 23	6♒13 4	14D 4.5	18 26.1	28 18.1	5 38.6	6 20.6	10 53.7	26 25.1	12 17.4	7 38.7
28 Sa	14 21 56	7 13 46	13♒ 8 59	20 9 13	14R 4.4	20 24.4	29 31.4	6 24.9	6 31.0	10 56.0	26 24.7	12 15.8	7 38.1
29 Su	14 25 53	8 12 5	27 13 47	4♓22 35	14 4.1	22 20.3	0♊44.6	7 11.2	6 41.3	10 58.3	26 24.4	12 14.2	7 37.5
30 M	14 29 50	9 10 23	11♓35 27	18 52 0	14 2.3	24 13.5	1 57.9	7 57.5	6 51.4	11 0.5	26 24.1	12 12.6	7 36.9

Astro Data Dy Hr Mn	Planet Ingress Dy Hr Mn	Last Aspect Dy Hr Mn	☽ Ingress Dy Hr Mn	Last Aspect Dy Hr Mn	☽ Ingress Dy Hr Mn	☽ Phases & Eclipses Dy Hr Mn
☽0N 8 0:38	♀ ♈ 10 18:28	1 3:05 ♅ △	♑ 1 6:38	1 16:06 ♀ ✶	♓ 1 20:42	6 10:31 ● 15♓23
♀0N 13 2:09	♂ ♓ 12 7:58	2 17:05 ♀ ✶	♒ 3 9:52	3 0:01 ♂ ☌	♈ 3 20:41	13 4:39 ☽ 22♊08
♃☍♅ 14 11:57	☿ ♓ 15 11:43	5 6:49 ♅ ☍	♓ 5 10:16	5 15:12 ♅ △	♉ 5 20:25	21 7:55 ○ 0♎13
♄⊼♇ 19 17:26	☉ ♈ 21 2:30	7 2:19 ♀ ☌	♈ 7 9:32	7 16:24 ♅ □	♊ 7 22:00	29 4:11 ☽ 7♑60
☽0S 22 2:28	♃ ♓ 25 22:07	9 5:50 ♅ △	♉ 9 9:40	9 21:03 ♅ ✶	♋ 10 3:12	
		11 11:24 ♂ □	♊ 11 12:35	12 0:54 ♂ △	♌ 12 12:36	4 19:45 ● 14♈33
☽0N 4 11:38	☿ ♈ 3 2:32	13 14:41 ♅ ✶	♋ 13 19:25	14 17:57 ♅ ☌	♍ 15 0:57	11 19:50 ☽ 21♋26
☿0N 5 13:00	♀ ♉ 3 23:05	15 19:28 ☉ △	♌ 16 5:56	17 10:19 ♂ ☍	♎ 17 13:54	20 0:33 ○ 29♎28
☽0S 18 8:56	☿ ♉ 18 4:10	18 15:16 ♃ ☍	♍ 18 18:33	20 0:33 ☉ ☍	♏ 20 1:37	27 12:59 ☽ 6♒47
♂0N 22 23:20	♂ ♈ 19 16:58	19 21:22 ♆ ✶	♎ 21 7:28	22 4:43 ♅ □	♐ 22 11:27	
	☉ ♉ 20 13:51	23 18:33 ♃ △	♏ 23 19:29	24 12:48 ♅ △	♑ 24 19:20	
	♀ ♊ 28 9:23	26 0:10 ♅ □	♐ 26 5:49	26 21:58 ♀ △	♒ 27 1:08	
		28 8:15 ♅ △	♑ 28 13:46	28 22:37 ♅ ☍	♓ 29 4:40	
		30 8:57 ♀ □	♒ 30 18:43			

Astro Data

1 MARCH 1962
Julian Day # 22705
Delta T 34.1 sec
SVP 05♓47'28"
Obliquity 23°26'33"
⚷ Chiron 6♓34.6
☽ Mean ☊ 16♌53.3

1 APRIL 1962
Julian Day # 22736
Delta T 34.1 sec
SVP 05♓47'26"
Obliquity 23°26'33"
⚷ Chiron 8♓31.0
☽ Mean ☊ 15♌14.8

LONGITUDE — MAY 1962

Day	Sid.Time	☉	0 hr ☽	Noon ☽	True ☊	☿	♀	♂	♃	♄	♅	♆	♇
1 Tu	14 33 46	10♉ 8 39	26♓11 46	3♈34 5	13♌58.1	26♉ 3.6	3♊11.1	8♈43.7	7♓ 1.5	11♒ 2.5	26♌23.9	12♏10.9	7♍36.3
2 W	14 37 43	11 6 54	10♈58 10	18 23 6	13R51.0	27 50.6	4 24.2	9 29.8	7 11.4	11 4.5	26R23.8	12R 9.3	7R35.8
3 Th	14 41 39	12 5 7	25 47 52	3♉11 25	13 41.5	29 34.3	5 37.4	10 16.0	7 21.2	11 6.4	26 23.7	12 7.7	7 35.3
4 F	14 45 36	13 3 19	10♉32 39	17 50 32	13 30.3	1♊14.5	6 50.5	11 2.1	7 30.9	11 8.2	26D23.6	12 6.0	7 34.8
5 Sa	14 49 32	14 1 29	25 4 8	2♊12 37	13 18.6	2 51.0	8 3.5	11 48.1	7 40.5	11 9.9	26 23.6	12 4.4	7 34.4
6 Su	14 53 29	14 59 37	9♊15 18	16 11 43	13 7.8	4 23.8	9 16.5	12 34.2	7 50.0	11 11.5	26 23.7	12 2.7	7 34.0
7 M	14 57 25	15 57 43	23 1 32	29 44 37	12 58.9	5 52.8	10 29.5	13 20.1	7 59.3	11 13.0	26 23.8	12 1.1	7 33.6
8 Tu	15 1 22	16 55 48	6♋21 2	12♋50 56	12 52.5	7 17.8	11 42.5	14 6.1	8 8.6	11 14.4	26 24.0	11 59.5	7 33.2
9 W	15 5 19	17 53 51	19 14 40	25 32 40	12 48.8	8 38.8	12 55.4	14 52.0	8 17.7	11 15.7	26 24.2	11 57.9	7 32.9
10 Th	15 9 15	18 51 52	1♌45 27	7♌53 36	12D47.2	9 55.8	14 8.3	15 37.8	8 26.6	11 16.9	26 24.5	11 56.2	7 32.6
11 F	15 13 12	19 49 51	13 57 46	19 58 37	12R46.9	11 8.6	15 21.1	16 23.6	8 35.5	11 18.0	26 24.8	11 54.6	7 32.3
12 Sa	15 17 8	20 47 48	25 56 49	1♍53 4	12 46.9	12 17.2	16 33.9	17 9.4	8 44.2	11 19.1	26 25.2	11 53.0	7 32.1
13 Su	15 21 5	21 45 43	7♍48 3	13 42 25	12 46.0	13 21.6	17 46.6	17 55.1	8 52.8	11 20.0	26 25.6	11 51.4	7 31.9
14 M	15 25 1	22 43 36	19 36 48	25 31 46	12 43.3	14 21.6	18 59.3	18 40.8	9 1.2	11 20.8	26 26.1	11 49.8	7 31.7
15 Tu	15 28 58	23 41 28	1♎27 54	7♎25 40	12 38.2	15 17.2	20 12.0	19 26.4	9 9.5	11 21.5	26 26.7	11 48.2	7 31.5
16 W	15 32 54	24 39 18	13 25 32	19 27 51	12 30.4	16 8.4	21 24.6	20 12.0	9 17.7	11 22.2	26 27.3	11 46.6	7 31.4
17 Th	15 36 51	25 37 6	25 32 58	1♏41 6	12 20.3	16 55.1	22 37.2	20 57.5	9 25.8	11 22.7	26 27.9	11 45.0	7 31.3
18 F	15 40 48	26 34 53	7♏52 28	14 7 9	12 8.5	17 37.1	23 49.7	21 43.0	9 33.7	11 23.1	26 28.6	11 43.5	7 31.3
19 Sa	15 44 44	27 32 39	20 25 15	26 46 43	11 56.0	18 14.6	25 2.2	22 28.5	9 41.4	11 23.5	26 29.4	11 41.9	7D31.2
20 Su	15 48 41	28 30 22	3♐11 33	9♐39 39	11 43.8	18 47.3	26 14.6	23 13.9	9 49.1	11 23.7	26 30.2	11 40.4	7 31.3
21 M	15 52 37	29 28 5	16 10 54	22 45 11	11 33.2	19 15.3	27 27.0	23 59.2	9 56.5	11R23.8	26 31.1	11 38.8	7 31.3
22 Tu	15 56 34	0♊25 47	29 22 21	6♑ 2 17	11 24.8	19 38.5	28 39.4	24 44.6	10 3.9	11 23.9	26 32.0	11 37.3	7 31.4
23 W	16 0 30	1 23 27	12♑44 54	19 30 4	11 19.2	19 56.9	29 51.7	25 29.8	10 11.1	11 23.8	26 33.0	11 35.8	7 31.4
24 Th	16 4 27	2 21 6	26 17 45	3♒ 7 54	11 16.3	20 10.5	1♋ 3.9	26 15.0	10 18.1	11 23.7	26 34.0	11 34.3	7 31.6
25 F	16 8 23	3 18 44	10♒ 0 31	16 55 34	11D15.5	20 19.4	2 16.1	27 0.2	10 25.0	11 23.4	26 35.0	11 32.8	7 31.7
26 Sa	16 12 20	4 16 21	23 53 4	0♓52 59	11R15.7	20R23.5	3 28.3	27 45.3	10 31.8	11 23.1	26 36.2	11 31.3	7 31.9
27 Su	16 16 17	5 13 58	7♓55 18	14 59 55	11 16.0	20 22.9	4 40.4	28 30.4	10 38.4	11 22.6	26 37.3	11 29.8	7 32.1
28 M	16 20 13	6 11 33	22 6 41	29 15 23	11 15.0	20 17.9	5 52.5	29 15.4	10 44.8	11 22.1	26 38.6	11 28.4	7 32.4
29 Tu	16 24 10	7 9 7	6♈25 42	13♈37 16	11 11.9	20 8.5	7 4.6	0♉ 0.4	10 51.1	11 21.5	26 39.8	11 26.9	7 32.6
30 W	16 28 6	8 6 41	20 49 33	28 2 0	11 6.5	19 54.9	8 16.6	0 45.3	10 57.2	11 20.7	26 41.2	11 25.5	7 32.9
31 Th	16 32 3	9 4 14	5♉13 57	12♉24 42	10 58.9	19 37.4	9 28.5	1 30.2	11 3.2	11 19.9	26 42.5	11 24.1	7 33.3

LONGITUDE — JUNE 1962

Day	Sid.Time	☉	0 hr ☽	Noon ☽	True ☊	☿	♀	♂	♃	♄	♅	♆	♇
1 F	16 35 59	10♊ 1 46	19♉33 32	26♉39 42	10♌49.7	19♊16.3	10♋40.4	2♉15.0	11♓ 9.0	11♒19.0	26♌44.0	11♏22.7	7♍33.7
2 Sa	16 39 56	10 59 17	3♊42 31	10♊41 21	10R40.1	18R52.1	11 52.3	2 59.8	11 14.6	11R18.0	26 45.4	11R21.3	7 34.0
3 Su	16 43 52	11 56 47	17 35 38	24 24 58	10 31.2	18 25.0	13 4.1	3 44.5	11 20.1	11 16.8	26 47.0	11 19.9	7 34.5
4 M	16 47 49	12 54 16	1♋ 8 59	7♋47 32	10 23.8	17 55.5	14 15.9	4 29.1	11 25.4	11 15.6	26 48.5	11 18.6	7 34.9
5 Tu	16 51 46	13 51 44	14 20 31	20 48 0	10 18.6	17 24.3	15 27.6	5 13.7	11 30.5	11 14.3	26 50.2	11 17.3	7 35.4
6 W	16 55 42	14 49 11	27 10 11	3♌27 20	10 15.7	16 51.7	16 39.3	5 58.3	11 35.5	11 12.9	26 51.8	11 16.0	7 35.9
7 Th	16 59 39	15 46 37	9♌39 49	15 48 6	10D14.8	16 18.3	17 50.9	6 42.7	11 40.3	11 11.5	26 53.6	11 14.7	7 36.5
8 F	17 3 35	16 44 1	21 52 41	27 54 8	10 15.3	15 44.8	19 2.4	7 27.2	11 44.9	11 9.9	26 55.3	11 13.4	7 37.1
9 Sa	17 7 32	17 41 25	3♍53 5	9♍50 8	10 16.4	15 11.6	20 13.9	8 11.5	11 49.4	11 8.2	26 57.1	11 12.2	7 37.7
10 Su	17 11 28	18 38 47	15 45 57	21 41 11	10R17.1	14 39.4	21 25.3	8 55.8	11 53.6	11 6.4	26 59.0	11 11.0	7 38.3
11 M	17 15 25	19 36 9	27 36 28	3♎32 27	10 16.8	14 8.7	22 36.7	9 40.0	11 57.7	11 4.6	27 0.9	11 9.8	7 39.0
12 Tu	17 19 21	20 33 29	9♎29 43	15 28 53	10 14.7	13 40.1	23 48.0	10 24.2	12 1.7	11 2.7	27 2.9	11 8.6	7 39.7
13 W	17 23 18	21 30 48	21 30 28	27 34 57	10 10.8	13 13.9	24 59.3	11 8.3	12 5.4	11 0.6	27 4.9	11 7.4	7 40.4
14 Th	17 27 15	22 28 7	3♏42 46	9♏54 18	10 5.0	12 50.7	26 10.5	11 52.4	12 9.0	10 58.5	27 6.9	11 6.3	7 41.1
15 F	17 31 11	23 25 25	16 9 50	22 29 35	9 57.9	12 30.9	27 21.6	12 36.4	12 12.4	10 56.3	27 9.0	11 5.2	7 41.9
16 Sa	17 35 8	24 22 42	28 53 42	5♐22 13	9 50.1	12 14.7	28 32.7	13 20.3	12 15.6	10 54.0	27 11.1	11 4.1	7 42.7
17 Su	17 39 4	25 19 58	11♐55 7	18 32 19	9 42.5	12 2.4	29 43.7	14 4.2	12 18.6	10 51.7	27 13.3	11 3.0	7 43.6
18 M	17 43 1	26 17 14	25 13 36	1♑58 44	9 35.9	11 54.4	0♌54.6	14 48.0	12 21.4	10 49.2	27 15.5	11 2.0	7 44.4
19 Tu	17 46 57	27 14 29	8♑47 27	15 39 25	9 30.9	11D50.7	2 5.5	15 31.7	12 24.1	10 46.7	27 17.8	11 1.0	7 45.3
20 W	17 50 54	28 11 43	22 34 15	29 31 37	9 27.8	11 51.5	3 16.3	16 15.4	12 26.6	10 44.1	27 20.0	10 60.0	7 46.2
21 Th	17 54 50	29 8 58	6♒31 9	13♒32 30	9D26.6	11 56.9	4 27.0	16 59.1	12 28.9	10 41.4	27 22.4	10 59.0	7 47.2
22 F	17 58 47	0♋ 6 12	20 35 19	27 39 19	9 27.0	12 7.0	5 37.7	17 42.6	12 31.0	10 38.7	27 24.8	10 58.1	7 48.2
23 Sa	18 2 44	1 3 26	4♓44 12	11♓49 42	9 28.2	12 21.8	6 48.3	18 26.1	12 32.9	10 35.8	27 27.2	10 57.1	7 49.2
24 Su	18 6 40	2 0 39	18 55 35	26 1 37	9 29.5	12 41.2	7 58.8	19 9.6	12 34.6	10 32.9	27 29.6	10 56.2	7 50.2
25 M	18 10 37	2 57 53	3♈ 7 34	10♈13 11	9R30.0	13 5.4	9 9.3	19 53.0	12 36.1	10 29.9	27 32.1	10 55.4	7 51.2
26 Tu	18 14 33	3 55 6	17 18 14	24 22 27	9 29.3	13 34.3	10 19.7	20 36.3	12 37.4	10 26.9	27 34.7	10 54.5	7 52.3
27 W	18 18 30	4 52 20	1♉25 33	8♉27 12	9 27.1	14 7.8	11 30.0	21 19.5	12 38.6	10 23.7	27 37.3	10 53.7	7 53.4
28 Th	18 22 26	5 49 34	15 27 5	22 24 52	9 23.5	14 45.8	12 40.3	22 2.7	12 39.5	10 20.5	27 39.9	10 52.9	7 54.6
29 F	18 26 23	6 46 48	29 20 12	6♊12 42	9 18.9	15 28.4	13 50.5	22 45.8	12 40.3	10 17.3	27 42.5	10 52.2	7 55.7
30 Sa	18 30 19	7 44 1	13♊ 2 4	19 47 58	9 14.0	16 15.4	15 0.6	23 28.9	12 40.8	10 13.9	27 45.2	10 51.5	7 56.9

Astro Data Dy Hr Mn	Planet Ingress Dy Hr Mn	Last Aspect Dy Hr Mn	☽ Ingress Dy Hr Mn	Last Aspect Dy Hr Mn	☽ Ingress Dy Hr Mn	☽ Phases & Eclipses Dy Hr Mn	Astro Data
☽0N 1 21:51	☿ ♊ 3 6:05	30 23:45 ☿ ⚹	♈ 1 6:12	1 12:09 ♅ □	♊ 1 17:40	4 4:25 ● 13♉14	1 MAY 1962
♃☍♇ 4 9:13	☉ ♊ 21 13:17	3 0:58 ♅ △	♉ 3 6:49	3 16:14 ♅ ⚹	♋ 3 21:56	11 12:44 ☽ 20♌21	Julian Day # 22766
♅ D 4 8:57	♀ ♋ 23 2:46	5 2:13 ♅ □	♊ 5 8:16	5 2:17 ♀ ☌	♌ 6 5:23	19 14:32 ○ 28♏08	Delta T 34.2 sec
☽0S 15 16:49	♂ ♉ 28 23:47	7 6:00 ♅ ⚹	♋ 7 12:28	8 10:04 ♅ ☌	♍ 8 16:12	26 19:05 ☽ 5♓02	SVP 05♓47'23"
♇ D 19 9:38		8 21:15 ☉ ⚹	♌ 9 20:35	10 12:45 ♀ ⚹	♎ 11 4:51		Obliquity 23°26'33"
♄ R 21 23:22	♀ ♌ 17 5:31	12 0:57 ♅ ☌	♍ 12 8:11	13 11:03 ♅ ⚹	♏ 13 16:45	2 13:27 ● 11♊31	⚷ Chiron 9♓59.5
☿ R 26 9:09	☉ ♋ 21 21:24	14 6:53 ☉ △	♎ 14 21:03	15 23:17 ♀ △	♐ 16 2:03	10 6:21 ☽ 18♍54	☽ Mean ☊ 13♌39.5
☽0N 29 6:07		17 1:48 ♅ ⚹	♏ 17 8:43	18 3:38 ♅ △	♑ 18 8:30	18 2:02 ○ 26♐22	
		19 14:32 ☉ ☍	♐ 19 18:02	19 12:26 ♂ △	♒ 20 12:49	24 23:42 ☽ 2♈57	1 JUNE 1962
♃⚺♄ 2 12:10		21 22:35 ♀ ☍	♑ 22 1:08	22 11:37 ♅ ☍	♓ 22 15:59		Julian Day # 22797
♃△♆ 2 23:30		23 23:55 ♂ □	♒ 24 6:31	24 0:25 ♂ ⚹	♈ 24 18:43		Delta T 34.2 sec
☽0S 12 1:43		26 7:01 ♂ ⚹	♓ 26 10:29	26 17:30 ♅ △	♉ 26 21:34		SVP 05♓47'19"
☿ D 19 7:45		27 20:58 ☿ □	♈ 28 13:15	28 21:10 ♅ □	♊ 29 1:09		Obliquity 23°26'32"
☽0N 25 12:36		30 9:46 ♅ △	♉ 30 15:17				⚷ Chiron 10♓48.3
							☽ Mean ☊ 12♌01.0

JULY 1962 LONGITUDE

Day	Sid.Time	☉	0 hr ☽	Noon ☽	True ☊	☿	♀	♂	♃	♄	♅	♆	♇
1 Su	18 34 16	8♋41 15	26♊30 8	3♋ 8 21	9♌ 9.4	17♊ 6.8	16♌10.6	24♉11.9	12♓41.2	10♒10.5	27♌47.9	10♏50.8	7♍58.1
2 M	18 38 13	9 38 29	9♋42 26	16 12 18	9R 5.8	18 2.6	17 20.5	24 54.8	12R 41.4	10R 7.1	27 50.7	10R 50.1	7 59.3
3 Tu	18 42 9	10 35 43	22 37 53	28 59 15	9 3.4	19 2.6	18 30.4	25 37.7	12 41.4	10 3.5	27 53.5	10 49.4	8 0.6
4 W	18 46 6	11 32 56	5♌16 30	11♌29 49	9D 2.3	20 6.8	19 40.2	26 20.4	12 41.1	9 60.0	27 56.3	10 48.8	8 1.9
5 Th	18 50 2	12 30 9	17 39 27	23 45 43	9 2.5	21 15.2	20 49.9	27 3.1	12 40.7	9 56.3	27 59.2	10 48.3	8 3.2
6 F	18 53 59	13 27 23	29 48 58	5♍49 39	9 3.7	22 27.8	21 59.5	27 45.8	12 40.1	9 52.6	28 2.1	10 47.7	8 4.5
7 Sa	18 57 55	14 24 36	11♍48 13	17 45 11	9 5.3	23 44.3	23 9.1	28 28.3	12 39.3	9 48.9	28 5.0	10 47.2	8 5.9
8 Su	19 1 52	15 21 48	23 41 6	29 36 31	9 6.9	25 4.9	24 18.5	29 10.8	12 38.3	9 45.0	28 8.0	10 46.7	8 7.2
9 M	19 5 48	16 19 1	5♎32 2	11♎28 15	9R 8.1	26 29.4	25 27.8	29 53.2	12 37.1	9 41.2	28 11.0	10 46.2	8 8.6
10 Tu	19 9 45	17 16 14	17 25 46	23 25 11	9 8.5	27 57.8	26 37.1	0♊35.6	12 35.7	9 37.3	28 14.0	10 45.8	8 10.1
11 W	19 13 42	18 13 26	29 27 4	5♏31 59	9 8.0	29 30.0	27 46.2	1 17.8	12 34.1	9 33.3	28 17.1	10 45.4	8 11.5
12 Th	19 17 38	19 10 39	11♏40 28	17 53 1	9 6.7	1♋ 5.9	28 55.3	2 0.0	12 32.4	9 29.3	28 20.2	10 45.0	8 13.0
13 F	19 21 35	20 7 51	24 10 2	0♐31 54	9 4.6	2 45.4	0♍ 4.2	2 42.1	12 30.4	9 25.3	28 23.3	10 44.7	8 14.5
14 Sa	19 25 31	21 5 4	6♐58 55	13 31 15	9 2.2	4 28.4	1 13.1	3 24.2	12 28.2	9 21.2	28 26.4	10 44.4	8 16.0
15 Su	19 29 28	22 2 16	20 9 3	26 52 18	8 59.8	6 14.8	2 21.8	4 6.2	12 25.9	9 17.1	28 29.6	10 44.1	8 17.5
16 M	19 33 24	22 59 29	3♑40 53	10♑34 36	8 57.7	8 4.4	3 30.4	4 48.1	12 23.4	9 12.9	28 32.8	10 43.8	8 19.0
17 Tu	19 37 21	23 56 42	17 33 7	24 36 2	8 56.2	9 56.9	4 38.9	5 29.9	12 20.7	9 8.7	28 36.0	10 43.6	8 20.6
18 W	19 41 17	24 53 56	1♒42 49	8♒52 54	8D 55.5	11 52.2	5 47.3	6 11.6	12 17.8	9 4.5	28 39.3	10 43.4	8 22.2
19 Th	19 45 14	25 51 10	16 5 37	23 20 20	8 55.5	13 50.0	6 55.6	6 53.3	12 14.7	9 0.2	28 42.6	10 43.3	8 23.8
20 F	19 49 11	26 48 24	0♓36 19	7♓52 54	8 56.0	15 50.1	8 3.7	7 34.9	12 11.4	8 55.9	28 45.9	10 43.2	8 25.4
21 Sa	19 53 7	27 45 39	15 9 24	22 25 13	8 56.9	17 52.1	9 11.8	8 16.4	12 8.0	8 51.6	28 49.2	10 43.1	8 27.1
22 Su	19 57 4	28 42 55	29 39 47	6♈52 33	8 57.7	19 55.8	10 19.7	8 57.9	12 4.3	8 47.3	28 52.5	10 43.0	8 28.7
23 M	20 1 0	29 40 11	14♈ 3 7	21 11 5	8 58.4	22 0.7	11 27.5	9 39.2	12 0.5	8 42.9	28 55.9	10D 43.0	8 30.4
24 Tu	20 4 57	0♌37 29	28 16 9	5♉18 5	8R 58.6	24 6.7	12 35.1	10 20.5	11 56.5	8 38.6	28 59.3	10 43.0	8 32.1
25 W	20 8 53	1 34 47	12♉16 42	19 11 52	8 58.5	26 13.3	13 42.7	11 1.8	11 52.4	8 34.2	29 2.7	10 43.0	8 33.8
26 Th	20 12 50	2 32 7	26 3 29	2♊51 29	8 58.1	28 20.3	14 50.1	11 42.9	11 48.0	8 29.7	29 6.1	10 43.1	8 35.6
27 F	20 16 46	3 29 27	9♊35 52	16 16 37	8 57.5	0♌27.4	15 57.4	12 24.0	11 43.5	8 25.3	29 9.6	10 43.2	8 37.3
28 Sa	20 20 43	4 26 49	22 53 44	29 27 16	8 57.0	2 34.2	17 4.5	13 5.0	11 38.9	8 20.9	29 13.1	10 43.3	8 39.1
29 Su	20 24 40	5 24 11	5♋57 16	12♋23 45	8 56.5	4 40.7	18 11.5	13 45.9	11 34.0	8 16.4	29 16.6	10 43.5	8 40.9
30 M	20 28 36	6 21 34	18 46 49	25 6 33	8 56.2	6 46.5	19 18.4	14 26.7	11 29.0	8 12.0	29 20.1	10 43.7	8 42.7
31 Tu	20 32 33	7 18 58	1♌23 2	7♌36 24	8D 56.1	8 51.4	20 25.1	15 7.4	11 23.9	8 7.5	29 23.6	10 43.9	8 44.5

AUGUST 1962 LONGITUDE

Day	Sid.Time	☉	0 hr ☽	Noon ☽	True ☊	☿	♀	♂	♃	♄	♅	♆	♇
1 W	20 36 29	8♌16 23	13♌46 48	19♌54 23	8♌56.1	10♌55.3	21♍31.7	15♊48.1	11♓18.6	8♒ 3.0	29♌27.2	10♏44.2	8♍46.3
2 Th	20 40 26	9 13 49	25 59 22	2♍ 1 59	8R 56.1	12 58.2	22 38.1	16 28.7	11R 13.1	7R 58.6	29 30.8	10 44.5	8 48.2
3 F	20 44 22	10 11 15	8♍ 2 28	14 1 9	8 56.0	14 59.7	23 44.4	17 9.1	11 7.5	7 54.1	29 34.3	10 44.8	8 50.0
4 Sa	20 48 19	11 8 43	19 58 21	25 54 26	8 55.8	16 60.0	24 50.5	17 49.5	11 1.7	7 49.7	29 37.9	10 45.2	8 51.9
5 Su	20 52 15	12 6 11	1♎49 47	7♎44 52	8 55.5	18 58.8	25 56.4	18 29.8	10 55.8	7 45.2	29 41.5	10 45.6	8 53.8
6 M	20 56 12	13 3 39	13 40 9	19 36 6	8 55.0	20 56.2	27 2.2	19 10.0	10 49.8	7 40.8	29 45.2	10 46.0	8 55.7
7 Tu	21 0 9	14 1 9	25 33 15	1♏32 8	8 54.6	22 52.1	28 7.8	19 50.2	10 43.6	7 36.3	29 48.8	10 46.5	8 57.6
8 W	21 4 5	14 58 39	7♏33 19	13 37 21	8D 54.3	24 46.5	29 13.2	20 30.2	10 37.3	7 31.9	29 52.5	10 47.0	8 59.5
9 Th	21 8 2	15 56 10	19 44 47	25 56 12	8 54.3	26 39.4	0♎18.4	21 10.2	10 30.9	7 27.5	29 56.1	10 47.5	9 1.4
10 F	21 11 58	16 53 42	2♐12 5	8♐32 58	8 54.6	28 30.7	1 23.4	21 50.0	10 24.3	7 23.2	29 59.8	10 48.0	9 3.4
11 Sa	21 15 55	17 51 15	14 59 16	21 31 23	8 55.2	0♍20.6	2 28.2	22 29.8	10 17.7	7 18.8	0♍ 3.5	10 48.6	9 5.3
12 Su	21 19 51	18 48 49	28 9 37	4♑54 9	8 56.0	2 8.9	3 32.9	23 9.5	10 10.9	7 14.5	0 7.2	10 49.3	9 7.3
13 M	21 23 48	19 46 24	11♑45 6	18 42 24	8 56.9	3 55.6	4 37.3	23 49.1	10 4.0	7 10.2	0 10.9	10 49.9	9 9.3
14 Tu	21 27 44	20 44 0	25 45 53	2♒55 12	8R 57.6	5 40.9	5 41.5	24 28.6	9 57.0	7 5.9	0 14.6	10 50.6	9 11.3
15 W	21 31 41	21 41 37	10♒ 9 51	17 29 13	8 57.8	7 24.7	6 45.4	25 8.0	9 50.0	7 1.7	0 18.3	10 51.3	9 13.2
16 Th	21 35 38	22 39 15	24 52 29	2♓18 46	8 57.4	9 7.0	7 49.2	25 47.3	9 42.8	6 57.4	0 22.0	10 52.0	9 15.2
17 F	21 39 34	23 36 54	9♓47 4	17 16 21	8 56.4	10 47.8	8 52.7	26 26.5	9 35.5	6 53.3	0 25.8	10 52.8	9 17.3
18 Sa	21 43 31	24 34 34	24 45 32	2♈13 35	8 54.7	12 27.2	9 55.9	27 5.7	9 28.2	6 49.1	0 29.5	10 53.6	9 19.3
19 Su	21 47 27	25 32 16	9♈39 31	17 2 27	8 52.7	14 5.2	10 59.0	27 44.7	9 20.8	6 45.0	0 33.2	10 54.5	9 21.3
20 M	21 51 24	26 30 0	24 21 37	1♉36 24	8 50.7	15 41.7	12 1.7	28 23.6	9 13.3	6 40.9	0 37.0	10 55.3	9 23.3
21 Tu	21 55 20	27 27 45	8♉46 19	15 51 1	8 49.2	17 16.7	13 4.2	29 2.5	9 5.7	6 36.9	0 40.7	10 56.2	9 25.4
22 W	21 59 17	28 25 32	22 50 20	29 44 11	8D 48.4	18 50.4	14 6.5	29 41.3	8 58.1	6 32.9	0 44.5	10 57.1	9 27.4
23 Th	22 3 13	29 23 21	6♊32 36	13♊15 44	8 48.4	20 22.6	15 8.5	0♋19.9	8 50.4	6 29.0	0 48.2	10 58.1	9 29.4
24 F	22 7 10	0♍21 12	19 53 47	26 27 1	8 49.3	21 53.4	16 10.2	0 58.5	8 42.7	6 25.1	0 52.0	10 59.1	9 31.5
25 Sa	22 11 7	1 19 4	2♋55 43	9♋20 12	8 50.7	23 22.8	17 11.6	1 37.0	8 34.9	6 21.3	0 55.8	11 0.1	9 33.6
26 Su	22 15 3	2 16 58	15 40 48	21 57 51	8 52.2	24 50.8	18 12.7	2 15.3	8 27.1	6 17.5	0 59.5	11 1.1	9 35.6
27 M	22 19 0	3 14 54	28 11 39	4♌22 31	8R 53.4	26 17.3	19 13.6	2 53.6	8 19.2	6 13.7	1 3.3	11 2.2	9 37.7
28 Tu	22 22 56	4 12 51	10♌30 43	16 36 33	8 53.8	27 42.3	20 14.1	3 31.8	8 11.3	6 10.1	1 7.0	11 3.3	9 39.8
29 W	22 26 53	5 10 50	22 40 15	28 42 4	8 53.0	29 5.8	21 14.3	4 9.8	8 3.4	6 6.4	1 10.8	11 4.5	9 41.8
30 Th	22 30 49	6 8 51	4♍42 13	10♍40 56	8 50.9	0♎27.9	22 14.2	4 47.8	7 55.5	6 2.9	1 14.5	11 5.6	9 43.9
31 F	22 34 46	7 6 53	16 38 27	22 34 58	8 47.4	1 48.3	23 13.7	5 25.6	7 47.6	5 59.4	1 18.3	11 6.8	9 46.0

Astro Data Dy Hr Mn	Planet Ingress Dy Hr Mn	Last Aspect Dy Hr Mn	☽ Ingress Dy Hr Mn	Last Aspect Dy Hr Mn	☽ Ingress Dy Hr Mn	☽ Phases & Eclipses Dy Hr Mn	Astro Data
♃ R 2 8:58	♂ ♊ 9 3:50	1 2:21 ♅ ⚹	♋ 1 6:19	2 7:01 ♅ ☌	♍ 2 7:57	1 23:52 ● 9♋38	1 JULY 1962
☽0S 9 10:33	☿ ♋ 11 7:36	3 5:59 ♂ ⚹	♌ 3 13:55	4 10:51 ♀ ☌	♎ 4 20:17	9 23:39 ☽ 17♎15	Julian Day # 22827
☽0N 22 18:37	♀ ♍ 12 22:32	5 20:27 ♅ ☌	♍ 6 0:22	7 8:36 ♅ ⚹	♏ 7 8:56	17 11:40 ○ 24♑25	Delta T 34.2 sec
♆ D 23 8:12	☉ ♌ 23 8:18	8 11:50 ♂ △	♎ 8 12:48	9 19:46 ♅ □	♐ 9 19:48	17 11:54 ☍ A 0.392	SVP 05♓47'13"
♄⚻♇ 25 1:14	☿ ♌ 26 18:50	11 0:07 ☿ △	♏ 11 1:05	11 14:30 ♂ ☍	♑ 12 3:18	24 4:18 ☽ 0♉48	Obliquity 23°26'32"
		13 8:00 ♅ □	♐ 13 11:00	12 22:24 ♆ ⚹	♒ 14 7:07	31 12:24 ● 7♌49	⚷ Chiron 10♓45.4R
☽0S 5 18:17	♀ ♎ 8 17:13	15 14:56 ♅ △	♑ 15 17:32	16 1:33 ♂ △	♓ 16 8:17	31 12:24:58 ☌ A 3'33"	☽ Mean ☊ 10♌25.7
♃△♆ 6 13:41	☿ ♍ 10 19:29	17 11:40 ☉ ☍	♒ 17 21:07	18 3:55 ♂ □	♈ 18 8:25		
♀0S 8 15:08	♅ ♍ 10 1:18	19 20:57 ♅ ☍	♓ 19 23:00	20 6:59 ♂ ⚹	♉ 20 9:20	8 15:55 ☽ 15♏37	1 AUGUST 1962
♃☍♇ 18 22:42	♂ ♋ 22 11:37	21 22:19 ☉ △	♈ 22 0:34	22 10:26 ☉ □	♊ 22 12:28	15 20:09 ○ 22♒30	Julian Day # 22858
☽0N 19 1:51	☉ ♍ 23 15:12	24 1:14 ♅ △	♉ 24 2:57	24 4:06 ☿ □	♋ 24 18:34	15 19:57 ☍ A 0.596	Delta T 34.3 sec
☿0S 28 15:00	☿ ♎ 29 15:48	26 5:23 ♅ □	♊ 26 6:57	26 19:50 ☿ ⚹	♌ 27 3:30	22 10:26 ☽ 28♉51	SVP 05♓47'08"
		28 11:37 ♅ ⚹	♋ 28 13:00	28 20:54 ♀ ⚹	♍ 29 14:36	30 3:09 ● 6♍16	Obliquity 23°26'33"
		30 1:05 ♀ ⚹	♌ 30 21:21				⚷ Chiron 9♓53.4R
							☽ Mean ☊ 8♌47.2

LONGITUDE — SEPTEMBER 1962

Day	Sid.Time	☉	0 hr ☽	Noon ☽	True ☊	☿	♀	♂	♃	♄	♅	♆	♇
1 Sa	22 38 42	8♍ 4 57	28♍30 44	4♎26 1	8♌42.7	3♎ 7.2	24♎12.8	6♋ 3.3	7♓39.7	5♒55.9	1♍22.0	11♏ 8.0	9♍48.1
2 Su	22 42 39	9 3 2	10♎21 3	16 16 9	8R37.4	4 24.4	25 11.6	6 41.0	7R31.7	5R52.6	1 25.7	11 9.3	9 50.1
3 M	22 46 36	10 1 9	22 11 38	28 7 52	8 31.9	5 40.0	26 10.0	7 18.5	7 23.8	5 49.3	1 29.5	11 10.5	9 52.2
4 Tu	22 50 32	10 59 17	4♏ 5 13	10♏ 4 6	8 26.9	6 53.7	27 8.1	7 55.9	7 15.9	5 46.0	1 33.2	11 11.8	9 54.3
5 W	22 54 29	11 57 27	16 4 58	22 8 18	8 22.9	8 5.7	28 5.7	8 33.1	7 8.0	5 42.9	1 36.9	11 13.2	9 56.4
6 Th	22 58 25	12 55 38	28 14 37	4♐24 25	8 20.2	9 15.7	29 2.8	9 10.3	7 0.1	5 39.8	1 40.6	11 14.5	9 58.4
7 F	23 2 22	13 53 51	10♐38 14	16 56 38	8D 19.1	10 23.7	29 59.6	9 47.3	6 52.3	5 36.8	1 44.3	11 15.9	10 0.5
8 Sa	23 6 18	14 52 6	23 20 7	29 49 13	8 19.4	11 29.6	0♏55.8	10 24.3	6 44.5	5 33.8	1 48.0	11 17.3	10 2.6
9 Su	23 10 15	15 50 22	6♑24 21	13♑ 5 56	8 20.6	12 33.3	1 51.6	11 1.1	6 36.8	5 30.9	1 51.7	11 18.7	10 4.7
10 M	23 14 11	16 48 39	19 54 16	26 49 34	8 22.1	13 34.6	2 46.9	11 37.8	6 29.1	5 28.2	1 55.4	11 20.2	10 6.7
11 Tu	23 18 8	17 46 58	3♒51 50	11♒ 1 1	8R23.0	14 33.3	3 41.7	12 14.4	6 21.5	5 25.5	1 59.0	11 21.7	10 8.8
12 W	23 22 5	18 45 19	18 16 46	25 38 38	8 22.7	15 29.4	4 36.0	12 50.8	6 13.9	5 22.8	2 2.7	11 23.2	10 10.9
13 Th	23 26 1	19 43 41	3♓ 5 53	10♓37 39	8 20.7	16 22.7	5 29.7	13 27.2	6 6.4	5 20.3	2 6.3	11 24.7	10 12.9
14 F	23 29 58	20 42 4	18 12 49	25 50 11	8 16.7	17 12.9	6 22.8	14 3.4	5 59.0	5 17.8	2 9.9	11 26.3	10 15.0
15 Sa	23 33 54	21 40 30	3♈28 26	11♈ 6 10	8 11.1	17 59.8	7 15.3	14 39.5	5 51.6	5 15.4	2 13.5	11 27.8	10 17.0
16 Su	23 37 51	22 38 58	18 42 4	26 14 51	8 4.6	18 43.1	8 7.2	15 15.4	5 44.3	5 13.1	2 17.1	11 29.4	10 19.1
17 M	23 41 47	23 37 27	3♉43 23	11♉ 6 43	7 58.0	19 22.7	8 58.5	15 51.3	5 37.1	5 10.9	2 20.7	11 31.1	10 21.1
18 Tu	23 45 44	24 35 59	18 24 4	25 34 55	7 52.2	19 58.2	9 49.1	16 27.0	5 30.0	5 8.8	2 24.2	11 32.7	10 23.2
19 W	23 49 40	25 34 33	2♊38 54	9♊35 53	7 48.1	20 29.3	10 39.1	17 2.6	5 23.1	5 6.7	2 27.8	11 34.4	10 25.2
20 Th	23 53 37	26 33 9	16 25 56	23 9 12	7D 45.8	20 55.6	11 28.3	17 38.1	5 16.2	5 4.8	2 31.3	11 36.1	10 27.2
21 F	23 57 33	27 31 48	29 46 0	6♋16 45	7 45.3	21 16.9	12 16.8	18 13.4	5 9.4	5 2.9	2 34.8	11 37.8	10 29.2
22 Sa	0 1 30	28 30 29	12♋41 55	19 2 0	7 46.1	21 32.7	13 4.6	18 48.6	5 2.7	5 1.2	2 38.3	11 39.5	10 31.2
23 Su	0 5 27	29 29 11	25 17 33	1♌29 5	7 47.2	21 42.7	13 51.5	19 23.6	4 56.2	4 59.5	2 41.7	11 41.3	10 33.2
24 M	0 9 23	0♎27 57	7♌37 8	13 42 13	7R47.8	21R46.5	14 37.7	19 58.5	4 49.7	4 57.9	2 45.2	11 43.1	10 35.2
25 Tu	0 13 20	1 26 44	19 44 47	25 45 18	7 47.0	21 43.6	15 23.0	20 33.3	4 43.4	4 56.4	2 48.6	11 44.9	10 37.2
26 W	0 17 16	2 25 33	1♍44 8	7♍41 42	7 44.0	21 33.9	16 7.4	21 7.9	4 37.2	4 55.0	2 52.0	11 46.7	10 39.1
27 Th	0 21 13	3 24 25	13 38 17	19 34 10	7 38.6	21 16.9	16 50.8	21 42.4	4 31.2	4 53.7	2 55.4	11 48.5	10 41.1
28 F	0 25 9	4 23 18	25 29 39	1♎24 55	7 30.7	20 52.5	17 33.4	22 16.7	4 25.3	4 52.5	2 58.7	11 50.4	10 43.0
29 Sa	0 29 6	5 22 14	7♎20 12	13 15 42	7 20.6	20 20.6	18 14.9	22 50.9	4 19.6	4 51.4	3 2.1	11 52.3	10 45.0
30 Su	0 33 2	6 21 12	19 11 34	25 8 1	7 9.3	19 41.2	18 55.4	23 24.9	4 14.0	4 50.4	3 5.4	11 54.2	10 46.9

LONGITUDE — OCTOBER 1962

Day	Sid.Time	☉	0 hr ☽	Noon ☽	True ☊	☿	♀	♂	♃	♄	♅	♆	♇
1 M	0 36 59	7♎20 11	1♏ 5 15	7♏ 3 27	6♌57.5	18♎54.7	19♏34.8	23♋58.8	4♓ 8.5	4♒49.4	3♍ 8.6	11♏56.1	10♍48.8
2 Tu	0 40 56	8 19 13	13 2 53	19 3 47	6R46.4	18R 1.4	20 13.0	24 32.5	4R 3.2	4R48.6	3 11.9	11 58.0	10 50.7
3 W	0 44 52	9 18 16	25 6 28	1♐11 16	6 36.8	17 2.3	20 50.1	25 6.0	3 58.1	4 47.9	3 15.1	11 59.9	10 52.6
4 Th	0 48 49	10 17 22	7♐18 32	13 28 42	6 29.6	15 58.2	21 26.0	25 39.4	3 53.1	4 47.3	3 18.3	12 1.9	10 54.5
5 F	0 52 45	11 16 29	19 42 11	25 59 27	6 24.9	14 50.5	22 0.5	26 12.6	3 48.3	4 46.8	3 21.5	12 3.9	10 56.3
6 Sa	0 56 42	12 15 38	2♑21 1	8♑47 22	6D 22.7	13 40.8	22 33.8	26 45.6	3 43.7	4 46.3	3 24.6	12 5.9	10 58.2
7 Su	1 0 38	13 14 48	15 18 59	21 56 22	6 22.3	12 30.9	23 5.6	27 18.5	3 39.3	4 46.0	3 27.7	12 7.9	10 60.0
8 M	1 4 35	14 14 1	28 39 54	5♒29 58	6R22.6	11 22.6	23 36.0	27 51.2	3 35.0	4 45.8	3 30.8	12 9.9	11 1.8
9 Tu	1 8 31	15 13 15	12♒26 49	19 30 34	6 22.7	10 17.9	24 4.9	28 23.7	3 30.9	4D 45.7	3 33.9	12 12.0	11 3.6
10 W	1 12 28	16 12 31	26 41 10	3♓58 23	6 21.2	9 18.6	24 32.2	28 56.0	3 27.0	4 45.7	3 36.9	12 14.0	11 5.4
11 Th	1 16 25	17 11 49	11♓21 47	18 50 41	6 17.3	8 26.4	24 57.9	29 28.2	3 23.2	4 45.8	3 39.8	12 16.1	11 7.2
12 F	1 20 21	18 11 8	26 24 12	4♈ 1 13	6 10.8	7 42.9	25 21.9	0♌ 0.1	3 19.7	4 45.9	3 42.8	12 18.2	11 8.9
13 Sa	1 24 18	19 10 29	11♈40 27	19 20 30	6 1.9	7 9.0	25 44.2	0 31.9	3 16.3	4 46.2	3 45.7	12 20.3	11 10.6
14 Su	1 28 14	20 9 53	26 59 53	4♉37 9	5 51.4	6 45.6	26 4.6	1 3.5	3 13.1	4 46.6	3 48.6	12 22.4	11 12.3
15 M	1 32 11	21 9 18	12♉10 55	19 39 57	5 40.6	6D 33.1	26 23.2	1 34.9	3 10.1	4 47.1	3 51.4	12 24.5	11 14.0
16 Tu	1 36 7	22 8 46	27 3 12	4♊19 50	5 30.9	6 31.7	26 39.8	2 6.2	3 7.3	4 47.7	3 54.2	12 26.6	11 15.7
17 W	1 40 4	23 8 16	11♊29 17	18 31 12	5 23.1	6 41.1	26 54.5	2 37.2	3 4.7	4 48.3	3 57.0	12 28.7	11 17.4
18 Th	1 44 0	24 7 48	25 25 28	2♋12 10	5 17.9	7 1.2	27 7.1	3 8.0	3 2.3	4 49.1	3 59.8	12 30.9	11 19.0
19 F	1 47 57	25 7 22	8♋51 32	15 23 59	5 15.2	7 31.2	27 17.6	3 38.6	3 0.1	4 50.0	4 2.5	12 33.1	11 20.6
20 Sa	1 51 54	26 6 59	21 49 59	28 10 6	5D 14.3	8 10.4	27 26.0	4 9.0	2 58.1	4 51.0	4 5.1	12 35.2	11 22.2
21 Su	1 55 50	27 6 38	4♌24 58	10♌35 13	5R 14.3	8 58.2	27 32.1	4 39.2	2 56.3	4 52.1	4 7.8	12 37.4	11 23.8
22 M	1 59 47	28 6 20	16 41 31	22 44 29	5 14.0	9 53.6	27 36.0	5 9.2	2 54.7	4 53.3	4 10.3	12 39.6	11 25.4
23 Tu	2 3 43	29 6 3	28 44 45	4♍42 54	5 12.1	10 55.9	27R37.6	5 39.0	2 53.3	4 54.6	4 12.9	12 41.8	11 26.9
24 W	2 7 40	0♏ 5 49	10♍39 29	16 35 1	5 7.9	12 4.2	27 36.8	6 8.5	2 52.1	4 56.0	4 15.4	12 44.0	11 28.4
25 Th	2 11 36	1 5 36	22 29 56	28 24 39	5 0.7	13 17.8	27 33.7	6 37.8	2 51.0	4 57.4	4 17.8	12 46.2	11 29.9
26 F	2 15 33	2 5 26	4♎19 32	10♎14 52	4 50.6	14 35.8	27 28.1	7 6.8	2 50.2	4 59.0	4 20.3	12 48.4	11 31.4
27 Sa	2 19 29	3 5 18	16 10 56	22 7 56	4 38.0	15 57.8	27 20.2	7 35.6	2 49.6	5 0.7	4 22.6	12 50.6	11 32.8
28 Su	2 23 26	4 5 12	28 6 4	4♏ 5 28	4 23.6	17 23.0	27 9.8	8 4.2	2 49.2	5 2.5	4 25.0	12 52.8	11 34.2
29 M	2 27 22	5 5 8	10♏ 6 17	16 8 37	4 8.7	18 51.0	26 57.1	8 32.5	2D 49.0	5 4.4	4 27.3	12 55.1	11 35.6
30 Tu	2 31 19	6 5 6	22 12 36	28 18 21	3 54.5	20 21.2	26 41.9	9 0.5	2 49.0	5 6.4	4 29.5	12 57.3	11 37.0
31 W	2 35 16	7 5 6	4♐26 1	10♐35 45	3 42.2	21 53.3	26 24.4	9 28.3	2 49.3	5 8.4	4 31.7	12 59.5	11 38.4

Astro Data (Dy Hr Mn)	Planet Ingress (Dy Hr Mn)	Last Aspect (Dy Hr Mn)	☽ Ingress (Dy Hr Mn)	Last Aspect (Dy Hr Mn)	☽ Ingress (Dy Hr Mn)	☽ Phases & Eclipses (Dy Hr Mn)	Astro Data
☽0S 2 0:41	♀ ♏ 7 0:11	30 12:51 ♆ ⚹	♎ 1 3:01	2 23:59 ♂ △	♐ 3 9:40	7 6:44 ☽ 14♐10	1 SEPTEMBER 1962
☽0N 15 11:13	☉ ♎ 23 12:35	3 8:45 ♀ ☌	♏ 3 15:46	4 15:26 ☿ ⚹	♑ 5 19:35	14 4:11 ○ 20♓52	Julian Day # 22889
♃⊻♄ 22 7:39		4 15:03 ☉ ⚹	♐ 6 3:26	7 22:30 ♂ ☍	♒ 8 2:22	20 19:36 ☽ 27♊21	Delta T 34.3 sec
☿ R 24 1:53	♂ ♌ 11 23:54	7 6:44 ☉ □	♑ 8 12:20	9 20:19 ♀ □	♓ 10 5:29	28 19:39 ● 5♎12	SVP 05♓47'05"
☽0S 29 6:26	☉ ♏ 23 21:40	9 18:09 ☉ △	♒ 10 17:26	11 22:19 ♀ △	♈ 12 5:41		Obliquity 23°26'34"
		11 19:06 ☿ △	♓ 12 19:02	13 12:33 ☉ ☍	♉ 14 4:43	6 19:54 ☽ 13♑05	⚷ Chiron 8♓30.1R
♃☍♅ 8 13:55		14 4:11 ☉ ☍	♈ 14 18:33	15 23:21 ♀ ☍	♊ 16 4:50	13 12:33 ○ 19♈42	☽ Mean ☊ 7♌08.7
♄ D 9 16:25		16 0:02 ☿ ☍	♉ 16 18:00	17 21:33 ☉ △	♋ 18 8:05	20 8:47 ☽ 26♋29	
☽0N 12 22:14		18 11:07 ☉ △	♊ 18 19:29	20 10:42 ♀ △	♌ 20 15:30	28 13:05 ● 4♏38	1 OCTOBER 1962
☿ D 15 15:04		20 19:36 ☉ □	♋ 21 0:26	23 0:47 ☉ ⚹	♍ 23 2:31		Julian Day # 22919
♀ R 23 4:14		23 8:49 ☉ ⚹	♌ 23 9:07	25 10:12 ♀ ⚹	♎ 25 15:14		Delta T 34.4 sec
☽0S 26 12:43		25 3:55 ☿ ⚹	♍ 25 20:31	26 23:30 ☿ ☌	♏ 28 3:49		SVP 05♓47'03"
♃ D 29 10:32		27 17:09 ♂ ⚹	♎ 28 9:08	30 8:39 ♀ ☌	♐ 30 15:19		Obliquity 23°26'34"
		30 8:57 ♂ □	♏ 30 21:49				⚷ Chiron 7♓09.0R
							☽ Mean ☊ 5♌33.3

NOVEMBER 1962 LONGITUDE

Day	Sid.Time	☉	0 hr ☽	Noon ☽	True ☊	☿	♀	♂	♃	♄	♅	♆	♇
1 Th	2 39 12	8♏ 5 8	16♐47 44	23♐ 2 12	3♌32.5	23♎26.8	26♏ 4.6	9♌55.9	2♓49.7	5♒10.6	4♍33.9	13♏ 1.8	11♍39.7
2 F	2 43 9	9 5 11	29 19 26	5♑39 42	3R25.9	25 1.6	25R42.5	10 23.1	2 50.3	5 12.9	4 36.0	13 4.0	11 41.0
3 Sa	2 47 5	10 5 16	12♑ 3 20	18 30 44	3 22.2	26 37.3	25 18.4	10 50.1	2 51.2	5 15.3	4 38.0	13 6.3	11 42.3
4 Su	2 51 2	11 5 23	25 2 14	1♒38 15	3D20.9	28 13.7	24 52.1	11 16.8	2 52.2	5 17.7	4 40.1	13 8.5	11 43.5
5 M	2 54 58	12 5 31	8♒19 10	15 5 19	3R20.7	29 50.6	24 24.0	11 43.2	2 53.4	5 20.3	4 42.0	13 10.8	11 44.8
6 Tu	2 58 55	13 5 40	21 57 0	28 54 25	3 20.6	1♏27.8	23 54.1	12 9.3	2 54.9	5 22.9	4 44.0	13 13.0	11 46.0
7 W	3 2 51	14 5 52	5♓57 41	13♓ 6 45	3 19.1	3 5.3	23 22.6	12 35.1	2 56.5	5 25.7	4 45.8	13 15.3	11 47.1
8 Th	3 6 48	15 6 4	20 21 25	27 41 18	3 15.3	4 42.9	22 49.7	13 0.6	2 58.4	5 28.5	4 47.7	13 17.5	11 48.3
9 F	3 10 45	16 6 18	5♈ 5 49	12♈34 11	3 8.9	6 20.6	22 15.6	13 25.8	3 0.4	5 31.4	4 49.4	13 19.7	11 49.4
10 Sa	3 14 41	17 6 33	20 5 25	27 38 23	2 59.9	7 58.2	21 40.5	13 50.7	3 2.7	5 34.5	4 51.2	13 22.0	11 50.5
11 Su	3 18 38	18 6 50	5♉11 51	12♉44 30	2 49.2	9 35.7	21 4.7	14 15.2	3 5.1	5 37.6	4 52.8	13 24.2	11 51.5
12 M	3 22 34	19 7 9	20 15 2	27 42 11	2 38.0	11 13.1	20 28.3	14 39.5	3 7.8	5 40.8	4 54.5	13 26.5	11 52.6
13 Tu	3 26 31	20 7 30	5♊ 4 51	12♊22 3	2 27.7	12 50.3	19 51.8	15 3.4	3 10.6	5 44.1	4 56.0	13 28.7	11 53.6
14 W	3 30 27	21 7 52	19 33 0	26 37 10	2 19.3	14 27.3	19 15.2	15 27.0	3 13.6	5 47.4	4 57.6	13 31.0	11 54.6
15 Th	3 34 24	22 8 16	3♋34 11	10♋23 56	2 13.6	16 4.2	18 38.9	15 50.2	3 16.9	5 50.9	4 59.0	13 33.2	11 55.5
16 F	3 38 20	23 8 42	17 6 28	23 41 58	2 10.4	17 40.8	18 3.2	16 13.1	3 20.3	5 54.5	5 0.5	13 35.4	11 56.4
17 Sa	3 42 17	24 9 10	0♌10 50	6♌33 30	2D 9.4	19 17.1	17 28.2	16 35.6	3 23.9	5 58.1	5 1.8	13 37.6	11 57.3
18 Su	3 46 14	25 9 39	12 50 31	19 2 29	2 9.7	20 53.3	16 54.2	16 57.8	3 27.7	6 1.8	5 3.1	13 39.9	11 58.2
19 M	3 50 10	26 10 11	25 10 4	1♍13 55	2R10.1	22 29.2	16 21.4	17 19.5	3 31.7	6 5.6	5 4.4	13 42.1	11 59.0
20 Tu	3 54 7	27 10 44	7♍14 43	13 13 7	2 9.6	24 4.9	15 50.1	17 40.9	3 35.9	6 9.5	5 5.6	13 44.3	11 59.8
21 W	3 58 3	28 11 19	19 9 46	25 5 16	2 7.1	25 40.4	15 20.4	18 1.9	3 40.3	6 13.5	5 6.8	13 46.5	12 0.6
22 Th	4 2 0	29 11 55	1♎ 0 13	6♎55 7	2 2.3	27 15.6	14 52.5	18 22.4	3 44.8	6 17.6	5 7.9	13 48.7	12 1.3
23 F	4 5 56	0♐12 33	12 50 29	18 46 44	1 54.8	28 50.7	14 26.5	18 42.6	3 49.6	6 21.7	5 8.9	13 50.8	12 2.1
24 Sa	4 9 53	1 13 13	24 44 15	0♏43 21	1 45.1	0♐25.6	14 2.7	19 2.3	3 54.5	6 25.9	5 9.9	13 53.0	12 2.7
25 Su	4 13 49	2 13 55	6♏44 20	12 47 23	1 33.9	2 0.3	13 40.9	19 21.6	3 59.6	6 30.2	5 10.8	13 55.2	12 3.4
26 M	4 17 46	3 14 38	18 52 41	25 0 22	1 22.1	3 34.9	13 21.5	19 40.4	4 4.9	6 34.6	5 11.7	13 57.3	12 4.0
27 Tu	4 21 43	4 15 22	1♐10 31	7♐23 12	1 10.8	5 9.4	13 4.4	19 58.8	4 10.3	6 39.1	5 12.6	13 59.5	12 4.6
28 W	4 25 39	5 16 8	13 38 26	19 56 16	1 1.0	6 43.7	12 49.7	20 16.7	4 16.0	6 43.6	5 13.3	14 1.6	12 5.2
29 Th	4 29 36	6 16 55	26 16 42	2♑39 48	0 53.4	8 17.9	12 37.5	20 34.2	4 21.8	6 48.2	5 14.0	14 3.7	12 5.7
30 F	4 33 32	7 17 43	9♑ 5 35	15 34 8	0 48.5	9 52.0	12 27.7	20 51.1	4 27.8	6 52.9	5 14.7	14 5.9	12 6.2

DECEMBER 1962 LONGITUDE

Day	Sid.Time	☉	0 hr ☽	Noon ☽	True ☊	☿	♀	♂	♃	♄	♅	♆	♇
1 Sa	4 37 29	8♐18 32	22♑ 5 31	28♑39 53	0♌46.2	11♐26.0	12♏20.4	21♌ 7.6	4♓34.0	6♒57.7	5♍15.3	14♏ 8.0	12♍ 6.6
2 Su	4 41 25	9 19 22	5♒17 20	11♒58 3	0D45.9	12 60.0	12R15.6	21 23.5	4 40.3	7 2.5	5 15.9	14 10.0	12 7.1
3 M	4 45 22	10 20 14	18 42 11	25 29 53	0 46.8	14 33.9	12D13.2	21 39.0	4 46.8	7 7.4	5 16.3	14 12.1	12 7.5
4 Tu	4 49 18	11 21 6	2♓21 20	9♓16 36	0R47.9	16 7.7	12 13.3	21 53.9	4 53.5	7 12.4	5 16.8	14 14.2	12 7.8
5 W	4 53 15	12 21 58	16 15 45	23 18 46	0 48.1	17 41.6	12 15.7	22 8.3	5 0.3	7 17.4	5 17.2	14 16.2	12 8.2
6 Th	4 57 12	13 22 52	0♈25 33	7♈35 52	0 46.7	19 15.4	12 20.5	22 22.1	5 7.3	7 22.5	5 17.5	14 18.3	12 8.5
7 F	5 1 8	14 23 46	14 49 22	22 5 34	0 43.3	20 49.2	12 27.7	22 35.4	5 14.5	7 27.7	5 17.7	14 20.3	12 8.7
8 Sa	5 5 5	15 24 41	29 23 54	6♉43 37	0 38.0	22 23.0	12 37.1	22 48.2	5 21.8	7 32.9	5 17.9	14 22.3	12 9.0
9 Su	5 9 1	16 25 36	14♉ 3 55	21 23 54	0 31.3	23 56.9	12 48.8	23 0.3	5 29.3	7 38.3	5 18.1	14 24.2	12 9.2
10 M	5 12 58	17 26 33	28 42 37	5♊59 10	0 24.1	25 30.7	13 2.6	23 11.9	5 36.9	7 43.6	5 18.2	14 26.2	12 9.4
11 Tu	5 16 54	18 27 30	13♊12 39	20 22 14	0 17.4	27 4.6	13 18.6	23 22.9	5 44.7	7 49.1	5R18.2	14 28.2	12 9.5
12 W	5 20 51	19 28 28	27 27 12	4♋26 58	0 12.0	28 38.5	13 36.6	23 33.3	5 52.7	7 54.6	5 18.2	14 30.1	12 9.6
13 Th	5 24 48	20 29 27	11♋21 5	18 9 16	0 8.5	0♑12.3	13 56.7	23 43.0	6 0.7	8 0.1	5 18.1	14 32.0	12 9.7
14 F	5 28 44	21 30 27	24 51 23	1♌27 24	0D 6.9	1 46.2	14 18.6	23 52.2	6 9.0	8 5.8	5 18.0	14 33.9	12R 9.7
15 Sa	5 32 41	22 31 28	7♌57 29	14 21 52	0 7.0	3 20.1	14 42.4	24 0.7	6 17.3	8 11.4	5 17.8	14 35.8	12 9.7
16 Su	5 36 37	23 32 30	20 40 53	26 55 0	0 8.4	4 53.9	15 8.1	24 8.5	6 25.9	8 17.2	5 17.6	14 37.6	12 9.7
17 M	5 40 34	24 33 33	3♍ 4 43	9♍10 34	0 10.1	6 27.6	15 35.5	24 15.6	6 34.5	8 23.0	5 17.3	14 39.5	12 9.7
18 Tu	5 44 30	25 34 36	15 13 9	21 13 5	0R11.6	8 1.2	16 4.5	24 22.1	6 43.3	8 28.8	5 16.9	14 41.3	12 9.6
19 W	5 48 27	26 35 40	27 11 1	3♎ 7 33	0 12.2	9 34.7	16 35.2	24 27.9	6 52.3	8 34.7	5 16.5	14 43.1	12 9.5
20 Th	5 52 23	27 36 46	9♎ 3 20	14 58 57	0 11.4	11 8.0	17 7.5	24 33.0	7 1.4	8 40.7	5 16.1	14 44.9	12 9.3
21 F	5 56 20	28 37 52	20 55 1	26 52 4	0 9.1	12 40.9	17 41.2	24 37.3	7 10.6	8 46.7	5 15.5	14 46.6	12 9.1
22 Sa	6 0 17	29 38 59	2♏50 37	8♏51 9	0 5.4	14 13.5	18 16.4	24 40.9	7 19.9	8 52.8	5 15.0	14 48.4	12 8.9
23 Su	6 4 13	0♑40 6	14 54 5	20 59 47	0 0.7	15 45.6	18 52.9	24 43.8	7 29.4	8 58.9	5 14.3	14 50.1	12 8.7
24 M	6 8 10	1 41 14	27 8 33	3♐20 39	29♋55.6	17 17.0	19 30.8	24 45.9	7 39.0	9 5.1	5 13.6	14 51.8	12 8.4
25 Tu	6 12 6	2 42 23	9♐36 16	15 55 31	29 50.6	18 47.7	20 10.0	24 47.3	7 48.8	9 11.3	5 12.9	14 53.4	12 8.1
26 W	6 16 3	3 43 33	22 18 28	28 45 8	29 46.3	20 17.5	20 50.3	24R47.9	7 58.6	9 17.5	5 12.1	14 55.1	12 7.8
27 Th	6 19 59	4 44 42	5♑15 28	11♑49 23	29 43.2	21 46.1	21 31.9	24 47.7	8 8.6	9 23.8	5 11.3	14 56.7	12 7.4
28 F	6 23 56	5 45 52	18 26 45	25 7 24	29D41.4	23 13.3	22 14.5	24 46.7	8 18.7	9 30.2	5 10.4	14 58.3	12 7.0
29 Sa	6 27 52	6 47 3	1♒51 11	8♒37 53	29 41.0	24 38.9	22 58.3	24 44.9	8 29.0	9 36.6	5 9.4	14 59.8	12 6.6
30 Su	6 31 49	7 48 13	15 27 20	22 19 20	29 41.7	26 2.3	23 43.0	24 42.4	8 39.3	9 43.0	5 8.4	15 1.4	12 6.1
31 M	6 35 46	8 49 23	29 13 41	6♓10 13	29 43.0	27 23.4	24 28.8	24 39.0	8 49.8	9 49.5	5 7.4	15 2.9	12 5.6

Astro Data Dy Hr Mn	Planet Ingress Dy Hr Mn	Last Aspect Dy Hr Mn	☽ Ingress Dy Hr Mn	Last Aspect Dy Hr Mn	☽ Ingress Dy Hr Mn	☽ Phases & Eclipses Dy Hr Mn
☽0N 9 9:11	☿ ♏ 5 2:20	1 14:37 ☿ ⚹	♑ 2 1:17	30 9:18 ♆ ⚹	♒ 1 14:26	5 7:15 ☽ 12♒24
☽0S 22 20:17	☉ ♐ 22 19:02	4 6:38 ☿ □	♒ 4 9:02	3 5:19 ♂ ☍	♓ 3 19:53	11 22:03 ○ 19♉02
	☿ ♐ 23 17:31	6 3:16 ♀ □	♓ 6 13:52	5 2:45 ☿ □	♈ 5 23:17	19 2:09 ☽ 26♌16
♀ D 3 11:26		8 3:55 ♀ △	♈ 8 15:45	7 13:01 ♂ △	♉ 8 0:59	27 6:29 ● 4♐32
☽0N 6 18:07	☿ ♑ 12 20:51	9 13:45 ♂ △	♉ 10 15:45	9 14:50 ♂ □	♊ 10 2:07	
♃☍♅ 7 11:01	☉ ♑ 22 8:15	12 0:21 ♀ ☍	♊ 12 15:43	12 2:17 ☿ ☍	♋ 12 4:21	4 16:48 ☽ 12♓04
♅ R 11 5:12	☊ ♋ 23 3:32	13 16:56 ♂ ⚹	♋ 14 17:49	13 5:36 ♆ △	♌ 14 9:20	11 9:27 ○ 18♊52
♇ R 14 21:45		16 11:54 ☉ △	♌ 16 23:40	16 6:42 ♂ ☌	♍ 16 17:59	18 22:42 ☽ 26♍32
☽0S 20 4:55		19 2:09 ☉ □	♍ 19 9:33	18 22:42 ☉ □	♎ 19 5:41	26 22:59 ● 4♑42
♂ R 26 6:11		21 20:00 ☉ ⚹	♎ 21 21:58	21 17:00 ☉ ⚹	♏ 21 18:18	
		23 12:12 ♂ ⚹	♏ 24 10:33	23 19:22 ♂ □	♐ 24 5:33	
		26 1:36 ♂ □	♐ 26 21:43	26 4:39 ♂ △	♑ 26 14:19	
		28 12:57 ♂ △	♑ 29 7:00	28 9:37 ☿ ☌	♒ 28 20:42	
				30 16:05 ♂ ☍	♓ 31 1:20	

Astro Data

1 NOVEMBER 1962
Julian Day # 22950
Delta T 34.4 sec
SVP 05♓47'00"
Obliquity 23°26'34"
⚷ Chiron 6♓16.3R
☽ Mean ☊ 3♌54.8

1 DECEMBER 1962
Julian Day # 22980
Delta T 34.4 sec
SVP 05♓46'55"
Obliquity 23°26'33"
⚷ Chiron 6♓14.6
☽ Mean ☊ 2♌19.5

LONGITUDE JANUARY 1963

Day	Sid.Time	☉	0 hr ☽	Noon ☽	True ☊	☿	♀	♂	♃	♄	♅	♆	♇
1 Tu	6 39 42	9♑50 33	13♓ 8 44	20♓ 9 4	29♋44.5	28♑41.6	25♏15.5	24♌34.8	9♓ 0.4	9♒56.0	5♍ 6.3	15♏ 4.4	12♍ 5.1
2 W	6 43 39	10 51 43	27 11 3	4♈14 28	29 45.6	29 56.5	26 3.2	24R 29.8	9 11.1	10 2.6	5R 5.1	15 5.9	12R 4.5
3 Th	6 47 35	11 52 53	11♈19 7	18 24 47	29R 46.1	1♒ 7.3	26 51.7	24 24.0	9 21.9	10 9.2	5 3.9	15 7.3	12 3.9
4 F	6 51 32	12 54 2	25 31 11	2♉38 1	29 45.7	2 13.6	27 41.0	24 17.3	9 32.8	10 15.8	5 2.6	15 8.7	12 3.3
5 Sa	6 55 28	13 55 11	9♉44 58	16 51 40	29 44.5	3 14.5	28 31.2	24 9.9	9 43.8	10 22.5	5 1.3	15 10.1	12 2.7
6 Su	6 59 25	14 56 20	23 57 40	1♊ 2 34	29 42.8	4 9.3	29 22.2	24 1.6	9 55.0	10 29.2	4 60.0	15 11.4	12 2.0
7 M	7 3 21	15 57 28	8♊ 5 54	15 7 11	29 40.8	4 57.1	0♐13.9	23 52.6	10 6.2	10 35.9	4 58.6	15 12.8	12 1.3
8 Tu	7 7 18	16 58 36	22 5 58	29 1 48	29 39.1	5 37.0	1 6.3	23 42.7	10 17.5	10 42.7	4 57.1	15 14.1	12 0.6
9 W	7 11 15	17 59 44	5♋54 16	12♋43 0	29 37.7	6 8.2	1 59.5	23 32.0	10 29.0	10 49.5	4 55.6	15 15.3	11 59.8
10 Th	7 15 11	19 0 52	19 27 41	26 8 5	29D 37.0	6 29.7	2 53.3	23 20.6	10 40.5	10 56.3	4 54.1	15 16.6	11 59.1
11 F	7 19 8	20 1 59	2♌44 1	9♌15 24	29 36.8	6R 40.7	3 47.8	23 8.3	10 52.1	11 3.2	4 52.5	15 17.8	11 58.3
12 Sa	7 23 4	21 3 6	15 42 13	22 4 33	29 37.2	6 40.6	4 43.0	22 55.3	11 3.8	11 10.1	4 50.9	15 19.0	11 57.4
13 Su	7 27 1	22 4 13	28 22 33	4♍36 27	29 37.9	6 28.8	5 38.7	22 41.5	11 15.7	11 17.0	4 49.2	15 20.1	11 56.6
14 M	7 30 57	23 5 19	10♍46 32	16 53 10	29 38.6	6 5.3	6 35.0	22 26.9	11 27.6	11 23.9	4 47.5	15 21.2	11 55.7
15 Tu	7 34 54	24 6 26	22 56 46	28 57 47	29 39.3	5 30.1	7 31.9	22 11.5	11 39.6	11 30.9	4 45.7	15 22.3	11 54.7
16 W	7 38 50	25 7 32	4♎56 44	10♎54 10	29 39.8	4 43.8	8 29.3	21 55.5	11 51.6	11 37.8	4 43.9	15 23.4	11 53.8
17 Th	7 42 47	26 8 38	16 50 37	22 46 42	29R 40.1	3 47.6	9 27.2	21 38.7	12 3.8	11 44.8	4 42.1	15 24.4	11 52.8
18 F	7 46 44	27 9 44	28 42 59	4♏40 5	29 40.1	2 42.9	10 25.7	21 21.3	12 16.0	11 51.9	4 40.2	15 25.4	11 51.8
19 Sa	7 50 40	28 10 49	10♏38 35	16 39 4	29 40.1	1 31.7	11 24.6	21 3.1	12 28.4	11 58.9	4 38.3	15 26.4	11 50.8
20 Su	7 54 37	29 11 54	22 42 5	28 48 10	29D 40.0	0 16.1	12 24.0	20 44.3	12 40.8	12 6.0	4 36.3	15 27.3	11 49.8
21 M	7 58 33	0♒12 59	4♐57 49	11♐11 27	29 40.0	28♑58.5	13 23.8	20 24.9	12 53.3	12 13.1	4 34.3	15 28.2	11 48.7
22 Tu	8 2 30	1 14 3	17 29 28	23 52 10	29 40.2	27 41.3	14 24.1	20 5.0	13 5.9	12 20.1	4 32.3	15 29.1	11 47.6
23 W	8 6 26	2 15 7	0♑19 46	6♑52 27	29 40.4	26 26.8	15 24.7	19 44.4	13 18.5	12 27.3	4 30.2	15 29.9	11 46.5
24 Th	8 10 23	3 16 11	13 30 14	20 13 6	29 40.7	25 16.9	16 25.8	19 23.3	13 31.2	12 34.4	4 28.1	15 30.7	11 45.4
25 F	8 14 19	4 17 14	27 0 53	3♒53 20	29R 40.8	24 13.2	17 27.2	19 1.8	13 44.0	12 41.5	4 26.0	15 31.5	11 44.3
26 Sa	8 18 16	5 18 16	10♒50 8	17 50 50	29 40.7	23 17.1	18 29.0	18 39.8	13 56.9	12 48.7	4 23.8	15 32.2	11 43.1
27 Su	8 22 13	6 19 17	24 54 56	2♓ 1 53	29 40.3	22 29.2	19 31.1	18 17.4	14 9.9	12 55.8	4 21.6	15 32.9	11 41.9
28 M	8 26 9	7 20 17	9♓11 5	16 21 53	29 39.5	21 50.0	20 33.6	17 54.6	14 22.9	13 3.0	4 19.4	15 33.6	11 40.7
29 Tu	8 30 6	8 21 16	23 33 41	0♈45 52	29 38.5	21 19.8	21 36.4	17 31.6	14 35.9	13 10.2	4 17.1	15 34.2	11 39.4
30 W	8 34 2	9 22 13	7♈57 51	15 9 6	29 37.4	20 58.5	22 39.5	17 8.2	14 49.1	13 17.3	4 14.8	15 34.8	11 38.2
31 Th	8 37 59	10 23 10	22 19 9	29 27 35	29 36.5	20 45.7	23 43.0	16 44.6	15 2.3	13 24.5	4 12.5	15 35.4	11 36.9

LONGITUDE FEBRUARY 1963

Day	Sid.Time	☉	0 hr ☽	Noon ☽	True ☊	☿	♀	♂	♃	♄	♅	♆	♇
1 F	8 41 55	11♒24 5	6♉34 4	13♉38 18	29♋36.0	20♑41.1	24♐46.7	16♌20.9	15♓15.6	13♒31.7	4♍10.2	15♏35.9	11♍35.6
2 Sa	8 45 52	12 24 59	20 40 5	27 39 14	29D 36.1	20D 44.3	25 50.6	15R 57.0	15 28.9	13 38.9	4R 7.8	15 36.4	11R 34.3
3 Su	8 49 48	13 25 52	4♊35 37	11♊29 8	29 36.8	20 54.7	26 54.9	15 33.0	15 42.3	13 46.1	4 5.4	15 36.9	11 33.0
4 M	8 53 45	14 26 43	18 19 43	25 7 20	29 37.9	21 11.7	27 59.4	15 9.0	15 55.7	13 53.3	4 3.0	15 37.3	11 31.6
5 Tu	8 57 42	15 27 33	1♋51 55	8♋33 27	29 39.2	21 35.0	29 4.2	14 45.0	16 9.2	14 0.5	4 0.6	15 37.7	11 30.3
6 W	9 1 38	16 28 22	15 11 53	21 47 12	29 40.3	22 3.9	0♑ 9.3	14 21.0	16 22.7	14 7.7	3 58.1	15 38.1	11 28.9
7 Th	9 5 35	17 29 9	28 19 22	4♌48 21	29R 40.8	22 38.0	1 14.5	13 57.2	16 36.3	14 14.8	3 55.6	15 38.4	11 27.5
8 F	9 9 31	18 29 55	11♌14 10	17 36 47	29 40.4	23 16.9	2 20.0	13 33.4	16 50.0	14 22.0	3 53.1	15 38.7	11 26.1
9 Sa	9 13 28	19 30 39	23 56 14	0♍12 33	29 38.9	24 0.2	3 25.8	13 9.9	17 3.7	14 29.2	3 50.6	15 39.0	11 24.7
10 Su	9 17 24	20 31 22	6♍25 50	12 36 10	29 36.4	24 47.4	4 31.7	12 46.6	17 17.4	14 36.4	3 48.1	15 39.2	11 23.3
11 M	9 21 21	21 32 4	18 43 43	24 48 40	29 33.0	25 38.3	5 37.9	12 23.5	17 31.2	14 43.5	3 45.6	15 39.4	11 21.8
12 Tu	9 25 17	22 32 45	0♎51 15	6♎51 46	29 29.1	26 32.6	6 44.3	12 0.8	17 45.0	14 50.7	3 43.0	15 39.6	11 20.4
13 W	9 29 14	23 33 24	12 50 32	18 47 56	29 25.1	27 29.9	7 50.9	11 38.4	17 58.9	14 57.8	3 40.4	15 39.7	11 18.9
14 Th	9 33 11	24 34 3	24 44 24	0♏40 23	29 21.5	28 30.0	8 57.7	11 16.4	18 12.8	15 5.0	3 37.8	15 39.8	11 17.4
15 F	9 37 7	25 34 40	6♏36 23	12 32 58	29 18.7	29 32.8	10 4.6	10 54.8	18 26.8	15 12.1	3 35.3	15 39.9	11 15.9
16 Sa	9 41 4	26 35 16	18 30 40	24 30 4	29D 17.2	0♒37.9	11 11.8	10 33.7	18 40.8	15 19.2	3 32.7	15R 39.9	11 14.4
17 Su	9 45 0	27 35 51	0♐31 48	6♐36 27	29 16.9	1 45.3	12 19.1	10 13.1	18 54.8	15 26.3	3 30.0	15 39.9	11 12.9
18 M	9 48 57	28 36 24	12 44 37	18 56 53	29 17.7	2 54.8	13 26.6	9 53.0	19 8.9	15 33.4	3 27.4	15 39.8	11 11.4
19 Tu	9 52 53	29 36 56	25 13 50	1♑35 58	29 19.3	4 6.2	14 34.3	9 33.5	19 23.0	15 40.4	3 24.8	15 39.8	11 9.9
20 W	9 56 50	0♓37 28	8♑ 3 43	14 37 29	29 21.0	5 19.5	15 42.1	9 14.6	19 37.1	15 47.5	3 22.2	15 39.7	11 8.3
21 Th	10 0 46	1 37 57	21 17 31	28 4 0	29R 22.2	6 34.4	16 50.1	8 56.3	19 51.3	15 54.5	3 19.5	15 39.5	11 6.8
22 F	10 4 43	2 38 26	4♒56 56	11♒56 11	29 22.3	7 51.0	17 58.2	8 38.6	20 5.5	16 1.5	3 16.9	15 39.3	11 5.3
23 Sa	10 8 40	3 38 52	19 1 28	26 12 18	29 20.9	9 9.2	19 6.4	8 21.6	20 19.8	16 8.5	3 14.3	15 39.1	11 3.7
24 Su	10 12 36	4 39 18	3♓28 4	10♓47 59	29 17.7	10 28.8	20 14.8	8 5.3	20 34.0	16 15.5	3 11.6	15 38.9	11 2.2
25 M	10 16 33	5 39 41	18 11 9	25 36 32	29 12.9	11 49.8	21 23.4	7 49.7	20 48.3	16 22.4	3 9.0	15 38.6	11 0.6
26 Tu	10 20 29	6 40 3	3♈ 3 4	10♈29 42	29 7.2	13 12.2	22 32.0	7 34.9	21 2.6	16 29.3	3 6.4	15 38.3	10 59.0
27 W	10 24 26	7 40 23	17 55 20	25 19 2	29 1.3	14 35.8	23 40.8	7 20.8	21 17.0	16 36.2	3 3.7	15 38.0	10 57.5
28 Th	10 28 22	8 40 41	2♉39 55	9♉57 15	28 56.1	16 0.8	24 49.6	7 7.4	21 31.3	16 43.1	3 1.1	15 37.6	10 55.9

Astro Data	Dy Hr Mn
☽0N	3 0:33
☿ R	11 11:46
♃⚺♄	13 6:25
☽0S	16 13:38
♃☍♇	16 3:59
♄⚻♇	17 23:55
☽0N	30 6:13
☿ D	1 1:58
♃△♆	2 14:05
☽0S	12 21:29
♆ R	16 6:05
♄□♆	18 21:48
☽0N	26 13:34

Planet Ingress	Dy Hr Mn
☿ ♒	2 1:10
♀ ♐	6 17:35
☉ ♒	20 18:54
☿ ♑	20 4:59
♀ ♑	5 20:36
☿ ♒	15 10:08
☉ ♓	19 9:09

Last Aspect Dy Hr Mn		☽ Ingress Dy Hr Mn
1 21:57	♀ △	♈ 2 4:48
3 21:56	♂ △	♉ 4 7:34
6 9:45	♀ ☍	♊ 6 10:14
8 2:45	♂ ⚹	♋ 8 13:41
9 23:08	☉ ☍	♌ 10 19:01
12 13:22	♂ ☌	♍ 13 3:07
15 2:31	☉ △	♎ 15 14:05
17 20:34	☉ □	♏ 18 2:35
20 13:56	☉ ⚹	♐ 20 14:20
22 4:46	♂ △	♑ 22 23:23
24 19:25	☿ ☌	♒ 25 5:14
26 14:07	♀ ⚹	♓ 27 8:35
28 20:29	♀ □	♈ 29 10:44
31 2:32	♀ △	♉ 31 12:55

Last Aspect Dy Hr Mn		☽ Ingress Dy Hr Mn
2 0:07	☿ △	♊ 2 16:03
4 18:35	♀ ☍	♋ 4 20:40
6 13:03	☿ ☍	♌ 7 3:06
8 14:52	☉ ☍	♍ 9 11:36
11 14:44	☿ △	♎ 11 22:18
14 8:20	☿ □	♏ 14 10:38
16 17:38	☉ □	♐ 16 22:57
19 8:59	☉ ⚹	♑ 19 9:00
20 21:23	♃ ⚹	♒ 21 15:23
22 19:06	♄ ☌	♓ 23 18:17
25 5:37	♀ ⚹	♈ 25 19:05
27 10:07	♀ □	♉ 27 19:38

☽ Phases & Eclipses Dy Hr Mn	
3 1:02	☽ 11♈55
9 23:08	○ 18♋59
9 23:19	☍ A 1.018
17 20:34	☽ 27♎01
25 13:42	● 4♒52
25 13:36:36	☌ A 0'25"
1 8:50	☽ 11♉46
8 14:52	○ 19♌08
16 17:38	☽ 27♏20
24 2:06	● 4♓45

Astro Data
1 JANUARY 1963
Julian Day # 23011
Delta T 34.5 sec
SVP 05♓46'50"
Obliquity 23°26'34"
⚷ Chiron 7♓06.6
☽ Mean ☊ 0♌41.0
1 FEBRUARY 1963
Julian Day # 23042
Delta T 34.5 sec
SVP 05♓46'45"
Obliquity 23°26'34"
⚷ Chiron 8♓41.1
☽ Mean ☊ 29♋02.5

MARCH 1963 LONGITUDE

Day	Sid.Time	☉	0 hr ☽	Noon☽	True ☊	☿	♀	♂	♃	♄	♅	♆	♇
1 F	10 32 19	9♓40 57	17♉10 27	24♉19 5	28♋52.3	17♒26.9	25♑58.6	6♌54.8	21♓45.7	16♒49.9	2♍58.5	15♏37.2	10♍54.3
2 Sa	10 36 15	10 41 11	1♊22 54	8♊21 44	28D 50.2	18 54.3	27 7.7	6R 43.0	22 0.1	16 56.7	2R 55.9	15R 36.7	10R 52.8
3 Su	10 40 12	11 41 23	15 15 35	22 4 33	28 49.9	20 22.9	28 16.9	6 32.0	22 14.5	17 3.5	2 53.3	15 36.3	10 51.2
4 M	10 44 9	12 41 32	28 48 47	5♋28 31	28 50.8	21 52.6	29 26.2	6 21.8	22 29.0	17 10.2	2 50.7	15 35.7	10 49.6
5 Tu	10 48 5	13 41 40	12♋ 4 0	18 35 33	28 52.2	23 23.4	0♒35.6	6 12.4	22 43.4	17 16.9	2 48.1	15 35.2	10 48.1
6 W	10 52 2	14 41 46	25 3 25	1♌27 54	28R 53.1	24 55.4	1 45.1	6 3.7	22 57.9	17 23.6	2 45.6	15 34.6	10 46.5
7 Th	10 55 58	15 41 49	7♌49 15	14 7 43	28 52.8	26 28.6	2 54.7	5 55.9	23 12.4	17 30.3	2 43.0	15 34.0	10 44.9
8 F	10 59 55	16 41 51	20 23 32	26 36 52	28 50.4	28 2.8	4 4.4	5 48.8	23 26.9	17 36.9	2 40.5	15 33.4	10 43.4
9 Sa	11 3 51	17 41 50	2♍47 53	8♍56 45	28 45.8	29 38.2	5 14.2	5 42.6	23 41.4	17 43.5	2 38.0	15 32.8	10 41.8
10 Su	11 7 48	18 41 47	15 3 35	21 8 32	28 38.7	1♓14.8	6 24.1	5 37.1	23 55.9	17 50.0	2 35.5	15 32.1	10 40.3
11 M	11 11 44	19 41 43	27 11 41	3♎13 13	28 29.8	2 52.4	7 34.0	5 32.4	24 10.4	17 56.5	2 33.0	15 31.4	10 38.7
12 Tu	11 15 41	20 41 36	9♎13 14	15 11 57	28 19.6	4 31.3	8 44.1	5 28.4	24 24.9	18 2.9	2 30.5	15 30.6	10 37.2
13 W	11 19 37	21 41 28	21 9 31	27 6 13	28 9.1	6 11.2	9 54.2	5 25.3	24 39.4	18 9.3	2 28.0	15 29.8	10 35.6
14 Th	11 23 34	22 41 18	3♏ 2 18	8♏58 5	27 59.2	7 52.4	11 4.4	5 22.9	24 54.0	18 15.7	2 25.6	15 29.0	10 34.1
15 F	11 27 31	23 41 6	14 53 56	20 50 16	27 50.8	9 34.7	12 14.7	5 21.2	25 8.5	18 22.0	2 23.2	15 28.2	10 32.6
16 Sa	11 31 27	24 40 52	26 47 32	2♐46 14	27 44.5	11 18.2	13 25.1	5D 20.3	25 23.0	18 28.3	2 20.8	15 27.3	10 31.0
17 Su	11 35 24	25 40 37	8♐46 54	14 50 7	27 40.6	13 2.9	14 35.5	5 20.2	25 37.6	18 34.6	2 18.5	15 26.4	10 29.5
18 M	11 39 20	26 40 20	20 56 28	27 6 35	27D 38.9	14 48.9	15 46.1	5 20.7	25 52.1	18 40.8	2 16.1	15 25.5	10 28.0
19 Tu	11 43 17	27 40 1	3♑21 5	9♑40 35	27 38.9	16 36.0	16 56.7	5 22.0	26 6.7	18 46.9	2 13.8	15 24.6	10 26.5
20 W	11 47 13	28 39 41	16 5 41	22 36 54	27R 39.6	18 24.5	18 7.3	5 24.0	26 21.2	18 53.0	2 11.5	15 23.6	10 25.1
21 Th	11 51 10	29 39 19	29 14 44	5♒59 33	27 40.0	20 14.1	19 18.0	5 26.7	26 35.7	18 59.1	2 9.3	15 22.6	10 23.6
22 F	11 55 6	0♈38 55	12♒51 36	19 50 59	27 38.9	22 5.0	20 28.8	5 30.1	26 50.3	19 5.1	2 7.1	15 21.6	10 22.1
23 Sa	11 59 3	1 38 29	26 57 37	4♓11 12	27 35.7	23 57.2	21 39.7	5 34.2	27 4.8	19 11.0	2 4.9	15 20.5	10 20.7
24 Su	12 3 0	2 38 1	11♓31 14	18 56 59	27 29.9	25 50.6	22 50.6	5 39.0	27 19.3	19 16.9	2 2.7	15 19.5	10 19.3
25 M	12 6 56	3 37 32	26 27 28	4♈ 1 34	27 21.8	27 45.3	24 1.5	5 44.4	27 33.8	19 22.8	2 0.6	15 18.4	10 17.8
26 Tu	12 10 53	4 37 0	11♈38 0	19 15 21	27 12.0	29 41.2	25 12.5	5 50.5	27 48.3	19 28.6	1 58.5	15 17.2	10 16.4
27 W	12 14 49	5 36 27	26 52 14	4♉27 17	27 1.7	1♈38.3	26 23.6	5 57.2	28 2.8	19 34.3	1 56.4	15 16.1	10 15.0
28 Th	12 18 46	6 35 51	11♉59 13	19 26 56	26 52.2	3 36.6	27 34.7	6 4.5	28 17.2	19 40.0	1 54.4	15 14.9	10 13.6
29 F	12 22 42	7 35 13	26 49 31	4♊ 6 17	26 44.6	5 36.0	28 45.9	6 12.5	28 31.7	19 45.6	1 52.4	15 13.7	10 12.3
30 Sa	12 26 39	8 34 32	11♊16 44	18 20 36	26 39.5	7 36.5	29 57.1	6 21.1	28 46.1	19 51.2	1 50.4	15 12.5	10 10.9
31 Su	12 30 35	9 33 50	25 17 50	2♋ 8 30	26 36.9	9 38.0	1♓ 8.3	6 30.3	29 0.5	19 56.7	1 48.5	15 11.3	10 9.6

APRIL 1963 LONGITUDE

Day	Sid.Time	☉	0 hr ☽	Noon☽	True ☊	☿	♀	♂	♃	♄	♅	♆	♇
1 M	12 34 32	10♈33 5	8♋52 51	15♋31 12	26♋36.1	11♈40.3	2♓19.6	6♌40.1	29♓14.9	20♒ 2.1	1♍46.6	15♏10.0	10♍ 8.3
2 Tu	12 38 29	11 32 18	22 3 58	28 31 37	26R 36.3	13 43.3	3 30.9	6 50.4	29 29.3	20 7.5	1R 44.8	15R 8.8	10R 7.0
3 W	12 42 25	12 31 28	4♌54 36	11♌13 26	26 36.1	15 47.0	4 42.2	7 1.3	29 43.7	20 12.8	1 42.9	15 7.5	10 5.7
4 Th	12 46 22	13 30 36	17 28 34	23 40 29	26 34.4	17 51.0	5 53.6	7 12.8	29 58.0	20 18.1	1 41.2	15 6.1	10 4.4
5 F	12 50 18	14 29 42	29 49 36	5♍56 18	26 30.4	19 55.2	7 5.1	7 24.8	0♈12.3	20 23.3	1 39.5	15 4.8	10 3.2
6 Sa	12 54 15	15 28 45	12♍ 0 56	18 3 47	26 23.5	21 59.4	8 16.6	7 37.3	0 26.6	20 28.4	1 37.8	15 3.5	10 2.0
7 Su	12 58 11	16 27 47	24 5 9	0♎ 5 16	26 13.7	24 3.3	9 28.1	7 50.3	0 40.9	20 33.4	1 36.1	15 2.1	10 0.8
8 M	13 2 8	17 26 46	6♎ 4 18	12 2 28	26 1.4	26 6.5	10 39.6	8 3.8	0 55.1	20 38.4	1 34.5	15 0.7	9 59.6
9 Tu	13 6 4	18 25 43	17 59 55	23 56 48	25 47.6	28 8.8	11 51.2	8 17.8	1 9.3	20 43.3	1 33.0	14 59.3	9 58.4
10 W	13 10 1	19 24 38	29 53 17	5♏49 31	25 33.2	0♉ 9.8	13 2.8	8 32.3	1 23.5	20 48.2	1 31.5	14 57.9	9 57.3
11 Th	13 13 58	20 23 31	11♏45 42	17 42 2	25 19.6	2 9.1	14 14.5	8 47.2	1 37.6	20 53.0	1 30.0	14 56.4	9 56.1
12 F	13 17 54	21 22 22	23 38 47	29 36 11	25 7.6	4 6.5	15 26.2	9 2.7	1 51.7	20 57.7	1 28.6	14 55.0	9 55.0
13 Sa	13 21 51	22 21 11	5♐34 36	11♐34 23	24 58.2	6 1.5	16 37.9	9 18.5	2 5.8	21 2.3	1 27.2	14 53.5	9 53.9
14 Su	13 25 47	23 19 59	17 35 56	23 39 43	24 51.7	7 53.9	17 49.7	9 34.8	2 19.9	21 6.9	1 25.9	14 52.0	9 52.9
15 M	13 29 44	24 18 45	29 46 14	5♑56 2	24 48.0	9 43.2	19 1.5	9 51.5	2 33.9	21 11.4	1 24.6	14 50.5	9 51.8
16 Tu	13 33 40	25 17 29	12♑ 9 39	18 27 40	24 46.5	11 29.2	20 13.3	10 8.7	2 47.9	21 15.8	1 23.3	14 49.0	9 50.8
17 W	13 37 37	26 16 11	24 50 41	1♒19 16	24 46.2	13 11.6	21 25.2	10 26.3	3 1.8	21 20.2	1 22.2	14 47.5	9 49.8
18 Th	13 41 33	27 14 52	7♒53 57	14 35 13	24 46.1	14 50.1	22 37.1	10 44.2	3 15.7	21 24.5	1 21.0	14 46.0	9 48.9
19 F	13 45 30	28 13 31	21 23 26	28 18 53	24 44.8	16 24.5	23 49.0	11 2.6	3 29.6	21 28.7	1 19.9	14 44.5	9 47.9
20 Sa	13 49 27	29 12 8	5♓21 40	12♓31 43	24 41.4	17 54.6	25 1.0	11 21.3	3 43.4	21 32.8	1 18.9	14 42.9	9 47.0
21 Su	13 53 23	0♉10 44	19 48 45	27 12 16	24 35.4	19 20.3	26 12.9	11 40.5	3 57.2	21 36.8	1 17.9	14 41.3	9 46.1
22 M	13 57 20	1 9 18	4♈41 29	12♈15 25	24 26.8	20 41.3	27 24.9	11 60.0	4 10.9	21 40.8	1 16.9	14 39.8	9 45.3
23 Tu	14 1 16	2 7 50	19 52 53	27 32 31	24 16.5	21 57.5	28 37.0	12 19.8	4 24.6	21 44.6	1 16.0	14 38.2	9 44.4
24 W	14 5 13	3 6 20	5♉12 52	12♉52 26	24 5.5	23 8.8	29 49.0	12 40.1	4 38.3	21 48.4	1 15.2	14 36.6	9 43.6
25 Th	14 9 9	4 4 49	20 29 46	28 3 31	23 55.1	24 15.1	1♈ 1.1	13 0.7	4 51.9	21 52.2	1 14.4	14 35.0	9 42.8
26 F	14 13 6	5 3 15	5♊32 31	12♊55 48	23 46.6	25 16.4	2 13.2	13 21.6	5 5.4	21 55.8	1 13.7	14 33.4	9 42.0
27 Sa	14 17 2	6 1 40	20 12 37	27 22 29	23 40.7	26 12.4	3 25.3	13 42.9	5 18.9	21 59.3	1 13.0	14 31.8	9 41.3
28 Su	14 20 59	7 0 2	4♋25 6	11♋20 26	23 37.4	27 3.2	4 37.4	14 4.5	5 32.4	22 2.8	1 12.4	14 30.2	9 40.6
29 M	14 24 55	7 58 23	18 8 34	24 49 48	23D 36.2	27 48.7	5 49.6	14 26.4	5 45.8	22 6.2	1 11.8	14 28.6	9 39.9
30 Tu	14 28 52	8 56 41	1♌24 30	7♌53 7	23R 36.2	28 28.7	7 1.7	14 48.7	5 59.1	22 9.5	1 11.2	14 26.9	9 39.3

Astro Data	Planet Ingress	Last Aspect	☽ Ingress	Last Aspect	☽ Ingress	☽ Phases & Eclipses	Astro Data
Dy Hr Mn	Dy Hr Mn	Dy Hr Mn	Dy Hr Mn	Dy Hr Mn	Dy Hr Mn	Dy Hr Mn	1 MARCH 1963
☽0S 12 4:13	♀ ♒ 4 11:41	1 16:07 ♀ △	♊ 1 21:39	2 14:04 ♃ △	♌ 2 14:45	2 17:17 ☽ 11♊25	Julian Day # 23070
♂ D 16 17:21	☿ ♓ 9 5:26	3 12:31 ♃ □	♋ 4 2:08	4 5:30 ♄ ☍	♍ 5 0:20	10 7:49 ○ 19♍01	Delta T 34.6 sec
☽0N 25 23:26	☉ ♈ 21 8:20	5 20:02 ♃ △	♌ 6 9:15	6 6:01 ♆ ⚹	♎ 7 11:49	18 12:08 ☽ 27♐10	SVP 05♓46'42"
☿0N 27 22:00	☿ ♈ 26 3:52	8 16:57 ☿ ☍	♍ 8 18:34	9 5:32 ♄ △	♏ 10 0:14	25 12:10 ● 4♈08	Obliquity 23°26'35"
	♀ ♓ 30 1:00	10 17:53 ♃ ☍	♎ 11 5:35	11 18:33 ♄ □	♐ 12 12:48		⚷ Chiron 10♓25.8
♃□♆ 4 12:28		12 17:54 ♄ △	♏ 13 17:51	14 12:21 ☉ △	♑ 15 0:27	1 3:15 ☽ 10♋41	☽ Mean ☊ 27♋33.6
☽0S 8 10:23	♃ ♈ 4 3:19	15 21:06 ♃ △	♐ 16 6:27	17 2:52 ☉ □	♒ 17 9:34	9 0:57 ○ 18♎28	
♃⚻♅ 10 12:14	☿ ♉ 9 22:03	18 12:08 ☉ □	♑ 18 17:35	19 12:44 ☉ ⚹	♓ 19 14:53	17 2:52 ☽ 26♑23	1 APRIL 1963
♃0N 14 16:03	☉ ♉ 20 19:36	21 0:48 ☉ ⚹	♒ 21 1:21	21 11:19 ♀ ☌	♈ 21 16:30	23 20:29 ● 2♉58	Julian Day # 23101
☽0N 22 10:34	♀ ♈ 24 3:39	22 14:16 ♀ ☌	♓ 23 5:04	23 2:56 ♄ ⚹	♉ 23 15:51	30 15:08 ☽ 9♌33	Delta T 34.6 sec
♀0N 27 5:01		25 2:22 ☿ ☌	♈ 25 5:38	25 6:24 ☿ ☌	♊ 25 15:06		SVP 05♓46'39"
		26 23:11 ♀ ⚹	♉ 27 4:57	27 2:58 ♄ △	♋ 27 16:27		Obliquity 23°26'35"
		29 3:28 ♀ □	♊ 29 5:13	29 18:22 ☿ ⚹	♌ 29 21:25		⚷ Chiron 12♓21.3
		31 6:36 ♃ □	♋ 31 8:13				☽ Mean ☊ 25♋55.1

LONGITUDE — MAY 1963

Day	Sid.Time	☉	0 hr ☽	Noon ☽	True ☊	☿	♀	♂	♃	♄	♅	♆	♇
1 W	14 32 49	9♉54 58	14♌16 13	20♌34 19	23♋36.2	29♉ 3.4	8♈13.9	15♌11.2	6♈12.4	22♒12.7	1♍10.8	14♏25.3	9♍38.6
2 Th	14 36 45	10 53 12	26 48 0	2♍57 52	23R 35.2	29 32.6	9 26.1	15 34.1	6 25.6	22 15.8	1R 10.3	14R 23.7	9R 38.1
3 F	14 40 42	11 51 24	9♍ 4 26	15 8 15	23 32.0	29 56.3	10 38.3	15 57.2	6 38.8	22 18.8	1 10.0	14 22.1	9 37.5
4 Sa	14 44 38	12 49 34	21 9 48	27 9 33	23 26.4	0♊14.6	11 50.5	16 20.6	6 51.9	22 21.8	1 9.7	14 20.4	9 36.9
5 Su	14 48 35	13 47 42	3♎ 7 55	9♎ 5 14	23 18.1	0 27.5	13 2.7	16 44.3	7 4.9	22 24.6	1 9.4	14 18.8	9 36.4
6 M	14 52 31	14 45 48	15 1 52	20 58 6	23 7.6	0R 35.0	14 15.0	17 8.3	7 17.9	22 27.4	1 9.2	14 17.1	9 35.9
7 Tu	14 56 28	15 43 53	26 54 10	2♏50 19	22 55.6	0 37.2	15 27.3	17 32.6	7 30.8	22 30.1	1 9.0	14 15.5	9 35.5
8 W	15 0 24	16 41 55	8♏46 43	14 43 35	22 43.1	0 34.4	16 39.5	17 57.1	7 43.7	22 32.7	1 8.9	14 13.9	9 35.1
9 Th	15 4 21	17 39 56	20 41 5	26 39 22	22 31.1	0 26.6	17 51.9	18 21.8	7 56.5	22 35.2	1D 8.9	14 12.3	9 34.7
10 F	15 8 18	18 37 56	2♐38 38	8♐39 4	22 20.8	0 14.2	19 4.2	18 46.8	8 9.2	22 37.6	1 8.9	14 10.6	9 34.3
11 Sa	15 12 14	19 35 54	14 40 54	20 44 21	22 12.6	29♉57.4	20 16.5	19 12.1	8 21.8	22 39.9	1 8.9	14 9.0	9 34.0
12 Su	15 16 11	20 33 50	26 49 42	2♑57 16	22 7.1	29 36.6	21 28.9	19 37.6	8 34.4	22 42.1	1 9.0	14 7.4	9 33.7
13 M	15 20 7	21 31 45	9♑ 7 24	15 20 27	22 4.2	29 12.1	22 41.3	20 3.3	8 46.9	22 44.2	1 9.2	14 5.8	9 33.4
14 Tu	15 24 4	22 29 39	21 36 51	27 57 1	22D 3.3	28 44.5	23 53.7	20 29.3	8 59.4	22 46.3	1 9.4	14 4.1	9 33.1
15 W	15 28 0	23 27 32	4♒21 25	10♒50 30	22 3.8	28 14.3	25 6.1	20 55.5	9 11.8	22 48.2	1 9.7	14 2.5	9 32.9
16 Th	15 31 57	24 25 23	17 24 42	24 4 26	22R 4.5	27 41.9	26 18.5	21 21.9	9 24.0	22 50.0	1 10.0	14 0.9	9 32.7
17 F	15 35 53	25 23 13	0♓50 3	7♓41 49	22 4.6	27 8.1	27 31.0	21 48.5	9 36.3	22 51.8	1 10.4	13 59.3	9 32.6
18 Sa	15 39 50	26 21 2	14 39 56	21 44 25	22 3.1	26 33.3	28 43.4	22 15.4	9 48.4	22 53.4	1 10.8	13 57.7	9 32.4
19 Su	15 43 47	27 18 50	28 55 8	6♈11 47	21 59.6	25 58.3	29 55.9	22 42.5	10 0.5	22 55.0	1 11.3	13 56.2	9 32.3
20 M	15 47 43	28 16 36	13♈33 51	21 0 38	21 54.0	25 23.5	1♉ 8.4	23 9.7	10 12.4	22 56.5	1 11.9	13 54.6	9 32.3
21 Tu	15 51 40	29 14 22	28 31 14	6♉ 4 35	21 46.9	24 49.7	2 20.9	23 37.2	10 24.3	22 57.8	1 12.5	13 53.0	9D 32.2
22 W	15 55 36	0♊12 6	13♉39 28	21 14 36	21 39.1	24 17.3	3 33.5	24 4.9	10 36.1	22 59.1	1 13.1	13 51.5	9 32.2
23 Th	15 59 33	1 9 49	28 48 40	6♊20 24	21 31.7	23 47.0	4 46.0	24 32.8	10 47.9	23 0.3	1 13.8	13 49.9	9 32.3
24 F	16 3 29	2 7 31	13♊48 36	21 12 13	21 25.7	23 19.2	5 58.6	25 0.9	10 59.5	23 1.3	1 14.6	13 48.4	9 32.3
25 Sa	16 7 26	3 5 12	28 30 22	5♋42 23	21 21.6	22 54.3	7 11.1	25 29.2	11 11.1	23 2.3	1 15.4	13 46.8	9 32.4
26 Su	16 11 22	4 2 51	12♋47 46	19 46 15	21D 19.6	22 32.8	8 23.7	25 57.7	11 22.5	23 3.2	1 16.2	13 45.3	9 32.5
27 M	16 15 19	5 0 29	26 37 44	3♌22 18	21 19.4	22 14.8	9 36.3	26 26.4	11 33.9	23 4.0	1 17.1	13 43.8	9 32.7
28 Tu	16 19 16	5 58 5	10♌ 0 10	16 31 39	21 20.3	22 0.8	10 48.9	26 55.2	11 45.2	23 4.6	1 18.1	13 42.3	9 32.9
29 W	16 23 12	6 55 40	22 57 12	29 17 17	21 21.6	21 50.9	12 1.5	27 24.2	11 56.3	23 5.2	1 19.1	13 40.9	9 33.1
30 Th	16 27 9	7 53 13	5♍32 28	11♍43 18	21R 22.4	21D 45.2	13 14.2	27 53.4	12 7.4	23 5.7	1 20.2	13 39.4	9 33.3
31 F	16 31 5	8 50 45	17 50 22	23 54 15	21 21.9	21 44.0	14 26.8	28 22.8	12 18.4	23 6.1	1 21.3	13 38.0	9 33.6

LONGITUDE — JUNE 1963

Day	Sid.Time	☉	0 hr ☽	Noon ☽	True ☊	☿	♀	♂	♃	♄	♅	♆	♇
1 Sa	16 35 2	9♊48 16	29♍55 32	5♎54 45	21♋19.9	21♉47.2	15♉39.4	28♌52.3	12♈29.3	23♒ 6.4	1♍22.5	13♏36.5	9♍33.9
2 Su	16 38 58	10 45 45	11♎52 26	17 49 4	21R 16.0	21 54.8	16 52.1	29 22.0	12 40.1	23 6.6	1 23.7	13R 35.1	9 34.2
3 M	16 42 55	11 43 13	23 45 6	29 40 58	21 10.7	22 7.0	18 4.8	29 51.9	12 50.7	23R 6.6	1 25.0	13 33.7	9 34.6
4 Tu	16 46 51	12 40 40	5♏37 2	11♏33 39	21 4.2	22 23.6	19 17.4	0♍21.9	13 1.3	23 6.6	1 26.3	13 32.3	9 35.0
5 W	16 50 48	13 38 6	17 31 7	23 29 43	20 57.4	22 44.7	20 30.1	0 52.1	13 11.8	23 6.5	1 27.7	13 31.0	9 35.4
6 Th	16 54 45	14 35 30	29 29 40	5♐31 11	20 50.9	23 10.1	21 42.9	1 22.4	13 22.1	23 6.3	1 29.1	13 29.6	9 35.9
7 F	16 58 41	15 32 54	11♐34 28	17 39 41	20 45.3	23 39.8	22 55.6	1 52.9	13 32.4	23 6.0	1 30.6	13 28.3	9 36.4
8 Sa	17 2 38	16 30 17	23 47 1	29 56 36	20 41.1	24 13.7	24 8.3	2 23.5	13 42.5	23 5.6	1 32.1	13 27.0	9 36.9
9 Su	17 6 34	17 27 39	6♑ 8 37	12♑23 14	20 38.5	24 51.7	25 21.1	2 54.3	13 52.6	23 5.1	1 33.7	13 25.7	9 37.4
10 M	17 10 31	18 25 1	18 40 38	25 1 0	20D 37.5	25 33.8	26 33.9	3 25.2	14 2.5	23 4.5	1 35.3	13 24.4	9 38.0
11 Tu	17 14 27	19 22 21	1♒24 32	7♒51 27	20 38.0	26 19.8	27 46.7	3 56.3	14 12.3	23 3.9	1 37.0	13 23.2	9 38.6
12 W	17 18 24	20 19 41	14 21 59	20 56 21	20 39.2	27 9.7	28 59.5	4 27.5	14 22.0	23 3.1	1 38.7	13 21.9	9 39.2
13 Th	17 22 21	21 17 1	27 34 48	4♓17 30	20 40.8	28 3.3	0♊12.3	4 58.8	14 31.6	23 2.2	1 40.4	13 20.7	9 39.9
14 F	17 26 17	22 14 20	11♓ 4 38	17 56 21	20R 42.0	29 0.7	1 25.2	5 30.3	14 41.0	23 1.2	1 42.2	13 19.5	9 40.6
15 Sa	17 30 14	23 11 39	24 52 43	1♈53 42	20 42.4	0♊ 1.7	2 38.0	6 1.9	14 50.4	23 0.1	1 44.1	13 18.3	9 41.3
16 Su	17 34 10	24 8 57	8♈59 11	16 8 59	20 41.7	1 6.3	3 50.9	6 33.6	14 59.6	22 59.0	1 46.0	13 17.2	9 42.0
17 M	17 38 7	25 6 15	23 22 44	0♉39 58	20 39.8	2 14.4	5 3.8	7 5.5	15 8.7	22 57.7	1 47.9	13 16.1	9 42.8
18 Tu	17 42 3	26 3 33	8♉ 0 5	15 22 22	20 37.1	3 25.9	6 16.7	7 37.5	15 17.6	22 56.4	1 49.9	13 15.0	9 43.6
19 W	17 46 0	27 0 50	22 46 0	0♊10 5	20 34.0	4 40.9	7 29.7	8 9.6	15 26.5	22 54.9	1 52.0	13 13.9	9 44.5
20 Th	17 49 56	27 58 7	7♊33 41	14 55 50	20 31.0	5 59.2	8 42.6	8 41.9	15 35.2	22 53.4	1 54.0	13 12.8	9 45.3
21 F	17 53 53	28 55 24	22 15 36	29 32 6	20 28.6	7 20.9	9 55.6	9 14.3	15 43.8	22 51.7	1 56.2	13 11.8	9 46.2
22 Sa	17 57 50	29 52 41	6♋44 33	13♋52 17	20D 27.1	8 45.8	11 8.6	9 46.8	15 52.2	22 50.0	1 58.3	13 10.8	9 47.2
23 Su	18 1 46	0♋49 57	20 54 46	27 51 34	20 26.7	10 14.0	12 21.6	10 19.5	16 0.5	22 48.2	2 0.6	13 9.8	9 48.1
24 M	18 5 43	1 47 12	4♌42 27	11♌27 17	20 27.1	11 45.4	13 34.7	10 52.3	16 8.7	22 46.3	2 2.8	13 8.9	9 49.1
25 Tu	18 9 39	2 44 27	18 6 5	24 38 59	20 28.2	13 20.0	14 47.7	11 25.2	16 16.7	22 44.3	2 5.1	13 7.9	9 50.1
26 W	18 13 36	3 41 42	1♍ 6 13	7♍28 7	20 29.5	14 57.8	16 0.8	11 58.2	16 24.6	22 42.2	2 7.4	13 7.0	9 51.1
27 Th	18 17 32	4 38 55	13 45 5	19 57 34	20 30.7	16 38.7	17 13.8	12 31.3	16 32.3	22 40.1	2 9.8	13 6.1	9 52.2
28 F	18 21 29	5 36 9	26 6 6	2♎11 11	20R 31.5	18 22.6	18 26.9	13 4.6	16 39.9	22 37.8	2 12.2	13 5.3	9 53.3
29 Sa	18 25 25	6 33 21	8♎13 24	14 13 19	20 31.7	20 9.4	19 40.0	13 37.9	16 47.4	22 35.5	2 14.7	13 4.5	9 54.4
30 Su	18 29 22	7 30 33	20 11 29	26 8 30	20 31.3	21 59.2	20 53.1	14 11.4	16 54.7	22 33.0	2 17.2	13 3.7	9 55.5

Astro Data	Dy Hr Mn
☽0S	5 16:48
♃∠♄	6 22:14
☿ R	6 22:30
♅ D	9 10:16
♃⊼♇	16 16:49
☽0N	19 20:57
♇ D	21 15:40
☿ D	30 18:52
☽0S	1 23:57
♄ R	3 9:39
♃⊼♆	6 15:27
☽0N	16 5:08
☽0S	29 7:50

Planet Ingress	Dy Hr Mn
☿ ♊	3 4:17
☿ ♉	10 20:39
♀ ♉	19 1:21
☉ ♊	21 18:58
♂ ♍	3 6:30
♀ ♊	12 19:57
☿ ♊	14 23:20
☉ ♋	22 3:04

Last Aspect Dy Hr Mn		☽ Ingress Dy Hr Mn
2 5:31	☿ □	♍ 2 6:13
3 10:27	♆ ✱	♎ 4 17:42
6 15:04	♄ △	♏ 7 6:16
9 3:50	♄ □	♐ 9 18:42
11 15:51	♄ ✱	♑ 12 6:13
14 12:59	☿ △	♒ 14 15:51
16 17:43	☿ □	♓ 16 22:32
18 21:08	☉ ✱	♈ 19 1:48
20 15:56	♂ △	♉ 21 2:21
22 17:01	♂ □	♊ 23 1:53
24 18:51	♂ ✱	♋ 25 2:29
26 16:28	☿ ✱	♌ 27 5:58
29 8:45	♂ ☌	♍ 29 13:22

Last Aspect Dy Hr Mn		☽ Ingress Dy Hr Mn
31 7:43	☿ △	♎ 1 0:09
2 22:42	♄ △	♏ 3 12:39
5 11:13	♄ □	♐ 6 1:01
7 22:39	♄ ✱	♑ 8 12:07
10 16:29	♀ △	♒ 10 21:22
13 0:55	☿ □	♓ 13 4:21
14 20:53	☉ □	♈ 15 8:46
17 3:03	☉ ✱	♉ 17 10:54
19 0:14	♄ □	♊ 19 11:44
21 11:46	☉ ☌	♋ 21 12:46
22 15:33	♃ □	♌ 23 15:44
25 8:27	♄ ☍	♍ 25 21:56
27 7:26	♀ □	♎ 28 7:41
30 4:44	♄ △	♏ 30 19:48

☽ Phases & Eclipses Dy Hr Mn	
8 17:23	○ 17♏24
16 13:36	☽ 24♒58
23 4:00	● 1♊19
30 4:55	☽ 8♍05
7 8:31	○ 15♐53
14 20:53	☽ 23♓04
21 11:46	● 29♊23
28 20:24	☽ 6♎25

Astro Data

1 MAY 1963
Julian Day # 23131
Delta T 34.7 sec
SVP 05♓46'35"
Obliquity 23°26'35"
⚷ Chiron 13♓52.1
☽ Mean ☊ 24♋19.7

1 JUNE 1963
Julian Day # 23162
Delta T 34.7 sec
SVP 05♓46'31"
Obliquity 23°26'35"
⚷ Chiron 14♓46.4
☽ Mean ☊ 22♋41.2

JULY 1963 LONGITUDE

Day	Sid.Time	☉	0 hr ☽	Noon ☽	True ☊	☿	♀	♂	♃	♄	♅	♆	♇
1 M	18 33 19	8♋27 45	2♏ 4 52	8♏ 1 9	20♋30.4	23♊51.8	22♊ 6.3	14♍45.0	17♈ 1.8	22♒30.5	2♍19.7	13♏ 2.9	9♍56.7
2 Tu	18 37 15	9 24 57	13 57 49	19 55 23	20R 29.1	25 47.0	23 19.4	15 18.7	17 8.9	22R 28.0	2 22.3	13R 2.2	9 57.8
3 W	18 41 12	10 22 8	25 54 15	1♐54 49	20 27.7	27 44.8	24 32.6	15 52.5	17 15.7	22 25.3	2 24.9	13 1.4	9 59.1
4 Th	18 45 8	11 19 19	7♐57 29	14 2 32	20 26.4	29 44.9	25 45.8	16 26.4	17 22.4	22 22.5	2 27.6	13 0.8	10 0.3
5 F	18 49 5	12 16 30	20 10 15	26 20 53	20 25.3	1♋47.1	26 59.0	17 0.4	17 29.0	22 19.7	2 30.3	13 0.1	10 1.6
6 Sa	18 53 1	13 13 41	2♑34 37	8♑51 37	20 24.6	3 51.2	28 12.3	17 34.5	17 35.4	22 16.8	2 33.0	12 59.5	10 2.9
7 Su	18 56 58	14 10 51	15 11 59	21 35 47	20D 24.3	5 56.9	29 25.5	18 8.7	17 41.6	22 13.9	2 35.8	12 58.9	10 4.2
8 M	19 0 54	15 8 2	28 3 6	4♒33 54	20 24.3	8 4.0	0♋38.8	18 43.0	17 47.7	22 10.8	2 38.6	12 58.3	10 5.5
9 Tu	19 4 51	16 5 13	11♒ 8 13	17 45 59	20 24.6	10 12.1	1 52.1	19 17.4	17 53.6	22 7.7	2 41.4	12 57.8	10 6.9
10 W	19 8 48	17 2 24	24 27 9	1♓11 39	20 24.9	12 21.1	3 5.4	19 51.9	17 59.4	22 4.5	2 44.2	12 57.3	10 8.2
11 Th	19 12 44	17 59 36	7♓59 24	14 50 17	20 25.2	14 30.4	4 18.7	20 26.6	18 5.0	22 1.3	2 47.1	12 56.8	10 9.6
12 F	19 16 41	18 56 47	21 44 11	28 40 56	20 25.4	16 40.0	5 32.1	21 1.3	18 10.4	21 57.9	2 50.1	12 56.3	10 11.1
13 Sa	19 20 37	19 54 0	5♈40 25	12♈42 24	20 25.5	18 49.5	6 45.5	21 36.1	18 15.6	21 54.5	2 53.0	12 55.9	10 12.5
14 Su	19 24 34	20 51 12	19 46 41	26 53 1	20 25.5	20 58.6	7 58.9	22 11.0	18 20.7	21 51.1	2 56.0	12 55.5	10 14.0
15 M	19 28 30	21 48 26	4♉ 1 5	11♉10 34	20 25.5	23 7.2	9 12.3	22 46.0	18 25.6	21 47.6	2 59.0	12 55.2	10 15.5
16 Tu	19 32 27	22 45 40	18 21 6	25 32 14	20 25.6	25 14.9	10 25.8	23 21.1	18 30.4	21 44.0	3 2.1	12 54.9	10 17.0
17 W	19 36 23	23 42 55	2♊43 31	9♊54 28	20 25.9	27 21.6	11 39.3	23 56.3	18 35.0	21 40.3	3 5.2	12 54.6	10 18.5
18 Th	19 40 20	24 40 10	17 4 33	24 13 14	20 26.2	29 27.2	12 52.8	24 31.6	18 39.4	21 36.7	3 8.3	12 54.3	10 20.1
19 F	19 44 17	25 37 26	1♋19 58	8♋24 13	20 26.6	1♌31.4	14 6.3	25 7.0	18 43.6	21 32.9	3 11.5	12 54.1	10 21.7
20 Sa	19 48 13	26 34 43	15 25 28	22 23 16	20R 26.8	3 34.3	15 19.9	25 42.5	18 47.6	21 29.1	3 14.6	12 53.9	10 23.3
21 Su	19 52 10	27 32 0	29 17 10	6♌ 6 50	20 26.8	5 35.7	16 33.5	26 18.1	18 51.5	21 25.2	3 17.8	12 53.7	10 24.9
22 M	19 56 6	28 29 18	12♌51 59	19 32 25	20 26.3	7 35.4	17 47.1	26 53.8	18 55.2	21 21.3	3 21.1	12 53.6	10 26.5
23 Tu	20 0 3	29 26 36	26 8 0	2♍38 44	20 25.5	9 33.6	19 0.7	27 29.6	18 58.6	21 17.3	3 24.3	12 53.5	10 28.2
24 W	20 3 59	0♌23 55	9♍ 4 40	15 25 56	20 24.3	11 30.1	20 14.3	28 5.4	19 1.9	21 13.3	3 27.6	12 53.4	10 29.9
25 Th	20 7 56	1 21 13	21 42 47	27 55 30	20 22.9	13 24.9	21 28.0	28 41.4	19 5.1	21 9.3	3 30.9	12D 53.3	10 31.6
26 F	20 11 52	2 18 33	4♎ 4 27	10♎10 2	20 21.5	15 18.1	22 41.7	29 17.5	19 8.0	21 5.2	3 34.2	12 53.3	10 33.3
27 Sa	20 15 49	3 15 52	16 12 45	22 13 4	20 20.4	17 9.5	23 55.4	29 53.6	19 10.7	21 1.0	3 37.6	12 53.4	10 35.0
28 Su	20 19 46	4 13 13	28 11 34	4♏ 8 46	20D 19.8	18 59.2	25 9.1	0♎29.8	19 13.3	20 56.9	3 41.0	12 53.4	10 36.7
29 M	20 23 42	5 10 33	10♏ 5 17	16 1 40	20 19.7	20 47.2	26 22.8	1 6.2	19 15.6	20 52.6	3 44.4	12 53.5	10 38.5
30 Tu	20 27 39	6 7 54	21 58 32	27 56 26	20 20.3	22 33.5	27 36.6	1 42.6	19 17.8	20 48.4	3 47.8	12 53.6	10 40.3
31 W	20 31 35	7 5 16	3♐55 57	9♐57 36	20 21.5	24 18.1	28 50.4	2 19.0	19 19.8	20 44.1	3 51.2	12 53.8	10 42.1

AUGUST 1963 LONGITUDE

Day	Sid.Time	☉	0 hr ☽	Noon ☽	True ☊	☿	♀	♂	♃	♄	♅	♆	♇
1 Th	20 35 32	8♌ 2 39	16♐ 1 55	22♐ 9 21	20♋22.9	26♌ 1.0	0♌ 4.2	2♎55.6	19♈21.6	20♒39.8	3♍54.7	12♏54.0	10♍43.9
2 F	20 39 28	9 0 2	28 20 19	4♑35 13	20 24.2	27 42.2	1 18.0	3 32.3	19 23.2	20R 35.5	3 58.2	12 54.2	10 45.7
3 Sa	20 43 25	9 57 25	10♑54 20	17 17 54	20R 25.2	29 21.7	2 31.8	4 9.0	19 24.6	20 31.1	4 1.7	12 54.4	10 47.6
4 Su	20 47 21	10 54 50	23 46 5	0♒18 58	20 25.4	0♍59.6	3 45.7	4 45.8	19 25.8	20 26.7	4 5.2	12 54.7	10 49.4
5 M	20 51 18	11 52 15	6♒56 33	13 38 42	20 24.7	2 35.8	4 59.6	5 22.7	19 26.8	20 22.3	4 8.7	12 55.0	10 51.3
6 Tu	20 55 15	12 49 41	20 25 17	27 16 0	20 22.8	4 10.4	6 13.5	5 59.7	19 27.6	20 17.9	4 12.3	12 55.4	10 53.2
7 W	20 59 11	13 47 9	4♓10 32	11♓ 8 28	20 20.1	5 43.3	7 27.4	6 36.8	19 28.3	20 13.5	4 15.8	12 55.8	10 55.1
8 Th	21 3 8	14 44 37	18 9 22	25 12 45	20 16.8	7 14.5	8 41.4	7 14.0	19 28.7	20 9.0	4 19.4	12 56.2	10 57.0
9 F	21 7 4	15 42 6	2♈18 5	9♈24 52	20 13.3	8 44.0	9 55.4	7 51.2	19R 28.9	20 4.6	4 23.0	12 56.6	10 58.9
10 Sa	21 11 1	16 39 37	16 32 37	23 40 51	20 10.3	10 11.9	11 9.4	8 28.5	19 28.9	20 0.1	4 26.6	12 57.1	11 0.8
11 Su	21 14 57	17 37 9	0♉49 7	7♉57 3	20 8.2	11 38.1	12 23.4	9 5.9	19 28.8	19 55.6	4 30.3	12 57.6	11 2.8
12 M	21 18 54	18 34 43	15 4 16	22 10 29	20D 7.3	13 2.5	13 37.4	9 43.4	19 28.4	19 51.1	4 33.9	12 58.1	11 4.7
13 Tu	21 22 50	19 32 18	29 15 27	6♊18 55	20 7.5	14 25.2	14 51.5	10 20.9	19 27.8	19 46.6	4 37.6	12 58.7	11 6.7
14 W	21 26 47	20 29 55	13♊20 41	20 20 36	20 8.7	15 46.1	16 5.6	10 58.6	19 27.1	19 42.1	4 41.2	12 59.3	11 8.7
15 Th	21 30 44	21 27 33	27 18 28	4♋14 9	20 10.1	17 5.2	17 19.7	11 36.3	19 26.1	19 37.6	4 44.9	12 59.9	11 10.7
16 F	21 34 40	22 25 13	11♋ 7 29	17 58 18	20R 11.3	18 22.4	18 33.9	12 14.1	19 24.9	19 33.1	4 48.6	13 0.6	11 12.7
17 Sa	21 38 37	23 22 54	24 46 26	1♌31 42	20 11.5	19 37.8	19 48.0	12 52.0	19 23.6	19 28.6	4 52.3	13 1.3	11 14.7
18 Su	21 42 33	24 20 37	8♌13 55	14 52 57	20 10.2	20 51.1	21 2.2	13 30.0	19 22.0	19 24.2	4 56.0	13 2.0	11 16.7
19 M	21 46 30	25 18 21	21 28 36	28 0 46	20 7.2	22 2.4	22 16.4	14 8.1	19 20.2	19 19.7	4 59.7	13 2.8	11 18.7
20 Tu	21 50 26	26 16 6	4♍29 20	10♍54 13	20 2.6	23 11.5	23 30.6	14 46.2	19 18.3	19 15.2	5 3.5	13 3.6	11 20.8
21 W	21 54 23	27 13 52	17 15 24	23 32 56	19 56.6	24 18.5	24 44.9	15 24.4	19 16.1	19 10.8	5 7.2	13 4.4	11 22.8
22 Th	21 58 19	28 11 40	29 46 54	5♎57 26	19 49.9	25 23.1	25 59.1	16 2.7	19 13.8	19 6.4	5 10.9	13 5.2	11 24.9
23 F	22 2 16	29 9 29	12♎ 4 47	18 9 11	19 43.3	26 25.3	27 13.4	16 41.1	19 11.2	19 2.0	5 14.7	13 6.1	11 26.9
24 Sa	22 6 13	0♍ 7 20	24 10 59	0♏10 34	19 37.3	27 24.9	28 27.7	17 19.6	19 8.5	18 57.6	5 18.4	13 7.0	11 29.0
25 Su	22 10 9	1 5 11	6♏ 8 24	12 4 58	19 32.7	28 21.9	29 42.0	17 58.1	19 5.5	18 53.2	5 22.2	13 8.0	11 31.0
26 M	22 14 6	2 3 4	18 0 48	23 56 28	19 29.8	29 16.0	0♍56.3	18 36.7	19 2.4	18 48.9	5 25.9	13 8.9	11 33.1
27 Tu	22 18 2	3 0 59	29 52 34	5♐49 43	19D 28.6	0♎ 7.2	2 10.7	19 15.4	18 59.1	18 44.6	5 29.7	13 10.0	11 35.2
28 W	22 21 59	3 58 54	11♐48 32	17 49 41	19 28.9	0 55.1	3 25.0	19 54.2	18 55.6	18 40.4	5 33.5	13 11.0	11 37.3
29 Th	22 25 55	4 56 51	23 53 47	0♑ 1 26	19 30.0	1 39.7	4 39.4	20 33.1	18 51.9	18 36.1	5 37.2	13 12.0	11 39.4
30 F	22 29 52	5 54 49	6♑13 12	12 29 39	19 31.4	2 20.6	5 53.8	21 12.0	18 48.1	18 31.9	5 41.0	13 13.1	11 41.4
31 Sa	22 33 48	6 52 49	18 51 14	25 18 21	19R 32.1	2 57.8	7 8.2	21 51.0	18 44.0	18 27.8	5 44.8	13 14.3	11 43.5

Astro Data Dy Hr Mn	Planet Ingress Dy Hr Mn	Last Aspect Dy Hr Mn	☽ Ingress Dy Hr Mn	Last Aspect Dy Hr Mn	☽ Ingress Dy Hr Mn	☽ Phases & Eclipses Dy Hr Mn	Astro Data
♃⚼♅ 5 8:19	☿ ♋ 4 3:00	2 17:03 ♄ □	♐ 3 8:11	1 22:35 ☿ △	♑ 2 3:12	6 21:55 ○ 14♑06	1 JULY 1963
☽0N 13 11:06	♀ ♋ 7 11:18	5 14:40 ♀ ☍	♑ 5 19:03	3 15:57 ♃ □	♒ 4 11:25	6 22:02 ☍ P 0.706	Julian Day # 23192
♆ D 25 19:14	☿ ♌ 18 6:19	7 5:48 ♂ △	♒ 8 3:36	5 23:47 ♄ ☌	♓ 6 16:46	14 1:57 ☽ 20♈56	Delta T 34.7 sec
☽0S 26 15:55	☉ ♌ 23 13:59	9 19:46 ♄ ☌	♓ 10 9:53	7 15:04 ♆ △	♈ 8 20:07	20 20:43 ● 27♋24	SVP 05♓46'26"
♂0S 28 19:43	♂ ♎ 27 4:14	11 22:42 ♂ ☍	♈ 12 14:16	10 5:47 ♄ ✶	♉ 10 22:37	20 20:35:37 ☌ T 1'40"	Obliquity 23°26'35"
	♀ ♌ 31 22:38	14 3:30 ♄ ✶	♉ 14 17:15	12 8:02 ♄ □	♊ 13 1:16	28 13:13 ☽ 4♏45	⚷ Chiron 14♓50.4R
☽0N 9 16:25		16 13:30 ☿ ✶	♊ 16 19:27	14 13:10 ☉ ✶	♋ 15 4:39		☽ Mean ☊ 21♋05.9
♃ R 9 15:26	☿ ♍ 3 9:20	18 13:03 ♂ □	♋ 18 21:45	16 14:31 ♃ □	♌ 17 9:17	5 9:31 ○ 12♒15	1 AUGUST 1963
♃⚼♅ 10 14:40	☉ ♍ 23 20:58	20 20:43 ☉ ☌	♌ 21 1:15	19 7:35 ☉ ☌	♍ 19 15:40	12 6:21 ☽ 18♉50	Julian Day # 23223
♃✶♄ 18 18:56	♀ ♍ 25 5:49	22 15:13 ♄ ☍	♍ 23 7:06	21 14:44 ☿ ☌	♎ 22 0:25	19 7:35 ● 25♌37	Delta T 34.8 sec
☽0S 22 23:39	☿ ♎ 26 20:33	25 14:11 ♂ ☌	♎ 25 16:02	24 9:33 ♀ ✶	♏ 24 11:39	27 6:54 ☽ 3♐18	SVP 05♓46'21"
☿0S 22 10:11		27 17:11 ♀ □	♏ 28 3:38	26 1:37 ♄ □	♐ 27 0:15		Obliquity 23°26'35"
		30 12:38 ♀ △	♐ 30 16:08	28 17:01 ♂ ✶	♑ 29 11:57		⚷ Chiron 14♓05.2R
				31 5:53 ♂ □	♒ 31 20:37		☽ Mean ☊ 19♋27.4

LONGITUDE — SEPTEMBER 1963

Day	Sid.Time	☉	0 hr ☽	Noon ☽	True ☊	☿	♀	♂	♃	♄	♅	♆	♇
1 Su	22 37 45	7♍50 50	1♒51 19	8♒30 18	19♋31.3	3♎30.8	8♍22.6	22♎30.0	18♈39.8	18♒23.7	5♍48.5	13♏15.4	11♍45.6
2 M	22 41 42	8 48 52	15 15 23	22 6 29	19R28.6	3 59.6	9 37.0	23 9.2	18R35.4	18R19.6	5 52.3	13 16.6	11 47.7
3 Tu	22 45 38	9 46 56	29 3 23	6♓ 5 43	19 23.8	4 23.7	10 51.5	23 48.4	18 30.8	18 15.6	5 56.0	13 17.8	11 49.8
4 W	22 49 35	10 45 1	13♓12 56	20 24 23	19 17.1	4 42.9	12 5.9	24 27.7	18 26.1	18 11.6	5 59.8	13 19.0	11 51.9
5 Th	22 53 31	11 43 8	27 39 18	4♈56 49	19 9.1	4 57.0	13 20.4	25 7.1	18 21.2	18 7.7	6 3.5	13 20.3	11 54.0
6 F	22 57 28	12 41 17	12♈16 1	19 35 59	19 0.8	5R 5.5	14 34.9	25 46.5	18 16.1	18 3.8	6 7.3	13 21.6	11 56.1
7 Sa	23 1 24	13 39 28	26 55 48	4♉14 37	18 53.3	5 8.3	15 49.4	26 26.0	18 10.8	17 59.9	6 11.0	13 22.9	11 58.2
8 Su	23 5 21	14 37 41	11♉31 43	18 46 26	18 47.4	5 5.0	17 3.9	27 5.6	18 5.4	17 56.2	6 14.8	13 24.2	12 0.3
9 M	23 9 17	15 35 56	25 58 15	3♊ 6 47	18 43.6	4 55.4	18 18.4	27 45.3	17 59.9	17 52.4	6 18.5	13 25.6	12 2.4
10 Tu	23 13 14	16 34 13	10♊11 46	17 13 3	18D41.9	4 39.4	19 32.9	28 25.0	17 54.2	17 48.8	6 22.2	13 27.0	12 4.5
11 W	23 17 11	17 32 32	24 10 34	1♋ 4 21	18 41.9	4 16.8	20 47.5	29 4.8	17 48.3	17 45.2	6 26.0	13 28.4	12 6.6
12 Th	23 21 7	18 30 53	7♋54 29	14 41 3	18R42.6	3 47.6	22 2.1	29 44.7	17 42.3	17 41.6	6 29.7	13 29.8	12 8.7
13 F	23 25 4	19 29 17	21 24 14	28 4 8	18 42.9	3 11.9	23 16.7	0♏24.7	17 36.2	17 38.2	6 33.4	13 31.3	12 10.8
14 Sa	23 29 0	20 27 42	4♌40 54	11♌14 40	18 41.7	2 29.8	24 31.3	1 4.7	17 29.9	17 34.7	6 37.1	13 32.8	12 12.9
15 Su	23 32 57	21 26 10	17 45 31	24 13 31	18 38.2	1 42.0	25 45.9	1 44.9	17 23.4	17 31.4	6 40.7	13 34.3	12 15.0
16 M	23 36 53	22 24 39	0♍38 44	7♍ 1 12	18 32.1	0 48.9	27 0.5	2 25.1	17 16.9	17 28.1	6 44.4	13 35.9	12 17.0
17 Tu	23 40 50	23 23 11	13 20 55	19 37 54	18 23.2	29♍51.3	28 15.1	3 5.3	17 10.2	17 24.9	6 48.1	13 37.4	12 19.1
18 W	23 44 46	24 21 44	25 52 11	2♎ 3 46	18 12.3	28 50.4	29 29.8	3 45.7	17 3.4	17 21.8	6 51.7	13 39.0	12 21.2
19 Th	23 48 43	25 20 20	8♎12 43	14 19 7	18 0.0	27 47.3	0♎44.5	4 26.1	16 56.5	17 18.7	6 55.3	13 40.7	12 23.2
20 F	23 52 39	26 18 57	20 23 5	26 24 47	17 47.6	26 43.3	1 59.1	5 6.6	16 49.4	17 15.7	6 58.9	13 42.3	12 25.3
21 Sa	23 56 36	27 17 36	2♏24 26	8♏22 17	17 36.0	25 40.1	3 13.8	5 47.2	16 42.3	17 12.8	7 2.5	13 44.0	12 27.3
22 Su	0 0 33	28 16 17	14 18 41	20 14 0	17 26.3	24 39.2	4 28.5	6 27.8	16 35.0	17 10.0	7 6.1	13 45.6	12 29.4
23 M	0 4 29	29 14 59	26 8 40	2♐ 3 11	17 19.1	23 42.2	5 43.2	7 8.5	16 27.7	17 7.2	7 9.7	13 47.3	12 31.4
24 Tu	0 8 26	0♎13 44	7♐58 4	13 53 55	17 14.4	22 50.5	6 57.9	7 49.3	16 20.3	17 4.6	7 13.2	13 49.1	12 33.4
25 W	0 12 22	1 12 30	19 51 19	25 50 57	17 12.2	22 5.5	8 12.6	8 30.2	16 12.8	17 2.0	7 16.8	13 50.8	12 35.5
26 Th	0 16 19	2 11 18	1♑53 27	7♑59 31	17D11.7	21 28.5	9 27.3	9 11.1	16 5.2	16 59.5	7 20.3	13 52.6	12 37.5
27 F	0 20 15	3 10 8	14 9 49	20 24 59	17R11.8	21 0.3	10 42.0	9 52.1	15 57.5	16 57.1	7 23.8	13 54.4	12 39.5
28 Sa	0 24 12	4 8 59	26 45 40	3♒12 24	17 11.5	20 41.7	11 56.7	10 33.2	15 49.8	16 54.7	7 27.3	13 56.2	12 41.5
29 Su	0 28 8	5 7 52	9♒45 41	16 25 53	17 9.8	20D33.2	13 11.4	11 14.3	15 42.0	16 52.5	7 30.7	13 58.0	12 43.4
30 M	0 32 5	6 6 47	23 13 14	0♓ 7 50	17 5.7	20 34.9	14 26.1	11 55.6	15 34.2	16 50.3	7 34.1	13 59.9	12 45.4

LONGITUDE — OCTOBER 1963

Day	Sid.Time	☉	0 hr ☽	Noon ☽	True ☊	☿	♀	♂	♃	♄	♅	♆	♇
1 Tu	0 36 2	7♎ 5 44	7♓ 9 34	14♓18 8	16♋59.0	20♍46.8	15♎40.9	12♏36.8	15♈26.3	16♒48.3	7♍37.5	14♏ 1.8	12♍47.4
2 W	0 39 58	8 4 42	21 33 3	28 53 33	16R49.8	21 8.8	16 55.6	13 18.2	15R18.3	16R46.3	7 40.9	14 3.6	12 49.3
3 Th	0 43 55	9 3 42	6♈18 45	13♈47 34	16 39.0	21 40.4	18 10.3	13 59.6	15 10.3	16 44.4	7 44.3	14 5.5	12 51.2
4 F	0 47 51	10 2 45	21 18 47	28 51 8	16 27.6	22 21.2	19 25.1	14 41.1	15 2.3	16 42.6	7 47.6	14 7.5	12 53.2
5 Sa	0 51 48	11 1 49	6♉23 22	13♉54 13	16 17.0	23 10.6	20 39.8	15 22.6	14 54.3	16 40.9	7 50.9	14 9.4	12 55.1
6 Su	0 55 44	12 0 56	21 22 35	28 47 28	16 8.4	24 7.8	21 54.5	16 4.3	14 46.2	16 39.3	7 54.2	14 11.4	12 57.0
7 M	0 59 41	13 0 5	6♊ 8 6	13♊23 52	16 2.4	25 12.2	23 9.3	16 46.0	14 38.2	16 37.8	7 57.5	14 13.3	12 58.9
8 Tu	1 3 37	13 59 17	20 34 19	27 39 15	15 59.1	26 22.9	24 24.0	17 27.7	14 30.1	16 36.4	8 0.7	14 15.3	13 0.7
9 W	1 7 34	14 58 31	4♋38 35	11♋32 22	15 57.9	27 39.4	25 38.8	18 9.6	14 22.0	16 35.0	8 3.9	14 17.3	13 2.6
10 Th	1 11 31	15 57 47	18 20 46	25 4 3	15 57.8	29 0.7	26 53.6	18 51.5	14 13.9	16 33.8	8 7.1	14 19.3	13 4.4
11 F	1 15 27	16 57 5	1♌42 32	8♌16 32	15 57.4	0♎26.3	28 8.4	19 33.5	14 5.9	16 32.7	8 10.3	14 21.4	13 6.2
12 Sa	1 19 24	17 56 26	14 46 25	21 12 31	15 55.6	1 55.6	29 23.1	20 15.5	13 57.8	16 31.7	8 13.4	14 23.4	13 8.0
13 Su	1 23 20	18 55 49	27 35 11	3♍54 43	15 51.2	3 27.9	0♏37.9	20 57.7	13 49.8	16 30.7	8 16.5	14 25.5	13 9.8
14 M	1 27 17	19 55 14	10♍11 22	16 25 24	15 44.0	5 2.7	1 52.7	21 39.9	13 41.8	16 29.9	8 19.5	14 27.6	13 11.6
15 Tu	1 31 13	20 54 42	22 37 0	28 46 21	15 33.7	6 39.5	3 7.5	22 22.1	13 33.8	16 29.2	8 22.5	14 29.7	13 13.4
16 W	1 35 10	21 54 11	4♎53 35	10♎58 51	15 21.1	8 18.0	4 22.3	23 4.5	13 25.9	16 28.5	8 25.5	14 31.8	13 15.1
17 Th	1 39 6	22 53 43	17 2 14	23 3 53	15 6.9	9 57.8	5 37.1	23 46.9	13 18.0	16 28.0	8 28.5	14 33.9	13 16.8
18 F	1 43 3	23 53 17	29 3 53	5♏ 2 24	14 52.5	11 38.5	6 51.9	24 29.3	13 10.1	16 27.6	8 31.4	14 36.0	13 18.5
19 Sa	1 47 0	24 52 52	10♏59 34	16 55 34	14 39.0	13 19.9	8 6.7	25 11.9	13 2.4	16 27.2	8 34.3	14 38.1	13 20.2
20 Su	1 50 56	25 52 30	22 50 39	28 45 5	14 27.5	15 1.8	9 21.5	25 54.5	12 54.7	16 27.0	8 37.2	14 40.3	13 21.9
21 M	1 54 53	26 52 10	4♐39 10	10♐33 17	14 18.6	16 44.0	10 36.3	26 37.2	12 47.1	16D26.9	8 40.0	14 42.4	13 23.5
22 Tu	1 58 49	27 51 51	16 27 51	22 23 19	14 12.7	18 26.3	11 51.1	27 19.9	12 39.5	16 26.9	8 42.8	14 44.6	13 25.1
23 W	2 2 46	28 51 35	28 20 13	4♑19 6	14 9.5	20 8.5	13 5.9	28 2.8	12 32.0	16 27.0	8 45.5	14 46.8	13 26.7
24 Th	2 6 42	29 51 20	10♑20 34	16 25 15	14D 8.4	21 50.7	14 20.8	28 45.7	12 24.7	16 27.1	8 48.2	14 48.9	13 28.3
25 F	2 10 39	0♏51 7	22 33 47	28 46 51	14R 8.5	23 32.6	15 35.6	29 28.6	12 17.4	16 27.4	8 50.9	14 51.1	13 29.9
26 Sa	2 14 35	1 50 55	5♒ 5 6	11♒29 8	14 8.6	25 14.3	16 50.4	0♐11.6	12 10.2	16 27.8	8 53.5	14 53.3	13 31.4
27 Su	2 18 32	2 50 46	17 59 34	24 36 53	14 7.6	26 55.6	18 5.2	0 54.7	12 3.2	16 28.3	8 56.1	14 55.5	13 32.9
28 M	2 22 29	3 50 37	1♓21 30	8♓13 41	14 4.6	28 36.6	19 19.9	1 37.8	11 56.2	16 28.9	8 58.7	14 57.8	13 34.4
29 Tu	2 26 25	4 50 31	15 13 32	22 20 58	13 59.1	0♏17.2	20 34.7	2 21.0	11 49.4	16 29.6	9 1.2	14 60.0	13 35.9
30 W	2 30 22	5 50 26	29 35 41	6♈57 9	13 51.3	1 57.3	21 49.5	3 4.3	11 42.6	16 30.4	9 3.6	15 2.2	13 37.3
31 Th	2 34 18	6 50 23	14♈24 34	21 56 57	13 41.8	3 37.0	23 4.3	3 47.6	11 36.0	16 31.3	9 6.1	15 4.4	13 38.7

Astro Data	Planet Ingress	Last Aspect	☽ Ingress	Last Aspect	☽ Ingress	☽ Phases & Eclipses	Astro Data
Dy Hr Mn	Dy Hr Mn	Dy Hr Mn	Dy Hr Mn	Dy Hr Mn	Dy Hr Mn	Dy Hr Mn	1 SEPTEMBER 1963
☽0N 5 23:11	♂ ♏ 12 9:11	2 14:30 ♂ △	♓ 3 1:37	1 23:19 ☿ ☍	♈ 2 13:48	3 19:33 ○ 10♓34	Julian Day # 23254
☿ R 6 23:09	☿ ♍ 16 20:29	4 0:10 ♆ △	♈ 5 3:52	3 20:42 ♀ ☍	♉ 4 13:50	10 11:42 ☽ 17♊03	Delta T 34.8 sec
♃✶♄ 12 6:14	♀ ♎ 18 9:43	6 23:09 ♂ ☍	♉ 7 5:02	6 4:47 ☿ △	♊ 6 13:58	17 20:51 ● 24♍14	SVP 05♓46'17"
☽0S 19 6:43	☉ ♎ 23 18:24	8 10:34 ♄ □	♊ 9 6:45	8 10:47 ☿ □	♋ 8 16:01	26 0:38 ☽ 2♑13	Obliquity 23°26'36"
♀0S 20 19:25		11 8:57 ♂ △	♋ 11 10:08	10 16:52 ♀ □	♌ 10 20:54		⚷ Chiron 12♓45.8R
☿0N 22 6:27	☿ ♎ 10 16:44	13 3:43 ♀ ✶	♌ 13 15:30	12 10:49 ♂ □	♍ 13 4:34	3 4:44 ○ 9♈15	☽ Mean ☊ 17♋48.9
☿ D 29 8:04	♀ ♏ 12 11:50	14 23:34 ♄ ☍	♍ 15 22:47	14 23:29 ♂ ✶	♎ 15 14:24	9 19:27 ☽ 15♋47	
☽0N 3 8:30	☉ ♏ 24 3:29	18 7:48 ♀ ☌	♎ 18 8:00	17 12:43 ☉ ☌	♏ 18 1:53	17 12:43 ● 23♎25	1 OCTOBER 1963
♃⊼♆ 9 11:08	♂ ♐ 25 17:31	19 17:50 ♄ △	♏ 20 19:10	20 6:37 ♂ ☌	♐ 20 14:32	25 17:20 ☽ 1♒34	Julian Day # 23284
☿0S 13 16:55	☿ ♏ 28 19:54	23 6:53 ☉ ✶	♐ 23 7:50	23 1:09 ☉ ✶	♑ 23 3:21		Delta T 34.9 sec
☽0S 16 13:14		25 4:15 ☿ □	♑ 25 20:15	25 14:08 ♂ ✶	♒ 25 14:20		SVP 05♓46'15"
♃⊼♇ 17 2:55		27 12:46 ☿ △	♒ 28 6:03	27 18:27 ☿ △	♓ 27 21:36		Obliquity 23°26'37"
♄ D 21 16:22		29 12:45 ♄ ☌	♓ 30 11:47	29 9:54 ♀ △	♈ 30 0:40		⚷ Chiron 11♓24.0R
☽0N 30 19:43							☽ Mean ☊ 16♋13.6

NOVEMBER 1963 LONGITUDE

Day	Sid.Time	☉	0 hr ☽	Noon ☽	True ☊	☿	♀	♂	♃	♄	♅	♆	♇
1 F	2 38 15	7♏50 21	29♈33 6	7♉11 41	13♋31.6	5♏16.2	24♏19.1	4♐31.0	11♈29.6	16♒32.3	9♍ 8.5	15♏ 6.6	13♍40.1
2 Sa	2 42 11	8 50 22	14♉51 15	22 30 22	13R22.0	6 55.1	25 33.9	5 14.5	11R23.3	16 33.4	9 10.8	15 8.9	13 41.5
3 Su	2 46 8	9 50 24	0♊ 7 37	7♊41 45	13 14.1	8 33.4	26 48.6	5 58.0	11 17.1	16 34.6	9 13.1	15 11.1	13 42.9
4 M	2 50 4	10 50 29	15 11 37	22 36 17	13 8.7	10 11.3	28 3.4	6 41.6	11 11.0	16 35.9	9 15.3	15 13.4	13 44.2
5 Tu	2 54 1	11 50 35	29 55 4	7♋ 7 28	13D 5.9	11 48.8	29 18.2	7 25.2	11 5.1	16 37.4	9 17.6	15 15.6	13 45.5
6 W	2 57 57	12 50 44	14♋13 12	21 12 12	13 5.2	13 25.9	0♐33.0	8 8.9	10 59.4	16 38.9	9 19.7	15 17.9	13 46.8
7 Th	3 1 54	13 50 54	28 4 30	4♌50 21	13 5.7	15 2.6	1 47.7	8 52.7	10 53.8	16 40.5	9 21.8	15 20.1	13 48.0
8 F	3 5 51	14 51 7	11♌30 2	18 3 58	13R 6.4	16 38.9	3 2.5	9 36.6	10 48.4	16 42.2	9 23.9	15 22.4	13 49.2
9 Sa	3 9 47	15 51 22	24 32 33	0♍56 16	13 6.0	18 14.7	4 17.3	10 20.5	10 43.1	16 44.0	9 25.9	15 24.6	13 50.4
10 Su	3 13 44	16 51 39	7♍15 35	13 30 59	13 3.8	19 50.3	5 32.1	11 4.4	10 38.0	16 45.9	9 27.9	15 26.9	13 51.6
11 M	3 17 40	17 51 57	19 42 55	25 51 47	12 59.2	21 25.5	6 46.9	11 48.5	10 33.1	16 47.9	9 29.9	15 29.1	13 52.7
12 Tu	3 21 37	18 52 18	1♎58 1	8♎ 1 56	12 52.3	23 0.3	8 1.6	12 32.6	10 28.3	16 50.0	9 31.7	15 31.4	13 53.8
13 W	3 25 33	19 52 40	14 3 54	20 4 12	12 43.3	24 34.8	9 16.4	13 16.7	10 23.7	16 52.2	9 33.6	15 33.6	13 54.9
14 Th	3 29 30	20 53 5	26 3 5	2♏ 0 47	12 33.1	26 9.1	10 31.2	14 1.0	10 19.3	16 54.5	9 35.3	15 35.8	13 56.0
15 F	3 33 26	21 53 31	7♏57 31	13 53 29	12 22.6	27 43.0	11 45.9	14 45.2	10 15.1	16 56.9	9 37.1	15 38.1	13 57.0
16 Sa	3 37 23	22 53 59	19 48 53	25 43 53	12 12.8	29 16.7	13 0.7	15 29.6	10 11.1	16 59.4	9 38.8	15 40.3	13 58.0
17 Su	3 41 20	23 54 28	1♐38 42	7♐33 33	12 4.5	0♐50.1	14 15.5	16 14.0	10 7.2	17 2.0	9 40.4	15 42.6	13 59.0
18 M	3 45 16	24 54 59	13 28 39	19 24 16	11 58.2	2 23.3	15 30.3	16 58.5	10 3.6	17 4.7	9 42.0	15 44.8	13 59.9
19 Tu	3 49 13	25 55 32	25 20 41	1♑18 14	11 54.3	3 56.3	16 45.0	17 43.0	10 0.1	17 7.5	9 43.5	15 47.0	14 0.8
20 W	3 53 9	26 56 6	7♑17 18	13 18 15	11D52.7	5 29.0	17 59.8	18 27.6	9 56.8	17 10.4	9 45.0	15 49.2	14 1.7
21 Th	3 57 6	27 56 41	19 21 34	25 27 41	11 52.8	7 1.5	19 14.5	19 12.2	9 53.8	17 13.4	9 46.4	15 51.5	14 2.6
22 F	4 1 2	28 57 17	1♒37 9	7♒50 27	11 54.1	8 33.8	20 29.3	19 56.9	9 50.9	17 16.4	9 47.8	15 53.7	14 3.4
23 Sa	4 4 59	29 57 55	14 8 10	20 30 49	11 55.6	10 5.9	21 44.0	20 41.7	9 48.2	17 19.6	9 49.1	15 55.9	14 4.2
24 Su	4 8 56	0♐58 34	26 58 56	3♓33 0	11R56.6	11 37.8	22 58.7	21 26.5	9 45.8	17 22.8	9 50.4	15 58.1	14 4.9
25 M	4 12 52	1 59 14	10♓13 27	17 0 38	11 56.3	13 9.6	24 13.5	22 11.3	9 43.5	17 26.2	9 51.6	16 0.2	14 5.7
26 Tu	4 16 49	2 59 55	23 54 46	0♈55 58	11 54.4	14 41.1	25 28.2	22 56.2	9 41.5	17 29.6	9 52.7	16 2.4	14 6.4
27 W	4 20 45	4 0 37	8♈ 4 8	15 19 1	11 50.8	16 12.4	26 42.9	23 41.2	9 39.6	17 33.1	9 53.8	16 4.6	14 7.0
28 Th	4 24 42	5 1 20	22 40 9	0♉ 6 50	11 45.9	17 43.4	27 57.6	24 26.2	9 38.0	17 36.7	9 54.9	16 6.8	14 7.7
29 F	4 28 38	6 2 4	7♉38 12	15 13 11	11 40.4	19 14.3	29 12.2	25 11.3	9 36.5	17 40.4	9 55.9	16 8.9	14 8.3
30 Sa	4 32 35	7 2 50	22 50 33	0♊28 59	11 35.2	20 44.9	0♑26.9	25 56.4	9 35.3	17 44.2	9 56.8	16 11.0	14 8.9

DECEMBER 1963 LONGITUDE

Day	Sid.Time	☉	0 hr ☽	Noon ☽	True ☊	☿	♀	♂	♃	♄	♅	♆	♇
1 Su	4 36 31	8♐ 3 36	8♊ 7 9	15♊43 41	11♋30.9	22♐15.2	1♑41.6	26♐41.6	9♈34.3	17♒48.0	9♍57.7	16♏13.2	14♍ 9.4
2 M	4 40 28	9 4 24	23 17 20	0♋46 57	11R28.1	23 45.1	2 56.2	27 26.8	9R33.5	17 52.0	9 58.5	16 15.3	14 9.9
3 Tu	4 44 25	10 5 13	8♋11 34	15 30 22	11D27.0	25 14.7	4 10.9	28 12.1	9 32.9	17 56.0	9 59.3	16 17.4	14 10.4
4 W	4 48 21	11 6 3	22 42 48	29 48 26	11 27.3	26 43.9	5 25.5	28 57.5	9 32.5	18 0.1	10 0.0	16 19.5	14 10.8
5 Th	4 52 18	12 6 55	6♌47 6	13♌38 46	11 28.6	28 12.6	6 40.1	29 42.9	9D32.3	18 4.3	10 0.7	16 21.6	14 11.3
6 F	4 56 14	13 7 48	20 23 34	27 1 43	11 30.3	29 40.7	7 54.7	0♑28.3	9 32.3	18 8.6	10 1.3	16 23.6	14 11.6
7 Sa	5 0 11	14 8 42	3♍33 36	9♍59 38	11R31.6	1♑ 8.1	9 9.4	1 13.8	9 32.5	18 13.0	10 1.9	16 25.7	14 12.0
8 Su	5 4 7	15 9 37	16 20 17	22 36 4	11 32.0	2 34.8	10 24.0	1 59.4	9 32.9	18 17.4	10 2.3	16 27.7	14 12.3
9 M	5 8 4	16 10 34	28 47 32	4♎55 12	11 31.3	4 0.6	11 38.5	2 45.0	9 33.6	18 21.9	10 2.8	16 29.7	14 12.6
10 Tu	5 12 0	17 11 32	10♎59 38	17 1 19	11 29.4	5 25.2	12 53.1	3 30.6	9 34.4	18 26.5	10 3.2	16 31.7	14 12.9
11 W	5 15 57	18 12 31	23 0 46	28 58 27	11 26.4	6 48.7	14 7.7	4 16.3	9 35.5	18 31.2	10 3.5	16 33.7	14 13.1
12 Th	5 19 54	19 13 31	4♏54 49	10♏50 14	11 22.7	8 10.6	15 22.3	5 2.1	9 36.7	18 35.9	10 3.8	16 35.7	14 13.3
13 F	5 23 50	20 14 32	16 45 7	22 39 48	11 18.9	9 30.8	16 36.8	5 47.9	9 38.2	18 40.7	10 4.0	16 37.7	14 13.4
14 Sa	5 27 47	21 15 34	28 34 34	4♐29 45	11 15.3	10 49.0	17 51.3	6 33.7	9 39.9	18 45.6	10 4.1	16 39.6	14 13.5
15 Su	5 31 43	22 16 37	10♐25 35	16 22 18	11 12.4	12 4.8	19 5.9	7 19.6	9 41.8	18 50.6	10 4.2	16 41.5	14 13.6
16 M	5 35 40	23 17 41	22 20 10	28 19 22	11 10.3	13 17.8	20 20.4	8 5.5	9 43.9	18 55.6	10R 4.3	16 43.4	14 13.7
17 Tu	5 39 36	24 18 46	4♑20 8	10♑22 41	11D 9.3	14 27.7	21 34.9	8 51.5	9 46.2	19 0.7	10 4.2	16 45.3	14R13.7
18 W	5 43 33	25 19 51	16 27 15	22 34 3	11 9.2	15 33.8	22 49.4	9 37.6	9 48.7	19 5.9	10 4.2	16 47.2	14 13.7
19 Th	5 47 29	26 20 57	28 43 21	4♒55 25	11 9.9	16 35.5	24 3.8	10 23.6	9 51.4	19 11.2	10 4.0	16 49.0	14 13.7
20 F	5 51 26	27 22 3	11♒10 30	17 28 56	11 11.1	17 32.3	25 18.3	11 9.8	9 54.3	19 16.5	10 3.8	16 50.9	14 13.6
21 Sa	5 55 23	28 23 9	23 51 0	0♓17 1	11 12.4	18 23.4	26 32.7	11 55.9	9 57.4	19 21.8	10 3.6	16 52.7	14 13.5
22 Su	5 59 19	29 24 16	6♓47 17	13 22 8	11 13.5	19 7.9	27 47.1	12 42.1	10 0.7	19 27.3	10 3.3	16 54.5	14 13.3
23 M	6 3 16	0♑25 23	20 1 48	26 46 33	11R14.1	19 45.1	29 1.5	13 28.4	10 4.2	19 32.8	10 2.9	16 56.2	14 13.2
24 Tu	6 7 12	1 26 30	3♈36 33	10♈31 56	11 14.3	20 14.1	0♒15.8	14 14.7	10 7.8	19 38.4	10 2.5	16 58.0	14 13.0
25 W	6 11 9	2 27 37	17 32 41	24 38 43	11 14.0	20 33.8	1 30.2	15 1.0	10 11.7	19 44.0	10 2.1	16 59.7	14 12.7
26 Th	6 15 5	3 28 44	1♉49 49	9♉ 5 38	11 13.3	20R43.5	2 44.5	15 47.3	10 15.8	19 49.7	10 1.5	17 1.4	14 12.5
27 F	6 19 2	4 29 52	16 25 41	23 49 17	11 12.5	20 42.4	3 58.8	16 33.7	10 20.1	19 55.4	10 1.0	17 3.1	14 12.2
28 Sa	6 22 58	5 30 59	1♊15 42	8♊44 1	11 11.8	20 29.9	5 13.0	17 20.2	10 24.5	20 1.2	10 0.3	17 4.7	14 11.8
29 Su	6 26 55	6 32 7	16 13 16	23 42 24	11 11.3	20 5.5	6 27.2	18 6.6	10 29.2	20 7.1	9 59.7	17 6.3	14 11.5
30 M	6 30 52	7 33 14	1♋10 21	8♋36 5	11D11.1	19 29.4	7 41.4	18 53.1	10 34.0	20 13.0	9 58.9	17 7.9	14 11.1
31 Tu	6 34 48	8 34 22	15 58 37	23 17 3	11 11.0	18 41.8	8 55.6	19 39.7	10 39.0	20 19.0	9 58.1	17 9.5	14 10.7

Astro Data Dy Hr Mn	Planet Ingress Dy Hr Mn	Last Aspect Dy Hr Mn	☽ Ingress Dy Hr Mn	Last Aspect Dy Hr Mn	☽ Ingress Dy Hr Mn	☽ Phases & Eclipses Dy Hr Mn	Astro Data
☽0S 12 19:36	♀ ♐ 5 13:25	31 3:23 ♄ ⚹	♉ 1 0:42	2 7:00 ♂ ☍	♋ 2 10:44	1 13:55 ○ 8♉25	1 NOVEMBER 1963
♃⊼♅ 22 18:44	☿ ♐ 16 11:07	2 18:18 ♀ ☍	♊ 2 23:48	3 13:20 ♆ △	♌ 4 12:20	8 6:37 ☽ 15♌08	Julian Day # 23315
☽0N 27 6:39	☉ ♐ 23 0:49	4 2:16 ♄ △	♋ 5 0:08	5 19:57 ♄ ☍	♍ 6 17:26	16 6:50 ● 23♏11	Delta T 34.9 sec
	♀ ♑ 29 15:21	6 1:51 ♆ △	♌ 7 3:24	8 0:14 ♆ ⚹	♎ 9 2:21	24 7:56 ☽ 1♓19	SVP 05♓46'12"
♃ D 5 10:11		8 10:42 ☿ □	♍ 9 10:14	10 14:56 ♄ △	♏ 11 14:04	30 23:54 ○ 8♊03	Obliquity 23°26'36"
☽0S 10 2:24	♂ ♑ 5 9:03	11 3:49 ☿ ⚹	♎ 11 20:07	13 3:56 ♄ □	♐ 14 2:53		⚷ Chiron 10♓25.9R
♅ R 16 5:12	☿ ♑ 6 5:17	13 5:37 ♄ △	♏ 14 7:57	16 2:06 ☉ ☌	♑ 16 15:21		☽ Mean ☊ 14♋35.1
♇ R 17 7:07	☉ ♑ 22 14:02	16 6:50 ☉ ☌	♐ 16 20:40	18 13:54 ♀ ☌	♒ 19 2:29	7 21:34 ☽ 15♍03	
♃⊼♅ 22 16:38	♀ ♒ 23 18:53	18 7:33 ♂ ☌	♑ 19 9:23	21 9:12 ☉ ⚹	♓ 21 11:28	16 2:06 ● 23♐23	1 DECEMBER 1963
☽0N 24 15:05		21 18:22 ☉ ⚹	♒ 21 20:51	23 17:34 ♀ ⚹	♈ 23 17:41	23 19:54 ☽ 1♈16	Julian Day # 23345
☿ R 26 9:40		23 15:48 ♀ ⚹	♓ 24 5:32	25 5:12 ☿ □	♉ 25 20:57	30 11:04 ○ 8♋01	Delta T 35.0 sec
		26 2:56 ♀ □	♈ 26 10:25	27 6:53 ☿ △	♊ 27 21:58	30 11:07 ☍T 1.335	SVP 05♓46'07"
		28 9:19 ♀ △	♉ 28 11:49	29 6:17 ♄ △	♋ 29 22:07		Obliquity 23°26'36"
		29 15:56 ♄ □	♊ 30 11:14	31 6:22 ♂ ☍	♌ 31 23:09		⚷ Chiron 10♓16.4
							☽ Mean ☊ 12♋59.8

LONGITUDE — JANUARY 1964

Day	Sid.Time	☉	0 hr ☽	Noon ☽	True ☊	☿	♀	♂	♃	♄	♅	♆	♇
1 W	6 38 45	9♑35 30	0♌30 37	7♌38 39	11♋11.1	17♑43.7	10♒ 9.7	20♑26.3	10♈44.2	20♒25.0	9♍57.3	17♏11.1	14♍10.2
2 Th	6 42 41	10 36 38	14 40 41	21 36 23	11R 11.2	16R 36.6	11 23.8	21 12.9	10 49.6	20 31.1	9R 56.4	17 12.6	14R 9.7
3 F	6 46 38	11 37 47	28 25 36	5♍ 8 17	11 11.2	15 22.4	12 37.9	21 59.5	10 55.1	20 37.2	9 55.4	17 14.1	14 9.2
4 Sa	6 50 34	12 38 55	11♍44 34	18 14 39	11 11.1	14 3.5	13 51.9	22 46.2	11 0.9	20 43.4	9 54.4	17 15.6	14 8.7
5 Su	6 54 31	13 40 4	24 38 52	0♎57 38	11 10.9	12 42.4	15 5.9	23 32.9	11 6.8	20 49.7	9 53.4	17 17.0	14 8.1
6 M	6 58 27	14 41 13	7♎11 26	13 20 47	11D 10.8	11 21.8	16 19.9	24 19.7	11 12.8	20 55.9	9 52.3	17 18.4	14 7.5
7 Tu	7 2 24	15 42 22	19 26 14	25 28 23	11 10.7	10 4.3	17 33.8	25 6.4	11 19.1	21 2.3	9 51.1	17 19.8	14 6.9
8 W	7 6 21	16 43 31	1♏27 49	7♏25 7	11 10.9	8 52.1	18 47.7	25 53.3	11 25.5	21 8.6	9 49.9	17 21.2	14 6.2
9 Th	7 10 17	17 44 41	13 20 53	19 15 40	11 11.4	7 46.9	20 1.6	26 40.1	11 32.1	21 15.0	9 48.6	17 22.5	14 5.5
10 F	7 14 14	18 45 50	25 10 1	1♐ 4 28	11 12.2	6 50.2	21 15.4	27 27.0	11 38.8	21 21.5	9 47.3	17 23.8	14 4.8
11 Sa	7 18 10	19 47 0	6♐59 28	12 55 29	11 13.2	6 2.9	22 29.2	28 13.9	11 45.7	21 28.0	9 46.0	17 25.1	14 4.0
12 Su	7 22 7	20 48 9	18 52 55	24 52 9	11 14.1	5 25.3	23 43.0	29 0.8	11 52.8	21 34.6	9 44.6	17 26.4	14 3.3
13 M	7 26 3	21 49 19	0♑53 31	6♑57 16	11R 14.8	4 57.6	24 56.7	29 47.8	12 0.1	21 41.1	9 43.1	17 27.6	14 2.5
14 Tu	7 30 0	22 50 28	13 3 40	19 12 55	11 15.0	4 39.6	26 10.4	0♒34.8	12 7.5	21 47.8	9 41.6	17 28.8	14 1.6
15 W	7 33 57	23 51 36	25 25 11	1♒40 34	11 14.5	4D 30.9	27 24.0	1 21.8	12 15.0	21 54.4	9 40.1	17 29.9	14 0.8
16 Th	7 37 53	24 52 45	7♒59 11	14 21 6	11 13.4	4 31.0	28 37.6	2 8.9	12 22.8	22 1.1	9 38.5	17 31.1	13 59.9
17 F	7 41 50	25 53 52	20 46 21	27 14 58	11 11.6	4 39.2	29 51.1	2 56.0	12 30.6	22 7.9	9 36.9	17 32.2	13 59.0
18 Sa	7 45 46	26 54 59	3♓46 55	10♓22 15	11 9.3	4 55.0	1♓ 4.6	3 43.1	12 38.6	22 14.6	9 35.2	17 33.3	13 58.0
19 Su	7 49 43	27 56 5	17 0 54	23 42 53	11 6.8	5 17.8	2 18.1	4 30.2	12 46.8	22 21.4	9 33.5	17 34.3	13 57.1
20 M	7 53 39	28 57 11	0♈28 10	7♈16 43	11 4.6	5 46.8	3 31.4	5 17.3	12 55.1	22 28.3	9 31.7	17 35.3	13 56.1
21 Tu	7 57 36	29 58 15	14 8 29	21 3 26	11 3.0	6 21.5	4 44.8	6 4.5	13 3.6	22 35.1	9 29.9	17 36.3	13 55.1
22 W	8 1 32	0♒59 19	28 1 28	5♉ 2 30	11D 2.3	7 1.3	5 58.0	6 51.6	13 12.2	22 42.0	9 28.1	17 37.2	13 54.0
23 Th	8 5 29	2 0 22	12♉ 6 24	19 12 58	11 2.6	7 45.9	7 11.2	7 38.8	13 20.9	22 49.0	9 26.2	17 38.1	13 53.0
24 F	8 9 25	3 1 23	26 21 57	3♊33 5	11 3.7	8 34.6	8 24.4	8 26.0	13 29.8	22 55.9	9 24.3	17 39.0	13 51.9
25 Sa	8 13 22	4 2 24	10♊45 58	18 0 10	11 5.1	9 27.2	9 37.5	9 13.3	13 38.9	23 2.9	9 22.3	17 39.9	13 50.8
26 Su	8 17 19	5 3 24	25 15 10	2♋30 23	11 6.5	10 23.2	10 50.5	10 0.5	13 48.0	23 9.9	9 20.3	17 40.7	13 49.6
27 M	8 21 15	6 4 23	9♋45 12	16 58 56	11R 7.1	11 22.3	12 3.4	10 47.8	13 57.3	23 16.9	9 18.3	17 41.5	13 48.5
28 Tu	8 25 12	7 5 20	24 10 53	1♌20 21	11 6.6	12 24.3	13 16.3	11 35.1	14 6.7	23 24.0	9 16.2	17 42.2	13 47.3
29 W	8 29 8	8 6 17	8♌26 41	15 29 14	11 4.6	13 28.9	14 29.1	12 22.3	14 16.3	23 31.0	9 14.1	17 42.9	13 46.1
30 Th	8 33 5	9 7 13	22 27 26	29 20 50	11 1.3	14 35.8	15 41.8	13 9.6	14 25.9	23 38.1	9 12.0	17 43.6	13 44.9
31 F	8 37 1	10 8 7	6♍ 9 3	12♍51 50	10 56.8	15 44.8	16 54.5	13 57.0	14 35.7	23 45.2	9 9.8	17 44.3	13 43.7

LONGITUDE — FEBRUARY 1964

Day	Sid.Time	☉	0 hr ☽	Noon ☽	True ☊	☿	♀	♂	♃	♄	♅	♆	♇
1 Sa	8 40 58	11♒ 9 1	19♍29 3	26♍ 0 40	10♋51.8	16♑55.8	18♓ 7.1	14♒44.3	14♈45.6	23♒52.3	9♍ 7.6	17♏44.9	13♍42.4
2 Su	8 44 55	12 9 54	2♎26 48	8♎47 39	10R 46.8	18 8.7	19 19.6	15 31.6	14 55.7	23 59.5	9R 5.4	17 45.5	13R 41.1
3 M	8 48 51	13 10 46	15 3 30	21 14 45	10 42.6	19 23.2	20 32.0	16 19.0	15 5.8	24 6.6	9 3.2	17 46.0	13 39.8
4 Tu	8 52 48	14 11 37	27 21 51	3♏25 21	10 39.5	20 39.3	21 44.4	17 6.3	15 16.1	24 13.8	9 0.9	17 46.5	13 38.5
5 W	8 56 44	15 12 28	9♏25 46	15 23 45	10D 38.0	21 56.9	22 56.6	17 53.7	15 26.5	24 21.0	8 58.6	17 47.0	13 37.2
6 Th	9 0 41	16 13 17	21 19 55	27 14 54	10 37.9	23 15.9	24 8.8	18 41.1	15 37.0	24 28.2	8 56.2	17 47.5	13 35.8
7 F	9 4 37	17 14 6	3♐ 9 21	9♐ 3 55	10 39.1	24 36.1	25 20.9	19 28.5	15 47.6	24 35.4	8 53.8	17 47.9	13 34.5
8 Sa	9 8 34	18 14 54	14 59 13	20 55 53	10 40.8	25 57.6	26 32.9	20 15.9	15 58.4	24 42.6	8 51.5	17 48.3	13 33.1
9 Su	9 12 30	19 15 41	26 54 28	2♑55 31	10 42.5	27 20.2	27 44.9	21 3.3	16 9.2	24 49.8	8 49.0	17 48.6	13 31.7
10 M	9 16 27	20 16 27	8♑59 32	15 6 56	10R 43.3	28 44.0	28 56.7	21 50.7	16 20.1	24 57.1	8 46.6	17 48.9	13 30.3
11 Tu	9 20 24	21 17 11	21 18 5	27 33 19	10 42.7	0♒ 8.9	0♈ 8.5	22 38.2	16 31.2	25 4.3	8 44.2	17 49.2	13 28.9
12 W	9 24 20	22 17 55	3♒52 49	10♒16 44	10 40.2	1 34.8	1 20.2	23 25.6	16 42.3	25 11.5	8 41.7	17 49.5	13 27.5
13 Th	9 28 17	23 18 37	16 45 8	23 17 58	10 35.6	3 1.7	2 31.7	24 13.0	16 53.6	25 18.8	8 39.2	17 49.7	13 26.0
14 F	9 32 13	24 19 17	29 55 7	6♓36 24	10 29.2	4 29.6	3 43.2	25 0.5	17 5.0	25 26.0	8 36.7	17 49.8	13 24.5
15 Sa	9 36 10	25 19 57	13♓21 31	20 10 11	10 21.5	5 58.5	4 54.6	25 47.9	17 16.4	25 33.3	8 34.1	17 50.0	13 23.1
16 Su	9 40 6	26 20 34	27 1 59	3♈56 33	10 13.4	7 28.3	6 5.8	26 35.4	17 28.0	25 40.5	8 31.6	17 50.1	13 21.6
17 M	9 44 3	27 21 10	10♈53 28	17 52 20	10 5.8	8 59.0	7 17.0	27 22.8	17 39.6	25 47.8	8 29.0	17 50.2	13 20.1
18 Tu	9 47 59	28 21 45	24 52 44	1♉54 21	9 59.7	10 30.7	8 28.0	28 10.2	17 51.3	25 55.0	8 26.5	17R 50.2	13 18.6
19 W	9 51 56	29 22 17	8♉56 51	15 59 57	9 55.7	12 3.4	9 39.0	28 57.7	18 3.1	26 2.3	8 23.9	17 50.2	13 17.1
20 Th	9 55 52	0♓22 48	23 3 27	0♊ 7 8	9D 53.8	13 36.9	10 49.8	29 45.1	18 15.1	26 9.5	8 21.3	17 50.2	13 15.5
21 F	9 59 49	1 23 17	7♊10 50	14 14 25	9 53.7	15 11.4	12 0.5	0♓32.5	18 27.0	26 16.8	8 18.7	17 50.1	13 14.0
22 Sa	10 3 46	2 23 44	21 17 45	28 20 40	9 54.5	16 46.8	13 11.0	1 19.9	18 39.1	26 24.0	8 16.1	17 50.0	13 12.5
23 Su	10 7 42	3 24 9	5♋23 2	12♋24 38	9R 55.4	18 23.2	14 21.5	2 7.3	18 51.3	26 31.2	8 13.5	17 49.9	13 10.9
24 M	10 11 39	4 24 33	19 25 15	26 24 37	9 55.1	20 0.5	15 31.8	2 54.7	19 3.5	26 38.4	8 10.9	17 49.7	13 9.4
25 Tu	10 15 35	5 24 54	3♌22 26	10♌18 20	9 52.7	21 38.8	16 41.9	3 42.1	19 15.9	26 45.6	8 8.2	17 49.5	13 7.8
26 W	10 19 32	6 25 14	17 11 58	24 2 57	9 47.8	23 18.1	17 52.0	4 29.5	19 28.3	26 52.8	8 5.6	17 49.3	13 6.3
27 Th	10 23 28	7 25 31	0♍50 52	7♍35 23	9 40.3	24 58.3	19 1.9	5 16.9	19 40.7	27 0.0	8 3.0	17 49.0	13 4.7
28 F	10 27 25	8 25 47	14 16 8	20 52 51	9 30.7	26 39.5	20 11.6	6 4.3	19 53.3	27 7.2	8 0.3	17 48.7	13 3.1
29 Sa	10 31 21	9 26 1	27 25 18	3♎53 21	9 19.9	28 21.8	21 21.2	6 51.6	20 5.9	27 14.3	7 57.7	17 48.4	13 1.6

Astro Data Dy Hr Mn	Planet Ingress Dy Hr Mn	Last Aspect Dy Hr Mn	☽ Ingress Dy Hr Mn	Last Aspect Dy Hr Mn	☽ Ingress Dy Hr Mn	☽ Phases & Eclipses Dy Hr Mn	Astro Data
☽0S 6 10:02	♂ ♒ 13 6:13	2 10:11 ♄ ☍	♍ 3 2:48	31 21:16 ♀ ☍	♎ 1 19:25	6 15:58 ☽ 15♎22	1 JANUARY 1964
☿ D 15 11:42	♀ ♓ 17 2:54	4 21:48 ♂ △	♎ 5 10:10	3 17:47 ♄ △	♏ 4 5:12	14 20:43 ● 23♑43	Julian Day # 23376
☽0N 20 20:43	☉ ♒ 21 0:41	7 12:03 ♂ □	♏ 7 21:04	6 6:26 ♄ □	♐ 6 17:35	14 20:29:31 ◐ P 0.559	Delta T 35.0 sec
♃⚻♇ 26 3:45		10 4:58 ♂ ✶	♐ 10 9:49	9 1:52 ♀ □	♑ 9 6:11	22 5:29 ☽ 1♉13	SVP 05♓46'01"
	☿ ♒ 10 21:30	12 10:48 ♀ ✶	♑ 12 22:14	10 17:16 ♆ ✶	♒ 11 16:39	28 23:23 ○ 8♌05	Obliquity 23°26'36"
☽0S 2 18:23	♀ ♈ 10 21:09	14 20:43 ☉ ☌	♒ 15 8:48	13 15:48 ♄ ☌	♓ 14 0:09		⚷ Chiron 10♓59.9
♀0N 11 23:59	☉ ♓ 19 14:57	17 2:33 ♄ ☌	♓ 17 17:04	15 7:54 ♆ △	♈ 16 5:10		☽ Mean ☊ 11♋21.3
☽0N 17 1:48	♂ ♓ 20 7:33	19 21:06 ☉ ✶	♈ 19 23:10	18 6:25 ☉ ✶	♉ 18 8:45	5 12:42 ☽ 15♏45	
♃⚻♆ 17 21:42	☿ ♓ 29 22:50	21 14:46 ♄ ✶	♉ 22 3:23	20 5:19 ♄ □	♊ 20 11:48	13 13:01 ● 23♒52	1 FEBRUARY 1964
♆ R 18 14:29		23 18:12 ♄ □	♊ 24 6:05	22 8:46 ♄ △	♋ 22 14:49	20 13:24 ☽ 0♊57	Julian Day # 23407
		25 20:31 ♄ △	♋ 26 7:51	23 23:22 ♃ □	♌ 24 18:11	27 12:39 ○ 7♍57	Delta T 35.1 sec
		27 13:11 ♆ △	♌ 28 9:45	26 17:08 ♄ ☍	♍ 26 22:30		SVP 05♓45'56"
		30 2:04 ♄ ☍	♍ 30 13:09	28 6:25 ♆ ✶	♎ 29 4:46		Obliquity 23°26'37"
							⚷ Chiron 12♓27.7
							☽ Mean ☊ 9♋42.8

MARCH 1964 LONGITUDE

Day	Sid.Time	☉	0 hr ☽	Noon ☽	True ☊	☿	♀	♂	♃	♄	♅	♆	♇
1 Su	10 35 18	10♓26 14	10♎16 56	16♎36 6	9♋ 8.9	0♓ 5.1	22♈30.6	7♓39.0	20♈18.6	27♒21.5	7♍55.1	17♏48.0	12♍60.0
2 M	10 39 15	11 26 24	22 50 58	29 1 44	8R 58.8	1 49.4	23 39.9	8 26.3	20 31.3	27 28.6	7R 52.5	17R 47.6	12R 58.4
3 Tu	10 43 11	12 26 34	5♏ 8 43	11♏12 17	8 50.5	3 34.8	24 49.1	9 13.6	20 44.1	27 35.7	7 49.8	17 47.2	12 56.8
4 W	10 47 8	13 26 41	17 12 53	23 11 3	8 44.6	5 21.2	25 58.0	10 1.0	20 57.0	27 42.8	7 47.2	17 46.8	12 55.2
5 Th	10 51 4	14 26 47	29 7 19	5♐ 2 20	8 41.1	7 8.7	27 6.9	10 48.3	21 10.0	27 49.8	7 44.6	17 46.3	12 53.7
6 F	10 55 1	15 26 52	10♐56 43	16 51 8	8D 39.7	8 57.3	28 15.5	11 35.6	21 23.0	27 56.9	7 42.0	17 45.8	12 52.1
7 Sa	10 58 57	16 26 55	22 46 18	28 42 52	8 39.8	10 47.1	29 24.0	12 22.8	21 36.1	28 3.9	7 39.4	17 45.2	12 50.5
8 Su	11 2 54	17 26 56	4♑41 33	10♑43 0	8R 40.2	12 37.9	0♉32.3	13 10.1	21 49.2	28 10.9	7 36.8	17 44.6	12 48.9
9 M	11 6 50	18 26 56	16 47 51	22 56 43	8 40.0	14 29.7	1 40.5	13 57.4	22 2.4	28 17.9	7 34.2	17 44.0	12 47.4
10 Tu	11 10 47	19 26 54	29 10 6	5♒28 30	8 38.1	16 22.7	2 48.4	14 44.6	22 15.7	28 24.8	7 31.7	17 43.4	12 45.8
11 W	11 14 44	20 26 50	11♒52 16	18 21 41	8 33.8	18 16.7	3 56.2	15 31.8	22 29.0	28 31.8	7 29.1	17 42.7	12 44.2
12 Th	11 18 40	21 26 45	24 56 54	1♓37 56	8 26.7	20 11.8	5 3.8	16 19.0	22 42.4	28 38.7	7 26.6	17 42.0	12 42.7
13 F	11 22 37	22 26 37	8♓24 39	15 16 49	8 17.2	22 7.8	6 11.2	17 6.2	22 55.8	28 45.5	7 24.1	17 41.2	12 41.1
14 Sa	11 26 33	23 26 28	22 14 0	29 15 42	8 5.8	24 4.8	7 18.4	17 53.4	23 9.3	28 52.4	7 21.6	17 40.5	12 39.6
15 Su	11 30 30	24 26 17	6♈21 15	13♈29 57	7 53.8	26 2.6	8 25.5	18 40.5	23 22.8	28 59.2	7 19.1	17 39.7	12 38.0
16 M	11 34 26	25 26 4	20 41 1	27 53 39	7 42.4	28 1.2	9 32.2	19 27.6	23 36.4	29 5.9	7 16.6	17 38.9	12 36.5
17 Tu	11 38 23	26 25 48	5♉ 7 5	12♉20 34	7 32.8	0♈ 0.5	10 38.8	20 14.7	23 50.0	29 12.7	7 14.1	17 38.0	12 34.9
18 W	11 42 19	27 25 31	19 33 26	26 45 9	7 25.9	2 0.2	11 45.2	21 1.8	24 3.7	29 19.4	7 11.7	17 37.1	12 33.4
19 Th	11 46 16	28 25 11	3♊55 12	11♊ 3 16	7 21.7	4 0.3	12 51.3	21 48.8	24 17.4	29 26.1	7 9.3	17 36.2	12 31.9
20 F	11 50 13	29 24 49	18 9 5	25 12 28	7D 20.0	6 0.6	13 57.2	22 35.9	24 31.1	29 32.7	7 6.9	17 35.3	12 30.4
21 Sa	11 54 9	0♈24 25	2♋13 20	9♋11 40	7R 19.8	8 0.8	15 2.9	23 22.9	24 44.9	29 39.3	7 4.6	17 34.3	12 28.9
22 Su	11 58 6	1 23 59	16 7 28	23 0 46	7 19.7	10 0.7	16 8.3	24 9.8	24 58.8	29 45.9	7 2.2	17 33.3	12 27.4
23 M	12 2 2	2 23 30	29 51 37	6♌40 1	7 18.4	11 59.9	17 13.4	24 56.8	25 12.6	29 52.4	6 59.9	17 32.3	12 26.0
24 Tu	12 5 59	3 22 58	13♌26 0	20 9 31	7 14.8	13 58.2	18 18.3	25 43.7	25 26.5	29 58.8	6 57.7	17 31.3	12 24.5
25 W	12 9 55	4 22 25	26 50 33	3♍28 59	7 8.4	15 55.2	19 22.9	26 30.6	25 40.5	0♓ 5.3	6 55.4	17 30.2	12 23.1
26 Th	12 13 52	5 21 49	10♍ 4 44	16 37 40	6 59.0	17 50.5	20 27.2	27 17.4	25 54.4	0 11.7	6 53.2	17 29.2	12 21.6
27 F	12 17 48	6 21 11	23 7 38	29 34 32	6 47.1	19 43.7	21 31.3	28 4.2	26 8.4	0 18.0	6 51.0	17 28.0	12 20.2
28 Sa	12 21 45	7 20 31	5♎58 13	12♎18 37	6 33.7	21 34.4	22 35.0	28 51.0	26 22.5	0 24.3	6 48.8	17 26.9	12 18.8
29 Su	12 25 42	8 19 49	18 35 39	24 49 22	6 20.1	23 22.2	23 38.4	29 37.8	26 36.5	0 30.6	6 46.7	17 25.8	12 17.4
30 M	12 29 38	9 19 5	0♏59 47	7♏ 7 1	6 7.3	25 6.7	24 41.6	0♈24.5	26 50.6	0 36.8	6 44.6	17 24.6	12 16.0
31 Tu	12 33 35	10 18 18	13 11 17	19 12 48	5 56.4	26 47.5	25 44.4	1 11.2	27 4.8	0 42.9	6 42.5	17 23.4	12 14.7

APRIL 1964 LONGITUDE

Day	Sid.Time	☉	0 hr ☽	Noon ☽	True ☊	☿	♀	♂	♃	♄	♅	♆	♇
1 W	12 37 31	11♈17 31	25♏11 54	1♐ 8 59	5♋48.2	28♈24.2	26♉46.8	1♈57.9	27♈18.9	0♓49.1	6♍40.5	17♏22.1	12♍13.3
2 Th	12 41 28	12 16 41	7♐ 4 29	12 58 54	5R 42.8	29 56.4	27 49.0	2 44.5	27 33.1	0 55.1	6R 38.5	17R 20.9	12R 12.0
3 F	12 45 24	13 15 49	18 52 48	24 46 46	5 39.9	1♉23.9	28 50.8	3 31.1	27 47.3	1 1.1	6 36.5	17 19.6	12 10.7
4 Sa	12 49 21	14 14 56	0♑41 27	6♑37 31	5D 39.0	2 46.2	29 52.2	4 17.7	28 1.5	1 7.1	6 34.6	17 18.4	12 9.4
5 Su	12 53 17	15 14 1	12 35 38	18 36 31	5R 39.0	4 3.2	0♊53.3	5 4.3	28 15.7	1 13.0	6 32.7	17 17.0	12 8.1
6 M	12 57 14	16 13 4	24 40 50	0♒49 17	5 38.8	5 14.6	1 54.0	5 50.8	28 30.0	1 18.9	6 30.9	17 15.7	12 6.9
7 Tu	13 1 10	17 12 5	7♒ 2 30	13 21 4	5 37.3	6 20.1	2 54.3	6 37.2	28 44.3	1 24.7	6 29.1	17 14.4	12 5.6
8 W	13 5 7	18 11 5	19 45 31	26 16 17	5 33.7	7 19.7	3 54.3	7 23.7	28 58.6	1 30.4	6 27.3	17 13.0	12 4.4
9 Th	13 9 4	19 10 3	2♓53 40	9♓37 52	5 27.6	8 13.2	4 53.8	8 10.1	29 12.9	1 36.1	6 25.6	17 11.6	12 3.2
10 F	13 13 0	20 8 58	16 28 53	23 26 36	5 19.1	9 0.3	5 52.9	8 56.5	29 27.2	1 41.8	6 23.9	17 10.2	12 2.0
11 Sa	13 16 57	21 7 52	0♈30 38	7♈40 30	5 8.7	9 41.2	6 51.5	9 42.8	29 41.5	1 47.3	6 22.3	17 8.8	12 0.8
12 Su	13 20 53	22 6 45	14 55 30	22 14 47	4 57.5	10 15.6	7 49.7	10 29.1	29 55.9	1 52.8	6 20.7	17 7.4	11 59.7
13 M	13 24 50	23 5 35	29 37 22	7♉ 2 12	4 46.8	10 43.5	8 47.5	11 15.4	0♉10.3	1 58.3	6 19.1	17 5.9	11 58.6
14 Tu	13 28 46	24 4 23	14♉28 11	21 54 15	4 37.7	11 5.0	9 44.8	12 1.6	0 24.6	2 3.7	6 17.6	17 4.5	11 57.5
15 W	13 32 43	25 3 9	29 19 23	6♊42 40	4 31.1	11 20.1	10 41.5	12 47.7	0 39.0	2 9.0	6 16.1	17 3.0	11 56.4
16 Th	13 36 39	26 1 53	14♊ 3 18	21 20 37	4 27.2	11R 28.8	11 37.8	13 33.9	0 53.4	2 14.3	6 14.7	17 1.5	11 55.4
17 F	13 40 36	27 0 35	28 34 8	5♋43 31	4D 25.8	11 31.3	12 33.5	14 20.0	1 7.8	2 19.5	6 13.3	17 0.0	11 54.4
18 Sa	13 44 33	27 59 15	12♋48 31	19 49 4	4 25.8	11 27.8	13 28.7	15 6.0	1 22.2	2 24.6	6 12.0	16 58.5	11 53.4
19 Su	13 48 29	28 57 52	26 45 10	3♌36 54	4R 26.2	11 18.4	14 23.3	15 52.0	1 36.6	2 29.7	6 10.7	16 57.0	11 52.4
20 M	13 52 26	29 56 27	10♌24 24	17 7 50	4 25.7	11 3.7	15 17.2	16 38.0	1 51.0	2 34.7	6 9.5	16 55.5	11 51.4
21 Tu	13 56 22	0♉55 0	23 47 25	0♍23 20	4 23.5	10 43.8	16 10.6	17 23.9	2 5.4	2 39.6	6 8.3	16 53.9	11 50.5
22 W	14 0 19	1 53 31	6♍55 45	13 24 53	4 18.8	10 19.3	17 3.3	18 9.8	2 19.8	2 44.4	6 7.1	16 52.4	11 49.6
23 Th	14 4 15	2 51 59	19 50 51	26 13 47	4 11.6	9 50.6	17 55.4	18 55.6	2 34.2	2 49.2	6 6.0	16 50.8	11 48.7
24 F	14 8 12	3 50 26	2♎33 49	8♎51 2	4 2.3	9 18.4	18 46.7	19 41.4	2 48.6	2 53.9	6 5.0	16 49.2	11 47.9
25 Sa	14 12 8	4 48 50	15 5 30	21 17 20	3 51.8	8 43.3	19 37.4	20 27.1	3 3.0	2 58.6	6 4.0	16 47.6	11 47.0
26 Su	14 16 5	5 47 12	27 26 35	3♏33 21	3 40.9	8 5.9	20 27.3	21 12.8	3 17.4	3 3.1	6 3.1	16 46.0	11 46.2
27 M	14 20 2	6 45 33	9♏37 45	15 39 55	3 30.8	7 27.0	21 16.4	21 58.4	3 31.8	3 7.6	6 2.2	16 44.4	11 45.5
28 Tu	14 23 58	7 43 52	21 40 1	27 38 15	3 22.2	6 47.3	22 4.8	22 44.0	3 46.2	3 12.1	6 1.3	16 42.8	11 44.7
29 W	14 27 55	8 42 9	3♐34 53	9♐30 11	3 15.7	6 7.6	22 52.3	23 29.6	4 0.5	3 16.4	6 0.5	16 41.2	11 44.0
30 Th	14 31 51	9 40 24	15 24 30	21 18 14	3 11.7	5 28.5	23 39.0	24 15.1	4 14.9	3 20.7	5 59.8	16 39.6	11 43.3

Astro Data

	Dy Hr Mn
☽0S	1 2:50
♃⚼♅	11 0:09
☽0N	15 8:54
☿0N	18 2:08
☽0S	28 10:38
♃⚼♇	31 15:22
♂0N	1 1:53
☽0N	11 18:34
☿ R	16 21:50
☽0S	24 17:27
♃⚹♄	24 13:05

Planet Ingress

		Dy Hr Mn
♀	♉	7 12:38
☿	♈	16 23:54
☉	♈	20 14:10
♄	♓	24 4:17
♂	♈	29 11:24
☿	♉	2 0:57
♀	♊	4 3:03
♃	♉	12 6:52
☉	♉	20 1:27

Last Aspect / ☽ Ingress (March)

Last Aspect Dy Hr Mn		☽ Ingress Dy Hr Mn
2 9:04	♄ △	♏ 2 13:54
4 21:22	♄ □	♐ 5 1:47
7 10:48	♄ ⚹	♑ 7 14:35
9 10:26	♃ □	♒ 10 1:35
12 6:43	♄ ☌	♓ 12 9:05
14 3:41	☿ ☌	♈ 14 13:15
16 14:07	♄ ⚹	♉ 16 15:30
18 16:26	♄ □	♊ 18 17:26
20 19:34	♄ △	♋ 20 20:11
22 15:42	♃ □	♌ 23 0:15
24 21:52	♃ △	♍ 25 5:42
27 9:47	♂ ☍	♎ 27 12:48
29 15:46	♃ ☍	♏ 29 22:03

Last Aspect / ☽ Ingress (April)

Last Aspect Dy Hr Mn		☽ Ingress Dy Hr Mn
1 3:29	♀ ☍	♐ 1 9:41
3 18:29	♃ △	♑ 3 22:36
6 7:38	♃ □	♒ 6 10:24
8 17:14	♃ ⚹	♓ 8 18:47
10 1:12	♆ △	♈ 10 23:08
12 12:37	☉ ☌	♉ 13 0:37
14 4:12	♆ ☍	♊ 15 1:06
16 21:13	☉ ⚹	♋ 17 2:23
19 4:09	☉ □	♌ 19 5:40
20 11:47	♂ △	♍ 21 11:17
22 20:08	♀ □	♎ 23 19:08
25 11:03	♂ ☍	♏ 26 5:01
27 14:07	♆ ☌	♐ 28 16:46

☽ Phases & Eclipses

Dy Hr Mn		
6 10:00	☽	15♐52
14 2:14	●	23♓32
20 20:39	☽	0♋16
28 2:48	○	7♎27
5 5:45	☽	15♑28
12 12:37	●	22♈38
19 4:09	☽	29♋08
26 17:50	○	6♏31

Astro Data

1 MARCH 1964
Julian Day # 23436
Delta T 35.1 sec
SVP 05♓45'53"
Obliquity 23°26'38"
⚷ Chiron 14♓12.4
☽ Mean ☊ 8♋10.7

1 APRIL 1964
Julian Day # 23467
Delta T 35.2 sec
SVP 05♓45'50"
Obliquity 23°26'38"
⚷ Chiron 16♓06.5
☽ Mean ☊ 6♋32.2

LONGITUDE — MAY 1964

Day	Sid.Time	☉	0 hr ☽	Noon ☽	True ☊	☿	♀	♂	♃	♄	♅	♆	♇
1 F	14 35 48	10♉38 38	27♐11 48	3♑ 5 40	3♋ 9.9	4♉50.6	24♊24.7	25♈ 0.6	4♉29.2	3♓24.9	5♍59.1	16♏38.0	11♍42.6
2 Sa	14 39 44	11 36 50	9♑ 0 23	14 56 30	3D 9.8	4R14.8	25 9.6	25 46.0	4 43.6	3 29.0	5R58.5	16R36.4	11R42.0
3 Su	14 43 41	12 35 1	20 54 36	26 55 18	3 10.8	3 41.4	25 53.5	26 31.4	4 57.9	3 33.0	5 57.9	16 34.8	11 41.4
4 M	14 47 37	13 33 10	2♒59 14	9♒ 7 3	3R12.0	3 11.1	26 36.4	27 16.7	5 12.2	3 37.0	5 57.3	16 33.1	11 40.8
5 Tu	14 51 34	14 31 18	15 19 23	21 36 51	3 12.5	2 44.3	27 18.4	28 2.0	5 26.5	3 40.9	5 56.9	16 31.5	11 40.3
6 W	14 55 31	15 29 25	28 0 1	4♓29 24	3 11.7	2 21.2	27 59.2	28 47.2	5 40.8	3 44.7	5 56.4	16 29.9	11 39.7
7 Th	14 59 27	16 27 30	11♓ 5 25	17 48 25	3 9.0	2 2.3	28 39.0	29 32.4	5 55.1	3 48.4	5 56.1	16 28.2	11 39.2
8 F	15 3 24	17 25 33	24 38 35	1♈35 56	3 4.5	1 47.8	29 17.6	0♉17.5	6 9.3	3 52.0	5 55.7	16 26.6	11 38.8
9 Sa	15 7 20	18 23 35	8♈40 21	15 51 29	2 58.6	1 37.7	29 55.0	1 2.6	6 23.6	3 55.5	5 55.5	16 25.0	11 38.3
10 Su	15 11 17	19 21 36	23 8 47	0♉31 33	2 52.0	1D32.3	0♋31.2	1 47.7	6 37.8	3 59.0	5 55.2	16 23.3	11 37.9
11 M	15 15 13	20 19 35	7♉58 52	15 29 40	2 45.5	1 31.5	1 6.1	2 32.6	6 52.0	4 2.4	5 55.1	16 21.7	11 37.5
12 Tu	15 19 10	21 17 33	23 2 47	0♊37 1	2 40.0	1 35.3	1 39.7	3 17.6	7 6.1	4 5.7	5 55.0	16 20.1	11 37.2
13 W	15 23 6	22 15 30	8♊11 7	15 43 55	2 36.2	1 43.8	2 12.0	4 2.5	7 20.3	4 8.9	5D54.9	16 18.4	11 36.9
14 Th	15 27 3	23 13 24	23 14 17	0♋41 17	2D34.2	1 56.9	2 42.8	4 47.3	7 34.4	4 12.0	5 54.9	16 16.8	11 36.6
15 F	15 31 0	24 11 18	8♋ 4 5	15 22 3	2 34.0	2 14.4	3 12.1	5 32.1	7 48.5	4 15.0	5 55.0	16 15.2	11 36.3
16 Sa	15 34 56	25 9 9	22 34 41	29 41 41	2 35.0	2 36.4	3 39.8	6 16.8	8 2.5	4 18.0	5 55.1	16 13.6	11 36.1
17 Su	15 38 53	26 6 59	6♌42 54	13♌38 17	2 36.4	3 2.6	4 6.0	7 1.5	8 16.6	4 20.8	5 55.2	16 12.0	11 35.9
18 M	15 42 49	27 4 47	20 27 55	27 11 59	2R37.4	3 33.0	4 30.5	7 46.1	8 30.6	4 23.6	5 55.5	16 10.4	11 35.8
19 Tu	15 46 46	28 2 33	3♍50 42	10♍24 23	2 37.5	4 7.5	4 53.2	8 30.7	8 44.5	4 26.2	5 55.7	16 8.8	11 35.6
20 W	15 50 42	29 0 17	16 53 20	23 17 53	2 36.1	4 45.9	5 14.2	9 15.2	8 58.5	4 28.8	5 56.0	16 7.2	11 35.5
21 Th	15 54 39	29 58 0	29 38 22	5♎55 9	2 33.2	5 28.0	5 33.3	9 59.6	9 12.4	4 31.3	5 56.4	16 5.6	11 35.4
22 F	15 58 35	0♊55 42	12♎ 8 33	18 18 52	2 29.1	6 13.9	5 50.4	10 44.0	9 26.2	4 33.7	5 56.8	16 4.1	11D35.4
23 Sa	16 2 32	1 53 21	24 26 24	0♏31 27	2 24.1	7 3.4	6 5.6	11 28.4	9 40.1	4 36.0	5 57.3	16 2.5	11 35.4
24 Su	16 6 29	2 51 0	6♏34 16	12 35 6	2 19.0	7 56.3	6 18.8	12 12.6	9 53.8	4 38.2	5 57.9	16 0.9	11 35.4
25 M	16 10 25	3 48 37	18 34 12	24 31 49	2 14.2	8 52.6	6 29.9	12 56.9	10 7.6	4 40.3	5 58.5	15 59.4	11 35.5
26 Tu	16 14 22	4 46 12	0♐28 11	6♐23 31	2 10.3	9 52.1	6 38.8	13 41.0	10 21.3	4 42.3	5 59.1	15 57.9	11 35.5
27 W	16 18 18	5 43 47	12 18 6	18 12 11	2 7.5	10 54.8	6 45.5	14 25.2	10 35.0	4 44.2	5 59.8	15 56.4	11 35.7
28 Th	16 22 15	6 41 20	24 6 3	0♑ 0 0	2D 6.0	12 0.7	6 50.0	15 9.2	10 48.6	4 46.1	6 0.5	15 54.9	11 35.8
29 F	16 26 11	7 38 53	5♑54 23	11 49 32	2 5.8	13 9.5	6R52.2	15 53.3	11 2.2	4 47.8	6 1.3	15 53.4	11 36.0
30 Sa	16 30 8	8 36 24	17 45 52	23 43 47	2 6.6	14 21.3	6 52.0	16 37.2	11 15.7	4 49.4	6 2.2	15 51.9	11 36.2
31 Su	16 34 4	9 33 55	29 43 44	5♒46 11	2 8.0	15 36.1	6 49.5	17 21.1	11 29.2	4 51.0	6 3.1	15 50.4	11 36.4

LONGITUDE — JUNE 1964

Day	Sid.Time	☉	0 hr ☽	Noon ☽	True ☊	☿	♀	♂	♃	♄	♅	♆	♇
1 M	16 38 1	10♊31 24	11♒51 37	18♒ 0 34	2♋ 9.6	16♉53.6	6♋44.6	18♉ 5.0	11♉42.7	4♓52.4	6♍ 4.1	15♏49.0	11♍36.7
2 Tu	16 41 58	11 28 53	24 13 31	0♓31 1	2 11.0	18 14.0	6R37.3	18 48.8	11 56.1	4 53.8	6 5.1	15R47.5	11 37.0
3 W	16 45 54	12 26 21	6♓53 33	13 21 36	2R11.8	19 37.2	6 27.6	19 32.5	12 9.4	4 55.0	6 6.1	15 46.1	11 37.3
4 Th	16 49 51	13 23 48	19 55 34	26 35 51	2 11.7	21 3.2	6 15.5	20 16.2	12 22.7	4 56.2	6 7.2	15 44.7	11 37.7
5 F	16 53 47	14 21 15	3♈22 41	10♈16 16	2 10.9	22 31.8	6 1.0	20 59.9	12 36.0	4 57.2	6 8.4	15 43.3	11 38.1
6 Sa	16 57 44	15 18 40	17 16 37	24 23 36	2 9.4	24 3.2	5 44.2	21 43.4	12 49.2	4 58.2	6 9.6	15 41.9	11 38.5
7 Su	17 1 40	16 16 6	1♉36 57	8♉56 11	2 7.5	25 37.2	5 25.0	22 27.0	13 2.3	4 59.0	6 10.9	15 40.6	11 38.9
8 M	17 5 37	17 13 30	16 20 40	23 49 34	2 5.6	27 14.0	5 3.6	23 10.4	13 15.4	4 59.8	6 12.2	15 39.2	11 39.4
9 Tu	17 9 33	18 10 55	1♊21 57	8♊56 41	2 4.1	28 53.3	4 40.0	23 53.9	13 28.5	5 0.5	6 13.6	15 37.9	11 39.9
10 W	17 13 30	19 8 18	16 32 37	24 8 31	2 3.1	0♊35.4	4 14.4	24 37.2	13 41.4	5 1.0	6 15.0	15 36.6	11 40.5
11 Th	17 17 27	20 5 41	1♋43 12	9♋15 29	2D 2.8	2 20.0	3 46.8	25 20.5	13 54.4	5 1.5	6 16.5	15 35.3	11 41.0
12 F	17 21 23	21 3 3	16 44 21	24 8 50	2 3.0	4 7.2	3 17.3	26 3.8	14 7.2	5 1.9	6 18.0	15 34.1	11 41.6
13 Sa	17 25 20	22 0 24	1♌28 11	8♌41 46	2 3.7	5 57.0	2 46.2	26 46.9	14 20.0	5 2.1	6 19.5	15 32.8	11 42.3
14 Su	17 29 16	22 57 44	15 49 11	22 50 8	2 4.5	7 49.3	2 13.5	27 30.1	14 32.7	5 2.3	6 21.2	15 31.6	11 42.9
15 M	17 33 13	23 55 3	29 44 32	6♍32 22	2 5.2	9 44.0	1 39.4	28 13.1	14 45.4	5R 2.3	6 22.8	15 30.4	11 43.6
16 Tu	17 37 9	24 52 21	13♍13 49	19 49 8	2R 5.6	11 41.1	1 4.2	28 56.1	14 58.0	5 2.3	6 24.5	15 29.2	11 44.3
17 W	17 41 6	25 49 39	26 18 37	2♎42 41	2 5.8	13 40.5	0 28.1	29 39.1	15 10.5	5 2.2	6 26.3	15 28.0	11 45.1
18 Th	17 45 3	26 46 55	9♎ 1 44	15 16 16	2 5.6	15 42.0	29♊51.2	0♊21.9	15 23.0	5 1.9	6 28.1	15 26.9	11 45.9
19 F	17 48 59	27 44 11	21 26 44	27 33 37	2 5.3	17 45.5	29 13.8	1 4.8	15 35.4	5 1.6	6 29.9	15 25.8	11 46.7
20 Sa	17 52 56	28 41 26	3♏37 24	9♏38 33	2 4.9	19 50.8	28 36.2	1 47.5	15 47.7	5 1.2	6 31.8	15 24.7	11 47.5
21 Su	17 56 52	29 38 40	15 37 29	21 34 40	2 4.5	21 57.7	27 58.5	2 30.2	15 59.9	5 0.7	6 33.8	15 23.6	11 48.4
22 M	18 0 49	0♋35 54	27 30 29	3♐25 19	2 4.3	24 6.0	27 21.1	3 12.9	16 12.1	5 0.0	6 35.8	15 22.6	11 49.3
23 Tu	18 4 45	1 33 7	9♐19 32	15 13 28	2D 4.2	26 15.4	26 44.2	3 55.5	16 24.2	4 59.3	6 37.8	15 21.6	11 50.2
24 W	18 8 42	2 30 20	21 7 26	27 1 44	2R 4.2	28 25.7	26 8.0	4 38.0	16 36.2	4 58.5	6 39.9	15 20.6	11 51.1
25 Th	18 12 38	3 27 32	2♑56 41	8♑52 32	2 4.2	0♋36.6	25 32.8	5 20.4	16 48.1	4 57.6	6 42.0	15 19.6	11 52.1
26 F	18 16 35	4 24 44	14 49 34	20 48 4	2 4.2	2 47.8	24 58.7	6 2.9	16 60.0	4 56.6	6 44.2	15 18.7	11 53.1
27 Sa	18 20 32	5 21 56	26 48 18	2♒50 33	2 4.0	4 59.1	24 26.0	6 45.2	17 11.7	4 55.5	6 46.4	15 17.8	11 54.2
28 Su	18 24 28	6 19 8	8♒55 6	15 2 14	2 3.5	7 10.1	23 54.9	7 27.5	17 23.4	4 54.3	6 48.6	15 16.9	11 55.2
29 M	18 28 25	7 16 19	21 12 17	27 25 31	2 3.0	9 20.6	23 25.4	8 9.7	17 35.0	4 53.0	6 50.9	15 16.0	11 56.3
30 Tu	18 32 21	8 13 31	3♓42 18	10♓ 2 56	2 2.3	11 30.3	22 57.8	8 51.9	17 46.6	4 51.6	6 53.2	15 15.2	11 57.4

Astro Data Dy Hr Mn	Planet Ingress Dy Hr Mn	Last Aspect Dy Hr Mn	☽ Ingress Dy Hr Mn	Last Aspect Dy Hr Mn	☽ Ingress Dy Hr Mn	☽ Phases & Eclipses Dy Hr Mn	Astro Data
♃△♅ 7 1:35	♂ ♉ 7 14:41	30 19:14 ♂ △	♑ 1 5:42	1 12:54 ♂ □	♓ 2 11:01	4 22:20 ☽ 14♒27	1 MAY 1964
☽0N 9 5:20	♀ ♋ 9 3:16	3 11:57 ♂ □	♒ 3 18:06	4 2:17 ☿ ✶	♈ 4 18:03	11 21:02 ● 21♉10	Julian Day # 23497
☿ D 10 16:08	☉ ♊ 21 0:50	6 1:33 ♂ ✶	♓ 6 3:43	5 20:24 ☉ ✶	♉ 6 21:20	18 12:42 ☽ 27♌35	Delta T 35.3 sec
♅ D 13 11:26		8 8:25 ♀ □	♈ 8 9:16	8 19:34 ☿ ☌	♊ 8 21:50	26 9:29 ○ 5♐09	SVP 05♓45'47"
☽0S 21 23:39	☿ ♊ 9 15:45	8 9:16 ☽ T	♉ 10 11:09	10 4:22 ☉ ☌	♋ 10 21:16		Obliquity 23°26'37"
♇ D 22 21:29	♀ ♊ 17 18:17	11 21:02 ☉ ☌	♊ 12 11:01	12 15:54 ♂ ✶	♌ 12 21:35	3 11:07 ☽ 12♓53	⚷ Chiron 17♓38.5
♀ R 29 10:29	♂ ♊ 17 11:43	13 5:27 ♇ □	♋ 14 10:53	14 21:11 ♂ □	♍ 15 0:27	10 4:22 ● 19♊19	☽ Mean ☊ 4♋56.8
♃△♇ 31 13:04	☉ ♋ 21 8:57	16 4:38 ☉ ✶	♌ 16 12:31	17 6:37 ♂ △	♎ 17 6:54	10 4:33:33 P 0.755	
	☿ ♋ 24 17:17	18 12:42 ☉ □	♍ 18 17:02	19 14:33 ♀ △	♏ 19 16:49	16 23:02 ☽ 25♍47	1 JUNE 1964
☽0N 5 15:08		21 0:40 ☉ △	♎ 21 0:41	21 0:46 ♃ ☍	♐ 22 5:03	25 1:08 ○ 3♑30	Julian Day # 23528
♄ R 15 3:25		21 11:34 ♀ □	♏ 23 10:58	24 9:42 ♀ ☍	♑ 24 18:02	25 1:06 T 1.556	Delta T 35.3 sec
☽0S 18 5:58		24 18:50 ♆ ☌	♐ 25 23:03	26 4:27 ♃ △	♒ 27 6:22		SVP 05♓45'42"
♃☍♆ 18 6:59		26 22:34 ♇ □	♑ 28 12:00	29 4:08 ♀ △	♓ 29 16:56		Obliquity 23°26'37"
		29 21:32 ♂ △	♒ 31 0:32				⚷ Chiron 18♓36.3
							☽ Mean ☊ 3♋18.3

JULY 1964 LONGITUDE

Day	Sid.Time	☉	0 hr ☽	Noon ☽	True ☊	☿	♀	♂	♃	♄	♅	♆	♇
1 W	18 36 18	9♋10 43	16♓27 45	22♓57 5	2♋ 1.6	13♋39.1	22♊32.2	9♊34.0	17♉58.0	4♓50.1	6♍55.6	15♏14.4	11♍58.5
2 Th	18 40 14	10 7 54	29 31 12	6♈10 24	2D 1.1	15 46.7	22R 8.8	10 16.1	18 9.4	4R48.5	6 58.0	15R13.6	11 59.7
3 F	18 44 11	11 5 6	12♈54 54	19 44 52	2 1.0	17 53.1	21 47.5	10 58.1	18 20.6	4 46.9	7 0.5	15 12.8	12 0.9
4 Sa	18 48 7	12 2 18	26 40 25	3♉41 33	2 1.2	19 57.9	21 28.5	11 40.0	18 31.8	4 45.1	7 3.0	15 12.1	12 2.1
5 Su	18 52 4	12 59 31	10♉48 10	18 0 3	2 1.9	22 1.2	21 11.8	12 21.9	18 42.9	4 43.3	7 5.5	15 11.4	12 3.4
6 M	18 56 1	13 56 44	25 16 50	2♊38 3	2 2.8	24 2.8	20 57.5	13 3.7	18 53.8	4 41.3	7 8.1	15 10.7	12 4.6
7 Tu	18 59 57	14 53 57	10♊ 3 3	17 31 4	2 3.7	26 2.7	20 45.6	13 45.5	19 4.7	4 39.3	7 10.7	15 10.1	12 5.9
8 W	19 3 54	15 51 11	25 1 12	2♋32 27	2R 4.2	28 0.7	20 36.0	14 27.2	19 15.5	4 37.2	7 13.3	15 9.5	12 7.2
9 Th	19 7 50	16 48 25	10♋ 3 47	17 34 7	2 4.2	29 56.9	20 28.9	15 8.9	19 26.2	4 35.0	7 16.0	15 8.9	12 8.6
10 F	19 11 47	17 45 39	25 2 20	2♌27 27	2 3.4	1♌51.3	20 24.1	15 50.5	19 36.8	4 32.7	7 18.8	15 8.3	12 9.9
11 Sa	19 15 43	18 42 53	9♌48 30	17 4 39	2 1.9	3 43.7	20D 21.7	16 32.0	19 47.3	4 30.3	7 21.5	15 7.8	12 11.3
12 Su	19 19 40	19 40 7	24 15 15	1♍19 44	1 59.8	5 34.2	20 21.6	17 13.5	19 57.6	4 27.8	7 24.3	15 7.3	12 12.7
13 M	19 23 36	20 37 21	8♍17 45	15 9 7	1 57.4	7 22.8	20 23.8	17 54.9	20 7.9	4 25.3	7 27.1	15 6.9	12 14.2
14 Tu	19 27 33	21 34 35	21 53 46	28 31 50	1 55.2	9 9.5	20 28.2	18 36.2	20 18.1	4 22.7	7 30.0	15 6.4	12 15.6
15 W	19 31 30	22 31 50	5♎ 3 30	11♎29 8	1 53.4	10 54.3	20 34.8	19 17.5	20 28.1	4 19.9	7 32.9	15 6.0	12 17.1
16 Th	19 35 26	23 29 4	17 49 6	24 3 56	1D 52.5	12 37.1	20 43.6	19 58.7	20 38.1	4 17.2	7 35.8	15 5.6	12 18.6
17 F	19 39 23	24 26 18	0♏14 7	6♏20 15	1 52.5	14 18.1	20 54.5	20 39.8	20 47.9	4 14.3	7 38.8	15 5.3	12 20.1
18 Sa	19 43 19	25 23 33	12 22 54	18 22 39	1 53.4	15 57.1	21 7.4	21 20.9	20 57.6	4 11.3	7 41.8	15 5.0	12 21.7
19 Su	19 47 16	26 20 48	24 20 5	0♐15 48	1 54.9	17 34.2	21 22.3	22 1.9	21 7.2	4 8.3	7 44.8	15 4.7	12 23.2
20 M	19 51 12	27 18 3	6♐10 20	12 4 12	1 56.6	19 9.4	21 39.1	22 42.9	21 16.7	4 5.2	7 47.9	15 4.5	12 24.8
21 Tu	19 55 9	28 15 18	17 57 56	23 52 0	1 58.0	20 42.7	21 57.8	23 23.8	21 26.0	4 2.1	7 51.0	15 4.3	12 26.4
22 W	19 59 5	29 12 34	29 46 48	5♑42 45	1R 58.7	22 14.1	22 18.3	24 4.6	21 35.3	3 58.8	7 54.1	15 4.1	12 28.1
23 Th	20 3 2	0♌ 9 50	11♑40 12	17 39 28	1 58.3	23 43.5	22 40.5	24 45.4	21 44.4	3 55.5	7 57.2	15 3.9	12 29.7
24 F	20 6 59	1 7 7	23 40 51	29 44 33	1 56.6	25 11.0	23 4.5	25 26.1	21 53.4	3 52.1	8 0.4	15 3.8	12 31.4
25 Sa	20 10 55	2 4 24	5♒50 49	11♒59 48	1 53.5	26 36.5	23 30.1	26 6.8	22 2.2	3 48.7	8 3.6	15 3.7	12 33.1
26 Su	20 14 52	3 1 42	18 11 39	24 26 31	1 49.1	27 60.0	23 57.3	26 47.4	22 11.0	3 45.2	8 6.8	15 3.7	12 34.8
27 M	20 18 48	3 59 1	0♓44 29	7♓ 5 39	1 44.0	29 21.4	24 26.0	27 27.9	22 19.6	3 41.6	8 10.1	15D 3.6	12 36.5
28 Tu	20 22 45	4 56 20	13 30 6	19 57 56	1 38.6	0♍40.8	24 56.2	28 8.4	22 28.1	3 38.0	8 13.4	15 3.6	12 38.2
29 W	20 26 41	5 53 41	26 29 11	3♈ 3 58	1 33.6	1 58.0	25 27.8	28 48.8	22 36.4	3 34.3	8 16.7	15 3.7	12 40.0
30 Th	20 30 38	6 51 2	9♈42 21	16 24 24	1 29.7	3 13.1	26 0.8	29 29.1	22 44.6	3 30.6	8 20.0	15 3.8	12 41.8
31 F	20 34 34	7 48 24	23 10 11	29 59 47	1 27.2	4 26.0	26 35.1	0♋ 9.4	22 52.7	3 26.7	8 23.3	15 3.9	12 43.6

AUGUST 1964 LONGITUDE

Day	Sid.Time	☉	0 hr ☽	Noon ☽	True ☊	☿	♀	♂	♃	♄	♅	♆	♇
1 Sa	20 38 31	8♌45 48	6♉53 14	13♉50 32	1♋26.2	5♍36.6	27♊10.7	0♋49.7	23♉ 0.7	3♓22.9	8♍26.7	15♏ 4.0	12♍45.4
2 Su	20 42 28	9 43 13	20 51 40	27 56 33	1D 26.6	6 44.8	27 47.5	1 29.8	23 8.5	3R19.0	8 30.1	15 4.2	12 47.2
3 M	20 46 24	10 40 39	5♊ 5 2	12♊16 52	1 27.9	7 50.5	28 25.5	2 10.0	23 16.1	3 15.0	8 33.5	15 4.4	12 49.0
4 Tu	20 50 21	11 38 6	19 31 45	26 49 13	1R 29.1	8 53.7	29 4.6	2 50.0	23 23.7	3 11.0	8 37.0	15 4.6	12 50.9
5 W	20 54 17	12 35 35	4♋ 8 46	11♋29 43	1 29.5	9 54.3	29 44.9	3 30.0	23 31.0	3 6.9	8 40.4	15 4.9	12 52.8
6 Th	20 58 14	13 33 4	18 51 22	26 12 53	1 28.3	10 52.1	0♋26.1	4 9.9	23 38.3	3 2.8	8 43.9	15 5.2	12 54.6
7 F	21 2 10	14 30 35	3♌33 25	10♌52 3	1 25.3	11 46.9	1 8.4	4 49.8	23 45.3	2 58.7	8 47.4	15 5.5	12 56.5
8 Sa	21 6 7	15 28 7	18 7 55	25 20 11	1 20.2	12 38.8	1 51.6	5 29.6	23 52.3	2 54.5	8 51.0	15 5.9	12 58.5
9 Su	21 10 3	16 25 40	2♍28 5	9♍30 57	1 13.7	13 27.4	2 35.8	6 9.3	23 59.0	2 50.3	8 54.5	15 6.3	13 0.4
10 M	21 14 0	17 23 14	16 28 15	23 19 37	1 6.3	14 12.7	3 20.8	6 49.0	24 5.6	2 46.0	8 58.1	15 6.7	13 2.3
11 Tu	21 17 57	18 20 49	0♎ 4 48	6♎43 43	0 59.0	14 54.5	4 6.7	7 28.6	24 12.1	2 41.7	9 1.6	15 7.1	13 4.3
12 W	21 21 53	19 18 25	13 16 24	19 43 3	0 52.8	15 32.6	4 53.4	8 8.1	24 18.4	2 37.3	9 5.2	15 7.6	13 6.2
13 Th	21 25 50	20 16 2	26 3 59	2♏19 34	0 48.1	16 6.7	5 41.0	8 47.5	24 24.5	2 33.0	9 8.8	15 8.2	13 8.2
14 F	21 29 46	21 13 39	8♏30 19	14 36 46	0 45.3	16 36.7	6 29.3	9 26.9	24 30.5	2 28.6	9 12.5	15 8.7	13 10.2
15 Sa	21 33 43	22 11 18	20 39 30	26 39 10	0D 44.3	17 2.3	7 18.3	10 6.3	24 36.3	2 24.2	9 16.1	15 9.3	13 12.2
16 Su	21 37 39	23 8 58	2♐36 26	8♐31 55	0 44.7	17 23.4	8 8.1	10 45.5	24 42.0	2 19.7	9 19.7	15 9.9	13 14.2
17 M	21 41 36	24 6 39	14 26 19	20 20 15	0 45.8	17 39.6	8 58.6	11 24.7	24 47.5	2 15.3	9 23.4	15 10.6	13 16.2
18 Tu	21 45 32	25 4 21	26 14 22	2♑ 9 15	0R 46.7	17 50.8	9 49.7	12 3.8	24 52.8	2 10.8	9 27.1	15 11.2	13 18.2
19 W	21 49 29	26 2 4	8♑ 5 27	14 3 31	0 46.5	17R 56.8	10 41.5	12 42.9	24 57.9	2 6.3	9 30.8	15 12.0	13 20.3
20 Th	21 53 26	26 59 48	20 3 53	26 6 58	0 44.5	17 57.3	11 33.9	13 21.9	25 2.9	2 1.8	9 34.5	15 12.7	13 22.3
21 F	21 57 22	27 57 33	2♒13 8	8♒22 39	0 40.2	17 52.2	12 27.0	14 0.8	25 7.7	1 57.3	9 38.2	15 13.5	13 24.4
22 Sa	22 1 19	28 55 20	14 35 44	20 52 33	0 33.6	17 41.3	13 20.6	14 39.7	25 12.4	1 52.8	9 41.9	15 14.3	13 26.4
23 Su	22 5 15	29 53 8	27 13 10	3♓37 35	0 25.0	17 24.6	14 14.8	15 18.5	25 16.8	1 48.2	9 45.6	15 15.1	13 28.5
24 M	22 9 12	0♍50 57	10♓ 5 45	16 37 35	0 14.9	17 2.0	15 9.6	15 57.2	25 21.1	1 43.7	9 49.3	15 16.0	13 30.6
25 Tu	22 13 8	1 48 48	23 12 55	29 51 33	0 4.4	16 33.6	16 4.9	16 35.9	25 25.2	1 39.2	9 53.1	15 16.9	13 32.6
26 W	22 17 5	2 46 41	6♈33 19	13♈17 58	29♊54.5	15 59.6	17 0.7	17 14.5	25 29.1	1 34.6	9 56.8	15 17.8	13 34.7
27 Th	22 21 1	3 44 35	20 5 17	26 55 6	29 46.2	15 20.2	17 57.0	17 53.0	25 32.9	1 30.1	10 0.6	15 18.8	13 36.8
28 F	22 24 58	4 42 31	3♉47 13	10♉41 28	29 40.2	14 36.0	18 53.9	18 31.5	25 36.4	1 25.6	10 4.3	15 19.8	13 38.9
29 Sa	22 28 55	5 40 29	17 37 44	24 35 54	29 36.7	13 47.4	19 51.2	19 9.9	25 39.8	1 21.0	10 8.1	15 20.8	13 41.0
30 Su	22 32 51	6 38 29	1♊35 54	8♊37 37	29D 35.4	12 55.2	20 49.0	19 48.2	25 43.0	1 16.5	10 11.8	15 21.8	13 43.1
31 M	22 36 48	7 36 30	15 40 59	22 45 54	29R 35.5	12 0.3	21 47.2	20 26.5	25 46.0	1 12.0	10 15.6	15 22.9	13 45.2

Astro Data Dy Hr Mn	Planet Ingress Dy Hr Mn
☽0N 2 22:37	☿ ♌ 9 0:38
♀ D 11 13:00	☉ ♌ 22 19:53
☽0S 15 13:06	☿ ♍ 27 11:35
♆ D 27 7:01	♂ ♋ 30 18:23
☽0N 30 3:56	
	♀ ♋ 5 8:53
☽0S 11 21:12	☉ ♍ 23 2:51
☿ R 19 14:14	☊ ♊ 25 10:22
☽0N 26 8:53	

Last Aspect Dy Hr Mn	☽ Ingress Dy Hr Mn
1 10:54 ♀ □	♈ 2 0:52
3 15:12 ♀ ✱	♉ 4 5:42
5 21:39 ☿ ✱	♊ 6 7:43
7 17:00 ♀ ☌	♋ 8 7:57
9 15:10 ♃ ✱	♌ 10 8:01
11 17:28 ♀ ✱	♍ 12 9:44
13 23:23 ☉ ✱	♎ 14 14:41
16 11:47 ☉ □	♏ 16 23:32
19 4:25 ☉ △	♐ 19 11:28
21 11:43 ♂ ☍	♑ 22 0:27
23 20:24 ♃ △	♒ 24 12:30
26 21:03 ☿ ☍	♓ 26 22:36
29 4:29 ♂ □	♈ 29 6:25
31 6:17 ♀ ✱	♉ 31 12:00

Last Aspect Dy Hr Mn	☽ Ingress Dy Hr Mn
2 3:55 ♃ ☌	♊ 2 15:28
4 16:27 ♀ ☌	♋ 4 17:13
6 7:52 ♃ ✱	♌ 6 18:11
8 9:38 ♃ □	♍ 8 19:50
10 13:28 ♃ △	♎ 10 23:51
12 12:09 ☉ ✱	♏ 13 7:31
15 7:57 ♃ ☍	♐ 15 18:44
17 21:25 ☉ △	♑ 18 7:38
20 9:57 ♃ △	♒ 20 19:39
22 20:19 ♃ □	♓ 23 5:13
25 4:01 ♃ ✱	♈ 25 12:15
26 19:57 ♀ □	♉ 27 17:24
29 13:53 ♃ ☌	♊ 29 21:16

☽ Phases & Eclipses Dy Hr Mn	
2 20:31	☽ 10♈57
9 11:31	● 17♋16
9 11:17:16	✔ P 0.322
16 11:47	☽ 23♎57
24 15:58	○ 1♒45
1 3:29	☽ 8♉54
7 19:17	● 15♌17
15 3:19	☽ 22♏19
23 5:25	○ 0♓06
30 9:15	☽ 7♊01

Astro Data

1 JULY 1964
Julian Day # 23558
Delta T 35.4 sec
SVP 05♓45'37"
Obliquity 23°26'37"
⚷ Chiron 18♓45.3R
☽ Mean ☊ 1♋43.0

1 AUGUST 1964
Julian Day # 23589
Delta T 35.4 sec
SVP 05♓45'32"
Obliquity 23°26'38"
⚷ Chiron 18♓05.3R
☽ Mean ☊ 0♋04.6

LONGITUDE SEPTEMBER 1964

Day	Sid.Time	☉	0 hr ☽	Noon ☽	True ☊	☿	♀	♂	♃	♄	♅	♆	♇
1 Tu	22 40 44	8♍34 34	29♊52 13	6♋59 45	29♊35.7	11♍ 3.6	22♋45.8	21♋ 4.7	25♉48.8	1♓ 7.5	10♍19.4	15♏24.0	13♍47.3
2 W	22 44 41	9 32 40	14♋ 8 15	21 17 23	29R 35.0	10R 6.4	23 44.9	21 42.8	25 51.5	1R 3.1	10 23.1	15 25.1	13 49.4
3 Th	22 48 37	10 30 47	28 26 46	5♌35 55	29 32.3	9 9.8	24 44.4	22 20.9	25 53.9	0 58.6	10 26.9	15 26.3	13 51.6
4 F	22 52 34	11 28 57	12♌44 18	19 51 20	29 26.8	8 15.1	25 44.3	22 58.8	25 56.1	0 54.2	10 30.7	15 27.5	13 53.7
5 Sa	22 56 30	12 27 8	26 56 22	3♍58 47	29 18.6	7 23.4	26 44.5	23 36.7	25 58.2	0 49.8	10 34.5	15 28.7	13 55.8
6 Su	23 0 27	13 25 21	10♍57 56	17 53 14	29 8.2	6 36.1	27 45.2	24 14.6	26 0.0	0 45.4	10 38.2	15 30.0	13 57.9
7 M	23 4 24	14 23 36	24 44 12	1♎30 22	28 56.4	5 54.3	28 46.1	24 52.3	26 1.7	0 41.0	10 42.0	15 31.2	14 0.0
8 Tu	23 8 20	15 21 53	8♎11 26	14 47 11	28 44.6	5 19.0	29 47.5	25 30.0	26 3.1	0 36.7	10 45.8	15 32.5	14 2.2
9 W	23 12 17	16 20 11	21 17 32	27 42 32	28 33.9	4 51.1	0♌49.1	26 7.6	26 4.4	0 32.4	10 49.5	15 33.9	14 4.3
10 Th	23 16 13	17 18 31	4♏ 2 20	10♏17 11	28 25.2	4 31.2	1 51.1	26 45.2	26 5.4	0 28.1	10 53.3	15 35.2	14 6.4
11 F	23 20 10	18 16 52	16 27 29	22 33 39	28 19.1	4D 20.0	2 53.4	27 22.6	26 6.3	0 23.9	10 57.0	15 36.6	14 8.5
12 Sa	23 24 6	19 15 15	28 36 13	4♐35 45	28 15.4	4 17.8	3 56.1	28 0.0	26 7.0	0 19.7	11 0.8	15 38.0	14 10.6
13 Su	23 28 3	20 13 40	10♐32 54	16 28 19	28D 13.9	4 24.8	4 59.0	28 37.3	26 7.4	0 15.6	11 4.5	15 39.5	14 12.7
14 M	23 31 59	21 12 6	22 22 40	28 16 40	28R 13.7	4 41.1	6 2.2	29 14.6	26R 7.7	0 11.5	11 8.3	15 40.9	14 14.9
15 Tu	23 35 56	22 10 34	4♑11 0	10♑ 6 20	28 13.6	5 6.5	7 5.7	29 51.7	26 7.7	0 7.5	11 12.0	15 42.4	14 17.0
16 W	23 39 53	23 9 4	16 3 22	22 2 42	28 12.7	5 41.0	8 9.5	0♌28.8	26 7.6	0 3.5	11 15.7	15 43.9	14 19.1
17 Th	23 43 49	24 7 35	28 4 56	4♒10 36	28 9.9	6 24.0	9 13.6	1 5.8	26 7.2	29♒59.5	11 19.4	15 45.5	14 21.2
18 F	23 47 46	25 6 8	10♒20 11	16 34 5	28 4.7	7 15.3	10 18.0	1 42.7	26 6.7	29 55.6	11 23.1	15 47.0	14 23.3
19 Sa	23 51 42	26 4 43	22 52 35	29 15 56	27 56.7	8 14.3	11 22.6	2 19.5	26 6.0	29 51.8	11 26.8	15 48.6	14 25.4
20 Su	23 55 39	27 3 19	5♓44 14	12♓17 28	27 46.3	9 20.5	12 27.4	2 56.3	26 5.0	29 48.0	11 30.5	15 50.2	14 27.4
21 M	23 59 35	28 1 57	18 55 34	25 38 17	27 34.2	10 33.1	13 32.6	3 32.9	26 3.9	29 44.3	11 34.1	15 51.8	14 29.5
22 Tu	0 3 32	29 0 37	2♈25 21	9♈16 20	27 21.5	11 51.7	14 37.9	4 9.5	26 2.5	29 40.6	11 37.8	15 53.5	14 31.6
23 W	0 7 28	29 59 19	16 10 48	23 8 15	27 9.5	13 15.6	15 43.5	4 46.0	26 1.0	29 37.0	11 41.4	15 55.2	14 33.6
24 Th	0 11 25	0♎58 3	0♉ 8 9	7♉ 9 57	26 59.3	14 44.1	16 49.4	5 22.5	25 59.2	29 33.5	11 45.0	15 56.8	14 35.7
25 F	0 15 21	1 56 50	14 13 11	21 17 22	26 51.8	16 16.6	17 55.5	5 58.8	25 57.3	29 30.0	11 48.6	15 58.6	14 37.8
26 Sa	0 19 18	2 55 38	28 22 5	5♊26 59	26 47.1	17 52.5	19 1.8	6 35.1	25 55.1	29 26.6	11 52.2	16 0.3	14 39.8
27 Su	0 23 15	3 54 29	12♊31 48	19 36 18	26 45.0	19 31.3	20 8.4	7 11.3	25 52.8	29 23.3	11 55.8	16 2.1	14 41.8
28 M	0 27 11	4 53 22	26 40 19	3♋43 43	26 44.6	21 12.5	21 15.2	7 47.4	25 50.3	29 20.0	11 59.4	16 3.9	14 43.9
29 Tu	0 31 8	5 52 18	10♋46 24	17 48 17	26 44.6	22 55.5	22 22.2	8 23.4	25 47.5	29 16.8	12 2.9	16 5.7	14 45.9
30 W	0 35 4	6 51 16	24 49 17	1♌49 16	26 43.6	24 40.1	23 29.4	8 59.3	25 44.6	29 13.7	12 6.4	16 7.5	14 47.9

LONGITUDE OCTOBER 1964

Day	Sid.Time	☉	0 hr ☽	Noon ☽	True ☊	☿	♀	♂	♃	♄	♅	♆	♇
1 Th	0 39 1	7♎50 16	8♌48 7	15♌45 38	26♊40.7	26♍25.7	24♌36.8	9♌35.2	25♉41.5	29♒10.6	12♍ 9.9	16♏ 9.3	14♍49.9
2 F	0 42 57	8 49 18	22 41 37	29 35 48	26R 35.0	28 12.2	25 44.4	10 10.9	25R 38.2	29R 7.7	12 13.4	16 11.2	14 51.9
3 Sa	0 46 54	9 48 23	6♍27 51	13♍17 29	26 26.6	29 59.1	26 52.1	10 46.6	25 34.6	29 4.8	12 16.9	16 13.1	14 53.8
4 Su	0 50 50	10 47 30	20 4 20	26 48 3	26 15.7	1♎46.4	28 0.1	11 22.2	25 30.9	29 2.0	12 20.3	16 15.0	14 55.8
5 M	0 54 47	11 46 39	3♎28 20	10♎ 4 52	26 3.5	3 33.7	29 8.3	11 57.6	25 27.0	28 59.2	12 23.7	16 16.9	14 57.7
6 Tu	0 58 44	12 45 50	16 37 26	23 5 50	25 51.1	5 20.9	0♍16.6	12 33.0	25 23.0	28 56.6	12 27.1	16 18.8	14 59.7
7 W	1 2 40	13 45 3	29 29 59	5♏49 51	25 39.8	7 7.9	1 25.1	13 8.3	25 18.7	28 54.0	12 30.5	16 20.8	15 1.6
8 Th	1 6 37	14 44 18	12♏ 5 31	18 17 7	25 30.4	8 54.6	2 33.8	13 43.5	25 14.3	28 51.6	12 33.9	16 22.7	15 3.5
9 F	1 10 33	15 43 35	24 24 54	0♐29 10	25 23.6	10 40.9	3 42.7	14 18.6	25 9.6	28 49.2	12 37.2	16 24.7	15 5.4
10 Sa	1 14 30	16 42 54	6♐30 20	12 28 50	25 19.5	12 26.7	4 51.7	14 53.5	25 4.9	28 46.9	12 40.5	16 26.7	15 7.3
11 Su	1 18 26	17 42 14	18 25 13	24 20 2	25D 17.7	14 11.9	6 0.8	15 28.4	24 59.9	28 44.7	12 43.7	16 28.7	15 9.1
12 M	1 22 23	18 41 37	0♑13 53	6♑ 7 27	25 17.6	15 56.5	7 10.2	16 3.2	24 54.8	28 42.6	12 47.0	16 30.8	15 11.0
13 Tu	1 26 19	19 41 1	12 1 23	17 56 22	25R 18.1	17 40.6	8 19.6	16 37.9	24 49.5	28 40.6	12 50.2	16 32.8	15 12.8
14 W	1 30 16	20 40 28	23 53 6	29 52 15	25 18.3	19 23.9	9 29.2	17 12.4	24 44.0	28 38.6	12 53.4	16 34.9	15 14.6
15 Th	1 34 13	21 39 56	5♒54 30	12♒ 0 30	25 17.1	21 6.6	10 39.0	17 46.9	24 38.4	28 36.8	12 56.6	16 36.9	15 16.4
16 F	1 38 9	22 39 25	18 10 48	24 25 59	25 13.9	22 48.7	11 48.9	18 21.3	24 32.6	28 35.1	12 59.7	16 39.0	15 18.2
17 Sa	1 42 6	23 38 57	0♓46 28	7♓12 38	25 8.4	24 30.1	12 59.0	18 55.5	24 26.7	28 33.4	13 2.8	16 41.1	15 19.9
18 Su	1 46 2	24 38 30	13 44 44	20 22 54	25 0.7	26 10.8	14 9.2	19 29.6	24 20.6	28 31.9	13 5.8	16 43.2	15 21.7
19 M	1 49 59	25 38 5	27 7 7	3♈57 16	24 51.4	27 50.9	15 19.5	20 3.7	24 14.4	28 30.4	13 8.9	16 45.3	15 23.4
20 Tu	1 53 55	26 37 42	10♈53 1	17 53 58	24 41.4	29 30.4	16 30.0	20 37.6	24 8.0	28 29.1	13 11.9	16 47.5	15 25.1
21 W	1 57 52	27 37 21	24 59 33	2♉ 9 4	24 31.9	1♏ 9.2	17 40.5	21 11.4	24 1.5	28 27.8	13 14.8	16 49.6	15 26.8
22 Th	2 1 48	28 37 1	9♉21 47	16 36 53	24 23.9	2 47.4	18 51.3	21 45.1	23 54.9	28 26.6	13 17.8	16 51.8	15 28.5
23 F	2 5 45	29 36 44	23 53 32	1♊10 55	24 18.1	4 25.0	20 2.1	22 18.7	23 48.1	28 25.6	13 20.7	16 53.9	15 30.1
24 Sa	2 9 42	0♏36 29	8♊28 17	15 44 55	24 14.8	6 2.0	21 13.1	22 52.1	23 41.3	28 24.6	13 23.5	16 56.1	15 31.7
25 Su	2 13 38	1 36 17	23 0 11	0♋13 36	24D 13.7	7 38.5	22 24.2	23 25.5	23 34.3	28 23.8	13 26.4	16 58.3	15 33.3
26 M	2 17 35	2 36 6	7♋24 45	14 33 17	24 14.2	9 14.4	23 35.5	23 58.7	23 27.2	28 23.0	13 29.2	17 0.5	15 34.9
27 Tu	2 21 31	3 35 58	21 39 0	28 41 44	24R 15.2	10 49.8	24 46.8	24 31.8	23 19.9	28 22.4	13 31.9	17 2.7	15 36.5
28 W	2 25 28	4 35 52	5♌41 24	12♌37 58	24 15.7	12 24.7	25 58.3	25 4.8	23 12.6	28 21.8	13 34.6	17 4.9	15 38.0
29 Th	2 29 24	5 35 48	19 31 24	26 21 43	24 14.8	13 59.1	27 9.9	25 37.7	23 5.2	28 21.4	13 37.3	17 7.1	15 39.5
30 F	2 33 21	6 35 47	3♍ 8 56	9♍53 3	24 11.8	15 33.1	28 21.6	26 10.4	22 57.7	28 21.0	13 39.9	17 9.3	15 41.0
31 Sa	2 37 17	7 35 47	16 34 5	23 12 1	24 6.7	17 6.5	29 33.3	26 43.0	22 50.1	28 20.8	13 42.5	17 11.5	15 42.5

Astro Data	Planet Ingress	Last Aspect	☽ Ingress	Last Aspect	☽ Ingress	☽ Phases & Eclipses	Astro Data
Dy Hr Mn	Dy Hr Mn	Dy Hr Mn	Dy Hr Mn	Dy Hr Mn	Dy Hr Mn	Dy Hr Mn	1 SEPTEMBER 1964
☽0S 8 5:50	♀ ♌ 8 4:53	30 20:43 ♇ □	♋ 1 0:13	2 11:09 ♄ ☍	♍ 2 12:42	6 4:34 ● 13♍36	Julian Day # 23620
☿ D 11 17:48	♂ ♌ 15 5:22	2 19:43 ♃ ✶	♌ 3 2:36	4 9:39 ♃ △	♎ 4 17:44	13 21:24 ☽ 21♐06	Delta T 35.5 sec
♃ R 14 19:01	♄ ♒ 16 21:04	4 22:21 ♃ □	♍ 5 5:12	6 22:53 ♄ △	♏ 7 0:57	21 17:31 ○ 28♓45	SVP 05♓45'28"
☽0N 22 15:32	☉ ♎ 23 0:17	7 7:43 ♀ ✶	♎ 7 9:19	9 8:40 ♄ □	♐ 9 11:02	28 15:01 ☽ 5♋30	Obliquity 23°26'39"
		9 9:30 ♂ □	♏ 9 16:19	11 20:55 ♄ ✶	♑ 11 23:32		⚷ Chiron 16♓49.2R
☽0S 5 14:11	☿ ♎ 3 0:12	11 22:44 ♂ △	♐ 12 2:47	14 1:42 ♃ △	♒ 14 12:15	5 16:20 ● 12♎27	☽ Mean ☊ 28♊26.1
☿0S 5 6:46	♀ ♍ 5 18:10	13 21:24 ☉ □	♑ 14 15:30	16 19:50 ♄ ☌	♓ 16 22:33	13 16:56 ☽ 20♑23	
☽0N 20 0:46	☿ ♏ 20 7:11	16 20:07 ♃ △	♒ 17 3:47	18 18:56 ♃ ✶	♈ 19 5:05	21 4:45 ○ 27♈49	1 OCTOBER 1964
	☉ ♏ 23 9:21	19 13:03 ♄ ☌	♓ 19 13:22	21 5:49 ♄ ✶	♉ 21 8:24	27 21:59 ☽ 4♌31	Julian Day # 23650
	♀ ♎ 31 8:54	21 17:31 ☉ ☍	♈ 21 19:44	23 7:27 ♄ □	♊ 23 10:03		Delta T 35.6 sec
		23 23:01 ♄ ✶	♉ 23 23:46	25 8:57 ♄ △	♋ 25 11:37		SVP 05♓45'25"
		26 1:49 ♄ □	♊ 26 2:46	27 5:49 ♀ ✶	♌ 27 14:14		Obliquity 23°26'39"
		28 4:30 ♄ △	♋ 28 5:39	29 15:31 ♄ ☍	♍ 29 18:25		⚷ Chiron 15♓27.4R
		30 1:34 ♃ ✶	♌ 30 8:52				☽ Mean ☊ 26♊50.7

NOVEMBER 1964 LONGITUDE

Day	Sid.Time	☉	0 hr ☽	Noon ☽	True ☊	☿	♀	♂	♃	♄	♅	♆	♇
1 Su	2 41 14	8♏35 50	29♍46 49	6♎18 28	23♊59.8	18♏39.5	0♎45.2	27♌15.4	22♉42.4	28♒20.6	13♍45.1	17♏13.7	15♍44.0
2 M	2 45 11	9 35 54	12♎46 56	19 12 10	23R 51.8	20 12.1	1 57.2	27 47.8	22R 34.7	28D 20.6	13 47.6	17 16.0	15 45.4
3 Tu	2 49 7	10 36 1	25 34 10	1♏52 54	23 43.7	21 44.2	3 9.3	28 19.9	22 26.8	28 20.7	13 50.1	17 18.2	15 46.8
4 W	2 53 4	11 36 10	8♏ 8 24	14 20 43	23 36.2	23 16.0	4 21.5	28 52.0	22 18.9	28 20.8	13 52.5	17 20.4	15 48.1
5 Th	2 57 0	12 36 20	20 29 55	26 36 9	23 30.1	24 47.3	5 33.8	29 23.9	22 11.0	28 21.1	13 54.9	17 22.7	15 49.5
6 F	3 0 57	13 36 32	2♐39 35	8♐40 27	23 25.9	26 18.2	6 46.2	29 55.6	22 3.0	28 21.5	13 57.3	17 24.9	15 50.8
7 Sa	3 4 53	14 36 46	14 39 2	20 35 39	23D 23.7	27 48.7	7 58.7	0♍27.2	21 54.9	28 22.0	13 59.6	17 27.2	15 52.1
8 Su	3 8 50	15 37 2	26 30 41	2♑24 35	23 23.3	29 18.7	9 11.2	0 58.6	21 46.8	28 22.6	14 1.8	17 29.4	15 53.4
9 M	3 12 46	16 37 19	8♑17 48	14 10 52	23 24.3	0♐48.4	10 23.8	1 29.9	21 38.7	28 23.3	14 4.1	17 31.7	15 54.6
10 Tu	3 16 43	17 37 38	20 4 20	25 58 48	23 26.0	2 17.6	11 36.5	2 1.1	21 30.6	28 24.1	14 6.2	17 33.9	15 55.8
11 W	3 20 40	18 37 58	1♒54 53	7♒53 11	23 27.7	3 46.4	12 49.3	2 32.0	21 22.4	28 25.0	14 8.4	17 36.2	15 57.0
12 Th	3 24 36	19 38 20	13 54 23	19 59 6	23R 28.9	5 14.8	14 2.2	3 2.8	21 14.3	28 26.0	14 10.4	17 38.4	15 58.2
13 F	3 28 33	20 38 43	26 7 58	2♓21 36	23 28.9	6 42.7	15 15.1	3 33.5	21 6.1	28 27.1	14 12.5	17 40.7	15 59.3
14 Sa	3 32 29	21 39 7	8♓40 32	15 5 18	23 27.5	8 10.0	16 28.1	4 3.9	20 57.9	28 28.3	14 14.4	17 42.9	16 0.4
15 Su	3 36 26	22 39 33	21 36 17	28 13 51	23 24.7	9 36.8	17 41.2	4 34.2	20 49.7	28 29.6	14 16.4	17 45.2	16 1.5
16 M	3 40 22	23 40 0	4♈58 10	11♈49 19	23 20.8	11 3.0	18 54.3	5 4.4	20 41.6	28 31.1	14 18.3	17 47.4	16 2.6
17 Tu	3 44 19	24 40 28	18 47 12	25 51 35	23 16.4	12 28.6	20 7.6	5 34.3	20 33.4	28 32.6	14 20.1	17 49.7	16 3.6
18 W	3 48 15	25 40 58	3♉ 2 1	10♉17 56	23 12.0	13 53.5	21 20.8	6 4.1	20 25.3	28 34.2	14 21.9	17 51.9	16 4.6
19 Th	3 52 12	26 41 29	17 38 33	25 3 1	23 8.4	15 17.6	22 34.2	6 33.7	20 17.2	28 35.9	14 23.6	17 54.1	16 5.5
20 F	3 56 9	27 42 2	2♊30 19	9♊59 25	23 5.9	16 40.8	23 47.6	7 3.1	20 9.2	28 37.8	14 25.3	17 56.4	16 6.5
21 Sa	4 0 5	28 42 37	17 29 15	24 58 43	23D 4.8	18 3.0	25 1.1	7 32.3	20 1.2	28 39.7	14 26.9	17 58.6	16 7.4
22 Su	4 4 2	29 43 12	2♋26 51	9♋52 41	23 4.9	19 24.2	26 14.6	8 1.4	19 53.2	28 41.7	14 28.5	18 0.8	16 8.2
23 M	4 7 58	0♐43 50	17 15 27	24 34 26	23 6.0	20 44.1	27 28.2	8 30.2	19 45.4	28 43.9	14 30.1	18 3.0	16 9.1
24 Tu	4 11 55	1 44 29	1♌49 7	8♌59 5	23 7.4	22 2.5	28 41.9	8 58.9	19 37.5	28 46.1	14 31.5	18 5.2	16 9.9
25 W	4 15 51	2 45 10	16 4 4	23 3 55	23 8.7	23 19.4	29 55.6	9 27.3	19 29.8	28 48.4	14 33.0	18 7.4	16 10.7
26 Th	4 19 48	3 45 52	29 58 35	6♍48 7	23R 9.3	24 34.4	1♏ 9.4	9 55.5	19 22.1	28 50.8	14 34.4	18 9.6	16 11.4
27 F	4 23 44	4 46 36	13♍32 38	20 12 19	23 9.2	25 47.3	2 23.3	10 23.6	19 14.4	28 53.4	14 35.7	18 11.8	16 12.2
28 Sa	4 27 41	5 47 22	26 47 21	3♎18 0	23 8.1	26 57.8	3 37.2	10 51.4	19 6.9	28 56.0	14 37.0	18 14.0	16 12.9
29 Su	4 31 38	6 48 9	9♎44 31	16 7 9	23 6.3	28 5.6	4 51.1	11 19.0	18 59.5	28 58.7	14 38.2	18 16.1	16 13.5
30 M	4 35 34	7 48 57	22 26 10	28 41 50	23 4.0	29 10.2	6 5.1	11 46.3	18 52.1	29 1.5	14 39.3	18 18.3	16 14.1

DECEMBER 1964 LONGITUDE

Day	Sid.Time	☉	0 hr ☽	Noon ☽	True ☊	☿	♀	♂	♃	♄	♅	♆	♇
1 Tu	4 39 31	8♐49 47	4♏54 22	11♏ 4 1	23♊ 1.7	0♑11.1	7♏19.2	12♍13.5	18♉44.9	29♒ 4.4	14♍40.4	18♏20.4	16♍14.7
2 W	4 43 27	9 50 39	17 11 1	23 15 36	22R 59.7	1 8.0	8 33.2	12 40.3	18R 37.7	29 7.4	14 41.5	18 22.6	16 15.3
3 Th	4 47 24	10 51 31	29 17 57	5♐18 18	22 58.1	2 0.0	9 47.4	13 7.0	18 30.7	29 10.5	14 42.5	18 24.7	16 15.8
4 F	4 51 20	11 52 25	11♐16 53	17 13 55	22D 57.2	2 46.8	11 1.6	13 33.4	18 23.8	29 13.7	14 43.4	18 26.8	16 16.3
5 Sa	4 55 17	12 53 20	23 9 38	29 4 18	22 56.9	3 27.4	12 15.8	13 59.5	18 17.0	29 17.0	14 44.3	18 28.9	16 16.8
6 Su	4 59 13	13 54 16	4♑58 13	10♑51 39	22 57.2	4 1.1	13 30.0	14 25.4	18 10.4	29 20.4	14 45.2	18 31.0	16 17.2
7 M	5 3 10	14 55 13	16 44 58	22 38 30	22 57.8	4 27.1	14 44.3	14 51.1	18 3.9	29 23.8	14 45.9	18 33.1	16 17.6
8 Tu	5 7 7	15 56 10	28 32 40	4♒27 52	22 58.6	4 44.6	15 58.6	15 16.4	17 57.5	29 27.4	14 46.7	18 35.1	16 18.0
9 W	5 11 3	16 57 9	10♒24 34	16 23 15	22 59.4	4R 52.6	17 13.0	15 41.5	17 51.3	29 31.0	14 47.3	18 37.2	16 18.3
10 Th	5 15 0	17 58 8	22 24 25	28 28 35	22 60.0	4 50.4	18 27.4	16 6.3	17 45.2	29 34.8	14 47.9	18 39.2	16 18.6
11 F	5 18 56	18 59 8	4♓36 19	10♓48 8	23 0.3	4 37.4	19 41.8	16 30.8	17 39.3	29 38.6	14 48.5	18 41.2	16 18.9
12 Sa	5 22 53	20 0 8	17 4 36	23 26 13	23R 0.5	4 12.9	20 56.2	16 55.1	17 33.5	29 42.5	14 49.0	18 43.2	16 19.1
13 Su	5 26 49	21 1 8	29 53 28	6♈26 50	23 0.5	3 36.9	22 10.7	17 19.0	17 27.9	29 46.5	14 49.4	18 45.2	16 19.3
14 M	5 30 46	22 2 10	13♈ 6 39	19 53 12	23D 0.4	2 49.6	23 25.2	17 42.6	17 22.4	29 50.6	14 49.8	18 47.1	16 19.5
15 Tu	5 34 42	23 3 11	26 46 39	3♉47 3	23 0.3	1 51.7	24 39.7	18 6.0	17 17.1	29 54.7	14 50.1	18 49.1	16 19.6
16 W	5 38 39	24 4 13	10♉54 16	18 8 1	23 0.4	0 44.5	25 54.3	18 29.0	17 12.0	29 59.0	14 50.4	18 51.0	16 19.7
17 Th	5 42 36	25 5 16	25 27 48	2♊53 0	23 0.6	29♐29.7	27 8.9	18 51.7	17 7.1	0♓ 3.3	14 50.6	18 52.9	16 19.8
18 F	5 46 32	26 6 19	10♊22 47	17 56 8	23R 0.7	28 9.6	28 23.5	19 14.1	17 2.3	0 7.7	14 50.7	18 54.8	16R 19.8
19 Sa	5 50 29	27 7 23	25 31 57	3♋ 9 2	23 0.8	26 46.9	29 38.1	19 36.1	16 57.7	0 12.2	14 50.8	18 56.7	16 19.9
20 Su	5 54 25	28 8 27	10♋46 8	18 22 0	23 0.6	25 24.5	0♐52.8	19 57.8	16 53.3	0 16.8	14R 50.9	18 58.6	16 19.8
21 M	5 58 22	29 9 32	25 55 26	3♌25 21	23 0.2	24 4.9	2 7.5	20 19.2	16 49.1	0 21.4	14 50.9	19 0.4	16 19.8
22 Tu	6 2 18	0♑10 38	10♌50 45	18 10 52	22 59.4	22 50.8	3 22.2	20 40.2	16 45.1	0 26.2	14 50.8	19 2.2	16 19.7
23 W	6 6 15	1 11 44	25 25 4	2♍32 54	22 58.5	21 44.1	4 36.9	21 0.9	16 41.2	0 30.9	14 50.7	19 4.0	16 19.6
24 Th	6 10 12	2 12 50	9♍34 5	16 28 34	22 57.6	20 46.6	5 51.7	21 21.2	16 37.6	0 35.8	14 50.5	19 5.8	16 19.4
25 F	6 14 8	3 13 58	23 16 21	29 57 37	22D 57.0	19 59.0	7 6.4	21 41.1	16 34.1	0 40.8	14 50.2	19 7.5	16 19.2
26 Sa	6 18 5	4 15 5	6♎32 40	13♎ 1 51	22 56.8	19 22.1	8 21.2	22 0.6	16 30.9	0 45.8	14 49.9	19 9.3	16 19.0
27 Su	6 22 1	5 16 14	19 25 35	25 44 20	22 57.2	18 55.9	9 36.1	22 19.7	16 27.8	0 50.9	14 49.6	19 11.0	16 18.7
28 M	6 25 58	6 17 23	1♏58 34	8♏ 8 47	22 58.1	18 40.2	10 50.9	22 38.4	16 24.9	0 56.0	14 49.2	19 12.7	16 18.5
29 Tu	6 29 54	7 18 33	14 15 29	20 19 8	22 59.4	18D 34.5	12 5.8	22 56.7	16 22.2	1 1.3	14 48.7	19 14.3	16 18.1
30 W	6 33 51	8 19 43	26 20 12	2♐19 7	23 0.8	18 38.2	13 20.6	23 14.6	16 19.8	1 6.6	14 48.2	19 15.9	16 17.8
31 Th	6 37 47	9 20 53	8♐16 18	14 12 6	23 2.0	18 50.6	14 35.5	23 32.0	16 17.5	1 11.9	14 47.6	19 17.6	16 17.4

Astro Data Dy Hr Mn	Planet Ingress Dy Hr Mn	Last Aspect Dy Hr Mn	☽ Ingress Dy Hr Mn	Last Aspect Dy Hr Mn	☽ Ingress Dy Hr Mn	☽ Phases & Eclipses Dy Hr Mn
☽0S 1 21:27	♂ ♍ 6 3:20	31 11:14 ♃ △	♎ 1 0:24	2 23:45 ♄ □	♐ 3 1:24	4 7:16 ● 11♏54
♄ D 1 20:44	☿ ♐ 8 11:02	3 5:28 ♂ ⚹	♏ 3 8:25	5 12:29 ♄ ⚹	♑ 5 13:53	12 12:20 ☽ 20♒09
♀0S 3 10:20	☉ ♐ 22 6:39	5 18:20 ♂ □	♐ 5 18:43	7 3:41 ♆ ⚹	♒ 8 2:57	19 15:43 ○ 27♉21
☽0N 16 11:32	♀ ♏ 25 1:25	8 3:48 ♄ ⚹	♑ 8 7:06	10 14:15 ♄ ☌	♓ 10 15:00	26 7:10 ☽ 4♍04
☽0S 29 3:33	☿ ♑ 30 19:30	10 2:53 ♃ △	♒ 10 20:08	12 8:06 ♀ △	♈ 13 0:12	
		13 4:30 ♄ ☌	♓ 13 7:28	15 5:25 ♄ ⚹	♉ 15 5:33	4 1:18 ● 11♐56
♃☍♆ 3 16:01	☿ ♐ 16 14:31	15 2:05 ☉ △	♈ 15 15:10	17 2:59 ♀ ☍	♊ 17 7:21	4 1:31:21 P 0.752
☿ R 9 7:05	♄ ♓ 16 5:39	17 16:32 ♄ ⚹	♉ 17 18:57	19 2:41 ☉ ☍	♋ 19 7:02	12 6:01 ☽ 20♓15
☽0N 13 21:28	♀ ♐ 19 7:02	19 17:45 ♄ □	♊ 19 19:58	20 14:53 ♂ ⚹	♌ 21 6:31	19 2:41 ○ 27♊14
♇ R 18 18:39	☉ ♑ 21 19:50	21 17:57 ♄ △	♋ 21 20:04	22 18:17 ☿ △	♍ 23 7:41	19 2:37 T 1.175
♅ R 20 6:45		23 18:20 ♀ □	♌ 23 20:59	24 21:07 ♂ ☌	♎ 25 12:04	25 19:27 ☽ 4♎03
☽0S 26 9:29		25 22:01 ♄ ☍	♍ 26 0:02	26 23:06 ☿ ⚹	♏ 27 20:11	
☿ D 29 2:15		28 0:21 ☿ □	♎ 28 5:54	29 17:40 ♂ ⚹	♐ 30 7:20	
♃△♇ 31 1:19		30 14:04 ☿ ⚹	♏ 30 14:31			

Astro Data

1 NOVEMBER 1964
Julian Day # 23681
Delta T 35.6 sec
SVP 05♓45'21"
Obliquity 23°26'39"
⚷ Chiron 14♓25.8R
☽ Mean ☊ 25♊12.2

1 DECEMBER 1964
Julian Day # 23711
Delta T 35.7 sec
SVP 05♓45'17"
Obliquity 23°26'39"
⚷ Chiron 14♓10.7
☽ Mean ☊ 23♊36.9

LONGITUDE JANUARY 1965

Day	Sid.Time	☉	0 hr ☽	Noon ☽	True ☊	☿	♀	♂	♃	♄	♅	♆	♇
1 F	6 41 44	10♑22 3	20♐ 6 54	26♐ 1 1	23♊ 2.6	19♐11.0	15♐50.4	23♍49.0	16♉15.4	1♓17.4	14♍47.0	19♏19.2	16♍17.0
2 Sa	6 45 41	11 23 14	1♑54 45	7♑48 23	23R 2.4	19 38.6	17 5.3	24 5.5	16R13.6	1 22.9	14R46.3	19 20.7	16R16.5
3 Su	6 49 37	12 24 25	13 42 10	19 36 22	23 1.1	20 12.7	18 20.3	24 21.6	16 11.9	1 28.4	14 45.6	19 22.3	16 16.1
4 M	6 53 34	13 25 36	25 31 14	1♒26 59	22 58.7	20 52.6	19 35.2	24 37.2	16 10.5	1 34.1	14 44.8	19 23.8	16 15.6
5 Tu	6 57 30	14 26 47	7♒23 53	13 22 11	22 55.5	21 37.7	20 50.2	24 52.3	16 9.3	1 39.8	14 43.9	19 25.3	16 15.0
6 W	7 1 27	15 27 57	19 22 8	25 24 2	22 51.5	22 27.5	22 5.1	25 6.9	16 8.2	1 45.5	14 43.0	19 26.7	16 14.5
7 Th	7 5 23	16 29 7	1♓28 12	7♓34 56	22 47.5	23 21.5	23 20.1	25 21.0	16 7.4	1 51.3	14 42.1	19 28.1	16 13.9
8 F	7 9 20	17 30 17	13 44 36	19 57 34	22 43.7	24 19.1	24 35.1	25 34.6	16 6.8	1 57.2	14 41.1	19 29.5	16 13.2
9 Sa	7 13 16	18 31 27	26 14 13	2♈34 57	22 40.8	25 20.0	25 50.0	25 47.6	16 6.4	2 3.1	14 40.0	19 30.9	16 12.6
10 Su	7 17 13	19 32 35	9♈ 0 11	15 30 18	22D39.0	26 23.9	27 5.0	26 0.2	16D 6.2	2 9.1	14 38.9	19 32.3	16 11.9
11 M	7 21 10	20 33 44	22 5 42	28 46 44	22 38.5	27 30.5	28 20.0	26 12.2	16 6.3	2 15.1	14 37.8	19 33.6	16 11.2
12 Tu	7 25 6	21 34 51	5♉33 41	12♉26 48	22 39.2	28 39.4	29 35.0	26 23.6	16 6.5	2 21.2	14 36.6	19 34.9	16 10.4
13 W	7 29 3	22 35 58	19 26 11	26 31 53	22 40.6	29 50.4	0♑50.0	26 34.5	16 6.9	2 27.4	14 35.3	19 36.1	16 9.7
14 Th	7 32 59	23 37 5	3♊43 45	11♊ 1 31	22 42.2	1♑ 3.3	2 5.0	26 44.8	16 7.6	2 33.6	14 34.0	19 37.4	16 8.9
15 F	7 36 56	24 38 11	18 24 42	25 52 39	22R43.1	2 18.0	3 20.0	26 54.5	16 8.4	2 39.8	14 32.6	19 38.6	16 8.0
16 Sa	7 40 52	25 39 16	3♋24 33	10♋59 23	22 42.8	3 34.3	4 35.0	27 3.6	16 9.5	2 46.1	14 31.2	19 39.7	16 7.2
17 Su	7 44 49	26 40 21	18 36 2	26 13 15	22 40.8	4 52.0	5 50.0	27 12.1	16 10.8	2 52.5	14 29.8	19 40.9	16 6.3
18 M	7 48 45	27 41 25	3♌49 43	11♌24 8	22 37.1	6 11.0	7 5.0	27 20.0	16 12.2	2 58.9	14 28.3	19 42.0	16 5.4
19 Tu	7 52 42	28 42 28	18 55 16	26 21 58	22 31.9	7 31.3	8 20.1	27 27.3	16 13.9	3 5.3	14 26.8	19 43.1	16 4.5
20 W	7 56 39	29 43 31	3♍43 15	10♍58 18	22 26.1	8 52.7	9 35.1	27 33.9	16 15.8	3 11.8	14 25.2	19 44.1	16 3.5
21 Th	8 0 35	0♒44 33	18 6 33	25 7 35	22 20.3	10 15.2	10 50.1	27 39.9	16 17.8	3 18.3	14 23.6	19 45.2	16 2.5
22 F	8 4 32	1 45 35	2♎ 1 12	8♎47 27	22 15.5	11 38.6	12 5.2	27 45.2	16 20.1	3 24.9	14 21.9	19 46.2	16 1.5
23 Sa	8 8 28	2 46 36	15 26 27	21 58 31	22 12.1	13 3.0	13 20.2	27 49.8	16 22.6	3 31.5	14 20.2	19 47.1	16 0.5
24 Su	8 12 25	3 47 37	28 24 6	4♏43 41	22D10.5	14 28.3	14 35.3	27 53.8	16 25.2	3 38.1	14 18.4	19 48.0	15 59.4
25 M	8 16 21	4 48 38	10♏57 50	17 7 12	22 10.5	15 54.5	15 50.3	27 57.0	16 28.1	3 44.8	14 16.6	19 48.9	15 58.3
26 Tu	8 20 18	5 49 38	23 12 22	29 14 1	22 11.7	17 21.5	17 5.4	27 59.6	16 31.2	3 51.6	14 14.8	19 49.8	15 57.2
27 W	8 24 14	6 50 37	5♐12 47	11♐ 9 16	22 13.3	18 49.3	18 20.4	28 1.4	16 34.4	3 58.3	14 12.9	19 50.6	15 56.1
28 Th	8 28 11	7 51 36	17 4 3	22 57 44	22R14.4	20 17.8	19 35.5	28R 2.4	16 37.9	4 5.1	14 11.0	19 51.4	15 54.9
29 F	8 32 8	8 52 34	28 50 47	4♑43 43	22 14.3	21 47.1	20 50.5	28 2.8	16 41.5	4 12.0	14 9.0	19 52.2	15 53.8
30 Sa	8 36 4	9 53 31	10♑36 56	16 30 51	22 12.3	23 17.2	22 5.6	28 2.4	16 45.3	4 18.8	14 7.0	19 52.9	15 52.6
31 Su	8 40 1	10 54 28	22 25 46	28 22 1	22 7.9	24 48.0	23 20.7	28 1.2	16 49.4	4 25.7	14 5.0	19 53.6	15 51.4

LONGITUDE FEBRUARY 1965

Day	Sid.Time	☉	0 hr ☽	Noon ☽	True ☊	☿	♀	♂	♃	♄	♅	♆	♇
1 M	8 43 57	11♒55 23	4♒19 49	10♒19 23	22♊ 1.1	26♑19.5	24♑35.7	27♍59.2	16♉53.6	4♓32.7	14♍ 2.9	19♏54.3	15♍50.1
2 Tu	8 47 54	12 56 18	16 20 55	22 24 33	21R52.4	27 51.8	25 50.8	27R56.5	16 58.0	4 39.6	14R 0.8	19 54.9	15R48.9
3 W	8 51 50	13 57 11	28 30 25	4♓38 37	21 42.2	29 24.8	27 5.9	27 53.0	17 2.6	4 46.6	13 58.7	19 55.5	15 47.6
4 Th	8 55 47	14 58 3	10♓49 17	17 2 31	21 31.6	0♒58.5	28 20.9	27 48.7	17 7.3	4 53.6	13 56.5	19 56.1	15 46.3
5 F	8 59 43	15 58 54	23 18 25	29 37 9	21 21.6	2 33.0	29 36.0	27 43.7	17 12.3	5 0.7	13 54.3	19 56.6	15 45.0
6 Sa	9 3 40	16 59 43	5♈58 51	12♈23 41	21 13.0	4 8.2	0♒51.0	27 37.8	17 17.4	5 7.8	13 52.1	19 57.1	15 43.7
7 Su	9 7 37	18 0 31	18 51 53	25 23 38	21 6.7	5 44.2	2 6.0	27 31.1	17 22.7	5 14.8	13 49.8	19 57.6	15 42.3
8 M	9 11 33	19 1 18	1♉59 13	8♉38 51	21 2.9	7 20.9	3 21.1	27 23.7	17 28.2	5 22.0	13 47.6	19 58.0	15 40.9
9 Tu	9 15 30	20 2 2	15 22 47	22 11 16	21D 1.4	8 58.5	4 36.1	27 15.5	17 33.8	5 29.1	13 45.2	19 58.4	15 39.6
10 W	9 19 26	21 2 46	29 4 30	6♊ 2 37	21 1.5	10 36.8	5 51.1	27 6.5	17 39.6	5 36.3	13 42.9	19 58.8	15 38.2
11 Th	9 23 23	22 3 28	13♊ 5 41	20 13 40	21R 2.2	12 15.9	7 6.1	26 56.7	17 45.6	5 43.4	13 40.5	19 59.1	15 36.8
12 F	9 27 19	23 4 8	27 26 25	4♋43 38	21 2.3	13 55.8	8 21.1	26 46.2	17 51.8	5 50.6	13 38.2	19 59.4	15 35.3
13 Sa	9 31 16	24 4 46	12♋ 4 52	19 29 29	21 0.5	15 36.6	9 36.1	26 34.8	17 58.1	5 57.8	13 35.8	19 59.6	15 33.9
14 Su	9 35 12	25 5 23	26 56 41	4♌25 33	20 56.3	17 18.2	10 51.1	26 22.8	18 4.6	6 5.1	13 33.3	19 59.9	15 32.4
15 M	9 39 9	26 5 59	11♌55 1	19 23 58	20 49.3	19 0.7	12 6.1	26 9.9	18 11.3	6 12.3	13 30.9	20 0.0	15 31.0
16 Tu	9 43 6	27 6 32	26 51 11	4♍15 33	20 40.0	20 44.1	13 21.1	25 56.3	18 18.1	6 19.5	13 28.4	20 0.2	15 29.5
17 W	9 47 2	28 7 4	11♍35 57	18 51 26	20 29.3	22 28.3	14 36.0	25 42.0	18 25.0	6 26.8	13 25.9	20 0.3	15 28.0
18 Th	9 50 59	29 7 35	26 1 9	3♎ 4 29	20 18.5	24 13.5	15 51.0	25 27.0	18 32.1	6 34.1	13 23.4	20 0.4	15 26.5
19 F	9 54 55	0♓ 8 4	10♎ 1 0	16 50 26	20 8.7	25 59.5	17 6.0	25 11.2	18 39.4	6 41.4	13 20.9	20 0.5	15 25.0
20 Sa	9 58 52	1 8 32	23 32 44	0♏ 8 2	20 0.9	27 46.5	18 20.9	24 54.8	18 46.8	6 48.7	13 18.3	20R 0.5	15 23.5
21 Su	10 2 48	2 8 59	6♏36 36	12 58 49	19 55.7	29 34.4	19 35.9	24 37.7	18 54.4	6 56.0	13 15.8	20 0.5	15 22.0
22 M	10 6 45	3 9 24	19 15 11	25 26 18	19 52.9	1♓23.2	20 50.8	24 20.0	19 2.1	7 3.3	13 13.2	20 0.4	15 20.4
23 Tu	10 10 41	4 9 48	1♐32 48	7♐35 21	19D52.0	3 13.0	22 5.8	24 1.6	19 10.0	7 10.6	13 10.7	20 0.3	15 18.9
24 W	10 14 38	5 10 10	13 34 39	19 31 24	19R52.1	5 3.6	23 20.7	23 42.6	19 18.0	7 17.9	13 8.1	20 0.2	15 17.3
25 Th	10 18 35	6 10 31	25 26 19	1♑20 3	19 52.1	6 55.1	24 35.6	23 23.0	19 26.2	7 25.2	13 5.5	20 0.1	15 15.8
26 F	10 22 31	7 10 51	7♑13 16	13 6 34	19 50.8	8 47.4	25 50.6	23 2.9	19 34.5	7 32.5	13 2.9	19 59.9	15 14.2
27 Sa	10 26 28	8 11 9	19 0 32	24 55 41	19 47.4	10 40.5	27 5.5	22 42.3	19 42.9	7 39.9	13 0.3	19 59.7	15 12.6
28 Su	10 30 24	9 11 26	0♒52 28	6♒51 18	19 41.2	12 34.3	28 20.4	22 21.2	19 51.5	7 47.2	12 57.6	19 59.4	15 11.1

Astro Data

	Dy Hr Mn
☽0N	10 4:42
♃ D	10 9:33
♃△♇	14 18:40
☽0S	22 16:41
♂ R	28 22:38
☽0N	6 9:39
☽0S	19 1:40
♆ R	20 1:23
♃☍♆	28 21:20

Planet Ingress

	Dy Hr Mn
♀ ♑	12 8:00
☿ ♑	13 3:12
☉ ♒	20 6:29
☿ ♒	3 9:02
♀ ♒	5 7:41
☉ ♓	18 20:48
☿ ♓	21 5:40

Last Aspect / ☽ Ingress

Last Aspect Dy Hr Mn		☽ Ingress Dy Hr Mn
1 7:42	♂ □	♑ 1 20:06
3 22:08	♂ △	♒ 4 9:04
6 6:38	☿ ✶	♓ 6 21:06
8 23:09	♀ □	♈ 9 7:08
11 12:21	♀ △	♉ 11 14:10
13 12:13	♂ △	♊ 13 17:48
15 13:47	♂ □	♋ 15 18:35
17 13:40	♂ ✶	♌ 17 17:57
19 1:17	♆ □	♍ 19 17:55
21 16:30	♂ ☌	♎ 21 20:28
22 19:47	♀ □	♏ 24 3:01
26 9:33	♂ ✶	♐ 26 13:32
28 22:22	♂ □	♑ 29 2:21
31 11:16	♂ △	♒ 31 15:18

Last Aspect / ☽ Ingress

Last Aspect Dy Hr Mn		☽ Ingress Dy Hr Mn
2 7:05	♆ □	♓ 3 2:56
5 8:21	♂ ☍	♈ 5 12:43
6 22:17	☉ ✶	♉ 7 20:24
9 20:38	♂ △	♊ 10 1:36
11 22:54	♂ □	♋ 12 4:14
13 23:06	♂ ✶	♌ 14 4:54
16 0:27	☉ ☍	♍ 16 5:05
17 23:03	♂ ☌	♎ 18 6:45
20 8:54	☿ △	♏ 20 11:45
22 9:36	♂ ✶	♐ 22 20:57
24 22:05	♀ ✶	♑ 25 9:17
27 7:17	♂ △	♒ 27 22:14

☽ Phases & Eclipses

Dy Hr Mn	
2 21:07	● 12♑17
10 20:59	☽ 20♈26
17 13:37	○ 27♋15
24 11:07	☽ 4♏16
1 16:36	● 12♒37
9 8:53	☽ 20♉25
16 0:27	○ 27♌08
23 5:39	☽ 4♐24

Astro Data

1 JANUARY 1965
Julian Day # 23742
Delta T 35.7 sec
SVP 05♓45'11"
Obliquity 23°26'39"
⚷ Chiron 14♓48.0
☽ Mean ☊ 21♊58.4

1 FEBRUARY 1965
Julian Day # 23773
Delta T 35.8 sec
SVP 05♓45'06"
Obliquity 23°26'39"
⚷ Chiron 16♓10.5
☽ Mean ☊ 20♊20.0

MARCH 1965 LONGITUDE

Day	Sid.Time	☉	0 hr ☽	Noon ☽	True ☊	☿	♀	♂	♃	♄	♅	♆	♇
1 M	10 34 21	10♓11 41	12♒52 32	18♒56 26	19♊32.0	14♓28.7	29♒35.3	21♍59.6	20♉ 0.2	7♓54.5	12♍55.0	19♏59.2	15♍ 9.5
2 Tu	10 38 17	11 11 54	25 3 14	1♓13 3	19R 20.3	16 23.7	0♓50.2	21R 37.7	20 9.0	8 1.8	12R 52.4	19R 58.8	15R 7.9
3 W	10 42 14	12 12 6	7♓26 0	13 42 7	19 6.9	18 19.1	2 5.1	21 15.3	20 18.0	8 9.1	12 49.8	19 58.5	15 6.3
4 Th	10 46 10	13 12 16	20 1 24	26 23 47	18 52.8	20 14.7	3 19.9	20 52.7	20 27.1	8 16.4	12 47.1	19 58.1	15 4.7
5 F	10 50 7	14 12 23	2♈49 12	9♈17 34	18 39.2	22 10.4	4 34.8	20 29.7	20 36.3	8 23.7	12 44.5	19 57.7	15 3.1
6 Sa	10 54 4	15 12 29	15 48 47	22 22 47	18 27.5	24 6.0	5 49.6	20 6.6	20 45.6	8 31.0	12 41.9	19 57.2	15 1.5
7 Su	10 58 0	16 12 33	28 59 29	5♉38 52	18 18.5	26 1.1	7 4.5	19 43.2	20 55.1	8 38.3	12 39.2	19 56.8	14 60.0
8 M	11 1 57	17 12 35	12♉20 54	19 5 37	18 12.5	27 55.6	8 19.3	19 19.7	21 4.7	8 45.6	12 36.6	19 56.3	14 58.4
9 Tu	11 5 53	18 12 35	25 53 4	2♊43 18	18 9.4	29 49.1	9 34.1	18 56.1	21 14.4	8 52.9	12 34.0	19 55.7	14 56.8
10 W	11 9 50	19 12 33	9♊36 25	16 32 29	18 8.4	1♈41.3	10 48.9	18 32.4	21 24.3	9 0.1	12 31.4	19 55.2	14 55.2
11 Th	11 13 46	20 12 28	23 31 33	0♋33 39	18 8.3	3 31.6	12 3.7	18 8.7	21 34.2	9 7.4	12 28.8	19 54.6	14 53.6
12 F	11 17 43	21 12 22	7♋38 43	14 46 39	18 7.8	5 19.8	13 18.5	17 45.1	21 44.3	9 14.6	12 26.2	19 53.9	14 52.0
13 Sa	11 21 39	22 12 13	21 57 12	29 10 4	18 5.6	7 5.3	14 33.2	17 21.5	21 54.4	9 21.8	12 23.6	19 53.3	14 50.5
14 Su	11 25 36	23 12 2	6♌24 47	13♌40 46	18 0.8	8 47.7	15 48.0	16 58.1	22 4.7	9 29.0	12 21.1	19 52.6	14 48.9
15 M	11 29 33	24 11 48	20 57 23	28 13 50	17 53.2	10 26.5	17 2.7	16 34.8	22 15.1	9 36.2	12 18.5	19 51.8	14 47.3
16 Tu	11 33 29	25 11 32	5♍29 16	12♍42 51	17 43.0	12 1.1	18 17.4	16 11.8	22 25.6	9 43.3	12 16.0	19 51.1	14 45.8
17 W	11 37 26	26 11 15	19 53 42	27 0 58	17 31.3	13 31.1	19 32.1	15 49.0	22 36.2	9 50.5	12 13.4	19 50.3	14 44.2
18 Th	11 41 22	27 10 55	4♎ 3 56	11♎ 1 57	17 19.2	14 56.1	20 46.8	15 26.4	22 46.8	9 57.6	12 10.9	19 49.5	14 42.7
19 F	11 45 19	28 10 33	17 54 31	24 41 15	17 8.1	16 15.5	22 1.5	15 4.2	22 57.6	10 4.7	12 8.4	19 48.7	14 41.1
20 Sa	11 49 15	29 10 9	1♏21 56	7♏56 33	16 59.0	17 28.9	23 16.1	14 42.4	23 8.5	10 11.8	12 5.9	19 47.8	14 39.6
21 Su	11 53 12	0♈ 9 44	14 25 9	20 47 58	16 52.5	18 36.0	24 30.8	14 21.0	23 19.5	10 18.8	12 3.4	19 46.9	14 38.1
22 M	11 57 8	1 9 17	27 5 20	3♐17 41	16 48.7	19 36.4	25 45.4	14 0.0	23 30.6	10 25.8	12 1.0	19 46.0	14 36.6
23 Tu	12 1 5	2 8 48	9♐25 31	15 29 26	16D 47.1	20 29.9	27 0.0	13 39.5	23 41.7	10 32.8	11 58.6	19 45.0	14 35.1
24 W	12 5 1	3 8 17	21 30 4	27 28 4	16 46.9	21 16.1	28 14.6	13 19.5	23 53.0	10 39.8	11 56.2	19 44.1	14 33.6
25 Th	12 8 58	4 7 44	3♑24 6	9♑18 54	16R 47.2	21 54.9	29 29.2	13 0.1	24 4.4	10 46.7	11 53.8	19 43.1	14 32.1
26 F	12 12 55	5 7 10	15 13 7	21 7 28	16 46.7	22 26.1	0♈43.8	12 41.2	24 15.8	10 53.7	11 51.4	19 42.1	14 30.6
27 Sa	12 16 51	6 6 34	27 2 33	2♒59 2	16 44.6	22 49.7	1 58.4	12 22.9	24 27.3	11 0.5	11 49.1	19 41.0	14 29.2
28 Su	12 20 48	7 5 56	8♒57 28	14 58 24	16 40.1	23 5.6	3 13.0	12 5.2	24 38.9	11 7.4	11 46.8	19 39.9	14 27.7
29 M	12 24 44	8 5 16	21 2 17	27 9 32	16 33.1	23R 13.9	4 27.5	11 48.1	24 50.6	11 14.2	11 44.5	19 38.8	14 26.3
30 Tu	12 28 41	9 4 35	3♓20 28	9♓35 21	16 23.7	23 14.8	5 42.1	11 31.8	25 2.4	11 21.0	11 42.3	19 37.7	14 24.9
31 W	12 32 37	10 3 51	15 54 20	22 17 31	16 12.7	23 8.5	6 56.6	11 16.1	25 14.3	11 27.8	11 40.0	19 36.6	14 23.4

APRIL 1965 LONGITUDE

Day	Sid.Time	☉	0 hr ☽	Noon ☽	True ☊	☿	♀	♂	♃	♄	♅	♆	♇
1 Th	12 36 34	11♈ 3 6	28♓44 54	5♈16 23	16♊ 0.9	22♈55.2	8♈11.1	11♍ 1.1	25♉26.2	11♓34.5	11♍37.9	19♏35.4	14♍22.1
2 F	12 40 30	12 2 18	11♈51 49	18 31 0	15R 49.6	22R 35.5	9 25.6	10R 46.9	25 38.2	11 41.2	11R 35.7	19R 34.2	14R 20.7
3 Sa	12 44 27	13 1 29	25 13 40	1♉59 30	15 39.9	22 9.8	10 40.1	10 33.4	25 50.3	11 47.8	11 33.6	19 33.0	14 19.3
4 Su	12 48 24	14 0 37	8♉48 13	15 39 29	15 32.4	21 38.7	11 54.5	10 20.7	26 2.5	11 54.4	11 31.5	19 31.7	14 18.0
5 M	12 52 20	14 59 43	22 32 59	29 28 26	15 27.6	21 2.9	13 9.0	10 8.7	26 14.7	12 1.0	11 29.4	19 30.5	14 16.6
6 Tu	12 56 17	15 58 48	6♊25 35	13♊24 14	15D 25.5	20 23.3	14 23.4	9 57.5	26 27.0	12 7.5	11 27.4	19 29.2	14 15.3
7 W	13 0 13	16 57 50	20 24 10	27 25 14	15 25.2	19 40.5	15 37.8	9 47.1	26 39.4	12 14.0	11 25.4	19 27.9	14 14.0
8 Th	13 4 10	17 56 49	4♋27 19	11♋30 17	15 25.9	18 55.6	16 52.2	9 37.5	26 51.8	12 20.4	11 23.4	19 26.6	14 12.8
9 F	13 8 6	18 55 47	18 34 1	25 38 22	15R 26.4	18 9.4	18 6.6	9 28.6	27 4.3	12 26.8	11 21.5	19 25.3	14 11.5
10 Sa	13 12 3	19 54 42	2♌43 11	9♌48 15	15 25.7	17 22.8	19 20.9	9 20.6	27 16.9	12 33.2	11 19.6	19 23.9	14 10.3
11 Su	13 15 59	20 53 34	16 53 20	23 58 6	15 22.9	16 36.7	20 35.3	9 13.4	27 29.5	12 39.5	11 17.8	19 22.6	14 9.1
12 M	13 19 56	21 52 24	1♍ 2 13	8♍ 5 16	15 18.0	15 51.9	21 49.6	9 6.9	27 42.2	12 45.7	11 16.0	19 21.2	14 7.9
13 Tu	13 23 53	22 51 12	15 6 47	22 6 17	15 11.0	15 9.3	23 3.9	9 1.2	27 54.9	12 51.9	11 14.2	19 19.8	14 6.7
14 W	13 27 49	23 49 58	29 3 18	5♎57 20	15 2.8	14 29.5	24 18.2	8 56.4	28 7.7	12 58.1	11 12.5	19 18.3	14 5.6
15 Th	13 31 46	24 48 42	12♎47 56	19 34 41	14 54.3	13 53.2	25 32.4	8 52.3	28 20.6	13 4.2	11 10.8	19 16.9	14 4.4
16 F	13 35 42	25 47 24	26 17 15	2♏55 21	14 46.4	13 20.7	26 46.7	8 48.9	28 33.5	13 10.2	11 9.1	19 15.4	14 3.3
17 Sa	13 39 39	26 46 3	9♏28 48	15 57 31	14 39.9	12 52.6	28 0.9	8 46.4	28 46.4	13 16.2	11 7.5	19 14.0	14 2.2
18 Su	13 43 35	27 44 41	22 21 31	28 40 54	14 35.5	12 29.1	29 15.1	8 44.6	28 59.4	13 22.2	11 6.0	19 12.5	14 1.2
19 M	13 47 32	28 43 17	4♐55 51	11♐ 6 40	14D 33.1	12 10.5	0♉29.3	8D 43.5	29 12.5	13 28.0	11 4.5	19 11.0	14 0.1
20 Tu	13 51 28	29 41 52	17 13 41	23 17 21	14 32.7	11 57.0	1 43.5	8 43.2	29 25.6	13 33.9	11 3.0	19 9.5	13 59.1
21 W	13 55 25	0♉40 24	29 18 8	5♑16 35	14 33.5	11 48.5	2 57.7	8 43.6	29 38.8	13 39.7	11 1.6	19 8.0	13 58.1
22 Th	13 59 22	1 38 55	11♑13 15	17 8 46	14 35.0	11D 45.1	4 11.9	8 44.8	29 52.0	13 45.4	11 0.2	19 6.5	13 57.2
23 F	14 3 18	2 37 25	23 3 44	28 58 48	14R 36.4	11 46.8	5 26.0	8 46.7	0♊ 5.2	13 51.1	10 58.9	19 4.9	13 56.2
24 Sa	14 7 15	3 35 52	4♒54 37	10♒51 49	14 36.9	11 53.4	6 40.1	8 49.3	0 18.5	13 56.7	10 57.6	19 3.4	13 55.3
25 Su	14 11 11	4 34 19	16 51 1	22 52 49	14 35.9	12 5.0	7 54.3	8 52.6	0 31.9	14 2.2	10 56.3	19 1.8	13 54.4
26 M	14 15 8	5 32 43	28 57 47	5♓ 6 26	14 33.4	12 21.3	9 8.4	8 56.6	0 45.2	14 7.7	10 55.1	19 0.2	13 53.6
27 Tu	14 19 4	6 31 6	11♓19 14	17 36 34	14 29.3	12 42.2	10 22.4	9 1.2	0 58.7	14 13.1	10 54.0	18 58.7	13 52.7
28 W	14 23 1	7 29 27	23 58 45	0♈26 0	14 23.9	13 7.5	11 36.5	9 6.6	1 12.1	14 18.5	10 52.9	18 57.1	13 51.9
29 Th	14 26 57	8 27 47	6♈58 27	13 36 7	14 18.0	13 37.1	12 50.6	9 12.6	1 25.6	14 23.8	10 51.8	18 55.5	13 51.1
30 F	14 30 54	9 26 5	20 18 55	27 6 41	14 12.1	14 10.9	14 4.6	9 19.3	1 39.1	14 29.0	10 50.8	18 53.9	13 50.3

Astro Data (Dy Hr Mn)

☽0N	5 14:44
☿0N	9 9:03
☽0S	18 11:25
♀0N	28 0:32
☿ R	29 14:52
☽0N	1 21:49
♄☍♅	1 9:07
☽0S	14 20:18
♂ D	19 21:56
☿ D	22 4:00
♄☍♇	23 18:57
☽0N	29 6:55

Planet Ingress (Dy Hr Mn)

♀ ♓	1 7:55
☿ ♈	9 2:19
☉ ♈	20 20:05
♀ ♈	25 9:54
♀ ♉	18 14:31
☉ ♉	20 7:26
♃ ♊	22 14:32

Last Aspect / ☽ Ingress (Dy Hr Mn)

Last Aspect	☽ Ingress
1 14:16 ♃ □	♓ 2 9:38
4 1:34 ♂ ☍	♈ 4 18:45
4 18:45 ☽ T	♉ 7 1:49
8 15:42 ♃ ☌	♊ 9 7:14
10 17:52 ☉ □	♋ 11 11:03
13 0:27 ☉ △	♌ 13 13:23
15 2:10 ♃ □	♍ 15 14:55
17 11:24 ☉ ☍	♎ 17 17:04
18 20:48 ☿ ☍	♏ 19 21:32
21 21:10 ☉ △	♐ 22 5:37
24 15:09 ♀ □	♑ 24 17:07
26 18:40 ♃ △	♒ 27 5:59
29 7:36 ♃ □	♓ 29 17:32

Last Aspect / ☽ Ingress (Dy Hr Mn)

Last Aspect	☽ Ingress
31 17:46 ♃ ⚹	♈ 1 2:19
2 18:43 ☿ ☌	♉ 3 8:29
5 6:30 ♃ ☌	♊ 5 12:55
6 22:49 ☿ ⚹	♋ 7 16:24
9 14:39 ♃ ⚹	♌ 9 19:24
11 18:15 ♃ □	♍ 11 22:14
13 22:22 ♃ △	♎ 14 1:38
16 0:58 ♀ ☍	♏ 16 6:42
18 12:49 ♃ ☍	♐ 18 14:31
19 17:38 ♇ □	♑ 21 1:24
22 15:57 ♆ ⚹	♒ 23 14:04
25 4:20 ♆ □	♓ 26 2:02
27 14:34 ♆ △	♈ 28 11:12
29 12:33 ☿ ☌	♉ 30 17:04

☽ Phases & Eclipses (Dy Hr Mn)

3 9:56	●	12♓37
10 17:52	☽	19♊57
17 11:24	○	26♍40
25 1:37	☽	4♑12
2 0:21	●	12♈03
9 0:40	☽	18♋57
15 23:02	○	25♎45
23 21:07	☽	3♒29

Astro Data

1 MARCH 1965
Julian Day # 23801
Delta T 35.9 sec
SVP 05♓45'02"
Obliquity 23°26'40"
⚷ Chiron 17♓48.3
☽ Mean ☊ 18♊51.0

1 APRIL 1965
Julian Day # 23832
Delta T 35.9 sec
SVP 05♓44'59"
Obliquity 23°26'40"
⚷ Chiron 19♓41.3
☽ Mean ☊ 17♊12.5

LONGITUDE — MAY 1965

Day	Sid.Time	☉	0 hr ☽	Noon☽	True☊	☿	♀	♂	♃	♄	♅	♆	♇
1 Sa	14 34 51	10♉24 21	3♉59 7	10♉55 49	14♊ 7.1	14♈48.5	15♉18.7	9♍26.6	1♊52.7	14♓34.2	10♍49.9	18♏52.3	13♍49.6
2 Su	14 38 47	11 22 36	17 56 21	25 0 10	14R 3.5	15 30.0	16 32.7	9 34.6	2 6.3	14 39.3	10R49.0	18R50.7	13R48.9
3 M	14 42 44	12 20 48	2♊ 6 45	9♊15 28	14D 1.4	16 15.1	17 46.7	9 43.2	2 19.9	14 44.3	10 48.1	18 49.0	13 48.2
4 Tu	14 46 40	13 19 0	16 25 45	23 37 1	14 0.9	17 3.7	19 0.7	9 52.4	2 33.6	14 49.3	10 47.4	18 47.4	13 47.6
5 W	14 50 37	14 17 9	0♋48 43	8♋ 0 22	14 1.7	17 55.6	20 14.6	10 2.2	2 47.3	14 54.2	10 46.6	18 45.8	13 47.0
6 Th	14 54 33	15 15 16	15 11 29	22 21 40	14 3.1	18 50.8	21 28.6	10 12.6	3 1.0	14 59.0	10 45.9	18 44.2	13 46.4
7 F	14 58 30	16 13 22	29 30 33	6♌37 51	14 4.4	19 49.0	22 42.5	10 23.6	3 14.7	15 3.7	10 45.3	18 42.5	13 45.8
8 Sa	15 2 26	17 11 25	13♌43 18	20 46 39	14R 5.2	20 50.2	23 56.4	10 35.2	3 28.5	15 8.4	10 44.7	18 40.9	13 45.3
9 Su	15 6 23	18 9 27	27 47 43	4♍46 20	14 4.9	21 54.3	25 10.3	10 47.3	3 42.3	15 13.0	10 44.2	18 39.3	13 44.8
10 M	15 10 20	19 7 26	11♍42 20	18 35 33	14 3.5	23 1.2	26 24.2	11 0.0	3 56.1	15 17.6	10 43.7	18 37.7	13 44.3
11 Tu	15 14 16	20 5 24	25 25 52	2♎13 9	14 1.0	24 10.8	27 38.1	11 13.2	4 10.0	15 22.0	10 43.2	18 36.0	13 43.8
12 W	15 18 13	21 3 20	8♎57 16	15 38 6	13 57.9	25 23.0	28 51.9	11 26.9	4 23.8	15 26.4	10 42.9	18 34.4	13 43.4
13 Th	15 22 9	22 1 14	22 15 32	28 49 31	13 54.6	26 37.8	0♊ 5.7	11 41.2	4 37.7	15 30.7	10 42.5	18 32.8	13 43.0
14 F	15 26 6	22 59 6	5♏19 57	11♏46 48	13 51.5	27 55.0	1 19.6	11 55.9	4 51.6	15 34.9	10 42.3	18 31.1	13 42.7
15 Sa	15 30 2	23 56 57	18 10 4	24 29 46	13 49.2	29 14.7	2 33.4	12 11.2	5 5.5	15 39.0	10 42.0	18 29.5	13 42.4
16 Su	15 33 59	24 54 46	0♐45 59	6♐58 50	13 47.7	0♉36.8	3 47.1	12 26.9	5 19.4	15 43.1	10 41.9	18 27.9	13 42.1
17 M	15 37 55	25 52 34	13 8 27	19 15 4	13D47.2	2 1.3	5 0.9	12 43.1	5 33.3	15 47.1	10 41.8	18 26.3	13 41.8
18 Tu	15 41 52	26 50 21	25 18 55	1♑20 19	13 47.6	3 28.1	6 14.6	12 59.7	5 47.3	15 51.0	10D41.7	18 24.7	13 41.6
19 W	15 45 49	27 48 6	7♑19 36	13 17 9	13 48.6	4 57.2	7 28.4	13 16.8	6 1.2	15 54.8	10 41.7	18 23.1	13 41.4
20 Th	15 49 45	28 45 51	19 13 24	25 8 49	13 49.9	6 28.6	8 42.1	13 34.3	6 15.2	15 58.6	10 41.7	18 21.5	13 41.2
21 F	15 53 42	29 43 34	1♒ 3 53	6♒59 9	13 51.2	8 2.3	9 55.8	13 52.3	6 29.2	16 2.2	10 41.8	18 19.9	13 41.0
22 Sa	15 57 38	0♊41 16	12 55 9	18 52 28	13 52.2	9 38.3	11 9.5	14 10.7	6 43.2	16 5.8	10 42.0	18 18.3	13 40.9
23 Su	16 1 35	1 38 56	24 51 40	0♓53 19	13R52.8	11 16.5	12 23.2	14 29.5	6 57.2	16 9.3	10 42.2	18 16.7	13 40.8
24 M	16 5 31	2 36 36	6♓58 2	13 6 21	13 52.9	12 56.9	13 36.9	14 48.8	7 11.2	16 12.7	10 42.5	18 15.1	13 40.8
25 Tu	16 9 28	3 34 15	19 18 49	25 35 55	13 52.5	14 39.6	14 50.5	15 8.4	7 25.2	16 16.0	10 42.8	18 13.6	13D40.8
26 W	16 13 24	4 31 53	1♈58 8	8♈25 49	13 51.7	16 24.6	16 4.2	15 28.4	7 39.2	16 19.2	10 43.1	18 12.0	13 40.8
27 Th	16 17 21	5 29 29	14 59 17	21 38 44	13 50.7	18 11.8	17 17.8	15 48.8	7 53.2	16 22.4	10 43.6	18 10.4	13 40.8
28 F	16 21 18	6 27 5	28 24 18	5♉15 55	13 49.7	20 1.2	18 31.5	16 9.6	8 7.2	16 25.4	10 44.0	18 8.9	13 40.9
29 Sa	16 25 14	7 24 40	12♉13 27	19 16 38	13 49.0	21 52.8	19 45.1	16 30.8	8 21.3	16 28.4	10 44.6	18 7.4	13 41.0
30 Su	16 29 11	8 22 14	26 25 1	3♊38 3	13 48.5	23 46.7	20 58.7	16 52.4	8 35.3	16 31.3	10 45.1	18 5.9	13 41.1
31 M	16 33 7	9 19 47	10♊55 4	18 15 18	13D48.3	25 42.7	22 12.3	17 14.3	8 49.3	16 34.0	10 45.8	18 4.4	13 41.3

LONGITUDE — JUNE 1965

Day	Sid.Time	☉	0 hr ☽	Noon☽	True☊	☿	♀	♂	♃	♄	♅	♆	♇
1 Tu	16 37 4	10♊17 20	25♊37 55	3♋ 1 59	13♊48.4	27♉40.8	23♊25.8	17♍36.5	9♊ 3.3	16♓36.7	10♍46.5	18♏ 2.9	13♍41.5
2 W	16 41 0	11 14 50	10♋26 37	17 50 54	13 48.5	29 40.9	24 39.4	17 59.1	9 17.3	16 39.3	10 47.2	18R 1.4	13 41.7
3 Th	16 44 57	12 12 20	25 13 58	2♌35 3	13 48.7	1♊43.0	25 53.0	18 22.1	9 31.4	16 41.9	10 48.0	17 60.0	13 42.0
4 F	16 48 53	13 9 49	9♌53 25	17 8 29	13R48.8	3 46.9	27 6.5	18 45.4	9 45.4	16 44.3	10 48.9	17 58.5	13 42.3
5 Sa	16 52 50	14 7 16	24 19 45	1♍26 51	13 48.9	5 52.6	28 20.0	19 9.0	9 59.4	16 46.6	10 49.8	17 57.1	13 42.6
6 Su	16 56 47	15 4 42	8♍29 30	15 27 32	13D48.8	7 59.8	29 33.5	19 32.9	10 13.3	16 48.8	10 50.7	17 55.7	13 43.0
7 M	17 0 43	16 2 7	22 20 54	29 9 34	13 48.8	10 8.4	0♋47.0	19 57.2	10 27.3	16 50.9	10 51.7	17 54.3	13 43.3
8 Tu	17 4 40	16 59 30	5♎53 37	12♎33 11	13 49.0	12 18.2	2 0.5	20 21.7	10 41.3	16 53.0	10 52.8	17 52.9	13 43.8
9 W	17 8 36	17 56 53	19 8 25	25 39 30	13 49.3	14 29.0	3 13.9	20 46.6	10 55.2	16 54.9	10 53.9	17 51.5	13 44.2
10 Th	17 12 33	18 54 14	2♏ 6 39	8♏30 4	13 49.7	16 40.4	4 27.4	21 11.7	11 9.2	16 56.8	10 55.0	17 50.2	13 44.7
11 F	17 16 29	19 51 35	14 50 0	21 6 38	13 50.3	18 52.3	5 40.8	21 37.2	11 23.1	16 58.5	10 56.3	17 48.8	13 45.2
12 Sa	17 20 26	20 48 54	27 20 13	3♐30 57	13 50.8	21 4.4	6 54.2	22 2.9	11 37.0	17 0.2	10 57.5	17 47.5	13 45.7
13 Su	17 24 22	21 46 13	9♐39 3	15 44 44	13R51.1	23 16.3	8 7.6	22 28.9	11 50.9	17 1.7	10 58.8	17 46.2	13 46.3
14 M	17 28 19	22 43 31	21 48 14	27 49 45	13 51.0	25 27.9	9 20.9	22 55.1	12 4.8	17 3.2	11 0.2	17 45.0	13 46.9
15 Tu	17 32 16	23 40 49	3♑49 32	9♑47 48	13 50.5	27 38.8	10 34.3	23 21.6	12 18.6	17 4.5	11 1.6	17 43.7	13 47.5
16 W	17 36 12	24 38 5	15 44 51	21 40 55	13 49.4	29 48.8	11 47.6	23 48.4	12 32.4	17 5.8	11 3.1	17 42.5	13 48.2
17 Th	17 40 9	25 35 22	27 36 21	3♒31 27	13 47.9	1♋57.8	13 1.0	24 15.5	12 46.3	17 7.0	11 4.6	17 41.3	13 48.9
18 F	17 44 5	26 32 38	9♒26 34	15 22 7	13 46.1	4 5.4	14 14.3	24 42.8	13 0.0	17 8.0	11 6.1	17 40.1	13 49.6
19 Sa	17 48 2	27 29 53	21 18 28	27 16 6	13 44.3	6 11.5	15 27.6	25 10.3	13 13.8	17 9.0	11 7.7	17 38.9	13 50.3
20 Su	17 51 58	28 27 9	3♓15 27	9♓17 2	13 42.6	8 15.9	16 40.9	25 38.1	13 27.6	17 9.9	11 9.4	17 37.8	13 51.1
21 M	17 55 55	29 24 24	15 21 20	21 28 53	13 41.4	10 18.6	17 54.1	26 6.1	13 41.3	17 10.7	11 11.1	17 36.6	13 51.9
22 Tu	17 59 51	0♋21 38	27 40 13	3♈55 50	13D40.8	12 19.4	19 7.4	26 34.3	13 55.0	17 11.3	11 12.8	17 35.5	13 52.7
23 W	18 3 48	1 18 53	10♈16 16	16 42 0	13 41.0	14 18.3	20 20.6	27 2.8	14 8.6	17 11.9	11 14.6	17 34.5	13 53.6
24 Th	18 7 45	2 16 7	23 13 27	29 51 0	13 41.9	16 15.1	21 33.9	27 31.5	14 22.3	17 12.4	11 16.5	17 33.4	13 54.5
25 F	18 11 41	3 13 22	6♉34 57	13♉25 30	13 43.2	18 9.9	22 47.1	28 0.5	14 35.9	17 12.7	11 18.4	17 32.4	13 55.4
26 Sa	18 15 38	4 10 36	20 22 42	27 26 30	13 44.5	20 2.6	24 0.3	28 29.7	14 49.5	17 13.0	11 20.3	17 31.4	13 56.4
27 Su	18 19 34	5 7 51	4♊36 41	11♊52 49	13R45.4	21 53.1	25 13.5	28 59.1	15 3.0	17 13.2	11 22.3	17 30.4	13 57.3
28 M	18 23 31	6 5 5	19 14 21	26 40 32	13 45.5	23 41.5	26 26.7	29 28.7	15 16.5	17R13.3	11 24.3	17 29.4	13 58.3
29 Tu	18 27 27	7 2 20	4♋10 26	11♋43 2	13 44.6	25 27.7	27 39.8	29 58.5	15 30.0	17 13.2	11 26.4	17 28.5	13 59.4
30 W	18 31 24	7 59 34	19 17 11	26 51 40	13 42.5	27 11.8	28 53.0	0♎28.6	15 43.5	17 13.1	11 28.5	17 27.6	14 0.4

Astro Data (Dy Hr Mn)	Planet Ingress (Dy Hr Mn)	Last Aspect (Dy Hr Mn)	☽ Ingress (Dy Hr Mn)	Last Aspect (Dy Hr Mn)	☽ Ingress (Dy Hr Mn)	☽ Phases & Eclipses (Dy Hr Mn)	Astro Data
☽0S 12 3:25	♀ ♊ 12 22:08	2 1:32 ♆ ☍	♊ 2 20:26	31 20:06 ♀ ☌	♋ 1 7:05	1 11:56 ● 10♉53	1 MAY 1965
♅ D 18 14:32	☿ ♉ 15 13:19	4 1:07 ☿ ⚹	♋ 4 22:39	2 12:33 ♂ ⚹	♌ 3 7:46	8 6:20 ☽ 17♌27	Julian Day # 23862
♇ D 25 5:21	☉ ♊ 21 6:50	6 11:31 ♀ ⚹	♌ 7 0:50	5 7:22 ♀ ⚹	♍ 5 9:33	15 11:52 ○ 24♏26	Delta T 36.0 sec
☽0N 26 16:36		8 19:04 ♀ □	♍ 9 3:47	6 19:41 ♂ ☌	♎ 7 13:29	23 14:40 ☽ 2♓14	SVP 05♓44'56"
	☿ ♊ 2 3:47	11 4:16 ♀ △	♎ 11 8:04	8 21:39 ☉ △	♏ 9 20:04	30 21:12 ● 9♊13	Obliquity 23°26'40"
☽0S 8 9:06	♀ ♋ 6 8:39	13 8:50 ☿ ☍	♏ 13 14:10	11 13:26 ♂ ⚹	♐ 12 5:10	30 21:16:55 ☌ T 5'15"	⚷ Chiron 21♓15.2
♃□♅ 8 21:29	☿ ♋ 16 2:04	15 11:52 ☉ ☍	♐ 15 22:32	14 8:54 ☿ ☍	♑ 14 16:20		☽ Mean ☊ 15♊37.1
♃□♇ 21 19:49	☉ ♋ 21 14:56	17 5:13 ♄ □	♑ 18 9:20	16 16:57 ♂ △	♒ 17 4:51	6 12:11 ☽ 15♍34	1 JUNE 1965
☽0N 23 1:10	♂ ♎ 29 1:12	20 21:03 ☉ △	♒ 20 21:50	19 13:33 ☉ △	♓ 19 17:29	14 1:59 ○ 22♐48	Julian Day # 23893
♄ R 28 5:32	♀ ♌ 30 21:59	22 10:50 ♆ □	♓ 23 10:14	21 21:48 ♂ ☍	♈ 22 4:29	14 1:49 ☍P 0.177	Delta T 36.1 sec
♂0S 30 13:14		24 21:55 ♆ △	♈ 25 20:19	23 20:39 ♀ □	♉ 24 12:16	22 5:36 ☽ 0♈35	SVP 05♓44'51"
		27 4:36 ♀ ⚹	♉ 28 2:48	26 14:16 ♂ △	♊ 26 16:18	29 4:52 ● 7♋14	Obliquity 23°26'40"
		29 18:54 ☿ ☌	♊ 30 5:58	28 17:04 ♂ □	♋ 28 17:20		⚷ Chiron 22♓17.7
				30 16:32 ♀ ☌	♌ 30 16:59		☽ Mean ☊ 13♊58.7

JULY 1965 LONGITUDE

Day	Sid.Time	☉	0 hr ☽	Noon ☽	True ☊	☿	♀	♂	♃	♄	♅	♆	♇
1 Th	18 35 21	8♋56 48	4♌25 16	11♌56 50	13♊39.5	28♋53.7	0♌ 6.1	0♎58.8	15♊56.9	17♓12.9	11♍30.7	17♏26.7	14♍ 1.5
2 F	18 39 17	9 54 2	19 25 16	26 49 35	13R 36.1	0♌33.3	1 19.3	1 29.3	16 10.2	17R 12.5	11 32.9	17R 25.9	14 2.6
3 Sa	18 43 14	10 51 15	4♍ 9 1	11♍22 54	13 32.7	2 10.8	2 32.4	1 59.9	16 23.6	17 12.1	11 35.1	17 25.1	14 3.8
4 Su	18 47 10	11 48 28	18 30 47	25 32 25	13 30.0	3 46.2	3 45.4	2 30.8	16 36.9	17 11.6	11 37.4	17 24.3	14 5.0
5 M	18 51 7	12 45 41	2♎27 39	9♎16 33	13D 28.4	5 19.3	4 58.5	3 1.8	16 50.1	17 11.0	11 39.7	17 23.5	14 6.1
6 Tu	18 55 3	13 42 53	15 59 16	22 36 3	13 28.1	6 50.1	6 11.5	3 33.1	17 3.3	17 10.2	11 42.1	17 22.7	14 7.4
7 W	18 59 0	14 40 5	29 7 15	5♏33 15	13 28.8	8 18.8	7 24.5	4 4.5	17 16.4	17 9.4	11 44.5	17 22.0	14 8.6
8 Th	19 2 56	15 37 17	11♏54 29	18 11 24	13 30.2	9 45.2	8 37.5	4 36.1	17 29.6	17 8.5	11 47.0	17 21.4	14 9.9
9 F	19 6 53	16 34 29	24 24 27	0♐34 5	13 31.8	11 9.2	9 50.5	5 7.9	17 42.6	17 7.5	11 49.4	17 20.7	14 11.2
10 Sa	19 10 50	17 31 41	6♐40 44	12 44 49	13R 33.0	12 31.0	11 3.5	5 39.9	17 55.6	17 6.3	11 52.0	17 20.1	14 12.5
11 Su	19 14 46	18 28 52	18 46 43	24 46 47	13 33.0	13 50.4	12 16.4	6 12.0	18 8.6	17 5.1	11 54.5	17 19.5	14 13.8
12 M	19 18 43	19 26 4	0♑45 22	6♑42 45	13 31.6	15 7.5	13 29.3	6 44.3	18 21.5	17 3.8	11 57.2	17 18.9	14 15.2
13 Tu	19 22 39	20 23 16	12 39 13	18 35 3	13 28.4	16 22.0	14 42.2	7 16.8	18 34.4	17 2.4	11 59.8	17 18.4	14 16.6
14 W	19 26 36	21 20 29	24 30 28	0♒25 42	13 23.6	17 34.1	15 55.0	7 49.4	18 47.2	17 0.9	12 2.5	17 17.9	14 18.0
15 Th	19 30 32	22 17 41	6♒21 1	12 16 36	13 17.3	18 43.5	17 7.9	8 22.3	18 59.9	16 59.3	12 5.2	17 17.4	14 19.5
16 F	19 34 29	23 14 54	18 12 44	24 9 38	13 10.1	19 50.3	18 20.7	8 55.2	19 12.6	16 57.7	12 8.0	17 16.9	14 20.9
17 Sa	19 38 25	24 12 8	0♓ 7 36	6♓ 6 54	13 2.8	20 54.4	19 33.5	9 28.4	19 25.3	16 55.9	12 10.7	17 16.5	14 22.4
18 Su	19 42 22	25 9 22	12 7 52	18 10 50	12 56.0	21 55.7	20 46.3	10 1.7	19 37.8	16 54.0	12 13.6	17 16.1	14 23.9
19 M	19 46 19	26 6 36	24 16 11	0♈24 20	12 50.3	22 54.0	21 59.0	10 35.1	19 50.4	16 52.1	12 16.4	17 15.8	14 25.4
20 Tu	19 50 15	27 3 51	6♈35 43	12 50 46	12 46.4	23 49.2	23 11.7	11 8.7	20 2.8	16 50.0	12 19.3	17 15.5	14 27.0
21 W	19 54 12	28 1 7	19 9 58	25 33 47	12D 44.3	24 41.3	24 24.4	11 42.5	20 15.2	16 47.9	12 22.2	17 15.2	14 28.6
22 Th	19 58 8	28 58 24	2♉ 2 42	8♉37 9	12 44.0	25 30.2	25 37.1	12 16.4	20 27.6	16 45.6	12 25.2	17 14.9	14 30.2
23 F	20 2 5	29 55 42	15 17 33	22 4 14	12 44.7	26 15.5	26 49.8	12 50.5	20 39.8	16 43.3	12 28.2	17 14.7	14 31.8
24 Sa	20 6 1	0♌53 0	28 57 28	5♊57 24	12R 45.9	26 57.3	28 2.4	13 24.7	20 52.0	16 40.9	12 31.2	17 14.5	14 33.4
25 Su	20 9 58	1 50 20	13♊ 4 1	20 17 11	12 46.5	27 35.4	29 15.1	13 59.1	21 4.2	16 38.4	12 34.3	17 14.3	14 35.1
26 M	20 13 54	2 47 40	27 36 32	5♋ 1 33	12 45.6	28 9.6	0♍27.7	14 33.6	21 16.3	16 35.9	12 37.4	17 14.2	14 36.7
27 Tu	20 17 51	3 45 2	12♋31 27	20 5 17	12 42.7	28 39.7	1 40.2	15 8.3	21 28.3	16 33.2	12 40.5	17 14.1	14 38.4
28 W	20 21 48	4 42 24	27 41 56	5♌20 8	12 37.6	29 5.6	2 52.8	15 43.1	21 40.2	16 30.5	12 43.6	17 14.0	14 40.2
29 Th	20 25 44	5 39 47	12♌58 30	20 35 41	12 30.7	29 27.0	4 5.3	16 18.1	21 52.1	16 27.6	12 46.8	17D 14.0	14 41.9
30 F	20 29 41	6 37 10	28 10 18	5♍41 6	12 22.7	29 43.9	5 17.8	16 53.2	22 3.8	16 24.7	12 50.0	17 13.9	14 43.6
31 Sa	20 33 37	7 34 34	13♍ 7 0	20 27 4	12 14.8	29 56.0	6 30.3	17 28.5	22 15.5	16 21.8	12 53.2	17 14.0	14 45.4

AUGUST 1965 LONGITUDE

Day	Sid.Time	☉	0 hr ☽	Noon ☽	True ☊	☿	♀	♂	♃	♄	♅	♆	♇
1 Su	20 37 34	8♌31 59	27♍40 37	4♎47 8	12♊ 7.9	0♍ 3.1	7♍42.7	18♎ 3.9	22♊27.2	16♓18.7	12♍56.5	17♏14.0	14♍47.2
2 M	20 41 30	9 29 25	11♎46 23	18 38 18	12R 2.7	0R 5.3	8 55.1	18 39.4	22 38.7	16R 15.6	12 59.8	17 14.1	14 49.0
3 Tu	20 45 27	10 26 51	25 22 59	2♏ 0 43	11 59.7	0 2.2	10 7.5	19 15.1	22 50.2	16 12.4	13 3.1	17 14.2	14 50.8
4 W	20 49 23	11 24 17	8♏31 52	14 56 56	11D 58.6	29♌53.9	11 19.9	19 50.9	23 1.5	16 9.1	13 6.4	17 14.4	14 52.6
5 Th	20 53 20	12 21 45	21 16 26	27 30 58	11 58.8	29 40.4	12 32.2	20 26.8	23 12.8	16 5.7	13 9.7	17 14.6	14 54.5
6 F	20 57 17	13 19 13	3♐41 7	9♐47 30	11R 59.5	29 21.6	13 44.5	21 2.9	23 24.0	16 2.3	13 13.1	17 14.8	14 56.4
7 Sa	21 1 13	14 16 42	15 50 42	21 51 18	11 59.7	28 57.7	14 56.7	21 39.1	23 35.2	15 58.8	13 16.5	17 15.0	14 58.2
8 Su	21 5 10	15 14 11	27 49 50	3♑46 48	11 58.4	28 28.8	16 8.9	22 15.4	23 46.2	15 55.3	13 19.9	17 15.3	15 0.1
9 M	21 9 6	16 11 42	9♑42 39	15 37 50	11 54.9	27 55.2	17 21.1	22 51.8	23 57.1	15 51.7	13 23.4	17 15.6	15 2.1
10 Tu	21 13 3	17 9 14	21 32 42	27 27 36	11 48.8	27 17.3	18 33.2	23 28.4	24 8.0	15 48.0	13 26.9	17 16.0	15 4.0
11 W	21 16 59	18 6 46	3♒22 48	9♒18 35	11 40.1	26 35.5	19 45.3	24 5.1	24 18.7	15 44.3	13 30.3	17 16.4	15 5.9
12 Th	21 20 56	19 4 20	15 15 9	21 12 42	11 29.4	25 50.5	20 57.4	24 41.9	24 29.4	15 40.5	13 33.8	17 16.8	15 7.9
13 F	21 24 52	20 1 54	27 11 25	3♓11 27	11 17.2	25 2.9	22 9.4	25 18.8	24 40.0	15 36.6	13 37.4	17 17.2	15 9.8
14 Sa	21 28 49	20 59 30	9♓12 58	15 16 8	11 4.7	24 13.6	23 21.4	25 55.9	24 50.4	15 32.7	13 40.9	17 17.7	15 11.8
15 Su	21 32 46	21 57 7	21 21 7	27 28 6	10 52.8	23 23.3	24 33.4	26 33.0	25 0.8	15 28.7	13 44.5	17 18.2	15 13.8
16 M	21 36 42	22 54 46	3♈37 18	9♈48 58	10 42.7	22 33.2	25 45.3	27 10.3	25 11.1	15 24.7	13 48.0	17 18.8	15 15.8
17 Tu	21 40 39	23 52 26	16 3 23	22 20 50	10 34.9	21 44.0	26 57.2	27 47.7	25 21.2	15 20.7	13 51.6	17 19.3	15 17.8
18 W	21 44 35	24 50 7	28 41 40	5♉ 6 16	10 29.8	20 56.9	28 9.0	28 25.3	25 31.3	15 16.5	13 55.2	17 19.9	15 19.8
19 Th	21 48 32	25 47 50	11♉34 59	18 8 15	10 27.3	20 12.8	29 20.8	29 2.9	25 41.3	15 12.4	13 58.9	17 20.6	15 21.9
20 F	21 52 28	26 45 35	24 46 25	1♊29 52	10D 26.6	19 32.6	0♎32.6	29 40.7	25 51.1	15 8.2	14 2.5	17 21.2	15 23.9
21 Sa	21 56 25	27 43 22	8♊18 55	15 13 49	10R 26.7	18 57.3	1 44.3	0♏18.5	26 0.9	15 4.0	14 6.2	17 21.9	15 25.9
22 Su	22 0 21	28 41 10	22 14 42	29 21 38	10 26.3	18 27.6	2 56.0	0 56.5	26 10.5	14 59.7	14 9.8	17 22.7	15 28.0
23 M	22 4 18	29 39 0	6♋34 27	13♋52 51	10 24.4	18 4.2	4 7.7	1 34.6	26 20.0	14 55.4	14 13.5	17 23.4	15 30.1
24 Tu	22 8 15	0♍36 52	21 16 22	28 44 16	10 20.1	17 47.7	5 19.3	2 12.8	26 29.4	14 51.0	14 17.2	17 24.2	15 32.2
25 W	22 12 11	1 34 45	6♌15 40	13♌49 29	10 13.0	17D 38.6	6 30.9	2 51.2	26 38.7	14 46.6	14 20.9	17 25.0	15 34.2
26 Th	22 16 8	2 32 40	21 24 30	28 59 24	10 3.6	17 37.1	7 42.4	3 29.6	26 47.9	14 42.2	14 24.6	17 25.9	15 36.3
27 F	22 20 4	3 30 36	6♍32 51	14♍ 3 33	9 52.7	17 43.7	8 53.9	4 8.2	26 56.9	14 37.8	14 28.3	17 26.8	15 38.4
28 Sa	22 24 1	4 28 34	21 30 14	28 51 52	9 41.6	17 58.3	10 5.4	4 46.9	27 5.9	14 33.3	14 32.1	17 27.7	15 40.5
29 Su	22 27 57	5 26 34	6♎ 7 32	13♎16 33	9 31.7	18 21.0	11 16.8	5 25.7	27 14.7	14 28.8	14 35.8	17 28.6	15 42.6
30 M	22 31 54	6 24 35	20 18 29	27 13 3	9 23.8	18 51.9	12 28.1	6 4.5	27 23.4	14 24.3	14 39.5	17 29.6	15 44.8
31 Tu	22 35 50	7 22 37	4♏ 0 15	10♏40 13	9 18.4	19 30.8	13 39.5	6 43.6	27 31.9	14 19.7	14 43.3	17 30.6	15 46.9

Astro Data	Dy Hr Mn
☽0S	5 14:43
♃□♄	6 11:55
♃⊼♆	7 9:43
☽0N	20 7:41
♆ D	29 17:41
☽0S	1 21:41
☿ R	1 21:56
☽0N	16 12:42
♄☍♇	17 11:12
♀0S	20 23:56
☿ D	25 16:24
♄☍♅	28 3:36
☽0S	29 6:33

Planet Ingress	Dy Hr Mn
☿ ♌	1 15:55
☉ ♌	23 1:48
♀ ♍	25 14:51
☿ ♍	31 11:24
☿ ♌	3 8:09
♀ ♎	19 13:06
♂ ♏	20 12:16
☉ ♍	23 8:43

Last Aspect Dy Hr Mn		☽ Ingress Dy Hr Mn
1 20:48	♆ □	♍ 2 17:11
3 22:08	♆ ✶	♎ 4 19:43
6 1:57	♃ △	♏ 7 1:38
8 10:23	☿ ☌	♐ 9 10:53
10 22:43	♃ ☍	♑ 11 22:29
13 17:01	☉ ☍	♒ 14 11:08
16 3:37	☿ ☍	♓ 16 23:45
19 3:55	☉ △	♈ 19 11:13
21 17:53	☉ □	♉ 21 20:14
23 22:16	☉ □	♊ 24 1:48
26 0:56	☿ ✶	♋ 26 3:53
27 7:29	♆ △	♌ 28 3:37
30 2:31	☿ ☌	♍ 30 2:55

Last Aspect Dy Hr Mn		☽ Ingress Dy Hr Mn
31 15:11	♃ □	♎ 1 3:54
3 8:20	☿ ✶	♏ 3 8:20
5 15:48	☿ □	♐ 5 16:49
8 1:15	☿ △	♑ 8 4:22
10 4:08	♂ □	♒ 10 17:09
12 20:02	♂ △	♓ 13 5:37
15 7:18	♃ □	♈ 15 16:57
17 23:28	♂ ☍	♉ 18 2:27
20 3:50	☉ □	♊ 20 9:20
22 11:39	☉ ✶	♋ 22 13:04
23 17:44	♆ △	♌ 24 14:01
26 8:37	♃ ✶	♍ 26 13:36
28 9:12	♃ □	♎ 28 13:52
30 12:26	♃ △	♏ 30 16:54

☽ Phases & Eclipses Dy Hr Mn	
5 19:36	☽ 13♎32
13 17:01	○ 21♑04
21 17:53	☽ 28♈44
28 11:45	● 5♌10
4 5:47	☽ 11♏38
12 8:22	○ 19♒24
20 3:50	☽ 26♉55
26 18:50	● 3♍18

Astro Data

1 JULY 1965
Julian Day # 23923
Delta T 36.1 sec
SVP 05♓44'45"
Obliquity 23°26'40"
⚷ Chiron 22♓32.9R
☽ Mean ☊ 12♊23.4

1 AUGUST 1965
Julian Day # 23954
Delta T 36.2 sec
SVP 05♓44'40"
Obliquity 23°26'41"
⚷ Chiron 21♓59.3R
☽ Mean ☊ 10♊44.9

LONGITUDE — SEPTEMBER 1965

Day	Sid.Time	☉	0 hr ☽	Noon ☽	True ☊	☿	♀	♂	♃	♄	♅	♆	♇
1 W	22 39 47	8♍20 40	17♏13 14	23♏39 43	9♊15.6	20♌17.4	14♎50.7	7♏22.7	27♊40.3	14♓15.2	14♍47.0	17♏31.6	15♍49.0
2 Th	22 43 44	9 18 45	0♐ 0 12	6♐15 16	9R14.6	21 11.6	16 2.0	8 1.9	27 48.6	14R10.6	14 50.8	17 32.7	15 51.1
3 F	22 47 40	10 16 52	12 25 32	18 31 41	9 14.5	22 12.9	17 13.1	8 41.2	27 56.8	14 6.1	14 54.6	17 33.8	15 53.3
4 Sa	22 51 37	11 15 0	24 34 23	0♑34 16	9 14.2	23 21.0	18 24.2	9 20.6	28 4.8	14 1.5	14 58.3	17 34.9	15 55.4
5 Su	22 55 33	12 13 9	6♑31 59	12 28 11	9 12.5	24 35.5	19 35.3	10 0.1	28 12.7	13 56.9	15 2.1	17 36.1	15 57.5
6 M	22 59 30	13 11 20	18 23 24	24 18 12	9 8.5	25 55.9	20 46.3	10 39.8	28 20.4	13 52.3	15 5.9	17 37.3	15 59.7
7 Tu	23 3 26	14 9 32	0♒13 3	6♒ 8 24	9 1.9	27 21.6	21 57.3	11 19.5	28 28.0	13 47.7	15 9.7	17 38.5	16 1.8
8 W	23 7 23	15 7 46	12 4 39	18 2 6	8 52.5	28 52.3	23 8.1	11 59.3	28 35.5	13 43.1	15 13.4	17 39.7	16 4.0
9 Th	23 11 19	16 6 2	24 1 4	0♓ 1 45	8 40.8	0♍27.2	24 19.0	12 39.2	28 42.8	13 38.5	15 17.2	17 41.0	16 6.1
10 F	23 15 16	17 4 19	6♓ 4 22	12 9 1	8 27.6	2 5.9	25 29.8	13 19.2	28 50.0	13 33.9	15 21.0	17 42.3	16 8.2
11 Sa	23 19 13	18 2 38	18 15 51	24 24 57	8 13.9	3 47.8	26 40.5	13 59.3	28 57.0	13 29.4	15 24.8	17 43.6	16 10.4
12 Su	23 23 9	19 0 58	0♈36 21	6♈50 8	8 1.0	5 32.5	27 51.1	14 39.5	29 3.9	13 24.8	15 28.5	17 44.9	16 12.5
13 M	23 27 6	19 59 21	13 6 22	19 25 6	7 49.8	7 19.4	29 1.7	15 19.9	29 10.7	13 20.3	15 32.3	17 46.3	16 14.6
14 Tu	23 31 2	20 57 45	25 46 26	2♉10 29	7 41.2	9 8.1	0♏12.2	16 0.3	29 17.2	13 15.7	15 36.1	17 47.7	16 16.8
15 W	23 34 59	21 56 12	8♉37 22	15 7 16	7 35.5	10 58.2	1 22.7	16 40.7	29 23.7	13 11.2	15 39.8	17 49.1	16 18.9
16 Th	23 38 55	22 54 41	21 40 23	28 16 56	7 32.5	12 49.4	2 33.1	17 21.3	29 30.0	13 6.7	15 43.6	17 50.5	16 21.1
17 F	23 42 52	23 53 12	4♊57 8	11♊41 15	7D31.6	14 41.2	3 43.5	18 2.0	29 36.1	13 2.2	15 47.3	17 52.0	16 23.2
18 Sa	23 46 48	24 51 45	18 29 29	25 22 3	7R31.8	16 33.4	4 53.7	18 42.8	29 42.0	12 57.8	15 51.1	17 53.5	16 25.3
19 Su	23 50 45	25 50 20	2♋19 4	9♋20 37	7 31.7	18 25.8	6 4.0	19 23.7	29 47.8	12 53.3	15 54.8	17 55.0	16 27.4
20 M	23 54 42	26 48 58	16 26 40	23 37 4	7 30.3	20 18.1	7 14.1	20 4.7	29 53.5	12 48.9	15 58.6	17 56.6	16 29.6
21 Tu	23 58 38	27 47 38	0♌51 32	8♌ 9 36	7 26.7	22 10.2	8 24.2	20 45.8	29 59.0	12 44.6	16 2.3	17 58.2	16 31.7
22 W	0 2 35	28 46 20	15 30 40	22 54 0	7 20.6	24 1.9	9 34.2	21 26.9	0♋ 4.3	12 40.3	16 6.0	17 59.8	16 33.8
23 Th	0 6 31	29 45 4	0♍18 43	7♍43 48	7 12.1	25 53.0	10 44.2	22 8.2	0 9.4	12 36.0	16 9.7	18 1.4	16 35.9
24 F	0 10 28	0♎43 50	15 8 12	22 30 49	7 2.2	27 43.6	11 54.1	22 49.5	0 14.4	12 31.7	16 13.4	18 3.0	16 38.0
25 Sa	0 14 24	1 42 38	29 50 38	7♎ 6 37	6 52.0	29 33.5	13 3.9	23 31.0	0 19.2	12 27.5	16 17.1	18 4.7	16 40.1
26 Su	0 18 21	2 41 29	14♎17 55	21 23 48	6 42.7	1♎22.6	14 13.6	24 12.5	0 23.8	12 23.3	16 20.8	18 6.4	16 42.1
27 M	0 22 17	3 40 21	28 23 42	5♏17 14	6 35.2	3 11.0	15 23.3	24 54.2	0 28.2	12 19.2	16 24.4	18 8.1	16 44.2
28 Tu	0 26 14	4 39 15	12♏ 4 11	18 44 33	6 30.2	4 58.5	16 32.9	25 35.9	0 32.5	12 15.1	16 28.1	18 9.8	16 46.3
29 W	0 30 10	5 38 11	25 18 26	1♐46 5	6D27.6	6 45.2	17 42.4	26 17.7	0 36.6	12 11.1	16 31.7	18 11.6	16 48.3
30 Th	0 34 7	6 37 9	8♐ 7 53	14 24 18	6 27.0	8 31.0	18 51.8	26 59.6	0 40.5	12 7.1	16 35.3	18 13.4	16 50.4

LONGITUDE — OCTOBER 1965

Day	Sid.Time	☉	0 hr ☽	Noon ☽	True ☊	☿	♀	♂	♃	♄	♅	♆	♇
1 F	0 38 4	7♎36 9	20♐35 52	26♐43 11	6♊27.6	10♎15.9	20♏ 1.1	27♏41.6	0♋44.2	12♓ 3.2	16♍38.9	18♏15.2	16♍52.4
2 Sa	0 42 0	8 35 10	2♑46 53	8♑47 37	6R28.4	12 0.0	21 10.3	28 23.7	0 47.8	11R59.3	16 42.5	18 17.0	16 54.5
3 Su	0 45 57	9 34 13	14 46 3	20 42 49	6 28.4	13 43.2	22 19.5	29 5.8	0 51.1	11 55.5	16 46.1	18 18.8	16 56.5
4 M	0 49 53	10 33 18	26 38 35	2♒33 57	6 26.8	15 25.6	23 28.5	29 48.1	0 54.3	11 51.8	16 49.6	18 20.7	16 58.5
5 Tu	0 53 50	11 32 25	8♒29 30	14 25 48	6 23.1	17 7.1	24 37.5	0♐30.4	0 57.3	11 48.1	16 53.2	18 22.5	17 0.5
6 W	0 57 46	12 31 33	20 23 20	26 22 33	6 17.2	18 47.8	25 46.3	1 12.8	1 0.1	11 44.5	16 56.7	18 24.4	17 2.5
7 Th	1 1 43	13 30 44	2♓23 51	8♓27 35	6 9.3	20 27.7	26 55.1	1 55.3	1 2.7	11 40.9	17 0.2	18 26.3	17 4.4
8 F	1 5 39	14 29 56	14 34 0	20 43 22	6 0.2	22 6.8	28 3.7	2 37.9	1 5.1	11 37.4	17 3.6	18 28.3	17 6.4
9 Sa	1 9 36	15 29 10	26 55 47	3♈11 24	5 50.5	23 45.1	29 12.2	3 20.5	1 7.3	11 34.0	17 7.1	18 30.2	17 8.3
10 Su	1 13 33	16 28 26	9♈30 15	15 52 20	5 41.4	25 22.6	0♐20.6	4 3.3	1 9.4	11 30.7	17 10.5	18 32.2	17 10.3
11 M	1 17 29	17 27 44	22 17 38	28 46 3	5 33.6	26 59.4	1 28.9	4 46.1	1 11.2	11 27.4	17 13.9	18 34.1	17 12.2
12 Tu	1 21 26	18 27 4	5♉17 33	11♉52 1	5 27.8	28 35.5	2 37.1	5 29.0	1 12.9	11 24.2	17 17.3	18 36.1	17 14.1
13 W	1 25 22	19 26 26	18 29 21	25 9 29	5 24.2	0♏10.9	3 45.1	6 11.9	1 14.3	11 21.1	17 20.6	18 38.1	17 16.0
14 Th	1 29 19	20 25 50	1♊52 21	8♊37 52	5D22.8	1 45.6	4 53.0	6 55.0	1 15.6	11 18.1	17 24.0	18 40.2	17 17.8
15 F	1 33 15	21 25 17	15 26 0	22 16 44	5 23.1	3 19.6	6 0.8	7 38.1	1 16.6	11 15.1	17 27.3	18 42.2	17 19.7
16 Sa	1 37 12	22 24 46	29 10 3	6♋ 5 54	5 24.4	4 52.9	7 8.5	8 21.3	1 17.5	11 12.2	17 30.5	18 44.3	17 21.5
17 Su	1 41 8	23 24 18	13♋ 4 17	20 5 7	5R25.6	6 25.6	8 16.0	9 4.6	1 18.2	11 9.4	17 33.8	18 46.3	17 23.4
18 M	1 45 5	24 23 51	27 8 18	4♌13 42	5 26.0	7 57.6	9 23.4	9 48.0	1 18.6	11 6.7	17 37.0	18 48.4	17 25.2
19 Tu	1 49 2	25 23 27	11♌21 6	18 30 12	5 24.9	9 29.1	10 30.7	10 31.4	1R18.9	11 4.1	17 40.2	18 50.5	17 26.9
20 W	1 52 58	26 23 6	25 40 38	2♍51 58	5 22.0	10 59.8	11 37.8	11 14.9	1 19.0	11 1.5	17 43.4	18 52.6	17 28.7
21 Th	1 56 55	27 22 46	10♍ 3 39	17 15 6	5 17.5	12 30.0	12 44.8	11 58.5	1 18.8	10 59.1	17 46.5	18 54.7	17 30.5
22 F	2 0 51	28 22 29	24 25 40	1♎34 40	5 12.0	13 59.6	13 51.6	12 42.2	1 18.5	10 56.7	17 49.6	18 56.8	17 32.2
23 Sa	2 4 48	29 22 14	8♎41 27	15 45 19	5 6.1	15 28.5	14 58.3	13 26.0	1 18.0	10 54.4	17 52.7	18 59.0	17 33.9
24 Su	2 8 44	0♏22 1	22 45 41	29 41 59	5 0.8	16 56.8	16 4.8	14 9.8	1 17.2	10 52.3	17 55.7	19 1.1	17 35.6
25 M	2 12 41	1 21 50	6♏33 46	13♏20 39	4 56.6	18 24.4	17 11.1	14 53.7	1 16.3	10 50.2	17 58.8	19 3.3	17 37.3
26 Tu	2 16 37	2 21 40	20 2 25	26 38 54	4 54.0	19 51.4	18 17.3	15 37.7	1 15.1	10 48.2	18 1.7	19 5.5	17 38.9
27 W	2 20 34	3 21 33	3♐10 6	9♐36 6	4D53.0	21 17.7	19 23.3	16 21.8	1 13.7	10 46.3	18 4.7	19 7.6	17 40.5
28 Th	2 24 31	4 21 28	15 57 5	22 13 20	4 53.5	22 43.3	20 29.1	17 5.9	1 12.2	10 44.5	18 7.6	19 9.8	17 42.2
29 F	2 28 27	5 21 25	28 25 14	4♑33 11	4 54.9	24 8.2	21 34.7	17 50.1	1 10.4	10 42.8	18 10.5	19 12.0	17 43.7
30 Sa	2 32 24	6 21 23	10♑37 41	16 39 17	4 56.7	25 32.3	22 40.1	18 34.4	1 8.5	10 41.2	18 13.3	19 14.2	17 45.3
31 Su	2 36 20	7 21 23	22 38 33	28 36 4	4 58.3	26 55.6	23 45.3	19 18.7	1 6.3	10 39.6	18 16.1	19 16.4	17 46.9

Astro Data Dy Hr Mn	Planet Ingress Dy Hr Mn	Last Aspect Dy Hr Mn	☽ Ingress Dy Hr Mn	Last Aspect Dy Hr Mn	☽ Ingress Dy Hr Mn	☽ Phases & Eclipses Dy Hr Mn	Astro Data
☽0N 12 17:49	☿ ♍ 8 17:14	1 6:06 ☿ □	♐ 1 24:00	30 16:45 ♇ □	♑ 1 18:29	2 19:27 ☽ 10♐06	1 SEPTEMBER 1965
☽0S 25 16:32	♀ ♏ 13 19:50	4 7:05 ♃ ☍	♑ 4 10:51	3 16:54 ♀ ✶	♒ 4 6:48	10 23:32 ○ 18♓01	Julian Day # 23985
☿0S 27 1:04	♃ ♋ 21 4:39	6 5:22 ♀ □	♒ 6 23:34	6 11:56 ♀ □	♓ 6 19:14	18 11:58 ☽ 25♊21	Delta T 36.3 sec
	☉ ♎ 23 6:06	9 9:28 ♃ △	♓ 9 11:57	9 4:48 ♀ △	♈ 9 5:54	25 3:18 ● 1♎51	SVP 05♓44'36"
♅☌♇ 9 20:11	☿ ♎ 25 5:49	11 21:00 ♃ □	♈ 11 22:50	11 9:57 ☿ ☍	♉ 11 14:16		Obliquity 23°26'41"
☽0N 10 0:36		14 6:39 ♃ ✶	♉ 14 7:56	13 0:16 ♆ ☍	♊ 13 20:40	2 12:37 ☽ 9♑06	⚷ Chiron 20♓47.4R
♃ R 19 19:32	♂ ♐ 4 6:46	16 2:26 ☉ △	♊ 16 15:06	15 11:19 ☉ △	♋ 16 1:27	10 14:14 ○ 17♈04	☽ Mean ☊ 9♊06.4
☽0S 23 2:01	♀ ♐ 9 16:46	18 19:38 ♃ ☌	♋ 18 20:01	17 19:00 ☉ □	♌ 18 4:51	17 19:00 ☽ 24♋11	
	☿ ♏ 12 21:15	20 18:34 ☉ ✶	♌ 20 22:35	20 1:16 ☉ ✶	♍ 20 7:13	24 14:11 ● 0♏57	1 OCTOBER 1965
	☉ ♏ 23 15:10	22 10:07 ♂ □	♍ 22 23:30	21 14:49 ♆ ✶	♎ 22 9:21		Julian Day # 24015
		24 23:28 ☿ ☌	♎ 25 0:15	23 11:35 ♀ ✶	♏ 24 12:31		Delta T 36.3 sec
		25 3:18 ☉ ☌	♏ 27 2:47	25 23:38 ☿ ☌	♐ 26 18:09		SVP 05♓44'33"
		29 1:56 ♂ ☌	♐ 29 8:42	28 9:30 ♀ ☌	♑ 29 3:05		Obliquity 23°26'42"
				31 9:45 ☿ ✶	♒ 31 14:49		⚷ Chiron 19♓25.7R
							☽ Mean ☊ 7♊31.1

NOVEMBER 1965

LONGITUDE

Day	Sid.Time	☉	0 hr ☽	Noon ☽	True ☊	☿	♀	♂	♃	♄	♅	♆	♇
1 M	2 40 17	8♏21 24	4♒32 27	10♒28 19	4♊59.2	28♏18.1	24♐50.3	20♐ 3.1	1♋ 4.0	10♓38.2	18♍18.9	19♏18.6	17♍48.4
2 Tu	2 44 13	9 21 27	16 24 18	22 20 59	4R59.0	29 39.6	25 55.1	20 47.6	1R 1.4	10R36.9	18 21.6	19 20.9	17 49.9
3 W	2 48 10	10 21 32	28 18 58	4♓18 48	4 57.6	1♐ 0.0	26 59.6	21 32.1	0 58.7	10 35.7	18 24.3	19 23.1	17 51.3
4 Th	2 52 6	11 21 38	10♓21 0	16 26 4	4 55.2	2 19.4	28 3.9	22 16.7	0 55.7	10 34.6	18 26.9	19 25.3	17 52.8
5 F	2 56 3	12 21 46	22 34 26	28 46 27	4 52.1	3 37.6	29 7.9	23 1.4	0 52.6	10 33.6	18 29.5	19 27.6	17 54.2
6 Sa	3 0 0	13 21 55	5♈ 2 27	11♈22 39	4 48.6	4 54.5	0♑11.7	23 46.1	0 49.3	10 32.7	18 32.1	19 29.8	17 55.6
7 Su	3 3 56	14 22 6	17 47 13	24 16 14	4 45.2	6 10.0	1 15.2	24 30.9	0 45.8	10 31.9	18 34.6	19 32.0	17 57.0
8 M	3 7 53	15 22 18	0♉49 44	7♉27 37	4 42.4	7 23.8	2 18.4	25 15.8	0 42.1	10 31.2	18 37.1	19 34.3	17 58.3
9 Tu	3 11 49	16 22 33	14 9 44	20 55 54	4 40.4	8 35.8	3 21.3	26 0.7	0 38.2	10 30.6	18 39.5	19 36.5	17 59.6
10 W	3 15 46	17 22 49	27 45 48	4♊39 9	4D39.5	9 45.8	4 23.9	26 45.7	0 34.1	10 30.1	18 41.9	19 38.8	18 0.9
11 Th	3 19 42	18 23 7	11♊35 34	18 34 41	4 39.4	10 53.6	5 26.3	27 30.7	0 29.9	10 29.8	18 44.3	19 41.0	18 2.2
12 F	3 23 39	19 23 27	25 36 4	2♋39 19	4 40.2	11 58.9	6 28.2	28 15.8	0 25.5	10 29.5	18 46.6	19 43.3	18 3.4
13 Sa	3 27 35	20 23 48	9♋44 2	16 49 50	4 41.3	13 1.3	7 29.9	29 1.0	0 20.9	10 29.3	18 48.8	19 45.5	18 4.7
14 Su	3 31 32	21 24 12	23 56 20	1♌ 3 11	4 42.4	14 0.5	8 31.2	29 46.2	0 16.1	10D29.2	18 51.1	19 47.8	18 5.8
15 M	3 35 29	22 24 37	8♌10 4	15 16 39	4 43.2	14 56.1	9 32.2	0♑31.5	0 11.1	10 29.3	18 53.2	19 50.0	18 7.0
16 Tu	3 39 25	23 25 5	22 22 41	29 27 52	4R43.6	15 47.7	10 32.8	1 16.8	0 6.0	10 29.4	18 55.4	19 52.3	18 8.1
17 W	3 43 22	24 25 34	6♍31 56	13♍34 38	4 43.3	16 34.6	11 33.1	2 2.2	0 0.7	10 29.7	18 57.5	19 54.5	18 9.2
18 Th	3 47 18	25 26 5	20 35 43	27 34 57	4 42.7	17 16.4	12 32.9	2 47.7	29♊55.2	10 30.0	18 59.5	19 56.8	18 10.3
19 F	3 51 15	26 26 38	4♎32 3	11♎26 47	4 41.7	17 52.4	13 32.3	3 33.2	29 49.6	10 30.5	19 1.5	19 59.0	18 11.4
20 Sa	3 55 11	27 27 12	18 18 54	25 8 10	4 40.7	18 21.9	14 31.4	4 18.8	29 43.9	10 31.0	19 3.4	20 1.3	18 12.4
21 Su	3 59 8	28 27 49	1♏54 22	8♏37 15	4 39.9	18 44.2	15 29.9	5 4.4	29 37.9	10 31.7	19 5.3	20 3.5	18 13.4
22 M	4 3 4	29 28 27	15 16 40	21 52 27	4 39.3	18 58.5	16 28.1	5 50.1	29 31.8	10 32.5	19 7.2	20 5.7	18 14.3
23 Tu	4 7 1	0♐29 6	28 24 29	4♐52 41	4D39.1	19R 4.1	17 25.8	6 35.9	29 25.6	10 33.4	19 8.9	20 8.0	18 15.2
24 W	4 10 58	1 29 47	11♐17 3	17 37 34	4 39.1	19 0.1	18 22.9	7 21.7	29 19.3	10 34.4	19 10.7	20 10.2	18 16.1
25 Th	4 14 54	2 30 30	23 54 22	0♑ 7 33	4 39.2	18 46.0	19 19.6	8 7.5	29 12.8	10 35.5	19 12.4	20 12.4	18 17.0
26 F	4 18 51	3 31 13	6♑17 20	12 23 58	4 39.4	18 21.2	20 15.7	8 53.4	29 6.1	10 36.7	19 14.0	20 14.6	18 17.8
27 Sa	4 22 47	4 31 58	18 27 45	24 29 2	4R39.5	17 45.6	21 11.3	9 39.4	28 59.4	10 38.0	19 15.6	20 16.8	18 18.6
28 Su	4 26 44	5 32 44	0♒28 15	6♒25 50	4 39.4	16 59.1	22 6.3	10 25.4	28 52.5	10 39.4	19 17.2	20 19.0	18 19.4
29 M	4 30 40	6 33 31	12 22 16	18 18 5	4 39.3	16 2.4	23 0.7	11 11.5	28 45.5	10 40.9	19 18.6	20 21.2	18 20.1
30 Tu	4 34 37	7 34 19	24 13 50	0♓10 4	4 39.1	14 56.4	23 54.5	11 57.6	28 38.4	10 42.5	19 20.1	20 23.4	18 20.9

DECEMBER 1965

LONGITUDE

Day	Sid.Time	☉	0 hr ☽	Noon ☽	True ☊	☿	♀	♂	♃	♄	♅	♆	♇
1 W	4 38 33	8♐35 7	6♓ 7 23	12♓ 6 23	4♊39.0	13♐42.8	24♑47.6	12♑43.7	28♊31.2	10♓44.3	19♍21.5	20♏25.6	18♍21.5
2 Th	4 42 30	9 35 57	18 7 38	24 11 45	4D39.0	12R23.6	25 40.0	13 29.9	28R23.9	10 46.1	19 22.8	20 27.7	18 22.2
3 F	4 46 27	10 36 48	0♈19 17	6♈30 46	4 39.4	11 1.2	26 31.7	14 16.1	28 16.5	10 48.0	19 24.0	20 29.9	18 22.8
4 Sa	4 50 23	11 37 39	12 46 41	19 7 29	4 40.0	9 38.6	27 22.7	15 2.4	28 8.9	10 50.1	19 25.3	20 32.0	18 23.4
5 Su	4 54 20	12 38 31	25 33 32	2♉ 5 8	4 40.7	8 18.4	28 12.9	15 48.7	28 1.4	10 52.2	19 26.4	20 34.1	18 23.9
6 M	4 58 16	13 39 24	8♉42 29	15 25 40	4 41.6	7 3.4	29 2.2	16 35.1	27 53.7	10 54.4	19 27.5	20 36.2	18 24.4
7 Tu	5 2 13	14 40 18	22 14 39	29 9 17	4R42.2	5 55.7	29 50.8	17 21.5	27 46.0	10 56.8	19 28.6	20 38.3	18 24.9
8 W	5 6 9	15 41 13	6♊ 9 18	13♊14 17	4 42.4	4 57.3	0♒38.4	18 7.9	27 38.2	10 59.2	19 29.6	20 40.4	18 25.4
9 Th	5 10 6	16 42 9	20 23 40	27 36 51	4 42.0	4 9.2	1 25.2	18 54.4	27 30.3	11 1.7	19 30.5	20 42.5	18 25.8
10 F	5 14 2	17 43 6	4♋53 4	12♋11 31	4 41.0	3 32.2	2 11.0	19 40.9	27 22.4	11 4.4	19 31.4	20 44.6	18 26.2
11 Sa	5 17 59	18 44 4	19 31 21	26 51 43	4 39.4	3 6.6	2 55.8	20 27.5	27 14.4	11 7.1	19 32.3	20 46.6	18 26.5
12 Su	5 21 56	19 45 3	4♌11 46	11♌30 43	4 37.5	2D52.2	3 39.6	21 14.1	27 6.4	11 9.9	19 33.1	20 48.7	18 26.9
13 M	5 25 52	20 46 3	18 47 51	26 2 31	4 35.5	2 48.4	4 22.3	22 0.7	26 58.3	11 12.9	19 33.8	20 50.7	18 27.1
14 Tu	5 29 49	21 47 4	3♍14 13	10♍22 31	4 34.0	2 54.7	5 3.9	22 47.4	26 50.2	11 15.9	19 34.4	20 52.7	18 27.4
15 W	5 33 45	22 48 5	17 27 8	24 27 51	4D33.2	3 10.3	5 44.4	23 34.1	26 42.1	11 19.0	19 35.1	20 54.7	18 27.6
16 Th	5 37 42	23 49 8	1♎24 32	8♎17 11	4 33.3	3 34.4	6 23.7	24 20.9	26 34.0	11 22.2	19 35.6	20 56.7	18 27.8
17 F	5 41 38	24 50 12	15 5 48	21 50 29	4 34.2	4 6.1	7 1.7	25 7.6	26 25.8	11 25.5	19 36.1	20 58.6	18 28.0
18 Sa	5 45 35	25 51 17	28 31 21	5♏ 8 31	4 35.6	4 44.6	7 38.4	25 54.5	26 17.6	11 28.9	19 36.5	21 0.5	18 28.1
19 Su	5 49 32	26 52 23	11♏42 8	18 12 22	4 37.2	5 29.2	8 13.8	26 41.3	26 9.5	11 32.4	19 36.9	21 2.5	18 28.2
20 M	5 53 28	27 53 29	24 39 21	1♐ 3 14	4R38.4	6 19.2	8 47.8	27 28.2	26 1.3	11 36.0	19 37.3	21 4.4	18 28.2
21 Tu	5 57 25	28 54 36	7♐24 8	13 42 10	4 38.7	7 13.9	9 20.3	28 15.1	25 53.1	11 39.6	19 37.5	21 6.3	18R28.3
22 W	6 1 21	29 55 44	19 57 27	26 10 6	4 37.8	8 12.8	9 51.3	29 2.0	25 45.0	11 43.4	19 37.7	21 8.1	18 28.2
23 Th	6 5 18	0♑56 53	2♑20 13	8♑27 56	4 35.4	9 15.4	10 20.7	29 49.0	25 36.9	11 47.2	19 37.9	21 10.0	18 28.2
24 F	6 9 14	1 58 1	14 33 22	20 36 41	4 31.6	10 21.2	10 48.5	0♒36.0	25 28.8	11 51.2	19 38.0	21 11.8	18 28.1
25 Sa	6 13 11	2 59 10	26 38 3	2♒37 40	4 26.7	11 29.8	11 14.6	1 23.1	25 20.8	11 55.2	19R38.0	21 13.6	18 28.0
26 Su	6 17 7	4 0 20	8♒35 47	14 32 42	4 21.2	12 41.0	11 38.8	2 10.1	25 12.8	11 59.3	19 38.0	21 15.4	18 27.9
27 M	6 21 4	5 1 29	20 28 42	26 24 11	4 15.6	13 54.4	12 1.3	2 57.2	25 4.8	12 3.5	19 38.0	21 17.1	18 27.7
28 Tu	6 25 1	6 2 39	2♓19 32	8♓15 12	4 10.6	15 9.7	12 21.8	3 44.3	24 56.9	12 7.8	19 37.8	21 18.9	18 27.5
29 W	6 28 57	7 3 48	14 11 40	20 9 28	4 6.6	16 26.7	12 40.4	4 31.4	24 49.1	12 12.2	19 37.6	21 20.6	18 27.2
30 Th	6 32 54	8 4 57	26 9 9	2♈11 17	4 4.2	17 45.3	12 56.9	5 18.6	24 41.4	12 16.6	19 37.4	21 22.3	18 27.0
31 F	6 36 50	9 6 7	8♈16 29	14 25 21	4D 3.4	19 5.2	13 11.3	6 5.8	24 33.7	12 21.1	19 37.1	21 24.0	18 26.7

Astro Data Dy Hr Mn	Planet Ingress Dy Hr Mn
☽0N 6 9:19	☿ ♐ 2 6:04
♄ D 14 3:17	♀ ♑ 5 19:36
☽0S 19 9:30	♂ ♑ 14 7:19
☿ R 23 2:15	♃ ♊ 17 3:08
	☉ ♐ 22 12:29
☽0N 3 18:44	
☿ D 12 20:40	♀ ♒ 7 4:37
☽0S 16 14:57	☉ ♑ 22 1:40
♇ R 21 5:05	♂ ♒ 23 5:36
♅ R 25 6:06	
☽0N 31 2:59	

Last Aspect Dy Hr Mn	☽ Ingress Dy Hr Mn	Last Aspect Dy Hr Mn	☽ Ingress Dy Hr Mn
2 21:05 ♀ ⚹	♓ 3 3:23	2 20:03 ♃ □	♈ 2 23:22
5 13:52 ♀ □	♈ 5 14:21	5 5:14 ♀ □	♉ 5 8:11
7 13:12 ♂ △	♉ 7 22:29	6 21:11 ♆ ☍	♊ 7 13:27
9 9:41 ♆ ☍	♊ 10 3:54	9 11:43 ♃ ☌	♋ 9 15:57
12 4:47 ♂ ☍	♋ 12 7:29	11 2:03 ♆ △	♌ 11 17:08
13 19:24 ☉ △	♌ 14 10:13	13 13:25 ♃ ⚹	♍ 13 18:35
16 1:54 ☉ □	♍ 16 12:54	15 15:42 ♃ □	♎ 15 21:33
18 15:55 ♃ □	♎ 18 16:10	17 20:02 ♃ △	♏ 18 2:40
20 19:59 ♃ △	♏ 20 20:37	20 5:37 ♂ ⚹	♐ 20 10:01
22 8:47 ♆ ☌	♐ 23 2:56	22 11:04 ♃ ☍	♑ 22 19:27
25 10:09 ♃ ☍	♑ 25 11:45	24 13:12 ♆ ⚹	♒ 25 6:44
27 5:52 ♀ ☌	♒ 27 23:03	27 9:13 ♃ △	♓ 27 19:17
30 8:50 ♃ △	♓ 30 11:40	29 21:07 ♃ □	♈ 30 7:40

☽ Phases & Eclipses Dy Hr Mn	Astro Data
1 8:26 ☽ 8♒42	1 NOVEMBER 1965
9 4:15 ○ 16♉33	Julian Day # 24046
16 1:54 ☽ 23♌30	Delta T 36.4 sec
23 4:10 ● 0♐40	SVP 05♓44'30"
23 4:14:15 A 4'02"	Obliquity 23°26'41"
	⚷ Chiron 18♓20.0R
1 5:24 ☽ 8♓49	☽ Mean ☊ 5♊52.6
8 17:21 ○ 16♊25	1 DECEMBER 1965
8 17:10 A 0.882	Julian Day # 24076
15 9:52 ☽ 23♍13	Delta T 36.5 sec
22 21:03 ● 0♑49	SVP 05♓44'25"
31 1:46 ☽ 9♈11	Obliquity 23°26'41"
	⚷ Chiron 17♓58.1
	☽ Mean ☊ 4♊17.3

LONGITUDE — JANUARY 1966

Day	Sid.Time	☉	0 hr ☽	Noon ☽	True ☊	☿	♀	♂	♃	♄	♅	♆	♇
1 Sa	6 40 47	10♑ 7 16	20♈38 29	26♈56 28	4♊ 3.9	20♐26.3	13♒23.5	6♒52.9	24♊26.1	12♓25.7	19♍36.8	21♏25.6	18♍26.3
2 Su	6 44 43	11 8 25	3♉19 51	9♉49 10	4 5.3	21 48.6	13 33.5	7 40.1	24R18.5	12 30.4	19R36.3	21 27.2	18R26.0
3 M	6 48 40	12 9 33	16 24 51	23 7 13	4 7.0	23 11.8	13 41.2	8 27.4	24 11.1	12 35.2	19 35.9	21 28.8	18 25.5
4 Tu	6 52 36	13 10 42	29 56 31	6♊52 50	4R 8.0	24 36.0	13 46.5	9 14.6	24 3.8	12 40.0	19 35.4	21 30.4	18 25.1
5 W	6 56 33	14 11 50	13♊56 5	21 6 1	4 7.7	26 0.9	13R49.4	10 1.9	23 56.5	12 45.0	19 34.8	21 31.9	18 24.7
6 Th	7 0 30	15 12 58	28 22 10	5♋43 52	4 5.4	27 26.7	13 49.8	10 49.1	23 49.4	12 49.9	19 34.2	21 33.5	18 24.2
7 F	7 4 26	16 14 6	13♋10 18	20 40 26	4 1.2	28 53.2	13 47.8	11 36.4	23 42.4	12 55.0	19 33.5	21 35.0	18 23.6
8 Sa	7 8 23	17 15 14	28 13 6	5♌47 4	3 55.2	0♑20.3	13 43.2	12 23.7	23 35.5	13 0.2	19 32.7	21 36.4	18 23.1
9 Su	7 12 19	18 16 22	13♌21 2	20 53 44	3 48.3	1 48.0	13 36.1	13 11.0	23 28.8	13 5.4	19 32.0	21 37.9	18 22.5
10 M	7 16 16	19 17 29	28 24 0	5♍50 44	3 41.2	3 16.4	13 26.5	13 58.3	23 22.1	13 10.6	19 31.1	21 39.3	18 21.9
11 Tu	7 20 12	20 18 37	13♍13 3	20 30 14	3 35.0	4 45.4	13 14.4	14 45.7	23 15.6	13 16.0	19 30.2	21 40.7	18 21.2
12 W	7 24 9	21 19 44	27 41 44	4♎47 15	3 30.5	6 14.9	12 59.8	15 33.0	23 9.2	13 21.4	19 29.3	21 42.0	18 20.6
13 Th	7 28 5	22 20 51	11♎46 36	18 39 50	3D28.1	7 44.9	12 42.8	16 20.3	23 2.9	13 26.9	19 28.3	21 43.4	18 19.9
14 F	7 32 2	23 21 58	25 27 3	2♏ 8 32	3 27.5	9 15.5	12 23.4	17 7.7	22 56.8	13 32.4	19 27.2	21 44.7	18 19.1
15 Sa	7 35 59	24 23 5	8♏44 35	15 15 37	3 28.3	10 46.7	12 1.6	17 55.1	22 50.9	13 38.0	19 26.1	21 45.9	18 18.4
16 Su	7 39 55	25 24 12	21 42 2	28 4 16	3R29.4	12 18.3	11 37.7	18 42.5	22 45.1	13 43.7	19 25.0	21 47.2	18 17.6
17 M	7 43 52	26 25 19	4♐22 44	10♐37 50	3 30.0	13 50.5	11 11.6	19 29.8	22 39.4	13 49.5	19 23.8	21 48.4	18 16.7
18 Tu	7 47 48	27 26 25	16 49 59	22 59 31	3 28.9	15 23.2	10 43.6	20 17.2	22 33.9	13 55.3	19 22.5	21 49.6	18 15.9
19 W	7 51 45	28 27 32	29 6 45	5♑11 58	3 25.6	16 56.5	10 13.8	21 4.6	22 28.6	14 1.1	19 21.2	21 50.8	18 15.0
20 Th	7 55 41	29 28 37	11♑15 25	17 17 19	3 19.5	18 30.3	9 42.3	21 52.1	22 23.4	14 7.1	19 19.9	21 51.9	18 14.1
21 F	7 59 38	0♒29 42	23 17 51	29 17 11	3 10.9	20 4.6	9 9.3	22 39.5	22 18.4	14 13.0	19 18.5	21 53.0	18 13.2
22 Sa	8 3 35	1 30 47	5♒15 29	11♒12 55	3 0.1	21 39.6	8 35.1	23 26.9	22 13.6	14 19.1	19 17.0	21 54.0	18 12.2
23 Su	8 7 31	2 31 50	17 9 36	23 5 44	2 47.9	23 15.1	7 59.8	24 14.3	22 9.0	14 25.2	19 15.5	21 55.1	18 11.3
24 M	8 11 28	3 32 53	29 1 31	4♓57 8	2 35.5	24 51.1	7 23.8	25 1.7	22 4.5	14 31.3	19 14.0	21 56.1	18 10.3
25 Tu	8 15 24	4 33 55	10♓52 52	16 49 0	2 23.8	26 27.8	6 47.1	25 49.1	22 0.2	14 37.5	19 12.4	21 57.0	18 9.2
26 W	8 19 21	5 34 56	22 45 51	28 43 50	2 13.9	28 5.1	6 10.2	26 36.5	21 56.1	14 43.8	19 10.8	21 58.0	18 8.2
27 Th	8 23 17	6 35 56	4♈43 20	10♈44 51	2 6.4	29 43.0	5 33.1	27 23.9	21 52.2	14 50.1	19 9.1	21 58.9	18 7.1
28 F	8 27 14	7 36 55	16 48 53	22 55 59	2 1.6	1♒21.5	4 56.3	28 11.3	21 48.5	14 56.4	19 7.4	21 59.8	18 6.0
29 Sa	8 31 10	8 37 52	29 6 44	5♉21 44	1D59.4	3 0.7	4 19.9	28 58.7	21 44.9	15 2.8	19 5.6	22 0.6	18 4.8
30 Su	8 35 7	9 38 49	11♉41 34	18 6 51	1 58.9	4 40.6	3 44.2	29 46.1	21 41.6	15 9.3	19 3.8	22 1.4	18 3.7
31 M	8 39 3	10 39 44	24 38 10	1♊16 0	1R59.3	6 21.1	3 9.5	0♓33.5	21 38.4	15 15.8	19 2.0	22 2.2	18 2.5

LONGITUDE — FEBRUARY 1966

Day	Sid.Time	☉	0 hr ☽	Noon ☽	True ☊	☿	♀	♂	♃	♄	♅	♆	♇
1 Tu	8 43 0	11♒40 38	8♊ 0 48	14♊52 54	1♊59.3	8♒ 2.4	2♒35.9	1♓20.9	21♊35.5	15♓22.3	19♍ 0.1	22♏ 2.9	18♍ 1.3
2 W	8 46 57	12 41 30	21 52 28	28 59 33	1R57.8	9 44.3	2R 3.7	2 8.2	21R32.7	15 28.9	18R58.2	22 3.7	18R 0.1
3 Th	8 50 53	13 42 22	6♋13 55	13♋35 9	1 53.9	11 27.0	1 33.1	2 55.6	21 30.2	15 35.6	18 56.2	22 4.3	17 58.9
4 F	8 54 50	14 43 12	21 2 37	28 35 23	1 47.2	13 10.4	1 4.2	3 42.9	21 27.8	15 42.2	18 54.3	22 5.0	17 57.6
5 Sa	8 58 46	15 44 0	6♌12 20	13♌52 9	1 38.0	14 54.6	0 37.2	4 30.3	21 25.6	15 49.0	18 52.2	22 5.6	17 56.4
6 Su	9 2 43	16 44 48	21 33 22	29 14 29	1 27.2	16 39.4	0 12.4	5 17.6	21 23.7	15 55.7	18 50.2	22 6.2	17 55.1
7 M	9 6 39	17 45 34	6♍53 58	14♍30 23	1 16.1	18 25.0	29♑49.7	6 4.9	21 21.9	16 2.5	18 48.1	22 6.7	17 53.8
8 Tu	9 10 36	18 46 19	22 2 29	29 29 9	1 5.9	20 11.4	29 29.3	6 52.2	21 20.3	16 9.3	18 45.9	22 7.2	17 52.4
9 W	9 14 33	19 47 3	6♎49 32	14♎ 3 2	0 57.9	21 58.4	29 11.2	7 39.5	21 18.9	16 16.2	18 43.8	22 7.7	17 51.1
10 Th	9 18 29	20 47 46	21 9 16	28 8 6	0 52.5	23 46.1	28 55.6	8 26.7	21 17.8	16 23.1	18 41.6	22 8.1	17 49.7
11 F	9 22 26	21 48 28	4♏59 35	11♏43 57	0 49.7	25 34.4	28 42.5	9 14.0	21 16.8	16 30.0	18 39.4	22 8.6	17 48.3
12 Sa	9 26 22	22 49 9	18 21 32	24 52 49	0 48.8	27 23.4	28 31.9	10 1.2	21 16.0	16 37.0	18 37.1	22 8.9	17 46.9
13 Su	9 30 19	23 49 48	1♐18 17	7♐38 32	0 48.8	29 12.9	28 23.8	10 48.4	21 15.5	16 44.0	18 34.8	22 9.3	17 45.5
14 M	9 34 15	24 50 27	13 54 8	20 5 40	0 48.4	1♓ 2.9	28 18.1	11 35.6	21 15.1	16 51.0	18 32.5	22 9.6	17 44.1
15 Tu	9 38 12	25 51 5	26 13 42	2♑18 48	0 46.3	2 53.2	28D15.0	12 22.8	21D14.9	16 58.1	18 30.2	22 9.9	17 42.7
16 W	9 42 8	26 51 41	8♑21 26	14 22 4	0 41.7	4 43.8	28 14.3	13 10.0	21 15.0	17 5.1	18 27.8	22 10.1	17 41.2
17 Th	9 46 5	27 52 16	20 21 9	26 19 1	0 34.1	6 34.5	28 16.1	13 57.2	21 15.2	17 12.3	18 25.5	22 10.3	17 39.7
18 F	9 50 2	28 52 50	2♒16 1	8♒12 24	0 23.4	8 25.2	28 20.2	14 44.3	21 15.7	17 19.4	18 23.1	22 10.5	17 38.2
19 Sa	9 53 58	29 53 22	14 8 25	20 4 18	0 10.2	10 15.6	28 26.6	15 31.4	21 16.3	17 26.5	18 20.6	22 10.6	17 36.8
20 Su	9 57 55	0♓53 53	26 0 11	1♓56 16	29♉55.4	12 5.5	28 35.3	16 18.5	21 17.2	17 33.7	18 18.2	22 10.7	17 35.2
21 M	10 1 51	1 54 22	7♓52 42	13 49 36	29 40.1	13 54.6	28 46.2	17 5.6	21 18.2	17 40.9	18 15.7	22 10.8	17 33.7
22 Tu	10 5 48	2 54 49	19 47 9	25 45 32	29 25.7	15 42.6	28 59.3	17 52.6	21 19.5	17 48.2	18 13.2	22R10.8	17 32.2
23 W	10 9 44	3 55 15	1♈44 56	7♈45 35	29 13.2	17 29.1	29 14.4	18 39.6	21 20.9	17 55.4	18 10.7	22 10.8	17 30.7
24 Th	10 13 41	4 55 39	13 47 46	19 51 47	29 3.4	19 13.7	29 31.6	19 26.6	21 22.5	18 2.7	18 8.2	22 10.8	17 29.1
25 F	10 17 37	5 56 1	25 57 59	2♉ 6 47	28 56.8	20 56.1	29 50.7	20 13.6	21 24.4	18 10.0	18 5.7	22 10.7	17 27.6
26 Sa	10 21 34	6 56 21	8♉18 37	14 33 57	28 53.1	22 35.5	0♒11.7	21 0.6	21 26.4	18 17.2	18 3.1	22 10.6	17 26.0
27 Su	10 25 30	7 56 40	20 53 18	27 17 10	28D51.7	24 11.7	0 34.5	21 47.5	21 28.6	18 24.6	18 0.5	22 10.5	17 24.4
28 M	10 29 27	8 56 56	3♊46 6	10♊20 35	28R51.5	25 43.9	0 59.1	22 34.4	21 31.1	18 31.9	17 58.0	22 10.3	17 22.9

Astro Data

	Dy Hr Mn
♀ R	5 16:21
☽0S	12 20:18
♃⚻♆	25 14:56
☽0N	27 9:13
☽0S	9 3:52
♀ D	15 18:41
♃ D	15 6:57
♄☍♇	20 4:11
♆ R	22 10:42
☽0N	23 14:19
♄☍♅	24 13:30

Planet Ingress

	Dy Hr Mn
☿ ♑	7 18:26
☉ ♒	20 12:20
☿ ♒	27 4:10
♂ ♓	30 7:01
♀ ♑	6 12:46
☿ ♓	13 10:17
☉ ♓	19 2:38
☊ ♉	19 16:40
♀ ♒	25 10:55

Last Aspect / ☽ Ingress (January)

Last Aspect Dy Hr Mn		☽ Ingress Dy Hr Mn
1 7:10	♃ ✶	♉ 1 17:46
3 9:06	♆ ☍	♊ 4 0:06
5 22:19	☿ ☍	♋ 6 2:40
7 13:28	♆ △	♌ 8 2:50
9 16:00	♃ ✶	♍ 10 2:34
11 16:28	♃ □	♎ 12 3:53
13 20:00	☉ □	♏ 14 8:08
16 7:34	☉ ✶	♐ 16 15:39
18 11:05	♃ ☍	♑ 19 1:45
20 21:10	♆ ✶	♒ 21 13:26
23 15:20	♂ ☌	♓ 24 1:58
26 12:24	☿ ✶	♈ 26 14:33
28 23:44	♂ ✶	♉ 29 1:43
30 19:14	♆ ☍	♊ 31 9:43

Last Aspect / ☽ Ingress (February)

Last Aspect Dy Hr Mn		☽ Ingress Dy Hr Mn
1 23:26	♃ ☌	♋ 2 13:41
4 1:40	♆ △	♌ 4 14:14
6 0:51	♆ □	♍ 6 13:11
8 11:45	♀ △	♎ 8 12:50
10 13:10	♀ □	♏ 10 15:15
12 19:26	☿ □	♐ 12 21:33
14 23:12	☉ ✶	♑ 15 7:26
17 16:01	♀ ☌	♒ 17 19:26
19 16:16	♆ □	♓ 20 8:05
22 18:52	♀ ✶	♈ 22 20:30
25 7:48	♀ □	♉ 25 7:53
27 7:05	☿ ✶	♊ 27 17:03

☽ Phases & Eclipses

Dy Hr Mn	
7 5:16	○ 16♋28
13 20:00	☽ 23♎12
21 15:46	● 1♒10
29 19:48	☽ 9♉28
5 15:58	○ 16♌24
12 8:53	☽ 23♏12
20 10:49	● 1♓21
28 10:15	☽ 9♊23

Astro Data

1 JANUARY 1966
Julian Day # 24107
Delta T 36.5 sec
SVP 05♓44'19"
Obliquity 23°26'41"
⚷ Chiron 18♓27.9
☽ Mean ☊ 2♊38.8

1 FEBRUARY 1966
Julian Day # 24138
Delta T 36.6 sec
SVP 05♓44'14"
Obliquity 23°26'42"
⚷ Chiron 19♓44.2
☽ Mean ☊ 1♊00.3

MARCH 1966

LONGITUDE

Day	Sid.Time	☉	0 hr ☽	Noon ☽	True ☊	☿	♀	♂	♃	♄	♅	♆	♇
1 Tu	10 33 24	9♓57 10	17♊ 1 7	23♊48 4	28♉51.4	27♓11.5	1♒25.4	23♓21.2	21♊33.7	18♓39.2	17♍55.4	22♏10.1	17♍21.3
2 W	10 37 20	10 57 23	0♋41 46	7♋42 24	28R50.1	28 34.1	1 53.3	24 8.1	21 36.5	18 46.6	17R52.8	22R 9.9	17R19.7
3 Th	10 41 17	11 57 33	14 49 59	22 4 21	28 46.7	29 51.0	2 22.8	24 54.8	21 39.5	18 53.9	17 50.2	22 9.6	17 18.1
4 F	10 45 13	12 57 41	29 25 8	6♌51 42	28 40.6	1♈ 1.5	2 53.8	25 41.6	21 42.7	19 1.3	17 47.6	22 9.3	17 16.6
5 Sa	10 49 10	13 57 47	14♌23 14	21 58 40	28 32.0	2 5.2	3 26.3	26 28.3	21 46.0	19 8.7	17 45.0	22 9.0	17 15.0
6 Su	10 53 6	14 57 51	29 36 45	7♍16 6	28 21.8	3 1.6	4 0.2	27 15.0	21 49.6	19 16.1	17 42.4	22 8.6	17 13.4
7 M	10 57 3	15 57 53	14♍55 16	22 32 47	28 10.9	3 50.1	4 35.5	28 1.7	21 53.3	19 23.4	17 39.7	22 8.2	17 11.8
8 Tu	11 0 59	16 57 54	0♎ 7 15	7♎37 24	28 0.9	4 30.4	5 12.1	28 48.3	21 57.2	19 30.8	17 37.1	22 7.8	17 10.2
9 W	11 4 56	17 57 52	15 2 10	22 20 39	27 52.8	5 2.1	5 49.9	29 34.9	22 1.3	19 38.2	17 34.5	22 7.3	17 8.6
10 Th	11 8 53	18 57 48	29 32 14	6♏36 30	27 47.3	5 25.1	6 28.9	0♈21.5	22 5.6	19 45.6	17 31.9	22 6.8	17 7.0
11 F	11 12 49	19 57 43	13♏33 17	20 22 36	27 44.4	5 39.2	7 9.2	1 8.0	22 10.0	19 53.0	17 29.3	22 6.3	17 5.4
12 Sa	11 16 46	20 57 37	27 4 39	3♐39 45	27D43.6	5R44.5	7 50.5	1 54.5	22 14.6	20 0.4	17 26.6	22 5.7	17 3.8
13 Su	11 20 42	21 57 28	10♐ 8 22	16 31 0	27 43.9	5 41.0	8 32.9	2 41.0	22 19.4	20 7.8	17 24.0	22 5.2	17 2.2
14 M	11 24 39	22 57 18	22 48 15	29 0 44	27R44.3	5 29.0	9 16.3	3 27.4	22 24.4	20 15.2	17 21.4	22 4.5	17 0.6
15 Tu	11 28 35	23 57 7	5♑ 9 4	11♑13 52	27 43.6	5 8.9	10 0.7	4 13.8	22 29.5	20 22.6	17 18.8	22 3.9	16 59.0
16 W	11 32 32	24 56 53	17 15 46	23 15 19	27 41.0	4 41.3	10 46.1	5 0.2	22 34.8	20 30.0	17 16.2	22 3.2	16 57.5
17 Th	11 36 28	25 56 38	29 13 6	5♒ 9 36	27 35.9	4 6.9	11 32.4	5 46.5	22 40.3	20 37.4	17 13.6	22 2.5	16 55.9
18 F	11 40 25	26 56 21	11♒ 5 18	17 0 36	27 28.4	3 26.5	12 19.5	6 32.8	22 45.9	20 44.8	17 11.0	22 1.8	16 54.3
19 Sa	11 44 22	27 56 3	22 55 54	28 51 31	27 18.7	2 41.1	13 7.5	7 19.0	22 51.7	20 52.1	17 8.5	22 1.0	16 52.7
20 Su	11 48 18	28 55 42	4♓47 43	10♓44 47	27 7.6	1 51.8	13 56.2	8 5.3	22 57.7	20 59.5	17 5.9	22 0.2	16 51.2
21 M	11 52 15	29 55 20	16 42 54	22 42 15	26 56.0	0 59.6	14 45.8	8 51.4	23 3.8	21 6.8	17 3.4	21 59.4	16 49.6
22 Tu	11 56 11	0♈54 55	28 43 0	4♈45 17	26 45.0	0 5.8	15 36.0	9 37.6	23 10.0	21 14.2	17 0.8	21 58.5	16 48.1
23 W	12 0 8	1 54 28	10♈49 16	16 55 4	26 35.6	29♓11.5	16 27.0	10 23.7	23 16.5	21 21.5	16 58.3	21 57.7	16 46.5
24 Th	12 4 4	2 54 0	23 2 51	29 12 46	26 28.3	28 17.8	17 18.6	11 9.7	23 23.0	21 28.8	16 55.8	21 56.7	16 45.0
25 F	12 8 1	3 53 29	5♉25 1	11♉39 49	26 23.6	27 25.9	18 10.9	11 55.7	23 29.8	21 36.1	16 53.3	21 55.8	16 43.5
26 Sa	12 11 57	4 52 56	17 57 25	24 18 5	26D21.4	26 36.5	19 3.8	12 41.7	23 36.6	21 43.4	16 50.9	21 54.8	16 42.0
27 Su	12 15 54	5 52 21	0♊42 7	7♊ 9 50	26 21.1	25 50.7	19 57.3	13 27.6	23 43.7	21 50.7	16 48.4	21 53.9	16 40.5
28 M	12 19 51	6 51 44	13 41 34	20 17 40	26 22.0	25 8.9	20 51.4	14 13.5	23 50.9	21 57.9	16 46.0	21 52.8	16 39.0
29 Tu	12 23 47	7 51 5	26 58 27	3♋44 11	26R23.1	24 31.9	21 46.1	14 59.3	23 58.2	22 5.1	16 43.6	21 51.8	16 37.5
30 W	12 27 44	8 50 23	10♋35 7	17 31 24	26 23.6	24 0.0	22 41.3	15 45.1	24 5.6	22 12.4	16 41.2	21 50.7	16 36.1
31 Th	12 31 40	9 49 39	24 33 6	1♌40 9	26 22.5	23 33.6	23 37.0	16 30.9	24 13.2	22 19.5	16 38.9	21 49.7	16 34.6

APRIL 1966

LONGITUDE

Day	Sid.Time	☉	0 hr ☽	Noon ☽	True ☊	☿	♀	♂	♃	♄	♅	♆	♇
1 F	12 35 37	10♈48 52	8♌52 21	16♌ 9 18	26♉19.5	23♓12.7	24♒33.2	17♈16.6	24♊21.0	22♓26.7	16♍36.6	21♏48.6	16♍33.2
2 Sa	12 39 33	11 48 3	23 30 29	0♍55 11	26R14.9	22R57.6	25 29.8	18 2.2	24 28.9	22 33.9	16R34.3	21R47.4	16R31.8
3 Su	12 43 30	12 47 12	8♍22 33	15 51 34	26 8.8	22 48.1	26 27.0	18 47.9	24 36.9	22 41.0	16 32.0	21 46.3	16 30.4
4 M	12 47 26	13 46 19	23 21 8	0♎50 8	26 2.3	22D44.3	27 24.6	19 33.4	24 45.0	22 48.1	16 29.7	21 45.1	16 29.0
5 Tu	12 51 23	14 45 23	8♎17 24	15 41 49	25 56.1	22 46.0	28 22.6	20 18.9	24 53.3	22 55.1	16 27.5	21 43.9	16 27.6
6 W	12 55 20	15 44 25	23 2 22	0♏18 11	25 51.2	22 53.2	29 21.1	21 4.4	25 1.7	23 2.2	16 25.3	21 42.7	16 26.3
7 Th	12 59 16	16 43 25	7♏28 30	14 32 47	25 48.0	23 5.5	0♓19.9	21 49.8	25 10.2	23 9.2	16 23.2	21 41.4	16 24.9
8 F	13 3 13	17 42 24	21 30 39	28 21 54	25D46.6	23 22.8	1 19.2	22 35.2	25 18.8	23 16.1	16 21.0	21 40.1	16 23.6
9 Sa	13 7 9	18 41 20	5♐ 6 28	11♐44 30	25 46.9	23 44.9	2 18.8	23 20.5	25 27.6	23 23.1	16 18.9	21 38.9	16 22.3
10 Su	13 11 6	19 40 15	18 16 13	24 41 57	25 48.2	24 11.7	3 18.9	24 5.8	25 36.5	23 30.0	16 16.9	21 37.6	16 21.0
11 M	13 15 2	20 39 8	1♑ 2 10	7♑17 20	25 49.8	24 42.7	4 19.2	24 51.0	25 45.5	23 36.9	16 14.9	21 36.2	16 19.8
12 Tu	13 18 59	21 38 0	13 28 1	19 34 48	25R51.0	25 18.0	5 19.9	25 36.2	25 54.6	23 43.8	16 12.9	21 34.9	16 18.5
13 W	13 22 55	22 36 50	25 38 15	1♒39 1	25 51.3	25 57.2	6 21.0	26 21.4	26 3.9	23 50.6	16 10.9	21 33.5	16 17.3
14 Th	13 26 52	23 35 37	7♒37 39	13 34 46	25 50.3	26 40.1	7 22.3	27 6.5	26 13.2	23 57.4	16 9.0	21 32.2	16 16.1
15 F	13 30 49	24 34 24	19 30 55	25 26 38	25 47.8	27 26.6	8 24.0	27 51.5	26 22.7	24 4.1	16 7.1	21 30.8	16 14.9
16 Sa	13 34 45	25 33 8	1♓22 25	7♓18 43	25 44.0	28 16.6	9 26.0	28 36.5	26 32.3	24 10.8	16 5.2	21 29.3	16 13.7
17 Su	13 38 42	26 31 51	13 15 59	19 14 34	25 39.4	29 9.7	10 28.2	29 21.5	26 42.0	24 17.5	16 3.4	21 27.9	16 12.6
18 M	13 42 38	27 30 31	25 14 50	1♈17 4	25 34.4	0♈ 5.9	11 30.7	0♉ 6.4	26 51.7	24 24.1	16 1.7	21 26.5	16 11.5
19 Tu	13 46 35	28 29 10	7♈21 31	13 28 23	25 29.6	1 5.1	12 33.5	0 51.3	27 1.6	24 30.7	15 59.9	21 25.0	16 10.4
20 W	13 50 31	29 27 48	19 37 52	25 50 5	25 25.6	2 7.1	13 36.6	1 36.1	27 11.6	24 37.2	15 58.2	21 23.5	16 9.3
21 Th	13 54 28	0♉26 23	2♉ 5 10	8♉23 11	25 22.6	3 11.8	14 39.8	2 20.8	27 21.8	24 43.7	15 56.6	21 22.0	16 8.2
22 F	13 58 24	1 24 56	14 44 14	21 8 22	25D21.0	4 19.0	15 43.4	3 5.5	27 32.0	24 50.2	15 55.0	21 20.5	16 7.2
23 Sa	14 2 21	2 23 28	27 35 38	4♊ 6 5	25 20.6	5 28.8	16 47.1	3 50.2	27 42.3	24 56.6	15 53.4	21 19.0	16 6.2
24 Su	14 6 17	3 21 57	10♊39 47	17 16 45	25 21.2	6 40.9	17 51.1	4 34.8	27 52.7	25 3.0	15 51.9	21 17.5	16 5.2
25 M	14 10 14	4 20 25	23 57 3	0♋40 44	25 22.5	7 55.4	18 55.2	5 19.4	28 3.2	25 9.3	15 50.4	21 16.0	16 4.2
26 Tu	14 14 11	5 18 50	7♋27 50	14 18 22	25 23.9	9 12.1	19 59.6	6 3.9	28 13.8	25 15.6	15 49.0	21 14.4	16 3.3
27 W	14 18 7	6 17 14	21 12 20	28 9 42	25 25.1	10 31.0	21 4.2	6 48.4	28 24.4	25 21.8	15 47.6	21 12.9	16 2.4
28 Th	14 22 4	7 15 35	5♌10 23	12♌14 15	25R25.6	11 52.1	22 9.0	7 32.8	28 35.2	25 28.0	15 46.3	21 11.3	16 1.5
29 F	14 26 0	8 13 54	19 21 4	26 30 35	25 25.3	13 15.2	23 14.0	8 17.1	28 46.1	25 34.1	15 45.0	21 9.7	16 0.7
30 Sa	14 29 57	9 12 11	3♍42 25	10♍56 8	25 24.3	14 40.4	24 19.1	9 1.4	28 57.0	25 40.2	15 43.8	21 8.2	15 59.9

Astro Data Dy Hr Mn	Planet Ingress Dy Hr Mn	Last Aspect Dy Hr Mn	☽ Ingress Dy Hr Mn	Last Aspect Dy Hr Mn	☽ Ingress Dy Hr Mn	☽ Phases & Eclipses Dy Hr Mn
☿0N 1 12:30	☿ ♈ 3 2:57	1 19:55 ☿ □	♋ 1 22:48	2 3:27 ♀ ☍	♍ 2 10:31	7 1:45 ○ 16♍02
☽0S 8 13:57	♂ ♈ 9 12:55	3 17:36 ♂ △	♌ 4 0:57	4 2:16 ♃ □	♎ 4 10:40	14 0:19 ☽ 22♐58
♃⚻♆ 10 6:05	☉ ♈ 21 1:53	5 12:16 ♆ □	♍ 6 0:36	6 11:11 ♀ △	♏ 6 11:30	22 4:46 ● 1♈07
♂0N 11 15:08	☿ ♓ 22 2:34	7 21:48 ♂ ☍	♎ 7 23:48	8 3:20 ☿ △	♐ 8 14:54	29 20:43 ☽ 8♋42
☿ R 12 2:18		9 11:32 ♃ △	♏ 10 0:47	10 13:52 ♃ ☍	♑ 10 22:02	
☽0N 22 19:54	♀ ♓ 6 15:53	11 15:04 ♆ ☌	♐ 12 5:18	13 1:32 ♂ □	♒ 13 8:42	5 11:13 ○ 15♎13
☿0S 27 19:26	☿ ♈ 17 21:31	14 0:19 ☉ □	♑ 14 13:55	15 18:02 ♂ ⚹	♓ 15 21:13	12 17:28 ☽ 22♑21
♄△♆ 27 9:17	♂ ♉ 17 20:35	16 16:48 ☉ ⚹	♒ 17 1:35	18 3:16 ♃ □	♈ 18 9:27	20 20:35 ● 0♉18
	☉ ♉ 20 13:12	18 23:51 ♃ △	♓ 19 14:19	20 14:49 ♃ ⚹	♉ 20 20:00	28 3:49 ☽ 7♌25
♅☌♇ 4 20:43		21 12:50 ♃ □	♈ 22 2:33	22 19:03 ♄ ⚹	♊ 23 4:27	
☿ D 4 4:25		24 0:40 ♃ ⚹	♉ 24 13:32	25 7:25 ♃ ☌	♋ 25 10:48	
☽0S 5 0:46		26 15:24 ☿ ⚹	♊ 26 22:41	27 7:14 ♄ △	♌ 27 15:09	
☽0N 19 2:50		28 19:49 ☿ □	♋ 29 5:23	29 15:58 ♃ ⚹	♍ 29 17:50	
☿0N 23 16:40		30 22:22 ☿ △	♌ 31 9:12			

Astro Data

1 MARCH 1966
Julian Day # 24166
Delta T 36.7 sec
SVP 05♓44'10"
Obliquity 23°26'42"
⚷ Chiron 21♓18.4
☽ Mean ☊ 29♉31.3

1 APRIL 1966
Julian Day # 24197
Delta T 36.8 sec
SVP 05♓44'06"
Obliquity 23°26'43"
⚷ Chiron 23♓10.3
☽ Mean ☊ 27♉52.8

LONGITUDE — MAY 1966

Day	Sid.Time	☉	0 hr ☽	Noon ☽	True ☊	☿	♀	♂	♃	♄	♅	♆	♇
1 Su	14 33 53	10♉10 26	18♍11 11	25♍27 0	25♉22.7	16♈ 7.6	25♓24.4	9♉45.6	29♊ 8.0	25♓46.2	15♍42.6	21♏ 6.6	15♍59.1
2 M	14 37 50	11 8 39	2♎42 53	9♎58 10	25R 20.9	17 36.7	26 29.9	10 29.8	29 19.1	25 52.1	15R 41.4	21R 5.0	15R 58.3
3 Tu	14 41 46	12 6 50	17 12 6	24 23 59	25 19.2	19 7.9	27 35.6	11 13.9	29 30.3	25 58.0	15 40.3	21 3.4	15 57.5
4 W	14 45 43	13 4 59	1♏33 7	8♏38 52	25 18.0	20 41.0	28 41.4	11 58.0	29 41.6	26 3.9	15 39.3	21 1.8	15 56.8
5 Th	14 49 40	14 3 6	15 40 37	22 37 55	25D 17.3	22 16.0	29 47.5	12 42.1	29 52.9	26 9.6	15 38.3	21 0.2	15 56.1
6 F	14 53 36	15 1 11	29 30 22	6♐17 40	25 17.2	23 53.0	0♈53.6	13 26.0	0♋ 4.4	26 15.4	15 37.3	20 58.5	15 55.5
7 Sa	14 57 33	15 59 16	12♐59 40	19 36 17	25 17.5	25 32.0	1 59.9	14 10.0	0 15.9	26 21.0	15 36.4	20 56.9	15 54.8
8 Su	15 1 29	16 57 18	26 7 34	2♑33 39	25 18.2	27 12.8	3 6.4	14 53.8	0 27.4	26 26.7	15 35.6	20 55.3	15 54.2
9 M	15 5 26	17 55 19	8♑54 46	15 11 14	25 19.0	28 55.6	4 13.0	15 37.7	0 39.1	26 32.2	15 34.8	20 53.7	15 53.7
10 Tu	15 9 22	18 53 19	21 23 26	27 31 47	25 19.7	0♉40.3	5 19.8	16 21.4	0 50.8	26 37.7	15 34.0	20 52.1	15 53.1
11 W	15 13 19	19 51 18	3♒36 47	9♒38 58	25 20.1	2 27.0	6 26.7	17 5.2	1 2.6	26 43.1	15 33.3	20 50.4	15 52.6
12 Th	15 17 16	20 49 15	15 38 51	21 37 0	25R 20.4	4 15.6	7 33.8	17 48.8	1 14.4	26 48.5	15 32.7	20 48.8	15 52.1
13 F	15 21 12	21 47 10	27 34 2	3♓30 29	25 20.4	6 6.2	8 40.9	18 32.5	1 26.3	26 53.8	15 32.1	20 47.2	15 51.6
14 Sa	15 25 9	22 45 5	9♓26 57	15 23 58	25 20.2	7 58.7	9 48.2	19 16.0	1 38.3	26 59.0	15 31.6	20 45.5	15 51.2
15 Su	15 29 5	23 42 58	21 22 6	27 21 51	25 20.1	9 53.1	10 55.6	19 59.5	1 50.3	27 4.2	15 31.1	20 43.9	15 50.8
16 M	15 33 2	24 40 50	3♈23 41	9♈28 5	25D 19.9	11 49.4	12 3.2	20 43.0	2 2.5	27 9.3	15 30.6	20 42.3	15 50.4
17 Tu	15 36 58	25 38 40	15 35 24	21 46 1	25 19.9	13 47.7	13 10.8	21 26.4	2 14.6	27 14.3	15 30.2	20 40.6	15 50.1
18 W	15 40 55	26 36 30	28 0 13	4♉18 15	25 20.0	15 47.7	14 18.6	22 9.8	2 26.8	27 19.3	15 29.9	20 39.0	15 49.8
19 Th	15 44 51	27 34 18	10♉40 17	17 6 27	25 20.1	17 49.6	15 26.5	22 53.1	2 39.1	27 24.1	15 29.6	20 37.4	15 49.5
20 F	15 48 48	28 32 5	23 36 46	0♊11 14	25R 20.2	19 53.2	16 34.4	23 36.4	2 51.5	27 29.0	15 29.4	20 35.8	15 49.3
21 Sa	15 52 44	29 29 51	6♊49 47	13 32 17	25 20.1	21 58.4	17 42.5	24 19.6	3 3.9	27 33.7	15 29.2	20 34.2	15 49.0
22 Su	15 56 41	0♊27 35	20 18 32	27 8 18	25 19.8	24 5.1	18 50.7	25 2.7	3 16.3	27 38.4	15 29.1	20 32.6	15 48.9
23 M	16 0 38	1 25 18	4♋ 1 19	10♋57 17	25 19.3	26 13.2	19 59.0	25 45.9	3 28.8	27 43.0	15D 29.0	20 31.0	15 48.7
24 Tu	16 4 34	2 22 59	17 55 51	24 56 42	25 18.5	28 22.5	21 7.3	26 28.9	3 41.4	27 47.5	15 29.0	20 29.4	15 48.6
25 W	16 8 31	3 20 39	1♌59 27	9♌ 3 46	25 17.7	0♊32.7	22 15.8	27 11.9	3 54.0	27 51.9	15 29.1	20 27.8	15 48.5
26 Th	16 12 27	4 18 18	16 9 17	23 15 40	25 17.0	2 43.8	23 24.3	27 54.8	4 6.6	27 56.3	15 29.2	20 26.2	15 48.4
27 F	16 16 24	5 15 55	0♍22 35	7♍29 43	25D 16.6	4 55.4	24 32.9	28 37.7	4 19.3	28 0.6	15 29.3	20 24.7	15D 48.4
28 Sa	16 20 20	6 13 30	14 36 44	21 43 19	25 16.7	7 7.3	25 41.6	29 20.6	4 32.1	28 4.8	15 29.5	20 23.1	15 48.4
29 Su	16 24 17	7 11 4	28 49 11	5♎54 2	25 17.2	9 19.2	26 50.4	0♊ 3.3	4 44.9	28 8.9	15 29.8	20 21.6	15 48.4
30 M	16 28 14	8 8 36	12♎57 32	19 59 25	25 18.1	11 30.9	27 59.3	0 46.1	4 57.7	28 12.9	15 30.1	20 20.0	15 48.5
31 Tu	16 32 10	9 6 7	26 59 20	3♏57 2	25 19.1	13 42.1	29 8.2	1 28.7	5 10.6	28 16.9	15 30.4	20 18.5	15 48.6

LONGITUDE — JUNE 1966

Day	Sid.Time	☉	0 hr ☽	Noon ☽	True ☊	☿	♀	♂	♃	♄	♅	♆	♇
1 W	16 36 7	10♊ 3 37	10♏52 10	17♏44 29	25♉20.0	15♊52.4	0♉17.2	2♊11.4	5♋23.5	28♓20.8	15♍30.8	20♏17.0	15♍48.7
2 Th	16 40 3	11 1 6	24 33 41	1♐19 32	25R 20.4	18 1.7	1 26.4	2 53.9	5 36.4	28 24.6	15 31.3	20R 15.5	15 48.9
3 F	16 44 0	11 58 33	8♐ 1 47	14 40 15	25 20.0	20 9.7	2 35.5	3 36.4	5 49.4	28 28.3	15 31.8	20 14.0	15 49.1
4 Sa	16 47 56	12 56 0	21 14 48	27 45 20	25 18.8	22 16.2	3 44.8	4 18.9	6 2.4	28 31.9	15 32.4	20 12.5	15 49.3
5 Su	16 51 53	13 53 26	4♑11 49	10♑34 16	25 16.7	24 21.0	4 54.1	5 1.3	6 15.5	28 35.5	15 33.0	20 11.0	15 49.5
6 M	16 55 49	14 50 51	16 52 46	23 7 29	25 14.0	26 23.9	6 3.6	5 43.7	6 28.6	28 38.9	15 33.7	20 9.6	15 49.8
7 Tu	16 59 46	15 48 15	29 18 36	5♒26 23	25 10.9	28 24.9	7 13.0	6 26.0	6 41.7	28 42.3	15 34.5	20 8.2	15 50.1
8 W	17 3 43	16 45 38	11♒31 12	17 33 25	25 7.9	0♋23.7	8 22.6	7 8.2	6 54.8	28 45.6	15 35.3	20 6.7	15 50.5
9 Th	17 7 39	17 43 1	23 33 28	29 31 49	25 5.4	2 20.3	9 32.2	7 50.4	7 8.0	28 48.8	15 36.1	20 5.3	15 50.9
10 F	17 11 36	18 40 23	5♓28 59	11♓25 31	25 3.6	4 14.5	10 42.0	8 32.6	7 21.2	28 51.9	15 37.0	20 3.9	15 51.3
11 Sa	17 15 32	19 37 45	17 21 59	23 18 58	25D 2.9	6 6.5	11 51.7	9 14.7	7 34.5	28 55.0	15 37.9	20 2.6	15 51.7
12 Su	17 19 29	20 35 6	29 17 4	5♈16 52	25 3.2	7 56.0	13 1.6	9 56.7	7 47.7	28 57.9	15 38.9	20 1.2	15 52.2
13 M	17 23 25	21 32 26	11♈18 58	17 23 56	25 4.3	9 43.1	14 11.5	10 38.8	8 1.0	29 0.7	15 40.0	19 59.9	15 52.7
14 Tu	17 27 22	22 29 47	23 32 19	29 44 38	25 5.9	11 27.7	15 21.4	11 20.7	8 14.3	29 3.5	15 41.1	19 58.5	15 53.2
15 W	17 31 18	23 27 6	6♉ 1 20	12♉22 48	25 7.5	13 9.8	16 31.5	12 2.6	8 27.7	29 6.1	15 42.2	19 57.2	15 53.8
16 Th	17 35 15	24 24 26	18 49 24	25 21 19	25R 8.5	14 49.5	17 41.6	12 44.5	8 41.0	29 8.7	15 43.4	19 56.0	15 54.4
17 F	17 39 12	25 21 45	1♊58 44	8♊41 40	25 8.5	16 26.6	18 51.7	13 26.3	8 54.4	29 11.2	15 44.7	19 54.7	15 55.0
18 Sa	17 43 8	26 19 4	15 30 1	22 23 36	25 7.0	18 1.2	20 2.0	14 8.0	9 7.8	29 13.6	15 46.0	19 53.4	15 55.6
19 Su	17 47 5	27 16 22	29 22 3	6♋24 55	25 4.2	19 33.2	21 12.2	14 49.8	9 21.3	29 15.8	15 47.3	19 52.2	15 56.3
20 M	17 51 1	28 13 39	13♋31 41	20 41 40	25 0.0	21 2.7	22 22.6	15 31.4	9 34.7	29 18.0	15 48.7	19 51.0	15 57.0
21 Tu	17 54 58	29 10 57	27 54 10	5♌ 8 27	24 55.1	22 29.5	23 33.0	16 13.0	9 48.2	29 20.1	15 50.2	19 49.9	15 57.8
22 W	17 58 54	0♋ 8 13	12♌23 43	19 39 15	24 50.1	23 53.8	24 43.4	16 54.6	10 1.7	29 22.1	15 51.7	19 48.7	15 58.6
23 Th	18 2 51	1 5 29	26 54 20	4♍ 8 18	24 45.7	25 15.3	25 53.9	17 36.1	10 15.1	29 24.0	15 53.2	19 47.6	15 59.4
24 F	18 6 47	2 2 44	11♍20 38	18 30 49	24 42.6	26 34.2	27 4.4	18 17.5	10 28.6	29 25.8	15 54.8	19 46.5	16 0.2
25 Sa	18 10 44	2 59 58	25 38 30	2♎43 24	24D 41.0	27 50.4	28 15.0	18 58.9	10 42.1	29 27.5	15 56.5	19 45.4	16 1.1
26 Su	18 14 41	3 57 12	9♎45 18	16 44 5	24 40.9	29 3.7	29 25.6	19 40.3	10 55.7	29 29.1	15 58.2	19 44.3	16 1.9
27 M	18 18 37	4 54 25	23 39 41	0♏32 6	24 41.9	0♌14.2	0♊36.3	20 21.6	11 9.2	29 30.6	15 59.9	19 43.3	16 2.9
28 Tu	18 22 34	5 51 38	7♏21 19	14 7 23	24 43.2	1 21.8	1 47.1	21 2.8	11 22.7	29 32.0	16 1.7	19 42.2	16 3.8
29 W	18 26 30	6 48 50	20 50 21	27 30 15	24R 44.1	2 26.3	2 57.9	21 44.0	11 36.3	29 33.3	16 3.5	19 41.2	16 4.8
30 Th	18 30 27	7 46 2	4♐ 7 7	10♐40 59	24 43.8	3 27.8	4 8.7	22 25.1	11 49.8	29 34.5	16 5.4	19 40.3	16 5.8

Astro Data	Planet Ingress	Last Aspect	☽ Ingress	Last Aspect	☽ Ingress	☽ Phases & Eclipses	Astro Data
Dy Hr Mn	Dy Hr Mn	Dy Hr Mn	Dy Hr Mn	Dy Hr Mn	Dy Hr Mn	Dy Hr Mn	1 MAY 1966
☽0S 2 10:09	♀ ♈ 5 4:33	1 18:19 ♃ □	♎ 1 19:31	2 6:51 ♄ △	♐ 2 9:38	4 21:00 ○ 13♏56	Julian Day # 24227
♀0N 8 5:15	♃ ♋ 5 14:52	3 20:50 ♃ △	♏ 3 21:23	4 13:30 ♄ □	♑ 4 16:10	4 21:11 ◐ A 0.916	Delta T 36.8 sec
☽0N 16 10:51	☿ ♉ 9 14:48	5 18:16 ♄ △	♐ 6 0:52	6 22:49 ♄ ✶	♒ 7 1:21	12 11:19 ☽ 21♒17	SVP 05♓44'03"
♅ D 23 16:37	☉ ♊ 21 12:32	8 2:19 ☿ △	♑ 8 7:12	8 17:04 ♆ □	♓ 9 12:57	20 9:42 ● 28♉55	Obliquity 23°26'43"
♇ D 27 11:12	☿ ♊ 24 17:59	10 10:18 ♄ ✶	♒ 10 16:52	11 23:21 ♄ ☌	♈ 12 1:26	20 9:38:24 ◐ A 0'04"	⚷ Chiron 24♓45.9
☽0S 29 17:02	♂ ♊ 28 22:07	12 11:19 ☉ □	♓ 13 4:55	13 21:48 ☉ ✶	♉ 14 12:30	27 8:50 ☽ 5♍37	☽ Mean ☊ 26♉17.5
♃□♆ 31 13:11	♀ ♉ 31 18:00	15 11:30 ♄ ☌	♈ 15 17:15	16 18:57 ♄ ✶	♊ 16 20:26		
		16 18:49 ♀ ☌	♉ 18 3:49	18 23:49 ♄ □	♋ 19 1:05	3 7:40 ○ 12♐17	1 JUNE 1966
☽0N 12 18:58	☿ ♋ 7 19:11	20 9:42 ☉ ☌	♊ 20 11:40	21 2:23 ♄ △	♌ 21 3:29	11 4:58 ☽ 19♓50	Julian Day # 24258
☽0S 25 22:07	☉ ♋ 21 20:33	22 12:57 ♄ □	♋ 22 17:00	22 22:11 ♀ □	♍ 23 5:08	18 20:09 ● 27♊07	Delta T 36.9 sec
♅☌♇ 30 9:48	☿ ♌ 26 19:05	24 16:57 ♄ △	♌ 24 20:37	25 6:28 ♄ ☍	♎ 25 7:23	25 13:22 ☽ 3♎32	SVP 05♓43'58"
	♀ ♊ 26 11:40	26 20:54 ♂ □	♍ 26 23:22	26 17:58 ♂ △	♏ 27 11:04		Obliquity 23°26'42"
		28 22:51 ♄ ☍	♎ 29 2:00	29 15:44 ♄ △	♐ 29 16:31		⚷ Chiron 25♓52.8
		31 4:02 ♀ ☍	♏ 31 5:11				☽ Mean ☊ 24♉39.0

JULY 1966 LONGITUDE

Day	Sid.Time	☉	0 hr ☽	Noon ☽	True ☊	☿	♀	♂	♃	♄	♅	♆	♇
1 F	18 34 23	8♋43 14	17♐11 52	23♐39 46	24♉41.7	4♌26.1	5♊19.6	23♊ 6.2	12♋ 3.4	29♓35.7	16♍ 7.4	19♏39.3	16♍ 6.8
2 Sa	18 38 20	9 40 25	0♑ 4 41	6♑26 37	24R 37.5	5 21.2	6 30.6	23 47.3	12 16.9	29 36.7	16 9.3	19R 38.4	16 7.9
3 Su	18 42 17	10 37 36	12 45 35	19 1 36	24 31.3	6 12.9	7 41.6	24 28.3	12 30.5	29 37.6	16 11.4	19 37.5	16 9.0
4 M	18 46 13	11 34 48	25 14 44	1♒25 2	24 23.5	7 1.1	8 52.6	25 9.2	12 44.0	29 38.4	16 13.4	19 36.7	16 10.1
5 Tu	18 50 10	12 31 59	7♒32 38	13 37 41	24 14.9	7 45.6	10 3.7	25 50.1	12 57.6	29 39.1	16 15.5	19 35.8	16 11.2
6 W	18 54 6	13 29 10	19 40 24	25 41 1	24 6.2	8 26.5	11 14.9	26 31.0	13 11.1	29 39.7	16 17.7	19 35.0	16 12.4
7 Th	18 58 3	14 26 21	1♓39 51	7♓37 15	23 58.4	9 3.5	12 26.1	27 11.8	13 24.7	29 40.2	16 19.9	19 34.3	16 13.6
8 F	19 1 59	15 23 33	13 33 38	19 29 27	23 52.0	9 36.5	13 37.4	27 52.5	13 38.3	29 40.6	16 22.1	19 33.5	16 14.8
9 Sa	19 5 56	16 20 45	25 25 11	1♈21 24	23 47.6	10 5.4	14 48.7	28 33.2	13 51.8	29 40.9	16 24.4	19 32.8	16 16.1
10 Su	19 9 52	17 17 57	7♈18 40	13 17 35	23D 45.2	10 30.1	16 0.1	29 13.9	14 5.3	29 41.2	16 26.7	19 32.1	16 17.3
11 M	19 13 49	18 15 10	19 18 46	25 22 52	23 44.6	10 50.3	17 11.5	29 54.5	14 18.9	29R 41.3	16 29.1	19 31.4	16 18.6
12 Tu	19 17 46	19 12 23	1♉30 31	7♉42 20	23 45.2	11 6.0	18 23.0	0♋35.1	14 32.4	29 41.3	16 31.5	19 30.8	16 19.9
13 W	19 21 42	20 9 37	13 58 55	20 20 49	23R 46.1	11 17.2	19 34.5	1 15.6	14 45.9	29 41.2	16 33.9	19 30.1	16 21.3
14 Th	19 25 39	21 6 51	26 48 33	3♊22 29	23 46.4	11R 23.6	20 46.1	1 56.1	14 59.5	29 41.0	16 36.4	19 29.6	16 22.7
15 F	19 29 35	22 4 6	10♊ 2 58	16 50 8	23 45.1	11 25.3	21 57.7	2 36.5	15 13.0	29 40.7	16 38.9	19 29.0	16 24.1
16 Sa	19 33 32	23 1 22	23 44 2	0♋44 31	23 41.8	11 22.1	23 9.4	3 16.9	15 26.5	29 40.3	16 41.5	19 28.5	16 25.5
17 Su	19 37 28	23 58 38	7♋51 16	15 3 47	23 36.1	11 14.1	24 21.1	3 57.3	15 39.9	29 39.8	16 44.1	19 28.0	16 26.9
18 M	19 41 25	24 55 54	22 21 20	29 43 6	23 28.4	11 1.3	25 32.9	4 37.6	15 53.4	29 39.2	16 46.7	19 27.5	16 28.4
19 Tu	19 45 21	25 53 11	7♌ 8 5	14♌35 10	23 19.3	10 43.9	26 44.7	5 17.8	16 6.9	29 38.5	16 49.4	19 27.1	16 29.9
20 W	19 49 18	26 50 29	22 3 14	29 31 8	23 10.0	10 22.0	27 56.6	5 58.0	16 20.3	29 37.7	16 52.1	19 26.7	16 31.4
21 Th	19 53 15	27 47 46	6♍57 45	14♍22 7	23 1.5	9 55.7	29 8.5	6 38.1	16 33.7	29 36.8	16 54.9	19 26.3	16 32.9
22 F	19 57 11	28 45 4	21 43 22	29 0 46	22 54.9	9 25.4	0♋20.4	7 18.2	16 47.1	29 35.8	16 57.7	19 26.0	16 34.5
23 Sa	20 1 8	29 42 22	6♎13 47	13♎22 2	22 50.6	8 51.6	1 32.4	7 58.3	17 0.5	29 34.7	17 0.5	19 25.7	16 36.1
24 Su	20 5 4	0♌39 40	20 25 19	27 23 32	22D 48.6	8 14.5	2 44.4	8 38.3	17 13.8	29 33.5	17 3.4	19 25.4	16 37.7
25 M	20 9 1	1 36 59	4♏16 45	11♏ 5 5	22 48.2	7 34.9	3 56.5	9 18.3	17 27.2	29 32.2	17 6.2	19 25.2	16 39.3
26 Tu	20 12 57	2 34 18	17 48 45	24 28 1	22R 48.6	6 53.2	5 8.7	9 58.2	17 40.5	29 30.8	17 9.2	19 25.0	16 40.9
27 W	20 16 54	3 31 37	1♐ 3 9	7♐34 27	22 48.4	6 10.2	6 20.8	10 38.0	17 53.7	29 29.3	17 12.1	19 24.8	16 42.6
28 Th	20 20 50	4 28 57	14 2 12	20 26 40	22 46.6	5 26.6	7 33.0	11 17.8	18 7.0	29 27.7	17 15.1	19 24.6	16 44.3
29 F	20 24 47	5 26 18	26 48 7	3♑ 6 45	22 42.5	4 43.2	8 45.3	11 57.6	18 20.2	29 26.0	17 18.1	19 24.5	16 46.0
30 Sa	20 28 44	6 23 39	9♑22 46	15 36 20	22 35.6	4 0.7	9 57.6	12 37.3	18 33.4	29 24.3	17 21.2	19 24.4	16 47.7
31 Su	20 32 40	7 21 0	21 47 34	27 56 37	22 26.0	3 20.0	11 10.0	13 17.0	18 46.6	29 22.4	17 24.3	19 24.4	16 49.5

AUGUST 1966 LONGITUDE

Day	Sid.Time	☉	0 hr ☽	Noon ☽	True ☊	☿	♀	♂	♃	♄	♅	♆	♇
1 M	20 36 37	8♌18 23	4♒ 3 33	10♒ 8 30	22♉14.3	2♌41.9	12♋22.4	13♋56.6	18♋59.7	29♓20.4	17♍27.4	19♏24.3	16♍51.2
2 Tu	20 40 33	9 15 46	16 11 35	22 12 54	22R 1.3	2R 7.0	13 34.8	14 36.2	19 12.8	29R 18.4	17 30.5	19D 24.4	16 53.0
3 W	20 44 30	10 13 10	28 12 36	4♓10 52	21 48.1	1 36.0	14 47.3	15 15.8	19 25.9	29 16.2	17 33.7	19 24.4	16 54.8
4 Th	20 48 26	11 10 35	10♓ 7 55	16 3 59	21 35.9	1 9.7	15 59.9	15 55.2	19 38.9	29 14.0	17 36.9	19 24.5	16 56.6
5 F	20 52 23	12 8 1	21 59 23	27 54 27	21 25.5	0 48.5	17 12.5	16 34.7	19 51.9	29 11.7	17 40.1	19 24.6	16 58.4
6 Sa	20 56 19	13 5 28	3♈49 35	9♈45 14	21 17.6	0 32.9	18 25.1	17 14.1	20 4.9	29 9.3	17 43.4	19 24.7	17 0.3
7 Su	21 0 16	14 2 57	15 41 53	21 40 4	21 12.4	0D 23.4	19 37.8	17 53.5	20 17.8	29 6.8	17 46.6	19 24.9	17 2.1
8 M	21 4 13	15 0 26	27 40 23	3♉43 24	21 9.7	0 20.2	20 50.5	18 32.8	20 30.7	29 4.2	17 49.9	19 25.1	17 4.0
9 Tu	21 8 9	15 57 57	9♉49 48	16 0 12	21 8.8	0 23.6	22 3.3	19 12.1	20 43.6	29 1.5	17 53.3	19 25.3	17 5.9
10 W	21 12 6	16 55 30	22 15 15	28 35 36	21 8.8	0 33.8	23 16.2	19 51.3	20 56.4	28 58.8	17 56.6	19 25.6	17 7.8
11 Th	21 16 2	17 53 4	5♊ 1 50	11♊34 29	21 8.4	0 51.0	24 29.0	20 30.5	21 9.2	28 56.0	17 60.0	19 25.9	17 9.7
12 F	21 19 59	18 50 39	18 14 1	25 0 46	21 6.6	1 15.1	25 42.0	21 9.7	21 21.9	28 53.0	18 3.4	19 26.2	17 11.7
13 Sa	21 23 55	19 48 16	1♋54 56	8♋56 33	21 2.6	1 46.2	26 55.0	21 48.8	21 34.6	28 50.1	18 6.8	19 26.6	17 13.6
14 Su	21 27 52	20 45 54	16 5 26	23 21 12	20 56.0	2 24.3	28 8.0	22 27.8	21 47.2	28 47.0	18 10.3	19 27.0	17 15.6
15 M	21 31 48	21 43 33	0♌43 13	8♌10 39	20 47.0	3 9.2	29 21.1	23 6.9	21 59.8	28 43.8	18 13.7	19 27.4	17 17.6
16 Tu	21 35 45	22 41 14	15 42 26	23 17 22	20 36.4	4 0.9	0♌34.2	23 45.8	22 12.3	28 40.6	18 17.2	19 27.9	17 19.6
17 W	21 39 42	23 38 56	0♍54 6	8♍31 13	20 25.3	4 59.1	1 47.3	24 24.8	22 24.8	28 37.3	18 20.7	19 28.4	17 21.6
18 Th	21 43 38	24 36 39	16 7 22	23 41 13	20 15.2	6 3.8	3 0.5	25 3.6	22 37.2	28 33.9	18 24.3	19 28.9	17 23.6
19 F	21 47 35	25 34 24	1♎11 35	8♎37 28	20 7.0	7 14.6	4 13.8	25 42.5	22 49.6	28 30.5	18 27.8	19 29.5	17 25.6
20 Sa	21 51 31	26 32 9	15 58 5	23 12 50	20 1.4	8 31.3	5 27.0	26 21.3	23 1.9	28 26.9	18 31.4	19 30.0	17 27.7
21 Su	21 55 28	27 29 56	0♏21 21	7♏23 27	19 58.5	9 53.5	6 40.4	27 0.0	23 14.2	28 23.4	18 34.9	19 30.7	17 29.7
22 M	21 59 24	28 27 44	14 19 9	21 8 34	19D 57.5	11 20.9	7 53.7	27 38.7	23 26.4	28 19.7	18 38.5	19 31.3	17 31.8
23 Tu	22 3 21	29 25 33	27 51 57	4♐29 41	19R 57.5	12 53.1	9 7.1	28 17.4	23 38.5	28 16.0	18 42.1	19 32.0	17 33.8
24 W	22 7 17	0♍23 23	11♐ 2 7	17 29 43	19 57.2	14 29.8	10 20.6	28 56.0	23 50.6	28 12.2	18 45.8	19 32.7	17 35.9
25 Th	22 11 14	1 21 15	23 52 54	0♑12 8	19 55.4	16 10.4	11 34.0	29 34.5	24 2.6	28 8.4	18 49.4	19 33.5	17 38.0
26 F	22 15 11	2 19 7	6♑27 50	12 40 24	19 51.4	17 54.5	12 47.6	0♌13.1	24 14.6	28 4.5	18 53.1	19 34.2	17 40.1
27 Sa	22 19 7	3 17 1	18 50 13	24 57 37	19 44.6	19 41.7	14 1.1	0 51.5	24 26.5	28 0.5	18 56.7	19 35.1	17 42.2
28 Su	22 23 4	4 14 57	1♒ 2 52	7♒ 6 16	19 35.1	21 31.6	15 14.7	1 29.9	24 38.3	27 56.5	19 0.4	19 35.9	17 44.3
29 M	22 27 0	5 12 53	13 8 2	19 8 23	19 23.5	23 23.6	16 28.3	2 8.3	24 50.1	27 52.5	19 4.1	19 36.8	17 46.4
30 Tu	22 30 57	6 10 51	25 7 29	1♓ 5 31	19 10.6	25 17.4	17 42.0	2 46.7	25 1.8	27 48.4	19 7.8	19 37.7	17 48.5
31 W	22 34 53	7 8 51	7♓ 2 39	12 59 2	18 57.4	27 12.5	18 55.7	3 25.0	25 13.4	27 44.2	19 11.5	19 38.6	17 50.6

Astro Data	Dy Hr Mn
☽0N	10 2:16
♄ R	11 13:03
☿ R	14 20:14
♃✱♇	20 22:26
☽0S	23 3:23
♃✱♅	23 0:02
♆ D	1 4:30
♃△♆	2 21:13
☽0N	6 8:26
☿ D	7 23:42
☽0S	19 10:43

Planet Ingress	Dy Hr Mn
♂ ♋	11 3:15
♀ ♋	21 17:11
☉ ♌	23 7:23
♀ ♌	15 12:47
☉ ♍	23 14:18
♂ ♌	25 15:52

Last Aspect Dy Hr Mn		☽ Ingress	Dy Hr Mn
1 23:07	♄ □	♑	1 23:51
4 8:33	♄ ✱	♒	4 9:14
6 14:29	♂ △	♓	6 20:39
9 8:37	♄ ☌	♈	9 9:16
10 21:43	☉ □	♉	11 21:03
14 5:16	♄ ✱	♊	14 5:51
16 10:10	♄ □	♋	16 10:44
18 11:53	♄ △	♌	18 12:27
20 10:18	♀ ✱	♍	20 12:46
22 12:57	♄ ☍	♎	22 13:38
23 18:28	♃ □	♏	24 16:32
26 21:09	♄ △	♐	26 22:04
29 4:59	♄ □	♑	29 6:04
31 14:46	♄ ✱	♒	31 16:02

Last Aspect Dy Hr Mn		☽ Ingress	Dy Hr Mn
2 6:24	♆ □	♓	3 3:36
5 14:34	♄ ☌	♈	5 16:15
7 9:25	♃ □	♉	8 4:38
10 12:41	♄ ✱	♊	10 14:38
12 18:41	♄ □	♋	12 20:41
14 21:35	♀ ☌	♌	14 22:50
16 11:48	☉ ☌	♍	16 22:35
18 19:43	♄ ☍	♎	18 22:05
20 18:50	☉ ✱	♏	20 23:24
23 3:02	☉ □	♐	23 3:51
25 8:02	♄ □	♑	25 11:37
27 17:54	♄ ✱	♒	27 21:56
30 0:24	☿ ☍	♓	30 9:48

☽ Phases & Eclipses Dy Hr Mn	
2 19:36	○ 10♑27
10 21:43	☽ 18♈10
18 4:30	● 25♋07
24 19:00	☽ 1♏25
1 9:05	○ 8♒40
9 12:55	☽ 16♉29
16 11:48	● 23♌10
23 3:02	☽ 29♏33
31 0:14	○ 7♓09

Astro Data

1 JULY 1966
Julian Day # 24288
Delta T 37.0 sec
SVP 05♓43'53"
Obliquity 23°26'42"
⚷ Chiron 26♓13.8R
☽ Mean ☊ 23♉03.7

1 AUGUST 1966
Julian Day # 24319
Delta T 37.1 sec
SVP 05♓43'47"
Obliquity 23°26'43"
⚷ Chiron 25♓46.6R
☽ Mean ☊ 21♉25.3

LONGITUDE — SEPTEMBER 1966

Day	Sid.Time	☉	0 hr ☽	Noon ☽	True ☊	☿	♀	♂	♃	♄	♅	♆	♇
1 Th	22 38 50	8♍ 6 52	18♓54 52	24♓50 20	18♉45.2	29♌ 8.6	20♌ 9.5	4♌ 3.2	25♋25.0	27♓40.0	19♍15.2	19♏39.6	17♍52.8
2 F	22 42 46	9 4 55	0♈45 40	6♈41 7	18R 34.8	1♍ 5.3	21 23.3	4 41.4	25 36.4	27R 35.8	19 19.0	19 40.5	17 54.9
3 Sa	22 46 43	10 2 59	12 36 58	18 33 32	18 26.9	3 2.4	22 37.1	5 19.6	25 47.8	27 31.5	19 22.7	19 41.6	17 57.1
4 Su	22 50 40	11 1 6	24 31 14	0♉30 26	18 21.7	4 59.6	23 51.0	5 57.7	25 59.2	27 27.2	19 26.5	19 42.6	17 59.2
5 M	22 54 36	11 59 14	6♉31 38	12 35 19	18D 19.1	6 56.6	25 4.9	6 35.8	26 10.4	27 22.8	19 30.2	19 43.7	18 1.3
6 Tu	22 58 33	12 57 24	18 42 1	24 52 19	18 18.4	8 53.2	26 18.9	7 13.8	26 21.6	27 18.4	19 34.0	19 44.8	18 3.5
7 W	23 2 29	13 55 37	1♊ 6 46	7♊26 0	18 18.8	10 49.4	27 32.9	7 51.8	26 32.7	27 14.0	19 37.7	19 45.9	18 5.7
8 Th	23 6 26	14 53 51	13 50 33	20 21 0	18R 19.3	12 44.9	28 46.9	8 29.7	26 43.7	27 9.5	19 41.5	19 47.1	18 7.8
9 F	23 10 22	15 52 7	26 57 50	3♋41 29	18 18.7	14 39.7	0♍ 1.0	9 7.7	26 54.6	27 5.0	19 45.3	19 48.3	18 10.0
10 Sa	23 14 19	16 50 26	10♋32 16	17 30 20	18 16.3	16 33.6	1 15.1	9 45.5	27 5.5	27 0.5	19 49.1	19 49.5	18 12.1
11 Su	23 18 15	17 48 46	24 35 43	1♌48 13	18 11.7	18 26.6	2 29.3	10 23.3	27 16.2	26 55.9	19 52.8	19 50.8	18 14.3
12 M	23 22 12	18 47 9	9♌ 7 25	16 32 41	18 5.0	20 18.6	3 43.5	11 1.1	27 26.9	26 51.4	19 56.6	19 52.1	18 16.5
13 Tu	23 26 9	19 45 34	24 3 11	1♍37 49	17 56.8	22 9.6	4 57.7	11 38.8	27 37.4	26 46.8	20 0.4	19 53.4	18 18.6
14 W	23 30 5	20 44 0	9♍15 21	16 54 26	17 48.0	23 59.6	6 12.0	12 16.5	27 47.9	26 42.2	20 4.2	19 54.7	18 20.8
15 Th	23 34 2	21 42 29	24 33 39	2♎11 34	17 39.8	25 48.5	7 26.3	12 54.2	27 58.3	26 37.5	20 8.0	19 56.1	18 23.0
16 F	23 37 58	22 40 59	9♎46 50	17 18 15	17 33.3	27 36.4	8 40.6	13 31.7	28 8.6	26 32.9	20 11.7	19 57.4	18 25.1
17 Sa	23 41 55	23 39 31	24 44 47	2♏ 5 34	17 29.0	29 23.2	9 54.9	14 9.3	28 18.8	26 28.3	20 15.5	19 58.9	18 27.3
18 Su	23 45 51	24 38 5	9♏20 1	16 27 42	17D 27.0	1♎ 9.0	11 9.3	14 46.8	28 28.9	26 23.6	20 19.3	20 0.3	18 29.4
19 M	23 49 48	25 36 40	23 28 25	0♐22 10	17 26.9	2 53.7	12 23.7	15 24.2	28 38.9	26 19.0	20 23.1	20 1.8	18 31.6
20 Tu	23 53 44	26 35 18	7♐ 9 4	13 49 24	17 27.8	4 37.4	13 38.2	16 1.6	28 48.8	26 14.3	20 26.8	20 3.2	18 33.7
21 W	23 57 41	27 33 57	20 23 31	26 51 51	17R 28.8	6 20.0	14 52.7	16 39.0	28 58.6	26 9.7	20 30.6	20 4.8	18 35.9
22 Th	0 1 38	28 32 37	3♑14 54	9♑33 9	17 28.9	8 1.6	16 7.2	17 16.2	29 8.2	26 5.0	20 34.4	20 6.3	18 38.0
23 F	0 5 34	29 31 19	15 47 9	21 57 25	17 27.3	9 42.3	17 21.7	17 53.5	29 17.8	26 0.4	20 38.1	20 7.9	18 40.2
24 Sa	0 9 31	0♎30 3	28 4 26	4♒ 8 42	17 23.8	11 21.9	18 36.2	18 30.7	29 27.3	25 55.7	20 41.9	20 9.5	18 42.3
25 Su	0 13 27	1 28 49	10♒10 40	16 10 45	17 18.4	13 0.6	19 50.8	19 7.8	29 36.6	25 51.1	20 45.6	20 11.1	18 44.4
26 M	0 17 24	2 27 36	22 9 20	28 6 46	17 11.2	14 38.4	21 5.4	19 44.9	29 45.9	25 46.5	20 49.3	20 12.7	18 46.5
27 Tu	0 21 20	3 26 26	4♓ 3 22	9♓59 26	17 3.1	16 15.2	22 20.1	20 22.0	29 55.0	25 41.9	20 53.1	20 14.4	18 48.6
28 W	0 25 17	4 25 17	15 55 12	21 50 55	16 54.8	17 51.2	23 34.7	20 59.0	0♌ 4.0	25 37.3	20 56.8	20 16.0	18 50.7
29 Th	0 29 13	5 24 10	27 46 48	3♈43 4	16 47.0	19 26.2	24 49.4	21 35.9	0 12.9	25 32.8	21 0.5	20 17.7	18 52.8
30 F	0 33 10	6 23 4	9♈39 55	15 37 35	16 40.5	21 0.3	26 4.1	22 12.8	0 21.7	25 28.3	21 4.2	20 19.5	18 54.9

LONGITUDE — OCTOBER 1966

Day	Sid.Time	☉	0 hr ☽	Noon ☽	True ☊	☿	♀	♂	♃	♄	♅	♆	♇
1 Sa	0 37 6	7♎22 1	21♈36 15	27♈36 11	16♉35.8	22♎33.6	27♍18.8	22♌49.7	0♌30.3	25♓23.7	21♍ 7.8	20♏21.2	18♍57.0
2 Su	0 41 3	8 21 0	3♉37 37	9♉40 51	16R 33.0	24 6.0	28 33.6	23 26.5	0 38.8	25R 19.3	21 11.5	20 23.0	18 59.1
3 M	0 45 0	9 20 2	15 46 10	21 53 55	16D 32.1	25 37.6	29 48.4	24 3.3	0 47.2	25 14.8	21 15.2	20 24.8	19 1.1
4 Tu	0 48 56	10 19 5	28 4 28	4♊18 11	16 32.7	27 8.3	1♎ 3.2	24 40.0	0 55.5	25 10.4	21 18.8	20 26.6	19 3.2
5 W	0 52 53	11 18 11	10♊35 30	16 56 50	16 34.1	28 38.2	2 18.0	25 16.6	1 3.7	25 6.0	21 22.4	20 28.4	19 5.2
6 Th	0 56 49	12 17 19	23 22 36	29 53 14	16 35.8	0♏ 7.2	3 32.9	25 53.3	1 11.7	25 1.7	21 26.0	20 30.2	19 7.3
7 F	1 0 46	13 16 29	6♋29 8	13♋10 38	16R 36.9	1 35.4	4 47.7	26 29.8	1 19.6	24 57.4	21 29.6	20 32.1	19 9.3
8 Sa	1 4 42	14 15 42	19 58 2	26 51 31	16 37.0	3 2.8	6 2.6	27 6.3	1 27.3	24 53.1	21 33.2	20 34.0	19 11.3
9 Su	1 8 39	15 14 57	3♌51 11	10♌57 0	16 35.6	4 29.2	7 17.6	27 42.8	1 35.0	24 48.9	21 36.7	20 35.9	19 13.3
10 M	1 12 35	16 14 14	18 8 44	25 26 2	16 33.0	5 54.8	8 32.5	28 19.2	1 42.4	24 44.7	21 40.3	20 37.8	19 15.3
11 Tu	1 16 32	17 13 34	2♍48 20	10♍14 55	16 29.3	7 19.5	9 47.5	28 55.6	1 49.8	24 40.6	21 43.8	20 39.7	19 17.2
12 W	1 20 29	18 12 56	17 44 52	25 17 9	16 25.2	8 43.3	11 2.5	29 31.9	1 57.0	24 36.5	21 47.3	20 41.7	19 19.2
13 Th	1 24 25	19 12 20	2♎50 37	10♎24 5	16 21.4	10 6.1	12 17.5	0♍ 8.1	2 4.0	24 32.5	21 50.8	20 43.7	19 21.1
14 F	1 28 22	20 11 46	17 56 19	25 26 9	16 18.4	11 27.9	13 32.5	0 44.3	2 10.9	24 28.6	21 54.2	20 45.7	19 23.1
15 Sa	1 32 18	21 11 14	2♏52 29	10♏14 22	16D 16.5	12 48.7	14 47.6	1 20.5	2 17.7	24 24.7	21 57.7	20 47.7	19 25.0
16 Su	1 36 15	22 10 44	17 30 59	24 41 42	16 16.0	14 8.3	16 2.6	1 56.5	2 24.3	24 20.8	22 1.1	20 49.7	19 26.9
17 M	1 40 11	23 10 16	1♐46 4	8♐43 48	16 16.6	15 26.8	17 17.7	2 32.5	2 30.8	24 17.0	22 4.5	20 51.7	19 28.8
18 Tu	1 44 8	24 9 50	15 34 48	22 19 5	16 17.9	16 44.1	18 32.8	3 8.5	2 37.1	24 13.3	22 7.8	20 53.8	19 30.6
19 W	1 48 4	25 9 26	28 56 52	5♑28 25	16 19.5	18 0.0	19 47.9	3 44.4	2 43.2	24 9.7	22 11.2	20 55.8	19 32.5
20 Th	1 52 1	26 9 4	11♑54 6	18 14 23	16 20.7	19 14.5	21 3.0	4 20.2	2 49.2	24 6.1	22 14.5	20 57.9	19 34.3
21 F	1 55 58	27 8 43	24 29 45	0♒40 44	16R 21.3	20 27.5	22 18.2	4 56.0	2 55.1	24 2.6	22 17.8	20 60.0	19 36.1
22 Sa	1 59 54	28 8 24	6♒47 55	12 51 49	16 21.1	21 38.8	23 33.3	5 31.7	3 0.7	23 59.1	22 21.0	21 2.1	19 37.9
23 Su	2 3 51	29 8 7	18 53 1	24 52 2	16 20.0	22 48.2	24 48.5	6 7.4	3 6.3	23 55.8	22 24.3	21 4.2	19 39.7
24 M	2 7 47	0♏ 7 51	0♓49 26	6♓45 40	16 18.2	23 55.7	26 3.6	6 43.0	3 11.6	23 52.5	22 27.5	21 6.3	19 41.4
25 Tu	2 11 44	1 7 37	12 41 15	18 36 36	16 16.0	25 0.9	27 18.8	7 18.5	3 16.8	23 49.3	22 30.6	21 8.5	19 43.2
26 W	2 15 40	2 7 25	24 32 7	0♈28 12	16 13.7	26 3.7	28 34.0	7 54.0	3 21.8	23 46.1	22 33.8	21 10.6	19 44.9
27 Th	2 19 37	3 7 15	6♈25 9	12 23 19	16 11.5	27 3.8	29 49.1	8 29.4	3 26.7	23 43.1	22 36.9	21 12.8	19 46.6
28 F	2 23 33	4 7 6	18 22 56	24 24 17	16 9.9	28 0.9	1♏ 4.3	9 4.7	3 31.3	23 40.1	22 40.0	21 14.9	19 48.3
29 Sa	2 27 30	5 6 59	0♉27 34	6♉33 0	16 8.8	28 54.7	2 19.6	9 40.0	3 35.8	23 37.2	22 43.0	21 17.1	19 49.9
30 Su	2 31 27	6 6 54	12 40 45	18 51 0	16D 8.4	29 44.9	3 34.8	10 15.2	3 40.2	23 34.4	22 46.0	21 19.3	19 51.6
31 M	2 35 23	7 6 52	25 3 55	1♊19 39	16 8.5	0♐30.9	4 50.0	10 50.3	3 44.3	23 31.7	22 49.0	21 21.5	19 53.2

Astro Data	Dy Hr Mn
☽0N	2 13:57
♃△♄	9 16:13
♅✱♆	10 4:28
☽0S	15 20:32
☿0S	18 15:53
☽0N	29 19:44
♀0S	5 19:39
☽0S	13 7:32
☽0N	27 2:25

Planet Ingress	Dy Hr Mn
☿ ♍	1 10:35
♀ ♍	8 23:40
☿ ♎	17 8:19
☉ ♎	23 11:43
♃ ♌	27 13:19
♀ ♎	3 3:44
☿ ♏	5 22:03
♂ ♍	12 18:37
☉ ♏	23 20:51
♀ ♏	27 3:28
☿ ♐	30 7:38

Last Aspect Dy Hr Mn		☽ Ingress Dy Hr Mn
1 17:38	♄ ☌	♈ 1 22:27
4 2:59	♃ □	♉ 4 10:59
6 16:36	♄ ✱	♊ 6 21:52
9 0:13	♄ □	♋ 9 5:26
11 4:32	♃ ☌	♌ 11 9:01
12 17:21	♆ □	♍ 13 9:26
15 5:25	♃ ✱	♎ 15 8:33
17 5:52	♃ □	♏ 17 8:34
19 9:06	♃ △	♐ 19 11:21
21 14:25	☉ □	♑ 21 17:52
24 2:45	♃ ☍	♒ 24 3:48
25 20:05	♆ □	♓ 26 15:48
28 19:31	♄ ☌	♈ 29 4:29

Last Aspect Dy Hr Mn		☽ Ingress Dy Hr Mn
1 2:35	♂ △	♉ 1 16:47
3 18:25	♄ ✱	♊ 4 3:43
6 4:52	♂ ✱	♋ 6 12:12
8 8:32	♄ △	♌ 8 17:25
10 17:26	♂ ☌	♍ 10 19:27
12 10:53	♄ ☍	♎ 12 19:29
14 3:52	☉ ☌	♏ 14 19:21
16 11:22	♄ △	♐ 16 20:59
18 16:34	☉ ✱	♑ 19 1:55
21 5:34	☉ □	♒ 21 10:41
23 13:16	♀ △	♓ 23 22:20
26 3:23	☿ △	♈ 26 11:03
26 17:58	♃ △	♉ 28 23:05
30 21:03	♄ ✱	♊ 31 9:28

☽ Phases & Eclipses Dy Hr Mn	
8 2:07	☽ 14♊59
14 19:13	● 21♍31
21 14:25	☽ 28♐09
29 16:47	○ 6♈05
7 13:08	☽ 13♋49
14 3:52	● 20♎21
21 5:34	☽ 27♑23
29 10:00	○ 5♉32
29 10:12	☍ A 0.952

Astro Data

1 SEPTEMBER 1966
Julian Day # 24350
Delta T 37.1 sec
SVP 05♓43'43"
Obliquity 23°26'43"
⚷ Chiron 24♓38.9R
☽ Mean ☊ 19♉46.8

1 OCTOBER 1966
Julian Day # 24380
Delta T 37.2 sec
SVP 05♓43'40"
Obliquity 23°26'44"
⚷ Chiron 23♓17.8R
☽ Mean ☊ 18♉11.4

NOVEMBER 1966 LONGITUDE

Day	Sid.Time	☉	0 hr ☽	Noon ☽	True ☊	☿	♀	♂	♃	♄	♅	♆	♇
1 Tu	2 39 20	8♏ 6 51	7♊38 21	14♊ 0 10	16♉ 8.9	1♐12.4	6♏ 5.3	11♍25.4	3♌48.3	23♓29.0	22♍51.9	21♏23.7	19♍54.8
2 W	2 43 16	9 6 52	20 25 18	26 53 51	16 9.6	1 48.9	7 20.5	12 0.5	3 52.1	23R 26.5	22 54.9	21 25.9	19 56.3
3 Th	2 47 13	10 6 56	3♋26 2	10♋ 1 58	16 10.3	2 19.7	8 35.8	12 35.4	3 55.8	23 24.0	22 57.7	21 28.1	19 57.9
4 F	2 51 9	11 7 1	16 41 48	23 25 40	16 10.9	2 44.4	9 51.0	13 10.3	3 59.2	23 21.7	23 0.6	21 30.3	19 59.4
5 Sa	2 55 6	12 7 9	0♌13 41	7♌ 5 53	16R 11.2	3 2.1	11 6.3	13 45.1	4 2.5	23 19.4	23 3.4	21 32.5	20 0.9
6 Su	2 59 2	13 7 18	14 2 18	21 2 53	16 11.3	3R 12.4	12 21.6	14 19.9	4 5.6	23 17.2	23 6.2	21 34.8	20 2.4
7 M	3 2 59	14 7 30	28 7 30	5♍15 57	16 11.2	3 14.5	13 36.9	14 54.5	4 8.5	23 15.2	23 8.9	21 37.0	20 3.8
8 Tu	3 6 56	15 7 44	12♍27 55	19 43 0	16 11.1	3 7.8	14 52.2	15 29.2	4 11.2	23 13.2	23 11.6	21 39.3	20 5.2
9 W	3 10 52	16 7 59	27 0 41	4♎20 22	16D 11.0	2 51.7	16 7.6	16 3.7	4 13.7	23 11.3	23 14.2	21 41.5	20 6.6
10 Th	3 14 49	17 8 17	11♎41 20	19 2 49	16 11.1	2 25.8	17 22.9	16 38.1	4 16.1	23 9.5	23 16.8	21 43.7	20 8.0
11 F	3 18 45	18 8 37	26 24 1	3♏44 2	16 11.2	1 49.9	18 38.2	17 12.5	4 18.2	23 7.8	23 19.4	21 46.0	20 9.3
12 Sa	3 22 42	19 8 58	11♏ 2 4	18 17 16	16R 11.3	1 4.0	19 53.6	17 46.8	4 20.2	23 6.2	23 21.9	21 48.2	20 10.7
13 Su	3 26 38	20 9 22	25 28 53	2♐36 14	16 11.3	0 8.6	21 8.9	18 21.0	4 21.9	23 4.7	23 24.4	21 50.5	20 12.0
14 M	3 30 35	21 9 47	9♐38 43	16 35 54	16 11.0	29♏ 4.6	22 24.3	18 55.2	4 23.5	23 3.3	23 26.9	21 52.7	20 13.2
15 Tu	3 34 31	22 10 13	23 27 26	0♑13 7	16 10.4	27 53.1	23 39.7	19 29.2	4 24.8	23 2.0	23 29.3	21 55.0	20 14.5
16 W	3 38 28	23 10 41	6♑52 52	13 26 45	16 9.6	26 36.2	24 55.0	20 3.2	4 26.0	23 0.9	23 31.6	21 57.3	20 15.7
17 Th	3 42 25	24 11 11	19 54 54	26 17 36	16 8.6	25 15.9	26 10.4	20 37.1	4 27.0	22 59.8	23 34.0	21 59.5	20 16.9
18 F	3 46 21	25 11 42	2♒35 10	8♒48 4	16 7.7	23 54.9	27 25.8	21 10.8	4 27.8	22 58.8	23 36.2	22 1.8	20 18.0
19 Sa	3 50 18	26 12 14	14 56 45	21 1 45	16 7.0	22 35.9	28 41.2	21 44.5	4 28.4	22 57.9	23 38.5	22 4.0	20 19.1
20 Su	3 54 14	27 12 47	27 3 38	3♓ 2 59	16D 6.7	21 21.4	29 56.5	22 18.2	4 28.7	22 57.2	23 40.6	22 6.3	20 20.2
21 M	3 58 11	28 13 21	9♓ 0 24	14 56 29	16 7.0	20 13.9	1♐11.9	22 51.7	4R 28.9	22 56.5	23 42.8	22 8.5	20 21.3
22 Tu	4 2 7	29 13 57	20 51 49	26 47 0	16 7.8	19 15.2	2 27.3	23 25.1	4 28.9	22 56.0	23 44.8	22 10.7	20 22.3
23 W	4 6 4	0♐14 34	2♈42 36	8♈39 8	16 9.0	18 26.8	3 42.6	23 58.5	4 28.7	22 55.5	23 46.9	22 13.0	20 23.4
24 Th	4 10 0	1 15 12	14 37 8	20 37 1	16 10.5	17 49.6	4 58.0	24 31.7	4 28.3	22 55.2	23 48.9	22 15.2	20 24.3
25 F	4 13 57	2 15 51	26 39 15	2♉44 12	16 11.8	17 24.1	6 13.4	25 4.8	4 27.7	22 54.9	23 50.8	22 17.4	20 25.3
26 Sa	4 17 54	3 16 31	8♉52 11	15 3 29	16R 12.6	17D 10.2	7 28.8	25 37.9	4 26.9	22D 54.8	23 52.7	22 19.7	20 26.2
27 Su	4 21 50	4 17 13	21 18 17	27 36 47	16 12.7	17 7.5	8 44.1	26 10.9	4 25.9	22 54.8	23 54.6	22 21.9	20 27.1
28 M	4 25 47	5 17 56	3♊59 2	10♊25 7	16 11.8	17 15.5	9 59.5	26 43.7	4 24.7	22 54.9	23 56.3	22 24.1	20 27.9
29 Tu	4 29 43	6 18 40	16 54 59	23 28 35	16 9.9	17 33.3	11 14.9	27 16.5	4 23.3	22 55.1	23 58.1	22 26.3	20 28.8
30 W	4 33 40	7 19 26	0♋ 5 48	6♋46 29	16 7.1	18 0.2	12 30.3	27 49.2	4 21.7	22 55.4	23 59.8	22 28.5	20 29.6

DECEMBER 1966 LONGITUDE

Day	Sid.Time	☉	0 hr ☽	Noon ☽	True ☊	☿	♀	♂	♃	♄	♅	♆	♇
1 Th	4 37 36	8♐20 13	13♋30 28	20♋17 32	16♉ 3.7	18♏35.2	13♐45.7	28♍21.7	4♌19.9	22♓55.8	24♍ 1.4	22♏30.7	20♍30.3
2 F	4 41 33	9 21 2	27 7 29	4♌ 0 4	16R 0.2	19 17.5	15 1.1	28 54.2	4R 17.9	22 56.3	24 3.0	22 32.9	20 31.1
3 Sa	4 45 30	10 21 51	10♌55 4	17 52 17	15 57.2	20 6.2	16 16.4	29 26.5	4 15.7	22 57.0	24 4.6	22 35.1	20 31.8
4 Su	4 49 26	11 22 42	24 51 28	1♍52 26	15 55.0	21 0.5	17 31.8	29 58.8	4 13.4	22 57.7	24 6.1	22 37.2	20 32.4
5 M	4 53 23	12 23 35	8♍54 58	15 58 53	15D 54.1	21 59.8	18 47.2	0♎30.9	4 10.8	22 58.6	24 7.5	22 39.4	20 33.1
6 Tu	4 57 19	13 24 29	23 3 58	0♎ 9 59	15 54.3	23 3.5	20 2.6	1 2.9	4 8.0	22 59.5	24 8.9	22 41.5	20 33.7
7 W	5 1 16	14 25 24	7♎16 44	14 23 55	15 55.5	24 10.8	21 18.0	1 34.8	4 5.1	23 0.6	24 10.2	22 43.7	20 34.2
8 Th	5 5 12	15 26 20	21 31 15	28 38 23	15 57.1	25 21.5	22 33.4	2 6.6	4 1.9	23 1.7	24 11.5	22 45.8	20 34.8
9 F	5 9 9	16 27 18	5♏44 59	12♏50 36	15R 58.4	26 34.9	23 48.8	2 38.3	3 58.6	23 3.0	24 12.7	22 47.9	20 35.3
10 Sa	5 13 5	17 28 17	19 54 49	26 57 9	15 58.7	27 50.8	25 4.2	3 9.8	3 55.0	23 4.4	24 13.9	22 50.0	20 35.8
11 Su	5 17 2	18 29 17	3♐57 6	10♐54 13	15 57.4	29 8.8	26 19.6	3 41.2	3 51.3	23 5.9	24 15.0	22 52.1	20 36.2
12 M	5 20 59	19 30 18	17 48 2	24 38 6	15 54.4	0♐28.6	27 35.0	4 12.5	3 47.4	23 7.4	24 16.1	22 54.1	20 36.6
13 Tu	5 24 55	20 31 19	1♑24 4	8♑ 5 37	15 49.7	1 50.0	28 50.4	4 43.7	3 43.3	23 9.1	24 17.1	22 56.2	20 37.0
14 W	5 28 52	21 32 22	14 42 31	21 14 38	15 43.7	3 12.7	0♑ 5.8	5 14.7	3 39.1	23 10.9	24 18.0	22 58.3	20 37.3
15 Th	5 32 48	22 33 25	27 41 55	4♒ 4 25	15 37.0	4 36.7	1 21.2	5 45.6	3 34.6	23 12.9	24 18.9	23 0.3	20 37.6
16 F	5 36 45	23 34 29	10♒22 16	16 35 43	15 30.5	6 1.6	2 36.6	6 16.3	3 30.0	23 14.9	24 19.7	23 2.3	20 37.9
17 Sa	5 40 41	24 35 33	22 45 4	28 50 44	15 24.9	7 27.4	3 52.0	6 46.9	3 25.3	23 17.0	24 20.5	23 4.3	20 38.1
18 Su	5 44 38	25 36 38	4♓53 9	10♓52 51	15 20.8	8 54.0	5 7.4	7 17.3	3 20.3	23 19.2	24 21.2	23 6.3	20 38.3
19 M	5 48 34	26 37 43	16 50 25	22 46 25	15D 18.4	10 21.3	6 22.8	7 47.6	3 15.2	23 21.5	24 21.9	23 8.2	20 38.5
20 Tu	5 52 31	27 38 48	28 41 30	4♈36 18	15 17.8	11 49.2	7 38.2	8 17.8	3 9.9	23 23.9	24 22.5	23 10.2	20 38.7
21 W	5 56 28	28 39 53	10♈31 30	16 27 44	15 18.5	13 17.7	8 53.5	8 47.8	3 4.5	23 26.5	24 23.1	23 12.1	20 38.8
22 Th	6 0 24	29 40 59	22 25 40	28 25 54	15 20.0	14 46.6	10 8.9	9 17.6	2 58.9	23 29.1	24 23.6	23 14.0	20 38.8
23 F	6 4 21	0♑42 5	4♉29 3	10♉35 39	15R 21.5	16 16.0	11 24.2	9 47.3	2 53.1	23 31.8	24 24.0	23 15.9	20R 38.9
24 Sa	6 8 17	1 43 11	16 46 14	23 1 12	15 22.0	17 45.8	12 39.6	10 16.8	2 47.2	23 34.6	24 24.4	23 17.8	20 38.9
25 Su	6 12 14	2 44 18	29 20 56	5♊45 42	15 20.9	19 16.0	13 54.9	10 46.2	2 41.2	23 37.5	24 24.7	23 19.6	20 38.8
26 M	6 16 10	3 45 24	12♊15 39	18 50 52	15 17.6	20 46.5	15 10.3	11 15.4	2 35.0	23 40.6	24 25.0	23 21.5	20 38.8
27 Tu	6 20 7	4 46 31	25 31 17	2♋16 45	15 12.1	22 17.4	16 25.6	11 44.5	2 28.7	23 43.7	24 25.2	23 23.3	20 38.7
28 W	6 24 3	5 47 39	9♋ 6 57	16 1 30	15 4.6	23 48.6	17 40.9	12 13.3	2 22.3	23 46.9	24 25.4	23 25.1	20 38.6
29 Th	6 28 0	6 48 46	22 59 54	0♌ 1 37	14 55.7	25 20.1	18 56.2	12 42.0	2 15.7	23 50.2	24 25.5	23 26.8	20 38.4
30 F	6 31 57	7 49 54	7♌ 6 1	14 12 27	14 46.6	26 52.0	20 11.6	13 10.6	2 9.1	23 53.6	24R 25.5	23 28.6	20 38.2
31 Sa	6 35 53	8 51 2	21 20 17	28 28 53	14 38.3	28 24.2	21 26.9	13 38.9	2 2.2	23 57.1	24 25.5	23 30.3	20 38.0

Astro Data

	Dy Hr Mn
☿ R	6 17:55
♄☍♅	8 8:20
☽0S	9 17:24
♃ R	21 10:22
☽0N	23 9:56
☿ D	26 17:49
♄ D	26 15:33
☽0S	7 0:26
♂0S	12 6:03
☽0N	20 17:37
♇ R	23 15:37
♅ R	30 7:30

Planet Ingress

	Dy Hr Mn
☿ ♏	13 3:26
♀ ♐	20 1:06
☉ ♐	22 18:14
♂ ♎	4 0:55
☿ ♐	11 15:27
♀ ♑	13 22:09
☉ ♑	22 7:28

Last Aspect / ☽ Ingress

Last Aspect Dy Hr Mn		☽ Ingress Dy Hr Mn
2 5:36	♄ □	♋ 2 17:43
4 11:51	♄ △	♌ 4 23:36
6 12:56	♆ □	♍ 7 3:10
8 17:47	♅ ☌	♎ 9 4:54
9 11:51	♃ ⚹	♏ 11 5:53
13 7:19	☿ ☌	♐ 13 7:36
15 0:03	♅ □	♑ 15 11:37
17 13:04	♀ ⚹	♒ 17 19:03
20 0:20	☉ □	♓ 20 5:53
22 5:52	♅ ☍	♈ 22 18:31
23 3:34	♃ △	♉ 25 6:37
27 9:42	♂ △	♊ 27 16:31
29 19:42	♂ □	♋ 29 23:50

Last Aspect / ☽ Ingress

Last Aspect Dy Hr Mn		☽ Ingress Dy Hr Mn
2 3:14	♂ ⚹	♌ 2 5:02
3 20:09	♆ □	♍ 4 8:48
6 1:50	♅ ☌	♎ 6 11:43
8 1:55	♀ ⚹	♏ 8 14:18
10 14:54	☿ ☌	♐ 10 17:13
12 18:59	♀ ☌	♑ 12 21:30
14 17:41	♅ △	♒ 15 4:19
17 3:57	☉ ⚹	♓ 17 14:17
19 21:41	☉ □	♈ 20 2:39
21 6:24	☿ △	♉ 22 15:07
24 14:39	♅ △	♊ 25 1:14
26 22:02	♅ □	♋ 27 7:58
29 2:27	♅ ⚹	♌ 29 11:57
31 13:18	☿ △	♍ 31 14:33

☽ Phases & Eclipses

Dy Hr Mn	
5 22:18	☽ 13♌03
12 14:26	● 19♏45
12 14:22:50	● T 1'58"
20 0:20	☽ 27♒14
28 2:40	○ 5♊25
5 6:22	☽ 12♍40
12 3:13	● 19♐38
19 21:41	☽ 27♓33
27 17:43	○ 5♋32

Astro Data

1 NOVEMBER 1966
Julian Day # 24411
Delta T 37.3 sec
SVP 05♓43'36"
Obliquity 23°26'43"
⚷ Chiron 22♓08.4R
☽ Mean ☊ 16♉32.9

1 DECEMBER 1966
Julian Day # 24441
Delta T 37.4 sec
SVP 05♓43'31"
Obliquity 23°26'43"
⚷ Chiron 21♓40.3R
☽ Mean ☊ 14♉57.6

LONGITUDE — JANUARY 1967

Day	Sid.Time	☉	0 hr ☽	Noon ☽	True ☊	☿	♀	♂	♃	♄	♅	♆	♇
1 Su	6 39 50	9♑52 10	5♍37 41	12♍46 9	14♉31.6	29♐56.7	22♑42.2	14♎ 7.0	1♌55.3	24♓ 0.7	24♍25.4	23♏32.0	20♍37.7
2 M	6 43 46	10 53 19	19 53 53	27 0 31	14R27.3	1♑29.5	23 57.4	14 35.0	1R48.3	24 4.3	24R25.3	23 33.7	20R37.4
3 Tu	6 47 43	11 54 28	4♎ 5 46	11♎ 9 27	14D25.2	3 2.7	25 12.7	15 2.8	1 41.2	24 8.1	24 25.1	23 35.4	20 37.1
4 W	6 51 39	12 55 37	18 11 25	25 11 36	14 25.1	4 36.2	26 28.0	15 30.4	1 33.9	24 12.0	24 24.9	23 37.0	20 36.8
5 Th	6 55 36	13 56 47	2♏ 9 56	9♏ 6 24	14R25.8	6 10.0	27 43.3	15 57.7	1 26.6	24 15.9	24 24.6	23 38.6	20 36.4
6 F	6 59 32	14 57 57	16 0 58	22 53 34	14 26.2	7 44.3	28 58.6	16 24.9	1 19.2	24 19.9	24 24.3	23 40.2	20 36.0
7 Sa	7 3 29	15 59 7	29 44 10	6♐32 39	14 25.1	9 18.9	0♒13.8	16 51.8	1 11.7	24 24.1	24 23.8	23 41.7	20 35.5
8 Su	7 7 26	17 0 17	13♐18 55	20 2 48	14 21.6	10 53.8	1 29.1	17 18.6	1 4.1	24 28.3	24 23.4	23 43.3	20 35.0
9 M	7 11 22	18 1 28	26 44 7	3♑22 40	14 15.2	12 29.2	2 44.3	17 45.1	0 56.4	24 32.6	24 22.9	23 44.8	20 34.5
10 Tu	7 15 19	19 2 38	9♑58 14	16 30 38	14 6.1	14 5.1	3 59.6	18 11.3	0 48.7	24 36.9	24 22.3	23 46.3	20 34.0
11 W	7 19 15	20 3 48	22 59 40	29 25 11	13 54.7	15 41.3	5 14.8	18 37.4	0 40.9	24 41.4	24 21.7	23 47.7	20 33.4
12 Th	7 23 12	21 4 57	5♒47 4	12♒ 5 17	13 42.0	17 18.0	6 30.0	19 3.2	0 33.1	24 46.0	24 21.0	23 49.1	20 32.8
13 F	7 27 8	22 6 7	18 19 51	24 30 49	13 29.3	18 55.1	7 45.2	19 28.7	0 25.2	24 50.6	24 20.3	23 50.5	20 32.1
14 Sa	7 31 5	23 7 15	0♓38 23	6♓42 45	13 17.7	20 32.7	9 0.4	19 54.0	0 17.2	24 55.3	24 19.5	23 51.9	20 31.5
15 Su	7 35 2	24 8 23	12 44 15	18 43 15	13 8.1	22 10.8	10 15.6	20 19.1	0 9.3	25 0.1	24 18.6	23 53.3	20 30.8
16 M	7 38 58	25 9 31	24 40 12	0♈35 35	13 1.1	23 49.4	11 30.8	20 43.9	0 1.3	25 4.9	24 17.7	23 54.6	20 30.1
17 Tu	7 42 55	26 10 38	6♈30 0	12 24 0	12 56.9	25 28.6	12 45.9	21 8.4	29♋53.3	25 9.9	24 16.8	23 55.9	20 29.3
18 W	7 46 51	27 11 44	18 18 17	24 13 29	12D55.0	27 8.2	14 1.0	21 32.6	29 45.2	25 14.9	24 15.8	23 57.1	20 28.5
19 Th	7 50 48	28 12 49	0♉10 18	6♉ 9 26	12 54.6	28 48.4	15 16.1	21 56.6	29 37.2	25 20.0	24 14.7	23 58.3	20 27.7
20 F	7 54 44	29 13 53	12 11 36	18 17 28	12R54.8	0♒29.1	16 31.2	22 20.3	29 29.1	25 25.2	24 13.6	23 59.5	20 26.9
21 Sa	7 58 41	0♒14 57	24 27 42	0♊42 53	12 54.3	2 10.3	17 46.3	22 43.7	29 21.0	25 30.4	24 12.5	24 0.7	20 26.0
22 Su	8 2 37	1 15 59	7♊ 3 36	13 30 17	12 52.1	3 52.1	19 1.4	23 6.9	29 13.0	25 35.7	24 11.3	24 1.8	20 25.1
23 M	8 6 34	2 17 1	20 3 17	26 42 50	12 47.4	5 34.4	20 16.4	23 29.7	29 5.0	25 41.1	24 10.0	24 3.0	20 24.2
24 Tu	8 10 31	3 18 2	3♋29 1	10♋21 46	12 39.9	7 17.2	21 31.4	23 52.2	28 57.0	25 46.5	24 8.7	24 4.0	20 23.2
25 W	8 14 27	4 19 2	17 20 47	24 25 40	12 29.9	9 0.6	22 46.4	24 14.4	28 49.0	25 52.1	24 7.4	24 5.1	20 22.3
26 Th	8 18 24	5 20 1	1♌35 47	8♌50 22	12 18.0	10 44.4	24 1.4	24 36.3	28 41.0	25 57.6	24 6.0	24 6.1	20 21.3
27 F	8 22 20	6 20 59	16 8 33	23 29 19	12 5.7	12 28.7	25 16.3	24 57.9	28 33.1	26 3.3	24 4.5	24 7.1	20 20.2
28 Sa	8 26 17	7 21 56	0♍51 39	8♍14 29	11 54.2	14 13.3	26 31.3	25 19.2	28 25.2	26 9.0	24 3.1	24 8.0	20 19.2
29 Su	8 30 13	8 22 53	15 36 51	22 57 50	11 44.7	15 58.3	27 46.2	25 40.1	28 17.3	26 14.8	24 1.5	24 9.0	20 18.1
30 M	8 34 10	9 23 48	0♎16 38	7♎32 36	11 38.0	17 43.6	29 1.1	26 0.6	28 9.6	26 20.6	23 59.9	24 9.8	20 17.0
31 Tu	8 38 6	10 24 43	14 45 14	21 54 9	11 34.2	19 29.1	0♓15.9	26 20.9	28 1.8	26 26.5	23 58.3	24 10.7	20 15.9

LONGITUDE — FEBRUARY 1967

Day	Sid.Time	☉	0 hr ☽	Noon ☽	True ☊	☿	♀	♂	♃	♄	♅	♆	♇
1 W	8 42 3	11♒25 37	28♎59 9	6♏ 0 8	11♉32.7	21♒14.6	1♓30.8	26♎40.7	27♋54.2	26♓32.5	23♍56.6	24♏11.5	20♍14.7
2 Th	8 46 0	12 26 31	12♏57 5	19 50 6	11R32.5	23 0.0	2 45.6	27 0.2	27R46.6	26 38.5	23R54.9	24 12.3	20R13.6
3 F	8 49 56	13 27 24	26 39 19	3♐24 54	11 32.2	24 45.3	4 0.4	27 19.3	27 39.0	26 44.6	23 53.2	24 13.1	20 12.4
4 Sa	8 53 53	14 28 16	10♐ 7 2	16 45 55	11 30.5	26 30.0	5 15.2	27 38.0	27 31.6	26 50.7	23 51.4	24 13.8	20 11.2
5 Su	8 57 49	15 29 7	23 21 42	29 54 31	11 26.3	28 14.2	6 30.0	27 56.3	27 24.3	26 56.9	23 49.6	24 14.5	20 9.9
6 M	9 1 46	16 29 58	6♑24 30	12♑51 44	11 19.0	29 57.3	7 44.7	28 14.2	27 17.0	27 3.1	23 47.7	24 15.2	20 8.7
7 Tu	9 5 42	17 30 47	19 16 15	25 38 5	11 8.8	1♓39.2	8 59.4	28 31.7	27 9.8	27 9.4	23 45.8	24 15.8	20 7.4
8 W	9 9 39	18 31 35	1♒57 15	8♒13 44	10 56.0	3 19.5	10 14.1	28 48.7	27 2.8	27 15.8	23 43.8	24 16.4	20 6.1
9 Th	9 13 35	19 32 22	14 27 33	20 38 41	10 41.9	4 57.8	11 28.8	29 5.3	26 55.8	27 22.2	23 41.8	24 16.9	20 4.8
10 F	9 17 32	20 33 8	26 47 11	2♓53 7	10 27.5	6 33.5	12 43.4	29 21.4	26 49.0	27 28.6	23 39.8	24 17.5	20 3.5
11 Sa	9 21 29	21 33 52	8♓56 34	14 57 41	10 14.2	8 6.2	13 58.0	29 37.1	26 42.2	27 35.1	23 37.8	24 18.0	20 2.1
12 Su	9 25 25	22 34 35	20 56 40	26 53 47	10 3.0	9 35.2	15 12.6	29 52.4	26 35.6	27 41.7	23 35.7	24 18.4	20 0.8
13 M	9 29 22	23 35 16	2♈49 21	8♈43 43	9 54.5	11 0.1	16 27.1	0♏ 7.1	26 29.1	27 48.3	23 33.5	24 18.8	19 59.4
14 Tu	9 33 18	24 35 56	14 37 19	20 30 39	9 49.0	12 20.0	17 41.6	0 21.4	26 22.8	27 54.9	23 31.4	24 19.2	19 58.0
15 W	9 37 15	25 36 34	26 24 14	2♉18 40	9 46.1	13 34.4	18 56.1	0 35.1	26 16.6	28 1.6	23 29.2	24 19.6	19 56.6
16 Th	9 41 11	26 37 11	8♉14 34	14 12 34	9D45.3	14 42.4	20 10.5	0 48.4	26 10.5	28 8.3	23 27.0	24 19.9	19 55.1
17 F	9 45 8	27 37 46	20 13 22	26 17 40	9R45.5	15 43.4	21 24.9	1 1.1	26 4.6	28 15.1	23 24.7	24 20.2	19 53.7
18 Sa	9 49 4	28 38 19	2♊26 8	8♊39 28	9 45.6	16 36.8	22 39.3	1 13.4	25 58.8	28 21.9	23 22.4	24 20.4	19 52.2
19 Su	9 53 1	29 38 50	14 58 18	21 23 13	9 44.5	17 21.8	23 53.6	1 25.1	25 53.2	28 28.8	23 20.1	24 20.7	19 50.8
20 M	9 56 58	0♓39 20	27 54 46	4♋33 19	9 41.3	17 57.8	25 7.9	1 36.2	25 47.7	28 35.6	23 17.8	24 20.8	19 49.3
21 Tu	10 0 54	1 39 47	11♋19 10	18 12 27	9 35.7	18 24.5	26 22.2	1 46.8	25 42.4	28 42.6	23 15.5	24 21.0	19 47.8
22 W	10 4 51	2 40 13	25 13 5	2♌20 50	9 27.7	18 41.4	27 36.4	1 56.8	25 37.2	28 49.5	23 13.1	24 21.1	19 46.3
23 Th	10 8 47	3 40 37	9♌35 12	16 55 31	9 17.9	18R48.2	28 50.5	2 6.3	25 32.2	28 56.5	23 10.7	24 21.2	19 44.8
24 F	10 12 44	4 41 0	24 20 53	1♍50 15	9 7.6	18 45.1	0♈ 4.7	2 15.1	25 27.4	29 3.5	23 8.3	24R21.3	19 43.2
25 Sa	10 16 40	5 41 20	9♍22 24	16 56 6	8 57.7	18 32.0	1 18.7	2 23.4	25 22.7	29 10.6	23 5.8	24 21.3	19 41.7
26 Su	10 20 37	6 41 39	24 30 2	2♎ 2 58	8 49.6	18 9.5	2 32.8	2 31.1	25 18.2	29 17.7	23 3.4	24 21.2	19 40.1
27 M	10 24 33	7 41 56	9♎33 44	17 1 17	8 43.9	17 37.9	3 46.8	2 38.1	25 13.9	29 24.8	23 0.9	24 21.2	19 38.6
28 Tu	10 28 30	8 42 11	24 24 48	1♏43 35	8 40.9	16 58.3	5 0.7	2 44.5	25 9.7	29 31.9	22 58.4	24 21.1	19 37.0

Astro Data

	Dy Hr Mn
☽0S	3 5:12
♄☍♅	6 22:54
☽0N	17 0:48
♅⚹♆	25 22:52
☽0S	30 10:33
♃△♄	7 0:42
☽0N	13 7:20
☿ R	23 4:26
♆ R	24 22:06
♀0N	25 20:00
☽0S	26 18:48

Planet Ingress

	Dy Hr Mn
☿ ♑	1 0:52
♀ ♒	6 19:36
♃ ♋	16 3:50
☿ ♒	19 17:05
☉ ♒	20 18:08
♀ ♓	30 18:53
☿ ♓	6 0:38
♂ ♏	12 12:20
☉ ♓	19 8:24
♀ ♈	23 22:30

Last Aspect / ☽ Ingress

Last Aspect Dy Hr Mn		☽ Ingress Dy Hr Mn
2 7:38	♅ ☌	♎ 2 17:04
4 15:35	♀ □	♏ 4 20:16
6 14:38	♅ ⚹	♐ 7 0:28
8 20:02	♄ □	♑ 9 5:53
11 3:11	♄ ⚹	♒ 11 13:05
13 10:43	♆ □	♓ 13 22:45
16 10:43	♃ △	♈ 16 10:48
18 22:54	♃ □	♉ 18 23:39
21 9:18	♃ ⚹	♊ 21 10:38
23 10:14	♄ □	♋ 23 17:51
25 19:11	♃ ☌	♌ 25 21:20
27 16:17	♀ ☍	♍ 27 22:36
29 20:33	♃ ⚹	♎ 29 23:33

Last Aspect / ☽ Ingress

Last Aspect Dy Hr Mn		☽ Ingress Dy Hr Mn
31 22:10	♃ □	♏ 1 1:44
3 1:45	♃ △	♐ 3 5:55
5 10:17	☿ ⚹	♑ 5 12:10
7 17:53	♂ □	♒ 7 20:17
10 5:10	♂ △	♓ 10 6:19
12 13:45	♄ ☌	♈ 12 18:17
14 23:45	♃ □	♉ 15 7:19
17 15:59	♄ ⚹	♊ 17 19:16
20 1:15	♄ □	♋ 20 3:48
22 6:09	♄ △	♌ 22 8:04
24 0:01	♆ □	♍ 24 9:04
26 7:41	♄ ☍	♎ 26 8:44
28 1:13	♃ □	♏ 28 9:09

☽ Phases & Eclipses

Dy Hr Mn	
3 14:19	☽ 12♎31
10 18:06	● 19♑49
18 19:41	☽ 28♈02
26 6:40	○ 5♌37
1 23:03	☽ 12♏24
9 10:44	● 19♒60
17 15:56	☽ 28♉18
24 17:43	○ 5♍26

Astro Data

1 JANUARY 1967
Julian Day # 24472
Delta T 37.4 sec
SVP 05♓43'25"
Obliquity 23°26'43"
⚷ Chiron 22♓03.0
☽ Mean ☊ 13♉19.2

1 FEBRUARY 1967
Julian Day # 24503
Delta T 37.5 sec
SVP 05♓43'20"
Obliquity 23°26'44"
⚷ Chiron 23♓13.2
☽ Mean ☊ 11♉40.7

MARCH 1967 LONGITUDE

Day	Sid.Time	☉	0 hr ☽	Noon ☽	True ☊	☿	♀	♂	♃	♄	♅	♆	♇
1 W	10 32 27	9♓42 25	8♏57 8	16♏ 5 10	8♉40.1	16♓11.5	6♈14.6	2♏50.3	25♋ 5.7	29♓39.1	22♍55.9	24♏21.0	19♍35.5
2 Th	10 36 23	10 42 38	23 7 31	0♐ 4 11	8D40.6	15R18.9	7 28.5	2 55.4	25R 1.9	29 46.3	22R53.3	24R20.8	19R33.9
3 F	10 40 20	11 42 49	6♐55 17	13 41 0	8R41.3	14 21.7	8 42.3	2 59.8	24 58.3	29 53.5	22 50.8	24 20.6	19 32.3
4 Sa	10 44 16	12 42 59	20 21 37	26 57 24	8 41.1	13 21.5	9 56.1	3 3.5	24 54.9	0♈ 0.7	22 48.2	24 20.4	19 30.7
5 Su	10 48 13	13 43 7	3♑28 43	9♑55 53	8 39.1	12 19.7	11 9.8	3 6.6	24 51.6	0 8.0	22 45.7	24 20.2	19 29.1
6 M	10 52 9	14 43 14	16 19 15	22 39 6	8 34.8	11 17.8	12 23.5	3 9.0	24 48.5	0 15.3	22 43.1	24 19.9	19 27.5
7 Tu	10 56 6	15 43 19	28 55 44	5♒ 9 26	8 28.2	10 17.1	13 37.1	3 10.6	24 45.7	0 22.6	22 40.5	24 19.6	19 25.9
8 W	11 0 2	16 43 22	11♒20 26	17 28 57	8 19.6	9 19.1	14 50.7	3R11.5	24 43.0	0 30.0	22 37.9	24 19.2	19 24.3
9 Th	11 3 59	17 43 23	23 35 11	29 39 17	8 9.9	8 24.7	16 4.3	3 11.7	24 40.5	0 37.3	22 35.3	24 18.8	19 22.7
10 F	11 7 56	18 43 23	5♓41 27	11♓41 49	7 59.9	7 34.8	17 17.8	3 11.1	24 38.2	0 44.7	22 32.7	24 18.4	19 21.1
11 Sa	11 11 52	19 43 21	17 40 35	23 37 53	7 50.7	6 50.3	18 31.2	3 9.8	24 36.0	0 52.0	22 30.1	24 18.0	19 19.5
12 Su	11 15 49	20 43 17	29 33 56	5♈28 57	7 43.0	6 11.7	19 44.6	3 7.7	24 34.1	0 59.4	22 27.5	24 17.5	19 17.9
13 M	11 19 45	21 43 11	11♈23 10	17 16 53	7 37.3	5 39.2	20 58.0	3 4.9	24 32.4	1 6.9	22 24.9	24 17.0	19 16.3
14 Tu	11 23 42	22 43 3	23 10 23	29 4 2	7 33.9	5 13.2	22 11.3	3 1.3	24 30.8	1 14.3	22 22.2	24 16.4	19 14.7
15 W	11 27 38	23 42 52	4♉58 15	10♉53 27	7D32.6	4 53.6	23 24.5	2 56.9	24 29.5	1 21.7	22 19.6	24 15.9	19 13.1
16 Th	11 31 35	24 42 40	16 50 7	22 48 47	7 33.0	4 40.5	24 37.7	2 51.8	24 28.3	1 29.1	22 17.0	24 15.3	19 11.5
17 F	11 35 31	25 42 26	28 49 59	4♊54 18	7 34.4	4D33.7	25 50.8	2 45.9	24 27.4	1 36.6	22 14.4	24 14.6	19 9.9
18 Sa	11 39 28	26 42 9	11♊ 2 21	17 14 42	7 35.9	4 33.1	27 3.9	2 39.2	24 26.6	1 44.1	22 11.8	24 14.0	19 8.3
19 Su	11 43 24	27 41 50	23 31 58	29 54 44	7R36.9	4 38.4	28 16.9	2 31.8	24 26.1	1 51.5	22 9.2	24 13.3	19 6.7
20 M	11 47 21	28 41 29	6♋23 33	12♋58 51	7 36.7	4 49.4	29 29.8	2 23.6	24 25.7	1 59.0	22 6.6	24 12.5	19 5.1
21 Tu	11 51 18	29 41 6	19 41 4	26 30 27	7 34.9	5 5.7	0♉42.7	2 14.6	24D25.5	2 6.5	22 4.0	24 11.8	19 3.6
22 W	11 55 14	0♈40 40	3♌27 9	10♌31 8	7 31.5	5 27.2	1 55.5	2 4.9	24 25.5	2 14.0	22 1.4	24 11.0	19 2.0
23 Th	11 59 11	1 40 12	17 42 10	24 59 50	7 26.9	5 53.5	3 8.3	1 54.4	24 25.8	2 21.4	21 58.8	24 10.2	19 0.4
24 F	12 3 7	2 39 42	2♍23 30	9♍52 21	7 21.7	6 24.4	4 20.9	1 43.1	24 26.2	2 28.9	21 56.3	24 9.4	18 58.9
25 Sa	12 7 4	3 39 9	17 25 22	25 1 22	7 16.6	6 59.6	5 33.5	1 31.2	24 26.8	2 36.4	21 53.7	24 8.5	18 57.3
26 Su	12 11 0	4 38 34	2♎39 6	10♎17 14	7 12.5	7 38.9	6 46.1	1 18.4	24 27.6	2 43.9	21 51.2	24 7.6	18 55.8
27 M	12 14 57	5 37 58	17 54 27	25 29 31	7 9.7	8 22.0	7 58.6	1 5.0	24 28.5	2 51.3	21 48.6	24 6.7	18 54.3
28 Tu	12 18 53	6 37 19	3♏ 1 16	10♏28 43	7D 8.6	9 8.6	9 11.0	0 50.9	24 29.7	2 58.8	21 46.1	24 5.7	18 52.7
29 W	12 22 50	7 36 38	17 51 3	25 7 36	7 8.9	9 58.7	10 23.3	0 36.0	24 31.0	3 6.3	21 43.6	24 4.8	18 51.2
30 Th	12 26 47	8 35 56	2♐17 57	9♐21 48	7 10.1	10 52.0	11 35.5	0 20.5	24 32.6	3 13.7	21 41.2	24 3.8	18 49.7
31 F	12 30 43	9 35 12	16 19 5	23 9 48	7 11.6	11 48.3	12 47.7	0 4.3	24 34.3	3 21.2	21 38.7	24 2.7	18 48.3

APRIL 1967 LONGITUDE

Day	Sid.Time	☉	0 hr ☽	Noon ☽	True ☊	☿	♀	♂	♃	♄	♅	♆	♇
1 Sa	12 34 40	10♈34 26	29♐54 8	6♑32 21	7♉12.8	12♓47.5	13♉59.9	29♎47.4	24♋36.2	3♈28.6	21♍36.3	24♏ 1.7	18♍46.8
2 Su	12 38 36	11 33 38	13♑ 4 45	19 31 46	7R13.2	13 49.4	15 11.9	29R29.9	24 38.3	3 36.1	21R33.8	24R 0.6	18R45.3
3 M	12 42 33	12 32 49	25 53 47	2♒11 16	7 12.5	14 53.8	16 23.9	29 11.9	24 40.6	3 43.5	21 31.5	23 59.5	18 43.9
4 Tu	12 46 29	13 31 58	8♒24 40	14 34 25	7 10.7	16 0.8	17 35.8	28 53.2	24 43.1	3 50.9	21 29.1	23 58.4	18 42.4
5 W	12 50 26	14 31 5	20 40 58	26 44 43	7 7.9	17 10.1	18 47.7	28 34.0	24 45.7	3 58.4	21 26.7	23 57.3	18 41.0
6 Th	12 54 22	15 30 10	2♓46 5	8♓45 26	7 4.5	18 21.6	19 59.4	28 14.3	24 48.6	4 5.7	21 24.4	23 56.1	18 39.6
7 F	12 58 19	16 29 13	14 43 7	20 39 27	7 0.9	19 35.3	21 11.1	27 54.0	24 51.6	4 13.1	21 22.1	23 54.9	18 38.2
8 Sa	13 2 16	17 28 15	26 34 45	2♈29 18	6 57.6	20 51.1	22 22.7	27 33.4	24 54.8	4 20.5	21 19.8	23 53.7	18 36.9
9 Su	13 6 12	18 27 14	8♈23 24	14 17 17	6 55.0	22 8.9	23 34.2	27 12.3	24 58.1	4 27.8	21 17.6	23 52.4	18 35.5
10 M	13 10 9	19 26 11	20 11 13	26 5 29	6 53.3	23 28.6	24 45.7	26 50.9	25 1.7	4 35.2	21 15.3	23 51.2	18 34.2
11 Tu	13 14 5	20 25 7	2♉ 0 20	7♉56 3	6D52.5	24 50.3	25 57.1	26 29.1	25 5.4	4 42.5	21 13.2	23 49.9	18 32.9
12 W	13 18 2	21 24 0	13 52 55	19 51 15	6 52.5	26 13.7	27 8.3	26 7.0	25 9.3	4 49.8	21 11.0	23 48.6	18 31.5
13 Th	13 21 58	22 22 52	25 51 22	1♊53 38	6 53.3	27 39.0	28 19.6	25 44.7	25 13.4	4 57.0	21 8.9	23 47.3	18 30.3
14 F	13 25 55	23 21 41	7♊58 24	14 6 5	6 54.4	29 6.1	29 30.7	25 22.2	25 17.6	5 4.3	21 6.8	23 46.0	18 29.0
15 Sa	13 29 51	24 20 28	20 17 4	26 31 48	6 55.6	0♈34.9	0♊41.7	24 59.5	25 22.0	5 11.5	21 4.7	23 44.6	18 27.8
16 Su	13 33 48	25 19 13	2♋50 42	9♋14 11	6 56.6	2 5.4	1 52.6	24 36.8	25 26.6	5 18.7	21 2.7	23 43.2	18 26.5
17 M	13 37 45	26 17 56	15 42 40	22 16 33	6R57.3	3 37.6	3 3.5	24 13.9	25 31.3	5 25.9	21 0.7	23 41.9	18 25.3
18 Tu	13 41 41	27 16 36	28 56 9	5♌41 45	6 57.5	5 11.5	4 14.2	23 51.1	25 36.2	5 33.1	20 58.7	23 40.5	18 24.2
19 W	13 45 38	28 15 14	12♌33 33	19 31 38	6 57.2	6 47.1	5 24.9	23 28.3	25 41.3	5 40.2	20 56.8	23 39.0	18 23.0
20 Th	13 49 34	29 13 50	26 35 58	3♍46 22	6 56.6	8 24.3	6 35.4	23 5.5	25 46.5	5 47.3	20 54.9	23 37.6	18 21.9
21 F	13 53 31	0♉12 24	11♍ 2 30	18 23 52	6 55.9	10 3.2	7 45.8	22 42.9	25 51.9	5 54.3	20 53.1	23 36.2	18 20.8
22 Sa	13 57 27	1 10 55	25 49 48	3♎19 29	6 55.2	11 43.8	8 56.2	22 20.4	25 57.4	6 1.4	20 51.3	23 34.7	18 19.7
23 Su	14 1 24	2 9 24	10♎51 58	18 26 9	6 54.7	13 26.0	10 6.4	21 58.1	26 3.1	6 8.4	20 49.5	23 33.2	18 18.6
24 M	14 5 20	3 7 52	26 0 55	3♏35 4	6D54.4	15 10.0	11 16.5	21 36.1	26 8.9	6 15.3	20 47.8	23 31.7	18 17.6
25 Tu	14 9 17	4 6 17	11♏ 7 28	18 36 59	6 54.4	16 55.6	12 26.5	21 14.4	26 14.9	6 22.3	20 46.1	23 30.2	18 16.5
26 W	14 13 14	5 4 41	26 2 37	3♐23 29	6 54.4	18 42.9	13 36.4	20 53.0	26 21.0	6 29.2	20 44.4	23 28.7	18 15.5
27 Th	14 17 10	6 3 3	10♐38 50	17 48 6	6R54.5	20 32.0	14 46.2	20 31.9	26 27.3	6 36.0	20 42.8	23 27.2	18 14.6
28 F	14 21 7	7 1 23	24 50 54	1♑47 0	6 54.6	22 22.7	15 55.9	20 11.3	26 33.7	6 42.9	20 41.3	23 25.6	18 13.6
29 Sa	14 25 3	7 59 42	8♑36 19	15 18 56	6 54.5	24 15.2	17 5.5	19 51.0	26 40.3	6 49.6	20 39.8	23 24.1	18 12.7
30 Su	14 29 0	8 58 0	21 55 2	28 24 54	6 54.4	26 9.3	18 14.9	19 31.3	26 47.0	6 56.4	20 38.3	23 22.5	18 11.8

Astro Data	Dy Hr Mn	Planet Ingress	Dy Hr Mn	Last Aspect Dy Hr Mn		☽ Ingress Dy Hr Mn	Last Aspect Dy Hr Mn		☽ Ingress Dy Hr Mn	☽ Phases & Eclipses Dy Hr Mn		Astro Data
												1 MARCH 1967
♂ R	8 17:44	♄ ♈	3 21:32	2 11:35	♄ △	♐ 2 11:53	31 23:48	♂ ⚹	♑ 1 0:11	3 9:10	☽ 12♐06	Julian Day # 24531
☽ 0 N	12 13:28	♀ ♉	20 9:56	4 4:25	♅ □	♑ 4 17:35	3 6:08	♂ □	♒ 3 7:49	11 4:30	● 19♓55	Delta T 37.6 sec
☿ D	17 14:27	☉ ♈	21 7:37	6 16:03	♃ ☍	♒ 7 2:03	5 15:12	♂ △	♓ 5 18:29	19 8:31	☽ 28♊03	SVP 05♓43'16"
♃ D	21 9:16	♂ ♎	31 6:10	9 1:26	♆ □	♓ 9 12:41	7 20:36	♃ △	♈ 8 6:57	26 3:21	○ 4♎47	Obliquity 23°26'44"
☽ 0 S	26 5:36			11 13:55	♃ △	♈ 12 0:53	10 13:08	♂ ☍	♉ 10 19:56			⚷ Chiron 24♓43.9
		☿ ♈	14 14:38	14 2:44	♃ □	♉ 14 13:54	13 5:27	♀ ☌	♊ 13 8:15	1 20:58	☽ 11♑26	☽ Mean ☊ 10♉11.7
☽ 0 N	8 19:35	♀ ♊	14 9:54	16 17:13	☉ ⚹	♊ 17 2:19	15 8:47	♂ △	♋ 15 18:37	9 22:20	● 19♈22	
♄ 0 N	12 13:50	☉ ♉	20 18:55	19 9:53	♀ ⚹	♋ 19 12:10	17 20:48	☉ □	♌ 18 1:54	17 20:48	☽ 27♋09	1 APRIL 1967
☿ 0 N	18 11:13			21 8:22	♃ ☌	♌ 21 18:04	20 4:45	☉ △	♍ 20 5:43	24 12:03	○ 3♏37	Julian Day # 24562
☽ 0 S	22 16:40			23 10:38	♆ □	♍ 23 20:08	22 0:12	♃ ⚹	♎ 22 6:41	24 12:06	☍T 1.336	Delta T 37.6 sec
				25 11:06	♃ ⚹	♎ 25 19:50	24 0:13	♃ □	♏ 24 6:19			SVP 05♓43'13"
				27 10:24	♃ □	♏ 27 19:10	26 0:30	♃ △	♐ 26 6:27			Obliquity 23°26'44"
				29 11:01	♃ △	♐ 29 20:08	27 19:08	☿ △	♑ 28 8:54			⚷ Chiron 26♓34.6
							30 9:10	☿ □	♒ 30 14:57			☽ Mean ☊ 8♉33.2

LONGITUDE MAY 1967

Day	Sid.Time	☉	0 hr ☽	Noon ☽	True ☊	☿	♀	♂	♃	♄	♅	♆	♇
1 M	14 32 56	9♉56 15	4♒48 57	11♒ 7 36	6♉54.3	28♈ 5.2	19♊24.3	19♎12.0	26♋53.9	7♈ 3.1	20♍36.9	23♏21.0	18♍10.9
2 Tu	14 36 53	10 54 30	17 21 21	23 30 44	6D 54.3	0♉ 2.8	20 33.5	18R 53.3	27 0.9	7 9.8	20R 35.5	23R 19.4	18R 10.1
3 W	14 40 49	11 52 42	29 36 18	5♓38 35	6 54.5	2 2.0	21 42.6	18 35.2	27 8.0	7 16.4	20 34.1	23 17.8	18 9.3
4 Th	14 44 46	12 50 53	11♓38 9	17 35 31	6 55.0	4 2.9	22 51.6	18 17.6	27 15.2	7 23.0	20 32.8	23 16.2	18 8.5
5 F	14 48 43	13 49 3	23 31 13	29 25 45	6 55.7	6 5.3	24 0.4	18 0.7	27 22.6	7 29.6	20 31.6	23 14.6	18 7.7
6 Sa	14 52 39	14 47 11	5♈19 34	11♈13 7	6 56.5	8 9.3	25 9.2	17 44.4	27 30.2	7 36.1	20 30.4	23 13.0	18 7.0
7 Su	14 56 36	15 45 18	17 6 48	23 1 1	6 57.2	10 14.7	26 17.7	17 28.8	27 37.8	7 42.5	20 29.2	23 11.4	18 6.3
8 M	15 0 32	16 43 23	28 56 7	4♉52 24	6R 57.7	12 21.4	27 26.2	17 13.9	27 45.6	7 48.9	20 28.1	23 9.8	18 5.6
9 Tu	15 4 29	17 41 27	10♉50 10	16 49 42	6 57.8	14 29.3	28 34.5	16 59.7	27 53.5	7 55.3	20 27.1	23 8.2	18 5.0
10 W	15 8 25	18 39 29	22 51 14	28 55 0	6 57.3	16 38.2	29 42.7	16 46.3	28 1.6	8 1.6	20 26.1	23 6.6	18 4.3
11 Th	15 12 22	19 37 29	5♊ 1 12	11♊10 4	6 56.3	18 48.0	0♋50.8	16 33.6	28 9.7	8 7.8	20 25.1	23 4.9	18 3.8
12 F	15 16 18	20 35 28	17 21 46	23 36 30	6 54.6	20 58.4	1 58.7	16 21.7	28 18.0	8 14.0	20 24.2	23 3.3	18 3.2
13 Sa	15 20 15	21 33 25	29 54 26	6♋15 47	6 52.6	23 9.2	3 6.5	16 10.6	28 26.4	8 20.2	20 23.4	23 1.7	18 2.7
14 Su	15 24 12	22 31 21	12♋40 44	19 9 26	6 50.5	25 20.1	4 14.1	16 0.2	28 35.0	8 26.3	20 22.6	23 0.0	18 2.2
15 M	15 28 8	23 29 15	25 42 6	2♌18 52	6 48.5	27 30.9	5 21.5	15 50.7	28 43.6	8 32.4	20 21.8	22 58.4	18 1.7
16 Tu	15 32 5	24 27 7	8♌59 56	15 45 24	6 47.2	29 41.3	6 28.8	15 42.0	28 52.4	8 38.4	20 21.1	22 56.8	18 1.2
17 W	15 36 1	25 24 57	22 35 23	29 29 56	6D 46.6	1♊51.0	7 35.9	15 34.1	29 1.2	8 44.3	20 20.4	22 55.2	18 0.8
18 Th	15 39 58	26 22 45	6♍29 4	13♍32 41	6 46.8	3 59.7	8 42.9	15 26.9	29 10.2	8 50.2	20 19.8	22 53.5	18 0.5
19 F	15 43 54	27 20 32	20 40 40	27 52 45	6 47.7	6 7.1	9 49.6	15 20.7	29 19.3	8 56.0	20 19.3	22 51.9	18 0.1
20 Sa	15 47 51	28 18 17	5♎ 8 35	12♎27 42	6 49.0	8 13.1	10 56.2	15 15.2	29 28.5	9 1.7	20 18.8	22 50.3	17 59.8
21 Su	15 51 47	29 16 0	19 49 31	27 13 22	6 50.2	10 17.3	12 2.6	15 10.5	29 37.8	9 7.4	20 18.4	22 48.7	17 59.5
22 M	15 55 44	0♊13 42	4♏38 28	12♏ 3 56	6R 50.8	12 19.5	13 8.8	15 6.6	29 47.2	9 13.1	20 18.0	22 47.1	17 59.2
23 Tu	15 59 41	1 11 23	19 28 53	26 52 21	6 50.4	14 19.6	14 14.9	15 3.6	29 56.7	9 18.7	20 17.6	22 45.4	17 59.0
24 W	16 3 37	2 9 2	4♐13 24	11♐31 9	6 48.8	16 17.3	15 20.7	15 1.3	0♌ 6.3	9 24.2	20 17.3	22 43.8	17 58.8
25 Th	16 7 34	3 6 40	18 44 46	25 53 33	6 46.0	18 12.6	16 26.3	14 59.8	0 16.0	9 29.6	20 17.1	22 42.2	17 58.6
26 F	16 11 30	4 4 17	2♑56 54	9♑54 21	6 42.3	20 5.4	17 31.7	14D 59.1	0 25.8	9 35.0	20 16.9	22 40.7	17 58.5
27 Sa	16 15 27	5 1 52	16 45 36	23 30 29	6 38.2	21 55.4	18 36.9	14 59.2	0 35.7	9 40.3	20 16.8	22 39.1	17 58.4
28 Su	16 19 23	5 59 27	0♒ 8 59	6♒41 13	6 34.3	23 42.8	19 41.9	15 0.1	0 45.7	9 45.6	20D 16.7	22 37.5	17 58.3
29 M	16 23 20	6 57 1	13 7 26	19 27 58	6 31.1	25 27.3	20 46.6	15 1.7	0 55.7	9 50.8	20 16.7	22 35.9	17D 58.3
30 Tu	16 27 17	7 54 34	25 43 14	1♓53 44	6 29.0	27 9.0	21 51.2	15 4.0	1 5.9	9 55.9	20 16.7	22 34.4	17 58.3
31 W	16 31 13	8 52 6	8♓ 0 2	14 2 41	6D 28.3	28 47.7	22 55.5	15 7.2	1 16.2	10 1.0	20 16.8	22 32.8	17 58.3

LONGITUDE JUNE 1967

Day	Sid.Time	☉	0 hr ☽	Noon ☽	True ☊	☿	♀	♂	♃	♄	♅	♆	♇
1 Th	16 35 10	9♊49 37	20♓ 2 20	25♓59 35	6♉28.7	0♋23.6	23♋59.6	15♎11.0	1♌26.5	10♈ 5.9	20♍17.0	22♏31.3	17♍58.3
2 F	16 39 6	10 47 7	1♈55 4	7♈49 25	6 30.1	1 56.4	25 3.4	15 15.6	1 37.0	10 10.8	20 17.2	22R 29.7	17 58.4
3 Sa	16 43 3	11 44 37	13 43 12	19 37 2	6 31.8	3 26.3	26 7.0	15 20.9	1 47.5	10 15.7	20 17.4	22 28.2	17 58.5
4 Su	16 46 59	12 42 5	25 31 28	1♉27 0	6R 33.2	4 53.2	27 10.3	15 26.9	1 58.1	10 20.4	20 17.7	22 26.7	17 58.7
5 M	16 50 56	13 39 33	7♉24 6	13 23 13	6 33.8	6 17.0	28 13.4	15 33.6	2 8.8	10 25.1	20 18.0	22 25.2	17 58.9
6 Tu	16 54 52	14 37 0	19 24 44	25 28 58	6 32.9	7 37.7	29 16.2	15 41.1	2 19.6	10 29.7	20 18.5	22 23.7	17 59.1
7 W	16 58 49	15 34 27	1♊36 13	7♊46 41	6 30.3	8 55.2	0♌18.7	15 49.2	2 30.4	10 34.3	20 18.9	22 22.2	17 59.3
8 Th	17 2 45	16 31 53	14 0 32	20 17 53	6 25.8	10 9.6	1 21.0	15 58.0	2 41.3	10 38.7	20 19.4	22 20.8	17 59.6
9 F	17 6 42	17 29 18	26 38 49	3♋ 3 19	6 19.9	11 20.8	2 22.9	16 7.4	2 52.3	10 43.1	20 20.0	22 19.3	17 59.9
10 Sa	17 10 39	18 26 42	9♋31 23	16 2 57	6 12.9	12 28.7	3 24.6	16 17.6	3 3.4	10 47.4	20 20.6	22 17.9	18 0.2
11 Su	17 14 35	19 24 5	22 37 55	29 16 13	6 5.7	13 33.2	4 25.9	16 28.3	3 14.6	10 51.6	20 21.3	22 16.5	18 0.6
12 M	17 18 32	20 21 27	5♌57 42	12♌42 17	5 59.0	14 34.3	5 27.0	16 39.7	3 25.8	10 55.8	20 22.0	22 15.1	18 1.0
13 Tu	17 22 28	21 18 48	19 29 49	26 20 13	5 53.7	15 31.9	6 27.7	16 51.8	3 37.1	10 59.8	20 22.8	22 13.7	18 1.4
14 W	17 26 25	22 16 9	3♍13 23	10♍ 9 13	5 50.2	16 25.9	7 28.0	17 4.4	3 48.5	11 3.8	20 23.6	22 12.4	18 1.9
15 Th	17 30 21	23 13 28	17 7 37	24 8 30	5D 48.6	17 16.2	8 28.0	17 17.6	3 59.9	11 7.7	20 24.5	22 11.0	18 2.4
16 F	17 34 18	24 10 46	1♎11 44	8♎17 12	5 48.6	18 2.7	9 27.6	17 31.5	4 11.4	11 11.5	20 25.4	22 9.7	18 2.9
17 Sa	17 38 15	25 8 4	15 24 43	22 34 4	5 49.6	18 45.4	10 26.8	17 45.9	4 23.0	11 15.3	20 26.4	22 8.4	18 3.5
18 Su	17 42 11	26 5 20	29 44 58	6♏57 5	5R 50.4	19 24.1	11 25.7	18 0.8	4 34.6	11 18.9	20 27.5	22 7.1	18 4.1
19 M	17 46 8	27 2 36	14♏ 9 58	21 23 8	5 50.3	19 58.7	12 24.1	18 16.3	4 46.3	11 22.4	20 28.6	22 5.8	18 4.7
20 Tu	17 50 4	27 59 51	28 36 1	5♐48 0	5 48.3	20 29.1	13 22.1	18 32.4	4 58.0	11 25.9	20 29.7	22 4.6	18 5.3
21 W	17 54 1	28 57 5	12♐58 26	20 6 36	5 44.1	20 55.2	14 19.7	18 49.0	5 9.8	11 29.3	20 30.9	22 3.3	18 6.0
22 Th	17 57 57	29 54 19	27 11 51	4♑13 32	5 37.6	21 16.9	15 16.8	19 6.1	5 21.7	11 32.6	20 32.1	22 2.1	18 6.7
23 F	18 1 54	0♋51 33	11♑11 3	18 3 54	5 29.4	21 34.2	16 13.5	19 23.7	5 33.6	11 35.8	20 33.4	22 0.9	18 7.5
24 Sa	18 5 50	1 48 46	24 51 41	1♒34 6	5 20.3	21 47.0	17 9.7	19 41.8	5 45.6	11 38.9	20 34.8	21 59.8	18 8.2
25 Su	18 9 47	2 45 59	8♒10 59	14 42 17	5 11.2	21 55.2	18 5.4	20 0.4	5 57.6	11 41.9	20 36.2	21 58.6	18 9.0
26 M	18 13 44	3 43 12	21 8 4	27 28 32	5 3.2	21R 58.8	19 0.6	20 19.5	6 9.7	11 44.9	20 37.6	21 57.5	18 9.9
27 Tu	18 17 40	4 40 24	3♓43 58	9♓54 46	4 57.0	21 57.8	19 55.2	20 39.0	6 21.8	11 47.7	20 39.1	21 56.4	18 10.7
28 W	18 21 37	5 37 37	16 1 24	22 4 23	4 52.9	21 52.3	20 49.4	20 59.0	6 34.0	11 50.5	20 40.7	21 55.3	18 11.6
29 Th	18 25 33	6 34 49	28 4 19	4♈ 1 48	4D 50.9	21 42.3	21 42.9	21 19.5	6 46.2	11 53.1	20 42.2	21 54.3	18 12.5
30 F	18 29 30	7 32 2	9♈57 31	15 52 7	4 50.5	21 28.0	22 35.9	21 40.4	6 58.5	11 55.7	20 43.9	21 53.3	18 13.5

Astro Data	Planet Ingress	Last Aspect	☽ Ingress	Last Aspect	☽ Ingress	☽ Phases & Eclipses	Astro Data
Dy Hr Mn	Dy Hr Mn	Dy Hr Mn	Dy Hr Mn	Dy Hr Mn	Dy Hr Mn	Dy Hr Mn	1 MAY 1967
☽0N 6 1:54	☿ ♉ 1 23:26	2 11:36 ♆ □	♓ 3 0:47	1 8:45 ♀ △	♈ 1 20:07	1 10:33 ☽ 10♒22	Julian Day # 24592
♄⚼♆ 10 15:07	♀ ♋ 10 6:05	5 7:55 ♃ △	♈ 5 13:10	4 3:40 ♀ □	♉ 4 9:04	9 14:55 ● 18♉18	Delta T 37.7 sec
☽0S 20 1:45	☿ ♊ 16 3:27	7 21:36 ♃ □	♉ 8 2:09	6 5:54 ♆ ☍	♊ 6 20:52	9 14:42:09 ◐ P 0.720	SVP 05♓43'09"
♂ D 26 9:29	☉ ♊ 21 18:18	10 10:21 ♃ ✶	♊ 10 14:08	8 12:03 ♅ □	♋ 9 6:18	17 5:18 ☽ 25♌38	Obliquity 23°26'44"
♅ D 28 21:37	♃ ♌ 23 8:20	12 5:51 ♅ □	♋ 13 0:11	10 23:21 ♆ △	♌ 11 13:19	23 20:22 ○ 2♐00	⚷ Chiron 28♓11.8
♇ D 29 20:30	☿ ♋ 31 18:02	15 5:34 ♃ ☌	♌ 15 7:49	13 4:48 ♆ □	♍ 13 18:24	31 1:52 ☽ 8♓57	☽ Mean ☊ 6♉57.9
		17 5:18 ☉ □	♍ 17 12:52	15 11:12 ☉ □	♎ 15 21:58		
☽0N 2 8:32	♀ ♌ 6 16:48	19 14:33 ♃ ✶	♎ 19 15:31	17 17:27 ☉ △	♏ 18 0:25	8 5:13 ● 16♊44	1 JUNE 1967
♃∠♇ 9 16:54	☉ ♋ 22 2:23	21 16:04 ♃ □	♏ 21 16:30	19 13:10 ♆ ☌	♐ 20 2:20	15 11:12 ☽ 23♍40	Julian Day # 24623
☽0S 16 8:02		23 5:18 ♆ ☌	♐ 23 17:06	21 12:42 ♅ □	♑ 22 4:46	22 4:57 ○ 0♑06	Delta T 37.8 sec
♃∠♅ 22 23:40		25 2:34 ♅ □	♑ 25 18:58	23 18:56 ♆ ✶	♒ 24 9:11	29 18:39 ☽ 7♈19	SVP 05♓43'04"
☿ R 26 6:51		27 10:27 ♆ ✶	♒ 27 23:44	26 1:33 ♆ □	♓ 26 16:49		Obliquity 23°26'44"
☽0N 29 15:28		30 3:12 ☿ △	♓ 30 8:18	28 11:41 ♆ △	♈ 29 3:53		⚷ Chiron 29♓22.8
							☽ Mean ☊ 5♉19.4

JULY 1967 LONGITUDE

Day	Sid.Time	☉	0 hr ☽	Noon ☽	True ☊	☿	♀	♂	♃	♄	♅	♆	♇
1 Sa	18 33 26	8♋29 15	21♈46 16	27♈40 40	4♉51.0	21♋ 9.5	23♌28.3	22♎ 1.8	7♌10.8	11♈58.1	20♍45.6	21♏52.3	18♍14.4
2 Su	18 37 23	9 26 27	3♉35 56	9♉32 43	4R51.5	20R47.2	24 20.1	22 23.5	7 23.2	12 0.5	20 47.3	21R51.3	18 15.4
3 M	18 41 19	10 23 40	15 31 37	21 33 11	4 50.9	20 21.3	25 11.3	22 45.7	7 35.6	12 2.8	20 49.1	21 50.3	18 16.4
4 Tu	18 45 16	11 20 54	27 37 55	3♊46 17	4 48.5	19 52.1	26 1.8	23 8.4	7 48.0	12 5.0	20 50.9	21 49.4	18 17.5
5 W	18 49 13	12 18 7	9♊58 37	16 15 15	4 43.8	19 20.1	26 51.6	23 31.4	8 0.5	12 7.1	20 52.8	21 48.5	18 18.6
6 Th	18 53 9	13 15 21	22 36 21	29 2 4	4 36.5	18 45.9	27 40.7	23 54.8	8 13.1	12 9.1	20 54.7	21 47.6	18 19.7
7 F	18 57 6	14 12 34	5♋32 23	12♋ 7 15	4 27.0	18 9.8	28 29.1	24 18.7	8 25.6	12 10.9	20 56.7	21 46.8	18 20.8
8 Sa	19 1 2	15 9 48	18 46 29	25 29 51	4 16.1	17 32.6	29 16.7	24 42.9	8 38.3	12 12.7	20 58.7	21 45.9	18 22.0
9 Su	19 4 59	16 7 2	2♌17 0	9♌ 7 36	4 4.7	16 54.8	0♍ 3.5	25 7.5	8 50.9	12 14.4	21 0.7	21 45.2	18 23.2
10 M	19 8 55	17 4 16	16 1 12	22 57 22	3 54.1	16 17.0	0 49.5	25 32.5	9 3.6	12 16.0	21 2.8	21 44.4	18 24.4
11 Tu	19 12 52	18 1 30	29 55 42	6♍55 45	3 45.2	15 40.0	1 34.6	25 57.8	9 16.3	12 17.5	21 5.0	21 43.6	18 25.7
12 W	19 16 48	18 58 44	13♍57 8	20 59 31	3 38.9	15 4.3	2 18.9	26 23.5	9 29.1	12 18.9	21 7.2	21 42.9	18 27.0
13 Th	19 20 45	19 55 57	28 2 37	5♎ 6 11	3 35.2	14 30.7	3 2.2	26 49.6	9 41.9	12 20.2	21 9.4	21 42.3	18 28.3
14 F	19 24 42	20 53 11	12♎10 1	19 13 57	3D33.7	13 59.6	3 44.6	27 16.0	9 54.7	12 21.4	21 11.7	21 41.6	18 29.6
15 Sa	19 28 38	21 50 25	26 17 51	3♏21 37	3R33.5	13 31.8	4 25.9	27 42.7	10 7.5	12 22.5	21 14.0	21 41.0	18 30.9
16 Su	19 32 35	22 47 38	10♏25 7	17 28 12	3 33.5	13 7.6	5 6.2	28 9.8	10 20.4	12 23.4	21 16.4	21 40.4	18 32.3
17 M	19 36 31	23 44 52	24 30 44	1♐32 28	3 32.3	12 47.5	5 45.4	28 37.2	10 33.3	12 24.3	21 18.8	21 39.8	18 33.7
18 Tu	19 40 28	24 42 6	8♐33 11	15 32 35	3 28.9	12 32.0	6 23.5	29 4.9	10 46.2	12 25.1	21 21.2	21 39.3	18 35.1
19 W	19 44 24	25 39 20	22 30 18	29 25 59	3 22.9	12 21.4	7 0.4	29 32.9	10 59.1	12 25.8	21 23.7	21 38.8	18 36.6
20 Th	19 48 21	26 36 35	6♑19 12	13♑ 9 34	3 14.0	12D16.0	7 36.1	0♏ 1.3	11 12.1	12 26.4	21 26.2	21 38.3	18 38.0
21 F	19 52 18	27 33 50	19 56 40	26 40 8	3 3.1	12 16.0	8 10.5	0 29.9	11 25.1	12 26.9	21 28.8	21 37.9	18 39.5
22 Sa	19 56 14	28 31 5	3♒19 37	9♒54 51	2 50.8	12 21.6	8 43.6	0 58.8	11 38.1	12 27.2	21 31.4	21 37.4	18 41.1
23 Su	20 0 11	29 28 21	16 25 40	22 51 57	2 38.6	12 33.0	9 15.4	1 28.0	11 51.1	12 27.5	21 34.0	21 37.1	18 42.6
24 M	20 4 7	0♌25 37	29 13 40	5♓30 56	2 27.4	12 50.1	9 45.7	1 57.5	12 4.2	12 27.7	21 36.7	21 36.7	18 44.2
25 Tu	20 8 4	1 22 54	11♓43 53	17 52 49	2 18.3	13 13.1	10 14.6	2 27.3	12 17.2	12R27.7	21 39.4	21 36.4	18 45.7
26 W	20 12 0	2 20 12	23 58 5	0♈ 0 4	2 11.7	13 42.0	10 41.9	2 57.3	12 30.3	12 27.7	21 42.1	21 36.1	18 47.4
27 Th	20 15 57	3 17 31	5♈59 18	11 56 18	2 7.7	14 16.9	11 7.7	3 27.6	12 43.4	12 27.6	21 44.9	21 35.8	18 49.0
28 F	20 19 53	4 14 51	17 51 41	23 46 4	2 5.8	14 57.5	11 31.8	3 58.2	12 56.5	12 27.3	21 47.7	21 35.6	18 50.6
29 Sa	20 23 50	5 12 11	29 40 8	5♉34 33	2 5.4	15 44.1	11 54.3	4 29.1	13 9.6	12 27.0	21 50.5	21 35.4	18 52.3
30 Su	20 27 47	6 9 33	11♉30 0	17 27 10	2 5.3	16 36.3	12 15.0	5 0.2	13 22.8	12 26.6	21 53.4	21 35.2	18 54.0
31 M	20 31 43	7 6 56	23 26 45	29 29 23	2 4.6	17 34.3	12 34.0	5 31.5	13 35.9	12 26.0	21 56.3	21 35.1	18 55.7

AUGUST 1967 LONGITUDE

Day	Sid.Time	☉	0 hr ☽	Noon ☽	True ☊	☿	♀	♂	♃	♄	♅	♆	♇
1 Tu	20 35 40	8♌ 4 20	5♊35 41	11♊46 12	2♉ 2.2	18♋37.8	12♍51.1	6♏ 3.1	13♌49.1	12♈25.4	21♍59.3	21♏35.0	18♍57.4
2 W	20 39 36	9 1 45	18 1 27	24 21 49	1R57.5	19 46.8	13 6.2	6 35.0	14 2.3	12R24.6	22 2.3	21R34.9	18 59.2
3 Th	20 43 33	9 59 11	0♋47 39	7♋19 9	1 50.3	21 1.2	13 19.5	7 7.1	14 15.4	12 23.8	22 5.3	21D34.9	19 0.9
4 F	20 47 29	10 56 38	13 56 23	20 39 19	1 40.7	22 20.6	13 30.6	7 39.5	14 28.6	12 22.8	22 8.3	21 34.9	19 2.7
5 Sa	20 51 26	11 54 7	27 27 47	4♌21 27	1 29.5	23 45.1	13 39.7	8 12.1	14 41.8	12 21.8	22 11.4	21 34.9	19 4.5
6 Su	20 55 22	12 51 36	11♌19 52	18 22 29	1 17.8	25 14.3	13 46.7	8 44.9	14 55.0	12 20.6	22 14.5	21 35.0	19 6.4
7 M	20 59 19	13 49 6	25 28 39	2♍37 41	1 6.7	26 48.0	13 51.4	9 18.0	15 8.2	12 19.4	22 17.7	21 35.1	19 8.2
8 Tu	21 3 16	14 46 37	9♍48 48	17 1 17	0 57.5	28 26.0	13R54.0	9 51.2	15 21.4	12 18.0	22 20.8	21 35.2	19 10.1
9 W	21 7 12	15 44 9	24 14 26	1♎27 33	0 50.9	0♌ 8.0	13 54.2	10 24.8	15 34.6	12 16.6	22 24.0	21 35.3	19 11.9
10 Th	21 11 9	16 41 42	8♎40 5	15 51 30	0 47.0	1 53.5	13 52.1	10 58.5	15 47.8	12 15.0	22 27.3	21 35.5	19 13.8
11 F	21 15 5	17 39 16	23 1 26	0♏ 9 32	0D45.4	3 42.3	13 47.7	11 32.5	16 0.9	12 13.4	22 30.5	21 35.7	19 15.7
12 Sa	21 19 2	18 36 51	7♏15 36	14 19 27	0R45.3	5 34.1	13 40.8	12 6.6	16 14.1	12 11.6	22 33.8	21 36.0	19 17.6
13 Su	21 22 58	19 34 26	21 20 59	28 20 8	0 45.5	7 28.3	13 31.6	12 41.0	16 27.3	12 9.8	22 37.1	21 36.3	19 19.6
14 M	21 26 55	20 32 2	5♐16 53	12♐11 11	0 44.7	9 24.6	13 20.0	13 15.6	16 40.5	12 7.9	22 40.4	21 36.6	19 21.5
15 Tu	21 30 51	21 29 40	19 3 0	25 52 19	0 41.9	11 22.7	13 6.0	13 50.4	16 53.7	12 5.8	22 43.8	21 36.9	19 23.5
16 W	21 34 48	22 27 18	2♑39 3	9♑23 6	0 36.7	13 22.2	12 49.6	14 25.4	17 6.8	12 3.7	22 47.1	21 37.3	19 25.5
17 Th	21 38 45	23 24 58	16 4 23	22 42 46	0 28.9	15 22.6	12 30.9	15 0.5	17 20.0	12 1.5	22 50.5	21 37.7	19 27.5
18 F	21 42 41	24 22 38	29 18 6	5♒50 16	0 19.0	17 23.7	12 9.9	15 35.9	17 33.1	11 59.2	22 54.0	21 38.2	19 29.5
19 Sa	21 46 38	25 20 20	12♒19 8	18 44 35	0 8.1	19 25.1	11 46.8	16 11.5	17 46.2	11 56.8	22 57.4	21 38.7	19 31.5
20 Su	21 50 34	26 18 3	25 6 33	1♓24 59	29♈57.0	21 26.6	11 21.5	16 47.2	17 59.4	11 54.3	23 0.9	21 39.2	19 33.5
21 M	21 54 31	27 15 47	7♓39 55	13 51 23	29 46.9	23 28.0	10 54.3	17 23.1	18 12.5	11 51.8	23 4.4	21 39.7	19 35.5
22 Tu	21 58 27	28 13 33	19 59 33	26 4 35	29 38.6	25 28.9	10 25.2	17 59.2	18 25.5	11 49.1	23 7.9	21 40.3	19 37.6
23 W	22 2 24	29 11 20	2♈ 6 44	8♈ 6 19	29 32.7	27 29.2	9 54.4	18 35.5	18 38.6	11 46.4	23 11.4	21 40.9	19 39.7
24 Th	22 6 20	0♍ 9 8	14 3 44	19 59 23	29 29.2	29 28.8	9 22.1	19 12.0	18 51.7	11 43.5	23 14.9	21 41.5	19 41.7
25 F	22 10 17	1 6 59	25 53 47	1♉47 27	29D27.8	1♍27.5	8 48.5	19 48.6	19 4.7	11 40.6	23 18.5	21 42.2	19 43.8
26 Sa	22 14 14	2 4 51	7♉40 57	13 34 55	29 28.0	3 25.3	8 13.6	20 25.4	19 17.7	11 37.6	23 22.1	21 42.9	19 45.9
27 Su	22 18 10	3 2 44	19 29 59	25 26 48	29 28.9	5 22.0	7 37.9	21 2.4	19 30.7	11 34.6	23 25.7	21 43.6	19 48.0
28 M	22 22 7	4 0 40	1♊26 2	7♊28 21	29R29.6	7 17.6	7 1.5	21 39.5	19 43.7	11 31.4	23 29.3	21 44.4	19 50.1
29 Tu	22 26 3	4 58 38	13 34 25	19 44 52	29 29.3	9 12.0	6 24.5	22 16.8	19 56.7	11 28.2	23 32.9	21 45.2	19 52.2
30 W	22 30 0	5 56 37	26 0 16	2♋21 9	29 27.2	11 5.2	5 47.4	22 54.3	20 9.6	11 24.9	23 36.5	21 46.0	19 54.3
31 Th	22 33 56	6 54 38	8♋47 58	15 21 5	29 23.0	12 57.2	5 10.2	23 32.0	20 22.5	11 21.5	23 40.2	21 46.9	19 56.5

Astro Data	Planet Ingress	Last Aspect	☽ Ingress	Last Aspect	☽ Ingress	☽ Phases & Eclipses	Astro Data
Dy Hr Mn	Dy Hr Mn	Dy Hr Mn	Dy Hr Mn	Dy Hr Mn	Dy Hr Mn	Dy Hr Mn	1 JULY 1967
☽0S 13 12:41	♀ ♍ 8 22:11	1 3:44 ♀ △	♉ 1 16:43	2 7:39 ♅ □	♋ 2 22:32	7 17:00 ● 14♋53	Julian Day # 24653
☿ D 20 12:01	♂ ♏ 19 22:56	3 20:37 ♀ □	♊ 4 4:39	4 16:42 ☿ ☌	♌ 5 4:26	14 15:53 ☽ 21♎31	Delta T 37.9 sec
♅✶♆ 24 0:23	☉ ♌ 23 13:16	6 10:07 ♀ ✶	♋ 6 13:47	6 17:26 ♆ □	♍ 7 7:36	21 14:39 ○ 28♑09	SVP 05♓42'58"
♃△♄ 25 19:15		8 10:56 ♂ □	♌ 8 19:58	8 20:56 ♅ ☌	♎ 9 9:34	29 12:14 ☽ 5♉41	Obliquity 23°26'44"
♄ R 25 4:08	☿ ♌ 8 22:09	10 16:58 ♂ ✶	♍ 11 0:07	10 14:22 ☉ ✶	♏ 11 11:44		⚷ Chiron 29♓49.6
☽0N 26 22:34	☊ ♈ 19 17:22	12 13:13 ♆ ✶	♎ 13 3:20	13 2:11 ♅ ✶	♐ 13 14:52	6 2:48 ● 12♌58	☽ Mean ☊ 3♉44.1
	☉ ♍ 23 20:12	15 2:29 ♂ ☌	♏ 15 6:17	15 6:29 ♅ □	♑ 15 19:18	12 20:44 ☽ 19♏27	
♆ D 3 15:20	☿ ♍ 24 6:17	16 22:36 ☉ △	♐ 17 9:22	17 12:17 ♅ △	♒ 18 1:17	20 2:27 ○ 26♒24	1 AUGUST 1967
♀ R 8 14:29		19 12:38 ♂ ✶	♑ 19 12:59	20 2:27 ☉ ☍	♓ 20 9:18	28 5:35 ☽ 4♊14	Julian Day # 24684
☽0S 9 18:01		21 14:39 ☉ ☍	♒ 21 17:59	22 6:13 ♅ ☍	♈ 22 19:47		Delta T 37.9 sec
☽0N 23 5:36		23 9:40 ♆ □	♓ 24 1:28	24 9:54 ♃ △	♉ 25 8:21		SVP 05♓42'53"
♃⊻♇ 28 14:10		25 19:30 ♅ ☍	♈ 26 12:00	27 7:58 ♅ △	♊ 27 21:08		Obliquity 23°26'44"
		27 17:44 ☿ □	♉ 29 0:40	29 19:24 ♅ □	♋ 30 7:34		⚷ Chiron 29♓28.5R
		30 20:59 ♅ △	♊ 31 13:00				☽ Mean ☊ 2♉05.6

Day	Sid.Time	☉	0 hr ☽	Noon ☽	True ☊	☿	♀	♂	♃	♄	♅	♆	♇
1 F	22 37 53	7♍52 41	22♋ 0 43	28♋46 59	29♈17.0	14♍47.9	4♍33.3	24♏ 9.8	20♌35.4	11♈18.0	23♍43.9	21♏47.8	19♍58.6
2 Sa	22 41 49	8 50 46	5♌39 49	12♌39 1	29R 9.6	16 37.4	3R56.9	24 47.8	20 48.2	11R14.5	23 47.5	21 48.7	20 0.8
3 Su	22 45 46	9 48 53	19 44 10	26 54 46	29 1.6	18 25.7	3 21.1	25 25.9	21 1.1	11 10.9	23 51.2	21 49.6	20 2.9
4 M	22 49 43	10 47 1	4♍10 4	11♍29 17	28 53.9	20 12.7	2 46.3	26 4.2	21 13.8	11 7.2	23 54.9	21 50.6	20 5.1
5 Tu	22 53 39	11 45 12	18 51 29	26 15 40	28 47.6	21 58.5	2 12.6	26 42.6	21 26.6	11 3.5	23 58.7	21 51.6	20 7.2
6 W	22 57 36	12 43 23	3♎40 51	11♎ 6 2	28 43.3	23 43.0	1 40.3	27 21.2	21 39.3	10 59.7	24 2.4	21 52.7	20 9.4
7 Th	23 1 32	13 41 37	18 30 18	25 52 49	28D41.1	25 26.4	1 9.4	27 60.0	21 52.0	10 55.8	24 6.1	21 53.7	20 11.6
8 F	23 5 29	14 39 52	3♏12 51	10♏29 47	28 40.7	27 8.6	0 40.3	28 38.9	22 4.7	10 51.9	24 9.9	21 54.8	20 13.7
9 Sa	23 9 25	15 38 8	17 43 10	24 52 37	28 41.6	28 49.6	0 12.9	29 18.0	22 17.3	10 47.9	24 13.6	21 55.9	20 15.9
10 Su	23 13 22	16 36 26	1♐57 55	8♐58 56	28 42.9	0♎29.5	29♌47.5	29 57.2	22 29.9	10 43.9	24 17.4	21 57.1	20 18.1
11 M	23 17 18	17 34 46	15 55 36	22 47 56	28R43.6	2 8.2	29 24.2	0♐36.5	22 42.4	10 39.8	24 21.1	21 58.3	20 20.3
12 Tu	23 21 15	18 33 7	29 36 2	6♑19 59	28 43.0	3 45.8	29 3.0	1 16.0	22 54.9	10 35.7	24 24.9	21 59.5	20 22.4
13 W	23 25 12	19 31 30	12♑59 55	19 36 0	28 40.8	5 22.3	28 44.1	1 55.6	23 7.4	10 31.5	24 28.7	22 0.7	20 24.6
14 Th	23 29 8	20 29 54	26 8 21	2♒37 7	28 36.8	6 57.6	28 27.5	2 35.4	23 19.8	10 27.2	24 32.5	22 2.0	20 26.8
15 F	23 33 5	21 28 20	9♒ 2 27	15 24 29	28 31.5	8 31.9	28 13.3	3 15.2	23 32.1	10 22.9	24 36.2	22 3.3	20 29.0
16 Sa	23 37 1	22 26 47	21 43 20	27 59 7	28 25.3	10 5.1	28 1.4	3 55.3	23 44.5	10 18.6	24 40.0	22 4.6	20 31.2
17 Su	23 40 58	23 25 17	4♓11 59	10♓22 1	28 19.1	11 37.3	27 52.0	4 35.4	23 56.7	10 14.2	24 43.8	22 6.0	20 33.4
18 M	23 44 54	24 23 47	16 29 23	22 34 13	28 13.4	13 8.3	27 45.0	5 15.7	24 8.9	10 9.8	24 47.6	22 7.4	20 35.5
19 Tu	23 48 51	25 22 20	28 36 41	4♈37 0	28 8.9	14 38.3	27 40.5	5 56.1	24 21.1	10 5.4	24 51.4	22 8.8	20 37.7
20 W	23 52 47	26 20 55	10♈35 22	16 32 3	28 5.9	16 7.2	27D38.3	6 36.6	24 33.2	10 0.9	24 55.1	22 10.2	20 39.9
21 Th	23 56 44	27 19 32	22 27 20	28 21 33	28D 4.5	17 35.1	27 38.6	7 17.2	24 45.3	9 56.4	24 58.9	22 11.6	20 42.1
22 F	0 0 40	28 18 11	4♉15 4	10♉ 8 18	28 4.5	19 1.9	27 41.2	7 58.0	24 57.3	9 51.8	25 2.7	22 13.1	20 44.2
23 Sa	0 4 37	29 16 52	16 1 41	21 55 41	28 5.6	20 27.5	27 46.1	8 38.9	25 9.3	9 47.3	25 6.5	22 14.6	20 46.4
24 Su	0 8 34	0♎15 35	27 50 50	3♊47 41	28 7.3	21 52.1	27 53.3	9 19.9	25 21.2	9 42.7	25 10.3	22 16.1	20 48.6
25 M	0 12 30	1 14 20	9♊46 47	15 48 43	28 9.0	23 15.5	28 2.7	10 1.0	25 33.0	9 38.1	25 14.0	22 17.7	20 50.7
26 Tu	0 16 27	2 13 8	21 54 6	28 3 32	28R10.3	24 37.8	28 14.3	10 42.2	25 44.8	9 33.4	25 17.8	22 19.3	20 52.9
27 W	0 20 23	3 11 58	4♋17 35	10♋36 49	28 10.7	25 58.8	28 27.9	11 23.6	25 56.5	9 28.8	25 21.6	22 20.9	20 55.0
28 Th	0 24 20	4 10 50	17 1 45	23 32 51	28 10.1	27 18.7	28 43.7	12 5.1	26 8.2	9 24.1	25 25.3	22 22.5	20 57.2
29 F	0 28 16	5 9 44	0♌10 29	6♌54 55	28 8.4	28 37.2	29 1.4	12 46.7	26 19.8	9 19.4	25 29.1	22 24.1	20 59.3
30 Sa	0 32 13	6 8 41	13 46 18	20 44 38	28 5.9	29 54.4	29 21.0	13 28.4	26 31.3	9 14.7	25 32.8	22 25.8	21 1.4

LONGITUDE OCTOBER 1967

Day	Sid.Time	☉	0 hr ☽	Noon ☽	True ☊	☿	♀	♂	♃	♄	♅	♆	♇
1 Su	0 36 9	7♎ 7 40	27♌49 46	5♍ 1 21	28♈ 3.0	1♏10.2	29♌42.6	14♐10.2	26♌42.7	9♈10.0	25♍36.6	22♏27.5	21♍ 3.6
2 M	0 40 6	8 6 41	12♍18 52	19 41 37	28R 0.2	2 24.4	0♍ 5.9	14 52.1	26 54.1	9R 5.3	25 40.3	22 29.2	21 5.7
3 Tu	0 44 3	9 5 45	27 8 46	4♎39 18	27 57.9	3 37.1	0 30.9	15 34.2	27 5.4	9 0.6	25 44.0	22 31.0	21 7.8
4 W	0 47 59	10 4 50	12♎12 9	19 46 7	27 56.5	4 48.2	0 57.7	16 16.3	27 16.7	8 55.8	25 47.7	22 32.7	21 9.9
5 Th	0 51 56	11 3 57	27 20 4	4♏52 50	27D56.0	5 57.4	1 26.0	16 58.6	27 27.9	8 51.1	25 51.4	22 34.5	21 12.0
6 F	0 55 52	12 3 7	12♏23 21	19 50 38	27 56.3	7 4.7	1 55.9	17 41.0	27 39.0	8 46.4	25 55.1	22 36.3	21 14.0
7 Sa	0 59 49	13 2 18	27 13 52	4♐32 20	27 57.2	8 10.0	2 27.3	18 23.5	27 50.0	8 41.7	25 58.8	22 38.1	21 16.1
8 Su	1 3 45	14 1 31	11♐45 32	18 53 4	27 58.4	9 12.9	3 0.2	19 6.0	28 0.9	8 37.0	26 2.4	22 40.0	21 18.2
9 M	1 7 42	15 0 46	25 54 44	2♑50 26	27 59.3	10 13.5	3 34.4	19 48.7	28 11.8	8 32.4	26 6.1	22 41.8	21 20.2
10 Tu	1 11 38	16 0 3	9♑40 12	16 24 11	27R59.9	11 11.4	4 10.0	20 31.5	28 22.5	8 27.7	26 9.7	22 43.7	21 22.3
11 W	1 15 35	16 59 22	23 2 34	29 35 38	27 59.9	12 6.4	4 46.9	21 14.4	28 33.2	8 23.1	26 13.3	22 45.6	21 24.3
12 Th	1 19 32	17 58 42	6♒ 3 43	12♒27 9	27 59.4	12 58.2	5 25.1	21 57.4	28 43.8	8 18.4	26 16.9	22 47.5	21 26.3
13 F	1 23 28	18 58 4	18 46 18	25 1 33	27 58.5	13 46.6	6 4.4	22 40.4	28 54.4	8 13.8	26 20.5	22 49.4	21 28.3
14 Sa	1 27 25	19 57 28	1♓13 15	7♓21 46	27 57.4	14 31.1	6 44.9	23 23.6	29 4.8	8 9.3	26 24.1	22 51.4	21 30.3
15 Su	1 31 21	20 56 53	13 27 28	19 30 40	27 56.3	15 11.5	7 26.6	24 6.8	29 15.1	8 4.7	26 27.6	22 53.4	21 32.2
16 M	1 35 18	21 56 20	25 31 42	1♈30 50	27 55.5	15 47.2	8 9.3	24 50.2	29 25.4	8 0.2	26 31.1	22 55.3	21 34.2
17 Tu	1 39 14	22 55 50	7♈28 24	13 24 40	27 54.9	16 17.9	8 53.1	25 33.6	29 35.5	7 55.7	26 34.6	22 57.3	21 36.1
18 W	1 43 11	23 55 21	19 19 53	25 14 20	27D54.6	16 43.1	9 37.9	26 17.1	29 45.6	7 51.3	26 38.1	22 59.3	21 38.0
19 Th	1 47 7	24 54 54	1♉ 8 18	7♉ 2 2	27 54.5	17 2.3	10 23.7	27 0.7	29 55.5	7 46.9	26 41.6	23 1.4	21 39.9
20 F	1 51 4	25 54 29	12 55 49	18 49 57	27 54.6	17 14.9	11 10.4	27 44.4	0♍ 5.4	7 42.5	26 45.0	23 3.4	21 41.8
21 Sa	1 55 1	26 54 7	24 44 45	0♊40 33	27 54.8	17R20.3	11 58.0	28 28.1	0 15.2	7 38.2	26 48.4	23 5.5	21 43.7
22 Su	1 58 57	27 53 46	6♊37 41	12 36 33	27R54.8	17 18.1	12 46.5	29 12.0	0 24.8	7 33.9	26 51.8	23 7.5	21 45.6
23 M	2 2 54	28 53 28	18 37 31	24 41 2	27 54.8	17 7.7	13 35.9	29 55.9	0 34.4	7 29.7	26 55.2	23 9.6	21 47.4
24 Tu	2 6 50	29 53 12	0♋47 32	6♋57 28	27 54.6	16 48.6	14 26.1	0♑39.9	0 43.8	7 25.5	26 58.5	23 11.7	21 49.2
25 W	2 10 47	0♏52 58	13 11 18	19 29 30	27 54.4	16 20.7	15 17.0	1 24.0	0 53.2	7 21.4	27 1.8	23 13.8	21 51.0
26 Th	2 14 43	1 52 47	25 52 33	2♌20 52	27D54.2	15 43.7	16 8.7	2 8.2	1 2.4	7 17.3	27 5.1	23 16.0	21 52.8
27 F	2 18 40	2 52 38	8♌54 53	15 34 56	27 54.2	14 57.7	17 1.2	2 52.4	1 11.5	7 13.3	27 8.4	23 18.1	21 54.6
28 Sa	2 22 36	3 52 30	22 21 18	29 14 12	27 54.5	14 3.2	17 54.3	3 36.7	1 20.6	7 9.4	27 11.6	23 20.2	21 56.3
29 Su	2 26 33	4 52 25	6♍13 41	13♍19 42	27 55.0	13 0.9	18 48.1	4 21.1	1 29.5	7 5.5	27 14.8	23 22.4	21 58.0
30 M	2 30 30	5 52 23	20 32 3	27 50 20	27 55.7	11 52.0	19 42.6	5 5.6	1 38.2	7 1.6	27 18.0	23 24.5	21 59.7
31 Tu	2 34 26	6 52 22	5♎14 2	12♎42 24	27 56.4	10 38.1	20 37.7	5 50.2	1 46.9	6 57.9	27 21.2	23 26.7	22 1.4

Astro Data Dy Hr Mn	Planet Ingress Dy Hr Mn	Last Aspect Dy Hr Mn	☽ Ingress Dy Hr Mn	Last Aspect Dy Hr Mn	☽ Ingress Dy Hr Mn	☽ Phases & Eclipses Dy Hr Mn	Astro Data
☽0S 6 1:51	☿ ♎ 9 16:53	1 4:01 ♂ △	♌ 1 14:08	1 3:14 ♀ ☌	♍ 1 3:38	4 11:37 ● 11♍15	1 SEPTEMBER 1967
♃□♆ 7 3:32	♀ ♌ 9 11:58	3 9:58 ♂ □	♍ 3 17:07	2 21:43 ♅ ☌	♎ 3 4:34	11 3:06 ☽ 17♐42	Julian Day # 24715
☿0S 10 9:39	♂ ♐ 10 1:44	5 13:18 ♂ ✶	♎ 5 18:03	5 0:13 ♃ ✶	♏ 5 4:14	18 16:59 ○ 25♓05	Delta T 38.0 sec
☽0N 19 12:20	☉ ♎ 23 17:38	7 5:33 ♃ ✶	♏ 7 18:44	7 1:00 ♃ □	♐ 7 4:32	26 21:44 ☽ 3♋06	SVP 05♓42'48"
♀ D 20 9:34	☿ ♏ 30 1:46	9 20:25 ♂ ☌	♐ 9 20:40	9 3:59 ♃ △	♑ 9 7:04		Obliquity 23°26'45"
♃⊼♄ 21 16:05		11 23:03 ♀ △	♑ 12 0:43	11 5:50 ♅ △	♒ 11 12:45	3 20:24 ● 9♎56	⚷ Chiron 28♓25.3R
♃⊻♅ 22 15:52	♀ ♍ 1 18:07	13 21:03 ♅ △	♒ 14 7:08	13 19:47 ♃ ☍	♓ 13 21:38	10 12:11 ☽ 16♑30	☽ Mean ☊ 0♉27.1
	♃ ♍ 19 10:51	16 11:55 ♀ ☍	♓ 16 15:53	16 1:59 ♅ ☍	♈ 16 8:58	18 10:11 ○ 24♈21	
☽0S 3 12:13	♂ ♑ 23 2:14	18 16:59 ☉ ☍	♈ 19 2:46	18 21:30 ♃ △	♉ 18 21:41	18 10:15 ☍T 1.143	1 OCTOBER 1967
☽0N 16 18:38	☉ ♏ 24 2:44	21 10:34 ♀ △	♉ 21 15:20	21 4:12 ♅ △	♊ 21 10:38	26 12:04 ☽ 2♌23	Julian Day # 24745
♄⊼♆ 16 18:06		24 0:05 ♀ □	♊ 24 4:21	23 22:04 ☉ △	♋ 23 22:27		Delta T 38.1 sec
☿ R 21 5:15		26 12:34 ♀ ✶	♋ 26 15:45	26 2:16 ♅ ✶	♌ 26 7:40		SVP 05♓42'45"
☽0S 30 23:19		28 20:54 ☿ □	♌ 28 23:41	28 1:44 ♆ □	♍ 28 13:19		Obliquity 23°26'45"
				30 11:09 ♅ ☌	♎ 30 15:31		⚷ Chiron 27♓05.0R
							☽ Mean ☊ 28♈51.8

NOVEMBER 1967 LONGITUDE

Day	Sid.Time	☉	0 hr ☽	Noon ☽	True ☊	☿	♀	♂	♃	♄	♅	♆	♇
1 W	2 38 23	7♏52 23	20♎14 33	27♎49 27	27♈56.8	9♏21.2	21♍33.4	6♑34.8	1♍55.5	6♈54.2	27♍24.3	23♏28.9	22♍ 3.1
2 Th	2 42 19	8 52 27	5♏25 56	13♏ 2 48	27R 56.8	8R 3.5	22 29.7	7 19.5	2 3.9	6R 50.5	27 27.4	23 31.1	22 4.7
3 F	2 46 16	9 52 32	20 38 47	28 12 40	27 56.2	6 47.4	23 26.6	8 4.3	2 12.2	6 47.0	27 30.4	23 33.3	22 6.3
4 Sa	2 50 12	10 52 39	5♐43 18	13♐ 9 38	27 55.0	5 35.4	24 24.0	8 49.1	2 20.3	6 43.5	27 33.4	23 35.5	22 7.9
5 Su	2 54 9	11 52 48	20 30 46	27 46 1	27 53.3	4 29.7	25 21.9	9 34.0	2 28.4	6 40.1	27 36.4	23 37.7	22 9.5
6 M	2 58 5	12 52 59	4♑54 48	11♑56 48	27 51.4	3 32.3	26 20.3	10 19.0	2 36.3	6 36.7	27 39.4	23 39.9	22 11.0
7 Tu	3 2 2	13 53 11	18 51 50	25 39 55	27 49.7	2 44.7	27 19.3	11 4.1	2 44.1	6 33.5	27 42.3	23 42.2	22 12.6
8 W	3 5 59	14 53 25	2♒21 9	8♒55 49	27 48.5	2 8.0	28 18.7	11 49.2	2 51.7	6 30.3	27 45.2	23 44.4	22 14.1
9 Th	3 9 55	15 53 40	15 24 17	21 46 59	27D 48.0	1 42.8	29 18.5	12 34.3	2 59.2	6 27.2	27 48.0	23 46.6	22 15.5
10 F	3 13 52	16 53 56	28 4 25	4♓17 5	27 48.4	1D 29.3	0♎18.8	13 19.6	3 6.6	6 24.2	27 50.8	23 48.9	22 17.0
11 Sa	3 17 48	17 54 14	10♓25 34	16 30 25	27 49.6	1 27.3	1 19.5	14 4.9	3 13.9	6 21.3	27 53.6	23 51.1	22 18.4
12 Su	3 21 45	18 54 34	22 32 10	28 31 22	27 51.2	1 36.3	2 20.7	14 50.2	3 20.9	6 18.4	27 56.3	23 53.3	22 19.8
13 M	3 25 41	19 54 54	4♈28 31	10♈24 7	27 52.8	1 55.6	3 22.2	15 35.6	3 27.9	6 15.7	27 59.0	23 55.6	22 21.2
14 Tu	3 29 38	20 55 17	16 18 37	22 12 27	27R 54.2	2 24.5	4 24.2	16 21.0	3 34.7	6 13.0	28 1.7	23 57.8	22 22.5
15 W	3 33 34	21 55 40	28 6 0	3♉59 37	27 54.7	3 2.0	5 26.5	17 6.5	3 41.4	6 10.5	28 4.3	24 0.1	22 23.8
16 Th	3 37 31	22 56 6	9♉53 37	15 48 20	27 54.0	3 47.3	6 29.2	17 52.1	3 47.9	6 8.0	28 6.9	24 2.3	22 25.1
17 F	3 41 28	23 56 33	21 44 0	27 40 52	27 52.0	4 39.5	7 32.3	18 37.7	3 54.3	6 5.6	28 9.4	24 4.6	22 26.4
18 Sa	3 45 24	24 57 1	3♊39 10	9♊39 7	27 48.7	5 37.7	8 35.7	19 23.4	4 0.5	6 3.3	28 11.9	24 6.8	22 27.6
19 Su	3 49 21	25 57 31	15 40 55	21 44 47	27 44.2	6 41.2	9 39.5	20 9.1	4 6.5	6 1.1	28 14.3	24 9.1	22 28.8
20 M	3 53 17	26 58 3	27 50 53	3♋59 28	27 39.0	7 49.3	10 43.5	20 54.8	4 12.5	5 59.0	28 16.7	24 11.4	22 30.0
21 Tu	3 57 14	27 58 37	10♋10 44	16 24 57	27 33.7	9 1.3	11 48.0	21 40.6	4 18.2	5 57.0	28 19.1	24 13.6	22 31.2
22 W	4 1 10	28 59 12	22 42 20	29 3 10	27 28.8	10 16.6	12 52.7	22 26.5	4 23.8	5 55.1	28 21.4	24 15.9	22 32.3
23 Th	4 5 7	29 59 49	5♌27 43	11♌56 19	27 25.0	11 34.9	13 57.7	23 12.4	4 29.3	5 53.3	28 23.7	24 18.1	22 33.4
24 F	4 9 3	1♐ 0 27	18 29 13	25 6 44	27 22.7	12 55.6	15 3.1	23 58.3	4 34.5	5 51.6	28 25.9	24 20.4	22 34.5
25 Sa	4 13 0	2 1 7	1♍49 8	8♍36 40	27D 21.9	14 18.4	16 8.7	24 44.3	4 39.6	5 50.0	28 28.1	24 22.6	22 35.5
26 Su	4 16 57	3 1 49	15 29 30	22 27 46	27 22.5	15 42.9	17 14.5	25 30.3	4 44.6	5 48.6	28 30.3	24 24.8	22 36.5
27 M	4 20 53	4 2 32	29 31 30	6♎40 37	27 23.9	17 8.9	18 20.7	26 16.4	4 49.4	5 47.2	28 32.3	24 27.1	22 37.5
28 Tu	4 24 50	5 3 17	13♎54 55	21 14 3	27R 25.3	18 36.1	19 27.1	27 2.5	4 54.0	5 45.9	28 34.4	24 29.3	22 38.4
29 W	4 28 46	6 4 4	28 37 28	6♏ 4 31	27 25.8	20 4.4	20 33.7	27 48.6	4 58.4	5 44.7	28 36.4	24 31.5	22 39.3
30 Th	4 32 43	7 4 52	13♏34 22	21 6 0	27 24.8	21 33.5	21 40.6	28 34.8	5 2.7	5 43.6	28 38.3	24 33.7	22 40.2

DECEMBER 1967 LONGITUDE

Day	Sid.Time	☉	0 hr ☽	Noon ☽	True ☊	☿	♀	♂	♃	♄	♅	♆	♇
1 F	4 36 39	8♐ 5 41	28♏38 22	6♐10 17	27♈21.8	23♏ 3.3	22♎47.8	29♑21.1	5♍ 6.8	5♈42.6	28♍40.2	24♏36.0	22♍41.1
2 Sa	4 40 36	9 6 32	13♐40 33	21 7 59	27R 16.8	24 33.8	23 55.1	0♒ 7.3	5 10.7	5R 41.8	28 42.1	24 38.2	22 41.9
3 Su	4 44 32	10 7 24	28 31 31	5♑50 8	27 10.2	26 4.7	25 2.7	0 53.6	5 14.5	5 41.0	28 43.9	24 40.4	22 42.7
4 M	4 48 29	11 8 17	13♑ 3 0	20 9 30	27 2.9	27 36.0	26 10.4	1 40.0	5 18.0	5 40.4	28 45.6	24 42.5	22 43.4
5 Tu	4 52 26	12 9 11	27 9 9	4♒ 1 41	26 55.9	29 7.6	27 18.4	2 26.4	5 21.4	5 39.8	28 47.3	24 44.7	22 44.1
6 W	4 56 22	13 10 6	10♒47 3	17 25 19	26 50.0	0♐39.5	28 26.6	3 12.8	5 24.6	5 39.4	28 49.0	24 46.9	22 44.8
7 Th	5 0 19	14 11 1	23 56 44	0♓21 42	26 45.8	2 11.7	29 34.9	3 59.2	5 27.6	5 39.1	28 50.6	24 49.1	22 45.5
8 F	5 4 15	15 11 57	6♓40 40	12 54 11	26D 43.6	3 44.0	0♏43.4	4 45.7	5 30.5	5 38.9	28 52.1	24 51.2	22 46.1
9 Sa	5 8 12	16 12 54	19 2 52	25 7 22	26 43.2	5 16.5	1 52.1	5 32.2	5 33.1	5D 38.8	28 53.6	24 53.3	22 46.7
10 Su	5 12 8	17 13 52	1♈ 8 20	7♈ 6 28	26 44.0	6 49.1	3 1.0	6 18.7	5 35.6	5 38.8	28 55.0	24 55.5	22 47.3
11 M	5 16 5	18 14 50	13 2 23	18 56 46	26 45.3	8 21.9	4 10.1	7 5.2	5 37.9	5 38.9	28 56.4	24 57.6	22 47.8
12 Tu	5 20 2	19 15 48	24 50 13	0♉43 20	26R 46.1	9 54.8	5 19.3	7 51.8	5 40.0	5 39.1	28 57.7	24 59.7	22 48.3
13 W	5 23 58	20 16 48	6♉36 38	12 30 38	26 45.5	11 27.7	6 28.7	8 38.4	5 41.9	5 39.5	28 59.0	25 1.8	22 48.7
14 Th	5 27 55	21 17 48	18 25 47	24 22 28	26 42.9	13 0.8	7 38.2	9 25.0	5 43.6	5 39.9	29 0.2	25 3.9	22 49.2
15 F	5 31 51	22 18 49	0♊21 2	6♊21 47	26 37.7	14 34.0	8 47.9	10 11.6	5 45.1	5 40.5	29 1.4	25 5.9	22 49.6
16 Sa	5 35 48	23 19 50	12 24 55	18 30 39	26 30.0	16 7.3	9 57.7	10 58.2	5 46.5	5 41.1	29 2.5	25 8.0	22 49.9
17 Su	5 39 44	24 20 52	24 39 6	0♋50 21	26 20.1	17 40.7	11 7.7	11 44.9	5 47.6	5 41.9	29 3.6	25 10.0	22 50.3
18 M	5 43 41	25 21 55	7♋ 4 29	13 21 30	26 8.9	19 14.3	12 17.8	12 31.5	5 48.6	5 42.8	29 4.6	25 12.0	22 50.5
19 Tu	5 47 37	26 22 58	19 41 25	26 4 13	25 57.3	20 48.0	13 28.1	13 18.2	5 49.3	5 43.8	29 5.6	25 14.0	22 50.8
20 W	5 51 34	27 24 2	2♌29 54	8♌58 29	25 46.5	22 21.8	14 38.5	14 4.9	5 49.9	5 44.9	29 6.4	25 16.0	22 51.0
21 Th	5 55 31	28 25 7	15 29 58	22 4 24	25 37.4	23 55.8	15 49.0	14 51.6	5 50.3	5 46.1	29 7.3	25 18.0	22 51.2
22 F	5 59 27	29 26 13	28 41 50	5♍22 21	25 30.7	25 30.0	16 59.7	15 38.4	5R 50.5	5 47.4	29 8.1	25 19.9	22 51.4
23 Sa	6 3 24	0♑27 19	12♍ 6 4	18 53 5	25 26.7	27 4.3	18 10.5	16 25.1	5 50.4	5 48.8	29 8.8	25 21.9	22 51.5
24 Su	6 7 20	1 28 26	25 43 33	2♎37 34	25D 25.2	28 38.9	19 21.4	17 11.9	5 50.2	5 50.4	29 9.5	25 23.8	22 51.6
25 M	6 11 17	2 29 33	9♎35 14	16 36 35	25 25.2	0♑13.6	20 32.4	17 58.6	5 49.8	5 52.0	29 10.1	25 25.7	22 51.7
26 Tu	6 15 13	3 30 42	23 41 37	0♏50 14	25R 25.5	1 48.6	21 43.5	18 45.4	5 49.2	5 53.7	29 10.6	25 27.6	22R 51.7
27 W	6 19 10	4 31 51	8♏ 2 13	15 17 14	25 25.0	3 23.9	22 54.7	19 32.2	5 48.4	5 55.6	29 11.1	25 29.4	22 51.7
28 Th	6 23 6	5 33 0	22 34 51	29 54 28	25 22.3	4 59.4	24 6.0	20 19.0	5 47.4	5 57.5	29 11.6	25 31.3	22 51.6
29 F	6 27 3	6 34 10	7♐15 21	14♐36 40	25 16.9	6 35.2	25 17.5	21 5.8	5 46.2	5 59.6	29 12.0	25 33.1	22 51.6
30 Sa	6 31 0	7 35 21	21 57 31	29 16 55	25 8.6	8 11.3	26 29.0	21 52.6	5 44.8	6 1.8	29 12.3	25 34.9	22 51.5
31 Su	6 34 56	8 36 32	6♑33 53	13♑47 28	24 57.9	9 47.6	27 40.6	22 39.4	5 43.3	6 4.1	29 12.6	25 36.7	22 51.3

Astro Data Dy Hr Mn	Planet Ingress Dy Hr Mn	Last Aspect Dy Hr Mn	☽ Ingress Dy Hr Mn	Last Aspect Dy Hr Mn	☽ Ingress Dy Hr Mn	☽ Phases & Eclipses Dy Hr Mn	Astro Data
☿ D 10 16:16	♀ ♎ 9 16:32	31 2:47 ♄ ☍	♏ 1 15:26	1 1:12 ♂ ⚹	♐ 1 2:10	2 5:48 ● 9♏07	1 NOVEMBER 1967
♀0S 12 3:36	☉ ♐ 23 0:04	3 10:55 ♅ ⚹	♐ 3 14:51	3 0:20 ♅ □	♑ 3 2:25	2 5:38:17 ☽ T non-C	Julian Day # 24776
☽0N 13 0:37		5 11:47 ♅ □	♑ 5 15:44	5 3:51 ☿ ⚹	♒ 5 4:57	9 1:00 ☽ 15♒56	Delta T 38.1 sec
♄0S 18 9:01	♂ ♒ 1 20:12	7 16:09 ♀ △	♒ 7 19:45	7 1:37 ♆ □	♓ 7 11:19	17 4:53 ○ 24♉09	SVP 05♓42'42"
☽0S 27 8:37	☿ ♐ 5 13:41	9 15:50 ♆ □	♓ 10 3:42	9 19:33 ♅ ☍	♈ 9 21:43	25 0:23 ☽ 2♍02	Obliquity 23°26'45"
	♀ ♏ 7 8:48	12 10:52 ♅ ☍	♈ 12 14:58	11 11:34 ☉ △	♉ 12 10:32		⚷ Chiron 25♓52.6R
♄ D 9 10:27	☉ ♑ 22 13:16	14 0:05 ♂ □	♉ 15 3:52	14 21:20 ♅ △	♊ 14 23:18	1 16:10 ● 8♐47	☽ Mean ☊ 27♈13.3
☽0N 10 6:46	☿ ♑ 24 20:33	17 13:00 ♅ △	♊ 17 16:40	17 8:34 ♅ □	♋ 17 10:23	8 17:57 ☽ 15♓58	
♃⊼♄ 11 12:45		20 0:51 ♅ □	♋ 20 4:13	19 17:40 ♅ ⚹	♌ 19 19:21	16 23:21 ○ 24♊19	1 DECEMBER 1967
♄0N 20 1:00		22 12:54 ☉ △	♌ 22 13:47	22 1:27 ☉ △	♍ 22 2:21	24 10:48 ☽ 1♎56	Julian Day # 24806
♃ R 22 10:02		24 10:38 ♆ □	♍ 24 20:46	24 5:59 ♅ ☌	♎ 24 7:27	31 3:38 ● 8♑46	Delta T 38.2 sec
♃⊼♄ 23 22:15		26 22:20 ♅ ☌	♎ 27 0:48	25 15:10 ♂ △	♏ 26 10:36		SVP 05♓42'37"
☽0S 24 14:48		28 22:37 ♂ □	♏ 29 2:13	28 10:50 ♅ ⚹	♐ 28 12:09		Obliquity 23°26'44"
♇ R 26 4:48				30 11:53 ♅ □	♑ 30 13:11		⚷ Chiron 25♓18.6R
							☽ Mean ☊ 25♈38.0

LONGITUDE JANUARY 1968

Day	Sid.Time	☉	0 hr ☽	Noon ☽	True ☊	☿	♀	♂	♃	♄	♅	♆	♇
1 M	6 38 53	9♑37 43	20♑56 48	28♑ 1 6	24♈45.8	11♑24.3	28♏52.3	23♒26.2	5♍41.5	6♈ 6.4	29♍12.8	25♏38.5	22♍51.1
2 Tu	6 42 49	10 38 54	4♒59 45	11♒52 17	24R 33.8	13 1.4	0♐ 4.1	24 13.1	5R 39.5	6 8.9	29 13.0	25 40.2	22R 50.9
3 W	6 46 46	11 40 5	18 38 24	25 17 59	24 23.0	14 38.7	1 16.0	24 59.9	5 37.4	6 11.5	29 13.1	25 41.9	22 50.7
4 Th	6 50 42	12 41 15	1♓51 4	8♓17 51	24 14.5	16 16.4	2 27.9	25 46.7	5 35.0	6 14.2	29R 13.1	25 43.6	22 50.4
5 F	6 54 39	13 42 26	14 38 39	20 53 53	24 8.7	17 54.4	3 39.9	26 33.6	5 32.5	6 17.0	29 13.1	25 45.3	22 50.1
6 Sa	6 58 35	14 43 36	27 4 5	3♈ 9 50	24 5.5	19 32.8	4 52.0	27 20.4	5 29.7	6 19.8	29 13.0	25 46.9	22 49.8
7 Su	7 2 32	15 44 45	9♈11 48	15 10 38	24D 4.4	21 11.5	6 4.2	28 7.2	5 26.8	6 22.8	29 12.9	25 48.5	22 49.4
8 M	7 6 29	16 45 55	21 7 5	27 1 49	24R 4.3	22 50.5	7 16.4	28 54.0	5 23.7	6 25.9	29 12.7	25 50.1	22 49.0
9 Tu	7 10 25	17 47 4	2♉55 34	8♉49 1	24 4.1	24 29.8	8 28.7	29 40.8	5 20.4	6 29.1	29 12.5	25 51.7	22 48.5
10 W	7 14 22	18 48 12	14 42 50	20 37 39	24 2.6	26 9.4	9 41.0	0♓27.7	5 16.9	6 32.4	29 12.2	25 53.2	22 48.1
11 Th	7 18 18	19 49 20	26 34 3	2♊32 34	23 59.0	27 49.3	10 53.5	1 14.4	5 13.3	6 35.7	29 11.8	25 54.7	22 47.6
12 F	7 22 15	20 50 28	8♊33 41	14 37 49	23 52.6	29 29.4	12 5.9	2 1.2	5 9.4	6 39.2	29 11.4	25 56.2	22 47.0
13 Sa	7 26 11	21 51 35	20 45 17	26 56 23	23 43.3	1♒ 9.7	13 18.5	2 48.0	5 5.4	6 42.8	29 11.0	25 57.7	22 46.5
14 Su	7 30 8	22 52 42	3♋11 15	9♋30 1	23 31.5	2 50.2	14 31.1	3 34.8	5 1.3	6 46.4	29 10.4	25 59.1	22 45.9
15 M	7 34 5	23 53 48	15 52 42	22 19 14	23 18.0	4 30.6	15 43.7	4 21.5	4 56.9	6 50.2	29 9.9	26 0.5	22 45.2
16 Tu	7 38 1	24 54 53	28 49 30	5♌23 19	23 3.9	6 11.0	16 56.4	5 8.3	4 52.4	6 54.0	29 9.3	26 1.9	22 44.6
17 W	7 41 58	25 55 59	12♌ 0 28	18 40 43	22 50.7	7 51.3	18 9.2	5 55.0	4 47.7	6 57.9	29 8.6	26 3.3	22 43.9
18 Th	7 45 54	26 57 3	25 23 45	2♍ 9 22	22 39.4	9 31.2	19 22.0	6 41.7	4 42.9	7 1.9	29 7.8	26 4.6	22 43.2
19 F	7 49 51	27 58 8	8♍57 16	15 47 15	22 30.9	11 10.7	20 34.9	7 28.4	4 37.8	7 6.1	29 7.1	26 5.9	22 42.5
20 Sa	7 53 47	28 59 11	22 39 9	29 32 48	22 25.5	12 49.5	21 47.8	8 15.1	4 32.7	7 10.2	29 6.2	26 7.2	22 41.7
21 Su	7 57 44	0♒ 0 15	6♎28 7	13♎25 1	22 22.9	14 27.5	23 0.8	9 1.8	4 27.4	7 14.5	29 5.3	26 8.4	22 40.9
22 M	8 1 40	1 1 18	20 23 27	27 23 25	22 22.2	16 4.3	24 13.8	9 48.4	4 21.9	7 18.9	29 4.4	26 9.6	22 40.0
23 Tu	8 5 37	2 2 21	4♏24 52	11♏27 45	22 22.2	17 39.6	25 26.9	10 35.1	4 16.2	7 23.3	29 3.4	26 10.8	22 39.2
24 W	8 9 34	3 3 23	18 32 0	25 37 27	22 21.5	19 13.1	26 40.0	11 21.7	4 10.5	7 27.9	29 2.3	26 12.0	22 38.3
25 Th	8 13 30	4 4 25	2♐43 55	9♐51 7	22 18.9	20 44.3	27 53.2	12 8.3	4 4.6	7 32.5	29 1.2	26 13.1	22 37.4
26 F	8 17 27	5 5 27	16 58 40	24 6 7	22 13.5	22 12.8	29 6.4	12 54.9	3 58.5	7 37.2	29 0.1	26 14.2	22 36.4
27 Sa	8 21 23	6 6 28	1♑12 57	8♑18 36	22 5.3	23 38.0	0♑19.6	13 41.5	3 52.3	7 42.0	28 58.9	26 15.2	22 35.5
28 Su	8 25 20	7 7 28	15 22 24	22 23 43	21 54.6	24 59.3	1 32.9	14 28.0	3 46.0	7 46.8	28 57.6	26 16.3	22 34.5
29 M	8 29 16	8 8 28	29 21 56	6♒16 27	21 42.4	26 16.0	2 46.2	15 14.6	3 39.6	7 51.8	28 56.4	26 17.3	22 33.5
30 Tu	8 33 13	9 9 27	13♒ 6 44	19 52 21	21 30.1	27 27.5	3 59.5	16 1.1	3 33.0	7 56.8	28 55.0	26 18.2	22 32.4
31 W	8 37 9	10 10 24	26 32 58	3♓ 8 22	21 18.9	28 32.9	5 12.9	16 47.6	3 26.3	8 1.9	28 53.6	26 19.2	22 31.4

LONGITUDE FEBRUARY 1968

Day	Sid.Time	☉	0 hr ☽	Noon ☽	True ☊	☿	♀	♂	♃	♄	♅	♆	♇
1 Th	8 41 6	11♒11 21	9♓38 27	16♓ 3 15	21♈ 9.9	29♒31.5	6♑26.3	17♓34.1	3♍19.5	8♈ 7.0	28♍52.2	26♏20.1	22♍30.3
2 F	8 45 3	12 12 16	22 22 54	28 37 40	21R 3.5	0♓22.5	7 39.7	18 20.5	3R 12.6	8 12.3	28R 50.7	26 20.9	22R 29.1
3 Sa	8 48 59	13 13 10	4♈47 54	10♈54 3	20 59.8	1 4.9	8 53.1	19 6.9	3 5.6	8 17.6	28 49.1	26 21.8	22 28.0
4 Su	8 52 56	14 14 3	16 56 36	22 56 8	20D 58.5	1 38.2	10 6.6	19 53.3	2 58.5	8 23.0	28 47.6	26 22.6	22 26.8
5 M	8 56 52	15 14 54	28 53 17	4♉48 42	20 58.6	2 1.6	11 20.1	20 39.7	2 51.4	8 28.4	28 45.9	26 23.3	22 25.6
6 Tu	9 0 49	16 15 44	10♉43 2	16 37 1	20R 59.2	2R 14.5	12 33.6	21 26.0	2 44.1	8 34.0	28 44.3	26 24.1	22 24.4
7 W	9 4 45	17 16 32	22 31 18	28 26 36	20 59.1	2 16.6	13 47.1	22 12.3	2 36.7	8 39.6	28 42.6	26 24.8	22 23.2
8 Th	9 8 42	18 17 19	4♊23 35	10♊22 52	20 57.6	2 7.8	15 0.7	22 58.6	2 29.3	8 45.2	28 40.8	26 25.5	22 22.0
9 F	9 12 38	19 18 5	16 25 3	22 30 42	20 53.8	1 48.0	16 14.3	23 44.9	2 21.8	8 51.0	28 39.0	26 26.1	22 20.7
10 Sa	9 16 35	20 18 49	28 40 18	4♋54 14	20 47.6	1 17.8	17 27.9	24 31.1	2 14.2	8 56.8	28 37.2	26 26.7	22 19.4
11 Su	9 20 32	21 19 32	11♋12 51	17 36 23	20 39.3	0 37.8	18 41.5	25 17.3	2 6.6	9 2.6	28 35.3	26 27.3	22 18.1
12 M	9 24 28	22 20 13	24 4 57	0♌38 35	20 29.4	29♒48.9	19 55.1	26 3.4	1 58.9	9 8.5	28 33.4	26 27.8	22 16.8
13 Tu	9 28 25	23 20 52	7♌17 10	14 0 33	20 18.9	28 52.7	21 8.8	26 49.6	1 51.2	9 14.5	28 31.5	26 28.3	22 15.4
14 W	9 32 21	24 21 30	20 48 25	27 40 24	20 8.9	27 50.5	22 22.4	27 35.6	1 43.5	9 20.5	28 29.5	26 28.8	22 14.1
15 Th	9 36 18	25 22 7	4♍36 2	11♍34 50	20 0.4	26 44.1	23 36.1	28 21.7	1 35.7	9 26.6	28 27.5	26 29.2	22 12.7
16 F	9 40 14	26 22 42	18 36 15	25 39 45	19 54.2	25 35.5	24 49.8	29 7.7	1 27.8	9 32.8	28 25.4	26 29.7	22 11.3
17 Sa	9 44 11	27 23 16	2♎44 48	9♎50 54	19 50.5	24 26.4	26 3.6	29 53.7	1 20.0	9 39.0	28 23.3	26 30.0	22 9.9
18 Su	9 48 7	28 23 48	16 57 37	24 4 32	19D 49.2	23 18.6	27 17.3	0♈39.6	1 12.1	9 45.3	28 21.2	26 30.4	22 8.4
19 M	9 52 4	29 24 19	1♏11 18	8♏17 39	19 49.6	22 13.8	28 31.1	1 25.6	1 4.2	9 51.6	28 19.1	26 30.7	22 7.0
20 Tu	9 56 1	0♓24 49	15 23 20	22 28 9	19 50.7	21 13.2	29 44.9	2 11.4	0 56.3	9 58.0	28 16.9	26 30.9	22 5.5
21 W	9 59 57	1 25 18	29 31 57	6♐34 35	19R 51.4	20 18.0	0♒58.7	2 57.3	0 48.4	10 4.4	28 14.7	26 31.2	22 4.0
22 Th	10 3 54	2 25 45	13♐35 55	20 35 49	19 50.8	19 29.1	2 12.5	3 43.1	0 40.5	10 10.9	28 12.4	26 31.4	22 2.6
23 F	10 7 50	3 26 11	27 34 6	4♑30 38	19 48.3	18 47.1	3 26.3	4 28.9	0 32.6	10 17.4	28 10.2	26 31.5	22 1.1
24 Sa	10 11 47	4 26 36	11♑25 11	18 17 32	19 43.8	18 12.3	4 40.2	5 14.6	0 24.7	10 24.0	28 7.9	26 31.7	21 59.6
25 Su	10 15 43	5 27 0	25 7 28	1♒54 42	19 37.4	17 44.8	5 54.0	6 0.3	0 16.8	10 30.6	28 5.6	26 31.8	21 58.0
26 M	10 19 40	6 27 22	8♒39 0	15 20 5	19 30.0	17 24.8	7 7.9	6 46.0	0 9.0	10 37.3	28 3.2	26 31.8	21 56.5
27 Tu	10 23 36	7 27 42	21 57 45	28 31 46	19 22.4	17 12.0	8 21.8	7 31.6	0 1.2	10 44.0	28 0.8	26R 31.9	21 55.0
28 W	10 27 33	8 28 0	5♓ 1 59	11♓28 18	19 15.4	17D 6.2	9 35.7	8 17.2	29♌53.4	10 50.8	27 58.4	26 31.9	21 53.4
29 Th	10 31 30	9 28 17	17 50 39	24 9 3	19 9.9	17 7.1	10 49.6	9 2.8	29 45.6	10 57.6	27 56.0	26 31.8	21 51.8

Astro Data

	Dy Hr Mn
♅ R	4 6:14
☽0N	6 13:41
☽0S	20 19:15
☽0N	2 21:30
☿ R	6 16:40
☽0S	17 1:02
♂0N	18 18:25
♆ R	27 8:55
☿ D	28 8:36

Planet Ingress

	Dy Hr Mn
♀ ♐	1 22:37
♂ ♓	9 9:49
☿ ♒	12 7:19
☉ ♒	20 23:54
♀ ♑	26 17:35
☿ ♓	1 12:57
☿ ♒	11 18:54
♂ ♈	17 3:18
☉ ♓	19 14:09
♀ ♒	20 4:55
♃ ♌	27 3:33

Last Aspect / ☽ Ingress (January)

Last Aspect Dy Hr Mn		☽ Ingress Dy Hr Mn
1 14:43	♀ ⚹	♒ 1 15:23
3 12:45	♆ □	♓ 3 20:35
6 4:13	♅ ☍	♈ 6 5:45
8 16:55	♂ ⚹	♉ 8 18:02
11 5:17	♅ △	♊ 11 6:54
13 16:19	♅ □	♋ 13 17:54
16 0:36	♅ ⚹	♌ 16 2:09
18 1:13	♆ □	♍ 18 8:11
20 11:54	☉ △	♎ 20 12:47
22 7:13	♀ ⚹	♏ 22 16:28
24 17:45	♅ ⚹	♐ 24 19:23
26 20:14	♅ □	♑ 26 21:57
28 23:16	♅ △	♒ 29 1:06
31 3:56	☿ ☌	♓ 31 6:16

Last Aspect / ☽ Ingress (February)

Last Aspect Dy Hr Mn		☽ Ingress Dy Hr Mn
2 12:24	♅ ☍	♈ 2 14:39
3 18:07	☉ ⚹	♉ 5 2:15
7 12:30	♅ △	♊ 7 15:09
9 23:54	♅ □	♋ 10 2:34
12 8:11	♅ ⚹	♌ 12 10:50
14 11:23	☿ ☍	♍ 14 16:02
16 18:54	♂ ☍	♎ 16 19:21
18 20:46	☉ △	♏ 18 22:00
20 21:49	♅ ⚹	♐ 21 0:48
23 1:02	♅ □	♑ 23 4:12
25 5:13	♅ △	♒ 25 8:37
27 14:36	♃ ☍	♓ 27 14:42
29 19:12	♅ ☍	♈ 29 23:14

☽ Phases & Eclipses

Dy Hr Mn	
7 14:23	☽ 16♈21
15 16:11	○ 24♋35
22 19:38	☽ 1♏51
29 16:29	● 8♒50
6 12:20	☽ 16♉47
14 6:43	○ 24♌38
21 3:28	☽ 1♐34
28 6:56	● 8♓45

Astro Data

1 JANUARY 1968
Julian Day # 24837
Delta T 38.3 sec
SVP 05♓42'30"
Obliquity 23°26'44"
⚷ Chiron 25♓34.3
☽ Mean ☊ 23♈59.5

1 FEBRUARY 1968
Julian Day # 24868
Delta T 38.4 sec
SVP 05♓42'24"
Obliquity 23°26'45"
⚷ Chiron 26♓38.7
☽ Mean ☊ 22♈21.1

MARCH 1968 — LONGITUDE

Day	Sid.Time	☉	0 hr ☽	Noon ☽	True ☊	☿	♀	♂	♃	♄	♅	♆	♇
1 F	10 35 26	10♓28 32	0♈23 35	6♈34 25	19♈ 6.1	17♒14.4	12♒ 3.5	9♈48.3	29♌38.0	11♈ 4.4	27♍53.6	26♏31.8	21♍50.3
2 Sa	10 39 23	11 28 45	12 41 45	18 45 52	19D 4.4	17 27.7	13 17.4	10 33.8	29R30.3	11 11.3	27R51.1	26R31.6	21R48.7
3 Su	10 43 19	12 28 56	24 47 9	0♉46 0	19 4.3	17 46.7	14 31.3	11 19.2	29 22.8	11 18.2	27 48.6	26 31.5	21 47.1
4 M	10 47 16	13 29 5	6♉42 52	12 38 16	19 5.5	18 11.1	15 45.2	12 4.6	29 15.3	11 25.2	27 46.1	26 31.3	21 45.5
5 Tu	10 51 12	14 29 13	18 32 44	24 26 53	19 7.2	18 40.3	16 59.1	12 49.9	29 7.8	11 32.2	27 43.6	26 31.1	21 43.9
6 W	10 55 9	15 29 18	0♊21 19	6♊16 39	19 8.9	19 14.2	18 13.0	13 35.2	29 0.5	11 39.2	27 41.1	26 30.9	21 42.3
7 Th	10 59 5	16 29 21	12 13 32	18 12 35	19R 9.9	19 52.4	19 26.9	14 20.5	28 53.2	11 46.3	27 38.6	26 30.6	21 40.7
8 F	11 3 2	17 29 22	24 14 27	0♋19 45	19 9.8	20 34.6	20 40.8	15 5.7	28 46.0	11 53.4	27 36.0	26 30.3	21 39.1
9 Sa	11 6 59	18 29 20	6♋29 3	12 42 52	19 8.3	21 20.6	21 54.8	15 50.9	28 39.0	12 0.5	27 33.5	26 30.0	21 37.5
10 Su	11 10 55	19 29 17	19 1 43	25 25 58	19 5.4	22 10.0	23 8.7	16 36.0	28 32.0	12 7.7	27 30.9	26 29.6	21 35.9
11 M	11 14 52	20 29 11	1♌55 56	8♌31 51	19 1.6	23 2.7	24 22.6	17 21.1	28 25.1	12 14.9	27 28.3	26 29.2	21 34.3
12 Tu	11 18 48	21 29 4	15 13 48	22 1 44	18 57.2	23 58.5	25 36.5	18 6.2	28 18.3	12 22.1	27 25.7	26 28.8	21 32.7
13 W	11 22 45	22 28 54	28 55 31	5♍54 50	18 53.0	24 57.1	26 50.5	18 51.1	28 11.6	12 29.3	27 23.1	26 28.3	21 31.1
14 Th	11 26 41	23 28 41	12♍59 15	20 8 14	18 49.4	25 58.4	28 4.4	19 36.1	28 5.0	12 36.6	27 20.5	26 27.8	21 29.5
15 F	11 30 38	24 28 27	27 21 7	4♎37 10	18 47.0	27 2.2	29 18.3	20 21.0	27 58.6	12 43.9	27 17.9	26 27.3	21 27.8
16 Sa	11 34 34	25 28 11	11♎55 34	19 15 31	18D45.8	28 8.4	0♓32.3	21 5.8	27 52.3	12 51.2	27 15.3	26 26.7	21 26.2
17 Su	11 38 31	26 27 53	26 36 11	3♏56 45	18 45.8	29 16.8	1 46.2	21 50.6	27 46.1	12 58.6	27 12.7	26 26.1	21 24.6
18 M	11 42 28	27 27 33	11♏16 28	18 34 40	18 46.7	0♓27.5	3 0.1	22 35.4	27 40.0	13 5.9	27 10.1	26 25.5	21 23.0
19 Tu	11 46 24	28 27 12	25 50 44	3♐ 4 10	18 48.1	1 40.1	4 14.1	23 20.1	27 34.0	13 13.3	27 7.5	26 24.9	21 21.4
20 W	11 50 21	29 26 49	10♐14 32	17 21 32	18 49.3	2 54.7	5 28.0	24 4.8	27 28.2	13 20.7	27 4.9	26 24.2	21 19.8
21 Th	11 54 17	0♈26 24	24 24 55	1♑24 31	18R50.1	4 11.2	6 42.0	24 49.4	27 22.6	13 28.2	27 2.3	26 23.5	21 18.2
22 F	11 58 14	1 25 57	8♑20 14	15 12 2	18 50.0	5 29.6	7 56.0	25 34.0	27 17.1	13 35.6	26 59.7	26 22.7	21 16.6
23 Sa	12 2 10	2 25 29	21 59 54	28 43 54	18 49.2	6 49.6	9 9.9	26 18.5	27 11.7	13 43.1	26 57.1	26 22.0	21 15.1
24 Su	12 6 7	3 24 59	5♒24 3	12♒ 0 28	18 47.7	8 11.3	10 23.9	27 3.0	27 6.5	13 50.5	26 54.5	26 21.2	21 13.5
25 M	12 10 3	4 24 27	18 33 12	25 2 23	18 45.7	9 34.7	11 37.8	27 47.5	27 1.4	13 58.0	26 51.9	26 20.4	21 11.9
26 Tu	12 14 0	5 23 53	1♓28 5	7♓50 25	18 43.7	10 59.7	12 51.8	28 31.9	26 56.5	14 5.5	26 49.3	26 19.5	21 10.4
27 W	12 17 57	6 23 17	14 9 29	20 25 24	18 41.9	12 26.2	14 5.7	29 16.2	26 51.7	14 13.0	26 46.7	26 18.6	21 8.8
28 Th	12 21 53	7 22 39	26 38 19	2♈48 21	18 40.6	13 54.2	15 19.7	0♉ 0.5	26 47.1	14 20.6	26 44.2	26 17.7	21 7.3
29 F	12 25 50	8 22 0	8♈55 39	15 0 25	18D39.9	15 23.8	16 33.6	0 44.8	26 42.7	14 28.1	26 41.6	26 16.8	21 5.7
30 Sa	12 29 46	9 21 18	21 2 50	27 3 8	18 39.7	16 54.8	17 47.6	1 29.0	26 38.4	14 35.6	26 39.1	26 15.8	21 4.2
31 Su	12 33 43	10 20 34	3♉ 1 35	8♉58 27	18 40.0	18 27.3	19 1.5	2 13.2	26 34.3	14 43.2	26 36.5	26 14.8	21 2.7

APRIL 1968 — LONGITUDE

Day	Sid.Time	☉	0 hr ☽	Noon ☽	True ☊	☿	♀	♂	♃	♄	♅	♆	♇
1 M	12 37 39	11♈19 48	14♉54 6	20♉48 51	18♈40.6	20♓ 1.3	20♓15.5	2♉57.3	26♌30.4	14♈50.7	26♍34.0	26♏13.8	21♍ 1.2
2 Tu	12 41 36	12 19 0	26 43 7	2♊37 20	18 41.4	21 36.7	21 29.4	3 41.3	26R26.6	14 58.3	26R31.5	26R12.8	20R59.7
3 W	12 45 32	13 18 10	8♊31 57	14 27 27	18 42.0	23 13.6	22 43.3	4 25.4	26 23.1	15 5.8	26 29.1	26 11.7	20 58.2
4 Th	12 49 29	14 17 17	20 24 22	26 23 14	18 42.5	24 51.9	23 57.2	5 9.3	26 19.7	15 13.4	26 26.6	26 10.6	20 56.8
5 F	12 53 25	15 16 22	2♋24 36	8♋29 3	18 42.8	26 31.7	25 11.2	5 53.2	26 16.5	15 21.0	26 24.2	26 9.5	20 55.3
6 Sa	12 57 22	16 15 25	14 37 7	20 49 23	18R42.9	28 12.9	26 25.1	6 37.1	26 13.4	15 28.5	26 21.8	26 8.4	20 53.9
7 Su	13 1 19	17 14 26	27 6 23	3♌28 37	18 42.9	29 55.6	27 39.0	7 20.9	26 10.6	15 36.1	26 19.4	26 7.2	20 52.5
8 M	13 5 15	18 13 24	9♌56 32	16 30 31	18D42.8	1♈39.8	28 52.9	8 4.7	26 7.9	15 43.6	26 17.0	26 6.1	20 51.1
9 Tu	13 9 12	19 12 20	23 10 52	29 57 47	18 42.8	3 25.4	0♈ 6.7	8 48.4	26 5.4	15 51.2	26 14.7	26 4.8	20 49.7
10 W	13 13 8	20 11 13	6♍51 21	13♍51 29	18 43.0	5 12.5	1 20.6	9 32.1	26 3.1	15 58.8	26 12.3	26 3.6	20 48.3
11 Th	13 17 5	21 10 5	20 58 0	28 10 30	18 43.1	7 1.1	2 34.5	10 15.7	26 1.0	16 6.3	26 10.0	26 2.4	20 47.0
12 F	13 21 1	22 8 54	5♎28 27	12♎51 9	18R43.3	8 51.3	3 48.4	10 59.3	25 59.0	16 13.8	26 7.8	26 1.1	20 45.6
13 Sa	13 24 58	23 7 41	20 17 46	27 47 20	18 43.4	10 42.9	5 2.2	11 42.8	25 57.2	16 21.4	26 5.5	25 59.8	20 44.3
14 Su	13 28 54	24 6 26	5♏18 48	12♏51 3	18 43.2	12 36.1	6 16.1	12 26.2	25 55.7	16 28.9	26 3.3	25 58.5	20 43.0
15 M	13 32 51	25 5 9	20 22 58	27 53 27	18 42.8	14 30.8	7 29.9	13 9.6	25 54.3	16 36.4	26 1.1	25 57.2	20 41.8
16 Tu	13 36 48	26 3 51	5♐21 30	12♐46 11	18 42.1	16 27.0	8 43.8	13 53.0	25 53.1	16 43.9	25 59.0	25 55.9	20 40.5
17 W	13 40 44	27 2 30	20 6 42	27 22 24	18 41.2	18 24.7	9 57.6	14 36.3	25 52.1	16 51.4	25 56.8	25 54.5	20 39.3
18 Th	13 44 41	28 1 8	4♑32 49	11♑37 36	18 40.3	20 24.0	11 11.5	15 19.6	25 51.2	16 58.9	25 54.7	25 53.1	20 38.1
19 F	13 48 37	28 59 45	18 36 34	25 29 38	18D39.7	22 24.6	12 25.3	16 2.8	25 50.6	17 6.3	25 52.7	25 51.7	20 36.9
20 Sa	13 52 34	29 58 20	2♒16 53	8♒58 28	18 39.6	24 26.7	13 39.2	16 46.0	25 50.1	17 13.8	25 50.7	25 50.3	20 35.7
21 Su	13 56 30	0♉56 53	15 34 37	22 5 38	18 39.9	26 30.0	14 53.0	17 29.1	25D49.9	17 21.2	25 48.7	25 48.9	20 34.5
22 M	14 0 27	1 55 24	28 31 51	4♓53 37	18 40.8	28 34.7	16 6.8	18 12.2	25 49.8	17 28.7	25 46.7	25 47.5	20 33.4
23 Tu	14 4 23	2 53 54	11♓11 18	17 25 18	18 42.0	0♉40.4	17 20.7	18 55.2	25 49.9	17 36.1	25 44.8	25 46.0	20 32.3
24 W	14 8 20	3 52 22	23 35 59	29 43 41	18 43.2	2 47.2	18 34.5	19 38.2	25 50.2	17 43.4	25 42.9	25 44.5	20 31.2
25 Th	14 12 17	4 50 48	5♈48 46	11♈51 33	18 44.2	4 54.8	19 48.3	20 21.1	25 50.6	17 50.8	25 41.0	25 43.0	20 30.1
26 F	14 16 13	5 49 13	17 52 21	23 51 26	18R44.7	7 3.1	21 2.1	21 4.0	25 51.3	17 58.1	25 39.2	25 41.5	20 29.1
27 Sa	14 20 10	6 47 35	29 49 6	5♉45 35	18 44.3	9 11.9	22 15.9	21 46.9	25 52.1	18 5.5	25 37.5	25 40.0	20 28.1
28 Su	14 24 6	7 45 56	11♉41 11	17 36 7	18 42.9	11 20.9	23 29.7	22 29.7	25 53.1	18 12.7	25 35.7	25 38.5	20 27.1
29 M	14 28 3	8 44 16	23 30 39	29 25 4	18 40.6	13 29.8	24 43.5	23 12.4	25 54.3	18 20.0	25 34.0	25 37.0	20 26.1
30 Tu	14 31 59	9 42 33	5♊19 36	11♊14 35	18 37.5	15 38.4	25 57.3	23 55.1	25 55.7	18 27.3	25 32.4	25 35.4	20 25.2

Astro Data	Planet Ingress	Last Aspect	☽ Ingress	Last Aspect	☽ Ingress	☽ Phases & Eclipses
Dy Hr Mn	Dy Hr Mn	Dy Hr Mn	Dy Hr Mn	Dy Hr Mn	Dy Hr Mn	Dy Hr Mn
☽0N 1 5:34	♀ ♓ 15 13:32	3 9:07 ♃ △	♉ 3 10:27	1 23:37 ♅ △	♊ 2 6:40	7 9:20 ☽ 16♊53
♄⚼♆ 4 20:32	☿ ♓ 17 14:45	5 21:18 ♃ □	♊ 5 23:17	4 12:04 ♅ □	♋ 4 19:13	14 18:52 ○ 24♍16
☽0S 15 9:44	☉ ♈ 20 13:22	8 8:51 ♃ ✶	♋ 8 11:21	7 1:08 ♀ △	♌ 7 5:28	21 11:07 ☽ 0♑54
♃⚼♄ 16 1:50	♂ ♉ 27 23:43	10 15:49 ♅ ✶	♌ 10 20:27	9 5:09 ♃ ☌	♍ 9 12:04	28 22:48 ● 8♈19
☽0N 28 12:52		12 22:45 ♅ ☌	♍ 13 1:51	11 8:39 ♅ ☌	♎ 11 15:01	28 22:59:51 ✔ P 0.899
♃⚺♅ 29 14:45	☿ ♈ 7 1:01	14 23:55 ♅ ☌	♎ 15 4:23	13 9:03 ♃ ✶	♏ 13 15:32	
☿0N 9 22:13	♀ ♈ 8 21:48	17 4:45 ☿ △	♏ 17 5:33	15 8:59 ♅ ✶	♐ 15 15:23	6 3:27 ☽ 16♋24
♃□♆ 9 11:30	☉ ♉ 20 0:41	19 4:39 ☉ △	♐ 19 6:53	17 12:17 ☉ △	♑ 17 16:23	13 4:52 ○ 23♎20
☽0S 11 20:23	☿ ♉ 22 16:18	21 5:02 ♃ △	♑ 21 9:34	19 19:35 ☉ □	♒ 19 19:57	13 4:47 ✔ T 1.111
♀0N 11 18:11		23 8:47 ♅ △	♒ 23 14:16	22 0:06 ♅ ✶	♓ 22 2:46	19 19:35 ☽ 29♑48
♃□♆ 20 4:24		25 18:10 ♂ ✶	♓ 25 21:15	24 4:11 ♆ △	♈ 24 12:32	27 15:21 ● 7♉25
♃⚺♅ 20 7:37		28 0:11 ♅ ☍	♈ 28 6:32	26 16:02 ♃ △	♉ 27 0:22	
♅✶♆ 20 13:50		30 11:07 ♃ △	♉ 30 17:55	29 4:52 ♃ □	♊ 29 13:11	
♃ D 21 23:26	☽0N 24 18:57					

Astro Data

1 MARCH 1968
Julian Day # 24897
Delta T 38.4 sec
SVP 05♓42'21"
Obliquity 23°26'45"
⚷ Chiron 28♓09.4
☽ Mean ☊ 20♈48.9

1 APRIL 1968
Julian Day # 24928
Delta T 38.5 sec
SVP 05♓42'17"
Obliquity 23°26'45"
⚷ Chiron 29♓58.9
☽ Mean ☊ 19♈10.4

LONGITUDE — MAY 1968

Day	Sid.Time	☉	0 hr ☽	Noon ☽	True ☊	☿	♀	♂	♃	♄	♅	♆	♇
1 W	14 35 56	10♉40 49	17♊10 17	23♊ 7 4	18♈33.9	17♉46.5	27♈11.1	24♉37.8	25♌57.3	18♈34.5	25♍30.8	25♏33.9	20♍24.3
2 Th	14 39 52	11 39 3	29 5 17	5♋ 5 19	18R 30.2	19 53.6	28 24.9	25 20.4	25 59.1	18 41.7	25R 29.2	25R 32.3	20R 23.4
3 F	14 43 49	12 37 14	11♋ 7 33	17 12 28	18 26.9	21 59.5	29 38.7	26 2.9	26 1.0	18 48.8	25 27.7	25 30.8	20 22.6
4 Sa	14 47 46	13 35 24	23 20 29	29 32 6	18 24.3	24 3.9	0♉52.4	26 45.4	26 3.1	18 56.0	25 26.2	25 29.2	20 21.7
5 Su	14 51 42	14 33 32	5♌47 47	12♌ 8 1	18D 22.9	26 6.5	2 6.2	27 27.9	26 5.4	19 3.1	25 24.8	25 27.6	20 20.9
6 M	14 55 39	15 31 38	18 33 18	25 4 4	18 22.6	28 7.0	3 19.9	28 10.3	26 7.9	19 10.1	25 23.4	25 26.0	20 20.1
7 Tu	14 59 35	16 29 42	1♍40 44	8♍23 40	18 23.4	0♊ 5.2	4 33.7	28 52.6	26 10.5	19 17.2	25 22.1	25 24.4	20 19.4
8 W	15 3 32	17 27 44	15 13 8	22 9 36	18 24.7	2 0.9	5 47.4	29 34.9	26 13.3	19 24.2	25 20.8	25 22.8	20 18.7
9 Th	15 7 28	18 25 44	29 12 12	6♎21 45	18 26.2	3 53.9	7 1.1	0♊17.2	26 16.3	19 31.1	25 19.5	25 21.2	20 18.0
10 F	15 11 25	19 23 42	13♎37 39	20 59 27	18R 27.1	5 43.9	8 14.8	0 59.4	26 19.5	19 38.0	25 18.3	25 19.6	20 17.3
11 Sa	15 15 21	20 21 38	28 26 31	5♏57 58	18 26.8	7 30.9	9 28.5	1 41.5	26 22.8	19 44.9	25 17.2	25 18.0	20 16.7
12 Su	15 19 18	21 19 33	13♏32 49	21 9 55	18 25.1	9 14.8	10 42.3	2 23.6	26 26.3	19 51.8	25 16.1	25 16.3	20 16.1
13 M	15 23 15	22 17 26	28 47 58	6♐25 41	18 21.8	10 55.3	11 56.0	3 5.7	26 30.0	19 58.6	25 15.0	25 14.7	20 15.5
14 Tu	15 27 11	23 15 18	14♐ 1 43	21 34 50	18 17.3	12 32.5	13 9.7	3 47.7	26 33.8	20 5.4	25 14.0	25 13.1	20 15.0
15 W	15 31 8	24 13 9	29 3 53	6♑27 51	18 12.2	14 6.3	14 23.4	4 29.7	26 37.8	20 12.1	25 13.0	25 11.5	20 14.4
16 Th	15 35 4	25 10 58	13♑45 57	20 57 33	18 7.3	15 36.5	15 37.1	5 11.6	26 42.0	20 18.8	25 12.1	25 9.8	20 14.0
17 F	15 39 1	26 8 46	28 2 16	4♒59 52	18 3.2	17 3.3	16 50.8	5 53.5	26 46.3	20 25.4	25 11.3	25 8.2	20 13.5
18 Sa	15 42 57	27 6 33	11♒50 21	18 33 51	18 0.5	18 26.3	18 4.5	6 35.3	26 50.8	20 32.1	25 10.5	25 6.6	20 13.1
19 Su	15 46 54	28 4 18	25 10 38	1♓41 5	17D 59.4	19 45.8	19 18.2	7 17.1	26 55.4	20 38.6	25 9.7	25 5.0	20 12.7
20 M	15 50 51	29 2 3	8♓ 5 38	14 24 48	17 59.7	21 1.5	20 31.8	7 58.8	27 0.2	20 45.1	25 9.0	25 3.3	20 12.3
21 Tu	15 54 47	29 59 46	20 39 8	26 49 11	18 0.9	22 13.5	21 45.5	8 40.5	27 5.1	20 51.6	25 8.3	25 1.7	20 12.0
22 W	15 58 44	0♊57 28	2♈55 33	8♈58 44	18 2.4	23 21.6	22 59.2	9 22.2	27 10.2	20 58.0	25 7.7	25 0.1	20 11.7
23 Th	16 2 40	1 55 9	14 59 17	20 57 43	18R 3.3	24 25.9	24 12.9	10 3.8	27 15.5	21 4.4	25 7.2	24 58.5	20 11.4
24 F	16 6 37	2 52 49	26 54 29	2♉50 2	18 2.9	25 26.2	25 26.6	10 45.3	27 20.9	21 10.7	25 6.6	24 56.9	20 11.1
25 Sa	16 10 33	3 50 28	8♉44 44	14 38 59	18 0.6	26 22.6	26 40.3	11 26.9	27 26.4	21 17.0	25 6.2	24 55.3	20 10.9
26 Su	16 14 30	4 48 6	20 33 4	26 27 17	17 56.3	27 14.9	27 54.0	12 8.3	27 32.1	21 23.2	25 5.8	24 53.7	20 10.7
27 M	16 18 26	5 45 43	2♊21 55	8♊17 11	17 49.8	28 3.0	29 7.7	12 49.8	27 38.0	21 29.3	25 5.4	24 52.1	20 10.6
28 Tu	16 22 23	6 43 19	14 13 18	20 10 29	17 41.6	28 46.9	0♊21.4	13 31.2	27 44.0	21 35.4	25 5.2	24 50.5	20 10.5
29 W	16 26 20	7 40 54	26 8 56	2♋ 8 50	17 32.3	29 26.5	1 35.1	14 12.5	27 50.1	21 41.5	25 4.9	24 48.9	20 10.4
30 Th	16 30 16	8 38 27	8♋10 25	14 13 54	17 22.8	0♋ 1.8	2 48.8	14 53.8	27 56.4	21 47.5	25 4.7	24 47.3	20 10.3
31 F	16 34 13	9 35 59	20 19 32	26 27 33	17 13.9	0 32.6	4 2.4	15 35.1	28 2.8	21 53.4	25 4.6	24 45.8	20D 10.3

LONGITUDE — JUNE 1968

Day	Sid.Time	☉	0 hr ☽	Noon ☽	True ☊	☿	♀	♂	♃	♄	♅	♆	♇
1 Sa	16 38 9	10♊33 30	2♌38 17	8♌52 2	17♈ 6.6	0♋58.9	5♊16.1	16♊16.3	28♌ 9.4	21♈59.3	25♍ 4.5	24♏44.2	20♍10.3
2 Su	16 42 6	11 31 0	15 9 9	21 30 0	17R 1.2	1 20.6	6 29.8	16 57.4	28 16.1	22 5.1	25D 4.5	24R 42.7	20 10.4
3 M	16 46 2	12 28 28	27 54 59	4♍24 29	16 58.1	1 37.8	7 43.5	17 38.6	28 22.9	22 10.9	25 4.5	24 41.1	20 10.4
4 Tu	16 49 59	13 25 55	10♍58 53	17 38 36	16D 57.0	1 50.3	8 57.2	18 19.6	28 29.9	22 16.6	25 4.6	24 39.6	20 10.5
5 W	16 53 55	14 23 21	24 23 56	1♎15 10	16 57.3	1 58.2	10 10.8	19 0.7	28 37.0	22 22.2	25 4.7	24 38.1	20 10.7
6 Th	16 57 52	15 20 46	8♎12 32	15 16 6	16R 58.0	2R 1.4	11 24.5	19 41.7	28 44.2	22 27.8	25 4.9	24 36.6	20 10.9
7 F	17 1 49	16 18 9	22 25 50	29 41 32	16 58.2	2 0.2	12 38.2	20 22.6	28 51.6	22 33.3	25 5.1	24 35.1	20 11.1
8 Sa	17 5 45	17 15 32	7♏ 2 48	14♏29 4	16 56.6	1 54.5	13 51.8	21 3.5	28 59.1	22 38.7	25 5.4	24 33.6	20 11.3
9 Su	17 9 42	18 12 53	21 59 34	29 33 19	16 52.9	1 44.5	15 5.5	21 44.4	29 6.7	22 44.1	25 5.8	24 32.1	20 11.5
10 M	17 13 38	19 10 14	7♐ 9 11	14♐45 56	16 46.7	1 30.3	16 19.2	22 25.2	29 14.4	22 49.4	25 6.2	24 30.7	20 11.8
11 Tu	17 17 35	20 7 33	22 22 13	29 56 41	16 38.5	1 12.3	17 32.8	23 6.0	29 22.3	22 54.6	25 6.6	24 29.3	20 12.2
12 W	17 21 31	21 4 52	7♑28 3	14♑55 5	16 29.2	0 50.7	18 46.5	23 46.7	29 30.2	22 59.8	25 7.1	24 27.9	20 12.5
13 Th	17 25 28	22 2 11	22 16 47	29 32 17	16 19.9	0 25.9	20 0.2	24 27.4	29 38.3	23 4.9	25 7.7	24 26.5	20 12.9
14 F	17 29 24	22 59 29	6♒40 57	13♒42 22	16 11.8	29♊58.2	21 13.9	25 8.0	29 46.5	23 9.9	25 8.3	24 25.1	20 13.3
15 Sa	17 33 21	23 56 46	20 36 20	27 22 51	16 5.5	29 28.2	22 27.5	25 48.6	29 54.8	23 14.9	25 9.0	24 23.7	20 13.8
16 Su	17 37 18	24 54 3	4♓ 2 6	10♓34 23	16 1.6	28 56.3	23 41.2	26 29.2	0♍ 3.3	23 19.8	25 9.7	24 22.3	20 14.3
17 M	17 41 14	25 51 19	17 0 9	23 19 56	15D 59.8	28 23.0	24 54.9	27 9.7	0 11.8	23 24.6	25 10.4	24 21.0	20 14.8
18 Tu	17 45 11	26 48 36	29 34 18	5♈43 54	15 59.5	27 48.9	26 8.6	27 50.2	0 20.5	23 29.3	25 11.3	24 19.7	20 15.3
19 W	17 49 7	27 45 52	11♈49 24	17 51 25	15R 59.7	27 14.6	27 22.3	28 30.7	0 29.2	23 34.0	25 12.1	24 18.4	20 15.9
20 Th	17 53 4	28 43 7	23 50 38	29 47 40	15 59.6	26 40.7	28 36.0	29 11.1	0 38.1	23 38.5	25 13.1	24 17.1	20 16.5
21 F	17 57 0	29 40 23	5♉43 7	11♉37 33	15 57.9	26 7.7	29 49.7	29 51.5	0 47.1	23 43.1	25 14.0	24 15.8	20 17.2
22 Sa	18 0 57	0♋37 39	17 31 28	23 25 21	15 54.0	25 36.3	1♋ 3.5	0♋31.8	0 56.2	23 47.5	25 15.1	24 14.6	20 17.8
23 Su	18 4 53	1 34 54	29 19 38	5♊14 40	15 47.4	25 6.9	2 17.2	1 12.2	1 5.3	23 51.8	25 16.1	24 13.4	20 18.5
24 M	18 8 50	2 32 9	11♊10 48	17 8 18	15 38.1	24 40.1	3 30.9	1 52.4	1 14.6	23 56.1	25 17.3	24 12.2	20 19.3
25 Tu	18 12 47	3 29 24	23 7 24	29 8 17	15 26.5	24 16.3	4 44.7	2 32.7	1 24.0	24 0.3	25 18.5	24 11.0	20 20.0
26 W	18 16 43	4 26 38	5♋11 7	11♋16 2	15 13.6	23 55.9	5 58.4	3 12.9	1 33.5	24 4.4	25 19.7	24 9.9	20 20.8
27 Th	18 20 40	5 23 53	17 23 7	23 32 30	15 0.3	23 39.4	7 12.1	3 53.0	1 43.1	24 8.4	25 21.0	24 8.7	20 21.6
28 F	18 24 36	6 21 7	29 44 15	5♌58 29	14 47.7	23 26.9	8 25.9	4 33.2	1 52.8	24 12.4	25 22.3	24 7.6	20 22.5
29 Sa	18 28 33	7 18 21	12♌15 19	18 34 52	14 37.0	23 18.8	9 39.6	5 13.2	2 2.5	24 16.2	25 23.7	24 6.5	20 23.4
30 Su	18 32 29	8 15 34	24 57 18	1♍22 48	14 28.8	23D 15.2	10 53.4	5 53.3	2 12.4	24 20.0	25 25.1	24 5.5	20 24.3

Astro Data Dy Hr Mn	Planet Ingress Dy Hr Mn	Last Aspect Dy Hr Mn	☽ Ingress Dy Hr Mn	Last Aspect Dy Hr Mn	☽ Ingress Dy Hr Mn	☽ Phases & Eclipses Dy Hr Mn	Astro Data
☽0S 9 6:41	♀ ♉ 3 6:56	1 22:30 ♀ ⚹	♋ 2 1:50	3 0:52 ♃ ☌	♍ 3 3:52	5 17:54 ☽ 15♌17	1 MAY 1968
♅⚹♆ 12 11:51	☿ ♊ 6 22:56	4 7:02 ♂ ⚹	♌ 4 12:54	5 1:12 ♅ ☌	♎ 5 9:49	12 13:05 ○ 21♏51	Julian Day # 24958
♄⚻♇ 15 7:47	♂ ♊ 8 14:14	6 20:38 ☿ □	♍ 6 20:58	7 10:43 ♃ ⚹	♏ 7 12:30	19 5:44 ☽ 28♒18	Delta T 38.6 sec
☽0N 22 0:20	☉ ♊ 21 0:06	8 17:29 ♆ ⚹	♎ 9 1:21	9 11:24 ♃ □	♐ 9 12:42	27 7:30 ● 6♊04	SVP 05♓42'14"
♇ D 31 4:01	♀ ♊ 27 17:02	10 20:41 ♃ ⚹	♏ 11 2:30	11 11:11 ♃ △	♑ 11 12:05		Obliquity 23°26'45"
	☿ ♋ 29 22:44	12 20:22 ♃ □	♐ 13 1:53	13 4:42 ♅ △	♒ 13 12:46	4 4:47 ☽ 13♍37	⚷ Chiron 1♈37.0
♅ D 2 0:36		14 20:04 ♃ △	♑ 15 1:31	15 15:09 ☿ △	♓ 15 16:42	10 20:13 ○ 19♐59	☽ Mean ☊ 17♈35.1
☽0S 5 14:49	☿ ♊ 13 22:32	16 20:32 ☉ △	♒ 17 3:22	17 20:45 ☿ □	♈ 18 0:50	17 18:14 ☽ 26♓35	
☿ R 6 5:16	♃ ♍ 15 14:43	19 5:44 ☉ □	♓ 19 8:53	20 11:25 ♂ ⚹	♉ 20 12:25	25 22:24 ● 4♋23	1 JUNE 1968
☽0N 18 6:04	☉ ♋ 21 8:13	21 8:43 ♅ ☍	♈ 21 18:14	22 15:44 ♅ △	♊ 23 1:22		Julian Day # 24989
♄⚻♆ 27 1:27	♀ ♋ 21 3:20	24 0:54 ♃ △	♉ 24 6:15	25 4:22 ♅ □	♋ 25 13:43		Delta T 38.7 sec
☿ D 30 6:09	♂ ♋ 21 5:03	26 16:40 ♀ ☌	♊ 26 19:12	27 15:32 ♅ ⚹	♌ 28 0:30		SVP 05♓42'08"
		29 6:57 ☿ ☌	♋ 29 7:43	29 22:50 ♄ △	♍ 30 9:26		Obliquity 23°26'44"
		31 9:18 ♅ ⚹	♌ 31 18:53				⚷ Chiron 2♈50.8
							☽ Mean ☊ 15♈56.6

JULY 1968 — LONGITUDE

Day	Sid.Time	☉	0 hr ☽	Noon ☽	True ☊	☿	♀	♂	♃	♄	♅	♆	♇
1 M	18 36 26	9♋12 47	7♍51 36	14♍23 55	14♈23.5	23♊16.4	12♋ 7.2	6♋33.3	2♍22.4	24♈23.7	25♍26.6	24♏ 4.4	20♍25.2
2 Tu	18 40 22	10 9 59	21 0 1	27 40 10	14R 20.7	23 22.4	13 20.9	7 13.3	2 32.4	24 27.2	25 28.2	24R 3.4	20 26.2
3 W	18 44 19	11 7 12	4♎24 38	11♎13 40	14 19.9	23 33.4	14 34.7	7 53.2	2 42.5	24 30.7	25 29.7	24 2.4	20 27.2
4 Th	18 48 16	12 4 24	18 7 29	25 6 12	14 19.8	23 49.3	15 48.4	8 33.1	2 52.7	24 34.2	25 31.4	24 1.5	20 28.2
5 F	18 52 12	13 1 35	2♏ 9 53	9♏18 28	14 19.3	24 10.2	17 2.2	9 12.9	3 3.0	24 37.5	25 33.0	24 0.5	20 29.3
6 Sa	18 56 9	13 58 47	16 31 47	23 49 28	14 17.1	24 36.2	18 16.0	9 52.8	3 13.4	24 40.7	25 34.8	23 59.6	20 30.4
7 Su	19 0 5	14 55 58	1♐11 1	8♐35 46	14 12.6	25 7.2	19 29.8	10 32.5	3 23.9	24 43.9	25 36.5	23 58.7	20 31.5
8 M	19 4 2	15 53 9	16 2 50	23 31 17	14 5.3	25 43.1	20 43.5	11 12.3	3 34.4	24 46.9	25 38.4	23 57.9	20 32.6
9 Tu	19 7 58	16 50 20	0♑59 59	8♑27 47	13 55.8	26 24.0	21 57.3	11 52.0	3 45.1	24 49.9	25 40.2	23 57.0	20 33.8
10 W	19 11 55	17 47 31	15 53 32	23 16 6	13 45.0	27 9.8	23 11.1	12 31.7	3 55.8	24 52.8	25 42.1	23 56.2	20 35.0
11 Th	19 15 52	18 44 43	0♒34 27	7♒47 40	13 34.0	28 0.5	24 24.9	13 11.3	4 6.5	24 55.5	25 44.1	23 55.4	20 36.2
12 F	19 19 48	19 41 54	14 55 0	21 55 56	13 24.1	28 55.9	25 38.7	13 50.9	4 17.4	24 58.2	25 46.1	23 54.7	20 37.4
13 Sa	19 23 45	20 39 6	28 50 5	5♓37 17	13 16.3	29 56.1	26 52.5	14 30.5	4 28.3	25 0.8	25 48.1	23 54.0	20 38.7
14 Su	19 27 41	21 36 18	12♓17 34	18 51 6	13 10.9	1♋ 1.0	28 6.3	15 10.1	4 39.3	25 3.3	25 50.2	23 53.3	20 40.0
15 M	19 31 38	22 33 31	25 18 11	1♈39 15	13 8.1	2 10.5	29 20.1	15 49.6	4 50.3	25 5.7	25 52.4	23 52.6	20 41.3
16 Tu	19 35 34	23 30 45	7♈54 49	14 5 29	13D 7.1	3 24.5	0♌33.9	16 29.1	5 1.5	25 8.0	25 54.5	23 52.0	20 42.7
17 W	19 39 31	24 27 59	20 11 51	26 14 36	13R 7.1	4 43.0	1 47.7	17 8.5	5 12.7	25 10.2	25 56.8	23 51.3	20 44.0
18 Th	19 43 27	25 25 14	2♉14 23	8♉11 54	13 7.0	6 5.8	3 1.5	17 47.9	5 23.9	25 12.3	25 59.0	23 50.8	20 45.4
19 F	19 47 24	26 22 29	14 7 48	20 2 44	13 5.7	7 33.0	4 15.4	18 27.3	5 35.3	25 14.3	26 1.3	23 50.2	20 46.9
20 Sa	19 51 21	27 19 45	25 57 18	1♊52 3	13 2.4	9 4.3	5 29.2	19 6.7	5 46.7	25 16.2	26 3.7	23 49.7	20 48.3
21 Su	19 55 17	28 17 2	7♊47 33	13 44 15	12 56.7	10 39.7	6 43.1	19 46.0	5 58.1	25 18.0	26 6.1	23 49.2	20 49.8
22 M	19 59 14	29 14 20	19 42 36	25 42 56	12 48.4	12 18.9	7 56.9	20 25.3	6 9.6	25 19.8	26 8.5	23 48.7	20 51.3
23 Tu	20 3 10	0♌11 39	1♋45 34	7♋50 46	12 37.9	14 1.8	9 10.8	21 4.6	6 21.2	25 21.4	26 11.0	23 48.3	20 52.8
24 W	20 7 7	1 8 58	13 58 43	20 9 32	12 26.0	15 48.2	10 24.6	21 43.8	6 32.9	25 22.9	26 13.5	23 47.9	20 54.4
25 Th	20 11 3	2 6 18	26 23 19	2♌40 7	12 13.6	17 37.9	11 38.5	22 23.0	6 44.6	25 24.3	26 16.0	23 47.5	20 55.9
26 F	20 15 0	3 3 39	8♌59 55	15 22 43	12 2.0	19 30.6	12 52.4	23 2.2	6 56.3	25 25.6	26 18.6	23 47.2	20 57.5
27 Sa	20 18 56	4 1 0	21 48 28	28 17 7	11 52.1	21 26.0	14 6.3	23 41.4	7 8.1	25 26.8	26 21.3	23 46.9	20 59.1
28 Su	20 22 53	4 58 22	4♍48 38	11♍22 58	11 44.6	23 23.8	15 20.2	24 20.5	7 20.0	25 27.9	26 23.9	23 46.6	21 0.8
29 M	20 26 50	5 55 44	18 0 8	24 40 8	11 39.8	25 23.6	16 34.0	24 59.6	7 31.9	25 28.9	26 26.6	23 46.4	21 2.4
30 Tu	20 30 46	6 53 7	1♎22 59	8♎ 8 45	11D 37.6	27 25.2	17 47.9	25 38.6	7 43.9	25 29.8	26 29.4	23 46.2	21 4.1
31 W	20 34 43	7 50 31	14 57 29	21 49 16	11 37.2	29 28.2	19 1.8	26 17.6	7 55.9	25 30.5	26 32.1	23 46.0	21 5.8

AUGUST 1968 — LONGITUDE

Day	Sid.Time	☉	0 hr ☽	Noon ☽	True ☊	☿	♀	♂	♃	♄	♅	♆	♇
1 Th	20 38 39	8♌47 55	28♎44 10	5♏42 12	11♈37.7	1♌32.2	20♌15.7	26♋56.6	8♍ 7.9	25♈31.2	26♍34.9	23♏45.8	21♍ 7.5
2 F	20 42 36	9 45 20	12♏43 23	19 47 39	11R 37.9	3 36.9	21 29.6	27 35.6	8 20.0	25 31.8	26 37.8	23R 45.7	21 9.2
3 Sa	20 46 32	10 42 45	26 54 52	4♐ 4 48	11 36.8	5 42.1	22 43.5	28 14.5	8 32.2	25 32.3	26 40.7	23 45.6	21 11.0
4 Su	20 50 29	11 40 11	11♐17 8	18 31 25	11 33.7	7 47.3	23 57.3	28 53.4	8 44.4	25 32.6	26 43.6	23 45.6	21 12.8
5 M	20 54 25	12 37 38	25 47 6	3♑ 3 32	11 28.3	9 52.4	25 11.2	29 32.3	8 56.6	25 32.9	26 46.5	23D 45.6	21 14.6
6 Tu	20 58 22	13 35 6	10♑19 59	17 35 38	11 21.0	11 57.1	26 25.1	0♌11.1	9 8.9	25 33.1	26 49.5	23 45.6	21 16.4
7 W	21 2 19	14 32 34	24 49 41	2♒ 1 16	11 12.4	14 1.2	27 39.0	0 50.0	9 21.2	25R 33.1	26 52.5	23 45.6	21 18.2
8 Th	21 6 15	15 30 3	9♒ 9 36	16 13 58	11 3.6	16 4.6	28 52.9	1 28.7	9 33.6	25 33.1	26 55.6	23 45.7	21 20.0
9 F	21 10 12	16 27 34	23 13 43	0♓ 8 21	10 55.7	18 6.8	0♍ 6.7	2 7.5	9 46.0	25 33.0	26 58.6	23 45.8	21 21.9
10 Sa	21 14 8	17 25 5	6♓57 28	13 40 51	10 49.5	20 8.1	1 20.6	2 46.2	9 58.4	25 32.7	27 1.7	23 45.9	21 23.8
11 Su	21 18 5	18 22 37	20 18 23	26 50 6	10 45.4	22 8.2	2 34.5	3 24.9	10 10.9	25 32.3	27 4.9	23 46.1	21 25.7
12 M	21 22 1	19 20 11	3♈16 11	9♈36 52	10D 43.5	24 7.1	3 48.4	4 3.6	10 23.4	25 31.9	27 8.0	23 46.3	21 27.6
13 Tu	21 25 58	20 17 46	15 52 32	22 3 39	10 43.3	26 4.7	5 2.2	4 42.3	10 35.9	25 31.3	27 11.2	23 46.6	21 29.5
14 W	21 29 54	21 15 23	28 10 42	4♉14 15	10 44.2	28 0.9	6 16.1	5 20.9	10 48.5	25 30.7	27 14.4	23 46.8	21 31.5
15 Th	21 33 51	22 13 1	10♉14 55	16 13 20	10 45.5	29 55.8	7 30.0	5 59.5	11 1.1	25 29.9	27 17.7	23 47.1	21 33.4
16 F	21 37 48	23 10 41	22 10 7	28 5 55	10R 46.1	1♍49.2	8 43.9	6 38.1	11 13.7	25 29.0	27 21.0	23 47.5	21 35.4
17 Sa	21 41 44	24 8 22	4♊ 1 23	9♊57 8	10 45.5	3 41.2	9 57.7	7 16.6	11 26.4	25 28.0	27 24.2	23 47.8	21 37.4
18 Su	21 45 41	25 6 5	15 53 45	21 51 48	10 43.2	5 31.8	11 11.6	7 55.2	11 39.1	25 27.0	27 27.6	23 48.2	21 39.4
19 M	21 49 37	26 3 50	27 51 49	3♋54 17	10 39.1	7 21.0	12 25.5	8 33.7	11 51.8	25 25.8	27 30.9	23 48.7	21 41.4
20 Tu	21 53 34	27 1 36	9♋59 37	16 8 10	10 33.2	9 8.8	13 39.4	9 12.1	12 4.6	25 24.5	27 34.3	23 49.1	21 43.4
21 W	21 57 30	27 59 24	22 20 15	28 36 5	10 26.3	10 55.1	14 53.3	9 50.6	12 17.3	25 23.1	27 37.7	23 49.6	21 45.5
22 Th	22 1 27	28 57 13	4♌55 51	11♌19 36	10 18.9	12 40.1	16 7.1	10 29.0	12 30.1	25 21.7	27 41.1	23 50.1	21 47.5
23 F	22 5 23	29 55 4	17 47 22	24 19 7	10 11.9	14 23.7	17 21.0	11 7.4	12 42.9	25 20.1	27 44.6	23 50.7	21 49.6
24 Sa	22 9 20	0♍52 56	0♍54 42	7♍34 0	10 6.0	16 5.9	18 34.9	11 45.8	12 55.8	25 18.4	27 48.0	23 51.3	21 51.7
25 Su	22 13 17	1 50 50	14 16 46	21 2 49	10 1.8	17 46.8	19 48.8	12 24.2	13 8.6	25 16.6	27 51.5	23 51.9	21 53.8
26 M	22 17 13	2 48 45	27 51 51	4♎43 38	9D 59.4	19 26.3	21 2.6	13 2.5	13 21.5	25 14.7	27 55.0	23 52.6	21 55.9
27 Tu	22 21 10	3 46 41	11♎37 53	18 34 21	9 58.8	21 4.5	22 16.5	13 40.8	13 34.4	25 12.8	27 58.5	23 53.3	21 58.0
28 W	22 25 6	4 44 39	25 32 48	2♏33 0	9 59.6	22 41.4	23 30.4	14 19.1	13 47.3	25 10.7	28 2.1	23 54.0	22 0.1
29 Th	22 29 3	5 42 38	9♏34 43	16 37 46	10 0.9	24 17.0	24 44.2	14 57.4	14 0.2	25 8.5	28 5.6	23 54.7	22 2.2
30 F	22 32 59	6 40 39	23 41 56	0♐47 0	10R 2.3	25 51.3	25 58.1	15 35.6	14 13.1	25 6.3	28 9.2	23 55.5	22 4.3
31 Sa	22 36 56	7 38 41	7♐52 46	14 58 59	10 2.8	27 24.2	27 11.9	16 13.8	14 26.1	25 3.9	28 12.8	23 56.3	22 6.5

Astro Data Dy Hr Mn	Planet Ingress Dy Hr Mn	Last Aspect Dy Hr Mn	☽ Ingress Dy Hr Mn	Last Aspect Dy Hr Mn	☽ Ingress Dy Hr Mn	☽ Phases & Eclipses Dy Hr Mn	Astro Data
☽0S 2 20:27	☿ ♋ 13 1:30	2 8:04 ♅ ☌	♎ 2 16:10	31 20:45 ♂ □	♏ 1 2:11	3 12:42 ☽ 11♎37	1 JULY 1968
☽0N 15 13:04	♀ ♌ 15 12:59	4 11:08 ♄ ☍	♏ 4 20:20	3 2:20 ♂ △	♐ 3 5:11	10 3:18 ○ 17♑55	Julian Day # 25019
☽0S 30 1:03	☉ ♌ 22 19:07	6 14:54 ♅ ⚹	♐ 6 22:05	5 1:38 ♅ □	♑ 5 6:57	17 9:11 ☽ 24♈50	Delta T 38.7 sec
	☿ ♌ 31 6:11	8 16:15 ☿ ☍	♑ 8 22:24	7 3:25 ♅ △	♒ 7 8:37	25 11:49 ● 2♌35	SVP 05♓42'02"
♆ D 5 1:17		10 16:01 ♅ △	♒ 10 23:03	9 4:01 ♄ ⚹	♓ 9 11:45		Obliquity 23°26'45"
♄ R 7 2:22	♂ ♌ 5 17:07	12 17:19 ♄ ⚹	♓ 13 2:03	11 12:30 ♅ ☍	♈ 11 17:53	1 18:34 ☽ 9♏32	⚷ Chiron 3♈21.6
☽0N 11 21:18	♀ ♍ 8 21:49	15 8:25 ♀ △	♈ 15 8:51	13 23:37 ☿ △	♉ 14 3:36	8 11:32 ○ 15♒58	☽ Mean ☊ 14♈21.3
♃⚼♄ 12 15:35	☿ ♍ 15 0:53	17 9:53 ♄ ☌	♉ 17 19:30	16 10:32 ♅ △	♊ 16 15:51	16 2:13 ☽ 23♉16	
☽0S 26 6:45	☉ ♍ 23 2:03	20 3:02 ☉ ⚹	♊ 20 8:13	18 23:18 ♅ □	♋ 19 4:15	23 23:57 ● 0♍53	1 AUGUST 1968
		22 12:54 ♅ □	♋ 22 20:31	21 10:11 ♅ ⚹	♌ 21 14:40	30 23:34 ☽ 7♐38	Julian Day # 25050
		24 23:46 ♅ ⚹	♌ 25 6:55	23 13:50 ♄ △	♍ 23 22:21		Delta T 38.8 sec
		27 6:46 ♄ △	♍ 27 15:10	26 0:06 ♅ ☌	♎ 26 3:45		SVP 05♓41'57"
		29 15:40 ☿ ⚹	♎ 29 21:32	27 23:22 ♄ ☍	♏ 28 7:38		Obliquity 23°26'45"
				30 7:35 ♅ ⚹	♐ 30 10:40		⚷ Chiron 3♈05.1R
							☽ Mean ☊ 12♈42.9

LONGITUDE SEPTEMBER 1968

Day	Sid.Time	☉	0 hr ☽	Noon ☽	True ☊	☿	♀	♂	♃	♄	♅	♆	♇
1 Su	22 40 52	8♍36 44	22♐ 5 23	29♐11 40	10♈ 2.1	28♍55.9	28♍25.7	16♌52.0	14♍39.0	25♈ 1.5	28♍16.4	23♏57.2	22♍ 8.6
2 M	22 44 49	9 34 49	6♑17 31	13♑22 33	10R 0.0	0♎26.3	29 39.5	17 30.1	14 52.0	24R58.9	28 20.0	23 58.0	22 10.8
3 Tu	22 48 46	10 32 55	20 26 22	27 28 34	9 56.8	1 55.4	0♎53.3	18 8.2	15 5.0	24 56.3	28 23.7	23 59.0	22 12.9
4 W	22 52 42	11 31 3	4♒28 41	11♒26 19	9 52.8	3 23.2	2 7.1	18 46.3	15 18.0	24 53.6	28 27.3	23 59.9	22 15.1
5 Th	22 56 39	12 29 12	18 21 1	25 12 24	9 48.6	4 49.6	3 20.9	19 24.4	15 30.9	24 50.8	28 31.0	24 0.9	22 17.3
6 F	23 0 35	13 27 22	2♓ 0 6	8♓43 49	9 44.9	6 14.8	4 34.7	20 2.5	15 43.9	24 47.9	28 34.7	24 1.8	22 19.5
7 Sa	23 4 32	14 25 34	15 23 18	21 58 24	9 42.0	7 38.5	5 48.5	20 40.5	15 56.9	24 44.9	28 38.4	24 2.9	22 21.6
8 Su	23 8 28	15 23 48	28 29 1	4♈55 8	9D 40.4	9 0.9	7 2.2	21 18.5	16 9.9	24 41.9	28 42.1	24 3.9	22 23.8
9 M	23 12 25	16 22 4	11♈16 49	17 34 14	9 40.0	10 21.9	8 16.0	21 56.5	16 22.9	24 38.8	28 45.8	24 5.0	22 26.0
10 Tu	23 16 21	17 20 22	23 47 35	29 57 10	9 40.6	11 41.4	9 29.7	22 34.5	16 35.9	24 35.5	28 49.5	24 6.1	22 28.2
11 W	23 20 18	18 18 41	6♉ 3 21	12♉ 6 31	9 41.9	12 59.4	10 43.5	23 12.4	16 48.9	24 32.3	28 53.3	24 7.3	22 30.4
12 Th	23 24 15	19 17 3	18 7 9	24 5 44	9 43.5	14 15.9	11 57.2	23 50.3	17 1.9	24 28.9	28 57.0	24 8.4	22 32.6
13 F	23 28 11	20 15 27	0♊ 2 49	5♊58 57	9 44.9	15 30.7	13 10.9	24 28.2	17 14.9	24 25.4	29 0.7	24 9.6	22 34.8
14 Sa	23 32 8	21 13 53	11 54 44	17 50 45	9R 45.9	16 43.9	14 24.6	25 6.1	17 27.9	24 21.9	29 4.5	24 10.8	22 37.0
15 Su	23 36 4	22 12 21	23 47 36	29 45 53	9 46.2	17 55.4	15 38.3	25 44.0	17 40.9	24 18.3	29 8.3	24 12.1	22 39.2
16 M	23 40 1	23 10 51	5♋46 10	11♋49 2	9 45.7	19 4.9	16 52.0	26 21.8	17 53.8	24 14.7	29 12.0	24 13.4	22 41.4
17 Tu	23 43 57	24 9 24	17 55 0	24 4 34	9 44.5	20 12.6	18 5.7	26 59.6	18 6.8	24 10.9	29 15.8	24 14.7	22 43.6
18 W	23 47 54	25 7 59	0♌18 12	6♌36 15	9 42.8	21 18.1	19 19.4	27 37.4	18 19.8	24 7.1	29 19.6	24 16.0	22 45.8
19 Th	23 51 50	26 6 35	12 59 4	19 26 52	9 40.9	22 21.5	20 33.1	28 15.2	18 32.7	24 3.3	29 23.4	24 17.4	22 48.0
20 F	23 55 47	27 5 14	25 59 49	2♍37 57	9 39.1	23 22.5	21 46.8	28 53.0	18 45.7	23 59.3	29 27.2	24 18.8	22 50.2
21 Sa	23 59 44	28 3 55	9♍21 14	16 9 33	9 37.6	24 21.0	23 0.4	29 30.7	18 58.6	23 55.3	29 31.0	24 20.2	22 52.4
22 Su	0 3 40	29 2 38	23 2 37	0♎ 0 7	9 36.6	25 16.7	24 14.1	0♍ 8.4	19 11.5	23 51.3	29 34.7	24 21.6	22 54.6
23 M	0 7 37	0♎ 1 23	7♎ 1 38	14 6 39	9D 36.3	26 9.6	25 27.7	0 46.1	19 24.4	23 47.2	29 38.5	24 23.1	22 56.8
24 Tu	0 11 33	1 0 10	21 14 38	28 24 58	9 36.4	26 59.3	26 41.4	1 23.8	19 37.3	23 43.0	29 42.3	24 24.6	22 59.0
25 W	0 15 30	1 58 58	5♏37 2	12♏50 12	9 36.9	27 45.7	27 55.0	2 1.4	19 50.1	23 38.8	29 46.1	24 26.1	23 1.2
26 Th	0 19 26	2 57 49	20 3 52	27 17 25	9 37.5	28 28.3	29 8.6	2 39.0	20 3.0	23 34.5	29 49.9	24 27.7	23 3.4
27 F	0 23 23	3 56 41	4♐30 21	11♐42 7	9 38.1	29 7.0	0♏22.2	3 16.6	20 15.8	23 30.2	29 53.7	24 29.2	23 5.5
28 Sa	0 27 19	4 55 36	18 52 19	26 0 33	9 38.4	29 41.3	1 35.8	3 54.2	20 28.6	23 25.8	29 57.5	24 30.8	23 7.7
29 Su	0 31 16	5 54 32	3♑ 6 30	10♑ 9 54	9R 38.6	0♏10.9	2 49.4	4 31.7	20 41.4	23 21.4	0♎ 1.2	24 32.5	23 9.9
30 M	0 35 13	6 53 29	17 10 31	24 8 12	9 38.5	0 35.5	4 2.9	5 9.2	20 54.2	23 17.0	0 5.0	24 34.1	23 12.0

LONGITUDE OCTOBER 1968

Day	Sid.Time	☉	0 hr ☽	Noon ☽	True ☊	☿	♀	♂	♃	♄	♅	♆	♇
1 Tu	0 39 9	7♎52 29	1♒ 2 48	7♒54 13	9♈38.4	0♏54.5	5♏16.5	5♍46.7	21♍ 6.9	23♈12.5	0♎ 8.8	24♏35.8	23♍14.2
2 W	0 43 6	8 51 30	14 42 22	21 27 13	9D 38.3	1 7.6	6 30.0	6 24.2	21 19.6	23R 8.0	0 12.5	24 37.4	23 16.3
3 Th	0 47 2	9 50 32	28 8 41	4♓46 47	9 38.3	1R 14.3	7 43.5	7 1.6	21 32.2	23 3.4	0 16.3	24 39.1	23 18.5
4 F	0 50 59	10 49 37	11♓21 28	17 52 44	9 38.3	1 14.2	8 57.0	7 39.1	21 44.9	22 58.8	0 20.0	24 40.9	23 20.6
5 Sa	0 54 55	11 48 43	24 20 36	0♈45 6	9 38.5	1 6.8	10 10.4	8 16.5	21 57.5	22 54.2	0 23.8	24 42.6	23 22.7
6 Su	0 58 52	12 47 52	7♈ 6 15	13 24 9	9R 38.5	0 51.9	11 23.9	8 53.8	22 10.1	22 49.6	0 27.5	24 44.4	23 24.8
7 M	1 2 48	13 47 2	19 38 52	25 50 31	9 38.5	0 29.1	12 37.3	9 31.2	22 22.6	22 44.9	0 31.2	24 46.2	23 26.9
8 Tu	1 6 45	14 46 15	1♉59 16	8♉ 5 18	9 38.2	29♎58.2	13 50.8	10 8.5	22 35.1	22 40.2	0 34.9	24 48.0	23 29.0
9 W	1 10 41	15 45 29	14 8 51	20 10 10	9 37.5	29 19.3	15 4.2	10 45.9	22 47.6	22 35.5	0 38.6	24 49.8	23 31.1
10 Th	1 14 38	16 44 46	26 9 33	2♊ 7 22	9 36.6	28 32.5	16 17.6	11 23.1	23 0.0	22 30.8	0 42.3	24 51.7	23 33.2
11 F	1 18 35	17 44 5	8♊ 3 58	13 59 49	9 35.5	27 38.4	17 30.9	12 0.4	23 12.4	22 26.0	0 46.0	24 53.5	23 35.2
12 Sa	1 22 31	18 43 27	19 55 20	25 51 1	9 34.4	26 37.7	18 44.3	12 37.7	23 24.8	22 21.3	0 49.7	24 55.4	23 37.3
13 Su	1 26 28	19 42 50	1♋47 23	7♋44 59	9 33.5	25 31.4	19 57.6	13 14.9	23 37.1	22 16.5	0 53.3	24 57.3	23 39.3
14 M	1 30 24	20 42 16	13 44 22	19 46 7	9D 32.9	24 21.1	21 11.0	13 52.1	23 49.4	22 11.8	0 56.9	24 59.3	23 41.3
15 Tu	1 34 21	21 41 45	25 50 48	1♌59 1	9 32.8	23 8.4	22 24.3	14 29.3	24 1.6	22 7.0	1 0.6	25 1.2	23 43.3
16 W	1 38 17	22 41 15	8♌11 17	14 28 10	9 33.3	21 55.3	23 37.6	15 6.5	24 13.8	22 2.2	1 4.2	25 3.2	23 45.3
17 Th	1 42 14	23 40 48	20 50 8	27 17 38	9 34.3	20 43.9	24 50.9	15 43.6	24 25.9	21 57.4	1 7.7	25 5.1	23 47.3
18 F	1 46 10	24 40 23	3♍51 2	10♍30 35	9 35.5	19 36.3	26 4.2	16 20.7	24 38.0	21 52.7	1 11.3	25 7.1	23 49.3
19 Sa	1 50 7	25 40 0	17 16 28	24 8 42	9 36.7	18 34.6	27 17.4	16 57.8	24 50.1	21 47.9	1 14.9	25 9.1	23 51.2
20 Su	1 54 4	26 39 40	1♎ 7 13	8♎11 45	9R 37.5	17 40.4	28 30.7	17 34.9	25 2.0	21 43.1	1 18.4	25 11.2	23 53.2
21 M	1 58 0	27 39 21	15 21 54	22 37 6	9 37.6	16 55.5	29 43.9	18 11.9	25 14.0	21 38.4	1 21.9	25 13.2	23 55.1
22 Tu	2 1 57	28 39 5	29 56 38	7♏19 41	9 36.7	16 20.7	0♐57.1	18 49.0	25 25.9	21 33.7	1 25.4	25 15.3	23 57.0
23 W	2 5 53	29 38 51	14♏45 16	22 12 24	9 34.9	15 57.0	2 10.3	19 25.9	25 37.7	21 28.9	1 28.8	25 17.3	23 58.9
24 Th	2 9 50	0♏38 38	29 40 1	7♐ 7 5	9 32.3	15D 44.6	3 23.5	20 2.9	25 49.5	21 24.3	1 32.3	25 19.4	24 0.7
25 F	2 13 46	1 38 28	14♐32 35	21 55 38	9 29.3	15 43.5	4 36.7	20 39.9	26 1.2	21 19.6	1 35.7	25 21.5	24 2.6
26 Sa	2 17 43	2 38 19	29 15 24	6♑31 15	9 26.4	15 53.4	5 49.8	21 16.8	26 12.8	21 14.9	1 39.1	25 23.6	24 4.4
27 Su	2 21 39	3 38 12	13♑42 38	20 49 11	9 24.2	16 13.9	7 2.9	21 53.7	26 24.4	21 10.3	1 42.5	25 25.7	24 6.2
28 M	2 25 36	4 38 7	27 50 40	4♒46 59	9D 23.1	16 44.3	8 16.0	22 30.5	26 35.9	21 5.8	1 45.8	25 27.9	24 8.0
29 Tu	2 29 33	5 38 3	11♒38 8	18 24 13	9 23.0	17 23.7	9 29.1	23 7.3	26 47.4	21 1.2	1 49.1	25 30.0	24 9.8
30 W	2 33 29	6 38 1	25 5 26	1♓41 59	9 24.0	18 11.3	10 42.1	23 44.1	26 58.7	20 56.7	1 52.4	25 32.1	24 11.5
31 Th	2 37 26	7 38 0	8♓14 8	14 42 13	9 25.6	19 6.3	11 55.1	24 20.9	27 10.1	20 52.2	1 55.7	25 34.3	24 13.3

Astro Data	Dy Hr Mn
☿0S	1 11:56
♀0S	4 7:44
☽0N	8 5:57
♄⊼♆	16 6:07
☽0S	22 14:53
♄⊼♇	30 17:52
☿ R	3 11:40
☽0N	5 13:46
♃⊼♄	8 7:07
♃☌♇	13 5:11
☽0S	20 0:57
♃⚹♆	20 22:06
☿ D	24 14:17
♅0S	25 17:12

Planet Ingress	Dy Hr Mn
☿ ♎	1 16:59
♀ ♎	2 6:39
♂ ♍	21 18:39
☉ ♎	22 23:26
♀ ♏	26 16:45
☿ ♏	28 14:40
♅ ♎	28 16:08
☿ ♎	7 22:46
♀ ♐	21 5:16
☉ ♏	23 8:30

Last Aspect Dy Hr Mn		☽ Ingress Dy Hr Mn
1 12:56	☿ □	♑ 1 13:22
3 13:38	♅ △	♒ 3 16:19
5 11:20	♄ ⚹	♓ 5 20:27
8 0:24	♅ ☍	♈ 8 2:49
10 1:33	♄ ☌	♉ 10 12:06
12 21:54	♅ △	♊ 12 23:54
15 10:48	♅ □	♋ 15 12:28
17 22:07	♅ ⚹	♌ 17 23:25
20 5:30	♂ ☌	♍ 20 7:15
22 11:19	♅ ☌	♎ 22 12:00
24 10:11	☿ ☌	♏ 24 14:39
26 16:18	♅ ⚹	♐ 26 16:30
28 7:37	♄ △	♑ 28 18:44
30 12:46	♆ ⚹	♒ 30 22:11

Last Aspect Dy Hr Mn		☽ Ingress Dy Hr Mn
2 17:43	♆ □	♓ 3 3:21
5 0:41	♆ △	♈ 5 10:35
7 5:57	♄ ☌	♉ 7 20:07
9 21:23	♆ ☍	♊ 10 7:43
12 12:26	☿ △	♋ 12 20:23
14 22:22	♆ △	♌ 15 8:08
17 8:15	♀ □	♍ 17 16:58
19 19:06	♀ ⚹	♎ 19 22:05
21 21:44	☉ ☌	♏ 22 0:05
23 17:44	♃ ⚹	♐ 24 0:32
25 18:56	♃ □	♑ 26 1:13
27 21:50	♃ △	♒ 28 3:43
30 0:48	♆ □	♓ 30 8:54

☽ Phases & Eclipses Dy Hr Mn	
6 22:07	○ 14♓21
14 20:31	☽ 22♊04
22 11:08	● 29♍30
22 11:18:06	✔T 0'40"
29 5:07	☽ 6♑07
6 11:46	○ 13♈17
6 11:42	☍T 1.169
14 15:05	☽ 21♋20
21 21:44	● 28♎33
28 12:40	☽ 5♒10

Astro Data

1 SEPTEMBER 1968
Julian Day # 25081
Delta T 38.9 sec
SVP 05♓41'53"
Obliquity 23°26'45"
⚷ Chiron 2♈05.3R
☽ Mean ☊ 11♈04.4

1 OCTOBER 1968
Julian Day # 25111
Delta T 39.0 sec
SVP 05♓41'49"
Obliquity 23°26'46"
⚷ Chiron 0♈46.0R
☽ Mean ☊ 9♈29.0

NOVEMBER 1968 LONGITUDE

Day	Sid.Time	☉	0 hr ☽	Noon ☽	True ☊	☿	♀	♂	♃	♄	♅	♆	♇
1 F	2 41 22	8♏38 1	21♓ 6 29	27♓27 15	9♈27.2	20♎ 7.7	13♐ 8.1	24♍57.7	27♍21.3	20♈47.8	1♎58.9	25♏36.5	24♍15.0
2 Sa	2 45 19	9 38 3	3♈44 48	9♈59 24	9R 28.3	21 14.8	14 21.1	25 34.4	27 32.5	20R 43.4	2 2.1	25 38.7	24 16.7
3 Su	2 49 15	10 38 7	16 11 19	22 20 45	9 28.2	22 26.9	15 34.0	26 11.1	27 43.6	20 39.0	2 5.3	25 40.8	24 18.3
4 M	2 53 12	11 38 13	28 27 56	4♉33 4	9 26.6	23 43.2	16 46.9	26 47.7	27 54.6	20 34.8	2 8.5	25 43.0	24 20.0
5 Tu	2 57 8	12 38 21	10♉36 20	16 37 54	9 23.2	25 3.1	17 59.7	27 24.4	28 5.5	20 30.5	2 11.6	25 45.2	24 21.6
6 W	3 1 5	13 38 31	22 37 57	28 36 41	9 18.2	26 26.0	19 12.6	28 1.0	28 16.4	20 26.3	2 14.7	25 47.4	24 23.2
7 Th	3 5 2	14 38 42	4♊34 16	10♊30 57	9 12.0	27 51.6	20 25.4	28 37.5	28 27.2	20 22.2	2 17.7	25 49.7	24 24.7
8 F	3 8 58	15 38 56	16 26 58	22 22 34	9 5.0	29 19.2	21 38.2	29 14.1	28 37.9	20 18.1	2 20.8	25 51.9	24 26.3
9 Sa	3 12 55	16 39 11	28 18 3	4♋13 46	8 58.0	0♏48.6	22 50.9	29 50.6	28 48.6	20 14.1	2 23.7	25 54.1	24 27.8
10 Su	3 16 51	17 39 28	10♋10 5	16 7 26	8 51.6	2 19.5	24 3.6	0♎27.1	28 59.1	20 10.1	2 26.7	25 56.3	24 29.3
11 M	3 20 48	18 39 47	22 6 14	28 7 0	8 46.6	3 51.5	25 16.3	1 3.6	29 9.6	20 6.2	2 29.6	25 58.6	24 30.8
12 Tu	3 24 44	19 40 8	4♌10 15	10♌16 31	8 43.3	5 24.4	26 28.9	1 40.0	29 19.9	20 2.4	2 32.5	26 0.8	24 32.3
13 W	3 28 41	20 40 31	16 26 22	22 40 24	8D 41.9	6 58.1	27 41.6	2 16.5	29 30.2	19 58.6	2 35.4	26 3.1	24 33.7
14 Th	3 32 37	21 40 56	28 59 11	5♍23 17	8 42.0	8 32.4	28 54.1	2 52.8	29 40.4	19 54.9	2 38.2	26 5.3	24 35.1
15 F	3 36 34	22 41 23	11♍53 14	18 29 29	8 43.2	10 7.0	0♑ 6.7	3 29.2	29 50.5	19 51.3	2 41.0	26 7.6	24 36.5
16 Sa	3 40 31	23 41 51	25 12 28	2♎ 2 26	8R 44.6	11 42.0	1 19.2	4 5.5	0♎ 0.5	19 47.7	2 43.7	26 9.8	24 37.8
17 Su	3 44 27	24 42 21	8♎59 35	16 3 55	8 45.2	13 17.2	2 31.7	4 41.8	0 10.4	19 44.3	2 46.4	26 12.1	24 39.1
18 M	3 48 24	25 42 54	23 15 14	0♏33 9	8 44.3	14 52.5	3 44.1	5 18.1	0 20.2	19 40.9	2 49.0	26 14.3	24 40.4
19 Tu	3 52 20	26 43 28	7♏57 4	15 26 10	8 41.2	16 28.0	4 56.5	5 54.3	0 30.0	19 37.5	2 51.7	26 16.6	24 41.7
20 W	3 56 17	27 44 3	22 59 26	0♐35 41	8 35.9	18 3.4	6 8.8	6 30.5	0 39.6	19 34.3	2 54.2	26 18.8	24 42.9
21 Th	4 0 13	28 44 40	8♐13 34	15 51 43	8 28.8	19 38.8	7 21.2	7 6.6	0 49.1	19 31.2	2 56.8	26 21.1	24 44.1
22 F	4 4 10	29 45 19	23 28 44	1♑ 3 16	8 20.6	21 14.1	8 33.4	7 42.7	0 58.5	19 28.1	2 59.3	26 23.4	24 45.3
23 Sa	4 8 7	0♐45 59	8♑34 5	16 0 9	8 12.6	22 49.4	9 45.7	8 18.8	1 7.8	19 25.1	3 1.7	26 25.6	24 46.4
24 Su	4 12 3	1 46 40	23 20 35	0♒34 46	8 5.7	24 24.6	10 57.9	8 54.9	1 17.0	19 22.2	3 4.1	26 27.9	24 47.6
25 M	4 16 0	2 47 22	7♒42 16	14 42 53	8 0.7	25 59.7	12 10.0	9 30.9	1 26.0	19 19.4	3 6.5	26 30.1	24 48.7
26 Tu	4 19 56	3 48 6	21 36 35	28 23 32	7D 57.9	27 34.7	13 22.1	10 6.8	1 35.0	19 16.7	3 8.8	26 32.4	24 49.7
27 W	4 23 53	4 48 50	5♓ 3 59	11♓38 19	7 57.2	29 9.5	14 34.1	10 42.7	1 43.8	19 14.1	3 11.1	26 34.6	24 50.7
28 Th	4 27 49	5 49 35	18 7 0	24 30 30	7 57.7	0♐44.3	15 46.0	11 18.6	1 52.5	19 11.6	3 13.3	26 36.8	24 51.7
29 F	4 31 46	6 50 21	0♈49 22	7♈ 4 6	7R 58.5	2 18.9	16 57.9	11 54.5	2 1.1	19 9.1	3 15.5	26 39.1	24 52.7
30 Sa	4 35 42	7 51 8	13 15 15	19 23 16	7 58.6	3 53.5	18 9.7	12 30.3	2 9.6	19 6.8	3 17.6	26 41.3	24 53.6

DECEMBER 1968 LONGITUDE

Day	Sid.Time	☉	0 hr ☽	Noon ☽	True ☊	☿	♀	♂	♃	♄	♅	♆	♇
1 Su	4 39 39	8♐51 56	25♈28 39	1♉31 49	7♈56.9	5♐27.9	19♑21.5	13♎ 6.0	2♎18.0	19♈ 4.6	3♎19.7	26♏43.5	24♍54.5
2 M	4 43 36	9 52 45	7♉33 9	13 32 59	7R 52.7	7 2.3	20 33.2	13 41.7	2 26.2	19R 2.4	3 21.8	26 45.7	24 55.4
3 Tu	4 47 32	10 53 36	19 31 38	25 29 21	7 45.7	8 36.7	21 44.8	14 17.4	2 34.4	19 0.4	3 23.8	26 47.9	24 56.3
4 W	4 51 29	11 54 27	1♊26 23	7♊22 56	7 36.0	10 10.9	22 56.3	14 53.1	2 42.3	18 58.5	3 25.7	26 50.1	24 57.1
5 Th	4 55 25	12 55 19	13 19 10	19 15 16	7 24.1	11 45.2	24 7.8	15 28.7	2 50.2	18 56.6	3 27.6	26 52.3	24 57.8
6 F	4 59 22	13 56 12	25 11 23	1♋ 7 41	7 10.9	13 19.4	25 19.2	16 4.2	2 57.9	18 54.9	3 29.5	26 54.5	24 58.6
7 Sa	5 3 18	14 57 7	7♋ 4 21	13 1 34	6 57.4	14 53.6	26 30.5	16 39.7	3 5.5	18 53.3	3 31.3	26 56.7	24 59.3
8 Su	5 7 15	15 58 2	18 59 34	24 58 36	6 45.0	16 27.8	27 41.7	17 15.2	3 13.0	18 51.8	3 33.0	26 58.9	24 60.0
9 M	5 11 11	16 58 59	0♌58 57	7♌ 0 59	6 34.4	18 2.1	28 52.9	17 50.6	3 20.4	18 50.4	3 34.7	27 1.0	25 0.6
10 Tu	5 15 8	17 59 56	13 5 2	19 11 33	6 26.4	19 36.4	0♒ 4.0	18 26.0	3 27.5	18 49.0	3 36.4	27 3.2	25 1.3
11 W	5 19 5	19 0 55	25 21 0	1♍33 52	6 21.3	21 10.8	1 14.9	19 1.4	3 34.6	18 47.8	3 38.0	27 5.3	25 1.8
12 Th	5 23 1	20 1 55	7♍50 40	14 11 59	6 18.8	22 45.2	2 25.8	19 36.7	3 41.5	18 46.7	3 39.5	27 7.4	25 2.4
13 F	5 26 58	21 2 55	20 38 19	27 10 15	6D 18.2	24 19.7	3 36.6	20 11.9	3 48.3	18 45.7	3 41.0	27 9.5	25 2.9
14 Sa	5 30 54	22 3 57	3♎48 16	10♎32 49	6R 18.3	25 54.3	4 47.3	20 47.1	3 54.9	18 44.9	3 42.4	27 11.6	25 3.4
15 Su	5 34 51	23 5 0	17 24 14	24 22 48	6 18.0	27 29.0	5 57.9	21 22.3	4 1.4	18 44.1	3 43.8	27 13.7	25 3.8
16 M	5 38 47	24 6 4	1♏28 33	8♏41 25	6 15.9	29 3.9	7 8.4	21 57.4	4 7.7	18 43.4	3 45.2	27 15.8	25 4.3
17 Tu	5 42 44	25 7 9	16 1 3	23 26 56	6 11.3	0♑38.9	8 18.8	22 32.4	4 13.9	18 42.9	3 46.4	27 17.8	25 4.6
18 W	5 46 40	26 8 15	0♐58 15	8♐33 58	6 3.7	2 14.0	9 29.1	23 7.4	4 19.9	18 42.4	3 47.7	27 19.9	25 5.0
19 Th	5 50 37	27 9 21	16 12 52	23 53 33	5 53.7	3 49.2	10 39.3	23 42.3	4 25.8	18 42.1	3 48.8	27 21.9	25 5.3
20 F	5 54 34	28 10 29	1♑34 31	9♑14 14	5 42.2	5 24.6	11 49.4	24 17.2	4 31.5	18 41.9	3 50.0	27 23.9	25 5.6
21 Sa	5 58 30	29 11 37	16 51 14	24 24 9	5 30.5	7 0.2	12 59.4	24 52.1	4 37.1	18D 41.7	3 51.0	27 25.9	25 5.8
22 Su	6 2 27	0♑12 45	1♒51 48	9♒13 14	5 20.1	8 35.8	14 9.2	25 26.8	4 42.5	18 41.7	3 52.0	27 27.9	25 6.1
23 M	6 6 23	1 13 53	16 27 43	23 34 49	5 11.9	10 11.6	15 18.9	26 1.5	4 47.7	18 41.9	3 53.0	27 29.9	25 6.2
24 Tu	6 10 20	2 15 2	0♓34 16	7♓26 5	5 6.6	11 47.4	16 28.5	26 36.2	4 52.8	18 42.1	3 53.9	27 31.8	25 6.4
25 W	6 14 16	3 16 10	14 10 26	20 47 38	5 3.9	13 23.3	17 37.9	27 10.7	4 57.7	18 42.4	3 54.7	27 33.7	25 6.5
26 Th	6 18 13	4 17 19	27 18 9	3♈42 30	5 3.0	14 59.3	18 47.2	27 45.3	5 2.5	18 42.9	3 55.5	27 35.6	25 6.6
27 F	6 22 10	5 18 27	10♈ 1 18	16 15 9	5 3.0	16 35.2	19 56.4	28 19.7	5 7.0	18 43.4	3 56.2	27 37.5	25R 6.6
28 Sa	6 26 6	6 19 36	22 24 44	28 30 38	5 2.4	18 11.1	21 5.3	28 54.1	5 11.4	18 44.1	3 56.9	27 39.4	25 6.6
29 Su	6 30 3	7 20 44	4♉33 30	10♉33 55	5 0.1	19 46.8	22 14.2	29 28.4	5 15.7	18 44.9	3 57.5	27 41.2	25 6.6
30 M	6 33 59	8 21 53	16 32 25	22 29 32	4 55.3	21 22.4	23 22.8	0♏ 2.7	5 19.7	18 45.8	3 58.0	27 43.1	25 6.5
31 Tu	6 37 56	9 23 1	28 25 41	4♊21 17	4 47.4	22 57.6	24 31.3	0 36.9	5 23.6	18 46.8	3 58.5	27 44.9	25 6.4

Astro Data Dy Hr Mn	Planet Ingress Dy Hr Mn	Last Aspect Dy Hr Mn	☽ Ingress Dy Hr Mn	Last Aspect Dy Hr Mn	☽ Ingress Dy Hr Mn	☽ Phases & Eclipses Dy Hr Mn	Astro Data
☽0N 1 19:59	☿ ♏ 8 11:00	1 11:59 ♃ ☍	♈ 1 16:51	30 11:26 ♄ ☌	♉ 1 8:58	5 4:25 ○ 12♉49	1 NOVEMBER 1968
♂0S 14 11:43	♂ ♎ 9 6:10	3 13:36 ☿ ☍	♉ 4 3:01	3 14:41 ♆ ☍	♊ 3 21:06	13 8:53 ☽ 21♌03	Julian Day # 25142
☽0S 16 11:03	♀ ♑ 14 21:48	6 11:30 ♃ △	♊ 6 14:48	5 23:34 ♇ □	♋ 6 9:43	20 8:01 ● 28♏04	Delta T 39.0 sec
☽0N 29 1:02	♃ ♎ 15 22:44	9 3:18 ♂ □	♋ 9 3:26	8 19:21 ♀ ☍	♌ 8 22:02	26 23:30 ☽ 4♓48	SVP 05♓41'45"
	☉ ♐ 22 5:49	11 14:17 ♃ ⚹	♌ 11 15:45	11 3:23 ♆ □	♍ 11 8:59		Obliquity 23°26'45"
♃0S 4 6:55	☿ ♐ 27 12:47	13 23:49 ♀ △	♍ 14 1:55	13 12:01 ♆ ⚹	♎ 13 17:08	4 23:07 ○ 12♊53	⚷ Chiron 29♓31.5R
♃☌♅ 11 15:00		16 1:42 ♆ ⚹	♎ 16 8:26	15 19:26 ☿ ⚹	♏ 15 21:31	13 0:49 ☽ 21♍05	☽ Mean ☊ 7♈50.5
☽0S 13 19:04	♀ ♒ 9 22:40	17 18:05 ♄ ☍	♏ 18 11:06	17 18:12 ♆ ☌	♐ 17 22:28	19 18:19 ● 27♐56	
♄ D 21 11:38	☿ ♑ 16 14:11	20 8:01 ☉ ☌	♐ 20 11:04	19 18:19 ☉ ☌	♑ 19 21:32	26 14:14 ☽ 4♈54	1 DECEMBER 1968
☽0N 26 6:38	☉ ♑ 21 19:00	22 2:01 ♇ □	♑ 22 10:19	21 16:54 ♆ ⚹	♒ 21 20:59		Julian Day # 25172
♇ R 27 17:05	♂ ♏ 29 22:07	24 5:10 ♆ ⚹	♒ 24 11:02	23 18:45 ♆ □	♓ 23 23:01		Delta T 39.1 sec
		26 11:57 ☿ □	♓ 26 14:52	26 0:33 ♆ △	♈ 26 5:02		SVP 05♓41'41"
		28 16:02 ♆ △	♈ 28 22:26	28 13:24 ♂ ☍	♉ 28 14:57		Obliquity 23°26'45"
				30 22:37 ♆ ☍	♊ 31 3:11		⚷ Chiron 28♓53.5R
							☽ Mean ☊ 6♈15.2

LONGITUDE — JANUARY 1969

Day	Sid.Time	☉	0 hr ☽	Noon ☽	True ☊	☿	♀	♂	♃	♄	♅	♆	♇
1 W	6 41 52	10♑24 10	10♊16 42	16♊12 15	4♈36.7	24♑32.5	25♒39.6	1♏11.0	5♎27.3	18♈47.9	3♎59.0	27♏46.7	25♍ 6.3
2 Th	6 45 49	11 25 18	22 8 10	28 4 40	4R 23.5	26 6.8	26 47.7	1 45.1	5 30.9	18 49.1	3 59.4	27 48.4	25R 6.2
3 F	6 49 45	12 26 26	4♋ 1 58	10♋ 0 12	4 8.8	27 40.3	27 55.6	2 19.0	5 34.3	18 50.4	3 59.7	27 50.2	25 6.0
4 Sa	6 53 42	13 27 35	15 59 30	22 0 1	3 53.9	29 12.9	29 3.4	2 53.0	5 37.5	18 51.9	3 60.0	27 51.9	25 5.7
5 Su	6 57 39	14 28 43	28 1 50	4♌ 5 8	3 39.9	0♒44.4	0♓10.9	3 26.8	5 40.5	18 53.4	4 0.2	27 53.6	25 5.5
6 M	7 1 35	15 29 51	10♌10 1	16 16 42	3 27.9	2 14.5	1 18.2	4 0.6	5 43.3	18 55.1	4 0.4	27 55.3	25 5.2
7 Tu	7 5 32	16 30 59	22 25 21	28 36 13	3 18.6	3 42.8	2 25.4	4 34.3	5 45.9	18 56.8	4 0.5	27 56.9	25 4.9
8 W	7 9 28	17 32 8	4♍49 35	11♍ 5 46	3 12.5	5 9.0	3 32.2	5 7.9	5 48.4	18 58.7	4R 0.5	27 58.6	25 4.5
9 Th	7 13 25	18 33 16	17 25 7	23 48 1	3 9.3	6 32.6	4 38.9	5 41.5	5 50.7	19 0.7	4 0.5	28 0.2	25 4.1
10 F	7 17 21	19 34 24	0♎14 54	6♎46 11	3D 8.3	7 53.3	5 45.3	6 15.0	5 52.8	19 2.7	4 0.4	28 1.7	25 3.7
11 Sa	7 21 18	20 35 32	13 22 16	20 3 35	3R 8.4	9 10.3	6 51.5	6 48.4	5 54.7	19 4.9	4 0.3	28 3.3	25 3.2
12 Su	7 25 14	21 36 40	26 50 29	3♏43 15	3 8.5	10 23.2	7 57.5	7 21.7	5 56.4	19 7.2	4 0.1	28 4.8	25 2.8
13 M	7 29 11	22 37 48	10♏42 5	17 47 2	3 7.2	11 31.2	9 3.2	7 54.9	5 58.0	19 9.6	3 59.9	28 6.3	25 2.2
14 Tu	7 33 8	23 38 56	24 58 1	2♐14 45	3 3.6	12 33.5	10 8.6	8 28.1	5 59.3	19 12.1	3 59.6	28 7.8	25 1.7
15 W	7 37 4	24 40 4	9♐36 46	17 3 23	2 57.4	13 29.3	11 13.8	9 1.1	6 0.5	19 14.7	3 59.3	28 9.3	25 1.1
16 Th	7 41 1	25 41 12	24 33 42	2♑ 6 39	2 48.8	14 17.9	12 18.7	9 34.1	6 1.4	19 17.4	3 58.9	28 10.7	25 0.5
17 F	7 44 57	26 42 20	9♑41 2	17 15 32	2 38.7	14 58.2	13 23.3	10 7.0	6 2.2	19 20.2	3 58.4	28 12.1	24 59.9
18 Sa	7 48 54	27 43 27	24 48 48	2♒19 31	2 28.2	15 29.4	14 27.7	10 39.7	6 2.8	19 23.1	3 57.9	28 13.4	24 59.2
19 Su	7 52 50	28 44 33	9♒46 27	17 8 32	2 18.6	15 50.8	15 31.7	11 12.4	6 3.2	19 26.2	3 57.3	28 14.8	24 58.5
20 M	7 56 47	29 45 39	24 24 51	1♓34 42	2 11.1	16R 1.5	16 35.4	11 45.0	6R 3.4	19 29.3	3 56.7	28 16.1	24 57.8
21 Tu	8 0 43	0♒46 44	8♓37 36	15 33 18	2 6.1	16 0.9	17 38.8	12 17.5	6 3.4	19 32.5	3 56.0	28 17.4	24 57.0
22 W	8 4 40	1 47 48	22 21 44	29 3 0	2D 3.7	15 48.9	18 41.8	12 49.8	6 3.2	19 35.8	3 55.3	28 18.6	24 56.2
23 Th	8 8 37	2 48 51	5♈37 22	12♈ 5 15	2 3.4	15 25.2	19 44.5	13 22.1	6 2.8	19 39.2	3 54.5	28 19.9	24 55.4
24 F	8 12 33	3 49 53	18 27 6	24 43 31	2 4.1	14 50.3	20 46.8	13 54.2	6 2.3	19 42.7	3 53.7	28 21.0	24 54.5
25 Sa	8 16 30	4 50 54	0♉55 5	7♉ 2 27	2R 4.8	14 4.7	21 48.7	14 26.3	6 1.5	19 46.3	3 52.8	28 22.2	24 53.6
26 Su	8 20 26	5 51 54	13 6 16	19 7 11	2 4.6	13 9.7	22 50.2	14 58.2	6 0.5	19 50.0	3 51.8	28 23.3	24 52.7
27 M	8 24 23	6 52 53	25 5 49	1♊ 2 48	2 2.5	12 6.8	23 51.3	15 30.1	5 59.4	19 53.8	3 50.8	28 24.4	24 51.8
28 Tu	8 28 19	7 53 51	6♊58 42	12 54 2	1 58.2	10 57.7	24 52.0	16 1.8	5 58.1	19 57.6	3 49.8	28 25.5	24 50.8
29 W	8 32 16	8 54 47	18 49 20	24 45 2	1 51.6	9 44.6	25 52.3	16 33.4	5 56.5	20 1.6	3 48.7	28 26.6	24 49.9
30 Th	8 36 12	9 55 43	0♋41 31	6♋39 8	1 43.0	8 29.7	26 52.1	17 4.8	5 54.8	20 5.7	3 47.5	28 27.6	24 48.9
31 F	8 40 9	10 56 37	12 38 12	18 38 58	1 33.2	7 15.1	27 51.4	17 36.2	5 52.9	20 9.8	3 46.3	28 28.6	24 47.8

LONGITUDE — FEBRUARY 1969

Day	Sid.Time	☉	0 hr ☽	Noon ☽	True ☊	☿	♀	♂	♃	♄	♅	♆	♇
1 Sa	8 44 6	11♒57 30	24♋41 37	0♌46 20	1♈23.1	6♒ 3.0	28♓50.2	18♏ 7.4	5♎50.8	20♈14.0	3♎45.1	28♏29.5	24♍46.8
2 Su	8 48 2	12 58 22	6♌53 15	13 2 27	1R 13.5	4R 55.1	29 48.5	18 38.6	5R 48.6	20 18.4	3R 43.8	28 30.4	24R 45.7
3 M	8 51 59	13 59 13	19 14 2	25 28 4	1 5.5	3 53.0	0♈46.3	19 9.6	5 46.1	20 22.8	3 42.5	28 31.3	24 44.6
4 Tu	8 55 55	15 0 3	1♍44 37	8♍ 3 45	0 59.5	2 57.7	1 43.6	19 40.4	5 43.4	20 27.3	3 41.1	28 32.2	24 43.4
5 W	8 59 52	16 0 51	14 25 34	20 50 8	0 55.8	2 10.1	2 40.3	20 11.2	5 40.6	20 31.8	3 39.6	28 33.0	24 42.3
6 Th	9 3 48	17 1 39	27 17 36	3♎48 5	0D 54.3	1 30.6	3 36.4	20 41.8	5 37.6	20 36.5	3 38.2	28 33.8	24 41.1
7 F	9 7 45	18 2 25	10♎21 45	16 58 46	0 54.6	0 59.5	4 31.9	21 12.2	5 34.4	20 41.2	3 36.6	28 34.5	24 39.9
8 Sa	9 11 41	19 3 11	23 39 20	0♏23 37	0 55.9	0 36.8	5 26.8	21 42.5	5 31.0	20 46.1	3 35.1	28 35.2	24 38.7
9 Su	9 15 38	20 3 55	7♏11 46	14 3 57	0 57.3	0 22.2	6 21.1	22 12.7	5 27.5	20 51.0	3 33.4	28 35.9	24 37.4
10 M	9 19 35	21 4 39	21 0 14	28 0 39	0R 58.0	0D 15.4	7 14.6	22 42.8	5 23.8	20 55.9	3 31.8	28 36.6	24 36.1
11 Tu	9 23 31	22 5 22	5♐ 5 8	12♐13 30	0 57.2	0 16.1	8 7.6	23 12.6	5 19.9	21 1.0	3 30.1	28 37.2	24 34.9
12 W	9 27 28	23 6 3	19 25 29	26 40 40	0 54.7	0 23.8	8 59.8	23 42.4	5 15.8	21 6.1	3 28.3	28 37.8	24 33.5
13 Th	9 31 24	24 6 44	3♑58 30	11♑18 20	0 50.6	0 38.1	9 51.2	24 11.9	5 11.6	21 11.4	3 26.6	28 38.3	24 32.2
14 F	9 35 21	25 7 23	18 39 23	26 0 48	0 45.4	0 58.5	10 41.9	24 41.3	5 7.2	21 16.6	3 24.7	28 38.9	24 30.9
15 Sa	9 39 17	26 8 1	3♒21 38	10♒40 59	0 39.9	1 24.5	11 31.8	25 10.6	5 2.6	21 22.0	3 22.9	28 39.4	24 29.5
16 Su	9 43 14	27 8 38	17 57 53	25 11 28	0 34.8	1 55.7	12 20.9	25 39.6	4 57.9	21 27.4	3 21.0	28 39.8	24 28.1
17 M	9 47 11	28 9 13	2♓20 58	9♓25 41	0 30.8	2 31.6	13 9.1	26 8.5	4 53.0	21 32.9	3 19.0	28 40.2	24 26.7
18 Tu	9 51 7	29 9 47	16 25 5	23 18 46	0 28.4	3 12.0	13 56.4	26 37.2	4 47.9	21 38.5	3 17.0	28 40.6	24 25.3
19 W	9 55 4	0♓10 19	0♈ 6 29	6♈48 7	0D 27.6	3 56.5	14 42.8	27 5.7	4 42.7	21 44.2	3 15.0	28 41.0	24 23.9
20 Th	9 59 0	1 10 49	13 23 44	19 53 27	0 28.2	4 44.7	15 28.3	27 34.1	4 37.4	21 49.9	3 13.0	28 41.3	24 22.4
21 F	10 2 57	2 11 18	26 17 34	2♉36 26	0 29.7	5 36.3	16 12.7	28 2.2	4 31.9	21 55.6	3 10.9	28 41.6	24 21.0
22 Sa	10 6 53	3 11 44	8♉50 30	15 0 15	0 31.4	6 31.2	16 56.0	28 30.2	4 26.3	22 1.5	3 8.8	28 41.8	24 19.5
23 Su	10 10 50	4 12 9	21 6 14	27 9 2	0 32.9	7 28.9	17 38.3	28 57.9	4 20.5	22 7.4	3 6.6	28 42.0	24 18.0
24 M	10 14 46	5 12 32	3♊ 9 16	9♊ 7 31	0R 33.6	8 29.5	18 19.5	29 25.5	4 14.6	22 13.4	3 4.4	28 42.2	24 16.5
25 Tu	10 18 43	6 12 53	15 4 24	21 0 31	0 33.3	9 32.5	18 59.4	29 52.8	4 8.6	22 19.4	3 2.2	28 42.4	24 15.0
26 W	10 22 39	7 13 12	26 56 27	2♋52 46	0 31.8	10 38.0	19 38.1	0♐19.9	4 2.4	22 25.5	3 0.0	28 42.5	24 13.5
27 Th	10 26 36	8 13 29	8♋49 59	14 48 35	0 29.3	11 45.7	20 15.6	0 46.9	3 56.1	22 31.7	2 57.7	28 42.5	24 11.9
28 F	10 30 33	9 13 44	20 49 3	26 51 45	0 26.1	12 55.4	20 51.7	1 13.6	3 49.7	22 37.9	2 55.5	28R 42.6	24 10.4

Astro Data Dy Hr Mn	Planet Ingress Dy Hr Mn	Last Aspect Dy Hr Mn	☽ Ingress Dy Hr Mn	Last Aspect Dy Hr Mn	☽ Ingress Dy Hr Mn	☽ Phases & Eclipses Dy Hr Mn	Astro Data
♅ R 8 7:28	☿ ♒ 4 12:18	2 10:24 ♀ △	♋ 2 15:53	1 8:54 ♀ △	♌ 1 10:29	3 18:28 ○ 13♋13	1 JANUARY 1969
☽0S 10 0:31	♀ ♓ 4 20:07	4 23:44 ♆ △	♌ 5 3:55	3 17:52 ♆ □	♍ 3 20:40	11 14:00 ☽ 21♎11	Julian Day # 25203
☿ R 20 10:56	☉ ♒ 20 5:38	7 10:45 ♆ □	♍ 7 14:42	6 2:21 ♆ ✶	♎ 6 5:00	18 4:59 ● 27♑56	Delta T 39.2 sec
♃ R 20 12:29		9 19:53 ♆ ✶	♎ 9 23:32	7 18:47 ♄ ☍	♏ 8 11:18	25 8:23 ☽ 5♉12	SVP 05♓41'35"
☽0N 22 14:22	♀ ♈ 2 4:45	11 14:00 ☉ □	♏ 12 5:32	10 13:02 ♆ ☌	♐ 10 15:23		Obliquity 23°26'44"
♀0N 31 5:32	☉ ♓ 18 19:55	14 5:14 ♆ ☌	♐ 14 8:19	12 8:29 ♇ □	♑ 12 17:28	2 12:56 ○ 13♌31	⚷ Chiron 29♓04.3
	♂ ♐ 25 6:21	16 0:43 ♇ □	♑ 16 8:39	14 16:19 ♆ ✶	♒ 14 18:30	10 0:08 ☽ 21♏05	☽ Mean ☊ 4♈36.8
☽0S 6 5:17		18 5:27 ♆ ✶	♒ 18 8:17	16 17:49 ♆ □	♓ 16 20:03	16 16:25 ● 27♒50	1 FEBRUARY 1969
☿ D 10 9:38		20 6:27 ♆ □	♓ 20 9:20	18 21:28 ♆ △	♈ 18 23:48	24 4:30 ☽ 5♊24	Julian Day # 25234
☽0N 18 23:57		22 10:41 ♆ △	♈ 22 13:43	20 15:44 ♄ ☌	♉ 21 7:02		Delta T 39.3 sec
♆ R 28 20:20		24 2:24 ♄ ☌	♉ 24 22:13	23 16:14 ♂ ☍	♊ 23 17:41		SVP 05♓41'29"
		27 6:41 ♆ ☍	♊ 27 9:53	25 18:31 ♇ □	♋ 26 6:11		Obliquity 23°26'45"
		29 15:34 ♀ □	♋ 29 22:36	28 15:39 ♆ △	♌ 28 18:12		⚷ Chiron 0♈04.2
							☽ Mean ☊ 2♈58.3

MARCH 1969 LONGITUDE

Day	Sid.Time	☉	0 hr ☽	Noon ☽	True ☊	☿	♀	♂	♃	♄	♅	♆	♇
1 Sa	10 34 29	10♓13 58	2♌57 3	9♌ 5 16	0♈22.7	14♒ 7.1	21♈26.4	1♐40.0	3♎43.2	22♈44.1	2♎53.1	28♏42.6	24♍ 8.8
2 Su	10 38 26	11 14 9	15 16 39	21 31 22	0R 19.5	15 20.7	21 59.7	2 6.3	3R 36.6	22 50.4	2R 50.8	28R 42.6	24R 7.3
3 M	10 42 22	12 14 18	27 49 35	4♍11 23	0 16.9	16 36.1	22 31.5	2 32.3	3 29.8	22 56.8	2 48.4	28 42.5	24 5.7
4 Tu	10 46 19	13 14 25	10♍36 48	17 5 49	0 15.0	17 53.1	23 1.7	2 58.1	3 23.0	23 3.2	2 46.0	28 42.4	24 4.1
5 W	10 50 15	14 14 31	23 38 24	0♎14 27	0D 14.2	19 11.7	23 30.3	3 23.7	3 16.1	23 9.7	2 43.6	28 42.3	24 2.5
6 Th	10 54 12	15 14 34	6♎53 53	13 36 34	0 14.1	20 31.9	23 57.3	3 49.0	3 9.1	23 16.3	2 41.2	28 42.2	24 0.9
7 F	10 58 8	16 14 36	20 22 20	27 11 2	0 14.8	21 53.6	24 22.5	4 14.0	3 2.0	23 22.8	2 38.7	28 42.0	23 59.3
8 Sa	11 2 5	17 14 36	4♏ 2 30	10♏56 34	0 15.8	23 16.7	24 46.0	4 38.8	2 54.8	23 29.5	2 36.3	28 41.7	23 57.7
9 Su	11 6 2	18 14 35	17 53 3	24 51 46	0 16.9	24 41.2	25 7.6	5 3.3	2 47.5	23 36.1	2 33.8	28 41.5	23 56.1
10 M	11 9 58	19 14 32	1♐52 32	8♐55 9	0 17.8	26 7.1	25 27.3	5 27.6	2 40.2	23 42.9	2 31.3	28 41.2	23 54.5
11 Tu	11 13 55	20 14 27	15 59 24	23 5 2	0R 18.2	27 34.3	25 45.1	5 51.6	2 32.8	23 49.6	2 28.8	28 40.9	23 52.9
12 W	11 17 51	21 14 21	0♑11 47	7♑19 20	0 18.1	29 2.8	26 0.8	6 15.3	2 25.4	23 56.5	2 26.2	28 40.5	23 51.3
13 Th	11 21 48	22 14 13	14 27 23	21 35 31	0 17.6	0♓32.6	26 14.4	6 38.6	2 17.8	24 3.3	2 23.7	28 40.1	23 49.7
14 F	11 25 44	23 14 4	28 43 22	5♒50 29	0 16.9	2 3.7	26 25.9	7 1.7	2 10.3	24 10.2	2 21.2	28 39.7	23 48.0
15 Sa	11 29 41	24 13 53	12♒56 24	20 0 39	0 16.1	3 36.1	26 35.2	7 24.5	2 2.7	24 17.2	2 18.6	28 39.3	23 46.4
16 Su	11 33 37	25 13 40	27 2 45	4♓ 2 15	0 15.5	5 9.7	26 42.3	7 47.0	1 55.0	24 24.1	2 16.0	28 38.8	23 44.8
17 M	11 37 34	26 13 25	10♓58 41	17 51 39	0 15.1	6 44.5	26 47.0	8 9.1	1 47.3	24 31.2	2 13.4	28 38.3	23 43.2
18 Tu	11 41 31	27 13 8	24 40 48	1♈25 50	0D 14.9	8 20.6	26R 49.4	8 30.9	1 39.6	24 38.2	2 10.8	28 37.7	23 41.6
19 W	11 45 27	28 12 49	8♈ 6 30	14 42 40	0 14.9	9 58.0	26 49.4	8 52.3	1 31.8	24 45.3	2 8.2	28 37.2	23 39.9
20 Th	11 49 24	29 12 28	21 14 14	27 41 13	0 15.0	11 36.6	26 46.9	9 13.4	1 24.1	24 52.4	2 5.6	28 36.6	23 38.3
21 F	11 53 20	0♈12 5	4♉ 3 42	10♉21 50	0R 15.0	13 16.4	26 42.0	9 34.1	1 16.3	24 59.6	2 3.0	28 35.9	23 36.7
22 Sa	11 57 17	1 11 40	16 35 52	22 46 7	0 14.9	14 57.5	26 34.6	9 54.5	1 8.5	25 6.8	2 0.4	28 35.3	23 35.1
23 Su	12 1 13	2 11 12	28 52 55	4♊56 41	0 14.8	16 39.9	26 24.7	10 14.5	1 0.8	25 14.0	1 57.8	28 34.6	23 33.5
24 M	12 5 10	3 10 43	10♊57 55	16 57 6	0 14.5	18 23.6	26 12.3	10 34.1	0 53.0	25 21.3	1 55.2	28 33.8	23 31.9
25 Tu	12 9 6	4 10 11	22 54 46	28 51 29	0 14.3	20 8.5	25 57.4	10 53.4	0 45.2	25 28.6	1 52.6	28 33.1	23 30.3
26 W	12 13 3	5 9 37	4♋47 50	10♋44 24	0D 14.2	21 54.8	25 40.0	11 12.2	0 37.5	25 35.9	1 50.0	28 32.3	23 28.7
27 Th	12 17 0	6 9 0	16 41 45	22 40 30	0 14.3	23 42.4	25 20.3	11 30.6	0 29.8	25 43.2	1 47.4	28 31.5	23 27.1
28 F	12 20 56	7 8 22	28 41 11	4♌44 22	0 14.7	25 31.3	24 58.2	11 48.7	0 22.1	25 50.6	1 44.8	28 30.6	23 25.6
29 Sa	12 24 53	8 7 41	10♌50 34	17 0 14	0 15.4	27 21.6	24 33.9	12 6.3	0 14.4	25 58.0	1 42.2	28 29.8	23 24.0
30 Su	12 28 49	9 6 57	23 13 49	29 31 40	0 16.3	29 13.2	24 7.4	12 23.4	0 6.8	26 5.4	1 39.6	28 28.9	23 22.5
31 M	12 32 46	10 6 12	5♍54 6	12♍21 21	0 17.1	1♈ 6.2	23 38.9	12 40.2	29♍59.2	26 12.8	1 37.1	28 28.0	23 20.9

APRIL 1969 LONGITUDE

Day	Sid.Time	☉	0 hr ☽	Noon ☽	True ☊	☿	♀	♂	♃	♄	♅	♆	♇
1 Tu	12 36 42	11♈ 5 24	18♍53 32	25♍30 44	0♈17.8	3♈ 0.5	23♈ 8.6	12♐56.5	29♍51.7	26♈20.2	1♎34.5	28♏27.0	23♍19.4
2 W	12 40 39	12 4 34	2♎12 53	8♎59 52	0R 18.0	4 56.1	22R 36.5	13 12.3	29R 44.3	26 27.7	1R 31.9	28R 26.0	23R 17.8
3 Th	12 44 35	13 3 41	15 51 26	22 47 16	0 17.6	6 53.1	22 3.0	13 27.6	29 36.8	26 35.2	1 29.4	28 25.0	23 16.3
4 F	12 48 32	14 2 47	29 46 58	6♏50 2	0 16.5	8 51.4	21 28.1	13 42.5	29 29.5	26 42.7	1 26.9	28 24.0	23 14.8
5 Sa	12 52 29	15 1 51	13♏55 57	21 4 8	0 14.8	10 50.9	20 52.1	13 56.9	29 22.2	26 50.2	1 24.3	28 23.0	23 13.3
6 Su	12 56 25	16 0 53	28 13 58	5♐24 52	0 12.8	12 51.7	20 15.3	14 10.8	29 15.0	26 57.8	1 21.8	28 21.9	23 11.9
7 M	13 0 22	16 59 53	12♐36 14	19 47 31	0 10.8	14 53.6	19 37.9	14 24.2	29 7.9	27 5.3	1 19.4	28 20.8	23 10.4
8 Tu	13 4 18	17 58 52	26 58 11	4♑ 7 49	0 9.2	16 56.6	19 0.1	14 37.0	29 0.8	27 12.9	1 16.9	28 19.7	23 9.0
9 W	13 8 15	18 57 49	11♑15 59	18 22 22	0D 8.2	19 0.5	18 22.2	14 49.4	28 53.9	27 20.5	1 14.4	28 18.5	23 7.5
10 Th	13 12 11	19 56 44	25 26 40	2♒28 41	0 8.2	21 5.3	17 44.5	15 1.1	28 47.0	27 28.1	1 12.0	28 17.4	23 6.1
11 F	13 16 8	20 55 38	9♒28 14	16 25 11	0 8.9	23 10.7	17 7.1	15 12.3	28 40.2	27 35.7	1 9.6	28 16.2	23 4.7
12 Sa	13 20 4	21 54 29	23 19 26	0♓10 52	0 10.2	25 16.6	16 30.4	15 22.9	28 33.6	27 43.3	1 7.2	28 15.0	23 3.3
13 Su	13 24 1	22 53 19	6♓59 26	13 45 4	0 11.7	27 22.8	15 54.6	15 33.0	28 27.0	27 50.9	1 4.8	28 13.7	23 2.0
14 M	13 27 58	23 52 7	20 27 42	27 7 16	0R 12.7	29 29.0	15 19.9	15 42.4	28 20.6	27 58.5	1 2.5	28 12.5	23 0.6
15 Tu	13 31 54	24 50 53	3♈43 42	10♈16 58	0 13.0	1♉34.9	14 46.5	15 51.2	28 14.2	28 6.2	1 0.2	28 11.2	22 59.3
16 W	13 35 51	25 49 38	16 47 0	23 13 47	0 12.0	3 40.3	14 14.6	15 59.4	28 8.0	28 13.8	0 57.9	28 9.9	22 58.0
17 Th	13 39 47	26 48 20	29 37 15	5♉57 27	0 9.7	5 44.8	13 44.4	16 6.9	28 1.9	28 21.4	0 55.6	28 8.6	22 56.7
18 F	13 43 44	27 47 0	12♉14 24	18 28 11	0 6.1	7 48.2	13 15.9	16 13.8	27 55.9	28 29.1	0 53.4	28 7.3	22 55.4
19 Sa	13 47 40	28 45 39	24 38 54	0♊46 42	0 1.4	9 50.0	12 49.5	16 20.1	27 50.1	28 36.7	0 51.1	28 5.9	22 54.2
20 Su	13 51 37	29 44 16	6♊51 48	12 54 28	29♓56.3	11 50.0	12 25.1	16 25.7	27 44.4	28 44.4	0 49.0	28 4.5	22 52.9
21 M	13 55 33	0♉42 50	18 55 0	24 53 45	29 51.2	13 47.9	12 2.9	16 30.6	27 38.8	28 52.0	0 46.8	28 3.2	22 51.7
22 Tu	13 59 30	1 41 22	0♋51 8	6♋47 36	29 46.8	15 43.2	11 43.0	16 34.8	27 33.4	28 59.6	0 44.7	28 1.8	22 50.5
23 W	14 3 27	2 39 53	12 43 37	18 39 44	29 43.5	17 35.8	11 25.4	16 38.4	27 28.1	29 7.3	0 42.6	28 0.3	22 49.4
24 Th	14 7 23	3 38 21	24 36 30	0♌34 31	29D 41.7	19 25.3	11 10.2	16 41.2	27 22.9	29 14.9	0 40.5	27 58.9	22 48.2
25 F	14 11 20	4 36 47	6♌34 21	12 36 38	29 41.2	21 11.5	10 57.4	16 43.4	27 17.9	29 22.5	0 38.5	27 57.5	22 47.1
26 Sa	14 15 16	5 35 11	18 41 59	24 50 59	29 42.0	22 54.3	10 47.0	16 44.8	27 13.1	29 30.1	0 36.5	27 56.0	22 46.0
27 Su	14 19 13	6 33 32	1♍ 4 12	7♍22 12	29 43.5	24 33.3	10 39.1	16R 45.5	27 8.4	29 37.7	0 34.5	27 54.5	22 44.9
28 M	14 23 9	7 31 52	13 45 28	20 14 24	29 45.0	26 8.5	10 33.5	16 45.5	27 3.9	29 45.3	0 32.6	27 53.0	22 43.9
29 Tu	14 27 6	8 30 9	26 49 21	3♎30 33	29R 45.9	27 39.7	10D 30.4	16 44.7	26 59.5	29 52.9	0 30.7	27 51.5	22 42.8
30 W	14 31 2	9 28 25	10♎18 4	17 11 54	29 45.5	29 6.7	10 29.7	16 43.3	26 55.3	0♉ 0.5	0 28.9	27 50.0	22 41.8

Astro Data	Dy Hr Mn
♃0N	2 7:27
☽0S	5 11:38
♄⊼♇	11 9:19
♃☌♅	11 19:40
☽0N	18 9:32
♀ R	18 11:49
♅0N	26 23:23
☽0S	1 20:09
☿0N	1 13:27
☽0N	14 17:17
♄⊼♆	15 13:33
♃⊼♄	15 13:55
♃⚹♆	15 14:34
♂ R	27 11:24

Planet Ingress	Dy Hr Mn
☿ ♓	12 15:19
☉ ♈	20 19:08
☿ ♈	30 9:59
♃ ♍	30 21:37
☿ ♉	14 5:55
☊ ♓	19 6:52
☉ ♉	20 6:27
♄ ♉	29 22:24
☿ ♊	30 15:18
☽0S	29 5:39
♀ D	29 19:20

Last Aspect Dy Hr Mn		☽ Ingress	Dy Hr Mn
3 1:40	♆ □	♍	3 4:07
5 9:13	♆ ⚹	♎	5 11:34
7 7:17	♀ ☍	♏	7 16:56
9 18:33	♆ ☌	♐	9 20:48
11 21:50	☿ ⚹	♑	11 23:40
13 23:54	♆ ⚹	♒	14 2:09
16 2:44	♆ □	♓	16 5:04
18 7:00	♆ △	♈	18 9:27
20 10:15	♀ ☌	♉	20 16:20
22 23:24	♆ ☍	♊	23 2:12
25 6:00	♀ ⚹	♋	25 14:18
27 23:39	♆ △	♌	28 2:37
30 10:00	♆ □	♍	30 12:54

Last Aspect Dy Hr Mn		☽ Ingress	Dy Hr Mn
1 19:37	♃ ☌	♎	1 20:03
3 18:42	♄ ☍	♏	4 0:22
6 1:41	♃ ⚹	♐	6 2:57
8 3:24	♃ □	♑	8 5:04
10 5:39	♃ △	♒	10 7:46
12 8:36	♆ □	♓	12 11:41
14 14:06	♃ ☍	♈	14 17:13
16 21:36	♄ ☌	♉	17 0:43
19 6:44	♆ ☍	♊	19 10:28
21 20:13	♄ ⚹	♋	21 22:17
24 9:26	♄ □	♌	24 10:51
26 21:12	♄ △	♍	26 21:57
29 1:52	♆ ⚹	♎	29 5:44

☽ Phases & Eclipses Dy Hr Mn	
4 5:17	○ 13♍28
11 7:44	☽ 20♐34
18 4:51	● 27♓25
18 4:54:18	☌ A 0'26"
26 0:48	☽ 5♋12
2 18:45	○ 12♎51
2 18:32	☍ A 0.703
9 13:58	☽ 19♑32
16 18:16	● 26♈34
24 19:45	☽ 4♌26

Astro Data

1 MARCH 1969
Julian Day # 25262
Delta T 39.4 sec
SVP 05♓41'25"
Obliquity 23°26'45"
⚷ Chiron 1♈28.8
☽ Mean ☊ 1♈29.3

1 APRIL 1969
Julian Day # 25293
Delta T 39.4 sec
SVP 05♓41'21"
Obliquity 23°26'46"
⚷ Chiron 3♈17.2
☽ Mean ☊ 29♓50.8

LONGITUDE — MAY 1969

Day	Sid.Time	☉	0 hr ☽	Noon ☽	True ☊	☿	♀	♂	♃	♄	♅	♆	♇
1 Th	14 34 59	10♉26 38	24♎11 50	1♏17 32	29♓43.3	0♊29.5	10♈31.3	16♐41.0	26♍51.3	0♉ 8.1	0♎27.1	27♏48.5	22♍40.8
2 F	14 38 55	11 24 50	8♏28 29	15 43 59	29R 39.2	1 48.0	10 35.3	16R 38.0	26R 47.4	0 15.6	0R 25.3	27R 46.9	22R 39.9
3 Sa	14 42 52	12 23 0	23 3 16	0♐25 23	29 33.6	3 2.1	10 41.5	16 34.3	26 43.7	0 23.2	0 23.6	27 45.4	22 39.0
4 Su	14 46 49	13 21 9	7♐49 21	15 14 7	29 27.1	4 11.6	10 49.9	16 29.8	26 40.1	0 30.7	0 21.9	27 43.8	22 38.1
5 M	14 50 45	14 19 16	22 38 42	0♑ 2 6	29 20.5	5 16.6	11 0.6	16 24.6	26 36.7	0 38.2	0 20.2	27 42.3	22 37.2
6 Tu	14 54 42	15 17 21	7♑23 25	14 41 53	29 14.7	6 16.9	11 13.3	16 18.6	26 33.5	0 45.7	0 18.6	27 40.7	22 36.3
7 W	14 58 38	16 15 25	21 56 52	29 7 53	29 10.5	7 12.6	11 28.1	16 11.8	26 30.5	0 53.2	0 17.1	27 39.1	22 35.5
8 Th	15 2 35	17 13 28	6♒14 33	13♒16 42	29D 8.2	8 3.5	11 44.8	16 4.3	26 27.6	1 0.6	0 15.6	27 37.6	22 34.7
9 F	15 6 31	18 11 29	20 14 13	27 7 7	29 7.7	8 49.5	12 3.5	15 56.0	26 25.0	1 8.1	0 14.1	27 36.0	22 34.0
10 Sa	15 10 28	19 9 29	3♓55 31	10♓39 34	29 8.4	9 30.7	12 24.0	15 46.9	26 22.4	1 15.5	0 12.6	27 34.4	22 33.2
11 Su	15 14 25	20 7 28	17 19 28	23 55 28	29R 9.4	10 6.9	12 46.3	15 37.1	26 20.1	1 22.9	0 11.2	27 32.8	22 32.5
12 M	15 18 21	21 5 25	0♈27 48	6♈56 42	29 9.9	10 38.2	13 10.4	15 26.6	26 18.0	1 30.2	0 9.9	27 31.1	22 31.8
13 Tu	15 22 18	22 3 21	13 22 22	19 45 3	29 8.9	11 4.4	13 36.1	15 15.3	26 16.0	1 37.6	0 8.6	27 29.5	22 31.2
14 W	15 26 14	23 1 16	26 4 53	2♉22 3	29 5.7	11 25.7	14 3.4	15 3.3	26 14.2	1 44.9	0 7.3	27 27.9	22 30.5
15 Th	15 30 11	23 59 9	8♉36 40	14 48 53	29 0.0	11 41.9	14 32.2	14 50.6	26 12.6	1 52.2	0 6.1	27 26.3	22 30.0
16 F	15 34 7	24 57 1	20 58 46	27 6 27	28 52.0	11 53.1	15 2.5	14 37.2	26 11.1	1 59.4	0 5.0	27 24.7	22 29.4
17 Sa	15 38 4	25 54 51	3♊12 1	9♊15 36	28 42.2	11R 59.4	15 34.3	14 23.2	26 9.9	2 6.7	0 3.8	27 23.0	22 28.9
18 Su	15 42 0	26 52 40	15 17 19	21 17 22	28 31.3	12 0.8	16 7.4	14 8.5	26 8.8	2 13.9	0 2.8	27 21.4	22 28.4
19 M	15 45 57	27 50 28	27 15 54	3♋13 12	28 20.3	11 57.5	16 41.8	13 53.2	26 7.9	2 21.1	0 1.8	27 19.8	22 27.9
20 Tu	15 49 54	28 48 14	9♋ 9 30	15 5 10	28 10.3	11 49.6	17 17.4	13 37.4	26 7.2	2 28.2	0 0.8	27 18.2	22 27.4
21 W	15 53 50	29 45 59	21 0 32	26 56 2	28 2.0	11 37.4	17 54.3	13 20.9	26 6.7	2 35.3	29♍59.9	27 16.5	22 27.0
22 Th	15 57 47	0♊43 42	2♌52 9	8♌49 22	27 55.9	11 21.0	18 32.3	13 4.0	26 6.4	2 42.4	29 59.0	27 14.9	22 26.6
23 F	16 1 43	1 41 23	14 48 15	20 49 23	27 52.3	11 0.9	19 11.5	12 46.5	26D 6.2	2 49.4	29 58.2	27 13.3	22 26.3
24 Sa	16 5 40	2 39 3	26 53 22	3♍ 0 50	27D 50.8	10 37.3	19 51.7	12 28.6	26 6.2	2 56.4	29 57.4	27 11.7	22 26.0
25 Su	16 9 36	3 36 41	9♍12 25	15 28 45	27 50.7	10 10.7	20 33.0	12 10.2	26 6.4	3 3.4	29 56.7	27 10.0	22 25.7
26 M	16 13 33	4 34 18	21 50 27	28 18 4	27R 51.2	9 41.6	21 15.2	11 51.5	26 6.8	3 10.3	29 56.1	27 8.4	22 25.4
27 Tu	16 17 29	5 31 54	4♎52 7	11♎32 59	27 51.1	9 10.5	21 58.4	11 32.4	26 7.4	3 17.2	29 55.4	27 6.8	22 25.2
28 W	16 21 26	6 29 27	18 20 59	25 16 14	27 49.5	8 37.9	22 42.6	11 13.0	26 8.2	3 24.0	29 54.9	27 5.2	22 25.0
29 Th	16 25 23	7 27 0	2♏18 45	9♏28 16	27 45.6	8 4.4	23 27.6	10 53.3	26 9.1	3 30.8	29 54.4	27 3.6	22 24.8
30 F	16 29 19	8 24 31	16 44 23	24 6 27	27 39.2	7 30.6	24 13.5	10 33.4	26 10.2	3 37.6	29 53.9	27 2.0	22 24.7
31 Sa	16 33 16	9 22 1	1♐33 34	9♐ 4 43	27 30.7	6 57.0	25 0.2	10 13.3	26 11.5	3 44.3	29 53.5	27 0.5	22 24.6

LONGITUDE — JUNE 1969

Day	Sid.Time	☉	0 hr ☽	Noon ☽	True ☊	☿	♀	♂	♃	♄	♅	♆	♇
1 Su	16 37 12	10♊19 31	16♐38 40	24♐14 7	27♓20.7	6♊24.3	25♈47.7	9♐53.1	26♍13.0	3♉51.0	29♍53.1	26♏58.9	22♍24.5
2 M	16 41 9	11 16 59	1♑49 43	9♑24 7	27R 10.6	5R 53.0	26 35.9	9R 32.7	26 14.6	3 57.6	29R 52.8	26R 57.3	22D 24.5
3 Tu	16 45 5	12 14 26	16 56 5	24 24 30	27 1.4	5 23.6	27 24.9	9 12.3	26 16.4	4 4.2	29 52.6	26 55.8	22 24.5
4 W	16 49 2	13 11 52	1♒48 24	9♒ 7 4	26 54.2	4 56.6	28 14.7	8 51.9	26 18.4	4 10.8	29 52.4	26 54.2	22 24.5
5 Th	16 52 58	14 9 18	16 19 56	23 26 42	26 49.5	4 32.5	29 5.1	8 31.5	26 20.6	4 17.3	29 52.3	26 52.7	22 24.6
6 F	16 56 55	15 6 43	0♓27 13	7♓21 29	26 47.2	4 11.6	29 56.1	8 11.1	26 22.9	4 23.7	29 52.2	26 51.1	22 24.7
7 Sa	17 0 52	16 4 7	14 9 41	20 52 4	26 46.5	3 54.3	0♉47.8	7 50.9	26 25.4	4 30.1	29D 52.1	26 49.6	22 24.8
8 Su	17 4 48	17 1 31	27 28 58	4♈ 0 47	26 46.6	3 40.9	1 40.1	7 30.8	26 28.1	4 36.4	29 52.1	26 48.1	22 24.9
9 M	17 8 45	17 58 54	10♈27 58	16 50 54	26 46.1	3 31.5	2 33.0	7 10.9	26 30.9	4 42.7	29 52.2	26 46.6	22 25.1
10 Tu	17 12 41	18 56 17	23 10 4	29 25 49	26 43.9	3D 26.4	3 26.5	6 51.3	26 33.9	4 49.0	29 52.3	26 45.1	22 25.3
11 W	17 16 38	19 53 39	5♉38 34	11♉48 39	26 39.3	3 25.7	4 20.5	6 31.9	26 37.1	4 55.1	29 52.5	26 43.7	22 25.6
12 Th	17 20 34	20 51 1	17 56 23	24 2 3	26 31.8	3 29.5	5 15.0	6 12.9	26 40.4	5 1.3	29 52.7	26 42.2	22 25.9
13 F	17 24 31	21 48 22	0♊ 5 51	6♊ 8 2	26 21.5	3 37.8	6 10.1	5 54.3	26 44.0	5 7.3	29 53.0	26 40.8	22 26.2
14 Sa	17 28 27	22 45 42	12 8 46	18 8 14	26 9.0	3 50.7	7 5.6	5 36.1	26 47.6	5 13.3	29 53.3	26 39.3	22 26.5
15 Su	17 32 24	23 43 2	24 6 34	0♋ 3 56	25 55.2	4 8.1	8 1.6	5 18.4	26 51.5	5 19.3	29 53.7	26 37.9	22 26.9
16 M	17 36 21	24 40 21	6♋ 0 29	11 56 26	25 41.3	4 30.1	8 58.0	5 1.2	26 55.5	5 25.2	29 54.2	26 36.5	22 27.3
17 Tu	17 40 17	25 37 40	17 51 56	23 47 16	25 28.4	4 56.5	9 54.9	4 44.6	26 59.7	5 31.0	29 54.7	26 35.2	22 27.8
18 W	17 44 14	26 34 58	29 42 40	5♌38 26	25 17.4	5 27.4	10 52.1	4 28.5	27 4.0	5 36.8	29 55.2	26 33.8	22 28.2
19 Th	17 48 10	27 32 15	11♌34 57	17 32 36	25 9.0	6 2.6	11 49.8	4 13.0	27 8.5	5 42.5	29 55.8	26 32.5	22 28.8
20 F	17 52 7	28 29 32	23 31 50	29 33 7	25 3.5	6 42.2	12 47.9	3 58.2	27 13.1	5 48.1	29 56.5	26 31.1	22 29.3
21 Sa	17 56 3	29 26 48	5♍37 0	11♍44 3	25 0.6	7 26.0	13 46.4	3 44.0	27 17.9	5 53.7	29 57.2	26 29.8	22 29.9
22 Su	18 0 0	0♋24 3	17 54 50	24 9 58	24D 59.6	8 14.0	14 45.2	3 30.6	27 22.9	5 59.2	29 57.9	26 28.5	22 30.5
23 M	18 3 57	1 21 17	0♎30 4	6♎55 43	24R 59.5	9 6.1	15 44.3	3 17.8	27 28.0	6 4.7	29 58.7	26 27.3	22 31.1
24 Tu	18 7 53	2 18 31	13 27 29	20 5 51	24 59.2	10 2.2	16 43.9	3 5.8	27 33.2	6 10.0	29 59.6	26 26.0	22 31.7
25 W	18 11 50	3 15 44	26 51 16	3♏43 59	24 57.6	11 2.3	17 43.7	2 54.6	27 38.6	6 15.4	0♎ 0.5	26 24.8	22 32.4
26 Th	18 15 46	4 12 57	10♏44 9	17 51 45	24 53.9	12 6.3	18 43.9	2 44.1	27 44.2	6 20.6	0 1.5	26 23.6	22 33.2
27 F	18 19 43	5 10 9	25 6 32	2♐28 0	24 47.7	13 14.2	19 44.4	2 34.5	27 49.9	6 25.8	0 2.5	26 22.4	22 33.9
28 Sa	18 23 39	6 7 21	9♐55 27	17 27 57	24 39.2	14 25.9	20 45.2	2 25.6	27 55.7	6 30.9	0 3.6	26 21.2	22 34.7
29 Su	18 27 36	7 4 33	25 4 20	2♑43 17	24 29.2	15 41.3	21 46.3	2 17.5	28 1.7	6 35.9	0 4.7	26 20.1	22 35.5
30 M	18 31 32	8 1 44	10♑23 23	18 3 9	24 18.9	17 0.5	22 47.7	2 10.3	28 7.8	6 40.8	0 5.9	26 19.0	22 36.4

Astro Data Dy Hr Mn	Planet Ingress Dy Hr Mn	Last Aspect Dy Hr Mn	☽ Ingress Dy Hr Mn	Last Aspect Dy Hr Mn	☽ Ingress Dy Hr Mn	☽ Phases & Eclipses Dy Hr Mn
♄⊼♅ 3 1:05	♅ ♍ 20 20:57	30 11:09 ♂ ⚹	♏ 1 9:50	1 20:55 ♅ □	♑ 1 21:07	2 5:13 ○ 11♏37
☽0N 11 22:53	☉ ♊ 21 5:50	3 7:39 ♆ ☌	♐ 3 11:19	3 20:51 ♅ △	♒ 3 21:03	8 20:12 ☽ 18♒02
☿ R 17 19:06		5 6:25 ♃ □	♑ 5 11:57	5 23:03 ♀ ⚹	♓ 5 23:13	16 8:26 ● 25♉17
♃ D 23 8:20	♀ ♉ 6 1:48	7 9:30 ♆ ⚹	♒ 7 13:28	8 4:22 ♅ ☍	♈ 8 4:36	24 12:15 ☽ 3♍08
☽0S 26 14:27	☉ ♋ 21 13:55	9 12:49 ♆ □	♓ 9 17:04	9 15:18 ☉ ⚹	♉ 10 13:06	31 13:18 ○ 9♐54
	♅ ♎ 24 10:29	11 18:36 ♆ △	♈ 11 23:09	12 23:34 ♅ △	♊ 12 23:48	
♇ D 2 14:01		13 3:29 ♂ △	♉ 14 7:28	15 11:40 ♅ □	♋ 15 11:52	7 3:39 ☽ 16♓13
♅ D 7 6:34		16 12:34 ♆ ☍	♊ 16 17:41	18 0:25 ♅ ⚹	♌ 18 0:35	14 23:09 ● 23♊41
☽0N 8 3:37		18 21:43 ♃ □	♋ 19 5:30	20 10:45 ☉ ⚹	♍ 20 12:53	23 1:44 ☽ 1♎25
☿ D 10 15:48		21 18:11 ♅ ⚹	♌ 21 18:12	22 23:01 ♅ ☌	♎ 22 23:03	29 20:04 ○ 7♑52
♃⚹♆ 12 8:36		24 0:36 ♆ □	♍ 24 6:07	23 17:14 ☿ △	♏ 25 5:31	
☽0S 22 21:28		26 14:59 ♆ ⚹	♎ 26 15:07	27 4:29 ♃ ⚹	♐ 27 8:00	
		28 8:01 ♀ ☍	♏ 28 20:05	29 4:40 ♃ □	♑ 29 7:44	
		30 21:20 ♅ ⚹	♐ 30 21:30			

Astro Data

1 MAY 1969
Julian Day # 25323
Delta T 39.5 sec
SVP 05♓41'18"
Obliquity 23°26'45"
⚷ Chiron 4♈56.7
☽ Mean ☊ 28♓15.5

1 JUNE 1969
Julian Day # 25354
Delta T 39.6 sec
SVP 05♓41'13"
Obliquity 23°26'44"
⚷ Chiron 6♈14.4
☽ Mean ☊ 26♓37.0

JULY 1969 LONGITUDE

Day	Sid.Time	☉	0 hr ☽	Noon ☽	True ☊	☿	♀	♂	♃	♄	♅	♆	♇
1 Tu	18 35 29	8♋58 55	25♑41 10	3♒16 4	24♓ 9.5	18♊23.4	23♉49.4	2♐ 3.8	28♍14.0	6♉45.7	0♎ 7.1	26♏17.9	22♍37.2
2 W	18 39 26	9 56 6	10♒46 39	18 11 57	24R 2.0	19 49.9	24 51.4	1R 58.2	28 20.4	6 50.5	0 8.4	26R 16.8	22 38.1
3 Th	18 43 22	10 53 17	25 31 11	2♓43 47	23 57.0	21 20.0	25 53.6	1 53.4	28 27.0	6 55.3	0 9.7	26 15.8	22 39.1
4 F	18 47 19	11 50 29	9♓49 26	16 48 2	23 54.5	22 53.6	26 56.1	1 49.5	28 33.6	6 59.9	0 11.1	26 14.7	22 40.0
5 Sa	18 51 15	12 47 40	23 39 37	0♈24 24	23D 53.9	24 30.7	27 58.9	1 46.3	28 40.4	7 4.5	0 12.5	26 13.7	22 41.0
6 Su	18 55 12	13 44 52	7♈ 2 43	13 34 59	23R 54.1	26 11.2	29 1.9	1 44.0	28 47.4	7 9.0	0 14.0	26 12.7	22 42.0
7 M	18 59 8	14 42 4	20 1 40	26 23 16	23 54.1	27 55.0	0♊ 5.1	1 42.6	28 54.4	7 13.4	0 15.5	26 11.8	22 43.1
8 Tu	19 3 5	15 39 16	2♉40 20	8♉53 22	23 52.8	29 42.0	1 8.6	1D 41.9	29 1.6	7 17.7	0 17.1	26 10.9	22 44.2
9 W	19 7 1	16 36 29	15 2 55	21 9 26	23 49.4	1♋32.1	2 12.3	1 42.2	29 8.9	7 22.0	0 18.7	26 10.0	22 45.3
10 Th	19 10 58	17 33 42	27 13 23	3♊15 13	23 43.5	3 25.0	3 16.3	1 43.2	29 16.4	7 26.2	0 20.3	26 9.1	22 46.4
11 F	19 14 55	18 30 56	9♊15 17	15 13 57	23 35.1	5 20.7	4 20.4	1 45.1	29 23.9	7 30.3	0 22.1	26 8.2	22 47.6
12 Sa	19 18 51	19 28 10	21 11 31	27 8 16	23 24.7	7 18.9	5 24.8	1 47.7	29 31.6	7 34.3	0 23.8	26 7.4	22 48.8
13 Su	19 22 48	20 25 25	3♋ 4 26	9♋ 0 15	23 13.2	9 19.4	6 29.3	1 51.3	29 39.4	7 38.2	0 25.6	26 6.6	22 50.0
14 M	19 26 44	21 22 39	14 55 54	20 51 36	23 1.5	11 21.8	7 34.1	1 55.6	29 47.4	7 42.0	0 27.5	26 5.9	22 51.2
15 Tu	19 30 41	22 19 55	26 47 32	2♌43 53	22 50.6	13 26.0	8 39.0	2 0.7	29 55.4	7 45.8	0 29.4	26 5.1	22 52.5
16 W	19 34 37	23 17 10	8♌40 53	14 38 44	22 41.5	15 31.7	9 44.2	2 6.6	0♎ 3.6	7 49.4	0 31.3	26 4.4	22 53.8
17 Th	19 38 34	24 14 26	20 37 43	26 38 5	22 34.6	17 38.4	10 49.5	2 13.4	0 11.9	7 53.0	0 33.3	26 3.7	22 55.1
18 F	19 42 30	25 11 42	2♍40 10	8♍44 20	22 30.2	19 46.0	11 55.0	2 20.9	0 20.3	7 56.5	0 35.4	26 3.1	22 56.5
19 Sa	19 46 27	26 8 58	14 50 57	21 0 27	22D 28.2	21 54.0	13 0.6	2 29.1	0 28.8	7 59.9	0 37.4	26 2.5	22 57.8
20 Su	19 50 24	27 6 14	27 13 17	3♎29 56	22 28.0	24 2.2	14 6.5	2 38.2	0 37.4	8 3.2	0 39.6	26 1.9	22 59.2
21 M	19 54 20	28 3 31	9♎50 55	16 16 41	22 28.8	26 10.4	15 12.5	2 48.0	0 46.1	8 6.4	0 41.7	26 1.3	23 0.7
22 Tu	19 58 17	29 0 48	22 47 45	29 24 33	22R 29.6	28 18.2	16 18.6	2 58.5	0 55.0	8 9.5	0 44.0	26 0.8	23 2.1
23 W	20 2 13	29 58 5	6♏ 7 30	12♏56 53	22 29.6	0♌25.5	17 25.0	3 9.7	1 3.9	8 12.5	0 46.2	26 0.2	23 3.6
24 Th	20 6 10	0♌55 23	19 52 55	26 55 41	22 28.0	2 32.0	18 31.4	3 21.7	1 13.0	8 15.4	0 48.5	25 59.8	23 5.1
25 F	20 10 6	1 52 41	4♐ 5 5	11♐20 50	22 24.5	4 37.5	19 38.1	3 34.4	1 22.1	8 18.3	0 50.9	25 59.3	23 6.6
26 Sa	20 14 3	2 49 59	18 42 26	26 9 13	22 19.1	6 41.9	20 44.9	3 47.7	1 31.4	8 21.0	0 53.2	25 58.9	23 8.1
27 Su	20 17 59	3 47 18	3♑40 17	11♑14 34	22 12.5	8 45.0	21 51.8	4 1.8	1 40.7	8 23.6	0 55.7	25 58.5	23 9.7
28 M	20 21 56	4 44 37	18 50 51	26 27 50	22 5.5	10 46.9	22 58.9	4 16.4	1 50.2	8 26.2	0 58.1	25 58.2	23 11.3
29 Tu	20 25 53	5 41 57	4♒ 4 11	11♒38 34	21 59.0	12 47.3	24 6.1	4 31.8	1 59.7	8 28.6	1 0.6	25 57.9	23 12.9
30 W	20 29 49	6 39 18	19 9 45	26 36 39	21 53.9	14 46.2	25 13.5	4 47.7	2 9.3	8 31.0	1 3.2	25 57.6	23 14.6
31 Th	20 33 46	7 36 40	3♓58 18	11♓13 59	21 50.8	16 43.6	26 21.0	5 4.3	2 19.1	8 33.2	1 5.8	25 57.3	23 16.2

AUGUST 1969 LONGITUDE

Day	Sid.Time	☉	0 hr ☽	Noon ☽	True ☊	☿	♀	♂	♃	♄	♅	♆	♇
1 F	20 37 42	8♌34 2	18♓23 10	25♓25 30	21♓49.5	18♌39.4	27♊28.7	5♐21.5	2♎28.9	8♉35.4	1♎ 8.4	25♏57.1	23♍17.9
2 Sa	20 41 39	9 31 26	2♈20 51	9♈ 9 14	21D 49.8	20 33.7	28 36.5	5 39.3	2 38.8	8 37.4	1 11.0	25R 56.9	23 19.6
3 Su	20 45 35	10 28 50	15 50 50	22 25 55	21 51.1	22 26.3	29 44.4	5 57.6	2 48.8	8 39.4	1 13.7	25 56.7	23 21.3
4 M	20 49 32	11 26 16	28 54 53	5♉18 12	21 52.4	24 17.3	0♋52.5	6 16.6	2 58.9	8 41.3	1 16.4	25 56.6	23 23.0
5 Tu	20 53 28	12 23 44	11♉36 21	17 49 54	21R 53.0	26 6.8	2 0.7	6 36.1	3 9.1	8 43.0	1 19.2	25 56.5	23 24.8
6 W	20 57 25	13 21 12	23 59 24	0♊ 5 25	21 52.4	27 54.7	3 9.0	6 56.2	3 19.3	8 44.7	1 22.0	25 56.4	23 26.6
7 Th	21 1 22	14 18 42	6♊ 8 28	12 9 6	21 50.2	29 40.9	4 17.5	7 16.8	3 29.7	8 46.2	1 24.8	25D 56.4	23 28.4
8 F	21 5 18	15 16 13	18 7 50	24 5 7	21 46.4	1♍25.6	5 26.1	7 37.9	3 40.1	8 47.7	1 27.7	25 56.4	23 30.2
9 Sa	21 9 15	16 13 45	0♋ 1 25	5♋57 7	21 41.3	3 8.7	6 34.8	7 59.6	3 50.6	8 49.0	1 30.6	25 56.4	23 32.0
10 Su	21 13 11	17 11 19	11 52 37	17 48 14	21 35.4	4 50.3	7 43.7	8 21.8	4 1.2	8 50.2	1 33.6	25 56.5	23 33.9
11 M	21 17 8	18 8 54	23 44 17	29 41 2	21 29.2	6 30.3	8 52.6	8 44.6	4 11.9	8 51.4	1 36.5	25 56.6	23 35.8
12 Tu	21 21 4	19 6 30	5♌38 45	11♌37 39	21 23.6	8 8.8	10 1.7	9 7.8	4 22.6	8 52.4	1 39.5	25 56.7	23 37.7
13 W	21 25 1	20 4 7	17 37 57	23 39 51	21 18.9	9 45.8	11 10.9	9 31.5	4 33.5	8 53.3	1 42.6	25 56.8	23 39.6
14 Th	21 28 58	21 1 46	29 43 33	5♍49 15	21 15.6	11 21.2	12 20.1	9 55.7	4 44.4	8 54.1	1 45.7	25 57.0	23 41.5
15 F	21 32 54	21 59 25	11♍57 9	18 7 28	21D 13.8	12 55.1	13 29.5	10 20.4	4 55.3	8 54.8	1 48.7	25 57.3	23 43.4
16 Sa	21 36 51	22 57 6	24 20 26	0♎36 17	21 13.5	14 27.5	14 39.0	10 45.5	5 6.4	8 55.5	1 51.9	25 57.5	23 45.4
17 Su	21 40 47	23 54 48	6♎55 17	13 17 42	21 14.3	15 58.4	15 48.6	11 11.1	5 17.5	8 56.0	1 55.0	25 57.8	23 47.3
18 M	21 44 44	24 52 31	19 43 48	26 13 54	21 15.7	17 27.7	16 58.4	11 37.2	5 28.7	8 56.3	1 58.2	25 58.1	23 49.3
19 Tu	21 48 40	25 50 15	2♏48 15	9♏27 8	21 17.3	18 55.5	18 8.2	12 3.6	5 39.9	8 56.6	2 1.4	25 58.5	23 51.3
20 W	21 52 37	26 48 1	16 10 47	22 59 24	21R 18.4	20 21.7	19 18.1	12 30.6	5 51.3	8 56.8	2 4.7	25 58.8	23 53.3
21 Th	21 56 33	27 45 47	29 53 5	6♐51 53	21 18.7	21 46.4	20 28.1	12 57.9	6 2.6	8R 56.9	2 7.9	25 59.3	23 55.4
22 F	22 0 30	28 43 35	13♐55 45	21 4 31	21 18.0	23 9.4	21 38.2	13 25.6	6 14.1	8 56.9	2 11.2	25 59.7	23 57.4
23 Sa	22 4 27	29 41 24	28 17 51	5♑35 21	21 16.4	24 30.8	22 48.4	13 53.8	6 25.6	8 56.7	2 14.6	26 0.2	23 59.5
24 Su	22 8 23	0♍39 13	12♑56 24	20 20 17	21 14.1	25 50.5	23 58.7	14 22.3	6 37.2	8 56.5	2 17.9	26 0.7	24 1.5
25 M	22 12 20	1 37 5	27 46 11	5♒13 10	21 11.5	27 8.5	25 9.1	14 51.2	6 48.8	8 56.2	2 21.3	26 1.3	24 3.6
26 Tu	22 16 16	2 34 57	12♒40 14	20 6 21	21 9.2	28 24.7	26 19.7	15 20.4	7 0.5	8 55.7	2 24.7	26 1.8	24 5.7
27 W	22 20 13	3 32 51	27 30 32	4♓51 47	21 7.4	29 39.1	27 30.3	15 50.1	7 12.2	8 55.1	2 28.1	26 2.5	24 7.8
28 Th	22 24 9	4 30 46	12♓ 9 16	19 22 10	21D 6.5	0♎51.7	28 41.0	16 20.0	7 24.0	8 54.5	2 31.5	26 3.1	24 9.9
29 F	22 28 6	5 28 43	26 29 53	3♈31 54	21 6.4	2 2.2	29 51.7	16 50.3	7 35.9	8 53.7	2 35.0	26 3.8	24 12.0
30 Sa	22 32 2	6 26 41	10♈27 53	17 17 40	21 6.9	3 10.7	1♌ 2.6	17 21.0	7 47.8	8 52.8	2 38.5	26 4.5	24 14.2
31 Su	22 35 59	7 24 42	24 1 9	0♉38 28	21 8.0	4 17.0	2 13.6	17 52.0	7 59.7	8 51.9	2 42.0	26 5.2	24 16.3

Astro Data Dy Hr Mn	Planet Ingress Dy Hr Mn	Last Aspect Dy Hr Mn	☽ Ingress Dy Hr Mn	Last Aspect Dy Hr Mn	☽ Ingress Dy Hr Mn	☽ Phases & Eclipses Dy Hr Mn	Astro Data
☽0N 5 9:26	♀ ♊ 6 22:04	1 4:03 ♃ △	♒ 1 6:49	1 16:55 ♀ □	♈ 1 19:54	6 13:17 ☽ 14♈17	1 JULY 1969
♂ D 8 6:07	☿ ♋ 8 3:58	3 1:14 ♆ □	♓ 3 7:26	3 14:00 ☿ △	♉ 4 2:02	14 14:11 ● 21♋57	Julian Day # 25384
♄□♇ 17 23:47	♃ ♎ 15 13:29	5 8:59 ♃ ☍	♈ 5 11:16	6 9:01 ☿ □	♊ 6 11:49	22 12:09 ☽ 29♎30	Delta T 39.7 sec
☽0S 20 2:52	☿ ♌ 22 19:11	7 17:21 ☿ ✱	♉ 7 18:53	8 10:51 ♇ □	♋ 8 23:57	29 2:45 ○ 5♒49	SVP 05♓41'06"
♃☌♅ 20 7:57	☉ ♌ 23 0:48	10 4:07 ♃ △	♊ 10 5:31	11 4:27 ♆ △	♌ 11 12:38		Obliquity 23°26'44"
☽0N 1 17:28		12 17:01 ♃ □	♋ 12 17:47	13 16:32 ♆ □	♍ 14 0:32	5 1:38 ☽ 12♉28	⚷ Chiron 6♈50.7
♃0S 2 12:38	♀ ♋ 3 5:30	15 6:24 ♃ ✱	♌ 15 6:29	16 3:07 ♆ ✱	♎ 16 10:51	13 5:16 ● 20♌17	☽ Mean ☊ 25♓01.7
♆ D 7 14:55	☿ ♍ 7 4:21	17 10:51 ♆ □	♍ 17 18:42	18 10:16 ☉ ✱	♏ 18 18:54	20 20:03 ☽ 27♏36	
♅0S 11 1:29	☉ ♍ 23 7:43	19 23:45 ☉ ✱	♎ 20 5:20	20 20:03 ☉ □	♐ 21 0:12	27 10:32 ○ 3♓58	1 AUGUST 1969
☽0S 16 7:56	☿ ♎ 27 6:50	22 12:09 ☉ □	♏ 22 13:04	23 2:28 ☉ △	♑ 23 2:49	27 10:48 ☍ A 0.013	Julian Day # 25415
♄□♇ 21 17:46	♀ ♌ 29 2:48	24 10:25 ♆ ☌	♐ 24 17:10	24 22:54 ☿ △	♒ 25 3:36		Delta T 39.8 sec
♄ R 21 5:44		26 7:10 ♇ □	♑ 26 18:09	26 21:37 ♆ □	♓ 27 4:03		SVP 05♓41'01"
☿0S 25 8:41		28 11:13 ♆ ✱	♒ 28 17:34	28 23:16 ♆ △	♈ 29 5:57		Obliquity 23°26'45"
☽0N 29 3:18		30 10:57 ♆ □	♓ 30 17:30	30 12:35 ♂ △	♉ 31 10:50		⚷ Chiron 6♈40.2R
							☽ Mean ☊ 23♓23.3

LONGITUDE — SEPTEMBER 1969

Day	Sid.Time	☉	0 hr ☽	Noon ☽	True ☊	☿	♀	♂	♃	♄	♅	♆	♇
1 M	22 39 55	8♍22 44	7♉ 9 46	13♉35 22	21♓ 9.1	5♎21.1	3♌24.7	18♐23.3	8♎11.7	8♉50.8	2♎45.5	26♏ 6.0	24♍18.4
2 Tu	22 43 52	9 20 48	19 55 39	26 11 2	21 10.0	6 22.8	4 35.9	18 54.9	8 23.8	8R 49.6	2 49.0	26 6.8	24 20.6
3 W	22 47 49	10 18 54	2♊22 2	8♊29 10	21R 10.6	7 22.0	5 47.2	19 26.9	8 35.9	8 48.3	2 52.6	26 7.6	24 22.7
4 Th	22 51 45	11 17 2	14 32 59	20 34 4	21 10.7	8 18.6	6 58.5	19 59.1	8 48.0	8 47.0	2 56.1	26 8.4	24 24.9
5 F	22 55 42	12 15 12	26 32 58	2♋30 15	21 10.4	9 12.3	8 10.0	20 31.7	9 0.2	8 45.5	2 59.7	26 9.3	24 27.1
6 Sa	22 59 38	13 13 24	8♋26 29	14 22 11	21 9.7	10 3.0	9 21.5	21 4.6	9 12.4	8 43.9	3 3.3	26 10.3	24 29.3
7 Su	23 3 35	14 11 38	20 17 52	26 14 0	21 8.8	10 50.5	10 33.1	21 37.7	9 24.7	8 42.2	3 7.0	26 11.2	24 31.5
8 M	23 7 31	15 9 54	2♌11 3	8♌ 9 24	21 8.0	11 34.6	11 44.8	22 11.1	9 37.1	8 40.4	3 10.6	26 12.2	24 33.7
9 Tu	23 11 28	16 8 12	14 9 27	20 11 31	21 7.2	12 15.0	12 56.6	22 44.9	9 49.4	8 38.5	3 14.3	26 13.2	24 35.9
10 W	23 15 24	17 6 31	26 15 55	2♍22 53	21 6.7	12 51.5	14 8.5	23 18.9	10 1.8	8 36.5	3 17.9	26 14.2	24 38.1
11 Th	23 19 21	18 4 53	8♍32 38	14 45 22	21 6.4	13 23.7	15 20.4	23 53.2	10 14.3	8 34.4	3 21.6	26 15.3	24 40.3
12 F	23 23 18	19 3 16	21 1 13	27 20 17	21D 6.4	13 51.5	16 32.5	24 27.7	10 26.8	8 32.2	3 25.3	26 16.4	24 42.5
13 Sa	23 27 14	20 1 42	3♎42 41	10♎ 8 27	21 6.4	14 14.4	17 44.6	25 2.5	10 39.3	8 29.9	3 29.0	26 17.5	24 44.7
14 Su	23 31 11	21 0 9	16 37 37	23 10 14	21R 6.4	14 32.1	18 56.7	25 37.6	10 51.8	8 27.6	3 32.7	26 18.7	24 46.9
15 M	23 35 7	21 58 38	29 46 16	6♏25 44	21 6.4	14 44.3	20 9.0	26 12.9	11 4.4	8 25.1	3 36.5	26 19.9	24 49.1
16 Tu	23 39 4	22 57 8	13♏ 8 36	19 54 49	21 6.2	14R 50.7	21 21.3	26 48.5	11 17.0	8 22.5	3 40.2	26 21.1	24 51.4
17 W	23 43 0	23 55 40	26 44 21	3♐37 6	21 6.0	14 50.9	22 33.7	27 24.3	11 29.7	8 19.9	3 43.9	26 22.3	24 53.6
18 Th	23 46 57	24 54 14	10♐33 1	17 31 57	21 5.7	14 44.5	23 46.2	28 0.4	11 42.4	8 17.1	3 47.7	26 23.6	24 55.8
19 F	23 50 53	25 52 50	24 33 46	1♑38 15	21D 5.6	14 31.4	24 58.7	28 36.6	11 55.1	8 14.3	3 51.4	26 24.9	24 58.0
20 Sa	23 54 50	26 51 27	8♑45 11	15 54 16	21 5.7	14 11.3	26 11.3	29 13.2	12 7.8	8 11.4	3 55.2	26 26.2	25 0.3
21 Su	23 58 47	27 50 6	23 5 10	0♒17 27	21 6.1	13 44.1	27 24.0	29 49.9	12 20.6	8 8.4	3 59.0	26 27.6	25 2.5
22 M	0 2 43	28 48 47	7♒30 41	14 44 21	21 6.7	13 9.7	28 36.8	0♑26.8	12 33.3	8 5.3	4 2.8	26 29.0	25 4.7
23 Tu	0 6 40	29 47 29	21 57 52	29 10 40	21 7.4	12 28.4	29 49.6	1 4.0	12 46.1	8 2.1	4 6.5	26 30.4	25 6.9
24 W	0 10 36	0♎46 13	6♓22 7	13♓31 36	21 8.0	11 40.5	1♍ 2.5	1 41.3	12 59.0	7 58.8	4 10.3	26 31.8	25 9.1
25 Th	0 14 33	1 44 59	20 38 29	27 42 13	21R 8.3	10 46.6	2 15.4	2 18.9	13 11.8	7 55.5	4 14.1	26 33.3	25 11.4
26 F	0 18 29	2 43 46	4♈42 15	11♈38 7	21 8.0	9 47.4	3 28.4	2 56.6	13 24.7	7 52.1	4 17.9	26 34.8	25 13.6
27 Sa	0 22 26	3 42 36	18 29 25	25 15 52	21 7.1	8 44.1	4 41.5	3 34.5	13 37.5	7 48.6	4 21.7	26 36.3	25 15.8
28 Su	0 26 22	4 41 28	1♉57 13	8♉33 24	21 5.6	7 37.9	5 54.7	4 12.6	13 50.4	7 45.0	4 25.5	26 37.8	25 18.0
29 M	0 30 19	5 40 21	15 4 23	21 30 16	21 3.6	6 30.3	7 7.9	4 50.9	14 3.4	7 41.4	4 29.2	26 39.3	25 20.2
30 Tu	0 34 16	6 39 18	27 51 14	4♊ 7 32	21 1.5	5 23.2	8 21.2	5 29.4	14 16.3	7 37.7	4 33.0	26 40.9	25 22.4

LONGITUDE — OCTOBER 1969

Day	Sid.Time	☉	0 hr ☽	Noon ☽	True ☊	☿	♀	♂	♃	♄	♅	♆	♇
1 W	0 38 12	7♎38 16	10♊19 32	16♊27 37	20♓59.5	4♎18.1	9♍34.5	6♑ 8.1	14♎29.2	7♉33.9	4♎36.8	26♏42.5	25♍24.6
2 Th	0 42 9	8 37 17	22 32 17	28 34 0	20R 57.9	3R 16.9	10 47.9	6 46.9	14 42.2	7R 30.0	4 40.6	26 44.2	25 26.7
3 F	0 46 5	9 36 20	4♋33 21	10♋30 54	20D 57.1	2 21.3	12 1.4	7 25.9	14 55.2	7 26.1	4 44.4	26 45.8	25 28.9
4 Sa	0 50 2	10 35 25	16 27 14	22 22 58	20 57.1	1 32.9	13 14.9	8 5.0	15 8.1	7 22.1	4 48.2	26 47.5	25 31.1
5 Su	0 53 58	11 34 33	28 18 42	4♌15 2	20 58.0	0 52.8	14 28.5	8 44.4	15 21.1	7 18.1	4 52.0	26 49.2	25 33.2
6 M	0 57 55	12 33 43	10♌12 33	16 11 48	20 59.4	0 22.2	15 42.2	9 23.9	15 34.1	7 14.0	4 55.7	26 50.9	25 35.4
7 Tu	1 1 51	13 32 55	22 13 19	28 17 37	21 1.1	0 1.8	16 55.9	10 3.5	15 47.1	7 9.8	4 59.5	26 52.7	25 37.5
8 W	1 5 48	14 32 9	4♍25 7	10♍36 13	21 2.6	29♍52.0	18 9.7	10 43.3	16 0.1	7 5.6	5 3.2	26 54.4	25 39.7
9 Th	1 9 45	15 31 25	16 51 15	23 10 29	21R 3.4	29D 52.9	19 23.5	11 23.3	16 13.2	7 1.3	5 7.0	26 56.2	25 41.8
10 F	1 13 41	16 30 44	29 34 7	6♎ 2 14	21 3.2	0♎ 4.5	20 37.3	12 3.4	16 26.2	6 57.0	5 10.7	26 58.0	25 43.9
11 Sa	1 17 38	17 30 5	12♎34 53	19 11 59	21 1.7	0 26.4	21 51.3	12 43.7	16 39.2	6 52.6	5 14.5	26 59.8	25 46.0
12 Su	1 21 34	18 29 28	25 53 25	2♏38 59	20 58.9	0 58.1	23 5.2	13 24.1	16 52.2	6 48.1	5 18.2	27 1.7	25 48.1
13 M	1 25 31	19 28 53	9♏28 21	16 21 13	20 54.9	1 39.1	24 19.3	14 4.6	17 5.2	6 43.7	5 21.9	27 3.5	25 50.2
14 Tu	1 29 27	20 28 20	23 17 11	0♐15 48	20 50.3	2 28.5	25 33.3	14 45.3	17 18.2	6 39.2	5 25.6	27 5.4	25 52.3
15 W	1 33 24	21 27 48	7♐16 40	14 19 19	20 45.8	3 25.6	26 47.4	15 26.2	17 31.2	6 34.6	5 29.3	27 7.3	25 54.3
16 Th	1 37 20	22 27 19	21 23 19	28 28 16	20 41.9	4 29.5	28 1.6	16 7.1	17 44.2	6 30.0	5 33.0	27 9.2	25 56.4
17 F	1 41 17	23 26 52	5♑33 47	12♑39 32	20 39.1	5 39.6	29 15.8	16 48.2	17 57.2	6 25.4	5 36.6	27 11.2	25 58.4
18 Sa	1 45 14	24 26 26	19 45 14	26 50 36	20D 37.9	6 55.1	0♎30.1	17 29.5	18 10.2	6 20.8	5 40.3	27 13.1	26 0.4
19 Su	1 49 10	25 26 2	3♒55 24	10♒59 26	20 38.1	8 15.1	1 44.3	18 10.8	18 23.2	6 16.1	5 43.9	27 15.1	26 2.4
20 M	1 53 7	26 25 39	18 2 31	25 4 28	20 39.3	9 39.1	2 58.7	18 52.3	18 36.2	6 11.4	5 47.5	27 17.1	26 4.4
21 Tu	1 57 3	27 25 18	2♓ 5 6	9♓ 4 12	20 40.8	11 6.4	4 13.0	19 33.8	18 49.1	6 6.6	5 51.1	27 19.1	26 6.4
22 W	2 1 0	28 24 59	16 1 34	22 57 0	20R 41.7	12 36.6	5 27.4	20 15.5	19 2.1	6 1.9	5 54.7	27 21.1	26 8.4
23 Th	2 4 56	29 24 42	29 50 13	6♈40 58	20 41.5	14 9.0	6 41.9	20 57.3	19 15.0	5 57.1	5 58.3	27 23.1	26 10.3
24 F	2 8 53	0♏24 26	13♈28 59	20 13 59	20 39.4	15 43.3	7 56.3	21 39.2	19 27.9	5 52.3	6 1.8	27 25.2	26 12.2
25 Sa	2 12 49	1 24 13	26 55 43	3♉33 56	20 35.2	17 19.1	9 10.9	22 21.2	19 40.8	5 47.5	6 5.4	27 27.2	26 14.1
26 Su	2 16 46	2 24 1	10♉ 8 25	16 39 2	20 29.2	18 56.1	10 25.4	23 3.3	19 53.7	5 42.7	6 8.9	27 29.3	26 16.0
27 M	2 20 43	3 23 51	23 5 39	29 28 13	20 21.8	20 34.0	11 40.0	23 45.5	20 6.5	5 37.9	6 12.4	27 31.4	26 17.9
28 Tu	2 24 39	4 23 44	5♊46 46	12♊ 1 24	20 13.7	22 12.5	12 54.6	24 27.8	20 19.4	5 33.0	6 15.8	27 33.5	26 19.8
29 W	2 28 36	5 23 38	18 12 17	24 19 40	20 5.8	23 51.6	14 9.3	25 10.1	20 32.2	5 28.2	6 19.3	27 35.6	26 21.6
30 Th	2 32 32	6 23 35	0♋23 52	6♋25 16	19 58.9	25 30.9	15 24.0	25 52.6	20 45.0	5 23.4	6 22.7	27 37.7	26 23.4
31 F	2 36 29	7 23 33	12 24 19	18 21 31	19 53.6	27 10.4	16 38.8	26 35.2	20 57.7	5 18.6	6 26.1	27 39.9	26 25.2

Astro Data Dy Hr Mn	Planet Ingress Dy Hr Mn	Last Aspect Dy Hr Mn	☽ Ingress Dy Hr Mn	Last Aspect Dy Hr Mn	☽ Ingress Dy Hr Mn	☽ Phases & Eclipses Dy Hr Mn	Astro Data
♃⚻♄ 3 22:08	♂ ♑ 21 6:35	2 11:53 ♆ ☍	♊ 2 19:23	2 5:48 ♇ □	♋ 2 14:52	3 16:58 ☽ 10♊60	1 SEPTEMBER 1969
☽0S 12 14:05	☉ ♎ 23 5:07	4 19:46 ♇ □	♋ 5 6:57	4 20:58 ♆ △	♌ 5 3:25	11 19:56 ● 18♍53	Julian Day # 25446
♃∠♆ 16 8:33	♀ ♍ 23 3:26	7 11:55 ♆ △	♌ 7 19:36	7 9:14 ♆ □	♍ 7 15:21	11 19:58:19 ☌ A 3'11"	Delta T 39.9 sec
☿ R 16 12:41		9 23:57 ♆ □	♍ 10 7:20	9 19:07 ♆ ⚹	♎ 10 0:48	19 2:24 ☽ 25♐59	SVP 05♓40'57"
☽0N 25 13:16	☿ ♍ 7 2:57	12 10:00 ♆ ⚹	♎ 12 17:01	11 9:39 ☉ ☌	♏ 12 7:19	25 20:21 ○ 2♈35	Obliquity 23°26'45"
	☿ ♎ 9 26:45	14 17:15 ♂ ⚹	♏ 15 0:25	14 6:34 ♆ ☌	♐ 14 11:33	25 20:10 ☍ A 0.901	⚷ Chiron 5♈45.1R
☿0N 7 0:26	♀ ♎ 17 14:17	16 23:21 ♆ ☌	♐ 17 5:42	16 12:19 ♀ □	♑ 16 14:35		☽ Mean ☊ 21♓44.8
☿ D 8 9:53	☉ ♏ 23 14:11	19 7:11 ♂ ☌	♑ 19 9:14	18 12:40 ♆ ⚹	♒ 18 17:21	3 11:05 ☽ 10♋04	
☽0S 9 21:54		21 8:29 ☉ △	♒ 21 11:31	20 15:49 ♆ □	♓ 20 20:26	11 9:39 ● 17♎54	1 OCTOBER 1969
☿0S 15 16:14		23 7:34 ♆ □	♓ 23 13:22	22 19:43 ♆ △	♈ 23 0:17	18 8:32 ☽ 24♑48	Julian Day # 25476
♀0S 20 11:28		25 10:04 ♆ △	♈ 25 15:55	24 15:20 ♂ □	♉ 25 5:32	25 8:44 ○ 1♉46	Delta T 39.9 sec
☽0N 22 21:29		26 15:20 ♃ ☍	♉ 27 20:29	27 8:21 ♆ ☍	♊ 27 13:00		SVP 05♓40'54"
♄⚻♅ 22 20:35		29 21:46 ♆ ☍	♊ 30 4:05	29 16:03 ♇ □	♋ 29 23:13		Obliquity 23°26'45"
							⚷ Chiron 4♈27.2R
							☽ Mean ☊ 20♓09.4

NOVEMBER 1969 LONGITUDE

Day	Sid.Time	☉	0 hr ☽	Noon ☽	True ☊	☿	♀	♂	♃	♄	♅	♆	♇
1 Sa	2 40 25	8♏23 34	24♋17 24	0♌12 34	19♓50.3	28♎50.0	17♎53.5	27♑17.8	21♎10.5	5♉13.7	6♎29.5	27♏42.0	26♍27.0
2 Su	2 44 22	9 23 37	6♌ 7 38	12 3 15	19D 49.0	0♏29.5	19 8.3	28 0.5	21 23.2	5R 8.9	6 32.8	27 44.2	26 28.8
3 M	2 48 18	10 23 42	18 0 3	23 58 44	19 49.2	2 8.9	20 23.2	28 43.4	21 35.9	5 4.1	6 36.1	27 46.4	26 30.5
4 Tu	2 52 15	11 23 49	29 59 56	6♍ 4 17	19 50.3	3 48.1	21 38.1	29 26.3	21 48.6	4 59.3	6 39.4	27 48.5	26 32.2
5 W	2 56 12	12 23 59	12♍12 25	18 24 53	19R 51.4	5 27.1	22 53.0	0♒ 9.2	22 1.2	4 54.5	6 42.7	27 50.7	26 33.9
6 Th	3 0 8	13 24 10	24 42 11	1♎ 4 47	19 51.5	7 5.8	24 7.9	0 52.3	22 13.8	4 49.8	6 46.0	27 52.9	26 35.6
7 F	3 4 5	14 24 23	7♎33 1	14 7 7	19 49.9	8 44.3	25 22.9	1 35.5	22 26.3	4 45.0	6 49.2	27 55.1	26 37.2
8 Sa	3 8 1	15 24 38	20 47 11	27 33 14	19 45.9	10 22.5	26 37.8	2 18.7	22 38.9	4 40.3	6 52.3	27 57.3	26 38.8
9 Su	3 11 58	16 24 55	4♏25 3	11♏22 22	19 39.5	12 0.3	27 52.9	3 2.0	22 51.3	4 35.6	6 55.5	27 59.5	26 40.4
10 M	3 15 54	17 25 14	18 24 41	25 31 26	19 31.0	13 37.8	29 7.9	3 45.3	23 3.8	4 31.0	6 58.6	28 1.8	26 42.0
11 Tu	3 19 51	18 25 35	2♐41 53	9♐55 14	19 21.3	15 15.0	0♏23.0	4 28.8	23 16.2	4 26.3	7 1.7	28 4.0	26 43.6
12 W	3 23 47	19 25 57	17 10 39	24 27 13	19 11.4	16 51.9	1 38.0	5 12.3	23 28.6	4 21.8	7 4.8	28 6.2	26 45.1
13 Th	3 27 44	20 26 21	1♑44 7	9♑ 0 32	19 2.6	18 28.5	2 53.1	5 55.9	23 40.9	4 17.2	7 7.8	28 8.5	26 46.6
14 F	3 31 41	21 26 47	16 15 44	23 29 7	18 55.7	20 4.7	4 8.3	6 39.5	23 53.2	4 12.7	7 10.8	28 10.7	26 48.1
15 Sa	3 35 37	22 27 13	0♒40 10	7♒48 31	18 51.3	21 40.7	5 23.4	7 23.2	24 5.4	4 8.2	7 13.8	28 13.0	26 49.5
16 Su	3 39 34	23 27 41	14 53 53	21 56 8	18D 49.3	23 16.3	6 38.6	8 7.0	24 17.6	4 3.8	7 16.7	28 15.2	26 51.0
17 M	3 43 30	24 28 10	28 55 10	5♓51 0	18 49.1	24 51.7	7 53.7	8 50.8	24 29.7	3 59.4	7 19.6	28 17.5	26 52.4
18 Tu	3 47 27	25 28 41	12♓43 41	19 33 18	18R 49.5	26 26.8	9 8.9	9 34.7	24 41.8	3 55.1	7 22.4	28 19.7	26 53.7
19 W	3 51 23	26 29 12	26 19 58	3♈ 3 46	18 49.4	28 1.7	10 24.1	10 18.6	24 53.8	3 50.8	7 25.2	28 22.0	26 55.1
20 Th	3 55 20	27 29 45	9♈44 47	16 23 6	18 47.6	29 36.4	11 39.3	11 2.6	25 5.8	3 46.6	7 28.0	28 24.2	26 56.4
21 F	3 59 16	28 30 19	22 58 44	29 31 41	18 43.1	1♐10.8	12 54.6	11 46.6	25 17.7	3 42.4	7 30.7	28 26.5	26 57.7
22 Sa	4 3 13	29 30 55	6♉ 1 58	12♉29 31	18 35.7	2 45.0	14 9.8	12 30.6	25 29.6	3 38.3	7 33.4	28 28.7	26 58.9
23 Su	4 7 10	0♐31 32	18 54 16	25 16 11	18 25.5	4 19.1	15 25.1	13 14.7	25 41.4	3 34.3	7 36.1	28 31.0	27 0.2
24 M	4 11 6	1 32 10	1♊35 11	7♊51 15	18 13.1	5 53.0	16 40.3	13 58.9	25 53.1	3 30.3	7 38.7	28 33.2	27 1.4
25 Tu	4 15 3	2 32 49	14 4 21	20 14 32	17 59.5	7 26.7	17 55.6	14 43.1	26 4.8	3 26.4	7 41.3	28 35.5	27 2.6
26 W	4 18 59	3 33 31	26 21 51	2♋26 26	17 46.0	9 0.3	19 10.9	15 27.3	26 16.5	3 22.6	7 43.8	28 37.7	27 3.7
27 Th	4 22 56	4 34 13	8♋28 28	14 28 12	17 33.6	10 33.8	20 26.3	16 11.5	26 28.0	3 18.8	7 46.3	28 40.0	27 4.8
28 F	4 26 52	5 34 57	20 25 57	26 22 4	17 23.5	12 7.1	21 41.6	16 55.8	26 39.5	3 15.1	7 48.8	28 42.2	27 5.9
29 Sa	4 30 49	6 35 42	2♌17 0	8♌11 13	17 16.0	13 40.4	22 56.9	17 40.2	26 50.9	3 11.5	7 51.2	28 44.5	27 7.0
30 Su	4 34 45	7 36 29	14 5 17	19 59 46	17 11.3	15 13.6	24 12.3	18 24.5	27 2.3	3 7.9	7 53.5	28 46.7	27 8.0

DECEMBER 1969 LONGITUDE

Day	Sid.Time	☉	0 hr ☽	Noon ☽	True ☊	☿	♀	♂	♃	♄	♅	♆	♇
1 M	4 38 42	8♐37 17	25♌55 18	1♍52 33	17♓ 9.1	16♐46.7	25♏27.7	19♒ 8.9	27♎13.6	3♉ 4.5	7♎55.9	28♏49.0	27♍ 9.0
2 Tu	4 42 39	9 38 7	7♍52 11	13 54 55	17R 8.6	18 19.7	26 43.1	19 53.3	27 24.8	3R 1.1	7 58.1	28 51.2	27 9.9
3 W	4 46 35	10 38 58	20 1 27	26 12 27	17 8.6	19 52.7	27 58.5	20 37.8	27 36.0	2 57.7	8 0.4	28 53.4	27 10.9
4 Th	4 50 32	11 39 50	2♎28 35	8♎50 27	17 7.9	21 25.6	29 13.9	21 22.2	27 47.0	2 54.5	8 2.6	28 55.6	27 11.8
5 F	4 54 28	12 40 44	15 18 36	21 53 26	17 5.6	22 58.4	0♐29.3	22 6.8	27 58.0	2 51.4	8 4.7	28 57.8	27 12.6
6 Sa	4 58 25	13 41 39	28 35 17	5♏24 19	17 0.6	24 31.1	1 44.7	22 51.3	28 8.9	2 48.3	8 6.8	29 0.1	27 13.5
7 Su	5 2 21	14 42 35	12♏20 31	19 23 41	16 52.9	26 3.8	3 0.2	23 35.9	28 19.8	2 45.3	8 8.8	29 2.2	27 14.3
8 M	5 6 18	15 43 33	26 33 24	3♐49 3	16 42.6	27 36.3	4 15.6	24 20.5	28 30.5	2 42.5	8 10.8	29 4.4	27 15.1
9 Tu	5 10 14	16 44 32	11♐ 9 50	18 34 45	16 30.7	29 8.7	5 31.1	25 5.1	28 41.2	2 39.7	8 12.8	29 6.6	27 15.8
10 W	5 14 11	17 45 31	26 2 41	3♑32 26	16 18.4	0♑40.9	6 46.5	25 49.7	28 51.8	2 37.0	8 14.7	29 8.8	27 16.5
11 Th	5 18 8	18 46 32	11♑ 2 45	18 32 25	16 7.2	2 12.9	8 2.0	26 34.4	29 2.3	2 34.4	8 16.5	29 11.0	27 17.2
12 F	5 22 4	19 47 33	26 0 19	3♒25 27	15 58.2	3 44.7	9 17.5	27 19.1	29 12.7	2 31.9	8 18.3	29 13.1	27 17.8
13 Sa	5 26 1	20 48 35	10♒46 59	18 4 13	15 52.1	5 16.1	10 33.0	28 3.8	29 23.0	2 29.5	8 20.1	29 15.2	27 18.4
14 Su	5 29 57	21 49 37	25 16 43	2♓24 9	15 48.8	6 47.2	11 48.4	28 48.5	29 33.2	2 27.2	8 21.8	29 17.4	27 19.0
15 M	5 33 54	22 50 40	9♓26 24	16 23 26	15D 47.8	8 17.8	13 3.9	29 33.2	29 43.4	2 25.0	8 23.4	29 19.5	27 19.5
16 Tu	5 37 50	23 51 43	23 15 23	0♈ 2 27	15R 47.7	9 47.8	14 19.4	0♓18.0	29 53.4	2 22.9	8 25.0	29 21.6	27 20.1
17 W	5 41 47	24 52 46	6♈44 52	13 22 57	15 47.3	11 17.1	15 34.9	1 2.7	0♏ 3.3	2 20.9	8 26.6	29 23.7	27 20.5
18 Th	5 45 44	25 53 50	19 57 0	26 27 18	15 45.3	12 45.5	16 50.3	1 47.5	0 13.2	2 19.0	8 28.0	29 25.8	27 21.0
19 F	5 49 40	26 54 54	2♉54 11	9♉17 53	15 40.8	14 13.0	18 5.8	2 32.2	0 22.9	2 17.2	8 29.5	29 27.8	27 21.4
20 Sa	5 53 37	27 55 59	15 38 39	21 56 41	15 33.2	15 39.2	19 21.3	3 17.0	0 32.5	2 15.5	8 30.9	29 29.9	27 21.7
21 Su	5 57 33	28 57 3	28 12 9	4♊25 11	15 22.8	17 4.0	20 36.8	4 1.8	0 42.1	2 14.0	8 32.2	29 31.9	27 22.1
22 M	6 1 30	29 58 9	10♊35 55	16 44 26	15 10.1	18 27.0	21 52.3	4 46.5	0 51.5	2 12.5	8 33.5	29 33.9	27 22.4
23 Tu	6 5 26	0♑59 14	22 50 50	28 55 11	14 56.2	19 47.9	23 7.8	5 31.3	1 0.8	2 11.1	8 34.7	29 35.9	27 22.6
24 W	6 9 23	2 0 20	4♋57 35	10♋58 9	14 42.2	21 6.4	24 23.2	6 16.1	1 10.0	2 9.9	8 35.9	29 37.9	27 22.9
25 Th	6 13 19	3 1 27	16 57 1	22 54 22	14 29.4	22 22.1	25 38.7	7 0.9	1 19.1	2 8.7	8 37.0	29 39.9	27 23.1
26 F	6 17 16	4 2 34	28 50 23	4♌45 20	14 18.7	23 34.4	26 54.2	7 45.6	1 28.1	2 7.7	8 38.0	29 41.8	27 23.3
27 Sa	6 21 13	5 3 41	10♌39 33	16 33 21	14 10.7	24 42.8	28 9.7	8 30.4	1 36.9	2 6.7	8 39.1	29 43.8	27 23.4
28 Su	6 25 9	6 4 48	22 27 9	28 21 25	14 5.7	25 46.6	29 25.2	9 15.2	1 45.7	2 5.9	8 40.0	29 45.7	27 23.5
29 M	6 29 6	7 5 56	4♍16 40	10♍13 26	14D 3.2	26 45.2	0♑40.7	9 59.9	1 54.3	2 5.2	8 40.9	29 47.6	27 23.5
30 Tu	6 33 2	8 7 5	16 12 19	22 13 58	14 2.8	27 37.7	1 56.2	10 44.7	2 2.8	2 4.6	8 41.7	29 49.5	27R 23.6
31 W	6 36 59	9 8 13	28 19 0	4♎28 6	14R 3.3	28 23.4	3 11.7	11 29.4	2 11.2	2 4.1	8 42.5	29 51.3	27 23.6

Astro Data Dy Hr Mn	Planet Ingress Dy Hr Mn	Last Aspect Dy Hr Mn	☽ Ingress Dy Hr Mn	Last Aspect Dy Hr Mn	☽ Ingress Dy Hr Mn	☽ Phases & Eclipses Dy Hr Mn	Astro Data
☽0S 6 6:44	☿ ♏ 1 16:53	1 10:43 ☿ □	♌ 1 11:35	1 5:52 ♆ □	♍ 1 8:14	2 7:14 ☽ 9♌42	1 NOVEMBER 1969
☽0N 19 3:10	♂ ♒ 4 18:51	3 19:38 ♆ □	♍ 4 0:00	3 17:12 ♆ ✶	♎ 3 19:17	9 22:11 ● 17♏21	Julian Day # 25507
♃⊻♇ 30 13:14	♀ ♏ 10 16:40	6 6:01 ♆ ✶	♎ 6 9:59	5 23:13 ♃ ☌	♏ 6 2:30	16 15:45 ☽ 24♒07	Delta T 40.0 sec
	☿ ♐ 20 6:00	8 11:25 ♀ ☌	♏ 8 16:18	8 4:11 ♆ ☌	♐ 8 5:43	23 23:54 ○ 1♊32	SVP 05♓40'50"
☽0S 3 15:08	☉ ♐ 22 11:31	10 16:15 ♆ ☌	♐ 10 19:30	10 4:34 ♃ ✶	♑ 10 6:20		Obliquity 23°26'45"
♃⊻♆ 12 1:11		12 15:49 ♇ □	♑ 12 21:08	12 5:14 ♃ □	♒ 12 6:27	2 3:50 ☽ 9♍48	⚷ Chiron 3♈10.3R
☽0N 16 7:42	♀ ♐ 4 14:41	14 19:53 ♆ ✶	♒ 14 22:53	14 7:16 ♃ △	♓ 14 7:56	9 9:42 ● 17♐09	☽ Mean ☊ 18♓30.9
☽0S 30 22:00	☿ ♑ 9 13:21	16 22:55 ♆ □	♓ 17 1:52	16 10:49 ♆ △	♈ 16 11:56	16 1:09 ☽ 23♓55	
♃☍♄ 30 4:44	♂ ♓ 15 14:22	19 3:38 ♆ △	♈ 19 6:32	18 11:54 ☉ △	♉ 18 18:35	23 17:35 ○ 1♋44	1 DECEMBER 1969
♇ R 30 8:08	♃ ♏ 16 15:55	21 4:18 ♃ ☍	♉ 21 12:52	21 2:34 ♆ ☍	♊ 21 3:28	31 22:52 ☽ 10♎06	Julian Day # 25537
	☉ ♑ 22 0:44	23 18:13 ♆ ☍	♊ 23 20:59	23 8:57 ♇ □	♋ 23 14:08		Delta T 40.1 sec
	♀ ♑ 28 11:04	26 1:23 ♇ □	♋ 26 7:10	26 1:45 ♆ △	♌ 26 2:21		SVP 05♓40'45"
		28 16:47 ♆ △	♌ 28 19:22	28 14:53 ♆ □	♍ 28 15:20		Obliquity 23°26'44"
				31 3:01 ♆ ✶	♎ 31 3:18		⚷ Chiron 2♈27.0R
							☽ Mean ☊ 16♓55.6

LONGITUDE — JANUARY 1970

Day	Sid.Time	☉	0 hr ☽	Noon ☽	True ☊	☿	♀	♂	♃	♄	♅	♆	♇
1 Th	6 40 55	10♑ 9 23	10♎41 56	17♎ 1 10	14♓ 3.7	29♑ 1.3	4♑27.2	12♓14.2	2♏19.5	2♉ 3.7	8♎43.2	29♏53.2	27♍23.5
2 F	6 44 52	11 10 32	23 26 24	29 58 11	14R 2.9	29 30.5	5 42.7	12 58.9	2 27.6	2R 3.5	8 43.9	29 55.0	27R23.5
3 Sa	6 48 48	12 11 42	6♏36 59	13♏23 10	14 0.1	29 50.2	6 58.2	13 43.7	2 35.7	2D 3.3	8 44.5	29 56.8	27 23.4
4 Su	6 52 45	13 12 52	20 16 56	27 18 19	13 54.9	29R59.5	8 13.7	14 28.4	2 43.5	2 3.3	8 45.1	29 58.5	27 23.2
5 M	6 56 42	14 14 3	4♐27 9	11♐43 1	13 47.5	29 57.7	9 29.2	15 13.1	2 51.3	2 3.3	8 45.6	0♐ 0.3	27 23.0
6 Tu	7 0 38	15 15 13	19 5 20	26 33 13	13 38.5	29 44.2	10 44.7	15 57.8	2 58.9	2 3.5	8 46.0	0 2.0	27 22.8
7 W	7 4 35	16 16 24	4♑ 5 37	11♑41 20	13 29.0	29 18.8	12 0.2	16 42.6	3 6.4	2 3.8	8 46.4	0 3.7	27 22.6
8 Th	7 8 31	17 17 35	19 19 1	26 57 16	13 20.1	28 41.8	13 15.7	17 27.3	3 13.8	2 4.2	8 46.8	0 5.4	27 22.3
9 F	7 12 28	18 18 45	4♒34 41	12♒ 9 57	13 13.0	27 53.6	14 31.2	18 12.0	3 21.0	2 4.8	8 47.0	0 7.1	27 22.0
10 Sa	7 16 24	19 19 55	19 41 53	27 9 27	13 8.4	26 55.3	15 46.7	18 56.6	3 28.1	2 5.4	8 47.2	0 8.7	27 21.7
11 Su	7 20 21	20 21 5	4♓31 51	11♓48 27	13D 6.2	25 48.4	17 2.2	19 41.3	3 35.0	2 6.1	8 47.4	0 10.4	27 21.3
12 M	7 24 18	21 22 14	18 58 50	26 2 47	13 6.0	24 35.0	18 17.7	20 26.0	3 41.8	2 7.0	8 47.5	0 11.9	27 20.9
13 Tu	7 28 14	22 23 22	3♈ 0 16	9♈51 22	13 6.9	23 17.4	19 33.1	21 10.6	3 48.4	2 8.0	8R47.5	0 13.5	27 20.5
14 W	7 32 11	23 24 30	16 36 18	23 15 23	13R 7.9	21 58.0	20 48.6	21 55.2	3 54.9	2 9.0	8 47.5	0 15.0	27 20.0
15 Th	7 36 7	24 25 37	29 48 58	6♉17 29	13 8.0	20 39.5	22 4.1	22 39.8	4 1.2	2 10.2	8 47.5	0 16.6	27 19.5
16 F	7 40 4	25 26 43	12♉41 20	19 0 58	13 6.3	19 24.0	23 19.5	23 24.4	4 7.4	2 11.5	8 47.3	0 18.0	27 18.9
17 Sa	7 44 0	26 27 48	25 16 49	1♊29 17	13 2.4	18 13.7	24 35.0	24 9.0	4 13.5	2 13.0	8 47.2	0 19.5	27 18.4
18 Su	7 47 57	27 28 53	7♊38 45	13 45 35	12 56.5	17 10.2	25 50.4	24 53.5	4 19.4	2 14.5	8 46.9	0 20.9	27 17.8
19 M	7 51 53	28 29 57	19 50 6	25 52 35	12 49.0	16 14.7	27 5.8	25 38.0	4 25.1	2 16.1	8 46.6	0 22.3	27 17.1
20 Tu	7 55 50	29 31 1	1♋53 20	7♋52 33	12 40.5	15 28.1	28 21.2	26 22.5	4 30.7	2 17.9	8 46.3	0 23.7	27 16.5
21 W	7 59 47	0♒32 3	13 50 30	19 47 22	12 31.9	14 50.7	29 36.6	27 7.0	4 36.1	2 19.7	8 45.9	0 25.1	27 15.8
22 Th	8 3 43	1 33 5	25 43 21	1♌38 39	12 24.0	14 22.7	0♒52.1	27 51.5	4 41.3	2 21.7	8 45.4	0 26.4	27 15.1
23 F	8 7 40	2 34 6	7♌33 29	13 28 4	12 17.5	14 3.9	2 7.5	28 35.9	4 46.4	2 23.7	8 44.9	0 27.7	27 14.3
24 Sa	8 11 36	3 35 6	19 22 37	25 17 25	12 12.9	13D53.9	3 22.8	29 20.3	4 51.4	2 25.9	8 44.3	0 29.0	27 13.6
25 Su	8 15 33	4 36 6	1♍12 45	7♍ 8 55	12D10.3	13 52.3	4 38.2	0♈ 4.6	4 56.1	2 28.2	8 43.7	0 30.2	27 12.7
26 M	8 19 29	5 37 5	13 6 18	19 5 17	12 9.6	13 58.6	5 53.6	0 49.0	5 0.7	2 30.6	8 43.0	0 31.4	27 11.9
27 Tu	8 23 26	6 38 3	25 6 16	1♎ 9 46	12 10.4	14 12.2	7 9.0	1 33.3	5 5.2	2 33.1	8 42.3	0 32.6	27 11.0
28 W	8 27 22	7 39 0	7♎16 13	13 26 11	12 12.0	14 32.5	8 24.3	2 17.6	5 9.5	2 35.7	8 41.5	0 33.7	27 10.1
29 Th	8 31 19	8 39 57	19 40 10	25 58 42	12 13.7	14 59.0	9 39.7	3 1.9	5 13.6	2 38.3	8 40.7	0 34.8	27 9.2
30 F	8 35 16	9 40 53	2♏22 21	8♏51 35	12R15.0	15 31.1	10 55.0	3 46.1	5 17.5	2 41.1	8 39.8	0 35.9	27 8.3
31 Sa	8 39 12	10 41 48	15 26 53	22 8 38	12 15.1	16 8.3	12 10.4	4 30.3	5 21.2	2 44.0	8 38.9	0 37.0	27 7.3

LONGITUDE — FEBRUARY 1970

Day	Sid.Time	☉	0 hr ☽	Noon ☽	True ☊	☿	♀	♂	♃	♄	♅	♆	♇
1 Su	8 43 9	11♒42 43	28♏57 9	5♐52 36	12♓13.9	16♑50.2	13♒25.7	5♈14.5	5♏24.8	2♉47.0	8♎37.9	0♐38.0	27♍ 6.3
2 M	8 47 5	12 43 37	12♐55 2	20 4 20	12R11.3	17 36.3	14 41.0	5 58.6	5 28.2	2 50.1	8R36.8	0 39.0	27R 5.3
3 Tu	8 51 2	13 44 31	27 20 9	4♑41 59	12 7.7	18 26.4	15 56.4	6 42.8	5 31.5	2 53.4	8 35.7	0 40.0	27 4.2
4 W	8 54 58	14 45 23	12♑ 9 8	19 40 41	12 3.6	19 19.9	17 11.7	7 26.9	5 34.5	2 56.7	8 34.6	0 40.9	27 3.1
5 Th	8 58 55	15 46 15	27 15 32	4♒52 30	11 59.7	20 16.6	18 27.0	8 11.0	5 37.4	3 0.1	8 33.4	0 41.8	27 2.0
6 F	9 2 51	16 47 5	12♒30 18	20 7 37	11 56.7	21 16.3	19 42.3	8 55.0	5 40.1	3 3.6	8 32.2	0 42.7	27 0.9
7 Sa	9 6 48	17 47 54	27 43 8	5♓15 40	11D54.8	22 18.7	20 57.6	9 39.0	5 42.6	3 7.1	8 30.9	0 43.5	26 59.8
8 Su	9 10 45	18 48 42	12♓44 8	20 7 35	11 54.3	23 23.5	22 12.8	10 23.0	5 44.9	3 10.8	8 29.5	0 44.3	26 58.6
9 M	9 14 41	19 49 28	27 25 17	4♈36 42	11 54.8	24 30.6	23 28.1	11 7.0	5 47.0	3 14.6	8 28.1	0 45.1	26 57.4
10 Tu	9 18 38	20 50 13	11♈41 27	18 39 21	11 56.1	25 39.7	24 43.3	11 50.9	5 49.0	3 18.5	8 26.7	0 45.8	26 56.2
11 W	9 22 34	21 50 56	25 30 23	2♉14 40	11 57.6	26 50.9	25 58.6	12 34.8	5 50.7	3 22.5	8 25.2	0 46.5	26 54.9
12 Th	9 26 31	22 51 38	8♉52 27	15 24 5	11 58.8	28 3.8	27 13.8	13 18.7	5 52.3	3 26.5	8 23.7	0 47.2	26 53.7
13 F	9 30 27	23 52 18	21 49 56	28 10 30	11R59.3	29 18.5	28 29.0	14 2.5	5 53.7	3 30.7	8 22.1	0 47.8	26 52.4
14 Sa	9 34 24	24 52 57	4♊26 16	10♊37 44	11 59.0	0♒34.7	29 44.1	14 46.3	5 54.9	3 34.9	8 20.5	0 48.4	26 51.1
15 Su	9 38 20	25 53 33	16 45 27	22 49 54	11 57.9	1 52.4	0♓59.3	15 30.1	5 55.9	3 39.2	8 18.9	0 49.0	26 49.7
16 M	9 42 17	26 54 8	28 51 35	4♋51 1	11 56.2	3 11.6	2 14.4	16 13.8	5 56.8	3 43.7	8 17.2	0 49.5	26 48.4
17 Tu	9 46 14	27 54 42	10♋48 38	16 44 52	11 54.1	4 32.1	3 29.6	16 57.5	5 57.4	3 48.2	8 15.4	0 50.0	26 47.0
18 W	9 50 10	28 55 14	22 40 7	28 34 46	11 51.9	5 53.9	4 44.7	17 41.1	5 57.9	3 52.7	8 13.6	0 50.5	26 45.7
19 Th	9 54 7	29 55 43	4♌29 9	10♌23 36	11 50.0	7 17.0	5 59.8	18 24.7	5R58.1	3 57.4	8 11.8	0 50.9	26 44.3
20 F	9 58 3	0♓56 12	16 18 23	22 13 49	11 48.5	8 41.3	7 14.8	19 8.3	5 58.2	4 2.2	8 10.0	0 51.3	26 42.9
21 Sa	10 2 0	1 56 38	28 10 7	4♍ 7 34	11 47.6	10 6.7	8 29.9	19 51.8	5 58.1	4 7.0	8 8.1	0 51.7	26 41.4
22 Su	10 5 56	2 57 3	10♍ 6 23	16 6 49	11D47.3	11 33.3	9 44.9	20 35.3	5 57.8	4 11.9	8 6.1	0 52.0	26 40.0
23 M	10 9 53	3 57 26	22 9 6	28 13 29	11 47.5	13 1.0	10 60.0	21 18.8	5 57.3	4 16.9	8 4.2	0 52.3	26 38.5
24 Tu	10 13 49	4 57 48	4♎20 12	10♎29 31	11 47.9	14 29.7	12 15.0	22 2.2	5 56.6	4 22.0	8 2.1	0 52.6	26 37.0
25 W	10 17 46	5 58 8	16 41 44	22 57 7	11 48.6	15 59.6	13 29.9	22 45.6	5 55.8	4 27.1	8 0.1	0 52.8	26 35.6
26 Th	10 21 43	6 58 27	29 15 58	5♏38 36	11 49.2	17 30.5	14 44.9	23 28.9	5 54.7	4 32.3	7 58.0	0 53.0	26 34.1
27 F	10 25 39	7 58 44	12♏ 5 18	18 36 24	11 49.6	19 2.5	15 59.9	24 12.2	5 53.5	4 37.6	7 55.9	0 53.2	26 32.5
28 Sa	10 29 36	8 59 0	25 12 9	1♐52 50	11 49.9	20 35.5	17 14.8	24 55.5	5 52.0	4 43.0	7 53.8	0 53.3	26 31.0

Astro Data	Planet Ingress	Last Aspect	☽ Ingress	Last Aspect	☽ Ingress	☽ Phases & Eclipses	Astro Data
Dy Hr Mn	Dy Hr Mn	Dy Hr Mn	Dy Hr Mn	Dy Hr Mn	Dy Hr Mn	Dy Hr Mn	1 JANUARY 1970
♄ D 3 21:06	☿ ♒ 4 4:24	2 11:29 ☿ □	♏ 2 12:03	31 20:46 ♇ ⚹	♐ 1 1:50	7 20:35 ● 17♑09	Julian Day # 25568
☿ R 4 8:10	☿ ♑ 4 11:54	4 16:32 ♆ ☌	♐ 4 16:33	2 23:34 ♇ □	♑ 3 4:22	14 13:18 ☽ 23♈58	Delta T 40.2 sec
☽0N 12 13:51	♆ ♐ 4 19:52	6 13:19 ♇ □	♑ 6 17:30	4 23:39 ♇ △	♒ 5 4:19	22 12:55 ○ 2♌06	SVP 05♓40'39"
♅ R 13 6:09	☉ ♒ 20 11:24	8 14:02 ☿ ☌	♒ 8 16:47	6 12:21 ♀ ☌	♓ 7 3:37	30 14:38 ☽ 10♏18	Obliquity 23°26'44"
☿ D 24 16:38	♀ ♒ 21 7:26	9 6:39 ♅ △	♓ 10 16:37	8 23:14 ♇ ☍	♈ 9 4:17		⚷ Chiron 2♈31.2
♂0N 26 1:42	♂ ♈ 24 21:29	12 14:14 ♇ ☍	♈ 12 18:48	11 2:36 ☿ □	♉ 11 7:59	6 7:13 ● 17♒05	☽ Mean ☊ 15♓17.2
☽0S 27 3:37		14 13:18 ☉ □	♉ 15 0:20	13 13:59 ♀ □	♊ 13 15:29	13 4:10 ☽ 24♉03	
	☿ ♒ 13 13:08	17 3:54 ♇ △	♊ 17 9:07	15 19:55 ♇ □	♋ 16 2:17	21 8:19 ○ 2♍18	1 FEBRUARY 1970
☽0N 8 23:05	♀ ♓ 14 5:04	19 14:48 ♇ □	♋ 19 20:13	18 8:17 ♇ ⚹	♌ 18 14:53	21 8:30 ☍ P 0.046	Julian Day # 25599
♃ R 19 21:58	☉ ♓ 19 1:42	22 4:37 ♂ △	♌ 22 8:40	20 6:07 ♂ △	♍ 21 3:42		Delta T 40.3 sec
☽0S 23 9:14		23 2:25 ♅ ⚹	♍ 24 21:33	23 8:52 ♇ ☌	♎ 23 15:30		SVP 05♓40'33"
		27 4:07 ♇ ☌	♎ 27 9:42	25 12:21 ♂ ☍	♏ 26 1:23		Obliquity 23°26'44"
		28 14:38 ☿ □	♏ 29 19:34	28 2:22 ♇ ⚹	♐ 28 8:38		⚷ Chiron 3♈25.5
							☽ Mean ☊ 13♓38.7

MARCH 1970 LONGITUDE

Day	Sid.Time	☉	0 hr ☽	Noon ☽	True ☊	☿	♀	♂	♃	♄	♅	♆	♇
1 Su	10 33 32	9♓59 14	8♐38 39	15♐29 46	11♓49.9	22♒ 9.6	18♓29.7	25♈38.7	5♏50.4	4♉48.4	7♎51.6	0♐53.4	26♍29.5
2 M	10 37 29	10 59 27	22 26 15	29 28 7	11D49.9	23 44.8	19 44.6	26 21.9	5R48.6	4 54.0	7R49.4	0 53.4	26R27.9
3 Tu	10 41 25	11 59 39	6♑35 14	13♑47 21	11 49.9	25 21.0	20 59.5	27 5.1	5 46.6	4 59.5	7 47.2	0R53.5	26 26.4
4 W	10 45 22	12 59 49	21 4 6	28 24 57	11 50.0	26 58.2	22 14.4	27 48.2	5 44.5	5 5.2	7 44.9	0 53.5	26 24.8
5 Th	10 49 18	13 59 57	5♒49 17	13♒16 17	11 50.1	28 36.5	23 29.2	28 31.3	5 42.1	5 10.9	7 42.6	0 53.4	26 23.2
6 F	10 53 15	15 0 4	20 45 4	28 14 40	11 50.4	0♓15.9	24 44.0	29 14.4	5 39.6	5 16.7	7 40.3	0 53.4	26 21.6
7 Sa	10 57 12	16 0 9	5♓44 1	13♓12 6	11R50.5	1 56.4	25 58.9	29 57.4	5 36.8	5 22.6	7 38.0	0 53.2	26 20.1
8 Su	11 1 8	17 0 12	20 37 51	28 0 17	11 50.5	3 38.0	27 13.6	0♉40.3	5 33.9	5 28.5	7 35.6	0 53.1	26 18.5
9 M	11 5 5	18 0 13	5♈18 32	12♈31 50	11 50.2	5 20.7	28 28.4	1 23.3	5 30.9	5 34.5	7 33.2	0 52.9	26 16.8
10 Tu	11 9 1	19 0 12	19 39 32	26 41 11	11 49.5	7 4.5	29 43.1	2 6.2	5 27.6	5 40.6	7 30.8	0 52.7	26 15.2
11 W	11 12 58	20 0 9	3♉36 27	10♉25 10	11 48.5	8 49.4	0♈57.9	2 49.0	5 24.2	5 46.7	7 28.4	0 52.5	26 13.6
12 Th	11 16 54	21 0 4	17 7 20	23 43 4	11 47.4	10 35.5	2 12.6	3 31.9	5 20.5	5 52.8	7 26.0	0 52.2	26 12.0
13 F	11 20 51	21 59 57	0♊12 36	6♊36 17	11 46.4	12 22.7	3 27.2	4 14.6	5 16.8	5 59.1	7 23.5	0 51.9	26 10.4
14 Sa	11 24 47	22 59 48	12 54 31	19 7 47	11D45.7	14 11.1	4 41.9	4 57.4	5 12.8	6 5.4	7 21.0	0 51.6	26 8.7
15 Su	11 28 44	23 59 36	25 16 38	1♋21 37	11 45.5	16 0.7	5 56.5	5 40.1	5 8.7	6 11.7	7 18.5	0 51.2	26 7.1
16 M	11 32 41	24 59 23	7♋23 19	13 22 20	11 45.9	17 51.5	7 11.1	6 22.7	5 4.4	6 18.1	7 16.0	0 50.8	26 5.5
17 Tu	11 36 37	25 59 7	19 19 15	25 14 40	11 46.8	19 43.5	8 25.6	7 5.3	5 0.0	6 24.6	7 13.5	0 50.3	26 3.9
18 W	11 40 34	26 58 48	1♌ 9 7	7♌ 3 9	11 48.1	21 36.6	9 40.2	7 47.9	4 55.4	6 31.1	7 11.0	0 49.9	26 2.2
19 Th	11 44 30	27 58 28	12 57 18	18 52 1	11 49.6	23 30.9	10 54.7	8 30.4	4 50.7	6 37.6	7 8.4	0 49.4	26 0.6
20 F	11 48 27	28 58 5	24 47 45	0♍44 55	11 50.8	25 26.4	12 9.1	9 12.9	4 45.8	6 44.2	7 5.8	0 48.9	25 59.0
21 Sa	11 52 23	29 57 40	6♍43 53	12 44 57	11R51.6	27 23.0	13 23.6	9 55.4	4 40.7	6 50.9	7 3.3	0 48.3	25 57.3
22 Su	11 56 20	0♈57 13	18 48 26	24 54 32	11 51.5	29 20.6	14 38.0	10 37.8	4 35.5	6 57.6	7 0.7	0 47.7	25 55.7
23 M	12 0 16	1 56 44	1♎ 3 30	7♎15 28	11 50.4	1♈19.3	15 52.4	11 20.1	4 30.2	7 4.4	6 58.1	0 47.1	25 54.1
24 Tu	12 4 13	2 56 13	13 30 34	19 48 54	11 48.3	3 19.0	17 6.8	12 2.4	4 24.7	7 11.2	6 55.5	0 46.4	25 52.5
25 W	12 8 9	3 55 40	26 10 33	2♏35 34	11 45.3	5 19.5	18 21.1	12 44.7	4 19.1	7 18.0	6 52.9	0 45.7	25 50.9
26 Th	12 12 6	4 55 5	9♏ 3 58	15 35 46	11 41.7	7 20.7	19 35.4	13 26.9	4 13.3	7 24.9	6 50.3	0 45.0	25 49.2
27 F	12 16 3	5 54 28	22 10 58	28 49 36	11 38.0	9 22.6	20 49.7	14 9.1	4 7.4	7 31.8	6 47.7	0 44.3	25 47.6
28 Sa	12 19 59	6 53 49	5♐31 37	12♐17 3	11 34.8	11 24.9	22 3.9	14 51.3	4 1.4	7 38.8	6 45.1	0 43.5	25 46.0
29 Su	12 23 56	7 53 9	19 5 51	25 58 0	11 32.4	13 27.5	23 18.2	15 33.4	3 55.3	7 45.8	6 42.5	0 42.7	25 44.5
30 M	12 27 52	8 52 27	2♑53 28	9♑52 11	11D31.2	15 30.1	24 32.4	16 15.5	3 49.0	7 52.9	6 39.9	0 41.9	25 42.9
31 Tu	12 31 49	9 51 43	16 54 3	23 58 55	11 31.2	17 32.5	25 46.5	16 57.5	3 42.7	7 59.9	6 37.3	0 41.1	25 41.3

APRIL 1970 LONGITUDE

Day	Sid.Time	☉	0 hr ☽	Noon ☽	True ☊	☿	♀	♂	♃	♄	♅	♆	♇
1 W	12 35 45	10♈50 57	1♒ 6 38	8♒16 55	11♓32.2	19♈34.4	27♈ 0.7	17♉39.5	3♏36.2	8♉ 7.1	6♎34.8	0♐40.2	25♍39.7
2 Th	12 39 42	11 50 10	15 29 27	22 43 52	11 33.7	21 35.4	28 14.8	18 21.4	3R29.6	8 14.2	6R32.2	0R39.3	25R38.2
3 F	12 43 38	12 49 21	29 59 40	7♓16 19	11R35.0	23 35.2	29 28.9	19 3.4	3 22.9	8 21.4	6 29.6	0 38.3	25 36.6
4 Sa	12 47 35	13 48 30	14♓33 10	21 49 33	11 35.3	25 33.6	0♉43.0	19 45.2	3 16.1	8 28.7	6 27.0	0 37.4	25 35.1
5 Su	12 51 32	14 47 37	29 4 45	6♈18 0	11 34.2	27 30.0	1 57.0	20 27.1	3 9.2	8 35.9	6 24.4	0 36.4	25 33.6
6 M	12 55 28	15 46 42	13♈28 34	20 35 45	11 31.4	29 24.1	3 11.0	21 8.9	3 2.3	8 43.2	6 21.9	0 35.4	25 32.0
7 Tu	12 59 25	16 45 45	27 38 53	4♉37 24	11 27.0	1♉15.6	4 25.0	21 50.6	2 55.2	8 50.5	6 19.3	0 34.3	25 30.5
8 W	13 3 21	17 44 46	11♉30 50	18 18 49	11 21.4	3 4.0	5 38.9	22 32.4	2 48.1	8 57.9	6 16.8	0 33.3	25 29.1
9 Th	13 7 18	18 43 45	25 1 8	1♊37 46	11 15.2	4 49.0	6 52.8	23 14.0	2 40.9	9 5.3	6 14.2	0 32.2	25 27.6
10 F	13 11 14	19 42 42	8♊ 8 27	14 33 36	11 9.3	6 30.4	8 6.7	23 55.7	2 33.6	9 12.7	6 11.7	0 31.1	25 26.1
11 Sa	13 15 11	20 41 37	20 53 24	27 8 11	11 4.3	8 7.7	9 20.6	24 37.3	2 26.3	9 20.1	6 9.2	0 29.9	25 24.7
12 Su	13 19 7	21 40 29	3♋18 23	9♋24 29	11 0.8	9 40.6	10 34.4	25 18.9	2 18.9	9 27.6	6 6.8	0 28.8	25 23.2
13 M	13 23 4	22 39 19	15 27 3	21 26 40	10D59.0	11 9.1	11 48.2	26 0.4	2 11.5	9 35.1	6 4.3	0 27.6	25 21.8
14 Tu	13 27 1	23 38 7	27 23 59	3♌19 37	10 58.8	12 32.7	13 1.9	26 41.9	2 4.0	9 42.6	6 1.8	0 26.4	25 20.4
15 W	13 30 57	24 36 52	9♌14 14	15 8 29	10 59.7	13 51.4	14 15.6	27 23.3	1 56.4	9 50.1	5 59.4	0 25.2	25 19.0
16 Th	13 34 54	25 35 36	21 2 59	26 58 22	11 1.2	15 4.9	15 29.3	28 4.7	1 48.9	9 57.6	5 57.0	0 23.9	25 17.7
17 F	13 38 50	26 34 17	2♍55 13	8♍54 6	11R 2.5	16 13.1	16 42.9	28 46.1	1 41.3	10 5.2	5 54.6	0 22.7	25 16.3
18 Sa	13 42 47	27 32 56	14 55 31	20 59 55	11 2.7	17 15.9	17 56.5	29 27.4	1 33.7	10 12.8	5 52.3	0 21.4	25 15.0
19 Su	13 46 43	28 31 32	27 7 42	3♎19 13	11 1.2	18 13.1	19 10.1	0♊ 8.6	1 26.0	10 20.4	5 49.9	0 20.1	25 13.7
20 M	13 50 40	29 30 7	9♎34 44	15 54 24	10 57.7	19 4.7	20 23.6	0 49.9	1 18.4	10 28.0	5 47.6	0 18.8	25 12.4
21 Tu	13 54 36	0♉28 40	22 18 21	28 46 35	10 52.1	19 50.5	21 37.1	1 31.1	1 10.7	10 35.6	5 45.3	0 17.4	25 11.1
22 W	13 58 33	1 27 10	5♏19 4	11♏55 40	10 44.6	20 30.6	22 50.5	2 12.2	1 3.0	10 43.2	5 43.0	0 16.1	25 9.9
23 Th	14 2 30	2 25 39	18 36 11	25 20 21	10 35.9	21 4.8	24 4.0	2 53.3	0 55.3	10 50.9	5 40.8	0 14.7	25 8.7
24 F	14 6 26	3 24 6	2♐ 7 53	8♐58 25	10 27.0	21 33.2	25 17.3	3 34.4	0 47.7	10 58.5	5 38.6	0 13.3	25 7.4
25 Sa	14 10 23	4 22 32	15 51 39	22 47 12	10 18.9	21 55.7	26 30.7	4 15.4	0 40.0	11 6.2	5 36.4	0 11.9	25 6.3
26 Su	14 14 19	5 20 56	29 44 44	6♑43 57	10 12.3	22 12.5	27 44.0	4 56.4	0 32.4	11 13.9	5 34.2	0 10.5	25 5.1
27 M	14 18 16	6 19 18	13♑44 33	20 46 17	10 7.9	22 23.4	28 57.3	5 37.4	0 24.8	11 21.6	5 32.1	0 9.0	25 4.0
28 Tu	14 22 12	7 17 39	27 48 57	4♒52 22	10D 5.8	22R28.7	0♊10.5	6 18.3	0 17.2	11 29.2	5 30.0	0 7.6	25 2.8
29 W	14 26 9	8 15 58	11♒56 22	19 0 48	10 5.4	22 28.4	1 23.7	6 59.2	0 9.6	11 36.9	5 28.0	0 6.1	25 1.7
30 Th	14 30 5	9 14 15	26 5 31	3♓10 21	10R 6.1	22 22.8	2 36.9	7 40.1	0 2.1	11 44.6	5 25.9	0 4.6	25 0.7

Astro Data	Planet Ingress	Last Aspect	☽ Ingress	Last Aspect	☽ Ingress	☽ Phases & Eclipses	Astro Data
Dy Hr Mn	Dy Hr Mn	Dy Hr Mn	Dy Hr Mn	Dy Hr Mn	Dy Hr Mn	Dy Hr Mn	1 MARCH 1970
♆ R 3 9:00	☿ ♓ 5 20:10	2 7:05 ♂ △	♑ 2 12:54	2 23:04 ♀ ⚹	♓ 3 0:01	1 2:33 ☽ 10♐06	Julian Day # 25627
☽0N 8 10:05	♂ ♉ 7 1:28	4 11:34 ♂ □	♒ 4 14:34	4 18:11 ♇ ☍	♈ 5 1:32	7 17:42 ● 16♓44	Delta T 40.3 sec
♃☍♄ 8 14:26	♀ ♈ 10 5:25	6 14:17 ♂ ⚹	♓ 6 14:49	6 4:09 ☉ ☌	♉ 7 4:02	7 17:37:49 ● T 3'28"	SVP 05♓40'29"
♀0N 12 12:52	☉ ♈ 21 0:56	8 11:44 ♀ ☌	♈ 8 15:16	9 0:48 ♇ △	♊ 9 9:02	14 21:16 ☽ 23♊53	Obliquity 23°26'44"
☽0S 22 15:48	☿ ♈ 22 7:59	9 3:42 ♅ ☍	♉ 10 17:43	11 8:39 ♇ □	♋ 11 17:33	23 1:52 ○ 2♎01	⚷ Chiron 4♈46.8
♄⚻♅ 22 7:58		12 16:32 ♇ △	♊ 12 23:37	13 22:30 ♂ ⚹	♌ 14 5:16	30 11:04 ☽ 9♑20	☽ Mean ☊ 12♓09.7
☿0N 23 19:37	♀ ♉ 3 10:05	15 1:39 ♇ □	♋ 15 9:18	16 15:07 ♂ □	♍ 16 18:07		
	☿ ♉ 6 7:40	17 14:45 ☉ △	♌ 17 21:40	18 20:18 ♇ ☌	♎ 19 5:35	6 4:09 ● 15♈57	1 APRIL 1970
☽0N 4 20:16	♂ ♊ 18 18:59	18 19:21 ♀ △	♍ 20 10:30	19 16:47 ♅ ☌	♏ 21 14:15	13 15:44 ☽ 23♋18	Julian Day # 25658
☽0S 18 23:18	☉ ♉ 20 12:15	22 13:58 ♇ ☌	♎ 22 21:56	23 11:38 ♇ ⚹	♐ 23 20:15	21 16:21 ○ 1♏09	Delta T 40.4 sec
♄Q♇ 18 6:02	♀ ♊ 27 20:33	24 7:37 ♀ ☍	♏ 25 7:10	25 15:59 ♇ □	♑ 26 0:26	28 17:18 ☽ 7♒60	SVP 05♓40'25"
☿ R 28 10:51	♃ ♎ 30 6:44	27 6:31 ♇ ⚹	♐ 27 14:07	27 19:18 ♇ △	♒ 28 3:43		Obliquity 23°26'44"
♃⚺♆ 29 13:57		29 11:35 ♇ □	♑ 29 19:00	29 17:46 ☿ □	♓ 30 6:37		⚷ Chiron 6♈33.9
		31 16:27 ♀ □	♒ 31 22:08				☽ Mean ☊ 10♓31.2

LONGITUDE — MAY 1970

Day	Sid.Time	☉	0 hr ☽	Noon ☽	True ☊	☿	♀	♂	♃	♄	♅	♆	♇
1 F	14 34 2	10♉12 31	10♓15 8	17♓19 39	10♓ 6.5	22♉12.1	3♊50.0	8♊20.9	29♎54.6	11♉52.3	5♎24.0	0♐ 3.1	24♍59.6
2 Sa	14 37 59	11 10 46	24 23 36	1♈26 42	10R 5.7	21R 56.6	5 3.2	9 1.7	29R 47.2	12 0.1	5R 22.0	0R 1.6	24R 58.6
3 Su	14 41 55	12 8 59	8♈28 35	15 28 51	10 2.7	21 36.7	6 16.2	9 42.4	29 39.8	12 7.8	5 20.1	0 0.1	24 57.6
4 M	14 45 52	13 7 10	22 27 2	29 22 43	9 57.1	21 12.7	7 29.3	10 23.1	29 32.5	12 15.5	5 18.2	29♏58.6	24 56.6
5 Tu	14 49 48	14 5 20	6♉15 25	13♉ 4 43	9 48.9	20 45.2	8 42.3	11 3.8	29 25.2	12 23.2	5 16.3	29 57.0	24 55.7
6 W	14 53 45	15 3 29	19 50 10	26 31 28	9 38.7	20 14.7	9 55.2	11 44.4	29 18.0	12 30.9	5 14.5	29 55.5	24 54.8
7 Th	14 57 41	16 1 35	3♊ 8 18	9♊40 30	9 27.5	19 41.6	11 8.1	12 25.1	29 10.9	12 38.6	5 12.7	29 53.9	24 53.9
8 F	15 1 38	16 59 40	16 7 57	22 30 40	9 16.5	19 6.8	12 21.0	13 5.6	29 3.9	12 46.3	5 11.0	29 52.3	24 53.0
9 Sa	15 5 34	17 57 44	28 48 44	5♋ 2 21	9 6.5	18 30.7	13 33.9	13 46.2	28 56.9	12 54.0	5 9.3	29 50.8	24 52.2
10 Su	15 9 31	18 55 45	11♋11 49	17 17 30	8 58.6	17 54.0	14 46.7	14 26.7	28 50.0	13 1.7	5 7.7	29 49.2	24 51.4
11 M	15 13 28	19 53 45	23 19 50	29 19 21	8 53.1	17 17.4	15 59.5	15 7.1	28 43.3	13 9.4	5 6.1	29 47.6	24 50.6
12 Tu	15 17 24	20 51 42	5♌16 36	11♌12 12	8 50.0	16 41.5	17 12.2	15 47.6	28 36.6	13 17.0	5 4.5	29 46.0	24 49.8
13 W	15 21 21	21 49 38	17 6 48	23 1 3	8D 48.9	16 7.0	18 24.9	16 28.0	28 30.0	13 24.7	5 3.0	29 44.4	24 49.1
14 Th	15 25 17	22 47 32	28 55 39	4♍51 16	8R 48.9	15 34.4	19 37.5	17 8.3	28 23.5	13 32.3	5 1.5	29 42.8	24 48.4
15 F	15 29 14	23 45 25	10♍48 36	16 48 18	8 49.0	15 4.2	20 50.1	17 48.6	28 17.2	13 40.0	5 0.0	29 41.2	24 47.7
16 Sa	15 33 10	24 43 15	22 51 0	28 57 17	8 48.2	14 36.8	22 2.6	18 28.9	28 10.9	13 47.6	4 58.6	29 39.6	24 47.1
17 Su	15 37 7	25 41 4	5♎ 7 42	11♎22 42	8 45.7	14 12.8	23 15.1	19 9.2	28 4.8	13 55.2	4 57.3	29 37.9	24 46.5
18 M	15 41 3	26 38 51	17 42 41	24 7 56	8 40.6	13 52.4	24 27.6	19 49.4	27 58.8	14 2.8	4 56.0	29 36.3	24 45.9
19 Tu	15 45 0	27 36 37	0♏38 38	7♏14 52	8 33.0	13 36.0	25 40.0	20 29.5	27 52.9	14 10.4	4 54.7	29 34.7	24 45.3
20 W	15 48 57	28 34 21	13 56 33	20 43 29	8 23.1	13 23.7	26 52.3	21 9.7	27 47.1	14 17.9	4 53.5	29 33.1	24 44.8
21 Th	15 52 53	29 32 4	27 35 24	4♐31 49	8 11.7	13 15.8	28 4.6	21 49.8	27 41.5	14 25.5	4 52.4	29 31.5	24 44.3
22 F	15 56 50	0♊29 45	11♐32 14	18 36 2	7 59.9	13D 12.2	29 16.9	22 29.9	27 36.0	14 33.0	4 51.2	29 29.8	24 43.9
23 Sa	16 0 46	1 27 25	25 42 33	2♑51 5	7 49.0	13 13.2	0♋29.1	23 9.9	27 30.6	14 40.5	4 50.2	29 28.2	24 43.4
24 Su	16 4 43	2 25 4	10♑ 0 57	17 11 29	7 40.0	13 18.8	1 41.3	23 49.9	27 25.4	14 48.0	4 49.2	29 26.6	24 43.0
25 M	16 8 39	3 22 42	24 22 7	1♒32 17	7 33.5	13 28.8	2 53.4	24 29.9	27 20.3	14 55.5	4 48.2	29 25.0	24 42.7
26 Tu	16 12 36	4 20 19	8♒41 33	15 49 35	7 29.8	13 43.3	4 5.5	25 9.9	27 15.4	15 2.9	4 47.3	29 23.3	24 42.3
27 W	16 16 32	5 17 55	22 56 5	0♓ 0 51	7 28.4	14 2.3	5 17.5	25 49.8	27 10.6	15 10.3	4 46.4	29 21.7	24 42.0
28 Th	16 20 29	6 15 30	7♓ 3 47	14 4 46	7 28.2	14 25.7	6 29.5	26 29.7	27 5.9	15 17.7	4 45.6	29 20.1	24 41.7
29 F	16 24 26	7 13 5	21 3 46	28 0 44	7 27.9	14 53.3	7 41.5	27 9.5	27 1.5	15 25.1	4 44.8	29 18.5	24 41.5
30 Sa	16 28 22	8 10 38	4♈55 39	11♈48 27	7 26.4	15 25.1	8 53.3	27 49.4	26 57.1	15 32.4	4 44.1	29 16.9	24 41.3
31 Su	16 32 19	9 8 10	18 39 3	25 27 23	7 22.6	16 0.9	10 5.2	28 29.2	26 52.9	15 39.7	4 43.4	29 15.3	24 41.1

LONGITUDE — JUNE 1970

Day	Sid.Time	☉	0 hr ☽	Noon ☽	True ☊	☿	♀	♂	♃	♄	♅	♆	♇
1 M	16 36 15	10♊ 5 42	2♉13 18	8♉56 39	7♓16.0	16♉40.8	11♋17.0	29♊ 8.9	26♎48.9	15♉47.0	4♎42.8	29♏13.7	24♍40.9
2 Tu	16 40 12	11 3 13	15 37 14	22 14 52	7R 6.6	17 24.5	12 28.7	29 48.7	26R 45.1	15 54.3	4R 42.2	29R 12.1	24R 40.8
3 W	16 44 8	12 0 43	28 49 22	5♊20 32	6 55.1	18 12.0	13 40.4	0♋28.4	26 41.4	16 1.5	4 41.7	29 10.5	24 40.7
4 Th	16 48 5	12 58 12	11♊48 13	18 12 18	6 42.3	19 3.2	14 52.1	1 8.1	26 37.9	16 8.7	4 41.2	29 9.0	24 40.7
5 F	16 52 2	13 55 40	24 32 42	0♋49 23	6 29.6	19 57.9	16 3.7	1 47.7	26 34.5	16 15.8	4 40.8	29 7.4	24D 40.7
6 Sa	16 55 58	14 53 8	7♋ 2 26	13 11 57	6 18.0	20 56.1	17 15.2	2 27.4	26 31.3	16 23.0	4 40.4	29 5.9	24 40.7
7 Su	16 59 55	15 50 34	19 18 7	25 21 13	6 8.5	21 57.8	18 26.7	3 7.0	26 28.3	16 30.0	4 40.1	29 4.3	24 40.7
8 M	17 3 51	16 47 59	1♌21 34	7♌19 34	6 1.5	23 2.8	19 38.2	3 46.6	26 25.5	16 37.1	4 39.9	29 2.8	24 40.8
9 Tu	17 7 48	17 45 23	13 15 41	19 10 25	5 57.3	24 11.0	20 49.5	4 26.1	26 22.8	16 44.1	4 39.7	29 1.3	24 40.9
10 W	17 11 44	18 42 46	25 4 21	0♍58 5	5D 55.3	25 22.5	22 0.8	5 5.6	26 20.3	16 51.1	4 39.5	28 59.7	24 41.0
11 Th	17 15 41	19 40 8	6♍52 15	12 47 31	5 54.9	26 37.1	23 12.1	5 45.1	26 18.0	16 58.0	4 39.4	28 58.2	24 41.2
12 F	17 19 37	20 37 29	18 44 34	24 44 5	5R 55.0	27 54.9	24 23.3	6 24.6	26 15.9	17 4.9	4D 39.3	28 56.8	24 41.4
13 Sa	17 23 34	21 34 49	0♎46 45	6♎53 14	5 54.7	29 15.8	25 34.4	7 4.0	26 13.9	17 11.7	4 39.4	28 55.3	24 41.7
14 Su	17 27 31	22 32 8	13 4 9	19 20 6	5 53.0	0♊39.7	26 45.5	7 43.4	26 12.2	17 18.5	4 39.4	28 53.8	24 41.9
15 M	17 31 27	23 29 26	25 41 35	2♏ 9 1	5 49.1	2 6.6	27 56.5	8 22.8	26 10.6	17 25.3	4 39.5	28 52.4	24 42.2
16 Tu	17 35 24	24 26 43	8♏42 44	15 22 55	5 42.9	3 36.5	29 7.4	9 2.1	26 9.2	17 32.0	4 39.7	28 50.9	24 42.6
17 W	17 39 20	25 24 0	22 9 38	29 2 46	5 34.4	5 9.5	0♌18.2	9 41.4	26 7.9	17 38.7	4 39.9	28 49.5	24 42.9
18 Th	17 43 17	26 21 16	6♐ 2 3	13♐ 7 2	5 24.5	6 45.3	1 29.0	10 20.7	26 6.9	17 45.3	4 40.2	28 48.1	24 43.3
19 F	17 47 13	27 18 31	20 17 8	27 31 37	5 14.2	8 24.1	2 39.8	10 60.0	26 6.0	17 51.8	4 40.5	28 46.7	24 43.8
20 Sa	17 51 10	28 15 46	4♑49 37	12♑10 12	5 4.5	10 5.8	3 50.4	11 39.2	26 5.3	17 58.4	4 40.9	28 45.4	24 44.2
21 Su	17 55 6	29 13 0	19 32 25	26 55 15	4 56.5	11 50.4	5 1.0	12 18.4	26 4.8	18 4.8	4 41.3	28 44.0	24 44.7
22 M	17 59 3	0♋10 14	4♒17 49	11♒39 14	4 51.0	13 37.8	6 11.5	12 57.6	26 4.4	18 11.3	4 41.8	28 42.7	24 45.2
23 Tu	18 3 0	1 7 27	18 58 45	26 15 44	4 47.9	15 27.9	7 21.9	13 36.8	26D 4.3	18 17.6	4 42.3	28 41.4	24 45.8
24 W	18 6 56	2 4 41	3♓29 41	10♓40 12	4D 47.0	17 20.7	8 32.3	14 15.9	26 4.3	18 24.0	4 42.9	28 40.1	24 46.4
25 Th	18 10 53	3 1 54	17 47 3	24 50 3	4 47.4	19 16.1	9 42.6	14 55.1	26 4.5	18 30.2	4 43.6	28 38.8	24 47.0
26 F	18 14 49	3 59 7	1♈49 9	8♈44 21	4R 47.9	21 13.9	10 52.8	15 34.2	26 4.9	18 36.4	4 44.3	28 37.5	24 47.7
27 Sa	18 18 46	4 56 20	15 35 42	22 23 17	4 47.4	23 14.0	12 2.9	16 13.2	26 5.4	18 42.6	4 45.0	28 36.3	24 48.3
28 Su	18 22 42	5 53 34	29 7 13	5♉47 37	4 45.1	25 16.3	13 13.0	16 52.3	26 6.1	18 48.7	4 45.8	28 35.1	24 49.0
29 M	18 26 39	6 50 47	12♉24 35	18 58 13	4 40.5	27 20.4	14 22.9	17 31.3	26 7.1	18 54.7	4 46.7	28 33.9	24 49.8
30 Tu	18 30 35	7 48 1	25 28 36	1♊55 49	4 33.7	29 26.3	15 32.8	18 10.4	26 8.1	19 0.7	4 47.6	28 32.7	24 50.6

Astro Data Dy Hr Mn	Planet Ingress Dy Hr Mn	Last Aspect Dy Hr Mn	☽ Ingress Dy Hr Mn	Last Aspect Dy Hr Mn	☽ Ingress Dy Hr Mn	☽ Phases & Eclipses Dy Hr Mn	Astro Data
☽0N 2 3:50	♆ ♏ 3 1:34	2 0:59 ♇ ☍	♈ 2 9:32	3 0:39 ♆ ☍	♊ 3 2:10	5 14:51 ● 14♉41	1 MAY 1970
☽0S 16 7:06	☉ ♊ 21 11:37	4 12:11 ♃ ☍	♉ 4 13:05	5 3:51 ♃ △	♋ 5 10:25	13 10:26 ☽ 22♌15	Julian Day # 25688
☿ D 22 6:47	♀ ♋ 22 14:19	6 18:07 ♆ ☍	♊ 6 18:17	7 19:23 ♆ △	♌ 7 21:17	21 3:38 ○ 29♏41	Delta T 40.5 sec
☽0N 29 8:57		9 0:16 ♃ △	♋ 9 2:17	10 7:58 ♆ □	♍ 10 10:02	27 22:32 ☽ 6♓12	SVP 05♓40'22"
	♂ ♋ 2 6:50	11 12:55 ♆ △	♌ 11 13:22	12 20:37 ☿ △	♎ 12 22:28		Obliquity 23°26'44"
♇ D 5 2:24	☿ ♊ 13 12:46	14 1:35 ♆ □	♍ 14 2:10	15 4:37 ♀ □	♏ 15 8:02	4 2:21 ● 13♊04	⚷ Chiron 8♈14.7
☽0S 12 14:28	♀ ♌ 16 17:49	16 13:21 ♆ ✶	♎ 16 14:02	17 11:36 ♆ ☌	♐ 17 13:39	12 4:06 ☽ 20♍47	☽ Mean ☊ 8♓55.9
♅ D 12 9:40	☉ ♋ 21 19:43	18 18:58 ♃ ☌	♏ 18 22:49	19 12:27 ☉ ☍	♑ 19 16:04	19 12:27 ○ 27♐48	
♃ D 23 9:44	☿ ♋ 30 6:22	21 3:38 ☉ ☍	♐ 21 4:11	21 14:56 ♆ ✶	♒ 21 17:00	26 4:01 ☽ 4♈09	1 JUNE 1970
☽0N 25 13:37		23 3:01 ♃ ✶	♑ 23 7:13	23 16:00 ♆ □	♓ 23 18:11		Julian Day # 25719
		25 8:26 ♆ ✶	♒ 25 9:25	25 18:31 ♆ △	♈ 25 20:52		Delta T 40.6 sec
		27 10:52 ♆ □	♓ 27 11:59	27 18:36 ♃ ☍	♉ 28 1:35		SVP 05♓40'17"
		29 14:13 ♆ △	♈ 29 15:27	30 5:41 ♆ ☍	♊ 30 8:24		Obliquity 23°26'43"
		31 18:16 ♂ ✶	♉ 31 20:03				⚷ Chiron 9♈36.2
							☽ Mean ☊ 7♓17.4

JULY 1970 LONGITUDE

Day	Sid.Time	☉	0 hr ☽	Noon ☽	True ☊	☿	♀	♂	♃	♄	♅	♆	♇
1 W	18 34 32	8♋45 14	8♊19 54	14♊40 54	4♓25.0	1♋33.7	16♌42.7	18♋49.4	26♎ 9.4	19♉ 6.6	4♎48.5	28♏31.5	24♍51.4
2 Th	18 38 29	9 42 28	20 58 53	27 13 53	4R15.4	3 42.2	17 52.4	19 28.3	26 10.9	19 12.5	4 49.5	28R30.4	24 52.2
3 F	18 42 25	10 39 41	3♋25 58	9♋35 13	4 5.7	5 51.7	19 2.1	20 7.3	26 12.5	19 18.3	4 50.6	28 29.3	24 53.1
4 Sa	18 46 22	11 36 55	15 41 43	21 45 38	3 56.9	8 1.7	20 11.7	20 46.2	26 14.3	19 24.0	4 51.7	28 28.2	24 54.0
5 Su	18 50 18	12 34 8	27 47 7	3♌46 25	3 49.7	10 12.1	21 21.1	21 25.1	26 16.3	19 29.7	4 52.9	28 27.2	24 54.9
6 M	18 54 15	13 31 22	9♌43 46	15 39 28	3 44.7	12 22.5	22 30.5	22 4.0	26 18.4	19 35.3	4 54.1	28 26.1	24 55.8
7 Tu	18 58 11	14 28 35	21 33 55	27 27 29	3 41.8	14 32.7	23 39.8	22 42.9	26 20.8	19 40.8	4 55.3	28 25.1	24 56.8
8 W	19 2 8	15 25 48	3♍20 38	9♍13 52	3D40.9	16 42.4	24 49.1	23 21.8	26 23.3	19 46.3	4 56.7	28 24.1	24 57.8
9 Th	19 6 4	16 23 1	15 7 42	21 2 43	3 41.5	18 51.4	25 58.2	24 0.6	26 25.9	19 51.7	4 58.0	28 23.2	24 58.9
10 F	19 10 1	17 20 14	26 59 31	2♎58 44	3 42.8	20 59.4	27 7.2	24 39.4	26 28.8	19 57.0	4 59.4	28 22.2	24 60.0
11 Sa	19 13 58	18 17 27	9♎ 0 58	15 6 54	3R44.0	23 6.3	28 16.1	25 18.2	26 31.8	20 2.3	5 0.9	28 21.3	25 1.1
12 Su	19 17 54	19 14 40	21 17 9	27 32 19	3 44.4	25 11.9	29 24.9	25 57.0	26 35.0	20 7.4	5 2.4	28 20.4	25 2.2
13 M	19 21 51	20 11 53	3♏52 59	10♏19 40	3 43.3	27 16.2	0♍33.6	26 35.7	26 38.3	20 12.6	5 4.0	28 19.6	25 3.3
14 Tu	19 25 47	21 9 6	16 52 47	23 32 41	3 40.6	29 18.9	1 42.1	27 14.4	26 41.8	20 17.6	5 5.6	28 18.7	25 4.5
15 W	19 29 44	22 6 19	0♐19 34	7♐13 29	3 36.4	1♌20.1	2 50.6	27 53.2	26 45.5	20 22.6	5 7.2	28 17.9	25 5.7
16 Th	19 33 40	23 3 32	14 14 21	21 21 52	3 30.9	3 19.5	3 58.9	28 31.9	26 49.3	20 27.5	5 8.9	28 17.1	25 7.0
17 F	19 37 37	24 0 45	28 35 35	5♑54 49	3 25.0	5 17.3	5 7.2	29 10.5	26 53.3	20 32.3	5 10.7	28 16.4	25 8.2
18 Sa	19 41 34	24 57 58	13♑18 48	20 46 31	3 19.4	7 13.3	6 15.3	29 49.2	26 57.5	20 37.0	5 12.5	28 15.7	25 9.5
19 Su	19 45 30	25 55 12	28 16 56	5♒48 53	3 14.8	9 7.6	7 23.3	0♌27.8	27 1.8	20 41.7	5 14.3	28 15.0	25 10.9
20 M	19 49 27	26 52 27	13♒21 14	20 52 51	3 11.8	11 0.0	8 31.1	1 6.5	27 6.3	20 46.3	5 16.2	28 14.3	25 12.2
21 Tu	19 53 23	27 49 41	28 22 40	5♓49 44	3D10.6	12 50.7	9 38.8	1 45.1	27 11.0	20 50.8	5 18.2	28 13.7	25 13.6
22 W	19 57 20	28 46 57	13♓13 12	20 32 26	3 10.8	14 39.6	10 46.4	2 23.6	27 15.7	20 55.2	5 20.1	28 13.1	25 15.0
23 Th	20 1 16	29 44 13	27 46 52	4♈56 10	3 11.9	16 26.6	11 53.9	3 2.2	27 20.7	20 59.5	5 22.2	28 12.5	25 16.4
24 F	20 5 13	0♌41 30	12♈ 0 5	18 58 31	3 13.3	18 11.9	13 1.2	3 40.8	27 25.8	21 3.8	5 24.2	28 11.9	25 17.8
25 Sa	20 9 9	1 38 48	25 51 29	2♉39 4	3R14.3	19 55.5	14 8.4	4 19.3	27 31.0	21 8.0	5 26.4	28 11.4	25 19.3
26 Su	20 13 6	2 36 7	9♉21 26	15 58 48	3 14.2	21 37.2	15 15.5	4 57.9	27 36.4	21 12.0	5 28.5	28 10.9	25 20.8
27 M	20 17 3	3 33 26	22 31 26	28 59 37	3 12.9	23 17.2	16 22.4	5 36.4	27 42.0	21 16.0	5 30.7	28 10.5	25 22.3
28 Tu	20 20 59	4 30 47	5♊23 37	11♊43 44	3 10.2	24 55.4	17 29.1	6 14.9	27 47.7	21 20.0	5 33.0	28 10.0	25 23.9
29 W	20 24 56	5 28 9	18 0 17	24 13 31	3 6.6	26 31.9	18 35.8	6 53.4	27 53.5	21 23.8	5 35.2	28 9.6	25 25.4
30 Th	20 28 52	6 25 32	0♋23 42	6♋31 7	3 2.3	28 6.6	19 42.2	7 31.9	27 59.5	21 27.5	5 37.6	28 9.3	25 27.0
31 F	20 32 49	7 22 56	12 36 0	18 38 35	2 58.0	29 39.5	20 48.6	8 10.4	28 5.6	21 31.2	5 40.0	28 8.9	25 28.6

AUGUST 1970 LONGITUDE

Day	Sid.Time	☉	0 hr ☽	Noon ☽	True ☊	☿	♀	♂	♃	♄	♅	♆	♇
1 Sa	20 36 45	8♌20 21	24♋39 7	0♌37 49	2♓54.1	1♍10.7	21♍54.7	8♌48.8	28♎11.9	21♉34.8	5♎42.4	28♏ 8.6	25♍30.3
2 Su	20 40 42	9 17 47	6♌34 57	12 30 44	2R51.1	2 40.1	23 0.7	9 27.3	28 18.3	21 38.2	5 44.8	28R 8.3	25 31.9
3 M	20 44 38	10 15 13	18 25 25	24 19 18	2 49.2	4 7.6	24 6.6	10 5.7	28 24.9	21 41.6	5 47.3	28 8.1	25 33.6
4 Tu	20 48 35	11 12 40	0♍12 41	6♍ 5 51	2D48.4	5 33.4	25 12.2	10 44.1	28 31.6	21 44.9	5 49.9	28 7.9	25 35.3
5 W	20 52 32	12 10 8	11 59 10	17 53 0	2 48.6	6 57.3	26 17.7	11 22.6	28 38.4	21 48.1	5 52.4	28 7.7	25 37.1
6 Th	20 56 28	13 7 37	23 47 46	29 43 53	2 49.7	8 19.4	27 23.0	12 0.9	28 45.4	21 51.2	5 55.0	28 7.6	25 38.8
7 F	21 0 25	14 5 7	5♎41 50	11♎42 4	2 51.1	9 39.6	28 28.1	12 39.3	28 52.5	21 54.2	5 57.7	28 7.4	25 40.6
8 Sa	21 4 21	15 2 38	17 45 7	23 51 31	2 52.6	10 57.8	29 33.0	13 17.7	28 59.7	21 57.1	6 0.4	28 7.4	25 42.3
9 Su	21 8 18	16 0 9	0♏ 1 47	6♏16 28	2 53.7	12 14.0	0♎37.8	13 56.1	29 7.1	21 59.9	6 3.1	28 7.3	25 44.1
10 M	21 12 14	16 57 42	12 36 4	19 1 6	2R54.3	13 28.1	1 42.3	14 34.4	29 14.5	22 2.6	6 5.8	28D 7.3	25 46.0
11 Tu	21 16 11	17 55 15	25 32 1	2♐ 9 13	2 54.2	14 40.1	2 46.6	15 12.8	29 22.2	22 5.2	6 8.6	28 7.3	25 47.8
12 W	21 20 7	18 52 49	8♐53 0	15 43 34	2 53.5	15 49.9	3 50.7	15 51.1	29 29.9	22 7.8	6 11.5	28 7.3	25 49.7
13 Th	21 24 4	19 50 24	22 41 1	29 45 17	2 52.3	16 57.5	4 54.5	16 29.4	29 37.8	22 10.2	6 14.3	28 7.4	25 51.6
14 F	21 28 1	20 48 0	6♑56 7	14♑13 9	2 50.8	18 2.6	5 58.2	17 7.7	29 45.8	22 12.5	6 17.2	28 7.5	25 53.5
15 Sa	21 31 57	21 45 37	21 35 46	29 3 13	2 49.5	19 5.3	7 1.5	17 46.0	29 53.9	22 14.7	6 20.2	28 7.7	25 55.4
16 Su	21 35 54	22 43 15	6♒34 37	14♒ 8 53	2 48.4	20 5.4	8 4.7	18 24.3	0♏ 2.1	22 16.9	6 23.1	28 7.9	25 57.3
17 M	21 39 50	23 40 54	21 44 52	29 21 23	2D47.9	21 2.8	9 7.6	19 2.5	0 10.4	22 18.9	6 26.1	28 8.1	25 59.2
18 Tu	21 43 47	24 38 35	6♓57 13	14♓31 10	2 47.8	21 57.3	10 10.2	19 40.8	0 18.9	22 20.8	6 29.2	28 8.3	26 1.2
19 W	21 47 43	25 36 16	22 2 9	29 29 10	2 48.0	22 48.9	11 12.5	20 19.0	0 27.4	22 22.6	6 32.2	28 8.6	26 3.2
20 Th	21 51 40	26 33 59	6♈51 23	14♈ 8 7	2 48.5	23 37.2	12 14.6	20 57.3	0 36.1	22 24.3	6 35.3	28 8.9	26 5.2
21 F	21 55 36	27 31 44	21 18 51	28 23 14	2 49.0	24 22.2	13 16.4	21 35.5	0 44.9	22 25.9	6 38.4	28 9.2	26 7.2
22 Sa	21 59 33	28 29 31	5♉21 6	12♉12 25	2 49.4	25 3.7	14 18.0	22 13.8	0 53.8	22 27.4	6 41.6	28 9.6	26 9.2
23 Su	22 3 30	29 27 19	18 57 15	25 35 50	2R49.7	25 41.4	15 19.2	22 52.0	1 2.8	22 28.8	6 44.8	28 10.0	26 11.2
24 M	22 7 26	0♍25 9	2♊ 8 26	8♊35 26	2 49.7	26 15.2	16 20.1	23 30.2	1 11.9	22 30.1	6 48.0	28 10.4	26 13.3
25 Tu	22 11 23	1 23 1	14 57 13	21 14 15	2 49.7	26 44.7	17 20.7	24 8.4	1 21.1	22 31.3	6 51.2	28 10.9	26 15.3
26 W	22 15 19	2 20 54	27 26 58	3♋35 51	2D49.6	27 9.8	18 21.1	24 46.6	1 30.5	22 32.4	6 54.5	28 11.4	26 17.4
27 Th	22 19 16	3 18 50	9♋41 22	15 43 59	2 49.6	27 30.2	19 21.0	25 24.8	1 39.9	22 33.4	6 57.8	28 11.9	26 19.5
28 F	22 23 12	4 16 47	21 44 7	27 42 13	2 49.7	27 45.5	20 20.7	26 3.0	1 49.4	22 34.3	7 1.1	28 12.5	26 21.6
29 Sa	22 27 9	5 14 46	3♌38 40	9♌33 50	2 50.0	27 55.7	21 20.0	26 41.2	1 59.1	22 35.0	7 4.4	28 13.1	26 23.7
30 Su	22 31 5	6 12 46	15 28 6	21 21 47	2 50.2	28R 0.3	22 18.9	27 19.4	2 8.8	22 35.7	7 7.8	28 13.7	26 25.8
31 M	22 35 2	7 10 48	27 15 13	3♍ 8 41	2R50.4	27 59.2	23 17.4	27 57.6	2 18.6	22 36.2	7 11.2	28 14.3	26 28.0

Astro Data Dy Hr Mn	Planet Ingress Dy Hr Mn	Last Aspect Dy Hr Mn	☽ Ingress Dy Hr Mn	Last Aspect Dy Hr Mn	☽ Ingress Dy Hr Mn	☽ Phases & Eclipses Dy Hr Mn	Astro Data
☽0S 9 21:06	♀ ♍ 12 12:16	2 10:00 ♃ △	♋ 2 17:21	1 7:11 ♃ □	♌ 1 10:44	3 15:18 ● 11♋16	1 JULY 1970
♄□♅ 10 15:12	☿ ♌ 14 8:06	5 1:20 ♆ △	♌ 5 4:26	3 20:32 ♃ ✶	♍ 3 23:34	11 19:43 ☽ 19♎04	Julian Day # 25749
☽0N 22 20:06	♂ ♌ 18 6:43	7 13:56 ♆ □	♍ 7 17:11	6 8:45 ♆ ✶	♎ 6 12:32	18 19:58 ○ 25♑46	Delta T 40.7 sec
♃⊻♆ 31 12:01	☉ ♌ 23 6:37	10 2:46 ♆ ✶	♎ 10 6:02	8 22:13 ♃ ☌	♏ 8 23:57	25 11:00 ☽ 2♉05	SVP 05♓40'11"
	☿ ♍ 31 5:21	12 10:13 ♃ ☌	♏ 12 16:41	11 4:43 ♆ ☌	♐ 11 8:07		Obliquity 23°26'43"
☽0S 6 3:06		14 20:26 ♆ ☌	♐ 14 23:26	13 11:54 ♃ ✶	♑ 13 12:25	2 5:58 ● 9♌32	⚷ Chiron 10♈17.9
♀0S 8 5:44	♀ ♎ 8 9:59	16 21:10 ♃ ✶	♑ 17 2:19	15 13:28 ♃ □	♒ 15 13:31	10 8:50 ☽ 17♏19	☽ Mean ☊ 5♓42.1
♆ D 10 2:21	♃ ♏ 15 17:57	18 23:57 ♆ ✶	♒ 19 2:44	17 10:04 ♆ □	♓ 17 13:01	17 3:15 ○ 23♒49	
☽0N 19 5:16	☉ ♍ 23 13:34	20 23:46 ♆ □	♓ 21 2:36	19 9:50 ♆ △	♈ 19 12:50	17 3:23 ☍ P 0.408	1 AUGUST 1970
☿0S 20 12:14		23 3:30 ☉ △	♈ 23 3:42	21 11:19 ☉ △	♉ 21 14:46	23 20:34 ☽ 0♊17	Julian Day # 25780
☿ R 30 7:27		25 2:56 ♃ ☍	♉ 25 7:18	23 16:42 ♆ ☍	♊ 23 20:03	31 22:01 ● 8♍04	Delta T 40.8 sec
		27 10:28 ♆ ☍	♊ 27 13:53	25 23:26 ☿ □	♋ 26 4:58	31 21:54:49 ☌ A 6'48"	SVP 05♓40'05"
		29 19:17 ♃ △	♋ 29 23:14	28 13:02 ♆ △	♌ 28 16:38		Obliquity 23°26'43"
				31 2:01 ♆ □	♍ 31 5:36		⚷ Chiron 10♈13.5R
							☽ Mean ☊ 4♓03.7

LONGITUDE — SEPTEMBER 1970

Day	Sid.Time	☉	0 hr ☽	Noon ☽	True ☊	☿	♀	♂	♃	♄	♅	♆	♇
1 Tu	22 38 59	8♍ 8 52	9♍ 2 29	14♍56 53	2♓50.4	27♍52.1	24♎15.6	28♌35.8	2♏28.6	22♉36.7	7♎14.6	28♏15.0	26♍30.1
2 W	22 42 55	9 6 57	20 52 11	26 48 38	2R 50.1	27R 38.9	25 13.4	29 14.0	2 38.6	22 37.0	7 18.0	28 15.8	26 32.3
3 Th	22 46 52	10 5 4	2♎46 32	8♎46 10	2 49.4	27 19.5	26 10.7	29 52.1	2 48.7	22 37.2	7 21.5	28 16.5	26 34.4
4 F	22 50 48	11 3 13	14 47 50	20 51 50	2 48.4	26 53.7	27 7.6	0♍30.3	2 58.9	22R 37.4	7 25.0	28 17.3	26 36.6
5 Sa	22 54 45	12 1 23	26 58 30	3♏ 8 10	2 47.2	26 21.8	28 4.1	1 8.4	3 9.2	22 37.4	7 28.4	28 18.1	26 38.8
6 Su	22 58 41	12 59 34	9♏21 12	15 37 56	2 45.9	25 43.8	29 0.1	1 46.6	3 19.6	22 37.3	7 32.0	28 18.9	26 41.0
7 M	23 2 38	13 57 48	21 58 46	28 24 2	2 44.8	25 0.2	29 55.6	2 24.7	3 30.0	22 37.1	7 35.5	28 19.8	26 43.1
8 Tu	23 6 34	14 56 2	4♐54 7	11♐29 21	2D 44.1	24 11.3	0♏50.7	3 2.9	3 40.6	22 36.8	7 39.1	28 20.7	26 45.3
9 W	23 10 31	15 54 19	18 10 0	24 56 21	2 43.9	23 18.0	1 45.2	3 41.0	3 51.2	22 36.3	7 42.6	28 21.7	26 47.6
10 Th	23 14 28	16 52 36	1♑48 33	8♑46 43	2 44.3	22 21.0	2 39.1	4 19.1	4 1.9	22 35.8	7 46.2	28 22.6	26 49.8
11 F	23 18 24	17 50 56	15 50 48	23 0 42	2 45.2	21 21.4	3 32.6	4 57.2	4 12.7	22 35.2	7 49.8	28 23.6	26 52.0
12 Sa	23 22 21	18 49 17	0♒16 6	7♒36 36	2 46.3	20 20.4	4 25.4	5 35.4	4 23.6	22 34.4	7 53.5	28 24.7	26 54.2
13 Su	23 26 17	19 47 39	15 1 36	22 30 21	2 47.4	19 19.4	5 17.6	6 13.5	4 34.6	22 33.6	7 57.1	28 25.7	26 56.4
14 M	23 30 14	20 46 3	0♓ 1 58	7♓35 27	2R 47.9	18 19.7	6 9.2	6 51.6	4 45.6	22 32.6	8 0.7	28 26.8	26 58.7
15 Tu	23 34 10	21 44 29	15 9 40	22 43 30	2 47.6	17 22.8	7 0.1	7 29.7	4 56.7	22 31.6	8 4.4	28 27.9	27 0.9
16 W	23 38 7	22 42 56	0♈15 44	7♈45 16	2 46.3	16 30.1	7 50.4	8 7.8	5 7.9	22 30.4	8 8.1	28 29.1	27 3.1
17 Th	23 42 3	23 41 25	15 11 1	22 32 2	2 44.1	15 43.0	8 39.9	8 45.9	5 19.1	22 29.1	8 11.8	28 30.2	27 5.4
18 F	23 46 0	24 39 57	29 47 32	6♉55 53	2 41.2	15 2.6	9 28.7	9 24.0	5 30.4	22 27.8	8 15.5	28 31.4	27 7.6
19 Sa	23 49 56	25 38 30	13♉59 36	20 55 26	2 38.1	14 30.0	10 16.8	10 2.0	5 41.8	22 26.3	8 19.2	28 32.7	27 9.8
20 Su	23 53 53	26 37 6	27 44 17	4♊26 12	2 35.3	14 6.1	11 4.1	10 40.1	5 53.3	22 24.7	8 22.9	28 33.9	27 12.1
21 M	23 57 50	27 35 44	11♊ 1 22	17 30 6	2 33.3	13 51.4	11 50.6	11 18.2	6 4.8	22 23.0	8 26.6	28 35.2	27 14.3
22 Tu	0 1 46	28 34 25	23 52 49	0♋10 0	2D 32.2	13D 46.4	12 36.2	11 56.3	6 16.4	22 21.3	8 30.4	28 36.5	27 16.6
23 W	0 5 43	29 33 7	6♋22 11	12 29 56	2 32.3	13 51.2	13 21.0	12 34.4	6 28.1	22 19.4	8 34.1	28 37.9	27 18.8
24 Th	0 9 39	0♎31 52	18 33 52	24 34 34	2 33.4	14 5.9	14 4.9	13 12.5	6 39.8	22 17.4	8 37.9	28 39.2	27 21.1
25 F	0 13 36	1 30 39	0♌32 39	6♌28 41	2 35.1	14 30.3	14 47.8	13 50.6	6 51.6	22 15.3	8 41.7	28 40.6	27 23.3
26 Sa	0 17 32	2 29 28	12 23 14	18 16 51	2 36.8	15 4.0	15 29.7	14 28.7	7 3.4	22 13.1	8 45.4	28 42.1	27 25.5
27 Su	0 21 29	3 28 19	24 10 2	0♍ 3 15	2R 38.1	15 46.7	16 10.7	15 6.8	7 15.3	22 10.8	8 49.2	28 43.5	27 27.8
28 M	0 25 25	4 27 13	5♍56 56	11 51 27	2 38.4	16 37.8	16 50.5	15 44.9	7 27.3	22 8.5	8 53.0	28 45.0	27 30.0
29 Tu	0 29 22	5 26 8	17 47 12	23 44 27	2 37.2	17 36.6	17 29.3	16 23.0	7 39.3	22 6.0	8 56.8	28 46.5	27 32.2
30 W	0 33 19	6 25 6	29 43 29	5♎44 33	2 34.4	18 42.5	18 6.9	17 1.1	7 51.4	22 3.4	9 0.5	28 48.0	27 34.5

LONGITUDE — OCTOBER 1970

Day	Sid.Time	☉	0 hr ☽	Noon ☽	True ☊	☿	♀	♂	♃	♄	♅	♆	♇
1 Th	0 37 15	7♎24 6	11♎47 51	17♎53 34	2♓29.9	19♍54.9	18♏43.4	17♍39.2	8♏ 3.5	22♉ 0.7	9♎ 4.3	28♏49.5	27♍36.7
2 F	0 41 12	8 23 8	24 1 50	0♏12 48	2R 24.1	21 12.9	19 18.5	18 17.2	8 15.7	21R 58.0	9 8.1	28 51.1	27 38.9
3 Sa	0 45 8	9 22 11	6♏26 36	12 43 20	2 17.5	22 36.0	19 52.4	18 55.3	8 27.9	21 55.1	9 11.9	28 52.7	27 41.1
4 Su	0 49 5	10 21 17	19 3 7	25 26 6	2 10.8	24 3.4	20 24.9	19 33.4	8 40.2	21 52.2	9 15.7	28 54.3	27 43.3
5 M	0 53 1	11 20 25	1♐52 23	8♐22 6	2 4.8	25 34.6	20 56.1	20 11.5	8 52.6	21 49.1	9 19.5	28 56.0	27 45.5
6 Tu	0 56 58	12 19 34	14 55 26	21 32 29	2 0.1	27 8.8	21 25.7	20 49.6	9 4.9	21 46.0	9 23.3	28 57.6	27 47.7
7 W	1 0 54	13 18 45	28 13 27	4♑58 28	1 57.2	28 45.7	21 53.9	21 27.7	9 17.4	21 42.8	9 27.1	28 59.3	27 49.9
8 Th	1 4 51	14 17 58	11♑47 41	18 41 12	1D 56.0	0♎24.7	22 20.4	22 5.7	9 29.8	21 39.5	9 30.9	29 1.0	27 52.1
9 F	1 8 48	15 17 13	25 39 5	2♒41 22	1 56.4	2 5.3	22 45.3	22 43.8	9 42.4	21 36.2	9 34.6	29 2.8	27 54.2
10 Sa	1 12 44	16 16 30	9♒47 58	16 58 43	1 57.6	3 47.3	23 8.5	23 21.9	9 54.9	21 32.7	9 38.4	29 4.5	27 56.4
11 Su	1 16 41	17 15 48	24 13 23	1♓31 32	1R 58.7	5 30.2	23 29.9	23 60.0	10 7.5	21 29.2	9 42.2	29 6.3	27 58.5
12 M	1 20 37	18 15 8	8♓52 41	16 16 10	1 58.7	7 13.8	23 49.4	24 38.0	10 20.1	21 25.6	9 45.9	29 8.1	28 0.7
13 Tu	1 24 34	19 14 29	23 41 13	1♈ 6 55	1 56.9	8 57.8	24 7.1	25 16.1	10 32.8	21 21.9	9 49.7	29 9.9	28 2.8
14 W	1 28 30	20 13 53	8♈32 20	15 56 26	1 52.8	10 42.2	24 22.8	25 54.2	10 45.5	21 18.2	9 53.4	29 11.7	28 4.9
15 Th	1 32 27	21 13 18	23 18 12	0♉36 39	1 46.6	12 26.5	24 36.4	26 32.2	10 58.3	21 14.4	9 57.2	29 13.6	28 7.0
16 F	1 36 23	22 12 46	7♉50 52	15 0 2	1 38.9	14 10.9	24 48.0	27 10.3	11 11.0	21 10.5	10 0.9	29 15.5	28 9.1
17 Sa	1 40 20	23 12 16	22 3 30	29 0 47	1 30.4	15 55.0	24 57.4	27 48.4	11 23.8	21 6.5	10 4.6	29 17.4	28 11.2
18 Su	1 44 17	24 11 48	5♊51 31	12♊35 33	1 22.2	17 38.9	25 4.7	28 26.5	11 36.7	21 2.5	10 8.3	29 19.3	28 13.3
19 M	1 48 13	25 11 22	19 12 53	25 43 41	1 15.2	19 22.4	25 9.7	29 4.5	11 49.6	20 58.4	10 12.1	29 21.2	28 15.3
20 Tu	1 52 10	26 10 59	2♋ 8 14	8♋26 56	1 10.2	21 5.5	25R 12.4	29 42.6	12 2.5	20 54.3	10 15.7	29 23.2	28 17.4
21 W	1 56 6	27 10 37	14 40 15	20 48 47	1 7.3	22 48.2	25 12.7	0♎20.7	12 15.4	20 50.1	10 19.4	29 25.1	28 19.4
22 Th	2 0 3	28 10 18	26 53 7	2♌53 56	1D 6.3	24 30.4	25 10.8	0 58.8	12 28.4	20 45.8	10 23.1	29 27.1	28 21.4
23 F	2 3 59	29 10 2	8♌51 53	14 47 41	1 6.7	26 12.0	25 6.4	1 36.9	12 41.3	20 41.5	10 26.7	29 29.1	28 23.4
24 Sa	2 7 56	0♏ 9 47	20 41 58	26 35 26	1R 7.6	27 53.2	24 59.6	2 15.0	12 54.4	20 37.1	10 30.4	29 31.1	28 25.4
25 Su	2 11 52	1 9 35	2♍28 43	8♍22 25	1 8.0	29 33.8	24 50.5	2 53.1	13 7.4	20 32.7	10 34.0	29 33.1	28 27.4
26 M	2 15 49	2 9 25	14 17 7	20 13 19	1 7.0	1♏13.9	24 38.9	3 31.2	13 20.4	20 28.2	10 37.6	29 35.2	28 29.3
27 Tu	2 19 46	3 9 17	26 11 30	2♎12 6	1 3.8	2 53.5	24 24.9	4 9.3	13 33.5	20 23.7	10 41.2	29 37.2	28 31.3
28 W	2 23 42	4 9 11	8♎15 26	14 21 48	0 57.9	4 32.5	24 8.6	4 47.4	13 46.6	20 19.1	10 44.7	29 39.3	28 33.2
29 Th	2 27 39	5 9 7	20 31 25	26 44 26	0 49.5	6 11.0	23 50.0	5 25.5	13 59.7	20 14.5	10 48.3	29 41.4	28 35.1
30 F	2 31 35	6 9 5	3♏ 0 57	9♏20 58	0 38.9	7 49.0	23 29.1	6 3.6	14 12.8	20 9.9	10 51.8	29 43.5	28 37.0
31 Sa	2 35 32	7 9 5	15 44 29	22 11 23	0 26.9	9 26.4	23 6.0	6 41.7	14 26.0	20 5.2	10 55.3	29 45.6	28 38.8

Astro Data (Dy Hr Mn)	Planet Ingress (Dy Hr Mn)	Last Aspect (Dy Hr Mn)	☽ Ingress (Dy Hr Mn)	Last Aspect (Dy Hr Mn)	☽ Ingress (Dy Hr Mn)	☽ Phases & Eclipses (Dy Hr Mn)	Astro Data
☽0S 2 8:59	♂ ♍ 3 4:57	2 14:56 ♆ ⚹	♎ 2 18:25	30 18:35 ♅ ☌	♏ 2 11:35	8 19:38 ☽ 15♐44	1 SEPTEMBER 1970
♄ R 4 13:57	♀ ♏ 7 1:54	5 2:19 ♀ ☌	♏ 5 5:54	4 18:31 ♆ ☌	♐ 4 20:31	15 11:09 ○ 22♓12	Julian Day # 25811
♄⊼♅ 7 9:48	☉ ♎ 23 10:59	7 11:53 ♆ ☌	♐ 7 14:58	7 1:06 ☿ □	♑ 7 3:10	22 9:42 ☽ 28♊58	Delta T 40.8 sec
☿0N 11 2:50		9 15:18 ♇ □	♑ 9 20:51	9 5:49 ♆ ⚹	♒ 9 7:26	30 14:31 ● 7♎01	SVP 05♓40'01"
☽0N 15 16:09	☿ ♎ 7 18:04	11 20:56 ♆ ⚹	♒ 11 23:34	11 8:03 ♆ □	♓ 11 9:30		Obliquity 23°26'44"
☿ D 22 0:17	♂ ♎ 20 10:57	13 21:28 ♆ □	♓ 13 23:57	13 8:52 ♆ △	♈ 13 10:12	8 4:43 ☽ 14♑30	⚷ Chiron 9♈23.3R
☽0S 29 15:13	☉ ♏ 23 20:04	15 21:10 ♆ △	♈ 15 23:35	14 20:21 ☉ ☍	♉ 15 11:00	14 20:21 ○ 21♈04	☽ Mean ☊ 2♓25.2
♃⊻♅ 8 2:46	☿ ♏ 25 6:16	16 12:40 ♅ ☍	♉ 18 0:21	17 12:31 ♆ ☍	♊ 17 13:43	22 2:47 ☽ 28♋17	
☿0S 10 8:57		20 1:28 ♆ ☍	♊ 20 4:02	19 19:12 ♂ □	♋ 19 19:59	30 6:28 ● 6♏25	1 OCTOBER 1970
☽0N 13 2:35		22 9:42 ☉ □	♋ 22 11:41	22 5:07 ♆ △	♌ 22 6:12		Julian Day # 25841
♀ R 20 15:57		24 20:14 ♆ △	♌ 24 22:54	24 18:01 ♆ □	♍ 24 18:57		Delta T 40.9 sec
♂0S 24 11:44		27 9:19 ♆ □	♍ 27 11:53	27 6:53 ♆ ⚹	♎ 27 7:37		SVP 05♓39'58"
☽0S 26 22:00		29 22:09 ♆ ⚹	♎ 30 0:33	28 4:56 ♅ ☌	♏ 29 18:15		Obliquity 23°26'44"
♃∠♇ 26 19:12							⚷ Chiron 8♈07.1R
							☽ Mean ☊ 0♓49.8

NOVEMBER 1970 LONGITUDE

Day	Sid.Time	☉	0 hr ☽	Noon ☽	True ☊	☿	♀	♂	♃	♄	♅	♆	♇
1 Su	2 39 28	8♏ 9 7	28♏41 36	5♐14 57	0♓14.7	11♏ 3.4	22♏40.8	7♎19.8	14♏39.2	20♉ 0.5	10♎58.8	29♏47.7	28♍40.7
2 M	2 43 25	9 9 11	11♐51 19	18 30 31	0R 3.4	12 40.0	22R13.7	7 57.9	14 52.3	19R55.8	11 2.3	29 49.9	28 42.5
3 Tu	2 47 21	10 9 17	25 12 26	1♑56 55	29♒54.2	14 16.0	21 44.8	8 36.0	15 5.5	19 51.0	11 5.7	29 52.0	28 44.3
4 W	2 51 18	11 9 24	8♑43 54	15 33 17	29 47.5	15 51.7	21 14.2	9 14.1	15 18.7	19 46.2	11 9.2	29 54.2	28 46.1
5 Th	2 55 15	12 9 33	22 25 2	29 19 9	29 43.7	17 26.9	20 42.1	9 52.2	15 31.9	19 41.4	11 12.6	29 56.3	28 47.9
6 F	2 59 11	13 9 43	6♒15 36	13♒14 25	29D 42.2	19 1.7	20 8.7	10 30.3	15 45.1	19 36.6	11 15.9	29 58.5	28 49.6
7 Sa	3 3 8	14 9 55	20 15 33	27 19 0	29R 42.1	20 36.1	19 34.1	11 8.4	15 58.3	19 31.7	11 19.3	0♐ 0.7	28 51.3
8 Su	3 7 4	15 10 8	4♓24 39	11♓32 23	29 42.2	22 10.1	18 58.7	11 46.5	16 11.6	19 26.9	11 22.6	0 2.9	28 53.0
9 M	3 11 1	16 10 23	18 41 57	25 53 2	29 41.0	23 43.8	18 22.7	12 24.6	16 24.8	19 22.0	11 25.9	0 5.1	28 54.7
10 Tu	3 14 57	17 10 39	3♈ 5 14	10♈18 1	29 37.6	25 17.1	17 46.2	13 2.7	16 38.0	19 17.1	11 29.2	0 7.3	28 56.4
11 W	3 18 54	18 10 56	17 30 48	24 42 53	29 31.3	26 50.1	17 9.6	13 40.8	16 51.2	19 12.3	11 32.4	0 9.5	28 58.0
12 Th	3 22 50	19 11 15	1♉53 32	9♉ 1 59	29 22.1	28 22.7	16 33.1	14 18.9	17 4.4	19 7.4	11 35.6	0 11.7	28 59.6
13 F	3 26 47	20 11 36	16 7 29	23 9 19	29 10.7	29 55.1	15 57.0	14 57.0	17 17.7	19 2.5	11 38.8	0 13.9	29 1.2
14 Sa	3 30 44	21 11 58	0♊ 6 49	6♊59 27	28 58.1	1♐27.2	15 21.5	15 35.1	17 30.9	18 57.6	11 42.0	0 16.2	29 2.7
15 Su	3 34 40	22 12 23	13 46 45	20 28 27	28 45.7	2 58.9	14 46.9	16 13.2	17 44.1	18 52.7	11 45.1	0 18.4	29 4.3
16 M	3 38 37	23 12 49	27 4 21	3♋34 27	28 34.7	4 30.4	14 13.4	16 51.3	17 57.3	18 47.9	11 48.2	0 20.6	29 5.8
17 Tu	3 42 33	24 13 16	9♋58 51	16 17 48	28 26.0	6 1.6	13 41.2	17 29.4	18 10.5	18 43.0	11 51.2	0 22.9	29 7.2
18 W	3 46 30	25 13 46	22 31 37	28 40 46	28 20.0	7 32.5	13 10.5	18 7.5	18 23.7	18 38.2	11 54.3	0 25.1	29 8.7
19 Th	3 50 26	26 14 17	4♌45 45	10♌47 10	28 16.7	9 3.1	12 41.5	18 45.7	18 36.9	18 33.4	11 57.2	0 27.4	29 10.1
20 F	3 54 23	27 14 50	16 45 39	22 41 52	28 15.4	10 33.4	12 14.4	19 23.8	18 50.0	18 28.6	12 0.2	0 29.7	29 11.5
21 Sa	3 58 19	28 15 25	28 36 31	4♍30 19	28 15.2	12 3.4	11 49.3	20 1.9	19 3.2	18 23.8	12 3.1	0 31.9	29 12.9
22 Su	4 2 16	29 16 1	10♍23 57	16 18 9	28 15.0	13 33.1	11 26.3	20 40.0	19 16.4	18 19.0	12 6.0	0 34.2	29 14.2
23 M	4 6 13	0♐16 39	22 13 33	28 10 50	28 13.6	15 2.5	11 5.6	21 18.1	19 29.5	18 14.3	12 8.9	0 36.4	29 15.6
24 Tu	4 10 9	1 17 19	4♎10 35	10♎13 21	28 10.1	16 31.4	10 47.2	21 56.3	19 42.6	18 9.6	12 11.7	0 38.7	29 16.9
25 W	4 14 6	2 18 0	16 19 37	22 29 48	28 3.8	17 59.9	10 31.2	22 34.4	19 55.7	18 4.9	12 14.4	0 40.9	29 18.1
26 Th	4 18 2	3 18 43	28 44 15	5♏ 3 12	27 54.7	19 28.0	10 17.6	23 12.5	20 8.8	18 0.3	12 17.2	0 43.2	29 19.3
27 F	4 21 59	4 19 28	11♏26 47	17 55 3	27 43.2	20 55.6	10 6.5	23 50.6	20 21.9	17 55.7	12 19.9	0 45.4	29 20.5
28 Sa	4 25 55	5 20 14	24 27 57	1♐ 5 18	27 30.1	22 22.5	9 57.9	24 28.8	20 34.9	17 51.1	12 22.5	0 47.7	29 21.7
29 Su	4 29 52	6 21 1	7♐46 53	14 32 21	27 16.7	23 48.9	9 51.7	25 6.9	20 47.9	17 46.6	12 25.2	0 50.0	29 22.9
30 M	4 33 48	7 21 50	21 21 20	28 13 24	27 4.2	25 14.4	9 48.1	25 45.0	21 0.9	17 42.2	12 27.7	0 52.2	29 24.0

DECEMBER 1970 LONGITUDE

Day	Sid.Time	☉	0 hr ☽	Noon ☽	True ☊	☿	♀	♂	♃	♄	♅	♆	♇
1 Tu	4 37 45	8♐22 40	5♑ 8 5	12♑ 4 57	26♒53.7	26♐39.1	9♏46.8	26♎23.1	21♏13.9	17♉37.8	12♎30.3	0♐54.5	29♍25.1
2 W	4 41 42	9 23 31	19 3 34	26 3 32	26R46.2	28 2.7	9D 48.0	27 1.3	21 26.8	17R33.4	12 32.8	0 56.7	29 26.1
3 Th	4 45 38	10 24 23	3♒ 4 29	10♒ 6 9	26 41.7	29 25.2	9 51.6	27 39.4	21 39.7	17 29.1	12 35.2	0 58.9	29 27.1
4 F	4 49 35	11 25 15	17 8 16	24 10 41	26D 39.8	0♑46.4	9 57.5	28 17.5	21 52.6	17 24.8	12 37.6	1 1.2	29 28.1
5 Sa	4 53 31	12 26 9	1♓13 14	8♓15 49	26R 39.6	2 6.0	10 5.8	28 55.6	22 5.5	17 20.6	12 40.0	1 3.4	29 29.1
6 Su	4 57 28	13 27 3	15 18 21	22 20 46	26 39.7	3 23.7	10 16.2	29 33.7	22 18.3	17 16.5	12 42.3	1 5.6	29 30.0
7 M	5 1 24	14 27 58	29 22 57	6♈24 47	26 38.9	4 39.4	10 28.9	0♏11.8	22 31.0	17 12.4	12 44.6	1 7.8	29 30.9
8 Tu	5 5 21	15 28 53	13♈26 7	20 26 43	26 36.0	5 52.7	10 43.7	0 49.9	22 43.8	17 8.4	12 46.8	1 10.0	29 31.8
9 W	5 9 18	16 29 49	27 26 21	4♉24 41	26 30.3	7 3.1	11 0.6	1 28.0	22 56.5	17 4.5	12 49.0	1 12.2	29 32.6
10 Th	5 13 14	17 30 46	11♉21 20	18 15 56	26 22.0	8 10.3	11 19.5	2 6.1	23 9.1	17 0.7	12 51.1	1 14.4	29 33.4
11 F	5 17 11	18 31 44	25 8 4	1♊57 16	26 11.4	9 13.8	11 40.3	2 44.2	23 21.8	16 56.9	12 53.2	1 16.6	29 34.2
12 Sa	5 21 7	19 32 42	8♊43 10	15 25 21	25 59.8	10 13.0	12 3.1	3 22.3	23 34.4	16 53.1	12 55.3	1 18.8	29 34.9
13 Su	5 25 4	20 33 42	22 3 32	28 37 26	25 48.1	11 7.2	12 27.7	4 0.3	23 46.9	16 49.5	12 57.3	1 21.0	29 35.6
14 M	5 29 0	21 34 42	5♋ 6 52	11♋31 47	25 37.6	11 55.8	12 54.1	4 38.4	23 59.4	16 46.0	12 59.2	1 23.1	29 36.3
15 Tu	5 32 57	22 35 43	17 52 10	24 8 6	25 29.3	12 37.9	13 22.2	5 16.5	24 11.8	16 42.5	13 1.1	1 25.3	29 36.9
16 W	5 36 53	23 36 45	0♌19 49	6♌27 35	25 23.5	13 12.9	13 51.9	5 54.6	24 24.2	16 39.1	13 2.9	1 27.4	29 37.5
17 Th	5 40 50	24 37 47	12 31 46	18 32 47	25 20.3	13 39.6	14 23.3	6 32.7	24 36.6	16 35.8	13 4.7	1 29.5	29 38.1
18 F	5 44 47	25 38 51	24 31 9	0♍27 26	25D 19.4	13 57.4	14 56.2	7 10.8	24 48.9	16 32.5	13 6.5	1 31.6	29 38.6
19 Sa	5 48 43	26 39 55	6♍22 12	12 16 8	25 19.8	14R 5.3	15 30.5	7 48.9	25 1.1	16 29.4	13 8.2	1 33.7	29 39.1
20 Su	5 52 40	27 41 0	18 9 51	24 4 4	25R 20.8	14 2.5	16 6.3	8 26.9	25 13.3	16 26.3	13 9.8	1 35.8	29 39.6
21 M	5 56 36	28 42 6	29 59 27	5♎56 41	25 21.2	13 48.5	16 43.4	9 5.0	25 25.5	16 23.4	13 11.4	1 37.9	29 40.0
22 Tu	6 0 33	29 43 12	11♎56 27	17 59 24	25 20.2	13 22.7	17 21.9	9 43.1	25 37.6	16 20.5	13 13.0	1 39.9	29 40.4
23 W	6 4 29	0♑44 20	24 6 7	0♏17 10	25 17.2	12 45.3	18 1.6	10 21.2	25 49.6	16 17.7	13 14.5	1 42.0	29 40.7
24 Th	6 8 26	1 45 28	6♏33 3	12 54 9	25 12.0	11 56.5	18 42.5	10 59.2	26 1.6	16 15.0	13 15.9	1 44.0	29 41.1
25 F	6 12 22	2 46 37	19 20 47	25 53 10	25 4.7	10 57.2	19 24.6	11 37.3	26 13.5	16 12.4	13 17.3	1 46.0	29 41.4
26 Sa	6 16 19	3 47 46	2♐31 22	9♐15 19	24 56.0	9 49.0	20 7.7	12 15.4	26 25.3	16 9.9	13 18.6	1 48.0	29 41.6
27 Su	6 20 16	4 48 56	16 4 52	22 59 39	24 46.9	8 33.7	20 52.0	12 53.4	26 37.1	16 7.5	13 19.9	1 50.0	29 41.8
28 M	6 24 12	5 50 6	29 59 15	7♑ 3 7	24 38.2	7 13.7	21 37.3	13 31.5	26 48.8	16 5.2	13 21.1	1 51.9	29 42.0
29 Tu	6 28 9	6 51 17	14♑10 36	21 20 59	24 31.1	5 51.7	22 23.5	14 9.5	27 0.5	16 3.0	13 22.3	1 53.9	29 42.2
30 W	6 32 5	7 52 27	28 33 32	5♒47 30	24 26.1	4 30.3	23 10.7	14 47.5	27 12.1	16 1.0	13 23.4	1 55.8	29 42.3
31 Th	6 36 2	8 53 38	13♒ 2 10	20 16 51	24D 23.5	3 12.4	23 58.8	15 25.6	27 23.6	15 59.0	13 24.5	1 57.7	29 42.4

Astro Data Dy Hr Mn	Planet Ingress Dy Hr Mn	Last Aspect Dy Hr Mn	☽ Ingress Dy Hr Mn	Last Aspect Dy Hr Mn	☽ Ingress Dy Hr Mn	☽ Phases & Eclipses Dy Hr Mn	Astro Data
☽0N 9 10:32	☊ ♒ 2 8:13	1 2:02 ♆ ☌	♐ 1 2:24	2 17:48 ♇ △	♒ 2 18:45	6 12:47 ☽ 13♒42	1 NOVEMBER 1970
♃☍♄ 18 19:20	♆ ♐ 6 16:30	3 6:19 ♇ □	♑ 3 8:32	4 19:54 ♂ △	♓ 4 21:55	13 7:28 ○ 20♉30	Julian Day # 25872
☽0S 23 5:09	☿ ♐ 13 1:16	5 13:07 ♆ ⚹	♒ 5 13:11	7 0:14 ♇ ☍	♈ 7 1:03	20 23:13 ☽ 28♌13	Delta T 41.0 sec
	☉ ♐ 22 17:25	7 0:39 ☿ □	♓ 7 16:33	8 3:46 ☉ △	♉ 9 4:24	28 21:14 ● 6♐14	SVP 05♓39'55"
♀ D 1 0:03		9 17:05 ♇ ☍	♈ 9 18:52	11 7:48 ♇ △	♊ 11 8:33		Obliquity 23°26'43"
☽0N 6 15:43	☿ ♑ 3 10:14	10 17:20 ♂ ☍	♉ 11 20:50	13 13:48 ♇ □	♋ 13 14:32	5 20:36 ☽ 13♓18	⚷ Chiron 6♈48.1R
☿ R 19 5:59	♂ ♏ 6 16:34	13 22:09 ♇ △	♊ 13 23:48	15 22:38 ♇ ⚹	♌ 15 23:21	12 21:03 ○ 20♊26	☽ Mean ☊ 29♒11.3
☽0S 20 12:24	☉ ♑ 22 6:36	16 3:43 ♇ □	♋ 16 5:23	18 2:29 ☉ △	♍ 18 11:04	20 21:09 ☽ 28♍35	
		18 12:56 ♇ ⚹	♌ 18 14:36	20 23:21 ♇ ☌	♎ 21 0:01	28 10:43 ● 6♑17	1 DECEMBER 1970
		20 23:13 ☉ □	♍ 21 2:50	22 2:44 ☿ □	♏ 23 11:27		Julian Day # 25902
		23 14:11 ♇ ☌	♎ 23 15:39	25 18:54 ♇ ⚹	♐ 25 19:28		Delta T 41.1 sec
		25 12:48 ♂ ☌	♏ 26 2:25	27 23:31 ♇ □	♑ 28 0:01		SVP 05♓39'49"
		28 8:54 ♇ ⚹	♐ 28 10:02	30 1:54 ♇ △	♒ 30 2:24		Obliquity 23°26'42"
		30 14:04 ♇ □	♑ 30 15:05				⚷ Chiron 5♈59.7R
							☽ Mean ☊ 27♒36.0

LONGITUDE JANUARY 1971

Day	Sid.Time	☉	0 hr ☽	Noon ☽	True ☊	☿	♀	♂	♃	♄	♅	♆	♇
1 F	6 39 58	9♑54 49	27♒30 55	4♓43 51	24♒23.0	2♑ 0.0	24♏47.7	16♏ 3.6	27♏35.0	15♉57.1	13♎25.5	1♐59.6	29♍42.5
2 Sa	6 43 55	10 55 59	11♓55 13	19 4 37	24D 23.9	0R 55.1	25 37.5	16 41.6	27 46.3	15R 55.3	13 26.4	2 1.5	29R 42.5
3 Su	6 47 51	11 57 9	26 11 48	3♈16 33	24 25.2	29♐59.1	26 28.1	17 19.6	27 57.6	15 53.7	13 27.3	2 3.3	29 42.4
4 M	6 51 48	12 58 19	10♈18 42	17 18 10	24R 26.1	29 12.9	27 19.4	17 57.5	28 8.8	15 52.1	13 28.1	2 5.1	29 42.4
5 Tu	6 55 45	13 59 29	24 14 51	1♉ 8 44	24 25.6	28 36.8	28 11.5	18 35.5	28 19.9	15 50.7	13 28.9	2 6.9	29 42.3
6 W	6 59 41	15 0 38	7♉59 46	14 47 55	24 23.3	28 11.0	29 4.3	19 13.5	28 31.0	15 49.3	13 29.6	2 8.7	29 42.2
7 Th	7 3 38	16 1 47	21 33 7	28 15 20	24 19.2	27 55.1	29 57.8	19 51.4	28 41.9	15 48.1	13 30.3	2 10.5	29 42.0
8 F	7 7 34	17 2 55	4♊54 31	11♊30 36	24 13.7	27D 48.8	0♐51.9	20 29.4	28 52.8	15 47.0	13 30.9	2 12.2	29 41.8
9 Sa	7 11 31	18 4 4	18 3 30	24 33 9	24 7.3	27 51.5	1 46.7	21 7.3	29 3.6	15 46.0	13 31.5	2 14.0	29 41.6
10 Su	7 15 27	19 5 11	0♋59 30	7♋22 31	24 0.9	28 2.5	2 42.1	21 45.3	29 14.3	15 45.1	13 32.0	2 15.7	29 41.4
11 M	7 19 24	20 6 19	13 42 12	19 58 32	23 55.2	28 21.1	3 38.1	22 23.2	29 24.9	15 44.3	13 32.4	2 17.3	29 41.1
12 Tu	7 23 21	21 7 26	26 11 35	2♌21 27	23 50.7	28 46.7	4 34.7	23 1.1	29 35.5	15 43.6	13 32.8	2 19.0	29 40.8
13 W	7 27 17	22 8 33	8♌28 16	14 32 16	23 47.8	29 18.6	5 31.8	23 39.0	29 45.9	15 43.0	13 33.1	2 20.6	29 40.4
14 Th	7 31 14	23 9 39	20 33 39	26 32 44	23D 46.7	29 56.2	6 29.4	24 16.9	29 56.2	15 42.6	13 33.4	2 22.2	29 40.0
15 F	7 35 10	24 10 46	2♍29 51	8♍25 25	23 47.0	0♑38.9	7 27.6	24 54.8	0♐ 6.5	15 42.2	13 33.6	2 23.8	29 39.6
16 Sa	7 39 7	25 11 51	14 19 53	20 13 42	23 48.3	1 26.2	8 26.3	25 32.7	0 16.6	15 42.0	13 33.8	2 25.3	29 39.1
17 Su	7 43 3	26 12 57	26 7 25	2♎ 1 35	23 50.2	2 17.6	9 25.4	26 10.5	0 26.7	15D 41.9	13 33.9	2 26.8	29 38.6
18 M	7 47 0	27 14 2	7♎56 48	13 53 39	23 52.0	3 12.8	10 25.0	26 48.4	0 36.6	15 41.9	13R 33.9	2 28.3	29 38.1
19 Tu	7 50 56	28 15 7	19 52 47	25 54 48	23R 53.2	4 11.3	11 25.0	27 26.2	0 46.5	15 42.0	13 33.9	2 29.8	29 37.6
20 W	7 54 53	29 16 12	2♏ 0 20	8♏10 0	23 53.5	5 12.8	12 25.5	28 4.1	0 56.2	15 42.2	13 33.8	2 31.3	29 37.0
21 Th	7 58 50	0♒17 16	14 24 22	20 43 57	23 52.7	6 17.0	13 26.4	28 41.9	1 5.8	15 42.5	13 33.7	2 32.7	29 36.4
22 F	8 2 46	1 18 21	27 9 15	3♐40 38	23 50.8	7 23.7	14 27.7	29 19.7	1 15.4	15 43.0	13 33.5	2 34.1	29 35.7
23 Sa	8 6 43	2 19 24	10♐18 23	17 2 43	23 48.1	8 32.6	15 29.3	29 57.5	1 24.8	15 43.6	13 33.3	2 35.4	29 35.1
24 Su	8 10 39	3 20 27	23 53 37	0♑51 2	23 45.0	9 43.6	16 31.3	0♐35.3	1 34.1	15 44.2	13 33.0	2 36.8	29 34.4
25 M	8 14 36	4 21 30	7♑54 40	15 4 7	23 42.1	10 56.4	17 33.7	1 13.1	1 43.3	15 45.0	13 32.6	2 38.1	29 33.6
26 Tu	8 18 32	5 22 32	22 18 48	29 37 59	23 39.7	12 10.9	18 36.4	1 50.9	1 52.4	15 45.9	13 32.2	2 39.4	29 32.9
27 W	8 22 29	6 23 33	7♒ 0 50	14♒26 25	23 38.1	13 27.0	19 39.4	2 28.6	2 1.4	15 47.0	13 31.8	2 40.6	29 32.1
28 Th	8 26 25	7 24 34	21 53 44	29 21 45	23D 37.5	14 44.5	20 42.7	3 6.3	2 10.2	15 48.1	13 31.3	2 41.8	29 31.2
29 F	8 30 22	8 25 33	6♓49 27	14♓15 53	23 37.8	16 3.4	21 46.3	3 44.0	2 18.9	15 49.3	13 30.7	2 43.0	29 30.4
30 Sa	8 34 19	9 26 31	21 40 10	29 1 31	23 38.7	17 23.5	22 50.2	4 21.7	2 27.5	15 50.7	13 30.1	2 44.2	29 29.5
31 Su	8 38 15	10 27 28	6♈19 17	13♈32 55	23 39.8	18 44.8	23 54.4	4 59.3	2 36.0	15 52.1	13 29.4	2 45.3	29 28.6

LONGITUDE FEBRUARY 1971

Day	Sid.Time	☉	0 hr ☽	Noon ☽	True ☊	☿	♀	♂	♃	♄	♅	♆	♇
1 M	8 42 12	11♒28 23	20♈42 3	27♈46 22	23♒40.8	20♑ 7.2	24♐58.9	5♐37.0	2♐44.4	15♉53.7	13♎28.7	2♐46.4	29♍27.6
2 Tu	8 46 8	12 29 18	4♉45 44	11♉40 5	23R 41.4	21 30.7	26 3.6	6 14.6	2 52.6	15 55.4	13R 27.9	2 47.5	29R 26.7
3 W	8 50 5	13 30 11	18 29 27	25 13 56	23 41.4	22 55.2	27 8.5	6 52.2	3 0.7	15 57.2	13 27.1	2 48.5	29 25.7
4 Th	8 54 1	14 31 2	1♊53 40	8♊28 53	23 41.0	24 20.7	28 13.7	7 29.8	3 8.6	15 59.1	13 26.2	2 49.5	29 24.7
5 F	8 57 58	15 31 53	14 59 47	21 26 37	23 40.2	25 47.1	29 19.1	8 7.3	3 16.5	16 1.1	13 25.2	2 50.5	29 23.6
6 Sa	9 1 54	16 32 41	27 49 37	4♋ 9 2	23 39.3	27 14.4	0♑24.8	8 44.9	3 24.2	16 3.2	13 24.2	2 51.4	29 22.6
7 Su	9 5 51	17 33 29	10♋25 8	16 38 9	23 38.3	28 42.6	1 30.7	9 22.4	3 31.7	16 5.5	13 23.2	2 52.3	29 21.5
8 M	9 9 48	18 34 15	22 48 18	28 55 50	23 37.6	0♒11.7	2 36.8	9 59.9	3 39.2	16 7.8	13 22.1	2 53.2	29 20.3
9 Tu	9 13 44	19 34 59	5♌ 0 56	11♌ 3 52	23 37.2	1 41.7	3 43.1	10 37.3	3 46.5	16 10.2	13 21.0	2 54.1	29 19.2
10 W	9 17 41	20 35 43	17 4 48	23 4 0	23D 37.0	3 12.5	4 49.6	11 14.8	3 53.6	16 12.8	13 19.8	2 54.9	29 18.0
11 Th	9 21 37	21 36 24	29 1 40	4♍58 3	23 36.9	4 44.2	5 56.3	11 52.2	4 0.6	16 15.4	13 18.5	2 55.7	29 16.8
12 F	9 25 34	22 37 5	10♍53 26	16 48 4	23 37.0	6 16.7	7 3.2	12 29.6	4 7.5	16 18.2	13 17.2	2 56.4	29 15.6
13 Sa	9 29 30	23 37 44	22 42 16	28 36 22	23R 37.1	7 50.1	8 10.3	13 7.0	4 14.2	16 21.0	13 15.9	2 57.1	29 14.4
14 Su	9 33 27	24 38 22	4♎30 43	10♎25 43	23 37.0	9 24.3	9 17.6	13 44.4	4 20.8	16 24.0	13 14.5	2 57.8	29 13.1
15 M	9 37 23	25 38 59	16 21 47	22 19 21	23 36.8	10 59.4	10 25.0	14 21.7	4 27.2	16 27.0	13 13.1	2 58.5	29 11.9
16 Tu	9 41 20	26 39 34	28 18 55	4♏20 57	23 36.5	12 35.3	11 32.6	14 59.0	4 33.5	16 30.2	13 11.6	2 59.1	29 10.6
17 W	9 45 17	27 40 8	10♏25 59	16 34 32	23 36.1	14 12.2	12 40.4	15 36.3	4 39.6	16 33.4	13 10.1	2 59.7	29 9.2
18 Th	9 49 13	28 40 41	22 47 9	29 4 21	23D 35.9	15 49.9	13 48.3	16 13.6	4 45.6	16 36.8	13 8.5	3 0.2	29 7.9
19 F	9 53 10	29 41 13	5♐26 39	11♐54 31	23 35.9	17 28.5	14 56.4	16 50.9	4 51.4	16 40.2	13 6.9	3 0.7	29 6.5
20 Sa	9 57 6	0♓41 44	18 28 24	25 8 38	23 36.2	19 8.0	16 4.6	17 28.1	4 57.1	16 43.8	13 5.3	3 1.2	29 5.2
21 Su	10 1 3	1 42 13	1♑55 30	8♑49 10	23 36.8	20 48.4	17 13.0	18 5.3	5 2.6	16 47.4	13 3.6	3 1.7	29 3.8
22 M	10 4 59	2 42 41	15 49 39	22 56 49	23 37.6	22 29.8	18 21.5	18 42.4	5 7.9	16 51.2	13 1.8	3 2.1	29 2.4
23 Tu	10 8 56	3 43 7	0♒10 24	7♒29 55	23 38.4	24 12.1	19 30.2	19 19.5	5 13.1	16 55.0	13 0.1	3 2.5	29 0.9
24 W	10 12 52	4 43 32	14 54 43	22 23 58	23R 39.0	25 55.4	20 38.9	19 56.6	5 18.1	16 58.9	12 58.2	3 2.8	28 59.5
25 Th	10 16 49	5 43 56	29 56 43	7♓31 49	23 39.0	27 39.7	21 47.8	20 33.7	5 23.0	17 3.0	12 56.4	3 3.1	28 58.0
26 F	10 20 46	6 44 18	15♓ 8 6	22 44 18	23 38.4	29 24.9	22 56.8	21 10.7	5 27.7	17 7.1	12 54.5	3 3.4	28 56.6
27 Sa	10 24 42	7 44 37	0♈19 12	7♈51 36	23 37.1	1♓11.2	24 5.9	21 47.6	5 32.2	17 11.3	12 52.6	3 3.6	28 55.1
28 Su	10 28 39	8 44 56	15 20 25	22 44 42	23 35.3	2 58.4	25 15.2	22 24.6	5 36.5	17 15.6	12 50.6	3 3.8	28 53.6

Astro Data Dy Hr Mn	Planet Ingress Dy Hr Mn	Last Aspect Dy Hr Mn	☽ Ingress Dy Hr Mn	Last Aspect Dy Hr Mn	☽ Ingress Dy Hr Mn	☽ Phases & Eclipses Dy Hr Mn	Astro Data
♇ R 1 21:59	☿ ♐ 2 23:36	1 0:07 ♃ □	♓ 1 4:08	1 7:51 ♀ △	♉ 1 15:49	4 4:55 ☽ 13♈11	1 JANUARY 1971
☽0N 2 20:24	♀ ♐ 7 1:00	3 6:03 ☿ □	♈ 3 6:26	3 19:31 ♇ △	♊ 3 20:34	11 13:20 ○ 20♋40	Julian Day # 25933
♃∠♅ 5 20:49	☿ ♑ 14 2:16	5 7:20 ☿ △	♉ 5 10:00	6 2:56 ♇ □	♋ 6 4:07	19 18:08 ☽ 29♎01	Delta T 41.2 sec
☿ D 8 4:36	♃ ♐ 14 8:49	7 14:36 ♇ △	♊ 7 15:08	8 12:47 ♇ ✶	♌ 8 14:06	26 22:55 ● 6♒21	SVP 05♓39'43"
♃✶♇ 12 11:46	☉ ♒ 20 17:13	9 21:34 ♇ □	♋ 9 22:09	10 7:41 ☉ ☍	♍ 11 1:58		Obliquity 23°26'42"
☽0S 16 19:29	♂ ♐ 23 1:34	12 6:46 ♇ ✶	♌ 12 7:24	13 13:16 ♇ ☌	♎ 13 14:50	2 14:31 ☽ 13♉06	⚷ Chiron 5♈57.6
♄ D 17 13:01		14 7:52 ♂ □	♍ 14 18:57	15 20:23 ☉ △	♏ 16 3:22	10 7:41 ○ 20♌55	☽ Mean ☊ 25♒57.6
♅ R 18 6:54	♀ ♑ 5 14:57	17 7:09 ♇ ☌	♎ 17 7:53	18 12:14 ☉ □	♐ 18 13:45	10 7:45 ◑T 1.308	
☽0N 30 3:32	☿ ♒ 7 20:51	19 18:08 ☉ □	♏ 19 20:04	20 18:58 ♇ □	♑ 20 20:37	18 12:14 ☽ 29♏12	1 FEBRUARY 1971
	☉ ♓ 19 7:27	22 4:31 ♇ ✶	♐ 22 5:16	22 22:05 ♇ △	♒ 22 23:43	25 9:49 ● 6♓09	Julian Day # 25964
♃☌♆ 1 6:49	☿ ♓ 26 7:57	24 9:48 ♇ □	♑ 24 10:33	24 19:54 ☿ ☌	♓ 25 0:05	25 9:37:26 ◐P 0.787	Delta T 41.3 sec
☽0S 13 2:17		26 11:51 ♇ △	♒ 26 12:36	26 21:47 ♇ ☍	♈ 26 23:30		SVP 05♓39'38"
☽0N 26 13:45		27 21:57 ♀ ✶	♓ 28 13:01	28 17:28 ♀ □	♉ 28 23:54		Obliquity 23°26'42"
		30 12:45 ♇ ☍	♈ 30 13:36				⚷ Chiron 6♈46.2
							☽ Mean ☊ 24♒19.1

MARCH 1971 — LONGITUDE

Day	Sid.Time	☉	0 hr ☽	Noon ☽	True ☊	☿	♀	♂	♃	♄	♅	♆	♇
1 M	10 32 35	9♓45 12	0♉ 3 40	7♉16 42	23♒33.2	4♓46.7	26♑24.5	23♐ 1.5	5♐40.7	17♉19.9	12♎48.6	3♐ 4.0	28♍52.0
2 Tu	10 36 32	10 45 26	14 23 23	21 23 29	23R31.3	6 36.0	27 33.9	23 38.3	5 44.7	17 24.4	12R46.5	3 4.2	28R50.5
3 W	10 40 28	11 45 38	28 16 55	5♊ 3 44	23 30.0	8 26.3	28 43.4	24 15.1	5 48.5	17 29.0	12 44.5	3 4.3	28 49.0
4 Th	10 44 25	12 45 48	11♊44 9	18 18 28	23D29.5	10 17.6	29 53.0	24 51.9	5 52.2	17 33.6	12 42.4	3 4.4	28 47.4
5 F	10 48 21	13 45 56	24 47 1	1♋10 15	23 29.9	12 9.9	1♒ 2.7	25 28.6	5 55.7	17 38.3	12 40.2	3R 4.4	28 45.9
6 Sa	10 52 18	14 46 2	7♋28 39	13 42 40	23 31.0	14 3.2	2 12.5	26 5.3	5 59.0	17 43.1	12 38.1	3 4.4	28 44.3
7 Su	10 56 15	15 46 6	19 52 48	25 59 33	23 32.6	15 57.3	3 22.4	26 42.0	6 2.1	17 48.0	12 35.9	3 4.4	28 42.7
8 M	11 0 11	16 46 7	2♌ 3 21	8♌ 4 42	23 34.3	17 52.4	4 32.4	27 18.6	6 5.0	17 53.0	12 33.7	3 4.3	28 41.1
9 Tu	11 4 8	17 46 7	14 3 58	20 1 36	23R35.5	19 48.3	5 42.4	27 55.1	6 7.8	17 58.0	12 31.4	3 4.2	28 39.5
10 W	11 8 4	18 46 4	25 57 56	1♍53 18	23 35.8	21 44.9	6 52.6	28 31.7	6 10.4	18 3.2	12 29.1	3 4.1	28 37.9
11 Th	11 12 1	19 46 0	7♍48 2	13 42 24	23 34.9	23 42.2	8 2.8	29 8.1	6 12.8	18 8.4	12 26.8	3 3.9	28 36.3
12 F	11 15 57	20 45 53	19 36 41	25 31 8	23 32.6	25 40.0	9 13.1	29 44.6	6 15.1	18 13.6	12 24.5	3 3.7	28 34.7
13 Sa	11 19 54	21 45 45	1♎25 59	7♎21 29	23 28.9	27 38.2	10 23.4	0♑20.9	6 17.1	18 19.0	12 22.1	3 3.5	28 33.1
14 Su	11 23 50	22 45 34	13 17 51	19 15 20	23 24.1	29 36.5	11 33.9	0 57.3	6 19.0	18 24.4	12 19.8	3 3.3	28 31.5
15 M	11 27 47	23 45 22	25 14 12	1♏14 42	23 18.6	1♈34.9	12 44.4	1 33.6	6 20.6	18 29.9	12 17.4	3 3.0	28 29.8
16 Tu	11 31 44	24 45 8	7♏17 8	13 21 48	23 13.1	3 32.9	13 55.0	2 9.8	6 22.1	18 35.4	12 14.9	3 2.6	28 28.2
17 W	11 35 40	25 44 52	19 29 3	25 39 13	23 8.0	5 30.5	15 5.7	2 46.0	6 23.4	18 41.1	12 12.5	3 2.3	28 26.6
18 Th	11 39 37	26 44 34	1♐52 43	8♐ 9 56	23 4.1	7 27.1	16 16.4	3 22.1	6 24.6	18 46.8	12 10.0	3 1.9	28 24.9
19 F	11 43 33	27 44 15	14 31 16	20 57 10	23 1.6	9 22.6	17 27.2	3 58.2	6 25.5	18 52.6	12 7.6	3 1.5	28 23.3
20 Sa	11 47 30	28 43 54	27 28 2	4♑ 4 16	23D 0.7	11 16.5	18 38.1	4 34.3	6 26.3	18 58.4	12 5.1	3 1.0	28 21.6
21 Su	11 51 26	29 43 31	10♑46 13	17 34 11	23 1.1	13 8.4	19 49.0	5 10.2	6 26.8	19 4.3	12 2.6	3 0.5	28 20.0
22 M	11 55 23	0♈43 7	24 28 24	1♒29 0	23 2.5	14 57.8	20 60.0	5 46.1	6 27.2	19 10.3	12 0.1	3 0.0	28 18.4
23 Tu	11 59 19	1 42 41	8♒35 58	15 49 8	23 3.9	16 44.5	22 11.0	6 22.0	6R27.4	19 16.3	11 57.5	2 59.5	28 16.7
24 W	12 3 16	2 42 13	23 8 12	0♓32 39	23R 4.5	18 27.8	23 22.1	6 57.8	6 27.4	19 22.4	11 55.0	2 58.9	28 15.1
25 Th	12 7 13	3 41 43	8♓ 1 46	15 34 40	23 3.6	20 7.3	24 33.3	7 33.5	6 27.2	19 28.6	11 52.4	2 58.3	28 13.5
26 F	12 11 9	4 41 11	23 10 17	0♈47 26	23 0.8	21 42.7	25 44.4	8 9.1	6 26.8	19 34.8	11 49.9	2 57.7	28 11.8
27 Sa	12 15 6	5 40 37	8♈24 49	16 1 5	22 56.1	23 13.5	26 55.7	8 44.7	6 26.2	19 41.1	11 47.3	2 57.0	28 10.2
28 Su	12 19 2	6 40 1	23 34 55	1♉ 5 7	22 49.8	24 39.3	28 7.0	9 20.2	6 25.5	19 47.4	11 44.7	2 56.3	28 8.6
29 M	12 22 59	7 39 23	8♉30 32	15 50 14	22 42.8	25 59.8	29 18.3	9 55.6	6 24.5	19 53.8	11 42.1	2 55.6	28 7.0
30 Tu	12 26 55	8 38 43	23 3 29	0♊ 9 45	22 36.1	27 14.6	0♓29.7	10 30.9	6 23.4	20 0.2	11 39.5	2 54.8	28 5.3
31 W	12 30 52	9 38 1	7♊ 8 44	14 0 18	22 30.5	28 23.4	1 41.1	11 6.2	6 22.1	20 6.7	11 37.0	2 54.0	28 3.7

APRIL 1971 — LONGITUDE

Day	Sid.Time	☉	0 hr ☽	Noon ☽	True ☊	☿	♀	♂	♃	♄	♅	♆	♇
1 Th	12 34 48	10♈37 16	20♊44 33	27♊21 40	22♒26.6	29♈26.0	2♓52.5	11♑41.4	6♐20.6	20♉13.3	11♎34.4	2♐53.2	28♍ 2.2
2 F	12 38 45	11 36 29	3♋52 3	10♋16 8	22D24.6	0♉22.2	4 4.0	12 16.5	6R18.9	20 19.9	11R31.8	2R52.4	28R 0.6
3 Sa	12 42 42	12 35 40	16 34 27	22 47 37	22 24.4	1 11.7	5 15.5	12 51.5	6 17.0	20 26.6	11 29.2	2 51.5	27 59.0
4 Su	12 46 38	13 34 49	28 56 14	5♌ 0 57	22 25.3	1 54.4	6 27.1	13 26.5	6 14.9	20 33.3	11 26.6	2 50.6	27 57.4
5 M	12 50 35	14 33 55	11♌ 2 22	17 1 7	22R26.4	2 30.3	7 38.7	14 1.3	6 12.7	20 40.0	11 24.0	2 49.7	27 55.9
6 Tu	12 54 31	15 32 58	22 57 48	28 52 58	22 27.0	2 59.2	8 50.3	14 36.1	6 10.3	20 46.8	11 21.4	2 48.7	27 54.3
7 W	12 58 28	16 32 0	4♍47 9	10♍40 49	22 26.0	3 21.1	10 1.9	15 10.8	6 7.7	20 53.7	11 18.8	2 47.8	27 52.8
8 Th	13 2 24	17 30 59	16 34 25	22 28 21	22 23.0	3 36.1	11 13.6	15 45.3	6 4.9	21 0.6	11 16.2	2 46.8	27 51.2
9 F	13 6 21	18 29 56	28 22 57	4♎18 31	22 17.5	3R44.2	12 25.3	16 19.8	6 1.9	21 7.5	11 13.7	2 45.7	27 49.7
10 Sa	13 10 17	19 28 51	10♎15 19	16 13 36	22 9.6	3 45.7	13 37.1	16 54.2	5 58.8	21 14.5	11 11.1	2 44.7	27 48.2
11 Su	13 14 14	20 27 44	22 13 31	28 15 16	21 59.7	3 40.6	14 48.9	17 28.6	5 55.5	21 21.5	11 8.6	2 43.6	27 46.7
12 M	13 18 10	21 26 35	4♏18 59	10♏24 47	21 48.6	3 29.3	16 0.7	18 2.8	5 52.0	21 28.5	11 6.0	2 42.5	27 45.2
13 Tu	13 22 7	22 25 24	16 32 50	22 43 13	21 37.3	3 12.2	17 12.6	18 36.9	5 48.4	21 35.6	11 3.5	2 41.4	27 43.8
14 W	13 26 4	23 24 11	28 56 7	5♐11 40	21 26.7	2 49.7	18 24.4	19 10.9	5 44.5	21 42.8	11 1.0	2 40.2	27 42.3
15 Th	13 30 0	24 22 56	11♐30 3	17 51 29	21 17.8	2 22.2	19 36.4	19 44.8	5 40.6	21 49.9	10 58.5	2 39.1	27 40.9
16 F	13 33 57	25 21 40	24 16 10	0♑44 22	21 11.3	1 50.5	20 48.3	20 18.6	5 36.4	21 57.1	10 56.0	2 37.9	27 39.5
17 Sa	13 37 53	26 20 22	7♑16 22	13 52 26	21 7.4	1 15.1	22 0.3	20 52.3	5 32.1	22 4.4	10 53.5	2 36.7	27 38.1
18 Su	13 41 50	27 19 2	20 32 53	27 17 58	21D 5.7	0 36.8	23 12.3	21 25.9	5 27.7	22 11.7	10 51.0	2 35.5	27 36.7
19 M	13 45 46	28 17 41	4♒ 7 57	11♒ 3 2	21 5.6	29♈56.3	24 24.3	21 59.3	5 23.0	22 19.0	10 48.6	2 34.2	27 35.4
20 Tu	13 49 43	29 16 18	18 3 21	25 8 54	21R 6.0	29 14.5	25 36.4	22 32.7	5 18.2	22 26.3	10 46.2	2 32.9	27 34.0
21 W	13 53 39	0♉14 53	2♓19 38	9♓35 17	21 5.6	28 32.0	26 48.5	23 5.9	5 13.3	22 33.7	10 43.8	2 31.6	27 32.7
22 Th	13 57 36	1 13 26	16 55 28	24 19 36	21 3.4	27 49.8	28 0.6	23 38.9	5 8.2	22 41.1	10 41.4	2 30.3	27 31.4
23 F	14 1 33	2 11 58	1♈46 57	9♈16 35	20 58.6	27 8.5	29 12.7	24 11.9	5 3.0	22 48.5	10 39.0	2 29.0	27 30.1
24 Sa	14 5 29	3 10 28	16 47 28	24 18 25	20 51.1	26 28.9	0♈24.9	24 44.7	4 57.6	22 55.9	10 36.7	2 27.6	27 28.8
25 Su	14 9 26	4 8 56	1♉48 14	9♉15 42	20 41.4	25 51.6	1 37.0	25 17.3	4 52.1	23 3.4	10 34.3	2 26.3	27 27.6
26 M	14 13 22	5 7 23	16 39 40	23 59 3	20 30.6	25 17.2	2 49.2	25 49.8	4 46.5	23 10.9	10 32.1	2 24.9	27 26.3
27 Tu	14 17 19	6 5 48	1♊12 57	8♊20 39	20 19.8	24 46.2	4 1.4	26 22.1	4 40.7	23 18.5	10 29.8	2 23.5	27 25.1
28 W	14 21 15	7 4 11	15 21 38	22 15 32	20 10.3	24 19.0	5 13.7	26 54.3	4 34.8	23 26.0	10 27.5	2 22.1	27 23.9
29 Th	14 25 12	8 2 31	29 2 16	5♋41 52	20 3.0	23 55.9	6 25.9	27 26.3	4 28.8	23 33.6	10 25.3	2 20.6	27 22.8
30 F	14 29 8	9 0 50	12♋14 34	18 40 43	19 58.1	23 37.3	7 38.2	27 58.2	4 22.6	23 41.2	10 23.2	2 19.2	27 21.7

Astro Data Dy Hr Mn	Planet Ingress Dy Hr Mn	Last Aspect Dy Hr Mn	☽ Ingress Dy Hr Mn	Last Aspect Dy Hr Mn	☽ Ingress Dy Hr Mn	☽ Phases & Eclipses Dy Hr Mn
♆ R 5 18:08	♀ ♒ 4 2:24	3 0:56 ♇ △	♊ 3 3:01	1 13:13 ♇ □	♋ 1 16:51	4 2:01 ☽ 12♊51
☽0S 12 8:41	♂ ♑ 12 10:11	5 7:27 ♇ □	♋ 5 9:47	3 22:05 ♇ ⚹	♌ 4 2:05	12 2:34 ○ 20♍52
☿0N 14 23:45	☿ ♈ 14 4:46	7 17:20 ♇ ⚹	♌ 7 19:55	5 19:33 ♄ □	♍ 6 14:16	20 2:30 ☽ 28♐50
♃ R 23 11:33	☉ ♈ 21 6:38	10 5:28 ♂ △	♍ 10 8:10	8 22:53 ♇ ☌	♎ 9 3:17	26 19:23 ● 5♈29
☽0N 26 1:05	♀ ♓ 29 14:02	12 18:10 ♇ ☌	♎ 12 21:06	10 20:10 ☉ ☍	♏ 11 15:28	
		13 22:03 ♅ ☌	♏ 15 9:31	13 21:38 ♇ ⚹	♐ 14 2:03	2 15:46 ☽ 12♋15
☽0S 8 14:45	☿ ♉ 1 14:11	17 17:21 ♇ ⚹	♐ 17 20:23	16 6:17 ♇ □	♑ 16 10:38	10 20:10 ○ 20♎18
☿ R 9 17:11	☿ ♈ 18 21:52	20 2:30 ☉ □	♑ 20 4:37	18 12:58 ☉ □	♒ 18 16:46	18 12:58 ☽ 27♑51
☽0N 22 10:58	☉ ♉ 20 17:54	22 6:34 ♇ △	♒ 22 9:29	20 17:58 ☿ ⚹	♓ 20 20:08	25 4:02 ● 4♉19
♀0N 26 16:54	♀ ♈ 23 15:44	24 0:25 ♀ ☌	♓ 24 11:07	22 19:30 ♀ ☌	♈ 22 21:08	
		26 7:54 ♇ ☍	♈ 26 10:45	24 14:51 ☿ ☌	♉ 24 21:06	
		28 7:52 ♀ ⚹	♉ 28 10:15	26 17:41 ♇ △	♊ 26 21:58	
		30 8:28 ♇ △	♊ 30 11:43	28 21:03 ♇ □	♋ 29 1:43	

Astro Data

1 MARCH 1971
Julian Day # 25992
Delta T 41.3 sec
SVP 05♓39'34"
Obliquity 23°26'43"
⚷ Chiron 8♈04.1
☽ Mean ☊ 22♒50.1

1 APRIL 1971
Julian Day # 26023
Delta T 41.4 sec
SVP 05♓39'30"
Obliquity 23°26'42"
⚷ Chiron 9♈50.0
☽ Mean ☊ 21♒11.6

LONGITUDE — MAY 1971

Day	Sid.Time	☉	0 hr ☽	Noon ☽	True ☊	☿	♀	♂	♃	♄	♅	♆	♇
1 Sa	14 33 5	9♉59 7	25♋ 0 47	1♌15 19	19♒55.7	23♈23.3	8♈50.4	28♑29.9	4♐16.4	23♉48.8	10♎21.0	2♐17.7	27♍20.5
2 Su	14 37 2	10 57 21	7♌24 56	13 30 17	19D 54.9	23R 14.0	10 2.7	29 1.4	4R 10.0	23 56.4	10R 18.9	2R 16.3	27R 19.5
3 M	14 40 58	11 55 34	19 32 3	25 30 56	19R 55.0	23D 9.5	11 15.0	29 32.8	4 3.5	24 4.1	10 16.8	2 14.8	27 18.4
4 Tu	14 44 55	12 53 44	1♍27 35	7♍22 41	19 54.6	23 9.8	12 27.3	0♒ 3.9	3 56.9	24 11.7	10 14.7	2 13.3	27 17.3
5 W	14 48 51	13 51 53	13 16 51	19 10 43	19 52.8	23 14.9	13 39.6	0 34.9	3 50.2	24 19.4	10 12.7	2 11.8	27 16.3
6 Th	14 52 48	14 49 59	25 4 48	0♎59 39	19 48.8	23 24.7	14 52.0	1 5.8	3 43.4	24 27.1	10 10.7	2 10.2	27 15.3
7 F	14 56 44	15 48 4	6♎55 42	12 53 22	19 42.0	23 39.2	16 4.3	1 36.4	3 36.6	24 34.8	10 8.8	2 8.7	27 14.4
8 Sa	15 0 41	16 46 7	18 53 0	24 54 52	19 32.6	23 58.2	17 16.7	2 6.8	3 29.6	24 42.5	10 6.8	2 7.2	27 13.4
9 Su	15 4 37	17 44 8	0♏59 12	7♏ 6 12	19 20.8	24 21.6	18 29.1	2 37.1	3 22.6	24 50.2	10 5.0	2 5.6	27 12.5
10 M	15 8 34	18 42 7	13 15 58	19 28 35	19 7.7	24 49.3	19 41.5	3 7.1	3 15.5	24 57.9	10 3.1	2 4.0	27 11.6
11 Tu	15 12 31	19 40 5	25 44 5	2♐ 2 29	18 54.2	25 21.2	20 53.9	3 36.9	3 8.3	25 5.6	10 1.3	2 2.5	27 10.8
12 W	15 16 27	20 38 2	8♐23 45	14 47 53	18 41.5	25 57.1	22 6.3	4 6.6	3 1.1	25 13.4	9 59.5	2 0.9	27 9.9
13 Th	15 20 24	21 35 57	21 14 50	27 44 37	18 30.8	26 36.8	23 18.8	4 36.0	2 53.8	25 21.1	9 57.8	1 59.3	27 9.1
14 F	15 24 20	22 33 50	4♑17 13	10♑52 39	18 22.7	27 20.3	24 31.3	5 5.2	2 46.4	25 28.9	9 56.1	1 57.7	27 8.4
15 Sa	15 28 17	23 31 42	17 30 59	24 12 18	18 17.5	28 7.3	25 43.8	5 34.1	2 39.0	25 36.6	9 54.4	1 56.1	27 7.6
16 Su	15 32 13	24 29 33	0♒56 40	7♒44 14	18 14.9	28 57.9	26 56.3	6 2.8	2 31.5	25 44.4	9 52.8	1 54.5	27 6.9
17 M	15 36 10	25 27 23	14 35 6	21 29 23	18 14.2	29 51.8	28 8.8	6 31.3	2 24.0	25 52.2	9 51.3	1 52.9	27 6.2
18 Tu	15 40 6	26 25 11	28 27 9	5♓28 28	18 14.2	0♉48.9	29 21.3	6 59.5	2 16.5	25 59.9	9 49.7	1 51.3	27 5.6
19 W	15 44 3	27 22 59	12♓33 17	19 41 28	18 13.6	1 49.2	0♉33.9	7 27.5	2 8.9	26 7.7	9 48.2	1 49.7	27 4.9
20 Th	15 48 0	28 20 45	26 52 50	4♈ 7 0	18 11.3	2 52.5	1 46.4	7 55.2	2 1.3	26 15.5	9 46.8	1 48.1	27 4.3
21 F	15 51 56	29 18 30	11♈23 32	18 41 49	18 6.6	3 58.8	2 59.0	8 22.6	1 53.7	26 23.2	9 45.4	1 46.4	27 3.7
22 Sa	15 55 53	0♊16 14	26 1 9	3♉20 41	17 59.2	5 8.0	4 11.6	8 49.7	1 46.0	26 31.0	9 44.0	1 44.8	27 3.2
23 Su	15 59 49	1 13 57	10♉39 33	17 56 48	17 49.5	6 19.9	5 24.2	9 16.5	1 38.4	26 38.7	9 42.7	1 43.2	27 2.7
24 M	16 3 46	2 11 39	25 11 32	2♊22 49	17 38.6	7 34.6	6 36.8	9 43.0	1 30.8	26 46.5	9 41.5	1 41.6	27 2.2
25 Tu	16 7 42	3 9 20	9♊29 52	16 32 0	17 27.7	8 52.0	7 49.5	10 9.2	1 23.1	26 54.2	9 40.2	1 39.9	27 1.8
26 W	16 11 39	4 6 59	23 28 37	0♋19 20	17 17.8	10 12.0	9 2.1	10 35.1	1 15.5	27 1.9	9 39.1	1 38.3	27 1.3
27 Th	16 15 35	5 4 37	7♋ 3 54	13 42 13	17 10.0	11 34.6	10 14.8	11 0.7	1 7.8	27 9.7	9 38.0	1 36.7	27 1.0
28 F	16 19 32	6 2 14	20 14 22	26 40 31	17 4.8	12 59.8	11 27.5	11 25.9	1 0.2	27 17.4	9 36.9	1 35.1	27 0.6
29 Sa	16 23 29	6 59 49	3♌ 1 1	9♌16 15	17 2.0	14 27.5	12 40.1	11 50.8	0 52.7	27 25.1	9 35.9	1 33.5	27 0.3
30 Su	16 27 25	7 57 23	15 26 45	21 33 4	17D 1.1	15 57.8	13 52.8	12 15.3	0 45.1	27 32.8	9 34.9	1 31.8	26 60.0
31 M	16 31 22	8 54 55	27 35 49	3♍35 38	17 1.4	17 30.5	15 5.5	12 39.5	0 37.6	27 40.4	9 34.0	1 30.2	26 59.7

LONGITUDE — JUNE 1971

Day	Sid.Time	☉	0 hr ☽	Noon ☽	True ☊	☿	♀	♂	♃	♄	♅	♆	♇
1 Tu	16 35 18	9♊52 26	9♍33 13	15♍29 12	17♒ 1.7	19♉ 5.7	16♉18.2	13♒ 3.3	0♐30.1	27♉48.1	9♎33.1	1♐28.6	26♍59.5
2 W	16 39 15	10 49 56	21 24 17	27 19 6	17R 1.1	20 43.4	17 30.9	13 26.8	0R 22.7	27 55.7	9R 32.2	1R 27.0	26R 59.3
3 Th	16 43 11	11 47 25	3♎14 17	9♎10 26	16 58.8	22 23.6	18 43.7	13 49.9	0 15.3	28 3.4	9 31.5	1 25.4	26 59.1
4 F	16 47 8	12 44 52	15 8 7	21 7 50	16 54.2	24 6.2	19 56.4	14 12.5	0 7.9	28 11.0	9 30.7	1 23.8	26 59.0
5 Sa	16 51 4	13 42 18	27 10 1	3♏15 6	16 47.4	25 51.3	21 9.2	14 34.8	0 0.7	28 18.6	9 30.0	1 22.3	26 58.9
6 Su	16 55 1	14 39 43	9♏23 23	15 35 9	16 38.5	27 38.8	22 21.9	14 56.7	29♏53.5	28 26.1	9 29.4	1 20.7	26 58.8
7 M	16 58 58	15 37 7	21 50 34	28 9 45	16 28.3	29 28.7	23 34.7	15 18.2	29 46.3	28 33.7	9 28.8	1 19.1	26D 58.8
8 Tu	17 2 54	16 34 30	4♐32 45	10♐59 32	16 17.8	1♊21.0	24 47.5	15 39.3	29 39.3	28 41.2	9 28.3	1 17.6	26 58.8
9 W	17 6 51	17 31 52	17 30 3	24 4 8	16 7.9	3 15.6	26 0.3	15 59.9	29 32.3	28 48.7	9 27.8	1 16.0	26 58.8
10 Th	17 10 47	18 29 13	0♑41 38	7♑22 21	15 59.5	5 12.5	27 13.2	16 20.1	29 25.4	28 56.2	9 27.4	1 14.5	26 58.9
11 F	17 14 44	19 26 34	14 6 3	20 52 33	15 53.4	7 11.6	28 26.0	16 39.8	29 18.6	29 3.7	9 27.1	1 13.0	26 59.0
12 Sa	17 18 40	20 23 54	27 41 36	4♒33 2	15 49.7	9 12.8	29 38.9	16 59.0	29 11.8	29 11.1	9 26.7	1 11.4	26 59.1
13 Su	17 22 37	21 21 13	11♒26 39	18 22 18	15D 48.3	11 16.0	0♊51.7	17 17.8	29 5.2	29 18.5	9 26.5	1 9.9	26 59.2
14 M	17 26 34	22 18 32	25 19 52	2♓19 13	15 48.5	13 21.0	2 4.6	17 36.0	28 58.7	29 25.9	9 26.3	1 8.4	26 59.4
15 Tu	17 30 30	23 15 50	9♓20 15	16 22 50	15 49.4	15 27.7	3 17.6	17 53.8	28 52.3	29 33.3	9 26.1	1 7.0	26 59.6
16 W	17 34 27	24 13 8	23 26 51	0♈32 9	15R 50.0	17 35.8	4 30.5	18 11.0	28 45.9	29 40.6	9 26.0	1 5.5	26 59.9
17 Th	17 38 23	25 10 25	7♈38 32	14 45 45	15 49.3	19 45.2	5 43.4	18 27.7	28 39.7	29 47.9	9D 25.9	1 4.0	27 0.2
18 F	17 42 20	26 7 43	21 53 29	29 1 24	15 46.8	21 55.6	6 56.4	18 43.9	28 33.6	29 55.1	9 25.9	1 2.6	27 0.5
19 Sa	17 46 16	27 5 0	6♉ 9 2	13♉15 57	15 42.2	24 6.7	8 9.4	18 59.4	28 27.7	0♊ 2.4	9 26.0	1 1.2	27 0.8
20 Su	17 50 13	28 2 17	20 21 35	27 25 23	15 36.0	26 18.2	9 22.4	19 14.4	28 21.8	0 9.6	9 26.1	0 59.8	27 1.2
21 M	17 54 9	28 59 34	4♊26 49	11♊25 18	15 28.8	28 30.0	10 35.4	19 28.8	28 16.1	0 16.7	9 26.2	0 58.4	27 1.6
22 Tu	17 58 6	29 56 50	18 20 19	25 11 26	15 21.5	0♋41.6	11 48.5	19 42.6	28 10.5	0 23.8	9 26.4	0 57.0	27 2.1
23 W	18 2 3	0♋54 6	1♋58 13	8♋40 23	15 14.9	2 52.9	13 1.5	19 55.8	28 5.1	0 30.9	9 26.7	0 55.6	27 2.6
24 Th	18 5 59	1 51 22	15 17 43	21 50 6	15 9.8	5 3.5	14 14.6	20 8.4	27 59.7	0 38.0	9 27.0	0 54.3	27 3.1
25 F	18 9 56	2 48 37	28 17 31	4♌40 4	15 6.5	7 13.3	15 27.7	20 20.3	27 54.6	0 45.0	9 27.4	0 53.0	27 3.6
26 Sa	18 13 52	3 45 52	10♌57 57	17 11 25	15D 5.1	9 22.0	16 40.8	20 31.6	27 49.5	0 52.0	9 27.8	0 51.7	27 4.2
27 Su	18 17 49	4 43 6	23 20 50	29 26 37	15 5.3	11 29.4	17 53.9	20 42.2	27 44.7	0 58.9	9 28.3	0 50.4	27 4.8
28 M	18 21 45	5 40 19	5♍29 16	11♍29 17	15 6.6	13 35.3	19 7.0	20 52.1	27 39.9	1 5.8	9 28.8	0 49.1	27 5.5
29 Tu	18 25 42	6 37 33	17 27 14	23 23 45	15 8.2	15 39.7	20 20.2	21 1.4	27 35.4	1 12.6	9 29.4	0 47.8	27 6.1
30 W	18 29 38	7 34 45	29 19 24	5♎14 50	15R 9.4	17 42.5	21 33.4	21 10.0	27 30.9	1 19.4	9 30.0	0 46.6	27 6.8

Astro Data Dy Hr Mn	Planet Ingress Dy Hr Mn
☿ D 3 10:25	♂ ♒ 3 20:57
☽0S 5 20:51	☿ ♉ 17 3:32
♄□♅ 10 13:03	♀ ♉ 18 12:48
☽0N 19 18:01	☉ ♊ 21 17:15
♃☌♆ 22 4:57	
♄△♇ 25 22:14	♃ ♏ 5 2:12
	☿ ♊ 7 6:45
☽0S 2 3:23	♀ ♊ 12 6:58
♇ D 7 15:16	♄ ♊ 18 16:09
♃☍♄ 12 1:14	☿ ♋ 21 16:25
☽0N 15 22:58	☉ ♋ 22 1:20
♅ D 17 14:51	
♄☍♆ 25 23:05	
☽0S 29 10:31	

Last Aspect Dy Hr Mn	☽ Ingress Dy Hr Mn	Last Aspect Dy Hr Mn	☽ Ingress Dy Hr Mn
1 6:58 ♂ ☍	♌ 1 9:34	2 13:23 ♄ △	♎ 2 17:26
3 9:11 ♄ □	♍ 3 21:03	3 22:05 ♂ △	♏ 5 5:36
6 4:25 ♇ ☌	♎ 6 9:59	7 14:54 ♃ ☌	♐ 7 15:28
8 10:27 ☿ ☍	♏ 8 22:03	9 17:17 ♇ □	♑ 9 22:45
11 2:45 ♇ ✶	♐ 11 8:08	12 3:46 ♀ △	♒ 12 4:03
13 10:54 ♇ □	♑ 13 16:09	14 7:07 ♄ □	♓ 14 8:01
15 20:15 ☿ □	♒ 15 22:19	16 10:38 ♄ ✶	♈ 16 11:06
18 1:42 ♀ ✶	♓ 18 2:39	18 7:38 ☉ ✶	♉ 18 13:39
20 2:37 ☉ ✶	♈ 20 5:11	20 13:31 ♃ ☍	♊ 20 16:24
20 21:19 ♅ ☍	♉ 22 6:31	22 15:16 ♇ □	♋ 22 20:30
24 3:04 ♇ △	♊ 24 8:01	24 23:17 ♃ △	♌ 25 3:12
26 6:11 ♇ □	♋ 26 11:26	27 8:35 ♃ □	♍ 27 13:06
28 13:17 ♄ ✶	♌ 28 18:16	29 20:22 ♃ ✶	♎ 30 1:22
31 0:09 ♄ □	♍ 31 4:48		

☽ Phases & Eclipses Dy Hr Mn		
2 7:34	☽	11♌16
10 11:24	○	19♏10
17 20:15	☽	26♒16
24 12:32	●	2♊42
1 0:42	☽	9♍54
9 0:04	○	17♐32
16 1:24	☽	24♓16
22 21:57	●	0♋49
30 18:11	☽	8♎18

Astro Data

1 MAY 1971
Julian Day # 26053
Delta T 41.5 sec
SVP 05♓39'26"
Obliquity 23°26'42"
⚷ Chiron 11♈32.1
☽ Mean ☊ 19♒36.3

1 JUNE 1971
Julian Day # 26084
Delta T 41.6 sec
SVP 05♓39'22"
Obliquity 23°26'41"
⚷ Chiron 12♈57.4
☽ Mean ☊ 17♒57.8

JULY 1971 — LONGITUDE

Day	Sid.Time	☉	0 hr ☽	Noon ☽	True ☊	☿	♀	♂	♃	♄	♅	♆	♇
1 Th	18 33 35	8♋31 57	11♎10 41	17♎ 7 33	15♒ 9.7	19♋43.4	22♊46.5	21♒17.9	27♏26.7	1♊26.2	9♎30.7	0♐45.4	27♍ 7.6
2 F	18 37 32	9 29 9	23 6 3	29 6 45	15R 8.7	21 42.5	23 59.7	21 25.2	27R22.6	1 32.9	9 31.4	0R44.2	27 8.3
3 Sa	18 41 28	10 26 21	5♏10 12	11♏16 55	15 6.2	23 39.6	25 13.0	21 31.7	27 18.6	1 39.5	9 32.2	0 43.1	27 9.1
4 Su	18 45 25	11 23 32	17 27 19	23 41 49	15 2.4	25 34.8	26 26.2	21 37.5	27 14.9	1 46.1	9 33.1	0 41.9	27 9.9
5 M	18 49 21	12 20 43	0♐ 0 44	6♐24 17	14 57.6	27 28.1	27 39.4	21 42.5	27 11.3	1 52.7	9 34.0	0 40.8	27 10.8
6 Tu	18 53 18	13 17 54	12 52 38	19 25 50	14 52.5	29 19.3	28 52.7	21 46.9	27 7.8	1 59.2	9 34.9	0 39.7	27 11.7
7 W	18 57 14	14 15 5	26 3 53	2♑46 39	14 47.7	1♌ 8.5	0♋ 6.0	21 50.5	27 4.5	2 5.7	9 35.9	0 38.6	27 12.6
8 Th	19 1 11	15 12 16	9♑33 55	16 25 25	14 43.7	2 55.8	1 19.3	21 53.3	27 1.4	2 12.1	9 37.0	0 37.6	27 13.5
9 F	19 5 8	16 9 27	23 20 47	0♒19 37	14 41.0	4 40.9	2 32.6	21 55.5	26 58.5	2 18.4	9 38.1	0 36.6	27 14.5
10 Sa	19 9 4	17 6 38	7♒21 27	14 25 49	14D 39.6	6 24.1	3 46.0	21 56.8	26 55.8	2 24.7	9 39.2	0 35.6	27 15.5
11 Su	19 13 1	18 3 49	21 32 12	28 40 6	14 39.6	8 5.3	4 59.4	21R 57.4	26 53.2	2 31.0	9 40.4	0 34.6	27 16.6
12 M	19 16 57	19 1 0	5♓49 4	12♓58 37	14 40.5	9 44.4	6 12.8	21 57.2	26 50.8	2 37.1	9 41.7	0 33.6	27 17.6
13 Tu	19 20 54	19 58 12	20 8 20	27 17 49	14 41.9	11 21.5	7 26.2	21 56.3	26 48.5	2 43.3	9 43.0	0 32.7	27 18.7
14 W	19 24 50	20 55 24	4♈26 43	11♈34 41	14 43.1	12 56.5	8 39.6	21 54.6	26 46.5	2 49.3	9 44.3	0 31.8	27 19.8
15 Th	19 28 47	21 52 37	18 41 26	25 46 41	14R 43.8	14 29.6	9 53.1	21 52.1	26 44.6	2 55.3	9 45.7	0 30.9	27 21.0
16 F	19 32 43	22 49 51	2♉50 11	9♉51 42	14 43.5	16 0.6	11 6.6	21 48.8	26 42.9	3 1.3	9 47.2	0 30.1	27 22.2
17 Sa	19 36 40	23 47 5	16 51 0	23 47 53	14 42.3	17 29.5	12 20.1	21 44.7	26 41.4	3 7.2	9 48.7	0 29.3	27 23.4
18 Su	19 40 37	24 44 21	0♊42 7	7♊33 31	14 40.3	18 56.4	13 33.6	21 39.9	26 40.0	3 13.0	9 50.2	0 28.5	27 24.6
19 M	19 44 33	25 41 36	14 21 53	21 7 2	14 37.8	20 21.2	14 47.2	21 34.3	26 38.9	3 18.8	9 51.8	0 27.7	27 25.9
20 Tu	19 48 30	26 38 53	27 48 48	4♋27 4	14 35.3	21 43.9	16 0.8	21 28.0	26 37.9	3 24.5	9 53.4	0 27.0	27 27.1
21 W	19 52 26	27 36 10	11♋ 1 41	17 32 35	14 33.0	23 4.3	17 14.4	21 20.9	26 37.1	3 30.1	9 55.1	0 26.3	27 28.5
22 Th	19 56 23	28 33 27	23 59 43	0♌23 5	14 31.4	24 22.6	18 28.0	21 13.2	26 36.5	3 35.7	9 56.9	0 25.6	27 29.8
23 F	20 0 19	29 30 46	6♌42 43	12 58 44	14D 30.5	25 38.7	19 41.7	21 4.7	26 36.1	3 41.2	9 58.7	0 24.9	27 31.2
24 Sa	20 4 16	0♌28 4	19 11 15	25 20 27	14 30.4	26 52.4	20 55.3	20 55.5	26D 35.9	3 46.6	10 0.5	0 24.3	27 32.6
25 Su	20 8 12	1 25 23	1♍26 36	7♍29 59	14 31.0	28 3.7	22 9.0	20 45.7	26 35.8	3 51.9	10 2.4	0 23.7	27 34.0
26 M	20 12 9	2 22 43	13 30 56	19 29 50	14 31.9	29 12.6	23 22.7	20 35.3	26 35.9	3 57.2	10 4.3	0 23.1	27 35.4
27 Tu	20 16 6	3 20 3	25 27 7	1♎23 15	14 33.0	0♍18.9	24 36.4	20 24.2	26 36.3	4 2.4	10 6.3	0 22.6	27 36.9
28 W	20 20 2	4 17 23	7♎18 44	13 14 4	14 34.1	1 22.7	25 50.2	20 12.6	26 36.7	4 7.6	10 8.3	0 22.1	27 38.4
29 Th	20 23 59	5 14 44	19 9 49	25 6 33	14 34.8	2 23.7	27 4.0	20 0.4	26 37.4	4 12.6	10 10.4	0 21.6	27 39.9
30 F	20 27 55	6 12 6	1♏ 4 50	7♏ 5 16	14R 35.2	3 21.8	28 17.8	19 47.7	26 38.3	4 17.6	10 12.5	0 21.2	27 41.5
31 Sa	20 31 52	7 9 28	13 8 24	19 14 49	14 35.2	4 17.1	29 31.6	19 34.6	26 39.3	4 22.5	10 14.6	0 20.8	27 43.0

AUGUST 1971 — LONGITUDE

Day	Sid.Time	☉	0 hr ☽	Noon ☽	True ☊	☿	♀	♂	♃	♄	♅	♆	♇
1 Su	20 35 48	8♌ 6 50	25♏25 2	1♐39 34	14♒34.8	5♍ 9.2	0♌45.4	19♒21.0	26♏40.6	4♊27.3	10♎16.8	0♐20.4	27♍44.6
2 M	20 39 45	9 4 14	7♐58 53	14 23 22	14R 34.3	5 58.1	1 59.2	19R 6.9	26 42.0	4 32.1	10 19.1	0R20.0	27 46.2
3 Tu	20 43 41	10 1 38	20 53 21	27 29 4	14 33.8	6 43.6	3 13.1	18 52.6	26 43.6	4 36.8	10 21.3	0 19.7	27 47.9
4 W	20 47 38	10 59 2	4♑10 39	10♑58 8	14 33.3	7 25.6	4 27.0	18 37.9	26 45.3	4 41.4	10 23.7	0 19.4	27 49.5
5 Th	20 51 35	11 56 28	17 51 26	24 50 20	14 33.0	8 3.9	5 40.9	18 22.9	26 47.3	4 45.9	10 26.0	0 19.2	27 51.2
6 F	20 55 31	12 53 54	1♒54 28	9♒ 3 23	14D 32.9	8 38.3	6 54.8	18 7.6	26 49.4	4 50.3	10 28.4	0 18.9	27 52.9
7 Sa	20 59 28	13 51 21	16 16 30	23 33 7	14R 32.8	9 8.5	8 8.8	17 52.1	26 51.7	4 54.7	10 30.9	0 18.8	27 54.6
8 Su	21 3 24	14 48 49	0♓52 29	8♓13 44	14 32.8	9 34.5	9 22.7	17 36.5	26 54.2	4 58.9	10 33.4	0 18.6	27 56.4
9 M	21 7 21	15 46 18	15 36 3	22 58 34	14 32.8	9 56.0	10 36.7	17 20.7	26 56.8	5 3.1	10 35.9	0 18.5	27 58.1
10 Tu	21 11 17	16 43 48	0♈20 26	7♈40 52	14 32.6	10 12.8	11 50.7	17 4.9	26 59.6	5 7.2	10 38.4	0 18.4	27 59.9
11 W	21 15 14	17 41 20	14 59 10	22 14 42	14 32.3	10 24.8	13 4.8	16 48.9	27 2.6	5 11.2	10 41.0	0 18.3	28 1.7
12 Th	21 19 10	18 38 53	29 26 58	6♉35 31	14 32.0	10R 31.6	14 18.8	16 33.0	27 5.8	5 15.2	10 43.7	0D 18.2	28 3.6
13 F	21 23 7	19 36 28	13♉40 3	20 40 22	14D 31.9	10 33.2	15 32.9	16 17.2	27 9.1	5 19.0	10 46.4	0 18.2	28 5.4
14 Sa	21 27 4	20 34 4	27 36 19	4♊27 53	14 31.9	10 29.4	16 47.0	16 1.4	27 12.6	5 22.7	10 49.1	0 18.3	28 7.3
15 Su	21 31 0	21 31 42	11♊15 3	17 57 55	14 32.2	10 20.1	18 1.1	15 45.7	27 16.3	5 26.4	10 51.8	0 18.3	28 9.2
16 M	21 34 57	22 29 21	24 36 35	1♋11 11	14 32.8	10 5.3	19 15.3	15 30.3	27 20.1	5 30.0	10 54.6	0 18.4	28 11.1
17 Tu	21 38 53	23 27 2	7♋41 55	14 8 55	14 33.6	9 44.8	20 29.4	15 15.1	27 24.2	5 33.4	10 57.4	0 18.6	28 13.0
18 W	21 42 50	24 24 44	20 32 23	26 52 30	14 34.4	9 18.9	21 43.6	15 0.1	27 28.3	5 36.8	11 0.3	0 18.7	28 14.9
19 Th	21 46 46	25 22 27	3♌ 9 26	9♌23 23	14R 35.0	8 47.6	22 57.8	14 45.5	27 32.7	5 40.1	11 3.2	0 18.9	28 16.9
20 F	21 50 43	26 20 13	15 34 32	21 43 2	14 35.3	8 11.3	24 12.1	14 31.2	27 37.2	5 43.3	11 6.1	0 19.1	28 18.8
21 Sa	21 54 39	27 17 59	27 49 6	3♍52 55	14 34.9	7 30.3	25 26.3	14 17.4	27 41.9	5 46.4	11 9.1	0 19.4	28 20.8
22 Su	21 58 36	28 15 47	9♍54 42	15 54 40	14 33.8	6 45.1	26 40.6	14 4.0	27 46.7	5 49.4	11 12.1	0 19.7	28 22.8
23 M	22 2 33	29 13 36	21 53 3	27 50 8	14 32.1	5 56.4	27 54.9	13 51.1	27 51.7	5 52.3	11 15.1	0 20.0	28 24.8
24 Tu	22 6 29	0♍11 26	3♎46 12	9♎41 35	14 29.9	5 4.9	29 9.2	13 38.7	27 56.8	5 55.1	11 18.1	0 20.3	28 26.9
25 W	22 10 26	1 9 18	15 36 37	21 31 42	14 27.3	4 11.5	0♍23.5	13 26.9	28 2.1	5 57.8	11 21.2	0 20.7	28 28.9
26 Th	22 14 22	2 7 11	27 27 15	3♏23 43	14 24.8	3 17.3	1 37.8	13 15.7	28 7.6	6 0.4	11 24.3	0 21.1	28 31.0
27 F	22 18 19	3 5 6	9♏21 35	15 21 20	14 22.7	2 23.3	2 52.2	13 5.1	28 13.2	6 2.9	11 27.5	0 21.6	28 33.0
28 Sa	22 22 15	4 3 1	21 23 30	27 28 39	14 21.3	1 30.6	4 6.5	12 55.1	28 19.0	6 5.3	11 30.7	0 22.1	28 35.1
29 Su	22 26 12	5 0 58	3♐37 18	9♐50 2	14D 20.7	0 40.4	5 20.9	12 45.9	28 24.9	6 7.6	11 33.9	0 22.6	28 37.2
30 M	22 30 8	5 58 57	16 7 22	22 29 49	14 21.0	29♌53.8	6 35.3	12 37.4	28 31.0	6 9.8	11 37.1	0 23.1	28 39.3
31 Tu	22 34 5	6 56 57	28 57 52	5♑31 57	14 22.1	29 11.9	7 49.7	12 29.5	28 37.2	6 11.9	11 40.3	0 23.7	28 41.5

Astro Data (Dy Hr Mn)

	Dy Hr Mn
♃✶♇	5 2:33
♂ R	11 6:30
☽0N	13 4:02
♃ D	24 19:09
☽0S	26 18:00
☽0N	9 11:10
☿ R	12 19:13
♆ D	12 15:14
☽0S	23 1:14

Planet Ingress (Dy Hr Mn)

	Dy Hr Mn
☿ ♌	6 8:53
♀ ♋	6 22:02
☉ ♌	23 12:15
☿ ♍	26 17:03
♀ ♌	31 9:15
☉ ♍	23 19:15
♀ ♍	24 16:25
☿ ♌	29 20:41

Last Aspect / ☽ Ingress (July)

Last Aspect Dy Hr Mn		☽ Ingress Dy Hr Mn
2 2:00	♀ △	♏ 2 13:46
4 18:40	♃ ☌	♐ 4 23:59
7 2:04	♇ □	♑ 7 7:03
9 6:43	♇ △	♒ 9 11:26
11 8:59	♃ □	♓ 11 14:14
13 12:02	♇ ☍	♈ 13 16:32
15 5:47	☉ □	♉ 15 19:10
17 18:16	♇ △	♊ 17 22:47
19 23:21	♇ □	♋ 20 3:56
22 9:15	☉ ☌	♌ 22 11:16
24 16:38	☿ ☌	♍ 24 21:09
27 4:23	♇ ☌	♎ 27 9:12
29 17:46	♀ □	♏ 29 21:50

Last Aspect / ☽ Ingress (August)

Last Aspect Dy Hr Mn		☽ Ingress Dy Hr Mn
1 4:30	♇ ✶	♐ 1 8:49
3 12:35	♇ □	♑ 3 16:32
5 17:10	♇ △	♒ 5 20:47
7 17:29	♃ □	♓ 7 22:34
9 20:10	♇ ☍	♈ 9 23:27
11 4:46	☉ △	♉ 12 0:55
14 0:54	♇ △	♊ 14 4:10
16 6:31	♇ □	♋ 16 9:50
18 14:39	♇ ✶	♌ 18 17:57
20 23:46	♃ □	♍ 21 4:19
23 13:12	♇ ☌	♎ 23 16:22
24 19:41	♂ △	♏ 26 5:09
28 14:13	♇ ✶	♐ 28 16:56
31 0:25	☿ △	♑ 31 1:54

☽ Phases & Eclipses (Dy Hr Mn)

Dy Hr Mn	
8 10:37	○ 15♑38
15 5:47	☽ 22♈06
22 9:15	● 28♋56
22 9:31:08	● P 0.069
30 11:07	☽ 6♏39
6 19:42	○ 13♒41
6 19:43	● T 1.728
13 10:55	☽ 20♉03
20 22:53	● 27♌15
20 22:38:50	● P 0.508
29 2:56	☽ 5♐08

Astro Data

1 JULY 1971
Julian Day # 26114
Delta T 41.7 sec
SVP 05♓39'16"
Obliquity 23°26'41"
⚷ Chiron 13♈44.4
☽ Mean ☊ 16♒22.5

1 AUGUST 1971
Julian Day # 26145
Delta T 41.8 sec
SVP 05♓39'11"
Obliquity 23°26'41"
⚷ Chiron 13♈46.1R
☽ Mean ☊ 14♒44.0

LONGITUDE — SEPTEMBER 1971

Day	Sid.Time	☉	0 hr ☽	Noon ☽	True ☊	☿	♀	♂	♃	♄	♅	♆	♇
1 W	22 38 2	7♍54 58	12♑12 23	18♑59 26	14♒23.6	28♌35.6	9♍ 4.1	12♒22.4	28♏43.6	6♊13.9	11♎43.6	0♐24.3	28♍43.6
2 Th	22 41 58	8 53 0	25 53 14	2♒53 45	14 25.0	28R 5.8	10 18.5	12R16.1	28 50.1	6 15.8	11 46.9	0 25.0	28 45.7
3 F	22 45 55	9 51 4	10♒ 0 50	17 14 9	14R25.8	27 43.2	11 33.0	12 10.6	28 56.7	6 17.6	11 50.3	0 25.7	28 47.9
4 Sa	22 49 51	10 49 10	24 33 11	1♓57 13	14 25.5	27 28.5	12 47.4	12 5.8	29 3.5	6 19.3	11 53.6	0 26.4	28 50.1
5 Su	22 53 48	11 47 17	9♓25 25	16 56 44	14 24.0	27D 22.1	14 1.9	12 1.7	29 10.5	6 20.9	11 57.0	0 27.1	28 52.2
6 M	22 57 44	12 45 25	24 30 4	2♈ 4 12	14 21.2	27 24.2	15 16.3	11 58.5	29 17.5	6 22.3	12 0.4	0 27.9	28 54.4
7 Tu	23 1 41	13 43 35	9♈37 55	17 10 1	14 17.4	27 35.2	16 30.8	11 56.1	29 24.7	6 23.7	12 3.8	0 28.7	28 56.6
8 W	23 5 37	14 41 48	24 39 23	2♉ 5 1	14 13.2	27 54.9	17 45.3	11 54.4	29 32.1	6 25.0	12 7.3	0 29.5	28 58.8
9 Th	23 9 34	15 40 2	9♉26 4	16 41 50	14 9.2	28 23.4	18 59.8	11D 53.5	29 39.6	6 26.1	12 10.8	0 30.4	29 1.0
10 F	23 13 31	16 38 18	23 51 50	0♊55 45	14 6.2	29 0.5	20 14.4	11 53.5	29 47.2	6 27.2	12 14.3	0 31.2	29 3.2
11 Sa	23 17 27	17 36 37	7♊53 25	14 44 52	14D 4.4	29 45.8	21 28.9	11 54.2	29 54.9	6 28.1	12 17.8	0 32.2	29 5.4
12 Su	23 21 24	18 34 58	21 30 13	28 9 41	14 4.0	0♍39.1	22 43.5	11 55.8	0♐ 2.8	6 28.9	12 21.3	0 33.1	29 7.6
13 M	23 25 20	19 33 21	4♋43 36	11♋12 20	14 4.8	1 39.8	23 58.1	11 58.1	0 10.8	6 29.7	12 24.9	0 34.1	29 9.9
14 Tu	23 29 17	20 31 46	17 36 18	23 55 56	14 6.3	2 47.5	25 12.7	12 1.2	0 18.9	6 30.3	12 28.4	0 35.1	29 12.1
15 W	23 33 13	21 30 13	0♌11 39	6♌23 53	14 7.8	4 1.7	26 27.3	12 5.2	0 27.2	6 30.8	12 32.0	0 36.2	29 14.4
16 Th	23 37 10	22 28 42	12 33 3	18 39 31	14R 8.6	5 21.8	27 41.9	12 9.9	0 35.6	6 31.2	12 35.6	0 37.2	29 16.6
17 F	23 41 6	23 27 13	24 43 39	0♍45 48	14 8.0	6 47.1	28 56.5	12 15.4	0 44.1	6 31.5	12 39.2	0 38.3	29 18.9
18 Sa	23 45 3	24 25 46	6♍46 14	12 45 15	14 5.6	8 17.1	0♎11.1	12 21.7	0 52.7	6 31.6	12 42.9	0 39.5	29 21.1
19 Su	23 48 59	25 24 21	18 43 5	24 39 58	14 1.1	9 51.2	1 25.8	12 28.8	1 1.4	6R31.7	12 46.5	0 40.6	29 23.4
20 M	23 52 56	26 22 58	0♎36 7	6♎31 45	13 54.8	11 28.8	2 40.4	12 36.6	1 10.3	6 31.7	12 50.2	0 41.8	29 25.6
21 Tu	23 56 53	27 21 37	12 27 5	18 22 19	13 47.0	13 9.4	3 55.1	12 45.3	1 19.3	6 31.5	12 53.9	0 43.0	29 27.9
22 W	0 0 49	28 20 18	24 17 41	0♏13 26	13 38.4	14 52.4	5 9.7	12 54.6	1 28.4	6 31.3	12 57.5	0 44.3	29 30.1
23 Th	0 4 46	29 19 1	6♏ 9 50	12 7 12	13 29.8	16 37.4	6 24.4	13 4.8	1 37.6	6 30.9	13 1.2	0 45.6	29 32.4
24 F	0 8 42	0♎17 45	18 5 51	24 6 9	13 22.0	18 24.0	7 39.1	13 15.6	1 46.9	6 30.4	13 4.9	0 46.9	29 34.7
25 Sa	0 12 39	1 16 32	0♐ 8 31	6♐13 23	13 15.8	20 11.7	8 53.8	13 27.2	1 56.3	6 29.8	13 8.7	0 48.2	29 36.9
26 Su	0 16 35	2 15 20	12 21 12	18 32 31	13 11.6	22 0.3	10 8.5	13 39.5	2 5.9	6 29.1	13 12.4	0 49.5	29 39.2
27 M	0 20 32	3 14 10	24 47 48	1♑ 7 36	13D 9.5	23 49.4	11 23.2	13 52.5	2 15.5	6 28.3	13 16.1	0 50.9	29 41.4
28 Tu	0 24 28	4 13 2	7♑32 28	14 2 53	13 9.1	25 38.8	12 37.9	14 6.2	2 25.3	6 27.4	13 19.9	0 52.3	29 43.7
29 W	0 28 25	5 11 55	20 39 20	27 22 14	13 9.9	27 28.3	13 52.6	14 20.6	2 35.1	6 26.4	13 23.6	0 53.8	29 46.0
30 Th	0 32 22	6 10 50	4♒11 57	11♒ 8 40	13R10.9	29 17.6	15 7.3	14 35.6	2 45.1	6 25.2	13 27.4	0 55.2	29 48.2

LONGITUDE — OCTOBER 1971

Day	Sid.Time	☉	0 hr ☽	Noon ☽	True ☊	☿	♀	♂	♃	♄	♅	♆	♇
1 F	0 36 18	7♎ 9 47	18♒12 28	25♒23 18	13♒11.1	1♎ 6.7	16♎22.0	14♒51.3	2♐55.1	6♊24.0	13♎31.2	0♐56.7	29♍50.5
2 Sa	0 40 15	8 8 46	2♓40 52	10♓ 4 39	13R 9.5	2 55.5	17 36.7	15 7.6	3 5.3	6R22.7	13 34.9	0 58.2	29 52.7
3 Su	0 44 11	9 7 46	17 33 58	25 7 52	13 5.7	4 43.7	18 51.4	15 24.5	3 15.5	6 21.2	13 38.7	0 59.8	29 55.0
4 M	0 48 8	10 6 48	2♈45 13	10♈24 42	12 59.5	6 31.4	20 6.1	15 42.1	3 25.9	6 19.7	13 42.5	1 1.3	29 57.2
5 Tu	0 52 4	11 5 52	18 4 57	25 44 29	12 51.5	8 18.4	21 20.9	16 0.2	3 36.3	6 18.0	13 46.3	1 2.9	29 59.4
6 W	0 56 1	12 4 59	3♉21 52	10♉55 46	12 42.5	10 4.8	22 35.6	16 18.8	3 46.8	6 16.2	13 50.1	1 4.5	0♎ 1.6
7 Th	0 59 57	13 4 7	18 24 59	25 48 31	12 33.7	11 50.5	23 50.3	16 38.1	3 57.5	6 14.4	13 53.9	1 6.2	0 3.9
8 F	1 3 54	14 3 18	3♊ 5 35	10♊15 39	12 26.2	13 35.5	25 5.0	16 57.9	4 8.2	6 12.4	13 57.6	1 7.8	0 6.1
9 Sa	1 7 51	15 2 32	17 18 22	24 13 40	12 20.8	15 19.8	26 19.8	17 18.2	4 19.0	6 10.3	14 1.4	1 9.5	0 8.3
10 Su	1 11 47	16 1 47	1♋ 1 36	7♋42 26	12 17.7	17 3.3	27 34.5	17 39.0	4 29.9	6 8.2	14 5.2	1 11.2	0 10.5
11 M	1 15 44	17 1 5	14 16 33	20 44 23	12D 16.6	18 46.0	28 49.3	18 0.4	4 40.9	6 5.9	14 9.0	1 12.9	0 12.7
12 Tu	1 19 40	18 0 25	27 6 30	3♌23 28	12 16.8	20 28.1	0♏ 4.0	18 22.2	4 51.9	6 3.5	14 12.8	1 14.7	0 14.9
13 W	1 23 37	18 59 48	9♌35 52	15 44 20	12R 17.3	22 9.3	1 18.8	18 44.6	5 3.1	6 1.1	14 16.6	1 16.4	0 17.0
14 Th	1 27 33	19 59 13	21 49 26	27 51 44	12 16.9	23 49.9	2 33.5	19 7.4	5 14.3	5 58.5	14 20.4	1 18.2	0 19.2
15 F	1 31 30	20 58 40	3♍51 45	9♍50 0	12 14.7	25 29.7	3 48.3	19 30.7	5 25.6	5 55.9	14 24.1	1 20.0	0 21.4
16 Sa	1 35 26	21 58 9	15 46 54	21 42 53	12 9.8	27 8.9	5 3.1	19 54.5	5 37.0	5 53.1	14 27.9	1 21.9	0 23.5
17 Su	1 39 23	22 57 40	27 38 17	3♎33 24	12 2.1	28 47.3	6 17.8	20 18.7	5 48.5	5 50.3	14 31.7	1 23.7	0 25.6
18 M	1 43 20	23 57 14	9♎28 31	15 23 53	11 51.7	0♏25.1	7 32.6	20 43.4	6 0.0	5 47.3	14 35.4	1 25.6	0 27.8
19 Tu	1 47 16	24 56 50	21 19 40	27 16 4	11 39.0	2 2.3	8 47.4	21 8.5	6 11.6	5 44.3	14 39.2	1 27.5	0 29.9
20 W	1 51 13	25 56 27	3♏13 15	9♏11 21	11 25.1	3 38.8	10 2.2	21 34.0	6 23.3	5 41.2	14 42.9	1 29.4	0 32.0
21 Th	1 55 9	26 56 7	15 10 33	21 10 11	11 11.2	5 14.7	11 17.0	21 60.0	6 35.1	5 38.0	14 46.6	1 31.3	0 34.0
22 F	1 59 6	27 55 49	27 12 53	3♐16 25	10 58.3	6 50.0	12 31.7	22 26.3	6 46.9	5 34.7	14 50.4	1 33.2	0 36.1
23 Sa	2 3 2	28 55 33	9♐21 50	15 29 25	10 47.4	8 24.7	13 46.5	22 53.1	6 58.8	5 31.3	14 54.1	1 35.2	0 38.2
24 Su	2 6 59	29 55 18	21 39 28	27 52 21	10 39.3	9 58.8	15 1.3	23 20.2	7 10.8	5 27.8	14 57.8	1 37.2	0 40.2
25 M	2 10 55	0♏55 5	4♑ 8 28	10♑28 13	10 34.2	11 32.4	16 16.1	23 47.8	7 22.8	5 24.3	15 1.5	1 39.2	0 42.2
26 Tu	2 14 52	1 54 54	16 52 4	23 20 29	10 31.7	13 5.4	17 30.9	24 15.6	7 34.9	5 20.7	15 5.1	1 41.2	0 44.3
27 W	2 18 49	2 54 45	29 53 55	6♒32 50	10 31.0	14 37.9	18 45.6	24 43.9	7 47.1	5 17.0	15 8.8	1 43.2	0 46.3
28 Th	2 22 45	3 54 37	13♒17 37	20 8 38	10 31.0	16 9.9	20 0.4	25 12.5	7 59.3	5 13.2	15 12.5	1 45.2	0 48.2
29 F	2 26 42	4 54 31	27 6 6	4♓10 9	10 30.4	17 41.4	21 15.2	25 41.4	8 11.6	5 9.4	15 16.1	1 47.3	0 50.2
30 Sa	2 30 38	5 54 27	11♓20 44	18 37 39	10 27.9	19 12.3	22 29.9	26 10.6	8 24.0	5 5.5	15 19.7	1 49.3	0 52.1
31 Su	2 34 35	6 54 24	26 0 25	3♈28 26	10 22.9	20 42.8	23 44.7	26 40.2	8 36.4	5 1.5	15 23.3	1 51.4	0 54.1

Astro Data	Dy Hr Mn
♃✶♇	1 0:06
☽0N	5 20:52
☿ D	5 6:02
♂ D	9 13:51
♃☌♆	16 5:29
☽0S	19 7:45
♄ R	19 2:17
♀0S	20 5:56
☿0S	2 10:59
☽0N	3 7:51
☽0S	16 13:28
♃☍♄	17 2:58
☽0N	30 17:53

Planet Ingress	Dy Hr Mn
☿ ♍	11 6:45
♃ ♐	11 15:33
♀ ♎	17 20:25
☉ ♎	23 16:45
☿ ♎	30 9:19
♇ ♎	5 6:17
♀ ♏	11 22:43
☿ ♏	17 17:49
☉ ♏	24 1:53

Last Aspect Dy Hr Mn		☽ Ingress Dy Hr Mn
2 5:07	♃ ✶	♒ 2 7:04
4 7:23	♃ □	♓ 4 8:51
6 7:39	♃ △	♈ 6 8:43
8 5:24	☿ △	♉ 8 8:37
10 10:08	♃ ☍	♊ 10 10:25
12 13:48	♇ □	♋ 12 15:21
14 22:09	♇ ✶	♌ 14 23:38
16 0:05	♅ ✶	♍ 17 10:29
19 21:37	♇ ☌	♎ 19 22:47
21 0:55	♅ ☌	♏ 22 11:33
24 22:57	♇ ✶	♐ 24 23:43
27 9:19	♇ □	♑ 27 9:53
29 16:17	♇ △	♒ 29 16:39

Last Aspect Dy Hr Mn		☽ Ingress Dy Hr Mn
30 20:35	♀ △	♓ 1 19:37
3 19:35	♇ ☍	♈ 3 19:40
5 5:34	♀ ☍	♉ 5 18:42
6 21:04	♂ □	♊ 7 18:53
9 17:16	♀ △	♋ 9 22:10
11 9:35	☿ □	♌ 12 5:30
14 4:37	☿ ✶	♍ 14 16:16
15 4:08	♄ □	♎ 17 4:47
19 7:59	☉ ☌	♏ 19 17:31
21 14:09	♂ □	♐ 22 5:31
24 3:23	♂ ✶	♑ 24 16:05
26 1:20	♀ ✶	♒ 27 0:11
28 21:30	♂ ☌	♓ 29 4:57
30 20:00	♀ △	♈ 31 6:26

☽ Phases & Eclipses Dy Hr Mn	
5 4:02	○ 11♓57
11 18:23	☽ 18♊21
19 14:42	● 26♍00
27 17:17	☽ 3♑57
4 12:19	○ 10♈37
11 5:29	☽ 17♋15
19 7:59	● 25♎17
27 5:54	☽ 3♒09

Astro Data

1 SEPTEMBER 1971
Julian Day # 26176
Delta T 41.9 sec
SVP 05♓39'06"
Obliquity 23°26'41"
⚷ Chiron 13♈00.9R
☽ Mean ☊ 13♒05.6

1 OCTOBER 1971
Julian Day # 26206
Delta T 42.0 sec
SVP 05♓39'03"
Obliquity 23°26'41"
⚷ Chiron 11♈46.8R
☽ Mean ☊ 11♒30.2

NOVEMBER 1971 LONGITUDE

Day	Sid.Time	☉	0 hr ☽	Noon ☽	True ☊	☿	♀	♂	♃	♄	♅	♆	♇
1 M	2 38 31	7♏54 23	11♈ 0 46	18♈36 23	10♒15.1	22♏12.7	24♏59.4	27♒10.0	8♐48.8	4♊57.5	15♎26.9	1♐53.5	0♎56.0
2 Tu	2 42 28	8 54 23	26 13 59	3♉52 13	10R 4.9	23 42.1	26 14.2	27 40.2	9 1.3	4R53.3	15 30.5	1 55.6	0 57.9
3 W	2 46 24	9 54 26	11♉29 38	19 4 49	9 53.4	25 11.1	27 28.9	28 10.6	9 13.9	4 49.2	15 34.0	1 57.7	0 59.7
4 Th	2 50 21	10 54 30	26 36 25	4♊ 3 12	9 41.9	26 39.5	28 43.7	28 41.4	9 26.5	4 44.9	15 37.5	1 59.9	1 1.6
5 F	2 54 18	11 54 36	11♊24 11	18 38 33	9 31.8	28 7.4	29 58.4	29 12.3	9 39.2	4 40.7	15 41.0	2 2.0	1 3.4
6 Sa	2 58 14	12 54 45	25 45 44	2♋45 25	9 24.1	29 34.7	1♐13.2	29 43.6	9 51.9	4 36.3	15 44.5	2 4.2	1 5.2
7 Su	3 2 11	13 54 55	9♋37 29	16 22 1	9 19.1	1♐ 1.5	2 27.9	0♓15.1	10 4.6	4 31.9	15 48.0	2 6.3	1 7.0
8 M	3 6 7	14 55 7	22 59 18	29 29 42	9 16.6	2 27.6	3 42.7	0 46.9	10 17.4	4 27.5	15 51.4	2 8.5	1 8.8
9 Tu	3 10 4	15 55 22	5♌53 44	12♌11 58	9 15.9	3 53.1	4 57.4	1 18.9	10 30.3	4 23.0	15 54.9	2 10.7	1 10.5
10 W	3 14 0	16 55 38	18 25 3	24 33 37	9 15.9	5 18.0	6 12.1	1 51.1	10 43.2	4 18.4	15 58.3	2 12.9	1 12.3
11 Th	3 17 57	17 55 57	0♍38 21	6♍39 55	9 15.4	6 42.1	7 26.9	2 23.6	10 56.1	4 13.8	16 1.6	2 15.1	1 14.0
12 F	3 21 53	18 56 17	12 38 58	18 36 6	9 13.2	8 5.4	8 41.6	2 56.3	11 9.1	4 9.2	16 5.0	2 17.3	1 15.7
13 Sa	3 25 50	19 56 39	24 31 54	0♎26 54	9 8.6	9 27.8	9 56.3	3 29.2	11 22.1	4 4.5	16 8.3	2 19.5	1 17.3
14 Su	3 29 47	20 57 3	6♎21 36	12 16 26	9 1.1	10 49.2	11 11.1	4 2.4	11 35.2	3 59.8	16 11.6	2 21.7	1 18.9
15 M	3 33 43	21 57 29	18 11 47	24 7 58	8 50.7	12 9.6	12 25.8	4 35.7	11 48.3	3 55.1	16 14.9	2 23.9	1 20.6
16 Tu	3 37 40	22 57 57	0♏ 5 17	6♏ 3 58	8 38.1	13 28.8	13 40.6	5 9.3	12 1.4	3 50.3	16 18.1	2 26.1	1 22.1
17 W	3 41 36	23 58 27	12 4 11	18 6 5	8 24.2	14 46.6	14 55.3	5 43.1	12 14.6	3 45.5	16 21.3	2 28.4	1 23.7
18 Th	3 45 33	24 58 58	24 9 49	0♐15 27	8 10.1	16 2.9	16 10.0	6 17.1	12 27.8	3 40.7	16 24.5	2 30.6	1 25.2
19 F	3 49 29	25 59 31	6♐23 5	12 32 48	7 57.1	17 17.5	17 24.7	6 51.3	12 41.0	3 35.8	16 27.6	2 32.9	1 26.7
20 Sa	3 53 26	27 0 5	18 44 41	24 58 50	7 46.1	18 30.2	18 39.5	7 25.6	12 54.3	3 30.9	16 30.8	2 35.1	1 28.2
21 Su	3 57 22	28 0 41	1♑15 23	7♑34 28	7 37.8	19 40.7	19 54.2	8 0.2	13 7.6	3 26.1	16 33.9	2 37.4	1 29.7
22 M	4 1 19	29 1 18	13 56 17	20 21 4	7 32.6	20 48.7	21 8.9	8 34.9	13 20.9	3 21.2	16 36.9	2 39.6	1 31.1
23 Tu	4 5 16	0♐ 1 56	26 49 2	3♒20 29	7D 30.2	21 53.8	22 23.6	9 9.9	13 34.3	3 16.2	16 39.9	2 41.9	1 32.5
24 W	4 9 12	1 2 36	9♒55 43	16 35 1	7 29.7	22 55.8	23 38.3	9 44.9	13 47.6	3 11.3	16 42.9	2 44.1	1 33.9
25 Th	4 13 9	2 3 16	23 18 43	0♓ 7 3	7R 30.1	23 54.1	24 53.0	10 20.2	14 1.0	3 6.4	16 45.9	2 46.4	1 35.2
26 F	4 17 5	3 3 58	7♓ 0 15	13 58 28	7 30.3	24 48.2	26 7.7	10 55.6	14 14.5	3 1.5	16 48.8	2 48.7	1 36.5
27 Sa	4 21 2	4 4 41	21 1 45	28 10 2	7 29.0	25 37.6	27 22.3	11 31.1	14 27.9	2 56.5	16 51.7	2 50.9	1 37.8
28 Su	4 24 58	5 5 24	5♈23 5	12♈40 33	7 25.5	26 21.6	28 37.0	12 6.8	14 41.4	2 51.6	16 54.5	2 53.2	1 39.1
29 M	4 28 55	6 6 9	20 1 52	27 26 18	7 19.5	26 59.6	29 51.6	12 42.7	14 54.8	2 46.7	16 57.3	2 55.4	1 40.3
30 Tu	4 32 51	7 6 55	4♉52 59	12♉20 54	7 11.4	27 30.8	1♑ 6.3	13 18.6	15 8.3	2 41.8	17 0.1	2 57.7	1 41.5

DECEMBER 1971 LONGITUDE

Day	Sid.Time	☉	0 hr ☽	Noon ☽	True ☊	☿	♀	♂	♃	♄	♅	♆	♇
1 W	4 36 48	8♐ 7 42	19♉48 56	27♉15 57	7♒ 2.0	27♐54.4	2♑20.9	13♓54.7	15♐21.8	2♊36.9	17♎ 2.8	2♐59.9	1♎42.7
2 Th	4 40 45	9 8 30	4♊40 46	12♊ 2 17	6R52.5	28 9.6	3 35.5	14 31.0	15 35.3	2R32.0	17 5.5	3 2.2	1 43.8
3 F	4 44 41	10 9 19	19 19 31	26 31 35	6 44.1	28R15.5	4 50.1	15 7.3	15 48.9	2 27.2	17 8.2	3 4.4	1 44.9
4 Sa	4 48 38	11 10 9	3♋37 49	10♋37 41	6 37.6	28 11.5	6 4.7	15 43.8	16 2.4	2 22.3	17 10.8	3 6.7	1 46.0
5 Su	4 52 34	12 11 1	17 30 54	24 17 17	6 33.5	27 56.8	7 19.3	16 20.4	16 16.0	2 17.5	17 13.4	3 8.9	1 47.1
6 M	4 56 31	13 11 54	0♌56 55	7♌29 57	6D 31.7	27 30.9	8 33.9	16 57.1	16 29.5	2 12.7	17 15.9	3 11.2	1 48.1
7 Tu	5 0 27	14 12 48	13 56 43	20 17 38	6 31.8	26 53.8	9 48.4	17 33.9	16 43.1	2 7.9	17 18.4	3 13.4	1 49.1
8 W	5 4 24	15 13 43	26 33 13	2♍44 2	6 32.9	26 5.6	11 3.0	18 10.8	16 56.7	2 3.2	17 20.8	3 15.6	1 50.0
9 Th	5 8 20	16 14 40	8♍50 41	14 53 50	6R 34.0	25 7.0	12 17.5	18 47.8	17 10.3	1 58.5	17 23.3	3 17.8	1 51.0
10 F	5 12 17	17 15 37	20 54 7	26 52 11	6 34.2	23 59.2	13 32.1	19 24.9	17 23.9	1 53.8	17 25.6	3 20.1	1 51.9
11 Sa	5 16 14	18 16 36	2♎48 41	8♎44 15	6 32.8	22 44.0	14 46.6	20 2.1	17 37.4	1 49.2	17 27.9	3 22.3	1 52.7
12 Su	5 20 10	19 17 36	14 39 27	20 34 52	6 29.4	21 23.6	16 1.1	20 39.5	17 51.0	1 44.6	17 30.2	3 24.4	1 53.5
13 M	5 24 7	20 18 37	26 31 0	2♏28 20	6 23.8	20 0.8	17 15.6	21 16.9	18 4.6	1 40.1	17 32.4	3 26.6	1 54.3
14 Tu	5 28 3	21 19 40	8♏27 16	14 28 10	6 16.6	18 38.3	18 30.1	21 54.4	18 18.2	1 35.6	17 34.6	3 28.8	1 55.1
15 W	5 32 0	22 20 43	20 31 21	26 37 4	6 8.2	17 18.8	19 44.6	22 32.0	18 31.8	1 31.1	17 36.7	3 31.0	1 55.8
16 Th	5 35 56	23 21 47	2♐45 30	8♐56 49	5 59.6	16 4.9	20 59.0	23 9.7	18 45.4	1 26.7	17 38.8	3 33.1	1 56.5
17 F	5 39 53	24 22 52	15 11 5	21 28 23	5 51.6	14 58.8	22 13.5	23 47.5	18 59.0	1 22.4	17 40.9	3 35.3	1 57.2
18 Sa	5 43 50	25 23 57	27 48 44	4♑12 6	5 45.0	14 2.0	23 27.9	24 25.3	19 12.5	1 18.1	17 42.9	3 37.4	1 57.8
19 Su	5 47 46	26 25 4	10♑38 27	17 7 47	5 40.2	13 15.5	24 42.3	25 3.3	19 26.1	1 13.9	17 44.8	3 39.6	1 58.4
20 M	5 51 43	27 26 11	23 40 2	0♒15 10	5D 37.6	12 39.9	25 56.7	25 41.3	19 39.7	1 9.7	17 46.7	3 41.7	1 58.9
21 Tu	5 55 39	28 27 18	6♒53 9	13 33 59	5 36.9	12 15.3	27 11.1	26 19.4	19 53.2	1 5.6	17 48.5	3 43.8	1 59.5
22 W	5 59 36	29 28 25	20 17 40	27 4 12	5 37.7	12D 1.4	28 25.4	26 57.6	20 6.7	1 1.6	17 50.3	3 45.9	1 60.0
23 Th	6 3 32	0♑29 33	3♓53 37	10♓45 55	5 39.2	11 57.8	29 39.8	27 35.9	20 20.3	0 57.6	17 52.1	3 48.0	2 0.4
24 F	6 7 29	1 30 41	17 41 8	24 39 14	5 40.7	12 3.8	0♒54.1	28 14.2	20 33.8	0 53.7	17 53.8	3 50.0	2 0.8
25 Sa	6 11 25	2 31 49	1♈40 10	8♈43 49	5R 41.4	12 18.6	2 8.3	28 52.6	20 47.2	0 49.9	17 55.4	3 52.1	2 1.2
26 Su	6 15 22	3 32 57	15 50 1	22 58 31	5 40.7	12 41.5	3 22.6	29 31.0	21 0.7	0 46.2	17 57.0	3 54.1	2 1.6
27 M	6 19 19	4 34 5	0♉ 9 0	7♉21 1	5 38.6	13 11.6	4 36.8	0♈ 9.5	21 14.1	0 42.5	17 58.5	3 56.1	2 1.9
28 Tu	6 23 15	5 35 13	14 34 6	21 47 37	5 35.2	13 48.3	5 51.0	0 48.1	21 27.5	0 38.9	18 0.0	3 58.1	2 2.2
29 W	6 27 12	6 36 21	29 0 58	6♊13 25	5 30.9	14 30.9	7 5.2	1 26.7	21 40.9	0 35.4	18 1.4	4 0.1	2 2.4
30 Th	6 31 8	7 37 29	13♊24 16	20 32 47	5 26.5	15 18.7	8 19.3	2 5.4	21 54.3	0 32.0	18 2.8	4 2.1	2 2.6
31 F	6 35 5	8 38 37	27 38 17	4♋40 9	5 22.6	16 11.0	9 33.4	2 44.1	22 7.7	0 28.7	18 4.2	4 4.0	2 2.8

Astro Data	Dy Hr Mn
☽0S	12 19:00
☽0N	27 1:16
♄☍♆	27 18:50
☿ R	3 2:33
♄□♅	5 13:31
☽0S	10 1:21
♃✶♅	10 3:45
♄△♇	10 8:39
☿ D	22 20:47
☽0N	24 6:20
♂0N	27 16:45

Planet Ingress	Dy Hr Mn
♀ ♐	5 0:30
☿ ♐	6 6:59
♂ ♓	6 12:31
☉ ♐	22 23:14
♀ ♑	29 2:41
☉ ♑	22 12:24
♀ ♒	23 6:32
♂ ♈	26 18:04

Last Aspect Dy Hr Mn		☽ Ingress Dy Hr Mn
2 2:20	♂ ✶	♉ 2 5:55
4 3:43	♀ ☍	♊ 4 5:27
6 7:02	♂ △	♋ 6 7:15
7 11:02	♅ □	♌ 8 12:56
9 20:51	☉ □	♍ 10 22:44
12 13:51	☉ ✶	♎ 13 11:05
14 20:02	♅ ☌	♏ 15 23:49
18 1:46	☉ ☌	♐ 18 11:30
19 23:49	♀ ☌	♑ 20 21:36
22 5:02	♅ □	♒ 23 5:52
25 3:04	♀ ✶	♓ 25 11:48
27 11:41	♀ □	♈ 27 15:04
29 11:43	☿ △	♉ 29 16:08

Last Aspect Dy Hr Mn		☽ Ingress Dy Hr Mn
30 14:07	♂ ✶	♊ 1 16:25
3 14:53	☿ ☍	♋ 3 17:51
4 23:29	♅ □	♌ 5 22:17
7 23:10	☿ △	♍ 8 6:40
10 5:37	☿ □	♎ 10 18:19
12 12:14	☿ ✶	♏ 13 7:01
15 4:11	♂ △	♐ 15 18:37
17 19:03	☉ ☌	♑ 18 4:07
20 4:36	♀ ☌	♒ 20 11:32
21 23:40	♃ ✶	♓ 22 17:10
24 19:00	♃ ☌	♈ 24 21:09
26 8:51	♃ △	♉ 26 23:45
27 8:08	♀ □	♊ 29 1:38
30 14:31	♃ ☍	♋ 31 4:01

☽ Phases & Eclipses Dy Hr Mn		
2 21:19	○	9♉48
9 20:51	☽	16♌48
18 1:46	●	25♏03
25 16:37	☽	2♓45
2 7:48	○	9♊28
9 16:02	☽	16♍55
17 19:03	●	25♐11
25 1:35	☽	2♈36
31 20:20	○	9♋30

Astro Data

1 NOVEMBER 1971
Julian Day # 26237
Delta T 42.1 sec
SVP 05♓39'00"
Obliquity 23°26'41"
⚷ Chiron 10♈26.0R
☽ Mean ☊ 9♒51.7

1 DECEMBER 1971
Julian Day # 26267
Delta T 42.1 sec
SVP 05♓38'55"
Obliquity 23°26'40"
⚷ Chiron 9♈32.8R
☽ Mean ☊ 8♒16.4

LONGITUDE JANUARY 1972

Day	Sid.Time	☉	0 hr ☽	Noon ☽	True ☊	☿	♀	♂	♃	♄	♅	♆	♇
1 Sa	6 39 1	9♑39 46	11♋37 49	18♋30 49	5♒19.6	17♐ 7.5	10♒47.4	3♈22.8	22♐21.0	0♊25.5	18♎ 5.4	4♐ 5.9	2♎ 2.9
2 Su	6 42 58	10 40 54	25 18 48	2♌ 1 31	5D 18.0	18 7.7	12 1.5	4 1.6	22 34.3	0R 22.3	18 6.6	4 7.9	2 3.1
3 M	6 46 54	11 42 3	8♌38 52	15 10 49	5 17.7	19 11.0	13 15.5	4 40.5	22 47.5	0 19.2	18 7.8	4 9.8	2 3.1
4 Tu	6 50 51	12 43 11	21 37 30	27 59 5	5 18.5	20 17.2	14 29.4	5 19.3	23 0.8	0 16.2	18 8.9	4 11.6	2R 3.2
5 W	6 54 48	13 44 20	4♍15 52	10♍28 14	5 20.0	21 26.0	15 43.4	5 58.3	23 14.0	0 13.4	18 10.0	4 13.5	2 3.2
6 Th	6 58 44	14 45 29	16 36 38	22 41 31	5 21.7	22 37.0	16 57.2	6 37.2	23 27.1	0 10.6	18 11.0	4 15.3	2 3.1
7 F	7 2 41	15 46 38	28 43 28	4♎43 1	5 23.1	23 50.1	18 11.1	7 16.2	23 40.3	0 7.9	18 11.9	4 17.1	2 3.1
8 Sa	7 6 37	16 47 47	10♎40 46	16 37 20	5R 24.0	25 4.9	19 24.9	7 55.3	23 53.4	0 5.3	18 12.8	4 18.9	2 3.0
9 Su	7 10 34	17 48 56	22 33 19	28 29 20	5 24.1	26 21.4	20 38.7	8 34.3	24 6.4	0 2.8	18 13.6	4 20.7	2 2.8
10 M	7 14 30	18 50 6	4♏25 58	10♏23 48	5 23.3	27 39.4	21 52.4	9 13.4	24 19.5	0 0.4	18 14.4	4 22.5	2 2.7
11 Tu	7 18 27	19 51 15	16 23 23	22 25 13	5 21.8	28 58.7	23 6.1	9 52.6	24 32.4	29♉58.1	18 15.1	4 24.2	2 2.5
12 W	7 22 23	20 52 25	28 29 46	4♐37 29	5 19.8	0♑19.3	24 19.8	10 31.8	24 45.4	29 55.9	18 15.8	4 25.9	2 2.2
13 Th	7 26 20	21 53 34	10♐48 42	17 3 45	5 17.7	1 40.9	25 33.4	11 11.0	24 58.3	29 53.8	18 16.4	4 27.6	2 2.0
14 F	7 30 17	22 54 43	23 22 51	29 46 10	5 15.7	3 3.6	26 47.0	11 50.2	25 11.1	29 51.8	18 17.0	4 29.2	2 1.7
15 Sa	7 34 13	23 55 52	6♑13 49	12♑45 48	5 14.1	4 27.2	28 0.5	12 29.5	25 23.9	29 49.9	18 17.5	4 30.9	2 1.3
16 Su	7 38 10	24 57 1	19 22 4	26 2 30	5 13.2	5 51.8	29 14.0	13 8.8	25 36.7	29 48.1	18 17.9	4 32.5	2 1.0
17 M	7 42 6	25 58 9	2♒46 54	9♒35 2	5D 12.8	7 17.1	0♓27.5	13 48.1	25 49.4	29 46.5	18 18.3	4 34.1	2 0.6
18 Tu	7 46 3	26 59 17	16 26 36	23 21 17	5 12.9	8 43.3	1 40.8	14 27.5	26 2.1	29 44.9	18 18.6	4 35.6	2 0.1
19 W	7 49 59	28 0 24	0♓18 43	7♓18 31	5 13.4	10 10.2	2 54.2	15 6.9	26 14.7	29 43.4	18 18.9	4 37.2	1 59.7
20 Th	7 53 56	29 1 30	14 20 19	21 23 43	5 14.1	11 37.8	4 7.5	15 46.3	26 27.2	29 42.1	18 19.1	4 38.7	1 59.2
21 F	7 57 52	0♒ 2 35	28 28 22	5♈33 54	5 14.6	13 6.1	5 20.7	16 25.7	26 39.7	29 40.9	18 19.2	4 40.2	1 58.6
22 Sa	8 1 49	1 3 40	12♈39 58	19 46 15	5 15.0	14 35.1	6 33.8	17 5.2	26 52.1	29 39.7	18 19.3	4 41.6	1 58.0
23 Su	8 5 46	2 4 43	26 52 26	3♉58 16	5R 15.2	16 4.8	7 46.9	17 44.7	27 4.5	29 38.7	18R 19.4	4 43.0	1 57.4
24 M	8 9 42	3 5 45	11♉ 3 26	18 7 40	5 15.2	17 35.1	8 60.0	18 24.2	27 16.8	29 37.8	18 19.4	4 44.4	1 56.8
25 Tu	8 13 39	4 6 47	25 10 44	2♊12 21	5 15.1	19 6.0	10 12.9	19 3.7	27 29.1	29 37.1	18 19.3	4 45.8	1 56.2
26 W	8 17 35	5 7 47	9♊12 16	16 10 13	5D 15.0	20 37.6	11 25.8	19 43.2	27 41.3	29 36.4	18 19.2	4 47.2	1 55.5
27 Th	8 21 32	6 8 46	23 5 56	29 59 10	5 15.1	22 9.9	12 38.6	20 22.7	27 53.4	29 35.8	18 19.0	4 48.5	1 54.7
28 F	8 25 28	7 9 45	6♋49 39	13♋37 9	5 15.2	23 42.8	13 51.4	21 2.2	28 5.5	29 35.4	18 18.8	4 49.8	1 54.0
29 Sa	8 29 25	8 10 42	20 21 26	27 2 18	5 15.4	25 16.3	15 4.1	21 41.8	28 17.4	29 35.1	18 18.5	4 51.0	1 53.2
30 Su	8 33 22	9 11 38	3♌39 34	10♌13 7	5R 15.5	26 50.5	16 16.7	22 21.3	28 29.4	29 34.9	18 18.1	4 52.3	1 52.4
31 M	8 37 18	10 12 33	16 42 49	23 8 40	5 15.4	28 25.4	17 29.2	23 0.9	28 41.2	29D 34.7	18 17.7	4 53.5	1 51.6

LONGITUDE FEBRUARY 1972

Day	Sid.Time	☉	0 hr ☽	Noon ☽	True ☊	☿	♀	♂	♃	♄	♅	♆	♇
1 Tu	8 41 15	11♒13 27	29♌30 39	5♍48 51	5♒15.0	0♒ 0.9	18♓41.6	23♈40.5	28♐53.0	29♉34.8	18♎17.3	4♐54.6	1♎50.7
2 W	8 45 11	12 14 20	12♍ 3 22	18 14 24	5R 14.3	1 37.1	19 54.0	24 20.0	29 4.7	29 34.9	18R 16.7	4 55.8	1R 49.8
3 Th	8 49 8	13 15 12	24 22 11	0♎27 2	5 13.2	3 14.1	21 6.2	24 59.6	29 16.3	29 35.1	18 16.2	4 56.9	1 48.9
4 F	8 53 4	14 16 3	6♎29 16	12 29 19	5 12.0	4 51.7	22 18.4	25 39.2	29 27.9	29 35.5	18 15.5	4 58.0	1 47.9
5 Sa	8 57 1	15 16 53	18 27 37	24 24 40	5 10.7	6 30.1	23 30.5	26 18.8	29 39.4	29 35.9	18 14.9	4 59.0	1 46.9
6 Su	9 0 57	16 17 43	0♏20 57	6♏17 3	5 9.7	8 9.2	24 42.6	26 58.4	29 50.7	29 36.5	18 14.1	5 0.0	1 45.9
7 M	9 4 54	17 18 31	12 13 32	18 10 59	5D 9.1	9 49.1	25 54.5	27 38.0	0♑ 2.1	29 37.2	18 13.4	5 1.0	1 44.9
8 Tu	9 8 51	18 19 19	24 10 0	0♐11 11	5 9.2	11 29.7	27 6.3	28 17.6	0 13.3	29 38.0	18 12.5	5 2.0	1 43.8
9 W	9 12 47	19 20 5	6♐15 6	12 22 20	5 9.8	13 11.2	28 18.1	28 57.2	0 24.4	29 38.9	18 11.6	5 2.9	1 42.8
10 Th	9 16 44	20 20 51	18 33 25	24 48 51	5 10.9	14 53.4	29 29.8	29 36.8	0 35.5	29 39.9	18 10.7	5 3.8	1 41.6
11 F	9 20 40	21 21 35	1♑ 9 5	7♑34 29	5 12.3	16 36.5	0♈41.3	0♉16.4	0 46.5	29 41.1	18 9.7	5 4.7	1 40.5
12 Sa	9 24 37	22 22 19	14 5 21	20 41 53	5 13.7	18 20.4	1 52.8	0 56.0	0 57.4	29 42.3	18 8.7	5 5.5	1 39.4
13 Su	9 28 33	23 23 1	27 24 10	4♒12 12	5R 14.5	20 5.1	3 4.2	1 35.6	1 8.2	29 43.7	18 7.6	5 6.3	1 38.2
14 M	9 32 30	24 23 42	11♒ 5 49	18 4 44	5 14.6	21 50.6	4 15.4	2 15.3	1 18.9	29 45.2	18 6.4	5 7.1	1 37.0
15 Tu	9 36 26	25 24 22	25 8 33	2♓16 43	5 13.6	23 37.0	5 26.6	2 54.9	1 29.5	29 46.7	18 5.3	5 7.8	1 35.7
16 W	9 40 23	26 25 0	9♓28 35	16 43 27	5 11.6	25 24.3	6 37.6	3 34.5	1 40.0	29 48.4	18 4.0	5 8.5	1 34.5
17 Th	9 44 20	27 25 36	24 0 29	1♈18 51	5 8.7	27 12.3	7 48.6	4 14.1	1 50.4	29 50.2	18 2.7	5 9.1	1 33.2
18 F	9 48 16	28 26 11	8♈37 43	15 56 16	5 5.4	29 1.2	8 59.4	4 53.8	2 0.7	29 52.2	18 1.4	5 9.8	1 31.9
19 Sa	9 52 13	29 26 44	23 13 44	0♉29 25	5 2.2	0♓50.9	10 10.1	5 33.4	2 10.9	29 54.2	18 0.0	5 10.4	1 30.6
20 Su	9 56 9	0♓27 15	7♉42 44	14 53 12	4 59.6	2 41.3	11 20.7	6 13.0	2 21.0	29 56.3	17 58.6	5 10.9	1 29.3
21 M	10 0 6	1 27 45	22 0 26	29 4 8	4D 58.1	4 32.5	12 31.2	6 52.6	2 31.0	29 58.6	17 57.1	5 11.5	1 27.9
22 Tu	10 4 2	2 28 13	6♊ 4 10	13♊ 0 24	4 57.8	6 24.3	13 41.5	7 32.2	2 40.9	0♊ 0.9	17 55.6	5 12.0	1 26.5
23 W	10 7 59	3 28 38	19 52 51	26 41 31	4 58.7	8 16.7	14 51.7	8 11.8	2 50.7	0 3.4	17 54.0	5 12.4	1 25.1
24 Th	10 11 55	4 29 2	3♋26 31	10♋ 7 57	5 0.2	10 9.6	16 1.7	8 51.4	3 0.3	0 5.9	17 52.4	5 12.9	1 23.7
25 F	10 15 52	5 29 24	16 45 55	23 20 34	5 1.8	12 2.9	17 11.6	9 31.0	3 9.9	0 8.6	17 50.8	5 13.2	1 22.3
26 Sa	10 19 49	6 29 44	29 52 1	6♌20 23	5R 2.8	13 56.4	18 21.4	10 10.6	3 19.3	0 11.4	17 49.1	5 13.6	1 20.9
27 Su	10 23 45	7 30 2	12♌45 46	19 8 16	5 2.7	15 50.0	19 31.0	10 50.1	3 28.7	0 14.2	17 47.3	5 13.9	1 19.4
28 M	10 27 42	8 30 18	25 27 58	1♍44 55	5 0.9	17 43.5	20 40.5	11 29.7	3 37.9	0 17.2	17 45.6	5 14.2	1 17.9
29 Tu	10 31 38	9 30 32	7♍59 14	14 10 58	4 57.3	19 36.6	21 49.8	12 9.2	3 47.0	0 20.3	17 43.8	5 14.5	1 16.5

Astro Data Dy Hr Mn	Planet Ingress Dy Hr Mn	Last Aspect Dy Hr Mn	☽ Ingress Dy Hr Mn	Last Aspect Dy Hr Mn	☽ Ingress Dy Hr Mn	☽ Phases & Eclipses Dy Hr Mn	Astro Data
♇ R 4 14:44	♄ ♉ 10 3:43	1 11:17 ♅ □	♌ 2 8:22	1 0:08 ♄ □	♍ 1 0:56	8 13:31 ☽ 17♎22	1 JANUARY 1972
☽0S 6 9:07	☿ ♑ 11 18:18	4 2:39 ♃ △	♍ 4 15:50	3 10:18 ♄ △	♎ 3 11:06	16 10:52 ● 25♑25	Julian Day # 26298
☽0N 20 11:38	♀ ♓ 16 15:01	6 13:45 ♃ □	♎ 7 2:33	5 22:58 ♃ ✶	♏ 5 23:18	16 11:02:37 ✔ A 1'53"	Delta T 42.2 sec
♅ R 23 5:26	☉ ♒ 20 22:59	9 8:38 ☿ ✶	♏ 9 15:03	8 10:55 ♄ ☍	♐ 8 11:38	23 9:29 ☽ 2♉29	SVP 05♓38'49"
♄ D 31 10:22	☿ ♒ 31 23:46	12 2:49 ♄ ☍	♐ 12 2:57	10 3:45 ☉ ✶	♑ 10 21:50	30 10:58 ○ 9♌39	Obliquity 23°26'39"
		14 7:05 ♀ ✶	♑ 14 12:26	13 4:08 ♄ △	♒ 13 4:36	30 10:53 ☍ T 1.050	⚷ Chiron 9♈24.4
☽0S 2 17:46	♃ ♑ 6 19:36	16 18:40 ♄ △	♒ 16 19:04	15 7:49 ♄ □	♓ 15 8:11		☽ Mean ☊ 6♒38.0
♃⊼♄ 4 16:28	♀ ♈ 10 10:08	18 22:59 ♄ □	♓ 18 23:28	17 9:36 ♄ ✶	♈ 17 9:51	7 11:11 ☽ 17♏47	
♀0N 11 12:10	♂ ♉ 10 14:04	21 2:03 ♄ ✶	♈ 21 2:35	19 11:02 ☉ ✶	♉ 19 11:11	15 0:29 ● 25♒26	1 FEBRUARY 1972
♃□♇ 15 12:46	☿ ♓ 18 12:53	23 0:21 ♃ △	♉ 23 5:17	21 13:35 ♄ ☌	♊ 21 13:35	21 17:20 ☽ 2♊11	Julian Day # 26329
☽0N 16 19:27	☉ ♓ 19 13:11	25 7:34 ♄ ☌	♊ 25 8:14	22 20:32 ♅ △	♋ 23 17:52	29 3:12 ○ 9♍39	Delta T 42.3 sec
	♄ ♊ 21 14:52	27 8:28 ♃ ☍	♋ 27 12:01	25 1:58 ♅ □	♌ 26 0:15		SVP 05♓38'43"
		29 16:36 ♄ ✶	♌ 29 17:21	27 14:00 ♀ △	♍ 28 8:39		Obliquity 23°26'40"
							⚷ Chiron 10♈07.4
							☽ Mean ☊ 4♒59.5

MARCH 1972 — LONGITUDE

Day	Sid.Time	☉	0 hr ☽	Noon ☽	True ☊	☿	♀	♂	♃	♄	♅	♆	♇
1 W	10 35 35	10♓30 45	20♍20 13	26♍27 6	4♒52.1	21♓29.1	22♈58.9	12♉48.8	3♑56.0	0♊23.4	17♎41.9	5♐14.7	1♎15.0
2 Th	10 39 31	11 30 55	2♎31 44	8♎34 18	4R45.6	23 20.7	24 7.9	13 28.3	4 4.8	0 26.7	17R40.0	5 14.9	1R13.4
3 F	10 43 28	12 31 4	14 35 0	20 34 3	4 38.4	25 11.0	25 16.7	14 7.8	4 13.5	0 30.1	17 38.1	5 15.1	1 11.9
4 Sa	10 47 24	13 31 12	26 31 46	2♏28 27	4 31.2	26 59.6	26 25.4	14 47.3	4 22.2	0 33.5	17 36.1	5 15.2	1 10.4
5 Su	10 51 21	14 31 18	8♏24 30	14 20 19	4 24.9	28 46.1	27 33.9	15 26.8	4 30.6	0 37.1	17 34.1	5 15.3	1 8.8
6 M	10 55 17	15 31 22	20 16 23	26 13 11	4 20.0	0♈30.1	28 42.2	16 6.3	4 39.0	0 40.8	17 32.1	5 15.3	1 7.3
7 Tu	10 59 14	16 31 24	2♐11 16	8♐11 13	4 16.8	2 11.0	29 50.3	16 45.7	4 47.2	0 44.5	17 30.0	5R15.4	1 5.7
8 W	11 3 11	17 31 25	14 13 36	20 19 4	4D15.5	3 48.3	0♉58.2	17 25.2	4 55.3	0 48.4	17 27.9	5 15.3	1 4.1
9 Th	11 7 7	18 31 25	26 28 13	2♑41 40	4 15.8	5 21.4	2 6.0	18 4.6	5 3.3	0 52.3	17 25.8	5 15.3	1 2.5
10 F	11 11 4	19 31 22	9♑ 0 0	15 23 48	4 17.0	6 50.0	3 13.6	18 44.1	5 11.1	0 56.3	17 23.7	5 15.2	1 0.9
11 Sa	11 15 0	20 31 18	21 53 32	28 29 39	4R18.3	8 13.3	4 21.0	19 23.5	5 18.8	1 0.4	17 21.5	5 15.1	0 59.3
12 Su	11 18 57	21 31 13	5♒12 28	12♒ 2 11	4 18.9	9 31.0	5 28.1	20 2.9	5 26.4	1 4.7	17 19.2	5 15.0	0 57.7
13 M	11 22 53	22 31 5	18 58 50	26 2 19	4 17.9	10 42.5	6 35.1	20 42.3	5 33.8	1 9.0	17 17.0	5 14.8	0 56.1
14 Tu	11 26 50	23 30 56	3♓12 18	10♓28 18	4 14.8	11 47.3	7 41.9	21 21.7	5 41.1	1 13.4	17 14.7	5 14.6	0 54.4
15 W	11 30 46	24 30 45	17 49 37	25 15 20	4 9.4	12 45.1	8 48.5	22 1.1	5 48.2	1 17.8	17 12.4	5 14.3	0 52.8
16 Th	11 34 43	25 30 32	2♈44 24	10♈15 41	4 2.2	13 35.5	9 54.8	22 40.5	5 55.2	1 22.4	17 10.1	5 14.1	0 51.2
17 F	11 38 40	26 30 16	17 47 56	25 19 53	3 54.0	14 18.1	11 0.9	23 19.8	6 2.0	1 27.0	17 7.7	5 13.7	0 49.5
18 Sa	11 42 36	27 29 59	2♉50 19	10♉18 8	3 45.8	14 52.9	12 6.8	23 59.2	6 8.7	1 31.8	17 5.4	5 13.4	0 47.9
19 Su	11 46 33	28 29 40	17 42 21	25 2 8	3 38.7	15 19.5	13 12.4	24 38.5	6 15.3	1 36.6	17 3.0	5 13.0	0 46.2
20 M	11 50 29	29 29 18	2♊16 53	9♊26 8	3 33.5	15 38.0	14 17.8	25 17.8	6 21.6	1 41.5	17 0.6	5 12.6	0 44.6
21 Tu	11 54 26	0♈28 55	16 29 38	23 27 19	3 30.5	15R48.3	15 22.9	25 57.1	6 27.9	1 46.5	16 58.1	5 12.2	0 42.9
22 W	11 58 22	1 28 28	0♋19 12	7♋ 5 29	3D29.6	15 50.5	16 27.8	26 36.4	6 34.0	1 51.5	16 55.7	5 11.7	0 41.3
23 Th	12 2 19	2 28 0	13 46 25	20 22 20	3 30.0	15 44.8	17 32.4	27 15.7	6 39.9	1 56.7	16 53.2	5 11.2	0 39.7
24 F	12 6 15	3 27 29	26 53 35	3♌20 34	3R30.8	15 31.6	18 36.7	27 55.0	6 45.7	2 1.9	16 50.7	5 10.7	0 38.0
25 Sa	12 10 12	4 26 56	9♌43 41	16 3 18	3 30.7	15 11.3	19 40.7	28 34.2	6 51.3	2 7.2	16 48.2	5 10.1	0 36.4
26 Su	12 14 9	5 26 20	22 19 46	28 33 25	3 29.0	14 44.3	20 44.5	29 13.4	6 56.7	2 12.5	16 45.7	5 9.5	0 34.7
27 M	12 18 5	6 25 43	4♍44 34	10♍53 28	3 24.7	14 11.4	21 47.9	29 52.7	7 2.0	2 18.0	16 43.2	5 8.9	0 33.1
28 Tu	12 22 2	7 25 3	17 0 20	23 5 23	3 17.7	13 33.3	22 51.0	0♊31.8	7 7.1	2 23.5	16 40.7	5 8.3	0 31.5
29 W	12 25 58	8 24 20	29 8 47	5♎10 42	3 8.1	12 50.9	23 53.7	1 11.0	7 12.1	2 29.0	16 38.1	5 7.6	0 29.8
30 Th	12 29 55	9 23 36	11♎11 15	17 10 37	2 56.5	12 5.2	24 56.2	1 50.2	7 16.9	2 34.7	16 35.6	5 6.9	0 28.2
31 F	12 33 51	10 22 50	23 8 54	29 6 18	2 43.7	11 17.1	25 58.3	2 29.3	7 21.5	2 40.4	16 33.0	5 6.1	0 26.6

APRIL 1972 — LONGITUDE

Day	Sid.Time	☉	0 hr ☽	Noon ☽	True ☊	☿	♀	♂	♃	♄	♅	♆	♇
1 Sa	12 37 48	11♈22 2	5♏ 2 58	10♏59 8	2♒30.8	10♈27.5	27♉ 0.0	3♊ 8.4	7♑25.9	2♊46.2	16♎30.4	5♐ 5.3	0♎25.0
2 Su	12 41 44	12 21 12	16 55 2	22 50 57	2R19.0	9R37.7	28 1.4	3 47.5	7 30.2	2 52.0	16R27.9	5R 4.5	0R23.3
3 M	12 45 41	13 20 20	28 47 13	4♐44 12	2 9.1	8 48.4	29 2.4	4 26.6	7 34.4	2 58.0	16 25.3	5 3.7	0 21.7
4 Tu	12 49 38	14 19 26	10♐42 21	16 42 6	2 1.7	8 0.7	0♊ 3.0	5 5.7	7 38.3	3 3.9	16 22.7	5 2.9	0 20.2
5 W	12 53 34	15 18 30	22 43 58	28 48 31	1 57.0	7 15.4	1 3.3	5 44.7	7 42.1	3 10.0	16 20.1	5 2.0	0 18.6
6 Th	12 57 31	16 17 33	4♑56 19	11♑ 7 59	1 54.8	6 33.2	2 3.1	6 23.8	7 45.7	3 16.1	16 17.5	5 1.1	0 17.0
7 F	13 1 27	17 16 34	17 24 7	23 45 21	1D54.3	5 54.8	3 2.5	7 2.8	7 49.1	3 22.3	16 15.0	5 0.1	0 15.4
8 Sa	13 5 24	18 15 33	0♒12 16	6♒45 24	1R54.4	5 20.6	4 1.5	7 41.8	7 52.4	3 28.5	16 12.4	4 59.2	0 13.9
9 Su	13 9 20	19 14 30	13 25 15	20 12 13	1 54.0	4 51.1	5 0.0	8 20.8	7 55.4	3 34.8	16 9.8	4 58.2	0 12.3
10 M	13 13 17	20 13 26	27 6 31	4♓ 8 18	1 52.0	4 26.5	5 58.1	8 59.8	7 58.3	3 41.1	16 7.2	4 57.2	0 10.8
11 Tu	13 17 13	21 12 19	11♓17 26	18 33 38	1 47.6	4 7.2	6 55.8	9 38.8	8 1.0	3 47.5	16 4.6	4 56.1	0 9.3
12 W	13 21 10	22 11 11	25 56 22	3♈24 50	1 40.5	3 53.1	7 52.9	10 17.7	8 3.5	3 54.0	16 2.0	4 55.1	0 7.8
13 Th	13 25 7	23 10 1	10♈58 3	18 34 48	1 31.0	3 44.4	8 49.5	10 56.6	8 5.9	4 0.5	15 59.5	4 54.0	0 6.3
14 F	13 29 3	24 8 49	26 13 44	3♉53 23	1 20.1	3D41.0	9 45.7	11 35.6	8 8.0	4 7.1	15 56.9	4 52.9	0 4.8
15 Sa	13 33 0	25 7 35	11♉32 18	19 9 1	1 9.0	3 42.9	10 41.3	12 14.5	8 10.0	4 13.7	15 54.4	4 51.7	0 3.3
16 Su	13 36 56	26 6 20	26 42 15	4♊10 52	0 59.1	3 49.9	11 36.3	12 53.4	8 11.8	4 20.3	15 51.8	4 50.6	0 1.9
17 M	13 40 53	27 5 2	11♊33 54	18 50 39	0 51.4	4 1.8	12 30.7	13 32.3	8 13.4	4 27.1	15 49.3	4 49.4	0 0.5
18 Tu	13 44 49	28 3 42	26 0 41	3♋ 3 42	0 46.4	4 18.7	13 24.6	14 11.1	8 14.8	4 33.8	15 46.8	4 48.2	29♍59.0
19 W	13 48 46	29 2 19	9♋59 42	16 48 47	0 43.9	4 40.1	14 17.8	14 50.0	8 16.0	4 40.7	15 44.3	4 47.0	29 57.6
20 Th	13 52 42	0♉ 0 55	23 31 13	0♌ 7 23	0 43.2	5 6.1	15 10.4	15 28.8	8 17.0	4 47.5	15 41.8	4 45.7	29 56.3
21 F	13 56 39	0 59 28	6♌37 43	13 2 45	0 43.2	5 36.4	16 2.3	16 7.6	8 17.9	4 54.4	15 39.3	4 44.5	29 54.9
22 Sa	14 0 36	1 57 59	19 22 59	25 38 57	0 42.5	6 10.7	16 53.5	16 46.4	8 18.6	5 1.4	15 36.9	4 43.2	29 53.6
23 Su	14 4 32	2 56 28	1♍51 12	8♍ 0 13	0 40.2	6 49.1	17 44.0	17 25.2	8 19.0	5 8.4	15 34.4	4 41.9	29 52.2
24 M	14 8 29	3 54 54	14 6 29	20 10 25	0 35.4	7 31.2	18 33.8	18 3.9	8 19.3	5 15.4	15 32.0	4 40.6	29 50.9
25 Tu	14 12 25	4 53 19	26 12 25	2♎12 52	0 27.7	8 16.9	19 22.7	18 42.7	8R19.4	5 22.5	15 29.6	4 39.2	29 49.6
26 W	14 16 22	5 51 41	8♎12 2	14 10 12	0 17.2	9 6.0	20 10.9	19 21.4	8 19.3	5 29.6	15 27.2	4 37.9	29 48.4
27 Th	14 20 18	6 50 2	20 7 37	26 4 29	0 4.6	9 58.4	20 58.2	20 0.1	8 19.0	5 36.7	15 24.9	4 36.5	29 47.1
28 F	14 24 15	7 48 21	2♏ 0 59	7♏57 18	29♑50.7	10 54.0	21 44.7	20 38.8	8 18.6	5 43.9	15 22.5	4 35.1	29 45.9
29 Sa	14 28 11	8 46 38	13 53 34	19 50 0	29 36.7	11 52.6	22 30.2	21 17.4	8 17.9	5 51.1	15 20.2	4 33.7	29 44.7
30 Su	14 32 8	9 44 53	25 46 44	1♐44 0	29 23.8	12 54.1	23 14.8	21 56.1	8 17.1	5 58.4	15 17.9	4 32.3	29 43.5

Astro Data	Dy Hr Mn
☽0S	1 1:53
☿0N	5 11:44
♆ R	7 5:19
♃⚺♆	10 12:31
♄△♇	10 19:15
☽0N	15 5:38
☿ R	21 18:38
♄⚼♅	22 13:10
☽0S	28 8:27
☽0N	11 16:14
☿ D	14 3:29
♄☍♆	19 18:47
☽0S	24 13:41
♃ R	25 0:19

Planet Ingress	Dy Hr Mn
☿ ♈	5 16:59
♀ ♉	7 3:25
☉ ♈	20 12:21
♂ ♊	27 4:30
♀ ♊	3 22:48
♇ ♍	17 7:45
☉ ♉	19 23:37
☊ ♑	27 8:04

Last Aspect Dy Hr Mn		☽ Ingress Dy Hr Mn
1 2:39	☿ ☍	♎ 1 19:00
3 23:46	♀ ☍	♏ 4 7:00
5 15:05	♂ ☍	♐ 6 19:36
8 7:05	☉ □	♑ 9 6:49
10 21:17	☉ ⚹	♒ 11 14:43
13 3:06	♂ □	♓ 13 18:39
15 11:35	☉ ☌	♈ 15 19:37
16 22:56	♅ ☍	♉ 17 19:27
19 19:01	☉ ⚹	♊ 19 20:12
21 0:49	♅ △	♋ 21 23:26
24 2:00	♂ ⚹	♌ 24 5:46
26 14:02	♂ □	♍ 26 14:48
28 12:37	♀ △	♎ 29 1:42
30 10:47	♅ ☌	♏ 31 13:48

Last Aspect Dy Hr Mn		☽ Ingress Dy Hr Mn
3 0:34	♀ ☍	♐ 3 2:27
4 11:19	♅ ⚹	♑ 5 14:20
6 23:44	☉ □	♒ 7 23:37
9 11:06	☉ ⚹	♓ 10 4:58
10 21:08	♂ □	♈ 12 6:32
13 20:31	☉ ☌	♉ 14 5:54
14 18:42	♃ △	♊ 16 5:16
18 6:44	♇ □	♋ 18 6:46
20 11:38	♇ ⚹	♌ 20 11:46
21 18:56	♀ ⚹	♍ 22 20:24
25 7:13	♇ ☌	♎ 25 7:34
27 1:49	♀ △	♏ 27 19:56
30 7:57	♇ ⚹	♐ 30 8:31

☽ Phases & Eclipses Dy Hr Mn	
8 7:05	☽ 17♐49
15 11:35	● 24♓60
22 2:12	☽ 1♋34
29 20:05	○ 9♎14
6 23:44	☽ 17♑16
13 20:31	● 24♈00
20 12:45	☽ 0♌32
28 12:44	○ 8♏19

Astro Data

1 MARCH 1972
Julian Day # 26358
Delta T 42.4 sec
SVP 05♓38'39"
Obliquity 23°26'40"
⚷ Chiron 11♈24.9
☽ Mean ☊ 3♒27.3

1 APRIL 1972
Julian Day # 26389
Delta T 42.5 sec
SVP 05♓38'36"
Obliquity 23°26'40"
⚷ Chiron 13♈09.8
☽ Mean ☊ 1♒48.8

Day	Sid.Time	☉	0 hr ☽	Noon ☽	True ☊	☿	♀	♂	♃	♄	♅	♆	♇
1 M	14 36 4	10♉43 6	7♐42 0	13♐41 0	29♑12.8	13♈58.5	23♊58.5	22♊34.7	8♑16.1	6♊ 5.7	15♎15.7	4♐30.8	29♍42.4
2 Tu	14 40 1	11 41 18	19 41 17	25 43 11	29R 4.5	15 5.5	24 41.1	23 13.4	8R14.8	6 13.0	15R13.4	4R29.4	29R41.2
3 W	14 43 58	12 39 28	1♑47 6	7♑53 25	28 59.0	16 15.1	25 22.7	23 52.0	8 13.4	6 20.4	15 11.2	4 27.9	29 40.1
4 Th	14 47 54	13 37 37	14 2 36	20 15 10	28 56.2	17 27.3	26 3.3	24 30.6	8 11.9	6 27.7	15 9.1	4 26.4	29 39.0
5 F	14 51 51	14 35 45	26 31 36	2♒52 26	28D 55.3	18 41.9	26 42.7	25 9.1	8 10.1	6 35.2	15 6.9	4 25.0	29 38.0
6 Sa	14 55 47	15 33 50	9♒18 15	15 49 31	28R 55.5	19 58.9	27 20.9	25 47.7	8 8.1	6 42.6	15 4.8	4 23.4	29 37.0
7 Su	14 59 44	16 31 55	22 26 46	29 10 24	28 55.4	21 18.3	27 58.0	26 26.2	8 6.0	6 50.1	15 2.7	4 21.9	29 35.9
8 M	15 3 40	17 29 58	6♓ 0 46	12♓58 4	28 54.2	22 39.9	28 33.8	27 4.8	8 3.7	6 57.6	15 0.6	4 20.4	29 35.0
9 Tu	15 7 37	18 27 59	20 2 25	27 13 39	28 50.8	24 3.8	29 8.3	27 43.3	8 1.2	7 5.1	14 58.6	4 18.9	29 34.0
10 W	15 11 34	19 26 0	4♈31 30	11♈55 24	28 45.0	25 29.8	29 41.5	28 21.8	7 58.5	7 12.6	14 56.6	4 17.3	29 33.1
11 Th	15 15 30	20 23 59	19 24 35	26 58 5	28 37.0	26 58.1	0♋13.3	29 0.3	7 55.6	7 20.2	14 54.7	4 15.8	29 32.1
12 F	15 19 27	21 21 56	4♉34 42	12♉13 9	28 27.5	28 28.4	0 43.6	29 38.8	7 52.6	7 27.8	14 52.7	4 14.2	29 31.3
13 Sa	15 23 23	22 19 53	19 51 59	27 29 47	28 17.8	0♉ 1.0	1 12.4	0♋17.2	7 49.3	7 35.4	14 50.8	4 12.6	29 30.4
14 Su	15 27 20	23 17 48	5♊ 5 10	12♊36 50	28 9.0	1 35.6	1 39.7	0 55.7	7 45.9	7 43.0	14 49.0	4 11.0	29 29.6
15 M	15 31 16	24 15 41	20 3 41	27 24 47	28 2.2	3 12.4	2 5.4	1 34.2	7 42.4	7 50.7	14 47.2	4 9.4	29 28.8
16 Tu	15 35 13	25 13 33	4♋39 26	11♋47 10	27 57.7	4 51.2	2 29.4	2 12.6	7 38.6	7 58.4	14 45.4	4 7.8	29 28.0
17 W	15 39 9	26 11 23	18 47 44	25 41 3	27D 55.6	6 32.2	2 51.6	2 51.0	7 34.7	8 6.1	14 43.7	4 6.2	29 27.3
18 Th	15 43 6	27 9 11	2♌27 15	9♌ 6 36	27 55.4	8 15.2	3 12.0	3 29.4	7 30.6	8 13.8	14 42.0	4 4.6	29 26.6
19 F	15 47 3	28 6 57	15 39 28	22 6 19	27 56.0	10 0.4	3 30.6	4 7.8	7 26.4	8 21.5	14 40.3	4 3.0	29 25.9
20 Sa	15 50 59	29 4 42	28 27 39	4♍44 3	27R 56.5	11 47.7	3 47.2	4 46.2	7 22.0	8 29.2	14 38.7	4 1.4	29 25.3
21 Su	15 54 56	0♊ 2 25	10♍56 5	17 4 20	27 55.9	13 37.0	4 1.9	5 24.6	7 17.4	8 36.9	14 37.1	3 59.8	29 24.6
22 M	15 58 52	1 0 7	23 9 22	29 11 44	27 53.3	15 28.4	4 14.5	6 2.9	7 12.7	8 44.7	14 35.6	3 58.2	29 24.0
23 Tu	16 2 49	1 57 47	5♎11 56	11♎10 28	27 48.6	17 22.0	4 24.9	6 41.2	7 7.8	8 52.4	14 34.1	3 56.6	29 23.5
24 W	16 6 45	2 55 26	17 7 47	23 4 16	27 41.6	19 17.5	4 33.2	7 19.6	7 2.8	9 0.2	14 32.7	3 54.9	29 22.9
25 Th	16 10 42	3 53 3	29 0 18	4♏56 12	27 33.0	21 15.1	4 39.3	7 57.9	6 57.7	9 8.0	14 31.3	3 53.3	29 22.4
26 F	16 14 38	4 50 38	10♏52 15	16 48 43	27 23.3	23 14.7	4 43.1	8 36.2	6 52.4	9 15.8	14 29.9	3 51.7	29 22.0
27 Sa	16 18 35	5 48 13	22 45 49	28 43 46	27 13.4	25 16.1	4R44.6	9 14.4	6 46.9	9 23.5	14 28.6	3 50.1	29 21.5
28 Su	16 22 32	6 45 46	4♐42 45	10♐42 56	27 4.3	27 19.4	4 43.7	9 52.7	6 41.3	9 31.3	14 27.3	3 48.4	29 21.1
29 M	16 26 28	7 43 18	16 44 31	22 47 40	26 56.7	29 24.5	4 40.5	10 31.0	6 35.6	9 39.1	14 26.1	3 46.8	29 20.8
30 Tu	16 30 25	8 40 50	28 52 36	4♑59 31	26 51.1	1♊31.1	4 34.8	11 9.2	6 29.8	9 46.9	14 24.9	3 45.2	29 20.4
31 W	16 34 21	9 38 20	11♑ 8 39	17 20 16	26 47.7	3 39.1	4 26.8	11 47.4	6 23.8	9 54.7	14 23.8	3 43.6	29 20.1

LONGITUDE JUNE 1972

Day	Sid.Time	☉	0 hr ☽	Noon ☽	True ☊	☿	♀	♂	♃	♄	♅	♆	♇
1 Th	16 38 18	10♊35 49	23♑34 38	29♑52 6	26♑46.4	5♊48.5	4♋16.3	12♋25.6	6♑17.7	10♊ 2.5	14♎22.7	3♐42.0	29♍19.8
2 F	16 42 14	11 33 17	6♒12 59	12♒37 38	26D 46.7	7 58.8	4R 3.4	13 3.8	6R11.5	10 10.3	14R21.7	3R40.4	29R19.6
3 Sa	16 46 11	12 30 45	19 6 24	25 39 41	26 47.9	10 10.0	3 48.1	13 42.0	6 5.1	10 18.1	14 20.7	3 38.8	29 19.4
4 Su	16 50 7	13 28 11	2♓17 48	9♓ 1 4	26R 49.1	12 21.8	3 30.4	14 20.2	5 58.7	10 25.9	14 19.8	3 37.2	29 19.2
5 M	16 54 4	14 25 37	15 49 44	22 43 59	26 49.6	14 33.9	3 10.5	14 58.4	5 52.1	10 33.7	14 18.9	3 35.6	29 19.0
6 Tu	16 58 1	15 23 3	29 43 55	6♈49 28	26 48.7	16 46.0	2 48.3	15 36.6	5 45.5	10 41.5	14 18.1	3 34.0	29 18.9
7 W	17 1 57	16 20 28	14♈ 0 27	21 16 32	26 46.1	18 57.8	2 24.0	16 14.7	5 38.7	10 49.3	14 17.3	3 32.4	29 18.8
8 Th	17 5 54	17 17 52	28 37 12	6♉ 1 46	26 42.0	21 9.2	1 57.7	16 52.9	5 31.9	10 57.0	14 16.5	3 30.8	29 18.7
9 F	17 9 50	18 15 16	13♉29 23	20 59 4	26 36.8	23 19.8	1 29.4	17 31.1	5 24.9	11 4.8	14 15.8	3 29.3	29D 18.7
10 Sa	17 13 47	19 12 39	28 29 44	6♊ 0 14	26 31.4	25 29.4	0 59.4	18 9.2	5 17.9	11 12.6	14 15.2	3 27.7	29 18.7
11 Su	17 17 43	20 10 2	13♊29 24	20 56 6	26 26.4	27 37.7	0 27.7	18 47.3	5 10.8	11 20.3	14 14.6	3 26.2	29 18.8
12 M	17 21 40	21 7 24	28 19 18	5♋38 4	26 22.6	29 44.6	29♊54.6	19 25.5	5 3.6	11 28.1	14 14.1	3 24.7	29 18.8
13 Tu	17 25 36	22 4 45	12♋51 37	19 59 20	26D 20.3	1♋49.9	29 20.2	20 3.6	4 56.3	11 35.8	14 13.6	3 23.1	29 18.9
14 W	17 29 33	23 2 5	27 0 48	3♌55 45	26 19.7	3 53.4	28 44.7	20 41.7	4 49.0	11 43.5	14 13.2	3 21.6	29 19.1
15 Th	17 33 30	23 59 25	10♌44 5	17 25 52	26 20.3	5 55.0	28 8.3	21 19.8	4 41.6	11 51.2	14 12.8	3 20.1	29 19.3
16 F	17 37 26	24 56 43	24 1 16	0♍30 37	26 21.7	7 54.6	27 31.3	21 57.9	4 34.2	11 58.9	14 12.5	3 18.6	29 19.5
17 Sa	17 41 23	25 54 1	6♍54 17	13 12 44	26 23.3	9 52.2	26 53.9	22 36.0	4 26.7	12 6.5	14 12.2	3 17.2	29 19.7
18 Su	17 45 19	26 51 18	19 26 28	25 36 2	26R 24.4	11 47.5	26 16.3	23 14.1	4 19.2	12 14.2	14 12.0	3 15.7	29 20.0
19 M	17 49 16	27 48 34	1♎42 1	7♎44 57	26 24.5	13 40.7	25 38.7	23 52.1	4 11.6	12 21.8	14 11.8	3 14.3	29 20.3
20 Tu	17 53 12	28 45 49	13 45 27	19 44 2	26 23.5	15 31.6	25 1.5	24 30.2	4 4.0	12 29.4	14 11.7	3 12.8	29 20.6
21 W	17 57 9	29 43 4	25 41 16	1♏37 39	26 21.3	17 20.3	24 24.9	25 8.3	3 56.4	12 37.0	14D 11.6	3 11.4	29 21.0
22 Th	18 1 5	0♋40 18	7♏33 41	13 29 49	26 18.1	19 6.7	23 49.0	25 46.3	3 48.8	12 44.6	14 11.6	3 10.0	29 21.4
23 F	18 5 2	1 37 31	19 26 27	25 23 58	26 14.3	20 50.8	23 14.1	26 24.3	3 41.1	12 52.1	14 11.6	3 8.6	29 21.8
24 Sa	18 8 59	2 34 44	1♐22 44	7♐23 3	26 10.4	22 32.6	22 40.4	27 2.4	3 33.5	12 59.6	14 11.7	3 7.2	29 22.3
25 Su	18 12 55	3 31 56	13 25 10	19 29 20	26 6.7	24 12.0	22 8.2	27 40.4	3 25.8	13 7.1	14 11.9	3 5.9	29 22.8
26 M	18 16 52	4 29 8	25 35 46	1♑44 39	26 3.8	25 49.2	21 37.5	28 18.4	3 18.1	13 14.6	14 12.1	3 4.6	29 23.3
27 Tu	18 20 48	5 26 20	7♑56 7	14 10 21	26 1.8	27 24.0	21 8.6	28 56.4	3 10.4	13 22.0	14 12.3	3 3.3	29 23.9
28 W	18 24 45	6 23 32	20 27 26	26 47 31	26D 0.9	28 56.4	20 41.6	29 34.4	3 2.8	13 29.4	14 12.6	3 2.0	29 24.4
29 Th	18 28 41	7 20 43	3♒10 41	9♒37 5	26 0.9	0♌26.5	20 16.6	0♌12.4	2 55.1	13 36.8	14 13.0	3 0.7	29 25.1
30 F	18 32 38	8 17 54	16 6 47	22 39 55	26 1.7	1 54.3	19 53.8	0 50.4	2 47.5	13 44.2	14 13.4	2 59.4	29 25.7

Astro Data	Dy Hr Mn
☽0N	9 1:14
♃⊼♄	14 6:13
☽0S	21 18:56
♀ R	27 3:14
☽0N	5 7:52
♇ D	9 5:44
☽0S	18 1:30
♅ D	21 17:28
♃⊻♆	28 3:05

Planet Ingress	Dy Hr Mn
♀ ♋	10 13:51
☿ ♉	12 23:45
♂ ♋	12 13:14
☉ ♊	20 23:00
☿ ♊	29 6:46
♀ ♊	11 20:08
☿ ♋	12 2:56
☉ ♋	21 7:06
☿ ♌	28 16:52
♂ ♌	28 16:09

Last Aspect Dy Hr Mn		☽ Ingress Dy Hr Mn
2 19:50	♇ □	♑ 2 20:29
5 5:53	♇ △	♒ 5 6:35
7 10:19	♀ △	♓ 7 13:28
9 15:51	♇ ☍	♈ 9 16:35
11 15:53	♂ ✶	♉ 11 16:47
13 15:10	♇ △	♊ 13 15:57
15 15:24	♇ □	♋ 15 16:16
17 18:39	♇ ✶	♌ 17 19:38
20 1:16	☉ □	♍ 20 2:56
22 12:24	♇ ☌	♎ 22 13:36
23 18:48	♅ ☌	♏ 25 2:01
27 13:15	♇ ✶	♐ 27 14:33
30 0:55	♇ □	♑ 30 2:13

Last Aspect Dy Hr Mn		☽ Ingress Dy Hr Mn
1 10:58	♇ △	♒ 1 12:15
2 15:12	♅ △	♓ 3 19:52
5 23:17	♇ ☍	♈ 6 0:27
7 9:39	♀ ✶	♉ 8 2:15
10 1:18	♇ △	♊ 10 2:24
12 2:43	☿ ☌	♋ 12 2:45
14 3:59	♇ ✶	♌ 14 5:10
16 6:09	♀ ✶	♍ 16 11:03
18 19:20	♇ ☌	♎ 18 20:39
20 22:50	♂ □	♏ 21 8:43
23 19:58	♇ ✶	♐ 23 21:14
26 7:25	♇ □	♑ 26 8:36
28 16:56	♇ △	♒ 28 18:02

☽ Phases & Eclipses Dy Hr Mn	
6 12:26	☽ 16♒04
13 4:08	● 22♉30
20 1:16	☽ 29♌08
28 4:28	○ 6♐56
4 21:22	☽ 14♓19
11 11:30	● 20♊38
18 15:41	☽ 27♍29
26 18:46	○ 5♑14

Astro Data

1 MAY 1972
Julian Day # 26419
Delta T 42.6 sec
SVP 05♓38'33"
Obliquity 23°26'39"
⚷ Chiron 14♈53.0
☽ Mean ☊ 0♒13.5

1 JUNE 1972
Julian Day # 26450
Delta T 42.7 sec
SVP 05♓38'28"
Obliquity 23°26'38"
⚷ Chiron 16♈21.0
☽ Mean ☊ 28♑35.0

JULY 1972 — LONGITUDE

Day	Sid.Time	☉	0 hr ☽	Noon ☽	True ☊	☿	♀	♂	♃	♄	♅	♆	♇
1 Sa	18 36 35	9♋15 6	29♒16 34	5♓56 50	26♑ 2.9	3♌19.6	19♊33.1	1♌28.4	2♑39.9	13♊51.5	14♎13.9	2♐58.2	29♍26.4
2 Su	18 40 31	10 12 17	12♓40 49	19 28 34	26 4.1	4 42.4	19R 14.8	2 6.4	2R 32.3	13 58.8	14 14.4	2R 57.0	29 27.1
3 M	18 44 28	11 9 29	26 20 7	3♈15 28	26 5.1	6 2.8	18 58.8	2 44.4	2 24.8	14 6.1	14 15.0	2 55.8	29 27.9
4 Tu	18 48 24	12 6 40	10♈14 34	17 17 19	26R 5.5	7 20.7	18 45.2	3 22.4	2 17.3	14 13.3	14 15.6	2 54.6	29 28.7
5 W	18 52 21	13 3 52	24 23 30	1♉32 52	26 5.3	8 36.1	18 34.0	4 0.4	2 9.8	14 20.5	14 16.2	2 53.4	29 29.5
6 Th	18 56 17	14 1 5	8♉45 4	15 59 39	26 4.5	9 48.8	18 25.3	4 38.4	2 2.4	14 27.6	14 17.0	2 52.3	29 30.3
7 F	19 0 14	14 58 18	23 16 5	0♊33 44	26 3.4	10 58.8	18 18.9	5 16.3	1 55.1	14 34.8	14 17.7	2 51.2	29 31.2
8 Sa	19 4 10	15 55 31	7♊51 57	15 9 58	26 2.2	12 6.1	18 14.9	5 54.3	1 47.8	14 41.8	14 18.6	2 50.1	29 32.1
9 Su	19 8 7	16 52 45	22 27 2	29 42 24	26 1.1	13 10.6	18D 13.2	6 32.3	1 40.6	14 48.9	14 19.5	2 49.0	29 33.0
10 M	19 12 4	17 49 58	6♋55 17	14♋ 4 59	26 0.4	14 12.2	18 13.9	7 10.3	1 33.5	14 55.9	14 20.4	2 48.0	29 34.0
11 Tu	19 16 0	18 47 13	21 10 52	28 12 23	26D 0.1	15 10.7	18 16.9	7 48.3	1 26.4	15 2.9	14 21.4	2 47.0	29 35.0
12 W	19 19 57	19 44 27	5♌ 9 5	12♌ 0 35	26 0.1	16 6.1	18 22.1	8 26.3	1 19.4	15 9.8	14 22.4	2 46.0	29 36.0
13 Th	19 23 53	20 41 41	18 46 42	25 27 18	26 0.4	16 58.3	18 29.4	9 4.2	1 12.5	15 16.7	14 23.5	2 45.0	29 37.1
14 F	19 27 50	21 38 56	2♍ 2 22	8♍32 2	26 0.9	17 47.2	18 38.9	9 42.2	1 5.7	15 23.5	14 24.7	2 44.1	29 38.2
15 Sa	19 31 46	22 36 10	14 56 28	21 15 58	26 1.3	18 32.5	18 50.5	10 20.2	0 59.0	15 30.3	14 25.8	2 43.2	29 39.3
16 Su	19 35 43	23 33 25	27 30 53	3♎41 39	26 1.6	19 14.2	19 4.1	10 58.2	0 52.4	15 37.0	14 27.1	2 42.3	29 40.4
17 M	19 39 39	24 30 40	9♎48 44	15 52 38	26 1.7	19 52.2	19 19.6	11 36.2	0 46.0	15 43.7	14 28.4	2 41.4	29 41.6
18 Tu	19 43 36	25 27 54	21 53 54	27 53 5	26 1.8	20 26.2	19 37.1	12 14.1	0 39.6	15 50.3	14 29.7	2 40.6	29 42.8
19 W	19 47 33	26 25 10	3♏50 45	9♏47 29	26 1.8	20 56.1	19 56.4	12 52.1	0 33.3	15 56.9	14 31.1	2 39.8	29 44.0
20 Th	19 51 29	27 22 25	15 43 51	21 40 24	26 1.8	21 21.8	20 17.4	13 30.1	0 27.2	16 3.5	14 32.6	2 39.0	29 45.2
21 F	19 55 26	28 19 41	27 37 40	3♐36 10	26 2.0	21 43.1	20 40.3	14 8.0	0 21.1	16 9.9	14 34.0	2 38.3	29 46.5
22 Sa	19 59 22	29 16 57	9♐36 22	15 38 44	26 2.3	21 59.8	21 4.7	14 46.0	0 15.2	16 16.4	14 35.6	2 37.5	29 47.8
23 Su	20 3 19	0♌14 13	21 43 41	27 51 32	26 2.7	22 11.8	21 30.8	15 24.0	0 9.5	16 22.8	14 37.2	2 36.9	29 49.2
24 M	20 7 15	1 11 30	4♑ 2 39	10♑17 16	26 3.1	22R 19.1	21 58.5	16 2.0	0 3.8	16 29.1	14 38.8	2 36.2	29 50.5
25 Tu	20 11 12	2 8 47	16 35 35	22 57 46	26R 3.5	22 21.4	22 27.6	16 39.9	29♐58.3	16 35.4	14 40.5	2 35.6	29 51.9
26 W	20 15 8	3 6 5	29 23 53	5♒54 0	26 3.5	22 18.6	22 58.3	17 17.9	29 53.0	16 41.6	14 42.2	2 34.9	29 53.3
27 Th	20 19 5	4 3 24	12♒28 5	19 6 2	26 3.3	22 10.9	23 30.3	17 55.9	29 47.8	16 47.7	14 44.0	2 34.4	29 54.8
28 F	20 23 2	5 0 43	25 47 46	2♓33 5	26 2.6	21 58.0	24 3.7	18 33.9	29 42.7	16 53.8	14 45.8	2 33.8	29 56.3
29 Sa	20 26 58	5 58 3	9♓21 47	16 13 38	26 1.5	21 40.2	24 38.3	19 11.8	29 37.8	16 59.8	14 47.7	2 33.3	29 57.7
30 Su	20 30 55	6 55 24	23 8 23	0♈ 5 43	26 0.2	21 17.5	25 14.3	19 49.8	29 33.0	17 5.8	14 49.6	2 32.8	29 59.3
31 M	20 34 51	7 52 46	7♈ 5 22	14 7 2	25 58.9	20 50.2	25 51.4	20 27.8	29 28.4	17 11.7	14 51.6	2 32.3	0♎ 0.8

AUGUST 1972 — LONGITUDE

Day	Sid.Time	☉	0 hr ☽	Noon ☽	True ☊	☿	♀	♂	♃	♄	♅	♆	♇
1 Tu	20 38 48	8♌50 9	21♈10 24	28♈15 10	25♑57.9	20♌18.4	26♊29.8	21♌ 5.8	29♐23.9	17♊17.6	14♎53.6	2♐31.9	0♎ 2.4
2 W	20 42 44	9 47 33	5♉21 3	12♉27 43	25D 57.4	19R 42.6	27 9.2	21 43.8	29R 19.6	17 23.4	14 55.6	2R 31.5	0 3.9
3 Th	20 46 41	10 44 59	19 34 53	26 42 14	25 57.5	19 3.2	27 49.7	22 21.8	29 15.5	17 29.1	14 57.7	2 31.1	0 5.6
4 F	20 50 37	11 42 25	3♊49 28	10♊56 16	25 58.2	18 20.8	28 31.3	22 59.8	29 11.5	17 34.7	14 59.9	2 30.8	0 7.2
5 Sa	20 54 34	12 39 54	18 2 16	25 7 10	25 59.3	17 36.1	29 13.8	23 37.9	29 7.7	17 40.3	15 2.0	2 30.5	0 8.8
6 Su	20 58 31	13 37 23	2♋10 36	9♋12 11	26 0.5	16 49.7	29 57.4	24 15.9	29 4.1	17 45.8	15 4.3	2 30.2	0 10.5
7 M	21 2 27	14 34 54	16 11 34	23 8 24	26R 1.4	16 2.4	0♋41.8	24 53.9	29 0.6	17 51.3	15 6.5	2 30.0	0 12.2
8 Tu	21 6 24	15 32 25	0♌ 2 18	6♌52 56	26 1.6	15 15.2	1 27.1	25 32.0	28 57.3	17 56.7	15 8.9	2 29.8	0 14.0
9 W	21 10 20	16 29 58	13 40 1	20 23 17	26 0.8	14 28.9	2 13.3	26 10.0	28 54.2	18 2.0	15 11.2	2 29.6	0 15.7
10 Th	21 14 17	17 27 32	27 2 29	3♍37 29	25 58.9	13 44.4	3 0.3	26 48.1	28 51.3	18 7.2	15 13.6	2 29.4	0 17.5
11 F	21 18 13	18 25 7	10♍ 8 10	16 34 31	25 56.1	13 2.5	3 48.1	27 26.1	28 48.5	18 12.4	15 16.0	2 29.3	0 19.3
12 Sa	21 22 10	19 22 43	22 56 35	29 14 28	25 52.6	12 24.2	4 36.6	28 4.2	28 45.9	18 17.4	15 18.5	2 29.2	0 21.1
13 Su	21 26 6	20 20 20	5♎28 22	11♎38 33	25 48.8	11 50.2	5 25.9	28 42.3	28 43.5	18 22.5	15 21.0	2 29.2	0 22.9
14 M	21 30 3	21 17 58	17 45 20	23 49 6	25 45.3	11 21.3	6 15.9	29 20.4	28 41.3	18 27.4	15 23.6	2D 29.2	0 24.7
15 Tu	21 34 0	22 15 37	29 50 17	5♏49 23	25 42.4	10 58.0	7 6.6	29 58.4	28 39.3	18 32.2	15 26.2	2 29.2	0 26.6
16 W	21 37 56	23 13 17	11♏46 55	17 43 27	25 40.6	10 41.0	7 57.9	0♍36.5	28 37.4	18 37.0	15 28.8	2 29.2	0 28.5
17 Th	21 41 53	24 10 58	23 39 32	29 35 48	25D 40.0	10D 30.8	8 49.9	1 14.6	28 35.8	18 41.7	15 31.5	2 29.3	0 30.4
18 F	21 45 49	25 8 40	5♐32 51	11♐31 16	25 40.4	10 27.5	9 42.5	1 52.7	28 34.3	18 46.3	15 34.2	2 29.4	0 32.3
19 Sa	21 49 46	26 6 23	17 31 41	23 34 39	25 41.8	10 31.7	10 35.7	2 30.9	28 33.0	18 50.8	15 36.9	2 29.6	0 34.3
20 Su	21 53 42	27 4 8	29 40 45	5♑50 30	25 43.5	10 43.3	11 29.4	3 9.0	28 31.9	18 55.3	15 39.7	2 29.7	0 36.2
21 M	21 57 39	28 1 53	12♑ 4 21	18 22 43	25 45.0	11 2.6	12 23.8	3 47.1	28 31.0	18 59.6	15 42.5	2 30.0	0 38.2
22 Tu	22 1 35	28 59 40	24 45 58	1♒14 19	25R 45.6	11 29.5	13 18.7	4 25.2	28 30.3	19 3.9	15 45.4	2 30.2	0 40.2
23 W	22 5 32	29 57 28	7♒47 57	14 26 56	25 45.0	12 4.1	14 14.1	5 3.4	28 29.8	19 8.1	15 48.3	2 30.5	0 42.2
24 Th	22 9 29	0♍55 17	21 11 12	28 0 34	25 42.8	12 46.1	15 10.0	5 41.5	28 29.4	19 12.2	15 51.2	2 30.8	0 44.2
25 F	22 13 25	1 53 8	4♓54 46	11♓53 25	25 39.0	13 35.5	16 6.4	6 19.7	28D 29.3	19 16.2	15 54.1	2 31.1	0 46.3
26 Sa	22 17 22	2 51 0	18 55 59	26 1 55	25 33.9	14 32.0	17 3.3	6 57.9	28 29.3	19 20.1	15 57.1	2 31.5	0 48.3
27 Su	22 21 18	3 48 54	3♈10 33	10♈21 14	25 28.1	15 35.3	18 0.7	7 36.1	28 29.5	19 24.0	16 0.1	2 31.9	0 50.4
28 M	22 25 15	4 46 50	17 33 14	24 45 52	25 22.4	16 45.2	18 58.6	8 14.2	28 29.9	19 27.7	16 3.2	2 32.3	0 52.5
29 Tu	22 29 11	5 44 47	1♉58 30	9♉10 32	25 17.5	18 1.2	19 56.8	8 52.4	28 30.5	19 31.4	16 6.2	2 32.8	0 54.5
30 W	22 33 8	6 42 46	16 21 27	23 30 47	25 14.1	19 23.0	20 55.6	9 30.7	28 31.3	19 34.9	16 9.3	2 33.3	0 56.6
31 Th	22 37 4	7 40 47	0♊38 11	7♊43 24	25D 12.4	20 50.1	21 54.7	10 8.9	28 32.3	19 38.4	16 12.5	2 33.8	0 58.8

Astro Data	Planet Ingress	Last Aspect	☽ Ingress	Last Aspect	☽ Ingress	☽ Phases & Eclipses	Astro Data
Dy Hr Mn	Dy Hr Mn	Dy Hr Mn	Dy Hr Mn	Dy Hr Mn	Dy Hr Mn	Dy Hr Mn	1 JULY 1972
☽0N 2 13:05	☉ ♌ 22 18:03	30 6:45 ♀ △	♓ 1 1:18	1 13:52 ♃ △	♉ 1 14:57	4 3:25 ☽ 12♈15	Julian Day # 26480
♄△♅ 4 8:22	♃ ♐ 24 16:43	3 5:27 ♇ ☍	♈ 3 6:22	3 4:54 ♂ □	♊ 3 17:33	10 19:39 ● 18♋37	Delta T 42.8 sec
♀ D 9 4:55	♇ ♎ 30 11:42	4 14:17 ♀ ⚹	♉ 5 9:25	5 20:01 ♀ ☌	♋ 5 20:18	10 19:45:53 ● T 2'36"	SVP 05♓38'22"
☽0S 15 9:43		7 10:18 ♇ △	♊ 7 11:05	6 22:08 ♅ □	♌ 7 23:56	18 7:46 ☽ 25♎46	Obliquity 23°26'38"
☿ R 24 23:02	♀ ♋ 6 1:26	9 11:45 ♇ □	♋ 9 12:29	10 3:17 ♃ △	♍ 10 5:23	26 7:24 ○ 3♒24	⚷ Chiron 17♈12.1
♃□♇ 25 22:43	♂ ♍ 15 0:59	11 14:23 ♇ ⚹	♌ 11 15:05	12 11:03 ♃ □	♎ 12 13:27	26 7:16 ● P 0.543	☽ Mean ☊ 26♑59.7
☽0N 29 18:42	☉ ♍ 23 1:03	12 23:29 ♀ ⚹	♍ 13 20:16	15 0:17 ♂ ⚹	♏ 15 0:19		
		16 4:11 ♇ ☌	♎ 16 4:49	17 1:09 ☉ □	♐ 17 12:49	2 8:02 ☽ 10♉07	1 AUGUST 1972
☽0S 11 18:42		18 7:46 ☉ □	♏ 18 16:15	19 21:45 ♃ ☌	♑ 20 0:38	9 5:26 ● 16♌43	Julian Day # 26511
♆ D 14 3:09		21 4:20 ♇ ⚹	♐ 21 4:46	21 6:58 ♅ □	♒ 22 9:43	17 1:09 ☽ 24♏14	Delta T 42.9 sec
☿ D 17 22:38		23 15:51 ♇ □	♑ 23 16:10	24 12:50 ♃ ⚹	♓ 24 15:28	24 18:22 ○ 1♓40	SVP 05♓38'17"
♃ D 25 8:01		26 0:55 ♇ △	♒ 26 1:07	26 16:08 ♃ □	♈ 26 18:40	31 12:48 ☽ 8♊12	Obliquity 23°26'38"
☽0N 26 2:10		28 6:56 ♃ ⚹	♓ 28 7:29	28 18:14 ♃ △	♉ 28 20:43		⚷ Chiron 17♈18.5R
		30 11:00 ♃ □	♈ 30 11:50	30 8:13 ♀ ⚹	♊ 30 22:56		☽ Mean ☊ 25♑21.2

LONGITUDE SEPTEMBER 1972

Day	Sid.Time	☉	0 hr ☽	Noon ☽	True ☊	☿	♀	♂	♃	♄	♅	♆	♇
1 F	22 41 1	8♍38 50	14♊46 12	21♊46 27	25♑12.3	22♌21.9	22♋54.3	10♍47.1	28♐33.5	19♊41.8	16♎15.7	2♐34.4	1♎ 0.9
2 Sa	22 44 58	9 36 55	28 44 5	5♋39 2	25 13.3	23 58.2	23 54.2	11 25.4	28 34.8	19 45.1	16 18.8	2 35.0	1 3.0
3 Su	22 48 54	10 35 3	12♋31 16	19 20 48	25R 14.6	25 38.2	24 54.5	12 3.7	28 36.3	19 48.3	16 22.1	2 35.6	1 5.2
4 M	22 52 51	11 33 12	26 7 35	2♌51 37	25 15.1	27 21.6	25 55.2	12 42.0	28 38.1	19 51.4	16 25.3	2 36.3	1 7.4
5 Tu	22 56 47	12 31 22	9♌32 51	16 11 15	25 14.1	29 7.8	26 56.3	13 20.3	28 40.0	19 54.4	16 28.6	2 36.9	1 9.5
6 W	23 0 44	13 29 35	22 46 45	29 19 16	25 11.0	0♍56.4	27 57.7	13 58.6	28 42.0	19 57.3	16 31.9	2 37.7	1 11.7
7 Th	23 4 40	14 27 50	5♍48 44	12♍15 5	25 5.7	2 46.8	28 59.4	14 36.9	28 44.3	20 0.0	16 35.2	2 38.4	1 13.9
8 F	23 8 37	15 26 6	18 38 14	24 58 9	24 58.2	4 38.8	0♌ 1.4	15 15.3	28 46.8	20 2.7	16 38.6	2 39.2	1 16.1
9 Sa	23 12 33	16 24 24	1♎14 51	7♎28 21	24 49.1	6 31.9	1 3.8	15 53.6	28 49.4	20 5.3	16 42.0	2 40.0	1 18.3
10 Su	23 16 30	17 22 44	13 38 43	19 46 7	24 39.4	8 25.7	2 6.5	16 32.0	28 52.2	20 7.8	16 45.4	2 40.9	1 20.5
11 M	23 20 27	18 21 5	25 50 43	1♏52 46	24 29.8	10 19.9	3 9.5	17 10.4	28 55.3	20 10.2	16 48.8	2 41.7	1 22.8
12 Tu	23 24 23	19 19 28	7♏52 35	13 50 31	24 21.4	12 14.4	4 12.7	17 48.7	28 58.4	20 12.5	16 52.2	2 42.7	1 25.0
13 W	23 28 20	20 17 53	19 47 1	25 42 32	24 14.9	14 8.8	5 16.3	18 27.2	29 1.8	20 14.7	16 55.7	2 43.6	1 27.2
14 Th	23 32 16	21 16 20	1♐37 36	7♐32 47	24 10.5	16 3.0	6 20.1	19 5.6	29 5.4	20 16.8	16 59.2	2 44.6	1 29.5
15 F	23 36 13	22 14 48	13 28 41	19 25 55	24D 8.3	17 56.7	7 24.2	19 44.0	29 9.1	20 18.7	17 2.7	2 45.6	1 31.7
16 Sa	23 40 9	23 13 18	25 25 9	1♑27 2	24 7.9	19 50.0	8 28.6	20 22.5	29 13.0	20 20.6	17 6.2	2 46.6	1 34.0
17 Su	23 44 6	24 11 49	7♑32 14	13 41 23	24 8.5	21 42.5	9 33.2	21 0.9	29 17.1	20 22.4	17 9.8	2 47.7	1 36.3
18 M	23 48 2	25 10 23	19 55 6	26 13 59	24R 9.1	23 34.4	10 38.1	21 39.4	29 21.3	20 24.0	17 13.3	2 48.8	1 38.5
19 Tu	23 51 59	26 8 57	2♒38 32	9♒ 9 11	24 8.9	25 25.4	11 43.2	22 17.9	29 25.7	20 25.6	17 16.9	2 49.9	1 40.8
20 W	23 55 56	27 7 34	15 46 15	22 29 57	24 6.8	27 15.6	12 48.6	22 56.4	29 30.3	20 27.0	17 20.5	2 51.0	1 43.1
21 Th	23 59 52	28 6 12	29 20 19	6♓17 16	24 2.4	29 4.8	13 54.2	23 34.9	29 35.1	20 28.4	17 24.1	2 52.2	1 45.3
22 F	0 3 49	29 4 52	13♓20 30	20 29 33	23 55.5	0♎53.2	15 0.1	24 13.4	29 40.0	20 29.6	17 27.8	2 53.4	1 47.6
23 Sa	0 7 45	0♎ 3 33	27 43 46	5♈ 2 21	23 46.5	2 40.6	16 6.1	24 52.0	29 45.1	20 30.7	17 31.4	2 54.6	1 49.9
24 Su	0 11 42	1 2 17	12♈24 21	19 48 43	23 36.4	4 27.1	17 12.5	25 30.5	29 50.3	20 31.7	17 35.1	2 55.9	1 52.2
25 M	0 15 38	2 1 3	27 14 23	4♉40 14	23 26.2	6 12.6	18 19.0	26 9.1	29 55.8	20 32.6	17 38.7	2 57.2	1 54.4
26 Tu	0 19 35	2 59 51	12♉ 5 12	19 28 20	23 17.2	7 57.1	19 25.7	26 47.7	0♑ 1.3	20 33.4	17 42.4	2 58.5	1 56.7
27 W	0 23 31	3 58 41	26 48 47	4♊ 5 52	23 10.4	9 40.8	20 32.7	27 26.3	0 7.1	20 34.1	17 46.1	2 59.8	1 59.0
28 Th	0 27 28	4 57 34	11♊19 1	18 27 52	23 6.0	11 23.5	21 39.9	28 5.0	0 13.0	20 34.7	17 49.8	3 1.2	2 1.3
29 F	0 31 24	5 56 29	25 32 11	2♋31 53	23D 4.0	13 5.3	22 47.3	28 43.6	0 19.0	20 35.1	17 53.5	3 2.6	2 3.6
30 Sa	0 35 21	6 55 26	9♋26 59	16 17 35	23 3.7	14 46.2	23 54.8	29 22.3	0 25.2	20 35.5	17 57.3	3 4.0	2 5.8

LONGITUDE OCTOBER 1972

Day	Sid.Time	☉	0 hr ☽	Noon ☽	True ☊	☿	♀	♂	♃	♄	♅	♆	♇
1 Su	0 39 18	7♎54 25	23♋ 3 51	29♋46 2	23♑ 3.9	16♎26.2	25♌ 2.6	0♎ 1.0	0♑31.6	20♊35.7	18♎ 1.0	3♐ 5.5	2♎ 8.1
2 M	0 43 14	8 53 27	6♌24 21	12♌59 3	23R 3.3	18 5.4	26 10.6	0 39.7	0 38.1	20R 35.9	18 4.7	3 7.0	2 10.4
3 Tu	0 47 11	9 52 31	19 30 23	25 58 33	23 0.8	19 43.7	27 18.7	1 18.4	0 44.8	20 35.9	18 8.5	3 8.5	2 12.7
4 W	0 51 7	10 51 38	2♍23 46	8♍46 10	22 55.6	21 21.2	28 27.0	1 57.2	0 51.6	20 35.8	18 12.3	3 10.0	2 14.9
5 Th	0 55 4	11 50 46	15 5 54	21 23 4	22 47.5	22 57.8	29 35.5	2 36.0	0 58.6	20 35.6	18 16.0	3 11.5	2 17.2
6 F	0 59 0	12 49 57	27 37 44	3♎49 59	22 36.5	24 33.7	0♍44.2	3 14.8	1 5.7	20 35.3	18 19.8	3 13.1	2 19.4
7 Sa	1 2 57	13 49 9	9♎59 52	16 7 27	22 23.4	26 8.8	1 53.0	3 53.6	1 13.0	20 34.9	18 23.6	3 14.7	2 21.7
8 Su	1 6 53	14 48 24	22 12 48	28 16 0	22 9.2	27 43.1	3 2.0	4 32.4	1 20.4	20 34.3	18 27.3	3 16.3	2 23.9
9 M	1 10 50	15 47 41	4♏17 11	10♏16 30	21 55.2	29 16.7	4 11.2	5 11.2	1 28.0	20 33.7	18 31.1	3 18.0	2 26.2
10 Tu	1 14 47	16 47 0	16 14 9	22 10 24	21 42.5	0♏49.5	5 20.5	5 50.1	1 35.7	20 32.9	18 34.9	3 19.7	2 28.4
11 W	1 18 43	17 46 21	28 5 33	3♐59 57	21 32.1	2 21.6	6 30.0	6 29.0	1 43.5	20 32.0	18 38.7	3 21.3	2 30.6
12 Th	1 22 40	18 45 43	9♐54 2	15 48 13	21 24.4	3 53.0	7 39.6	7 7.9	1 51.5	20 31.1	18 42.5	3 23.1	2 32.8
13 F	1 26 36	19 45 8	21 43 4	27 39 7	21 19.6	5 23.6	8 49.3	7 46.8	1 59.6	20 30.0	18 46.3	3 24.8	2 35.0
14 Sa	1 30 33	20 44 35	3♑36 59	9♑37 18	21 17.3	6 53.5	9 59.2	8 25.8	2 7.8	20 28.8	18 50.0	3 26.6	2 37.2
15 Su	1 34 29	21 44 3	15 40 44	21 47 57	21 16.7	8 22.7	11 9.3	9 4.7	2 16.2	20 27.5	18 53.8	3 28.3	2 39.4
16 M	1 38 26	22 43 33	27 59 39	4♒16 29	21 16.6	9 51.2	12 19.5	9 43.7	2 24.7	20 26.1	18 57.6	3 30.1	2 41.6
17 Tu	1 42 22	23 43 4	10♒39 5	17 8 2	21 16.0	11 19.0	13 29.8	10 22.7	2 33.4	20 24.6	19 1.4	3 32.0	2 43.8
18 W	1 46 19	24 42 38	23 43 50	0♓26 52	21 13.6	12 46.0	14 40.2	11 1.7	2 42.1	20 22.9	19 5.2	3 33.8	2 45.9
19 Th	1 50 16	25 42 13	7♓17 23	14 15 27	21 8.9	14 12.2	15 50.8	11 40.8	2 51.0	20 21.2	19 8.9	3 35.7	2 48.1
20 F	1 54 12	26 41 50	21 20 58	28 33 36	21 1.5	15 37.7	17 1.5	12 19.8	3 0.0	20 19.4	19 12.7	3 37.5	2 50.2
21 Sa	1 58 9	27 41 28	5♈52 48	13♈17 45	20 51.7	17 2.3	18 12.3	12 58.9	3 9.2	20 17.4	19 16.5	3 39.4	2 52.3
22 Su	2 2 5	28 41 9	20 47 29	28 20 48	20 40.5	18 26.2	19 23.2	13 38.0	3 18.4	20 15.4	19 20.2	3 41.3	2 54.4
23 M	2 6 2	29 40 51	5♉56 25	13♉32 57	20 29.1	19 49.1	20 34.3	14 17.1	3 27.8	20 13.3	19 24.0	3 43.3	2 56.5
24 Tu	2 9 58	0♏40 36	21 9 1	28 43 18	20 18.9	21 11.2	21 45.5	14 56.2	3 37.3	20 11.0	19 27.7	3 45.2	2 58.6
25 W	2 13 55	1 40 23	6♊14 35	13♊41 51	20 11.0	22 32.2	22 56.8	15 35.4	3 46.9	20 8.7	19 31.4	3 47.2	3 0.7
26 Th	2 17 51	2 40 12	21 4 15	28 21 8	20 5.8	23 52.3	24 8.2	16 14.6	3 56.7	20 6.2	19 35.1	3 49.2	3 2.7
27 F	2 21 48	3 40 3	5♋32 6	12♋36 54	20 3.2	25 11.2	25 19.8	16 53.8	4 6.5	20 3.7	19 38.9	3 51.2	3 4.8
28 Sa	2 25 45	4 39 57	19 35 30	26 27 59	20D 2.6	26 28.9	26 31.4	17 33.0	4 16.5	20 1.1	19 42.6	3 53.2	3 6.8
29 Su	2 29 41	5 39 52	3♌14 33	9♌55 30	20R 2.7	27 45.3	27 43.2	18 12.3	4 26.5	19 58.3	19 46.2	3 55.2	3 8.8
30 M	2 33 38	6 39 50	16 31 13	23 2 4	20 2.4	29 0.3	28 55.0	18 51.6	4 36.7	19 55.5	19 49.9	3 57.3	3 10.8
31 Tu	2 37 34	7 39 50	29 28 29	5♍50 52	20 0.4	0♐13.8	0♎ 7.0	19 30.9	4 47.0	19 52.6	19 53.6	3 59.3	3 12.8

Astro Data Dy Hr Mn	Planet Ingress Dy Hr Mn	Last Aspect Dy Hr Mn	☽ Ingress Dy Hr Mn	Last Aspect Dy Hr Mn	☽ Ingress Dy Hr Mn	☽ Phases & Eclipses Dy Hr Mn	Astro Data
☽0S 8 3:03	☿ ♍ 5 11:36	1 23:44 ♃ ☍	♋ 2 2:11	30 15:00 ♅ □	♌ 1 12:25	7 17:28 ● 15♍10	1 SEPTEMBER 1972
☽0N 22 11:34	♀ ♌ 7 23:27	3 23:36 ♀ ☌	♌ 4 6:54	3 15:54 ♀ ☌	♍ 3 19:31	15 19:13 ☽ 23♐02	Julian Day # 26542
☿0S 23 2:48	☿ ♎ 21 12:11	6 10:53 ♃ △	♍ 6 13:15	5 10:29 ♄ □	♎ 6 4:35	23 4:07 ○ 0♈14	Delta T 43.0 sec
	☉ ♎ 22 22:33	8 19:20 ♃ □	♎ 8 21:36	8 12:32 ☿ ☌	♏ 8 15:27	29 19:16 ☽ 6♋44	SVP 05♓38'13"
♅∠♆ 2 23:39	♃ ♑ 25 18:19	11 6:08 ♃ ⚹	♏ 11 8:15	8 23:47 ♀ ⚹	♐ 11 3:52		Obliquity 23°26'38"
♄ R 2 16:25	♂ ♎ 30 23:23	13 1:08 ☉ ⚹	♐ 13 20:42	12 21:32 ♄ ☍	♑ 13 16:44	7 8:08 ● 14♎09	⚷ Chiron 16♈37.1R
♂0S 4 6:34		16 7:37 ♃ ☌	♑ 16 9:07	15 12:55 ☉ □	♒ 16 3:51	15 12:55 ☽ 22♑16	☽ Mean ☊ 23♑42.7
☽0S 5 9:43	♀ ♍ 5 8:33	18 10:50 ☉ △	♒ 18 19:04	18 1:54 ☉ △	♓ 18 11:12	22 13:25 ○ 29♈15	
♃□♇ 18 13:31	☿ ♏ 9 11:11	21 0:26 ♃ ⚹	♓ 21 1:09	19 22:17 ♄ □	♈ 20 14:22	29 4:41 ☽ 5♌52	1 OCTOBER 1972
☽0N 19 21:45	☉ ♏ 23 7:41	23 3:21 ♃ □	♈ 23 3:44	22 13:25 ☉ ☍	♉ 22 14:37		Julian Day # 26572
♃⚻♅ 25 0:50	☿ ♐ 30 19:27	25 4:22 ♃ △	♉ 25 4:27	24 1:03 ♀ △	♊ 24 14:02		Delta T 43.1 sec
♄△♅ 30 20:25	♀ ♎ 30 21:40	27 1:04 ♂ △	♊ 27 5:14	26 5:29 ♀ □	♋ 26 14:44		SVP 05♓38'10"
		29 5:43 ♂ □	♋ 29 7:39	28 13:16 ☿ △	♌ 28 18:14		Obliquity 23°26'38"
				30 6:14 ♄ ⚹	♍ 31 0:59		⚷ Chiron 15♈24.6R
							☽ Mean ☊ 22♑07.4

NOVEMBER 1972 LONGITUDE

Day	Sid.Time	☉	0 hr ☽	Noon ☽	True ☊	☿	♀	♂	♃	♄	♅	♆	♇
1 W	2 41 31	8♏39 52	12♍ 9 38	18♍25 8	19♑55.9	1♐25.5	1♎19.1	20♎10.2	4♑57.4	19♊49.6	19♎57.2	4♐ 1.4	3♎14.7
2 Th	2 45 27	9 39 56	24 37 43	0♎47 42	19R 48.6	2 35.4	2 31.3	20 49.5	5 7.8	19R 46.5	20 0.9	4 3.5	3 16.6
3 F	2 49 24	10 40 2	6♎55 20	13 0 53	19 38.6	3 43.1	3 43.5	21 28.9	5 18.4	19 43.3	20 4.5	4 5.6	3 18.6
4 Sa	2 53 20	11 40 10	19 4 32	25 6 28	19 26.6	4 48.5	4 55.9	22 8.3	5 29.1	19 40.0	20 8.1	4 7.7	3 20.5
5 Su	2 57 17	12 40 21	1♏ 6 52	7♏ 5 52	19 13.5	5 51.3	6 8.3	22 47.7	5 39.9	19 36.6	20 11.7	4 9.8	3 22.3
6 M	3 1 14	13 40 33	13 3 38	19 0 18	19 0.5	6 51.1	7 20.8	23 27.2	5 50.8	19 33.2	20 15.2	4 12.0	3 24.2
7 Tu	3 5 10	14 40 47	24 56 3	0♐51 4	18 48.7	7 47.7	8 33.5	24 6.7	6 1.8	19 29.6	20 18.8	4 14.1	3 26.0
8 W	3 9 7	15 41 2	6♐45 35	12 39 51	18 39.0	8 40.6	9 46.2	24 46.1	6 12.9	19 26.0	20 22.3	4 16.3	3 27.9
9 Th	3 13 3	16 41 20	18 34 9	24 28 50	18 31.9	9 29.4	10 58.9	25 25.7	6 24.0	19 22.3	20 25.8	4 18.5	3 29.7
10 F	3 17 0	17 41 39	0♑24 17	6♑20 55	18 27.5	10 13.6	12 11.8	26 5.2	6 35.3	19 18.6	20 29.3	4 20.6	3 31.4
11 Sa	3 20 56	18 41 59	12 19 13	18 19 43	18D 25.6	10 52.6	13 24.7	26 44.7	6 46.7	19 14.7	20 32.8	4 22.8	3 33.2
12 Su	3 24 53	19 42 21	24 22 56	0♒29 30	18 25.6	11 25.8	14 37.7	27 24.3	6 58.1	19 10.8	20 36.2	4 25.0	3 34.9
13 M	3 28 49	20 42 45	6♒40 0	12 55 3	18 26.4	11 52.6	15 50.8	28 3.9	7 9.6	19 6.8	20 39.6	4 27.2	3 36.6
14 Tu	3 32 46	21 43 9	19 15 17	25 41 17	18R 27.1	12 12.2	17 3.9	28 43.5	7 21.3	19 2.8	20 43.0	4 29.4	3 38.3
15 W	3 36 43	22 43 35	2♓13 36	8♓52 43	18 26.7	12R 24.0	18 17.1	29 23.2	7 33.0	18 58.6	20 46.4	4 31.7	3 40.0
16 Th	3 40 39	23 44 3	15 39 1	22 32 46	18 24.3	12 27.1	19 30.4	0♏ 2.8	7 44.7	18 54.5	20 49.7	4 33.9	3 41.6
17 F	3 44 36	24 44 31	29 34 2	6♈42 44	18 19.8	12 21.0	20 43.7	0 42.5	7 56.6	18 50.2	20 53.0	4 36.1	3 43.2
18 Sa	3 48 32	25 45 1	13♈58 35	21 21 2	18 13.4	12 5.0	21 57.1	1 22.2	8 8.5	18 45.9	20 56.3	4 38.3	3 44.8
19 Su	3 52 29	26 45 33	28 49 19	6♉22 27	18 5.6	11 38.6	23 10.6	2 2.0	8 20.5	18 41.5	20 59.6	4 40.6	3 46.4
20 M	3 56 25	27 46 6	13♉59 17	21 38 28	17 57.5	11 1.7	24 24.1	2 41.7	8 32.6	18 37.1	21 2.8	4 42.8	3 47.9
21 Tu	4 0 22	28 46 40	29 18 36	6♊58 15	17 50.1	10 14.4	25 37.7	3 21.5	8 44.8	18 32.7	21 6.0	4 45.1	3 49.4
22 W	4 4 18	29 47 15	14♊36 0	22 10 36	17 44.4	9 17.1	26 51.4	4 1.3	8 57.0	18 28.2	21 9.2	4 47.3	3 50.9
23 Th	4 8 15	0♐47 53	29 40 52	7♋ 5 52	17 40.9	8 10.9	28 5.1	4 41.1	9 9.3	18 23.6	21 12.3	4 49.6	3 52.4
24 F	4 12 12	1 48 32	14♋24 53	21 37 21	17D 39.5	6 57.3	29 18.8	5 21.0	9 21.7	18 19.0	21 15.5	4 51.8	3 53.8
25 Sa	4 16 8	2 49 12	28 43 0	5♌41 41	17 39.9	5 38.3	0♏32.7	6 0.9	9 34.1	18 14.3	21 18.5	4 54.1	3 55.2
26 Su	4 20 5	3 49 54	12♌33 27	19 18 29	17 41.2	4 16.5	1 46.5	6 40.8	9 46.6	18 9.7	21 21.6	4 56.4	3 56.6
27 M	4 24 1	4 50 38	25 57 6	2♍29 40	17R 42.4	2 54.5	3 0.5	7 20.7	9 59.2	18 4.9	21 24.6	4 58.6	3 57.9
28 Tu	4 27 58	5 51 23	8♍56 38	15 18 28	17 42.8	1 35.0	4 14.4	8 0.7	10 11.8	18 0.2	21 27.6	5 0.9	3 59.2
29 W	4 31 54	6 52 9	21 35 42	27 48 49	17 41.5	0 20.7	5 28.5	8 40.7	10 24.5	17 55.4	21 30.5	5 3.1	4 0.5
30 Th	4 35 51	7 52 58	3♎58 19	10♎ 4 41	17 38.4	29♏13.9	6 42.6	9 20.7	10 37.3	17 50.5	21 33.5	5 5.4	4 1.8

DECEMBER 1972 LONGITUDE

Day	Sid.Time	☉	0 hr ☽	Noon ☽	True ☊	☿	♀	♂	♃	♄	♅	♆	♇
1 F	4 39 47	8♐53 47	16♎ 8 22	22♎ 9 48	17♑33.5	28♏16.4	7♏56.7	10♏ 0.7	10♑50.1	17♊45.7	21♎36.3	5♐ 7.6	4♎ 3.0
2 Sa	4 43 44	9 54 38	28 9 21	4♏ 7 25	17R 27.1	27R 29.4	9 10.9	10 40.8	11 3.0	17R 40.8	21 39.2	5 9.9	4 4.2
3 Su	4 47 41	10 55 31	10♏ 4 17	16 0 16	17 20.0	26 53.7	10 25.1	11 20.9	11 15.9	17 35.9	21 42.0	5 12.2	4 5.4
4 M	4 51 37	11 56 24	21 55 39	27 50 39	17 12.9	26 29.5	11 39.3	12 1.0	11 28.9	17 31.0	21 44.8	5 14.4	4 6.5
5 Tu	4 55 34	12 57 19	3♐45 31	9♐40 28	17 6.4	26D 16.7	12 53.6	12 41.1	11 41.9	17 26.1	21 47.5	5 16.7	4 7.6
6 W	4 59 30	13 58 15	15 35 43	21 31 29	17 1.3	26 14.7	14 7.9	13 21.3	11 55.0	17 21.2	21 50.2	5 18.9	4 8.7
7 Th	5 3 27	14 59 12	27 27 59	3♑25 29	16 57.7	26 23.0	15 22.3	14 1.5	12 8.2	17 16.2	21 52.8	5 21.1	4 9.8
8 F	5 7 23	16 0 10	9♑24 13	15 24 29	16D 55.9	26 40.7	16 36.7	14 41.7	12 21.4	17 11.3	21 55.4	5 23.4	4 10.8
9 Sa	5 11 20	17 1 9	21 26 34	27 30 51	16 55.7	27 7.0	17 51.1	15 21.9	12 34.6	17 6.3	21 58.0	5 25.6	4 11.8
10 Su	5 15 16	18 2 9	3♒37 40	9♒47 26	16 56.8	27 41.1	19 5.6	16 2.2	12 47.9	17 1.3	22 0.5	5 27.8	4 12.7
11 M	5 19 13	19 3 9	16 0 34	22 17 29	16 58.4	28 22.0	20 20.1	16 42.5	13 1.2	16 56.4	22 3.0	5 30.0	4 13.6
12 Tu	5 23 10	20 4 10	28 38 40	5♓ 4 33	17 0.2	29 9.1	21 34.6	17 22.8	13 14.6	16 51.4	22 5.5	5 32.3	4 14.5
13 W	5 27 6	21 5 11	11♓35 33	18 12 6	17R 1.4	0♐ 1.5	22 49.2	18 3.1	13 28.0	16 46.5	22 7.9	5 34.5	4 15.4
14 Th	5 31 3	22 6 13	24 54 31	1♈43 6	17 1.7	0 58.7	24 3.7	18 43.4	13 41.5	16 41.6	22 10.2	5 36.6	4 16.2
15 F	5 34 59	23 7 15	8♈38 1	15 39 20	17 0.9	2 0.1	25 18.3	19 23.8	13 55.0	16 36.7	22 12.5	5 38.8	4 17.0
16 Sa	5 38 56	24 8 18	22 46 57	0♉ 0 38	16 59.0	3 5.1	26 32.9	20 4.2	14 8.5	16 31.8	22 14.8	5 41.0	4 17.7
17 Su	5 42 52	25 9 21	7♉19 57	14 44 17	16 56.3	4 13.2	27 47.6	20 44.6	14 22.1	16 26.9	22 17.0	5 43.2	4 18.4
18 M	5 46 49	26 10 24	22 12 52	29 44 43	16 53.3	5 24.2	29 2.2	21 25.1	14 35.7	16 22.0	22 19.2	5 45.3	4 19.1
19 Tu	5 50 45	27 11 28	7♊18 47	14♊53 52	16 50.6	6 37.6	0♐16.9	22 5.5	14 49.3	16 17.2	22 21.3	5 47.5	4 19.8
20 W	5 54 42	28 12 33	22 28 45	0♋ 2 11	16 48.6	7 53.1	1 31.6	22 46.0	15 3.0	16 12.4	22 23.4	5 49.6	4 20.4
21 Th	5 58 39	29 13 38	7♋32 59	15 0 6	16D 47.5	9 10.4	2 46.4	23 26.6	15 16.7	16 7.7	22 25.4	5 51.7	4 21.0
22 F	6 2 35	0♑14 44	22 22 20	29 39 31	16 47.4	10 29.4	4 1.1	24 7.1	15 30.4	16 2.9	22 27.4	5 53.8	4 21.5
23 Sa	6 6 32	1 15 50	6♌50 26	13♌54 49	16 48.1	11 49.9	5 15.9	24 47.7	15 44.2	15 58.3	22 29.4	5 55.9	4 22.0
24 Su	6 10 28	2 16 56	20 52 26	27 43 12	16 49.2	13 11.6	6 30.7	25 28.3	15 57.9	15 53.6	22 31.2	5 58.0	4 22.5
25 M	6 14 25	3 18 3	4♍27 9	11♍ 4 29	16 50.5	14 34.4	7 45.5	26 8.9	16 11.8	15 49.0	22 33.1	6 0.1	4 23.0
26 Tu	6 18 21	4 19 11	17 35 30	24 0 36	16 51.4	15 58.3	9 0.4	26 49.6	16 25.6	15 44.4	22 34.9	6 2.1	4 23.4
27 W	6 22 18	5 20 19	0♎20 13	6♎34 53	16R 52.0	17 23.0	10 15.3	27 30.3	16 39.4	15 39.9	22 36.6	6 4.2	4 23.8
28 Th	6 26 15	6 21 28	12 45 8	18 51 30	16 51.9	18 48.5	11 30.1	28 11.0	16 53.3	15 35.4	22 38.3	6 6.2	4 24.1
29 F	6 30 11	7 22 38	24 54 35	0♏54 55	16 51.4	20 14.8	12 45.0	28 51.7	17 7.2	15 31.0	22 39.9	6 8.2	4 24.4
30 Sa	6 34 8	8 23 48	6♏53 3	12 49 31	16 50.5	21 41.7	13 60.0	29 32.5	17 21.1	15 26.6	22 41.5	6 10.2	4 24.7
31 Su	6 38 4	9 24 58	18 44 50	24 39 26	16 49.5	23 9.3	15 14.9	0♐13.3	17 35.1	15 22.3	22 43.0	6 12.2	4 24.9

Astro Data	Planet Ingress	Last Aspect	☽ Ingress	Last Aspect	☽ Ingress	☽ Phases & Eclipses	Astro Data
Dy Hr Mn	Dy Hr Mn	Dy Hr Mn	Dy Hr Mn	Dy Hr Mn	Dy Hr Mn	Dy Hr Mn	1 NOVEMBER 1972
☽0S 1 14:47	♂ ♏ 15 22:17	1 14:39 ♄ □	♎ 2 10:27	1 10:56 ♅ ☌	♏ 2 3:42	6 1:21 ● 13♏44	Julian Day # 26603
♀0S 2 22:55	☉ ♐ 22 5:03	4 6:26 ♂ ☌	♏ 4 21:46	4 9:03 ☿ ☌	♐ 4 16:22	14 5:01 ☽ 21♒56	Delta T 43.2 sec
☿ R 15 20:27	♀ ♏ 24 13:23	6 1:21 ☉ ☌	♐ 7 10:16	6 12:41 ♅ ✶	♑ 7 5:06	20 23:07 ○ 28♉44	SVP 05♓38'06"
☽0N 16 6:51	☿ ♏ 29 7:08	9 14:44 ♂ ✶	♑ 9 23:11	9 11:44 ☿ ✶	♒ 9 16:53	27 17:45 ☽ 5♍36	Obliquity 23°26'38"
☽0S 28 19:49		12 6:18 ♂ □	♒ 12 11:02	12 1:01 ☿ □	♓ 12 2:33		⚷ Chiron 14♈02.6R
	☿ ♐ 12 23:20	14 18:32 ♂ △	♓ 14 19:56	13 22:21 ♀ △	♈ 14 8:59	5 20:24 ● 13♐49	☽ Mean ☊ 20♑28.9
☿ D 5 16:23	♀ ♐ 18 18:34	16 15:08 ☉ △	♈ 17 0:44	16 2:26 ☉ △	♉ 16 11:59	13 18:36 ☽ 21♓52	
☽0N 13 13:47	☉ ♑ 21 18:13	18 14:08 ♀ ☍	♉ 19 1:53	18 11:51 ♀ ☍	♊ 18 12:24	20 9:45 ○ 28♊37	1 DECEMBER 1972
♃⊼♄ 23 18:20	♂ ♐ 30 16:12	20 23:07 ☉ ☍	♊ 21 1:05	20 9:45 ☉ ☍	♋ 20 11:57	27 10:27 ☽ 5♎47	Julian Day # 26633
☽0S 26 2:50		22 21:12 ♀ △	♋ 23 0:31	22 3:00 ♂ △	♌ 22 12:34		Delta T 43.3 sec
		24 11:26 ♅ □	♌ 25 2:12	24 8:27 ♂ □	♍ 24 16:03		SVP 05♓38'02"
		26 15:45 ♅ ✶	♍ 27 7:24	26 18:18 ♂ ✶	♎ 26 23:21		Obliquity 23°26'37"
		29 15:29 ☿ ✶	♎ 29 16:15	28 19:32 ♅ ☌	♏ 29 10:10		⚷ Chiron 13♈06.0R
				30 21:36 ♃ ✶	♐ 31 22:51		☽ Mean ☊ 18♑53.6

LONGITUDE JANUARY 1973

Day	Sid.Time	☉	0 hr ☽	Noon ☽	True ☊	☿	♀	♂	♃	♄	♅	♆	♇
1 M	6 42 1	10♑26 8	0♐33 48	6♐28 18	16♑48.4	24♐37.4	16♐29.8	0♐54.1	17♑49.0	15♊18.1	22♎44.5	6♐14.1	4♎25.1
2 Tu	6 45 57	11 27 19	12 23 21	18 19 16	16R 47.6	26 6.1	17 44.8	1 34.9	18 3.0	15R 13.9	22 45.9	6 16.1	4 25.3
3 W	6 49 54	12 28 30	24 16 22	0♑14 55	16 47.0	27 35.3	18 59.8	2 15.8	18 16.9	15 9.7	22 47.3	6 18.0	4 25.4
4 Th	6 53 50	13 29 42	6♑15 11	12 17 24	16D 46.7	29 4.9	20 14.7	2 56.7	18 30.9	15 5.7	22 48.6	6 19.9	4 25.5
5 F	6 57 47	14 30 53	18 21 44	24 28 25	16 46.7	0♑35.0	21 29.7	3 37.6	18 44.9	15 1.7	22 49.9	6 21.8	4 25.6
6 Sa	7 1 44	15 32 4	0♒37 37	6♒49 29	16 46.7	2 5.6	22 44.7	4 18.5	18 58.9	14 57.8	22 51.1	6 23.6	4R 25.6
7 Su	7 5 40	16 33 15	13 4 12	19 21 56	16R 46.8	3 36.6	23 59.8	4 59.5	19 13.0	14 53.9	22 52.3	6 25.5	4 25.6
8 M	7 9 37	17 34 25	25 42 50	2♓ 7 6	16 46.8	5 8.1	25 14.8	5 40.5	19 27.0	14 50.2	22 53.4	6 27.3	4 25.6
9 Tu	7 13 33	18 35 35	8♓34 52	15 6 20	16 46.6	6 40.0	26 29.8	6 21.5	19 41.0	14 46.5	22 54.4	6 29.1	4 25.5
10 W	7 17 30	19 36 45	21 41 38	28 20 58	16 46.3	8 12.3	27 44.8	7 2.5	19 55.0	14 42.9	22 55.4	6 30.9	4 25.4
11 Th	7 21 26	20 37 54	5♈ 4 27	11♈52 12	16 46.1	9 45.1	28 59.8	7 43.5	20 9.0	14 39.3	22 56.4	6 32.6	4 25.2
12 F	7 25 23	21 39 2	18 44 18	25 40 47	16D 45.9	11 18.3	0♑14.9	8 24.6	20 23.1	14 35.9	22 57.2	6 34.4	4 25.0
13 Sa	7 29 19	22 40 10	2♉41 35	9♉46 37	16 46.0	12 51.9	1 29.9	9 5.7	20 37.1	14 32.5	22 58.1	6 36.1	4 24.8
14 Su	7 33 16	23 41 18	16 55 40	24 8 26	16 46.4	14 26.1	2 44.9	9 46.8	20 51.1	14 29.3	22 58.8	6 37.8	4 24.6
15 M	7 37 13	24 42 24	1♊24 31	8♊43 24	16 47.0	16 0.7	3 60.0	10 27.9	21 5.2	14 26.1	22 59.6	6 39.5	4 24.3
16 Tu	7 41 9	25 43 30	16 4 27	23 26 57	16 47.8	17 35.8	5 15.0	11 9.1	21 19.2	14 23.0	23 0.2	6 41.1	4 24.0
17 W	7 45 6	26 44 35	0♋50 8	8♋13 7	16 48.5	19 11.4	6 30.1	11 50.3	21 33.2	14 20.0	23 0.8	6 42.7	4 23.6
18 Th	7 49 2	27 45 40	15 35 1	22 54 57	16R 48.8	20 47.5	7 45.1	12 31.5	21 47.2	14 17.1	23 1.4	6 44.3	4 23.3
19 F	7 52 59	28 46 44	0♌12 3	7♌25 30	16 48.5	22 24.1	9 0.2	13 12.8	22 1.2	14 14.3	23 1.9	6 45.9	4 22.8
20 Sa	7 56 55	29 47 47	14 34 35	21 38 40	16 47.6	24 1.3	10 15.2	13 54.0	22 15.2	14 11.6	23 2.3	6 47.4	4 22.4
21 Su	8 0 52	0♒48 49	28 37 16	5♍30 2	16 45.9	25 39.1	11 30.3	14 35.3	22 29.1	14 9.0	23 2.7	6 49.0	4 21.9
22 M	8 4 48	1 49 51	12♍16 44	18 57 16	16 43.9	27 17.4	12 45.4	15 16.6	22 43.1	14 6.4	23 3.0	6 50.5	4 21.4
23 Tu	8 8 45	2 50 53	25 31 42	2♎ 0 12	16 41.6	28 56.3	14 0.4	15 58.0	22 57.0	14 4.0	23 3.3	6 51.9	4 20.8
24 W	8 12 42	3 51 54	8♎23 1	14 40 31	16 39.6	0♒35.8	15 15.5	16 39.3	23 11.0	14 1.7	23 3.5	6 53.4	4 20.3
25 Th	8 16 38	4 52 54	20 53 10	27 1 27	16 38.1	2 16.0	16 30.6	17 20.7	23 24.9	13 59.5	23 3.6	6 54.8	4 19.6
26 F	8 20 35	5 53 54	3♏ 5 55	9♏ 7 10	16D 37.4	3 56.7	17 45.7	18 2.2	23 38.8	13 57.4	23 3.7	6 56.2	4 19.0
27 Sa	8 24 31	6 54 53	15 5 47	21 2 24	16 37.6	5 38.2	19 0.8	18 43.6	23 52.7	13 55.4	23R 3.8	6 57.5	4 18.3
28 Su	8 28 28	7 55 52	26 57 39	2♐52 7	16 38.7	7 20.2	20 15.8	19 25.1	24 6.5	13 53.5	23 3.7	6 58.8	4 17.6
29 M	8 32 24	8 56 50	8♐46 24	14 41 6	16 40.3	9 2.9	21 30.9	20 6.6	24 20.4	13 51.7	23 3.7	7 0.1	4 16.9
30 Tu	8 36 21	9 57 48	20 36 45	26 33 51	16 42.1	10 46.3	22 46.0	20 48.1	24 34.2	13 50.0	23 3.5	7 1.4	4 16.1
31 W	8 40 17	10 58 44	2♑32 52	8♑34 15	16 43.6	12 30.4	24 1.1	21 29.6	24 48.0	13 48.4	23 3.4	7 2.7	4 15.3

LONGITUDE FEBRUARY 1973

Day	Sid.Time	☉	0 hr ☽	Noon ☽	True ☊	☿	♀	♂	♃	♄	♅	♆	♇
1 Th	8 44 14	11♒59 40	14♑38 21	20♑45 29	16♑44.4	14♒15.0	25♑16.2	22♐11.2	25♑ 1.7	13♊46.9	23♎ 3.1	7♐ 3.9	4♎14.5
2 F	8 48 11	13 0 35	26 55 56	3♒ 9 53	16R 43.9	16 0.3	26 31.3	22 52.8	25 15.5	13R 45.6	23R 2.8	7 5.1	4R 13.7
3 Sa	8 52 7	14 1 29	9♒27 30	15 48 51	16 42.1	17 46.3	27 46.4	23 34.4	25 29.2	13 44.3	23 2.5	7 6.2	4 12.8
4 Su	8 56 4	15 2 21	22 13 58	28 42 49	16 38.8	19 32.7	29 1.5	24 16.0	25 42.8	13 43.2	23 2.1	7 7.3	4 11.9
5 M	9 0 0	16 3 13	5♓15 20	11♓51 24	16 34.4	21 19.8	0♒16.5	24 57.7	25 56.5	13 42.1	23 1.6	7 8.4	4 10.9
6 Tu	9 3 57	17 4 3	18 30 53	25 13 36	16 29.3	23 7.3	1 31.6	25 39.4	26 10.1	13 41.2	23 1.1	7 9.5	4 9.9
7 W	9 7 53	18 4 52	1♈59 22	8♈47 59	16 24.1	24 55.2	2 46.7	26 21.1	26 23.7	13 40.4	23 0.5	7 10.5	4 8.9
8 Th	9 11 50	19 5 39	15 39 15	22 33 0	16 19.6	26 43.4	4 1.7	27 2.8	26 37.2	13 39.7	22 59.9	7 11.5	4 7.9
9 F	9 15 46	20 6 25	29 29 1	6♉27 10	16 16.4	28 31.8	5 16.8	27 44.5	26 50.7	13 39.2	22 59.2	7 12.5	4 6.9
10 Sa	9 19 43	21 7 9	13♉27 16	20 29 10	16D 14.7	0♓20.4	6 31.8	28 26.3	27 4.2	13 38.7	22 58.5	7 13.4	4 5.8
11 Su	9 23 40	22 7 52	27 32 41	4♊37 41	16 14.6	2 8.8	7 46.9	29 8.0	27 17.6	13 38.4	22 57.7	7 14.3	4 4.7
12 M	9 27 36	23 8 33	11♊43 57	18 51 17	16 15.6	3 57.0	9 1.9	29 49.8	27 31.0	13 38.1	22 56.9	7 15.2	4 3.6
13 Tu	9 31 33	24 9 12	25 59 24	3♋ 8 1	16 17.1	5 44.7	10 16.9	0♑31.6	27 44.3	13D 38.0	22 56.0	7 16.1	4 2.4
14 W	9 35 29	25 9 50	10♋16 45	17 25 13	16R 18.2	7 31.6	11 31.9	1 13.5	27 57.6	13 38.0	22 55.0	7 16.9	4 1.2
15 Th	9 39 26	26 10 26	24 32 57	1♌39 26	16 18.0	9 17.4	12 47.0	1 55.3	28 10.8	13 38.1	22 54.1	7 17.6	4 0.1
16 F	9 43 22	27 11 0	8♌44 9	15 46 32	16 16.0	11 1.9	14 2.0	2 37.2	28 24.0	13 38.3	22 53.0	7 18.4	3 58.8
17 Sa	9 47 19	28 11 33	22 46 2	29 42 8	16 11.9	12 44.5	15 16.9	3 19.1	28 37.2	13 38.7	22 51.9	7 19.1	3 57.6
18 Su	9 51 15	29 12 4	6♍34 21	13♍22 15	16 5.9	14 24.9	16 31.9	4 1.0	28 50.3	13 39.1	22 50.8	7 19.8	3 56.3
19 M	9 55 12	0♓12 33	20 5 29	26 43 48	15 58.4	16 2.5	17 46.9	4 43.0	29 3.3	13 39.7	22 49.6	7 20.4	3 55.0
20 Tu	9 59 9	1 13 1	3♎17 4	9♎45 13	15 50.3	17 36.9	19 1.9	5 25.0	29 16.3	13 40.3	22 48.4	7 21.0	3 53.7
21 W	10 3 5	2 13 28	16 8 20	22 26 34	15 42.4	19 7.3	20 16.8	6 7.0	29 29.2	13 41.1	22 47.1	7 21.6	3 52.4
22 Th	10 7 2	3 13 53	28 40 10	4♏49 30	15 35.7	20 33.3	21 31.8	6 49.0	29 42.1	13 42.0	22 45.7	7 22.2	3 51.1
23 F	10 10 58	4 14 17	10♏55 0	16 57 8	15 30.6	21 54.2	22 46.8	7 31.0	29 55.0	13 43.0	22 44.4	7 22.7	3 49.7
24 Sa	10 14 55	5 14 39	22 56 28	28 53 37	15 27.7	23 9.3	24 1.7	8 13.1	0♒ 7.7	13 44.1	22 42.9	7 23.1	3 48.3
25 Su	10 18 51	6 15 0	4♐49 11	10♐43 50	15D 26.6	24 18.0	25 16.7	8 55.2	0 20.4	13 45.4	22 41.5	7 23.6	3 46.9
26 M	10 22 48	7 15 20	16 38 14	22 33 3	15 27.1	25 19.7	26 31.6	9 37.3	0 33.1	13 46.7	22 40.0	7 24.0	3 45.5
27 Tu	10 26 44	8 15 38	28 28 57	4♑26 36	15 28.2	26 13.8	27 46.5	10 19.4	0 45.7	13 48.2	22 38.4	7 24.4	3 44.0
28 W	10 30 41	9 15 55	10♑26 36	16 29 33	15R 29.2	26 59.7	29 1.5	11 1.5	0 58.2	13 49.7	22 36.8	7 24.7	3 42.6

Astro Data Dy Hr Mn	Planet Ingress Dy Hr Mn	Last Aspect Dy Hr Mn	☽ Ingress Dy Hr Mn	Last Aspect Dy Hr Mn	☽ Ingress Dy Hr Mn	☽ Phases & Eclipses Dy Hr Mn	Astro Data
♇ R 6 6:56	☿ ♑ 4 14:41	3 7:37 ☿ ☌	♑ 3 11:30	1 23:07 ♀ ☌	♒ 2 5:55	4 15:42 ● 14♑10	1 JANUARY 1973
☽0N 9 19:17	♀ ♑ 11 19:15	5 8:48 ♅ □	♒ 5 22:47	4 4:00 ♂ ✶	♓ 4 14:22	4 15:45:37 ☌ A 7'49"	Julian Day # 26664
♃∠♆ 17 18:27	☉ ♒ 20 4:48	7 23:01 ♀ ✶	♓ 8 8:03	6 13:55 ♃ ✶	♈ 6 20:29	12 5:27 ☽ 21♈53	Delta T 43.4 sec
☽0S 22 12:20	☿ ♒ 23 15:23	10 12:03 ♀ □	♈ 10 14:57	8 22:06 ☿ ✶	♉ 9 0:53	18 21:28 ○ 28♋40	SVP 05♓37'56"
♃□♅ 23 10:53		12 7:19 ♅ ☍	♉ 12 19:24	10 23:34 ♃ △	♊ 11 4:10	18 21:17 ☍ A 0.866	Obliquity 23°26'36"
♅ R 27 5:30	♀ ♒ 4 18:43	14 12:06 ☉ △	♊ 14 21:41	12 20:41 ☉ △	♋ 13 6:44	26 6:05 ☽ 6♏09	⚷ Chiron 12♈52.9
	☿ ♓ 9 19:30	16 11:17 ♅ △	♋ 16 22:39	15 6:13 ♃ ☍	♌ 15 9:12		☽ Mean ☊ 17♑15.1
☽0N 6 1:18	♂ ♑ 12 5:51	18 21:28 ☉ ☍	♌ 18 23:40	17 10:07 ☉ ☍	♍ 17 12:31	3 9:23 ● 14♒25	
♄ D 13 12:49	☉ ♓ 18 19:01	20 14:24 ♅ ✶	♍ 21 2:23	19 16:31 ♃ △	♎ 19 17:58	10 14:05 ☽ 21♉43	1 FEBRUARY 1973
♃⚼♄ 17 2:48	♃ ♒ 23 9:28	23 7:13 ☿ △	♎ 23 8:16	22 2:02 ♃ □	♏ 22 2:35	17 10:07 ○ 28♌37	Julian Day # 26695
☽0S 18 22:36	♀ ♓ 28 18:45	25 5:01 ♃ □	♏ 25 17:52	24 2:27 ♀ □	♐ 24 14:14	25 3:10 ☽ 6♐23	Delta T 43.5 sec
☿0N 26 19:10		27 18:06 ♃ ✶	♐ 28 6:10	26 22:24 ♀ ✶	♑ 27 3:04		SVP 05♓37'50"
		30 4:56 ♅ ✶	♑ 30 18:54				Obliquity 23°26'36"
							⚷ Chiron 13♈31.8
							☽ Mean ☊ 15♑36.7

MARCH 1973 LONGITUDE

Day	Sid.Time	☉	0 hr ☽	Noon ☽	True ☊	☿	♀	♂	♃	♄	♅	♆	♇
1 Th	10 34 38	10♓16 10	22♑35 59	28♑46 22	15♑29.0	27♓37.1	0♓16.4	11♑43.7	1♒10.7	13♊51.4	22♎35.1	7♐25.0	3♎41.1
2 F	10 38 34	11 16 23	5♒ 1 9	11♒20 37	15R27.0	28 5.4	1 31.3	12 25.9	1 23.1	13 53.2	22R33.5	7 25.3	3R39.6
3 Sa	10 42 31	12 16 35	17 45 1	24 14 30	15 22.5	28 24.6	2 46.2	13 8.1	1 35.4	13 55.1	22 31.7	7 25.5	3 38.1
4 Su	10 46 27	13 16 45	0♓49 4	7♓28 38	15 15.6	28R34.3	4 1.1	13 50.3	1 47.6	13 57.1	22 30.0	7 25.8	3 36.6
5 M	10 50 24	14 16 54	14 13 1	21 1 54	15 6.6	28 34.7	5 16.0	14 32.5	1 59.8	13 59.2	22 28.2	7 25.9	3 35.1
6 Tu	10 54 20	15 17 0	27 54 53	4♈51 30	14 56.4	28 25.9	6 30.8	15 14.8	2 11.9	14 1.4	22 26.3	7 26.1	3 33.5
7 W	10 58 17	16 17 5	11♈51 11	18 53 23	14 45.9	28 8.1	7 45.7	15 57.1	2 24.0	14 3.8	22 24.4	7 26.2	3 32.0
8 Th	11 2 13	17 17 7	25 57 30	3♉ 2 58	14 36.4	27 42.0	9 0.5	16 39.3	2 35.9	14 6.2	22 22.5	7 26.2	3 30.4
9 F	11 6 10	18 17 8	10♉ 9 15	17 15 50	14 29.0	27 8.2	10 15.4	17 21.6	2 47.8	14 8.7	22 20.5	7R26.3	3 28.9
10 Sa	11 10 7	19 17 6	24 22 18	1♊28 19	14 24.0	26 27.6	11 30.2	18 3.9	2 59.6	14 11.4	22 18.5	7 26.3	3 27.3
11 Su	11 14 3	20 17 2	8♊33 35	15 37 54	14D21.5	25 41.1	12 45.0	18 46.2	3 11.3	14 14.1	22 16.5	7 26.2	3 25.7
12 M	11 18 0	21 16 56	22 41 6	29 43 5	14 21.0	24 49.9	13 59.8	19 28.6	3 22.9	14 17.0	22 14.5	7 26.2	3 24.1
13 Tu	11 21 56	22 16 48	6♋43 46	13♋43 5	14R21.3	23 55.2	15 14.5	20 10.9	3 34.5	14 19.9	22 12.4	7 26.1	3 22.5
14 W	11 25 53	23 16 38	20 40 58	27 37 20	14 21.3	22 58.4	16 29.3	20 53.3	3 45.9	14 23.0	22 10.2	7 26.0	3 20.9
15 Th	11 29 49	24 16 25	4♌32 5	11♌25 5	14 19.8	22 0.7	17 44.0	21 35.7	3 57.3	14 26.1	22 8.1	7 25.8	3 19.2
16 F	11 33 46	25 16 10	18 16 9	25 5 4	14 15.7	21 3.5	18 58.8	22 18.1	4 8.6	14 29.4	22 5.9	7 25.6	3 17.6
17 Sa	11 37 42	26 15 52	1♍51 36	8♍35 30	14 8.8	20 7.8	20 13.5	23 0.5	4 19.8	14 32.7	22 3.7	7 25.4	3 16.0
18 Su	11 41 39	27 15 33	15 16 28	21 54 15	13 59.1	19 14.8	21 28.2	23 42.9	4 30.9	14 36.2	22 1.4	7 25.1	3 14.3
19 M	11 45 36	28 15 12	28 28 36	4♎59 17	13 47.3	18 25.3	22 42.8	24 25.3	4 41.9	14 39.7	21 59.2	7 24.8	3 12.7
20 Tu	11 49 32	29 14 48	11♎26 10	17 49 7	13 34.4	17 40.3	23 57.5	25 7.8	4 52.8	14 43.4	21 56.9	7 24.5	3 11.0
21 W	11 53 29	0♈14 23	24 8 6	0♏23 10	13 21.7	17 0.2	25 12.2	25 50.2	5 3.7	14 47.1	21 54.6	7 24.1	3 9.4
22 Th	11 57 25	1 13 55	6♏34 26	12 42 7	13 10.3	16 25.5	26 26.8	26 32.7	5 14.4	14 50.9	21 52.2	7 23.7	3 7.7
23 F	12 1 22	2 13 26	18 46 28	24 47 51	13 1.0	15 56.7	27 41.4	27 15.2	5 25.0	14 54.8	21 49.9	7 23.3	3 6.1
24 Sa	12 5 18	3 12 55	0♐46 43	6♐43 31	12 54.4	15 33.8	28 56.1	27 57.7	5 35.5	14 58.8	21 47.5	7 22.8	3 4.4
25 Su	12 9 15	4 12 22	12 38 50	18 33 14	12 50.4	15 16.9	0♈10.7	28 40.3	5 46.0	15 2.9	21 45.1	7 22.4	3 2.8
26 M	12 13 11	5 11 48	24 27 22	0♑21 52	12 48.7	15 6.1	1 25.3	29 22.8	5 56.3	15 7.1	21 42.7	7 21.8	3 1.1
27 Tu	12 17 8	6 11 11	6♑17 28	12 14 49	12 48.4	15D 1.1	2 39.8	0♒ 5.4	6 6.5	15 11.4	21 40.2	7 21.3	2 59.5
28 W	12 21 5	7 10 33	18 14 39	24 17 37	12 48.3	15 2.0	3 54.4	0 47.9	6 16.6	15 15.8	21 37.8	7 20.7	2 57.8
29 Th	12 25 1	8 9 53	0♒24 25	6♒35 37	12 47.5	15 8.5	5 9.0	1 30.5	6 26.6	15 20.2	21 35.3	7 20.1	2 56.2
30 F	12 28 58	9 9 12	12 51 50	19 13 31	12 44.8	15 20.4	6 23.5	2 13.1	6 36.5	15 24.8	21 32.8	7 19.5	2 54.5
31 Sa	12 32 54	10 8 28	25 41 4	2♓14 46	12 39.6	15 37.4	7 38.0	2 55.7	6 46.3	15 29.4	21 30.3	7 18.8	2 52.9

APRIL 1973 LONGITUDE

Day	Sid.Time	☉	0 hr ☽	Noon ☽	True ☊	☿	♀	♂	♃	♄	♅	♆	♇
1 Su	12 36 51	11♈ 7 43	8♓54 47	15♓41 7	12♑31.7	15♓59.3	8♈52.5	3♒38.2	6♒55.9	15♊34.1	21♎27.8	7♐18.1	2♎51.2
2 M	12 40 47	12 6 55	22 33 35	29 31 54	12R21.4	16 26.0	10 7.0	4 20.8	7 5.5	15 38.9	21R25.2	7R17.4	2R49.6
3 Tu	12 44 44	13 6 6	6♈35 35	13♈44 0	12 9.5	16 57.0	11 21.5	5 3.4	7 14.9	15 43.7	21 22.7	7 16.6	2 48.0
4 W	12 48 40	14 5 15	20 56 23	28 11 54	11 57.3	17 32.3	12 36.0	5 46.1	7 24.2	15 48.7	21 20.2	7 15.8	2 46.3
5 Th	12 52 37	15 4 21	5♉29 38	12♉48 38	11 46.1	18 11.5	13 50.4	6 28.7	7 33.4	15 53.7	21 17.6	7 15.0	2 44.7
6 F	12 56 33	16 3 26	20 7 59	27 26 50	11 37.1	18 54.6	15 4.9	7 11.3	7 42.5	15 58.8	21 15.0	7 14.2	2 43.1
7 Sa	13 0 30	17 2 28	4♊44 25	12♊ 0 3	11 30.8	19 41.2	16 19.3	7 53.9	7 51.4	16 4.0	21 12.5	7 13.3	2 41.5
8 Su	13 4 27	18 1 28	19 13 13	26 23 30	11 27.4	20 31.1	17 33.7	8 36.5	8 0.2	16 9.3	21 9.9	7 12.4	2 39.9
9 M	13 8 23	19 0 26	3♋30 37	10♋34 23	11D26.1	21 24.3	18 48.1	9 19.1	8 8.9	16 14.6	21 7.3	7 11.5	2 38.4
10 Tu	13 12 20	19 59 22	17 34 45	24 31 41	11R26.1	22 20.5	20 2.4	10 1.7	8 17.5	16 20.0	21 4.7	7 10.5	2 36.8
11 W	13 16 16	20 58 15	1♌25 15	8♌15 31	11 25.8	23 19.7	21 16.8	10 44.3	8 25.9	16 25.5	21 2.2	7 9.6	2 35.2
12 Th	13 20 13	21 57 6	15 2 37	21 46 38	11 24.1	24 21.5	22 31.1	11 26.9	8 34.2	16 31.1	20 59.6	7 8.6	2 33.7
13 F	13 24 9	22 55 54	28 27 40	5♍ 5 47	11 20.1	25 26.1	23 45.4	12 9.5	8 42.4	16 36.7	20 57.0	7 7.5	2 32.2
14 Sa	13 28 6	23 54 40	11♍41 2	18 13 27	11 13.2	26 33.1	24 59.7	12 52.1	8 50.4	16 42.4	20 54.4	7 6.5	2 30.6
15 Su	13 32 2	24 53 24	24 43 1	1♎ 9 43	11 3.7	27 42.6	26 14.0	13 34.8	8 58.3	16 48.2	20 51.8	7 5.4	2 29.1
16 M	13 35 59	25 52 6	7♎33 32	13 54 25	10 52.0	28 54.4	27 28.2	14 17.4	9 6.1	16 54.0	20 49.3	7 4.3	2 27.6
17 Tu	13 39 56	26 50 46	20 12 21	26 27 18	10 39.3	0♈ 8.5	28 42.4	14 60.0	9 13.7	16 59.9	20 46.7	7 3.2	2 26.2
18 W	13 43 52	27 49 24	2♏39 18	8♏48 24	10 26.7	1 24.7	29 56.6	15 42.6	9 21.1	17 5.8	20 44.1	7 2.0	2 24.7
19 Th	13 47 49	28 48 0	14 54 42	20 58 19	10 15.2	2 43.1	1♉10.8	16 25.2	9 28.5	17 11.9	20 41.6	7 0.9	2 23.2
20 F	13 51 45	29 46 34	26 59 28	2♐58 25	10 5.8	4 3.5	2 25.0	17 7.8	9 35.7	17 17.9	20 39.1	6 59.7	2 21.8
21 Sa	13 55 42	0♉45 6	8♐55 27	14 50 58	9 58.9	5 25.9	3 39.2	17 50.4	9 42.7	17 24.1	20 36.5	6 58.5	2 20.4
22 Su	13 59 38	1 43 37	20 45 22	26 39 9	9 54.8	6 50.3	4 53.3	18 33.0	9 49.6	17 30.3	20 34.0	6 57.2	2 19.0
23 M	14 3 35	2 42 6	2♑32 50	8♑26 59	9D52.9	8 16.6	6 7.5	19 15.6	9 56.3	17 36.6	20 31.5	6 56.0	2 17.6
24 Tu	14 7 31	3 40 33	14 22 13	20 19 10	9 52.7	9 44.9	7 21.6	19 58.2	10 2.9	17 42.9	20 29.0	6 54.7	2 16.3
25 W	14 11 28	4 38 59	26 18 30	2♒20 54	9R53.3	11 14.9	8 35.7	20 40.7	10 9.4	17 49.3	20 26.5	6 53.4	2 14.9
26 Th	14 15 25	5 37 23	8♒27 2	14 37 33	9 53.5	12 46.9	9 49.8	21 23.3	10 15.7	17 55.7	20 24.1	6 52.1	2 13.6
27 F	14 19 21	6 35 45	20 53 6	27 14 16	9 52.4	14 20.6	11 3.9	22 5.8	10 21.8	18 2.2	20 21.6	6 50.8	2 12.3
28 Sa	14 23 18	7 34 6	3♓41 34	10♓15 26	9 49.4	15 56.2	12 17.9	22 48.4	10 27.8	18 8.7	20 19.2	6 49.4	2 11.0
29 Su	14 27 14	8 32 26	16 56 10	23 43 56	9 44.1	17 33.7	13 32.0	23 30.9	10 33.6	18 15.3	20 16.7	6 48.1	2 9.7
30 M	14 31 11	9 30 43	0♈38 45	7♈40 27	9 36.8	19 12.9	14 46.0	24 13.4	10 39.2	18 22.0	20 14.4	6 46.7	2 8.5

Astro Data	Planet Ingress	Last Aspect	☽ Ingress	Last Aspect	☽ Ingress	☽ Phases & Eclipses	Astro Data
Dy Hr Mn	Dy Hr Mn	Dy Hr Mn	Dy Hr Mn	Dy Hr Mn	Dy Hr Mn	Dy Hr Mn	1 MARCH 1973
☿ R 4 12:58	☉ ♈ 20 18:12	1 10:11 ☿ ✶	♒ 1 14:22	1 12:56 ☿ ☌	♈ 2 12:48	5 0:07 ● 14♓17	Julian Day # 26723
☽0N 5 9:06	♀ ♈ 24 20:34	3 8:50 ♅ △	♓ 3 22:31	4 0:39 ♅ ☍	♉ 4 14:58	11 21:26 ☽ 21♊11	Delta T 43.6 sec
♅∠♆ 6 2:57	♂ ♒ 26 20:59	6 0:53 ♅ ☌	♈ 6 3:37	5 21:53 ♅ ✶	♊ 6 16:12	18 23:33 ○ 28♍14	SVP 05♓37'47"
♆ R 9 14:32		7 17:56 ♅ ☍	♉ 8 6:51	8 3:14 ♅ △	♋ 8 18:04	26 23:46 ☽ 6♑11	Obliquity 23°26'37"
♃△♇ 12 2:04	☿ ♈ 16 21:17	10 3:21 ☿ ✶	♊ 10 9:31	10 8:50 ☿ △	♌ 10 21:31		⚷ Chiron 14♈43.8
☿0S 14 21:03	♀ ♉ 18 1:05	12 3:26 ☿ □	♋ 12 12:29	12 14:41 ♀ △	♍ 13 2:47	3 11:45 ● 13♈35	☽ Mean ☊ 14♑07.7
☽0S 18 7:25	☉ ♉ 20 5:30	14 4:50 ☉ △	♌ 14 16:07	15 6:07 ☿ ☍	♎ 15 9:50	10 4:28 ☽ 20♋10	
♀0N 27 11:02		16 6:43 ♅ ✶	♍ 16 20:42	17 18:10 ♀ ☍	♏ 17 18:51	17 13:51 ○ 27♎25	1 APRIL 1973
☿ D 27 8:19		18 23:33 ☉ ☍	♎ 19 2:48	19 3:10 ♂ □	♐ 20 6:02	25 17:59 ☽ 5♒23	Julian Day # 26754
☽0N 1 18:18		21 3:27 ♂ □	♏ 21 11:15	21 23:37 ♅ ✶	♑ 22 18:49		Delta T 43.6 sec
♃✶♆ 3 4:01		23 19:52 ♀ △	♐ 23 22:26	24 12:17 ♅ □	♒ 25 7:21		SVP 05♓37'44"
☽0S 14 13:44		25 18:26 ♅ ✶	♑ 26 11:16	27 2:26 ♂ ☌	♓ 27 17:10		Obliquity 23°26'37"
☿0N 21 14:34		28 6:42 ♅ □	♒ 28 23:12	29 2:22 ♄ □	♈ 29 22:53		⚷ Chiron 16♈27.4
☽0N 29 3:33		30 16:17 ♅ △	♓ 31 7:55				☽ Mean ☊ 12♑29.2

LONGITUDE — MAY 1973

Day	Sid.Time	☉	0 hr ☽	Noon ☽	True ☊	☿	♀	♂	♃	♄	♅	♆	♇
1 Tu	14 35 7	10♉28 59	14♈48 41	22♈ 2 53	9♑28.0	20♈53.9	16♉ 0.1	24♒55.9	10♒44.7	18♊28.7	20♎12.0	6♐45.3	2♎ 7.3
2 W	14 39 4	11 27 14	29 22 20	6♉46 6	9R 18.8	22 36.8	17 14.1	25 38.4	10 50.1	18 35.4	20R 9.6	6R 43.9	2R 6.1
3 Th	14 43 0	12 25 27	14♉13 10	21 42 24	9 10.3	24 21.5	18 28.1	26 20.8	10 55.2	18 42.2	20 7.3	6 42.4	2 4.9
4 F	14 46 57	13 23 38	29 12 40	6♊42 46	9 3.4	26 8.0	19 42.0	27 3.2	11 0.2	18 49.1	20 5.0	6 41.0	2 3.7
5 Sa	14 50 54	14 21 48	14♊11 39	21 38 17	8 58.8	27 56.3	20 56.0	27 45.6	11 5.0	18 56.0	20 2.7	6 39.5	2 2.6
6 Su	14 54 50	15 19 55	29 1 50	6♋21 35	8D 56.5	29 46.5	22 9.9	28 28.0	11 9.7	19 2.9	20 0.4	6 38.1	2 1.5
7 M	14 58 47	16 18 1	13♋36 58	20 47 36	8 56.2	1♉38.5	23 23.9	29 10.4	11 14.2	19 9.9	19 58.2	6 36.6	2 0.4
8 Tu	15 2 43	17 16 5	27 53 14	4♌53 46	8 57.0	3 32.4	24 37.8	29 52.7	11 18.5	19 16.9	19 56.0	6 35.1	1 59.4
9 W	15 6 40	18 14 7	11♌49 12	18 39 37	8R 57.9	5 28.0	25 51.7	0♓35.0	11 22.6	19 23.9	19 53.8	6 33.6	1 58.3
10 Th	15 10 36	19 12 7	25 25 10	2♍ 6 4	8 57.9	7 25.5	27 5.5	1 17.2	11 26.6	19 31.0	19 51.7	6 32.0	1 57.3
11 F	15 14 33	20 10 4	8♍42 33	15 14 53	8 56.2	9 24.7	28 19.4	1 59.5	11 30.4	19 38.2	19 49.6	6 30.5	1 56.4
12 Sa	15 18 29	21 8 0	21 43 18	28 8 4	8 52.5	11 25.7	29 33.2	2 41.7	11 34.0	19 45.4	19 47.5	6 29.0	1 55.4
13 Su	15 22 26	22 5 55	4♎29 24	10♎47 32	8 46.8	13 28.3	0♊47.0	3 23.8	11 37.4	19 52.6	19 45.4	6 27.4	1 54.5
14 M	15 26 23	23 3 47	17 2 40	23 15 0	8 39.6	15 32.6	2 0.8	4 6.0	11 40.7	19 59.8	19 43.4	6 25.8	1 53.6
15 Tu	15 30 19	24 1 38	29 24 41	5♏31 55	8 31.6	17 38.3	3 14.6	4 48.1	11 43.8	20 7.1	19 41.4	6 24.3	1 52.7
16 W	15 34 16	24 59 28	11♏36 50	17 39 36	8 23.6	19 45.5	4 28.4	5 30.1	11 46.6	20 14.4	19 39.4	6 22.7	1 51.9
17 Th	15 38 12	25 57 15	23 40 24	29 39 25	8 16.4	21 53.9	5 42.1	6 12.2	11 49.4	20 21.7	19 37.5	6 21.1	1 51.0
18 F	15 42 9	26 55 2	5♐36 51	11♐32 56	8 10.5	24 3.4	6 55.9	6 54.2	11 51.9	20 29.1	19 35.6	6 19.5	1 50.2
19 Sa	15 46 5	27 52 47	17 27 55	23 22 7	8 6.5	26 13.7	8 9.6	7 36.1	11 54.2	20 36.5	19 33.8	6 17.9	1 49.5
20 Su	15 50 2	28 50 31	29 15 51	5♑ 9 28	8D 4.4	28 24.7	9 23.3	8 18.1	11 56.4	20 44.0	19 32.0	6 16.3	1 48.8
21 M	15 53 58	29 48 14	11♑ 3 24	16 58 5	8 4.0	0♊36.2	10 37.0	8 59.9	11 58.4	20 51.4	19 30.2	6 14.7	1 48.1
22 Tu	15 57 55	0♊45 55	22 53 59	28 51 39	8 4.9	2 47.8	11 50.7	9 41.8	12 0.2	20 58.9	19 28.5	6 13.1	1 47.4
23 W	16 1 52	1 43 35	4♒51 35	10♒54 23	8 6.5	4 59.3	13 4.3	10 23.6	12 1.8	21 6.4	19 26.8	6 11.5	1 46.7
24 Th	16 5 48	2 41 15	17 0 38	23 10 55	8 8.1	7 10.4	14 18.0	11 5.3	12 3.2	21 14.0	19 25.1	6 9.9	1 46.1
25 F	16 9 45	3 38 53	29 25 49	5♓45 54	8R 9.0	9 20.9	15 31.6	11 47.0	12 4.4	21 21.5	19 23.5	6 8.2	1 45.5
26 Sa	16 13 41	4 36 30	12♓11 43	18 43 43	8 8.9	11 30.4	16 45.2	12 28.7	12 5.5	21 29.1	19 21.9	6 6.6	1 45.0
27 Su	16 17 38	5 34 6	25 22 19	2♈ 7 48	8 7.3	13 38.7	17 58.9	13 10.3	12 6.3	21 36.7	19 20.4	6 5.0	1 44.5
28 M	16 21 34	6 31 42	9♈ 0 20	15 59 56	8 4.5	15 45.6	19 12.5	13 51.8	12 7.0	21 44.4	19 18.9	6 3.4	1 44.0
29 Tu	16 25 31	7 29 16	23 6 28	0♉19 35	8 0.7	17 50.8	20 26.0	14 33.3	12 7.4	21 52.0	19 17.4	6 1.7	1 43.5
30 W	16 29 27	8 26 50	7♉38 46	15 3 18	7 56.5	19 54.2	21 39.6	15 14.7	12R 7.7	21 59.7	19 16.0	6 0.1	1 43.1
31 Th	16 33 24	9 24 23	22 32 17	0♊ 4 41	7 52.5	21 55.6	22 53.2	15 56.0	12 7.8	22 7.4	19 14.7	5 58.5	1 42.7

LONGITUDE — JUNE 1973

Day	Sid.Time	☉	0 hr ☽	Noon ☽	True ☊	☿	♀	♂	♃	♄	♅	♆	♇
1 F	16 37 21	10♊21 55	7♊39 21	15♊15 3	7♑49.4	23♊54.8	24♊ 6.7	16♓37.3	12♒ 7.7	22♊15.1	19♎13.3	5♐56.9	1♎42.3
2 Sa	16 41 17	11 19 26	22 50 34	0♋24 42	7R 47.5	25 51.7	25 20.3	17 18.5	12R 7.4	22 22.8	19R 12.1	5R 55.3	1R 42.0
3 Su	16 45 14	12 16 55	7♋56 18	15 24 23	7D 46.9	27 46.3	26 33.8	17 59.6	12 6.9	22 30.5	19 10.9	5 53.7	1 41.7
4 M	16 49 10	13 14 24	22 48 5	0♌ 6 43	7 47.4	29 38.4	27 47.3	18 40.7	12 6.2	22 38.3	19 9.7	5 52.0	1 41.4
5 Tu	16 53 7	14 11 52	7♌19 44	14 26 47	7 48.6	1♋27.9	29 0.8	19 21.7	12 5.3	22 46.0	19 8.6	5 50.4	1 41.2
6 W	16 57 3	15 9 18	21 27 40	28 22 19	7 50.0	3 14.9	0♋14.3	20 2.5	12 4.2	22 53.8	19 7.5	5 48.8	1 41.0
7 Th	17 1 0	16 6 43	5♍10 50	11♍53 21	7R 51.0	4 59.3	1 27.8	20 43.4	12 3.0	23 1.6	19 6.4	5 47.2	1 40.8
8 F	17 4 57	17 4 7	18 30 7	25 1 28	7 51.4	6 41.0	2 41.2	21 24.1	12 1.5	23 9.4	19 5.4	5 45.7	1 40.7
9 Sa	17 8 53	18 1 29	1♎27 44	7♎49 19	7 50.8	8 20.1	3 54.6	22 4.7	11 59.9	23 17.1	19 4.5	5 44.1	1 40.5
10 Su	17 12 50	18 58 51	14 6 37	20 20 1	7 49.4	9 56.4	5 8.0	22 45.3	11 58.1	23 24.9	19 3.6	5 42.5	1 40.5
11 M	17 16 46	19 56 12	26 29 56	2♏36 46	7 47.2	11 30.1	6 21.4	23 25.7	11 56.0	23 32.7	19 2.8	5 40.9	1D 40.4
12 Tu	17 20 43	20 53 31	8♏40 52	14 42 37	7 44.8	13 1.0	7 34.8	24 6.1	11 53.8	23 40.6	19 2.0	5 39.4	1 40.4
13 W	17 24 39	21 50 50	20 42 20	26 40 22	7 42.3	14 29.2	8 48.1	24 46.4	11 51.5	23 48.4	19 1.2	5 37.8	1 40.4
14 Th	17 28 36	22 48 8	2♐37 1	8♐32 34	7 40.1	15 54.5	10 1.5	25 26.6	11 48.9	23 56.2	19 0.5	5 36.3	1 40.5
15 F	17 32 32	23 45 26	14 27 19	20 21 33	7 38.5	17 17.1	11 14.8	26 6.7	11 46.2	24 4.0	18 59.9	5 34.8	1 40.6
16 Sa	17 36 29	24 42 42	26 15 31	2♑ 9 31	7D 37.5	18 36.8	12 28.1	26 46.7	11 43.2	24 11.8	18 59.3	5 33.3	1 40.7
17 Su	17 40 26	25 39 58	8♑ 3 50	13 58 46	7 37.3	19 53.6	13 41.4	27 26.6	11 40.1	24 19.6	18 58.8	5 31.8	1 40.9
18 M	17 44 22	26 37 14	19 54 36	25 51 41	7 37.5	21 7.4	14 54.7	28 6.4	11 36.9	24 27.4	18 58.3	5 30.3	1 41.0
19 Tu	17 48 19	27 34 29	1♒50 20	7♒50 57	7 38.2	22 18.3	16 7.9	28 46.1	11 33.4	24 35.2	18 57.8	5 28.8	1 41.3
20 W	17 52 15	28 31 44	13 53 53	19 59 33	7 39.1	23 26.1	17 21.2	29 25.6	11 29.8	24 43.0	18 57.5	5 27.3	1 41.5
21 Th	17 56 12	29 28 58	26 8 23	2♓20 47	7 40.0	24 30.8	18 34.4	0♈ 5.1	11 25.9	24 50.9	18 57.1	5 25.9	1 41.8
22 F	18 0 8	0♋26 13	8♓37 12	14 58 5	7 40.7	25 32.2	19 47.6	0 44.4	11 22.0	24 58.6	18 56.8	5 24.4	1 42.1
23 Sa	18 4 5	1 23 27	21 23 51	27 54 53	7R 41.0	26 30.4	21 0.8	1 23.7	11 17.8	25 6.4	18 56.6	5 23.0	1 42.5
24 Su	18 8 1	2 20 40	4♈31 34	11♈14 11	7 41.1	27 25.2	22 14.0	2 2.8	11 13.5	25 14.2	18 56.4	5 21.6	1 42.8
25 M	18 11 58	3 17 54	18 2 58	24 58 3	7 41.0	28 16.6	23 27.2	2 41.7	11 9.0	25 22.0	18 56.3	5 20.2	1 43.2
26 Tu	18 15 55	4 15 8	1♉59 26	9♉ 7 0	7 40.7	29 4.3	24 40.3	3 20.5	11 4.4	25 29.8	18D 56.2	5 18.8	1 43.7
27 W	18 19 51	5 12 22	16 20 29	23 39 28	7 40.4	29 48.4	25 53.5	3 59.2	10 59.6	25 37.5	18 56.2	5 17.4	1 44.2
28 Th	18 23 48	6 9 36	1♊ 3 20	8♊31 21	7 40.3	0♌28.6	27 6.6	4 37.8	10 54.6	25 45.2	18 56.2	5 16.1	1 44.7
29 F	18 27 44	7 6 50	16 2 36	23 36 5	7D 40.2	1 5.0	28 19.7	5 16.1	10 49.5	25 53.0	18 56.3	5 14.8	1 45.2
30 Sa	18 31 41	8 4 5	1♋10 42	8♋45 15	7R 40.2	1 37.3	29 32.8	5 54.4	10 44.2	26 0.7	18 56.4	5 13.5	1 45.8

Astro Data

	Dy Hr Mn
☽0S	11 18:32
♄△♅	12 5:28
☽0N	26 11:41
♃ R	30 22:10
☽0S	7 23:54
♇ D	11 20:11
☽0N	22 18:21
♅ D	26 22:00
♃♇♄	28 17:30

Planet Ingress

	Dy Hr Mn
☿ ♉	6 2:55
♂ ♓	8 4:09
♀ ♊	12 8:42
☿ ♊	20 17:24
☉ ♊	21 4:54
☿ ♋	4 4:42
♀ ♋	5 19:20
♂ ♈	20 20:54
☉ ♋	21 13:01
☿ ♌	27 6:42
♀ ♌	30 8:55

Last Aspect / ☽ Ingress (May)

Last Aspect Dy Hr Mn		☽ Ingress Dy Hr Mn
1 17:35	♂ ⚹	♉ 2 1:01
3 20:23	♂ □	♊ 4 1:16
6 1:23	☿ ⚹	♋ 6 1:35
7 17:57	♀ ⚹	♌ 8 3:36
10 3:18	♀ □	♍ 10 8:13
11 22:49	☉ △	♎ 12 15:31
14 5:45	♄ △	♏ 15 1:09
17 4:58	☉ ☍	♐ 17 12:41
19 6:27	♄ ☍	♑ 20 1:30
21 17:06	♅ □	♒ 22 14:17
24 8:19	♄ △	♓ 25 1:05
26 17:10	♄ □	♈ 27 8:14
28 21:54	♄ ⚹	♉ 29 11:28
30 12:54	♂ ⚹	♊ 31 11:53

Last Aspect / ☽ Ingress (June)

Last Aspect Dy Hr Mn		☽ Ingress Dy Hr Mn
2 5:29	☿ ☌	♋ 2 11:21
3 18:05	♅ □	♌ 4 11:49
6 2:30	♄ ⚹	♍ 6 14:51
8 8:38	♄ □	♎ 8 21:16
10 18:11	♄ △	♏ 11 6:52
13 8:40	♂ △	♐ 13 18:43
16 1:07	♂ □	♑ 16 7:37
18 17:29	♂ ⚹	♒ 18 20:19
21 7:01	☉ △	♓ 21 7:29
23 10:09	☿ △	♈ 23 15:48
25 18:45	☿ □	♉ 25 20:37
27 17:02	♀ ⚹	♊ 27 22:18
29 15:45	♄ ☌	♋ 29 22:08

☽ Phases & Eclipses

Dy Hr Mn	
2 20:55	● 12♉18
9 12:07	☽ 18♌43
17 4:58	○ 26♏09
25 8:40	☽ 3♓60
1 4:34	● 10♊33
7 21:11	☽ 16♍57
15 20:35	○ 24♐35
15 20:50	☍ A 0.468
23 19:45	☽ 2♈11
30 11:39	● 8♋32
30 11:37:57	☌ T 7'04"

Astro Data

1 MAY 1973
Julian Day # 26784
Delta T 43.7 sec
SVP 05♓37'40"
Obliquity 23°26'36"
⚷ Chiron 18♈11.8
☽ Mean ☊ 10♑53.8

1 JUNE 1973
Julian Day # 26815
Delta T 43.8 sec
SVP 05♓37'36"
Obliquity 23°26'35"
⚷ Chiron 19♈43.6
☽ Mean ☊ 9♑15.4

JULY 1973

LONGITUDE

Day	Sid.Time	☉	0 hr ☽	Noon ☽	True ☊	☿	♀	♂	♃	♄	♅	♆	♇
1 Su	18 35 37	9♋ 1 18	16♋18 37	23♋49 37	7♑40.2	2♌ 5.4	0♌45.9	6♈32.4	10♒38.8	26♊ 8.4	18♎56.6	5♐12.2	1♎46.4
2 M	18 39 34	9 58 32	1♌17 15	8♌40 32	7R40.1	2 29.2	1 59.0	7 10.4	10R33.3	26 16.1	18 56.9	5R10.9	1 47.1
3 Tu	18 43 30	10 55 46	15 58 41	23 11 3	7 39.8	2 48.6	3 12.0	7 48.1	10 27.6	26 23.8	18 57.2	5 9.7	1 47.7
4 W	18 47 27	11 52 59	0♍17 11	7♍16 45	7 39.4	3 3.6	4 25.1	8 25.7	10 21.7	26 31.4	18 57.5	5 8.4	1 48.4
5 Th	18 51 24	12 50 12	14 9 36	20 55 47	7 38.9	3 13.9	5 38.1	9 3.0	10 15.7	26 39.0	18 57.9	5 7.2	1 49.2
6 F	18 55 20	13 47 24	27 35 24	4♎ 8 42	7 38.5	3R19.6	6 51.1	9 40.3	10 9.6	26 46.6	18 58.4	5 6.0	1 49.9
7 Sa	18 59 17	14 44 37	10♎36 1	16 57 47	7D38.3	3 20.6	8 4.0	10 17.3	10 3.4	26 54.2	18 58.9	5 4.9	1 50.7
8 Su	19 3 13	15 41 49	23 14 27	29 26 32	7 38.3	3 16.8	9 17.0	10 54.1	9 57.1	27 1.8	18 59.4	5 3.7	1 51.6
9 M	19 7 10	16 39 1	5♏34 32	11♏39 0	7 38.7	3 8.4	10 29.9	11 30.8	9 50.6	27 9.3	19 0.1	5 2.6	1 52.4
10 Tu	19 11 6	17 36 13	17 40 28	23 39 27	7 39.5	2 55.4	11 42.8	12 7.2	9 44.0	27 16.8	19 0.7	5 1.5	1 53.3
11 W	19 15 3	18 33 25	29 36 28	5♐32 0	7 40.5	2 38.0	12 55.7	12 43.5	9 37.4	27 24.3	19 1.4	5 0.4	1 54.2
12 Th	19 18 59	19 30 37	11♐26 31	17 20 27	7 41.6	2 16.2	14 8.5	13 19.6	9 30.6	27 31.8	19 2.2	4 59.4	1 55.2
13 F	19 22 56	20 27 49	23 14 12	29 8 10	7 42.5	1 50.4	15 21.3	13 55.5	9 23.7	27 39.2	19 3.0	4 58.4	1 56.2
14 Sa	19 26 53	21 25 1	5♑ 2 41	10♑58 6	7R42.9	1 20.9	16 34.1	14 31.1	9 16.7	27 46.6	19 3.9	4 57.4	1 57.2
15 Su	19 30 49	22 22 14	16 54 41	22 52 43	7 42.7	0 48.1	17 46.9	15 6.6	9 9.7	27 54.0	19 4.8	4 56.4	1 58.2
16 M	19 34 46	23 19 27	28 52 29	4♒54 12	7 41.8	0 12.5	18 59.7	15 41.8	9 2.5	28 1.3	19 5.8	4 55.4	1 59.3
17 Tu	19 38 42	24 16 40	10♒58 6	17 4 25	7 40.1	29♋34.6	20 12.4	16 16.8	8 55.3	28 8.6	19 6.8	4 54.5	2 0.4
18 W	19 42 39	25 13 53	23 13 22	29 25 8	7 37.7	28 54.9	21 25.1	16 51.6	8 48.0	28 15.9	19 7.9	4 53.6	2 1.5
19 Th	19 46 35	26 11 7	5♓39 58	11♓58 3	7 35.0	28 14.3	22 37.8	17 26.1	8 40.6	28 23.2	19 9.0	4 52.7	2 2.7
20 F	19 50 32	27 8 22	18 19 38	24 44 55	7 32.3	27 33.2	23 50.4	18 0.4	8 33.2	28 30.4	19 10.2	4 51.9	2 3.9
21 Sa	19 54 28	28 5 37	1♈14 7	7♈47 28	7 30.0	26 52.6	25 3.0	18 34.4	8 25.7	28 37.5	19 11.4	4 51.1	2 5.1
22 Su	19 58 25	29 2 54	14 25 10	21 7 24	7 28.4	26 13.0	26 15.6	19 8.2	8 18.2	28 44.7	19 12.7	4 50.3	2 6.3
23 M	20 2 22	0♌ 0 11	27 54 20	4♉46 4	7D27.7	25 35.2	27 28.2	19 41.7	8 10.6	28 51.8	19 14.0	4 49.5	2 7.6
24 Tu	20 6 18	0 57 29	11♉42 40	18 44 8	7 28.0	24 59.9	28 40.8	20 14.9	8 2.9	28 58.8	19 15.4	4 48.8	2 8.9
25 W	20 10 15	1 54 48	25 50 22	3♊ 1 11	7 29.1	24 27.8	29 53.3	20 47.9	7 55.2	29 5.9	19 16.9	4 48.1	2 10.2
26 Th	20 14 11	2 52 7	10♊16 17	17 35 13	7 30.5	23 59.5	1♍ 5.8	21 20.6	7 47.5	29 12.8	19 18.3	4 47.4	2 11.6
27 F	20 18 8	3 49 28	24 57 27	2♋22 18	7R31.6	23 35.5	2 18.3	21 52.9	7 39.8	29 19.8	19 19.9	4 46.7	2 13.0
28 Sa	20 22 4	4 46 50	9♋48 58	17 16 35	7 32.0	23 16.3	3 30.8	22 25.0	7 32.0	29 26.7	19 21.4	4 46.1	2 14.4
29 Su	20 26 1	5 44 13	24 44 11	2♌10 44	7 31.2	23 2.4	4 43.2	22 56.7	7 24.2	29 33.5	19 23.1	4 45.5	2 15.8
30 M	20 29 57	6 41 36	9♌35 15	16 56 44	7 28.9	22D54.1	5 55.6	23 28.1	7 16.4	29 40.3	19 24.7	4 44.9	2 17.3
31 Tu	20 33 54	7 39 1	24 14 17	1♍27 5	7 25.4	22 51.6	7 8.0	23 59.2	7 8.6	29 47.1	19 26.5	4 44.4	2 18.8

AUGUST 1973

LONGITUDE

Day	Sid.Time	☉	0 hr ☽	Noon ☽	True ☊	☿	♀	♂	♃	♄	♅	♆	♇
1 W	20 37 51	8♌36 26	8♍34 28	15♍35 52	7♑20.9	22♋55.3	8♍20.3	24♈30.0	7♒ 0.8	29♊53.8	19♎28.2	4♐43.9	2♎20.3
2 Th	20 41 47	9 33 51	22 30 57	29 19 29	7R16.2	23 5.2	9 32.7	25 0.4	6R53.0	0♋ 0.5	19 30.0	4R43.4	2 21.8
3 F	20 45 44	10 31 17	6♎ 1 25	12♎36 50	7 11.9	23 21.5	10 45.0	25 30.4	6 45.3	0 7.1	19 31.9	4 43.0	2 23.4
4 Sa	20 49 40	11 28 44	19 5 58	25 29 7	7 8.6	23 44.3	11 57.2	26 0.1	6 37.5	0 13.6	19 33.8	4 42.6	2 25.0
5 Su	20 53 37	12 26 12	1♏46 45	7♏59 19	7D 6.5	24 13.6	13 9.4	26 29.4	6 29.8	0 20.1	19 35.8	4 42.2	2 26.6
6 M	20 57 33	13 23 40	14 7 24	20 11 35	7 6.0	24 49.4	14 21.6	26 58.3	6 22.1	0 26.6	19 37.8	4 41.8	2 28.2
7 Tu	21 1 30	14 21 9	26 12 29	2♐10 43	7 6.6	25 31.7	15 33.8	27 26.9	6 14.4	0 33.0	19 39.8	4 41.5	2 29.9
8 W	21 5 26	15 18 39	8♐ 6 56	14 1 44	7 8.1	26 20.3	16 45.9	27 55.1	6 6.8	0 39.3	19 41.9	4 41.2	2 31.5
9 Th	21 9 23	16 16 10	19 55 44	25 49 29	7 9.7	27 15.2	17 57.9	28 22.9	5 59.2	0 45.6	19 44.0	4 41.0	2 33.2
10 F	21 13 20	17 13 42	1♑43 33	7♑38 26	7R10.8	28 16.2	19 10.0	28 50.2	5 51.7	0 51.8	19 46.2	4 40.7	2 35.0
11 Sa	21 17 16	18 11 14	13 34 36	19 32 29	7 10.7	29 23.3	20 22.0	29 17.2	5 44.3	0 58.0	19 48.4	4 40.5	2 36.7
12 Su	21 21 13	19 8 48	25 32 26	1♒34 47	7 9.0	0♌36.1	21 33.9	29 43.7	5 36.9	1 4.1	19 50.7	4 40.4	2 38.5
13 M	21 25 9	20 6 23	7♒39 49	13 47 45	7 5.3	1 54.4	22 45.9	0♉ 9.8	5 29.6	1 10.2	19 53.0	4 40.3	2 40.3
14 Tu	21 29 6	21 3 58	19 58 45	26 12 56	6 59.7	3 18.1	23 57.7	0 35.4	5 22.3	1 16.1	19 55.3	4 40.2	2 42.1
15 W	21 33 2	22 1 35	2♓30 24	8♓51 10	6 52.7	4 46.8	25 9.6	1 0.6	5 15.1	1 22.1	19 57.7	4 40.1	2 43.9
16 Th	21 36 59	22 59 13	15 15 16	21 42 40	6 44.7	6 20.1	26 21.4	1 25.4	5 8.0	1 27.9	20 0.1	4D40.0	2 45.8
17 F	21 40 55	23 56 53	28 13 20	4♈47 14	6 36.8	7 57.8	27 33.1	1 49.6	5 1.0	1 33.7	20 2.6	4 40.0	2 47.6
18 Sa	21 44 52	24 54 34	11♈24 18	18 4 30	6 29.6	9 39.5	28 44.8	2 13.4	4 54.1	1 39.4	20 5.1	4 40.1	2 49.5
19 Su	21 48 49	25 52 16	24 47 48	1♉34 8	6 24.0	11 24.7	29 56.5	2 36.6	4 47.3	1 45.1	20 7.6	4 40.1	2 51.4
20 M	21 52 45	26 50 0	8♉23 32	15 15 57	6 20.4	13 13.0	1♎ 8.1	2 59.3	4 40.6	1 50.7	20 10.2	4 40.2	2 53.3
21 Tu	21 56 42	27 47 46	22 11 22	29 9 46	6D18.8	15 4.1	2 19.7	3 21.5	4 34.0	1 56.2	20 12.9	4 40.3	2 55.3
22 W	22 0 38	28 45 34	6♊11 7	13♊15 20	6 18.8	16 57.5	3 31.3	3 43.2	4 27.5	2 1.7	20 15.5	4 40.5	2 57.2
23 Th	22 4 35	29 43 23	20 22 16	27 31 46	6 19.7	18 52.7	4 42.8	4 4.3	4 21.1	2 7.1	20 18.2	4 40.7	2 59.2
24 F	22 8 31	0♍41 15	4♋43 32	11♋57 14	6R20.3	20 49.4	5 54.3	4 24.8	4 14.9	2 12.4	20 20.9	4 40.9	3 1.2
25 Sa	22 12 28	1 39 8	19 12 26	26 28 33	6 19.7	22 47.2	7 5.7	4 44.7	4 8.7	2 17.6	20 23.7	4 41.2	3 3.2
26 Su	22 16 24	2 37 2	3♌45 0	11♌ 1 3	6 17.0	24 45.7	8 17.1	5 4.1	4 2.7	2 22.8	20 26.5	4 41.5	3 5.3
27 M	22 20 21	3 34 58	18 15 57	25 28 55	6 11.8	26 44.7	9 28.5	5 22.8	3 56.9	2 27.9	20 29.4	4 41.8	3 7.3
28 Tu	22 24 18	4 32 56	2♍39 8	9♍45 52	6 4.3	28 43.8	10 39.8	5 40.9	3 51.2	2 32.9	20 32.2	4 42.1	3 9.4
29 W	22 28 14	5 30 55	16 48 24	23 46 8	5 55.1	0♍42.8	11 51.0	5 58.3	3 45.6	2 37.8	20 35.2	4 42.5	3 11.4
30 Th	22 32 11	6 28 56	0♎38 35	7♎25 23	5 45.2	2 41.5	13 2.2	6 15.1	3 40.1	2 42.7	20 38.1	4 42.9	3 13.5
31 F	22 36 7	7 26 58	14 6 18	20 41 16	5 35.6	4 39.7	14 13.4	6 31.2	3 34.8	2 47.5	20 41.1	4 43.4	3 15.6

Astro Data	Dy Hr Mn
♂0N	1 2:19
☽0S	5 7:26
☿ R	6 17:00
☽0N	20 0:12
☿ D	30 21:47
☽0S	1 17:03
♅∠♆	7 17:14
☽0N	16 6:19
♆ D	16 16:06
♀0S	20 11:28
♃⚹♆	20 1:20
☽0S	29 3:17

Planet Ingress	Dy Hr Mn
☿ ♋	16 8:03
☉ ♌	22 23:56
♀ ♍	25 2:13
♄ ♋	1 22:20
☿ ♌	11 12:21
♂ ♉	12 14:56
♀ ♎	19 1:10
☉ ♍	23 6:53
☿ ♍	28 15:22

Last Aspect Dy Hr Mn		☽ Ingress Dy Hr Mn
1 4:12	♅ □	♌ 1 21:55
3 17:34	♄ ⚹	♍ 3 23:31
5 22:31	♄ □	♎ 6 4:23
8 7:23	♄ △	♏ 8 13:05
9 23:51	☉ △	♐ 11 0:48
13 9:05	♄ ☍	♑ 13 13:45
15 11:56	☉ ☍	♒ 16 2:15
18 9:52	♄ △	♓ 18 13:07
20 19:09	♄ □	♈ 20 21:43
23 1:42	♄ ⚹	♉ 23 3:41
24 21:46	☿ ⚹	♊ 25 6:58
27 7:08	♄ ☌	♋ 27 8:10
28 21:18	☿ ☌	♌ 29 8:29
31 9:17	♄ ⚹	♍ 31 9:34

Last Aspect Dy Hr Mn		☽ Ingress Dy Hr Mn
2 1:01	☿ ⚹	♎ 2 13:12
4 13:30	♂ ☍	♏ 4 20:35
6 22:33	☿ △	♐ 7 7:37
9 17:54	♂ △	♑ 9 20:30
12 8:39	♂ □	♒ 12 8:52
14 2:16	☉ ☍	♓ 14 19:14
16 22:39	♀ ☍	♈ 17 3:16
19 2:03	☉ △	♉ 19 9:14
21 10:22	☉ □	♊ 21 13:26
22 23:53	♅ △	♋ 23 16:08
25 1:58	♅ □	♌ 25 17:49
27 16:22	☿ ☌	♍ 27 19:33
28 5:12	♂ △	♎ 29 22:52

☽ Phases & Eclipses Dy Hr Mn	
7 8:26	☽ 15♎05
15 11:56	○ 22♑51
15 11:39	☍ A 0.104
23 3:58	☽ 0♉10
29 18:59	● 6♌30
5 22:27	☽ 13♏20
14 2:16	○ 21♒09
21 10:22	☽ 28♉13
28 3:25	● 4♍41

Astro Data

1 JULY 1973
Julian Day # 26845
Delta T 43.9 sec
SVP 05♓37'30"
Obliquity 23°26'35"
⚷ Chiron 20♈40.1
☽ Mean ☊ 7♑40.1

1 AUGUST 1973
Julian Day # 26876
Delta T 44.0 sec
SVP 05♓37'25"
Obliquity 23°26'35"
⚷ Chiron 20♈52.9R
☽ Mean ☊ 6♑01.6

LONGITUDE SEPTEMBER 1973

Day	Sid.Time	☉	0 hr ☽	Noon ☽	True ☊	☿	♀	♂	♃	♄	♅	♆	♇
1 Sa	22 40 4	8♍25 2	27♎10 20	3♏33 41	5♑27.5	6♍37.2	15♎24.5	6♉46.6	3♒29.7	2♋52.1	20♎44.1	4♐43.9	3♎17.7
2 Su	22 44 0	9 23 7	9♏51 37	16 4 31	5R21.3	8 34.0	16 35.6	7 1.4	3R24.7	2 56.8	20 47.1	4 44.4	3 19.9
3 M	22 47 57	10 21 14	22 12 54	28 17 17	5 17.5	10 29.8	17 46.6	7 15.5	3 19.9	3 1.3	20 50.2	4 44.9	3 22.0
4 Tu	22 51 53	11 19 22	4♐18 17	10♐16 32	5D15.8	12 24.7	18 57.5	7 28.8	3 15.2	3 5.7	20 53.3	4 45.5	3 24.1
5 W	22 55 50	12 17 32	16 12 43	22 7 30	5 15.7	14 18.6	20 8.4	7 41.4	3 10.7	3 10.1	20 56.4	4 46.1	3 26.3
6 Th	22 59 47	13 15 43	28 1 35	3♑55 37	5R16.1	16 11.4	21 19.3	7 53.3	3 6.4	3 14.4	20 59.6	4 46.8	3 28.5
7 F	23 3 43	14 13 55	9♑50 17	15 46 11	5 16.2	18 3.1	22 30.0	8 4.5	3 2.3	3 18.5	21 2.8	4 47.5	3 30.7
8 Sa	23 7 40	15 12 9	21 43 56	27 44 3	5 14.9	19 53.7	23 40.8	8 14.9	2 58.3	3 22.6	21 6.0	4 48.2	3 32.9
9 Su	23 11 36	16 10 25	3♒47 4	9♒53 22	5 11.4	21 43.2	24 51.4	8 24.5	2 54.5	3 26.7	21 9.2	4 48.9	3 35.1
10 M	23 15 33	17 8 42	16 3 21	22 17 17	5 5.4	23 31.5	26 2.0	8 33.3	2 50.8	3 30.6	21 12.5	4 49.7	3 37.3
11 Tu	23 19 29	18 7 1	28 35 22	4♓57 43	4 56.8	25 18.6	27 12.5	8 41.4	2 47.4	3 34.4	21 15.8	4 50.5	3 39.5
12 W	23 23 26	19 5 21	11♓24 21	17 55 14	4 46.1	27 4.6	28 23.0	8 48.6	2 44.1	3 38.1	21 19.1	4 51.3	3 41.7
13 Th	23 27 22	20 3 44	24 30 12	1♈ 9 4	4 34.1	28 49.5	29 33.4	8 55.0	2 41.0	3 41.8	21 22.5	4 52.2	3 44.0
14 F	23 31 19	21 2 8	7♈51 33	14 37 20	4 22.0	0♎33.3	0♏43.7	9 0.6	2 38.1	3 45.3	21 25.8	4 53.1	3 46.2
15 Sa	23 35 16	22 0 34	21 26 5	28 17 27	4 10.9	2 16.0	1 54.0	9 5.4	2 35.4	3 48.8	21 29.2	4 54.0	3 48.5
16 Su	23 39 12	22 59 2	5♉11 5	12♉ 6 39	4 1.9	3 57.6	3 4.2	9 9.3	2 32.8	3 52.2	21 32.7	4 55.0	3 50.7
17 M	23 43 9	23 57 32	19 3 51	26 2 27	3 55.5	5 38.2	4 14.3	9 12.4	2 30.5	3 55.4	21 36.1	4 55.9	3 53.0
18 Tu	23 47 5	24 56 5	3♊ 2 13	10♊ 2 59	3 52.0	7 17.7	5 24.3	9 14.6	2 28.3	3 58.6	21 39.6	4 57.0	3 55.3
19 W	23 51 2	25 54 39	17 4 37	24 7 1	3D50.6	8 56.2	6 34.3	9R15.9	2 26.4	4 1.7	21 43.0	4 58.0	3 57.5
20 Th	23 54 58	26 53 16	1♋10 5	8♋13 44	3R50.5	10 33.7	7 44.3	9 16.3	2 24.6	4 4.7	21 46.5	4 59.1	3 59.8
21 F	23 58 55	27 51 56	15 17 50	22 22 16	3 50.3	12 10.1	8 54.1	9 15.8	2 23.0	4 7.5	21 50.1	5 0.2	4 2.1
22 Sa	0 2 51	28 50 37	29 26 50	6♌31 17	3 48.6	13 45.6	10 3.9	9 14.4	2 21.6	4 10.3	21 53.6	5 1.3	4 4.4
23 Su	0 6 48	29 49 21	13♌35 20	20 38 36	3 44.6	15 20.2	11 13.6	9 12.2	2 20.4	4 13.0	21 57.2	5 2.5	4 6.7
24 M	0 10 45	0♎48 7	27 40 39	4♍41 2	3 37.7	16 53.7	12 23.2	9 9.0	2 19.4	4 15.6	22 0.7	5 3.7	4 9.0
25 Tu	0 14 41	1 46 54	11♍39 14	18 34 43	3 28.0	18 26.4	13 32.8	9 4.9	2 18.6	4 18.0	22 4.3	5 4.9	4 11.3
26 W	0 18 38	2 45 44	25 27 0	2♎15 35	3 16.2	19 58.1	14 42.2	8 59.9	2 18.0	4 20.4	22 7.9	5 6.1	4 13.6
27 Th	0 22 34	3 44 36	9♎ 0 4	15 40 5	3 3.4	21 28.8	15 51.6	8 54.0	2 17.6	4 22.7	22 11.6	5 7.4	4 15.9
28 F	0 26 31	4 43 30	22 15 22	28 45 47	2 50.8	22 58.6	17 0.9	8 47.3	2D17.4	4 24.8	22 15.2	5 8.7	4 18.2
29 Sa	0 30 27	5 42 26	5♏11 15	11♏31 51	2 39.8	24 27.5	18 10.2	8 39.7	2 17.4	4 26.9	22 18.9	5 10.1	4 20.4
30 Su	0 34 24	6 41 24	17 47 44	23 59 9	2 31.0	25 55.4	19 19.3	8 31.2	2 17.6	4 28.8	22 22.5	5 11.4	4 22.7

LONGITUDE OCTOBER 1973

Day	Sid.Time	☉	0 hr ☽	Noon ☽	True ☊	☿	♀	♂	♃	♄	♅	♆	♇
1 M	0 38 20	7♎40 24	0♐ 6 29	6♐10 8	2♑25.0	27♎22.4	20♏28.3	8♉21.8	2♒18.0	4♋30.6	22♎26.2	5♐12.8	4♎25.0
2 Tu	0 42 17	8 39 25	12 10 37	18 8 30	2R21.6	28 48.4	21 37.3	8R11.7	2 18.5	4 32.4	22 29.9	5 14.2	4 27.3
3 W	0 46 13	9 38 29	24 4 24	29 58 58	2D20.3	0♏13.4	22 46.1	8 0.7	2 19.3	4 34.0	22 33.6	5 15.7	4 29.6
4 Th	0 50 10	10 37 34	5♑52 52	11♑46 49	2R20.1	1 37.4	23 54.9	7 49.0	2 20.3	4 35.5	22 37.3	5 17.1	4 31.9
5 F	0 54 7	11 36 41	17 41 28	23 37 34	2 20.0	3 0.4	25 3.5	7 36.5	2 21.5	4 36.9	22 41.0	5 18.6	4 34.2
6 Sa	0 58 3	12 35 50	29 35 45	5♒36 42	2 19.0	4 22.3	26 12.0	7 23.2	2 22.9	4 38.2	22 44.8	5 20.1	4 36.5
7 Su	1 2 0	13 35 0	11♒41 0	17 49 14	2 15.9	5 43.1	27 20.5	7 9.3	2 24.4	4 39.4	22 48.5	5 21.7	4 38.8
8 M	1 5 56	14 34 12	24 1 53	0♓19 22	2 10.4	7 2.7	28 28.8	6 54.6	2 26.2	4 40.5	22 52.3	5 23.2	4 41.0
9 Tu	1 9 53	15 33 26	6♓42 0	13 10 0	2 2.3	8 21.1	29 36.9	6 39.3	2 28.1	4 41.4	22 56.0	5 24.8	4 43.3
10 W	1 13 49	16 32 42	19 43 28	26 22 24	1 52.0	9 38.3	0♐45.0	6 23.4	2 30.3	4 42.3	22 59.8	5 26.4	4 45.6
11 Th	1 17 46	17 32 0	3♈ 6 37	9♈55 53	1 40.3	10 54.1	1 52.9	6 6.9	2 32.6	4 43.1	23 3.5	5 28.1	4 47.8
12 F	1 21 42	18 31 19	16 49 47	23 47 50	1 28.4	12 8.4	3 0.7	5 49.9	2 35.2	4 43.7	23 7.3	5 29.7	4 50.1
13 Sa	1 25 39	19 30 41	0♉49 29	7♉54 4	1 17.4	13 21.2	4 8.4	5 32.3	2 37.9	4 44.2	23 11.1	5 31.4	4 52.3
14 Su	1 29 36	20 30 5	15 0 58	22 9 29	1 8.5	14 32.3	5 15.9	5 14.3	2 40.8	4 44.6	23 14.9	5 33.1	4 54.6
15 M	1 33 32	21 29 31	29 19 0	6♊28 56	1 2.3	15 41.6	6 23.3	4 55.8	2 43.9	4 44.9	23 18.6	5 34.8	4 56.8
16 Tu	1 37 29	22 29 0	13♊38 44	20 47 58	0 58.9	16 49.0	7 30.6	4 37.0	2 47.2	4 45.1	23 22.4	5 36.6	4 59.0
17 W	1 41 25	23 28 30	27 56 15	5♋ 3 18	0D57.8	17 54.2	8 37.7	4 17.8	2 50.6	4R45.2	23 26.2	5 38.4	5 1.2
18 Th	1 45 22	24 28 3	12♋ 8 54	19 12 53	0R58.0	18 57.2	9 44.7	3 58.3	2 54.3	4 45.2	23 30.0	5 40.2	5 3.4
19 F	1 49 18	25 27 39	26 15 9	3♌15 36	0 58.3	19 57.6	10 51.5	3 38.5	2 58.1	4 45.0	23 33.8	5 42.0	5 5.6
20 Sa	1 53 15	26 27 16	10♌14 11	17 10 49	0 57.5	20 55.1	11 58.1	3 18.6	3 2.2	4 44.8	23 37.5	5 43.8	5 7.8
21 Su	1 57 11	27 26 56	24 5 27	0♍57 58	0 54.7	21 49.7	13 4.6	2 58.4	3 6.4	4 44.4	23 41.3	5 45.7	5 10.0
22 M	2 1 8	28 26 38	7♍48 16	14 36 11	0 49.2	22 40.8	14 11.0	2 38.2	3 10.8	4 43.9	23 45.1	5 47.5	5 12.1
23 Tu	2 5 5	29 26 22	21 21 33	28 4 11	0 41.3	23 28.1	15 17.1	2 17.9	3 15.3	4 43.3	23 48.9	5 49.4	5 14.3
24 W	2 9 1	0♏26 9	4♎43 52	11♎20 24	0 31.5	24 11.3	16 23.1	1 57.7	3 20.1	4 42.6	23 52.6	5 51.3	5 16.4
25 Th	2 12 58	1 25 57	17 53 35	24 23 15	0 20.7	24 49.9	17 28.9	1 37.4	3 25.0	4 41.8	23 56.4	5 53.3	5 18.5
26 F	2 16 54	2 25 48	0♏49 16	7♏11 32	0 10.1	25 23.4	18 34.6	1 17.3	3 30.1	4 40.9	24 0.1	5 55.2	5 20.6
27 Sa	2 20 51	3 25 41	13 30 2	19 44 46	0 0.7	25 51.3	19 40.0	0 57.4	3 35.4	4 39.9	24 3.9	5 57.2	5 22.7
28 Su	2 24 47	4 25 35	25 55 51	2♐ 3 27	29♐53.3	26 13.0	20 45.2	0 37.7	3 40.8	4 38.7	24 7.6	5 59.1	5 24.8
29 M	2 28 44	5 25 32	8♐ 7 48	14 9 12	29 48.3	26 27.8	21 50.3	0 18.3	3 46.5	4 37.4	24 11.4	6 1.1	5 26.9
30 Tu	2 32 40	6 25 30	20 8 2	26 4 42	29D45.8	26R35.3	22 55.1	29♈59.2	3 52.2	4 36.1	24 15.1	6 3.1	5 28.9
31 W	2 36 37	7 25 30	1♑59 43	7♑53 37	29 45.2	26 34.8	23 59.6	29 40.4	3 58.2	4 34.6	24 18.8	6 5.2	5 31.0

Astro Data	Dy Hr Mn
♃△♇	2 16:40
♃⚻♄	5 1:47
☽0N	12 13:32
☿0S	14 18:13
♄□♇	14 17:18
♂ R	19 23:19
☽0S	25 12:16
♃ D	28 13:26
♄□♇	7 12:56
☽0N	9 21:58
♄ R	17 5:50
☽0S	22 18:51
☿ R	30 10:29

Planet Ingress	Dy Hr Mn
☿ ♎	13 16:16
♀ ♏	13 9:05
☉ ♎	23 4:21
☿ ♏	2 20:12
♀ ♐	9 8:08
☉ ♏	23 13:30
☊ ♐	27 2:02
♂ ♈	29 22:56

Last Aspect Dy Hr Mn		☽ Ingress	Dy Hr Mn
31 12:02	♅ ☌	♏	1 5:17
1 23:01	☉ ⚹	♐	3 15:24
5 9:38	♅ ⚹	♑	6 4:01
8 4:20	♀ □	♒	8 16:30
10 21:07	♀ △	♓	11 2:40
13 8:59	☿ ☍	♈	13 9:56
15 0:06	♅ ☍	♉	15 14:59
17 9:03	☉ △	♊	17 18:48
19 16:11	☉ □	♋	19 22:01
21 22:54	☉ ⚹	♌	22 0:56
23 14:17	♅ ⚹	♍	24 3:58
25 3:34	♀ ⚹	♎	26 8:00
28 1:30	☿ ☌	♏	28 14:18
30 3:15	♀ ☌	♐	30 23:47

Last Aspect Dy Hr Mn		☽ Ingress	Dy Hr Mn
2 20:55	♅ ⚹	♑	3 12:02
5 16:28	♀ ⚹	♒	6 0:49
8 9:20	♀ □	♓	8 11:23
9 3:26	☿ △	♈	10 18:29
12 10:53	♅ ☍	♉	12 22:36
13 23:07	☿ ☍	♊	15 1:09
16 16:24	♅ △	♋	17 3:28
18 22:33	☉ □	♌	19 6:25
21 6:19	☉ ⚹	♍	21 10:19
23 3:59	☿ ⚹	♎	23 15:28
25 11:13	♅ ☌	♏	25 22:28
28 0:34	☿ ☌	♐	28 7:57
30 19:24	♂ △	♑	30 19:57

☽ Phases & Eclipses Dy Hr Mn	
4 15:22	☽ 11♐57
12 15:16	○ 19♓42
19 16:11	☽ 26♊34
26 13:54	● 3♎20
4 10:32	☽ 11♑04
12 3:09	○ 18♈39
18 22:33	☽ 25♋24
26 3:17	● 2♏34

Astro Data

1 SEPTEMBER 1973
Julian Day # 26907
Delta T 44.1 sec
SVP 05♓37'21"
Obliquity 23°26'35"
⚷ Chiron 20♈17.0R
☽ Mean ☊ 4♑23.1

1 OCTOBER 1973
Julian Day # 26937
Delta T 44.2 sec
SVP 05♓37'18"
Obliquity 23°26'35"
⚷ Chiron 19♈07.1R
☽ Mean ☊ 2♑47.7

NOVEMBER 1973 LONGITUDE

Day	Sid.Time	☉	0 hr ☽	Noon ☽	True ☊	☿	♀	♂	♃	♄	♅	♆	♇
1 Th	2 40 34	8♏25 31	13♑46 57	19♑40 22	29♐46.0	26♏25.6	25♐ 4.0	29♈22.1	4♒ 4.3	4♋33.0	24♎22.5	6♐ 7.2	5♎33.0
2 F	2 44 30	9 25 35	25 34 29	1♒29 58	29 47.3	26R 7.4	26 8.1	29R 4.2	4 10.6	4R31.3	24 26.2	6 9.3	5 35.0
3 Sa	2 48 27	10 25 39	7♒27 30	13 27 45	29R48.2	25 39.7	27 12.0	28 46.8	4 17.1	4 29.5	24 29.9	6 11.3	5 37.0
4 Su	2 52 23	11 25 46	19 31 22	25 39 0	29 47.8	25 2.3	28 15.5	28 29.9	4 23.7	4 27.6	24 33.6	6 13.4	5 38.9
5 M	2 56 20	12 25 54	1♓51 16	8♓ 8 41	29 45.7	24 15.4	29 18.9	28 13.6	4 30.5	4 25.6	24 37.2	6 15.5	5 40.9
6 Tu	3 0 16	13 26 3	14 31 44	21 0 48	29 41.6	23 19.4	0♑21.9	27 57.9	4 37.4	4 23.5	24 40.9	6 17.6	5 42.8
7 W	3 4 13	14 26 14	27 36 10	4♈17 59	29 35.8	22 15.2	1 24.6	27 42.9	4 44.5	4 21.3	24 44.5	6 19.8	5 44.7
8 Th	3 8 9	15 26 27	11♈ 6 15	18 0 50	29 28.8	21 4.0	2 27.1	27 28.5	4 51.7	4 19.0	24 48.1	6 21.9	5 46.6
9 F	3 12 6	16 26 41	25 1 27	2♉ 7 37	29 21.4	19 47.7	3 29.2	27 14.7	4 59.1	4 16.6	24 51.7	6 24.0	5 48.4
10 Sa	3 16 3	17 26 56	9♉18 44	16 34 5	29 14.6	18 28.5	4 31.0	27 1.7	5 6.7	4 14.1	24 55.3	6 26.2	5 50.3
11 Su	3 19 59	18 27 14	23 52 49	1♊14 2	29 9.1	17 8.7	5 32.4	26 49.4	5 14.4	4 11.5	24 58.8	6 28.3	5 52.1
12 M	3 23 56	19 27 33	8♊36 48	16 0 10	29 5.5	15 51.0	6 33.5	26 37.8	5 22.2	4 8.8	25 2.4	6 30.5	5 53.9
13 Tu	3 27 52	20 27 54	23 23 14	0♋45 10	29D 4.0	14 37.9	7 34.2	26 27.0	5 30.2	4 6.0	25 5.9	6 32.7	5 55.7
14 W	3 31 49	21 28 17	8♋ 5 13	15 22 44	29 4.1	13 31.8	8 34.6	26 16.9	5 38.4	4 3.1	25 9.4	6 34.9	5 57.5
15 Th	3 35 45	22 28 42	22 37 14	29 48 16	29 5.3	12 34.5	9 34.6	26 7.6	5 46.6	4 0.1	25 12.9	6 37.1	5 59.2
16 F	3 39 42	23 29 9	6♌55 34	13♌58 56	29 6.8	11 47.5	10 34.2	25 59.1	5 55.0	3 57.0	25 16.3	6 39.3	6 0.9
17 Sa	3 43 38	24 29 38	20 58 14	27 53 27	29R 7.7	11 11.8	11 33.3	25 51.3	6 3.6	3 53.8	25 19.8	6 41.5	6 2.6
18 Su	3 47 35	25 30 8	4♍44 37	11♍31 46	29 7.4	10 47.7	12 32.0	25 44.4	6 12.3	3 50.6	25 23.2	6 43.7	6 4.3
19 M	3 51 32	26 30 40	18 15 0	24 54 25	29 5.5	10D35.3	13 30.3	25 38.3	6 21.1	3 47.2	25 26.6	6 46.0	6 5.9
20 Tu	3 55 28	27 31 14	1♎30 9	8♎ 2 18	29 2.1	10 34.2	14 28.2	25 33.0	6 30.1	3 43.8	25 29.9	6 48.2	6 7.5
21 W	3 59 25	28 31 50	14 30 58	20 56 17	28 57.6	10 43.9	15 25.5	25 28.5	6 39.2	3 40.3	25 33.3	6 50.4	6 9.1
22 Th	4 3 21	29 32 27	27 18 20	3♏37 13	28 52.5	11 3.6	16 22.4	25 24.8	6 48.4	3 36.7	25 36.6	6 52.7	6 10.7
23 F	4 7 18	0♐33 6	9♏53 3	16 5 55	28 47.4	11 32.5	17 18.7	25 21.9	6 57.8	3 33.0	25 39.9	6 54.9	6 12.2
24 Sa	4 11 14	1 33 47	22 15 56	28 23 13	28 42.9	12 9.6	18 14.5	25 19.9	7 7.2	3 29.2	25 43.1	6 57.2	6 13.7
25 Su	4 15 11	2 34 29	4♐27 56	10♐30 15	28 39.5	12 54.1	19 9.7	25 18.7	7 16.8	3 25.4	25 46.4	6 59.4	6 15.2
26 M	4 19 7	3 35 13	16 30 22	22 28 30	28 37.5	13 45.1	20 4.4	25D 18.3	7 26.6	3 21.5	25 49.6	7 1.7	6 16.7
27 Tu	4 23 4	4 35 57	28 24 56	4♑19 58	28D 36.9	14 41.8	20 58.4	25 18.7	7 36.4	3 17.5	25 52.7	7 4.0	6 18.1
28 W	4 27 1	5 36 43	10♑13 57	16 7 17	28 37.4	15 43.5	21 51.9	25 19.9	7 46.4	3 13.5	25 55.9	7 6.2	6 19.5
29 Th	4 30 57	6 37 30	22 0 22	27 53 41	28 38.7	16 49.6	22 44.6	25 21.9	7 56.5	3 9.4	25 59.0	7 8.5	6 20.9
30 F	4 34 54	7 38 19	3♒47 44	9♒43 2	28 40.5	17 59.3	23 36.7	25 24.6	8 6.7	3 5.2	26 2.1	7 10.7	6 22.2

DECEMBER 1973 LONGITUDE

Day	Sid.Time	☉	0 hr ☽	Noon ☽	True ☊	☿	♀	♂	♃	♄	♅	♆	♇
1 Sa	4 38 50	8♐39 8	15♒40 10	21♒39 41	28♐42.2	19♏12.3	24♑28.0	25♈28.2	8♒17.1	3♋ 0.9	26♎ 5.1	7♐13.0	6♎23.6
2 Su	4 42 47	9 39 58	27 42 13	3♓48 20	28 43.4	20 28.1	25 18.6	25 32.5	8 27.5	2R56.6	26 8.1	7 15.3	6 24.8
3 M	4 46 43	10 40 48	9♓58 39	16 13 45	28R43.8	21 46.3	26 8.4	25 37.6	8 38.1	2 52.3	26 11.1	7 17.5	6 26.1
4 Tu	4 50 40	11 41 40	22 34 11	29 0 27	28 43.5	23 6.5	26 57.4	25 43.4	8 48.7	2 47.8	26 14.0	7 19.8	6 27.3
5 W	4 54 36	12 42 33	5♈32 59	12♈12 7	28 42.3	24 28.4	27 45.5	25 49.9	8 59.5	2 43.4	26 16.9	7 22.0	6 28.5
6 Th	4 58 33	13 43 26	18 58 6	25 51 2	28 40.6	25 51.9	28 32.8	25 57.1	9 10.3	2 38.9	26 19.8	7 24.3	6 29.7
7 F	5 2 30	14 44 20	2♉50 54	9♉57 28	28 38.7	27 16.6	29 19.1	26 5.1	9 21.3	2 34.3	26 22.6	7 26.5	6 30.8
8 Sa	5 6 26	15 45 15	17 10 22	24 29 2	28 36.9	28 42.4	0♒ 4.4	26 13.7	9 32.4	2 29.7	26 25.4	7 28.8	6 31.9
9 Su	5 10 23	16 46 11	1♊52 45	9♊20 39	28 35.5	0♐ 9.1	0 48.8	26 23.0	9 43.6	2 25.0	26 28.2	7 31.0	6 33.0
10 M	5 14 19	17 47 7	16 51 41	24 24 47	28D 34.8	1 36.7	1 32.1	26 33.0	9 54.9	2 20.3	26 30.9	7 33.3	6 34.1
11 Tu	5 18 16	18 48 5	1♋58 46	9♋32 29	28 34.6	3 4.9	2 14.3	26 43.6	10 6.2	2 15.6	26 33.6	7 35.5	6 35.1
12 W	5 22 12	19 49 3	17 4 47	24 34 36	28 35.0	4 33.7	2 55.3	26 54.8	10 17.7	2 10.9	26 36.3	7 37.7	6 36.0
13 Th	5 26 9	20 50 3	2♌ 1 1	9♌23 13	28 35.6	6 3.0	3 35.2	27 6.6	10 29.3	2 6.1	26 38.9	7 39.9	6 37.0
14 F	5 30 5	21 51 3	16 40 30	23 52 25	28 36.3	7 32.8	4 13.9	27 19.0	10 40.9	2 1.2	26 41.4	7 42.1	6 37.9
15 Sa	5 34 2	22 52 5	0♍58 35	7♍58 50	28 36.8	9 3.0	4 51.3	27 32.1	10 52.7	1 56.4	26 43.9	7 44.3	6 38.8
16 Su	5 37 59	23 53 7	14 53 6	21 41 25	28R37.1	10 33.5	5 27.3	27 45.6	11 4.5	1 51.5	26 46.4	7 46.5	6 39.6
17 M	5 41 55	24 54 10	28 23 58	5♎ 0 58	28 37.2	12 4.4	6 2.0	27 59.8	11 16.4	1 46.6	26 48.9	7 48.7	6 40.5
18 Tu	5 45 52	25 55 15	11♎32 43	17 59 33	28 37.1	13 35.5	6 35.3	28 14.5	11 28.4	1 41.7	26 51.2	7 50.9	6 41.2
19 W	5 49 48	26 56 20	24 21 49	0♏39 55	28 36.9	15 7.0	7 7.0	28 29.8	11 40.5	1 36.7	26 53.6	7 53.1	6 42.0
20 Th	5 53 45	27 57 26	6♏54 12	13 5 4	28D 36.7	16 38.6	7 37.3	28 45.6	11 52.7	1 31.8	26 55.9	7 55.2	6 42.7
21 F	5 57 41	28 58 33	19 12 51	25 17 55	28 36.7	18 10.5	8 5.9	29 1.9	12 4.9	1 26.8	26 58.2	7 57.4	6 43.4
22 Sa	6 1 38	29 59 40	1♐20 35	7♐21 10	28 36.8	19 42.7	8 32.8	29 18.7	12 17.3	1 21.9	27 0.4	7 59.5	6 44.0
23 Su	6 5 35	1♑ 0 49	13 19 58	19 17 16	28 37.0	21 15.1	8 58.1	29 36.0	12 29.7	1 16.9	27 2.5	8 1.6	6 44.6
24 M	6 9 31	2 1 57	25 13 18	1♑ 8 22	28R37.1	22 47.7	9 21.5	29 53.8	12 42.2	1 11.9	27 4.7	8 3.8	6 45.2
25 Tu	6 13 28	3 3 6	7♑ 2 43	12 56 35	28 37.1	24 20.5	9 43.0	0♉12.1	12 54.8	1 7.0	27 6.7	8 5.9	6 45.8
26 W	6 17 24	4 4 16	18 50 15	24 43 59	28 36.8	25 53.6	10 2.7	0 30.9	13 7.4	1 2.0	27 8.8	8 8.0	6 46.3
27 Th	6 21 21	5 5 25	0♒38 4	6♒32 48	28 36.1	27 26.9	10 20.3	0 50.1	13 20.1	0 57.1	27 10.7	8 10.0	6 46.7
28 F	6 25 17	6 6 35	12 28 32	18 25 36	28 35.1	29 0.4	10 35.9	1 9.8	13 32.9	0 52.1	27 12.7	8 12.1	6 47.2
29 Sa	6 29 14	7 7 45	24 24 23	0♓25 17	28 33.9	0♑34.3	10 49.3	1 29.9	13 45.8	0 47.2	27 14.5	8 14.1	6 47.6
30 Su	6 33 10	8 8 55	6♓28 43	12 35 10	28 32.6	2 8.4	11 0.6	1 50.4	13 58.7	0 42.3	27 16.4	8 16.2	6 48.0
31 M	6 37 7	9 10 5	18 45 4	24 58 55	28 31.5	3 42.8	11 9.5	2 11.3	14 11.7	0 37.4	27 18.2	8 18.2	6 48.3

Astro Data	Dy Hr Mn
♃⚻♄	4 10:50
☽0N	6 6:53
♃△♇	16 20:33
☽0S	18 23:42
☿ D	19 14:14
♃⚹♆	22 14:31
♂ D	26 0:06
☽0N	3 15:12
☽0S	16 5:14
☽0N	30 22:20

Planet Ingress	Dy Hr Mn
♀ ♑	5 15:39
☉ ♐	22 10:54
♀ ♒	7 21:37
☿ ♐	8 21:29
☉ ♑	22 0:08
♂ ♉	24 8:09
☿ ♑	28 15:14

Last Aspect Dy Hr Mn		☽ Ingress Dy Hr Mn
2 6:55	♂ □	♒ 2 8:58
4 18:39	♀ ⚹	♓ 4 20:26
6 15:02	☿ △	♈ 7 4:19
9 3:43	♂ ☌	♉ 9 8:25
10 14:27	☉ ☍	♊ 11 9:59
13 4:56	♂ ⚹	♋ 13 10:46
15 5:47	♂ □	♌ 15 12:20
17 8:23	♂ △	♍ 17 15:41
19 16:08	☉ ⚹	♎ 19 21:15
21 20:47	♅ ☌	♏ 22 5:06
23 15:31	♀ ⚹	♐ 24 15:11
26 18:51	♅ ⚹	♑ 27 3:13
29 8:09	♅ □	♒ 29 16:17

Last Aspect Dy Hr Mn		☽ Ingress Dy Hr Mn
1 20:53	♅ △	♓ 2 4:32
4 8:45	♀ ⚹	♈ 4 13:50
6 17:37	♀ □	♉ 6 19:08
8 20:54	☿ ☍	♊ 8 20:58
10 15:34	♂ ⚹	♋ 10 20:52
12 15:58	♂ □	♌ 12 20:44
14 18:04	♂ △	♍ 14 22:20
16 17:13	☉ □	♎ 17 2:53
19 8:01	♂ ☍	♏ 19 10:44
20 9:49	♃ □	♐ 21 21:20
24 3:46	♅ ⚹	♑ 24 9:41
26 16:57	♅ □	♒ 26 22:43
29 5:41	♅ △	♓ 29 11:10
30 3:36	☉ ⚹	♈ 31 21:34

☽ Phases & Eclipses Dy Hr Mn	
3 6:29	☽ 10♒42
10 14:27	○ 18♉03
17 6:34	☽ 24♌46
24 19:55	● 2♐24
3 1:29	☽ 10♓45
10 1:35	○ 17♊51
10 1:44	☍ P 0.101
16 17:13	☽ 24♍37
24 15:07	● 2♑40
24 15:02:00	☌ A 12'02"

Astro Data
1 NOVEMBER 1973
Julian Day # 26968
Delta T 44.3 sec
SVP 05♓37'15"
Obliquity 23°26'34"
⚷ Chiron 17♈43.9R
☽ Mean ☊ 1♑09.2
1 DECEMBER 1973
Julian Day # 26998
Delta T 44.4 sec
SVP 05♓37'10"
Obliquity 23°26'33"
⚷ Chiron 16♈42.7R
☽ Mean ☊ 29♐33.9

LONGITUDE JANUARY 1974

Day	Sid.Time	☉	0 hr ☽	Noon ☽	True ☊	☿	♀	♂	♃	♄	♅	♆	♇
1 Tu	6 41 4	10♑11 14	1♈17 12	7♈40 23	28♐30.8	5♑17.5	11♒16.2	2♉32.6	14♒24.7	0♋32.5	27♎19.9	8♐20.2	6♎48.6
2 W	6 45 0	11 12 24	14 8 56	20 43 17	28D 30.6	6 52.5	11 20.5	2 54.3	14 37.8	0R 27.7	27 21.6	8 22.2	6 48.8
3 Th	6 48 57	12 13 33	27 23 47	4♉10 45	28 31.1	8 27.8	11R 22.3	3 16.4	14 51.0	0 22.9	27 23.2	8 24.1	6 49.1
4 F	6 52 53	13 14 42	11♉ 4 23	18 4 45	28 32.1	10 3.5	11 21.7	3 38.9	15 4.2	0 18.1	27 24.8	8 26.1	6 49.3
5 Sa	6 56 50	14 15 51	25 11 49	2♊25 22	28 33.3	11 39.5	11 18.6	4 1.7	15 17.5	0 13.3	27 26.3	8 28.0	6 49.4
6 Su	7 0 46	15 16 59	9♊45 0	17 10 9	28 34.4	13 15.9	11 13.0	4 24.9	15 30.8	0 8.6	27 27.8	8 29.9	6 49.5
7 M	7 4 43	16 18 7	24 40 4	2♋13 47	28R 35.1	14 52.7	11 4.8	4 48.4	15 44.2	0 3.9	27 29.2	8 31.8	6 49.6
8 Tu	7 8 39	17 19 15	9♋50 15	17 28 14	28 34.8	16 29.9	10 54.1	5 12.3	15 57.6	29♊59.3	27 30.5	8 33.7	6 49.7
9 W	7 12 36	18 20 23	25 6 29	2♌43 40	28 33.5	18 7.6	10 40.9	5 36.4	16 11.1	29 54.7	27 31.9	8 35.5	6R 49.7
10 Th	7 16 33	19 21 30	10♌18 31	17 49 50	28 31.3	19 45.6	10 25.2	6 0.9	16 24.7	29 50.2	27 33.1	8 37.4	6 49.7
11 F	7 20 29	20 22 38	25 16 34	2♍37 49	28 28.3	21 24.1	10 7.0	6 25.6	16 38.3	29 45.7	27 34.3	8 39.2	6 49.6
12 Sa	7 24 26	21 23 45	9♍52 50	17 1 8	28 25.1	23 3.1	9 46.5	6 50.7	16 51.9	29 41.3	27 35.5	8 41.0	6 49.5
13 Su	7 28 22	22 24 52	24 2 23	0♎56 27	28 22.3	24 42.5	9 23.7	7 16.0	17 5.6	29 36.9	27 36.6	8 42.7	6 49.4
14 M	7 32 19	23 25 59	7♎43 22	14 23 20	28 20.2	26 22.3	8 58.7	7 41.7	17 19.3	29 32.6	27 37.6	8 44.5	6 49.3
15 Tu	7 36 15	24 27 5	20 56 39	27 23 43	28D 19.2	28 2.6	8 31.7	8 7.6	17 33.1	29 28.3	27 38.6	8 46.2	6 49.1
16 W	7 40 12	25 28 12	3♏45 2	10♏ 1 6	28 19.4	29 43.4	8 2.8	8 33.7	17 46.9	29 24.1	27 39.5	8 47.9	6 48.8
17 Th	7 44 8	26 29 19	16 12 31	22 19 49	28 20.7	1♒24.6	7 32.1	9 0.2	18 0.7	29 19.9	27 40.4	8 49.6	6 48.6
18 F	7 48 5	27 30 25	28 23 35	4♐24 24	28 22.5	3 6.3	6 59.9	9 26.8	18 14.6	29 15.8	27 41.2	8 51.2	6 48.3
19 Sa	7 52 2	28 31 31	10♐22 47	16 19 16	28 24.3	4 48.3	6 26.4	9 53.8	18 28.5	29 11.8	27 42.0	8 52.9	6 48.0
20 Su	7 55 58	29 32 36	22 14 19	28 8 23	28R 25.5	6 30.8	5 51.6	10 21.0	18 42.5	29 7.9	27 42.7	8 54.5	6 47.6
21 M	7 59 55	0♒33 42	4♑ 1 53	9♑55 11	28 25.5	8 13.5	5 16.0	10 48.4	18 56.5	29 4.0	27 43.4	8 56.1	6 47.2
22 Tu	8 3 51	1 34 46	15 48 38	21 42 30	28 23.9	9 56.5	4 39.7	11 16.1	19 10.5	29 0.2	27 44.0	8 57.6	6 46.8
23 W	8 7 48	2 35 50	27 37 6	3♒32 38	28 20.5	11 39.8	4 2.9	11 44.0	19 24.6	28 56.5	27 44.5	8 59.1	6 46.3
24 Th	8 11 44	3 36 53	9♒29 22	15 27 28	28 15.4	13 23.1	3 26.0	12 12.1	19 38.7	28 52.9	27 45.0	9 0.7	6 45.8
25 F	8 15 41	4 37 56	21 27 9	27 28 36	28 9.0	15 6.4	2 49.1	12 40.4	19 52.8	28 49.4	27 45.4	9 2.1	6 45.3
26 Sa	8 19 37	5 38 57	3♓32 1	9♓37 37	28 1.7	16 49.7	2 12.5	13 9.0	20 7.0	28 45.9	27 45.8	9 3.6	6 44.7
27 Su	8 23 34	6 39 58	15 45 34	21 56 9	27 54.3	18 32.6	1 36.6	13 37.7	20 21.1	28 42.5	27 46.1	9 5.0	6 44.1
28 M	8 27 31	7 40 57	28 9 36	4♈26 12	27 47.7	20 15.1	1 1.4	14 6.7	20 35.3	28 39.2	27 46.4	9 6.4	6 43.5
29 Tu	8 31 27	8 41 55	10♈46 14	17 10 2	27 42.6	21 56.9	0 27.3	14 35.8	20 49.6	28 36.0	27 46.6	9 7.8	6 42.8
30 W	8 35 24	9 42 53	23 37 55	0♉10 14	27 39.2	23 37.8	29♑54.4	15 5.1	21 3.8	28 32.9	27 46.7	9 9.1	6 42.2
31 Th	8 39 20	10 43 49	6♉47 20	13 29 30	27D 37.8	25 17.4	29 23.0	15 34.7	21 18.1	28 29.9	27 46.8	9 10.4	6 41.4

LONGITUDE FEBRUARY 1974

Day	Sid.Time	☉	0 hr ☽	Noon ☽	True ☊	☿	♀	♂	♃	♄	♅	♆	♇
1 F	8 43 17	11♒44 43	20♉17 2	27♉10 10	27♐38.1	26♒55.4	28♑53.3	16♉ 4.4	21♒32.3	28♊26.9	27♎46.8	9♐11.7	6♎40.7
2 Sa	8 47 13	12 45 37	4♊ 9 2	11♊13 42	27 39.3	28 31.5	28R 25.4	16 34.3	21 46.6	28R 24.1	27R 46.8	9 13.0	6R 39.9
3 Su	8 51 10	13 46 29	18 24 5	25 39 58	27R 40.4	0♓ 5.0	27 59.4	17 4.3	22 0.9	28 21.4	27 46.7	9 14.2	6 39.1
4 M	8 55 6	14 47 19	3♋ 0 57	10♋26 29	27 40.6	1 35.6	27 35.6	17 34.5	22 15.3	28 18.7	27 46.6	9 15.4	6 38.3
5 Tu	8 59 3	15 48 9	17 55 49	25 28 2	27 39.0	3 2.7	27 14.0	18 4.9	22 29.6	28 16.2	27 46.4	9 16.5	6 37.4
6 W	9 3 0	16 48 57	3♌ 2 4	10♌36 43	27 35.0	4 25.6	26 54.7	18 35.4	22 43.9	28 13.7	27 46.2	9 17.7	6 36.5
7 Th	9 6 56	17 49 43	18 10 45	25 42 51	27 28.8	5 43.6	26 37.8	19 6.1	22 58.3	28 11.4	27 45.9	9 18.8	6 35.6
8 F	9 10 53	18 50 28	3♍11 48	10♍36 28	27 21.0	6 56.1	26 23.3	19 36.9	23 12.7	28 9.1	27 45.5	9 19.9	6 34.6
9 Sa	9 14 49	19 51 13	17 55 49	25 9 2	27 12.4	8 2.3	26 11.3	20 7.8	23 27.0	28 7.0	27 45.1	9 20.9	6 33.6
10 Su	9 18 46	20 51 56	2♎15 30	9♎14 48	27 4.1	9 1.4	26 1.8	20 38.9	23 41.4	28 5.0	27 44.7	9 21.9	6 32.6
11 M	9 22 42	21 52 37	16 6 42	22 51 13	26 57.1	9 52.7	25 54.9	21 10.1	23 55.8	28 3.0	27 44.1	9 22.9	6 31.6
12 Tu	9 26 39	22 53 18	29 28 28	5♏58 48	26 52.2	10 35.5	25 50.4	21 41.5	24 10.2	28 1.2	27 43.6	9 23.9	6 30.5
13 W	9 30 35	23 53 58	12♏22 37	18 40 27	26 49.4	11 9.1	25D 48.4	22 13.0	24 24.6	27 59.5	27 42.9	9 24.8	6 29.4
14 Th	9 34 32	24 54 37	24 52 53	1♐ 0 34	26D 48.6	11 33.0	25 48.8	22 44.6	24 39.0	27 57.9	27 42.3	9 25.7	6 28.3
15 F	9 38 29	25 55 14	7♐ 4 9	13 4 21	26 49.1	11R 46.8	25 51.7	23 16.3	24 53.4	27 56.4	27 41.5	9 26.5	6 27.2
16 Sa	9 42 25	26 55 50	19 1 50	24 57 14	26R 50.0	11 50.2	25 56.9	23 48.2	25 7.8	27 55.0	27 40.8	9 27.3	6 26.0
17 Su	9 46 22	27 56 26	0♑51 14	6♑44 24	26 50.1	11 43.1	26 4.5	24 20.1	25 22.2	27 53.7	27 39.9	9 28.1	6 24.8
18 M	9 50 18	28 56 59	12 37 19	18 30 29	26 48.7	11 25.7	26 14.3	24 52.2	25 36.6	27 52.5	27 39.0	9 28.9	6 23.6
19 Tu	9 54 15	29 57 32	24 24 24	0♒19 28	26 44.8	10 58.5	26 26.3	25 24.5	25 51.0	27 51.5	27 38.1	9 29.6	6 22.4
20 W	9 58 11	0♓58 3	6♒16 2	12 14 26	26 38.2	10 22.0	26 40.4	25 56.8	26 5.3	27 50.5	27 37.1	9 30.3	6 21.1
21 Th	10 2 8	1 58 33	18 14 55	24 17 41	26 29.0	9 37.3	26 56.6	26 29.2	26 19.7	27 49.7	27 36.1	9 31.0	6 19.9
22 F	10 6 4	2 59 1	0♓22 53	6♓30 38	26 17.5	8 45.5	27 14.7	27 1.7	26 34.1	27 49.0	27 35.0	9 31.6	6 18.6
23 Sa	10 10 1	3 59 27	12 41 1	18 54 5	26 4.8	7 47.9	27 34.8	27 34.4	26 48.4	27 48.4	27 33.8	9 32.2	6 17.2
24 Su	10 13 58	4 59 51	25 9 52	1♈28 24	25 51.8	6 46.2	27 56.8	28 7.1	27 2.8	27 47.9	27 32.6	9 32.7	6 15.9
25 M	10 17 54	6 0 14	7♈49 41	14 13 47	25 39.9	5 42.0	28 20.6	28 40.0	27 17.1	27 47.5	27 31.4	9 33.3	6 14.5
26 Tu	10 21 51	7 0 35	20 40 43	27 10 36	25 29.9	4 36.8	28 46.1	29 12.9	27 31.4	27 47.2	27 30.1	9 33.8	6 13.2
27 W	10 25 47	8 0 55	3♉43 30	10♉19 33	25 22.7	3 32.4	29 13.2	29 46.0	27 45.7	27D 47.0	27 28.8	9 34.2	6 11.8
28 Th	10 29 44	9 1 12	16 58 55	23 41 46	25 18.3	2 30.1	29 42.0	0♊19.1	27 60.0	27 47.0	27 27.4	9 34.6	6 10.3

Astro Data	Planet Ingress	Last Aspect	☽ Ingress	Last Aspect	☽ Ingress	☽ Phases & Eclipses	Astro Data
Dy Hr Mn	Dy Hr Mn	Dy Hr Mn	Dy Hr Mn	Dy Hr Mn	Dy Hr Mn	Dy Hr Mn	1 JANUARY 1974
♀ R 3 6:07	♄ ♊ 7 20:27	2 23:59 ♅ ☍	♉ 3 4:38	1 14:29 ♀ △	♊ 1 16:53	1 18:06 ☽ 10♈57	Julian Day # 27029
♃⚼♄ 4 18:29	☿ ♒ 16 3:56	4 6:59 ♃ □	♊ 5 8:00	3 16:21 ♄ ☌	♋ 3 19:06	8 12:36 ○ 17♋51	Delta T 44.5 sec
♇ R 9 0:53	☉ ♒ 20 10:46	7 4:29 ♅ △	♋ 7 8:28	5 15:39 ♅ □	♌ 5 19:11	15 7:04 ☽ 24♎45	SVP 05♓37'05"
☽0S 12 13:37	♀ ♑ 29 19:51	9 3:49 ♅ □	♌ 9 7:42	7 15:55 ♄ ⚹	♍ 7 18:52	23 11:02 ● 3♒04	Obliquity 23°26'33"
☽0N 27 4:38		11 7:16 ♄ ⚹	♍ 11 7:41	9 16:57 ♄ □	♎ 9 20:10	31 7:39 ☽ 11♉03	⚷ Chiron 16♈23.3
♃⚼♇ 1 13:19	☿ ♓ 2 22:42	13 9:38 ♄ □	♎ 13 10:21	11 21:21 ♄ △	♏ 12 0:58		☽ Mean ☊ 27♐55.4
♅ R 1 2:57	☉ ♓ 19 0:59	15 15:49 ♄ △	♏ 15 16:54	14 1:49 ♀ ⚹	♐ 14 10:01	6 23:24 ○ 17♌48	
☽0S 9 0:31	♂ ♊ 27 10:11	17 22:05 ☉ ⚹	♐ 18 3:12	16 17:59 ♄ ☍	♑ 16 22:16	14 0:04 ☽ 24♏55	1 FEBRUARY 1974
♀ D 13 7:28	♀ ♒ 28 14:25	20 13:57 ♄ ☍	♑ 20 15:47	19 6:33 ♅ □	♒ 19 11:21	22 5:34 ● 3♓13	Julian Day # 27060
☿ R 15 19:45		23 0:15 ♅ □	♒ 23 4:50	21 18:57 ♄ △	♓ 21 23:15		Delta T 44.6 sec
☽0N 23 11:01		25 14:36 ♄ △	♓ 25 17:00	24 5:53 ♂ ⚹	♈ 24 9:12		SVP 05♓37'00"
♃△♅ 25 22:00		28 0:57 ♄ □	♈ 28 3:32	26 15:27 ♀ □	♉ 26 17:11		Obliquity 23°26'33"
♃△♄ 27 2:13		30 11:04 ♀ □	♉ 30 11:41	28 19:59 ♃ □	♊ 28 23:10		⚷ Chiron 16♈56.4
♄ D 27 21:13							☽ Mean ☊ 26♐17.0

MARCH 1974 LONGITUDE

Day	Sid.Time	☉	0 hr ☽	Noon ☽	True ☊	☿	♀	♂	♃	♄	♅	♆	♇
1 F	10 33 40	10♓ 1 27	0♊28 16	7♊18 37	25♐16.5	1♓31.2	0♒12.3	0♊52.3	28♒14.2	27♊47.1	27♎26.0	9♐35.0	6♎ 8.9
2 Sa	10 37 37	11 1 40	14 12 57	21 11 23	25R16.2	0R36.9	0 44.1	1 25.6	28 28.5	27 47.3	27R24.5	9 35.4	6R 7.5
3 Su	10 41 33	12 1 52	28 14 0	5♋20 43	25 16.3	29♒47.9	1 17.3	1 59.0	28 42.7	27 47.5	27 23.0	9 35.7	6 6.0
4 M	10 45 30	13 2 1	12♋31 27	19 45 53	25 15.4	29 5.1	1 51.9	2 32.5	28 56.9	27 48.0	27 21.4	9 36.0	6 4.5
5 Tu	10 49 27	14 2 8	27 3 39	4♌24 11	25 12.4	28 28.7	2 27.9	3 6.0	29 11.1	27 48.5	27 19.8	9 36.3	6 3.0
6 W	10 53 23	15 2 12	11♌46 48	19 10 38	25 6.7	27 59.1	3 5.1	3 39.6	29 25.2	27 49.1	27 18.2	9 36.5	6 1.5
7 Th	10 57 20	16 2 15	26 34 45	3♍58 8	24 58.1	27 36.3	3 43.5	4 13.3	29 39.4	27 49.9	27 16.5	9 36.7	5 60.0
8 F	11 1 16	17 2 16	11♍19 44	18 38 30	24 47.2	27 20.4	4 23.1	4 47.0	29 53.4	27 50.7	27 14.8	9 36.8	5 58.4
9 Sa	11 5 13	18 2 14	25 53 26	3♎ 3 39	24 35.2	27D11.1	5 3.9	5 20.9	0♓ 7.5	27 51.7	27 13.0	9 36.9	5 56.9
10 Su	11 9 9	19 2 11	10♎ 8 25	17 7 8	24 23.4	27 8.4	5 45.7	5 54.7	0 21.5	27 52.8	27 11.2	9 37.0	5 55.3
11 M	11 13 6	20 2 6	23 59 24	0♏44 59	24 13.0	27 12.0	6 28.7	6 28.7	0 35.5	27 54.0	27 9.4	9 37.1	5 53.8
12 Tu	11 17 2	21 2 0	7♏23 51	13 56 6	24 4.9	27 21.5	7 12.6	7 2.7	0 49.5	27 55.3	27 7.5	9R37.1	5 52.2
13 W	11 20 59	22 1 51	20 21 59	26 41 53	23 59.5	27 36.6	7 57.5	7 36.8	1 3.5	27 56.7	27 5.6	9 37.1	5 50.6
14 Th	11 24 56	23 1 41	2♐56 17	9♐ 5 45	23 56.7	27 57.1	8 43.3	8 10.9	1 17.4	27 58.2	27 3.6	9 37.0	5 49.0
15 F	11 28 52	24 1 30	15 10 54	21 12 25	23 55.7	28 22.7	9 30.0	8 45.1	1 31.2	27 59.8	27 1.6	9 36.9	5 47.4
16 Sa	11 32 49	25 1 17	27 10 58	3♑ 7 17	23 55.6	28 52.9	10 17.6	9 19.4	1 45.1	28 1.6	26 59.6	9 36.8	5 45.7
17 Su	11 36 45	26 1 1	9♑ 2 2	14 55 55	23 55.2	29 27.6	11 6.0	9 53.7	1 58.9	28 3.4	26 57.6	9 36.7	5 44.1
18 M	11 40 42	27 0 45	20 49 36	26 43 43	23 53.5	0♓ 6.5	11 55.2	10 28.1	2 12.6	28 5.4	26 55.5	9 36.5	5 42.5
19 Tu	11 44 38	28 0 26	2♒38 52	8♒35 35	23 49.5	0 49.2	12 45.1	11 2.5	2 26.3	28 7.4	26 53.4	9 36.3	5 40.8
20 W	11 48 35	29 0 6	14 34 22	20 35 38	23 42.8	1 35.6	13 35.8	11 37.0	2 40.0	28 9.6	26 51.2	9 36.0	5 39.2
21 Th	11 52 31	29 59 43	26 39 45	2♓47 1	23 33.3	2 25.4	14 27.2	12 11.6	2 53.6	28 11.9	26 49.0	9 35.8	5 37.6
22 F	11 56 28	0♈59 19	8♓57 38	15 11 46	23 21.4	3 18.4	15 19.2	12 46.2	3 7.2	28 14.3	26 46.8	9 35.4	5 35.9
23 Sa	12 0 24	1 58 53	21 29 30	27 50 49	23 8.2	4 14.5	16 11.9	13 20.8	3 20.8	28 16.8	26 44.6	9 35.1	5 34.2
24 Su	12 4 21	2 58 25	4♈15 41	10♈43 59	22 54.6	5 13.4	17 5.2	13 55.5	3 34.2	28 19.3	26 42.3	9 34.7	5 32.6
25 M	12 8 18	3 57 55	17 15 36	23 50 20	22 42.0	6 15.0	17 59.1	14 30.3	3 47.7	28 22.0	26 40.0	9 34.3	5 30.9
26 Tu	12 12 14	4 57 23	0♉28 2	7♉ 8 30	22 31.4	7 19.2	18 53.5	15 5.1	4 1.1	28 24.8	26 37.7	9 33.9	5 29.2
27 W	12 16 11	5 56 49	13 51 33	20 37 3	22 23.7	8 25.8	19 48.5	15 40.0	4 14.4	28 27.7	26 35.4	9 33.4	5 27.6
28 Th	12 20 7	6 56 12	27 24 53	4♊14 57	22 18.9	9 34.6	20 44.0	16 14.9	4 27.7	28 30.7	26 33.0	9 32.9	5 25.9
29 F	12 24 4	7 55 34	11♊ 7 12	18 1 34	22D16.8	10 45.7	21 40.1	16 49.8	4 40.9	28 33.8	26 30.7	9 32.4	5 24.3
30 Sa	12 28 0	8 54 53	24 58 5	1♋56 43	22 16.4	11 58.9	22 36.6	17 24.8	4 54.1	28 37.0	26 28.3	9 31.8	5 22.6
31 Su	12 31 57	9 54 9	8♋57 27	16 0 14	22R16.6	13 14.1	23 33.6	17 59.9	5 7.2	28 40.3	26 25.8	9 31.2	5 20.9

APRIL 1974 LONGITUDE

Day	Sid.Time	☉	0 hr ☽	Noon ☽	True ☊	☿	♀	♂	♃	♄	♅	♆	♇
1 M	12 35 53	10♈53 24	23♋ 4 59	0♌11 34	22♐16.1	14♓31.3	24♒31.0	18♊34.9	5♓20.2	28♊43.7	26♎23.4	9♐30.6	5♎19.3
2 Tu	12 39 50	11 52 35	7♌19 45	14 29 13	22R13.8	15 50.3	25 28.9	19 10.0	5 33.2	28 47.2	26R21.0	9R29.9	5R17.6
3 W	12 43 47	12 51 45	21 39 35	28 50 23	22 8.9	17 11.2	26 27.1	19 45.2	5 46.1	28 50.8	26 18.5	9 29.2	5 16.0
4 Th	12 47 43	13 50 52	6♍ 1 0	13♍10 50	22 1.6	18 33.8	27 25.9	20 20.4	5 59.0	28 54.5	26 16.0	9 28.5	5 14.4
5 F	12 51 40	14 49 57	20 19 11	27 25 21	21 52.1	19 58.1	28 24.9	20 55.6	6 11.8	28 58.3	26 13.5	9 27.8	5 12.7
6 Sa	12 55 36	15 49 0	4♎28 37	11♎28 21	21 41.5	21 24.2	29 24.4	21 30.8	6 24.5	29 2.1	26 11.0	9 27.0	5 11.1
7 Su	12 59 33	16 48 0	18 23 57	25 14 54	21 30.9	22 51.9	0♓24.3	22 6.1	6 37.2	29 6.1	26 8.5	9 26.2	5 9.5
8 M	13 3 29	17 46 59	2♏ 0 49	8♏41 24	21 21.5	24 21.3	1 24.5	22 41.4	6 49.8	29 10.1	26 6.0	9 25.4	5 7.8
9 Tu	13 7 26	18 45 56	15 16 32	21 46 11	21 14.1	25 52.3	2 25.1	23 16.8	7 2.3	29 14.3	26 3.4	9 24.5	5 6.2
10 W	13 11 22	19 44 51	28 10 27	4♐29 33	21 9.2	27 24.8	3 26.0	23 52.2	7 14.8	29 18.5	26 0.9	9 23.6	5 4.6
11 Th	13 15 19	20 43 44	10♐43 47	16 53 35	21D 6.7	28 59.0	4 27.2	24 27.6	7 27.2	29 22.8	25 58.3	9 22.7	5 3.0
12 F	13 19 16	21 42 35	22 59 24	29 1 48	21 6.2	0♈34.8	5 28.8	25 3.0	7 39.5	29 27.2	25 55.8	9 21.8	5 1.5
13 Sa	13 23 12	22 41 25	5♑ 1 22	10♑58 43	21 6.8	2 12.1	6 30.6	25 38.5	7 51.7	29 31.7	25 53.2	9 20.8	4 59.9
14 Su	13 27 9	23 40 12	16 54 31	22 49 26	21R 7.7	3 51.0	7 32.8	26 14.0	8 3.9	29 36.2	25 50.6	9 19.8	4 58.3
15 M	13 31 5	24 38 58	28 44 8	4♒39 16	21 7.8	5 31.5	8 35.2	26 49.5	8 16.0	29 40.9	25 48.1	9 18.8	4 56.8
16 Tu	13 35 2	25 37 43	10♒35 30	16 33 26	21 6.4	7 13.6	9 37.9	27 25.1	8 28.0	29 45.6	25 45.5	9 17.8	4 55.2
17 W	13 38 58	26 36 25	22 33 41	28 36 45	21 3.0	8 57.2	10 40.9	28 0.7	8 39.9	29 50.4	25 42.9	9 16.7	4 53.7
18 Th	13 42 55	27 35 6	4♓43 9	10♓53 18	20 57.5	10 42.5	11 44.1	28 36.3	8 51.7	29 55.3	25 40.3	9 15.6	4 52.2
19 F	13 46 51	28 33 45	17 7 32	23 26 8	20 50.1	12 29.4	12 47.5	29 12.0	9 3.5	0♋ 0.3	25 37.8	9 14.5	4 50.7
20 Sa	13 50 48	29 32 22	29 49 16	6♈17 3	20 41.4	14 17.8	13 51.2	29 47.6	9 15.1	0 5.4	25 35.2	9 13.4	4 49.2
21 Su	13 54 45	0♉30 58	12♈49 28	19 26 24	20 32.4	16 7.9	14 55.2	0♋23.4	9 26.7	0 10.5	25 32.6	9 12.2	4 47.8
22 M	13 58 41	1 29 32	26 7 43	2♉53 7	20 24.0	17 59.7	15 59.3	0 59.1	9 38.2	0 15.7	25 30.1	9 11.0	4 46.3
23 Tu	14 2 38	2 28 4	9♉42 18	16 34 54	20 17.0	19 53.0	17 3.7	1 34.9	9 49.6	0 21.0	25 27.5	9 9.8	4 44.9
24 W	14 6 34	3 26 34	23 30 30	0♊28 41	20 12.0	21 48.0	18 8.2	2 10.7	10 0.9	0 26.3	25 25.0	9 8.6	4 43.5
25 Th	14 10 31	4 25 2	7♊29 1	14 31 5	20D 9.3	23 44.6	19 13.0	2 46.5	10 12.1	0 31.8	25 22.4	9 7.4	4 42.1
26 F	14 14 27	5 23 28	21 34 31	28 38 57	20 8.7	25 42.8	20 17.9	3 22.3	10 23.3	0 37.3	25 19.9	9 6.1	4 40.7
27 Sa	14 18 24	6 21 52	5♋44 3	12♋49 34	20 9.4	27 42.5	21 23.0	3 58.2	10 34.3	0 42.8	25 17.4	9 4.8	4 39.3
28 Su	14 22 20	7 20 14	19 55 13	27 0 48	20 10.6	29 43.9	22 28.4	4 34.1	10 45.2	0 48.5	25 14.9	9 3.5	4 38.0
29 M	14 26 17	8 18 33	4♌ 6 6	11♌10 55	20R11.5	1♉46.6	23 33.8	5 10.0	10 56.0	0 54.2	25 12.4	9 2.2	4 36.7
30 Tu	14 30 14	9 16 51	18 15 3	25 18 16	20 11.3	3 50.8	24 39.5	5 46.0	11 6.8	0 60.0	25 9.9	9 0.9	4 35.4

Astro Data

	Dy Hr Mn
☽0S	8 11:37
☿ D	9 22:16
♆ R	12 1:20
☽0N	22 18:06
♃⊼♇	31 22:27
☽0S	4 20:34
☿0N	15 1:01
☽0N	19 1:54
♃□♆	19 20:41
♃⊡♅	25 18:04

Planet Ingress

	Dy Hr Mn
☿ ♒	2 17:49
♃ ♓	8 11:11
☿ ♓	17 20:11
☉ ♈	21 0:07
♀ ♓	6 14:17
☿ ♈	11 15:20
♄ ♋	18 22:33
☉ ♉	20 11:19
♂ ♋	20 8:18
☿ ♉	28 3:10

Last Aspect / ☽ Ingress (March)

Last Aspect Dy Hr Mn		☽ Ingress Dy Hr Mn
3 2:31	☿ △	♋ 3 3:00
5 0:26	♅ □	♌ 5 4:49
7 5:04	♃ ☍	♍ 7 5:33
9 3:17	♄ □	♎ 9 6:52
11 6:56	♄ △	♏ 11 10:40
13 14:07	☿ □	♐ 13 18:20
16 3:36	☿ ✶	♑ 16 5:41
18 13:44	☉ ✶	♒ 18 18:38
21 3:02	♄ △	♓ 21 6:33
23 12:51	♄ □	♈ 23 16:02
25 20:17	♄ ✶	♉ 25 23:09
27 11:20	♀ □	♊ 28 4:33
30 6:18	♄ ☌	♋ 30 8:40

Last Aspect / ☽ Ingress (April)

Last Aspect Dy Hr Mn		☽ Ingress Dy Hr Mn
1 5:34	♅ □	♌ 1 11:41
3 12:04	♄ ✶	♍ 3 13:56
5 14:42	♄ □	♎ 5 16:22
7 18:55	♄ △	♏ 7 20:25
9 22:22	☿ △	♐ 10 3:27
12 12:55	♄ ☍	♑ 12 13:56
14 18:04	♅ □	♒ 15 2:34
17 14:31	♄ △	♓ 17 14:44
19 23:57	♂ □	♈ 20 0:20
21 22:53	♅ ☍	♉ 22 6:53
23 13:55	♀ ✶	♊ 24 11:11
26 8:10	☿ ✶	♋ 26 14:17
28 8:59	♅ □	♌ 28 17:03
30 11:44	♅ ✶	♍ 30 20:00

☽ Phases & Eclipses

Dy Hr Mn	
1 18:03	☽ 10♊47
8 10:03	○ 17♍27
15 19:15	☽ 24♐49
23 21:24	● 2♈52
31 1:44	☽ 9♋58
6 21:00	○ 16♎41
14 14:57	☽ 24♑17
22 10:16	● 1♉55
29 7:39	☽ 8♌37

Astro Data

1 MARCH 1974
Julian Day # 27088
Delta T 44.7 sec
SVP 05♓36'56"
Obliquity 23°26'33"
⚷ Chiron 18♈04.8
☽ Mean ☊ 24♐48.0

1 APRIL 1974
Julian Day # 27119
Delta T 44.7 sec
SVP 05♓36'53"
Obliquity 23°26'33"
⚷ Chiron 19♈47.0
☽ Mean ☊ 23♐09.5

LONGITUDE — MAY 1974

Day	Sid.Time	☉	0 hr ☽	Noon ☽	True ☊	☿	♀	♂	♃	♄	♅	♆	♇
1 W	14 34 10	10♉15 6	2♏20 23	9♏21 6	20♍ 9.3	5♉56.3	25♓45.3	6♊21.9	11♓17.4	1♋ 5.8	25♎ 7.5	8♐59.5	4♎34.1
2 Th	14 38 7	11 13 20	16 20 11	23 17 19	20R 5.7	8 3.0	26 51.3	6 57.9	11 27.9	1 11.7	25R 5.0	8 58.1	4 32.8
3 F	14 42 3	12 11 31	0♎12 11	7♎ 4 29	20 0.7	10 10.8	27 57.4	7 33.9	11 38.3	1 17.7	25 2.6	8 56.7	4 31.6
4 Sa	14 46 0	13 9 40	13 53 52	20 40 4	19 54.9	12 19.5	29 3.7	8 9.9	11 48.6	1 23.7	25 0.2	8 55.3	4 30.3
5 Su	14 49 56	14 7 48	27 22 46	4♏ 1 44	19 49.0	14 28.9	0♈10.1	8 46.0	11 58.8	1 29.8	24 57.8	8 53.9	4 29.2
6 M	14 53 53	15 5 54	10♏36 47	17 7 46	19 43.8	16 38.8	1 16.7	9 22.0	12 8.8	1 36.0	24 55.4	8 52.5	4 28.0
7 Tu	14 57 49	16 3 58	23 34 36	29 57 17	19 39.9	18 49.0	2 23.4	9 58.1	12 18.8	1 42.2	24 53.1	8 51.0	4 26.8
8 W	15 1 46	17 2 0	6♐15 52	12♐30 30	19D 36.7	20 59.1	3 30.3	10 34.2	12 28.7	1 48.4	24 50.7	8 49.5	4 25.7
9 Th	15 5 43	18 0 1	18 41 22	24 48 46	19 37.2	23 9.0	4 37.3	11 10.3	12 38.4	1 54.8	24 48.4	8 48.1	4 24.6
10 F	15 9 39	18 58 1	0♑53 1	6♑54 30	19 37.2	25 18.3	5 44.4	11 46.4	12 48.1	2 1.2	24 46.2	8 46.6	4 23.5
11 Sa	15 13 36	19 55 59	12 53 41	18 51 2	19 38.6	27 26.8	6 51.7	12 22.6	12 57.6	2 7.6	24 43.9	8 45.1	4 22.5
12 Su	15 17 32	20 53 56	24 47 4	0♒42 23	19 40.4	29 34.1	7 59.0	12 58.7	13 7.0	2 14.1	24 41.7	8 43.6	4 21.5
13 M	15 21 29	21 51 51	6♒37 32	12 33 8	19 42.0	1♊40.0	9 6.6	13 34.9	13 16.2	2 20.6	24 39.5	8 42.0	4 20.4
14 Tu	15 25 25	22 49 45	18 29 47	24 28 49	19R42.8	3 44.2	10 14.2	14 11.1	13 25.4	2 27.2	24 37.3	8 40.5	4 19.5
15 W	15 29 22	23 47 38	0♓28 41	6♓32 8	19 42.7	5 46.5	11 21.9	14 47.3	13 34.4	2 33.9	24 35.2	8 38.9	4 18.5
16 Th	15 33 18	24 45 30	12 39 0	18 49 49	19 41.5	7 46.7	12 29.8	15 23.6	13 43.3	2 40.6	24 33.0	8 37.4	4 17.6
17 F	15 37 15	25 43 20	25 5 4	1♈25 8	19 39.3	9 44.5	13 37.8	15 59.8	13 52.0	2 47.3	24 30.9	8 35.8	4 16.7
18 Sa	15 41 12	26 41 9	7♈50 22	14 21 1	19 36.3	11 39.7	14 45.8	16 36.1	14 0.7	2 54.1	24 28.9	8 34.2	4 15.8
19 Su	15 45 8	27 38 57	20 57 15	27 39 7	19 33.1	13 32.4	15 54.0	17 12.4	14 9.2	3 1.0	24 26.9	8 32.7	4 15.0
20 M	15 49 5	28 36 44	4♉26 31	11♉19 17	19 30.0	15 22.2	17 2.3	17 48.7	14 17.6	3 7.8	24 24.9	8 31.1	4 14.2
21 Tu	15 53 1	29 34 30	18 17 8	25 19 38	19 27.5	17 9.2	18 10.6	18 25.1	14 25.8	3 14.8	24 22.9	8 29.5	4 13.4
22 W	15 56 58	0♊32 14	2♊26 17	9♊36 29	19 25.9	18 53.1	19 19.1	19 1.4	14 33.9	3 21.8	24 21.0	8 27.9	4 12.6
23 Th	16 0 54	1 29 57	16 49 35	24 4 52	19D25.2	20 34.1	20 27.6	19 37.8	14 41.9	3 28.8	24 19.1	8 26.3	4 11.9
24 F	16 4 51	2 27 39	1♋23 36	8♋39 5	19 25.4	22 12.0	21 36.3	20 14.2	14 49.7	3 35.8	24 17.3	8 24.7	4 11.2
25 Sa	16 8 47	3 25 19	15 56 35	23 13 28	19 26.4	23 46.7	22 45.0	20 50.6	14 57.4	3 42.9	24 15.4	8 23.0	4 10.6
26 Su	16 12 44	4 22 58	0♌29 7	7♌43 0	19 27.5	25 18.2	23 53.8	21 27.0	15 4.9	3 50.1	24 13.7	8 21.4	4 9.9
27 M	16 16 41	5 20 35	14 54 38	22 2 38	19 28.9	26 46.6	25 2.7	22 3.5	15 12.3	3 57.2	24 11.9	8 19.8	4 9.3
28 Tu	16 20 37	6 18 11	29 9 41	6♍12 33	19R29.1	28 11.6	26 11.6	22 40.0	15 19.5	4 4.5	24 10.2	8 18.2	4 8.8
29 W	16 24 34	7 15 45	13♍12 12	20 7 58	19 29.1	29 33.3	27 20.6	23 16.4	15 26.6	4 11.7	24 8.6	8 16.6	4 8.2
30 Th	16 28 30	8 13 18	27 0 19	3♎49 0	19 28.6	0♋51.7	28 29.7	23 52.9	15 33.5	4 19.0	24 7.0	8 14.9	4 7.7
31 F	16 32 27	9 10 49	10♎34 1	17 15 21	19 27.6	2 6.7	29 38.9	24 29.4	15 40.3	4 26.3	24 5.4	8 13.3	4 7.2

LONGITUDE — JUNE 1974

Day	Sid.Time	☉	0 hr ☽	Noon ☽	True ☊	☿	♀	♂	♃	♄	♅	♆	♇
1 Sa	16 36 23	10♊ 8 19	23♎53 2	0♏27 7	19♍26.5	3♋18.3	0♉48.2	25♊ 5.9	15♓47.0	4♋33.6	24♎ 3.9	8♐11.7	4♎ 6.8
2 Su	16 40 20	11 5 48	6♏57 38	13 24 39	19R25.4	4 26.3	1 57.5	25 42.5	15 53.4	4 41.0	24R 2.4	8R10.1	4R 6.3
3 M	16 44 16	12 3 16	19 48 15	26 8 31	19 24.5	5 30.8	3 6.9	26 19.0	15 59.8	4 48.4	24 0.9	8 8.4	4 6.0
4 Tu	16 48 13	13 0 42	2♐25 33	8♐39 28	19 23.9	6 31.7	4 16.3	26 55.6	16 5.9	4 55.8	23 59.5	8 6.8	4 5.6
5 W	16 52 10	13 58 8	14 50 25	20 58 33	19D23.6	7 28.9	5 25.9	27 32.2	16 12.0	5 3.3	23 58.1	8 5.2	4 5.3
6 Th	16 56 6	14 55 33	27 4 4	3♑ 7 12	19 23.6	8 22.3	6 35.5	28 8.8	16 17.8	5 10.8	23 56.8	8 3.6	4 5.0
7 F	17 0 3	15 52 57	9♑ 8 11	15 7 17	19 23.9	9 11.8	7 45.2	28 45.4	16 23.5	5 18.3	23 55.6	8 2.0	4 4.7
8 Sa	17 3 59	16 50 20	21 4 51	27 1 13	19 24.1	9 57.4	8 54.9	29 22.0	16 29.0	5 25.8	23 54.3	8 0.4	4 4.5
9 Su	17 7 56	17 47 42	2♒56 45	8♒51 54	19 24.4	10 39.0	10 4.7	29 58.6	16 34.5	5 33.4	23 53.2	7 58.8	4 4.3
10 M	17 11 52	18 45 4	14 47 5	20 42 48	19R24.5	11 16.5	11 14.6	0♋35.3	16 39.6	5 41.0	23 52.0	7 57.2	4 4.1
11 Tu	17 15 49	19 42 25	26 39 32	2♓37 49	19 24.5	11 49.7	12 24.6	1 11.9	16 44.6	5 48.6	23 50.9	7 55.6	4 4.0
12 W	17 19 45	20 39 45	8♓38 12	14 41 14	19 24.5	12 18.7	13 34.6	1 48.6	16 49.5	5 56.2	23 49.9	7 54.0	3.9
13 Th	17 23 42	21 37 6	20 47 27	26 57 26	19D24.4	12 43.3	14 44.7	2 25.3	16 54.2	6 3.8	23 48.9	7 52.5	3.8
14 F	17 27 39	22 34 25	3♈11 41	9♈30 44	19 24.5	13 3.4	15 54.8	3 2.1	16 58.7	6 11.5	23 47.9	7 50.9	4D 3.8
15 Sa	17 31 35	23 31 44	15 55 2	22 25 0	19 24.7	13 19.1	17 5.0	3 38.8	17 3.0	6 19.2	23 47.0	7 49.4	3.8
16 Su	17 35 32	24 29 3	29 0 57	5♉43 8	19 25.1	13 30.2	18 15.2	4 15.6	17 7.2	6 26.9	23 46.2	7 47.8	3.8
17 M	17 39 28	25 26 22	12♉31 42	19 26 39	19 25.2	13R36.7	19 25.6	4 52.3	17 11.2	6 34.6	23 45.4	7 46.3	3.9
18 Tu	17 43 25	26 23 40	26 27 51	3♊35 3	19 26.2	13 38.7	20 35.9	5 29.1	17 15.0	6 42.3	23 44.6	7 44.8	4.0
19 W	17 47 21	27 20 58	10♊47 20	18 12 31	19R26.6	13 36.2	21 46.4	6 5.9	17 18.6	6 50.0	23 43.9	7 43.2	4.1
20 Th	17 51 18	28 18 15	25 27 30	2♋52 52	19 26.6	13 29.3	22 56.9	6 42.8	17 22.1	6 57.8	23 43.3	7 41.7	4.3
21 F	17 55 14	29 15 33	10♋20 42	17 49 57	19 26.2	13 18.1	24 7.4	7 19.6	17 25.3	7 5.6	23 42.7	7 40.3	4.5
22 Sa	17 59 11	0♋12 49	25 19 33	2♌49 8	19 25.3	13 2.7	25 18.0	7 56.5	17 28.4	7 13.3	23 42.2	7 38.8	4.7
23 Su	18 3 8	1 10 5	10♌15 42	17 40 18	19 24.1	12 43.8	26 28.6	8 33.4	17 31.3	7 21.1	23 41.7	7 37.3	5.0
24 M	18 7 4	2 7 21	25 1 27	2♍18 28	19 22.7	12 20.4	27 39.3	9 10.3	17 34.0	7 28.9	23 41.2	7 35.9	5.3
25 Tu	18 11 1	3 4 35	9♍30 47	16 37 59	19 21.4	11 54.1	28 50.0	9 47.2	17 36.5	7 36.7	23 40.8	7 34.4	5.6
26 W	18 14 57	4 1 49	23 40 23	0♎36 10	19D20.6	11 24.9	0♊ 0.8	10 24.2	17 38.9	7 44.5	23 40.5	7 33.0	6.0
27 Th	18 18 54	4 59 3	7♎27 1	14 12 25	19 20.8	10 53.3	1 11.6	11 1.1	17 41.0	7 52.3	23 40.2	7 31.6	6.4
28 F	18 22 50	5 56 15	20 52 24	27 27 40	19 20.8	10 19.7	2 22.5	11 38.1	17 43.0	8 0.1	23 40.0	7 30.2	6.8
29 Sa	18 26 47	6 53 28	3♏57 24	10♏23 57	19 21.9	9 44.6	3 33.4	12 15.0	17 44.7	8 7.9	23 39.8	7 28.9	7.3
30 Su	18 30 43	7 50 40	16 45 46	23 3 47	19 23.3	9 8.8	4 44.4	12 52.0	17 46.3	8 15.7	23 39.6	7 27.5	7.8

Astro Data

Astro Data Dy Hr Mn	Planet Ingress Dy Hr Mn	Last Aspect Dy Hr Mn	☽ Ingress Dy Hr Mn	Last Aspect Dy Hr Mn	☽ Ingress Dy Hr Mn	☽ Phases & Eclipses Dy Hr Mn
☽0S 2 2:48	♀ ♈ 4 20:21	2 19:45 ♀ ♂	♎ 2 23:39	1 2:19 ♂ ♂	♏ 1 11:10	6 8:55 ○ 15♏27
♀0N 7 21:16	☿ ♊ 12 4:55	4 19:41 ♅ ♂	♏ 5 4:43	3 12:58 ♂ △	♐ 3 19:21	14 9:29 ◑ 23♒13
☽0N 16 10:00	☉ ♊ 21 10:36	6 13:20 ♀ □	♐ 7 12:05	5 17:51 ♅ ⚹	♑ 6 5:48	21 20:34 ● 0♊24
♄□♅ 28 13:14	☿ ♋ 29 8:03	9 11:57 ♅ ⚹	♑ 9 22:15	8 17:40 ♀ ♂	♒ 8 18:02	28 13:03 ◐ 6♍49
☽0S 29 7:48	♀ ♉ 31 7:19	11 23:49 ♅ □	♒ 12 10:34	10 18:21 ♅ △	♓ 11 6:43	
		14 12:16 ♅ △	♓ 14 23:03	13 1:45 ☉ ♂	♈ 13 17:52	4 22:10 ○ 13♐54
☽0N 12 17:53	♂ ♋ 9 0:54	17 1:19 ☉ ⚹	♈ 17 10:34	15 15:00 ♀ ⚹	♉ 16 1:46	4 22:10 ⚹P 0.827
♇ D 14 13:16	☉ ♋ 21 18:38	19 6:16 ♀ ♂	♉ 19 16:10	17 13:04 ♀ ♂	Ⅱ 18 5:59	13 1:45 ◑ 21♒41
☿ R 17 22:38	♀ ♊ 25 23:44	21 0:14 ♂ ⚹	Ⅱ 21 19:54	20 4:56 ♂ ♂	♋ 20 7:21	20 4:56 ● 28♊30
♄⚹♆ 24 18:08		23 12:22 ♅ △	♋ 23 21:46	21 23:57 ♀ ⚹	♌ 22 7:30	20 4:47:20 ✦T 5'09"
☽0S 25 13:51		25 13:41 ♀ □	♌ 25 23:12	24 4:42 ♀ □	♍ 24 8:11	26 19:20 ◐ 4♎48
		27 22:11 ♅ ⚹	♍ 28 1:25	25 13:42 ♃ ♂	♎ 26 10:57	
		29 18:17 ♂ ⚹	♎ 30 5:16	28 5:04 ♅ ♂	♏ 28 16:40	

Astro Data

1 MAY 1974
Julian Day # 27149
Delta T 44.8 sec
SVP 05♓36'50"
Obliquity 23°26'32"
δ Chiron 21♈32.7
☽ Mean Ω 21♐34.2

1 JUNE 1974
Julian Day # 27180
Delta T 44.9 sec
SVP 05♓36'45"
Obliquity 23°26'31"
δ Chiron 23♈08.3
☽ Mean Ω 19♐55.7

JULY 1974 LONGITUDE

Day	Sid.Time	☉	0 hr ☽	Noon ☽	True ☊	☿	♀	♂	♃	♄	♅	♆	♇
1 M	18 34 40	8♋47 51	29♏18 22	5♐29 50	19♐24.6	8♋32.7	5♊55.4	13♌29.1	17♓47.7	8♋23.5	23♎39.6	7♐26.2	4♎ 8.3
2 Tu	18 38 37	9 45 3	11♐38 30	17 44 38	19R 25.5	7R 57.0	7 6.5	14 6.1	17 48.9	8 31.3	23D 39.5	7R 24.9	4 8.9
3 W	18 42 33	10 42 14	23 48 33	29 50 31	19 25.6	7 22.3	8 17.6	14 43.1	17 49.9	8 39.2	23 39.6	7 23.6	4 9.5
4 Th	18 46 30	11 39 25	5♑50 46	11♑49 34	19 24.7	6 49.3	9 28.8	15 20.2	17 50.7	8 47.0	23 39.6	7 22.3	4 10.1
5 F	18 50 26	12 36 36	17 47 9	23 43 45	19 22.7	6 18.4	10 40.0	15 57.3	17 51.3	8 54.8	23 39.8	7 21.0	4 10.7
6 Sa	18 54 23	13 33 47	29 39 38	5♒35 3	19 19.6	5 50.3	11 51.3	16 34.4	17 51.7	9 2.6	23 39.9	7 19.8	4 11.4
7 Su	18 58 19	14 30 58	11♒30 15	17 25 33	19 15.7	5 25.5	13 2.6	17 11.5	17R 52.0	9 10.4	23 40.2	7 18.6	4 12.1
8 M	19 2 16	15 28 9	23 21 14	29 17 38	19 11.3	5 4.3	14 14.0	17 48.6	17 52.0	9 18.1	23 40.5	7 17.4	4 12.9
9 Tu	19 6 12	16 25 20	5♓15 8	11♓14 6	19 7.0	4 47.3	15 25.4	18 25.8	17 51.8	9 25.9	23 40.8	7 16.2	4 13.7
10 W	19 10 9	17 22 32	17 14 58	23 18 10	19 3.3	4 34.6	16 36.9	19 2.9	17 51.5	9 33.7	23 41.2	7 15.1	4 14.5
11 Th	19 14 6	18 19 44	29 24 10	5♈33 27	19 0.6	4 26.7	17 48.4	19 40.1	17 50.9	9 41.4	23 41.6	7 13.9	4 15.3
12 F	19 18 2	19 16 57	11♈46 33	18 3 56	18D 59.1	4D 23.8	18 60.0	20 17.3	17 50.2	9 49.2	23 42.1	7 12.8	4 16.2
13 Sa	19 21 59	20 14 10	24 26 8	0♉53 37	18 58.9	4 25.9	20 11.6	20 54.5	17 49.3	9 56.9	23 42.7	7 11.7	4 17.1
14 Su	19 25 55	21 11 23	7♉26 50	14 6 12	18 59.8	4 33.4	21 23.3	21 31.8	17 48.1	10 4.6	23 43.3	7 10.7	4 18.1
15 M	19 29 52	22 8 38	20 52 0	27 44 29	19 1.2	4 46.2	22 35.0	22 9.1	17 46.8	10 12.4	23 43.9	7 9.6	4 19.0
16 Tu	19 33 48	23 5 53	4♊43 45	11♊49 45	19 2.6	5 4.5	23 46.7	22 46.4	17 45.3	10 20.1	23 44.6	7 8.6	4 20.0
17 W	19 37 45	24 3 8	19 2 17	26 20 57	19R 3.2	5 28.3	24 58.6	23 23.7	17 43.5	10 27.7	23 45.4	7 7.6	4 21.1
18 Th	19 41 42	25 0 24	3♋45 10	11♋14 10	19 2.4	5 57.5	26 10.4	24 1.0	17 41.6	10 35.4	23 46.2	7 6.6	4 22.1
19 F	19 45 38	25 57 41	18 46 58	26 22 28	19 0.0	6 32.2	27 22.3	24 38.4	17 39.5	10 43.1	23 47.1	7 5.7	4 23.2
20 Sa	19 49 35	26 54 58	3♌59 26	11♌36 33	18 56.0	7 12.4	28 34.3	25 15.8	17 37.2	10 50.7	23 48.0	7 4.8	4 24.3
21 Su	19 53 31	27 52 16	19 12 30	26 46 2	18 50.7	7 58.0	29 46.3	25 53.2	17 34.7	10 58.3	23 49.0	7 3.9	4 25.5
22 M	19 57 28	28 49 33	4♍15 56	11♍41 12	18 45.0	8 48.9	0♋58.3	26 30.6	17 32.1	11 5.9	23 50.0	7 3.0	4 26.7
23 Tu	20 1 24	29 46 52	19 0 58	26 14 35	18 39.6	9 45.1	2 10.4	27 8.0	17 29.2	11 13.4	23 51.0	7 2.2	4 27.9
24 W	20 5 21	0♌44 10	3♎21 35	10♎21 44	18 35.4	10 46.6	3 22.6	27 45.5	17 26.1	11 21.0	23 52.2	7 1.4	4 29.1
25 Th	20 9 17	1 41 29	17 14 57	24 1 20	18 32.7	11 53.2	4 34.7	28 23.0	17 22.9	11 28.5	23 53.3	7 0.6	4 30.4
26 F	20 13 14	2 38 48	0♏41 7	7♏14 38	18D 31.7	13 4.8	5 46.9	29 0.5	17 19.5	11 36.0	23 54.6	6 59.9	4 31.7
27 Sa	20 17 11	3 36 8	13 42 18	20 4 37	18 32.1	14 21.3	6 59.2	29 38.0	17 15.9	11 43.4	23 55.8	6 59.1	4 33.0
28 Su	20 21 7	4 33 28	26 22 4	2♐35 12	18 33.3	15 42.7	8 11.5	0♍15.5	17 12.1	11 50.9	23 57.1	6 58.4	4 34.3
29 M	20 25 4	5 30 48	8♐44 33	14 50 37	18R 34.5	17 8.7	9 23.8	0 53.1	17 8.1	11 58.3	23 58.5	6 57.8	4 35.7
30 Tu	20 29 0	6 28 9	20 53 56	26 54 56	18 34.9	18 39.3	10 36.2	1 30.7	17 4.0	12 5.6	23 59.9	6 57.1	4 37.1
31 W	20 32 57	7 25 31	2♑54 5	8♑51 47	18 33.7	20 14.1	11 48.7	2 8.3	16 59.7	12 13.0	24 1.4	6 56.5	4 38.5

AUGUST 1974 LONGITUDE

Day	Sid.Time	☉	0 hr ☽	Noon ☽	True ☊	☿	♀	♂	♃	♄	♅	♆	♇
1 Th	20 36 53	8♌22 53	14♑48 24	20♑44 15	18♐30.5	21♋53.0	13♋ 1.1	2♍45.9	16♓55.2	12♋20.3	24♎ 2.9	6♐56.0	4♎40.0
2 F	20 40 50	9 20 16	26 39 39	2♒34 52	18R 25.0	23 35.8	14 13.7	3 23.6	16R 50.6	12 27.6	24 4.5	6R 55.4	4 41.5
3 Sa	20 44 46	10 17 40	8♒30 8	14 25 40	18 17.4	25 22.1	15 26.2	4 1.2	16 45.8	12 34.8	24 6.1	6 54.9	4 43.0
4 Su	20 48 43	11 15 5	20 21 41	26 18 23	18 8.2	27 11.7	16 38.8	4 38.9	16 40.8	12 42.0	24 7.8	6 54.4	4 44.5
5 M	20 52 40	12 12 31	2♓15 58	8♓14 38	17 58.1	29 4.2	17 51.5	5 16.6	16 35.7	12 49.2	24 9.5	6 53.9	4 46.0
6 Tu	20 56 36	13 9 57	14 14 37	20 16 9	17 48.0	0♌59.3	19 4.2	5 54.4	16 30.4	12 56.3	24 11.2	6 53.5	4 47.6
7 W	21 0 33	14 7 25	26 19 31	2♈24 59	17 38.9	2 56.6	20 17.0	6 32.1	16 25.0	13 3.4	24 13.0	6 53.1	4 49.2
8 Th	21 4 29	15 4 54	8♈32 53	14 43 35	17 31.5	4 55.8	21 29.8	7 9.9	16 19.4	13 10.5	24 14.9	6 52.7	4 50.8
9 F	21 8 26	16 2 24	20 57 28	27 14 56	17 26.2	6 56.5	22 42.6	7 47.7	16 13.7	13 17.5	24 16.8	6 52.4	4 52.5
10 Sa	21 12 22	16 59 56	3♉36 26	10♉ 2 25	17 23.3	8 58.3	23 55.5	8 25.5	16 7.8	13 24.5	24 18.7	6 52.1	4 54.2
11 Su	21 16 19	17 57 29	16 33 20	23 9 37	17D 22.4	11 0.8	25 8.4	9 3.4	16 1.8	13 31.4	24 20.7	6 51.8	4 55.9
12 M	21 20 15	18 55 4	29 51 39	6♊39 47	17 22.7	13 3.9	26 21.4	9 41.3	15 55.7	13 38.3	24 22.8	6 51.6	4 57.6
13 Tu	21 24 12	19 52 40	13♊34 18	20 35 20	17R 23.3	15 7.1	27 34.5	10 19.2	15 49.4	13 45.1	24 24.8	6 51.4	4 59.3
14 W	21 28 9	20 50 17	27 42 53	4♋56 50	17 22.9	17 10.2	28 47.6	10 57.1	15 43.0	13 51.9	24 27.0	6 51.2	5 1.1
15 Th	21 32 5	21 47 56	12♋16 48	19 42 16	17 20.8	19 12.9	0♌ 0.7	11 35.1	15 36.4	13 58.7	24 29.1	6 51.0	5 2.9
16 F	21 36 2	22 45 37	27 12 28	4♌46 25	17 16.1	21 15.2	1 13.9	12 13.1	15 29.8	14 5.4	24 31.3	6 50.9	5 4.7
17 Sa	21 39 58	23 43 19	12♌23 0	20 0 54	17 9.0	23 16.7	2 27.1	12 51.1	15 23.0	14 12.1	24 33.6	6 50.8	5 6.5
18 Su	21 43 55	24 41 2	27 38 45	5♍15 9	17 0.0	25 17.3	3 40.3	13 29.2	15 16.1	14 18.7	24 35.9	6 50.8	5 8.4
19 M	21 47 51	25 38 46	12♍48 45	20 18 15	16 50.1	27 17.0	4 53.6	14 7.2	15 9.1	14 25.2	24 38.2	6D 50.8	5 10.2
20 Tu	21 51 48	26 36 32	27 42 36	5♎ 0 51	16 40.4	29 15.5	6 7.0	14 45.3	15 2.0	14 31.7	24 40.6	6 50.8	5 12.1
21 W	21 55 44	27 34 19	12♎12 21	19 16 37	16 32.2	1♍13.0	7 20.3	15 23.5	14 54.9	14 38.2	24 43.0	6 50.8	5 14.0
22 Th	21 59 41	28 32 7	26 13 27	3♏ 2 48	16 26.2	3 9.1	8 33.8	16 1.6	14 47.6	14 44.6	24 45.5	6 50.9	5 16.0
23 F	22 3 37	29 29 56	9♏44 49	16 19 50	16 22.6	5 4.1	9 47.2	16 39.8	14 40.2	14 50.9	24 48.0	6 51.0	5 17.9
24 Sa	22 7 34	0♍27 46	22 48 15	29 10 36	16D 21.1	6 57.7	11 0.7	17 18.0	14 32.8	14 57.2	24 50.5	6 51.1	5 19.9
25 Su	22 11 31	1 25 38	5♐27 27	11♐39 26	16R 20.9	8 50.0	12 14.2	17 56.2	14 25.3	15 3.4	24 53.1	6 51.3	5 21.9
26 M	22 15 27	2 23 31	17 47 11	23 51 20	16 21.1	10 41.0	13 27.8	18 34.5	14 17.7	15 9.6	24 55.7	6 51.5	5 23.9
27 Tu	22 19 24	3 21 25	29 52 32	5♑51 23	16 20.4	12 30.7	14 41.4	19 12.8	14 10.1	15 15.7	24 58.3	6 51.8	5 25.9
28 W	22 23 20	4 19 20	11♑48 27	17 44 17	16 17.9	14 19.1	15 55.1	19 51.1	14 2.4	15 21.7	25 1.0	6 52.1	5 27.9
29 Th	22 27 17	5 17 17	23 39 21	29 34 8	16 12.9	16 6.1	17 8.7	20 29.4	13 54.7	15 27.7	25 3.8	6 52.4	5 30.0
30 F	22 31 13	6 15 15	5♒28 59	11♒24 18	16 5.1	17 51.8	18 22.5	21 7.8	13 46.9	15 33.6	25 6.5	6 52.7	5 32.0
31 Sa	22 35 10	7 13 14	17 20 20	23 17 22	15 54.7	19 36.3	19 36.2	21 46.1	13 39.1	15 39.4	25 9.3	6 53.1	5 34.1

Astro Data	Planet Ingress	Last Aspect	☽ Ingress	Last Aspect	☽ Ingress	☽ Phases & Eclipses	Astro Data
Dy Hr Mn	Dy Hr Mn	Dy Hr Mn	Dy Hr Mn	Dy Hr Mn	Dy Hr Mn	Dy Hr Mn	1 JULY 1974
♅ D 2 0:16	♀ ♋ 21 4:34	30 1:55 ♃ △	♐ 1 1:20	1 18:45 ♅ □	♒ 2 6:46	4 12:40 ○ 12♑10	Julian Day # 27210
♃ R 7 16:13	☉ ♌ 23 5:30	2 23:42 ♅ ✶	♑ 3 12:19	4 7:38 ♅ △	♓ 4 19:26	12 15:28 ☽ 19♈54	Delta T 45.0 sec
☽0N 10 1:11	♂ ♍ 27 14:04	5 11:52 ♅ □	♒ 6 0:41	6 10:41 ♀ △	♈ 7 7:15	19 12:06 ● 26♋27	SVP 05♓36'40"
☿ D 12 1:56		8 0:39 ♅ △	♓ 8 13:25	9 6:22 ♅ ☍	♉ 9 17:13	26 3:51 ☽ 2♏48	Obliquity 23°26'31"
☽0S 22 22:16	☿ ♌ 5 11:42	10 1:13 ♃ ☌	♈ 11 1:10	11 17:07 ♀ ✶	♊ 12 0:15		⚷ Chiron 24♈10.3
	♀ ♌ 14 23:47	12 22:39 ♅ ☍	♉ 13 10:21	13 18:31 ♅ △	♋ 14 3:49	3 3:57 ○ 10♒27	☽ Mean ☊ 18♐20.4
☽0N 6 7:49	☿ ♍ 20 9:04	15 2:25 ☉ ✶	♊ 15 15:54	15 19:42 ♅ □	♌ 16 4:26	11 2:46 ☽ 18♉04	
☽0S 19 8:44	☉ ♍ 23 12:29	17 10:37 ♀ ☌	♋ 17 17:56	17 19:44 ☿ ☌	♍ 18 3:42	17 19:02 ● 24♌29	1 AUGUST 1974
♆ D 19 3:38		19 12:06 ☉ ☌	♌ 19 17:43	19 3:42 ♃ ☍	♎ 20 3:45	24 15:38 ☽ 1♐05	Julian Day # 27241
♃△♄ 22 5:19		21 11:03 ♂ ☌	♍ 21 17:10	22 4:21 ☉ ✶	♏ 22 6:37		Delta T 45.1 sec
		22 21:29 ♃ ☍	♎ 23 18:19	23 13:16 ♂ ✶	♐ 24 13:34		SVP 05♓36'35"
		25 20:49 ♂ ✶	♏ 25 22:45	26 14:11 ♅ ✶	♑ 27 0:15		Obliquity 23°26'31"
		27 6:39 ♃ △	♐ 28 7:00	29 2:52 ♅ □	♒ 29 12:53		⚷ Chiron 24♈29.7R
		30 6:11 ♅ ✶	♑ 30 18:11				☽ Mean ☊ 16♐41.9

LONGITUDE — SEPTEMBER 1974

Day	Sid.Time	☉	0 hr ☽	Noon ☽	True ☊	☿	♀	♂	♃	♄	♅	♆	♇
1 Su	22 39 6	8♍11 15	29♒15 37	5♓15 15	15♐42.2	21♍19.5	20♌50.0	22♍24.6	13♓31.2	15♋45.2	25♎12.2	6♐53.5	5♎36.2
2 M	22 43 3	9 9 18	11♓16 26	17 19 17	15R 28.5	23 1.4	22 3.9	23 3.0	13R 23.3	15 50.9	25 15.0	6 53.9	5 38.3
3 Tu	22 47 0	10 7 22	23 23 56	29 30 30	15 14.7	24 42.0	23 17.7	23 41.5	13 15.4	15 56.6	25 17.9	6 54.4	5 40.4
4 W	22 50 56	11 5 28	5♈39 5	11♈49 51	15 2.1	26 21.5	24 31.7	24 20.0	13 7.5	16 2.2	25 20.9	6 54.9	5 42.5
5 Th	22 54 53	12 3 36	18 2 56	24 18 32	14 51.6	27 59.7	25 45.6	24 58.5	12 59.5	16 7.7	25 23.8	6 55.4	5 44.7
6 F	22 58 49	13 1 45	0♉36 51	6♉58 7	14 43.8	29 36.7	26 59.6	25 37.0	12 51.6	16 13.1	25 26.8	6 56.0	5 46.8
7 Sa	23 2 46	13 59 57	13 22 38	19 50 42	14 39.0	1♎12.5	28 13.6	26 15.6	12 43.6	16 18.5	25 29.9	6 56.6	5 49.0
8 Su	23 6 42	14 58 11	26 22 39	2♊58 48	14 36.6	2 47.2	29 27.7	26 54.3	12 35.7	16 23.8	25 32.9	6 57.2	5 51.2
9 M	23 10 39	15 56 26	9♊39 31	16 25 6	14 36.0	4 20.7	0♍41.8	27 32.9	12 27.8	16 29.0	25 36.0	6 57.9	5 53.4
10 Tu	23 14 35	16 54 44	23 15 50	0♋11 55	14 36.0	5 53.0	1 56.0	28 11.6	12 19.9	16 34.2	25 39.1	6 58.5	5 55.6
11 W	23 18 32	17 53 4	7♋13 28	14 20 30	14 35.2	7 24.2	3 10.2	28 50.3	12 12.0	16 39.3	25 42.3	6 59.3	5 57.8
12 Th	23 22 29	18 51 26	21 32 52	28 50 15	14 32.6	8 54.2	4 24.4	29 29.1	12 4.1	16 44.3	25 45.5	7 0.0	6 0.0
13 F	23 26 25	19 49 50	6♌12 9	13♌37 54	14 27.4	10 23.1	5 38.6	0♎ 7.9	11 56.3	16 49.2	25 48.7	7 0.8	6 2.3
14 Sa	23 30 22	20 48 16	21 6 38	28 37 19	14 19.5	11 50.7	6 52.9	0 46.7	11 48.5	16 54.0	25 51.9	7 1.6	6 4.5
15 Su	23 34 18	21 46 45	6♍ 8 48	13♍39 51	14 9.4	13 17.2	8 7.3	1 25.5	11 40.8	16 58.8	25 55.2	7 2.5	6 6.7
16 M	23 38 15	22 45 15	21 9 12	28 35 39	13 58.2	14 42.5	9 21.6	2 4.4	11 33.1	17 3.4	25 58.5	7 3.4	6 9.0
17 Tu	23 42 11	23 43 47	5♎58 2	13♎15 24	13 47.2	16 6.6	10 36.0	2 43.3	11 25.5	17 8.0	26 1.8	7 4.3	6 11.3
18 W	23 46 8	24 42 20	20 26 53	27 31 54	13 37.6	17 29.5	11 50.4	3 22.3	11 17.9	17 12.5	26 5.1	7 5.2	6 13.5
19 Th	23 50 4	25 40 56	4♏30 0	11♏21 1	13 30.2	18 51.1	13 4.9	4 1.2	11 10.5	17 17.0	26 8.5	7 6.2	6 15.8
20 F	23 54 1	26 39 33	18 4 54	24 41 48	13 25.6	20 11.3	14 19.3	4 40.3	11 3.1	17 21.3	26 11.9	7 7.2	6 18.1
21 Sa	23 57 58	27 38 12	1♐12 3	7♐36 2	13D 23.3	21 30.2	15 33.8	5 19.3	10 55.8	17 25.5	26 15.3	7 8.2	6 20.4
22 Su	0 1 54	28 36 53	13 54 17	20 7 22	13 22.8	22 47.7	16 48.4	5 58.4	10 48.5	17 29.7	26 18.7	7 9.3	6 22.7
23 M	0 5 51	29 35 36	26 15 55	2♑20 36	13R 23.0	24 3.8	18 2.9	6 37.5	10 41.4	17 33.8	26 22.2	7 10.4	6 25.0
24 Tu	0 9 47	0♎34 20	8♑22 5	14 21 2	13 22.8	25 18.3	19 17.5	7 16.6	10 34.4	17 37.8	26 25.7	7 11.5	6 27.3
25 W	0 13 44	1 33 6	20 18 5	26 13 54	13 21.1	26 31.1	20 32.1	7 55.8	10 27.5	17 41.7	26 29.2	7 12.7	6 29.6
26 Th	0 17 40	2 31 53	2♒ 9 3	8♒ 4 6	13 17.3	27 42.3	21 46.7	8 35.0	10 20.6	17 45.5	26 32.7	7 13.8	6 31.9
27 F	0 21 37	3 30 43	13 59 33	19 55 53	13 10.8	28 51.7	23 1.4	9 14.2	10 13.9	17 49.2	26 36.2	7 15.1	6 34.2
28 Sa	0 25 33	4 29 34	25 53 29	1♓52 42	13 1.8	29 59.1	24 16.0	9 53.5	10 7.4	17 52.8	26 39.8	7 16.3	6 36.5
29 Su	0 29 30	5 28 26	7♓53 51	13 57 10	12 50.9	1♏ 4.4	25 30.7	10 32.8	10 0.9	17 56.3	26 43.3	7 17.5	6 38.8
30 M	0 33 27	6 27 21	20 2 50	26 10 59	12 38.8	2 7.6	26 45.5	11 12.1	9 54.6	17 59.7	26 46.9	7 18.8	6 41.1

LONGITUDE — OCTOBER 1974

Day	Sid.Time	☉	0 hr ☽	Noon ☽	True ☊	☿	♀	♂	♃	♄	♅	♆	♇
1 Tu	0 37 23	7♎26 18	2♈21 43	8♈35 6	12♐26.6	3♏ 8.4	28♍ 0.2	11♎51.5	9♓48.4	18♋ 3.0	26♎50.5	7♐20.2	6♎43.4
2 W	0 41 20	8 25 17	14 51 10	21 9 56	12R 15.4	4 6.5	29 15.0	12 30.9	9R 42.3	18 6.3	26 54.2	7 21.5	6 45.8
3 Th	0 45 16	9 24 17	27 31 23	3♉55 33	12 6.1	5 1.9	0♎29.8	13 10.3	9 36.4	18 9.4	26 57.8	7 22.9	6 48.1
4 F	0 49 13	10 23 20	10♉22 25	16 52 2	11 59.4	5 54.3	1 44.6	13 49.8	9 30.6	18 12.4	27 1.4	7 24.3	6 50.4
5 Sa	0 53 9	11 22 25	23 24 27	29 59 45	11 55.4	6 43.4	2 59.4	14 29.3	9 25.0	18 15.4	27 5.1	7 25.7	6 52.7
6 Su	0 57 6	12 21 33	6♊38 1	13♊19 22	11D 53.8	7 28.9	4 14.3	15 8.8	9 19.5	18 18.2	27 8.8	7 27.2	6 55.0
7 M	1 1 2	13 20 42	20 3 57	26 51 54	11 53.9	8 10.5	5 29.2	15 48.4	9 14.2	18 20.9	27 12.5	7 28.6	6 57.3
8 Tu	1 4 59	14 19 54	3♋43 20	10♋38 22	11R 54.7	8 47.8	6 44.1	16 28.0	9 9.0	18 23.6	27 16.2	7 30.1	6 59.6
9 W	1 8 55	15 19 9	17 37 3	24 39 24	11 55.0	9 20.4	7 59.0	17 7.6	9 4.0	18 26.1	27 19.9	7 31.7	7 1.9
10 Th	1 12 52	16 18 26	1♌45 18	8♌54 34	11 53.9	9 47.9	9 14.0	17 47.3	8 59.2	18 28.5	27 23.6	7 33.2	7 4.2
11 F	1 16 49	17 17 45	16 6 55	23 21 55	11 50.7	10 9.9	10 29.0	18 27.1	8 54.5	18 30.9	27 27.3	7 34.8	7 6.5
12 Sa	1 20 45	18 17 6	0♍39 0	7♍57 31	11 45.4	10 25.9	11 44.0	19 6.8	8 50.0	18 33.1	27 31.0	7 36.4	7 8.8
13 Su	1 24 42	19 16 29	15 16 41	22 35 39	11 38.1	10R 35.3	12 59.0	19 46.6	8 45.7	18 35.2	27 34.8	7 38.0	7 11.1
14 M	1 28 38	20 15 55	29 53 31	7♎ 9 21	11 29.9	10 37.7	14 14.0	20 26.5	8 41.5	18 37.2	27 38.5	7 39.7	7 13.3
15 Tu	1 32 35	21 15 23	14♎22 16	21 31 37	11 21.6	10 32.5	15 29.1	21 6.3	8 37.6	18 39.1	27 42.3	7 41.4	7 15.6
16 W	1 36 31	22 14 53	28 36 10	5♏35 49	11 14.4	10 19.4	16 44.1	21 46.3	8 33.8	18 40.9	27 46.0	7 43.1	7 17.9
17 Th	1 40 28	23 14 25	12♏29 55	19 18 9	11 9.0	9 58.0	17 59.2	22 26.2	8 30.2	18 42.6	27 49.8	7 44.8	7 20.1
18 F	1 44 24	24 13 59	26 0 22	2♐36 31	11 5.8	9 27.9	19 14.3	23 6.2	8 26.8	18 44.1	27 53.6	7 46.5	7 22.4
19 Sa	1 48 21	25 13 35	9♐ 6 45	15 31 16	11D 4.6	8 49.3	20 29.4	23 46.2	8 23.6	18 45.6	27 57.4	7 48.3	7 24.6
20 Su	1 52 18	26 13 12	21 50 25	28 4 38	11 5.1	8 2.2	21 44.5	24 26.3	8 20.6	18 46.9	28 1.1	7 50.1	7 26.8
21 M	1 56 14	27 12 52	4♑14 26	10♑20 21	11 6.5	7 7.0	22 59.7	25 6.4	8 17.8	18 48.2	28 4.9	7 51.9	7 29.0
22 Tu	2 0 11	28 12 33	16 22 58	22 22 56	11 7.9	6 4.7	24 14.8	25 46.5	8 15.1	18 49.3	28 8.7	7 53.7	7 31.2
23 W	2 4 7	29 12 16	28 20 53	4♒17 27	11R 8.6	4 56.3	25 30.0	26 26.7	8 12.7	18 50.3	28 12.5	7 55.5	7 33.4
24 Th	2 8 4	0♏12 0	10♒13 16	16 8 57	11 7.9	3 43.4	26 45.1	27 6.9	8 10.5	18 51.2	28 16.2	7 57.4	7 35.6
25 F	2 12 0	1 11 47	22 5 6	28 2 17	11 5.6	2 28.0	28 0.3	27 47.2	8 8.4	18 52.0	28 20.0	7 59.3	7 37.8
26 Sa	2 15 57	2 11 35	4♓ 1 1	10♓ 1 48	11 1.5	1 12.1	29 15.5	28 27.4	8 6.6	18 52.7	28 23.8	8 1.2	7 39.9
27 Su	2 19 53	3 11 24	16 5 2	22 11 6	10 56.0	29♎58.0	0♏30.7	29 7.7	8 5.0	18 53.3	28 27.6	8 3.1	7 42.1
28 M	2 23 50	4 11 16	28 20 19	4♈32 56	10 49.6	28 48.2	1 45.9	29 48.1	8 3.5	18 53.8	28 31.3	8 5.0	7 44.2
29 Tu	2 27 47	5 11 9	10♈49 8	17 9 2	10 43.0	27 44.7	3 1.1	0♏28.5	8 2.3	18 54.1	28 35.1	8 7.0	7 46.3
30 W	2 31 43	6 11 4	23 32 41	0♉ 0 5	10 36.9	26 49.3	4 16.3	1 8.9	8 1.3	18 54.3	28 38.8	8 9.0	7 48.4
31 Th	2 35 40	7 11 1	6♉31 11	13 5 51	10 32.0	26 3.7	5 31.5	1 49.4	8 0.5	18R 54.5	28 42.6	8 11.0	7 50.5

Astro Data	Dy Hr Mn
☽0N	2 14:06
☿0S	6 14:44
☽0S	15 19:32
♂0S	15 13:04
♃⚼♅	19 4:22
☽0N	29 20:38
♀0S	5 6:12
☽0S	13 4:47
☿ R	13 19:48
☽0N	27 3:52
♃□♆	27 13:09
♄ R	31 14:56

Planet Ingress	Dy Hr Mn
☿ ♎	6 5:48
♀ ♍	8 10:28
♂ ♎	12 19:08
☉ ♎	23 9:58
☿ ♏	28 0:20
♀ ♎	2 14:27
☉ ♏	23 19:11
☿ ♎	26 23:21
♀ ♏	26 14:12
♂ ♏	28 7:05

Last Aspect Dy Hr Mn		☽ Ingress Dy Hr Mn
31 15:49	♅ △	♓ 1 1:29
3 2:58	☿ ☍	♈ 3 12:58
5 16:22	♀ △	♉ 5 22:50
8 6:12	♀ □	♊ 8 6:36
10 8:58	♂ □	♋ 10 11:40
12 13:40	♂ ✶	♌ 12 13:54
14 7:38	♅ ✶	♍ 14 14:12
16 2:45	☉ ☌	♎ 16 14:17
18 9:34	♅ ☌	♏ 18 16:14
20 16:52	☉ ✶	♐ 20 21:46
23 7:08	☉ □	♑ 23 7:22
25 13:59	☿ □	♒ 25 19:38
28 1:33	♅ △	♓ 28 8:14
30 14:36	♀ ☍	♈ 30 19:25

Last Aspect Dy Hr Mn		☽ Ingress Dy Hr Mn
2 22:56	♅ ☍	♉ 3 4:39
4 14:31	♄ ✶	♊ 5 12:00
7 12:40	♅ △	♋ 7 17:30
9 16:36	♅ □	♌ 9 21:03
11 18:49	♅ ✶	♍ 11 22:56
13 5:26	♄ ✶	♎ 14 0:11
15 22:34	♅ ☌	♏ 16 2:23
17 10:58	♄ △	♐ 18 7:14
20 11:57	♅ ✶	♑ 20 15:44
23 1:53	☉ □	♒ 23 3:20
25 13:20	♀ △	♓ 25 15:57
27 5:32	♄ △	♈ 28 3:13
30 9:32	♅ ☍	♉ 30 12:00

☽ Phases & Eclipses Dy Hr Mn		
1 19:25	○	8♓58
9 12:01	☽	16♊26
16 2:45	●	22♍52
23 7:08	☽	29♐53
1 10:38	○	7♈52
8 19:46	☽	15♋09
15 12:25	●	21♎46
23 1:53	☽	29♑17
31 1:19	○	7♉14

Astro Data

1 SEPTEMBER 1974
Julian Day # 27272
Delta T 45.2 sec
SVP 05♓36'31"
Obliquity 23°26'31"
⚷ Chiron 23♈59.6R
☽ Mean ☊ 15♐03.4

1 OCTOBER 1974
Julian Day # 27302
Delta T 45.2 sec
SVP 05♓36'29"
Obliquity 23°26'31"
⚷ Chiron 22♈52.6R
☽ Mean ☊ 13♐28.0

NOVEMBER 1974 LONGITUDE

Day	Sid.Time	☉	0 hr ☽	Noon ☽	True ☊	☿	♀	♂	♃	♄	♅	♆	♇
1 F	2 39 36	8♏10 59	19♉43 57	26♉25 19	10♐28.7	25♎28.8	6♏46.8	2♏29.9	7♓59.9	18♋54.5	28♎46.3	8♐13.0	7♎52.6
2 Sa	2 43 33	9 11 0	3♊ 9 46	9♊57 4	10D 27.1	25R 5.3	8 2.0	3 10.4	7R 59.5	18R 54.4	28 50.1	8 15.0	7 54.6
3 Su	2 47 29	10 11 3	16 47 2	23 39 27	10 27.0	24D 53.4	9 17.3	3 51.0	7D 59.2	18 54.2	28 53.8	8 17.0	7 56.7
4 M	2 51 26	11 11 8	0♋34 8	7♋30 54	10 28.1	24 53.0	10 32.6	4 31.6	7 59.2	18 53.9	28 57.5	8 19.1	7 58.7
5 Tu	2 55 22	12 11 15	14 29 35	21 29 59	10 29.6	25 3.6	11 47.8	5 12.3	7 59.4	18 53.4	29 1.2	8 21.1	8 0.7
6 W	2 59 19	13 11 24	28 31 57	5♌35 18	10 31.0	25 24.6	13 3.1	5 53.0	7 59.9	18 52.9	29 4.9	8 23.2	8 2.7
7 Th	3 3 16	14 11 35	12♌39 51	19 45 22	10R 31.7	25 55.3	14 18.4	6 33.8	8 0.5	18 52.2	29 8.6	8 25.3	8 4.7
8 F	3 7 12	15 11 48	26 51 37	3♍58 18	10 31.2	26 34.6	15 33.7	7 14.6	8 1.3	18 51.4	29 12.3	8 27.4	8 6.6
9 Sa	3 11 9	16 12 3	11♍ 5 6	18 11 40	10 29.6	27 21.9	16 49.0	7 55.4	8 2.3	18 50.6	29 15.9	8 29.5	8 8.6
10 Su	3 15 5	17 12 20	25 17 34	2♎22 21	10 27.0	28 16.1	18 4.3	8 36.3	8 3.5	18 49.6	29 19.6	8 31.7	8 10.5
11 M	3 19 2	18 12 39	9♎25 35	16 26 47	10 23.8	29 16.5	19 19.7	9 17.2	8 4.9	18 48.5	29 23.2	8 33.8	8 12.4
12 Tu	3 22 58	19 13 0	23 25 27	0♏21 8	10 20.5	0♏22.2	20 35.0	9 58.1	8 6.6	18 47.2	29 26.8	8 35.9	8 14.3
13 W	3 26 55	20 13 23	7♏13 25	14 1 55	10 17.8	1 32.6	21 50.4	10 39.1	8 8.4	18 45.9	29 30.5	8 38.1	8 16.1
14 Th	3 30 51	21 13 48	20 46 19	27 26 21	10 15.8	2 46.9	23 5.7	11 20.2	8 10.4	18 44.5	29 34.0	8 40.3	8 17.9
15 F	3 34 48	22 14 14	4♐ 1 53	10♐32 48	10D 14.8	4 4.6	24 21.1	12 1.3	8 12.7	18 42.9	29 37.6	8 42.5	8 19.8
16 Sa	3 38 45	23 14 42	16 59 6	23 20 53	10 14.9	5 25.2	25 36.4	12 42.4	8 15.1	18 41.3	29 41.2	8 44.6	8 21.5
17 Su	3 42 41	24 15 11	29 38 17	5♑51 35	10 15.6	6 48.3	26 51.8	13 23.5	8 17.7	18 39.5	29 44.7	8 46.8	8 23.3
18 M	3 46 38	25 15 42	12♑ 1 4	18 7 7	10 16.9	8 13.4	28 7.1	14 4.7	8 20.6	18 37.6	29 48.2	8 49.1	8 25.1
19 Tu	3 50 34	26 16 14	24 10 9	0♒10 40	10 18.3	9 40.1	29 22.5	14 46.0	8 23.6	18 35.7	29 51.7	8 51.3	8 26.8
20 W	3 54 31	27 16 48	6♒ 9 10	12 6 13	10 19.5	11 8.3	0♐37.9	15 27.3	8 26.8	18 33.6	29 55.2	8 53.5	8 28.5
21 Th	3 58 27	28 17 22	18 2 23	23 58 16	10R 20.3	12 37.6	1 53.2	16 8.6	8 30.3	18 31.4	29 58.6	8 55.7	8 30.1
22 F	4 2 24	29 17 58	29 54 27	5♓51 33	10 20.6	14 7.9	3 8.6	16 49.9	8 33.9	18 29.1	0♏ 2.1	8 57.9	8 31.8
23 Sa	4 6 20	0♐18 35	11♓50 8	17 50 49	10 20.3	15 39.0	4 24.0	17 31.3	8 37.7	18 26.7	0 5.5	9 0.2	8 33.4
24 Su	4 10 17	1 19 13	23 54 8	0♈ 0 36	10 19.5	17 10.7	5 39.3	18 12.7	8 41.7	18 24.2	0 8.9	9 2.4	8 35.0
25 M	4 14 14	2 19 53	6♈10 43	12 24 53	10 18.6	18 42.9	6 54.7	18 54.2	8 45.9	18 21.7	0 12.2	9 4.7	8 36.6
26 Tu	4 18 10	3 20 33	18 43 28	25 6 47	10 17.6	20 15.5	8 10.1	19 35.7	8 50.3	18 19.0	0 15.5	9 6.9	8 38.1
27 W	4 22 7	4 21 15	1♉35 2	8♉ 8 20	10 16.7	21 48.4	9 25.4	20 17.3	8 54.8	18 16.2	0 18.8	9 9.2	8 39.6
28 Th	4 26 3	5 21 58	14 46 44	21 30 10	10 16.1	23 21.5	10 40.8	20 58.9	8 59.6	18 13.3	0 22.1	9 11.4	8 41.1
29 F	4 30 0	6 22 42	28 18 28	5♊11 22	10D 15.8	24 54.8	11 56.2	21 40.5	9 4.5	18 10.4	0 25.4	9 13.7	8 42.6
30 Sa	4 33 56	7 23 27	12♊ 8 32	19 9 32	10 15.7	26 28.3	13 11.5	22 22.2	9 9.6	18 7.3	0 28.6	9 15.9	8 44.0

DECEMBER 1974 LONGITUDE

Day	Sid.Time	☉	0 hr ☽	Noon ☽	True ☊	☿	♀	♂	♃	♄	♅	♆	♇
1 Su	4 37 53	8♐24 14	26♊13 53	3♋21 0	10♐15.8	28♏ 1.8	14♐26.9	23♏ 3.9	9♓14.9	18♋ 4.2	0♏31.8	9♐18.2	8♎45.4
2 M	4 41 49	9 25 1	10♋30 19	17 41 12	10R 15.9	29 35.5	15 42.3	23 45.6	9 20.4	18R 0.9	0 34.9	9 20.5	8 46.8
3 Tu	4 45 46	10 25 51	24 53 5	2♌ 5 20	10 15.9	1♐ 9.1	16 57.6	24 27.4	9 26.0	17 57.6	0 38.1	9 22.7	8 48.1
4 W	4 49 43	11 26 41	9♌17 25	16 28 47	10 15.9	2 42.8	18 13.0	25 9.3	9 31.9	17 54.2	0 41.2	9 25.0	8 49.4
5 Th	4 53 39	12 27 33	23 39 1	0♍47 41	10 15.7	4 16.6	19 28.4	25 51.2	9 37.8	17 50.7	0 44.2	9 27.3	8 50.7
6 F	4 57 36	13 28 26	7♍54 25	14 58 58	10D 15.6	5 50.3	20 43.8	26 33.1	9 44.0	17 47.1	0 47.3	9 29.5	8 52.0
7 Sa	5 1 32	14 29 20	22 1 5	29 0 34	10 15.6	7 24.1	21 59.1	27 15.0	9 50.3	17 43.5	0 50.3	9 31.8	8 53.2
8 Su	5 5 29	15 30 16	5♎57 17	12♎51 7	10 15.9	8 57.9	23 14.5	27 57.1	9 56.8	17 39.7	0 53.3	9 34.0	8 54.4
9 M	5 9 25	16 31 13	19 41 58	26 29 47	10 16.4	10 31.7	24 29.9	28 39.1	10 3.5	17 35.9	0 56.2	9 36.3	8 55.6
10 Tu	5 13 22	17 32 12	3♏14 29	9♏56 3	10 17.1	12 5.6	25 45.3	29 21.2	10 10.4	17 32.0	0 59.1	9 38.5	8 56.7
11 W	5 17 18	18 33 11	16 34 24	23 9 32	10 17.8	13 39.5	27 0.7	0♐ 3.4	10 17.4	17 28.1	1 2.0	9 40.8	8 57.8
12 Th	5 21 15	19 34 12	29 41 24	6♐ 9 59	10R 18.4	15 13.4	28 16.0	0 45.5	10 24.5	17 24.0	1 4.8	9 43.0	8 58.9
13 F	5 25 12	20 35 13	12♐35 17	18 57 19	10 18.6	16 47.5	29 31.4	1 27.8	10 31.8	17 19.9	1 7.6	9 45.2	8 59.9
14 Sa	5 29 8	21 36 15	25 16 5	1♑31 41	10 18.1	18 21.5	0♑46.8	2 10.0	10 39.3	17 15.8	1 10.3	9 47.5	9 0.9
15 Su	5 33 5	22 37 19	7♑44 11	13 53 44	10 17.1	19 55.7	2 2.2	2 52.3	10 47.0	17 11.6	1 13.0	9 49.7	9 1.9
16 M	5 37 1	23 38 22	20 0 28	26 4 38	10 15.3	21 30.0	3 17.6	3 34.7	10 54.8	17 7.3	1 15.7	9 51.9	9 2.9
17 Tu	5 40 58	24 39 27	2♒ 6 28	8♒ 6 16	10 13.1	23 4.3	4 33.0	4 17.1	11 2.7	17 2.9	1 18.4	9 54.1	9 3.8
18 W	5 44 54	25 40 31	14 4 22	20 1 11	10 10.7	24 38.8	5 48.3	4 59.5	11 10.8	16 58.5	1 20.9	9 56.3	9 4.7
19 Th	5 48 51	26 41 36	25 57 9	1♓52 42	10 8.3	26 13.5	7 3.7	5 42.0	11 19.1	16 54.1	1 23.5	9 58.5	9 5.5
20 F	5 52 47	27 42 42	7♓48 22	13 44 41	10 6.4	27 48.3	8 19.1	6 24.5	11 27.5	16 49.5	1 26.0	10 0.7	9 6.3
21 Sa	5 56 44	28 43 48	19 42 13	25 41 33	10D 5.2	29 23.3	9 34.4	7 7.0	11 36.0	16 45.0	1 28.5	10 2.9	9 7.1
22 Su	6 0 41	29 44 54	1♈43 16	7♈47 58	10 5.0	0♑58.4	10 49.8	7 49.6	11 44.7	16 40.4	1 30.9	10 5.0	9 7.8
23 M	6 4 37	0♑46 0	13 56 15	20 8 41	10 5.6	2 33.8	12 5.1	8 32.2	11 53.5	16 35.7	1 33.3	10 7.2	9 8.5
24 Tu	6 8 34	1 47 6	26 25 49	2♉48 10	10 6.9	4 9.3	13 20.4	9 14.8	12 2.5	16 31.1	1 35.6	10 9.3	9 9.2
25 W	6 12 30	2 48 13	9♉16 8	15 50 7	10 8.5	5 45.1	14 35.8	9 57.5	12 11.6	16 26.3	1 37.9	10 11.4	9 9.8
26 Th	6 16 27	3 49 20	22 30 22	29 17 1	10 10.0	7 21.2	15 51.1	10 40.3	12 20.8	16 21.6	1 40.1	10 13.6	9 10.4
27 F	6 20 23	4 50 27	6♊10 7	13♊ 9 31	10R 10.8	8 57.5	17 6.4	11 23.1	12 30.1	16 16.8	1 42.4	10 15.7	9 11.0
28 Sa	6 24 20	5 51 34	20 14 55	27 25 53	10 10.6	10 34.0	18 21.7	12 5.9	12 39.6	16 12.0	1 44.5	10 17.8	9 11.6
29 Su	6 28 17	6 52 41	4♋41 48	12♋ 1 54	10 8.9	12 10.8	19 37.0	12 48.7	12 49.3	16 7.1	1 46.6	10 19.9	9 12.1
30 M	6 32 13	7 53 49	19 25 17	26 50 59	10 5.9	13 47.8	20 52.3	13 31.6	12 59.0	16 2.3	1 48.7	10 21.9	9 12.5
31 Tu	6 36 10	8 54 56	4♌17 55	11♌45 3	10 1.9	15 25.1	22 7.6	14 14.6	13 8.9	15 57.4	1 50.7	10 24.0	9 13.0

Astro Data

	Dy Hr Mn
☿ D	3 12:51
♃ D	3 12:13
♃⊼♇	4 6:48
☽0S	9 11:31
♃⊼♇	20 22:15
☽0N	23 11:54
♃□♆	2 0:35
☽0S	6 16:46
☽0N	20 20:18

Planet Ingress

	Dy Hr Mn
☿ ♏	11 16:05
♀ ♐	19 11:56
♅ ♏	21 9:30
☉ ♐	22 16:38
☿ ♐	2 6:17
♂ ♐	10 22:05
♀ ♑	13 9:06
☿ ♑	21 9:16
☉ ♑	22 5:56

Last Aspect / ☽ Ingress

Last Aspect Dy Hr Mn		☽ Ingress Dy Hr Mn
31 22:31	♄ ⚹	♊ 1 18:23
3 21:12	♅ △	♋ 3 23:01
6 0:56	♅ □	♌ 6 2:30
8 3:58	♅ ⚹	♍ 8 5:18
9 13:05	♄ ⚹	♎ 10 7:58
12 10:28	♅ ☌	♏ 12 11:23
14 4:36	♀ ☌	♐ 14 16:39
17 0:12	♅ ⚹	♑ 17 0:42
19 11:37	♀ ⚹	♒ 19 11:39
21 22:39	☉ □	♓ 22 0:11
23 13:09	♄ △	♈ 24 11:59
25 23:14	♄ □	♉ 26 21:05
28 17:16	☿ ☍	♊ 29 2:58

Last Aspect / ☽ Ingress

Last Aspect Dy Hr Mn		☽ Ingress Dy Hr Mn
30 1:59	♀ ☍	♋ 1 6:22
2 23:15	♂ △	♌ 3 8:31
5 3:53	♂ □	♍ 5 10:40
7 9:27	♂ ⚹	♎ 7 13:42
9 9:20	♀ ⚹	♏ 9 18:13
11 1:37	♄ △	♐ 12 0:34
13 16:25	☉ ☌	♑ 14 9:04
15 18:21	♄ ☍	♒ 16 19:48
19 1:38	☉ ⚹	♓ 19 8:12
21 19:43	☉ □	♈ 21 20:35
23 5:07	♄ □	♉ 24 6:45
25 13:01	♄ ⚹	♊ 26 13:15
27 11:00	♃ □	♋ 28 16:15
30 2:34	♀ ☍	♌ 30 17:05

☽ Phases & Eclipses

Dy Hr Mn	
7 2:47	☽ 14♌19
14 0:53	● 21♏16
21 22:39	☽ 29♒15
29 15:10	○ 7♊01
29 15:13	☍T 1.289
6 10:10	☽ 13♍54
13 16:25	● 21♐17
13 16:12:29	☌P 0.827
21 19:43	☽ 29♓34
29 3:51	○ 7♋02

Astro Data

1 NOVEMBER 1974
Julian Day # 27333
Delta T 45.3 sec
SVP 05♓36'26"
Obliquity 23°26'31"
⚷ Chiron 21♈28.4R
☽ Mean ☊ 11♐49.5

1 DECEMBER 1974
Julian Day # 27363
Delta T 45.4 sec
SVP 05♓36'21"
Obliquity 23°26'30"
⚷ Chiron 20♈22.8R
☽ Mean ☊ 10♐14.2

LONGITUDE — JANUARY 1975

Day	Sid.Time	☉	0 hr ☽	Noon ☽	True ☊	☿	♀	♂	♃	♄	♅	♆	♇
1 W	6 40 6	9♑56 4	19♌11 18	26♌35 42	9♐57.5	17♑ 2.6	23♑22.9	14♐57.6	13♓18.9	15♋52.5	1♏52.7	10♐26.0	9♎13.4
2 Th	6 44 3	10 57 12	3♍57 22	11♍15 32	9R 53.3	18 40.4	24 38.1	15 40.6	13 29.0	15R 47.5	1 54.6	10 28.0	9 13.7
3 F	6 47 59	11 58 21	18 29 36	25 39 6	9 50.0	20 18.3	25 53.4	16 23.6	13 39.2	15 42.6	1 56.5	10 30.0	9 14.0
4 Sa	6 51 56	12 59 30	2♎43 44	9♎43 20	9D 48.0	21 56.5	27 8.6	17 6.8	13 49.6	15 37.7	1 58.3	10 32.0	9 14.3
5 Su	6 55 52	14 0 39	16 37 51	23 27 22	9 47.6	23 34.8	28 23.9	17 49.9	14 0.1	15 32.7	2 0.0	10 34.0	9 14.6
6 M	6 59 49	15 1 48	0♏12 0	6♏51 59	9 48.4	25 13.2	29 39.1	18 33.1	14 10.7	15 27.7	2 1.8	10 35.9	9 14.8
7 Tu	7 3 46	16 2 58	13 27 34	19 59 3	9 50.0	26 51.6	0♒54.4	19 16.3	14 21.4	15 22.8	2 3.4	10 37.9	9 15.0
8 W	7 7 42	17 4 8	26 26 43	2♐50 50	9 51.5	28 30.0	2 9.6	19 59.6	14 32.2	15 17.8	2 5.1	10 39.8	9 15.1
9 Th	7 11 39	18 5 18	9♐11 43	15 29 36	9R 52.3	0♒ 8.3	3 24.8	20 42.9	14 43.1	15 12.8	2 6.6	10 41.7	9 15.3
10 F	7 15 35	19 6 28	21 44 44	27 57 19	9 51.5	1 46.4	4 40.0	21 26.3	14 54.1	15 7.9	2 8.1	10 43.6	9 15.3
11 Sa	7 19 32	20 7 37	4♑ 7 33	10♑15 36	9 48.7	3 24.1	5 55.2	22 9.7	15 5.3	15 3.0	2 9.6	10 45.4	9R 15.4
12 Su	7 23 28	21 8 47	16 21 38	22 25 46	9 43.8	5 1.3	7 10.4	22 53.1	15 16.5	14 58.0	2 11.0	10 47.3	9 15.4
13 M	7 27 25	22 9 56	28 28 9	4♒28 57	9 36.9	6 37.8	8 25.6	23 36.6	15 27.9	14 53.1	2 12.4	10 49.1	9 15.4
14 Tu	7 31 21	23 11 5	10♒28 18	16 26 23	9 28.5	8 13.4	9 40.8	24 20.1	15 39.3	14 48.2	2 13.7	10 50.9	9 15.3
15 W	7 35 18	24 12 13	22 23 24	28 19 35	9 19.4	9 47.9	10 55.9	25 3.6	15 50.8	14 43.4	2 14.9	10 52.7	9 15.2
16 Th	7 39 15	25 13 21	4♓15 13	10♓10 36	9 10.4	11 20.8	12 11.1	25 47.2	16 2.5	14 38.5	2 16.1	10 54.4	9 15.1
17 F	7 43 11	26 14 28	16 6 5	22 2 4	9 2.3	12 51.9	13 26.2	26 30.8	16 14.2	14 33.7	2 17.3	10 56.2	9 14.9
18 Sa	7 47 8	27 15 35	27 59 0	3♈57 22	8 56.0	14 20.7	14 41.3	27 14.5	16 26.0	14 28.9	2 18.4	10 57.9	9 14.7
19 Su	7 51 4	28 16 40	9♈57 40	16 0 30	8 51.8	15 46.9	15 56.4	27 58.2	16 37.9	14 24.2	2 19.4	10 59.6	9 14.5
20 M	7 55 1	29 17 45	22 6 25	28 16 3	8D 49.7	17 9.8	17 11.5	28 41.9	16 50.0	14 19.4	2 20.4	11 1.2	9 14.2
21 Tu	7 58 57	0♒18 49	4♉30 0	10♉48 52	8 49.5	18 28.9	18 26.5	29 25.7	17 2.0	14 14.8	2 21.3	11 2.9	9 13.9
22 W	8 2 54	1 19 52	17 13 16	23 43 43	8 50.4	19 43.6	19 41.6	0♑ 9.4	17 14.2	14 10.1	2 22.2	11 4.5	9 13.5
23 Th	8 6 50	2 20 54	0♊20 44	7♊ 4 42	8R 51.4	20 53.0	20 56.6	0 53.3	17 26.5	14 5.5	2 23.0	11 6.1	9 13.2
24 F	8 10 47	3 21 55	13 55 53	20 54 27	8 51.6	21 56.4	22 11.6	1 37.2	17 38.8	14 1.0	2 23.7	11 7.6	9 12.7
25 Sa	8 14 44	4 22 56	28 0 19	5♋13 16	8 49.9	22 53.0	23 26.5	2 21.1	17 51.3	13 56.5	2 24.4	11 9.2	9 12.3
26 Su	8 18 40	5 23 55	12♋32 50	19 58 20	8 45.9	23 42.0	24 41.5	3 5.0	18 3.8	13 52.1	2 25.1	11 10.7	9 11.8
27 M	8 22 37	6 24 53	27 28 52	5♌ 3 19	8 39.4	24 22.5	25 56.4	3 49.0	18 16.3	13 47.7	2 25.7	11 12.2	9 11.3
28 Tu	8 26 33	7 25 50	12♌40 25	20 18 47	8 31.0	24 53.7	27 11.3	4 33.0	18 29.0	13 43.3	2 26.2	11 13.7	9 10.8
29 W	8 30 30	8 26 47	27 57 0	5♍33 38	8 21.5	25 14.8	28 26.2	5 17.1	18 41.7	13 39.1	2 26.7	11 15.1	9 10.2
30 Th	8 34 26	9 27 42	13♍ 7 23	20 37 3	8 12.2	25R 25.3	29 41.0	6 1.1	18 54.5	13 34.9	2 27.1	11 16.5	9 9.6
31 F	8 38 23	10 28 37	28 1 40	5♎20 25	8 4.2	25 24.8	0♓55.9	6 45.3	19 7.4	13 30.7	2 27.5	11 17.9	9 9.0

LONGITUDE — FEBRUARY 1975

Day	Sid.Time	☉	0 hr ☽	Noon ☽	True ☊	☿	♀	♂	♃	♄	♅	♆	♇
1 Sa	8 42 19	11♒29 31	12♎32 47	19♎38 25	7♐58.5	25♒12.9	2♓10.7	7♑29.4	19♓20.3	13♋26.6	2♏27.8	11♐19.2	9♎ 8.3
2 Su	8 46 16	12 30 24	26 37 12	3♏29 10	7R 55.1	24R 49.9	3 25.5	8 13.6	19 33.3	13R 22.6	2 28.0	11 20.5	9R 7.6
3 M	8 50 13	13 31 17	10♏14 32	16 53 38	7D 53.9	24 16.0	4 40.2	8 57.9	19 46.4	13 18.7	2 28.2	11 21.8	9 6.9
4 Tu	8 54 9	14 32 9	23 26 51	29 54 40	7 54.1	23 32.2	5 55.0	9 42.2	19 59.5	13 14.8	2 28.4	11 23.1	9 6.1
5 W	8 58 6	15 33 0	6♐17 34	12♐36 6	7R 54.5	22 39.4	7 9.7	10 26.5	20 12.7	13 11.0	2 28.5	11 24.4	9 5.3
6 Th	9 2 2	16 33 50	18 50 44	25 2 0	7 54.0	21 39.2	8 24.4	11 10.8	20 26.0	13 7.3	2R 28.5	11 25.6	9 4.5
7 F	9 5 59	17 34 39	1♑10 20	7♑16 10	7 51.4	20 33.2	9 39.1	11 55.2	20 39.3	13 3.6	2 28.5	11 26.7	9 3.7
8 Sa	9 9 55	18 35 27	13 19 53	19 21 50	7 46.2	19 23.5	10 53.7	12 39.6	20 52.7	13 0.0	2 28.4	11 27.9	9 2.8
9 Su	9 13 52	19 36 14	25 22 18	1♒21 34	7 37.9	18 11.9	12 8.3	13 24.1	21 6.1	12 56.6	2 28.3	11 29.0	9 1.9
10 M	9 17 48	20 37 0	7♒19 51	13 17 20	7 26.8	17 0.5	13 22.9	14 8.6	21 19.6	12 53.2	2 28.1	11 30.1	9 0.9
11 Tu	9 21 45	21 37 44	19 14 13	25 10 37	7 13.5	15 51.1	14 37.5	14 53.1	21 33.2	12 49.8	2 27.8	11 31.2	8 60.0
12 W	9 25 42	22 38 28	1♓ 6 43	7♓ 2 40	6 59.0	14 45.4	15 52.0	15 37.6	21 46.8	12 46.6	2 27.5	11 32.2	8 59.0
13 Th	9 29 38	23 39 9	12 58 38	18 54 47	6 44.5	13 44.8	17 6.5	16 22.2	22 0.4	12 43.5	2 27.1	11 33.2	8 57.9
14 F	9 33 35	24 39 50	24 51 22	0♈48 37	6 31.2	12 50.4	18 21.0	17 6.8	22 14.1	12 40.4	2 26.7	11 34.1	8 56.9
15 Sa	9 37 31	25 40 28	6♈46 49	12 46 19	6 20.2	12 2.9	19 35.4	17 51.5	22 27.9	12 37.5	2 26.3	11 35.1	8 55.8
16 Su	9 41 28	26 41 6	18 47 30	24 50 46	6 11.9	11 22.9	20 49.8	18 36.1	22 41.7	12 34.6	2 25.7	11 36.0	8 54.7
17 M	9 45 24	27 41 41	0♉56 36	7♉ 5 32	6 6.7	10 50.6	22 4.2	19 20.8	22 55.5	12 31.8	2 25.2	11 36.8	8 53.6
18 Tu	9 49 21	28 42 15	13 18 5	19 34 49	6 4.1	10 26.1	23 18.5	20 5.6	23 9.4	12 29.2	2 24.5	11 37.7	8 52.4
19 W	9 53 17	29 42 47	25 56 21	2♊23 14	6 3.4	10 9.3	24 32.8	20 50.3	23 23.3	12 26.6	2 23.9	11 38.5	8 51.3
20 Th	9 57 14	0♓43 17	8♊56 1	15 35 15	6 3.4	9D 59.9	25 47.0	21 35.1	23 37.3	12 24.1	2 23.1	11 39.2	8 50.1
21 F	10 1 11	1 43 46	22 21 19	29 14 34	6 2.8	9 57.8	27 1.2	22 19.9	23 51.3	12 21.8	2 22.3	11 40.0	8 48.8
22 Sa	10 5 7	2 44 12	6♋15 12	13♋23 13	6 0.4	10 2.4	28 15.4	23 4.8	24 5.3	12 19.5	2 21.5	11 40.7	8 47.6
23 Su	10 9 4	3 44 37	20 38 26	28 0 26	5 55.5	10 13.4	29 29.5	23 49.6	24 19.4	12 17.3	2 20.6	11 41.4	8 46.3
24 M	10 13 0	4 44 59	5♌28 34	13♌ 1 54	5 47.8	10 30.5	0♈43.6	24 34.5	24 33.5	12 15.3	2 19.7	11 42.0	8 45.0
25 Tu	10 16 57	5 45 20	20 39 20	28 19 31	5 37.8	10 53.2	1 57.6	25 19.5	24 47.6	12 13.3	2 18.7	11 42.6	8 43.7
26 W	10 20 53	6 45 39	6♍ 1 0	13♍42 16	5 26.4	11 21.1	3 11.6	26 4.4	25 1.8	12 11.5	2 17.6	11 43.2	8 42.4
27 Th	10 24 50	7 45 57	21 21 46	28 58 6	5 15.0	11 53.8	4 25.5	26 49.4	25 16.0	12 9.7	2 16.5	11 43.7	8 41.0
28 F	10 28 46	8 46 12	6♎29 56	13♎56 11	5 4.9	12 31.1	5 39.4	27 34.4	25 30.2	12 8.1	2 15.4	11 44.2	8 39.7

Astro Data Dy Hr Mn	Planet Ingress Dy Hr Mn	Last Aspect Dy Hr Mn	☽ Ingress Dy Hr Mn	Last Aspect Dy Hr Mn	☽ Ingress Dy Hr Mn	☽ Phases & Eclipses Dy Hr Mn	Astro Data
☽0S 2 23:10	♀ ♒ 6 6:39	31 16:50 ♂ △	♍ 1 17:32	1 21:00 ☿ △	♏ 2 5:53	4 19:04 ☽ 13♎48	1 JANUARY 1975
♃△♄ 10 20:34	☿ ♒ 8 21:58	3 13:36 ♀ △	♎ 3 19:21	4 0:09 ☿ □	♐ 4 12:10	12 10:20 ● 21♑35	Julian Day # 27394
♇ R 11 17:39	☉ ♒ 20 16:36	5 22:55 ♀ □	♏ 5 23:39	6 5:00 ☿ ✱	♑ 6 21:42	20 15:14 ☽ 29♈57	Delta T 45.5 sec
☽0N 17 4:18	♂ ♑ 21 18:49	8 4:24 ☿ ✱	♐ 8 6:39	8 15:18 ♃ ✱	♒ 9 9:16	27 15:09 ○ 7♌03	SVP 05♓36'15"
♃□♅ 22 16:39	♀ ♓ 30 6:05	9 23:22 ♂ ☌	♑ 10 15:58	11 5:17 ☉ ☌	♓ 11 21:45		Obliquity 23°26'29"
☽0S 30 8:26		12 10:20 ☉ ☌	♒ 13 3:03	13 18:36 ♃ ☌	♈ 14 10:22	3 6:23 ☽ 13♏47	⚷ Chiron 19♈57.1
☿ R 30 10:48	☉ ♓ 19 6:50	15 5:45 ♂ ✱	♓ 15 15:23	16 17:03 ☉ ✱	♉ 16 22:09	11 5:17 ● 21♒51	☽ Mean ☊ 8♐35.7
	♀ ♈ 23 9:53	17 22:24 ♂ □	♈ 18 4:03	18 21:06 ♀ ✱	♊ 19 7:35	19 7:38 ☽ 0♊02	
♅ R 6 1:48		20 15:14 ☉ □	♉ 20 15:21	21 8:57 ♀ □	♋ 21 13:18	26 1:15 ○ 6♍49	1 FEBRUARY 1975
☽0N 13 11:23		22 5:07 ☿ □	♊ 22 23:23	23 6:07 ♃ △	♌ 23 15:13		Julian Day # 27425
☿ D 20 19:27		24 15:34 ♀ △	♋ 25 3:20	24 9:54 ♆ △	♍ 25 14:37		Delta T 45.6 sec
♀0N 25 7:04		26 9:03 ♃ △	♌ 27 4:00	27 9:03 ♂ △	♎ 27 13:38		SVP 05♓36'10"
☽0S 26 19:47		29 0:50 ♀ ☍	♍ 29 3:14				Obliquity 23°26'30"
		30 9:23 ♃ ☍	♎ 31 3:13				⚷ Chiron 20♈24.2
							☽ Mean ☊ 6♐57.3

MARCH 1975 LONGITUDE

Day	Sid.Time	☉	0 hr ☽	Noon ☽	True ☊	☿	♀	♂	♃	♄	♅	♆	♇
1 Sa	10 32 43	9♓46 26	21♎16 1	28♎28 47	4♐57.2	13♒12.5	6♈53.2	28♑19.4	25♓44.5	12♋ 6.6	2♏14.2	11♐44.7	8♎38.3
2 Su	10 36 39	10 46 39	5♏34 8	12♏31 55	4R52.2	13 57.8	8 7.0	29 4.5	25 58.8	12R 5.1	2R13.0	11 45.1	8R36.9
3 M	10 40 36	11 46 50	19 22 12	26 5 12	4 49.8	14 46.7	9 20.8	29 49.6	26 13.1	12 3.8	2 11.7	11 45.5	8 35.4
4 Tu	10 44 33	12 47 0	2♐41 19	9♐10 58	4 49.2	15 38.9	10 34.5	0♒34.7	26 27.4	12 2.6	2 10.4	11 45.9	8 34.0
5 W	10 48 29	13 47 8	15 34 44	21 53 10	4 49.2	16 34.2	11 48.2	1 19.9	26 41.7	12 1.5	2 9.0	11 46.2	8 32.5
6 Th	10 52 26	14 47 14	28 6 55	4♑16 33	4 48.6	17 32.5	13 1.8	2 5.1	26 56.1	12 0.5	2 7.6	11 46.6	8 31.1
7 F	10 56 22	15 47 19	10♑22 42	16 25 56	4 46.3	18 33.4	14 15.4	2 50.3	27 10.5	11 59.6	2 6.1	11 46.8	8 29.6
8 Sa	11 0 19	16 47 23	22 26 48	28 25 47	4 41.4	19 36.8	15 28.9	3 35.5	27 24.9	11 58.9	2 4.6	11 47.1	8 28.1
9 Su	11 4 15	17 47 24	4♒23 21	10♒19 54	4 33.7	20 42.7	16 42.4	4 20.8	27 39.4	11 58.2	2 3.1	11 47.3	8 26.5
10 M	11 8 12	18 47 24	16 15 49	22 11 25	4 23.2	21 50.8	17 55.8	5 6.0	27 53.8	11 57.7	2 1.5	11 47.4	8 25.0
11 Tu	11 12 8	19 47 22	28 6 58	4♓ 2 42	4 10.5	23 1.0	19 9.2	5 51.3	28 8.3	11 57.2	1 59.8	11 47.6	8 23.5
12 W	11 16 5	20 47 19	9♓58 49	15 55 31	3 56.6	24 13.2	20 22.5	6 36.7	28 22.8	11 56.9	1 58.1	11 47.7	8 21.9
13 Th	11 20 2	21 47 13	21 52 57	27 51 15	3 42.7	25 27.3	21 35.7	7 22.0	28 37.3	11 56.7	1 56.4	11 47.7	8 20.3
14 F	11 23 58	22 47 6	3♈50 35	9♈51 7	3 29.8	26 43.2	22 48.9	8 7.4	28 51.8	11D56.6	1 54.6	11R47.8	8 18.7
15 Sa	11 27 55	23 46 56	15 53 1	21 56 29	3 19.1	28 0.9	24 2.1	8 52.7	29 6.3	11 56.6	1 52.8	11 47.8	8 17.1
16 Su	11 31 51	24 46 44	28 1 44	4♉ 9 3	3 11.1	29 20.3	25 15.2	9 38.1	29 20.8	11 56.7	1 51.0	11 47.7	8 15.5
17 M	11 35 48	25 46 31	10♉18 43	16 31 6	3 6.0	0♓41.3	26 28.2	10 23.5	29 35.3	11 57.0	1 49.1	11 47.7	8 13.9
18 Tu	11 39 44	26 46 15	22 46 33	29 5 29	3D 3.6	2 3.8	27 41.2	11 9.0	29 49.8	11 57.3	1 47.2	11 47.6	8 12.3
19 W	11 43 41	27 45 57	5♊28 20	11♊55 34	3 3.1	3 27.9	28 54.1	11 54.4	0♈ 4.4	11 57.8	1 45.3	11 47.4	8 10.7
20 Th	11 47 37	28 45 37	18 27 37	25 4 55	3R 3.6	4 53.5	0♉ 7.0	12 39.9	0 18.9	11 58.4	1 43.3	11 47.2	8 9.0
21 F	11 51 34	29 45 14	1♋47 53	8♋36 50	3 3.9	6 20.5	1 19.8	13 25.3	0 33.4	11 59.1	1 41.3	11 47.1	8 7.4
22 Sa	11 55 31	0♈44 49	15 32 0	22 33 32	3 2.9	7 48.9	2 32.5	14 10.8	0 48.0	11 59.9	1 39.2	11 46.8	8 5.7
23 Su	11 59 27	1 44 22	29 41 24	6♌55 25	2 59.8	9 18.8	3 45.1	14 56.3	1 2.5	12 0.8	1 37.1	11 46.6	8 4.1
24 M	12 3 24	2 43 53	14♌15 10	21 40 4	2 54.4	10 50.0	4 57.7	15 41.9	1 17.0	12 1.8	1 35.0	11 46.3	8 2.4
25 Tu	12 7 20	3 43 21	29 9 19	6♍41 54	2 47.0	12 22.6	6 10.2	16 27.4	1 31.6	12 3.0	1 32.9	11 45.9	8 0.8
26 W	12 11 17	4 42 47	14♍16 41	21 52 23	2 38.3	13 56.6	7 22.7	17 12.9	1 46.1	12 4.2	1 30.7	11 45.6	7 59.1
27 Th	12 15 13	5 42 10	29 27 39	7♎ 1 9	2 29.4	15 31.9	8 35.0	17 58.5	2 0.6	12 5.6	1 28.5	11 45.2	7 57.4
28 F	12 19 10	6 41 32	14♎31 36	21 57 51	2 21.5	17 8.6	9 47.3	18 44.1	2 15.1	12 7.0	1 26.3	11 44.7	7 55.8
29 Sa	12 23 6	7 40 52	29 18 54	6♏33 57	2 15.5	18 46.7	10 59.5	19 29.7	2 29.6	12 8.6	1 24.0	11 44.3	7 54.1
30 Su	12 27 3	8 40 10	13♏42 23	20 43 50	2 11.7	20 26.1	12 11.7	20 15.3	2 44.1	12 10.3	1 21.7	11 43.8	7 52.4
31 M	12 31 0	9 39 26	27 38 7	4♐25 14	2D10.2	22 7.0	13 23.8	21 0.9	2 58.6	12 12.1	1 19.4	11 43.3	7 50.8

APRIL 1975 LONGITUDE

Day	Sid.Time	☉	0 hr ☽	Noon ☽	True ☊	☿	♀	♂	♃	♄	♅	♆	♇
1 Tu	12 34 56	10♈38 40	11♐ 5 22	17♐38 48	2♐10.4	23♓49.2	14♉35.8	21♒46.5	3♈13.1	12♋14.0	1♏17.1	11♐42.7	7♎49.1
2 W	12 38 53	11 37 52	24 5 57	0♑27 19	2 11.5	25 32.8	15 47.7	22 32.2	3 27.5	12 16.0	1R14.8	11R42.1	7R47.4
3 Th	12 42 49	12 37 3	6♑43 26	12 54 54	2R12.5	27 17.8	16 59.5	23 17.8	3 42.0	12 18.1	1 12.4	11 41.5	7 45.8
4 F	12 46 46	13 36 12	19 2 20	25 6 21	2 12.5	29 4.2	18 11.3	24 3.5	3 56.4	12 20.3	1 10.0	11 40.9	7 44.1
5 Sa	12 50 42	14 35 19	1♒ 7 33	7♒ 6 32	2 10.8	0♈52.0	19 23.0	24 49.2	4 10.8	12 22.6	1 7.6	11 40.2	7 42.5
6 Su	12 54 39	15 34 24	13 3 51	19 0 2	2 7.2	2 41.3	20 34.6	25 34.8	4 25.2	12 25.0	1 5.2	11 39.5	7 40.8
7 M	12 58 35	16 33 28	24 55 35	0♓50 58	2 1.6	4 32.0	21 46.2	26 20.5	4 39.6	12 27.5	1 2.7	11 38.8	7 39.2
8 Tu	13 2 32	17 32 29	6♓46 35	12 42 48	1 54.4	6 24.2	22 57.6	27 6.2	4 53.9	12 30.1	1 0.3	11 38.0	7 37.5
9 W	13 6 28	18 31 29	18 39 56	24 38 17	1 46.3	8 17.8	24 9.0	27 51.9	5 8.3	12 32.9	0 57.8	11 37.2	7 35.9
10 Th	13 10 25	19 30 27	0♈38 4	6♈39 32	1 38.0	10 12.8	25 20.3	28 37.6	5 22.6	12 35.7	0 55.3	11 36.4	7 34.2
11 F	13 14 22	20 29 23	12 42 50	18 48 8	1 30.4	12 9.3	26 31.5	29 23.3	5 36.9	12 38.6	0 52.8	11 35.6	7 32.6
12 Sa	13 18 18	21 28 16	24 55 34	1♉ 5 16	1 24.2	14 7.2	27 42.7	0♓ 9.0	5 51.1	12 41.6	0 50.3	11 34.7	7 31.0
13 Su	13 22 15	22 27 8	7♉17 22	13 31 59	1 19.7	16 6.5	28 53.7	0 54.7	6 5.4	12 44.8	0 47.8	11 33.8	7 29.4
14 M	13 26 11	23 25 58	19 49 16	26 9 22	1D17.2	18 7.2	0♊ 4.7	1 40.5	6 19.6	12 48.0	0 45.2	11 32.9	7 27.8
15 Tu	13 30 8	24 24 46	2♊32 27	8♊58 42	1 16.6	20 9.2	1 15.5	2 26.2	6 33.8	12 51.3	0 42.7	11 31.9	7 26.2
16 W	13 34 4	25 23 32	15 28 19	22 1 30	1 17.3	22 12.4	2 26.3	3 11.9	6 47.9	12 54.7	0 40.1	11 30.9	7 24.7
17 Th	13 38 1	26 22 15	28 38 29	5♋19 28	1 18.8	24 16.7	3 36.9	3 57.6	7 2.0	12 58.2	0 37.6	11 29.9	7 23.1
18 F	13 41 57	27 20 57	12♋ 4 38	18 54 10	1 20.3	26 22.1	4 47.5	4 43.3	7 16.1	13 1.8	0 35.0	11 28.9	7 21.5
19 Sa	13 45 54	28 19 36	25 48 9	2♌46 40	1R21.0	28 28.3	5 58.0	5 28.9	7 30.2	13 5.5	0 32.5	11 27.9	7 20.0
20 Su	13 49 51	29 18 13	9♌49 39	16 56 57	1 20.6	0♉35.3	7 8.3	6 14.6	7 44.2	13 9.3	0 29.9	11 26.8	7 18.5
21 M	13 53 47	0♉16 47	24 8 21	1♍23 25	1 18.8	2 42.8	8 18.6	7 0.3	7 58.2	13 13.2	0 27.3	11 25.7	7 17.0
22 Tu	13 57 44	1 15 19	8♍41 40	16 2 26	1 15.8	4 50.6	9 28.7	7 46.0	8 12.1	13 17.2	0 24.8	11 24.6	7 15.5
23 W	14 1 40	2 13 49	23 24 58	0♎48 24	1 12.0	6 58.5	10 38.8	8 31.6	8 26.0	13 21.2	0 22.2	11 23.4	7 14.0
24 Th	14 5 37	3 12 17	8♎11 50	15 34 17	1 7.9	9 6.2	11 48.7	9 17.3	8 39.9	13 25.4	0 19.6	11 22.2	7 12.5
25 F	14 9 33	4 10 43	22 54 48	0♏12 28	1 4.3	11 13.4	12 58.5	10 2.9	8 53.7	13 29.6	0 17.1	11 21.1	7 11.1
26 Sa	14 13 30	5 9 7	7♏26 27	14 35 59	1 1.6	13 19.9	14 8.2	10 48.6	9 7.5	13 33.9	0 14.5	11 19.8	7 9.6
27 Su	14 17 26	6 7 30	21 40 28	28 39 25	1D 0.2	15 25.2	15 17.8	11 34.2	9 21.2	13 38.3	0 12.0	11 18.6	7 8.2
28 M	14 21 23	7 5 50	5♐32 31	12♐19 34	1 0.0	17 29.1	16 27.2	12 19.8	9 34.9	13 42.8	0 9.4	11 17.4	7 6.8
29 Tu	14 25 20	8 4 9	19 0 31	25 35 28	1 0.8	19 31.3	17 36.6	13 5.5	9 48.5	13 47.4	0 6.9	11 16.1	7 5.4
30 W	14 29 16	9 2 27	2♑ 4 35	8♑28 11	1 2.2	21 31.5	18 45.8	13 51.1	10 2.1	13 52.1	0 4.4	11 14.8	7 4.1

Astro Data	Planet Ingress	Last Aspect	☽ Ingress	Last Aspect	☽ Ingress	☽ Phases & Eclipses	Astro Data
Dy Hr Mn	Dy Hr Mn	Dy Hr Mn	Dy Hr Mn	Dy Hr Mn	Dy Hr Mn	Dy Hr Mn	1 MARCH 1975
☽0N 12 17:40	♂ ♒ 3 5:32	1 12:24 ♂ □	♏ 1 14:33	2 3:09 ☿ □	♑ 2 11:08	4 20:20 ☽ 13♐38	Julian Day # 27453
♄ D 14 8:32	☿ ♓ 16 11:50	3 12:28 ♃ △	♐ 3 19:05	3 22:09 ♀ △	♒ 4 21:45	12 23:47 ● 21♓47	Delta T 45.6 sec
♆ R 14 10:02	♃ ♈ 18 16:47	5 21:40 ♃ □	♑ 6 3:39	7 3:04 ♂ ☌	♓ 7 10:17	20 20:05 ☽ 29♊35	SVP 05♓36'07"
♃⊼♅ 25 1:53	♀ ♉ 19 21:42	8 10:10 ♃ ⚹	♒ 8 15:09	9 12:14 ♀ ⚹	♈ 9 22:44	27 10:36 ○ 6♎08	Obliquity 23°26'30"
☽0S 26 6:54	☉ ♈ 21 5:57	10 12:32 ☿ ☌	♓ 11 3:49	11 16:39 ☉ ☌	♉ 12 9:53		⚷ Chiron 21♈29.0
♃0N 28 22:42		13 13:49 ♃ ☌	♈ 13 16:18	13 10:32 ♄ ⚹	♊ 14 19:14	3 12:25 ☽ 13♑08	☽ Mean ☊ 5♐28.3
	☿ ♈ 4 12:28	16 2:53 ☿ ⚹	♉ 16 3:52	16 19:34 ☉ ⚹	♋ 17 2:27	11 16:39 ● 21♈10	
☿0N 7 1:51	♂ ♓ 11 19:15	18 13:39 ♃ ⚹	♊ 18 13:43	19 5:26 ☿ □	♌ 19 7:14	19 4:41 ☽ 28♋31	1 APRIL 1975
☽0N 8 23:47	♀ ♊ 13 22:26	20 20:05 ☉ □	♋ 20 20:48	20 2:44 ♆ △	♍ 21 9:42	25 19:55 ○ 4♏59	Julian Day # 27484
♃☍♇ 18 8:20	☿ ♉ 19 17:20	21 17:53 ♄ ☌	♌ 23 0:31	22 7:32 ♄ ⚹	♎ 23 10:41		Delta T 45.7 sec
☽0S 22 15:52	☉ ♉ 20 17:07	24 2:28 ♂ ☍	♍ 25 1:21	24 8:32 ♄ □	♏ 25 11:39		SVP 05♓36'04"
		25 23:25 ☿ ☍	♎ 27 0:51	26 11:34 ☿ ☍	♐ 27 14:20		Obliquity 23°26'29"
		28 7:08 ♂ △	♏ 29 1:08	28 21:14 ♀ ☍	♑ 29 20:08		⚷ Chiron 23♈09.6
		30 13:04 ☿ △	♐ 31 4:10				☽ Mean ☊ 3♐49.8

LONGITUDE — MAY 1975

Day	Sid.Time	☉	0 hr ☽	Noon ☽	True ☊	☿	♀	♂	♃	♄	♅	♆	♇
1 Th	14 33 13	10♉ 0 42	14♑46 40	21♑ 0 26	1♐ 3.7	23♉29.4	19♊54.9	14♓36.7	10♈15.7	13♋56.8	0♏ 1.9	11♐13.5	7♎ 2.7
2 F	14 37 9	10 58 56	27 10 1	3♒15 57	1 5.0	25 24.7	21 3.8	15 22.3	10 29.2	14 1.6	29♎59.4	11R 12.2	7R 1.4
3 Sa	14 41 6	11 57 9	9♒18 47	15 19 7	1R 5.6	27 17.2	22 12.7	16 7.9	10 42.6	14 6.5	29R56.9	11 10.8	7 0.1
4 Su	14 45 2	12 55 20	21 17 31	27 14 35	1 5.4	29 6.8	23 21.4	16 53.4	10 56.0	14 11.5	29 54.4	11 9.4	6 58.8
5 M	14 48 59	13 53 30	3♓10 52	9♓ 6 55	1 4.3	0♊53.2	24 29.9	17 39.0	11 9.4	14 16.5	29 51.9	11 8.1	6 57.6
6 Tu	14 52 55	14 51 38	15 3 16	21 0 26	1 2.6	2 36.2	25 38.4	18 24.5	11 22.7	14 21.6	29 49.4	11 6.7	6 56.3
7 W	14 56 52	15 49 45	26 58 51	2♈58 57	1 0.5	4 15.8	26 46.7	19 10.0	11 35.9	14 26.8	29 47.0	11 5.2	6 55.1
8 Th	15 0 49	16 47 50	9♈ 1 6	15 5 40	0 58.3	5 51.8	27 54.9	19 55.5	11 49.1	14 32.1	29 44.6	11 3.8	6 53.9
9 F	15 4 45	17 45 54	21 12 56	27 23 8	0 56.3	7 24.1	29 2.9	20 41.0	12 2.2	14 37.5	29 42.2	11 2.4	6 52.8
10 Sa	15 8 42	18 43 56	3♉36 29	9♉53 7	0 54.8	8 52.7	0♋10.8	21 26.4	12 15.2	14 42.9	29 39.8	11 0.9	6 51.6
11 Su	15 12 38	19 41 57	16 13 10	22 36 42	0 53.8	10 17.4	1 18.5	22 11.9	12 28.2	14 48.4	29 37.4	10 59.4	6 50.5
12 M	15 16 35	20 39 56	29 3 44	5♊34 17	0D 53.5	11 38.2	2 26.1	22 57.3	12 41.2	14 53.9	29 35.1	10 57.9	6 49.4
13 Tu	15 20 31	21 37 54	12♊ 8 20	18 45 49	0 53.6	12 55.1	3 33.5	23 42.6	12 54.0	14 59.6	29 32.8	10 56.4	6 48.3
14 W	15 24 28	22 35 50	25 26 40	2♋10 47	0 54.2	14 7.9	4 40.8	24 28.0	13 6.8	15 5.3	29 30.5	10 54.9	6 47.3
15 Th	15 28 24	23 33 45	8♋58 5	15 48 27	0 54.8	15 16.6	5 47.9	25 13.3	13 19.6	15 11.0	29 28.2	10 53.4	6 46.2
16 F	15 32 21	24 31 37	22 41 44	29 37 49	0 55.5	16 21.2	6 54.8	25 58.6	13 32.2	15 16.9	29 25.9	10 51.9	6 45.2
17 Sa	15 36 18	25 29 28	6♌36 31	13♌37 40	0 56.0	17 21.6	8 1.6	26 43.8	13 44.8	15 22.8	29 23.7	10 50.3	6 44.3
18 Su	15 40 14	26 27 18	20 41 3	27 46 25	0R 56.2	18 17.7	9 8.1	27 29.1	13 57.4	15 28.7	29 21.5	10 48.8	6 43.3
19 M	15 44 11	27 25 5	4♍53 32	12♍ 2 3	0 56.2	19 9.4	10 14.5	28 14.3	14 9.8	15 34.8	29 19.3	10 47.2	6 42.4
20 Tu	15 48 7	28 22 51	19 11 38	26 21 54	0 56.0	19 56.7	11 20.7	28 59.4	14 22.2	15 40.8	29 17.2	10 45.6	6 41.5
21 W	15 52 4	29 20 35	3♎32 23	10♎42 38	0 55.9	20 39.5	12 26.7	29 44.5	14 34.5	15 47.0	29 15.1	10 44.1	6 40.7
22 Th	15 56 0	0♊18 17	17 52 9	25 0 24	0D 55.7	21 17.8	13 32.5	0♈29.6	14 46.7	15 53.2	29 13.0	10 42.5	6 39.8
23 F	15 59 57	1 15 58	2♏ 6 53	9♏11 4	0 55.7	21 51.5	14 38.1	1 14.7	14 58.9	15 59.4	29 10.9	10 40.9	6 39.0
24 Sa	16 3 53	2 13 37	16 12 27	23 10 33	0 55.8	22 20.6	15 43.5	1 59.7	15 10.9	16 5.7	29 8.9	10 39.3	6 38.2
25 Su	16 7 50	3 11 15	0♐ 4 57	6♐55 18	0R 55.8	22 44.9	16 48.7	2 44.7	15 22.9	16 12.1	29 6.9	10 37.7	6 37.5
26 M	16 11 47	4 8 52	13 41 17	20 22 43	0 55.8	23 4.5	17 53.6	3 29.6	15 34.8	16 18.5	29 5.0	10 36.1	6 36.8
27 Tu	16 15 43	5 6 28	26 59 25	3♑31 21	0 55.5	23 19.3	18 58.3	4 14.6	15 46.6	16 25.0	29 3.1	10 34.5	6 36.1
28 W	16 19 40	6 4 3	9♑58 34	16 21 9	0 55.0	23 29.4	20 2.8	4 59.4	15 58.4	16 31.5	29 1.2	10 32.8	6 35.4
29 Th	16 23 36	7 1 36	22 39 18	28 53 18	0 54.3	23R34.8	21 7.1	5 44.3	16 10.0	16 38.1	28 59.4	10 31.2	6 34.8
30 F	16 27 33	7 59 9	5♒ 3 27	11♒10 10	0 53.5	23 35.6	22 11.1	6 29.1	16 21.6	16 44.7	28 57.5	10 29.6	6 34.2
31 Sa	16 31 29	8 56 41	17 13 53	23 15 4	0 52.7	23 31.9	23 14.8	7 13.9	16 33.1	16 51.4	28 55.8	10 28.0	6 33.7

LONGITUDE — JUNE 1975

Day	Sid.Time	☉	0 hr ☽	Noon ☽	True ☊	☿	♀	♂	♃	♄	♅	♆	♇
1 Su	16 35 26	9♊54 12	29♒14 14	5♓11 58	0♐52.2	23♊23.7	24♋18.3	7♈58.6	16♈44.5	16♋58.1	28♎54.0	10♐26.4	6♎33.1
2 M	16 39 22	10 51 42	11♓ 8 47	17 5 18	0D 52.0	23R11.3	25 21.6	8 43.2	16 55.7	17 4.9	28R52.3	10R24.7	6R32.6
3 Tu	16 43 19	11 49 11	23 2 4	28 59 41	0 52.2	22 55.0	26 24.6	9 27.9	17 6.9	17 11.7	28 50.7	10 23.1	6 32.1
4 W	16 47 16	12 46 39	4♈58 42	10♈59 40	0 52.9	22 35.0	27 27.3	10 12.5	17 18.0	17 18.6	28 49.1	10 21.5	6 31.7
5 Th	16 51 12	13 44 7	17 3 7	23 9 33	0 54.0	22 11.7	28 29.7	10 57.0	17 29.1	17 25.5	28 47.5	10 19.9	6 31.3
6 F	16 55 9	14 41 34	29 19 23	5♉33 2	0 55.2	21 45.4	29 31.9	11 41.5	17 40.0	17 32.4	28 45.9	10 18.2	6 30.9
7 Sa	16 59 5	15 39 0	11♉50 50	18 13 4	0 56.2	21 16.6	0♌33.7	12 25.9	17 50.8	17 39.4	28 44.4	10 16.6	6 30.5
8 Su	17 3 2	16 36 26	24 39 55	1♊11 30	0R 56.9	20 45.9	1 35.3	13 10.3	18 1.5	17 46.5	28 43.0	10 15.0	6 30.2
9 M	17 6 58	17 33 51	7♊47 51	14 28 56	0 56.9	20 13.6	2 36.5	13 54.6	18 12.1	17 53.5	28 41.6	10 13.4	6 29.9
10 Tu	17 10 55	18 31 15	21 14 34	28 4 33	0 56.0	19 40.4	3 37.4	14 38.9	18 22.6	18 0.6	28 40.2	10 11.8	6 29.7
11 W	17 14 51	19 28 39	4♋58 34	11♋56 14	0 54.3	19 6.8	4 38.0	15 23.1	18 33.0	18 7.8	28 38.9	10 10.2	6 29.5
12 Th	17 18 48	20 26 1	18 57 6	26 0 41	0 52.0	18 33.3	5 38.2	16 7.2	18 43.3	18 15.0	28 37.6	10 8.6	6 29.3
13 F	17 22 45	21 23 23	3♌ 6 28	10♌13 54	0 49.3	18 0.7	6 38.1	16 51.3	18 53.4	18 22.2	28 36.4	10 7.0	6 29.1
14 Sa	17 26 41	22 20 44	17 22 28	24 31 40	0 46.7	17 29.4	7 37.6	17 35.3	19 3.5	18 29.4	28 35.2	10 5.4	6 29.0
15 Su	17 30 38	23 18 3	1♍40 59	8♍49 59	0 44.6	16 60.0	8 36.8	18 19.3	19 13.5	18 36.7	28 34.1	10 3.9	6 28.9
16 M	17 34 34	24 15 22	15 58 17	23 5 31	0D 43.5	16 32.9	9 35.5	19 3.1	19 23.3	18 44.1	28 33.0	10 2.3	6 28.9
17 Tu	17 38 31	25 12 40	0♎11 23	7♎15 37	0 43.3	16 8.6	10 33.8	19 47.0	19 33.0	18 51.4	28 31.9	10 0.7	6D 28.9
18 W	17 42 27	26 9 57	14 18 0	21 18 21	0 44.1	15 47.5	11 31.7	20 30.7	19 42.6	18 58.8	28 30.9	9 59.2	6 28.9
19 Th	17 46 24	27 7 13	28 16 30	5♏12 17	0 45.5	15 30.0	12 29.2	21 14.4	19 52.1	19 6.2	28 30.0	9 57.6	6 28.9
20 F	17 50 20	28 4 28	12♏ 5 33	18 56 12	0 46.9	15 16.4	13 26.2	21 58.0	20 1.4	19 13.6	28 29.1	9 56.1	6 29.0
21 Sa	17 54 17	29 1 43	25 44 4	2♐29 2	0R 47.8	15 6.9	14 22.7	22 41.6	20 10.7	19 21.1	28 28.2	9 54.6	6 29.1
22 Su	17 58 14	29 58 57	9♐10 57	15 49 43	0 47.6	15D 1.8	15 18.8	23 25.0	20 19.8	19 28.6	28 27.4	9 53.1	6 29.3
23 M	18 2 10	0♋56 10	22 25 11	28 57 16	0 46.0	15 1.1	16 14.3	24 8.5	20 28.8	19 36.1	28 26.7	9 51.6	6 29.4
24 Tu	18 6 7	1 53 24	5♑25 52	11♑50 58	0 43.0	15 5.1	17 9.3	24 51.8	20 37.6	19 43.6	28 26.0	9 50.1	6 29.6
25 W	18 10 3	2 50 36	18 12 32	24 30 35	0 38.6	15 13.8	18 3.8	25 35.1	20 46.4	19 51.2	28 25.3	9 48.7	6 29.9
26 Th	18 14 0	3 47 49	0♒45 13	6♒56 33	0 33.2	15 27.3	18 57.8	26 18.3	20 55.0	19 58.7	28 24.7	9 47.2	6 30.2
27 F	18 17 56	4 45 1	13 4 46	19 10 7	0 27.5	15 45.5	19 51.2	27 1.4	21 3.4	20 6.3	28 24.2	9 45.8	6 30.5
28 Sa	18 21 53	5 42 13	25 12 54	1♓13 27	0 22.0	16 8.5	20 44.0	27 44.4	21 11.8	20 13.9	28 23.7	9 44.3	6 30.8
29 Su	18 25 50	6 39 25	7♓12 11	13 9 32	0 17.4	16 36.3	21 36.1	28 27.4	21 20.0	20 21.6	28 23.2	9 42.9	6 31.2
30 M	18 29 46	7 36 37	19 6 1	25 2 9	0 14.1	17 8.7	22 27.7	29 10.3	21 28.0	20 29.2	28 22.8	9 41.5	6 31.6

Astro Data

Astro Data	Dy Hr Mn
♃△♆	4 21:51
☽0N	6 6:34
☽0S	19 22:26
♂0N	26 9:01
☿ R	29 16:00
☽0N	2 14:24
♃□♄	4 3:02
☽0S	16 4:03
♇ D	17 4:03
☿ D	22 15:18
☽0N	29 22:53

Planet Ingress

Planet Ingress	Dy Hr Mn
♅ ♎	1 17:49
☿ ♊	4 11:55
♀ ♋	9 20:11
☉ ♊	21 16:24
♂ ♈	21 8:14
♀ ♌	6 10:54
☉ ♋	22 0:26

Last Aspect / ☽ Ingress

Last Aspect Dy Hr Mn		☽ Ingress Dy Hr Mn
2 5:31	♅ □	♒ 2 5:34
4 17:19	♅ △	♓ 4 17:34
6 23:33	♀ □	♈ 7 6:03
9 16:44	♀ ✶	♉ 9 17:03
11 11:56	♂ ✶	♊ 12 1:44
14 7:14	♅ △	♋ 14 8:08
16 11:38	♅ □	♌ 16 12:38
18 14:38	♅ ✶	♍ 18 15:45
20 17:18	♂ ☍	♎ 20 18:05
22 19:03	♅ ☌	♏ 22 20:25
23 23:48	♄ △	♐ 24 23:51
27 3:46	♅ ✶	♑ 27 5:31
29 12:10	♅ □	♒ 29 14:09

Last Aspect Dy Hr Mn		☽ Ingress Dy Hr Mn
31 23:20	♅ △	♓ 1 1:32
3 7:27	♀ △	♈ 3 14:01
6 0:26	♀ □	♉ 6 1:19
7 11:03	♄ ✶	♊ 8 9:49
10 13:01	♅ △	♋ 10 15:21
12 16:24	♅ □	♌ 12 18:45
14 18:47	♅ ✶	♍ 14 21:11
16 14:58	☉ □	♎ 16 23:41
19 0:23	♅ ☌	♏ 19 2:59
20 12:38	♄ △	♐ 21 7:34
23 11:03	♄ ✶	♑ 23 13:56
25 19:30	♅ □	♒ 25 22:33
28 6:20	♅ △	♓ 28 9:33
30 2:50	♄ △	♈ 30 22:02

☽ Phases & Eclipses

Dy Hr Mn	
3 5:44	☽ 12♒11
11 7:05	● 19♉59
11 7:16:44	• P 0.864
18 10:29	☽ 26♌53
25 5:51	○ 3♐25
25 5:48	• T 1.426
1 23:22	☽ 10♓50
9 18:49	● 18♊19
16 14:58	☽ 24♍51
23 16:54	○ 1♑36

Astro Data

1 MAY 1975
Julian Day # 27514
Delta T 45.8 sec
SVP 05♓36'01"
Obliquity 23°26'29"
⚷ Chiron 24♈56.5
☽ Mean ☊ 2♐14.4

1 JUNE 1975
Julian Day # 27545
Delta T 45.9 sec
SVP 05♓35'57"
Obliquity 23°26'28"
⚷ Chiron 26♈36.0
☽ Mean ☊ 0♐35.9

JULY 1975 LONGITUDE

Day	Sid.Time	☉	0 hr ☽	Noon ☽	True ☊	☿	♀	♂	♃	♄	♅	♆	♇
1 Tu	18 33 43	8♋33 49	0♈58 29	6♈55 37	0♐12.3	17♊45.9	23♌18.6	29♈53.1	21♈36.0	20♋36.9	28♎22.5	9♐40.2	6♎32.0
2 W	18 37 39	9 31 2	12 54 10	18 54 44	0D 12.0	18 27.7	24 8.8	0♉35.8	21 43.8	20 44.6	28R 22.2	9R 38.8	6 32.5
3 Th	18 41 36	10 28 14	24 57 56	1♉ 4 23	0 12.9	19 14.0	24 58.4	1 18.4	21 51.4	20 52.3	28 21.9	9 37.5	6 33.0
4 F	18 45 32	11 25 27	7♉14 40	13 29 20	0 14.3	20 4.9	25 47.2	2 1.0	21 58.9	20 60.0	28 21.7	9 36.1	6 33.6
5 Sa	18 49 29	12 22 40	19 48 53	26 13 45	0R 15.6	21 0.2	26 35.3	2 43.5	22 6.3	21 7.7	28 21.6	9 34.8	6 34.1
6 Su	18 53 25	13 19 53	2♊44 18	9♊20 47	0 16.0	21 59.9	27 22.6	3 25.8	22 13.5	21 15.4	28 21.5	9 33.5	6 34.7
7 M	18 57 22	14 17 6	16 3 22	22 52 2	0 14.9	23 4.0	28 9.1	4 8.1	22 20.5	21 23.2	28D 21.5	9 32.3	6 35.4
8 Tu	19 1 19	15 14 20	29 46 40	6♋46 59	0 11.8	24 12.4	28 54.8	4 50.3	22 27.4	21 30.9	28 21.5	9 31.0	6 36.1
9 W	19 5 15	16 11 34	13♋52 32	21 2 46	0 6.9	25 24.9	29 39.6	5 32.4	22 34.2	21 38.7	28 21.6	9 29.8	6 36.8
10 Th	19 9 12	17 8 47	28 16 57	5♌34 16	0 0.4	26 41.7	0♍23.5	6 14.4	22 40.8	21 46.5	28 21.7	9 28.6	6 37.5
11 F	19 13 8	18 6 1	12♌53 49	20 14 40	29♏53.1	28 2.5	1 6.5	6 56.2	22 47.2	21 54.2	28 21.9	9 27.4	6 38.3
12 Sa	19 17 5	19 3 15	27 35 53	4♍56 32	29 46.0	29 27.4	1 48.5	7 38.0	22 53.5	22 2.0	28 22.1	9 26.2	6 39.1
13 Su	19 21 1	20 0 29	12♍15 47	19 32 55	29 39.9	0♋56.2	2 29.4	8 19.7	22 59.6	22 9.8	28 22.4	9 25.1	6 39.9
14 M	19 24 58	20 57 43	26 47 17	3♎58 25	29 35.7	2 29.0	3 9.4	9 1.2	23 5.5	22 17.6	28 22.7	9 24.0	6 40.7
15 Tu	19 28 54	21 54 57	11♎ 5 57	18 9 37	29D 33.4	4 5.4	3 48.2	9 42.7	23 11.3	22 25.4	28 23.1	9 22.9	6 41.6
16 W	19 32 51	22 52 11	25 9 18	2♏ 4 59	29 32.9	5 45.6	4 25.9	10 24.0	23 17.0	22 33.1	28 23.5	9 21.8	6 42.6
17 Th	19 36 48	23 49 25	8♏56 42	15 44 32	29 33.6	7 29.3	5 2.4	11 5.3	23 22.4	22 40.9	28 24.0	9 20.7	6 43.5
18 F	19 40 44	24 46 39	22 28 38	29 9 10	29R 34.4	9 16.3	5 37.7	11 46.4	23 27.7	22 48.7	28 24.6	9 19.7	6 44.5
19 Sa	19 44 41	25 43 53	5♐46 17	12♐20 9	29 34.4	11 6.5	6 11.6	12 27.4	23 32.8	22 56.5	28 25.2	9 18.7	6 45.5
20 Su	19 48 37	26 41 8	18 50 55	25 18 42	29 32.7	12 59.6	6 44.3	13 8.3	23 37.8	23 4.3	28 25.8	9 17.7	6 46.6
21 M	19 52 34	27 38 22	1♑43 37	8♑ 5 45	29 28.7	14 55.5	7 15.6	13 49.1	23 42.6	23 12.1	28 26.5	9 16.8	6 47.6
22 Tu	19 56 30	28 35 38	14 25 11	20 41 57	29 22.1	16 53.8	7 45.4	14 29.7	23 47.2	23 19.8	28 27.3	9 15.8	6 48.8
23 W	20 0 27	29 32 53	26 56 7	3♒ 7 44	29 13.3	18 54.2	8 13.7	15 10.3	23 51.6	23 27.6	28 28.1	9 14.9	6 49.9
24 Th	20 4 23	0♌30 9	9♒16 53	15 23 38	29 2.8	20 56.5	8 40.5	15 50.7	23 55.9	23 35.3	28 28.9	9 14.1	6 51.1
25 F	20 8 20	1 27 26	21 28 7	27 30 28	28 51.5	23 0.3	9 5.7	16 31.0	23 60.0	23 43.1	28 29.8	9 13.2	6 52.3
26 Sa	20 12 17	2 24 44	3♓30 53	9♓29 36	28 40.5	25 5.2	9 29.2	17 11.2	24 3.9	23 50.8	28 30.8	9 12.4	6 53.5
27 Su	20 16 13	3 22 2	15 26 54	21 23 7	28 30.6	27 11.0	9 51.0	17 51.3	24 7.6	23 58.5	28 31.8	9 11.6	6 54.7
28 M	20 20 10	4 19 21	27 18 39	3♈13 54	28 22.7	29 17.4	10 11.1	18 31.2	24 11.1	24 6.2	28 32.8	9 10.8	6 56.0
29 Tu	20 24 6	5 16 41	9♈ 9 24	15 5 39	28 17.1	1♌24.0	10 29.3	19 11.0	24 14.5	24 13.9	28 34.0	9 10.1	6 57.3
30 W	20 28 3	6 14 2	21 3 13	27 2 42	28 14.0	3 30.6	10 45.7	19 50.7	24 17.6	24 21.6	28 35.1	9 9.4	6 58.6
31 Th	20 31 59	7 11 24	3♉ 4 45	9♉10 0	28D 12.8	5 36.8	11 0.1	20 30.2	24 20.6	24 29.3	28 36.3	9 8.7	6 60.0

AUGUST 1975 LONGITUDE

Day	Sid.Time	☉	0 hr ☽	Noon ☽	True ☊	☿	♀	♂	♃	♄	♅	♆	♇
1 F	20 35 56	8♌ 8 47	15♉19 6	21♉32 42	28♏12.9	7♌42.5	11♍12.5	21♉ 9.6	24♈23.4	24♋37.0	28♎37.6	9♐ 8.0	7♎ 1.4
2 Sa	20 39 52	9 6 11	27 51 25	4♊15 50	28R 13.1	9 47.5	11 22.8	21 48.9	24 26.0	24 44.6	28 38.9	9R 7.4	7 2.8
3 Su	20 43 49	10 3 37	10♊46 27	17 23 44	28 12.6	11 51.6	11 31.1	22 28.0	24 28.4	24 52.2	28 40.3	9 6.8	7 4.3
4 M	20 47 46	11 1 3	24 7 57	0♋59 19	28 10.2	13 54.7	11 37.2	23 7.0	24 30.7	24 59.8	28 41.7	9 6.3	7 5.7
5 Tu	20 51 42	11 58 31	7♋57 48	15 3 15	28 5.4	15 56.6	11 41.1	23 45.8	24 32.7	25 7.4	28 43.1	9 5.7	7 7.2
6 W	20 55 39	12 56 0	22 15 16	29 33 15	27 58.1	17 57.2	11R 42.7	24 24.4	24 34.5	25 15.0	28 44.6	9 5.2	7 8.7
7 Th	20 59 35	13 53 30	6♌56 26	14♌23 48	27 48.6	19 56.5	11 42.1	25 2.9	24 36.2	25 22.5	28 46.2	9 4.7	7 10.3
8 F	21 3 32	14 51 1	21 54 13	29 26 28	27 38.0	21 54.4	11 39.1	25 41.3	24 37.6	25 30.0	28 47.8	9 4.3	7 11.9
9 Sa	21 7 28	15 48 33	6♍59 16	14♍31 20	27 27.5	23 50.8	11 33.8	26 19.5	24 38.9	25 37.5	28 49.5	9 3.9	7 13.5
10 Su	21 11 25	16 46 6	22 1 29	29 28 38	27 18.3	25 45.8	11 26.1	26 57.5	24 39.9	25 45.0	28 51.2	9 3.5	7 15.1
11 M	21 15 21	17 43 39	6♎51 52	14♎10 26	27 11.3	27 39.3	11 16.0	27 35.3	24 40.8	25 52.4	28 52.9	9 3.1	7 16.7
12 Tu	21 19 18	18 41 14	21 23 49	28 31 40	27 6.9	29 31.3	11 3.6	28 13.0	24 41.4	25 59.8	28 54.7	9 2.8	7 18.4
13 W	21 23 15	19 38 50	5♏33 47	12♏30 11	27 4.9	1♍21.8	10 48.7	28 50.5	24 41.9	26 7.2	28 56.5	9 2.5	7 20.1
14 Th	21 27 11	20 36 26	19 20 58	26 6 20	27 4.5	3 10.8	10 31.5	29 27.8	24R 42.2	26 14.5	28 58.4	9 2.3	7 21.8
15 F	21 31 8	21 34 4	2♐46 35	9♐22 2	27 4.5	4 58.3	10 12.0	0♊ 5.0	24 42.2	26 21.9	29 0.4	9 2.0	7 23.6
16 Sa	21 35 4	22 31 42	15 53 4	22 20 3	27 3.6	6 44.3	9 50.3	0 42.0	24 42.1	26 29.1	29 2.4	9 1.9	7 25.3
17 Su	21 39 1	23 29 21	28 43 20	5♑ 3 16	27 0.8	8 28.8	9 26.4	1 18.7	24 41.7	26 36.4	29 4.4	9 1.7	7 27.1
18 M	21 42 57	24 27 2	11♑20 11	17 34 20	26 55.4	10 11.9	9 0.5	1 55.4	24 41.2	26 43.6	29 6.5	9 1.6	7 28.9
19 Tu	21 46 54	25 24 43	23 46 0	29 55 23	26 47.1	11 53.6	8 32.6	2 31.8	24 40.5	26 50.8	29 8.6	9 1.5	7 30.7
20 W	21 50 50	26 22 26	6♒ 2 40	12♒ 8 2	26 36.2	13 33.8	8 2.9	3 8.0	24 39.6	26 57.9	29 10.7	9 1.4	7 32.6
21 Th	21 54 47	27 20 10	18 11 37	24 13 33	26 23.3	15 12.5	7 31.5	3 44.1	24 38.4	27 5.1	29 12.9	9D 1.4	7 34.4
22 F	21 58 44	28 17 55	0♓13 58	6♓13 0	26 9.4	16 49.9	6 58.6	4 19.9	24 37.1	27 12.1	29 15.2	9 1.4	7 36.3
23 Sa	22 2 40	29 15 42	12 10 49	18 7 35	25 55.8	18 25.9	6 24.5	4 55.6	24 35.6	27 19.1	29 17.5	9 1.4	7 38.2
24 Su	22 6 37	0♍13 30	24 3 30	29 58 48	25 43.4	20 0.5	5 49.3	5 31.0	24 33.9	27 26.1	29 19.8	9 1.4	7 40.2
25 M	22 10 33	1 11 20	5♈53 48	11♈48 48	25 33.2	21 33.6	5 13.2	6 6.2	24 31.9	27 33.1	29 22.1	9 1.5	7 42.1
26 Tu	22 14 30	2 9 11	17 44 10	23 40 21	25 25.7	23 5.4	4 36.5	6 41.3	24 29.8	27 40.0	29 24.5	9 1.7	7 44.1
27 W	22 18 26	3 7 4	29 37 48	5♉37 3	25 21.0	24 35.8	3 59.3	7 16.1	24 27.5	27 46.8	29 27.0	9 1.8	7 46.0
28 Th	22 22 23	4 4 59	11♉38 38	17 43 10	25 18.8	26 4.8	3 22.1	7 50.7	24 25.0	27 53.7	29 29.5	9 2.0	7 48.0
29 F	22 26 19	5 2 56	23 51 14	0♊ 3 30	25 18.2	27 32.4	2 44.9	8 25.1	24 22.3	28 0.4	29 32.0	9 2.2	7 50.1
30 Sa	22 30 16	6 0 54	6♊20 35	12 43 7	25 18.3	28 58.6	2 8.0	8 59.2	24 19.4	28 7.2	29 34.6	9 2.5	7 52.1
31 Su	22 34 12	6 58 55	19 11 40	25 46 47	25 17.8	0♎23.4	1 31.7	9 33.2	24 16.3	28 13.8	29 37.2	9 2.8	7 54.1

Astro Data	Planet Ingress	Last Aspect	☽ Ingress	Last Aspect	☽ Ingress	☽ Phases & Eclipses	Astro Data
Dy Hr Mn	Dy Hr Mn	Dy Hr Mn	Dy Hr Mn	Dy Hr Mn	Dy Hr Mn	Dy Hr Mn	1 JULY 1975
♅ D 7 3:59	♂ ♉ 1 3:53	3 6:42 ♅ ☍	♉ 3 9:54	1 18:02 ♄ ✶	♊ 2 4:02	1 16:37 ☽ 9♈13	Julian Day # 27575
☽0S 13 10:41	♀ ♍ 9 11:06	5 13:29 ♀ □	♊ 5 18:58	4 8:01 ♅ △	♋ 4 10:17	9 4:10 ● 16♋21	Delta T 46.0 sec
☽0N 27 7:09	☊ ♏ 10 1:20	7 22:25 ♀ ✶	♋ 8 0:23	6 10:42 ♅ □	♌ 6 12:44	15 19:47 ☽ 22♎42	SVP 05♓35'52"
♃♇♆ 27 22:24	☿ ♋ 12 8:56	10 0:08 ♅ □	♌ 10 2:50	8 11:00 ♅ ✶	♍ 8 12:53	23 5:28 ○ 29♑46	Obliquity 23°26'28"
♄♇♆ 28 13:02	☉ ♌ 23 11:22	12 3:22 ☿ ✶	♍ 12 3:55	10 8:17 ♂ △	♎ 10 12:51	31 8:48 ☽ 7♉32	⚷ Chiron 27♈43.6
♃□♄ 29 2:50	☿ ♌ 28 8:05	13 16:28 ♄ ✶	♎ 14 5:21	12 12:41 ♅ ☌	♏ 12 14:30		☽ Mean ☊ 29♏00.6
		16 5:36 ♅ ☌	♏ 16 8:23	14 18:54 ♂ ☍	♐ 14 18:59	7 11:57 ● 14♌22	
♀ R 6 5:21	☿ ♍ 12 6:12	18 4:26 ☉ △	♐ 18 13:32	17 0:40 ♅ ✶	♑ 17 2:25	14 2:24 ☽ 20♏42	1 AUGUST 1975
☽0S 9 19:25	♂ ♊ 14 20:47	20 17:50 ♅ ✶	♑ 20 20:46	19 10:30 ♅ □	♒ 19 12:09	21 19:48 ○ 28♒08	Julian Day # 27606
♃ R 14 19:32	☉ ♍ 23 18:24	23 5:28 ☉ ☍	♒ 23 5:56	21 22:02 ♅ △	♓ 21 23:32	29 23:20 ☽ 5♊59	Delta T 46.0 sec
♆ D 21 14:53	☿ ♎ 30 17:20	25 13:59 ♅ △	♓ 25 16:58	24 6:55 ♄ △	♈ 24 12:02		SVP 05♓35'47"
☽0N 23 14:27		28 4:53 ☿ △	♈ 28 5:27	26 23:38 ♅ ☍	♉ 27 0:45		Obliquity 23°26'28"
☿0S 29 23:02		30 15:06 ♅ ☍	♉ 30 17:53	29 8:07 ♄ ✶	♊ 29 11:53		⚷ Chiron 28♈09.8
				31 18:58 ♅ △	♋ 31 19:35		☽ Mean ☊ 27♏22.2

LONGITUDE SEPTEMBER 1975

Day	Sid.Time	☉	0 hr ☽	Noon ☽	True ☊	☿	♀	♂	♃	♄	♅	♆	♇
1 M	22 38 9	7♍56 57	2♋28 54	9♋18 20	25♏15.8	1♎46.7	0♍56.2	10♊ 6.9	24♈13.1	28♋20.5	29♎39.8	9♐ 3.1	7♎56.2
2 Tu	22 42 6	8 55 2	16 15 17	23 19 44	25R11.5	3 8.5	0R21.7	10 40.3	24R 9.6	28 27.0	29 42.5	9 3.5	7 58.3
3 W	22 46 2	9 53 8	0♌31 29	7♌50 7	25 4.7	4 28.8	29♌48.5	11 13.5	24 6.0	28 33.6	29 45.2	9 3.8	8 0.4
4 Th	22 49 59	10 51 16	15 14 57	22 45 6	24 55.7	5 47.5	29 16.6	11 46.4	24 2.1	28 40.0	29 48.0	9 4.3	8 2.5
5 F	22 53 55	11 49 26	0♍19 28	7♍56 46	24 45.5	7 4.6	28 46.4	12 19.1	23 58.1	28 46.5	29 50.8	9 4.7	8 4.6
6 Sa	22 57 52	12 47 37	15 35 37	23 14 34	24 35.1	8 20.1	28 17.8	12 51.5	23 53.9	28 52.8	29 53.6	9 5.2	8 6.8
7 Su	23 1 48	13 45 50	0♎52 13	8♎27 12	24 26.0	9 33.8	27 51.2	13 23.7	23 49.5	28 59.1	29 56.5	9 5.7	8 8.9
8 M	23 5 45	14 44 5	15 58 20	23 24 37	24 19.0	10 45.7	27 26.6	13 55.5	23 45.0	29 5.4	29 59.4	9 6.3	8 11.1
9 Tu	23 9 41	15 42 22	0♏45 13	7♏59 35	24 14.7	11 55.7	27 4.0	14 27.1	23 40.2	29 11.6	0♏ 2.3	9 6.9	8 13.3
10 W	23 13 38	16 40 40	15 7 21	22 8 22	24D 12.7	13 3.7	26 43.7	14 58.4	23 35.3	29 17.7	0 5.3	9 7.5	8 15.4
11 Th	23 17 35	17 38 59	29 2 37	5♐50 18	24 12.5	14 9.6	26 25.6	15 29.4	23 30.3	29 23.8	0 8.3	9 8.1	8 17.6
12 F	23 21 31	18 37 21	12♐31 40	19 7 7	24R12.9	15 13.4	26 9.9	16 0.1	23 25.0	29 29.8	0 11.3	9 8.8	8 19.9
13 Sa	23 25 28	19 35 44	25 37 4	2♑ 1 58	24 12.9	16 14.7	25 56.5	16 30.5	23 19.6	29 35.7	0 14.3	9 9.5	8 22.1
14 Su	23 29 24	20 34 8	8♑22 19	14 38 37	24 11.3	17 13.6	25 45.5	17 0.6	23 14.1	29 41.6	0 17.4	9 10.2	8 24.3
15 M	23 33 21	21 32 34	20 51 18	27 0 51	24 7.5	18 9.8	25 37.0	17 30.4	23 8.4	29 47.4	0 20.5	9 11.0	8 26.6
16 Tu	23 37 17	22 31 1	3♒ 7 40	9♒12 9	24 1.2	19 3.1	25 30.8	17 59.9	23 2.5	29 53.2	0 23.7	9 11.8	8 28.8
17 W	23 41 14	23 29 30	15 14 37	21 15 25	23 52.6	19 53.4	25 27.1	18 29.1	22 56.5	29 58.8	0 26.9	9 12.7	8 31.1
18 Th	23 45 10	24 28 1	27 14 49	3♓13 4	23 42.3	20 40.3	25D 25.7	18 57.9	22 50.4	0♌ 4.5	0 30.1	9 13.5	8 33.3
19 F	23 49 7	25 26 34	9♓10 24	15 7 0	23 31.1	21 23.8	25 26.7	19 26.4	22 44.1	0 10.0	0 33.3	9 14.4	8 35.6
20 Sa	23 53 4	26 25 8	21 3 4	26 58 48	23 20.0	22 3.4	25 30.0	19 54.6	22 37.7	0 15.5	0 36.6	9 15.4	8 37.9
21 Su	23 57 0	27 23 45	2♈54 23	8♈50 1	23 10.0	22 38.8	25 35.7	20 22.4	22 31.2	0 20.9	0 39.8	9 16.3	8 40.2
22 M	0 0 57	28 22 23	14 45 56	20 42 20	23 1.9	23 9.9	25 43.5	20 49.8	22 24.5	0 26.2	0 43.1	9 17.3	8 42.5
23 Tu	0 4 53	29 21 4	26 39 32	2♉37 48	22 56.0	23 36.1	25 53.6	21 16.9	22 17.7	0 31.4	0 46.5	9 18.3	8 44.8
24 W	0 8 50	0♎19 46	8♉37 30	14 39 0	22 52.7	23 57.2	26 5.8	21 43.7	22 10.8	0 36.6	0 49.8	9 19.4	8 47.1
25 Th	0 12 46	1 18 31	20 42 42	26 49 5	22D 51.5	24 12.7	26 20.1	22 10.0	22 3.8	0 41.7	0 53.2	9 20.4	8 49.4
26 F	0 16 43	2 17 18	2♊58 36	9♊11 47	22 51.9	24R22.2	26 36.5	22 36.0	21 56.7	0 46.8	0 56.6	9 21.6	8 51.7
27 Sa	0 20 39	3 16 7	15 29 10	21 51 15	22 53.1	24 25.5	26 54.8	23 1.6	21 49.4	0 51.7	1 0.1	9 22.7	8 54.0
28 Su	0 24 36	4 14 58	28 18 35	4♋51 38	22R54.0	24 22.0	27 15.0	23 26.8	21 42.1	0 56.6	1 3.5	9 23.9	8 56.3
29 M	0 28 33	5 13 52	11♋30 52	18 16 38	22 54.0	24 11.4	27 37.1	23 51.5	21 34.7	1 1.4	1 7.0	9 25.1	8 58.7
30 Tu	0 32 29	6 12 48	25 9 11	2♌ 8 41	22 52.4	23 53.5	28 1.0	24 15.8	21 27.2	1 6.1	1 10.5	9 26.3	9 1.0

LONGITUDE OCTOBER 1975

Day	Sid.Time	☉	0 hr ☽	Noon ☽	True ☊	☿	♀	♂	♃	♄	♅	♆	♇
1 W	0 36 26	7♎11 47	9♌15 5	16♌28 11	22♏48.8	23♎28.0	28♌26.5	24♊39.7	21♈19.6	1♌10.7	1♏14.0	9♐27.5	9♎ 3.3
2 Th	0 40 22	8 10 47	23 47 33	1♍12 34	22R43.5	22R54.9	28 53.8	25 3.2	21R11.9	1 15.2	1 17.5	9 28.8	9 5.6
3 F	0 44 19	9 9 50	8♍42 25	16 16 3	22 37.2	22 14.2	29 22.7	25 26.2	21 4.2	1 19.7	1 21.1	9 30.1	9 8.0
4 Sa	0 48 15	10 8 55	23 52 18	1♎29 52	22 30.6	21 26.3	29 53.1	25 48.7	20 56.4	1 24.1	1 24.6	9 31.4	9 10.3
5 Su	0 52 12	11 8 2	9♎ 7 24	16 43 33	22 24.8	20 31.5	0♍24.9	26 10.7	20 48.5	1 28.4	1 28.2	9 32.8	9 12.6
6 M	0 56 8	12 7 12	24 17 3	1♏46 42	22 20.4	19 30.9	0 58.3	26 32.3	20 40.6	1 32.6	1 31.8	9 34.2	9 15.0
7 Tu	1 0 5	13 6 23	9♏11 31	16 30 40	22D 17.9	18 25.4	1 33.0	26 53.4	20 32.6	1 36.7	1 35.4	9 35.6	9 17.3
8 W	1 4 1	14 5 36	23 43 32	0♐49 43	22 17.2	17 16.5	2 9.0	27 13.9	20 24.6	1 40.7	1 39.0	9 37.1	9 19.6
9 Th	1 7 58	15 4 51	7♐48 59	14 41 17	22 18.0	16 5.8	2 46.3	27 34.0	20 16.6	1 44.6	1 42.7	9 38.5	9 21.9
10 F	1 11 55	16 4 8	21 26 45	28 5 36	22 19.5	14 55.2	3 24.8	27 53.5	20 8.5	1 48.4	1 46.3	9 40.0	9 24.3
11 Sa	1 15 51	17 3 27	4♑38 11	11♑ 4 55	22 20.9	13 46.7	4 4.5	28 12.5	20 0.5	1 52.2	1 50.0	9 41.5	9 26.6
12 Su	1 19 48	18 2 47	17 26 18	23 42 50	22R21.5	12 42.1	4 45.4	28 30.9	19 52.4	1 55.8	1 53.7	9 43.1	9 28.9
13 M	1 23 44	19 2 9	29 55 3	6♒ 3 30	22 20.9	11 43.4	5 27.4	28 48.8	19 44.3	1 59.4	1 57.4	9 44.7	9 31.2
14 Tu	1 27 41	20 1 33	12♒ 8 42	18 11 11	22 18.8	10 52.3	6 10.4	29 6.1	19 36.2	2 2.8	2 1.1	9 46.3	9 33.5
15 W	1 31 37	21 0 59	24 11 26	0♓ 9 55	22 15.2	10 10.1	6 54.5	29 22.8	19 28.1	2 6.2	2 4.8	9 47.9	9 35.8
16 Th	1 35 34	22 0 26	6♓ 7 6	12 3 21	22 10.6	9 38.0	7 39.5	29 39.0	19 20.0	2 9.5	2 8.5	9 49.5	9 38.1
17 F	1 39 30	22 59 56	17 59 2	23 54 31	22 5.3	9 16.6	8 25.5	29 54.5	19 11.9	2 12.6	2 12.2	9 51.2	9 40.4
18 Sa	1 43 27	23 59 27	29 50 6	5♈46 3	22 0.1	9D 6.2	9 12.5	0♋ 9.4	19 3.9	2 15.7	2 16.0	9 52.9	9 42.7
19 Su	1 47 24	24 59 0	11♈42 38	17 40 4	21 55.5	9 7.0	10 0.3	0 23.7	18 55.8	2 18.7	2 19.7	9 54.6	9 44.9
20 M	1 51 20	25 58 35	23 38 36	29 38 26	21 51.8	9 18.7	10 49.0	0 37.4	18 47.9	2 21.5	2 23.5	9 56.3	9 47.2
21 Tu	1 55 17	26 58 12	5♉39 46	11♉42 49	21 49.5	9 40.9	11 38.5	0 50.5	18 39.9	2 24.3	2 27.2	9 58.1	9 49.4
22 W	1 59 13	27 57 51	17 47 49	23 54 59	21D 48.4	10 12.8	12 28.9	1 2.8	18 32.0	2 26.9	2 31.0	9 59.8	9 51.7
23 Th	2 3 10	28 57 32	0♊ 4 34	6♊16 50	21 48.6	10 53.9	13 20.0	1 14.5	18 24.2	2 29.5	2 34.7	10 1.6	9 53.9
24 F	2 7 6	29 57 16	12 32 3	18 50 31	21 49.7	11 43.2	14 11.8	1 25.5	18 16.4	2 32.0	2 38.5	10 3.4	9 56.2
25 Sa	2 11 3	0♏57 1	25 12 33	1♋38 27	21 51.2	12 39.9	15 4.4	1 35.8	18 8.7	2 34.3	2 42.3	10 5.3	9 58.4
26 Su	2 14 59	1 56 49	8♋ 8 33	14 43 8	21 52.7	13 43.2	15 57.7	1 45.4	18 1.0	2 36.6	2 46.1	10 7.1	10 0.6
27 M	2 18 56	2 56 39	21 22 31	28 6 55	21R53.8	14 52.3	16 51.7	1 54.3	17 53.5	2 38.7	2 49.8	10 9.0	10 2.8
28 Tu	2 22 53	3 56 31	4♌56 32	11♌51 29	21 54.2	16 6.5	17 46.3	2 2.4	17 46.0	2 40.8	2 53.6	10 10.9	10 5.0
29 W	2 26 49	4 56 26	18 51 48	25 57 23	21 53.7	17 24.9	18 41.5	2 9.8	17 38.6	2 42.7	2 57.4	10 12.8	10 7.1
30 Th	2 30 46	5 56 22	3♍ 8 2	10♍23 23	21 52.5	18 47.1	19 37.4	2 16.3	17 31.3	2 44.5	3 1.1	10 14.8	10 9.3
31 F	2 34 42	6 56 21	17 42 56	25 6 4	21 50.7	20 12.3	20 33.8	2 22.1	17 24.0	2 46.2	3 4.9	10 16.7	10 11.4

Astro Data	Planet Ingress	Last Aspect	☽ Ingress	Last Aspect	☽ Ingress	☽ Phases & Eclipses	Astro Data
Dy Hr Mn	Dy Hr Mn	Dy Hr Mn	Dy Hr Mn	Dy Hr Mn	Dy Hr Mn	Dy Hr Mn	1 SEPTEMBER 1975
♃⚼♆ 3 12:02	♀ ♌ 2 15:34	2 22:43 ♅ □	♌ 2 23:08	2 8:33 ♀ ☌	♍ 2 10:03	5 19:19 ● 12♍36	Julian Day # 27637
☽0S 6 5:56	♅ ♏ 8 5:14	4 23:15 ♅ ⚹	♍ 4 23:29	4 3:08 ♂ □	♎ 4 9:39	12 11:59 ☽ 19♐06	Delta T 46.1 sec
♀ D 18 1:46	♄ ♌ 17 4:56	6 21:01 ♄ ⚹	♎ 6 22:38	6 3:41 ♂ △	♏ 6 9:09	20 11:50 ○ 26♓54	SVP 05♓35'43"
☽0N 19 20:40	☉ ♎ 23 15:55	8 21:25 ♄ □	♏ 8 22:46	6 11:41 ♄ □	♐ 8 10:35	28 11:46 ☽ 4♋44	Obliquity 23°26'28"
☿ R 26 23:46		11 0:37 ♄ △	♐ 11 1:41	10 11:55 ♂ ☍	♑ 10 15:29		⚷ Chiron 27♈45.9R
	♀ ♍ 4 5:19	13 0:36 ♀ △	♑ 13 8:11	12 4:35 ♃ □	♒ 13 0:10	5 3:23 ● 11♎16	☽ Mean ☊ 25♏43.7
☽0S 3 16:47	♂ ♋ 17 8:44	15 17:35 ♄ ☍	♒ 15 17:51	15 10:40 ♂ △	♓ 15 11:40	12 1:15 ☽ 18♑06	
♄□♅ 4 18:10	☉ ♏ 24 1:06	17 20:21 ♀ ☍	♓ 18 5:32	16 7:30 ♆ □	♈ 18 0:20	20 5:06 ○ 26♈11	1 OCTOBER 1975
☽0N 17 2:29		20 11:50 ☉ ☍	♈ 20 18:07	20 5:06 ☉ ☍	♉ 20 12:43	27 22:07 ☽ 3♌52	Julian Day # 27667
♄□♅ 17 14:01		22 22:26 ♀ △	♉ 23 6:43	21 12:44 ♀ △	♊ 22 23:51		Delta T 46.2 sec
☿ D 18 10:15		25 11:18 ♀ □	♊ 25 18:13	24 10:49 ♃ ⚹	♋ 25 8:57		SVP 05♓35'41"
☽0S 31 2:15		27 21:59 ♀ ⚹	♋ 28 3:07	26 17:48 ♃ □	♌ 27 15:20		Obliquity 23°26'28"
		29 21:52 ☿ □	♌ 30 8:20	28 21:56 ♃ △	♍ 29 18:47		⚷ Chiron 26♈42.2R
				31 4:57 ♀ ☌	♎ 31 19:55		☽ Mean ☊ 24♏08.3

NOVEMBER 1975 LONGITUDE

Day	Sid.Time	☉	0 hr ☽	Noon ☽	True ☊	☿	♀	♂	♃	♄	♅	♆	♇
1 Sa	2 38 39	7♏56 22	2♎31 58	9♎59 45	21♏48.9	21♎40.1	21♍30.8	2♋27.1	17♈16.9	2♌47.8	3♏ 8.7	10♐18.7	10♎13.6
2 Su	2 42 35	8 56 25	17 28 26	24 56 58	21R 47.3	23 10.1	22 28.3	2 31.3	17R 9.9	2 49.3	3 12.4	10 20.6	10 15.7
3 M	2 46 32	9 56 30	2♏24 17	9♏49 22	21 46.2	24 41.8	23 26.4	2 34.7	17 3.1	2 50.7	3 16.2	10 22.6	10 17.8
4 Tu	2 50 28	10 56 37	17 11 13	24 28 58	21D 45.7	26 14.9	24 24.9	2 37.2	16 56.3	2 52.0	3 19.9	10 24.7	10 19.8
5 W	2 54 25	11 56 46	1♐41 51	8♐49 14	21 45.8	27 49.2	25 24.0	2 38.9	16 49.7	2 53.1	3 23.7	10 26.7	10 21.9
6 Th	2 58 22	12 56 57	15 50 41	22 45 51	21 46.3	29 24.3	26 23.5	2R 39.8	16 43.2	2 54.2	3 27.4	10 28.7	10 24.0
7 F	3 2 18	13 57 9	29 34 38	6♑16 59	21 47.1	1♏ 0.1	27 23.4	2 39.8	16 36.8	2 55.1	3 31.1	10 30.8	10 26.0
8 Sa	3 6 15	14 57 23	12♑53 2	19 23 2	21 47.8	2 36.4	28 23.8	2 38.9	16 30.6	2 55.9	3 34.9	10 32.9	10 28.0
9 Su	3 10 11	15 57 38	25 47 17	2♒ 6 13	21 48.4	4 13.0	29 24.7	2 37.2	16 24.5	2 56.7	3 38.6	10 35.0	10 30.0
10 M	3 14 8	16 57 55	8♒20 18	14 30 3	21R 48.7	5 49.9	0♎25.9	2 34.6	16 18.6	2 57.3	3 42.3	10 37.1	10 32.0
11 Tu	3 18 4	17 58 13	20 36 1	26 38 47	21 48.8	7 26.9	1 27.5	2 31.1	16 12.8	2 57.7	3 46.0	10 39.2	10 34.0
12 W	3 22 1	18 58 33	2♓38 54	8♓36 57	21 48.7	9 3.9	2 29.6	2 26.8	16 7.2	2 58.1	3 49.7	10 41.3	10 35.9
13 Th	3 25 57	19 58 54	14 33 31	20 29 8	21 48.5	10 40.9	3 32.0	2 21.6	16 1.7	2 58.4	3 53.3	10 43.4	10 37.8
14 F	3 29 54	20 59 16	26 24 19	2♈19 35	21D 48.3	12 17.9	4 34.7	2 15.5	15 56.4	2R 58.5	3 57.0	10 45.6	10 39.7
15 Sa	3 33 51	21 59 40	8♈15 24	14 12 12	21 48.3	13 54.7	5 37.9	2 8.6	15 51.3	2 58.6	4 0.6	10 47.7	10 41.6
16 Su	3 37 47	23 0 5	20 10 21	26 10 14	21 48.4	15 31.4	6 41.3	2 0.8	15 46.3	2 58.5	4 4.2	10 49.9	10 43.5
17 M	3 41 44	24 0 32	2♉12 10	8♉16 25	21 48.5	17 7.9	7 45.1	1 52.1	15 41.6	2 58.3	4 7.8	10 52.1	10 45.3
18 Tu	3 45 40	25 1 0	14 23 14	20 32 48	21R 48.7	18 44.2	8 49.3	1 42.5	15 37.0	2 58.0	4 11.4	10 54.3	10 47.1
19 W	3 49 37	26 1 30	26 45 17	3♊ 0 50	21 48.7	20 20.4	9 53.7	1 32.1	15 32.5	2 57.6	4 15.0	10 56.5	10 48.9
20 Th	3 53 33	27 2 2	9♊19 33	15 41 29	21 48.5	21 56.3	10 58.5	1 20.9	15 28.3	2 57.1	4 18.6	10 58.7	10 50.7
21 F	3 57 30	28 2 35	22 6 44	28 35 17	21 47.9	23 32.0	12 3.5	1 8.8	15 24.2	2 56.4	4 22.1	11 0.9	10 52.4
22 Sa	4 1 26	29 3 9	5♋ 7 13	11♋42 29	21 47.1	25 7.6	13 8.9	0 55.9	15 20.4	2 55.7	4 25.7	11 3.1	10 54.1
23 Su	4 5 23	0♐ 3 45	18 21 8	25 3 8	21 46.1	26 42.9	14 14.5	0 42.2	15 16.7	2 54.8	4 29.2	11 5.3	10 55.9
24 M	4 9 20	1 4 23	1♌48 28	8♌37 8	21 45.0	28 18.1	15 20.4	0 27.6	15 13.2	2 53.8	4 32.6	11 7.6	10 57.5
25 Tu	4 13 16	2 5 3	15 29 4	22 24 12	21 44.2	29 53.1	16 26.6	0 12.3	15 9.9	2 52.8	4 36.1	11 9.8	10 59.2
26 W	4 17 13	3 5 44	29 22 29	6♍23 46	21D 43.7	1♐28.0	17 33.1	29♊56.2	15 6.8	2 51.6	4 39.6	11 12.0	11 0.8
27 Th	4 21 9	4 6 27	13♍27 55	20 34 42	21 43.8	3 2.7	18 39.7	29 39.4	15 3.9	2 50.3	4 43.0	11 14.3	11 2.4
28 F	4 25 6	5 7 11	27 43 52	4♎55 5	21 44.5	4 37.2	19 46.7	29 21.9	15 1.2	2 48.8	4 46.4	11 16.5	11 4.0
29 Sa	4 29 2	6 7 57	12♎ 7 57	19 22 1	21 45.6	6 11.7	20 53.8	29 3.7	14 58.7	2 47.3	4 49.7	11 18.8	11 5.5
30 Su	4 32 59	7 8 45	26 36 45	3♏51 33	21 46.8	7 46.0	22 1.2	28 44.8	14 56.4	2 45.7	4 53.1	11 21.0	11 7.0

DECEMBER 1975 LONGITUDE

Day	Sid.Time	☉	0 hr ☽	Noon ☽	True ☊	☿	♀	♂	♃	♄	♅	♆	♇
1 M	4 36 55	8♐ 9 34	11♏ 5 49	18♏18 52	21♏47.6	9♐20.3	23♎ 8.8	28♊25.3	14♈54.3	2♌44.0	4♏56.4	11♐23.3	11♎ 8.5
2 Tu	4 40 52	9 10 24	25 30 0	2♐38 35	21R 47.8	10 54.5	24 16.6	28R 5.3	14R 52.4	2R 42.1	4 59.7	11 25.5	11 10.0
3 W	4 44 49	10 11 16	9♐43 57	16 45 30	21 47.1	12 28.6	25 24.7	27 44.7	14 50.7	2 40.2	5 3.0	11 27.8	11 11.4
4 Th	4 48 45	11 12 8	23 42 44	0♑35 12	21 45.3	14 2.7	26 32.9	27 23.5	14 49.3	2 38.1	5 6.2	11 30.1	11 12.8
5 F	4 52 42	12 13 2	7♑22 33	14 4 35	21 42.6	15 36.7	27 41.3	27 2.0	14 48.0	2 35.9	5 9.4	11 32.3	11 14.2
6 Sa	4 56 38	13 13 57	20 41 9	27 12 16	21 39.3	17 10.7	28 49.9	26 40.0	14 47.0	2 33.7	5 12.6	11 34.6	11 15.6
7 Su	5 0 35	14 14 53	3♒38 2	9♒58 40	21 35.8	18 44.8	29 58.6	26 17.7	14 46.1	2 31.3	5 15.8	11 36.9	11 16.9
8 M	5 4 31	15 15 49	16 14 26	22 25 44	21 32.6	20 18.8	1♏ 7.6	25 55.0	14 45.5	2 28.8	5 18.9	11 39.1	11 18.2
9 Tu	5 8 28	16 16 46	28 33 2	4♓36 48	21 30.2	21 52.9	2 16.7	25 32.1	14 45.0	2 26.3	5 22.0	11 41.4	11 19.4
10 W	5 12 24	17 17 44	10♓37 36	16 36 2	21D 28.9	23 26.9	3 25.9	25 8.9	14D 44.8	2 23.6	5 25.0	11 43.6	11 20.6
11 Th	5 16 21	18 18 42	22 32 42	28 28 13	21 28.8	25 1.1	4 35.3	24 45.6	14 44.8	2 20.9	5 28.1	11 45.9	11 21.8
12 F	5 20 18	19 19 41	4♈23 13	10♈18 20	21 29.7	26 35.2	5 44.9	24 22.2	14 45.0	2 18.0	5 31.1	11 48.1	11 23.0
13 Sa	5 24 14	20 20 41	16 14 11	22 11 20	21 31.4	28 9.4	6 54.6	23 58.8	14 45.4	2 15.0	5 34.0	11 50.4	11 24.1
14 Su	5 28 11	21 21 41	28 10 23	4♉11 50	21 33.3	29 43.7	8 4.5	23 35.3	14 46.1	2 12.0	5 36.9	11 52.6	11 25.2
15 M	5 32 7	22 22 42	10♉16 11	16 23 52	21R 34.8	1♑18.0	9 14.5	23 11.8	14 46.9	2 8.9	5 39.8	11 54.9	11 26.3
16 Tu	5 36 4	23 23 43	22 35 14	28 50 36	21 35.3	2 52.3	10 24.7	22 48.4	14 47.9	2 5.7	5 42.7	11 57.1	11 27.3
17 W	5 40 0	24 24 45	5♊10 12	11♊34 11	21 34.4	4 26.6	11 35.0	22 25.2	14 49.2	2 2.4	5 45.5	11 59.3	11 28.4
18 Th	5 43 57	25 25 48	18 2 37	24 35 29	21 31.8	6 1.0	12 45.4	22 2.2	14 50.6	1 59.0	5 48.3	12 1.5	11 29.3
19 F	5 47 53	26 26 51	1♋12 40	7♋54 1	21 27.6	7 35.3	13 55.9	21 39.4	14 52.3	1 55.5	5 51.0	12 3.8	11 30.3
20 Sa	5 51 50	27 27 55	14 39 17	21 28 8	21 22.0	9 9.6	15 6.6	21 16.8	14 54.2	1 51.9	5 53.7	12 6.0	11 31.2
21 Su	5 55 47	28 28 59	28 20 13	5♌15 9	21 15.7	10 43.7	16 17.4	20 54.6	14 56.2	1 48.3	5 56.4	12 8.2	11 32.1
22 M	5 59 43	29 30 4	12♌12 31	19 11 54	21 9.5	12 17.8	17 28.3	20 32.7	14 58.5	1 44.6	5 59.0	12 10.3	11 32.9
23 Tu	6 3 40	0♑31 10	26 12 53	3♍15 6	21 4.1	13 51.6	18 39.4	20 11.3	15 1.0	1 40.8	6 1.6	12 12.5	11 33.7
24 W	6 7 36	1 32 16	10♍18 13	17 21 54	21 0.3	15 25.1	19 50.5	19 50.3	15 3.6	1 36.9	6 4.1	12 14.7	11 34.5
25 Th	6 11 33	2 33 23	24 25 55	1♎30 1	20D 58.4	16 58.3	21 1.8	19 29.7	15 6.5	1 33.0	6 6.6	12 16.8	11 35.2
26 F	6 15 29	3 34 31	8♎34 0	15 37 43	20 58.2	18 30.9	22 13.1	19 9.7	15 9.6	1 29.0	6 9.1	12 19.0	11 35.9
27 Sa	6 19 26	4 35 39	22 41 1	29 43 43	20 59.2	20 3.0	23 24.6	18 50.2	15 12.8	1 24.9	6 11.5	12 21.1	11 36.6
28 Su	6 23 22	5 36 48	6♏45 40	13♏46 42	21 0.5	21 34.2	24 36.1	18 31.3	15 16.3	1 20.8	6 13.9	12 23.2	11 37.2
29 M	6 27 19	6 37 57	20 46 34	27 45 4	21R 1.2	23 4.5	25 47.8	18 13.1	15 19.9	1 16.6	6 16.2	12 25.4	11 37.8
30 Tu	6 31 16	7 39 8	4♐41 54	11♐36 45	21 0.3	24 33.6	26 59.5	17 55.5	15 23.8	1 12.3	6 18.5	12 27.5	11 38.4
31 W	6 35 12	8 40 18	18 29 18	25 19 12	20 57.2	26 1.3	28 11.4	17 38.5	15 27.8	1 8.0	6 20.7	12 29.5	11 38.9

Astro Data Dy Hr Mn	Planet Ingress Dy Hr Mn	Last Aspect Dy Hr Mn	☽ Ingress Dy Hr Mn	Last Aspect Dy Hr Mn	☽ Ingress Dy Hr Mn	☽ Phases & Eclipses Dy Hr Mn
♂ R 6 12:01	☿ ♏ 6 8:58	2 10:10 ☿ ☌	♏ 2 20:07	30 13:45 ♅ ☌	♐ 2 7:33	3 13:05 ● 10♏29
♀0S 12 2:56	♀ ♎ 9 13:52	4 12:45 ♀ ⚹	♐ 4 21:10	4 6:15 ♂ ☍	♑ 4 10:58	3 13:15:06 • P 0.959
☽0N 13 9:06	☉ ♐ 22 22:31	6 19:09 ♀ □	♑ 7 0:45	6 16:29 ♀ □	♒ 6 17:12	10 18:21 ☽ 17♒44
♄ R 14 19:25	☿ ♐ 25 1:44	9 7:28 ♀ △	♒ 9 7:59	8 18:15 ♂ △	♓ 9 2:52	18 22:28 ○ 25♉58
☽0S 27 9:29	♂ ♊ 25 18:30	10 18:21 ☉ □	♓ 11 18:42	11 5:46 ☿ □	♈ 11 15:06	18 22:23 ☍ T 1.064
		13 12:00 ☉ △	♈ 14 7:17	14 3:34 ☿ △	♉ 14 3:39	26 6:52 ☽ 3♍23
☽0N 10 17:15	♀ ♏ 7 0:29	15 15:13 ♃ ☌	♉ 16 19:38	14 21:46 ♀ ☍	♊ 16 14:12	
♃ D 10 12:39	☿ ♑ 14 4:10	18 22:28 ☉ ☍	♊ 19 6:14	18 14:39 ☉ ☍	♋ 18 21:49	3 0:50 ● 10♐13
☽0S 24 15:30	☉ ♑ 22 11:46	20 11:32 ♃ ⚹	♋ 21 14:36	20 0:53 ♀ △	♌ 21 2:54	10 14:39 ☽ 17♓55
		23 16:58 ☿ △	♌ 23 20:48	22 13:57 ♂ ⚹	♍ 23 6:28	18 14:39 ○ 26♊03
		26 0:57 ♂ ⚹	♍ 26 1:04	24 17:42 ♀ ⚹	♎ 25 9:27	25 14:52 ☽ 3♎11
		28 2:41 ♂ □	♎ 28 3:48	26 18:58 ☿ □	♏ 27 12:28	
		30 3:27 ♂ △	♏ 30 5:37	29 9:27 ♀ ☌	♐ 29 15:53	
				30 22:33 ♂ ☍	♑ 31 20:16	

Astro Data

1 NOVEMBER 1975
Julian Day # 27698
Delta T 46.3 sec
SVP 05♓35'38"
Obliquity 23°26'27"
⚷ Chiron 25♈17.5R
☽ Mean ☊ 22♏29.8

1 DECEMBER 1975
Julian Day # 27728
Delta T 46.4 sec
SVP 05♓35'34"
Obliquity 23°26'26"
⚷ Chiron 24♈07.5R
☽ Mean ☊ 20♏54.5

LONGITUDE — JANUARY 1976

Day	Sid.Time	☉	0 hr ☽	Noon ☽	True ☊	☿	♀	♂	♃	♄	♅	♆	♇
1 Th	6 39 9	9♑41 29	2♑ 6 6	8♑49 39	20♏51.6	27♑27.1	29♏23.3	17♊22.3	15♈32.1	1♌ 3.6	6♏22.9	12♐31.6	11♎39.4
2 F	6 43 5	10 42 40	15 29 34	22 5 33	20R43.9	28 50.9	0♐35.3	17R 6.8	15 36.5	0R59.2	6 25.1	12 33.7	11 39.9
3 Sa	6 47 2	11 43 50	28 37 25	5♒ 5 2	20 34.5	0♒12.1	1 47.4	16 52.0	15 41.1	0 54.7	6 27.2	12 35.7	11 40.3
4 Su	6 50 58	12 45 1	11♒28 19	17 47 18	20 24.6	1 30.3	2 59.5	16 38.0	15 45.9	0 50.1	6 29.2	12 37.8	11 40.7
5 M	6 54 55	13 46 12	24 2 6	0♓12 54	20 15.0	2 45.0	4 11.7	16 24.8	15 50.9	0 45.6	6 31.2	12 39.8	11 41.0
6 Tu	6 58 51	14 47 22	6♓20 0	12 23 44	20 6.7	3 55.6	5 24.0	16 12.4	15 56.1	0 40.9	6 33.2	12 41.8	11 41.4
7 W	7 2 48	15 48 32	18 24 33	24 22 55	20 0.4	5 1.3	6 36.3	16 0.8	16 1.4	0 36.3	6 35.1	12 43.7	11 41.6
8 Th	7 6 45	16 49 42	0♈19 24	6♈14 35	19 56.4	6 1.4	7 48.7	15 50.0	16 7.0	0 31.6	6 36.9	12 45.7	11 41.9
9 F	7 10 41	17 50 51	12 9 6	18 3 36	19D54.7	6 55.2	9 1.2	15 40.0	16 12.7	0 26.8	6 38.7	12 47.6	11 42.1
10 Sa	7 14 38	18 52 0	23 58 46	29 55 16	19 54.6	7 41.7	10 13.7	15 30.8	16 18.5	0 22.0	6 40.5	12 49.6	11 42.3
11 Su	7 18 34	19 53 8	5♉53 49	11♉55 4	19 55.4	8 20.1	11 26.3	15 22.5	16 24.6	0 17.2	6 42.2	12 51.5	11 42.4
12 M	7 22 31	20 54 16	17 59 39	24 8 10	19R56.0	8 49.4	12 38.9	15 15.0	16 30.8	0 12.4	6 43.9	12 53.4	11 42.5
13 Tu	7 26 27	21 55 23	0♊21 12	6♊39 13	19 55.5	9 8.8	13 51.6	15 8.3	16 37.2	0 7.6	6 45.5	12 55.2	11 42.6
14 W	7 30 24	22 56 30	13 2 37	19 31 43	19 52.9	9R17.6	15 4.4	15 2.4	16 43.8	0 2.7	6 47.0	12 57.1	11R42.6
15 Th	7 34 20	23 57 36	26 6 41	2♋47 34	19 47.7	9 15.0	16 17.2	14 57.4	16 50.5	29♋57.8	6 48.5	12 58.9	11 42.6
16 F	7 38 17	24 58 41	9♋34 17	16 26 37	19 40.0	9 0.8	17 30.1	14 53.2	16 57.4	29 52.9	6 50.0	13 0.7	11 42.6
17 Sa	7 42 14	25 59 46	23 24 11	0♌26 28	19 30.0	8 34.8	18 43.0	14 49.7	17 4.5	29 48.0	6 51.4	13 2.5	11 42.5
18 Su	7 46 10	27 0 51	7♌32 49	14 42 31	19 18.9	7 57.3	19 55.9	14 47.1	17 11.7	29 43.1	6 52.7	13 4.3	11 42.4
19 M	7 50 7	28 1 55	21 54 46	29 8 43	19 7.7	7 9.1	21 8.9	14 45.2	17 19.1	29 38.1	6 54.0	13 6.0	11 42.3
20 Tu	7 54 3	29 2 58	6♍23 33	13♍38 28	18 57.7	6 11.3	22 22.0	14D44.2	17 26.6	29 33.2	6 55.3	13 7.7	11 42.1
21 W	7 58 0	0♒ 4 1	20 52 45	28 5 45	18 49.9	5 5.4	23 35.1	14 43.9	17 34.3	29 28.3	6 56.5	13 9.4	11 41.9
22 Th	8 1 56	1 5 4	5♎16 57	12♎25 57	18 44.9	3 53.6	24 48.2	14 44.3	17 42.1	29 23.3	6 57.6	13 11.1	11 41.6
23 F	8 5 53	2 6 6	19 32 27	26 36 14	18D42.5	2 38.0	26 1.4	14 45.5	17 50.1	29 18.4	6 58.7	13 12.7	11 41.3
24 Sa	8 9 50	3 7 8	3♏37 13	10♏35 22	18 41.9	1 20.9	27 14.6	14 47.5	17 58.2	29 13.5	6 59.7	13 14.4	11 41.0
25 Su	8 13 46	4 8 10	17 30 43	24 23 18	18R42.1	0 4.7	28 27.9	14 50.2	18 6.5	29 8.5	7 0.7	13 16.0	11 40.7
26 M	8 17 43	5 9 11	1♐13 13	8♐ 0 31	18 41.6	28♑51.6	29 41.2	14 53.6	18 15.0	29 3.6	7 1.6	13 17.5	11 40.3
27 Tu	8 21 39	6 10 11	14 45 16	21 27 31	18 39.2	27 43.3	0♑54.6	14 57.7	18 23.5	28 58.7	7 2.4	13 19.1	11 39.9
28 W	8 25 36	7 11 11	28 7 14	4♑44 24	18 34.1	26 41.4	2 8.0	15 2.6	18 32.2	28 53.9	7 3.2	13 20.6	11 39.4
29 Th	8 29 32	8 12 10	11♑18 58	17 50 50	18 25.8	25 47.1	3 21.4	15 8.1	18 41.1	28 49.0	7 4.0	13 22.1	11 38.9
30 F	8 33 29	9 13 9	24 19 54	0♒46 2	18 14.7	25 1.0	4 34.8	15 14.3	18 50.1	28 44.2	7 4.7	13 23.6	11 38.4
31 Sa	8 37 25	10 14 6	7♒ 9 9	13 29 10	18 1.3	24 23.6	5 48.3	15 21.2	18 59.2	28 39.4	7 5.3	13 25.1	11 37.9

LONGITUDE — FEBRUARY 1976

Day	Sid.Time	☉	0 hr ☽	Noon ☽	True ☊	☿	♀	♂	♃	♄	♅	♆	♇
1 Su	8 41 22	11♒15 3	19♒45 59	25♒59 37	17♏47.0	23♑55.0	7♑ 1.8	15♊28.7	19♈ 8.5	28♋34.6	7♏ 5.9	13♐26.5	11♎37.3
2 M	8 45 19	12 15 58	2♓10 4	8♓17 27	17R32.9	23R35.0	8 15.3	15 36.9	19 17.8	28R29.9	7 6.4	13 27.9	11R36.7
3 Tu	8 49 15	13 16 52	14 21 54	20 23 38	17 20.3	23D23.5	9 28.9	15 45.7	19 27.4	28 25.2	7 6.9	13 29.2	11 36.0
4 W	8 53 12	14 17 45	26 22 56	2♈20 10	17 10.1	23 20.0	10 42.4	15 55.1	19 37.0	28 20.5	7 7.3	13 30.6	11 35.3
5 Th	8 57 8	15 18 37	8♈15 43	14 10 6	17 2.8	23 24.0	11 56.0	16 5.2	19 46.8	28 15.9	7 7.7	13 31.9	11 34.6
6 F	9 1 5	16 19 27	20 3 50	25 57 29	16 58.4	23 35.1	13 9.6	16 15.8	19 56.7	28 11.3	7 8.0	13 33.1	11 33.9
7 Sa	9 5 1	17 20 16	1♉51 42	7♉47 7	16 56.4	23 52.7	14 23.3	16 27.0	20 6.7	28 6.8	7 8.2	13 34.4	11 33.1
8 Su	9 8 58	18 21 4	13 44 26	19 44 21	16 55.9	24 16.4	15 36.9	16 38.8	20 16.8	28 2.3	7 8.4	13 35.6	11 32.3
9 M	9 12 54	19 21 50	25 47 35	1♊54 49	16 55.8	24 45.7	16 50.6	16 51.1	20 27.1	27 57.8	7 8.5	13 36.8	11 31.5
10 Tu	9 16 51	20 22 34	8♊ 6 43	14 23 57	16 55.0	25 20.1	18 4.3	17 4.0	20 37.4	27 53.5	7R 8.6	13 38.0	11 30.6
11 W	9 20 47	21 23 17	20 47 3	27 16 31	16 52.3	25 59.1	19 18.0	17 17.4	20 47.9	27 49.1	7 8.6	13 39.1	11 29.7
12 Th	9 24 44	22 23 58	3♋52 44	10♋35 55	16 47.1	26 42.5	20 31.7	17 31.4	20 58.5	27 44.9	7 8.6	13 40.2	11 28.8
13 F	9 28 41	23 24 38	17 26 12	24 23 27	16 39.2	27 29.7	21 45.4	17 45.8	21 9.2	27 40.7	7 8.5	13 41.3	11 27.9
14 Sa	9 32 37	24 25 16	1♌27 25	8♌37 36	16 28.9	28 20.6	22 59.2	18 0.7	21 20.0	27 36.5	7 8.4	13 42.3	11 26.9
15 Su	9 36 34	25 25 53	15 53 19	23 13 45	16 17.2	29 14.8	24 13.0	18 16.1	21 30.9	27 32.5	7 8.2	13 43.3	11 25.9
16 M	9 40 30	26 26 28	0♍37 52	8♍ 4 35	16 5.3	0♒12.1	25 26.7	18 32.0	21 41.9	27 28.5	7 7.9	13 44.3	11 24.8
17 Tu	9 44 27	27 27 1	15 32 44	23 1 8	15 54.6	1 12.1	26 40.5	18 48.3	21 53.0	27 24.5	7 7.6	13 45.2	11 23.8
18 W	9 48 23	28 27 34	0♎28 40	7♎54 20	15 46.1	2 14.8	27 54.4	19 5.1	22 4.3	27 20.6	7 7.2	13 46.1	11 22.7
19 Th	9 52 20	29 28 4	15 17 12	22 36 34	15 40.4	3 19.9	29 8.2	19 22.3	22 15.6	27 16.8	7 6.8	13 47.0	11 21.6
20 F	9 56 16	0♓28 34	29 51 51	7♏ 2 38	15 37.5	4 27.2	0♒22.0	19 39.9	22 27.0	27 13.1	7 6.4	13 47.9	11 20.4
21 Sa	10 0 13	1 29 2	14♏ 8 41	21 9 54	15D36.7	5 36.6	1 35.9	19 57.9	22 38.5	27 9.5	7 5.8	13 48.7	11 19.3
22 Su	10 4 10	2 29 29	28 6 18	4♐57 58	15R36.9	6 48.0	2 49.8	20 16.4	22 50.1	27 5.9	7 5.3	13 49.5	11 18.1
23 M	10 8 6	3 29 55	11♐45 6	18 27 55	15 36.7	8 1.2	4 3.7	20 35.2	23 1.8	27 2.4	7 4.6	13 50.2	11 16.9
24 Tu	10 12 3	4 30 20	25 6 40	1♑41 36	15 35.0	9 16.2	5 17.6	20 54.4	23 13.5	26 59.0	7 3.9	13 50.9	11 15.7
25 W	10 15 59	5 30 43	8♑12 57	14 40 59	15 30.7	10 32.8	6 31.5	21 14.0	23 25.4	26 55.7	7 3.2	13 51.6	11 14.4
26 Th	10 19 56	6 31 4	21 5 52	27 27 48	15 23.7	11 50.9	7 45.5	21 34.0	23 37.4	26 52.5	7 2.4	13 52.3	11 13.1
27 F	10 23 52	7 31 25	3♒46 55	10♒ 3 22	15 14.0	13 10.6	8 59.4	21 54.3	23 49.4	26 49.3	7 1.6	13 52.9	11 11.8
28 Sa	10 27 49	8 31 43	16 17 14	22 28 36	15 2.4	14 31.7	10 13.4	22 15.0	24 1.5	26 46.3	7 0.7	13 53.5	11 10.5
29 Su	10 31 45	9 32 0	28 37 33	4♓44 11	14 49.7	15 54.1	11 27.3	22 36.1	24 13.7	26 43.3	6 59.8	13 54.0	11 9.2

Astro Data

	Dy Hr Mn
☽0N	7 2:34
☿ R	14 6:42
♇ R	14 11:41
☽0S	20 22:29
♂ D	20 21:27
♄□♆	2 7:56
☽0N	3 11:40
☿ D	3 22:57
♅ R	10 22:11
☽0S	17 7:46

Planet Ingress

	Dy Hr Mn
♀ ♐	1 12:14
☿ ♒	2 20:22
♄ ♋	14 13:17
☉ ♒	20 22:25
☿ ♑	25 1:30
♀ ♑	26 6:09
☿ ♒	15 19:03
☉ ♓	19 12:40
♀ ♒	19 16:50

Last Aspect / ☽ Ingress (January)

Last Aspect Dy Hr Mn		☽ Ingress Dy Hr Mn
2 0:13	♃ □	♒ 3 2:33
4 9:38	♂ △	♓ 5 11:35
6 19:17	♂ □	♈ 7 23:21
9 12:40	☉ □	♉ 10 12:10
12 6:13	☉ △	♊ 12 23:19
14 6:54	♃ ✶	♋ 15 7:00
17 10:51	♄ ☌	♌ 17 11:15
18 22:37	♀ △	♍ 19 13:25
21 14:13	♄ ✶	♎ 21 15:10
23 16:31	♄ □	♏ 23 17:48
25 20:13	♄ △	♐ 25 21:51
27 6:34	♃ △	♑ 28 3:24
30 8:09	♄ ☍	♒ 30 10:34

Last Aspect / ☽ Ingress (February)

Last Aspect Dy Hr Mn		☽ Ingress Dy Hr Mn
31 22:47	♃ ✶	♓ 1 19:47
4 3:55	♄ △	♈ 4 7:17
6 16:26	♄ □	♉ 6 20:13
9 4:15	♄ ✶	♊ 9 8:16
11 1:13	☉ △	♋ 11 16:59
13 18:23	☿ ☍	♌ 13 21:32
15 16:43	☉ ☍	♍ 15 22:59
17 19:29	♀ △	♎ 17 23:14
19 19:38	♄ □	♏ 20 0:14
21 22:16	♄ △	♐ 22 3:18
23 20:32	♃ △	♑ 24 8:54
26 10:50	♄ ☍	♒ 26 16:48
28 15:16	♃ ✶	♓ 29 2:42

☽ Phases & Eclipses

Dy Hr Mn	
1 14:40	● 10♑19
9 12:40	☽ 18♈23
17 4:47	○ 26♋12
23 23:04	☽ 3♏05
31 6:20	● 10♒30
8 10:05	☽ 18♉47
15 16:43	○ 26♌08
22 8:16	☽ 2♐50
29 23:25	● 10♓31

Astro Data

1 JANUARY 1976
Julian Day # 27759
Delta T 46.5 sec
SVP 05♓35'28"
Obliquity 23°26'26"
⚷ Chiron 23♈35.4R
☽ Mean ☊ 19♏16.0

1 FEBRUARY 1976
Julian Day # 27790
Delta T 46.5 sec
SVP 05♓35'23"
Obliquity 23°26'26"
⚷ Chiron 23♈56.4
☽ Mean ☊ 17♏37.5

MARCH 1976 LONGITUDE

Day	Sid.Time	☉	0 hr ☽	Noon ☽	True ☊	☿	♀	♂	♃	♄	♅	♆	♇
1 M	10 35 42	10♓32 15	10♓48 33	16♓50 48	14♏37.2	17♒17.9	12♒41.3	22♊57.5	24♈26.0	26♋40.4	6♏58.8	13♐54.6	11♎ 7.8
2 Tu	10 39 39	11 32 28	22 51 2	28 49 27	14R 26.0	18 43.0	13 55.2	23 19.2	24 38.4	26R 37.6	6R 57.7	13 55.1	11R 6.4
3 W	10 43 35	12 32 40	4♈46 14	10♈41 38	14 16.8	20 9.4	15 9.2	23 41.2	24 50.8	26 35.0	6 56.6	13 55.5	11 5.0
4 Th	10 47 32	13 32 49	16 35 58	22 29 34	14 10.3	21 37.0	16 23.2	24 3.6	25 3.3	26 32.4	6 55.5	13 55.9	11 3.6
5 F	10 51 28	14 32 57	28 22 51	4♉16 16	14 6.5	23 5.7	17 37.2	24 26.2	25 15.9	26 29.9	6 54.3	13 56.3	11 2.2
6 Sa	10 55 25	15 33 2	10♉10 18	16 5 30	14D 5.0	24 35.7	18 51.1	24 49.2	25 28.5	26 27.5	6 53.1	13 56.7	11 0.7
7 Su	10 59 21	16 33 6	22 2 28	28 1 47	14 5.2	26 6.9	20 5.1	25 12.4	25 41.3	26 25.2	6 51.8	13 57.0	10 59.2
8 M	11 3 18	17 33 8	4♊ 4 7	10♊10 7	14 6.1	27 39.2	21 19.1	25 36.0	25 54.1	26 23.0	6 50.4	13 57.3	10 57.7
9 Tu	11 7 14	18 33 7	16 20 26	22 35 45	14R 6.8	29 12.7	22 33.1	25 59.8	26 6.9	26 20.9	6 49.1	13 57.5	10 56.2
10 W	11 11 11	19 33 4	28 56 39	5♋23 44	14 6.3	0♓47.3	23 47.1	26 23.9	26 19.8	26 18.9	6 47.6	13 57.7	10 54.7
11 Th	11 15 8	20 32 59	11♋57 28	18 38 18	14 4.0	2 23.2	25 1.0	26 48.3	26 32.8	26 17.1	6 46.2	13 57.9	10 53.2
12 F	11 19 4	21 32 52	25 26 28	2♌22 6	13 59.6	4 0.1	26 15.0	27 12.9	26 45.9	26 15.3	6 44.7	13 58.1	10 51.6
13 Sa	11 23 1	22 32 42	9♌25 8	16 35 19	13 53.3	5 38.3	27 29.0	27 37.7	26 59.0	26 13.6	6 43.1	13 58.2	10 50.1
14 Su	11 26 57	23 32 31	23 52 11	1♍15 2	13 45.7	7 17.6	28 43.0	28 2.8	27 12.1	26 12.1	6 41.5	13 58.2	10 48.5
15 M	11 30 54	24 32 17	8♍42 59	16 14 58	13 37.8	8 58.1	29 57.0	28 28.2	27 25.3	26 10.6	6 39.9	13R 58.3	10 46.9
16 Tu	11 34 50	25 32 1	23 49 47	1♎26 8	13 30.5	10 39.8	1♓10.9	28 53.8	27 38.6	26 9.3	6 38.2	13 58.3	10 45.3
17 W	11 38 47	26 31 43	9♎ 2 42	16 38 11	13 24.8	12 22.6	2 24.9	29 19.5	27 51.9	26 8.0	6 36.5	13 58.3	10 43.7
18 Th	11 42 43	27 31 23	24 11 22	1♏41 11	13 21.2	14 6.8	3 38.9	29 45.6	28 5.3	26 6.9	6 34.7	13 58.2	10 42.1
19 F	11 46 40	28 31 1	9♏ 6 44	16 27 14	13D 19.8	15 52.1	4 52.9	0♋11.8	28 18.7	26 5.9	6 32.9	13 58.1	10 40.5
20 Sa	11 50 36	29 30 38	23 42 11	0♐51 12	13 20.1	17 38.7	6 6.9	0 38.2	28 32.2	26 4.9	6 31.1	13 58.0	10 38.9
21 Su	11 54 33	0♈30 13	7♐54 5	14 50 50	13 21.3	19 26.6	7 20.9	1 4.9	28 45.7	26 4.1	6 29.2	13 57.9	10 37.3
22 M	11 58 30	1 29 46	21 41 29	28 26 16	13R 22.5	21 15.7	8 34.9	1 31.7	28 59.3	26 3.4	6 27.3	13 57.7	10 35.6
23 Tu	12 2 26	2 29 18	5♑ 5 26	11♑39 19	13 22.9	23 6.1	9 48.9	1 58.7	29 12.9	26 2.8	6 25.4	13 57.5	10 34.0
24 W	12 6 23	3 28 48	18 8 16	24 32 40	13 21.8	24 57.8	11 2.9	2 26.0	29 26.6	26 2.4	6 23.4	13 57.2	10 32.3
25 Th	12 10 19	4 28 16	0♒52 54	7♒ 9 21	13 18.9	26 50.8	12 16.9	2 53.4	29 40.3	26 2.0	6 21.4	13 56.9	10 30.7
26 F	12 14 16	5 27 42	13 22 22	19 32 19	13 14.3	28 45.1	13 30.9	3 21.0	29 54.0	26 1.7	6 19.4	13 56.6	10 29.0
27 Sa	12 18 12	6 27 6	25 39 31	1♓44 16	13 8.3	0♈40.6	14 44.9	3 48.8	0♉ 7.8	26D 1.6	6 17.3	13 56.3	10 27.3
28 Su	12 22 9	7 26 28	7♓46 51	13 47 31	13 1.7	2 37.4	15 58.9	4 16.8	0 21.6	26 1.6	6 15.2	13 55.9	10 25.6
29 M	12 26 5	8 25 49	19 46 30	25 44 3	12 55.1	4 35.4	17 12.9	4 45.0	0 35.5	26 1.6	6 13.0	13 55.5	10 24.0
30 Tu	12 30 2	9 25 7	1♈40 23	7♈35 43	12 49.2	6 34.5	18 26.8	5 13.3	0 49.4	26 1.8	6 10.9	13 55.0	10 22.3
31 W	12 33 59	10 24 24	13 30 17	19 24 19	12 44.6	8 34.8	19 40.8	5 41.8	1 3.3	26 2.1	6 8.7	13 54.6	10 20.6

APRIL 1976 LONGITUDE

Day	Sid.Time	☉	0 hr ☽	Noon ☽	True ☊	☿	♀	♂	♃	♄	♅	♆	♇
1 Th	12 37 55	11♈23 38	25♈18 5	1♉11 51	12♏41.5	10♈36.2	20♓54.8	6♋10.4	1♉17.3	26♋ 2.5	6♏ 6.5	13♐54.0	10♎18.9
2 F	12 41 52	12 22 51	7♉ 5 55	13 0 37	12D 40.1	12 38.5	22 8.8	6 39.3	1 31.3	26 3.0	6R 4.2	13R 53.5	10R 17.3
3 Sa	12 45 48	13 22 1	18 56 18	24 53 23	12 40.1	14 41.6	23 22.7	7 8.2	1 45.3	26 3.7	6 1.9	13 52.9	10 15.6
4 Su	12 49 45	14 21 9	0♊52 17	6♊53 27	12 41.2	16 45.4	24 36.7	7 37.4	1 59.4	26 4.4	5 59.6	13 52.3	10 13.9
5 M	12 53 41	15 20 15	12 57 23	19 4 35	12 42.9	18 49.8	25 50.7	8 6.7	2 13.4	26 5.3	5 57.3	13 51.7	10 12.3
6 Tu	12 57 38	16 19 19	25 15 35	1♋30 54	12 44.6	20 54.4	27 4.6	8 36.1	2 27.5	26 6.2	5 55.0	13 51.1	10 10.6
7 W	13 1 34	17 18 20	7♋51 4	14 16 37	12R 45.8	22 59.2	28 18.6	9 5.7	2 41.7	26 7.3	5 52.6	13 50.4	10 8.9
8 Th	13 5 31	18 17 19	20 47 59	27 25 35	12 46.1	25 3.8	29 32.5	9 35.4	2 55.8	26 8.5	5 50.2	13 49.7	10 7.3
9 F	13 9 28	19 16 16	4♌ 9 47	11♌ 0 48	12 45.3	27 8.0	0♈46.4	10 5.2	3 10.0	26 9.8	5 47.8	13 48.9	10 5.6
10 Sa	13 13 24	20 15 10	17 58 45	25 3 35	12 43.5	29 11.5	2 0.3	10 35.2	3 24.2	26 11.2	5 45.4	13 48.1	10 4.0
11 Su	13 17 21	21 14 2	2♍15 5	9♍32 51	12 41.1	1♉13.8	3 14.2	11 5.3	3 38.4	26 12.7	5 43.0	13 47.3	10 2.3
12 M	13 21 17	22 12 52	16 56 18	24 24 41	12 38.3	3 14.8	4 28.1	11 35.6	3 52.6	26 14.3	5 40.5	13 46.5	10 0.7
13 Tu	13 25 14	23 11 40	1♎57 1	9♎32 14	12 35.7	5 14.0	5 42.0	12 5.9	4 6.9	26 16.0	5 38.1	13 45.6	9 59.1
14 W	13 29 10	24 10 25	17 9 8	24 46 28	12 33.8	7 11.0	6 55.9	12 36.4	4 21.2	26 17.8	5 35.6	13 44.7	9 57.5
15 Th	13 33 7	25 9 8	2♏22 58	9♏57 24	12D 32.7	9 5.7	8 9.8	13 7.0	4 35.4	26 19.7	5 33.1	13 43.8	9 55.9
16 F	13 37 3	26 7 50	17 28 39	24 55 41	12 32.6	10 57.5	9 23.7	13 37.7	4 49.7	26 21.8	5 30.6	13 42.9	9 54.3
17 Sa	13 41 0	27 6 30	2♐17 40	9♐33 55	12 33.2	12 46.2	10 37.6	14 8.5	5 4.0	26 23.9	5 28.1	13 41.9	9 52.7
18 Su	13 44 57	28 5 8	16 43 55	23 47 22	12 34.2	14 31.6	11 51.4	14 39.5	5 18.3	26 26.1	5 25.6	13 40.9	9 51.1
19 M	13 48 53	29 3 44	0♑44 6	7♑34 6	12 35.3	16 13.3	13 5.3	15 10.5	5 32.7	26 28.5	5 23.0	13 39.9	9 49.5
20 Tu	13 52 50	0♉ 2 19	14 17 31	20 54 33	12 36.2	17 51.2	14 19.2	15 41.7	5 47.0	26 30.9	5 20.5	13 38.9	9 48.0
21 W	13 56 46	1 0 52	27 25 33	3♒50 55	12R 36.6	19 25.0	15 33.0	16 12.9	6 1.3	26 33.5	5 17.9	13 37.8	9 46.4
22 Th	14 0 43	1 59 24	10♒11 4	16 26 29	12 36.5	20 54.5	16 46.9	16 44.3	6 15.7	26 36.1	5 15.4	13 36.7	9 44.9
23 F	14 4 39	2 57 53	22 37 39	28 45 5	12 36.0	22 19.6	18 0.8	17 15.7	6 30.1	26 38.8	5 12.8	13 35.6	9 43.4
24 Sa	14 8 36	3 56 22	4♓49 15	10♓50 39	12 35.1	23 40.1	19 14.6	17 47.3	6 44.4	26 41.7	5 10.3	13 34.5	9 41.9
25 Su	14 12 32	4 54 48	16 49 45	22 46 59	12 34.0	24 56.0	20 28.5	18 19.0	6 58.8	26 44.6	5 7.7	13 33.3	9 40.4
26 M	14 16 29	5 53 13	28 42 46	4♈37 30	12 33.0	26 7.0	21 42.3	18 50.8	7 13.1	26 47.7	5 5.2	13 32.2	9 39.0
27 Tu	14 20 26	6 51 36	10♈31 34	16 25 17	12 32.2	27 13.2	22 56.1	19 22.6	7 27.5	26 50.8	5 2.6	13 31.0	9 37.5
28 W	14 24 22	7 49 57	22 19 0	28 13 0	12 31.6	28 14.4	24 10.0	19 54.6	7 41.9	26 54.0	5 0.1	13 29.7	9 36.1
29 Th	14 28 19	8 48 17	4♉ 7 36	10♉ 3 3	12D 31.4	29 10.6	25 23.8	20 26.6	7 56.2	26 57.4	4 57.5	13 28.5	9 34.7
30 F	14 32 15	9 46 35	15 59 38	21 57 37	12 31.3	0♊ 1.6	26 37.6	20 58.8	8 10.6	27 0.8	4 55.0	13 27.2	9 33.3

Astro Data Dy Hr Mn	Planet Ingress Dy Hr Mn	Last Aspect Dy Hr Mn	☽ Ingress Dy Hr Mn	Last Aspect Dy Hr Mn	☽ Ingress Dy Hr Mn	☽ Phases & Eclipses Dy Hr Mn	Astro Data
☽0N 1 19:18	☿ ♓ 9 12:02	2 7:33 ♄ △	♈ 2 14:22	1 1:31 ♄ □	♉ 1 9:34	9 4:38 ☽ 18♊45	1 MARCH 1976
♃□♄ 9 22:34	♀ ♓ 15 0:59	4 20:11 ♄ □	♉ 5 3:18	3 14:22 ♄ ⚹	♊ 3 22:15	16 2:53 ○ 25♍39	Julian Day # 27819
☽0S 15 18:41	♂ ♋ 18 13:15	7 9:22 ☿ □	♊ 7 15:56	6 3:53 ♀ □	♋ 6 9:06	22 18:54 ☽ 2♑17	Delta T 46.6 sec
♆ R 15 20:39	☉ ♈ 20 11:50	9 19:03 ♂ ☌	♋ 10 1:59	8 9:42 ♄ ☌	♌ 8 16:36	30 17:08 ● 10♈07	SVP 05♓35'20"
♃⚼♆ 21 21:12	☿ ♈ 26 15:36	12 2:21 ♃ □	♌ 12 7:55	10 4:10 ☉ △	♍ 10 20:16		Obliquity 23°26'27"
♄ D 27 19:58	♃ ♉ 26 10:25	14 8:37 ♀ ☍	♍ 14 9:59	12 14:57 ♄ ⚹	♎ 12 20:54	7 19:02 ☽ 18♋05	⚷ Chiron 25♈00.0
☿0N 28 12:23		16 8:14 ♂ □	♎ 16 9:44	14 14:26 ♄ □	♏ 14 20:14	14 11:49 ○ 24♎39	☽ Mean ☊ 16♏05.4
☽0N 29 1:20	♀ ♈ 8 8:56	18 9:10 ♂ △	♏ 18 9:17	16 14:22 ♄ △	♐ 16 20:15	21 7:14 ☽ 1♒19	
	☿ ♉ 10 9:29	20 10:28 ☉ △	♐ 20 10:34	18 20:52 ☉ △	♑ 18 22:43	29 10:19 ● 9♉13	1 APRIL 1976
♀0N 11 5:08	☉ ♉ 19 23:03	22 13:13 ♃ △	♑ 22 14:48	20 22:23 ♄ ☍	♒ 21 4:47	29 10:23:30 ✔ A 6'41"	Julian Day # 27850
☽0S 12 5:27	☿ ♊ 29 23:11	24 21:39 ♃ □	♒ 24 22:19	22 23:20 ☿ □	♓ 23 14:28		Delta T 46.7 sec
♃☍♅ 18 10:16		26 1:06 ♆ ⚹	♓ 27 8:34	25 20:06 ♄ △	♈ 26 2:37		SVP 05♓35'17"
☽0N 25 6:56		29 12:36 ♄ △	♈ 29 20:37	28 9:22 ♄ □	♉ 28 15:37		Obliquity 23°26'27"
							⚷ Chiron 26♈39.7
							☽ Mean ☊ 14♏26.8

LONGITUDE — MAY 1976

Day	Sid.Time	☉	0 hr ☽	Noon ☽	True ☊	☿	♀	♂	♃	♄	♅	♆	♇
1 Sa	14 36 12	10♉44 51	27♉57 15	3♊58 49	12♏31.4	0♊47.5	27♈51.4	21♋31.0	8♉24.9	27♋ 4.3	4♏52.4	13♐25.9	9♎31.9
2 Su	14 40 8	11 43 5	10♊ 2 34	16 8 49	12R 31.5	1 28.1	29 5.2	22 3.4	8 39.3	27 7.9	4R 49.9	13R 24.6	9R 30.5
3 M	14 44 5	12 41 18	22 17 51	28 29 57	12 31.6	2 3.5	0♉19.0	22 35.8	8 53.6	27 11.6	4 47.3	13 23.3	9 29.2
4 Tu	14 48 1	13 39 29	4♋45 28	11♋ 4 41	12 31.5	2 33.5	1 32.8	23 8.3	9 8.0	27 15.4	4 44.8	13 22.0	9 27.8
5 W	14 51 58	14 37 37	17 27 57	23 55 34	12 31.3	2 58.2	2 46.6	23 40.9	9 22.3	27 19.3	4 42.3	13 20.6	9 26.5
6 Th	14 55 55	15 35 44	0♌27 52	7♌ 5 7	12 31.1	3 17.6	4 0.4	24 13.6	9 36.6	27 23.3	4 39.8	13 19.2	9 25.3
7 F	14 59 51	16 33 49	13 47 34	20 35 25	12D 31.0	3 31.6	5 14.2	24 46.3	9 50.9	27 27.3	4 37.3	13 17.8	9 24.0
8 Sa	15 3 48	17 31 52	27 28 47	4♍27 44	12 31.1	3 40.4	6 27.9	25 19.2	10 5.2	27 31.5	4 34.8	13 16.4	9 22.8
9 Su	15 7 44	18 29 52	11♍32 11	18 41 59	12 31.4	3R 44.0	7 41.7	25 52.1	10 19.5	27 35.7	4 32.4	13 15.0	9 21.6
10 M	15 11 41	19 27 51	25 56 49	3♎16 14	12 31.9	3 42.6	8 55.4	26 25.1	10 33.7	27 40.0	4 29.9	13 13.6	9 20.4
11 Tu	15 15 37	20 25 48	10♎39 40	18 6 24	12 32.6	3 36.2	10 9.1	26 58.1	10 48.0	27 44.4	4 27.5	13 12.1	9 19.2
12 W	15 19 34	21 23 44	25 35 35	3♏ 6 16	12 33.1	3 25.3	11 22.9	27 31.2	11 2.2	27 48.9	4 25.1	13 10.6	9 18.1
13 Th	15 23 30	22 21 37	10♏37 25	18 7 59	12R 33.4	3 9.9	12 36.6	28 4.4	11 16.4	27 53.4	4 22.7	13 9.2	9 16.9
14 F	15 27 27	23 19 29	25 36 52	3♐ 3 4	12 33.2	2 50.5	13 50.3	28 37.7	11 30.6	27 58.1	4 20.3	13 7.7	9 15.8
15 Sa	15 31 23	24 17 20	10♐25 34	17 43 33	12 32.4	2 27.4	15 4.0	29 11.0	11 44.7	28 2.8	4 18.0	13 6.2	9 14.8
16 Su	15 35 20	25 15 10	24 56 14	2♑ 3 4	12 31.1	2 1.0	16 17.8	29 44.4	11 58.9	28 7.6	4 15.6	13 4.7	9 13.7
17 M	15 39 17	26 12 58	9♑ 3 36	15 57 35	12 29.5	1 31.9	17 31.5	0♌17.9	12 13.0	28 12.5	4 13.3	13 3.1	9 12.7
18 Tu	15 43 13	27 10 44	22 44 54	29 25 35	12 27.7	1 0.5	18 45.2	0 51.4	12 27.1	28 17.4	4 11.0	13 1.6	9 11.7
19 W	15 47 10	28 8 30	5♒59 49	12♒27 50	12 26.2	0 27.5	19 58.9	1 25.0	12 41.2	28 22.5	4 8.8	13 0.0	9 10.8
20 Th	15 51 6	29 6 14	18 50 3	25 6 53	12D 25.2	29♉53.3	21 12.6	1 58.7	12 55.2	28 27.6	4 6.5	12 58.5	9 9.8
21 F	15 55 3	0♊ 3 58	1♓18 52	7♓26 31	12 24.9	29 18.7	22 26.3	2 32.4	13 9.3	28 32.8	4 4.3	12 56.9	9 8.9
22 Sa	15 58 59	1 1 40	13 30 25	19 31 10	12 25.4	28 44.2	23 40.0	3 6.2	13 23.2	28 38.0	4 2.1	12 55.3	9 8.0
23 Su	16 2 56	1 59 21	25 29 20	1♈25 31	12 26.5	28 10.4	24 53.7	3 40.1	13 37.2	28 43.3	3 59.9	12 53.8	9 7.2
24 M	16 6 52	2 57 1	7♈20 17	13 14 10	12 28.0	27 38.0	26 7.5	4 14.0	13 51.1	28 48.7	3 57.8	12 52.2	9 6.3
25 Tu	16 10 49	3 54 40	19 7 42	25 1 23	12 29.6	27 7.3	27 21.2	4 48.0	14 5.0	28 54.2	3 55.7	12 50.6	9 5.5
26 W	16 14 46	4 52 19	0♉55 40	6♉50 59	12R 30.8	26 39.0	28 34.9	5 22.1	14 18.9	28 59.7	3 53.6	12 49.0	9 4.8
27 Th	16 18 42	5 49 56	12 47 42	18 46 10	12 31.3	26 13.4	29 48.6	5 56.2	14 32.8	29 5.3	3 51.6	12 47.4	9 4.0
28 F	16 22 39	6 47 32	24 46 41	0♊49 33	12 30.7	25 51.1	1♊ 2.3	6 30.4	14 46.5	29 11.0	3 49.5	12 45.8	9 3.3
29 Sa	16 26 35	7 45 7	6♊54 58	13 3 8	12 28.9	25 32.3	2 16.0	7 4.6	15 0.3	29 16.8	3 47.6	12 44.1	9 2.6
30 Su	16 30 32	8 42 41	19 14 14	25 28 23	12 25.9	25 17.2	3 29.7	7 38.9	15 14.0	29 22.6	3 45.6	12 42.5	9 2.0
31 M	16 34 28	9 40 13	1♋45 43	8♋ 6 19	12 21.9	25 6.2	4 43.4	8 13.3	15 27.7	29 28.4	3 43.7	12 40.9	9 1.4

LONGITUDE — JUNE 1976

Day	Sid.Time	☉	0 hr ☽	Noon ☽	True ☊	☿	♀	♂	♃	♄	♅	♆	♇
1 Tu	16 38 25	10♊37 45	14♋30 16	20♋57 38	12♏17.4	24♉59.4	5♊57.1	8♌47.7	15♉41.4	29♋34.4	3♏41.8	12♐39.3	9♎ 0.8
2 W	16 42 22	11 35 15	27 28 28	4♌ 2 50	12R 13.0	24D 57.0	7 10.8	9 22.2	15 55.0	29 40.3	3R 40.0	12R 37.7	9R 0.2
3 Th	16 46 18	12 32 44	10♌40 47	17 22 22	12 9.2	24 59.0	8 24.5	9 56.7	16 8.5	29 46.4	3 38.2	12 36.0	8 59.7
4 F	16 50 15	13 30 12	24 7 36	0♍56 33	12 6.4	25 5.4	9 38.2	10 31.3	16 22.0	29 52.5	3 36.4	12 34.4	8 59.2
5 Sa	16 54 11	14 27 39	7♍49 13	14 45 36	12D 5.1	25 16.4	10 51.9	11 6.0	16 35.5	29 58.7	3 34.7	12 32.8	8 58.7
6 Su	16 58 8	15 25 4	21 45 38	28 49 15	12 5.0	25 31.8	12 5.6	11 40.7	16 48.9	0♌ 4.9	3 33.0	12 31.2	8 58.3
7 M	17 2 4	16 22 28	5♎56 17	13♎ 6 33	12 6.0	25 51.6	13 19.2	12 15.4	17 2.3	0 11.2	3 31.3	12 29.5	8 57.9
8 Tu	17 6 1	17 19 51	20 19 44	27 35 27	12 7.4	26 15.9	14 32.9	12 50.2	17 15.6	0 17.5	3 29.7	12 27.9	8 57.5
9 W	17 9 57	18 17 13	4♏53 13	12♏12 29	12R 8.5	26 44.5	15 46.6	13 25.1	17 28.9	0 23.9	3 28.1	12 26.3	8 57.2
10 Th	17 13 54	19 14 34	19 32 35	26 52 46	12 8.4	27 17.4	17 0.3	13 60.0	17 42.1	0 30.3	3 26.6	12 24.7	8 56.9
11 F	17 17 51	20 11 54	4♐12 15	11♐30 13	12 6.8	27 54.4	18 14.0	14 34.9	17 55.3	0 36.8	3 25.1	12 23.1	8 56.6
12 Sa	17 21 47	21 9 13	18 45 50	25 58 17	12 3.4	28 35.6	19 27.6	15 9.9	18 8.4	0 43.4	3 23.6	12 21.5	8 56.3
13 Su	17 25 44	22 6 32	3♑ 6 49	10♑10 45	11 58.3	29 20.7	20 41.3	15 45.0	18 21.4	0 50.0	3 22.2	12 19.9	8 56.1
14 M	17 29 40	23 3 50	17 9 33	24 2 45	11 52.1	0♊ 9.9	21 55.0	16 20.1	18 34.4	0 56.6	3 20.9	12 18.3	8 56.0
15 Tu	17 33 37	24 1 7	0♒50 3	7♒31 18	11 45.5	1 2.9	23 8.7	16 55.2	18 47.4	1 3.3	3 19.6	12 16.7	8 55.8
16 W	17 37 33	24 58 24	14 6 28	20 35 39	11 39.3	1 59.7	24 22.4	17 30.4	19 0.3	1 10.0	3 18.3	12 15.1	8 55.7
17 Th	17 41 30	25 55 41	26 59 4	3♓17 4	11 34.3	3 0.2	25 36.1	18 5.6	19 13.1	1 16.8	3 17.0	12 13.6	8 55.6
18 F	17 45 26	26 52 57	9♓30 4	15 38 33	11 30.8	4 4.3	26 49.8	18 40.9	19 25.8	1 23.6	3 15.9	12 12.0	8D 55.6
19 Sa	17 49 23	27 50 12	21 43 4	27 44 13	11D 29.2	5 12.1	28 3.5	19 16.3	19 38.5	1 30.5	3 14.7	12 10.5	8 55.6
20 Su	17 53 20	28 47 28	3♈42 38	9♈38 58	11 29.1	6 23.4	29 17.2	19 51.7	19 51.2	1 37.4	3 13.6	12 8.9	8 55.6
21 M	17 57 16	29 44 43	15 33 51	21 27 57	11 30.0	7 38.3	0♋30.9	20 27.1	20 3.8	1 44.3	3 12.6	12 7.4	8 55.6
22 Tu	18 1 13	0♋41 59	27 21 54	3♉16 19	11 31.3	8 56.6	1 44.7	21 2.6	20 16.3	1 51.3	3 11.6	12 5.9	8 55.7
23 W	18 5 9	1 39 14	9♉11 47	15 8 52	11R 32.1	10 18.3	2 58.4	21 38.2	20 28.7	1 58.3	3 10.6	12 4.3	8 55.9
24 Th	18 9 6	2 36 29	21 8 3	27 9 50	11 31.6	11 43.4	4 12.1	22 13.8	20 41.1	2 5.4	3 9.7	12 2.8	8 56.0
25 F	18 13 2	3 33 43	3♊14 35	9♊22 39	11 29.2	13 11.8	5 25.8	22 49.4	20 53.4	2 12.5	3 8.9	12 1.4	8 56.2
26 Sa	18 16 59	4 30 58	15 34 18	21 49 45	11 24.7	14 43.5	6 39.6	23 25.1	21 5.6	2 19.7	3 8.1	11 59.9	8 56.4
27 Su	18 20 55	5 28 13	28 9 8	4♋32 31	11 17.9	16 18.5	7 53.3	24 0.8	21 17.7	2 26.8	3 7.3	11 58.4	8 56.7
28 M	18 24 52	6 25 27	10♋59 52	17 31 7	11 9.4	17 56.8	9 7.1	24 36.6	21 29.8	2 34.1	3 6.6	11 57.0	8 57.0
29 Tu	18 28 49	7 22 41	24 6 9	0♌44 46	10 60.0	19 38.2	10 20.8	25 12.5	21 41.8	2 41.3	3 5.9	11 55.5	8 57.3
30 W	18 32 45	8 19 55	7♌26 46	14 11 53	10 50.5	21 22.7	11 34.6	25 48.4	21 53.7	2 48.6	3 5.3	11 54.1	8 57.6

Astro Data

	Dy Hr Mn
♃⊼♇	5 6:32
☽0S	9 14:36
☿ R	9 5:04
♄□♆	15 12:48
♃⊼♆	20 5:00
☽0N	22 13:37
☿ D	2 1:20
☽0S	5 21:51
☽0N	18 21:59
♇ D	18 21:43

Planet Ingress

	Dy Hr Mn
♀ ♉	2 17:49
♂ ♌	16 11:10
☿ ♉	19 19:21
☉ ♊	20 22:21
♀ ♊	27 3:43
♄ ♌	5 5:08
☿ ♊	13 19:20
♀ ♋	20 13:56
☉ ♋	21 6:24

Last Aspect / ☽ Ingress

Last Aspect Dy Hr Mn		☽ Ingress Dy Hr Mn
30 22:14	♄ ⚹	♊ 1 4:05
2 6:37	♆ ☍	♋ 3 14:53
5 18:21	♄ ☌	♌ 5 23:09
7 5:17	☉ □	♍ 8 4:21
10 2:51	♄ ⚹	♎ 10 6:39
12 3:34	♄ □	♏ 12 7:03
14 5:02	♂ △	♐ 14 7:04
15 4:23	♆ ☌	♑ 16 8:31
18 10:01	♄ ☍	♒ 18 13:02
20 21:22	☉ □	♓ 20 21:27
23 6:35	♄ △	♈ 23 9:07
25 20:03	♄ □	♉ 25 22:07
28 8:49	♄ ⚹	♊ 28 10:22
29 11:21	♆ ☍	♋ 30 20:39

Last Aspect / ☽ Ingress

Last Aspect Dy Hr Mn		☽ Ingress Dy Hr Mn
2 4:03	♄ ☌	♌ 2 4:37
4 1:43	☿ □	♍ 4 10:21
6 6:34	☿ △	♎ 6 14:00
7 18:40	☉ △	♏ 8 15:58
10 13:13	☿ ☍	♐ 10 17:07
12 4:15	☉ ☍	♑ 12 18:45
14 2:29	♃ △	♒ 14 22:31
16 21:51	☉ △	♓ 17 5:43
19 14:05	♀ □	♈ 19 16:32
21 10:28	♂ △	♉ 22 5:21
24 2:18	♂ □	♊ 24 17:37
26 15:46	♂ ⚹	♋ 27 3:29
28 19:34	♃ ⚹	♌ 29 10:39

☽ Phases & Eclipses

Dy Hr Mn	
7 5:17	☽ 16♌47
13 20:04	○ 23♏10
13 19:54	☍ P 0.122
20 21:22	☽ 29♒58
29 1:47	● 7♊49
5 12:20	☽ 14♍57
12 4:15	○ 21♐19
19 13:15	☽ 28♓22
27 14:50	● 6♋04

Astro Data

1 MAY 1976
Julian Day # 27880
Delta T 46.8 sec
SVP 05♓35'15"
Obliquity 23°26'26"
⚷ Chiron 28♈27.9
☽ Mean ☊ 12♏51.5

1 JUNE 1976
Julian Day # 27911
Delta T 46.9 sec
SVP 05♓35'10"
Obliquity 23°26'25"
⚷ Chiron 0♉10.6
☽ Mean ☊ 11♏13.0

JULY 1976 LONGITUDE

Day	Sid.Time	☉	0 hr ☽	Noon ☽	True ☊	☿	♀	♂	♃	♄	♅	♆	♇
1 Th	18 36 42	9♋17 8	20♌59 54	27♌50 32	10♏42.0	23♊10.2	12♋48.4	26♌24.3	22♉ 5.6	2♌55.9	3♏ 4.8	11♐52.7	8♎58.0
2 F	18 40 38	10 14 21	4♍43 33	11♍38 44	10R35.4	25 0.7	14 2.1	27 0.3	22 17.3	3 3.2	3R 4.3	11R51.3	8 58.5
3 Sa	18 44 35	11 11 34	18 35 53	25 34 48	10 31.1	26 53.9	15 15.9	27 36.3	22 29.0	3 10.6	3 3.8	11 50.0	8 58.9
4 Su	18 48 31	12 8 46	2♎35 22	9♎37 25	10D29.0	28 49.8	16 29.7	28 12.4	22 40.6	3 18.0	3 3.4	11 48.6	8 59.4
5 M	18 52 28	13 5 58	16 40 51	23 45 31	10 28.7	0♋48.1	17 43.4	28 48.5	22 52.1	3 25.4	3 3.1	11 47.3	8 59.9
6 Tu	18 56 24	14 3 10	0♏51 18	7♏57 59	10R29.2	2 48.8	18 57.2	29 24.6	23 3.5	3 32.8	3 2.8	11 46.0	9 0.5
7 W	19 0 21	15 0 22	15 5 24	22 13 15	10 29.3	4 51.5	20 11.0	0♍ 0.8	23 14.8	3 40.3	3 2.5	11 44.7	9 1.1
8 Th	19 4 18	15 57 33	29 21 12	6♐28 53	10 28.0	6 56.0	21 24.7	0 37.1	23 26.1	3 47.8	3 2.3	11 43.4	9 1.7
9 F	19 8 14	16 54 45	13♐35 50	20 41 33	10 24.4	9 2.0	22 38.5	1 13.4	23 37.2	3 55.3	3 2.2	11 42.1	9 2.3
10 Sa	19 12 11	17 51 56	27 45 29	4♑47 4	10 18.2	11 9.2	23 52.3	1 49.7	23 48.3	4 2.8	3 2.1	11 40.9	9 3.0
11 Su	19 16 7	18 49 7	11♑45 44	18 40 56	10 9.6	13 17.4	25 6.1	2 26.1	23 59.2	4 10.4	3D 2.1	11 39.7	9 3.7
12 M	19 20 4	19 46 19	25 32 10	2♒19 1	9 59.2	15 26.3	26 19.9	3 2.5	24 10.1	4 18.0	3 2.1	11 38.5	9 4.5
13 Tu	19 24 0	20 43 31	9♒ 1 6	15 38 12	9 48.0	17 35.5	27 33.7	3 38.9	24 20.8	4 25.5	3 2.1	11 37.3	9 5.3
14 W	19 27 57	21 40 43	22 10 9	28 36 57	9 37.2	19 44.7	28 47.4	4 15.4	24 31.5	4 33.2	3 2.2	11 36.1	9 6.1
15 Th	19 31 53	22 37 55	4♓58 40	11♓15 30	9 27.9	21 53.7	0♌ 1.2	4 52.0	24 42.1	4 40.8	3 2.4	11 35.0	9 6.9
16 F	19 35 50	23 35 8	17 27 44	23 35 46	9 20.6	24 2.3	1 15.0	5 28.6	24 52.5	4 48.4	3 2.6	11 33.9	9 7.8
17 Sa	19 39 47	24 32 22	29 40 1	5♈41 3	9 15.8	26 10.2	2 28.8	6 5.2	25 2.9	4 56.1	3 2.9	11 32.8	9 8.7
18 Su	19 43 43	25 29 36	11♈39 26	17 35 46	9 13.4	28 17.2	3 42.7	6 41.9	25 13.2	5 3.7	3 3.2	11 31.7	9 9.6
19 M	19 47 40	26 26 51	23 30 44	29 25 0	9D12.6	0♌23.1	4 56.5	7 18.6	25 23.3	5 11.4	3 3.6	11 30.7	9 10.6
20 Tu	19 51 36	27 24 7	5♉19 14	11♉14 9	9R12.6	2 27.8	6 10.3	7 55.4	25 33.3	5 19.1	3 4.0	11 29.7	9 11.6
21 W	19 55 33	28 21 23	17 10 23	23 8 38	9 12.5	4 31.2	7 24.1	8 32.2	25 43.3	5 26.8	3 4.5	11 28.7	9 12.6
22 Th	19 59 29	29 18 41	29 9 29	5♊13 31	9 11.1	6 33.1	8 38.0	9 9.0	25 53.1	5 34.5	3 5.0	11 27.7	9 13.7
23 F	20 3 26	0♌15 59	11♊21 17	17 33 13	9 7.6	8 33.5	9 51.8	9 45.9	26 2.8	5 42.2	3 5.6	11 26.8	9 14.8
24 Sa	20 7 22	1 13 18	23 49 43	0♋11 3	9 1.6	10 32.4	11 5.7	10 22.9	26 12.4	5 49.9	3 6.3	11 25.9	9 15.9
25 Su	20 11 19	2 10 37	6♋37 25	13 8 54	8 53.0	12 29.7	12 19.5	10 59.9	26 21.9	5 57.7	3 7.0	11 25.0	9 17.1
26 M	20 15 16	3 7 58	19 45 29	26 27 0	8 42.3	14 25.3	13 33.4	11 37.0	26 31.2	6 5.4	3 7.7	11 24.1	9 18.2
27 Tu	20 19 12	4 5 19	3♌13 12	10♌ 3 45	8 30.3	16 19.2	14 47.2	12 14.0	26 40.5	6 13.1	3 8.5	11 23.3	9 19.5
28 W	20 23 9	5 2 41	16 58 12	23 56 1	8 18.2	18 11.5	16 1.1	12 51.2	26 49.6	6 20.9	3 9.4	11 22.5	9 20.7
29 Th	20 27 5	6 0 4	0♍56 42	7♍59 38	8 7.3	20 2.1	17 15.0	13 28.4	26 58.6	6 28.6	3 10.3	11 21.7	9 22.0
30 F	20 31 2	6 57 27	15 4 16	22 10 3	7 58.6	21 51.0	18 28.8	14 5.6	27 7.4	6 36.4	3 11.2	11 20.9	9 23.3
31 Sa	20 34 58	7 54 51	29 16 30	6♎23 10	7 52.6	23 38.2	19 42.7	14 42.9	27 16.1	6 44.1	3 12.2	11 20.2	9 24.6

AUGUST 1976 LONGITUDE

Day	Sid.Time	☉	0 hr ☽	Noon ☽	True ☊	☿	♀	♂	♃	♄	♅	♆	♇
1 Su	20 38 55	8♌52 15	13♎29 42	20♎35 47	7♏49.3	25♌23.8	20♌56.5	15♍20.2	27♉24.7	6♌51.8	3♏13.3	11♐19.5	9♎25.9
2 M	20 42 51	9 49 40	27 41 11	4♏45 43	7R48.1	27 7.7	22 10.4	15 57.5	27 33.2	6 59.6	3 14.4	11R18.8	9 27.3
3 Tu	20 46 48	10 47 5	11♏49 16	18 51 43	7 48.0	28 49.9	23 24.3	16 34.9	27 41.5	7 7.3	3 15.5	11 18.2	9 28.7
4 W	20 50 45	11 44 32	25 52 59	2♐52 58	7 47.7	0♍30.5	24 38.1	17 12.4	27 49.7	7 15.0	3 16.7	11 17.6	9 30.1
5 Th	20 54 41	12 42 1	9♐51 34	16 48 40	7 45.8	2 9.4	25 52.0	17 49.9	27 57.8	7 22.8	3 18.0	11 17.0	9 31.6
6 F	20 58 38	13 39 26	23 44 5	0♑37 37	7 41.6	3 46.8	27 5.9	18 27.4	28 5.7	7 30.5	3 19.3	11 16.5	9 33.1
7 Sa	21 2 34	14 36 55	7♑29 3	14 18 6	7 34.7	5 22.5	28 19.7	19 5.0	28 13.5	7 38.2	3 20.6	11 15.9	9 34.6
8 Su	21 6 31	15 34 24	21 4 30	27 47 56	7 25.1	6 56.5	29 33.6	19 42.6	28 21.2	7 45.9	3 22.0	11 15.5	9 36.2
9 M	21 10 27	16 31 54	4♒28 7	11♒ 4 48	7 13.6	8 29.0	0♍47.4	20 20.2	28 28.7	7 53.6	3 23.5	11 15.0	9 37.7
10 Tu	21 14 24	17 29 25	17 37 44	24 6 44	7 1.2	9 59.8	2 1.3	20 57.9	28 36.0	8 1.3	3 25.0	11 14.6	9 39.3
11 W	21 18 20	18 26 58	0♓31 41	6♓52 33	6 49.2	11 28.9	3 15.1	21 35.7	28 43.2	8 8.9	3 26.6	11 14.2	9 40.9
12 Th	21 22 17	19 24 31	13 9 20	19 22 9	6 38.6	12 56.5	4 28.9	22 13.5	28 50.3	8 16.6	3 28.1	11 13.8	9 42.6
13 F	21 26 14	20 22 6	25 31 11	1♈36 43	6 30.2	14 22.3	5 42.8	22 51.3	28 57.2	8 24.2	3 29.8	11 13.5	9 44.2
14 Sa	21 30 10	21 19 42	7♈39 5	13 38 41	6 24.4	15 46.5	6 56.6	23 29.2	29 4.0	8 31.8	3 31.5	11 13.2	9 45.9
15 Su	21 34 7	22 17 19	19 36 1	25 31 35	6 21.1	17 8.9	8 10.5	24 7.1	29 10.6	8 39.4	3 33.2	11 12.9	9 47.6
16 M	21 38 3	23 14 58	1♉26 0	7♉19 51	6D19.9	18 29.6	9 24.3	24 45.1	29 17.0	8 47.0	3 35.0	11 12.6	9 49.3
17 Tu	21 42 0	24 12 39	13 13 47	19 8 30	6 20.0	19 48.5	10 38.1	25 23.1	29 23.3	8 54.6	3 36.8	11 12.4	9 51.1
18 W	21 45 56	25 10 21	25 4 39	1♊ 2 56	6R20.2	21 5.5	11 52.0	26 1.2	29 29.5	9 2.2	3 38.7	11 12.2	9 52.9
19 Th	21 49 53	26 8 5	7♊ 4 1	13 8 35	6 19.7	22 20.7	13 5.8	26 39.3	29 35.5	9 9.7	3 40.6	11 12.1	9 54.7
20 F	21 53 49	27 5 50	19 17 13	25 30 31	6 17.4	23 33.9	14 19.7	27 17.4	29 41.3	9 17.2	3 42.6	11 12.0	9 56.5
21 Sa	21 57 46	28 3 37	1♋48 58	8♋13 1	6 13.0	24 45.1	15 33.5	27 55.6	29 46.9	9 24.7	3 44.6	11 11.9	9 58.3
22 Su	22 1 43	29 1 26	14 42 57	21 18 59	6 6.2	25 54.2	16 47.3	28 33.9	29 52.4	9 32.2	3 46.7	11 11.8	10 0.2
23 M	22 5 39	29 59 16	28 1 12	4♌49 32	5 57.3	27 1.1	18 1.2	29 12.2	29 57.7	9 39.6	3 48.8	11D11.8	10 2.1
24 Tu	22 9 36	0♍57 8	11♌43 43	18 43 26	5 47.2	28 5.7	19 15.0	29 50.5	0♊ 2.9	9 47.0	3 51.0	11 11.8	10 4.0
25 W	22 13 32	1 55 1	25 48 7	2♍57 9	5 36.9	29 8.0	20 28.8	0♎28.9	0 7.9	9 54.4	3 53.1	11 11.9	10 5.9
26 Th	22 17 29	2 52 56	10♍ 9 47	17 25 11	5 27.6	0♎ 7.7	21 42.6	1 7.4	0 12.7	10 1.8	3 55.4	11 12.0	10 7.9
27 F	22 21 25	3 50 53	24 42 31	2♎ 0 54	5 20.2	1 4.7	22 56.5	1 45.9	0 17.3	10 9.1	3 57.7	11 12.1	10 9.8
28 Sa	22 25 22	4 48 50	9♎19 31	16 37 35	5 15.2	1 58.9	24 10.3	2 24.4	0 21.7	10 16.4	3 60.0	11 12.2	10 11.8
29 Su	22 29 18	5 46 50	23 54 25	1♏ 9 27	5D12.8	2 50.1	25 24.1	3 3.0	0 26.0	10 23.7	4 2.3	11 12.4	10 13.8
30 M	22 33 15	6 44 50	8♏22 12	15 32 17	5 12.3	3 38.2	26 37.9	3 41.6	0 30.1	10 30.9	4 4.7	11 12.6	10 15.8
31 Tu	22 37 11	7 42 52	22 39 27	29 43 30	5 12.9	4 22.9	27 51.7	4 20.3	0 34.0	10 38.1	4 7.2	11 12.8	10 17.9

Astro Data	Planet Ingress	Last Aspect	☽ Ingress	Last Aspect	☽ Ingress	☽ Phases & Eclipses	Astro Data
Dy Hr Mn	Dy Hr Mn	Dy Hr Mn	Dy Hr Mn	Dy Hr Mn	Dy Hr Mn	Dy Hr Mn	1 JULY 1976
♄□♅ 2 3:15	☿ ♋ 4 14:18	1 9:55 ♂ ☌	♍ 1 15:46	1 22:55 ☿ ⚹	♏ 2 3:55	4 17:28 ☽ 12♎50	Julian Day # 27941
☽0S 3 4:09	♂ ♍ 6 23:27	3 16:32 ☿ □	♎ 3 19:34	4 3:22 ♃ ☍	♐ 4 7:03	11 13:09 ○ 19♑20	Delta T 47.0 sec
♃⚼♇ 11 10:43	♀ ♌ 14 23:36	5 21:27 ♂ ⚹	♏ 5 22:33	6 6:25 ♀ △	♑ 6 10:54	19 6:29 ☽ 26♈42	SVP 05♓35'05"
♅ D 11 6:05	☿ ♌ 18 19:35	7 13:55 ♃ ☍	♐ 8 1:05	8 13:07 ♃ △	♒ 8 15:57	27 1:39 ● 4♌09	Obliquity 23°26'25"
☽0N 16 7:27	☉ ♌ 22 17:18	8 20:48 ♆ ☌	♑ 10 3:49	10 20:34 ♃ □	♓ 10 23:00		⚷ Chiron 1♉22.9
☽0S 30 10:58		12 1:32 ♀ ☍	♒ 12 7:53	13 6:49 ♃ ⚹	♈ 13 8:49	2 22:06 ☽ 10♏43	☽ Mean ☊ 9♏37.7
	☿ ♍ 3 16:41	14 4:26 ♃ □	♓ 14 14:36	15 5:55 ☉ △	♉ 15 21:05	9 23:43 ○ 17♒29	
☽0N 12 16:40	♀ ♍ 8 8:36	16 15:36 ☿ △	♈ 17 0:40	18 8:57 ♃ ☌	♊ 18 9:54	18 0:12 ☽ 25♉11	1 AUGUST 1976
☿0S 22 10:27	☉ ♍ 23 0:18	19 6:29 ☉ □	♉ 19 13:11	20 16:17 ☉ ⚹	♋ 20 20:34	25 11:01 ● 2♍22	Julian Day # 27972
♆ D 23 2:04	♃ ♊ 23 10:24	22 0:20 ☉ ⚹	♊ 22 1:40	23 3:28 ♃ ⚹	♌ 23 3:31		Delta T 47.1 sec
☽0S 26 19:22	♂ ♎ 24 5:55	23 0:11 ♆ ☍	♋ 24 11:39	23 23:05 ♆ △	♍ 25 7:04		SVP 05♓35'01"
♂0S 26 12:23	☿ ♎ 25 20:52	26 12:16 ♃ ⚹	♌ 26 18:19	26 20:50 ♀ ☌	♎ 27 8:42		Obliquity 23°26'25"
♄⚹♇ 27 3:17		28 17:09 ♃ □	♍ 28 22:23	28 3:05 ♆ ⚹	♏ 29 10:05		⚷ Chiron 1♉54.6
		30 20:35 ♃ △	♎ 31 1:13	31 9:40 ♀ ⚹	♐ 31 12:28		☽ Mean ☊ 7♏59.2

LONGITUDE SEPTEMBER 1976

Day	Sid.Time	☉	0 hr ☽	Noon ☽	True ☊	☿	♀	♂	♃	♄	♅	♆	♇
1 W	22 41 8	8♍40 55	6♐44 20	13♐41 55	5♏13.5	5♎ 3.9	29♍ 5.5	4♎59.0	0♊37.8	10♌45.3	4♏ 9.7	11♐13.1	10♎19.9
2 Th	22 45 5	9 39 0	20 36 13	27 27 17	5R13.0	5 41.2	0♎19.2	5 37.8	0 41.3	10 52.4	4 12.2	11 13.4	10 22.0
3 F	22 49 1	10 37 6	4♑15 7	10♑59 46	5 10.5	6 14.3	1 33.0	6 16.6	0 44.7	10 59.5	4 14.8	11 13.8	10 24.1
4 Sa	22 52 58	11 35 14	17 41 15	24 19 35	5 5.9	6 43.1	2 46.8	6 55.5	0 47.8	11 6.6	4 17.4	11 14.1	10 26.2
5 Su	22 56 54	12 33 23	0♒54 48	7♒26 51	4 59.1	7 7.3	4 0.5	7 34.4	0 50.8	11 13.6	4 20.0	11 14.5	10 28.3
6 M	23 0 51	13 31 33	13 55 44	20 21 27	4 50.8	7 26.5	5 14.2	8 13.3	0 53.6	11 20.6	4 22.7	11 15.0	10 30.4
7 Tu	23 4 47	14 29 45	26 43 57	3♓ 3 16	4 41.8	7 40.5	6 27.9	8 52.3	0 56.2	11 27.5	4 25.4	11 15.5	10 32.6
8 W	23 8 44	15 27 59	9♓19 23	15 32 21	4 33.0	7R48.9	7 41.7	9 31.4	0 58.7	11 34.4	4 28.1	11 16.0	10 34.7
9 Th	23 12 40	16 26 14	21 42 16	27 49 13	4 25.2	7 51.4	8 55.4	10 10.4	1 0.9	11 41.2	4 30.9	11 16.5	10 36.9
10 F	23 16 37	17 24 31	3♈53 23	9♈54 58	4 19.2	7 47.8	10 9.0	10 49.6	1 2.9	11 48.0	4 33.7	11 17.1	10 39.1
11 Sa	23 20 34	18 22 50	15 54 13	21 51 27	4 15.3	7 37.8	11 22.7	11 28.8	1 4.8	11 54.8	4 36.6	11 17.6	10 41.2
12 Su	23 24 30	19 21 11	27 47 3	3♉41 23	4D13.4	7 21.2	12 36.4	12 8.0	1 6.4	12 1.5	4 39.5	11 18.3	10 43.4
13 M	23 28 27	20 19 34	9♉34 56	15 28 12	4 13.3	6 57.9	13 50.1	12 47.3	1 7.9	12 8.2	4 42.4	11 18.9	10 45.7
14 Tu	23 32 23	21 17 59	21 21 44	27 16 5	4 14.4	6 27.8	15 3.7	13 26.6	1 9.1	12 14.8	4 45.3	11 19.6	10 47.9
15 W	23 36 20	22 16 27	3♊11 52	9♊ 9 42	4 16.0	5 51.2	16 17.4	14 6.0	1 10.2	12 21.4	4 48.3	11 20.4	10 50.1
16 Th	23 40 16	23 14 56	15 10 15	21 14 8	4R17.3	5 8.1	17 31.0	14 45.4	1 11.0	12 27.9	4 51.3	11 21.1	10 52.4
17 F	23 44 13	24 13 28	27 22 0	3♋34 27	4 17.5	4 19.1	18 44.6	15 24.9	1 11.7	12 34.3	4 54.4	11 21.9	10 54.6
18 Sa	23 48 9	25 12 1	9♋52 5	16 15 24	4 16.4	3 24.7	19 58.2	16 4.4	1 12.2	12 40.7	4 57.5	11 22.7	10 56.9
19 Su	23 52 6	26 10 37	22 44 52	29 20 50	4 13.6	2 26.0	21 11.9	16 44.0	1R12.4	12 47.1	5 0.6	11 23.6	10 59.2
20 M	23 56 3	27 9 16	6♌ 3 33	12♌53 6	4 9.4	1 23.8	22 25.5	17 23.6	1 12.5	12 53.4	5 3.7	11 24.5	11 1.5
21 Tu	23 59 59	28 7 56	19 49 27	26 52 24	4 4.2	0 19.6	23 39.1	18 3.3	1 12.3	12 59.7	5 6.9	11 25.4	11 3.8
22 W	0 3 56	29 6 38	4♍ 1 32	11♍16 19	3 58.7	29♍14.7	24 52.6	18 43.1	1 12.0	13 5.8	5 10.1	11 26.3	11 6.1
23 Th	0 7 52	0♎ 5 23	18 36 0	25 59 45	3 53.6	28 10.8	26 6.2	19 22.8	1 11.4	13 12.0	5 13.3	11 27.3	11 8.4
24 F	0 11 49	1 4 9	3♎26 33	10♎55 22	3 49.7	27 9.4	27 19.8	20 2.7	1 10.7	13 18.0	5 16.6	11 28.3	11 10.7
25 Sa	0 15 45	2 2 58	18 25 6	25 54 42	3 47.3	26 12.2	28 33.3	20 42.6	1 9.7	13 24.0	5 19.9	11 29.3	11 13.0
26 Su	0 19 42	3 1 48	3♏23 7	10♏49 25	3D46.5	25 20.7	29 46.9	21 22.5	1 8.5	13 30.0	5 23.2	11 30.4	11 15.3
27 M	0 23 38	4 0 40	18 12 46	25 32 28	3 47.1	24 36.3	1♏ 0.4	22 2.5	1 7.2	13 35.9	5 26.5	11 31.5	11 17.6
28 Tu	0 27 35	4 59 35	2♐47 58	9♐58 50	3 48.4	24 0.1	2 13.9	22 42.5	1 5.6	13 41.7	5 29.8	11 32.6	11 20.0
29 W	0 31 32	5 58 30	17 4 48	24 5 41	3 49.9	23 33.1	3 27.4	23 22.6	1 3.9	13 47.4	5 33.2	11 33.8	11 22.3
30 Th	0 35 28	6 57 28	1♑ 1 26	7♑52 6	3R50.8	23 15.9	4 40.9	24 2.7	1 1.9	13 53.1	5 36.6	11 35.0	11 24.6

LONGITUDE OCTOBER 1976

Day	Sid.Time	☉	0 hr ☽	Noon ☽	True ☊	☿	♀	♂	♃	♄	♅	♆	♇
1 F	0 39 25	7♎56 27	14♑37 46	21♑18 37	3♏50.8	23♍ 9.0	5♏54.4	24♎42.9	0♊59.7	13♌58.7	5♏40.0	11♐36.2	11♎27.0
2 Sa	0 43 21	8 55 28	27 54 51	4♒26 40	3R49.5	23D12.4	7 7.9	25 23.1	0R57.4	14 4.2	5 43.5	11 37.4	11 29.3
3 Su	0 47 18	9 54 31	10♒54 21	17 18 7	3 47.2	23 26.2	8 21.3	26 3.4	0 54.8	14 9.7	5 47.0	11 38.7	11 31.7
4 M	0 51 14	10 53 36	23 38 14	29 54 57	3 44.1	23 50.1	9 34.7	26 43.7	0 52.1	14 15.1	5 50.4	11 40.0	11 34.0
5 Tu	0 55 11	11 52 42	6♓ 8 29	12♓19 4	3 40.5	24 23.6	10 48.1	27 24.1	0 49.1	14 20.4	5 53.9	11 41.3	11 36.4
6 W	0 59 7	12 51 50	18 26 57	24 32 19	3 37.1	25 6.1	12 1.5	28 4.5	0 46.0	14 25.7	5 57.5	11 42.7	11 38.7
7 Th	1 3 4	13 51 0	0♈35 23	6♈36 22	3 34.1	25 57.1	13 14.8	28 45.0	0 42.6	14 30.9	6 1.0	11 44.0	11 41.0
8 F	1 7 0	14 50 13	12 35 30	18 33 0	3 32.0	26 55.7	14 28.2	29 25.5	0 39.1	14 36.0	6 4.6	11 45.4	11 43.4
9 Sa	1 10 57	15 49 27	24 29 7	0♉24 6	3D30.8	28 1.3	15 41.5	0♏ 6.1	0 35.4	14 41.0	6 8.1	11 46.9	11 45.7
10 Su	1 14 54	16 48 43	6♉18 14	12 11 50	3 30.6	29 13.1	16 54.8	0 46.7	0 31.5	14 45.9	6 11.7	11 48.3	11 48.1
11 M	1 18 50	17 48 1	18 5 14	23 58 48	3 31.1	0♎30.3	18 8.1	1 27.4	0 27.4	14 50.8	6 15.3	11 49.8	11 50.4
12 Tu	1 22 47	18 47 22	29 52 56	5♊48 3	3 32.2	1 52.2	19 21.4	2 8.1	0 23.2	14 55.6	6 18.9	11 51.3	11 52.7
13 W	1 26 43	19 46 45	11♊44 36	17 43 6	3 33.5	3 18.1	20 34.7	2 48.9	0 18.7	15 0.3	6 22.6	11 52.9	11 55.1
14 Th	1 30 40	20 46 10	23 44 1	29 47 54	3 34.8	4 47.6	21 47.9	3 29.8	0 14.1	15 4.9	6 26.2	11 54.4	11 57.4
15 F	1 34 36	21 45 38	5♋55 17	12♋ 6 44	3 35.7	6 19.8	23 1.1	4 10.6	0 9.3	15 9.5	6 29.9	11 56.0	11 59.7
16 Sa	1 38 33	22 45 7	18 22 46	24 43 55	3R36.2	7 54.5	24 14.4	4 51.6	0 4.4	15 13.9	6 33.6	11 57.6	12 2.0
17 Su	1 42 29	23 44 39	1♌10 41	7♌43 29	3 36.2	9 31.0	25 27.6	5 32.6	29♉59.2	15 18.3	6 37.3	11 59.2	12 4.4
18 M	1 46 26	24 44 14	14 22 42	21 8 37	3 35.7	11 9.1	26 40.7	6 13.6	29 53.9	15 22.6	6 41.0	12 0.9	12 6.7
19 Tu	1 50 23	25 43 50	28 1 23	5♍ 1 2	3 34.9	12 48.4	27 53.9	6 54.7	29 48.4	15 26.8	6 44.7	12 2.6	12 9.0
20 W	1 54 19	26 43 29	12♍ 7 28	19 20 21	3 34.0	14 28.5	29 7.1	7 35.9	29 42.8	15 30.9	6 48.4	12 4.3	12 11.3
21 Th	1 58 16	27 43 10	26 39 15	4♎ 3 30	3 33.3	16 9.3	0♐20.2	8 17.1	29 37.0	15 34.9	6 52.1	12 6.0	12 13.5
22 F	2 2 12	28 42 53	11♎32 17	19 4 38	3 32.8	17 50.5	1 33.3	8 58.3	29 31.1	15 38.8	6 55.8	12 7.7	12 15.8
23 Sa	2 6 9	29 42 39	26 39 27	4♏15 33	3D32.6	19 32.0	2 46.4	9 39.7	29 25.0	15 42.7	6 59.6	12 9.5	12 18.1
24 Su	2 10 5	0♏42 26	11♏51 43	19 26 44	3 32.6	21 13.6	3 59.5	10 21.0	29 18.7	15 46.4	7 3.3	12 11.3	12 20.3
25 M	2 14 2	1 42 16	26 59 27	4♐28 47	3 32.7	22 55.1	5 12.5	11 2.4	29 12.4	15 50.0	7 7.1	12 13.1	12 22.6
26 Tu	2 17 58	2 42 7	11♐53 49	19 13 45	3R32.8	24 36.5	6 25.6	11 43.9	29 5.8	15 53.6	7 10.8	12 14.9	12 24.8
27 W	2 21 55	3 42 0	26 27 59	3♑36 3	3 32.9	26 17.8	7 38.6	12 25.4	28 59.2	15 57.1	7 14.6	12 16.8	12 27.1
28 Th	2 25 52	4 41 54	10♑37 43	17 32 50	3 32.8	27 58.8	8 51.6	13 7.0	28 52.4	16 0.4	7 18.3	12 18.7	12 29.3
29 F	2 29 48	5 41 51	24 21 27	1♒ 3 43	3D32.7	29 39.4	10 4.6	13 48.6	28 45.5	16 3.7	7 22.1	12 20.5	12 31.5
30 Sa	2 33 45	6 41 49	7♒39 53	14 10 16	3 32.7	1♏19.7	11 17.5	14 30.3	28 38.5	16 6.8	7 25.9	12 22.4	12 33.7
31 Su	2 37 41	7 41 48	20 35 15	26 55 17	3 32.8	2 59.6	12 30.4	15 12.0	28 31.4	16 9.9	7 29.6	12 24.4	12 35.9

Astro Data	Planet Ingress	Last Aspect	☽ Ingress	Last Aspect	☽ Ingress	☽ Phases & Eclipses	Astro Data
Dy Hr Mn	Dy Hr Mn	Dy Hr Mn	Dy Hr Mn	Dy Hr Mn	Dy Hr Mn	Dy Hr Mn	1 SEPTEMBER 1976
♀0S 3 18:35	♀ ♎ 1 17:44	1 7:43 ♆ ☌	♑ 2 16:29	1 19:09 ♂ □	♒ 2 3:49	1 3:35 ☽ 8♐50	Julian Day # 28003
♄△♆ 5 3:32	☿ ♍ 21 7:15	3 12:12 ☉ △	♒ 4 22:20	4 6:14 ♂ △	♓ 4 12:10	8 12:52 ○ 15♓59	Delta T 47.2 sec
☿ R 8 22:04	☉ ♎ 22 21:48	5 19:09 ♄ ☍	♓ 7 6:11	6 14:04 ☿ ☍	♈ 6 22:50	16 17:20 ☽ 23♊57	SVP 05♓34'57"
☽0N 9 0:30	♀ ♏ 26 4:17	8 12:52 ☉ ☍	♈ 9 16:18	8 4:55 ☉ ☍	♉ 9 11:11	23 19:55 ● 0♎54	Obliquity 23°26'25"
♃ R 19 18:39		10 15:55 ♄ △	♉ 12 4:30	11 0:07 ♀ ☍	♊ 12 0:14	30 11:12 ☽ 7♑25	⚷ Chiron 1♉35.5R
☽0S 23 5:24	♂ ♏ 8 20:23	13 23:52 ☉ △	♊ 14 17:32	13 17:34 ☉ △	♋ 14 12:24		☽ Mean ☊ 6♏20.7
☿0N 25 11:40	☿ ♎ 10 14:47	16 17:20 ☉ □	♋ 17 5:07	16 21:49 ♃ ✱	♌ 16 21:49	8 4:55 ○ 15♈02	
	♃ ♉ 16 20:24	19 6:46 ☉ ✱	♌ 19 13:11	19 3:04 ♃ □	♍ 19 3:25	16 8:59 ☽ 23♋07	1 OCTOBER 1976
☿ D 1 3:59	♀ ♐ 20 17:22	21 7:09 ♀ ✱	♍ 21 17:16	21 4:47 ♃ △	♎ 21 5:26	23 5:10 ● 29♎55	Julian Day # 28033
☽0N 6 6:46	☉ ♏ 23 6:58	23 14:31 ☿ ☌	♎ 23 18:28	23 5:10 ☉ ☌	♏ 23 5:17	23 5:12:58 • T 4'47"	Delta T 47.3 sec
♆✱♇ 10 7:07	☿ ♏ 29 4:55	25 17:41 ♀ ☌	♏ 25 18:34	25 3:31 ♃ ☍	♐ 25 4:49	29 22:05 ☽ 6♒37	SVP 05♓34'54"
☿0S 13 20:32		27 10:01 ☿ ✱	♐ 27 19:21	26 23:41 ☿ ✱	♑ 27 5:55		Obliquity 23°26'25"
☽0S 20 16:04		29 11:18 ♂ ✱	♑ 29 22:13	29 7:47 ♃ △	♒ 29 10:05		⚷ Chiron 0♉34.5R
				31 14:55 ♃ □	♓ 31 17:53		☽ Mean ☊ 4♏45.4

NOVEMBER 1976 LONGITUDE

Day	Sid.Time	☉	0 hr ☽	Noon ☽	True ☊	☿	♀	♂	♃	♄	♅	♆	♇
1 M	2 41 38	8♏41 49	3♓10 48	9♓22 16	3♏33.1	4♏39.2	13♐43.3	15♏53.8	28♉24.2	16♌12.9	7♏33.4	12♐26.3	12♎38.0
2 Tu	2 45 34	9 41 52	15 30 10	21 34 56	3 33.7	6 18.3	14 56.1	16 35.6	28R 16.8	16 15.7	7 37.1	12 28.3	12 40.2
3 W	2 49 31	10 41 56	27 37 2	3♈36 52	3 34.5	7 57.0	16 9.0	17 17.5	28 9.4	16 18.5	7 40.9	12 30.2	12 42.3
4 Th	2 53 27	11 42 2	9♈34 50	15 31 18	3 35.2	9 35.3	17 21.7	17 59.4	28 1.9	16 21.1	7 44.7	12 32.2	12 44.4
5 F	2 57 24	12 42 9	21 26 39	27 21 11	3 35.8	11 13.1	18 34.5	18 41.4	27 54.3	16 23.7	7 48.4	12 34.2	12 46.5
6 Sa	3 1 21	13 42 19	3♉15 13	9♉ 9 3	3R 36.1	12 50.6	19 47.2	19 23.4	27 46.6	16 26.1	7 52.2	12 36.3	12 48.6
7 Su	3 5 17	14 42 30	15 2 56	20 57 9	3 35.8	14 27.7	20 59.9	20 5.5	27 38.8	16 28.5	7 55.9	12 38.3	12 50.7
8 M	3 9 14	15 42 43	26 51 58	2♊47 38	3 34.9	16 4.4	22 12.5	20 47.6	27 31.0	16 30.7	7 59.6	12 40.4	12 52.8
9 Tu	3 13 10	16 42 58	8♊44 25	14 42 35	3 33.4	17 40.6	23 25.2	21 29.8	27 23.1	16 32.9	8 3.4	12 42.4	12 54.8
10 W	3 17 7	17 43 14	20 42 26	26 44 14	3 31.3	19 16.6	24 37.7	22 12.1	27 15.2	16 34.9	8 7.1	12 44.5	12 56.8
11 Th	3 21 3	18 43 33	2♋48 19	8♋55 2	3 29.0	20 52.2	25 50.3	22 54.3	27 7.2	16 36.8	8 10.8	12 46.6	12 58.8
12 F	3 25 0	19 43 53	15 4 43	21 17 44	3 26.7	22 27.5	27 2.8	23 36.7	26 59.1	16 38.7	8 14.5	12 48.7	13 0.8
13 Sa	3 28 56	20 44 15	27 34 30	3♌55 22	3 24.7	24 2.4	28 15.3	24 19.1	26 51.0	16 40.4	8 18.3	12 50.8	13 2.8
14 Su	3 32 53	21 44 40	10♌20 45	16 51 2	3D 23.4	25 37.1	29 27.7	25 1.5	26 42.9	16 42.0	8 21.9	12 53.0	13 4.8
15 M	3 36 50	22 45 6	23 26 36	0♍ 7 44	3 23.0	27 11.4	0♑40.1	25 44.0	26 34.8	16 43.5	8 25.6	12 55.1	13 6.7
16 Tu	3 40 46	23 45 34	6♍54 45	13 47 49	3 23.5	28 45.6	1 52.5	26 26.6	26 26.6	16 44.8	8 29.3	12 57.3	13 8.6
17 W	3 44 43	24 46 3	20 47 4	27 52 28	3 24.7	0♐19.4	3 4.8	27 9.2	26 18.4	16 46.1	8 33.0	12 59.4	13 10.5
18 Th	3 48 39	25 46 35	5♎ 3 53	12♎21 1	3 26.1	1 53.0	4 17.1	27 51.9	26 10.3	16 47.3	8 36.6	13 1.6	13 12.3
19 F	3 52 36	26 47 8	19 43 24	27 10 24	3R 27.3	3 26.5	5 29.3	28 34.6	26 2.1	16 48.3	8 40.2	13 3.8	13 14.2
20 Sa	3 56 32	27 47 44	4♏41 11	12♏14 49	3 27.8	4 59.7	6 41.5	29 17.4	25 53.9	16 49.3	8 43.9	13 6.0	13 16.0
21 Su	4 0 29	28 48 21	19 50 10	27 26 3	3 27.0	6 32.7	7 53.7	0♐ 0.2	25 45.7	16 50.1	8 47.5	13 8.2	13 17.8
22 M	4 4 25	29 48 59	5♐ 1 15	12♐34 29	3 24.9	8 5.5	9 5.8	0 43.1	25 37.6	16 50.8	8 51.1	13 10.4	13 19.6
23 Tu	4 8 22	0♐49 39	20 4 35	27 30 26	3 21.5	9 38.1	10 17.9	1 26.0	25 29.4	16 51.4	8 54.6	13 12.6	13 21.3
24 W	4 12 19	1 50 20	4♑51 6	12♑ 5 47	3 17.4	11 10.6	11 29.9	2 9.0	25 21.3	16 51.9	8 58.2	13 14.8	13 23.1
25 Th	4 16 15	2 51 3	19 13 54	26 15 2	3 13.0	12 42.9	12 41.8	2 52.0	25 13.3	16 52.3	9 1.7	13 17.1	13 24.8
26 F	4 20 12	3 51 46	3♒ 8 59	9♒55 45	3 9.1	14 15.1	13 53.7	3 35.1	25 5.3	16 52.5	9 5.2	13 19.3	13 26.5
27 Sa	4 24 8	4 52 31	16 35 26	23 8 19	3 6.2	15 47.1	15 5.6	4 18.2	24 57.3	16R 52.7	9 8.7	13 21.5	13 28.1
28 Su	4 28 5	5 53 16	29 34 48	5♓55 20	3D 4.7	17 18.9	16 17.3	5 1.4	24 49.4	16 52.7	9 12.2	13 23.8	13 29.7
29 M	4 32 1	6 54 2	12♓10 28	18 20 47	3 4.7	18 50.5	17 29.0	5 44.6	24 41.6	16 52.6	9 15.7	13 26.0	13 31.3
30 Tu	4 35 58	7 54 50	24 26 54	0♈29 25	3 5.8	20 21.9	18 40.7	6 27.9	24 33.8	16 52.4	9 19.1	13 28.3	13 32.9

DECEMBER 1976 LONGITUDE

Day	Sid.Time	☉	0 hr ☽	Noon ☽	True ☊	☿	♀	♂	♃	♄	♅	♆	♇
1 W	4 39 54	8♐55 38	6♈28 59	12♈26 10	3♏ 7.5	21♐53.1	19♑52.3	7♐11.2	24♉26.1	16♌52.1	9♏22.5	13♐30.5	13♎34.5
2 Th	4 43 51	9 56 27	18 21 35	24 15 45	3 9.2	23 24.1	21 3.8	7 54.6	24R 18.5	16R 51.7	9 25.9	13 32.8	13 36.0
3 F	4 47 48	10 57 18	0♉ 9 13	6♉ 2 27	3R 10.2	24 54.8	22 15.2	8 38.0	24 11.0	16 51.2	9 29.2	13 35.1	13 37.5
4 Sa	4 51 44	11 58 9	11 55 53	17 49 54	3 9.8	26 25.3	23 26.5	9 21.5	24 3.5	16 50.5	9 32.6	13 37.3	13 38.9
5 Su	4 55 41	12 59 1	23 44 53	29 41 8	3 7.6	27 55.3	24 37.8	10 5.0	23 56.2	16 49.8	9 35.9	13 39.6	13 40.4
6 M	4 59 37	13 59 54	5♊38 53	11♊38 25	3 3.3	29 25.0	25 49.0	10 48.6	23 49.0	16 48.9	9 39.2	13 41.8	13 41.8
7 Tu	5 3 34	15 0 48	17 39 54	23 43 30	2 57.0	0♑54.2	27 0.0	11 32.2	23 41.9	16 47.9	9 42.4	13 44.1	13 43.2
8 W	5 7 30	16 1 43	29 49 23	5♋57 39	2 49.3	2 22.8	28 11.1	12 15.9	23 34.8	16 46.9	9 45.7	13 46.4	13 44.5
9 Th	5 11 27	17 2 40	12♋ 8 27	18 21 52	2 40.7	3 50.7	29 22.0	12 59.6	23 28.0	16 45.7	9 48.9	13 48.6	13 45.8
10 F	5 15 23	18 3 37	24 38 3	0♌57 7	2 32.2	5 17.9	0♒32.8	13 43.4	23 21.2	16 44.4	9 52.0	13 50.9	13 47.1
11 Sa	5 19 20	19 4 35	7♌19 12	13 44 28	2 24.5	6 44.1	1 43.5	14 27.2	23 14.6	16 42.9	9 55.2	13 53.2	13 48.4
12 Su	5 23 17	20 5 34	20 13 6	26 45 17	2 18.6	8 9.3	2 54.2	15 11.1	23 8.0	16 41.4	9 58.3	13 55.4	13 49.6
13 M	5 27 13	21 6 35	3♍21 15	10♍ 1 13	2 14.8	9 33.1	4 4.7	15 55.0	23 1.7	16 39.8	10 1.4	13 57.7	13 50.8
14 Tu	5 31 10	22 7 36	16 45 22	23 33 57	2D 13.1	10 55.4	5 15.1	16 39.0	22 55.4	16 38.1	10 4.4	13 59.9	13 52.0
15 W	5 35 6	23 8 38	0♎27 6	7♎24 57	2 13.1	12 16.0	6 25.4	17 23.0	22 49.4	16 36.2	10 7.4	14 2.2	13 53.1
16 Th	5 39 3	24 9 42	14 27 34	21 34 53	2 14.1	13 34.4	7 35.7	18 7.1	22 43.4	16 34.3	10 10.4	14 4.4	13 54.2
17 F	5 42 59	25 10 46	28 46 47	6♏ 2 57	2R 14.9	14 50.4	8 45.8	18 51.2	22 37.7	16 32.2	10 13.4	14 6.6	13 55.3
18 Sa	5 46 56	26 11 51	13♏22 59	20 46 17	2 14.5	16 3.6	9 55.8	19 35.4	22 32.0	16 30.1	10 16.3	14 8.9	13 56.3
19 Su	5 50 52	27 12 58	28 12 7	5♐39 37	2 11.8	17 13.3	11 5.7	20 19.6	22 26.6	16 27.8	10 19.1	14 11.1	13 57.3
20 M	5 54 49	28 14 5	13♐ 7 46	20 35 30	2 6.6	18 19.2	12 15.4	21 3.9	22 21.3	16 25.5	10 22.0	14 13.3	13 58.3
21 Tu	5 58 46	29 15 12	28 1 42	5♑25 14	1 59.0	19 20.6	13 25.1	21 48.2	22 16.2	16 23.0	10 24.8	14 15.5	13 59.2
22 W	6 2 42	0♑16 20	12♑45 2	20 0 9	1 49.6	20 16.8	14 34.6	22 32.6	22 11.2	16 20.5	10 27.6	14 17.7	14 0.1
23 Th	6 6 39	1 17 29	27 9 46	4♒13 12	1 39.5	21 7.1	15 43.9	23 17.0	22 6.5	16 17.8	10 30.3	14 19.9	14 1.0
24 F	6 10 35	2 18 38	11♒10 1	17 59 55	1 29.9	21 50.6	16 53.2	24 1.5	22 1.9	16 15.1	10 33.0	14 22.1	14 1.8
25 Sa	6 14 32	3 19 46	24 42 48	1♓18 46	1 21.9	22 26.4	18 2.3	24 46.0	21 57.5	16 12.2	10 35.6	14 24.3	14 2.6
26 Su	6 18 28	4 20 55	7♓48 2	14 10 57	1 16.1	22 53.7	19 11.2	25 30.5	21 53.2	16 9.3	10 38.2	14 26.4	14 3.4
27 M	6 22 25	5 22 4	20 28 1	26 39 47	1 12.7	23 11.5	20 19.9	26 15.1	21 49.2	16 6.2	10 40.8	14 28.6	14 4.1
28 Tu	6 26 21	6 23 13	2♈46 51	8♈49 53	1D 11.5	23R 19.1	21 28.5	26 59.7	21 45.4	16 3.1	10 43.3	14 30.7	14 4.8
29 W	6 30 18	7 24 22	14 49 35	20 46 38	1 11.6	23 15.6	22 37.0	27 44.4	21 41.7	15 59.9	10 45.8	14 32.8	14 5.5
30 Th	6 34 15	8 25 31	26 41 45	2♉35 36	1R 12.1	23 0.4	23 45.2	28 29.1	21 38.3	15 56.6	10 48.3	14 35.0	14 6.1
31 F	6 38 11	9 26 39	8♉28 51	14 22 8	1 12.0	22 33.5	24 53.3	29 13.9	21 35.0	15 53.2	10 50.7	14 37.1	14 6.7

Astro Data

	Dy Hr Mn
☽0 N	2 12:26
♃□♇	5 18:59
☽0 S	17 1:53
♄ R	27 18:46
☽0 N	29 19:15
♆✶♇	5 22:00
☽0 S	14 9:52
☽0 N	27 4:11
☿ R	28 4:34

Planet Ingress

	Dy Hr Mn
♀ ♑	14 10:42
☿ ♐	16 19:02
♂ ♐	20 23:53
☉ ♐	22 4:22
☿ ♑	6 9:25
♀ ♒	9 12:53
☉ ♑	21 17:35

Last Aspect / ☽ Ingress

Last Aspect Dy Hr Mn		☽ Ingress Dy Hr Mn
3 1:04	♃ ✶	♈ 3 4:46
4 17:31	♀ △	♉ 5 17:23
8 1:18	♃ ☌	♊ 8 6:21
10 8:41	♀ ☍	♋ 10 18:28
12 22:38	♃ ✶	♌ 13 4:36
15 7:39	☿ □	♍ 15 11:46
17 11:21	♂ ✶	♎ 17 15:34
18 19:16	♄ ✶	♏ 19 16:32
21 15:11	☉ ☌	♐ 21 16:03
22 18:50	♄ △	♑ 23 16:03
25 10:08	♃ △	♒ 25 18:30
27 15:13	♃ □	♓ 28 0:47
30 0:13	♃ ✶	♈ 30 11:01

Last Aspect / ☽ Ingress

Last Aspect Dy Hr Mn		☽ Ingress Dy Hr Mn
2 11:45	☿ △	♉ 2 23:41
5 1:59	♀ △	♊ 5 12:38
6 22:17	♄ ✶	♋ 8 0:21
9 21:35	♃ ✶	♌ 10 10:12
12 5:19	♃ □	♍ 12 17:55
14 10:48	♃ △	♎ 14 23:13
16 17:33	☉ ✶	♏ 17 2:01
18 14:46	♃ ☍	♐ 19 2:54
21 2:08	☉ ☌	♑ 21 3:12
22 15:34	♃ △	♒ 23 4:48
25 0:06	♂ ✶	♓ 25 9:36
27 11:55	♂ □	♈ 27 18:32
30 3:53	♂ △	♉ 30 6:43

☽ Phases & Eclipses

Dy Hr Mn	
6 23:15	○ 14♉41
6 23:01	☊ A 0.838
14 22:39	☽ 22♌42
21 15:11	● 29♏27
28 12:59	☽ 6♓26
6 18:15	○ 14♊46
14 10:14	☽ 22♍34
21 2:08	● 29♐21
28 7:48	☽ 6♈43

Astro Data

1 NOVEMBER 1976
Julian Day # 28064
Delta T 47.3 sec
SVP 05♓34'51"
Obliquity 23°26'25"
⚷ Chiron 29♈09.3R
☽ Mean ☊ 3♏06.9

1 DECEMBER 1976
Julian Day # 28094
Delta T 47.4 sec
SVP 05♓34'47"
Obliquity 23°26'24"
⚷ Chiron 27♈56.1R
☽ Mean ☊ 1♏31.5

LONGITUDE JANUARY 1977

Day	Sid.Time	☉	0 hr ☽	Noon ☽	True ☊	☿	♀	♂	♃	♄	♅	♆	♇
1 Sa	6 42 8	10♑27 48	20♉16 0	26♉11 2	1♏10.1	21♑54.7	26♒ 1.2	29♐58.7	21♉32.0	15♌49.8	10♏53.0	14♐39.1	14♎ 7.3
2 Su	6 46 4	11 28 57	2♊ 7 41	8♊ 6 25	1R 5.7	21R 4.8	27 8.9	0♑43.6	21R29.1	15R46.2	10 55.3	14 41.2	14 7.8
3 M	6 50 1	12 30 5	14 7 33	20 11 26	0 58.5	20 4.7	28 16.3	1 28.4	21 26.4	15 42.6	10 57.6	14 43.3	14 8.3
4 Tu	6 53 57	13 31 13	26 18 16	2♋28 14	0 48.5	18 56.0	29 23.6	2 13.4	21 24.0	15 38.9	10 59.8	14 45.3	14 8.8
5 W	6 57 54	14 32 22	8♋41 26	14 57 55	0 36.3	17 40.8	0♓30.7	2 58.4	21 21.7	15 35.1	11 2.0	14 47.4	14 9.2
6 Th	7 1 50	15 33 30	21 17 41	27 40 41	0 22.9	16 21.5	1 37.5	3 43.4	21 19.7	15 31.3	11 4.1	14 49.4	14 9.6
7 F	7 5 47	16 34 38	4♌ 6 48	10♌35 58	0 9.4	15 0.7	2 44.1	4 28.5	21 17.8	15 27.4	11 6.2	14 51.4	14 9.9
8 Sa	7 9 44	17 35 45	17 8 3	23 42 55	29♎57.1	13 41.0	3 50.4	5 13.6	21 16.2	15 23.4	11 8.3	14 53.4	14 10.2
9 Su	7 13 40	18 36 53	0♍20 28	7♍ 0 38	29 47.1	12 24.8	4 56.6	5 58.7	21 14.7	15 19.3	11 10.3	14 55.3	14 10.5
10 M	7 17 37	19 38 1	13 43 21	20 28 36	29 39.9	11 14.3	6 2.4	6 43.9	21 13.5	15 15.2	11 12.2	14 57.3	14 10.7
11 Tu	7 21 33	20 39 8	27 16 22	4♎ 6 43	29 35.7	10 11.1	7 8.0	7 29.1	21 12.5	15 11.0	11 14.1	14 59.2	14 10.9
12 W	7 25 30	21 40 16	10♎59 40	17 55 18	29D34.0	9 16.5	8 13.4	8 14.4	21 11.6	15 6.8	11 15.9	15 1.1	14 11.1
13 Th	7 29 26	22 41 24	24 53 40	1♏54 48	29R33.7	8 31.3	9 18.5	8 59.7	21 11.0	15 2.5	11 17.7	15 3.0	14 11.2
14 F	7 33 23	23 42 31	8♏58 39	16 5 8	29 33.6	7 55.7	10 23.3	9 45.1	21 10.6	14 58.1	11 19.5	15 4.9	14 11.3
15 Sa	7 37 19	24 43 39	23 14 7	0♐25 17	29 32.2	7 29.9	11 27.8	10 30.5	21D10.4	14 53.7	11 21.2	15 6.8	14 11.4
16 Su	7 41 16	25 44 46	7♐38 17	14 52 36	29 28.4	7 13.6	12 32.0	11 15.9	21 10.4	14 49.3	11 22.8	15 8.6	14R11.4
17 M	7 45 13	26 45 53	22 7 39	29 22 42	29 21.6	7D 6.4	13 35.9	12 1.4	21 10.7	14 44.8	11 24.4	15 10.4	14 11.4
18 Tu	7 49 9	27 47 0	6♑36 59	13♑49 41	29 11.9	7 7.8	14 39.5	12 47.0	21 11.1	14 40.2	11 26.0	15 12.2	14 11.4
19 W	7 53 6	28 48 7	20 59 55	28 6 54	28 60.0	7 17.1	15 42.7	13 32.5	21 11.7	14 35.6	11 27.5	15 14.0	14 11.3
20 Th	7 57 2	29 49 12	5♒ 9 51	12♒ 8 6	28 47.0	7 33.8	16 45.7	14 18.1	21 12.6	14 31.0	11 28.9	15 15.8	14 11.2
21 F	8 0 59	0♒50 17	19 1 6	25 48 26	28 34.4	7 57.2	17 48.2	15 3.8	21 13.6	14 26.3	11 30.3	15 17.5	14 11.0
22 Sa	8 4 55	1 51 22	2♓29 51	9♓ 5 14	28 23.5	8 26.7	18 50.4	15 49.4	21 14.8	14 21.6	11 31.6	15 19.2	14 10.8
23 Su	8 8 52	2 52 25	15 34 37	21 58 10	28 14.9	9 1.9	19 52.2	16 35.1	21 16.3	14 16.8	11 32.9	15 20.9	14 10.6
24 M	8 12 48	3 53 27	28 16 11	4♈29 5	28 9.3	9 42.0	20 53.7	17 20.9	21 18.0	14 12.1	11 34.1	15 22.5	14 10.4
25 Tu	8 16 45	4 54 29	10♈37 21	16 41 33	28 6.3	10 26.8	21 54.7	18 6.6	21 19.8	14 7.3	11 35.3	15 24.2	14 10.1
26 W	8 20 42	5 55 29	22 42 19	28 40 18	28D 5.3	11 15.7	22 55.3	18 52.4	21 21.9	14 2.5	11 36.4	15 25.8	14 9.7
27 Th	8 24 38	6 56 28	4♉36 11	10♉30 42	28R 5.3	12 8.3	23 55.4	19 38.3	21 24.2	13 57.6	11 37.5	15 27.4	14 9.4
28 F	8 28 35	7 57 26	16 24 31	22 18 23	28 5.1	13 4.3	24 55.1	20 24.1	21 26.6	13 52.8	11 38.5	15 28.9	14 9.0
29 Sa	8 32 31	8 58 23	28 12 56	4♊ 8 51	28 3.5	14 3.4	25 54.3	21 10.0	21 29.3	13 47.9	11 39.5	15 30.5	14 8.6
30 Su	8 36 28	9 59 19	10♊ 6 43	16 7 8	27 59.8	15 5.3	26 53.0	21 56.0	21 32.1	13 43.0	11 40.4	15 32.0	14 8.1
31 M	8 40 24	11 0 13	22 10 34	28 17 29	27 53.4	16 9.8	27 51.2	22 41.9	21 35.2	13 38.1	11 41.2	15 33.5	14 7.6

LONGITUDE FEBRUARY 1977

Day	Sid.Time	☉	0 hr ☽	Noon ☽	True ☊	☿	♀	♂	♃	♄	♅	♆	♇
1 Tu	8 44 21	12♒ 1 7	4♋28 14	10♋43 6	27♎44.3	17♑16.5	28♓48.9	23♑27.9	21♉38.5	13♌33.2	11♏42.0	15♐34.9	14♎ 7.1
2 W	8 48 17	13 1 59	17 2 16	23 25 51	27R33.0	18 25.5	29 46.0	24 14.0	21 41.9	13R28.3	11 42.7	15 36.3	14R 6.5
3 Th	8 52 14	14 2 50	29 53 51	6♌26 11	27 20.3	19 36.4	0♈42.6	25 0.0	21 45.5	13 23.4	11 43.4	15 37.7	14 5.9
4 F	8 56 11	15 3 39	13♌ 2 40	19 43 5	27 7.5	20 49.1	1 38.5	25 46.1	21 49.3	13 18.5	11 44.0	15 39.1	14 5.3
5 Sa	9 0 7	16 4 28	26 27 6	3♍14 24	26 55.7	22 3.6	2 33.9	26 32.2	21 53.3	13 13.6	11 44.6	15 40.5	14 4.7
6 Su	9 4 4	17 5 15	10♍ 4 35	16 57 16	26 46.1	23 19.6	3 28.6	27 18.4	21 57.5	13 8.7	11 45.1	15 41.8	14 4.0
7 M	9 8 0	18 6 1	23 52 6	0♎48 43	26 39.2	24 37.1	4 22.7	28 4.5	22 1.9	13 3.8	11 45.6	15 43.1	14 3.2
8 Tu	9 11 57	19 6 46	7♎46 49	14 46 6	26 35.3	25 56.0	5 16.1	28 50.7	22 6.5	12 58.9	11 46.0	15 44.3	14 2.5
9 W	9 15 53	20 7 30	21 46 22	28 47 26	26D33.9	27 16.2	6 8.8	29 37.0	22 11.2	12 54.1	11 46.4	15 45.6	14 1.7
10 Th	9 19 50	21 8 14	5♏49 9	12♏51 26	26 34.0	28 37.6	7 0.7	0♒23.2	22 16.1	12 49.3	11 46.6	15 46.8	14 0.9
11 F	9 23 46	22 8 56	19 54 9	26 57 13	26R34.4	0♒ 0.3	7 51.9	1 9.5	22 21.2	12 44.4	11 46.9	15 47.9	14 0.0
12 Sa	9 27 43	23 9 37	4♐ 0 31	11♐ 3 55	26 34.0	1 24.1	8 42.4	1 55.9	22 26.5	12 39.7	11 47.1	15 49.1	13 59.2
13 Su	9 31 40	24 10 17	18 7 15	25 10 16	26 31.5	2 49.0	9 32.0	2 42.2	22 31.9	12 34.9	11 47.2	15 50.2	13 58.3
14 M	9 35 36	25 10 56	2♑12 41	9♑14 9	26 26.6	4 15.0	10 20.8	3 28.6	22 37.5	12 30.1	11R47.3	15 51.3	13 57.3
15 Tu	9 39 33	26 11 34	16 14 18	23 12 40	26 19.2	5 42.0	11 8.7	4 15.0	22 43.3	12 25.4	11 47.3	15 52.3	13 56.4
16 W	9 43 29	27 12 10	0♒ 8 48	7♒ 2 15	26 9.9	7 10.1	11 55.7	5 1.4	22 49.3	12 20.8	11 47.3	15 53.4	13 55.4
17 Th	9 47 26	28 12 45	13 52 32	20 39 13	25 59.6	8 39.1	12 41.8	5 47.9	22 55.4	12 16.1	11 47.2	15 54.3	13 54.4
18 F	9 51 22	29 13 19	27 21 57	4♓ 0 25	25 49.4	10 9.2	13 26.9	6 34.3	23 1.7	12 11.5	11 47.0	15 55.3	13 53.3
19 Sa	9 55 19	0♓13 51	10♓34 21	17 3 40	25 40.5	11 40.1	14 11.0	7 20.8	23 8.2	12 7.0	11 46.8	15 56.2	13 52.3
20 Su	9 59 15	1 14 21	23 28 17	29 48 15	25 33.6	13 12.1	14 54.0	8 7.3	23 14.8	12 2.5	11 46.5	15 57.1	13 51.2
21 M	10 3 12	2 14 50	6♈ 3 45	12♈15 1	25 29.2	14 45.0	15 35.9	8 53.9	23 21.6	11 58.0	11 46.2	15 58.0	13 50.1
22 Tu	10 7 9	3 15 17	18 22 21	24 26 10	25D27.1	16 18.9	16 16.7	9 40.4	23 28.5	11 53.6	11 45.9	15 58.8	13 48.9
23 W	10 11 5	4 15 42	0♉26 57	6♉25 13	25 26.9	17 53.8	16 56.3	10 27.0	23 35.6	11 49.3	11 45.4	15 59.6	13 47.7
24 Th	10 15 2	5 16 6	12 21 32	18 16 31	25 27.9	19 29.6	17 34.7	11 13.6	23 42.8	11 45.0	11 45.0	16 0.4	13 46.5
25 F	10 18 58	6 16 27	24 10 48	0♊ 5 3	25 29.2	21 6.4	18 11.7	12 0.2	23 50.2	11 40.7	11 44.4	16 1.1	13 45.3
26 Sa	10 22 55	7 16 46	5♊59 56	11 56 6	25R30.0	22 44.1	18 47.4	12 46.8	23 57.8	11 36.5	11 43.8	16 1.8	13 44.1
27 Su	10 26 51	8 17 4	17 54 15	23 54 59	25 29.4	24 22.9	19 21.7	13 33.4	24 5.5	11 32.4	11 43.2	16 2.5	13 42.8
28 M	10 30 48	9 17 19	29 58 54	6♋ 6 35	25 26.9	26 2.6	19 54.6	14 20.1	24 13.3	11 28.4	11 42.5	16 3.1	13 41.5

Astro Data	Planet Ingress	Last Aspect	☽ Ingress	Last Aspect	☽ Ingress	☽ Phases & Eclipses	Astro Data
Dy Hr Mn	Dy Hr Mn	Dy Hr Mn	Dy Hr Mn	Dy Hr Mn	Dy Hr Mn	Dy Hr Mn	1 JANUARY 1977
☽0S 10 16:32	♂ ♑ 1 0:42	1 12:54 ♀ □	♊ 1 19:43	2 14:21 ♂ ☍	♌ 3 0:11	5 12:10 ○ 15♋03	Julian Day # 28125
♄△♆ 12 21:54	♀ ♓ 4 13:01	4 6:37 ♀ △	♋ 4 7:12	4 15:50 ♃ □	♍ 5 6:17	12 19:55 ☽ 22♎31	Delta T 47.5 sec
♃ D 15 10:56	☊ ♎ 7 18:06	6 0:04 ♃ ✶	♌ 6 16:20	7 7:42 ♂ △	♎ 7 10:36	19 14:11 ● 29♑24	SVP 05♓34'42"
♇ R 16 7:05	☉ ♒ 20 4:14	8 7:32 ♃ □	♍ 8 23:23	9 10:24 ♀ ☍	♏ 9 14:04	27 5:11 ☽ 7♉10	Obliquity 23°26'24"
☿ D 17 8:01		10 13:18 ♃ △	♎ 11 4:48	11 4:12 ♃ ☍	♐ 11 17:11		⚷ Chiron 27♈18.9R
☽0N 23 14:35	♀ ♈ 2 5:54	12 19:55 ☉ □	♏ 13 8:44	13 11:06 ☉ ✶	♑ 13 20:14	4 3:56 ○ 15♌14	☽ Mean ☊ 29♎53.1
♄✶♇ 24 9:05	♂ ♒ 9 11:57	15 2:41 ☉ ✶	♐ 15 11:18	15 11:14 ♃ △	♒ 15 23:45	11 4:07 ☽ 22♏19	
♀0N 31 0:16	☿ ♒ 10 23:55	16 12:28 ♆ ☌	♑ 17 13:02	18 3:37 ☉ ☌	♓ 18 4:45	18 3:37 ● 29♒22	1 FEBRUARY 1977
	☉ ♓ 18 18:30	19 14:11 ☉ ☌	♒ 19 15:12	19 23:34 ♃ ✶	♈ 20 12:22	26 2:50 ☽ 7♊24	Julian Day # 28156
☽0S 6 23:33		21 3:53 ♃ □	♓ 21 19:30	21 19:39 ♀ ☌	♉ 22 23:06		Delta T 47.6 sec
♅ R 14 19:50		23 10:42 ♃ ✶	♈ 24 3:19	24 23:18 ♃ ☌	♊ 25 11:50		SVP 05♓34'37"
☽0N 20 0:33		25 15:49 ♂ □	♉ 26 14:41	27 14:59 ☿ △	♋ 28 0:02		Obliquity 23°26'24"
♄□♅ 24 0:03		28 18:53 ♀ ✶	♊ 29 3:37				⚷ Chiron 27♈35.2
		31 12:06 ♀ □	♋ 31 15:20				☽ Mean ☊ 28♎14.6

MARCH 1977 LONGITUDE

Day	Sid.Time	☉	0 hr ☽	Noon ☽	True ☊	☿	♀	♂	♃	♄	♅	♆	♇
1 Tu	10 34 44	10♓17 33	12♋18 32	18♋35 10	25♎22.6	27♒43.4	20♈25.9	15♒ 6.7	24♉21.3	11♌24.4	11♏41.8	16♐ 3.7	13♎40.2
2 W	10 38 41	11 17 45	24 56 52	1♌23 52	25R16.6	29 25.2	20 55.6	15 53.4	24 29.4	11R20.5	11R41.0	16 4.3	13R38.9
3 Th	10 42 38	12 17 54	7♌56 20	14 34 19	25 9.4	1♓ 8.1	21 23.8	16 40.1	24 37.7	11 16.6	11 40.2	16 4.8	13 37.5
4 F	10 46 34	13 18 1	21 17 44	28 6 23	25 2.0	2 52.0	21 50.2	17 26.8	24 46.1	11 12.8	11 39.3	16 5.3	13 36.2
5 Sa	10 50 31	14 18 7	4♍59 57	11♍58 3	24 55.1	4 36.9	22 14.9	18 13.5	24 54.6	11 9.1	11 38.3	16 5.8	13 34.8
6 Su	10 54 27	15 18 10	19 0 9	26 5 41	24 49.6	6 23.0	22 37.7	19 0.2	25 3.3	11 5.5	11 37.3	16 6.2	13 33.4
7 M	10 58 24	16 18 12	3♎14 0	10♎24 28	24 45.9	8 10.1	22 58.7	19 47.0	25 12.0	11 2.0	11 36.3	16 6.6	13 31.9
8 Tu	11 2 20	17 18 12	17 36 25	24 49 12	24D44.1	9 58.4	23 17.8	20 33.7	25 21.0	10 58.5	11 35.2	16 7.0	13 30.5
9 W	11 6 17	18 18 10	2♏ 2 13	9♏14 56	24 44.1	11 47.8	23 34.8	21 20.5	25 30.0	10 55.1	11 34.0	16 7.3	13 29.0
10 Th	11 10 13	19 18 7	16 26 49	23 37 30	24 45.2	13 38.3	23 49.8	22 7.2	25 39.2	10 51.8	11 32.9	16 7.6	13 27.5
11 F	11 14 10	20 18 2	0♐46 35	7♐53 47	24 46.7	15 29.9	24 2.7	22 54.0	25 48.5	10 48.6	11 31.6	16 7.9	13 26.1
12 Sa	11 18 7	21 17 55	14 58 53	22 1 41	24R47.8	17 22.6	24 13.4	23 40.8	25 57.9	10 45.4	11 30.3	16 8.1	13 24.5
13 Su	11 22 3	22 17 47	29 2 2	5♑59 47	24 47.7	19 16.4	24 21.9	24 27.6	26 7.5	10 42.4	11 29.0	16 8.3	13 23.0
14 M	11 26 0	23 17 37	12♑54 52	19 47 8	24 46.3	21 11.3	24 28.1	25 14.5	26 17.1	10 39.4	11 27.6	16 8.5	13 21.5
15 Tu	11 29 56	24 17 26	26 36 32	3♒22 57	24 43.4	23 7.2	24 31.9	26 1.3	26 26.9	10 36.5	11 26.2	16 8.6	13 19.9
16 W	11 33 53	25 17 13	10♒ 6 18	16 46 29	24 39.4	25 4.2	24R33.4	26 48.1	26 36.8	10 33.8	11 24.8	16 8.7	13 18.4
17 Th	11 37 49	26 16 58	23 23 24	29 56 59	24 34.7	27 2.0	24 32.5	27 34.9	26 46.8	10 31.1	11 23.3	16 8.8	13 16.8
18 F	11 41 46	27 16 41	6♓27 10	12♓53 52	24 30.2	29 0.7	24 29.2	28 21.8	26 56.9	10 28.5	11 21.7	16R 8.8	13 15.2
19 Sa	11 45 42	28 16 22	19 17 6	25 36 50	24 26.2	1♈ 0.1	24 23.4	29 8.6	27 7.1	10 26.0	11 20.1	16 8.8	13 13.6
20 Su	11 49 39	29 16 1	1♈53 7	8♈ 6 4	24 23.2	3 0.2	24 15.1	29 55.5	27 17.5	10 23.6	11 18.5	16 8.7	13 12.0
21 M	11 53 35	0♈15 38	14 15 46	20 22 25	24D21.6	5 0.7	24 4.3	0♓42.3	27 27.9	10 21.3	11 16.8	16 8.7	13 10.4
22 Tu	11 57 32	1 15 13	26 26 15	2♉27 31	24 21.2	7 1.6	23 51.0	1 29.2	27 38.4	10 19.1	11 15.1	16 8.6	13 8.7
23 W	12 1 29	2 14 46	8♉26 34	14 23 46	24 21.9	9 2.5	23 35.2	2 16.0	27 49.1	10 17.0	11 13.3	16 8.4	13 7.1
24 Th	12 5 25	3 14 17	20 19 31	26 14 18	24 23.2	11 3.2	23 17.1	3 2.8	27 59.8	10 15.0	11 11.5	16 8.2	13 5.5
25 F	12 9 22	4 13 46	2♊ 8 35	8♊ 2 55	24 24.9	13 3.5	22 56.6	3 49.7	28 10.7	10 13.1	11 9.7	16 8.0	13 3.8
26 Sa	12 13 18	5 13 12	13 57 51	19 53 59	24 26.5	15 3.1	22 33.7	4 36.5	28 21.6	10 11.3	11 7.8	16 7.8	13 2.2
27 Su	12 17 15	6 12 36	25 51 52	1♋52 9	24R27.5	17 1.6	22 8.7	5 23.3	28 32.6	10 9.6	11 5.9	16 7.5	13 0.5
28 M	12 21 11	7 11 58	7♋55 25	14 2 15	24 27.9	18 58.7	21 41.5	6 10.2	28 43.8	10 8.1	11 4.0	16 7.2	12 58.8
29 Tu	12 25 8	8 11 18	20 13 14	26 28 54	24 27.4	20 53.9	21 12.4	6 57.0	28 55.0	10 6.6	11 2.0	16 6.9	12 57.2
30 W	12 29 4	9 10 35	2♌49 44	9♌16 10	24 26.3	22 46.9	20 41.5	7 43.8	29 6.3	10 5.2	11 0.0	16 6.5	12 55.5
31 Th	12 33 1	10 9 50	15 48 31	22 27 4	24 24.7	24 37.3	20 9.0	8 30.6	29 17.7	10 3.9	10 58.0	16 6.1	12 53.8

APRIL 1977 LONGITUDE

Day	Sid.Time	☉	0 hr ☽	Noon ☽	True ☊	☿	♀	♂	♃	♄	♅	♆	♇
1 F	12 36 58	11♈ 9 2	29♌11 56	6♍ 3 7	24♎22.8	26♈24.7	19♈34.9	9♓17.4	29♉29.2	10♌ 2.8	10♏55.9	16♐ 5.7	12♎52.1
2 Sa	12 40 54	12 8 12	13♍ 0 30	20 3 48	24R21.2	28 8.6	18R59.7	10 4.2	29 40.7	10R 1.7	10R53.8	16R 5.2	12R50.5
3 Su	12 44 51	13 7 20	27 12 37	4♎26 23	24 19.9	29 48.7	18 23.4	10 50.9	29 52.3	10 0.8	10 51.7	16 4.7	12 48.8
4 M	12 48 47	14 6 26	11♎44 24	19 5 53	24D19.1	1♉24.7	17 46.3	11 37.7	0♊ 4.1	9 59.9	10 49.5	16 4.2	12 47.1
5 Tu	12 52 44	15 5 30	26 29 56	3♏55 38	24 18.9	2 56.2	17 8.6	12 24.5	0 15.9	9 59.2	10 47.3	16 3.7	12 45.4
6 W	12 56 40	16 4 32	11♏22 0	18 48 6	24 19.2	4 22.9	16 30.7	13 11.2	0 27.7	9 58.6	10 45.1	16 3.1	12 43.7
7 Th	13 0 37	17 3 32	26 13 2	3♐35 55	24 19.8	5 44.5	15 52.8	13 58.0	0 39.7	9 58.1	10 42.9	16 2.5	12 42.1
8 F	13 4 33	18 2 31	10♐56 3	18 12 47	24 20.4	7 0.8	15 15.1	14 44.7	0 51.7	9 57.7	10 40.6	16 1.8	12 40.4
9 Sa	13 8 30	19 1 27	25 25 35	2♑34 3	24 20.9	8 11.6	14 37.9	15 31.4	1 3.8	9 57.4	10 38.3	16 1.2	12 38.7
10 Su	13 12 27	20 0 22	9♑37 54	16 36 59	24R21.2	9 16.6	14 1.5	16 18.1	1 16.0	9 57.2	10 36.0	16 0.5	12 37.1
11 M	13 16 23	20 59 16	23 31 11	0♒20 32	24 21.2	10 15.8	13 26.0	17 4.9	1 28.2	9D57.1	10 33.7	15 59.7	12 35.4
12 Tu	13 20 20	21 58 7	7♒ 5 7	13 45 2	24 21.1	11 9.0	12 51.7	17 51.5	1 40.5	9 57.1	10 31.4	15 59.0	12 33.8
13 W	13 24 16	22 56 57	20 20 29	26 51 39	24 21.0	11 56.1	12 18.8	18 38.2	1 52.9	9 57.3	10 29.0	15 58.2	12 32.1
14 Th	13 28 13	23 55 45	3♓18 46	9♓42 4	24D20.9	12 36.9	11 47.4	19 24.9	2 5.3	9 57.5	10 26.6	15 57.4	12 30.5
15 F	13 32 9	24 54 31	16 1 47	22 18 10	24 20.9	13 11.5	11 17.9	20 11.5	2 17.8	9 57.9	10 24.2	15 56.5	12 28.8
16 Sa	13 36 6	25 53 15	28 31 25	4♈41 47	24 21.0	13 39.8	10 50.2	20 58.1	2 30.4	9 58.3	10 21.7	15 55.6	12 27.2
17 Su	13 40 2	26 51 58	10♈49 29	16 54 45	24 21.2	14 1.9	10 24.5	21 44.8	2 43.0	9 58.9	10 19.3	15 54.7	12 25.6
18 M	13 43 59	27 50 39	22 57 48	28 58 50	24R21.3	14 17.6	10 1.0	22 31.3	2 55.7	9 59.6	10 16.8	15 53.8	12 24.0
19 Tu	13 47 55	28 49 17	4♉58 7	10♉55 52	24 21.2	14 27.2	9 39.7	23 17.9	3 8.4	10 0.4	10 14.4	15 52.9	12 22.4
20 W	13 51 52	29 47 54	16 52 21	22 47 50	24 20.8	14R30.7	9 20.7	24 4.5	3 21.2	10 1.3	10 11.9	15 51.9	12 20.8
21 Th	13 55 49	0♉46 29	28 42 38	4♊37 2	24 20.2	14 28.3	9 4.1	24 51.0	3 34.1	10 2.3	10 9.4	15 50.9	12 19.2
22 F	13 59 45	1 45 2	10♊31 24	16 26 7	24 19.2	14 20.2	8 49.8	25 37.5	3 47.0	10 3.4	10 6.9	15 49.8	12 17.6
23 Sa	14 3 42	2 43 33	22 21 34	28 18 12	24 18.1	14 6.8	8 38.0	26 23.9	3 59.9	10 4.6	10 4.4	15 48.8	12 16.1
24 Su	14 7 38	3 42 2	4♋16 27	10♋16 50	24 16.9	13 48.4	8 28.6	27 10.4	4 13.0	10 5.9	10 1.8	15 47.7	12 14.5
25 M	14 11 35	4 40 28	16 19 50	22 25 58	24 16.0	13 25.3	8 21.6	27 56.8	4 26.0	10 7.4	9 59.3	15 46.6	12 13.0
26 Tu	14 15 31	5 38 53	28 35 46	4♌49 46	24D15.4	12 58.1	8 17.1	28 43.2	4 39.1	10 8.9	9 56.8	15 45.5	12 11.5
27 W	14 19 28	6 37 16	11♌ 8 29	17 32 25	24 15.4	12 27.3	8D14.9	29 29.6	4 52.3	10 10.6	9 54.2	15 44.3	12 10.0
28 Th	14 23 24	7 35 36	24 2 1	0♍37 41	24 15.9	11 53.5	8 15.2	0♈15.9	5 5.5	10 12.3	9 51.7	15 43.2	12 8.5
29 F	14 27 21	8 33 54	7♍19 44	14 8 25	24 16.8	11 17.4	8 17.7	1 2.2	5 18.7	10 14.2	9 49.2	15 42.0	12 7.1
30 Sa	14 31 18	9 32 10	21 3 51	28 6 0	24 18.0	10 39.7	8 22.5	1 48.5	5 32.0	10 16.1	9 46.6	15 40.8	12 5.6

Astro Data	Planet Ingress	Last Aspect	☽ Ingress	Last Aspect	☽ Ingress	☽ Phases & Eclipses	Astro Data
Dy Hr Mn	Dy Hr Mn	Dy Hr Mn	Dy Hr Mn	Dy Hr Mn	Dy Hr Mn	Dy Hr Mn	1 MARCH 1977
☽0S 6 8:10	☿ ♓ 2 8:09	1 23:08 ♃ ⚹	♌ 2 9:25	1 0:31 ♃ □	♍ 1 1:25	5 17:13 ○ 15♍01	Julian Day # 28184
♀ R 16 3:01	☿ ♈ 18 11:56	4 6:12 ♃ □	♍ 4 15:19	3 4:30 ♃ △	♎ 3 4:39	12 11:35 ☽ 21♐47	Delta T 47.7 sec
♆ R 18 7:35	☉ ♈ 20 17:42	6 10:21 ♃ △	♎ 6 18:34	4 9:26 ♀ ☍	♏ 5 5:40	19 18:33 ● 29♓02	SVP 05♓34'34"
☽0N 19 8:37	♂ ♓ 20 2:19	8 9:40 ♀ ☍	♏ 8 20:37	6 3:06 ♂ △	♐ 7 6:08	27 22:27 ☽ 7♋08	Obliquity 23°26'24"
☿0N 19 16:57		10 15:34 ♃ ☍	♐ 10 22:42	8 12:34 ☉ △	♑ 9 7:40		⚷ Chiron 28♈33.2
♃⚼♇ 24 10:50	☿ ♉ 3 2:46	12 15:55 ♀ △	♑ 13 1:40	10 19:15 ☉ □	♒ 11 11:24	4 4:09 ○ 14♎17	☽ Mean ☊ 26♎45.6
	♃ ♊ 3 15:42	14 23:43 ♃ △	♒ 15 6:00	13 5:10 ☉ ⚹	♓ 13 17:49	4 4:18 • P 0.193	
☽0S 2 18:15	☉ ♉ 20 4:57	17 8:09 ♂ ☌	♓ 17 12:06	15 8:29 ♂ ☌	♈ 16 2:52	10 19:15 ☽ 20♑48	1 APRIL 1977
♄ D 11 5:41	♂ ♈ 27 15:46	19 18:33 ☉ ☌	♈ 19 20:23	18 10:35 ☉ ☌	♉ 18 14:02	18 10:35 ● 28♈17	Julian Day # 28215
☽0N 15 14:48		21 18:58 ♀ ☌	♉ 22 7:05	20 15:37 ♂ ⚹	♊ 21 2:37	18 10:30:42 • A 7'04"	Delta T 47.8 sec
☿ R 20 2:09		24 15:49 ♃ ☌	♊ 24 19:39	23 8:44 ♂ □	♋ 23 15:25	26 14:42 ☽ 6♌15	SVP 05♓34'32"
♄□♅ 22 22:26		26 16:47 ♀ ⚹	♋ 27 8:16	26 0:15 ♂ △	♌ 26 2:43		Obliquity 23°26'24"
♀ D 27 9:49		29 16:52 ♃ ⚹	♌ 29 18:40	27 8:38 ♆ △	♍ 28 10:52		⚷ Chiron 0♉11.2
☽0S 30 4:40				29 14:42 ♆ □	♎ 30 15:13		☽ Mean ☊ 25♎07.1

LONGITUDE — MAY 1977

Day	Sid.Time	☉	0 hr ☽	Noon ☽	True ☊	☿	♀	♂	♃	♄	♅	♆	♇
1 Su	14 35 14	10♉30 24	5♎14 42	12♎29 37	24♎19.0	10♉ 1.0	8♈29.6	2♈34.7	5♊45.3	10♌18.2	9♏44.1	15♐39.5	12♎ 4.2
2 M	14 39 11	11 28 37	19 50 13	27 15 49	24R19.6	9R22.0	8 38.9	3 20.9	5 58.6	10 20.4	9R41.5	15R38.3	12R 2.8
3 Tu	14 43 7	12 26 47	4♏45 33	12♏18 25	24 19.4	8 43.5	8 50.3	4 7.1	6 12.0	10 22.6	9 39.0	15 37.0	12 1.4
4 W	14 47 4	13 24 56	19 53 18	27 28 58	24 18.3	8 6.2	9 3.8	4 53.3	6 25.4	10 25.0	9 36.4	15 35.7	11 60.0
5 Th	14 51 0	14 23 3	5♐ 4 14	12♐37 50	24 16.3	7 30.5	9 19.3	5 39.4	6 38.9	10 27.4	9 33.9	15 34.4	11 58.6
6 F	14 54 57	15 21 8	20 8 40	27 35 41	24 13.7	6 57.2	9 36.7	6 25.5	6 52.4	10 30.0	9 31.4	15 33.1	11 57.3
7 Sa	14 58 53	16 19 12	4♑58 0	12♑14 53	24 11.0	6 26.8	9 56.1	7 11.6	7 5.9	10 32.7	9 28.8	15 31.7	11 56.0
8 Su	15 2 50	17 17 15	19 25 48	26 30 23	24 8.5	5 59.7	10 17.3	7 57.6	7 19.5	10 35.4	9 26.3	15 30.4	11 54.7
9 M	15 6 47	18 15 16	3♒28 27	10♒19 58	24 6.7	5 36.2	10 40.3	8 43.6	7 33.1	10 38.3	9 23.8	15 29.0	11 53.4
10 Tu	15 10 43	19 13 16	17 5 3	23 43 55	24D 6.0	5 16.7	11 5.0	9 29.6	7 46.7	10 41.2	9 21.3	15 27.6	11 52.1
11 W	15 14 40	20 11 15	0♓16 53	6♓44 19	24 6.3	5 1.5	11 31.3	10 15.5	8 0.4	10 44.3	9 18.8	15 26.2	11 50.9
12 Th	15 18 36	21 9 12	13 6 40	19 24 23	24 7.5	4 50.7	11 59.3	11 1.4	8 14.0	10 47.4	9 16.3	15 24.7	11 49.7
13 F	15 22 33	22 7 8	25 37 56	1♈47 48	24 9.2	4D44.4	12 28.7	11 47.3	8 27.7	10 50.7	9 13.9	15 23.3	11 48.5
14 Sa	15 26 29	23 5 2	7♈54 26	13 58 16	24 10.7	4 42.7	12 59.6	12 33.1	8 41.5	10 54.0	9 11.4	15 21.8	11 47.3
15 Su	15 30 26	24 2 56	19 59 44	25 59 14	24R11.6	4 45.6	13 31.9	13 18.9	8 55.2	10 57.4	9 9.0	15 20.3	11 46.2
16 M	15 34 22	25 0 48	1♉57 8	7♉53 45	24 11.4	4 53.1	14 5.6	14 4.6	9 9.0	11 0.9	9 6.5	15 18.9	11 45.1
17 Tu	15 38 19	25 58 39	13 49 24	19 44 24	24 9.7	5 5.2	14 40.5	14 50.3	9 22.8	11 4.5	9 4.1	15 17.4	11 44.0
18 W	15 42 16	26 56 28	25 38 59	1♊33 25	24 6.4	5 21.8	15 16.7	15 36.0	9 36.6	11 8.2	9 1.8	15 15.8	11 42.9
19 Th	15 46 12	27 54 16	7♊27 57	13 22 49	24 1.7	5 42.8	15 54.1	16 21.6	9 50.4	11 12.0	8 59.4	15 14.3	11 41.9
20 F	15 50 9	28 52 3	19 18 16	25 14 32	23 55.7	6 8.1	16 32.7	17 7.2	10 4.3	11 15.9	8 57.0	15 12.8	11 40.8
21 Sa	15 54 5	29 49 48	1♋11 53	7♋10 36	23 49.3	6 37.6	17 12.3	17 52.7	10 18.2	11 19.9	8 54.7	15 11.2	11 39.9
22 Su	15 58 2	0♊47 32	13 10 58	19 13 19	23 42.8	7 11.2	17 53.0	18 38.2	10 32.0	11 23.9	8 52.4	15 9.7	11 38.9
23 M	16 1 58	1 45 14	25 18 0	1♌25 23	23 37.2	7 48.8	18 34.7	19 23.6	10 45.9	11 28.1	8 50.1	15 8.1	11 38.0
24 Tu	16 5 55	2 42 55	7♌35 53	13 49 54	23 32.9	8 30.2	19 17.4	20 9.0	10 59.8	11 32.3	8 47.8	15 6.6	11 37.1
25 W	16 9 51	3 40 34	20 7 55	26 30 20	23 30.2	9 15.3	20 1.0	20 54.3	11 13.8	11 36.6	8 45.6	15 5.0	11 36.2
26 Th	16 13 48	4 38 12	2♍57 38	9♍30 15	23D29.3	10 4.1	20 45.6	21 39.6	11 27.7	11 41.0	8 43.4	15 3.4	11 35.3
27 F	16 17 45	5 35 48	16 8 34	22 52 58	23 29.7	10 56.3	21 31.0	22 24.8	11 41.6	11 45.4	8 41.2	15 1.8	11 34.5
28 Sa	16 21 41	6 33 22	29 43 43	6♎41 0	23 30.9	11 52.0	22 17.2	23 10.0	11 55.5	11 50.0	8 39.0	15 0.2	11 33.7
29 Su	16 25 38	7 30 56	13♎44 53	20 55 18	23R32.0	12 51.0	23 4.2	23 55.2	12 9.5	11 54.6	8 36.9	14 58.6	11 32.9
30 M	16 29 34	8 28 28	28 12 0	5♏34 31	23 32.3	13 53.3	23 52.1	24 40.2	12 23.4	11 59.3	8 34.8	14 57.0	11 32.2
31 Tu	16 33 31	9 25 58	13♏ 2 14	20 34 19	23 30.8	14 58.7	24 40.6	25 25.3	12 37.4	12 4.1	8 32.7	14 55.4	11 31.5

LONGITUDE — JUNE 1977

Day	Sid.Time	☉	0 hr ☽	Noon ☽	True ☊	☿	♀	♂	♃	♄	♅	♆	♇
1 W	16 37 27	10♊23 28	28♏ 9 44	5♐47 19	23♎27.4	16♉ 7.2	25♈29.9	26♈10.3	12♊51.3	12♌ 9.0	8♏30.7	14♐53.8	11♎30.8
2 Th	16 41 24	11 20 56	13♐25 46	21 3 43	23R22.0	17 18.7	26 19.9	26 55.2	13 5.3	12 13.9	8R28.7	14R52.2	11R30.2
3 F	16 45 20	12 18 24	28 39 48	6♑12 45	23 15.2	18 33.2	27 10.6	27 40.1	13 19.3	12 18.9	8 26.7	14 50.5	11 29.6
4 Sa	16 49 17	13 15 50	13♑41 21	21 4 36	23 7.9	19 50.6	28 1.9	28 24.9	13 33.2	12 24.0	8 24.8	14 48.9	11 29.0
5 Su	16 53 14	14 13 16	28 21 39	5♒31 54	23 0.9	21 11.0	28 53.8	29 9.7	13 47.2	12 29.2	8 22.9	14 47.3	11 28.4
6 M	16 57 10	15 10 41	12♒34 57	19 30 37	22 55.3	22 34.1	29 46.4	29 54.4	14 1.1	12 34.4	8 21.0	14 45.7	11 27.9
7 Tu	17 1 7	16 8 5	26 18 54	2♓59 59	22 51.5	24 0.1	0♉39.5	0♉39.1	14 15.1	12 39.7	8 19.2	14 44.1	11 27.4
8 W	17 5 3	17 5 29	9♓34 11	16 1 55	22D49.6	25 28.9	1 33.2	1 23.7	14 29.0	12 45.0	8 17.4	14 42.4	11 27.0
9 Th	17 9 0	18 2 52	22 23 41	28 40 3	22 49.4	27 0.5	2 27.4	2 8.3	14 43.0	12 50.5	8 15.6	14 40.8	11 26.5
10 F	17 12 56	19 0 15	4♈51 38	10♈59 2	22 50.2	28 34.8	3 22.2	2 52.8	14 56.9	12 56.0	8 13.8	14 39.2	11 26.1
11 Sa	17 16 53	19 57 37	17 2 51	23 3 43	22R51.0	0♊11.8	4 17.4	3 37.3	15 10.8	13 1.6	8 12.2	14 37.6	11 25.8
12 Su	17 20 49	20 54 58	29 2 11	4♉58 49	22 50.9	1 51.6	5 13.2	4 21.7	15 24.7	13 7.2	8 10.5	14 36.0	11 25.4
13 M	17 24 46	21 52 19	10♉54 8	16 48 34	22 49.1	3 34.1	6 9.4	5 6.0	15 38.6	13 12.9	8 8.9	14 34.3	11 25.1
14 Tu	17 28 43	22 49 40	22 42 35	28 36 32	22 45.1	5 19.3	7 6.0	5 50.3	15 52.5	13 18.7	8 7.3	14 32.7	11 24.9
15 W	17 32 39	23 47 0	4♊30 47	10♊25 38	22 38.5	7 7.1	8 3.1	6 34.5	16 6.4	13 24.5	8 5.8	14 31.1	11 24.6
16 Th	17 36 36	24 44 20	16 21 19	22 18 5	22 29.6	8 57.5	9 0.6	7 18.7	16 20.3	13 30.4	8 4.3	14 29.5	11 24.4
17 F	17 40 32	25 41 39	28 16 7	4♋15 37	22 18.8	10 50.4	9 58.5	8 2.8	16 34.1	13 36.3	8 2.8	14 28.0	11 24.3
18 Sa	17 44 29	26 38 57	10♋16 44	16 19 37	22 7.0	12 45.8	10 56.7	8 46.8	16 48.0	13 42.3	8 1.4	14 26.4	11 24.1
19 Su	17 48 25	27 36 15	22 24 27	28 31 22	21 55.3	14 43.6	11 55.4	9 30.8	17 1.8	13 48.4	8 0.1	14 24.8	11 24.0
20 M	17 52 22	28 33 32	4♌40 35	10♌52 16	21 44.7	16 43.6	12 54.4	10 14.7	17 15.6	13 54.5	7 58.7	14 23.2	11 24.0
21 Tu	17 56 18	29 30 49	17 6 41	23 24 4	21 36.0	18 45.8	13 53.8	10 58.5	17 29.4	14 0.7	7 57.5	14 21.7	11D23.9
22 W	18 0 15	0♋28 5	29 44 43	6♍ 8 56	21 29.8	20 49.8	14 53.4	11 42.3	17 43.2	14 7.0	7 56.2	14 20.1	11 23.9
23 Th	18 4 12	1 25 20	12♍37 4	19 9 26	21 26.1	22 55.7	15 53.5	12 26.0	17 56.9	14 13.3	7 55.1	14 18.6	11 24.0
24 F	18 8 8	2 22 35	25 46 25	2♎28 21	21D24.7	25 3.0	16 53.8	13 9.6	18 10.6	14 19.6	7 53.9	14 17.1	11 24.0
25 Sa	18 12 5	3 19 49	9♎15 32	16 8 14	21R24.6	27 11.7	17 54.4	13 53.1	18 24.3	14 26.0	7 52.8	14 15.5	11 24.1
26 Su	18 16 1	4 17 2	23 6 37	0♏10 46	21 24.8	29 21.4	18 55.4	14 36.6	18 38.0	14 32.5	7 51.8	14 14.0	11 24.3
27 M	18 19 58	5 14 15	7♏20 38	14 36 1	21 24.0	1♋31.8	19 56.6	15 20.0	18 51.6	14 39.0	7 50.8	14 12.5	11 24.4
28 Tu	18 23 54	6 11 27	21 56 31	29 21 36	21 21.3	3 42.7	20 58.1	16 3.4	19 5.2	14 45.5	7 49.8	14 11.1	11 24.6
29 W	18 27 51	7 8 39	6♐50 28	14♐22 12	21 16.0	5 53.7	21 59.9	16 46.7	19 18.8	14 52.1	7 48.9	14 9.6	11 24.9
30 Th	18 31 47	8 5 51	21 55 41	29 29 43	21 8.2	8 4.7	23 2.0	17 29.9	19 32.3	14 58.7	7 48.1	14 8.1	11 25.1

Astro Data	Planet Ingress	Last Aspect	☽ Ingress	Last Aspect	☽ Ingress	☽ Phases & Eclipses	Astro Data
Dy Hr Mn	Dy Hr Mn	Dy Hr Mn	Dy Hr Mn	Dy Hr Mn	Dy Hr Mn	Dy Hr Mn	1 MAY 1977
♂0N 1 6:24	☉ ♊ 21 4:14	1 17:10 ♆ ⚹	♏ 2 16:24	31 3:21 ☿ ☍	♐ 1 2:54	3 13:03 ○ 12♏58	Julian Day # 28245
☽0N 12 20:36		3 13:03 ☉ ☍	♐ 4 15:59	2 22:21 ♂ △	♑ 3 2:07	10 4:08 ☽ 19♒23	Delta T 47.9 sec
☿ D 13 20:51	♀ ♉ 6 6:10	5 16:40 ♆ ☌	♑ 6 15:54	5 1:24 ♂ □	♒ 5 2:44	18 2:51 ● 27♉03	SVP 05♓34'29"
♃⚻♅ 15 20:23	♂ ♉ 6 3:00	7 20:09 ☉ △	♒ 8 18:00	6 19:24 ☿ □	♓ 7 6:35	26 3:20 ☽ 4♍46	Obliquity 23°26'24"
♄⚹♇ 24 22:09	☿ ♊ 10 21:07	10 4:08 ☉ □	♓ 10 23:29	9 10:04 ☿ ⚹	♈ 9 14:34		⚷ Chiron 2♉00.5
♃△♇ 26 12:27	☉ ♋ 21 12:14	12 16:39 ☉ ⚹	♈ 13 8:29	11 6:18 ☉ ⚹	♉ 12 1:56	1 20:31 ○ 11♐13	☽ Mean ☊ 23♎31.7
☽0S 27 14:10	☿ ♋ 26 7:07	14 14:44 ♆ △	♉ 15 20:04	13 4:44 ♄ □	♊ 14 14:50	8 15:07 ☽ 17♓42	
♃⚹♄ 27 9:47		18 2:51 ☉ ☌	♊ 18 8:50	16 18:23 ☉ ☌	♋ 17 3:28	16 18:23 ● 25♊28	1 JUNE 1977
		19 19:16 ♂ ⚹	♋ 20 21:35	18 2:14 ♇ □	♌ 19 14:53	24 12:44 ☽ 2♎53	Julian Day # 28276
♃☍♆ 8 20:41		22 11:34 ♂ □	♌ 23 9:13	21 3:47 ☿ ⚹	♍ 22 0:29		Delta T 47.9 sec
☽0N 9 3:41		25 1:33 ♂ △	♍ 25 18:31	23 22:27 ☿ □	♎ 24 7:35		SVP 05♓34'25"
♇ D 21 13:21		26 22:00 ♆ □	♎ 28 0:28	25 16:11 ♃ △	♏ 26 11:42		Obliquity 23°26'23"
☽0S 23 22:07		29 17:53 ♂ ☍	♏ 30 2:57	27 22:18 ♀ ☍	♐ 28 13:02		⚷ Chiron 3♉47.3
♄△♆ 23 16:13				29 20:09 ♃ ☍	♑ 30 12:48		☽ Mean ☊ 21♎53.2

JULY 1977 — LONGITUDE

Day	Sid.Time	☉	0 hr ☽	Noon ☽	True ☊	☿	♀	♂	♃	♄	♅	♆	♇
1 F	18 35 44	9♋ 3 2	7♑ 3 0	14♑34 15	20♎58.4	10♋15.3	24♉ 4.3	18♉13.0	19♊45.9	15♌ 5.4	7♏47.3	14♐ 6.7	11♎25.4
2 Sa	18 39 41	10 0 14	22 2 13	29 25 46	20R 47.8	12 25.3	25 6.9	18 56.1	19 59.3	15 12.2	7R 46.5	14R 5.3	11 25.8
3 Su	18 43 37	10 57 25	6♒43 54	13♒55 50	20 37.5	14 34.5	26 9.8	19 39.1	20 12.8	15 18.9	7 45.8	14 3.9	11 26.1
4 M	18 47 34	11 54 36	21 0 58	27 58 57	20 28.6	16 42.6	27 12.9	20 22.1	20 26.2	15 25.8	7 45.2	14 2.5	11 26.5
5 Tu	18 51 30	12 51 47	4♓49 36	11♓32 56	20 22.0	18 49.5	28 16.2	21 4.9	20 39.6	15 32.6	7 44.5	14 1.1	11 27.0
6 W	18 55 27	13 48 59	18 9 11	24 38 39	20 17.9	20 55.0	29 19.8	21 47.7	20 52.9	15 39.5	7 44.0	13 59.7	11 27.4
7 Th	18 59 23	14 46 11	1♈ 1 48	7♈19 11	20 16.0	22 59.1	0♊23.6	22 30.5	21 6.3	15 46.5	7 43.5	13 58.4	11 27.9
8 F	19 3 20	15 43 23	13 31 23	19 39 3	20 15.6	25 1.5	1 27.6	23 13.1	21 19.5	15 53.4	7 43.0	13 57.1	11 28.5
9 Sa	19 7 16	16 40 36	25 42 52	1♉43 30	20 15.5	27 2.2	2 31.8	23 55.7	21 32.8	16 0.4	7 42.6	13 55.7	11 29.0
10 Su	19 11 13	17 37 49	7♉41 37	13 37 50	20 14.8	29 1.2	3 36.2	24 38.2	21 46.0	16 7.5	7 42.3	13 54.5	11 29.6
11 M	19 15 10	18 35 2	19 32 49	25 27 6	20 12.4	0♌58.4	4 40.9	25 20.6	21 59.1	16 14.6	7 41.9	13 53.2	11 30.2
12 Tu	19 19 6	19 32 16	1♊21 16	7♊15 46	20 7.5	2 53.7	5 45.7	26 2.9	22 12.2	16 21.7	7 41.7	13 51.9	11 30.9
13 W	19 23 3	20 29 30	13 11 4	19 7 33	19 59.9	4 47.2	6 50.7	26 45.2	22 25.3	16 28.9	7 41.5	13 50.7	11 31.6
14 Th	19 26 59	21 26 45	25 5 32	1♋ 5 20	19 49.7	6 38.9	7 55.9	27 27.4	22 38.3	16 36.1	7 41.3	13 49.5	11 32.3
15 F	19 30 56	22 24 1	7♋ 7 8	13 11 9	19 37.5	8 28.6	9 1.3	28 9.5	22 51.2	16 43.3	7 41.2	13 48.3	11 33.1
16 Sa	19 34 52	23 21 16	19 17 31	25 26 18	19 24.1	10 16.5	10 6.9	28 51.5	23 4.2	16 50.5	7D 41.2	13 47.1	11 33.9
17 Su	19 38 49	24 18 32	1♌37 37	7♌51 30	19 10.7	12 2.5	11 12.6	29 33.5	23 17.0	16 57.8	7 41.2	13 46.0	11 34.7
18 M	19 42 46	25 15 49	14 7 59	20 27 7	18 58.5	13 46.6	12 18.6	0♊15.3	23 29.8	17 5.1	7 41.3	13 44.9	11 35.6
19 Tu	19 46 42	26 13 5	26 48 57	3♍13 33	18 48.3	15 28.8	13 24.6	0 57.1	23 42.6	17 12.5	7 41.4	13 43.8	11 36.5
20 W	19 50 39	27 10 22	9♍41 0	16 11 24	18 41.0	17 9.1	14 30.9	1 38.8	23 55.3	17 19.8	7 41.5	13 42.7	11 37.4
21 Th	19 54 35	28 7 39	22 44 53	29 21 39	18 36.5	18 47.6	15 37.2	2 20.4	24 7.9	17 27.2	7 41.8	13 41.6	11 38.3
22 F	19 58 32	29 4 57	6♎ 1 50	12♎45 40	18D 34.4	20 24.2	16 43.8	3 1.9	24 20.5	17 34.6	7 42.0	13 40.6	11 39.3
23 Sa	20 2 28	0♌ 2 15	19 33 20	26 24 59	18R 34.0	21 59.0	17 50.5	3 43.3	24 33.1	17 42.1	7 42.3	13 39.6	11 40.3
24 Su	20 6 25	0 59 33	3♏20 47	10♏20 49	18 34.1	23 31.8	18 57.3	4 24.6	24 45.5	17 49.5	7 42.7	13 38.6	11 41.4
25 M	20 10 21	1 56 51	17 25 4	24 33 28	18 33.4	25 2.8	20 4.3	5 5.9	24 57.9	17 57.0	7 43.1	13 37.7	11 42.5
26 Tu	20 14 18	2 54 10	1♐45 46	9♐ 1 38	18 30.9	26 31.9	21 11.4	5 47.0	25 10.3	18 4.5	7 43.6	13 36.8	11 43.6
27 W	20 18 15	3 51 29	16 20 33	23 41 53	18 25.9	27 59.0	22 18.7	6 28.1	25 22.6	18 12.0	7 44.2	13 35.9	11 44.7
28 Th	20 22 11	4 48 49	1♑ 4 51	8♑28 32	18 18.4	29 24.2	23 26.1	7 9.0	25 34.8	18 19.6	7 44.7	13 35.0	11 45.9
29 F	20 26 8	5 46 9	15 51 58	23 14 6	18 9.0	0♍47.4	24 33.6	7 49.9	25 46.9	18 27.1	7 45.4	13 34.1	11 47.1
30 Sa	20 30 4	6 43 30	0♒33 54	7♒50 24	17 58.7	2 8.7	25 41.3	8 30.7	25 59.0	18 34.7	7 46.1	13 33.3	11 48.3
31 Su	20 34 1	7 40 52	15 2 40	22 9 56	17 48.5	3 27.9	26 49.1	9 11.4	26 11.0	18 42.3	7 46.8	13 32.5	11 49.5

AUGUST 1977 — LONGITUDE

Day	Sid.Time	☉	0 hr ☽	Noon ☽	True ☊	☿	♀	♂	♃	♄	♅	♆	♇
1 M	20 37 57	8♌38 14	29♒11 33	6♓ 7 5	17♎39.7	4♍45.0	27♊57.0	9♊52.0	26♊23.0	18♌49.9	7♏47.6	13♐31.8	11♎50.8
2 Tu	20 41 54	9 35 37	12♓56 13	19 38 50	17R 33.1	5 60.0	29 5.1	10 32.6	26 34.8	18 57.5	7 48.4	13R 31.0	11 52.1
3 W	20 45 50	10 33 2	26 14 59	2♈44 50	17 28.9	7 12.7	0♋13.3	11 13.0	26 46.6	19 5.1	7 49.3	13 30.3	11 53.5
4 Th	20 49 47	11 30 27	9♈ 8 42	15 27 0	17D 27.0	8 23.2	1 21.7	11 53.3	26 58.4	19 12.7	7 50.3	13 29.6	11 54.8
5 F	20 53 43	12 27 54	21 40 14	27 48 57	17 26.8	9 31.4	2 30.1	12 33.6	27 10.0	19 20.3	7 51.3	13 29.0	11 56.2
6 Sa	20 57 40	13 25 22	3♉53 46	9♉55 20	17R 27.3	10 37.2	3 38.7	13 13.7	27 21.6	19 28.0	7 52.3	13 28.3	11 57.6
7 Su	21 1 37	14 22 51	15 54 18	21 51 21	17 27.6	11 40.4	4 47.5	13 53.8	27 33.1	19 35.7	7 53.4	13 27.7	11 59.1
8 M	21 5 33	15 20 22	27 47 7	3♊42 15	17 26.8	12 41.0	5 56.3	14 33.7	27 44.5	19 43.3	7 54.5	13 27.2	12 0.6
9 Tu	21 9 30	16 17 54	9♊37 22	15 33 2	17 24.0	13 38.8	7 5.2	15 13.6	27 55.8	19 51.0	7 55.7	13 26.6	12 2.1
10 W	21 13 26	17 15 27	21 29 48	27 28 9	17 19.0	14 33.8	8 14.3	15 53.3	28 7.1	19 58.7	7 57.0	13 26.1	12 3.6
11 Th	21 17 23	18 13 1	3♋28 32	9♋31 20	17 11.7	15 25.8	9 23.5	16 33.0	28 18.2	20 6.3	7 58.3	13 25.7	12 5.1
12 F	21 21 19	19 10 37	15 36 52	21 45 23	17 2.6	16 14.6	10 32.8	17 12.5	28 29.3	20 14.0	7 59.6	13 25.2	12 6.7
13 Sa	21 25 16	20 8 14	27 57 5	4♌12 7	16 52.6	17 0.1	11 42.2	17 51.9	28 40.3	20 21.7	8 1.0	13 24.8	12 8.3
14 Su	21 29 12	21 5 53	10♌30 32	16 52 21	16 42.4	17 42.0	12 51.7	18 31.3	28 51.2	20 29.4	8 2.5	13 24.4	12 10.0
15 M	21 33 9	22 3 32	23 17 34	29 46 6	16 33.1	18 20.2	14 1.3	19 10.5	29 2.0	20 37.1	8 4.0	13 24.1	12 11.6
16 Tu	21 37 6	23 1 13	6♍17 50	12♍52 42	16 25.5	18 54.6	15 11.1	19 49.6	29 12.7	20 44.7	8 5.5	13 23.7	12 13.3
17 W	21 41 2	23 58 55	19 30 32	26 11 14	16 20.2	19 24.8	16 20.9	20 28.6	29 23.3	20 52.4	8 7.1	13 23.4	12 15.0
18 Th	21 44 59	24 56 39	2♎54 41	9♎40 48	16 17.3	19 50.6	17 30.8	21 7.5	29 33.8	21 0.1	8 8.8	13 23.2	12 16.7
19 F	21 48 55	25 54 23	16 29 28	23 20 39	16D 16.4	20 11.8	18 40.8	21 46.2	29 44.3	21 7.8	8 10.4	13 23.0	12 18.5
20 Sa	21 52 52	26 52 9	0♏14 17	7♏10 20	16 17.0	20 28.3	19 50.9	22 24.9	29 54.6	21 15.4	8 12.2	13 22.8	12 20.2
21 Su	21 56 48	27 49 55	14 8 45	21 9 27	16 18.1	20 39.6	21 1.1	23 3.4	0♋ 4.8	21 23.1	8 14.0	13 22.6	12 22.0
22 M	22 0 45	28 47 43	28 12 22	5♐17 22	16R 18.7	20R 45.6	22 11.4	23 41.9	0 14.9	21 30.7	8 15.8	13 22.5	12 23.9
23 Tu	22 4 41	29 45 32	12♐24 14	19 32 45	16 18.0	20 46.2	23 21.8	24 20.2	0 24.9	21 38.4	8 17.7	13 22.4	12 25.7
24 W	22 8 38	0♍43 22	26 42 33	3♑53 14	16 15.5	20 41.0	24 32.3	24 58.4	0 34.8	21 46.0	8 19.6	13 22.3	12 27.6
25 Th	22 12 35	1 41 13	11♑ 4 20	18 15 17	16 11.1	20 30.0	25 42.9	25 36.4	0 44.6	21 53.6	8 21.6	13D 22.3	12 29.4
26 F	22 16 31	2 39 6	25 25 28	2♒34 15	16 5.3	20 13.0	26 53.6	26 14.4	0 54.3	22 1.2	8 23.6	13 22.3	12 31.3
27 Sa	22 20 28	3 37 0	9♒40 58	16 44 58	15 58.7	19 50.1	28 4.3	26 52.2	1 3.9	22 8.8	8 25.6	13 22.3	12 33.3
28 Su	22 24 24	4 34 55	23 45 38	0♓42 25	15 52.2	19 21.2	29 15.2	27 29.9	1 13.3	22 16.4	8 27.7	13 22.4	12 35.2
29 M	22 28 21	5 32 51	7♓34 49	14 22 28	15 46.5	18 46.6	0♌26.2	28 7.5	1 22.7	22 23.9	8 29.9	13 22.5	12 37.2
30 Tu	22 32 17	6 30 50	21 5 4	27 42 29	15 42.4	18 6.6	1 37.2	28 44.9	1 31.9	22 31.5	8 32.1	13 22.6	12 39.1
31 W	22 36 14	7 28 49	4♈14 39	10♈41 37	15D 40.1	17 21.5	2 48.3	29 22.3	1 41.0	22 39.0	8 34.3	13 22.7	12 41.1

Astro Data	Dy Hr Mn
☽ 0 N	6 12:42
♃ ♇ ♅	14 5:37
♅ D	16 8:41
☽ 0 S	21 4:50
☽ 0 N	2 22:52
☽ 0 S	17 11:25
☿ 0 S	22 3:56
☿ R	22 14:19
♆ D	25 12:07
☿ 0 N	27 14:27
☽ 0 N	30 8:49

Planet Ingress	Dy Hr Mn
♀ ♊	6 15:09
☿ ♌	10 12:00
♂ ♊	17 15:13
☉ ♌	22 23:04
☿ ♍	28 10:15
♀ ♋	2 19:19
♃ ♋	20 12:42
☉ ♍	23 6:00
♀ ♌	28 15:09

Last Aspect Dy Hr Mn		☽ Ingress Dy Hr Mn
2 5:22	♀ △	♒ 2 12:56
4 11:33	♀ □	♓ 4 15:31
6 7:06	♂ ⚹	♈ 6 22:03
9 3:09	☿ □	♉ 9 8:33
11 12:32	♂ ☌	♊ 11 21:15
13 18:59	♃ ☌	♋ 14 9:50
16 19:45	♂ ⚹	♌ 16 20:51
18 18:03	♃ ⚹	♍ 19 5:58
21 10:32	☉ ⚹	♎ 21 13:09
23 8:53	♃ △	♏ 23 18:13
25 14:18	☿ □	♐ 25 21:04
27 20:59	☿ △	♑ 27 22:15
28 17:22	♇ □	♒ 29 23:04

Last Aspect Dy Hr Mn		☽ Ingress Dy Hr Mn
31 21:41	♀ △	♓ 1 1:23
3 0:59	♃ □	♈ 3 6:54
5 10:54	♃ ⚹	♉ 5 16:18
7 7:31	♄ □	♊ 8 4:29
10 13:31	♃ ☌	♋ 10 17:04
12 1:19	☿ ⚹	♌ 13 3:57
15 10:48	♃ ⚹	♍ 15 12:26
17 17:57	♃ □	♎ 17 18:49
19 23:25	♃ △	♏ 19 23:35
22 1:04	☉ □	♐ 22 3:03
23 20:58	♂ ☍	♑ 24 5:30
26 2:41	♀ ☍	♒ 26 7:41
28 6:45	♂ △	♓ 28 10:46
30 14:36	♂ □	♈ 30 16:11

☽ Phases & Eclipses Dy Hr Mn		
1 3:24	○	9♑11
8 4:39	☽	15♈54
16 8:36	●	23♋42
23 19:38	☽	0♏49
30 10:52	○	7♒09
6 20:40	☽	14♉15
14 21:31	●	21♌58
22 1:04	☽	28♏50
28 20:10	○	5♓24

Astro Data

1 JULY 1977
Julian Day # 28306
Delta T 48.0 sec
SVP 05♓34'20"
Obliquity 23°26'23"
⚷ Chiron 5♉05.6
☽ Mean ☊ 20♎17.9

1 AUGUST 1977
Julian Day # 28337
Delta T 48.1 sec
SVP 05♓34'15"
Obliquity 23°26'23"
⚷ Chiron 5♉44.8
☽ Mean ☊ 18♎39.5

LONGITUDE SEPTEMBER 1977

Day	Sid.Time	☉	0 hr ☽	Noon ☽	True ☊	☿	♀	♂	♃	♄	♅	♆	♇
1 Th	22 40 10	8♍26 51	17♈ 3 33	23♈20 42	15♎39.5	16♍32.0	3♌59.6	29♊59.5	1♋50.0	22♌46.5	8♏36.5	13♐22.9	12♎43.2
2 F	22 44 7	9 24 54	29 33 25	5♉42 6	15 40.3	15R38.8	5 10.9	0♋36.6	1 58.9	22 54.0	8 38.9	13 23.2	12 45.2
3 Sa	22 48 4	10 23 0	11♉47 14	17 49 20	15 41.8	14 42.8	6 22.3	1 13.5	2 7.6	23 1.4	8 41.2	13 23.4	12 47.2
4 Su	22 52 0	11 21 7	23 48 58	29 46 42	15 43.5	13 45.1	7 33.8	1 50.3	2 16.2	23 8.9	8 43.6	13 23.7	12 49.3
5 M	22 55 57	12 19 16	5♊43 11	11♊39 1	15R44.6	12 46.8	8 45.4	2 27.0	2 24.7	23 16.3	8 46.0	13 24.0	12 51.4
6 Tu	22 59 53	13 17 27	17 34 49	23 31 11	15 44.7	11 49.2	9 57.0	3 3.6	2 33.1	23 23.7	8 48.5	13 24.4	12 53.5
7 W	23 3 50	14 15 41	29 28 45	5♋28 3	15 43.6	10 53.6	11 8.8	3 40.0	2 41.3	23 31.1	8 51.0	13 24.8	12 55.6
8 Th	23 7 46	15 13 56	11♋29 40	17 34 3	15 41.0	10 1.3	12 20.6	4 16.3	2 49.4	23 38.4	8 53.6	13 25.2	12 57.7
9 F	23 11 43	16 12 13	23 41 41	29 52 57	15 37.4	9 13.5	13 32.5	4 52.4	2 57.4	23 45.7	8 56.2	13 25.7	12 59.9
10 Sa	23 15 39	17 10 32	6♌ 8 11	12♌27 37	15 33.0	8 31.5	14 44.5	5 28.4	3 5.3	23 53.0	8 58.8	13 26.1	13 2.0
11 Su	23 19 36	18 8 53	18 51 28	25 19 49	15 28.4	7 56.2	15 56.6	6 4.2	3 13.0	24 0.3	9 1.5	13 26.7	13 4.2
12 M	23 23 33	19 7 17	1♍52 42	8♍30 2	15 24.2	7 28.5	17 8.8	6 39.9	3 20.5	24 7.5	9 4.2	13 27.2	13 6.4
13 Tu	23 27 29	20 5 42	15 11 42	21 57 29	15 20.9	7 9.2	18 21.0	7 15.4	3 27.9	24 14.7	9 6.9	13 27.8	13 8.6
14 W	23 31 26	21 4 8	28 47 7	5♎40 16	15 18.8	6D58.8	19 33.3	7 50.8	3 35.2	24 21.8	9 9.7	13 28.4	13 10.8
15 Th	23 35 22	22 2 37	12♎36 35	19 35 41	15D18.0	6 57.6	20 45.6	8 26.0	3 42.3	24 29.0	9 12.5	13 29.1	13 13.0
16 F	23 39 19	23 1 7	26 37 8	3♏40 33	15 18.3	7 5.8	21 58.1	9 1.1	3 49.3	24 36.1	9 15.4	13 29.7	13 15.3
17 Sa	23 43 15	23 59 40	10♏45 30	17 51 37	15 19.3	7 23.5	23 10.6	9 36.0	3 56.1	24 43.1	9 18.3	13 30.5	13 17.5
18 Su	23 47 12	24 58 14	24 58 31	2♐ 5 50	15 20.7	7 50.4	24 23.2	10 10.7	4 2.8	24 50.1	9 21.2	13 31.2	13 19.8
19 M	23 51 8	25 56 49	9♐13 15	16 20 26	15 21.9	8 26.3	25 35.8	10 45.3	4 9.3	24 57.1	9 24.1	13 32.0	13 22.0
20 Tu	23 55 5	26 55 26	23 27 8	0♑33 1	15R22.5	9 10.9	26 48.5	11 19.6	4 15.7	25 4.0	9 27.1	13 32.8	13 24.3
21 W	23 59 1	27 54 5	7♑37 51	14 41 20	15 22.3	10 3.7	28 1.3	11 53.9	4 21.9	25 10.9	9 30.1	13 33.6	13 26.6
22 Th	0 2 58	28 52 46	21 43 14	28 43 16	15 21.3	11 4.0	29 14.2	12 27.9	4 27.9	25 17.8	9 33.2	13 34.5	13 28.9
23 F	0 6 55	29 51 28	5♒41 10	12♒36 40	15 19.7	12 11.5	0♍27.1	13 1.8	4 33.8	25 24.6	9 36.2	13 35.4	13 31.2
24 Sa	0 10 51	0♎50 12	19 29 32	26 19 28	15 17.8	13 25.2	1 40.1	13 35.5	4 39.5	25 31.4	9 39.3	13 36.3	13 33.5
25 Su	0 14 48	1 48 57	3♓ 6 16	9♓49 42	15 15.9	14 44.8	2 53.1	14 9.0	4 45.1	25 38.1	9 42.5	13 37.3	13 35.8
26 M	0 18 44	2 47 45	16 29 35	23 5 46	15 14.4	16 9.4	4 6.2	14 42.3	4 50.5	25 44.8	9 45.6	13 38.3	13 38.1
27 Tu	0 22 41	3 46 34	29 38 7	6♈ 6 35	15 13.4	17 38.4	5 19.4	15 15.5	4 55.7	25 51.4	9 48.8	13 39.3	13 40.4
28 W	0 26 37	4 45 25	12♈31 8	18 51 49	15D12.9	19 11.3	6 32.6	15 48.4	5 0.8	25 58.0	9 52.0	13 40.4	13 42.8
29 Th	0 30 34	5 44 19	25 8 43	1♉21 59	15 13.1	20 47.4	7 45.9	16 21.2	5 5.7	26 4.5	9 55.3	13 41.4	13 45.1
30 F	0 34 30	6 43 14	7♉31 50	13 38 31	15 13.6	22 26.2	8 59.3	16 53.8	5 10.4	26 11.0	9 58.6	13 42.6	13 47.4

LONGITUDE OCTOBER 1977

Day	Sid.Time	☉	0 hr ☽	Noon ☽	True ☊	☿	♀	♂	♃	♄	♅	♆	♇
1 Sa	0 38 27	7♎42 12	19♉42 20	25♉43 40	15♎14.4	24♍ 7.2	10♍12.7	17♋26.2	5♋15.0	26♌17.4	10♏ 1.9	13♐43.7	13♎49.8
2 Su	0 42 24	8 41 11	1♊42 55	7♊40 32	15 15.1	25 49.9	11 26.2	17 58.4	5 19.4	26 23.8	10 5.2	13 44.9	13 52.1
3 M	0 46 20	9 40 13	13 37 0	19 32 50	15 15.8	27 34.1	12 39.7	18 30.4	5 23.6	26 30.1	10 8.5	13 46.1	13 54.5
4 Tu	0 50 17	10 39 18	25 28 35	1♋24 48	15 16.2	29 19.2	13 53.3	19 2.2	5 27.6	26 36.3	10 11.9	13 47.3	13 56.8
5 W	0 54 13	11 38 25	7♋22 6	13 21 1	15R16.4	1♎ 5.0	15 7.0	19 33.7	5 31.4	26 42.6	10 15.3	13 48.5	13 59.2
6 Th	0 58 10	12 37 34	19 22 10	25 26 7	15 16.4	2 51.3	16 20.7	20 5.1	5 35.1	26 48.7	10 18.7	13 49.8	14 1.6
7 F	1 2 6	13 36 45	1♌33 25	7♌44 36	15 16.3	4 37.8	17 34.5	20 36.2	5 38.6	26 54.8	10 22.1	13 51.1	14 3.9
8 Sa	1 6 3	14 35 58	14 0 9	20 20 29	15D16.2	6 24.3	18 48.3	21 7.2	5 41.9	27 0.8	10 25.6	13 52.5	14 6.3
9 Su	1 9 59	15 35 14	26 46 0	3♍16 57	15 16.2	8 10.8	20 2.2	21 37.8	5 45.0	27 6.8	10 29.1	13 53.9	14 8.6
10 M	1 13 56	16 34 32	9♍53 34	16 35 55	15 16.3	9 57.0	21 16.1	22 8.3	5 47.9	27 12.7	10 32.6	13 55.2	14 11.0
11 Tu	1 17 53	17 33 52	23 24 0	0♎17 40	15 16.4	11 42.9	22 30.1	22 38.5	5 50.7	27 18.5	10 36.1	13 56.7	14 13.4
12 W	1 21 49	18 33 15	7♎16 40	14 20 36	15R16.6	13 28.3	23 44.1	23 8.5	5 53.2	27 24.3	10 39.6	13 58.1	14 15.7
13 Th	1 25 46	19 32 39	21 28 58	28 41 10	15 16.6	15 13.3	24 58.2	23 38.2	5 55.6	27 30.0	10 43.2	13 59.6	14 18.1
14 F	1 29 42	20 32 6	5♏56 30	13♏14 11	15 16.3	16 57.8	26 12.3	24 7.6	5 57.7	27 35.7	10 46.7	14 1.1	14 20.4
15 Sa	1 33 39	21 31 34	20 33 26	27 53 25	15 15.8	18 41.7	27 26.5	24 36.8	5 59.7	27 41.2	10 50.3	14 2.6	14 22.8
16 Su	1 37 35	22 31 5	5♐13 18	12♐32 20	15 15.0	20 24.9	28 40.7	25 5.8	6 1.4	27 46.7	10 53.9	14 4.2	14 25.1
17 M	1 41 32	23 30 37	19 49 48	27 5 4	15 14.2	22 7.6	29 55.0	25 34.4	6 3.0	27 52.2	10 57.6	14 5.7	14 27.5
18 Tu	1 45 28	24 30 11	4♑17 36	11♑26 57	15 13.4	23 49.6	1♎ 9.3	26 2.8	6 4.4	27 57.5	11 1.2	14 7.3	14 29.8
19 W	1 49 25	25 29 47	18 32 46	25 34 49	15D12.9	25 31.0	2 23.6	26 31.0	6 5.6	28 2.8	11 4.8	14 9.0	14 32.1
20 Th	1 53 22	26 29 24	2♒32 56	9♒27 2	15 12.9	27 11.8	3 38.0	26 58.8	6 6.6	28 8.0	11 8.5	14 10.6	14 34.5
21 F	1 57 18	27 29 4	16 17 7	23 3 12	15 13.4	28 52.0	4 52.4	27 26.4	6 7.3	28 13.2	11 12.2	14 12.3	14 36.8
22 Sa	2 1 15	28 28 44	29 45 22	6♓23 44	15 14.4	0♏31.5	6 6.9	27 53.6	6 7.9	28 18.2	11 15.8	14 14.0	14 39.1
23 Su	2 5 11	29 28 27	12♓58 24	19 29 32	15 15.6	2 10.4	7 21.3	28 20.6	6 8.3	28 23.2	11 19.5	14 15.7	14 41.4
24 M	2 9 8	0♏28 11	25 57 14	2♈21 39	15 16.7	3 48.7	8 35.9	28 47.3	6R 8.5	28 28.1	11 23.2	14 17.4	14 43.7
25 Tu	2 13 4	1 27 57	8♈42 56	15 1 11	15R17.4	5 26.5	9 50.4	29 13.6	6 8.5	28 32.9	11 26.9	14 19.2	14 46.0
26 W	2 17 1	2 27 45	21 16 34	27 29 11	15 17.4	7 3.7	11 5.0	29 39.7	6 8.3	28 37.7	11 30.6	14 20.9	14 48.2
27 Th	2 20 57	3 27 35	3♉39 11	9♉46 43	15 16.5	8 40.3	12 19.7	0♌ 5.4	6 7.8	28 42.3	11 34.4	14 22.7	14 50.5
28 F	2 24 54	4 27 27	15 51 55	21 55 0	15 14.6	10 16.5	13 34.3	0 30.8	6 7.2	28 46.9	11 38.1	14 24.6	14 52.8
29 Sa	2 28 50	5 27 20	27 56 8	3♊55 34	15 11.8	11 52.1	14 49.0	0 55.9	6 6.4	28 51.4	11 41.8	14 26.4	14 55.0
30 Su	2 32 47	6 27 16	9♊53 32	15 50 21	15 8.3	13 27.2	16 3.8	1 20.6	6 5.4	28 55.8	11 45.6	14 28.3	14 57.3
31 M	2 36 44	7 27 14	21 46 20	27 41 51	15 4.5	15 1.8	17 18.5	1 45.0	6 4.2	29 0.2	11 49.3	14 30.2	14 59.5

Astro Data Dy Hr Mn	Planet Ingress Dy Hr Mn	Last Aspect Dy Hr Mn	☽ Ingress Dy Hr Mn	Last Aspect Dy Hr Mn	☽ Ingress Dy Hr Mn	☽ Phases & Eclipses Dy Hr Mn	Astro Data
☽0S 13 19:06	♂ ♋ 1 0:20	1 11:01 ♄ △	♉ 2 0:52	1 13:14 ♄ □	♊ 1 20:33	5 14:33 ☽ 12♊55	1 SEPTEMBER 1977
☿ D 14 15:04	♀ ♍ 22 15:05	3 22:39 ♄ □	♊ 4 12:27	4 9:07 ☿ □	♋ 4 9:09	13 9:23 ● 20♍29	Julian Day # 28368
☽0N 26 17:16	☉ ♎ 23 3:29	6 11:52 ♄ ✶	♋ 7 1:03	6 1:29 ♂ ☌	♌ 6 20:58	20 6:18 ☽ 27♐11	Delta T 48.2 sec
♆✶♇ 26 3:11		8 8:02 ☉ ✶	♌ 9 12:14	9 0:39 ♄ ☌	♍ 9 5:59	27 8:17 ○ 4♈07	SVP 05♓34'12"
	☿ ♎ 4 9:16	11 9:38 ♄ ☌	♍ 11 20:34	10 22:37 ♂ ✶	♎ 11 11:29	27 8:29 ☍ A 0.901	Obliquity 23°26'23"
☿0S 6 17:54	♀ ♎ 17 1:37	13 9:23 ☉ ☌	♎ 14 2:07	13 10:06 ♄ ✶	♏ 13 14:11		⚷ Chiron 5♉32.7R
☽0S 11 4:27	☿ ♏ 21 16:23	15 20:32 ♄ ✶	♏ 16 5:45	15 12:18 ♀ ✶	♐ 15 15:27	5 9:21 ☽ 12♋01	☽ Mean ☊ 17♎00.9
♀0S 19 22:39	☉ ♏ 23 12:41	17 23:59 ☉ ✶	♐ 18 8:28	17 13:23 ♄ △	♑ 17 16:51	12 20:31 ● 19♎24	
☽0N 24 0:01	♂ ♌ 26 18:56	20 6:18 ☉ □	♑ 20 11:04	19 14:04 ♂ ☍	♒ 19 19:36	12 20:26:39 ☌ T 2'37"	1 OCTOBER 1977
♃ R 24 10:13		22 13:12 ☉ △	♒ 22 14:12	21 21:31 ☉ △	♓ 22 0:26	19 12:46 ☽ 26♑01	Julian Day # 28398
		24 10:41 ♄ ☍	♓ 24 18:30	24 5:29 ♂ △	♈ 24 7:34	26 23:35 ○ 3♉27	Delta T 48.3 sec
		25 23:19 ☿ ☍	♈ 27 0:40	26 16:48 ♂ □	♉ 26 16:53		SVP 05♓34'10"
		29 1:48 ♄ △	♉ 29 9:21	29 1:51 ♄ □	♊ 29 4:08		Obliquity 23°26'23"
				31 14:44 ♄ ✶	♋ 31 16:40		⚷ Chiron 4♉36.0R
							☽ Mean ☊ 15♎25.6

NOVEMBER 1977 LONGITUDE

Day	Sid.Time	☉	0 hr ☽	Noon ☽	True ☊	☿	♀	♂	♃	♄	♅	♆	♇
1 Tu	2 40 40	8♏27 14	3♋37 19	9♋33 9	15♎ 0.9	16♏36.0	18♎33.3	2♌ 9.1	6♋ 2.8	29♌ 4.4	11♏53.1	14♐32.1	15♎ 1.7
2 W	2 44 37	9 27 16	15 29 50	21 27 53	14R 58.0	18 9.8	19 48.2	2 32.8	6R 1.2	29 8.6	11 56.8	14 34.0	15 3.9
3 Th	2 48 33	10 27 21	27 27 50	3♌30 14	14 56.0	19 43.1	21 3.0	2 56.1	5 59.3	29 12.6	12 0.6	14 35.9	15 6.1
4 F	2 52 30	11 27 27	9♌35 40	15 44 43	14D 55.2	21 16.0	22 17.9	3 19.0	5 57.3	29 16.6	12 4.3	14 37.9	15 8.3
5 Sa	2 56 26	12 27 35	21 57 57	28 15 56	14 55.5	22 48.4	23 32.9	3 41.6	5 55.1	29 20.5	12 8.1	14 39.8	15 10.4
6 Su	3 0 23	13 27 46	4♍39 12	11♍ 8 14	14 56.8	24 20.5	24 47.8	4 3.7	5 52.7	29 24.3	12 11.8	14 41.8	15 12.6
7 M	3 4 19	14 27 58	17 43 28	24 25 13	14 58.5	25 52.2	26 2.8	4 25.4	5 50.1	29 28.0	12 15.6	14 43.8	15 14.7
8 Tu	3 8 16	15 28 12	1♎13 43	8♎ 9 3	14R 59.9	27 23.6	27 17.8	4 46.8	5 47.3	29 31.6	12 19.3	14 45.8	15 16.8
9 W	3 12 13	16 28 29	15 11 9	22 19 48	15 0.5	28 54.5	28 32.9	5 7.7	5 44.3	29 35.1	12 23.1	14 47.9	15 18.9
10 Th	3 16 9	17 28 47	29 34 35	6♏54 52	14 59.7	0♐25.1	29 47.9	5 28.1	5 41.1	29 38.5	12 26.8	14 49.9	15 21.0
11 F	3 20 6	18 29 8	14♏19 53	21 48 40	14 57.3	1 55.3	1♏ 3.0	5 48.2	5 37.7	29 41.9	12 30.6	14 52.0	15 23.1
12 Sa	3 24 2	19 29 30	29 20 7	6♐53 4	14 53.3	3 25.1	2 18.1	6 7.7	5 34.1	29 45.1	12 34.3	14 54.1	15 25.1
13 Su	3 27 59	20 29 53	14♐26 17	21 58 31	14 48.1	4 54.6	3 33.3	6 26.8	5 30.3	29 48.2	12 38.0	14 56.2	15 27.2
14 M	3 31 55	21 30 19	29 28 37	6♑55 30	14 42.5	6 23.6	4 48.4	6 45.5	5 26.4	29 51.2	12 41.8	14 58.3	15 29.2
15 Tu	3 35 52	22 30 45	14♑18 16	21 36 8	14 37.3	7 52.2	6 3.6	7 3.6	5 22.3	29 54.2	12 45.5	15 0.4	15 31.2
16 W	3 39 48	23 31 13	28 48 35	5♒55 12	14 33.4	9 20.3	7 18.7	7 21.3	5 17.9	29 57.0	12 49.2	15 2.5	15 33.2
17 Th	3 43 45	24 31 43	12♒55 47	19 50 17	14D 31.0	10 48.0	8 33.9	7 38.4	5 13.4	29 59.7	12 52.9	15 4.7	15 35.1
18 F	3 47 42	25 32 13	26 38 49	3♓21 34	14 30.4	12 15.1	9 49.1	7 55.1	5 8.8	0♍ 2.3	12 56.6	15 6.8	15 37.1
19 Sa	3 51 38	26 32 45	9♓58 50	16 30 57	14 31.1	13 41.7	11 4.4	8 11.2	5 3.9	0 4.8	13 0.3	15 9.0	15 39.0
20 Su	3 55 35	27 33 18	22 58 20	29 21 23	14 32.6	15 7.6	12 19.6	8 26.8	4 58.9	0 7.2	13 4.0	15 11.1	15 40.9
21 M	3 59 31	28 33 52	5♈40 32	11♈56 10	14R 33.9	16 32.9	13 34.9	8 41.9	4 53.7	0 9.5	13 7.6	15 13.3	15 42.7
22 Tu	4 3 28	29 34 27	18 8 41	24 18 26	14 34.1	17 57.4	14 50.1	8 56.4	4 48.4	0 11.7	13 11.3	15 15.5	15 44.6
23 W	4 7 24	0♐35 4	0♉25 47	6♉31 0	14 32.7	19 21.0	16 5.4	9 10.4	4 42.9	0 13.8	13 14.9	15 17.7	15 46.4
24 Th	4 11 21	1 35 42	12 34 22	18 36 8	14 29.0	20 43.7	17 20.7	9 23.8	4 37.2	0 15.8	13 18.5	15 19.9	15 48.2
25 F	4 15 17	2 36 21	24 36 31	0♊35 41	14 22.9	22 5.2	18 36.0	9 36.6	4 31.4	0 17.7	13 22.1	15 22.1	15 50.0
26 Sa	4 19 14	3 37 2	6♊33 50	12 31 9	14 14.7	23 25.5	19 51.3	9 48.8	4 25.4	0 19.5	13 25.7	15 24.3	15 51.8
27 Su	4 23 11	4 37 44	18 27 47	24 23 56	14 5.0	24 44.3	21 6.6	10 0.4	4 19.3	0 21.1	13 29.3	15 26.6	15 53.5
28 M	4 27 7	5 38 27	0♋19 48	6♋15 36	13 54.4	26 1.5	22 22.0	10 11.4	4 13.0	0 22.7	13 32.9	15 28.8	15 55.2
29 Tu	4 31 4	6 39 12	12 11 35	18 8 1	13 44.1	27 16.8	23 37.3	10 21.8	4 6.6	0 24.2	13 36.4	15 31.0	15 56.9
30 W	4 35 0	7 39 58	24 5 15	0♌ 3 38	13 34.9	28 30.0	24 52.7	10 31.5	4 0.1	0 25.5	13 39.9	15 33.3	15 58.5

DECEMBER 1977 LONGITUDE

Day	Sid.Time	☉	0 hr ☽	Noon ☽	True ☊	☿	♀	♂	♃	♄	♅	♆	♇
1 Th	4 38 57	8♐40 46	6♌ 3 34	12♌ 5 30	13♎27.6	29♐40.7	26♏ 8.1	10♌40.6	3♋53.5	0♍26.7	13♏43.4	15♐35.5	16♎ 0.2
2 F	4 42 53	9 41 35	18 9 56	24 17 22	13R 22.6	0♑48.5	27 23.5	10 49.0	3R 46.7	0 27.9	13 46.9	15 37.8	16 1.8
3 Sa	4 46 50	10 42 25	0♍28 21	6♍43 28	13D 20.0	1 53.1	28 38.9	10 56.7	3 39.8	0 28.9	13 50.4	15 40.0	16 3.3
4 Su	4 50 46	11 43 17	13 3 18	19 28 25	13 19.4	2 53.9	29 54.3	11 3.7	3 32.7	0 29.8	13 53.8	15 42.3	16 4.9
5 M	4 54 43	12 44 10	25 59 21	2♎36 38	13 20.0	3 50.5	1♐ 9.7	11 10.0	3 25.6	0 30.5	13 57.2	15 44.6	16 6.4
6 Tu	4 58 40	13 45 4	9♎20 41	16 11 50	13R 20.7	4 42.1	2 25.2	11 15.6	3 18.4	0 31.2	14 0.6	15 46.8	16 7.9
7 W	5 2 36	14 46 0	23 10 17	0♏16 5	13 20.3	5 28.2	3 40.6	11 20.5	3 11.0	0 31.8	14 4.0	15 49.1	16 9.4
8 Th	5 6 33	15 46 57	7♏29 4	14 48 53	13 18.0	6 7.9	4 56.1	11 24.6	3 3.6	0 32.2	14 7.4	15 51.3	16 10.8
9 F	5 10 29	16 47 55	22 14 55	29 46 20	13 13.0	6 40.5	6 11.5	11 28.0	2 56.1	0 32.6	14 10.7	15 53.6	16 12.2
10 Sa	5 14 26	17 48 55	7♐22 3	15♐ 0 51	13 5.5	7 5.1	7 27.0	11 30.6	2 48.4	0 32.8	14 14.0	15 55.9	16 13.6
11 Su	5 18 22	18 49 55	22 41 17	0♑21 55	12 55.9	7 20.9	8 42.5	11 32.4	2 40.8	0R 32.9	14 17.3	15 58.1	16 15.0
12 M	5 22 19	19 50 56	8♑ 1 13	15 37 45	12 45.4	7R 27.0	9 58.0	11R 33.4	2 33.0	0 32.9	14 20.5	16 0.4	16 16.3
13 Tu	5 26 15	20 51 58	23 10 13	0♒37 29	12 35.4	7 22.6	11 13.4	11 33.6	2 25.2	0 32.8	14 23.7	16 2.7	16 17.6
14 W	5 30 12	21 53 0	7♒58 40	15 13 4	12 26.9	7 7.1	12 28.9	11 33.1	2 17.3	0 32.6	14 26.9	16 4.9	16 18.8
15 Th	5 34 9	22 54 3	22 20 17	29 20 7	12 20.8	6 40.0	13 44.4	11 31.7	2 9.3	0 32.2	14 30.1	16 7.2	16 20.1
16 F	5 38 5	23 55 7	6♓12 35	12♓57 50	12 17.3	6 1.4	14 59.9	11 29.5	2 1.3	0 31.8	14 33.2	16 9.4	16 21.3
17 Sa	5 42 2	24 56 10	19 36 14	26 8 11	12D 16.0	5 11.6	16 15.4	11 26.5	1 53.3	0 31.2	14 36.3	16 11.7	16 22.4
18 Su	5 45 58	25 57 14	2♈34 14	8♈54 54	12R 16.0	4 11.3	17 30.9	11 22.7	1 45.2	0 30.5	14 39.4	16 13.9	16 23.6
19 M	5 49 55	26 58 19	15 10 48	21 22 32	12 16.1	3 2.1	18 46.4	11 18.1	1 37.1	0 29.8	14 42.4	16 16.2	16 24.7
20 Tu	5 53 51	27 59 23	27 30 40	3♉35 45	12 15.2	1 45.9	20 1.9	11 12.6	1 29.0	0 28.9	14 45.4	16 18.4	16 25.7
21 W	5 57 48	29 0 28	9♉38 19	15 38 52	12 12.0	0 25.1	21 17.4	11 6.3	1 20.9	0 27.9	14 48.4	16 20.6	16 26.8
22 Th	6 1 44	0♑ 1 34	21 37 48	27 35 33	12 6.1	29♐ 2.4	22 32.9	10 59.2	1 12.7	0 26.7	14 51.3	16 22.8	16 27.8
23 F	6 5 41	1 2 39	3♊32 27	9♊28 47	11 57.1	27 40.5	23 48.3	10 51.3	1 4.6	0 25.5	14 54.2	16 25.0	16 28.7
24 Sa	6 9 38	2 3 45	15 24 50	21 20 47	11 45.3	26 22.2	25 3.8	10 42.5	0 56.4	0 24.2	14 57.1	16 27.2	16 29.7
25 Su	6 13 34	3 4 52	27 16 52	3♋13 13	11 31.3	25 9.8	26 19.3	10 32.9	0 48.3	0 22.8	14 59.9	16 29.4	16 30.6
26 M	6 17 31	4 5 58	9♋10 0	15 7 21	11 16.3	24 5.3	27 34.8	10 22.5	0 40.2	0 21.2	15 2.7	16 31.6	16 31.4
27 Tu	6 21 27	5 7 5	21 5 25	27 4 23	11 1.4	23 10.0	28 50.3	10 11.2	0 32.1	0 19.6	15 5.4	16 33.8	16 32.3
28 W	6 25 24	6 8 13	3♌ 4 23	9♌ 5 40	10 47.9	22 24.8	0♑ 5.8	9 59.2	0 24.0	0 17.8	15 8.1	16 36.0	16 33.1
29 Th	6 29 20	7 9 20	15 8 26	21 13 0	10 36.7	21 50.3	1 21.3	9 46.4	0 15.9	0 16.0	15 10.8	16 38.1	16 33.8
30 F	6 33 17	8 10 28	27 19 40	3♍28 49	10 28.4	21 26.2	2 36.8	9 32.7	0 7.9	0 14.0	15 13.4	16 40.3	16 34.6
31 Sa	6 37 14	9 11 36	9♍40 51	15 56 12	10 23.3	21D 12.5	3 52.3	9 18.3	29♊59.9	0 11.9	15 16.0	16 42.4	16 35.3

Astro Data	Dy Hr Mn
☽0S	7 14:56
☽0N	20 6:08
☽0S	5 1:07
♄ R	11 12:11
☿ R	12 2:11
♂ R	12 19:12
☽0N	17 13:25
♆✶♇	25 20:28
♃✶♄	28 23:52
♃⚻♅	29 11:30
☿ D	31 22:02

Planet Ingress	Dy Hr Mn
☿ ♐	9 17:20
♀ ♏	10 3:52
♄ ♍	17 2:41
☉ ♐	22 10:07
☿ ♑	1 6:43
♀ ♐	4 1:49
☉ ♑	21 23:23
☿ ♐	21 7:18
♀ ♑	27 22:09
♃ ♊	30 23:50

Last Aspect Dy Hr Mn		☽ Ingress	Dy Hr Mn
2 9:40	♀ □	♌	3 5:03
5 14:06	♄ ☌	♍	5 15:17
7 16:25	☿ ✶	♎	7 21:51
10 0:24	♀ ☌	♏	10 0:42
12 0:40	♄ □	♐	12 1:03
14 0:36	♄ △	♑	14 0:50
15 14:31	☉ ✶	♒	16 2:00
17 21:52	☉ □	♓	18 5:58
20 9:20	☉ △	♈	20 13:13
21 23:35	☿ △	♉	22 23:09
24 10:36	♀ ☍	♊	25 10:48
27 14:14	☿ ☍	♋	27 23:20
30 1:47	♀ △	♌	30 11:53

Last Aspect Dy Hr Mn		☽ Ingress	Dy Hr Mn
2 20:04	♀ □	♍	2 23:05
4 4:59	♆ □	♎	5 7:18
6 11:54	♇ ☌	♏	7 11:33
8 10:55	♅ ☌	♐	9 12:22
10 17:33	☉ ☌	♑	11 11:26
12 13:02	♇ □	♒	13 10:59
15 1:02	☉ ✶	♓	15 13:09
17 10:37	☉ □	♈	17 19:11
20 1:02	☉ △	♉	20 4:54
21 10:21	♅ ☍	♊	22 16:51
24 21:50	♀ ☍	♋	25 5:30
26 14:50	♇ □	♌	27 17:52
29 12:46	☿ △	♍	30 5:13

☽ Phases & Eclipses Dy Hr Mn	
4 3:58	☽ 11♌37
11 7:09	● 18♏47
17 21:52	☽ 25♒27
25 17:31	○ 3♊21
3 21:16	☽ 11♍36
10 17:33	● 18♐34
17 10:37	☽ 25♓23
25 12:49	○ 3♋37

Astro Data

1 NOVEMBER 1977
Julian Day # 28429
Delta T 48.4 sec
SVP 05♓34'07"
Obliquity 23°26'23"
⚷ Chiron 3♉10.9R
☽ Mean ☊ 13♎47.1

1 DECEMBER 1977
Julian Day # 28459
Delta T 48.4 sec
SVP 05♓34'03"
Obliquity 23°26'22"
⚷ Chiron 1♉53.5R
☽ Mean ☊ 12♎11.8

LONGITUDE — JANUARY 1978

Day	Sid.Time	☉	0 hr ☽	Noon ☽	True ☊	☿	♀	♂	♃	♄	♅	♆	♇
1 Su	6 41 10	10♑12 45	22♍15 22	28♍38 51	10♎20.8	21♐ 8.5	5♑ 7.8	9♌ 3.1	29♊52.0	0♍ 9.8	15♏18.6	16♐44.5	16♎35.9
2 M	6 45 7	11 13 54	5♎ 7 9	11♎40 47	10R 20.1	21 13.8	6 23.3	8R 47.2	29R 44.2	0R 7.5	15 21.1	16 46.6	16 36.5
3 Tu	6 49 3	12 15 3	18 20 13	25 5 52	10 20.1	21 27.5	7 38.8	8 30.5	29 36.4	0 5.1	15 23.6	16 48.7	16 37.1
4 W	6 53 0	13 16 13	1♏58 5	8♏57 6	10 19.3	21 48.9	8 54.3	8 13.2	29 28.6	0 2.7	15 26.0	16 50.8	16 37.7
5 Th	6 56 56	14 17 23	16 2 58	23 15 36	10 16.6	22 17.3	10 9.8	7 55.1	29 21.0	0 0.1	15 28.4	16 52.9	16 38.2
6 F	7 0 53	15 18 33	0♐34 42	7♐59 43	10 11.2	22 52.0	11 25.3	7 36.4	29 13.4	29♌57.4	15 30.7	16 54.9	16 38.7
7 Sa	7 4 49	16 19 44	15 29 54	23 4 15	10 3.0	23 32.4	12 40.8	7 17.1	29 5.9	29 54.7	15 33.0	16 57.0	16 39.2
8 Su	7 8 46	17 20 54	0♑41 34	8♑20 31	9 52.5	24 17.9	13 56.3	6 57.1	28 58.5	29 51.8	15 35.3	16 59.0	16 39.6
9 M	7 12 43	18 22 5	15 59 37	23 37 26	9 40.8	25 7.9	15 11.8	6 36.6	28 51.2	29 48.9	15 37.5	17 1.0	16 39.9
10 Tu	7 16 39	19 23 15	1♒12 29	8♒43 28	9 29.3	26 2.0	16 27.3	6 15.6	28 44.0	29 45.8	15 39.7	17 3.0	16 40.3
11 W	7 20 36	20 24 24	16 9 14	23 28 50	9 19.4	26 59.7	17 42.8	5 54.0	28 36.9	29 42.7	15 41.8	17 5.0	16 40.6
12 Th	7 24 32	21 25 34	0♓41 33	7♓46 57	9 11.9	28 0.7	18 58.3	5 32.0	28 29.9	29 39.5	15 43.9	17 7.0	16 40.9
13 F	7 28 29	22 26 42	14 44 46	21 34 59	9 7.2	29 4.5	20 13.8	5 9.6	28 23.1	29 36.2	15 45.9	17 8.9	16 41.1
14 Sa	7 32 25	23 27 51	28 17 48	4♈53 30	9D 5.1	0♑10.9	21 29.2	4 46.9	28 16.3	29 32.8	15 47.9	17 10.8	16 41.3
15 Su	7 36 22	24 28 58	11♈22 32	17 45 26	9 4.7	1 19.7	22 44.7	4 23.8	28 9.7	29 29.4	15 49.8	17 12.7	16 41.5
16 M	7 40 18	25 30 5	24 2 48	0♉15 16	9R 5.0	2 30.5	24 0.2	4 0.4	28 3.3	29 25.8	15 51.7	17 14.6	16 41.6
17 Tu	7 44 15	26 31 10	6♉23 29	12 28 5	9 4.5	3 43.3	25 15.6	3 36.8	27 56.9	29 22.2	15 53.5	17 16.5	16 41.7
18 W	7 48 12	27 32 16	18 29 44	24 29 2	9 2.4	4 57.8	26 31.0	3 13.1	27 50.7	29 18.5	15 55.3	17 18.3	16 41.7
19 Th	7 52 8	28 33 20	0♊26 33	6♊22 50	8 57.7	6 13.9	27 46.5	2 49.2	27 44.7	29 14.8	15 57.0	17 20.1	16R 41.7
20 F	7 56 5	29 34 24	12 18 23	18 13 38	8 50.4	7 31.5	29 1.9	2 25.2	27 38.8	29 10.9	15 58.7	17 21.9	16 41.7
21 Sa	8 0 1	0♒35 26	24 8 59	0♋ 4 45	8 40.3	8 50.4	0♒17.3	2 1.1	27 33.0	29 7.0	16 0.3	17 23.7	16 41.7
22 Su	8 3 58	1 36 28	6♋ 1 16	11 58 45	8 28.4	10 10.5	1 32.7	1 37.1	27 27.4	29 3.1	16 1.9	17 25.5	16 41.6
23 M	8 7 54	2 37 29	17 57 25	23 57 27	8 15.3	11 31.8	2 48.1	1 13.1	27 22.0	28 59.0	16 3.4	17 27.2	16 41.5
24 Tu	8 11 51	3 38 30	29 58 59	6♌ 2 8	8 2.3	12 54.1	4 3.5	0 49.2	27 16.7	28 54.9	16 4.9	17 28.9	16 41.3
25 W	8 15 47	4 39 29	12♌ 7 1	18 13 45	7 50.5	14 17.5	5 18.9	0 25.5	27 11.6	28 50.8	16 6.3	17 30.6	16 41.1
26 Th	8 19 44	5 40 28	24 22 25	0♍33 10	7 40.7	15 41.8	6 34.3	0 1.9	27 6.7	28 46.5	16 7.7	17 32.3	16 40.9
27 F	8 23 41	6 41 26	6♍46 9	13 1 32	7 33.6	17 7.0	7 49.6	29♋38.6	27 1.9	28 42.3	16 9.0	17 33.9	16 40.6
28 Sa	8 27 37	7 42 23	19 19 31	25 40 21	7 29.4	18 33.2	9 5.0	29 15.5	26 57.3	28 37.9	16 10.3	17 35.6	16 40.3
29 Su	8 31 34	8 43 19	2♎ 4 17	8♎31 39	7D 27.6	20 0.2	10 20.3	28 52.8	26 52.9	28 33.5	16 11.5	17 37.2	16 40.0
30 M	8 35 30	9 44 15	15 2 44	21 37 53	7 27.7	21 28.0	11 35.7	28 30.4	26 48.7	28 29.1	16 12.7	17 38.7	16 39.6
31 Tu	8 39 27	10 45 10	28 17 25	5♏ 1 39	7 28.6	22 56.6	12 51.0	28 8.4	26 44.6	28 24.6	16 13.8	17 40.3	16 39.2

LONGITUDE — FEBRUARY 1978

Day	Sid.Time	☉	0 hr ☽	Noon ☽	True ☊	☿	♀	♂	♃	♄	♅	♆	♇
1 W	8 43 23	11♒46 4	11♏50 50	18♏45 12	7♎29.1	24♑26.0	14♒ 6.4	27♋46.8	26♊40.8	28♌20.1	16♏14.8	17♐41.8	16♎38.8
2 Th	8 47 20	12 46 58	25 44 51	2♐49 47	7R 28.3	25 56.1	15 21.7	27R 25.7	26R 37.1	28R 15.5	16 15.8	17 43.3	16R 38.3
3 F	8 51 16	13 47 51	9♐59 53	17 14 50	7 25.4	27 27.1	16 37.0	27 5.2	26 33.6	28 10.9	16 16.8	17 44.8	16 37.8
4 Sa	8 55 13	14 48 43	24 34 13	1♑57 21	7 20.3	28 58.8	17 52.3	26 45.1	26 30.3	28 6.3	16 17.7	17 46.2	16 37.3
5 Su	8 59 10	15 49 34	9♑23 28	16 51 35	7 13.3	0♒31.3	19 7.6	26 25.6	26 27.2	28 1.6	16 18.5	17 47.6	16 36.7
6 M	9 3 6	16 50 24	24 20 39	1♒49 31	7 5.2	2 4.5	20 22.9	26 6.8	26 24.3	27 56.9	16 19.3	17 49.0	16 36.1
7 Tu	9 7 3	17 51 14	9♒17 0	16 41 57	6 57.1	3 38.5	21 38.2	25 48.5	26 21.6	27 52.2	16 20.0	17 50.4	16 35.5
8 W	9 10 59	18 52 2	24 3 17	1♓20 4	6 50.0	5 13.3	22 53.4	25 30.9	26 19.0	27 47.4	16 20.7	17 51.7	16 34.8
9 Th	9 14 56	19 52 48	8♓31 28	15 36 52	6 44.8	6 48.9	24 8.7	25 14.0	26 16.7	27 42.7	16 21.3	17 53.0	16 34.1
10 F	9 18 52	20 53 33	22 35 49	29 28 4	6 41.7	8 25.2	25 23.9	24 57.9	26 14.6	27 37.9	16 21.9	17 54.3	16 33.4
11 Sa	9 22 49	21 54 17	6♈13 33	12♈52 21	6D 40.7	10 2.4	26 39.1	24 42.4	26 12.7	27 33.0	16 22.4	17 55.5	16 32.6
12 Su	9 26 45	22 54 59	19 24 39	25 50 50	6 41.4	11 40.3	27 54.3	24 27.7	26 10.9	27 28.2	16 22.8	17 56.7	16 31.8
13 M	9 30 42	23 55 40	2♉11 20	8♉26 39	6 42.8	13 19.1	29 9.5	24 13.7	26 9.4	27 23.3	16 23.2	17 57.9	16 31.0
14 Tu	9 34 38	24 56 18	14 37 20	20 44 1	6R 44.2	14 58.7	0♓24.7	24 0.5	26 8.1	27 18.5	16 23.6	17 59.1	16 30.2
15 W	9 38 35	25 56 56	26 47 19	2♊47 51	6 44.7	16 39.2	1 39.9	23 48.1	26 7.0	27 13.6	16 23.8	18 0.2	16 29.3
16 Th	9 42 32	26 57 31	8♊46 16	14 43 9	6 43.8	18 20.5	2 55.0	23 36.5	26 6.0	27 8.8	16 24.1	18 1.3	16 28.4
17 F	9 46 28	27 58 5	20 39 6	26 34 41	6 41.2	20 2.7	4 10.1	23 25.6	26 5.3	27 3.9	16 24.2	18 2.4	16 27.4
18 Sa	9 50 25	28 58 37	2♋30 25	8♋26 47	6 36.8	21 45.9	5 25.2	23 15.6	26 4.8	26 59.1	16 24.4	18 3.4	16 26.5
19 Su	9 54 21	29 59 7	14 24 14	20 23 8	6 31.1	23 29.9	6 40.3	23 6.4	26 4.5	26 54.2	16R 24.4	18 4.4	16 25.5
20 M	9 58 18	0♓59 36	26 23 50	2♌26 39	6 24.5	25 14.8	7 55.4	22 57.9	26D 4.4	26 49.4	16 24.4	18 5.4	16 24.4
21 Tu	10 2 14	2 0 2	8♌31 48	14 39 29	6 17.9	27 0.7	9 10.4	22 50.3	26 4.5	26 44.5	16 24.4	18 6.3	16 23.4
22 W	10 6 11	3 0 27	20 49 53	27 3 5	6 11.9	28 47.5	10 25.5	22 43.4	26 4.8	26 39.7	16 24.3	18 7.2	16 22.3
23 Th	10 10 7	4 0 51	3♍19 10	9♍38 12	6 7.0	0♓35.2	11 40.5	22 37.3	26 5.3	26 34.9	16 24.1	18 8.1	16 21.2
24 F	10 14 4	5 1 12	16 0 14	22 25 15	6 3.8	2 23.9	12 55.5	22 32.1	26 5.9	26 30.1	16 23.9	18 8.9	16 20.1
25 Sa	10 18 1	6 1 32	28 53 16	5♎24 20	6D 2.2	4 13.5	14 10.4	22 27.6	26 6.8	26 25.4	16 23.6	18 9.7	16 18.9
26 Su	10 21 57	7 1 51	11♎58 25	18 35 33	6 2.1	6 4.1	15 25.4	22 23.9	26 7.9	26 20.6	16 23.3	18 10.5	16 17.7
27 M	10 25 54	8 2 8	25 15 47	1♏59 7	6 3.1	7 55.6	16 40.3	22 20.9	26 9.2	26 15.9	16 23.0	18 11.3	16 16.5
28 Tu	10 29 50	9 2 23	8♏45 35	15 35 14	6 4.7	9 47.9	17 55.2	22 18.7	26 10.6	26 11.2	16 22.5	18 12.0	16 15.3

Astro Data Dy Hr Mn	Planet Ingress Dy Hr Mn	Last Aspect Dy Hr Mn	☽ Ingress Dy Hr Mn	Last Aspect Dy Hr Mn	☽ Ingress Dy Hr Mn	☽ Phases & Eclipses Dy Hr Mn	Astro Data
☽0S 1 9:39	♄ ♌ 5 0:47	1 14:08 ♃ □	♎ 1 14:31	2 4:15 ♄ □	♐ 2 7:13	2 12:07 ☽ 11♎45	1 JANUARY 1978
☽0N 13 22:55	☿ ♑ 13 20:07	3 19:43 ♃ △	♏ 3 20:35	4 5:43 ♄ △	♑ 4 8:50	9 4:00 ● 18♑32	Julian Day # 28490
♇ R 19 0:46	☉ ♒ 20 10:04	5 22:59 ♄ □	♐ 5 23:03	6 2:47 ♂ ☍	♒ 6 9:04	16 3:03 ☽ 25♈38	Delta T 48.5 sec
☽0S 28 16:31	♀ ♒ 20 18:29	7 22:42 ♄ △	♑ 7 22:55	8 6:07 ♄ ☍	♓ 8 9:47	24 7:56 ○ 3♌59	SVP 05♓33'57"
	♂ ♋ 26 1:59	9 4:00 ☉ ☌	♒ 9 22:05	10 6:20 ♃ □	♈ 10 12:56	31 23:51 ☽ 11♏46	Obliquity 23°26'22"
☽0N 10 9:52		11 22:16 ♄ ☍	♓ 11 22:50	12 17:37 ♀ ⚹	♉ 12 19:50		⚷ Chiron 1♉09.5R
♅ R 19 15:25	☿ ♒ 4 15:54	13 23:57 ♃ □	♈ 14 3:05	15 0:52 ♄ □	♊ 15 6:24	7 14:54 ● 18♒29	☽ Mean ☊ 10♎33.3
♅⊻♇ 20 0:05	♀ ♓ 13 16:07	16 10:21 ♄ △	♉ 16 11:30	17 16:12 ☉ △	♋ 17 18:56	14 22:11 ☽ 25♉52	
♃ D 20 1:24	☉ ♓ 19 0:21	18 21:36 ♄ □	♊ 18 23:06	19 17:14 ♂ ☌	♌ 20 7:10	23 1:26 ○ 4♍04	1 FEBRUARY 1978
☽0S 24 23:05	☿ ♓ 22 16:11	21 10:00 ♄ ⚹	♋ 21 11:50	22 11:11 ♄ ☌	♍ 22 17:39		Julian Day # 28521
♃⚹♄ 28 2:11		22 21:28 ♇ □	♌ 24 0:02	24 18:51 ♃ □	♎ 25 2:03		Delta T 48.6 sec
		26 8:30 ♄ ☌	♍ 26 10:56	27 1:47 ♄ ⚹	♏ 27 8:28		SVP 05♓33'53"
		28 18:12 ♂ ⚹	♎ 28 20:08				Obliquity 23°26'22"
		31 0:13 ♄ ⚹	♏ 31 3:04				⚷ Chiron 1♉19.0
							☽ Mean ☊ 8♎54.8

MARCH 1978 LONGITUDE

Day	Sid.Time	☉	0 hr ☽	Noon ☽	True ☊	☿	♀	♂	♃	♄	♅	♆	♇
1 W	10 33 47	10♓ 2 37	22♏28 4	29♏24 5	6♎ 6.2	11♓41.1	19♓10.1	22♋17.3	26♊12.3	26♌ 6.6	16♏22.0	18♐12.7	16♎14.1
2 Th	10 37 43	11 2 49	6♐23 13	13♐25 24	6R 7.0	13 35.0	20 25.0	22D 16.6	26 14.2	26R 1.9	16R 21.5	18 13.3	16R 12.8
3 F	10 41 40	12 3 1	20 30 28	27 38 11	6 6.9	15 29.7	21 39.9	22 16.7	26 16.2	25 57.4	16 20.9	18 13.9	16 11.5
4 Sa	10 45 36	13 3 10	4♑48 16	12♑ 0 19	6 5.6	17 25.0	22 54.7	22 17.5	26 18.5	25 52.8	16 20.3	18 14.5	16 10.2
5 Su	10 49 33	14 3 18	19 13 51	26 28 19	6 3.4	19 20.8	24 9.6	22 19.0	26 20.9	25 48.3	16 19.6	18 15.1	16 8.8
6 M	10 53 30	15 3 25	3♒43 6	10♒57 30	6 0.6	21 17.0	25 24.4	22 21.2	26 23.5	25 43.8	16 18.9	18 15.6	16 7.5
7 Tu	10 57 26	16 3 30	18 10 49	25 22 20	5 57.7	23 13.3	26 39.2	22 24.2	26 26.4	25 39.4	16 18.1	18 16.1	16 6.1
8 W	11 1 23	17 3 33	2♓31 18	9♓37 6	5 55.2	25 9.7	27 53.9	22 27.8	26 29.4	25 35.1	16 17.2	18 16.5	16 4.7
9 Th	11 5 19	18 3 34	16 39 4	23 36 43	5 53.4	27 5.9	29 8.7	22 32.1	26 32.6	25 30.8	16 16.3	18 16.9	16 3.3
10 F	11 9 16	19 3 33	0♈29 36	7♈17 24	5D 52.6	29 1.6	0♈23.4	22 37.2	26 35.9	25 26.5	16 15.4	18 17.3	16 1.8
11 Sa	11 13 12	20 3 30	13 59 55	20 37 2	5 52.7	0♈56.5	1 38.1	22 42.8	26 39.5	25 22.3	16 14.4	18 17.6	16 0.4
12 Su	11 17 9	21 3 26	27 8 47	3♉35 18	5 53.4	2 50.3	2 52.8	22 49.1	26 43.2	25 18.2	16 13.3	18 18.0	15 58.9
13 M	11 21 5	22 3 19	9♉56 46	16 13 31	5 54.6	4 42.6	4 7.4	22 56.1	26 47.2	25 14.1	16 12.2	18 18.2	15 57.4
14 Tu	11 25 2	23 3 10	22 25 55	28 34 24	5 55.9	6 33.0	5 22.1	23 3.7	26 51.3	25 10.1	16 11.1	18 18.5	15 55.9
15 W	11 28 59	24 2 59	4♊39 28	10♊41 38	5 56.9	8 21.1	6 36.7	23 11.9	26 55.5	25 6.1	16 9.9	18 18.7	15 54.4
16 Th	11 32 55	25 2 46	16 41 27	22 39 31	5R 57.5	10 6.3	7 51.2	23 20.8	27 0.0	25 2.2	16 8.7	18 18.9	15 52.9
17 F	11 36 52	26 2 30	28 36 24	4♋32 43	5 57.7	11 48.3	9 5.8	23 30.2	27 4.6	24 58.4	16 7.4	18 19.0	15 51.3
18 Sa	11 40 48	27 2 12	10♋29 2	16 25 56	5 57.4	13 26.5	10 20.3	23 40.2	27 9.4	24 54.7	16 6.1	18 19.1	15 49.8
19 Su	11 44 45	28 1 52	22 23 58	28 23 39	5 56.7	15 0.5	11 34.8	23 50.7	27 14.4	24 51.0	16 4.7	18 19.2	15 48.2
20 M	11 48 41	29 1 30	4♌25 30	10♌29 57	5 55.8	16 29.7	12 49.2	24 1.8	27 19.6	24 47.4	16 3.3	18R 19.2	15 46.6
21 Tu	11 52 38	0♈ 1 6	16 37 24	22 48 14	5 54.9	17 53.9	14 3.7	24 13.5	27 24.9	24 43.9	16 1.8	18 19.3	15 45.0
22 W	11 56 34	1 0 39	29 2 45	5♍21 10	5 54.2	19 12.4	15 18.1	24 25.7	27 30.3	24 40.5	16 0.3	18 19.2	15 43.4
23 Th	12 0 31	2 0 10	11♍43 40	18 10 21	5 53.7	20 24.9	16 32.4	24 38.4	27 36.0	24 37.1	15 58.8	18 19.2	15 41.8
24 F	12 4 27	2 59 39	24 41 17	1♎16 25	5D 53.5	21 31.2	17 46.8	24 51.6	27 41.8	24 33.8	15 57.2	18 19.1	15 40.2
25 Sa	12 8 24	3 59 6	7♎55 39	14 38 52	5 53.5	22 30.7	19 1.1	25 5.3	27 47.7	24 30.6	15 55.5	18 19.0	15 38.6
26 Su	12 12 21	4 58 30	21 25 50	28 16 17	5R 53.5	23 23.4	20 15.3	25 19.5	27 53.8	24 27.5	15 53.9	18 18.8	15 36.9
27 M	12 16 17	5 57 53	5♏ 9 57	12♏ 6 30	5 53.5	24 9.0	21 29.6	25 34.1	28 0.1	24 24.5	15 52.2	18 18.6	15 35.3
28 Tu	12 20 14	6 57 14	19 5 34	26 6 48	5 53.5	24 47.3	22 43.8	25 49.3	28 6.5	24 21.6	15 50.4	18 18.4	15 33.6
29 W	12 24 10	7 56 34	3♐ 9 50	10♐14 19	5 53.3	25 18.1	23 58.0	26 4.8	28 13.1	24 18.7	15 48.6	18 18.1	15 31.9
30 Th	12 28 7	8 55 51	17 19 52	24 26 8	5 53.1	25 41.5	25 12.2	26 20.8	28 19.8	24 16.0	15 46.8	18 17.9	15 30.3
31 F	12 32 3	9 55 7	1♑32 48	8♑39 33	5D 52.9	25 57.5	26 26.3	26 37.3	28 26.6	24 13.3	15 44.9	18 17.5	15 28.6

APRIL 1978 LONGITUDE

Day	Sid.Time	☉	0 hr ☽	Noon ☽	True ☊	☿	♀	♂	♃	♄	♅	♆	♇
1 Sa	12 36 0	10♈54 21	15♑46 3	22♑52 1	5♎52.9	26♈ 6.0	27♈40.4	26♋54.2	28♊33.7	24♌10.7	15♏43.0	18♐17.2	15♎26.9
2 Su	12 39 56	11 53 34	29 57 10	7♒ 1 12	5 53.1	26R 7.3	28 54.5	27 11.4	28 40.8	24R 8.2	15R 41.1	18R 16.8	15R 25.3
3 M	12 43 53	12 52 44	14♒ 3 50	21 4 48	5 53.6	26 1.5	0♉ 8.6	27 29.1	28 48.1	24 5.9	15 39.2	18 16.4	15 23.6
4 Tu	12 47 50	13 51 53	28 3 48	5♓ 0 34	5 54.3	25 49.1	1 22.6	27 47.2	28 55.5	24 3.6	15 37.2	18 15.9	15 21.9
5 W	12 51 46	14 51 0	11♓54 49	18 46 17	5 55.0	25 30.3	2 36.6	28 5.7	29 3.1	24 1.4	15 35.1	18 15.5	15 20.2
6 Th	12 55 43	15 50 5	25 34 42	2♈19 50	5R 55.6	25 5.6	3 50.5	28 24.6	29 10.8	23 59.3	15 33.1	18 15.0	15 18.5
7 F	12 59 39	16 49 8	9♈ 1 29	15 39 26	5 55.7	24 35.7	5 4.5	28 43.9	29 18.7	23 57.3	15 31.0	18 14.4	15 16.9
8 Sa	13 3 36	17 48 9	22 13 34	28 43 48	5 55.2	24 1.2	6 18.4	29 3.5	29 26.7	23 55.4	15 28.8	18 13.8	15 15.2
9 Su	13 7 32	18 47 8	5♉10 4	11♉32 23	5 54.1	23 22.8	7 32.3	29 23.5	29 34.8	23 53.6	15 26.7	18 13.2	15 13.5
10 M	13 11 29	19 46 5	17 50 51	24 5 34	5 52.4	22 41.4	8 46.1	29 43.8	29 43.0	23 51.9	15 24.5	18 12.6	15 11.8
11 Tu	13 15 25	20 45 0	0♊16 44	6♊24 38	5 50.3	21 57.7	9 59.9	0♌ 4.5	29 51.4	23 50.3	15 22.3	18 12.0	15 10.1
12 W	13 19 22	21 43 53	12 29 33	18 31 52	5 48.0	21 12.7	11 13.7	0 25.5	29 59.9	23 48.8	15 20.1	18 11.3	15 8.5
13 Th	13 23 19	22 42 43	24 31 59	0♋30 23	5 45.8	20 27.2	12 27.4	0 46.9	0♋ 8.6	23 47.5	15 17.8	18 10.5	15 6.8
14 F	13 27 15	23 41 32	6♋27 32	12 23 59	5 44.2	19 42.2	13 41.2	1 8.5	0 17.3	23 46.2	15 15.5	18 9.8	15 5.1
15 Sa	13 31 12	24 40 18	18 20 18	24 17 2	5D 43.2	18 58.3	14 54.8	1 30.5	0 26.2	23 45.0	15 13.2	18 9.0	15 3.5
16 Su	13 35 8	25 39 2	0♌14 48	6♌14 12	5 43.2	18 16.4	16 8.5	1 52.8	0 35.2	23 43.9	15 10.9	18 8.2	15 1.8
17 M	13 39 5	26 37 44	12 15 47	18 20 10	5 43.9	17 37.1	17 22.1	2 15.4	0 44.3	23 43.0	15 8.5	18 7.4	15 0.2
18 Tu	13 43 1	27 36 23	24 27 53	0♍39 29	5 45.3	17 1.1	18 35.6	2 38.3	0 53.5	23 42.1	15 6.2	18 6.5	14 58.5
19 W	13 46 58	28 35 0	6♍55 25	13 16 7	5 46.9	16 28.8	19 49.1	3 1.4	1 2.8	23 41.4	15 3.8	18 5.6	14 56.9
20 Th	13 50 54	29 33 35	19 41 57	26 13 10	5 48.3	16 0.8	21 2.6	3 24.9	1 12.3	23 40.7	15 1.4	18 4.7	14 55.3
21 F	13 54 51	0♉32 8	2♎49 57	9♎32 23	5R 49.0	15 37.2	22 16.1	3 48.6	1 21.8	23 40.2	14 59.0	18 3.8	14 53.7
22 Sa	13 58 47	1 30 39	16 20 23	23 13 48	5 48.7	15 18.3	23 29.5	4 12.5	1 31.5	23 39.8	14 56.5	18 2.8	14 52.1
23 Su	14 2 44	2 29 8	0♏12 19	7♏15 32	5 47.1	15 4.4	24 42.8	4 36.8	1 41.2	23 39.5	14 54.1	18 1.8	14 50.5
24 M	14 6 41	3 27 35	14 22 54	21 33 46	5 44.2	14 55.4	25 56.2	5 1.2	1 51.1	23 39.2	14 51.6	18 0.8	14 48.9
25 Tu	14 10 37	4 26 0	28 47 26	6♐ 3 7	5 40.4	14D 51.5	27 9.5	5 26.0	2 1.1	23D 39.1	14 49.2	17 59.8	14 47.3
26 W	14 14 34	5 24 24	13♐20 0	20 37 18	5 36.1	14 52.6	28 22.7	5 50.9	2 11.1	23 39.1	14 46.7	17 58.7	14 45.8
27 Th	14 18 30	6 22 46	27 54 15	5♑10 8	5 32.1	14 58.6	29 35.9	6 16.1	2 21.3	23 39.2	14 44.2	17 57.6	14 44.3
28 F	14 22 27	7 21 6	12♑24 19	19 36 16	5 28.9	15 9.5	0♊49.1	6 41.6	2 31.6	23 39.4	14 41.7	17 56.5	14 42.7
29 Sa	14 26 23	8 19 25	26 45 32	3♒51 47	5D 27.0	15 25.1	2 2.3	7 7.3	2 41.9	23 39.8	14 39.2	17 55.4	14 41.2
30 Su	14 30 20	9 17 43	10♒54 47	17 54 21	5 26.5	15 45.3	3 15.4	7 33.2	2 52.4	23 40.2	14 36.7	17 54.2	14 39.7

Astro Data Dy Hr Mn	Planet Ingress Dy Hr Mn	Last Aspect Dy Hr Mn	☽ Ingress Dy Hr Mn	Last Aspect Dy Hr Mn	☽ Ingress Dy Hr Mn	☽ Phases & Eclipses Dy Hr Mn	Astro Data
♂ D 2 9:56	♀ ♈ 9 16:29	1 6:17 ♄ □	♐ 1 13:02	1 22:04 ♀ □	♒ 2 0:05	2 8:34 ☽ 11♐24	1 MARCH 1978
☽0N 9 20:22	☿ ♈ 10 12:10	3 9:44 ♃ ☍	♑ 3 15:58	4 1:30 ♃ △	♓ 4 3:20	9 2:36 ● 18♓10	Julian Day # 28549
☿0N 10 22:48	☉ ♈ 20 23:34	5 8:56 ♀ ⚹	♒ 5 17:51	6 6:27 ♃ □	♈ 6 7:51	16 18:21 ☽ 25♊48	Delta T 48.7 sec
♀0N 11 23:44		7 13:50 ♃ △	♓ 7 19:45	8 13:28 ♃ ⚹	♉ 8 14:21	24 16:20 ○ 3♎40	SVP 05♓33'50"
♆ R 20 18:47	♀ ♉ 2 21:14	9 21:01 ☿ ☌	♈ 9 23:08	10 11:32 ♄ □	♊ 10 23:27	24 16:22 ☍T 1.452	Obliquity 23°26'23"
☽0S 24 6:47	♂ ♌ 10 18:50	11 23:13 ♃ ⚹	♉ 12 5:18	12 22:31 ♄ ⚹	♋ 13 10:59	31 15:11 ☽ 10♑33	⚷ Chiron 2♉12.7
	♃ ♋ 12 0:12	14 5:18 ♄ □	♊ 14 14:48	15 13:56 ☉ □	♌ 15 23:30		☽ Mean ☊ 7♎25.8
☿ R 1 16:17	☉ ♉ 20 10:50	16 20:53 ♃ ☌	♋ 17 2:49	18 6:38 ☉ △	♍ 18 10:44	7 15:15 ● 17♈27	
☽0N 6 5:00	♀ ♊ 27 7:53	19 12:17 ☉ △	♌ 19 15:12	20 2:45 ♀ △	♎ 20 18:53	7 15:02:58 ☌ P 0.788	1 APRIL 1978
♃□♅ 13 20:08		21 21:02 ♃ ⚹	♍ 22 1:49	22 12:45 ♄ ⚹	♏ 22 23:39	15 13:56 ☽ 25♋14	Julian Day # 28580
☽0S 20 16:03		24 5:32 ♃ □	♎ 24 9:41	24 21:03 ♀ ☍	♐ 25 2:00	23 4:11 ○ 2♏39	Delta T 48.8 sec
☿ D 25 6:48		26 11:26 ♃ △	♏ 26 15:01	26 17:00 ♄ △	♑ 27 3:27	29 21:02 ☽ 9♒11	SVP 05♓33'47"
♄ D 25 12:16		28 11:43 ♂ △	♐ 28 18:37	28 4:39 ☿ □	♒ 29 5:28		Obliquity 23°26'23"
♅⚺♇ 26 22:37		30 18:43 ♃ ☍	♑ 30 21:23				⚷ Chiron 3♉48.7
							☽ Mean ☊ 5♎47.3

LONGITUDE — MAY 1978

Day	Sid.Time	☉	0 hr ☽	Noon ☽	True ☊	☿	♀	♂	♃	♄	♅	♆	♇
1 M	14 34 17	10♉15 58	24♒50 26	1♓43 0	5♎27.2	16♈ 9.9	4♊28.5	7♌59.3	3♋ 2.9	23♌40.7	14♏34.1	17♐53.0	14♎38.2
2 Tu	14 38 13	11 14 13	8♓32 5	15 17 44	5 28.6	16 38.9	5 41.5	8 25.6	3 13.5	23 41.4	14R31.6	17R51.8	14R36.8
3 W	14 42 10	12 12 26	22 0 2	28 39 5	5 30.0	17 12.0	6 54.5	8 52.2	3 24.3	23 42.1	14 29.1	17 50.6	14 35.3
4 Th	14 46 6	13 10 37	5♈14 56	11♈47 41	5R30.6	17 49.0	8 7.5	9 18.9	3 35.1	23 42.9	14 26.5	17 49.4	14 33.9
5 F	14 50 3	14 8 47	18 17 24	24 44 8	5 29.8	18 29.9	9 20.4	9 45.9	3 46.0	23 43.9	14 24.0	17 48.1	14 32.5
6 Sa	14 53 59	15 6 55	1♉ 7 55	7♉28 49	5 27.2	19 14.4	10 33.3	10 13.1	3 57.0	23 45.0	14 21.5	17 46.8	14 31.1
7 Su	14 57 56	16 5 2	13 46 51	20 2 5	5 22.6	20 2.4	11 46.2	10 40.4	4 8.0	23 46.1	14 18.9	17 45.5	14 29.7
8 M	15 1 52	17 3 7	26 14 34	2♊24 23	5 16.3	20 53.9	12 59.0	11 8.0	4 19.2	23 47.4	14 16.4	17 44.2	14 28.3
9 Tu	15 5 49	18 1 11	8♊31 39	14 36 30	5 8.7	21 48.6	14 11.8	11 35.7	4 30.4	23 48.8	14 13.9	17 42.8	14 27.0
10 W	15 9 45	18 59 12	20 39 7	26 39 45	5 0.6	22 46.4	15 24.5	12 3.7	4 41.7	23 50.3	14 11.3	17 41.5	14 25.7
11 Th	15 13 42	19 57 12	2♋38 39	8♋36 8	4 52.8	23 47.2	16 37.2	12 31.8	4 53.1	23 51.9	14 8.8	17 40.1	14 24.4
12 F	15 17 39	20 55 11	14 32 36	20 28 26	4 46.0	24 51.0	17 49.8	13 0.1	5 4.6	23 53.5	14 6.3	17 38.7	14 23.1
13 Sa	15 21 35	21 53 7	26 24 8	2♌20 10	4 40.9	25 57.6	19 2.5	13 28.6	5 16.1	23 55.3	14 3.8	17 37.3	14 21.8
14 Su	15 25 32	22 51 2	8♌17 6	14 15 30	4 37.7	27 6.9	20 15.0	13 57.3	5 27.7	23 57.2	14 1.3	17 35.9	14 20.6
15 M	15 29 28	23 48 55	20 15 59	26 19 9	4D36.4	28 18.9	21 27.5	14 26.1	5 39.4	23 59.2	13 58.8	17 34.5	14 19.4
16 Tu	15 33 25	24 46 46	2♍25 38	8♍36 3	4 36.6	29 33.5	22 40.0	14 55.1	5 51.1	24 1.3	13 56.3	17 33.0	14 18.2
17 W	15 37 21	25 44 36	14 51 2	21 11 8	4 37.7	0♉50.6	23 52.4	15 24.3	6 2.9	24 3.5	13 53.8	17 31.5	14 17.1
18 Th	15 41 18	26 42 24	27 36 53	4♎ 8 44	4R38.6	2 10.3	25 4.8	15 53.6	6 14.8	24 5.8	13 51.4	17 30.1	14 15.9
19 F	15 45 14	27 40 10	10♎47 4	17 32 7	4 38.7	3 32.4	26 17.1	16 23.0	6 26.7	24 8.2	13 48.9	17 28.6	14 14.8
20 Sa	15 49 11	28 37 54	24 24 0	1♏22 41	4 37.0	4 56.8	27 29.4	16 52.7	6 38.7	24 10.7	13 46.5	17 27.1	14 13.7
21 Su	15 53 8	29 35 37	8♏27 55	15 39 18	4 33.1	6 23.7	28 41.6	17 22.4	6 50.8	24 13.3	13 44.1	17 25.5	14 12.6
22 M	15 57 4	0♊33 19	22 56 14	0♐17 56	4 27.0	7 53.0	29 53.8	17 52.3	7 2.9	24 16.0	13 41.7	17 24.0	14 11.6
23 Tu	16 1 1	1 30 59	7♐43 27	15 11 42	4 19.2	9 24.5	1♋ 5.9	18 22.4	7 15.1	24 18.8	13 39.3	17 22.5	14 10.6
24 W	16 4 57	2 28 38	22 41 31	0♑11 44	4 10.5	10 58.5	2 18.0	18 52.6	7 27.3	24 21.7	13 37.0	17 20.9	14 9.6
25 Th	16 8 54	3 26 16	7♑41 8	15 8 39	4 2.1	12 34.7	3 30.1	19 22.9	7 39.6	24 24.6	13 34.6	17 19.4	14 8.7
26 F	16 12 50	4 23 53	22 33 15	29 54 7	3 55.0	14 13.2	4 42.0	19 53.4	7 51.9	24 27.7	13 32.3	17 17.8	14 7.7
27 Sa	16 16 47	5 21 29	7♒10 34	14♒22 6	3 49.8	15 54.1	5 54.0	20 24.0	8 4.3	24 30.9	13 30.0	17 16.2	14 6.8
28 Su	16 20 43	6 19 4	21 28 23	28 29 16	3 46.9	17 37.2	7 5.9	20 54.7	8 16.8	24 34.1	13 27.7	17 14.7	14 6.0
29 M	16 24 40	7 16 38	5♓24 45	12♓14 54	3D46.0	19 22.7	8 17.7	21 25.6	8 29.3	24 37.4	13 25.5	17 13.1	14 5.1
30 Tu	16 28 37	8 14 11	18 59 55	25 40 4	3 46.2	21 10.4	9 29.5	21 56.6	8 41.8	24 40.9	13 23.2	17 11.5	14 4.3
31 W	16 32 33	9 11 44	2♈15 39	8♈47 1	3R46.7	23 0.4	10 41.2	22 27.8	8 54.4	24 44.4	13 21.0	17 9.9	14 3.5

LONGITUDE — JUNE 1978

Day	Sid.Time	☉	0 hr ☽	Noon ☽	True ☊	☿	♀	♂	♃	♄	♅	♆	♇
1 Th	16 36 30	10♊ 9 15	15♈14 28	21♈38 22	3♎46.1	24♉52.7	11♋52.9	22♌59.0	9♋ 7.1	24♌48.0	13♏18.8	17♐ 8.3	14♎ 2.7
2 F	16 40 26	11 6 46	27 59 0	4♉16 39	3R43.6	26 47.2	13 4.5	23 30.4	9 19.8	24 51.7	13R16.7	17R 6.7	14R 2.0
3 Sa	16 44 23	12 4 16	10♉31 36	16 44 2	3 38.6	28 43.9	14 16.1	24 1.9	9 32.5	24 55.5	13 14.6	17 5.0	14 1.3
4 Su	16 48 19	13 1 45	22 54 11	29 2 12	3 30.8	0♊42.6	15 27.6	24 33.6	9 45.3	24 59.4	13 12.5	17 3.4	14 0.6
5 M	16 52 16	13 59 14	5♊ 8 13	11♊12 24	3 20.5	2 43.5	16 39.1	25 5.3	9 58.1	25 3.3	13 10.4	17 1.8	13 60.0
6 Tu	16 56 12	14 56 41	17 14 52	23 15 44	3 8.4	4 46.3	17 50.5	25 37.2	10 11.0	25 7.4	13 8.4	17 0.2	13 59.4
7 W	17 0 9	15 54 8	29 15 9	5♋13 17	2 55.4	6 50.9	19 1.9	26 9.2	10 23.9	25 11.5	13 6.4	16 58.6	13 58.8
8 Th	17 4 6	16 51 33	11♋10 19	17 6 29	2 42.7	8 57.2	20 13.2	26 41.3	10 36.8	25 15.7	13 4.4	16 56.9	13 58.3
9 F	17 8 2	17 48 58	23 2 1	28 57 14	2 31.2	11 5.0	21 24.5	27 13.6	10 49.8	25 20.0	13 2.5	16 55.3	13 57.7
10 Sa	17 11 59	18 46 22	4♌52 29	10♌48 10	2 21.9	13 14.1	22 35.6	27 45.9	11 2.8	25 24.4	13 0.5	16 53.7	13 57.3
11 Su	17 15 55	19 43 44	16 44 43	22 42 37	2 15.3	15 24.3	23 46.8	28 18.4	11 15.8	25 28.9	12 58.7	16 52.1	13 56.8
12 M	17 19 52	20 41 6	28 42 25	4♍44 41	2 11.2	17 35.3	24 57.8	28 50.9	11 28.9	25 33.4	12 56.8	16 50.5	13 56.4
13 Tu	17 23 48	21 38 27	10♍50 1	16 59 3	2D 9.4	19 47.0	26 8.8	29 23.6	11 42.0	25 38.0	12 55.0	16 48.8	13 56.0
14 W	17 27 45	22 35 47	23 12 23	29 30 41	2R 9.1	21 58.9	27 19.8	29 56.4	11 55.1	25 42.7	12 53.3	16 47.2	13 55.6
15 Th	17 31 41	23 33 5	5♎54 34	12♎24 34	2 9.1	24 10.9	28 30.6	0♍29.3	12 8.3	25 47.5	12 51.6	16 45.6	13 55.3
16 F	17 35 38	24 30 23	19 1 12	25 44 53	2 8.3	26 22.7	29 41.4	1 2.3	12 21.5	25 52.3	12 49.9	16 44.0	13 55.0
17 Sa	17 39 35	25 27 40	2♏35 55	9♏34 25	2 5.8	28 33.9	0♌52.1	1 35.3	12 34.7	25 57.3	12 48.2	16 42.4	13 54.8
18 Su	17 43 31	26 24 57	16 40 20	23 53 25	2 0.9	0♋44.4	2 2.7	2 8.5	12 47.9	26 2.2	12 46.6	16 40.8	13 54.5
19 M	17 47 28	27 22 12	1♐13 11	8♐38 55	1 53.4	2 54.0	3 13.3	2 41.8	13 1.2	26 7.3	12 45.0	16 39.2	13 54.3
20 Tu	17 51 24	28 19 27	16 9 41	23 44 21	1 43.8	5 2.3	4 23.8	3 15.2	13 14.5	26 12.4	12 43.5	16 37.6	13 54.2
21 W	17 55 21	29 16 42	1♑21 36	9♑ 0 2	1 33.2	7 9.2	5 34.2	3 48.7	13 27.8	26 17.7	12 42.0	16 36.1	13 54.1
22 Th	17 59 17	0♋13 56	16 38 15	24 14 49	1 22.6	9 14.6	6 44.6	4 22.2	13 41.1	26 22.9	12 40.6	16 34.5	13 54.0
23 F	18 3 14	1 11 9	1♒48 27	9♒17 59	1 13.4	11 18.3	7 54.8	4 55.9	13 54.5	26 28.3	12 39.2	16 32.9	13 53.9
24 Sa	18 7 11	2 8 23	16 42 29	24 1 11	1 6.5	13 20.1	9 5.0	5 29.6	14 7.9	26 33.7	12 37.8	16 31.4	13D53.9
25 Su	18 11 7	3 5 36	1♓13 36	8♓19 24	1 2.2	15 20.1	10 15.1	6 3.5	14 21.2	26 39.2	12 36.5	16 29.8	13 53.9
26 M	18 15 4	4 2 49	15 18 30	22 10 57	1 0.2	17 18.2	11 25.1	6 37.4	14 34.6	26 44.7	12 35.2	16 28.3	13 53.9
27 Tu	18 19 0	5 0 2	28 56 58	5♈36 50	0 59.8	19 14.2	12 35.1	7 11.4	14 48.1	26 50.3	12 34.0	16 26.8	13 54.0
28 W	18 22 57	5 57 15	12♈10 59	18 39 50	0 59.7	21 8.2	13 44.9	7 45.5	15 1.5	26 56.0	12 32.8	16 25.3	13 54.1
29 Th	18 26 53	6 54 29	25 3 51	1♉23 33	0 58.8	23 0.1	14 54.7	8 19.7	15 14.9	27 1.7	12 31.7	16 23.8	13 54.2
30 F	18 30 50	7 51 42	7♉39 22	13 51 47	0 56.1	24 49.9	16 4.4	8 54.0	15 28.4	27 7.5	12 30.6	16 22.3	13 54.4

Astro Data Dy Hr Mn	Planet Ingress Dy Hr Mn	Last Aspect Dy Hr Mn	☽ Ingress Dy Hr Mn	Last Aspect Dy Hr Mn	☽ Ingress Dy Hr Mn	☽ Phases & Eclipses Dy Hr Mn	Astro Data
☽0N 3 11:48	☿ ♉ 16 8:20	30 21:59 ♄ ☍	♓ 1 9:00	1 18:03 ♄ △	♉ 2 3:50	7 4:47 ● 16♉17	1 MAY 1978
☽0S 18 2:10	☉ ♊ 21 10:08	2 16:34 ♆ □	♈ 3 14:27	4 4:06 ♄ □	♊ 4 13:53	15 7:39 ☽ 24♌07	Julian Day # 28610
☽0N 30 18:06	♀ ♋ 22 2:03	5 10:08 ♄ △	♉ 5 21:52	6 17:30 ♂ ✶	♋ 7 1:30	22 13:17 ○ 1♐05	Delta T 48.9 sec
		7 19:14 ♄ □	♊ 8 7:18	8 20:20 ♀ ☌	♌ 9 14:07	29 3:30 ☽ 7♓25	SVP 05♓33'44"
♃∠♄ 5 14:14	☿ ♊ 3 15:26	10 6:22 ♄ ✶	♋ 10 18:41	12 0:18 ♂ ☌	♍ 12 2:35		Obliquity 23°26'22"
☽0S 14 11:53	♂ ♍ 14 2:38	12 23:01 ☿ □	♌ 13 7:17	14 8:41 ♀ ✶	♎ 14 12:55	5 19:01 ● 14♊45	⚷ Chiron 5♉39.2
♃△♅ 17 21:50	♀ ♌ 16 6:19	15 17:44 ☿ △	♍ 15 19:15	16 15:37 ☿ △	♏ 16 19:28	13 22:44 ☽ 22♍33	☽ Mean ☊ 4♎12.0
♃□♇ 22 22:58	☿ ♋ 17 15:49	17 22:11 ☉ △	♎ 18 4:24	18 15:37 ♄ □	♐ 18 22:01	20 20:30 ○ 29♐08	
♇ D 24 7:42	☉ ♋ 21 18:10	20 5:50 ♀ △	♏ 20 9:39	20 20:30 ☉ ☍	♑ 20 21:52	27 11:44 ☽ 5♈28	1 JUNE 1978
☽0N 27 1:26		22 2:11 ♄ □	♐ 22 11:31	21 19:42 ♇ □	♒ 22 21:07		Julian Day # 28641
		24 2:41 ♄ △	♑ 24 11:41	24 16:19 ♄ ☍	♓ 24 21:57		Delta T 49.0 sec
		25 10:23 ♇ □	♒ 26 12:10	26 4:02 ☿ △	♈ 27 1:53		SVP 05♓33'40"
		28 5:18 ♄ ☍	♓ 28 14:36	29 3:44 ♄ △	♉ 29 9:21		Obliquity 23°26'22"
		30 4:31 ☿ ✶	♈ 30 19:52				⚷ Chiron 7♉30.1
							☽ Mean ☊ 2♎33.5

JULY 1978 LONGITUDE

Day	Sid.Time	☉	0 hr ☽	Noon ☽	True ☊	☿	♀	♂	♃	♄	♅	♆	♇
1 Sa	18 34 46	8♋48 56	20♉ 1 14	26♉ 8 5	0♎50.8	26♋37.6	17♌14.0	9♍28.4	15♋41.8	27♌13.4	12♏29.5	16♐20.8	13♎54.6
2 Su	18 38 43	9 46 9	2♊12 43	8♊15 27	0R42.7	28 23.1	18 23.6	10 2.9	15 55.3	27 19.3	12R28.5	16R19.3	13 54.9
3 M	18 42 40	10 43 23	14 16 32	20 16 15	0 32.0	0♌ 6.6	19 33.0	10 37.5	16 8.8	27 25.3	12 27.6	16 17.9	13 55.1
4 Tu	18 46 36	11 40 37	26 14 49	2♋12 24	0 19.5	1 47.8	20 42.4	11 12.1	16 22.3	27 31.3	12 26.7	16 16.5	13 55.5
5 W	18 50 33	12 37 50	8♋ 9 13	14 5 25	0 6.0	3 27.0	21 51.6	11 46.9	16 35.8	27 37.4	12 25.8	16 15.0	13 55.8
6 Th	18 54 29	13 35 4	20 1 12	25 56 43	29♍52.7	5 4.0	23 0.8	12 21.7	16 49.3	27 43.5	12 25.0	16 13.6	13 56.2
7 F	18 58 26	14 32 18	1♌52 11	7♌47 50	29 40.8	6 38.9	24 9.8	12 56.6	17 2.8	27 49.7	12 24.3	16 12.3	13 56.6
8 Sa	19 2 22	15 29 32	13 43 54	19 40 41	29 31.0	8 11.6	25 18.8	13 31.6	17 16.3	27 56.0	12 23.6	16 10.9	13 57.0
9 Su	19 6 19	16 26 45	25 38 31	1♍37 46	29 23.8	9 42.1	26 27.7	14 6.7	17 29.8	28 2.3	12 22.9	16 9.5	13 57.5
10 M	19 10 15	17 23 59	7♍38 51	13 42 13	29 19.4	11 10.4	27 36.4	14 41.9	17 43.4	28 8.6	12 22.3	16 8.2	13 58.0
11 Tu	19 14 12	18 21 13	19 48 22	25 57 50	29D 17.4	12 36.5	28 45.1	15 17.1	17 56.8	28 15.1	12 21.7	16 6.9	13 58.6
12 W	19 18 9	19 18 26	2♎11 10	8♎28 56	29 17.1	14 0.4	29 53.6	15 52.5	18 10.4	28 21.5	12 21.2	16 5.6	13 59.1
13 Th	19 22 5	20 15 40	14 51 42	21 20 2	29R17.4	15 22.0	1♍ 2.1	16 27.9	18 23.9	28 28.0	12 20.8	16 4.3	13 59.7
14 F	19 26 2	21 12 53	27 54 28	4♏35 25	29 17.3	16 41.3	2 10.4	17 3.3	18 37.4	28 34.6	12 20.4	16 3.0	14 0.4
15 Sa	19 29 58	22 10 7	11♏23 17	18 18 19	29 15.8	17 58.2	3 18.5	17 38.9	18 50.9	28 41.2	12 20.0	16 1.8	14 1.1
16 Su	19 33 55	23 7 20	25 20 36	2♐30 4	29 12.2	19 12.8	4 26.6	18 14.6	19 4.3	28 47.8	12 19.7	16 0.6	14 1.8
17 M	19 37 51	24 4 34	9♐46 26	17 9 10	29 6.4	20 24.8	5 34.6	18 50.3	19 17.8	28 54.5	12 19.4	15 59.4	14 2.5
18 Tu	19 41 48	25 1 48	24 37 34	2♑10 38	28 58.6	21 34.3	6 42.4	19 26.1	19 31.3	29 1.2	12 19.2	15 58.2	14 3.3
19 W	19 45 44	25 59 2	9♑47 14	17 26 3	28 49.7	22 41.2	7 50.0	20 1.9	19 44.7	29 8.0	12 19.1	15 57.1	14 4.1
20 Th	19 49 41	26 56 17	25 5 41	2♒44 42	28 40.8	23 45.3	8 57.6	20 37.9	19 58.2	29 14.8	12 19.0	15 55.9	14 4.9
21 F	19 53 38	27 53 32	10♒21 41	17 55 20	28 33.0	24 46.7	10 5.0	21 13.9	20 11.6	29 21.7	12D 18.9	15 54.8	14 5.8
22 Sa	19 57 34	28 50 47	25 24 31	2♓48 15	28 27.1	25 45.2	11 12.2	21 50.0	20 25.0	29 28.5	12 19.0	15 53.7	14 6.7
23 Su	20 1 31	29 48 3	10♓ 5 48	17 16 40	28 23.6	26 40.6	12 19.4	22 26.1	20 38.4	29 35.5	12 19.0	15 52.7	14 7.6
24 M	20 5 27	0♌45 20	24 20 30	1♈17 14	28D 22.3	27 32.9	13 26.3	23 2.4	20 51.8	29 42.4	12 19.1	15 51.6	14 8.6
25 Tu	20 9 24	1 42 38	8♈ 6 55	14 49 46	28 22.5	28 22.0	14 33.2	23 38.7	21 5.2	29 49.4	12 19.3	15 50.6	14 9.6
26 W	20 13 20	2 39 57	21 26 6	27 56 20	28R 23.3	29 7.7	15 39.8	24 15.1	21 18.6	29 56.5	12 19.5	15 49.6	14 10.6
27 Th	20 17 17	3 37 16	4♉20 58	10♉40 31	28 23.8	29 49.8	16 46.4	24 51.5	21 31.9	0♍ 3.5	12 19.7	15 48.6	14 11.7
28 F	20 21 13	4 34 37	16 55 30	23 6 29	28 22.9	0♍28.2	17 52.7	25 28.1	21 45.2	0 10.6	12 20.1	15 47.7	14 12.8
29 Sa	20 25 10	5 31 59	29 13 59	5♊18 31	28 20.2	1 2.7	18 59.0	26 4.7	21 58.5	0 17.8	12 20.4	15 46.8	14 13.9
30 Su	20 29 7	6 29 21	11♊20 36	17 20 40	28 15.3	1 33.1	20 5.0	26 41.4	22 11.8	0 24.9	12 20.8	15 45.9	14 15.0
31 M	20 33 3	7 26 45	23 19 8	29 16 24	28 8.4	1 59.3	21 10.9	27 18.1	22 25.1	0 32.1	12 21.3	15 45.0	14 16.2

AUGUST 1978 LONGITUDE

Day	Sid.Time	☉	0 hr ☽	Noon ☽	True ☊	☿	♀	♂	♃	♄	♅	♆	♇
1 Tu	20 37 0	8♌24 10	5♋12 48	11♋ 8 40	27♍59.9	2♍21.1	22♍16.6	27♍55.0	22♋38.3	0♍39.4	12♏21.8	15♐44.2	14♎17.4
2 W	20 40 56	9 21 36	17 4 15	22 59 50	27R50.8	2 38.3	23 22.2	28 31.9	22 51.5	0 46.6	12 22.4	15R43.4	14 18.6
3 Th	20 44 53	10 19 2	28 55 39	4♌51 54	27 41.7	2 50.8	24 27.6	29 8.8	23 4.7	0 53.9	12 23.1	15 42.6	14 19.9
4 F	20 48 49	11 16 30	10♌48 47	16 46 31	27 33.5	2R 58.2	25 32.8	29 45.9	23 17.8	1 1.2	12 23.7	15 41.9	14 21.2
5 Sa	20 52 46	12 13 58	22 45 19	28 45 22	27 27.0	3 0.6	26 37.8	0♎23.0	23 30.9	1 8.5	12 24.5	15 41.1	14 22.5
6 Su	20 56 42	13 11 28	4♍46 56	10♍50 15	27 22.5	2 57.8	27 42.6	1 0.2	23 44.0	1 15.9	12 25.3	15 40.4	14 23.9
7 M	21 0 39	14 8 58	16 55 37	23 3 18	27D 20.0	2 49.7	28 47.2	1 37.5	23 57.1	1 23.3	12 26.1	15 39.8	14 25.3
8 Tu	21 4 36	15 6 29	29 13 41	5♎27 6	27 19.5	2 36.3	29 51.6	2 14.9	24 10.1	1 30.7	12 27.0	15 39.1	14 26.7
9 W	21 8 32	16 4 1	11♎43 57	18 4 38	27 20.3	2 17.5	0♎55.8	2 52.3	24 23.1	1 38.1	12 27.9	15 38.5	14 28.1
10 Th	21 12 29	17 1 34	24 29 34	0♏59 9	27 21.7	1 53.5	1 59.7	3 29.8	24 36.0	1 45.5	12 28.9	15 37.9	14 29.6
11 F	21 16 25	17 59 8	7♏33 48	14 13 52	27R 22.9	1 24.4	3 3.5	4 7.3	24 48.9	1 53.0	12 30.0	15 37.4	14 31.1
12 Sa	21 20 22	18 56 42	20 59 39	27 51 24	27 23.3	0 50.5	4 7.0	4 44.9	25 1.8	2 0.4	12 31.0	15 36.9	14 32.6
13 Su	21 24 18	19 54 18	4♐49 13	11♐53 8	27 22.4	0 12.1	5 10.3	5 22.6	25 14.6	2 7.9	12 32.2	15 36.4	14 34.1
14 M	21 28 15	20 51 54	19 3 0	26 18 29	27 19.9	29♌29.8	6 13.3	6 0.4	25 27.4	2 15.4	12 33.4	15 35.9	14 35.7
15 Tu	21 32 11	21 49 31	3♑39 7	11♑ 4 13	27 16.0	28 44.1	7 16.1	6 38.2	25 40.2	2 23.0	12 34.6	15 35.5	14 37.3
16 W	21 36 8	22 47 10	18 32 58	26 4 20	27 11.4	27 55.7	8 18.6	7 16.1	25 52.9	2 30.5	12 35.9	15 35.1	14 38.9
17 Th	21 40 5	23 44 49	3♒37 15	11♒10 31	27 6.6	27 5.4	9 20.8	7 54.1	26 5.6	2 38.0	12 37.3	15 34.7	14 40.5
18 F	21 44 1	24 42 30	18 42 54	26 13 14	27 2.4	26 14.1	10 22.7	8 32.1	26 18.2	2 45.6	12 38.7	15 34.4	14 42.2
19 Sa	21 47 58	25 40 12	3♓40 23	11♓ 3 21	26 59.4	25 22.9	11 24.4	9 10.2	26 30.7	2 53.2	12 40.1	15 34.1	14 43.9
20 Su	21 51 54	26 37 55	18 21 16	25 33 29	26D 57.8	24 32.7	12 25.7	9 48.4	26 43.2	3 0.7	12 41.6	15 33.8	14 45.6
21 M	21 55 51	27 35 39	2♈39 27	9♈38 51	26 57.7	23 44.5	13 26.8	10 26.6	26 55.7	3 8.3	12 43.1	15 33.6	14 47.4
22 Tu	21 59 47	28 33 25	16 31 33	23 17 32	26 58.6	22 59.4	14 27.5	11 4.9	27 8.1	3 15.9	12 44.7	15 33.4	14 49.1
23 W	22 3 44	29 31 13	29 56 58	6♉30 4	27 0.1	22 18.3	15 28.0	11 43.3	27 20.5	3 23.5	12 46.4	15 33.2	14 50.9
24 Th	22 7 40	0♍29 3	12♉57 13	19 18 51	27 1.6	21 42.2	16 28.0	12 21.7	27 32.8	3 31.1	12 48.0	15 33.0	14 52.7
25 F	22 11 37	1 26 54	25 35 26	1♊47 31	27R 2.5	21 11.9	17 27.8	13 0.2	27 45.1	3 38.7	12 49.8	15 32.9	14 54.5
26 Sa	22 15 33	2 24 47	7♊55 38	14 0 22	27 2.5	20 48.1	18 27.2	13 38.8	27 57.3	3 46.3	12 51.5	15 32.8	14 56.4
27 Su	22 19 30	3 22 42	20 2 14	26 1 49	27 1.5	20 31.4	19 26.3	14 17.4	28 9.4	3 53.9	12 53.4	15 32.8	14 58.3
28 M	22 23 27	4 20 39	1♋59 39	7♋56 14	26 59.4	20D 22.2	20 25.0	14 56.1	28 21.5	4 1.5	12 55.2	15D 32.8	15 0.2
29 Tu	22 27 23	5 18 37	13 52 2	19 47 32	26 56.5	20 21.0	21 23.3	15 34.9	28 33.5	4 9.1	12 57.1	15 32.8	15 2.1
30 W	22 31 20	6 16 37	25 43 7	1♌39 12	26 53.2	20 27.9	22 21.2	16 13.8	28 45.5	4 16.7	12 59.1	15 32.8	15 4.0
31 Th	22 35 16	7 14 39	7♌36 6	13 34 10	26 49.9	20 43.2	23 18.7	16 52.7	28 57.4	4 24.3	13 1.1	15 32.9	15 6.0

Astro Data

	Dy Hr Mn
♃⊼♆	3 14:36
☽0S	11 20:09
♄∠♇	18 8:19
♅ D	21 10:04
☽0N	24 10:30
☿ R	4 23:07
♂0S	6 4:49
♀0S	7 20:35
☽0S	8 2:51
☽0N	20 20:52
☿ D	28 15:41
♆ D	28 0:54

Planet Ingress

	Dy Hr Mn
☿ ♌	2 22:28
☊ ♍	5 10:41
♀ ♍	12 2:14
☉ ♌	23 5:00
♄ ♍	26 12:01
☿ ♍	27 6:10
♂ ♎	4 9:07
♀ ♎	8 3:08
☿ ♌	13 7:05
☉ ♍	23 11:57

Last Aspect / ☽ Ingress

Last Aspect Dy Hr Mn		☽ Ingress Dy Hr Mn
1 15:10	☿ ⚹	♊ 1 19:37
4 2:35	♄ ⚹	♋ 4 7:33
5 17:24	♃ ☌	♌ 6 20:13
9 4:51	♄ ☌	♍ 9 8:44
10 20:55	☉ ⚹	♎ 11 19:48
14 1:13	♄ ⚹	♏ 14 3:47
16 5:51	♄ □	♐ 16 7:50
18 7:03	♄ △	♑ 18 8:33
20 3:05	☉ ☍	♒ 20 7:41
22 6:38	♄ ☍	♓ 22 7:26
23 21:40	♂ ☍	♈ 24 9:46
26 15:03	☿ △	♉ 26 15:50
28 17:29	♂ △	♊ 29 1:31
31 8:28	♂ □	♋ 31 13:28

Last Aspect / ☽ Ingress

Last Aspect Dy Hr Mn		☽ Ingress Dy Hr Mn
3 0:28	♂ ⚹	♌ 3 2:10
4 9:49	♆ △	♍ 5 14:29
8 1:20	♀ ☌	♎ 8 1:30
10 0:12	♃ □	♏ 10 10:11
12 7:11	♃ △	♐ 12 15:43
14 16:23	☿ △	♑ 14 18:03
16 11:52	♃ ☍	♒ 16 18:15
18 11:22	☿ ☍	♓ 18 18:04
20 14:10	♃ △	♈ 20 19:29
22 23:10	☉ △	♉ 23 0:06
25 4:14	♃ ⚹	♊ 25 8:31
27 0:57	☿ ⚹	♋ 27 19:59
30 6:15	♃ ☌	♌ 30 8:40

☽ Phases & Eclipses

Dy Hr Mn		
5 9:50	●	13♋01
13 10:49	☽	20♎41
20 3:05	○	27♑04
26 22:31	☽	3♉34
4 1:01	●	11♌19
11 20:06	☽	18♏47
18 10:14	○	25♒07
25 12:18	☽	1♊57

Astro Data

1 JULY 1978
Julian Day # 28671
Delta T 49.1 sec
SVP 05♓33'36"
Obliquity 23°26'22"
⚷ Chiron 8♉54.7
☽ Mean ☊ 0♎58.2

1 AUGUST 1978
Julian Day # 28702
Delta T 49.1 sec
SVP 05♓33'31"
Obliquity 23°26'22"
⚷ Chiron 9♉41.7
☽ Mean ☊ 29♍19.7

LONGITUDE SEPTEMBER 1978

Day	Sid.Time	☉	0 hr ☽	Noon☽	True☊	☿	♀	♂	♃	♄	♅	♆	♇
1 F	22 39 13	8♍12 43	19♌33 39	25♌34 50	26♍47.0	21♌ 6.7	24♎15.8	17♎31.7	29♋ 9.3	4♍31.9	13♏ 3.2	15♐33.0	15♎ 8.0
2 Sa	22 43 9	9 10 48	1♍37 55	7♍43 8	26R44.8	21 38.5	25 12.4	18 10.7	29 21.0	4 39.5	13 5.2	15 33.2	15 9.9
3 Su	22 47 6	10 8 55	13 50 39	20 0 39	26 43.5	22 18.4	26 8.6	18 49.8	29 32.7	4 47.1	13 7.4	15 33.3	15 12.0
4 M	22 51 2	11 7 4	26 13 17	2♎28 44	26D43.0	23 6.2	27 4.3	19 29.0	29 44.4	4 54.7	13 9.6	15 33.5	15 14.0
5 Tu	22 54 59	12 5 14	8♎47 9	15 8 41	26 43.4	24 1.5	27 59.6	20 8.3	29 55.9	5 2.3	13 11.8	15 33.8	15 16.0
6 W	22 58 56	13 3 26	21 33 30	28 1 45	26 44.2	25 4.1	28 54.3	20 47.6	0♌ 7.4	5 9.9	13 14.1	15 34.1	15 18.1
7 Th	23 2 52	14 1 39	4♏33 37	11♏ 9 14	26 45.3	26 13.4	29 48.5	21 27.0	0 18.8	5 17.4	13 16.4	15 34.4	15 20.2
8 F	23 6 49	14 59 54	17 48 46	24 32 20	26 46.4	27 29.0	0♏42.2	22 6.5	0 30.2	5 25.0	13 18.7	15 34.7	15 22.3
9 Sa	23 10 45	15 58 11	1♐20 3	8♐11 58	26 47.1	28 50.4	1 35.3	22 46.0	0 41.4	5 32.5	13 21.1	15 35.1	15 24.4
10 Su	23 14 42	16 56 29	15 8 7	22 8 27	26R47.4	0♍17.0	2 27.8	23 25.6	0 52.6	5 40.0	13 23.5	15 35.5	15 26.5
11 M	23 18 38	17 54 48	29 12 49	6♑21 2	26 47.3	1 48.4	3 19.7	24 5.3	1 3.7	5 47.5	13 26.0	15 35.9	15 28.7
12 Tu	23 22 35	18 53 9	13♑32 46	20 47 38	26 46.7	3 23.9	4 10.9	24 45.0	1 14.7	5 55.0	13 28.5	15 36.4	15 30.8
13 W	23 26 31	19 51 32	28 5 6	5♒24 33	26 46.0	5 3.0	5 1.5	25 24.8	1 25.6	6 2.5	13 31.1	15 36.9	15 33.0
14 Th	23 30 28	20 49 56	12♒45 18	20 6 35	26 45.3	6 45.2	5 51.4	26 4.7	1 36.5	6 9.9	13 33.7	15 37.5	15 35.2
15 F	23 34 25	21 48 22	27 27 33	4♓47 23	26 44.8	8 29.9	6 40.6	26 44.6	1 47.3	6 17.4	13 36.3	15 38.0	15 37.4
16 Sa	23 38 21	22 46 49	12♓ 5 14	19 20 19	26 44.4	10 16.7	7 29.0	27 24.6	1 57.9	6 24.8	13 39.0	15 38.6	15 39.6
17 Su	23 42 18	23 45 18	26 31 51	3♈39 10	26D44.3	12 5.2	8 16.7	28 4.6	2 8.5	6 32.2	13 41.6	15 39.3	15 41.8
18 M	23 46 14	24 43 49	10♈41 44	17 39 5	26 44.4	13 54.9	9 3.5	28 44.7	2 19.0	6 39.6	13 44.4	15 39.9	15 44.1
19 Tu	23 50 11	25 42 23	24 30 53	1♉16 57	26 44.5	15 45.6	9 49.5	29 24.9	2 29.4	6 46.9	13 47.2	15 40.6	15 46.3
20 W	23 54 7	26 40 58	7♉57 11	14 31 39	26R44.6	17 36.8	10 34.7	0♏ 5.1	2 39.7	6 54.2	13 50.0	15 41.4	15 48.6
21 Th	23 58 4	27 39 35	21 0 28	27 23 54	26 44.5	19 28.3	11 19.0	0 45.4	2 49.9	7 1.5	13 52.8	15 42.1	15 50.8
22 F	0 2 0	28 38 15	3♊42 18	9♊56 1	26 44.4	21 19.9	12 2.3	1 25.8	3 0.1	7 8.8	13 55.7	15 42.9	15 53.1
23 Sa	0 5 57	29 36 57	16 5 34	22 11 25	26 44.2	23 11.4	12 44.7	2 6.3	3 10.1	7 16.1	13 58.6	15 43.7	15 55.4
24 Su	0 9 53	0♎35 41	28 14 8	4♋14 17	26D44.1	25 2.7	13 26.1	2 46.8	3 20.0	7 23.3	14 1.5	15 44.6	15 57.7
25 M	0 13 50	1 34 27	10♋12 25	16 9 9	26 44.1	26 53.5	14 6.4	3 27.3	3 29.8	7 30.5	14 4.5	15 45.5	16 0.0
26 Tu	0 17 47	2 33 15	22 5 2	28 0 40	26 44.5	28 43.8	14 45.6	4 8.0	3 39.5	7 37.6	14 7.5	15 46.4	16 2.3
27 W	0 21 43	3 32 6	3♌56 35	9♌53 19	26 45.0	0♎33.5	15 23.8	4 48.7	3 49.1	7 44.8	14 10.5	15 47.3	16 4.7
28 Th	0 25 40	4 30 59	15 51 21	21 51 11	26 45.8	2 22.5	16 0.7	5 29.5	3 58.6	7 51.9	14 13.6	15 48.3	16 7.0
29 F	0 29 36	5 29 54	27 53 12	3♍57 48	26 46.7	4 10.7	16 36.4	6 10.3	4 8.0	7 58.9	14 16.7	15 49.3	16 9.3
30 Sa	0 33 33	6 28 51	10♍ 5 19	16 16 2	26 47.4	5 58.2	17 10.9	6 51.2	4 17.3	8 5.9	14 19.8	15 50.4	16 11.7

LONGITUDE OCTOBER 1978

Day	Sid.Time	☉	0 hr ☽	Noon☽	True☊	☿	♀	♂	♃	♄	♅	♆	♇
1 Su	0 37 29	7♎27 51	22♍30 10	28♍47 55	26♍47.8	7♎44.9	17♏44.1	7♏32.2	4♌26.5	8♍12.9	14♏23.0	15♐51.4	16♎14.0
2 M	0 41 26	8 26 52	5♎ 9 23	11♎34 39	26R47.7	9 30.8	18 15.8	8 13.3	4 35.5	8 19.9	14 26.2	15 52.5	16 16.4
3 Tu	0 45 22	9 25 56	18 3 43	24 36 34	26 47.0	11 15.8	18 46.2	8 54.4	4 44.4	8 26.8	14 29.4	15 53.7	16 18.7
4 W	0 49 19	10 25 1	1♏13 6	7♏53 13	26 45.6	13 0.0	19 15.1	9 35.6	4 53.2	8 33.7	14 32.6	15 54.8	16 21.1
5 Th	0 53 16	11 24 8	14 36 45	21 23 32	26 43.8	14 43.4	19 42.4	10 16.8	5 1.9	8 40.5	14 35.9	15 56.0	16 23.4
6 F	0 57 12	12 23 18	28 13 21	5♐ 6 1	26 41.7	16 26.0	20 8.1	10 58.1	5 10.5	8 47.3	14 39.2	15 57.2	16 25.8
7 Sa	1 1 9	13 22 29	12♐ 1 17	18 58 56	26 39.7	18 7.7	20 32.2	11 39.5	5 18.9	8 54.0	14 42.5	15 58.5	16 28.2
8 Su	1 5 5	14 21 42	25 58 44	3♑ 0 27	26 38.1	19 48.6	20 54.5	12 21.0	5 27.3	9 0.7	14 45.9	15 59.7	16 30.5
9 M	1 9 2	15 20 57	10♑ 3 50	17 8 40	26D37.4	21 28.7	21 15.0	13 2.5	5 35.4	9 7.4	14 49.2	16 1.1	16 32.9
10 Tu	1 12 58	16 20 13	24 14 41	1♒21 38	26 37.4	23 8.1	21 33.7	13 44.0	5 43.5	9 14.0	14 52.6	16 2.4	16 35.3
11 W	1 16 55	17 19 32	8♒29 13	15 37 9	26 38.3	24 46.7	21 50.4	14 25.7	5 51.4	9 20.6	14 56.0	16 3.7	16 37.7
12 Th	1 20 51	18 18 51	22 45 6	29 52 42	26 39.7	26 24.5	22 5.1	15 7.4	5 59.2	9 27.1	14 59.5	16 5.1	16 40.0
13 F	1 24 48	19 18 13	6♓59 33	14♓ 5 16	26 41.0	28 1.6	22 17.8	15 49.1	6 6.9	9 33.5	15 2.9	16 6.5	16 42.4
14 Sa	1 28 45	20 17 36	21 9 23	28 13 11	26R41.9	29 38.0	22 28.3	16 30.9	6 14.4	9 39.9	15 6.4	16 8.0	16 44.8
15 Su	1 32 41	21 17 2	5♈11 4	12♈ 7 44	26 41.7	1♏13.7	22 36.7	17 12.8	6 21.7	9 46.3	15 9.9	16 9.4	16 47.1
16 M	1 36 38	22 16 29	19 1 3	25 50 38	26 40.3	2 48.8	22 42.9	17 54.7	6 29.0	9 52.6	15 13.4	16 10.9	16 49.5
17 Tu	1 40 34	23 15 58	2♉36 8	9♉17 18	26 37.5	4 23.2	22 46.7	18 36.8	6 36.1	9 58.8	15 16.9	16 12.4	16 51.9
18 W	1 44 31	24 15 30	15 53 55	22 25 52	26 33.6	5 56.9	22R48.3	19 18.8	6 43.0	10 5.0	15 20.4	16 14.0	16 54.2
19 Th	1 48 27	25 15 3	28 53 8	5♊15 46	26 28.9	7 30.0	22 47.5	20 1.0	6 49.8	10 11.1	15 24.0	16 15.5	16 56.6
20 F	1 52 24	26 14 39	11♊33 53	17 47 44	26 24.0	9 2.5	22 44.3	20 43.2	6 56.5	10 17.2	15 27.6	16 17.1	16 58.9
21 Sa	1 56 20	27 14 17	23 57 37	0♋ 3 53	26 19.6	10 34.4	22 38.8	21 25.4	7 3.0	10 23.2	15 31.2	16 18.7	17 1.3
22 Su	2 0 17	28 13 57	6♋ 6 59	12 7 24	26 16.1	12 5.6	22 30.8	22 7.7	7 9.4	10 29.2	15 34.8	16 20.4	17 3.6
23 M	2 4 14	29 13 39	18 5 40	24 2 22	26 13.9	13 36.3	22 20.4	22 50.1	7 15.6	10 35.1	15 38.4	16 22.0	17 6.0
24 Tu	2 8 10	0♏13 24	29 58 5	5♌53 28	26D13.2	15 6.4	22 7.6	23 32.6	7 21.7	10 40.9	15 42.0	16 23.7	17 8.3
25 W	2 12 7	1 13 11	11♌49 7	17 45 42	26 13.7	16 35.9	21 52.4	24 15.1	7 27.5	10 46.7	15 45.7	16 25.4	17 10.6
26 Th	2 16 3	2 13 0	23 43 48	29 44 4	26 15.2	18 4.8	21 34.9	24 57.7	7 33.3	10 52.4	15 49.4	16 27.1	17 12.9
27 F	2 20 0	3 12 51	5♍47 4	11♍53 21	26 16.9	19 33.1	21 15.1	25 40.3	7 38.9	10 58.0	15 53.0	16 28.9	17 15.3
28 Sa	2 23 56	4 12 44	18 3 26	24 17 44	26R18.3	21 0.8	20 53.1	26 23.1	7 44.3	11 3.6	15 56.7	16 30.7	17 17.6
29 Su	2 27 53	5 12 40	0♎36 38	7♎ 0 26	26 18.5	22 27.9	20 29.0	27 5.8	7 49.5	11 9.1	16 0.4	16 32.5	17 19.8
30 M	2 31 49	6 12 37	13 29 19	20 3 24	26 17.0	23 54.4	20 2.8	27 48.7	7 54.6	11 14.5	16 4.1	16 34.3	17 22.1
31 Tu	2 35 46	7 12 37	26 42 39	3♏26 58	26 13.6	25 20.1	19 34.8	28 31.6	7 59.5	11 19.9	16 7.8	16 36.1	17 24.4

Astro Data Dy Hr Mn	Planet Ingress Dy Hr Mn	Last Aspect Dy Hr Mn	☽ Ingress Dy Hr Mn	Last Aspect Dy Hr Mn	☽ Ingress Dy Hr Mn	☽ Phases & Eclipses Dy Hr Mn	Astro Data
							1 SEPTEMBER 1978
☽0S 4 8:57	♃ ♌ 5 8:30	1 10:11 ♀ ⚹	♍ 1 20:46	30 14:25 ♀ ⚹	♎ 1 14:17	2 16:09 ● 9♍50	Julian Day # 28733
♃□♆ 8 10:01	♀ ♏ 7 5:07	4 6:52 ♃ ⚹	♎ 4 7:15	2 20:46 ♇ ☌	♏ 3 21:48	10 3:20 ☽ 17♐05	Delta T 49.2 sec
♆⚹♇ 15 9:20	☿ ♍ 9 19:23	6 14:38 ♀ ☌	♏ 6 15:38	5 9:19 ♀ ☌	♐ 6 3:07	16 19:01 ○ 23♓33	SVP 05♓33'27"
☽0N 17 7:19	♂ ♏ 19 20:57	8 19:06 ☿ □	♐ 8 21:39	7 11:59 ☿ ⚹	♑ 8 6:52	16 19:04 ☍T 1.327	Obliquity 23°26'23"
☿0S 28 13:45	☉ ♎ 23 9:25	10 14:53 ♂ ⚹	♑ 11 1:20	9 21:53 ☿ □	♒ 10 9:42	24 5:07 ☽ 0♋48	⚷ Chiron 9♉37.2R
	☿ ♎ 26 16:40	12 19:24 ♂ □	♒ 13 3:09	12 6:57 ☿ △	♓ 12 12:12		☽ Mean ☊ 27♍41.2
☽0S 1 15:55		14 22:46 ♂ △	♓ 15 4:09	14 2:16 ♀ △	♈ 14 15:06	2 6:41 ● 8♎43	
☽0N 14 16:37	☿ ♏ 14 5:30	16 19:01 ☉ ☍	♈ 17 5:50	16 6:10 ☉ ☍	♉ 16 19:22	2 6:27:54 ☌P 0.691	1 OCTOBER 1978
♀ R 18 3:58	☉ ♏ 23 18:37	19 9:08 ♂ ☍	♉ 19 9:43	18 12:41 ♀ ☍	♊ 19 2:05	9 9:38 ☽ 15♑45	Julian Day # 28763
☽0S 29 0:41		21 13:32 ☉ △	♊ 21 16:56	21 7:00 ☉ △	♋ 21 11:52	16 6:10 ○ 22♈32	Delta T 49.3 sec
		23 16:30 ☿ □	♋ 24 3:31	23 10:10 ♂ △	♌ 24 0:04	24 0:34 ☽ 0♌15	SVP 05♓33'25"
		26 15:55 ☿ ⚹	♌ 26 16:02	26 2:37 ♂ □	♍ 26 12:32	31 20:06 ● 8♏03	Obliquity 23°26'23"
		28 0:31 ♇ ⚹	♍ 29 4:11	28 16:57 ♂ ⚹	♎ 28 22:51		⚷ Chiron 8♉45.4R
				30 7:08 ♇ ☌	♏ 31 5:53		☽ Mean ☊ 26♍05.8

NOVEMBER 1978 LONGITUDE

Day	Sid.Time	☉	0 hr ☽	Noon ☽	True ☊	☿	♀	♂	♃	♄	♅	♆	♇
1 W	2 39 42	8♏12 38	10♏16 5	17♏ 9 41	26♍ 8.3	26♏45.2	19♏ 5.1	29♏14.6	8♌ 4.3	11♍25.2	16♏11.5	16♐38.0	17♎26.7
2 Th	2 43 39	9 12 42	24 7 18	1♐ 8 26	26R 1.6	28 9.5	18R33.7	29 57.6	8 8.8	11 30.4	16 15.2	16 39.8	17 28.9
3 F	2 47 36	10 12 47	8♐12 30	15 18 51	25 54.2	29 33.0	18 1.0	0♐40.7	8 13.2	11 35.5	16 19.0	16 41.7	17 31.1
4 Sa	2 51 32	11 12 54	22 26 51	29 35 53	25 47.0	0♐55.7	17 27.1	1 23.9	8 17.5	11 40.6	16 22.7	16 43.6	17 33.4
5 Su	2 55 29	12 13 3	6♑45 20	13♑54 41	25 41.0	2 17.5	16 52.2	2 7.1	8 21.5	11 45.6	16 26.4	16 45.6	17 35.6
6 M	2 59 25	13 13 13	21 3 26	28 11 10	25 36.8	3 38.3	16 16.5	2 50.3	8 25.4	11 50.5	16 30.2	16 47.5	17 37.8
7 Tu	3 3 22	14 13 25	5♒17 36	12♒22 26	25D34.7	4 58.0	15 40.3	3 33.7	8 29.1	11 55.3	16 33.9	16 49.5	17 40.0
8 W	3 7 18	15 13 38	19 25 31	26 26 42	25 34.4	6 16.5	15 3.8	4 17.1	8 32.6	12 0.1	16 37.7	16 51.5	17 42.1
9 Th	3 11 15	16 13 52	3♓25 54	10♓23 4	25 35.3	7 33.7	14 27.3	5 0.5	8 35.9	12 4.8	16 41.4	16 53.5	17 44.3
10 F	3 15 11	17 14 8	17 18 8	24 11 4	25R36.3	8 49.4	13 51.0	5 44.0	8 39.0	12 9.3	16 45.2	16 55.5	17 46.4
11 Sa	3 19 8	18 14 26	1♈ 1 48	7♈50 16	25 36.4	10 3.6	13 15.1	6 27.6	8 42.0	12 13.8	16 48.9	16 57.5	17 48.6
12 Su	3 23 5	19 14 45	14 36 21	21 19 56	25 34.7	11 15.9	12 40.0	7 11.2	8 44.8	12 18.3	16 52.7	16 59.6	17 50.7
13 M	3 27 1	20 15 5	28 0 53	4♉39 1	25 30.5	12 26.1	12 5.8	7 54.9	8 47.4	12 22.6	16 56.4	17 1.6	17 52.8
14 Tu	3 30 58	21 15 27	11♉14 11	17 46 12	25 23.8	13 34.1	11 32.9	8 38.7	8 49.8	12 26.8	17 0.1	17 3.7	17 54.8
15 W	3 34 54	22 15 51	24 14 55	0♊40 13	25 14.7	14 39.6	11 1.3	9 22.5	8 52.0	12 31.0	17 3.9	17 5.8	17 56.9
16 Th	3 38 51	23 16 16	7♊ 2 1	13 20 15	25 4.0	15 42.1	10 31.3	10 6.3	8 54.0	12 35.1	17 7.6	17 7.9	17 58.9
17 F	3 42 47	24 16 43	19 34 58	25 46 13	24 52.8	16 41.3	10 3.0	10 50.3	8 55.8	12 39.1	17 11.3	17 10.0	18 1.0
18 Sa	3 46 44	25 17 12	1♋54 10	7♋59 1	24 41.9	17 36.8	9 36.7	11 34.2	8 57.5	12 43.0	17 15.1	17 12.1	18 3.0
19 Su	3 50 40	26 17 42	14 1 4	20 0 40	24 32.6	18 28.2	9 12.5	12 18.3	8 58.9	12 46.8	17 18.8	17 14.2	18 4.9
20 M	3 54 37	27 18 14	25 58 13	1♌54 13	24 25.3	19 14.8	8 50.4	13 2.4	9 0.2	12 50.5	17 22.5	17 16.4	18 6.9
21 Tu	3 58 34	28 18 48	7♌49 11	13 43 42	24 20.6	19 56.1	8 30.7	13 46.5	9 1.2	12 54.1	17 26.2	17 18.5	18 8.8
22 W	4 2 30	29 19 24	19 38 23	25 33 53	24D18.2	20 31.4	8 13.3	14 30.7	9 2.1	12 57.6	17 29.9	17 20.7	18 10.8
23 Th	4 6 27	0♐20 1	1♍30 52	7♍30 0	24 17.7	20 60.0	7 58.3	15 15.0	9 2.8	13 1.1	17 33.6	17 22.9	18 12.7
24 F	4 10 23	1 20 40	13 32 1	19 37 33	24R18.1	21 21.1	7 45.7	15 59.3	9 3.2	13 4.4	17 37.2	17 25.1	18 14.5
25 Sa	4 14 20	2 21 20	25 47 16	2♎ 1 48	24 18.4	21R33.9	7 35.7	16 43.7	9R 3.5	13 7.6	17 40.9	17 27.3	18 16.4
26 Su	4 18 16	3 22 3	8♎21 41	14 47 24	24 17.5	21 37.8	7 28.1	17 28.2	9 3.6	13 10.8	17 44.5	17 29.5	18 18.2
27 M	4 22 13	4 22 46	21 19 20	27 57 46	24 14.4	21 31.8	7 23.1	18 12.7	9 3.4	13 13.8	17 48.2	17 31.7	18 20.0
28 Tu	4 26 9	5 23 32	4♏42 47	11♏34 23	24 8.7	21 15.5	7D20.5	18 57.2	9 3.1	13 16.8	17 51.8	17 33.9	18 21.8
29 W	4 30 6	6 24 18	18 32 20	25 36 15	24 0.3	20 48.4	7 20.4	19 41.9	9 2.6	13 19.6	17 55.4	17 36.1	18 23.6
30 Th	4 34 3	7 25 7	2♐45 35	9♐59 37	23 49.7	20 10.2	7 22.7	20 26.5	9 1.9	13 22.3	17 59.0	17 38.4	18 25.3

DECEMBER 1978 LONGITUDE

Day	Sid.Time	☉	0 hr ☽	Noon ☽	True ☊	☿	♀	♂	♃	♄	♅	♆	♇
1 F	4 37 59	8♐25 56	17♐17 27	24♐38 7	23♍38.0	19♐21.2	7♏27.4	21♐11.3	9♌ 0.9	13♍25.0	18♏ 2.6	17♐40.6	18♎27.0
2 Sa	4 41 56	9 26 47	2♑ 0 36	9♑23 50	23R26.5	18R22.1	7 34.4	21 56.0	8R59.8	13 27.5	18 6.2	17 42.9	18 28.7
3 Su	4 45 52	10 27 39	16 46 47	24 8 30	23 16.4	17 14.1	7 43.7	22 40.9	8 58.5	13 30.0	18 9.7	17 45.1	18 30.4
4 M	4 49 49	11 28 31	1♒28 9	8♒45 1	23 8.8	15 58.7	7 55.2	23 25.8	8 57.0	13 32.3	18 13.3	17 47.4	18 32.0
5 Tu	4 53 45	12 29 25	15 58 32	23 8 18	23 4.1	14 38.4	8 8.8	24 10.7	8 55.3	13 34.5	18 16.8	17 49.6	18 33.6
6 W	4 57 42	13 30 19	0♓14 3	7♓15 41	23 1.9	13 15.7	8 24.6	24 55.7	8 53.3	13 36.6	18 20.3	17 51.9	18 35.2
7 Th	5 1 38	14 31 14	14 13 8	21 6 30	23 1.5	11 53.3	8 42.4	25 40.7	8 51.2	13 38.6	18 23.7	17 54.1	18 36.8
8 F	5 5 35	15 32 9	27 55 56	4♈41 35	23 1.4	10 34.1	9 2.1	26 25.8	8 48.9	13 40.5	18 27.2	17 56.4	18 38.3
9 Sa	5 9 32	16 33 5	11♈23 39	18 2 22	23 0.5	9 20.6	9 23.9	27 11.0	8 46.4	13 42.3	18 30.6	17 58.7	18 39.8
10 Su	5 13 28	17 34 2	24 37 55	1♉10 27	22 57.5	8 15.0	9 47.4	27 56.2	8 43.7	13 44.0	18 34.0	18 0.9	18 41.2
11 M	5 17 25	18 35 0	7♉40 9	14 7 6	22 51.6	7 18.9	10 12.8	28 41.4	8 40.8	13 45.6	18 37.4	18 3.2	18 42.7
12 Tu	5 21 21	19 35 58	20 31 23	26 53 3	22 42.5	6 33.3	10 39.9	29 26.7	8 37.8	13 47.1	18 40.8	18 5.5	18 44.1
13 W	5 25 18	20 36 57	3♊12 9	9♊28 40	22 30.7	5 58.9	11 8.7	0♑12.0	8 34.5	13 48.5	18 44.1	18 7.7	18 45.5
14 Th	5 29 14	21 37 57	15 42 37	21 54 0	22 16.8	5 35.8	11 39.1	0 57.4	8 31.1	13 49.7	18 47.4	18 10.0	18 46.8
15 F	5 33 11	22 38 58	28 2 52	4♋ 9 15	22 2.1	5D23.6	12 11.1	1 42.8	8 27.4	13 50.9	18 50.7	18 12.2	18 48.1
16 Sa	5 37 7	23 39 59	10♋13 14	16 14 57	21 47.8	5 21.9	12 44.6	2 28.3	8 23.6	13 51.9	18 53.9	18 14.5	18 49.4
17 Su	5 41 4	24 41 1	22 14 34	28 12 20	21 35.0	5 30.0	13 19.5	3 13.8	8 19.6	13 52.9	18 57.2	18 16.8	18 50.7
18 M	5 45 1	25 42 4	4♌ 8 30	10♌ 3 27	21 24.8	5 47.1	13 55.8	3 59.4	8 15.5	13 53.7	19 0.4	18 19.0	18 51.9
19 Tu	5 48 57	26 43 7	15 57 33	21 51 17	21 17.4	6 12.5	14 33.5	4 45.0	8 11.1	13 54.4	19 3.5	18 21.3	18 53.1
20 W	5 52 54	27 44 12	27 45 9	3♍39 42	21 13.0	6 45.2	15 12.5	5 30.7	8 6.6	13 55.0	19 6.7	18 23.5	18 54.3
21 Th	5 56 50	28 45 17	9♍35 34	15 33 23	21D11.0	7 24.5	15 52.7	6 16.4	8 1.9	13 55.5	19 9.8	18 25.7	18 55.4
22 F	6 0 47	29 46 23	21 33 49	27 37 33	21R10.6	8 9.6	16 34.1	7 2.2	7 57.0	13 55.9	19 12.9	18 28.0	18 56.5
23 Sa	6 4 43	0♑47 29	3♎45 17	9♎57 43	21 10.7	9 0.0	17 16.6	7 48.0	7 52.0	13 56.1	19 15.9	18 30.2	18 57.6
24 Su	6 8 40	1 48 37	16 15 31	22 39 17	21 9.9	9 55.0	18 0.3	8 33.8	7 46.8	13R56.3	19 18.9	18 32.4	18 58.6
25 M	6 12 36	2 49 45	29 9 35	5♏46 51	21 7.4	10 54.1	18 45.0	9 19.7	7 41.4	13 56.3	19 21.9	18 34.6	18 59.6
26 Tu	6 16 33	3 50 53	12♏31 27	19 23 31	21 2.3	11 56.7	19 30.7	10 5.7	7 35.9	13 56.2	19 24.9	18 36.8	19 0.6
27 W	6 20 30	4 52 3	26 23 4	3♐29 53	20 54.5	13 2.4	20 17.4	10 51.7	7 30.2	13 56.1	19 27.8	18 39.1	19 1.5
28 Th	6 24 26	5 53 13	10♐43 33	18 3 25	20 44.5	14 11.0	21 5.0	11 37.7	7 24.4	13 55.8	19 30.7	18 41.2	19 2.4
29 F	6 28 23	6 54 23	25 28 37	2♑58 5	20 33.1	15 22.0	21 53.5	12 23.8	7 18.4	13 55.4	19 33.5	18 43.4	19 3.3
30 Sa	6 32 19	7 55 34	10♑30 37	18 4 55	20 21.7	16 35.2	22 42.9	13 9.9	7 12.3	13 54.9	19 36.4	18 45.6	19 4.1
31 Su	6 36 16	8 56 44	25 39 39	3♒13 29	20 11.7	17 50.3	23 33.1	13 56.1	7 6.1	13 54.2	19 39.1	18 47.8	19 4.9

Astro Data Dy Hr Mn	Planet Ingress Dy Hr Mn
☽0N 11 0:12	♂ ♐ 2 1:20
♅⊻♆ 16 3:53	☿ ♐ 3 7:48
☽0S 25 10:55	☉ ♐ 22 16:05
☿ R 25 21:42	
♃ R 25 20:30	♂ ♑ 12 17:39
♀ D 28 13:10	☉ ♑ 22 5:21
☽0N 8 6:48	
♅⊻♇ 13 17:00	
☿ D 15 15:57	
☽0S 22 21:03	
♄ R 24 21:12	

Last Aspect Dy Hr Mn	☽ Ingress Dy Hr Mn
2 7:40 ☿ ☌	♐ 2 10:03
3 15:45 ♇ ⚹	♑ 4 12:40
5 18:14 ♇ □	♒ 6 15:04
7 21:03 ♇ △	♓ 8 18:06
9 23:53 ☉ △	♈ 10 22:11
12 5:47 ♇ ☍	♉ 13 3:35
14 20:00 ☉ ☍	♊ 15 10:45
16 20:58 ♇ △	♋ 17 20:16
20 2:57 ☉ △	♌ 20 8:09
22 1:53 ☿ △	♍ 22 20:57
24 15:41 ☿ □	♎ 25 8:07
27 0:22 ☿ ⚹	♏ 27 15:39
28 22:57 ♅ ☌	♐ 29 19:23

Last Aspect Dy Hr Mn	☽ Ingress Dy Hr Mn
1 6:43 ♂ ☌	♑ 1 20:44
3 2:49 ♇ □	♒ 3 21:35
5 14:31 ♂ ⚹	♓ 5 23:36
7 21:12 ♂ □	♈ 8 3:40
10 6:25 ♂ △	♉ 10 9:50
11 20:31 ♅ ☍	♊ 12 17:54
14 12:31 ☉ ☍	♋ 15 3:50
16 17:23 ♅ △	♌ 17 15:37
19 23:58 ☉ △	♍ 20 4:34
21 19:18 ♅ ⚹	♎ 22 16:40
24 5:08 ♇ ☌	♏ 25 1:32
26 12:56 ♀ ☌	♐ 27 6:07
28 13:37 ♇ ⚹	♑ 29 7:15
30 20:28 ♀ ⚹	♒ 31 6:53

☽ Phases & Eclipses Dy Hr Mn	
7 16:18	☽ 14♒54
14 20:00	○ 22♉06
22 21:24	☽ 0♍13
30 8:19	● 7♐46
7 0:34	☽ 14♓33
14 12:31	○ 22♊10
22 17:41	☽ 0♎31
29 19:36	● 7♑44

Astro Data

1 NOVEMBER 1978
Julian Day # 28794
Delta T 49.4 sec
SVP 05♓33'23"
Obliquity 23°26'22"
⚷ Chiron 7♉20.9R
☽ Mean ☊ 24♍27.3

1 DECEMBER 1978
Julian Day # 28824
Delta T 49.5 sec
SVP 05♓33'18"
Obliquity 23°26'22"
⚷ Chiron 5♉59.5R
☽ Mean ☊ 22♍52.0

LONGITUDE — JANUARY 1979

Day	Sid.Time	☉	0 hr ☽	Noon ☽	True ☊	☿	♀	♂	♃	♄	♅	♆	♇
1 M	6 40 12	9♑57 55	10♒45 13	18♒13 46	20♍ 4.0	19♐ 7.1	24♏24.0	14♑42.3	6♌59.7	13♍53.5	19♏41.9	18♐49.9	19♎ 5.7
2 Tu	6 44 9	10 59 6	25 38 11	2♓57 45	19R 59.2	20 25.4	25 15.8	15 28.5	6R 53.2	13R 52.7	19 44.6	18 52.1	19 6.4
3 W	6 48 6	12 0 16	10♓11 58	17 20 28	19D 57.0	21 45.0	26 8.2	16 14.8	6 46.6	13 51.7	19 47.2	18 54.2	19 7.1
4 Th	6 52 2	13 1 26	24 23 8	1♈19 56	19 56.7	23 5.9	27 1.3	17 1.1	6 39.8	13 50.6	19 49.8	18 56.3	19 7.8
5 F	6 55 59	14 2 36	8♈11 0	14 56 33	19R 57.2	24 27.9	27 55.1	17 47.4	6 32.9	13 49.5	19 52.4	18 58.4	19 8.4
6 Sa	6 59 55	15 3 45	21 36 53	28 12 21	19 57.1	25 50.9	28 49.6	18 33.8	6 26.0	13 48.2	19 55.0	19 0.5	19 9.0
7 Su	7 3 52	16 4 54	4♉43 17	11♉10 5	19 55.3	27 14.9	29 44.7	19 20.2	6 18.9	13 46.8	19 57.4	19 2.6	19 9.5
8 M	7 7 48	17 6 3	17 33 6	23 52 40	19 51.2	28 39.6	0♐40.4	20 6.7	6 11.7	13 45.3	19 59.9	19 4.6	19 10.0
9 Tu	7 11 45	18 7 11	0♊ 9 7	6♊22 44	19 44.3	0♑ 5.2	1 36.6	20 53.2	6 4.4	13 43.7	20 2.3	19 6.7	19 10.5
10 W	7 15 41	19 8 19	12 33 45	18 42 26	19 35.0	1 31.5	2 33.4	21 39.7	5 57.0	13 42.0	20 4.7	19 8.7	19 11.0
11 Th	7 19 38	20 9 27	24 48 56	0♋53 27	19 24.0	2 58.5	3 30.8	22 26.2	5 49.6	13 40.2	20 7.0	19 10.7	19 11.4
12 F	7 23 35	21 10 34	6♋56 8	12 57 7	19 12.2	4 26.1	4 28.7	23 12.8	5 42.1	13 38.3	20 9.3	19 12.7	19 11.7
13 Sa	7 27 31	22 11 41	18 56 34	24 54 37	19 0.6	5 54.4	5 27.1	23 59.4	5 34.5	13 36.3	20 11.5	19 14.7	19 12.1
14 Su	7 31 28	23 12 47	0♌51 26	6♌47 11	18 50.4	7 23.3	6 26.0	24 46.1	5 26.8	13 34.2	20 13.7	19 16.7	19 12.4
15 M	7 35 24	24 13 53	12 42 7	18 36 28	18 42.2	8 52.7	7 25.3	25 32.7	5 19.1	13 32.0	20 15.9	19 18.6	19 12.6
16 Tu	7 39 21	25 14 59	24 30 30	0♍24 34	18 36.4	10 22.8	8 25.1	26 19.5	5 11.3	13 29.7	20 18.0	19 20.6	19 12.9
17 W	7 43 17	26 16 4	6♍19 2	12 14 19	18 33.2	11 53.4	9 25.4	27 6.2	5 3.4	13 27.3	20 20.0	19 22.5	19 13.1
18 Th	7 47 14	27 17 9	18 10 52	24 9 12	18D 32.3	13 24.6	10 26.0	27 53.0	4 55.5	13 24.8	20 22.0	19 24.4	19 13.2
19 F	7 51 10	28 18 13	0♎ 9 52	6♎13 26	18 32.9	14 56.3	11 27.1	28 39.7	4 47.6	13 22.2	20 24.0	19 26.2	19 13.3
20 Sa	7 55 7	29 19 18	12 20 30	18 31 41	18 34.2	16 28.6	12 28.5	29 26.6	4 39.6	13 19.5	20 25.9	19 28.1	19 13.4
21 Su	7 59 4	0♒20 21	24 47 37	1♏ 8 53	18R 35.2	18 1.4	13 30.4	0♒13.4	4 31.6	13 16.7	20 27.8	19 29.9	19R 13.5
22 M	8 3 0	1 21 25	7♏36 5	14 9 43	18 35.2	19 34.9	14 32.6	1 0.3	4 23.6	13 13.8	20 29.6	19 31.7	19 13.5
23 Tu	8 6 57	2 22 28	20 50 14	27 37 58	18 33.4	21 8.9	15 35.1	1 47.2	4 15.6	13 10.9	20 31.4	19 33.5	19 13.5
24 W	8 10 53	3 23 31	4♐33 7	11♐35 42	18 29.7	22 43.5	16 38.0	2 34.2	4 7.6	13 7.8	20 33.1	19 35.3	19 13.4
25 Th	8 14 50	4 24 33	18 45 33	26 2 19	18 24.2	24 18.6	17 41.2	3 21.1	3 59.5	13 4.7	20 34.7	19 37.0	19 13.3
26 F	8 18 46	5 25 35	3♑25 23	10♑53 58	18 17.6	25 54.4	18 44.7	4 8.1	3 51.5	13 1.5	20 36.4	19 38.8	19 13.2
27 Sa	8 22 43	6 26 36	18 27 1	26 3 23	18 10.8	27 30.9	19 48.5	4 55.1	3 43.4	12 58.1	20 37.9	19 40.5	19 13.0
28 Su	8 26 39	7 27 36	3♒41 44	11♒20 42	18 4.7	29 7.9	20 52.6	5 42.2	3 35.4	12 54.8	20 39.4	19 42.2	19 12.8
29 M	8 30 36	8 28 36	18 58 55	26 35 3	18 0.1	0♒45.6	21 57.0	6 29.2	3 27.4	12 51.3	20 40.9	19 43.8	19 12.6
30 Tu	8 34 33	9 29 34	4♓ 7 53	11♓36 22	17D 57.4	2 23.9	23 1.6	7 16.3	3 19.4	12 47.7	20 42.3	19 45.4	19 12.3
31 W	8 38 29	10 30 31	18 59 37	26 16 59	17 56.7	4 3.0	24 6.5	8 3.4	3 11.5	12 44.1	20 43.7	19 47.0	19 12.0

LONGITUDE — FEBRUARY 1979

Day	Sid.Time	☉	0 hr ☽	Noon ☽	True ☊	☿	♀	♂	♃	♄	♅	♆	♇
1 Th	8 42 26	11♒31 27	3♈27 59	10♈32 21	17♍57.5	5♒42.7	25♐11.6	8♒50.5	3♌ 3.6	12♍40.4	20♏45.0	19♐48.6	19♎11.7
2 F	8 46 22	12 32 22	17 29 58	24 20 55	17 59.0	7 23.1	26 17.0	9 37.7	2R 55.8	12R 36.6	20 46.2	19 50.2	19R 11.3
3 Sa	8 50 19	13 33 15	1♉ 5 22	7♉43 36	18 0.4	9 4.2	27 22.6	10 24.8	2 48.0	12 32.8	20 47.4	19 51.7	19 10.9
4 Su	8 54 15	14 34 8	14 15 59	20 42 57	18R 1.0	10 46.1	28 28.4	11 12.0	2 40.2	12 28.9	20 48.6	19 53.2	19 10.4
5 M	8 58 12	15 34 58	27 4 55	3♊22 23	18 0.3	12 28.7	29 34.5	11 59.2	2 32.5	12 24.9	20 49.7	19 54.7	19 10.0
6 Tu	9 2 8	16 35 47	9♊35 48	15 45 39	17 58.1	14 12.0	0♑40.7	12 46.4	2 24.9	12 20.9	20 50.7	19 56.1	19 9.4
7 W	9 6 5	17 36 35	21 52 22	27 56 23	17 54.5	15 56.1	1 47.2	13 33.6	2 17.4	12 16.8	20 51.7	19 57.6	19 8.9
8 Th	9 10 2	18 37 21	3♋58 7	9♋57 54	17 49.8	17 41.0	2 53.8	14 20.8	2 9.9	12 12.7	20 52.6	19 59.0	19 8.3
9 F	9 13 58	19 38 6	15 56 7	21 53 3	17 44.6	19 26.6	4 0.6	15 8.0	2 2.6	12 8.5	20 53.5	20 0.3	19 7.7
10 Sa	9 17 55	20 38 50	27 49 2	3♌44 18	17 39.5	21 13.0	5 7.7	15 55.3	1 55.3	12 4.2	20 54.3	20 1.7	19 7.1
11 Su	9 21 51	21 39 32	9♌39 7	15 33 44	17 35.0	23 0.1	6 14.9	16 42.5	1 48.1	11 59.9	20 55.1	20 3.0	19 6.4
12 M	9 25 48	22 40 12	21 28 23	27 23 18	17 31.6	24 47.9	7 22.3	17 29.8	1 41.0	11 55.5	20 55.8	20 4.3	19 5.7
13 Tu	9 29 44	23 40 52	3♍18 44	9♍14 55	17 29.4	26 36.5	8 29.8	18 17.1	1 34.0	11 51.1	20 56.5	20 5.5	19 5.0
14 W	9 33 41	24 41 29	15 12 9	21 10 40	17D 28.6	28 25.6	9 37.5	19 4.3	1 27.2	11 46.7	20 57.1	20 6.8	19 4.2
15 Th	9 37 37	25 42 6	27 10 49	3♎12 55	17 28.9	0♓15.4	10 45.4	19 51.6	1 20.4	11 42.2	20 57.6	20 8.0	19 3.4
16 F	9 41 34	26 42 41	9♎17 20	15 24 27	17 30.0	2 5.8	11 53.5	20 38.9	1 13.7	11 37.6	20 58.1	20 9.1	19 2.6
17 Sa	9 45 31	27 43 15	21 34 39	27 48 23	17 31.6	3 56.6	13 1.6	21 26.3	1 7.2	11 33.1	20 58.5	20 10.3	19 1.7
18 Su	9 49 27	28 43 48	4♏ 6 5	10♏28 11	17 33.2	5 47.7	14 10.0	22 13.6	1 0.8	11 28.5	20 58.9	20 11.4	19 0.8
19 M	9 53 24	29 44 19	16 55 7	23 27 18	17 34.3	7 39.1	15 18.5	23 0.9	0 54.6	11 23.8	20 59.3	20 12.5	18 59.9
20 Tu	9 57 20	0♓44 49	0♐ 5 6	6♐48 50	17R 34.7	9 30.6	16 27.1	23 48.2	0 48.4	11 19.2	20 59.5	20 13.5	18 59.0
21 W	10 1 17	1 45 18	13 38 45	20 34 58	17 34.4	11 21.9	17 35.8	24 35.6	0 42.4	11 14.5	20 59.8	20 14.5	18 58.0
22 Th	10 5 13	2 45 46	27 37 30	4♑46 14	17 33.4	13 13.0	18 44.7	25 22.9	0 36.6	11 9.8	20 59.9	20 15.5	18 57.0
23 F	10 9 10	3 46 12	12♑ 0 53	19 20 58	17 31.8	15 3.4	19 53.7	26 10.3	0 30.9	11 5.0	21 0.0	20 16.5	18 55.9
24 Sa	10 13 6	4 46 37	26 45 52	4♒14 47	17 30.2	16 53.0	21 2.8	26 57.6	0 25.3	11 0.3	21R 0.1	20 17.4	18 54.9
25 Su	10 17 3	5 47 0	11♒46 45	19 20 42	17 28.7	18 41.4	22 12.1	27 45.0	0 19.9	10 55.5	21 0.1	20 18.3	18 53.8
26 M	10 20 59	6 47 22	26 55 28	4♓29 52	17 27.6	20 28.1	23 21.4	28 32.4	0 14.7	10 50.7	21 0.0	20 19.1	18 52.7
27 Tu	10 24 56	7 47 42	12♓ 2 41	19 32 46	17D 27.2	22 12.9	24 30.9	29 19.7	0 9.6	10 45.9	20 59.9	20 20.0	18 51.6
28 W	10 28 53	8 48 1	26 59 6	4♈20 44	17 27.2	23 55.1	25 40.4	0♓ 7.1	0 4.7	10 41.1	20 59.7	20 20.8	18 50.4

Astro Data	Dy Hr Mn
☽0N	4 14:09
♆⚹♇	11 9:29
☽0S	19 5:34
♃☍♆	21 4:13
♇ R	21 20:47
☽0N	31 23:29
☽0S	15 12:13
♅ R	24 11:58
☽0N	28 10:23

Planet Ingress	Dy Hr Mn
♀ ♐	7 6:38
☿ ♑	8 22:33
☉ ♒	20 16:00
♂ ♒	20 17:07
☿ ♒	28 12:49
♀ ♑	5 9:16
☿ ♓	14 20:38
☉ ♓	19 6:13
♂ ♓	27 20:25
♃ ♋	28 23:35

Last Aspect Dy Hr Mn		☽ Ingress Dy Hr Mn
1 23:21	♀ □	♓ 2 7:08
4 4:51	♀ △	♈ 4 9:41
6 8:36	☿ △	♉ 6 15:17
8 5:09	♂ △	♊ 8 23:42
10 12:56	♇ △	♋ 11 10:14
13 10:51	♂ ☍	♌ 13 22:16
15 15:25	♅ □	♍ 16 11:10
18 20:48	♂ △	♎ 18 23:40
20 13:51	♆ ⚹	♏ 21 9:51
23 0:38	☿ ⚹	♐ 23 16:08
25 1:26	♆ ☌	♑ 25 18:27
27 15:59	☿ ☌	♒ 27 18:12
29 5:02	♀ ⚹	♓ 29 17:25
31 9:05	♀ □	♈ 31 18:11

Last Aspect Dy Hr Mn		☽ Ingress Dy Hr Mn
2 16:47	♀ △	♉ 2 22:03
4 12:12	♅ ☍	♊ 5 5:33
6 20:14	♆ ☍	♋ 7 16:06
9 10:00	♅ △	♌ 10 4:25
12 7:58	☿ ☍	♍ 12 17:18
14 11:33	♅ ⚹	♎ 15 5:37
17 12:52	☉ △	♏ 17 16:12
19 11:55	♂ □	♐ 19 23:51
21 19:58	♂ ⚹	♑ 22 4:00
23 14:41	♅ ⚹	♒ 24 5:12
26 2:42	♂ ☌	♓ 26 4:52
27 21:42	♀ ⚹	♈ 28 4:54

☽ Phases & Eclipses Dy Hr Mn	
5 11:15	☽ 14♈31
13 7:09	○ 22♋30
21 11:23	☽ 0♏49
28 6:20	● 7♒44
4 0:36	☽ 14♉36
12 2:39	○ 22♌47
20 1:17	☽ 0♐48
26 16:45	● 7♓29
26 16:54:16	☌ T 2'49"

Astro Data

1 JANUARY 1979
Julian Day # 28855
Delta T 49.6 sec
SVP 05♓33'13"
Obliquity 23°26'21"
⚷ Chiron 5♉08.5R
☽ Mean ☊ 21♍13.5

1 FEBRUARY 1979
Julian Day # 28886
Delta T 49.7 sec
SVP 05♓33'08"
Obliquity 23°26'22"
⚷ Chiron 5♉10.9
☽ Mean ☊ 19♍35.0

MARCH 1979 LONGITUDE

Day	Sid.Time	☉	0 hr ☽	Noon ☽	True ☊	☿	♀	♂	♃	♄	♅	♆	♇
1 Th	10 32 49	9♓48 17	11♈36 55	18♈47 4	17♍27.7	25♓34.4	26♑50.0	0♓54.4	29♋59.9	10♍36.3	20♏59.5	20♐21.5	18♎49.2
2 F	10 36 46	10 48 32	25 50 44	2♉47 41	17 28.3	27 10.1	27 59.8	1 41.8	29R55.3	10R31.5	20R59.3	20 22.2	18R48.0
3 Sa	10 40 42	11 48 44	9♉37 51	16 21 17	17 28.9	28 41.8	29 9.6	2 29.1	29 50.9	10 26.7	20 58.9	20 22.9	18 46.8
4 Su	10 44 39	12 48 55	22 58 9	29 28 47	17 29.4	0♈ 8.7	0♒19.5	3 16.5	29 46.7	10 21.9	20 58.5	20 23.6	18 45.5
5 M	10 48 35	13 49 4	5♊53 32	12♊12 53	17R29.6	1 30.4	1 29.5	4 3.8	29 42.6	10 17.1	20 58.1	20 24.2	18 44.2
6 Tu	10 52 32	14 49 10	18 27 18	24 37 19	17 29.6	2 46.3	2 39.6	4 51.1	29 38.7	10 12.3	20 57.6	20 24.8	18 42.9
7 W	10 56 28	15 49 14	0♋43 30	6♋46 23	17 29.6	3 55.8	3 49.7	5 38.4	29 35.0	10 7.5	20 57.1	20 25.4	18 41.6
8 Th	11 0 25	16 49 16	12 46 32	18 44 28	17D29.5	4 58.4	4 60.0	6 25.7	29 31.5	10 2.7	20 56.5	20 25.9	18 40.2
9 F	11 4 22	17 49 16	24 40 44	0♌35 48	17 29.5	5 53.6	6 10.3	7 13.0	29 28.2	9 58.0	20 55.8	20 26.4	18 38.9
10 Sa	11 8 18	18 49 14	6♌30 9	12 24 14	17 29.6	6 40.9	7 20.7	8 0.3	29 25.0	9 53.3	20 55.1	20 26.9	18 37.5
11 Su	11 12 15	19 49 10	18 18 26	24 13 8	17 29.8	7 20.2	8 31.1	8 47.6	29 22.1	9 48.6	20 54.4	20 27.3	18 36.1
12 M	11 16 11	20 49 4	0♍ 8 42	6♍ 5 25	17 30.0	7 50.9	9 41.7	9 34.8	29 19.3	9 43.9	20 53.6	20 27.7	18 34.7
13 Tu	11 20 8	21 48 55	12 3 36	18 3 30	17R30.2	8 13.1	10 52.3	10 22.1	29 16.7	9 39.2	20 52.8	20 28.1	18 33.2
14 W	11 24 4	22 48 45	24 5 21	0♎ 9 23	17 30.2	8 26.5	12 2.9	11 9.3	29 14.3	9 34.6	20 51.9	20 28.4	18 31.8
15 Th	11 28 1	23 48 33	6♎15 47	12 24 46	17 29.9	8R31.3	13 13.7	11 56.5	29 12.1	9 30.0	20 50.9	20 28.7	18 30.3
16 F	11 31 57	24 48 18	18 36 30	24 51 10	17 29.2	8 27.5	14 24.5	12 43.8	29 10.0	9 25.5	20 49.9	20 28.9	18 28.8
17 Sa	11 35 54	25 48 2	1♏ 8 56	7♏30 0	17 28.2	8 15.4	15 35.3	13 31.0	29 8.2	9 20.9	20 48.9	20 29.2	18 27.3
18 Su	11 39 51	26 47 45	13 54 31	20 22 40	17 27.0	7 55.5	16 46.3	14 18.1	29 6.6	9 16.5	20 47.8	20 29.4	18 25.8
19 M	11 43 47	27 47 25	26 54 38	3♐30 34	17 25.7	7 28.3	17 57.3	15 5.3	29 5.1	9 12.0	20 46.6	20 29.5	18 24.2
20 Tu	11 47 44	28 47 4	10♐10 37	16 54 57	17 24.7	6 54.5	19 8.3	15 52.5	29 3.8	9 7.6	20 45.4	20 29.6	18 22.7
21 W	11 51 40	29 46 41	23 43 38	0♑36 45	17D24.2	6 14.9	20 19.4	16 39.6	29 2.8	9 3.3	20 44.2	20 29.7	18 21.1
22 Th	11 55 37	0♈46 16	7♑34 20	14 36 18	17 24.2	5 30.4	21 30.6	17 26.7	29 1.9	8 59.0	20 42.9	20 29.8	18 19.5
23 F	11 59 33	1 45 49	21 42 32	28 52 49	17 24.8	4 42.1	22 41.8	18 13.9	29 1.2	8 54.7	20 41.6	20R29.8	18 17.9
24 Sa	12 3 30	2 45 21	6♒ 6 50	13♒24 9	17 25.8	3 51.1	23 53.1	19 0.9	29 0.7	8 50.5	20 40.2	20 29.8	18 16.4
25 Su	12 7 26	3 44 51	20 44 15	28 6 27	17 27.0	2 58.4	25 4.4	19 48.0	29 0.4	8 46.4	20 38.8	20 29.8	18 14.7
26 M	12 11 23	4 44 19	5♓30 3	12♓54 13	17R27.9	2 5.3	26 15.8	20 35.1	29D 0.3	8 42.3	20 37.3	20 29.7	18 13.1
27 Tu	12 15 19	5 43 46	20 18 4	27 40 42	17 28.2	1 12.8	27 27.2	21 22.1	29 0.4	8 38.3	20 35.8	20 29.6	18 11.5
28 W	12 19 16	6 43 10	5♈ 1 12	12♈18 41	17 27.5	0 21.8	28 38.7	22 9.1	29 0.7	8 34.3	20 34.3	20 29.5	18 9.8
29 Th	12 23 13	7 42 32	19 32 20	26 41 25	17 25.8	29♓33.5	29 50.2	22 56.1	29 1.2	8 30.4	20 32.7	20 29.3	18 8.2
30 F	12 27 9	8 41 52	3♉45 20	10♉43 35	17 23.1	28 48.4	1♓ 1.7	23 43.1	29 1.8	8 26.6	20 31.1	20 29.1	18 6.5
31 Sa	12 31 6	9 41 10	17 35 49	24 21 52	17 19.9	28 7.4	2 13.3	24 30.0	29 2.7	8 22.9	20 29.4	20 28.8	18 4.9

APRIL 1979 LONGITUDE

Day	Sid.Time	☉	0 hr ☽	Noon ☽	True ☊	☿	♀	♂	♃	♄	♅	♆	♇
1 Su	12 35 2	10♈40 26	1♊ 1 38	7♊35 14	17♍16.6	27♓30.9	3♓24.9	25♓16.9	29♋ 3.8	8♍19.2	20♏27.7	20♐28.6	18♎ 3.2
2 M	12 38 59	11 39 39	14 2 49	20 24 44	17R13.6	26R59.4	4 36.5	26 3.8	29 5.0	8R15.6	20R25.9	20R28.3	18R 1.6
3 Tu	12 42 55	12 38 51	26 41 20	2♋53 6	17 11.5	26 33.2	5 48.2	26 50.7	29 6.4	8 12.0	20 24.2	20 27.9	17 59.9
4 W	12 46 52	13 38 0	9♋ 0 34	15 4 18	17D10.4	26 12.5	6 59.9	27 37.5	29 8.1	8 8.5	20 22.3	20 27.5	17 58.2
5 Th	12 50 48	14 37 6	21 4 52	27 2 55	17 10.5	25 57.4	8 11.6	28 24.3	29 9.9	8 5.2	20 20.5	20 27.1	17 56.5
6 F	12 54 45	15 36 11	2♌59 4	8♌53 56	17 11.6	25 47.8	9 23.4	29 11.1	29 11.8	8 1.9	20 18.6	20 26.7	17 54.8
7 Sa	12 58 42	16 35 13	14 48 7	20 42 13	17 13.3	25D43.9	10 35.2	29 57.8	29 14.0	7 58.6	20 16.7	20 26.3	17 53.2
8 Su	13 2 38	17 34 12	26 36 48	2♍32 23	17 15.1	25 45.4	11 47.0	0♈44.5	29 16.4	7 55.5	20 14.7	20 25.8	17 51.5
9 M	13 6 35	18 33 10	8♍29 28	14 28 30	17R16.4	25 52.2	12 58.9	1 31.2	29 18.9	7 52.4	20 12.7	20 25.2	17 49.8
10 Tu	13 10 31	19 32 5	20 29 54	26 34 0	17 16.7	26 4.2	14 10.8	2 17.8	29 21.6	7 49.4	20 10.7	20 24.7	17 48.1
11 W	13 14 28	20 30 58	2♎41 8	8♎51 31	17 15.5	26 21.1	15 22.7	3 4.4	29 24.5	7 46.5	20 8.6	20 24.1	17 46.4
12 Th	13 18 24	21 29 49	15 5 21	21 22 46	17 12.7	26 42.8	16 34.6	3 51.0	29 27.6	7 43.7	20 6.5	20 23.5	17 44.7
13 F	13 22 21	22 28 38	27 43 50	4♏ 8 35	17 8.4	27 9.1	17 46.6	4 37.5	29 30.8	7 41.0	20 4.4	20 22.8	17 43.0
14 Sa	13 26 17	23 27 25	10♏36 59	17 8 59	17 2.8	27 39.7	18 58.6	5 24.0	29 34.3	7 38.4	20 2.3	20 22.2	17 41.4
15 Su	13 30 14	24 26 10	23 44 29	0♐23 20	16 56.5	28 14.5	20 10.6	6 10.5	29 37.9	7 35.9	20 0.1	20 21.4	17 39.7
16 M	13 34 11	25 24 54	7♐ 5 25	13 50 33	16 50.3	28 53.3	21 22.7	6 57.0	29 41.6	7 33.4	19 57.9	20 20.7	17 38.0
17 Tu	13 38 7	26 23 35	20 38 36	27 29 25	16 45.0	29 35.8	22 34.8	7 43.4	29 45.6	7 31.1	19 55.7	20 20.0	17 36.4
18 W	13 42 4	27 22 15	4♑22 50	11♑18 42	16 41.1	0♈22.0	23 46.9	8 29.8	29 49.7	7 28.8	19 53.4	20 19.2	17 34.7
19 Th	13 46 0	28 20 54	18 16 55	25 17 20	16D39.0	1 11.5	24 59.0	9 16.1	29 53.9	7 26.7	19 51.2	20 18.4	17 33.0
20 F	13 49 57	29 19 30	2♒19 49	9♒24 13	16 38.5	2 4.3	26 11.2	10 2.4	29 58.4	7 24.6	19 48.9	20 17.5	17 31.4
21 Sa	13 53 53	0♉18 5	16 30 23	23 38 6	16 39.3	3 0.2	27 23.4	10 48.7	0♌ 3.0	7 22.6	19 46.6	20 16.6	17 29.8
22 Su	13 57 50	1 16 38	0♓47 8	7♓57 11	16 40.6	3 59.1	28 35.6	11 34.9	0 7.8	7 20.7	19 44.2	20 15.7	17 28.1
23 M	14 1 46	2 15 10	15 7 53	22 18 50	16R41.3	5 0.9	29 47.8	12 21.1	0 12.7	7 19.0	19 41.9	20 14.8	17 26.5
24 Tu	14 5 43	3 13 40	29 29 32	6♈39 27	16 40.6	6 5.3	1♈ 0.1	13 7.3	0 17.8	7 17.3	19 39.5	20 13.9	17 24.9
25 W	14 9 40	4 12 8	13♈48 0	20 54 35	16 37.9	7 12.4	2 12.4	13 53.4	0 23.0	7 15.7	19 37.1	20 12.9	17 23.3
26 Th	14 13 36	5 10 35	27 58 34	4♉59 21	16 33.0	8 22.0	3 24.7	14 39.5	0 28.4	7 14.3	19 34.7	20 11.9	17 21.7
27 F	14 17 33	6 9 0	11♉56 22	18 49 7	16 26.0	9 34.0	4 37.0	15 25.5	0 34.0	7 12.9	19 32.3	20 10.8	17 20.1
28 Sa	14 21 29	7 7 22	25 37 10	2♊20 11	16 17.7	10 48.4	5 49.3	16 11.5	0 39.7	7 11.6	19 29.8	20 9.8	17 18.5
29 Su	14 25 26	8 5 43	8♊57 59	15 30 25	16 8.8	12 5.1	7 1.6	16 57.5	0 45.6	7 10.5	19 27.4	20 8.7	17 17.0
30 M	14 29 22	9 4 3	21 57 31	28 19 25	16 0.5	13 24.0	8 14.0	17 43.4	0 51.6	7 9.4	19 24.9	20 7.6	17 15.4

Astro Data	Planet Ingress	Last Aspect	☽ Ingress	Last Aspect	☽ Ingress	☽ Phases & Eclipses	Astro Data
Dy Hr Mn	Dy Hr Mn	Dy Hr Mn	Dy Hr Mn	Dy Hr Mn	Dy Hr Mn	Dy Hr Mn	1 MARCH 1979
☿0N 2 20:25	☿ ♈ 3 21:32	2 6:59 ♃ □	♉ 2 7:09	3 0:19 ♂ □	♋ 3 6:24	5 16:23 ☽ 14♊30	Julian Day # 28914
☽0S 14 18:16	♀ ♒ 3 17:18	4 12:29 ♃ ✶	♊ 4 12:58	5 16:19 ♃ ☌	♌ 5 17:58	13 21:14 ○ 22♍42	Delta T 49.7 sec
☿ R 15 1:15	☉ ♈ 21 5:22	6 3:48 ♆ ☍	♋ 6 22:34	7 11:27 ♆ △	♍ 8 6:52	13 21:08 P 0.854	SVP 05♓33'05"
♆ R 23 7:35	☿ ♓ 28 10:39	9 9:40 ♃ ☌	♌ 9 10:47	10 17:34 ♃ ✶	♎ 10 18:45	21 11:22 ☽ 0♑15	Obliquity 23°26'23"
♃ D 26 0:55	♀ ♓ 29 3:18	11 5:16 ♅ □	♍ 11 23:42	13 3:22 ♃ □	♏ 13 4:16	28 3:00 ● 6♈51	⚷ Chiron 5♉59.9
☽0N 27 21:14		14 10:09 ♃ ✶	♎ 14 11:42	15 10:41 ♃ △	♐ 15 11:18		☽ Mean ☊ 18♍06.0
♅×♆ 31 9:36	♂ ♈ 7 1:08	16 20:11 ♃ □	♏ 16 21:49	17 10:51 ☉ △	♑ 17 16:23	4 9:57 ☽ 14♋03	
☿0S 2 0:56	☿ ♈ 17 12:48	19 3:58 ♃ △	♐ 19 5:38	19 19:58 ♃ ☍	♒ 19 20:02	12 13:15 ○ 22♎02	1 APRIL 1979
☿ D 7 5:21	☉ ♉ 20 16:35	20 18:19 ♆ ☌	♑ 21 10:56	21 6:21 ♆ ✶	♓ 21 22:41	19 18:30 ☽ 29♑06	Julian Day # 28945
♂0N 9 21:12	♃ ♌ 20 8:29	23 12:13 ♃ ☍	♒ 23 13:52	23 8:32 ♆ □	♈ 24 0:51	26 13:15 ● 5♉43	Delta T 49.8 sec
☽0S 11 1:17	♀ ♈ 23 4:02	25 7:41 ♀ ☌	♓ 25 15:04	25 10:49 ♆ △	♉ 26 3:27		SVP 05♓33'03"
☽0N 24 6:36		27 14:10 ♃ △	♈ 27 15:47	27 13:13 ♅ ☍	♊ 28 7:49		Obliquity 23°26'23"
☿0N 24 1:50		29 15:57 ♃ □	♉ 29 17:36	29 20:35 ♆ ☍	♋ 30 15:11		⚷ Chiron 7♉33.7
♀0N 26 5:03		31 20:26 ♃ ✶	♊ 31 22:08				☽ Mean ☊ 16♍27.5

LONGITUDE — MAY 1979

Day	Sid.Time	☉	0 hr ☽	Noon ☽	True ☊	☿	♀	♂	♃	♄	♅	♆	♇
1 Tu	14 33 19	10♉ 2 20	4♋36 20	10♋48 36	15♍53.5	14♈45.1	9♈26.3	18♈29.3	0♌57.8	7♍ 8.4	19♏22.4	20♐ 6.5	17♎13.9
2 W	14 37 15	11 0 35	16 56 37	23 0 52	15R48.4	16 8.3	10 38.7	19 15.1	1 4.1	7R 7.6	19R19.9	20R 5.3	17R12.4
3 Th	14 41 12	11 58 48	29 1 54	5♌ 0 19	15 45.5	17 33.6	11 51.1	20 0.9	1 10.6	7 6.9	19 17.5	20 4.2	17 10.9
4 F	14 45 9	12 56 59	10♌56 44	16 51 48	15D44.4	19 0.9	13 3.5	20 46.6	1 17.2	7 6.2	19 14.9	20 3.0	17 9.4
5 Sa	14 49 5	13 55 8	22 46 12	28 40 35	15 44.8	20 30.3	14 15.9	21 32.3	1 23.9	7 5.7	19 12.4	20 1.8	17 8.0
6 Su	14 53 2	14 53 15	4♍35 37	10♍31 57	15R45.6	22 1.7	15 28.4	22 17.9	1 30.8	7 5.2	19 9.9	20 0.5	17 6.5
7 M	14 56 58	15 51 20	16 30 13	22 31 1	15 46.1	23 35.0	16 40.8	23 3.5	1 37.8	7 4.9	19 7.4	19 59.3	17 5.1
8 Tu	15 0 55	16 49 24	28 34 52	4♎42 16	15 45.2	25 10.4	17 53.2	23 49.1	1 45.0	7 4.7	19 4.9	19 58.0	17 3.7
9 W	15 4 51	17 47 25	10♎53 39	17 9 21	15 42.3	26 47.7	19 5.7	24 34.6	1 52.2	7D 4.6	19 2.4	19 56.7	17 2.3
10 Th	15 8 48	18 45 25	23 29 39	29 54 43	15 36.9	28 27.0	20 18.2	25 20.0	1 59.7	7 4.6	18 59.8	19 55.4	17 0.9
11 F	15 12 44	19 43 23	6♏24 36	12♏59 19	15 29.2	0♉ 8.3	21 30.7	26 5.4	2 7.2	7 4.7	18 57.3	19 54.1	16 59.5
12 Sa	15 16 41	20 41 19	19 38 42	26 22 32	15 19.6	1 51.5	22 43.2	26 50.8	2 14.9	7 4.9	18 54.8	19 52.7	16 58.2
13 Su	15 20 37	21 39 14	3♐10 30	10♐ 2 14	15 8.9	3 36.8	23 55.7	27 36.1	2 22.7	7 5.2	18 52.3	19 51.4	16 56.9
14 M	15 24 34	22 37 7	16 57 16	23 55 6	14 58.3	5 24.0	25 8.2	28 21.3	2 30.6	7 5.6	18 49.7	19 50.0	16 55.6
15 Tu	15 28 31	23 34 59	0♑55 16	7♑57 15	14 48.8	7 13.2	26 20.8	29 6.5	2 38.7	7 6.1	18 47.2	19 48.6	16 54.3
16 W	15 32 27	24 32 50	15 0 34	22 4 47	14 41.4	9 4.4	27 33.4	29 51.7	2 46.8	7 6.7	18 44.7	19 47.2	16 53.1
17 Th	15 36 24	25 30 39	29 9 31	6♒14 27	14 36.6	10 57.5	28 46.0	0♉36.8	2 55.1	7 7.4	18 42.2	19 45.7	16 51.8
18 F	15 40 20	26 28 27	13♒19 19	20 23 52	14 34.2	12 52.6	29 58.6	1 21.9	3 3.5	7 8.2	18 39.7	19 44.3	16 50.6
19 Sa	15 44 17	27 26 15	27 27 59	4♓31 29	14D33.6	14 49.7	1♉11.2	2 6.9	3 12.1	7 9.2	18 37.2	19 42.8	16 49.4
20 Su	15 48 13	28 24 1	11♓34 17	18 36 17	14R33.8	16 48.6	2 23.8	2 51.9	3 20.7	7 10.2	18 34.7	19 41.4	16 48.3
21 M	15 52 10	29 21 45	25 37 21	2♈37 21	14 33.4	18 49.4	3 36.4	3 36.8	3 29.5	7 11.3	18 32.3	19 39.9	16 47.2
22 Tu	15 56 6	0♊19 29	9♈36 7	16 33 26	14 31.4	20 52.0	4 49.1	4 21.6	3 38.3	7 12.6	18 29.8	19 38.4	16 46.0
23 W	16 0 3	1 17 12	23 29 5	0♉22 45	14 26.9	22 56.3	6 1.8	5 6.5	3 47.3	7 13.9	18 27.4	19 36.9	16 44.9
24 Th	16 4 0	2 14 54	7♉14 8	14 2 53	14 19.6	25 2.3	7 14.5	5 51.2	3 56.4	7 15.3	18 24.9	19 35.3	16 43.9
25 F	16 7 56	3 12 34	20 48 41	27 31 10	14 9.6	27 9.6	8 27.2	6 35.9	4 5.6	7 16.9	18 22.5	19 33.8	16 42.9
26 Sa	16 11 53	4 10 14	4♊10 2	10♊45 1	13 57.8	29 18.3	9 39.9	7 20.6	4 14.9	7 18.5	18 20.1	19 32.3	16 41.8
27 Su	16 15 49	5 7 52	17 15 55	23 42 35	13 45.2	1♊28.1	10 52.6	8 5.2	4 24.3	7 20.3	18 17.7	19 30.7	16 40.9
28 M	16 19 46	6 5 29	0♋ 4 58	6♋23 4	13 33.1	3 38.9	12 5.3	8 49.7	4 33.8	7 22.1	18 15.3	19 29.2	16 39.9
29 Tu	16 23 42	7 3 4	12 37 2	18 47 2	13 22.4	5 50.3	13 18.1	9 34.2	4 43.4	7 24.1	18 13.0	19 27.6	16 39.0
30 W	16 27 39	8 0 39	24 53 22	0♌56 23	13 14.1	8 2.1	14 30.8	10 18.7	4 53.1	7 26.1	18 10.6	19 26.0	16 38.1
31 Th	16 31 36	8 58 12	6♌56 32	12 54 17	13 8.4	10 14.2	15 43.6	11 3.1	5 2.9	7 28.3	18 8.3	19 24.4	16 37.2

LONGITUDE — JUNE 1979

Day	Sid.Time	☉	0 hr ☽	Noon ☽	True ☊	☿	♀	♂	♃	♄	♅	♆	♇
1 F	16 35 32	9♊55 44	18♌50 14	24♌44 56	13♍ 5.2	12♊26.1	16♉56.3	11♉47.4	5♌12.8	7♍30.5	18♏ 6.0	19♐22.8	16♎36.4
2 Sa	16 39 29	10 53 14	0♍39 3	6♍33 14	13R 4.0	14 37.7	18 9.1	12 31.6	5 22.8	7 32.9	18R 3.8	19R21.2	16R35.6
3 Su	16 43 25	11 50 43	12 28 11	18 24 34	13 3.8	16 48.6	19 21.9	13 15.8	5 32.9	7 35.3	18 1.5	19 19.6	16 34.8
4 M	16 47 22	12 48 11	24 23 5	0♎24 24	13 3.6	18 58.6	20 34.7	13 60.0	5 43.1	7 37.9	17 59.3	19 18.0	16 34.0
5 Tu	16 51 18	13 45 37	6♎29 10	12 37 59	13 2.3	21 7.4	21 47.5	14 44.1	5 53.3	7 40.5	17 57.1	19 16.4	16 33.3
6 W	16 55 15	14 43 3	18 51 25	25 9 57	12 59.1	23 14.9	23 0.3	15 28.1	6 3.7	7 43.2	17 54.9	19 14.8	16 32.6
7 Th	16 59 11	15 40 27	1♏33 58	8♏ 3 46	12 53.5	25 20.7	24 13.2	16 12.1	6 14.1	7 46.1	17 52.8	19 13.2	16 31.9
8 F	17 3 8	16 37 50	14 39 30	21 21 14	12 45.3	27 24.9	25 26.0	16 56.0	6 24.6	7 49.0	17 50.7	19 11.6	16 31.3
9 Sa	17 7 4	17 35 13	28 8 52	5♐ 2 7	12 35.0	29 27.1	26 38.9	17 39.8	6 35.2	7 52.0	17 48.6	19 10.0	16 30.7
10 Su	17 11 1	18 32 34	12♐ 0 37	19 3 51	12 23.5	1♋27.3	27 51.8	18 23.6	6 45.9	7 55.1	17 46.5	19 8.3	16 30.1
11 M	17 14 58	19 29 54	26 11 9	3♑21 47	12 12.0	3 25.3	29 4.6	19 7.4	6 56.7	7 58.3	17 44.5	19 6.7	16 29.6
12 Tu	17 18 54	20 27 14	10♑34 57	17 49 52	12 1.7	5 21.2	0♊17.6	19 51.1	7 7.5	8 1.6	17 42.5	19 5.1	16 29.1
13 W	17 22 51	21 24 34	25 5 40	2♒21 37	11 53.5	7 14.7	1 30.5	20 34.7	7 18.4	8 4.9	17 40.6	19 3.5	16 28.6
14 Th	17 26 47	22 21 52	9♒36 59	16 51 10	11 48.1	9 5.9	2 43.4	21 18.3	7 29.4	8 8.4	17 38.6	19 1.9	16 28.1
15 F	17 30 44	23 19 10	24 3 39	1♓14 2	11 45.3	10 54.7	3 56.4	22 1.8	7 40.5	8 11.9	17 36.7	19 0.2	16 27.7
16 Sa	17 34 40	24 16 28	8♓21 59	15 27 20	11D44.4	12 41.2	5 9.3	22 45.3	7 51.6	8 15.6	17 34.9	18 58.6	16 27.4
17 Su	17 38 37	25 13 46	22 29 55	29 29 40	11R44.5	14 25.2	6 22.3	23 28.7	8 2.8	8 19.3	17 33.0	18 57.0	16 27.0
18 M	17 42 34	26 11 3	6♈26 35	13♈20 40	11 44.2	16 6.8	7 35.3	24 12.0	8 14.1	8 23.1	17 31.2	18 55.4	16 26.7
19 Tu	17 46 30	27 8 20	20 11 56	27 0 25	11 42.4	17 45.9	8 48.4	24 55.3	8 25.4	8 27.0	17 29.5	18 53.8	16 26.4
20 W	17 50 27	28 5 36	3♉46 6	10♉28 59	11 38.3	19 22.5	10 1.4	25 38.5	8 36.8	8 30.9	17 27.8	18 52.2	16 26.1
21 Th	17 54 23	29 2 53	17 9 2	23 46 13	11 31.5	20 56.7	11 14.5	26 21.7	8 48.3	8 35.0	17 26.1	18 50.6	16 25.9
22 F	17 58 20	0♋ 0 9	0♊20 26	6♊51 37	11 22.2	22 28.3	12 27.6	27 4.8	8 59.9	8 39.1	17 24.4	18 49.0	16 25.7
23 Sa	18 2 16	0 57 25	13 19 40	19 44 31	11 11.1	23 57.5	13 40.7	27 47.8	9 11.5	8 43.4	17 22.8	18 47.4	16 25.6
24 Su	18 6 13	1 54 41	26 6 5	2♋24 21	10 59.3	25 24.1	14 53.8	28 30.8	9 23.1	8 47.7	17 21.3	18 45.9	16 25.5
25 M	18 10 9	2 51 56	8♋39 18	14 50 59	10 47.8	26 48.2	16 6.9	29 13.7	9 34.9	8 52.1	17 19.7	18 44.3	16 25.4
26 Tu	18 14 6	3 49 11	20 59 29	27 4 58	10 37.7	28 9.6	17 20.1	29 56.6	9 46.7	8 56.5	17 18.3	18 42.7	16 25.3
27 W	18 18 3	4 46 26	3♌ 7 37	9♌ 7 43	10 29.7	29 28.4	18 33.2	0♊39.4	9 58.5	9 1.1	17 16.8	18 41.2	16D25.3
28 Th	18 21 59	5 43 40	15 5 36	21 1 38	10 24.2	0♌44.5	19 46.4	1 22.1	10 10.4	9 5.7	17 15.4	18 39.7	16 25.3
29 F	18 25 56	6 40 54	26 56 17	2♍50 3	10 21.2	1 57.9	20 59.6	2 4.8	10 22.4	9 10.4	17 14.1	18 38.1	16 25.4
30 Sa	18 29 52	7 38 7	8♍43 27	14 37 5	10D20.3	3 8.5	22 12.8	2 47.4	10 34.4	9 15.1	17 12.7	18 36.6	16 25.4

Astro Data (Dy Hr Mn)	Planet Ingress (Dy Hr Mn)	Last Aspect (Dy Hr Mn)	☽ Ingress (Dy Hr Mn)	Last Aspect (Dy Hr Mn)	☽ Ingress (Dy Hr Mn)	☽ Phases & Eclipses (Dy Hr Mn)	Astro Data
☽0S 8 9:53	☿ ♉ 10 22:03	2 4:51 ♂ □	♌ 3 1:56	1 1:06 ♆ △	♍ 1 22:41	4 4:25 ☽ 13♌08	1 MAY 1979
♄ D 9 14:53	♂ ♉ 16 4:25	4 21:19 ♂ △	♍ 5 14:41	3 15:30 ♀ △	♎ 4 11:12	12 2:01 ○ 20♏46	Julian Day # 28975
☽0N 21 14:09	♀ ♉ 18 0:29	7 6:57 ♆ □	♎ 8 2:48	6 10:02 ☿ △	♏ 6 21:05	18 23:57 ☽ 27♒26	Delta T 49.9 sec
♃□♆ 27 13:59	☉ ♊ 21 15:54	10 10:40 ☿ ☍	♏ 10 12:10	8 21:06 ♀ ☍	♐ 9 3:15	26 0:00 ● 4♊10	SVP 05♓33'00"
	☿ ♊ 26 7:44	12 2:01 ☉ ☍	♐ 12 18:25	10 12:06 ♆ ☌	♑ 11 6:23		Obliquity 23°26'22"
☽0S 4 19:33		14 20:43 ♂ △	♑ 14 22:25	12 16:09 ♂ △	♒ 13 8:06	2 22:37 ☽ 11♍47	⚷ Chiron 9♉25.3
☽0N 17 20:42	☿ ♋ 9 6:32	16 23:16 ♀ □	♒ 17 1:26	14 22:41 ☉ △	♓ 15 9:56	10 11:55 ○ 19♐01	☽ Mean ☊ 14♍52.2
♃⚺♄ 19 5:00	♀ ♊ 11 18:13	18 23:57 ☉ □	♓ 19 4:18	17 5:01 ☉ □	♈ 17 12:52	17 5:01 ☽ 25♓26	
♇ D 27 1:26	☉ ♋ 21 23:56	21 6:53 ☉ ⚹	♈ 21 7:30	19 13:10 ☉ ⚹	♉ 19 17:18	24 11:58 ● 2♋23	1 JUNE 1979
	♂ ♊ 26 1:55	22 17:18 ♆ △	♉ 23 11:20	21 17:41 ♂ ☌	♊ 21 23:23		Julian Day # 29006
	☿ ♌ 27 9:51	25 13:31 ☿ ☌	♊ 25 16:28	23 10:12 ♆ ☍	♋ 24 7:24		Delta T 50.0 sec
		27 4:10 ♆ ☍	♋ 27 23:51	26 15:52 ☿ ☌	♌ 26 17:47		SVP 05♓32'56"
		29 10:51 ♅ △	♌ 30 10:08	28 10:33 ♀ ⚹	♍ 29 6:14		Obliquity 23°26'22"
							⚷ Chiron 11♉20.3
							☽ Mean ☊ 13♍13.7

JULY 1979 LONGITUDE

Day	Sid.Time	☉	0 hr ☽	Noon ☽	True ☊	☿	♀	♂	♃	♄	♅	♆	♇
1 Su	18 33 49	8♋35 20	20♍31 33	26♍27 31	10♍20.6	4♌16.2	23♊26.0	3♊29.9	10♌46.5	9♍20.0	17♏11.5	18♐35.1	16♎25.6
2 M	18 37 45	9 32 33	2♎25 38	8♎26 34	10R21.3	5 20.9	24 39.3	4 12.4	10 58.6	9 24.9	17R10.2	18R33.6	16 25.7
3 Tu	18 41 42	10 29 45	14 31 0	20 39 35	10 21.4	6 22.6	25 52.5	4 54.8	11 10.7	9 29.9	17 9.1	18 32.1	16 25.9
4 W	18 45 38	11 26 57	26 52 55	3♏11 36	10 20.1	7 21.3	27 5.8	5 37.1	11 22.9	9 34.9	17 7.9	18 30.7	16 26.1
5 Th	18 49 35	12 24 8	9♏36 9	16 6 57	10 16.9	8 16.6	28 19.1	6 19.4	11 35.2	9 40.1	17 6.8	18 29.2	16 26.4
6 F	18 53 32	13 21 20	22 44 21	29 28 31	10 11.6	9 8.7	29 32.4	7 1.6	11 47.5	9 45.3	17 5.8	18 27.8	16 26.6
7 Sa	18 57 28	14 18 31	6♐19 30	13♐17 9	10 4.5	9 57.3	0♋45.7	7 43.7	11 59.9	9 50.5	17 4.8	18 26.3	16 27.0
8 Su	19 1 25	15 15 42	20 21 11	27 31 6	9 56.3	10 42.3	1 59.1	8 25.8	12 12.2	9 55.9	17 3.9	18 24.9	16 27.3
9 M	19 5 21	16 12 53	4♑46 16	12♑5 53	9 47.9	11 23.7	3 12.4	9 7.8	12 24.7	10 1.3	17 3.0	18 23.5	16 27.7
10 Tu	19 9 18	17 10 4	19 29 0	26 54 38	9 40.4	12 1.2	4 25.8	9 49.8	12 37.1	10 6.7	17 2.1	18 22.2	16 28.1
11 W	19 13 14	18 7 16	4♒21 43	11♒49 11	9 34.5	12 34.8	5 39.2	10 31.7	12 49.7	10 12.3	17 1.3	18 20.8	16 28.6
12 Th	19 17 11	19 4 27	19 16 0	26 41 16	9 30.9	13 4.2	6 52.6	11 13.5	13 2.2	10 17.8	17 0.6	18 19.5	16 29.1
13 F	19 21 7	20 1 39	4♓4 7	11♓23 51	9D29.3	13 29.4	8 6.1	11 55.3	13 14.8	10 23.5	16 59.8	18 18.1	16 29.6
14 Sa	19 25 4	20 58 51	18 39 55	25 51 53	9 29.5	13 50.2	9 19.6	12 37.0	13 27.4	10 29.2	16 59.2	18 16.8	16 30.1
15 Su	19 29 1	21 56 4	2♈59 27	10♈2 26	9 30.5	14 6.5	10 33.0	13 18.6	13 40.1	10 35.0	16 58.6	18 15.5	16 30.7
16 M	19 32 57	22 53 18	17 0 48	23 54 31	9R31.4	14 18.2	11 46.6	14 0.2	13 52.8	10 40.8	16 58.0	18 14.3	16 31.3
17 Tu	19 36 54	23 50 32	0♉43 41	7♉28 27	9 31.3	14R25.2	13 0.1	14 41.7	14 5.5	10 46.7	16 57.5	18 13.0	16 32.0
18 W	19 40 50	24 47 47	14 8 56	20 45 20	9 29.6	14 27.3	14 13.7	15 23.1	14 18.2	10 52.6	16 57.0	18 11.8	16 32.7
19 Th	19 44 47	25 45 2	27 17 50	3♊46 36	9 26.0	14 24.6	15 27.2	16 4.5	14 31.0	10 58.6	16 56.6	18 10.6	16 33.4
20 F	19 48 43	26 42 18	10♊11 51	16 33 43	9 20.7	14 17.1	16 40.9	16 45.8	14 43.8	11 4.7	16 56.3	18 9.4	16 34.1
21 Sa	19 52 40	27 39 35	22 52 23	29 7 58	9 14.1	14 4.7	17 54.5	17 27.1	14 56.7	11 10.8	16 56.0	18 8.2	16 34.9
22 Su	19 56 36	28 36 53	5♋20 39	11♋30 33	9 6.9	13 47.5	19 8.1	18 8.3	15 9.6	11 17.0	16 55.7	18 7.1	16 35.7
23 M	20 0 33	29 34 11	17 37 48	23 42 34	8 59.9	13 25.7	20 21.8	18 49.4	15 22.5	11 23.2	16 55.5	18 6.0	16 36.6
24 Tu	20 4 30	0♌31 30	29 45 2	5♌45 21	8 53.8	12 59.5	21 35.5	19 30.4	15 35.4	11 29.5	16 55.4	18 4.9	16 37.5
25 W	20 8 26	1 28 50	11♌43 45	17 40 28	8 49.1	12 29.2	22 49.2	20 11.4	15 48.3	11 35.8	16 55.3	18 3.8	16 38.4
26 Th	20 12 23	2 26 10	23 35 46	29 29 58	8 46.2	11 55.1	24 3.0	20 52.3	16 1.3	11 42.2	16D55.2	18 2.7	16 39.3
27 F	20 16 19	3 23 30	5♍23 24	11♍16 28	8D45.0	11 17.7	25 16.7	21 33.1	16 14.3	11 48.6	16 55.2	18 1.7	16 40.3
28 Sa	20 20 16	4 20 51	17 9 35	23 3 12	8 45.2	10 37.6	26 30.5	22 13.9	16 27.3	11 55.1	16 55.3	18 0.7	16 41.3
29 Su	20 24 12	5 18 13	28 57 49	4♎53 58	8 46.5	9 55.3	27 44.3	22 54.6	16 40.3	12 1.6	16 55.4	17 59.7	16 42.3
30 M	20 28 9	6 15 35	10♎52 13	16 53 8	8 48.2	9 11.5	28 58.1	23 35.2	16 53.4	12 8.2	16 55.5	17 58.8	16 43.4
31 Tu	20 32 5	7 12 58	22 57 19	29 5 22	8 49.7	8 27.0	0♌11.9	24 15.8	17 6.4	12 14.8	16 55.7	17 57.8	16 44.5

AUGUST 1979 LONGITUDE

Day	Sid.Time	☉	0 hr ☽	Noon ☽	True ☊	☿	♀	♂	♃	♄	♅	♆	♇
1 W	20 36 2	8♌10 21	5♏17 53	11♏35 26	8♍50.5	7♌42.6	1♌25.8	24♊56.2	17♌19.5	12♍21.4	16♏56.0	17♐56.9	16♎45.6
2 Th	20 39 59	9 7 45	17 58 34	24 27 45	8R50.2	6R59.1	2 39.7	25 36.6	17 32.6	12 28.1	16 56.3	17R56.1	16 46.8
3 F	20 43 55	10 5 9	1♐3 26	7♐45 53	8 48.6	6 17.3	3 53.6	26 17.0	17 45.7	12 34.8	16 56.7	17 55.2	16 48.0
4 Sa	20 47 52	11 2 34	14 35 21	21 31 51	8 46.0	5 37.9	5 7.5	26 57.2	17 58.8	12 41.6	16 57.1	17 54.4	16 49.2
5 Su	20 51 48	12 0 0	28 35 17	5♑45 23	8 42.6	5 1.8	6 21.4	27 37.4	18 11.9	12 48.4	16 57.6	17 53.6	16 50.4
6 M	20 55 45	12 57 27	13♑1 42	20 23 33	8 39.0	4 29.7	7 35.3	28 17.6	18 25.0	12 55.2	16 58.1	17 52.8	16 51.7
7 Tu	20 59 41	13 54 54	27 50 9	5♒20 30	8 35.7	4 2.3	8 49.3	28 57.6	18 38.1	13 2.1	16 58.7	17 52.1	16 53.0
8 W	21 3 38	14 52 23	12♒53 33	20 28 7	8 33.3	3 40.1	10 3.3	29 37.6	18 51.3	13 9.1	16 59.3	17 51.4	16 54.4
9 Th	21 7 34	15 49 52	28 3 0	5♓37 2	8D32.0	3 23.6	11 17.3	0♋17.5	19 4.4	13 16.0	16 60.0	17 50.7	16 55.7
10 F	21 11 31	16 47 22	13♓9 6	20 38 10	8 31.7	3 13.3	12 31.3	0 57.3	19 17.6	13 23.0	17 0.7	17 50.1	16 57.1
11 Sa	21 15 28	17 44 54	28 3 21	5♈23 54	8 32.4	3D 9.5	13 45.4	1 37.1	19 30.7	13 30.0	17 1.5	17 49.4	16 58.5
12 Su	21 19 24	18 42 27	12♈39 15	19 48 58	8 33.6	3 12.5	14 59.4	2 16.8	19 43.9	13 37.1	17 2.3	17 48.8	16 60.0
13 M	21 23 21	19 40 1	26 52 48	3♉50 35	8 34.9	3 22.5	16 13.5	2 56.4	19 57.0	13 44.1	17 3.2	17 48.3	17 1.5
14 Tu	21 27 17	20 37 37	10♉42 21	17 28 12	8R35.8	3 39.6	17 27.6	3 36.0	20 10.2	13 51.3	17 4.1	17 47.7	17 3.0
15 W	21 31 14	21 35 15	24 8 19	0♊42 58	8 36.0	4 3.8	18 41.8	4 15.5	20 23.4	13 58.4	17 5.1	17 47.2	17 4.5
16 Th	21 35 10	22 32 54	7♊12 27	13 37 8	8 35.5	4 35.2	19 55.9	4 54.9	20 36.5	14 5.6	17 6.2	17 46.8	17 6.0
17 F	21 39 7	23 30 34	19 57 21	26 13 30	8 34.2	5 13.7	21 10.1	5 34.2	20 49.7	14 12.8	17 7.3	17 46.3	17 7.6
18 Sa	21 43 3	24 28 16	2♋25 57	8♋35 4	8 32.5	5 59.2	22 24.3	6 13.5	21 2.8	14 20.0	17 8.4	17 45.9	17 9.2
19 Su	21 47 0	25 26 0	14 41 13	20 44 44	8 30.6	6 51.6	23 38.5	6 52.7	21 16.0	14 27.2	17 9.6	17 45.5	17 10.9
20 M	21 50 57	26 23 45	26 45 58	2♌45 12	8 28.8	7 50.6	24 52.8	7 31.8	21 29.1	14 34.5	17 10.8	17 45.2	17 12.5
21 Tu	21 54 53	27 21 32	8♌42 45	14 38 55	8 27.3	8 56.2	26 7.0	8 10.8	21 42.2	14 41.8	17 12.1	17 44.8	17 14.2
22 W	21 58 50	28 19 20	20 33 57	26 28 10	8 26.2	10 7.9	27 21.3	8 49.8	21 55.4	14 49.1	17 13.5	17 44.6	17 15.9
23 Th	22 2 46	29 17 9	2♍21 49	8♍15 12	8D25.7	11 25.5	28 35.6	9 28.6	22 8.5	14 56.5	17 14.8	17 44.3	17 17.6
24 F	22 6 43	0♍15 0	14 8 36	20 2 18	8 25.7	12 48.7	29 49.9	10 7.4	22 21.6	15 3.8	17 16.3	17 44.1	17 19.4
25 Sa	22 10 39	1 12 52	25 56 37	1♎51 55	8 26.1	14 17.0	1♍4.2	10 46.1	22 34.7	15 11.2	17 17.8	17 43.9	17 21.2
26 Su	22 14 36	2 10 46	7♎48 31	13 46 49	8 26.6	15 50.1	2 18.5	11 24.8	22 47.7	15 18.6	17 19.3	17 43.7	17 23.0
27 M	22 18 32	3 8 40	19 47 13	25 50 7	8 27.3	17 27.5	3 32.9	12 3.3	23 0.8	15 26.0	17 20.9	17 43.6	17 24.8
28 Tu	22 22 29	4 6 37	1♏55 58	8♏5 14	8 27.8	19 8.7	4 47.3	12 41.8	23 13.8	15 33.4	17 22.5	17 43.5	17 26.6
29 W	22 26 25	5 4 34	14 18 22	20 35 51	8 28.1	20 53.3	6 1.6	13 20.2	23 26.8	15 40.9	17 24.2	17 43.4	17 28.5
30 Th	22 30 22	6 2 33	26 58 7	3♐25 38	8R28.3	22 40.9	7 16.0	13 58.5	23 39.8	15 48.3	17 25.9	17D43.4	17 30.4
31 F	22 34 19	7 0 34	9♐58 47	16 37 56	8 28.3	24 30.9	8 30.4	14 36.7	23 52.8	15 55.8	17 27.7	17 43.4	17 32.3

Astro Data

	Dy Hr Mn
☽0S	2 4:59
☽0N	15 3:42
☿ R	17 22:42
♅ D	26 10:59
☽0S	29 13:05
♃✶♇	29 4:03
♃□♅	30 4:03
♃△♆	3 16:27
☽0N	11 12:14
☿ D	11 1:32
♅⚺♇	16 6:02
☽0S	25 19:33
♆ D	30 11:14

Planet Ingress

	Dy Hr Mn
♀ ♋	6 9:02
☉ ♌	23 10:49
♀ ♌	30 20:07
♂ ♋	8 13:28
☉ ♍	23 17:47
♀ ♍	24 3:16

Last Aspect / ☽ Ingress

Last Aspect Dy Hr Mn		☽ Ingress Dy Hr Mn
1 6:34	♀ □	♎ 1 19:08
4 0:27	♀ △	♏ 4 5:57
5 13:48	♅ ☌	♐ 6 12:56
7 20:44	♆ ☌	♑ 8 16:07
9 20:02	♅ ✶	♒ 10 16:59
11 22:29	♆ ✶	♓ 12 17:23
14 4:07	☉ △	♈ 14 18:57
16 10:59	☉ □	♉ 16 22:43
18 20:56	☉ ✶	♊ 19 5:00
20 15:00	♆ ☍	♋ 21 13:40
23 5:59	♀ ☌	♌ 24 0:30
25 18:08	♂ ✶	♍ 26 13:01
28 21:14	♀ ✶	♎ 29 2:06
31 2:43	♂ △	♏ 31 13:46

Last Aspect / ☽ Ingress

Last Aspect Dy Hr Mn		☽ Ingress Dy Hr Mn
1 23:11	♃ □	♐ 2 22:05
4 22:17	♂ ☍	♑ 5 2:23
6 6:26	♅ ✶	♒ 7 3:28
8 9:35	♃ ☍	♓ 9 3:05
10 7:30	♆ □	♈ 11 3:10
12 12:03	♃ △	♉ 13 5:21
14 19:02	☉ □	♊ 15 10:41
17 7:21	☉ ✶	♋ 17 19:17
19 4:56	♇ □	♌ 20 6:28
22 17:10	☉ ☌	♍ 22 19:11
24 7:19	♆ □	♎ 25 8:13
27 6:32	♃ ✶	♏ 27 20:12
29 17:41	♃ □	♐ 30 5:39

☽ Phases & Eclipses

Dy Hr Mn	
2 15:24	☽ 10♎09
9 19:59	○ 17♑01
16 10:59	☽ 23♈19
24 1:41	● 0♌36
1 5:57	☽ 8♏25
8 3:21	○ 15♒00
14 19:02	☽ 21♉23
22 17:10	● 29♌01
22 17:21:48	☉ A 6'03"
30 18:09	☽ 6♐46

Astro Data

1 JULY 1979
Julian Day # 29036
Delta T 50.1 sec
SVP 05♓32'51"
Obliquity 23°26'22"
⚷ Chiron 12♉51.5
☽ Mean ☊ 11♍38.4

1 AUGUST 1979
Julian Day # 29067
Delta T 50.1 sec
SVP 05♓32'47"
Obliquity 23°26'22"
⚷ Chiron 13♉46.8
☽ Mean ☊ 9♍59.9

LONGITUDE SEPTEMBER 1979

Day	Sid.Time	☉	0 hr ☽	Noon ☽	True ☊	☿	♀	♂	♃	♄	♅	♆	♇
1 Sa	22 38 15	7♍58 35	23♐23 22	0♑15 16	8♍28.3	26♌22.9	9♍44.9	15♋14.8	24♌ 5.8	16♍ 3.3	17♏29.5	17♐43.4	17♎34.2
2 Su	22 42 12	8 56 38	7♑13 43	14 18 40	8D 28.3	28 16.5	10 59.3	15 52.9	24 18.7	16 10.7	17 31.4	17 43.5	17 36.2
3 M	22 46 8	9 54 43	21 29 56	28 47 9	8 28.4	0♍11.3	12 13.7	16 30.9	24 31.6	16 18.2	17 33.3	17 43.6	17 38.2
4 Tu	22 50 5	10 52 49	6♒ 9 46	13♒37 7	8 28.6	2 7.0	13 28.2	17 8.8	24 44.5	16 25.7	17 35.3	17 43.7	17 40.1
5 W	22 54 1	11 50 56	21 8 19	28 42 24	8 28.8	4 3.2	14 42.6	17 46.6	24 57.4	16 33.3	17 37.3	17 43.9	17 42.2
6 Th	22 57 58	12 49 5	6♓18 13	13♓54 36	8R 28.9	5 59.6	15 57.1	18 24.3	25 10.2	16 40.8	17 39.3	17 44.1	17 44.2
7 F	23 1 54	13 47 15	21 30 21	29 4 16	8 28.9	7 56.1	17 11.6	19 1.9	25 23.0	16 48.3	17 41.4	17 44.3	17 46.2
8 Sa	23 5 51	14 45 27	6♈35 12	14♈ 2 7	8 28.5	9 52.3	18 26.1	19 39.5	25 35.8	16 55.8	17 43.5	17 44.6	17 48.3
9 Su	23 9 48	15 43 41	21 24 9	28 40 32	8 27.8	11 48.1	19 40.6	20 16.9	25 48.5	17 3.3	17 45.7	17 44.9	17 50.4
10 M	23 13 44	16 41 57	5♉50 42	12♉54 17	8 26.9	13 43.4	20 55.1	20 54.3	26 1.2	17 10.9	17 47.9	17 45.2	17 52.5
11 Tu	23 17 41	17 40 16	19 51 3	26 40 58	8 25.9	15 38.0	22 9.7	21 31.6	26 13.9	17 18.4	17 50.2	17 45.5	17 54.6
12 W	23 21 37	18 38 36	3♊24 7	10♊ 0 42	8 25.2	17 31.8	23 24.2	22 8.8	26 26.6	17 25.9	17 52.5	17 45.9	17 56.7
13 Th	23 25 34	19 36 58	16 31 2	22 55 32	8D 24.8	19 24.8	24 38.8	22 45.9	26 39.2	17 33.4	17 54.8	17 46.4	17 58.8
14 F	23 29 30	20 35 23	29 14 39	5♋28 52	8 24.9	21 16.8	25 53.3	23 23.0	26 51.7	17 41.0	17 57.2	17 46.8	18 1.0
15 Sa	23 33 27	21 33 50	11♋38 43	17 44 45	8 25.6	23 7.9	27 7.9	23 59.9	27 4.3	17 48.5	17 59.6	17 47.3	18 3.2
16 Su	23 37 23	22 32 18	23 47 29	29 47 28	8 26.7	24 58.1	28 22.5	24 36.7	27 16.8	17 56.0	18 2.1	17 47.8	18 5.4
17 M	23 41 20	23 30 49	5♌45 11	11♌41 10	8 28.1	26 47.2	29 37.1	25 13.5	27 29.2	18 3.5	18 4.6	17 48.4	18 7.6
18 Tu	23 45 17	24 29 22	17 35 50	23 29 39	8 29.4	28 35.2	0♎51.8	25 50.2	27 41.6	18 11.0	18 7.1	17 49.0	18 9.8
19 W	23 49 13	25 27 57	29 23 1	5♍16 18	8R 30.3	0♎22.3	2 6.4	26 26.7	27 54.0	18 18.5	18 9.7	17 49.6	18 12.0
20 Th	23 53 10	26 26 34	11♍ 9 52	17 4 0	8 30.5	2 8.3	3 21.0	27 3.2	28 6.3	18 26.0	18 12.3	17 50.2	18 14.2
21 F	23 57 6	27 25 13	22 59 2	28 55 13	8 29.8	3 53.3	4 35.7	27 39.5	28 18.6	18 33.5	18 15.0	17 50.9	18 16.5
22 Sa	0 1 3	28 23 54	4♎52 49	10♎52 4	8 28.1	5 37.3	5 50.3	28 15.8	28 30.8	18 40.9	18 17.7	17 51.6	18 18.8
23 Su	0 4 59	29 22 37	16 53 11	22 56 25	8 25.5	7 20.3	7 5.0	28 52.0	28 43.0	18 48.4	18 20.4	17 52.4	18 21.0
24 M	0 8 56	0♎21 22	29 1 58	5♏10 5	8 22.1	9 2.3	8 19.7	29 28.0	28 55.1	18 55.8	18 23.2	17 53.2	18 23.3
25 Tu	0 12 52	1 20 9	11♏21 0	17 34 57	8 18.4	10 43.3	9 34.3	0♌ 4.0	29 7.2	19 3.3	18 26.0	17 54.0	18 25.6
26 W	0 16 49	2 18 57	23 52 11	0♐12 58	8 14.8	12 23.3	10 49.0	0 39.8	29 19.2	19 10.7	18 28.8	17 54.8	18 27.9
27 Th	0 20 45	3 17 47	6♐37 35	13 6 18	8 11.8	14 2.5	12 3.7	1 15.6	29 31.1	19 18.1	18 31.7	17 55.7	18 30.2
28 F	0 24 42	4 16 39	19 39 23	26 17 6	8 9.8	15 40.7	13 18.4	1 51.2	29 43.1	19 25.4	18 34.6	17 56.6	18 32.5
29 Sa	0 28 39	5 15 33	2♑59 42	9♑47 23	8D 9.0	17 18.0	14 33.1	2 26.7	29 54.9	19 32.8	18 37.6	17 57.5	18 34.9
30 Su	0 32 35	6 14 29	16 40 19	23 38 34	8 9.3	18 54.4	15 47.8	3 2.1	0♍ 6.7	19 40.1	18 40.5	17 58.5	18 37.2

LONGITUDE OCTOBER 1979

Day	Sid.Time	☉	0 hr ☽	Noon ☽	True ☊	☿	♀	♂	♃	♄	♅	♆	♇
1 M	0 36 32	7♎13 26	0♒42 8	7♒50 56	8♍10.5	20♎29.9	17♎ 2.5	3♌37.4	0♍18.4	19♍47.5	18♏43.5	17♐59.5	18♎39.5
2 Tu	0 40 28	8 12 25	15 4 45	22 23 12	8 12.0	22 4.6	18 17.2	4 12.6	0 30.1	19 54.7	18 46.6	18 0.5	18 41.9
3 W	0 44 25	9 11 26	29 45 47	7♓11 51	8R 13.1	23 38.4	19 31.8	4 47.7	0 41.6	20 2.0	18 49.6	18 1.6	18 44.2
4 Th	0 48 21	10 10 28	14♓40 37	22 11 9	8 13.2	25 11.3	20 46.5	5 22.7	0 53.2	20 9.3	18 52.7	18 2.7	18 46.6
5 F	0 52 18	11 9 32	29 42 25	7♈13 19	8 11.7	26 43.5	22 1.2	5 57.6	1 4.6	20 16.5	18 55.8	18 3.8	18 49.0
6 Sa	0 56 14	12 8 38	14♈42 44	22 9 33	8 8.6	28 14.8	23 15.9	6 32.3	1 16.0	20 23.7	18 59.0	18 4.9	18 51.3
7 Su	1 0 11	13 7 47	29 32 42	6♉51 15	8 4.1	29 45.3	24 30.6	7 6.9	1 27.3	20 30.8	19 2.2	18 6.1	18 53.7
8 M	1 4 8	14 6 57	14♉ 4 23	21 11 25	7 58.6	1♏15.0	25 45.3	7 41.4	1 38.6	20 37.9	19 5.4	18 7.3	18 56.1
9 Tu	1 8 4	15 6 10	28 11 53	5♊ 5 30	7 53.0	2 43.9	27 0.1	8 15.8	1 49.8	20 45.1	19 8.6	18 8.5	18 58.5
10 W	1 12 1	16 5 25	11♊52 8	18 31 50	7 47.9	4 12.0	28 14.8	8 50.1	2 0.9	20 52.1	19 11.9	18 9.8	19 0.8
11 Th	1 15 57	17 4 42	25 4 46	1♋31 17	7 44.1	5 39.3	29 29.5	9 24.3	2 11.9	20 59.2	19 15.2	18 11.1	19 3.2
12 F	1 19 54	18 4 2	7♋51 48	14 6 48	7D 41.9	7 5.7	0♏44.2	9 58.3	2 22.8	21 6.2	19 18.5	18 12.4	19 5.6
13 Sa	1 23 50	19 3 24	20 16 51	26 22 36	7 41.3	8 31.3	1 58.9	10 32.2	2 33.7	21 13.2	19 21.8	18 13.8	19 8.0
14 Su	1 27 47	20 2 48	2♌24 39	8♌23 39	7 42.0	9 55.9	3 13.7	11 6.0	2 44.5	21 20.1	19 25.2	18 15.1	19 10.4
15 M	1 31 43	21 2 15	14 20 16	20 15 8	7 43.5	11 19.8	4 28.4	11 39.7	2 55.2	21 27.0	19 28.5	18 16.5	19 12.8
16 Tu	1 35 40	22 1 44	26 8 51	2♍ 2 1	7R 44.9	12 42.6	5 43.1	12 13.2	3 5.8	21 33.9	19 31.9	18 18.0	19 15.2
17 W	1 39 37	23 1 15	7♍55 11	13 48 52	7 45.6	14 4.5	6 57.9	12 46.6	3 16.4	21 40.7	19 35.4	18 19.4	19 17.5
18 Th	1 43 33	24 0 48	19 43 32	25 39 36	7 44.7	15 25.4	8 12.6	13 19.8	3 26.8	21 47.5	19 38.8	18 20.9	19 19.9
19 F	1 47 30	25 0 23	1♎37 27	7♎37 23	7 41.7	16 45.2	9 27.4	13 52.9	3 37.2	21 54.2	19 42.3	18 22.4	19 22.3
20 Sa	1 51 26	26 0 1	13 39 42	19 44 35	7 36.5	18 3.8	10 42.1	14 25.9	3 47.4	22 0.9	19 45.8	18 23.9	19 24.7
21 Su	1 55 23	26 59 40	25 52 13	2♏ 2 44	7 29.2	19 21.3	11 56.9	14 58.7	3 57.6	22 7.6	19 49.3	18 25.5	19 27.0
22 M	1 59 19	27 59 22	8♏16 13	14 32 43	7 20.3	20 37.4	13 11.6	15 31.3	4 7.7	22 14.2	19 52.8	18 27.0	19 29.4
23 Tu	2 3 16	28 59 5	20 52 16	27 14 52	7 10.6	21 52.1	14 26.4	16 3.9	4 17.7	22 20.7	19 56.3	18 28.6	19 31.8
24 W	2 7 12	29 58 51	3♐40 32	10♐ 9 15	7 1.0	23 5.3	15 41.1	16 36.2	4 27.5	22 27.2	19 59.9	18 30.3	19 34.1
25 Th	2 11 9	0♏58 38	16 41 2	23 15 54	6 52.6	24 16.8	16 55.9	17 8.4	4 37.3	22 33.7	20 3.5	18 31.9	19 36.5
26 F	2 15 6	1 58 27	29 53 53	6♑35 2	6 46.1	25 26.5	18 10.6	17 40.5	4 47.0	22 40.1	20 7.0	18 33.6	19 38.8
27 Sa	2 19 2	2 58 18	13♑19 25	20 7 7	6 41.9	26 34.1	19 25.4	18 12.4	4 56.6	22 46.5	20 10.7	18 35.3	19 41.2
28 Su	2 22 59	3 58 10	26 58 12	3♒52 46	6D 40.1	27 39.5	20 40.1	18 44.1	5 6.0	22 52.8	20 14.3	18 37.0	19 43.5
29 M	2 26 55	4 58 5	10♒50 51	17 52 27	6 40.0	28 42.5	21 54.8	19 15.6	5 15.4	22 59.1	20 17.9	18 38.8	19 45.8
30 Tu	2 30 52	5 58 0	24 57 34	2♓ 6 2	6R 40.7	29 42.8	23 9.6	19 47.0	5 24.6	23 5.3	20 21.5	18 40.5	19 48.2
31 W	2 34 48	6 57 57	9♓17 41	16 32 11	6 41.0	0♐40.0	24 24.3	20 18.3	5 33.8	23 11.4	20 25.2	18 42.3	19 50.5

Astro Data	Dy Hr Mn
♆✶♇	5 22:36
☽0N	7 22:24
♅⊻♆	8 13:22
♄□♆	14 19:58
♄✶♅	17 5:13
♄⊻♇	17 18:20
♀0S	19 16:41
☿0S	20 4:39
☽0S	22 1:20
♅⊻♇	24 5:28
☽0N	5 9:20
☽0S	19 7:54
♃∠♇	24 21:19

Planet Ingress	Dy Hr Mn
☿ ♍	2 21:39
♀ ♎	17 7:21
☿ ♎	18 18:59
☉ ♎	23 15:16
♂ ♌	24 21:21
♃ ♍	29 10:23
☿ ♏	7 3:55
♀ ♏	11 9:48
☉ ♏	24 0:28
☿ ♐	30 7:06

Last Aspect Dy Hr Mn		☽ Ingress Dy Hr Mn
1 6:05	☿ △	♑ 1 11:34
2 17:33	♇ □	♒ 3 13:59
5 6:09	♃ ☍	♓ 5 14:03
6 19:55	♂ △	♈ 7 13:29
9 7:22	♃ △	♉ 9 14:12
11 11:23	♃ □	♊ 11 17:54
13 19:23	♃ ✶	♋ 14 1:27
16 10:13	♀ ✶	♌ 16 12:25
18 20:55	♃ ☌	♍ 19 1:15
21 9:58	♂ ✶	♎ 21 14:11
24 0:54	♂ □	♏ 24 1:54
26 10:29	♃ □	♐ 26 11:36
28 18:26	♃ △	♑ 28 18:40
30 5:13	♄ △	♒ 30 22:49

Last Aspect Dy Hr Mn		☽ Ingress Dy Hr Mn
2 12:52	☿ △	♓ 3 0:23
4 8:50	♄ ☍	♈ 5 0:28
7 0:23	☿ ☍	♉ 7 0:45
8 11:09	♄ △	♊ 9 3:07
11 9:05	♀ △	♋ 11 9:09
13 1:51	♄ ✶	♌ 13 19:12
15 14:51	☉ ✶	♍ 16 7:51
18 4:13	♄ ☌	♎ 18 20:44
21 2:23	☉ ☌	♏ 21 8:02
23 2:48	♄ ✶	♐ 23 17:09
25 10:49	♄ □	♑ 26 0:11
28 1:18	☿ ✶	♒ 28 5:16
29 20:40	♀ □	♓ 30 8:29

☽ Phases & Eclipses Dy Hr Mn	
6 10:59	○ 13♓16
6 10:54	•T 1.094
13 6:15	☽ 19♊52
21 9:47	● 27♍49
29 4:20	☽ 5♑26
5 19:35	○ 11♈58
12 21:24	☽ 18♋57
21 2:23	● 27♎06
28 13:06	☽ 4♒31

Astro Data

1 SEPTEMBER 1979
Julian Day # 29098
Delta T 50.2 sec
SVP 05♓32'43"
Obliquity 23°26'23"
⚷ Chiron 13♉50.5R
☽ Mean ☊ 8♍21.4

1 OCTOBER 1979
Julian Day # 29128
Delta T 50.3 sec
SVP 05♓32'41"
Obliquity 23°26'23"
⚷ Chiron 13♉04.4R
☽ Mean ☊ 6♍46.0

NOVEMBER 1979 LONGITUDE

Day	Sid.Time	☉	0 hr ☽	Noon ☽	True ☊	☿	♀	♂	♃	♄	♅	♆	♇
1 Th	2 38 45	7♏57 56	23♓49 6	1♈ 7 53	6♍39.8	1♐33.8	25♏39.0	20♌49.3	5♍42.8	23♍17.5	20♏28.9	18♐44.1	19♎52.8
2 F	2 42 41	8 57 57	8♈27 52	15 48 17	6R36.2	2 23.9	26 53.7	21 20.2	5 51.7	23 23.5	20 32.5	18 46.0	19 55.1
3 Sa	2 46 38	9 57 59	23 8 16	0♉26 55	6 30.0	3 9.8	28 8.5	21 50.9	6 0.5	23 29.5	20 36.2	18 47.8	19 57.3
4 Su	2 50 34	10 58 3	7♉43 17	14 56 28	6 21.3	3 51.1	29 23.2	22 21.4	6 9.2	23 35.4	20 39.9	18 49.7	19 59.6
5 M	2 54 31	11 58 9	22 5 37	29 9 59	6 10.8	4 27.1	0♐37.9	22 51.8	6 17.8	23 41.3	20 43.6	18 51.5	20 1.9
6 Tu	2 58 28	12 58 16	6♊ 8 56	13♊ 2 0	5 59.8	4 57.4	1 52.6	23 21.9	6 26.2	23 47.1	20 47.3	18 53.5	20 4.1
7 W	3 2 24	13 58 26	19 48 50	26 29 18	5 49.5	5 21.3	3 7.3	23 51.9	6 34.5	23 52.8	20 51.0	18 55.4	20 6.3
8 Th	3 6 21	14 58 38	3♋ 3 23	9♋31 14	5 40.7	5 38.1	4 22.0	24 21.7	6 42.7	23 58.5	20 54.7	18 57.3	20 8.6
9 F	3 10 17	15 58 51	15 53 6	22 9 24	5 34.3	5R47.2	5 36.7	24 51.3	6 50.8	24 4.1	20 58.5	18 59.3	20 10.8
10 Sa	3 14 14	16 59 7	28 20 36	4♌27 16	5 30.5	5 47.8	6 51.4	25 20.7	6 58.7	24 9.6	21 2.2	19 1.3	20 13.0
11 Su	3 18 10	17 59 25	10♌30 1	16 29 30	5D28.8	5 39.5	8 6.1	25 49.9	7 6.5	24 15.1	21 5.9	19 3.2	20 15.1
12 M	3 22 7	18 59 44	22 26 26	28 21 29	5 28.6	5 21.5	9 20.8	26 18.9	7 14.2	24 20.5	21 9.6	19 5.3	20 17.3
13 Tu	3 26 3	20 0 6	4♍15 23	10♍ 8 48	5R28.8	4 53.5	10 35.5	26 47.7	7 21.8	24 25.8	21 13.4	19 7.3	20 19.5
14 W	3 30 0	21 0 29	16 2 26	21 56 54	5 28.4	4 15.4	11 50.2	27 16.2	7 29.2	24 31.0	21 17.1	19 9.3	20 21.6
15 Th	3 33 57	22 0 54	27 52 49	3♎50 44	5 26.2	3 27.2	13 4.8	27 44.5	7 36.4	24 36.2	21 20.8	19 11.4	20 23.7
16 F	3 37 53	23 1 21	9♎51 10	15 54 33	5 21.5	2 29.5	14 19.5	28 12.7	7 43.6	24 41.3	21 24.6	19 13.4	20 25.8
17 Sa	3 41 50	24 1 50	22 1 15	28 11 33	5 14.0	1 23.3	15 34.2	28 40.5	7 50.6	24 46.3	21 28.3	19 15.5	20 27.9
18 Su	3 45 46	25 2 21	4♏25 42	10♏43 48	5 3.7	0 10.0	16 48.9	29 8.2	7 57.4	24 51.3	21 32.1	19 17.6	20 30.0
19 M	3 49 43	26 2 53	17 5 54	23 32 0	4 51.3	28♏51.7	18 3.6	29 35.6	8 4.1	24 56.2	21 35.8	19 19.7	20 32.0
20 Tu	3 53 39	27 3 27	0♐ 1 58	6♐35 38	4 37.7	27 30.7	19 18.3	0♍ 2.7	8 10.7	25 1.0	21 39.5	19 21.8	20 34.0
21 W	3 57 36	28 4 3	13 12 48	19 53 12	4 24.2	26 9.6	20 32.9	0 29.6	8 17.1	25 5.7	21 43.2	19 24.0	20 36.0
22 Th	4 1 32	29 4 40	26 36 33	3♑22 33	4 12.1	24 51.1	21 47.6	0 56.2	8 23.3	25 10.3	21 47.0	19 26.1	20 38.0
23 F	4 5 29	0♐ 5 18	10♑10 57	17 1 29	4 2.5	23 37.9	23 2.3	1 22.6	8 29.4	25 14.9	21 50.7	19 28.3	20 40.0
24 Sa	4 9 26	1 5 58	23 53 56	0♒48 7	3 55.8	22 32.1	24 16.9	1 48.7	8 35.4	25 19.4	21 54.4	19 30.4	20 41.9
25 Su	4 13 22	2 6 38	7♒43 53	14 41 8	3 52.1	21 35.7	25 31.6	2 14.6	8 41.1	25 23.8	21 58.1	19 32.6	20 43.9
26 M	4 17 19	3 7 20	21 39 49	28 39 52	3 50.7	20 49.8	26 46.2	2 40.1	8 46.8	25 28.1	22 1.8	19 34.8	20 45.8
27 Tu	4 21 15	4 8 3	5♓41 16	12♓43 56	3 50.6	20 15.3	28 0.8	3 5.4	8 52.2	25 32.3	22 5.5	19 37.0	20 47.7
28 W	4 25 12	5 8 46	19 47 50	26 52 49	3 50.2	19 52.4	29 15.5	3 30.4	8 57.5	25 36.4	22 9.1	19 39.2	20 49.5
29 Th	4 29 8	6 9 31	3♈58 43	11♈ 5 17	3 48.4	19D41.1	0♑30.1	3 55.1	9 2.7	25 40.5	22 12.8	19 41.4	20 51.4
30 F	4 33 5	7 10 17	18 12 12	25 19 3	3 44.0	19 40.7	1 44.7	4 19.5	9 7.7	25 44.4	22 16.4	19 43.6	20 53.2

DECEMBER 1979 LONGITUDE

Day	Sid.Time	☉	0 hr ☽	Noon ☽	True ☊	☿	♀	♂	♃	♄	♅	♆	♇
1 Sa	4 37 1	8♐11 3	2♉25 21	9♉30 34	3♍36.6	19♏50.8	2♑59.2	4♍43.6	9♍12.5	25♍48.3	22♏20.1	19♐45.9	20♎55.0
2 Su	4 40 58	9 11 51	16 34 5	23 35 18	3R26.4	20 10.4	4 13.8	5 7.4	9 17.1	25 52.1	22 23.7	19 48.1	20 56.7
3 M	4 44 55	10 12 40	0♊33 35	7♊28 21	3 14.3	20 38.8	5 28.4	5 30.9	9 21.6	25 55.7	22 27.3	19 50.3	20 58.5
4 Tu	4 48 51	11 13 30	14 19 4	21 5 15	3 1.3	21 15.1	6 42.9	5 54.1	9 25.9	25 59.3	22 30.9	19 52.6	21 0.2
5 W	4 52 48	12 14 21	27 46 35	4♋22 46	2 48.9	21 58.3	7 57.4	6 16.9	9 30.0	26 2.8	22 34.5	19 54.8	21 1.9
6 Th	4 56 44	13 15 13	10♋53 43	17 19 23	2 38.1	22 47.8	9 12.0	6 39.4	9 34.0	26 6.2	22 38.1	19 57.1	21 3.5
7 F	5 0 41	14 16 6	23 39 54	29 55 29	2 29.9	23 42.7	10 26.5	7 1.6	9 37.8	26 9.6	22 41.6	19 59.3	21 5.2
8 Sa	5 4 37	15 17 1	6♌ 6 27	12♌13 13	2 24.4	24 42.3	11 41.0	7 23.4	9 41.4	26 12.8	22 45.1	20 1.6	21 6.8
9 Su	5 8 34	16 17 57	18 16 16	24 16 10	2 21.6	25 46.2	12 55.5	7 44.8	9 44.8	26 15.9	22 48.7	20 3.8	21 8.4
10 M	5 12 31	17 18 53	0♍13 32	6♍ 9 0	2D20.8	26 53.6	14 9.9	8 5.9	9 48.1	26 18.9	22 52.2	20 6.1	21 9.9
11 Tu	5 16 27	18 19 51	12 3 15	17 56 59	2R20.9	28 4.2	15 24.4	8 26.6	9 51.1	26 21.8	22 55.6	20 8.4	21 11.4
12 W	5 20 24	19 20 51	23 50 54	29 45 43	2 20.9	29 17.5	16 38.8	8 47.0	9 54.0	26 24.7	22 59.1	20 10.6	21 12.9
13 Th	5 24 20	20 21 51	5♎42 6	11♎40 42	2 19.8	0♐33.2	17 53.3	9 6.9	9 56.7	26 27.4	23 2.5	20 12.9	21 14.4
14 F	5 28 17	21 22 52	17 42 11	23 47 5	2 16.5	1 50.9	19 7.7	9 26.4	9 59.3	26 30.0	23 5.9	20 15.2	21 15.8
15 Sa	5 32 13	22 23 54	29 55 56	6♏ 9 11	2 10.6	3 10.4	20 22.1	9 45.5	10 1.6	26 32.5	23 9.3	20 17.4	21 17.3
16 Su	5 36 10	23 24 58	12♏27 11	18 50 11	2 2.2	4 31.4	21 36.5	10 4.2	10 3.7	26 34.9	23 12.7	20 19.7	21 18.6
17 M	5 40 6	24 26 2	25 18 21	1♐51 43	1 51.7	5 53.8	22 50.9	10 22.5	10 5.7	26 37.3	23 16.0	20 22.0	21 20.0
18 Tu	5 44 3	25 27 7	8♐30 13	15 13 39	1 39.9	7 17.4	24 5.2	10 40.3	10 7.5	26 39.5	23 19.4	20 24.2	21 21.3
19 W	5 48 0	26 28 13	22 1 44	28 54 3	1 28.1	8 41.9	25 19.6	10 57.7	10 9.0	26 41.6	23 22.7	20 26.5	21 22.6
20 Th	5 51 56	27 29 20	5♑50 8	12♑49 27	1 17.5	10 7.4	26 33.9	11 14.6	10 10.4	26 43.6	23 25.9	20 28.7	21 23.9
21 F	5 55 53	28 30 27	19 51 24	26 55 26	1 9.0	11 33.7	27 48.2	11 31.1	10 11.6	26 45.5	23 29.2	20 31.0	21 25.1
22 Sa	5 59 49	29 31 34	4♒ 0 58	11♒ 7 27	1 3.3	13 0.7	29 2.5	11 47.1	10 12.6	26 47.3	23 32.4	20 33.2	21 26.3
23 Su	6 3 46	0♑32 42	18 14 25	25 21 25	1D 0.4	14 28.3	0♒16.8	12 2.5	10 13.4	26 49.0	23 35.6	20 35.5	21 27.5
24 M	6 7 42	1 33 50	2♓28 7	9♓34 14	0 59.7	15 56.4	1 31.0	12 17.5	10 14.0	26 50.5	23 38.7	20 37.7	21 28.6
25 Tu	6 11 39	2 34 58	16 39 30	23 43 47	1 0.3	17 25.1	2 45.2	12 32.0	10 14.4	26 52.0	23 41.9	20 40.0	21 29.7
26 W	6 15 35	3 36 6	0♈46 56	7♈48 51	1R 0.9	18 54.2	3 59.4	12 45.9	10R14.6	26 53.3	23 45.0	20 42.2	21 30.7
27 Th	6 19 32	4 37 14	14 49 25	21 48 34	1 0.5	20 23.8	5 13.6	12 59.4	10 14.7	26 54.6	23 48.0	20 44.4	21 31.8
28 F	6 23 29	5 38 22	28 46 10	5♉42 5	0 58.0	21 53.7	6 27.7	13 12.3	10 14.5	26 55.7	23 51.1	20 46.6	21 32.8
29 Sa	6 27 25	6 39 30	12♉36 10	19 28 12	0 53.2	23 24.1	7 41.8	13 24.6	10 14.1	26 56.8	23 54.1	20 48.8	21 33.7
30 Su	6 31 22	7 40 38	26 17 59	3♊ 5 16	0 46.1	24 54.8	8 55.8	13 36.4	10 13.6	26 57.7	23 57.0	20 51.0	21 34.7
31 M	6 35 18	8 41 46	9♊49 46	16 31 16	0 37.4	26 25.9	10 9.9	13 47.6	10 12.8	26 58.5	23 60.0	20 53.2	21 35.6

Astro Data

	Dy Hr Mn
☽0N	1 19:31
☿ R	9 13:55
☽0S	15 16:12
☽0N	29 3:51
☿ D	29 12:41
☽0S	13 1:51
☽0N	26 10:32
♃ R	26 14:59

Planet Ingress

	Dy Hr Mn
♀ ♐	4 11:50
☿ ♏	18 3:08
♂ ♍	19 21:36
☉ ♐	22 21:54
♀ ♑	28 14:20
☿ ♐	12 13:34
☉ ♑	22 11:10
♀ ♒	22 18:35

Last Aspect / ☽ Ingress

Last Aspect Dy Hr Mn	☽ Ingress Dy Hr Mn
1 3:17 ♀ △	♈ 1 10:09
2 21:49 ♂ △	♉ 3 11:16
5 2:43 ♄ △	♊ 5 13:25
7 7:33 ♂ ✱	♋ 7 18:24
9 15:49 ♄ ✱	♌ 10 3:14
12 8:11 ♂ ☌	♍ 12 15:20
14 17:20 ♄ ☌	♎ 15 4:16
17 13:26 ♂ ✱	♏ 17 15:29
19 19:48 ☿ ☌	♐ 19 23:56
21 21:26 ♄ □	♑ 22 6:01
24 2:30 ♄ △	♒ 24 10:37
26 9:37 ♀ ✱	♓ 26 14:17
28 9:53 ♄ ☍	♈ 28 17:17
30 4:32 ♇ ☍	♉ 30 19:54

Last Aspect / ☽ Ingress

Last Aspect Dy Hr Mn	☽ Ingress Dy Hr Mn
2 15:59 ♄ △	♊ 2 23:02
4 20:52 ♄ □	♋ 5 4:01
7 4:47 ♄ ✱	♌ 7 12:09
9 16:34 ☿ □	♍ 9 23:33
12 12:21 ☿ ✱	♎ 12 12:29
14 7:56 ☉ ✱	♏ 15 0:08
17 2:26 ♄ ✱	♐ 17 8:36
19 8:23 ☉ ☌	♑ 19 13:55
21 14:47 ♀ ☌	♒ 21 17:13
23 9:04 ♅ □	♓ 23 19:50
25 17:22 ♄ ☍	♈ 25 22:40
27 11:32 ♇ ☍	♉ 28 2:08
30 1:10 ♄ △	♊ 30 6:32

☽ Phases & Eclipses

Dy Hr Mn	
4 5:47	○ 11♉13
11 16:24	☽ 18♌41
19 18:04	● 26♏48
26 21:09	☽ 4♓01
3 18:08	○ 10♊59
11 13:59	☽ 18♍55
19 8:23	● 26♐50
26 5:11	☽ 3♈49

Astro Data

1 NOVEMBER 1979
Julian Day # 29159
Delta T 50.4 sec
SVP 05♓32'38"
Obliquity 23°26'23"
⚷ Chiron 11♉41.2R
☽ Mean ☊ 5♍07.5

1 DECEMBER 1979
Julian Day # 29189
Delta T 50.5 sec
SVP 05♓32'34"
Obliquity 23°26'22"
⚷ Chiron 10♉16.1R
☽ Mean ☊ 3♍32.2

LONGITUDE JANUARY 1980

Day	Sid.Time	☉	0 hr ☽	Noon ☽	True ☊	☿	♀	♂	♃	♄	♅	♆	♇
1 Tu	6 39 15	9♑42 54	23♊ 9 28	29♊44 10	0♍27.9	27♐57.4	11♒23.8	13♍58.3	10♍11.9	26♍59.2	24♏ 2.9	20♐55.4	21♎36.4
2 W	6 43 11	10 44 2	6♋15 11	12♋42 20	0R 18.8	29 29.2	12 37.8	14 8.3	10R 10.7	26 59.8	24 5.7	20 57.5	21 37.3
3 Th	6 47 8	11 45 10	19 5 34	25 24 50	0 10.9	1♑ 1.3	13 51.7	14 17.8	10 9.4	27 0.3	24 8.6	20 59.7	21 38.1
4 F	6 51 4	12 46 18	1♌40 13	7♌51 48	0 4.9	2 33.8	15 5.6	14 26.7	10 7.9	27 0.7	24 11.3	21 1.8	21 38.8
5 Sa	6 55 1	13 47 27	13 59 48	20 4 28	0 1.2	4 6.7	16 19.4	14 34.9	10 6.2	27 1.0	24 14.1	21 4.0	21 39.5
6 Su	6 58 58	14 48 35	26 6 9	2♍ 5 15	29♌59.7	5 39.9	17 33.2	14 42.5	10 4.3	27R 1.1	24 16.8	21 6.1	21 40.2
7 M	7 2 54	15 49 43	8♍ 2 12	13 57 32	29D 59.9	7 13.5	18 47.0	14 49.4	10 2.2	27 1.2	24 19.5	21 8.2	21 40.9
8 Tu	7 6 51	16 50 52	19 51 48	25 45 34	0♍ 1.2	8 47.5	20 0.7	14 55.7	9 59.9	27 1.1	24 22.1	21 10.3	21 41.5
9 W	7 10 47	17 52 0	1♎39 28	7♎34 10	0 2.9	10 21.9	21 14.4	15 1.3	9 57.4	27 0.9	24 24.7	21 12.4	21 42.1
10 Th	7 14 44	18 53 9	13 30 17	19 28 31	0R 4.1	11 56.6	22 28.0	15 6.2	9 54.7	27 0.7	24 27.3	21 14.4	21 42.6
11 F	7 18 40	19 54 18	25 29 29	1♏33 52	0 4.0	13 31.9	23 41.6	15 10.5	9 51.9	27 0.3	24 29.8	21 16.5	21 43.1
12 Sa	7 22 37	20 55 26	7♏42 15	13 55 12	0 2.4	15 7.5	24 55.2	15 14.0	9 48.8	26 59.8	24 32.3	21 18.5	21 43.6
13 Su	7 26 33	21 56 35	20 13 14	26 36 47	29♌59.1	16 43.6	26 8.7	15 16.8	9 45.6	26 59.2	24 34.7	21 20.6	21 44.1
14 M	7 30 30	22 57 44	3♐ 6 11	9♐41 40	29 54.2	18 20.2	27 22.2	15 18.9	9 42.2	26 58.4	24 37.1	21 22.6	21 44.5
15 Tu	7 34 27	23 58 52	16 23 21	23 11 13	29 48.4	19 57.2	28 35.6	15 20.2	9 38.6	26 57.6	24 39.5	21 24.6	21 44.8
16 W	7 38 23	25 0 0	0♑ 5 6	7♑ 4 40	29 42.4	21 34.8	29 49.0	15R 20.8	9 34.8	26 56.7	24 41.8	21 26.5	21 45.2
17 Th	7 42 20	26 1 8	14 9 30	21 18 59	29 36.9	23 12.8	1♓ 2.3	15 20.6	9 30.9	26 55.6	24 44.1	21 28.5	21 45.5
18 F	7 46 16	27 2 16	28 32 26	5♒49 5	29 32.6	24 51.4	2 15.6	15 19.6	9 26.7	26 54.5	24 46.3	21 30.4	21 45.7
19 Sa	7 50 13	28 3 23	13♒ 8 4	20 28 31	29 29.9	26 30.5	3 28.8	15 17.9	9 22.4	26 53.2	24 48.5	21 32.4	21 46.0
20 Su	7 54 9	29 4 29	27 49 34	5♓10 24	29D 29.0	28 10.1	4 41.9	15 15.4	9 18.0	26 51.9	24 50.6	21 34.3	21 46.1
21 M	7 58 6	0♒ 5 34	12♓30 14	19 48 23	29 29.4	29 50.3	5 55.0	15 12.1	9 13.3	26 50.4	24 52.7	21 36.1	21 46.3
22 Tu	8 2 2	1 6 39	27 4 16	4♈17 24	29 30.8	1♒31.1	7 8.1	15 8.0	9 8.5	26 48.8	24 54.7	21 38.0	21 46.4
23 W	8 5 59	2 7 42	11♈27 22	18 33 54	29 32.3	3 12.4	8 21.0	15 3.2	9 3.5	26 47.2	24 56.7	21 39.8	21 46.5
24 Th	8 9 56	3 8 45	25 36 46	2♉35 53	29R 33.4	4 54.3	9 33.9	14 57.5	8 58.4	26 45.4	24 58.6	21 41.7	21R 46.5
25 F	8 13 52	4 9 46	9♉31 9	16 22 33	29 33.5	6 36.8	10 46.8	14 51.0	8 53.1	26 43.5	25 0.5	21 43.5	21 46.5
26 Sa	8 17 49	5 10 47	23 10 9	29 53 58	29 32.3	8 19.8	11 59.5	14 43.8	8 47.7	26 41.5	25 2.4	21 45.2	21 46.5
27 Su	8 21 45	6 11 46	6♊34 5	13♊10 34	29 30.1	10 3.4	13 12.2	14 35.7	8 42.1	26 39.4	25 4.2	21 47.0	21 46.4
28 M	8 25 42	7 12 45	19 43 32	26 13 3	29 27.0	11 47.5	14 24.8	14 26.9	8 36.4	26 37.3	25 5.9	21 48.7	21 46.3
29 Tu	8 29 38	8 13 42	2♋39 11	9♋ 2 3	29 23.6	13 32.1	15 37.4	14 17.3	8 30.6	26 35.0	25 7.6	21 50.5	21 46.2
30 W	8 33 35	9 14 38	15 21 44	21 38 19	29 20.2	15 17.1	16 49.8	14 6.9	8 24.6	26 32.6	25 9.3	21 52.1	21 46.0
31 Th	8 37 31	10 15 33	27 51 54	4♌ 2 36	29 17.4	17 2.6	18 2.2	13 55.7	8 18.4	26 30.2	25 10.9	21 53.8	21 45.8

LONGITUDE FEBRUARY 1980

Day	Sid.Time	☉	0 hr ☽	Noon ☽	True ☊	☿	♀	♂	♃	♄	♅	♆	♇
1 F	8 41 28	11♒16 27	10♌10 34	16♌15 55	29♌15.4	18♒48.4	19♓14.5	13♍43.7	8♍12.2	26♍27.6	25♏12.4	21♐55.4	21♎45.6
2 Sa	8 45 25	12 17 20	22 18 52	28 19 36	29D 14.4	20 34.5	20 26.7	13R 31.0	8R 5.8	26R 25.0	25 13.9	21 57.1	21R 45.3
3 Su	8 49 21	13 18 12	4♍18 23	10♍15 29	29 14.3	22 20.7	21 38.8	13 17.5	7 59.3	26 22.2	25 15.4	21 58.7	21 45.0
4 M	8 53 18	14 19 3	16 11 12	22 5 55	29 15.0	24 7.0	22 50.8	13 3.2	7 52.7	26 19.4	25 16.8	22 0.2	21 44.7
5 Tu	8 57 14	15 19 52	28 0 1	3♎53 54	29 16.2	25 53.2	24 2.8	12 48.3	7 45.9	26 16.5	25 18.1	22 1.8	21 44.3
6 W	9 1 11	16 20 41	9♎48 4	15 42 59	29 17.5	27 39.1	25 14.6	12 32.6	7 39.1	26 13.5	25 19.4	22 3.3	21 43.9
7 Th	9 5 7	17 21 29	21 39 11	27 37 14	29 18.8	29 24.5	26 26.3	12 16.2	7 32.1	26 10.4	25 20.6	22 4.8	21 43.4
8 F	9 9 4	18 22 16	3♏37 41	9♏41 7	29 19.7	1♓ 9.2	27 38.0	11 59.1	7 25.1	26 7.2	25 21.8	22 6.2	21 42.9
9 Sa	9 13 0	19 23 2	15 48 8	21 59 17	29R 20.1	2 52.8	28 49.6	11 41.3	7 17.9	26 4.0	25 22.9	22 7.7	21 42.4
10 Su	9 16 57	20 23 47	28 15 10	4♐36 16	29 20.0	4 35.1	0♈ 1.0	11 23.0	7 10.7	26 0.6	25 24.0	22 9.1	21 41.9
11 M	9 20 54	21 24 31	11♐ 3 5	17 36 1	29 19.5	6 15.6	1 12.4	11 3.9	7 3.4	25 57.2	25 25.1	22 10.5	21 41.3
12 Tu	9 24 50	22 25 14	24 15 24	1♑ 1 27	29 18.8	7 54.0	2 23.6	10 44.4	6 56.0	25 53.7	25 26.0	22 11.8	21 40.7
13 W	9 28 47	23 25 56	7♑54 15	14 53 46	29 18.0	9 29.7	3 34.8	10 24.2	6 48.6	25 50.2	25 26.9	22 13.1	21 40.0
14 Th	9 32 43	24 26 37	21 59 47	29 11 56	29 17.4	11 2.1	4 45.8	10 3.5	6 41.0	25 46.5	25 27.8	22 14.4	21 39.3
15 F	9 36 40	25 27 16	6♒29 40	13♒52 16	29 17.0	12 30.8	5 56.8	9 42.3	6 33.4	25 42.8	25 28.6	22 15.7	21 38.6
16 Sa	9 40 36	26 27 55	21 18 55	28 48 37	29D 16.8	13 55.0	7 7.6	9 20.7	6 25.8	25 39.0	25 29.4	22 17.0	21 37.9
17 Su	9 44 33	27 28 31	6♓20 18	13♓52 50	29 16.8	15 14.2	8 18.3	8 58.6	6 18.1	25 35.2	25 30.1	22 18.2	21 37.1
18 M	9 48 29	28 29 6	21 25 7	28 56 0	29R 16.8	16 27.6	9 28.9	8 36.2	6 10.3	25 31.3	25 30.7	22 19.4	21 36.3
19 Tu	9 52 26	29 29 40	6♈24 30	13♈49 39	29 16.9	17 34.4	10 39.4	8 13.5	6 2.6	25 27.3	25 31.3	22 20.5	21 35.5
20 W	9 56 23	0♓30 11	21 10 40	28 26 55	29 16.8	18 34.2	11 49.7	7 50.4	5 54.7	25 23.3	25 31.8	22 21.6	21 34.6
21 Th	10 0 19	1 30 41	5♉37 53	12♉43 14	29 16.6	19 26.1	12 59.9	7 27.1	5 46.9	25 19.2	25 32.3	22 22.7	21 33.7
22 F	10 4 16	2 31 9	19 42 47	26 36 27	29D 16.4	20 9.6	14 10.0	7 3.6	5 39.0	25 15.0	25 32.7	22 23.8	21 32.8
23 Sa	10 8 12	3 31 35	3♊24 19	10♊ 6 30	29 16.3	20 44.1	15 19.9	6 40.0	5 31.2	25 10.8	25 33.1	22 24.8	21 31.8
24 Su	10 12 9	4 32 0	16 43 16	23 14 52	29 16.5	21 9.3	16 29.7	6 16.2	5 23.3	25 6.6	25 33.4	22 25.8	21 30.8
25 M	10 16 5	5 32 22	29 41 40	6♋ 3 59	29 16.9	21 24.7	17 39.3	5 52.4	5 15.4	25 2.3	25 33.7	22 26.8	21 29.8
26 Tu	10 20 2	6 32 42	12♋22 13	18 36 43	29 17.5	21R 30.3	18 48.8	5 28.6	5 7.5	24 57.9	25 33.9	22 27.7	21 28.8
27 W	10 23 58	7 33 1	24 47 52	0♌56 0	29 18.4	21 26.0	19 58.1	5 4.7	4 59.6	24 53.5	25 34.1	22 28.6	21 27.7
28 Th	10 27 55	8 33 17	7♌ 1 29	13 4 38	29 19.2	21 12.1	21 7.3	4 41.0	4 51.7	24 49.1	25 34.1	22 29.5	21 26.6
29 F	10 31 52	9 33 32	19 5 44	25 5 6	29R 19.8	20 48.9	22 16.3	4 17.4	4 43.9	24 44.6	25R 34.2	22 30.3	21 25.5

Astro Data	Planet Ingress	Last Aspect	☽ Ingress	Last Aspect	☽ Ingress	☽ Phases & Eclipses	Astro Data
Dy Hr Mn	Dy Hr Mn	Dy Hr Mn	Dy Hr Mn	Dy Hr Mn	Dy Hr Mn	Dy Hr Mn	1 JANUARY 1980
♄ R 6 22:42	☿ ♑ 2 8:02	1 9:54 ☿ ☍	♋ 1 12:29	2 5:50 ♅ □	♍ 2 15:21	2 9:02 ○ 11♋07	Julian Day # 29220
☽0S 9 11:25	☊ ♌ 5 14:56	3 15:03 ♄ ⚹	♌ 3 20:47	4 20:30 ♄ ☌	♎ 5 4:04	10 11:50 ☽ 19♎23	Delta T 50.5 sec
♂ R 16 6:18	☊ ♍ 7 2:35	5 20:21 ♅ □	♍ 6 7:48	7 0:52 ♆ ⚹	♏ 7 16:46	17 21:19 ● 26♑55	SVP 05♓32'28"
☽0N 22 17:20	☊ ♌ 12 18:20	8 14:34 ♄ ☌	♎ 8 20:38	9 19:45 ♄ ⚹	♐ 10 3:19	24 13:58 ☽ 3♉44	Obliquity 23°26'22"
♇ R 24 15:49	♀ ♓ 16 3:37	10 20:01 ♀ △	♏ 11 8:55	12 2:55 ♄ □	♑ 12 10:12		⚷ Chiron 9♉17.9R
♆⚹♇ 26 16:36	☉ ♒ 20 21:49	13 12:41 ♄ ⚹	♐ 13 18:17	14 6:17 ♄ △	♒ 14 13:20	1 2:21 ○ 11♌22	☽ Mean ☊ 1♍53.7
	☿ ♒ 21 2:18	15 23:29 ♀ ⚹	♑ 15 23:51	16 8:51 ☉ ☌	♓ 16 13:54	9 7:35 ☽ 19♏42	
☽0S 5 19:33		17 21:19 ☉ ☌	♒ 18 2:25	18 6:32 ♅ △	♈ 18 13:42	16 8:51 ● 26♒50	1 FEBRUARY 1980
♀0N 11 0:49	☿ ♓ 7 8:07	19 19:07 ♅ □	♓ 20 3:33	20 1:57 ♆ △	♉ 20 14:35	16 8:53:11 ● T 4'08"	Julian Day # 29251
♃∠♇ 14 5:55	♀ ♈ 9 23:39	21 23:34 ♄ ☍	♈ 22 4:52	22 10:09 ♅ ☍	♊ 22 17:58	23 0:14 ☽ 3♊32	Delta T 50.6 sec
♄⚹♅ 18 2:55	☉ ♓ 19 12:02	23 17:27 ♇ ☍	♉ 24 7:31	24 15:22 ♄ □	♋ 25 0:34		SVP 05♓32'23"
☽0N 19 1:58		26 6:15 ♄ △	♊ 26 12:11	27 1:30 ♅ △	♌ 27 10:10		Obliquity 23°26'23"
☿ R 26 1:33		28 12:43 ♄ □	♋ 28 19:02	29 12:58 ♅ □	♍ 29 21:53		⚷ Chiron 9♉12.7
♅ R 29 6:40		30 21:23 ♄ ⚹	♌ 31 4:08				☽ Mean ☊ 0♍15.2

MARCH 1980 LONGITUDE

Day	Sid.Time	☉	0 hr ☽	Noon ☽	True ☊	☿	♀	♂	♃	♄	♅	♆	♇
1 Sa	10 35 48	10♓33 44	1♍ 3 0	6♍59 41	29♌20.0	20♓17.0	23♈25.1	3♍53.9	4♍36.1	24♍40.1	25♏34.2	22♐31.1	21♎24.4
2 Su	10 39 45	11 33 55	12 55 25	18 50 27	29R 19.6	19R 37.2	24 33.8	3R 30.6	4R 28.3	24R 35.6	25R 34.1	22 31.9	21R 23.2
3 M	10 43 41	12 34 4	24 45 2	0♎39 26	29 18.5	18 50.7	25 42.3	3 7.6	4 20.5	24 31.0	25 34.0	22 32.6	21 22.0
4 Tu	10 47 38	13 34 11	6♎33 55	12 28 47	29 16.7	17 58.5	26 50.6	2 44.8	4 12.8	24 26.4	25 33.8	22 33.3	21 20.8
5 W	10 51 34	14 34 17	18 24 18	24 20 49	29 14.4	17 2.1	27 58.7	2 22.4	4 5.1	24 21.8	25 33.6	22 34.0	21 19.5
6 Th	10 55 31	15 34 21	0♏18 41	6♏18 16	29 11.8	16 2.7	29 6.6	2 0.3	3 57.5	24 17.1	25 33.3	22 34.7	21 18.3
7 F	10 59 27	16 34 23	12 19 59	18 24 14	29 9.3	15 1.9	0♉14.4	1 38.6	3 50.0	24 12.5	25 33.0	22 35.3	21 17.0
8 Sa	11 3 24	17 34 23	24 31 29	0♐42 12	29 7.2	14 1.1	1 21.9	1 17.4	3 42.5	24 7.8	25 32.6	22 35.9	21 15.7
9 Su	11 7 20	18 34 22	6♐56 52	13 15 57	29 5.8	13 1.7	2 29.3	0 56.6	3 35.0	24 3.1	25 32.1	22 36.4	21 14.4
10 M	11 11 17	19 34 20	19 39 56	26 9 17	29D 5.3	12 4.7	3 36.4	0 36.4	3 27.7	23 58.3	25 31.7	22 36.9	21 13.0
11 Tu	11 15 14	20 34 15	2♑44 24	9♑25 40	29 5.8	11 11.4	4 43.4	0 16.6	3 20.4	23 53.6	25 31.1	22 37.4	21 11.6
12 W	11 19 10	21 34 9	16 13 23	23 7 43	29 7.0	10 22.7	5 50.1	29♌57.5	3 13.2	23 48.9	25 30.5	22 37.8	21 10.2
13 Th	11 23 7	22 34 2	0♒ 8 45	7♒16 26	29 8.4	9 39.1	6 56.7	29 38.9	3 6.1	23 44.1	25 29.9	22 38.3	21 8.8
14 F	11 27 3	23 33 53	14 30 32	21 50 38	29 9.7	9 1.2	8 3.0	29 20.9	2 59.0	23 39.4	25 29.2	22 38.6	21 7.4
15 Sa	11 31 0	24 33 41	29 16 7	6♓46 14	29R 10.3	8 29.4	9 9.1	29 3.6	2 52.1	23 34.6	25 28.4	22 39.0	21 6.0
16 Su	11 34 56	25 33 28	14♓20 1	21 56 21	29 9.6	8 4.0	10 14.9	28 47.0	2 45.3	23 29.9	25 27.6	22 39.3	21 4.5
17 M	11 38 53	26 33 14	29 34 0	7♈11 41	29 7.6	7 44.8	11 20.5	28 31.0	2 38.6	23 25.1	25 26.8	22 39.6	21 3.0
18 Tu	11 42 49	27 32 57	14♈48 4	22 21 55	29 4.2	7 32.0	12 25.9	28 15.8	2 32.0	23 20.4	25 25.8	22 39.8	21 1.5
19 W	11 46 46	28 32 38	29 52 2	7♉17 22	29 0.1	7D 25.5	13 31.0	28 1.3	2 25.5	23 15.6	25 24.9	22 40.0	20 60.0
20 Th	11 50 43	29 32 16	14♉37 4	21 50 28	28 55.7	7 25.0	14 35.8	27 47.5	2 19.1	23 10.9	25 23.9	22 40.2	20 58.5
21 F	11 54 39	0♈31 53	28 57 5	5♊56 39	28 51.8	7 30.3	15 40.4	27 34.5	2 12.9	23 6.2	25 22.8	22 40.3	20 56.9
22 Sa	11 58 36	1 31 27	12♊49 6	19 34 29	28 49.0	7 41.3	16 44.7	27 22.2	2 6.8	23 1.6	25 21.7	22 40.4	20 55.4
23 Su	12 2 32	2 30 59	26 13 3	2♋45 8	28D 47.5	7 57.6	17 48.7	27 10.8	2 0.8	22 56.9	25 20.6	22 40.5	20 53.8
24 M	12 6 29	3 30 29	9♋11 10	15 31 38	28 47.5	8 18.9	18 52.4	27 0.1	1 55.0	22 52.3	25 19.4	22R 40.5	20 52.2
25 Tu	12 10 25	4 29 57	21 47 4	27 58 3	28 48.6	8 45.1	19 55.8	26 50.2	1 49.3	22 47.6	25 18.2	22 40.6	20 50.6
26 W	12 14 22	5 29 22	4♌ 5 7	10♌ 8 52	28 50.3	9 15.8	20 58.8	26 41.1	1 43.7	22 43.1	25 16.9	22 40.5	20 49.0
27 Th	12 18 18	6 28 44	16 9 48	22 8 29	28 51.8	9 50.8	22 1.6	26 32.8	1 38.3	22 38.5	25 15.6	22 40.5	20 47.4
28 F	12 22 15	7 28 5	28 5 23	4♍ 0 58	28R 52.5	10 29.9	23 4.0	26 25.2	1 33.1	22 34.0	25 14.2	22 40.4	20 45.8
29 Sa	12 26 12	8 27 23	9♍55 38	15 49 48	28 51.8	11 12.7	24 6.0	26 18.5	1 28.0	22 29.5	25 12.8	22 40.3	20 44.2
30 Su	12 30 8	9 26 39	21 43 47	27 37 54	28 49.3	11 59.2	25 7.7	26 12.5	1 23.0	22 25.1	25 11.3	22 40.1	20 42.5
31 M	12 34 5	10 25 53	3♎32 27	9♎27 40	28 44.7	12 49.1	26 9.1	26 7.3	1 18.2	22 20.7	25 9.8	22 39.9	20 40.9

APRIL 1980 LONGITUDE

Day	Sid.Time	☉	0 hr ☽	Noon ☽	True ☊	☿	♀	♂	♃	♄	♅	♆	♇
1 Tu	12 38 1	11♈25 5	15♎23 48	21♎21 1	28♌38.2	13♓42.1	27♉10.0	26♌ 2.9	1♍13.6	22♍16.3	25♏ 8.3	22♐39.7	20♎39.2
2 W	12 41 58	12 24 15	27 19 34	3♏19 37	28R 30.4	14 38.2	28 10.6	25R 59.3	1R 9.1	22R 12.0	25R 6.7	22R 39.4	20R 37.5
3 Th	12 45 54	13 23 23	9♏21 22	15 25 2	28 21.8	15 37.2	29 10.8	25 56.4	1 4.8	22 7.7	25 5.0	22 39.1	20 35.9
4 F	12 49 51	14 22 28	21 30 49	27 38 57	28 13.4	16 39.0	0♊10.5	25 54.3	1 0.6	22 3.5	25 3.4	22 38.8	20 34.2
5 Sa	12 53 47	15 21 33	3♐49 43	10♐ 3 22	28 5.8	17 43.3	1 9.8	25 52.9	0 56.6	21 59.3	25 1.7	22 38.5	20 32.5
6 Su	12 57 44	16 20 35	16 20 14	22 40 38	27 60.0	18 50.2	2 8.7	25D 52.3	0 52.8	21 55.2	24 59.9	22 38.1	20 30.8
7 M	13 1 40	17 19 35	29 4 55	5♑33 27	27 56.1	19 59.4	3 7.2	25 52.4	0 49.2	21 51.2	24 58.2	22 37.7	20 29.2
8 Tu	13 5 37	18 18 34	12♑ 6 37	18 44 44	27D 54.4	21 10.9	4 5.1	25 53.2	0 45.7	21 47.2	24 56.3	22 37.2	20 27.5
9 W	13 9 34	19 17 31	25 28 10	2♒17 12	27 54.4	22 24.5	5 2.6	25 54.8	0 42.4	21 43.2	24 54.5	22 36.7	20 25.8
10 Th	13 13 30	20 16 27	9♒12 3	16 12 51	27 55.2	23 40.3	5 59.7	25 57.0	0 39.3	21 39.3	24 52.6	22 36.2	20 24.1
11 F	13 17 27	21 15 20	23 19 37	0♓32 13	27R 56.0	24 58.2	6 56.2	26 0.0	0 36.4	21 35.5	24 50.7	22 35.7	20 22.4
12 Sa	13 21 23	22 14 12	7♓50 23	15 13 38	27 55.7	26 18.0	7 52.1	26 3.7	0 33.6	21 31.8	24 48.7	22 35.1	20 20.7
13 Su	13 25 20	23 13 2	22 41 18	0♈12 33	27 53.5	27 39.7	8 47.6	26 8.0	0 31.1	21 28.1	24 46.7	22 34.5	20 19.0
14 M	13 29 16	24 11 50	7♈46 22	15 21 35	27 48.8	29 3.3	9 42.5	26 13.0	0 28.7	21 24.5	24 44.7	22 33.9	20 17.3
15 Tu	13 33 13	25 10 36	22 56 56	0♉31 7	27 41.8	0♈28.8	10 36.8	26 18.7	0 26.5	21 20.9	24 42.7	22 33.2	20 15.7
16 W	13 37 9	26 9 21	8♉ 2 50	15 30 51	27 33.2	1 56.1	11 30.5	26 25.1	0 24.4	21 17.4	24 40.6	22 32.5	20 14.0
17 Th	13 41 6	27 8 3	22 54 3	0♊11 32	27 24.0	3 25.1	12 23.5	26 32.0	0 22.6	21 14.0	24 38.5	22 31.8	20 12.3
18 F	13 45 3	28 6 43	7♊22 31	14 26 31	27 15.2	4 55.9	13 16.0	26 39.7	0 21.0	21 10.7	24 36.3	22 31.1	20 10.6
19 Sa	13 48 59	29 5 21	21 23 12	28 12 28	27 8.1	6 28.4	14 7.7	26 47.9	0 19.5	21 7.5	24 34.2	22 30.3	20 9.0
20 Su	13 52 56	0♉ 3 57	4♋54 24	11♋29 14	27 3.0	8 2.6	14 58.8	26 56.8	0 18.2	21 4.3	24 32.0	22 29.5	20 7.3
21 M	13 56 52	1 2 31	17 57 21	24 19 13	27 0.3	9 38.6	15 49.1	27 6.2	0 17.1	21 1.2	24 29.8	22 28.7	20 5.6
22 Tu	14 0 49	2 1 3	0♌35 24	6♌46 32	26D 59.4	11 16.2	16 38.7	27 16.3	0 16.2	20 58.2	24 27.5	22 27.8	20 4.0
23 W	14 4 45	2 59 32	12 53 15	18 56 12	26 59.7	12 55.5	17 27.5	27 26.9	0 15.5	20 55.3	24 25.2	22 26.9	20 2.4
24 Th	14 8 42	3 57 59	24 56 5	0♍53 31	27R 0.2	14 36.6	18 15.4	27 38.1	0 15.0	20 52.5	24 23.0	22 26.0	20 0.7
25 F	14 12 38	4 56 25	6♍49 9	12 43 35	26 59.7	16 19.4	19 2.6	27 49.8	0 14.6	20 49.8	24 20.6	22 25.1	19 59.1
26 Sa	14 16 35	5 54 47	18 37 21	24 31 0	26 57.5	18 3.8	19 48.8	28 2.1	0D 14.5	20 47.1	24 18.3	22 24.1	19 57.5
27 Su	14 20 32	6 53 8	0♎24 59	6♎19 42	26 52.8	19 50.0	20 34.1	28 14.9	0 14.5	20 44.5	24 16.0	22 23.1	19 55.9
28 M	14 24 28	7 51 27	12 15 33	18 12 50	26 45.4	21 38.0	21 18.5	28 28.2	0 14.7	20 42.1	24 13.6	22 22.1	19 54.3
29 Tu	14 28 25	8 49 44	24 11 49	0♏12 43	26 35.4	23 27.6	22 1.9	28 42.0	0 15.1	20 39.7	24 11.2	22 21.0	19 52.7
30 W	14 32 21	9 47 59	6♏15 43	12 20 57	26 23.5	25 19.1	22 44.3	28 56.3	0 15.7	20 37.4	24 8.8	22 20.0	19 51.1

Astro Data	Planet Ingress	Last Aspect	☽ Ingress	Last Aspect	☽ Ingress	☽ Phases & Eclipses	Astro Data
Dy Hr Mn	Dy Hr Mn	Dy Hr Mn	Dy Hr Mn	Dy Hr Mn	Dy Hr Mn	Dy Hr Mn	1 MARCH 1980
☽0S 4 2:04	♀ ♉ 6 18:54	3 1:39 ♅ ⚹	♎ 3 10:40	1 21:20 ♂ ⚹	♏ 2 5:21	1 21:00 ○ 11♍26	Julian Day # 29280
☽0N 17 12:33	♂ ♌ 11 20:46	5 21:20 ♀ ☍	♏ 5 23:22	4 8:35 ♂ □	♐ 4 16:35	1 20:45 ☍ A 0.654	Delta T 50.7 sec
☿ D 19 13:59	☉ ♈ 20 11:10	8 1:59 ♅ ☌	♐ 8 10:38	6 18:00 ♂ △	♑ 7 1:43	9 23:49 ☽ 19♐34	SVP 05♓32'20"
♆ R 24 17:42		10 7:56 ♄ □	♑ 10 19:02	8 23:00 ♅ ⚹	♒ 9 8:00	16 18:56 ● 26♓21	Obliquity 23°26'23"
♄□♆ 26 13:32	♀ ♊ 3 19:46	12 16:05 ♅ ⚹	♒ 12 23:45	11 4:29 ♂ ☍	♓ 11 11:07	23 12:31 ☽ 3♋02	⚷ Chiron 9♉58.8
☽0S 31 8:01	☿ ♈ 14 15:58	14 23:40 ♂ ☍	♓ 15 1:10	13 8:45 ☿ ☌	♈ 13 11:40	31 15:14 ○ 11♎03	☽ Mean ☊ 28♌43.1
	☉ ♉ 19 22:23	16 18:56 ☉ ☌	♈ 17 0:41	15 5:22 ♂ △	♉ 15 11:11		
♂ D 6 8:27		18 21:05 ♂ △	♉ 19 0:13	17 6:01 ♂ □	♊ 17 11:41	8 12:06 ☽ 18♑48	1 APRIL 1980
☽0N 13 23:40		20 21:42 ♂ □	♊ 21 1:47	19 14:38 ☉ ⚹	♋ 19 15:11	15 3:46 ● 25♈20	Julian Day # 29311
☿0N 18 17:26		23 1:44 ♂ ⚹	♋ 23 6:55	21 12:18 ♅ △	♌ 21 22:52	22 2:59 ☽ 2♌08	Delta T 50.7 sec
♃ D 26 8:47		25 6:48 ♅ △	♌ 25 15:58	24 5:31 ♂ ☌	♍ 24 10:12	30 7:35 ○ 10♏06	SVP 05♓32'18"
☽0S 27 14:41		27 20:40 ♂ ☌	♍ 28 3:52	26 11:32 ♅ ⚹	♎ 26 23:09		Obliquity 23°26'24"
		30 7:34 ♀ △	♎ 30 16:49	29 9:10 ♂ ⚹	♏ 29 11:35		⚷ Chiron 11♉31.1
							☽ Mean ☊ 27♌04.6

LONGITUDE — MAY 1980

Day	Sid.Time	☉	0 hr ☽	Noon ☽	True ☊	☿	♀	♂	♃	♄	♅	♆	♇
1 Th	14 36 18	10♉46 13	18♏28 32	24♏38 33	26♌10.6	27♈12.2	23♊25.6	29♌11.1	0♍16.4	20♍35.2	24♏ 6.4	22♐18.9	19♎49.6
2 F	14 40 14	11 44 25	0♐51 3	7♐ 6 8	25R57.7	29 7.1	24 5.9	29 26.4	0 17.4	20R33.1	24R 4.0	22R17.8	19R48.0
3 Sa	14 44 11	12 42 35	13 23 51	19 44 16	25 46.1	1♉ 3.7	24 44.9	29 42.1	0 18.5	20 31.0	24 1.5	22 16.6	19 46.5
4 Su	14 48 7	13 40 43	26 7 31	2♑33 41	25 36.5	3 2.1	25 22.8	29 58.3	0 19.8	20 29.1	23 59.1	22 15.5	19 45.0
5 M	14 52 4	14 38 50	9♑ 2 57	15 35 28	25 29.7	5 2.1	25 59.5	0♍15.0	0 21.3	20 27.3	23 56.6	22 14.3	19 43.5
6 Tu	14 56 1	15 36 56	22 11 26	28 51 4	25 25.7	7 3.8	26 34.9	0 32.0	0 23.0	20 25.6	23 54.2	22 13.1	19 42.0
7 W	14 59 57	16 35 0	5♒34 36	12♒22 15	25D24.0	9 7.0	27 9.0	0 49.5	0 24.8	20 24.0	23 51.7	22 11.9	19 40.6
8 Th	15 3 54	17 33 3	19 14 12	26 10 37	25R23.7	11 11.7	27 41.8	1 7.5	0 26.8	20 22.4	23 49.2	22 10.7	19 39.1
9 F	15 7 50	18 31 4	3♓11 36	10♓17 8	25 23.6	13 17.9	28 13.1	1 25.8	0 29.0	20 21.0	23 46.7	22 9.4	19 37.7
10 Sa	15 11 47	19 29 4	17 27 7	24 41 20	25 22.4	15 25.3	28 43.0	1 44.5	0 31.4	20 19.7	23 44.2	22 8.1	19 36.3
11 Su	15 15 43	20 27 3	1♈59 22	9♈20 42	25 19.2	17 33.9	29 11.3	2 3.6	0 34.0	20 18.4	23 41.7	22 6.8	19 34.9
12 M	15 19 40	21 25 0	16 44 37	24 10 16	25 13.2	19 43.4	29 38.0	2 23.2	0 36.7	20 17.3	23 39.2	22 5.5	19 33.5
13 Tu	15 23 36	22 22 56	1♉36 40	9♉ 2 47	25 4.6	21 53.6	0♋ 3.2	2 43.1	0 39.6	20 16.3	23 36.6	22 4.1	19 32.1
14 W	15 27 33	23 20 51	16 27 30	23 49 41	24 53.9	24 4.5	0 26.6	3 3.4	0 42.6	20 15.3	23 34.1	22 2.8	19 30.8
15 Th	15 31 30	24 18 45	1♊ 8 19	8♊22 25	24 42.4	26 15.5	0 48.3	3 24.0	0 45.9	20 14.5	23 31.6	22 1.4	19 29.5
16 F	15 35 26	25 16 36	15 31 11	22 33 58	24 31.3	28 26.7	1 8.2	3 45.0	0 49.3	20 13.8	23 29.1	22 0.0	19 28.2
17 Sa	15 39 23	26 14 27	29 30 17	6♋19 53	24 21.8	0♊37.5	1 26.2	4 6.4	0 52.9	20 13.2	23 26.6	21 58.6	19 26.9
18 Su	15 43 19	27 12 15	13♋ 2 38	19 38 39	24 14.7	2 47.9	1 42.2	4 28.1	0 56.6	20 12.7	23 24.1	21 57.2	19 25.7
19 M	15 47 16	28 10 3	26 8 7	2♌31 25	24 10.2	4 57.4	1 56.3	4 50.2	1 0.5	20 12.2	23 21.6	21 55.8	19 24.4
20 Tu	15 51 12	29 7 48	8♌49 0	15 1 24	24 8.0	7 5.8	2 8.2	5 12.6	1 4.6	20 11.9	23 19.1	21 54.3	19 23.2
21 W	15 55 9	0♊ 5 32	21 9 14	27 13 8	24 7.4	9 12.9	2 18.1	5 35.3	1 8.8	20 11.7	23 16.6	21 52.8	19 22.1
22 Th	15 59 5	1 3 14	3♍13 47	9♍11 53	24 7.4	11 18.3	2 25.8	5 58.3	1 13.2	20D11.6	23 14.1	21 51.4	19 20.9
23 F	16 3 2	2 0 54	15 8 5	21 3 3	24 6.8	13 22.0	2 31.2	6 21.7	1 17.8	20 11.6	23 11.6	21 49.9	19 19.8
24 Sa	16 6 59	2 58 33	26 57 28	2♎51 54	24 4.8	15 23.6	2R34.3	6 45.3	1 22.5	20 11.7	23 9.1	21 48.4	19 18.7
25 Su	16 10 55	3 56 11	8♎46 57	14 43 9	24 0.4	17 23.0	2 35.1	7 9.3	1 27.4	20 11.9	23 6.7	21 46.9	19 17.6
26 M	16 14 52	4 53 47	20 40 57	26 40 47	23 53.5	19 20.1	2 33.5	7 33.5	1 32.4	20 12.2	23 4.2	21 45.3	19 16.5
27 Tu	16 18 48	5 51 22	2♏43 1	8♏47 55	23 44.1	21 14.7	2 29.6	7 58.0	1 37.6	20 12.7	23 1.8	21 43.8	19 15.5
28 W	16 22 45	6 48 55	14 55 45	21 6 40	23 32.6	23 6.8	2 23.2	8 22.8	1 42.9	20 13.2	22 59.3	21 42.2	19 14.5
29 Th	16 26 41	7 46 27	27 20 46	3♐38 7	23 20.1	24 56.2	2 14.4	8 47.9	1 48.4	20 13.8	22 56.9	21 40.7	19 13.5
30 F	16 30 38	8 43 58	9♐58 43	16 22 32	23 7.7	26 42.9	2 3.1	9 13.2	1 54.0	20 14.5	22 54.5	21 39.1	19 12.5
31 Sa	16 34 34	9 41 28	22 49 29	29 19 30	22 56.4	28 26.8	1 49.4	9 38.8	1 59.8	20 15.3	22 52.2	21 37.6	19 11.6

LONGITUDE — JUNE 1980

Day	Sid.Time	☉	0 hr ☽	Noon ☽	True ☊	☿	♀	♂	♃	♄	♅	♆	♇
1 Su	16 38 31	10♊38 57	5♑52 28	12♑28 17	22♌47.1	0♋ 7.9	1♋33.4	10♍ 4.6	2♍ 5.7	20♍16.3	22♏49.8	21♐36.0	19♎10.7
2 M	16 42 28	11 36 25	19 6 53	25 48 11	22R40.5	1 46.2	1R14.9	10 30.7	2 11.7	20 17.3	22R47.5	21R34.4	19R 9.9
3 Tu	16 46 24	12 33 53	2♒32 8	9♒18 44	22 36.7	3 21.6	0 54.2	10 57.1	2 17.9	20 18.4	22 45.2	21 32.8	19 9.0
4 W	16 50 21	13 31 19	16 7 58	22 59 51	22D35.2	4 54.1	0 31.3	11 23.7	2 24.3	20 19.7	22 42.9	21 31.2	19 8.2
5 Th	16 54 17	14 28 45	29 54 25	6♓51 41	22 35.2	6 23.7	0 6.3	11 50.5	2 30.8	20 21.0	22 40.6	21 29.6	19 7.4
6 F	16 58 14	15 26 10	13♓51 39	20 54 17	22R35.5	7 50.3	29♊39.2	12 17.6	2 37.4	20 22.4	22 38.3	21 28.0	19 6.7
7 Sa	17 2 10	16 23 34	27 59 30	5♈ 7 7	22 35.0	9 13.9	29 10.3	12 44.9	2 44.1	20 23.9	22 36.1	21 26.4	19 6.0
8 Su	17 6 7	17 20 58	12♈16 54	19 28 31	22 32.7	10 34.5	28 39.6	13 12.4	2 51.0	20 25.6	22 33.9	21 24.8	19 5.3
9 M	17 10 3	18 18 22	26 41 31	3♉55 22	22 28.1	11 52.1	28 7.4	13 40.2	2 58.0	20 27.3	22 31.7	21 23.2	19 4.6
10 Tu	17 14 0	19 15 45	11♉ 9 26	18 23 0	22 21.2	13 6.5	27 33.8	14 8.1	3 5.2	20 29.1	22 29.5	21 21.5	19 4.0
11 W	17 17 57	20 13 7	25 35 19	2♊45 37	22 12.4	14 17.8	26 59.0	14 36.3	3 12.4	20 31.1	22 27.4	21 19.9	19 3.4
12 Th	17 21 53	21 10 29	9♊53 8	16 57 8	22 2.9	15 25.9	26 23.2	15 4.8	3 19.8	20 33.1	22 25.3	21 18.3	19 2.8
13 F	17 25 50	22 7 50	23 56 57	0♋52 4	21 53.6	16 30.6	25 46.6	15 33.4	3 27.4	20 35.2	22 23.2	21 16.7	19 2.3
14 Sa	17 29 46	23 5 10	7♋42 0	14 26 29	21 45.6	17 32.1	25 9.4	16 2.2	3 35.0	20 37.4	22 21.1	21 15.1	19 1.8
15 Su	17 33 43	24 2 30	21 5 18	27 38 26	21 39.6	18 30.0	24 32.0	16 31.3	3 42.8	20 39.8	22 19.1	21 13.4	19 1.3
16 M	17 37 39	24 59 49	4♌ 5 59	10♌28 7	21 35.9	19 24.5	23 54.4	17 0.6	3 50.7	20 42.2	22 17.1	21 11.8	19 0.8
17 Tu	17 41 36	25 57 7	16 45 9	22 57 30	21D34.4	20 15.3	23 17.0	17 30.0	3 58.7	20 44.7	22 15.2	21 10.2	19 0.4
18 W	17 45 32	26 54 25	29 5 39	5♍10 6	21 34.5	21 2.5	22 40.0	17 59.7	4 6.9	20 47.3	22 13.2	21 8.6	19 0.1
19 Th	17 49 29	27 51 41	11♍11 27	17 10 19	21 35.4	21 45.8	22 3.6	18 29.5	4 15.1	20 50.0	22 11.3	21 7.0	18 59.7
20 F	17 53 26	28 48 57	23 7 20	29 3 10	21R36.3	22 25.1	21 28.1	18 59.5	4 23.5	20 52.8	22 9.5	21 5.4	18 59.4
21 Sa	17 57 22	29 46 12	4♎58 27	10♎53 50	21 36.3	23 0.5	20 53.6	19 29.7	4 32.0	20 55.6	22 7.7	21 3.8	18 59.1
22 Su	18 1 19	0♋43 27	16 49 57	22 47 22	21 34.8	23 31.7	20 20.4	20 0.1	4 40.6	20 58.6	22 5.9	21 2.2	18 58.9
23 M	18 5 15	1 40 40	28 46 41	4♏48 24	21 31.3	23 58.6	19 48.7	20 30.7	4 49.3	21 1.7	22 4.1	21 0.6	18 58.7
24 Tu	18 9 12	2 37 54	10♏52 58	17 0 50	21 25.9	24 21.2	19 18.6	21 1.4	4 58.1	21 4.8	22 2.4	20 59.0	18 58.5
25 W	18 13 8	3 35 6	23 12 19	29 27 43	21 19.0	24 39.4	18 50.3	21 32.3	5 7.0	21 8.1	22 0.7	20 57.4	18 58.3
26 Th	18 17 5	4 32 19	5♐47 11	12♐10 53	21 11.2	24 53.1	18 23.9	22 3.4	5 16.0	21 11.4	21 59.1	20 55.9	18 58.2
27 F	18 21 1	5 29 30	18 38 49	25 10 59	21 3.2	25 2.1	17 59.6	22 34.7	5 25.1	21 14.8	21 57.5	20 54.3	18 58.1
28 Sa	18 24 58	6 26 42	1♑47 15	8♑27 28	20 56.0	25R 6.6	17 37.4	23 6.1	5 34.3	21 18.3	21 55.9	20 52.7	18D58.1
29 Su	18 28 55	7 23 53	15 11 23	21 58 45	20 50.3	25 6.5	17 17.5	23 37.6	5 43.7	21 21.9	21 54.4	20 51.2	18 58.1
30 M	18 32 51	8 21 5	28 49 15	5♒42 34	20 46.4	25 1.7	16 59.8	24 9.4	5 53.1	21 25.6	21 53.0	20 49.7	18 58.1

Astro Data	Planet Ingress	Last Aspect	☽ Ingress	Last Aspect	☽ Ingress	☽ Phases & Eclipses	Astro Data
Dy Hr Mn	Dy Hr Mn	Dy Hr Mn	Dy Hr Mn	Dy Hr Mn	Dy Hr Mn	Dy Hr Mn	1 MAY 1980
☽0N 11 9:38	☿ ♉ 2 10:56	1 21:13 ♂ □	♐ 1 22:22	2 6:35 ♅ ⚹	♒ 2 19:29	7 20:51 ☽ 17♒25	Julian Day # 29341
♄ D 22 11:50	♂ ♍ 4 2:27	3 22:32 ♀ ☍	♑ 4 7:14	4 11:28 ♅ □	♓ 5 0:10	14 12:00 ● 23♉50	Delta T 50.8 sec
☽0S 24 22:41	♀ ♋ 12 20:53	6 3:05 ♅ ⚹	♒ 6 14:03	7 1:55 ♀ □	♈ 7 3:23	21 19:16 ☽ 0♍52	SVP 05♓32'15"
♀ R 24 20:10	☿ ♊ 16 17:06	8 15:11 ♀ △	♓ 8 18:33	9 2:17 ♀ ⚹	♉ 9 5:29	29 21:28 ○ 8♐38	Obliquity 23°26'23"
	☉ ♊ 20 21:42	10 19:15 ♀ □	♈ 10 20:44	10 18:47 ♅ ☍	♊ 11 7:22		⚷ Chiron 13♉24.1
☽0N 7 17:36	☿ ♋ 31 22:05	12 8:38 ♆ △	♉ 12 21:24	13 3:01 ♀ ☌	♋ 13 10:29	6 2:53 ☽ 15♓33	☽ Mean ☊ 25♌29.2
♃∠♇ 17 4:49		14 14:34 ☿ ☌	♊ 14 22:07	15 2:14 ♅ △	♌ 15 16:22	12 20:38 ● 21♊60	
☽0S 21 7:37	♀ ♊ 5 5:44	16 11:01 ♆ ☍	♋ 17 0:52	17 19:21 ☉ ⚹	♍ 18 1:47	20 12:32 ☽ 29♍19	1 JUNE 1980
♄□♆ 22 18:21	☉ ♋ 21 5:47	19 4:06 ☉ ⚹	♌ 19 7:14	20 12:32 ☉ □	♎ 20 13:55	28 9:02 ○ 6♑48	Julian Day # 29372
☿ R 28 11:12		21 4:10 ♅ □	♍ 21 17:32	22 14:02 ☿ □	♏ 23 2:26		Delta T 50.9 sec
♇ D 28 20:09		23 16:18 ♅ ⚹	♎ 24 6:11	25 2:51 ☿ △	♐ 25 13:02		SVP 05♓32'11"
		26 2:09 ♆ ⚹	♏ 26 18:37	27 7:32 ♂ □	♑ 27 20:46		Obliquity 23°26'23"
		28 15:34 ♅ ☌	♐ 29 5:05	29 17:25 ☿ ☍	♒ 30 2:04		⚷ Chiron 15♉23.2
		31 11:56 ☿ ☍	♑ 31 13:14				☽ Mean ☊ 23♌50.7

JULY 1980 — LONGITUDE

Day	Sid.Time	☉	0 hr ☽	Noon ☽	True ☊	☿	♀	♂	♃	♄	♅	♆	♇
1 Tu	18 36 48	9♋18 16	12♒38 24	19♒36 24	20♌44.5	24♋52.5	16♊44.6	24♍41.2	6♍ 2.6	21♍29.4	21♏51.5	20♐48.2	18♎58.2
2 W	18 40 44	10 15 27	26 36 17	3♓37 46	20D 44.4	24R 38.8	16R 31.7	25 13.3	6 12.2	21 33.2	21R 50.1	20R 46.6	18 58.2
3 Th	18 44 41	11 12 38	10♓40 34	17 44 27	20 45.4	24 20.9	16 21.2	25 45.5	6 21.9	21 37.1	21 48.8	20 45.1	18 58.4
4 F	18 48 37	12 9 50	24 49 10	1♈54 31	20 46.7	23 58.9	16 13.2	26 17.8	6 31.7	21 41.2	21 47.5	20 43.7	18 58.5
5 Sa	18 52 34	13 7 1	9♈ 0 16	16 6 12	20R 47.6	23 33.3	16 7.5	26 50.3	6 41.6	21 45.2	21 46.2	20 42.2	18 58.7
6 Su	18 56 30	14 4 13	23 12 5	0♉17 39	20 47.3	23 4.3	16D 4.3	27 22.9	6 51.6	21 49.4	21 45.0	20 40.7	18 58.9
7 M	19 0 27	15 1 26	7♉22 36	14 26 37	20 45.6	22 32.3	16 3.4	27 55.7	7 1.6	21 53.7	21 43.8	20 39.3	18 59.2
8 Tu	19 4 24	15 58 39	21 29 23	28 30 30	20 42.3	21 57.9	16 4.8	28 28.7	7 11.8	21 58.0	21 42.7	20 37.8	18 59.5
9 W	19 8 20	16 55 52	5♊29 36	12♊26 16	20 37.9	21 21.5	16 8.5	29 1.8	7 22.0	22 2.4	21 41.6	20 36.4	18 59.8
10 Th	19 12 17	17 53 6	19 20 9	26 10 50	20 32.9	20 43.7	16 14.4	29 35.0	7 32.4	22 6.9	21 40.5	20 35.0	19 0.2
11 F	19 16 13	18 50 20	2♋58 0	9♋41 20	20 28.1	20 5.2	16 22.5	0♎ 8.4	7 42.8	22 11.4	21 39.5	20 33.6	19 0.6
12 Sa	19 20 10	19 47 34	16 20 36	22 55 38	20 23.9	19 26.7	16 32.7	0 41.9	7 53.3	22 16.1	21 38.6	20 32.3	19 1.0
13 Su	19 24 6	20 44 49	29 26 17	5♌52 33	20 21.0	18 48.7	16 45.0	1 15.6	8 3.8	22 20.8	21 37.7	20 30.9	19 1.4
14 M	19 28 3	21 42 4	12♌14 28	18 32 9	20D 19.5	18 12.0	16 59.3	1 49.4	8 14.5	22 25.6	21 36.8	20 29.6	19 1.9
15 Tu	19 31 59	22 39 19	24 45 48	0♍55 41	20 19.3	17 37.1	17 15.5	2 23.3	8 25.2	22 30.4	21 36.0	20 28.3	19 2.5
16 W	19 35 56	23 36 34	7♍ 2 8	13 5 31	20 20.2	17 4.8	17 33.6	2 57.4	8 36.0	22 35.4	21 35.3	20 27.0	19 3.0
17 Th	19 39 53	24 33 49	19 6 17	25 4 56	20 21.7	16 35.7	17 53.6	3 31.6	8 46.9	22 40.4	21 34.6	20 25.7	19 3.6
18 F	19 43 49	25 31 4	1♎ 1 59	6♎58 0	20 23.4	16 10.1	18 15.2	4 5.9	8 57.9	22 45.4	21 33.9	20 24.4	19 4.2
19 Sa	19 47 46	26 28 20	12 53 32	18 49 11	20 24.7	15 48.8	18 38.6	4 40.4	9 8.9	22 50.6	21 33.3	20 23.2	19 4.9
20 Su	19 51 42	27 25 36	24 45 35	0♏43 18	20R 25.4	15 32.0	19 3.7	5 14.9	9 20.0	22 55.8	21 32.8	20 22.0	19 5.6
21 M	19 55 39	28 22 52	6♏42 56	12 45 4	20 25.1	15 20.2	19 30.3	5 49.7	9 31.1	23 1.1	21 32.3	20 20.8	19 6.3
22 Tu	19 59 35	29 20 9	18 50 15	24 58 59	20 23.9	15D 13.6	19 58.4	6 24.5	9 42.3	23 6.4	21 31.8	20 19.6	19 7.1
23 W	20 3 32	0♌17 25	1♐11 46	7♐29 0	20 21.9	15 12.5	20 28.1	6 59.5	9 53.6	23 11.8	21 31.4	20 18.4	19 7.9
24 Th	20 7 28	1 14 43	13 51 0	20 18 5	20 19.4	15 17.1	20 59.1	7 34.5	10 5.0	23 17.3	21 31.0	20 17.3	19 8.7
25 F	20 11 25	2 12 0	26 50 23	3♑28 1	20 16.8	15 27.6	21 31.6	8 9.7	10 16.4	23 22.8	21 30.7	20 16.2	19 9.6
26 Sa	20 15 22	3 9 18	10♑10 56	16 59 3	20 14.4	15 44.0	22 5.4	8 45.0	10 27.9	23 28.4	21 30.5	20 15.1	19 10.5
27 Su	20 19 18	4 6 37	23 52 8	0♒49 50	20 12.6	16 6.5	22 40.4	9 20.5	10 39.4	23 34.0	21 30.3	20 14.1	19 11.4
28 M	20 23 15	5 3 57	7♒51 46	14 57 25	20D 11.6	16 35.0	23 16.7	9 56.0	10 51.0	23 39.7	21 30.1	20 13.0	19 12.3
29 Tu	20 27 11	6 1 17	22 6 13	29 17 34	20 11.3	17 9.5	23 54.2	10 31.7	11 2.7	23 45.5	21 30.0	20 12.0	19 13.3
30 W	20 31 8	6 58 38	6♓30 49	13♓45 18	20 11.7	17 50.1	24 32.9	11 7.4	11 14.4	23 51.3	21D 30.0	20 11.0	19 14.3
31 Th	20 35 4	7 55 59	21 0 24	28 15 29	20 12.5	18 36.7	25 12.6	11 43.3	11 26.1	23 57.2	21 30.0	20 10.0	19 15.4

AUGUST 1980 — LONGITUDE

Day	Sid.Time	☉	0 hr ☽	Noon ☽	True ☊	☿	♀	♂	♃	♄	♅	♆	♇
1 F	20 39 1	8♌53 22	5♈29 58	12♈43 18	20♌13.4	19♋29.1	25♊53.4	12♎19.3	11♍38.0	24♍ 3.2	21♏30.0	20♐ 9.1	19♎16.4
2 Sa	20 42 57	9 50 46	19 55 2	27 4 45	20 14.2	20 27.4	26 35.3	12 55.4	11 49.8	24 9.1	21 30.1	20R 8.2	19 17.6
3 Su	20 46 54	10 48 11	4♉12 5	11♉16 45	20R 14.6	21 31.4	27 18.1	13 31.6	12 1.7	24 15.2	21 30.3	20 7.3	19 18.7
4 M	20 50 51	11 45 38	18 18 30	25 17 9	20 14.6	22 40.9	28 1.9	14 8.0	12 13.7	24 21.3	21 30.5	20 6.4	19 19.9
5 Tu	20 54 47	12 43 6	2♊18 33	9♊ 4 36	20 14.3	23 55.9	28 46.6	14 44.4	12 25.7	24 27.4	21 30.8	20 5.6	19 21.1
6 W	20 58 44	13 40 35	15 53 14	22 38 22	20 13.7	25 16.1	29 32.2	15 21.0	12 37.8	24 33.7	21 31.1	20 4.8	19 22.3
7 Th	21 2 40	14 38 5	29 19 59	5♋58 3	20 13.0	26 41.3	0♋18.6	15 57.6	12 49.9	24 39.9	21 31.4	20 4.0	19 23.5
8 F	21 6 37	15 35 37	12♋32 36	19 3 36	20 12.4	28 11.3	1 5.9	16 34.4	13 2.1	24 46.2	21 31.9	20 3.3	19 24.8
9 Sa	21 10 33	16 33 10	25 31 7	1♌55 11	20 12.0	29 45.8	1 53.9	17 11.3	13 14.3	24 52.6	21 32.3	20 2.5	19 26.2
10 Su	21 14 30	17 30 44	8♌15 51	14 33 13	20D 11.7	1♌24.6	2 42.7	17 48.3	13 26.6	24 59.0	21 32.8	20 1.8	19 27.5
11 M	21 18 26	18 28 19	20 47 23	26 58 29	20 11.7	3 7.2	3 32.2	18 25.4	13 38.9	25 5.4	21 33.4	20 1.2	19 28.9
12 Tu	21 22 23	19 25 55	3♍ 6 42	9♍12 12	20R 11.7	4 53.4	4 22.5	19 2.6	13 51.2	25 11.9	21 34.0	20 0.5	19 30.3
13 W	21 26 20	20 23 33	15 15 15	21 16 5	20 11.7	6 42.7	5 13.3	19 39.9	14 3.6	25 18.4	21 34.7	19 59.9	19 31.7
14 Th	21 30 16	21 21 11	27 15 3	3♎12 27	20 11.6	8 34.8	6 4.9	20 17.4	14 16.0	25 25.0	21 35.5	19 59.3	19 33.2
15 F	21 34 13	22 18 51	9♎ 8 42	15 4 12	20 11.4	10 29.3	6 57.1	20 54.9	14 28.4	25 31.6	21 36.2	19 58.8	19 34.7
16 Sa	21 38 9	23 16 31	20 59 23	26 54 46	20 11.1	12 25.8	7 49.8	21 32.5	14 40.9	25 38.3	21 37.1	19 58.3	19 36.2
17 Su	21 42 6	24 14 13	2♏50 49	8♏48 6	20 10.8	14 23.9	8 43.2	22 10.2	14 53.4	25 45.0	21 37.9	19 57.8	19 37.7
18 M	21 46 2	25 11 56	14 47 8	20 48 30	20D 10.5	16 23.1	9 37.1	22 48.1	15 6.0	25 51.7	21 38.9	19 57.3	19 39.3
19 Tu	21 49 59	26 9 40	26 52 45	3♐ 0 28	20 10.4	18 23.3	10 31.6	23 26.0	15 18.6	25 58.5	21 39.9	19 56.9	19 40.9
20 W	21 53 55	27 7 25	9♐12 11	15 28 25	20 10.5	20 23.9	11 26.7	24 4.0	15 31.2	26 5.3	21 40.9	19 56.5	19 42.5
21 Th	21 57 52	28 5 11	21 49 40	28 16 21	20 11.0	22 24.8	12 22.2	24 42.2	15 43.8	26 12.2	21 42.0	19 56.1	19 44.1
22 F	22 1 49	29 2 58	4♑48 51	11♑27 26	20 11.8	24 25.7	13 18.2	25 20.4	15 56.5	26 19.1	21 43.1	19 55.8	19 45.8
23 Sa	22 5 45	0♍ 0 47	18 12 18	25 3 30	20 12.6	26 26.3	14 14.8	25 58.7	16 9.2	26 26.0	21 44.3	19 55.5	19 47.5
24 Su	22 9 42	0 58 36	2♒ 0 57	9♒ 4 29	20 13.4	28 26.4	15 11.8	26 37.1	16 21.9	26 32.9	21 45.6	19 55.2	19 49.2
25 M	22 13 38	1 56 27	16 13 41	23 28 5	20R 13.8	0♍25.9	16 9.3	27 15.6	16 34.7	26 39.9	21 46.8	19 55.0	19 51.0
26 Tu	22 17 35	2 54 20	0♓47 1	8♓ 9 40	20 13.6	2 24.6	17 7.2	27 54.2	16 47.4	26 46.9	21 48.2	19 54.8	19 52.7
27 W	22 21 31	3 52 14	15 35 10	23 2 31	20 12.8	4 22.4	18 5.5	28 32.9	17 0.2	26 54.0	21 49.6	19 54.6	19 54.5
28 Th	22 25 28	4 50 9	0♈30 42	7♈58 40	20 11.4	6 19.2	19 4.3	29 11.7	17 13.0	27 1.0	21 51.0	19 54.5	19 56.3
29 F	22 29 24	5 48 6	15 25 26	22 50 3	20 9.6	8 14.9	20 3.5	29 50.5	17 25.9	27 8.1	21 52.5	19 54.3	19 58.1
30 Sa	22 33 21	6 46 5	0♉11 40	7♉29 34	20 7.6	10 9.5	21 3.1	0♏29.5	17 38.7	27 15.3	21 54.0	19 54.3	20 0.0
31 Su	22 37 18	7 44 6	14 43 10	21 52 1	20 6.0	12 3.0	22 3.1	1 8.6	17 51.6	27 22.4	21 55.6	19D 54.2	20 1.9

Astro Data

	Dy Hr Mn
☽0N	4 23:58
♄✱♅	5 4:16
♀ D	6 21:15
♂0S	12 5:07
☽0S	18 16:28
☿ D	22 16:37
♅ D	30 11:39
☽0N	1 6:15
☽0S	15 0:16
♆✱♇	27 1:11
☽0N	28 14:02
♆ D	31 23:39

Planet Ingress

	Dy Hr Mn
♂ ♎	10 17:59
☉ ♌	22 16:42
♀ ♋	6 14:25
☿ ♌	9 3:31
☉ ♍	22 23:41
☿ ♍	24 18:47
♂ ♏	29 5:50

Last Aspect / ☽ Ingress

Last Aspect Dy Hr Mn		☽ Ingress Dy Hr Mn
1 15:50	♅ □	♓ 2 5:48
4 2:36	♂ ☍	♈ 4 8:46
5 23:47	☿ □	♉ 6 11:30
8 12:26	♂ △	♊ 8 14:33
10 4:53	♄ □	♋ 10 18:44
12 10:52	♄ ✱	♌ 13 1:03
14 17:54	♅ □	♍ 15 10:11
17 11:55	☉ ✱	♎ 17 21:55
20 5:51	☉ □	♏ 20 10:33
22 8:25	♄ ✱	♐ 22 21:42
24 17:37	♄ □	♑ 25 5:45
26 23:28	♄ △	♒ 27 10:34
29 3:09	♀ △	♓ 29 13:11
31 7:18	♀ □	♈ 31 14:53

Last Aspect / ☽ Ingress

Last Aspect Dy Hr Mn		☽ Ingress Dy Hr Mn
2 11:46	♀ ✱	♉ 2 16:55
4 10:28	♄ △	♊ 4 20:10
6 15:33	♄ □	♋ 7 1:12
8 22:47	♄ ✱	♌ 9 8:23
11 1:29	♅ □	♍ 11 17:54
13 20:17	♄ ☌	♎ 14 5:32
16 5:02	☉ ✱	♏ 16 18:15
18 22:28	☉ □	♐ 19 6:08
21 12:35	☉ △	♑ 21 15:11
23 14:30	♄ △	♒ 23 20:32
25 19:04	♂ △	♓ 25 22:43
27 18:21	♄ ☍	♈ 27 23:11
29 8:02	♀ □	♉ 29 23:41

☽ Phases & Eclipses

Dy Hr Mn	
5 7:27	☽ 13♈25
12 6:46	● 20♋04
20 5:51	☽ 27♎40
27 18:54	○ 4♒52
27 19:08	☍ A 0.253
3 12:00	☽ 11♉17
10 19:09	● 18♌17
10 19:11:30	☌ A 3'23"
18 22:28	☽ 26♏06
26 3:42	○ 3♓03
26 3:30	☍ A 0.709

Astro Data

1 JULY 1980
Julian Day # 29402
Delta T 51.0 sec
SVP 05♓32'06"
Obliquity 23°26'23"
⚷ Chiron 17♉00.3
☽ Mean ☊ 22♌15.4

1 AUGUST 1980
Julian Day # 29433
Delta T 51.0 sec
SVP 05♓32'01"
Obliquity 23°26'23"
⚷ Chiron 18♉03.1
☽ Mean ☊ 20♌36.9

LONGITUDE SEPTEMBER 1980

Day	Sid.Time	☉	0 hr ☽	Noon ☽	True ☊	☿	♀	♂	♃	♄	♅	♆	♇
1 M	22 41 14	8♍42 9	28♉55 49	5♊54 23	20♌ 4.9	13♍55.3	23♋ 3.5	1♏47.7	18♍ 4.5	27♍29.6	21♏57.2	19♐54.2	20♎ 3.8
2 Tu	22 45 11	9 40 14	12♊47 40	19 35 43	20D 4.7	15 46.3	24 4.2	2 27.0	18 17.4	27 36.8	21 58.9	19 54.2	20 5.7
3 W	22 49 7	10 38 21	26 18 40	2♋56 42	20 5.3	17 36.2	25 5.3	3 6.3	18 30.3	27 44.0	22 0.6	19 54.3	20 7.6
4 Th	22 53 4	11 36 30	9♋30 6	15 59 7	20 6.6	19 24.8	26 6.8	3 45.8	18 43.2	27 51.3	22 2.4	19 54.3	20 9.6
5 F	22 57 0	12 34 41	22 24 2	28 45 11	20 8.1	21 12.3	27 8.6	4 25.3	18 56.2	27 58.5	22 4.2	19 54.5	20 11.6
6 Sa	23 0 57	13 32 53	5♌ 2 52	11♌17 21	20 9.5	22 58.5	28 10.7	5 4.9	19 9.1	28 5.8	22 6.1	19 54.6	20 13.6
7 Su	23 4 53	14 31 8	17 28 56	23 37 52	20R 10.2	24 43.5	29 13.1	5 44.6	19 22.1	28 13.1	22 8.0	19 54.8	20 15.6
8 M	23 8 50	15 29 24	29 44 24	5♍48 47	20 9.8	26 27.4	0♌15.8	6 24.4	19 35.1	28 20.4	22 9.9	19 55.0	20 17.6
9 Tu	23 12 47	16 27 43	11♍51 13	17 51 56	20 8.2	28 10.1	1 18.9	7 4.3	19 48.1	28 27.8	22 11.9	19 55.2	20 19.7
10 W	23 16 43	17 26 3	23 51 8	29 49 3	20 5.2	29 51.6	2 22.2	7 44.3	20 1.0	28 35.1	22 14.0	19 55.5	20 21.8
11 Th	23 20 40	18 24 24	5♎45 53	11♎41 53	20 1.0	1♎32.0	3 25.8	8 24.4	20 14.0	28 42.5	22 16.0	19 55.8	20 23.9
12 F	23 24 36	19 22 48	17 37 17	23 32 24	19 55.9	3 11.3	4 29.7	9 4.6	20 27.0	28 49.8	22 18.2	19 56.2	20 26.0
13 Sa	23 28 33	20 21 13	29 27 30	5♏22 57	19 50.5	4 49.4	5 33.8	9 44.9	20 40.0	28 57.2	22 20.3	19 56.6	20 28.1
14 Su	23 32 29	21 19 40	11♏19 6	17 16 21	19 45.3	6 26.5	6 38.2	10 25.2	20 53.0	29 4.6	22 22.6	19 57.0	20 30.2
15 M	23 36 26	22 18 9	23 15 8	29 15 55	19 41.0	8 2.5	7 42.9	11 5.6	21 6.0	29 12.0	22 24.8	19 57.4	20 32.4
16 Tu	23 40 22	23 16 40	5♐19 12	11♐25 31	19 38.0	9 37.5	8 47.8	11 46.2	21 19.0	29 19.5	22 27.1	19 57.9	20 34.6
17 W	23 44 19	24 15 12	17 35 22	23 49 20	19D 36.4	11 11.4	9 52.9	12 26.8	21 32.0	29 26.9	22 29.5	19 58.4	20 36.8
18 Th	23 48 15	25 13 45	0♑ 7 57	6♑31 45	19 36.3	12 44.2	10 58.3	13 7.5	21 45.0	29 34.3	22 31.8	19 58.9	20 39.0
19 F	23 52 12	26 12 21	13 1 15	19 36 53	19 37.3	14 16.0	12 4.0	13 48.2	21 58.0	29 41.8	22 34.3	19 59.5	20 41.2
20 Sa	23 56 9	27 10 58	26 19 2	3♒ 8 0	19 38.8	15 46.8	13 9.8	14 29.1	22 10.9	29 49.2	22 36.7	20 0.1	20 43.4
21 Su	0 0 5	28 9 37	10♒ 3 58	17 6 56	19R 40.0	17 16.5	14 15.9	15 10.0	22 23.9	29 56.7	22 39.2	20 0.8	20 45.6
22 M	0 4 2	29 8 17	24 16 47	1♓33 11	19 40.3	18 45.2	15 22.2	15 51.1	22 36.9	0♎ 4.1	22 41.8	20 1.4	20 47.9
23 Tu	0 7 58	0♎ 6 59	8♓55 35	16 23 15	19 38.9	20 12.9	16 28.7	16 32.2	22 49.8	0 11.5	22 44.4	20 2.1	20 50.2
24 W	0 11 55	1 5 43	23 55 16	1♈30 31	19 35.6	21 39.5	17 35.5	17 13.3	23 2.7	0 19.0	22 47.0	20 2.9	20 52.4
25 Th	0 15 51	2 4 29	9♈ 7 46	16 45 40	19 30.5	23 5.0	18 42.4	17 54.6	23 15.7	0 26.4	22 49.6	20 3.6	20 54.7
26 F	0 19 48	3 3 17	24 22 52	1♉58 2	19 24.3	24 29.4	19 49.6	18 35.9	23 28.6	0 33.9	22 52.3	20 4.4	20 57.0
27 Sa	0 23 44	4 2 7	9♉29 56	16 57 29	19 17.6	25 52.8	20 56.9	19 17.4	23 41.5	0 41.3	22 55.0	20 5.2	20 59.3
28 Su	0 27 41	5 0 59	24 19 44	1♊35 58	19 11.5	27 15.0	22 4.5	19 58.9	23 54.3	0 48.7	22 57.8	20 6.1	21 1.6
29 M	0 31 38	5 59 54	8♊45 43	15 48 39	19 6.8	28 36.0	23 12.2	20 40.5	24 7.2	0 56.2	23 0.6	20 7.0	21 3.9
30 Tu	0 35 34	6 58 51	22 44 41	29 33 52	19 3.9	29 55.8	24 20.1	21 22.1	24 20.1	1 3.6	23 3.4	20 7.9	21 6.3

LONGITUDE OCTOBER 1980

Day	Sid.Time	☉	0 hr ☽	Noon ☽	True ☊	☿	♀	♂	♃	♄	♅	♆	♇
1 W	0 39 31	7♎57 50	6♋16 25	12♋52 39	19♌ 2.9	1♏14.4	25♌28.3	22♏ 3.9	24♍32.9	1♎11.0	23♏ 6.3	20♐ 8.9	21♎ 8.6
2 Th	0 43 27	8 56 51	19 22 59	25 47 53	19D 3.3	2 31.6	26 36.6	22 45.7	24 45.7	1 18.4	23 9.2	20 9.9	21 11.0
3 F	0 47 24	9 55 55	2♌ 7 51	8♌23 25	19 4.5	3 47.4	27 45.1	23 27.7	24 58.5	1 25.8	23 12.1	20 10.9	21 13.3
4 Sa	0 51 20	10 55 1	14 35 5	20 43 22	19R 5.4	5 1.8	28 53.7	24 9.7	25 11.2	1 33.2	23 15.1	20 11.9	21 15.7
5 Su	0 55 17	11 54 10	26 48 46	2♍51 42	19 5.1	6 14.6	0♍ 2.6	24 51.7	25 24.0	1 40.6	23 18.1	20 13.0	21 18.0
6 M	0 59 13	12 53 20	8♍52 38	14 51 55	19 3.0	7 25.7	1 11.5	25 33.9	25 36.7	1 48.0	23 21.1	20 14.1	21 20.4
7 Tu	1 3 10	13 52 33	20 49 53	26 46 52	18 58.4	8 35.1	2 20.7	26 16.1	25 49.4	1 55.3	23 24.2	20 15.2	21 22.8
8 W	1 7 7	14 51 48	2♎43 6	8♎38 52	18 51.2	9 42.5	3 30.0	26 58.5	26 2.0	2 2.7	23 27.3	20 16.4	21 25.2
9 Th	1 11 3	15 51 5	14 34 20	20 29 44	18 41.8	10 47.9	4 39.4	27 40.9	26 14.6	2 10.0	23 30.4	20 17.6	21 27.6
10 F	1 15 0	16 50 24	26 25 15	2♏21 3	18 30.8	11 51.0	5 49.0	28 23.3	26 27.2	2 17.3	23 33.5	20 18.8	21 29.9
11 Sa	1 18 56	17 49 45	8♏17 20	14 14 19	18 19.0	12 51.7	6 58.8	29 5.9	26 39.8	2 24.6	23 36.7	20 20.1	21 32.3
12 Su	1 22 53	18 49 8	20 12 12	26 11 14	18 7.5	13 49.7	8 8.7	29 48.5	26 52.3	2 31.8	23 39.9	20 21.3	21 34.7
13 M	1 26 49	19 48 33	2♐11 43	8♐13 56	17 57.3	14 44.8	9 18.7	0♐31.3	27 4.8	2 39.1	23 43.1	20 22.6	21 37.1
14 Tu	1 30 46	20 48 0	14 18 17	20 25 7	17 49.2	15 36.7	10 28.9	1 14.0	27 17.2	2 46.3	23 46.4	20 24.0	21 39.5
15 W	1 34 42	21 47 28	26 34 53	2♑48 3	17 43.7	16 25.0	11 39.2	1 56.9	27 29.6	2 53.5	23 49.7	20 25.3	21 41.9
16 Th	1 38 39	22 46 59	9♑ 5 6	15 26 33	17 40.6	17 9.5	12 49.6	2 39.9	27 42.0	3 0.7	23 53.0	20 26.7	21 44.3
17 F	1 42 36	23 46 31	21 52 54	28 24 41	17D 39.7	17 49.8	14 0.2	3 22.9	27 54.3	3 7.8	23 56.3	20 28.1	21 46.7
18 Sa	1 46 32	24 46 5	5♒ 2 23	11♒46 24	17R 39.9	18 25.3	15 10.8	4 5.9	28 6.6	3 15.0	23 59.7	20 29.6	21 49.1
19 Su	1 50 29	25 45 41	18 37 6	25 34 43	17 40.2	18 55.7	16 21.6	4 49.1	28 18.9	3 22.1	24 3.0	20 31.1	21 51.5
20 M	1 54 25	26 45 18	2♓39 21	9♓50 57	17 39.4	19 20.5	17 32.5	5 32.3	28 31.1	3 29.1	24 6.4	20 32.5	21 53.9
21 Tu	1 58 22	27 44 57	17 9 14	24 33 43	17 36.5	19 39.1	18 43.6	6 15.6	28 43.2	3 36.1	24 9.9	20 34.1	21 56.3
22 W	2 2 18	28 44 38	2♈ 3 42	9♈38 12	17 30.9	19 50.9	19 54.7	6 59.0	28 55.3	3 43.1	24 13.3	20 35.6	21 58.7
23 Th	2 6 15	29 44 20	17 16 5	24 56 2	17 22.7	19R 55.4	21 6.0	7 42.4	29 7.3	3 50.1	24 16.8	20 37.2	22 1.0
24 F	2 10 11	0♏44 5	2♉36 35	10♉16 17	17 12.6	19 52.0	22 17.4	8 25.9	29 19.3	3 57.1	24 20.2	20 38.8	22 3.4
25 Sa	2 14 8	1 43 51	17 53 37	25 27 15	17 1.7	19 40.2	23 28.9	9 9.5	29 31.3	4 4.0	24 23.7	20 40.4	22 5.8
26 Su	2 18 4	2 43 40	2♊55 57	10♊18 42	16 51.4	19 19.7	24 40.5	9 53.1	29 43.2	4 10.8	24 27.2	20 42.0	22 8.2
27 M	2 22 1	3 43 31	17 34 44	24 43 28	16 42.8	18 50.0	25 52.2	10 36.9	29 55.0	4 17.7	24 30.8	20 43.7	22 10.5
28 Tu	2 25 58	4 43 24	1♋44 38	8♋38 8	16 36.7	18 11.1	27 4.1	11 20.7	0♎ 6.8	4 24.4	24 34.3	20 45.4	22 12.9
29 W	2 29 54	5 43 19	15 24 6	22 2 48	16 33.2	17 23.1	28 16.0	12 4.5	0 18.5	4 31.2	24 37.9	20 47.1	22 15.2
30 Th	2 33 51	6 43 17	28 34 38	5♌ 0 7	16D 31.8	16 26.6	29 28.1	12 48.4	0 30.2	4 37.9	24 41.5	20 48.8	22 17.6
31 F	2 37 47	7 43 16	11♌19 50	17 34 24	16R 31.6	15 22.4	0♎40.2	13 32.4	0 41.8	4 44.6	24 45.1	20 50.6	22 19.9

Astro Data Dy Hr Mn	Planet Ingress Dy Hr Mn	Last Aspect Dy Hr Mn	☽ Ingress Dy Hr Mn	Last Aspect Dy Hr Mn	☽ Ingress Dy Hr Mn	☽ Phases & Eclipses Dy Hr Mn
♃□♆ 9 13:35	♀ ♌ 7 17:57	31 21:32 ♄ △	♊ 1 1:50	2 10:13 ♃ ✶	♌ 2 19:57	1 18:08 ☽ 9♊26
☿0S 10 21:36	☿ ♎ 10 2:00	3 2:35 ♄ □	♋ 3 6:39	4 19:55 ♂ □	♍ 5 6:19	9 10:00 ● 16♍52
☽0S 11 6:51	♄ ♎ 21 10:47	5 10:38 ♄ ✶	♌ 5 14:22	7 11:39 ♂ ✶	♎ 7 18:30	17 13:54 ☽ 24♐49
♃⊻♇ 11 21:41	☉ ♎ 22 21:09	7 9:06 ♅ □	♍ 8 0:31	9 14:00 ♇ ☌	♏ 10 7:15	24 12:08 ○ 1♈35
♃✶♅ 22 11:22	☿ ♏ 30 1:16	10 9:37 ♄ ☌	♎ 10 12:22	12 13:36 ♃ ✶	♐ 12 19:37	
☽0N 24 23:58		12 5:43 ♇ ☌	♏ 13 1:06	15 1:48 ♃ □	♑ 15 6:37	1 3:18 ☽ 8♋06
	♀ ♍ 4 23:07	15 12:00 ♄ ✶	♐ 15 13:28	17 11:15 ♃ △	♒ 17 14:54	9 2:50 ● 15♎58
☽0S 8 12:51	♂ ♐ 12 6:27	17 22:56 ♄ □	♑ 17 23:45	19 13:15 ☉ △	♓ 19 19:31	17 3:47 ☽ 23♑56
☽0N 22 11:16	☉ ♏ 23 6:18	20 6:15 ♄ △	♒ 20 6:31	21 18:55 ♃ ☍	♈ 21 20:43	23 20:52 ○ 0♉36
☿ R 23 1:59	♃ ♎ 27 10:10	21 21:21 ♅ □	♓ 22 9:27	23 7:27 ♇ ☍	♉ 23 19:55	30 16:33 ☽ 7♌25
	♀ ♎ 30 10:38	23 22:35 ♃ ☍	♈ 24 9:37	25 18:45 ♃ △	♊ 25 19:17	
		26 0:11 ☿ ☍	♉ 26 8:53	27 15:14 ♀ □	♋ 27 21:00	
		27 23:18 ♃ △	♊ 28 9:21	30 1:49 ♀ ✶	♌ 30 2:38	
		30 3:02 ♀ ✶	♋ 30 12:46			

Astro Data

1 SEPTEMBER 1980
Julian Day # 29464
Delta T 51.1 sec
SVP 05♓31'58"
Obliquity 23°26'24"
⚷ Chiron 18♉14.1R
☽ Mean ☊ 18♌58.4

1 OCTOBER 1980
Julian Day # 29494
Delta T 51.2 sec
SVP 05♓31'55"
Obliquity 23°26'24"
⚷ Chiron 17♉32.9R
☽ Mean ☊ 17♌23.1

NOVEMBER 1980 LONGITUDE

Day	Sid.Time	☉	0 hr ☽	Noon ☽	True ☊	☿	♀	♂	♃	♄	♅	♆	♇
1 Sa	2 41 44	8♏43 18	23♌44 27	29♌50 38	16♌31.5	14♏11.7	1♎52.4	14♐16.5	0♎53.3	4♎51.2	24♏48.7	20♐52.4	22♎22.2
2 Su	2 45 40	9 43 21	5♍53 35	11♍53 54	16R 30.3	12R 56.4	3 4.8	15 0.6	1 4.8	4 57.8	24 52.3	20 54.2	22 24.6
3 M	2 49 37	10 43 27	17 52 9	23 48 53	16 26.9	11 38.5	4 17.2	15 44.8	1 16.2	5 4.4	24 55.9	20 56.0	22 26.9
4 Tu	2 53 33	11 43 35	29 44 35	5♎39 40	16 20.7	10 20.4	5 29.7	16 29.1	1 27.5	5 10.9	24 59.6	20 57.8	22 29.2
5 W	2 57 30	12 43 45	11♎34 32	17 29 31	16 11.5	9 4.5	6 42.3	17 13.4	1 38.8	5 17.3	25 3.2	20 59.7	22 31.5
6 Th	3 1 27	13 43 57	23 24 53	29 20 55	15 59.5	7 53.2	7 55.0	17 57.8	1 50.0	5 23.7	25 6.9	21 1.6	22 33.7
7 F	3 5 23	14 44 10	5♏17 48	11♏15 42	15 45.4	6 48.9	9 7.7	18 42.3	2 1.1	5 30.0	25 10.6	21 3.5	22 36.0
8 Sa	3 9 20	15 44 26	17 14 46	23 15 9	15 30.4	5 53.3	10 20.6	19 26.8	2 12.2	5 36.3	25 14.3	21 5.4	22 38.3
9 Su	3 13 16	16 44 43	29 16 57	5♐20 18	15 15.7	5 8.0	11 33.5	20 11.5	2 23.1	5 42.6	25 17.9	21 7.3	22 40.5
10 M	3 17 13	17 45 2	11♐25 20	17 32 13	15 2.5	4 33.7	12 46.5	20 56.1	2 34.0	5 48.8	25 21.6	21 9.3	22 42.7
11 Tu	3 21 9	18 45 23	23 41 7	29 52 15	14 51.7	4 11.1	13 59.6	21 40.9	2 44.8	5 54.9	25 25.3	21 11.2	22 44.9
12 W	3 25 6	19 45 45	6♑ 5 53	12♑22 17	14 43.9	4D 0.2	15 12.7	22 25.6	2 55.6	6 1.0	25 29.1	21 13.2	22 47.1
13 Th	3 29 2	20 46 9	18 41 48	25 4 47	14 39.2	4 0.7	16 25.9	23 10.5	3 6.2	6 7.0	25 32.8	21 15.2	22 49.3
14 F	3 32 59	21 46 34	1♒31 38	8♒ 2 44	14 37.1	4 12.0	17 39.2	23 55.4	3 16.8	6 13.0	25 36.5	21 17.2	22 51.5
15 Sa	3 36 56	22 47 1	14 38 32	21 19 23	14 36.7	4 33.4	18 52.5	24 40.4	3 27.3	6 18.9	25 40.2	21 19.3	22 53.7
16 Su	3 40 52	23 47 28	28 5 41	4♓57 43	14 36.7	5 4.1	20 5.9	25 25.4	3 37.7	6 24.8	25 43.9	21 21.3	22 55.8
17 M	3 44 49	24 47 57	11♓55 42	18 59 44	14 35.8	5 43.1	21 19.3	26 10.5	3 48.0	6 30.6	25 47.7	21 23.4	22 57.9
18 Tu	3 48 45	25 48 27	26 9 44	3♈25 30	14 32.9	6 29.6	22 32.8	26 55.6	3 58.2	6 36.3	25 51.4	21 25.5	23 0.0
19 W	3 52 42	26 48 59	10♈46 36	18 12 25	14 27.4	7 22.8	23 46.4	27 40.8	4 8.3	6 41.9	25 55.1	21 27.6	23 2.1
20 Th	3 56 38	27 49 31	25 42 6	3♉14 39	14 19.2	8 21.7	25 0.0	28 26.1	4 18.3	6 47.5	25 58.8	21 29.7	23 4.2
21 F	4 0 35	28 50 5	10♉48 51	18 23 27	14 9.0	9 25.7	26 13.7	29 11.4	4 28.2	6 53.1	26 2.6	21 31.8	23 6.2
22 Sa	4 4 31	29 50 41	25 57 5	3♊28 25	13 57.8	10 34.0	27 27.5	29 56.8	4 38.0	6 58.5	26 6.3	21 33.9	23 8.3
23 Su	4 8 28	0♐51 18	10♊56 12	18 19 17	13 47.0	11 46.1	28 41.3	0♑42.2	4 47.8	7 3.9	26 10.0	21 36.1	23 10.3
24 M	4 12 25	1 51 56	25 36 44	2♋47 46	13 37.8	13 1.5	29 55.1	1 27.7	4 57.4	7 9.3	26 13.7	21 38.2	23 12.3
25 Tu	4 16 21	2 52 36	9♋51 53	16 48 45	13 31.0	14 19.6	1♏ 9.0	2 13.2	5 6.9	7 14.5	26 17.4	21 40.4	23 14.2
26 W	4 20 18	3 53 18	23 38 15	0♌20 29	13 27.0	15 40.1	2 23.0	2 58.8	5 16.4	7 19.7	26 21.1	21 42.5	23 16.2
27 Th	4 24 14	4 54 1	6♌55 41	13 24 13	13D 25.3	17 2.6	3 37.0	3 44.4	5 25.7	7 24.8	26 24.8	21 44.7	23 18.1
28 F	4 28 11	5 54 45	19 46 35	26 3 20	13 25.3	18 26.7	4 51.1	4 30.1	5 34.9	7 29.9	26 28.5	21 46.9	23 20.0
29 Sa	4 32 7	6 55 31	2♍15 5	8♍22 29	13R 25.7	19 52.3	6 5.2	5 15.8	5 44.0	7 34.8	26 32.2	21 49.1	23 21.9
30 Su	4 36 4	7 56 18	14 26 12	20 26 55	13 25.6	21 19.1	7 19.4	6 1.6	5 53.0	7 39.7	26 35.9	21 51.3	23 23.8

DECEMBER 1980 LONGITUDE

Day	Sid.Time	☉	0 hr ☽	Noon ☽	True ☊	☿	♀	♂	♃	♄	♅	♆	♇
1 M	4 40 0	8♐57 7	26♍25 16	2♎21 54	13♌23.9	22♏46.9	8♏33.6	6♑47.5	6♎ 1.8	7♎44.5	26♏39.6	21♐53.5	23♎25.6
2 Tu	4 43 57	9 57 58	8♎17 25	14 12 22	13R 19.8	24 15.5	9 47.8	7 33.4	6 10.6	7 49.3	26 43.2	21 55.8	23 27.4
3 W	4 47 54	10 58 49	20 7 17	26 2 37	13 13.1	25 44.9	11 2.1	8 19.3	6 19.2	7 53.9	26 46.9	21 58.0	23 29.2
4 Th	4 51 50	11 59 43	1♏58 47	7♏56 10	13 4.1	27 14.8	12 16.4	9 5.3	6 27.7	7 58.5	26 50.5	22 0.2	23 31.0
5 F	4 55 47	13 0 37	13 55 5	19 55 45	12 53.1	28 45.3	13 30.8	9 51.4	6 36.1	8 3.0	26 54.1	22 2.5	23 32.7
6 Sa	4 59 43	14 1 32	25 58 24	2♐ 3 12	12 41.3	0♐16.1	14 45.2	10 37.5	6 44.4	8 7.4	26 57.7	22 4.7	23 34.5
7 Su	5 3 40	15 2 29	8♐10 15	14 19 40	12 29.6	1 47.3	15 59.6	11 23.6	6 52.6	8 11.7	27 1.3	22 7.0	23 36.2
8 M	5 7 36	16 3 27	20 31 30	26 45 47	12 19.0	3 18.8	17 14.1	12 9.8	7 0.6	8 16.0	27 4.9	22 9.2	23 37.8
9 Tu	5 11 33	17 4 26	3♑ 2 34	9♑21 55	12 10.5	4 50.6	18 28.6	12 56.1	7 8.5	8 20.2	27 8.5	22 11.5	23 39.5
10 W	5 15 29	18 5 25	15 43 52	22 8 29	12 4.6	6 22.6	19 43.1	13 42.3	7 16.3	8 24.2	27 12.1	22 13.8	23 41.1
11 Th	5 19 26	19 6 25	28 35 52	5♒ 6 9	12 1.3	7 54.8	20 57.7	14 28.7	7 23.9	8 28.2	27 15.6	22 16.0	23 42.7
12 F	5 23 23	20 7 26	11♒39 28	18 16 0	12D 0.4	9 27.1	22 12.3	15 15.0	7 31.4	8 32.1	27 19.1	22 18.3	23 44.2
13 Sa	5 27 19	21 8 28	24 55 55	1♓39 24	12 1.0	10 59.6	23 26.9	16 1.5	7 38.7	8 35.9	27 22.6	22 20.6	23 45.8
14 Su	5 31 16	22 9 30	8♓26 40	15 17 51	12 2.1	12 32.2	24 41.5	16 47.9	7 46.0	8 39.6	27 26.1	22 22.8	23 47.3
15 M	5 35 12	23 10 32	22 13 5	29 12 26	12R 2.8	14 5.0	25 56.1	17 34.4	7 53.0	8 43.3	27 29.6	22 25.1	23 48.7
16 Tu	5 39 9	24 11 35	6♈15 53	13♈23 18	12 2.1	15 37.9	27 10.8	18 20.9	7 60.0	8 46.8	27 33.0	22 27.3	23 50.2
17 W	5 43 5	25 12 38	20 34 27	27 48 58	11 59.4	17 11.0	28 25.5	19 7.5	8 6.8	8 50.2	27 36.4	22 29.6	23 51.6
18 Th	5 47 2	26 13 41	5♉ 6 20	12♉25 56	11 54.7	18 44.1	29 40.2	19 54.1	8 13.4	8 53.6	27 39.8	22 31.9	23 52.9
19 F	5 50 58	27 14 45	19 47 0	27 8 41	11 48.5	20 17.5	0♐55.0	20 40.7	8 19.9	8 56.8	27 43.2	22 34.1	23 54.3
20 Sa	5 54 55	28 15 49	4♊30 1	11♊50 4	11 41.3	21 51.0	2 9.7	21 27.4	8 26.3	8 60.0	27 46.5	22 36.4	23 55.6
21 Su	5 58 52	29 16 54	19 7 50	26 22 26	11 34.4	23 24.6	3 24.5	22 14.1	8 32.5	9 3.0	27 49.9	22 38.7	23 56.9
22 M	6 2 48	0♑17 59	3♋33 0	10♋38 49	11 28.4	24 58.5	4 39.3	23 0.8	8 38.5	9 6.0	27 53.2	22 40.9	23 58.2
23 Tu	6 6 45	1 19 5	17 39 18	24 34 0	11 24.2	26 32.5	5 54.1	23 47.6	8 44.4	9 8.9	27 56.4	22 43.2	23 59.4
24 W	6 10 41	2 20 11	1♌22 38	8♌ 5 5	11D 21.9	28 6.7	7 9.0	24 34.4	8 50.2	9 11.6	27 59.7	22 45.4	24 0.6
25 Th	6 14 38	3 21 17	14 41 21	21 11 35	11 21.5	29 41.2	8 23.8	25 21.2	8 55.8	9 14.3	28 2.9	22 47.7	24 1.8
26 F	6 18 34	4 22 24	27 36 4	3♍55 10	11 22.5	1♑15.9	9 38.7	26 8.1	9 1.2	9 16.9	28 6.1	22 49.9	24 2.9
27 Sa	6 22 31	5 23 32	10♍ 9 18	16 19 1	11 24.2	2 50.8	10 53.6	26 55.0	9 6.5	9 19.3	28 9.3	22 52.1	24 4.0
28 Su	6 26 28	6 24 40	22 24 52	28 27 27	11 25.8	4 26.0	12 8.5	27 42.0	9 11.6	9 21.7	28 12.4	22 54.3	24 5.0
29 M	6 30 24	7 25 48	4♎27 24	10♎25 19	11R 26.7	6 1.5	13 23.5	28 28.9	9 16.6	9 24.0	28 15.5	22 56.6	24 6.1
30 Tu	6 34 21	8 26 57	16 21 52	22 17 38	11 26.4	7 37.3	14 38.4	29 15.9	9 21.3	9 26.1	28 18.6	22 58.8	24 7.1
31 W	6 38 17	9 28 7	28 13 15	4♏ 9 17	11 24.6	9 13.4	15 53.4	0♒ 2.9	9 26.0	9 28.2	28 21.7	23 1.0	24 8.0

Astro Data	Dy Hr Mn
♄0S	1 12:51
♀0S	2 11:46
☽0S	4 19:22
♃0S	10 4:08
☿ D	12 10:56
☽0N	18 22:03
☽0S	2 3:06
☽0N	16 6:33
☽0S	29 11:54
♃☌♄	31 21:25

Planet Ingress	Dy Hr Mn
☉ ♐	22 3:41
♂ ♑	22 1:42
♀ ♏	24 1:35
☿ ♐	5 19:45
♀ ♐	18 6:21
☉ ♑	21 16:56
☿ ♑	25 4:46
♂ ♒	30 22:30

Last Aspect Dy Hr Mn		☽ Ingress	Dy Hr Mn
1 2:06	♅ □	♍	1 12:19
3 14:20	♅ ⚹	♎	4 0:31
5 22:16	♇ ☌	♏	6 13:19
8 16:02	♅ ☌	♐	9 1:25
10 22:10	♇ ⚹	♑	11 12:15
13 12:56	♅ ⚹	♒	13 21:10
15 19:49	♅ □	♓	16 3:21
18 1:20	♂ □	♈	18 6:22
20 4:35	♂ △	♉	20 6:51
22 0:15	♅ ☍	♊	22 6:27
23 20:01	♇ △	♋	24 7:18
26 4:51	♅ △	♌	26 11:23
28 12:52	♅ □	♍	28 19:37

Last Aspect Dy Hr Mn		☽ Ingress	Dy Hr Mn
1 0:29	♅ ⚹	♎	1 7:13
3 6:50	♇ ☌	♏	3 20:00
6 1:58	♅ ☌	♐	6 7:57
8 6:00	♇ ⚹	♑	8 18:12
10 21:31	♅ ⚹	♒	11 2:36
13 4:24	♅ □	♓	13 9:03
15 9:06	♅ △	♈	15 13:21
17 8:16	☉ △	♉	17 15:36
19 12:59	♅ ☍	♊	19 16:39
21 7:59	♇ △	♋	21 18:03
23 18:00	♅ △	♌	23 21:34
26 0:57	♅ □	♍	26 4:32
28 11:33	♅ ⚹	♎	28 15:05
30 15:43	♇ ☌	♏	31 3:36

☽ Phases & Eclipses Dy Hr Mn		
7 20:43	●	15♏36
15 15:47	☽	23♒27
22 6:39	○	0♊07
29 9:59	☽	7♍21
7 14:35	●	15♐40
15 1:47	☽	23♓15
21 18:08	○	0♋03
29 6:32	☽	7♎42

Astro Data

1 NOVEMBER 1980
Julian Day # 29525
Delta T 51.2 sec
SVP 05♓31'52"
Obliquity 23°26'24"
⚷ Chiron 16♉10.9R
☽ Mean ☊ 15♌44.6

1 DECEMBER 1980
Julian Day # 29555
Delta T 51.3 sec
SVP 05♓31'48"
Obliquity 23°26'24"
⚷ Chiron 14♉42.6R
☽ Mean ☊ 14♌09.3

LONGITUDE — JANUARY 1981

Day	Sid.Time	☉	0 hr ☽	Noon ☽	True ☊	☿	♀	♂	♃	♄	♅	♆	♇
1 Th	6 42 14	10♑29 16	10♏ 6 16	16♏ 4 43	11♌21.4	10♑49.8	17♐ 8.4	0♒50.0	9♎30.4	9♎30.1	28♏24.7	23♐ 3.2	24♎ 9.0
2 F	6 46 10	11 30 27	22 5 5	28 7 47	11R 16.9	12 26.5	18 23.4	1 37.1	9 34.7	9 32.0	28 27.7	23 5.3	24 9.9
3 Sa	6 50 7	12 31 37	4♐13 10	10♐21 32	11 11.9	14 3.6	19 38.4	2 24.2	9 38.8	9 33.7	28 30.6	23 7.5	24 10.7
4 Su	6 54 3	13 32 48	16 33 7	22 48 6	11 6.7	15 41.1	20 53.4	3 11.3	9 42.7	9 35.4	28 33.5	23 9.7	24 11.6
5 M	6 58 0	14 33 58	29 6 37	5♑28 42	11 2.1	17 18.9	22 8.4	3 58.5	9 46.5	9 36.9	28 36.4	23 11.8	24 12.3
6 Tu	7 1 57	15 35 9	11♑54 24	18 23 38	10 58.5	18 57.1	23 23.4	4 45.7	9 50.1	9 38.3	28 39.3	23 14.0	24 13.1
7 W	7 5 53	16 36 20	24 56 22	1♒32 28	10 56.2	20 35.7	24 38.5	5 32.9	9 53.5	9 39.7	28 42.1	23 16.1	24 13.8
8 Th	7 9 50	17 37 30	8♒11 49	14 54 16	10D 55.3	22 14.6	25 53.5	6 20.1	9 56.7	9 40.9	28 44.9	23 18.2	24 14.5
9 F	7 13 46	18 38 40	21 39 39	28 27 48	10 55.6	23 53.9	27 8.6	7 7.4	9 59.8	9 42.0	28 47.6	23 20.3	24 15.2
10 Sa	7 17 43	19 39 50	5♓18 35	12♓11 49	10 56.8	25 33.5	28 23.7	7 54.6	10 2.6	9 43.0	28 50.3	23 22.4	24 15.8
11 Su	7 21 39	20 40 59	19 7 21	26 5 2	10 58.3	27 13.5	29 38.7	8 41.9	10 5.3	9 43.9	28 52.9	23 24.5	24 16.4
12 M	7 25 36	21 42 7	3♈ 4 44	10♈ 6 16	10 59.6	28 53.8	0♑53.8	9 29.2	10 7.8	9 44.6	28 55.6	23 26.5	24 16.9
13 Tu	7 29 32	22 43 15	17 9 28	24 14 7	11R 0.3	0♒34.4	2 8.8	10 16.5	10 10.1	9 45.3	28 58.1	23 28.6	24 17.4
14 W	7 33 29	23 44 22	1♉20 0	8♉26 50	11 0.3	2 15.3	3 23.9	11 3.9	10 12.3	9 45.9	29 0.7	23 30.6	24 17.9
15 Th	7 37 26	24 45 29	15 34 20	22 42 7	10 59.4	3 56.3	4 39.0	11 51.2	10 14.2	9 46.3	29 3.2	23 32.6	24 18.3
16 F	7 41 22	25 46 35	29 49 48	6♊56 56	10 57.8	5 37.4	5 54.1	12 38.6	10 16.0	9 46.7	29 5.6	23 34.6	24 18.7
17 Sa	7 45 19	26 47 40	14♊ 3 4	21 7 41	10 55.9	7 18.6	7 9.1	13 25.9	10 17.5	9 46.9	29 8.1	23 36.6	24 19.1
18 Su	7 49 15	27 48 44	28 10 18	5♋10 25	10 54.1	8 59.8	8 24.2	14 13.3	10 18.9	9R 47.0	29 10.4	23 38.6	24 19.4
19 M	7 53 12	28 49 48	12♋ 7 33	19 1 15	10 52.6	10 40.7	9 39.3	15 0.7	10 20.1	9 47.0	29 12.8	23 40.5	24 19.7
20 Tu	7 57 8	29 50 51	25 51 9	2♌36 55	10 51.6	12 21.4	10 54.4	15 48.1	10 21.1	9 47.0	29 15.1	23 42.4	24 20.0
21 W	8 1 5	0♒51 53	9♌18 17	15 55 5	10D 51.2	14 1.5	12 9.4	16 35.5	10 22.0	9 46.8	29 17.3	23 44.4	24 20.2
22 Th	8 5 1	1 52 54	22 27 14	28 54 42	10 51.4	15 40.9	13 24.5	17 22.9	10 22.6	9 46.5	29 19.5	23 46.2	24 20.4
23 F	8 8 58	2 53 55	5♍17 35	11♍36 3	10 52.0	17 19.4	14 39.6	18 10.4	10 23.0	9 46.1	29 21.7	23 48.1	24 20.5
24 Sa	8 12 55	3 54 56	17 50 19	24 0 42	10 52.7	18 56.7	15 54.7	18 57.8	10R 23.3	9 45.5	29 23.8	23 50.0	24 20.6
25 Su	8 16 51	4 55 55	0♎ 7 34	6♎11 21	10 53.5	20 32.4	17 9.8	19 45.2	10 23.3	9 44.9	29 25.8	23 51.8	24 20.7
26 M	8 20 48	5 56 54	12 12 31	18 11 36	10 54.1	22 6.1	18 24.9	20 32.7	10 23.2	9 44.2	29 27.9	23 53.6	24R 20.7
27 Tu	8 24 44	6 57 53	24 9 7	0♏ 5 39	10 54.4	23 37.4	19 40.0	21 20.2	10 22.9	9 43.3	29 29.8	23 55.4	24 20.7
28 W	8 28 41	7 58 51	6♏ 1 47	11 58 7	10R 54.5	25 5.8	20 55.1	22 7.6	10 22.4	9 42.4	29 31.7	23 57.2	24 20.7
29 Th	8 32 37	8 59 48	17 55 15	23 53 45	10 54.5	26 30.7	22 10.2	22 55.1	10 21.7	9 41.3	29 33.6	23 58.9	24 20.6
30 F	8 36 34	10 0 45	29 54 13	5♐57 11	10D 54.4	27 51.6	23 25.3	23 42.5	10 20.8	9 40.2	29 35.5	24 0.6	24 20.5
31 Sa	8 40 30	11 1 41	12♐ 3 11	18 12 40	10 54.4	29 7.7	24 40.4	24 30.0	10 19.7	9 38.9	29 37.2	24 2.3	24 20.4

LONGITUDE — FEBRUARY 1981

Day	Sid.Time	☉	0 hr ☽	Noon ☽	True ☊	☿	♀	♂	♃	♄	♅	♆	♇
1 Su	8 44 27	12♒ 2 36	24♐26 6	0♑43 49	10♌54.5	0♓18.3	25♑55.5	25♒17.5	10♎18.4	9♎37.6	29♏39.0	24♐ 4.0	24♎20.2
2 M	8 48 24	13 3 30	7♑ 6 7	13 33 15	10 54.7	1 22.6	27 10.6	26 5.0	10R 16.9	9R 36.1	29 40.6	24 5.7	24R 20.0
3 Tu	8 52 20	14 4 24	20 5 19	26 42 23	10 54.9	2 19.9	28 25.7	26 52.5	10 15.3	9 34.5	29 42.3	24 7.3	24 19.7
4 W	8 56 17	15 5 16	3♒24 25	10♒11 14	10R 55.1	3 9.3	29 40.8	27 39.9	10 13.4	9 32.9	29 43.9	24 8.9	24 19.5
5 Th	9 0 13	16 6 7	17 2 37	23 58 14	10 55.1	3 50.1	0♒55.9	28 27.4	10 11.4	9 31.1	29 45.4	24 10.5	24 19.1
6 F	9 4 10	17 6 57	0♓57 40	8♓ 0 27	10 54.8	4 21.5	2 11.0	29 14.9	10 9.1	9 29.2	29 46.9	24 12.0	24 18.8
7 Sa	9 8 6	18 7 46	15 6 2	22 13 52	10 54.2	4 43.0	3 26.1	0♓ 2.4	10 6.7	9 27.2	29 48.3	24 13.5	24 18.4
8 Su	9 12 3	19 8 33	29 23 21	6♈33 54	10 53.3	4R 54.0	4 41.2	0 49.8	10 4.1	9 25.2	29 49.7	24 15.0	24 18.0
9 M	9 15 59	20 9 19	13♈44 55	20 55 53	10 52.2	4 54.2	5 56.3	1 37.3	10 1.3	9 23.0	29 51.0	24 16.5	24 17.5
10 Tu	9 19 56	21 10 4	28 6 16	5♉15 39	10 51.2	4 43.6	7 11.3	2 24.7	9 58.4	9 20.7	29 52.3	24 18.0	24 17.0
11 W	9 23 53	22 10 46	12♉23 38	19 29 51	10D 50.5	4 22.2	8 26.4	3 12.2	9 55.2	9 18.4	29 53.5	24 19.4	24 16.5
12 Th	9 27 49	23 11 27	26 34 4	3♊36 2	10 50.4	3 50.7	9 41.4	3 59.6	9 51.9	9 15.9	29 54.6	24 20.8	24 16.0
13 F	9 31 46	24 12 7	10♊35 34	17 32 33	10 50.9	3 9.7	10 56.5	4 47.0	9 48.4	9 13.4	29 55.8	24 22.1	24 15.4
14 Sa	9 35 42	25 12 45	24 26 49	1♋18 19	10 51.8	2 20.3	12 11.5	5 34.4	9 44.7	9 10.7	29 56.8	24 23.5	24 14.7
15 Su	9 39 39	26 13 21	8♋ 6 58	14 52 41	10 53.1	1 23.7	13 26.5	6 21.8	9 40.9	9 8.0	29 57.8	24 24.8	24 14.1
16 M	9 43 35	27 13 55	21 35 23	28 15 3	10 54.3	0 21.7	14 41.6	7 9.2	9 36.9	9 5.2	29 58.8	24 26.1	24 13.4
17 Tu	9 47 32	28 14 28	4♌51 36	11♌24 58	10R 55.0	29♒15.9	15 56.6	7 56.5	9 32.7	9 2.3	29 59.7	24 27.3	24 12.7
18 W	9 51 28	29 14 59	17 55 7	24 22 1	10 55.0	28 8.0	17 11.6	8 43.9	9 28.3	8 59.3	0♐ 0.5	24 28.6	24 11.9
19 Th	9 55 25	0♓15 28	0♍45 40	7♍ 6 2	10 53.9	27 0.0	18 26.6	9 31.2	9 23.8	8 56.3	0 1.3	24 29.8	24 11.2
20 F	9 59 22	1 15 56	13 23 12	19 37 12	10 51.8	25 53.4	19 41.5	10 18.5	9 19.1	8 53.1	0 2.1	24 30.9	24 10.3
21 Sa	10 3 18	2 16 22	25 48 9	1♎56 13	10 48.7	24 49.9	20 56.5	11 5.9	9 14.3	8 49.9	0 2.7	24 32.0	24 9.5
22 Su	10 7 15	3 16 47	8♎ 1 36	14 4 31	10 45.0	23 50.7	22 11.5	11 53.1	9 9.3	8 46.6	0 3.4	24 33.1	24 8.6
23 M	10 11 11	4 17 10	20 5 18	26 4 17	10 41.0	22 56.8	23 26.5	12 40.4	9 4.2	8 43.2	0 3.9	24 34.2	24 7.7
24 Tu	10 15 8	5 17 32	2♏ 1 50	7♏58 25	10 37.3	22 9.2	24 41.4	13 27.7	8 58.9	8 39.8	0 4.5	24 35.3	24 6.8
25 W	10 19 4	6 17 52	13 54 30	19 50 35	10 34.3	21 28.3	25 56.4	14 14.9	8 53.4	8 36.3	0 4.9	24 36.3	24 5.8
26 Th	10 23 1	7 18 11	25 47 14	1♐45 0	10 32.4	20 54.5	27 11.3	15 2.1	8 47.9	8 32.7	0 5.3	24 37.3	24 4.8
27 F	10 26 57	8 18 29	7♐44 30	13 46 19	10D 31.7	20 28.0	28 26.3	15 49.3	8 42.2	8 29.0	0 5.7	24 38.2	24 3.8
28 Sa	10 30 54	9 18 45	19 51 4	25 59 21	10 32.2	20 8.7	29 41.2	16 36.5	8 36.3	8 25.3	0 6.0	24 39.1	24 2.8

Astro Data	Planet Ingress	Last Aspect	☽ Ingress	Last Aspect	☽ Ingress	☽ Phases & Eclipses	Astro Data
Dy Hr Mn	Dy Hr Mn	Dy Hr Mn	Dy Hr Mn	Dy Hr Mn	Dy Hr Mn	Dy Hr Mn	1 JANUARY 1981
☽0N 12 12:46	♀ ♑ 11 6:48	2 12:42 ♅ ☌	♐ 2 15:42	1 1:45 ♂ ⚹	♑ 1 10:37	6 7:24 ● 15♑54	Julian Day # 29586
♄ R 18 16:58	☿ ♒ 12 15:48	4 14:40 ♇ ⚹	♑ 5 1:41	3 17:25 ♅ ⚹	♒ 3 17:55	13 10:10 ☽ 23♈09	Delta T 51.4 sec
♃ R 24 19:23	☉ ♒ 20 3:36	7 6:52 ♅ ⚹	♒ 7 9:12	5 21:59 ♅ □	♓ 5 22:21	20 7:39 ○ 0♌10	SVP 05♓31'43"
☽0S 25 20:50	☿ ♓ 31 17:35	9 12:37 ♅ □	♓ 9 14:42	8 0:44 ♅ △	♈ 8 1:01	20 7:50 ☍ A 1.014	Obliquity 23°26'24"
♇ R 26 12:51		11 16:52 ♅ △	♈ 11 18:43	9 17:37 ♆ △	♉ 10 3:11	28 4:19 ☽ 8♏10	⚷ Chiron 13♉38.4R
	♀ ♒ 4 6:07	13 12:06 ♇ ☍	♉ 13 21:45	12 5:42 ♅ ☍	♊ 12 5:51		☽ Mean ☊ 12♌30.8
☽0N 8 18:44	♂ ♓ 6 22:48	15 22:45 ♅ ☍	♊ 16 0:17	14 1:26 ☉ △	♋ 14 9:43	4 22:14 ● 16♒02	
☿ R 8 12:31	☿ ♒ 16 8:02	17 17:26 ♇ △	♋ 18 3:08	16 15:09 ♅ △	♌ 16 15:10	4 22:08:31 ☌ A 0'33"	1 FEBRUARY 1981
♆⚹♇ 9 12:26	♅ ♐ 17 8:52	20 6:02 ♅ △	♌ 20 7:21	18 17:30 ☿ ☍	♍ 18 22:34	11 17:49 ☽ 22♉56	Julian Day # 29617
☽0S 22 4:56	☉ ♓ 18 17:52	22 12:49 ♅ □	♍ 22 14:02	20 21:32 ♆ □	♎ 21 8:12	18 22:58 ○ 0♍13	Delta T 51.4 sec
	♀ ♓ 28 6:01	24 22:38 ♅ ⚹	♎ 24 23:45	23 9:00 ♆ ⚹	♏ 23 19:54	27 1:14 ☽ 8♐22	SVP 05♓31'38"
		27 0:23 ♇ ☌	♏ 27 11:49	26 3:09 ♀ □	♐ 26 8:29		Obliquity 23°26'24"
		29 23:23 ♅ ☌	♐ 30 0:12	28 9:24 ♆ ☌	♑ 28 19:46		⚷ Chiron 13♉26.8
							☽ Mean ☊ 10♌52.3

MARCH 1981 LONGITUDE

Day	Sid.Time	☉	0 hr ☽	Noon ☽	True ☊	☿	♀	♂	♃	♄	♅	♆	♇
1 Su	10 34 51	10♓19 0	2♑11 45	8♑28 48	10♌33.5	19♒56.5	0♓56.1	17♓23.7	8♎30.3	8♎21.5	0♐ 6.3	24♐40.0	24♎ 1.7
2 M	10 38 47	11 19 13	14 51 0	21 18 48	10 35.3	19D 51.2	2 11.0	18 10.8	8R 24.2	8R 17.6	0 6.5	24 40.9	24R 0.6
3 Tu	10 42 44	12 19 24	27 52 34	4♒32 32	10R 36.8	19 52.5	3 25.9	18 57.9	8 18.0	8 13.7	0 6.6	24 41.7	23 59.5
4 W	10 46 40	13 19 34	11♒18 50	18 11 30	10 37.3	20 0.1	4 40.9	19 45.0	8 11.6	8 9.7	0 6.7	24 42.5	23 58.4
5 Th	10 50 37	14 19 43	25 10 21	2♓15 5	10 36.5	20 13.6	5 55.7	20 32.1	8 5.1	8 5.6	0R 6.7	24 43.2	23 57.2
6 F	10 54 33	15 19 49	9♓25 14	16 40 9	10 33.9	20 32.8	7 10.6	21 19.2	7 58.5	8 1.5	0 6.7	24 44.0	23 56.0
7 Sa	10 58 30	16 19 54	23 59 5	1♈21 8	10 29.7	20 57.2	8 25.5	22 6.2	7 51.9	7 57.4	0 6.6	24 44.7	23 54.8
8 Su	11 2 26	17 19 56	8♈45 17	16 10 32	10 24.3	21 26.5	9 40.3	22 53.2	7 45.1	7 53.2	0 6.5	24 45.3	23 53.5
9 M	11 6 23	18 19 57	23 35 49	1♉ 0 7	10 18.5	22 0.4	10 55.2	23 40.2	7 38.2	7 48.9	0 6.3	24 45.9	23 52.2
10 Tu	11 10 19	19 19 56	8♉22 32	15 42 12	10 13.0	22 38.5	12 10.0	24 27.1	7 31.2	7 44.6	0 6.1	24 46.5	23 50.9
11 W	11 14 16	20 19 52	22 58 27	0♊10 44	10 8.6	23 20.7	13 24.8	25 14.0	7 24.1	7 40.3	0 5.8	24 47.1	23 49.6
12 Th	11 18 13	21 19 46	7♊18 38	14 21 55	10 6.0	24 6.6	14 39.6	26 0.9	7 17.0	7 35.9	0 5.4	24 47.6	23 48.3
13 F	11 22 9	22 19 39	21 20 25	28 14 10	10D 5.1	24 55.9	15 54.4	26 47.7	7 9.7	7 31.5	0 5.0	24 48.1	23 46.9
14 Sa	11 26 6	23 19 28	5♋ 3 13	11♋47 45	10 5.6	25 48.5	17 9.2	27 34.6	7 2.4	7 27.1	0 4.6	24 48.6	23 45.6
15 Su	11 30 2	24 19 16	18 27 57	25 4 5	10 6.9	26 44.2	18 23.9	28 21.4	6 55.1	7 22.6	0 4.1	24 49.0	23 44.2
16 M	11 33 59	25 19 1	1♌36 23	8♌ 5 7	10R 8.1	27 42.7	19 38.7	29 8.1	6 47.6	7 18.1	0 3.5	24 49.4	23 42.7
17 Tu	11 37 55	26 18 45	14 30 33	20 52 55	10 8.3	28 43.9	20 53.4	29 54.8	6 40.2	7 13.5	0 2.9	24 49.7	23 41.3
18 W	11 41 52	27 18 25	27 12 24	3♍29 14	10 6.8	29 47.7	22 8.1	0♈41.5	6 32.6	7 8.9	0 2.3	24 50.1	23 39.9
19 Th	11 45 48	28 18 4	9♍43 33	15 55 30	10 3.0	0♓53.8	23 22.8	1 28.2	6 25.0	7 4.4	0 1.5	24 50.4	23 38.4
20 F	11 49 45	29 17 41	22 5 14	28 12 50	9 56.9	2 2.2	24 37.5	2 14.8	6 17.4	6 59.7	0 0.8	24 50.6	23 36.9
21 Sa	11 53 42	0♈17 15	4♎18 27	10♎22 12	9 48.7	3 12.8	25 52.1	3 1.3	6 9.8	6 55.1	29♏60.0	24 50.8	23 35.4
22 Su	11 57 38	1 16 48	16 24 11	22 24 35	9 39.0	4 25.5	27 6.8	3 47.9	6 2.1	6 50.5	29 59.1	24 51.0	23 33.9
23 M	12 1 35	2 16 18	28 23 33	4♏21 19	9 28.6	5 40.1	28 21.4	4 34.4	5 54.4	6 45.8	29 58.2	24 51.2	23 32.4
24 Tu	12 5 31	3 15 47	10♏18 8	16 14 15	9 18.6	6 56.7	29 36.0	5 20.9	5 46.6	6 41.1	29 57.3	24 51.3	23 30.8
25 W	12 9 28	4 15 14	22 10 3	28 5 53	9 9.8	8 15.0	0♈50.6	6 7.3	5 38.9	6 36.4	29 56.3	24 51.4	23 29.2
26 Th	12 13 24	5 14 39	4♐ 2 12	9♐59 27	9 2.9	9 35.2	2 5.2	6 53.7	5 31.1	6 31.8	29 55.2	24 51.5	23 27.7
27 F	12 17 21	6 14 2	15 58 9	21 58 53	8 58.3	10 57.0	3 19.8	7 40.1	5 23.4	6 27.1	29 54.1	24R 51.5	23 26.1
28 Sa	12 21 17	7 13 24	28 2 11	4♑ 8 43	8D 56.0	12 20.5	4 34.4	8 26.4	5 15.6	6 22.4	29 53.0	24 51.5	23 24.5
29 Su	12 25 14	8 12 44	10♑19 3	16 33 51	8 55.6	13 45.7	5 48.9	9 12.7	5 7.9	6 17.7	29 51.8	24 51.4	23 22.9
30 M	12 29 11	9 12 2	22 53 43	29 19 14	8 56.1	15 12.4	7 3.5	9 59.0	5 0.2	6 13.0	29 50.5	24 51.4	23 21.3
31 Tu	12 33 7	10 11 18	5♒50 56	12♒29 16	8R 56.7	16 40.7	8 18.0	10 45.2	4 52.5	6 8.3	29 49.2	24 51.3	23 19.6

APRIL 1981 LONGITUDE

Day	Sid.Time	☉	0 hr ☽	Noon ☽	True ☊	☿	♀	♂	♃	♄	♅	♆	♇
1 W	12 37 4	11♈10 32	19♒14 36	26♒ 7 9	8♌56.3	18♓10.5	9♈32.5	11♈31.4	4♎44.8	6♎ 3.7	29♏47.9	24♐51.1	23♎18.0
2 Th	12 41 0	12 9 45	3♓ 6 59	10♓13 58	8R 54.0	19 41.9	10 47.0	12 17.5	4R 37.1	5R 59.0	29R 46.5	24R 50.9	23R 16.4
3 F	12 44 57	13 8 55	17 27 48	24 47 55	8 49.2	21 14.7	12 1.5	13 3.6	4 29.5	5 54.4	29 45.1	24 50.7	23 14.7
4 Sa	12 48 53	14 8 4	2♈13 34	9♈43 46	8 41.8	22 49.1	13 16.0	13 49.6	4 21.9	5 49.7	29 43.7	24 50.5	23 13.0
5 Su	12 52 50	15 7 11	17 17 22	24 53 5	8 32.6	24 24.9	14 30.4	14 35.7	4 14.4	5 45.1	29 42.2	24 50.2	23 11.4
6 M	12 56 46	16 6 16	2♉29 32	10♉ 5 21	8 22.5	26 2.2	15 44.9	15 21.6	4 6.9	5 40.5	29 40.6	24 49.9	23 9.7
7 Tu	13 0 43	17 5 18	17 39 13	25 9 53	8 12.7	27 41.0	16 59.3	16 7.6	3 59.5	5 36.0	29 39.0	24 49.6	23 8.0
8 W	13 4 39	18 4 19	2♊36 19	9♊57 38	8 4.4	29 21.3	18 13.7	16 53.5	3 52.1	5 31.4	29 37.4	24 49.2	23 6.3
9 Th	13 8 36	19 3 17	17 13 12	24 22 35	7 58.5	1♈ 3.0	19 28.1	17 39.3	3 44.8	5 26.9	29 35.7	24 48.8	23 4.7
10 F	13 12 33	20 2 13	1♋25 32	8♋22 0	7 55.1	2 46.3	20 42.5	18 25.1	3 37.6	5 22.5	29 34.0	24 48.4	23 3.0
11 Sa	13 16 29	21 1 7	15 12 6	21 56 5	7D 53.8	4 31.0	21 56.8	19 10.9	3 30.5	5 18.0	29 32.3	24 47.9	23 1.3
12 Su	13 20 26	21 59 58	28 34 15	5♌ 7 1	7R 53.8	6 17.3	23 11.1	19 56.6	3 23.4	5 13.6	29 30.5	24 47.4	22 59.6
13 M	13 24 22	22 58 47	11♌34 49	17 58 8	7 53.9	8 5.1	24 25.4	20 42.2	3 16.4	5 9.3	29 28.7	24 46.9	22 57.9
14 Tu	13 28 19	23 57 34	24 17 24	0♍33 6	7 52.9	9 54.4	25 39.7	21 27.8	3 9.5	5 5.0	29 26.8	24 46.3	22 56.2
15 W	13 32 15	24 56 18	6♍45 39	12 55 26	7 49.8	11 45.2	26 54.0	22 13.4	3 2.8	5 0.7	29 25.0	24 45.7	22 54.5
16 Th	13 36 12	25 55 1	19 2 50	25 8 10	7 43.9	13 37.6	28 8.3	22 58.9	2 56.1	4 56.5	29 23.0	24 45.1	22 52.8
17 F	13 40 8	26 53 41	1♎11 42	7♎13 41	7 35.2	15 31.6	29 22.5	23 44.3	2 49.5	4 52.3	29 21.1	24 44.5	22 51.1
18 Sa	13 44 5	27 52 19	13 14 20	19 13 51	7 23.8	17 27.1	0♉36.7	24 29.8	2 43.0	4 48.1	29 19.1	24 43.8	22 49.5
19 Su	13 48 2	28 50 55	25 12 23	1♏10 6	7 10.6	19 24.1	1 50.9	25 15.1	2 36.7	4 44.1	29 17.1	24 43.1	22 47.8
20 M	13 51 58	29 49 29	7♏ 7 9	13 3 41	6 56.4	21 22.7	3 5.1	26 0.4	2 30.4	4 40.0	29 15.0	24 42.4	22 46.1
21 Tu	13 55 55	0♉48 2	18 59 54	24 55 58	6 42.6	23 22.7	4 19.2	26 45.7	2 24.3	4 36.1	29 13.0	24 41.6	22 44.4
22 W	13 59 51	1 46 32	0♐52 7	6♐48 37	6 30.1	25 24.2	5 33.4	27 30.9	2 18.3	4 32.2	29 10.9	24 40.8	22 42.8
23 Th	14 3 48	2 45 1	12 45 46	18 43 55	6 19.9	27 27.1	6 47.5	28 16.1	2 12.4	4 28.3	29 8.7	24 40.0	22 41.1
24 F	14 7 44	3 43 28	24 43 26	0♑44 46	6 12.5	29 31.3	8 1.6	29 1.3	2 6.7	4 24.5	29 6.6	24 39.2	22 39.4
25 Sa	14 11 41	4 41 53	6♑48 24	12 54 50	6 8.0	1♉36.7	9 15.7	29 46.3	2 1.1	4 20.8	29 4.4	24 38.3	22 37.8
26 Su	14 15 37	5 40 17	19 4 39	25 18 24	6 5.9	3 43.2	10 29.8	0♉31.4	1 55.6	4 17.1	29 2.2	24 37.4	22 36.2
27 M	14 19 34	6 38 39	1♒36 41	8♒ 0 6	6 5.3	5 50.7	11 43.9	1 16.4	1 50.3	4 13.5	28 60.0	24 36.5	22 34.5
28 Tu	14 23 31	7 37 0	14 29 13	21 4 34	6 5.3	7 58.9	12 57.9	2 1.3	1 45.1	4 10.0	28 57.7	24 35.5	22 32.9
29 W	14 27 27	8 35 19	27 46 36	4♓35 43	6 4.5	10 7.8	14 12.0	2 46.2	1 40.1	4 6.6	28 55.4	24 34.5	22 31.3
30 Th	14 31 24	9 33 37	11♓32 8	18 35 55	6 1.9	12 17.0	15 26.0	3 31.0	1 35.2	4 3.2	28 53.1	24 33.5	22 29.7

Astro Data Dy Hr Mn	Planet Ingress Dy Hr Mn	Last Aspect Dy Hr Mn	☽ Ingress Dy Hr Mn	Last Aspect Dy Hr Mn	☽ Ingress Dy Hr Mn	☽ Phases & Eclipses Dy Hr Mn	Astro Data
☿ D 2 7:06	♂ ♈ 17 2:40	2 16:56 ♇ □	♒ 3 3:51	1 18:18 ♅ □	♓ 1 18:41	6 10:31 ● 15♓46	1 MARCH 1981
♃☌♄ 4 19:05	☿ ♓ 18 4:33	4 23:14 ♆ ⚹	♓ 5 8:12	3 19:59 ♅ △	♈ 3 20:25	13 1:51 ☽ 22♊24	Julian Day # 29645
♅ R 5 1:47	☉ ♈ 20 17:03	7 1:14 ♆ □	♈ 7 9:48	5 11:55 ♆ △	♉ 5 20:04	20 15:22 ○ 29♍56	Delta T 51.5 sec
☽0N 8 2:42	♅ ♏ 20 23:26	9 1:54 ♆ △	♉ 9 10:22	7 19:11 ♅ ☍	♊ 7 19:47	28 19:34 ☽ 8♑02	SVP 05♓31'35"
♂0N 19 9:29	♀ ♈ 24 7:43	11 3:58 ♂ ⚹	♊ 11 11:42	9 12:44 ♆ ☍	♋ 9 21:34		Obliquity 23°26'25"
☽0S 21 11:54		13 10:03 ♂ □	♋ 13 15:06	12 1:42 ♅ △	♌ 12 2:36	4 20:19 ● 14♈58	⚷ Chiron 14♉06.5
♀0N 26 21:59	☿ ♈ 8 9:11	15 19:10 ♂ △	♌ 15 21:02	14 9:51 ♅ □	♍ 14 10:56	11 11:11 ☽ 21♋29	☽ Mean ☊ 9♌23.3
♆ R 27 6:08	♀ ♉ 17 12:08	17 19:29 ♆ △	♍ 18 5:20	16 20:21 ♅ ⚹	♎ 16 21:38	19 7:59 ○ 29♎10	
♄0N 30 23:42	☉ ♉ 20 4:19	20 15:22 ☉ ☍	♎ 20 15:31	19 7:59 ☉ ☍	♏ 19 9:39	27 10:14 ☽ 7♒04	1 APRIL 1981
	☿ ♉ 24 5:31	22 16:54 ♆ ⚹	♏ 23 3:14	21 20:36 ♅ ☌	♐ 21 22:15		Julian Day # 29676
☽0N 4 12:57	♂ ♉ 25 7:17	25 15:42 ♅ ☌	♐ 25 15:51	24 9:08 ♂ △	♑ 24 10:31		Delta T 51.6 sec
♃0N 9 17:30		27 17:43 ♆ ☌	♑ 28 3:52	26 19:04 ♅ ⚹	♒ 26 20:57		SVP 05♓31'32"
☿0N 11 9:40		30 12:57 ♅ ⚹	♒ 30 13:15	29 2:02 ♅ □	♓ 29 3:56		Obliquity 23°26'25"
☽0S 17 18:14							⚷ Chiron 15♉36.0
							☽ Mean ☊ 7♌44.8

LONGITUDE — MAY 1981

Day	Sid.Time	☉	0 hr ☽	Noon ☽	True ☊	☿	♀	♂	♃	♄	♅	♆	♇
1 F	14 35 20	10♉31 53	25♓46 59	3♈ 4 59	5♌56.8	14♉26.3	16♉40.0	4♉15.8	1♎30.5	3♎59.9	28♏50.8	24♐32.5	22♎28.1
2 Sa	14 39 17	11 30 7	10♈29 22	17 59 19	5R49.1	16 35.5	17 54.0	5 0.6	1R25.9	3R56.6	28R48.5	24R31.5	22R26.5
3 Su	14 43 13	12 28 20	25 33 48	3♉11 36	5 39.4	18 44.3	19 8.0	5 45.3	1 21.4	3 53.5	28 46.1	24 30.4	22 24.9
4 M	14 47 10	13 26 31	10♉51 19	18 31 31	5 28.5	20 52.3	20 22.0	6 29.9	1 17.2	3 50.4	28 43.7	24 29.3	22 23.4
5 Tu	14 51 6	14 24 41	26 10 41	3♊47 24	5 17.8	22 59.3	21 35.9	7 14.5	1 13.1	3 47.4	28 41.3	24 28.2	22 21.8
6 W	14 55 3	15 22 49	11♊20 21	18 48 25	5 8.6	25 5.0	22 49.8	7 59.0	1 9.1	3 44.5	28 38.9	24 27.0	22 20.3
7 Th	14 59 0	16 20 55	26 10 41	3♋26 27	5 1.8	27 9.0	24 3.8	8 43.5	1 5.4	3 41.6	28 36.5	24 25.8	22 18.8
8 F	15 2 56	17 18 59	10♋35 15	17 36 53	4 57.6	29 11.2	25 17.7	9 28.0	1 1.8	3 38.9	28 34.1	24 24.7	22 17.3
9 Sa	15 6 53	18 17 2	24 31 18	1♌18 40	4D 55.8	1♊11.2	26 31.6	10 12.3	0 58.3	3 36.2	28 31.6	24 23.4	22 15.8
10 Su	15 10 49	19 15 2	7♌59 14	14 33 25	4R55.5	3 8.9	27 45.4	10 56.7	0 55.1	3 33.7	28 29.2	24 22.2	22 14.4
11 M	15 14 46	20 13 1	21 1 41	27 24 33	4 55.7	5 4.0	28 59.3	11 40.9	0 52.0	3 31.2	28 26.7	24 21.0	22 12.9
12 Tu	15 18 42	21 10 58	3♍42 34	9♍56 18	4 55.0	6 56.3	0♊13.1	12 25.2	0 49.1	3 28.8	28 24.2	24 19.7	22 11.5
13 W	15 22 39	22 8 52	16 6 18	22 13 6	4 52.7	8 45.7	1 26.9	13 9.3	0 46.3	3 26.5	28 21.7	24 18.4	22 10.1
14 Th	15 26 35	23 6 45	28 17 12	4♎19 5	4 47.8	10 32.1	2 40.7	13 53.4	0 43.8	3 24.2	28 19.3	24 17.1	22 8.7
15 F	15 30 32	24 4 37	10♎19 11	16 17 52	4 40.4	12 15.4	3 54.5	14 37.5	0 41.4	3 22.1	28 16.8	24 15.8	22 7.3
16 Sa	15 34 29	25 2 26	22 15 31	28 12 24	4 30.5	13 55.4	5 8.2	15 21.5	0 39.2	3 20.1	28 14.3	24 14.4	22 5.9
17 Su	15 38 25	26 0 14	4♏ 8 49	10♏ 4 59	4 18.9	15 32.1	6 21.9	16 5.4	0 37.1	3 18.1	28 11.8	24 13.0	22 4.6
18 M	15 42 22	26 58 1	16 1 9	21 57 28	4 6.4	17 5.4	7 35.7	16 49.3	0 35.3	3 16.3	28 9.3	24 11.7	22 3.3
19 Tu	15 46 18	27 55 46	27 54 8	3♐51 20	3 54.2	18 35.4	8 49.4	17 33.1	0 33.6	3 14.5	28 6.8	24 10.3	22 2.0
20 W	15 50 15	28 53 30	9♐49 15	15 48 3	3 43.2	20 1.8	10 3.0	18 16.9	0 32.1	3 12.9	28 4.3	24 8.9	22 0.7
21 Th	15 54 11	29 51 12	21 47 58	27 49 13	3 34.2	21 24.7	11 16.7	19 0.6	0 30.8	3 11.3	28 1.7	24 7.4	21 59.5
22 F	15 58 8	0♊48 54	3♑52 4	9♑56 50	3 27.8	22 44.0	12 30.4	19 44.3	0 29.7	3 9.9	27 59.2	24 6.0	21 58.2
23 Sa	16 2 4	1 46 34	16 3 50	22 13 26	3 24.0	23 59.7	13 44.0	20 27.9	0 28.7	3 8.5	27 56.7	24 4.5	21 57.0
24 Su	16 6 1	2 44 13	28 26 4	4♒42 8	3D 22.5	25 11.8	14 57.6	21 11.5	0 28.0	3 7.2	27 54.3	24 3.1	21 55.9
25 M	16 9 58	3 41 51	11♒ 2 7	17 26 28	3 22.6	26 20.1	16 11.3	21 55.0	0 27.4	3 6.1	27 51.8	24 1.6	21 54.7
26 Tu	16 13 54	4 39 28	23 55 40	0♓30 10	3R23.3	27 24.6	17 24.9	22 38.5	0 27.0	3 5.0	27 49.3	24 0.1	21 53.6
27 W	16 17 51	5 37 4	7♓10 24	13 56 42	3 23.7	28 25.3	18 38.4	23 21.9	0D 26.7	3 4.0	27 46.8	23 58.6	21 52.5
28 Th	16 21 47	6 34 39	20 49 20	27 48 28	3 22.8	29 22.0	19 52.0	24 5.3	0 26.7	3 3.1	27 44.3	23 57.1	21 51.4
29 F	16 25 44	7 32 13	4♈54 6	12♈ 6 4	3 19.9	0♋14.8	21 5.6	24 48.6	0 26.8	3 2.4	27 41.9	23 55.5	21 50.3
30 Sa	16 29 40	8 29 47	19 24 2	26 47 26	3 14.9	1 3.6	22 19.1	25 31.8	0 27.1	3 1.7	27 39.4	23 54.0	21 49.3
31 Su	16 33 37	9 27 19	4♉15 31	11♉47 19	3 8.2	1 48.2	23 32.7	26 15.1	0 27.6	3 1.1	27 37.0	23 52.4	21 48.3

LONGITUDE — JUNE 1981

Day	Sid.Time	☉	0 hr ☽	Noon ☽	True ☊	☿	♀	♂	♃	♄	♅	♆	♇
1 M	16 37 33	10♊24 51	19♉21 43	26♉57 29	3♌ 0.5	2♋28.6	24♊46.2	26♉58.2	0♎28.3	3♎ 0.6	27♏34.5	23♐50.9	21♎47.3
2 Tu	16 41 30	11 22 22	4♊33 18	12♊ 7 49	2R52.8	3 4.7	25 59.7	27 41.3	0 29.2	3R 0.3	27R32.1	23R49.3	21R46.4
3 W	16 45 27	12 19 52	19 39 46	27 7 58	2 46.2	3 36.4	27 13.2	28 24.4	0 30.2	3 0.0	27 29.7	23 47.7	21 45.4
4 Th	16 49 23	13 17 21	4♋31 23	11♋49 11	2 41.3	4 3.8	28 26.7	29 7.3	0 31.4	2 59.8	27 27.3	23 46.2	21 44.6
5 F	16 53 20	14 14 49	19 0 42	26 5 30	2D 38.6	4 26.6	29 40.2	29 50.3	0 32.8	2D 59.8	27 25.0	23 44.6	21 43.7
6 Sa	16 57 16	15 12 16	3♌ 3 20	9♌54 10	2 37.8	4 44.8	0♋53.6	0♊33.2	0 34.4	2 59.8	27 22.6	23 43.0	21 42.9
7 Su	17 1 13	16 9 41	16 38 6	23 15 21	2 38.4	4 58.5	2 7.0	1 16.0	0 36.1	2 60.0	27 20.3	23 41.4	21 42.1
8 M	17 5 9	17 7 6	29 46 18	6♍11 22	2 39.6	5 7.6	3 20.5	1 58.7	0 38.1	3 0.2	27 18.0	23 39.8	21 41.3
9 Tu	17 9 6	18 4 29	12♍31 4	18 45 57	2R40.6	5R12.1	4 33.9	2 41.5	0 40.2	3 0.6	27 15.7	23 38.2	21 40.5
10 W	17 13 2	19 1 51	24 56 34	1♎ 3 30	2 40.6	5 12.0	5 47.2	3 24.1	0 42.4	3 1.0	27 13.4	23 36.6	21 39.8
11 Th	17 16 59	19 59 12	7♎ 7 19	13 8 35	2 39.0	5 7.4	7 0.6	4 6.7	0 44.9	3 1.5	27 11.2	23 34.9	21 39.1
12 F	17 20 56	20 56 32	19 7 50	25 5 34	2 35.6	4 58.5	8 13.9	4 49.2	0 47.5	3 2.2	27 8.9	23 33.3	21 38.5
13 Sa	17 24 52	21 53 51	1♏ 2 15	6♏58 20	2 30.5	4 45.5	9 27.3	5 31.7	0 50.3	3 2.9	27 6.7	23 31.7	21 37.8
14 Su	17 28 49	22 51 10	12 54 13	18 50 15	2 24.2	4 28.4	10 40.6	6 14.1	0 53.2	3 3.8	27 4.6	23 30.1	21 37.2
15 M	17 32 45	23 48 27	24 46 47	0♐44 4	2 17.3	4 7.7	11 53.9	6 56.5	0 56.4	3 4.7	27 2.4	23 28.5	21 36.7
16 Tu	17 36 42	24 45 44	6♐42 24	12 41 59	2 10.4	3 43.6	13 7.1	7 38.8	0 59.7	3 5.8	27 0.3	23 26.8	21 36.1
17 W	17 40 38	25 43 0	18 43 2	24 45 45	2 4.3	3 16.5	14 20.4	8 21.1	1 3.1	3 7.0	26 58.2	23 25.2	21 35.6
18 Th	17 44 35	26 40 16	0♑50 19	6♑56 54	1 59.5	2 46.8	15 33.6	9 3.3	1 6.7	3 8.2	26 56.1	23 23.6	21 35.2
19 F	17 48 31	27 37 31	13 5 40	19 16 48	1 56.3	2 15.1	16 46.8	9 45.5	1 10.5	3 9.6	26 54.1	23 22.0	21 34.7
20 Sa	17 52 28	28 34 45	25 30 31	1♒46 59	1D 54.8	1 41.8	18 0.0	10 27.6	1 14.5	3 11.0	26 52.1	23 20.4	21 34.3
21 Su	17 56 25	29 31 59	8♒ 6 27	14 29 7	1 54.7	1 7.5	19 13.2	11 9.6	1 18.6	3 12.6	26 50.1	23 18.8	21 34.0
22 M	18 0 21	0♋29 13	20 55 16	27 25 7	1 55.8	0 32.9	20 26.4	11 51.6	1 22.8	3 14.2	26 48.1	23 17.2	21 33.6
23 Tu	18 4 18	1 26 27	3♓58 57	10♓37 0	1 57.3	29♊58.4	21 39.5	12 33.6	1 27.2	3 15.9	26 46.2	23 15.6	21 33.3
24 W	18 8 14	2 23 41	17 19 30	24 6 39	1 58.7	29 24.6	22 52.7	13 15.5	1 31.8	3 17.8	26 44.3	23 14.0	21 33.0
25 Th	18 12 11	3 20 54	0♈58 35	7♈55 21	1R59.4	28 52.3	24 5.8	13 57.3	1 36.5	3 19.7	26 42.5	23 12.4	21 32.8
26 F	18 16 7	4 18 8	14 56 59	22 3 19	1 59.0	28 21.9	25 18.9	14 39.1	1 41.4	3 21.7	26 40.7	23 10.8	21 32.6
27 Sa	18 20 4	5 15 21	29 14 9	6♉29 5	1 57.5	27 53.9	26 32.0	15 20.8	1 46.4	3 23.9	26 38.9	23 9.2	21 32.4
28 Su	18 24 0	6 12 35	13♉47 38	21 9 8	1 54.9	27 28.8	27 45.1	16 2.5	1 51.6	3 26.1	26 37.1	23 7.6	21 32.2
29 M	18 27 57	7 9 49	28 32 51	5♊57 54	1 51.8	27 7.1	28 58.1	16 44.2	1 57.0	3 28.4	26 35.4	23 6.1	21 32.1
30 Tu	18 31 54	8 7 3	13♊23 22	20 48 13	1 48.6	26 49.1	0♌11.2	17 25.8	2 2.4	3 30.8	26 33.8	23 4.5	21 32.1

Astro Data (Dy Hr Mn)	Planet Ingress (Dy Hr Mn)	Last Aspect (Dy Hr Mn)	☽ Ingress (Dy Hr Mn)	Last Aspect (Dy Hr Mn)	☽ Ingress (Dy Hr Mn)	☽ Phases & Eclipses (Dy Hr Mn)	Astro Data
☽0N 2 0:05	☿ ♊ 8 9:42	1 5:03 ♅ △	♈ 1 6:57	1 12:56 ♅ ☍	♊ 1 16:48	4 4:19 ● 13♉37	1 MAY 1981
☽0S 15 0:45	♀ ♊ 11 19:45	2 22:20 ♆ △	♉ 3 6:59	3 13:14 ♀ ☌	♋ 3 16:38	10 22:22 ☽ 20♌09	Julian Day # 29706
♃ D 27 18:26	☉ ♊ 21 3:39	5 3:56 ♅ ☍	♊ 5 6:01	5 14:14 ♅ △	♌ 5 18:43	19 0:04 ○ 27♏56	Delta T 51.6 sec
☽0N 29 10:08	☿ ♋ 28 17:04	6 21:09 ♆ ☍	♋ 7 6:18	7 19:26 ♅ □	♍ 8 0:25	26 21:00 ☽ 5♓30	SVP 05♓31'29"
		9 7:02 ♅ △	♌ 9 9:40	10 4:27 ♅ ⚹	♎ 10 9:55		Obliquity 23°26'25"
♄ D 5 2:12	♀ ♋ 5 6:29	11 16:37 ♀ □	♍ 11 16:55	12 8:53 ♆ ⚹	♏ 12 21:54	2 11:32 ● 11♊50	⚷ Chiron 17♉29.8
☿ R 9 11:36	♂ ♊ 5 5:26	14 0:04 ♅ ⚹	♎ 14 3:24	15 4:33 ♅ ☌	♐ 15 10:31	9 11:33 ☽ 18♍32	☽ Mean ☊ 6♌09.5
☽0S 11 8:04	☉ ♋ 21 11:45	16 3:59 ♆ ⚹	♏ 16 15:37	17 15:04 ☉ ☍	♑ 17 22:21	17 15:04 ○ 26♐19	
☽0N 25 17:56	☿ ♊ 22 22:51	19 0:25 ♅ ☌	♐ 19 4:14	20 2:36 ♅ ⚹	♒ 20 8:36	25 4:25 ☽ 3♈31	1 JUNE 1981
	♀ ♌ 29 20:20	21 4:38 ♆ ☌	♑ 21 16:20	22 10:50 ♅ □	♓ 22 16:44		Julian Day # 29737
		23 22:59 ♅ ⚹	♒ 24 3:01	24 20:28 ☿ □	♈ 24 22:18		Delta T 51.7 sec
		26 7:06 ♅ □	♓ 26 11:05	26 21:50 ☿ ⚹	♉ 27 1:16		SVP 05♓31'25"
		28 15:38 ☿ □	♈ 28 15:44	29 0:45 ♀ ⚹	♊ 29 2:21		Obliquity 23°26'24"
		30 7:18 ♆ △	♉ 30 17:10				⚷ Chiron 19♉33.4
							☽ Mean ☊ 4♌31.0

JULY 1981 LONGITUDE

Day	Sid.Time	☉	0 hr ☽	Noon ☽	True ☊	☿	♀	♂	♃	♄	♅	♆	♇
1 W	18 35 50	9♋ 4 16	28♊11 30	5♋32 15	1♌45.8	26♊35.2	1♌24.2	18♊ 7.3	2♎ 8.1	3♎33.3	26♏32.1	23♐ 3.0	21♎32.0
2 Th	18 39 47	10 1 30	12♋49 34	20 2 39	1R 43.9	26R 25.7	2 37.2	18 48.8	2 13.8	3 35.9	26R 30.5	23R 1.4	21D 32.0
3 F	18 43 43	10 58 44	27 10 51	4♌13 36	1D 43.1	26D 20.7	3 50.2	19 30.2	2 19.8	3 38.6	26 29.0	22 59.9	21 32.0
4 Sa	18 47 40	11 55 57	11♌10 32	18 1 25	1 43.3	26 20.5	5 3.2	20 11.6	2 25.8	3 41.4	26 27.5	22 58.4	21 32.1
5 Su	18 51 36	12 53 11	24 46 9	1♍24 46	1 44.2	26 25.3	6 16.1	20 52.9	2 32.0	3 44.3	26 26.0	22 56.9	21 32.2
6 M	18 55 33	13 50 24	7♍57 25	14 24 22	1 45.5	26 35.0	7 29.1	21 34.1	2 38.4	3 47.3	26 24.6	22 55.4	21 32.3
7 Tu	18 59 30	14 47 37	20 45 59	27 2 39	1 46.8	26 49.8	8 42.0	22 15.3	2 44.9	3 50.3	26 23.2	22 53.9	21 32.5
8 W	19 3 26	15 44 49	3♎14 52	9♎23 8	1 47.7	27 9.6	9 54.9	22 56.5	2 51.5	3 53.5	26 21.8	22 52.4	21 32.7
9 Th	19 7 23	16 42 2	15 28 1	21 30 3	1R 48.1	27 34.7	11 7.7	23 37.6	2 58.2	3 56.7	26 20.5	22 51.0	21 32.9
10 F	19 11 19	17 39 14	27 29 49	3♏27 53	1 47.9	28 4.8	12 20.6	24 18.6	3 5.1	4 0.0	26 19.3	22 49.5	21 33.2
11 Sa	19 15 16	18 36 26	9♏24 48	15 21 6	1 47.0	28 40.0	13 33.4	24 59.6	3 12.1	4 3.4	26 18.0	22 48.1	21 33.5
12 Su	19 19 12	19 33 39	21 17 18	27 13 54	1 45.7	29 20.3	14 46.2	25 40.5	3 19.3	4 6.9	26 16.9	22 46.7	21 33.8
13 M	19 23 9	20 30 51	3♐11 21	9♐10 4	1 44.2	0♋ 5.7	15 58.9	26 21.4	3 26.5	4 10.5	26 15.8	22 45.3	21 34.2
14 Tu	19 27 5	21 28 3	15 10 27	21 12 50	1 42.7	0 56.0	17 11.7	27 2.2	3 33.9	4 14.2	26 14.7	22 43.9	21 34.6
15 W	19 31 2	22 25 16	27 17 32	3♑24 49	1 41.4	1 51.2	18 24.4	27 43.0	3 41.5	4 17.9	26 13.6	22 42.6	21 35.0
16 Th	19 34 59	23 22 29	9♑34 54	15 47 59	1 40.5	2 51.3	19 37.0	28 23.7	3 49.1	4 21.7	26 12.7	22 41.2	21 35.5
17 F	19 38 55	24 19 42	22 4 13	28 23 42	1D 40.0	3 56.3	20 49.7	29 4.3	3 56.9	4 25.7	26 11.7	22 39.9	21 36.0
18 Sa	19 42 52	25 16 56	4♒46 33	11♒12 47	1 39.9	5 5.9	22 2.3	29 45.0	4 4.8	4 29.6	26 10.8	22 38.6	21 36.5
19 Su	19 46 48	26 14 10	17 42 29	24 15 37	1 40.1	6 20.2	23 14.9	0♋25.5	4 12.8	4 33.7	26 10.0	22 37.3	21 37.1
20 M	19 50 45	27 11 24	0♓52 11	7♓32 10	1 40.5	7 39.1	24 27.5	1 6.0	4 20.9	4 37.9	26 9.2	22 36.1	21 37.7
21 Tu	19 54 41	28 8 39	14 15 31	21 2 12	1 40.8	9 2.4	25 40.1	1 46.5	4 29.1	4 42.1	26 8.4	22 34.8	21 38.3
22 W	19 58 38	29 5 55	27 52 7	4♈45 11	1 41.1	10 30.1	26 52.6	2 26.9	4 37.5	4 46.4	26 7.7	22 33.6	21 39.0
23 Th	20 2 34	0♌ 3 12	11♈41 17	18 40 18	1 41.3	12 2.0	28 5.1	3 7.2	4 45.9	4 50.8	26 7.1	22 32.4	21 39.7
24 F	20 6 31	1 0 29	25 42 2	2♉46 18	1 41.4	13 38.0	29 17.5	3 47.5	4 54.5	4 55.2	26 6.5	22 31.2	21 40.4
25 Sa	20 10 28	1 57 48	9♉52 51	17 1 23	1 41.4	15 17.9	0♍30.0	4 27.8	5 3.2	4 59.8	26 5.9	22 30.0	21 41.2
26 Su	20 14 24	2 55 7	24 11 34	1♊22 59	1 41.4	17 1.6	1 42.4	5 8.0	5 12.0	5 4.4	26 5.4	22 28.9	21 42.0
27 M	20 18 21	3 52 28	8♊35 12	15 47 44	1 41.6	18 48.6	2 54.8	5 48.2	5 20.9	5 9.1	26 4.9	22 27.7	21 42.8
28 Tu	20 22 17	4 49 49	23 0 2	0♋11 32	1 41.8	20 38.9	4 7.2	6 28.3	5 29.9	5 13.8	26 4.5	22 26.6	21 43.7
29 W	20 26 14	5 47 12	7♋21 40	14 29 51	1 42.1	22 32.2	5 19.5	7 8.3	5 39.0	5 18.6	26 4.2	22 25.6	21 44.6
30 Th	20 30 10	6 44 35	21 35 30	28 38 5	1R 42.4	24 28.0	6 31.8	7 48.3	5 48.2	5 23.5	26 3.9	22 24.5	21 45.5
31 F	20 34 7	7 41 59	5♌37 5	12♌32 5	1 42.5	26 26.2	7 44.1	8 28.3	5 57.5	5 28.5	26 3.6	22 23.5	21 46.5

AUGUST 1981 LONGITUDE

Day	Sid.Time	☉	0 hr ☽	Noon ☽	True ☊	☿	♀	♂	♃	♄	♅	♆	♇
1 Sa	20 38 3	8♌39 24	19♌22 41	26♌ 8 37	1♌42.2	28♋26.3	8♍56.4	9♋ 8.2	6♎ 6.9	5♎33.5	26♏ 3.4	22♐22.5	21♎47.5
2 Su	20 42 0	9 36 50	2♍49 40	9♍25 45	1R 41.6	0♌28.0	10 8.6	9 48.0	6 16.4	5 38.7	26R 3.3	22R 21.5	21 48.5
3 M	20 45 57	10 34 17	15 56 49	22 22 58	1 40.6	2 30.9	11 20.8	10 27.8	6 26.1	5 43.8	26 3.2	22 20.6	21 49.5
4 Tu	20 49 53	11 31 44	28 44 22	5♎ 1 15	1 39.3	4 34.8	12 32.9	11 7.5	6 35.8	5 49.1	26D 3.1	22 19.6	21 50.6
5 W	20 53 50	12 29 12	11♎13 56	17 22 47	1 38.0	6 39.2	13 45.1	11 47.2	6 45.6	5 54.4	26 3.1	22 18.7	21 51.7
6 Th	20 57 46	13 26 41	23 28 16	29 30 50	1 36.9	8 44.0	14 57.1	12 26.8	6 55.4	5 59.7	26 3.2	22 17.9	21 52.9
7 F	21 1 43	14 24 10	5♏31 2	11♏29 24	1D 36.2	10 48.7	16 9.2	13 6.4	7 5.4	6 5.2	26 3.3	22 17.0	21 54.1
8 Sa	21 5 39	15 21 41	17 26 30	23 22 55	1 36.0	12 53.1	17 21.2	13 45.9	7 15.5	6 10.7	26 3.4	22 16.2	21 55.3
9 Su	21 9 36	16 19 12	29 19 14	5♐16 3	1 36.4	14 57.1	18 33.2	14 25.4	7 25.6	6 16.2	26 3.7	22 15.4	21 56.5
10 M	21 13 32	17 16 44	11♐13 55	17 13 24	1 37.4	17 0.4	19 45.1	15 4.8	7 35.9	6 21.8	26 3.9	22 14.6	21 57.8
11 Tu	21 17 29	18 14 17	23 15 2	29 19 17	1 38.7	19 2.8	20 57.0	15 44.2	7 46.2	6 27.5	26 4.2	22 13.9	21 59.1
12 W	21 21 26	19 11 51	5♑26 38	11♑37 28	1 40.1	21 4.3	22 8.8	16 23.5	7 56.6	6 33.2	26 4.6	22 13.2	22 0.4
13 Th	21 25 22	20 9 26	17 52 10	24 10 59	1 41.3	23 4.7	23 20.7	17 2.7	8 7.1	6 39.0	26 5.0	22 12.5	22 1.8
14 F	21 29 19	21 7 2	0♒34 10	7♒ 1 51	1R 41.7	25 3.9	24 32.4	17 41.9	8 17.7	6 44.9	26 5.5	22 11.9	22 3.1
15 Sa	21 33 15	22 4 39	13 34 6	20 10 54	1 41.3	27 1.8	25 44.1	18 21.1	8 28.3	6 50.8	26 6.0	22 11.2	22 4.6
16 Su	21 37 12	23 2 17	26 52 8	3♓37 40	1 39.9	28 58.4	26 55.8	19 0.2	8 39.1	6 56.7	26 6.6	22 10.6	22 6.0
17 M	21 41 8	23 59 56	10♓27 12	17 20 27	1 37.5	0♍53.7	28 7.4	19 39.2	8 49.9	7 2.7	26 7.2	22 10.1	22 7.5
18 Tu	21 45 5	24 57 37	24 17 1	1♈16 29	1 34.4	2 47.6	29 19.0	20 18.2	9 0.7	7 8.8	26 7.9	22 9.5	22 9.0
19 W	21 49 1	25 55 19	8♈18 25	15 22 20	1 31.1	4 40.1	0♎30.6	20 57.2	9 11.7	7 14.9	26 8.6	22 9.0	22 10.5
20 Th	21 52 58	26 53 3	22 27 45	29 34 15	1 27.9	6 31.2	1 42.1	21 36.1	9 22.7	7 21.0	26 9.4	22 8.6	22 12.0
21 F	21 56 54	27 50 49	6♉41 22	13♉48 43	1 25.5	8 20.9	2 53.5	22 14.9	9 33.8	7 27.2	26 10.2	22 8.1	22 13.6
22 Sa	22 0 51	28 48 36	20 55 56	28 2 41	1D 24.2	10 9.3	4 5.0	22 53.7	9 44.9	7 33.5	26 11.1	22 7.7	22 15.2
23 Su	22 4 48	29 46 25	5♊ 8 41	12♊13 41	1 24.1	11 56.2	5 16.3	23 32.5	9 56.2	7 39.8	26 12.0	22 7.3	22 16.8
24 M	22 8 44	0♍44 16	19 17 26	26 19 45	1 25.0	13 41.8	6 27.7	24 11.2	10 7.5	7 46.2	26 13.0	22 7.0	22 18.5
25 Tu	22 12 41	1 42 9	3♋20 26	10♋19 16	1 26.4	15 26.0	7 38.9	24 49.8	10 18.8	7 52.6	26 14.1	22 6.6	22 20.2
26 W	22 16 37	2 40 3	17 16 6	24 10 41	1 27.8	17 8.9	8 50.2	25 28.4	10 30.3	7 59.0	26 15.1	22 6.4	22 21.9
27 Th	22 20 34	3 37 59	1♌ 2 52	7♌52 24	1R 28.4	18 50.5	10 1.4	26 6.9	10 41.8	8 5.5	26 16.3	22 6.1	22 23.6
28 F	22 24 30	4 35 57	14 39 5	21 22 42	1 27.7	20 30.7	11 12.5	26 45.4	10 53.3	8 12.0	26 17.5	22 5.9	22 25.3
29 Sa	22 28 27	5 33 56	28 3 3	4♍39 57	1 25.4	22 9.6	12 23.6	27 23.9	11 4.9	8 18.6	26 18.7	22 5.7	22 27.1
30 Su	22 32 23	6 31 57	11♍13 14	17 42 47	1 21.3	23 47.3	13 34.7	28 2.2	11 16.6	8 25.2	26 20.0	22 5.5	22 28.9
31 M	22 36 20	7 30 0	24 8 31	0♎30 25	1 15.9	25 23.6	14 45.7	28 40.6	11 28.3	8 31.8	26 21.3	22 5.4	22 30.7

Astro Data	Planet Ingress	Last Aspect	☽ Ingress	Last Aspect	☽ Ingress	☽ Phases & Eclipses	Astro Data
Dy Hr Mn	Dy Hr Mn	Dy Hr Mn	Dy Hr Mn	Dy Hr Mn	Dy Hr Mn	Dy Hr Mn	1 JULY 1981
♇ D 1 16:12	☿ ♋ 12 21:08	30 21:25 ☿ ☌	♋ 1 2:57	1 11:51 ♅ □	♍ 1 18:54	1 19:03 ● 9♋50	Julian Day # 29767
☿ D 3 12:58	♂ ♋ 18 8:54	2 22:49 ♅ △	♌ 3 4:47	3 18:55 ♅ ⚹	♎ 4 2:24	9 2:39 ☽ 16♎48	Delta T 51.8 sec
☽0S 8 16:10	☉ ♌ 22 22:40	5 3:00 ☿ ⚹	♍ 5 9:26	5 21:41 ♆ ⚹	♏ 6 12:58	17 4:39 ○ 24♑31	SVP 05♓31'20"
♃0S 8 15:37	♀ ♍ 24 14:04	7 11:53 ☿ □	♎ 7 17:42	8 17:25 ♅ ☌	♐ 9 1:22	17 4:47 ☍ P 0.548	Obliquity 23°26'24"
☽0N 22 23:46		10 1:14 ☿ △	♏ 10 5:02	10 21:59 ♆ ☌	♑ 11 13:20	24 9:40 ☽ 1♉24	⚷ Chiron 21♉17.8
♃☌♄ 24 4:16	☿ ♌ 1 18:30	12 10:04 ♅ ☌	♐ 12 17:35	13 15:36 ♅ ⚹	♒ 13 22:56	31 3:52 ● 7♌51	☽ Mean ☊ 2♌55.7
♄0S 29 6:47	☿ ♍ 16 12:47	15 0:53 ♂ ☍	♑ 15 5:19	16 4:23 ☿ ☍	♓ 16 5:34	31 3:45:44 ☌ T 2'03"	
	♀ ♎ 18 13:44	17 7:50 ♅ ⚹	♒ 17 15:02	18 9:27 ♀ ☍	♈ 18 9:49		1 AUGUST 1981
♅ D 4 10:50	☉ ♍ 23 5:38	19 15:27 ♅ □	♓ 19 22:26	20 8:01 ☉ △	♉ 20 12:43	7 19:26 ☽ 15♏11	Julian Day # 29798
☽0S 5 0:34		22 2:19 ☉ △	♈ 22 3:43	22 14:16 ☉ □	♊ 22 15:18	15 16:37 ○ 22♒45	Delta T 51.8 sec
♆⚹♇ 18 6:55		24 6:40 ♀ △	♉ 24 7:18	24 5:09 ♇ △	♋ 24 18:17	22 14:16 ☽ 29♉23	SVP 05♓31'14"
☽0N 19 5:18		26 3:10 ♅ ☍	♊ 26 9:42	26 15:38 ♅ △	♌ 26 22:10	29 14:43 ● 6♍10	Obliquity 23°26'25"
♀0S 19 23:26		27 23:04 ♆ ☍	♋ 28 11:41	28 20:51 ♅ □	♍ 29 3:32		⚷ Chiron 22♉30.2
♃∠♅ 30 7:47		30 7:36 ♅ △	♌ 30 14:20	31 8:59 ♂ ⚹	♎ 31 11:02		☽ Mean ☊ 1♌17.2

LONGITUDE SEPTEMBER 1981

Day	Sid.Time	☉	0 hr ☽	Noon ☽	True ☊	☿	♀	♂	♃	♄	♅	♆	♇
1 Tu	22 40 17	8♍28 4	6♎48 31	13♎ 2 54	1♌ 9.5	26♍58.7	15♎56.6	29♋18.8	11♎40.1	8♎38.5	26♏22.7	22♐ 5.3	22♎32.6
2 W	22 44 13	9 26 9	19 13 45	25 21 17	1R 2.9	28 32.6	17 7.5	29 57.0	11 52.0	8 45.3	26 24.1	22R 5.2	22 34.5
3 Th	22 48 10	10 24 16	1♏25 47	7♏27 38	0 56.7	0♎ 5.1	18 18.4	0♌35.2	12 3.9	8 52.0	26 25.6	22D 5.2	22 36.3
4 F	22 52 6	11 22 25	13 27 13	19 25 0	0 51.8	1 36.4	19 29.2	1 13.3	12 15.8	8 58.8	26 27.1	22 5.2	22 38.3
5 Sa	22 56 3	12 20 35	25 21 30	1♐17 16	0 48.4	3 6.5	20 39.9	1 51.3	12 27.8	9 5.7	26 28.7	22 5.2	22 40.2
6 Su	22 59 59	13 18 47	7♐12 54	13 8 59	0D 46.7	4 35.2	21 50.5	2 29.3	12 39.9	9 12.5	26 30.4	22 5.3	22 42.1
7 M	23 3 56	14 17 0	19 6 9	25 5 2	0 46.6	6 2.7	23 1.2	3 7.3	12 52.0	9 19.4	26 32.0	22 5.4	22 44.1
8 Tu	23 7 52	15 15 15	1♑ 6 16	7♑10 30	0 47.7	7 29.0	24 11.7	3 45.1	13 4.1	9 26.3	26 33.7	22 5.5	22 46.1
9 W	23 11 49	16 13 31	13 18 18	19 30 15	0 49.1	8 53.9	25 22.2	4 23.0	13 16.3	9 33.3	26 35.5	22 5.7	22 48.1
10 Th	23 15 46	17 11 48	25 46 52	2♒ 8 37	0R 50.1	10 17.5	26 32.6	5 0.7	13 28.6	9 40.3	26 37.3	22 5.9	22 50.1
11 F	23 19 42	18 10 8	8♒35 51	15 8 51	0 49.9	11 39.7	27 42.9	5 38.4	13 40.8	9 47.3	26 39.2	22 6.1	22 52.2
12 Sa	23 23 39	19 8 28	21 47 47	28 32 43	0 47.9	13 0.5	28 53.2	6 16.1	13 53.2	9 54.3	26 41.1	22 6.4	22 54.3
13 Su	23 27 35	20 6 51	5♓23 30	12♓19 56	0 43.8	14 19.9	0♏ 3.4	6 53.7	14 5.5	10 1.4	26 43.0	22 6.7	22 56.3
14 M	23 31 32	21 5 15	19 21 36	26 27 58	0 37.7	15 37.9	1 13.5	7 31.2	14 17.9	10 8.5	26 45.0	22 7.0	22 58.4
15 Tu	23 35 28	22 3 41	3♈38 24	10♈52 6	0 30.0	16 54.3	2 23.6	8 8.7	14 30.4	10 15.6	26 47.1	22 7.4	23 0.6
16 W	23 39 25	23 2 9	18 8 16	25 25 59	0 21.7	18 9.1	3 33.5	8 46.1	14 42.8	10 22.7	26 49.2	22 7.8	23 2.7
17 Th	23 43 21	24 0 39	2♉44 23	10♉ 2 37	0 13.8	19 22.3	4 43.4	9 23.5	14 55.4	10 29.9	26 51.3	22 8.2	23 4.8
18 F	23 47 18	24 59 12	17 19 53	24 35 29	0 7.2	20 33.7	5 53.3	10 0.8	15 7.9	10 37.1	26 53.5	22 8.7	23 7.0
19 Sa	23 51 15	25 57 46	1♊48 50	8♊59 27	0 2.7	21 43.3	7 3.0	10 38.1	15 20.5	10 44.3	26 55.7	22 9.2	23 9.2
20 Su	23 55 11	26 56 23	16 6 59	23 11 12	0D 0.3	22 51.0	8 12.7	11 15.3	15 33.1	10 51.5	26 57.9	22 9.7	23 11.4
21 M	23 59 8	27 55 2	0♋11 57	7♋ 9 13	29♋59.8	23 56.6	9 22.3	11 52.4	15 45.8	10 58.7	27 0.2	22 10.3	23 13.6
22 Tu	0 3 4	28 53 43	14 2 59	20 53 21	0♌ 0.4	25 0.0	10 31.8	12 29.5	15 58.4	11 6.0	27 2.6	22 10.8	23 15.8
23 W	0 7 1	29 52 27	27 40 23	4♌24 13	0R 1.0	26 1.1	11 41.3	13 6.6	16 11.1	11 13.3	27 4.9	22 11.5	23 18.1
24 Th	0 10 57	0♎51 12	11♌ 4 58	17 42 43	0 0.5	26 59.7	12 50.7	13 43.6	16 23.9	11 20.6	27 7.4	22 12.1	23 20.3
25 F	0 14 54	1 50 0	24 17 35	0♍49 35	29♋57.9	27 55.5	13 59.9	14 20.5	16 36.7	11 27.8	27 9.8	22 12.8	23 22.6
26 Sa	0 18 50	2 48 50	7♍18 47	13 45 11	29 52.7	28 48.5	15 9.2	14 57.3	16 49.4	11 35.2	27 12.3	22 13.5	23 24.9
27 Su	0 22 47	3 47 42	20 8 48	26 29 36	29 44.8	29 38.2	16 18.3	15 34.1	17 2.3	11 42.5	27 14.9	22 14.3	23 27.1
28 M	0 26 44	4 46 36	2♎47 36	9♎ 2 46	29 34.5	0♏24.6	17 27.3	16 10.9	17 15.1	11 49.8	27 17.4	22 15.1	23 29.4
29 Tu	0 30 40	5 45 33	15 15 7	21 24 43	29 22.5	1 7.2	18 36.2	16 47.5	17 28.0	11 57.1	27 20.0	22 15.9	23 31.7
30 W	0 34 37	6 44 31	27 31 38	3♏35 59	29 10.0	1 45.9	19 45.1	17 24.1	17 40.8	12 4.5	27 22.7	22 16.7	23 34.1

LONGITUDE OCTOBER 1981

Day	Sid.Time	☉	0 hr ☽	Noon ☽	True ☊	☿	♀	♂	♃	♄	♅	♆	♇
1 Th	0 38 33	7♎43 31	9♏37 57	15♏37 45	28♋58.1	2♏20.1	20♏53.8	18♌ 0.7	17♎53.7	12♎11.9	27♏25.4	22♐17.6	23♎36.4
2 F	0 42 30	8 42 33	21 35 42	27 32 6	28R 47.7	2 49.5	22 2.5	18 37.1	18 6.6	12 19.2	27 28.1	22 18.5	23 38.7
3 Sa	0 46 26	9 41 37	3♐27 23	9♐22 0	28 39.6	3 13.8	23 11.0	19 13.5	18 19.6	12 26.6	27 30.9	22 19.4	23 41.1
4 Su	0 50 23	10 40 43	15 16 26	21 11 16	28 34.2	3 32.5	24 19.4	19 49.9	18 32.5	12 33.9	27 33.7	22 20.4	23 43.4
5 M	0 54 19	11 39 50	27 7 4	3♑ 4 30	28 31.2	3 45.2	25 27.7	20 26.2	18 45.5	12 41.3	27 36.5	22 21.4	23 45.8
6 Tu	0 58 16	12 39 0	9♑ 4 11	15 6 49	28D 30.3	3R 51.3	26 35.9	21 2.4	18 58.5	12 48.7	27 39.4	22 22.5	23 48.1
7 W	1 2 12	13 38 11	21 13 5	27 23 39	28R 30.3	3 50.4	27 44.0	21 38.5	19 11.4	12 56.1	27 42.3	22 23.5	23 50.5
8 Th	1 6 9	14 37 24	3♒39 9	10♒ 0 13	28 30.3	3 42.2	28 52.0	22 14.6	19 24.4	13 3.4	27 45.2	22 24.6	23 52.9
9 F	1 10 6	15 36 38	16 27 23	23 1 8	28 29.2	3 26.2	29 59.8	22 50.6	19 37.4	13 10.8	27 48.1	22 25.7	23 55.3
10 Sa	1 14 2	16 35 55	29 41 46	6♓29 33	28 25.9	3 2.2	1♐ 7.5	23 26.5	19 50.5	13 18.2	27 51.1	22 26.9	23 57.7
11 Su	1 17 59	17 35 13	13♓24 29	20 26 28	28 20.1	2 29.9	2 15.1	24 2.4	20 3.5	13 25.5	27 54.2	22 28.1	24 0.0
12 M	1 21 55	18 34 33	27 35 10	4♈50 0	28 11.6	1 49.5	3 22.5	24 38.2	20 16.5	13 32.9	27 57.2	22 29.3	24 2.4
13 Tu	1 25 52	19 33 55	12♈10 15	19 34 59	28 1.1	1 1.1	4 29.8	25 13.9	20 29.5	13 40.2	28 0.3	22 30.5	24 4.8
14 W	1 29 48	20 33 19	27 3 6	4♉33 25	27 49.6	0 5.3	5 36.9	25 49.5	20 42.5	13 47.6	28 3.4	22 31.8	24 7.2
15 Th	1 33 45	21 32 45	12♉ 4 41	19 35 40	27 38.4	29♎ 2.9	6 43.9	26 25.1	20 55.6	13 54.9	28 6.6	22 33.1	24 9.6
16 F	1 37 41	22 32 13	27 5 9	4♊32 5	27 28.9	27 55.2	7 50.7	27 0.7	21 8.6	14 2.2	28 9.7	22 34.4	24 12.0
17 Sa	1 41 38	23 31 44	11♊55 33	19 14 47	27 21.9	26 43.5	8 57.4	27 36.1	21 21.6	14 9.5	28 12.9	22 35.7	24 14.4
18 Su	1 45 35	24 31 16	26 29 14	3♋38 31	27 17.6	25 29.8	10 3.9	28 11.5	21 34.6	14 16.8	28 16.1	22 37.1	24 16.8
19 M	1 49 31	25 30 52	10♋42 27	17 40 58	27 15.7	24 16.1	11 10.2	28 46.8	21 47.7	14 24.1	28 19.4	22 38.5	24 19.3
20 Tu	1 53 28	26 30 29	24 34 8	1♌22 9	27 15.4	23 4.5	12 16.4	29 22.0	22 0.7	14 31.4	28 22.7	22 40.0	24 21.7
21 W	1 57 24	27 30 9	8♌ 5 16	14 43 45	27 15.2	21 57.3	13 22.4	29 57.2	22 13.7	14 38.7	28 26.0	22 41.4	24 24.1
22 Th	2 1 21	28 29 51	21 17 58	27 48 14	27 14.0	20 56.4	14 28.2	0♍32.2	22 26.7	14 45.9	28 29.3	22 42.9	24 26.5
23 F	2 5 17	29 29 35	4♍14 51	10♍38 10	27 10.7	20 3.6	15 33.8	1 7.2	22 39.7	14 53.1	28 32.6	22 44.4	24 28.9
24 Sa	2 9 14	0♏29 21	16 58 25	23 15 51	27 4.4	19 20.4	16 39.3	1 42.2	22 52.7	15 0.3	28 36.0	22 45.9	24 31.3
25 Su	2 13 10	1 29 10	29 30 42	5♎43 6	26 55.1	18 47.7	17 44.5	2 17.0	23 5.7	15 7.5	28 39.4	22 47.5	24 33.7
26 M	2 17 7	2 29 1	11♎53 14	18 1 12	26 43.1	18 26.3	18 49.6	2 51.7	23 18.7	15 14.7	28 42.8	22 49.1	24 36.0
27 Tu	2 21 4	3 28 53	24 7 7	0♏11 5	26 29.2	18D 16.2	19 54.4	3 26.4	23 31.6	15 21.8	28 46.2	22 50.7	24 38.4
28 W	2 25 0	4 28 48	6♏13 12	12 13 34	26 14.6	18 17.5	20 59.0	4 1.0	23 44.5	15 29.0	28 49.7	22 52.3	24 40.8
29 Th	2 28 57	5 28 45	18 12 20	24 9 40	26 0.6	18 29.8	22 3.4	4 35.5	23 57.5	15 36.1	28 53.2	22 54.0	24 43.2
30 F	2 32 53	6 28 43	0♐ 5 44	6♐ 0 48	25 48.2	18 52.5	23 7.6	5 9.9	24 10.4	15 43.1	28 56.7	22 55.7	24 45.6
31 Sa	2 36 50	7 28 43	11 55 8	17 49 4	25 38.3	19 24.8	24 11.5	5 44.2	24 23.3	15 50.2	29 0.2	22 57.4	24 47.9

Astro Data	Planet Ingress	Last Aspect	☽ Ingress	Last Aspect	☽ Ingress	☽ Phases & Eclipses	Astro Data
Dy Hr Mn	Dy Hr Mn	Dy Hr Mn	Dy Hr Mn	Dy Hr Mn	Dy Hr Mn	Dy Hr Mn	1 SEPTEMBER 1981
☽0S 1 8:39	☿ ♎ 2 22:40	2 6:33 ♇ ☌	♏ 2 21:10	2 11:55 ♅ ☌	♐ 2 16:59	6 13:26 ☽ 13♐51	Julian Day # 29829
☿0S 2 22:03	♂ ♌ 2 1:52	5 2:16 ♅ ☌	♐ 5 9:24	4 17:12 ♇ ✶	♑ 5 5:49	14 3:09 ○ 21♓13	Delta T 51.9 sec
♆ D 3 11:07	♀ ♏ 12 22:51	7 8:43 ♀ ✶	♑ 7 21:48	7 13:55 ♀ ✶	♒ 7 17:01	20 19:47 ☽ 27♊45	SVP 05♓31'11"
☽0N 15 12:33	☊ ♋ 20 7:21	10 1:36 ♅ ✶	♒ 10 7:59	9 20:42 ♅ □	♓ 10 0:32	28 4:07 ● 4♎57	Obliquity 23°26'26"
☽0S 28 16:01	☊ ♌ 21 10:22	12 13:47 ♀ △	♓ 12 14:34	12 0:37 ♅ △	♈ 12 4:01		⚷ Chiron 22♉51.2R
	☉ ♎ 23 3:05	14 12:30 ♅ △	♈ 14 17:55	14 4:33 ☿ ☍	♉ 14 4:43	6 7:45 ☽ 12♑58	☽ Mean ☊ 29♋38.7
♄∠♅ 3 22:29	☊ ♋ 24 6:29	16 8:06 ♇ ☍	♉ 16 19:30	16 1:44 ♅ ☍	♊ 16 4:41	13 12:49 ○ 20♈06	
☿ R 6 9:15	☿ ♏ 27 11:02	18 15:51 ♅ ☍	♊ 18 20:59	18 2:58 ♂ ✶	♋ 18 5:52	20 3:40 ☽ 26♋40	1 OCTOBER 1981
☽0N 12 22:20		20 19:47 ☉ □	♋ 20 23:39	20 6:44 ♅ △	♌ 20 9:34	27 20:13 ● 4♏19	Julian Day # 29859
♃✶♆ 23 9:50	♀ ♐ 9 0:04	22 22:57 ♅ △	♌ 23 4:08	22 14:24 ☉ ✶	♍ 22 16:05		Delta T 52.0 sec
☽0S 25 22:40	☿ ♎ 14 2:09	25 7:09 ☿ ✶	♍ 25 10:29	24 22:21 ♅ ✶	♎ 25 0:56		SVP 05♓31'09"
☿ D 27 9:10	♂ ♍ 21 1:56	27 13:29 ♅ ✶	♎ 27 18:40	27 1:02 ♇ ☌	♏ 27 11:38		Obliquity 23°26'26"
	☉ ♏ 23 12:13	29 16:12 ♇ ☌	♏ 30 4:53	29 21:39 ♅ ☌	♐ 29 23:48		⚷ Chiron 22♉17.6R
							☽ Mean ☊ 28♋03.3

NOVEMBER 1981 — LONGITUDE

Day	Sid.Time	☉	0 hr ☽	Noon ☽	True ☊	☿	♀	♂	♃	♄	♅	♆	♇
1 Su	2 40 46	8♏28 46	23♐43 0	29♐37 22	25♋31.3	20♎ 5.9	25♐15.2	6♍18.4	24♎36.1	15♎57.2	29♏ 3.7	22♐59.1	24♎50.3
2 M	2 44 43	9 28 49	5♑32 38	11♑29 22	25R 27.2	20 54.9	26 18.6	6 52.6	24 49.0	16 4.2	29 7.2	23 0.8	24 52.6
3 Tu	2 48 39	10 28 55	17 28 7	23 29 31	25D 25.5	21 51.1	27 21.7	7 26.6	25 1.8	16 11.1	29 10.8	23 2.6	24 55.0
4 W	2 52 36	11 29 2	29 34 11	5♒42 49	25 25.3	22 53.5	28 24.6	8 0.6	25 14.6	16 18.1	29 14.4	23 4.4	24 57.3
5 Th	2 56 33	12 29 11	11♒56 4	18 14 35	25R 25.6	24 1.3	29 27.1	8 34.4	25 27.4	16 25.0	29 18.0	23 6.2	24 59.7
6 F	3 0 29	13 29 21	24 39 0	1♓ 9 53	25 25.0	25 13.8	0♑29.4	9 8.2	25 40.1	16 31.8	29 21.6	23 8.1	25 2.0
7 Sa	3 4 26	14 29 32	7♓47 45	14 32 59	25 22.8	26 30.4	1 31.3	9 41.8	25 52.8	16 38.6	29 25.2	23 9.9	25 4.3
8 Su	3 8 22	15 29 45	21 25 49	28 26 20	25 18.1	27 50.3	2 32.9	10 15.4	26 5.5	16 45.4	29 28.8	23 11.8	25 6.6
9 M	3 12 19	16 30 0	5♈34 25	12♈49 43	25 11.0	29 13.2	3 34.1	10 48.9	26 18.1	16 52.2	29 32.4	23 13.7	25 8.9
10 Tu	3 16 15	17 30 16	20 11 40	27 39 27	25 1.8	0♏38.5	4 35.0	11 22.2	26 30.7	16 58.9	29 36.1	23 15.6	25 11.1
11 W	3 20 12	18 30 34	5♉12 2	12♉48 11	24 51.6	2 5.9	5 35.5	11 55.5	26 43.3	17 5.6	29 39.7	23 17.5	25 13.4
12 Th	3 24 8	19 30 53	20 26 34	28 5 45	24 41.5	3 34.9	6 35.7	12 28.6	26 55.9	17 12.2	29 43.4	23 19.4	25 15.6
13 F	3 28 5	20 31 14	5♊44 19	13♊20 51	24 32.8	5 5.3	7 35.4	13 1.7	27 8.4	17 18.8	29 47.1	23 21.4	25 17.9
14 Sa	3 32 2	21 31 37	20 54 8	28 23 4	24 26.4	6 36.8	8 34.7	13 34.6	27 20.8	17 25.3	29 50.8	23 23.4	25 20.1
15 Su	3 35 58	22 32 1	5♋46 47	13♋ 4 36	24 22.6	8 9.2	9 33.6	14 7.5	27 33.3	17 31.8	29 54.4	23 25.4	25 22.3
16 M	3 39 55	23 32 28	20 16 4	27 20 57	24D 21.2	9 42.3	10 32.1	14 40.2	27 45.7	17 38.3	29 58.1	23 27.4	25 24.5
17 Tu	3 43 51	24 32 56	4♌19 11	11♌10 52	24 21.4	11 16.0	11 30.1	15 12.9	27 58.0	17 44.7	0♐ 1.8	23 29.4	25 26.7
18 W	3 47 48	25 33 26	17 56 12	24 35 31	24R 22.1	12 50.1	12 27.6	15 45.4	28 10.3	17 51.1	0 5.5	23 31.5	25 28.8
19 Th	3 51 44	26 33 58	1♍ 9 13	7♍37 42	24 22.3	14 24.5	13 24.6	16 17.8	28 22.6	17 57.4	0 9.3	23 33.5	25 31.0
20 F	3 55 41	27 34 32	14 1 27	20 20 54	24 20.8	15 59.1	14 21.2	16 50.1	28 34.8	18 3.7	0 13.0	23 35.6	25 33.1
21 Sa	3 59 37	28 35 8	26 36 31	2♎48 45	24 17.0	17 33.8	15 17.2	17 22.2	28 47.0	18 9.9	0 16.7	23 37.7	25 35.2
22 Su	4 3 34	29 35 45	8♎57 58	15 4 35	24 10.8	19 8.7	16 12.6	17 54.3	28 59.1	18 16.1	0 20.4	23 39.8	25 37.3
23 M	4 7 31	0♐36 24	21 8 54	27 11 15	24 2.3	20 43.6	17 7.5	18 26.2	29 11.1	18 22.2	0 24.1	23 41.9	25 39.4
24 Tu	4 11 27	1 37 4	3♏11 54	9♏11 6	23 52.4	22 18.5	18 1.8	18 57.9	29 23.2	18 28.2	0 27.8	23 44.0	25 41.4
25 W	4 15 24	2 37 46	15 9 3	21 5 58	23 41.8	23 53.4	18 55.5	19 29.6	29 35.1	18 34.2	0 31.5	23 46.2	25 43.5
26 Th	4 19 20	3 38 29	27 2 2	2♐57 27	23 31.5	25 28.2	19 48.5	20 1.1	29 47.0	18 40.2	0 35.2	23 48.3	25 45.5
27 F	4 23 17	4 39 14	8♐52 23	14 47 4	23 22.5	27 3.0	20 40.9	20 32.5	29 58.9	18 46.1	0 39.0	23 50.5	25 47.5
28 Sa	4 27 13	5 40 0	20 41 41	26 36 29	23 15.5	28 37.7	21 32.6	21 3.8	0♏10.6	18 51.9	0 42.7	23 52.7	25 49.5
29 Su	4 31 10	6 40 48	2♑31 45	8♑27 47	23 10.7	0♐12.4	22 23.5	21 34.9	0 22.4	18 57.6	0 46.4	23 54.8	25 51.4
30 M	4 35 6	7 41 36	14 24 55	20 23 33	23D 8.3	1 46.9	23 13.7	22 5.8	0 34.0	19 3.4	0 50.1	23 57.0	25 53.4

DECEMBER 1981 — LONGITUDE

Day	Sid.Time	☉	0 hr ☽	Noon ☽	True ☊	☿	♀	♂	♃	♄	♅	♆	♇
1 Tu	4 39 3	8♐42 26	26♑24 6	2♒27 1	23♋ 7.9	3♐21.4	24♑ 3.1	22♍36.6	0♏45.6	19♎ 9.0	0♐53.8	23♐59.2	25♎55.3
2 W	4 43 0	9 43 16	8♒32 49	14 42 0	23 8.9	4 55.8	24 51.7	23 7.3	0 57.2	19 14.6	0 57.5	24 1.4	25 57.2
3 Th	4 46 56	10 44 8	20 55 7	27 12 44	23 10.4	6 30.2	25 39.4	23 37.8	1 8.6	19 20.1	1 1.1	24 3.6	25 59.0
4 F	4 50 53	11 45 0	3♓35 24	10♓ 3 39	23R 11.7	8 4.5	26 26.2	24 8.2	1 20.0	19 25.5	1 4.8	24 5.9	26 0.9
5 Sa	4 54 49	12 45 53	16 37 58	23 18 47	23 11.9	9 38.7	27 12.1	24 38.4	1 31.3	19 30.9	1 8.5	24 8.1	26 2.7
6 Su	4 58 46	13 46 46	0♈ 6 27	7♈ 1 10	23 10.6	11 12.9	27 57.0	25 8.5	1 42.6	19 36.2	1 12.1	24 10.3	26 4.5
7 M	5 2 42	14 47 41	14 3 2	21 11 57	23 7.6	12 47.1	28 40.9	25 38.3	1 53.7	19 41.4	1 15.8	24 12.6	26 6.3
8 Tu	5 6 39	15 48 36	28 27 37	5♉49 33	23 3.1	14 21.3	29 23.7	26 8.1	2 4.8	19 46.6	1 19.4	24 14.8	26 8.0
9 W	5 10 35	16 49 32	13♉17 1	20 49 6	22 57.6	15 55.5	0♒ 5.4	26 37.6	2 15.9	19 51.7	1 23.0	24 17.1	26 9.7
10 Th	5 14 32	17 50 28	28 24 42	6♊ 2 36	22 52.1	17 29.8	0 45.9	27 7.0	2 26.8	19 56.7	1 26.6	24 19.3	26 11.4
11 F	5 18 29	18 51 26	13♊41 26	21 19 52	22 47.4	19 4.1	1 25.2	27 36.2	2 37.7	20 1.7	1 30.2	24 21.6	26 13.1
12 Sa	5 22 25	19 52 24	28 56 31	6♋30 9	22 44.0	20 38.4	2 3.3	28 5.3	2 48.5	20 6.6	1 33.8	24 23.8	26 14.7
13 Su	5 26 22	20 53 24	13♋59 39	21 24 1	22D 42.2	22 12.8	2 40.0	28 34.2	2 59.2	20 11.4	1 37.4	24 26.1	26 16.3
14 M	5 30 18	21 54 24	28 42 31	5♌54 35	22 42.1	23 47.3	3 15.5	29 2.9	3 9.8	20 16.1	1 40.9	24 28.4	26 17.9
15 Tu	5 34 15	22 55 25	12♌59 50	19 58 7	22 43.1	25 22.0	3 49.5	29 31.4	3 20.3	20 20.7	1 44.5	24 30.6	26 19.5
16 W	5 38 11	23 56 27	26 49 24	3♍33 50	22 44.7	26 56.7	4 22.0	29 59.7	3 30.8	20 25.3	1 48.0	24 32.9	26 21.0
17 Th	5 42 8	24 57 30	10♍11 41	16 43 19	22 46.2	28 31.6	4 53.0	0♎27.9	3 41.1	20 29.8	1 51.5	24 35.2	26 22.5
18 F	5 46 4	25 58 33	23 9 8	29 29 38	22R 47.0	0♑ 6.6	5 22.4	0 55.8	3 51.4	20 34.2	1 55.0	24 37.4	26 24.0
19 Sa	5 50 1	26 59 38	5♎45 20	11♎56 45	22 46.7	1 41.7	5 50.3	1 23.5	4 1.5	20 38.5	1 58.4	24 39.7	26 25.4
20 Su	5 53 58	28 0 44	18 4 26	24 8 53	22 45.2	3 17.1	6 16.4	1 51.1	4 11.6	20 42.8	2 1.9	24 42.0	26 26.8
21 M	5 57 54	29 1 50	0♏10 37	6♏10 8	22 42.5	4 52.5	6 40.7	2 18.4	4 21.6	20 46.9	2 5.3	24 44.2	26 28.2
22 Tu	6 1 51	0♑ 2 57	12 7 52	18 4 16	22 39.0	6 28.2	7 3.2	2 45.5	4 31.5	20 51.0	2 8.7	24 46.5	26 29.6
23 W	6 5 47	1 4 5	23 59 42	29 54 33	22 35.2	8 4.0	7 23.9	3 12.3	4 41.2	20 55.0	2 12.1	24 48.8	26 30.9
24 Th	6 9 44	2 5 13	5♐49 9	11♐43 47	22 31.4	9 40.0	7 42.6	3 39.0	4 50.9	20 58.9	2 15.5	24 51.0	26 32.2
25 F	6 13 40	3 6 22	17 38 45	23 34 18	22 28.2	11 16.2	7 59.2	4 5.4	5 0.5	21 2.7	2 18.8	24 53.3	26 33.4
26 Sa	6 17 37	4 7 31	29 30 41	5♑28 7	22 25.8	12 52.5	8 13.8	4 31.6	5 10.0	21 6.4	2 22.1	24 55.5	26 34.7
27 Su	6 21 33	5 8 41	11♑26 49	17 27 2	22D 24.4	14 28.9	8 26.2	4 57.5	5 19.3	21 10.1	2 25.4	24 57.8	26 35.9
28 M	6 25 30	6 9 51	23 28 58	29 32 53	22 24.0	16 5.4	8 36.5	5 23.2	5 28.6	21 13.6	2 28.7	25 0.0	26 37.0
29 Tu	6 29 27	7 11 1	5♒39 0	11♒47 36	22 24.5	17 41.9	8 44.4	5 48.7	5 37.7	21 17.1	2 31.9	25 2.3	26 38.1
30 W	6 33 23	8 12 11	17 58 58	24 13 23	22 25.5	19 18.5	8 50.0	6 13.9	5 46.7	21 20.4	2 35.1	25 4.5	26 39.2
31 Th	6 37 20	9 13 21	0♓31 11	6♓52 41	22 26.8	20 55.0	8R 53.2	6 38.8	5 55.6	21 23.7	2 38.3	25 6.7	26 40.3

Astro Data

	Dy Hr Mn
♃☌♇	2 8:25
☽0N	9 9:40
☽0S	22 5:07
♃⚺♅	2 0:56
☽0N	6 20:15
☽0S	19 12:06
♂0S	27 17:06
♀ R	31 19:45

Planet Ingress

	Dy Hr Mn
♀ ♑	5 12:39
☿ ♏	9 13:14
♅ ♐	16 12:03
☉ ♐	22 9:36
♃ ♏	27 2:19
☿ ♐	28 20:52
♀ ♒	8 20:52
♂ ♎	16 0:14
☿ ♑	17 22:21
☉ ♑	21 22:51

Last Aspect / ☽ Ingress

Last Aspect Dy Hr Mn		☽ Ingress Dy Hr Mn
1 3:26	♀ ☌	♑ 1 12:46
3 23:21	♅ ⚹	♒ 4 0:51
6 8:44	♅ □	♓ 6 9:52
8 13:49	♅ △	♈ 8 14:39
10 10:19	♃ ☍	♉ 10 15:44
12 14:37	♅ ☍	♊ 12 14:59
14 10:29	♃ △	♋ 14 14:37
16 12:54	♃ □	♌ 16 16:32
18 18:49	♃ ⚹	♍ 18 21:53
21 4:09	☉ ⚹	♎ 21 6:33
23 16:15	♃ ☌	♏ 23 17:36
25 20:21	☿ ☌	♐ 26 6:00
28 10:26	♇ ⚹	♑ 28 18:53

Last Aspect / ☽ Ingress

Last Aspect Dy Hr Mn		☽ Ingress Dy Hr Mn
30 23:02	♇ □	♒ 1 7:09
3 9:42	♇ △	♓ 3 17:16
5 20:00	♀ ⚹	♈ 5 23:49
8 1:36	♀ □	♉ 8 2:31
9 21:53	♂ △	♊ 10 2:30
11 22:36	♂ □	♋ 12 1:40
14 0:35	♂ ⚹	♌ 14 2:08
16 0:15	☿ △	♍ 16 5:38
18 5:47	☉ □	♎ 18 12:58
20 21:30	☉ ⚹	♏ 20 23:39
21 13:27	♀ □	♐ 23 12:11
25 18:04	♇ ⚹	♑ 26 0:59
28 6:13	♇ □	♒ 28 12:53
30 16:40	♇ △	♓ 30 23:01

☽ Phases & Eclipses

Dy Hr Mn	
5 1:09	☽ 12♒32
11 22:26	○ 19♉27
18 14:54	☽ 26♌11
26 14:38	● 4♐16
4 16:22	☽ 12♓27
11 8:41	○ 19♊14
18 5:47	☽ 26♍13
26 10:10	● 4♑33

Astro Data

1 NOVEMBER 1981
Julian Day # 29890
Delta T 52.0 sec
SVP 05♓31'06"
Obliquity 23°26'26"
⚷ Chiron 20♉58.4R
☽ Mean ☊ 26♋24.8

1 DECEMBER 1981
Julian Day # 29920
Delta T 52.1 sec
SVP 05♓31'01"
Obliquity 23°26'26"
⚷ Chiron 19♉27.1R
☽ Mean ☊ 24♋49.5

LONGITUDE JANUARY 1982

Day	Sid.Time	☉	0 hr ☽	Noon ☽	True ☊	☿	♀	♂	♃	♄	♅	♆	♇
1 F	6 41 16	10♑14 31	13♓18 13	19♓48 6	22♋28.0	22♑31.4	8♒54.0	7♎ 3.4	6♏ 4.4	21♎26.8	2♐41.4	25♐ 8.9	26♎41.3
2 Sa	6 45 13	11 15 40	26 22 41	3♈ 2 13	22 28.9	24 7.7	8R 52.4	7 27.8	6 13.1	21 29.9	2 44.5	25 11.1	26 42.3
3 Su	6 49 9	12 16 50	9♈46 58	16 37 8	22R 29.2	25 43.6	8 48.2	7 51.9	6 21.6	21 32.9	2 47.6	25 13.3	26 43.3
4 M	6 53 6	13 17 59	23 32 48	0♉34 1	22 29.1	27 19.0	8 41.5	8 15.7	6 30.1	21 35.7	2 50.7	25 15.5	26 44.2
5 Tu	6 57 2	14 19 8	7♉40 39	14 52 30	22 28.5	28 53.9	8 32.2	8 39.3	6 38.4	21 38.5	2 53.7	25 17.7	26 45.1
6 W	7 0 59	15 20 16	22 9 10	29 30 8	22 27.8	0♒28.1	8 20.4	9 2.5	6 46.5	21 41.2	2 56.7	25 19.8	26 46.0
7 Th	7 4 56	16 21 24	6♊54 45	14♊22 12	22 27.0	2 1.3	8 6.1	9 25.4	6 54.6	21 43.8	2 59.7	25 22.0	26 46.8
8 F	7 8 52	17 22 32	21 51 33	29 21 49	22 26.4	3 33.3	7 49.4	9 48.1	7 2.5	21 46.3	3 2.6	25 24.1	26 47.6
9 Sa	7 12 49	18 23 40	6♋51 54	14♋20 44	22 26.0	5 3.7	7 30.2	10 10.4	7 10.3	21 48.7	3 5.5	25 26.3	26 48.3
10 Su	7 16 45	19 24 47	21 47 16	29 10 28	22D 25.9	6 32.4	7 8.7	10 32.4	7 18.0	21 51.0	3 8.4	25 28.4	26 49.0
11 M	7 20 42	20 25 54	6♌29 27	13♌43 25	22 26.0	7 58.8	6 44.9	10 54.1	7 25.5	21 53.1	3 11.2	25 30.5	26 49.7
12 Tu	7 24 38	21 27 1	20 51 47	27 54 1	22 26.1	9 22.5	6 18.9	11 15.5	7 32.9	21 55.2	3 14.0	25 32.6	26 50.4
13 W	7 28 35	22 28 7	4♍49 51	11♍39 5	22R 26.1	10 43.1	5 51.0	11 36.5	7 40.2	21 57.2	3 16.7	25 34.7	26 51.0
14 Th	7 32 32	23 29 14	18 21 45	24 57 56	22 26.1	11 59.9	5 21.3	11 57.1	7 47.3	21 59.1	3 19.4	25 36.7	26 51.6
15 F	7 36 28	24 30 20	1♎27 54	7♎51 59	22 25.9	13 12.3	4 49.8	12 17.5	7 54.3	22 0.9	3 22.1	25 38.8	26 52.1
16 Sa	7 40 25	25 31 26	14 10 37	20 24 16	22 25.7	14 19.6	4 16.9	12 37.4	8 1.1	22 2.5	3 24.8	25 40.8	26 52.6
17 Su	7 44 21	26 32 31	26 33 28	2♏38 47	22D 25.7	15 21.0	3 42.8	12 57.0	8 7.8	22 4.1	3 27.4	25 42.8	26 53.1
18 M	7 48 18	27 33 37	8♏40 49	14 40 8	22 25.8	16 15.6	3 7.6	13 16.1	8 14.3	22 5.6	3 29.9	25 44.9	26 53.5
19 Tu	7 52 14	28 34 42	20 37 20	26 32 59	22 26.2	17 2.7	2 31.6	13 34.9	8 20.7	22 6.9	3 32.4	25 46.8	26 53.9
20 W	7 56 11	29 35 47	2♐27 39	8♐21 52	22 26.9	17 41.3	1 55.0	13 53.3	8 27.0	22 8.2	3 34.9	25 48.8	26 54.3
21 Th	8 0 7	0♒36 52	14 16 8	20 10 57	22 27.8	18 10.6	1 18.1	14 11.3	8 33.1	22 9.3	3 37.4	25 50.8	26 54.6
22 F	8 4 4	1 37 56	26 6 43	2♑ 3 52	22 28.7	18 29.8	0 41.2	14 28.9	8 39.0	22 10.3	3 39.8	25 52.7	26 54.9
23 Sa	8 8 1	2 38 59	8♑ 2 44	14 3 39	22 29.5	18R 38.2	0 4.5	14 46.0	8 44.8	22 11.3	3 42.1	25 54.6	26 55.1
24 Su	8 11 57	3 40 2	20 6 54	26 12 43	22R 29.9	18 35.4	29♑28.2	15 2.7	8 50.4	22 12.1	3 44.4	25 56.5	26 55.3
25 M	8 15 54	4 41 5	2♒21 17	8♒32 47	22 29.7	18 21.1	28 52.6	15 18.9	8 55.9	22 12.8	3 46.7	25 58.4	26 55.5
26 Tu	8 19 50	5 42 6	14 47 21	21 5 4	22 28.8	17 55.2	28 18.0	15 34.7	9 1.2	22 13.4	3 48.9	26 0.3	26 55.7
27 W	8 23 47	6 43 6	27 26 1	3♓50 17	22 27.2	17 18.4	27 44.5	15 50.0	9 6.4	22 13.9	3 51.1	26 2.1	26 55.8
28 Th	8 27 43	7 44 6	10♓17 52	16 48 49	22 25.0	16 31.3	27 12.4	16 4.8	9 11.3	22 14.3	3 53.2	26 3.9	26 55.8
29 F	8 31 40	8 45 4	23 23 9	0♈ 0 52	22 22.6	15 35.1	26 41.9	16 19.2	9 16.2	22 14.6	3 55.3	26 5.7	26R 55.9
30 Sa	8 35 36	9 46 2	6♈42 0	13 26 32	22 20.3	14 31.4	26 13.1	16 33.0	9 20.8	22 14.8	3 57.4	26 7.5	26 55.9
31 Su	8 39 33	10 46 57	20 14 27	27 5 46	22 18.4	13 22.1	25 46.2	16 46.3	9 25.3	22R 14.9	3 59.4	26 9.3	26 55.8

LONGITUDE FEBRUARY 1982

Day	Sid.Time	☉	0 hr ☽	Noon ☽	True ☊	☿	♀	♂	♃	♄	♅	♆	♇
1 M	8 43 30	11♒47 52	4♉ 0 25	10♉58 22	22♋17.4	12♒ 9.3	25♑21.3	16♎59.1	9♏29.6	22♎14.8	4♐ 1.3	26♐11.0	26♎55.7
2 Tu	8 47 26	12 48 46	17 59 31	25 3 43	22D 17.3	10R 55.1	24R 58.6	17 11.4	9 33.8	22R 14.7	4 3.2	26 12.7	26R 55.6
3 W	8 51 23	13 49 38	2♊10 48	9♊20 31	22 18.1	9 41.7	24 38.1	17 23.2	9 37.7	22 14.4	4 5.1	26 14.4	26 55.5
4 Th	8 55 19	14 50 28	16 32 32	23 46 29	22 19.4	8 30.9	24 19.9	17 34.4	9 41.5	22 14.1	4 6.9	26 16.0	26 55.3
5 F	8 59 16	15 51 18	1♋ 1 52	8♋18 10	22 20.9	7 24.6	24 4.2	17 45.0	9 45.2	22 13.6	4 8.6	26 17.7	26 55.1
6 Sa	9 3 12	16 52 6	15 34 45	22 50 57	22R 21.8	6 24.1	23 50.9	17 55.1	9 48.6	22 13.1	4 10.3	26 19.3	26 54.8
7 Su	9 7 9	17 52 52	0♌ 6 4	7♌19 21	22 21.8	5 30.4	23 40.1	18 4.7	9 51.9	22 12.4	4 12.0	26 20.9	26 54.6
8 M	9 11 5	18 53 38	14 30 5	21 37 33	22 20.4	4 44.4	23 31.7	18 13.6	9 55.0	22 11.6	4 13.6	26 22.5	26 54.2
9 Tu	9 15 2	19 54 21	28 41 7	5♍40 12	22 17.6	4 6.4	23 25.9	18 21.9	9 57.9	22 10.7	4 15.2	26 24.0	26 53.9
10 W	9 18 59	20 55 4	12♍34 20	19 23 9	22 13.5	3 36.6	23D 22.6	18 29.6	10 0.7	22 9.8	4 16.7	26 25.5	26 53.5
11 Th	9 22 55	21 55 45	26 6 23	2♎43 55	22 8.7	3 15.0	23 21.7	18 36.7	10 3.3	22 8.7	4 18.1	26 27.0	26 53.1
12 F	9 26 52	22 56 25	9♎15 44	15 41 59	22 3.7	3 1.4	23 23.2	18 43.2	10 5.6	22 7.5	4 19.5	26 28.4	26 52.6
13 Sa	9 30 48	23 57 4	22 2 51	28 18 40	21 59.2	2D 55.5	23 27.2	18 49.0	10 7.8	22 6.2	4 20.9	26 29.9	26 52.1
14 Su	9 34 45	24 57 42	4♏29 51	10♏36 51	21 55.8	2 56.9	23 33.5	18 54.1	10 9.9	22 4.8	4 22.2	26 31.3	26 51.6
15 M	9 38 41	25 58 19	16 40 13	22 40 31	21D 53.8	3 5.2	23 42.1	18 58.6	10 11.7	22 3.3	4 23.5	26 32.7	26 51.0
16 Tu	9 42 38	26 58 55	28 38 22	4♐34 24	21 53.3	3 19.8	23 52.9	19 2.4	10 13.3	22 1.7	4 24.7	26 34.0	26 50.4
17 W	9 46 34	27 59 29	10♐29 17	16 23 37	21 54.1	3 40.5	24 5.9	19 5.5	10 14.8	22 0.0	4 25.8	26 35.3	26 49.8
18 Th	9 50 31	29 0 2	22 18 5	28 13 17	21 55.7	4 6.8	24 21.0	19 7.9	10 16.1	21 58.2	4 26.9	26 36.6	26 49.1
19 F	9 54 28	0♓ 0 34	4♑ 9 49	10♑ 8 16	21 57.4	4 38.1	24 38.2	19 9.6	10 17.2	21 56.3	4 28.0	26 37.9	26 48.4
20 Sa	9 58 24	1 1 5	16 9 8	22 12 54	21R 58.6	5 14.2	24 57.3	19R 10.6	10 18.1	21 54.3	4 28.9	26 39.1	26 47.7
21 Su	10 2 21	2 1 34	28 20 0	4♒30 46	21 58.6	5 54.6	25 18.3	19 10.8	10 18.8	21 52.3	4 29.9	26 40.3	26 47.0
22 M	10 6 17	3 2 1	10♒45 30	17 4 25	21 56.8	6 39.1	25 41.2	19 10.3	10 19.3	21 50.1	4 30.8	26 41.5	26 46.2
23 Tu	10 10 14	4 2 28	23 27 38	29 55 12	21 52.9	7 27.3	26 5.9	19 9.0	10 19.6	21 47.8	4 31.6	26 42.7	26 45.4
24 W	10 14 10	5 2 52	6♓27 5	13♓ 3 11	21 47.1	8 18.9	26 32.2	19 7.0	10R 19.8	21 45.4	4 32.4	26 43.8	26 44.5
25 Th	10 18 7	6 3 15	19 43 17	26 27 9	21 39.8	9 13.7	27 0.2	19 4.2	10 19.7	21 43.0	4 33.1	26 44.9	26 43.6
26 F	10 22 3	7 3 36	3♈14 29	10♈ 4 56	21 31.8	10 11.5	27 29.8	19 0.6	10 19.5	21 40.4	4 33.8	26 45.9	26 42.7
27 Sa	10 26 0	8 3 55	16 58 8	23 53 44	21 24.0	11 12.0	28 0.9	18 56.3	10 19.1	21 37.8	4 34.4	26 47.0	26 41.8
28 Su	10 29 56	9 4 12	0♉51 21	7♉50 38	21 17.3	12 15.0	28 33.5	18 51.1	10 18.4	21 35.1	4 34.9	26 47.9	26 40.8

Astro Data	Planet Ingress	Last Aspect	☽ Ingress	Last Aspect	☽ Ingress	☽ Phases & Eclipses	Astro Data
Dy Hr Mn	Dy Hr Mn	Dy Hr Mn	Dy Hr Mn	Dy Hr Mn	Dy Hr Mn	Dy Hr Mn	1 JANUARY 1982
☽0N 3 4:08	☿ ♒ 5 16:49	1 21:50 ♆ □	♈ 2 6:33	2 11:34 ♀ △	♊ 2 20:20	3 4:45 ☽ 12♈29	Julian Day # 29951
☽0S 15 20:07	☉ ♒ 20 9:31	4 7:17 ♆ △	♉ 4 11:02	4 17:12 ♇ △	♋ 4 22:18	9 19:53 ○ 19♋14	Delta T 52.2 sec
☿ R 23 6:03	♀ ♑ 23 2:56	5 11:55 ☉ △	♊ 6 12:49	6 18:43 ♇ □	♌ 6 23:50	9 19:56 ☍ T 1.331	SVP 05♓30'55"
♇ R 29 8:18		8 7:54 ♇ △	♋ 8 13:01	8 20:57 ♇ ✶	♍ 9 2:15	16 23:58 ☽ 26♎32	Obliquity 23°26'26"
☽0N 30 9:33	☉ ♓ 18 23:47	10 8:10 ♇ □	♌ 10 13:21	11 0:37 ♆ □	♎ 11 7:02	25 4:56 ● 4♒54	⚷ Chiron 18♉15.1R
♄ R 31 3:46		12 10:11 ♇ ✶	♍ 12 15:37	13 9:13 ♇ ☌	♏ 13 15:16	25 4:41:59 ☌ P 0.566	☽ Mean ☊ 23♋11.0
		14 13:13 ♆ □	♎ 14 21:17	15 20:21 ☉ □	♐ 16 2:45		
♀ D 10 20:38		17 0:38 ♇ ☌	♏ 17 6:46	18 14:50 ☉ ✶	♑ 18 15:36	1 14:28 ☽ 12♉25	1 FEBRUARY 1982
☽0S 12 5:00		19 17:38 ☉ ✶	♐ 19 19:00	20 20:58 ♇ □	♒ 21 3:15	8 7:57 ○ 19♌14	Julian Day # 29982
☿ D 13 7:18		22 1:37 ♇ ✶	♑ 22 7:51	23 6:08 ♇ △	♓ 23 12:09	15 20:21 ☽ 26♏50	Delta T 52.2 sec
♂ R 20 19:13		24 17:32 ♀ ☌	♒ 24 19:25	25 13:28 ♀ ✶	♈ 25 18:17	23 21:13 ● 4♓56	SVP 05♓30'51"
♆✶♇ 24 8:50		26 23:03 ♇ △	♓ 27 4:49	27 19:53 ♀ □	♉ 27 22:32		Obliquity 23°26'26"
♃ R 24 5:42		29 5:48 ♀ ✶	♈ 29 11:58				⚷ Chiron 17♉54.6
☽0N 26 14:58		31 11:43 ♇ ☍	♉ 31 17:03				☽ Mean ☊ 21♋32.5

MARCH 1982 LONGITUDE

Day	Sid.Time	☉	0 hr ☽	Noon ☽	True ☊	☿	♀	♂	♃	♄	♅	♆	♇
1 M	10 33 53	10♓ 4 28	14♉51 16	21♉52 58	21♋12.5	13♒20.4	29♑ 7.4	18♎45.3	10♏17.6	21♎32.3	4♐35.4	26♐48.9	26♎39.8
2 Tu	10 37 50	11 4 41	28 55 30	5♊58 40	21D 9.8	14 28.0	29 42.7	18R38.6	10R16.6	21R29.4	4 35.9	26 49.8	26R38.8
3 W	10 41 46	12 4 52	13♊ 2 16	20 6 8	21 9.1	15 37.8	0♒19.3	18 31.2	10 15.4	21 26.4	4 36.3	26 50.7	26 37.8
4 Th	10 45 43	13 5 2	27 10 9	4♋14 9	21 9.8	16 49.5	0 57.2	18 23.0	10 14.1	21 23.3	4 36.6	26 51.6	26 36.7
5 F	10 49 39	14 5 9	11♋17 59	18 21 27	21R10.8	18 3.1	1 36.2	18 14.0	10 12.5	21 20.2	4 36.9	26 52.4	26 35.6
6 Sa	10 53 36	15 5 14	25 24 19	2♌26 21	21 11.0	19 18.4	2 16.4	18 4.2	10 10.8	21 17.0	4 37.1	26 53.3	26 34.5
7 Su	10 57 32	16 5 17	9♌27 13	16 26 34	21 9.5	20 35.5	2 57.8	17 53.7	10 8.9	21 13.7	4 37.3	26 54.0	26 33.3
8 M	11 1 29	17 5 17	23 24 1	0♍19 10	21 5.6	21 54.2	3 40.1	17 42.5	10 6.8	21 10.3	4 37.5	26 54.8	26 32.1
9 Tu	11 5 25	18 5 16	7♍11 35	14 0 50	20 59.1	23 14.5	4 23.5	17 30.5	10 4.5	21 6.9	4R37.5	26 55.5	26 30.9
10 W	11 9 22	19 5 13	20 46 33	27 28 21	20 50.3	24 36.3	5 7.9	17 17.7	10 2.0	21 3.4	4 37.5	26 56.1	26 29.7
11 Th	11 13 19	20 5 8	4♎ 5 58	10♎39 9	20 40.0	25 59.5	5 53.3	17 4.2	9 59.3	20 59.8	4 37.5	26 56.8	26 28.4
12 F	11 17 15	21 5 1	17 7 47	23 31 49	20 29.1	27 24.2	6 39.6	16 50.0	9 56.5	20 56.2	4 37.4	26 57.4	26 27.2
13 Sa	11 21 12	22 4 52	29 51 17	6♏ 6 21	20 18.8	28 50.2	7 26.7	16 35.1	9 53.5	20 52.5	4 37.3	26 58.0	26 25.9
14 Su	11 25 8	23 4 41	12♏17 14	18 24 15	20 10.0	0♓17.7	8 14.7	16 19.5	9 50.3	20 48.7	4 37.1	26 58.5	26 24.5
15 M	11 29 5	24 4 29	24 27 48	0♐28 23	20 3.4	1 46.4	9 3.5	16 3.2	9 46.9	20 44.9	4 36.8	26 59.0	26 23.2
16 Tu	11 33 1	25 4 15	6♐26 29	12 22 43	19 59.2	3 16.5	9 53.1	15 46.2	9 43.4	20 41.0	4 36.5	26 59.5	26 21.8
17 W	11 36 58	26 3 59	18 17 41	24 12 3	19D57.3	4 47.9	10 43.4	15 28.6	9 39.7	20 37.0	4 36.2	26 59.9	26 20.5
18 Th	11 40 54	27 3 42	0♑ 6 30	6♑ 1 41	19 57.0	6 20.6	11 34.4	15 10.4	9 35.8	20 33.0	4 35.8	27 0.3	26 19.1
19 F	11 44 51	28 3 23	11 58 20	17 57 6	19R57.4	7 54.5	12 26.2	14 51.6	9 31.8	20 29.0	4 35.3	27 0.7	26 17.6
20 Sa	11 48 48	29 3 2	23 58 38	0♒ 3 35	19 57.6	9 29.8	13 18.6	14 32.3	9 27.6	20 24.9	4 34.8	27 1.1	26 16.2
21 Su	11 52 44	0♈ 2 39	6♒12 31	12 25 56	19 56.3	11 6.3	14 11.6	14 12.4	9 23.2	20 20.7	4 34.2	27 1.4	26 14.8
22 M	11 56 41	1 2 15	18 44 17	25 7 56	19 52.9	12 44.1	15 5.3	13 52.0	9 18.7	20 16.5	4 33.6	27 1.6	26 13.3
23 Tu	12 0 37	2 1 49	1♓37 6	8♓11 56	19 46.8	14 23.1	15 59.5	13 31.1	9 14.0	20 12.2	4 33.0	27 1.9	26 11.8
24 W	12 4 34	3 1 20	14 52 26	21 38 28	19 38.1	16 3.5	16 54.3	13 9.8	9 9.2	20 7.9	4 32.2	27 2.1	26 10.3
25 Th	12 8 30	4 0 50	28 29 44	5♈25 52	19 27.3	17 45.2	17 49.6	12 48.1	9 4.2	20 3.6	4 31.5	27 2.3	26 8.8
26 F	12 12 27	5 0 18	12♈26 21	19 30 32	19 15.5	19 28.1	18 45.4	12 26.1	8 59.0	19 59.2	4 30.7	27 2.4	26 7.2
27 Sa	12 16 23	5 59 44	26 37 44	3♉47 13	19 3.8	21 12.4	19 41.8	12 3.8	8 53.7	19 54.8	4 29.8	27 2.5	26 5.7
28 Su	12 20 20	6 59 7	10♉58 15	18 10 4	18 53.5	22 58.0	20 38.6	11 41.2	8 48.3	19 50.4	4 28.9	27 2.6	26 4.1
29 M	12 24 17	7 58 29	25 22 1	2♊33 29	18 45.6	24 45.0	21 35.9	11 18.3	8 42.7	19 45.9	4 27.9	27R 2.6	26 2.5
30 Tu	12 28 13	8 57 48	9♊43 56	16 52 57	18 40.5	26 33.3	22 33.6	10 55.3	8 37.0	19 41.4	4 26.9	27 2.6	26 0.9
31 W	12 32 10	9 57 5	24 0 12	1♋ 5 28	18 38.0	28 23.0	23 31.7	10 32.2	8 31.2	19 36.9	4 25.8	27 2.6	25 59.3

APRIL 1982 LONGITUDE

Day	Sid.Time	☉	0 hr ☽	Noon ☽	True ☊	☿	♀	♂	♃	♄	♅	♆	♇
1 Th	12 36 6	10♈56 20	8♋ 8 35	15♋ 9 27	18♋37.4	0♈14.0	24♒30.3	10♎ 9.0	8♏25.2	19♎32.4	4♐24.7	27♐ 2.5	25♎57.7
2 F	12 40 3	11 55 32	22 8 3	29 4 23	18R37.4	2 6.4	25 29.2	9R45.7	8R19.1	19R27.8	4R23.6	27R 2.4	25R56.1
3 Sa	12 43 59	12 54 42	5♌58 27	12♌50 16	18 36.6	4 0.2	26 28.6	9 22.5	8 12.9	19 23.2	4 22.4	27 2.3	25 54.5
4 Su	12 47 56	13 53 50	19 39 48	26 27 2	18 34.0	5 55.3	27 28.3	8 59.3	8 6.6	19 18.6	4 21.2	27 2.2	25 52.8
5 M	12 51 52	14 52 55	3♍11 55	9♍54 21	18 28.7	7 51.8	28 28.4	8 36.2	8 0.2	19 14.0	4 19.9	27 2.0	25 51.2
6 Tu	12 55 49	15 51 58	16 34 12	23 11 19	18 20.5	9 49.7	29 28.8	8 13.2	7 53.6	19 9.4	4 18.5	27 1.7	25 49.5
7 W	12 59 45	16 50 59	29 45 33	6♎16 45	18 9.6	11 48.9	0♓29.6	7 50.4	7 47.0	19 4.8	4 17.2	27 1.5	25 47.9
8 Th	13 3 42	17 49 57	12♎44 44	19 9 23	17 56.8	13 49.3	1 30.7	7 27.9	7 40.3	19 0.2	4 15.7	27 1.2	25 46.2
9 F	13 7 39	18 48 54	25 30 36	1♏48 20	17 43.3	15 50.9	2 32.1	7 5.5	7 33.4	18 55.5	4 14.3	27 0.9	25 44.5
10 Sa	13 11 35	19 47 49	8♏ 2 35	14 13 24	17 30.2	17 53.7	3 33.8	6 43.5	7 26.5	18 50.9	4 12.8	27 0.5	25 42.8
11 Su	13 15 32	20 46 41	20 20 56	26 25 24	17 18.8	19 57.5	4 35.8	6 21.9	7 19.5	18 46.3	4 11.2	27 0.1	25 41.2
12 M	13 19 28	21 45 32	2♐27 2	8♐26 13	17 9.8	22 2.2	5 38.1	6 0.6	7 12.4	18 41.6	4 9.6	26 59.7	25 39.5
13 Tu	13 23 25	22 44 21	14 23 19	20 18 50	17 3.5	24 7.7	6 40.7	5 39.7	7 5.3	18 37.0	4 8.0	26 59.3	25 37.8
14 W	13 27 21	23 43 9	26 13 16	2♑ 7 12	16 60.0	26 13.8	7 43.6	5 19.3	6 58.0	18 32.4	4 6.4	26 58.8	25 36.1
15 Th	13 31 18	24 41 54	8♑ 1 15	13 56 3	16D58.5	28 20.3	8 46.7	4 59.4	6 50.8	18 27.8	4 4.7	26 58.3	25 34.4
16 F	13 35 14	25 40 38	19 52 17	25 50 37	16R58.3	0♉26.9	9 50.1	4 39.9	6 43.4	18 23.2	4 2.9	26 57.7	25 32.7
17 Sa	13 39 11	26 39 20	1♒51 47	7♒56 26	16 58.3	2 33.5	10 53.7	4 21.1	6 36.0	18 18.7	4 1.1	26 57.2	25 31.0
18 Su	13 43 8	27 38 1	14 5 16	20 18 53	16 57.3	4 39.7	11 57.6	4 2.8	6 28.5	18 14.1	3 59.3	26 56.6	25 29.3
19 M	13 47 4	28 36 40	26 37 51	3♓ 2 42	16 54.5	6 45.3	13 1.7	3 45.1	6 21.0	18 9.6	3 57.5	26 55.9	25 27.6
20 Tu	13 51 1	29 35 17	9♓33 48	16 11 28	16 49.2	8 49.9	14 6.0	3 28.0	6 13.5	18 5.1	3 55.6	26 55.3	25 25.9
21 W	13 54 57	0♉33 52	22 55 49	29 46 52	16 41.4	10 53.1	15 10.5	3 11.6	6 5.9	18 0.6	3 53.7	26 54.6	25 24.3
22 Th	13 58 54	1 32 26	6♈44 25	13♈48 6	16 31.6	12 54.8	16 15.2	2 55.9	5 58.3	17 56.2	3 51.7	26 53.9	25 22.6
23 F	14 2 50	2 30 58	20 57 24	28 11 37	16 20.5	14 54.4	17 20.1	2 40.9	5 50.6	17 51.7	3 49.7	26 53.1	25 20.9
24 Sa	14 6 47	3 29 28	5♉29 53	12♉51 15	16 9.5	16 51.9	18 25.2	2 26.6	5 43.0	17 47.4	3 47.7	26 52.4	25 19.2
25 Su	14 10 43	4 27 56	20 14 42	27 39 12	15 59.7	18 46.7	19 30.5	2 13.0	5 35.3	17 43.0	3 45.7	26 51.5	25 17.5
26 M	14 14 40	5 26 22	5♊ 3 41	12♊27 13	15 52.2	20 38.7	20 36.0	2 0.2	5 27.7	17 38.7	3 43.6	26 50.7	25 15.9
27 Tu	14 18 37	6 24 46	19 48 55	27 8 3	15 47.3	22 27.7	21 41.6	1 48.2	5 20.0	17 34.4	3 41.5	26 49.9	25 14.2
28 W	14 22 33	7 23 9	4♋24 2	11♋36 23	15D45.0	24 13.3	22 47.4	1 37.0	5 12.3	17 30.2	3 39.4	26 49.0	25 12.6
29 Th	14 26 30	8 21 29	18 44 48	25 49 5	15 44.6	25 55.4	23 53.4	1 26.5	5 4.7	17 26.0	3 37.2	26 48.1	25 10.9
30 F	14 30 26	9 19 47	2♌49 10	9♌45 2	15R45.0	27 33.9	24 59.5	1 16.8	4 57.0	17 21.9	3 35.1	26 47.1	25 9.3

Astro Data Dy Hr Mn	Planet Ingress Dy Hr Mn	Last Aspect Dy Hr Mn	☽ Ingress Dy Hr Mn	Last Aspect Dy Hr Mn	☽ Ingress Dy Hr Mn	☽ Phases & Eclipses Dy Hr Mn	Astro Data
♅ R 9 19:41	♀ ♒ 2 11:25	2 1:24 ♀ △	♊ 2 1:50	2 6:33 ♇ □	♌ 2 13:36	2 22:15 ☽ 12♊00	1 MARCH 1982
☽0S 11 13:52	☿ ♓ 13 19:11	3 23:28 ♆ ☍	♋ 4 4:48	4 14:55 ♀ ☍	♍ 4 18:18	9 20:45 ○ 18♍57	Julian Day # 30010
☽0N 25 22:32	☉ ♈ 20 22:56	6 1:59 ♇ □	♌ 6 7:50	6 19:00 ♆ □	♎ 7 0:26	17 17:15 ☽ 26♐47	Delta T 52.3 sec
♆ R 29 16:38	☿ ♈ 31 20:59	8 6:05 ♆ △	♍ 8 11:27	9 2:51 ♆ ✶	♏ 9 8:33	25 10:17 ● 4♈26	SVP 05♓30'47"
		10 11:03 ♆ □	♎ 10 16:34	9 22:51 ♃ ☌	♐ 11 19:07		Obliquity 23°26'27"
☿0N 3 3:12	♀ ♓ 6 12:20	12 21:49 ☿ △	♏ 13 0:17	14 1:33 ♆ ☌	♑ 14 7:41	1 5:08 ☽ 11♋09	⚷ Chiron 18♉28.0
♄∠♅ 3 5:59	☿ ♉ 15 18:54	14 23:09 ☉ △	♐ 15 11:03	16 12:42 ☉ □	♒ 16 20:18	8 10:18 ○ 18♎15	☽ Mean ☊ 20♋03.6
☽0S 7 21:48	☉ ♉ 20 10:07	17 17:42 ♆ ☌	♑ 17 23:47	19 4:02 ☉ ✶	♓ 19 6:20	16 12:42 ☽ 26♑12	
♂0N 11 20:12		20 10:54 ☉ ✶	♒ 20 11:53	21 6:59 ♆ □	♈ 21 12:23	23 20:29 ● 3♉21	1 APRIL 1982
☽0N 22 8:23		22 15:32 ♆ ✶	♓ 22 21:01	23 9:50 ♆ △	♉ 23 14:59	30 12:07 ☽ 9♌49	Julian Day # 30041
		24 21:28 ♆ □	♈ 25 2:37	24 22:43 ♀ ✶	♊ 25 15:48		Delta T 52.4 sec
		27 0:42 ♆ △	♉ 27 5:39	27 11:29 ♆ ☍	♋ 27 16:43		SVP 05♓30'44"
		28 22:50 ☿ ✶	♊ 29 7:44	29 13:48 ☿ ✶	♌ 29 19:09		Obliquity 23°26'27"
		31 8:31 ☿ □	♋ 31 10:09				⚷ Chiron 19♉54.0
							☽ Mean ☊ 18♋25.1

LONGITUDE — MAY 1982

Day	Sid.Time	☉	0 hr ☽	Noon ☽	True ☊	☿	♀	♂	♃	♄	♅	♆	♇
1 Sa	14 34 23	10♉18 3	16♌36 47	23♌24 31	15♋45.0	29♉ 8.6	26♓ 5.7	1♎ 8.0	4♏49.4	17♎17.8	3♐32.9	26♐46.2	25♎ 7.7
2 Su	14 38 19	11 16 17	0♍ 8 25	6♍48 37	15R43.4	0♊39.3	27 12.1	0R59.9	4R41.8	17R13.8	3R30.6	26R45.2	25R 6.1
3 M	14 42 16	12 14 29	13 25 18	19 58 36	15 39.6	2 5.9	28 18.7	0 52.6	4 34.3	17 9.8	3 28.4	26 44.2	25 4.5
4 Tu	14 46 12	13 12 39	26 28 41	2♎55 40	15 33.3	3 28.4	29 25.4	0 46.2	4 26.7	17 5.9	3 26.1	26 43.1	25 2.9
5 W	14 50 9	14 10 46	9♎19 37	15 40 39	15 24.7	4 46.6	0♈32.2	0 40.5	4 19.3	17 2.0	3 23.8	26 42.1	25 1.3
6 Th	14 54 6	15 8 52	21 58 49	28 14 10	15 14.5	6 0.6	1 39.2	0 35.6	4 11.8	16 58.2	3 21.5	26 41.0	24 59.7
7 F	14 58 2	16 6 57	4♏26 47	10♏36 44	15 3.7	7 10.1	2 46.3	0 31.5	4 4.4	16 54.4	3 19.2	26 39.9	24 58.2
8 Sa	15 1 59	17 4 59	16 44 5	22 48 58	14 53.2	8 15.2	3 53.5	0 28.2	3 57.1	16 50.8	3 16.8	26 38.7	24 56.6
9 Su	15 5 55	18 3 0	28 51 29	4♐51 51	14 44.0	9 15.8	5 0.8	0 25.7	3 49.8	16 47.1	3 14.4	26 37.6	24 55.1
10 M	15 9 52	19 1 0	10♐50 16	16 47 0	14 36.8	10 11.7	6 8.3	0 24.0	3 42.6	16 43.6	3 12.1	26 36.4	24 53.6
11 Tu	15 13 48	19 58 58	22 42 21	28 36 40	14 32.0	11 3.1	7 15.9	0D 23.0	3 35.5	16 40.1	3 9.7	26 35.2	24 52.1
12 W	15 17 45	20 56 54	4♑30 23	10♑23 56	14D 29.5	11 49.7	8 23.6	0 22.8	3 28.5	16 36.7	3 7.3	26 34.0	24 50.6
13 Th	15 21 41	21 54 49	16 17 48	22 12 34	14 28.9	12 31.5	9 31.5	0 23.3	3 21.5	16 33.3	3 4.8	26 32.7	24 49.1
14 F	15 25 38	22 52 43	28 8 45	4♒ 7 0	14 29.6	13 8.6	10 39.4	0 24.6	3 14.6	16 30.0	3 2.4	26 31.5	24 47.7
15 Sa	15 29 35	23 50 36	10♒ 7 56	16 12 11	14 30.8	13 40.7	11 47.5	0 26.7	3 7.8	16 26.8	2 60.0	26 30.2	24 46.3
16 Su	15 33 31	24 48 27	22 20 24	28 33 13	14R31.6	14 8.0	12 55.6	0 29.4	3 1.1	16 23.7	2 57.5	26 28.9	24 44.9
17 M	15 37 28	25 46 17	4♓51 14	11♓15 1	14 31.2	14 30.3	14 3.9	0 32.9	2 54.5	16 20.6	2 55.0	26 27.6	24 43.5
18 Tu	15 41 24	26 44 6	17 45 5	24 21 48	14 29.1	14 47.7	15 12.2	0 37.1	2 47.9	16 17.7	2 52.6	26 26.2	24 42.1
19 W	15 45 21	27 41 54	1♈ 5 30	7♈56 19	14 25.1	15 0.2	16 20.7	0 42.0	2 41.5	16 14.8	2 50.1	26 24.9	24 40.7
20 Th	15 49 17	28 39 40	14 54 16	21 59 9	14 19.5	15 7.8	17 29.2	0 47.6	2 35.2	16 12.0	2 47.6	26 23.5	24 39.4
21 F	15 53 14	29 37 26	29 10 37	6♉28 5	14 12.9	15R10.6	18 37.9	0 53.9	2 29.0	16 9.2	2 45.1	26 22.1	24 38.1
22 Sa	15 57 10	0♊35 10	13♉50 48	21 17 51	14 6.1	15 8.7	19 46.6	1 0.9	2 23.0	16 6.6	2 42.6	26 20.7	24 36.8
23 Su	16 1 7	1 32 53	28 48 10	6♊20 35	14 0.1	15 2.2	20 55.4	1 8.5	2 17.0	16 4.0	2 40.1	26 19.3	24 35.5
24 M	16 5 4	2 30 35	13♊53 55	21 26 57	13 55.6	14 51.3	22 4.3	1 16.9	2 11.2	16 1.5	2 37.6	26 17.9	24 34.3
25 Tu	16 9 0	3 28 16	28 58 33	6♋27 40	13 52.9	14 36.3	23 13.3	1 25.8	2 5.5	15 59.1	2 35.1	26 16.4	24 33.0
26 W	16 12 57	4 25 55	13♋53 22	21 14 54	13D 52.1	14 17.5	24 22.3	1 35.4	1 60.0	15 56.8	2 32.6	26 15.0	24 31.8
27 Th	16 16 53	5 23 33	28 31 38	5♌43 10	13 52.7	13 55.1	25 31.4	1 45.7	1 54.6	15 54.6	2 30.1	26 13.5	24 30.7
28 F	16 20 50	6 21 9	12♌49 12	19 49 36	13 54.1	13 29.7	26 40.6	1 56.5	1 49.3	15 52.5	2 27.7	26 12.0	24 29.5
29 Sa	16 24 46	7 18 44	26 44 20	3♍33 31	13R55.3	13 1.5	27 49.9	2 8.0	1 44.2	15 50.5	2 25.2	26 10.5	24 28.4
30 Su	16 28 43	8 16 17	10♍17 17	16 55 54	13 55.7	12 31.2	28 59.2	2 20.0	1 39.2	15 48.5	2 22.7	26 9.0	24 27.3
31 M	16 32 39	9 13 49	23 29 36	29 58 44	13 54.7	11 59.2	0♉ 8.6	2 32.6	1 34.3	15 46.7	2 20.2	26 7.5	24 26.2

LONGITUDE — JUNE 1982

Day	Sid.Time	☉	0 hr ☽	Noon ☽	True ☊	☿	♀	♂	♃	♄	♅	♆	♇
1 Tu	16 36 36	10♊11 19	6♎23 34	12♎44 27	13♋52.3	11♊26.1	1♉18.1	2♎45.8	1♏29.6	15♎44.9	2♐17.7	26♐ 5.9	24♎25.1
2 W	16 40 33	11 8 49	19 1 42	25 15 36	13R48.4	10R52.5	2 27.6	2 59.6	1R25.1	15R43.3	2R15.3	26R 4.4	24R24.1
3 Th	16 44 29	12 6 17	1♏26 27	7♏34 31	13 43.6	10 18.9	3 37.2	3 13.9	1 20.7	15 41.7	2 12.8	26 2.8	24 23.1
4 F	16 48 26	13 3 44	13 40 4	19 43 22	13 38.4	9 46.0	4 46.8	3 28.7	1 16.5	15 40.2	2 10.4	26 1.3	24 22.1
5 Sa	16 52 22	14 1 9	25 44 37	1♐44 5	13 33.3	9 14.3	5 56.6	3 44.1	1 12.4	15 38.8	2 8.0	25 59.7	24 21.2
6 Su	16 56 19	14 58 34	7♐41 58	13 38 32	13 28.9	8 44.3	7 6.4	3 59.9	1 8.5	15 37.6	2 5.5	25 58.1	24 20.3
7 M	17 0 15	15 55 58	19 34 0	25 28 37	13 25.7	8 16.5	8 16.2	4 16.3	1 4.8	15 36.4	2 3.1	25 56.5	24 19.4
8 Tu	17 4 12	16 53 21	1♑22 41	7♑16 28	13 23.7	7 51.5	9 26.2	4 33.2	1 1.2	15 35.3	2 0.8	25 54.9	24 18.5
9 W	17 8 8	17 50 43	13 10 17	19 4 30	13D 23.1	7 29.5	10 36.2	4 50.5	0 57.8	15 34.3	1 58.4	25 53.3	24 17.7
10 Th	17 12 5	18 48 5	24 59 29	0♒55 38	13 23.6	7 11.0	11 46.2	5 8.3	0 54.6	15 33.4	1 56.0	25 51.7	24 16.9
11 F	17 16 2	19 45 26	6♒53 23	12 53 13	13 24.9	6 56.3	12 56.3	5 26.6	0 51.5	15 32.6	1 53.7	25 50.1	24 16.1
12 Sa	17 19 58	20 42 46	18 55 35	25 1 1	13 26.5	6 45.6	14 6.5	5 45.4	0 48.6	15 31.9	1 51.4	25 48.5	24 15.4
13 Su	17 23 55	21 40 6	1♓10 3	7♓23 11	13 28.0	6D 39.1	15 16.7	6 4.6	0 45.8	15 31.4	1 49.1	25 46.9	24 14.6
14 M	17 27 51	22 37 25	13 40 58	20 3 54	13R29.0	6 37.0	16 27.0	6 24.2	0 43.3	15 30.9	1 46.8	25 45.3	24 14.0
15 Tu	17 31 48	23 34 44	26 32 27	3♈ 7 3	13 29.2	6 39.4	17 37.4	6 44.2	0 40.9	15 30.5	1 44.5	25 43.7	24 13.3
16 W	17 35 44	24 32 2	9♈48 3	16 35 42	13 28.5	6 46.4	18 47.8	7 4.7	0 38.7	15 30.2	1 42.3	25 42.1	24 12.7
17 Th	17 39 41	25 29 21	23 30 9	0♉31 24	13 27.1	6 57.9	19 58.3	7 25.6	0 36.7	15 30.0	1 40.1	25 40.4	24 12.1
18 F	17 43 37	26 26 39	7♉39 19	14 53 33	13 25.2	7 14.0	21 8.8	7 46.9	0 34.8	15D 29.9	1 37.9	25 38.8	24 11.5
19 Sa	17 47 34	27 23 56	22 13 36	29 38 48	13 23.2	7 34.7	22 19.4	8 8.6	0 33.1	15 29.9	1 35.7	25 37.2	24 11.0
20 Su	17 51 31	28 21 14	7♊ 8 18	14♊41 6	13 21.4	8 0.0	23 30.0	8 30.7	0 31.6	15 30.0	1 33.5	25 35.6	24 10.5
21 M	17 55 27	29 18 31	22 16 4	29 52 3	13 20.1	8 29.8	24 40.7	8 53.2	0 30.3	15 30.2	1 31.4	25 34.0	24 10.0
22 Tu	17 59 24	0♋15 47	7♋27 48	15♋ 2 9	13D 19.5	9 4.1	25 51.4	9 16.1	0 29.2	15 30.5	1 29.3	25 32.4	24 9.6
23 W	18 3 20	1 13 4	22 33 56	0♌ 2 9	13 19.6	9 42.8	27 2.2	9 39.4	0 28.2	15 30.9	1 27.3	25 30.7	24 9.2
24 Th	18 7 17	2 10 19	7♌25 53	14 44 24	13 20.2	10 25.8	28 13.0	10 3.0	0 27.5	15 31.4	1 25.2	25 29.1	24 8.8
25 F	18 11 13	3 7 34	21 57 8	29 3 40	13 21.0	11 13.0	29 23.9	10 27.0	0 26.9	15 32.0	1 23.2	25 27.5	24 8.5
26 Sa	18 15 10	4 4 49	6♍ 3 47	12♍57 23	13 21.8	12 4.5	0♊34.8	10 51.3	0 26.5	15 32.7	1 21.3	25 25.9	24 8.2
27 Su	18 19 7	5 2 3	19 44 31	26 25 21	13 22.4	13 0.1	1 45.8	11 16.0	0D 26.2	15 33.5	1 19.3	25 24.3	24 7.9
28 M	18 23 3	5 59 16	3♎ 0 8	9♎29 13	13R22.6	13 59.8	2 56.8	11 41.0	0 26.2	15 34.4	1 17.4	25 22.7	24 7.7
29 Tu	18 27 0	6 56 29	15 52 58	22 11 49	13 22.6	15 3.5	4 7.8	12 6.4	0 26.3	15 35.4	1 15.5	25 21.2	24 7.5
30 W	18 30 56	7 53 41	28 26 13	4♏36 39	13 22.2	16 11.2	5 18.9	12 32.1	0 26.6	15 36.5	1 13.7	25 19.6	24 7.3

Astro Data

	Dy Hr Mn
☽0S	5 4:37
♀0N	7 13:34
♂ D	11 18:35
♃⚻♅	16 20:33
☽0N	19 18:59
☿ R	21 2:05
♂0S	26 22:43
☽0S	1 10:49
☿ D	13 23:20
☽0N	16 4:23
♄ D	18 11:05
♃ D	27 18:16
☽0S	28 17:19

Planet Ingress

	Dy Hr Mn
☿ ♊	1 13:29
♀ ♈	4 12:27
☉ ♊	21 9:23
♀ ♉	30 21:02
☉ ♋	21 17:23
♀ ♊	25 12:13

Last Aspect / ☽ Ingress

Last Aspect Dy Hr Mn		☽ Ingress Dy Hr Mn
1 17:57	♆ △	♍ 1 23:45
4 5:59	♀ ☍	♎ 4 6:32
6 9:00	♆ ⚹	♏ 6 15:24
8 0:45	☉ ☍	♐ 9 2:17
11 7:52	♆ ☌	♑ 11 14:50
13 17:15	♇ □	♒ 14 3:44
16 8:00	♆ ⚹	♓ 16 14:46
18 17:30	☉ ⚹	♈ 18 22:04
20 19:20	♆ △	♉ 21 1:22
21 5:25	♃ ☍	♊ 23 1:54
24 19:42	♆ ☍	♋ 25 1:38
26 18:36	♀ □	♌ 27 2:27
29 2:05	♀ △	♍ 29 5:43
31 4:51	♆ □	♎ 31 12:02

Last Aspect / ☽ Ingress

Last Aspect Dy Hr Mn		☽ Ingress Dy Hr Mn
2 13:33	♆ ⚹	♏ 2 21:12
3 4:42	♀ ☍	♐ 5 8:31
7 12:55	♆ ☌	♑ 7 21:12
9 22:34	♇ □	♒ 10 10:08
12 13:31	♆ ⚹	♓ 12 21:44
14 22:30	♆ □	♈ 15 6:20
17 3:43	♆ △	♉ 17 11:07
19 0:10	♀ ☌	♊ 19 12:34
21 11:52	☉ ☌	♋ 21 12:13
23 7:47	♀ ⚹	♌ 23 11:57
25 5:53	♆ △	♍ 25 13:36
27 10:09	♆ □	♎ 27 18:30
29 18:01	♆ ⚹	♏ 30 3:02

☽ Phases & Eclipses

Dy Hr Mn		
8 0:45	○	17♏07
16 5:11	☽	25♒01
23 4:40	●	1♊44
29 20:07	☽	8♍07
6 15:59	○	15♐37
14 18:06	☽	23♓21
21 11:52	●	29♊47
21 12:03:42	✔	P 0.617
28 5:56	☽	6♎13

Astro Data

1 MAY 1982
Julian Day # 30071
Delta T 52.4 sec
SVP 05♓30'41"
Obliquity 23°26'27"
⚷ Chiron 21♉48.4
☽ Mean ☊ 16♋49.7

1 JUNE 1982
Julian Day # 30102
Delta T 52.5 sec
SVP 05♓30'37"
Obliquity 23°26'27"
⚷ Chiron 23♉56.6
☽ Mean ☊ 15♋11.2

JULY 1982 LONGITUDE

Day	Sid.Time	☉	0 hr ☽	Noon ☽	True ☊	☿	♀	♂	♃	♄	♅	♆	♇
1 Th	18 34 53	8♋50 53	10♏43 34	16♏47 26	13♋21.7	17♊22.8	6♊30.1	12♎58.1	0♏27.1	15♎37.8	1♐11.9	25♐18.0	24♎ 7.2
2 F	18 38 49	9 48 5	22 48 42	28 47 47	13R 21.3	18 38.2	7 41.3	13 24.4	0 27.8	15 39.1	1R 10.1	25R 16.5	24R 7.1
3 Sa	18 42 46	10 45 16	4♐45 7	10♐41 3	13 20.9	19 57.5	8 52.5	13 51.0	0 28.7	15 40.5	1 8.4	25 14.9	24 7.0
4 Su	18 46 42	11 42 27	16 36 0	22 30 16	13 20.6	21 20.6	10 3.8	14 17.9	0 29.7	15 42.0	1 6.7	25 13.4	24D 6.9
5 M	18 50 39	12 39 38	28 24 13	4♑18 8	13D 20.5	22 47.4	11 15.1	14 45.1	0 30.9	15 43.5	1 5.0	25 11.8	24 6.9
6 Tu	18 54 36	13 36 49	10♑12 20	16 7 5	13R 20.5	24 17.9	12 26.5	15 12.6	0 32.3	15 45.2	1 3.4	25 10.3	24 7.0
7 W	18 58 32	14 34 0	22 2 41	27 59 25	13 20.5	25 52.0	13 37.9	15 40.4	0 33.9	15 47.0	1 1.8	25 8.8	24 7.0
8 Th	19 2 29	15 31 11	3♒57 32	9♒57 21	13 20.4	27 29.6	14 49.4	16 8.5	0 35.6	15 48.9	1 0.3	25 7.3	24 7.1
9 F	19 6 25	16 28 23	15 59 8	22 3 12	13 20.2	29 10.7	16 1.0	16 36.8	0 37.5	15 50.9	0 58.8	25 5.8	24 7.3
10 Sa	19 10 22	17 25 34	28 9 52	4♓19 26	13 19.7	0♋55.1	17 12.5	17 5.4	0 39.6	15 53.0	0 57.3	25 4.4	24 7.4
11 Su	19 14 18	18 22 46	10♓32 15	16 48 40	13 19.2	2 42.7	18 24.1	17 34.3	0 41.8	15 55.1	0 55.9	25 2.9	24 7.6
12 M	19 18 15	19 19 58	23 9 1	29 33 39	13 18.6	4 33.4	19 35.8	18 3.4	0 44.3	15 57.4	0 54.5	25 1.5	24 7.9
13 Tu	19 22 11	20 17 11	6♈ 2 54	12♈37 5	13 18.1	6 26.9	20 47.5	18 32.8	0 46.9	15 59.7	0 53.2	25 0.0	24 8.1
14 W	19 26 8	21 14 24	19 16 29	26 1 22	13D 17.8	8 23.2	21 59.3	19 2.4	0 49.6	16 2.2	0 51.9	24 58.6	24 8.4
15 Th	19 30 5	22 11 37	2♉51 52	9♉48 6	13 18.0	10 21.9	23 11.1	19 32.3	0 52.6	16 4.7	0 50.6	24 57.2	24 8.8
16 F	19 34 1	23 8 52	16 50 4	23 57 39	13 18.5	12 22.8	24 23.0	20 2.4	0 55.7	16 7.3	0 49.4	24 55.8	24 9.1
17 Sa	19 37 58	24 6 7	1♊10 37	8♊28 34	13 19.3	14 25.6	25 34.9	20 32.8	0 59.0	16 10.1	0 48.2	24 54.4	24 9.5
18 Su	19 41 54	25 3 23	15 51 0	23 17 12	13 20.2	16 30.1	26 46.8	21 3.4	1 2.4	16 12.9	0 47.1	24 53.1	24 10.0
19 M	19 45 51	26 0 39	0♋46 22	8♋17 36	13R 20.8	18 35.8	27 58.8	21 34.3	1 6.0	16 15.8	0 46.0	24 51.8	24 10.5
20 Tu	19 49 47	26 57 56	15 49 50	23 21 59	13 21.0	20 42.5	29 10.9	22 5.4	1 9.8	16 18.8	0 45.0	24 50.4	24 11.0
21 W	19 53 44	27 55 14	0♌52 57	8♌21 39	13 20.6	22 50.0	0♋23.0	22 36.7	1 13.8	16 21.9	0 44.0	24 49.1	24 11.5
22 Th	19 57 40	28 52 32	15 47 1	23 8 8	13 19.4	24 57.7	1 35.1	23 8.2	1 17.9	16 25.0	0 43.1	24 47.9	24 12.1
23 F	20 1 37	29 49 50	0♍24 11	7♍34 30	13 17.5	27 5.6	2 47.3	23 40.0	1 22.1	16 28.3	0 42.2	24 46.6	24 12.7
24 Sa	20 5 34	0♌47 9	14 38 35	21 36 7	13 15.3	29 13.3	3 59.5	24 12.0	1 26.6	16 31.6	0 41.3	24 45.4	24 13.3
25 Su	20 9 30	1 44 28	28 26 54	5♎10 57	13 13.1	1♌20.5	5 11.8	24 44.2	1 31.1	16 35.0	0 40.5	24 44.2	24 14.0
26 M	20 13 27	2 41 47	11♎48 23	18 19 27	13 11.3	3 27.0	6 24.1	25 16.7	1 35.9	16 38.6	0 39.8	24 43.0	24 14.7
27 Tu	20 17 23	3 39 7	24 44 30	1♏ 3 57	13D 10.2	5 32.8	7 36.4	25 49.3	1 40.8	16 42.2	0 39.1	24 41.8	24 15.5
28 W	20 21 20	4 36 28	7♏18 18	13 28 6	13 9.9	7 37.4	8 48.8	26 22.1	1 45.8	16 45.8	0 38.5	24 40.6	24 16.2
29 Th	20 25 16	5 33 48	19 33 54	25 36 17	13 10.6	9 41.0	10 1.2	26 55.2	1 51.0	16 49.6	0 37.9	24 39.5	24 17.0
30 F	20 29 13	6 31 10	1♐35 50	7♐33 8	13 11.9	11 43.2	11 13.7	27 28.4	1 56.4	16 53.4	0 37.3	24 38.4	24 17.9
31 Sa	20 33 9	7 28 32	13 28 45	19 23 12	13 13.6	13 44.1	12 26.2	28 1.8	2 1.9	16 57.4	0 36.8	24 37.3	24 18.7

AUGUST 1982 LONGITUDE

Day	Sid.Time	☉	0 hr ☽	Noon ☽	True ☊	☿	♀	♂	♃	♄	♅	♆	♇
1 Su	20 37 6	8♌25 54	25♐17 2	1♑10 43	13♋15.1	15♌43.6	13♋38.8	28♎35.5	2♏ 7.6	17♎ 1.4	0♐36.4	24♐36.2	24♎19.6
2 M	20 41 3	9 23 18	7♑ 4 43	12 59 25	13R 16.1	17 41.6	14 51.4	29 9.3	2 13.4	17 5.5	0R 36.0	24R 35.2	24 20.6
3 Tu	20 44 59	10 20 42	18 55 13	24 52 28	13 16.2	19 38.1	16 4.0	29 43.3	2 19.3	17 9.6	0 35.6	24 34.2	24 21.6
4 W	20 48 56	11 18 6	0♒51 28	6♒52 29	13 14.9	21 33.0	17 16.7	0♏17.5	2 25.4	17 13.9	0 35.3	24 33.2	24 22.6
5 Th	20 52 52	12 15 32	12 55 44	19 1 27	13 12.3	23 26.3	18 29.4	0 51.8	2 31.6	17 18.2	0 35.1	24 32.2	24 23.6
6 F	20 56 49	13 12 59	25 9 48	1♓20 56	13 8.4	25 18.1	19 42.2	1 26.4	2 38.0	17 22.6	0 34.9	24 31.3	24 24.6
7 Sa	21 0 45	14 10 26	7♓35 0	13 52 7	13 3.5	27 8.3	20 55.0	2 1.1	2 44.5	17 27.0	0 34.7	24 30.4	24 25.7
8 Su	21 4 42	15 7 55	20 12 23	26 35 55	12 58.3	28 56.9	22 7.9	2 36.0	2 51.2	17 31.6	0 34.6	24 29.5	24 26.9
9 M	21 8 38	16 5 25	3♈ 2 50	9♈33 13	12 53.2	0♍43.9	23 20.8	3 11.0	2 57.9	17 36.2	0D 34.6	24 28.6	24 28.0
10 Tu	21 12 35	17 2 56	16 7 5	22 44 51	12 48.9	2 29.4	24 33.7	3 46.2	3 4.9	17 40.8	0 34.6	24 27.8	24 29.2
11 W	21 16 32	18 0 28	29 26 20	6♉11 42	12 46.0	4 13.4	25 46.7	4 21.6	3 11.9	17 45.6	0 34.6	24 27.0	24 30.4
12 Th	21 20 28	18 58 2	13♉ 1 4	19 54 30	12D 44.6	5 55.8	26 59.8	4 57.2	3 19.1	17 50.4	0 34.7	24 26.2	24 31.7
13 F	21 24 25	19 55 38	26 52 0	3♊53 34	12 44.6	7 36.7	28 12.9	5 32.9	3 26.4	17 55.3	0 34.9	24 25.4	24 32.9
14 Sa	21 28 21	20 53 15	10♊59 7	18 8 29	12 45.6	9 16.1	29 26.0	6 8.8	3 33.9	18 0.3	0 35.1	24 24.7	24 34.2
15 Su	21 32 18	21 50 53	25 21 25	2♋37 33	12 47.0	10 54.0	0♌39.2	6 44.9	3 41.4	18 5.3	0 35.4	24 24.0	24 35.6
16 M	21 36 14	22 48 34	9♋56 26	17 17 28	12R 47.8	12 30.4	1 52.4	7 21.1	3 49.1	18 10.4	0 35.7	24 23.4	24 36.9
17 Tu	21 40 11	23 46 15	24 39 59	2♌ 3 10	12 47.3	14 5.3	3 5.7	7 57.5	3 57.0	18 15.6	0 36.1	24 22.7	24 38.3
18 W	21 44 7	24 43 58	9♌26 11	16 48 6	12 45.0	15 38.8	4 19.0	8 34.1	4 4.9	18 20.8	0 36.5	24 22.1	24 39.8
19 Th	21 48 4	25 41 43	24 7 59	1♍24 55	12 40.7	17 10.7	5 32.3	9 10.8	4 13.0	18 26.1	0 36.9	24 21.5	24 41.2
20 F	21 52 1	26 39 28	8♍38 3	15 46 36	12 34.7	18 41.2	6 45.7	9 47.6	4 21.2	18 31.5	0 37.5	24 21.0	24 42.7
21 Sa	21 55 57	27 37 15	22 49 54	29 47 27	12 27.6	20 10.1	7 59.2	10 24.6	4 29.5	18 36.9	0 38.0	24 20.5	24 44.2
22 Su	21 59 54	28 35 3	6♎38 53	13♎23 58	12 20.3	21 37.6	9 12.6	11 1.8	4 37.9	18 42.4	0 38.7	24 20.0	24 45.7
23 M	22 3 50	29 32 53	20 2 39	26 35 1	12 13.8	23 3.5	10 26.2	11 39.1	4 46.5	18 47.9	0 39.3	24 19.5	24 47.3
24 Tu	22 7 47	0♍30 43	3♏ 1 18	9♏21 47	12 8.6	24 27.8	11 39.7	12 16.6	4 55.1	18 53.5	0 40.1	24 19.1	24 48.9
25 W	22 11 43	1 28 35	15 36 57	21 47 16	12 5.3	25 50.6	12 53.3	12 54.2	5 3.9	18 59.2	0 40.9	24 18.7	24 50.5
26 Th	22 15 40	2 26 28	27 53 18	3♐55 41	12D 3.9	27 11.8	14 6.9	13 31.9	5 12.8	19 4.9	0 41.7	24 18.3	24 52.1
27 F	22 19 36	3 24 23	9♐55 3	15 52 3	12 4.0	28 31.4	15 20.6	14 9.8	5 21.8	19 10.7	0 42.6	24 18.0	24 53.8
28 Sa	22 23 33	4 22 19	21 47 21	27 41 36	12 5.0	29 49.2	16 34.3	14 47.9	5 30.9	19 16.5	0 43.5	24 17.7	24 55.5
29 Su	22 27 30	5 20 16	3♑35 26	9♑29 29	12R 6.1	1♎ 5.3	17 48.0	15 26.0	5 40.1	19 22.4	0 44.5	24 17.4	24 57.2
30 M	22 31 26	6 18 14	15 24 18	21 20 28	12 6.3	2 19.7	19 1.8	16 4.3	5 49.4	19 28.3	0 45.5	24 17.2	24 58.9
31 Tu	22 35 23	7 16 14	27 18 27	3♒18 43	12 5.0	3 32.1	20 15.6	16 42.8	5 58.8	19 34.3	0 46.6	24 17.0	25 0.7

Astro Data Dy Hr Mn	Planet Ingress Dy Hr Mn
♇ D 4 13:11	☿ ♋ 9 11:26
♄∠♅ 11 5:02	♀ ♋ 20 16:21
☽0N 13 11:28	☉ ♌ 23 4:15
♃⊻♅ 14 12:45	☿ ♌ 24 8:48
☽0S 26 0:51	
	♂ ♏ 3 11:45
☽0N 9 16:41	☿ ♍ 8 14:06
♆✶♇ 9 7:14	♀ ♌ 14 11:09
♅ D 9 10:21	☉ ♍ 23 11:15
☽0S 22 9:28	☿ ♎ 28 3:22
☿0S 26 14:41	

Last Aspect Dy Hr Mn	☽ Ingress Dy Hr Mn
30 19:59 ☉ △	♐ 2 14:25
4 17:29 ♆ ☌	♑ 5 3:15
7 4:11 ♇ □	♒ 7 16:03
9 17:57 ♆ ✶	♓ 10 3:35
12 3:31 ♆ □	♈ 12 12:49
14 10:08 ♆ △	♉ 14 19:00
16 11:24 ☉ ✶	♊ 16 22:03
18 19:09 ♀ ☌	♋ 18 22:46
20 18:57 ☉ ☌	♌ 20 22:35
22 14:43 ♆ △	♍ 22 23:20
24 17:29 ♆ □	♎ 25 2:45
27 2:08 ♂ ☌	♏ 27 9:58
28 3:14 ♀ △	♐ 29 20:48

Last Aspect Dy Hr Mn	☽ Ingress Dy Hr Mn
1 7:04 ♂ ✶	♑ 1 9:36
3 10:59 ♇ □	♒ 3 22:17
6 0:19 ☿ ☍	♓ 6 9:23
8 8:03 ♆ □	♈ 8 18:21
10 16:48 ♀ □	♉ 11 1:00
13 2:32 ♀ ✶	♊ 13 5:22
14 22:44 ♇ △	♋ 15 7:40
16 23:57 ♇ □	♌ 17 8:40
19 2:45 ☉ ☌	♍ 19 9:40
21 2:35 ♆ □	♎ 21 12:22
23 8:42 ♇ ☌	♏ 23 18:21
25 22:28 ☿ ✶	♐ 26 4:11
28 6:23 ♇ ✶	♑ 28 16:42
30 19:23 ♇ □	♒ 31 5:23

☽ Phases & Eclipses Dy Hr Mn	
6 7:32	○ 13♑55
6 7:31	T 1.718
14 3:47	☽ 21♈23
20 18:57	● 27♋43
20 18:43:49	P 0.464
27 18:22	☽ 4♏23
4 22:34	○ 12♒12
12 11:08	☽ 19♉25
19 2:45	● 25♌48
26 9:49	☽ 2♐50

Astro Data

1 JULY 1982
Julian Day # 30132
Delta T 52.6 sec
SVP 05♓30'32"
Obliquity 23°26'27"
⚷ Chiron 25♉48.7
☽ Mean ☊ 13♋35.9

1 AUGUST 1982
Julian Day # 30163
Delta T 52.6 sec
SVP 05♓30'27"
Obliquity 23°26'28"
⚷ Chiron 27♉11.5
☽ Mean ☊ 11♋57.5

LONGITUDE — SEPTEMBER 1982

Day	Sid.Time	☉	0 hr ☽	Noon ☽	True ☊	☿	♀	♂	♃	♄	♅	♆	♇
1 W	22 39 19	8♍14 15	9♒21 39	15♒27 35	12♋ 1.5	4♎42.6	21♌29.4	17♏21.3	6♏ 8.3	19♎40.4	0♐47.8	24♐16.8	25♎ 2.4
2 Th	22 43 16	9 12 18	21 36 46	27 49 26	11R 55.7	5 51.1	22 43.3	18 0.0	6 17.9	19 46.5	0 49.0	24R 16.7	25 4.3
3 F	22 47 12	10 10 22	4♓ 5 41	10♓25 35	11 47.6	6 57.4	23 57.2	18 38.9	6 27.7	19 52.6	0 50.2	24 16.6	25 6.1
4 Sa	22 51 9	11 8 28	16 49 10	23 16 22	11 37.9	8 1.5	25 11.2	19 17.8	6 37.5	19 58.8	0 51.5	24 16.5	25 7.9
5 Su	22 55 5	12 6 35	29 47 6	6♈21 13	11 27.4	9 3.3	26 25.1	19 56.9	6 47.4	20 5.0	0 52.8	24D 16.4	25 9.8
6 M	22 59 2	13 4 44	12♈58 33	19 38 58	11 17.1	10 2.5	27 39.2	20 36.1	6 57.4	20 11.3	0 54.2	24 16.4	25 11.7
7 Tu	23 2 58	14 2 55	26 22 14	3♉ 8 13	11 8.2	10 59.1	28 53.2	21 15.4	7 7.5	20 17.6	0 55.6	24 16.4	25 13.6
8 W	23 6 55	15 1 9	9♉56 44	16 47 39	11 1.3	11 52.9	0♍ 7.3	21 54.9	7 17.6	20 24.0	0 57.1	24 16.5	25 15.6
9 Th	23 10 52	15 59 24	23 40 51	0♊36 16	10 56.9	12 43.7	1 21.5	22 34.4	7 27.9	20 30.4	0 58.6	24 16.6	25 17.5
10 F	23 14 48	16 57 41	7♊33 48	14 33 24	10D 54.9	13 31.3	2 35.6	23 14.1	7 38.3	20 36.9	1 0.2	24 16.7	25 19.5
11 Sa	23 18 45	17 56 1	21 35 0	28 38 32	10 54.6	14 15.4	3 49.9	23 54.0	7 48.7	20 43.4	1 1.8	24 16.8	25 21.5
12 Su	23 22 41	18 54 22	5♋43 54	12♋50 56	10R 55.0	14 55.8	5 4.1	24 33.9	7 59.3	20 49.9	1 3.5	24 17.0	25 23.5
13 M	23 26 38	19 52 46	19 59 26	27 9 7	10 54.8	15 32.3	6 18.4	25 14.0	8 9.9	20 56.5	1 5.2	24 17.2	25 25.6
14 Tu	23 30 34	20 51 12	4♌19 39	11♌30 33	10 52.8	16 4.5	7 32.7	25 54.2	8 20.6	21 3.1	1 7.0	24 17.5	25 27.6
15 W	23 34 31	21 49 40	18 41 20	25 51 23	10 48.4	16 32.2	8 47.1	26 34.5	8 31.4	21 9.8	1 8.8	24 17.8	25 29.7
16 Th	23 38 27	22 48 10	3♍ 0 4	10♍ 6 41	10 41.2	16 55.0	10 1.5	27 14.9	8 42.3	21 16.5	1 10.7	24 18.1	25 31.8
17 F	23 42 24	23 46 42	17 10 34	24 11 4	10 31.4	17 12.6	11 15.9	27 55.4	8 53.2	21 23.2	1 12.6	24 18.4	25 33.9
18 Sa	23 46 21	24 45 16	1♎ 7 32	7♎59 28	10 20.0	17 24.6	12 30.3	28 36.1	9 4.3	21 30.0	1 14.5	24 18.8	25 36.0
19 Su	23 50 17	25 43 51	14 46 25	21 28 4	10 8.1	17R 30.6	13 44.8	29 16.8	9 15.4	21 36.8	1 16.5	24 19.2	25 38.2
20 M	23 54 14	26 42 29	28 4 13	4♏34 49	9 57.0	17 30.3	14 59.3	29 57.7	9 26.6	21 43.6	1 18.5	24 19.7	25 40.3
21 Tu	23 58 10	27 41 8	10♏59 55	17 19 42	9 47.6	17 23.4	16 13.8	0♐38.7	9 37.8	21 50.5	1 20.6	24 20.1	25 42.5
22 W	0 2 7	28 39 49	23 34 28	29 44 36	9 40.6	17 9.6	17 28.4	1 19.8	9 49.1	21 57.4	1 22.8	24 20.6	25 44.7
23 Th	0 6 3	29 38 32	5♐50 35	11♐52 56	9 36.2	16 48.7	18 42.9	2 1.0	10 0.5	22 4.3	1 24.9	24 21.2	25 46.9
24 F	0 10 0	0♎37 17	17 52 17	23 49 16	9 34.1	16 20.5	19 57.5	2 42.4	10 12.0	22 11.2	1 27.1	24 21.8	25 49.1
25 Sa	0 13 56	1 36 3	29 44 32	5♑38 48	9 33.6	15 45.1	21 12.2	3 23.8	10 23.6	22 18.2	1 29.4	24 22.4	25 51.4
26 Su	0 17 53	2 34 51	11♑32 44	17 27 4	9 33.6	15 2.6	22 26.8	4 5.3	10 35.2	22 25.2	1 31.7	24 23.0	25 53.6
27 M	0 21 50	3 33 41	23 22 26	29 19 31	9 33.0	14 13.5	23 41.5	4 47.0	10 46.8	22 32.2	1 34.0	24 23.7	25 55.9
28 Tu	0 25 46	4 32 33	5♒18 56	11♒21 14	9 30.9	13 18.2	24 56.2	5 28.7	10 58.6	22 39.3	1 36.4	24 24.4	25 58.2
29 W	0 29 43	5 31 26	17 26 58	23 36 34	9 26.4	12 17.7	26 10.9	6 10.5	11 10.3	22 46.3	1 38.8	24 25.1	26 0.4
30 Th	0 33 39	6 30 21	29 50 25	6♓ 8 47	9 19.3	11 13.1	27 25.7	6 52.5	11 22.2	22 53.4	1 41.3	24 25.9	26 2.7

LONGITUDE — OCTOBER 1982

Day	Sid.Time	☉	0 hr ☽	Noon ☽	True ☊	☿	♀	♂	♃	♄	♅	♆	♇
1 F	0 37 36	7♎29 18	12♓31 52	18♓59 46	9♋ 9.5	10♎ 5.8	28♍40.4	7♐34.5	11♏34.1	23♎ 0.6	1♐43.8	24♐26.7	26♎ 5.0
2 Sa	0 41 32	8 28 17	25 32 27	2♈ 9 49	8R 57.7	8R 57.3	29 55.2	8 16.6	11 46.1	23 7.7	1 46.3	24 27.5	26 7.3
3 Su	0 45 29	9 27 18	8♈51 38	15 37 37	8 44.8	7 49.4	1♎10.0	8 58.8	11 58.1	23 14.8	1 48.9	24 28.4	26 9.7
4 M	0 49 25	10 26 20	22 27 22	29 20 26	8 32.3	6 44.0	2 24.8	9 41.1	12 10.2	23 22.0	1 51.5	24 29.3	26 12.0
5 Tu	0 53 22	11 25 25	6♉16 23	13♉14 41	8 21.2	5 42.8	3 39.7	10 23.5	12 22.3	23 29.2	1 54.1	24 30.2	26 14.3
6 W	0 57 19	12 24 32	20 14 52	27 16 28	8 12.5	4 47.6	4 54.6	11 6.0	12 34.5	23 36.4	1 56.8	24 31.2	26 16.7
7 Th	1 1 15	13 23 42	4♊19 5	11♊22 21	8 6.7	3 59.9	6 9.5	11 48.6	12 46.7	23 43.6	1 59.5	24 32.2	26 19.1
8 F	1 5 12	14 22 54	18 25 58	25 29 41	8 3.7	3 21.1	7 24.4	12 31.3	12 59.0	23 50.8	2 2.3	24 33.2	26 21.4
9 Sa	1 9 8	15 22 8	2♋33 18	9♋36 42	8 2.8	2 52.0	8 39.3	13 14.1	13 11.4	23 58.1	2 5.1	24 34.2	26 23.8
10 Su	1 13 5	16 21 24	16 39 46	23 42 24	8 2.7	2 33.3	9 54.3	13 57.0	13 23.8	24 5.3	2 7.9	24 35.3	26 26.2
11 M	1 17 1	17 20 43	0♌44 31	7♌46 1	8 2.3	2D 25.4	11 9.3	14 40.0	13 36.2	24 12.6	2 10.8	24 36.4	26 28.6
12 Tu	1 20 58	18 20 4	14 46 45	21 46 34	8 0.2	2 28.4	12 24.3	15 23.0	13 48.7	24 19.8	2 13.7	24 37.6	26 31.0
13 W	1 24 54	19 19 28	28 45 15	5♍42 32	7 55.5	2 42.1	13 39.3	16 6.2	14 1.2	24 27.1	2 16.6	24 38.7	26 33.4
14 Th	1 28 51	20 18 53	12♍38 6	19 31 37	7 48.0	3 6.0	14 54.3	16 49.4	14 13.8	24 34.4	2 19.6	24 39.9	26 35.7
15 F	1 32 48	21 18 21	26 22 43	3♎10 59	7 37.8	3 39.7	16 9.4	17 32.7	14 26.4	24 41.7	2 22.6	24 41.2	26 38.2
16 Sa	1 36 44	22 17 51	9♎56 5	16 37 37	7 25.9	4 22.4	17 24.5	18 16.1	14 39.1	24 49.0	2 25.6	24 42.4	26 40.6
17 Su	1 40 41	23 17 23	23 15 18	29 48 51	7 13.3	5 13.3	18 39.5	18 59.6	14 51.8	24 56.3	2 28.6	24 43.7	26 43.0
18 M	1 44 37	24 16 57	6♏18 7	12♏42 58	7 1.4	6 11.8	19 54.6	19 43.2	15 4.5	25 3.6	2 31.7	24 45.0	26 45.4
19 Tu	1 48 34	25 16 33	19 3 23	25 19 28	6 51.2	7 16.9	21 9.8	20 26.9	15 17.3	25 10.9	2 34.8	24 46.3	26 47.8
20 W	1 52 30	26 16 11	1♐31 23	7♐39 22	6 43.5	8 27.9	22 24.9	21 10.7	15 30.1	25 18.2	2 38.0	24 47.7	26 50.2
21 Th	1 56 27	27 15 51	13 43 46	19 45 0	6 38.4	9 44.0	23 40.0	21 54.5	15 42.9	25 25.5	2 41.1	24 49.1	26 52.6
22 F	2 0 23	28 15 33	25 43 32	1♑39 55	6D 36.0	11 4.4	24 55.2	22 38.4	15 55.8	25 32.8	2 44.3	24 50.5	26 55.0
23 Sa	2 4 20	29 15 17	7♑34 44	13 28 37	6 35.4	12 28.7	26 10.3	23 22.4	16 8.7	25 40.1	2 47.5	24 52.0	26 57.4
24 Su	2 8 16	0♏15 2	19 22 13	25 16 12	6 35.8	13 56.1	27 25.5	24 6.5	16 21.6	25 47.4	2 50.8	24 53.5	26 59.9
25 M	2 12 13	1 14 49	1♒11 18	7♒ 8 10	6R 36.2	15 26.1	28 40.7	24 50.6	16 34.6	25 54.7	2 54.1	24 55.0	27 2.3
26 Tu	2 16 10	2 14 38	13 7 29	19 9 57	6 35.5	16 58.3	29 55.9	25 34.9	16 47.6	26 2.0	2 57.4	24 56.5	27 4.7
27 W	2 20 6	3 14 28	25 16 9	1♓26 41	6 32.9	18 32.3	1♏11.1	26 19.2	17 0.6	26 9.2	3 0.7	24 58.0	27 7.1
28 Th	2 24 3	4 14 20	7♓42 3	14 2 42	6 28.1	20 7.6	2 26.3	27 3.5	17 13.6	26 16.5	3 4.0	24 59.6	27 9.5
29 F	2 27 59	5 14 14	20 28 58	27 1 4	6 20.9	21 44.1	3 41.5	27 48.0	17 26.7	26 23.7	3 7.4	25 1.2	27 11.9
30 Sa	2 31 56	6 14 9	3♈39 8	10♈23 7	6 11.9	23 21.4	4 56.7	28 32.5	17 39.7	26 31.0	3 10.8	25 2.8	27 14.3
31 Su	2 35 52	7 14 6	17 12 52	24 8 3	6 1.9	24 59.3	6 11.9	29 17.1	17 52.8	26 38.2	3 14.2	25 4.5	27 16.7

Astro Data

	Dy Hr Mn
☽0N	5 21:52
♆ D	5 23:36
☽0S	18 18:32
♃∠♆	19 8:35
☿ R	19 11:03
☽0N	3 4:56
♀0S	4 17:08
☿ D	11 5:22
♄✶♆	14 21:50
☽0S	16 3:05
☽0N	30 14:26

Planet Ingress

	Dy Hr Mn
♀ ♍	7 21:38
♂ ♐	20 1:20
☉ ♎	23 8:46
♀ ♎	2 1:32
☉ ♏	23 17:58
♀ ♏	26 1:19
♂ ♑	31 23:05

Last Aspect / ☽ Ingress

Last Aspect Dy Hr Mn		☽ Ingress Dy Hr Mn
2 6:43	♇ △	♓ 2 16:11
4 13:51	♆ □	♈ 5 0:24
7 4:55	♀ △	♉ 7 6:27
8 21:59	♂ ☍	♊ 9 10:57
11 6:26	♇ △	♋ 11 14:18
13 9:13	♂ △	♌ 13 16:46
15 13:51	♂ □	♍ 15 18:57
17 19:24	♂ ✶	♎ 17 22:03
19 19:37	♇ ☌	♏ 20 3:32
22 10:45	☉ ✶	♐ 22 12:30
24 16:06	♇ ✶	♑ 25 0:31
27 5:11	♇ □	♒ 27 13:21
29 16:41	♇ △	♓ 30 0:18

Last Aspect / ☽ Ingress

Last Aspect Dy Hr Mn		☽ Ingress Dy Hr Mn
1 22:01	♆ □	♈ 2 8:06
4 6:33	♇ ☍	♉ 4 13:09
5 10:39	♃ ☍	♊ 6 16:39
8 13:30	♇ △	♋ 8 19:39
10 16:42	♇ □	♌ 10 22:44
12 20:12	♇ ✶	♍ 13 2:09
14 21:01	♆ □	♎ 15 6:23
17 6:20	♇ ☌	♏ 17 12:21
18 16:44	♃ ☌	♐ 19 21:02
22 5:35	☉ ✶	♑ 22 8:38
24 18:19	♀ □	♒ 24 21:36
27 3:37	♇ △	♓ 27 9:12
29 14:13	♂ △	♈ 29 17:25
31 22:00	♂ △	♉ 31 22:04

☽ Phases & Eclipses

Dy Hr Mn	
3 12:28	○ 10♓41
10 17:19	☽ 17♊40
17 12:09	● 24♍16
25 4:07	☽ 1♑46
3 1:09	○ 9♈30
9 23:26	☽ 16♋20
17 0:04	● 23♎18
25 0:08	☽ 1♒15

Astro Data

1 SEPTEMBER 1982
Julian Day # 30194
Delta T 52.7 sec
SVP 05♓30'23"
Obliquity 23°26'28"
⚷ Chiron 27♉43.6
☽ Mean ☊ 10♋19.0

1 OCTOBER 1982
Julian Day # 30224
Delta T 52.8 sec
SVP 05♓30'20"
Obliquity 23°26'29"
⚷ Chiron 27♉18.8R
☽ Mean ☊ 8♋43.6

NOVEMBER 1982 LONGITUDE

Day	Sid.Time	☉	0 hr ☽	Noon ☽	True ☊	☿	♀	♂	♃	♄	♅	♆	♇
1 M	2 39 49	8♏14 5	1♉ 8 14	8♉12 52	5♋51.9	26♎37.7	7♏27.2	0♑ 1.7	18♏ 6.0	26♎45.4	3♐17.6	25♐ 6.1	27♎19.0
2 Tu	2 43 45	9 14 6	15 21 16	22 32 42	5R43.1	28 16.4	8 42.4	0 46.4	18 19.1	26 52.6	3 21.0	25 7.8	27 21.4
3 W	2 47 42	10 14 9	29 46 24	7♊ 1 34	5 36.3	29 55.2	9 57.7	1 31.2	18 32.2	26 59.8	3 24.5	25 9.5	27 23.8
4 Th	2 51 39	11 14 13	14♊17 25	21 33 14	5 32.0	1♏34.0	11 12.9	2 16.1	18 45.4	27 6.9	3 28.0	25 11.3	27 26.2
5 F	2 55 35	12 14 20	28 48 23	6♋ 2 16	5D30.1	3 12.9	12 28.2	3 1.0	18 58.6	27 14.1	3 31.5	25 13.0	27 28.5
6 Sa	2 59 32	13 14 29	13♋14 25	20 24 28	5 30.1	4 51.6	13 43.5	3 46.0	19 11.8	27 21.2	3 35.0	25 14.8	27 30.9
7 Su	3 3 28	14 14 40	27 32 7	4♌37 9	5 31.1	6 30.2	14 58.8	4 31.0	19 25.0	27 28.3	3 38.5	25 16.6	27 33.2
8 M	3 7 25	15 14 53	11♌39 27	18 38 55	5R31.9	8 8.5	16 14.1	5 16.1	19 38.2	27 35.4	3 42.1	25 18.5	27 35.5
9 Tu	3 11 21	16 15 8	25 35 31	2♍29 12	5 31.5	9 46.7	17 29.4	6 1.3	19 51.5	27 42.5	3 45.7	25 20.3	27 37.9
10 W	3 15 18	17 15 25	9♍19 58	16 7 49	5 29.3	11 24.6	18 44.7	6 46.5	20 4.7	27 49.5	3 49.2	25 22.2	27 40.2
11 Th	3 19 14	18 15 44	22 52 43	29 34 39	5 24.9	13 2.2	20 0.0	7 31.8	20 17.9	27 56.5	3 52.8	25 24.1	27 42.5
12 F	3 23 11	19 16 5	6♎13 34	12♎49 24	5 18.5	14 39.5	21 15.3	8 17.2	20 31.2	28 3.5	3 56.4	25 26.0	27 44.8
13 Sa	3 27 8	20 16 28	19 22 7	25 51 39	5 10.8	16 16.5	22 30.7	9 2.6	20 44.5	28 10.5	4 0.1	25 27.9	27 47.0
14 Su	3 31 4	21 16 53	2♏17 55	8♏40 53	5 2.5	17 53.3	23 46.0	9 48.1	20 57.7	28 17.4	4 3.7	25 29.8	27 49.3
15 M	3 35 1	22 17 19	15 0 31	21 16 49	4 54.6	19 29.7	25 1.4	10 33.6	21 11.0	28 24.3	4 7.3	25 31.8	27 51.6
16 Tu	3 38 57	23 17 47	27 29 51	3♐39 40	4 47.9	21 5.9	26 16.7	11 19.2	21 24.2	28 31.2	4 11.0	25 33.7	27 53.8
17 W	3 42 54	24 18 17	9♐46 25	15 50 17	4 43.0	22 41.8	27 32.1	12 4.9	21 37.5	28 38.1	4 14.6	25 35.7	27 56.0
18 Th	3 46 50	25 18 49	21 51 29	27 50 19	4 40.1	24 17.5	28 47.4	12 50.6	21 50.8	28 44.9	4 18.3	25 37.8	27 58.3
19 F	3 50 47	26 19 21	3♑47 8	9♑42 19	4D39.1	25 52.8	0♐ 2.8	13 36.4	22 4.0	28 51.6	4 22.0	25 39.8	28 0.4
20 Sa	3 54 43	27 19 55	15 36 19	21 29 37	4 39.7	27 28.0	1 18.2	14 22.2	22 17.3	28 58.4	4 25.7	25 41.8	28 2.6
21 Su	3 58 40	28 20 31	27 22 46	3♒16 19	4 41.3	29 2.9	2 33.5	15 8.1	22 30.5	29 5.1	4 29.3	25 43.9	28 4.8
22 M	4 2 37	29 21 8	9♒10 52	15 7 3	4 43.1	0♐37.6	3 48.9	15 54.0	22 43.7	29 11.8	4 33.0	25 45.9	28 7.0
23 Tu	4 6 33	0♐21 45	21 5 30	27 6 52	4R44.5	2 12.1	5 4.3	16 40.0	22 57.0	29 18.4	4 36.7	25 48.0	28 9.1
24 W	4 10 30	1 22 24	3♓11 47	9♓20 53	4 44.9	3 46.5	6 19.6	17 26.0	23 10.2	29 25.0	4 40.4	25 50.1	28 11.2
25 Th	4 14 26	2 23 4	15 34 46	21 53 59	4 44.0	5 20.6	7 35.0	18 12.1	23 23.4	29 31.5	4 44.1	25 52.2	28 13.3
26 F	4 18 23	3 23 46	28 19 1	4♈50 17	4 41.6	6 54.7	8 50.3	18 58.2	23 36.5	29 38.0	4 47.8	25 54.4	28 15.4
27 Sa	4 22 19	4 24 28	11♈28 4	18 12 34	4 38.0	8 28.6	10 5.7	19 44.3	23 49.7	29 44.5	4 51.5	25 56.5	28 17.4
28 Su	4 26 16	5 25 11	25 3 49	2♉ 1 43	4 33.6	10 2.3	11 21.1	20 30.5	24 2.9	29 50.9	4 55.2	25 58.6	28 19.5
29 M	4 30 12	6 25 55	9♉ 5 58	16 16 10	4 29.1	11 36.0	12 36.4	21 16.7	24 16.0	29 57.2	4 58.9	26 0.8	28 21.5
30 Tu	4 34 9	7 26 41	23 31 41	0♊51 46	4 25.1	13 9.6	13 51.8	22 3.0	24 29.1	0♏ 3.6	5 2.6	26 3.0	28 23.5

DECEMBER 1982 LONGITUDE

Day	Sid.Time	☉	0 hr ☽	Noon ☽	True ☊	☿	♀	♂	♃	♄	♅	♆	♇
1 W	4 38 6	8♐27 28	8♊15 32	15♊42 1	4♋22.1	14♐43.1	15♐ 7.1	22♑49.3	24♏42.2	0♏ 9.8	5♐ 6.3	26♐ 5.1	28♎25.5
2 Th	4 42 2	9 28 16	23 10 10	0♋38 57	4D20.4	16 16.5	16 22.5	23 35.7	24 55.3	0 16.1	5 10.0	26 7.3	28 27.4
3 F	4 45 59	10 29 5	8♋ 7 19	15 34 19	4 20.1	17 49.9	17 37.9	24 22.1	25 8.3	0 22.2	5 13.7	26 9.5	28 29.4
4 Sa	4 49 55	11 29 56	22 59 3	0♌20 43	4 20.9	19 23.2	18 53.2	25 8.5	25 21.4	0 28.3	5 17.4	26 11.7	28 31.3
5 Su	4 53 52	12 30 47	7♌38 43	14 52 30	4 22.2	20 56.5	20 8.6	25 55.0	25 34.4	0 34.4	5 21.1	26 13.9	28 33.2
6 M	4 57 48	13 31 40	22 1 42	29 6 3	4 23.6	22 29.8	21 23.9	26 41.5	25 47.4	0 40.4	5 24.8	26 16.2	28 35.0
7 Tu	5 1 45	14 32 35	6♍ 5 26	12♍59 47	4R24.6	24 3.0	22 39.3	27 28.0	26 0.3	0 46.4	5 28.4	26 18.4	28 36.9
8 W	5 5 42	15 33 31	19 49 10	26 33 41	4 24.7	25 36.1	23 54.7	28 14.6	26 13.2	0 52.3	5 32.1	26 20.6	28 38.7
9 Th	5 9 38	16 34 27	3♎13 29	9♎48 48	4 23.9	27 9.2	25 10.0	29 1.2	26 26.1	0 58.1	5 35.8	26 22.9	28 40.5
10 F	5 13 35	17 35 26	16 19 49	22 46 48	4 22.4	28 42.3	26 25.4	29 47.8	26 39.0	1 3.9	5 39.4	26 25.1	28 42.3
11 Sa	5 17 31	18 36 25	29 9 59	5♏29 35	4 20.2	0♑15.2	27 40.8	0♒34.5	26 51.8	1 9.7	5 43.1	26 27.3	28 44.0
12 Su	5 21 28	19 37 25	11♏45 52	17 59 3	4 17.9	1 48.1	28 56.2	1 21.2	27 4.6	1 15.3	5 46.7	26 29.6	28 45.7
13 M	5 25 24	20 38 27	24 9 20	0♐16 57	4 15.7	3 20.8	0♑11.5	2 7.9	27 17.3	1 20.9	5 50.3	26 31.9	28 47.4
14 Tu	5 29 21	21 39 29	6♐22 6	12 24 59	4 13.9	4 53.3	1 26.9	2 54.7	27 30.0	1 26.5	5 53.9	26 34.1	28 49.1
15 W	5 33 17	22 40 32	18 25 49	24 24 48	4 12.7	6 25.6	2 42.3	3 41.5	27 42.7	1 31.9	5 57.5	26 36.4	28 50.7
16 Th	5 37 14	23 41 37	0♑22 10	6♑18 10	4D12.2	7 57.6	3 57.6	4 28.3	27 55.3	1 37.4	6 1.1	26 38.7	28 52.4
17 F	5 41 11	24 42 41	12 13 3	18 7 6	4 12.3	9 29.2	5 13.0	5 15.1	28 7.9	1 42.7	6 4.7	26 40.9	28 53.9
18 Sa	5 45 7	25 43 47	24 0 38	29 53 59	4 12.9	11 0.3	6 28.4	6 2.0	28 20.5	1 48.0	6 8.2	26 43.2	28 55.5
19 Su	5 49 4	26 44 52	5♒47 31	11♒41 39	4 13.6	12 30.9	7 43.7	6 48.9	28 33.0	1 53.2	6 11.8	26 45.5	28 57.0
20 M	5 53 0	27 45 59	17 36 49	23 33 28	4 14.5	14 0.8	8 59.1	7 35.8	28 45.4	1 58.3	6 15.3	26 47.7	28 58.5
21 Tu	5 56 57	28 47 5	29 32 7	5♓33 15	4 15.2	15 29.8	10 14.4	8 22.8	28 57.8	2 3.4	6 18.8	26 50.0	29 0.0
22 W	6 0 53	29 48 12	11♓37 25	17 45 11	4 15.6	16 57.7	11 29.8	9 9.7	29 10.2	2 8.4	6 22.3	26 52.3	29 1.4
23 Th	6 4 50	0♑49 19	23 57 5	0♈13 40	4R15.8	18 24.4	12 45.1	9 56.7	29 22.5	2 13.3	6 25.7	26 54.5	29 2.9
24 F	6 8 46	1 50 26	6♈35 27	13 2 57	4 15.9	19 49.6	14 0.4	10 43.7	29 34.7	2 18.1	6 29.2	26 56.8	29 4.2
25 Sa	6 12 43	2 51 33	19 36 34	26 16 41	4 15.8	21 13.0	15 15.7	11 30.7	29 46.9	2 22.9	6 32.6	26 59.1	29 5.6
26 Su	6 16 40	3 52 40	3♉ 3 34	9♉57 23	4D15.7	22 34.2	16 31.0	12 17.7	29 59.0	2 27.6	6 36.0	27 1.3	29 6.9
27 M	6 20 36	4 53 47	16 58 8	24 5 40	4 15.7	23 52.9	17 46.3	13 4.7	0♐11.1	2 32.2	6 39.4	27 3.6	29 8.2
28 Tu	6 24 33	5 54 55	1♊19 43	8♊39 45	4 15.9	25 8.6	19 1.6	13 51.8	0 23.1	2 36.8	6 42.7	27 5.8	29 9.4
29 W	6 28 29	6 56 2	16 5 6	23 34 57	4 16.0	26 20.8	20 16.9	14 38.8	0 35.0	2 41.2	6 46.1	27 8.1	29 10.7
30 Th	6 32 26	7 57 10	1♋ 8 16	8♋43 57	4R16.2	27 28.9	21 32.2	15 25.9	0 46.9	2 45.6	6 49.4	27 10.3	29 11.9
31 F	6 36 22	8 58 18	16 20 47	23 57 31	4 16.1	28 32.3	22 47.5	16 13.0	0 58.8	2 49.9	6 52.7	27 12.6	29 13.0

Astro Data	Planet Ingress	Last Aspect	☽ Ingress	Last Aspect	☽ Ingress	☽ Phases & Eclipses
Dy Hr Mn	Dy Hr Mn	Dy Hr Mn	Dy Hr Mn	Dy Hr Mn	Dy Hr Mn	Dy Hr Mn
♄☌♇ 8 0:38	☿ ♏ 3 1:10	2 5:02 ♃ ☍	♊ 3 0:23	2 8:30 ♇ △	♋ 2 10:58	1 12:57 ○ 8♉46
☽0S 12 10:17	♀ ♐ 18 23:07	4 21:47 ♇ △	♋ 5 1:59	4 9:02 ♇ □	♌ 4 11:26	8 6:38 ☽ 15♌32
☽0N 27 1:05	☿ ♐ 21 14:28	7 0:02 ♇ □	♌ 7 4:10	6 11:09 ♇ ⚹	♍ 6 13:32	15 15:10 ● 22♏56
	☉ ♐ 22 15:23	9 3:42 ♄ ⚹	♍ 9 7:40	8 15:57 ♂ △	♎ 8 18:11	23 20:06 ☽ 1♓13
♃⊻♆ 8 16:40	♄ ♏ 29 10:28	11 4:31 ♆ □	♎ 11 12:46	10 23:11 ♇ ☌	♏ 11 1:34	
☽0S 9 16:19		13 16:27 ♄ ☌	♏ 13 19:42	13 6:14 ♃ ☌	♐ 13 11:27	1 0:21 ○ 8♊28
♃⊻♇ 21 4:48	☿ ♑ 10 20:04	15 21:22 ♀ ☌	♐ 16 4:52	15 20:58 ♇ ⚹	♑ 15 23:15	7 15:53 ☽ 15♍13
☽0N 24 10:30	♂ ♒ 10 6:17	18 13:58 ♄ ⚹	♑ 18 16:21	18 10:02 ♇ □	♒ 18 12:12	15 9:18 ● 23♐04
	♀ ♑ 12 20:20	21 3:56 ☿ ⚹	♒ 21 5:20	20 22:56 ♇ △	♓ 21 0:56	15 9:31:19 • P 0.735
	☉ ♑ 22 4:38	23 16:29 ♄ △	♓ 23 17:43	23 10:33 ♃ △	♈ 23 11:34	23 14:17 ☽ 1♈26
	♃ ♐ 26 1:57	25 19:30 ♆ □	♈ 26 3:07	25 17:02 ♇ ☍	♉ 25 18:37	30 11:33 ○ 8♋27
		28 8:19 ♄ ☍	♉ 28 8:31	27 12:47 ☿ △	♊ 27 21:49	30 11:29 • T 1.182
		30 1:36 ♃ ☍	♊ 30 10:36	29 20:55 ♇ △	♋ 29 22:12	
				31 20:33 ☿ ☍	♌ 31 21:33	

Astro Data

1 NOVEMBER 1982
Julian Day # 30255
Delta T 52.8 sec
SVP 05♓30'17"
Obliquity 23°26'29"
⚷ Chiron 26♉03.8R
☽ Mean ☊ 7♋05.1

1 DECEMBER 1982
Julian Day # 30285
Delta T 52.9 sec
SVP 05♓30'12"
Obliquity 23°26'28"
⚷ Chiron 24♉30.0R
☽ Mean ☊ 5♋29.8

LONGITUDE — JANUARY 1983

Day	Sid.Time	☉	0 hr ☽	Noon ☽	True ☊	☿	♀	♂	♃	♄	♅	♆	♇
1 Sa	6 40 19	9♑59 26	1♌32 55	9♌ 5 48	4♋15.7	29♑30.1	24♑ 2.7	17♒ 0.1	1♐10.5	2♏54.1	6♐56.0	27♐14.8	29♎14.1
2 Su	6 44 15	11 0 34	16 35 6	23 59 53	4R15.1	0♒21.7	25 18.0	17 47.2	1 22.2	2 58.3	6 59.2	27 17.0	29 15.2
3 M	6 48 12	12 1 43	1♍19 20	8♍32 54	4 14.2	1 6.1	26 33.2	18 34.3	1 33.8	3 2.3	7 2.4	27 19.2	29 16.3
4 Tu	6 52 9	13 2 51	15 40 7	22 40 45	4 13.3	1 42.5	27 48.5	19 21.4	1 45.4	3 6.3	7 5.6	27 21.4	29 17.3
5 W	6 56 5	14 4 0	29 34 44	6♎22 7	4 12.5	2 9.9	29 3.7	20 8.5	1 56.9	3 10.1	7 8.7	27 23.6	29 18.3
6 Th	7 0 2	15 5 9	13♎ 3 5	19 37 55	4D12.2	2 27.5	0♒18.9	20 55.6	2 8.3	3 13.9	7 11.9	27 25.8	29 19.3
7 F	7 3 58	16 6 18	26 6 58	2♏30 40	4 12.4	2R34.5	1 34.1	21 42.7	2 19.6	3 17.6	7 15.0	27 28.0	29 20.2
8 Sa	7 7 55	17 7 28	8♏49 28	15 3 49	4 13.1	2 30.2	2 49.3	22 29.9	2 30.9	3 21.2	7 18.0	27 30.2	29 21.1
9 Su	7 11 51	18 8 37	21 14 14	27 21 11	4 14.3	2 14.1	4 4.5	23 17.0	2 42.1	3 24.8	7 21.1	27 32.3	29 21.9
10 M	7 15 48	19 9 47	3♐25 6	9♐26 28	4 15.7	1 46.2	5 19.7	24 4.1	2 53.2	3 28.2	7 24.1	27 34.5	29 22.8
11 Tu	7 19 44	20 10 57	15 25 42	21 23 10	4 17.0	1 6.7	6 34.9	24 51.3	3 4.2	3 31.5	7 27.1	27 36.6	29 23.6
12 W	7 23 41	21 12 6	27 19 16	3♑14 19	4R17.9	0 16.4	7 50.0	25 38.4	3 15.1	3 34.8	7 30.0	27 38.8	29 24.3
13 Th	7 27 38	22 13 15	9♑ 8 38	15 2 32	4 17.9	29♑16.3	9 5.2	26 25.6	3 26.0	3 38.0	7 32.9	27 40.9	29 25.0
14 F	7 31 34	23 14 24	20 56 15	26 50 4	4 17.0	28 8.2	10 20.4	27 12.7	3 36.7	3 41.0	7 35.8	27 43.0	29 25.7
15 Sa	7 35 31	24 15 33	2♒44 14	8♒39 0	4 15.0	26 54.2	11 35.5	27 59.9	3 47.4	3 44.0	7 38.6	27 45.1	29 26.4
16 Su	7 39 27	25 16 41	14 34 35	20 31 16	4 12.0	25 36.5	12 50.6	28 47.0	3 58.0	3 46.9	7 41.4	27 47.1	29 27.0
17 M	7 43 24	26 17 48	26 29 17	2♓28 56	4 8.3	24 17.7	14 5.7	29 34.1	4 8.5	3 49.6	7 44.2	27 49.2	29 27.5
18 Tu	7 47 20	27 18 55	8♓30 30	14 34 18	4 4.2	23 0.1	15 20.8	0♓21.3	4 18.9	3 52.3	7 46.9	27 51.2	29 28.1
19 W	7 51 17	28 20 1	20 40 42	26 50 2	4 0.3	21 46.1	16 35.9	1 8.4	4 29.2	3 54.9	7 49.6	27 53.3	29 28.6
20 Th	7 55 13	29 21 7	3♈ 2 42	9♈19 6	3 57.0	20 37.6	17 50.9	1 55.5	4 39.4	3 57.4	7 52.3	27 55.3	29 29.0
21 F	7 59 10	0♒22 11	15 39 40	22 4 48	3 54.8	19 36.0	19 5.9	2 42.6	4 49.5	3 59.7	7 54.9	27 57.3	29 29.5
22 Sa	8 3 7	1 23 14	28 34 55	5♉10 26	3D53.9	18 42.6	20 20.9	3 29.7	4 59.5	4 2.0	7 57.5	27 59.3	29 29.8
23 Su	8 7 3	2 24 17	11♉51 40	18 38 57	3 54.2	17 57.9	21 35.9	4 16.8	5 9.4	4 4.2	8 0.0	28 1.2	29 30.2
24 M	8 11 0	3 25 18	25 32 31	2♊32 27	3 55.5	17 22.3	22 50.9	5 3.8	5 19.2	4 6.3	8 2.5	28 3.2	29 30.5
25 Tu	8 14 56	4 26 19	9♊38 48	16 51 23	3 57.1	16 56.0	24 5.8	5 50.9	5 28.9	4 8.3	8 5.0	28 5.1	29 30.8
26 W	8 18 53	5 27 18	24 9 55	1♋33 54	3R58.3	16 38.7	25 20.8	6 37.9	5 38.5	4 10.1	8 7.4	28 7.0	29 31.0
27 Th	8 22 49	6 28 17	9♋ 2 39	16 35 18	3 58.5	16D30.0	26 35.7	7 25.0	5 47.9	4 11.9	8 9.8	28 8.9	29 31.3
28 F	8 26 46	7 29 14	24 10 51	1♌48 5	3 57.2	16 29.5	27 50.5	8 12.0	5 57.3	4 13.6	8 12.1	28 10.8	29 31.4
29 Sa	8 30 43	8 30 11	9♌25 46	17 2 34	3 54.1	16 36.7	29 5.4	8 59.0	6 6.6	4 15.2	8 14.4	28 12.6	29 31.6
30 Su	8 34 39	9 31 6	24 37 10	2♍ 8 21	3 49.4	16 51.0	0♓20.2	9 45.9	6 15.7	4 16.6	8 16.6	28 14.4	29 31.7
31 M	8 38 36	10 32 1	9♍34 57	16 56 0	3 43.8	17 11.8	1 35.0	10 32.9	6 24.7	4 18.0	8 18.8	28 16.2	29 31.7

LONGITUDE — FEBRUARY 1983

Day	Sid.Time	☉	0 hr ☽	Noon ☽	True ☊	☿	♀	♂	♃	♄	♅	♆	♇
1 Tu	8 42 32	11♒32 54	24♍10 45	1♎18 36	3♋37.9	17♑38.7	2♓49.8	11♓19.8	6♐33.6	4♏19.3	8♐21.0	28♐18.0	29♎31.8
2 W	8 46 29	12 33 47	8♎19 11	15 12 21	3R32.7	18 11.2	4 4.5	12 6.7	6 42.4	4 20.4	8 23.1	28 19.8	29R31.7
3 Th	8 50 25	13 34 39	21 58 8	28 36 42	3 28.8	18 48.6	5 19.2	12 53.6	6 51.1	4 21.5	8 25.2	28 21.5	29 31.7
4 F	8 54 22	14 35 30	5♏ 8 23	11♏33 37	3D26.7	19 30.7	6 33.9	13 40.5	6 59.6	4 22.4	8 27.2	28 23.2	29 31.6
5 Sa	8 58 18	15 36 21	17 52 56	24 6 53	3 26.2	20 16.9	7 48.6	14 27.4	7 8.1	4 23.3	8 29.2	28 24.9	29 31.5
6 Su	9 2 15	16 37 10	0♐16 5	6♐21 12	3 27.0	21 6.9	9 3.3	15 14.2	7 16.4	4 24.0	8 31.1	28 26.6	29 31.4
7 M	9 6 12	17 37 59	12 22 50	18 21 37	3 28.5	22 0.5	10 17.9	16 1.0	7 24.5	4 24.6	8 33.0	28 28.3	29 31.2
8 Tu	9 10 8	18 38 47	24 18 10	0♑13 3	3R29.9	22 57.2	11 32.5	16 47.8	7 32.6	4 25.2	8 34.8	28 29.9	29 31.0
9 W	9 14 5	19 39 33	6♑ 6 49	11 59 59	3 30.3	23 56.8	12 47.0	17 34.6	7 40.5	4 25.6	8 36.6	28 31.5	29 30.7
10 Th	9 18 1	20 40 19	17 52 59	23 46 14	3 29.0	24 59.1	14 1.6	18 21.4	7 48.3	4 25.9	8 38.3	28 33.1	29 30.4
11 F	9 21 58	21 41 3	29 40 8	5♒34 59	3 25.4	26 3.8	15 16.1	19 8.1	7 55.9	4 26.1	8 40.0	28 34.6	29 30.1
12 Sa	9 25 54	22 41 46	11♒31 4	17 28 38	3 19.5	27 10.8	16 30.6	19 54.8	8 3.4	4R26.2	8 41.7	28 36.1	29 29.7
13 Su	9 29 51	23 42 28	23 27 53	29 29 0	3 11.4	28 20.0	17 45.0	20 41.5	8 10.8	4 26.2	8 43.2	28 37.6	29 29.3
14 M	9 33 47	24 43 8	5♓32 8	11♓37 25	3 1.7	29 31.0	18 59.4	21 28.2	8 18.0	4 26.1	8 44.8	28 39.1	29 28.9
15 Tu	9 37 44	25 43 47	17 44 58	23 54 55	2 51.2	0♒43.9	20 13.8	22 14.8	8 25.1	4 25.9	8 46.3	28 40.6	29 28.4
16 W	9 41 40	26 44 25	0♈ 7 23	6♈22 31	2 40.9	1 58.6	21 28.2	23 1.4	8 32.0	4 25.6	8 47.7	28 42.0	29 27.9
17 Th	9 45 37	27 45 0	12 40 28	19 1 25	2 31.7	3 14.8	22 42.5	23 48.0	8 38.8	4 25.1	8 49.1	28 43.4	29 27.4
18 F	9 49 34	28 45 34	25 25 34	1♉53 9	2 24.6	4 32.5	23 56.7	24 34.5	8 45.5	4 24.6	8 50.4	28 44.7	29 26.8
19 Sa	9 53 30	29 46 6	8♉24 25	14 59 38	2 19.9	5 51.7	25 11.0	25 21.0	8 52.0	4 24.0	8 51.7	28 46.1	29 26.2
20 Su	9 57 27	0♓46 37	21 39 3	28 22 58	2D17.7	7 12.3	26 25.2	26 7.5	8 58.3	4 23.2	8 52.9	28 47.4	29 25.6
21 M	10 1 23	1 47 5	5♊11 37	12♊ 5 12	2 17.3	8 34.2	27 39.3	26 53.9	9 4.5	4 22.4	8 54.1	28 48.6	29 24.9
22 Tu	10 5 20	2 47 32	19 3 52	26 7 41	2R18.0	9 57.3	28 53.4	27 40.4	9 10.6	4 21.5	8 55.2	28 49.9	29 24.2
23 W	10 9 16	3 47 57	3♋16 36	10♋30 26	2 18.4	11 21.7	0♈ 7.5	28 26.7	9 16.5	4 20.4	8 56.3	28 51.1	29 23.5
24 Th	10 13 13	4 48 20	17 48 51	25 11 22	2 17.4	12 47.3	1 21.5	29 13.1	9 22.2	4 19.3	8 57.3	28 52.3	29 22.7
25 F	10 17 9	5 48 41	2♌37 19	10♌ 5 51	2 14.2	14 14.0	2 35.5	29 59.4	9 27.8	4 18.0	8 58.3	28 53.5	29 21.9
26 Sa	10 21 6	6 49 0	17 36 0	25 6 40	2 8.2	15 41.9	3 49.4	0♈45.6	9 33.2	4 16.7	8 59.2	28 54.6	29 21.1
27 Su	10 25 3	7 49 17	2♍36 39	10♍ 4 46	1 59.8	17 10.9	5 3.2	1 31.9	9 38.5	4 15.2	9 0.1	28 55.7	29 20.3
28 M	10 28 59	8 49 33	17 29 50	24 50 45	1 49.6	18 41.0	6 17.1	2 18.1	9 43.6	4 13.7	9 0.9	28 56.8	29 19.4

Astro Data	Dy Hr Mn
☽0S	5 22:30
☿ R	7 3:00
♃⊻♄	14 13:20
☽0N	20 17:15
☿ D	27 13:26
♇ R	1 5:52
☽0S	2 6:18
♄ R	12 11:18
☽0N	16 22:10
♃☌♅	18 22:42
♀0N	24 18:24
♂0N	26 19:50

Planet Ingress	Dy Hr Mn
☿ ♒	1 13:32
♀ ♒	5 17:58
☿ ♑	12 6:55
♂ ♓	17 13:10
☉ ♒	20 15:17
♀ ♓	29 17:31
☿ ♒	14 9:36
☉ ♓	19 5:31
♀ ♈	22 21:35
♂ ♈	25 0:19

Last Aspect Dy Hr Mn		☽ Ingress Dy Hr Mn
2 20:37	♇ ⚹	♍ 2 21:49
4 23:00	♀ △	♎ 5 0:44
7 6:02	♇ ☌	♏ 7 7:16
9 4:17	♂ □	♐ 9 17:14
12 4:14	♇ ⚹	♑ 12 5:26
14 17:17	♇ □	♒ 14 18:26
17 6:37	♂ ☌	♓ 17 7:02
19 16:15	☉ ⚹	♈ 19 18:08
22 1:41	♇ ☍	♉ 22 2:36
23 18:52	♀ □	♊ 24 7:40
26 8:42	♇ △	♋ 26 9:28
28 8:25	♇ □	♌ 28 9:10
30 7:49	♇ ⚹	♍ 30 8:35

Last Aspect Dy Hr Mn		☽ Ingress Dy Hr Mn
1 6:56	♆ □	♎ 1 9:47
3 13:40	♇ ☌	♏ 3 14:32
5 4:55	☿ ⚹	♐ 5 23:28
8 10:34	♇ ⚹	♑ 8 11:33
10 23:40	♇ □	♒ 11 0:40
13 12:00	♇ △	♓ 13 13:02
15 21:15	♆ □	♈ 15 23:46
18 7:29	♇ ☍	♉ 18 8:30
20 9:22	♀ ⚹	♊ 20 14:52
22 18:14	♀ □	♋ 22 18:31
24 19:32	♂ △	♌ 24 19:47
26 18:46	♇ ⚹	♍ 26 19:49
28 18:47	♆ □	♎ 28 20:30

☽ Phases & Eclipses Dy Hr Mn	
6 4:00	☽ 15♎15
14 5:08	● 23♑27
22 5:33	☽ 1♉37
28 22:26	○ 8♌26
4 19:17	☽ 15♏24
13 0:32	● 23♒44
20 17:32	☽ 1♊31
27 8:58	○ 8♍12

Astro Data

1 JANUARY 1983
Julian Day # 30316
Delta T 53.0 sec
SVP 05♓30'06"
Obliquity 23°26'28"
⚷ Chiron 23♉10.1R
☽ Mean ☊ 3♋51.3

1 FEBRUARY 1983
Julian Day # 30347
Delta T 53.0 sec
SVP 05♓30'01"
Obliquity 23°26'29"
⚷ Chiron 22♉39.9
☽ Mean ☊ 2♋12.8

MARCH 1983 LONGITUDE

Day	Sid.Time	☉	0 hr ☽	Noon ☽	True ☊	☿	♀	♂	♃	♄	♅	♆	♇
1 Tu	10 32 56	9♓49 46	2♎ 6 32	9♎16 24	1♋38.9	20♒12.1	7♈30.8	3♈ 4.2	9♐48.5	4♏12.1	9♐ 1.7	28♐57.8	29♎18.5
2 W	10 36 52	10 49 58	16 19 44	23 16 6	1R 28.7	21 44.4	8 44.6	3 50.3	9 53.3	4R 10.3	9 2.4	28 58.8	29R 17.5
3 Th	10 40 49	11 50 9	0♏ 5 17	6♏47 17	1 20.3	23 17.8	9 58.2	4 36.4	9 57.9	4 8.5	9 3.0	28 59.8	29 16.6
4 F	10 44 45	12 50 18	13 22 15	19 50 27	1 14.3	24 52.2	11 11.9	5 22.5	10 2.3	4 6.6	9 3.6	29 0.7	29 15.6
5 Sa	10 48 42	13 50 25	26 12 19	2♐28 22	1 10.7	26 27.7	12 25.5	6 8.5	10 6.6	4 4.5	9 4.1	29 1.7	29 14.5
6 Su	10 52 38	14 50 31	8♐39 13	14 45 29	1D 9.3	28 4.3	13 39.0	6 54.4	10 10.7	4 2.4	9 4.6	29 2.5	29 13.5
7 M	10 56 35	15 50 35	20 47 51	26 47 2	1R 9.3	29 42.0	14 52.5	7 40.4	10 14.6	4 0.2	9 5.1	29 3.4	29 12.4
8 Tu	11 0 32	16 50 38	2♑43 44	8♑38 37	1 9.4	1♓20.8	16 5.9	8 26.3	10 18.4	3 57.9	9 5.5	29 4.2	29 11.3
9 W	11 4 28	17 50 39	14 32 22	20 25 36	1 8.7	3 0.7	17 19.3	9 12.1	10 21.9	3 55.5	9 5.8	29 5.0	29 10.2
10 Th	11 8 25	18 50 39	26 18 56	2♒12 54	1 6.0	4 41.7	18 32.6	9 58.0	10 25.3	3 53.1	9 6.1	29 5.8	29 9.0
11 F	11 12 21	19 50 37	8♒ 8 2	14 4 45	1 0.8	6 23.9	19 45.9	10 43.8	10 28.6	3 50.5	9 6.3	29 6.5	29 7.8
12 Sa	11 16 18	20 50 33	20 3 27	26 4 27	0 52.7	8 7.1	20 59.1	11 29.5	10 31.6	3 47.8	9 6.4	29 7.2	29 6.6
13 Su	11 20 14	21 50 27	2♓ 8 1	8♓14 22	0 41.8	9 51.6	22 12.3	12 15.2	10 34.5	3 45.1	9 6.6	29 7.8	29 5.4
14 M	11 24 11	22 50 19	14 23 37	20 35 53	0 28.9	11 37.2	23 25.4	13 0.9	10 37.2	3 42.3	9R 6.6	29 8.4	29 4.1
15 Tu	11 28 7	23 50 9	26 51 10	3♈ 9 31	0 15.0	13 24.0	24 38.5	13 46.5	10 39.7	3 39.4	9 6.6	29 9.0	29 2.8
16 W	11 32 4	24 49 58	9♈30 51	15 55 8	0 1.1	15 11.9	25 51.5	14 32.1	10 42.0	3 36.4	9 6.6	29 9.6	29 1.5
17 Th	11 36 1	25 49 44	22 22 19	28 52 19	29♊48.7	17 1.1	27 4.4	15 17.6	10 44.1	3 33.3	9 6.5	29 10.1	29 0.2
18 F	11 39 57	26 49 28	5♉25 7	12♉ 0 39	29 38.7	18 51.5	28 17.3	16 3.1	10 46.1	3 30.2	9 6.3	29 10.6	28 58.9
19 Sa	11 43 54	27 49 10	18 38 56	25 20 0	29 31.7	20 43.1	29 30.1	16 48.5	10 47.9	3 26.9	9 6.1	29 11.1	28 57.5
20 Su	11 47 50	28 48 50	2♊ 3 54	8♊50 43	29 27.6	22 35.9	0♉42.9	17 33.9	10 49.4	3 23.6	9 5.8	29 11.5	28 56.1
21 M	11 51 47	29 48 28	15 40 32	22 33 28	29 26.0	24 29.9	1 55.6	18 19.3	10 50.8	3 20.3	9 5.5	29 11.9	28 54.7
22 Tu	11 55 43	0♈48 3	29 29 36	6♋29 1	29 25.7	26 25.1	3 8.2	19 4.6	10 52.1	3 16.9	9 5.2	29 12.2	28 53.3
23 W	11 59 40	1 47 36	13♋31 42	20 37 36	29 25.5	28 21.4	4 20.7	19 49.9	10 53.1	3 13.4	9 4.7	29 12.6	28 51.9
24 Th	12 3 36	2 47 7	27 46 35	4♌58 24	29 24.1	0♈18.9	5 33.2	20 35.1	10 53.9	3 9.8	9 4.3	29 12.8	28 50.4
25 F	12 7 33	3 46 35	12♌12 41	19 28 56	29 20.3	2 17.5	6 45.6	21 20.2	10 54.6	3 6.1	9 3.7	29 13.1	28 48.9
26 Sa	12 11 30	4 46 1	26 46 32	4♍ 4 45	29 13.8	4 17.0	7 57.9	22 5.3	10 55.0	3 2.5	9 3.2	29 13.3	28 47.4
27 Su	12 15 26	5 45 25	11♍22 46	18 39 42	29 4.6	6 17.6	9 10.2	22 50.4	10R 55.3	2 58.7	9 2.5	29 13.5	28 45.9
28 M	12 19 23	6 44 47	25 54 37	3♎ 6 39	28 53.4	8 18.9	10 22.3	23 35.4	10 55.4	2 54.9	9 1.9	29 13.7	28 44.4
29 Tu	12 23 19	7 44 6	10♎14 57	17 18 44	28 41.4	10 21.0	11 34.4	24 20.4	10 55.3	2 51.0	9 1.1	29 13.8	28 42.9
30 W	12 27 16	8 43 23	24 17 22	1♏10 22	28 30.0	12 23.6	12 46.4	25 5.3	10 55.0	2 47.1	9 0.4	29 13.9	28 41.3
31 Th	12 31 12	9 42 39	7♏57 23	14 38 13	28 20.2	14 26.6	13 58.4	25 50.2	10 54.6	2 43.1	8 59.5	29 13.9	28 39.7

APRIL 1983 LONGITUDE

Day	Sid.Time	☉	0 hr ☽	Noon ☽	True ☊	☿	♀	♂	♃	♄	♅	♆	♇
1 F	12 35 9	10♈41 52	21♏12 50	27♏41 22	28♊12.9	16♈29.8	15♉10.3	26♈35.0	10♐53.9	2♏39.1	8♐58.7	29♐14.0	28♎38.2
2 Sa	12 39 5	11 41 4	4♐ 4 3	10♐21 16	28R 8.3	18 32.9	16 22.0	27 19.8	10R 53.1	2R 35.0	8R 57.8	29R 13.9	28R 36.6
3 Su	12 43 2	12 40 14	16 33 26	22 41 6	28D 6.1	20 35.7	17 33.7	28 4.5	10 52.1	2 30.8	8 56.8	29 13.9	28 35.0
4 M	12 46 58	13 39 22	28 44 53	4♑45 24	28 5.6	22 37.9	18 45.4	28 49.2	10 50.8	2 26.7	8 55.8	29 13.8	28 33.3
5 Tu	12 50 55	14 38 29	10♑43 19	16 39 20	28R 5.8	24 39.1	19 56.9	29 33.9	10 49.4	2 22.5	8 54.7	29 13.7	28 31.7
6 W	12 54 52	15 37 34	22 34 9	28 28 25	28 5.6	26 39.0	21 8.4	0♉18.5	10 47.9	2 18.2	8 53.6	29 13.6	28 30.1
7 Th	12 58 48	16 36 37	4♒22 50	10♒18 0	28 4.1	28 37.2	22 19.8	1 3.0	10 46.1	2 13.9	8 52.5	29 13.4	28 28.5
8 F	13 2 45	17 35 38	16 14 34	22 13 4	28 0.4	0♉33.4	23 31.1	1 47.5	10 44.1	2 9.6	8 51.3	29 13.2	28 26.8
9 Sa	13 6 41	18 34 37	28 14 1	4♓17 51	27 54.2	2 27.2	24 42.3	2 32.0	10 42.0	2 5.2	8 50.0	29 13.0	28 25.1
10 Su	13 10 38	19 33 34	10♓24 58	16 35 40	27 45.5	4 18.2	25 53.4	3 16.4	10 39.7	2 0.8	8 48.7	29 12.7	28 23.5
11 M	13 14 34	20 32 30	22 50 11	29 8 41	27 34.9	6 6.1	27 4.5	4 0.7	10 37.2	1 56.4	8 47.4	29 12.4	28 21.8
12 Tu	13 18 31	21 31 24	5♈31 12	11♈57 45	27 23.3	7 50.5	28 15.4	4 45.1	10 34.5	1 51.9	8 46.0	29 12.0	28 20.1
13 W	13 22 27	22 30 15	18 28 16	25 2 34	27 11.6	9 31.2	29 26.3	5 29.3	10 31.6	1 47.4	8 44.6	29 11.7	28 18.4
14 Th	13 26 24	23 29 5	1♉40 29	8♉21 46	27 1.2	11 7.8	0♊37.0	6 13.5	10 28.6	1 42.9	8 43.1	29 11.3	28 16.8
15 F	13 30 21	24 27 53	15 6 9	21 53 22	26 52.8	12 40.2	1 47.7	6 57.7	10 25.4	1 38.4	8 41.6	29 10.8	28 15.1
16 Sa	13 34 17	25 26 39	28 43 6	5♊35 8	26 47.1	14 8.0	2 58.3	7 41.8	10 22.0	1 33.9	8 40.0	29 10.4	28 13.4
17 Su	13 38 14	26 25 22	12♊29 12	19 25 6	26 44.0	15 31.1	4 8.8	8 25.9	10 18.4	1 29.3	8 38.5	29 9.9	28 11.7
18 M	13 42 10	27 24 4	26 22 39	3♋21 43	26D 43.1	16 49.2	5 19.2	9 9.9	10 14.7	1 24.8	8 36.8	29 9.3	28 10.0
19 Tu	13 46 7	28 22 43	10♋22 9	17 23 51	26 43.6	18 2.4	6 29.4	9 53.8	10 10.8	1 20.2	8 35.2	29 8.8	28 8.3
20 W	13 50 3	29 21 20	24 26 43	1♌30 37	26R 44.3	19 10.3	7 39.6	10 37.7	10 6.7	1 15.7	8 33.5	29 8.2	28 6.6
21 Th	13 54 0	0♉19 55	8♌35 25	15 40 56	26 44.1	20 12.9	8 49.7	11 21.6	10 2.5	1 11.1	8 31.7	29 7.6	28 4.9
22 F	13 57 56	1 18 28	22 46 57	29 53 10	26 42.1	21 10.1	9 59.6	12 5.4	9 58.1	1 6.5	8 30.0	29 6.9	28 3.2
23 Sa	14 1 53	2 16 58	6♍59 15	14♍ 4 48	26 38.0	22 1.8	11 9.4	12 49.1	9 53.6	1 1.9	8 28.1	29 6.3	28 1.5
24 Su	14 5 50	3 15 26	21 9 20	28 12 23	26 31.7	22 47.9	12 19.1	13 32.8	9 48.9	0 57.3	8 26.3	29 5.6	27 59.8
25 M	14 9 46	4 13 52	5♎13 25	12♎11 53	26 23.8	23 28.4	13 28.7	14 16.5	9 44.0	0 52.8	8 24.4	29 4.8	27 58.2
26 Tu	14 13 43	5 12 16	19 7 17	25 59 7	26 15.3	24 3.1	14 38.2	15 0.1	9 39.0	0 48.2	8 22.5	29 4.1	27 56.5
27 W	14 17 39	6 10 38	2♏46 59	9♏30 29	26 7.1	24 32.2	15 47.5	15 43.6	9 33.9	0 43.7	8 20.5	29 3.3	27 54.8
28 Th	14 21 36	7 8 59	16 9 23	22 43 28	26 0.1	24 55.6	16 56.7	16 27.1	9 28.6	0 39.1	8 18.6	29 2.5	27 53.1
29 F	14 25 32	8 7 17	29 12 42	5♐37 4	25 55.0	25 13.2	18 5.8	17 10.5	9 23.2	0 34.6	8 16.6	29 1.6	27 51.5
30 Sa	14 29 29	9 5 34	11♐56 43	18 11 51	25 51.9	25 25.3	19 14.7	17 53.9	9 17.6	0 30.1	8 14.5	29 0.7	27 49.8

Astro Data Dy Hr Mn	Planet Ingress Dy Hr Mn	Last Aspect Dy Hr Mn	☽ Ingress Dy Hr Mn	Last Aspect Dy Hr Mn	☽ Ingress Dy Hr Mn	☽ Phases & Eclipses Dy Hr Mn	Astro Data
☽0S 1 15:53	☿ ♓ 7 4:24	2 22:34 ♇ ☌	♏ 2 23:51	31 11:52 ♀ ☍	♐ 1 16:20	6 13:16 ☽ 15♐24	1 MARCH 1983
♆✶♇ 11 16:59	☊ ♊ 16 2:05	5 0:34 ☿ □	♐ 5 7:15	4 0:58 ♆ ☌	♑ 4 2:30	14 17:43 ● 23♓35	Julian Day # 30375
♅ R 14 13:04	♀ ♉ 19 9:51	7 16:51 ♇ ✶	♑ 7 18:29	6 12:02 ♇ □	♒ 6 15:06	22 2:25 ☽ 0♋54	Delta T 53.1 sec
☽0N 16 3:33	☉ ♈ 21 4:39	10 5:46 ♇ □	♒ 10 7:30	9 1:57 ♆ ✶	♓ 9 3:30	28 19:27 ○ 7♎33	SVP 05♓29'58"
☿0N 25 10:26	☿ ♈ 23 20:09	12 18:03 ♆ ✶	♓ 12 19:47	11 12:07 ♆ □	♈ 11 13:37		Obliquity 23°26'30"
♃ R 27 23:56		15 4:23 ♆ □	♈ 15 6:00	13 19:31 ♆ △	♉ 13 20:59	5 8:38 ☽ 14♑60	⚷ Chiron 23♉06.1
☽0S 29 1:54	♂ ♉ 5 14:03	17 12:33 ♆ △	♉ 17 14:04	14 19:08 ☿ ☌	♊ 16 2:15	13 7:58 ● 22♈50	☽ Mean ☊ 0♋43.9
	☿ ♉ 7 17:04	19 17:45 ☉ ✶	♊ 19 20:20	18 4:47 ♆ ☍	♋ 18 6:14	20 8:58 ☽ 29♋43	
♆ R 1 4:27	♀ ♊ 13 11:26	21 23:30 ♆ ☍	♋ 22 0:52	20 8:58 ☉ □	♌ 20 9:26	27 6:31 ○ 6♏26	1 APRIL 1983
☽0N 12 10:56	☉ ♉ 20 15:50	24 1:46 ♇ □	♌ 24 3:43	22 10:41 ♆ △	♍ 22 12:12		Julian Day # 30406
☽0S 25 10:44		26 4:01 ♆ △	♍ 26 5:18	24 13:30 ♆ □	♎ 24 15:04		Delta T 53.2 sec
		28 5:31 ♆ □	♎ 28 6:48	26 17:25 ♆ ✶	♏ 26 19:04		SVP 05♓29'55"
		30 8:36 ♆ ✶	♏ 30 9:57	28 16:27 ☿ ☍	♐ 29 1:28		Obliquity 23°26'30"
							⚷ Chiron 24♉27.8
							☽ Mean ☊ 29♊05.4

LONGITUDE — MAY 1983

Day	Sid.Time	☉	0 hr ☽	Noon ☽	True ☊	☿	♀	♂	♃	♄	♅	♆	♇
1 Su	14 33 25	10♉ 3 50	24♐22 46	0♑29 52	25♊50.9	25♉31.7	20♊23.6	18♉37.3	9♐11.9	0♏25.6	8♐12.5	28♐59.9	27♎48.2
2 M	14 37 22	11 2 3	6♑33 34	12 34 23	25D 51.4	25R 32.8	21 32.3	19 20.6	9R 6.1	0R 21.1	8R 10.4	28R 58.9	27R 46.5
3 Tu	14 41 19	12 0 16	18 32 52	24 29 36	25 52.7	25 28.5	22 40.8	20 3.8	9 0.1	0 16.7	8 8.3	28 58.0	27 44.9
4 W	14 45 15	12 58 26	0♒25 11	6♒20 16	25 54.1	25 19.3	23 49.2	20 47.0	8 54.1	0 12.3	8 6.1	28 57.0	27 43.3
5 Th	14 49 12	13 56 35	12 15 29	18 11 28	25R 54.9	25 5.2	24 57.5	21 30.1	8 47.9	0 7.9	8 3.9	28 56.0	27 41.6
6 F	14 53 8	14 54 43	24 8 52	0♓ 8 16	25 54.4	24 46.7	26 5.7	22 13.2	8 41.6	0 3.5	8 1.7	28 55.0	27 40.0
7 Sa	14 57 5	15 52 49	6♓10 17	12 15 28	25 52.3	24 24.2	27 13.6	22 56.3	8 35.1	29♎59.2	7 59.5	28 53.9	27 38.5
8 Su	15 1 1	16 50 54	18 24 17	24 37 11	25 48.6	23 58.0	28 21.5	23 39.3	8 28.6	29 54.9	7 57.3	28 52.9	27 36.9
9 M	15 4 58	17 48 58	0♈54 33	7♈16 39	25 43.5	23 28.8	29 29.2	24 22.2	8 22.0	29 50.6	7 55.0	28 51.8	27 35.3
10 Tu	15 8 54	18 47 0	13 43 43	20 15 50	25 37.5	22 56.9	0♋36.7	25 5.1	8 15.3	29 46.4	7 52.7	28 50.6	27 33.7
11 W	15 12 51	19 45 0	26 53 0	3♉35 9	25 31.5	22 23.1	1 44.1	25 48.0	8 8.4	29 42.3	7 50.4	28 49.5	27 32.2
12 Th	15 16 48	20 42 59	10♉22 4	17 13 29	25 26.0	21 47.9	2 51.4	26 30.8	8 1.5	29 38.1	7 48.1	28 48.3	27 30.7
13 F	15 20 44	21 40 57	24 9 0	1♊ 8 13	25 21.7	21 12.0	3 58.4	27 13.5	7 54.5	29 34.0	7 45.7	28 47.1	27 29.2
14 Sa	15 24 41	22 38 53	8♊10 36	15 15 39	25 19.1	20 36.0	5 5.3	27 56.2	7 47.5	29 30.0	7 43.4	28 45.9	27 27.7
15 Su	15 28 37	23 36 48	22 22 50	29 31 34	25D 18.0	20 0.5	6 12.0	28 38.9	7 40.3	29 26.0	7 41.0	28 44.7	27 26.2
16 M	15 32 34	24 34 41	6♋41 20	13♋51 39	25 18.4	19 26.2	7 18.6	29 21.5	7 33.1	29 22.1	7 38.6	28 43.4	27 24.7
17 Tu	15 36 30	25 32 32	21 2 2	28 12 4	25 19.6	18 53.5	8 25.0	0♊ 4.0	7 25.8	29 18.2	7 36.2	28 42.2	27 23.3
18 W	15 40 27	26 30 22	5♌21 23	12♌29 38	25 21.0	18 23.1	9 31.1	0 46.5	7 18.5	29 14.4	7 33.8	28 40.9	27 21.8
19 Th	15 44 23	27 28 10	19 36 32	26 41 50	25R 22.0	17 55.4	10 37.1	1 29.0	7 11.1	29 10.6	7 31.4	28 39.6	27 20.4
20 F	15 48 20	28 25 56	3♍45 18	10♍46 43	25 22.1	17 30.9	11 42.9	2 11.4	7 3.6	29 6.9	7 28.9	28 38.3	27 19.0
21 Sa	15 52 17	29 23 40	17 45 53	24 42 37	25 21.1	17 9.8	12 48.4	2 53.7	6 56.2	29 3.3	7 26.5	28 36.9	27 17.7
22 Su	15 56 13	0♊21 23	1♎36 45	8♎28 7	25 18.9	16 52.6	13 53.8	3 36.0	6 48.6	28 59.7	7 24.0	28 35.5	27 16.3
23 M	16 0 10	1 19 4	15 16 31	22 1 49	25 15.9	16 39.4	14 58.9	4 18.3	6 41.1	28 56.2	7 21.5	28 34.2	27 15.0
24 Tu	16 4 6	2 16 43	28 43 51	5♏22 30	25 12.5	16 30.4	16 3.8	5 0.4	6 33.5	28 52.8	7 19.1	28 32.8	27 13.7
25 W	16 8 3	3 14 22	11♏57 37	18 29 8	25 9.2	16D 25.8	17 8.5	5 42.6	6 25.9	28 49.4	7 16.6	28 31.4	27 12.4
26 Th	16 11 59	4 11 59	24 57 0	1♐21 11	25 6.5	16 25.6	18 12.9	6 24.7	6 18.3	28 46.1	7 14.1	28 29.9	27 11.1
27 F	16 15 56	5 9 34	7♐41 42	13 58 37	25 4.7	16 30.0	19 17.1	7 6.7	6 10.7	28 42.9	7 11.6	28 28.5	27 9.9
28 Sa	16 19 52	6 7 9	20 12 3	26 22 10	25D 3.9	16 38.8	20 21.1	7 48.7	6 3.0	28 39.7	7 9.2	28 27.0	27 8.6
29 Su	16 23 49	7 4 42	2♑29 11	8♑33 22	25 3.9	16 52.2	21 24.8	8 30.7	5 55.4	28 36.6	7 6.7	28 25.6	27 7.4
30 M	16 27 46	8 2 15	14 35 1	20 34 30	25 4.8	17 10.0	22 28.2	9 12.6	5 47.8	28 33.6	7 4.2	28 24.1	27 6.3
31 Tu	16 31 42	8 59 46	26 32 13	2♒28 36	25 6.0	17 32.2	23 31.4	9 54.4	5 40.1	28 30.7	7 1.7	28 22.6	27 5.1

LONGITUDE — JUNE 1983

Day	Sid.Time	☉	0 hr ☽	Noon ☽	True ☊	☿	♀	♂	♃	♄	♅	♆	♇
1 W	16 35 39	9♊57 17	8♒24 9	14♒19 22	25♊ 7.4	17♉58.7	24♋34.3	10♊36.2	5♐32.5	28♎27.8	6♐59.2	28♐21.1	27♎ 4.0
2 Th	16 39 35	10 54 46	20 14 47	26 10 58	25 8.6	18 29.5	25 37.0	11 18.0	5R 24.9	28R 25.0	6R 56.7	28R 19.6	27R 2.9
3 F	16 43 32	11 52 15	2♓ 8 29	8♓ 7 55	25R 9.4	19 4.3	26 39.3	11 59.7	5 17.4	28 22.3	6 54.3	28 18.0	27 1.8
4 Sa	16 47 28	12 49 43	14 9 51	20 14 52	25 9.6	19 43.2	27 41.3	12 41.4	5 9.8	28 19.7	6 51.8	28 16.5	27 0.7
5 Su	16 51 25	13 47 10	26 23 31	2♈36 20	25 9.3	20 26.0	28 43.1	13 23.0	5 2.3	28 17.2	6 49.3	28 15.0	26 59.7
6 M	16 55 21	14 44 37	8♈53 48	15 16 20	25 8.5	21 12.7	29 44.5	14 4.6	4 54.9	28 14.7	6 46.9	28 13.4	26 58.7
7 Tu	16 59 18	15 42 3	21 44 19	28 18 2	25 7.4	22 3.1	0♌45.6	14 46.1	4 47.4	28 12.4	6 44.4	28 11.8	26 57.7
8 W	17 3 15	16 39 28	4♉57 39	11♉43 15	25 6.3	22 57.2	1 46.4	15 27.6	4 40.1	28 10.1	6 42.0	28 10.3	26 56.8
9 Th	17 7 11	17 36 53	18 34 48	25 32 8	25 5.4	23 54.8	2 46.9	16 9.1	4 32.8	28 7.9	6 39.5	28 8.7	26 55.9
10 F	17 11 8	18 34 17	2♊34 55	9♊42 44	25 4.7	24 56.0	3 47.0	16 50.5	4 25.5	28 5.8	6 37.1	28 7.1	26 55.0
11 Sa	17 15 4	19 31 40	16 55 3	24 11 10	25D 4.4	26 0.5	4 46.8	17 31.8	4 18.3	28 3.8	6 34.7	28 5.5	26 54.1
12 Su	17 19 1	20 29 3	1♋30 21	8♋51 45	25 4.4	27 8.5	5 46.2	18 13.1	4 11.2	28 1.9	6 32.3	28 3.9	26 53.3
13 M	17 22 57	21 26 25	16 14 32	23 37 48	25 4.6	28 19.7	6 45.2	18 54.4	4 4.2	28 0.0	6 29.9	28 2.3	26 52.5
14 Tu	17 26 54	22 23 46	1♌ 0 42	8♌22 24	25 4.8	29 34.2	7 43.8	19 35.6	3 57.2	27 58.3	6 27.6	28 0.7	26 51.7
15 W	17 30 51	23 21 6	15 42 10	22 59 20	25 5.1	0♊51.8	8 42.0	20 16.8	3 50.4	27 56.6	6 25.2	27 59.1	26 51.0
16 Th	17 34 47	24 18 26	0♍13 19	7♍23 41	25R 5.2	2 12.7	9 39.8	20 57.9	3 43.6	27 55.1	6 22.9	27 57.5	26 50.3
17 F	17 38 44	25 15 44	14 30 2	21 32 9	25D 5.2	3 36.6	10 37.1	21 39.0	3 36.9	27 53.6	6 20.6	27 55.9	26 49.6
18 Sa	17 42 40	26 13 1	28 29 51	5♎23 5	25 5.2	5 3.7	11 34.0	22 20.0	3 30.3	27 52.3	6 18.3	27 54.2	26 48.9
19 Su	17 46 37	27 10 18	12♎11 48	18 56 6	25 5.2	6 33.9	12 30.4	23 1.0	3 23.8	27 51.0	6 16.0	27 52.6	26 48.3
20 M	17 50 33	28 7 33	25 36 4	2♏11 50	25 5.4	8 7.1	13 26.3	23 41.9	3 17.5	27 49.8	6 13.8	27 51.0	26 47.7
21 Tu	17 54 30	29 4 48	8♏43 34	15 11 27	25 5.8	9 43.3	14 21.7	24 22.8	3 11.2	27 48.8	6 11.5	27 49.4	26 47.2
22 W	17 58 26	0♋ 2 2	21 35 40	27 56 25	25 6.2	11 22.6	15 16.6	25 3.7	3 5.0	27 47.8	6 9.3	27 47.8	26 46.6
23 Th	18 2 23	0 59 16	4♐13 53	10♐28 17	25 6.7	13 4.8	16 10.9	25 44.5	2 59.0	27 46.9	6 7.1	27 46.1	26 46.1
24 F	18 6 20	1 56 29	16 39 49	22 48 39	25R 7.0	14 49.9	17 4.7	26 25.2	2 53.1	27 46.1	6 5.0	27 44.5	26 45.7
25 Sa	18 10 16	2 53 42	28 55 1	4♑59 7	25 7.1	16 37.8	17 57.9	27 5.9	2 47.3	27 45.4	6 2.9	27 42.9	26 45.2
26 Su	18 14 13	3 50 55	11♑ 1 9	17 1 22	25 6.8	18 28.6	18 50.5	27 46.6	2 41.7	27 44.8	6 0.8	27 41.3	26 44.8
27 M	18 18 9	4 48 7	23 0 0	28 57 19	25 6.0	20 22.0	19 42.5	28 27.2	2 36.2	27 44.4	5 58.7	27 39.7	26 44.5
28 Tu	18 22 6	5 45 19	4♒53 36	10♒49 11	25 4.7	22 18.0	20 33.8	29 7.8	2 30.8	27 44.0	5 56.6	27 38.1	26 44.1
29 W	18 26 2	6 42 31	16 44 23	22 39 34	25 3.1	24 16.4	21 24.5	29 48.4	2 25.6	27 43.7	5 54.6	27 36.5	26 43.8
30 Th	18 29 59	7 39 42	28 35 9	4♓31 33	25 1.4	26 17.1	22 14.5	0♋28.9	2 20.5	27 43.5	5 52.6	27 34.9	26 43.6

Astro Data	Planet Ingress	Last Aspect	☽ Ingress	Last Aspect	☽ Ingress	☽ Phases & Eclipses	Astro Data
Dy Hr Mn	Dy Hr Mn	Dy Hr Mn	Dy Hr Mn	Dy Hr Mn	Dy Hr Mn	Dy Hr Mn	1 MAY 1983
☿ R 1 16:36	♄ ♎ 6 19:31	1 9:02 ♆ ☌	♑ 1 11:01	2 16:27 ♄ △	♓ 2 19:42	5 3:43 ☽ 14♒06	Julian Day # 30436
☽0N 9 20:02	♀ ♋ 9 10:56	3 18:33 ♇ □	♒ 3 23:09	5 4:55 ♀ △	♈ 5 6:59	12 19:25 ● 21♉30	Delta T 53.2 sec
♃☌♅ 14 20:35	♂ ♊ 16 21:43	6 9:33 ♆ ⚹	♓ 6 11:43	7 11:48 ♄ ☍	♉ 7 15:05	19 14:17 ☽ 28♌03	SVP 05♓29'52"
☽0S 22 17:40	☉ ♊ 21 15:06	8 21:02 ♀ □	♈ 8 22:16	9 9:56 ☿ ☌	♊ 9 19:37	26 18:48 ○ 4♐57	Obliquity 23°26'30"
☿ D 25 12:49		11 5:02 ♄ ☍	♉ 11 5:36	11 18:23 ♆ ☍	♋ 11 21:32		⚷ Chiron 26♉22.5
	♀ ♌ 6 6:04	13 5:35 ♂ ☌	♊ 13 10:03	13 21:26 ☿ ⚹	♌ 13 22:21	3 21:07 ☽ 12♓43	☽ Mean ☊ 27♊30.0
☽0N 6 5:26	☿ ♊ 14 8:06	15 11:47 ♄ △	♋ 15 12:48	15 20:14 ♆ △	♍ 15 23:38	11 4:37 ● 19♊43	
♄⚹♆ 7 17:32	☉ ♋ 21 23:09	17 13:47 ♄ □	♌ 17 15:01	17 22:58 ♆ □	♎ 18 2:36	11 4:42:41 ● T 5'11"	1 JUNE 1983
☽0S 18 23:18	♂ ♋ 29 6:54	19 16:08 ♄ ⚹	♍ 19 17:37	20 4:56 ☉ △	♏ 20 7:59	17 19:46 ☽ 26♍03	Julian Day # 30467
♄⚹♆ 21 23:01		21 18:45 ♆ □	♎ 21 21:11	21 11:15 ♀ □	♐ 22 15:55	25 8:32 ○ 3♑14	Delta T 53.3 sec
		24 0:16 ♄ ☌	♏ 24 2:17	24 21:43 ♄ ⚹	♑ 25 2:08	25 8:22 ● P 0.335	SVP 05♓29'47"
		25 10:23 ♀ △	♐ 26 9:27	27 9:32 ♄ □	♒ 27 14:07		Obliquity 23°26'29"
		28 16:25 ♄ ⚹	♑ 28 19:07	29 22:15 ♄ △	♓ 30 2:52		⚷ Chiron 28♉35.3
		31 3:58 ♄ □	♒ 31 7:00				☽ Mean ☊ 25♊51.5

JULY 1983 LONGITUDE

Day	Sid.Time	☉	0 hr ☽	Noon ☽	True ☊	☿	♀	♂	♃	♄	♅	♆	♇
1 F	18 33 55	8♋36 54	10♓29 13	16♓28 39	24♊59.8	28♊19.9	23♌ 3.7	1♋ 9.3	2♐15.5	27♎43.4	5♐50.6	27♐33.3	26♎43.3
2 Sa	18 37 52	9 34 6	22 30 20	28 34 47	24R58.5	0♋24.6	23 52.3	1 49.7	2R10.7	27D43.4	5R48.7	27R31.8	26R43.1
3 Su	18 41 49	10 31 18	4♈42 33	10♈54 10	24D57.8	2 30.8	24 40.0	2 30.1	2 6.0	27 43.5	5 46.8	27 30.2	26 43.0
4 M	18 45 45	11 28 30	17 10 8	23 30 59	24 57.8	4 38.4	25 27.0	3 10.5	2 1.5	27 43.7	5 44.9	27 28.6	26 42.8
5 Tu	18 49 42	12 25 42	29 57 11	6♉29 10	24 58.4	6 47.1	26 13.2	3 50.8	1 57.2	27 44.0	5 43.1	27 27.1	26 42.7
6 W	18 53 38	13 22 55	13♉ 7 17	19 51 50	24 59.6	8 56.6	26 58.5	4 31.0	1 53.0	27 44.3	5 41.3	27 25.5	26 42.7
7 Th	18 57 35	14 20 8	26 42 58	3♊40 44	25 0.9	11 6.5	27 43.0	5 11.3	1 48.9	27 44.8	5 39.5	27 24.0	26D42.6
8 F	19 1 31	15 17 21	10♊45 3	17 55 38	25 2.0	13 16.7	28 26.5	5 51.4	1 45.1	27 45.4	5 37.8	27 22.4	26 42.6
9 Sa	19 5 28	16 14 35	25 12 4	2♋33 45	25R 2.5	15 26.8	29 9.1	6 31.6	1 41.4	27 46.1	5 36.1	27 20.9	26 42.7
10 Su	19 9 24	17 11 49	9♋59 53	17 29 35	25 1.9	17 36.5	29 50.8	7 11.7	1 37.8	27 46.9	5 34.5	27 19.4	26 42.7
11 M	19 13 21	18 9 3	25 1 46	2♌35 18	25 0.3	19 45.6	0♍31.4	7 51.8	1 34.5	27 47.8	5 32.8	27 17.9	26 42.8
12 Tu	19 17 18	19 6 17	10♌ 8 59	17 41 38	24 57.7	21 54.0	1 10.9	8 31.8	1 31.3	27 48.8	5 31.3	27 16.5	26 43.0
13 W	19 21 14	20 3 32	25 12 7	2♍39 23	24 54.5	24 1.3	1 49.3	9 11.8	1 28.2	27 49.9	5 29.7	27 15.0	26 43.1
14 Th	19 25 11	21 0 46	10♍ 2 30	17 20 43	24 51.2	26 7.4	2 26.6	9 51.7	1 25.4	27 51.1	5 28.2	27 13.5	26 43.3
15 F	19 29 7	21 58 0	24 33 26	1♎40 14	24 48.3	28 12.2	3 2.7	10 31.6	1 22.7	27 52.4	5 26.8	27 12.1	26 43.6
16 Sa	19 33 4	22 55 14	8♎40 53	15 35 17	24 46.4	0♌15.6	3 37.5	11 11.5	1 20.2	27 53.7	5 25.4	27 10.7	26 43.9
17 Su	19 37 0	23 52 29	22 23 30	29 5 42	24D45.7	2 17.5	4 11.0	11 51.3	1 17.9	27 55.2	5 24.0	27 9.3	26 44.2
18 M	19 40 57	24 49 43	5♏42 7	12♏13 8	24 46.1	4 17.7	4 43.2	12 31.1	1 15.7	27 56.8	5 22.6	27 7.9	26 44.5
19 Tu	19 44 53	25 46 57	18 39 5	25 0 26	24 47.3	6 16.3	5 14.0	13 10.9	1 13.8	27 58.5	5 21.4	27 6.5	26 44.9
20 W	19 48 50	26 44 12	1♐17 34	7♐30 57	24 49.0	8 13.2	5 43.3	13 50.6	1 12.0	28 0.2	5 20.1	27 5.1	26 45.3
21 Th	19 52 47	27 41 27	13 41 0	19 48 8	24R50.3	10 8.3	6 11.1	14 30.2	1 10.4	28 2.1	5 18.9	27 3.8	26 45.7
22 F	19 56 43	28 38 43	25 52 43	1♑55 9	24 50.8	12 1.7	6 37.3	15 9.8	1 9.0	28 4.0	5 17.8	27 2.5	26 46.2
23 Sa	20 0 40	29 35 58	7♑55 44	13 54 47	24 50.0	13 53.3	7 1.9	15 49.4	1 7.8	28 6.1	5 16.6	27 1.2	26 46.7
24 Su	20 4 36	0♌33 15	19 52 36	25 49 27	24 47.4	15 43.2	7 24.9	16 29.0	1 6.7	28 8.2	5 15.6	26 59.9	26 47.3
25 M	20 8 33	1 30 31	1♒45 35	7♒41 13	24 43.2	17 31.3	7 46.1	17 8.5	1 5.8	28 10.5	5 14.6	26 58.6	26 47.9
26 Tu	20 12 29	2 27 49	13 36 36	19 31 58	24 37.5	19 17.7	8 5.4	17 48.0	1 5.1	28 12.8	5 13.6	26 57.4	26 48.5
27 W	20 16 26	3 25 7	25 27 31	1♓23 33	24 30.7	21 2.2	8 23.0	18 27.4	1 4.6	28 15.2	5 12.6	26 56.1	26 49.1
28 Th	20 20 22	4 22 26	7♓20 17	13 18 2	24 23.4	22 45.1	8 38.6	19 6.8	1 4.3	28 17.7	5 11.8	26 54.9	26 49.8
29 F	20 24 19	5 19 45	19 17 5	25 17 47	24 16.5	24 26.2	8 52.2	19 46.2	1D 4.2	28 20.3	5 10.9	26 53.7	26 50.5
30 Sa	20 28 16	6 17 6	1♈20 30	7♈25 37	24 10.6	26 5.5	9 3.8	20 25.5	1 4.2	28 23.0	5 10.1	26 52.6	26 51.2
31 Su	20 32 12	7 14 27	13 33 36	19 44 52	24 6.2	27 43.2	9 13.4	21 4.8	1 4.4	28 25.8	5 9.4	26 51.4	26 52.0

AUGUST 1983 LONGITUDE

Day	Sid.Time	☉	0 hr ☽	Noon ☽	True ☊	☿	♀	♂	♃	♄	♅	♆	♇
1 M	20 36 9	8♌11 50	25♈59 54	2♉19 11	24♊ 3.6	29♌19.1	9♍20.8	21♋44.1	1♐ 4.8	28♎28.7	5♐ 8.7	26♐50.3	26♎52.8
2 Tu	20 40 5	9 9 13	8♉43 12	15 12 28	24D 2.8	0♍53.3	9 26.0	22 23.3	1 5.4	28 31.6	5R 8.0	26R49.2	26 53.7
3 W	20 44 2	10 6 38	21 47 23	28 28 24	24 3.3	2 25.7	9R29.0	23 2.5	1 6.2	28 34.7	5 7.4	26 48.1	26 54.5
4 Th	20 47 58	11 4 4	5♊15 49	12♊ 9 54	24 4.4	3 56.5	9 29.7	23 41.7	1 7.1	28 37.8	5 6.9	26 47.1	26 55.4
5 F	20 51 55	12 1 32	19 10 47	26 18 25	24R 5.3	5 25.4	9 28.2	24 20.8	1 8.3	28 41.0	5 6.4	26 46.0	26 56.4
6 Sa	20 55 51	12 59 0	3♋32 38	10♋53 1	24 5.1	6 52.7	9 24.3	24 59.9	1 9.6	28 44.3	5 6.0	26 45.0	26 57.4
7 Su	20 59 48	13 56 30	18 19 0	25 49 46	24 3.0	8 18.1	9 18.0	25 39.0	1 11.1	28 47.7	5 5.6	26 44.1	26 58.4
8 M	21 3 45	14 54 1	3♌24 19	11♌ 1 29	23 58.7	9 41.8	9 9.4	26 18.0	1 12.8	28 51.2	5 5.2	26 43.1	26 59.4
9 Tu	21 7 41	15 51 33	18 39 59	26 18 25	23 52.4	11 3.6	8 58.5	26 57.0	1 14.6	28 54.7	5 4.9	26 42.2	27 0.5
10 W	21 11 38	16 49 6	3♍55 24	11♍29 37	23 44.8	12 23.5	8 45.1	27 36.0	1 16.7	28 58.4	5 4.7	26 41.3	27 1.6
11 Th	21 15 34	17 46 40	18 59 49	26 24 56	23 36.8	13 41.5	8 29.4	28 14.9	1 18.9	29 2.1	5 4.5	26 40.4	27 2.7
12 F	21 19 31	18 44 15	3♎44 5	10♎56 38	23 29.5	14 57.6	8 11.4	28 53.8	1 21.3	29 5.9	5 4.3	26 39.6	27 3.9
13 Sa	21 23 27	19 41 51	18 2 8	25 0 22	23 23.8	16 11.6	7 51.1	29 32.7	1 23.8	29 9.8	5 4.2	26 38.7	27 5.1
14 Su	21 27 24	20 39 28	1♏51 18	8♏35 6	23 20.1	17 23.6	7 28.6	0♌11.5	1 26.6	29 13.8	5D 4.2	26 38.0	27 6.3
15 M	21 31 20	21 37 5	15 12 2	21 42 32	23D18.5	18 33.3	7 4.0	0 50.3	1 29.5	29 17.8	5 4.2	26 37.2	27 7.5
16 Tu	21 35 17	22 34 44	28 7 3	4♐26 9	23 18.4	19 40.8	6 37.4	1 29.0	1 32.6	29 21.9	5 4.3	26 36.4	27 8.8
17 W	21 39 14	23 32 24	10♐40 25	16 50 26	23 19.1	20 46.0	6 8.8	2 7.7	1 35.9	29 26.1	5 4.4	26 35.7	27 10.1
18 Th	21 43 10	24 30 5	22 56 47	29 0 3	23R19.6	21 48.7	5 38.5	2 46.4	1 39.3	29 30.4	5 4.6	26 35.1	27 11.5
19 F	21 47 7	25 27 46	5♑ 0 47	10♑59 31	23 18.9	22 48.9	5 6.6	3 25.0	1 43.0	29 34.8	5 4.8	26 34.4	27 12.8
20 Sa	21 51 3	26 25 29	16 56 43	22 52 49	23 16.2	23 46.4	4 33.3	4 3.7	1 46.7	29 39.2	5 5.0	26 33.8	27 14.2
21 Su	21 55 0	27 23 14	28 48 14	4♒43 19	23 10.9	24 41.0	3 58.7	4 42.2	1 50.7	29 43.7	5 5.4	26 33.2	27 15.7
22 M	21 58 56	28 20 59	10♒38 22	16 33 41	23 3.1	25 32.6	3 23.1	5 20.8	1 54.8	29 48.3	5 5.7	26 32.6	27 17.1
23 Tu	22 2 53	29 18 46	22 29 28	28 25 57	22 53.0	26 21.1	2 46.8	5 59.3	1 59.1	29 52.9	5 6.2	26 32.1	27 18.6
24 W	22 6 49	0♍16 34	4♓23 20	10♓21 45	22 41.1	27 6.3	2 9.8	6 37.8	2 3.5	29 57.6	5 6.6	26 31.6	27 20.1
25 Th	22 10 46	1 14 23	16 21 25	22 22 27	22 28.6	27 47.9	1 32.6	7 16.2	2 8.1	0♏ 2.4	5 7.2	26 31.1	27 21.7
26 F	22 14 43	2 12 14	28 25 3	4♈29 25	22 16.4	28 25.7	0 55.2	7 54.6	2 12.9	0 7.3	5 7.7	26 30.7	27 23.2
27 Sa	22 18 39	3 10 7	10♈35 44	16 44 14	22 5.6	28 59.6	0 18.0	8 33.0	2 17.8	0 12.2	5 8.4	26 30.3	27 24.8
28 Su	22 22 36	4 8 1	22 55 13	29 8 59	21 57.0	29 29.2	29♌41.3	9 11.4	2 22.9	0 17.2	5 9.0	26 29.9	27 26.4
29 M	22 26 32	5 5 57	5♉25 51	11♉46 12	21 51.0	29 54.3	29 5.1	9 49.7	2 28.2	0 22.2	5 9.8	26 29.5	27 28.1
30 Tu	22 30 29	6 3 55	18 10 24	24 38 54	21 47.6	0♎14.7	28 29.9	10 28.0	2 33.6	0 27.4	5 10.6	26 29.2	27 29.7
31 W	22 34 25	7 1 55	1♊12 6	7♊50 24	21D46.4	0 30.1	27 55.7	11 6.3	2 39.1	0 32.6	5 11.4	26 28.9	27 31.4

Astro Data Dy Hr Mn	Planet Ingress Dy Hr Mn	Last Aspect Dy Hr Mn	☽ Ingress Dy Hr Mn	Last Aspect Dy Hr Mn	☽ Ingress Dy Hr Mn	☽ Phases & Eclipses Dy Hr Mn	Astro Data
♄ D 1 12:31	☿ ♋ 1 19:18	2 9:55 ♆ □	♈ 2 14:47	1 7:13 ☿ △	♉ 1 7:37	3 12:12 ☽ 11♈00	1 JULY 1983
☽0N 3 13:37	♀ ♍ 10 5:25	4 19:53 ♄ ☍	♉ 5 0:05	3 2:23 ♂ ✶	♊ 3 14:43	10 12:18 ● 17♋41	Julian Day # 30497
♇ D 7 11:25	☿ ♌ 15 20:57	7 1:50 ♀ □	♊ 7 5:41	5 16:01 ♄ △	♋ 5 18:09	17 2:50 ☽ 23♎59	Delta T 53.4 sec
☽0S 16 5:09	☉ ♌ 23 10:04	9 6:47 ♀ ✶	♋ 9 7:50	7 16:46 ♄ □	♌ 7 18:37	24 23:27 ○ 1♒29	SVP 05♓29'41"
♃ D 29 7:04		11 4:24 ♄ □	♌ 11 7:54	9 16:10 ♄ ✶	♍ 9 17:49		Obliquity 23°26'30"
☽0N 30 19:53	☿ ♍ 1 10:22	13 4:14 ♄ ✶	♍ 13 7:43	11 15:41 ♂ ✶	♎ 11 17:51	2 0:52 ☽ 9♉11	⚷ Chiron 0♊35.6
♆✶♇ 30 16:40	♂ ♌ 13 16:54	15 7:10 ☿ ✶	♎ 15 9:10	13 19:21 ♄ ☌	♏ 13 20:44	8 19:18 ● 15♌40	☽ Mean ☊ 24♊16.2
	☉ ♍ 23 17:07	17 9:54 ♄ ☌	♏ 17 13:38	15 12:47 ☉ □	♐ 16 3:33	15 12:47 ☽ 22♏08	
♀ R 3 19:44	♄ ♏ 24 11:53	19 14:35 ☉ △	♐ 19 21:31	18 13:05 ♄ ✶	♑ 18 13:59	23 14:59 ○ 29♒55	1 AUGUST 1983
☽0S 12 12:36	♀ ♌ 27 11:43	22 4:21 ♄ ✶	♑ 22 8:11	21 1:53 ♄ □	♒ 21 2:25	31 11:22 ☽ 7♊29	Julian Day # 30528
♅ D 14 7:11	☿ ♎ 29 6:07	24 16:44 ♄ □	♒ 24 20:26	23 15:01 ♄ △	♓ 23 15:10		Delta T 53.4 sec
♀0S 21 3:01		27 5:40 ♄ △	♓ 27 9:11	26 0:01 ☿ ☍	♈ 26 3:08		SVP 05♓29'37"
☽0N 27 0:55		29 15:09 ♆ □	♈ 29 21:21	28 12:26 ♀ △	♉ 28 13:38		Obliquity 23°26'30"
				30 18:16 ♀ □	♊ 30 21:49		⚷ Chiron 2♊09.6
							☽ Mean ☊ 22♊37.8

Day	Sid.Time	☉	0 hr ☽	Noon ☽	True ☊	☿	♀	♂	♃	♄	♅	♆	♇
1 Th	22 38 22	7♍59 57	14♊34 11	21♊23 46	21♊46.4	0♎40.2	27♌22.9	11♌44.5	2♐44.8	0♏37.8	5♐12.3	26♐28.7	27♎33.1
2 F	22 42 18	8 58 0	28 19 24	5♋21 14	21R 46.3	0R 44.7	26R 51.5	12 22.7	2 50.7	0 43.1	5 13.2	26R 28.4	27 34.9
3 Sa	22 46 15	9 56 6	12♋29 16	19 43 21	21 45.1	0 43.3	26 21.8	13 0.9	2 56.7	0 48.5	5 14.2	26 28.3	27 36.7
4 Su	22 50 12	10 54 14	27 3 7	4♌28 3	21 41.7	0 36.0	25 53.9	13 39.1	3 2.9	0 53.9	5 15.2	26 28.1	27 38.5
5 M	22 54 8	11 52 24	11♌57 23	19 30 8	21 35.5	0 22.4	25 28.0	14 17.2	3 9.2	0 59.4	5 16.3	26 28.0	27 40.3
6 Tu	22 58 5	12 50 35	27 5 13	4♍41 20	21 26.8	0 2.4	25 4.1	14 55.3	3 15.6	1 5.0	5 17.5	26 27.9	27 42.1
7 W	23 2 1	13 48 48	12♍17 8	19 51 15	21 16.3	29♍36.1	24 42.4	15 33.3	3 22.2	1 10.6	5 18.7	26 27.8	27 44.0
8 Th	23 5 58	14 47 3	27 22 22	4♎49 14	21 5.1	29 3.4	24 22.9	16 11.3	3 29.0	1 16.3	5 19.9	26D 27.8	27 45.9
9 F	23 9 54	15 45 20	12♎10 49	19 26 14	20 54.6	28 24.7	24 5.7	16 49.3	3 35.9	1 22.0	5 21.2	26 27.8	27 47.8
10 Sa	23 13 51	16 43 38	26 34 50	3♏36 13	20 45.9	27 40.1	23 50.9	17 27.3	3 42.9	1 27.8	5 22.5	26 27.8	27 49.7
11 Su	23 17 47	17 41 58	10♏30 10	17 16 41	20 39.7	26 50.2	23 38.4	18 5.2	3 50.1	1 33.7	5 23.9	26 27.9	27 51.6
12 M	23 21 44	18 40 19	23 55 58	0♐28 19	20 36.1	25 55.8	23 28.3	18 43.1	3 57.4	1 39.6	5 25.3	26 28.0	27 53.6
13 Tu	23 25 41	19 38 42	6♐54 12	13 14 9	20 34.6	24 57.7	23 20.6	19 21.0	4 4.9	1 45.5	5 26.8	26 28.1	27 55.6
14 W	23 29 37	20 37 7	19 28 45	25 38 39	20 34.3	23 57.0	23 15.3	19 58.8	4 12.4	1 51.5	5 28.4	26 28.3	27 57.6
15 Th	23 33 34	21 35 33	1♑44 31	7♑47 0	20 34.2	22 55.0	23D 12.4	20 36.6	4 20.2	1 57.6	5 29.9	26 28.5	27 59.6
16 F	23 37 30	22 34 1	13 46 46	19 44 27	20 33.0	21 53.1	23 11.9	21 14.3	4 28.0	2 3.7	5 31.6	26 28.7	28 1.7
17 Sa	23 41 27	23 32 30	25 40 39	1♒35 54	20 29.8	20 52.7	23 13.7	21 52.1	4 36.0	2 9.8	5 33.2	26 29.0	28 3.8
18 Su	23 45 23	24 31 2	7♒30 46	13 25 40	20 24.0	19 55.3	23 17.8	22 29.8	4 44.1	2 16.0	5 35.0	26 29.3	28 5.8
19 M	23 49 20	25 29 34	19 21 3	25 17 17	20 15.3	19 2.3	23 24.2	23 7.4	4 52.3	2 22.2	5 36.7	26 29.6	28 7.9
20 Tu	23 53 16	26 28 9	1♓14 40	7♓13 27	20 4.1	18 15.2	23 32.8	23 45.1	5 0.7	2 28.5	5 38.5	26 30.0	28 10.1
21 W	23 57 13	27 26 45	13 13 53	19 16 7	19 51.1	17 35.2	23 43.6	24 22.7	5 9.1	2 34.8	5 40.4	26 30.4	28 12.2
22 Th	0 1 10	28 25 24	25 20 17	1♈26 31	19 37.3	17 3.2	23 56.5	25 0.2	5 17.7	2 41.2	5 42.3	26 30.8	28 14.3
23 F	0 5 6	29 24 4	7♈34 52	13 45 26	19 23.8	16 40.2	24 11.4	25 37.8	5 26.5	2 47.6	5 44.3	26 31.3	28 16.5
24 Sa	0 9 3	0♎22 46	19 58 17	26 13 30	19 11.7	16D 26.6	24 28.3	26 15.3	5 35.3	2 54.1	5 46.3	26 31.8	28 18.7
25 Su	0 12 59	1 21 30	2♉31 9	8♉51 23	19 2.1	16 22.9	24 47.2	26 52.7	5 44.2	3 0.6	5 48.3	26 32.3	28 20.9
26 M	0 16 56	2 20 17	15 14 20	21 40 9	18 55.2	16 29.3	25 8.0	27 30.2	5 53.3	3 7.1	5 50.4	26 32.9	28 23.1
27 Tu	0 20 52	3 19 5	28 9 4	4♊41 18	18 51.3	16 45.6	25 30.6	28 7.6	6 2.5	3 13.7	5 52.5	26 33.5	28 25.3
28 W	0 24 49	4 17 56	11♊17 6	17 56 44	18D 49.7	17 11.7	25 55.0	28 45.0	6 11.8	3 20.3	5 54.7	26 34.1	28 27.6
29 Th	0 28 45	5 16 50	24 40 28	1♋28 33	18R 49.6	17 47.1	26 21.1	29 22.4	6 21.2	3 26.9	5 56.9	26 34.8	28 29.8
30 F	0 32 42	6 15 45	8♋21 12	15 18 33	18 49.8	18 31.4	26 48.9	29 59.7	6 30.7	3 33.6	5 59.1	26 35.4	28 32.1

LONGITUDE OCTOBER 1983

Day	Sid.Time	☉	0 hr ☽	Noon ☽	True ☊	☿	♀	♂	♃	♄	♅	♆	♇
1 Sa	0 36 38	7♎14 43	22♋20 41	29♋27 33	18♊49.0	19♍24.1	27♌18.2	0♍37.0	6♐40.3	3♏40.3	6♐ 1.4	26♐36.2	28♎34.4
2 Su	0 40 35	8 13 44	6♌38 59	13♌54 40	18R 46.2	20 24.3	27 49.1	1 14.3	6 50.1	3 47.1	6 3.8	26 36.9	28 36.7
3 M	0 44 32	9 12 46	21 14 7	28 36 40	18 40.9	21 31.5	28 21.5	1 51.5	6 59.9	3 53.9	6 6.1	26 37.7	28 39.0
4 Tu	0 48 28	10 11 51	6♍ 1 33	13♍27 48	18 33.1	22 44.9	28 55.2	2 28.7	7 9.9	4 0.7	6 8.6	26 38.5	28 41.3
5 W	0 52 25	11 10 58	20 54 22	28 20 10	18 23.5	24 3.8	29 30.4	3 5.9	7 19.9	4 7.5	6 11.0	26 39.4	28 43.6
6 Th	0 56 21	12 10 7	5♎44 3	13♎ 4 56	18 13.1	25 27.5	0♍ 6.8	3 43.0	7 30.0	4 14.4	6 13.5	26 40.3	28 45.9
7 F	1 0 18	13 9 18	20 21 48	27 33 48	18 3.2	26 55.4	0 44.5	4 20.1	7 40.3	4 21.3	6 16.0	26 41.2	28 48.3
8 Sa	1 4 14	14 8 31	4♏40 10	11♏40 22	17 55.0	28 26.7	1 23.4	4 57.2	7 50.6	4 28.2	6 18.6	26 42.1	28 50.6
9 Su	1 8 11	15 7 47	18 34 4	25 21 2	17 49.0	0♎ 1.1	2 3.5	5 34.2	8 1.1	4 35.2	6 21.2	26 43.1	28 53.0
10 M	1 12 7	16 7 4	2♐ 1 19	8♐35 1	17 45.6	1 37.8	2 44.8	6 11.2	8 11.6	4 42.1	6 23.9	26 44.1	28 55.4
11 Tu	1 16 4	17 6 23	15 2 27	21 24 0	17D 44.4	3 16.5	3 27.1	6 48.2	8 22.2	4 49.2	6 26.6	26 45.1	28 57.7
12 W	1 20 1	18 5 44	27 40 9	3♑51 29	17 44.7	4 56.8	4 10.4	7 25.1	8 33.0	4 56.2	6 29.3	26 46.2	29 0.1
13 Th	1 23 57	19 5 6	9♑58 34	16 2 5	17R 45.5	6 38.3	4 54.8	8 2.0	8 43.8	5 3.2	6 32.0	26 47.3	29 2.5
14 F	1 27 54	20 4 31	22 2 40	28 0 59	17 45.9	8 20.7	5 40.1	8 38.9	8 54.7	5 10.3	6 34.8	26 48.4	29 4.9
15 Sa	1 31 50	21 3 57	3♒57 41	9♒53 25	17 44.8	10 3.6	6 26.4	9 15.7	9 5.7	5 17.4	6 37.7	26 49.6	29 7.3
16 Su	1 35 47	22 3 25	15 48 45	21 44 18	17 41.7	11 47.0	7 13.6	9 52.5	9 16.7	5 24.5	6 40.5	26 50.8	29 9.7
17 M	1 39 43	23 2 54	27 40 34	3♓38 3	17 36.4	13 30.6	8 1.7	10 29.2	9 27.9	5 31.6	6 43.4	26 52.0	29 12.1
18 Tu	1 43 40	24 2 26	9♓37 11	15 38 21	17 28.9	15 14.3	8 50.6	11 5.9	9 39.1	5 38.7	6 46.3	26 53.2	29 14.5
19 W	1 47 36	25 1 59	21 41 51	27 47 58	17 19.9	16 57.8	9 40.3	11 42.6	9 50.4	5 45.9	6 49.3	26 54.5	29 16.9
20 Th	1 51 33	26 1 34	3♈56 53	10♈ 8 46	17 10.1	18 41.2	10 30.8	12 19.2	10 1.8	5 53.0	6 52.3	26 55.8	29 19.3
21 F	1 55 30	27 1 11	16 23 43	22 41 45	17 0.5	20 24.3	11 22.1	12 55.8	10 13.3	6 0.2	6 55.3	26 57.1	29 21.7
22 Sa	1 59 26	28 0 50	29 2 54	5♉27 8	16 52.0	22 7.0	12 14.1	13 32.4	10 24.8	6 7.4	6 58.3	26 58.5	29 24.2
23 Su	2 3 23	29 0 31	11♉54 24	18 24 38	16 45.3	23 49.4	13 6.8	14 8.9	10 36.5	6 14.6	7 1.4	26 59.9	29 26.6
24 M	2 7 19	0♏ 0 14	24 57 46	1♊33 45	16 40.8	25 31.4	14 0.3	14 45.4	10 48.2	6 21.8	7 4.5	27 1.3	29 29.0
25 Tu	2 11 16	1 0 0	8♊12 32	14 54 3	16D 38.6	27 12.8	14 54.3	15 21.9	10 59.9	6 29.0	7 7.7	27 2.7	29 31.4
26 W	2 15 12	1 59 47	21 38 18	28 25 17	16 38.4	28 53.8	15 49.1	15 58.3	11 11.8	6 36.2	7 10.8	27 4.2	29 33.8
27 Th	2 19 9	2 59 37	5♋15 0	12♋ 7 27	16 39.4	0♏34.3	16 44.4	16 34.7	11 23.7	6 43.4	7 14.0	27 5.7	29 36.3
28 F	2 23 5	3 59 29	19 2 40	26 0 36	16 40.8	2 14.3	17 40.4	17 11.1	11 35.7	6 50.6	7 17.2	27 7.2	29 38.7
29 Sa	2 27 2	4 59 23	3♌ 1 15	10♌ 4 29	16R 41.5	3 53.8	18 37.0	17 47.4	11 47.7	6 57.9	7 20.5	27 8.7	29 41.1
30 Su	2 30 59	5 59 19	17 10 12	24 18 8	16 41.0	5 32.8	19 34.1	18 23.7	11 59.8	7 5.1	7 23.7	27 10.3	29 43.5
31 M	2 34 55	6 59 18	1♍28 1	8♍39 26	16 38.7	7 11.3	20 31.7	18 59.9	12 12.0	7 12.4	7 27.0	27 11.9	29 45.9

Astro Data	Dy Hr Mn
☿ R	2 6:41
☽0S	8 21:59
♆ D	8 11:00
☿0N	15 13:23
♀ D	15 17:22
☽0N	23 6:19
☿ D	24 20:49
♃☌♅	25 13:55
☽0S	6 8:19
☿0S	11 17:35
☽0N	20 13:22

Planet Ingress	Dy Hr Mn
☿ ♍	6 2:30
☉ ♎	23 14:42
♂ ♍	30 0:12
♀ ♍	5 19:35
☿ ♎	8 23:44
☉ ♏	23 23:54
☿ ♏	26 15:47

Last Aspect Dy Hr Mn		☽ Ingress Dy Hr Mn
1 22:43	♇ △	♋ 2 2:53
4 0:58	♇ □	♌ 4 4:47
6 0:58	♇ ⚹	♍ 6 4:36
8 2:36	☿ ☌	♎ 8 4:13
10 2:07	♇ ☌	♏ 10 5:49
12 3:24	☿ ⚹	♐ 12 11:08
14 16:35	♇ ⚹	♑ 14 20:34
17 4:51	♇ □	♒ 17 8:46
19 17:47	♇ △	♓ 19 21:30
22 6:36	☉ ☍	♈ 22 9:10
24 16:02	♇ ☍	♉ 24 19:12
26 23:57	♂ □	♊ 27 3:24
29 8:42	♂ ⚹	♋ 29 9:24

Last Aspect Dy Hr Mn		☽ Ingress Dy Hr Mn
1 10:32	♇ □	♌ 1 12:54
3 12:06	♇ ⚹	♍ 3 14:15
5 9:18	♆ □	♎ 5 14:42
7 14:07	♇ ☌	♏ 7 16:06
8 0:30	♂ ⚹	♐ 9 20:21
12 2:35	♇ ⚹	♑ 12 4:30
14 14:12	♇ □	♒ 14 16:00
17 3:05	♇ △	♓ 17 4:41
19 10:16	♆ □	♈ 19 16:18
22 0:40	♇ ☍	♉ 22 1:47
23 4:21	♂ △	♊ 24 9:10
26 14:38	☿ △	♋ 26 14:47
28 18:17	♇ □	♌ 28 18:50
30 21:09	♇ ⚹	♍ 30 21:33

☽ Phases & Eclipses Dy Hr Mn	
7 2:35	● 13♍55
14 2:24	☽ 20♐43
22 6:36	○ 28♓42
29 20:05	☽ 6♋06
6 11:16	● 12♎38
13 19:42	☽ 19♑54
21 21:53	○ 27♈56
29 3:37	☽ 5♌08

Astro Data

1 SEPTEMBER 1983
Julian Day # 30559
Delta T 53.5 sec
SVP 05♓29'33"
Obliquity 23°26'31"
⚷ Chiron 2♊54.2
☽ Mean ☊ 20♊59.3

1 OCTOBER 1983
Julian Day # 30589
Delta T 53.6 sec
SVP 05♓29'29"
Obliquity 23°26'31"
⚷ Chiron 2♊39.9R
☽ Mean ☊ 19♊23.9

NOVEMBER 1983 LONGITUDE

Day	Sid.Time	☉	0 hr ☽	Noon ☽	True ☊	☿	♀	♂	♃	♄	♅	♆	♇
1 Tu	2 38 52	7♏59 19	15♍51 54	23♍ 4 52	16♊34.7	8♏49.3	21♍29.9	19♍36.1	12♐24.2	7♏19.6	7♐30.3	27♐13.5	29♎48.3
2 W	2 42 48	8 59 21	0♎17 42	7♎29 42	16R 29.4	10 26.9	22 28.5	20 12.3	12 36.5	7 26.8	7 33.7	27 15.1	29 50.7
3 Th	2 46 45	9 59 26	14 40 9	21 48 20	16 23.5	12 3.9	23 27.7	20 48.4	12 48.9	7 34.1	7 37.0	27 16.8	29 53.1
4 F	2 50 41	10 59 33	28 53 34	5♏55 11	16 17.8	13 40.6	24 27.3	21 24.4	13 1.3	7 41.3	7 40.4	27 18.5	29 55.5
5 Sa	2 54 38	11 59 42	12♏52 38	19 45 25	16 13.1	15 16.8	25 27.4	22 0.5	13 13.8	7 48.5	7 43.8	27 20.2	29 57.9
6 Su	2 58 34	12 59 53	26 33 11	3♐15 41	16 9.9	16 52.5	26 27.9	22 36.5	13 26.3	7 55.8	7 47.2	27 21.9	0♏ 0.3
7 M	3 2 31	14 0 5	9♐52 47	16 24 28	16D 8.4	18 27.9	27 28.8	23 12.4	13 38.9	8 3.0	7 50.7	27 23.7	0 2.6
8 Tu	3 6 28	15 0 20	22 50 50	29 12 6	16 8.4	20 2.9	28 30.2	23 48.3	13 51.6	8 10.2	7 54.1	27 25.4	0 5.0
9 W	3 10 24	16 0 35	5♑28 33	11♑40 35	16 9.5	21 37.5	29 31.9	24 24.2	14 4.2	8 17.4	7 57.6	27 27.2	0 7.4
10 Th	3 14 21	17 0 53	17 48 37	23 53 11	16 11.3	23 11.7	0♎34.0	24 60.0	14 17.0	8 24.6	8 1.1	27 29.0	0 9.7
11 F	3 18 17	18 1 12	29 54 48	5♒54 5	16 13.0	24 45.6	1 36.5	25 35.7	14 29.8	8 31.8	8 4.6	27 30.9	0 12.0
12 Sa	3 22 14	19 1 32	11♒51 37	17 48 1	16R 14.2	26 19.2	2 39.4	26 11.4	14 42.6	8 39.0	8 8.2	27 32.7	0 14.4
13 Su	3 26 10	20 1 54	23 43 54	29 39 53	16 14.3	27 52.5	3 42.6	26 47.1	14 55.5	8 46.1	8 11.7	27 34.6	0 16.7
14 M	3 30 7	21 2 17	5♓36 35	11♓34 34	16 13.3	29 25.5	4 46.1	27 22.7	15 8.4	8 53.3	8 15.3	27 36.5	0 19.0
15 Tu	3 34 3	22 2 41	17 34 22	23 36 31	16 11.2	0♐58.2	5 50.0	27 58.2	15 21.4	9 0.4	8 18.8	27 38.4	0 21.3
16 W	3 38 0	23 3 7	29 41 30	5♈49 42	16 8.2	2 30.6	6 54.1	28 33.8	15 34.4	9 7.5	8 22.4	27 40.4	0 23.6
17 Th	3 41 57	24 3 34	12♈ 1 29	18 17 10	16 4.6	4 2.7	7 58.6	29 9.2	15 47.4	9 14.6	8 26.0	27 42.3	0 25.8
18 F	3 45 53	25 4 3	24 36 57	1♉ 0 59	16 1.1	5 34.6	9 3.4	29 44.6	16 0.5	9 21.6	8 29.6	27 44.3	0 28.1
19 Sa	3 49 50	26 4 33	7♉29 22	14 2 4	15 57.9	7 6.2	10 8.5	0♎20.0	16 13.7	9 28.7	8 33.2	27 46.3	0 30.3
20 Su	3 53 46	27 5 4	20 39 3	27 20 8	15 55.6	8 37.5	11 13.9	0 55.3	16 26.8	9 35.7	8 36.9	27 48.3	0 32.6
21 M	3 57 43	28 5 37	4♊ 5 9	10♊53 49	15D 54.3	10 8.7	12 19.6	1 30.6	16 40.0	9 42.7	8 40.5	27 50.3	0 34.8
22 Tu	4 1 39	29 6 12	17 45 50	24 40 52	15 53.9	11 39.5	13 25.5	2 5.8	16 53.2	9 49.7	8 44.2	27 52.3	0 37.0
23 W	4 5 36	0♐ 6 48	1♋38 34	8♋38 34	15 54.4	13 10.1	14 31.7	2 40.9	17 6.5	9 56.7	8 47.8	27 54.4	0 39.2
24 Th	4 9 32	1 7 26	15 40 28	22 43 55	15 55.4	14 40.4	15 38.2	3 16.0	17 19.8	10 3.6	8 51.5	27 56.4	0 41.3
25 F	4 13 29	2 8 6	29 48 33	6♌54 2	15 56.6	16 10.4	16 44.9	3 51.1	17 33.1	10 10.5	8 55.1	27 58.5	0 43.5
26 Sa	4 17 26	3 8 47	14♌ 0 3	21 6 16	15 57.6	17 40.0	17 51.9	4 26.1	17 46.5	10 17.4	8 58.8	28 0.6	0 45.6
27 Su	4 21 22	4 9 29	28 12 26	5♍18 14	15R 58.2	19 9.4	18 59.1	5 1.1	17 59.8	10 24.2	9 2.5	28 2.7	0 47.7
28 M	4 25 19	5 10 14	12♍23 26	19 27 44	15 58.1	20 38.3	20 6.5	5 36.0	18 13.2	10 31.1	9 6.2	28 4.8	0 49.8
29 Tu	4 29 15	6 10 59	26 30 53	3♎32 37	15 57.6	22 6.7	21 14.1	6 10.8	18 26.7	10 37.9	9 9.9	28 7.0	0 51.9
30 W	4 33 12	7 11 47	10♎32 39	17 30 44	15 56.7	23 34.7	22 22.0	6 45.6	18 40.1	10 44.6	9 13.6	28 9.1	0 54.0

DECEMBER 1983 LONGITUDE

Day	Sid.Time	☉	0 hr ☽	Noon ☽	True ☊	☿	♀	♂	♃	♄	♅	♆	♇
1 Th	4 37 8	8♐12 36	24♎26 33	1♏19 51	15♊55.7	25♐ 2.1	23♎30.1	7♎20.3	18♐53.6	10♏51.3	9♐17.2	28♐11.3	0♏56.0
2 F	4 41 5	9 13 26	8♏10 21	14 57 48	15R 54.8	26 28.9	24 38.3	7 54.9	19 7.1	10 58.0	9 21.0	28 13.4	0 58.1
3 Sa	4 45 1	10 14 18	21 41 57	28 22 35	15 54.1	27 54.9	25 46.8	8 29.5	19 20.6	11 4.7	9 24.6	28 15.6	1 0.1
4 Su	4 48 58	11 15 11	4♐59 33	11♐32 41	15D 53.7	29 20.0	26 55.4	9 4.0	19 34.1	11 11.3	9 28.3	28 17.8	1 2.0
5 M	4 52 55	12 16 5	18 1 54	24 27 10	15 53.7	0♑44.1	28 4.2	9 38.5	19 47.7	11 17.9	9 32.0	28 20.0	1 4.0
6 Tu	4 56 51	13 17 0	0♑48 31	7♑ 6 1	15 53.8	2 7.0	29 13.2	10 12.9	20 1.3	11 24.4	9 35.7	28 22.2	1 5.9
7 W	5 0 48	14 17 56	13 19 48	19 30 6	15 53.9	3 28.6	0♏22.4	10 47.2	20 14.8	11 30.9	9 39.4	28 24.4	1 7.9
8 Th	5 4 44	15 18 54	25 37 8	1♒41 16	15R 54.1	4 48.6	1 31.7	11 21.5	20 28.4	11 37.3	9 43.1	28 26.6	1 9.8
9 F	5 8 41	16 19 51	7♒42 49	13 42 15	15 54.1	6 6.7	2 41.2	11 55.6	20 42.0	11 43.7	9 46.7	28 28.8	1 11.6
10 Sa	5 12 37	17 20 50	19 39 59	25 36 32	15 54.0	7 22.7	3 50.8	12 29.7	20 55.6	11 50.1	9 50.4	28 31.1	1 13.5
11 Su	5 16 34	18 21 49	1♓32 27	7♓28 15	15 53.8	8 36.1	5 0.6	13 3.8	21 9.3	11 56.4	9 54.1	28 33.3	1 15.3
12 M	5 20 30	19 22 49	13 24 33	19 21 54	15D 53.7	9 46.7	6 10.5	13 37.7	21 22.9	12 2.7	9 57.7	28 35.6	1 17.1
13 Tu	5 24 27	20 23 49	25 20 56	1♈22 14	15 53.6	10 53.9	7 20.5	14 11.6	21 36.5	12 8.9	10 1.4	28 37.8	1 18.9
14 W	5 28 24	21 24 50	7♈26 22	13 33 53	15 53.9	11 57.2	8 30.7	14 45.4	21 50.1	12 15.1	10 5.0	28 40.1	1 20.6
15 Th	5 32 20	22 25 52	19 45 21	26 1 13	15 54.4	12 56.0	9 41.1	15 19.2	22 3.7	12 21.2	10 8.7	28 42.3	1 22.3
16 F	5 36 17	23 26 54	2♉21 55	8♉47 50	15 55.1	13 49.7	10 51.5	15 52.8	22 17.4	12 27.3	10 12.3	28 44.6	1 24.0
17 Sa	5 40 13	24 27 56	15 19 13	21 56 15	15 56.0	14 37.6	12 2.1	16 26.4	22 31.0	12 33.3	10 15.9	28 46.8	1 25.7
18 Su	5 44 10	25 28 59	28 39 2	5♊27 31	15 56.7	15 18.7	13 12.8	16 59.9	22 44.6	12 39.2	10 19.5	28 49.1	1 27.3
19 M	5 48 6	26 30 2	12♊21 33	19 20 49	15R 57.1	15 52.4	14 23.6	17 33.3	22 58.3	12 45.1	10 23.1	28 51.4	1 28.9
20 Tu	5 52 3	27 31 7	26 24 56	3♋33 21	15 56.9	16 17.6	15 34.6	18 6.6	23 11.9	12 51.0	10 26.7	28 53.6	1 30.5
21 W	5 56 0	28 32 11	10♋45 27	18 0 30	15 56.1	16 33.5	16 45.6	18 39.9	23 25.5	12 56.8	10 30.2	28 55.9	1 32.1
22 Th	5 59 56	29 33 16	25 17 43	2♌36 17	15 54.7	16R 39.2	17 56.8	19 13.1	23 39.1	13 2.5	10 33.8	28 58.2	1 33.6
23 F	6 3 53	0♑34 22	9♌55 22	17 14 11	15 52.9	16 34.1	19 8.1	19 46.1	23 52.7	13 8.2	10 37.3	29 0.5	1 35.1
24 Sa	6 7 49	1 35 29	24 31 57	1♍47 59	15 50.9	16 17.4	20 19.5	20 19.1	24 6.3	13 13.8	10 40.8	29 2.7	1 36.6
25 Su	6 11 46	2 36 36	9♍ 1 43	16 12 37	15 49.2	15 49.0	21 31.0	20 52.0	24 19.9	13 19.4	10 44.3	29 5.0	1 38.0
26 M	6 15 42	3 37 43	23 20 18	0♎24 29	15D 48.1	15 8.9	22 42.5	21 24.9	24 33.5	13 24.9	10 47.8	29 7.3	1 39.4
27 Tu	6 19 39	4 38 52	7♎24 57	14 21 37	15 47.8	14 17.6	23 54.2	21 57.6	24 47.0	13 30.3	10 51.3	29 9.5	1 40.8
28 W	6 23 35	5 40 0	21 14 25	28 3 23	15 48.4	13 16.1	25 6.0	22 30.2	25 0.6	13 35.7	10 54.7	29 11.8	1 42.1
29 Th	6 27 32	6 41 10	4♏48 34	11♏30 6	15 49.7	12 6.2	26 17.9	23 2.8	25 14.1	13 41.0	10 58.2	29 14.0	1 43.5
30 F	6 31 29	7 42 20	18 8 3	24 42 34	15 51.3	10 49.7	27 29.8	23 35.2	25 27.6	13 46.2	11 1.6	29 16.3	1 44.7
31 Sa	6 35 25	8 43 30	1♐13 46	7♐41 46	15 52.7	9 29.2	28 41.9	24 7.5	25 41.1	13 51.3	11 5.0	29 18.5	1 46.0

Astro Data	Dy Hr Mn
☽0S	2 17:46
♄⊻♅	3 18:24
♀0S	12 1:36
♃∠♇	14 23:46
☽0N	16 22:07
♂0S	24 10:19
☽0S	30 0:59
☽0N	14 7:14
☿ R	22 0:53
☽0S	27 6:18

Planet Ingress		Dy Hr Mn
♇	♏	5 21:17
♀	♎	9 10:52
☿	♐	14 8:56
♂	♎	18 10:26
☉	♐	22 21:18
☿	♑	4 11:22
♀	♏	6 16:15
☉	♑	22 10:30

Last Aspect Dy Hr Mn			☽ Ingress	Dy Hr Mn
1 18:56	♆	□	♎	1 23:31
4 1:46	♇	☌	♏	4 1:53
5 23:50	♀	⚹	♐	6 6:09
8 11:37	♀	□	♑	8 13:31
10 14:57	♂	△	♒	11 0:10
13 9:38	☿	□	♓	13 12:41
15 21:40	♂	☍	♈	16 0:36
18 5:53	♆	△	♉	18 10:06
20 12:29	☉	☍	♊	20 16:45
22 17:33	♆	☍	♋	22 21:10
23 23:56	♀	□	♌	25 0:19
26 23:44	♆	△	♍	27 3:02
29 2:44	♆	□	♎	29 5:57

Last Aspect Dy Hr Mn			☽ Ingress	Dy Hr Mn
1 6:32	♆	⚹	♏	1 9:41
2 4:58	♄	☌	♐	3 14:56
5 20:41	♀	⚹	♑	5 22:28
6 20:28	♄	⚹	♒	8 8:39
10 17:56	♆	⚹	♓	10 20:53
13 6:34	♆	□	♈	13 9:17
15 17:09	♆	△	♉	15 19:33
16 22:39	☿	△	♊	18 2:23
20 4:11	♆	☍	♋	20 6:02
21 13:36	♂	□	♌	22 7:44
24 7:28	♆	△	♍	24 9:01
26 9:50	♆	□	♎	26 11:18
28 14:03	♆	⚹	♏	28 15:27
30 18:51	♀	☌	♐	30 21:44

☽ Phases & Eclipses Dy Hr Mn	
4 22:21	● 11♏56
12 15:49	☽ 19♒41
20 12:29	○ 27♉37
27 10:50	☽ 4♍37
4 12:26	● 11♐47
4 12:30:22	● A 4'01"
12 13:09	☽ 19♓56
20 2:00	○ 27♊36
20 1:49	○ A 0.889
26 18:52	☽ 4♎26

Astro Data

1 NOVEMBER 1983
Julian Day # 30620
Delta T 53.7 sec
SVP 05♓29'26"
Obliquity 23°26'31"
⚷ Chiron 1♊30.7R
☽ Mean ☊ 17♊45.4

1 DECEMBER 1983
Julian Day # 30650
Delta T 53.7 sec
SVP 05♓29'21"
Obliquity 23°26'31"
⚷ Chiron 29♉55.3R
☽ Mean ☊ 16♊10.1

LONGITUDE — JANUARY 1984

Day	Sid.Time	☉	0 hr ☽	Noon ☽	True ☊	☿	♀	♂	♃	♄	♅	♆	♇
1 Su	6 39 22	9♑44 41	14♐ 6 42	20♐28 38	15♊53.3	8♑ 7.4	29♏54.0	24♎39.7	25♐54.6	13♏56.4	11♐ 8.3	29♐20.8	1♏47.2
2 M	6 43 18	10 45 52	26 47 42	3♑ 3 58	15R 52.9	6R 47.0	1♐ 6.2	25 11.9	26 8.0	14 1.5	11 11.7	29 23.0	1 48.4
3 Tu	6 47 15	11 47 4	9♑17 32	15 28 29	15 51.0	5 30.4	2 18.4	25 43.9	26 21.5	14 6.4	11 15.0	29 25.3	1 49.6
4 W	6 51 11	12 48 15	21 36 57	27 43 3	15 47.7	4 19.9	3 30.8	26 15.8	26 34.9	14 11.3	11 18.3	29 27.5	1 50.7
5 Th	6 55 8	13 49 26	3♒46 56	9♒48 46	15 43.2	3 17.1	4 43.2	26 47.6	26 48.3	14 16.1	11 21.6	29 29.7	1 51.8
6 F	6 59 4	14 50 37	15 48 45	21 47 10	15 37.8	2 23.4	5 55.7	27 19.2	27 1.6	14 20.8	11 24.8	29 31.9	1 52.8
7 Sa	7 3 1	15 51 48	27 44 18	3♓40 27	15 32.2	1 39.4	7 8.2	27 50.8	27 14.9	14 25.5	11 28.0	29 34.1	1 53.9
8 Su	7 6 58	16 52 58	9♓36 1	15 31 25	15 26.9	1 5.5	8 20.8	28 22.2	27 28.2	14 30.1	11 31.2	29 36.3	1 54.9
9 M	7 10 54	17 54 8	21 27 7	27 23 36	15 22.6	0 41.7	9 33.4	28 53.5	27 41.5	14 34.6	11 34.4	29 38.5	1 55.8
10 Tu	7 14 51	18 55 18	3♈21 24	9♈21 5	15 19.7	0 27.7	10 46.1	29 24.7	27 54.7	14 39.0	11 37.5	29 40.7	1 56.7
11 W	7 18 47	19 56 27	15 23 15	21 28 30	15D 18.3	0D 23.0	11 58.8	29 55.7	28 7.9	14 43.3	11 40.6	29 42.9	1 57.6
12 Th	7 22 44	20 57 35	27 37 26	3♉50 40	15 18.4	0 27.0	13 11.6	0♏26.6	28 21.0	14 47.6	11 43.7	29 45.0	1 58.5
13 F	7 26 40	21 58 43	10♉ 8 46	16 32 18	15 19.6	0 39.2	14 24.5	0 57.4	28 34.1	14 51.7	11 46.7	29 47.2	1 59.3
14 Sa	7 30 37	22 59 50	23 1 47	29 37 36	15 21.3	0 58.7	15 37.4	1 28.1	28 47.2	14 55.8	11 49.7	29 49.3	2 0.1
15 Su	7 34 33	24 0 57	6♊20 7	13♊ 9 32	15R 22.6	1 25.0	16 50.4	1 58.6	29 0.2	14 59.8	11 52.7	29 51.4	2 0.8
16 M	7 38 30	25 2 3	20 5 54	27 9 9	15 22.8	1 57.5	18 3.4	2 29.0	29 13.2	15 3.8	11 55.7	29 53.5	2 1.5
17 Tu	7 42 27	26 3 9	4♋18 58	11♋34 53	15 21.3	2 35.5	19 16.4	2 59.2	29 26.2	15 7.6	11 58.6	29 55.6	2 2.2
18 W	7 46 23	27 4 14	18 56 14	26 22 10	15 17.8	3 18.5	20 29.5	3 29.3	29 39.1	15 11.3	12 1.5	29 57.7	2 2.8
19 Th	7 50 20	28 5 18	3♌51 39	11♌23 32	15 12.4	4 6.0	21 42.6	3 59.3	29 52.0	15 15.0	12 4.3	29 59.8	2 3.4
20 F	7 54 16	29 6 22	18 56 35	26 29 32	15 5.7	4 57.5	22 55.8	4 29.1	0♑ 4.8	15 18.6	12 7.2	0♑ 1.8	2 4.0
21 Sa	7 58 13	0♒ 7 25	4♍ 1 10	11♍30 19	14 58.6	5 52.7	24 9.0	4 58.8	0 17.5	15 22.1	12 9.9	0 3.8	2 4.5
22 Su	8 2 9	1 8 28	18 55 56	26 17 12	14 52.0	6 51.1	25 22.3	5 28.3	0 30.2	15 25.5	12 12.7	0 5.9	2 5.0
23 M	8 6 6	2 9 30	3♎33 23	10♎44 1	14 46.8	7 52.6	26 35.6	5 57.6	0 42.9	15 28.8	12 15.4	0 7.9	2 5.5
24 Tu	8 10 2	3 10 32	17 48 48	24 47 35	14 43.6	8 56.7	27 49.0	6 26.8	0 55.5	15 32.0	12 18.0	0 9.8	2 5.9
25 W	8 13 59	4 11 33	1♏40 24	8♏27 23	14D 42.4	10 3.3	29 2.3	6 55.8	1 8.1	15 35.1	12 20.7	0 11.8	2 6.3
26 Th	8 17 56	5 12 34	15 8 49	21 44 59	14 42.8	11 12.1	0♑15.8	7 24.7	1 20.6	15 38.2	12 23.3	0 13.8	2 6.7
27 F	8 21 52	6 13 34	28 16 16	4♐43 5	14 43.9	12 22.9	1 29.2	7 53.4	1 33.0	15 41.1	12 25.8	0 15.7	2 7.0
28 Sa	8 25 49	7 14 34	11♐ 5 50	17 24 55	14R 44.8	13 35.6	2 42.7	8 21.9	1 45.4	15 43.9	12 28.3	0 17.6	2 7.2
29 Su	8 29 45	8 15 33	23 40 44	29 53 37	14 44.4	14 50.0	3 56.2	8 50.2	1 57.7	15 46.7	12 30.8	0 19.5	2 7.5
30 M	8 33 42	9 16 32	6♑ 3 55	12♑11 56	14 41.9	16 5.9	5 9.8	9 18.3	2 10.0	15 49.4	12 33.3	0 21.4	2 7.7
31 Tu	8 37 38	10 17 29	18 17 54	24 22 4	14 36.9	17 23.3	6 23.4	9 46.3	2 22.2	15 51.9	12 35.7	0 23.3	2 7.9

LONGITUDE — FEBRUARY 1984

Day	Sid.Time	☉	0 hr ☽	Noon ☽	True ☊	☿	♀	♂	♃	♄	♅	♆	♇
1 W	8 41 35	11♒18 26	0♒24 37	6♒25 44	14♊29.2	18♑42.1	7♑37.0	10♏14.0	2♑34.3	15♏54.4	12♐38.0	0♑25.1	2♏ 8.0
2 Th	8 45 32	12 19 22	12 25 34	18 24 16	14R 19.1	20 2.2	8 50.6	10 41.6	2 46.4	15 56.7	12 40.3	0 26.9	2 8.1
3 F	8 49 28	13 20 16	24 22 0	0♓18 54	14 7.4	21 23.4	10 4.3	11 8.9	2 58.4	15 59.0	12 42.6	0 28.7	2 8.2
4 Sa	8 53 25	14 21 10	6♓15 10	12 10 58	13 55.0	22 45.8	11 17.9	11 36.1	3 10.3	16 1.2	12 44.8	0 30.5	2R 8.2
5 Su	8 57 21	15 22 2	18 6 34	24 2 12	13 43.0	24 9.3	12 31.6	12 3.0	3 22.1	16 3.2	12 47.0	0 32.2	2 8.2
6 M	9 1 18	16 22 53	29 58 11	5♈54 52	13 32.5	25 33.8	13 45.3	12 29.7	3 33.9	16 5.2	12 49.1	0 34.0	2 8.1
7 Tu	9 5 14	17 23 42	11♈52 40	17 52 0	13 24.2	26 59.3	14 59.1	12 56.2	3 45.6	16 7.0	12 51.2	0 35.7	2 8.0
8 W	9 9 11	18 24 30	23 53 22	29 57 18	13 18.5	28 25.8	16 12.8	13 22.4	3 57.2	16 8.8	12 53.2	0 37.4	2 7.9
9 Th	9 13 7	19 25 17	6♉ 4 22	12♉15 8	13 15.4	29 53.3	17 26.6	13 48.4	4 8.8	16 10.5	12 55.2	0 39.0	2 7.7
10 F	9 17 4	20 26 2	18 30 14	24 50 17	13D 14.5	1♒21.6	18 40.3	14 14.2	4 20.2	16 12.0	12 57.2	0 40.6	2 7.5
11 Sa	9 21 0	21 26 45	1♊15 51	7♊47 32	13R 14.7	2 50.9	19 54.1	14 39.8	4 31.6	16 13.5	12 59.1	0 42.3	2 7.3
12 Su	9 24 57	22 27 27	14 25 50	21 11 10	13 15.0	4 21.0	21 7.9	15 5.1	4 42.9	16 14.8	13 0.9	0 43.8	2 7.1
13 M	9 28 54	23 28 8	28 3 50	5♋ 4 2	13 14.2	5 52.0	22 21.8	15 30.1	4 54.1	16 16.1	13 2.7	0 45.4	2 6.8
14 Tu	9 32 50	24 28 46	12♋11 42	19 26 38	13 11.2	7 23.9	23 35.6	15 54.9	5 5.3	16 17.2	13 4.5	0 46.9	2 6.4
15 W	9 36 47	25 29 23	26 48 23	4♌16 14	13 5.5	8 56.7	24 49.5	16 19.5	5 16.3	16 18.3	13 6.2	0 48.5	2 6.1
16 Th	9 40 43	26 29 59	11♌49 15	19 26 17	12 57.2	10 30.4	26 3.3	16 43.7	5 27.3	16 19.2	13 7.9	0 49.9	2 5.7
17 F	9 44 40	27 30 33	27 6 0	4♍46 56	12 46.9	12 4.9	27 17.2	17 7.8	5 38.1	16 20.1	13 9.5	0 51.4	2 5.2
18 Sa	9 48 36	28 31 5	12♍27 34	20 6 25	12 35.8	13 40.4	28 31.1	17 31.5	5 48.9	16 20.8	13 11.1	0 52.8	2 4.8
19 Su	9 52 33	29 31 35	27 42 5	5♎13 18	12 25.2	15 16.7	29 45.0	17 54.9	5 59.6	16 21.4	13 12.6	0 54.2	2 4.2
20 M	9 56 29	0♓32 5	12♎39 3	19 58 30	12 16.4	16 53.9	0♒58.9	18 18.1	6 10.2	16 22.0	13 14.0	0 55.6	2 3.7
21 Tu	10 0 26	1 32 33	27 11 6	4♏16 30	12 10.1	18 32.0	2 12.8	18 41.0	6 20.6	16 22.4	13 15.4	0 56.9	2 3.1
22 W	10 4 23	2 32 59	11♏14 35	18 5 27	12 6.4	20 11.1	3 26.8	19 3.6	6 31.0	16 22.7	13 16.8	0 58.3	2 2.5
23 Th	10 8 19	3 33 25	24 49 19	1♐26 33	12D 5.0	21 51.1	4 40.7	19 25.8	6 41.3	16 22.9	13 18.1	0 59.6	2 1.9
24 F	10 12 16	4 33 49	7♐57 37	14 23 1	12R 4.8	23 32.1	5 54.7	19 47.7	6 51.5	16R 23.0	13 19.4	1 0.8	2 1.2
25 Sa	10 16 12	5 34 12	20 43 20	26 59 6	12 4.7	25 14.0	7 8.7	20 9.4	7 1.6	16 23.1	13 20.6	1 2.0	2 0.5
26 Su	10 20 9	6 34 33	3♑10 55	9♑19 19	12 3.3	26 57.0	8 22.7	20 30.6	7 11.6	16 23.0	13 21.8	1 3.3	1 59.8
27 M	10 24 5	7 34 53	15 24 49	21 27 54	11 59.7	28 40.9	9 36.7	20 51.6	7 21.5	16 22.8	13 22.9	1 4.4	1 59.0
28 Tu	10 28 2	8 35 11	27 29 0	3♒28 32	11 53.2	0♓25.8	10 50.7	21 12.1	7 31.2	16 22.5	13 23.9	1 5.6	1 58.2
29 W	10 31 58	9 35 28	9♒26 50	15 24 12	11 43.6	2 11.7	12 4.7	21 32.3	7 40.9	16 22.1	13 24.9	1 6.7	1 57.4

Astro Data

Astro Data	Dy Hr Mn
☽0N	10 15:06
♄∠♆	10 19:01
☿ D	11 0:37
♃☌♆	19 17:24
♃∠♄	21 11:45
☽0S	23 12:01
♃✶♇	29 19:29
♇ R	4 2:05
☽0N	6 21:10
☽0S	19 20:12
♄ R	24 14:36

Planet Ingress

Planet Ingress	Dy Hr Mn
♀ ♐	1 2:00
♂ ♏	11 3:20
♃ ♑	19 15:04
♆ ♑	19 2:51
☉ ♒	20 21:05
♀ ♑	25 18:51
☿ ♒	9 1:50
☉ ♓	19 11:16
♀ ♒	19 4:53
☿ ♓	27 18:07

Last Aspect / ☽ Ingress

Last Aspect Dy Hr Mn		☽ Ingress Dy Hr Mn
2 4:57	♆ ☌	♑ 2 6:07
4 9:33	♂ □	♒ 4 16:30
7 3:43	♆ ✶	♓ 7 4:34
9 16:35	♆ □	♈ 9 17:15
12 4:08	♆ △	♉ 12 4:36
13 23:56	☉ △	♊ 14 12:40
16 16:39	♆ ☍	♋ 16 16:47
18 14:05	☉ ☍	♌ 18 17:50
20 6:54	♀ △	♍ 20 17:35
22 11:27	♀ □	♎ 22 18:07
24 18:56	♀ ✶	♏ 24 21:04
26 0:53	♄ ☌	♐ 27 3:12
28 2:37	♅ ☌	♑ 29 12:12
30 22:00	☿ ☌	♒ 31 23:11

Last Aspect / ☽ Ingress

Last Aspect Dy Hr Mn		☽ Ingress Dy Hr Mn
2 7:05	♄ □	♓ 3 11:22
5 13:53	☿ ✶	♈ 6 0:04
8 10:13	☿ □	♉ 8 12:05
10 4:00	☉ □	♊ 10 21:39
12 15:22	☉ △	♋ 13 3:20
14 20:30	♀ ☍	♌ 15 5:09
17 0:41	☉ ☍	♍ 17 4:32
19 3:33	♀ △	♎ 19 3:39
20 7:49	☿ △	♏ 21 4:44
22 17:56	☿ □	♐ 23 9:22
25 10:00	☿ ✶	♑ 25 17:49
27 11:07	♂ ✶	♒ 28 5:02

☽ Phases & Eclipses

Dy Hr Mn		
3 5:16	●	12♑00
11 9:48	☽	20♈21
18 14:05	○	27♋40
25 4:48	☽	4♏24
1 23:46	●	12♒19
10 4:00	☽	20♉36
17 0:41	○	27♌32
23 17:12	☽	4♐17

Astro Data

1 JANUARY 1984
Julian Day # 30681
Delta T 53.8 sec
SVP 05♓29'16"
Obliquity 23°26'31"
⚷ Chiron 28♉27.2R
☽ Mean ☊ 14♊31.6

1 FEBRUARY 1984
Julian Day # 30712
Delta T 53.8 sec
SVP 05♓29'10"
Obliquity 23°26'32"
⚷ Chiron 27♉46.4R
☽ Mean ☊ 12♊53.2

MARCH 1984 — LONGITUDE

Day	Sid.Time	☉	0 hr ☽	Noon ☽	True ☊	☿	♀	♂	♃	♄	♅	♆	♇
1 Th	10 35 55	10♓35 43	21♒20 54	27♒17 10	11♊31.3	3♓58.7	13♒18.8	21♏52.2	7♑50.4	16♏21.5	13♐25.9	1♑ 7.8	1♏56.6
2 F	10 39 52	11 35 57	3♓13 11	9♓ 9 7	11R17.0	5 46.7	14 32.8	22 11.6	7 59.9	16R20.9	13 26.8	1 8.8	1R55.7
3 Sa	10 43 48	12 36 8	15 5 9	21 1 25	11 1.9	7 35.8	15 46.8	22 30.7	8 9.2	16 20.2	13 27.6	1 9.9	1 54.7
4 Su	10 47 45	13 36 18	26 58 5	2♈55 19	10 47.1	9 25.9	17 0.8	22 49.4	8 18.4	16 19.4	13 28.4	1 10.8	1 53.8
5 M	10 51 41	14 36 26	8♈53 18	14 52 15	10 33.9	11 17.0	18 14.9	23 7.7	8 27.4	16 18.5	13 29.1	1 11.8	1 52.8
6 Tu	10 55 38	15 36 32	20 52 25	26 54 7	10 23.2	13 9.2	19 28.9	23 25.5	8 36.4	16 17.5	13 29.8	1 12.7	1 51.8
7 W	10 59 34	16 36 35	2♉57 39	9♉ 3 26	10 15.6	15 2.3	20 42.9	23 43.0	8 45.2	16 16.3	13 30.4	1 13.6	1 50.8
8 Th	11 3 31	17 36 37	15 11 51	21 23 23	10 10.9	16 56.5	21 57.0	23 60.0	8 53.9	16 15.1	13 31.0	1 14.5	1 49.7
9 F	11 7 27	18 36 37	27 38 32	3♊57 48	10 8.8	18 51.6	23 11.0	24 16.5	9 2.5	16 13.8	13 31.5	1 15.3	1 48.6
10 Sa	11 11 24	19 36 35	10♊21 45	16 50 54	10 8.4	20 47.5	24 25.1	24 32.6	9 11.0	16 12.4	13 32.0	1 16.1	1 47.5
11 Su	11 15 21	20 36 30	23 25 46	0♋ 6 50	10 8.4	22 44.3	25 39.1	24 48.3	9 19.3	16 10.9	13 32.4	1 16.9	1 46.4
12 M	11 19 17	21 36 23	6♋54 28	13 49 0	10 7.7	24 41.8	26 53.1	25 3.5	9 27.5	16 9.3	13 32.8	1 17.6	1 45.2
13 Tu	11 23 14	22 36 14	20 50 34	27 59 10	10 5.1	26 39.9	28 7.2	25 18.2	9 35.6	16 7.6	13 33.1	1 18.3	1 44.0
14 W	11 27 10	23 36 3	5♌14 36	12♌36 27	9 60.0	28 38.5	29 21.2	25 32.5	9 43.5	16 5.8	13 33.4	1 19.0	1 42.8
15 Th	11 31 7	24 35 49	20 4 4	27 36 33	9 52.3	0♈37.5	0♓35.2	25 46.2	9 51.3	16 3.9	13 33.6	1 19.6	1 41.6
16 F	11 35 3	25 35 34	5♍12 49	12♍51 34	9 42.5	2 36.5	1 49.3	25 59.5	9 58.9	16 1.9	13 33.7	1 20.2	1 40.3
17 Sa	11 39 0	26 35 16	20 31 23	28 10 49	9 31.8	4 35.4	3 3.3	26 12.2	10 6.4	15 59.8	13 33.8	1 20.8	1 39.1
18 Su	11 42 56	27 34 56	5♎48 24	13♎22 44	9 21.5	6 34.0	4 17.3	26 24.4	10 13.8	15 57.7	13R33.8	1 21.4	1 37.8
19 M	11 46 53	28 34 34	20 52 35	28 16 53	9 12.7	8 31.9	5 31.3	26 36.1	10 21.1	15 55.4	13 33.8	1 21.9	1 36.4
20 Tu	11 50 50	29 34 10	5♏34 49	12♏45 46	9 6.2	10 28.9	6 45.4	26 47.2	10 28.2	15 53.1	13 33.8	1 22.3	1 35.1
21 W	11 54 46	0♈33 44	19 49 24	26 45 32	9 2.4	12 24.5	7 59.4	26 57.8	10 35.1	15 50.6	13 33.7	1 22.8	1 33.7
22 Th	11 58 43	1 33 17	3♐34 15	10♐15 45	9D 1.0	14 18.4	9 13.4	27 7.8	10 41.9	15 48.1	13 33.5	1 23.2	1 32.3
23 F	12 2 39	2 32 48	16 50 24	23 18 38	9 1.0	16 10.1	10 27.5	27 17.2	10 48.6	15 45.5	13 33.3	1 23.6	1 30.9
24 Sa	12 6 36	3 32 17	29 41 0	5♑58 5	9R 1.5	17 59.3	11 41.5	27 26.0	10 55.1	15 42.8	13 33.0	1 23.9	1 29.5
25 Su	12 10 32	4 31 45	12♑10 28	18 18 48	9 1.3	19 45.5	12 55.5	27 34.2	11 1.4	15 40.1	13 32.7	1 24.2	1 28.1
26 M	12 14 29	5 31 11	24 23 40	0♒25 41	8 59.4	21 28.3	14 9.6	27 41.8	11 7.7	15 37.2	13 32.3	1 24.5	1 26.6
27 Tu	12 18 25	6 30 35	6♒25 24	12 22 22	8 55.2	23 7.3	15 23.6	27 48.7	11 13.7	15 34.3	13 31.9	1 24.7	1 25.1
28 W	12 22 22	7 29 57	18 20 2	24 15 54	8 48.4	24 41.9	16 37.6	27 55.0	11 19.6	15 31.3	13 31.4	1 24.9	1 23.6
29 Th	12 26 19	8 29 17	0♓11 19	6♓ 6 41	8 39.4	26 12.0	17 51.7	28 0.6	11 25.3	15 28.2	13 30.8	1 25.1	1 22.1
30 F	12 30 15	9 28 35	12 2 17	17 58 24	8 28.7	27 37.0	19 5.7	28 5.6	11 30.9	15 25.0	13 30.3	1 25.2	1 20.6
31 Sa	12 34 12	10 27 51	23 55 16	29 53 6	8 17.1	28 56.7	20 19.7	28 9.9	11 36.3	15 21.8	13 29.6	1 25.3	1 19.0

APRIL 1984 — LONGITUDE

Day	Sid.Time	☉	0 hr ☽	Noon ☽	True ☊	☿	♀	♂	♃	♄	♅	♆	♇
1 Su	12 38 8	11♈27 6	5♈52 3	11♈52 18	8♊ 5.9	0♉10.7	21♓33.7	28♏13.5	11♑41.6	15♏18.5	13♐28.9	1♑25.4	1♏17.5
2 M	12 42 5	12 26 18	17 54 0	23 57 18	7R55.8	1 18.8	22 47.7	28 16.3	11 46.6	15R15.1	13R28.2	1R25.4	1R15.9
3 Tu	12 46 1	13 25 28	0♉ 2 21	6♉ 9 20	7 47.8	2 20.8	24 1.7	28 18.5	11 51.6	15 11.6	13 27.4	1 25.4	1 14.3
4 W	12 49 58	14 24 36	12 18 25	18 29 51	7 42.2	3 16.4	25 15.7	28 20.0	11 56.3	15 8.1	13 26.6	1 25.4	1 12.7
5 Th	12 53 54	15 23 42	24 43 50	1♊ 0 41	7 39.1	4 5.6	26 29.7	28R20.7	12 0.9	15 4.5	13 25.7	1 25.3	1 11.1
6 F	12 57 51	16 22 46	7♊20 40	13 44 8	7D38.2	4 48.1	27 43.7	28 20.7	12 5.3	15 0.9	13 24.8	1 25.3	1 9.5
7 Sa	13 1 47	17 21 48	20 11 26	26 42 54	7 38.7	5 23.9	28 57.7	28 20.0	12 9.6	14 57.2	13 23.8	1 25.1	1 7.9
8 Su	13 5 44	18 20 47	3♋18 54	9♋59 46	7 39.9	5 53.0	0♈11.6	28 18.6	12 13.6	14 53.4	13 22.8	1 25.0	1 6.2
9 M	13 9 41	19 19 44	16 45 48	23 37 15	7R40.7	6 15.2	1 25.6	28 16.3	12 17.5	14 49.6	13 21.7	1 24.8	1 4.6
10 Tu	13 13 37	20 18 39	0♌34 14	7♌36 50	7 40.2	6 30.7	2 39.6	28 13.4	12 21.3	14 45.8	13 20.6	1 24.6	1 2.9
11 W	13 17 34	21 17 31	14 44 56	21 58 19	7 37.9	6R39.5	3 53.5	28 9.7	12 24.8	14 41.8	13 19.4	1 24.3	1 1.3
12 Th	13 21 30	22 16 21	29 16 34	6♍39 6	7 33.8	6 41.8	5 7.4	28 5.2	12 28.2	14 37.9	13 18.2	1 24.0	0 59.6
13 F	13 25 27	23 15 9	14♍ 5 10	21 33 51	7 28.1	6 37.7	6 21.4	27 60.0	12 31.4	14 33.8	13 17.0	1 23.7	0 58.0
14 Sa	13 29 23	24 13 54	29 4 7	6♎34 49	7 21.6	6 27.5	7 35.3	27 54.0	12 34.4	14 29.8	13 15.7	1 23.3	0 56.3
15 Su	13 33 20	25 12 38	14♎ 4 47	21 32 51	7 15.2	6 11.6	8 49.2	27 47.2	12 37.2	14 25.7	13 14.3	1 22.9	0 54.6
16 M	13 37 16	26 11 19	28 57 53	6♏18 52	7 9.8	5 50.3	10 3.1	27 39.7	12 39.9	14 21.5	13 12.9	1 22.5	0 52.9
17 Tu	13 41 13	27 9 59	13♏34 55	20 45 20	7 5.9	5 24.2	11 17.0	27 31.5	12 42.4	14 17.3	13 11.5	1 22.1	0 51.2
18 W	13 45 10	28 8 36	27 49 34	4♐47 17	7D 4.0	4 53.9	12 30.9	27 22.4	12 44.7	14 13.1	13 10.0	1 21.6	0 49.5
19 Th	13 49 6	29 7 12	11♐38 17	18 22 35	7 3.7	4 19.8	13 44.8	27 12.7	12 46.8	14 8.8	13 8.5	1 21.1	0 47.8
20 F	13 53 3	0♉ 5 46	25 0 17	1♑31 41	7 4.7	3 42.8	14 58.7	27 2.2	12 48.7	14 4.5	13 7.0	1 20.5	0 46.1
21 Sa	13 56 59	1 4 19	7♑57 7	14 17 3	7 6.2	3 3.6	16 12.5	26 50.9	12 50.5	14 0.2	13 5.4	1 20.0	0 44.4
22 Su	14 0 56	2 2 50	20 31 59	26 42 29	7 7.6	2 22.9	17 26.4	26 38.9	12 52.0	13 55.8	13 3.8	1 19.4	0 42.8
23 M	14 4 52	3 1 19	2♒49 7	8♒52 28	7R 8.3	1 41.4	18 40.3	26 26.1	12 53.4	13 51.4	13 2.1	1 18.8	0 41.1
24 Tu	14 8 49	3 59 46	14 53 10	20 51 47	7 7.6	1 0.1	19 54.2	26 12.7	12 54.6	13 47.0	13 0.4	1 18.1	0 39.4
25 W	14 12 45	4 58 12	26 48 53	2♓45 2	7 5.5	0 19.5	21 8.0	25 58.6	12 55.6	13 42.6	12 58.7	1 17.4	0 37.7
26 Th	14 16 42	5 56 37	8♓40 44	14 36 29	7 2.1	29♈40.4	22 21.9	25 43.7	12 56.4	13 38.1	12 56.9	1 16.7	0 36.0
27 F	14 20 39	6 54 59	20 32 43	26 29 52	6 57.6	29 3.4	23 35.8	25 28.3	12 57.0	13 33.6	12 55.1	1 15.9	0 34.3
28 Sa	14 24 35	7 53 20	2♈28 15	8♈28 14	6 52.5	28 29.2	24 49.6	25 12.1	12 57.4	13 29.1	12 53.2	1 15.2	0 32.6
29 Su	14 28 32	8 51 39	14 30 6	20 34 4	6 47.5	27 58.2	26 3.5	24 55.4	12R57.7	13 24.6	12 51.3	1 14.4	0 30.9
30 M	14 32 28	9 49 57	26 40 21	2♉49 8	6 43.1	27 30.8	27 17.3	24 38.1	12 57.7	13 20.1	12 49.4	1 13.5	0 29.3

Astro Data Dy Hr Mn	Planet Ingress Dy Hr Mn	Last Aspect Dy Hr Mn	☽ Ingress Dy Hr Mn	Last Aspect Dy Hr Mn	☽ Ingress Dy Hr Mn	☽ Phases & Eclipses Dy Hr Mn	Astro Data
☽0N 5 2:26	☿ ♈ 14 16:27	1 1:05 ♂ □	♓ 1 17:29	1 15:12 ♅ △	♉ 2 23:55	2 18:31 ● 12♓22	1 MARCH 1984
♄∠♆ 8 7:10	♀ ♓ 14 12:35	3 15:25 ♂ △	♈ 4 6:07	5 6:55 ♂ ☍	♊ 5 10:04	10 18:27 ☽ 20♊23	Julian Day # 30741
☿0N 15 14:28	☉ ♈ 20 10:24	5 20:54 ♀ ✶	♉ 6 18:09	7 17:46 ♀ □	♋ 7 17:59	17 10:10 ○ 27♍01	Delta T 53.9 sec
☽0S 18 6:42	☿ ♉ 31 20:25	8 17:25 ♂ ☍	♊ 9 4:30	9 19:59 ♂ △	♌ 9 23:01	24 7:58 ☽ 3♑52	SVP 05♓29'06"
♅ R 18 6:13		11 4:25 ♀ △	♋ 11 11:48	11 22:04 ♂ □	♍ 12 1:11		Obliquity 23°26'32"
♆✶♇ 27 5:34	♀ ♈ 7 20:13	13 11:21 ☿ △	♌ 13 15:21	13 22:09 ♂ ✶	♎ 14 1:29	1 12:10 ● 11♈57	⚷ Chiron 28♉05.9
☽0N 1 8:15	☉ ♉ 19 21:38	15 9:13 ♂ □	♍ 15 15:47	15 19:11 ☉ ☍	♏ 16 1:41	9 4:51 ☽ 19♋32	☽ Mean ☊ 11♊21.0
♆ R 2 14:05	☿ ♈ 25 11:49	17 10:10 ☉ ☍	♎ 17 14:51	17 23:14 ♂ ☌	♐ 18 3:44	15 19:11 ○ 25♎60	
♂ R 5 12:22		18 12:18 ♅ ✶	♏ 19 14:49	19 4:06 ♀ △	♑ 20 9:10	23 0:26 ☽ 3♒02	1 APRIL 1984
♀0N 10 16:14		21 12:31 ♂ ☌	♐ 21 17:41	22 11:41 ♂ ✶	♒ 22 18:27		Julian Day # 30772
☿ R 11 20:24		22 22:34 ♅ △	♑ 24 0:36	24 22:20 ♂ □	♓ 25 6:26		Delta T 53.9 sec
☽0S 14 17:33		26 6:37 ♂ ✶	♒ 26 11:09	27 9:43 ♂ △	♈ 27 19:03		SVP 05♓29'03"
♃⊻♅ 26 4:49		28 19:33 ♂ □	♓ 28 23:37	30 1:36 ☿ ☌	♉ 30 6:30		Obliquity 23°26'33"
☽0N 28 15:16	♃ R 29 18:37	31 8:35 ♂ △	♈ 31 12:14				⚷ Chiron 29♉24.1
							☽ Mean ☊ 9♊42.5

LONGITUDE — MAY 1984

Day	Sid.Time	☉	0 hr ☽	Noon ☽	True ☊	☿	♀	♂	♃	♄	♅	♆	♇
1 Tu	14 36 25	10♉48 13	9♉ 0 33	15♉14 44	6♊39.7	27♈ 7.5	28♈31.1	24♏20.2	12♑57.6	13♏15.6	12♐47.5	1♑12.7	0♏27.6
2 W	14 40 21	11 46 27	21 31 46	27 51 46	6R37.6	26R48.5	29 45.0	24R 1.8	12R57.3	13R11.0	12R45.5	1R11.8	0R25.9
3 Th	14 44 18	12 44 40	4♊14 48	10♊40 57	6D36.7	26 34.0	0♉58.8	23 42.9	12 56.8	13 6.5	12 43.5	1 10.9	0 24.3
4 F	14 48 14	13 42 50	17 10 18	23 42 55	6 37.1	26 24.1	2 12.6	23 23.5	12 56.1	13 2.0	12 41.5	1 9.9	0 22.6
5 Sa	14 52 11	14 40 59	0♋18 53	6♋58 18	6 38.2	26D18.9	3 26.4	23 3.8	12 55.2	12 57.4	12 39.4	1 9.0	0 21.0
6 Su	14 56 8	15 39 6	13 41 13	20 27 43	6 39.6	26 18.5	4 40.2	22 43.6	12 54.1	12 52.9	12 37.3	1 8.0	0 19.4
7 M	15 0 4	16 37 11	27 17 50	4♌11 36	6 40.9	26 22.8	5 54.0	22 23.1	12 52.8	12 48.4	12 35.2	1 7.0	0 17.8
8 Tu	15 4 1	17 35 15	11♌ 8 59	18 9 54	6R41.7	26 31.9	7 7.8	22 2.3	12 51.4	12 43.9	12 33.0	1 5.9	0 16.2
9 W	15 7 57	18 33 16	25 14 14	2♍21 45	6 41.7	26 45.5	8 21.6	21 41.3	12 49.7	12 39.4	12 30.9	1 4.9	0 14.6
10 Th	15 11 54	19 31 15	9♍32 9	16 45 4	6 40.9	27 3.6	9 35.3	21 20.0	12 47.9	12 34.9	12 28.7	1 3.8	0 13.0
11 F	15 15 50	20 29 12	24 0 0	1♎16 24	6 39.4	27 26.2	10 49.1	20 58.6	12 45.9	12 30.4	12 26.5	1 2.7	0 11.4
12 Sa	15 19 47	21 27 7	8♎33 38	15 50 58	6 37.5	27 53.1	12 2.8	20 37.0	12 43.7	12 26.0	12 24.2	1 1.5	0 9.9
13 Su	15 23 43	22 25 1	23 7 41	0♏23 1	6 35.7	28 24.1	13 16.6	20 15.4	12 41.3	12 21.5	12 21.9	1 0.4	0 8.3
14 M	15 27 40	23 22 53	7♏36 12	14 46 32	6 34.2	28 59.2	14 30.3	19 53.7	12 38.8	12 17.1	12 19.7	0 59.2	0 6.8
15 Tu	15 31 37	24 20 43	21 53 19	28 56 0	6 33.3	29 38.1	15 44.0	19 32.0	12 36.0	12 12.7	12 17.4	0 58.0	0 5.3
16 W	15 35 33	25 18 33	5♐54 3	12♐47 6	6D33.0	0♉20.8	16 57.8	19 10.4	12 33.1	12 8.4	12 15.0	0 56.8	0 3.8
17 Th	15 39 30	26 16 20	19 34 51	26 17 10	6 33.2	1 7.2	18 11.5	18 48.9	12 30.1	12 4.0	12 12.7	0 55.6	0 2.3
18 F	15 43 26	27 14 7	2♑53 59	9♑25 22	6 33.8	1 57.1	19 25.2	18 27.5	12 26.8	11 59.7	12 10.4	0 54.3	0 0.9
19 Sa	15 47 23	28 11 52	15 51 28	22 12 33	6 34.6	2 50.4	20 38.9	18 6.2	12 23.4	11 55.5	12 8.0	0 53.0	29♎59.4
20 Su	15 51 19	29 9 36	28 28 56	4♒41 1	6 35.4	3 47.0	21 52.7	17 45.2	12 19.8	11 51.2	12 5.6	0 51.7	29 58.0
21 M	15 55 16	0♊ 7 19	10♒49 15	16 54 8	6 36.0	4 46.7	23 6.4	17 24.5	12 16.0	11 47.0	12 3.2	0 50.4	29 56.6
22 Tu	15 59 12	1 5 0	22 56 11	28 55 58	6R36.3	5 49.6	24 20.1	17 4.0	12 12.0	11 42.9	12 0.8	0 49.1	29 55.2
23 W	16 3 9	2 2 41	4♓54 4	10♓51 1	6 36.4	6 55.5	25 33.8	16 43.9	12 7.9	11 38.8	11 58.4	0 47.7	29 53.8
24 Th	16 7 6	3 0 20	16 47 25	22 43 51	6 36.2	8 4.3	26 47.5	16 24.2	12 3.7	11 34.7	11 56.0	0 46.4	29 52.5
25 F	16 11 2	3 57 59	28 40 50	4♈38 54	6 36.0	9 16.0	28 1.2	16 4.9	11 59.2	11 30.7	11 53.5	0 45.0	29 51.1
26 Sa	16 14 59	4 55 36	10♈38 34	16 40 18	6 35.8	10 30.4	29 15.0	15 46.1	11 54.6	11 26.7	11 51.1	0 43.6	29 49.8
27 Su	16 18 55	5 53 13	22 44 31	28 51 36	6D35.6	11 47.7	0♊28.7	15 27.8	11 49.9	11 22.8	11 48.6	0 42.1	29 48.5
28 M	16 22 52	6 50 49	5♉ 1 54	11♉15 41	6 35.6	13 7.6	1 42.4	15 10.0	11 45.0	11 18.9	11 46.1	0 40.7	29 47.2
29 Tu	16 26 48	7 48 23	17 33 12	23 54 35	6 35.7	14 30.2	2 56.1	14 52.8	11 39.9	11 15.1	11 43.7	0 39.3	29 46.0
30 W	16 30 45	8 45 57	0♊19 58	6♊49 24	6R35.7	15 55.4	4 9.8	14 36.2	11 34.7	11 11.3	11 41.2	0 37.8	29 44.8
31 Th	16 34 41	9 43 30	13 22 52	20 0 19	6 35.7	17 23.2	5 23.5	14 20.3	11 29.3	11 7.6	11 38.7	0 36.3	29 43.6

LONGITUDE — JUNE 1984

Day	Sid.Time	☉	0 hr ☽	Noon ☽	True ☊	☿	♀	♂	♃	♄	♅	♆	♇
1 F	16 38 38	10♊41 1	26♊41 36	3♋26 35	6♊35.6	18♉53.6	6♊37.3	14♏ 5.0	11♑23.9	11♏ 4.0	11♐36.3	0♑34.8	29♎42.4
2 Sa	16 42 35	11 38 32	10♋15 3	17 6 44	6R35.2	20 26.6	7 51.0	13R50.4	11R18.2	11R 0.4	11R33.8	0R33.3	29R41.3
3 Su	16 46 31	12 36 1	24 1 24	0♌58 44	6 34.5	22 2.1	9 4.7	13 36.5	11 12.5	10 56.9	11 31.3	0 31.8	29 40.1
4 M	16 50 28	13 33 29	7♌58 26	15 0 11	6 33.8	23 40.1	10 18.4	13 23.4	11 6.6	10 53.4	11 28.8	0 30.3	29 39.0
5 Tu	16 54 24	14 30 56	22 3 39	29 8 32	6 33.1	25 20.7	11 32.1	13 11.0	11 0.6	10 50.0	11 26.4	0 28.8	29 38.0
6 W	16 58 21	15 28 22	6♍14 30	13♍21 13	6D32.7	27 3.8	12 45.8	12 59.4	10 54.4	10 46.7	11 23.9	0 27.2	29 36.9
7 Th	17 2 17	16 25 46	20 28 24	27 35 43	6 32.6	28 49.4	13 59.5	12 48.6	10 48.1	10 43.4	11 21.4	0 25.7	29 35.9
8 F	17 6 14	17 23 10	4♎42 51	11♎49 29	6 32.9	0♊37.5	15 13.2	12 38.5	10 41.8	10 40.2	11 18.9	0 24.1	29 34.9
9 Sa	17 10 11	18 20 32	18 55 17	25 59 55	6 33.7	2 28.0	16 26.9	12 29.3	10 35.3	10 37.1	11 16.5	0 22.5	29 33.9
10 Su	17 14 7	19 17 53	3♏ 3 3	10♏ 4 20	6 34.7	4 20.9	17 40.6	12 20.9	10 28.7	10 34.1	11 14.0	0 21.0	29 33.0
11 M	17 18 4	20 15 13	17 3 26	24 0 0	6 35.6	6 16.2	18 54.2	12 13.3	10 22.0	10 31.1	11 11.6	0 19.4	29 32.0
12 Tu	17 22 0	21 12 32	0♐53 43	7♐44 17	6R36.2	8 13.8	20 7.9	12 6.5	10 15.2	10 28.3	11 9.2	0 17.8	29 31.2
13 W	17 25 57	22 9 51	14 31 23	21 14 48	6 36.1	10 13.5	21 21.6	12 0.6	10 8.4	10 25.4	11 6.8	0 16.2	29 30.3
14 Th	17 29 53	23 7 8	27 54 19	4♑29 47	6 35.2	12 15.4	22 35.3	11 55.5	10 1.4	10 22.7	11 4.4	0 14.6	29 29.5
15 F	17 33 50	24 4 25	11♑ 1 5	17 28 12	6 33.5	14 19.2	23 49.0	11 51.2	9 54.4	10 20.1	11 2.0	0 13.0	29 28.7
16 Sa	17 37 46	25 1 42	23 51 8	0♒10 0	6 31.1	16 24.8	25 2.7	11 47.7	9 47.2	10 17.5	10 59.6	0 11.4	29 27.9
17 Su	17 41 43	25 58 58	6♒24 58	12 36 15	6 28.3	18 32.0	26 16.4	11 45.0	9 40.0	10 15.0	10 57.2	0 9.8	29 27.2
18 M	17 45 40	26 56 14	18 44 8	24 48 58	6 25.4	20 40.5	27 30.1	11 43.2	9 32.8	10 12.6	10 54.9	0 8.2	29 26.5
19 Tu	17 49 36	27 53 29	0♓51 10	6♓51 10	6 22.8	22 50.2	28 43.8	11D42.2	9 25.4	10 10.3	10 52.5	0 6.6	29 25.8
20 W	17 53 33	28 50 44	12 49 28	18 46 35	6 20.9	25 0.8	29 57.5	11 42.0	9 18.1	10 8.1	10 50.2	0 4.9	29 25.1
21 Th	17 57 29	29 47 59	24 43 6	0♈39 33	6D19.9	27 12.0	1♋11.2	11 42.6	9 10.6	10 5.9	10 47.9	0 3.3	29 24.5
22 F	18 1 26	0♋45 14	6♈36 33	12 34 41	6 20.0	29 23.5	2 25.0	11 44.0	9 3.1	10 3.9	10 45.6	0 1.7	29 23.9
23 Sa	18 5 22	1 42 28	18 34 33	24 36 44	6 20.9	1♋35.1	3 38.7	11 46.2	8 55.6	10 1.9	10 43.3	0 0.1	29 23.3
24 Su	18 9 19	2 39 43	0♉41 48	6♉50 17	6 22.4	3 46.4	4 52.4	11 49.1	8 48.0	9 60.0	10 41.1	29♐58.5	29 22.8
25 M	18 13 15	3 36 57	13 2 40	19 19 23	6 24.0	5 57.3	6 6.1	11 52.9	8 40.4	9 58.2	10 38.9	29 56.8	29 22.3
26 Tu	18 17 12	4 34 11	25 40 51	2♊ 7 20	6R25.3	8 7.4	7 19.9	11 57.5	8 32.7	9 56.5	10 36.7	29 55.2	29 21.9
27 W	18 21 9	5 31 25	8♊39 3	15 16 9	6 25.6	10 16.6	8 33.6	12 2.8	8 25.1	9 54.9	10 34.5	29 53.6	29 21.4
28 Th	18 25 5	6 28 40	21 58 37	28 46 22	6 24.8	12 24.6	9 47.4	12 8.9	8 17.4	9 53.4	10 32.3	29 52.0	29 21.0
29 F	18 29 2	7 25 54	5♋39 9	12♋36 40	6 22.4	14 31.3	11 1.1	12 15.7	8 9.7	9 51.9	10 30.2	29 50.4	29 20.7
30 Sa	18 32 58	8 23 8	19 38 27	26 43 58	6 18.8	16 36.5	12 14.9	12 23.3	8 2.0	9 50.6	10 28.1	29 48.8	29 20.3

Astro Data	Planet Ingress	Last Aspect	☽ Ingress	Last Aspect	☽ Ingress	☽ Phases & Eclipses	Astro Data
Dy Hr Mn	Dy Hr Mn	Dy Hr Mn	Dy Hr Mn	Dy Hr Mn	Dy Hr Mn	Dy Hr Mn	1 MAY 1984
♃✶♄ 5 15:40	♀ ♉ 2 4:53	2 4:38 ♂ ☍	♊ 2 16:02	1 5:22 ♇ △	♋ 1 5:54	1 3:45 ● 10♉57	Julian Day # 30802
☿ D 5 14:06	☿ ♉ 15 12:33	4 16:46 ☿ ✶	♋ 4 23:26	3 9:44 ♇ □	♌ 3 10:19	8 11:50 ☽ 18♌04	Delta T 54.0 sec
☽0S 12 2:40	♇ ♎ 18 14:18	6 22:23 ☿ □	♌ 7 4:43	5 12:49 ♇ ✶	♍ 5 13:27	15 4:29 ○ 24♏32	SVP 05♓29'00"
♄⚻♅ 12 19:11	☉ ♊ 20 20:58	9 2:37 ☿ △	♍ 9 8:02	6 16:42 ☉ □	♎ 7 16:03	15 4:40 ☍A 0.807	Obliquity 23°26'32"
☽0N 25 23:09	♀ ♊ 26 14:40	10 19:07 ♂ ✶	♎ 11 9:54	9 18:03 ♇ ☌	♏ 9 18:48	22 17:45 ☽ 1♓48	⚷ Chiron 1♊19.5
♃⚻♅ 27 12:31		13 9:04 ☿ ☍	♏ 13 11:22	10 15:45 ♂ ☌	♐ 11 22:26	30 16:48 ● 9♊26	☽ Mean ☊ 8♊07.2
	☿ ♊ 7 15:45	15 4:29 ☉ ☍	♐ 15 13:50	14 2:52 ♇ ✶	♑ 14 3:48	30 16:44:47 ☌A 0'11"	
☽0S 8 9:16	♀ ♋ 20 0:48	16 11:02 ♅ ☌	♑ 17 18:43	16 10:39 ♇ □	♒ 16 11:41		1 JUNE 1984
♃✶♄ 8 11:03	☉ ♋ 21 5:02	20 2:51 ♇ □	♒ 20 2:55	18 21:10 ♇ △	♓ 18 22:18	6 16:42 ☽ 16♍08	Julian Day # 30833
♂ D 19 18:16	☿ ♋ 22 6:39	22 13:57 ♇ △	♓ 22 14:09	21 6:09 ☿ □	♈ 21 10:40	13 14:42 ○ 22♐45	Delta T 54.0 sec
☽0N 22 7:04	♆ ♐ 23 1:15	24 22:31 ♀ ✶	♈ 25 2:39	23 22:35 ♆ △	♉ 23 22:38	13 14:26 ☍A 0.064	SVP 05♓28'55"
		27 13:50 ♇ ☍	♉ 27 14:13	24 21:45 ♂ ☍	♊ 26 8:04	21 11:10 ☽ 0♈15	Obliquity 23°26'32"
		28 19:02 ♂ ☍	♊ 29 23:23	28 13:53 ♆ ☍	♋ 28 14:09	29 3:18 ● 7♋34	⚷ Chiron 3♊37.1
				30 16:23 ♇ □	♌ 30 17:30		☽ Mean ☊ 6♊28.7

JULY 1984 LONGITUDE

Day	Sid.Time	☉	0 hr ☽	Noon ☽	True ☊	☿	♀	♂	♃	♄	♅	♆	♇
1 Su	18 36 55	9♋20 21	3♌52 36	11♌ 3 39	6♊14.1	18♋40.1	13♋28.7	12♏31.7	7♑54.3	9♏49.4	10♐26.1	29♐47.2	29♎20.0
2 M	18 40 51	10 17 35	18 16 25	25 30 12	6R 9.2	20 42.0	14 42.4	12 40.7	7R46.6	9R48.2	10R24.0	29R45.6	29R19.8
3 Tu	18 44 48	11 14 48	2♍44 16	9♍57 58	6 4.7	22 42.1	15 56.2	12 50.5	7 39.0	9 47.2	10 22.0	29 44.1	29 19.6
4 W	18 48 44	12 12 0	17 10 42	24 21 58	6 1.2	24 40.4	17 10.0	13 1.0	7 31.3	9 46.2	10 20.0	29 42.5	29 19.4
5 Th	18 52 41	13 9 13	1♎31 18	8♎38 22	5D 59.1	26 36.7	18 23.7	13 12.2	7 23.7	9 45.4	10 18.1	29 40.9	29 19.2
6 F	18 56 38	14 6 25	15 42 53	22 44 40	5 58.6	28 31.1	19 37.5	13 24.0	7 16.1	9 44.6	10 16.1	29 39.3	29 19.1
7 Sa	19 0 34	15 3 37	29 43 35	6♏39 34	5 59.3	0♌23.6	20 51.3	13 36.6	7 8.5	9 44.0	10 14.2	29 37.8	29 19.0
8 Su	19 4 31	16 0 48	13♏32 34	20 22 35	6 0.6	2 14.0	22 5.0	13 49.7	7 1.0	9 43.4	10 12.4	29 36.3	29 18.9
9 M	19 8 27	16 58 0	27 9 38	3♐53 41	6R 1.8	4 2.5	23 18.8	14 3.6	6 53.5	9 42.9	10 10.6	29 34.7	29D 18.9
10 Tu	19 12 24	17 55 11	10♐34 47	17 12 55	6 1.9	5 49.0	24 32.6	14 18.0	6 46.0	9 42.6	10 8.8	29 33.2	29 18.9
11 W	19 16 20	18 52 23	23 48 3	0♑20 12	6 0.5	7 33.6	25 46.4	14 33.1	6 38.6	9 42.3	10 7.0	29 31.7	29 18.9
12 Th	19 20 17	19 49 34	6♑49 19	13 15 22	5 57.1	9 16.1	27 0.1	14 48.7	6 31.3	9 42.1	10 5.3	29 30.2	29 19.0
13 F	19 24 13	20 46 46	19 38 21	25 58 15	5 51.7	10 56.7	28 13.9	15 5.0	6 24.1	9D 42.1	10 3.6	29 28.7	29 19.1
14 Sa	19 28 10	21 43 58	2♒15 5	8♒28 52	5 44.6	12 35.2	29 27.7	15 21.8	6 16.9	9 42.1	10 2.0	29 27.2	29 19.2
15 Su	19 32 7	22 41 11	14 39 43	20 47 44	5 36.3	14 11.8	0♌41.5	15 39.3	6 9.8	9 42.2	10 0.4	29 25.8	29 19.4
16 M	19 36 3	23 38 23	26 53 5	2♓55 59	5 27.8	15 46.4	1 55.3	15 57.2	6 2.7	9 42.4	9 58.8	29 24.3	29 19.6
17 Tu	19 40 0	24 35 37	8♓56 43	14 55 35	5 19.8	17 19.0	3 9.1	16 15.7	5 55.8	9 42.7	9 57.3	29 22.9	29 19.9
18 W	19 43 56	25 32 50	20 52 59	26 49 20	5 13.0	18 49.6	4 22.9	16 34.8	5 48.9	9 43.1	9 55.8	29 21.5	29 20.1
19 Th	19 47 53	26 30 5	2♈45 6	8♈40 49	5 8.1	20 18.2	5 36.7	16 54.3	5 42.1	9 43.7	9 54.3	29 20.1	29 20.4
20 F	19 51 49	27 27 20	14 37 2	20 34 21	5 5.2	21 44.8	6 50.5	17 14.4	5 35.5	9 44.3	9 52.9	29 18.7	29 20.8
21 Sa	19 55 46	28 24 36	26 33 21	2♉34 42	5D 4.2	23 9.2	8 4.3	17 35.0	5 28.9	9 45.0	9 51.6	29 17.3	29 21.2
22 Su	19 59 42	29 21 53	8♉39 1	14 46 56	5 4.5	24 31.6	9 18.1	17 56.1	5 22.4	9 45.8	9 50.2	29 16.0	29 21.6
23 M	20 3 39	0♌19 10	20 59 5	27 16 3	5 5.5	25 51.9	10 31.9	18 17.7	5 16.0	9 46.7	9 48.9	29 14.6	29 22.0
24 Tu	20 7 36	1 16 29	3♊38 22	10♊ 6 31	5R 6.1	27 10.0	11 45.7	18 39.8	5 9.8	9 47.7	9 47.7	29 13.3	29 22.5
25 W	20 11 32	2 13 48	16 40 52	23 21 43	5 5.5	28 25.9	12 59.6	19 2.4	5 3.7	9 48.8	9 46.5	29 12.0	29 23.0
26 Th	20 15 29	3 11 8	0♋ 9 10	7♋ 3 15	5 2.9	29 39.5	14 13.4	19 25.4	4 57.7	9 50.0	9 45.4	29 10.7	29 23.6
27 F	20 19 25	4 8 29	14 3 46	21 10 23	4 58.0	0♍50.8	15 27.3	19 48.9	4 51.8	9 51.3	9 44.3	29 9.5	29 24.1
28 Sa	20 23 22	5 5 51	28 22 32	5♌39 33	4 51.0	1 59.6	16 41.1	20 12.8	4 46.0	9 52.6	9 43.2	29 8.2	29 24.8
29 Su	20 27 18	6 3 14	13♌ 0 31	20 24 30	4 42.3	3 6.0	17 54.9	20 37.2	4 40.4	9 54.1	9 42.2	29 7.0	29 25.4
30 M	20 31 15	7 0 37	27 50 23	5♍17 5	4 32.9	4 9.8	19 8.8	21 2.0	4 35.0	9 55.7	9 41.2	29 5.8	29 26.1
31 Tu	20 35 12	7 58 1	12♍43 29	20 8 34	4 24.1	5 10.9	20 22.6	21 27.3	4 29.6	9 57.4	9 40.3	29 4.7	29 26.8

AUGUST 1984 LONGITUDE

Day	Sid.Time	☉	0 hr ☽	Noon ☽	True ☊	☿	♀	♂	♃	♄	♅	♆	♇
1 W	20 39 8	8♌55 26	27♍31 21	4♎51 4	4♊16.8	6♍ 9.2	21♌36.5	21♏53.0	4♑24.4	9♏59.1	9♐39.4	29♐ 3.5	29♎27.6
2 Th	20 43 5	9 52 51	12♎ 7 2	19 18 45	4R 11.7	7 4.5	22 50.3	22 19.0	4R 19.4	10 1.0	9R 38.6	29R 2.4	29 28.3
3 F	20 47 1	10 50 17	26 25 54	3♏28 16	4 9.0	7 56.8	24 4.2	22 45.5	4 14.5	10 3.0	9 37.8	29 1.2	29 29.2
4 Sa	20 50 58	11 47 44	10♏25 50	17 18 37	4D 8.2	8 46.0	25 18.0	23 12.4	4 9.8	10 5.0	9 37.1	29 0.2	29 30.0
5 Su	20 54 54	12 45 11	24 6 45	0♐50 28	4R 8.4	9 31.7	26 31.8	23 39.7	4 5.2	10 7.2	9 36.4	28 59.1	29 30.9
6 M	20 58 51	13 42 39	7♐29 59	14 5 34	4 8.6	10 13.9	27 45.7	24 7.3	4 0.8	10 9.4	9 35.7	28 58.1	29 31.8
7 Tu	21 2 47	14 40 7	20 37 29	27 5 59	4 7.5	10 52.5	28 59.5	24 35.3	3 56.6	10 11.7	9 35.1	28 57.0	29 32.7
8 W	21 6 44	15 37 37	3♑31 19	9♑53 41	4 4.3	11 27.1	0♍13.3	25 3.7	3 52.5	10 14.2	9 34.6	28 56.1	29 33.7
9 Th	21 10 41	16 35 7	16 13 17	22 30 15	3 58.4	11 57.6	1 27.2	25 32.4	3 48.6	10 16.7	9 34.1	28 55.1	29 34.7
10 F	21 14 37	17 32 39	28 44 45	4♒56 52	3 49.7	12 23.9	2 41.0	26 1.5	3 44.8	10 19.3	9 33.7	28 54.2	29 35.8
11 Sa	21 18 34	18 30 11	11♒ 6 42	17 14 20	3 38.6	12 45.7	3 54.8	26 30.8	3 41.3	10 22.0	9 33.3	28 53.2	29 36.9
12 Su	21 22 30	19 27 44	23 19 53	29 23 26	3 26.0	13 2.7	5 8.6	27 0.6	3 37.8	10 24.8	9 33.0	28 52.4	29 38.0
13 M	21 26 27	20 25 19	5♓25 7	11♓25 4	3 12.8	13 14.8	6 22.4	27 30.6	3 34.6	10 27.6	9 32.7	28 51.5	29 39.1
14 Tu	21 30 23	21 22 55	17 23 28	23 20 34	3 0.1	13R 21.8	7 36.2	28 1.0	3 31.6	10 30.6	9 32.4	28 50.7	29 40.3
15 W	21 34 20	22 20 32	29 16 36	5♈11 54	2 49.1	13 23.5	8 50.0	28 31.7	3 28.7	10 33.6	9 32.2	28 49.8	29 41.4
16 Th	21 38 16	23 18 10	11♈ 6 51	17 1 50	2 40.4	13 19.8	10 3.8	29 2.6	3 26.0	10 36.7	9 32.1	28 49.1	29 42.7
17 F	21 42 13	24 15 50	22 57 20	28 53 53	2 34.4	13 10.4	11 17.6	29 33.9	3 23.5	10 40.0	9 32.0	28 48.3	29 43.9
18 Sa	21 46 9	25 13 32	4♉52 0	10♉52 19	2 31.0	12 55.4	12 31.4	0♐ 5.5	3 21.1	10 43.3	9D 32.0	28 47.6	29 45.2
19 Su	21 50 6	26 11 15	16 55 26	23 2 0	2D 29.6	12 34.7	13 45.2	0 37.4	3 19.0	10 46.6	9 32.0	28 46.9	29 46.5
20 M	21 54 3	27 8 59	29 12 41	5♊28 8	2R 29.5	12 8.5	14 59.0	1 9.5	3 17.0	10 50.1	9 32.0	28 46.2	29 47.9
21 Tu	21 57 59	28 6 46	11♊48 58	18 15 48	2 29.3	11 36.7	16 12.8	1 42.0	3 15.2	10 53.7	9 32.2	28 45.6	29 49.2
22 W	22 1 56	29 4 34	24 49 8	1♋29 25	2 28.1	10 59.8	17 26.6	2 14.7	3 13.6	10 57.3	9 32.3	28 45.0	29 50.7
23 Th	22 5 52	0♍ 2 24	8♋16 57	15 11 55	2 24.8	10 18.1	18 40.4	2 47.7	3 12.2	11 1.0	9 32.6	28 44.4	29 52.1
24 F	22 9 49	1 0 16	22 14 17	29 23 51	2 19.0	9 32.1	19 54.2	3 21.0	3 11.0	11 4.8	9 32.8	28 43.9	29 53.6
25 Sa	22 13 45	1 58 9	6♌40 10	14♌ 2 34	2 10.7	8 42.5	21 8.0	3 54.5	3 9.9	11 8.7	9 33.2	28 43.3	29 55.0
26 Su	22 17 42	2 56 4	21 30 11	29 1 55	2 0.4	7 50.1	22 21.8	4 28.3	3 9.1	11 12.7	9 33.5	28 42.8	29 56.6
27 M	22 21 39	3 54 0	6♍36 32	14♍12 42	1 49.2	6 55.7	23 35.5	5 2.4	3 8.4	11 16.7	9 34.0	28 42.4	29 58.1
28 Tu	22 25 35	4 51 58	21 49 3	29 24 11	1 38.5	6 0.5	24 49.3	5 36.7	3 7.9	11 20.8	9 34.4	28 42.0	29 59.7
29 W	22 29 32	5 49 57	6♎56 52	14♎25 57	1 29.5	5 5.5	26 3.1	6 11.3	3D 7.7	11 25.0	9 35.0	28 41.6	0♏ 1.3
30 Th	22 33 28	6 47 58	21 50 30	29 9 46	1 22.9	4 11.9	27 16.8	6 46.1	3 7.6	11 29.3	9 35.5	28 41.2	0 2.9
31 F	22 37 25	7 46 0	6♏23 13	13♏30 31	1 19.1	3 20.8	28 30.6	7 21.1	3 7.7	11 33.6	9 36.2	28 40.9	0 4.5

Astro Data	Planet Ingress	Last Aspect	☽ Ingress	Last Aspect	☽ Ingress	☽ Phases & Eclipses	Astro Data
Dy Hr Mn	Dy Hr Mn	Dy Hr Mn	Dy Hr Mn	Dy Hr Mn	Dy Hr Mn	Dy Hr Mn	1 JULY 1984
☽0S 5 14:17	☿ ♌ 6 18:56	2 19:02 ♆ △	♍ 2 19:28	1 2:30 ♆ □	♎ 1 4:03	5 21:04 ☽ 13♎59	Julian Day # 30863
♇ D 9 8:22	♀ ♌ 14 10:30	4 20:55 ♆ □	♎ 4 21:27	3 5:12 ♇ ☌	♏ 3 6:04	13 2:20 ○ 20♑52	Delta T 54.1 sec
♄ D 13 6:16	☉ ♌ 22 15:58	6 23:50 ♆ ⚹	♏ 7 0:28	5 4:44 ♀ □	♐ 5 10:30	21 4:01 ☽ 28♈34	SVP 05♓28'49"
♆⚹♇ 18 19:08	☿ ♍ 26 6:49	8 16:30 ♀ △	♐ 9 5:03	7 17:10 ♀ △	♑ 7 17:24	28 11:51 ● 5♌34	Obliquity 23°26'32"
☽0N 19 14:13		11 10:29 ♆ ☌	♑ 11 11:23	10 1:39 ♇ □	♒ 10 2:25		⚷ Chiron 5♊45.5
♄⊻♅ 24 0:26	♀ ♍ 7 19:40	13 18:23 ♇ □	♒ 13 19:41	12 12:30 ♇ △	♓ 12 13:13	4 2:33 ☽ 11♏54	☽ Mean ☊ 4♊53.4
	♂ ♐ 17 19:50	16 4:59 ♆ ⚹	♓ 16 6:10	14 23:06 ♆ □	♈ 15 1:28	11 15:43 ○ 19♒08	
☽0S 1 19:49	☉ ♍ 22 23:00	18 17:06 ♆ □	♈ 18 18:26	17 13:42 ♇ ☍	♉ 17 14:13	19 19:41 ☽ 26♉59	1 AUGUST 1984
☿ R 14 19:34	♇ ♏ 28 4:59	21 5:35 ♇ ☍	♉ 21 6:52	19 19:41 ☉ □	♊ 20 1:31	26 19:25 ● 3♍43	Julian Day # 30894
☽0N 15 20:25		23 10:25 ☿ □	♊ 23 17:10	22 9:04 ♇ △	♋ 22 9:20		Delta T 54.1 sec
♅ D 18 5:40		25 23:03 ☿ ⚹	♋ 25 23:44	24 12:51 ♇ □	♌ 24 13:00		SVP 05♓28'44"
☽0S 29 3:37		28 1:43 ♇ □	♌ 28 2:41	26 13:28 ♇ ⚹	♍ 26 13:32		Obliquity 23°26'33"
♃ D 29 23:02		30 2:34 ♇ ⚹	♍ 30 3:29	28 10:53 ♆ □	♎ 28 12:57		⚷ Chiron 7♊30.6
				30 11:13 ♆ ⚹	♏ 30 13:23		☽ Mean ☊ 3♊14.9

LONGITUDE — SEPTEMBER 1984

Day	Sid.Time	☉	0 hr ☽	Noon ☽	True ☊	☿	♀	♂	♃	♄	♅	♆	♇
1 Sa	22 41 21	8♍44 4	20♏31 33	27♏26 19	1♊17.5	2♍33.5	29♍44.3	7♐56.4	3♑ 8.0	11♏38.0	9♐36.9	28♐40.6	0♏ 6.2
2 Su	22 45 18	9 42 9	4♐14 59	10♐57 49	1R 17.3	1R 51.1	0♎58.0	8 32.0	3 8.5	11 42.5	9 37.6	28R 40.3	0 7.9
3 M	22 49 14	10 40 15	17 35 10	24 7 26	1 17.2	1 14.5	2 11.7	9 7.7	3 9.1	11 47.1	9 38.4	28 40.0	0 9.6
4 Tu	22 53 11	11 38 23	0♑35 0	6♑58 20	1 16.1	0 44.5	3 25.5	9 43.7	3 10.0	11 51.7	9 39.2	28 39.8	0 11.4
5 W	22 57 7	12 36 32	13 17 50	19 33 55	1 12.8	0 22.1	4 39.2	10 19.9	3 11.1	11 56.4	9 40.1	28 39.7	0 13.2
6 Th	23 1 4	13 34 43	25 46 57	1♒57 17	1 6.9	0 7.7	5 52.8	10 56.3	3 12.3	12 1.2	9 41.1	28 39.5	0 15.0
7 F	23 5 1	14 32 55	8♒ 5 13	14 11 2	0 58.1	0D 1.9	7 6.5	11 32.9	3 13.7	12 6.1	9 42.1	28 39.4	0 16.8
8 Sa	23 8 57	15 31 9	20 14 58	26 17 13	0 47.0	0 4.9	8 20.2	12 9.7	3 15.4	12 11.0	9 43.1	28 39.3	0 18.6
9 Su	23 12 54	16 29 24	2♓17 58	8♓17 24	0 34.3	0 16.8	9 33.8	12 46.7	3 17.2	12 16.0	9 44.2	28D 39.3	0 20.5
10 M	23 16 50	17 27 41	14 15 41	20 12 58	0 20.9	0 37.6	10 47.4	13 23.9	3 19.1	12 21.0	9 45.3	28 39.3	0 22.4
11 Tu	23 20 47	18 26 0	26 9 24	2♈ 5 11	0 8.2	1 7.4	12 1.1	14 1.3	3 21.3	12 26.1	9 46.5	28 39.3	0 24.3
12 W	23 24 43	19 24 21	8♈ 0 30	13 55 37	29♉56.9	1 45.7	13 14.7	14 38.8	3 23.7	12 31.3	9 47.8	28 39.4	0 26.2
13 Th	23 28 40	20 22 43	19 50 46	25 46 17	29 48.1	2 32.4	14 28.3	15 16.6	3 26.2	12 36.5	9 49.1	28 39.4	0 28.2
14 F	23 32 36	21 21 8	1♉42 30	7♉39 49	29 41.9	3 27.0	15 41.9	15 54.5	3 28.9	12 41.8	9 50.4	28 39.6	0 30.2
15 Sa	23 36 33	22 19 35	13 38 40	19 39 33	29 38.4	4 29.1	16 55.5	16 32.7	3 31.8	12 47.2	9 51.8	28 39.7	0 32.2
16 Su	23 40 30	23 18 3	25 42 59	1♊49 31	29D 37.1	5 38.0	18 9.0	17 11.0	3 34.9	12 52.6	9 53.2	28 39.9	0 34.2
17 M	23 44 26	24 16 34	7♊59 44	14 14 14	29 37.3	6 53.3	19 22.6	17 49.5	3 38.2	12 58.1	9 54.7	28 40.1	0 36.2
18 Tu	23 48 23	25 15 8	20 33 37	26 58 30	29R 37.8	8 14.3	20 36.1	18 28.1	3 41.6	13 3.6	9 56.2	28 40.4	0 38.3
19 W	23 52 19	26 13 43	3♋29 24	10♋ 6 50	29 37.6	9 40.5	21 49.7	19 6.9	3 45.3	13 9.2	9 57.8	28 40.6	0 40.3
20 Th	23 56 16	27 12 21	16 51 13	23 42 50	29 35.9	11 11.1	23 3.2	19 45.9	3 49.1	13 14.9	9 59.5	28 41.0	0 42.4
21 F	0 0 12	28 11 1	0♌41 51	7♌48 13	29 32.0	12 45.7	24 16.8	20 25.1	3 53.0	13 20.6	10 1.1	28 41.3	0 44.5
22 Sa	0 4 9	29 9 43	15 1 44	22 21 56	29 25.8	14 23.5	25 30.3	21 4.4	3 57.2	13 26.4	10 2.9	28 41.7	0 46.7
23 Su	0 8 5	0♎ 8 27	29 48 9	7♍19 28	29 17.8	16 4.2	26 43.8	21 43.9	4 1.5	13 32.2	10 4.6	28 42.1	0 48.8
24 M	0 12 2	1 7 13	14♍54 46	22 32 47	29 9.0	17 47.2	27 57.3	22 23.6	4 6.0	13 38.1	10 6.4	28 42.6	0 51.0
25 Tu	0 15 59	2 6 2	0♎12 9	7♎51 25	29 0.3	19 32.0	29 10.8	23 3.4	4 10.7	13 44.0	10 8.3	28 43.0	0 53.1
26 W	0 19 55	3 4 52	15 29 10	23 4 5	28 53.0	21 18.2	0♏24.2	23 43.4	4 15.5	13 50.0	10 10.2	28 43.5	0 55.3
27 Th	0 23 52	4 3 44	0♏34 58	8♏ 0 49	28 47.8	23 5.5	1 37.7	24 23.5	4 20.5	13 56.0	10 12.2	28 44.1	0 57.5
28 F	0 27 48	5 2 38	15 20 51	22 34 27	28D 44.9	24 53.5	2 51.1	25 3.8	4 25.7	14 2.1	10 14.2	28 44.7	0 59.7
29 Sa	0 31 45	6 1 35	29 41 18	6♐41 12	28 44.2	26 41.9	4 4.6	25 44.2	4 31.0	14 8.2	10 16.2	28 45.3	1 2.0
30 Su	0 35 41	7 0 32	13♐34 10	20 20 22	28 44.8	28 30.6	5 18.0	26 24.7	4 36.6	14 14.4	10 18.3	28 45.9	1 4.2

LONGITUDE — OCTOBER 1984

Day	Sid.Time	☉	0 hr ☽	Noon ☽	True ☊	☿	♀	♂	♃	♄	♅	♆	♇
1 M	0 39 38	7♎59 32	27♐ 0 6	3♑33 43	28♉45.9	0♎19.3	6♏31.4	27♐ 5.4	4♑42.2	14♏20.6	10♐20.4	28♐46.6	1♏ 6.5
2 Tu	0 43 34	8 58 33	10♑ 1 39	16 24 25	28R 46.4	2 7.9	7 44.8	27 46.3	4 48.1	14 26.9	10 22.6	28 47.3	1 8.8
3 W	0 47 31	9 57 37	22 42 29	28 56 24	28 45.4	3 56.2	8 58.1	28 27.3	4 54.1	14 33.2	10 24.8	28 48.1	1 11.1
4 Th	0 51 28	10 56 41	5♒ 6 40	11♒13 45	28 42.5	5 44.1	10 11.5	29 8.4	5 0.2	14 39.6	10 27.1	28 48.8	1 13.4
5 F	0 55 24	11 55 48	17 18 8	23 20 15	28 37.5	7 31.5	11 24.8	29 49.6	5 6.5	14 46.0	10 29.4	28 49.6	1 15.7
6 Sa	0 59 21	12 54 57	29 20 29	5♓19 14	28 30.7	9 18.4	12 38.1	0♑31.0	5 13.0	14 52.4	10 31.7	28 50.5	1 18.0
7 Su	1 3 17	13 54 7	11♓16 48	17 13 30	28 22.7	11 4.6	13 51.4	1 12.5	5 19.6	14 58.9	10 34.1	28 51.4	1 20.3
8 M	1 7 14	14 53 19	23 9 36	29 5 20	28 14.1	12 50.2	15 4.7	1 54.0	5 26.4	15 5.4	10 36.5	28 52.2	1 22.6
9 Tu	1 11 10	15 52 33	5♈ 0 57	10♈56 39	28 5.9	14 35.1	16 17.9	2 35.8	5 33.3	15 11.9	10 38.9	28 53.2	1 25.0
10 W	1 15 7	16 51 49	16 52 39	22 49 9	27 58.8	16 19.3	17 31.2	3 17.6	5 40.3	15 18.5	10 41.4	28 54.1	1 27.3
11 Th	1 19 3	17 51 7	28 46 22	4♉44 33	27 53.3	18 2.8	18 44.4	3 59.5	5 47.5	15 25.1	10 44.0	28 55.1	1 29.7
12 F	1 23 0	18 50 27	10♉43 54	16 44 44	27 49.8	19 45.6	19 57.6	4 41.6	5 54.9	15 31.8	10 46.5	28 56.1	1 32.1
13 Sa	1 26 57	19 49 50	22 47 18	28 51 58	27D 48.3	21 27.7	21 10.8	5 23.8	6 2.4	15 38.5	10 49.2	28 57.2	1 34.5
14 Su	1 30 53	20 49 14	4♊59 5	11♊ 9 1	27 48.4	23 9.1	22 23.9	6 6.0	6 10.0	15 45.2	10 51.8	28 58.3	1 36.8
15 M	1 34 50	21 48 41	17 22 11	23 39 1	27 49.6	24 49.7	23 37.0	6 48.4	6 17.8	15 51.9	10 54.5	28 59.4	1 39.2
16 Tu	1 38 46	22 48 11	29 59 59	6♋25 30	27 51.3	26 29.7	24 50.2	7 30.9	6 25.7	15 58.7	10 57.2	29 0.5	1 41.6
17 W	1 42 43	23 47 42	12♋56 1	19 31 56	27R 52.7	28 9.0	26 3.3	8 13.5	6 33.8	16 5.5	10 60.0	29 1.7	1 44.0
18 Th	1 46 39	24 47 16	26 13 37	3♌ 1 23	27 53.1	29 47.6	27 16.4	8 56.2	6 42.0	16 12.4	11 2.8	29 2.9	1 46.5
19 F	1 50 36	25 46 52	9♌55 23	16 55 44	27 52.3	1♏25.6	28 29.4	9 39.0	6 50.3	16 19.2	11 5.6	29 4.1	1 48.9
20 Sa	1 54 32	26 46 31	24 2 22	1♍15 3	27 50.0	3 3.0	29 42.5	10 21.9	6 58.8	16 26.1	11 8.4	29 5.4	1 51.3
21 Su	1 58 29	27 46 11	8♍33 23	15 56 48	27 46.6	4 39.7	0♐55.5	11 4.9	7 7.4	16 33.0	11 11.3	29 6.7	1 53.7
22 M	2 2 26	28 45 54	23 24 30	0♎55 33	27 42.5	6 15.8	2 8.5	11 48.0	7 16.1	16 40.0	11 14.2	29 8.0	1 56.1
23 Tu	2 6 22	29 45 39	8♎28 53	16 3 19	27 38.4	7 51.4	3 21.5	12 31.1	7 25.0	16 46.9	11 17.2	29 9.3	1 58.5
24 W	2 10 19	0♏45 26	23 37 38	1♏10 34	27 34.9	9 26.4	4 34.5	13 14.4	7 33.9	16 53.9	11 20.2	29 10.7	2 1.0
25 Th	2 14 15	1 45 15	8♏40 57	16 7 41	27 32.6	11 0.9	5 47.5	13 57.8	7 43.0	17 0.9	11 23.2	29 12.1	2 3.4
26 F	2 18 12	2 45 7	23 29 48	0♐46 30	27D 31.6	12 34.8	7 0.4	14 41.3	7 52.3	17 8.0	11 26.3	29 13.5	2 5.8
27 Sa	2 22 8	3 45 0	7♐57 12	15 1 25	27 31.8	14 8.2	8 13.3	15 24.8	8 1.6	17 15.0	11 29.3	29 15.0	2 8.2
28 Su	2 26 5	4 44 55	21 58 56	28 49 39	27 33.0	15 41.1	9 26.2	16 8.5	8 11.1	17 22.1	11 32.4	29 16.5	2 10.7
29 M	2 30 1	5 44 51	5♑33 37	12♑11 4	27 34.5	17 13.5	10 39.1	16 52.2	8 20.7	17 29.2	11 35.6	29 18.0	2 13.1
30 Tu	2 33 58	6 44 50	18 42 17	25 7 39	27 35.9	18 45.4	11 51.9	17 36.0	8 30.4	17 36.3	11 38.7	29 19.5	2 15.5
31 W	2 37 55	7 44 50	1♒27 38	7♒42 45	27R 36.7	20 16.8	13 4.7	18 19.9	8 40.2	17 43.4	11 41.9	29 21.1	2 17.9

Astro Data (Dy Hr Mn)

	Dy Hr Mn
♀0S	3 5:39
☿ D	7 4:02
♆ D	9 22:14
☽0N	12 2:08
♄∠♆	24 19:43
☽0S	25 13:51
☿0S	2 23:14
☽0N	9 8:07
☽0S	23 0:58

Planet Ingress (Dy Hr Mn)

	Dy Hr Mn
♀ ♎	1 5:07
☊ ♉	11 17:01
☉ ♎	22 20:33
♀ ♏	25 16:05
☿ ♎	30 19:44
♂ ♑	5 6:02
☿ ♏	18 3:01
♀ ♐	20 5:45
☉ ♏	23 5:46

Last Aspect / ☽ Ingress

Last Aspect Dy Hr Mn		☽ Ingress Dy Hr Mn
31 8:45	♄ ☌	♐ 1 16:30
3 20:25	♆ ☌	♑ 3 22:55
4 22:35	☉ △	♒ 6 8:11
8 16:43	♆ ⚹	♓ 8 19:24
11 5:03	♆ □	♈ 11 7:47
13 17:50	♆ △	♉ 13 20:33
15 18:49	☉ △	♊ 16 8:26
18 15:09	♆ ☍	♋ 18 17:36
20 19:23	☉ ⚹	♌ 20 22:49
22 22:14	♆ △	♍ 23 0:19
24 21:40	♆ □	♎ 24 23:41
26 21:02	♆ ⚹	♏ 26 23:04
28 18:12	☿ ⚹	♐ 29 0:32

Last Aspect / ☽ Ingress

Last Aspect Dy Hr Mn		☽ Ingress Dy Hr Mn
1 3:14	♆ ☌	♑ 1 5:28
2 8:22	♄ ⚹	♒ 3 14:03
5 23:00	♆ ⚹	♓ 6 1:19
8 11:34	♆ □	♈ 8 13:51
11 0:18	♆ △	♉ 11 2:28
12 20:27	♀ ☍	♊ 13 14:14
15 22:08	♆ ☍	♋ 16 0:00
18 2:03	♀ △	♌ 18 6:41
20 8:26	♆ △	♍ 20 9:56
22 9:09	♆ □	♎ 22 10:32
24 8:50	♆ ⚹	♏ 24 10:08
25 13:33	♆ ☌	♐ 26 10:43
28 12:49	♆ ☌	♑ 28 14:05
30 0:07	☿ ⚹	♒ 30 21:13

☽ Phases & Eclipses

Dy Hr Mn	
2 10:30	☽ 10♐08
10 7:01	○ 17♓45
18 9:31	☽ 25♊38
25 3:11	● 2♎14
1 21:52	☽ 8♑53
9 23:58	○ 16♈52
17 21:14	☽ 24♋40
24 12:08	● 1♏16
31 13:07	☽ 8♒18

Astro Data

1 SEPTEMBER 1984
Julian Day # 30925
Delta T 54.2 sec
SVP 05♓28'40"
Obliquity 23°26'33"
⚷ Chiron 8♊27.3
☽ Mean ☊ 1♊36.4

1 OCTOBER 1984
Julian Day # 30955
Delta T 54.2 sec
SVP 05♓28'37"
Obliquity 23°26'34"
⚷ Chiron 8♊23.4R
☽ Mean ☊ 0♊01.1

NOVEMBER 1984 LONGITUDE

Day	Sid.Time	☉	0 hr ☽	Noon ☽	True ☊	☿	♀	♂	♃	♄	♅	♆	♇
1 Th	2 41 51	8♏44 51	13♒53 31	20♒ 0 30	27♉36.8	21♏47.7	14♐17.5	19♑ 3.8	8♑50.2	17♏50.5	11♐45.1	29♐22.7	2♏20.4
2 F	2 45 48	9 44 54	26 4 15	2♓ 5 19	27R35.9	23 18.2	15 30.2	19 47.9	9 0.2	17 57.6	11 48.4	29 24.3	2 22.8
3 Sa	2 49 44	10 44 59	8♓ 4 14	14 1 32	27 34.3	24 48.2	16 42.9	20 32.0	9 10.4	18 4.8	11 51.6	29 25.9	2 25.2
4 Su	2 53 41	11 45 5	19 57 41	25 53 9	27 32.1	26 17.8	17 55.6	21 16.1	9 20.6	18 11.9	11 54.9	29 27.5	2 27.6
5 M	2 57 37	12 45 13	1♈48 22	7♈43 44	27 29.7	27 46.8	19 8.2	22 0.4	9 31.0	18 19.1	11 58.2	29 29.2	2 30.0
6 Tu	3 1 34	13 45 22	13 39 36	19 36 17	27 27.4	29 15.4	20 20.8	22 44.7	9 41.4	18 26.2	12 1.6	29 30.9	2 32.4
7 W	3 5 30	14 45 33	25 34 7	1♉33 20	27 25.5	0♐43.4	21 33.4	23 29.0	9 52.0	18 33.4	12 4.9	29 32.6	2 34.8
8 Th	3 9 27	15 45 46	7♉34 12	13 36 55	27 24.2	2 10.9	22 45.9	24 13.5	10 2.7	18 40.6	12 8.3	29 34.4	2 37.1
9 F	3 13 23	16 46 1	19 41 41	25 48 43	27D 23.5	3 37.9	23 58.4	24 58.0	10 13.5	18 47.8	12 11.7	29 36.1	2 39.5
10 Sa	3 17 20	17 46 17	1♊58 11	8♊10 14	27 23.4	5 4.3	25 10.9	25 42.5	10 24.3	18 54.9	12 15.1	29 37.9	2 41.9
11 Su	3 21 17	18 46 35	14 25 4	20 42 50	27 23.8	6 30.1	26 23.3	26 27.1	10 35.3	19 2.1	12 18.5	29 39.7	2 44.2
12 M	3 25 13	19 46 55	27 3 43	3♋27 55	27 24.5	7 55.2	27 35.7	27 11.8	10 46.4	19 9.3	12 22.0	29 41.6	2 46.6
13 Tu	3 29 10	20 47 17	9♋55 35	16 26 55	27 25.2	9 19.7	28 48.0	27 56.5	10 57.5	19 16.5	12 25.5	29 43.4	2 48.9
14 W	3 33 6	21 47 41	23 2 6	29 41 17	27 25.8	10 43.3	0♑ 0.3	28 41.3	11 8.8	19 23.7	12 29.0	29 45.3	2 51.3
15 Th	3 37 3	22 48 7	6♌24 39	13♌12 18	27 26.3	12 6.0	1 12.5	29 26.1	11 20.1	19 30.9	12 32.5	29 47.2	2 53.6
16 F	3 40 59	23 48 35	20 4 19	27 0 43	27R26.4	13 27.8	2 24.8	0♒11.0	11 31.6	19 38.0	12 36.0	29 49.1	2 55.9
17 Sa	3 44 56	24 49 4	4♍ 1 29	11♍ 6 29	27 26.4	14 48.5	3 36.9	0 55.9	11 43.1	19 45.2	12 39.5	29 51.0	2 58.2
18 Su	3 48 53	25 49 35	18 15 30	25 28 14	27 26.3	16 8.0	4 49.0	1 40.9	11 54.7	19 52.4	12 43.1	29 53.0	3 0.5
19 M	3 52 49	26 50 8	2♎44 14	10♎ 2 59	27D 26.2	17 26.2	6 1.1	2 25.9	12 6.4	19 59.5	12 46.6	29 54.9	3 2.7
20 Tu	3 56 46	27 50 43	17 23 50	24 46 3	27 26.2	18 42.8	7 13.2	3 11.0	12 18.1	20 6.7	12 50.2	29 56.9	3 5.0
21 W	4 0 42	28 51 20	2♏ 8 51	9♏31 20	27 26.3	19 57.7	8 25.2	3 56.1	12 30.0	20 13.8	12 53.8	29 58.9	3 7.2
22 Th	4 4 39	29 51 58	16 52 38	24 11 53	27R26.4	21 10.7	9 37.1	4 41.3	12 41.9	20 21.0	12 57.4	0♑ 0.9	3 9.5
23 F	4 8 35	0♐52 38	1♐28 12	8♐40 50	27 26.4	22 21.4	10 49.0	5 26.5	12 53.9	20 28.1	13 1.0	0 2.9	3 11.7
24 Sa	4 12 32	1 53 19	15 49 3	22 52 17	27 26.2	23 29.6	12 0.8	6 11.7	13 6.0	20 35.2	13 4.6	0 5.0	3 13.9
25 Su	4 16 28	2 54 2	29 50 3	6♑42 3	27 25.8	24 34.8	13 12.6	6 57.0	13 18.2	20 42.3	13 8.3	0 7.0	3 16.1
26 M	4 20 25	3 54 46	13♑28 4	20 8 2	27 25.1	25 36.8	14 24.3	7 42.4	13 30.4	20 49.4	13 11.9	0 9.1	3 18.3
27 Tu	4 24 22	4 55 31	26 42 1	3♒10 12	27 24.1	26 35.0	15 36.0	8 27.8	13 42.7	20 56.4	13 15.6	0 11.2	3 20.4
28 W	4 28 18	5 56 17	9♒32 51	15 50 20	27 23.2	27 28.9	16 47.6	9 13.2	13 55.1	21 3.5	13 19.2	0 13.3	3 22.6
29 Th	4 32 15	6 57 4	22 3 6	28 11 37	27 22.4	28 17.9	17 59.1	9 58.6	14 7.6	21 10.5	13 22.9	0 15.4	3 24.7
30 F	4 36 11	7 57 52	4♓16 27	10♓18 10	27D 22.0	29 1.3	19 10.5	10 44.1	14 20.1	21 17.5	13 26.5	0 17.6	3 26.8

DECEMBER 1984 LONGITUDE

Day	Sid.Time	☉	0 hr ☽	Noon ☽	True ☊	☿	♀	♂	♃	♄	♅	♆	♇
1 Sa	4 40 8	8♐58 41	16♓17 20	22♓14 34	27♉22.1	29♐38.5	20♑21.9	11♒29.6	14♑32.7	21♏24.5	13♐30.2	0♑19.7	3♏28.9
2 Su	4 44 4	9 59 31	28 10 29	4♈ 5 39	27 22.7	0♑ 8.6	21 33.2	12 15.2	14 45.3	21 31.4	13 33.9	0 21.8	3 30.9
3 M	4 48 1	11 0 22	10♈ 0 40	15 56 5	27 23.9	0 30.9	22 44.4	13 0.7	14 58.0	21 38.3	13 37.5	0 24.0	3 33.0
4 Tu	4 51 57	12 1 13	21 52 25	27 50 10	27 25.2	0R 44.5	23 55.6	13 46.3	15 10.8	21 45.2	13 41.2	0 26.2	3 35.0
5 W	4 55 54	13 2 6	3♉49 47	9♉51 42	27 26.6	0 48.6	25 6.6	14 31.9	15 23.6	21 52.1	13 44.9	0 28.3	3 37.0
6 Th	4 59 51	14 2 59	15 56 16	22 3 47	27R27.7	0 42.4	26 17.6	15 17.5	15 36.5	21 59.0	13 48.5	0 30.5	3 39.0
7 F	5 3 47	15 3 53	28 14 32	4♊28 43	27 28.0	0 25.3	27 28.4	16 3.2	15 49.5	22 5.8	13 52.2	0 32.7	3 40.9
8 Sa	5 7 44	16 4 49	10♊46 29	17 7 55	27 27.5	29♐56.9	28 39.2	16 48.8	16 2.5	22 12.6	13 55.9	0 34.9	3 42.9
9 Su	5 11 40	17 5 45	23 33 4	0♋ 1 56	27 25.9	29 17.1	29 49.9	17 34.5	16 15.5	22 19.4	13 59.6	0 37.2	3 44.8
10 M	5 15 37	18 6 42	6♋34 27	13 10 31	27 23.4	28 26.3	1♒ 0.5	18 20.2	16 28.6	22 26.1	14 3.3	0 39.4	3 46.7
11 Tu	5 19 33	19 7 40	19 50 0	26 32 46	27 20.2	27 25.3	2 10.9	19 6.0	16 41.8	22 32.8	14 6.9	0 41.6	3 48.5
12 W	5 23 30	20 8 40	3♌18 37	10♌ 7 23	27 16.7	26 15.4	3 21.3	19 51.7	16 55.0	22 39.5	14 10.6	0 43.9	3 50.4
13 Th	5 27 26	21 9 40	16 58 51	23 52 51	27 13.4	24 58.7	4 31.6	20 37.4	17 8.2	22 46.1	14 14.3	0 46.1	3 52.2
14 F	5 31 23	22 10 41	0♍49 10	7♍47 38	27 10.9	23 37.5	5 41.7	21 23.2	17 21.5	22 52.7	14 17.9	0 48.3	3 54.0
15 Sa	5 35 20	23 11 43	14 48 4	21 50 17	27D 9.4	22 14.4	6 51.8	22 9.0	17 34.9	22 59.2	14 21.6	0 50.6	3 55.8
16 Su	5 39 16	24 12 46	28 54 6	5♎59 18	27 9.2	20 52.4	8 1.7	22 54.8	17 48.3	23 5.8	14 25.2	0 52.8	3 57.5
17 M	5 43 13	25 13 51	13♎ 5 42	20 13 1	27 10.1	19 34.1	9 11.5	23 40.6	18 1.7	23 12.2	14 28.8	0 55.1	3 59.2
18 Tu	5 47 9	26 14 56	27 21 0	4♏29 20	27 11.6	18 22.0	10 21.2	24 26.4	18 15.2	23 18.7	14 32.5	0 57.4	4 0.9
19 W	5 51 6	27 16 2	11♏37 39	18 45 33	27 13.1	17 18.0	11 30.7	25 12.2	18 28.7	23 25.1	14 36.1	0 59.6	4 2.6
20 Th	5 55 2	28 17 9	25 52 34	2♐58 14	27R13.8	16 23.6	12 40.2	25 58.0	18 42.3	23 31.4	14 39.7	1 1.9	4 4.2
21 F	5 58 59	29 18 16	10♐ 2 3	17 3 28	27 13.2	15 39.6	13 49.5	26 43.9	18 55.9	23 37.7	14 43.3	1 4.2	4 5.8
22 Sa	6 2 55	0♑19 25	24 1 59	0♑57 6	27 10.9	15 6.5	14 58.6	27 29.7	19 9.5	23 44.0	14 46.9	1 6.5	4 7.4
23 Su	6 6 52	1 20 34	7♑48 23	14 35 25	27 6.7	14 44.2	16 7.6	28 15.6	19 23.2	23 50.2	14 50.5	1 8.7	4 9.0
24 M	6 10 49	2 21 43	21 17 54	27 55 35	27 1.1	14D 32.5	17 16.5	29 1.5	19 36.9	23 56.4	14 54.0	1 11.0	4 10.5
25 Tu	6 14 45	3 22 52	4♒28 20	10♒56 6	26 54.7	14 30.8	18 25.2	29 47.3	19 50.6	24 2.5	14 57.6	1 13.3	4 12.0
26 W	6 18 42	4 24 2	17 18 58	23 37 4	26 48.1	14 38.4	19 33.8	0♓33.2	20 4.3	24 8.6	15 1.1	1 15.5	4 13.5
27 Th	6 22 38	5 25 11	29 50 40	6♓ 0 5	26 42.1	14 54.7	20 42.1	1 19.1	20 18.1	24 14.6	15 4.6	1 17.8	4 14.9
28 F	6 26 35	6 26 21	12♓ 5 45	18 8 8	26 37.5	15 18.7	21 50.3	2 4.9	20 31.9	24 20.5	15 8.1	1 20.1	4 16.3
29 Sa	6 30 31	7 27 31	24 7 46	0♈ 5 13	26 34.5	15 49.8	22 58.4	2 50.8	20 45.8	24 26.4	15 11.6	1 22.3	4 17.7
30 Su	6 34 28	8 28 40	6♈ 1 7	11 56 6	26D 33.3	16 27.2	24 6.2	3 36.7	20 59.6	24 32.3	15 15.1	1 24.6	4 19.0
31 M	6 38 25	9 29 50	17 50 49	23 45 55	26 33.7	17 10.3	25 13.8	4 22.5	21 13.5	24 38.1	15 18.5	1 26.9	4 20.3

Astro Data Dy Hr Mn	Planet Ingress Dy Hr Mn	Last Aspect Dy Hr Mn	☽ Ingress Dy Hr Mn	Last Aspect Dy Hr Mn	☽ Ingress Dy Hr Mn	☽ Phases & Eclipses Dy Hr Mn
☽0N 5 14:51	☿ ♐ 6 12:09	2 6:39 ♆ ✶	♓ 2 7:50	1 10:25 ♄ △	♈ 2 3:42	8 17:43 ○ 16♉30
☽0S 19 10:33	♀ ♑ 13 23:54	4 19:17 ♆ □	♈ 4 20:20	4 4:36 ♀ □	♉ 4 16:20	8 17:55 A 0.899
♃⊻♅ 23 20:04	♂ ♒ 15 18:09	7 8:00 ♆ △	♉ 7 8:53	6 22:21 ♀ △	♊ 7 3:24	16 6:59 ☽ 24♌06
	♆ ♑ 21 13:17	9 11:01 ♂ △	♊ 9 20:10	9 10:01 ☿ ☍	♋ 9 11:56	22 22:57 ● 0♐50
☽0N 2 22:15	☉ ♐ 22 3:11	12 4:57 ♆ ☍	♋ 12 5:31	11 4:54 ♄ △	♌ 11 18:08	22 22:53:22 T 1'60"
☿ R 4 21:46		14 10:48 ♂ ☍	♌ 14 12:34	13 12:40 ☿ △	♍ 13 22:35	30 8:01 ☽ 8♓18
☽0S 16 17:10	☿ ♑ 1 16:29	16 16:51 ♆ △	♍ 16 17:08	15 15:25 ☉ □	♎ 16 1:52	
☿ D 24 16:11	☿ ♐ 7 21:46	18 19:20 ♆ □	♎ 18 19:29	17 22:00 ☉ ✶	♏ 18 4:27	8 10:53 ○ 16♊32
☽0N 30 5:49	♀ ♒ 9 3:26	20 20:28 ♆ ✶	♏ 20 20:31	20 0:10 ♂ □	♐ 20 6:58	15 15:25 ☽ 23♍51
	☉ ♑ 21 16:23	22 5:44 ♄ ☌	♐ 22 21:34	22 6:21 ♂ ✶	♑ 22 10:21	22 11:47 ● 0♑49
	♂ ♓ 25 6:38	24 14:11 ☿ ☌	♑ 25 0:17	24 4:48 ♄ ✶	♒ 24 15:47	30 5:27 ☽ 8♈43
		26 13:22 ♄ ✶	♒ 27 6:06	26 13:07 ♄ □	♓ 27 0:18	
		29 13:00 ☿ ✶	♓ 29 15:33	29 0:38 ♄ △	♈ 29 11:49	

Astro Data

1 NOVEMBER 1984
Julian Day # 30986
Delta T 54.2 sec
SVP 05♓28'33"
Obliquity 23°26'33"
⚷ Chiron 7♊20.3R
☽ Mean ☊ 28♉22.6

1 DECEMBER 1984
Julian Day # 31016
Delta T 54.3 sec
SVP 05♓28'28"
Obliquity 23°26'33"
⚷ Chiron 5♊44.1R
☽ Mean ☊ 26♉47.3

LONGITUDE — JANUARY 1985

Day	Sid.Time	☉	0 hr ☽	Noon ☽	True ☊	☿	♀	♂	♃	♄	♅	♆	♇
1 Tu	6 42 21	10♑30 59	29♈42 4	5♉39 54	26♉35.0	17♐58.4	26♒21.3	5♓ 8.4	21♑27.4	24♏43.8	15♐21.9	1♑29.1	4♏21.6
2 W	6 46 18	11 32 8	11♉40 2	17 43 4	26 36.6	18 51.1	27 28.5	5 54.2	21 41.4	24 49.5	15 25.3	1 31.4	4 22.9
3 Th	6 50 14	12 33 17	23 49 32	29 59 56	26R 37.6	19 47.7	28 35.5	6 40.0	21 55.3	24 55.1	15 28.7	1 33.6	4 24.1
4 F	6 54 11	13 34 26	6♊14 40	12♊34 4	26 37.1	20 47.8	29 42.3	7 25.9	22 9.3	25 0.7	15 32.1	1 35.8	4 25.3
5 Sa	6 58 7	14 35 35	18 58 25	25 27 51	26 34.6	21 51.1	0♓48.8	8 11.7	22 23.2	25 6.2	15 35.4	1 38.1	4 26.4
6 Su	7 2 4	15 36 43	2♋ 2 26	8♋42 5	26 29.8	22 57.2	1 55.1	8 57.5	22 37.2	25 11.6	15 38.8	1 40.3	4 27.6
7 M	7 6 0	16 37 52	15 26 37	22 15 47	26 22.9	24 5.9	3 1.2	9 43.3	22 51.2	25 17.0	15 42.0	1 42.5	4 28.6
8 Tu	7 9 57	17 39 0	29 9 9	6♌ 6 17	26 14.4	25 16.7	4 7.0	10 29.0	23 5.3	25 22.3	15 45.3	1 44.7	4 29.7
9 W	7 13 54	18 40 8	13♌ 6 38	20 9 36	26 5.2	26 29.6	5 12.5	11 14.8	23 19.3	25 27.5	15 48.6	1 46.9	4 30.7
10 Th	7 17 50	19 41 16	27 14 35	4♍20 59	25 56.4	27 44.2	6 17.8	12 0.5	23 33.3	25 32.7	15 51.8	1 49.1	4 31.7
11 F	7 21 47	20 42 24	11♍28 12	18 35 44	25 49.0	29 0.5	7 22.8	12 46.2	23 47.4	25 37.8	15 55.0	1 51.3	4 32.7
12 Sa	7 25 43	21 43 31	25 43 5	2♎49 51	25 43.7	0♑18.2	8 27.5	13 32.0	24 1.4	25 42.9	15 58.2	1 53.5	4 33.6
13 Su	7 29 40	22 44 39	9♎55 44	17 0 29	25 40.9	1 37.3	9 31.9	14 17.6	24 15.5	25 47.8	16 1.3	1 55.6	4 34.5
14 M	7 33 36	23 45 46	24 3 54	1♏ 5 52	25D 40.1	2 57.7	10 36.0	15 3.3	24 29.6	25 52.7	16 4.4	1 57.8	4 35.3
15 Tu	7 37 33	24 46 54	8♏ 6 17	15 5 7	25 40.6	4 19.1	11 39.8	15 49.0	24 43.6	25 57.5	16 7.5	1 59.9	4 36.1
16 W	7 41 29	25 48 1	22 2 18	28 57 47	25R 41.2	5 41.6	12 43.3	16 34.6	24 57.7	26 2.3	16 10.5	2 2.0	4 36.9
17 Th	7 45 26	26 49 8	5♐51 29	12♐43 19	25 40.8	7 5.1	13 46.5	17 20.3	25 11.8	26 7.0	16 13.6	2 4.1	4 37.6
18 F	7 49 23	27 50 15	19 33 9	26 20 49	25 38.3	8 29.5	14 49.3	18 5.9	25 25.8	26 11.6	16 16.6	2 6.2	4 38.3
19 Sa	7 53 19	28 51 22	3♑ 6 7	9♑48 51	25 33.1	9 54.8	15 51.7	18 51.5	25 39.9	26 16.1	16 19.5	2 8.3	4 39.0
20 Su	7 57 16	29 52 28	16 28 47	23 5 39	25 25.0	11 20.9	16 53.8	19 37.1	25 54.0	26 20.6	16 22.5	2 10.4	4 39.7
21 M	8 1 12	0♒53 33	29 39 14	6♒ 9 20	25 14.4	12 47.7	17 55.5	20 22.6	26 8.0	26 24.9	16 25.4	2 12.5	4 40.3
22 Tu	8 5 9	1 54 38	12♒35 47	18 58 28	25 2.1	14 15.3	18 56.8	21 8.2	26 22.1	26 29.2	16 28.2	2 14.5	4 40.8
23 W	8 9 5	2 55 42	25 17 20	1♓32 25	24 49.4	15 43.7	19 57.7	21 53.7	26 36.1	26 33.4	16 31.0	2 16.5	4 41.3
24 Th	8 13 2	3 56 45	7♓43 48	13 51 39	24 37.4	17 12.7	20 58.2	22 39.2	26 50.2	26 37.5	16 33.8	2 18.5	4 41.8
25 F	8 16 58	4 57 48	19 56 13	25 57 50	24 27.1	18 42.4	21 58.2	23 24.6	27 4.2	26 41.6	16 36.6	2 20.5	4 42.3
26 Sa	8 20 55	5 58 49	1♈56 54	7♈53 52	24 19.2	20 12.8	22 57.8	24 10.1	27 18.2	26 45.6	16 39.3	2 22.5	4 42.7
27 Su	8 24 52	6 59 49	13 49 16	19 43 39	24 14.1	21 43.9	23 56.9	24 55.5	27 32.2	26 49.4	16 42.0	2 24.5	4 43.1
28 M	8 28 48	8 0 48	25 37 40	1♉31 58	24 11.5	23 15.7	24 55.5	25 40.9	27 46.2	26 53.2	16 44.6	2 26.4	4 43.4
29 Tu	8 32 45	9 1 45	7♉27 12	13 24 6	24D 10.8	24 48.1	25 53.6	26 26.2	28 0.1	26 56.9	16 47.2	2 28.3	4 43.7
30 W	8 36 41	10 2 42	19 23 20	25 25 37	24R 11.0	26 21.2	26 51.2	27 11.6	28 14.1	27 0.5	16 49.8	2 30.2	4 44.0
31 Th	8 40 38	11 3 37	1♊31 37	7♊41 59	24 10.8	27 55.0	27 48.2	27 56.9	28 28.0	27 4.1	16 52.3	2 32.1	4 44.2

LONGITUDE — FEBRUARY 1985

Day	Sid.Time	☉	0 hr ☽	Noon ☽	True ☊	☿	♀	♂	♃	♄	♅	♆	♇
1 F	8 44 34	12♒ 4 31	13♊57 19	20♊18 8	24♉ 9.3	29♑29.5	28♓44.6	28♓42.1	28♑41.9	27♏ 7.5	16♐54.8	2♑34.0	4♏44.4
2 Sa	8 48 31	13 5 24	26 44 52	3♋17 51	24R 5.5	1♒ 4.6	29 40.4	29 27.4	28 55.8	27 10.9	16 57.3	2 35.8	4 44.6
3 Su	8 52 27	14 6 16	9♋57 18	16 43 15	23 59.0	2 40.5	0♈35.6	0♈12.6	29 9.6	27 14.1	16 59.7	2 37.7	4 44.7
4 M	8 56 24	15 7 6	23 35 36	0♌34 4	23 49.8	4 17.1	1 30.2	0 57.7	29 23.5	27 17.3	17 2.0	2 39.5	4 44.8
5 Tu	9 0 21	16 7 55	7♌38 13	14 47 26	23 38.4	5 54.4	2 24.1	1 42.9	29 37.3	27 20.4	17 4.4	2 41.3	4R 44.9
6 W	9 4 17	17 8 43	22 0 56	29 17 52	23 26.1	7 32.5	3 17.3	2 28.0	29 51.1	27 23.4	17 6.6	2 43.0	4 44.9
7 Th	9 8 14	18 9 29	6♍37 16	13♍58 8	23 14.1	9 11.3	4 9.8	3 13.1	0♒ 4.8	27 26.3	17 8.9	2 44.8	4 44.9
8 F	9 12 10	19 10 15	21 19 28	28 40 19	23 3.8	10 50.9	5 1.6	3 58.1	0 18.5	27 29.1	17 11.1	2 46.5	4 44.8
9 Sa	9 16 7	20 10 59	5♎59 50	13♎17 16	22 56.0	12 31.3	5 52.6	4 43.1	0 32.2	27 31.8	17 13.2	2 48.2	4 44.7
10 Su	9 20 3	21 11 42	20 32 1	27 43 36	22 51.2	14 12.5	6 42.7	5 28.0	0 45.9	27 34.4	17 15.3	2 49.8	4 44.6
11 M	9 24 0	22 12 24	4♏51 42	11♏56 6	22 48.9	15 54.5	7 32.1	6 13.0	0 59.5	27 36.9	17 17.4	2 51.5	4 44.4
12 Tu	9 27 56	23 13 5	18 56 43	25 53 34	22 48.4	17 37.4	8 20.6	6 57.9	1 13.1	27 39.4	17 19.4	2 53.1	4 44.2
13 W	9 31 53	24 13 45	2♐46 44	9♐36 18	22 48.3	19 21.1	9 8.3	7 42.7	1 26.7	27 41.7	17 21.4	2 54.7	4 44.0
14 Th	9 35 50	25 14 24	16 22 27	23 5 20	22 47.3	21 5.6	9 55.0	8 27.6	1 40.2	27 43.9	17 23.3	2 56.3	4 43.8
15 F	9 39 46	26 15 2	29 45 7	6♑21 54	22 44.1	22 51.1	10 40.7	9 12.4	1 53.7	27 46.1	17 25.2	2 57.8	4 43.4
16 Sa	9 43 43	27 15 39	12♑55 50	19 26 58	22 38.1	24 37.4	11 25.5	9 57.1	2 7.1	27 48.1	17 27.0	2 59.3	4 43.1
17 Su	9 47 39	28 16 14	25 55 21	2♒21 1	22 28.9	26 24.5	12 9.3	10 41.9	2 20.5	27 50.0	17 28.8	3 0.8	4 42.7
18 M	9 51 36	29 16 48	8♒43 57	15 4 9	22 17.1	28 12.5	12 51.9	11 26.6	2 33.9	27 51.9	17 30.5	3 2.3	4 42.3
19 Tu	9 55 32	0♓17 21	21 21 34	27 36 13	22 3.4	0♓ 1.4	13 33.5	12 11.2	2 47.2	27 53.6	17 32.2	3 3.8	4 41.9
20 W	9 59 29	1 17 52	3♓48 4	9♓57 10	21 49.1	1 51.1	14 13.9	12 55.8	3 0.5	27 55.2	17 33.9	3 5.2	4 41.4
21 Th	10 3 25	2 18 21	16 3 34	22 7 23	21 35.4	3 41.7	14 53.1	13 40.4	3 13.7	27 56.8	17 35.5	3 6.6	4 40.9
22 F	10 7 22	3 18 48	28 8 47	4♈ 7 57	21 23.5	5 33.0	15 31.0	14 25.0	3 26.9	27 58.2	17 37.0	3 7.9	4 40.4
23 Sa	10 11 19	4 19 14	10♈ 5 11	16 0 48	21 14.1	7 25.0	16 7.7	15 9.5	3 40.0	27 59.5	17 38.5	3 9.2	4 39.8
24 Su	10 15 15	5 19 38	21 55 11	27 48 48	21 7.7	9 17.7	16 43.0	15 53.9	3 53.1	28 0.8	17 39.9	3 10.5	4 39.2
25 M	10 19 12	6 20 0	3♉42 8	9♉35 45	21 4.1	11 10.9	17 16.8	16 38.4	4 6.1	28 1.9	17 41.3	3 11.8	4 38.5
26 Tu	10 23 8	7 20 20	15 30 14	21 26 14	21D 2.7	13 4.7	17 49.2	17 22.8	4 19.0	28 2.9	17 42.7	3 13.1	4 37.8
27 W	10 27 5	8 20 39	27 24 23	3♊25 24	21R 2.7	14 58.8	18 20.1	18 7.1	4 31.9	28 3.8	17 43.9	3 14.3	4 37.1
28 Th	10 31 1	9 20 55	9♊29 58	15 38 46	21 2.9	16 53.1	18 49.4	18 51.4	4 44.8	28 4.7	17 45.2	3 15.5	4 36.4

Astro Data Dy Hr Mn	Planet Ingress Dy Hr Mn	Last Aspect Dy Hr Mn	☽ Ingress Dy Hr Mn	Last Aspect Dy Hr Mn	☽ Ingress Dy Hr Mn	☽ Phases & Eclipses Dy Hr Mn
☽0S 12 21:52	♀ ♓ 4 6:23	31 16:32 ♀ ✶	♉ 1 0:36	2 5:48 ♀ □	♋ 2 5:59	7 2:16 ○ 16♋44
♃✶♄ 22 17:26	☿ ♑ 11 18:25	3 10:12 ♀ □	♊ 3 12:00	4 10:09 ♃ ☍	♌ 4 11:02	13 23:27 ☽ 23♎44
☽0N 26 13:02	☉ ♒ 20 2:58	5 5:50 ☿ ☍	♋ 5 20:18	6 8:54 ♄ □	♍ 6 13:09	21 2:28 ● 0♒60
♀0N 30 19:34		7 17:23 ♄ △	♌ 8 1:28	8 10:05 ♄ ✶	♎ 8 14:10	29 3:29 ☽ 9♉11
	☿ ♒ 1 7:43	10 0:55 ☿ △	♍ 10 4:40	10 1:11 ☉ △	♏ 10 15:49	
♂0N 4 1:55	♀ ♈ 2 8:29	11 24:00 ♄ ✶	♎ 12 7:13	12 15:06 ♄ ☌	♐ 12 19:09	5 15:19 ○ 16♌47
♇ R 5 23:57	♂ ♈ 2 17:19	14 0:44 ♃ □	♏ 14 10:07	14 17:10 ☉ ✶	♑ 15 0:27	12 7:57 ☽ 23♏33
☽0S 9 3:37	♃ ♒ 6 15:35	16 7:02 ☉ ✶	♐ 16 13:48	17 3:34 ♄ ✶	♒ 17 7:36	19 18:43 ● 1♓05
♃∠♅ 17 17:04	☉ ♓ 18 17:07	17 21:17 ♂ □	♑ 18 18:29	19 12:35 ♄ □	♓ 19 16:38	27 23:41 ☽ 9♊20
♃⚺♆ 20 9:30	☿ ♓ 18 23:41	20 18:02 ♄ ✶	♒ 21 0:38	21 23:39 ♄ △	♈ 22 3:43	
☽0N 22 19:46		23 2:26 ♄ □	♓ 23 9:02	23 15:20 ♅ △	♉ 24 16:27	
♃□♇ 27 9:13		25 14:30 ♃ ✶	♈ 25 20:05	27 1:19 ♄ ☍	♊ 27 5:11	
		28 4:27 ♃ □	♉ 28 8:53			
		30 17:53 ♃ △	♊ 30 21:01			

Astro Data

1 JANUARY 1985
Julian Day # 31047
Delta T 54.3 sec
SVP 05♓28'23"
Obliquity 23°26'33"
⚷ Chiron 4♊08.9R
☽ Mean ☊ 25♉08.8

1 FEBRUARY 1985
Julian Day # 31078
Delta T 54.4 sec
SVP 05♓28'17"
Obliquity 23°26'34"
⚷ Chiron 3♊18.2R
☽ Mean ☊ 23♉30.3

MARCH 1985 — LONGITUDE

Day	Sid.Time	☉	0 hr ☽	Noon ☽	True ☊	☿	♀	♂	♃	♄	♅	♆	♇
1 F	10 34 58	10♓21 9	21♊52 29	28♊11 44	21♉ 2.3	18♓47.4	19♈17.0	19♈35.7	4♒57.5	28♏ 5.4	17♐46.4	3♑16.6	4♏35.6
2 Sa	10 38 54	11 21 22	4♋37 7	11♋ 9 6	20R 59.9	20 41.6	19 42.9	20 19.9	5 10.3	28 6.0	17 47.5	3 17.8	4R 34.8
3 Su	10 42 51	12 21 32	17 48 5	24 34 19	20 55.1	22 35.3	20 7.1	21 4.1	5 22.9	28 6.5	17 48.6	3 18.9	4 34.0
4 M	10 46 48	13 21 40	1♌27 53	8♌28 42	20 47.9	24 28.3	20 29.4	21 48.2	5 35.5	28 6.9	17 49.6	3 19.9	4 33.1
5 Tu	10 50 44	14 21 46	15 36 29	22 50 43	20 38.6	26 20.2	20 49.8	22 32.3	5 48.1	28 7.2	17 50.6	3 21.0	4 32.3
6 W	10 54 41	15 21 50	0♍10 42	7♍35 32	20 28.4	28 10.8	21 8.2	23 16.3	6 0.5	28 7.4	17 51.5	3 22.0	4 31.3
7 Th	10 58 37	16 21 52	15 4 9	22 35 24	20 18.2	29 59.5	21 24.6	24 0.3	6 12.9	28R 7.6	17 52.4	3 22.9	4 30.4
8 F	11 2 34	17 21 52	0♎ 8 0	7♎40 43	20 9.4	1♈45.9	21 38.9	24 44.3	6 25.2	28 7.6	17 53.2	3 23.9	4 29.4
9 Sa	11 6 30	18 21 51	15 12 21	22 41 47	20 2.7	3 29.7	21 51.0	25 28.2	6 37.5	28 7.5	17 54.0	3 24.8	4 28.4
10 Su	11 10 27	19 21 47	0♏ 8 1	7♏30 16	19 58.8	5 10.2	22 1.0	26 12.0	6 49.7	28 7.3	17 54.7	3 25.7	4 27.4
11 M	11 14 23	20 21 42	14 47 54	22 0 28	19D 57.2	6 46.9	22 8.7	26 55.9	7 1.8	28 7.0	17 55.4	3 26.5	4 26.3
12 Tu	11 18 20	21 21 35	29 7 39	6♐ 9 22	19 57.3	8 19.4	22 14.0	27 39.6	7 13.8	28 6.6	17 56.0	3 27.3	4 25.2
13 W	11 22 17	22 21 27	13♐ 5 35	19 56 26	19R 58.1	9 47.2	22R 17.1	28 23.4	7 25.8	28 6.1	17 56.5	3 28.1	4 24.1
14 Th	11 26 13	23 21 17	26 42 5	3♑22 49	19 58.4	11 9.6	22 17.7	29 7.1	7 37.7	28 5.5	17 57.0	3 28.9	4 23.0
15 F	11 30 10	24 21 5	9♑58 54	16 30 39	19 57.1	12 26.3	22 15.9	29 50.7	7 49.5	28 4.7	17 57.5	3 29.6	4 21.8
16 Sa	11 34 6	25 20 52	22 58 22	29 22 22	19 53.6	13 36.8	22 11.7	0♉34.3	8 1.2	28 3.9	17 57.9	3 30.3	4 20.6
17 Su	11 38 3	26 20 37	5♒42 55	12♒ 0 18	19 47.8	14 40.6	22 4.9	1 17.9	8 12.9	28 3.0	17 58.2	3 30.9	4 19.4
18 M	11 41 59	27 20 20	18 14 45	24 26 29	19 39.9	15 37.4	21 55.7	2 1.4	8 24.4	28 2.0	17 58.5	3 31.6	4 18.2
19 Tu	11 45 56	28 20 1	0♓35 41	6♓42 33	19 30.5	16 26.8	21 44.0	2 44.9	8 35.9	28 0.9	17 58.8	3 32.1	4 16.9
20 W	11 49 52	29 19 41	12 47 13	18 49 52	19 20.6	17 8.7	21 29.9	3 28.3	8 47.3	27 59.7	17 58.9	3 32.7	4 15.6
21 Th	11 53 49	0♈19 18	24 50 38	0♈49 42	19 11.0	17 42.7	21 13.3	4 11.7	8 58.6	27 58.4	17 59.1	3 33.2	4 14.3
22 F	11 57 46	1 18 53	6♈47 13	12 43 24	19 2.7	18 8.8	20 54.3	4 55.1	9 9.8	27 57.0	17R 59.1	3 33.7	4 13.0
23 Sa	12 1 42	2 18 27	18 38 28	24 32 40	18 56.4	18 26.9	20 32.9	5 38.4	9 20.9	27 55.5	17 59.2	3 34.2	4 11.6
24 Su	12 5 39	3 17 58	0♉26 18	6♉19 43	18 52.2	18R 37.1	20 9.3	6 21.7	9 31.9	27 53.9	17 59.1	3 34.6	4 10.2
25 M	12 9 35	4 17 27	12 13 15	18 7 20	18D 50.3	18 39.3	19 43.6	7 4.9	9 42.9	27 52.3	17 59.0	3 35.0	4 8.9
26 Tu	12 13 32	5 16 54	24 2 27	29 59 3	18 50.1	18 34.0	19 15.8	7 48.1	9 53.7	27 50.5	17 58.9	3 35.3	4 7.4
27 W	12 17 28	6 16 18	5♊57 42	11♊58 57	18 51.2	18 21.2	18 46.1	8 31.2	10 4.4	27 48.6	17 58.7	3 35.6	4 6.0
28 Th	12 21 25	7 15 41	18 3 24	24 11 40	18 52.8	18 1.5	18 14.6	9 14.3	10 15.1	27 46.6	17 58.5	3 35.9	4 4.6
29 F	12 25 21	8 15 1	0♋24 19	6♋42 0	18R 54.0	17 35.4	17 41.6	9 57.3	10 25.6	27 44.6	17 58.2	3 36.2	4 3.1
30 Sa	12 29 18	9 14 19	13 5 16	19 34 39	18 54.3	17 3.5	17 7.2	10 40.3	10 36.0	27 42.5	17 57.9	3 36.4	4 1.6
31 Su	12 33 15	10 13 35	26 10 37	2♌53 32	18 53.0	16 26.6	16 31.6	11 23.3	10 46.3	27 40.2	17 57.5	3 36.6	4 0.1

APRIL 1985 — LONGITUDE

Day	Sid.Time	☉	0 hr ☽	Noon ☽	True ☊	☿	♀	♂	♃	♄	♅	♆	♇
1 M	12 37 11	11♈12 48	9♌43 39	16♌41 5	18♉50.1	15♈45.4	15♈55.1	12♉ 6.2	10♒56.6	27♏37.9	17♐57.0	3♑36.7	3♏58.6
2 Tu	12 41 8	12 11 58	23 45 46	0♍57 26	18R 45.8	15R 0.9	15R 17.8	12 49.0	11 6.7	27R 35.5	17R 56.5	3 36.9	3R 57.1
3 W	12 45 4	13 11 7	8♍15 39	15 39 44	18 40.7	14 14.0	14 40.1	13 31.8	11 16.7	27 33.0	17 56.0	3 36.9	3 55.5
4 Th	12 49 1	14 10 13	23 8 50	0♎41 54	18 35.4	13 25.7	14 2.1	14 14.6	11 26.5	27 30.4	17 55.4	3 37.0	3 54.0
5 F	12 52 57	15 9 17	8♎17 47	15 55 12	18 30.9	12 37.0	13 24.3	14 57.3	11 36.3	27 27.8	17 54.7	3R 37.0	3 52.4
6 Sa	12 56 54	16 8 19	23 32 51	1♏ 9 26	18 27.5	11 48.8	12 46.7	15 39.9	11 46.0	27 25.1	17 54.0	3 37.0	3 50.8
7 Su	13 0 50	17 7 19	8♏43 43	16 14 37	18D 25.8	11 2.0	12 9.7	16 22.5	11 55.5	27 22.2	17 53.3	3 37.0	3 49.2
8 M	13 4 47	18 6 17	23 41 9	1♐ 2 33	18 25.6	10 17.4	11 33.5	17 5.1	12 5.0	27 19.3	17 52.5	3 36.9	3 47.6
9 Tu	13 8 43	19 5 13	8♐18 12	15 27 41	18 26.5	9 35.8	10 58.3	17 47.6	12 14.3	27 16.4	17 51.7	3 36.8	3 46.0
10 W	13 12 40	20 4 8	22 30 47	29 27 23	18 28.0	8 57.8	10 24.4	18 30.1	12 23.5	27 13.3	17 50.8	3 36.6	3 44.4
11 Th	13 16 37	21 3 1	6♑17 33	13♑ 1 28	18 29.4	8 23.9	9 52.0	19 12.6	12 32.5	27 10.2	17 49.8	3 36.5	3 42.8
12 F	13 20 33	22 1 52	19 39 23	26 11 37	18R 30.1	7 54.6	9 21.3	19 54.9	12 41.5	27 7.0	17 48.8	3 36.2	3 41.1
13 Sa	13 24 30	23 0 42	2♒38 33	9♒ 0 37	18 29.7	7 30.0	8 52.3	20 37.3	12 50.3	27 3.8	17 47.8	3 36.0	3 39.5
14 Su	13 28 26	23 59 29	15 18 14	21 31 50	18 28.2	7 10.6	8 25.3	21 19.6	12 59.0	27 0.4	17 46.7	3 35.7	3 37.8
15 M	13 32 23	24 58 15	27 41 50	3♓48 40	18 25.7	6 56.3	8 0.4	22 1.9	13 7.6	26 57.0	17 45.6	3 35.4	3 36.1
16 Tu	13 36 19	25 56 59	9♓52 44	15 54 24	18 22.4	6 47.3	7 37.7	22 44.1	13 16.0	26 53.6	17 44.4	3 35.1	3 34.5
17 W	13 40 16	26 55 42	21 54 2	27 51 58	18 18.7	6D 43.6	7 17.3	23 26.3	13 24.3	26 50.0	17 43.2	3 34.7	3 32.8
18 Th	13 44 12	27 54 22	3♈48 31	9♈43 58	18 15.3	6 45.0	6 59.2	24 8.4	13 32.5	26 46.4	17 42.0	3 34.3	3 31.1
19 F	13 48 9	28 53 1	15 38 36	21 32 42	18 12.3	6 51.5	6 43.5	24 50.5	13 40.5	26 42.8	17 40.7	3 33.9	3 29.4
20 Sa	13 52 6	29 51 38	27 26 32	3♉20 21	18 10.2	7 3.0	6 30.2	25 32.6	13 48.4	26 39.1	17 39.3	3 33.4	3 27.7
21 Su	13 56 2	0♉50 12	9♉14 25	15 9 0	18D 9.1	7 19.3	6 19.3	26 14.6	13 56.2	26 35.3	17 37.9	3 32.9	3 26.0
22 M	13 59 59	1 48 45	21 4 25	27 0 57	18 8.9	7 40.2	6 10.9	26 56.5	14 3.8	26 31.5	17 36.5	3 32.4	3 24.3
23 Tu	14 3 55	2 47 17	2♊58 56	8♊58 42	18 9.4	8 5.6	6 4.9	27 38.5	14 11.3	26 27.6	17 35.0	3 31.8	3 22.6
24 W	14 7 52	3 45 46	15 0 37	21 5 5	18 10.5	8 35.4	6 1.3	28 20.3	14 18.6	26 23.7	17 33.5	3 31.3	3 20.9
25 Th	14 11 48	4 44 13	27 12 30	3♋23 19	18 11.7	9 9.2	6D 0.1	29 2.2	14 25.8	26 19.7	17 31.9	3 30.6	3 19.2
26 F	14 15 45	5 42 38	9♋37 57	15 56 51	18 12.9	9 47.1	6 1.2	29 44.0	14 32.8	26 15.7	17 30.3	3 30.0	3 17.5
27 Sa	14 19 41	6 41 1	22 20 27	28 49 11	18 13.7	10 28.7	6 4.7	0♊25.7	14 39.7	26 11.6	17 28.7	3 29.3	3 15.8
28 Su	14 23 38	7 39 21	5♌23 27	12♌ 3 34	18R 14.0	11 13.9	6 10.4	1 7.4	14 46.5	26 7.5	17 27.0	3 28.6	3 14.2
29 M	14 27 35	8 37 40	18 49 48	25 42 22	18 13.9	12 2.6	6 18.4	1 49.1	14 53.1	26 3.3	17 25.3	3 27.9	3 12.5
30 Tu	14 31 31	9 35 57	2♍41 18	9♍46 35	18 13.3	12 54.6	6 28.5	2 30.7	14 59.5	25 59.1	17 23.6	3 27.1	3 10.8

Astro Data	Dy Hr Mn	Planet Ingress	Dy Hr Mn	Last Aspect Dy Hr Mn		☽ Ingress Dy Hr Mn	Last Aspect Dy Hr Mn		☽ Ingress Dy Hr Mn	☽ Phases & Eclipses Dy Hr Mn	
☿0N	7 0:10	☿ ♈	7 0:07	28 19:21	♂ ⚹	♋ 1 15:23	2 6:23	♄ □	♍ 2 10:25	7 2:13	○ 16♍27
♄ R	7 12:38	♂ ♉	15 5:06	3 18:12	♄ △	♌ 3 21:28	4 6:55	♄ ⚹	♎ 4 10:54	13 17:34	☽ 23♐05
☽0S	8 12:21	☉ ♈	20 16:14	5 20:39	♄ □	♍ 5 23:43	5 15:07	♅ ⚹	♏ 6 10:10	21 11:59	● 0♈49
♀ R	13 18:17			7 20:49	♄ ⚹	♎ 7 23:47	8 5:54	♄ ☌	♐ 8 10:17	29 16:11	☽ 8♋55
☽0N	22 2:06	☉ ♉	20 3:26	9 17:19	♂ ☍	♏ 9 23:47	9 19:30	☉ △	♑ 10 12:57		
♅ R	22 22:02	♂ ♊	26 9:13	11 22:17	♄ ☌	♐ 12 1:29	12 13:39	♄ ⚹	♒ 12 19:04	5 11:32	○ 15♎38
☿ R	24 19:00			14 4:34	♂ △	♑ 14 5:55	14 22:33	♄ □	♓ 15 4:30	12 4:41	☽ 22♑13
				16 9:32	♄ ⚹	♒ 16 13:11	17 9:52	♄ △	♈ 17 16:18	20 5:22	● 0♉05
☽0S	4 23:19			18 18:58	♄ □	♓ 18 22:50	19 4:08	♅ △	♉ 20 5:12	28 4:25	☽ 7♌50
♆ R	5 1:27			21 6:15	♄ △	♈ 21 10:20	22 12:35	♂ ☌	♊ 22 18:01		
♆⚹♇	15 12:31			23 3:45	♀ ☌	♉ 23 23:06	24 5:02	♅ ☍	♋ 25 5:26		
☿ D	17 5:23			26 7:40	♄ ☍	♊ 26 12:02	27 7:07	♄ △	♌ 27 14:10		
☽0N	18 8:15			28 0:21	♀ ⚹	♋ 28 23:13	29 12:32	♄ □	♍ 29 19:24		
♀ D	25 0:09			31 2:41	♄ △	♌ 31 6:51					

Astro Data

1 MARCH 1985
Julian Day # 31106
Delta T 54.4 sec
SVP 05♓28'14"
Obliquity 23°26'34"
⚷ Chiron 3♊28.5
☽ Mean ☊ 22♉01.4

1 APRIL 1985
Julian Day # 31137
Delta T 54.5 sec
SVP 05♓28'10"
Obliquity 23°26'35"
⚷ Chiron 4♊40.4
☽ Mean ☊ 20♉22.9

LONGITUDE

Day	Sid.Time	☉	0 hr ☽	Noon ☽	True ☊	☿	♀	♂	♃	♄	♅	♆	♇
1 W	14 35 28	10♉34 11	16♍57 58	24♍15 8	18♉12.6	13♈49.7	6♈40.7	3♊12.2	15♒ 5.8	25♏54.9	17♐21.8	3♑26.3	3♏ 9.1
2 Th	14 39 24	11 32 23	1♎37 30	9♎ 4 24	18R 11.8	14 48.0	6 54.9	3 53.8	15 11.9	25R 50.7	17R 20.0	3R 25.5	3R 7.4
3 F	14 43 21	12 30 34	16 34 58	24 8 12	18 11.1	15 49.2	7 11.2	4 35.2	15 17.9	25 46.4	17 18.1	3 24.7	3 5.7
4 Sa	14 47 17	13 28 42	1♏43 1	9♏18 15	18 10.7	16 53.2	7 29.4	5 16.7	15 23.7	25 42.1	17 16.3	3 23.8	3 4.1
5 Su	14 51 14	14 26 49	16 52 42	24 25 13	18D 10.6	17 59.9	7 49.4	5 58.1	15 29.3	25 37.7	17 14.4	3 22.9	3 2.4
6 M	14 55 10	15 24 54	1♐54 41	9♐20 7	18 10.7	19 9.3	8 11.3	6 39.4	15 34.8	25 33.3	17 12.4	3 22.0	3 0.8
7 Tu	14 59 7	16 22 58	16 40 38	23 55 32	18 10.8	20 21.3	8 34.9	7 20.7	15 40.2	25 29.0	17 10.4	3 21.0	2 59.1
8 W	15 3 4	17 21 0	1♑ 4 17	8♑ 6 31	18R 11.0	21 35.8	9 0.2	8 2.0	15 45.3	25 24.5	17 8.4	3 20.1	2 57.5
9 Th	15 7 0	18 19 1	15 2 1	21 50 44	18 11.0	22 52.7	9 27.1	8 43.2	15 50.3	25 20.1	17 6.4	3 19.1	2 55.9
10 F	15 10 57	19 17 0	28 32 46	5♒ 8 20	18 10.9	24 11.9	9 55.6	9 24.4	15 55.2	25 15.7	17 4.3	3 18.0	2 54.3
11 Sa	15 14 53	20 14 59	11♒37 45	18 1 22	18D 10.9	25 33.5	10 25.6	10 5.5	15 59.8	25 11.2	17 2.3	3 17.0	2 52.7
12 Su	15 18 50	21 12 55	24 19 41	0♓33 10	18 10.8	26 57.4	10 57.1	10 46.7	16 4.3	25 6.7	17 0.1	3 15.9	2 51.1
13 M	15 22 46	22 10 51	6♓42 21	12 47 46	18 11.0	28 23.6	11 29.9	11 27.7	16 8.6	25 2.3	16 58.0	3 14.8	2 49.5
14 Tu	15 26 43	23 8 45	18 49 58	24 49 29	18 11.3	29 51.9	12 4.1	12 8.8	16 12.8	24 57.8	16 55.8	3 13.7	2 47.9
15 W	15 30 39	24 6 38	0♈46 51	6♈42 32	18 11.9	1♉22.5	12 39.6	12 49.7	16 16.7	24 53.3	16 53.6	3 12.6	2 46.4
16 Th	15 34 36	25 4 29	12 37 4	18 30 52	18 12.6	2 55.2	13 16.3	13 30.7	16 20.5	24 48.8	16 51.4	3 11.4	2 44.8
17 F	15 38 33	26 2 20	24 24 23	0♉17 59	18 13.3	4 30.1	13 54.1	14 11.6	16 24.2	24 44.3	16 49.2	3 10.2	2 43.3
18 Sa	15 42 29	27 0 9	6♉12 5	12 6 58	18 13.9	6 7.2	14 33.2	14 52.5	16 27.6	24 39.8	16 46.9	3 9.0	2 41.8
19 Su	15 46 26	27 57 56	18 3 0	24 0 26	18R 14.1	7 46.4	15 13.3	15 33.3	16 30.8	24 35.3	16 44.6	3 7.8	2 40.3
20 M	15 50 22	28 55 43	29 59 33	6♊ 0 37	18 13.8	9 27.8	15 54.4	16 14.1	16 33.9	24 30.8	16 42.3	3 6.5	2 38.8
21 Tu	15 54 19	29 53 28	12♊ 3 50	18 9 26	18 13.0	11 11.3	16 36.6	16 54.9	16 36.8	24 26.3	16 40.0	3 5.2	2 37.4
22 W	15 58 15	0♊51 12	24 17 38	0♋28 39	18 11.6	12 57.0	17 19.7	17 35.6	16 39.5	24 21.9	16 37.7	3 4.0	2 35.9
23 Th	16 2 12	1 48 54	6♋42 41	12 59 56	18 9.8	14 44.8	18 3.7	18 16.3	16 42.1	24 17.4	16 35.3	3 2.6	2 34.5
24 F	16 6 9	2 46 35	19 20 38	25 44 58	18 7.8	16 34.8	18 48.6	18 57.0	16 44.4	24 13.0	16 33.0	3 1.3	2 33.1
25 Sa	16 10 5	3 44 15	2♌13 10	8♌45 25	18 5.9	18 26.9	19 34.4	19 37.6	16 46.5	24 8.6	16 30.6	2 60.0	2 31.7
26 Su	16 14 2	4 41 53	15 21 55	22 2 50	18 4.4	20 21.1	20 21.0	20 18.1	16 48.5	24 4.2	16 28.2	2 58.6	2 30.3
27 M	16 17 58	5 39 29	28 48 21	5♍38 33	18D 3.6	22 17.4	21 8.4	20 58.7	16 50.3	23 59.9	16 25.8	2 57.2	2 29.0
28 Tu	16 21 55	6 37 4	12♍33 31	19 33 15	18 3.6	24 15.7	21 56.5	21 39.2	16 51.9	23 55.5	16 23.4	2 55.8	2 27.6
29 W	16 25 51	7 34 37	26 37 40	3♎46 37	18 4.3	26 16.0	22 45.4	22 19.6	16 53.3	23 51.2	16 21.0	2 54.4	2 26.3
30 Th	16 29 48	8 32 9	10♎59 49	18 16 53	18 5.5	28 18.2	23 35.0	23 0.0	16 54.5	23 46.9	16 18.5	2 53.0	2 25.0
31 F	16 33 44	9 29 40	25 37 20	3♏ 0 33	18 6.7	0♊22.2	24 25.2	23 40.4	16 55.5	23 42.7	16 16.1	2 51.6	2 23.8

LONGITUDE

JUNE 1985

Day	Sid.Time	☉	0 hr ☽	Noon ☽	True ☊	☿	♀	♂	♃	♄	♅	♆	♇
1 Sa	16 37 41	10♊27 9	10♏25 47	17♏52 14	18♉ 7.6	2♊27.9	25♈16.2	24♊20.7	16♒56.4	23♏38.5	16♐13.6	2♑50.1	2♏22.5
2 Su	16 41 38	11 24 38	25 18 58	2♐45 4	18R 7.6	4 35.1	26 7.7	25 1.1	16 57.0	23R 34.3	16R 11.2	2R 48.6	2R 21.3
3 M	16 45 34	12 22 5	10♐ 9 32	17 31 24	18 6.5	6 43.7	26 59.9	25 41.3	16 57.5	23 30.2	16 8.7	2 47.2	2 20.1
4 Tu	16 49 31	13 19 31	24 49 47	2♑ 3 51	18 4.1	8 53.5	27 52.7	26 21.5	16R 57.7	23 26.1	16 6.3	2 45.7	2 18.9
5 W	16 53 27	14 16 57	9♑12 52	16 16 16	18 0.8	11 4.3	28 46.0	27 1.7	16 57.8	23 22.0	16 3.8	2 44.2	2 17.8
6 Th	16 57 24	15 14 21	23 13 38	0♒ 4 39	17 57.0	13 15.7	29 39.9	27 41.9	16 57.7	23 18.0	16 1.3	2 42.7	2 16.7
7 F	17 1 20	16 11 45	6♒49 11	13 27 17	17 53.1	15 27.7	0♉34.4	28 22.0	16 57.4	23 14.1	15 58.9	2 41.1	2 15.6
8 Sa	17 5 17	17 9 8	19 59 4	26 24 47	17 49.8	17 39.8	1 29.3	29 2.1	16 56.9	23 10.1	15 56.4	2 39.6	2 14.5
9 Su	17 9 13	18 6 31	2♓44 50	8♓59 38	17 47.5	19 51.8	2 24.7	29 42.2	16 56.2	23 6.3	15 53.9	2 38.1	2 13.4
10 M	17 13 10	19 3 53	15 9 43	21 15 38	17D 46.4	22 3.5	3 20.7	0♋22.2	16 55.4	23 2.5	15 51.5	2 36.5	2 12.4
11 Tu	17 17 7	20 1 14	27 17 57	3♈17 20	17 46.6	24 14.5	4 17.0	1 2.2	16 54.3	22 58.7	15 49.0	2 34.9	2 11.4
12 W	17 21 3	20 58 35	9♈14 22	15 9 41	17 47.7	26 24.7	5 13.9	1 42.2	16 53.0	22 55.0	15 46.6	2 33.4	2 10.4
13 Th	17 25 0	21 55 55	21 3 53	26 57 35	17 49.4	28 33.7	6 11.1	2 22.1	16 51.6	22 51.3	15 44.1	2 31.8	2 9.5
14 F	17 28 56	22 53 15	2♉51 20	8♉45 40	17 51.0	0♋41.5	7 8.8	3 2.0	16 50.0	22 47.7	15 41.6	2 30.2	2 8.6
15 Sa	17 32 53	23 50 35	14 41 6	20 38 4	17R 51.9	2 47.7	8 6.9	3 41.9	16 48.1	22 44.2	15 39.2	2 28.6	2 7.7
16 Su	17 36 49	24 47 54	26 37 1	2♊38 17	17 51.5	4 52.3	9 5.3	4 21.7	16 46.1	22 40.8	15 36.8	2 27.0	2 6.8
17 M	17 40 46	25 45 13	8♊42 11	14 49 0	17 49.5	6 55.0	10 4.1	5 1.6	16 43.9	22 37.3	15 34.4	2 25.4	2 6.0
18 Tu	17 44 42	26 42 31	20 58 56	27 12 9	17 45.8	8 55.8	11 3.3	5 41.3	16 41.5	22 34.0	15 31.9	2 23.8	2 5.2
19 W	17 48 39	27 39 49	3♋28 46	9♋48 50	17 40.4	10 54.7	12 2.8	6 21.1	16 38.9	22 30.8	15 29.5	2 22.2	2 4.4
20 Th	17 52 36	28 37 6	16 12 23	22 39 25	17 33.8	12 51.4	13 2.7	7 0.8	16 36.2	22 27.6	15 27.2	2 20.6	2 3.7
21 F	17 56 32	29 34 23	29 9 53	5♌43 44	17 26.7	14 46.0	14 2.9	7 40.5	16 33.2	22 24.4	15 24.8	2 19.0	2 3.0
22 Sa	18 0 29	0♋31 39	12♌20 53	19 1 17	17 19.9	16 38.5	15 3.4	8 20.2	16 30.1	22 21.4	15 22.4	2 17.3	2 2.3
23 Su	18 4 25	1 28 54	25 44 49	2♍31 26	17 14.2	18 28.7	16 4.2	8 59.8	16 26.8	22 18.4	15 20.1	2 15.7	2 1.7
24 M	18 8 22	2 26 9	9♍21 3	16 13 37	17 10.1	20 16.7	17 5.2	9 39.4	16 23.3	22 15.5	15 17.7	2 14.1	2 1.0
25 Tu	18 12 18	3 23 23	23 9 3	0♎ 7 17	17D 7.9	22 2.5	18 6.6	10 19.0	16 19.7	22 12.7	15 15.4	2 12.5	2 0.5
26 W	18 16 15	4 20 37	7♎ 8 14	14 11 48	17 7.5	23 46.0	19 8.3	10 58.5	16 15.8	22 9.9	15 13.1	2 10.9	1 59.9
27 Th	18 20 11	5 17 50	21 17 52	28 26 14	17 8.2	25 27.2	20 10.2	11 38.0	16 11.8	22 7.2	15 10.9	2 9.2	1 59.4
28 F	18 24 8	6 15 2	5♏36 40	12♏48 51	17R 9.3	27 6.2	21 12.3	12 17.5	16 7.7	22 4.6	15 8.6	2 7.6	1 58.9
29 Sa	18 28 5	7 12 14	20 2 23	27 16 50	17 9.6	28 42.9	22 14.8	12 56.9	16 3.3	22 2.1	15 6.4	2 6.0	1 58.4
30 Su	18 32 1	8 9 26	4♐31 38	11♐46 11	17 8.4	0♌17.3	23 17.5	13 36.3	15 58.8	21 59.7	15 4.2	2 4.4	1 58.0

Astro Data	Dy Hr Mn
☽0S	2 10:10
☽0N	15 14:30
♃✶♅	21 15:11
☽0S	29 18:50
♃ R	4 22:24
☽0N	11 21:05
☽0S	26 0:48

Planet Ingress	Dy Hr Mn
☿ ♉	14 2:10
☉ ♊	21 2:43
☿ ♊	30 19:44
♀ ♉	6 8:53
♂ ♋	9 10:40
☿ ♋	13 16:11
☉ ♋	21 10:44
☿ ♌	29 19:34

Last Aspect Dy Hr Mn		☽ Ingress Dy Hr Mn
1 14:39	♄ ✶	♎ 1 21:22
3 1:09	♅ ✶	♏ 3 21:17
5 13:52	♄ ☌	♐ 5 20:56
7 6:38	☿ △	♑ 7 22:11
9 18:08	♄ ✶	♒ 10 2:38
12 5:42	☿ ✶	♓ 12 10:56
14 12:12	♄ △	♈ 14 22:25
16 8:36	♅ △	♉ 17 11:23
19 21:41	☉ ☌	♊ 20 0:01
21 10:07	♂ ☌	♋ 22 11:05
24 9:05	♄ △	♌ 24 19:54
26 15:31	♄ □	♍ 27 2:06
28 23:17	☿ △	♎ 29 5:41
30 21:55	♀ ☍	♏ 31 7:07

Last Aspect Dy Hr Mn		☽ Ingress Dy Hr Mn
1 21:12	♄ ☌	♐ 2 7:33
4 5:22	♀ △	♑ 4 8:34
6 0:08	♄ ✶	♒ 6 11:52
8 17:53	♂ △	♓ 8 18:46
10 16:34	☿ □	♈ 11 5:24
13 1:55	☉ ✶	♉ 13 18:11
15 16:09	♄ ☍	♊ 16 6:45
18 11:58	☉ ☌	♋ 18 17:22
20 11:35	♄ △	♌ 21 1:32
22 17:54	♄ □	♍ 23 7:32
24 22:23	♄ ✶	♎ 25 11:48
27 7:55	☿ □	♏ 27 14:37
29 16:08	☿ △	♐ 29 16:30

☽ Phases & Eclipses Dy Hr Mn	
4 19:53	○ 14♏17
4 19:56	☍ T 1.237
11 17:34	☽ 20♒57
19 21:41	● 28♉50
19 21:28:42	☌ P 0.841
27 12:56	☽ 6♍11
3 3:50	○ 12♐31
10 8:19	☽ 19♓24
18 11:58	● 27♊11
25 18:53	☽ 4♎08

Astro Data

1 MAY 1985
Julian Day # 31167
Delta T 54.5 sec
SVP 05♓28'06"
Obliquity 23°26'35"
⚷ Chiron 6♊35.0
☽ Mean ☊ 18♉47.6

1 JUNE 1985
Julian Day # 31198
Delta T 54.6 sec
SVP 05♓28'02"
Obliquity 23°26'34"
⚷ Chiron 8♊57.1
☽ Mean ☊ 17♉09.1

JULY 1985 LONGITUDE

Day	Sid.Time	☉	0 hr ☽	Noon ☽	True ☊	☿	♀	♂	♃	♄	♅	♆	♇
1 M	18 35 58	9♋ 6 37	18♐59 47	26♐11 44	17♉ 5.1	1♌49.3	24♉20.4	14♋15.7	15♒54.2	21♏57.4	15♐ 2.0	2♑ 2.8	1♏57.6
2 Tu	18 39 54	10 3 48	3♑21 19	10♑27 49	16R 59.5	3 19.1	25 23.6	14 55.0	15R 49.4	21R 55.1	14R 59.8	2R 1.2	1R 57.2
3 W	18 43 51	11 0 59	17 30 33	24 28 56	16 51.9	4 46.6	26 27.0	15 34.4	15 44.4	21 52.9	14 57.7	1 59.6	1 56.9
4 Th	18 47 47	11 58 10	1♒22 26	8♒10 40	16 43.2	6 11.6	27 30.6	16 13.7	15 39.3	21 50.8	14 55.6	1 58.0	1 56.6
5 F	18 51 44	12 55 21	14 53 21	21 30 19	16 34.2	7 34.3	28 34.5	16 53.0	15 34.0	21 48.8	14 53.5	1 56.4	1 56.4
6 Sa	18 55 41	13 52 32	28 1 34	4♓27 11	16 26.0	8 54.6	29 38.5	17 32.2	15 28.6	21 46.9	14 51.4	1 54.8	1 56.1
7 Su	18 59 37	14 49 44	10♓47 24	17 2 32	16 19.3	10 12.4	0♊42.8	18 11.4	15 23.0	21 45.1	14 49.4	1 53.3	1 55.9
8 M	19 3 34	15 46 55	23 13 1	29 19 18	16 14.6	11 27.6	1 47.3	18 50.6	15 17.3	21 43.4	14 47.4	1 51.7	1 55.8
9 Tu	19 7 30	16 44 7	5♈21 58	11♈21 36	16 12.0	12 40.3	2 52.0	19 29.8	15 11.5	21 41.7	14 45.4	1 50.2	1 55.6
10 W	19 11 27	17 41 20	17 18 51	23 14 23	16D 11.3	13 50.4	3 56.9	20 8.9	15 5.5	21 40.2	14 43.5	1 48.6	1 55.5
11 Th	19 15 23	18 38 32	29 8 50	5♉ 2 55	16 11.7	14 57.8	5 2.0	20 48.1	14 59.4	21 38.7	14 41.6	1 47.1	1 55.5
12 F	19 19 20	19 35 46	10♉57 16	16 52 32	16R 12.3	16 2.3	6 7.3	21 27.2	14 53.1	21 37.3	14 39.7	1 45.5	1D 55.4
13 Sa	19 23 16	20 32 59	22 49 20	28 48 17	16 12.2	17 4.0	7 12.7	22 6.2	14 46.8	21 36.0	14 37.8	1 44.0	1 55.4
14 Su	19 27 13	21 30 14	4♊49 52	10♊54 36	16 10.5	18 2.8	8 18.4	22 45.3	14 40.3	21 34.8	14 36.0	1 42.5	1 55.5
15 M	19 31 10	22 27 28	17 2 54	23 15 7	16 6.6	18 58.4	9 24.2	23 24.3	14 33.7	21 33.7	14 34.2	1 41.0	1 55.6
16 Tu	19 35 6	23 24 44	29 31 30	5♋52 14	16 0.1	19 50.9	10 30.1	24 3.4	14 27.0	21 32.7	14 32.5	1 39.5	1 55.7
17 W	19 39 3	24 22 0	12♋17 26	18 47 6	15 51.3	20 40.0	11 36.3	24 42.3	14 20.2	21 31.8	14 30.8	1 38.1	1 55.8
18 Th	19 42 59	25 19 16	25 21 8	1♌59 22	15 40.7	21 25.7	12 42.6	25 21.3	14 13.3	21 31.0	14 29.1	1 36.6	1 56.0
19 F	19 46 56	26 16 33	8♌41 35	15 27 27	15 29.4	22 7.8	13 49.0	26 0.3	14 6.3	21 30.3	14 27.5	1 35.2	1 56.2
20 Sa	19 50 52	27 13 50	22 16 38	29 8 45	15 18.4	22 46.1	14 55.6	26 39.2	13 59.2	21 29.7	14 25.9	1 33.8	1 56.4
21 Su	19 54 49	28 11 7	6♍ 3 24	13♍ 0 12	15 8.8	23 20.6	16 2.3	27 18.1	13 52.1	21 29.2	14 24.3	1 32.3	1 56.7
22 M	19 58 45	29 8 25	19 58 47	26 58 48	15 1.5	23 51.0	17 9.2	27 57.0	13 44.8	21 28.8	14 22.8	1 31.0	1 57.0
23 Tu	20 2 42	0♌ 5 43	3♎59 59	11♎ 2 4	14 56.9	24 17.1	18 16.2	28 35.8	13 37.5	21 28.4	14 21.3	1 29.6	1 57.4
24 W	20 6 39	1 3 1	18 4 51	25 8 9	14 54.8	24 38.9	19 23.4	29 14.6	13 30.1	21 28.2	14 19.9	1 28.2	1 57.8
25 Th	20 10 35	2 0 20	2♏11 51	9♏15 49	14 54.3	24 56.1	20 30.7	29 53.4	13 22.6	21D 28.1	14 18.5	1 26.9	1 58.2
26 F	20 14 32	2 57 38	16 19 55	23 24 3	14 54.4	25 8.6	21 38.1	0♌32.2	13 15.1	21 28.1	14 17.1	1 25.5	1 58.6
27 Sa	20 18 28	3 54 58	0♐28 1	7♐31 39	14 53.7	25 16.3	22 45.7	1 11.0	13 7.5	21 28.1	14 15.8	1 24.2	1 59.1
28 Su	20 22 25	4 52 18	14 34 42	21 36 52	14 51.3	25R 19.0	23 53.4	1 49.7	12 59.9	21 28.3	14 14.5	1 22.9	1 59.6
29 M	20 26 21	5 49 38	28 37 49	5♑37 8	14 46.2	25 16.6	25 1.3	2 28.4	12 52.2	21 28.6	14 13.3	1 21.7	2 0.2
30 Tu	20 30 18	6 46 59	12♑34 24	19 29 10	14 38.3	25 9.1	26 9.2	3 7.1	12 44.5	21 28.9	14 12.1	1 20.4	2 0.8
31 W	20 34 14	7 44 21	26 20 59	3♒ 9 24	14 28.0	24 56.5	27 17.3	3 45.8	12 36.8	21 29.4	14 11.0	1 19.2	2 1.4

AUGUST 1985 LONGITUDE

Day	Sid.Time	☉	0 hr ☽	Noon ☽	True ☊	☿	♀	♂	♃	♄	♅	♆	♇
1 Th	20 38 11	8♌41 43	9♒54 1	16♒34 29	14♉16.2	24♌38.8	28♊25.5	4♌24.5	12♒29.1	21♏29.9	14♐ 9.9	1♑18.0	2♏ 2.1
2 F	20 42 8	9 39 6	23 10 32	29 41 59	14R 3.9	24R 16.2	29 33.9	5 3.1	12R 21.3	21 30.6	14R 8.8	1R 16.8	2 2.7
3 Sa	20 46 4	10 36 30	6♓ 8 43	12♓30 45	13 52.3	23 48.7	0♋42.3	5 41.7	12 13.5	21 31.3	14 7.8	1 15.6	2 3.5
4 Su	20 50 1	11 33 55	18 48 11	25 1 12	13 42.4	23 16.7	1 50.9	6 20.3	12 5.7	21 32.2	14 6.8	1 14.5	2 4.2
5 M	20 53 57	12 31 22	1♈10 7	7♈15 17	13 35.0	22 40.5	2 59.6	6 58.9	11 57.9	21 33.1	14 5.9	1 13.4	2 5.0
6 Tu	20 57 54	13 28 49	13 17 9	19 16 14	13 30.3	22 0.6	4 8.5	7 37.4	11 50.1	21 34.1	14 5.1	1 12.3	2 5.8
7 W	21 1 50	14 26 17	25 13 7	1♉ 8 24	13 27.8	21 17.6	5 17.4	8 16.0	11 42.3	21 35.3	14 4.2	1 11.2	2 6.7
8 Th	21 5 47	15 23 47	7♉ 2 43	12 56 46	13 27.1	20 32.0	6 26.5	8 54.5	11 34.5	21 36.5	14 3.5	1 10.1	2 7.5
9 F	21 9 43	16 21 19	18 51 14	24 46 47	13 27.0	19 44.7	7 35.6	9 33.0	11 26.7	21 37.8	14 2.7	1 9.1	2 8.5
10 Sa	21 13 40	17 18 51	0♊44 7	6♊43 54	13 26.6	18 56.5	8 44.9	10 11.5	11 19.0	21 39.2	14 2.1	1 8.1	2 9.4
11 Su	21 17 37	18 16 25	12 46 46	18 53 19	13 24.8	18 8.2	9 54.3	10 50.0	11 11.3	21 40.8	14 1.4	1 7.1	2 10.4
12 M	21 21 33	19 14 1	25 4 5	1♋19 34	13 20.8	17 20.8	11 3.8	11 28.5	11 3.6	21 42.4	14 0.8	1 6.2	2 11.4
13 Tu	21 25 30	20 11 37	7♋40 7	14 6 2	13 14.2	16 35.1	12 13.5	12 6.9	10 56.0	21 44.1	14 0.3	1 5.2	2 12.5
14 W	21 29 26	21 9 16	20 37 30	27 14 34	13 5.2	15 52.2	13 23.2	12 45.4	10 48.4	21 45.9	13 59.8	1 4.3	2 13.5
15 Th	21 33 23	22 6 55	3♌57 10	10♌45 7	12 54.2	15 12.9	14 33.0	13 23.8	10 40.9	21 47.8	13 59.4	1 3.5	2 14.6
16 F	21 37 19	23 4 36	17 38 3	24 35 32	12 42.4	14 37.9	15 42.9	14 2.2	10 33.4	21 49.8	13 59.0	1 2.6	2 15.8
17 Sa	21 41 16	24 2 18	1♍37 1	8♍41 52	12 30.8	14 8.2	16 52.9	14 40.6	10 26.0	21 51.9	13 58.7	1 1.8	2 17.0
18 Su	21 45 12	25 0 2	15 49 25	22 58 57	12 20.7	13 44.3	18 3.1	15 19.0	10 18.6	21 54.0	13 58.4	1 1.0	2 18.2
19 M	21 49 9	25 57 46	0♎ 9 47	7♎21 15	12 13.0	13 26.8	19 13.3	15 57.3	10 11.4	21 56.3	13 58.2	1 0.2	2 19.4
20 Tu	21 53 6	26 55 32	14 32 44	21 43 43	12 8.1	13D 16.2	20 23.6	16 35.7	10 4.2	21 58.7	13 58.0	0 59.5	2 20.6
21 W	21 57 2	27 53 19	28 53 45	6♏ 2 27	12D 5.7	13 12.8	21 34.0	17 14.0	9 57.1	22 1.1	13 57.8	0 58.8	2 21.9
22 Th	22 0 59	28 51 7	13♏ 9 34	20 14 53	12 5.2	13 17.0	22 44.4	17 52.3	9 50.0	22 3.6	13 57.8	0 58.1	2 23.3
23 F	22 4 55	29 48 56	27 18 15	4♐19 35	12R 5.4	13 28.9	23 55.0	18 30.6	9 43.1	22 6.3	13D 57.7	0 57.4	2 24.6
24 Sa	22 8 52	0♍46 46	11♐18 49	18 15 53	12 5.1	13 48.6	25 5.7	19 8.9	9 36.3	22 9.0	13 57.8	0 56.8	2 26.0
25 Su	22 12 48	1 44 38	25 10 45	2♑ 3 22	12 3.1	14 16.1	26 16.4	19 47.2	9 29.6	22 11.8	13 57.8	0 56.2	2 27.4
26 M	22 16 45	2 42 30	8♑53 38	15 41 27	11 58.6	14 51.4	27 27.3	20 25.4	9 23.0	22 14.7	13 58.0	0 55.7	2 28.8
27 Tu	22 20 41	3 40 24	22 26 42	29 9 14	11 51.6	15 34.3	28 38.2	21 3.6	9 16.5	22 17.7	13 58.2	0 55.1	2 30.3
28 W	22 24 38	4 38 20	5♒48 52	12♒25 27	11 42.3	16 24.7	29 49.2	21 41.8	9 10.2	22 20.8	13 58.4	0 54.6	2 31.8
29 Th	22 28 35	5 36 16	18 58 48	25 28 45	11 31.5	17 22.2	1♌ 0.3	22 20.1	9 3.9	22 23.9	13 58.7	0 54.2	2 33.3
30 F	22 32 31	6 34 14	1♓55 12	8♓18 2	11 20.2	18 26.6	2 11.5	22 58.2	8 57.8	22 27.2	13 59.0	0 53.7	2 34.9
31 Sa	22 36 28	7 32 14	14 37 13	20 52 45	11 9.6	19 37.6	3 22.8	23 36.4	8 51.8	22 30.5	13 59.4	0 53.3	2 36.4

Astro Data Dy Hr Mn	Planet Ingress Dy Hr Mn	Last Aspect Dy Hr Mn	☽ Ingress Dy Hr Mn	Last Aspect Dy Hr Mn	☽ Ingress Dy Hr Mn	☽ Phases & Eclipses Dy Hr Mn
♆✶♇ 5 1:12	♀ ♊ 6 8:01	30 18:53 ♃ ✶	♑ 1 18:22	2 1:56 ☿ ☍	♓ 2 12:33	2 12:08 ○ 10♑33
☽0N 9 4:05	☉ ♌ 22 21:36	3 16:42 ♀ △	♒ 3 21:36	4 5:16 ♄ △	♈ 4 21:43	10 0:49 ☽ 17♈43
♇ D 12 8:40	♂ ♌ 25 4:04	6 3:16 ♀ □	♓ 6 3:40	6 16:32 ☿ △	♉ 7 9:41	17 23:56 ● 25♋19
♃✶♅ 14 21:32		7 21:05 ♄ △	♈ 8 13:20	9 5:38 ♄ ☍	♊ 9 22:31	24 23:39 ☽ 1♏59
☽0S 23 5:24	♀ ♋ 2 9:10	10 6:04 ♂ □	♉ 11 1:44	11 11:43 ☉ ✶	♋ 12 9:28	31 21:41 ○ 8♒36
♄ D 25 19:34	☉ ♍ 23 4:36	12 22:28 ♂ ✶	♊ 13 14:23	14 2:05 ♄ △	♌ 14 16:57	
☿ R 28 0:52	♀ ♌ 28 3:39	15 4:02 ☿ ✶	♋ 16 0:54	16 10:05 ☉ ☌	♍ 16 21:15	8 18:29 ☽ 16♉08
		18 0:00 ♂ ☌	♌ 18 8:25	18 10:13 ♄ ✶	♎ 18 23:44	16 10:05 ● 23♌29
☽0N 5 11:25		20 0:54 ☿ ☌	♍ 20 13:29	20 22:11 ☉ ✶	♏ 21 1:51	23 4:36 ☽ 0♐00
☽0S 19 11:01		22 16:51 ☉ ✶	♎ 22 17:10	22 17:42 ♀ △	♐ 23 4:36	30 9:27 ○ 6♓57
☿ D 20 22:48		24 19:54 ☿ □	♏ 24 20:16	24 14:11 ♂ △	♑ 25 8:24	
♅ D 23 0:19		26 15:07 ☿ □	♐ 26 23:12	27 12:09 ♀ ☍	♒ 27 13:31	
		28 18:17 ☿ △	♑ 29 2:21	29 6:30 ♂ ☍	♓ 29 20:25	
		30 15:29 ♄ ✶	♒ 31 6:25			

Astro Data

1 JULY 1985
Julian Day # 31228
Delta T 54.6 sec
SVP 05♓27'56"
Obliquity 23°26'34"
⚷ Chiron 11♊14.6
☽ Mean ☊ 15♉33.8

1 AUGUST 1985
Julian Day # 31259
Delta T 54.6 sec
SVP 05♓27'50"
Obliquity 23°26'35"
⚷ Chiron 13♊13.1
☽ Mean ☊ 13♉55.3

LONGITUDE SEPTEMBER 1985

Day	Sid.Time	☉	0 hr ☽	Noon ☽	True ☊	☿	♀	♂	♃	♄	♅	♆	♇
1 Su	22 40 24	8♍30 15	27♓ 4 43	3♈13 14	11♉ 0.5	20♌54.6	4♌34.2	24♌14.6	8♒46.0	22♏33.9	13♐59.8	0♑52.9	2♏38.0
2 M	22 44 21	9 28 18	9♈18 31	15 20 51	10R 53.7	22 17.4	5 45.6	24 52.7	8R 40.3	22 37.4	14 0.3	0R 52.6	2 39.7
3 Tu	22 48 17	10 26 23	21 20 32	27 17 59	10 49.4	23 45.3	6 57.1	25 30.9	8 34.7	22 41.0	14 0.8	0 52.3	2 41.3
4 W	22 52 14	11 24 30	3♉13 39	9♉ 8 3	10D 47.4	25 18.0	8 8.8	26 9.0	8 29.3	22 44.6	14 1.4	0 52.0	2 43.0
5 Th	22 56 10	12 22 38	15 1 43	20 55 15	10 47.1	26 54.8	9 20.5	26 47.1	8 24.0	22 48.4	14 2.1	0 51.7	2 44.7
6 F	23 0 7	13 20 49	26 49 17	2♊44 28	10 47.9	28 35.3	10 32.3	27 25.2	8 18.8	22 52.2	14 2.7	0 51.5	2 46.4
7 Sa	23 4 4	14 19 2	8♊41 27	14 40 54	10R 48.7	0♍19.0	11 44.1	28 3.3	8 13.9	22 56.1	14 3.5	0 51.3	2 48.2
8 Su	23 8 0	15 17 16	20 43 31	26 49 55	10 48.7	2 5.4	12 56.1	28 41.4	8 9.1	23 0.1	14 4.3	0 51.1	2 50.0
9 M	23 11 57	16 15 33	3♋ 0 45	9♋16 34	10 47.2	3 53.9	14 8.1	29 19.5	8 4.4	23 4.1	14 5.1	0 51.0	2 51.8
10 Tu	23 15 53	17 13 52	15 37 53	22 5 9	10 43.6	5 44.2	15 20.3	29 57.6	7 59.9	23 8.3	14 6.0	0 50.9	2 53.6
11 W	23 19 50	18 12 13	28 38 40	5♌18 38	10 38.0	7 35.9	16 32.5	0♍35.6	7 55.6	23 12.5	14 7.0	0 50.9	2 55.4
12 Th	23 23 46	19 10 36	12♌ 5 9	18 58 6	10 30.7	9 28.5	17 44.7	1 13.7	7 51.5	23 16.8	14 8.0	0D 50.8	2 57.3
13 F	23 27 43	20 9 0	25 57 15	3♍ 2 12	10 22.6	11 21.8	18 57.1	1 51.7	7 47.5	23 21.1	14 9.0	0 50.8	2 59.2
14 Sa	23 31 39	21 7 27	10♍12 23	17 27 5	10 14.5	13 15.4	20 9.5	2 29.8	7 43.7	23 25.6	14 10.1	0 50.9	3 1.1
15 Su	23 35 36	22 5 56	24 45 29	2♎ 6 39	10 7.5	15 9.2	21 22.0	3 7.8	7 40.1	23 30.1	14 11.3	0 50.9	3 3.1
16 M	23 39 33	23 4 26	9♎29 40	16 53 32	10 2.2	17 2.8	22 34.5	3 45.8	7 36.6	23 34.7	14 12.5	0 51.0	3 5.0
17 Tu	23 43 29	24 2 58	24 17 19	1♏40 8	9 59.2	18 56.2	23 47.2	4 23.8	7 33.4	23 39.3	14 13.7	0 51.2	3 7.0
18 W	23 47 26	25 1 32	9♏ 1 12	16 19 50	9D 58.2	20 49.1	24 59.8	5 1.8	7 30.3	23 44.1	14 15.0	0 51.3	3 9.0
19 Th	23 51 22	26 0 8	23 35 28	0♐47 41	9 58.7	22 41.5	26 12.6	5 39.8	7 27.4	23 48.8	14 16.3	0 51.5	3 11.0
20 F	23 55 19	26 58 46	7♐56 8	15 0 37	9 60.0	24 33.1	27 25.4	6 17.7	7 24.7	23 53.7	14 17.7	0 51.8	3 13.1
21 Sa	23 59 15	27 57 25	22 1 0	28 57 16	10R 1.0	26 24.1	28 38.3	6 55.7	7 22.2	23 58.6	14 19.2	0 52.1	3 15.1
22 Su	0 3 12	28 56 6	5♑49 25	12♑37 31	10 0.9	28 14.2	29 51.3	7 33.6	7 19.9	24 3.6	14 20.7	0 52.4	3 17.2
23 M	0 7 8	29 54 48	19 21 39	26 1 57	9 59.2	0♎ 3.5	1♍ 4.3	8 11.6	7 17.8	24 8.7	14 22.2	0 52.7	3 19.3
24 Tu	0 11 5	0♎53 32	2♒38 31	9♒11 29	9 55.7	1 52.0	2 17.3	8 49.5	7 15.9	24 13.8	14 23.8	0 53.1	3 21.4
25 W	0 15 2	1 52 18	15 40 57	22 7 3	9 50.7	3 39.5	3 30.5	9 27.4	7 14.1	24 19.0	14 25.4	0 53.5	3 23.6
26 Th	0 18 58	2 51 6	28 29 52	4♓49 31	9 44.6	5 26.1	4 43.7	10 5.3	7 12.6	24 24.3	14 27.1	0 53.9	3 25.7
27 F	0 22 55	3 49 55	11♓ 6 5	17 19 40	9 38.1	7 11.7	5 56.9	10 43.2	7 11.2	24 29.6	14 28.9	0 54.4	3 27.9
28 Sa	0 26 51	4 48 46	23 30 23	29 38 21	9 32.1	8 56.5	7 10.2	11 21.0	7 10.1	24 35.0	14 30.6	0 54.9	3 30.0
29 Su	0 30 48	5 47 39	5♈43 43	11♈46 38	9 27.0	10 40.3	8 23.6	11 58.9	7 9.1	24 40.4	14 32.4	0 55.4	3 32.2
30 M	0 34 44	6 46 34	17 47 18	23 45 56	9 23.4	12 23.3	9 37.0	12 36.8	7 8.4	24 45.9	14 34.3	0 56.0	3 34.4

LONGITUDE OCTOBER 1985

Day	Sid.Time	☉	0 hr ☽	Noon ☽	True ☊	☿	♀	♂	♃	♄	♅	♆	♇
1 Tu	0 38 41	7♎45 31	29♈42 49	5♉38 14	9♉21.4	14♎ 5.3	10♍50.5	13♍14.6	7♒ 7.8	24♏51.5	14♐36.2	0♑56.5	3♏36.7
2 W	0 42 37	8 44 31	11♉32 31	17 26 4	9D 21.0	15 46.5	12 4.1	13 52.5	7R 7.5	24 57.1	14 38.2	0 57.2	3 38.9
3 Th	0 46 34	9 43 32	23 19 17	29 12 38	9 21.8	17 26.8	13 17.7	14 30.3	7D 7.3	25 2.7	14 40.2	0 57.8	3 41.2
4 F	0 50 30	10 42 36	5♊ 6 37	11♊ 1 46	9 23.3	19 6.2	14 31.4	15 8.1	7 7.3	25 8.5	14 42.2	0 58.5	3 43.4
5 Sa	0 54 27	11 41 42	16 58 37	22 57 47	9 25.1	20 44.9	15 45.1	15 46.0	7 7.5	25 14.2	14 44.3	0 59.3	3 45.7
6 Su	0 58 24	12 40 51	28 59 50	5♋ 5 22	9 26.6	22 22.7	16 58.9	16 23.8	7 8.0	25 20.1	14 46.4	1 0.0	3 48.0
7 M	1 2 20	13 40 1	11♋15 1	17 29 22	9R 27.4	23 59.7	18 12.7	17 1.6	7 8.6	25 26.0	14 48.6	1 0.8	3 50.3
8 Tu	1 6 17	14 39 14	23 48 57	0♌14 18	9 27.1	25 35.9	19 26.6	17 39.4	7 9.4	25 31.9	14 50.8	1 1.6	3 52.6
9 W	1 10 13	15 38 30	6♌45 51	13 23 59	9 25.6	27 11.4	20 40.6	18 17.2	7 10.4	25 37.9	14 53.1	1 2.5	3 54.9
10 Th	1 14 10	16 37 47	20 8 56	27 0 49	9 23.3	28 46.2	21 54.6	18 55.0	7 11.7	25 43.9	14 55.4	1 3.4	3 57.3
11 F	1 18 6	17 37 7	3♍59 38	11♍ 5 11	9 20.4	0♏20.2	23 8.6	19 32.8	7 13.1	25 50.0	14 57.7	1 4.3	3 59.6
12 Sa	1 22 3	18 36 29	18 17 6	25 34 50	9 17.4	1 53.5	24 22.7	20 10.6	7 14.7	25 56.1	15 0.1	1 5.2	4 2.0
13 Su	1 25 59	19 35 54	2♎57 40	10♎24 45	9 14.8	3 26.0	25 36.9	20 48.3	7 16.5	26 2.3	15 2.5	1 6.2	4 4.3
14 M	1 29 56	20 35 20	17 55 4	25 27 31	9 12.9	4 57.9	26 51.1	21 26.1	7 18.5	26 8.5	15 5.0	1 7.2	4 6.7
15 Tu	1 33 53	21 34 48	3♏ 0 57	10♏34 13	9D 12.0	6 29.1	28 5.3	22 3.8	7 20.7	26 14.8	15 7.5	1 8.3	4 9.1
16 W	1 37 49	22 34 19	18 6 11	25 35 48	9 12.1	7 59.6	29 19.6	22 41.6	7 23.1	26 21.1	15 10.0	1 9.3	4 11.5
17 Th	1 41 46	23 33 51	3♐ 2 9	10♐24 24	9 12.9	9 29.5	0♎33.9	23 19.3	7 25.6	26 27.4	15 12.6	1 10.4	4 13.8
18 F	1 45 42	24 33 26	17 41 56	24 54 12	9 14.0	10 58.6	1 48.2	23 57.0	7 28.4	26 33.8	15 15.2	1 11.6	4 16.2
19 Sa	1 49 39	25 33 2	2♑ 0 54	9♑ 1 49	9 15.1	12 27.0	3 2.6	24 34.7	7 31.4	26 40.3	15 17.9	1 12.7	4 18.6
20 Su	1 53 35	26 32 40	15 56 53	22 46 8	9R 15.8	13 54.8	4 17.1	25 12.5	7 34.6	26 46.8	15 20.6	1 13.9	4 21.1
21 M	1 57 32	27 32 19	29 29 43	6♒ 7 50	9 16.0	15 21.8	5 31.5	25 50.1	7 37.9	26 53.3	15 23.3	1 15.1	4 23.5
22 Tu	2 1 28	28 32 0	12♒40 46	19 8 49	9 15.6	16 48.1	6 46.0	26 27.8	7 41.5	26 59.8	15 26.0	1 16.4	4 25.9
23 W	2 5 25	29 31 43	25 32 19	1♓51 39	9 14.8	18 13.7	8 0.6	27 5.5	7 45.2	27 6.4	15 28.8	1 17.7	4 28.3
24 Th	2 9 22	0♏31 27	8♓ 7 8	14 19 9	9 13.7	19 38.5	9 15.1	27 43.2	7 49.1	27 13.0	15 31.6	1 19.0	4 30.7
25 F	2 13 18	1 31 14	20 28 1	26 34 5	9 12.6	21 2.4	10 29.8	28 20.8	7 53.2	27 19.7	15 34.5	1 20.3	4 33.2
26 Sa	2 17 15	2 31 1	2♈37 40	8♈39 3	9 11.6	22 25.5	11 44.4	28 58.4	7 57.4	27 26.3	15 37.4	1 21.6	4 35.6
27 Su	2 21 11	3 30 51	14 38 33	20 36 25	9 10.8	23 47.8	12 59.1	29 36.1	8 1.9	27 33.1	15 40.3	1 23.0	4 38.0
28 M	2 25 8	4 30 43	26 32 57	2♉28 22	9 10.4	25 9.0	14 13.8	0♎13.7	8 6.5	27 39.8	15 43.3	1 24.4	4 40.4
29 Tu	2 29 4	5 30 36	8♉22 58	14 17 1	9D 10.3	26 29.3	15 28.5	0 51.3	8 11.3	27 46.6	15 46.2	1 25.9	4 42.9
30 W	2 33 1	6 30 32	20 10 46	26 4 30	9 10.4	27 48.5	16 43.3	1 28.9	8 16.3	27 53.4	15 49.3	1 27.4	4 45.3
31 Th	2 36 57	7 30 29	1♊58 32	7♊53 11	9 10.5	29 6.4	17 58.1	2 6.5	8 21.5	28 0.2	15 52.3	1 28.8	4 47.7

Astro Data	Planet Ingress	Last Aspect	☽ Ingress	Last Aspect	☽ Ingress	☽ Phases & Eclipses	Astro Data
Dy Hr Mn	Dy Hr Mn	Dy Hr Mn	Dy Hr Mn	Dy Hr Mn	Dy Hr Mn	Dy Hr Mn	1 SEPTEMBER 1985
☽0N 1 18:43	☿ ♍ 6 19:39	31 15:13 ♄ △	♈ 1 5:42	29 17:33 ♅ △	♉ 1 0:35	7 12:16 ☽ 14♊49	Julian Day # 31290
♆ D 12 9:17	♂ ♍ 10 1:31	3 8:52 ♂ △	♉ 3 17:28	3 3:33 ♄ ☍	♊ 3 13:36	14 19:20 ● 21♍55	Delta T 54.7 sec
☽0S 15 19:15	☿ ♎ 22 23:13	6 4:12 ☿ □	♊ 6 6:27	5 8:46 ☿ △	♋ 6 1:59	21 11:03 ☽ 28♐24	SVP 05♓27'46"
☿0S 24 15:42	♀ ♍ 22 2:53	8 16:28 ♂ ✶	♋ 8 18:10	8 3:50 ☿ □	♌ 8 11:33	29 0:08 ○ 5♈48	Obliquity 23°26'35"
☽0N 29 1:37	☉ ♎ 23 2:07	10 14:01 ♄ △	♌ 11 2:27	10 16:57 ☿ ✶	♍ 10 17:09		⚷ Chiron 14♊25.5
		12 19:32 ♄ □	♍ 13 6:52	12 12:40 ♄ ✶	♎ 12 19:12	7 5:04 ☽ 13♋53	☽ Mean ☊ 12♉16.8
♃ D 3 8:17	☿ ♏ 10 18:50	14 21:56 ♄ ✶	♎ 15 8:34	14 4:33 ☉ ☌	♏ 14 19:13	14 4:33 ● 20♎47	
☽0S 13 5:50	♀ ♎ 16 13:04	16 23:07 ♀ ✶	♏ 17 9:17	16 13:19 ♄ ☌	♐ 16 19:05	20 20:13 ☽ 27♑23	1 OCTOBER 1985
♀0S 19 9:52	☉ ♏ 23 11:22	19 4:45 ♀ □	♐ 19 10:40	18 12:16 ☉ ✶	♑ 18 20:35	28 17:38 ○ 5♉15	Julian Day # 31320
☽0N 26 7:55	♂ ♎ 27 15:16	21 12:33 ♀ △	♑ 21 13:49	20 20:13 ☉ □	♒ 21 0:54	28 17:42 •T 1.074	Delta T 54.7 sec
	☿ ♐ 31 16:44	23 8:39 ♄ ✶	♒ 23 19:11	23 8:12 ☉ △	♓ 23 8:27		SVP 05♓27'43"
		25 16:14 ♄ □	♓ 26 2:50	25 16:22 ♂ ☍	♈ 25 18:47		Obliquity 23°26'36"
		28 2:07 ♄ △	♈ 28 12:43	27 2:05 ♅ △	♉ 28 6:59		⚷ Chiron 14♊36.3R
				30 17:27 ☿ ☍	♊ 30 19:59		☽ Mean ☊ 10♉41.5

NOVEMBER 1985 LONGITUDE

Day	Sid.Time	☉	0 hr ☽	Noon ☽	True ☊	☿	♀	♂	♃	♄	♅	♆	♇
1 F	2 40 54	8♏30 29	13♊48 47	19♊45 42	9♉10.6	0♐23.1	19♎12.9	2♎44.1	8♒26.8	28♏ 7.0	15♐55.4	1♑30.4	4♏50.1
2 Sa	2 44 51	9 30 31	25 44 19	1♋45 2	9R 10.7	1 38.3	20 27.8	3 21.7	8 32.3	28 13.9	15 58.5	1 31.9	4 52.6
3 Su	2 48 47	10 30 34	7♋48 19	13 54 36	9 10.6	2 52.0	21 42.7	3 59.3	8 38.0	28 20.8	16 1.6	1 33.5	4 55.0
4 M	2 52 44	11 30 40	20 4 22	26 18 6	9 10.4	4 4.0	22 57.6	4 36.9	8 43.9	28 27.7	16 4.8	1 35.1	4 57.4
5 Tu	2 56 40	12 30 48	2♌36 16	8♌59 20	9D 10.2	5 14.1	24 12.6	5 14.5	8 49.9	28 34.7	16 8.0	1 36.7	4 59.8
6 W	3 0 37	13 30 58	15 27 47	22 2 0	9 10.1	6 22.0	25 27.6	5 52.0	8 56.1	28 41.7	16 11.2	1 38.3	5 2.2
7 Th	3 4 33	14 31 10	28 42 22	5♍29 9	9 10.3	7 27.6	26 42.6	6 29.6	9 2.4	28 48.6	16 14.4	1 40.0	5 4.6
8 F	3 8 30	15 31 24	12♍22 31	19 22 35	9 10.7	8 30.5	27 57.6	7 7.1	9 8.9	28 55.7	16 17.7	1 41.7	5 7.0
9 Sa	3 12 26	16 31 40	26 29 14	3♎42 15	9 11.3	9 30.4	29 12.7	7 44.6	9 15.6	29 2.7	16 20.9	1 43.4	5 9.4
10 Su	3 16 23	17 31 58	11♎ 1 15	18 25 38	9 12.0	10 26.9	0♏27.8	8 22.2	9 22.4	29 9.7	16 24.2	1 45.1	5 11.8
11 M	3 20 20	18 32 18	25 54 39	3♏27 22	9R 12.6	11 19.8	1 42.9	8 59.7	9 29.4	29 16.8	16 27.6	1 46.9	5 14.2
12 Tu	3 24 16	19 32 39	11♏ 2 45	18 39 37	9 12.8	12 8.3	2 58.0	9 37.2	9 36.6	29 23.8	16 30.9	1 48.7	5 16.6
13 W	3 28 13	20 33 3	26 16 43	3♐52 49	9 12.4	12 52.2	4 13.2	10 14.7	9 43.9	29 30.9	16 34.3	1 50.5	5 19.0
14 Th	3 32 9	21 33 28	11♐26 40	18 57 7	9 11.4	13 30.7	5 28.3	10 52.2	9 51.4	29 38.0	16 37.7	1 52.3	5 21.3
15 F	3 36 6	22 33 55	26 23 9	3♑43 54	9 9.9	14 3.3	6 43.5	11 29.6	9 59.0	29 45.1	16 41.1	1 54.1	5 23.7
16 Sa	3 40 2	23 34 24	10♑58 39	18 6 55	9 8.1	14 29.2	7 58.7	12 7.1	10 6.7	29 52.2	16 44.5	1 56.0	5 26.0
17 Su	3 43 59	24 34 53	25 8 21	2♒ 2 49	9 6.3	14 47.7	9 14.0	12 44.6	10 14.7	29 59.4	16 48.0	1 57.9	5 28.4
18 M	3 47 55	25 35 24	8♒50 21	15 31 4	9 4.9	14R 58.1	10 29.2	13 22.0	10 22.7	0♐ 6.5	16 51.5	1 59.8	5 30.7
19 Tu	3 51 52	26 35 56	22 5 17	28 33 22	9D 4.2	14 59.7	11 44.4	13 59.4	10 30.9	0 13.6	16 54.9	2 1.7	5 33.0
20 W	3 55 49	27 36 30	4♓55 44	11♓12 55	9 4.3	14 51.8	12 59.7	14 36.8	10 39.3	0 20.8	16 58.4	2 3.7	5 35.3
21 Th	3 59 45	28 37 4	17 25 25	23 33 48	9 5.2	14 33.7	14 15.0	15 14.2	10 47.8	0 27.9	17 2.0	2 5.6	5 37.6
22 F	4 3 42	29 37 40	29 38 36	5♈40 21	9 6.7	14 5.0	15 30.2	15 51.6	10 56.4	0 35.0	17 5.5	2 7.6	5 39.8
23 Sa	4 7 38	0♐38 16	11♈39 36	17 36 50	9 8.4	13 25.7	16 45.5	16 28.9	11 5.2	0 42.2	17 9.0	2 9.6	5 42.1
24 Su	4 11 35	1 38 55	23 32 32	29 27 8	9 9.9	12 35.9	18 0.8	17 6.3	11 14.0	0 49.3	17 12.6	2 11.6	5 44.3
25 M	4 15 31	2 39 34	5♉21 3	11♉14 40	9R 10.7	11 36.2	19 16.2	17 43.6	11 23.1	0 56.5	17 16.2	2 13.6	5 46.6
26 Tu	4 19 28	3 40 15	17 8 18	23 2 17	9 10.5	10 27.9	20 31.5	18 21.0	11 32.2	1 3.6	17 19.7	2 15.6	5 48.8
27 W	4 23 24	4 40 56	28 56 54	4♊52 25	9 9.0	9 12.6	21 46.8	18 58.3	11 41.5	1 10.7	17 23.3	2 17.7	5 51.0
28 Th	4 27 21	5 41 40	10♊49 4	16 47 4	9 6.1	7 52.5	23 2.2	19 35.6	11 51.0	1 17.9	17 26.9	2 19.8	5 53.2
29 F	4 31 18	6 42 24	22 46 38	28 47 59	9 1.9	6 30.1	24 17.6	20 12.9	12 0.5	1 25.0	17 30.5	2 21.8	5 55.4
30 Sa	4 35 14	7 43 10	4♋51 20	10♋56 53	8 56.9	5 8.2	25 32.9	20 50.2	12 10.2	1 32.1	17 34.2	2 23.9	5 57.5

DECEMBER 1985 LONGITUDE

Day	Sid.Time	☉	0 hr ☽	Noon ☽	True ☊	☿	♀	♂	♃	♄	♅	♆	♇
1 Su	4 39 11	8♐43 57	17♋ 4 51	23♋15 30	8♉51.5	3♐49.5	26♏48.3	21♎27.4	12♒20.0	1♐39.2	17♐37.8	2♑26.0	5♏59.6
2 M	4 43 7	9 44 46	29 29 5	5♌45 51	8R 46.4	2R 36.7	28 3.7	22 4.7	12 29.9	1 46.3	17 41.4	2 28.2	6 1.8
3 Tu	4 47 4	10 45 36	12♌ 6 7	18 30 10	8 42.2	1 31.9	29 19.2	22 41.9	12 39.9	1 53.4	17 45.1	2 30.3	6 3.9
4 W	4 51 0	11 46 27	24 58 20	1♍30 55	8 39.3	0 36.7	0♐34.6	23 19.2	12 50.1	2 0.5	17 48.7	2 32.5	6 5.9
5 Th	4 54 57	12 47 20	8♍ 8 15	14 50 35	8D 38.0	29♏52.3	1 50.0	23 56.4	13 0.3	2 7.6	17 52.4	2 34.6	6 8.0
6 F	4 58 54	13 48 14	21 38 8	28 31 18	8 38.1	29 19.2	3 5.5	24 33.6	13 10.7	2 14.7	17 56.0	2 36.8	6 10.1
7 Sa	5 2 50	14 49 9	5♎30 0	12♎34 20	8 39.3	28 57.6	4 20.9	25 10.8	13 21.2	2 21.7	17 59.7	2 38.9	6 12.1
8 Su	5 6 47	15 50 6	19 44 12	26 59 24	8 40.8	28D 47.1	5 36.4	25 48.0	13 31.8	2 28.7	18 3.3	2 41.1	6 14.1
9 M	5 10 43	16 51 4	4♏19 32	11♏44 2	8R 41.8	28 47.4	6 51.8	26 25.1	13 42.5	2 35.7	18 7.0	2 43.3	6 16.1
10 Tu	5 14 40	17 52 3	19 12 14	26 43 13	8 41.4	28 57.6	8 7.3	27 2.3	13 53.4	2 42.7	18 10.7	2 45.5	6 18.0
11 W	5 18 36	18 53 3	4♐15 58	11♐49 22	8 39.2	29 17.0	9 22.8	27 39.4	14 4.3	2 49.7	18 14.3	2 47.8	6 19.9
12 Th	5 22 33	19 54 4	19 22 12	26 53 15	8 34.9	29 44.6	10 38.3	28 16.5	14 15.3	2 56.7	18 18.0	2 50.0	6 21.9
13 F	5 26 29	20 55 6	4♑21 19	11♑45 17	8 28.8	0♐19.8	11 53.8	28 53.6	14 26.5	3 3.6	18 21.7	2 52.2	6 23.8
14 Sa	5 30 26	21 56 9	19 4 11	26 17 11	8 21.7	1 1.6	13 9.3	29 30.7	14 37.7	3 10.5	18 25.3	2 54.4	6 25.6
15 Su	5 34 23	22 57 12	3♒23 40	10♒23 10	8 14.5	1 49.3	14 24.8	0♏ 7.7	14 49.1	3 17.4	18 29.0	2 56.7	6 27.5
16 M	5 38 19	23 58 16	17 15 28	24 0 31	8 8.1	2 42.3	15 40.3	0 44.8	15 0.5	3 24.3	18 32.6	2 58.9	6 29.3
17 Tu	5 42 16	24 59 20	0♓38 26	7♓ 9 29	8 3.3	3 39.8	16 55.8	1 21.8	15 12.0	3 31.1	18 36.3	3 1.2	6 31.1
18 W	5 46 12	26 0 25	13 34 5	19 52 42	8 0.4	4 41.3	18 11.3	1 58.8	15 23.7	3 37.9	18 39.9	3 3.4	6 32.9
19 Th	5 50 9	27 1 30	26 5 54	2♈14 19	7D 59.4	5 46.3	19 26.8	2 35.7	15 35.4	3 44.7	18 43.6	3 5.7	6 34.6
20 F	5 54 5	28 2 35	8♈18 35	14 19 23	7 60.0	6 54.5	20 42.3	3 12.7	15 47.2	3 51.4	18 47.2	3 8.0	6 36.3
21 Sa	5 58 2	29 3 40	20 17 22	26 13 12	8 1.2	8 5.3	21 57.8	3 49.6	15 59.1	3 58.1	18 50.8	3 10.2	6 38.0
22 Su	6 1 58	0♑ 4 46	2♉ 7 31	8♉ 0 56	8R 2.3	9 18.5	23 13.3	4 26.5	16 11.1	4 4.8	18 54.5	3 12.5	6 39.7
23 M	6 5 55	1 5 52	13 54 1	19 47 18	8 2.3	10 33.8	24 28.8	5 3.3	16 23.1	4 11.5	18 58.1	3 14.8	6 41.3
24 Tu	6 9 52	2 6 58	25 41 14	1♊36 18	8 0.3	11 50.9	25 44.3	5 40.2	16 35.3	4 18.1	19 1.7	3 17.0	6 42.9
25 W	6 13 48	3 8 5	7♊32 50	13 31 12	7 56.0	13 9.6	26 59.8	6 17.0	16 47.5	4 24.6	19 5.2	3 19.3	6 44.5
26 Th	6 17 45	4 9 12	19 31 39	25 34 25	7 49.1	14 29.7	28 15.3	6 53.8	16 59.8	4 31.2	19 8.8	3 21.6	6 46.0
27 F	6 21 41	5 10 19	1♋39 40	7♋47 32	7 39.9	15 51.1	29 30.8	7 30.6	17 12.2	4 37.7	19 12.4	3 23.9	6 47.6
28 Sa	6 25 38	6 11 26	13 58 6	20 11 26	7 29.0	17 13.6	0♑46.3	8 7.4	17 24.7	4 44.2	19 15.9	3 26.1	6 49.0
29 Su	6 29 34	7 12 34	26 27 35	2♌46 32	7 17.4	18 37.1	2 1.8	8 44.1	17 37.2	4 50.6	19 19.5	3 28.4	6 50.5
30 M	6 33 31	8 13 41	9♌ 8 20	15 32 58	7 6.1	20 1.6	3 17.3	9 20.9	17 49.8	4 57.0	19 23.0	3 30.7	6 51.9
31 Tu	6 37 27	9 14 50	22 0 30	28 30 57	6 56.2	21 26.8	4 32.8	9 57.6	18 2.5	5 3.3	19 26.5	3 32.9	6 53.3

Astro Data Dy Hr Mn	Planet Ingress Dy Hr Mn	Last Aspect Dy Hr Mn	☽ Ingress Dy Hr Mn	Last Aspect Dy Hr Mn	☽ Ingress Dy Hr Mn	☽ Phases & Eclipses Dy Hr Mn	Astro Data
♂0S 1 1:13	♀ ♏ 9 15:08	1 12:10 ♀ △	♋ 2 8:31	1 20:58 ♀ △	♌ 2 0:59	5 20:07 ☽ 13♌21	1 NOVEMBER 1985
☽0S 9 16:47	♄ ♐ 17 2:09	4 16:17 ♄ △	♌ 4 19:04	3 20:48 ♂ ✶	♍ 4 9:14	12 14:20 ● 20♏09	Julian Day # 31351
☿ R 18 16:09	☉ ♐ 22 8:51	7 0:11 ♄ □	♍ 7 2:18	6 13:00 ☿ ✶	♎ 6 14:33	12 14:10:31 ✔ T 1'59"	Delta T 54.8 sec
☽0N 22 13:48		9 4:18 ♄ ✶	♎ 9 5:52	8 10:29 ♂ ☌	♏ 8 16:56	19 9:04 ☽ 26♒59	SVP 05♓27'40"
	♀ ♐ 3 13:00	10 8:46 ♅ ✶	♏ 11 6:31	10 15:53 ☿ ☌	♐ 10 17:13	27 12:42 ○ 5♊13	Obliquity 23°26'35"
☽0S 7 1:35	☿ ♏ 4 19:23	13 5:09 ♄ ☌	♐ 13 5:52	12 14:50 ♂ ✶	♑ 12 16:59		⚷ Chiron 13♊43.5R
☿ D 8 11:23	☿ ♐ 12 11:05	14 8:18 ♅ ☌	♑ 15 5:53	14 18:13 ♂ □	♒ 14 18:15	5 9:01 ☽ 13♍10	☽ Mean ☊ 9♉03.0
♄⚺♆ 10 14:07	♂ ♏ 14 18:59	16 22:58 ☉ ✶	♒ 17 8:25	16 12:55 ☉ ✶	♓ 16 22:50	12 0:54 ● 19♐56	
☽0N 19 19:58	☉ ♑ 21 22:08	19 9:04 ☉ □	♓ 19 14:42	19 1:58 ☉ □	♈ 19 7:37	19 1:58 ☽ 27♓06	1 DECEMBER 1985
	♀ ♑ 27 9:17	21 23:58 ☉ △	♈ 22 0:42	21 19:27 ☉ △	♉ 21 19:41	27 7:30 ○ 5♋29	Julian Day # 31381
		23 11:07 ♅ △	♉ 24 13:07	23 5:09 ♃ □	♊ 24 8:45		Delta T 54.8 sec
		26 7:43 ♀ ☍	♊ 27 2:08	26 19:17 ♀ ☍	♋ 26 20:44		SVP 05♓27'34"
		28 18:36 ♂ △	♋ 29 14:23	27 12:03 ♂ △	♌ 29 6:44		Obliquity 23°26'35"
				30 22:50 ☿ △	♍ 31 14:43		⚷ Chiron 12♊08.6R
							☽ Mean ☊ 7♉27.7

LONGITUDE — JANUARY 1986

Day	Sid.Time	☉	0 hr ☽	Noon ☽	True ☊	☿	♀	♂	♃	♄	♅	♆	♇
1 W	6 41 24	10♑15 58	5♍ 4 23	11♍40 55	6♉48.5	22♐52.8	5♑48.3	10♏34.2	18♒15.3	5♐ 9.6	19♐30.0	3♑35.2	6♏54.7
2 Th	6 45 21	11 17 7	18 20 39	25 3 44	6R43.6	24 19.5	7 3.8	11 10.9	18 28.1	5 15.9	19 33.5	3 37.5	6 56.1
3 F	6 49 17	12 18 16	1♎50 17	8♎40 29	6D41.2	25 46.8	8 19.3	11 47.5	18 41.0	5 22.1	19 37.0	3 39.7	6 57.4
4 Sa	6 53 14	13 19 25	15 34 27	22 32 18	6 40.7	27 14.8	9 34.8	12 24.1	18 53.9	5 28.2	19 40.4	3 42.0	6 58.6
5 Su	6 57 10	14 20 35	29 34 4	6♏39 44	6R41.1	28 43.3	10 50.3	13 0.7	19 7.0	5 34.3	19 43.8	3 44.2	6 59.9
6 M	7 1 7	15 21 45	13♏49 12	21 2 15	6 41.0	0♑12.3	12 5.8	13 37.2	19 20.1	5 40.4	19 47.2	3 46.4	7 1.1
7 Tu	7 5 3	16 22 55	28 18 29	5♐37 27	6 39.3	1 41.8	13 21.3	14 13.8	19 33.2	5 46.4	19 50.6	3 48.7	7 2.3
8 W	7 9 0	17 24 5	12♐58 30	20 20 52	6 35.0	3 11.9	14 36.8	14 50.3	19 46.4	5 52.4	19 54.0	3 50.9	7 3.4
9 Th	7 12 57	18 25 16	27 43 40	5♑ 5 56	6 27.7	4 42.4	15 52.3	15 26.7	19 59.7	5 58.3	19 57.3	3 53.1	7 4.6
10 F	7 16 53	19 26 26	12♑26 39	19 44 48	6 17.8	6 13.4	17 7.8	16 3.2	20 13.0	6 4.1	20 0.7	3 55.3	7 5.6
11 Sa	7 20 50	20 27 36	26 59 24	4♒ 9 34	6 6.2	7 44.9	18 23.3	16 39.5	20 26.4	6 9.9	20 4.0	3 57.5	7 6.7
12 Su	7 24 46	21 28 46	11♒14 32	18 13 40	5 54.1	9 16.8	19 38.8	17 15.9	20 39.9	6 15.7	20 7.2	3 59.7	7 7.7
13 M	7 28 43	22 29 56	25 6 31	1♓52 49	5 42.8	10 49.2	20 54.3	17 52.2	20 53.3	6 21.4	20 10.5	4 1.9	7 8.7
14 Tu	7 32 39	23 31 4	8♓32 27	15 5 30	5 33.5	12 22.1	22 9.7	18 28.5	21 6.9	6 27.0	20 13.7	4 4.1	7 9.6
15 W	7 36 36	24 32 12	21 32 11	27 52 49	5 26.8	13 55.4	23 25.2	19 4.7	21 20.5	6 32.5	20 16.9	4 6.3	7 10.6
16 Th	7 40 32	25 33 20	4♈ 7 52	10♈17 53	5 22.8	15 29.3	24 40.7	19 41.0	21 34.1	6 38.0	20 20.1	4 8.4	7 11.4
17 F	7 44 29	26 34 26	16 23 28	22 25 17	5D21.0	17 3.6	25 56.1	20 17.1	21 47.8	6 43.5	20 23.2	4 10.6	7 12.3
18 Sa	7 48 26	27 35 32	28 24 0	4♉20 21	5R20.7	18 38.4	27 11.6	20 53.3	22 1.5	6 48.9	20 26.3	4 12.7	7 13.1
19 Su	7 52 22	28 36 37	10♉15 2	16 8 46	5 20.7	20 13.8	28 27.0	21 29.4	22 15.3	6 54.2	20 29.4	4 14.8	7 13.8
20 M	7 56 19	29 37 41	22 2 12	27 56 1	5 19.8	21 49.7	29 42.4	22 5.4	22 29.1	6 59.4	20 32.5	4 16.9	7 14.6
21 Tu	8 0 15	0♒38 45	3♊50 49	9♊47 12	5 17.0	23 26.2	0♒57.8	22 41.4	22 43.0	7 4.6	20 35.5	4 19.0	7 15.3
22 W	8 4 12	1 39 47	15 45 39	21 46 39	5 11.5	25 3.2	2 13.3	23 17.4	22 56.8	7 9.7	20 38.5	4 21.1	7 15.9
23 Th	8 8 8	2 40 49	27 50 35	3♋57 46	5 3.2	26 40.7	3 28.7	23 53.3	23 10.8	7 14.8	20 41.5	4 23.1	7 16.6
24 F	8 12 5	3 41 50	10♋ 8 28	16 22 49	4 52.1	28 18.9	4 44.1	24 29.2	23 24.7	7 19.8	20 44.4	4 25.2	7 17.2
25 Sa	8 16 1	4 42 50	22 40 56	29 2 49	4 39.0	29 57.7	5 59.4	25 5.1	23 38.7	7 24.7	20 47.3	4 27.2	7 17.7
26 Su	8 19 58	5 43 49	5♌28 25	11♌57 37	4 25.0	1♒37.1	7 14.8	25 40.9	23 52.8	7 29.5	20 50.2	4 29.3	7 18.3
27 M	8 23 55	6 44 47	18 30 15	25 6 7	4 11.3	3 17.2	8 30.2	26 16.7	24 6.8	7 34.3	20 53.0	4 31.3	7 18.7
28 Tu	8 27 51	7 45 44	1♍44 59	8♍26 38	3 59.1	4 57.8	9 45.5	26 52.4	24 20.9	7 39.0	20 55.8	4 33.2	7 19.2
29 W	8 31 48	8 46 41	15 10 49	21 57 21	3 49.5	6 39.2	11 0.9	27 28.1	24 35.0	7 43.6	20 58.6	4 35.2	7 19.6
30 Th	8 35 44	9 47 36	28 46 3	5♎36 45	3 42.9	8 21.2	12 16.2	28 3.8	24 49.2	7 48.1	21 1.3	4 37.2	7 20.0
31 F	8 39 41	10 48 31	12♎29 22	19 23 50	3 39.4	10 3.9	13 31.6	28 39.4	25 3.3	7 52.6	21 4.0	4 39.1	7 20.3

LONGITUDE — FEBRUARY 1986

Day	Sid.Time	☉	0 hr ☽	Noon ☽	True ☊	☿	♀	♂	♃	♄	♅	♆	♇
1 Sa	8 43 37	11♒49 25	26♎20 6	3♏18 10	3♉38.1	11♒47.3	14♒46.9	29♏15.0	25♒17.5	7♐57.0	21♐ 6.6	4♑41.0	7♏20.6
2 Su	8 47 34	12 50 19	10♏17 59	17 19 34	3R38.0	13 31.4	16 2.2	29 50.5	25 31.8	8 1.3	21 9.3	4 42.9	7 20.9
3 M	8 51 30	13 51 12	24 22 52	1♐27 45	3 37.8	15 16.2	17 17.5	0♐25.9	25 46.0	8 5.5	21 11.8	4 44.8	7 21.1
4 Tu	8 55 27	14 52 4	8♐34 6	15 41 40	3 36.0	17 1.6	18 32.8	1 1.3	26 0.3	8 9.7	21 14.4	4 46.6	7 21.3
5 W	8 59 24	15 52 55	22 50 8	29 59 5	3 31.7	18 47.7	19 48.1	1 36.7	26 14.6	8 13.8	21 16.9	4 48.5	7 21.5
6 Th	9 3 20	16 53 46	7♑ 8 2	14♑16 25	3 24.6	20 34.4	21 3.4	2 12.0	26 28.9	8 17.8	21 19.3	4 50.3	7 21.6
7 F	9 7 17	17 54 35	21 23 35	28 28 52	3 14.8	22 21.7	22 18.7	2 47.3	26 43.2	8 21.7	21 21.8	4 52.1	7 21.7
8 Sa	9 11 13	18 55 24	5♒31 36	12♒31 6	3 3.1	24 9.5	23 33.9	3 22.5	26 57.6	8 25.5	21 24.2	4 53.8	7R21.7
9 Su	9 15 10	19 56 11	19 26 45	26 18 2	2 50.9	25 57.8	24 49.2	3 57.6	27 11.9	8 29.2	21 26.5	4 55.6	7 21.7
10 M	9 19 6	20 56 56	3♓ 4 28	9♓45 46	2 39.2	27 46.6	26 4.4	4 32.7	27 26.3	8 32.9	21 28.8	4 57.3	7 21.7
11 Tu	9 23 3	21 57 41	16 21 41	22 52 10	2 29.4	29 35.6	27 19.6	5 7.7	27 40.7	8 36.5	21 31.0	4 59.0	7 21.7
12 W	9 26 59	22 58 23	29 17 14	5♈37 5	2 22.1	1♓24.9	28 34.9	5 42.6	27 55.0	8 40.0	21 33.3	5 0.7	7 21.6
13 Th	9 30 56	23 59 5	11♈51 58	18 2 16	2 17.6	3 14.2	29 50.0	6 17.5	28 9.4	8 43.3	21 35.4	5 2.4	7 21.4
14 F	9 34 53	24 59 44	24 8 26	0♉11 0	2D15.6	5 3.3	1♓ 5.2	6 52.3	28 23.8	8 46.6	21 37.5	5 4.0	7 21.3
15 Sa	9 38 49	26 0 22	6♉10 34	12 7 45	2 15.3	6 52.2	2 20.4	7 27.0	28 38.3	8 49.9	21 39.6	5 5.6	7 21.1
16 Su	9 42 46	27 0 59	18 3 12	23 57 37	2R15.9	8 40.5	3 35.5	8 1.7	28 52.7	8 53.0	21 41.7	5 7.2	7 20.8
17 M	9 46 42	28 1 33	29 51 41	5♊46 6	2 16.1	10 27.9	4 50.6	8 36.3	29 7.1	8 56.0	21 43.6	5 8.7	7 20.5
18 Tu	9 50 39	29 2 6	11♊41 31	17 38 38	2 15.2	12 14.2	6 5.7	9 10.9	29 21.5	8 59.0	21 45.6	5 10.3	7 20.2
19 W	9 54 35	0♓ 2 37	23 38 2	29 40 19	2 12.1	13 58.9	7 20.8	9 45.4	29 35.9	9 1.8	21 47.5	5 11.8	7 19.9
20 Th	9 58 32	1 3 7	5♋46 1	11♋55 35	2 6.8	15 41.7	8 35.9	10 19.8	29 50.3	9 4.6	21 49.3	5 13.2	7 19.5
21 F	10 2 28	2 3 34	18 9 26	24 27 50	1 59.1	17 22.1	9 50.9	10 54.1	0♓ 4.8	9 7.2	21 51.1	5 14.7	7 19.1
22 Sa	10 6 25	3 4 0	0♌51 1	7♌19 6	1 49.6	18 59.5	11 6.0	11 28.3	0 19.2	9 9.8	21 52.9	5 16.1	7 18.7
23 Su	10 10 22	4 4 24	13 52 5	20 29 52	1 39.2	20 33.5	12 21.0	12 2.5	0 33.6	9 12.3	21 54.6	5 17.5	7 18.2
24 M	10 14 18	5 4 46	27 12 16	3♍59 0	1 28.9	22 3.5	13 36.0	12 36.6	0 48.0	9 14.7	21 56.3	5 18.9	7 17.7
25 Tu	10 18 15	6 5 7	10♍49 41	17 43 55	1 19.7	23 28.7	14 50.9	13 10.7	1 2.4	9 17.0	21 57.9	5 20.2	7 17.1
26 W	10 22 11	7 5 25	24 41 12	1♎41 4	1 12.6	24 48.7	16 5.9	13 44.6	1 16.8	9 19.1	21 59.4	5 21.6	7 16.5
27 Th	10 26 8	8 5 42	8♎42 59	15 46 30	1 8.0	26 2.8	17 20.8	14 18.5	1 31.1	9 21.2	22 0.9	5 22.8	7 15.9
28 F	10 30 4	9 5 58	22 51 10	29 56 32	1D 5.8	27 10.3	18 35.7	14 52.3	1 45.5	9 23.2	22 2.4	5 24.1	7 15.3

Astro Data

	Dy Hr Mn
♃∠♆	2 21:07
☽0S	3 7:19
♃✱♅	8 18:18
☽0N	16 3:11
♄⊻♇	23 9:49
☽0S	30 11:48
♇ R	8 20:15
☽0N	12 11:26
☽0S	26 17:58
☿0N	27 17:46

Planet Ingress

	Dy Hr Mn
☿ ♑	5 20:42
☉ ♒	20 8:46
♀ ♒	20 5:36
☿ ♒	25 0:33
♂ ♐	2 6:27
☿ ♓	11 5:21
♀ ♓	13 3:11
☉ ♓	18 22:58
♃ ♓	20 16:05

Last Aspect / ☽ Ingress (January)

Last Aspect Dy Hr Mn		☽ Ingress Dy Hr Mn
2 11:59	☿ □	♎ 2 20:45
4 22:24	☿ ✱	♏ 5 0:44
6 9:19	♃ □	♐ 7 2:47
8 11:19	♅ ☌	♑ 9 3:42
10 12:22	☉ ☌	♒ 11 5:01
12 16:30	♃ ☌	♓ 13 8:39
15 6:09	☉ ✱	♈ 15 16:03
17 22:13	☉ □	♉ 18 3:14
20 0:56	♃ □	♊ 20 16:12
22 14:36	♃ △	♋ 23 4:15
25 4:46	♂ △	♌ 25 13:47
27 14:48	♂ □	♍ 27 20:51
29 22:42	♂ ✱	♎ 30 2:10

Last Aspect / ☽ Ingress (February)

Last Aspect Dy Hr Mn		☽ Ingress Dy Hr Mn
31 22:10	♃ △	♏ 1 6:19
3 2:24	♃ □	♐ 3 9:32
5 5:49	♃ ✱	♑ 5 12:02
6 0:23	♇ ✱	♒ 7 14:35
9 13:50	♃ ☌	♓ 9 18:32
11 9:31	♅ □	♈ 12 1:21
14 8:37	♃ ✱	♉ 14 11:38
16 22:27	♃ □	♊ 17 0:17
19 12:06	♃ △	♋ 19 12:39
20 22:15	☿ △	♌ 21 22:25
23 14:34	♅ △	♍ 24 4:58
26 0:14	☿ ☍	♎ 26 9:07
27 22:37	♅ ✱	♏ 28 12:06

☽ Phases & Eclipses

Dy Hr Mn	
3 19:47	☽ 13♎09
10 12:22	● 19♑58
17 22:13	☽ 27♈31
26 0:31	○ 5♌45
2 4:41	☽ 13♏02
9 0:55	● 19♒59
16 19:55	☽ 27♉51
24 15:02	○ 5♍43

Astro Data

1 JANUARY 1986
Julian Day # 31412
Delta T 54.9 sec
SVP 05♓27'28"
Obliquity 23°26'35"
⚷ Chiron 10♊25.6R
☽ Mean ☊ 5♉49.2

1 FEBRUARY 1986
Julian Day # 31443
Delta T 54.9 sec
SVP 05♓27'23"
Obliquity 23°26'36"
⚷ Chiron 9♊22.0R
☽ Mean ☊ 4♉10.7

MARCH 1986 LONGITUDE

Day	Sid.Time	☉	0 hr ☽	Noon ☽	True ☊	☿	♀	♂	♃	♄	♅	♆	♇
1 Sa	10 34 1	10♓ 6 12	7♏ 2 17	14♏ 8 5	1♉ 5.7	28♓10.7	19♓50.6	15♐26.0	1♓59.8	9♐25.1	22♐ 3.8	5♑25.3	7♏14.6
2 Su	10 37 57	11 6 25	21 13 41	28 18 51	1 6.6	29 3.4	21 5.5	15 59.6	2 14.2	9 26.9	22 5.2	5 26.5	7R13.9
3 M	10 41 54	12 6 36	5♐23 26	12♐27 15	1R 7.6	29 48.0	22 20.3	16 33.2	2 28.5	9 28.6	22 6.5	5 27.7	7 13.1
4 Tu	10 45 51	13 6 45	19 30 9	26 32 0	1 7.6	0♈24.0	23 35.1	17 6.6	2 42.8	9 30.3	22 7.8	5 28.8	7 12.4
5 W	10 49 47	14 6 54	3♑32 37	10♑31 50	1 5.8	0 51.1	24 50.0	17 40.0	2 57.1	9 31.8	22 9.0	5 30.0	7 11.6
6 Th	10 53 44	15 7 0	17 29 26	24 25 11	1 2.0	1 9.1	26 4.8	18 13.2	3 11.4	9 33.2	22 10.2	5 31.0	7 10.7
7 F	10 57 40	16 7 5	1♒18 50	8♒10 5	0 56.3	1R17.9	27 19.5	18 46.4	3 25.7	9 34.5	22 11.3	5 32.1	7 9.9
8 Sa	11 1 37	17 7 9	14 58 39	21 44 15	0 49.2	1 17.5	28 34.3	19 19.5	3 39.9	9 35.7	22 12.3	5 33.1	7 9.0
9 Su	11 5 33	18 7 10	28 26 35	5♓ 5 25	0 41.6	1 8.1	29 49.0	19 52.4	3 54.1	9 36.8	22 13.3	5 34.1	7 8.1
10 M	11 9 30	19 7 10	11♓40 30	18 11 41	0 34.4	0 50.1	1♈ 3.7	20 25.3	4 8.3	9 37.8	22 14.3	5 35.1	7 7.1
11 Tu	11 13 26	20 7 8	24 38 50	1♈ 1 54	0 28.3	0 24.0	2 18.4	20 58.0	4 22.5	9 38.7	22 15.2	5 36.0	7 6.1
12 W	11 17 23	21 7 4	7♈20 54	13 35 56	0 23.9	29♓50.4	3 33.1	21 30.6	4 36.6	9 39.5	22 16.0	5 36.9	7 5.1
13 Th	11 21 20	22 6 58	19 47 10	25 54 49	0D 21.5	29 10.2	4 47.7	22 3.1	4 50.8	9 40.2	22 16.8	5 37.7	7 4.1
14 F	11 25 16	23 6 49	1♉59 12	8♉ 0 42	0 20.9	28 24.4	6 2.3	22 35.5	5 4.8	9 40.8	22 17.6	5 38.6	7 3.0
15 Sa	11 29 13	24 6 39	13 59 43	19 56 45	0 21.7	27 34.1	7 16.9	23 7.7	5 18.9	9 41.3	22 18.3	5 39.4	7 1.9
16 Su	11 33 9	25 6 27	25 52 18	1♊46 57	0 23.4	26 40.4	8 31.5	23 39.9	5 32.9	9 41.7	22 18.9	5 40.1	7 0.8
17 M	11 37 6	26 6 12	7♊41 16	13 35 54	0 25.2	25 44.8	9 46.0	24 11.9	5 46.9	9 41.9	22 19.5	5 40.9	6 59.6
18 Tu	11 41 2	27 5 55	19 31 27	25 28 34	0R 26.4	24 48.3	11 0.5	24 43.8	6 0.9	9 42.1	22 20.0	5 41.6	6 58.5
19 W	11 44 59	28 5 36	1♋27 54	7♋30 3	0 26.6	23 52.2	12 15.0	25 15.5	6 14.8	9R 42.2	22 20.5	5 42.2	6 57.3
20 Th	11 48 55	29 5 15	13 35 37	19 45 10	0 25.5	22 57.7	13 29.4	25 47.2	6 28.7	9 42.2	22 20.9	5 42.9	6 56.1
21 F	11 52 52	0♈ 4 51	25 59 14	2♌18 16	0 23.1	22 5.7	14 43.8	26 18.7	6 42.5	9 42.1	22 21.3	5 43.5	6 54.8
22 Sa	11 56 49	1 4 25	8♌42 39	15 12 39	0 19.5	21 17.3	15 58.2	26 50.0	6 56.3	9 41.9	22 21.6	5 44.0	6 53.6
23 Su	12 0 45	2 3 57	21 48 29	28 30 13	0 15.2	20 33.0	17 12.5	27 21.3	7 10.1	9 41.6	22 21.9	5 44.6	6 52.3
24 M	12 4 42	3 3 27	5♍17 47	12♍11 2	0 10.8	19 53.7	18 26.9	27 52.3	7 23.8	9 41.2	22 22.1	5 45.1	6 51.0
25 Tu	12 8 38	4 2 54	19 9 39	26 13 12	0 6.9	19 19.6	19 41.1	28 23.3	7 37.5	9 40.7	22 22.3	5 45.5	6 49.6
26 W	12 12 35	5 2 19	3♎21 9	10♎32 51	0 3.9	18 51.1	20 55.4	28 54.1	7 51.1	9 40.0	22 22.4	5 46.0	6 48.3
27 Th	12 16 31	6 1 42	17 47 35	25 4 36	0D 2.3	18 28.5	22 9.6	29 24.7	8 4.7	9 39.3	22R 22.4	5 46.4	6 46.9
28 F	12 20 28	7 1 4	2♏23 7	9♏42 19	0 1.9	18 11.8	23 23.8	29 55.2	8 18.2	9 38.5	22 22.4	5 46.7	6 45.5
29 Sa	12 24 24	8 0 23	17 1 28	24 19 51	0 2.5	18 1.0	24 38.0	0♑25.6	8 31.7	9 37.6	22 22.4	5 47.1	6 44.1
30 Su	12 28 21	8 59 40	1♐36 49	8♐51 49	0 3.7	17D 56.1	25 52.1	0 55.7	8 45.2	9 36.6	22 22.3	5 47.4	6 42.7
31 M	12 32 17	9 58 56	16 4 22	23 14 3	0 5.1	17 56.8	27 6.2	1 25.8	8 58.6	9 35.5	22 22.2	5 47.7	6 41.2

APRIL 1986 LONGITUDE

Day	Sid.Time	☉	0 hr ☽	Noon ☽	True ☊	☿	♀	♂	♃	♄	♅	♆	♇
1 Tu	12 36 14	10♈58 11	0♑20 34	7♑23 42	0♉ 6.0	18♓ 3.2	28♈20.3	1♑55.6	9♓11.9	9♐34.3	22♐22.0	5♑47.9	6♏39.8
2 W	12 40 11	11 57 23	14 23 15	21 19 8	0R 6.3	18 14.8	29 34.3	2 25.3	9 25.2	9R 33.0	22R 21.7	5 48.1	6R 38.3
3 Th	12 44 7	12 56 34	28 11 17	4♒59 40	0 5.7	18 31.6	0♉48.4	2 54.8	9 38.5	9 31.6	22 21.4	5 48.3	6 36.8
4 F	12 48 4	13 55 42	11♒44 20	18 25 16	0 4.4	18 53.3	2 2.4	3 24.1	9 51.6	9 30.2	22 21.0	5 48.4	6 35.3
5 Sa	12 52 0	14 54 49	25 2 33	1♓36 14	0 2.5	19 19.6	3 16.3	3 53.2	10 4.8	9 28.6	22 20.6	5 48.5	6 33.7
6 Su	12 55 57	15 53 55	8♓ 6 22	14 33 3	0 0.5	19 50.4	4 30.3	4 22.1	10 17.8	9 26.9	22 20.2	5 48.6	6 32.2
7 M	12 59 53	16 52 58	20 56 20	27 16 20	29♈58.5	20 25.4	5 44.2	4 50.8	10 30.8	9 25.1	22 19.7	5R 48.6	6 30.6
8 Tu	13 3 50	17 51 59	3♈33 7	9♈46 50	29 57.0	21 4.3	6 58.0	5 19.3	10 43.8	9 23.3	22 19.1	5 48.6	6 29.0
9 W	13 7 46	18 50 58	15 57 35	22 5 32	29 56.0	21 47.1	8 11.9	5 47.6	10 56.7	9 21.3	22 18.5	5 48.6	6 27.5
10 Th	13 11 43	19 49 56	28 10 51	4♉13 44	29D 55.7	22 33.4	9 25.7	6 15.6	11 9.5	9 19.3	22 17.8	5 48.5	6 25.9
11 F	13 15 40	20 48 51	10♉14 26	16 13 12	29 55.8	23 23.1	10 39.4	6 43.5	11 22.2	9 17.2	22 17.1	5 48.4	6 24.3
12 Sa	13 19 36	21 47 44	22 10 21	28 6 12	29 56.4	24 16.0	11 53.2	7 11.1	11 34.9	9 14.9	22 16.3	5 48.3	6 22.6
13 Su	13 23 33	22 46 36	4♊ 1 8	9♊55 34	29 57.1	25 12.0	13 6.9	7 38.5	11 47.5	9 12.6	22 15.5	5 48.1	6 21.0
14 M	13 27 29	23 45 25	15 49 56	21 44 41	29 57.9	26 11.0	14 20.5	8 5.6	12 0.1	9 10.3	22 14.7	5 47.9	6 19.4
15 Tu	13 31 26	24 44 12	27 40 22	3♋37 28	29 58.5	27 12.7	15 34.2	8 32.5	12 12.5	9 7.8	22 13.8	5 47.7	6 17.7
16 W	13 35 22	25 42 56	9♋36 33	15 38 10	29 58.9	28 17.1	16 47.8	8 59.2	12 24.9	9 5.2	22 12.8	5 47.5	6 16.1
17 Th	13 39 19	26 41 39	21 42 54	27 51 19	29R 59.1	29 24.0	18 1.3	9 25.6	12 37.3	9 2.6	22 11.8	5 47.2	6 14.4
18 F	13 43 15	27 40 19	4♌ 3 57	10♌21 21	29 59.1	0♈33.4	19 14.9	9 51.7	12 49.5	8 59.9	22 10.8	5 46.8	6 12.7
19 Sa	13 47 12	28 38 57	16 44 0	23 12 21	29 59.0	1 45.2	20 28.3	10 17.6	13 1.7	8 57.1	22 9.7	5 46.5	6 11.1
20 Su	13 51 9	29 37 33	29 46 45	6♍27 30	29D 58.9	2 59.2	21 41.8	10 43.2	13 13.8	8 54.2	22 8.6	5 46.1	6 9.4
21 M	13 55 5	0♉36 6	13♍14 45	20 8 35	29 58.9	4 15.4	22 55.2	11 8.5	13 25.8	8 51.3	22 7.4	5 45.7	6 7.7
22 Tu	13 59 2	1 34 37	27 8 53	4♎15 26	29 59.0	5 33.8	24 8.5	11 33.6	13 37.7	8 48.3	22 6.1	5 45.2	6 6.0
23 W	14 2 58	2 33 7	11♎27 50	18 45 32	29 59.2	6 54.3	25 21.8	11 58.4	13 49.5	8 45.2	22 4.9	5 44.8	6 4.3
24 Th	14 6 55	3 31 34	26 7 49	3♏33 50	29R 59.3	8 16.8	26 35.1	12 22.8	14 1.3	8 42.0	22 3.6	5 44.2	6 2.6
25 F	14 10 51	4 29 59	11♏ 2 38	18 33 12	29 59.2	9 41.3	27 48.4	12 47.0	14 13.0	8 38.8	22 2.2	5 43.7	6 0.9
26 Sa	14 14 48	5 28 23	26 4 25	3♐35 13	29 58.9	11 7.7	29 1.6	13 10.9	14 24.6	8 35.5	22 0.8	5 43.1	5 59.2
27 Su	14 18 44	6 26 45	11♐ 4 31	18 31 22	29 58.4	12 36.1	0♊14.7	13 34.5	14 36.1	8 32.1	21 59.4	5 42.5	5 57.6
28 M	14 22 41	7 25 5	25 54 52	3♑14 16	29 57.6	14 6.4	1 27.9	13 57.7	14 47.5	8 28.7	21 57.9	5 41.9	5 55.9
29 Tu	14 26 38	8 23 24	10♑28 56	17 38 27	29 56.8	15 38.6	2 41.0	14 20.6	14 58.8	8 25.2	21 56.4	5 41.3	5 54.2
30 W	14 30 34	9 21 41	24 42 27	1♒40 48	29 56.1	17 12.7	3 54.0	14 43.2	15 10.0	8 21.6	21 54.8	5 40.6	5 52.5

Astro Data	Planet Ingress	Last Aspect	☽ Ingress	Last Aspect	☽ Ingress	☽ Phases & Eclipses	Astro Data
Dy Hr Mn	Dy Hr Mn	Dy Hr Mn	Dy Hr Mn	Dy Hr Mn	Dy Hr Mn	Dy Hr Mn	1 MARCH 1986
♅∠♇ 6 7:03	☿ ♈ 3 7:22	2 14:01 ☿ △	♐ 2 14:51	2 6:47 ☿ ⚹	♒ 3 3:11	3 12:17 ☽ 12♐37	Julian Day # 31471
☿ R 7 10:56	♀ ♈ 9 3:32	4 7:39 ♀ □	♑ 4 17:56	4 19:06 ♅ ⚹	♓ 5 9:03	10 14:52 ● 19♓44	Delta T 54.9 sec
☽0N 11 19:45	☿ ♓ 11 17:36	6 16:22 ♀ ⚹	♒ 6 21:42	7 2:37 ♅ □	♈ 7 17:12	18 16:39 ☽ 27♊47	SVP 05♓27'19"
♀0N 11 10:33	☉ ♈ 20 22:03	8 12:51 ♅ ⚹	♓ 9 2:48	9 12:25 ♅ △	♉ 10 3:36	26 3:02 ○ 5♎10	Obliquity 23°26'36"
♃⚹♆ 16 13:03	♂ ♑ 28 3:47	10 19:32 ♅ □	♈ 11 10:03	12 4:35 ☿ ⚹	♊ 12 15:51		⚷ Chiron 9♊21.2
☿0S 19 20:42		13 4:53 ♅ △	♉ 13 20:04	14 22:59 ☿ □	♋ 15 4:42	1 19:30 ☽ 11♑46	☽ Mean ☊ 2♉41.8
♄ R 19 9:27	♀ ♉ 2 8:19	16 1:31 ☿ ⚹	♊ 16 8:23	17 10:35 ☉ □	♌ 17 16:10	9 6:08 ● 19♈06	
♃△♇ 21 19:36	☊ ♈ 6 5:29	18 16:39 ☉ □	♋ 18 21:04	19 23:42 ☉ △	♍ 20 0:24	9 6:20:27 • P 0.824	1 APRIL 1986
☽0S 26 2:57	☿ ♈ 17 12:33	20 17:00 ☿ △	♌ 21 7:38	21 18:23 ♀ △	♎ 22 4:50	17 10:35 ☽ 27♋08	Julian Day # 31502
♅ R 27 14:17	☉ ♉ 20 9:12	23 10:21 ♂ △	♍ 23 14:39	23 17:24 ♅ ⚹	♏ 24 6:15	24 12:46 ○ 4♏03	Delta T 55.0 sec
☿ D 30 8:42	♀ ♊ 26 19:10	25 16:15 ♂ □	♎ 25 18:22	26 5:08 ♀ ☍	♐ 26 6:16	24 12:43 • T 1.202	SVP 05♓27'16"
♃□♄ 2 12:49		27 19:49 ♂ ⚹	♏ 27 20:05	27 17:35 ♅ ☌	♑ 28 6:41		Obliquity 23°26'36"
♆ R 7 12:52	☽0S 22 13:29	29 1:37 ☿ △	♐ 29 21:20	29 9:42 ☿ □	♒ 30 9:06		⚷ Chiron 10♊25.0
☽0N 8 3:01	☿0N 22 13:40	31 20:17 ♀ △	♑ 31 23:25				☽ Mean ☊ 1♉03.3

LONGITUDE — MAY 1986

Day	Sid.Time	☉	0 hr ☽	Noon ☽	True ☊	☿	♀	♂	♃	♄	♅	♆	♇
1 Th	14 34 31	10♉19 57	8♒33 25	15♒20 23	29♈55.8	18♈48.6	5♊ 7.0	15♑ 5.4	15♓21.2	8♐18.0	21♐53.2	5♑39.8	5♏50.8
2 F	14 38 27	11 18 11	22 1 51	28 38 3	29D56.0	20 26.4	6 20.0	15 27.2	15 32.2	8R14.3	21R51.6	5R39.1	5R49.1
3 Sa	14 42 24	12 16 24	5♓ 9 15	11♓35 45	29 56.7	22 6.0	7 32.9	15 48.7	15 43.2	8 10.6	21 49.9	5 38.3	5 47.4
4 Su	14 46 20	13 14 35	17 57 56	24 16 7	29 57.7	23 47.6	8 45.8	16 9.7	15 54.0	8 6.8	21 48.2	5 37.5	5 45.7
5 M	14 50 17	14 12 44	0♈30 41	6♈41 57	29 59.0	25 30.9	9 58.7	16 30.4	16 4.7	8 2.9	21 46.5	5 36.7	5 44.1
6 Tu	14 54 13	15 10 52	12 50 17	18 55 59	0♉ 0.0	27 16.1	11 11.5	16 50.7	16 15.4	7 59.0	21 44.7	5 35.8	5 42.4
7 W	14 58 10	16 8 59	24 59 22	1♉ 0 43	0R 0.7	29 3.2	12 24.3	17 10.5	16 25.9	7 55.1	21 42.9	5 34.9	5 40.7
8 Th	15 2 7	17 7 4	7♉ 0 20	12 58 27	0 0.6	0♉52.2	13 37.0	17 30.0	16 36.3	7 51.1	21 41.0	5 34.0	5 39.1
9 F	15 6 3	18 5 8	18 55 20	24 51 14	29♈59.6	2 43.0	14 49.7	17 49.0	16 46.7	7 47.1	21 39.1	5 33.1	5 37.4
10 Sa	15 10 0	19 3 10	0♊46 25	6♊41 7	29 57.7	4 35.7	16 2.4	18 7.5	16 56.9	7 43.0	21 37.2	5 32.1	5 35.8
11 Su	15 13 56	20 1 10	12 35 38	18 30 13	29 55.0	6 30.3	17 15.0	18 25.6	17 7.0	7 38.9	21 35.3	5 31.1	5 34.1
12 M	15 17 53	20 59 9	24 25 11	0♋20 52	29 51.6	8 26.7	18 27.6	18 43.3	17 17.0	7 34.7	21 33.3	5 30.1	5 32.5
13 Tu	15 21 49	21 57 6	6♋17 36	12 15 45	29 48.1	10 24.9	19 40.1	19 0.4	17 26.8	7 30.5	21 31.3	5 29.1	5 30.9
14 W	15 25 46	22 55 1	18 15 43	24 17 57	29 44.7	12 24.9	20 52.6	19 17.1	17 36.6	7 26.3	21 29.2	5 28.0	5 29.3
15 Th	15 29 42	23 52 54	0♌22 53	6♌30 59	29 42.0	14 26.7	22 5.1	19 33.3	17 46.2	7 22.1	21 27.2	5 27.0	5 27.7
16 F	15 33 39	24 50 46	12 42 45	18 58 40	29 40.3	16 30.1	23 17.4	19 49.0	17 55.8	7 17.8	21 25.1	5 25.8	5 26.1
17 Sa	15 37 36	25 48 36	25 19 14	1♍44 56	29D39.7	18 35.2	24 29.8	20 4.2	18 5.2	7 13.5	21 23.0	5 24.7	5 24.6
18 Su	15 41 32	26 46 24	8♍16 13	14 53 29	29 40.1	20 41.6	25 42.1	20 18.8	18 14.5	7 9.1	21 20.8	5 23.6	5 23.0
19 M	15 45 29	27 44 11	21 37 6	28 27 19	29 41.4	22 49.5	26 54.3	20 32.9	18 23.6	7 4.8	21 18.7	5 22.4	5 21.5
20 Tu	15 49 25	28 41 56	5♎24 16	12♎27 58	29 42.9	24 58.5	28 6.5	20 46.5	18 32.6	7 0.4	21 16.5	5 21.2	5 19.9
21 W	15 53 22	29 39 39	19 38 18	26 54 57	29R44.0	27 8.5	29 18.7	20 59.6	18 41.5	6 56.0	21 14.3	5 20.0	5 18.4
22 Th	15 57 18	0♊37 20	4♏17 24	11♏44 59	29 44.2	29 19.3	0♋30.7	21 12.0	18 50.3	6 51.6	21 12.0	5 18.7	5 16.9
23 F	16 1 15	1 35 1	19 16 49	26 51 51	29 43.1	1♊30.7	1 42.8	21 23.9	18 59.0	6 47.1	21 9.8	5 17.5	5 15.5
24 Sa	16 5 11	2 32 40	4♐28 56	12♐ 6 46	29 40.4	3 42.4	2 54.8	21 35.3	19 7.5	6 42.7	21 7.5	5 16.2	5 14.0
25 Su	16 9 8	3 30 18	19 44 3	27 19 29	29 36.4	5 54.1	4 6.7	21 46.0	19 15.9	6 38.3	21 5.2	5 14.9	5 12.6
26 M	16 13 5	4 27 54	4♑51 49	12♑19 57	29 31.6	8 5.6	5 18.6	21 56.1	19 24.1	6 33.8	21 2.9	5 13.6	5 11.1
27 Tu	16 17 1	5 25 30	19 42 55	26 59 57	29 26.7	10 16.6	6 30.4	22 5.6	19 32.3	6 29.3	21 0.6	5 12.2	5 9.7
28 W	16 20 58	6 23 4	4♒10 30	11♒14 11	29 22.4	12 26.8	7 42.2	22 14.4	19 40.2	6 24.9	20 58.2	5 10.9	5 8.3
29 Th	16 24 54	7 20 38	18 10 50	25 0 28	29 19.3	14 35.9	8 53.9	22 22.6	19 48.1	6 20.4	20 55.9	5 9.5	5 7.0
30 F	16 28 51	8 18 11	1♓43 13	8♓19 23	29D17.7	16 43.8	10 5.5	22 30.2	19 55.8	6 16.0	20 53.5	5 8.1	5 5.6
31 Sa	16 32 47	9 15 43	14 49 21	21 13 34	29 17.7	18 50.1	11 17.2	22 37.0	20 3.3	6 11.5	20 51.1	5 6.7	5 4.3

LONGITUDE — JUNE 1986

Day	Sid.Time	☉	0 hr ☽	Noon ☽	True ☊	☿	♀	♂	♃	♄	♅	♆	♇
1 Su	16 36 44	10♊13 14	27♓32 32	3♈46 48	29♈18.7	20♊54.8	12♋28.7	22♑43.2	20♓10.8	6♐ 7.0	20♐48.7	5♑ 5.3	5♏ 3.0
2 M	16 40 41	11 10 44	9♈56 55	16 3 24	29 20.2	22 57.5	13 40.2	22 48.7	20 18.0	6R 2.6	20R46.3	5R 3.9	5R 1.7
3 Tu	16 44 37	12 8 13	22 6 49	28 7 39	29R21.3	24 58.2	14 51.7	22 53.5	20 25.1	5 58.2	20 43.9	5 2.4	5 0.4
4 W	16 48 34	13 5 42	4♉ 6 23	10♉ 3 29	29 21.5	26 56.6	16 3.1	22 57.5	20 32.1	5 53.7	20 41.5	5 1.0	4 59.2
5 Th	16 52 30	14 3 10	15 59 22	21 54 23	29 19.9	28 52.8	17 14.4	23 0.8	20 38.9	5 49.3	20 39.0	4 59.5	4 58.0
6 F	16 56 27	15 0 37	27 48 53	3♊43 10	29 16.3	0♋46.7	18 25.7	23 3.4	20 45.6	5 45.0	20 36.6	4 58.0	4 56.8
7 Sa	17 0 23	15 58 4	9♊37 32	15 32 13	29 10.6	2 38.1	19 36.9	23 5.3	20 52.1	5 40.6	20 34.1	4 56.5	4 55.6
8 Su	17 4 20	16 55 29	21 27 27	27 23 28	29 3.1	4 27.0	20 48.1	23R 6.4	20 58.5	5 36.2	20 31.7	4 55.0	4 54.4
9 M	17 8 16	17 52 54	3♋20 27	9♋18 37	28 54.3	6 13.3	21 59.2	23 6.7	21 4.7	5 31.9	20 29.2	4 53.5	4 53.3
10 Tu	17 12 13	18 50 18	15 18 11	21 19 23	28 44.9	7 57.1	23 10.3	23 6.3	21 10.7	5 27.6	20 26.8	4 51.9	4 52.2
11 W	17 16 10	19 47 41	27 22 26	3♌27 37	28 35.9	9 38.4	24 21.2	23 5.2	21 16.6	5 23.4	20 24.3	4 50.4	4 51.1
12 Th	17 20 6	20 45 3	9♌35 12	15 45 32	28 28.1	11 16.9	25 32.2	23 3.3	21 22.3	5 19.1	20 21.8	4 48.9	4 50.1
13 F	17 24 3	21 42 24	21 58 57	28 15 48	28 22.2	12 52.9	26 43.0	23 0.6	21 27.8	5 14.9	20 19.4	4 47.3	4 49.1
14 Sa	17 27 59	22 39 44	4♍36 31	11♍ 1 28	28 18.4	14 26.2	27 53.8	22 57.2	21 33.2	5 10.8	20 16.9	4 45.7	4 48.1
15 Su	17 31 56	23 37 3	17 31 5	24 5 48	28D16.8	15 56.8	29 4.5	22 53.1	21 38.4	5 6.7	20 14.5	4 44.1	4 47.1
16 M	17 35 52	24 34 21	0♎45 58	7♎31 56	28 16.7	17 24.7	0♌15.1	22 48.2	21 43.5	5 2.6	20 12.0	4 42.6	4 46.2
17 Tu	17 39 49	25 31 38	14 24 0	21 22 20	28R17.5	18 49.9	1 25.7	22 42.6	21 48.3	4 58.5	20 9.5	4 41.0	4 45.3
18 W	17 43 45	26 28 54	28 27 0	5♏37 58	28 18.0	20 12.4	2 36.2	22 36.2	21 53.0	4 54.5	20 7.1	4 39.4	4 44.4
19 Th	17 47 42	27 26 10	12♏54 57	20 17 32	28 17.1	21 32.0	3 46.6	22 29.1	21 57.6	4 50.6	20 4.7	4 37.8	4 43.5
20 F	17 51 39	28 23 25	27 45 6	5♐16 49	28 14.3	22 48.8	4 56.9	22 21.4	22 1.9	4 46.7	20 2.2	4 36.2	4 42.7
21 Sa	17 55 35	29 20 39	12♐51 39	20 28 26	28 9.0	24 2.7	6 7.1	22 12.9	22 6.1	4 42.8	19 59.8	4 34.6	4 41.9
22 Su	17 59 32	0♋17 53	28 5 53	5♑42 37	28 1.5	25 13.7	7 17.3	22 3.7	22 10.1	4 39.0	19 57.4	4 33.0	4 41.1
23 M	18 3 28	1 15 7	13♑17 17	20 48 35	27 52.6	26 21.7	8 27.4	21 53.9	22 14.0	4 35.3	19 55.0	4 31.3	4 40.4
24 Tu	18 7 25	2 12 20	28 15 20	5♒36 32	27 43.4	27 26.6	9 37.3	21 43.4	22 17.6	4 31.6	19 52.6	4 29.7	4 39.7
25 W	18 11 21	3 9 32	12♒51 22	19 59 15	27 34.9	28 28.3	10 47.3	21 32.2	22 21.1	4 27.9	19 50.2	4 28.1	4 39.0
26 Th	18 15 18	4 6 45	26 59 49	3♓52 53	27 28.0	29 26.8	11 57.1	21 20.4	22 24.4	4 24.3	19 47.9	4 26.5	4 38.4
27 F	18 19 14	5 3 57	10♓38 31	17 16 55	27 23.4	0♌22.0	13 6.8	21 8.0	22 27.5	4 20.8	19 45.5	4 24.9	4 37.7
28 Sa	18 23 11	6 1 10	23 48 26	0♈13 31	27 21.0	1 13.8	14 16.5	20 55.0	22 30.4	4 17.4	19 43.2	4 23.3	4 37.2
29 Su	18 27 8	6 58 22	6♈32 43	12 46 37	27D20.4	2 2.0	15 26.0	20 41.5	22 33.1	4 13.9	19 40.9	4 21.6	4 36.6
30 M	18 31 4	7 55 35	18 55 52	25 1 7	27R20.6	2 46.6	16 35.5	20 27.4	22 35.7	4 10.6	19 38.6	4 20.0	4 36.1

Astro Data

	Dy Hr Mn
☽0N	5 8:58
♆✶♇	16 15:35
☽0S	19 23:24
♃⚼♇	31 2:35
☽0N	1 14:17
♃□♅	5 0:13
♂ R	8 23:25
♆✶♇	9 9:35
☽0S	16 7:03
♄⚺♇	21 7:17
♄⚺♆	24 21:47
☽0N	28 20:12

Planet Ingress

		Dy Hr Mn
☊	♉	5 23:00
☿	♉	7 12:33
☊	♈	8 17:08
☉	♊	21 8:28
♀	♋	21 13:46
☿	♊	22 7:26
☿	♋	5 14:06
♀	♌	15 18:52
☉	♋	21 16:30
☿	♌	26 14:15

Last Aspect / ☽ Ingress

Last Aspect Dy Hr Mn		☽ Ingress Dy Hr Mn
1 23:42	♅ ✶	♓ 2 14:30
4 7:17	♅ □	♈ 4 23:01
7 9:31	☿ ☌	♉ 7 9:59
8 22:10	☉ ☌	♊ 9 22:26
11 18:12	♅ ☍	♋ 12 11:18
14 10:04	☉ ✶	♌ 14 23:15
17 1:00	☉ □	♍ 17 8:45
19 11:33	☉ △	♎ 19 14:41
21 2:39	♅ ✶	♏ 21 17:02
23 3:24	♂ ✶	♐ 23 16:57
25 2:08	♅ ☌	♑ 25 16:15
27 3:56	♂ ☌	♒ 27 17:00
29 4:48	♅ ✶	♓ 29 20:54

Last Aspect / ☽ Ingress

Last Aspect Dy Hr Mn		☽ Ingress Dy Hr Mn
31 14:45	♂ ✶	♈ 1 4:43
3 6:49	☿ ✶	♉ 3 15:45
5 14:18	♂ △	♊ 6 4:26
7 23:01	♃ □	♋ 8 17:16
10 17:22	♀ ☌	♌ 11 5:11
12 23:26	☉ ✶	♍ 13 15:18
15 12:00	☉ □	♎ 15 22:38
17 20:26	☉ △	♏ 18 2:36
19 15:24	♂ ✶	♐ 20 3:36
21 14:38	♃ □	♑ 22 3:00
23 22:35	☿ ☍	♒ 24 2:50
25 11:43	♅ ✶	♓ 26 5:12
27 21:35	♃ ☌	♈ 28 11:35
30 2:56	♂ □	♉ 30 21:54

☽ Phases & Eclipses

Dy Hr Mn		
1 3:22	☽	10♒28
8 22:10	●	18♉01
17 1:00	☽	25♌51
23 20:45	○	2♐25
30 12:55	☽	8♓49
7 14:00	●	16♊32
15 12:00	☽	24♍06
22 3:42	○	0♑27
29 0:53	☽	7♈00

Astro Data

1 MAY 1986
Julian Day # 31532
Delta T 55.0 sec
SVP 05♓27'11"
Obliquity 23°26'36"
⚷ Chiron 12♊17.7
☽ Mean ☊ 29♈27.9

1 JUNE 1986
Julian Day # 31563
Delta T 55.1 sec
SVP 05♓27'07"
Obliquity 23°26'36"
⚷ Chiron 14♊43.9
☽ Mean ☊ 27♈49.5

JULY 1986 LONGITUDE

Day	Sid.Time	☉	0 hr ☽	Noon ☽	True ☊	☿	♀	♂	♃	♄	♅	♆	♇
1 Tu	18 35 1	8♋52 48	1♉ 3 0	7♉ 2 10	27♈20.7	3♌27.4	17♌44.9	20♑12.8	22♓38.1	4♐ 7.3	19♐36.3	4♑18.4	4♏35.6
2 W	18 38 57	9 50 1	12 59 13	18 54 45	27R19.6	4 4.3	18 54.2	19R57.7	22 40.2	4R 4.1	19R34.0	4R16.8	4R35.1
3 Th	18 42 54	10 47 14	24 49 17	0♊43 20	27 16.5	4 37.2	20 3.4	19 42.2	22 42.2	4 1.0	19 31.8	4 15.2	4 34.7
4 F	18 46 50	11 44 27	6♊37 20	12 31 41	27 10.8	5 6.0	21 12.5	19 26.3	22 44.0	3 57.9	19 29.5	4 13.6	4 34.3
5 Sa	18 50 47	12 41 40	18 26 46	24 22 52	27 2.4	5 30.5	22 21.5	19 10.0	22 45.6	3 54.9	19 27.3	4 12.0	4 33.9
6 Su	18 54 43	13 38 54	0♋20 14	6♋19 7	26 51.5	5 50.6	23 30.4	18 53.4	22 47.0	3 52.0	19 25.2	4 10.4	4 33.6
7 M	18 58 40	14 36 7	12 19 41	18 22 4	26 38.9	6 6.2	24 39.2	18 36.6	22 48.2	3 49.2	19 23.0	4 8.8	4 33.3
8 Tu	19 2 37	15 33 21	24 26 26	0♌32 52	26 25.6	6 17.3	25 47.9	18 19.5	22 49.3	3 46.4	19 20.9	4 7.2	4 33.1
9 W	19 6 33	16 30 35	6♌41 30	12 52 26	26 12.7	6R23.7	26 56.5	18 2.2	22 50.1	3 43.7	19 18.8	4 5.6	4 32.8
10 Th	19 10 30	17 27 48	19 5 48	25 21 44	26 1.3	6 25.4	28 5.0	17 44.8	22 50.7	3 41.1	19 16.7	4 4.1	4 32.6
11 F	19 14 26	18 25 2	1♍40 23	8♍ 1 58	25 52.2	6 22.3	29 13.4	17 27.3	22 51.1	3 38.6	19 14.7	4 2.5	4 32.5
12 Sa	19 18 23	19 22 16	14 26 41	20 54 48	25 45.9	6 14.5	0♍21.7	17 9.8	22R51.4	3 36.2	19 12.6	4 0.9	4 32.4
13 Su	19 22 19	20 19 29	27 26 35	4♎ 2 19	25 42.4	6 2.0	1 29.8	16 52.3	22 51.4	3 33.8	19 10.6	3 59.4	4 32.3
14 M	19 26 16	21 16 43	10♎42 18	17 26 49	25D41.0	5 45.0	2 37.8	16 34.8	22 51.3	3 31.5	19 8.7	3 57.9	4 32.2
15 Tu	19 30 12	22 13 57	24 16 8	1♏10 27	25R40.8	5 23.5	3 45.7	16 17.5	22 50.9	3 29.3	19 6.7	3 56.3	4D32.2
16 W	19 34 9	23 11 10	8♏ 9 56	15 14 37	25 40.6	4 58.0	4 53.5	16 0.3	22 50.4	3 27.2	19 4.8	3 54.8	4 32.2
17 Th	19 38 6	24 8 24	22 24 24	29 39 6	25 39.1	4 28.6	6 1.1	15 43.3	22 49.6	3 25.2	19 3.0	3 53.3	4 32.2
18 F	19 42 2	25 5 38	6♐58 18	14♐21 27	25 35.4	3 55.7	7 8.6	15 26.5	22 48.7	3 23.2	19 1.1	3 51.8	4 32.3
19 Sa	19 45 59	26 2 52	21 47 49	29 16 29	25 29.1	3 19.8	8 15.9	15 10.1	22 47.6	3 21.4	18 59.3	3 50.4	4 32.4
20 Su	19 49 55	27 0 6	6♑46 26	14♑16 29	25 20.3	2 41.5	9 23.1	14 53.9	22 46.3	3 19.6	18 57.6	3 48.9	4 32.6
21 M	19 53 52	27 57 21	21 45 28	29 12 10	25 9.8	2 1.3	10 30.2	14 38.2	22 44.8	3 18.0	18 55.8	3 47.5	4 32.7
22 Tu	19 57 48	28 54 37	6♒35 26	13♒54 14	24 58.7	1 19.9	11 37.1	14 22.8	22 43.1	3 16.4	18 54.1	3 46.0	4 33.0
23 W	20 1 45	29 51 52	21 7 40	28 15 0	24 48.4	0 38.0	12 43.8	14 7.9	22 41.2	3 14.9	18 52.5	3 44.6	4 33.2
24 Th	20 5 42	0♌49 9	5♓15 45	12♓ 9 34	24 39.8	29♋56.3	13 50.4	13 53.4	22 39.1	3 13.5	18 50.8	3 43.2	4 33.5
25 F	20 9 38	1 46 26	18 56 20	25 36 5	24 33.6	29 15.6	14 56.9	13 39.4	22 36.8	3 12.2	18 49.3	3 41.8	4 33.8
26 Sa	20 13 35	2 43 44	2♈ 9 4	8♈35 35	24 30.0	28 36.6	16 3.2	13 26.0	22 34.3	3 11.0	18 47.7	3 40.5	4 34.2
27 Su	20 17 31	3 41 2	14 56 7	21 11 11	24D28.5	28 0.0	17 9.3	13 13.1	22 31.7	3 9.9	18 46.2	3 39.1	4 34.5
28 M	20 21 28	4 38 22	27 21 24	3♉27 25	24R28.2	27 26.6	18 15.2	13 0.9	22 28.8	3 8.8	18 44.7	3 37.8	4 34.9
29 Tu	20 25 24	5 35 43	9♉29 52	15 29 27	24 28.3	26 57.0	19 21.0	12 49.3	22 25.8	3 7.9	18 43.3	3 36.4	4 35.4
30 W	20 29 21	6 33 5	21 26 49	27 22 39	24 27.4	26 31.7	20 26.6	12 38.3	22 22.6	3 7.1	18 41.9	3 35.1	4 35.9
31 Th	20 33 17	7 30 28	3♊17 33	9♊12 7	24 24.8	26 11.4	21 32.1	12 28.0	22 19.1	3 6.3	18 40.6	3 33.9	4 36.4

AUGUST 1986 LONGITUDE

Day	Sid.Time	☉	0 hr ☽	Noon ☽	True ☊	☿	♀	♂	♃	♄	♅	♆	♇
1 F	20 37 14	8♌27 52	15♊ 6 54	21♊ 2 26	24♈19.8	25♋56.3	22♍37.3	12♑18.4	22♓15.6	3♐ 5.7	18♐39.2	3♑32.6	4♏37.0
2 Sa	20 41 11	9 25 17	26 59 8	2♋57 26	24R12.1	25R47.0	23 42.4	12R 9.6	22R11.8	3R 5.1	18R38.0	3R31.4	4 37.5
3 Su	20 45 7	10 22 44	8♋57 39	15 0 6	24 2.1	25D43.7	24 47.3	12 1.5	22 7.8	3 4.7	18 36.8	3 30.1	4 38.2
4 M	20 49 4	11 20 11	21 5 0	27 12 31	23 50.4	25 46.7	25 51.9	11 54.2	22 3.7	3 4.3	18 35.6	3 28.9	4 38.8
5 Tu	20 53 0	12 17 39	3♌22 48	9♌35 54	23 37.8	25 56.1	26 56.4	11 47.7	21 59.4	3 4.0	18 34.5	3 27.8	4 39.5
6 W	20 56 57	13 15 8	15 51 52	22 10 43	23 25.7	26 12.0	28 0.7	11 41.9	21 54.9	3 3.9	18 33.4	3 26.6	4 40.2
7 Th	21 0 53	14 12 39	28 32 27	4♍57 2	23 14.9	26 34.7	29 4.8	11 37.0	21 50.3	3D 3.8	18 32.3	3 25.5	4 41.0
8 F	21 4 50	15 10 10	11♍24 27	17 54 41	23 6.4	27 3.9	0♎ 8.6	11 32.9	21 45.5	3 3.8	18 31.3	3 24.4	4 41.8
9 Sa	21 8 46	16 7 42	24 27 45	1♎ 3 40	23 0.6	27 39.9	1 12.2	11 29.7	21 40.5	3 4.0	18 30.4	3 23.3	4 42.6
10 Su	21 12 43	17 5 15	7♎42 30	14 24 17	22 57.5	28 22.4	2 15.6	11 27.3	21 35.4	3 4.2	18 29.5	3 22.2	4 43.5
11 M	21 16 40	18 2 48	21 9 9	27 57 9	22D56.5	29 11.5	3 18.7	11 25.7	21 30.1	3 4.5	18 28.6	3 21.2	4 44.3
12 Tu	21 20 36	19 0 23	4♏48 26	11♏43 4	22 56.8	0♌ 6.9	4 21.6	11D25.0	21 24.6	3 4.9	18 27.8	3 20.1	4 45.3
13 W	21 24 33	19 57 59	18 41 6	25 42 33	22R57.2	1 8.6	5 24.3	11 25.2	21 19.0	3 5.4	18 27.0	3 19.1	4 46.2
14 Th	21 28 29	20 55 35	2♐47 21	9♐55 21	22 56.7	2 16.4	6 26.6	11 26.2	21 13.3	3 6.1	18 26.3	3 18.2	4 47.2
15 F	21 32 26	21 53 13	17 6 19	24 19 53	22 54.2	3 30.0	7 28.7	11 28.0	21 7.4	3 6.8	18 25.6	3 17.2	4 48.2
16 Sa	21 36 22	22 50 51	1♑35 34	8♑52 46	22 49.6	4 49.3	8 30.5	11 30.7	21 1.4	3 7.6	18 25.0	3 16.3	4 49.3
17 Su	21 40 19	23 48 31	16 10 48	23 28 51	22 42.7	6 13.8	9 32.0	11 34.2	20 55.2	3 8.5	18 24.5	3 15.4	4 50.4
18 M	21 44 15	24 46 11	0♒46 5	8♒ 1 36	22 34.4	7 43.3	10 33.2	11 38.6	20 49.0	3 9.5	18 23.9	3 14.6	4 51.5
19 Tu	21 48 12	25 43 53	15 14 32	22 24 5	22 25.4	9 17.5	11 34.1	11 43.7	20 42.5	3 10.6	18 23.5	3 13.7	4 52.6
20 W	21 52 9	26 41 36	29 29 28	6♓30 3	22 17.0	10 55.9	12 34.7	11 49.7	20 36.0	3 11.8	18 23.0	3 12.9	4 53.8
21 Th	21 56 5	27 39 20	13♓25 19	20 14 55	22 10.1	12 38.2	13 34.9	11 56.4	20 29.3	3 13.1	18 22.7	3 12.2	4 55.0
22 F	22 0 2	28 37 6	26 58 36	3♈36 17	22 5.2	14 23.9	14 34.8	12 3.9	20 22.6	3 14.5	18 22.3	3 11.4	4 56.2
23 Sa	22 3 58	29 34 53	10♈ 8 3	16 34 4	22D 2.5	16 12.6	15 34.4	12 12.2	20 15.7	3 16.0	18 22.1	3 10.7	4 57.5
24 Su	22 7 55	0♍32 42	22 54 38	29 10 9	22 1.8	18 3.9	16 33.6	12 21.3	20 8.7	3 17.5	18 21.8	3 10.0	4 58.8
25 M	22 11 51	1 30 32	5♉21 4	11♉27 56	22 2.4	19 57.4	17 32.4	12 31.1	20 1.6	3 19.2	18 21.7	3 9.3	5 0.1
26 Tu	22 15 48	2 28 24	17 31 20	23 31 51	22 3.6	21 52.5	18 30.9	12 41.6	19 54.4	3 21.0	18 21.6	3 8.7	5 1.5
27 W	22 19 44	3 26 19	29 30 9	5♊26 52	22R 4.5	23 49.0	19 28.9	12 52.9	19 47.2	3 22.8	18D21.5	3 8.1	5 2.8
28 Th	22 23 41	4 24 14	11♊22 38	17 18 6	22 4.3	25 46.4	20 26.6	13 5.0	19 39.8	3 24.8	18 21.5	3 7.5	5 4.2
29 F	22 27 38	5 22 12	23 13 52	29 10 32	22 2.5	27 44.5	21 23.8	13 17.7	19 32.4	3 26.8	18 21.5	3 6.9	5 5.7
30 Sa	22 31 34	6 20 12	5♋ 8 38	11♋ 8 41	21 58.7	29 42.9	22 20.6	13 31.2	19 24.8	3 29.0	18 21.6	3 6.4	5 7.2
31 Su	22 35 31	7 18 13	17 11 9	23 16 25	21 53.2	1♍41.3	23 17.0	13 45.3	19 17.2	3 31.2	18 21.7	3 5.9	5 8.7

Astro Data	Planet Ingress	Last Aspect	☽ Ingress	Last Aspect	☽ Ingress	☽ Phases & Eclipses	Astro Data
Dy Hr Mn	Dy Hr Mn	Dy Hr Mn	Dy Hr Mn	Dy Hr Mn	Dy Hr Mn	Dy Hr Mn	1 JULY 1986
♅∠♇ 1 9:15	♀ ♍ 11 16:23	2 19:41 ♃ ⚹	♊ 3 10:32	1 16:43 ♀ □	♋ 2 6:04	7 4:55 ● 14♋48	Julian Day # 31593
☿ R 9 20:27	☉ ♌ 23 3:24	5 8:46 ♀ ⚹	♋ 5 23:19	4 10:17 ♀ ⚹	♌ 4 17:26	14 20:10 ☽ 22♎05	Delta T 55.1 sec
♃ R 12 17:01	☿ ♋ 23 21:51	7 20:48 ♃ △	♌ 8 10:56	6 5:07 ♅ △	♍ 7 2:44	21 10:40 ○ 28♑23	SVP 05♓27'01"
☽0S 13 12:24		10 18:54 ♀ ☌	♍ 10 20:50	9 6:09 ☿ ⚹	♎ 9 10:05	28 15:34 ☽ 5♉16	Obliquity 23°26'35"
♇ D 15 6:31	♀ ♎ 7 20:46	12 15:35 ♃ ☍	♎ 13 4:40	11 15:11 ☿ □	♏ 11 15:36		⚷ Chiron 17♊10.9
☽0N 26 3:33	☿ ♌ 11 21:09	14 20:10 ☉ □	♏ 15 9:58	13 4:29 ♃ △	♐ 13 19:17	5 18:36 ● 13♌02	☽ Mean ☊ 26♈14.2
☿ D 3 0:48	☉ ♍ 23 10:26	17 3:05 ☉ △	♐ 17 12:34	15 8:31 ☉ △	♑ 15 21:22	13 2:21 ☽ 20♏04	
♀0S 7 11:44	☿ ♍ 30 3:28	19 1:36 ♃ □	♑ 19 13:10	17 7:44 ♃ ⚹	♒ 17 22:44	19 18:54 ○ 26♒29	1 AUGUST 1986
♄ D 7 4:50		21 10:40 ☉ ☍	♒ 21 13:17	19 18:54 ☉ ☍	♓ 20 0:52	27 8:39 ☽ 3♊47	Julian Day # 31624
☽0S 9 17:02		22 20:15 ♅ ⚹	♓ 23 14:59	21 12:20 ♃ ☌	♈ 22 5:27		Delta T 55.1 sec
♂ D 12 7:46		25 17:47 ☿ △	♈ 25 20:02	23 15:23 ♅ △	♉ 24 13:36		SVP 05♓26'56"
♄⚺♆ 20 13:16		28 0:10 ☿ □	♉ 28 5:11	26 10:21 ☿ □	♊ 27 1:00		Obliquity 23°26'36"
☽0N 22 12:13		30 9:58 ☿ ⚹	♊ 30 17:19	29 10:55 ☿ ⚹	♋ 29 13:40		⚷ Chiron 19♊23.9
♃⚻♇ 25 4:17	♅ D 27 21:16						☽ Mean ☊ 24♈35.7

LONGITUDE SEPTEMBER 1986

Day	Sid.Time	☉	0 hr ☽	Noon ☽	True ☊	☿	♀	♂	♃	♄	♅	♆	♇
1 M	22 39 27	8♍16 17	29♋24 51	5♌36 43	21♈46.3	3♍39.6	24♎12.9	14♑ 0.2	19♓ 9.6	3♐33.5	18♐21.9	3♑ 5.5	5♏10.2
2 Tu	22 43 24	9 14 22	11♌52 14	18 11 32	21R38.8	5 37.5	25 8.3	14 15.7	19R 1.9	3 35.9	18 22.1	3R 5.0	5 11.7
3 W	22 47 20	10 12 28	24 34 42	1♍ 1 44	21 31.3	7 34.8	26 3.2	14 31.9	18 54.1	3 38.4	18 22.4	3 4.6	5 13.3
4 Th	22 51 17	11 10 37	7♍32 35	14 7 9	21 24.8	9 31.4	26 57.6	14 48.7	18 46.3	3 41.0	18 22.8	3 4.3	5 14.9
5 F	22 55 13	12 8 47	20 45 16	27 26 46	21 19.8	11 27.3	27 51.5	15 6.2	18 38.4	3 43.7	18 23.1	3 3.9	5 16.5
6 Sa	22 59 10	13 6 59	4♎11 25	10♎59 1	21 16.7	13 22.2	28 44.9	15 24.3	18 30.5	3 46.5	18 23.6	3 3.6	5 18.2
7 Su	23 3 7	14 5 12	17 49 20	24 42 8	21D15.4	15 16.2	29 37.6	15 43.0	18 22.6	3 49.4	18 24.1	3 3.4	5 19.9
8 M	23 7 3	15 3 27	1♏37 12	8♏34 21	21 15.8	17 9.1	0♏29.8	16 2.4	18 14.7	3 52.3	18 24.6	3 3.1	5 21.6
9 Tu	23 11 0	16 1 44	15 33 23	22 34 6	21 17.0	19 1.0	1 21.4	16 22.3	18 6.7	3 55.3	18 25.2	3 2.9	5 23.3
10 W	23 14 56	17 0 2	29 36 21	6♐39 56	21 18.4	20 51.8	2 12.3	16 42.9	17 58.8	3 58.5	18 25.9	3 2.7	5 25.1
11 Th	23 18 53	17 58 22	13♐44 40	20 50 21	21R19.3	22 41.5	3 2.5	17 4.0	17 50.8	4 1.7	18 26.6	3 2.6	5 26.9
12 F	23 22 49	18 56 43	27 56 45	5♑ 3 34	21 19.1	24 30.1	3 52.0	17 25.6	17 42.8	4 5.0	18 27.3	3 2.5	5 28.7
13 Sa	23 26 46	19 55 6	12♑10 30	19 17 13	21 17.4	26 17.6	4 40.8	17 47.8	17 34.9	4 8.4	18 28.1	3 2.4	5 30.5
14 Su	23 30 42	20 53 30	26 23 17	3♒28 17	21 14.5	28 4.0	5 28.9	18 10.6	17 26.9	4 11.8	18 29.0	3D 2.4	5 32.4
15 M	23 34 39	21 51 56	10♒31 46	17 33 15	21 10.5	29 49.2	6 16.1	18 33.8	17 19.0	4 15.4	18 29.9	3 2.4	5 34.3
16 Tu	23 38 36	22 50 24	24 32 14	1♓28 18	21 6.2	1♎33.4	7 2.6	18 57.6	17 11.1	4 19.0	18 30.9	3 2.4	5 36.1
17 W	23 42 32	23 48 53	8♓20 59	15 9 55	21 2.2	3 16.5	7 48.2	19 21.8	17 3.2	4 22.7	18 31.9	3 2.4	5 38.1
18 Th	23 46 29	24 47 24	21 54 46	28 35 17	20 58.9	4 58.5	8 32.9	19 46.5	16 55.4	4 26.5	18 32.9	3 2.5	5 40.0
19 F	23 50 25	25 45 57	5♈11 16	11♈42 39	20 56.8	6 39.5	9 16.6	20 11.7	16 47.6	4 30.4	18 34.0	3 2.6	5 42.0
20 Sa	23 54 22	26 44 31	18 9 24	24 31 37	20D55.9	8 19.5	9 59.5	20 37.3	16 39.9	4 34.3	18 35.2	3 2.8	5 43.9
21 Su	23 58 18	27 43 8	0♉49 26	7♉ 3 6	20 56.2	9 58.4	10 41.3	21 3.4	16 32.2	4 38.4	18 36.4	3 3.0	5 46.0
22 M	0 2 15	28 41 47	13 12 55	19 19 15	20 57.3	11 36.4	11 22.1	21 29.9	16 24.6	4 42.5	18 37.6	3 3.2	5 48.0
23 Tu	0 6 11	29 40 29	25 22 32	1♊23 15	20 58.9	13 13.3	12 1.8	21 56.8	16 17.0	4 46.7	18 38.9	3 3.4	5 50.0
24 W	0 10 8	0♎39 12	7♊21 53	13 19 1	21 0.5	14 49.4	12 40.5	22 24.1	16 9.5	4 50.9	18 40.3	3 3.7	5 52.1
25 Th	0 14 4	1 37 58	19 15 12	25 11 1	21 1.7	16 24.4	13 17.9	22 51.9	16 2.1	4 55.3	18 41.7	3 4.0	5 54.2
26 F	0 18 1	2 36 46	1♋ 7 6	7♋ 4 1	21R 2.2	17 58.6	13 54.2	23 20.0	15 54.8	4 59.7	18 43.1	3 4.4	5 56.3
27 Sa	0 21 58	3 35 36	13 2 23	19 2 46	21 1.9	19 31.8	14 29.3	23 48.6	15 47.5	5 4.1	18 44.6	3 4.8	5 58.4
28 Su	0 25 54	4 34 28	25 5 44	1♌11 47	21 0.9	21 4.1	15 3.0	24 17.5	15 40.4	5 8.7	18 46.2	3 5.2	6 0.5
29 M	0 29 51	5 33 23	7♌21 26	13 35 5	20 59.2	22 35.5	15 35.4	24 46.8	15 33.3	5 13.3	18 47.8	3 5.7	6 2.7
30 Tu	0 33 47	6 32 20	19 53 8	26 15 51	20 57.2	24 6.0	16 6.4	25 16.4	15 26.4	5 18.0	18 49.4	3 6.1	6 4.8

LONGITUDE OCTOBER 1986

Day	Sid.Time	☉	0 hr ☽	Noon ☽	True ☊	☿	♀	♂	♃	♄	♅	♆	♇
1 W	0 37 44	7♎31 19	2♍43 28	9♍16 8	20♈55.2	25♎35.6	16♏36.0	25♑46.4	15♓19.5	5♐22.8	18♐51.1	3♑ 6.7	6♏ 7.0
2 Th	0 41 40	8 30 20	15 53 52	22 36 37	20R53.5	27 4.2	17 4.0	26 16.8	15R12.8	5 27.6	18 52.8	3 7.2	6 9.2
3 F	0 45 37	9 29 23	29 24 15	6♎16 30	20 52.2	28 32.0	17 30.5	26 47.5	15 6.2	5 32.5	18 54.6	3 7.8	6 11.4
4 Sa	0 49 33	10 28 28	13♎13 2	20 13 27	20D51.6	29 58.9	17 55.4	27 18.6	14 59.7	5 37.5	18 56.4	3 8.4	6 13.7
5 Su	0 53 30	11 27 36	27 17 15	4♏23 55	20 51.6	1♏24.8	18 18.5	27 49.9	14 53.4	5 42.5	18 58.3	3 9.0	6 15.9
6 M	0 57 27	12 26 45	11♏32 52	18 43 32	20 52.0	2 49.8	18 39.9	28 21.6	14 47.1	5 47.6	19 0.2	3 9.7	6 18.2
7 Tu	1 1 23	13 25 56	25 55 18	3♐ 7 36	20 52.6	4 13.7	18 59.6	28 53.7	14 41.1	5 52.8	19 2.2	3 10.4	6 20.4
8 W	1 5 20	14 25 10	10♐19 53	17 31 39	20 53.3	5 36.7	19 17.3	29 26.0	14 35.1	5 58.1	19 4.2	3 11.2	6 22.7
9 Th	1 9 16	15 24 25	24 42 25	1♑51 47	20 53.8	6 58.7	19 33.1	29 58.6	14 29.3	6 3.3	19 6.2	3 12.0	6 25.0
10 F	1 13 13	16 23 42	8♑59 24	16 4 55	20R54.0	8 19.5	19 46.8	0♒31.5	14 23.7	6 8.7	19 8.3	3 12.8	6 27.3
11 Sa	1 17 9	17 23 0	23 8 7	0♒ 8 45	20 54.0	9 39.3	19 58.5	1 4.7	14 18.2	6 14.1	19 10.5	3 13.6	6 29.6
12 Su	1 21 6	18 22 20	7♒ 6 39	14 1 41	20 53.9	10 57.8	20 8.0	1 38.2	14 12.9	6 19.6	19 12.7	3 14.5	6 32.0
13 M	1 25 2	19 21 42	20 53 42	27 42 37	20 53.7	12 15.1	20 15.4	2 11.9	14 7.7	6 25.1	19 14.9	3 15.4	6 34.3
14 Tu	1 28 59	20 21 6	4♓28 20	11♓10 48	20D53.6	13 31.0	20 20.5	2 45.9	14 2.7	6 30.7	19 17.1	3 16.3	6 36.6
15 W	1 32 56	21 20 31	17 49 56	24 25 42	20 53.6	14 45.5	20R23.3	3 20.1	13 57.9	6 36.4	19 19.4	3 17.3	6 39.0
16 Th	1 36 52	22 19 58	0♈58 5	7♈27 2	20 53.7	15 58.4	20 23.7	3 54.6	13 53.2	6 42.1	19 21.8	3 18.3	6 41.4
17 F	1 40 49	23 19 28	13 52 34	20 14 43	20R53.8	17 9.7	20 21.8	4 29.2	13 48.7	6 47.8	19 24.2	3 19.3	6 43.7
18 Sa	1 44 45	24 18 59	26 33 32	2♉49 4	20 53.8	18 19.2	20 17.4	5 4.2	13 44.4	6 53.6	19 26.6	3 20.4	6 46.1
19 Su	1 48 42	25 18 32	9♉ 1 28	15 10 51	20 53.6	19 26.8	20 10.7	5 39.3	13 40.3	6 59.5	19 29.1	3 21.4	6 48.5
20 M	1 52 38	26 18 7	21 17 26	27 21 25	20 53.1	20 32.2	20 1.5	6 14.7	13 36.3	7 5.4	19 31.6	3 22.6	6 50.9
21 Tu	1 56 35	27 17 45	3♊23 5	9♊22 45	20 52.3	21 35.3	19 49.9	6 50.2	13 32.6	7 11.4	19 34.1	3 23.7	6 53.3
22 W	2 0 31	28 17 24	15 20 46	21 17 32	20 51.3	22 35.8	19 35.9	7 26.0	13 29.0	7 17.4	19 36.7	3 24.9	6 55.7
23 Th	2 4 28	29 17 6	27 13 29	3♋ 9 4	20 50.3	23 33.5	19 19.6	8 2.0	13 25.6	7 23.4	19 39.3	3 26.1	6 58.1
24 F	2 8 25	0♏16 50	9♋ 4 48	15 1 13	20 49.3	24 28.0	19 0.9	8 38.2	13 22.4	7 29.6	19 41.9	3 27.3	7 0.5
25 Sa	2 12 21	1 16 37	20 58 52	26 58 18	20D48.6	25 19.1	18 39.9	9 14.5	13 19.4	7 35.7	19 44.6	3 28.6	7 2.9
26 Su	2 16 18	2 16 25	3♌ 0 7	9♌ 4 54	20 48.4	26 6.4	18 16.9	9 51.1	13 16.5	7 41.9	19 47.3	3 29.9	7 5.4
27 M	2 20 14	3 16 16	15 13 13	21 25 37	20 48.7	26 49.4	17 51.7	10 27.8	13 13.9	7 48.2	19 50.1	3 31.2	7 7.8
28 Tu	2 24 11	4 16 9	27 42 39	4♍ 4 46	20 49.5	27 27.7	17 24.6	11 4.7	13 11.5	7 54.4	19 52.9	3 32.5	7 10.2
29 W	2 28 7	5 16 4	10♍32 25	17 5 56	20 50.7	28 0.8	16 55.7	11 41.8	13 9.2	8 0.8	19 55.7	3 33.9	7 12.6
30 Th	2 32 4	6 16 1	23 45 35	0♎31 30	20 51.9	28 28.1	16 25.1	12 19.1	13 7.2	8 7.1	19 58.6	3 35.3	7 15.1
31 F	2 36 0	7 16 0	7♎23 44	14 22 7	20R52.9	28 49.1	15 53.0	12 56.5	13 5.4	8 13.6	20 1.5	3 36.7	7 17.5

Astro Data	Planet Ingress	Last Aspect	☽ Ingress	Last Aspect	☽ Ingress	☽ Phases & Eclipses	Astro Data
Dy Hr Mn	Dy Hr Mn	Dy Hr Mn	Dy Hr Mn	Dy Hr Mn	Dy Hr Mn	Dy Hr Mn	1 SEPTEMBER 1986
☽0S 5 23:00	♀ ♏ 7 10:15	31 13:01 ♀ □	♌ 1 1:08	2 19:13 ♂ △	♎ 3 1:03	4 7:10 ● 11♍28	Julian Day # 31655
♃□♅ 6 19:51	☿ ♎ 15 2:28	3 2:58 ♀ ⚹	♍ 3 10:06	5 0:57 ♂ □	♏ 5 4:35	11 7:41 ☽ 18♐17	Delta T 55.2 sec
♆ D 14 19:39	☉ ♎ 23 7:59	4 20:14 ♃ ☍	♎ 5 16:33	7 5:09 ♂ ⚹	♐ 7 6:48	18 5:34 ○ 25♓01	SVP 05♓26'51"
☿0S 16 6:46		7 1:01 ♅ ⚹	♏ 7 21:12	8 14:37 ♅ ☌	♑ 9 8:52	26 3:17 ☽ 2♋45	Obliquity 23°26'36"
☽0N 18 21:07	☿ ♏ 4 0:19	9 6:50 ☿ ⚹	♐ 10 0:40	10 18:33 ♀ ⚹	♒ 11 11:45		⚷ Chiron 20♊54.2
	♂ ♒ 9 1:01	11 17:21 ☿ □	♑ 12 3:28	12 22:52 ♀ □	♓ 13 16:03	3 18:55 ● 10♎16	☽ Mean ☊ 22♈57.2
☽0S 3 7:22	☉ ♏ 23 17:14	14 3:15 ☿ △	♒ 14 6:07	15 4:39 ♀ △	♈ 15 22:13	3 19:05:19 ✔ AT 0'00"	
♄⊻♇ 15 18:53		15 13:38 ♅ ⚹	♓ 16 9:27	17 19:22 ☉ ☍	♉ 18 6:35	10 13:28 ☽ 16♑57	1 OCTOBER 1986
♀ R 15 16:33		18 5:34 ☉ ☍	♈ 18 14:33	19 22:22 ☿ ☍	♊ 20 17:15	17 19:22 ○ 24♈07	Julian Day # 31685
☽0N 16 4:55		20 4:47 ♂ □	♉ 20 22:25	23 4:33 ☉ △	♋ 23 5:37	17 19:18 ☍T 1.246	Delta T 55.2 sec
☽0S 30 17:25		22 16:56 ♂ △	♊ 23 9:13	25 9:19 ☿ △	♌ 25 18:02	25 22:26 ☽ 2♌12	SVP 05♓26'48"
		24 22:52 ♅ ☍	♋ 25 21:44	27 23:30 ☿ □	♍ 28 4:20		Obliquity 23°26'37"
		27 22:21 ♂ ☍	♌ 28 9:39	30 8:37 ☿ ⚹	♎ 30 11:05		⚷ Chiron 21♊22.5R
		30 9:00 ☿ ⚹	♍ 30 18:57				☽ Mean ☊ 21♈21.9

NOVEMBER 1986 LONGITUDE

Day	Sid.Time	☉	0 hr ☽	Noon ☽	True ☊	☿	♀	♂	♃	♄	♅	♆	♇
1 Sa	2 39 57	8♏16 1	21♎26 25	28♎36 13	20♈53.3	29♏ 3.0	15♏19.7	13♒34.1	13♓ 3.8	8♐20.0	20♐ 4.4	3♑38.2	7♏19.9
2 Su	2 43 54	9 16 4	5♏50 55	13♏ 9 49	20R 52.8	29R 9.4	14R 45.3	14 11.9	13R 2.3	8 26.5	20 7.3	3 39.7	7 22.4
3 M	2 47 50	10 16 10	20 32 4	27 56 45	20 51.3	29 7.5	14 10.0	14 49.8	13 1.1	8 33.0	20 10.3	3 41.2	7 24.8
4 Tu	2 51 47	11 16 17	5♐22 50	12♐49 20	20 48.9	28 56.9	13 34.1	15 27.9	13 0.1	8 39.6	20 13.4	3 42.7	7 27.2
5 W	2 55 43	12 16 26	20 15 12	27 39 30	20 46.0	28 36.9	12 57.8	16 6.1	12 59.3	8 46.2	20 16.4	3 44.3	7 29.6
6 Th	2 59 40	13 16 36	5♑ 1 21	12♑19 58	20 43.1	28 7.2	12 21.3	16 44.5	12 58.7	8 52.8	20 19.5	3 45.9	7 32.1
7 F	3 3 36	14 16 48	19 34 44	26 45 10	20 40.6	27 27.8	11 44.9	17 23.0	12 58.3	8 59.5	20 22.6	3 47.5	7 34.5
8 Sa	3 7 33	15 17 2	3♒50 55	10♒51 46	20D 39.0	26 38.7	11 8.9	18 1.6	12D 58.1	9 6.2	20 25.7	3 49.1	7 36.9
9 Su	3 11 29	16 17 17	17 47 36	24 38 28	20 38.6	25 40.6	10 33.4	18 40.4	12 58.1	9 12.9	20 28.9	3 50.8	7 39.3
10 M	3 15 26	17 17 33	1♓24 27	8♓ 5 44	20 39.3	24 34.3	9 58.7	19 19.3	12 58.4	9 19.7	20 32.1	3 52.5	7 41.7
11 Tu	3 19 23	18 17 51	14 42 31	21 15 4	20 40.7	23 21.5	9 25.1	19 58.3	12 58.8	9 26.4	20 35.3	3 54.2	7 44.1
12 W	3 23 19	19 18 10	27 43 40	4♈ 8 34	20 42.4	22 3.9	8 52.7	20 37.5	12 59.4	9 33.3	20 38.5	3 55.9	7 46.5
13 Th	3 27 16	20 18 30	10♈30 3	16 48 23	20R 43.7	20 43.8	8 21.8	21 16.7	13 0.3	9 40.1	20 41.7	3 57.6	7 48.9
14 F	3 31 12	21 18 52	23 3 48	29 16 32	20 44.1	19 23.8	7 52.6	21 56.1	13 1.3	9 46.9	20 45.0	3 59.4	7 51.3
15 Sa	3 35 9	22 19 16	5♉26 48	11♉34 46	20 43.1	18 6.6	7 25.2	22 35.5	13 2.6	9 53.8	20 48.3	4 1.2	7 53.7
16 Su	3 39 5	23 19 41	17 40 38	23 44 34	20 40.3	16 54.6	6 59.7	23 15.1	13 4.0	10 0.7	20 51.7	4 3.0	7 56.1
17 M	3 43 2	24 20 8	29 46 44	5♊47 18	20 35.9	15 50.2	6 36.4	23 54.7	13 5.7	10 7.6	20 55.0	4 4.8	7 58.4
18 Tu	3 46 58	25 20 36	11♊46 26	17 44 21	20 30.0	14 55.0	6 15.3	24 34.5	13 7.6	10 14.6	20 58.4	4 6.7	8 0.8
19 W	3 50 55	26 21 6	23 41 16	29 37 25	20 23.2	14 10.4	5 56.5	25 14.3	13 9.6	10 21.6	21 1.8	4 8.6	8 3.1
20 Th	3 54 52	27 21 38	5♋33 5	11♋28 35	20 16.1	13 37.2	5 40.1	25 54.3	13 11.9	10 28.5	21 5.2	4 10.5	8 5.4
21 F	3 58 48	28 22 12	17 24 15	23 20 29	20 9.5	13 15.8	5 26.1	26 34.3	13 14.3	10 35.5	21 8.6	4 12.4	8 7.8
22 Sa	4 2 45	29 22 47	29 17 43	5♌16 24	20 4.0	13D 5.9	5 14.6	27 14.4	13 17.0	10 42.5	21 12.0	4 14.3	8 10.1
23 Su	4 6 41	0♐23 23	11♌17 3	17 20 12	20 0.1	13 7.2	5 5.6	27 54.6	13 19.9	10 49.6	21 15.5	4 16.3	8 12.4
24 M	4 10 38	1 24 2	23 26 25	29 36 16	19D 58.0	13 19.1	4 59.2	28 34.9	13 22.9	10 56.6	21 19.0	4 18.2	8 14.7
25 Tu	4 14 34	2 24 42	5♍50 22	12♍ 9 16	19 57.7	13 40.7	4 55.2	29 15.2	13 26.2	11 3.7	21 22.5	4 20.2	8 16.9
26 W	4 18 31	3 25 23	18 33 33	25 3 45	19 58.6	14 11.1	4D 53.7	29 55.6	13 29.6	11 10.7	21 26.0	4 22.2	8 19.2
27 Th	4 22 27	4 26 7	1♎40 20	8♎23 40	20 0.0	14 49.6	4 54.6	0♓36.1	13 33.3	11 17.8	21 29.5	4 24.2	8 21.4
28 F	4 26 24	5 26 52	15 14 4	22 11 38	20R 1.1	15 35.1	4 57.9	1 16.7	13 37.1	11 24.9	21 33.0	4 26.3	8 23.7
29 Sa	4 30 21	6 27 38	29 16 23	6♏28 4	20 0.8	16 26.9	5 3.7	1 57.4	13 41.1	11 32.0	21 36.6	4 28.3	8 25.9
30 Su	4 34 17	7 28 26	13♏46 19	21 10 27	19 58.5	17 24.2	5 11.7	2 38.1	13 45.3	11 39.1	21 40.1	4 30.4	8 28.1

DECEMBER 1986 LONGITUDE

Day	Sid.Time	☉	0 hr ☽	Noon ☽	True ☊	☿	♀	♂	♃	♄	♅	♆	♇
1 M	4 38 14	8♐29 15	28♏39 40	6♐12 53	19♈54.0	18♏26.4	5♏22.0	3♓18.9	13♓49.7	11♐46.2	21♐43.7	4♑32.4	8♏30.3
2 Tu	4 42 10	9 30 6	13♐48 55	21 26 26	19R 47.4	19 32.6	5 34.5	3 59.7	13 54.3	11 53.3	21 47.3	4 34.5	8 32.4
3 W	4 46 7	10 30 58	29 4 3	6♑40 22	19 39.5	20 42.5	5 49.1	4 40.7	13 59.1	12 0.4	21 50.9	4 36.7	8 34.6
4 Th	4 50 3	11 31 51	14♑14 5	21 44 0	19 31.2	21 55.5	6 5.9	5 21.7	14 4.1	12 7.6	21 54.5	4 38.8	8 36.7
5 F	4 54 0	12 32 45	29 9 7	6♒28 35	19 23.8	23 11.1	6 24.6	6 2.7	14 9.2	12 14.7	21 58.1	4 40.9	8 38.9
6 Sa	4 57 57	13 33 39	13♒41 49	20 48 26	19 18.0	24 29.1	6 45.3	6 43.8	14 14.5	12 21.8	22 1.7	4 43.0	8 41.0
7 Su	5 1 53	14 34 34	27 48 16	4♓41 18	19 14.5	25 49.0	7 7.8	7 25.0	14 20.0	12 28.9	22 5.4	4 45.2	8 43.0
8 M	5 5 50	15 35 30	11♓27 41	18 7 44	19D 13.1	27 10.6	7 32.2	8 6.2	14 25.7	12 36.0	22 9.0	4 47.4	8 45.1
9 Tu	5 9 46	16 36 27	24 41 49	1♈10 23	19 13.2	28 33.7	7 58.4	8 47.4	14 31.6	12 43.1	22 12.6	4 49.5	8 47.1
10 W	5 13 43	17 37 24	7♈33 55	13 52 56	19R 14.1	29 58.0	8 26.2	9 28.7	14 37.6	12 50.2	22 16.3	4 51.7	8 49.1
11 Th	5 17 39	18 38 22	20 7 56	26 19 26	19 14.6	1♐23.4	8 55.7	10 10.0	14 43.8	12 57.3	22 19.9	4 53.9	8 51.1
12 F	5 21 36	19 39 20	2♉27 54	8♉33 46	19 13.6	2 49.7	9 26.8	10 51.4	14 50.2	13 4.4	22 23.5	4 56.1	8 53.1
13 Sa	5 25 32	20 40 20	14 37 27	20 39 18	19 10.3	4 16.9	9 59.4	11 32.8	14 56.7	13 11.5	22 27.2	4 58.3	8 55.1
14 Su	5 29 29	21 41 19	26 39 40	2♊38 48	19 4.2	5 44.7	10 33.5	12 14.3	15 3.5	13 18.6	22 30.8	5 0.5	8 57.0
15 M	5 33 26	22 42 20	8♊36 57	14 34 21	18 55.4	7 13.1	11 9.1	12 55.8	15 10.3	13 25.6	22 34.5	5 2.8	8 58.9
16 Tu	5 37 22	23 43 21	20 31 12	26 27 38	18 44.2	8 42.1	11 46.0	13 37.3	15 17.4	13 32.7	22 38.1	5 5.0	9 0.8
17 W	5 41 19	24 44 23	2♋23 50	8♋19 58	18 31.3	10 11.5	12 24.2	14 18.8	15 24.6	13 39.7	22 41.8	5 7.2	9 2.7
18 Th	5 45 15	25 45 26	14 16 11	20 12 41	18 17.8	11 41.3	13 3.7	15 0.4	15 31.9	13 46.7	22 45.4	5 9.5	9 4.5
19 F	5 49 12	26 46 29	26 9 40	2♌ 7 21	18 4.8	13 11.5	13 44.4	15 42.0	15 39.4	13 53.7	22 49.1	5 11.7	9 6.3
20 Sa	5 53 8	27 47 33	8♌ 6 1	14 5 59	17 53.4	14 42.1	14 26.2	16 23.6	15 47.1	14 0.7	22 52.7	5 14.0	9 8.1
21 Su	5 57 5	28 48 38	20 7 37	26 11 17	17 44.5	16 13.0	15 9.2	17 5.3	15 54.9	14 7.7	22 56.4	5 16.3	9 9.9
22 M	6 1 1	29 49 44	2♍17 26	8♍26 34	17 38.3	17 44.2	15 53.3	17 47.0	16 2.9	14 14.7	23 0.0	5 18.5	9 11.6
23 Tu	6 4 58	0♑50 50	14 39 11	20 55 51	17 35.0	19 15.6	16 38.5	18 28.7	16 11.0	14 21.6	23 3.6	5 20.8	9 13.3
24 W	6 8 55	1 51 57	27 17 6	3♎43 31	17D 33.8	20 47.3	17 24.6	19 10.4	16 19.3	14 28.5	23 7.3	5 23.0	9 15.0
25 Th	6 12 51	2 53 4	10♎15 39	16 53 59	17R 33.8	22 19.3	18 11.7	19 52.1	16 27.7	14 35.4	23 10.9	5 25.3	9 16.7
26 F	6 16 48	3 54 12	23 38 59	0♏30 59	17 33.8	23 51.6	18 59.7	20 33.9	16 36.3	14 42.3	23 14.5	5 27.6	9 18.3
27 Sa	6 20 44	4 55 21	7♏30 13	14 36 44	17 32.5	25 24.1	19 48.6	21 15.7	16 45.0	14 49.1	23 18.1	5 29.9	9 19.9
28 Su	6 24 41	5 56 31	21 50 25	29 10 53	17 28.8	26 56.9	20 38.4	21 57.5	16 53.8	14 55.9	23 21.7	5 32.1	9 21.5
29 M	6 28 37	6 57 41	6♐37 35	14♐ 9 39	17 22.3	28 29.9	21 28.9	22 39.3	17 2.8	15 2.7	23 25.3	5 34.4	9 23.0
30 Tu	6 32 34	7 58 51	21 46 2	29 25 28	17 13.1	0♑ 3.3	22 20.3	23 21.2	17 11.9	15 9.5	23 28.8	5 36.7	9 24.6
31 W	6 36 30	9 0 2	7♑ 6 30	14♑47 38	17 2.0	1 36.9	23 12.3	24 3.1	17 21.2	15 16.2	23 32.4	5 39.0	9 26.1

Astro Data	Planet Ingress	Last Aspect	☽ Ingress	Last Aspect	☽ Ingress	☽ Phases & Eclipses	Astro Data
Dy Hr Mn	Dy Hr Mn	Dy Hr Mn	Dy Hr Mn	Dy Hr Mn	Dy Hr Mn	Dy Hr Mn	1 NOVEMBER 1986
☿ R 2 6:47	☉ ♐ 22 14:44	31 21:41 ♅ ⚹	♏ 1 14:19	30 6:20 ☿ ☌	♐ 1 2:08	2 6:02 ● 9♏31	Julian Day # 31716
♃ D 8 9:28	♂ ♓ 26 2:35	3 13:46 ☿ ☌	♐ 3 15:19	2 12:36 ♅ ☌	♑ 3 1:28	8 21:11 ☽ 16♒10	Delta T 55.2 sec
☽0N 12 10:55		5 0:02 ♅ ☌	♑ 5 15:48	4 13:26 ☿ ⚹	♒ 5 1:23	16 12:12 ○ 23♉50	SVP 05♓26'44"
☿ D 22 9:03	☿ ♐ 10 0:34	7 12:31 ☿ ⚹	♒ 7 17:28	6 20:12 ☿ □	♓ 7 3:48	24 16:50 ☽ 2♍07	Obliquity 23°26'36"
♀ D 26 2:46	☉ ♑ 22 4:02	9 12:49 ☿ □	♓ 9 21:30	9 8:00 ☿ △	♈ 9 9:49		⚷ Chiron 20♊43.3R
☽0S 27 3:07	☿ ♑ 29 23:09	11 14:28 ☿ △	♈ 12 4:14	11 4:16 ♅ △	♉ 11 19:10	1 16:43 ● 9♐12	☽ Mean ☊ 19♈43.4
		13 21:42 ♂ ⚹	♉ 14 13:24	13 0:39 ♃ ⚹	♊ 14 6:41	8 8:02 ☽ 15♓56	
☽0N 9 15:53		16 12:12 ☉ ☍	♊ 17 0:26	16 7:04 ☉ ☍	♋ 16 19:09	16 7:04 ○ 24♊01	1 DECEMBER 1986
☽0S 24 10:33		19 3:19 ♂ △	♋ 19 12:46	18 2:35 ♃ △	♌ 19 7:44	24 9:17 ☽ 2♎16	Julian Day # 31746
		22 0:11 ☉ △	♌ 22 1:25	21 18:44 ☉ △	♍ 21 19:30	31 3:10 ● 9♑08	Delta T 55.3 sec
		24 10:36 ♂ ☍	♍ 24 12:46	23 16:07 ♅ □	♎ 24 5:05		SVP 05♓26'39"
		26 5:21 ♅ □	♎ 26 20:59	26 0:25 ☿ ⚹	♏ 26 11:06		Obliquity 23°26'36"
		28 10:57 ♅ ⚹	♏ 29 1:13	28 0:12 ♂ △	♐ 28 13:20		⚷ Chiron 19♊12.5R
				30 2:42 ♅ ☌	♑ 30 12:54		☽ Mean ☊ 18♈08.1

LONGITUDE — JANUARY 1987

Day	Sid.Time	☉	0 hr ☽	Noon ☽	True ☊	☿	♀	♂	♃	♄	♅	♆	♇
1 Th	6 40 27	10♑ 1 13	22♑27 21	0♒ 4 10	16♈50.2	3♑10.8	24♏ 5.2	24♓44.9	17♓30.6	15♐22.9	23♐36.0	5♑41.2	9♏27.5
2 F	6 44 24	11 2 24	7♒36 44	15 3 55	16R 39.2	4 45.1	24 58.6	25 26.8	17 40.1	15 29.6	23 39.5	5 43.5	9 28.9
3 Sa	6 48 20	12 3 35	22 24 47	29 38 39	16 30.1	6 19.6	25 52.8	26 8.8	17 49.8	15 36.3	23 43.0	5 45.8	9 30.3
4 Su	6 52 17	13 4 45	6♓45 5	13♓43 55	16 23.7	7 54.5	26 47.6	26 50.7	17 59.5	15 42.9	23 46.5	5 48.0	9 31.7
5 M	6 56 13	14 5 56	20 35 8	27 18 56	16 20.1	9 29.7	27 43.0	27 32.6	18 9.5	15 49.4	23 50.0	5 50.3	9 33.0
6 Tu	7 0 10	15 7 6	3♈55 42	10♈25 51	16 18.8	11 5.3	28 38.9	28 14.5	18 19.5	15 56.0	23 53.5	5 52.5	9 34.3
7 W	7 4 6	16 8 15	16 49 58	23 8 36	16 18.6	12 41.3	29 35.5	28 56.5	18 29.6	16 2.5	23 56.9	5 54.8	9 35.6
8 Th	7 8 3	17 9 24	29 22 24	5♉32 1	16 18.3	14 17.7	0♐32.6	29 38.4	18 39.9	16 8.9	24 0.4	5 57.0	9 36.9
9 F	7 12 0	18 10 33	11♉38 2	17 41 4	16 16.8	15 54.4	1 30.2	0♈20.4	18 50.3	16 15.3	24 3.8	5 59.3	9 38.1
10 Sa	7 15 56	19 11 41	23 41 42	29 40 27	16 12.9	17 31.6	2 28.3	1 2.3	19 0.8	16 21.7	24 7.2	6 1.5	9 39.2
11 Su	7 19 53	20 12 49	5♊37 49	11♊34 13	16 6.1	19 9.3	3 27.0	1 44.3	19 11.4	16 28.0	24 10.6	6 3.7	9 40.4
12 M	7 23 49	21 13 57	17 30 2	23 25 38	15 56.3	20 47.3	4 26.1	2 26.2	19 22.2	16 34.3	24 13.9	6 5.9	9 41.5
13 Tu	7 27 46	22 15 4	29 21 16	5♋17 12	15 43.8	22 25.9	5 25.6	3 8.2	19 33.0	16 40.6	24 17.3	6 8.1	9 42.6
14 W	7 31 42	23 16 10	11♋13 39	17 10 47	15 29.5	24 4.9	6 25.6	3 50.1	19 43.9	16 46.8	24 20.6	6 10.3	9 43.6
15 Th	7 35 39	24 17 16	23 8 45	29 7 42	15 14.5	25 44.4	7 26.1	4 32.1	19 55.0	16 52.9	24 23.9	6 12.5	9 44.6
16 F	7 39 35	25 18 22	5♌ 7 45	11♌ 9 2	15 0.0	27 24.4	8 26.9	5 14.0	20 6.1	16 59.0	24 27.2	6 14.7	9 45.6
17 Sa	7 43 32	26 19 27	17 11 42	23 15 54	14 47.2	29 4.8	9 28.2	5 55.9	20 17.4	17 5.1	24 30.4	6 16.9	9 46.5
18 Su	7 47 29	27 20 32	29 21 51	5♍29 45	14 36.9	0♒45.8	10 29.8	6 37.8	20 28.8	17 11.1	24 33.6	6 19.0	9 47.4
19 M	7 51 25	28 21 36	11♍39 53	17 52 33	14 29.7	2 27.2	11 31.8	7 19.7	20 40.2	17 17.1	24 36.8	6 21.2	9 48.3
20 Tu	7 55 22	29 22 40	24 8 5	0♎26 53	14 25.5	4 9.1	12 34.2	8 1.6	20 51.8	17 23.0	24 40.0	6 23.3	9 49.2
21 W	7 59 18	0♒23 44	6♎49 20	13 15 53	14D 23.8	5 51.4	13 36.9	8 43.5	21 3.4	17 28.8	24 43.2	6 25.4	9 50.0
22 Th	8 3 15	1 24 47	19 46 58	26 23 3	14R 23.7	7 34.2	14 39.9	9 25.4	21 15.2	17 34.6	24 46.3	6 27.5	9 50.7
23 F	8 7 11	2 25 50	3♏ 4 32	9♏51 46	14 23.9	9 17.4	15 43.3	10 7.3	21 27.0	17 40.4	24 49.4	6 29.6	9 51.5
24 Sa	8 11 8	3 26 52	16 45 4	23 44 35	14 23.2	11 0.9	16 47.0	10 49.2	21 38.9	17 46.1	24 52.4	6 31.7	9 52.1
25 Su	8 15 4	4 27 54	0♐50 23	8♐ 2 21	14 20.6	12 44.7	17 51.0	11 31.0	21 51.0	17 51.7	24 55.5	6 33.8	9 52.8
26 M	8 19 1	5 28 56	15 20 10	22 43 19	14 15.4	14 28.6	18 55.3	12 12.9	22 3.1	17 57.3	24 58.5	6 35.9	9 53.4
27 Tu	8 22 58	6 29 57	0♑11 5	7♑42 33	14 7.6	16 12.8	19 59.8	12 54.7	22 15.3	18 2.8	25 1.4	6 37.9	9 54.0
28 W	8 26 54	7 30 57	15 16 34	22 51 55	13 57.9	17 56.9	21 4.6	13 36.6	22 27.5	18 8.2	25 4.4	6 39.9	9 54.6
29 Th	8 30 51	8 31 57	0♒27 14	8♒ 1 10	13 47.5	19 40.8	22 9.7	14 18.4	22 39.9	18 13.6	25 7.3	6 41.9	9 55.1
30 F	8 34 47	9 32 56	15 32 23	22 59 39	13 37.5	21 24.5	23 15.0	15 0.3	22 52.3	18 19.0	25 10.2	6 43.9	9 55.6
31 Sa	8 38 44	10 33 53	0♓21 53	7♓38 13	13 29.2	23 7.6	24 20.6	15 42.1	23 4.9	18 24.2	25 13.0	6 45.9	9 56.0

LONGITUDE — FEBRUARY 1987

Day	Sid.Time	☉	0 hr ☽	Noon ☽	True ☊	☿	♀	♂	♃	♄	♅	♆	♇
1 Su	8 42 40	11♒34 50	14♓47 58	21♓50 41	13♈23.3	24♒50.0	25♐26.3	16♈23.9	23♓17.5	18♐29.4	25♐15.8	6♑47.9	9♏56.4
2 M	8 46 37	12 35 45	28 46 8	5♈34 16	13R 20.0	26 31.4	26 32.3	17 5.7	23 30.1	18 34.6	25 18.6	6 49.8	9 56.8
3 Tu	8 50 33	13 36 39	12♈15 15	18 49 21	13D 19.0	28 11.5	27 38.5	17 47.4	23 42.9	18 39.6	25 21.3	6 51.7	9 57.1
4 W	8 54 30	14 37 32	25 16 58	1♉38 38	13 19.5	29 49.8	28 44.9	18 29.2	23 55.7	18 44.6	25 24.0	6 53.6	9 57.4
5 Th	8 58 27	15 38 23	7♉54 53	14 6 21	13R 20.3	1♓26.0	29 51.5	19 10.9	24 8.6	18 49.5	25 26.7	6 55.5	9 57.7
6 F	9 2 23	16 39 13	20 13 40	26 17 29	13 20.5	2 59.6	0♑58.3	19 52.7	24 21.5	18 54.4	25 29.3	6 57.4	9 57.9
7 Sa	9 6 20	17 40 1	2♊18 25	8♊17 7	13 19.1	4 30.0	2 5.3	20 34.4	24 34.6	18 59.2	25 31.9	6 59.2	9 58.1
8 Su	9 10 16	18 40 48	14 14 11	20 10 9	13 15.6	5 56.7	3 12.5	21 16.1	24 47.7	19 3.9	25 34.4	7 1.0	9 58.2
9 M	9 14 13	19 41 34	26 5 34	2♋ 0 54	13 9.7	7 19.1	4 19.8	21 57.7	25 0.8	19 8.5	25 37.0	7 2.8	9 58.4
10 Tu	9 18 9	20 42 18	7♋56 34	13 52 59	13 1.7	8 36.4	5 27.3	22 39.4	25 14.0	19 13.1	25 39.4	7 4.6	9 58.4
11 W	9 22 6	21 43 1	19 50 27	25 49 17	12 52.3	9 47.9	6 35.0	23 21.0	25 27.3	19 17.6	25 41.9	7 6.4	9R 58.5
12 Th	9 26 2	22 43 42	1♌49 41	7♌51 54	12 42.1	10 52.9	7 42.8	24 2.6	25 40.6	19 22.0	25 44.3	7 8.1	9 58.5
13 F	9 29 59	23 44 21	13 56 3	20 2 17	12 32.3	11 50.7	8 50.8	24 44.2	25 54.0	19 26.3	25 46.6	7 9.8	9 58.5
14 Sa	9 33 56	24 44 59	26 10 43	2♍21 25	12 23.6	12 40.5	9 59.0	25 25.7	26 7.4	19 30.6	25 48.9	7 11.5	9 58.4
15 Su	9 37 52	25 45 36	8♍34 31	14 50 3	12 16.8	13 21.6	11 7.2	26 7.3	26 20.9	19 34.8	25 51.2	7 13.2	9 58.3
16 M	9 41 49	26 46 11	21 8 8	27 28 53	12 12.3	13 53.5	12 15.7	26 48.8	26 34.5	19 38.9	25 53.4	7 14.8	9 58.2
17 Tu	9 45 45	27 46 45	3♎52 25	10♎18 52	12D 10.1	14 15.7	13 24.3	27 30.3	26 48.1	19 42.9	25 55.6	7 16.4	9 58.0
18 W	9 49 42	28 47 18	16 48 25	23 21 16	12 9.8	14R 27.8	14 33.0	28 11.7	27 1.7	19 46.8	25 57.7	7 18.0	9 57.8
19 Th	9 53 38	29 47 49	29 57 35	6♏37 36	12 10.9	14 29.6	15 41.8	28 53.2	27 15.4	19 50.7	25 59.8	7 19.6	9 57.5
20 F	9 57 35	0♓48 19	13♏21 31	20 9 30	12 12.3	14 21.0	16 50.8	29 34.6	27 29.2	19 54.5	26 1.9	7 21.1	9 57.3
21 Sa	10 1 31	1 48 48	27 1 43	3♐58 16	12R 13.3	14 2.4	17 59.9	0♉16.0	27 43.0	19 58.2	26 3.9	7 22.6	9 56.9
22 Su	10 5 28	2 49 15	10♐59 8	18 4 17	12 13.1	13 34.2	19 9.2	0 57.4	27 56.8	20 1.8	26 5.8	7 24.1	9 56.6
23 M	10 9 25	3 49 42	25 13 31	2♑26 31	12 11.3	12 57.2	20 18.5	1 38.7	28 10.7	20 5.3	26 7.8	7 25.6	9 56.2
24 Tu	10 13 21	4 50 7	9♑42 51	17 1 57	12 7.8	12 12.1	21 27.9	2 20.1	28 24.6	20 8.7	26 9.6	7 27.1	9 55.8
25 W	10 17 18	5 50 31	24 23 6	1♒45 29	12 2.9	11 20.4	22 37.5	3 1.4	28 38.6	20 12.1	26 11.5	7 28.5	9 55.4
26 Th	10 21 14	6 50 53	9♒ 8 12	16 30 18	11 57.4	10 23.2	23 47.2	3 42.7	28 52.6	20 15.3	26 13.2	7 29.9	9 54.9
27 F	10 25 11	7 51 13	23 50 47	1♓ 8 44	11 52.1	9 22.1	24 56.9	4 23.9	29 6.6	20 18.5	26 15.0	7 31.2	9 54.4
28 Sa	10 29 7	8 51 32	8♓23 15	15 33 30	11 47.7	8 18.8	26 6.8	5 5.2	29 20.7	20 21.6	26 16.7	7 32.5	9 53.8

Astro Data

	Dy Hr Mn
☽0N	5 21:49
♂0N	9 11:07
☽0S	20 15:44
♅∠♇	23 21:12
☽0N	2 6:08
♃⚼♇	8 19:31
♇ R	11 16:55
♃□♅	12 7:56
☽0S	16 20:39
☿ R	18 16:07

Planet Ingress

		Dy Hr Mn
♀	♐	7 10:20
♂	♈	8 12:20
☿	♒	17 13:08
☉	♒	20 14:40
☿	♓	4 2:31
♀	♑	5 3:03
☉	♓	19 4:50
♂	♉	20 14:44

Last Aspect / ☽ Ingress

Last Aspect Dy Hr Mn			☽ Ingress	Dy Hr Mn
1 3:47	♂	⚹	♒	1 11:53
3 6:07	♀	□	♓	3 12:36
5 13:41	♀	△	♈	5 16:51
7 13:36	♅	△	♉	8 1:13
9 14:30	♃	⚹	♊	10 12:39
12 13:42	♅	☍	♋	13 1:18
15 6:03	☿	☍	♌	15 13:45
17 14:31	♅	△	♍	18 1:15
20 10:51	☉	△	♎	20 11:09
22 9:07	♅	⚹	♏	22 18:30
24 8:33	♃	△	♐	24 22:35
26 15:41	♅	☌	♑	26 23:42
28 11:31	♃	⚹	♒	28 23:17
30 15:35	♅	⚹	♓	30 23:24

Last Aspect / ☽ Ingress

Last Aspect Dy Hr Mn			☽ Ingress	Dy Hr Mn
1 19:47	♀	□	♈	2 2:09
4 7:08	♀	△	♉	4 8:53
6 8:19	♃	⚹	♊	6 19:23
8 23:02	♅	☍	♋	9 7:55
11 11:29	♃	△	♌	11 20:21
13 23:17	♅	△	♍	14 7:26
16 10:29	♃	☍	♎	16 16:44
18 23:41	☉	△	♏	19 0:04
21 1:13	♃	△	♐	21 5:09
23 5:00	♃	□	♑	23 7:57
25 7:03	♃	⚹	♒	25 9:08
27 3:57	♅	⚹	♓	27 10:07

☽ Phases & Eclipses

Dy Hr Mn		
6 22:34	☽	16♈05
15 2:30	○	24♋24
22 22:45	☽	2♏23
29 13:45	●	9♒07
5 16:21	☽	16♉20
13 20:58	○	24♌37
21 8:56	☽	2♐11
28 0:51	●	8♓54

Astro Data

1 JANUARY 1987
Julian Day # 31777
Delta T 55.3 sec
SVP 05♓26'33"
Obliquity 23°26'36"
⚷ Chiron 17♊22.6R
☽ Mean ☊ 16♈29.6

1 FEBRUARY 1987
Julian Day # 31808
Delta T 55.4 sec
SVP 05♓26'27"
Obliquity 23°26'36"
⚷ Chiron 16♊05.0R
☽ Mean ☊ 14♈51.1

MARCH 1987 LONGITUDE

Day	Sid.Time	☉	0 hr ☽	Noon ☽	True ☊	☿	♀	♂	♃	♄	♅	♆	♇
1 Su	10 33 4	9♓51 49	22♓38 51	29♓38 44	11♈44.7	7♓14.7	27♑16.7	5♉46.4	29♓34.8	20♐24.6	26♐18.3	7♑33.8	9♏53.2
2 M	10 37 0	10 52 4	6♈32 47	13♈20 45	11D43.3	6R11.5	28 26.7	6 27.6	29 49.0	20 27.5	26 19.9	7 35.1	9R52.6
3 Tu	10 40 57	11 52 17	20 2 34	26 38 16	11 43.5	5 10.4	29 36.9	7 8.8	0♈ 3.1	20 30.3	26 21.4	7 36.3	9 51.9
4 W	10 44 54	12 52 29	3♉ 8 1	9♉32 8	11 44.7	4 12.8	0♒47.0	7 49.9	0 17.3	20 33.0	26 22.9	7 37.6	9 51.3
5 Th	10 48 50	13 52 38	15 50 59	22 5 1	11 46.4	3 19.7	1 57.3	8 31.1	0 31.6	20 35.6	26 24.3	7 38.7	9 50.5
6 F	10 52 47	14 52 45	28 14 44	4♊20 42	11 48.0	2 32.0	3 7.7	9 12.2	0 45.8	20 38.1	26 25.7	7 39.9	9 49.8
7 Sa	10 56 43	15 52 50	10♊23 30	16 23 44	11R49.0	1 50.1	4 18.1	9 53.2	1 0.1	20 40.6	26 27.0	7 41.0	9 49.0
8 Su	11 0 40	16 52 53	22 22 0	28 18 55	11 49.0	1 14.7	5 28.6	10 34.3	1 14.4	20 42.9	26 28.3	7 42.1	9 48.2
9 M	11 4 36	17 52 54	4♋15 3	10♋11 0	11 47.8	0 45.9	6 39.1	11 15.3	1 28.8	20 45.2	26 29.6	7 43.2	9 47.4
10 Tu	11 8 33	18 52 53	16 7 18	22 4 28	11 45.6	0 23.7	7 49.7	11 56.3	1 43.1	20 47.3	26 30.7	7 44.2	9 46.5
11 W	11 12 29	19 52 50	28 2 58	4♌ 3 16	11 42.6	0 8.3	9 0.4	12 37.3	1 57.5	20 49.4	26 31.9	7 45.2	9 45.6
12 Th	11 16 26	20 52 44	10♌ 5 44	16 10 43	11 39.2	29♒59.5	10 11.2	13 18.2	2 11.9	20 51.3	26 33.0	7 46.2	9 44.7
13 F	11 20 23	21 52 37	22 18 30	28 29 20	11 35.8	29D57.0	11 22.0	13 59.1	2 26.3	20 53.2	26 34.0	7 47.1	9 43.7
14 Sa	11 24 19	22 52 27	4♍43 24	11♍ 0 50	11 32.9	0♓ 0.8	12 32.9	14 40.0	2 40.7	20 54.9	26 35.0	7 48.0	9 42.7
15 Su	11 28 16	23 52 15	17 21 45	23 46 9	11 30.8	0 10.3	13 43.9	15 20.8	2 55.2	20 56.6	26 35.9	7 48.9	9 41.7
16 M	11 32 12	24 52 1	0♎14 5	6♎45 29	11D29.5	0 25.5	14 54.9	16 1.6	3 9.6	20 58.2	26 36.8	7 49.7	9 40.7
17 Tu	11 36 9	25 51 45	13 20 18	19 58 28	11 29.2	0 46.0	16 5.9	16 42.4	3 24.1	20 59.6	26 37.6	7 50.5	9 39.6
18 W	11 40 5	26 51 28	26 39 51	3♏24 22	11 29.7	1 11.4	17 17.1	17 23.1	3 38.6	21 1.0	26 38.4	7 51.3	9 38.5
19 Th	11 44 2	27 51 8	10♏11 52	17 2 14	11 30.6	1 41.6	18 28.3	18 3.9	3 53.0	21 2.3	26 39.1	7 52.1	9 37.4
20 F	11 47 58	28 50 47	23 55 19	0♐50 58	11 31.7	2 16.1	19 39.5	18 44.6	4 7.5	21 3.5	26 39.8	7 52.8	9 36.2
21 Sa	11 51 55	29 50 24	7♐49 3	14 49 22	11 32.7	2 54.8	20 50.8	19 25.2	4 22.1	21 4.5	26 40.4	7 53.5	9 35.1
22 Su	11 55 52	0♈49 59	21 51 45	28 56 0	11R33.3	3 37.4	22 2.1	20 5.9	4 36.6	21 5.5	26 40.9	7 54.1	9 33.9
23 M	11 59 48	1 49 33	6♑ 1 52	13♑ 9 4	11 33.4	4 23.6	23 13.5	20 46.5	4 51.1	21 6.4	26 41.5	7 54.7	9 32.7
24 Tu	12 3 45	2 49 5	20 17 17	27 26 11	11 33.0	5 13.3	24 25.0	21 27.1	5 5.6	21 7.2	26 41.9	7 55.3	9 31.4
25 W	12 7 41	3 48 35	4♒35 22	11♒44 22	11 32.3	6 6.2	25 36.5	22 7.7	5 20.2	21 7.9	26 42.3	7 55.9	9 30.2
26 Th	12 11 38	4 48 4	18 52 45	26 0 1	11 31.5	7 2.1	26 48.0	22 48.2	5 34.7	21 8.4	26 42.7	7 56.4	9 28.9
27 F	12 15 34	5 47 30	3♓ 5 38	10♓ 9 7	11 30.8	8 0.9	27 59.6	23 28.7	5 49.2	21 8.9	26 43.0	7 56.9	9 27.6
28 Sa	12 19 31	6 46 55	17 9 57	24 7 39	11 30.3	9 2.4	29 11.2	24 9.2	6 3.7	21 9.3	26 43.2	7 57.3	9 26.2
29 Su	12 23 27	7 46 17	1♈ 1 48	7♈52 2	11D30.0	10 6.5	0♓22.9	24 49.7	6 18.3	21 9.5	26 43.4	7 57.8	9 24.9
30 M	12 27 24	8 45 38	14 38 1	21 19 31	11 29.9	11 13.0	1 34.6	25 30.1	6 32.8	21 9.7	26 43.6	7 58.1	9 23.5
31 Tu	12 31 21	9 44 57	27 56 24	4♉28 33	11 30.0	12 21.9	2 46.3	26 10.5	6 47.3	21R 9.8	26 43.6	7 58.5	9 22.1

APRIL 1987 LONGITUDE

Day	Sid.Time	☉	0 hr ☽	Noon ☽	True ☊	☿	♀	♂	♃	♄	♅	♆	♇
1 W	12 35 17	10♈44 13	10♉56 1	17♉18 53	11♈30.1	13♓33.0	3♓58.1	26♉50.9	7♈ 1.8	21♐ 9.8	26♐43.7	7♑58.8	9♏20.7
2 Th	12 39 14	11 43 27	23 37 19	29 51 34	11R30.1	14 46.2	5 9.9	27 31.2	7 16.3	21R 9.6	26R43.7	7 59.1	9R19.2
3 F	12 43 10	12 42 39	6♊ 1 57	12♊ 8 52	11 30.0	16 1.4	6 21.7	28 11.6	7 30.8	21 9.4	26 43.6	7 59.3	9 17.8
4 Sa	12 47 7	13 41 49	18 12 44	24 14 1	11 29.8	17 18.7	7 33.6	28 51.9	7 45.3	21 9.1	26 43.5	7 59.6	9 16.3
5 Su	12 51 3	14 40 57	0♋13 15	6♋10 58	11 29.6	18 37.8	8 45.4	29 32.1	7 59.8	21 8.6	26 43.3	7 59.8	9 14.8
6 M	12 55 0	15 40 2	12 7 44	18 4 7	11D29.5	19 58.8	9 57.4	0♊12.4	8 14.3	21 8.1	26 43.1	7 59.9	9 13.3
7 Tu	12 58 56	16 39 5	24 0 44	29 58 8	11 29.5	21 21.6	11 9.3	0 52.6	8 28.7	21 7.5	26 42.8	8 0.0	9 11.8
8 W	13 2 53	17 38 6	5♌56 55	11♌57 38	11 29.9	22 46.1	12 21.3	1 32.8	8 43.2	21 6.8	26 42.5	8 0.1	9 10.3
9 Th	13 6 50	18 37 4	18 0 48	24 6 57	11 30.4	24 12.4	13 33.3	2 12.9	8 57.6	21 6.0	26 42.1	8 0.2	9 8.7
10 F	13 10 46	19 36 1	0♍16 32	6♍29 57	11 31.2	25 40.3	14 45.3	2 53.0	9 12.0	21 5.0	26 41.7	8R 0.2	9 7.2
11 Sa	13 14 43	20 34 54	12 47 33	19 9 39	11 32.1	27 10.0	15 57.3	3 33.1	9 26.4	21 4.0	26 41.2	8 0.2	9 5.6
12 Su	13 18 39	21 33 46	25 36 26	2♎ 8 3	11 32.8	28 41.2	17 9.4	4 13.2	9 40.7	21 2.9	26 40.7	8 0.1	9 4.0
13 M	13 22 36	22 32 35	8♎44 31	15 25 50	11R33.1	0♈14.1	18 21.5	4 53.2	9 55.1	21 1.7	26 40.1	8 0.0	9 2.4
14 Tu	13 26 32	23 31 23	22 11 50	29 2 18	11 33.0	1 48.6	19 33.6	5 33.2	10 9.4	21 0.4	26 39.5	7 59.9	9 0.8
15 W	13 30 29	24 30 8	5♏56 55	12♏55 19	11 32.1	3 24.8	20 45.7	6 13.2	10 23.7	20 59.0	26 38.8	7 59.8	8 59.2
16 Th	13 34 25	25 28 52	19 57 1	27 1 32	11 30.7	5 2.5	21 57.9	6 53.1	10 38.0	20 57.5	26 38.1	7 59.6	8 57.6
17 F	13 38 22	26 27 34	4♐ 8 18	11♐16 47	11 28.9	6 41.8	23 10.1	7 33.0	10 52.2	20 55.9	26 37.3	7 59.4	8 55.9
18 Sa	13 42 18	27 26 14	18 26 24	25 36 36	11 26.9	8 22.8	24 22.3	8 12.9	11 6.4	20 54.3	26 36.5	7 59.1	8 54.3
19 Su	13 46 15	28 24 52	2♑46 52	9♑56 43	11 25.2	10 5.4	25 34.5	8 52.8	11 20.6	20 52.5	26 35.6	7 58.9	8 52.6
20 M	13 50 12	29 23 29	17 5 44	24 13 31	11D24.0	11 49.6	26 46.8	9 32.6	11 34.8	20 50.7	26 34.7	7 58.6	8 51.0
21 Tu	13 54 8	0♉22 4	1♒19 45	8♒24 9	11 23.6	13 35.5	27 59.1	10 12.4	11 49.0	20 48.7	26 33.7	7 58.2	8 49.3
22 W	13 58 5	1 20 37	15 26 29	22 26 35	11 24.1	15 22.9	29 11.4	10 52.2	12 3.1	20 46.7	26 32.7	7 57.9	8 47.7
23 Th	14 2 1	2 19 9	29 24 17	6♓19 26	11 25.2	17 12.1	0♈23.8	11 32.0	12 17.2	20 44.6	26 31.7	7 57.5	8 46.0
24 F	14 5 58	3 17 39	13♓11 56	20 1 41	11 26.7	19 2.9	1 36.1	12 11.7	12 31.2	20 42.4	26 30.6	7 57.0	8 44.3
25 Sa	14 9 54	4 16 8	26 48 34	3♈32 29	11 27.9	20 55.3	2 48.5	12 51.4	12 45.2	20 40.1	26 29.4	7 56.5	8 42.6
26 Su	14 13 51	5 14 34	10♈13 22	16 51 5	11R28.5	22 49.4	4 0.9	13 31.1	12 59.2	20 37.7	26 28.2	7 56.1	8 40.9
27 M	14 17 47	6 12 59	23 25 35	29 56 47	11 28.0	24 45.1	5 13.3	14 10.8	13 13.1	20 35.3	26 27.0	7 55.5	8 39.2
28 Tu	14 21 44	7 11 23	6♉24 37	12♉49 4	11 26.2	26 42.5	6 25.7	14 50.4	13 27.0	20 32.7	26 25.7	7 55.0	8 37.5
29 W	14 25 41	8 9 44	19 10 6	25 27 46	11 23.1	28 41.5	7 38.1	15 30.0	13 40.9	20 30.1	26 24.4	7 54.4	8 35.8
30 Th	14 29 37	9 8 4	1♊42 9	7♊53 21	11 18.9	0♉42.1	8 50.6	16 9.6	13 54.7	20 27.4	26 23.0	7 53.8	8 34.1

Astro Data	Planet Ingress	Last Aspect	☽ Ingress	Last Aspect	☽ Ingress	☽ Phases & Eclipses	Astro Data
Dy Hr Mn	Dy Hr Mn	Dy Hr Mn	Dy Hr Mn	Dy Hr Mn	Dy Hr Mn	Dy Hr Mn	1 MARCH 1987
☽0N 1 16:08	♃ ♈ 2 18:41	1 12:06 ♃ ☌	♈ 1 12:37	2 7:55 ♂ ☌	♊ 2 12:16	7 11:58 ☽ 16♊23	Julian Day # 31836
☿ D 12 21:22	♀ ♒ 3 7:55	3 11:30 ♅ △	♉ 3 18:11	4 16:59 ♅ ☍	♋ 4 23:33	15 13:13 ○ 24♍25	Delta T 55.4 sec
♃0N 13 6:30	☿ ♒ 11 21:55	4 19:55 ☉ ✶	♊ 6 3:26	6 17:56 ☿ △	♌ 7 12:04	22 16:22 ☽ 1♑31	SVP 05♓26'23"
☽0S 16 3:16	☿ ♓ 13 8:37	8 8:18 ♅ ☍	♋ 8 15:24	9 17:03 ♅ △	♍ 9 23:28	29 12:46 ● 8♈18	Obliquity 23°26'37"
☽0N 29 1:43	☉ ♈ 21 3:52	10 6:05 ☉ △	♌ 11 3:54	12 6:26 ☿ ☍	♎ 12 8:06	29 12:48:52 ✓ AT 0'08"	⚷ Chiron 15♊50.9
♄ R 31 4:43	♀ ♓ 28 16:20	13 14:52 ☿ ☍	♍ 13 14:55	14 7:50 ♅ ✶	♏ 14 13:41		☽ Mean ☊ 13♈22.2
♅ R 1 4:35		15 17:17 ♅ □	♎ 15 23:34	16 3:45 ♀ △	♐ 16 17:02	6 7:48 ☽ 15♋59	
♃□♆ 4 23:54	♂ ♊ 5 16:37	17 23:57 ♅ ✶	♏ 18 5:57	18 16:10 ☉ △	♑ 18 19:21	14 2:31 ○ 23♎38	1 APRIL 1987
♃⊼♇ 9 16:47	☿ ♈ 12 20:23	20 9:12 ☉ △	♐ 20 10:32	20 17:49 ♀ ✶	♒ 20 21:45	14 2:19 ☍ A 0.777	Julian Day # 31867
♆ R 10 0:13	☉ ♉ 20 14:58	22 8:11 ♅ ☌	♑ 22 13:48	22 19:02 ♅ ✶	♓ 23 1:02	20 22:15 ☽ 0♒18	Delta T 55.4 sec
☽0S 12 11:47	♀ ♈ 22 16:07	24 2:03 ♂ △	♒ 24 16:18	24 23:26 ♅ □	♈ 25 5:41	28 1:34 ● 7♉15	SVP 05♓26'20"
☿0N 16 10:02	☿ ♉ 29 15:39	26 14:35 ♀ ☌	♓ 26 18:46	27 5:33 ♅ △	♉ 27 12:06		Obliquity 23°26'37"
☽0N 25 9:14		28 16:30 ♅ □	♈ 28 22:12	28 4:08 ♇ ☍	♊ 29 20:43		⚷ Chiron 16♊44.5
♀0N 25 16:56		30 21:47 ♅ △	♉ 31 3:46				☽ Mean ☊ 11♈43.7

LONGITUDE — MAY 1987

Day	Sid.Time	☉	0 hr ☽	Noon ☽	True ☊	☿	♀	♂	♃	♄	♅	♆	♇
1 F	14 33 34	10♉ 6 21	14♊ 1 32	20♊ 6 56	11♈14.1	2♉44.3	10♈ 3.0	16♊49.2	14♈ 8.5	20♐24.6	26♐21.6	7♑53.1	8♏32.4
2 Sa	14 37 30	11 4 37	26 9 49	2♋10 30	11R 9.1	4 47.9	11 15.5	17 28.7	14 22.2	20R 21.7	26R 20.2	7R 52.4	8R 30.7
3 Su	14 41 27	12 2 51	8♋ 9 21	14 6 49	11 4.6	6 52.9	12 28.0	18 8.2	14 35.9	20 18.8	26 18.7	7 51.7	8 29.1
4 M	14 45 23	13 1 3	20 3 20	25 59 25	11 1.1	8 59.2	13 40.5	18 47.7	14 49.5	20 15.8	26 17.1	7 51.0	8 27.4
5 Tu	14 49 20	13 59 13	1♌55 36	7♌52 28	10 58.8	11 6.6	14 53.0	19 27.2	15 3.1	20 12.7	26 15.6	7 50.2	8 25.7
6 W	14 53 17	14 57 21	13 50 35	19 50 35	10D 58.0	13 15.1	16 5.5	20 6.6	15 16.7	20 9.6	26 14.0	7 49.5	8 24.0
7 Th	14 57 13	15 55 27	25 53 2	1♍58 35	10 58.5	15 24.3	17 18.0	20 46.0	15 30.2	20 6.4	26 12.3	7 48.6	8 22.3
8 F	15 1 10	16 53 31	8♍ 7 49	14 21 17	10 59.8	17 34.3	18 30.5	21 25.4	15 43.6	20 3.1	26 10.7	7 47.8	8 20.6
9 Sa	15 5 6	17 51 33	20 39 31	27 2 59	11 1.5	19 44.6	19 43.1	22 4.7	15 57.0	19 59.7	26 8.9	7 46.9	8 19.0
10 Su	15 9 3	18 49 33	3♎32 5	10♎ 7 8	11R 2.6	21 55.1	20 55.6	22 44.1	16 10.3	19 56.3	26 7.2	7 46.0	8 17.3
11 M	15 12 59	19 47 32	16 48 20	23 35 46	11 2.7	24 5.4	22 8.2	23 23.4	16 23.6	19 52.8	26 5.4	7 45.1	8 15.6
12 Tu	15 16 56	20 45 28	0♏29 21	7♏28 53	11 1.2	26 15.3	23 20.8	24 2.6	16 36.8	19 49.3	26 3.6	7 44.1	8 14.0
13 W	15 20 52	21 43 24	14 34 0	21 44 11	10 57.8	28 24.6	24 33.4	24 41.9	16 50.0	19 45.7	26 1.7	7 43.2	8 12.4
14 Th	15 24 49	22 41 17	28 58 44	6♐16 53	10 52.8	0♊32.9	25 46.0	25 21.1	17 3.1	19 42.0	25 59.8	7 42.2	8 10.7
15 F	15 28 45	23 39 9	13♐37 44	21 0 18	10 46.6	2 39.9	26 58.6	26 0.3	17 16.1	19 38.3	25 57.9	7 41.1	8 9.1
16 Sa	15 32 42	24 37 0	28 23 37	5♑46 41	10 40.1	4 45.4	28 11.2	26 39.5	17 29.1	19 34.6	25 56.0	7 40.1	8 7.5
17 Su	15 36 39	25 34 49	13♑ 8 34	20 28 27	10 34.1	6 49.1	29 23.9	27 18.7	17 42.1	19 30.7	25 54.0	7 39.0	8 5.9
18 M	15 40 35	26 32 38	27 45 36	4♒59 25	10 29.4	8 50.8	0♉36.6	27 57.8	17 54.9	19 26.9	25 52.0	7 37.9	8 4.3
19 Tu	15 44 32	27 30 25	12♒ 9 26	19 15 21	10 26.5	10 50.4	1 49.2	28 36.9	18 7.7	19 23.0	25 50.0	7 36.8	8 2.7
20 W	15 48 28	28 28 11	26 16 57	3♓14 10	10D 25.4	12 47.5	3 1.9	29 16.0	18 20.5	19 19.0	25 47.9	7 35.7	8 1.2
21 Th	15 52 25	29 25 55	10♓ 7 1	16 55 35	10 25.8	14 42.1	4 14.6	29 55.1	18 33.1	19 15.0	25 45.8	7 34.5	7 59.6
22 F	15 56 21	0♊23 39	23 40 1	0♈20 30	10 26.8	16 34.1	5 27.4	0♋34.1	18 45.7	19 10.9	25 43.7	7 33.3	7 58.1
23 Sa	16 0 18	1 21 21	6♈57 15	13 30 27	10R 27.6	18 23.3	6 40.1	1 13.2	18 58.3	19 6.8	25 41.5	7 32.1	7 56.6
24 Su	16 4 15	2 19 3	20 0 19	26 27 3	10 27.2	20 9.6	7 52.8	1 52.2	19 10.7	19 2.7	25 39.4	7 30.9	7 55.1
25 M	16 8 11	3 16 43	2♉50 48	9♉11 43	10 24.9	21 53.0	9 5.6	2 31.2	19 23.1	18 58.5	25 37.2	7 29.6	7 53.6
26 Tu	16 12 8	4 14 23	15 29 56	21 45 34	10 20.2	23 33.4	10 18.4	3 10.2	19 35.4	18 54.3	25 35.0	7 28.4	7 52.1
27 W	16 16 4	5 12 1	27 58 42	4♊ 9 25	10 13.1	25 10.8	11 31.1	3 49.1	19 47.6	18 50.1	25 32.7	7 27.1	7 50.6
28 Th	16 20 1	6 9 38	10♊17 49	16 24 0	10 4.0	26 45.1	12 43.9	4 28.1	19 59.8	18 45.8	25 30.5	7 25.8	7 49.2
29 F	16 23 57	7 7 14	22 28 4	28 30 11	9 53.6	28 16.3	13 56.7	5 7.0	20 11.8	18 41.6	25 28.2	7 24.4	7 47.8
30 Sa	16 27 54	8 4 49	4♋30 30	10♋29 14	9 42.8	29 44.4	15 9.5	5 45.9	20 23.8	18 37.2	25 25.9	7 23.1	7 46.3
31 Su	16 31 50	9 2 23	16 26 38	22 22 59	9 32.5	1♋ 9.2	16 22.4	6 24.8	20 35.8	18 32.9	25 23.6	7 21.7	7 45.0

LONGITUDE — JUNE 1987

Day	Sid.Time	☉	0 hr ☽	Noon ☽	True ☊	☿	♀	♂	♃	♄	♅	♆	♇
1 M	16 35 47	9♊59 55	28♋18 39	4♌14 0	9♈23.8	2♋30.9	17♉35.2	7♋ 3.6	20♈47.6	18♐28.5	25♐21.3	7♑20.4	7♏43.6
2 Tu	16 39 44	10 57 26	10♌ 9 29	16 5 35	9R 17.1	3 49.3	18 48.0	7 42.5	20 59.3	18R 24.2	25R 18.9	7R 19.0	7R 42.2
3 W	16 43 40	11 54 55	22 2 50	28 1 48	9 12.9	5 4.3	20 0.9	8 21.3	21 11.0	18 19.8	25 16.6	7 17.5	7 40.9
4 Th	16 47 37	12 52 24	4♍ 3 5	10♍ 7 17	9D 10.8	6 16.0	21 13.7	9 0.1	21 22.5	18 15.4	25 14.2	7 16.1	7 39.6
5 F	16 51 33	13 49 51	16 15 4	22 27 2	9 10.4	7 24.3	22 26.6	9 38.9	21 34.0	18 10.9	25 11.8	7 14.7	7 38.3
6 Sa	16 55 30	14 47 17	28 43 51	5♎ 6 6	9R 10.9	8 29.1	23 39.5	10 17.6	21 45.4	18 6.5	25 9.4	7 13.2	7 37.1
7 Su	16 59 26	15 44 41	11♎34 19	18 9 1	9 11.1	9 30.3	24 52.4	10 56.4	21 56.7	18 2.1	25 7.0	7 11.8	7 35.8
8 M	17 3 23	16 42 5	24 50 33	1♏39 11	9 10.1	10 28.0	26 5.3	11 35.1	22 7.9	17 57.6	25 4.6	7 10.3	7 34.6
9 Tu	17 7 19	17 39 27	8♏35 3	15 38 3	9 7.1	11 21.9	27 18.2	12 13.8	22 19.0	17 53.2	25 2.2	7 8.8	7 33.4
10 W	17 11 16	18 36 49	22 47 57	0♐ 4 16	9 1.6	12 12.0	28 31.1	12 52.5	22 30.0	17 48.8	24 59.8	7 7.3	7 32.2
11 Th	17 15 13	19 34 10	7♐26 18	14 53 12	8 53.8	12 58.3	29 44.0	13 31.1	22 40.9	17 44.3	24 57.3	7 5.8	7 31.1
12 F	17 19 9	20 31 29	22 23 51	29 57 5	8 44.3	13 40.6	0♊57.0	14 9.8	22 51.7	17 39.9	24 54.9	7 4.2	7 30.0
13 Sa	17 23 6	21 28 49	7♑31 34	15♑ 6 0	8 34.1	14 18.8	2 10.0	14 48.4	23 2.4	17 35.5	24 52.4	7 2.7	7 28.9
14 Su	17 27 2	22 26 7	22 39 5	0♒ 9 37	8 24.5	14 52.9	3 22.9	15 27.0	23 13.0	17 31.0	24 50.0	7 1.2	7 27.8
15 M	17 30 59	23 23 25	7♒36 32	14 58 57	8 16.7	15 22.8	4 35.9	16 5.6	23 23.5	17 26.6	24 47.6	6 59.6	7 26.8
16 Tu	17 34 55	24 20 43	22 16 11	29 27 44	8 11.1	15 48.3	5 49.0	16 44.2	23 33.9	17 22.2	24 45.1	6 58.0	7 25.7
17 W	17 38 52	25 18 0	6♓33 20	13♓32 51	8 8.1	16 9.4	7 2.0	17 22.8	23 44.2	17 17.8	24 42.6	6 56.5	7 24.8
18 Th	17 42 48	26 15 16	20 26 21	27 13 58	8D 7.0	16 26.0	8 15.0	18 1.3	23 54.4	17 13.5	24 40.2	6 54.9	7 23.8
19 F	17 46 45	27 12 33	3♈55 59	10♈32 45	8R 7.0	16 38.1	9 28.1	18 39.9	24 4.5	17 9.1	24 37.7	6 53.3	7 22.8
20 Sa	17 50 42	28 9 49	17 4 37	23 32 1	8 6.8	16 45.6	10 41.2	19 18.4	24 14.4	17 4.8	24 35.3	6 51.7	7 21.9
21 Su	17 54 38	29 7 5	29 55 21	6♉15 1	8 5.3	16R 48.6	11 54.3	19 56.9	24 24.3	17 0.5	24 32.8	6 50.1	7 21.0
22 M	17 58 35	0♋ 4 21	12♉31 23	18 44 49	8 1.6	16 47.0	13 7.4	20 35.4	24 34.0	16 56.2	24 30.4	6 48.5	7 20.2
23 Tu	18 2 31	1 1 36	24 55 37	1♊ 4 4	7 55.1	16 41.0	14 20.5	21 13.9	24 43.6	16 52.0	24 28.0	6 46.9	7 19.4
24 W	18 6 28	1 58 52	7♊10 26	13 14 55	7 45.7	16 30.6	15 33.7	21 52.4	24 53.1	16 47.7	24 25.5	6 45.3	7 18.6
25 Th	18 10 24	2 56 7	19 17 42	25 18 57	7 34.0	16 16.0	16 46.9	22 30.9	25 2.5	16 43.6	24 23.1	6 43.7	7 17.8
26 F	18 14 21	3 53 22	1♋18 49	7♋17 29	7 20.6	15 57.4	18 0.0	23 9.3	25 11.7	16 39.4	24 20.7	6 42.1	7 17.1
27 Sa	18 18 18	4 50 36	13 15 3	19 11 44	7 6.6	15 35.0	19 13.2	23 47.8	25 20.9	16 35.3	24 18.3	6 40.4	7 16.4
28 Su	18 22 14	5 47 51	25 7 41	1♌ 3 8	6 53.3	15 9.1	20 26.5	24 26.2	25 29.9	16 31.2	24 15.9	6 38.8	7 15.7
29 M	18 26 11	6 45 5	6♌58 18	12 53 31	6 41.7	14 40.3	21 39.7	25 4.6	25 38.7	16 27.2	24 13.5	6 37.2	7 15.0
30 Tu	18 30 7	7 42 18	18 49 4	24 45 21	6 32.5	14 8.8	22 52.9	25 43.0	25 47.5	16 23.2	24 11.1	6 35.6	7 14.4

Astro Data

	Dy Hr Mn
☽0S	9 21:00
☽0N	22 14:37
♃△♄	23 12:26
☽0S	6 5:21
☽0N	18 19:24
♃△♅	21 16:52
☿ R	21 3:44

Planet Ingress

	Dy Hr Mn
☿ ♊	13 17:50
♀ ♉	17 11:56
☉ ♊	21 14:10
♂ ♋	21 3:01
☿ ♋	30 4:21
♀ ♊	11 5:15
☉ ♋	21 22:11

Last Aspect / ☽ Ingress

Last Aspect Dy Hr Mn	☽ Ingress Dy Hr Mn
2 0:21 ♅ ☍	♋ 2 7:39
3 13:14 ♃ □	♌ 4 20:06
7 0:38 ♅ △	♍ 7 8:07
9 10:18 ♅ △	♎ 9 17:29
11 16:19 ♅ ⚹	♏ 11 23:09
13 12:50 ☉ ☍	♐ 14 1:41
15 23:38 ♀ △	♑ 16 2:37
17 21:51 ☉ △	♒ 18 3:42
20 5:23 ♂ △	♓ 20 6:24
22 3:41 ♅ □	♈ 22 11:23
24 10:29 ♅ △	♉ 24 18:39
25 13:03 ♀ ☌	♊ 27 3:55
29 13:09 ♅ ☍	♋ 29 14:59

Last Aspect / ☽ Ingress

Last Aspect Dy Hr Mn	☽ Ingress Dy Hr Mn
31 8:32 ♃ □	♌ 1 3:25
3 6:28 ♅ △	♍ 3 15:56
5 17:13 ♅ □	♎ 6 2:24
8 0:25 ♅ ⚹	♏ 8 9:06
10 10:18 ♀ ☍	♐ 10 11:53
12 4:00 ♅ ☌	♑ 12 12:05
14 0:55 ♃ □	♒ 14 11:45
16 4:07 ♅ ⚹	♓ 16 12:54
18 11:03 ☉ □	♈ 18 16:56
20 22:22 ☉ ⚹	♉ 21 0:09
22 16:25 ♂ ⚹	♊ 23 9:54
25 11:36 ♃ ⚹	♋ 25 21:22
28 0:45 ♃ □	♌ 28 9:52
30 14:16 ♃ △	♍ 30 22:34

☽ Phases & Eclipses

Dy Hr Mn	
6 2:26	☽ 15♌03
13 12:50	○ 22♏14
20 4:02	☽ 28♒38
27 15:13	● 5♊49
4 18:53	☽ 13♍38
11 20:49	○ 20♐24
18 11:03	☽ 26♓42
26 5:37	● 4♋07

Astro Data

1 MAY 1987
Julian Day # 31897
Delta T 55.5 sec
SVP 05♓26'16"
Obliquity 23°26'36"
⚷ Chiron 18♊33.7
☽ Mean ☊ 10♈08.3

1 JUNE 1987
Julian Day # 31928
Delta T 55.5 sec
SVP 05♓26'11"
Obliquity 23°26'36"
⚷ Chiron 21♊03.3
☽ Mean ☊ 8♈29.9

JULY 1987 LONGITUDE

Day	Sid.Time	☉	0 hr ☽	Noon ☽	True ☊	☿	♀	♂	♃	♄	♅	♆	♇
1 W	18 34 4	8♋39 31	0♍42 47	6♍41 50	6♈26.1	13♋35.1	24♊ 6.2	26♋21.4	25♈56.1	16♐19.2	24♐ 8.8	6♑34.0	7♏13.8
2 Th	18 38 0	9 36 44	12 43 0	18 46 51	6R 22.3	12R 59.9	25 19.5	26 59.8	26 4.6	16R 15.3	24R 6.4	6R 32.3	7R 13.3
3 F	18 41 57	10 33 57	24 53 57	1♎ 4 55	6D 20.8	12 23.6	26 32.8	27 38.2	26 12.9	16 11.5	24 4.1	6 30.7	7 12.8
4 Sa	18 45 53	11 31 9	7♎20 22	13 40 55	6R 20.6	11 47.0	27 46.1	28 16.5	26 21.1	16 7.7	24 1.8	6 29.1	7 12.3
5 Su	18 49 50	12 28 21	20 7 10	26 39 39	6 20.5	11 10.5	28 59.4	28 54.9	26 29.2	16 3.9	23 59.5	6 27.5	7 11.8
6 M	18 53 47	13 25 32	3♏18 53	10♏ 5 14	6 19.4	10 35.0	0♋12.8	29 33.2	26 37.1	16 0.2	23 57.2	6 25.9	7 11.4
7 Tu	18 57 43	14 22 43	16 58 59	24 0 14	6 16.4	10 0.9	1 26.1	0♌11.5	26 44.9	15 56.6	23 55.0	6 24.3	7 11.0
8 W	19 1 40	15 19 55	1♐ 8 54	8♐24 41	6 11.0	9 28.8	2 39.5	0 49.8	26 52.5	15 53.0	23 52.7	6 22.7	7 10.7
9 Th	19 5 36	16 17 6	15 47 5	23 15 18	6 3.2	8 59.4	3 52.9	1 28.1	27 0.0	15 49.5	23 50.5	6 21.1	7 10.3
10 F	19 9 33	17 14 17	0♑48 22	8♑25 5	5 53.5	8 33.2	5 6.3	2 6.4	27 7.4	15 46.0	23 48.4	6 19.5	7 10.0
11 Sa	19 13 29	18 11 28	16 4 8	23 44 2	5 43.1	8 10.6	6 19.7	2 44.7	27 14.6	15 42.6	23 46.2	6 17.9	7 9.8
12 Su	19 17 26	19 8 39	1♒23 22	9♒ 0 41	5 33.2	7 52.1	7 33.2	3 23.0	27 21.7	15 39.3	23 44.1	6 16.4	7 9.6
13 M	19 21 22	20 5 51	16 34 42	24 4 15	5 24.9	7 38.1	8 46.6	4 1.3	27 28.6	15 36.0	23 41.9	6 14.8	7 9.4
14 Tu	19 25 19	21 3 2	1♓28 24	8♓46 25	5 19.0	7 28.8	10 0.1	4 39.5	27 35.3	15 32.8	23 39.8	6 13.2	7 9.2
15 W	19 29 16	22 0 15	15 57 49	23 2 19	5 15.7	7D 24.5	11 13.7	5 17.8	27 42.0	15 29.7	23 37.8	6 11.7	7 9.1
16 Th	19 33 12	22 57 27	29 59 50	6♈50 28	5D 14.5	7 25.4	12 27.2	5 56.0	27 48.4	15 26.6	23 35.7	6 10.1	7 9.0
17 F	19 37 9	23 54 41	13♈34 27	20 12 7	5R 14.5	7 31.7	13 40.7	6 34.2	27 54.7	15 23.6	23 33.7	6 8.6	7 8.9
18 Sa	19 41 5	24 51 55	26 43 53	3♉10 13	5 14.7	7 43.5	14 54.3	7 12.5	28 0.8	15 20.7	23 31.7	6 7.1	7D 8.9
19 Su	19 45 2	25 49 10	9♉31 37	15 48 38	5 13.9	8 0.8	16 7.9	7 50.7	28 6.8	15 17.8	23 29.8	6 5.6	7 8.9
20 M	19 48 58	26 46 25	22 1 44	28 11 26	5 11.1	8 23.8	17 21.6	8 28.9	28 12.6	15 15.1	23 27.9	6 4.1	7 9.0
21 Tu	19 52 55	27 43 41	4♊18 12	10♊22 27	5 6.0	8 52.3	18 35.2	9 7.1	28 18.3	15 12.4	23 26.0	6 2.6	7 9.0
22 W	19 56 51	28 40 58	16 24 36	22 25 0	4 58.2	9 26.6	19 48.9	9 45.3	28 23.7	15 9.7	23 24.1	6 1.1	7 9.2
23 Th	20 0 48	29 38 16	28 23 59	4♋21 50	4 48.3	10 6.4	21 2.6	10 23.5	28 29.1	15 7.2	23 22.3	5 59.7	7 9.3
24 F	20 4 45	0♌35 35	10♋18 47	16 15 6	4 36.9	10 51.7	22 16.3	11 1.8	28 34.2	15 4.8	23 20.5	5 58.2	7 9.5
25 Sa	20 8 41	1 32 54	22 10 58	28 6 36	4 25.0	11 42.6	23 30.0	11 40.0	28 39.2	15 2.4	23 18.7	5 56.8	7 9.7
26 Su	20 12 38	2 30 14	4♌ 2 10	9♌57 52	4 13.6	12 38.9	24 43.8	12 18.2	28 44.0	15 0.1	23 17.0	5 55.4	7 9.9
27 M	20 16 34	3 27 34	15 53 55	21 50 31	4 3.7	13 40.5	25 57.6	12 56.3	28 48.6	14 57.9	23 15.3	5 54.0	7 10.2
28 Tu	20 20 31	4 24 55	27 47 55	3♍46 24	3 55.9	14 47.5	27 11.4	13 34.5	28 53.0	14 55.8	23 13.7	5 52.6	7 10.5
29 W	20 24 27	5 22 16	9♍46 15	15 47 48	3 50.6	15 59.5	28 25.2	14 12.7	28 57.3	14 53.7	23 12.0	5 51.3	7 10.9
30 Th	20 28 24	6 19 39	21 51 27	27 57 37	3D 47.8	17 16.7	29 39.0	14 50.9	29 1.4	14 51.8	23 10.5	5 49.9	7 11.3
31 F	20 32 20	7 17 1	4♎ 6 44	10♎19 17	3 47.1	18 38.6	0♌52.9	15 29.1	29 5.3	14 49.9	23 8.9	5 48.6	7 11.7

AUGUST 1987 LONGITUDE

Day	Sid.Time	☉	0 hr ☽	Noon ☽	True ☊	☿	♀	♂	♃	♄	♅	♆	♇
1 Sa	20 36 17	8♌14 25	16♎35 46	22♎56 42	3♈47.6	20♋ 5.4	2♌ 6.7	16♌ 7.2	29♈ 9.0	14♐48.1	23♐ 7.4	5♑47.3	7♏12.2
2 Su	20 40 14	9 11 48	29 22 36	5♏53 58	3R 48.5	21 36.6	3 20.6	16 45.4	29 12.6	14R 46.4	23R 6.0	5R 46.0	7 12.6
3 M	20 44 10	10 9 13	12♏31 15	19 14 50	3 48.8	23 12.2	4 34.5	17 23.6	29 15.9	14 44.8	23 4.6	5 44.7	7 13.2
4 Tu	20 48 7	11 6 38	26 5 3	3♐ 2 4	3 47.8	24 51.9	5 48.5	18 1.7	29 19.1	14 43.3	23 3.2	5 43.5	7 13.7
5 W	20 52 3	12 4 4	10♐ 5 57	17 16 33	3 44.8	26 35.3	7 2.4	18 39.9	29 22.1	14 41.9	23 1.8	5 42.2	7 14.3
6 Th	20 56 0	13 1 31	24 33 34	1♑56 27	3 39.9	28 22.3	8 16.4	19 18.0	29 24.9	14 40.6	23 0.6	5 41.0	7 14.9
7 F	20 59 56	13 58 58	9♑24 30	16 56 44	3 33.5	0♌12.4	9 30.3	19 56.2	29 27.5	14 39.4	22 59.3	5 39.8	7 15.6
8 Sa	21 3 53	14 56 26	24 32 3	2♒ 9 12	3 26.3	2 5.4	10 44.3	20 34.3	29 29.9	14 38.3	22 58.1	5 38.7	7 16.3
9 Su	21 7 49	15 53 55	9♒46 50	17 23 37	3 19.5	4 0.8	11 58.3	21 12.5	29 32.1	14 37.2	22 56.9	5 37.5	7 17.0
10 M	21 11 46	16 51 25	24 58 12	2♓29 23	3 13.7	5 58.3	13 12.4	21 50.6	29 34.2	14 36.3	22 55.8	5 36.4	7 17.8
11 Tu	21 15 43	17 48 56	9♓56 3	17 17 19	3 9.8	7 57.5	14 26.4	22 28.7	29 36.0	14 35.4	22 54.7	5 35.3	7 18.6
12 W	21 19 39	18 46 29	24 32 29	1♈41 2	3D 7.8	9 58.1	15 40.5	23 6.9	29 37.7	14 34.7	22 53.7	5 34.2	7 19.4
13 Th	21 23 36	19 44 2	8♈42 41	15 37 19	3 7.7	11 59.6	16 54.6	23 45.0	29 39.1	14 34.0	22 52.7	5 33.2	7 20.3
14 F	21 27 32	20 41 37	22 25 0	29 5 54	3 8.6	14 1.8	18 8.7	24 23.2	29 40.4	14 33.4	22 51.8	5 32.1	7 21.1
15 Sa	21 31 29	21 39 14	5♉40 22	12♉ 8 47	3 10.0	16 4.4	19 22.8	25 1.3	29 41.5	14 33.0	22 50.9	5 31.1	7 22.1
16 Su	21 35 25	22 36 52	18 31 37	24 49 24	3R 10.9	18 7.0	20 37.0	25 39.5	29 42.3	14 32.6	22 50.0	5 30.1	7 23.0
17 M	21 39 22	23 34 32	1♊ 2 39	7♊11 55	3 10.7	20 9.4	21 51.2	26 17.6	29 43.0	14 32.3	22 49.2	5 29.2	7 24.0
18 Tu	21 43 18	24 32 13	13 17 47	19 20 45	3 8.9	22 11.4	23 5.4	26 55.8	29 43.5	14 32.1	22 48.5	5 28.2	7 25.0
19 W	21 47 15	25 29 56	25 21 21	1♋20 4	3 5.5	24 12.8	24 19.6	27 33.9	29R 43.8	14D 32.0	22 47.8	5 27.3	7 26.1
20 Th	21 51 12	26 27 40	7♋17 22	13 13 40	3 0.6	26 13.4	25 33.8	28 12.1	29 43.9	14 32.0	22 47.1	5 26.5	7 27.2
21 F	21 55 8	27 25 26	19 9 22	25 4 49	2 54.7	28 13.1	26 48.1	28 50.3	29 43.7	14 32.2	22 46.5	5 25.6	7 28.3
22 Sa	21 59 5	28 23 14	1♌ 0 21	6♌56 14	2 48.3	0♍11.9	28 2.4	29 28.4	29 43.4	14 32.4	22 46.0	5 24.8	7 29.4
23 Su	22 3 1	29 21 3	12 52 46	18 50 9	2 42.2	2 9.5	29 16.6	0♍ 6.6	29 42.9	14 32.7	22 45.4	5 24.0	7 30.6
24 M	22 6 58	0♍18 53	24 48 39	0♍48 27	2 37.0	4 5.9	0♍31.0	0 44.8	29 42.1	14 33.1	22 45.0	5 23.2	7 31.8
25 Tu	22 10 54	1 16 45	6♍49 46	12 52 49	2 33.1	6 1.2	1 45.3	1 22.9	29 41.2	14 33.6	22 44.6	5 22.5	7 33.0
26 W	22 14 51	2 14 38	18 57 47	25 4 54	2 30.7	7 55.2	2 59.6	2 1.1	29 40.1	14 34.2	22 44.2	5 21.8	7 34.3
27 Th	22 18 47	3 12 33	1♎14 24	7♎26 31	2D 29.9	9 47.9	4 14.0	2 39.3	29 38.7	14 34.9	22 43.9	5 21.1	7 35.6
28 F	22 22 44	4 10 29	13 41 32	19 59 44	2 30.3	11 39.3	5 28.3	3 17.5	29 37.2	14 35.6	22 43.6	5 20.4	7 36.9
29 Sa	22 26 41	5 8 27	26 21 24	2♏46 52	2 31.6	13 29.4	6 42.7	3 55.7	29 35.5	14 36.5	22 43.4	5 19.8	7 38.3
30 Su	22 30 37	6 6 26	9♏16 25	15 50 22	2 33.2	15 18.3	7 57.1	4 33.9	29 33.6	14 37.5	22 43.2	5 19.2	7 39.7
31 M	22 34 34	7 4 26	22 29 1	29 12 36	2 34.6	17 5.8	9 11.5	5 12.1	29 31.4	14 38.6	22 43.1	5 18.6	7 41.1

Astro Data

	Dy Hr Mn
☽0S	3 11:59
☿ D	15 7:51
☽0N	16 1:33
♇ D	18 6:10
☽0S	30 17:15
♃⚼♄	10 18:21
☽0N	12 10:04
♃ R	19 21:07
♄ D	19 8:53
☽0S	26 22:26
♃⚼♄	28 14:43

Planet Ingress

	Dy Hr Mn
♀ ♋	5 19:50
♂ ♌	6 16:46
☉ ♌	23 9:06
♀ ♌	30 6:49
☿ ♌	6 21:20
☿ ♍	21 21:36
♂ ♍	22 19:51
☉ ♍	23 16:10
♀ ♍	23 14:00

Last Aspect / ☽ Ingress

Last Aspect Dy Hr Mn		☽ Ingress Dy Hr Mn
3 5:37	♂ ✶	♎ 3 9:55
5 17:52	♀ △	♏ 5 18:03
6 19:10	☉ △	♐ 7 22:05
9 18:07	♃ △	♑ 9 22:43
11 17:38	♃ □	♒ 11 21:49
13 17:38	♃ ✶	♓ 13 21:36
15 12:59	♅ □	♈ 16 0:00
18 2:24	♃ ☌	♉ 18 6:04
20 10:00	☉ ✶	♊ 20 15:33
23 0:10	♃ ✶	♋ 23 3:13
25 13:11	♃ □	♌ 25 15:50
28 2:12	♃ △	♍ 28 4:26
30 2:35	♅ □	♎ 30 15:59

Last Aspect / ☽ Ingress

Last Aspect Dy Hr Mn		☽ Ingress Dy Hr Mn
1 23:41	♃ ☍	♏ 2 1:09
3 21:34	☿ △	♐ 4 6:47
6 7:56	♃ △	♑ 6 8:52
8 7:50	♃ □	♒ 8 8:37
10 7:21	♃ ✶	♓ 10 8:01
11 21:16	♅ □	♈ 12 9:09
14 13:04	♃ ☌	♉ 14 13:38
16 14:20	♂ □	♊ 16 21:59
19 8:46	♃ ✶	♋ 19 9:19
21 21:24	♃ □	♌ 21 21:58
24 9:47	♃ △	♍ 24 10:23
26 7:24	♅ □	♎ 26 21:35
29 6:03	♃ ☍	♏ 29 6:49
30 12:46	☿ ✶	♐ 31 13:24

☽ Phases & Eclipses

Dy Hr Mn	
4 8:34	☽ 11♎52
11 3:33	○ 18♑20
17 20:17	☽ 24♈43
25 20:38	● 2♌22
2 19:24	☽ 9♏58
9 10:17	○ 16♒19
16 8:25	☽ 22♉57
24 11:59	● 0♍48

Astro Data

1 JULY 1987
Julian Day # 31958
Delta T 55.6 sec
SVP 05♓26'05"
Obliquity 23°26'36"
⚷ Chiron 23♊40.0
☽ Mean ☊ 6♈54.6

1 AUGUST 1987
Julian Day # 31989
Delta T 55.6 sec
SVP 05♓26'00"
Obliquity 23°26'36"
⚷ Chiron 26♊08.7
☽ Mean ☊ 5♈16.1

LONGITUDE — SEPTEMBER 1987

Day	Sid.Time	☉	0 hr ☽	Noon ☽	True ☊	☿	♀	♂	♃	♄	♅	♆	♇
1 Tu	22 38 30	8♍ 2 28	6♐ 1 20	12♐55 20	2♈35.2	18♍52.1	10♍25.9	5♍50.3	29♈29.1	14♐39.8	22♐43.1	5♑18.1	7♏42.5
2 W	22 42 27	9 0 31	19 54 40	26 59 15	2R 34.8	20 37.1	11 40.4	6 28.5	29R 26.6	14 41.1	22D 43.1	5R 17.6	7 44.0
3 Th	22 46 23	9 58 35	4♑ 8 55	11♑23 20	2 33.4	22 20.8	12 54.8	7 6.7	29 23.9	14 42.5	22 43.1	5 17.1	7 45.5
4 F	22 50 20	10 56 41	18 42 0	26 4 21	2 31.2	24 3.3	14 9.2	7 44.9	29 21.0	14 43.9	22 43.2	5 16.7	7 47.0
5 Sa	22 54 16	11 54 49	3♒29 35	10♒56 50	2 28.6	25 44.5	15 23.7	8 23.1	29 17.9	14 45.5	22 43.4	5 16.3	7 48.6
6 Su	22 58 13	12 52 57	18 25 8	25 53 27	2 26.0	27 24.6	16 38.2	9 1.3	29 14.6	14 47.2	22 43.6	5 15.9	7 50.2
7 M	23 2 10	13 51 7	3♓20 43	10♓45 54	2 23.9	29 3.4	17 52.6	9 39.5	29 11.2	14 48.9	22 43.8	5 15.6	7 51.8
8 Tu	23 6 6	14 49 19	18 8 0	25 26 9	2 22.6	0♎41.1	19 7.1	10 17.8	29 7.5	14 50.8	22 44.1	5 15.2	7 53.4
9 W	23 10 3	15 47 33	2♈39 34	9♈47 37	2D 22.2	2 17.6	20 21.6	10 56.0	29 3.7	14 52.7	22 44.5	5 15.0	7 55.1
10 Th	23 13 59	16 45 48	16 49 50	23 45 52	2 22.6	3 53.0	21 36.1	11 34.2	28 59.7	14 54.7	22 44.9	5 14.7	7 56.8
11 F	23 17 56	17 44 6	0♉35 34	7♉18 54	2 23.5	5 27.2	22 50.7	12 12.5	28 55.5	14 56.8	22 45.3	5 14.5	7 58.5
12 Sa	23 21 52	18 42 25	13 55 59	20 27 0	2 24.7	7 0.3	24 5.2	12 50.7	28 51.1	14 59.1	22 45.8	5 14.3	8 0.2
13 Su	23 25 49	19 40 47	26 52 18	3♊12 15	2 25.7	8 32.2	25 19.7	13 29.0	28 46.5	15 1.4	22 46.4	5 14.1	8 2.0
14 M	23 29 45	20 39 11	9♊27 19	15 38 1	2 26.5	10 3.0	26 34.3	14 7.3	28 41.8	15 3.8	22 47.0	5 14.0	8 3.7
15 Tu	23 33 42	21 37 37	21 44 52	27 48 26	2R 26.7	11 32.7	27 48.9	14 45.6	28 36.9	15 6.3	22 47.6	5 13.9	8 5.6
16 W	23 37 39	22 36 5	3♋49 17	9♋48 0	2 26.5	13 1.3	29 3.4	15 23.9	28 31.9	15 8.9	22 48.3	5 13.8	8 7.4
17 Th	23 41 35	23 34 35	15 45 7	21 41 11	2 25.8	14 28.7	0♎18.0	16 2.2	28 26.6	15 11.5	22 49.1	5D 13.8	8 9.2
18 F	23 45 32	24 33 7	27 36 45	3♌32 17	2 24.9	15 55.0	1 32.6	16 40.5	28 21.2	15 14.3	22 49.9	5 13.8	8 11.1
19 Sa	23 49 28	25 31 42	9♌28 15	15 25 6	2 23.9	17 20.1	2 47.3	17 18.8	28 15.7	15 17.2	22 50.8	5 13.9	8 13.0
20 Su	23 53 25	26 30 18	21 23 14	27 22 59	2 23.0	18 44.0	4 1.9	17 57.2	28 10.0	15 20.1	22 51.7	5 13.9	8 14.9
21 M	23 57 21	27 28 57	3♍24 42	9♍28 40	2 22.4	20 6.8	5 16.5	18 35.5	28 4.1	15 23.1	22 52.7	5 14.0	8 16.9
22 Tu	0 1 18	28 27 38	15 35 6	21 44 15	2 22.0	21 28.2	6 31.1	19 13.9	27 58.1	15 26.2	22 53.7	5 14.2	8 18.9
23 W	0 5 14	29 26 20	27 56 16	4♎11 19	2D 21.8	22 48.4	7 45.8	19 52.2	27 51.9	15 29.4	22 54.7	5 14.3	8 20.8
24 Th	0 9 11	0♎25 5	10♎29 30	16 50 55	2 21.8	24 7.3	9 0.4	20 30.6	27 45.6	15 32.7	22 55.8	5 14.5	8 22.8
25 F	0 13 8	1 23 51	23 15 38	29 43 43	2R 21.9	25 24.8	10 15.1	21 9.0	27 39.2	15 36.1	22 57.0	5 14.8	8 24.9
26 Sa	0 17 4	2 22 40	6♏15 12	12♏50 7	2 21.9	26 40.8	11 29.7	21 47.4	27 32.6	15 39.6	22 58.2	5 15.0	8 26.9
27 Su	0 21 1	3 21 30	19 28 29	26 10 17	2 21.9	27 55.4	12 44.4	22 25.8	27 25.9	15 43.1	22 59.5	5 15.3	8 29.0
28 M	0 24 57	4 20 22	2♐55 33	9♐44 13	2 21.7	29 8.3	13 59.1	23 4.2	27 19.1	15 46.7	23 0.8	5 15.7	8 31.1
29 Tu	0 28 54	5 19 16	16 36 17	23 31 39	2 21.5	0♏19.6	15 13.8	23 42.6	27 12.2	15 50.4	23 2.2	5 16.0	8 33.2
30 W	0 32 50	6 18 12	0♑30 15	7♑31 56	2D 21.3	1 29.0	16 28.4	24 21.0	27 5.1	15 54.2	23 3.6	5 16.4	8 35.3

LONGITUDE — OCTOBER 1987

Day	Sid.Time	☉	0 hr ☽	Noon ☽	True ☊	☿	♀	♂	♃	♄	♅	♆	♇
1 Th	0 36 47	7♎17 10	14♑36 31	21♑43 46	2♈21.4	2♏36.6	17♎43.1	24♍59.5	26♈58.0	15♐58.1	23♐ 5.0	5♑16.9	8♏37.4
2 F	0 40 43	8 16 9	28 53 24	6♒ 5 4	2 21.6	3 42.1	18 57.8	25 37.9	26R 50.7	16 2.1	23 6.6	5 17.4	8 39.6
3 Sa	0 44 40	9 15 10	13♒18 19	20 32 40	2 22.1	4 45.3	20 12.5	26 16.4	26 43.4	16 6.1	23 8.1	5 17.9	8 41.8
4 Su	0 48 37	10 14 12	27 47 36	5♓ 2 30	2 22.8	5 46.2	21 27.2	26 54.8	26 36.0	16 10.2	23 9.7	5 18.4	8 43.9
5 M	0 52 33	11 13 16	12♓16 43	19 29 38	2 23.4	6 44.5	22 41.8	27 33.3	26 28.4	16 14.4	23 11.4	5 19.0	8 46.1
6 Tu	0 56 30	12 12 22	26 40 32	3♈48 49	2R 23.8	7 40.0	23 56.5	28 11.8	26 20.8	16 18.6	23 13.1	5 19.6	8 48.4
7 W	1 0 26	13 11 31	10♈53 50	17 55 3	2 23.8	8 32.5	25 11.2	28 50.3	26 13.2	16 22.9	23 14.8	5 20.2	8 50.6
8 Th	1 4 23	14 10 41	24 51 57	1♉44 9	2 23.1	9 21.6	26 25.9	29 28.8	26 5.4	16 27.4	23 16.6	5 20.9	8 52.8
9 F	1 8 19	15 9 53	8♉31 19	15 13 15	2 21.8	10 7.1	27 40.6	0♎ 7.3	25 57.6	16 31.8	23 18.4	5 21.5	8 55.1
10 Sa	1 12 16	16 9 8	21 49 52	28 21 9	2 20.1	10 48.6	28 55.2	0 45.8	25 49.7	16 36.4	23 20.3	5 22.3	8 57.4
11 Su	1 16 12	17 8 24	4♊47 13	11♊ 8 15	2 18.0	11 25.8	0♏ 9.9	1 24.4	25 41.8	16 41.0	23 22.2	5 23.0	8 59.6
12 M	1 20 9	18 7 43	17 24 33	23 36 28	2 16.0	11 58.2	1 24.6	2 2.9	25 33.9	16 45.7	23 24.2	5 23.8	9 1.9
13 Tu	1 24 6	19 7 5	29 44 26	5♋48 55	2 14.3	12 25.4	2 39.3	2 41.5	25 25.9	16 50.5	23 26.2	5 24.7	9 4.2
14 W	1 28 2	20 6 28	11♋50 28	17 49 38	2D 13.3	12 46.9	3 54.0	3 20.1	25 17.8	16 55.3	23 28.3	5 25.5	9 6.6
15 Th	1 31 59	21 5 54	23 47 0	29 43 10	2 13.1	13 2.3	5 8.7	3 58.7	25 9.7	17 0.2	23 30.4	5 26.4	9 8.9
16 F	1 35 55	22 5 23	5♌38 44	11♌34 19	2 13.7	13R 11.0	6 23.4	4 37.3	25 1.6	17 5.2	23 32.5	5 27.3	9 11.2
17 Sa	1 39 52	23 4 53	17 30 31	23 27 54	2 15.0	13 12.4	7 38.1	5 16.0	24 53.5	17 10.2	23 34.7	5 28.3	9 13.6
18 Su	1 43 48	24 4 26	29 27 1	5♍28 23	2 16.6	13 6.2	8 52.9	5 54.6	24 45.4	17 15.3	23 36.9	5 29.3	9 15.9
19 M	1 47 45	25 4 1	11♍32 30	17 39 47	2 18.2	12 51.8	10 7.6	6 33.3	24 37.3	17 20.5	23 39.2	5 30.3	9 18.3
20 Tu	1 51 41	26 3 38	23 50 36	0♎ 5 18	2R 19.4	12 28.9	11 22.3	7 12.0	24 29.2	17 25.7	23 41.5	5 31.3	9 20.7
21 W	1 55 38	27 3 17	6♎24 6	12 47 11	2 19.5	11 57.3	12 37.0	7 50.7	24 21.1	17 31.0	23 43.8	5 32.4	9 23.1
22 Th	1 59 34	28 2 58	19 14 40	25 46 32	2 18.5	11 16.9	13 51.7	8 29.4	24 13.0	17 36.3	23 46.2	5 33.5	9 25.5
23 F	2 3 31	29 2 42	2♏22 45	9♏ 3 10	2 16.1	10 27.9	15 6.4	9 8.1	24 4.9	17 41.8	23 48.6	5 34.6	9 27.8
24 Sa	2 7 28	0♏ 2 27	15 47 36	22 35 45	2 12.5	9 31.0	16 21.2	9 46.8	23 56.8	17 47.2	23 51.1	5 35.8	9 30.2
25 Su	2 11 24	1 2 15	29 27 18	6♐21 54	2 8.1	8 26.8	17 35.9	10 25.5	23 48.8	17 52.8	23 53.6	5 37.0	9 32.7
26 M	2 15 21	2 2 4	13♐19 9	20 18 38	2 3.5	7 16.9	18 50.6	11 4.3	23 40.9	17 58.4	23 56.2	5 38.2	9 35.1
27 Tu	2 19 17	3 1 55	27 19 57	4♑22 44	1 59.2	6 2.7	20 5.3	11 43.1	23 33.0	18 4.0	23 58.8	5 39.5	9 37.5
28 W	2 23 14	4 1 48	11♑26 35	18 31 10	1 56.0	4 46.4	21 20.0	12 21.9	23 25.1	18 9.7	24 1.4	5 40.7	9 39.9
29 Th	2 27 10	5 1 42	25 36 12	2♒41 22	1D 54.3	3 30.1	22 34.8	13 0.7	23 17.3	18 15.5	24 4.0	5 42.0	9 42.3
30 F	2 31 7	6 1 38	9♒46 28	16 51 15	1 54.0	2 16.2	23 49.5	13 39.5	23 9.6	18 21.3	24 6.7	5 43.4	9 44.8
31 Sa	2 35 4	7 1 36	23 55 32	0♓59 6	1 54.9	1 7.0	25 4.2	14 18.3	23 1.9	18 27.2	24 9.5	5 44.7	9 47.2

Astro Data Dy Hr Mn	Planet Ingress Dy Hr Mn	Last Aspect Dy Hr Mn	☽ Ingress Dy Hr Mn	Last Aspect Dy Hr Mn	☽ Ingress Dy Hr Mn	☽ Phases & Eclipses Dy Hr Mn
♅∠♇ 1 9:00	☿ ♎ 7 13:52	2 16:05 ♃ △	♑ 2 17:04	1 20:37 ♃ □	♒ 2 1:51	1 3:48 ☽ 8♐12
♅ D 1 14:23	♀ ♎ 16 18:12	4 17:15 ♃ □	♒ 4 18:22	3 22:02 ♃ ✱	♓ 4 3:39	7 18:13 ○ 14♓35
☽0N 8 20:16	☉ ♎ 23 13:45	6 17:20 ♃ ✱	♓ 6 18:37	6 2:40 ♂ ☍	♈ 6 5:35	14 23:44 ☽ 21♊37
☿0S 8 2:06	☿ ♏ 28 17:21	8 7:33 ♅ □	♈ 8 19:34	8 3:00 ♀ ☍	♉ 8 8:57	23 3:08 ● 29♍34
♆ D 17 8:23		10 21:04 ♃ ☌	♉ 10 22:57	9 3:00 ☿ ☍	♊ 10 15:03	23 3:11:26 ✔ A 3'49"
♀0S 19 3:20	♂ ♎ 8 19:27	12 20:47 ♀ △	♊ 13 5:54	12 15:39 ♃ ✱	♋ 13 0:31	30 10:39 ☽ 6♑44
☽0S 23 4:46	♀ ♏ 10 20:49	15 13:31 ♃ ✱	♋ 15 16:22	15 2:45 ♃ □	♌ 15 12:34	
	☉ ♏ 23 23:01	18 1:29 ♃ □	♌ 18 4:50	17 14:42 ♃ △	♍ 18 1:06	7 4:12 ○ 13♈22
☽0N 6 6:17		20 13:27 ♃ △	♍ 20 17:13	19 23:42 ♅ □	♎ 20 11:50	7 4:02 ☍ A 0.987
♂0S 12 8:49		23 3:08 ☉ ☌	♎ 23 3:58	22 17:28 ☉ ☌	♏ 22 19:41	14 18:06 ☽ 20♋51
☿ R 16 16:46		25 8:06 ♃ ☍	♏ 25 12:30	24 1:05 ♀ ☌	♐ 25 0:57	22 17:28 ● 28♎46
☽0S 20 12:36		27 5:34 ♂ ✱	♐ 27 18:49	26 18:15 ♅ ☌	♑ 27 4:33	29 17:10 ☽ 5♒45
♃△♅ 24 13:04		29 18:11 ♃ △	♑ 29 23:08	28 20:07 ♃ □	♒ 29 7:27	
				31 2:08 ♀ □	♓ 31 10:19	

Astro Data

1 SEPTEMBER 1987
Julian Day # 32020
Delta T 55.6 sec
SVP 05♓25'56"
Obliquity 23°26'37"
⚷ Chiron 27♊58.9
☽ Mean ☊ 3♈37.6

1 OCTOBER 1987
Julian Day # 32050
Delta T 55.7 sec
SVP 05♓25'52"
Obliquity 23°26'37"
⚷ Chiron 28♊48.0
☽ Mean ☊ 2♈02.3

NOVEMBER 1987 LONGITUDE

Day	Sid.Time	☉	0 hr ☽	Noon ☽	True ☊	☿	♀	♂	♃	♄	♅	♆	♇
1 Su	2 39 0	8♏ 1 35	8♓ 1 45	15♓ 3 18	1♈56.3	0♏ 4.7	26♏18.9	14♎57.1	22♈54.3	18♐33.1	24♐12.2	5♑46.1	9♏49.6
2 M	2 42 57	9 1 36	22 3 31	29 2 9	1R57.6	29♎11.0	27 33.5	15 36.0	22R46.8	18 39.1	24 15.0	5 47.6	9 52.1
3 Tu	2 46 53	10 1 38	5♈58 56	12♈53 35	1 57.9	28R27.5	28 48.2	16 14.8	22 39.4	18 45.1	24 17.8	5 49.0	9 54.5
4 W	2 50 50	11 1 42	19 45 49	26 35 17	1 56.5	27 54.9	0♐ 2.9	16 53.7	22 32.1	18 51.1	24 20.7	5 50.5	9 56.9
5 Th	2 54 46	12 1 48	3♉21 42	10♉ 4 46	1 53.1	27 33.9	1 17.6	17 32.6	22 24.9	18 57.2	24 23.6	5 52.0	9 59.3
6 F	2 58 43	13 1 55	16 44 13	23 19 48	1 47.8	27D 24.6	2 32.3	18 11.5	22 17.8	19 3.4	24 26.5	5 53.5	10 1.8
7 Sa	3 2 39	14 2 5	29 51 23	6♊18 48	1 40.8	27 26.6	3 46.9	18 50.4	22 10.8	19 9.6	24 29.5	5 55.0	10 4.2
8 Su	3 6 36	15 2 16	12♊42 2	19 1 6	1 32.9	27 39.5	5 1.6	19 29.3	22 3.9	19 15.8	24 32.5	5 56.6	10 6.6
9 M	3 10 33	16 2 30	25 16 8	1♋27 17	1 24.8	28 2.5	6 16.2	20 8.3	21 57.2	19 22.1	24 35.5	5 58.2	10 9.0
10 Tu	3 14 29	17 2 45	7♋34 49	13 39 6	1 17.5	28 35.0	7 30.9	20 47.2	21 50.5	19 28.5	24 38.5	5 59.8	10 11.5
11 W	3 18 26	18 3 2	19 40 30	25 39 30	1 11.7	29 15.9	8 45.6	21 26.2	21 44.0	19 34.8	24 41.6	6 1.5	10 13.9
12 Th	3 22 22	19 3 21	1♌36 37	7♌32 25	1 7.8	0♏ 4.4	10 0.2	22 5.2	21 37.7	19 41.2	24 44.7	6 3.2	10 16.3
13 F	3 26 19	20 3 42	13 27 30	19 22 29	1D 5.8	0 59.7	11 14.9	22 44.3	21 31.5	19 47.7	24 47.8	6 4.9	10 18.7
14 Sa	3 30 15	21 4 5	25 18 1	1♍14 47	1 5.6	2 0.8	12 29.5	23 23.3	21 25.4	19 54.2	24 51.0	6 6.6	10 21.1
15 Su	3 34 12	22 4 30	7♍13 26	13 14 38	1 6.6	3 7.1	13 44.2	24 2.4	21 19.4	20 0.7	24 54.2	6 8.3	10 23.5
16 M	3 38 8	23 4 56	19 19 0	25 27 9	1R 7.8	4 17.8	14 58.8	24 41.4	21 13.6	20 7.3	24 57.4	6 10.1	10 25.9
17 Tu	3 42 5	24 5 25	1♎39 38	7♎56 56	1 8.4	5 32.3	16 13.5	25 20.5	21 8.0	20 13.9	25 0.6	6 11.8	10 28.3
18 W	3 46 2	25 5 55	14 19 29	20 47 37	1 7.4	6 50.0	17 28.1	25 59.6	21 2.5	20 20.5	25 3.9	6 13.7	10 30.7
19 Th	3 49 58	26 6 27	27 21 31	4♏ 1 18	1 4.3	8 10.5	18 42.7	26 38.7	20 57.2	20 27.1	25 7.1	6 15.5	10 33.0
20 F	3 53 55	27 7 1	10♏46 54	17 38 10	0 58.6	9 33.3	19 57.4	27 17.9	20 52.1	20 33.8	25 10.4	6 17.3	10 35.4
21 Sa	3 57 51	28 7 37	24 34 45	1♐36 11	0 50.8	10 58.1	21 12.0	27 57.0	20 47.1	20 40.6	25 13.8	6 19.2	10 37.7
22 Su	4 1 48	29 8 14	8♐41 52	15 51 7	0 41.3	12 24.5	22 26.6	28 36.2	20 42.4	20 47.3	25 17.1	6 21.1	10 40.1
23 M	4 5 44	0♐ 8 52	23 3 9	0♑17 8	0 31.2	13 52.2	23 41.3	29 15.4	20 37.7	20 54.1	25 20.5	6 23.0	10 42.4
24 Tu	4 9 41	1 9 32	7♑32 13	14 47 37	0 21.8	15 21.1	24 55.9	29 54.6	20 33.3	21 0.9	25 23.9	6 24.9	10 44.7
25 W	4 13 37	2 10 13	22 2 33	29 16 22	0 14.0	16 50.9	26 10.5	0♏33.8	20 29.1	21 7.7	25 27.3	6 26.9	10 47.0
26 Th	4 17 34	3 10 55	6♒28 29	13♒38 26	0 8.7	18 21.5	27 25.1	1 13.0	20 25.0	21 14.6	25 30.7	6 28.8	10 49.3
27 F	4 21 31	4 11 38	20 45 52	27 50 33	0 5.8	19 52.7	28 39.7	1 52.2	20 21.2	21 21.5	25 34.1	6 30.8	10 51.6
28 Sa	4 25 27	5 12 22	4♓52 20	11♓51 11	0D 5.0	21 24.4	29 54.2	2 31.5	20 17.5	21 28.4	25 37.6	6 32.8	10 53.9
29 Su	4 29 24	6 13 7	18 47 4	25 40 2	0R 5.4	22 56.5	1♑ 8.8	3 10.8	20 14.0	21 35.3	25 41.1	6 34.8	10 56.2
30 M	4 33 20	7 13 53	2♈30 11	9♈17 34	0 5.6	24 28.9	2 23.4	3 50.0	20 10.7	21 42.2	25 44.5	6 36.8	10 58.4

DECEMBER 1987 LONGITUDE

Day	Sid.Time	☉	0 hr ☽	Noon ☽	True ☊	☿	♀	♂	♃	♄	♅	♆	♇
1 Tu	4 37 17	8♐14 40	16♈ 2 15	22♈44 19	0♈ 4.6	26♏ 1.6	3♑37.9	4♏29.3	20♈ 7.7	21♐49.2	25♐48.0	6♑38.9	11♏ 0.6
2 W	4 41 13	9 15 28	29 23 47	6♉ 0 39	0R 1.1	27 34.4	4 52.4	5 8.6	20R 4.8	21 56.2	25 51.6	6 40.9	11 2.8
3 Th	4 45 10	10 16 17	12♉34 52	19 6 25	29♓54.8	29 7.4	6 6.9	5 48.0	20 2.1	22 3.2	25 55.1	6 43.0	11 5.0
4 F	4 49 6	11 17 7	25 35 12	2♊ 1 7	29 45.5	0♐40.6	7 21.4	6 27.3	19 59.6	22 10.2	25 58.6	6 45.1	11 7.2
5 Sa	4 53 3	12 17 58	8♊24 7	14 44 6	29 33.8	2 13.8	8 35.9	7 6.7	19 57.3	22 17.2	26 2.2	6 47.2	11 9.4
6 Su	4 57 0	13 18 50	21 1 1	27 14 52	29 20.5	3 47.1	9 50.4	7 46.0	19 55.3	22 24.2	26 5.7	6 49.3	11 11.5
7 M	5 0 56	14 19 44	3♋25 38	9♋33 26	29 6.8	5 20.5	11 4.9	8 25.4	19 53.4	22 31.3	26 9.3	6 51.4	11 13.7
8 Tu	5 4 53	15 20 38	15 38 22	21 40 40	28 54.0	6 54.0	12 19.3	9 4.8	19 51.7	22 38.3	26 12.9	6 53.6	11 15.8
9 W	5 8 49	16 21 33	27 40 33	3♌38 23	28 43.0	8 27.5	13 33.7	9 44.3	19 50.3	22 45.4	26 16.5	6 55.7	11 17.9
10 Th	5 12 46	17 22 30	9♌34 31	15 29 26	28 34.6	10 1.0	14 48.1	10 23.7	19 49.0	22 52.5	26 20.1	6 57.9	11 20.0
11 F	5 16 42	18 23 28	21 23 37	27 17 37	28 29.0	11 34.6	16 2.6	11 3.2	19 48.0	22 59.5	26 23.7	7 0.0	11 22.0
12 Sa	5 20 39	19 24 26	3♍12 4	9♍ 7 35	28 26.0	13 8.2	17 16.9	11 42.6	19 47.1	23 6.6	26 27.3	7 2.2	11 24.0
13 Su	5 24 35	20 25 26	15 4 51	21 4 33	28D 25.0	14 41.9	18 31.3	12 22.1	19 46.5	23 13.7	26 30.9	7 4.4	11 26.1
14 M	5 28 32	21 26 27	27 7 24	3♎14 5	28R 25.0	16 15.7	19 45.7	13 1.7	19 46.1	23 20.8	26 34.6	7 6.6	11 28.1
15 Tu	5 32 29	22 27 29	9♎25 17	15 41 39	28 24.7	17 49.6	21 0.0	13 41.2	19D 45.9	23 27.9	26 38.2	7 8.8	11 30.0
16 W	5 36 25	23 28 32	22 3 46	28 32 10	28 23.0	19 23.6	22 14.3	14 20.7	19 45.9	23 35.0	26 41.8	7 11.0	11 32.0
17 Th	5 40 22	24 29 36	5♏ 7 14	11♏49 17	28 19.0	20 57.6	23 28.7	15 0.3	19 46.1	23 42.1	26 45.4	7 13.3	11 33.9
18 F	5 44 18	25 30 40	18 38 27	25 34 40	28 12.2	22 31.8	24 43.0	15 39.9	19 46.5	23 49.2	26 49.1	7 15.5	11 35.8
19 Sa	5 48 15	26 31 46	2♐37 43	9♐47 11	28 2.6	24 6.1	25 57.2	16 19.5	19 47.1	23 56.3	26 52.7	7 17.7	11 37.7
20 Su	5 52 11	27 32 53	17 2 24	24 22 34	27 51.1	25 40.6	27 11.5	16 59.1	19 47.9	24 3.4	26 56.4	7 20.0	11 39.6
21 M	5 56 8	28 34 0	1♑46 41	9♑13 39	27 38.7	27 15.3	28 25.7	17 38.7	19 49.0	24 10.5	27 0.0	7 22.2	11 41.4
22 Tu	6 0 5	29 35 8	16 42 16	24 11 20	27 26.8	28 50.1	29 40.0	18 18.4	19 50.3	24 17.6	27 3.6	7 24.5	11 43.2
23 W	6 4 1	0♑36 16	1♒39 40	9♒ 6 13	27 16.9	0♑25.1	0♒54.2	18 58.0	19 51.7	24 24.7	27 7.3	7 26.7	11 45.0
24 Th	6 7 58	1 37 24	16 30 0	23 50 14	27 9.6	2 0.3	2 8.3	19 37.7	19 53.4	24 31.8	27 10.9	7 29.0	11 46.8
25 F	6 11 54	2 38 32	1♓ 6 18	8♓17 46	27 5.3	3 35.8	3 22.5	20 17.4	19 55.3	24 38.8	27 14.5	7 31.3	11 48.5
26 Sa	6 15 51	3 39 41	15 24 20	22 25 55	27D 3.5	5 11.5	4 36.6	20 57.1	19 57.4	24 45.9	27 18.2	7 33.5	11 50.2
27 Su	6 19 47	4 40 49	29 22 30	6♈14 12	27R 3.3	6 47.4	5 50.7	21 36.8	19 59.6	24 52.9	27 21.8	7 35.8	11 51.9
28 M	6 23 44	5 41 58	13♈ 1 14	19 43 49	27 3.2	8 23.5	7 4.7	22 16.5	20 2.1	24 59.9	27 25.4	7 38.1	11 53.5
29 Tu	6 27 40	6 43 6	26 22 14	2♉56 47	27 1.9	9 60.0	8 18.7	22 56.2	20 4.8	25 6.9	27 29.0	7 40.4	11 55.2
30 W	6 31 37	7 44 14	9♉27 45	15 55 22	26 58.3	11 36.7	9 32.7	23 36.0	20 7.7	25 13.9	27 32.6	7 42.6	11 56.8
31 Th	6 35 34	8 45 23	22 19 54	28 41 33	26 51.9	13 13.7	10 46.7	24 15.7	20 10.8	25 20.9	27 36.2	7 44.9	11 58.3

Astro Data Dy Hr Mn	Planet Ingress Dy Hr Mn	Last Aspect Dy Hr Mn	☽ Ingress Dy Hr Mn	Last Aspect Dy Hr Mn	☽ Ingress Dy Hr Mn	☽ Phases & Eclipses Dy Hr Mn	Astro Data
☽0N 2 14:15	☿ ♎ 1 1:57	2 10:23 ♀ △	♈ 2 13:40	1 17:35 ♅ △	♉ 2 1:06	5 16:46 ○ 12♉44	1 NOVEMBER 1987
☿ D 6 7:39	♀ ♐ 3 23:04	4 13:57 ☿ ☍	♉ 4 18:02	2 21:15 ♇ ☍	♊ 4 8:13	13 14:38 ☽ 20♌41	Julian Day # 32081
♇0S 12 23:27	☿ ♏ 11 21:57	5 16:46 ☉ ☍	♊ 7 0:16	6 9:49 ♅ ☍	♋ 6 17:20	21 6:33 ● 28♏24	Delta T 55.7 sec
☽0S 16 21:11	☉ ♐ 22 20:29	9 5:35 ☿ △	♋ 9 9:10	8 8:22 ♃ □	♌ 9 4:40	28 0:37 ☽ 5♓14	SVP 05♓25'48"
♃△♄ 21 13:39	♂ ♏ 24 3:19	11 20:39 ☿ □	♌ 11 20:45	11 10:14 ♅ △	♍ 11 17:30		Obliquity 23°26'36"
☽0N 29 19:38	♀ ♑ 28 1:51	13 23:05 ♅ △	♍ 14 9:29	13 22:55 ♅ □	♎ 14 5:40	5 8:01 ○ 12♊38	⚷ Chiron 28♊26.6R
		16 11:05 ♅ □	♎ 16 20:48	16 8:39 ♅ ⚹	♏ 16 14:41	13 11:41 ☽ 20♍55	☽ Mean ☊ 0♈23.8
♅∠♇ 9 21:51	☊ ♓ 2 5:13	18 22:38 ♂ ☌	♏ 19 4:47	18 11:32 ♀ ⚹	♐ 18 19:33	20 18:25 ● 28♐20	
☽0S 14 5:08	☿ ♐ 3 13:33	21 6:33 ☉ ☌	♐ 21 9:16	20 18:25 ☉ ☌	♑ 20 21:08	27 10:01 ☽ 5♈06	1 DECEMBER 1987
♃ D 15 12:22	☉ ♑ 22 9:46	23 10:47 ♂ ⚹	♑ 23 11:32	22 5:02 ♃ □	♒ 22 21:20		Julian Day # 32111
☽0N 27 0:13	☿ ♑ 22 17:40	24 21:26 ♃ □	♒ 25 13:13	24 17:35 ♅ ⚹	♓ 24 22:10		Delta T 55.8 sec
	♀ ♒ 22 6:29	27 14:41 ♀ ⚹	♓ 27 15:40	26 20:30 ♅ □	♈ 27 1:05		SVP 05♓25'43"
		29 12:05 ♅ □	♈ 29 19:36	29 2:02 ♅ △	♉ 29 6:37		Obliquity 23°26'36"
				31 3:50 ♂ ☍	♊ 31 14:29		⚷ Chiron 27♊03.8R
							☽ Mean ☊ 28♓48.5

LONGITUDE — JANUARY 1988

Day	Sid.Time	☉	0 hr ☽	Noon ☽	True ☊	☿	♀	♂	♃	♄	♅	♆	♇
1 F	6 39 30	9♑46 31	5♊ 0 29	11♊16 51	26♓42.4	14♑51.0	12♒ 0.6	24♏55.5	20♈14.1	25♐27.9	27♐39.8	7♑47.2	11♏59.9
2 Sa	6 43 27	10 47 39	17 30 45	23 42 17	26R 30.5	16 28.5	13 14.5	25 35.3	20 17.6	25 34.8	27 43.4	7 49.4	12 1.4
3 Su	6 47 23	11 48 48	29 51 33	5♋58 35	26 16.9	18 6.4	14 28.3	26 15.1	20 21.2	25 41.8	27 46.9	7 51.7	12 2.9
4 M	6 51 20	12 49 56	12♋ 3 30	18 6 21	26 2.9	19 44.5	15 42.1	26 54.9	20 25.1	25 48.7	27 50.5	7 54.0	12 4.3
5 Tu	6 55 16	13 51 4	24 7 16	0♌ 6 22	25 49.6	21 22.9	16 55.8	27 34.8	20 29.2	25 55.6	27 54.0	7 56.2	12 5.7
6 W	6 59 13	14 52 12	6♌ 3 52	11 59 58	25 38.1	23 1.5	18 9.6	28 14.6	20 33.4	26 2.4	27 57.5	7 58.5	12 7.1
7 Th	7 3 9	15 53 21	17 54 55	23 49 5	25 29.1	24 40.3	19 23.2	28 54.5	20 37.9	26 9.3	28 1.0	8 0.8	12 8.5
8 F	7 7 6	16 54 29	29 42 47	5♍36 29	25 23.1	26 19.2	20 36.9	29 34.4	20 42.5	26 16.1	28 4.5	8 3.0	12 9.8
9 Sa	7 11 3	17 55 37	11♍30 39	17 25 48	25 19.8	27 58.3	21 50.4	0♐14.3	20 47.3	26 22.9	28 8.0	8 5.3	12 11.1
10 Su	7 14 59	18 56 45	23 22 30	29 21 22	25D 18.8	29 37.4	23 4.0	0 54.2	20 52.3	26 29.6	28 11.5	8 7.5	12 12.4
11 M	7 18 56	19 57 53	5♎23 2	11♎28 10	25 19.0	1♒16.5	24 17.5	1 34.1	20 57.4	26 36.3	28 14.9	8 9.8	12 13.6
12 Tu	7 22 52	20 59 2	17 37 27	23 51 32	25R 19.6	2 55.5	25 30.9	2 14.1	21 2.8	26 43.0	28 18.4	8 12.0	12 14.8
13 W	7 26 49	22 0 10	0♏11 4	6♏36 41	25 19.3	4 34.3	26 44.3	2 54.1	21 8.3	26 49.7	28 21.8	8 14.2	12 16.0
14 Th	7 30 45	23 1 18	13 8 54	19 48 11	25 17.3	6 12.6	27 57.7	3 34.1	21 14.0	26 56.4	28 25.2	8 16.4	12 17.1
15 F	7 34 42	24 2 26	26 34 51	3♐29 6	25 12.9	7 50.5	29 11.0	4 14.1	21 19.9	27 3.0	28 28.6	8 18.6	12 18.2
16 Sa	7 38 38	25 3 34	10♐30 55	17 40 7	25 6.2	9 27.6	0♓24.2	4 54.1	21 26.0	27 9.5	28 31.9	8 20.8	12 19.3
17 Su	7 42 35	26 4 42	24 56 16	2♑18 42	24 57.7	11 3.7	1 37.4	5 34.1	21 32.2	27 16.1	28 35.3	8 23.0	12 20.4
18 M	7 46 32	27 5 50	9♑46 35	17 18 49	24 48.2	12 38.6	2 50.6	6 14.1	21 38.6	27 22.6	28 38.6	8 25.2	12 21.4
19 Tu	7 50 28	28 6 57	24 54 10	2♒31 19	24 38.9	14 11.9	4 3.7	6 54.2	21 45.2	27 29.0	28 41.9	8 27.4	12 22.3
20 W	7 54 25	29 8 3	10♒ 8 53	17 45 29	24 31.1	15 43.3	5 16.7	7 34.3	21 51.9	27 35.5	28 45.2	8 29.6	12 23.3
21 Th	7 58 21	0♒ 9 9	25 19 51	2♓50 49	24 25.5	17 12.4	6 29.7	8 14.3	21 58.8	27 41.9	28 48.4	8 31.7	12 24.2
22 F	8 2 18	1 10 14	10♓17 25	17 38 52	24D 22.4	18 38.5	7 42.6	8 54.4	22 5.9	27 48.2	28 51.6	8 33.9	12 25.0
23 Sa	8 6 14	2 11 18	24 54 34	2♈ 4 10	24 21.5	20 1.3	8 55.4	9 34.5	22 13.1	27 54.5	28 54.8	8 36.0	12 25.9
24 Su	8 10 11	3 12 21	9♈ 7 26	16 4 22	24 22.2	21 20.1	10 8.2	10 14.6	22 20.5	28 0.7	28 58.0	8 38.1	12 26.7
25 M	8 14 8	4 13 23	22 55 4	29 39 45	24R 23.3	22 34.1	11 20.9	10 54.7	22 28.0	28 6.9	29 1.2	8 40.2	12 27.4
26 Tu	8 18 4	5 14 24	6♉18 43	12♉52 20	24 23.7	23 42.7	12 33.5	11 34.9	22 35.7	28 13.1	29 4.3	8 42.3	12 28.1
27 W	8 22 1	6 15 24	19 20 59	25 45 6	24 22.7	24 45.1	13 46.1	12 15.0	22 43.6	28 19.2	29 7.4	8 44.4	12 28.8
28 Th	8 25 57	7 16 22	2♊ 5 4	8♊21 20	24 19.7	25 40.5	14 58.5	12 55.1	22 51.6	28 25.3	29 10.4	8 46.4	12 29.5
29 F	8 29 54	8 17 20	14 34 15	20 44 12	24 14.5	26 28.0	16 10.9	13 35.3	22 59.7	28 31.3	29 13.5	8 48.5	12 30.1
30 Sa	8 33 50	9 18 17	26 51 31	2♋56 31	24 7.5	27 6.8	17 23.2	14 15.5	23 8.0	28 37.3	29 16.5	8 50.5	12 30.7
31 Su	8 37 47	10 19 12	8♋59 27	15 0 35	23 59.3	27 36.0	18 35.5	14 55.7	23 16.4	28 43.2	29 19.4	8 52.5	12 31.2

LONGITUDE — FEBRUARY 1988

Day	Sid.Time	☉	0 hr ☽	Noon ☽	True ☊	☿	♀	♂	♃	♄	♅	♆	♇
1 M	8 41 43	11♒20 6	21♋ 0 10	26♋58 22	23♓50.6	27♒55.2	19♓47.6	15♐35.9	23♈25.0	28♐49.1	29♐22.4	8♑54.5	12♏31.7
2 Tu	8 45 40	12 20 59	2♌55 26	8♌51 31	23R 42.4	28R 3.6	20 59.6	16 16.1	23 33.7	28 54.9	29 25.3	8 56.5	12 32.2
3 W	8 49 37	13 21 51	14 46 51	20 41 39	23 35.4	28 0.9	22 11.6	16 56.3	23 42.6	29 0.6	29 28.2	8 58.5	12 32.7
4 Th	8 53 33	14 22 42	26 36 6	2♍30 29	23 30.1	27 47.1	23 23.4	17 36.5	23 51.6	29 6.3	29 31.0	9 0.4	12 33.1
5 F	8 57 30	15 23 32	8♍25 2	14 20 6	23 26.8	27 22.2	24 35.2	18 16.8	24 0.7	29 12.0	29 33.8	9 2.4	12 33.4
6 Sa	9 1 26	16 24 21	20 15 58	26 13 3	23D 25.5	26 46.8	25 46.8	18 57.1	24 9.9	29 17.5	29 36.6	9 4.3	12 33.7
7 Su	9 5 23	17 25 8	2♎11 44	8♎12 28	23 25.8	26 1.7	26 58.4	19 37.3	24 19.3	29 23.1	29 39.4	9 6.2	12 34.0
8 M	9 9 19	18 25 55	14 15 44	20 22 2	23 27.2	25 8.1	28 9.9	20 17.6	24 28.8	29 28.5	29 42.1	9 8.0	12 34.3
9 Tu	9 13 16	19 26 41	26 31 55	2♏45 54	23 29.0	24 7.4	29 21.2	20 57.9	24 38.4	29 33.9	29 44.7	9 9.9	12 34.5
10 W	9 17 12	20 27 25	9♏ 4 32	15 28 22	23R 30.5	23 1.5	0♈32.5	21 38.2	24 48.2	29 39.3	29 47.4	9 11.7	12 34.7
11 Th	9 21 9	21 28 9	21 57 54	28 33 36	23 31.1	21 52.1	1 43.6	22 18.6	24 58.1	29 44.6	29 50.0	9 13.5	12 34.8
12 F	9 25 6	22 28 52	5♐15 51	12♐ 4 57	23 30.3	20 41.3	2 54.7	22 58.9	25 8.1	29 49.8	29 52.5	9 15.3	12 34.9
13 Sa	9 29 2	23 29 33	19 1 3	26 4 10	23 28.2	19 31.0	4 5.6	23 39.2	25 18.2	29 54.9	29 55.1	9 17.1	12 35.0
14 Su	9 32 59	24 30 14	3♑14 10	10♑30 42	23 24.9	18 22.9	5 16.4	24 19.6	25 28.4	0♑ 0.0	29 57.5	9 18.8	12R 35.1
15 M	9 36 55	25 30 54	17 53 13	25 20 57	23 20.9	17 18.6	6 27.1	24 60.0	25 38.8	0 5.1	29 60.0	9 20.5	12 35.1
16 Tu	9 40 52	26 31 32	2♒53 0	10♒28 15	23 16.9	16 19.5	7 37.7	25 40.4	25 49.3	0 10.0	0♑ 2.4	9 22.3	12 35.0
17 W	9 44 48	27 32 9	18 5 29	25 43 23	23 13.4	15 26.6	8 48.2	26 20.7	25 59.8	0 14.9	0 4.8	9 23.9	12 35.0
18 Th	9 48 45	28 32 44	3♓20 40	10♓56 2	23 11.1	14 40.5	9 58.5	27 1.1	26 10.5	0 19.7	0 7.1	9 25.6	12 34.9
19 F	9 52 41	29 33 18	18 28 18	25 56 23	23D 10.1	14 1.8	11 8.7	27 41.5	26 21.3	0 24.4	0 9.4	9 27.2	12 34.7
20 Sa	9 56 38	0♓33 50	3♈19 24	10♈36 38	23 10.3	13 30.7	12 18.8	28 21.9	26 32.2	0 29.1	0 11.6	9 28.8	12 34.5
21 Su	10 0 35	1 34 20	17 47 33	24 51 49	23 11.3	13 7.2	13 28.7	29 2.3	26 43.2	0 33.7	0 13.8	9 30.4	12 34.3
22 M	10 4 31	2 34 49	1♉49 15	8♉39 53	23 12.8	12 51.3	14 38.5	29 42.7	26 54.3	0 38.2	0 15.9	9 31.9	12 34.1
23 Tu	10 8 28	3 35 15	15 23 49	22 1 19	23 14.1	12D 42.7	15 48.2	0♑23.2	27 5.5	0 42.7	0 18.1	9 33.5	12 33.8
24 W	10 12 24	4 35 40	28 32 44	4♊58 27	23R 14.9	12 41.1	16 57.7	1 3.6	27 16.8	0 47.0	0 20.1	9 35.0	12 33.5
25 Th	10 16 21	5 36 3	11♊18 57	17 34 42	23 14.9	12 46.2	18 7.0	1 44.0	27 28.2	0 51.3	0 22.1	9 36.4	12 33.1
26 F	10 20 17	6 36 24	23 46 12	29 54 0	23 14.1	12 57.6	19 16.2	2 24.4	27 39.7	0 55.5	0 24.1	9 37.9	12 32.7
27 Sa	10 24 14	7 36 43	5♋58 34	12♋ 0 23	23 12.5	13 14.9	20 25.2	3 4.9	27 51.3	0 59.7	0 26.0	9 39.3	12 32.3
28 Su	10 28 10	8 37 0	17 59 57	23 57 42	23 10.5	13 37.8	21 34.1	3 45.3	28 3.0	1 3.7	0 27.9	9 40.7	12 31.8
29 M	10 32 7	9 37 15	29 54 2	5♌49 21	23 8.3	14 5.8	22 42.7	4 25.8	28 14.8	1 7.7	0 29.8	9 42.1	12 31.4

Astro Data Dy Hr Mn	Planet Ingress Dy Hr Mn	Last Aspect Dy Hr Mn	☽ Ingress Dy Hr Mn	Last Aspect Dy Hr Mn	☽ Ingress Dy Hr Mn	☽ Phases & Eclipses Dy Hr Mn
☽0S 10 11:41	♂ ♐ 8 15:24	2 19:55 ♅ ☍	♋ 3 0:17	1 4:54 ♃ □	♌ 1 18:06	4 1:40 ○ 12♋54
♄∠♇ 17 18:42	☿ ♒ 10 5:28	5 7:20 ♂ △	♌ 5 11:47	4 5:57 ♅ △	♍ 4 6:54	12 7:04 ☽ 21♎17
☽0N 23 6:54	♀ ♓ 15 16:04	7 23:42 ♂ □	♍ 8 0:35	6 18:53 ♅ □	♎ 6 19:36	19 5:26 ● 28♑21
	☉ ♒ 20 20:24	10 9:43 ♅ □	♎ 10 13:17	9 6:14 ♅ ✶	♏ 9 6:42	25 21:54 ☽ 5♉09
☿ R 2 6:18		12 20:33 ♅ ✶	♏ 12 23:39	10 23:50 ♅ □	♐ 11 14:36	
☽0S 6 17:19	♀ ♈ 9 13:04	15 4:59 ♀ □	♐ 15 5:58	13 18:34 ♄ ☌	♑ 13 18:36	2 20:52 ○ 13♌14
♀0N 10 13:21	♄ ♑ 13 23:50	17 5:59 ♅ ☌	♑ 17 8:15	15 12:37 ♃ □	♒ 15 19:25	10 23:01 ☽ 21♏26
♄☌♅ 13 1:00	♅ ♑ 15 0:07	19 5:26 ☉ ☌	♒ 19 8:02	17 15:54 ☉ ☌	♓ 17 18:44	17 15:54 ● 28♒12
♇ R 14 14:49	☉ ♓ 19 10:35	21 5:34 ♅ ✶	♓ 21 7:27	19 15:33 ♂ □	♈ 19 18:35	24 12:15 ☽ 5♊07
☽0N 19 16:39	♂ ♑ 22 10:15	23 6:43 ♅ □	♈ 23 8:31	21 20:09 ♂ △	♉ 21 20:50	
☿ D 23 17:30		25 10:53 ♅ △	♉ 25 12:36	22 19:13 ☿ □	♊ 24 2:42	
♇0N 26 23:17		27 10:56 ☿ □	♊ 27 20:02	26 7:44 ♃ ✶	♋ 26 12:12	
		30 4:47 ♅ ☍	♋ 30 6:11	28 20:36 ♃ □	♌ 29 0:12	

Astro Data

1 JANUARY 1988
Julian Day # 32142
Delta T 55.8 sec
SVP 05♓25'37"
Obliquity 23°26'36"
⚷ Chiron 25♊09.1R
☽ Mean ☊ 27♓10.0

1 FEBRUARY 1988
Julian Day # 32173
Delta T 55.8 sec
SVP 05♓25'31"
Obliquity 23°26'36"
⚷ Chiron 23♊36.6R
☽ Mean ☊ 25♓31.5

MARCH 1988 — LONGITUDE

Day	Sid.Time	☉	0 hr ☽	Noon ☽	True ☊	☿	♀	♂	♃	♄	♅	♆	♇
1 Tu	10 36 4	10♓37 29	11♌44 1	17♌38 22	23♓ 6.2	14♒38.6	23♈51.2	5♑ 6.2	28♈26.6	1♑11.6	0♑31.6	9♑43.4	12♏30.8
2 W	10 40 0	11 37 40	23 32 43	29 27 20	23R 4.6	15 15.8	24 59.6	5 46.7	28 38.5	1 15.4	0 33.3	9 44.7	12R30.3
3 Th	10 43 57	12 37 49	5♍22 31	11♍18 31	23 3.4	15 57.2	26 7.7	6 27.2	28 50.6	1 19.1	0 35.0	9 46.0	12 29.7
4 F	10 47 53	13 37 56	17 15 35	23 13 58	23D 2.9	16 42.4	27 15.6	7 7.6	29 2.7	1 22.8	0 36.6	9 47.3	12 29.1
5 Sa	10 51 50	14 38 2	29 13 54	5♎15 39	23 2.9	17 31.2	28 23.4	7 48.1	29 14.8	1 26.3	0 38.3	9 48.5	12 28.4
6 Su	10 55 46	15 38 6	11♎19 27	17 25 36	23 3.3	18 23.4	29 30.9	8 28.6	29 27.1	1 29.8	0 39.8	9 49.7	12 27.7
7 M	10 59 43	16 38 8	23 34 21	29 46 0	23 3.9	19 18.6	0♉38.3	9 9.1	29 39.4	1 33.2	0 41.3	9 50.8	12 27.0
8 Tu	11 3 39	17 38 8	6♏ 0 52	12♏19 16	23 4.6	20 16.7	1 45.4	9 49.6	29 51.8	1 36.5	0 42.8	9 52.0	12 26.2
9 W	11 7 36	18 38 7	18 41 31	25 7 57	23 5.1	21 17.6	2 52.4	10 30.1	0♉ 4.3	1 39.7	0 44.2	9 53.1	12 25.5
10 Th	11 11 32	19 38 4	1♐38 52	8♐14 35	23 5.4	22 20.9	3 59.1	11 10.6	0 16.9	1 42.9	0 45.5	9 54.2	12 24.7
11 F	11 15 29	20 38 0	14 55 22	21 41 26	23R 5.6	23 26.7	5 5.6	11 51.2	0 29.5	1 45.9	0 46.8	9 55.2	12 23.8
12 Sa	11 19 26	21 37 54	28 32 57	5♑29 59	23 5.6	24 34.8	6 11.9	12 31.7	0 42.2	1 48.9	0 48.1	9 56.2	12 23.0
13 Su	11 23 22	22 37 46	12♑32 32	19 40 26	23D 5.5	25 45.0	7 17.9	13 12.2	0 55.0	1 51.7	0 49.3	9 57.2	12 22.1
14 M	11 27 19	23 37 37	26 53 28	4♒11 12	23 5.6	26 57.2	8 23.7	13 52.7	1 7.8	1 54.5	0 50.5	9 58.2	12 21.1
15 Tu	11 31 15	24 37 26	11♒33 6	18 58 28	23 5.7	28 11.3	9 29.3	14 33.3	1 20.7	1 57.2	0 51.6	9 59.1	12 20.2
16 W	11 35 12	25 37 13	26 26 31	3♓56 18	23 5.8	29 27.3	10 34.6	15 13.8	1 33.6	1 59.8	0 52.6	9 60.0	12 19.2
17 Th	11 39 8	26 36 58	11♓26 48	18 56 59	23R 6.0	0♓45.1	11 39.7	15 54.3	1 46.7	2 2.3	0 53.6	10 0.9	12 18.2
18 F	11 43 5	27 36 42	26 25 44	3♈52 3	23 6.1	2 4.5	12 44.5	16 34.8	1 59.7	2 4.7	0 54.6	10 1.7	12 17.1
19 Sa	11 47 1	28 36 23	11♈14 54	18 33 25	23 5.9	3 25.7	13 49.0	17 15.3	2 12.9	2 7.0	0 55.5	10 2.5	12 16.0
20 Su	11 50 58	29 36 2	25 46 51	2♉54 35	23 5.4	4 48.4	14 53.3	17 55.8	2 26.1	2 9.2	0 56.3	10 3.2	12 14.9
21 M	11 54 55	0♈35 40	9♉56 9	16 51 15	23 4.5	6 12.6	15 57.3	18 36.3	2 39.3	2 11.3	0 57.1	10 4.0	12 13.8
22 Tu	11 58 51	1 35 15	23 39 45	0♊21 39	23 3.5	7 38.4	17 0.9	19 16.8	2 52.6	2 13.3	0 57.9	10 4.7	12 12.7
23 W	12 2 48	2 34 47	6♊57 6	13 26 21	23 2.5	9 5.6	18 4.3	19 57.3	3 6.0	2 15.2	0 58.6	10 5.3	12 11.5
24 Th	12 6 44	3 34 18	19 49 44	26 7 43	23 1.7	10 34.3	19 7.4	20 37.8	3 19.4	2 17.1	0 59.2	10 6.0	12 10.3
25 F	12 10 41	4 33 46	2♋20 46	8♋29 25	23D 1.4	12 4.5	20 10.1	21 18.3	3 32.8	2 18.8	0 59.8	10 6.6	12 9.1
26 Sa	12 14 37	5 33 12	14 34 14	20 35 48	23 1.6	13 36.0	21 12.5	21 58.7	3 46.3	2 20.4	1 0.4	10 7.1	12 7.8
27 Su	12 18 34	6 32 36	26 34 44	2♌31 34	23 2.3	15 9.0	22 14.5	22 39.2	3 59.9	2 22.0	1 0.8	10 7.7	12 6.6
28 M	12 22 30	7 31 57	8♌26 54	14 21 18	23 3.5	16 43.4	23 16.2	23 19.7	4 13.5	2 23.4	1 1.3	10 8.2	12 5.3
29 Tu	12 26 27	8 31 16	20 15 16	26 9 19	23 4.9	18 19.1	24 17.5	24 0.1	4 27.1	2 24.7	1 1.7	10 8.6	12 4.0
30 W	12 30 24	9 30 33	2♍ 3 54	7♍59 28	23 6.2	19 56.3	25 18.4	24 40.5	4 40.8	2 26.0	1 2.0	10 9.0	12 2.6
31 Th	12 34 20	10 29 47	13 56 24	19 55 3	23R 7.1	21 34.8	26 18.9	25 21.0	4 54.5	2 27.1	1 2.3	10 9.4	12 1.3

APRIL 1988 — LONGITUDE

Day	Sid.Time	☉	0 hr ☽	Noon ☽	True ☊	☿	♀	♂	♃	♄	♅	♆	♇
1 F	12 38 17	11♈28 59	25♍55 45	1♎58 46	23♓ 7.4	23♓14.7	27♉19.0	26♑ 1.4	5♉ 8.2	2♑28.2	1♑ 2.5	10♑ 9.8	11♏59.9
2 Sa	12 42 13	12 28 10	8♎ 4 20	14 12 39	23R 6.7	24 56.1	28 18.7	26 41.8	5 22.0	2 29.1	1 2.6	10 10.1	11R58.5
3 Su	12 46 10	13 27 18	20 23 54	26 38 12	23 4.9	26 38.8	29 18.0	27 22.2	5 35.9	2 30.0	1 2.8	10 10.4	11 57.1
4 M	12 50 6	14 26 24	2♏55 41	9♏16 26	23 2.3	28 23.0	0♊16.8	28 2.6	5 49.7	2 30.7	1R 2.8	10 10.7	11 55.7
5 Tu	12 54 3	15 25 28	15 40 30	22 7 57	22 58.9	0♈ 8.6	1 15.2	28 43.0	6 3.6	2 31.4	1 2.8	10 10.9	11 54.2
6 W	12 57 59	16 24 30	28 38 49	5♐13 8	22 55.3	1 55.6	2 13.1	29 23.4	6 17.5	2 31.9	1 2.8	10 11.1	11 52.7
7 Th	13 1 56	17 23 31	11♐50 57	18 32 16	22 51.9	3 44.1	3 10.5	0♒ 3.8	6 31.5	2 32.4	1 2.7	10 11.3	11 51.3
8 F	13 5 53	18 22 30	25 17 7	2♑ 5 30	22 49.3	5 34.1	4 7.4	0 44.2	6 45.5	2 32.7	1 2.6	10 11.4	11 49.8
9 Sa	13 9 49	19 21 27	8♑57 24	15 52 49	22D47.7	7 25.5	5 3.7	1 24.5	6 59.5	2 33.0	1 2.4	10 11.6	11 48.2
10 Su	13 13 46	20 20 22	22 51 42	29 53 56	22 47.3	9 18.5	5 59.6	2 4.9	7 13.5	2 33.2	1 2.2	10 11.6	11 46.7
11 M	13 17 42	21 19 16	6♒59 24	14♒ 7 54	22 48.0	11 12.9	6 54.9	2 45.2	7 27.6	2R33.2	1 1.9	10R11.7	11 45.2
12 Tu	13 21 39	22 18 8	21 19 10	28 32 52	22 49.4	13 8.7	7 49.6	3 25.5	7 41.7	2 33.2	1 1.5	10 11.7	11 43.6
13 W	13 25 35	23 16 58	5♓48 34	13♓ 5 45	22 50.8	15 6.1	8 43.8	4 5.8	7 55.8	2 33.0	1 1.1	10 11.6	11 42.0
14 Th	13 29 32	24 15 46	20 23 49	27 42 8	22R51.6	17 4.8	9 37.3	4 46.0	8 10.0	2 32.8	1 0.7	10 11.6	11 40.5
15 F	13 33 28	25 14 33	4♈59 56	12♈16 29	22 51.1	19 5.0	10 30.2	5 26.3	8 24.1	2 32.5	1 0.2	10 11.5	11 38.9
16 Sa	13 37 25	26 13 17	19 30 58	26 42 39	22 49.0	21 6.5	11 22.5	6 6.5	8 38.3	2 32.0	0 59.6	10 11.3	11 37.2
17 Su	13 41 22	27 12 0	3♉50 47	10♉54 42	22 45.2	23 9.3	12 14.1	6 46.7	8 52.5	2 31.5	0 59.0	10 11.2	11 35.6
18 M	13 45 18	28 10 41	17 53 49	24 47 40	22 40.1	25 13.4	13 4.9	7 26.8	9 6.7	2 30.8	0 58.4	10 11.0	11 34.0
19 Tu	13 49 15	29 9 20	1♊35 56	8♊18 22	22 34.2	27 18.5	13 55.1	8 7.0	9 21.0	2 30.1	0 57.7	10 10.7	11 32.4
20 W	13 53 11	0♉ 7 57	14 54 54	21 25 35	22 28.3	29 24.6	14 44.5	8 47.1	9 35.2	2 29.3	0 57.0	10 10.5	11 30.7
21 Th	13 57 8	1 6 31	27 50 35	4♋10 10	22 23.1	1♉31.6	15 33.1	9 27.1	9 49.5	2 28.4	0 56.2	10 10.2	11 29.1
22 F	14 1 4	2 5 4	10♋24 42	16 34 39	22 19.2	3 39.2	16 20.9	10 7.2	10 3.8	2 27.3	0 55.3	10 9.9	11 27.4
23 Sa	14 5 1	3 3 34	22 40 30	28 42 51	22D17.0	5 47.3	17 7.8	10 47.2	10 18.1	2 26.2	0 54.5	10 9.5	11 25.7
24 Su	14 8 57	4 2 2	4♌42 17	10♌39 26	22 16.3	7 55.6	17 53.9	11 27.1	10 32.4	2 25.0	0 53.5	10 9.1	11 24.1
25 M	14 12 54	5 0 28	16 34 56	22 29 28	22 17.0	10 3.9	18 39.0	12 7.1	10 46.7	2 23.7	0 52.5	10 8.7	11 22.4
26 Tu	14 16 51	5 58 52	28 23 38	4♍18 5	22 18.4	12 11.8	19 23.2	12 47.0	11 1.0	2 22.3	0 51.5	10 8.3	11 20.7
27 W	14 20 47	6 57 14	10♍13 26	16 10 15	22 19.8	14 19.1	20 6.3	13 26.8	11 15.3	2 20.8	0 50.4	10 7.8	11 19.0
28 Th	14 24 44	7 55 33	22 9 3	28 10 22	22R20.5	16 25.5	20 48.5	14 6.7	11 29.6	2 19.2	0 49.3	10 7.3	11 17.3
29 F	14 28 40	8 53 51	4♎14 36	10♎22 9	22 19.7	18 30.7	21 29.6	14 46.5	11 43.9	2 17.6	0 48.2	10 6.7	11 15.6
30 Sa	14 32 37	9 52 7	16 33 20	22 48 24	22 16.9	20 34.4	22 9.5	15 26.2	11 58.2	2 15.8	0 47.0	10 6.1	11 14.0

Astro Data	Planet Ingress	Last Aspect	☽ Ingress	Last Aspect	☽ Ingress	☽ Phases & Eclipses	Astro Data
Dy Hr Mn	Dy Hr Mn	Dy Hr Mn	Dy Hr Mn	Dy Hr Mn	Dy Hr Mn	Dy Hr Mn	1 MARCH 1988
☽0S 4 23:06	♀ ♉ 6 10:21	2 10:32 ♃ △	♍ 2 13:06	1 3:01 ♀ △	♎ 1 8:05	3 16:01 ○ 13♍18	Julian Day # 32202
♃△♅ 12 12:19	♃ ♉ 8 15:44	3 16:01 ☉ ☍	♎ 5 1:32	3 14:10 ♂ □	♏ 3 18:26	3 16:13 ☍ A 1.091	Delta T 55.9 sec
☽0N 18 3:48	☿ ♓ 16 10:09	7 11:59 ♃ ☍	♏ 7 12:27	6 1:26 ♂ ✶	♐ 6 2:29	11 10:56 ☽ 21♐05	SVP 05♓25'27"
♃△♄ 18 10:58	☉ ♈ 20 9:39	9 5:17 ☿ □	♐ 9 20:59	7 10:44 ☉ △	♑ 8 8:19	18 2:02 ● 27♓42	Obliquity 23°26'36"
		11 16:26 ☿ ✶	♑ 12 2:31	9 19:21 ☉ □	♒ 10 12:10	18 1:58:00 ☌ T 3'47"	⚷ Chiron 23♊07.0
☽0S 1 5:42	♀ ♊ 3 17:07	13 18:11 ☉ ✶	♒ 14 5:08	12 1:45 ☉ ✶	♓ 12 14:24	25 4:42 ☽ 4♋45	☽ Mean ☊ 23♓59.4
♅ R 4 19:25	☿ ♈ 4 22:04	16 5:17 ☿ ☌	♓ 16 5:42	13 9:41 ♇ △	♈ 14 15:47		
☿0N 7 14:28	♂ ♒ 6 21:44	18 2:02 ☉ ☌	♈ 18 5:45	16 12:00 ☉ ☌	♉ 16 17:31	2 9:21 ○ 12♎51	1 APRIL 1988
♄ R 11 2:08	☉ ♉ 19 20:45	19 10:20 ♂ □	♉ 20 7:05	17 13:08 ♇ ☍	♊ 18 21:10	9 19:21 ☽ 20♑09	Julian Day # 32233
♆ R 11 13:17	☿ ♉ 20 6:42	21 15:51 ♂ △	♊ 22 11:21	19 23:40 ♀ ☌	♋ 21 4:04	16 12:00 ● 26♈43	Delta T 55.9 sec
☽0N 14 13:44		23 4:27 ☿ □	♋ 24 19:27	22 2:01 ♇ △	♌ 23 14:34	23 22:32 ☽ 3♌58	SVP 05♓25'24"
♃△♆ 22 9:59		26 15:39 ♂ ☍	♌ 27 6:54	25 4:29 ♀ ✶	♍ 26 3:16		Obliquity 23°26'37"
♃☍♇ 27 5:37		29 8:59 ♀ □	♍ 29 19:49	27 21:09 ♀ □	♎ 28 15:37		⚷ Chiron 23♊49.7
☽0S 28 13:01							☽ Mean ☊ 22♓20.9

LONGITUDE — MAY 1988

Day	Sid.Time	☉	0 hr ☽	Noon ☽	True ☊	☿	♀	♂	♃	♄	♅	♆	♇
1 Su	14 36 33	10♉50 21	29♎ 7 30	5♏30 45	22♓12.0	22♉36.2	22♊48.3	16♒ 5.9	12♉12.6	2♑13.9	0♑45.7	10♑ 5.5	11♏12.3
2 M	14 40 30	11 48 33	11♏58 10	18 29 41	22R 5.2	24 36.0	23 25.9	16 45.6	12 26.9	2R12.0	0R44.4	10R 4.9	11R10.6
3 Tu	14 44 26	12 46 43	25 5 12	1♐44 31	21 57.0	26 33.3	24 2.3	17 25.3	12 41.2	2 10.0	0 43.1	10 4.2	11 8.9
4 W	14 48 23	13 44 52	8♐27 24	15 13 35	21 48.2	28 28.1	24 37.3	18 4.9	12 55.5	2 7.9	0 41.7	10 3.6	11 7.2
5 Th	14 52 20	14 42 59	22 2 46	28 54 39	21 39.8	0♊20.0	25 11.0	18 44.4	13 9.9	2 5.7	0 40.3	10 2.8	11 5.5
6 F	14 56 16	15 41 5	5♑48 55	12♑45 16	21 32.7	2 8.9	25 43.4	19 23.9	13 24.2	2 3.4	0 38.9	10 2.1	11 3.8
7 Sa	15 0 13	16 39 9	19 43 26	26 43 11	21 27.6	3 54.7	26 14.3	20 3.4	13 38.5	2 1.0	0 37.4	10 1.3	11 2.1
8 Su	15 4 9	17 37 12	3♒44 17	10♒46 33	21 24.7	5 37.1	26 43.7	20 42.8	13 52.8	1 58.6	0 35.8	10 0.5	11 0.5
9 M	15 8 6	18 35 13	17 49 50	24 53 58	21D23.9	7 16.1	27 11.5	21 22.2	14 7.1	1 56.0	0 34.3	9 59.7	10 58.8
10 Tu	15 12 2	19 33 13	1♓58 48	9♓ 4 12	21 24.3	8 51.6	27 37.8	22 1.5	14 21.4	1 53.4	0 32.6	9 58.8	10 57.1
11 W	15 15 59	20 31 12	16 9 57	23 15 52	21R24.9	10 23.4	28 2.4	22 40.7	14 35.7	1 50.7	0 31.0	9 57.9	10 55.4
12 Th	15 19 55	21 29 10	0♈21 42	7♈27 7	21 24.7	11 51.6	28 25.3	23 19.9	14 49.9	1 48.0	0 29.3	9 57.0	10 53.8
13 F	15 23 52	22 27 6	14 31 46	21 35 16	21 22.6	13 16.1	28 46.4	23 59.0	15 4.2	1 45.1	0 27.6	9 56.1	10 52.1
14 Sa	15 27 49	23 25 1	28 37 7	5♉36 52	21 18.0	14 36.7	29 5.7	24 38.1	15 18.4	1 42.2	0 25.8	9 55.1	10 50.5
15 Su	15 31 45	24 22 54	12♉34 1	19 28 4	21 10.9	15 53.4	29 23.1	25 17.1	15 32.7	1 39.2	0 24.0	9 54.1	10 48.8
16 M	15 35 42	25 20 47	26 18 32	3♊ 5 0	21 1.5	17 6.3	29 38.6	25 56.0	15 46.9	1 36.1	0 22.2	9 53.1	10 47.2
17 Tu	15 39 38	26 18 37	9♊47 8	16 24 37	20 50.8	18 15.1	29 52.0	26 34.8	16 1.1	1 33.0	0 20.4	9 52.1	10 45.6
18 W	15 43 35	27 16 27	22 57 18	29 25 5	20 39.8	19 19.9	0♋ 3.4	27 13.5	16 15.3	1 29.8	0 18.5	9 51.0	10 44.0
19 Th	15 47 31	28 14 14	5♋47 59	12♋ 6 7	20 29.6	20 20.6	0 12.6	27 52.2	16 29.4	1 26.5	0 16.5	9 49.9	10 42.4
20 F	15 51 28	29 12 1	18 19 43	24 29 6	20 21.1	21 17.1	0 19.6	28 30.8	16 43.6	1 23.2	0 14.6	9 48.8	10 40.8
21 Sa	15 55 24	0♊ 9 45	0♌34 39	6♌36 51	20 15.0	22 9.4	0 24.4	29 9.3	16 57.7	1 19.8	0 12.6	9 47.7	10 39.2
22 Su	15 59 21	1 7 28	12 36 14	18 33 22	20 11.3	22 57.3	0R26.9	29 47.7	17 11.8	1 16.3	0 10.6	9 46.6	10 37.7
23 M	16 3 18	2 5 10	24 28 53	0♍23 26	20D 9.7	23 40.9	0 27.0	0♓26.0	17 25.8	1 12.8	0 8.6	9 45.4	10 36.1
24 Tu	16 7 14	3 2 50	6♍17 42	12 12 21	20 9.4	24 20.0	0 24.8	1 4.3	17 39.9	1 9.2	0 6.5	9 44.2	10 34.6
25 W	16 11 11	4 0 28	18 8 5	24 5 33	20R 9.7	24 54.7	0 20.1	1 42.4	17 53.9	1 5.5	0 4.4	9 43.0	10 33.1
26 Th	16 15 7	4 58 5	0♎ 5 25	6♎ 8 18	20 9.3	25 24.7	0 13.0	2 20.4	18 7.9	1 1.8	0 2.3	9 41.7	10 31.5
27 F	16 19 4	5 55 40	12 14 45	18 25 18	20 7.4	25 50.1	0 3.5	2 58.4	18 21.8	0 58.1	0 0.1	9 40.5	10 30.1
28 Sa	16 23 0	6 53 14	24 40 24	1♏ 0 23	20 3.2	26 10.9	29♊51.6	3 36.2	18 35.8	0 54.3	29♐58.0	9 39.2	10 28.6
29 Su	16 26 57	7 50 46	7♏25 32	13 56 0	19 56.5	26 26.9	29 37.2	4 14.0	18 49.7	0 50.4	29 55.8	9 37.9	10 27.1
30 M	16 30 53	8 48 18	20 31 49	27 12 55	19 47.3	26 38.3	29 20.4	4 51.7	19 3.5	0 46.5	29 53.6	9 36.6	10 25.7
31 Tu	16 34 50	9 45 48	3♐59 6	10♐50 3	19 36.3	26R45.0	29 1.3	5 29.2	19 17.3	0 42.5	29 51.3	9 35.2	10 24.3

LONGITUDE — JUNE 1988

Day	Sid.Time	☉	0 hr ☽	Noon ☽	True ☊	☿	♀	♂	♃	♄	♅	♆	♇
1 W	16 38 47	10♊43 17	17♐45 19	24♐44 25	19♓24.5	26♊47.0	28♊39.9	6♓ 6.6	19♉31.1	0♑38.6	29♐49.1	9♑33.9	10♏22.9
2 Th	16 42 43	11 40 46	1♑46 44	8♑51 40	19R13.2	26R44.5	28R16.3	6 44.0	19 44.9	0R34.5	29R46.8	9R32.5	10R21.5
3 F	16 46 40	12 38 13	15 58 33	23 6 46	19 3.4	26 37.6	27 50.6	7 21.2	19 58.6	0 30.5	29 44.5	9 31.1	10 20.1
4 Sa	16 50 36	13 35 40	0♒15 41	7♒24 47	18 56.1	26 26.4	27 22.9	7 58.3	20 12.3	0 26.3	29 42.2	9 29.7	10 18.8
5 Su	16 54 33	14 33 5	14 33 34	21 41 40	18 51.5	26 11.2	26 53.3	8 35.2	20 26.0	0 22.2	29 39.9	9 28.3	10 17.5
6 M	16 58 29	15 30 30	28 48 43	5♓54 31	18 49.3	25 52.2	26 22.1	9 12.1	20 39.6	0 18.0	29 37.6	9 26.9	10 16.1
7 Tu	17 2 26	16 27 55	12♓58 53	20 1 41	18 48.8	25 29.8	25 49.3	9 48.8	20 53.2	0 13.8	29 35.2	9 25.4	10 14.9
8 W	17 6 23	17 25 18	27 2 49	4♈ 2 15	18 48.7	25 4.3	25 15.2	10 25.3	21 6.7	0 9.5	29 32.8	9 24.0	10 13.6
9 Th	17 10 19	18 22 42	10♈59 55	17 55 44	18 47.8	24 36.2	24 40.0	11 1.8	21 20.2	0 5.3	29 30.5	9 22.5	10 12.4
10 F	17 14 16	19 20 4	24 49 39	1♉41 31	18 44.9	24 5.8	24 3.8	11 38.0	21 33.6	0 1.0	29 28.1	9 21.0	10 11.1
11 Sa	17 18 12	20 17 27	8♉31 12	15 18 32	18 39.3	23 33.8	23 27.0	12 14.1	21 47.0	29♐56.6	29 25.7	9 19.5	10 9.9
12 Su	17 22 9	21 14 48	22 3 18	28 45 18	18 30.9	23 0.7	22 49.7	12 50.1	22 0.4	29 52.3	29 23.3	9 18.0	10 8.8
13 M	17 26 5	22 12 10	5♊24 16	12♊ 0 0	18 20.1	22 27.0	22 12.2	13 25.9	22 13.7	29 47.9	29 20.8	9 16.5	10 7.6
14 Tu	17 30 2	23 9 30	18 32 17	25 0 56	18 7.7	21 53.3	21 34.6	14 1.5	22 26.9	29 43.6	29 18.4	9 14.9	10 6.5
15 W	17 33 58	24 6 50	1♋25 50	7♋46 54	17 54.9	21 20.2	20 57.4	14 36.9	22 40.1	29 39.2	29 16.0	9 13.4	10 5.4
16 Th	17 37 55	25 4 10	14 4 7	20 17 33	17 42.9	20 48.3	20 20.5	15 12.2	22 53.2	29 34.8	29 13.5	9 11.8	10 4.4
17 F	17 41 52	26 1 28	26 27 19	2♌33 39	17 32.7	20 18.0	19 44.5	15 47.3	23 6.3	29 30.3	29 11.1	9 10.3	10 3.3
18 Sa	17 45 48	26 58 46	8♌36 50	14 37 13	17 25.0	19 49.9	19 9.3	16 22.2	23 19.4	29 25.9	29 8.7	9 8.7	10 2.3
19 Su	17 49 45	27 56 4	20 35 12	26 31 18	17 19.9	19 24.6	18 35.3	16 56.8	23 32.4	29 21.5	29 6.2	9 7.1	10 1.3
20 M	17 53 41	28 53 20	2♍26 2	8♍19 59	17 17.3	19 2.3	18 2.6	17 31.3	23 45.3	29 17.0	29 3.8	9 5.5	10 0.3
21 Tu	17 57 38	29 50 36	14 13 47	20 8 4	17D16.5	18 43.5	17 31.4	18 5.6	23 58.1	29 12.6	29 1.3	9 3.9	9 59.4
22 W	18 1 34	0♋47 51	26 3 30	2♎ 0 48	17R16.6	18 28.5	17 1.9	18 39.7	24 10.9	29 8.2	28 58.9	9 2.4	9 58.5
23 Th	18 5 31	1 45 5	8♎ 0 38	14 3 40	17 16.5	18 17.7	16 34.2	19 13.6	24 23.7	29 3.7	28 56.4	9 0.7	9 57.6
24 F	18 9 27	2 42 19	20 10 34	26 21 57	17 15.2	18D11.1	16 8.5	19 47.2	24 36.3	28 59.3	28 54.0	8 59.1	9 56.8
25 Sa	18 13 24	3 39 32	2♏38 21	9♏ 0 17	17 12.0	18 9.1	15 44.9	20 20.6	24 48.9	28 54.9	28 51.5	8 57.5	9 55.9
26 Su	18 17 21	4 36 44	15 28 9	22 2 13	17 6.4	18 11.7	15 23.4	20 53.8	25 1.5	28 50.5	28 49.1	8 55.9	9 55.1
27 M	18 21 17	5 33 57	28 42 38	5♐29 27	16 58.6	18 19.0	15 4.2	21 26.8	25 13.9	28 46.1	28 46.7	8 54.3	9 54.4
28 Tu	18 25 14	6 31 8	12♐22 31	19 21 32	16 48.9	18 31.2	14 47.3	21 59.5	25 26.3	28 41.7	28 44.3	8 52.7	9 53.7
29 W	18 29 10	7 28 20	26 26 1	3♑35 24	16 38.5	18 48.1	14 32.7	22 32.0	25 38.7	28 37.4	28 41.8	8 51.1	9 53.0
30 Th	18 33 7	8 25 31	10♑48 56	18 5 45	16 28.3	19 10.0	14 20.6	23 4.3	25 51.0	28 33.0	28 39.4	8 49.5	9 52.3

Astro Data Dy Hr Mn	Planet Ingress Dy Hr Mn	Last Aspect Dy Hr Mn	☽ Ingress Dy Hr Mn	Last Aspect Dy Hr Mn	☽ Ingress Dy Hr Mn	☽ Phases & Eclipses Dy Hr Mn	Astro Data
☽0N 11 20:55	☿ ♊ 4 19:40	30 11:21 ♀ △	♏ 1 1:39	1 20:37 ♅ ☌	♑ 1 20:58	1 23:41 ○ 11♏48	1 MAY 1988
♃⚼♅ 14 11:05	♀ ♋ 17 16:26	3 3:07 ☿ ☍	♐ 3 8:52	3 6:50 ♃ △	♒ 3 23:34	9 1:23 ☽ 18♒39	Julian Day # 32263
♃⚼♄ 18 19:59	☉ ♊ 20 19:57	5 5:43 ♀ ☍	♑ 5 13:54	6 1:22 ♅ ⚹	♓ 6 2:00	15 22:11 ● 25♉16	Delta T 56.0 sec
♀ R 22 13:26	♂ ♓ 22 7:42	6 18:19 ☉ △	♒ 7 17:37	8 4:16 ♅ □	♈ 8 5:04	23 16:49 ☽ 2♍46	SVP 05♓25'21"
☽0S 25 20:30	♀ ♊ 27 7:36	9 16:24 ♀ △	♓ 9 20:39	10 9:01 ♄ △	♉ 10 9:02	31 10:53 ○ 10♐12	Obliquity 23°26'36"
☿ R 31 22:43	♅ ♐ 27 1:21	11 20:38 ♀ □	♈ 11 23:23	11 23:55 ♃ ☌	♊ 12 14:14		⚷ Chiron 25♊34.8
		14 0:50 ♀ ⚹	♉ 14 2:22	14 20:41 ♄ ☍	♋ 14 21:19		☽ Mean ☊ 20♓45.6
☽0N 8 1:50	♄ ♐ 10 5:23	15 23:18 ♂ □	♊ 16 6:31	16 17:21 ♃ ⚹	♌ 17 6:57	7 6:22 ☽ 16♓43	
♃⚼♆ 21 9:42	☉ ♋ 21 3:57	18 8:20 ♂ △	♋ 18 13:05	19 17:39 ♄ △	♍ 19 19:03	14 9:14 ● 23♊32	1 JUNE 1988
☽0S 22 3:37		19 20:50 ♃ ⚹	♌ 20 22:51	22 6:10 ♄ □	♎ 22 7:57	22 10:23 ☽ 1♎13	Julian Day # 32294
☿ D 24 22:40		22 22:17 ☿ ⚹	♍ 23 11:12	24 16:56 ♄ ⚹	♏ 24 18:58	29 19:46 ○ 8♑15	Delta T 56.0 sec
♄☌♅ 26 17:04		25 14:15 ☿ □	♎ 25 23:49	26 17:40 ♃ ☍	♐ 27 2:18		SVP 05♓25'15"
		28 10:01 ♅ ⚹	♏ 28 10:06	29 3:48 ♅ ☌	♑ 29 6:00		Obliquity 23°26'35"
		29 21:17 ♃ ☍	♐ 30 16:57				⚷ Chiron 28♊07.5
							☽ Mean ☊ 19♓07.1

JULY 1988 LONGITUDE

Day	Sid.Time	☉	0 hr ☽	Noon ☽	True ☊	☿	♀	♂	♃	♄	♅	♆	♇
1 F	18 37 3	9♋22 42	25♑24 59	2♒45 40	16♓19.5	19♊36.7	14♊10.8	23♓36.2	26♉ 3.1	28♐28.7	28♐37.1	8♑47.8	9♏51.6
2 Sa	18 41 0	10 19 53	10♒ 6 54	17 27 48	16R13.0	20 8.2	14R 3.5	24 8.0	26 15.3	28R24.4	28R34.7	8R46.2	9R51.0
3 Su	18 44 56	11 17 4	24 47 33	2♓ 5 28	16 9.0	20 44.5	13 58.5	24 39.4	26 27.3	28 20.2	28 32.3	8 44.6	9 50.5
4 M	18 48 53	12 14 16	9♓20 58	16 33 36	16D 7.4	21 25.5	13D 55.9	25 10.6	26 39.3	28 15.9	28 29.9	8 43.0	9 49.9
5 Tu	18 52 50	13 11 27	23 43 1	0♈48 58	16 7.4	22 11.2	13 55.7	25 41.5	26 51.2	28 11.7	28 27.6	8 41.4	9 49.4
6 W	18 56 46	14 8 39	7♈51 20	14 50 2	16R 7.9	23 1.5	13 57.8	26 12.0	27 3.0	28 7.5	28 25.3	8 39.7	9 48.9
7 Th	19 0 43	15 5 51	21 45 6	28 36 33	16 7.9	23 56.5	14 2.2	26 42.3	27 14.7	28 3.4	28 22.9	8 38.1	9 48.4
8 F	19 4 39	16 3 3	5♉24 29	12♉ 8 56	16 6.3	24 55.9	14 8.8	27 12.2	27 26.4	27 59.2	28 20.6	8 36.5	9 48.0
9 Sa	19 8 36	17 0 16	18 50 2	25 27 49	16 2.4	25 59.8	14 17.6	27 41.8	27 37.9	27 55.2	28 18.4	8 34.9	9 47.6
10 Su	19 12 32	17 57 29	2♊ 2 23	8♊33 45	15 56.2	27 8.2	14 28.5	28 11.1	27 49.4	27 51.1	28 16.1	8 33.3	9 47.3
11 M	19 16 29	18 54 43	15 1 58	21 27 3	15 48.0	28 20.8	14 41.4	28 40.0	28 0.8	27 47.1	28 13.9	8 31.7	9 46.9
12 Tu	19 20 25	19 51 57	27 49 1	4♋ 7 54	15 38.5	29 37.8	14 56.4	29 8.6	28 12.1	27 43.2	28 11.6	8 30.1	9 46.7
13 W	19 24 22	20 49 12	10♋23 44	16 36 32	15 28.6	0♋58.9	15 13.2	29 36.8	28 23.4	27 39.3	28 9.4	8 28.6	9 46.4
14 Th	19 28 19	21 46 26	22 46 24	28 53 26	15 19.3	2 24.2	15 32.0	0♈ 4.6	28 34.5	27 35.4	28 7.2	8 27.0	9 46.2
15 F	19 32 15	22 43 41	4♌57 45	10♌59 33	15 11.5	3 53.6	15 52.5	0 32.0	28 45.5	27 31.6	28 5.1	8 25.4	9 46.0
16 Sa	19 36 12	23 40 57	16 59 3	22 56 32	15 5.6	5 26.8	16 14.8	0 59.1	28 56.5	27 27.9	28 3.0	8 23.9	9 45.8
17 Su	19 40 8	24 38 12	28 52 20	4♍46 48	15 2.0	7 3.9	16 38.7	1 25.7	29 7.3	27 24.2	28 0.8	8 22.3	9 45.7
18 M	19 44 5	25 35 28	10♍40 23	16 33 33	15D 0.5	8 44.8	17 4.3	1 51.9	29 18.1	27 20.5	27 58.8	8 20.8	9 45.6
19 Tu	19 48 1	26 32 44	22 26 48	28 20 41	15 0.7	10 29.1	17 31.5	2 17.7	29 28.7	27 16.9	27 56.7	8 19.3	9 45.6
20 W	19 51 58	27 30 0	4♎15 48	10♎12 46	15 1.8	12 16.8	18 0.1	2 43.0	29 39.2	27 13.4	27 54.7	8 17.8	9D 45.5
21 Th	19 55 55	28 27 16	16 12 13	22 14 46	15 3.1	14 7.6	18 30.2	3 7.9	29 49.7	27 9.9	27 52.7	8 16.3	9 45.5
22 F	19 59 51	29 24 33	28 21 6	4♏31 49	15R 3.7	16 1.4	19 1.8	3 32.4	0♊ 0.0	27 6.5	27 50.7	8 14.8	9 45.6
23 Sa	20 3 48	0♌21 50	10♏47 32	17 8 49	15 3.1	17 57.8	19 34.6	3 56.4	0 10.2	27 3.2	27 48.8	8 13.3	9 45.7
24 Su	20 7 44	1 19 8	23 36 10	0♐ 9 58	15 0.9	19 56.5	20 8.8	4 19.9	0 20.4	26 59.9	27 46.9	8 11.8	9 45.8
25 M	20 11 41	2 16 25	6♐50 33	13 38 5	14 56.9	21 57.2	20 44.3	4 42.9	0 30.4	26 56.7	27 45.0	8 10.4	9 45.9
26 Tu	20 15 37	3 13 44	20 32 36	27 33 57	14 51.6	23 59.7	21 20.9	5 5.5	0 40.3	26 53.6	27 43.1	8 8.9	9 46.1
27 W	20 19 34	4 11 2	4♑41 48	11♑55 41	14 45.6	26 3.6	21 58.7	5 27.5	0 50.1	26 50.5	27 41.3	8 7.5	9 46.3
28 Th	20 23 30	5 8 22	19 14 54	26 38 38	14 39.6	28 8.5	22 37.7	5 49.0	0 59.7	26 47.5	27 39.5	8 6.1	9 46.6
29 F	20 27 27	6 5 42	4♒ 5 53	11♒35 37	14 34.5	0♌14.1	23 17.7	6 10.0	1 9.3	26 44.6	27 37.8	8 4.7	9 46.9
30 Sa	20 31 24	7 3 2	19 6 41	26 37 58	14 30.8	2 20.1	23 58.8	6 30.5	1 18.8	26 41.7	27 36.1	8 3.4	9 47.2
31 Su	20 35 20	8 0 24	4♓ 8 23	11♓36 54	14D 28.8	4 26.3	24 41.0	6 50.4	1 28.1	26 39.0	27 34.4	8 2.0	9 47.6

AUGUST 1988 LONGITUDE

Day	Sid.Time	☉	0 hr ☽	Noon ☽	True ☊	☿	♀	♂	♃	♄	♅	♆	♇
1 M	20 39 17	8♌57 46	19♓ 2 36	26♓24 44	14♓28.6	6♌32.2	25♊24.0	7♈ 9.7	1♊37.3	26♐36.3	27♐32.8	8♑ 0.7	9♏47.9
2 Tu	20 43 13	9 55 9	3♈42 40	10♈55 54	14 29.4	8 37.8	26 8.1	7 28.5	1 46.4	26R33.6	27R31.2	7R59.3	9 48.4
3 W	20 47 10	10 52 34	18 4 7	25 7 5	14 30.8	10 42.8	26 53.0	7 46.6	1 55.3	26 31.1	27 29.6	7 58.0	9 48.8
4 Th	20 51 6	11 50 0	2♉ 4 45	8♉57 7	14R32.0	12 47.0	27 38.8	8 4.2	2 4.2	26 28.6	27 28.1	7 56.8	9 49.3
5 F	20 55 3	12 47 27	15 44 16	22 26 24	14 32.3	14 50.2	28 25.5	8 21.1	2 12.9	26 26.3	27 26.6	7 55.5	9 49.8
6 Sa	20 58 59	13 44 55	29 3 42	5♊36 24	14 31.3	16 52.4	29 13.0	8 37.3	2 21.5	26 24.0	27 25.2	7 54.2	9 50.4
7 Su	21 2 56	14 42 25	12♊ 4 48	18 29 7	14 29.0	18 53.3	0♋ 1.2	8 52.9	2 29.9	26 21.7	27 23.7	7 53.0	9 51.0
8 M	21 6 53	15 39 56	24 49 40	1♋ 6 40	14 25.5	20 53.0	0 50.2	9 7.8	2 38.2	26 19.6	27 22.4	7 51.8	9 51.6
9 Tu	21 10 49	16 37 28	7♋20 25	13 31 9	14 21.2	22 51.3	1 40.0	9 22.1	2 46.4	26 17.6	27 21.1	7 50.6	9 52.3
10 W	21 14 46	17 35 2	19 39 5	25 44 28	14 16.7	24 48.3	2 30.4	9 35.6	2 54.5	26 15.6	27 19.8	7 49.5	9 53.0
11 Th	21 18 42	18 32 37	1♌47 32	7♌48 28	14 12.5	26 43.8	3 21.5	9 48.4	3 2.4	26 13.7	27 18.5	7 48.3	9 53.7
12 F	21 22 39	19 30 13	13 47 31	19 44 55	14 9.0	28 37.9	4 13.2	10 0.5	3 10.2	26 11.9	27 17.3	7 47.2	9 54.5
13 Sa	21 26 35	20 27 50	25 40 54	1♍35 43	14 6.6	0♍30.5	5 5.6	10 11.8	3 17.8	26 10.3	27 16.2	7 46.1	9 55.2
14 Su	21 30 32	21 25 28	7♍29 40	13 23 2	14D 5.4	2 21.6	5 58.5	10 22.4	3 25.3	26 8.6	27 15.1	7 45.1	9 56.1
15 M	21 34 28	22 23 7	19 16 9	25 9 23	14 5.4	4 11.2	6 52.0	10 32.3	3 32.6	26 7.1	27 14.0	7 44.0	9 56.9
16 Tu	21 38 25	23 20 48	1♎ 3 6	6♎57 44	14 6.2	5 59.4	7 46.1	10 41.3	3 39.8	26 5.7	27 13.0	7 43.0	9 57.8
17 W	21 42 22	24 18 30	12 53 44	18 51 35	14 7.6	7 46.1	8 40.8	10 49.6	3 46.8	26 4.4	27 12.0	7 42.0	9 58.7
18 Th	21 46 18	25 16 12	24 51 46	0♏54 49	14 9.1	9 31.4	9 36.0	10 57.1	3 53.7	26 3.1	27 11.1	7 41.0	9 59.7
19 F	21 50 15	26 13 56	7♏ 1 16	13 11 42	14 10.4	11 15.2	10 31.6	11 3.7	4 0.4	26 2.0	27 10.2	7 40.1	10 0.7
20 Sa	21 54 11	27 11 41	19 26 37	25 46 33	14R11.2	12 57.6	11 27.8	11 9.6	4 7.0	26 1.0	27 9.4	7 39.2	10 1.7
21 Su	21 58 8	28 9 27	2♐12 2	8♐43 30	14 11.4	14 38.6	12 24.4	11 14.7	4 13.5	26 0.0	27 8.6	7 38.3	10 2.8
22 M	22 2 4	29 7 15	15 21 19	22 5 48	14 10.8	16 18.2	13 21.6	11 18.9	4 19.7	25 59.2	27 7.9	7 37.4	10 3.8
23 Tu	22 6 1	0♍ 5 3	28 57 9	5♑55 25	14 9.6	17 56.4	14 19.1	11 22.4	4 25.8	25 58.4	27 7.2	7 36.6	10 5.0
24 W	22 9 57	1 2 53	13♑ 0 30	20 12 9	14 8.1	19 33.3	15 17.1	11 25.0	4 31.8	25 57.7	27 6.5	7 35.8	10 6.1
25 Th	22 13 54	2 0 44	27 29 55	4♒53 12	14 6.6	21 8.7	16 15.5	11 26.7	4 37.6	25 57.2	27 5.9	7 35.0	10 7.3
26 F	22 17 51	2 58 36	12♒21 13	19 53 0	14 5.3	22 42.8	17 14.4	11R27.7	4 43.2	25 56.7	27 5.4	7 34.2	10 8.5
27 Sa	22 21 47	3 56 30	27 27 30	5♓ 3 32	14 4.5	24 15.6	18 13.6	11 27.8	4 48.6	25 56.3	27 4.9	7 33.5	10 9.7
28 Su	22 25 44	4 54 25	12♓39 55	20 15 25	14D 4.2	25 47.0	19 13.3	11 27.0	4 53.9	25 56.0	27 4.4	7 32.8	10 11.0
29 M	22 29 40	5 52 21	27 48 53	5♈19 14	14 4.4	27 17.0	20 13.3	11 25.4	4 59.1	25 55.8	27 4.0	7 32.2	10 12.3
30 Tu	22 33 37	6 50 20	12♈45 30	20 6 53	14 4.8	28 45.7	21 13.7	11 23.0	5 4.0	25D 55.8	27 3.7	7 31.5	10 13.6
31 W	22 37 33	7 48 20	27 22 44	4♉32 33	14 5.4	0♎12.9	22 14.5	11 19.7	5 8.8	25 55.8	27 3.4	7 30.9	10 15.0

Astro Data Dy Hr Mn	Planet Ingress Dy Hr Mn	Last Aspect Dy Hr Mn	☽ Ingress Dy Hr Mn	Last Aspect Dy Hr Mn	☽ Ingress Dy Hr Mn	☽ Phases & Eclipses Dy Hr Mn	Astro Data
♀ D 4 14:09	☿ ♋ 12 6:42	1 1:03 ♃ △	♒ 1 7:30	1 13:50 ♅ □	♈ 1 17:53	6 11:36 ☽ 14♈36	1 JULY 1988
☽0N 5 6:38	♂ ♈ 13 20:00	3 6:08 ♅ ⚹	♓ 3 8:33	3 16:03 ♅ △	♉ 3 20:24	13 21:53 ● 21♋41	Julian Day # 32324
♃⚻♄ 10 2:39	♃ ♊ 21 23:59	5 7:59 ♅ □	♈ 5 10:37	4 22:07 ☿ □	♊ 6 1:43	22 2:14 ☽ 29♎30	Delta T 56.0 sec
♃⚻♅ 11 23:05	☉ ♌ 22 14:51	7 11:34 ♅ △	♉ 7 14:27	8 4:50 ♅ ☍	♋ 8 9:52	29 3:25 ○ 6♒14	SVP 05♓25'09"
☽0S 19 10:09	☿ ♌ 28 21:19	9 16:41 ♂ ⚹	♊ 9 20:16	9 4:54 ♇ △	♌ 10 20:26		Obliquity 23°26'35"
♇ D 20 4:21		12 3:50 ☿ ☌	♋ 12 4:08	13 3:13 ♅ △	♍ 13 8:46	4 18:22 ☽ 12♉34	⚷ Chiron 0♋53.6
	♀ ♋ 6 23:24	14 11:33 ♃ ⚹	♌ 14 14:11	15 16:12 ♅ □	♎ 15 21:52	12 12:31 ● 20♌00	☽ Mean ☊ 17♓31.8
☽0N 1 13:30	☿ ♍ 12 17:29	17 0:31 ♃ □	♍ 17 2:17	18 4:37 ♅ ⚹	♏ 18 10:12	20 15:51 ☽ 27♏50	
☽0S 15 16:14	☉ ♍ 22 21:54	19 14:31 ♃ △	♎ 19 15:22	20 15:51 ☉ □	♐ 20 19:55	27 10:56 ○ 4♓23	1 AUGUST 1988
♂ R 26 14:40	☿ ♎ 30 20:25	22 2:14 ☉ □	♏ 22 3:13	22 20:49 ♅ ☌	♑ 23 1:49	27 11:05 ☍ P 0.291	Julian Day # 32355
☽0N 28 23:03		23 15:59 ☿ △	♐ 24 11:42	24 12:17 ☿ △	♒ 25 4:05		Delta T 56.1 sec
☿0S 30 7:50		26 12:14 ♅ ☌	♑ 26 16:07	26 23:24 ♅ ⚹	♓ 27 4:01		SVP 05♓25'04"
♄ D 30 10:06		28 16:46 ☿ ☍	♒ 28 17:25	28 23:04 ☿ ☍	♈ 29 3:29		Obliquity 23°26'36"
		30 13:31 ♅ ⚹	♓ 30 17:23	30 23:28 ♅ △	♉ 31 4:22		⚷ Chiron 3♋38.1
							☽ Mean ☊ 15♓53.3

LONGITUDE — SEPTEMBER 1988

Day	Sid.Time	☉	0 hr ☽	Noon ☽	True ☊	☿	♀	♂	♃	♄	♅	♆	♇
1 Th	22 41 30	8♍46 22	11♉36 4	18♉33 5	14♓ 5.9	1♎38.8	23♋15.6	11♈15.5	5♊13.4	25♐55.9	27♐ 3.1	7♑30.3	10♏16.4
2 F	22 45 26	9 44 26	25 23 37	2♊ 7 46	14 6.2	3 3.3	24 17.1	11R 10.6	5 17.8	25 56.1	27R 2.9	7R 29.8	10 17.8
3 Sa	22 49 23	10 42 32	8♊45 45	15 17 53	14R 6.4	4 26.4	25 18.9	11 4.7	5 22.1	25 56.4	27 2.8	7 29.2	10 19.2
4 Su	22 53 20	11 40 40	21 44 30	28 6 0	14 6.3	5 48.0	26 21.1	10 58.1	5 26.1	25 56.8	27 2.7	7 28.8	10 20.7
5 M	22 57 16	12 38 50	4♋22 51	10♋35 30	14 6.2	7 8.2	27 23.5	10 50.6	5 30.0	25 57.3	27D 2.7	7 28.3	10 22.2
6 Tu	23 1 13	13 37 2	16 44 23	22 49 58	14D 6.1	8 26.7	28 26.3	10 42.3	5 33.7	25 57.9	27 2.7	7 27.9	10 23.7
7 W	23 5 9	14 35 16	28 52 41	4♌52 59	14 6.1	9 43.7	29 29.4	10 33.3	5 37.3	25 58.6	27 2.7	7 27.5	10 25.3
8 Th	23 9 6	15 33 31	10♌51 14	16 47 51	14 6.2	10 59.1	0♌32.7	10 23.4	5 40.6	25 59.4	27 2.8	7 27.1	10 26.9
9 F	23 13 2	16 31 49	22 43 10	28 37 34	14 6.4	12 12.8	1 36.3	10 12.8	5 43.8	26 0.2	27 3.0	7 26.8	10 28.5
10 Sa	23 16 59	17 30 9	4♍31 20	10♍24 47	14R 6.6	13 24.7	2 40.3	10 1.5	5 46.7	26 1.2	27 3.2	7 26.5	10 30.1
11 Su	23 20 55	18 28 30	16 18 14	22 11 56	14 6.7	14 34.7	3 44.4	9 49.5	5 49.5	26 2.3	27 3.4	7 26.2	10 31.8
12 M	23 24 52	19 26 53	28 6 11	4♎ 1 15	14 6.5	15 42.7	4 48.9	9 36.9	5 52.1	26 3.5	27 3.8	7 26.0	10 33.5
13 Tu	23 28 49	20 25 18	9♎57 26	15 54 59	14 6.0	16 48.7	5 53.6	9 23.6	5 54.5	26 4.8	27 4.1	7 25.7	10 35.2
14 W	23 32 45	21 23 45	21 54 14	27 55 29	14 5.2	17 52.5	6 58.5	9 9.7	5 56.6	26 6.1	27 4.5	7 25.6	10 36.9
15 Th	23 36 42	22 22 14	3♏59 3	10♏ 5 17	14 4.1	18 53.9	8 3.7	8 55.2	5 58.6	26 7.6	27 5.0	7 25.4	10 38.7
16 F	23 40 38	23 20 44	16 14 32	22 27 11	14 2.9	19 52.9	9 9.1	8 40.2	6 0.4	26 9.2	27 5.5	7 25.3	10 40.5
17 Sa	23 44 35	24 19 16	28 43 37	5♐ 4 12	14 1.8	20 49.1	10 14.7	8 24.8	6 2.1	26 10.8	27 6.1	7 25.2	10 42.3
18 Su	23 48 31	25 17 50	11♐29 20	17 59 23	14 0.9	21 42.6	11 20.6	8 8.9	6 3.5	26 12.6	27 6.7	7D 25.2	10 44.1
19 M	23 52 28	26 16 25	24 34 42	1♑15 36	14D 0.6	22 32.9	12 26.7	7 52.6	6 4.7	26 14.5	27 7.4	7 25.2	10 46.0
20 Tu	23 56 24	27 15 2	8♑ 2 19	14 55 3	14 0.8	23 20.0	13 33.0	7 36.0	6 5.7	26 16.4	27 8.1	7 25.2	10 47.9
21 W	0 0 21	28 13 41	21 53 52	28 58 46	14 1.5	24 3.5	14 39.5	7 19.1	6 6.5	26 18.5	27 8.9	7 25.3	10 49.8
22 Th	0 4 18	29 12 21	6♒ 9 35	13♒26 0	14 2.6	24 43.1	15 46.2	7 1.9	6 7.1	26 20.6	27 9.7	7 25.4	10 51.7
23 F	0 8 14	0♎11 3	20 47 34	28 13 40	14 3.7	25 18.6	16 53.1	6 44.6	6 7.6	26 22.8	27 10.6	7 25.5	10 53.7
24 Sa	0 12 11	1 9 47	5♓43 30	13♓16 10	14R 4.5	25 49.5	18 0.2	6 27.0	6R 7.8	26 25.1	27 11.5	7 25.6	10 55.6
25 Su	0 16 7	2 8 32	20 50 35	28 25 38	14 4.5	26 15.6	19 7.6	6 9.4	6 7.8	26 27.6	27 12.5	7 25.8	10 57.6
26 M	0 20 4	3 7 20	6♈ 0 7	13♈32 51	14 3.6	26 36.5	20 15.1	5 51.7	6 7.6	26 30.1	27 13.5	7 26.0	10 59.6
27 Tu	0 24 0	4 6 9	21 2 42	28 28 34	14 1.7	26 51.7	21 22.8	5 33.9	6 7.2	26 32.7	27 14.6	7 26.3	11 1.6
28 W	0 27 57	5 5 1	5♉49 32	13♉ 4 48	13 59.1	27R 0.8	22 30.7	5 16.2	6 6.6	26 35.3	27 15.7	7 26.6	11 3.7
29 Th	0 31 53	6 3 55	20 13 48	27 16 3	13 56.1	27 3.5	23 38.8	4 58.6	6 5.8	26 38.1	27 16.9	7 26.9	11 5.8
30 F	0 35 50	7 2 51	4♊11 21	10♊59 36	13 53.2	26 59.3	24 47.1	4 41.0	6 4.9	26 41.0	27 18.1	7 27.2	11 7.8

LONGITUDE — OCTOBER 1988

Day	Sid.Time	☉	0 hr ☽	Noon ☽	True ☊	☿	♀	♂	♃	♄	♅	♆	♇
1 Sa	0 39 46	8♎ 1 49	17♊40 54	24♊15 28	13♓50.9	26♎47.9	25♌55.5	4♈23.7	6♊ 3.7	26♐43.9	27♐19.4	7♑27.6	11♏ 9.9
2 Su	0 43 43	9 0 50	0♋43 37	7♋ 5 48	13D 49.6	26R 29.0	27 4.1	4R 6.5	6R 2.3	26 47.0	27 20.7	7 28.1	11 12.1
3 M	0 47 40	9 59 53	13 22 30	19 34 16	13 49.4	26 2.4	28 12.9	3 49.6	6 0.7	26 50.1	27 22.1	7 28.5	11 14.2
4 Tu	0 51 36	10 58 58	25 41 40	1♌45 19	13 50.2	25 28.0	29 21.9	3 33.0	5 58.9	26 53.3	27 23.5	7 29.0	11 16.4
5 W	0 55 33	11 58 6	7♌45 49	13 43 44	13 51.7	24 45.9	0♍31.0	3 16.7	5 56.9	26 56.6	27 25.0	7 29.5	11 18.5
6 Th	0 59 29	12 57 16	19 39 40	25 34 10	13 53.5	23 56.4	1 40.3	3 0.9	5 54.7	26 60.0	27 26.5	7 30.1	11 20.7
7 F	1 3 26	13 56 28	1♍27 44	7♍20 53	13 55.0	23 0.2	2 49.7	2 45.4	5 52.3	27 3.5	27 28.1	7 30.6	11 22.9
8 Sa	1 7 22	14 55 42	13 14 4	19 7 41	13R 55.7	21 58.0	3 59.3	2 30.4	5 49.7	27 7.0	27 29.7	7 31.3	11 25.1
9 Su	1 11 19	15 54 58	25 2 7	0♎57 42	13 55.0	20 51.2	5 9.0	2 16.0	5 46.9	27 10.7	27 31.3	7 31.9	11 27.4
10 M	1 15 15	16 54 17	6♎54 44	12 53 28	13 52.8	19 41.0	6 18.9	2 2.0	5 44.0	27 14.4	27 33.0	7 32.6	11 29.6
11 Tu	1 19 12	17 53 38	18 54 10	24 57 0	13 48.8	18 29.4	7 28.9	1 48.7	5 40.8	27 18.2	27 34.8	7 33.3	11 31.9
12 W	1 23 9	18 53 0	1♏ 2 9	7♏ 9 46	13 43.4	17 18.2	8 39.0	1 36.0	5 37.4	27 22.1	27 36.6	7 34.0	11 34.1
13 Th	1 27 5	19 52 25	13 20 1	19 33 1	13 37.0	16 9.5	9 49.3	1 23.9	5 33.8	27 26.0	27 38.4	7 34.8	11 36.4
14 F	1 31 2	20 51 52	25 48 55	2♐ 7 50	13 30.3	15 5.2	10 59.7	1 12.5	5 30.1	27 30.1	27 40.3	7 35.6	11 38.7
15 Sa	1 34 58	21 51 20	8♐29 56	14 55 21	13 24.0	14 7.3	12 10.3	1 1.8	5 26.1	27 34.2	27 42.2	7 36.5	11 41.0
16 Su	1 38 55	22 50 51	21 24 15	27 56 50	13 18.8	13 17.4	13 20.9	0 51.9	5 22.0	27 38.4	27 44.2	7 37.4	11 43.4
17 M	1 42 51	23 50 23	4♑33 16	11♑13 44	13 15.2	12 36.8	14 31.7	0 42.6	5 17.7	27 42.7	27 46.2	7 38.3	11 45.7
18 Tu	1 46 48	24 49 57	17 58 25	24 47 29	13D 13.5	12 6.5	15 42.6	0 34.1	5 13.2	27 47.0	27 48.3	7 39.2	11 48.0
19 W	1 50 44	25 49 33	1♒41 3	8♒39 12	13 13.4	11 47.2	16 53.6	0 26.4	5 8.6	27 51.4	27 50.4	7 40.2	11 50.4
20 Th	1 54 41	26 49 11	15 41 57	22 49 15	13 14.4	11D 39.1	18 4.7	0 19.5	5 3.7	27 55.9	27 52.6	7 41.2	11 52.7
21 F	1 58 38	27 48 50	0♓ 0 55	7♓16 41	13R 15.6	11 42.2	19 16.0	0 13.4	4 58.7	28 0.5	27 54.8	7 42.2	11 55.1
22 Sa	2 2 34	28 48 31	14 36 5	21 58 36	13 16.2	11 56.1	20 27.3	0 8.0	4 53.5	28 5.2	27 57.0	7 43.3	11 57.5
23 Su	2 6 31	29 48 13	29 23 32	6♈50 2	13 15.1	12 20.3	21 38.8	0 3.5	4 48.2	28 9.9	27 59.3	7 44.4	11 59.9
24 M	2 10 27	0♏47 57	14♈17 11	21 43 59	13 11.9	12 54.2	22 50.4	29♓59.7	4 42.7	28 14.7	28 1.6	7 45.5	12 2.2
25 Tu	2 14 24	1 47 43	29 9 20	6♉32 12	13 6.5	13 36.9	24 2.1	29 56.8	4 37.0	28 19.5	28 4.0	7 46.6	12 4.6
26 W	2 18 20	2 47 32	13♉51 35	21 6 31	12 59.2	14 27.6	25 13.8	29 54.6	4 31.2	28 24.4	28 6.3	7 47.8	12 7.0
27 Th	2 22 17	3 47 22	28 16 13	5♊20 1	12 50.9	15 25.6	26 25.7	29 53.3	4 25.2	28 29.4	28 8.8	7 49.0	12 9.4
28 F	2 26 13	4 47 14	12♊17 26	19 8 10	12 42.5	16 29.9	27 37.7	29D 52.7	4 19.1	28 34.5	28 11.3	7 50.3	12 11.9
29 Sa	2 30 10	5 47 9	25 52 4	2♋29 9	12 35.1	17 39.7	28 49.8	29 52.9	4 12.9	28 39.6	28 13.8	7 51.5	12 14.3
30 Su	2 34 7	6 47 6	8♋59 38	15 23 49	12 29.3	18 54.3	0♎ 2.0	29 53.9	4 6.5	28 44.8	28 16.3	7 52.8	12 16.7
31 M	2 38 3	7 47 5	21 42 7	27 55 4	12 25.7	20 13.0	1 14.3	29 55.7	3 59.9	28 50.0	28 18.9	7 54.1	12 19.1

Astro Data Dy Hr Mn	Planet Ingress Dy Hr Mn	Last Aspect Dy Hr Mn	☽ Ingress Dy Hr Mn	Last Aspect Dy Hr Mn	☽ Ingress Dy Hr Mn	☽ Phases & Eclipses Dy Hr Mn	Astro Data
♇0S 5 6:57	♀ ♌ 7 11:37	1 21:53 ♀ ⚹	♊ 2 8:11	1 17:42 ♅ ☍	♋ 1 22:39	3 3:50 ☽ 10♊52	1 SEPTEMBER 1988
♅ D 5 9:41	☉ ♎ 22 19:29	4 10:00 ♅ ☍	♋ 4 15:37	3 23:34 ☿ □	♌ 4 8:31	11 4:49 ● 18♍40	Julian Day # 32386
☽0S 11 22:13		7 1:20 ♀ ☌	♌ 7 2:14	6 15:51 ♅ △	♍ 6 21:01	11 4:43:33 ✓ A 6'57"	Delta T 56.1 sec
♆ D 18 18:19	♀ ♍ 4 13:15	9 8:48 ♅ △	♍ 9 14:48	9 5:03 ♅ □	♎ 9 10:03	19 3:18 ☽ 26♐24	SVP 05♓25'00"
♃ R 24 13:58	☉ ♏ 23 4:44	11 21:53 ♅ □	♎ 12 3:51	11 17:14 ♅ ⚹	♏ 11 21:58	25 19:07 ○ 2♈55	Obliquity 23°26'36"
☽0N 25 10:06	♂ ♓ 23 22:01	14 10:19 ♅ ⚹	♏ 14 16:07	12 20:38 ♇ ☌	♐ 14 7:58		⚷ Chiron 5♋49.1
☿ R 28 21:37	♀ ♎ 29 23:20	16 14:52 ☉ ⚹	♐ 17 2:25	16 11:39 ♅ ☌	♑ 16 15:44	2 16:59 ☽ 9♋43	☽ Mean ☊ 14♓14.8
		19 4:36 ♅ ☌	♑ 19 9:45	18 13:01 ☉ □	♒ 18 21:05	10 21:49 ● 17♎48	
☽0S 9 4:26		21 11:31 ☉ △	♒ 21 13:43	20 20:39 ♄ ⚹	♓ 20 23:58	18 13:01 ☽ 25♑22	1 OCTOBER 1988
♄☌♅ 18 13:28		23 10:19 ♅ ⚹	♓ 23 14:51	22 22:00 ♄ □	♈ 23 0:59	25 4:36 ○ 1♉59	Julian Day # 32416
☿ D 20 5:22		25 10:05 ♅ □	♈ 25 14:29	24 22:39 ♄ △	♉ 25 1:22		Delta T 56.2 sec
☽0N 22 20:22		27 10:01 ♅ △	♉ 27 14:29	27 2:44 ♂ ⚹	♊ 27 2:55		SVP 05♓24'56"
♂ D 28 5:07		29 6:19 ♀ □	♊ 29 16:43	29 7:16 ♂ □	♋ 29 7:28		Obliquity 23°26'36"
				31 15:58 ♂ △	♌ 31 16:03		⚷ Chiron 7♋00.4
							☽ Mean ☊ 12♓39.5

NOVEMBER 1988 — LONGITUDE

Day	Sid.Time	☉	0 hr ☽	Noon ☽	True ☊	☿	♀	♂	♃	♄	♅	♆	♇
1 Tu	2 42 0	8♏47 6	4♌ 3 13	10♌ 7 13	12♓24.2	21♎35.3	2♎26.7	29♓58.3	3♊53.3	28♐55.4	28♐21.5	7♑55.5	12♏21.5
2 W	2 45 56	9 47 9	16 7 44	22 5 26	12D 24.3	23 0.5	3 39.2	0♈ 1.6	3R 46.5	29 0.7	28 24.2	7 56.9	12 24.0
3 Th	2 49 53	10 47 14	28 1 1	3♍55 9	12 25.1	24 28.1	4 51.8	0 5.7	3 39.5	29 6.2	28 26.9	7 58.3	12 26.4
4 F	2 53 49	11 47 21	9♍48 30	15 41 41	12R 25.8	25 57.8	6 4.4	0 10.6	3 32.5	29 11.7	28 29.6	7 59.7	12 28.8
5 Sa	2 57 46	12 47 30	21 35 19	27 29 56	12 25.4	27 29.1	7 17.1	0 16.2	3 25.4	29 17.2	28 32.4	8 1.2	12 31.3
6 Su	3 1 42	13 47 42	3♎26 2	9♎24 6	12 22.9	29 1.7	8 30.0	0 22.5	3 18.1	29 22.8	28 35.2	8 2.7	12 33.7
7 M	3 5 39	14 47 55	15 24 31	21 27 36	12 18.0	0♏35.5	9 42.9	0 29.6	3 10.7	29 28.5	28 38.0	8 4.2	12 36.1
8 Tu	3 9 36	15 48 10	27 33 38	3♏42 49	12 10.3	2 10.0	10 55.8	0 37.4	3 3.3	29 34.2	28 40.9	8 5.7	12 38.6
9 W	3 13 32	16 48 27	9♏55 17	16 11 7	12 0.3	3 45.3	12 8.9	0 46.0	2 55.7	29 40.0	28 43.8	8 7.3	12 41.0
10 Th	3 17 29	17 48 46	22 30 21	28 52 56	11 48.5	5 20.9	13 22.0	0 55.2	2 48.1	29 45.8	28 46.7	8 8.9	12 43.4
11 F	3 21 25	18 49 7	5♐18 48	11♐47 51	11 36.1	6 57.0	14 35.2	1 5.1	2 40.4	29 51.7	28 49.7	8 10.5	12 45.8
12 Sa	3 25 22	19 49 29	18 19 59	24 55 4	11 24.3	8 33.2	15 48.5	1 15.7	2 32.6	29 57.7	28 52.7	8 12.1	12 48.3
13 Su	3 29 18	20 49 53	1♑32 58	8♑13 35	11 14.1	10 9.6	17 1.8	1 27.0	2 24.7	0♑ 3.6	28 55.7	8 13.8	12 50.7
14 M	3 33 15	21 50 18	14 56 50	21 42 39	11 6.4	11 46.1	18 15.2	1 39.0	2 16.8	0 9.7	28 58.7	8 15.5	12 53.1
15 Tu	3 37 11	22 50 45	28 31 1	5♒21 54	11 1.5	13 22.5	19 28.6	1 51.6	2 8.9	0 15.8	29 1.8	8 17.2	12 55.5
16 W	3 41 8	23 51 13	12♒15 21	19 11 22	10D 59.2	14 58.9	20 42.1	2 4.8	2 0.8	0 21.9	29 4.9	8 18.9	12 57.9
17 Th	3 45 5	24 51 42	26 9 58	3♓11 11	10 58.8	16 35.2	21 55.7	2 18.6	1 52.8	0 28.1	29 8.1	8 20.7	13 0.3
18 F	3 49 1	25 52 13	10♓14 58	17 21 13	10R 58.9	18 11.4	23 9.3	2 33.1	1 44.7	0 34.3	29 11.2	8 22.4	13 2.7
19 Sa	3 52 58	26 52 44	24 29 47	1♈40 25	10 58.4	19 47.4	24 23.0	2 48.1	1 36.5	0 40.6	29 14.4	8 24.2	13 5.1
20 Su	3 56 54	27 53 17	8♈52 47	16 6 24	10 55.9	21 23.3	25 36.7	3 3.7	1 28.4	0 46.9	29 17.6	8 26.1	13 7.4
21 M	4 0 51	28 53 51	23 20 43	0♉35 5	10 50.7	22 59.0	26 50.5	3 19.9	1 20.2	0 53.2	29 20.8	8 27.9	13 9.8
22 Tu	4 4 47	29 54 27	7♉48 47	15 1 47	10 42.5	24 34.5	28 4.3	3 36.6	1 12.0	0 59.6	29 24.1	8 29.8	13 12.1
23 W	4 8 44	0♐55 4	22 10 56	29 17 47	10 31.8	26 9.9	29 18.2	3 53.9	1 3.9	1 6.0	29 27.4	8 31.6	13 14.5
24 Th	4 12 40	1 55 42	6♊20 50	13♊19 22	10 19.5	27 45.1	0♏32.2	4 11.6	0 55.7	1 12.5	29 30.7	8 33.5	13 16.8
25 F	4 16 37	2 56 21	20 12 50	27 0 49	10 6.9	29 20.2	1 46.2	4 29.9	0 47.5	1 19.0	29 34.0	8 35.5	13 19.2
26 Sa	4 20 34	3 57 3	3♋43 0	10♋19 15	9 55.3	0♐55.1	3 0.2	4 48.7	0 39.4	1 25.6	29 37.3	8 37.4	13 21.5
27 Su	4 24 30	4 57 45	16 49 33	23 14 3	9 45.7	2 29.8	4 14.3	5 7.9	0 31.2	1 32.1	29 40.7	8 39.3	13 23.8
28 M	4 28 27	5 58 29	29 32 59	5♌46 44	9 38.8	4 4.5	5 28.4	5 27.6	0 23.1	1 38.7	29 44.1	8 41.3	13 26.1
29 Tu	4 32 23	6 59 15	11♌55 46	18 0 37	9 34.6	5 39.0	6 42.6	5 47.8	0 15.0	1 45.4	29 47.5	8 43.3	13 28.4
30 W	4 36 20	8 0 2	24 1 54	0♍ 0 15	9 32.7	7 13.4	7 56.9	6 8.4	0 7.0	1 52.1	29 50.9	8 45.3	13 30.6

DECEMBER 1988 — LONGITUDE

Day	Sid.Time	☉	0 hr ☽	Noon ☽	True ☊	☿	♀	♂	♃	♄	♅	♆	♇
1 Th	4 40 16	9♐ 0 50	5♍56 22	11♍50 56	9♓32.2	8♐47.8	9♏11.1	6♈29.5	29♉59.0	1♑58.8	29♐54.3	8♑47.3	13♏32.9
2 F	4 44 13	10 1 40	17 44 40	23 38 16	9R 32.2	10 22.0	10 25.5	6 51.0	29R 51.0	2 5.5	29 57.8	8 49.4	13 35.1
3 Sa	4 48 9	11 2 31	29 32 27	5♎27 52	9 31.3	11 56.2	11 39.8	7 12.9	29 43.1	2 12.3	0♑ 1.2	8 51.4	13 37.4
4 Su	4 52 6	12 3 24	11♎25 9	17 24 53	9 28.5	13 30.4	12 54.2	7 35.2	29 35.3	2 19.1	0 4.7	8 53.5	13 39.6
5 M	4 56 3	13 4 18	23 27 37	29 33 49	9 23.2	15 4.6	14 8.6	7 58.0	29 27.5	2 25.9	0 8.2	8 55.6	13 41.8
6 Tu	4 59 59	14 5 13	5♏43 51	11♏58 3	9 14.9	16 38.7	15 23.1	8 21.1	29 19.8	2 32.7	0 11.7	8 57.7	13 43.9
7 W	5 3 56	15 6 10	18 16 39	24 39 45	9 4.1	18 12.9	16 37.6	8 44.6	29 12.2	2 39.6	0 15.2	8 59.8	13 46.1
8 Th	5 7 52	16 7 7	1♐ 7 24	7♐39 30	8 51.3	19 47.1	17 52.1	9 8.5	29 4.7	2 46.5	0 18.8	9 1.9	13 48.2
9 F	5 11 49	17 8 6	14 15 56	20 56 25	8 37.6	21 21.3	19 6.7	9 32.7	28 57.3	2 53.4	0 22.3	9 4.0	13 50.4
10 Sa	5 15 45	18 9 6	27 40 40	4♑28 17	8 24.5	22 55.5	20 21.3	9 57.3	28 50.0	3 0.3	0 25.9	9 6.2	13 52.5
11 Su	5 19 42	19 10 6	11♑18 54	18 12 5	8 13.1	24 29.8	21 35.9	10 22.3	28 42.7	3 7.3	0 29.4	9 8.3	13 54.6
12 M	5 23 39	20 11 7	25 7 24	2♒ 4 30	8 4.3	26 4.2	22 50.6	10 47.6	28 35.6	3 14.2	0 33.0	9 10.5	13 56.7
13 Tu	5 27 35	21 12 9	9♒ 3 0	16 2 36	7 58.6	27 38.6	24 5.3	11 13.2	28 28.6	3 21.2	0 36.6	9 12.7	13 58.7
14 W	5 31 32	22 13 12	23 3 3	0♓ 4 10	7 55.8	29 13.2	25 20.0	11 39.2	28 21.8	3 28.2	0 40.2	9 14.9	14 0.7
15 Th	5 35 28	23 14 14	7♓ 5 46	14 7 45	7D 55.1	0♑47.7	26 34.7	12 5.5	28 15.0	3 35.3	0 43.8	9 17.1	14 2.8
16 F	5 39 25	24 15 17	21 10 3	28 12 33	7R 55.3	2 22.4	27 49.4	12 32.1	28 8.4	3 42.3	0 47.4	9 19.3	14 4.7
17 Sa	5 43 21	25 16 21	5♈15 12	12♈17 52	7 55.0	3 57.1	29 4.2	12 58.9	28 1.9	3 49.3	0 51.0	9 21.5	14 6.7
18 Su	5 47 18	26 17 25	19 20 26	26 22 43	7 52.9	5 31.9	0♐18.9	13 26.1	27 55.6	3 56.4	0 54.6	9 23.7	14 8.7
19 M	5 51 14	27 18 29	3♉24 27	10♉25 20	7 48.4	7 6.8	1 33.7	13 53.5	27 49.4	4 3.4	0 58.2	9 25.9	14 10.6
20 Tu	5 55 11	28 19 33	17 25 2	24 23 8	7 41.0	8 41.6	2 48.5	14 21.2	27 43.3	4 10.5	1 1.9	9 28.2	14 12.5
21 W	5 59 8	29 20 38	1♊19 12	8♊12 45	7 31.2	10 16.5	4 3.4	14 49.2	27 37.4	4 17.6	1 5.5	9 30.4	14 14.4
22 Th	6 3 4	0♑21 44	15 3 20	21 50 30	7 19.8	11 51.3	5 18.2	15 17.4	27 31.7	4 24.7	1 9.1	9 32.7	14 16.2
23 F	6 7 1	1 22 49	28 33 52	5♋13 6	7 8.0	13 26.1	6 33.1	15 45.9	27 26.1	4 31.8	1 12.7	9 34.9	14 18.0
24 Sa	6 10 57	2 23 55	11♋47 54	18 18 7	6 57.1	15 0.7	7 48.0	16 14.6	27 20.7	4 38.8	1 16.3	9 37.2	14 19.8
25 Su	6 14 54	3 25 2	24 43 40	1♌ 4 33	6 47.9	16 35.1	9 2.9	16 43.6	27 15.5	4 45.9	1 20.0	9 39.4	14 21.6
26 M	6 18 50	4 26 9	7♌20 54	13 32 55	6 41.2	18 9.3	10 17.8	17 12.7	27 10.4	4 53.0	1 23.6	9 41.7	14 23.4
27 Tu	6 22 47	5 27 16	19 40 54	25 45 14	6 37.2	19 43.0	11 32.7	17 42.1	27 5.5	5 0.1	1 27.2	9 44.0	14 25.1
28 W	6 26 43	6 28 24	1♍46 23	7♍44 50	6D 35.6	21 16.3	12 47.7	18 11.7	27 0.7	5 7.2	1 30.8	9 46.2	14 26.8
29 Th	6 30 40	7 29 32	13 41 11	19 36 2	6 35.7	22 48.9	14 2.7	18 41.5	26 56.2	5 14.3	1 34.4	9 48.5	14 28.5
30 F	6 34 37	8 30 40	25 30 2	1♎23 51	6 36.6	24 20.7	15 17.6	19 11.5	26 51.8	5 21.4	1 38.0	9 50.8	14 30.1
31 Sa	6 38 33	9 31 49	7♎18 10	13 13 40	6R 37.3	25 51.6	16 32.6	19 41.8	26 47.6	5 28.5	1 41.6	9 53.0	14 31.8

Astro Data	Planet Ingress	Last Aspect	☽ Ingress	Last Aspect	☽ Ingress	☽ Phases & Eclipses	Astro Data
Dy Hr Mn	Dy Hr Mn	Dy Hr Mn	Dy Hr Mn	Dy Hr Mn	Dy Hr Mn	Dy Hr Mn	1 NOVEMBER 1988
♀0S 2 0:18	♂ ♈ 1 12:57	3 2:13 ♄ △	♍ 3 4:02	3 0:21 ♃ △	♎ 3 0:56	1 10:11 ☽ 9♌13	Julian Day # 32447
☽0S 5 11:02	☿ ♏ 6 14:57	5 15:45 ♄ □	♎ 5 17:04	4 4:49 ☿ ✶	♏ 5 12:51	9 14:20 ● 17♏24	Delta T 56.2 sec
♂0N 17 11:08	♄ ♑ 12 9:25	8 3:58 ♄ ✶	♏ 8 4:46	7 20:15 ♃ ☍	♐ 7 21:55	16 21:35 ☽ 24♒46	SVP 05♓24'52"
☽0N 19 3:53	☉ ♐ 22 2:12	9 14:20 ☉ ☌	♐ 10 14:06	9 14:26 ☿ ☌	♑ 10 4:07	23 15:53 ○ 1♊35	Obliquity 23°26'35"
♃⊼♄ 22 20:25	♀ ♏ 23 13:34	12 19:15 ♅ ☌	♑ 12 21:12	12 5:57 ♃ △	♒ 12 8:25		⚷ Chiron 6♋59.7R
	☿ ♐ 25 10:04	14 13:12 ☉ ✶	♒ 15 2:36	14 11:53 ☿ ✶	♓ 14 11:53	1 6:49 ☽ 9♍18	☽ Mean ☊ 11♓01.0
♃⊼♅ 1 9:48	♃ ♉ 30 20:54	17 5:06 ♅ ✶	♓ 17 6:34	16 12:27 ♀ △	♈ 16 15:03	9 5:36 ● 17♐22	
☽0S 2 17:59		19 7:58 ♅ □	♈ 19 9:12	18 12:46 ☉ △	♉ 18 18:11	16 5:40 ☽ 24♓30	1 DECEMBER 1988
☽0N 16 8:46	♅ ♑ 2 15:33	21 9:59 ♅ △	♉ 21 11:02	20 17:38 ♃ ☌	♊ 20 21:43	23 5:29 ○ 1♋37	Julian Day # 32477
☽0S 30 1:08	☿ ♑ 14 11:53	23 7:33 ♅ ☍	♊ 23 13:12	22 0:26 ♂ ✶	♋ 23 2:35	31 4:57 ☽ 9♎44	Delta T 56.3 sec
	♀ ♐ 17 17:56	25 16:37 ♅ ☍	♋ 25 17:19	25 4:44 ♃ ✶	♌ 25 9:57		SVP 05♓24'47"
	☉ ♑ 21 15:28	26 17:38 ♇ △	♌ 28 0:52	27 14:34 ♃ □	♍ 27 20:27		Obliquity 23°26'35"
		30 11:44 ♅ △	♍ 30 11:59	30 2:45 ♃ △	♎ 30 9:09		⚷ Chiron 5♋48.2R
							☽ Mean ☊ 9♓25.7

LONGITUDE JANUARY 1989

Day	Sid.Time	☉	0 hr ☽	Noon ☽	True ☊	☿	♀	♂	♃	♄	♅	♆	♇
1 Su	6 42 30	10♑32 59	19♎11 3	25♎10 57	6♓36.8	27♑21.1	17♐47.7	20♈12.2	26♉43.6	5♑35.6	1♑45.2	9♑55.3	14♏33.3
2 M	6 46 26	11 34 8	1♏14 2	7♏20 52	6R 34.5	28 49.2	19 2.7	20 42.8	26R 39.8	5 42.7	1 48.8	9 57.6	14 34.9
3 Tu	6 50 23	12 35 18	13 32 1	19 47 56	6 30.0	0♒15.4	20 17.7	21 13.6	26 36.2	5 49.8	1 52.4	9 59.9	14 36.4
4 W	6 54 19	13 36 29	26 8 59	2♐35 30	6 23.3	1 39.3	21 32.8	21 44.6	26 32.8	5 56.8	1 56.0	10 2.1	14 37.9
5 Th	6 58 16	14 37 39	9♐ 7 38	15 45 27	6 14.9	3 0.7	22 47.8	22 15.7	26 29.5	6 3.9	1 59.6	10 4.4	14 39.4
6 F	7 2 12	15 38 50	22 28 52	29 17 43	6 5.8	4 18.9	24 2.9	22 47.1	26 26.5	6 10.9	2 3.1	10 6.7	14 40.9
7 Sa	7 6 9	16 40 1	6♑11 39	13♑10 13	5 56.8	5 33.4	25 18.0	23 18.6	26 23.7	6 18.0	2 6.7	10 8.9	14 42.3
8 Su	7 10 6	17 41 11	20 12 55	27 19 5	5 48.9	6 43.5	26 33.1	23 50.3	26 21.0	6 25.0	2 10.2	10 11.2	14 43.7
9 M	7 14 2	18 42 22	4♒28 4	11♒39 9	5 43.1	7 48.6	27 48.2	24 22.1	26 18.6	6 32.0	2 13.7	10 13.5	14 45.0
10 Tu	7 17 59	19 43 32	18 51 37	26 4 47	5 39.6	8 47.9	29 3.3	24 54.1	26 16.4	6 39.0	2 17.2	10 15.7	14 46.4
11 W	7 21 55	20 44 41	3♓18 3	10♓30 48	5D 38.3	9 40.6	0♑18.4	25 26.3	26 14.4	6 46.0	2 20.7	10 18.0	14 47.7
12 Th	7 25 52	21 45 50	17 42 33	24 52 55	5 38.8	10 25.8	1 33.5	25 58.6	26 12.5	6 52.9	2 24.2	10 20.2	14 48.9
13 F	7 29 48	22 46 59	2♈ 1 31	9♈ 8 7	5 40.1	11 2.5	2 48.6	26 31.1	26 10.9	6 59.8	2 27.6	10 22.4	14 50.1
14 Sa	7 33 45	23 48 6	16 12 31	23 14 33	5R 41.2	11 29.9	4 3.7	27 3.7	26 9.5	7 6.8	2 31.1	10 24.7	14 51.3
15 Su	7 37 42	24 49 13	0♉14 7	7♉11 8	5 41.3	11 47.3	5 18.8	27 36.4	26 8.3	7 13.6	2 34.5	10 26.9	14 52.5
16 M	7 41 38	25 50 19	14 5 32	20 57 15	5 39.7	11R 53.7	6 33.9	28 9.3	26 7.3	7 20.5	2 37.9	10 29.1	14 53.6
17 Tu	7 45 35	26 51 25	27 46 14	4♊32 24	5 36.3	11 48.8	7 49.0	28 42.3	26 6.6	7 27.4	2 41.3	10 31.3	14 54.7
18 W	7 49 31	27 52 30	11♊15 40	17 55 57	5 31.3	11 32.2	9 4.1	29 15.4	26 6.0	7 34.2	2 44.7	10 33.5	14 55.8
19 Th	7 53 28	28 53 34	24 33 8	1♋ 7 9	5 25.2	11 3.9	10 19.2	29 48.6	26 5.6	7 41.0	2 48.1	10 35.7	14 56.8
20 F	7 57 24	29 54 37	7♋37 53	14 5 16	5 18.7	10 24.3	11 34.3	0♉22.0	26D 5.5	7 47.7	2 51.4	10 37.9	14 57.8
21 Sa	8 1 21	0♒55 39	20 29 15	26 49 48	5 12.7	9 34.3	12 49.4	0 55.5	26 5.5	7 54.5	2 54.7	10 40.0	14 58.8
22 Su	8 5 17	1 56 41	3♌ 6 55	9♌20 40	5 7.7	8 35.1	14 4.6	1 29.0	26 5.8	8 1.2	2 58.0	10 42.2	14 59.7
23 M	8 9 14	2 57 42	15 31 8	21 38 28	5 4.3	7 28.4	15 19.7	2 2.7	26 6.2	8 7.9	3 1.3	10 44.3	15 0.6
24 Tu	8 13 11	3 58 42	27 42 53	3♍44 37	5D 2.6	6 16.2	16 34.8	2 36.5	26 6.9	8 14.5	3 4.5	10 46.5	15 1.5
25 W	8 17 7	4 59 42	9♍43 59	15 41 21	5 2.4	5 0.7	17 49.9	3 10.3	26 7.8	8 21.1	3 7.7	10 48.6	15 2.3
26 Th	8 21 4	6 0 41	21 37 7	27 31 44	5 3.4	3 44.3	19 5.0	3 44.3	26 8.8	8 27.7	3 10.9	10 50.7	15 3.1
27 F	8 25 0	7 1 39	3♎25 43	9♎19 35	5 5.2	2 29.2	20 20.1	4 18.4	26 10.1	8 34.3	3 14.1	10 52.8	15 3.8
28 Sa	8 28 57	8 2 36	15 13 55	21 9 17	5 7.1	1 17.4	21 35.3	4 52.5	26 11.6	8 40.8	3 17.3	10 54.9	15 4.5
29 Su	8 32 53	9 3 33	27 6 19	3♏ 5 39	5 8.6	0 10.8	22 50.4	5 26.8	26 13.3	8 47.2	3 20.4	10 56.9	15 5.2
30 M	8 36 50	10 4 29	9♏ 7 53	15 13 39	5R 9.2	29♑10.6	24 5.5	6 1.1	26 15.1	8 53.7	3 23.5	10 59.0	15 5.9
31 Tu	8 40 46	11 5 25	21 23 33	27 38 10	5 8.7	28 18.0	25 20.6	6 35.6	26 17.2	9 0.1	3 26.5	11 1.0	15 6.5

LONGITUDE FEBRUARY 1989

Day	Sid.Time	☉	0 hr ☽	Noon ☽	True ☊	☿	♀	♂	♃	♄	♅	♆	♇
1 W	8 44 43	12♒ 6 20	3♐57 59	10♐23 28	5♓ 7.1	27♑33.7	26♑35.8	7♉10.1	26♉19.5	9♑ 6.4	3♑29.6	11♑ 3.1	15♏ 7.1
2 Th	8 48 40	13 7 14	16 55 1	23 32 52	5R 4.7	26R 57.8	27 50.9	7 44.7	26 22.0	9 12.8	3 32.6	11 5.1	15 7.6
3 F	8 52 36	14 8 7	0♑17 11	7♑ 8 0	5 1.7	26 30.7	29 6.0	8 19.4	26 24.7	9 19.0	3 35.6	11 7.1	15 8.1
4 Sa	8 56 33	15 9 0	14 5 12	21 8 29	4 58.6	26 12.0	0♒21.1	8 54.1	26 27.5	9 25.3	3 38.5	11 9.0	15 8.6
5 Su	9 0 29	16 9 51	28 17 26	5♒31 28	4 55.9	26D 1.6	1 36.2	9 29.0	26 30.6	9 31.4	3 41.4	11 11.0	15 9.0
6 M	9 4 26	17 10 41	12♒49 52	20 11 48	4 54.0	25 59.0	2 51.4	10 3.9	26 33.9	9 37.6	3 44.3	11 12.9	15 9.4
7 Tu	9 8 22	18 11 30	27 36 21	5♓ 2 32	4D 53.1	26 3.8	4 6.5	10 38.9	26 37.3	9 43.7	3 47.2	11 14.9	15 9.8
8 W	9 12 19	19 12 18	12♓29 22	19 55 52	4 53.1	26 15.6	5 21.6	11 14.0	26 41.0	9 49.7	3 50.0	11 16.8	15 10.1
9 Th	9 16 15	20 13 4	27 21 8	4♈44 17	4 53.8	26 33.7	6 36.7	11 49.1	26 44.8	9 55.7	3 52.8	11 18.6	15 10.4
10 F	9 20 12	21 13 49	12♈ 4 35	19 21 25	4 54.9	26 57.8	7 51.8	12 24.3	26 48.8	10 1.6	3 55.5	11 20.5	15 10.6
11 Sa	9 24 9	22 14 32	26 34 16	3♉42 45	4 55.9	27 27.3	9 6.8	12 59.6	26 53.0	10 7.5	3 58.2	11 22.3	15 10.8
12 Su	9 28 5	23 15 14	10♉46 36	17 45 41	4R 56.7	28 1.9	10 21.9	13 34.9	26 57.4	10 13.4	4 0.9	11 24.1	15 11.0
13 M	9 32 2	24 15 54	24 39 54	1♊29 19	4 56.9	28 41.1	11 37.0	14 10.3	27 2.0	10 19.1	4 3.5	11 25.9	15 11.1
14 Tu	9 35 58	25 16 32	8♊13 59	14 54 4	4 56.6	29 24.5	12 52.0	14 45.8	27 6.8	10 24.9	4 6.1	11 27.7	15 11.2
15 W	9 39 55	26 17 9	21 29 24	28 1 11	4 56.0	0♒11.8	14 7.1	15 21.3	27 11.7	10 30.5	4 8.7	11 29.5	15 11.3
16 Th	9 43 51	27 17 44	4♋28 39	10♋52 21	4 55.0	1 2.7	15 22.1	15 56.9	27 16.8	10 36.1	4 11.2	11 31.2	15R 11.3
17 F	9 47 48	28 18 17	17 12 30	23 29 21	4 54.1	1 56.8	16 37.1	16 32.5	27 22.1	10 41.7	4 13.7	11 32.9	15 11.3
18 Sa	9 51 44	29 18 48	29 43 6	5♌53 58	4 53.3	2 54.0	17 52.2	17 8.2	27 27.6	10 47.2	4 16.2	11 34.6	15 11.3
19 Su	9 55 41	0♓19 18	12♌ 2 11	18 7 56	4 52.7	3 54.0	19 7.2	17 43.9	27 33.2	10 52.6	4 18.6	11 36.3	15 11.2
20 M	9 59 38	1 19 46	24 11 25	0♍12 53	4D 52.4	4 56.6	20 22.2	18 19.6	27 39.0	10 58.0	4 21.0	11 37.9	15 11.1
21 Tu	10 3 34	2 20 12	6♍12 31	12 10 34	4 52.3	6 1.6	21 37.2	18 55.4	27 44.9	11 3.3	4 23.3	11 39.5	15 11.0
22 W	10 7 31	3 20 37	18 7 15	24 2 52	4 52.4	7 8.8	22 52.2	19 31.3	27 51.1	11 8.5	4 25.6	11 41.1	15 10.8
23 Th	10 11 27	4 21 0	29 57 42	5♎52 2	4R 52.4	8 18.2	24 7.1	20 7.2	27 57.4	11 13.7	4 27.8	11 42.7	15 10.6
24 F	10 15 24	5 21 22	11♎46 14	17 40 39	4 52.4	9 29.5	25 22.1	20 43.1	28 3.8	11 18.8	4 30.0	11 44.2	15 10.3
25 Sa	10 19 20	6 21 42	23 35 42	29 31 48	4 52.3	10 42.7	26 37.1	21 19.1	28 10.4	11 23.9	4 32.2	11 45.7	15 10.0
26 Su	10 23 17	7 22 1	5♏29 25	11♏29 2	4 52.0	11 57.6	27 52.0	21 55.1	28 17.2	11 28.9	4 34.3	11 47.2	15 9.7
27 M	10 27 13	8 22 18	17 31 9	23 36 18	4 51.7	13 14.2	29 7.0	22 31.1	28 24.1	11 33.8	4 36.4	11 48.7	15 9.3
28 Tu	10 31 10	9 22 34	29 45 1	5♐57 51	4D 51.5	14 32.4	0♓21.9	23 7.2	28 31.2	11 38.7	4 38.4	11 50.1	15 8.9

Astro Data Dy Hr Mn	Planet Ingress Dy Hr Mn	Last Aspect Dy Hr Mn	☽ Ingress Dy Hr Mn	Last Aspect Dy Hr Mn	☽ Ingress Dy Hr Mn	☽ Phases & Eclipses Dy Hr Mn	Astro Data
☽0N 12 13:39	☿ ♒ 2 19:41	1 18:34 ☿ □	♏ 1 21:34	1 16:27 ☉ ⚹	♑ 2 23:30	7 19:22 ● 17♑29	1 JANUARY 1989
☿ R 16 1:45	♀ ♑ 10 18:08	4 0:44 ♃ ☍	♐ 4 7:12	4 21:01 ♃ △	♒ 5 2:51	14 13:58 ☽ 24♈24	Julian Day # 32508
♃ D 20 6:13	♂ ♉ 19 8:11	6 3:03 ♀ ☌	♑ 6 13:14	6 22:24 ♃ □	♓ 7 3:52	21 21:34 ○ 1♌50	Delta T 56.3 sec
☽0S 26 8:20	☉ ♒ 20 2:07	8 10:20 ♃ △	♒ 8 16:31	8 23:01 ♃ ⚹	♈ 9 4:18	30 2:02 ☽ 10♏10	SVP 05♓24'41"
	☿ ♑ 29 4:06	10 12:18 ♃ □	♓ 10 18:31	11 1:32 ☿ □	♉ 11 5:45		Obliquity 23°26'35"
☿ D 5 20:07		12 14:12 ♃ ⚹	♈ 12 20:36	13 7:26 ☿ △	♊ 13 9:22	6 7:37 ● 17♒30	⚷ Chiron 3♋51.5R
☽0N 8 21:16	♀ ♒ 3 17:15	14 19:18 ♂ ☌	♉ 14 23:36	15 9:32 ☉ △	♋ 15 15:40	12 23:15 ☽ 24♉14	☽ Mean ☊ 7♓47.2
♇ R 16 9:46	☿ ♒ 14 18:11	16 22:15 ☉ △	♊ 17 3:57	17 19:36 ♃ ⚹	♌ 18 0:33	20 15:32 ○ 1♍59	
☽0S 22 15:15	☉ ♓ 18 16:21	18 0:29 ☿ △	♋ 19 9:57	20 6:56 ♃ □	♍ 20 11:34	20 15:35 ☍T 1.275	1 FEBRUARY 1989
	♀ ♓ 27 16:59	21 10:36 ♃ ⚹	♌ 21 18:02	22 19:53 ♃ △	♎ 23 0:05	28 20:08 ☽ 10♐13	Julian Day # 32539
		23 20:50 ♃ □	♍ 24 4:32	25 6:50 ♀ △	♏ 25 12:57		Delta T 56.3 sec
		26 9:12 ♃ △	♎ 26 17:01	27 21:35 ♃ ☍	♐ 28 0:29		SVP 05♓24'36"
		29 5:40 ☿ □	♏ 29 5:49				Obliquity 23°26'35"
		31 12:30 ☿ ⚹	♐ 31 16:30				⚷ Chiron 2♋05.0R
							☽ Mean ☊ 6♓08.8

MARCH 1989 LONGITUDE

Day	Sid.Time	☉	0 hr ☽	Noon ☽	True ☊	☿	♀	♂	♃	♄	♅	♆	♇
1 W	10 35 7	10♓22 48	12♐15 18	18♐37 54	4♓51.4	15♒52.1	1♓36.9	23♉43.3	28♉38.4	11♑43.4	4♑40.4	11♑51.5	15♏ 8.5
2 Th	10 39 3	11 23 1	25 6 6	1♑40 21	4 51.6	17 13.3	2 51.8	24 19.5	28 45.8	11 48.1	4 42.4	11 52.9	15R 8.1
3 F	10 43 0	12 23 12	8♑20 59	15 8 15	4 52.1	18 35.9	4 6.7	24 55.7	28 53.4	11 52.8	4 44.3	11 54.2	15 7.6
4 Sa	10 46 56	13 23 22	22 2 18	29 3 8	4 52.8	19 59.8	5 21.6	25 31.9	29 1.0	11 57.3	4 46.1	11 55.6	15 7.0
5 Su	10 50 53	14 23 30	6♒10 37	13♒24 26	4 53.6	21 25.0	6 36.5	26 8.2	29 8.9	12 1.8	4 47.9	11 56.9	15 6.5
6 M	10 54 49	15 23 37	20 44 5	28 8 55	4R 54.3	22 51.6	7 51.4	26 44.5	29 16.8	12 6.3	4 49.7	11 58.1	15 5.9
7 Tu	10 58 46	16 23 42	5♓38 4	13♓10 34	4 54.6	24 19.4	9 6.3	27 20.9	29 24.9	12 10.6	4 51.4	11 59.4	15 5.3
8 W	11 2 42	17 23 45	20 45 18	28 21 4	4 54.2	25 48.4	10 21.2	27 57.2	29 33.2	12 14.8	4 53.1	12 0.6	15 4.6
9 Th	11 6 39	18 23 46	5♈56 38	13♈30 48	4 53.2	27 18.7	11 36.0	28 33.6	29 41.6	12 19.0	4 54.7	12 1.8	15 3.9
10 F	11 10 36	19 23 45	21 2 24	28 30 22	4 51.5	28 50.1	12 50.8	29 10.1	29 50.1	12 23.1	4 56.3	12 2.9	15 3.2
11 Sa	11 14 32	20 23 42	5♉53 47	13♉11 53	4 49.6	0♓22.8	14 5.7	29 46.5	29 58.8	12 27.2	4 57.8	12 4.0	15 2.4
12 Su	11 18 29	21 23 36	20 24 7	27 30 5	4 47.6	1 56.6	15 20.5	0♊23.0	0♊ 7.5	12 31.1	4 59.3	12 5.1	15 1.6
13 M	11 22 25	22 23 29	4♊29 32	11♊22 26	4 46.1	3 31.7	16 35.3	0 59.6	0 16.5	12 35.0	5 0.7	12 6.2	15 0.8
14 Tu	11 26 22	23 23 20	18 8 51	24 48 59	4D 45.3	5 7.9	17 50.1	1 36.1	0 25.5	12 38.7	5 2.1	12 7.2	14 60.0
15 W	11 30 18	24 23 8	1♋23 7	7♋51 38	4 45.4	6 45.3	19 4.8	2 12.7	0 34.7	12 42.4	5 3.4	12 8.2	14 59.1
16 Th	11 34 15	25 22 54	14 14 56	20 33 30	4 46.3	8 23.9	20 19.6	2 49.3	0 44.0	12 46.1	5 4.7	12 9.2	14 58.2
17 F	11 38 11	26 22 38	26 47 46	2♌58 13	4 47.8	10 3.8	21 34.3	3 25.9	0 53.4	12 49.6	5 5.9	12 10.1	14 57.3
18 Sa	11 42 8	27 22 19	9♌ 5 20	15 9 33	4 49.4	11 44.8	22 49.0	4 2.5	1 2.9	12 53.0	5 7.1	12 11.0	14 56.3
19 Su	11 46 5	28 21 58	21 11 19	27 11 2	4 50.8	13 27.1	24 3.7	4 39.2	1 12.5	12 56.4	5 8.2	12 11.9	14 55.3
20 M	11 50 1	29 21 35	3♍ 9 4	9♍ 5 46	4R 51.5	15 10.5	25 18.4	5 15.8	1 22.3	12 59.7	5 9.3	12 12.7	14 54.3
21 Tu	11 53 58	0♈21 10	15 1 29	20 56 30	4 51.1	16 55.3	26 33.1	5 52.5	1 32.2	13 2.9	5 10.3	12 13.5	14 53.3
22 W	11 57 54	1 20 43	26 51 5	2♎45 31	4 49.3	18 41.3	27 47.7	6 29.2	1 42.2	13 5.9	5 11.3	12 14.3	14 52.2
23 Th	12 1 51	2 20 14	8♎40 3	14 34 54	4 46.1	20 28.6	29 2.4	7 5.9	1 52.2	13 9.0	5 12.2	12 15.0	14 51.1
24 F	12 5 47	3 19 42	20 30 20	26 26 35	4 41.7	22 17.1	0♈17.0	7 42.6	2 2.4	13 11.9	5 13.1	12 15.7	14 50.0
25 Sa	12 9 44	4 19 9	2♏23 53	8♏22 31	4 36.5	24 7.0	1 31.6	8 19.4	2 12.7	13 14.7	5 13.9	12 16.4	14 48.8
26 Su	12 13 40	5 18 34	14 22 46	20 24 56	4 31.0	25 58.2	2 46.2	8 56.1	2 23.1	13 17.5	5 14.7	12 17.1	14 47.6
27 M	12 17 37	6 17 57	26 29 21	2♐36 22	4 25.8	27 50.6	4 0.8	9 32.9	2 33.7	13 20.1	5 15.4	12 17.7	14 46.4
28 Tu	12 21 33	7 17 19	8♐46 21	14 59 42	4 21.6	29 44.4	5 15.4	10 9.7	2 44.3	13 22.7	5 16.1	12 18.3	14 45.2
29 W	12 25 30	8 16 38	21 16 51	27 38 14	4 18.6	1♈39.5	6 29.9	10 46.5	2 55.0	13 25.1	5 16.7	12 18.8	14 44.0
30 Th	12 29 27	9 15 56	4♑ 4 15	10♑35 22	4D 17.2	3 35.9	7 44.4	11 23.3	3 5.8	13 27.5	5 17.3	12 19.3	14 42.7
31 F	12 33 23	10 15 12	17 11 57	23 54 23	4 17.3	5 33.5	8 59.0	12 0.2	3 16.7	13 29.8	5 17.8	12 19.8	14 41.4

APRIL 1989 LONGITUDE

Day	Sid.Time	☉	0 hr ☽	Noon ☽	True ☊	☿	♀	♂	♃	♄	♅	♆	♇
1 Sa	12 37 20	11♈14 26	0♒42 57	7♒37 52	4♓18.4	7♈32.4	10♈13.5	12♊37.0	3♊27.7	13♑32.0	5♑18.2	12♑20.3	14♏40.1
2 Su	12 41 16	12 13 39	14 39 16	21 47 5	4 19.9	9 32.5	11 28.0	13 13.9	3 38.8	13 34.1	5 18.6	12 20.7	14R 38.8
3 M	12 45 13	13 12 49	29 1 9	6♓21 7	4R 20.9	11 33.6	12 42.5	13 50.7	3 50.0	13 36.1	5 19.0	12 21.1	14 37.4
4 Tu	12 49 9	14 11 58	13♓46 26	21 16 22	4 20.6	13 35.8	13 57.0	14 27.6	4 1.2	13 38.0	5 19.3	12 21.4	14 36.0
5 W	12 53 6	15 11 5	28 49 57	6♈26 8	4 18.6	15 38.9	15 11.4	15 4.5	4 12.6	13 39.8	5 19.6	12 21.7	14 34.6
6 Th	12 57 2	16 10 10	14♈ 3 40	21 41 14	4 14.6	17 42.8	16 25.9	15 41.5	4 24.0	13 41.5	5 19.8	12 22.0	14 33.2
7 F	13 0 59	17 9 13	29 17 31	6♉51 11	4 8.9	19 47.4	17 40.3	16 18.4	4 35.6	13 43.1	5 19.9	12 22.3	14 31.8
8 Sa	13 4 56	18 8 14	14♉21 1	21 45 56	4 2.3	21 52.4	18 54.7	16 55.3	4 47.2	13 44.6	5 20.0	12 22.5	14 30.3
9 Su	13 8 52	19 7 13	29 5 2	6♊17 35	3 55.5	23 57.7	20 9.1	17 32.3	4 58.9	13 46.1	5R 20.0	12 22.7	14 28.9
10 M	13 12 49	20 6 10	13♊23 7	20 21 21	3 49.5	26 3.0	21 23.4	18 9.3	5 10.6	13 47.4	5 20.0	12 22.8	14 27.4
11 Tu	13 16 45	21 5 4	27 12 12	3♋55 45	3 45.1	28 8.0	22 37.8	18 46.3	5 22.5	13 48.6	5 20.0	12 22.9	14 25.9
12 W	13 20 42	22 3 56	10♋32 17	17 2 9	3D 42.6	0♉12.4	23 52.1	19 23.2	5 34.4	13 49.7	5 19.9	12 23.0	14 24.4
13 Th	13 24 38	23 2 46	23 25 49	29 43 51	3 41.9	2 16.0	25 6.4	20 0.2	5 46.4	13 50.8	5 19.7	12R 23.1	14 22.9
14 F	13 28 35	24 1 34	5♌56 48	12♌ 5 19	3 42.5	4 18.4	26 20.7	20 37.2	5 58.5	13 51.7	5 19.5	12 23.1	14 21.3
15 Sa	13 32 31	25 0 19	18 10 0	24 11 29	3 43.7	6 19.3	27 35.0	21 14.2	6 10.6	13 52.5	5 19.2	12 23.1	14 19.8
16 Su	13 36 28	25 59 2	0♍10 22	6♍ 7 12	3R 44.5	8 18.2	28 49.3	21 51.3	6 22.8	13 53.3	5 18.9	12 23.0	14 18.2
17 M	13 40 25	26 57 43	12 2 34	17 56 57	3 44.2	10 14.9	0♉ 3.5	22 28.3	6 35.1	13 53.9	5 18.5	12 22.9	14 16.6
18 Tu	13 44 21	27 56 21	23 50 48	29 44 34	3 42.0	12 9.1	1 17.7	23 5.3	6 47.4	13 54.4	5 18.1	12 22.8	14 15.0
19 W	13 48 18	28 54 58	5♎38 36	11♎33 15	3 37.4	14 0.4	2 31.9	23 42.3	6 59.8	13 54.9	5 17.7	12 22.7	14 13.4
20 Th	13 52 14	29 53 32	17 28 48	23 25 30	3 30.3	15 48.6	3 46.1	24 19.4	7 12.2	13 55.2	5 17.1	12 22.5	14 11.8
21 F	13 56 11	0♉52 5	29 23 34	5♏23 11	3 21.2	17 33.3	5 0.2	24 56.4	7 24.8	13 55.5	5 16.6	12 22.3	14 10.2
22 Sa	14 0 7	1 50 35	11♏24 32	17 27 46	3 10.5	19 14.4	6 14.4	25 33.4	7 37.3	13R 55.6	5 16.0	12 22.0	14 8.5
23 Su	14 4 4	2 49 4	23 33 0	29 40 25	2 59.3	20 51.6	7 28.5	26 10.5	7 50.0	13 55.7	5 15.3	12 21.7	14 6.9
24 M	14 8 0	3 47 31	5♐50 8	12♐ 2 20	2 48.5	22 24.8	8 42.6	26 47.5	8 2.7	13 55.6	5 14.6	12 21.4	14 5.2
25 Tu	14 11 57	4 45 57	18 17 11	24 34 54	2 39.1	23 53.8	9 56.7	27 24.6	8 15.4	13 55.5	5 13.8	12 21.1	14 3.6
26 W	14 15 54	5 44 21	0♑55 42	7♑19 52	2 31.9	25 18.4	11 10.8	28 1.6	8 28.2	13 55.2	5 13.0	12 20.7	14 1.9
27 Th	14 19 50	6 42 43	13 47 40	20 19 23	2 27.1	26 38.5	12 24.8	28 38.7	8 41.1	13 54.9	5 12.2	12 20.3	14 0.2
28 F	14 23 47	7 41 4	26 55 22	3♒35 53	2D 24.8	27 54.0	13 38.9	29 15.8	8 54.0	13 54.4	5 11.3	12 19.9	13 58.6
29 Sa	14 27 43	8 39 23	10♒21 15	17 11 43	2 24.3	29 4.9	14 52.9	29 52.9	9 7.0	13 53.9	5 10.4	12 19.4	13 56.9
30 Su	14 31 40	9 37 40	24 7 30	1♓ 8 41	2R 24.7	0♊11.0	16 6.9	0♋29.9	9 20.0	13 53.3	5 9.4	12 18.9	13 55.2

Astro Data

	Dy Hr Mn
♄☌♆	3 10:46
☽0N	8 7:46
☽0S	21 21:38
♀0N	26 8:38
☿0N	30 2:43
☽0N	4 18:57
♅ R	9 8:54
♃⚻♅	10 18:59
♆ R	13 23:36
☽0S	18 3:33
♄ R	22 23:37

Planet Ingress

	Dy Hr Mn
☿ ♓	10 18:07
♂ ♊	11 8:51
♃ ♊	11 3:26
☉ ♈	20 15:28
♀ ♈	23 18:32
☿ ♈	28 3:16
☿ ♉	11 21:36
♀ ♉	16 22:52
☉ ♉	20 2:39
☿ ♊	29 19:53
♂ ♋	29 4:37

Last Aspect / ☽ Ingress (March)

Last Aspect Dy Hr Mn		☽ Ingress Dy Hr Mn
1 7:37	☿ ⚹	♑ 2 8:58
4 12:03	♃ △	♒ 4 13:36
6 13:57	♃ □	♓ 6 14:59
8 14:02	♃ ⚹	♈ 8 14:36
10 13:59	☿ ⚹	♉ 10 14:25
12 1:47	☉ ⚹	♊ 12 16:16
14 10:11	☉ □	♋ 14 21:27
16 23:07	☉ △	♌ 17 6:13
18 11:33	♇ □	♍ 19 17:39
22 2:09	♀ ☍	♎ 22 6:24
23 9:08	♄ □	♏ 24 19:10
27 3:09	☿ △	♐ 27 6:54
28 2:50	♂ ☍	♑ 29 16:25
30 19:28	♇ ⚹	♒ 31 22:45

Last Aspect / ☽ Ingress (April)

Last Aspect Dy Hr Mn		☽ Ingress Dy Hr Mn
1 23:59	♇ □	♓ 3 1:37
4 1:20	♇ △	♈ 5 1:51
6 6:39	☿ ☌	♉ 7 1:07
8 0:15	♇ ☍	♊ 9 1:31
11 1:57	☿ ⚹	♋ 11 4:58
13 3:31	♀ □	♌ 13 12:31
15 20:58	♀ △	♍ 15 23:39
17 22:22	♂ □	♎ 18 12:31
20 14:34	♂ △	♏ 21 1:13
22 17:54	☿ ☍	♐ 23 12:38
25 18:15	♂ ☍	♑ 25 22:15
28 1:57	☿ △	♒ 28 5:33
29 8:45	♀ □	♓ 30 10:03

☽ Phases & Eclipses

Dy Hr Mn	
7 18:19	● 17♓10
7 18:07:44	✔ P 0.827
14 10:11	☽ 23♊49
22 9:58	○ 1♎45
30 10:21	☽ 9♑42
6 3:33	● 16♈19
12 23:13	☽ 23♋01
21 3:13	○ 0♏60
28 20:46	☽ 8♒32

Astro Data

1 MARCH 1989
Julian Day # 32567
Delta T 56.4 sec
SVP 05♓24'32"
Obliquity 23°26'35"
⚷ Chiron 1♋19.2R
☽ Mean ☊ 4♓39.8

1 APRIL 1989
Julian Day # 32598
Delta T 56.4 sec
SVP 05♓24'28"
Obliquity 23°26'35"
⚷ Chiron 1♋44.9
☽ Mean ☊ 3♓01.3

LONGITUDE — MAY 1989

Day	Sid.Time	☉	0 hr ☽	Noon ☽	True ☊	☿	♀	♂	♃	♄	♅	♆	♇
1 M	14 35 36	10♉35 56	8♓15 19	15♓27 16	2♓24.7	1♊12.2	17♉20.9	1♋ 7.0	9♊33.0	13♑52.5	5♑ 8.3	12♑18.4	13♏53.5
2 Tu	14 39 33	11 34 11	22 44 15	0♈ 5 51	2R23.3	2 8.6	18 34.9	1 44.1	9 46.1	13R51.7	5R 7.2	12R17.8	13R51.8
3 W	14 43 29	12 32 24	7♈31 25	15 0 10	2 19.5	2 59.9	19 48.9	2 21.2	9 59.3	13 50.8	5 6.1	12 17.3	13 50.1
4 Th	14 47 26	13 30 35	22 31 8	0♉ 3 12	2 13.0	3 46.2	21 2.8	2 58.3	10 12.5	13 49.7	5 4.9	12 16.6	13 48.5
5 F	14 51 23	14 28 45	7♉35 10	15 5 47	2 4.2	4 27.4	22 16.8	3 35.5	10 25.7	13 48.6	5 3.7	12 16.0	13 46.8
6 Sa	14 55 19	15 26 53	22 33 50	29 58 8	1 53.8	5 3.5	23 30.7	4 12.6	10 39.0	13 47.4	5 2.5	12 15.3	13 45.1
7 Su	14 59 16	16 25 0	7♊17 38	14♊31 27	1 43.0	5 34.4	24 44.6	4 49.7	10 52.3	13 46.1	5 1.2	12 14.6	13 43.4
8 M	15 3 12	17 23 5	21 38 53	28 39 27	1 33.2	6 0.0	25 58.5	5 26.9	11 5.7	13 44.7	4 59.8	12 13.9	13 41.7
9 Tu	15 7 9	18 21 8	5♋32 51	12♋19 1	1 25.2	6 20.5	27 12.4	6 4.0	11 19.0	13 43.2	4 58.4	12 13.1	13 40.0
10 W	15 11 5	19 19 10	18 58 1	25 30 8	1 19.6	6 35.7	28 26.3	6 41.1	11 32.5	13 41.6	4 57.0	12 12.3	13 38.3
11 Th	15 15 2	20 17 9	1♌55 43	8♌15 17	1 16.5	6 45.8	29 40.1	7 18.3	11 45.9	13 40.0	4 55.5	12 11.5	13 36.7
12 F	15 18 58	21 15 7	14 29 23	20 38 38	1D 15.3	6R 50.7	0♊53.9	7 55.4	11 59.4	13 38.2	4 54.0	12 10.7	13 35.0
13 Sa	15 22 55	22 13 2	26 43 43	2♍45 18	1R 15.2	6 50.7	2 7.7	8 32.6	12 12.9	13 36.3	4 52.5	12 9.8	13 33.3
14 Su	15 26 52	23 10 56	8♍44 4	14 40 41	1 15.1	6 45.8	3 21.5	9 9.8	12 26.5	13 34.4	4 50.9	12 8.9	13 31.7
15 M	15 30 48	24 8 48	20 35 48	26 30 2	1 13.9	6 36.3	4 35.3	9 46.9	12 40.1	13 32.4	4 49.3	12 8.0	13 30.0
16 Tu	15 34 45	25 6 39	2♎23 58	8♎18 9	1 10.7	6 22.4	5 49.0	10 24.1	12 53.7	13 30.3	4 47.6	12 7.0	13 28.3
17 W	15 38 41	26 4 27	14 13 4	20 9 8	1 4.8	6 4.4	7 2.7	11 1.2	13 7.3	13 28.1	4 45.9	12 6.0	13 26.7
18 Th	15 42 38	27 2 14	26 6 46	2♏ 6 16	0 56.3	5 42.6	8 16.4	11 38.4	13 21.0	13 25.8	4 44.2	12 5.0	13 25.1
19 F	15 46 34	28 0 0	8♏ 7 56	14 11 57	0 45.2	5 17.5	9 30.1	12 15.6	13 34.6	13 23.4	4 42.4	12 4.0	13 23.4
20 Sa	15 50 31	28 57 44	20 18 29	26 27 40	0 32.5	4 49.5	10 43.8	12 52.7	13 48.3	13 21.0	4 40.6	12 3.0	13 21.8
21 Su	15 54 27	29 55 27	2♐39 35	8♐54 15	0 19.0	4 19.2	11 57.5	13 29.9	14 2.1	13 18.4	4 38.8	12 1.9	13 20.2
22 M	15 58 24	0♊53 9	15 11 42	21 31 56	0 5.9	3 46.9	13 11.1	14 7.1	14 15.8	13 15.8	4 36.9	12 0.8	13 18.6
23 Tu	16 2 21	1 50 49	27 54 57	4♑20 46	29♒54.5	3 13.4	14 24.7	14 44.2	14 29.6	13 13.1	4 35.0	11 59.7	13 17.1
24 W	16 6 17	2 48 28	10♑49 24	17 20 52	29 45.4	2 39.2	15 38.3	15 21.4	14 43.3	13 10.4	4 33.1	11 58.5	13 15.5
25 Th	16 10 14	3 46 6	23 55 16	0♒32 39	29 39.2	2 5.0	16 51.9	15 58.6	14 57.1	13 7.5	4 31.2	11 57.4	13 13.9
26 F	16 14 10	4 43 43	7♒13 10	13 56 56	29 35.8	1 31.2	18 5.5	16 35.8	15 11.0	13 4.6	4 29.2	11 56.2	13 12.4
27 Sa	16 18 7	5 41 19	20 44 5	27 34 47	29D 34.6	0 58.6	19 19.1	17 13.0	15 24.8	13 1.6	4 27.2	11 55.0	13 10.9
28 Su	16 22 3	6 38 54	4♓29 9	11♓27 17	29R 34.4	0 27.6	20 32.6	17 50.2	15 38.6	12 58.6	4 25.1	11 53.7	13 9.3
29 M	16 26 0	7 36 29	18 29 12	25 34 53	29 34.2	29♉58.7	21 46.1	18 27.4	15 52.5	12 55.5	4 23.1	11 52.5	13 7.8
30 Tu	16 29 57	8 34 2	2♈44 11	9♈56 50	29 32.6	29 32.5	22 59.7	19 4.6	16 6.3	12 52.3	4 21.0	11 51.2	13 6.3
31 W	16 33 53	9 31 35	17 12 29	24 30 36	29 28.8	29 9.3	24 13.2	19 41.8	16 20.2	12 49.0	4 18.8	11 49.9	13 4.9

LONGITUDE — JUNE 1989

Day	Sid.Time	☉	0 hr ☽	Noon ☽	True ☊	☿	♀	♂	♃	♄	♅	♆	♇
1 Th	16 37 50	10♊29 6	1♉50 31	9♉11 30	29♒22.3	28♉49.5	25♊26.7	20♋19.0	16♊34.1	12♑45.6	4♑16.7	11♑48.6	13♏ 3.4
2 F	16 41 46	11 26 37	16 32 38	23 52 59	29R 13.4	28R 33.4	26 40.2	20 56.2	16 48.0	12R 42.2	4R 14.5	11R 47.3	13R 2.0
3 Sa	16 45 43	12 24 8	1♊11 35	8♊27 28	29 2.9	28 21.3	27 53.6	21 33.5	17 1.9	12 38.8	4 12.3	11 46.0	13 0.6
4 Su	16 49 39	13 21 37	15 39 42	22 47 30	28 51.8	28 13.3	29 7.1	22 10.7	17 15.8	12 35.3	4 10.1	11 44.6	12 59.2
5 M	16 53 36	14 19 5	29 50 8	6♋47 5	28 41.6	28D 9.6	0♋20.5	22 48.0	17 29.7	12 31.7	4 7.9	11 43.2	12 57.8
6 Tu	16 57 32	15 16 33	13♋37 56	20 22 29	28 33.1	28 10.3	1 34.0	23 25.2	17 43.7	12 28.0	4 5.6	11 41.8	12 56.4
7 W	17 1 29	16 13 59	27 0 40	3♌32 35	28 27.0	28 15.5	2 47.4	24 2.5	17 57.6	12 24.4	4 3.4	11 40.4	12 55.1
8 Th	17 5 26	17 11 24	9♌58 28	16 18 38	28 23.4	28 25.2	4 0.8	24 39.7	18 11.5	12 20.6	4 1.1	11 39.0	12 53.8
9 F	17 9 22	18 8 48	22 33 34	28 43 46	28D 22.0	28 39.4	5 14.1	25 17.0	18 25.4	12 16.8	3 58.8	11 37.5	12 52.5
10 Sa	17 13 19	19 6 11	4♍49 50	10♍52 22	28 22.0	28 58.1	6 27.5	25 54.3	18 39.3	12 12.9	3 56.5	11 36.1	12 51.2
11 Su	17 17 15	20 3 33	16 52 2	22 49 31	28R 22.4	29 21.2	7 40.8	26 31.5	18 53.2	12 9.0	3 54.1	11 34.6	12 49.9
12 M	17 21 12	21 0 54	28 45 29	4♎40 34	28 22.1	29 48.7	8 54.1	27 8.8	19 7.1	12 5.1	3 51.8	11 33.1	12 48.7
13 Tu	17 25 8	21 58 14	10♎35 27	16 30 43	28 20.3	0♊20.5	10 7.4	27 46.1	19 21.0	12 1.1	3 49.4	11 31.6	12 47.5
14 W	17 29 5	22 55 33	22 26 58	28 24 45	28 16.4	0 56.5	11 20.7	28 23.4	19 34.9	11 57.1	3 47.0	11 30.1	12 46.3
15 Th	17 33 1	23 52 51	4♏24 31	10♏26 44	28 10.2	1 36.8	12 34.0	29 0.7	19 48.8	11 53.0	3 44.6	11 28.6	12 45.1
16 F	17 36 58	24 50 8	16 31 45	22 39 53	28 1.7	2 21.1	13 47.2	29 38.0	20 2.7	11 48.9	3 42.2	11 27.1	12 44.0
17 Sa	17 40 55	25 47 25	28 51 22	5♐ 6 22	27 51.7	3 9.5	15 0.4	0♌15.3	20 16.5	11 44.8	3 39.8	11 25.6	12 42.9
18 Su	17 44 51	26 44 41	11♐25 0	17 47 18	27 41.1	4 1.8	16 13.6	0 52.6	20 30.4	11 40.6	3 37.4	11 24.0	12 41.8
19 M	17 48 48	27 41 56	24 13 13	0♑42 42	27 30.7	4 58.0	17 26.8	1 29.9	20 44.2	11 36.4	3 35.0	11 22.4	12 40.7
20 Tu	17 52 44	28 39 11	7♑15 38	13 51 50	27 21.6	5 58.0	18 40.0	2 7.2	20 58.1	11 32.1	3 32.6	11 20.9	12 39.7
21 W	17 56 41	29 36 26	20 31 10	27 13 26	27 14.5	7 1.8	19 53.1	2 44.5	21 11.9	11 27.9	3 30.2	11 19.3	12 38.6
22 Th	18 0 37	0♋33 40	3♒58 28	10♒46 5	27 9.9	8 9.3	21 6.2	3 21.9	21 25.7	11 23.6	3 27.7	11 17.7	12 37.7
23 F	18 4 34	1 30 54	17 36 7	24 28 28	27D 7.7	9 20.4	22 19.4	3 59.2	21 39.5	11 19.3	3 25.3	11 16.2	12 36.7
24 Sa	18 8 30	2 28 7	1♓23 0	8♓19 38	27 7.4	10 35.1	23 32.4	4 36.5	21 53.3	11 14.9	3 22.8	11 14.6	12 35.8
25 Su	18 12 27	3 25 21	15 18 16	22 18 50	27 8.2	11 53.4	24 45.5	5 13.9	22 7.0	11 10.6	3 20.4	11 13.0	12 34.9
26 M	18 16 24	4 22 34	29 21 13	6♈25 19	27R 8.9	13 15.2	25 58.6	5 51.2	22 20.7	11 6.2	3 18.0	11 11.4	12 34.0
27 Tu	18 20 20	5 19 47	13♈30 58	20 37 58	27 8.7	14 40.4	27 11.6	6 28.6	22 34.5	11 1.8	3 15.5	11 9.7	12 33.1
28 W	18 24 17	6 17 1	27 46 2	4♉54 52	27 6.9	16 9.1	28 24.6	7 6.0	22 48.1	10 57.4	3 13.1	11 8.1	12 32.3
29 Th	18 28 13	7 14 14	12♉ 4 1	19 13 4	27 3.0	17 41.2	29 37.6	7 43.4	23 1.8	10 53.0	3 10.6	11 6.5	12 31.5
30 F	18 32 10	8 11 28	26 21 27	3♊28 36	26 57.2	19 16.7	0♌50.6	8 20.8	23 15.5	10 48.5	3 8.2	11 4.9	12 30.8

Astro Data Dy Hr Mn	Planet Ingress Dy Hr Mn	Last Aspect Dy Hr Mn	☽ Ingress Dy Hr Mn	Last Aspect Dy Hr Mn	☽ Ingress Dy Hr Mn	☽ Phases & Eclipses Dy Hr Mn	Astro Data
☽0N 2 4:23	♀ ♊ 11 6:28	1 16:32 ♀ ⚹	♈ 2 11:51	2 19:23 ☿ ☌	♊ 2 22:02	5 11:46 ● 14♉57	1 MAY 1989
♄⚹♇ 2 4:28	☉ ♊ 21 1:54	3 10:08 ♄ □	♉ 4 11:55	4 2:44 ♃ ☌	♋ 5 0:17	12 14:20 ☽ 21♌50	Julian Day # 32628
♃⚻♆ 12 18:46	☊ ♒ 22 11:56	6 1:40 ♀ ☌	♊ 6 12:03	7 2:18 ☿ ⚹	♌ 7 5:28	20 18:16 ○ 29♏42	Delta T 56.5 sec
☿ R 12 11:52	☿ ♉ 28 22:53	7 6:01 ♃ ☌	♋ 8 14:19	9 12:09 ☿ □	♍ 9 14:29	28 4:01 ☽ 6♓49	SVP 05♓24'25"
☽0S 15 9:27		10 19:18 ♀ ⚹	♌ 10 20:23	12 2:14 ☿ △	♎ 12 2:31		Obliquity 23°26'35"
♃⚻♇ 18 6:27	♀ ♋ 4 17:17	12 14:20 ☉ □	♍ 13 6:30	14 12:37 ♂ □	♏ 14 15:11	3 19:53 ● 13♊12	⚷ Chiron 3♋21.1
♃⚻♄ 18 7:13	☿ ♊ 12 8:56	15 7:51 ☉ △	♎ 15 19:07	15 18:00 ♀ △	♐ 17 2:12	11 6:59 ☽ 20♍20	☽ Mean ☊ 1♓26.0
♄⚹♇ 18 22:49	♂ ♌ 16 14:10	16 22:29 ♄ □	♏ 18 7:48	19 6:57 ☉ ☍	♑ 19 10:41	19 6:57 ○ 27♐59	
☽0N 29 11:00	☉ ♋ 21 9:53	20 18:16 ☉ ☍	♐ 20 18:52	20 22:45 ♀ ☍	♒ 21 16:57	26 9:09 ☽ 4♈44	1 JUNE 1989
	♀ ♌ 29 7:21	21 22:12 ♃ ☍	♑ 23 3:54	23 7:13 ♃ △	♓ 23 21:36		Julian Day # 32659
☿ D 5 8:07		24 8:46 ♂ ☍	♒ 25 11:01	25 17:42 ♀ △	♈ 26 1:06		Delta T 56.5 sec
☽0S 11 15:56		26 21:15 ♀ △	♓ 27 16:13	28 1:11 ♀ □	♉ 28 3:45		SVP 05♓24'20"
♄☌♆ 24 3:09		29 18:48 ☿ ⚹	♈ 29 19:25	29 0:46 ♇ ☍	♊ 30 6:08		Obliquity 23°26'34"
☽0N 25 15:48		31 12:35 ♀ ⚹	♉ 31 20:59				⚷ Chiron 5♋53.9
							☽ Mean ☊ 29♒47.5

JULY 1989 — LONGITUDE

Day	Sid.Time	☉	0 hr ☽	Noon ☽	True ☊	☿	♀	♂	♃	♄	♅	♆	♇
1 Sa	18 36 6	9♋ 8 42	10♊33 55	17♊36 48	26♒50.1	20♊55.4	2♌ 3.6	8♌58.2	23♊29.1	10♑44.1	3♑ 5.8	11♑ 3.3	12♏30.0
2 Su	18 40 3	10 5 56	24 36 39	1♋32 56	26R42.6	22 37.4	3 16.6	9 35.6	23 42.7	10R39.7	3R 3.4	11R 1.7	12R29.3
3 M	18 44 0	11 3 10	8♋25 8	15 12 53	26 35.6	24 22.5	4 29.5	10 13.0	23 56.3	10 35.2	3 1.0	11 0.0	12 28.7
4 Tu	18 47 56	12 0 24	21 55 50	28 33 47	26 29.9	26 10.6	5 42.4	10 50.5	24 9.8	10 30.8	2 58.5	10 58.4	12 28.0
5 W	18 51 53	12 57 38	5♌ 6 39	11♌34 25	26 25.9	28 1.7	6 55.3	11 27.9	24 23.3	10 26.4	2 56.2	10 56.8	12 27.4
6 Th	18 55 49	13 54 51	17 57 12	24 15 13	26D23.9	29 55.6	8 8.2	12 5.4	24 36.8	10 22.0	2 53.8	10 55.2	12 26.8
7 F	18 59 46	14 52 4	0♍28 45	6♍38 11	26 23.6	1♋52.1	9 21.0	12 42.8	24 50.3	10 17.5	2 51.4	10 53.6	12 26.3
8 Sa	19 3 42	15 49 18	12 43 58	18 46 35	26 24.6	3 51.1	10 33.9	13 20.3	25 3.7	10 13.1	2 49.0	10 51.9	12 25.8
9 Su	19 7 39	16 46 31	24 46 35	0♎44 33	26 26.1	5 52.2	11 46.7	13 57.8	25 17.0	10 8.7	2 46.7	10 50.3	12 25.3
10 M	19 11 35	17 43 44	6♎41 4	12 36 48	26 27.5	7 55.4	12 59.4	14 35.3	25 30.4	10 4.3	2 44.3	10 48.7	12 24.8
11 Tu	19 15 32	18 40 57	18 32 20	24 28 19	26R28.1	10 0.2	14 12.2	15 12.8	25 43.7	9 60.0	2 42.0	10 47.1	12 24.4
12 W	19 19 29	19 38 9	0♏25 21	6♏24 1	26 27.4	12 6.5	15 24.9	15 50.3	25 56.9	9 55.6	2 39.7	10 45.5	12 24.0
13 Th	19 23 25	20 35 22	12 24 55	18 28 34	26 25.2	14 13.9	16 37.6	16 27.8	26 10.2	9 51.3	2 37.4	10 43.9	12 23.7
14 F	19 27 22	21 32 35	24 35 26	0♐45 58	26 21.6	16 22.1	17 50.3	17 5.4	26 23.3	9 47.0	2 35.1	10 42.3	12 23.4
15 Sa	19 31 18	22 29 48	7♐ 0 31	13 19 24	26 17.0	18 30.8	19 2.9	17 42.9	26 36.5	9 42.7	2 32.9	10 40.7	12 23.1
16 Su	19 35 15	23 27 2	19 42 48	26 10 52	26 11.7	20 39.7	20 15.5	18 20.5	26 49.6	9 38.5	2 30.7	10 39.2	12 22.8
17 M	19 39 11	24 24 15	2♑43 39	9♑21 6	26 6.6	22 48.5	21 28.1	18 58.0	27 2.6	9 34.3	2 28.5	10 37.6	12 22.6
18 Tu	19 43 8	25 21 29	16 3 6	22 49 26	26 2.1	24 57.0	22 40.7	19 35.6	27 15.6	9 30.1	2 26.3	10 36.0	12 22.4
19 W	19 47 4	26 18 43	29 39 51	6♒33 59	25 58.7	27 5.0	23 53.2	20 13.2	27 28.6	9 25.9	2 24.1	10 34.5	12 22.3
20 Th	19 51 1	27 15 57	13♒31 26	20 31 49	25D56.8	29 12.2	25 5.7	20 50.8	27 41.5	9 21.8	2 22.0	10 33.0	12 22.1
21 F	19 54 58	28 13 12	27 34 39	4♓39 29	25 56.3	1♌18.4	26 18.2	21 28.4	27 54.4	9 17.7	2 19.8	10 31.4	12 22.0
22 Sa	19 58 54	29 10 28	11♓45 53	18 53 24	25 57.0	3 23.5	27 30.6	22 6.0	28 7.2	9 13.7	2 17.7	10 29.9	12 22.0
23 Su	20 2 51	0♌ 7 44	26 1 38	3♈10 10	25 58.3	5 27.3	28 43.0	22 43.6	28 20.0	9 9.7	2 15.7	10 28.4	12D22.0
24 M	20 6 47	1 5 1	10♈18 40	17 26 46	25 59.6	7 29.8	29 55.4	23 21.3	28 32.7	9 5.8	2 13.6	10 26.9	12 22.0
25 Tu	20 10 44	2 2 19	24 34 12	1♉40 39	26R 0.5	9 30.8	1♍ 7.8	23 58.9	28 45.3	9 1.8	2 11.6	10 25.4	12 22.0
26 W	20 14 40	2 59 39	8♉45 52	15 49 34	26 0.6	11 30.3	2 20.1	24 36.6	28 57.9	8 58.0	2 9.6	10 23.9	12 22.1
27 Th	20 18 37	3 56 59	22 51 30	29 51 27	25 59.6	13 28.2	3 32.4	25 14.3	29 10.5	8 54.2	2 7.7	10 22.5	12 22.2
28 F	20 22 33	4 54 20	6♊49 8	13♊44 20	25 57.8	15 24.6	4 44.7	25 52.0	29 23.0	8 50.4	2 5.7	10 21.0	12 22.4
29 Sa	20 26 30	5 51 42	20 36 49	27 26 20	25 55.3	17 19.3	5 56.9	26 29.7	29 35.4	8 46.7	2 3.8	10 19.6	12 22.6
30 Su	20 30 27	6 49 5	4♋12 41	10♋55 40	25 52.6	19 12.3	7 9.1	27 7.5	29 47.8	8 43.0	2 2.0	10 18.2	12 22.8
31 M	20 34 23	7 46 30	17 35 6	24 10 51	25 50.1	21 3.7	8 21.3	27 45.2	0♋ 0.1	8 39.5	2 0.1	10 16.8	12 23.0

AUGUST 1989 — LONGITUDE

Day	Sid.Time	☉	0 hr ☽	Noon ☽	True ☊	☿	♀	♂	♃	♄	♅	♆	♇
1 Tu	20 38 20	8♌43 55	0♌42 49	7♌10 55	25♒48.1	22♌53.5	9♍33.5	28♌23.0	0♋12.3	8♑35.9	1♑58.3	10♑15.4	12♏23.3
2 W	20 42 16	9 41 20	13 35 10	19 55 34	25D46.9	24 41.6	10 45.6	29 0.8	0 24.5	8R32.4	1R56.6	10R14.0	12 23.6
3 Th	20 46 13	10 38 47	26 12 14	2♍25 17	25 46.6	26 28.1	11 57.7	29 38.6	0 36.6	8 29.0	1 54.8	10 12.7	12 24.0
4 F	20 50 9	11 36 15	8♍34 57	14 41 27	25 46.9	28 12.9	13 9.7	0♍16.4	0 48.7	8 25.7	1 53.1	10 11.4	12 24.4
5 Sa	20 54 6	12 33 43	20 45 7	26 46 17	25 47.8	29 56.1	14 21.7	0 54.2	1 0.6	8 22.4	1 51.5	10 10.0	12 24.8
6 Su	20 58 2	13 31 12	2♎45 22	8♎42 48	25 49.0	1♍37.7	15 33.7	1 32.1	1 12.5	8 19.2	1 49.9	10 8.7	12 25.3
7 M	21 1 59	14 28 42	14 39 3	20 34 38	25 50.1	3 17.7	16 45.6	2 10.0	1 24.3	8 16.0	1 48.3	10 7.5	12 25.8
8 Tu	21 5 56	15 26 12	26 30 6	2♏25 59	25 51.0	4 56.1	17 57.5	2 47.8	1 36.1	8 12.9	1 46.7	10 6.2	12 26.3
9 W	21 9 52	16 23 44	8♏22 53	14 21 22	25R51.5	6 32.9	19 9.4	3 25.7	1 47.8	8 9.9	1 45.2	10 5.0	12 26.8
10 Th	21 13 49	17 21 16	20 22 1	26 25 24	25 51.6	8 8.1	20 21.2	4 3.6	1 59.4	8 7.0	1 43.7	10 3.8	12 27.4
11 F	21 17 45	18 18 49	2♐32 5	8♐42 36	25 51.3	9 41.7	21 33.0	4 41.6	2 10.9	8 4.1	1 42.3	10 2.6	12 28.1
12 Sa	21 21 42	19 16 24	14 57 26	21 17 2	25 50.8	11 13.7	22 44.7	5 19.5	2 22.3	8 1.4	1 40.9	10 1.4	12 28.7
13 Su	21 25 38	20 13 59	27 41 46	4♑11 57	25 50.1	12 44.1	23 56.4	5 57.5	2 33.7	7 58.7	1 39.6	10 0.3	12 29.4
14 M	21 29 35	21 11 35	10♑47 48	17 29 25	25 49.5	14 12.9	25 8.1	6 35.4	2 45.0	7 56.0	1 38.3	9 59.1	12 30.2
15 Tu	21 33 31	22 9 12	24 16 50	1♒ 9 56	25 49.1	15 40.1	26 19.7	7 13.4	2 56.2	7 53.5	1 37.0	9 58.0	12 30.9
16 W	21 37 28	23 6 50	8♒ 8 28	15 12 4	25 48.8	17 5.6	27 31.2	7 51.4	3 7.3	7 51.0	1 35.8	9 57.0	12 31.7
17 Th	21 41 25	24 4 29	22 20 18	29 32 32	25D48.7	18 29.5	28 42.7	8 29.5	3 18.3	7 48.6	1 34.6	9 55.9	12 32.6
18 F	21 45 21	25 2 10	6♓48 8	14♓ 6 19	25R48.7	19 51.7	29 54.2	9 7.5	3 29.2	7 46.3	1 33.5	9 54.9	12 33.4
19 Sa	21 49 18	25 59 52	21 26 18	28 47 16	25 48.7	21 12.2	1♎ 5.6	9 45.6	3 40.1	7 44.1	1 32.4	9 53.9	12 34.3
20 Su	21 53 14	26 57 35	6♈ 8 22	13♈28 49	25 48.7	22 30.9	2 16.9	10 23.6	3 50.8	7 42.0	1 31.3	9 52.9	12 35.2
21 M	21 57 11	27 55 20	20 47 52	28 4 53	25 48.5	23 47.8	3 28.2	11 1.7	4 1.5	7 39.9	1 30.3	9 51.9	12 36.2
22 Tu	22 1 7	28 53 7	5♉19 14	12♉30 28	25 48.3	25 2.8	4 39.5	11 39.9	4 12.0	7 37.9	1 29.3	9 51.0	12 37.2
23 W	22 5 4	29 50 55	19 38 10	26 42 3	25D48.1	26 15.9	5 50.7	12 18.0	4 22.5	7 36.1	1 28.4	9 50.1	12 38.2
24 Th	22 9 0	0♍48 45	3♊41 54	10♊37 36	25 48.0	27 27.0	7 1.9	12 56.2	4 32.9	7 34.3	1 27.6	9 49.2	12 39.2
25 F	22 12 57	1 46 37	17 29 7	24 16 26	25 48.2	28 36.1	8 13.0	13 34.4	4 43.1	7 32.6	1 26.7	9 48.3	12 40.3
26 Sa	22 16 54	2 44 31	0♋59 38	7♋38 47	25 48.7	29 43.0	9 24.1	14 12.6	4 53.3	7 31.0	1 26.0	9 47.5	12 41.5
27 Su	22 20 50	3 42 27	14 14 1	20 45 28	25 49.4	0♎47.6	10 35.1	14 50.8	5 3.4	7 29.5	1 25.3	9 46.7	12 42.6
28 M	22 24 47	4 40 24	27 13 17	3♌37 37	25 50.1	1 49.9	11 46.1	15 29.1	5 13.3	7 28.0	1 24.6	9 46.0	12 43.8
29 Tu	22 28 43	5 38 23	9♌58 37	16 16 27	25 50.8	2 49.6	12 57.0	16 7.4	5 23.2	7 26.7	1 23.9	9 45.2	12 45.0
30 W	22 32 40	6 36 23	22 31 16	28 43 14	25R51.2	3 46.7	14 7.9	16 45.7	5 32.9	7 25.5	1 23.4	9 44.5	12 46.2
31 Th	22 36 36	7 34 26	4♍52 31	10♍59 17	25 51.1	4 41.0	15 18.7	17 24.0	5 42.6	7 24.3	1 22.8	9 43.8	12 47.5

Astro Data	Planet Ingress	Last Aspect	☽ Ingress	Last Aspect	☽ Ingress	☽ Phases & Eclipses	Astro Data
Dy Hr Mn	Dy Hr Mn	Dy Hr Mn	Dy Hr Mn	Dy Hr Mn	Dy Hr Mn	Dy Hr Mn	1 JULY 1989
☽0S 8 23:11	☿ ♋ 6 0:55	1 22:26 ♃ ☌	♋ 2 9:19	3 6:59 ♂ ☌	♍ 3 7:19	3 4:59 ● 11♋15	Julian Day # 32689
♃□♇ 18 12:21	☿ ♌ 20 9:04	3 7:09 ♇ △	♌ 4 14:37	4 9:58 ♀ ☌	♎ 5 18:28	11 0:19 ☽ 18♎42	Delta T 56.6 sec
☽0N 22 21:01	☉ ♌ 22 20:45	6 12:55 ♃ ✶	♍ 6 23:04	6 23:37 ☉ ✶	♏ 8 7:05	18 17:42 ○ 26♑04	SVP 05♓24'14"
♇ D 23 3:54	♀ ♍ 24 1:31	9 1:02 ♃ □	♎ 9 10:30	9 23:58 ♀ ✶	♐ 10 19:02	25 13:31 ☽ 2♉35	Obliquity 23°26'33"
	♃ ♋ 30 23:50	11 14:49 ♃ △	♏ 11 23:09	12 16:16 ♀ □	♑ 13 4:16		⚷ Chiron 8♋48.7
☽0S 5 6:51		13 17:32 ☉ △	♐ 14 10:31	15 3:55 ♀ △	♒ 15 9:59	1 16:06 ● 9♌22	☽ Mean ☊ 28♒12.2
♃☍♅ 8 19:18	♂ ♍ 3 13:35	16 13:25 ♃ ☍	♑ 16 19:01	17 3:07 ☉ ☍	♓ 17 12:46	9 17:29 ☽ 17♏06	
☽0N 19 4:29	☿ ♍ 5 0:54	18 18:39 ☿ ☍	♒ 19 0:35	18 23:35 ☿ ☍	♈ 19 13:59	17 3:07 ○ 24♒12	1 AUGUST 1989
♀0S 19 11:05	♀ ♎ 18 1:58	21 0:34 ♃ △	♓ 21 4:07	21 12:34 ☉ △	♉ 21 15:10	17 3:08 T 1.598	Julian Day # 32720
☿0S 23 12:50	☉ ♍ 23 3:46	23 3:56 ♃ □	♈ 23 6:41	23 12:18 ☿ △	♊ 23 17:39	23 18:40 ☽ 0♊36	Delta T 56.6 sec
	☿ ♎ 26 6:14	25 7:10 ♃ ✶	♉ 25 9:10	25 21:30 ☿ □	♋ 25 22:13	31 5:45 ● 7♍48	SVP 05♓24'08"
		27 4:16 ♂ □	♊ 27 12:15	27 1:11 ♂ ✶	♌ 28 5:12	31 5:30:50 P 0.634	Obliquity 23°26'34"
		29 16:03 ♃ ☌	♋ 29 16:32	29 6:14 ♀ ✶	♍ 30 14:29		⚷ Chiron 11♋50.5
		30 14:37 ♇ △	♌ 31 22:41				☽ Mean ☊ 26♒33.7

LONGITUDE — SEPTEMBER 1989

Day	Sid.Time	☉	0 hr ☽	Noon ☽	True ☊	☿	♀	♂	♃	♄	♅	♆	♇
1 F	22 40 33	8♍32 29	17♍ 3 43	23♍ 6 2	25♒50.3	5♎32.3	16♎29.5	18♍ 2.3	5♋52.1	7♑23.3	1♑22.3	9♑43.2	12♏48.8
2 Sa	22 44 29	9 30 35	29 6 26	5♎ 5 11	25R48.8	6 20.4	17 40.2	18 40.7	6 1.5	7R22.3	1R21.9	9R42.5	12 50.1
3 Su	22 48 26	10 28 42	11♎ 2 33	16 58 49	25 46.8	7 5.2	18 50.9	19 19.1	6 10.8	7 21.5	1 21.5	9 41.9	12 51.5
4 M	22 52 23	11 26 50	22 54 20	28 49 28	25 44.5	7 46.4	20 1.5	19 57.5	6 20.0	7 20.7	1 21.2	9 41.4	12 52.9
5 Tu	22 56 19	12 25 0	4♏44 37	10♏40 12	25 42.0	8 23.8	21 12.0	20 35.9	6 29.0	7 20.0	1 20.9	9 40.8	12 54.3
6 W	23 0 16	13 23 12	16 36 42	22 34 35	25 39.8	8 57.0	22 22.5	21 14.4	6 38.0	7 19.5	1 20.7	9 40.3	12 55.7
7 Th	23 4 12	14 21 25	28 34 24	4♐36 40	25 38.2	9 25.8	23 32.9	21 52.9	6 46.8	7 19.0	1 20.5	9 39.8	12 57.2
8 F	23 8 9	15 19 40	10♐41 57	16 50 48	25D37.4	9 50.0	24 43.2	22 31.4	6 55.5	7 18.6	1 20.4	9 39.4	12 58.7
9 Sa	23 12 5	16 17 56	23 3 46	29 21 24	25 37.5	10 9.2	25 53.5	23 9.9	7 4.0	7 18.3	1 20.3	9 39.0	13 0.3
10 Su	23 16 2	17 16 14	5♑44 13	12♑12 41	25 38.4	10 23.1	27 3.7	23 48.4	7 12.4	7 18.2	1D20.3	9 38.6	13 1.8
11 M	23 19 58	18 14 33	18 47 13	25 28 7	25 39.8	10R31.3	28 13.8	24 27.0	7 20.7	7D18.1	1 20.3	9 38.3	13 3.4
12 Tu	23 23 55	19 12 54	2♒15 39	9♒ 9 54	25 41.2	10 33.6	29 23.9	25 5.6	7 28.9	7 18.1	1 20.4	9 37.9	13 5.0
13 W	23 27 52	20 11 16	16 10 50	23 18 15	25R42.3	10 29.6	0♏33.9	25 44.2	7 37.0	7 18.2	1 20.5	9 37.7	13 6.6
14 Th	23 31 48	21 9 40	0♓31 48	7♓50 55	25 42.5	10 19.2	1 43.8	26 22.8	7 44.9	7 18.4	1 20.6	9 37.4	13 8.3
15 F	23 35 45	22 8 6	15 14 53	22 42 50	25 41.4	10 2.0	2 53.6	27 1.5	7 52.6	7 18.7	1 20.9	9 37.2	13 10.0
16 Sa	23 39 41	23 6 33	0♈13 44	7♈46 27	25 39.1	9 37.9	4 3.4	27 40.2	8 0.2	7 19.2	1 21.1	9 37.0	13 11.7
17 Su	23 43 38	24 5 3	15 19 47	22 52 33	25 35.6	9 7.0	5 13.0	28 18.9	8 7.7	7 19.7	1 21.5	9 36.8	13 13.4
18 M	23 47 34	25 3 34	0♉23 35	7♉51 47	25 31.6	8 29.4	6 22.6	28 57.6	8 15.1	7 20.3	1 21.8	9 36.7	13 15.2
19 Tu	23 51 31	26 2 8	15 16 11	22 36 0	25 27.5	7 45.2	7 32.1	29 36.4	8 22.3	7 21.0	1 22.3	9 36.6	13 17.0
20 W	23 55 27	27 0 44	29 50 35	6♊59 28	25 24.1	6 55.0	8 41.5	0♎15.2	8 29.3	7 21.8	1 22.8	9 36.6	13 18.8
21 Th	23 59 24	27 59 22	14♊ 2 22	20 59 11	25 21.9	5 59.4	9 50.9	0 54.0	8 36.3	7 22.7	1 23.3	9D36.5	13 20.6
22 F	0 3 21	28 58 3	27 49 55	4♋34 42	25D21.1	4 59.4	11 0.1	1 32.8	8 43.0	7 23.7	1 23.9	9 36.5	13 22.5
23 Sa	0 7 17	29 56 45	11♋13 48	17 47 31	25 21.6	3 56.0	12 9.3	2 11.7	8 49.6	7 24.8	1 24.5	9 36.6	13 24.4
24 Su	0 11 14	0♎55 30	24 16 13	0♌40 17	25 22.9	2 50.7	13 18.4	2 50.6	8 56.1	7 26.0	1 25.2	9 36.6	13 26.3
25 M	0 15 10	1 54 17	7♌ 0 10	13 16 15	25 24.6	1 44.9	14 27.4	3 29.5	9 2.4	7 27.3	1 25.9	9 36.7	13 28.2
26 Tu	0 19 7	2 53 6	19 28 56	25 38 37	25R25.7	0 40.2	15 36.3	4 8.5	9 8.6	7 28.6	1 26.7	9 36.9	13 30.2
27 W	0 23 3	3 51 58	1♍45 40	7♍50 24	25 25.6	29♍38.4	16 45.1	4 47.5	9 14.5	7 30.1	1 27.6	9 37.1	13 32.1
28 Th	0 27 0	4 50 51	13 53 9	19 54 9	25 23.9	28 41.2	17 53.8	5 26.5	9 20.4	7 31.7	1 28.4	9 37.3	13 34.1
29 F	0 30 56	5 49 47	25 53 42	1♎52 0	25 20.1	27 50.0	19 2.4	6 5.5	9 26.0	7 33.4	1 29.4	9 37.5	13 36.1
30 Sa	0 34 53	6 48 45	7♎49 18	13 45 46	25 14.4	27 6.2	20 11.0	6 44.6	9 31.5	7 35.2	1 30.4	9 37.8	13 38.2

LONGITUDE — OCTOBER 1989

Day	Sid.Time	☉	0 hr ☽	Noon ☽	True ☊	☿	♀	♂	♃	♄	♅	♆	♇
1 Su	0 38 49	7♎47 44	19♎41 39	25♎37 7	25♒ 7.1	26♍31.0	21♏19.4	7♎23.7	9♋36.9	7♑37.0	1♑31.4	9♑38.1	13♏40.2
2 M	0 42 46	8 46 46	1♏32 24	7♏27 45	24R58.7	26R 5.3	22 27.7	8 2.8	9 42.0	7 39.0	1 32.5	9 38.4	13 42.3
3 Tu	0 46 43	9 45 50	13 23 24	19 19 38	24 50.0	25D49.6	23 35.9	8 42.0	9 47.0	7 41.1	1 33.6	9 38.8	13 44.4
4 W	0 50 39	10 44 55	25 16 47	1♐15 11	24 41.9	25 44.5	24 43.9	9 21.2	9 51.8	7 43.2	1 34.8	9 39.2	13 46.5
5 Th	0 54 36	11 44 3	7♐15 14	13 17 21	24 35.2	25 49.8	25 51.9	10 0.4	9 56.5	7 45.5	1 36.1	9 39.6	13 48.6
6 F	0 58 32	12 43 12	19 22 0	25 29 40	24 30.3	26 5.5	26 59.7	10 39.6	10 1.0	7 47.8	1 37.4	9 40.1	13 50.7
7 Sa	1 2 29	13 42 23	1♑40 52	7♑56 8	24 27.5	26 31.3	28 7.5	11 18.9	10 5.3	7 50.3	1 38.7	9 40.6	13 52.9
8 Su	1 6 25	14 41 36	14 16 2	20 41 5	24D26.6	27 6.7	29 15.0	11 58.2	10 9.4	7 52.8	1 40.1	9 41.1	13 55.1
9 M	1 10 22	15 40 51	27 11 49	3♒48 42	24 27.2	27 50.9	0♐22.5	12 37.5	10 13.3	7 55.4	1 41.5	9 41.7	13 57.3
10 Tu	1 14 18	16 40 7	10♒32 10	17 22 31	24 28.2	28 43.4	1 29.8	13 16.9	10 17.1	7 58.1	1 43.0	9 42.3	13 59.5
11 W	1 18 15	17 39 25	24 19 59	1♓24 37	24R28.8	29 43.4	2 36.9	13 56.2	10 20.7	8 0.9	1 44.5	9 42.9	14 1.7
12 Th	1 22 12	18 38 45	8♓36 17	15 54 42	24 28.0	0♎50.2	3 43.9	14 35.6	10 24.1	8 3.8	1 46.1	9 43.6	14 3.9
13 F	1 26 8	19 38 6	23 19 18	0♈49 21	24 25.0	2 2.8	4 50.8	15 15.1	10 27.3	8 6.8	1 47.7	9 44.3	14 6.1
14 Sa	1 30 5	20 37 30	8♈23 50	16 1 37	24 19.6	3 20.7	5 57.5	15 54.5	10 30.3	8 9.9	1 49.4	9 45.0	14 8.4
15 Su	1 34 1	21 36 55	23 41 21	1♉21 38	24 12.1	4 43.1	7 4.0	16 34.0	10 33.1	8 13.0	1 51.1	9 45.8	14 10.7
16 M	1 37 58	22 36 23	9♉ 0 58	16 37 58	24 3.3	6 9.3	8 10.4	17 13.6	10 35.8	8 16.3	1 52.9	9 46.6	14 13.0
17 Tu	1 41 54	23 35 53	24 11 18	1♊39 47	23 54.3	7 38.8	9 16.5	17 53.1	10 38.3	8 19.6	1 54.7	9 47.4	14 15.3
18 W	1 45 51	24 35 25	9♊ 2 29	16 18 37	23 46.3	9 11.0	10 22.5	18 32.7	10 40.5	8 23.0	1 56.6	9 48.3	14 17.6
19 Th	1 49 47	25 34 59	23 27 44	0♋29 31	23 40.1	10 45.4	11 28.4	19 12.3	10 42.6	8 26.5	1 58.5	9 49.2	14 19.9
20 F	1 53 44	26 34 36	7♋23 55	14 11 2	23 36.2	12 21.6	12 34.0	19 52.0	10 44.5	8 30.1	2 0.4	9 50.1	14 22.2
21 Sa	1 57 41	27 34 14	20 51 9	27 24 40	23D34.5	13 59.3	13 39.5	20 31.7	10 46.2	8 33.8	2 2.4	9 51.1	14 24.6
22 Su	2 1 37	28 33 55	3♌52 2	10♌13 49	23 34.4	15 38.0	14 44.7	21 11.4	10 47.7	8 37.5	2 4.4	9 52.1	14 26.9
23 M	2 5 34	29 33 39	16 30 34	22 42 53	23R34.9	17 17.6	15 49.8	21 51.2	10 49.0	8 41.3	2 6.5	9 53.1	14 29.3
24 Tu	2 9 30	0♏33 24	28 51 22	4♍56 35	23 34.9	18 57.7	16 54.6	22 31.0	10 50.1	8 45.3	2 8.6	9 54.1	14 31.6
25 W	2 13 27	1 33 12	10♍59 5	16 59 22	23 33.4	20 38.2	17 59.3	23 10.8	10 51.0	8 49.2	2 10.8	9 55.2	14 34.0
26 Th	2 17 23	2 33 2	22 57 54	28 55 7	23 29.5	22 19.0	19 3.7	23 50.6	10 51.7	8 53.3	2 13.0	9 56.3	14 36.4
27 F	2 21 20	3 32 54	4♎51 23	10♎47 4	23 22.7	23 59.9	20 7.9	24 30.5	10 52.2	8 57.5	2 15.2	9 57.4	14 38.8
28 Sa	2 25 16	4 32 48	16 42 25	22 37 42	23 13.1	25 40.7	21 11.8	25 10.4	10 52.5	9 1.7	2 17.5	9 58.6	14 41.2
29 Su	2 29 13	5 32 44	28 33 9	4♏28 56	23 1.0	27 21.4	22 15.5	25 50.4	10R52.6	9 6.0	2 19.8	9 59.8	14 43.6
30 M	2 33 10	6 32 42	10♏25 14	16 22 13	22 47.3	29 1.9	23 19.0	26 30.4	10 52.5	9 10.4	2 22.2	10 1.0	14 46.0
31 Tu	2 37 6	7 32 42	22 20 2	28 18 50	22 33.1	0♏42.2	24 22.2	27 10.4	10 52.2	9 14.9	2 24.6	10 2.3	14 48.4

Astro Data	Planet Ingress	Last Aspect	☽ Ingress	Last Aspect	☽ Ingress	☽ Phases & Eclipses	Astro Data
Dy Hr Mn	Dy Hr Mn	Dy Hr Mn	Dy Hr Mn	Dy Hr Mn	Dy Hr Mn	Dy Hr Mn	1 SEPTEMBER 1989
☽0S 1 14:12	♀ ♏ 12 12:22	1 2:03 ♂ ☌	♎ 2 1:47	30 3:39 ♆ □	♏ 1 20:53	8 9:49 ☽ 15♐44	Julian Day # 32751
♃☍♄ 10 16:19	♂ ♎ 19 14:38	3 17:31 ♀ ☌	♏ 4 14:23	4 0:56 ☿ ⚹	♐ 4 9:29	15 11:50 ○ 22♓37	Delta T 56.7 sec
♅ D 10 1:14	☉ ♎ 23 1:20	6 9:51 ♂ ⚹	♐ 7 2:51	6 13:36 ☿ □	♑ 6 20:45	22 2:10 ☽ 29♊03	SVP 05♓24'04"
☿ R 11 20:57	☿ ♍ 26 15:28	9 5:58 ♀ ⚹	♑ 9 13:13	9 1:16 ☿ △	♒ 9 5:07	29 21:47 ● 6♎43	Obliquity 23°26'34"
♄ D 11 7:10		11 18:30 ♀ □	♒ 11 20:02	10 11:36 ☉ △	♓ 11 9:37		⚷ Chiron 14♋26.0
☽0N 15 14:24	♀ ♐ 8 16:00	12 18:46 ♇ □	♓ 13 23:08	12 9:00 ♇ △	♈ 13 10:41	8 0:52 ☽ 14♑44	☽ Mean ☊ 24♒55.2
♆ D 21 6:53	☿ ♎ 11 6:11	15 19:44 ♂ ☍	♈ 15 23:38	14 20:32 ☉ ☍	♉ 15 9:52	14 20:32 ○ 21♈28	
♂0S 22 13:31	☉ ♏ 23 10:35	16 14:55 ♆ □	♉ 17 23:22	16 8:12 ♇ ☍	♊ 17 9:19	21 13:19 ☽ 28♋07	1 OCTOBER 1989
☽0S 28 20:39	☿ ♏ 30 13:53	19 18:57 ☉ △	♊ 20 0:16	19 3:52 ☉ △	♋ 19 11:09	29 15:27 ● 6♏11	Julian Day # 32781
☿0N 29 18:25		22 2:10 ☉ □	♋ 22 3:50	21 13:19 ☉ □	♌ 21 16:47		Delta T 56.7 sec
♃☍♆ 1 5:54		23 3:58 ♇ △	♌ 24 10:44	23 10:55 ♂ ⚹	♍ 24 2:15		SVP 05♓24'01"
☿ D 3 23:48		25 15:44 ♀ □	♍ 26 20:32	25 15:23 ♀ □	♎ 26 14:11		Obliquity 23°26'34"
☽0N 13 1:19	☽0S 26 2:12	29 3:39 ☿ ☌	♎ 29 8:15	28 21:11 ☿ ☌	♏ 29 2:56		⚷ Chiron 16♋05.8
☿0S 14 20:26	♃ R 29 0:03			30 8:48 ♇ ☌	♐ 31 15:23		☽ Mean ☊ 23♒19.9

NOVEMBER 1989 LONGITUDE

Day	Sid.Time	☉	0 hr ☽	Noon ☽	True ☊	☿	♀	♂	♃	♄	♅	♆	♇
1 W	2 41 3	8♏32 44	4♐18 49	10♐20 9	22♒19.6	2♏22.2	25♐25.1	27♎50.5	10♋51.7	9♑19.4	2♑27.1	10♑ 3.6	14♏50.8
2 Th	2 44 59	9 32 48	16 23 5	22 27 53	22R 7.9	4 1.9	26 27.7	28 30.5	10R51.0	9 24.0	2 29.5	10 4.9	14 53.2
3 F	2 48 56	10 32 53	28 34 49	4♑44 15	21 58.8	5 41.2	27 30.1	29 10.7	10 50.1	9 28.7	2 32.1	10 6.2	14 55.6
4 Sa	2 52 52	11 33 0	10♑56 34	17 12 10	21 52.6	7 20.2	28 32.1	29 50.8	10 49.0	9 33.4	2 34.6	10 7.6	14 58.1
5 Su	2 56 49	12 33 9	23 31 30	29 55 4	21 49.2	8 58.7	29 33.8	0♏31.0	10 47.7	9 38.3	2 37.2	10 9.0	15 0.5
6 M	3 0 45	13 33 19	6♒23 19	12♒56 46	21D48.0	10 36.9	0♑35.2	1 11.2	10 46.2	9 43.2	2 39.9	10 10.4	15 2.9
7 Tu	3 4 42	14 33 31	19 35 51	26 20 59	21R47.9	12 14.7	1 36.2	1 51.5	10 44.5	9 48.1	2 42.5	10 11.9	15 5.3
8 W	3 8 39	15 33 44	3♓12 31	10♓10 42	21 47.6	13 52.1	2 36.9	2 31.7	10 42.6	9 53.2	2 45.2	10 13.3	15 7.8
9 Th	3 12 35	16 33 58	17 15 37	24 27 12	21 45.9	15 29.1	3 37.2	3 12.0	10 40.5	9 58.2	2 48.0	10 14.8	15 10.2
10 F	3 16 32	17 34 14	1♈45 13	9♈ 9 10	21 41.9	17 5.8	4 37.1	3 52.4	10 38.2	10 3.4	2 50.7	10 16.4	15 12.6
11 Sa	3 20 28	18 34 31	16 38 22	24 11 52	21 35.0	18 42.1	5 36.6	4 32.7	10 35.7	10 8.6	2 53.5	10 17.9	15 15.1
12 Su	3 24 25	19 34 50	1♉48 34	9♉27 8	21 25.5	20 18.1	6 35.7	5 13.1	10 33.0	10 13.9	2 56.4	10 19.5	15 17.5
13 M	3 28 21	20 35 11	17 6 10	24 44 12	21 14.2	21 53.7	7 34.3	5 53.6	10 30.1	10 19.3	2 59.2	10 21.1	15 19.9
14 Tu	3 32 18	21 35 33	2♊19 47	9♊51 34	21 2.6	23 29.0	8 32.5	6 34.1	10 27.0	10 24.7	3 2.1	10 22.7	15 22.3
15 W	3 36 14	22 35 58	17 18 22	24 39 11	20 51.8	25 4.1	9 30.2	7 14.6	10 23.7	10 30.2	3 5.1	10 24.4	15 24.7
16 Th	3 40 11	23 36 23	1♋53 14	9♋ 0 0	20 43.1	26 38.8	10 27.4	7 55.1	10 20.3	10 35.7	3 8.0	10 26.1	15 27.2
17 F	3 44 8	24 36 51	15 59 11	22 50 43	20 37.1	28 13.3	11 24.2	8 35.7	10 16.6	10 41.3	3 11.0	10 27.8	15 29.6
18 Sa	3 48 4	25 37 21	29 34 44	6♌11 29	20 33.8	29 47.6	12 20.4	9 16.3	10 12.8	10 46.9	3 14.1	10 29.5	15 32.0
19 Su	3 52 1	26 37 52	12♌41 25	19 5 2	20D32.6	1♐21.6	13 16.0	9 57.0	10 8.8	10 52.6	3 17.1	10 31.2	15 34.4
20 M	3 55 57	27 38 25	25 22 55	1♍35 43	20R32.5	2 55.4	14 11.1	10 37.7	10 4.6	10 58.4	3 20.2	10 33.0	15 36.8
21 Tu	3 59 54	28 38 59	7♍44 6	13 48 43	20 32.3	4 29.0	15 5.7	11 18.4	10 0.2	11 4.2	3 23.3	10 34.8	15 39.1
22 W	4 3 50	29 39 36	19 50 14	25 49 17	20 30.7	6 2.4	15 59.6	11 59.2	9 55.6	11 10.1	3 26.4	10 36.6	15 41.5
23 Th	4 7 47	0♐40 14	1♎46 28	7♎42 20	20 27.0	7 35.7	16 52.9	12 40.0	9 50.9	11 16.0	3 29.6	10 38.4	15 43.9
24 F	4 11 43	1 40 54	13 37 26	19 32 12	20 20.4	9 8.7	17 45.5	13 20.8	9 46.0	11 22.0	3 32.8	10 40.3	15 46.2
25 Sa	4 15 40	2 41 35	25 27 5	1♏22 26	20 10.8	10 41.7	18 37.5	14 1.7	9 40.9	11 28.0	3 36.0	10 42.1	15 48.6
26 Su	4 19 37	3 42 18	7♏18 34	13 15 45	19 58.8	12 14.5	19 28.7	14 42.6	9 35.6	11 34.1	3 39.2	10 44.0	15 50.9
27 M	4 23 33	4 43 2	19 14 12	25 14 5	19 45.1	13 47.1	20 19.3	15 23.5	9 30.2	11 40.2	3 42.5	10 45.9	15 53.3
28 Tu	4 27 30	5 43 48	1♐15 33	7♐18 44	19 30.8	15 19.6	21 9.0	16 4.5	9 24.6	11 46.3	3 45.7	10 47.9	15 55.6
29 W	4 31 26	6 44 35	13 23 43	19 30 36	19 17.1	16 52.0	21 58.0	16 45.5	9 18.9	11 52.6	3 49.0	10 49.8	15 57.9
30 Th	4 35 23	7 45 24	25 39 28	1♑50 26	19 5.2	18 24.3	22 46.1	17 26.6	9 13.0	11 58.8	3 52.4	10 51.8	16 0.2

DECEMBER 1989 LONGITUDE

Day	Sid.Time	☉	0 hr ☽	Noon ☽	True ☊	☿	♀	♂	♃	♄	♅	♆	♇
1 F	4 39 19	8♐46 13	8♑ 3 37	14♑19 10	18♒55.8	19♐56.4	23♑33.3	18♏ 7.7	9♋ 7.0	12♑ 5.1	3♑55.7	10♑53.8	16♏ 2.5
2 Sa	4 43 16	9 47 4	20 37 15	26 58 7	18R49.5	21 28.4	24 19.7	18 48.8	9R 0.8	12 11.5	3 59.1	10 55.8	16 4.8
3 Su	4 47 13	10 47 56	3♒21 58	9♒49 7	18 46.0	23 0.2	25 5.1	19 29.9	8 54.5	12 17.9	4 2.4	10 57.8	16 7.1
4 M	4 51 9	11 48 48	16 19 52	22 54 32	18D44.9	24 31.8	25 49.5	20 11.1	8 48.0	12 24.3	4 5.8	10 59.8	16 9.3
5 Tu	4 55 6	12 49 41	29 33 27	6♓16 55	18 45.2	26 3.2	26 32.9	20 52.4	8 41.4	12 30.7	4 9.3	11 1.9	16 11.5
6 W	4 59 2	13 50 35	13♓ 5 15	19 58 39	18R45.6	27 34.4	27 15.1	21 33.6	8 34.7	12 37.2	4 12.7	11 3.9	16 13.8
7 Th	5 2 59	14 51 30	26 57 18	4♈ 1 13	18 44.9	29 5.3	27 56.3	22 14.9	8 27.9	12 43.8	4 16.1	11 6.0	16 16.0
8 F	5 6 55	15 52 25	11♈10 20	18 24 24	18 42.3	0♑35.8	28 36.3	22 56.2	8 20.9	12 50.4	4 19.6	11 8.1	16 18.2
9 Sa	5 10 52	16 53 21	25 43 0	3♉ 5 34	18 37.2	2 6.0	29 15.0	23 37.6	8 13.9	12 57.0	4 23.1	11 10.2	16 20.3
10 Su	5 14 48	17 54 18	10♉31 20	17 59 22	18 29.8	3 35.7	29 52.5	24 19.0	8 6.7	13 3.6	4 26.6	11 12.3	16 22.5
11 M	5 18 45	18 55 15	25 28 36	2♊57 54	18 20.7	5 4.8	0♒28.7	25 0.4	7 59.4	13 10.3	4 30.1	11 14.4	16 24.6
12 Tu	5 22 42	19 56 14	10♊26 3	17 51 53	18 11.1	6 33.3	1 3.4	25 41.8	7 52.1	13 17.0	4 33.6	11 16.6	16 26.7
13 W	5 26 38	20 57 13	25 14 16	2♋32 11	18 2.2	8 0.9	1 36.7	26 23.3	7 44.6	13 23.7	4 37.1	11 18.7	16 28.8
14 Th	5 30 35	21 58 13	9♋44 48	16 51 24	17 54.9	9 27.7	2 8.6	27 4.9	7 37.1	13 30.5	4 40.6	11 20.9	16 30.9
15 F	5 34 31	22 59 14	23 51 31	0♌44 51	17 49.9	10 53.3	2 38.8	27 46.5	7 29.4	13 37.3	4 44.2	11 23.1	16 33.0
16 Sa	5 38 28	24 0 15	7♌31 16	14 10 51	17D47.3	12 17.6	3 7.5	28 28.1	7 21.7	13 44.1	4 47.7	11 25.3	16 35.1
17 Su	5 42 24	25 1 18	20 43 48	27 10 27	17 46.8	13 40.3	3 34.5	29 9.7	7 14.0	13 50.9	4 51.3	11 27.5	16 37.1
18 M	5 46 21	26 2 21	3♍31 14	9♍46 42	17 47.7	15 1.2	3 59.7	29 51.4	7 6.1	13 57.8	4 54.9	11 29.7	16 39.1
19 Tu	5 50 17	27 3 25	15 57 23	22 3 57	17 48.9	16 19.9	4 23.2	0♐33.1	6 58.2	14 4.7	4 58.5	11 31.9	16 41.1
20 W	5 54 14	28 4 30	28 7 1	4♎ 7 15	17R49.5	17 36.0	4 44.8	1 14.9	6 50.3	14 11.6	5 2.1	11 34.1	16 43.0
21 Th	5 58 11	29 5 36	10♎ 5 18	16 1 48	17 48.7	18 49.2	5 4.5	1 56.7	6 42.3	14 18.5	5 5.6	11 36.3	16 45.0
22 F	6 2 7	0♑ 6 42	21 57 21	27 52 33	17 45.9	19 58.9	5 22.2	2 38.5	6 34.2	14 25.5	5 9.2	11 38.5	16 46.9
23 Sa	6 6 4	1 7 50	3♏47 56	9♏44 1	17 41.0	21 4.5	5 37.8	3 20.4	6 26.1	14 32.5	5 12.8	11 40.8	16 48.8
24 Su	6 10 0	2 8 58	15 41 14	21 39 59	17 34.2	22 5.4	5 51.4	4 2.3	6 18.0	14 39.5	5 16.4	11 43.0	16 50.6
25 M	6 13 57	3 10 6	27 40 39	3♐43 29	17 26.1	23 1.0	6 2.7	4 44.3	6 9.9	14 46.5	5 20.1	11 45.3	16 52.5
26 Tu	6 17 53	4 11 15	9♐48 46	15 56 39	17 17.4	23 50.3	6 11.9	5 26.2	6 1.8	14 53.5	5 23.7	11 47.5	16 54.3
27 W	6 21 50	5 12 25	22 7 18	28 20 48	17 9.0	24 32.6	6 18.7	6 8.3	5 53.6	15 0.5	5 27.3	11 49.8	16 56.1
28 Th	6 25 46	6 13 35	4♑37 12	10♑56 32	17 1.8	25 7.0	6 23.2	6 50.3	5 45.5	15 7.6	5 30.9	11 52.1	16 57.9
29 F	6 29 43	7 14 45	17 18 49	23 44 0	16 56.3	25 32.6	6R25.3	7 32.4	5 37.3	15 14.7	5 34.5	11 54.3	16 59.6
30 Sa	6 33 40	8 15 56	0♒12 7	6♒43 7	16 52.9	25R48.4	6 25.0	8 14.5	5 29.2	15 21.7	5 38.1	11 56.6	17 1.4
31 Su	6 37 36	9 17 6	13 16 59	19 53 46	16D51.5	25 53.7	6 22.2	8 56.7	5 21.1	15 28.8	5 41.7	11 58.9	17 3.1

Astro Data Dy Hr Mn	Planet Ingress Dy Hr Mn	Last Aspect Dy Hr Mn	☽ Ingress Dy Hr Mn	Last Aspect Dy Hr Mn	☽ Ingress Dy Hr Mn	☽ Phases & Eclipses Dy Hr Mn	Astro Data
☽0N 9 10:57	♂ ♏ 4 5:29	3 1:14 ♂ ⚹	♑ 3 2:46	2 7:28 ♀ ☌	♒ 2 17:42	6 14:11 ☽ 14♒09	1 NOVEMBER 1989
♄☌♆ 13 11:41	♀ ♑ 5 10:13	4 7:45 ♇ ⚹	♒ 5 12:09	4 16:53 ☿ ⚹	♓ 5 0:48	13 5:51 ○ 20♉50	Julian Day # 32812
♃☍♄ 14 6:27	☿ ♐ 18 3:10	6 15:52 ♇ □	♓ 7 18:25	7 4:04 ☿ □	♈ 7 5:11	20 4:44 ☽ 27♌50	Delta T 56.8 sec
♃☍♆ 14 20:53	☉ ♐ 22 8:05	8 22:45 ☉ △	♈ 9 21:08	9 6:01 ♀ □	♉ 9 6:59	28 9:41 ● 6♐08	SVP 05♓23'57"
☽0S 22 7:36		10 14:21 ♃ □	♉ 11 21:09	10 23:13 ♂ ☍	♊ 11 7:15		Obliquity 23°26'33"
	☿ ♑ 7 14:30	13 8:24 ☿ ☍	♊ 13 20:19	12 16:30 ☉ ☍	♋ 13 7:49	6 1:26 ☽ 13♓54	⚷ Chiron 16♋34.3R
☽0N 6 17:46	♀ ♒ 10 4:54	13 20:19 ☽ T	♋ 15 20:51	15 7:10 ♂ △	♌ 15 10:41	12 16:30 ○ 20♊38	☽ Mean ☊ 21♒41.4
☽0S 19 14:05	♂ ♐ 18 4:57	18 0:26 ☿ △	♌ 18 0:45	17 16:39 ♂ □	♍ 17 17:19	19 23:55 ☽ 28♍04	
♃☍♅ 29 5:45	☉ ♑ 21 21:22	20 4:44 ☉ □	♍ 20 8:54	19 23:55 ☉ □	♎ 20 3:45	28 3:20 ● 6♑22	1 DECEMBER 1989
♀ R 29 8:50		21 15:43 ♀ △	♎ 22 20:25	21 19:35 ☿ □	♏ 22 16:18		Julian Day # 32842
☿ R 30 23:29		24 9:03 ♀ □	♏ 25 9:13	24 13:57 ☿ ⚹	♐ 25 4:37		Delta T 56.8 sec
		27 2:20 ♀ ⚹	♐ 27 21:30	25 16:48 ♀ ⚹	♑ 27 15:10		SVP 05♓23'52"
		29 7:48 ☿ ☌	♑ 30 8:26	29 15:43 ☿ ☌	♒ 29 23:38		Obliquity 23°26'33"
							⚷ Chiron 15♋43.0R
							☽ Mean ☊ 20♒06.1

LONGITUDE — JANUARY 1990

Day	Sid.Time	☉	0 hr ☽	Noon ☽	True ☊	☿	♀	♂	♃	♄	♅	♆	♇
1 M	6 41 33	10♑18 16	26♒33 26	3♓16 4	16♒51.8	25♑47.7	6♒16.9	9♐38.9	5♋13.0	15♑35.9	5♑45.3	12♑ 1.2	17♏ 4.7
2 Tu	6 45 29	11 19 26	10♓ 1 40	16 50 18	16 53.2	25R30.0	6R 9.1	10 21.1	5R 4.9	15 43.0	5 48.9	12 3.4	17 6.4
3 W	6 49 26	12 20 36	23 42 0	0♈36 49	16 54.8	25 0.5	5 58.8	11 3.4	4 56.9	15 50.1	5 52.5	12 5.7	17 8.0
4 Th	6 53 22	13 21 46	7♈34 44	14 35 41	16R55.8	24 19.2	5 45.9	11 45.7	4 48.9	15 57.2	5 56.1	12 8.0	17 9.6
5 F	6 57 19	14 22 55	21 39 36	28 46 17	16 55.7	23 27.0	5 30.5	12 28.0	4 40.9	16 4.3	5 59.7	12 10.2	17 11.1
6 Sa	7 1 15	15 24 4	5♉55 28	13♉ 6 50	16 54.2	22 25.1	5 12.7	13 10.4	4 33.1	16 11.4	6 3.3	12 12.5	17 12.6
7 Su	7 5 12	16 25 13	20 19 54	27 34 9	16 51.2	21 15.0	4 52.5	13 52.8	4 25.2	16 18.5	6 6.8	12 14.8	17 14.1
8 M	7 9 9	17 26 21	4♊48 57	12♊ 3 37	16 47.2	19 59.1	4 30.0	14 35.2	4 17.5	16 25.6	6 10.4	12 17.1	17 15.6
9 Tu	7 13 5	18 27 29	19 17 26	26 29 37	16 42.8	18 39.6	4 5.3	15 17.6	4 9.8	16 32.8	6 14.0	12 19.3	17 17.1
10 W	7 17 2	19 28 36	3♋39 26	10♋46 10	16 38.6	17 19.3	3 38.5	16 0.1	4 2.2	16 39.9	6 17.5	12 21.6	17 18.5
11 Th	7 20 58	20 29 43	17 49 10	24 47 51	16 35.3	16 0.6	3 9.8	16 42.7	3 54.7	16 47.0	6 21.0	12 23.9	17 19.8
12 F	7 24 55	21 30 50	1♌41 45	8♌30 30	16 33.2	14 45.9	2 39.2	17 25.3	3 47.2	16 54.1	6 24.6	12 26.1	17 21.2
13 Sa	7 28 51	22 31 57	15 13 53	21 51 47	16D32.4	13 37.2	2 7.1	18 7.9	3 39.9	17 1.2	6 28.1	12 28.4	17 22.5
14 Su	7 32 48	23 33 3	28 24 11	4♍51 12	16 32.8	12 36.0	1 33.6	18 50.5	3 32.6	17 8.3	6 31.6	12 30.6	17 23.8
15 M	7 36 45	24 34 9	11♍13 4	17 30 4	16 34.1	11 43.5	0 58.9	19 33.2	3 25.5	17 15.3	6 35.1	12 32.8	17 25.0
16 Tu	7 40 41	25 35 14	23 42 36	29 51 6	16 35.8	11 0.2	0 23.2	20 15.9	3 18.5	17 22.4	6 38.5	12 35.1	17 26.3
17 W	7 44 38	26 36 20	5♎56 5	11♎58 6	16 37.4	10 26.6	29♑46.9	20 58.7	3 11.5	17 29.5	6 42.0	12 37.3	17 27.5
18 Th	7 48 34	27 37 25	17 57 43	23 55 31	16R38.5	10 2.6	29 10.1	21 41.5	3 4.7	17 36.5	6 45.4	12 39.5	17 28.6
19 F	7 52 31	28 38 30	29 52 7	5♏48 8	16 38.8	9 47.8	28 33.2	22 24.3	2 58.1	17 43.5	6 48.8	12 41.7	17 29.7
20 Sa	7 56 27	29 39 35	11♏44 10	17 40 47	16 38.3	9D42.0	27 56.3	23 7.1	2 51.5	17 50.6	6 52.3	12 43.9	17 30.8
21 Su	8 0 24	0♒40 39	23 38 35	29 38 5	16 37.0	9 44.5	27 19.7	23 50.0	2 45.1	17 57.6	6 55.6	12 46.1	17 31.9
22 M	8 4 20	1 41 43	5♐39 47	11♐44 10	16 35.1	9 54.8	26 43.8	24 33.0	2 38.8	18 4.6	6 59.0	12 48.3	17 32.9
23 Tu	8 8 17	2 42 46	17 51 37	24 2 29	16 33.0	10 12.3	26 8.6	25 16.0	2 32.7	18 11.5	7 2.4	12 50.5	17 33.9
24 W	8 12 14	3 43 49	0♑17 5	6♑35 38	16 30.9	10 36.3	25 34.6	25 59.0	2 26.7	18 18.5	7 5.7	12 52.6	17 34.8
25 Th	8 16 10	4 44 52	12 58 18	19 25 9	16 29.2	11 6.4	25 1.8	26 42.0	2 20.8	18 25.4	7 9.0	12 54.8	17 35.8
26 F	8 20 7	5 45 53	25 56 14	2♒31 28	16 28.0	11 41.9	24 30.5	27 25.1	2 15.1	18 32.4	7 12.3	12 56.9	17 36.7
27 Sa	8 24 3	6 46 54	9♒10 47	15 53 58	16D27.4	12 22.3	24 0.8	28 8.2	2 9.6	18 39.3	7 15.6	12 59.1	17 37.5
28 Su	8 28 0	7 47 54	22 40 48	29 31 2	16 27.3	13 7.2	23 33.0	28 51.3	2 4.2	18 46.1	7 18.8	13 1.2	17 38.3
29 M	8 31 56	8 48 53	6♓24 21	13♓20 26	16 27.7	13 56.2	23 7.1	29 34.5	1 59.0	18 53.0	7 22.0	13 3.3	17 39.1
30 Tu	8 35 53	9 49 50	20 18 56	27 19 30	16 28.3	14 48.9	22 43.3	0♑17.7	1 54.0	18 59.8	7 25.2	13 5.4	17 39.8
31 W	8 39 49	10 50 47	4♈21 47	11♈25 27	16 29.0	15 44.9	22 21.7	1 0.9	1 49.1	19 6.6	7 28.4	13 7.4	17 40.6

LONGITUDE — FEBRUARY 1990

Day	Sid.Time	☉	0 hr ☽	Noon ☽	True ☊	☿	♀	♂	♃	♄	♅	♆	♇
1 Th	8 43 46	11♒51 42	18♈30 10	25♈35 37	16♒29.4	16♑44.0	22♑ 2.5	1♑44.2	1♋44.4	19♑13.4	7♑31.6	13♑ 9.5	17♏41.2
2 F	8 47 43	12 52 36	2♉41 29	9♉47 30	16R29.7	17 45.8	21R45.5	2 27.5	1R39.9	19 20.1	7 34.7	13 11.5	17 41.9
3 Sa	8 51 39	13 53 29	16 53 21	23 58 47	16 29.7	18 50.2	21 31.0	3 10.8	1 35.5	19 26.8	7 37.8	13 13.6	17 42.5
4 Su	8 55 36	14 54 20	1♊ 3 29	8♊ 7 13	16 29.7	19 56.9	21 18.9	3 54.1	1 31.4	19 33.5	7 40.8	13 15.6	17 43.0
5 M	8 59 32	15 55 10	15 9 41	22 10 35	16D29.6	21 5.8	21 9.4	4 37.5	1 27.4	19 40.1	7 43.9	13 17.6	17 43.6
6 Tu	9 3 29	16 55 59	29 9 39	6♋ 6 35	16 29.6	22 16.6	21 2.2	5 20.9	1 23.6	19 46.7	7 46.9	13 19.6	17 44.1
7 W	9 7 25	17 56 46	13♋ 1 5	19 52 52	16 29.7	23 29.2	20 57.6	6 4.4	1 20.0	19 53.3	7 49.9	13 21.5	17 44.5
8 Th	9 11 22	18 57 31	26 41 40	3♌27 13	16 29.9	24 43.6	20D55.4	6 47.9	1 16.6	19 59.8	7 52.8	13 23.5	17 45.0
9 F	9 15 18	19 58 16	10♌ 9 18	16 47 43	16R30.0	25 59.5	20 55.7	7 31.4	1 13.4	20 6.3	7 55.7	13 25.4	17 45.3
10 Sa	9 19 15	20 58 58	23 22 19	29 53 0	16 30.0	27 17.0	20 58.4	8 14.9	1 10.4	20 12.8	7 58.6	13 27.3	17 45.7
11 Su	9 23 12	21 59 40	6♍19 42	12♍42 26	16 29.7	28 35.8	21 3.5	8 58.5	1 7.5	20 19.2	8 1.5	13 29.2	17 46.0
12 M	9 27 8	23 0 20	19 1 16	25 16 20	16 29.1	29 56.0	21 10.8	9 42.1	1 4.9	20 25.6	8 4.3	13 31.0	17 46.3
13 Tu	9 31 5	24 0 59	1♎27 49	7♎35 58	16 28.1	1♒17.5	21 20.5	10 25.8	1 2.4	20 32.0	8 7.1	13 32.9	17 46.5
14 W	9 35 1	25 1 37	13 41 6	19 43 35	16 27.0	2 40.1	21 32.3	11 9.4	1 0.2	20 38.3	8 9.8	13 34.7	17 46.7
15 Th	9 38 58	26 2 13	25 43 49	1♏42 16	16 25.7	4 4.0	21 46.3	11 53.1	0 58.1	20 44.5	8 12.5	13 36.5	17 46.9
16 F	9 42 54	27 2 48	7♏39 25	13 35 48	16 24.7	5 29.0	22 2.4	12 36.9	0 56.2	20 50.7	8 15.2	13 38.3	17 47.0
17 Sa	9 46 51	28 3 23	19 31 59	25 28 33	16D23.9	6 55.1	22 20.5	13 20.7	0 54.6	20 56.9	8 17.9	13 40.1	17 47.1
18 Su	9 50 47	29 3 55	1♐26 3	7♐25 8	16 23.8	8 22.2	22 40.6	14 4.5	0 53.1	21 3.0	8 20.5	13 41.8	17 47.2
19 M	9 54 44	0♓ 4 27	13 26 21	19 30 18	16 24.2	9 50.4	23 2.5	14 48.3	0 51.9	21 9.1	8 23.0	13 43.5	17R47.2
20 Tu	9 58 41	1 4 58	25 37 32	1♑48 36	16 25.2	11 19.7	23 26.3	15 32.2	0 50.8	21 15.1	8 25.6	13 45.2	17 47.2
21 W	10 2 37	2 5 27	8♑ 3 58	14 24 5	16 26.5	12 49.9	23 51.8	16 16.1	0 49.9	21 21.1	8 28.1	13 46.9	17 47.2
22 Th	10 6 34	3 5 54	20 49 17	27 19 53	16 27.9	14 21.1	24 19.1	16 60.0	0 49.3	21 27.0	8 30.5	13 48.6	17 47.1
23 F	10 10 30	4 6 21	3♒56 2	10♒37 50	16R29.0	15 53.4	24 47.9	17 43.9	0 48.8	21 32.9	8 33.0	13 50.2	17 47.0
24 Sa	10 14 27	5 6 45	17 25 15	24 18 7	16 29.3	17 26.6	25 18.3	18 27.9	0D48.6	21 38.7	8 35.4	13 51.8	17 46.8
25 Su	10 18 23	6 7 9	1♓16 10	8♓18 58	16 28.8	19 0.9	25 50.2	19 11.9	0 48.5	21 44.5	8 37.7	13 53.4	17 46.6
26 M	10 22 20	7 7 30	15 26 0	22 36 39	16 27.1	20 36.1	26 23.5	19 56.0	0 48.6	21 50.2	8 40.0	13 54.9	17 46.4
27 Tu	10 26 16	8 7 50	29 50 12	7♈ 5 52	16 24.6	22 12.3	26 58.2	20 40.0	0 49.0	21 55.9	8 42.3	13 56.4	17 46.1
28 W	10 30 13	9 8 7	14♈22 52	21 40 23	16 21.4	23 49.5	27 34.2	21 24.1	0 49.5	22 1.5	8 44.5	13 57.9	17 45.8

Astro Data

	Dy Hr Mn
☽0N	2 22:37
☽0S	15 22:14
♄✶♇	16 15:48
☿ D	20 4:32
♃⚼♇	22 19:49
☽0N	30 4:11
♀ D	8 9:16
☽0S	12 7:10
♇ R	19 6:30
♃ D	24 19:15
☽0N	26 12:18

Planet Ingress

	Dy Hr Mn
♀ ♑	16 15:23
☉ ♒	20 8:02
♂ ♑	29 14:10
☿ ♒	12 1:11
☉ ♓	18 22:14

Last Aspect / ☽ Ingress

Last Aspect Dy Hr Mn		☽ Ingress Dy Hr Mn
31 6:52	♇ □	♓ 1 6:10
3 2:11	☿ ✶	♈ 3 10:56
5 2:50	☿ □	♉ 5 14:04
7 1:24	☿ △	♊ 7 16:02
8 17:01	♂ ☍	♋ 9 17:52
11 4:57	☉ ☍	♌ 11 21:02
13 5:31	♂ △	♍ 14 2:57
16 3:59	☉ △	♎ 16 12:17
18 21:28	♀ □	♏ 19 0:16
21 7:02	♀ ✶	♐ 21 12:44
23 15:14	♀ ☌	♑ 23 23:27
25 21:29	♀ ☌	♒ 26 7:25
28 11:27	♂ ✶	♓ 28 12:51
30 4:01	♀ ✶	♈ 30 16:34

Last Aspect / ☽ Ingress

Last Aspect Dy Hr Mn		☽ Ingress Dy Hr Mn
1 5:52	♀ □	♉ 1 19:27
3 7:43	♀ △	♊ 3 22:12
5 1:24	☉ △	♋ 6 1:27
7 20:10	☿ ☍	♌ 8 5:51
9 19:16	☉ ☍	♍ 10 12:13
12 4:11	♀ △	♎ 12 21:09
15 0:40	☉ △	♏ 15 8:34
17 18:48	☉ □	♐ 17 21:07
18 15:50	☿ ✶	♑ 20 8:30
22 6:42	♀ ☌	♒ 22 16:52
24 0:38	♇ □	♓ 24 21:49
26 19:03	♀ ✶	♈ 27 0:16

☽ Phases & Eclipses

Dy Hr Mn	
4 10:40	☽ 13♈49
11 4:57	○ 20♋42
18 21:17	☽ 28♎32
26 19:20	● 6♒35
26 19:30:24	✔ A 2'03"
2 18:32	☽ 13♉40
9 19:16	○ 20♌47
9 19:11	✔ T 1.075
17 18:48	☽ 28♏51
25 8:54	● 6♓30

Astro Data

1 JANUARY 1990
Julian Day # 32873
Delta T 56.9 sec
SVP 05♓23'46"
Obliquity 23°26'32"
⚷ Chiron 13♋50.4R
☽ Mean ☊ 18♒27.6

1 FEBRUARY 1990
Julian Day # 32904
Delta T 56.9 sec
SVP 05♓23'41"
Obliquity 23°26'33"
⚷ Chiron 11♋49.8R
☽ Mean ☊ 16♒49.1

MARCH 1990 LONGITUDE

Day	Sid.Time	☉	0 hr ☽	Noon ☽	True ☊	☿	♀	♂	♃	♄	♅	♆	♇
1 Th	10 34 10	10♓ 8 23	28♈57 39	6♉13 56	16♒18.1	25♒27.8	28♑11.5	22♑ 8.2	0♋50.3	22♑ 7.0	8♑46.6	13♑59.4	17♏45.5
2 F	10 38 6	11 8 37	13♉28 35	20 41 2	16R15.3	27 7.0	28 50.0	22 52.4	0 51.2	22 12.5	8 48.8	14 0.8	17R45.2
3 Sa	10 42 3	12 8 49	27 50 48	4♊57 33	16 13.4	28 47.3	29 29.7	23 36.5	0 52.3	22 17.9	8 50.9	14 2.3	17 44.8
4 Su	10 45 59	13 8 59	12♊ 1 1	19 1 0	16D 12.7	0♓28.6	0♒10.5	24 20.7	0 53.7	22 23.3	8 52.9	14 3.7	17 44.3
5 M	10 49 56	14 9 7	25 57 25	2♋50 14	16 13.1	2 11.0	0 52.4	25 4.9	0 55.2	22 28.6	8 54.9	14 5.0	17 43.9
6 Tu	10 53 52	15 9 12	9♋39 29	16 25 14	16 14.4	3 54.5	1 35.4	25 49.1	0 56.9	22 33.8	8 56.9	14 6.4	17 43.4
7 W	10 57 49	16 9 16	23 7 32	29 46 30	16 16.1	5 39.1	2 19.3	26 33.4	0 58.9	22 39.0	8 58.8	14 7.7	17 42.8
8 Th	11 1 45	17 9 17	6♌22 14	12♌54 49	16R 17.4	7 24.7	3 4.2	27 17.6	1 1.0	22 44.1	9 0.7	14 9.0	17 42.3
9 F	11 5 42	18 9 16	19 24 20	25 50 53	16 17.7	9 11.5	3 50.0	28 1.9	1 3.3	22 49.1	9 2.5	14 10.2	17 41.7
10 Sa	11 9 39	19 9 14	2♍14 30	8♍35 17	16 16.5	10 59.4	4 36.8	28 46.3	1 5.8	22 54.1	9 4.3	14 11.4	17 41.0
11 Su	11 13 35	20 9 9	14 53 15	21 8 29	16 13.7	12 48.4	5 24.3	29 30.6	1 8.4	22 59.0	9 6.0	14 12.6	17 40.4
12 M	11 17 32	21 9 2	27 21 2	3♎31 1	16 9.1	14 38.6	6 12.7	0♒15.0	1 11.3	23 3.8	9 7.7	14 13.8	17 39.7
13 Tu	11 21 28	22 8 53	9♎38 30	15 43 39	16 3.0	16 29.9	7 1.9	0 59.4	1 14.3	23 8.6	9 9.3	14 14.9	17 39.0
14 W	11 25 25	23 8 42	21 46 38	27 47 38	15 56.1	18 22.3	7 51.9	1 43.8	1 17.6	23 13.2	9 10.9	14 16.0	17 38.2
15 Th	11 29 21	24 8 30	3♏46 56	9♏44 49	15 49.0	20 15.9	8 42.6	2 28.2	1 21.0	23 17.9	9 12.4	14 17.1	17 37.4
16 F	11 33 18	25 8 16	15 41 38	21 37 45	15 42.5	22 10.5	9 34.0	3 12.7	1 24.6	23 22.4	9 13.9	14 18.1	17 36.6
17 Sa	11 37 14	26 8 0	27 33 38	3♐29 45	15 37.2	24 6.3	10 26.1	3 57.2	1 28.4	23 26.9	9 15.4	14 19.1	17 35.8
18 Su	11 41 11	27 7 42	9♐26 36	15 24 46	15 33.5	26 3.1	11 18.9	4 41.7	1 32.3	23 31.3	9 16.8	14 20.1	17 34.9
19 M	11 45 8	28 7 23	21 24 48	27 27 20	15D 31.7	28 0.9	12 12.2	5 26.3	1 36.4	23 35.6	9 18.1	14 21.1	17 34.0
20 Tu	11 49 4	29 7 2	3♑32 58	9♑42 19	15 31.5	29 59.6	13 6.2	6 10.8	1 40.7	23 39.8	9 19.4	14 22.0	17 33.0
21 W	11 53 1	0♈ 6 39	15 56 0	22 14 36	15 32.5	1♈59.2	14 0.8	6 55.4	1 45.2	23 44.0	9 20.7	14 22.9	17 32.1
22 Th	11 56 57	1 6 15	28 38 40	5♒ 8 42	15 33.9	3 59.4	14 55.9	7 40.0	1 49.9	23 48.1	9 21.9	14 23.7	17 31.1
23 F	12 0 54	2 5 48	11♒45 5	18 28 7	15R 34.8	6 0.3	15 51.5	8 24.6	1 54.7	23 52.1	9 23.0	14 24.6	17 30.1
24 Sa	12 4 50	3 5 20	25 17 59	2♓14 42	15 34.5	8 1.6	16 47.7	9 9.3	1 59.7	23 56.1	9 24.1	14 25.3	17 29.0
25 Su	12 8 47	4 4 50	9♓18 8	16 27 56	15 32.1	10 3.1	17 44.3	9 53.9	2 4.8	23 59.9	9 25.2	14 26.1	17 27.9
26 M	12 12 43	5 4 18	23 43 34	1♈ 4 20	15 27.6	12 4.6	18 41.5	10 38.6	2 10.2	24 3.7	9 26.2	14 26.8	17 26.8
27 Tu	12 16 40	6 3 44	8♈29 19	15 57 30	15 21.1	14 5.8	19 39.0	11 23.3	2 15.7	24 7.4	9 27.1	14 27.5	17 25.7
28 W	12 20 36	7 3 8	23 27 43	0♉58 45	15 13.2	16 6.5	20 37.1	12 7.9	2 21.3	24 11.0	9 28.0	14 28.2	17 24.6
29 Th	12 24 33	8 2 30	8♉29 24	15 58 30	15 5.0	18 6.4	21 35.5	12 52.7	2 27.1	24 14.5	9 28.8	14 28.8	17 23.4
30 F	12 28 30	9 1 50	23 24 57	0♊47 51	14 57.5	20 5.0	22 34.3	13 37.4	2 33.1	24 17.9	9 29.6	14 29.4	17 22.2
31 Sa	12 32 26	10 1 8	8♊ 6 25	15 20 3	14 51.6	22 2.1	23 33.5	14 22.1	2 39.2	24 21.3	9 30.4	14 30.0	17 21.0

APRIL 1990 LONGITUDE

Day	Sid.Time	☉	0 hr ☽	Noon ☽	True ☊	☿	♀	♂	♃	♄	♅	♆	♇
1 Su	12 36 23	11♈ 0 23	22♊28 22	29♊31 7	14♒47.9	23♈57.2	24♒33.1	15♒ 6.8	2♋45.5	24♑24.5	9♑31.1	14♑30.5	17♏19.7
2 M	12 40 19	11 59 36	6♋28 15	13♋19 48	14D 46.4	25 50.0	25 33.1	15 51.6	2 52.0	24 27.7	9 31.7	14 31.0	17R 18.5
3 Tu	12 44 16	12 58 46	20 5 57	26 46 58	14 46.4	27 40.0	26 33.4	16 36.4	2 58.6	24 30.8	9 32.3	14 31.5	17 17.2
4 W	12 48 12	13 57 55	3♌23 8	9♌54 49	14R 47.2	29 26.9	27 34.1	17 21.1	3 5.3	24 33.8	9 32.8	14 31.9	17 15.9
5 Th	12 52 9	14 57 0	16 22 23	22 46 11	14 47.6	1♉10.3	28 35.1	18 5.9	3 12.2	24 36.7	9 33.3	14 32.3	17 14.5
6 F	12 56 5	15 56 4	29 6 35	5♍23 55	14 46.5	2 49.8	29 36.4	18 50.7	3 19.2	24 39.5	9 33.8	14 32.7	17 13.2
7 Sa	13 0 2	16 55 5	11♍38 28	17 50 30	14 43.3	4 25.1	0♓38.0	19 35.5	3 26.4	24 42.3	9 34.1	14 33.0	17 11.8
8 Su	13 3 59	17 54 4	24 0 16	0♎ 7 58	14 37.3	5 55.9	1 39.9	20 20.3	3 33.7	24 44.9	9 34.5	14 33.3	17 10.4
9 M	13 7 55	18 53 1	6♎13 47	12 17 53	14 28.7	7 21.9	2 42.1	21 5.1	3 41.1	24 47.4	9 34.7	14 33.5	17 9.0
10 Tu	13 11 52	19 51 56	18 20 23	24 21 26	14 17.8	8 42.9	3 44.6	21 49.9	3 48.7	24 49.9	9 35.0	14 33.8	17 7.5
11 W	13 15 48	20 50 49	0♏21 10	6♏19 45	14 5.5	9 58.6	4 47.3	22 34.8	3 56.4	24 52.3	9 35.1	14 34.0	17 6.1
12 Th	13 19 45	21 49 40	12 17 19	18 14 5	13 52.8	11 8.9	5 50.4	23 19.6	4 4.3	24 54.5	9 35.3	14 34.1	17 4.6
13 F	13 23 41	22 48 29	24 10 15	0♐ 6 6	13 40.7	12 13.5	6 53.6	24 4.5	4 12.3	24 56.7	9R 35.3	14 34.3	17 3.2
14 Sa	13 27 38	23 47 16	6♐ 1 56	11 58 5	13 30.2	13 12.4	7 57.2	24 49.3	4 20.4	24 58.8	9 35.4	14 34.4	17 1.7
15 Su	13 31 34	24 46 2	17 54 58	23 53 0	13 22.1	14 5.4	9 1.0	25 34.2	4 28.6	25 0.8	9 35.3	14 34.4	17 0.1
16 M	13 35 31	25 44 45	29 52 41	5♑54 32	13 16.7	14 52.5	10 5.0	26 19.1	4 37.0	25 2.7	9 35.2	14R 34.5	16 58.6
17 Tu	13 39 28	26 43 27	11♑59 9	18 7 6	13 13.8	15 33.5	11 9.2	27 3.9	4 45.5	25 4.5	9 35.1	14 34.5	16 57.1
18 W	13 43 24	27 42 8	24 19 0	0♒35 28	13D 12.8	16 8.4	12 13.7	27 48.8	4 54.1	25 6.2	9 34.9	14 34.4	16 55.5
19 Th	13 47 21	28 40 46	6♒57 8	13 24 35	13R 12.9	16 37.1	13 18.3	28 33.7	5 2.8	25 7.8	9 34.7	14 34.4	16 54.0
20 F	13 51 17	29 39 23	19 58 21	26 38 55	13 12.8	16 59.8	14 23.2	29 18.6	5 11.7	25 9.3	9 34.4	14 34.3	16 52.4
21 Sa	13 55 14	0♉37 58	3♓26 37	10♓21 42	13 11.5	17 16.3	15 28.3	0♓ 3.5	5 20.7	25 10.8	9 34.1	14 34.1	16 50.8
22 Su	13 59 10	1 36 32	17 24 14	24 34 5	13 8.0	17 26.8	16 33.5	0 48.4	5 29.8	25 12.1	9 33.7	14 34.0	16 49.2
23 M	14 3 7	2 35 4	1♈50 53	9♈14 4	13 1.8	17R 31.3	17 39.0	1 33.2	5 39.0	25 13.3	9 33.3	14 33.8	16 47.6
24 Tu	14 7 3	3 33 34	16 42 50	24 16 7	12 53.1	17 30.1	18 44.6	2 18.1	5 48.3	25 14.4	9 32.8	14 33.5	16 45.9
25 W	14 11 0	4 32 2	1♉52 43	9♉31 15	12 42.7	17 23.4	19 50.4	3 3.0	5 57.7	25 15.5	9 32.2	14 33.3	16 44.3
26 Th	14 14 57	5 30 29	17 10 17	24 48 21	12 31.6	17 11.3	20 56.3	3 47.8	6 7.3	25 16.4	9 31.7	14 33.0	16 42.7
27 F	14 18 53	6 28 54	2♊24 5	9♊56 11	12 21.3	16 54.3	22 2.4	4 32.7	6 16.9	25 17.2	9 31.0	14 32.7	16 41.0
28 Sa	14 22 50	7 27 17	17 23 34	24 45 22	12 12.8	16 32.7	23 8.7	5 17.5	6 26.7	25 18.0	9 30.3	14 32.3	16 39.4
29 Su	14 26 46	8 25 38	2♋ 0 55	9♋ 9 49	12 6.9	16 7.0	24 15.1	6 2.4	6 36.5	25 18.6	9 29.6	14 31.9	16 37.7
30 M	14 30 43	9 23 56	16 11 49	23 6 56	12 3.7	15 37.7	25 21.6	6 47.2	6 46.5	25 19.1	9 28.8	14 31.5	16 36.0

Astro Data	Dy Hr Mn
☽0S	11 15:15
☿0N	21 7:49
☽0N	25 22:29
♃□♇	28 11:15
☽0S	7 21:34
♅ R	13 22:21
♆ R	16 12:56
☽0N	22 8:42
☿ R	23 6:54

Planet Ingress	Dy Hr Mn
☿ ♓	3 17:14
♀ ♒	3 17:52
♂ ♒	11 15:54
☉ ♈	20 21:19
☿ ♈	20 0:04
☿ ♉	4 7:35
♀ ♓	6 9:13
☉ ♉	20 8:27
♂ ♓	20 22:09

Last Aspect Dy Hr Mn		☽ Ingress Dy Hr Mn
28 22:41	♀ □	♉ 1 1:43
3 2:55	♀ △	♊ 3 3:37
4 2:05	☉ □	♋ 5 7:02
7 6:33	♂ ☍	♌ 7 12:24
8 20:50	♇ □	♍ 9 19:47
11 15:39	♄ △	♎ 12 5:09
14 2:54	♄ □	♏ 14 16:25
16 20:51	☉ △	♐ 17 4:56
19 15:39	☿ □	♑ 19 17:01
21 14:53	♄ ☌	♒ 22 2:31
23 10:16	♇ □	♓ 24 8:09
26 0:33	♄ ⚹	♈ 26 10:15
28 1:09	♄ □	♉ 28 10:26
30 1:26	♄ △	♊ 30 10:42

Last Aspect Dy Hr Mn		☽ Ingress Dy Hr Mn
1 3:48	♀ △	♋ 1 12:50
3 15:44	☿ □	♌ 3 17:50
6 1:02	♀ ☍	♍ 6 1:42
8 1:27	♄ △	♎ 8 11:44
10 12:59	♄ □	♏ 10 23:18
13 1:34	♄ ⚹	♐ 13 11:48
15 16:24	♂ ⚹	♑ 16 0:15
18 7:03	☉ □	♒ 18 10:53
20 17:42	♂ ☌	♓ 20 17:57
22 13:04	♄ ⚹	♈ 22 20:58
24 13:33	♄ □	♉ 24 21:03
26 12:45	♄ △	♊ 26 20:12
28 10:08	♀ □	♋ 28 20:39

☽ Phases & Eclipses Dy Hr Mn	
4 2:05	☽ 13♊14
11 10:59	○ 20♍37
19 14:30	☽ 28♐43
26 19:48	● 5♈53
2 10:24	☽ 12♋25
10 3:18	○ 20♎00
18 7:03	☽ 27♑59
25 4:27	● 4♉43

Astro Data

1 MARCH 1990
Julian Day # 32932
Delta T 56.9 sec
SVP 05♓23'37"
Obliquity 23°26'33"
⚷ Chiron 10♋42.9R
☽ Mean ☊ 15♒20.2

1 APRIL 1990
Julian Day # 32963
Delta T 57.0 sec
SVP 05♓23'33"
Obliquity 23°26'33"
⚷ Chiron 10♋46.4
☽ Mean ☊ 13♒41.7

LONGITUDE MAY 1990

Day	Sid.Time	☉	0 hr ☽	Noon ☽	True ☊	☿	♀	♂	♃	♄	♅	♆	♇
1 Tu	14 34 39	10♉22 13	29♋55 18	6♌37 11	12♒ 2.4	15♉ 5.3	26♓28.3	7♓32.0	6♋56.5	25♑19.6	9♑28.0	14♑31.1	16♏34.4
2 W	14 38 36	11 20 28	13♌12 59	19 43 9	12R 2.3	14R30.4	27 35.1	8 16.8	7 6.7	25 19.9	9R27.1	14R30.6	16R32.7
3 Th	14 42 32	12 18 40	26 8 9	2♍28 30	12 2.0	13 53.8	28 42.1	9 1.6	7 17.0	25 20.2	9 26.2	14 30.1	16 31.0
4 F	14 46 29	13 16 51	8♍44 44	14 57 20	12 0.4	13 16.1	29 49.2	9 46.3	7 27.3	25R20.3	9 25.3	14 29.5	16 29.3
5 Sa	14 50 26	14 14 59	21 6 48	27 13 34	11 56.5	12 38.0	0♈56.4	10 31.1	7 37.7	25 20.3	9 24.3	14 28.9	16 27.7
6 Su	14 54 22	15 13 6	3♎18 2	9♎20 35	11 49.8	12 0.1	2 3.7	11 15.8	7 48.3	25 20.3	9 23.2	14 28.3	16 26.0
7 M	14 58 19	16 11 10	15 21 32	21 21 11	11 40.3	11 23.2	3 11.2	12 0.5	7 58.9	25 20.1	9 22.1	14 27.7	16 24.3
8 Tu	15 2 15	17 9 13	27 19 46	3♏17 31	11 28.3	10 47.8	4 18.7	12 45.2	8 9.6	25 19.9	9 21.0	14 27.0	16 22.6
9 W	15 6 12	18 7 14	9♏14 38	15 11 16	11 14.8	10 14.6	5 26.4	13 29.9	8 20.4	25 19.5	9 19.8	14 26.3	16 20.9
10 Th	15 10 8	19 5 14	21 7 37	27 3 51	11 0.8	9 44.0	6 34.2	14 14.6	8 31.2	25 19.1	9 18.5	14 25.6	16 19.2
11 F	15 14 5	20 3 12	3♐ 0 7	8♐56 37	10 47.5	9 16.6	7 42.2	14 59.3	8 42.2	25 18.6	9 17.3	14 24.9	16 17.5
12 Sa	15 18 1	21 1 9	14 53 33	20 51 11	10 35.8	8 52.6	8 50.2	15 43.9	8 53.2	25 17.9	9 16.0	14 24.1	16 15.9
13 Su	15 21 58	21 59 4	26 49 47	2♑49 40	10 26.6	8 32.6	9 58.3	16 28.6	9 4.4	25 17.2	9 14.6	14 23.3	16 14.2
14 M	15 25 55	22 56 58	8♑51 10	14 54 43	10 20.2	8 16.6	11 6.6	17 13.2	9 15.6	25 16.4	9 13.2	14 22.5	16 12.5
15 Tu	15 29 51	23 54 50	21 0 44	27 9 43	10 16.6	8 4.9	12 14.9	17 57.7	9 26.8	25 15.5	9 11.8	14 21.6	16 10.8
16 W	15 33 48	24 52 41	3♒22 10	9♒38 38	10D 15.2	7 57.7	13 23.3	18 42.3	9 38.2	25 14.4	9 10.3	14 20.7	16 9.2
17 Th	15 37 44	25 50 31	15 59 39	22 25 47	10R 15.1	7D 55.0	14 31.9	19 26.8	9 49.6	25 13.3	9 8.8	14 19.8	16 7.5
18 F	15 41 41	26 48 20	28 57 33	5♓35 27	10 15.2	7 56.9	15 40.5	20 11.4	10 1.1	25 12.1	9 7.2	14 18.9	16 5.9
19 Sa	15 45 37	27 46 8	12♓19 53	19 11 12	10 14.5	8 3.4	16 49.2	20 55.8	10 12.7	25 10.8	9 5.6	14 17.9	16 4.2
20 Su	15 49 34	28 43 54	26 9 34	3♈15 3	10 11.8	8 14.5	17 58.0	21 40.3	10 24.3	25 9.4	9 4.0	14 16.9	16 2.6
21 M	15 53 30	29 41 39	10♈27 29	17 46 31	10 6.8	8 30.0	19 6.9	22 24.7	10 36.0	25 8.0	9 2.3	14 15.9	16 1.0
22 Tu	15 57 27	0♊39 24	25 11 32	2♉41 45	9 59.5	8 50.0	20 15.9	23 9.1	10 47.8	25 6.4	9 0.6	14 14.9	15 59.3
23 W	16 1 24	1 37 7	10♉16 7	17 53 25	9 50.4	9 14.3	21 24.9	23 53.5	10 59.6	25 4.7	8 58.9	14 13.8	15 57.7
24 Th	16 5 20	2 34 49	25 32 19	3♊11 21	9 40.7	9 42.9	22 34.1	24 37.8	11 11.6	25 3.0	8 57.1	14 12.7	15 56.1
25 F	16 9 17	3 32 30	10♊49 7	18 24 13	9 31.4	10 15.5	23 43.3	25 22.1	11 23.5	25 1.1	8 55.3	14 11.6	15 54.5
26 Sa	16 13 13	4 30 10	25 55 25	3♋21 36	9 23.8	10 52.2	24 52.6	26 6.3	11 35.6	24 59.2	8 53.5	14 10.5	15 53.0
27 Su	16 17 10	5 27 48	10♋41 56	17 55 43	9 18.5	11 32.8	26 1.9	26 50.5	11 47.7	24 57.2	8 51.6	14 9.3	15 51.4
28 M	16 21 6	6 25 25	25 2 33	2♌ 2 14	9 15.6	12 17.2	27 11.3	27 34.7	11 59.8	24 55.1	8 49.7	14 8.2	15 49.8
29 Tu	16 25 3	7 23 1	8♌54 42	15 40 8	9D 14.8	13 5.2	28 20.8	28 18.8	12 12.0	24 52.9	8 47.8	14 7.0	15 48.3
30 W	16 29 0	8 20 35	22 18 48	28 51 6	9 15.2	13 56.8	29 30.4	29 2.8	12 24.3	24 50.6	8 45.8	14 5.7	15 46.8
31 Th	16 32 56	9 18 8	5♍17 30	11♍38 31	9R 15.8	14 51.9	0♉40.0	29 46.8	12 36.6	24 48.2	8 43.8	14 4.5	15 45.3

LONGITUDE JUNE 1990

Day	Sid.Time	☉	0 hr ☽	Noon ☽	True ☊	☿	♀	♂	♃	♄	♅	♆	♇
1 F	16 36 53	10♊15 39	17♍54 42	24♍ 6 38	9♒15.6	15♉50.3	1♉49.6	0♈30.8	12♋49.0	24♑45.8	8♑41.8	14♑ 3.2	15♏43.8
2 Sa	16 40 49	11 13 9	0♎14 53	6♎19 59	9R 13.7	16 52.1	2 59.4	1 14.7	13 1.4	24R43.2	8R39.8	14R 2.0	15R42.3
3 Su	16 44 46	12 10 37	12 22 28	18 22 51	9 9.6	17 57.1	4 9.2	1 58.6	13 13.9	24 40.6	8 37.7	14 0.7	15 40.8
4 M	16 48 42	13 8 5	24 21 35	0♏19 5	9 3.3	19 5.2	5 19.0	2 42.4	13 26.4	24 38.0	8 35.6	13 59.3	15 39.4
5 Tu	16 52 39	14 5 31	6♏15 45	12 11 54	8 55.0	20 16.4	6 28.9	3 26.2	13 38.9	24 35.2	8 33.5	13 58.0	15 37.9
6 W	16 56 35	15 2 56	18 7 52	24 3 55	8 45.4	21 30.7	7 38.9	4 9.9	13 51.5	24 32.4	8 31.3	13 56.7	15 36.5
7 Th	17 0 32	16 0 21	0♐ 0 17	5♐57 12	8 35.4	22 48.0	8 48.9	4 53.6	14 4.2	24 29.5	8 29.1	13 55.3	15 35.1
8 F	17 4 29	16 57 44	11 54 51	17 53 26	8 25.8	24 8.2	9 59.0	5 37.2	14 16.9	24 26.5	8 27.0	13 53.9	15 33.7
9 Sa	17 8 25	17 55 6	23 53 9	29 54 9	8 17.5	25 31.4	11 9.2	6 20.8	14 29.6	24 23.4	8 24.7	13 52.5	15 32.4
10 Su	17 12 22	18 52 28	5♑56 40	12♑ 0 54	8 11.1	26 57.4	12 19.4	7 4.3	14 42.4	24 20.3	8 22.5	13 51.1	15 31.0
11 M	17 16 18	19 49 49	18 7 5	24 15 28	8 7.0	28 26.4	13 29.7	7 47.7	14 55.2	24 17.1	8 20.3	13 49.7	15 29.7
12 Tu	17 20 15	20 47 9	0♒26 21	6♒40 3	8D 5.0	29 58.1	14 40.0	8 31.1	15 8.1	24 13.8	8 18.0	13 48.2	15 28.4
13 W	17 24 11	21 44 29	12 56 54	19 17 15	8 4.8	1♊32.7	15 50.4	9 14.4	15 21.0	24 10.5	8 15.7	13 46.7	15 27.2
14 Th	17 28 8	22 41 48	25 41 31	2♓10 3	8 5.7	3 10.1	17 0.9	9 57.7	15 33.9	24 7.1	8 13.4	13 45.3	15 25.9
15 F	17 32 4	23 39 7	8♓43 15	15 21 29	8 7.0	4 50.3	18 11.4	10 40.9	15 46.9	24 3.7	8 11.1	13 43.8	15 24.7
16 Sa	17 36 1	24 36 25	22 5 3	28 54 14	8R 7.8	6 33.3	19 21.9	11 24.0	15 59.9	24 0.2	8 8.7	13 42.3	15 23.5
17 Su	17 39 58	25 33 44	5♈49 13	12♈50 2	8 7.4	8 18.9	20 32.6	12 7.1	16 12.9	23 56.6	8 6.4	13 40.8	15 22.3
18 M	17 43 54	26 31 1	19 56 39	27 8 51	8 5.3	10 7.3	21 43.2	12 50.1	16 26.0	23 52.9	8 4.0	13 39.2	15 21.1
19 Tu	17 47 51	27 28 19	4♉26 15	11♉48 18	8 1.6	11 58.3	22 53.9	13 33.0	16 39.1	23 49.2	8 1.7	13 37.7	15 20.0
20 W	17 51 47	28 25 36	19 14 14	26 43 12	7 56.6	13 51.9	24 4.7	14 15.9	16 52.2	23 45.5	7 59.3	13 36.2	15 18.9
21 Th	17 55 44	29 22 54	4♊14 9	11♊45 56	7 51.0	15 48.0	25 15.5	14 58.6	17 5.3	23 41.7	7 56.9	13 34.6	15 17.8
22 F	17 59 40	0♋20 11	19 17 24	26 47 21	7 45.7	17 46.4	26 26.4	15 41.3	17 18.5	23 37.9	7 54.5	13 33.1	15 16.7
23 Sa	18 3 37	1 17 27	4♋14 38	11♋38 13	7 41.3	19 47.1	27 37.3	16 23.9	17 31.7	23 34.0	7 52.1	13 31.5	15 15.7
24 Su	18 7 33	2 14 43	18 57 9	26 10 42	7 38.5	21 49.8	28 48.3	17 6.5	17 45.0	23 30.0	7 49.7	13 29.9	15 14.7
25 M	18 11 30	3 11 59	3♌18 16	10♌19 28	7D 37.2	23 54.5	29 59.3	17 48.9	17 58.2	23 26.0	7 47.2	13 28.3	15 13.7
26 Tu	18 15 27	4 9 14	17 14 2	24 1 56	7 37.5	26 0.8	1♊10.4	18 31.2	18 11.5	23 22.0	7 44.8	13 26.7	15 12.7
27 W	18 19 23	5 6 29	0♍43 15	7♍18 12	7 38.7	28 8.5	2 21.5	19 13.5	18 24.8	23 17.9	7 42.4	13 25.1	15 11.8
28 Th	18 23 20	6 3 43	13 47 6	20 10 21	7 40.2	0♋17.5	3 32.6	19 55.6	18 38.1	23 13.8	7 40.0	13 23.5	15 10.9
29 F	18 27 16	7 0 56	26 28 25	2♎41 50	7R 41.5	2 27.3	4 43.8	20 37.7	18 51.4	23 9.6	7 37.5	13 21.9	15 10.0
30 Sa	18 31 13	7 58 9	8♎51 9	14 56 56	7 42.0	4 37.8	5 55.0	21 19.6	19 4.8	23 5.5	7 35.1	13 20.3	15 9.2

Astro Data	Planet Ingress	Last Aspect	☽ Ingress	Last Aspect	☽ Ingress	☽ Phases & Eclipses	Astro Data
Dy Hr Mn	Dy Hr Mn	Dy Hr Mn	Dy Hr Mn	Dy Hr Mn	Dy Hr Mn	Dy Hr Mn	1 MAY 1990
♄ R 4 22:43	♀ ♈ 4 3:52	30 17:21 ♀ △	♌ 1 0:08	1 13:14 ♄ △	♎ 1 23:31	1 20:18 ☽ 11♌11	Julian Day # 32993
☽0S 5 2:36	☉ ♊ 21 7:37	2 6:07 ♇ □	♍ 3 7:18	4 0:33 ♄ □	♏ 4 11:22	9 19:31 ○ 18♏54	Delta T 57.0 sec
♀0N 7 5:08	♀ ♉ 30 10:13	5 8:17 ♄ △	♎ 5 17:28	6 12:54 ♄ ✶	♐ 6 23:59	17 19:45 ☽ 26♒38	SVP 05♓23'30"
♃☍♅ 13 19:31	♂ ♈ 31 7:11	7 19:59 ♄ □	♏ 8 5:22	8 11:01 ☉ ☍	♑ 9 12:12	24 11:47 ● 3♊03	Obliquity 23°26'32"
☿ D 17 2:02		10 8:28 ♄ ✶	♐ 10 17:56	11 22:58 ☿ △	♒ 11 23:09	31 8:11 ☽ 9♍38	⚷ Chiron 12♋09.1
☽0N 19 17:09	☿ ♊ 12 0:29	12 1:48 ♂ □	♑ 13 6:21	13 17:57 ☉ △	♓ 14 8:00		☽ Mean ☊ 12♒06.4
	☉ ♋ 21 15:33	15 8:17 ♄ ☌	♒ 15 17:30	16 4:48 ☉ □	♈ 16 13:55	8 11:01 ○ 17♐24	
☽0S 1 7:52	♀ ♊ 25 0:14	17 19:45 ☉ □	♓ 18 1:54	18 11:44 ☉ ✶	♉ 18 16:43	16 4:48 ☽ 24♓48	1 JUNE 1990
♂0N 6 9:20	☿ ♋ 27 20:46	20 4:42 ☉ ✶	♈ 20 6:31	20 8:26 ♀ ☌	♊ 20 17:15	22 18:55 ● 1♋05	Julian Day # 33024
♃☍♆ 6 8:46		21 23:52 ♄ □	♉ 22 7:42	21 21:13 ☿ ☌	♋ 22 17:09	29 22:07 ☽ 7♎54	Delta T 57.1 sec
♃△♇ 13 10:27		23 23:14 ♄ △	♊ 24 7:00	24 17:53 ♀ ✶	♌ 24 18:25		SVP 05♓23'25"
☽0N 15 23:23		26 0:18 ♂ □	♋ 26 6:34	26 18:28 ☿ ✶	♍ 26 22:42		Obliquity 23°26'32"
☽0S 28 14:43		28 4:34 ♂ △	♌ 28 8:29	28 17:42 ♄ △	♎ 29 6:47		⚷ Chiron 14♋38.4
		29 12:13 ♇ □	♍ 30 14:08				☽ Mean ☊ 10♒27.9

JULY 1990 LONGITUDE

Day	Sid.Time	☉	0 hr ☽	Noon ☽	True ☊	☿	♀	♂	♃	♄	♅	♆	♇
1 Su	18 35 9	8♋55 22	20♎59 44	27♎ 0 7	7♒41.2	6♋48.6	7♊ 6.3	22♈ 1.5	19♋18.2	23♑ 1.2	7♑32.6	13♑18.7	15♏ 8.4
2 M	18 39 6	9 52 34	2♏58 39	8♏55 51	7R 39.3	8 59.4	8 17.6	22 43.2	19 31.5	22R 57.0	7R 30.2	13R 17.1	15R 7.6
3 Tu	18 43 2	10 49 46	14 52 12	20 48 12	7 36.2	11 10.1	9 28.9	23 24.9	19 44.9	22 52.7	7 27.8	13 15.5	15 6.8
4 W	18 46 59	11 46 58	26 44 16	2♐40 49	7 32.4	13 20.2	10 40.3	24 6.5	19 58.3	22 48.4	7 25.4	13 13.8	15 6.1
5 Th	18 50 56	12 44 9	8♐38 12	14 36 44	7 28.3	15 29.7	11 51.8	24 47.9	20 11.7	22 44.1	7 22.9	13 12.2	15 5.4
6 F	18 54 52	13 41 21	20 36 45	26 38 29	7 24.4	17 38.2	13 3.2	25 29.3	20 25.2	22 39.8	7 20.5	13 10.6	15 4.7
7 Sa	18 58 49	14 38 32	2♑42 10	8♑48 0	7 21.0	19 45.6	14 14.8	26 10.5	20 38.6	22 35.4	7 18.1	13 9.0	15 4.1
8 Su	19 2 45	15 35 43	14 56 11	21 6 53	7 18.6	21 51.7	15 26.4	26 51.7	20 52.0	22 31.0	7 15.7	13 7.4	15 3.5
9 M	19 6 42	16 32 55	27 20 13	3♒36 22	7D 17.3	23 56.4	16 38.0	27 32.7	21 5.5	22 26.6	7 13.3	13 5.7	15 2.9
10 Tu	19 10 38	17 30 6	9♒55 27	16 17 35	7 17.0	25 59.6	17 49.7	28 13.6	21 18.9	22 22.2	7 10.9	13 4.1	15 2.4
11 W	19 14 35	18 27 18	22 42 56	29 11 37	7 17.6	28 1.1	19 1.4	28 54.4	21 32.4	22 17.8	7 8.6	13 2.5	15 1.9
12 Th	19 18 31	19 24 30	5♓43 46	12♓19 32	7 18.7	0♌ 1.0	20 13.1	29 35.1	21 45.8	22 13.4	7 6.2	13 0.9	15 1.4
13 F	19 22 28	20 21 43	18 59 1	25 42 21	7 20.0	1 59.0	21 24.9	0♉15.7	21 59.3	22 8.9	7 3.8	12 59.3	15 0.9
14 Sa	19 26 25	21 18 56	2♈29 38	9♈20 54	7 21.1	3 55.3	22 36.8	0 56.1	22 12.8	22 4.5	7 1.5	12 57.7	15 0.5
15 Su	19 30 21	22 16 9	16 16 10	23 15 25	7R 21.7	5 49.8	23 48.7	1 36.4	22 26.2	22 0.0	6 59.2	12 56.1	15 0.1
16 M	19 34 18	23 13 23	0♉18 32	7♉25 18	7 21.7	7 42.5	25 0.7	2 16.6	22 39.7	21 55.6	6 56.9	12 54.5	14 59.8
17 Tu	19 38 14	24 10 38	14 35 29	21 48 40	7 21.0	9 33.3	26 12.7	2 56.7	22 53.2	21 51.2	6 54.6	12 52.9	14 59.4
18 W	19 42 11	25 7 54	29 4 24	6♊22 7	7 20.0	11 22.3	27 24.7	3 36.6	23 6.6	21 46.7	6 52.3	12 51.3	14 59.2
19 Th	19 46 7	26 5 10	13♊41 9	21 0 47	7 18.6	13 9.4	28 36.8	4 16.4	23 20.1	21 42.3	6 50.0	12 49.7	14 58.9
20 F	19 50 4	27 2 27	28 20 14	5♋38 43	7 17.4	14 54.6	29 48.9	4 56.0	23 33.5	21 37.9	6 47.8	12 48.2	14 58.7
21 Sa	19 54 1	27 59 45	12♋55 23	20 9 29	7 16.5	16 38.1	1♋ 1.1	5 35.5	23 47.0	21 33.5	6 45.6	12 46.6	14 58.5
22 Su	19 57 57	28 57 3	27 20 17	4♌27 6	7D 16.0	18 19.7	2 13.3	6 14.8	24 0.4	21 29.1	6 43.4	12 45.1	14 58.4
23 M	20 1 54	29 54 22	11♌29 23	18 26 41	7 15.9	19 59.4	3 25.6	6 54.0	24 13.9	21 24.7	6 41.2	12 43.5	14 58.2
24 Tu	20 5 50	0♌51 41	25 18 39	2♍ 5 4	7 16.1	21 37.3	4 37.9	7 33.0	24 27.3	21 20.3	6 39.0	12 42.0	14 58.2
25 W	20 9 47	1 49 1	8♍45 50	15 20 58	7 16.6	23 13.4	5 50.3	8 11.9	24 40.7	21 16.0	6 36.9	12 40.5	14 58.1
26 Th	20 13 43	2 46 21	21 50 36	28 14 56	7 17.1	24 47.7	7 2.6	8 50.6	24 54.1	21 11.7	6 34.8	12 39.0	14D 58.1
27 F	20 17 40	3 43 41	4♎34 17	10♎49 1	7 17.5	26 20.1	8 15.1	9 29.1	25 7.5	21 7.4	6 32.7	12 37.5	14 58.1
28 Sa	20 21 36	4 41 2	16 59 35	23 6 28	7 17.8	27 50.7	9 27.5	10 7.4	25 20.8	21 3.1	6 30.6	12 36.0	14 58.1
29 Su	20 25 33	5 38 24	29 10 11	5♏11 16	7R 17.9	29 19.4	10 40.0	10 45.6	25 34.2	20 58.9	6 28.6	12 34.6	14 58.2
30 M	20 29 30	6 35 45	11♏10 18	17 7 50	7D 17.9	0♍46.2	11 52.6	11 23.6	25 47.5	20 54.7	6 26.6	12 33.1	14 58.3
31 Tu	20 33 26	7 33 8	23 4 28	29 0 44	7 17.9	2 11.1	13 5.2	12 1.5	26 0.8	20 50.5	6 24.6	12 31.7	14 58.5

AUGUST 1990 LONGITUDE

Day	Sid.Time	☉	0 hr ☽	Noon ☽	True ☊	☿	♀	♂	♃	♄	♅	♆	♇
1 W	20 37 23	8♌30 31	4♐57 12	10♐54 23	7♒17.9	3♍34.1	14♋17.8	12♉39.1	26♋14.1	20♑46.4	6♑22.7	12♑30.2	14♏58.7
2 Th	20 41 19	9 27 55	16 52 48	22 52 53	7 18.1	4 55.1	15 30.5	13 16.6	26 27.4	20R 42.3	6R 20.8	12R 28.8	14 58.9
3 F	20 45 16	10 25 19	28 55 6	4♑59 49	7 18.4	6 14.1	16 43.2	13 53.9	26 40.6	20 38.2	6 18.9	12 27.4	14 59.2
4 Sa	20 49 12	11 22 44	11♑ 7 24	17 18 8	7 18.8	7 31.1	17 55.9	14 31.0	26 53.9	20 34.2	6 17.1	12 26.1	14 59.5
5 Su	20 53 9	12 20 10	23 32 17	29 50 2	7 19.1	8 45.9	19 8.7	15 7.9	27 7.1	20 30.3	6 15.2	12 24.7	14 59.8
6 M	20 57 5	13 17 37	6♒11 31	12♒36 51	7R 19.3	9 58.6	20 21.6	15 44.7	27 20.2	20 26.3	6 13.5	12 23.4	15 0.1
7 Tu	21 1 2	14 15 5	19 6 2	25 39 4	7 19.2	11 9.1	21 34.5	16 21.2	27 33.4	20 22.5	6 11.7	12 22.1	15 0.5
8 W	21 4 59	15 12 33	2♓15 54	8♓56 24	7 18.6	12 17.2	22 47.4	16 57.5	27 46.5	20 18.6	6 10.0	12 20.8	15 1.0
9 Th	21 8 55	16 10 3	15 40 27	22 27 51	7 17.8	13 22.9	24 0.3	17 33.6	27 59.6	20 14.9	6 8.3	12 19.5	15 1.4
10 F	21 12 52	17 7 34	29 18 24	6♈11 52	7 16.6	14 26.2	25 13.4	18 9.6	28 12.7	20 11.1	6 6.7	12 18.2	15 1.9
11 Sa	21 16 48	18 5 6	13♈ 8 1	20 6 35	7 15.4	15 26.8	26 26.4	18 45.3	28 25.7	20 7.5	6 5.0	12 17.0	15 2.4
12 Su	21 20 45	19 2 40	27 7 18	4♉ 9 54	7 14.3	16 24.7	27 39.5	19 20.7	28 38.7	20 3.9	6 3.5	12 15.7	15 3.0
13 M	21 24 41	20 0 15	11♉14 7	18 19 39	7D 13.7	17 19.8	28 52.7	19 56.0	28 51.7	20 0.3	6 1.9	12 14.5	15 3.6
14 Tu	21 28 38	20 57 51	25 26 14	2♊33 33	7 13.6	18 11.9	0♌ 5.9	20 31.0	29 4.6	19 56.8	6 0.4	12 13.3	15 4.2
15 W	21 32 34	21 55 30	9♊41 19	16 49 11	7 14.1	19 0.8	1 19.1	21 5.8	29 17.5	19 53.4	5 59.0	12 12.2	15 4.9
16 Th	21 36 31	22 53 9	23 56 50	1♋ 3 54	7 15.1	19 46.4	2 32.4	21 40.4	29 30.4	19 50.0	5 57.6	12 11.0	15 5.6
17 F	21 40 28	23 50 51	8♋10 0	15 14 45	7 16.2	20 28.5	3 45.7	22 14.6	29 43.2	19 46.7	5 56.2	12 9.9	15 6.3
18 Sa	21 44 24	24 48 34	22 17 45	29 18 35	7 17.2	21 6.9	4 59.1	22 48.7	29 56.0	19 43.5	5 54.9	12 8.8	15 7.1
19 Su	21 48 21	25 46 18	6♌16 52	13♌12 11	7R 17.7	21 41.4	6 12.5	23 22.5	0♌ 8.8	19 40.3	5 53.6	12 7.8	15 7.9
20 M	21 52 17	26 44 4	20 4 11	26 52 30	7 17.3	22 11.7	7 25.9	23 56.0	0 21.5	19 37.2	5 52.3	12 6.7	15 8.7
21 Tu	21 56 14	27 41 50	3♍36 53	10♍17 4	7 15.9	22 37.7	8 39.4	24 29.2	0 34.1	19 34.2	5 51.1	12 5.7	15 9.6
22 W	22 0 10	28 39 39	16 52 54	23 24 16	7 13.4	22 59.1	9 52.9	25 2.2	0 46.7	19 31.3	5 49.9	12 4.7	15 10.5
23 Th	22 4 7	29 37 28	29 51 10	6♎13 37	7 10.2	23 15.6	11 6.5	25 34.9	0 59.3	19 28.4	5 48.8	12 3.7	15 11.4
24 F	22 8 3	0♍35 19	12♎31 47	18 45 52	7 6.6	23 27.0	12 20.1	26 7.2	1 11.8	19 25.6	5 47.7	12 2.8	15 12.3
25 Sa	22 12 0	1 33 11	24 56 7	1♏ 2 55	7 3.1	23R 33.1	13 33.7	26 39.3	1 24.3	19 22.9	5 46.7	12 1.9	15 13.3
26 Su	22 15 57	2 31 5	7♏ 6 38	13 7 45	7 0.1	23 33.6	14 47.4	27 11.1	1 36.7	19 20.2	5 45.7	12 1.0	15 14.4
27 M	22 19 53	3 29 0	19 6 46	25 4 12	6 58.0	23 28.3	16 1.1	27 42.6	1 49.1	19 17.7	5 44.8	12 0.1	15 15.4
28 Tu	22 23 50	4 26 56	1♐ 0 38	6♐56 40	6D 57.1	23 17.1	17 14.9	28 13.8	2 1.4	19 15.2	5 43.9	11 59.3	15 16.5
29 W	22 27 46	5 24 53	12 52 53	18 49 54	6 57.3	22 59.9	18 28.6	28 44.7	2 13.7	19 12.8	5 43.0	11 58.5	15 17.6
30 Th	22 31 43	6 22 52	24 48 20	0♑48 46	6 58.4	22 36.5	19 42.5	29 15.2	2 25.9	19 10.5	5 42.2	11 57.7	15 18.8
31 F	22 35 39	7 20 52	6♑51 46	12 57 54	7 0.1	22 7.2	20 56.3	29 45.4	2 38.0	19 8.3	5 41.5	11 56.9	15 20.0

Astro Data	Dy Hr Mn
☽0N	13 4:29
♃☍♄	13 12:54
☽0S	25 23:17
♇ D	26 1:25
☽0N	9 10:15
☿0S	20 10:17
☽0S	22 8:31
☿ R	25 14:08

Planet Ingress	Dy Hr Mn
☿ ♌	11 23:48
♂ ♉	12 14:44
♀ ♋	20 3:41
☉ ♌	23 2:22
☿ ♍	29 11:10
♀ ♌	13 22:05
♃ ♌	18 7:30
☉ ♍	23 9:21
♂ ♊	31 11:40

Last Aspect Dy Hr Mn		☽ Ingress Dy Hr Mn
1 4:01	♄ □	♏ 1 18:01
3 16:06	♄ ⚹	♐ 4 6:35
6 10:18	♂ △	♑ 6 18:39
9 0:25	♂ □	♒ 9 5:07
11 12:06	♂ ⚹	♓ 11 13:29
13 5:38	♄ ⚹	♈ 13 19:36
15 14:09	♀ ⚹	♉ 15 23:29
17 17:02	☉ ⚹	♊ 18 1:32
20 2:39	♀ ☌	♋ 20 2:44
22 2:54	☉ ☌	♌ 22 4:29
23 16:40	☿ ☌	♍ 24 8:17
26 5:49	♃ ⚹	♎ 26 15:18
29 0:21	☿ ⚹	♏ 29 1:39
31 6:03	♃ △	♐ 31 14:00

Last Aspect Dy Hr Mn		☽ Ingress Dy Hr Mn
1 7:48	☉ △	♑ 3 2:09
5 6:57	♃ ☍	♒ 5 12:19
6 18:41	♂ □	♓ 7 19:54
9 22:03	♃ △	♈ 10 1:13
12 2:38	♃ □	♉ 12 4:55
14 6:14	♃ ⚹	♊ 14 7:41
15 22:05	☉ ⚹	♋ 16 10:12
18 0:55	♂ ⚹	♌ 18 13:11
20 12:39	☉ ☌	♍ 20 17:33
22 15:41	♂ △	♎ 23 0:17
24 13:14	♄ □	♏ 25 9:56
27 18:07	♂ ☍	♐ 27 21:57
29 19:45	☿ □	♑ 30 10:23

☽ Phases & Eclipses Dy Hr Mn	
8 1:23	○ 15♑39
15 11:04	☽ 22♈43
22 2:54	● 29♋04
22 3:02:08	•T 2'33"
29 14:01	☽ 6♏12
6 14:19	○ 13♒52
6 14:12	☍P 0.676
13 15:54	☽ 20♉38
20 12:39	● 27♌15
28 7:34	☽ 4♐45

Astro Data

1 JULY 1990
Julian Day # 33054
Delta T 57.1 sec
SVP 05♓23'19"
Obliquity 23°26'31"
⚷ Chiron 17♋39.9
☽ Mean ☊ 8♒52.6

1 AUGUST 1990
Julian Day # 33085
Delta T 57.2 sec
SVP 05♓23'14"
Obliquity 23°26'31"
⚷ Chiron 20♋58.5
☽ Mean ☊ 7♒14.1

LONGITUDE — SEPTEMBER 1990

Day	Sid.Time	☉	0 hr ☽	Noon ☽	True ☊	☿	♀	♂	♃	♄	♅	♆	♇
1 Sa	22 39 36	8♍18 53	19♑ 7 40	25♑21 31	7♒ 1.7	21♍31.9	22♌10.2	0♊15.3	2♌50.1	19♑ 6.1	5♑40.8	11♑56.2	15♏21.2
2 Su	22 43 32	9 16 56	1♒39 50	8♒ 2 56	7R 2.7	20R51.1	23 24.1	0 44.9	3 2.1	19R 4.1	5R40.1	11R55.5	15 22.4
3 M	22 47 29	10 15 0	14 31 4	21 4 23	7 2.6	20 5.2	24 38.1	1 14.1	3 14.1	19 2.1	5 39.5	11 54.8	15 23.7
4 Tu	22 51 26	11 13 6	27 42 54	4♓26 33	7 1.0	19 14.7	25 52.1	1 42.9	3 26.0	19 0.2	5 39.0	11 54.2	15 25.0
5 W	22 55 22	12 11 13	11♓15 9	18 8 26	6 57.7	18 20.5	27 6.1	2 11.4	3 37.8	18 58.4	5 38.4	11 53.6	15 26.3
6 Th	22 59 19	13 9 22	25 5 59	2♈ 7 20	6 53.0	17 23.4	28 20.1	2 39.5	3 49.6	18 56.7	5 38.0	11 53.0	15 27.7
7 F	23 3 15	14 7 33	9♈11 55	16 19 6	6 47.4	16 24.6	29 34.2	3 7.3	4 1.3	18 55.1	5 37.6	11 52.4	15 29.1
8 Sa	23 7 12	15 5 46	23 28 16	0♉38 44	6 41.6	15 25.3	0♍48.4	3 34.6	4 12.9	18 53.6	5 37.2	11 51.9	15 30.5
9 Su	23 11 8	16 4 0	7♉49 52	15 1 5	6 36.4	14 26.8	2 2.5	4 1.6	4 24.5	18 52.2	5 36.9	11 51.4	15 31.9
10 M	23 15 5	17 2 17	22 11 48	29 21 33	6 32.5	13 30.3	3 16.7	4 28.2	4 36.0	18 50.8	5 36.6	11 51.0	15 33.4
11 Tu	23 19 1	18 0 36	6♊29 57	13♊36 38	6D 30.2	12 37.4	4 31.0	4 54.3	4 47.4	18 49.6	5 36.4	11 50.5	15 34.9
12 W	23 22 58	18 58 57	20 41 22	27 43 57	6 29.6	11 49.3	5 45.2	5 20.1	4 58.8	18 48.5	5 36.2	11 50.1	15 36.4
13 Th	23 26 54	19 57 20	4♋44 15	11♋42 11	6 30.4	11 7.1	6 59.6	5 45.4	5 10.1	18 47.4	5 36.1	11 49.8	15 38.0
14 F	23 30 51	20 55 46	18 37 40	25 30 40	6 31.6	10 32.0	8 13.9	6 10.2	5 21.3	18 46.5	5D 36.1	11 49.4	15 39.6
15 Sa	23 34 48	21 54 13	2♌21 9	9♌ 9 2	6R 32.5	10 4.7	9 28.3	6 34.6	5 32.4	18 45.6	5 36.0	11 49.1	15 41.2
16 Su	23 38 44	22 52 43	15 54 18	22 36 50	6 32.2	9 46.1	10 42.7	6 58.5	5 43.4	18 44.8	5 36.1	11 48.9	15 42.8
17 M	23 42 41	23 51 14	29 16 35	5♍53 25	6 29.9	9D 36.6	11 57.1	7 22.0	5 54.4	18 44.2	5 36.2	11 48.6	15 44.5
18 Tu	23 46 37	24 49 47	12♍27 15	18 57 57	6 25.4	9 36.6	13 11.6	7 44.9	6 5.3	18 43.6	5 36.3	11 48.4	15 46.2
19 W	23 50 34	25 48 23	25 25 26	1♎49 37	6 18.6	9 46.1	14 26.1	8 7.4	6 16.1	18 43.1	5 36.5	11 48.2	15 47.9
20 Th	23 54 30	26 47 0	8♎10 27	14 27 54	6 10.1	10 5.3	15 40.6	8 29.3	6 26.8	18 42.8	5 36.7	11 48.1	15 49.6
21 F	23 58 27	27 45 39	20 42 2	26 52 54	6 0.6	10 33.7	16 55.1	8 50.7	6 37.4	18 42.5	5 37.0	11 48.0	15 51.4
22 Sa	0 2 23	28 44 20	3♏ 0 39	9♏ 5 30	5 50.9	11 11.2	18 9.7	9 11.6	6 47.9	18 42.3	5 37.4	11 47.9	15 53.2
23 Su	0 6 20	29 43 3	15 7 43	21 7 36	5 42.1	11 57.4	19 24.3	9 32.0	6 58.3	18D 42.3	5 37.8	11D 47.9	15 55.0
24 M	0 10 17	0♎41 48	27 5 33	3♐ 2 1	5 35.0	12 51.6	20 38.9	9 51.7	7 8.6	18 42.3	5 38.2	11 47.9	15 56.8
25 Tu	0 14 13	1 40 34	8♐57 29	14 52 31	5 30.0	13 53.4	21 53.6	10 11.0	7 18.9	18 42.4	5 38.7	11 47.9	15 58.7
26 W	0 18 10	2 39 23	20 47 39	26 43 32	5 27.1	15 2.1	23 8.3	10 29.6	7 29.0	18 42.6	5 39.3	11 47.9	16 0.6
27 Th	0 22 6	3 38 13	2♑40 48	8♑40 7	5D 26.3	16 17.0	24 23.0	10 47.7	7 39.1	18 43.0	5 39.9	11 48.0	16 2.5
28 F	0 26 3	4 37 4	14 42 7	20 47 29	5 26.7	17 37.4	25 37.7	11 5.2	7 49.0	18 43.4	5 40.5	11 48.2	16 4.4
29 Sa	0 29 59	5 35 58	26 56 51	3♒10 50	5R 27.5	19 2.7	26 52.4	11 22.0	7 58.8	18 43.9	5 41.2	11 48.3	16 6.4
30 Su	0 33 56	6 34 53	9♒30 0	15 54 50	5 27.6	20 32.2	28 7.2	11 38.3	8 8.6	18 44.6	5 42.0	11 48.5	16 8.3

LONGITUDE — OCTOBER 1990

Day	Sid.Time	☉	0 hr ☽	Noon ☽	True ☊	☿	♀	♂	♃	♄	♅	♆	♇
1 M	0 37 52	7♎33 50	22♒25 45	29♒ 3 2	5♒26.3	22♍ 5.4	29♍21.9	11♊53.9	8♌18.2	18♑45.3	5♑42.8	11♑48.7	16♏10.3
2 Tu	0 41 49	8 32 48	5♓46 53	12♓37 19	5R 22.7	23 41.6	0♎36.7	12 8.9	8 27.7	18 46.1	5 43.6	11 49.0	16 12.3
3 W	0 45 46	9 31 49	19 34 10	26 37 9	5 16.5	25 20.4	1 51.6	12 23.2	8 37.1	18 47.0	5 44.5	11 49.3	16 14.4
4 Th	0 49 42	10 30 51	3♈45 46	10♈59 21	5 8.1	27 1.1	3 6.4	12 36.9	8 46.4	18 48.0	5 45.5	11 49.6	16 16.4
5 F	0 53 39	11 29 55	18 17 6	25 38 4	4 58.2	28 43.5	4 21.2	12 49.8	8 55.6	18 49.2	5 46.5	11 50.0	16 18.5
6 Sa	0 57 35	12 29 2	3♉ 1 13	10♉25 31	4 47.8	0♎27.2	5 36.1	13 2.1	9 4.7	18 50.4	5 47.6	11 50.3	16 20.6
7 Su	1 1 32	13 28 11	17 49 53	25 13 20	4 38.2	2 11.7	6 51.0	13 13.7	9 13.7	18 51.7	5 48.7	11 50.8	16 22.7
8 M	1 5 28	14 27 22	2♊34 55	9♊53 52	4 30.4	3 56.9	8 5.9	13 24.6	9 22.5	18 53.1	5 49.8	11 51.2	16 24.8
9 Tu	1 9 25	15 26 35	17 9 32	24 21 25	4 25.2	5 42.5	9 20.9	13 34.7	9 31.2	18 54.6	5 51.0	11 51.7	16 26.9
10 W	1 13 21	16 25 50	1♋29 10	8♋32 37	4 22.4	7 28.2	10 35.8	13 44.1	9 39.8	18 56.2	5 52.3	11 52.2	16 29.1
11 Th	1 17 18	17 25 8	15 31 39	22 26 20	4D 21.6	9 14.0	11 50.8	13 52.7	9 48.3	18 57.9	5 53.6	11 52.8	16 31.2
12 F	1 21 15	18 24 29	29 16 45	6♌ 3 5	4R 21.7	10 59.7	13 5.8	14 0.5	9 56.7	18 59.7	5 54.9	11 53.4	16 33.4
13 Sa	1 25 11	19 23 51	12♌45 33	19 24 20	4 21.6	12 45.1	14 20.9	14 7.5	10 4.9	19 1.6	5 56.3	11 54.0	16 35.6
14 Su	1 29 8	20 23 16	25 59 42	2♍31 49	4 19.9	14 30.1	15 35.9	14 13.8	10 13.0	19 3.6	5 57.8	11 54.6	16 37.9
15 M	1 33 4	21 22 43	9♍ 0 54	15 27 6	4 15.7	16 14.8	16 50.9	14 19.2	10 21.0	19 5.7	5 59.3	11 55.3	16 40.1
16 Tu	1 37 1	22 22 12	21 50 32	28 11 18	4 8.5	17 59.0	18 6.0	14 23.7	10 28.8	19 7.9	6 0.8	11 56.0	16 42.3
17 W	1 40 57	23 21 44	4♎29 29	10♎45 8	3 58.4	19 42.7	19 21.1	14 27.5	10 36.5	19 10.2	6 2.4	11 56.8	16 44.6
18 Th	1 44 54	24 21 17	16 58 17	23 8 58	3 45.9	21 25.8	20 36.2	14 30.3	10 44.1	19 12.6	6 4.1	11 57.6	16 46.9
19 F	1 48 50	25 20 53	29 17 15	5♏23 10	3 32.0	23 8.4	21 51.3	14 32.3	10 51.5	19 15.0	6 5.7	11 58.4	16 49.1
20 Sa	1 52 47	26 20 31	11♏26 50	17 28 21	3 17.7	24 50.3	23 6.4	14R 33.5	10 58.8	19 17.6	6 7.5	11 59.2	16 51.4
21 Su	1 56 44	27 20 10	23 27 55	29 25 42	3 4.4	26 31.7	24 21.6	14 33.8	11 5.9	19 20.2	6 9.3	12 0.1	16 53.7
22 M	2 0 40	28 19 52	5♐22 0	11♐17 8	2 53.1	28 12.5	25 36.7	14 33.2	11 12.9	19 23.0	6 11.1	12 1.0	16 56.1
23 Tu	2 4 37	29 19 35	17 11 28	23 5 26	2 44.4	29 52.7	26 51.9	14 31.7	11 19.8	19 25.8	6 13.0	12 2.0	16 58.4
24 W	2 8 33	0♏19 20	28 59 32	4♑54 16	2 38.7	1♏32.3	28 7.1	14 29.3	11 26.5	19 28.8	6 14.9	12 2.9	17 0.7
25 Th	2 12 30	1 19 7	10♑50 15	16 48 5	2 35.6	3 11.3	29 22.2	14 26.0	11 33.1	19 31.8	6 16.8	12 3.9	17 3.1
26 F	2 16 26	2 18 56	22 48 25	28 51 56	2 34.5	4 49.7	0♏37.4	14 21.9	11 39.5	19 34.9	6 18.8	12 5.0	17 5.4
27 Sa	2 20 23	3 18 46	4♒59 20	11♒11 17	2 34.4	6 27.6	1 52.6	14 16.8	11 45.7	19 38.1	6 20.9	12 6.1	17 7.8
28 Su	2 24 19	4 18 38	17 28 26	23 51 27	2 34.1	8 4.9	3 7.8	14 10.9	11 51.8	19 41.4	6 23.0	12 7.1	17 10.2
29 M	2 28 16	5 18 32	0♓20 52	6♓57 11	2 32.4	9 41.7	4 23.0	14 4.1	11 57.8	19 44.7	6 25.1	12 8.3	17 12.5
30 Tu	2 32 13	6 18 27	13 40 45	20 31 48	2 28.5	11 18.0	5 38.2	13 56.4	12 3.5	19 48.2	6 27.3	12 9.4	17 14.9
31 W	2 36 9	7 18 24	27 30 22	4♈36 18	2 21.9	12 53.8	6 53.5	13 47.8	12 9.2	19 51.7	6 29.5	12 10.6	17 17.3

Astro Data	Dy Hr Mn
☿0N	3 8:08
☽0N	5 17:54
♅ D	14 18:29
♃⚻♅	15 7:55
☿ D	17 12:06
☽0S	18 16:51
♄ D	23 5:11
♆ D	23 18:37
☽0N	3 3:21
♀0S	4 3:38
☿0S	8 4:34
☽0S	15 23:15
♂ R	20 19:30
☽0N	30 13:12

Planet Ingress	Dy Hr Mn
♀ ♍	7 8:21
☉ ♎	23 6:56
♀ ♎	1 12:13
☿ ♎	5 17:44
☉ ♏	23 16:14
☿ ♏	23 1:46
♀ ♏	25 12:03
♃⚻♆	31 8:06

Last Aspect Dy Hr Mn	☽ Ingress Dy Hr Mn
1 4:25 ☿ △	♒ 1 20:51
3 20:20 ♀ ☍	♓ 4 4:06
5 13:25 ♄ ⚹	♈ 6 8:23
7 16:20 ♄ □	♉ 8 10:55
9 18:24 ♄ △	♊ 10 13:05
11 20:53 ☉ □	♋ 12 15:53
14 4:19 ☉ ⚹	♌ 14 19:52
15 23:40 ♇ □	♍ 17 1:19
19 0:46 ☉ ☌	♎ 19 8:34
20 20:09 ♄ □	♏ 21 18:06
23 9:32 ♀ ⚹	♐ 24 5:52
26 5:18 ♀ □	♑ 26 18:36
28 23:50 ♀ △	♒ 29 5:54

Last Aspect Dy Hr Mn	☽ Ingress Dy Hr Mn
30 12:27 ♇ □	♓ 1 13:42
3 11:09 ☿ ☍	♈ 3 17:42
5 0:53 ♄ □	♉ 5 19:06
7 1:40 ♄ △	♊ 7 19:47
8 20:57 ☉ △	♋ 9 21:29
11 5:58 ♄ ☍	♌ 12 1:16
13 12:57 ☉ ⚹	♍ 14 7:21
15 18:53 ♄ △	♎ 16 15:26
18 15:37 ☉ ☌	♏ 19 1:24
20 15:42 ♄ ⚹	♐ 21 13:09
23 22:01 ♀ ⚹	♑ 24 2:03
25 17:32 ♄ ☌	♒ 26 14:14
27 23:25 ♇ □	♓ 28 23:22
30 10:47 ♄ ⚹	♈ 31 4:14

☽ Phases & Eclipses Dy Hr Mn	
5 1:46	○ 12♓15
11 20:53	☽ 18♊51
19 0:46	● 25♍50
27 2:06	☽ 3♑43
4 12:02	○ 11♈00
11 3:31	☽ 17♋34
18 15:37	● 25♎00
26 20:26	☽ 3♒10

Astro Data

1 SEPTEMBER 1990
Julian Day # 33116
Delta T 57.2 sec
SVP 05♓23'10"
Obliquity 23°26'32"
⚷ Chiron 24♋00.0
☽ Mean ☊ 5♒35.6

1 OCTOBER 1990
Julian Day # 33146
Delta T 57.3 sec
SVP 05♓23'06"
Obliquity 23°26'32"
⚷ Chiron 26♋11.9
☽ Mean ☊ 4♒00.3

NOVEMBER 1990 LONGITUDE

Day	Sid.Time	☉	0 hr ☽	Noon ☽	True ☊	☿	♀	♂	♃	♄	♅	♆	♇
1 Th	2 40 6	8♏18 22	11♈49 15	19♈ 8 36	2♒12.7	14♏29.1	8♏ 8.7	13♊38.4	12♌14.6	19♑55.4	6♑31.7	12♑11.8	17♏19.7
2 F	2 44 2	9 18 23	26 33 33	4♉ 3 4	2R 1.8	16 4.0	9 23.9	13R 28.1	12 19.9	19 59.1	6 34.0	12 13.1	17 22.1
3 Sa	2 47 59	10 18 25	11♉35 58	19 10 58	1 50.2	17 38.4	10 39.2	13 16.9	12 25.1	20 2.9	6 36.4	12 14.3	17 24.5
4 Su	2 51 55	11 18 29	26 46 40	4♊21 45	1 39.3	19 12.4	11 54.4	13 5.0	12 30.0	20 6.8	6 38.8	12 15.6	17 26.9
5 M	2 55 52	12 18 35	11♊54 54	19 24 59	1 30.3	20 46.0	13 9.7	12 52.2	12 34.8	20 10.7	6 41.2	12 17.0	17 29.4
6 Tu	2 59 48	13 18 43	26 51 1	4♋12 11	1 24.0	22 19.2	14 24.9	12 38.6	12 39.5	20 14.8	6 43.6	12 18.3	17 31.8
7 W	3 3 45	14 18 53	11♋27 54	18 37 47	1 20.5	23 52.0	15 40.2	12 24.2	12 43.9	20 18.9	6 46.1	12 19.7	17 34.2
8 Th	3 7 42	15 19 5	25 41 39	2♌39 27	1D 19.3	25 24.4	16 55.5	12 9.0	12 48.2	20 23.1	6 48.6	12 21.1	17 36.6
9 F	3 11 38	16 19 19	9♌31 19	16 17 27	1R 19.3	26 56.5	18 10.8	11 53.1	12 52.3	20 27.4	6 51.2	12 22.6	17 39.0
10 Sa	3 15 35	17 19 36	22 58 9	29 33 46	1 19.3	28 28.2	19 26.1	11 36.5	12 56.3	20 31.7	6 53.8	12 24.0	17 41.5
11 Su	3 19 31	18 19 54	6♍ 4 43	12♍31 21	1 18.0	29 59.6	20 41.4	11 19.1	13 0.0	20 36.1	6 56.5	12 25.5	17 43.9
12 M	3 23 28	19 20 14	18 54 6	25 13 19	1 14.4	1♐30.6	21 56.7	11 1.1	13 3.6	20 40.6	6 59.1	12 27.0	17 46.3
13 Tu	3 27 24	20 20 36	1♎29 21	7♎42 32	1 8.0	3 1.3	23 12.0	10 42.5	13 7.0	20 45.2	7 1.8	12 28.6	17 48.7
14 W	3 31 21	21 21 0	13 53 8	20 1 24	0 58.9	4 31.7	24 27.3	10 23.2	13 10.2	20 49.9	7 4.6	12 30.2	17 51.2
15 Th	3 35 17	22 21 25	26 7 32	2♏11 45	0 47.4	6 1.7	25 42.7	10 3.4	13 13.2	20 54.6	7 7.4	12 31.7	17 53.6
16 F	3 39 14	23 21 53	8♏14 12	14 15 1	0 34.4	7 31.3	26 58.0	9 43.1	13 16.1	20 59.4	7 10.2	12 33.4	17 56.0
17 Sa	3 43 11	24 22 22	20 14 21	26 12 22	0 21.2	9 0.5	28 13.4	9 22.4	13 18.7	21 4.3	7 13.0	12 35.0	17 58.4
18 Su	3 47 7	25 22 53	2♐ 9 11	8♐ 5 0	0 8.7	10 29.4	29 28.7	9 1.2	13 21.2	21 9.2	7 15.9	12 36.7	18 0.8
19 M	3 51 4	26 23 25	14 0 0	19 54 24	29♑58.1	11 57.8	0♐44.1	8 39.6	13 23.5	21 14.2	7 18.8	12 38.4	18 3.2
20 Tu	3 55 0	27 23 59	25 48 29	1♑42 34	29 50.0	13 25.8	1 59.4	8 17.7	13 25.6	21 19.3	7 21.7	12 40.1	18 5.6
21 W	3 58 57	28 24 35	7♑36 59	13 32 9	29 44.7	14 53.3	3 14.8	7 55.6	13 27.5	21 24.5	7 24.7	12 41.8	18 8.0
22 Th	4 2 53	29 25 11	19 28 30	25 26 33	29D 42.0	16 20.3	4 30.1	7 33.2	13 29.2	21 29.7	7 27.7	12 43.6	18 10.4
23 F	4 6 50	0♐25 49	1♒26 49	7♒29 53	29 41.4	17 46.6	5 45.5	7 10.7	13 30.7	21 35.0	7 30.7	12 45.4	18 12.8
24 Sa	4 10 46	1 26 28	13 36 21	19 46 50	29 42.1	19 12.3	7 0.8	6 48.0	13 32.0	21 40.3	7 33.8	12 47.2	18 15.2
25 Su	4 14 43	2 27 8	26 1 58	2♓22 23	29R 42.9	20 37.2	8 16.2	6 25.3	13 33.1	21 45.7	7 36.9	12 49.0	18 17.6
26 M	4 18 40	3 27 49	8♓48 41	15 21 24	29 43.0	22 1.2	9 31.5	6 2.6	13 34.0	21 51.2	7 40.0	12 50.8	18 19.9
27 Tu	4 22 36	4 28 31	22 1 0	28 47 53	29 41.3	23 24.3	10 46.9	5 39.9	13 34.8	21 56.7	7 43.1	12 52.7	18 22.3
28 W	4 26 33	5 29 14	5♈42 16	12♈44 13	29 37.6	24 46.2	12 2.2	5 17.3	13 35.3	22 2.3	7 46.3	12 54.6	18 24.7
29 Th	4 30 29	6 29 58	19 53 38	27 10 9	29 31.7	26 6.9	13 17.6	4 54.8	13 35.6	22 7.9	7 49.5	12 56.5	18 27.0
30 F	4 34 26	7 30 44	4♉33 14	12♉ 2 3	29 24.2	27 26.2	14 32.9	4 32.6	13R 35.8	22 13.6	7 52.7	12 58.4	18 29.3

DECEMBER 1990 LONGITUDE

Day	Sid.Time	☉	0 hr ☽	Noon ☽	True ☊	☿	♀	♂	♃	♄	♅	♆	♇
1 Sa	4 38 22	8♐31 30	19♉35 37	27♉12 43	29♑16.0	28♐43.7	15♐48.3	4♊10.6	13♌35.7	22♑19.4	7♑55.9	13♑ 0.3	18♏31.6
2 Su	4 42 19	9 32 18	4♊52 1	12♊32 6	29R 8.1	29 59.3	17 3.6	3R 48.9	13R 35.5	22 25.2	7 59.2	13 2.3	18 33.9
3 M	4 46 15	10 33 6	20 11 31	27 48 55	29 1.7	1♑12.7	18 18.9	3 27.5	13 35.0	22 31.0	8 2.4	13 4.3	18 36.2
4 Tu	4 50 12	11 33 56	5♋23 1	12♋52 42	28 57.3	2 23.6	19 34.3	3 6.5	13 34.4	22 37.0	8 5.7	13 6.3	18 38.5
5 W	4 54 9	12 34 48	20 17 3	27 35 22	28D 55.2	3 31.5	20 49.6	2 45.8	13 33.5	22 42.9	8 9.1	13 8.3	18 40.8
6 Th	4 58 5	13 35 40	4♌47 10	11♌52 9	28 55.0	4 36.1	22 5.0	2 25.7	13 32.5	22 49.0	8 12.4	13 10.3	18 43.1
7 F	5 2 2	14 36 34	18 50 14	25 41 29	28 56.1	5 36.7	23 20.3	2 6.0	13 31.2	22 55.0	8 15.8	13 12.4	18 45.3
8 Sa	5 5 58	15 37 28	2♍26 5	9♍ 4 22	28 57.4	6 32.9	24 35.7	1 46.8	13 29.8	23 1.1	8 19.1	13 14.4	18 47.5
9 Su	5 9 55	16 38 25	15 36 41	22 3 30	28R 58.2	7 24.0	25 51.0	1 28.3	13 28.2	23 7.3	8 22.5	13 16.5	18 49.7
10 M	5 13 51	17 39 22	28 25 18	4♎42 33	28 57.5	8 9.3	27 6.4	1 10.3	13 26.3	23 13.5	8 25.9	13 18.6	18 51.9
11 Tu	5 17 48	18 40 20	10♎55 46	17 5 26	28 55.0	8 48.1	28 21.7	0 52.9	13 24.3	23 19.8	8 29.4	13 20.7	18 54.1
12 W	5 21 44	19 41 20	23 11 59	29 15 54	28 50.7	9 19.4	29 37.1	0 36.2	13 22.1	23 26.1	8 32.8	13 22.8	18 56.3
13 Th	5 25 41	20 42 21	5♏17 33	11♏17 20	28 44.7	9 42.5	0♑52.4	0 20.1	13 19.6	23 32.4	8 36.3	13 24.9	18 58.4
14 F	5 29 38	21 43 23	17 15 35	23 12 37	28 37.8	9R 56.5	2 7.8	0 4.8	13 17.0	23 38.8	8 39.7	13 27.0	19 0.6
15 Sa	5 33 34	22 44 25	29 8 43	5♐ 4 9	28 30.5	10 0.5	3 23.1	29♉50.2	13 14.2	23 45.3	8 43.2	13 29.2	19 2.7
16 Su	5 37 31	23 45 29	10♐59 8	16 53 54	28 23.7	9 53.7	4 38.5	29 36.4	13 11.2	23 51.7	8 46.7	13 31.3	19 4.8
17 M	5 41 27	24 46 33	22 48 40	28 43 40	28 18.0	9 35.7	5 53.8	29 23.3	13 8.0	23 58.2	8 50.2	13 33.5	19 6.9
18 Tu	5 45 24	25 47 39	4♑39 7	10♑35 14	28 13.8	9 6.0	7 9.2	29 11.0	13 4.7	24 4.8	8 53.8	13 35.7	19 8.9
19 W	5 49 20	26 48 44	16 32 17	22 30 32	28D 11.4	8 24.7	8 24.5	28 59.5	13 1.1	24 11.4	8 57.3	13 37.9	19 11.0
20 Th	5 53 17	27 49 50	28 30 17	4♒31 51	28 10.7	7 32.3	9 39.8	28 48.9	12 57.3	24 18.0	9 0.8	13 40.1	19 13.0
21 F	5 57 14	28 50 57	10♒35 36	16 41 55	28 11.4	6 29.9	10 55.2	28 39.0	12 53.4	24 24.7	9 4.4	13 42.3	19 15.0
22 Sa	6 1 10	29 52 4	22 51 12	29 3 56	28 12.9	5 18.9	12 10.5	28 30.0	12 49.3	24 31.3	9 7.9	13 44.5	19 17.0
23 Su	6 5 7	0♑53 11	5♓20 31	11♓41 28	28 14.7	4 1.5	13 25.8	28 21.8	12 45.0	24 38.1	9 11.5	13 46.7	19 18.9
24 M	6 9 3	1 54 18	18 7 12	24 38 12	28 16.2	2 40.1	14 41.1	28 14.4	12 40.6	24 44.8	9 15.1	13 49.0	19 20.8
25 Tu	6 13 0	2 55 25	1♈14 51	7♈57 30	28R 16.9	1 17.6	15 56.4	28 7.9	12 35.9	24 51.6	9 18.6	13 51.2	19 22.8
26 W	6 16 56	3 56 33	14 46 27	21 41 52	28 16.4	29♐56.5	17 11.7	28 2.2	12 31.1	24 58.4	9 22.2	13 53.5	19 24.6
27 Th	6 20 53	4 57 40	28 43 47	5♉52 6	28 14.9	28 39.6	18 27.0	27 57.4	12 26.1	25 5.2	9 25.8	13 55.7	19 26.5
28 F	6 24 49	5 58 48	13♉ 6 34	20 26 44	28 12.4	27 29.1	19 42.3	27 53.3	12 21.0	25 12.1	9 29.4	13 58.0	19 28.3
29 Sa	6 28 46	6 59 56	27 51 56	5♊21 22	28 9.5	26 26.8	20 57.6	27 50.1	12 15.7	25 19.0	9 33.0	14 0.2	19 30.2
30 Su	6 32 43	8 1 3	12♊54 4	20 28 54	28 6.6	25 33.8	22 12.8	27 47.7	12 10.3	25 25.9	9 36.6	14 2.5	19 31.9
31 M	6 36 39	9 2 11	28 4 40	5♋40 7	28 4.3	24 51.0	23 28.1	27 46.1	12 4.7	25 32.8	9 40.2	14 4.7	19 33.7

Astro Data Dy Hr Mn	Planet Ingress Dy Hr Mn	Last Aspect Dy Hr Mn	☽ Ingress Dy Hr Mn	Last Aspect Dy Hr Mn	☽ Ingress Dy Hr Mn	☽ Phases & Eclipses Dy Hr Mn
☽0S 12 4:05	☿ ♐ 11 0:06	1 13:19 ♄ □	♉ 2 5:31	1 4:20 ♄ △	♊ 1 16:23	2 21:48 ○ 10♉13
☽0N 26 21:45	♀ ♐ 18 9:58	3 13:25 ♄ △	♊ 4 5:06	2 20:48 ♄ ☍	♋ 3 15:27	9 13:02 ☽ 16♌52
♃ R 30 5:03	☊ ♑ 18 19:22	5 1:30 ♂ ☌	♋ 6 5:07	5 4:00 ♄ ☍	♌ 5 16:00	17 9:05 ● 24♏45
	☉ ♐ 22 13:47	7 23:27 ☿ △	♌ 8 7:24	7 8:39 ♀ △	♍ 7 19:39	25 13:11 ☽ 3♓00
☽0S 9 9:15		10 11:19 ☿ □	♍ 10 12:48	9 21:14 ♀ □	♎ 10 3:00	
♃⊼♆ 11 20:11	☿ ♑ 2 0:13	12 6:24 ♀ ⚹	♎ 12 21:08	12 0:28 ♄ □	♏ 12 13:28	2 7:50 ○ 9♊52
☿ R 14 21:08	♀ ♑ 12 7:18	14 13:40 ♄ □	♏ 15 7:39	15 1:22 ♂ ☍	♐ 15 1:44	9 2:04 ☽ 16♍44
☽0N 24 4:10	♂ ♉ 14 7:46	17 17:58 ♀ ☌	♐ 17 19:39	17 4:22 ☉ ☌	♑ 17 14:35	17 4:22 ● 24♐58
	☉ ♑ 22 3:07	18 22:46 ♃ △	♑ 20 8:31	20 0:37 ♂ △	♒ 20 2:59	25 3:16 ☽ 3♈04
	☿ ♐ 25 22:57	22 4:06 ♄ ☌	♒ 22 21:07	22 10:47 ♂ □	♓ 22 13:48	31 18:35 ○ 9♋50
		24 12:17 ☿ ⚹	♓ 25 7:32	24 18:25 ♂ ⚹	♈ 24 21:45	
		27 2:45 ☿ □	♈ 27 14:06	26 23:54 ☿ △	♉ 27 2:09	
		29 11:18 ☿ △	♉ 29 16:37	28 23:57 ♂ ☍	♊ 29 3:26	
				30 19:07 ☿ ☍	♋ 31 3:02	

Astro Data

1 NOVEMBER 1990
Julian Day # 33177
Delta T 57.3 sec
SVP 05♓23'03"
Obliquity 23°26'31"
⚷ Chiron 27♋16.6
☽ Mean ☊ 2♒21.8

1 DECEMBER 1990
Julian Day # 33207
Delta T 57.4 sec
SVP 05♓22'59"
Obliquity 23°26'30"
⚷ Chiron 26♋54.7R
☽ Mean ☊ 0♒46.5

LONGITUDE — JANUARY 1991

Day	Sid.Time	☉	0 hr ☽	Noon ☽	True ☊	☿	♀	♂	♃	♄	♅	♆	♇
1 Tu	6 40 36	10♑ 3 19	13♋14 1	20♋45 11	28♑ 2.9	24♐18.7	24♑43.3	27♉45.3	11♌58.9	25♑39.8	9♑43.8	14♑ 7.0	19♏35.5
2 W	6 44 32	11 4 27	28 12 31	5♌35 4	28D 2.4	23R 56.8	25 58.5	27D 45.3	11R 53.1	25 46.7	9 47.4	14 9.3	19 37.2
3 Th	6 48 29	12 5 35	12♌52 4	20 2 55	28 2.8	23D 45.0	27 13.8	27 46.0	11 47.0	25 53.7	9 51.0	14 11.6	19 38.9
4 F	6 52 25	13 6 43	27 7 10	4♍ 4 37	28 3.8	23 42.7	28 29.0	27 47.5	11 40.8	26 0.7	9 54.6	14 13.8	19 40.5
5 Sa	6 56 22	14 7 51	10♍55 10	17 38 54	28 5.1	23 49.4	29 44.2	27 49.8	11 34.5	26 7.8	9 58.2	14 16.1	19 42.1
6 Su	7 0 18	15 9 0	24 16 1	0♎46 50	28 6.2	24 4.3	0♒59.4	27 52.8	11 28.1	26 14.8	10 1.8	14 18.4	19 43.7
7 M	7 4 15	16 10 8	7♎11 44	13 31 12	28R 6.9	24 26.6	2 14.6	27 56.5	11 21.5	26 21.9	10 5.3	14 20.7	19 45.3
8 Tu	7 8 12	17 11 17	19 45 44	25 55 53	28 7.0	24 55.8	3 29.7	28 0.9	11 14.8	26 28.9	10 8.9	14 22.9	19 46.9
9 W	7 12 8	18 12 26	2♏ 2 11	8♏ 5 12	28 6.6	25 31.2	4 44.9	28 6.1	11 8.0	26 36.0	10 12.5	14 25.2	19 48.4
10 Th	7 16 5	19 13 35	14 5 29	20 3 36	28 5.9	26 12.0	6 0.1	28 12.0	11 1.1	26 43.1	10 16.1	14 27.5	19 49.9
11 F	7 20 1	20 14 45	26 0 2	1♐55 17	28 4.8	26 57.8	7 15.2	28 18.5	10 54.1	26 50.2	10 19.6	14 29.7	19 51.3
12 Sa	7 23 58	21 15 54	7♐49 49	13 44 4	28 3.7	27 48.0	8 30.4	28 25.7	10 46.9	26 57.3	10 23.2	14 32.0	19 52.8
13 Su	7 27 54	22 17 3	19 38 25	25 33 16	28 2.8	28 42.2	9 45.5	28 33.6	10 39.7	27 4.5	10 26.7	14 34.3	19 54.2
14 M	7 31 51	23 18 12	1♑28 54	7♑25 40	28 2.1	29 40.0	11 0.6	28 42.2	10 32.4	27 11.6	10 30.3	14 36.5	19 55.5
15 Tu	7 35 47	24 19 20	13 23 49	19 23 36	28 1.8	0♑40.9	12 15.7	28 51.4	10 25.0	27 18.7	10 33.8	14 38.8	19 56.9
16 W	7 39 44	25 20 28	25 25 15	1♒28 58	28D 1.6	1 44.6	13 30.8	29 1.2	10 17.5	27 25.9	10 37.3	14 41.0	19 58.2
17 Th	7 43 41	26 21 36	7♒34 57	13 43 23	28 1.7	2 51.0	14 45.9	29 11.6	10 9.9	27 33.0	10 40.8	14 43.3	19 59.5
18 F	7 47 37	27 22 43	19 54 28	26 8 22	28R 1.7	3 59.6	16 0.9	29 22.7	10 2.3	27 40.2	10 44.3	14 45.5	20 0.7
19 Sa	7 51 34	28 23 49	2♓25 16	8♓45 21	28 1.7	5 10.4	17 16.0	29 34.3	9 54.6	27 47.3	10 47.8	14 47.7	20 1.9
20 Su	7 55 30	29 24 55	15 8 49	21 35 51	28 1.6	6 23.0	18 31.0	29 46.5	9 46.8	27 54.4	10 51.2	14 50.0	20 3.1
21 M	7 59 27	0♒26 0	28 6 38	4♈41 23	28 1.4	7 37.4	19 46.0	29 59.3	9 39.0	28 1.6	10 54.7	14 52.2	20 4.2
22 Tu	8 3 23	1 27 4	11♈20 15	18 3 25	28 1.1	8 53.3	21 1.0	0♊12.7	9 31.1	28 8.7	10 58.1	14 54.4	20 5.4
23 W	8 7 20	2 28 7	24 50 59	1♉43 5	28D 0.9	10 10.7	22 15.9	0 26.5	9 23.2	28 15.8	11 1.5	14 56.6	20 6.4
24 Th	8 11 16	3 29 8	8♉39 43	15 40 52	28 0.9	11 29.5	23 30.9	0 40.9	9 15.3	28 22.9	11 4.9	14 58.8	20 7.5
25 F	8 15 13	4 30 9	22 46 25	29 56 8	28 1.2	12 49.5	24 45.8	0 55.9	9 7.3	28 30.1	11 8.3	15 0.9	20 8.5
26 Sa	8 19 10	5 31 9	7♊ 9 45	14♊26 47	28 1.7	14 10.7	26 0.7	1 11.3	8 59.3	28 37.2	11 11.7	15 3.1	20 9.5
27 Su	8 23 6	6 32 8	21 46 44	29 8 57	28 2.5	15 32.9	27 15.6	1 27.2	8 51.3	28 44.3	11 15.0	15 5.3	20 10.4
28 M	8 27 3	7 33 6	6♋32 39	13♋57 3	28 3.2	16 56.2	28 30.4	1 43.6	8 43.3	28 51.4	11 18.4	15 7.4	20 11.3
29 Tu	8 30 59	8 34 3	21 21 13	28 44 16	28R 3.7	18 20.5	29 45.2	2 0.4	8 35.3	28 58.5	11 21.7	15 9.5	20 12.2
30 W	8 34 56	9 34 58	6♌ 5 15	13♌23 18	28 3.6	19 45.7	1♓ 0.0	2 17.7	8 27.3	29 5.5	11 25.0	15 11.7	20 13.1
31 Th	8 38 52	10 35 53	20 37 36	27 47 22	28 2.9	21 11.9	2 14.8	2 35.5	8 19.3	29 12.6	11 28.2	15 13.8	20 13.9

LONGITUDE — FEBRUARY 1991

Day	Sid.Time	☉	0 hr ☽	Noon ☽	True ☊	☿	♀	♂	♃	♄	♅	♆	♇
1 F	8 42 49	11♒36 47	4♍52 2	11♍51 5	28♑ 1.6	22♑38.9	3♓29.5	2♊53.6	8♌11.3	29♑19.6	11♑31.5	15♑15.9	20♏14.6
2 Sa	8 46 45	12 37 39	18 44 9	25 31 3	27R 59.7	24 6.7	4 44.2	3 12.2	8R 3.3	29 26.6	11 34.7	15 17.9	20 15.4
3 Su	8 50 42	13 38 31	2♎11 42	8♎46 9	27 57.5	25 35.4	5 58.9	3 31.2	7 55.3	29 33.6	11 37.9	15 20.0	20 16.1
4 M	8 54 39	14 39 22	15 14 36	21 37 20	27 55.3	27 4.9	7 13.6	3 50.6	7 47.4	29 40.6	11 41.0	15 22.1	20 16.7
5 Tu	8 58 35	15 40 12	27 54 43	4♏ 7 14	27 53.7	28 35.2	8 28.2	4 10.4	7 39.5	29 47.6	11 44.2	15 24.1	20 17.4
6 W	9 2 32	16 41 1	10♏15 22	16 19 41	27D 52.7	0♒ 6.3	9 42.8	4 30.5	7 31.7	29 54.6	11 47.3	15 26.1	20 18.0
7 Th	9 6 28	17 41 49	22 20 47	28 19 16	27 52.6	1 38.3	10 57.4	4 51.0	7 23.9	0♒ 1.5	11 50.4	15 28.1	20 18.5
8 F	9 10 25	18 42 37	4♐15 45	10♐10 52	27 53.4	3 11.0	12 11.9	5 11.9	7 16.1	0 8.4	11 53.5	15 30.1	20 19.1
9 Sa	9 14 21	19 43 23	16 5 12	21 59 22	27 54.9	4 44.5	13 26.5	5 33.2	7 8.4	0 15.3	11 56.5	15 32.1	20 19.5
10 Su	9 18 18	20 44 9	27 53 55	3♑49 23	27 56.7	6 18.8	14 40.9	5 54.8	7 0.8	0 22.1	11 59.5	15 34.0	20 20.0
11 M	9 22 14	21 44 53	9♑46 16	15 45 1	27 58.3	7 53.9	15 55.4	6 16.7	6 53.2	0 29.0	12 2.5	15 36.0	20 20.4
12 Tu	9 26 11	22 45 36	21 46 4	27 49 46	27R 59.4	9 29.8	17 9.8	6 39.0	6 45.7	0 35.8	12 5.4	15 37.9	20 20.8
13 W	9 30 8	23 46 18	3♒56 26	10♒ 6 19	27 59.4	11 6.5	18 24.2	7 1.6	6 38.3	0 42.6	12 8.4	15 39.8	20 21.1
14 Th	9 34 4	24 46 59	16 19 36	22 36 27	27 58.1	12 44.1	19 38.6	7 24.5	6 31.0	0 49.3	12 11.2	15 41.7	20 21.4
15 F	9 38 1	25 47 38	28 56 56	5♓21 5	27 55.3	14 22.5	20 52.9	7 47.7	6 23.8	0 56.0	12 14.1	15 43.5	20 21.7
16 Sa	9 41 57	26 48 16	11♓48 54	18 20 19	27 51.3	16 1.8	22 7.2	8 11.2	6 16.7	1 2.7	12 16.9	15 45.3	20 22.0
17 Su	9 45 54	27 48 52	24 55 14	1♈33 33	27 46.4	17 41.9	23 21.5	8 35.0	6 9.7	1 9.4	12 19.7	15 47.2	20 22.2
18 M	9 49 50	28 49 26	8♈15 5	14 59 43	27 41.2	19 23.0	24 35.7	8 59.2	6 2.7	1 16.0	12 22.5	15 49.0	20 22.3
19 Tu	9 53 47	29 49 59	21 47 15	28 37 33	27 36.4	21 4.9	25 49.9	9 23.5	5 55.9	1 22.6	12 25.2	15 50.7	20 22.4
20 W	9 57 43	0♓50 30	5♉30 28	12♉25 49	27 32.6	22 47.7	27 4.0	9 48.2	5 49.2	1 29.1	12 27.9	15 52.5	20 22.5
21 Th	10 1 40	1 50 59	19 23 28	26 23 17	27D 30.4	24 31.5	28 18.1	10 13.1	5 42.7	1 35.7	12 30.5	15 54.2	20 22.6
22 F	10 5 37	2 51 27	3♊25 7	10♊28 49	27 29.7	26 16.2	29 32.1	10 38.3	5 36.2	1 42.1	12 33.1	15 55.9	20R 22.6
23 Sa	10 9 33	3 51 52	17 34 14	24 41 8	27 30.4	28 1.8	0♈46.2	11 3.8	5 29.9	1 48.6	12 35.7	15 57.6	20 22.6
24 Su	10 13 30	4 52 16	1♋49 19	8♋58 30	27 31.8	29 48.5	2 0.1	11 29.4	5 23.8	1 55.0	12 38.3	15 59.3	20 22.5
25 M	10 17 26	5 52 37	16 8 19	23 18 25	27R 33.1	1♓36.0	3 14.0	11 55.4	5 17.7	2 1.3	12 40.8	16 0.9	20 22.4
26 Tu	10 21 23	6 52 57	0♌28 19	7♌37 33	27 33.5	3 24.6	4 27.9	12 21.5	5 11.8	2 7.6	12 43.2	16 2.5	20 22.3
27 W	10 25 19	7 53 15	14 45 33	21 51 44	27 32.3	5 14.1	5 41.7	12 47.9	5 6.1	2 13.9	12 45.7	16 4.1	20 22.2
28 Th	10 29 16	8 53 30	28 55 32	5♍56 21	27 29.0	7 4.5	6 55.4	13 14.5	5 0.5	2 20.1	12 48.1	16 5.6	20 22.0

Astro Data Dy Hr Mn	Planet Ingress Dy Hr Mn	Last Aspect Dy Hr Mn	☽ Ingress Dy Hr Mn	Last Aspect Dy Hr Mn	☽ Ingress Dy Hr Mn	☽ Phases & Eclipses Dy Hr Mn	Astro Data
♂ D 1 12:49	♀ ♒ 5 5:03	1 23:16 ♂ ⚹	♌ 2 2:54	2 19:12 ♄ △	♎ 2 20:02	7 18:36 ☽ 16♎58	1 JANUARY 1991
☿ D 3 17:52	☿ ♑ 14 8:02	4 1:09 ♂ □	♍ 4 4:57	5 3:39 ♄ □	♏ 5 4:01	15 23:50 ● 25♑20	Julian Day # 33238
☽0S 5 16:47	☉ ♒ 20 13:47	6 6:40 ♂ △	♎ 6 10:33	6 19:55 ♇ ☌	♐ 7 15:23	15 23:52:53 ● A 7'36"	Delta T 57.4 sec
♃⊼♅ 14 4:40	♂ ♊ 21 1:15	8 13:12 ♄ □	♏ 8 19:59	9 8:05 ☉ ⚹	♑ 10 4:16	23 14:21 ☽ 3♉05	SVP 05♓22'52"
☽0N 20 9:33	♀ ♓ 29 4:44	11 4:43 ♂ ☍	♐ 11 8:06	11 21:10 ♇ ⚹	♒ 12 16:16	30 6:10 ○ 9♌51	Obliquity 23°26'30"
		13 20:00 ☿ ☌	♑ 13 21:00	14 17:32 ☉ ☌	♓ 15 1:59	30 5:59 ☍ A 0.881	⚷ Chiron 25♋15.5R
☽0S 2 2:46	☿ ♒ 5 22:20	16 7:14 ♂ △	♒ 16 9:04	16 20:52 ♀ ☌	♈ 17 9:11		☽ Mean ☊ 29♑08.0
☽0N 16 15:44	♄ ♒ 6 18:51	18 18:29 ♂ □	♓ 18 19:23	18 22:35 ☿ ⚹	♉ 19 14:24	6 13:52 ☽ 17♏16	
♇ R 22 1:27	☉ ♓ 19 3:58	20 23:51 ♄ ⚹	♈ 21 3:28	21 16:45 ♀ ⚹	♊ 21 18:10	14 17:32 ● 25♒31	1 FEBRUARY 1991
♀0N 24 5:30	♀ ♈ 22 9:02	23 6:02 ♄ □	♉ 23 9:01	23 20:08 ☿ △	♋ 23 20:56	21 22:58 ☽ 2♊49	Julian Day # 33269
	☿ ♓ 24 2:35	25 9:41 ♄ △	♊ 25 12:06	25 7:05 ♇ △	♌ 25 23:13	28 18:25 ○ 9♍40	Delta T 57.5 sec
		27 9:45 ♀ △	♋ 27 13:23	27 9:28 ♇ □	♍ 28 1:50		SVP 05♓22'47"
		29 12:29 ♄ ☍	♌ 29 14:03				Obliquity 23°26'30"
		30 23:20 ♇ □	♍ 31 15:44				⚷ Chiron 23♋05.3R
							☽ Mean ☊ 27♑29.5

MARCH 1991 — LONGITUDE

Day	Sid.Time	☉	0 hr ☽	Noon ☽	True ☊	☿	♀	♂	♃	♄	♅	♆	♇
1 F	10 33 12	9♓53 44	12♍53 38	19♍46 54	27♑23.7	8♓55.9	8♈ 9.2	13♊41.3	4♌55.0	2♒26.3	12♑50.4	16♑ 7.2	20♏21.7
2 Sa	10 37 9	10 53 57	26 35 40	3♎19 38	27R16.7	10 48.3	9 22.8	14 8.3	4R49.7	2 32.4	12 52.7	16 8.7	20R21.5
3 Su	10 41 6	11 54 7	9♎58 32	16 32 13	27 8.9	12 41.5	10 36.4	14 35.5	4 44.6	2 38.5	12 55.0	16 10.2	20 21.2
4 M	10 45 2	12 54 16	23 0 40	29 23 57	27 1.0	14 35.5	11 50.0	15 2.9	4 39.6	2 44.5	12 57.2	16 11.6	20 20.8
5 Tu	10 48 59	13 54 23	5♏42 16	11♏55 52	26 53.9	16 30.4	13 3.5	15 30.5	4 34.8	2 50.5	12 59.4	16 13.1	20 20.5
6 W	10 52 55	14 54 29	18 5 10	24 10 34	26 48.4	18 25.9	14 16.9	15 58.3	4 30.1	2 56.4	13 1.5	16 14.5	20 20.1
7 Th	10 56 52	15 54 33	0♐12 36	6♐11 50	26 44.8	20 22.0	15 30.3	16 26.3	4 25.7	3 2.3	13 3.6	16 15.8	20 19.6
8 F	11 0 48	16 54 36	12 8 53	18 4 21	26D43.2	22 18.6	16 43.7	16 54.4	4 21.3	3 8.1	13 5.7	16 17.2	20 19.2
9 Sa	11 4 45	17 54 37	23 58 56	29 53 17	26 43.3	24 15.6	17 57.0	17 22.8	4 17.2	3 13.9	13 7.7	16 18.5	20 18.7
10 Su	11 8 41	18 54 36	5♑48 4	11♑43 56	26 44.3	26 12.7	19 10.2	17 51.3	4 13.2	3 19.6	13 9.7	16 19.8	20 18.1
11 M	11 12 38	19 54 34	17 41 33	23 41 31	26R45.4	28 9.7	20 23.4	18 19.9	4 9.5	3 25.3	13 11.6	16 21.1	20 17.6
12 Tu	11 16 35	20 54 29	29 44 24	5♒50 44	26 45.8	0♈ 6.5	21 36.5	18 48.8	4 5.8	3 30.9	13 13.5	16 22.3	20 17.0
13 W	11 20 31	21 54 24	12♒ 0 58	18 15 30	26 44.4	2 2.7	22 49.6	19 17.8	4 2.4	3 36.5	13 15.3	16 23.5	20 16.3
14 Th	11 24 28	22 54 16	24 34 38	0♓58 35	26 40.8	3 57.9	24 2.6	19 47.0	3 59.2	3 41.9	13 17.1	16 24.7	20 15.7
15 F	11 28 24	23 54 7	7♓27 28	14 1 18	26 34.8	5 52.0	25 15.6	20 16.3	3 56.1	3 47.4	13 18.9	16 25.8	20 15.0
16 Sa	11 32 21	24 53 55	20 40 0	27 23 21	26 26.5	7 44.4	26 28.5	20 45.8	3 53.2	3 52.7	13 20.6	16 26.9	20 14.2
17 Su	11 36 17	25 53 42	4♈11 3	11♈ 2 44	26 16.6	9 34.7	27 41.3	21 15.4	3 50.5	3 58.0	13 22.2	16 28.0	20 13.5
18 M	11 40 14	26 53 27	17 57 57	24 56 10	26 6.2	11 22.6	28 54.1	21 45.2	3 48.0	4 3.3	13 23.8	16 29.1	20 12.7
19 Tu	11 44 10	27 53 9	1♉56 52	8♉59 29	25 56.3	13 7.6	0♉ 6.8	22 15.1	3 45.7	4 8.4	13 25.4	16 30.1	20 11.9
20 W	11 48 7	28 52 50	16 3 30	23 8 26	25 48.1	14 49.1	1 19.5	22 45.2	3 43.6	4 13.6	13 26.9	16 31.1	20 11.0
21 Th	11 52 4	29 52 28	0♊13 50	7♊19 18	25 42.2	16 26.7	2 32.0	23 15.4	3 41.7	4 18.6	13 28.3	16 32.1	20 10.1
22 F	11 56 0	0♈52 4	14 24 32	21 29 16	25 38.9	17 60.0	3 44.6	23 45.8	3 39.9	4 23.6	13 29.8	16 33.0	20 9.2
23 Sa	11 59 57	1 51 38	28 33 18	5♋36 31	25D37.8	19 28.5	4 57.0	24 16.2	3 38.4	4 28.5	13 31.1	16 33.9	20 8.3
24 Su	12 3 53	2 51 9	12♋38 46	19 39 59	25R38.0	20 51.8	6 9.4	24 46.8	3 37.0	4 33.3	13 32.4	16 34.8	20 7.3
25 M	12 7 50	3 50 38	26 40 5	3♌38 59	25 38.3	22 9.5	7 21.6	25 17.5	3 35.9	4 38.1	13 33.7	16 35.6	20 6.3
26 Tu	12 11 46	4 50 5	10♌36 32	17 32 38	25 37.4	23 21.2	8 33.9	25 48.4	3 34.9	4 42.8	13 34.9	16 36.4	20 5.3
27 W	12 15 43	5 49 29	24 27 4	1♍19 39	25 34.4	24 26.6	9 46.0	26 19.3	3 34.2	4 47.4	13 36.1	16 37.2	20 4.3
28 Th	12 19 39	6 48 51	8♍10 6	14 58 9	25 28.6	25 25.4	10 58.0	26 50.4	3 33.6	4 52.0	13 37.2	16 37.9	20 3.2
29 F	12 23 36	7 48 11	21 43 29	28 25 49	25 20.0	26 17.5	12 10.0	27 21.5	3 33.2	4 56.4	13 38.3	16 38.6	20 2.1
30 Sa	12 27 33	8 47 29	5♎ 4 49	11♎40 16	25 9.0	27 2.5	13 21.9	27 52.8	3D33.0	5 0.8	13 39.3	16 39.3	20 1.0
31 Su	12 31 29	9 46 45	18 11 53	24 39 33	24 56.6	27 40.4	14 33.7	28 24.2	3 33.0	5 5.2	13 40.3	16 40.0	19 59.8

APRIL 1991 — LONGITUDE

Day	Sid.Time	☉	0 hr ☽	Noon ☽	True ☊	☿	♀	♂	♃	♄	♅	♆	♇
1 M	12 35 26	10♈45 58	1♏ 3 7	7♏22 35	24♑43.9	28♈11.1	15♉45.4	28♊55.7	3♌33.1	5♒ 9.4	13♑41.2	16♑40.6	19♏58.6
2 Tu	12 39 22	11 45 10	13 38 1	19 49 31	24R32.2	28 34.4	16 57.1	29 27.2	3 33.5	5 13.6	13 42.0	16 41.1	19R57.4
3 W	12 43 19	12 44 20	25 57 19	2♐ 1 45	24 22.3	28 50.5	18 8.6	29 58.9	3 34.1	5 17.7	13 42.9	16 41.7	19 56.2
4 Th	12 47 15	13 43 28	8♐ 3 9	14 2 0	24 14.9	28R59.4	19 20.1	0♋30.7	3 34.8	5 21.7	13 43.6	16 42.2	19 55.0
5 F	12 51 12	14 42 34	19 58 47	25 54 5	24 10.2	29 1.2	20 31.5	1 2.6	3 35.8	5 25.6	13 44.3	16 42.7	19 53.7
6 Sa	12 55 8	15 41 39	1♑48 29	7♑42 39	24 7.9	28 56.1	21 42.8	1 34.5	3 36.9	5 29.5	13 45.0	16 43.1	19 52.4
7 Su	12 59 5	16 40 42	13 37 15	19 32 57	24 7.2	28 44.5	22 54.0	2 6.6	3 38.2	5 33.3	13 45.6	16 43.5	19 51.1
8 M	13 3 2	17 39 43	25 30 28	1♒30 30	24 7.2	28 26.7	24 5.2	2 38.7	3 39.7	5 37.0	13 46.2	16 43.9	19 49.8
9 Tu	13 6 58	18 38 42	7♒33 42	13 40 44	24 6.8	28 3.1	25 16.2	3 11.0	3 41.4	5 40.6	13 46.7	16 44.3	19 48.4
10 W	13 10 55	19 37 39	19 52 12	26 8 37	24 4.8	27 34.4	26 27.2	3 43.3	3 43.3	5 44.1	13 47.2	16 44.6	19 47.1
11 Th	13 14 51	20 36 35	2♓30 28	8♓58 7	24 0.5	27 1.2	27 38.0	4 15.7	3 45.3	5 47.6	13 47.6	16 44.9	19 45.7
12 F	13 18 48	21 35 28	15 31 50	22 11 42	23 53.5	26 24.1	28 48.8	4 48.2	3 47.6	5 50.9	13 47.9	16 45.1	19 44.3
13 Sa	13 22 44	22 34 20	28 57 43	5♈49 43	23 43.9	25 44.0	29 59.5	5 20.8	3 50.0	5 54.2	13 48.2	16 45.3	19 42.8
14 Su	13 26 41	23 33 10	12♈47 21	19 50 9	23 32.5	25 1.6	1♊10.1	5 53.5	3 52.6	5 57.4	13 48.5	16 45.5	19 41.4
15 M	13 30 37	24 31 58	26 57 28	4♉ 8 35	23 20.3	24 17.8	2 20.6	6 26.2	3 55.4	6 0.5	13 48.7	16 45.7	19 39.9
16 Tu	13 34 34	25 30 44	11♉22 40	18 38 50	23 8.7	23 33.5	3 30.9	6 59.0	3 58.3	6 3.5	13 48.8	16 45.8	19 38.4
17 W	13 38 30	26 29 29	25 56 12	3♊13 53	22 58.8	22 49.4	4 41.2	7 32.0	4 1.5	6 6.4	13 48.9	16 45.9	19 36.9
18 Th	13 42 27	27 28 11	10♊31 7	17 47 9	22 51.5	22 6.3	5 51.4	8 4.9	4 4.8	6 9.2	13R49.0	16 45.9	19 35.4
19 F	13 46 24	28 26 51	25 1 23	2♋13 20	22 47.1	21 25.1	7 1.5	8 38.0	4 8.3	6 12.0	13 49.0	16R45.9	19 33.9
20 Sa	13 50 20	29 25 29	9♋22 37	16 29 0	22D45.2	20 46.4	8 11.4	9 11.1	4 11.9	6 14.6	13 48.9	16 45.9	19 32.4
21 Su	13 54 17	0♉24 4	23 32 18	0♌32 27	22R44.9	20 10.7	9 21.3	9 44.3	4 15.8	6 17.2	13 48.8	16 45.9	19 30.8
22 M	13 58 13	1 22 37	7♌29 26	14 23 19	22 44.8	19 38.6	10 31.0	10 17.6	4 19.8	6 19.7	13 48.6	16 45.8	19 29.2
23 Tu	14 2 10	2 21 8	21 14 9	28 2 0	22 43.8	19 10.5	11 40.6	10 50.9	4 23.9	6 22.1	13 48.4	16 45.7	19 27.7
24 W	14 6 6	3 19 37	4♍46 58	11♍29 4	22 40.7	18 46.8	12 50.1	11 24.3	4 28.3	6 24.3	13 48.2	16 45.5	19 26.1
25 Th	14 10 3	4 18 4	18 8 21	24 44 50	22 34.9	18 27.7	13 59.4	11 57.8	4 32.8	6 26.5	13 47.9	16 45.3	19 24.5
26 F	14 13 59	5 16 28	1♎18 30	7♎49 18	22 26.3	18 13.4	15 8.6	12 31.3	4 37.4	6 28.6	13 47.5	16 45.1	19 22.9
27 Sa	14 17 56	6 14 50	14 17 12	20 42 7	22 15.4	18 3.9	16 17.7	13 4.9	4 42.3	6 30.6	13 47.1	16 44.9	19 21.2
28 Su	14 21 53	7 13 11	27 4 1	3♏22 51	22 3.0	17D59.4	17 26.7	13 38.5	4 47.2	6 32.5	13 46.6	16 44.6	19 19.6
29 M	14 25 49	8 11 30	9♏38 34	15 51 13	21 50.3	17 59.9	18 35.5	14 12.2	4 52.4	6 34.4	13 46.1	16 44.3	19 18.0
30 Tu	14 29 46	9 9 47	22 0 50	28 7 31	21 38.4	18 5.2	19 44.2	14 46.0	4 57.7	6 36.1	13 45.6	16 43.9	19 16.3

Astro Data	Dy Hr Mn
☽0S	1 13:09
☿0N	12 12:51
☽0N	15 23:37
♃☍♄	16 1:26
☽0S	28 21:40
♃ D	30 13:15
☿ R	4 18:09
☽0N	12 8:34
♅ R	18 10:33
♆ R	19 0:11
☽0S	25 3:37
☿ D	28 9:49

Planet Ingress	Dy Hr Mn
☿ ♈	11 22:40
♀ ♉	18 21:45
☉ ♈	21 3:02
♂ ♋	3 0:49
♀ ♊	13 0:10
☉ ♉	20 14:08

Last Aspect Dy Hr Mn		☽ Ingress Dy Hr Mn
1 13:01	♇ ✶	♎ 2 6:03
3 11:21	♆ □	♏ 4 13:08
6 4:25	♇ ☌	♐ 6 23:35
9 0:41	☿ □	♑ 9 12:14
11 6:01	♀ □	♒ 12 0:31
13 22:53	♀ ✶	♓ 14 10:11
16 8:10	☉ ☌	♈ 16 16:38
18 20:34	♀ ☌	♉ 18 20:40
20 23:21	☉ ✶	♊ 20 23:37
22 16:27	♂ ☌	♋ 23 2:27
24 15:30	☿ □	♌ 25 5:43
27 3:23	♂ ✶	♍ 27 9:41
29 10:29	♂ □	♎ 29 14:49
31 19:50	♂ △	♏ 31 22:01

Last Aspect Dy Hr Mn		☽ Ingress Dy Hr Mn
2 12:14	♇ ☌	♐ 3 7:59
5 18:13	☿ △	♑ 5 20:19
8 5:43	☿ □	♒ 8 9:00
10 14:07	☿ ✶	♓ 10 19:18
12 7:35	♇ △	♈ 13 1:49
14 19:45	☿ ☌	♉ 15 5:06
16 13:37	♇ ☍	♊ 17 6:41
19 6:07	☉ ✶	♋ 19 8:17
20 18:30	☿ □	♌ 21 11:04
22 20:53	♇ □	♍ 23 15:29
25 2:18	♇ ✶	♎ 25 21:36
27 7:00	☿ ☍	♏ 28 5:34
29 18:40	♇ ☌	♐ 30 15:42

☽ Phases & Eclipses Dy Hr Mn	
8 10:32	☽ 17♐21
16 8:10	● 25♓14
23 6:03	☽ 2♋07
30 7:17	○ 9♎05
7 6:45	☽ 16♑57
14 19:38	● 24♈21
21 12:39	☽ 0♌55
28 20:59	○ 8♏04

Astro Data

1 MARCH 1991
Julian Day # 33297
Delta T 57.5 sec
SVP 05♓22'43"
Obliquity 23°26'30"
⚷ Chiron 21♋35.5R
☽ Mean ☊ 26♑00.6

1 APRIL 1991
Julian Day # 33328
Delta T 57.5 sec
SVP 05♓22'40"
Obliquity 23°26'30"
⚷ Chiron 21♋10.9
☽ Mean ☊ 24♑22.0

LONGITUDE — MAY 1991

Day	Sid.Time	☉	0 hr ☽	Noon ☽	True ☊	☿	♀	♂	♃	♄	♅	♆	♇
1 W	14 33 42	10♉ 8 2	4♐11 25	10♐12 46	21♑28.3	18♈15.4	20♊52.7	15♋19.8	5♌ 3.1	6♒37.7	13♑45.0	16♑43.6	19♏14.7
2 Th	14 37 39	11 6 16	16 11 50	22 8 56	21R 20.7	18 30.2	22 1.2	15 53.7	5 8.7	6 39.2	13R 44.3	16R 43.2	19R 13.0
3 F	14 41 35	12 4 28	28 4 28	3♑58 53	21 15.7	18 49.7	23 9.4	16 27.6	5 14.5	6 40.7	13 43.6	16 42.7	19 11.4
4 Sa	14 45 32	13 2 38	9♑52 41	15 46 24	21D 13.2	19 13.6	24 17.5	17 1.6	5 20.4	6 42.0	13 42.9	16 42.3	19 9.7
5 Su	14 49 28	14 0 47	21 40 38	27 36 0	21 12.5	19 41.8	25 25.5	17 35.6	5 26.5	6 43.3	13 42.1	16 41.8	19 8.0
6 M	14 53 25	14 58 55	3♒33 9	9♒32 45	21 12.9	20 14.2	26 33.3	18 9.7	5 32.7	6 44.4	13 41.2	16 41.2	19 6.4
7 Tu	14 57 22	15 57 1	15 35 29	21 42 1	21R 13.3	20 50.5	27 41.0	18 43.8	5 39.0	6 45.5	13 40.4	16 40.7	19 4.7
8 W	15 1 18	16 55 6	27 53 1	4♓ 9 5	21 12.7	21 30.7	28 48.5	19 18.0	5 45.5	6 46.4	13 39.4	16 40.1	19 3.0
9 Th	15 5 15	17 53 9	10♓30 49	16 58 40	21 10.3	22 14.6	29 55.9	19 52.3	5 52.1	6 47.3	13 38.4	16 39.5	19 1.3
10 F	15 9 11	18 51 11	23 33 5	0♈14 18	21 5.7	23 2.1	1♋ 3.1	20 26.6	5 58.9	6 48.0	13 37.4	16 38.8	18 59.6
11 Sa	15 13 8	19 49 11	7♈ 2 29	13 57 36	20 59.0	23 52.9	2 10.1	21 0.9	6 5.8	6 48.7	13 36.4	16 38.1	18 58.0
12 Su	15 17 4	20 47 10	20 59 26	28 7 37	20 50.5	24 47.1	3 16.9	21 35.3	6 12.8	6 49.2	13 35.2	16 37.4	18 56.3
13 M	15 21 1	21 45 8	5♉21 34	12♉40 31	20 41.2	25 44.5	4 23.6	22 9.8	6 20.0	6 49.7	13 34.1	16 36.7	18 54.6
14 Tu	15 24 57	22 43 4	20 3 34	27 29 42	20 32.3	26 44.9	5 30.1	22 44.3	6 27.3	6 50.0	13 32.9	16 35.9	18 52.9
15 W	15 28 54	23 40 59	4♊57 19	12♊26 46	20 24.7	27 48.3	6 36.5	23 18.9	6 34.8	6 50.3	13 31.6	16 35.2	18 51.2
16 Th	15 32 51	24 38 53	19 55 27	27 22 51	20 19.2	28 54.6	7 42.6	23 53.5	6 42.4	6 50.5	13 30.3	16 34.3	18 49.6
17 F	15 36 47	25 36 45	4♋47 59	12♋10 4	20 16.1	0♉ 3.6	8 48.5	24 28.1	6 50.1	6R 50.5	13 29.0	16 33.5	18 47.9
18 Sa	15 40 44	26 34 35	19 28 26	26 42 35	20D 15.1	1 15.4	9 54.3	25 2.8	6 57.9	6 50.5	13 27.7	16 32.6	18 46.2
19 Su	15 44 40	27 32 23	3♌52 9	10♌56 56	20 15.6	2 29.9	10 59.8	25 37.6	7 5.9	6 50.4	13 26.2	16 31.7	18 44.6
20 M	15 48 37	28 30 10	17 56 49	24 51 48	20R 16.6	3 46.9	12 5.2	26 12.4	7 13.9	6 50.1	13 24.8	16 30.8	18 42.9
21 Tu	15 52 33	29 27 55	1♍42 0	8♍27 32	20 16.9	5 6.4	13 10.3	26 47.2	7 22.1	6 49.8	13 23.3	16 29.9	18 41.3
22 W	15 56 30	0♊25 38	15 8 38	21 45 28	20 15.8	6 28.5	14 15.2	27 22.1	7 30.5	6 49.4	13 21.8	16 28.9	18 39.6
23 Th	16 0 26	1 23 20	28 18 17	4♎47 19	20 12.8	7 53.0	15 19.8	27 57.0	7 38.9	6 48.9	13 20.2	16 27.9	18 38.0
24 F	16 4 23	2 21 0	11♎12 47	17 34 53	20 7.7	9 20.0	16 24.2	28 32.0	7 47.4	6 48.2	13 18.6	16 26.8	18 36.4
25 Sa	16 8 20	3 18 39	23 53 48	0♏ 9 43	20 0.9	10 49.3	17 28.4	29 7.0	7 56.1	6 47.5	13 17.0	16 25.8	18 34.8
26 Su	16 12 16	4 16 16	6♏22 49	12 33 13	19 53.0	12 21.1	18 32.3	29 42.0	8 4.9	6 46.7	13 15.3	16 24.7	18 33.1
27 M	16 16 13	5 13 52	18 41 5	24 46 34	19 44.8	13 55.2	19 35.9	0♌17.1	8 13.8	6 45.8	13 13.6	16 23.6	18 31.6
28 Tu	16 20 9	6 11 27	0♐49 49	6♐51 1	19 37.2	15 31.8	20 39.3	0 52.2	8 22.8	6 44.8	13 11.8	16 22.5	18 30.0
29 W	16 24 6	7 9 0	12 50 19	18 47 57	19 30.8	17 10.7	21 42.5	1 27.3	8 31.9	6 43.7	13 10.1	16 21.4	18 28.4
30 Th	16 28 2	8 6 33	24 44 10	0♑39 12	19 26.1	18 51.9	22 45.3	2 2.5	8 41.1	6 42.5	13 8.2	16 20.2	18 26.8
31 F	16 31 59	9 4 4	6♑33 24	12 27 5	19 23.3	20 35.5	23 47.9	2 37.8	8 50.4	6 41.3	13 6.4	16 19.0	18 25.3

LONGITUDE — JUNE 1991

Day	Sid.Time	☉	0 hr ☽	Noon ☽	True ☊	☿	♀	♂	♃	♄	♅	♆	♇
1 Sa	16 35 56	10♊ 1 35	18♑20 38	24♑14 30	19♑22.4	22♉21.5	24♋50.1	3♌13.0	8♌59.8	6♒39.9	13♑ 4.5	16♑17.8	18♏23.8
2 Su	16 39 52	10 59 4	0♒ 9 7	6♒ 5 0	19D 22.9	24 9.7	25 52.1	3 48.3	9 9.3	6R 38.4	13R 2.6	16R 16.6	18R 22.2
3 M	16 43 49	11 56 33	12 2 40	18 2 42	19 24.3	26 0.4	26 53.8	4 23.7	9 18.9	6 36.9	13 0.7	16 15.3	18 20.7
4 Tu	16 47 45	12 54 1	24 5 40	0♓12 9	19 26.0	27 53.2	27 55.1	4 59.1	9 28.6	6 35.2	12 58.7	16 14.1	18 19.2
5 W	16 51 42	13 51 28	6♓22 47	12 38 7	19R 27.2	29 48.4	28 56.1	5 34.5	9 38.4	6 33.5	12 56.7	16 12.8	18 17.8
6 Th	16 55 38	14 48 54	18 58 45	25 25 11	19 27.3	1♊45.7	29 56.8	6 9.9	9 48.3	6 31.6	12 54.7	16 11.5	18 16.3
7 F	16 59 35	15 46 20	1♈57 53	8♈37 15	19 26.2	3 45.2	0♌57.1	6 45.4	9 58.3	6 29.7	12 52.7	16 10.1	18 14.8
8 Sa	17 3 31	16 43 45	15 23 31	22 16 52	19 23.6	5 46.7	1 57.1	7 21.0	10 8.4	6 27.7	12 50.6	16 8.8	18 13.4
9 Su	17 7 28	17 41 9	29 17 15	6♉24 30	19 20.0	7 50.2	2 56.8	7 56.5	10 18.6	6 25.6	12 48.5	16 7.4	18 12.0
10 M	17 11 24	18 38 33	13♉38 14	20 57 53	19 15.7	9 55.4	3 56.0	8 32.2	10 28.8	6 23.4	12 46.3	16 6.1	18 10.6
11 Tu	17 15 21	19 35 57	28 22 44	5♊51 50	19 11.5	12 2.3	4 54.9	9 7.8	10 39.2	6 21.2	12 44.2	16 4.7	18 9.2
12 W	17 19 18	20 33 20	13♊24 9	20 58 31	19 7.9	14 10.6	5 53.4	9 43.5	10 49.6	6 18.8	12 42.0	16 3.2	18 7.9
13 Th	17 23 14	21 30 42	28 33 43	6♋ 8 33	19 5.5	16 20.2	6 51.4	10 19.2	11 0.1	6 16.4	12 39.8	16 1.8	18 6.6
14 F	17 27 11	22 28 4	13♋41 49	21 12 28	19D 4.4	18 30.7	7 49.1	10 55.0	11 10.7	6 13.9	12 37.6	16 0.4	18 5.2
15 Sa	17 31 7	23 25 24	28 39 30	6♌ 2 6	19 4.5	20 42.0	8 46.3	11 30.8	11 21.4	6 11.3	12 35.4	15 58.9	18 4.0
16 Su	17 35 4	24 22 44	13♌19 38	20 31 36	19 5.5	22 53.7	9 43.0	12 6.7	11 32.2	6 8.6	12 33.1	15 57.5	18 2.7
17 M	17 39 0	25 20 3	27 37 40	4♍37 41	19 6.9	25 5.7	10 39.3	12 42.5	11 43.0	6 5.9	12 30.9	15 56.0	18 1.4
18 Tu	17 42 57	26 17 21	11♍31 35	18 19 29	19 8.1	27 17.5	11 35.1	13 18.4	11 53.9	6 3.1	12 28.6	15 54.5	18 0.2
19 W	17 46 54	27 14 38	25 1 31	1♎37 57	19R 8.7	29 29.0	12 30.3	13 54.4	12 4.9	6 0.2	12 26.3	15 53.0	17 59.0
20 Th	17 50 50	28 11 54	8♎ 9 6	14 35 17	19 8.4	1♋39.9	13 25.1	14 30.4	12 16.0	5 57.2	12 23.9	15 51.5	17 57.8
21 F	17 54 47	29 9 10	20 56 55	27 14 20	19 7.2	3 49.9	14 19.3	15 6.4	12 27.1	5 54.1	12 21.6	15 49.9	17 56.7
22 Sa	17 58 43	0♋ 6 24	3♏27 57	9♏38 9	19 5.2	5 58.8	15 12.9	15 42.4	12 38.3	5 51.0	12 19.3	15 48.4	17 55.5
23 Su	18 2 40	1 3 39	15 45 17	21 49 43	19 2.6	8 6.5	16 5.9	16 18.5	12 49.6	5 47.8	12 16.9	15 46.8	17 54.4
24 M	18 6 36	2 0 52	27 51 48	3♐51 50	19 0.0	10 12.7	16 58.4	16 54.6	13 1.0	5 44.6	12 14.5	15 45.3	17 53.3
25 Tu	18 10 33	2 58 6	9♐50 8	15 47 1	18 57.6	12 17.3	17 50.2	17 30.7	13 12.4	5 41.2	12 12.2	15 43.7	17 52.3
26 W	18 14 29	3 55 18	21 42 45	27 37 36	18 55.6	14 20.2	18 41.3	18 6.9	13 23.8	5 37.8	12 9.8	15 42.1	17 51.3
27 Th	18 18 26	4 52 31	3♑31 52	9♑25 49	18 54.4	16 21.3	19 31.8	18 43.1	13 35.4	5 34.4	12 7.4	15 40.6	17 50.2
28 F	18 22 23	5 49 43	15 19 43	21 13 53	18D 53.8	18 20.5	20 21.5	19 19.3	13 47.0	5 30.9	12 5.0	15 39.0	17 49.3
29 Sa	18 26 19	6 46 55	27 8 35	3♒ 4 10	18 54.0	20 17.7	21 10.6	19 55.6	13 58.6	5 27.3	12 2.6	15 37.4	17 48.3
30 Su	18 30 16	7 44 6	9♒ 0 58	14 59 20	18 54.6	22 12.9	21 58.9	20 31.9	14 10.4	5 23.7	12 0.2	15 35.8	17 47.4

Astro Data Dy Hr Mn	Planet Ingress Dy Hr Mn	Last Aspect Dy Hr Mn	☽ Ingress Dy Hr Mn	Last Aspect Dy Hr Mn	☽ Ingress Dy Hr Mn	☽ Phases & Eclipses Dy Hr Mn	Astro Data
☽0N 9 17:20	♀ ♋ 9 1:28	2 12:59 ♀ ☍	♑ 3 3:55	1 14:28 ♀ ☍	♒ 1 23:42	7 0:46 ☽ 15♒59	1 MAY 1991
♃☍♄ 17 1:24	☿ ♉ 16 22:45	4 19:48 ☿ □	♒ 5 16:51	4 8:51 ☿ □	♓ 4 11:36	14 4:36 ● 22♉54	Julian Day # 33358
♄ R 17 4:05	☉ ♊ 21 13:20	8 1:57 ♀ △	♓ 8 4:04	5 22:40 ♇ △	♈ 6 20:25	20 19:46 ☽ 29♌18	Delta T 57.6 sec
☽0S 22 8:17	♂ ♌ 26 12:19	9 18:06 ♂ △	♈ 10 11:35	8 2:31 ☉ ✶	♉ 9 1:13	28 11:37 ○ 6♐39	SVP 05♓22'37"
		12 6:51 ☿ ☌	♉ 12 15:07	10 7:26 ♇ ☍	♊ 11 2:36		Obliquity 23°26'29"
☽0N 6 0:58	☿ ♊ 5 2:24	14 4:36 ☉ ☌	♊ 14 16:02	12 12:06 ☉ ☌	♋ 13 2:16	5 15:30 ☽ 14♓29	⚷ Chiron 22♋13.3
☽0S 18 13:53	♀ ♌ 6 1:16	16 15:40 ☿ ✶	♋ 16 16:14	14 7:00 ♇ △	♌ 15 2:10	12 12:06 ● 21♊02	☽ Mean ☊ 22♑46.7
♃⊼♅ 20 14:10	☿ ♋ 19 5:40	18 12:37 ☉ ✶	♌ 18 17:30	16 19:49 ☉ ✶	♍ 17 4:03	19 4:19 ☽ 27♍25	1 JUNE 1991
	☉ ♋ 21 21:19	20 19:46 ☉ □	♍ 20 21:00	19 4:19 ☉ □	♎ 19 9:01	27 2:58 ○ 4♑60	Julian Day # 33389
		22 23:19 ♂ ✶	♎ 23 3:08	21 16:58 ☉ △	♏ 21 17:18	27 3:15 ☍ A 0.312	Delta T 57.6 sec
		25 10:29 ♂ □	♏ 25 11:41	23 4:14 ♇ ☌	♐ 24 4:16		SVP 05♓22'32"
		27 1:58 ♀ △	♐ 27 22:21	25 17:24 ♀ △	♑ 26 16:49		Obliquity 23°26'28"
		28 15:15 ♃ △	♑ 30 10:40	28 7:21 ☿ ☍	♒ 29 5:47		⚷ Chiron 24♋33.3
							☽ Mean ☊ 21♑08.2

JULY 1991 LONGITUDE

Day	Sid.Time	☉	0 hr ☽	Noon ☽	True ☊	☿	♀	♂	♃	♄	♅	♆	♇
1 M	18 34 12	8♋41 18	20♒59 39	27♒ 2 19	18♑55.5	24♋ 6.1	22♌46.4	21♌ 8.3	14♌22.1	5♒20.0	11♑57.7	15♑34.2	17♏46.5
2 Tu	18 38 9	9 38 30	3♓ 7 45	9♓16 24	18 56.4	25 57.2	23 33.1	21 44.6	14 34.0	5R 16.3	11R 55.3	15R 32.6	17R 45.6
3 W	18 42 5	10 35 42	15 28 42	21 45 7	18 57.2	27 46.2	24 19.0	22 21.0	14 45.8	5 12.5	11 52.9	15 31.0	17 44.8
4 Th	18 46 2	11 32 53	28 6 6	4♈32 5	18 57.8	29 33.2	25 4.0	22 57.5	14 57.8	5 8.6	11 50.5	15 29.3	17 44.0
5 F	18 49 58	12 30 6	11♈ 3 29	17 40 38	18R 58.0	1♌18.1	25 48.1	23 33.9	15 9.8	5 4.7	11 48.0	15 27.7	17 43.2
6 Sa	18 53 55	13 27 18	24 23 51	1♉13 22	18 57.9	3 0.9	26 31.3	24 10.4	15 21.8	5 0.8	11 45.6	15 26.1	17 42.4
7 Su	18 57 52	14 24 31	8♉ 9 16	15 11 35	18 57.6	4 41.6	27 13.5	24 47.0	15 33.9	4 56.8	11 43.2	15 24.5	17 41.7
8 M	19 1 48	15 21 44	22 20 9	29 34 39	18 57.2	6 20.2	27 54.7	25 23.6	15 46.1	4 52.7	11 40.7	15 22.9	17 41.0
9 Tu	19 5 45	16 18 58	6♊54 39	14♊19 30	18 56.9	7 56.7	28 34.9	26 0.2	15 58.3	4 48.7	11 38.3	15 21.2	17 40.3
10 W	19 9 41	17 16 12	21 48 25	29 20 29	18 56.7	9 31.1	29 14.1	26 36.8	16 10.5	4 44.5	11 35.9	15 19.6	17 39.7
11 Th	19 13 38	18 13 26	6♋54 37	14♋29 42	18 56.6	11 3.3	29 52.1	27 13.5	16 22.8	4 40.4	11 33.5	15 18.0	17 39.1
12 F	19 17 34	19 10 41	22 4 34	29 38 2	18 56.6	12 33.5	0♍28.9	27 50.3	16 35.2	4 36.2	11 31.1	15 16.4	17 38.5
13 Sa	19 21 31	20 7 55	7♌ 8 58	14♌36 20	18 56.6	14 1.5	1 4.6	28 27.0	16 47.6	4 32.0	11 28.7	15 14.8	17 38.0
14 Su	19 25 28	21 5 10	21 59 13	29 16 50	18 56.5	15 27.4	1 38.9	29 3.8	16 60.0	4 27.7	11 26.3	15 13.1	17 37.5
15 M	19 29 24	22 2 25	6♍28 34	13♍34 0	18 56.2	16 51.0	2 12.0	29 40.6	17 12.4	4 23.4	11 23.9	15 11.5	17 37.0
16 Tu	19 33 21	22 59 40	20 32 50	27 24 58	18 55.8	18 12.4	2 43.7	0♍17.5	17 24.9	4 19.1	11 21.6	15 9.9	17 36.6
17 W	19 37 17	23 56 55	4♎10 25	10♎49 22	18 55.4	19 31.5	3 14.0	0 54.4	17 37.5	4 14.8	11 19.2	15 8.3	17 36.2
18 Th	19 41 14	24 54 10	17 22 3	23 48 51	18D 55.2	20 48.3	3 42.8	1 31.3	17 50.1	4 10.4	11 16.9	15 6.7	17 35.8
19 F	19 45 10	25 51 25	0♏10 10	6♏26 28	18 55.1	22 2.8	4 10.1	2 8.3	18 2.7	4 6.0	11 14.5	15 5.1	17 35.4
20 Sa	19 49 7	26 48 40	12 38 16	18 46 4	18 55.4	23 14.8	4 35.8	2 45.3	18 15.3	4 1.6	11 12.2	15 3.6	17 35.1
21 Su	19 53 3	27 45 56	24 50 24	0♐51 48	18 56.1	24 24.3	4 59.9	3 22.3	18 28.0	3 57.2	11 9.9	15 2.0	17 34.8
22 M	19 57 0	28 43 12	6♐50 46	12 47 47	18 57.0	25 31.2	5 22.3	3 59.4	18 40.7	3 52.8	11 7.7	15 0.4	17 34.6
23 Tu	20 0 57	29 40 28	18 43 21	24 37 53	18 58.0	26 35.4	5 42.9	4 36.5	18 53.4	3 48.4	11 5.4	14 58.8	17 34.4
24 W	20 4 53	0♌37 45	0♑31 50	6♑25 35	18 58.9	27 36.9	6 1.6	5 13.6	19 6.2	3 43.9	11 3.1	14 57.3	17 34.2
25 Th	20 8 50	1 35 2	12 19 30	18 13 55	18R 59.5	28 35.5	6 18.5	5 50.7	19 19.0	3 39.5	11 0.9	14 55.8	17 34.0
26 F	20 12 46	2 32 19	24 9 9	0♒ 5 30	18 59.5	29 31.2	6 33.4	6 27.9	19 31.8	3 35.0	10 58.7	14 54.2	17 33.9
27 Sa	20 16 43	3 29 38	6♒ 3 13	12 2 35	18 58.8	0♍23.7	6 46.4	7 5.1	19 44.7	3 30.5	10 56.5	14 52.7	17 33.8
28 Su	20 20 39	4 26 56	18 3 51	24 7 13	18 57.5	1 13.0	6 57.3	7 42.4	19 57.5	3 26.1	10 54.4	14 51.2	17D 33.8
29 M	20 24 36	5 24 16	0♓12 56	6♓21 15	18 55.4	1 58.9	7 6.0	8 19.7	20 10.4	3 21.6	10 52.2	14 49.7	17 33.8
30 Tu	20 28 32	6 21 37	12 32 21	18 46 31	18 52.9	2 41.2	7 12.7	8 57.0	20 23.4	3 17.2	10 50.1	14 48.2	17 33.8
31 W	20 32 29	7 18 58	25 3 57	1♈24 55	18 50.3	3 19.9	7 17.1	9 34.4	20 36.3	3 12.7	10 48.0	14 46.7	17 33.8

AUGUST 1991 LONGITUDE

Day	Sid.Time	☉	0 hr ☽	Noon ☽	True ☊	☿	♀	♂	♃	♄	♅	♆	♇
1 Th	20 36 26	8♌16 20	7♈49 38	14♈18 23	18♑47.9	3♍54.7	7♍19.2	10♍11.8	20♌49.3	3♒ 8.3	10♑45.9	14♑45.3	17♏33.9
2 F	20 40 22	9 13 44	20 51 23	27 28 52	18R 46.1	4 25.4	7R 19.1	10 49.2	21 2.2	3R 3.8	10R 43.9	14R 43.8	17 34.0
3 Sa	20 44 19	10 11 8	4♉11 3	10♉58 6	18D 45.2	4 51.9	7 16.6	11 26.6	21 15.2	2 59.4	10 41.9	14 42.4	17 34.2
4 Su	20 48 15	11 8 34	17 50 8	24 47 14	18 45.2	5 14.0	7 11.8	12 4.2	21 28.3	2 55.0	10 39.9	14 41.0	17 34.4
5 M	20 52 12	12 6 1	1♊49 23	8♊56 30	18 46.0	5 31.5	7 4.7	12 41.7	21 41.3	2 50.6	10 37.9	14 39.6	17 34.6
6 Tu	20 56 8	13 3 30	16 8 21	23 24 37	18 47.3	5 44.2	6 55.1	13 19.3	21 54.3	2 46.3	10 36.0	14 38.2	17 34.9
7 W	21 0 5	14 1 0	0♋44 50	8♋ 6 25	18 48.6	5R 51.9	6 43.3	13 56.9	22 7.4	2 41.9	10 34.1	14 36.8	17 35.2
8 Th	21 4 1	14 58 31	15 34 39	23 2 41	18R 49.4	5 54.5	6 29.0	14 34.6	22 20.5	2 37.6	10 32.2	14 35.5	17 35.5
9 F	21 7 58	15 56 3	0♌31 35	8♌ 0 21	18 49.0	5 51.9	6 12.5	15 12.3	22 33.6	2 33.3	10 30.4	14 34.2	17 35.8
10 Sa	21 11 55	16 53 36	15 27 56	22 53 17	18 47.3	5 43.8	5 53.6	15 50.0	22 46.7	2 29.1	10 28.6	14 32.8	17 36.2
11 Su	21 15 51	17 51 10	0♍15 26	7♍33 25	18 44.3	5 30.4	5 32.5	16 27.8	22 59.8	2 24.8	10 26.8	14 31.5	17 36.7
12 M	21 19 48	18 48 46	14 46 28	21 53 53	18 40.2	5 11.6	5 9.3	17 5.6	23 12.9	2 20.6	10 25.1	14 30.3	17 37.1
13 Tu	21 23 44	19 46 22	28 55 11	5♎50 0	18 35.7	4 47.4	4 44.0	17 43.4	23 26.0	2 16.5	10 23.4	14 29.0	17 37.6
14 W	21 27 41	20 43 59	12♎38 9	19 19 37	18 31.3	4 18.0	4 16.7	18 21.3	23 39.1	2 12.4	10 21.7	14 27.8	17 38.2
15 Th	21 31 37	21 41 37	25 54 31	2♏23 6	18 27.7	3 43.7	3 47.5	18 59.2	23 52.3	2 8.3	10 20.1	14 26.6	17 38.7
16 F	21 35 34	22 39 17	8♏45 43	15 2 49	18 25.3	3 4.9	3 16.7	19 37.1	24 5.4	2 4.2	10 18.5	14 25.4	17 39.3
17 Sa	21 39 30	23 36 57	21 14 55	27 22 34	18D 24.3	2 21.9	2 44.3	20 15.1	24 18.5	2 0.2	10 16.9	14 24.2	17 39.9
18 Su	21 43 27	24 34 38	3♐26 23	9♐26 59	18 24.7	1 35.4	2 10.6	20 53.2	24 31.7	1 56.3	10 15.4	14 23.0	17 40.6
19 M	21 47 24	25 32 21	15 24 58	21 21 0	18 26.0	0 46.2	1 35.7	21 31.2	24 44.8	1 52.4	10 14.0	14 21.9	17 41.3
20 Tu	21 51 20	26 30 4	27 15 39	3♑ 9 33	18 27.7	29♌55.0	0 59.9	22 9.3	24 57.9	1 48.5	10 12.5	14 20.8	17 42.0
21 W	21 55 17	27 27 49	9♑ 3 13	14 57 13	18R 29.0	29 2.7	0 23.3	22 47.4	25 11.1	1 44.7	10 11.1	14 19.7	17 42.8
22 Th	21 59 13	28 25 35	20 52 2	26 48 6	18 29.4	28 10.5	29♌46.2	23 25.6	25 24.2	1 41.0	10 9.8	14 18.7	17 43.6
23 F	22 3 10	29 23 22	2♒45 49	8♒45 34	18 28.3	27 19.2	29 8.9	24 3.8	25 37.3	1 37.3	10 8.5	14 17.6	17 44.4
24 Sa	22 7 6	0♍21 10	14 47 39	20 52 18	18 25.3	26 30.0	28 31.5	24 42.1	25 50.4	1 33.7	10 7.2	14 16.6	17 45.3
25 Su	22 11 3	1 18 59	26 59 45	3♓10 10	18 20.3	25 44.0	27 54.4	25 20.3	26 3.5	1 30.1	10 5.9	14 15.6	17 46.2
26 M	22 14 59	2 16 50	9♓23 40	15 40 19	18 13.8	25 2.1	27 17.8	25 58.6	26 16.6	1 26.6	10 4.8	14 14.7	17 47.1
27 Tu	22 18 56	3 14 43	22 0 10	28 23 16	18 6.1	24 25.4	26 41.9	26 37.0	26 29.7	1 23.1	10 3.6	14 13.8	17 48.1
28 W	22 22 52	4 12 37	4♈49 35	11♈19 8	17 58.1	23 54.6	26 6.9	27 15.4	26 42.8	1 19.7	10 2.5	14 12.8	17 49.1
29 Th	22 26 49	5 10 33	17 51 53	24 27 50	17 50.6	23 30.5	25 33.1	27 53.8	26 55.8	1 16.4	10 1.4	14 12.0	17 50.1
30 F	22 30 46	6 8 31	1♉ 6 57	7♉49 15	17 44.4	23 13.7	25 0.7	28 32.3	27 8.9	1 13.2	10 0.4	14 11.1	17 51.1
31 Sa	22 34 42	7 6 30	14 34 44	21 23 25	17 40.1	23D 4.6	24 29.8	29 10.8	27 21.9	1 10.0	9 59.5	14 10.3	17 52.2

Astro Data	Planet Ingress	Last Aspect	☽ Ingress	Last Aspect	☽ Ingress	☽ Phases & Eclipses	Astro Data
Dy Hr Mn	Dy Hr Mn	Dy Hr Mn	Dy Hr Mn	Dy Hr Mn	Dy Hr Mn	Dy Hr Mn	1 JULY 1991
☽0N 3 7:19	☿ ♌ 4 6:05	1 3:47 ♀ ☍	♓ 1 17:51	2 0:20 ♃ △	♉ 2 16:32	5 2:50 ☽ 12♈37	Julian Day # 33419
♃⊼♆ 6 7:29	♀ ♍ 11 5:06	4 3:09 ☿ △	♈ 4 3:33	4 6:24 ♃ □	♊ 4 20:54	11 19:06 ● 18♋59	Delta T 57.7 sec
☽0S 15 21:50	♂ ♍ 15 12:36	6 3:58 ♀ △	♉ 6 9:52	6 9:40 ♃ ✶	♋ 6 22:47	11 19:06:03 ☌T 6'53"	SVP 05♓22'26"
♃□♇ 16 21:33	☉ ♌ 23 8:11	8 9:42 ♀ □	♊ 8 12:42	8 3:14 ♇ △	♌ 8 23:09	18 15:11 ☽ 25♎30	Obliquity 23°26'28"
♇ D 28 23:47	☿ ♍ 26 13:00	10 12:21 ♀ ✶	♋ 10 13:03	10 12:00 ♃ ☌	♍ 10 23:35	26 18:24 ○ 3♒16	⚷ Chiron 27♋37.7
☽0N 30 13:06		11 19:06 ☉ ☌	♌ 12 12:35	12 4:47 ♇ ✶	♎ 13 1:52	26 18:08 ☍A 0.254	☽ Mean ☊ 19♑32.9
	☿ ♌ 19 21:40	14 12:09 ♂ ☌	♍ 14 13:12	14 20:12 ♃ ✶	♏ 15 7:34		
♀ R 1 10:35	♀ ♌ 21 15:06	16 4:34 ☉ ✶	♎ 16 16:34	17 6:05 ♃ □	♐ 17 17:11	3 11:25 ☽ 10♉38	1 AUGUST 1991
☿ R 7 23:58	☉ ♍ 23 15:13	18 15:11 ☉ □	♏ 18 23:41	20 5:02 ☿ △	♑ 20 5:34	10 2:28 ● 16♌60	Julian Day # 33450
☽0S 12 7:48		21 6:19 ☉ △	♐ 21 10:16	22 5:29 ♂ △	♒ 22 18:27	17 5:01 ☽ 23♏49	Delta T 57.7 sec
♃⚼♅ 21 0:06		23 17:31 ☿ △	♑ 23 22:55	25 1:42 ♀ ☍	♓ 25 5:51	25 9:07 ○ 1♓41	SVP 05♓22'21"
☽0N 26 19:17		25 10:39 ♇ ✶	♒ 26 11:49	27 9:08 ♂ ☍	♈ 27 15:01		Obliquity 23°26'28"
☿ D 31 14:35		28 3:50 ♃ ☍	♓ 28 23:35	29 16:44 ♃ △	♉ 29 22:00		⚷ Chiron 1♌11.1
		30 9:41 ♇ △	♈ 31 9:20				☽ Mean ☊ 17♑54.5

LONGITUDE SEPTEMBER 1991

Day	Sid.Time	☉	0 hr ☽	Noon ☽	True ☊	☿	♀	♂	♃	♄	♅	♆	♇
1 Su	22 38 39	8♍ 4 32	28♉15 19	5♊10 26	17♑37.9	23♌ 3.7	24♌ 0.6	29♍49.3	27♌34.9	1♒ 6.9	9♑58.5	14♑ 9.5	17♏53.4
2 M	22 42 35	9 2 35	12♊ 8 47	19 10 20	17D 37.4	23 11.2	23R 33.3	0♎27.9	27 47.9	1R 3.8	9R 57.7	14R 8.7	17 54.5
3 Tu	22 46 32	10 0 41	26 15 0	3♋22 39	17 38.2	23 27.2	23 8.0	1 6.6	28 0.9	1 0.8	9 56.8	14 8.0	17 55.7
4 W	22 50 28	10 58 48	10♋33 6	17 46 3	17R 39.0	23 51.7	22 44.9	1 45.2	28 13.9	0 58.0	9 56.1	14 7.3	17 56.9
5 Th	22 54 25	11 56 57	25 1 7	2♌17 48	17 39.0	24 24.6	22 23.9	2 24.0	28 26.8	0 55.1	9 55.3	14 6.6	17 58.1
6 F	22 58 21	12 55 9	9♌35 32	16 53 37	17 37.1	25 5.6	22 5.2	3 2.7	28 39.8	0 52.4	9 54.6	14 5.9	17 59.4
7 Sa	23 2 18	13 53 22	24 11 18	1♍27 46	17 32.8	25 54.6	21 48.8	3 41.5	28 52.7	0 49.7	9 54.0	14 5.3	18 0.7
8 Su	23 6 15	14 51 37	8♍42 10	15 53 42	17 26.2	26 51.2	21 34.7	4 20.4	29 5.6	0 47.1	9 53.4	14 4.7	18 2.0
9 M	23 10 11	15 49 53	23 1 33	0♎ 5 0	17 17.5	27 55.0	21 23.1	4 59.3	29 18.4	0 44.6	9 52.8	14 4.1	18 3.4
10 Tu	23 14 8	16 48 12	7♎ 3 27	13 56 24	17 7.8	29 5.5	21 13.9	5 38.2	29 31.2	0 42.2	9 52.3	14 3.6	18 4.8
11 W	23 18 4	17 46 32	20 43 30	27 24 34	16 58.1	0♍22.2	21 7.1	6 17.1	29 44.0	0 39.9	9 51.9	14 3.1	18 6.2
12 Th	23 22 1	18 44 53	3♏59 31	10♏28 27	16 49.5	1 44.6	21 2.6	6 56.2	29 56.8	0 37.7	9 51.5	14 2.6	18 7.7
13 F	23 25 57	19 43 17	16 51 35	23 9 14	16 42.7	3 12.1	21D 0.6	7 35.2	0♍ 9.6	0 35.5	9 51.2	14 2.2	18 9.1
14 Sa	23 29 54	20 41 42	29 21 49	5♐29 52	16 38.2	4 44.2	21 0.9	8 14.3	0 22.3	0 33.4	9 50.9	14 1.8	18 10.6
15 Su	23 33 50	21 40 9	11♐33 56	17 34 38	16D 35.9	6 20.2	21 3.5	8 53.4	0 34.9	0 31.4	9 50.6	14 1.4	18 12.2
16 M	23 37 47	22 38 37	23 32 39	29 28 37	16 35.4	7 59.7	21 8.4	9 32.6	0 47.6	0 29.6	9 50.4	14 1.0	18 13.7
17 Tu	23 41 44	23 37 7	5♑23 15	11♑17 13	16R 35.8	9 42.1	21 15.5	10 11.8	1 0.2	0 27.8	9 50.3	14 0.7	18 15.3
18 W	23 45 40	24 35 38	17 11 11	23 5 49	16 36.1	11 26.8	21 24.8	10 51.1	1 12.7	0 26.1	9 50.2	14 0.4	18 16.9
19 Th	23 49 37	25 34 12	29 1 42	4♒59 27	16 35.4	13 13.5	21 36.3	11 30.4	1 25.3	0 24.4	9D 50.1	14 0.2	18 18.6
20 F	23 53 33	26 32 47	10♒59 33	17 2 31	16 32.7	15 1.7	21 49.8	12 9.7	1 37.7	0 22.9	9 50.2	13 60.0	18 20.2
21 Sa	23 57 30	27 31 23	23 8 44	29 18 32	16 27.5	16 51.0	22 5.4	12 49.1	1 50.2	0 21.5	9 50.2	13 59.8	18 21.9
22 Su	0 1 26	28 30 1	5♓32 11	11♓49 52	16 19.6	18 41.0	22 23.0	13 28.5	2 2.6	0 20.1	9 50.3	13 59.6	18 23.6
23 M	0 5 23	29 28 42	18 11 41	24 37 39	16 9.4	20 31.6	22 42.4	14 7.9	2 14.9	0 18.9	9 50.5	13 59.5	18 25.4
24 Tu	0 9 19	0♎27 24	1♈ 7 41	7♈41 40	15 57.6	22 22.4	23 3.8	14 47.4	2 27.2	0 17.8	9 50.7	13 59.4	18 27.1
25 W	0 13 16	1 26 8	14 19 23	21 0 35	15 45.2	24 13.3	23 26.9	15 27.0	2 39.5	0 16.7	9 50.9	13 59.3	18 28.9
26 Th	0 17 13	2 24 54	27 44 58	4♉32 15	15 33.5	26 4.0	23 51.8	16 6.5	2 51.7	0 15.8	9 51.3	13D 59.3	18 30.7
27 F	0 21 9	3 23 42	11♉22 6	18 14 12	15 23.6	27 54.3	24 18.3	16 46.2	3 3.9	0 14.9	9 51.6	13 59.3	18 32.6
28 Sa	0 25 6	4 22 32	25 8 18	2♊ 4 7	15 16.2	29 44.3	24 46.5	17 25.8	3 16.0	0 14.1	9 52.0	13 59.4	18 34.4
29 Su	0 29 2	5 21 25	9♊ 1 27	16 0 9	15 11.6	1♎33.7	25 16.3	18 5.6	3 28.1	0 13.5	9 52.5	13 59.4	18 36.3
30 M	0 32 59	6 20 20	23 0 4	0♋ 1 6	15 9.6	3 22.5	25 47.6	18 45.3	3 40.1	0 12.9	9 53.0	13 59.5	18 38.2

LONGITUDE OCTOBER 1991

Day	Sid.Time	☉	0 hr ☽	Noon ☽	True ☊	☿	♀	♂	♃	♄	♅	♆	♇
1 Tu	0 36 55	7♎19 18	7♋ 3 9	14♋ 6 10	15♑ 9.1	5♎10.7	26♌20.4	19♎25.1	3♍52.1	0♒12.5	9♑53.6	13♑59.7	18♏40.1
2 W	0 40 52	8 18 18	21 10 2	28 14 40	15R 9.1	6 58.1	26 54.5	20 5.0	4 4.0	0R 12.1	9 54.2	13 59.8	18 42.1
3 Th	0 44 48	9 17 20	5♌19 53	12♌25 28	15 8.1	8 44.7	27 30.0	20 44.9	4 15.8	0 11.8	9 54.9	14 0.1	18 44.1
4 F	0 48 45	10 16 24	19 31 9	26 36 36	15 5.1	10 30.6	28 6.9	21 24.9	4 27.6	0 11.7	9 55.6	14 0.3	18 46.0
5 Sa	0 52 42	11 15 30	3♍41 23	10♍45 2	14 59.2	12 15.7	28 45.0	22 4.8	4 39.3	0D 11.6	9 56.4	14 0.6	18 48.0
6 Su	0 56 38	12 14 39	17 47 1	24 46 47	14 50.4	13 60.0	29 24.2	22 44.9	4 51.0	0 11.6	9 57.2	14 0.9	18 50.1
7 M	1 0 35	13 13 50	1♎43 47	8♎37 27	14 39.2	15 43.5	0♍ 4.7	23 25.0	5 2.6	0 11.8	9 58.1	14 1.2	18 52.1
8 Tu	1 4 31	14 13 3	15 27 17	22 12 51	14 26.5	17 26.2	0 46.2	24 5.1	5 14.2	0 12.0	9 59.0	14 1.6	18 54.2
9 W	1 8 28	15 12 18	28 53 46	5♏29 48	14 13.7	19 8.0	1 28.9	24 45.3	5 25.6	0 12.3	9 60.0	14 2.0	18 56.3
10 Th	1 12 24	16 11 35	12♏ 0 46	18 26 40	14 2.0	20 49.2	2 12.5	25 25.5	5 37.0	0 12.8	10 1.0	14 2.4	18 58.4
11 F	1 16 21	17 10 54	24 47 32	1♐ 3 34	13 52.4	22 29.5	2 57.2	26 5.8	5 48.4	0 13.3	10 2.1	14 2.9	19 0.5
12 Sa	1 20 17	18 10 15	7♐15 3	13 22 22	13 45.4	24 9.1	3 42.8	26 46.1	5 59.6	0 14.0	10 3.2	14 3.4	19 2.6
13 Su	1 24 14	19 9 38	19 25 57	25 26 22	13 41.2	25 47.9	4 29.4	27 26.4	6 10.8	0 14.7	10 4.4	14 4.0	19 4.8
14 M	1 28 11	20 9 2	1♑24 10	7♑19 59	13 39.3	27 26.0	5 16.8	28 6.8	6 21.9	0 15.5	10 5.6	14 4.5	19 7.0
15 Tu	1 32 7	21 8 29	13 14 30	19 8 22	13 38.8	29 3.4	6 5.1	28 47.3	6 32.9	0 16.5	10 6.9	14 5.1	19 9.1
16 W	1 36 4	22 7 57	25 2 19	0♒57 2	13 38.9	0♏40.1	6 54.2	29 27.8	6 43.9	0 17.5	10 8.2	14 5.8	19 11.3
17 Th	1 40 0	23 7 27	6♒53 12	12 51 31	13 38.2	2 16.2	7 44.1	0♏ 8.3	6 54.8	0 18.7	10 9.6	14 6.5	19 13.6
18 F	1 43 57	24 6 58	18 52 35	24 57 2	13 35.8	3 51.6	8 34.8	0 48.9	7 5.6	0 19.9	10 11.0	14 7.2	19 15.8
19 Sa	1 47 53	25 6 32	1♓ 5 23	7♓18 7	13 31.1	5 26.3	9 26.3	1 29.5	7 16.3	0 21.3	10 12.4	14 7.9	19 18.0
20 Su	1 51 50	26 6 7	13 35 37	19 58 12	13 23.7	7 0.4	10 18.4	2 10.2	7 26.9	0 22.7	10 14.0	14 8.7	19 20.3
21 M	1 55 46	27 5 44	26 26 2	2♈59 12	13 13.8	8 33.9	11 11.3	2 50.9	7 37.4	0 24.3	10 15.5	14 9.5	19 22.6
22 Tu	1 59 43	28 5 22	9♈37 40	16 21 16	13 2.3	10 6.8	12 4.9	3 31.7	7 47.9	0 25.9	10 17.1	14 10.3	19 24.8
23 W	2 3 39	29 5 3	23 9 43	0♉ 2 37	12 50.1	11 39.2	12 59.1	4 12.5	7 58.2	0 27.6	10 18.8	14 11.2	19 27.1
24 Th	2 7 36	0♏ 4 46	6♉59 30	13 59 49	12 38.5	13 10.9	13 53.9	4 53.3	8 8.5	0 29.5	10 20.5	14 12.0	19 29.4
25 F	2 11 33	1 4 30	21 2 57	28 8 16	12 28.6	14 42.1	14 49.4	5 34.2	8 18.7	0 31.4	10 22.2	14 13.0	19 31.7
26 Sa	2 15 29	2 4 17	5♊15 11	12♊23 5	12 21.2	16 12.7	15 45.4	6 15.1	8 28.8	0 33.4	10 24.0	14 13.9	19 34.1
27 Su	2 19 26	3 4 6	19 31 25	26 39 44	12 16.8	17 42.8	16 42.1	6 56.1	8 38.8	0 35.6	10 25.9	14 14.9	19 36.4
28 M	2 23 22	4 3 58	3♋47 36	10♋54 42	12D 14.9	19 12.3	17 39.3	7 37.2	8 48.7	0 37.8	10 27.7	14 16.0	19 38.7
29 Tu	2 27 19	5 3 51	18 0 47	25 5 39	12 14.7	20 41.2	18 37.0	8 18.3	8 58.5	0 40.1	10 29.7	14 17.0	19 41.1
30 W	2 31 15	6 3 47	2♌ 9 9	9♌11 12	12R 15.1	22 9.6	19 35.2	8 59.4	9 8.2	0 42.5	10 31.7	14 18.1	19 43.5
31 Th	2 35 12	7 3 44	16 11 42	23 10 35	12 14.8	23 37.3	20 34.0	9 40.6	9 17.8	0 45.0	10 33.7	14 19.2	19 45.8

Astro Data	Dy Hr Mn
♂0S	3 17:37
♃☍♆	7 22:28
☽0S	8 18:08
♀ D	13 8:56
♃⊼♄	14 18:17
♅ D	19 8:37
☽0N	23 2:32
♆ D	26 7:13
☿0S	30 2:19
♄ D	5 3:57
☽0S	6 2:53
☽0N	20 10:46

Planet Ingress	Dy Hr Mn
♂ ♎	1 6:38
☿ ♍	10 17:14
♃ ♍	12 6:00
☉ ♎	23 12:48
☿ ♎	28 3:26
♀ ♍	6 21:15
☿ ♏	15 14:01
♂ ♏	16 19:05
☉ ♏	23 22:05

Last Aspect Dy Hr Mn		☽ Ingress	Dy Hr Mn
1 2:52	♂ △	♊	1 3:02
3 3:02	♃ ✶	♋	3 6:19
4 12:19	♇ △	♌	5 8:13
7 7:51	♃ ☌	♍	7 9:35
8 15:37	♇ ✶	♎	9 11:51
11 16:29	♃ ✶	♏	11 16:42
13 7:53	♀ □	♐	14 1:14
15 22:01	☉ □	♑	16 13:04
18 16:23	☉ △	♒	19 1:58
20 21:53	♀ ☍	♓	21 13:20
23 5:06	☿ ☍	♈	23 21:56
25 16:52	♀ △	♉	26 3:59
27 23:21	♀ □	♊	28 8:25
30 4:58	♀ ✶	♋	30 11:58

Last Aspect Dy Hr Mn		☽ Ingress	Dy Hr Mn
1 22:04	♂ □	♌	2 14:58
4 15:14	♀ ☌	♍	4 17:45
6 1:48	♇ ✶	♎	6 21:00
8 16:09	♂ ☌	♏	9 2:00
10 13:02	♇ ☌	♐	11 9:58
13 16:59	♂ ✶	♑	13 21:10
16 9:32	♂ □	♒	16 10:04
18 11:17	☉ △	♓	18 21:53
20 10:51	♇ △	♈	21 6:33
23 11:08	☉ ☍	♉	23 11:55
24 21:25	♇ ☍	♊	25 15:09
26 18:55	♀ □	♋	27 17:37
29 5:03	☿ △	♌	29 20:20
31 14:15	☿ □	♍	31 23:47

☽ Phases & Eclipses Dy Hr Mn	
1 18:16	☽ 8♊49
8 11:01	● 15♍18
15 22:01	☽ 22♐34
23 22:40	○ 0♈24
1 0:30	☽ 7♋21
7 21:39	● 14♎07
15 17:33	☽ 21♑52
23 11:08	○ 29♈33
30 7:11	☽ 6♌22

Astro Data

1 SEPTEMBER 1991
Julian Day # 33481
Delta T 57.8 sec
SVP 05♓22'17"
Obliquity 23°26'28"
⚷ Chiron 4♌38.6
☽ Mean ☊ 16♑16.0

1 OCTOBER 1991
Julian Day # 33511
Delta T 57.8 sec
SVP 05♓22'14"
Obliquity 23°26'28"
⚷ Chiron 7♌25.3
☽ Mean ☊ 14♑40.6

NOVEMBER 1991 LONGITUDE

Day	Sid.Time	☉	0 hr ☽	Noon ☽	True ☊	☿	♀	♂	♃	♄	♅	♆	♇
1 F	2 39 8	8♏ 3 44	0♍ 7 46	7♍ 3 9	12♑12.8	25♏ 4.5	21♍33.2	10♏21.9	9♍27.3	0♒47.6	10♑35.7	14♑20.3	19♏48.2
2 Sa	2 43 5	9 3 47	13 56 36	20 47 59	12R 8.2	26 31.1	22 32.9	11 3.1	9 36.7	0 50.3	10 37.8	14 21.5	19 50.6
3 Su	2 47 2	10 3 51	27 37 6	4♎23 44	12 1.1	27 57.0	23 33.1	11 44.5	9 45.9	0 53.1	10 40.0	14 22.7	19 53.0
4 M	2 50 58	11 3 57	11♎ 7 39	17 48 38	11 51.8	29 22.3	24 33.7	12 25.9	9 55.1	0 56.0	10 42.2	14 23.9	19 55.4
5 Tu	2 54 55	12 4 5	24 26 24	1♏ 0 46	11 41.2	0♐46.8	25 34.7	13 7.3	10 4.1	0 58.9	10 44.4	14 25.2	19 57.8
6 W	2 58 51	13 4 15	7♏31 32	13 58 31	11 30.3	2 10.6	26 36.1	13 48.8	10 13.1	1 2.0	10 46.6	14 26.5	20 0.2
7 Th	3 2 48	14 4 28	20 21 39	26 40 52	11 20.3	3 33.6	27 37.9	14 30.3	10 21.9	1 5.1	10 49.0	14 27.8	20 2.6
8 F	3 6 44	15 4 41	2♐56 13	9♐ 7 48	11 12.1	4 55.6	28 40.1	15 11.9	10 30.6	1 8.4	10 51.3	14 29.2	20 5.0
9 Sa	3 10 41	16 4 57	15 15 48	21 20 26	11 6.3	6 16.7	29 42.7	15 53.5	10 39.2	1 11.7	10 53.7	14 30.5	20 7.4
10 Su	3 14 37	17 5 14	27 22 4	3♑21 2	11 2.9	7 36.7	0♎45.6	16 35.2	10 47.7	1 15.1	10 56.1	14 31.9	20 9.8
11 M	3 18 34	18 5 33	9♑17 50	15 12 56	11D 1.7	8 55.6	1 48.9	17 16.9	10 56.0	1 18.7	10 58.6	14 33.4	20 12.2
12 Tu	3 22 31	19 5 53	21 6 53	27 0 18	11 2.2	10 13.1	2 52.5	17 58.7	11 4.2	1 22.3	11 1.1	14 34.8	20 14.7
13 W	3 26 27	20 6 15	2♒53 47	8♒48 0	11 3.4	11 29.2	3 56.4	18 40.5	11 12.3	1 25.9	11 3.7	14 36.3	20 17.1
14 Th	3 30 24	21 6 38	14 43 37	20 41 18	11R 4.5	12 43.6	5 0.7	19 22.3	11 20.3	1 29.7	11 6.2	14 37.8	20 19.5
15 F	3 34 20	22 7 3	26 41 44	2♓45 34	11 4.6	13 56.2	6 5.2	20 4.3	11 28.1	1 33.5	11 8.8	14 39.4	20 21.9
16 Sa	3 38 17	23 7 29	8♓53 26	15 5 56	11 3.0	15 6.8	7 10.1	20 46.2	11 35.8	1 37.5	11 11.5	14 40.9	20 24.3
17 Su	3 42 13	24 7 56	21 23 35	27 46 50	10 59.5	16 15.0	8 15.2	21 28.2	11 43.3	1 41.5	11 14.2	14 42.5	20 26.8
18 M	3 46 10	25 8 24	4♈16 4	10♈51 32	10 54.1	17 20.6	9 20.6	22 10.2	11 50.8	1 45.6	11 16.9	14 44.1	20 29.2
19 Tu	3 50 6	26 8 54	17 33 21	24 21 30	10 47.3	18 23.2	10 26.3	22 52.3	11 58.0	1 49.8	11 19.7	14 45.7	20 31.6
20 W	3 54 3	27 9 25	1♉15 50	8♉16 2	10 39.8	19 22.4	11 32.2	23 34.5	12 5.2	1 54.0	11 22.4	14 47.4	20 34.0
21 Th	3 58 0	28 9 58	15 21 37	22 31 59	10 32.6	20 17.8	12 38.5	24 16.7	12 12.2	1 58.3	11 25.3	14 49.1	20 36.4
22 F	4 1 56	29 10 32	29 46 25	7♊ 4 6	10 26.5	21 8.9	13 44.9	24 58.9	12 19.1	2 2.7	11 28.1	14 50.8	20 38.8
23 Sa	4 5 53	0♐11 7	14♊24 8	21 45 36	10 22.1	21 55.2	14 51.7	25 41.2	12 25.8	2 7.2	11 31.0	14 52.5	20 41.2
24 Su	4 9 49	1 11 44	29 7 37	6♋29 19	10D 19.8	22 35.9	15 58.6	26 23.5	12 32.4	2 11.8	11 33.9	14 54.3	20 43.6
25 M	4 13 46	2 12 23	13♋49 53	21 8 39	10 19.3	23 10.4	17 5.8	27 5.9	12 38.8	2 16.4	11 36.9	14 56.0	20 46.0
26 Tu	4 17 42	3 13 3	28 25 0	5♌38 26	10 20.2	23 37.9	18 13.3	27 48.3	12 45.1	2 21.2	11 39.8	14 57.8	20 48.4
27 W	4 21 39	4 13 45	12♌48 35	19 55 10	10 21.7	23 57.8	19 20.9	28 30.8	12 51.2	2 25.9	11 42.8	14 59.6	20 50.7
28 Th	4 25 36	5 14 28	26 58 1	3♍57 1	10R 22.9	24R 9.1	20 28.8	29 13.3	12 57.2	2 30.8	11 45.9	15 1.5	20 53.1
29 F	4 29 32	6 15 13	10♍52 7	17 43 21	10 23.1	24 11.1	21 36.9	29 55.9	13 3.0	2 35.7	11 48.9	15 3.3	20 55.5
30 Sa	4 33 29	7 16 0	24 30 45	1♎14 24	10 21.8	24 3.1	22 45.2	0♐38.5	13 8.7	2 40.7	11 52.0	15 5.2	20 57.8

DECEMBER 1991 LONGITUDE

Day	Sid.Time	☉	0 hr ☽	Noon ☽	True ☊	☿	♀	♂	♃	♄	♅	♆	♇
1 Su	4 37 25	8♐16 48	7♎54 23	14♎30 47	10♑18.9	23♐44.4	23♎53.7	1♐21.2	13♍14.2	2♒45.8	11♑55.1	15♑ 7.1	21♏ 0.2
2 M	4 41 22	9 17 37	21 3 41	27 33 11	10R 14.7	23R 14.8	25 2.3	2 3.9	13 19.5	2 50.9	11 58.3	15 9.0	21 2.5
3 Tu	4 45 18	10 18 28	3♏59 21	10♏22 16	10 9.7	22 34.0	26 11.2	2 46.7	13 24.7	2 56.1	12 1.4	15 10.9	21 4.8
4 W	4 49 15	11 19 21	16 42 1	22 58 40	10 4.5	21 42.5	27 20.2	3 29.5	13 29.7	3 1.4	12 4.6	15 12.9	21 7.1
5 Th	4 53 11	12 20 14	29 12 18	5♐23 2	9 59.7	20 41.0	28 29.4	4 12.4	13 34.6	3 6.7	12 7.8	15 14.9	21 9.4
6 F	4 57 8	13 21 9	11♐30 59	17 36 16	9 55.9	19 30.9	29 38.7	4 55.3	13 39.2	3 12.1	12 11.0	15 16.9	21 11.7
7 Sa	5 1 5	14 22 5	23 39 4	29 39 35	9 53.4	18 14.0	0♏48.2	5 38.3	13 43.8	3 17.6	12 14.3	15 18.9	21 14.0
8 Su	5 5 1	15 23 1	5♑38 3	11♑34 44	9D 52.3	16 52.7	1 57.9	6 21.3	13 48.1	3 23.1	12 17.6	15 20.9	21 16.3
9 M	5 8 58	16 23 59	17 29 59	23 24 7	9 52.4	15 29.7	3 7.7	7 4.4	13 52.3	3 28.7	12 20.9	15 22.9	21 18.5
10 Tu	5 12 54	17 24 58	29 17 33	5♒10 43	9 53.6	14 7.9	4 17.7	7 47.5	13 56.3	3 34.3	12 24.2	15 25.0	21 20.7
11 W	5 16 51	18 25 57	11♒ 4 5	16 58 11	9 55.2	12 49.8	5 27.8	8 30.6	14 0.1	3 40.0	12 27.5	15 27.0	21 23.0
12 Th	5 20 47	19 26 56	22 53 33	28 50 44	9 57.0	11 38.1	6 38.0	9 13.8	14 3.7	3 45.8	12 30.9	15 29.1	21 25.2
13 F	5 24 44	20 27 57	4♓50 21	10♓53 0	9 58.4	10 34.7	7 48.4	9 57.1	14 7.2	3 51.6	12 34.3	15 31.2	21 27.4
14 Sa	5 28 40	21 28 58	16 59 16	23 9 46	9R 59.2	9 41.1	8 58.9	10 40.4	14 10.4	3 57.5	12 37.7	15 33.3	21 29.5
15 Su	5 32 37	22 29 59	29 25 5	5♈45 45	9 59.1	8 58.1	10 9.5	11 23.7	14 13.5	4 3.4	12 41.1	15 35.4	21 31.7
16 M	5 36 34	23 31 1	12♈12 16	18 45 4	9 58.2	8 26.3	11 20.2	12 7.1	14 16.5	4 9.4	12 44.5	15 37.6	21 33.8
17 Tu	5 40 30	24 32 3	25 24 28	2♉10 42	9 56.6	8 5.5	12 31.0	12 50.5	14 19.2	4 15.4	12 47.9	15 39.7	21 36.0
18 W	5 44 27	25 33 6	9♉ 3 51	16 3 51	9 54.7	7D 55.6	13 42.0	13 34.0	14 21.7	4 21.5	12 51.4	15 41.9	21 38.1
19 Th	5 48 23	26 34 9	23 10 30	0♊23 22	9 52.8	7 55.9	14 53.1	14 17.5	14 24.1	4 27.6	12 54.9	15 44.0	21 40.2
20 F	5 52 20	27 35 13	7♊41 55	15 5 23	9 51.2	8 5.7	16 4.3	15 1.0	14 26.3	4 33.8	12 58.3	15 46.2	21 42.2
21 Sa	5 56 16	28 36 17	22 32 54	0♋ 3 26	9 50.2	8 24.3	17 15.6	15 44.6	14 28.3	4 40.0	13 1.8	15 48.4	21 44.3
22 Su	6 0 13	29 37 22	7♋35 55	15 9 11	9D 49.8	8 50.8	18 27.0	16 28.3	14 30.1	4 46.3	13 5.3	15 50.6	21 46.3
23 M	6 4 9	0♑38 27	22 42 6	0♌13 32	9 50.0	9 24.5	19 38.5	17 12.0	14 31.7	4 52.6	13 8.9	15 52.8	21 48.3
24 Tu	6 8 6	1 39 33	7♌42 29	15 8 1	9 50.6	10 4.5	20 50.1	17 55.7	14 33.1	4 59.0	13 12.4	15 55.0	21 50.3
25 W	6 12 3	2 40 39	22 29 21	29 45 51	9 51.3	10 50.2	22 1.8	18 39.5	14 34.4	5 5.4	13 15.9	15 57.3	21 52.3
26 Th	6 15 59	3 41 46	6♍57 2	14♍ 2 36	9 51.9	11 41.0	23 13.6	19 23.4	14 35.4	5 11.8	13 19.5	15 59.5	21 54.2
27 F	6 19 56	4 42 53	21 2 20	27 56 11	9 52.3	12 36.2	24 25.5	20 7.3	14 36.3	5 18.3	13 23.0	16 1.7	21 56.1
28 Sa	6 23 52	5 44 1	4♎44 15	11♎26 39	9R 52.4	13 35.3	25 37.4	20 51.2	14 36.9	5 24.8	13 26.6	16 4.0	21 58.0
29 Su	6 27 49	6 45 10	18 3 38	24 35 28	9 52.3	14 38.0	26 49.5	21 35.2	14 37.4	5 31.4	13 30.1	16 6.2	21 59.9
30 M	6 31 45	7 46 19	1♏ 2 29	7♏25 2	9 52.2	15 43.7	28 1.6	22 19.2	14R 37.7	5 38.0	13 33.7	16 8.5	22 1.8
31 Tu	6 35 42	8 47 29	13 43 29	19 58 11	9 52.0	16 52.1	29 13.9	23 3.3	14 37.8	5 44.7	13 37.3	16 10.7	22 3.6

Astro Data	Planet Ingress	Last Aspect	☽ Ingress	Last Aspect	☽ Ingress	☽ Phases & Eclipses	Astro Data
Dy Hr Mn	Dy Hr Mn	Dy Hr Mn	Dy Hr Mn	Dy Hr Mn	Dy Hr Mn	Dy Hr Mn	1 NOVEMBER 1991
☽0S 2 9:05	☿ ♐ 4 10:41	3 0:39 ☿ ⚹	♎ 3 4:13	2 8:03 ♀ ☌	♏ 2 16:33	6 11:11 ● 13♏32	Julian Day # 33542
♀0S 11 22:41	♀ ♎ 9 6:37	4 5:52 ♆ □	♏ 5 10:09	4 8:28 ♇ ☌	♐ 5 1:32	14 14:02 ☽ 21♒42	Delta T 57.9 sec
♃△♅ 11 10:52	☉ ♐ 22 19:36	7 15:04 ♀ ⚹	♐ 7 18:21	6 14:18 ☿ ☌	♑ 7 12:41	21 22:56 ○ 29♉08	SVP 05♓22'10"
☽0N 16 19:15	♂ ♐ 29 2:19	8 14:52 ♃ □	♑ 10 5:16	9 7:46 ♇ ⚹	♒ 10 1:27	28 15:21 ☽ 5♍53	Obliquity 23°26'28"
☿ R 28 17:01		11 22:13 ♇ ⚹	♒ 12 18:06	11 21:01 ♇ □	♓ 12 14:19		⚷ Chiron 9♌12.6
☽0S 29 13:46	♀ ♏ 6 7:21	14 14:02 ☉ □	♓ 15 6:33	14 9:32 ☉ □	♈ 15 1:06	6 3:56 ● 13♐31	☽ Mean ☊ 13♑02.1
	☉ ♑ 22 8:54	17 5:37 ☉ △	♈ 17 16:08	16 22:18 ☉ △	♉ 17 8:10	14 9:32 ☽ 21♓53	
☽0N 14 3:04	♀ ♐ 31 15:19	19 1:36 ☿ △	♉ 19 21:49	18 21:28 ♇ ☍	♊ 19 11:21	21 10:23 ○ 29♊03	1 DECEMBER 1991
☿ D 18 11:12		21 22:56 ☉ ☍	♊ 22 0:22	21 10:23 ☉ ☍	♋ 21 11:55	21 10:33 ☍ P 0.087	Julian Day # 33572
☽0S 26 19:38		23 12:52 ☿ ☍	♋ 24 1:25	22 22:34 ♇ △	♌ 23 11:38	28 1:55 ☽ 5♎49	Delta T 57.9 sec
♃ R 30 21:34		25 22:56 ♂ △	♌ 26 2:37	24 23:11 ♀ □	♍ 25 12:23		SVP 05♓22'06"
		28 4:04 ♂ □	♍ 28 5:12	27 6:26 ♀ ⚹	♎ 27 15:37		Obliquity 23°26'27"
		29 23:12 ☿ □	♎ 30 9:47	29 6:51 ♂ ⚹	♏ 29 22:03		⚷ Chiron 9♌30.7R
							☽ Mean ☊ 11♑26.8

LONGITUDE JANUARY 1992

Day	Sid.Time	☉	0 hr ☽	Noon ☽	True ☊	☿	♀	♂	♃	♄	♅	♆	♇
1 W	6 39 38	9♑48 39	26♏ 9 29	2♐17 45	9♑51.9	18♐ 2.9	0♐26.2	23♐47.4	14♍37.6	5♒51.3	13♑40.8	16♑13.0	22♏ 5.4
2 Th	6 43 35	10 49 49	8♐23 18	14 26 27	9D 52.0	19 15.9	1 38.5	24 31.5	14R 37.3	5 58.0	13 44.4	16 15.2	22 7.2
3 F	6 47 32	11 51 0	20 27 29	26 26 42	9 52.2	20 30.8	2 51.0	25 15.7	14 36.8	6 4.8	13 48.0	16 17.5	22 8.9
4 Sa	6 51 28	12 52 11	2♑24 22	8♑20 44	9R 52.3	21 47.3	4 3.5	25 60.0	14 36.1	6 11.6	13 51.6	16 19.8	22 10.7
5 Su	6 55 25	13 53 22	14 16 4	20 10 37	9 52.3	23 5.4	5 16.0	26 44.3	14 35.2	6 18.4	13 55.2	16 22.1	22 12.4
6 M	6 59 21	14 54 32	26 4 37	1♒58 22	9 52.1	24 24.8	6 28.7	27 28.6	14 34.1	6 25.2	13 58.8	16 24.3	22 14.1
7 Tu	7 3 18	15 55 43	7♒52 7	13 46 9	9 51.6	25 45.5	7 41.4	28 13.0	14 32.8	6 32.1	14 2.3	16 26.6	22 15.7
8 W	7 7 14	16 56 53	19 40 49	25 36 26	9 50.7	27 7.3	8 54.1	28 57.4	14 31.3	6 38.9	14 5.9	16 28.9	22 17.3
9 Th	7 11 11	17 58 3	1♓33 21	7♓31 59	9 49.5	28 30.1	10 6.9	29 41.9	14 29.7	6 45.9	14 9.5	16 31.2	22 18.9
10 F	7 15 8	18 59 13	13 32 43	19 36 1	9 48.2	29 53.8	11 19.8	0♑26.4	14 27.8	6 52.8	14 13.1	16 33.4	22 20.5
11 Sa	7 19 4	20 0 22	25 42 20	1♈52 9	9 47.1	1♑18.4	12 32.7	1 10.9	14 25.7	6 59.8	14 16.7	16 35.7	22 22.0
12 Su	7 23 1	21 1 31	8♈ 5 58	14 24 15	9 46.2	2 43.8	13 45.6	1 55.5	14 23.5	7 6.7	14 20.2	16 38.0	22 23.5
13 M	7 26 57	22 2 39	20 47 31	27 16 14	9D 45.8	4 10.0	14 58.6	2 40.1	14 21.0	7 13.7	14 23.8	16 40.3	22 25.0
14 Tu	7 30 54	23 3 46	3♉50 48	10♉31 35	9 46.1	5 36.8	16 11.6	3 24.8	14 18.4	7 20.8	14 27.3	16 42.5	22 26.5
15 W	7 34 50	24 4 53	17 18 55	24 12 58	9 46.9	7 4.4	17 24.7	4 9.5	14 15.6	7 27.8	14 30.9	16 44.8	22 27.9
16 Th	7 38 47	25 5 59	1♊13 48	8♊21 22	9 48.1	8 32.6	18 37.8	4 54.2	14 12.6	7 34.9	14 34.4	16 47.0	22 29.3
17 F	7 42 43	26 7 5	15 35 25	22 55 33	9 49.3	10 1.4	19 51.0	5 39.0	14 9.4	7 41.9	14 38.0	16 49.3	22 30.6
18 Sa	7 46 40	27 8 10	0♋21 10	7♋51 29	9R 50.2	11 30.9	21 4.2	6 23.8	14 6.1	7 49.0	14 41.5	16 51.6	22 32.0
19 Su	7 50 37	28 9 14	15 25 32	23 2 13	9 50.3	13 0.9	22 17.5	7 8.6	14 2.5	7 56.1	14 45.0	16 53.8	22 33.3
20 M	7 54 33	29 10 18	0♌40 20	8♌18 34	9 49.4	14 31.6	23 30.8	7 53.5	13 58.8	8 3.3	14 48.5	16 56.0	22 34.5
21 Tu	7 58 30	0♒11 20	15 55 37	23 30 14	9 47.5	16 2.8	24 44.1	8 38.5	13 54.9	8 10.4	14 52.0	16 58.3	22 35.8
22 W	8 2 26	1 12 23	1♍ 1 12	8♍27 31	9 44.8	17 34.7	25 57.5	9 23.4	13 50.8	8 17.5	14 55.5	17 0.5	22 37.0
23 Th	8 6 23	2 13 24	15 48 15	23 2 45	9 41.6	19 7.1	27 10.9	10 8.4	13 46.6	8 24.7	14 59.0	17 2.7	22 38.1
24 F	8 10 19	3 14 25	0♎10 30	7♎11 13	9 38.6	20 40.1	28 24.4	10 53.5	13 42.2	8 31.8	15 2.4	17 4.9	22 39.3
25 Sa	8 14 16	4 15 26	14 4 46	20 51 14	9 36.2	22 13.7	29 37.8	11 38.6	13 37.6	8 39.0	15 5.9	17 7.1	22 40.4
26 Su	8 18 12	5 16 26	27 30 49	4♏ 3 49	9D 34.8	23 47.9	0♑51.4	12 23.7	13 32.8	8 46.1	15 9.3	17 9.3	22 41.4
27 M	8 22 9	6 17 26	10♏30 39	16 51 49	9 34.6	25 22.8	2 4.9	13 8.9	13 27.9	8 53.3	15 12.7	17 11.5	22 42.5
28 Tu	8 26 6	7 18 25	23 7 49	29 19 13	9 35.5	26 58.3	3 18.5	13 54.1	13 22.9	9 0.5	15 16.1	17 13.7	22 43.5
29 W	8 30 2	8 19 24	5♐26 35	11♐30 28	9 37.2	28 34.4	4 32.1	14 39.3	13 17.6	9 7.7	15 19.5	17 15.8	22 44.5
30 Th	8 33 59	9 20 22	17 31 27	23 30 1	9 39.0	0♒11.1	5 45.8	15 24.6	13 12.3	9 14.9	15 22.8	17 18.0	22 45.4
31 F	8 37 55	10 21 19	29 26 42	5♑21 58	9R 40.5	1 48.6	6 59.4	16 9.9	13 6.7	9 22.0	15 26.2	17 20.1	22 46.3

LONGITUDE FEBRUARY 1992

Day	Sid.Time	☉	0 hr ☽	Noon ☽	True ☊	☿	♀	♂	♃	♄	♅	♆	♇
1 Sa	8 41 52	11♒22 16	11♑16 14	17♑ 9 54	9♑41.0	3♒26.7	8♑13.1	16♑55.3	13♍ 1.1	9♒29.2	15♑29.5	17♑22.2	22♏47.2
2 Su	8 45 48	12 23 11	23 3 19	28 56 50	9R 40.0	5 5.5	9 26.9	17 40.7	12R 55.3	9 36.4	15 32.8	17 24.4	22 48.0
3 M	8 49 45	13 24 6	4♒50 44	10♒45 16	9 37.3	6 45.0	10 40.6	18 26.1	12 49.3	9 43.6	15 36.1	17 26.5	22 48.8
4 Tu	8 53 41	14 24 59	16 40 40	22 37 11	9 32.7	8 25.2	11 54.4	19 11.6	12 43.2	9 50.8	15 39.3	17 28.5	22 49.6
5 W	8 57 38	15 25 51	28 35 1	4♓34 20	9 26.7	10 6.2	13 8.1	19 57.1	12 37.0	9 57.9	15 42.6	17 30.6	22 50.3
6 Th	9 1 35	16 26 42	10♓35 23	16 38 20	9 19.7	11 47.9	14 21.9	20 42.6	12 30.6	10 5.1	15 45.8	17 32.7	22 51.0
7 F	9 5 31	17 27 32	22 43 25	28 50 51	9 12.3	13 30.4	15 35.8	21 28.1	12 24.2	10 12.2	15 49.0	17 34.7	22 51.6
8 Sa	9 9 28	18 28 20	5♈ 0 54	11♈13 50	9 5.4	15 13.7	16 49.6	22 13.7	12 17.6	10 19.4	15 52.1	17 36.7	22 52.3
9 Su	9 13 24	19 29 7	17 29 57	23 49 34	8 59.7	16 57.7	18 3.4	22 59.3	12 10.9	10 26.5	15 55.3	17 38.8	22 52.8
10 M	9 17 21	20 29 53	0♉13 2	6♉40 41	8 55.7	18 42.5	19 17.3	23 45.0	12 4.1	10 33.6	15 58.4	17 40.7	22 53.4
11 Tu	9 21 17	21 30 37	13 12 53	19 49 59	8D 53.6	20 28.1	20 31.2	24 30.7	11 57.2	10 40.7	16 1.5	17 42.7	22 53.9
12 W	9 25 14	22 31 19	26 32 19	3♊20 9	8 53.3	22 14.5	21 45.1	25 16.4	11 50.2	10 47.8	16 4.6	17 44.7	22 54.4
13 Th	9 29 10	23 32 0	10♊13 45	17 13 14	8 54.3	24 1.7	22 59.0	26 2.1	11 43.1	10 54.9	16 7.6	17 46.6	22 54.8
14 F	9 33 7	24 32 39	24 18 38	1♋29 54	8 55.6	25 49.6	24 12.9	26 47.8	11 35.9	11 2.0	16 10.6	17 48.5	22 55.2
15 Sa	9 37 4	25 33 16	8♋46 45	16 8 47	8R 56.2	27 38.3	25 26.8	27 33.6	11 28.6	11 9.0	16 13.6	17 50.5	22 55.6
16 Su	9 41 0	26 33 52	23 35 23	1♌ 5 47	8 55.3	29 27.7	26 40.7	28 19.4	11 21.3	11 16.0	16 16.5	17 52.3	22 56.0
17 M	9 44 57	27 34 26	8♌39 1	16 13 59	8 52.3	1♓17.7	27 54.7	29 5.3	11 13.8	11 23.0	16 19.4	17 54.2	22 56.3
18 Tu	9 48 53	28 34 58	23 49 26	1♍24 7	8 47.0	3 8.4	29 8.6	29 51.2	11 6.3	11 30.0	16 22.3	17 56.1	22 56.5
19 W	9 52 50	29 35 29	8♍56 43	16 25 59	8 39.7	4 59.6	0♒22.6	0♒37.0	10 58.8	11 37.0	16 25.2	17 57.9	22 56.7
20 Th	9 56 46	0♓35 58	23 50 46	1♎10 6	8 31.3	6 51.2	1 36.6	1 23.0	10 51.2	11 43.9	16 28.0	17 59.7	22 56.9
21 F	10 0 43	1 36 26	8♎23 10	15 29 22	8 22.9	8 43.2	2 50.6	2 8.9	10 43.5	11 50.8	16 30.8	18 1.5	22 57.1
22 Sa	10 4 39	2 36 53	22 28 18	29 19 47	8 15.5	10 35.3	4 4.6	2 54.9	10 35.8	11 57.7	16 33.6	18 3.2	22 57.2
23 Su	10 8 36	3 37 18	6♏ 3 51	12♏40 41	8 9.9	12 27.5	5 18.6	3 40.9	10 28.1	12 4.6	16 36.3	18 5.0	22 57.3
24 M	10 12 33	4 37 41	19 10 35	25 34 2	8 6.4	14 19.6	6 32.6	4 26.9	10 20.3	12 11.4	16 39.0	18 6.7	22R 57.3
25 Tu	10 16 29	5 38 4	1♐51 32	8♐ 3 42	8D 5.1	16 11.2	7 46.7	5 13.0	10 12.5	12 18.2	16 41.6	18 8.4	22 57.4
26 W	10 20 26	6 38 25	14 11 11	20 14 39	8 5.2	18 2.2	9 0.7	5 59.1	10 4.7	12 25.0	16 44.3	18 10.0	22 57.3
27 Th	10 24 22	7 38 45	26 14 46	2♑12 13	8 6.1	19 52.1	10 14.8	6 45.2	9 56.8	12 31.7	16 46.8	18 11.7	22 57.3
28 F	10 28 19	8 39 3	8♑ 7 39	14 1 41	8R 6.6	21 40.8	11 28.8	7 31.3	9 48.9	12 38.5	16 49.4	18 13.3	22 57.2
29 Sa	10 32 15	9 39 19	19 54 55	25 47 53	8 5.8	23 27.7	12 42.9	8 17.5	9 41.1	12 45.2	16 51.9	18 14.9	22 57.1

Astro Data Dy Hr Mn	Planet Ingress Dy Hr Mn	Last Aspect Dy Hr Mn	☽ Ingress Dy Hr Mn	Last Aspect Dy Hr Mn	☽ Ingress Dy Hr Mn	☽ Phases & Eclipses Dy Hr Mn	Astro Data
☽0N 10 9:52	♂ ♑ 9 9:47	31 16:05 ♇ ☌	♐ 1 7:30	1 23:29 ♇ ⚹	♒ 2 14:09	4 23:10 ● 13♑51	1 JANUARY 1992
♃△♅ 12 13:07	☿ ♑ 10 1:46	3 10:15 ♂ ☌	♑ 3 19:09	4 12:26 ♇ □	♓ 5 2:51	4 23:04:40 ✔ A 10'58"	Julian Day # 33603
☽0S 23 4:36	☉ ♒ 20 19:33	5 16:10 ♇ ⚹	♒ 6 7:59	7 0:16 ♇ △	♈ 7 14:15	13 2:32 ☽ 22♈09	Delta T 58.0 sec
	♀ ♑ 25 7:14	8 20:01 ♂ ⚹	♓ 8 20:52	9 11:05 ♂ □	♉ 9 23:36	19 21:28 ○ 29♋04	SVP 05♓22'00"
☽0N 6 16:08	☿ ♒ 29 21:15	10 17:26 ♇ △	♈ 11 8:22	11 21:37 ♂ △	♊ 12 6:08	26 15:27 ☽ 5♏56	Obliquity 23°26'26"
♃⊼♄ 16 8:43		13 2:32 ☉ □	♉ 13 17:00	14 2:55 ☿ △	♋ 14 9:31		⚷ Chiron 8♌18.2R
☽0S 19 15:49	☿ ♓ 16 7:04	15 12:42 ☉ △	♊ 15 21:55	16 7:59 ♂ ☍	♌ 16 10:15	3 19:00 ● 14♒12	☽ Mean ☊ 9♑48.3
♇ R 24 21:32	♀ ♒ 18 16:40	17 7:37 ♀ ☍	♋ 17 23:26	18 8:04 ☉ ☍	♍ 18 9:47	11 16:15 ☽ 22♉12	
	♂ ♒ 18 4:38	19 21:28 ☉ ☍	♌ 19 22:57	19 22:32 ♇ ⚹	♎ 20 10:04	18 8:04 ○ 28♌55	1 FEBRUARY 1992
	☉ ♓ 19 9:44	21 15:12 ♀ △	♍ 21 22:22	21 16:22 ♆ □	♏ 22 13:11	25 7:56 ☽ 5♐58	Julian Day # 33634
		23 20:43 ♀ □	♎ 23 23:42	24 7:04 ♇ ☌	♐ 24 20:26		Delta T 58.1 sec
		25 16:23 ☿ □	♏ 26 4:32	26 8:59 ☿ □	♑ 27 7:33		SVP 05♓21'55"
		28 8:32 ☿ ⚹	♐ 28 13:20	29 8:30 ☿ ⚹	♒ 29 20:34		Obliquity 23°26'26"
		29 15:26 ♃ □	♑ 31 1:07				⚷ Chiron 6♌07.9R
							☽ Mean ☊ 8♑09.9

MARCH 1992 LONGITUDE

Day	Sid.Time	☉	0 hr ☽	Noon ☽	True ☊	☿	♀	♂	♃	♄	♅	♆	♇
1 Su	10 36 12	10♓39 34	1♒41 6	7♒35 1	8♑ 2.8	25♓12.5	13♒57.0	9♒ 3.7	9♍33.2	12♒51.8	16♑54.4	18♑16.5	22♏56.9
2 M	10 40 8	11 39 48	13 30 1	19 26 28	7R 57.2	26 54.6	15 11.1	9 49.9	9R 25.3	12 58.4	16 56.8	18 18.0	22R 56.7
3 Tu	10 44 5	12 39 59	25 24 40	1♓24 51	7 48.9	28 33.5	16 25.2	10 36.1	9 17.4	13 5.0	16 59.2	18 19.5	22 56.5
4 W	10 48 2	13 40 9	7♓27 12	13 31 54	7 38.1	0♈ 8.8	17 39.3	11 22.3	9 9.6	13 11.5	17 1.6	18 21.0	22 56.2
5 Th	10 51 58	14 40 17	19 39 2	25 48 42	7 25.8	1 39.8	18 53.4	12 8.6	9 1.8	13 18.1	17 3.9	18 22.5	22 55.9
6 F	10 55 55	15 40 24	2♈ 0 57	8♈15 51	7 12.9	3 6.0	20 7.4	12 54.8	8 54.0	13 24.5	17 6.2	18 24.0	22 55.5
7 Sa	10 59 51	16 40 28	14 33 26	20 53 45	7 0.5	4 26.8	21 21.5	13 41.1	8 46.2	13 30.9	17 8.4	18 25.4	22 55.2
8 Su	11 3 48	17 40 30	27 16 52	3♉42 51	6 49.8	5 41.6	22 35.6	14 27.4	8 38.5	13 37.3	17 10.6	18 26.8	22 54.8
9 M	11 7 44	18 40 31	10♉11 50	16 43 55	6 41.6	6 50.0	23 49.7	15 13.8	8 30.8	13 43.7	17 12.7	18 28.1	22 54.3
10 Tu	11 11 41	19 40 29	23 19 18	29 58 8	6 36.3	7 51.5	25 3.8	16 0.1	8 23.2	13 50.0	17 14.9	18 29.4	22 53.8
11 W	11 15 37	20 40 25	6♊40 37	13♊26 58	6 33.6	8 45.6	26 17.9	16 46.4	8 15.6	13 56.2	17 16.9	18 30.7	22 53.3
12 Th	11 19 34	21 40 19	20 17 23	27 12 1	6D 32.9	9 31.9	27 32.0	17 32.8	8 8.1	14 2.4	17 19.0	18 32.0	22 52.8
13 F	11 23 30	22 40 10	4♋10 59	11♋14 20	6R 33.0	10 10.1	28 46.1	18 19.2	8 0.7	14 8.6	17 20.9	18 33.3	22 52.2
14 Sa	11 27 27	23 40 0	18 22 2	25 33 54	6 32.7	10 40.0	0♓ 0.2	19 5.6	7 53.3	14 14.7	17 22.9	18 34.5	22 51.6
15 Su	11 31 24	24 39 47	2♌49 40	10♌ 8 51	6 30.6	11 1.4	1 14.3	19 51.9	7 46.1	14 20.7	17 24.8	18 35.7	22 51.0
16 M	11 35 20	25 39 32	17 30 53	24 55 1	6 25.9	11 14.3	2 28.3	20 38.4	7 38.9	14 26.8	17 26.6	18 36.8	22 50.3
17 Tu	11 39 17	26 39 14	2♍20 20	9♍45 51	6 18.4	11R 18.7	3 42.4	21 24.8	7 31.7	14 32.7	17 28.4	18 38.0	22 49.6
18 W	11 43 13	27 38 54	17 10 31	24 33 14	6 8.4	11 14.8	4 56.5	22 11.2	7 24.7	14 38.6	17 30.2	18 39.1	22 48.9
19 Th	11 47 10	28 38 33	1♎52 54	9♎ 8 34	5 56.9	11 2.8	6 10.5	22 57.6	7 17.8	14 44.5	17 31.9	18 40.1	22 48.1
20 F	11 51 6	29 38 9	16 19 18	23 24 24	5 45.0	10 43.1	7 24.6	23 44.1	7 11.0	14 50.3	17 33.5	18 41.2	22 47.3
21 Sa	11 55 3	0♈37 43	0♏23 16	7♏15 33	5 34.2	10 16.4	8 38.7	24 30.5	7 4.2	14 56.0	17 35.2	18 42.2	22 46.5
22 Su	11 58 59	1 37 16	14 1 1	20 39 40	5 25.3	9 43.3	9 52.8	25 17.0	6 57.6	15 1.7	17 36.7	18 43.2	22 45.7
23 M	12 2 56	2 36 47	27 11 39	3♐37 14	5 19.1	9 4.5	11 6.8	26 3.5	6 51.1	15 7.3	17 38.3	18 44.1	22 44.8
24 Tu	12 6 53	3 36 16	9♐56 50	16 10 57	5 15.5	8 21.1	12 20.9	26 50.0	6 44.7	15 12.9	17 39.7	18 45.0	22 43.9
25 W	12 10 49	4 35 43	22 20 10	28 25 6	5 14.1	7 33.8	13 35.0	27 36.5	6 38.5	15 18.4	17 41.2	18 45.9	22 42.9
26 Th	12 14 46	5 35 9	4♑26 27	10♑24 54	5 13.8	6 44.0	14 49.0	28 23.0	6 32.3	15 23.9	17 42.6	18 46.8	22 42.0
27 F	12 18 42	6 34 33	16 21 9	22 15 53	5 13.7	5 52.5	16 3.1	29 9.5	6 26.3	15 29.3	17 43.9	18 47.6	22 41.0
28 Sa	12 22 39	7 33 55	28 9 47	4♒ 3 31	5 12.5	5 0.5	17 17.2	29 56.0	6 20.5	15 34.6	17 45.2	18 48.4	22 40.0
29 Su	12 26 35	8 33 15	9♒57 41	15 52 52	5 9.3	4 9.1	18 31.2	0♓42.5	6 14.7	15 39.9	17 46.4	18 49.1	22 38.9
30 M	12 30 32	9 32 33	21 49 35	27 48 19	5 3.5	3 19.1	19 45.3	1 29.0	6 9.1	15 45.1	17 47.6	18 49.9	22 37.8
31 Tu	12 34 28	10 31 49	3♓49 28	9♓53 23	4 54.9	2 31.6	20 59.4	2 15.5	6 3.7	15 50.2	17 48.7	18 50.6	22 36.7

APRIL 1992 LONGITUDE

Day	Sid.Time	☉	0 hr ☽	Noon ☽	True ☊	☿	♀	♂	♃	♄	♅	♆	♇
1 W	12 38 25	11♈31 4	16♓ 0 19	22♓10 30	4♑43.8	1♈47.4	22♒13.4	3♓ 2.1	5♍58.3	15♒55.3	17♑49.8	18♑51.2	22♏35.6
2 Th	12 42 22	12 30 16	28 24 4	4♈41 4	4R 30.9	1R 6.9	23 27.5	3 48.6	5R 53.2	16 0.3	17 50.9	18 51.8	22R 34.5
3 F	12 46 18	13 29 27	11♈ 1 31	17 25 23	4 17.3	0 31.0	24 41.5	4 35.1	5 48.2	16 5.2	17 51.9	18 52.4	22 33.3
4 Sa	12 50 15	14 28 35	23 52 34	0♉22 56	4 4.3	29♓59.8	25 55.5	5 21.6	5 43.3	16 10.1	17 52.8	18 53.0	22 32.1
5 Su	12 54 11	15 27 42	6♉56 22	13 32 42	3 52.9	29 33.9	27 9.6	6 8.1	5 38.6	16 14.9	17 53.7	18 53.5	22 30.8
6 M	12 58 8	16 26 46	20 11 47	26 53 30	3 44.1	29 13.3	28 23.6	6 54.7	5 34.1	16 19.6	17 54.5	18 54.0	22 29.6
7 Tu	13 2 4	17 25 48	3♊37 44	10♊24 24	3 38.3	28 58.1	29 37.6	7 41.2	5 29.7	16 24.3	17 55.3	18 54.5	22 28.3
8 W	13 6 1	18 24 48	17 13 27	24 4 53	3 35.3	28 48.5	0♈51.6	8 27.7	5 25.5	16 28.9	17 56.0	18 54.9	22 27.0
9 Th	13 9 57	19 23 46	0♋58 40	7♋54 50	3D 34.4	28D 44.4	2 5.6	9 14.2	5 21.5	16 33.4	17 56.7	18 55.3	22 25.7
10 F	13 13 54	20 22 42	14 53 23	21 54 18	3R 34.6	28 45.6	3 19.6	10 0.6	5 17.7	16 37.8	17 57.4	18 55.7	22 24.4
11 Sa	13 17 51	21 21 35	28 57 33	6♌ 3 2	3 34.4	28 52.1	4 33.6	10 47.1	5 14.0	16 42.2	17 57.9	18 56.0	22 23.1
12 Su	13 21 47	22 20 26	13♌10 35	20 19 57	3 32.9	29 3.7	5 47.5	11 33.6	5 10.5	16 46.5	17 58.5	18 56.3	22 21.7
13 M	13 25 44	23 19 14	27 30 47	4♍42 40	3 29.0	29 20.2	7 1.5	12 20.0	5 7.1	16 50.7	17 58.9	18 56.6	22 20.3
14 Tu	13 29 40	24 18 0	11♍55 2	19 7 17	3 22.6	29 41.5	8 15.5	13 6.5	5 4.0	16 54.8	17 59.4	18 56.8	22 18.9
15 W	13 33 37	25 16 44	26 18 43	3♎28 36	3 13.8	0♈ 7.3	9 29.4	13 52.9	5 1.0	16 58.8	17 59.7	18 57.0	22 17.4
16 Th	13 37 33	26 15 26	10♎36 12	17 40 46	3 3.6	0 37.5	10 43.3	14 39.3	4 58.2	17 2.8	18 0.1	18 57.1	22 16.0
17 F	13 41 30	27 14 5	24 41 38	1♏38 10	2 52.9	1 11.9	11 57.3	15 25.7	4 55.5	17 6.7	18 0.3	18 57.3	22 14.5
18 Sa	13 45 26	28 12 43	8♏29 54	15 16 24	2 43.1	1 50.2	13 11.2	16 12.1	4 53.1	17 10.5	18 0.6	18 57.4	22 13.1
19 Su	13 49 23	29 11 19	21 57 26	28 32 51	2 35.1	2 32.3	14 25.1	16 58.5	4 50.8	17 14.2	18 0.7	18 57.4	22 11.6
20 M	13 53 19	0♉ 9 53	5♐ 2 39	11♐26 59	2 29.4	3 18.0	15 39.0	17 44.9	4 48.7	17 17.9	18 0.9	18R 57.5	22 10.1
21 Tu	13 57 16	1 8 26	17 46 4	24 0 15	2 26.1	4 7.1	16 52.9	18 31.3	4 46.8	17 21.5	18R 0.9	18 57.5	22 8.5
22 W	14 1 13	2 6 56	0♑ 9 58	6♑15 42	2D 25.0	4 59.6	18 6.8	19 17.6	4 45.1	17 24.9	18 1.0	18 57.4	22 7.0
23 Th	14 5 9	3 5 25	12 18 1	18 17 32	2 25.3	5 55.1	19 20.7	20 4.0	4 43.6	17 28.3	18 0.9	18 57.4	22 5.5
24 F	14 9 6	4 3 53	24 14 52	0♒10 41	2R 26.2	6 53.7	20 34.6	20 50.3	4 42.2	17 31.6	18 0.9	18 57.3	22 3.9
25 Sa	14 13 2	5 2 19	6♒ 5 39	12 0 27	2 26.6	7 55.2	21 48.5	21 36.6	4 41.0	17 34.9	18 0.7	18 57.1	22 2.3
26 Su	14 16 59	6 0 43	17 55 42	23 52 4	2 25.7	8 59.4	23 2.4	22 22.9	4 40.1	17 38.0	18 0.6	18 57.0	22 0.7
27 M	14 20 55	6 59 5	29 50 9	5♓50 32	2 22.9	10 6.3	24 16.3	23 9.2	4 39.3	17 41.1	18 0.3	18 56.8	21 59.1
28 Tu	14 24 52	7 57 26	11♓53 42	18 0 8	2 18.0	11 15.7	25 30.1	23 55.4	4 38.6	17 44.0	18 0.0	18 56.5	21 57.5
29 W	14 28 48	8 55 45	24 10 15	0♈24 22	2 11.0	12 27.6	26 44.0	24 41.7	4 38.2	17 46.9	17 59.7	18 56.3	21 55.9
30 Th	14 32 45	9 54 3	6♈42 42	13 5 27	2 2.6	13 41.9	27 57.9	25 27.9	4D 38.0	17 49.7	17 59.3	18 56.0	21 54.3

Astro Data Dy Hr Mn	Planet Ingress Dy Hr Mn	Last Aspect Dy Hr Mn	☽ Ingress Dy Hr Mn	Last Aspect Dy Hr Mn	☽ Ingress Dy Hr Mn	☽ Phases & Eclipses Dy Hr Mn
☿0N 3 6:02	☿ ♈ 3 21:45	2 19:03 ♇ □	♓ 3 9:11	1 13:26 ♀ ☌	♈ 2 3:04	4 13:22 ● 14♓14
☽0N 4 22:31	♀ ♓ 13 23:57	5 6:24 ♇ △	♈ 5 20:07	3 14:43 ♆ □	♉ 4 11:18	12 2:36 ☽ 21♊47
☿ R 17 0:32	☉ ♈ 20 8:48	7 14:15 ♀ ✶	♉ 8 5:05	6 16:10 ♀ ✶	♊ 6 17:33	18 18:18 ○ 28♍24
☽0S 18 2:44	♂ ♓ 28 2:04	10 3:29 ♀ □	♊ 10 12:03	8 20:07 ♀ □	♋ 8 22:18	26 2:30 ☽ 5♑41
☽0N 1 5:26		12 13:48 ♀ △	♋ 12 16:50	10 23:51 ☿ △	♌ 11 1:46	
☿0S 6 18:18	☿ ♓ 3 23:52	14 9:30 ☉ △	♌ 14 19:20	12 16:29 ☉ △	♍ 13 4:09	3 5:01 ● 13♈42
☿ D 9 6:26	♀ ♈ 7 7:16	16 8:38 ♇ □	♍ 16 20:13	14 17:18 ♇ ✶	♎ 15 6:10	10 10:06 ☽ 20♋47
♀0N 10 3:05	☿ ♈ 14 17:35	18 18:18 ☉ ☍	♎ 18 20:55	17 4:43 ☉ ☍	♏ 17 9:10	17 4:43 ○ 27♎26
☽0S 14 11:12	☉ ♉ 19 19:57	20 13:18 ♂ △	♏ 20 23:20	19 0:26 ♇ ☌	♐ 19 14:40	24 21:40 ☽ 4♒57
♆ R 20 12:14		22 21:46 ♂ □	♐ 23 5:13	21 1:32 ♂ □	♑ 21 23:40	
♅ R 21 23:19		25 11:06 ♂ ✶	♑ 25 15:08	23 19:36 ♇ ✶	♒ 24 11:38	
☿0N 22 21:43		27 12:50 ♇ ✶	♒ 28 3:44	26 11:31 ♀ ✶	♓ 27 0:20	
☽0N 28 12:53		30 1:37 ♇ □	♓ 30 16:23	29 1:05 ♂ ☌	♈ 29 11:13	
♃ D 30 19:38						

Astro Data

1 MARCH 1992
Julian Day # 33663
Delta T 58.1 sec
SVP 05♓21'51"
Obliquity 23°26'27"
⚷ Chiron 4♌13.1R
☽ Mean ☊ 6♑37.7

1 APRIL 1992
Julian Day # 33694
Delta T 58.1 sec
SVP 05♓21'48"
Obliquity 23°26'27"
⚷ Chiron 3♌17.1R
☽ Mean ☊ 4♑59.2

LONGITUDE — MAY 1992

Day	Sid.Time	☉	0 hr ☽	Noon ☽	True ☊	☿	♀	♂	♃	♄	♅	♆	♇
1 F	14 36 42	10♉52 19	19♈32 41	26♈ 4 23	1♑53.5	14♈58.5	29♈11.7	26♓14.1	4♍37.9	17♒52.4	17♑58.9	18♑55.7	21♏52.7
2 Sa	14 40 38	11 50 34	2♉40 27	9♉20 42	1R 44.7	16 17.4	0♉25.6	27 0.2	4 38.0	17 55.0	17R 58.4	18R 55.3	21R 51.0
3 Su	14 44 35	12 48 46	16 4 54	22 52 44	1 37.1	17 38.5	1 39.4	27 46.4	4 38.4	17 57.5	17 57.9	18 54.9	21 49.4
4 M	14 48 31	13 46 58	29 43 53	6♊37 57	1 31.3	19 1.8	2 53.3	28 32.5	4 38.9	17 59.9	17 57.3	18 54.5	21 47.7
5 Tu	14 52 28	14 45 7	13♊34 34	20 33 21	1 27.8	20 27.2	4 7.1	29 18.6	4 39.5	18 2.2	17 56.7	18 54.0	21 46.1
6 W	14 56 24	15 43 14	27 33 56	4♋35 58	1D 26.4	21 54.6	5 20.9	0♈ 4.6	4 40.4	18 4.5	17 56.0	18 53.6	21 44.4
7 Th	15 0 21	16 41 20	11♋39 9	18 43 13	1 26.7	23 24.2	6 34.7	0 50.6	4 41.5	18 6.6	17 55.3	18 53.1	21 42.7
8 F	15 4 17	17 39 24	25 47 53	2♌52 57	1 27.8	24 55.8	7 48.5	1 36.6	4 42.7	18 8.6	17 54.5	18 52.5	21 41.1
9 Sa	15 8 14	18 37 26	9♌58 13	17 3 27	1R 28.9	26 29.5	9 2.3	2 22.6	4 44.1	18 10.6	17 53.7	18 51.9	21 39.4
10 Su	15 12 11	19 35 26	24 8 29	1♍13 5	1 29.1	28 5.1	10 16.1	3 8.5	4 45.7	18 12.4	17 52.9	18 51.3	21 37.7
11 M	15 16 7	20 33 23	8♍17 1	15 20 2	1 27.8	29 42.8	11 29.9	3 54.4	4 47.5	18 14.2	17 52.0	18 50.7	21 36.0
12 Tu	15 20 4	21 31 19	22 21 52	29 22 10	1 24.7	1♉22.5	12 43.7	4 40.3	4 49.4	18 15.9	17 51.0	18 50.0	21 34.4
13 W	15 24 0	22 29 14	6♎20 38	13♎16 53	1 20.1	3 4.2	13 57.4	5 26.1	4 51.5	18 17.4	17 50.0	18 49.3	21 32.7
14 Th	15 27 57	23 27 6	20 10 35	27 1 21	1 14.4	4 47.9	15 11.2	6 11.9	4 53.8	18 18.9	17 49.0	18 48.6	21 31.0
15 F	15 31 53	24 24 57	3♏48 51	10♏32 47	1 8.4	6 33.7	16 25.0	6 57.6	4 56.3	18 20.3	17 47.9	18 47.9	21 29.3
16 Sa	15 35 50	25 22 46	17 12 52	23 48 55	1 2.9	8 21.5	17 38.7	7 43.4	4 59.0	18 21.6	17 46.7	18 47.1	21 27.7
17 Su	15 39 46	26 20 34	0♐20 46	6♐48 20	0 58.5	10 11.3	18 52.4	8 29.1	5 1.8	18 22.7	17 45.6	18 46.3	21 26.0
18 M	15 43 43	27 18 20	13 11 36	19 30 41	0 55.5	12 3.1	20 6.2	9 14.7	5 4.8	18 23.8	17 44.4	18 45.5	21 24.3
19 Tu	15 47 40	28 16 6	25 45 41	1♑56 51	0D 54.2	13 56.9	21 19.9	10 0.3	5 7.9	18 24.8	17 43.1	18 44.6	21 22.7
20 W	15 51 36	29 13 49	8♑ 4 27	14 8 52	0 54.3	15 52.7	22 33.7	10 45.9	5 11.3	18 25.7	17 41.8	18 43.7	21 21.0
21 Th	15 55 33	0♊11 32	20 10 28	26 9 45	0 55.4	17 50.5	23 47.4	11 31.5	5 14.8	18 26.5	17 40.5	18 42.8	21 19.4
22 F	15 59 29	1 9 14	2♒ 7 11	8♒ 3 20	0 57.1	19 50.2	25 1.1	12 17.0	5 18.4	18 27.2	17 39.1	18 41.9	21 17.7
23 Sa	16 3 26	2 6 54	13 58 45	19 54 3	0 58.8	21 51.7	26 14.8	13 2.4	5 22.2	18 27.8	17 37.7	18 40.9	21 16.1
24 Su	16 7 22	3 4 33	25 49 49	1♓46 41	0R 59.9	23 55.0	27 28.6	13 47.9	5 26.2	18 28.3	17 36.2	18 39.9	21 14.4
25 M	16 11 19	4 2 12	7♓45 14	13 46 5	1 0.1	26 0.0	28 42.3	14 33.3	5 30.4	18 28.7	17 34.7	18 38.9	21 12.8
26 Tu	16 15 15	4 59 49	19 49 48	25 56 57	0 59.1	28 6.6	29 56.0	15 18.6	5 34.7	18 29.0	17 33.2	18 37.9	21 11.2
27 W	16 19 12	5 57 25	2♈ 8 2	8♈23 30	0 57.1	0♊14.6	1♊ 9.7	16 3.9	5 39.1	18 29.2	17 31.6	18 36.8	21 9.6
28 Th	16 23 9	6 55 1	14 43 45	21 9 5	0 54.2	2 23.8	2 23.5	16 49.2	5 43.8	18R 29.3	17 30.0	18 35.7	21 8.0
29 F	16 27 5	7 52 35	27 39 45	4♉15 52	0 50.9	4 34.1	3 37.2	17 34.4	5 48.6	18 29.3	17 28.3	18 34.6	21 6.4
30 Sa	16 31 2	8 50 9	10♉57 27	17 44 26	0 47.6	6 45.3	4 50.9	18 19.6	5 53.5	18 29.2	17 26.6	18 33.5	21 4.8
31 Su	16 34 58	9 47 42	24 36 37	1♊33 42	0 44.7	8 57.0	6 4.6	19 4.7	5 58.6	18 29.0	17 24.9	18 32.3	21 3.2

LONGITUDE — JUNE 1992

Day	Sid.Time	☉	0 hr ☽	Noon ☽	True ☊	☿	♀	♂	♃	♄	♅	♆	♇
1 M	16 38 55	10♊45 14	8♊35 15	15♊40 48	0♑42.7	11♊ 9.0	7♊18.4	19♈49.7	6♍ 3.8	18♒28.8	17♑23.2	18♑31.2	21♏ 1.7
2 Tu	16 42 51	11 42 44	22 49 45	0♋ 1 29	0D 41.7	13 21.1	8 32.1	20 34.8	6 9.2	18R 28.4	17R 21.4	18R 30.0	21R 0.1
3 W	16 46 48	12 40 14	7♋15 19	14 30 34	0 41.6	15 32.9	9 45.8	21 19.7	6 14.8	18 27.9	17 19.6	18 28.8	20 58.6
4 Th	16 50 45	13 37 43	21 46 33	29 2 37	0 42.3	17 44.3	10 59.5	22 4.6	6 20.5	18 27.3	17 17.7	18 27.5	20 57.1
5 F	16 54 41	14 35 10	6♌18 9	13♌32 35	0 43.4	19 54.9	12 13.2	22 49.5	6 26.3	18 26.6	17 15.8	18 26.3	20 55.6
6 Sa	16 58 38	15 32 37	20 45 24	27 56 11	0 44.5	22 4.5	13 27.0	23 34.3	6 32.3	18 25.9	17 13.9	18 25.0	20 54.1
7 Su	17 2 34	16 30 2	5♍ 4 32	12♍10 10	0R 45.3	24 12.9	14 40.7	24 19.0	6 38.4	18 25.0	17 12.0	18 23.7	20 52.6
8 M	17 6 31	17 27 25	19 12 50	26 12 20	0 45.5	26 19.7	15 54.4	25 3.7	6 44.7	18 24.0	17 10.0	18 22.4	20 51.2
9 Tu	17 10 27	18 24 48	3♎ 8 32	10♎ 1 19	0 45.2	28 25.0	17 8.1	25 48.3	6 51.1	18 23.0	17 8.0	18 21.0	20 49.7
10 W	17 14 24	19 22 10	16 50 37	23 36 23	0 44.3	0♋28.4	18 21.8	26 32.9	6 57.7	18 21.8	17 6.0	18 19.7	20 48.3
11 Th	17 18 20	20 19 30	0♏18 35	6♏57 14	0 43.1	2 29.9	19 35.5	27 17.4	7 4.3	18 20.5	17 3.9	18 18.3	20 46.9
12 F	17 22 17	21 16 50	13 32 19	20 3 52	0 41.8	4 29.3	20 49.2	28 1.9	7 11.2	18 19.2	17 1.8	18 16.9	20 45.5
13 Sa	17 26 14	22 14 9	26 31 54	2♐56 30	0 40.8	6 26.6	22 2.9	28 46.3	7 18.1	18 17.8	16 59.7	18 15.5	20 44.2
14 Su	17 30 10	23 11 27	9♐17 42	15 35 37	0 40.0	8 21.7	23 16.6	29 30.6	7 25.2	18 16.2	16 57.6	18 14.1	20 42.8
15 M	17 34 7	24 8 44	21 50 20	28 1 59	0D 39.6	10 14.5	24 30.3	0♉14.9	7 32.4	18 14.6	16 55.4	18 12.7	20 41.5
16 Tu	17 38 3	25 6 1	4♑10 45	10♑16 48	0 39.5	12 5.0	25 44.0	0 59.1	7 39.7	18 12.9	16 53.3	18 11.2	20 40.2
17 W	17 42 0	26 3 17	16 20 22	22 21 41	0 39.7	13 53.2	26 57.7	1 43.3	7 47.2	18 11.1	16 51.1	18 9.8	20 38.9
18 Th	17 45 56	27 0 32	28 21 5	4♒18 52	0 40.0	15 39.0	28 11.4	2 27.4	7 54.8	18 9.2	16 48.9	18 8.3	20 37.6
19 F	17 49 53	27 57 48	10♒15 24	16 11 5	0 40.4	17 22.4	29 25.1	3 11.4	8 2.5	18 7.3	16 46.6	18 6.8	20 36.4
20 Sa	17 53 49	28 55 2	22 6 20	28 1 38	0 40.6	19 3.4	0♋38.8	3 55.4	8 10.3	18 5.2	16 44.4	18 5.3	20 35.2
21 Su	17 57 46	29 52 17	3♓57 28	9♓54 21	0R 40.8	20 42.0	1 52.5	4 39.3	8 18.2	18 3.0	16 42.1	18 3.8	20 34.0
22 M	18 1 43	0♋49 31	15 52 48	21 53 24	0 40.8	22 18.2	3 6.2	5 23.1	8 26.3	18 0.8	16 39.8	18 2.3	20 32.8
23 Tu	18 5 39	1 46 45	27 56 40	4♈ 3 11	0D 40.8	23 51.9	4 19.9	6 6.9	8 34.5	17 58.5	16 37.5	18 0.7	20 31.6
24 W	18 9 36	2 43 59	10♈13 30	16 28 9	0 40.8	25 23.2	5 33.7	6 50.6	8 42.8	17 56.1	16 35.2	17 59.2	20 30.5
25 Th	18 13 32	3 41 13	22 47 36	29 12 21	0 40.9	26 52.0	6 47.4	7 34.3	8 51.2	17 53.6	16 32.9	17 57.6	20 29.4
26 F	18 17 29	4 38 28	5♉42 44	12♉19 7	0 41.2	28 18.4	8 1.1	8 17.9	8 59.7	17 51.0	16 30.5	17 56.1	20 28.3
27 Sa	18 21 25	5 35 42	19 1 42	25 50 35	0 41.7	29 42.2	9 14.9	9 1.4	9 8.3	17 48.4	16 28.2	17 54.5	20 27.3
28 Su	18 25 22	6 32 56	2♊45 46	9♊47 5	0 42.2	1♌ 3.5	10 28.6	9 44.8	9 17.1	17 45.6	16 25.8	17 52.9	20 26.2
29 M	18 29 18	7 30 10	16 54 15	24 6 49	0R 42.6	2 22.2	11 42.4	10 28.2	9 25.9	17 42.8	16 23.4	17 51.4	20 25.2
30 Tu	18 33 15	8 27 24	1♋24 12	8♋45 38	0 42.7	3 38.3	12 56.1	11 11.4	9 34.9	17 40.0	16 21.0	17 49.8	20 24.3

Astro Data

	Dy Hr Mn
♄⊻♅	3 3:21
♂0N	9 22:29
☽0S	11 17:01
☽0N	25 20:36
♄ R	28 13:36
♄⊻♆	4 8:34
☽0S	7 21:57
♄⊻♆	19 19:17
☽0N	22 4:12

Planet Ingress

	Dy Hr Mn
♀ ♉	1 15:41
♂ ♈	5 21:36
☿ ♉	11 4:10
☉ ♊	20 19:12
☿ ♊	26 21:16
♀ ♊	26 1:18
☿ ♋	9 18:27
♂ ♉	14 15:56
♀ ♋	19 11:22
☉ ♋	21 3:14
☿ ♌	27 5:11

Last Aspect / ☽ Ingress

Last Aspect Dy Hr Mn		☽ Ingress Dy Hr Mn
30 22:52	♆ □	♉ 1 19:09
3 21:48	♂ ✶	♊ 4 0:28
5 13:11	☿ ✶	♋ 6 4:09
7 22:21	☿ □	♌ 8 7:07
10 7:33	☿ △	♍ 10 9:56
11 22:39	♇ ✶	♎ 12 13:05
13 21:37	♆ □	♏ 14 17:15
16 16:03	☉ ☍	♐ 16 23:22
18 9:53	♄ ✶	♑ 19 8:13
21 8:04	♀ △	♒ 21 19:43
24 3:43	♀ □	♓ 24 8:25
26 19:35	☿ ✶	♈ 26 19:52
28 7:14	♆ □	♉ 29 4:16
30 17:49	♇ ☍	♊ 31 9:19

Last Aspect / ☽ Ingress

Last Aspect Dy Hr Mn		☽ Ingress Dy Hr Mn
1 20:01	♂ ✶	♋ 2 11:58
4 0:31	♂ □	♌ 4 13:35
6 4:57	♂ △	♍ 6 15:28
8 14:22	☿ □	♎ 8 18:33
10 18:16	♂ ☍	♏ 10 23:27
12 13:16	♇ ☌	♐ 13 6:29
15 5:43	♀ ☍	♑ 15 15:50
17 8:34	♇ ✶	♒ 18 3:19
20 15:01	☉ △	♓ 20 16:00
22 14:44	☿ △	♈ 23 4:03
25 8:37	☿ □	♉ 25 13:28
27 2:31	♇ ☍	♊ 27 19:14
29 1:21	♄ △	♋ 29 21:42

☽ Phases & Eclipses

Dy Hr Mn	
2 17:44	● 12♉34
9 15:44	☽ 19♌15
16 16:03	○ 26♏01
24 15:53	☽ 3♓43
1 3:57	● 10♊55
7 20:47	☽ 17♍20
15 4:50	○ 24♐20
15 4:57	☍ P 0.682
23 8:11	☽ 2♈06
30 12:18	● 8♋57
30 12:10:24	☌ T 5'20"

Astro Data

1 MAY 1992
Julian Day # 33724
Delta T 58.2 sec
SVP 05♓21'45"
Obliquity 23°26'26"
⚷ Chiron 3♌53.4
☽ Mean ☊ 3♑23.9

1 JUNE 1992
Julian Day # 33755
Delta T 58.2 sec
SVP 05♓21'40"
Obliquity 23°26'25"
⚷ Chiron 5♌57.9
☽ Mean ☊ 1♑45.4

JULY 1992 — LONGITUDE

Day	Sid.Time	☉	0 hr ☽	Noon ☽	True ☊	☿	♀	♂	♃	♄	♅	♆	♇
1 W	18 37 12	9♋24 38	16♋10 18	23♋37 14	0♑42.5	4♌51.7	14♋ 9.9	11♉54.7	9♍43.9	17♒37.0	16♑18.6	17♑48.2	20♏23.3
2 Th	18 41 8	10 21 51	1♌ 5 26	8♌33 53	0R 41.8	6 2.3	15 23.7	12 37.8	9 53.1	17R 34.0	16R 16.2	17R 46.6	20R 22.4
3 F	18 45 5	11 19 5	16 1 33	23 27 29	0 40.8	7 10.1	16 37.4	13 20.8	10 2.4	17 30.9	16 13.8	17 45.0	20 21.5
4 Sa	18 49 1	12 16 18	0♍50 46	8♍10 39	0 39.5	8 15.1	17 51.2	14 3.8	10 11.7	17 27.7	16 11.4	17 43.3	20 20.6
5 Su	18 52 58	13 13 31	15 26 28	22 37 42	0 38.3	9 17.0	19 5.0	14 46.7	10 21.2	17 24.4	16 9.0	17 41.7	20 19.8
6 M	18 56 54	14 10 44	29 43 58	6♎45 2	0 37.3	10 15.9	20 18.7	15 29.5	10 30.8	17 21.1	16 6.6	17 40.1	20 19.0
7 Tu	19 0 51	15 7 56	13♎40 47	20 31 12	0D 36.9	11 11.5	21 32.5	16 12.2	10 40.4	17 17.7	16 4.2	17 38.5	20 18.2
8 W	19 4 47	16 5 8	27 16 22	3♏56 27	0 37.2	12 3.9	22 46.3	16 54.9	10 50.2	17 14.3	16 1.7	17 36.9	20 17.5
9 Th	19 8 44	17 2 20	10♏31 41	17 2 18	0 38.1	12 52.9	24 0.0	17 37.4	10 60.0	17 10.8	15 59.3	17 35.2	20 16.7
10 F	19 12 41	17 59 32	23 28 37	29 50 55	0 39.3	13 38.4	25 13.8	18 19.9	11 9.9	17 7.2	15 56.9	17 33.6	20 16.0
11 Sa	19 16 37	18 56 44	6♐ 9 32	12♐24 46	0 40.7	14 20.2	26 27.6	19 2.3	11 19.9	17 3.6	15 54.5	17 32.0	20 15.4
12 Su	19 20 34	19 53 56	18 36 55	24 46 15	0R 41.7	14 58.2	27 41.3	19 44.6	11 30.0	16 59.9	15 52.1	17 30.4	20 14.8
13 M	19 24 30	20 51 8	0♑53 5	6♑57 39	0 42.1	15 32.3	28 55.1	20 26.8	11 40.2	16 56.1	15 49.7	17 28.8	20 14.2
14 Tu	19 28 27	21 48 21	13 0 12	19 1 0	0 41.6	16 2.2	0♌ 8.9	21 8.9	11 50.5	16 52.3	15 47.3	17 27.1	20 13.6
15 W	19 32 23	22 45 33	25 0 16	0♒58 14	0 40.0	16 28.0	1 22.7	21 51.0	12 0.9	16 48.5	15 44.9	17 25.5	20 13.1
16 Th	19 36 20	23 42 46	6♒55 9	12 51 16	0 37.4	16 49.4	2 36.4	22 33.0	12 11.3	16 44.6	15 42.5	17 23.9	20 12.6
17 F	19 40 16	24 39 59	18 46 49	24 42 6	0 33.8	17 6.2	3 50.2	23 14.8	12 21.8	16 40.6	15 40.1	17 22.3	20 12.1
18 Sa	19 44 13	25 37 13	0♓37 25	6♓33 4	0 29.7	17 18.4	5 4.0	23 56.6	12 32.4	16 36.6	15 37.7	17 20.7	20 11.6
19 Su	19 48 10	26 34 27	12 29 25	18 26 50	0 25.5	17 25.9	6 17.8	24 38.3	12 43.1	16 32.6	15 35.3	17 19.1	20 11.2
20 M	19 52 6	27 31 42	24 25 43	0♈26 31	0 21.7	17R 28.5	7 31.6	25 19.9	12 53.8	16 28.5	15 33.0	17 17.5	20 10.8
21 Tu	19 56 3	28 28 58	6♈29 41	12 35 43	0 18.8	17 26.3	8 45.4	26 1.4	13 4.6	16 24.4	15 30.6	17 15.9	20 10.5
22 W	19 59 59	29 26 14	18 45 6	24 58 22	0D 17.0	17 19.0	9 59.2	26 42.9	13 15.5	16 20.2	15 28.3	17 14.3	20 10.2
23 Th	20 3 56	0♌23 31	1♉16 1	7♉38 35	0 16.5	17 6.9	11 13.0	27 24.2	13 26.5	16 16.0	15 26.0	17 12.8	20 9.9
24 F	20 7 52	1 20 49	14 6 31	20 40 18	0 17.1	16 49.9	12 26.8	28 5.4	13 37.5	16 11.8	15 23.7	17 11.2	20 9.7
25 Sa	20 11 49	2 18 8	27 20 17	4♊ 6 48	0 18.4	16 28.3	13 40.6	28 46.6	13 48.7	16 7.5	15 21.4	17 9.6	20 9.4
26 Su	20 15 45	3 15 29	11♊ 0 3	18 0 6	0 19.9	16 2.1	14 54.4	29 27.6	13 59.8	16 3.2	15 19.1	17 8.1	20 9.3
27 M	20 19 42	4 12 50	25 6 54	2♋20 10	0R 20.8	15 31.6	16 8.2	0♊ 8.6	14 11.1	15 58.9	15 16.9	17 6.6	20 9.1
28 Tu	20 23 39	5 10 12	9♋39 30	17 4 16	0 20.6	14 57.3	17 22.0	0 49.4	14 22.4	15 54.5	15 14.6	17 5.0	20 9.0
29 W	20 27 35	6 7 34	24 33 39	2♌ 6 40	0 18.8	14 19.5	18 35.9	1 30.1	14 33.8	15 50.2	15 12.4	17 3.5	20 8.9
30 Th	20 31 32	7 4 58	9♌42 10	17 18 54	0 15.4	13 38.9	19 49.7	2 10.7	14 45.2	15 45.8	15 10.2	17 2.0	20D 8.9
31 F	20 35 28	8 2 22	24 55 35	2♍30 53	0 10.6	12 55.9	21 3.5	2 51.2	14 56.7	15 41.3	15 8.1	17 0.5	20 8.9

AUGUST 1992 — LONGITUDE

Day	Sid.Time	☉	0 hr ☽	Noon ☽	True ☊	☿	♀	♂	♃	♄	♅	♆	♇
1 Sa	20 39 25	8♌59 47	10♍ 3 35	17♍32 31	0♑ 5.1	12♌11.4	22♌17.3	3♊31.6	15♍ 8.3	15♒36.9	15♑ 5.9	16♑59.0	20♏ 8.9
2 Su	20 43 21	9 57 13	24 56 42	2♎15 19	29♐59.6	11R 26.0	23 31.2	4 11.9	15 19.9	15R 32.4	15R 3.8	16R 57.6	20 8.9
3 M	20 47 18	10 54 39	9♎27 47	16 33 39	29R 55.0	10 40.6	24 45.0	4 52.1	15 31.6	15 28.0	15 1.7	16 56.1	20 9.0
4 Tu	20 51 14	11 52 6	23 32 45	0♏25 1	29 51.8	9 56.0	25 58.8	5 32.2	15 43.3	15 23.5	14 59.6	16 54.7	20 9.2
5 W	20 55 11	12 49 34	7♏10 34	13 49 40	29D 50.4	9 13.0	27 12.6	6 12.1	15 55.1	15 19.0	14 57.5	16 53.2	20 9.3
6 Th	20 59 8	13 47 3	20 22 39	26 49 57	29 50.4	8 32.6	28 26.4	6 51.9	16 6.9	15 14.5	14 55.5	16 51.8	20 9.5
7 F	21 3 4	14 44 32	3♐12 1	9♐29 23	29 51.5	7 55.3	29 40.2	7 31.7	16 18.8	15 10.0	14 53.5	16 50.5	20 9.7
8 Sa	21 7 1	15 42 2	15 42 34	21 52 4	29 52.8	7 22.2	0♍54.0	8 11.3	16 30.8	15 5.6	14 51.5	16 49.1	20 10.0
9 Su	21 10 57	16 39 33	27 58 23	4♑ 2 0	29R 53.6	6 53.7	2 7.8	8 50.7	16 42.8	15 1.1	14 49.6	16 47.7	20 10.3
10 M	21 14 54	17 37 5	10♑ 3 23	16 2 55	29 53.0	6 30.6	3 21.6	9 30.1	16 54.8	14 56.6	14 47.7	16 46.4	20 10.6
11 Tu	21 18 50	18 34 37	22 1 1	27 58 0	29 50.5	6 13.3	4 35.4	10 9.3	17 6.9	14 52.1	14 45.8	16 45.1	20 11.0
12 W	21 22 47	19 32 11	3♒54 11	9♒49 52	29 45.8	6 2.4	5 49.2	10 48.5	17 19.0	14 47.6	14 43.9	16 43.8	20 11.4
13 Th	21 26 44	20 29 46	15 45 17	21 40 40	29 39.0	5D 58.1	7 3.0	11 27.5	17 31.2	14 43.2	14 42.1	16 42.5	20 11.8
14 F	21 30 40	21 27 22	27 36 14	3♓32 11	29 30.3	6 0.8	8 16.8	12 6.4	17 43.4	14 38.7	14 40.3	16 41.2	20 12.3
15 Sa	21 34 37	22 24 59	9♓28 44	15 26 5	29 20.5	6 10.6	9 30.5	12 45.1	17 55.7	14 34.3	14 38.6	16 40.0	20 12.8
16 Su	21 38 33	23 22 37	21 24 26	27 24 3	29 10.4	6 27.7	10 44.3	13 23.7	18 8.0	14 29.9	14 36.9	16 38.7	20 13.3
17 M	21 42 30	24 20 17	3♈25 10	9♈28 4	29 0.9	6 52.1	11 58.1	14 2.2	18 20.3	14 25.5	14 35.2	16 37.5	20 13.8
18 Tu	21 46 26	25 17 58	15 33 5	21 40 34	28 52.9	7 23.9	13 11.8	14 40.6	18 32.7	14 21.1	14 33.5	16 36.3	20 14.4
19 W	21 50 23	26 15 41	27 50 52	4♉ 4 26	28 47.0	8 2.9	14 25.6	15 18.9	18 45.1	14 16.8	14 31.9	16 35.2	20 15.1
20 Th	21 54 19	27 13 26	10♉21 41	16 43 5	28 43.3	8 49.1	15 39.4	15 57.0	18 57.6	14 12.4	14 30.3	16 34.0	20 15.7
21 F	21 58 16	28 11 12	23 9 7	29 40 13	28D 41.9	9 42.3	16 53.1	16 35.0	19 10.1	14 8.1	14 28.8	16 32.9	20 16.4
22 Sa	22 2 12	29 9 0	6♊16 51	12♊59 25	28 41.9	10 42.3	18 6.9	17 12.8	19 22.6	14 3.9	14 27.3	16 31.8	20 17.2
23 Su	22 6 9	0♍ 6 49	19 48 15	26 43 37	28R 42.6	11 48.8	19 20.6	17 50.5	19 35.2	13 59.6	14 25.9	16 30.7	20 17.9
24 M	22 10 6	1 4 41	3♋45 39	10♋54 20	28 42.7	13 1.5	20 34.3	18 28.1	19 47.8	13 55.4	14 24.4	16 29.7	20 18.7
25 Tu	22 14 2	2 2 34	18 9 29	25 30 42	28 41.2	14 20.1	21 48.1	19 5.5	20 0.4	13 51.3	14 23.1	16 28.7	20 19.6
26 W	22 17 59	3 0 29	2♌57 23	10♌28 45	28 37.5	15 44.3	23 1.8	19 42.8	20 13.0	13 47.1	14 21.7	16 27.7	20 20.4
27 Th	22 21 55	3 58 25	18 3 45	25 41 13	28 31.3	17 13.5	24 15.6	20 19.9	20 25.7	13 43.1	14 20.4	16 26.7	20 21.3
28 F	22 25 52	4 56 24	3♍19 48	10♍58 6	28 22.8	18 47.4	25 29.3	20 56.8	20 38.4	13 39.0	14 19.2	16 25.8	20 22.3
29 Sa	22 29 48	5 54 23	18 34 41	26 8 14	28 13.1	20 25.4	26 43.0	21 33.6	20 51.2	13 35.0	14 17.9	16 24.8	20 23.2
30 Su	22 33 45	6 52 24	3♎37 27	11♎ 1 18	28 3.2	22 7.2	27 56.7	22 10.3	21 3.9	13 31.1	14 16.8	16 23.9	20 24.2
31 M	22 37 41	7 50 27	18 18 55	25 29 38	27 54.5	23 52.3	29 10.4	22 46.8	21 16.7	13 27.2	14 15.6	16 23.1	20 25.2

Astro Data Dy Hr Mn	Planet Ingress Dy Hr Mn	Last Aspect Dy Hr Mn	☽ Ingress Dy Hr Mn	Last Aspect Dy Hr Mn	☽ Ingress Dy Hr Mn	☽ Phases & Eclipses Dy Hr Mn	Astro Data
☽0S 5 4:17	♀ ♌ 13 21:07	1 6:48 ♇ △	♌ 1 22:15	1 16:13 ♇ ✶	♎ 2 8:17	7 2:43 ☽ 15♎14	1 JULY 1992
☽0N 19 11:20	☉ ♌ 22 14:09	3 6:59 ♇ □	♍ 3 22:37	4 4:39 ♀ ✶	♏ 4 11:16	14 19:06 ○ 22♑34	Julian Day # 33785
☿ R 20 0:54	♂ ♊ 26 18:59	5 8:08 ♇ ✶	♎ 6 0:27	6 16:37 ♀ □	♐ 6 17:57	22 22:12 ☽ 0♉19	Delta T 58.3 sec
♇ D 30 21:34		7 15:11 ♀ □	♏ 8 4:53	8 1:35 ♃ □	♑ 9 4:00	29 19:35 ● 6♌54	SVP 05♓21'35"
♃△♅ 31 19:49	☊ ♐ 1 22:09	10 3:38 ♀ △	♐ 10 12:17	10 20:18 ♇ ✶	♒ 11 16:06		Obliquity 23°26'24"
	♀ ♍ 7 6:26	11 20:53 ♄ ✶	♑ 12 22:16	13 10:27 ☉ ☍	♓ 14 4:51	5 10:59 ☽ 13♏16	⚷ Chiron 9♌00.2
☽0S 1 13:06	☉ ♍ 22 21:10	14 19:06 ☉ ☍	♒ 15 10:03	15 21:37 ♇ △	♈ 16 17:11	13 10:27 ○ 20♒55	☽ Mean ☊ 0♑10.1
♃⊼♄ 2 18:39	♀ ♎ 31 16:09	17 9:37 ♂ □	♓ 17 22:44	18 20:40 ☉ △	♉ 19 4:10	21 10:01 ☽ 28♉35	
♃△♆ 9 8:52		20 6:44 ☉ △	♈ 20 11:07	21 10:01 ☉ □	♊ 21 12:36	28 2:42 ● 5♍03	1 AUGUST 1992
♄⊻♅ 13 9:27		21 21:15 ♅ △	♉ 22 21:36	22 23:37 ♃ □	♋ 23 17:36		Julian Day # 33816
☿ D 13 2:53		25 2:42 ♂ ☌	♊ 25 4:44	25 6:30 ♀ ✶	♌ 25 19:15		Delta T 58.3 sec
☽0N 15 17:54		26 8:38 ♄ △	♋ 27 8:08	27 3:44 ♂ ✶	♍ 27 18:46		SVP 05♓21'29"
♃✶♇ 26 15:03		28 16:57 ♇ △	♌ 29 8:39	29 14:05 ♀ ☌	♎ 29 18:11		Obliquity 23°26'25"
☽0S 28 23:46		30 17:22 ♀ ☌	♍ 31 8:01	31 10:36 ☿ ✶	♏ 31 19:38		⚷ Chiron 12♌44.2
							☽ Mean ☊ 28♐31.6

LONGITUDE SEPTEMBER 1992

Day	Sid.Time	☉	0 hr ☽	Noon ☽	True ☊	☿	♀	♂	♃	♄	♅	♆	♇
1 Tu	22 41 38	8♍48 31	2♏33 3	9♏28 59	27♐47.7	25♌40.1	0♎24.1	23♊23.1	21♍29.5	13♒23.3	14♑14.6	16♑22.2	20♏26.3
2 W	22 45 35	9 46 36	16 17 27	22 58 39	27R43.3	27 30.2	1 37.8	23 59.2	21 42.3	13R 19.6	14R 13.5	16R 21.4	20 27.4
3 Th	22 49 31	10 44 43	29 32 53	6♐ 0 38	27D 41.2	29 22.1	2 51.5	24 35.2	21 55.2	13 15.8	14 12.5	16 20.6	20 28.5
4 F	22 53 28	11 42 52	12♐22 25	18 38 49	27 40.8	1♍15.5	4 5.1	25 11.0	22 8.0	13 12.2	14 11.6	16 19.9	20 29.6
5 Sa	22 57 24	12 41 1	24 50 27	0♑57 58	27R 41.0	3 10.0	5 18.8	25 46.7	22 20.9	13 8.5	14 10.7	16 19.2	20 30.8
6 Su	23 1 21	13 39 13	7♑ 2 0	13 3 10	27 40.7	5 5.2	6 32.4	26 22.2	22 33.8	13 5.0	14 9.8	16 18.5	20 32.0
7 M	23 5 17	14 37 25	19 2 3	24 59 13	27 38.9	7 0.9	7 46.1	26 57.5	22 46.7	13 1.5	14 9.0	16 17.8	20 33.3
8 Tu	23 9 14	15 35 40	0♒55 11	6♒50 24	27 34.7	8 56.6	8 59.7	27 32.6	22 59.6	12 58.1	14 8.3	16 17.2	20 34.6
9 W	23 13 10	16 33 55	12 45 19	18 40 18	27 27.8	10 52.3	10 13.3	28 7.6	23 12.5	12 54.7	14 7.5	16 16.6	20 35.9
10 Th	23 17 7	17 32 13	24 35 40	0♓31 42	27 18.1	12 47.7	11 26.9	28 42.3	23 25.5	12 51.4	14 6.9	16 16.0	20 37.2
11 F	23 21 4	18 30 32	6♓28 39	12 26 43	27 6.0	14 42.7	12 40.4	29 16.9	23 38.4	12 48.2	14 6.3	16 15.4	20 38.6
12 Sa	23 25 0	19 28 53	18 26 3	24 26 50	26 52.5	16 37.1	13 54.0	29 51.3	23 51.4	12 45.1	14 5.7	16 14.9	20 39.9
13 Su	23 28 57	20 27 15	0♈29 11	6♈33 13	26 38.5	18 30.8	15 7.5	0♋25.5	24 4.3	12 42.0	14 5.2	16 14.4	20 41.4
14 M	23 32 53	21 25 40	12 39 4	18 46 52	26 25.3	20 23.7	16 21.1	0 59.5	24 17.3	12 39.0	14 4.7	16 13.9	20 42.8
15 Tu	23 36 50	22 24 6	24 56 47	1♉ 8 59	26 13.9	22 15.7	17 34.6	1 33.4	24 30.3	12 36.1	14 4.3	16 13.5	20 44.3
16 W	23 40 46	23 22 35	7♉23 42	13 41 9	26 5.1	24 6.9	18 48.1	2 7.0	24 43.3	12 33.2	14 3.9	16 13.1	20 45.8
17 Th	23 44 43	24 21 6	20 1 37	26 25 24	25 59.2	25 57.1	20 1.6	2 40.4	24 56.2	12 30.4	14 3.6	16 12.8	20 47.3
18 F	23 48 39	25 19 38	2♊52 52	9♊24 21	25 56.0	27 46.3	21 15.1	3 13.7	25 9.2	12 27.7	14 3.3	16 12.4	20 48.9
19 Sa	23 52 36	26 18 14	16 0 14	22 40 52	25 54.9	29 34.5	22 28.6	3 46.7	25 22.2	12 25.1	14 3.1	16 12.1	20 50.4
20 Su	23 56 33	27 16 51	29 26 35	6♋17 41	25 54.8	1♎21.8	23 42.0	4 19.5	25 35.2	12 22.6	14 2.9	16 11.8	20 52.1
21 M	0 0 29	28 15 31	13♋14 21	20 16 43	25 54.4	3 8.0	24 55.5	4 52.1	25 48.2	12 20.2	14 2.8	16 11.6	20 53.7
22 Tu	0 4 26	29 14 12	27 24 47	4♌38 21	25 52.5	4 53.2	26 8.9	5 24.4	26 1.2	12 17.8	14D 2.7	16 11.4	20 55.4
23 W	0 8 22	0♎12 56	11♌57 5	19 20 27	25 48.2	6 37.5	27 22.4	5 56.6	26 14.2	12 15.5	14 2.7	16 11.2	20 57.1
24 Th	0 12 19	1 11 43	26 47 42	4♍17 55	25 41.2	8 20.8	28 35.8	6 28.4	26 27.1	12 13.3	14 2.7	16 11.1	20 58.8
25 F	0 16 15	2 10 31	11♍50 2	19 22 49	25 31.7	10 3.1	29 49.2	7 0.1	26 40.1	12 11.2	14 2.8	16 11.0	21 0.5
26 Sa	0 20 12	3 9 21	26 55 1	4♎25 20	25 20.7	11 44.4	1♏ 2.6	7 31.5	26 53.1	12 9.2	14 2.9	16 10.9	21 2.3
27 Su	0 24 8	4 8 14	11♎52 31	19 15 25	25 9.4	13 24.9	2 16.0	8 2.7	27 6.0	12 7.3	14 3.1	16D 10.9	21 4.0
28 M	0 28 5	5 7 8	26 33 4	3♏44 39	24 59.1	15 4.4	3 29.4	8 33.6	27 19.0	12 5.5	14 3.3	16 10.9	21 5.9
29 Tu	0 32 1	6 6 5	10♏49 34	17 47 26	24 50.8	16 43.0	4 42.8	9 4.3	27 31.9	12 3.8	14 3.6	16 10.9	21 7.7
30 W	0 35 58	7 5 3	24 38 6	1♐21 34	24 45.2	18 20.7	5 56.1	9 34.7	27 44.8	12 2.1	14 3.9	16 10.9	21 9.6

LONGITUDE OCTOBER 1992

Day	Sid.Time	☉	0 hr ☽	Noon ☽	True ☊	☿	♀	♂	♃	♄	♅	♆	♇
1 Th	0 39 55	8♎ 4 3	7♐58 1	14♐27 47	24♐42.2	19♎57.5	7♏ 9.4	10♋ 4.8	27♍57.7	12♒ 0.6	14♑ 4.3	16♑11.0	21♏11.4
2 F	0 43 51	9 3 5	20 51 19	27 9 8	24D 41.2	21 33.5	8 22.7	10 34.7	28 10.6	11R 59.1	14 4.7	16 11.2	21 13.3
3 Sa	0 47 48	10 2 9	3♑21 50	9♑30 5	24R 41.3	23 8.7	9 36.0	11 4.2	28 23.4	11 57.8	14 5.2	16 11.3	21 15.3
4 Su	0 51 44	11 1 14	15 34 31	21 35 48	24 41.3	24 43.0	10 49.3	11 33.5	28 36.3	11 56.5	14 5.8	16 11.5	21 17.2
5 M	0 55 41	12 0 21	27 34 37	3♒31 37	24 40.2	26 16.5	12 2.6	12 2.6	28 49.1	11 55.4	14 6.4	16 11.7	21 19.2
6 Tu	0 59 37	12 59 30	9♒27 24	15 22 32	24 37.0	27 49.2	13 15.8	12 31.3	29 1.9	11 54.3	14 7.0	16 12.0	21 21.2
7 W	1 3 34	13 58 41	21 17 36	27 13 3	24 31.3	29 21.1	14 29.0	12 59.8	29 14.7	11 53.4	14 7.7	16 12.3	21 23.2
8 Th	1 7 30	14 57 53	3♓ 9 21	9♓ 6 52	24 22.9	0♏52.2	15 42.2	13 27.9	29 27.5	11 52.5	14 8.4	16 12.6	21 25.2
9 F	1 11 27	15 57 7	15 5 58	21 6 53	24 12.4	2 22.6	16 55.4	13 55.8	29 40.2	11 51.7	14 9.2	16 13.0	21 27.2
10 Sa	1 15 24	16 56 23	27 9 53	3♈15 7	24 0.3	3 52.2	18 8.5	14 23.3	29 52.9	11 51.1	14 10.1	16 13.4	21 29.3
11 Su	1 19 20	17 55 42	9♈22 43	15 32 47	23 47.8	5 20.9	19 21.7	14 50.5	0♎ 5.6	11 50.5	14 11.0	16 13.8	21 31.4
12 M	1 23 17	18 55 2	21 45 22	28 0 30	23 35.9	6 48.9	20 34.8	15 17.4	0 18.2	11 50.0	14 11.9	16 14.2	21 33.5
13 Tu	1 27 13	19 54 24	4♉18 14	10♉38 34	23 25.7	8 16.1	21 47.9	15 44.0	0 30.8	11 49.7	14 12.9	16 14.7	21 35.6
14 W	1 31 10	20 53 48	17 1 33	23 27 11	23 17.9	9 42.5	23 0.9	16 10.2	0 43.4	11 49.4	14 13.9	16 15.3	21 37.7
15 Th	1 35 6	21 53 15	29 55 34	6♊26 47	23 12.9	11 8.1	24 14.0	16 36.2	0 56.0	11 49.3	14 15.0	16 15.8	21 39.9
16 F	1 39 3	22 52 44	13♊ 0 55	19 38 6	23D 10.4	12 32.8	25 27.0	17 1.7	1 8.5	11D 49.2	14 16.2	16 16.4	21 42.0
17 Sa	1 42 59	23 52 15	26 18 32	3♋ 2 20	23 10.0	13 56.7	26 40.0	17 26.9	1 21.0	11 49.2	14 17.4	16 17.0	21 44.2
18 Su	1 46 56	24 51 48	9♋49 42	16 40 46	23 10.6	15 19.6	27 53.0	17 51.8	1 33.5	11 49.4	14 18.6	16 17.7	21 46.4
19 M	1 50 53	25 51 24	23 35 40	0♌34 27	23R 11.3	16 41.6	29 6.0	18 16.2	1 45.9	11 49.6	14 19.9	16 18.4	21 48.6
20 Tu	1 54 49	26 51 2	7♌37 9	14 43 39	23 10.8	18 2.6	0♐18.9	18 40.3	1 58.3	11 50.0	14 21.3	16 19.1	21 50.9
21 W	1 58 46	27 50 42	21 53 46	29 7 9	23 8.4	19 22.6	1 31.8	19 4.0	2 10.6	11 50.4	14 22.6	16 19.9	21 53.1
22 Th	2 2 42	28 50 25	6♍23 22	13♍41 49	23 3.7	20 41.4	2 44.8	19 27.3	2 22.9	11 51.0	14 24.1	16 20.6	21 55.3
23 F	2 6 39	29 50 9	21 1 47	28 22 27	22 57.0	21 59.0	3 57.6	19 50.2	2 35.1	11 51.6	14 25.6	16 21.5	21 57.6
24 Sa	2 10 35	0♏49 56	5♎42 55	13♎ 2 13	22 48.9	23 15.4	5 10.5	20 12.6	2 47.4	11 52.4	14 27.1	16 22.3	21 59.9
25 Su	2 14 32	1 49 45	20 19 24	27 33 34	22 40.4	24 30.3	6 23.4	20 34.7	2 59.5	11 53.2	14 28.7	16 23.2	22 2.2
26 M	2 18 28	2 49 36	4♏43 50	11♏49 29	22 32.7	25 43.7	7 36.2	20 56.3	3 11.6	11 54.2	14 30.3	16 24.1	22 4.5
27 Tu	2 22 25	3 49 30	18 49 54	25 44 36	22 26.5	26 55.4	8 49.0	21 17.4	3 23.7	11 55.2	14 32.0	16 25.1	22 6.8
28 W	2 26 22	4 49 25	2♐33 17	9♐15 48	22 22.5	28 5.3	10 1.8	21 38.1	3 35.7	11 56.4	14 33.7	16 26.0	22 9.1
29 Th	2 30 18	5 49 21	15 52 9	22 22 28	22D 20.6	29 13.2	11 14.5	21 58.3	3 47.7	11 57.7	14 35.5	16 27.0	22 11.4
30 F	2 34 15	6 49 20	28 47 1	5♑ 6 8	22 20.6	0♐18.8	12 27.2	22 18.1	3 59.6	11 59.0	14 37.3	16 28.1	22 13.8
31 Sa	2 38 11	7 49 20	11♑20 18	17 30 0	22 21.7	1 21.9	13 39.9	22 37.3	4 11.4	12 0.5	14 39.1	16 29.2	22 16.1

Astro Data	Planet Ingress	Last Aspect	☽ Ingress	Last Aspect	☽ Ingress	☽ Phases & Eclipses	Astro Data
Dy Hr Mn	Dy Hr Mn	Dy Hr Mn	Dy Hr Mn	Dy Hr Mn	Dy Hr Mn	Dy Hr Mn	1 SEPTEMBER 1992
♀0S 2 16:25	☿ ♍ 3 8:03	2 23:37 ☿ □	♐ 3 0:50	2 14:13 ♃ □	♑ 2 17:29	3 22:39 ☽ 11♐40	Julian Day # 33847
☽0N 12 0:07	♂ ♋ 12 6:05	5 1:55 ♂ ☍	♑ 5 10:06	5 2:33 ♃ △	♒ 5 4:53	12 2:17 ○ 19♓34	Delta T 58.4 sec
☿0S 20 17:23	☿ ♎ 19 5:41	7 7:41 ♃ △	♒ 7 22:08	7 0:11 ♇ □	♓ 7 17:38	19 19:53 ☽ 27♊07	SVP 05♓21'26"
♅ D 22 23:45	☉ ♎ 22 18:43	10 8:44 ♂ △	♓ 10 10:56	10 5:28 ♃ ☍	♈ 10 5:36	26 10:40 ● 3♎36	Obliquity 23°26'25"
☽0S 25 10:29	♀ ♏ 25 3:31	12 11:01 ♃ ☍	♈ 12 23:02	11 18:03 ☉ ☍	♉ 12 15:48		⚷ Chiron 16♌34.8
♃Q♄ 27 2:07		14 8:03 ♀ ☍	♉ 15 9:47	14 12:21 ♀ ☍	♊ 15 0:08	3 14:12 ☽ 10♑37	☽ Mean ☊ 26♐53.1
♆ D 27 18:35	☿ ♏ 7 10:13	17 12:57 ☿ △	♊ 17 18:40	16 19:17 ☉ △	♋ 17 6:36	11 18:03 ○ 18♈40	
	♃ ♎ 10 13:26	19 19:53 ☉ □	♋ 20 0:59	19 10:22 ♀ △	♌ 19 11:01	19 4:12 ☽ 26♋02	1 OCTOBER 1992
☽0N 9 6:28	♀ ♐ 19 17:47	22 3:16 ☉ ✶	♌ 22 4:19	21 10:37 ☉ ✶	♍ 21 13:27	25 20:34 ● 2♏41	Julian Day # 33877
♄ D 16 2:06	☉ ♏ 23 3:57	24 3:09 ♀ ✶	♍ 24 5:08	23 1:42 ☿ ✶	♎ 23 14:39		Delta T 58.5 sec
☽0S 22 19:19	☿ ♐ 29 17:02	25 23:57 ♃ ☌	♎ 26 4:55	25 0:26 ♂ □	♏ 25 16:04		SVP 05♓21'23"
♃0S 22 17:54		27 6:59 ♆ □	♏ 28 5:44	27 15:23 ☿ ☌	♐ 27 19:29		Obliquity 23°26'25"
		30 5:37 ♃ ✶	♐ 30 9:33	28 16:52 ♄ ✶	♑ 30 2:18		⚷ Chiron 19♌55.2
							☽ Mean ☊ 25♐17.8

NOVEMBER 1992 LONGITUDE

Day	Sid.Time	☉	0 hr ☽	Noon ☽	True ☊	☿	♀	♂	♃	♄	♅	♆	♇
1 Su	2 42 8	8♏49 22	23♑35 50	29♑38 22	22♐23.2	2♐22.3	14♐52.6	22♋56.1	4♎23.2	12♒ 2.1	14♑41.0	16♑30.3	22♏18.5
2 M	2 46 4	9 49 25	5♒38 16	11♒36 10	22R 24.2	3 19.6	16 5.2	23 14.4	4 34.9	12 3.7	14 43.0	16 31.4	22 20.9
3 Tu	2 50 1	10 49 30	17 32 41	23 28 29	22 24.0	4 13.5	17 17.8	23 32.1	4 46.6	12 5.5	14 45.0	16 32.6	22 23.2
4 W	2 53 57	11 49 37	29 24 9	5♓20 17	22 22.2	5 3.5	18 30.3	23 49.4	4 58.2	12 7.4	14 47.0	16 33.7	22 25.6
5 Th	2 57 54	12 49 45	11♓17 26	17 16 7	22 18.6	5 49.2	19 42.8	24 6.1	5 9.7	12 9.3	14 49.1	16 35.0	22 28.0
6 F	3 1 51	13 49 54	23 16 47	29 19 52	22 13.4	6 30.2	20 55.3	24 22.3	5 21.2	12 11.4	14 51.2	16 36.2	22 30.4
7 Sa	3 5 47	14 50 5	5♈25 43	11♈34 38	22 7.0	7 5.8	22 7.8	24 37.9	5 32.6	12 13.6	14 53.4	16 37.5	22 32.8
8 Su	3 9 44	15 50 18	17 46 50	24 2 31	22 0.3	7 35.4	23 20.2	24 52.9	5 44.0	12 15.8	14 55.6	16 38.8	22 35.2
9 M	3 13 40	16 50 33	0♉21 46	6♉44 38	21 53.8	7 58.5	24 32.5	25 7.4	5 55.2	12 18.2	14 57.8	16 40.1	22 37.6
10 Tu	3 17 37	17 50 49	13 11 8	19 41 11	21 48.3	8 14.3	25 44.8	25 21.3	6 6.4	12 20.6	15 0.1	16 41.5	22 40.0
11 W	3 21 33	18 51 7	26 14 42	2♊51 34	21 44.3	8R 22.1	26 57.1	25 34.6	6 17.6	12 23.2	15 2.4	16 42.9	22 42.4
12 Th	3 25 30	19 51 26	9♊31 37	16 14 41	21D 42.1	8 21.2	28 9.3	25 47.3	6 28.6	12 25.8	15 4.8	16 44.3	22 44.8
13 F	3 29 26	20 51 48	23 0 35	29 49 10	21 41.5	8 11.1	29 21.5	25 59.4	6 39.6	12 28.5	15 7.2	16 45.7	22 47.2
14 Sa	3 33 23	21 52 11	6♋40 15	13♋33 41	21 42.2	7 51.1	0♑33.7	26 10.8	6 50.5	12 31.4	15 9.6	16 47.2	22 49.6
15 Su	3 37 20	22 52 36	20 29 19	27 27 0	21 43.6	7 21.0	1 45.8	26 21.6	7 1.4	12 34.3	15 12.1	16 48.7	22 52.0
16 M	3 41 16	23 53 3	4♌26 35	11♌27 56	21 45.2	6 40.5	2 57.8	26 31.8	7 12.1	12 37.3	15 14.6	16 50.2	22 54.4
17 Tu	3 45 13	24 53 32	18 30 54	25 35 17	21R 46.2	5 49.9	4 9.8	26 41.2	7 22.8	12 40.4	15 17.2	16 51.8	22 56.9
18 W	3 49 9	25 54 3	2♍40 53	9♍47 27	21 46.2	4 49.9	5 21.8	26 50.0	7 33.4	12 43.6	15 19.8	16 53.4	22 59.3
19 Th	3 53 6	26 54 35	16 54 40	24 2 13	21 45.0	3 41.6	6 33.7	26 58.1	7 43.9	12 46.9	15 22.4	16 55.0	23 1.7
20 F	3 57 2	27 55 9	1♎ 9 42	8♎16 41	21 42.6	2 26.6	7 45.5	27 5.4	7 54.3	12 50.3	15 25.0	16 56.6	23 4.1
21 Sa	4 0 59	28 55 45	15 22 41	22 27 12	21 39.6	1 7.1	8 57.3	27 12.0	8 4.6	12 53.7	15 27.7	16 58.2	23 6.5
22 Su	4 4 55	29 56 23	29 29 44	6♏29 45	21 36.2	29♏45.4	10 9.1	27 17.9	8 14.8	12 57.3	15 30.5	16 59.9	23 8.9
23 M	4 8 52	0♐57 2	13♏26 47	20 20 21	21 33.2	28 24.4	11 20.8	27 23.0	8 25.0	13 0.9	15 33.2	17 1.6	23 11.3
24 Tu	4 12 49	1 57 43	27 10 4	3♐55 35	21 30.9	27 6.8	12 32.4	27 27.4	8 35.0	13 4.7	15 36.0	17 3.3	23 13.7
25 W	4 16 45	2 58 26	10♐36 38	17 13 4	21D 29.6	25 54.9	13 44.0	27 31.0	8 44.9	13 8.5	15 38.9	17 5.1	23 16.1
26 Th	4 20 42	3 59 9	23 44 46	0♑11 44	21 29.3	24 51.1	14 55.5	27 33.7	8 54.8	13 12.4	15 41.7	17 6.8	23 18.5
27 F	4 24 38	4 59 54	6♑34 4	12 51 57	21 29.8	23 57.0	16 7.0	27 35.8	9 4.5	13 16.4	15 44.6	17 8.6	23 20.9
28 Sa	4 28 35	6 0 40	19 5 37	25 15 23	21 31.0	23 13.8	17 18.4	27R 37.0	9 14.2	13 20.4	15 47.5	17 10.4	23 23.2
29 Su	4 32 31	7 1 28	1♒21 40	7♒24 53	21 32.4	22 41.9	18 29.7	27 37.3	9 23.7	13 24.6	15 50.5	17 12.3	23 25.6
30 M	4 36 28	8 2 16	13 25 31	19 24 7	21 33.7	22 21.7	19 40.9	27 36.9	9 33.2	13 28.8	15 53.5	17 14.1	23 28.0

DECEMBER 1992 LONGITUDE

Day	Sid.Time	☉	0 hr ☽	Noon ☽	True ☊	☿	♀	♂	♃	♄	♅	♆	♇
1 Tu	4 40 24	9♐ 3 5	25♒21 15	1♓17 28	21♐34.6	22♏12.8	20♑52.1	27♋35.7	9♎42.5	13♒33.1	15♑56.5	17♑16.0	23♏30.3
2 W	4 44 21	10 3 55	7♓13 24	13 9 37	21R 35.1	22D 14.8	22 3.1	27R 33.6	9 51.7	13 37.5	15 59.5	17 17.9	23 32.7
3 Th	4 48 18	11 4 45	19 6 44	25 5 20	21 34.9	22 26.9	23 14.1	27 30.7	10 0.8	13 42.0	16 2.6	17 19.8	23 35.0
4 F	4 52 14	12 5 37	1♈ 6 0	7♈ 9 17	21 34.3	22 48.2	24 25.0	27 26.9	10 9.8	13 46.5	16 5.7	17 21.7	23 37.3
5 Sa	4 56 11	13 6 29	13 15 42	19 25 41	21 33.4	23 18.1	25 35.9	27 22.3	10 18.7	13 51.1	16 8.8	17 23.6	23 39.6
6 Su	5 0 7	14 7 23	25 39 41	1♉58 2	21 32.4	23 55.5	26 46.6	27 16.9	10 27.5	13 55.8	16 11.9	17 25.6	23 41.9
7 M	5 4 4	15 8 17	8♉21 1	14 48 51	21 31.4	24 39.7	27 57.2	27 10.6	10 36.1	14 0.6	16 15.1	17 27.6	23 44.2
8 Tu	5 8 0	16 9 12	21 21 37	27 59 23	21 30.7	25 29.8	29 7.7	27 3.5	10 44.7	14 5.5	16 18.3	17 29.6	23 46.5
9 W	5 11 57	17 10 8	4♊42 3	11♊29 28	21 30.3	26 25.2	0♒18.1	26 55.5	10 53.1	14 10.4	16 21.5	17 31.6	23 48.8
10 Th	5 15 53	18 11 5	18 21 22	25 17 25	21D 30.1	27 25.1	1 28.4	26 46.7	11 1.4	14 15.4	16 24.7	17 33.6	23 51.0
11 F	5 19 50	19 12 2	2♋17 13	9♋20 17	21 30.1	28 29.1	2 38.6	26 37.1	11 9.5	14 20.4	16 28.0	17 35.7	23 53.3
12 Sa	5 23 47	20 13 1	16 26 4	23 34 2	21 30.3	29 36.6	3 48.7	26 26.6	11 17.6	14 25.6	16 31.3	17 37.7	23 55.5
13 Su	5 27 43	21 14 0	0♌43 36	7♌54 11	21R 30.3	0♐47.1	4 58.7	26 15.3	11 25.5	14 30.7	16 34.6	17 39.8	23 57.7
14 M	5 31 40	22 15 1	15 5 14	22 16 13	21 30.3	2 0.2	6 8.5	26 3.1	11 33.3	14 36.0	16 37.9	17 41.9	23 59.9
15 Tu	5 35 36	23 16 2	29 26 39	6♍36 5	21 30.2	3 15.7	7 18.2	25 50.2	11 40.9	14 41.3	16 41.2	17 44.0	24 2.1
16 W	5 39 33	24 17 5	13♍44 9	20 50 31	21D 30.1	4 33.1	8 27.8	25 36.4	11 48.4	14 46.7	16 44.6	17 46.1	24 4.2
17 Th	5 43 29	25 18 8	27 54 53	4♎57 1	21 30.0	5 52.3	9 37.3	25 21.8	11 55.8	14 52.2	16 48.0	17 48.2	24 6.4
18 F	5 47 26	26 19 12	11♎56 45	18 53 53	21 30.2	7 13.0	10 46.7	25 6.5	12 3.1	14 57.7	16 51.3	17 50.4	24 8.5
19 Sa	5 51 22	27 20 17	25 48 20	2♏39 58	21 30.6	8 35.1	11 55.9	24 50.4	12 10.2	15 3.3	16 54.7	17 52.5	24 10.6
20 Su	5 55 19	28 21 24	9♏28 41	16 14 24	21 31.2	9 58.3	13 4.9	24 33.6	12 17.2	15 8.9	16 58.2	17 54.7	24 12.7
21 M	5 59 16	29 22 30	22 57 3	29 36 33	21 32.0	11 22.5	14 13.9	24 16.0	12 24.0	15 14.6	17 1.6	17 56.9	24 14.8
22 Tu	6 3 12	0♑23 38	6♐12 51	12♐45 53	21 32.6	12 47.6	15 22.6	23 57.8	12 30.7	15 20.4	17 5.1	17 59.1	24 16.9
23 W	6 7 9	1 24 46	19 15 36	25 42 0	21R 32.9	14 13.6	16 31.2	23 38.9	12 37.2	15 26.2	17 8.5	18 1.3	24 18.9
24 Th	6 11 5	2 25 55	2♑ 5 3	8♑24 46	21 32.8	15 40.2	17 39.7	23 19.4	12 43.6	15 32.1	17 12.0	18 3.5	24 20.9
25 F	6 15 2	3 27 4	14 41 13	20 54 29	21 31.9	17 7.5	18 48.0	22 59.2	12 49.8	15 38.1	17 15.5	18 5.7	24 22.9
26 Sa	6 18 58	4 28 14	27 4 41	3♒11 59	21 30.4	18 35.4	19 56.1	22 38.6	12 55.9	15 44.0	17 19.0	18 7.9	24 24.9
27 Su	6 22 55	5 29 23	9♒16 37	15 18 49	21 28.4	20 3.8	21 4.1	22 17.4	13 1.8	15 50.1	17 22.5	18 10.1	24 26.9
28 M	6 26 52	6 30 33	21 18 55	27 17 16	21 26.0	21 32.7	22 11.8	21 55.7	13 7.6	15 56.2	17 26.0	18 12.4	24 28.8
29 Tu	6 30 48	7 31 42	3♓14 15	9♓10 20	21 23.6	23 2.1	23 19.4	21 33.6	13 13.2	16 2.3	17 29.5	18 14.6	24 30.7
30 W	6 34 45	8 32 52	15 5 59	21 1 43	21 21.5	24 31.9	24 26.8	21 11.1	13 18.7	16 8.5	17 33.1	18 16.8	24 32.6
31 Th	6 38 41	9 34 1	26 58 5	2♈55 40	21 20.0	26 2.1	25 33.9	20 48.3	13 24.0	16 14.8	17 36.6	18 19.1	24 34.5

Astro Data

	Dy Hr Mn
☽0N	5 13:27
☿ R	11 9:49
☽0S	19 1:33
♃∠♇	21 5:50
♂ R	28 23:31
☿ D	1 7:31
☽0N	2 21:12
☽0S	16 6:42
☽0N	30 5:24

Planet Ingress

	Dy Hr Mn
♀ ♑	13 12:48
☿ ♏	21 19:44
☉ ♐	22 1:26
♀ ♒	8 17:49
☿ ♐	12 8:05
☉ ♑	21 14:43

Last Aspect / ☽ Ingress

Last Aspect Dy Hr Mn		☽ Ingress Dy Hr Mn
31 22:39	♂ ☍	♒ 1 12:43
3 9:50	♇ □	♓ 4 1:13
6 2:13	♂ △	♈ 6 13:19
8 13:52	♂ □	♉ 8 23:19
10 22:46	♂ ⚹	♊ 11 6:49
13 12:16	♀ ☍	♋ 13 12:19
15 10:15	♂ ☌	♌ 15 16:23
17 11:39	☉ □	♍ 17 19:28
19 18:07	☉ ⚹	♎ 19 22:03
21 20:13	♂ □	♏ 22 0:52
24 0:31	♂ △	♐ 24 5:01
25 4:36	♄ ⚹	♑ 26 11:38
28 16:38	♂ ☍	♒ 28 21:19

Last Aspect / ☽ Ingress

Last Aspect Dy Hr Mn		☽ Ingress Dy Hr Mn
30 20:15	♇ □	♓ 1 9:23
3 16:46	♂ △	♈ 3 21:49
6 3:04	♂ □	♉ 6 8:16
8 15:24	♀ △	♊ 8 15:37
9 23:41	☉ ☍	♋ 10 20:05
12 16:36	♂ ☌	♌ 12 22:47
14 14:56	♇ □	♍ 15 0:56
16 19:44	♂ ⚹	♎ 17 3:33
19 2:53	☉ ⚹	♏ 19 7:20
21 2:20	♇ ☌	♐ 21 12:42
22 18:26	♀ ⚹	♑ 23 20:04
25 18:48	♇ ⚹	♒ 26 5:43
28 6:22	♇ □	♓ 28 17:28
30 21:51	☿ □	♈ 31 6:07

☽ Phases & Eclipses

Dy Hr Mn	
2 9:11	☽ 10♒12
10 9:20	○ 18♉14
17 11:39	☽ 25♌23
24 9:11	● 2♐21
2 6:17	☽ 10♓20
9 23:41	○ 18♊10
9 23:44	T 1.271
16 19:13	☽ 25♍06
24 0:43	● 2♑28
24 0:30:44	P 0.842

Astro Data

1 NOVEMBER 1992
Julian Day # 33908
Delta T 58.5 sec
SVP 05♓21'19"
Obliquity 23°26'24"
⚷ Chiron 22♌26.9
☽ Mean ☊ 23♐39.3

1 DECEMBER 1992
Julian Day # 33938
Delta T 58.6 sec
SVP 05♓21'15"
Obliquity 23°26'23"
⚷ Chiron 23♌31.9
☽ Mean ☊ 22♐03.9

LONGITUDE — JANUARY 1993

Day	Sid.Time	☉	0 hr ☽	Noon ☽	True ☊	☿	♀	♂	♃	♄	♅	♆	♇
1 F	6 42 38	10♑35 11	8♈55 1	14♈56 47	21♐19.4	27♐32.7	26♒40.9	20♋25.1	13♎29.1	16♒21.1	17♑40.2	18♑21.4	24♏36.3
2 Sa	6 46 34	11 36 20	21 1 31	27 9 51	21D 19.8	29 3.7	27 47.6	20R 1.7	13 34.1	16 27.4	17 43.7	18 23.6	24 38.1
3 Su	6 50 31	12 37 29	3♉22 20	9♉39 30	21 20.9	0♑35.1	28 54.1	19 38.1	13 38.9	16 33.8	17 47.3	18 25.9	24 39.9
4 M	6 54 27	13 38 38	16 1 51	22 29 50	21 22.5	2 6.9	0♓ 0.3	19 14.3	13 43.5	16 40.2	17 50.8	18 28.1	24 41.7
5 Tu	6 58 24	14 39 46	29 3 45	5♊43 54	21 24.1	3 39.0	1 6.3	18 50.4	13 48.0	16 46.7	17 54.4	18 30.4	24 43.4
6 W	7 2 21	15 40 54	12♊30 22	19 23 12	21R 25.2	5 11.5	2 12.0	18 26.5	13 52.3	16 53.2	17 58.0	18 32.7	24 45.2
7 Th	7 6 17	16 42 2	26 22 13	3♋27 9	21 25.4	6 44.5	3 17.5	18 2.5	13 56.4	16 59.7	18 1.5	18 35.0	24 46.9
8 F	7 10 14	17 43 10	10♋37 30	17 52 41	21 24.2	8 17.8	4 22.7	17 38.6	14 0.4	17 6.3	18 5.1	18 37.3	24 48.5
9 Sa	7 14 10	18 44 18	25 11 55	2♌34 19	21 21.7	9 51.5	5 27.6	17 14.7	14 4.2	17 12.9	18 8.7	18 39.5	24 50.2
10 Su	7 18 7	19 45 25	9♌58 56	17 24 44	21 18.0	11 25.6	6 32.2	16 51.0	14 7.8	17 19.6	18 12.3	18 41.8	24 51.8
11 M	7 22 3	20 46 32	24 50 40	2♍15 42	21 13.6	13 0.2	7 36.5	16 27.4	14 11.2	17 26.3	18 15.8	18 44.1	24 53.4
12 Tu	7 26 0	21 47 39	9♍38 56	16 59 28	21 9.2	14 35.2	8 40.5	16 4.1	14 14.5	17 33.0	18 19.4	18 46.3	24 54.9
13 W	7 29 56	22 48 46	24 16 37	1♎29 48	21 5.5	16 10.6	9 44.2	15 40.9	14 17.6	17 39.8	18 23.0	18 48.6	24 56.4
14 Th	7 33 53	23 49 52	8♎38 34	15 42 37	21 3.0	17 46.6	10 47.6	15 18.1	14 20.5	17 46.6	18 26.5	18 50.9	24 57.9
15 F	7 37 50	24 50 59	22 41 50	29 36 9	21D 2.0	19 23.0	11 50.6	14 55.7	14 23.2	17 53.4	18 30.1	18 53.2	24 59.4
16 Sa	7 41 46	25 52 5	6♏25 39	13♏10 28	21 2.5	20 59.9	12 53.3	14 33.6	14 25.7	18 0.3	18 33.6	18 55.4	25 0.8
17 Su	7 45 43	26 53 12	19 50 48	26 26 53	21 3.8	22 37.3	13 55.6	14 11.9	14 28.1	18 7.2	18 37.2	18 57.7	25 2.3
18 M	7 49 39	27 54 18	2♐58 59	9♐27 23	21 5.5	24 15.2	14 57.6	13 50.7	14 30.3	18 14.1	18 40.7	18 59.9	25 3.6
19 Tu	7 53 36	28 55 24	15 52 21	22 14 6	21R 6.6	25 53.7	15 59.1	13 30.1	14 32.3	18 21.1	18 44.2	19 2.2	25 5.0
20 W	7 57 32	29 56 29	28 32 55	4♑48 59	21 6.4	27 32.8	17 0.3	13 9.9	14 34.1	18 28.0	18 47.8	19 4.4	25 6.3
21 Th	8 1 29	0♒57 34	11♑ 2 30	17 13 38	21 4.4	29 12.4	18 1.0	12 50.3	14 35.7	18 35.0	18 51.3	19 6.7	25 7.6
22 F	8 5 25	1 58 39	23 22 31	29 29 19	21 0.3	0♒52.6	19 1.4	12 31.4	14 37.1	18 42.1	18 54.8	19 8.9	25 8.9
23 Sa	8 9 22	2 59 42	5♒34 8	11♒37 7	20 54.1	2 33.4	20 1.3	12 13.0	14 38.4	18 49.1	18 58.3	19 11.2	25 10.1
24 Su	8 13 19	4 0 45	17 38 25	23 38 11	20 46.2	4 14.8	21 0.7	11 55.4	14 39.4	18 56.2	19 1.8	19 13.4	25 11.3
25 M	8 17 15	5 1 47	29 36 34	5♓33 49	20 37.2	5 56.8	21 59.6	11 38.4	14 40.2	19 3.2	19 5.3	19 15.6	25 12.4
26 Tu	8 21 12	6 2 48	11♓30 9	17 25 52	20 28.1	7 39.3	22 58.1	11 22.1	14 40.9	19 10.3	19 8.7	19 17.8	25 13.5
27 W	8 25 8	7 3 48	23 21 16	29 16 44	20 19.7	9 22.5	23 56.0	11 6.6	14 41.4	19 17.5	19 12.2	19 20.0	25 14.6
28 Th	8 29 5	8 4 47	5♈12 41	11♈ 9 33	20 12.8	11 6.3	24 53.4	10 51.8	14R 41.7	19 24.6	19 15.6	19 22.2	25 15.7
29 F	8 33 1	9 5 45	17 7 52	23 8 9	20 7.8	12 50.6	25 50.3	10 37.7	14 41.8	19 31.7	19 19.0	19 24.4	25 16.7
30 Sa	8 36 58	10 6 42	29 10 58	5♉16 56	20D 5.1	14 35.5	26 46.5	10 24.5	14 41.6	19 38.9	19 22.4	19 26.5	25 17.7
31 Su	8 40 54	11 7 37	11♉26 39	17 40 44	20 4.3	16 20.8	27 42.2	10 12.0	14 41.4	19 46.1	19 25.8	19 28.7	25 18.7

LONGITUDE — FEBRUARY 1993

Day	Sid.Time	☉	0 hr ☽	Noon ☽	True ☊	☿	♀	♂	♃	♄	♅	♆	♇
1 M	8 44 51	12♒ 8 31	23♉59 49	0♊24 28	20♐ 4.9	18♒ 6.7	28♓37.3	10♋ 0.3	14♎40.9	19♒53.3	19♑29.2	19♑30.8	25♏19.6
2 Tu	8 48 48	13 9 24	6♊55 13	13 32 34	20R 6.0	19 53.0	29 31.7	9R 49.4	14R 40.2	20 0.5	19 32.5	19 32.9	25 20.5
3 W	8 52 44	14 10 16	20 16 53	27 8 26	20 6.6	21 39.6	0♈25.4	9 39.4	14 39.3	20 7.7	19 35.9	19 35.1	25 21.3
4 Th	8 56 41	15 11 6	4♋ 7 19	11♋13 28	20 5.7	23 26.5	1 18.4	9 30.1	14 38.3	20 14.9	19 39.2	19 37.2	25 22.2
5 F	9 0 37	16 11 55	18 26 37	25 46 17	20 2.6	25 13.5	2 10.7	9 21.6	14 37.0	20 22.1	19 42.5	19 39.3	25 23.0
6 Sa	9 4 34	17 12 43	3♌11 45	10♌42 6	19 57.0	27 0.6	3 2.3	9 14.0	14 35.6	20 29.3	19 45.8	19 41.3	25 23.7
7 Su	9 8 30	18 13 29	18 16 11	25 52 46	19 49.2	28 47.5	3 53.0	9 7.1	14 34.0	20 36.5	19 49.0	19 43.4	25 24.4
8 M	9 12 27	19 14 14	3♍30 27	11♍ 7 50	19 40.0	0♓34.0	4 43.0	9 1.1	14 32.2	20 43.8	19 52.2	19 45.5	25 25.1
9 Tu	9 16 23	20 14 57	18 43 31	26 16 15	19 30.5	2 20.1	5 32.1	8 55.8	14 30.2	20 51.0	19 55.5	19 47.5	25 25.8
10 W	9 20 20	21 15 40	3♎44 51	11♎ 8 24	19 22.0	4 5.3	6 20.3	8 51.3	14 28.0	20 58.2	19 58.6	19 49.5	25 26.4
11 Th	9 24 17	22 16 21	18 26 9	25 37 35	19 15.4	5 49.3	7 7.7	8 47.6	14 25.7	21 5.5	20 1.8	19 51.5	25 27.0
12 F	9 28 13	23 17 2	2♏42 24	9♏40 30	19 11.2	7 31.9	7 54.1	8 44.7	14 23.1	21 12.7	20 4.9	19 53.5	25 27.5
13 Sa	9 32 10	24 17 41	16 31 57	23 16 58	19D 9.3	9 12.7	8 39.5	8 42.6	14 20.4	21 19.9	20 8.1	19 55.5	25 28.0
14 Su	9 36 6	25 18 19	29 55 51	6♐29 2	19 9.2	10 51.0	9 23.9	8 41.2	14 17.5	21 27.1	20 11.1	19 57.4	25 28.5
15 M	9 40 3	26 18 57	12♐56 58	19 20 8	19R 9.6	12 26.6	10 7.3	8D 40.6	14 14.4	21 34.4	20 14.2	19 59.3	25 28.9
16 Tu	9 43 59	27 19 33	25 39 2	1♑54 9	19 9.6	13 58.8	10 49.6	8 40.7	14 11.1	21 41.6	20 17.2	20 1.3	25 29.3
17 W	9 47 56	28 20 8	8♑ 5 58	14 14 54	19 7.8	15 26.9	11 30.7	8 41.6	14 7.6	21 48.8	20 20.3	20 3.2	25 29.7
18 Th	9 51 52	29 20 41	20 21 22	26 25 44	19 3.6	16 50.5	12 10.7	8 43.2	14 4.0	21 56.0	20 23.2	20 5.0	25 30.0
19 F	9 55 49	0♓21 13	2♒28 18	8♒29 22	18 56.4	18 8.8	12 49.5	8 45.5	14 0.2	22 3.2	20 26.2	20 6.9	25 30.3
20 Sa	9 59 46	1 21 44	14 29 10	20 27 54	18 46.3	19 21.1	13 27.0	8 48.6	13 56.2	22 10.4	20 29.1	20 8.7	25 30.5
21 Su	10 3 42	2 22 13	26 25 46	2♓22 55	18 33.8	20 26.8	14 3.2	8 52.3	13 52.1	22 17.5	20 32.0	20 10.5	25 30.8
22 M	10 7 39	3 22 40	8♓19 31	14 15 42	18 19.7	21 25.2	14 38.0	8 56.8	13 47.8	22 24.7	20 34.9	20 12.3	25 31.0
23 Tu	10 11 35	4 23 6	20 11 39	26 7 31	18 5.2	22 15.6	15 11.4	9 1.9	13 43.3	22 31.8	20 37.7	20 14.1	25 31.1
24 W	10 15 32	5 23 30	2♈ 3 30	7♈59 52	17 51.5	22 57.6	15 43.3	9 7.7	13 38.7	22 39.0	20 40.5	20 15.8	25 31.2
25 Th	10 19 28	6 23 52	13 56 50	19 54 45	17 39.7	23 30.7	16 13.6	9 14.1	13 33.9	22 46.1	20 43.2	20 17.6	25 31.3
26 F	10 23 25	7 24 13	25 53 57	1♉54 50	17 30.5	23 54.4	16 42.4	9 21.2	13 28.9	22 53.2	20 46.0	20 19.3	25R 31.3
27 Sa	10 27 21	8 24 31	7♉57 51	14 3 30	17 24.3	24R 8.5	17 9.5	9 29.0	13 23.8	23 0.2	20 48.7	20 20.9	25 31.3
28 Su	10 31 18	9 24 48	20 12 19	26 24 51	17 20.9	24 13.0	17 34.8	9 37.3	13 18.6	23 7.3	20 51.3	20 22.6	25 31.3

Astro Data

	Dy Hr Mn
☽0S	12 13:29
♄⊻♅	25 13:20
☽0N	26 13:19
♄⊻♆	27 12:18
♃ R	28 23:09
♀0N	30 15:24
♅☌♆	2 8:11
☽0S	8 23:11
♂ D	15 7:43
☽0N	22 20:17
☿0N	26 14:52
♇ R	26 14:28
☿ R	27 22:54

Planet Ingress

	Dy Hr Mn
☿ ♑	2 14:47
♀ ♓	3 23:54
☉ ♒	20 1:23
☿ ♒	21 11:25
♀ ♈	2 12:37
☿ ♓	7 16:19
☉ ♓	18 15:35

Last Aspect / ☽ Ingress

Last Aspect Dy Hr Mn		☽ Ingress Dy Hr Mn
2 14:31	♀ ⚹	♉ 2 17:30
4 16:04	♇ ☍	♊ 5 1:42
6 7:43	♄ △	♋ 7 6:10
8 23:24	♇ △	♌ 9 7:49
11 0:04	♇ □	♍ 11 8:20
13 1:06	♇ ⚹	♎ 13 9:30
15 4:01	☉ □	♏ 15 12:42
17 13:53	☉ ⚹	♐ 17 18:30
19 4:42	♄ ⚹	♑ 20 2:46
22 3:29	♇ ⚹	♒ 22 13:00
24 15:08	♇ □	♓ 25 0:47
27 3:50	♇ △	♈ 27 13:28
29 4:51	♄ ⚹	♉ 30 1:37

Last Aspect / ☽ Ingress

Last Aspect Dy Hr Mn		☽ Ingress Dy Hr Mn
1 9:20	♀ ⚹	♊ 1 11:15
3 2:48	☿ △	♋ 3 16:56
5 11:23	♇ △	♌ 5 18:51
7 11:16	♇ □	♍ 7 18:29
9 10:40	♇ ⚹	♎ 9 17:58
11 6:52	☉ △	♏ 11 19:23
13 15:56	♇ ☌	♐ 14 0:08
16 3:29	☉ ⚹	♑ 16 8:20
18 10:10	♇ ⚹	♒ 18 19:05
20 22:09	♇ □	♓ 21 7:12
23 10:46	♇ △	♈ 23 19:50
25 17:54	♄ ⚹	♉ 26 8:11
28 10:17	♇ ☍	♊ 28 18:52

☽ Phases & Eclipses

Dy Hr Mn	
1 3:38	☽ 10♈44
8 12:37	○ 18♋15
15 4:01	☽ 25♎01
22 18:27	● 2♒46
30 23:20	☽ 11♉06
6 23:55	○ 18♌13
13 14:57	☽ 24♏55
21 13:05	● 2♓55

Astro Data

1 JANUARY 1993
Julian Day # 33969
Delta T 58.6 sec
SVP 05♓21'10"
Obliquity 23°26'23"
⚷ Chiron 22♌58.9R
☽ Mean ☊ 20♐25.5

1 FEBRUARY 1993
Julian Day # 34000
Delta T 58.6 sec
SVP 05♓21'05"
Obliquity 23°26'23"
⚷ Chiron 21♌03.0R
☽ Mean ☊ 18♐47.0

MARCH 1993 — LONGITUDE

Day	Sid.Time	☉	0 hr ☽	Noon ☽	True ☊	☿	♀	♂	♃	♄	♅	♆	♇
1 M	10 35 15	10♓25 3	2♊41 41	9♊ 3 24	17♐19.7	24♓ 7.7	17♈58.4	9♋46.3	13♎13.2	23♒14.3	20♑53.9	20♑24.2	25♏31.2
2 Tu	10 39 11	11 25 15	15 30 37	22 3 52	17R 19.6	23R 53.0	18 20.1	9 55.9	13R 7.6	23 21.4	20 56.5	20 25.8	25R 31.1
3 W	10 43 8	12 25 26	28 43 39	5♋30 24	17 19.3	23 29.3	18 39.9	10 6.0	13 1.9	23 28.3	20 59.1	20 27.4	25 31.0
4 Th	10 47 4	13 25 35	12♋24 25	19 25 52	17 17.7	22 57.2	18 57.6	10 16.8	12 56.1	23 35.3	21 1.6	20 29.0	25 30.8
5 F	10 51 1	14 25 41	26 34 45	3♌50 49	17 13.8	22 17.6	19 13.4	10 28.0	12 50.2	23 42.2	21 4.1	20 30.5	25 30.6
6 Sa	10 54 57	15 25 45	11♌13 37	18 42 28	17 7.2	21 31.4	19 27.0	10 39.9	12 44.1	23 49.2	21 6.5	20 32.0	25 30.4
7 Su	10 58 54	16 25 47	26 16 24	3♍54 14	16 57.9	20 39.8	19 38.4	10 52.2	12 37.9	23 56.0	21 8.9	20 33.5	25 30.1
8 M	11 2 50	17 25 47	11♍34 39	19 16 10	16 46.9	19 44.1	19 47.6	11 5.1	12 31.6	24 2.9	21 11.3	20 35.0	25 29.8
9 Tu	11 6 47	18 25 46	26 57 15	4♎36 22	16 35.5	18 45.7	19 54.5	11 18.4	12 25.2	24 9.7	21 13.6	20 36.4	25 29.4
10 W	11 10 44	19 25 42	12♎12 8	19 43 17	16 24.9	17 46.0	19 59.0	11 32.3	12 18.6	24 16.5	21 15.9	20 37.8	25 29.1
11 Th	11 14 40	20 25 36	27 8 45	4♏27 44	16 16.3	16 46.4	20R 1.2	11 46.6	12 12.0	24 23.3	21 18.1	20 39.2	25 28.7
12 F	11 18 37	21 25 29	11♏39 40	18 44 11	16 10.4	15 48.1	20 0.9	12 1.5	12 5.3	24 30.0	21 20.3	20 40.5	25 28.2
13 Sa	11 22 33	22 25 21	25 41 13	2♐30 50	16 7.2	14 52.3	19 58.2	12 16.7	11 58.4	24 36.7	21 22.5	20 41.8	25 27.7
14 Su	11 26 30	23 25 10	9♐13 18	15 48 57	16D 6.1	14 0.0	19 53.0	12 32.5	11 51.5	24 43.4	21 24.6	20 43.1	25 27.2
15 M	11 30 26	24 24 58	22 18 18	28 41 53	16R 6.0	13 12.2	19 45.4	12 48.7	11 44.4	24 50.0	21 26.7	20 44.4	25 26.7
16 Tu	11 34 23	25 24 44	5♑ 0 16	11♑14 3	16 5.8	12 29.5	19 35.2	13 5.3	11 37.3	24 56.6	21 28.7	20 45.6	25 26.1
17 W	11 38 19	26 24 29	17 23 50	23 30 12	16 4.1	11 52.4	19 22.6	13 22.3	11 30.1	25 3.2	21 30.7	20 46.8	25 25.5
18 Th	11 42 16	27 24 12	29 33 42	5♒34 52	16 0.2	11 21.2	19 7.5	13 39.8	11 22.9	25 9.7	21 32.7	20 48.0	25 24.9
19 F	11 46 13	28 23 53	11♒34 11	17 32 5	15 53.5	10 56.2	18 50.0	13 57.6	11 15.5	25 16.2	21 34.6	20 49.1	25 24.2
20 Sa	11 50 9	29 23 32	23 28 56	29 25 6	15 43.9	10 37.4	18 30.1	14 15.9	11 8.1	25 22.6	21 36.4	20 50.2	25 23.5
21 Su	11 54 6	0♈23 9	5♓20 53	11♓16 33	15 31.9	10 24.9	18 7.9	14 34.5	11 0.7	25 29.0	21 38.3	20 51.3	25 22.8
22 M	11 58 2	1 22 45	17 12 18	23 8 20	15 18.4	10D 18.5	17 43.5	14 53.6	10 53.1	25 35.3	21 40.0	20 52.4	25 22.0
23 Tu	12 1 59	2 22 18	29 4 51	5♈ 2 0	15 4.4	10 18.0	17 17.0	15 13.0	10 45.6	25 41.6	21 41.8	20 53.4	25 21.2
24 W	12 5 55	3 21 49	10♈59 56	16 58 48	14 51.2	10 23.4	16 48.5	15 32.8	10 38.0	25 47.9	21 43.4	20 54.4	25 20.4
25 Th	12 9 52	4 21 19	22 58 48	29 0 6	14 39.7	10 34.3	16 18.2	15 52.9	10 30.3	25 54.1	21 45.1	20 55.4	25 19.5
26 F	12 13 48	5 20 46	5♉ 2 56	11♉ 7 33	14 30.7	10 50.4	15 46.2	16 13.4	10 22.7	26 0.3	21 46.7	20 56.3	25 18.6
27 Sa	12 17 45	6 20 11	17 14 14	23 23 20	14 24.7	11 11.7	15 12.7	16 34.2	10 15.0	26 6.4	21 48.2	20 57.2	25 17.7
28 Su	12 21 41	7 19 34	29 35 11	5♊50 12	14 21.4	11 37.7	14 37.8	16 55.4	10 7.2	26 12.4	21 49.7	20 58.0	25 16.8
29 M	12 25 38	8 18 55	12♊ 8 49	18 31 29	14D 20.4	12 8.2	14 2.0	17 16.8	9 59.5	26 18.5	21 51.1	20 58.9	25 15.8
30 Tu	12 29 35	9 18 13	24 58 41	1♋30 53	14 20.6	12 43.0	13 25.2	17 38.7	9 51.8	26 24.4	21 52.5	20 59.7	25 14.8
31 W	12 33 31	10 17 29	8♋ 8 31	14 51 59	14R 21.1	13 21.8	12 47.8	18 0.8	9 44.0	26 30.3	21 53.9	21 0.5	25 13.8

APRIL 1993 — LONGITUDE

Day	Sid.Time	☉	0 hr ☽	Noon ☽	True ☊	☿	♀	♂	♃	♄	♅	♆	♇
1 Th	12 37 28	11♈16 43	21♋41 37	28♋37 39	14♐20.6	14♓ 4.4	12♈10.1	18♋23.2	9♎36.3	26♒36.2	21♑55.2	21♑ 1.2	25♏12.7
2 F	12 41 24	12 15 54	5♌40 11	12♌49 11	14R 18.4	14 50.7	11R 32.2	18 45.9	9R 28.6	26 42.0	21 56.4	21 1.9	25R 11.7
3 Sa	12 45 21	13 15 3	20 4 24	27 25 24	14 13.8	15 40.3	10 54.4	19 8.9	9 20.9	26 47.7	21 57.6	21 2.6	25 10.6
4 Su	12 49 17	14 14 10	4♍51 33	12♍22 0	14 7.1	16 33.1	10 17.1	19 32.2	9 13.2	26 53.4	21 58.8	21 3.2	25 9.4
5 M	12 53 14	15 13 14	19 55 41	27 31 26	13 58.7	17 29.1	9 40.4	19 55.7	9 5.5	26 59.0	21 59.9	21 3.8	25 8.3
6 Tu	12 57 10	16 12 17	5♎ 7 54	12♎43 46	13 49.8	18 27.9	9 4.5	20 19.5	8 57.8	27 4.6	22 0.9	21 4.4	25 7.1
7 W	13 1 7	17 11 17	20 17 38	27 48 16	13 41.5	19 29.4	8 29.8	20 43.6	8 50.2	27 10.1	22 1.9	21 4.9	25 5.9
8 Th	13 5 4	18 10 15	5♏14 30	12♏35 22	13 34.7	20 33.6	7 56.4	21 7.9	8 42.7	27 15.5	22 2.9	21 5.5	25 4.7
9 F	13 9 0	19 9 11	19 50 5	26 58 6	13 30.1	21 40.3	7 24.5	21 32.5	8 35.1	27 20.9	22 3.8	21 5.9	25 3.4
10 Sa	13 12 57	20 8 5	3♐59 4	10♐52 50	13D 27.9	22 49.5	6 54.4	21 57.3	8 27.7	27 26.2	22 4.7	21 6.4	25 2.2
11 Su	13 16 53	21 6 58	17 39 26	24 19 4	13 27.6	24 0.9	6 26.1	22 22.3	8 20.3	27 31.5	22 5.5	21 6.8	25 0.9
12 M	13 20 50	22 5 49	0♑52 3	7♑18 49	13 28.4	25 14.5	5 59.8	22 47.6	8 12.9	27 36.7	22 6.2	21 7.2	24 59.6
13 Tu	13 24 46	23 4 38	13 39 52	19 55 45	13R 29.5	26 30.3	5 35.7	23 13.1	8 5.6	27 41.8	22 6.9	21 7.5	24 58.2
14 W	13 28 43	24 3 26	26 7 3	2♒14 23	13 29.9	27 48.2	5 13.8	23 38.8	7 58.4	27 46.9	22 7.6	21 7.8	24 56.9
15 Th	13 32 39	25 2 12	8♒18 22	14 19 35	13 28.8	29 8.1	4 54.2	24 4.8	7 51.2	27 51.9	22 8.2	21 8.1	24 55.5
16 F	13 36 36	26 0 56	20 18 36	26 16 0	13 25.8	0♈29.9	4 37.0	24 30.9	7 44.1	27 56.8	22 8.8	21 8.4	24 54.1
17 Sa	13 40 33	26 59 38	2♓12 16	8♓ 7 53	13 20.8	1 53.6	4 22.2	24 57.3	7 37.2	28 1.7	22 9.3	21 8.6	24 52.7
18 Su	13 44 29	27 58 18	14 3 17	19 58 53	13 14.0	3 19.2	4 9.8	25 23.9	7 30.3	28 6.5	22 9.7	21 8.8	24 51.3
19 M	13 48 26	28 56 57	25 55 0	1♈51 59	13 6.1	4 46.7	3 59.9	25 50.7	7 23.4	28 11.2	22 10.1	21 8.9	24 49.9
20 Tu	13 52 22	29 55 34	7♈50 4	13 49 30	12 57.7	6 15.9	3 52.5	26 17.7	7 16.7	28 15.8	22 10.5	21 9.0	24 48.4
21 W	13 56 19	0♉54 9	19 50 30	25 53 14	12 49.7	7 47.0	3 47.5	26 44.9	7 10.1	28 20.4	22 10.8	21 9.1	24 46.9
22 Th	14 0 15	1 52 42	1♉57 51	8♉ 4 31	12 42.9	9 19.8	3D 44.9	27 12.3	7 3.6	28 24.9	22 11.0	21R 9.1	24 45.4
23 F	14 4 12	2 51 14	14 13 23	20 24 35	12 37.7	10 54.4	3 44.7	27 39.8	6 57.2	28 29.3	22 11.2	21 9.2	24 43.9
24 Sa	14 8 8	3 49 43	26 38 15	2♊54 34	12 34.6	12 30.7	3 46.8	28 7.6	6 51.0	28 33.7	22 11.4	21 9.1	24 42.4
25 Su	14 12 5	4 48 11	9♊13 43	15 35 53	12D 33.3	14 8.7	3 51.2	28 35.5	6 44.8	28 38.0	22 11.5	21 9.1	24 40.9
26 M	14 16 1	5 46 36	22 1 17	28 30 9	12 33.6	15 48.5	3 57.9	29 3.6	6 38.8	28 42.2	22R 11.5	21 9.0	24 39.3
27 Tu	14 19 58	6 45 0	5♋ 2 43	11♋39 14	12 34.9	17 30.1	4 6.7	29 31.9	6 32.9	28 46.3	22 11.5	21 8.9	24 37.8
28 W	14 23 55	7 43 21	18 19 56	25 5 1	12 36.4	19 13.4	4 17.7	0♌ 0.4	6 27.1	28 50.3	22 11.4	21 8.7	24 36.2
29 Th	14 27 51	8 41 41	1♌54 40	8♌49 0	12R 37.5	20 58.4	4 30.8	0 29.0	6 21.5	28 54.2	22 11.3	21 8.6	24 34.6
30 F	14 31 48	9 39 58	15 48 4	22 51 49	12 37.5	22 45.2	4 45.9	0 57.8	6 16.0	28 58.1	22 11.2	21 8.4	24 33.0

Astro Data	Planet Ingress	Last Aspect	☽ Ingress	Last Aspect	☽ Ingress	☽ Phases & Eclipses	Astro Data
Dy Hr Mn	Dy Hr Mn	Dy Hr Mn	Dy Hr Mn	Dy Hr Mn	Dy Hr Mn	Dy Hr Mn	1 MARCH 1993
☿0S 5 23:28	☉ ♈ 20 14:41	2 14:53 ☿ □	♋ 3 2:16	1 6:06 ♇ △	♌ 1 14:21	1 15:47 ☽ 11♊05	Julian Day # 34028
☽0S 8 10:35		4 22:13 ♇ △	♌ 5 5:40	3 11:03 ♄ ☍	♍ 3 16:10	8 9:46 ○ 17♍50	Delta T 58.7 sec
♀ R 11 9:28	☿ ♈ 15 15:18	6 22:47 ♇ □	♍ 7 5:52	5 8:13 ♇ ✶	♎ 5 15:54	15 4:17 ☽ 24♐36	SVP 05♓21'01"
♄□♇ 20 3:00	☉ ♉ 20 1:49	8 21:43 ♇ ✶	♎ 9 4:46	7 11:03 ♄ △	♏ 7 15:32	23 7:14 ● 2♈40	Obliquity 23°26'23"
☽0N 22 2:20	♂ ♌ 27 23:40	10 19:29 ♄ △	♏ 11 4:40	9 12:44 ♄ □	♐ 9 17:10	31 4:10 ☽ 10♋28	⚷ Chiron 18♌57.2R
☿ D 22 13:44		12 23:37 ♇ ☌	♐ 13 7:33	11 17:58 ♄ ✶	♑ 11 22:24		☽ Mean ☊ 17♐18.0
♃⚼♄ 23 6:51		15 4:46 ♄ ✶	♑ 15 14:28	14 3:41 ☿ ✶	♒ 14 7:36	6 18:43 ○ 16♎58	
♃∠♇ 26 14:18		17 19:20 ☉ ✶	♒ 18 0:52	16 15:30 ♄ ☌	♓ 16 19:33	13 19:39 ☽ 23♑53	1 APRIL 1993
☽0S 4 21:18		20 3:52 ♄ ☌	♓ 20 13:11	18 23:51 ♂ △	♈ 19 8:14	21 23:49 ● 1♉52	Julian Day # 34059
☽0N 18 8:11		22 16:29 ♇ △	♈ 23 1:51	21 16:57 ♄ ✶	♉ 21 20:08	29 12:40 ☽ 9♌12	Delta T 58.7 sec
☿0N 19 22:06		25 5:53 ♄ ✶	♉ 25 13:59	24 3:43 ♄ □	♊ 24 6:27		SVP 05♓20'58"
♀ D 22 14:14		27 17:25 ♄ □	♊ 28 0:48	26 12:26 ♄ △	♋ 26 14:45		Obliquity 23°26'23"
♆ R 22 22:32		30 2:39 ♄ △	♋ 30 9:14	28 11:08 ♇ △	♌ 28 20:39		⚷ Chiron 17♌23.3R
♅ R 26 10:03				30 22:22 ♄ ☍	♍ 30 24:00		☽ Mean ☊ 15♐39.5

LONGITUDE — MAY 1993

Day	Sid.Time	☉	0 hr ☽	Noon ☽	True ☊	☿	♀	♂	♃	♄	♅	♆	♇
1 Sa	14 35 44	10♉38 13	0♍ 0 6	7♍12 37	12♐36.2	24♈33.8	5♈ 2.9	1♌26.7	6♎10.6	29♒ 1.9	22♑11.0	21♑ 8.1	24♏31.4
2 Su	14 39 41	11 36 26	14 28 58	21 48 34	12R33.5	26 24.1	5 21.8	1 55.8	6R 5.4	29 5.6	22R10.7	21R 7.8	24R29.8
3 M	14 43 37	12 34 37	29 10 46	6♎34 43	12 29.8	28 16.2	5 42.6	2 25.1	6 0.3	29 9.2	22 10.4	21 7.5	24 28.2
4 Tu	14 47 34	13 32 46	13♎59 34	21 24 18	12 25.7	0♉10.1	6 5.2	2 54.5	5 55.4	29 12.8	22 10.0	21 7.2	24 26.6
5 W	14 51 30	14 30 53	28 47 57	6♏ 9 32	12 21.8	2 5.7	6 29.4	3 24.0	5 50.6	29 16.2	22 9.6	21 6.8	24 24.9
6 Th	14 55 27	15 28 58	13♏28 6	20 42 48	12 18.8	4 3.1	6 55.4	3 53.7	5 46.0	29 19.6	22 9.2	21 6.4	24 23.3
7 F	14 59 24	16 27 2	27 52 53	4♐57 46	12 16.9	6 2.2	7 22.9	4 23.5	5 41.6	29 22.9	22 8.7	21 6.0	24 21.6
8 Sa	15 3 20	17 25 4	11♐56 57	18 50 9	12D16.2	8 3.0	7 52.0	4 53.4	5 37.3	29 26.1	22 8.1	21 5.5	24 20.0
9 Su	15 7 17	18 23 5	25 37 11	2♑18 2	12 16.7	10 5.5	8 22.5	5 23.5	5 33.1	29 29.2	22 7.6	21 5.0	24 18.3
10 M	15 11 13	19 21 5	8♑52 49	15 21 44	12 18.0	12 9.5	8 54.5	5 53.7	5 29.2	29 32.3	22 6.9	21 4.5	24 16.7
11 Tu	15 15 10	20 19 2	21 45 7	28 3 22	12 19.5	14 15.0	9 27.9	6 24.1	5 25.3	29 35.2	22 6.2	21 3.9	24 15.0
12 W	15 19 6	21 16 59	4♒16 55	10♒26 18	12 20.9	16 21.8	10 2.6	6 54.6	5 21.7	29 38.1	22 5.5	21 3.3	24 13.3
13 Th	15 23 3	22 14 54	16 32 4	22 34 46	12R21.7	18 29.9	10 38.6	7 25.1	5 18.2	29 40.8	22 4.7	21 2.7	24 11.7
14 F	15 27 0	23 12 48	28 35 0	4♓33 19	12 21.7	20 39.1	11 15.8	7 55.9	5 14.9	29 43.5	22 3.9	21 2.1	24 10.0
15 Sa	15 30 56	24 10 41	10♓30 19	16 26 33	12 20.9	22 49.1	11 54.1	8 26.7	5 11.7	29 46.1	22 3.0	21 1.4	24 8.3
16 Su	15 34 53	25 8 32	22 22 34	28 18 52	12 19.3	24 59.9	12 33.6	8 57.7	5 8.8	29 48.6	22 2.1	21 0.7	24 6.7
17 M	15 38 49	26 6 23	4♈15 56	10♈14 13	12 17.2	27 11.0	13 14.2	9 28.8	5 6.0	29 50.9	22 1.1	20 60.0	24 5.0
18 Tu	15 42 46	27 4 12	16 14 8	22 16 2	12 14.8	29 22.3	13 55.8	9 60.0	5 3.3	29 53.3	22 0.1	20 59.2	24 3.3
19 W	15 46 42	28 2 0	28 20 16	4♉27 5	12 12.6	1♊33.6	14 38.3	10 31.3	5 0.9	29 55.5	21 59.0	20 58.4	24 1.6
20 Th	15 50 39	28 59 46	10♉36 45	16 49 26	12 10.8	3 44.4	15 21.9	11 2.8	4 58.6	29 57.6	21 57.9	20 57.6	23 60.0
21 F	15 54 35	29 57 31	23 5 19	29 24 29	12 9.6	5 54.6	16 6.3	11 34.3	4 56.5	29 59.6	21 56.8	20 56.8	23 58.3
22 Sa	15 58 32	0♊55 16	5♊47 2	12♊13 1	12D 9.0	8 3.9	16 51.7	12 6.0	4 54.6	0♓ 1.5	21 55.6	20 55.9	23 56.7
23 Su	16 2 28	1 52 58	18 42 26	25 15 17	12 9.0	10 12.0	17 37.8	12 37.8	4 52.9	0 3.4	21 54.3	20 55.0	23 55.0
24 M	16 6 25	2 50 40	1♋51 33	8♋31 12	12 9.4	12 18.6	18 24.8	13 9.7	4 51.3	0 5.1	21 53.1	20 54.1	23 53.4
25 Tu	16 10 22	3 48 20	15 14 10	22 0 22	12 10.1	14 23.6	19 12.6	13 41.6	4 50.0	0 6.7	21 51.8	20 53.1	23 51.7
26 W	16 14 18	4 45 58	28 49 45	5♌42 11	12 10.9	16 26.6	20 1.1	14 13.7	4 48.8	0 8.3	21 50.4	20 52.1	23 50.1
27 Th	16 18 15	5 43 35	12♌37 35	19 35 49	12 11.5	18 27.6	20 50.3	14 45.9	4 47.8	0 9.7	21 49.0	20 51.1	23 48.5
28 F	16 22 11	6 41 11	26 36 42	3♍40 2	12R11.8	20 26.4	21 40.2	15 18.3	4 46.9	0 11.1	21 47.6	20 50.1	23 46.8
29 Sa	16 26 8	7 38 45	10♍45 38	17 53 10	12 11.9	22 22.8	22 30.8	15 50.6	4 46.3	0 12.3	21 46.1	20 49.1	23 45.2
30 Su	16 30 4	8 36 18	25 2 22	2♎12 49	12 11.7	24 16.8	23 22.0	16 23.1	4 45.8	0 13.5	21 44.6	20 48.0	23 43.6
31 M	16 34 1	9 33 49	9♎24 8	16 35 51	12 11.5	26 8.2	24 13.8	16 55.7	4 45.6	0 14.5	21 43.0	20 46.9	23 42.0

LONGITUDE — JUNE 1993

Day	Sid.Time	☉	0 hr ☽	Noon ☽	True ☊	☿	♀	♂	♃	♄	♅	♆	♇
1 Tu	16 37 57	10♊31 19	23♎47 26	0♏58 22	12♐11.3	27♊56.9	25♈ 6.3	17♌28.4	4♎45.5	0♓15.5	21♑41.4	20♑45.8	23♏40.4
2 W	16 41 54	11 28 47	8♏ 8 4	15 16 0	12D11.2	29 43.0	25 59.3	18 1.2	4D45.5	0 16.3	21R39.8	20R44.6	23R38.9
3 Th	16 45 51	12 26 15	22 21 36	29 24 19	12 11.2	1♋26.4	26 52.8	18 34.0	4 45.8	0 17.1	21 38.1	20 43.5	23 37.3
4 F	16 49 47	13 23 41	6♐23 39	13♐19 10	12R11.2	3 7.0	27 47.0	19 7.0	4 46.2	0 17.7	21 36.5	20 42.3	23 35.7
5 Sa	16 53 44	14 21 7	20 10 30	26 57 19	12 11.2	4 44.8	28 41.6	19 40.0	4 46.9	0 18.3	21 34.7	20 41.1	23 34.2
6 Su	16 57 40	15 18 32	3♑39 24	10♑16 39	12 11.0	6 19.9	29 36.8	20 13.1	4 47.7	0 18.8	21 33.0	20 39.9	23 32.7
7 M	17 1 37	16 15 55	16 48 59	23 16 28	12 10.7	7 52.0	0♉32.4	20 46.4	4 48.6	0 19.2	21 31.2	20 38.6	23 31.2
8 Tu	17 5 33	17 13 18	29 39 14	5♒57 28	12 10.2	9 21.3	1 28.5	21 19.6	4 49.8	0 19.4	21 29.3	20 37.3	23 29.7
9 W	17 9 30	18 10 41	12♒11 28	18 21 36	12 9.5	10 47.7	2 25.1	21 53.0	4 51.1	0 19.6	21 27.5	20 36.1	23 28.2
10 Th	17 13 27	19 8 3	24 28 14	0♓31 51	12 8.8	12 11.2	3 22.1	22 26.5	4 52.6	0R19.7	21 25.6	20 34.8	23 26.7
11 F	17 17 23	20 5 24	6♓32 56	12 32 1	12 8.2	13 31.7	4 19.5	23 0.0	4 54.3	0 19.6	21 23.7	20 33.4	23 25.3
12 Sa	17 21 20	21 2 44	18 29 40	24 26 25	12D 7.9	14 49.2	5 17.4	23 33.7	4 56.2	0 19.5	21 21.7	20 32.1	23 23.9
13 Su	17 25 16	22 0 4	0♈22 53	6♈19 38	12 8.0	16 3.7	6 15.6	24 7.4	4 58.2	0 19.3	21 19.7	20 30.7	23 22.4
14 M	17 29 13	22 57 24	12 17 14	18 16 14	12 8.6	17 15.1	7 14.2	24 41.2	5 0.4	0 19.0	21 17.7	20 29.3	23 21.0
15 Tu	17 33 9	23 54 44	24 17 12	0♉20 37	12 9.5	18 23.4	8 13.2	25 15.0	5 2.8	0 18.5	21 15.7	20 27.9	23 19.7
16 W	17 37 6	24 52 3	6♉26 59	12 36 43	12 10.6	19 28.4	9 12.6	25 49.0	5 5.3	0 18.0	21 13.6	20 26.5	23 18.3
17 Th	17 41 2	25 49 21	18 50 12	25 7 44	12 11.7	20 30.1	10 12.3	26 23.0	5 8.0	0 17.4	21 11.6	20 25.1	23 16.9
18 F	17 44 59	26 46 39	1♊29 37	7♊55 59	12R12.5	21 28.5	11 12.3	26 57.1	5 10.9	0 16.7	21 9.4	20 23.7	23 15.6
19 Sa	17 48 56	27 43 57	14 26 59	21 2 36	12 12.8	22 23.4	12 12.6	27 31.3	5 14.0	0 15.9	21 7.3	20 22.2	23 14.3
20 Su	17 52 52	28 41 15	27 42 48	4♋27 27	12 12.2	23 14.7	13 13.3	28 5.6	5 17.2	0 15.0	21 5.2	20 20.8	23 13.0
21 M	17 56 49	29 38 32	11♋16 18	18 9 4	12 10.9	24 2.4	14 14.2	28 40.0	5 20.6	0 14.0	21 3.0	20 19.3	23 11.8
22 Tu	18 0 45	0♋35 48	25 5 24	2♌ 4 53	12 8.8	24 46.3	15 15.5	29 14.4	5 24.2	0 12.9	21 0.8	20 17.8	23 10.5
23 W	18 4 42	1 33 4	9♌ 7 3	16 11 26	12 6.3	25 26.4	16 17.0	29 48.9	5 27.9	0 11.7	20 58.6	20 16.3	23 9.3
24 Th	18 8 38	2 30 20	23 17 32	0♍24 51	12 3.7	26 2.5	17 18.8	0♍23.5	5 31.8	0 10.4	20 56.3	20 14.8	23 8.1
25 F	18 12 35	3 27 34	7♍32 56	14 41 19	12 1.6	26 34.4	18 20.8	0 58.1	5 35.8	0 9.0	20 54.1	20 13.2	23 7.0
26 Sa	18 16 31	4 24 48	21 49 36	28 57 24	12D 0.1	27 2.2	19 23.2	1 32.9	5 40.0	0 7.5	20 51.8	20 11.7	23 5.8
27 Su	18 20 28	5 22 2	6♎ 4 23	13♎10 15	11 59.7	27 25.6	20 25.7	2 7.6	5 44.4	0 5.9	20 49.5	20 10.1	23 4.7
28 M	18 24 25	6 19 15	20 14 44	27 17 37	12 0.2	27 44.7	21 28.5	2 42.5	5 48.9	0 4.3	20 47.2	20 8.6	23 3.6
29 Tu	18 28 21	7 16 27	4♏18 41	11♏17 44	12 1.4	27 59.2	22 31.5	3 17.4	5 53.6	0 2.5	20 44.9	20 7.0	23 2.5
30 W	18 32 18	8 13 39	18 14 36	25 9 6	12 2.9	28 9.1	23 34.8	3 52.4	5 58.4	0 0.7	20 42.6	20 5.4	23 1.5

Astro Data	Planet Ingress	Last Aspect	☽ Ingress	Last Aspect	☽ Ingress	☽ Phases & Eclipses	Astro Data
Dy Hr Mn	Dy Hr Mn	Dy Hr Mn	Dy Hr Mn	Dy Hr Mn	Dy Hr Mn	Dy Hr Mn	1 MAY 1993
☽0 S 2 5:39	☿ ♉ 3 21:54	2 16:21 ♇ ⚹	♎ 3 1:20	1 7:56 ☿ △	♏ 1 10:22	6 3:34 ○ 15♏38	Julian Day # 34089
☽0 N 15 14:46	☿ ♊ 18 6:53	5 0:46 ♄ △	♏ 5 1:57	3 2:08 ♇ ☌	♐ 3 13:01	13 12:20 ☽ 22♒45	Delta T 58.8 sec
☽0 S 29 11:46	☉ ♊ 21 1:02	7 2:32 ♄ □	♐ 7 3:34	5 16:12 ♀ △	♑ 5 17:26	21 14:07 ● 0♊31	SVP 05♓20'55"
	♄ ♓ 21 4:57	9 6:57 ♄ ⚹	♑ 9 7:51	7 12:26 ♇ ⚹	♒ 8 0:39	21 14:19:12 ☌ P 0.735	Obliquity 23°26'22"
♃ D 1 1:09		11 4:44 ♇ ⚹	♒ 11 15:44	9 21:59 ♇ □	♓ 10 10:57	28 18:21 ☽ 7♍25	⚷ Chiron 17♌20.5
♄ R 10 5:28	☿ ♋ 2 3:54	14 2:18 ♄ ☌	♓ 14 2:51	12 9:52 ♇ △	♈ 12 23:14		☽ Mean ☊ 14♐04.2
☽0 N 11 22:31	♀ ♉ 6 10:03	16 6:30 ☿ ⚹	♈ 16 15:24	15 2:01 ♂ △	♉ 15 11:19	4 13:02 ○ 13♐55	
☽0 S 25 17:19	☉ ♋ 21 9:00	19 3:08 ♄ ⚹	♉ 19 3:16	17 15:03 ♂ □	♊ 17 21:12	4 13:00 ☍T 1.562	1 JUNE 1993
	♂ ♍ 23 7:42	21 1:41 ♇ ☍	♊ 21 13:07	20 1:52 ☉ ☌	♋ 20 4:05	12 5:36 ☽ 21♓16	Julian Day # 34120
	♄ ♒ 30 8:30	22 21:53 ♀ ⚹	♋ 23 20:38	21 23:25 ☿ ☌	♌ 22 8:26	20 1:52 ● 28♊46	Delta T 58.8 sec
		25 15:15 ♇ △	♌ 26 2:03	23 23:44 ♇ □	♍ 24 11:18	26 22:43 ☽ 5♎19	SVP 05♓20'51"
		27 19:10 ♇ □	♍ 28 5:46	26 9:02 ☿ ⚹	♎ 26 13:45		Obliquity 23°26'21"
		29 22:32 ☿ □	♎ 30 8:18	28 13:01 ☿ □	♏ 28 16:37		⚷ Chiron 18♌55.3
				30 20:26 ♄ □	♐ 30 20:28		☽ Mean ☊ 12♐25.7

JULY 1993 LONGITUDE

Day	Sid.Time	☉	0 hr ☽	Noon ☽	True ☊	☿	♀	♂	♃	♄	♅	♆	♇
1 Th	18 36 14	9♋10 51	2♐ 1 3	8♐50 17	12♐ 4.0	28♋14.5	24♉38.3	4♍27.5	6♎ 3.4	29♒58.7	20♑40.2	20♑ 3.9	23♏ 0.5
2 F	18 40 11	10 8 2	15 36 38	22 19 56	12R 4.2	28R 15.1	25 42.0	5 2.6	6 8.5	29R 56.7	20R 37.9	20R 2.3	22R 59.5
3 Sa	18 44 7	11 5 13	29 0 0	5♑36 42	12 3.2	28 11.2	26 46.0	5 37.8	6 13.8	29 54.6	20 35.5	20 0.7	22 58.5
4 Su	18 48 4	12 2 24	12♑ 9 54	18 39 31	12 0.8	28 2.6	27 50.1	6 13.1	6 19.3	29 52.4	20 33.1	19 59.1	22 57.6
5 M	18 52 0	12 59 35	25 5 29	1♒27 47	11 56.9	27 49.6	28 54.5	6 48.4	6 24.8	29 50.1	20 30.7	19 57.5	22 56.6
6 Tu	18 55 57	13 56 46	7♒46 25	14 1 31	11 52.0	27 32.2	29 59.0	7 23.8	6 30.6	29 47.8	20 28.4	19 55.9	22 55.8
7 W	18 59 54	14 53 58	20 13 11	26 21 38	11 46.5	27 10.7	1♊ 3.8	7 59.3	6 36.4	29 45.3	20 26.0	19 54.3	22 54.9
8 Th	19 3 50	15 51 9	2♓27 8	8♓29 58	11 41.1	26 45.4	2 8.8	8 34.8	6 42.4	29 42.8	20 23.6	19 52.7	22 54.1
9 F	19 7 47	16 48 21	14 30 32	20 29 14	11 36.3	26 16.5	3 13.9	9 10.4	6 48.6	29 40.2	20 21.2	19 51.0	22 53.3
10 Sa	19 11 43	17 45 33	26 26 33	2♈22 59	11 32.7	25 44.5	4 19.2	9 46.1	6 54.9	29 37.5	20 18.7	19 49.4	22 52.5
11 Su	19 15 40	18 42 45	8♈19 5	14 15 26	11D 30.5	25 9.8	5 24.7	10 21.8	7 1.3	29 34.7	20 16.3	19 47.8	22 51.7
12 M	19 19 36	19 39 58	20 12 36	26 11 13	11 29.9	24 33.1	6 30.4	10 57.6	7 7.9	29 31.8	20 13.9	19 46.2	22 51.0
13 Tu	19 23 33	20 37 11	2♉11 54	8♉15 16	11 30.5	23 54.8	7 36.3	11 33.4	7 14.5	29 28.9	20 11.5	19 44.5	22 50.3
14 W	19 27 29	21 34 25	14 21 54	20 32 24	11 31.9	23 15.6	8 42.3	12 9.4	7 21.4	29 25.9	20 9.1	19 42.9	22 49.7
15 Th	19 31 26	22 31 40	26 47 17	3♊ 7 3	11 33.4	22 36.2	9 48.5	12 45.3	7 28.3	29 22.8	20 6.7	19 41.3	22 49.0
16 F	19 35 23	23 28 55	9♊32 7	16 2 48	11R 34.2	21 57.3	10 54.9	13 21.4	7 35.4	29 19.7	20 4.3	19 39.7	22 48.4
17 Sa	19 39 19	24 26 11	22 39 21	29 21 52	11 33.6	21 19.4	12 1.4	13 57.5	7 42.7	29 16.4	20 1.8	19 38.1	22 47.9
18 Su	19 43 16	25 23 27	6♋10 20	13♋ 4 38	11 31.3	20 43.4	13 8.0	14 33.7	7 50.0	29 13.1	19 59.4	19 36.4	22 47.3
19 M	19 47 12	26 20 44	20 4 25	27 9 16	11 27.0	20 9.8	14 14.8	15 10.0	7 57.5	29 9.8	19 57.0	19 34.8	22 46.8
20 Tu	19 51 9	27 18 1	4♌18 35	11♌31 41	11 21.0	19 39.4	15 21.8	15 46.3	8 5.1	29 6.3	19 54.6	19 33.2	22 46.4
21 W	19 55 5	28 15 19	18 47 44	26 5 53	11 14.0	19 12.5	16 28.9	16 22.7	8 12.8	29 2.8	19 52.3	19 31.6	22 45.9
22 Th	19 59 2	29 12 37	3♍25 14	10♍44 53	11 6.8	18 49.9	17 36.1	16 59.1	8 20.7	28 59.3	19 49.9	19 30.0	22 45.5
23 F	20 2 58	0♌ 9 55	18 3 58	25 21 42	11 0.4	18 31.8	18 43.4	17 35.6	8 28.6	28 55.6	19 47.5	19 28.4	22 45.2
24 Sa	20 6 55	1 7 14	2♎37 25	9♎50 31	10 55.5	18 18.8	19 50.9	18 12.2	8 36.7	28 52.0	19 45.2	19 26.8	22 44.8
25 Su	20 10 52	2 4 33	17 0 33	24 7 12	10 52.6	18D 11.0	20 58.5	18 48.8	8 44.9	28 48.2	19 42.8	19 25.3	22 44.5
26 M	20 14 48	3 1 52	1♏10 15	8♏ 9 33	10D 51.6	18 8.9	22 6.3	19 25.5	8 53.2	28 44.4	19 40.5	19 23.7	22 44.2
27 Tu	20 18 45	3 59 12	15 5 7	21 56 56	10 52.0	18 12.6	23 14.1	20 2.2	9 1.7	28 40.6	19 38.2	19 22.1	22 44.0
28 W	20 22 41	4 56 32	28 45 8	5♐29 48	10R 52.9	18 22.3	24 22.1	20 39.0	9 10.2	28 36.7	19 35.8	19 20.6	22 43.8
29 Th	20 26 38	5 53 53	12♐11 5	18 49 6	10 53.3	18 38.1	25 30.2	21 15.9	9 18.9	28 32.7	19 33.6	19 19.0	22 43.6
30 F	20 30 34	6 51 14	25 24 0	1♑55 51	10 52.3	19 0.1	26 38.5	21 52.8	9 27.6	28 28.7	19 31.3	19 17.5	22 43.5
31 Sa	20 34 31	7 48 36	8♑24 47	14 50 52	10 49.2	19 28.2	27 46.8	22 29.8	9 36.5	28 24.7	19 29.0	19 16.0	22 43.3

AUGUST 1993 LONGITUDE

Day	Sid.Time	☉	0 hr ☽	Noon ☽	True ☊	☿	♀	♂	♃	♄	♅	♆	♇
1 Su	20 38 27	8♌45 59	21♑14 8	27♑34 37	10♐43.6	20♋ 2.6	28♊55.3	23♍ 6.8	9♎45.5	28♒20.6	19♑26.8	19♑14.5	22♏43.3
2 M	20 42 24	9 43 22	3♒52 23	10♒ 7 27	10R 35.6	20 43.1	0♋ 3.9	23 43.9	9 54.6	28R 16.5	19R 24.6	19R 13.0	22D 43.2
3 Tu	20 46 21	10 40 46	16 19 51	22 29 39	10 25.6	21 29.8	1 12.6	24 21.1	10 3.7	28 12.3	19 22.4	19 11.5	22 43.2
4 W	20 50 17	11 38 11	28 36 56	4♓41 49	10 14.6	22 22.5	2 21.4	24 58.3	10 13.0	28 8.1	19 20.2	19 10.0	22 43.2
5 Th	20 54 14	12 35 37	10♓44 27	16 45 3	10 3.5	23 21.1	3 30.4	25 35.6	10 22.4	28 3.8	19 18.0	19 8.6	22 43.3
6 F	20 58 10	13 33 4	22 43 51	28 41 10	9 53.3	24 25.6	4 39.4	26 12.9	10 31.9	27 59.5	19 15.9	19 7.1	22 43.4
7 Sa	21 2 7	14 30 32	4♈37 21	10♈32 48	9 44.8	25 35.7	5 48.6	26 50.3	10 41.4	27 55.2	19 13.8	19 5.7	22 43.5
8 Su	21 6 3	15 28 2	16 28 0	22 23 25	9 38.6	26 51.4	6 57.9	27 27.7	10 51.1	27 50.9	19 11.7	19 4.3	22 43.7
9 M	21 10 0	16 25 33	28 19 38	4♉17 12	9 34.7	28 12.3	8 7.3	28 5.3	11 0.9	27 46.5	19 9.6	19 2.9	22 43.9
10 Tu	21 13 56	17 23 5	10♉16 46	16 18 58	9D 33.1	29 38.3	9 16.8	28 42.8	11 10.7	27 42.1	19 7.6	19 1.5	22 44.1
11 W	21 17 53	18 20 38	22 24 26	28 33 51	9 32.9	1♌ 9.1	10 26.4	29 20.5	11 20.7	27 37.7	19 5.6	19 0.1	22 44.3
12 Th	21 21 50	19 18 13	4♊47 50	11♊ 7 1	9R 33.3	2 44.4	11 36.1	29 58.2	11 30.7	27 33.2	19 3.6	18 58.8	22 44.6
13 F	21 25 46	20 15 50	17 31 58	24 3 10	9 33.1	4 23.9	12 45.9	0♎35.9	11 40.8	27 28.8	19 1.6	18 57.4	22 45.0
14 Sa	21 29 43	21 13 28	0♋41 2	7♋25 51	9 31.4	6 7.2	13 55.8	1 13.7	11 51.0	27 24.3	18 59.7	18 56.1	22 45.3
15 Su	21 33 39	22 11 7	14 17 44	21 16 40	9 27.4	7 54.0	15 5.8	1 51.6	12 1.3	27 19.8	18 57.8	18 54.8	22 45.7
16 M	21 37 36	23 8 48	28 22 27	5♌34 38	9 20.9	9 43.8	16 16.0	2 29.6	12 11.7	27 15.3	18 55.9	18 53.5	22 46.2
17 Tu	21 41 32	24 6 30	12♌52 35	20 15 30	9 12.0	11 36.2	17 26.2	3 7.6	12 22.2	27 10.8	18 54.1	18 52.3	22 46.6
18 W	21 45 29	25 4 14	27 42 22	5♍12 3	9 1.7	13 30.9	18 36.5	3 45.6	12 32.8	27 6.2	18 52.3	18 51.0	22 47.1
19 Th	21 49 25	26 1 58	12♍43 20	20 14 58	8 50.9	15 27.4	19 46.9	4 23.7	12 43.4	27 1.7	18 50.5	18 49.8	22 47.7
20 F	21 53 22	26 59 44	27 45 42	5♎14 25	8 41.1	17 25.4	20 57.3	5 1.9	12 54.1	26 57.2	18 48.8	18 48.6	22 48.2
21 Sa	21 57 19	27 57 32	12♎40 3	20 1 47	8 33.3	19 24.4	22 7.9	5 40.2	13 4.9	26 52.6	18 47.1	18 47.4	22 48.8
22 Su	22 1 15	28 55 20	27 18 55	4♏30 57	8 28.0	21 24.2	23 18.6	6 18.5	13 15.8	26 48.1	18 45.4	18 46.3	22 49.5
23 M	22 5 12	29 53 10	11♏37 37	18 38 44	8 25.2	23 24.4	24 29.3	6 56.8	13 26.7	26 43.6	18 43.8	18 45.2	22 50.1
24 Tu	22 9 8	0♍51 0	25 34 19	2♐24 30	8 24.3	25 24.6	25 40.1	7 35.2	13 37.7	26 39.1	18 42.2	18 44.1	22 50.8
25 W	22 13 5	1 48 52	9♐ 9 30	15 49 36	8 24.3	27 24.8	26 51.1	8 13.7	13 48.8	26 34.6	18 40.6	18 43.0	22 51.6
26 Th	22 17 1	2 46 46	22 25 7	28 56 23	8 23.9	29 24.6	28 2.1	8 52.2	13 59.9	26 30.1	18 39.1	18 41.9	22 52.3
27 F	22 20 58	3 44 40	5♑23 46	11♑47 36	8 21.9	1♍23.9	29 13.2	9 30.8	14 11.2	26 25.6	18 37.7	18 40.9	22 53.1
28 Sa	22 24 54	4 42 36	18 8 11	24 25 48	8 17.4	3 22.5	0♌24.3	10 9.5	14 22.4	26 21.1	18 36.2	18 39.9	22 54.0
29 Su	22 28 51	5 40 33	0♒40 44	6♒53 11	8 10.0	5 20.3	1 35.6	10 48.2	14 33.8	26 16.7	18 34.8	18 38.9	22 54.8
30 M	22 32 48	6 38 31	13 3 19	19 11 20	7 59.9	7 17.2	2 46.9	11 26.9	14 45.2	26 12.3	18 33.5	18 37.9	22 55.7
31 Tu	22 36 44	7 36 31	25 17 22	1♓21 31	7 47.5	9 13.0	3 58.3	12 5.7	14 56.7	26 7.9	18 32.1	18 37.0	22 56.6

Astro Data Dy Hr Mn	Planet Ingress Dy Hr Mn	Last Aspect Dy Hr Mn	☽ Ingress Dy Hr Mn	Last Aspect Dy Hr Mn	☽ Ingress Dy Hr Mn	☽ Phases & Eclipses Dy Hr Mn	Astro Data
☿ R 1 15:29	♀ ♊ 6 0:21	3 1:38 ♄ ⚹	♑ 3 1:49	1 3:44 ♂ △	♒ 1 16:36	3 23:45 ○ 12♑02	1 JULY 1993
☽0N 9 7:00	☉ ♌ 22 19:51	5 7:50 ♀ △	♒ 5 9:14	3 23:04 ♄ ☌	♓ 4 2:44	11 22:49 ☽ 19♈37	Julian Day # 34150
♃∠♇ 17 15:56		7 18:37 ♄ ☌	♓ 7 19:10	6 7:24 ♂ ☍	♈ 6 14:39	19 11:24 ● 26♋48	Delta T 58.8 sec
☽0S 23 0:10	♀ ♋ 1 22:38	9 22:39 ☿ △	♈ 10 7:11	8 23:43 ☿ □	♉ 9 3:22	26 3:25 ☽ 3♏10	SVP 05♓20'45"
☿ D 25 20:50	☿ ♌ 10 5:51	12 18:37 ♄ ⚹	♉ 12 19:37	11 14:13 ♂ △	♊ 11 14:47		Obliquity 23°26'21"
	♂ ♎ 12 1:10	15 4:55 ♄ □	♊ 15 6:07	13 18:07 ♄ △	♋ 13 22:46	2 12:10 ○ 10♒12	⚷ Chiron 21♌43.7
♇ D 2 19:28	☉ ♍ 23 2:50	17 11:47 ♄ △	♋ 17 13:08	15 14:32 ♇ △	♌ 16 2:43	10 15:19 ☽ 17♉60	☽ Mean ☊ 10♐50.4
☽0N 5 15:14	☿ ♍ 26 7:06	19 11:24 ☉ ☌	♌ 19 16:47	17 23:02 ♄ ☍	♍ 18 3:41	17 19:28 ● 24♌53	
♂0S 14 1:14	♀ ♌ 27 15:48	21 16:46 ♄ ☍	♍ 21 18:24	19 16:04 ♇ ⚹	♎ 20 3:35	24 9:57 ☽ 1♐15	1 AUGUST 1993
♃⚼♄ 16 5:41		23 7:42 ♇ ⚹	♎ 23 19:39	22 2:51 ☉ ⚹	♏ 22 4:27		Julian Day # 34181
☽0S 19 9:11		25 19:52 ♄ △	♏ 25 22:00	24 1:52 ♄ □	♐ 24 7:45		Delta T 58.9 sec
♅☌♆ 20 7:44		27 23:45 ♄ □	♐ 28 2:13	26 7:27 ♄ ⚹	♑ 26 13:58		SVP 05♓20'40"
		30 5:37 ♄ ⚹	♑ 30 8:27	28 9:05 ♇ ⚹	♒ 28 22:42		Obliquity 23°26'21"
				31 1:39 ♄ ☌	♓ 31 9:19		⚷ Chiron 25♌29.1
							☽ Mean ☊ 9♐11.9

LONGITUDE — SEPTEMBER 1993

Day	Sid.Time	☉	0 hr ☽	Noon ☽	True ☊	☿	♀	♂	♃	♄	♅	♆	♇
1 W	22 40 41	8♍34 32	7♓23 56	13♓24 44	7♐33.7	11♍ 7.8	5♌ 9.8	12♎44.6	15♎ 8.2	26♒ 3.5	18♑30.9	18♑36.1	22♏57.6
2 Th	22 44 37	9 32 35	19 24 2	25 22 0	7R 19.8	13 1.5	6 21.4	13 23.5	15 19.8	25R 59.1	18R 29.6	18R 35.2	22 58.6
3 F	22 48 34	10 30 40	1♈18 49	7♈14 42	7 6.8	14 54.0	7 33.1	14 2.5	15 31.5	25 54.8	18 28.4	18 34.4	22 59.6
4 Sa	22 52 30	11 28 47	13 9 54	19 4 43	6 55.7	16 45.4	8 44.8	14 41.6	15 43.2	25 50.5	18 27.3	18 33.5	23 0.7
5 Su	22 56 27	12 26 55	24 59 30	0♉54 38	6 47.3	18 35.6	9 56.7	15 20.7	15 55.0	25 46.3	18 26.2	18 32.7	23 1.8
6 M	23 0 23	13 25 5	6♉50 35	12 47 50	6 41.7	20 24.5	11 8.6	15 59.8	16 6.8	25 42.1	18 25.1	18 32.0	23 2.9
7 Tu	23 4 20	14 23 17	18 46 55	24 48 24	6 38.7	22 12.3	12 20.6	16 39.1	16 18.7	25 37.9	18 24.1	18 31.2	23 4.0
8 W	23 8 17	15 21 32	0♊52 55	7♊ 1 5	6D 37.7	23 59.0	13 32.7	17 18.3	16 30.6	25 33.8	18 23.1	18 30.5	23 5.2
9 Th	23 12 13	16 19 48	13 13 33	19 30 58	6R 37.6	25 44.4	14 44.8	17 57.7	16 42.6	25 29.7	18 22.2	18 29.8	23 6.4
10 F	23 16 10	17 18 6	25 53 56	2♋23 3	6 37.5	27 28.7	15 57.0	18 37.1	16 54.7	25 25.6	18 21.3	18 29.2	23 7.7
11 Sa	23 20 6	18 16 27	8♋58 51	15 41 44	6 36.0	29 11.8	17 9.4	19 16.6	17 6.8	25 21.7	18 20.5	18 28.5	23 8.9
12 Su	23 24 3	19 14 50	22 32 1	29 29 51	6 32.5	0♎53.8	18 21.7	19 56.1	17 18.9	25 17.7	18 19.7	18 27.9	23 10.2
13 M	23 27 59	20 13 14	6♌35 12	13♌47 48	6 26.4	2 34.7	19 34.2	20 35.7	17 31.1	25 13.8	18 18.9	18 27.4	23 11.6
14 Tu	23 31 56	21 11 41	21 7 12	28 32 41	6 18.0	4 14.5	20 46.7	21 15.3	17 43.4	25 10.0	18 18.3	18 26.8	23 12.9
15 W	23 35 52	22 10 10	6♍ 3 18	13♍37 55	6 7.9	5 53.2	21 59.3	21 55.0	17 55.6	25 6.2	18 17.6	18 26.3	23 14.3
16 Th	23 39 49	23 8 40	21 15 15	28 53 54	5 57.3	7 30.9	23 12.0	22 34.8	18 8.0	25 2.4	18 17.0	18 25.9	23 15.7
17 F	23 43 46	24 7 13	6♎32 25	14♎ 9 24	5 47.4	9 7.5	24 24.7	23 14.7	18 20.3	24 58.8	18 16.5	18 25.4	23 17.2
18 Sa	23 47 42	25 5 47	21 43 33	29 13 42	5 39.5	10 43.0	25 37.5	23 54.5	18 32.7	24 55.2	18 16.0	18 25.0	23 18.7
19 Su	23 51 39	26 4 23	6♏38 54	13♏58 24	5 34.1	12 17.6	26 50.4	24 34.5	18 45.2	24 51.6	18 15.5	18 24.6	23 20.2
20 M	23 55 35	27 3 1	21 11 39	28 18 21	5 31.4	13 51.1	28 3.3	25 14.5	18 57.7	24 48.1	18 15.1	18 24.3	23 21.7
21 Tu	23 59 32	28 1 41	5♐18 23	12♐11 46	5D 30.6	15 23.6	29 16.3	25 54.6	19 10.2	24 44.7	18 14.7	18 24.0	23 23.2
22 W	0 3 28	29 0 22	18 58 42	25 39 29	5R 30.9	16 55.1	0♍29.3	26 34.7	19 22.8	24 41.4	18 14.4	18 23.7	23 24.8
23 Th	0 7 25	29 59 5	2♑14 29	8♑44 8	5 31.2	18 25.6	1 42.4	27 14.9	19 35.4	24 38.1	18 14.2	18 23.4	23 26.4
24 F	0 11 21	0♎57 50	15 8 54	21 29 14	5 30.2	19 55.1	2 55.6	27 55.1	19 48.0	24 34.9	18 14.0	18 23.2	23 28.1
25 Sa	0 15 18	1 56 36	27 45 38	3♒58 31	5 27.1	21 23.6	4 8.8	28 35.4	20 0.6	24 31.8	18 13.8	18 23.0	23 29.7
26 Su	0 19 14	2 55 24	10♒ 8 20	16 15 29	5 21.6	22 51.0	5 22.1	29 15.8	20 13.3	24 28.7	18 13.7	18 22.9	23 31.4
27 M	0 23 11	3 54 14	22 20 19	28 23 10	5 13.5	24 17.5	6 35.4	29 56.2	20 26.0	24 25.8	18D 13.7	18 22.7	23 33.1
28 Tu	0 27 8	4 53 5	4♓24 18	10♓24 1	5 3.5	25 42.9	7 48.8	0♏36.7	20 38.8	24 22.9	18 13.7	18 22.7	23 34.9
29 W	0 31 4	5 51 59	16 22 32	22 20 2	4 52.3	27 7.2	9 2.3	1 17.2	20 51.5	24 20.1	18 13.7	18 22.6	23 36.6
30 Th	0 35 1	6 50 54	28 16 45	4♈12 51	4 40.9	28 30.5	10 15.8	1 57.8	21 4.3	24 17.3	18 13.8	18D 22.6	23 38.4

LONGITUDE — OCTOBER 1993

Day	Sid.Time	☉	0 hr ☽	Noon ☽	True ☊	☿	♀	♂	♃	♄	♅	♆	♇
1 F	0 38 57	7♎49 51	10♈ 8 31	16♈ 3 56	4♐30.2	29♎52.7	11♍29.4	2♏38.4	21♎17.2	24♒14.7	18♑14.0	18♑22.6	23♏40.2
2 Sa	0 42 54	8 48 50	21 59 20	27 54 54	4R 21.3	1♏13.7	12 43.0	3 19.1	21 30.0	24R 12.1	18 14.2	18 22.6	23 42.1
3 Su	0 46 50	9 47 52	3♉50 56	9♉47 41	4 14.5	2 33.5	13 56.7	3 59.9	21 42.9	24 9.6	18 14.4	18 22.7	23 43.9
4 M	0 50 47	10 46 56	15 45 29	21 44 41	4 10.3	3 52.1	15 10.4	4 40.7	21 55.7	24 7.2	18 14.8	18 22.8	23 45.8
5 Tu	0 54 43	11 46 1	27 45 42	3♊48 57	4D 8.4	5 9.4	16 24.2	5 21.6	22 8.6	24 4.9	18 15.1	18 22.9	23 47.7
6 W	0 58 40	12 45 9	9♊54 55	16 4 7	4 8.3	6 25.3	17 38.1	6 2.6	22 21.6	24 2.7	18 15.5	18 23.1	23 49.6
7 Th	1 2 37	13 44 20	22 17 4	28 34 18	4 9.3	7 39.7	18 52.0	6 43.6	22 34.5	24 0.6	18 16.0	18 23.3	23 51.5
8 F	1 6 33	14 43 33	4♋56 23	11♋23 51	4R 10.5	8 52.6	20 5.9	7 24.6	22 47.5	23 58.5	18 16.5	18 23.6	23 53.5
9 Sa	1 10 30	15 42 48	17 57 11	24 36 51	4 10.9	10 3.9	21 19.9	8 5.8	23 0.4	23 56.6	18 17.0	18 23.9	23 55.5
10 Su	1 14 26	16 42 5	1♌23 11	8♌16 28	4 9.8	11 13.4	22 34.0	8 46.9	23 13.4	23 54.7	18 17.7	18 24.2	23 57.5
11 M	1 18 23	17 41 25	15 16 48	22 24 8	4 6.8	12 21.0	23 48.1	9 28.2	23 26.4	23 52.9	18 18.3	18 24.5	23 59.5
12 Tu	1 22 19	18 40 46	29 38 14	6♍58 38	4 2.0	13 26.5	25 2.3	10 9.5	23 39.4	23 51.3	18 19.0	18 24.9	24 1.6
13 W	1 26 16	19 40 11	14♍24 41	21 55 30	3 55.8	14 29.7	26 16.5	10 50.9	23 52.4	23 49.7	18 19.8	18 25.3	24 3.6
14 Th	1 30 12	20 39 37	29 30 1	7♎ 7 1	3 49.0	15 30.5	27 30.7	11 32.3	24 5.5	23 48.2	18 20.6	18 25.7	24 5.7
15 F	1 34 9	21 39 6	14♎45 10	22 23 8	3 42.7	16 28.6	28 45.0	12 13.8	24 18.5	23 46.8	18 21.5	18 26.2	24 7.8
16 Sa	1 38 6	22 38 36	29 59 31	7♏33 4	3 37.6	17 23.8	29 59.3	12 55.4	24 31.5	23 45.5	18 22.4	18 26.7	24 9.9
17 Su	1 42 2	23 38 9	15♏ 2 36	22 27 10	3 34.4	18 15.7	1♎13.7	13 37.0	24 44.6	23 44.4	18 23.4	18 27.3	24 12.0
18 M	1 45 59	24 37 43	29 45 56	6♐58 21	3D 33.1	19 4.1	2 28.1	14 18.7	24 57.6	23 43.3	18 24.4	18 27.8	24 14.2
19 Tu	1 49 55	25 37 20	14♐ 4 0	21 2 43	3 33.4	19 48.5	3 42.6	15 0.4	25 10.7	23 42.3	18 25.4	18 28.5	24 16.3
20 W	1 53 52	26 36 58	27 54 28	4♑39 24	3 34.7	20 28.6	4 57.1	15 42.2	25 23.7	23 41.4	18 26.6	18 29.1	24 18.5
21 Th	1 57 48	27 36 38	11♑17 46	17 49 56	3 36.2	21 3.9	6 11.6	16 24.0	25 36.8	23 40.6	18 27.7	18 29.8	24 20.7
22 F	2 1 45	28 36 20	24 16 19	0♒37 24	3R 37.2	21 34.0	7 26.1	17 6.0	25 49.8	23 39.9	18 29.0	18 30.5	24 22.9
23 Sa	2 5 41	29 36 3	6♒53 42	13 5 45	3 37.0	21 58.3	8 40.7	17 47.9	26 2.9	23 39.4	18 30.2	18 31.2	24 25.2
24 Su	2 9 38	0♏35 48	19 14 6	25 19 15	3 35.3	22 16.2	9 55.3	18 29.9	26 15.9	23 38.9	18 31.5	18 32.0	24 27.4
25 M	2 13 35	1 35 35	1♓21 43	7♓21 59	3 32.1	22R 27.2	11 10.0	19 12.0	26 29.0	23 38.5	18 32.9	18 32.8	24 29.6
26 Tu	2 17 31	2 35 23	13 20 30	19 17 41	3 27.7	22 30.7	12 24.7	19 54.2	26 42.0	23 38.2	18 34.3	18 33.6	24 31.9
27 W	2 21 28	3 35 14	25 13 56	1♈ 9 36	3 22.5	22 26.1	13 39.4	20 36.3	26 55.0	23 38.1	18 35.8	18 34.5	24 34.2
28 Th	2 25 24	4 35 5	7♈ 5 1	13 0 28	3 17.1	22 12.9	14 54.1	21 18.6	27 8.0	23D 38.0	18 37.3	18 35.4	24 36.4
29 F	2 29 21	5 34 59	18 56 13	24 52 31	3 12.1	21 50.7	16 8.9	22 0.9	27 21.0	23 38.0	18 38.8	18 36.3	24 38.7
30 Sa	2 33 17	6 34 55	0♉49 36	6♉47 42	3 8.0	21 19.2	17 23.7	22 43.3	27 34.0	23 38.2	18 40.4	18 37.3	24 41.0
31 Su	2 37 14	7 34 52	12 47 1	18 47 46	3 5.1	20 38.4	18 38.6	23 25.7	27 46.9	23 38.4	18 42.1	18 38.3	24 43.4

Astro Data	Dy Hr Mn
☽0N	1 22:23
☿0S	12 9:35
☽0S	15 19:47
♃□♅	16 16:47
♃□♆	17 9:31
♅ D	27 12:29
☽0N	29 4:22
♆ D	30 6:09
♄□♇	9 6:37
♃△♄	12 19:28
☽0S	13 6:22
♃⊻♇	14 0:29
♀0S	18 20:52
♅☌♆	24 20:18

Planet Ingress	Dy Hr Mn
☿ ♎	11 11:18
♀ ♍	21 14:22
☉ ♎	23 0:22
♂ ♏	27 2:15
☿ ♏	1 2:09
♀ ♎	16 0:13
☉ ♏	23 9:37
☿ R	25 22:40
☽0N	26 9:57
♄ D	28 3:39

Last Aspect Dy Hr Mn		☽ Ingress Dy Hr Mn	
2 7:12	♇ △	♈	2 21:21
5 1:34	♄ ⚹	♉	5 10:09
7 13:34	♄ □	♊	7 22:16
10 3:24	☿ □	♋	10 7:37
12 1:06	♇ △	♌	12 12:51
14 6:32	♄ ☍	♍	14 14:20
16 3:10	☉ ☌	♎	16 13:44
18 6:46	♀ ⚹	♏	18 13:14
20 12:40	♀ □	♐	20 14:53
22 19:32	☉ □	♑	22 19:54
25 1:41	♂ □	♒	25 4:19
27 4:23	☿ △	♓	27 15:13
29 14:37	♇ △	♈	30 3:29

Last Aspect Dy Hr Mn		☽ Ingress Dy Hr Mn	
2 4:28	♄ ⚹	♉	2 16:13
4 16:42	♄ □	♊	5 4:27
7 3:18	♄ △	♋	7 14:42
9 10:48	♇ △	♌	9 21:34
11 14:41	♇ □	♍	12 0:36
13 20:35	♀ ☌	♎	14 0:47
15 15:15	♃ ☌	♏	16 0:01
17 14:53	♇ ☌	♐	18 0:23
19 21:33	☉ ⚹	♑	20 3:42
22 8:52	☉ □	♒	22 10:49
24 14:07	♃ △	♓	24 21:17
26 22:39	♇ △	♈	27 9:39
29 17:18	♃ ☍	♉	29 22:20

☽ Phases & Eclipses Dy Hr Mn		
1 2:33	○	8♓41
9 6:26	☽	16♊35
16 3:10	●	23♍16
22 19:32	☽	29♐48
30 18:54	○	7♈37
8 19:35	☽	15♋32
15 11:36	●	22♎08
22 8:52	☽	28♑58
30 12:38	○	7♉06

Astro Data

1 SEPTEMBER 1993
Julian Day # 34212
Delta T 58.9 sec
SVP 05♓20'37"
Obliquity 23°26'21"
⚷ Chiron 29♌36.8
☽ Mean ☊ 7♐33.4

1 OCTOBER 1993
Julian Day # 34242
Delta T 59.0 sec
SVP 05♓20'34"
Obliquity 23°26'21"
⚷ Chiron 3♍28.4
☽ Mean ☊ 5♐58.1

NOVEMBER 1993 LONGITUDE

Day	Sid.Time	☉	0 hr ☽	Noon ☽	True ☊	☿	♀	♂	♃	♄	♅	♆	♇
1 M	2 41 10	8♏34 52	24♉50 10	0♊54 28	3♐ 3.6	19♏48.4	19♎53.4	24♏ 8.2	27♎59.9	23♒38.8	18♑43.8	18♑39.3	24♏45.7
2 Tu	2 45 7	9 34 53	7♊ 0 53	13 9 42	3D 3.4	18R 49.8	21 8.3	24 50.7	28 12.8	23 39.2	18 45.5	18 40.4	24 48.0
3 W	2 49 3	10 34 57	19 21 12	25 35 39	3 4.2	17 43.6	22 23.3	25 33.3	28 25.7	23 39.8	18 47.3	18 41.5	24 50.4
4 Th	2 53 0	11 35 2	1♋53 24	8♋14 46	3 5.6	16 31.3	23 38.2	26 16.0	28 38.7	23 40.4	18 49.1	18 42.6	24 52.7
5 F	2 56 57	12 35 10	14 40 6	21 9 43	3 7.2	15 14.7	24 53.2	26 58.7	28 51.5	23 41.2	18 51.0	18 43.7	24 55.1
6 Sa	3 0 53	13 35 19	27 43 58	4♌23 8	3 8.5	13 55.9	26 8.2	27 41.5	29 4.4	23 42.1	18 52.9	18 44.9	24 57.4
7 Su	3 4 50	14 35 31	11♌ 7 29	17 57 13	3R 9.2	12 37.5	27 23.2	28 24.3	29 17.2	23 43.0	18 54.9	18 46.1	24 59.8
8 M	3 8 46	15 35 44	24 52 27	1♍53 13	3 9.0	11 21.9	28 38.3	29 7.2	29 30.1	23 44.1	18 56.9	18 47.4	25 2.2
9 Tu	3 12 43	16 36 0	8♍59 26	16 10 52	3 8.0	10 11.6	29 53.4	29 50.2	29 42.9	23 45.3	18 58.9	18 48.6	25 4.6
10 W	3 16 39	17 36 18	23 27 8	0♎47 42	3 6.4	9 8.8	1♏ 8.5	0♐33.2	29 55.6	23 46.5	19 1.0	18 49.9	25 7.0
11 Th	3 20 36	18 36 37	8♎11 56	15 38 59	3 4.5	8 15.2	2 23.6	1 16.3	0♏ 8.4	23 47.9	19 3.1	18 51.2	25 9.3
12 F	3 24 32	19 36 59	23 7 56	0♏37 45	3 2.7	7 32.2	3 38.8	1 59.4	0 21.1	23 49.4	19 5.3	18 52.6	25 11.7
13 Sa	3 28 29	20 37 23	8♏ 7 22	15 35 42	3 1.3	7 0.5	4 54.0	2 42.6	0 33.7	23 51.0	19 7.5	18 54.0	25 14.1
14 Su	3 32 26	21 37 48	23 1 39	0♐24 16	3D 0.6	6 40.5	6 9.2	3 25.8	0 46.4	23 52.7	19 9.8	18 55.4	25 16.5
15 M	3 36 22	22 38 15	7♐42 38	14 55 59	3 0.5	6D 32.2	7 24.4	4 9.2	0 59.0	23 54.4	19 12.1	18 56.8	25 18.9
16 Tu	3 40 19	23 38 43	22 3 44	29 5 23	3 0.9	6 35.1	8 39.6	4 52.5	1 11.6	23 56.3	19 14.4	18 58.3	25 21.4
17 W	3 44 15	24 39 13	6♑ 0 41	12♑49 28	3 1.6	6 48.6	9 54.9	5 36.0	1 24.1	23 58.3	19 16.8	18 59.8	25 23.8
18 Th	3 48 12	25 39 45	19 31 46	26 7 42	3 2.4	7 12.0	11 10.1	6 19.4	1 36.6	24 0.4	19 19.2	19 1.3	25 26.2
19 F	3 52 8	26 40 17	2♒37 32	9♒ 1 36	3 3.1	7 44.4	12 25.4	7 3.0	1 49.1	24 2.6	19 21.7	19 2.8	25 28.6
20 Sa	3 56 5	27 40 51	15 20 20	21 34 12	3 3.5	8 24.8	13 40.7	7 46.6	2 1.5	24 4.9	19 24.2	19 4.4	25 31.0
21 Su	4 0 2	28 41 26	27 43 45	3♓49 32	3R 3.6	9 12.5	14 56.0	8 30.2	2 13.9	24 7.3	19 26.7	19 6.0	25 33.4
22 M	4 3 58	29 42 2	9♓52 7	15 52 4	3 3.6	10 6.5	16 11.3	9 13.9	2 26.2	24 9.7	19 29.3	19 7.6	25 35.8
23 Tu	4 7 55	0♐42 39	21 49 58	27 46 23	3 3.4	11 6.0	17 26.6	9 57.6	2 38.5	24 12.3	19 31.9	19 9.2	25 38.2
24 W	4 11 51	1 43 18	3♈41 50	9♈36 52	3 3.2	12 10.4	18 41.9	10 41.4	2 50.7	24 15.0	19 34.5	19 10.9	25 40.6
25 Th	4 15 48	2 43 57	15 31 58	21 27 34	3D 3.1	13 19.0	19 57.3	11 25.3	3 2.9	24 17.8	19 37.2	19 12.6	25 43.0
26 F	4 19 44	3 44 38	27 24 7	3♉21 58	3 3.1	14 31.2	21 12.6	12 9.2	3 15.0	24 20.6	19 39.9	19 14.3	25 45.4
27 Sa	4 23 41	4 45 20	9♉21 30	15 23 0	3 3.2	15 46.5	22 28.0	12 53.2	3 27.1	24 23.6	19 42.6	19 16.0	25 47.8
28 Su	4 27 37	5 46 3	21 26 45	27 32 59	3R 3.4	17 4.5	23 43.3	13 37.2	3 39.1	24 26.6	19 45.4	19 17.8	25 50.1
29 M	4 31 34	6 46 48	3♊41 53	9♊53 38	3 3.5	18 24.7	24 58.7	14 21.2	3 51.1	24 29.8	19 48.2	19 19.6	25 52.5
30 Tu	4 35 30	7 47 33	16 8 21	22 26 9	3 3.3	19 46.9	26 14.1	15 5.4	4 3.1	24 33.0	19 51.1	19 21.4	25 54.9

DECEMBER 1993 LONGITUDE

Day	Sid.Time	☉	0 hr ☽	Noon ☽	True ☊	☿	♀	♂	♃	♄	♅	♆	♇
1 W	4 39 27	8♐48 20	28♊47 8	5♋11 21	3♐ 2.9	21♏10.6	27♏29.5	15♐49.5	4♏14.9	24♒36.4	19♑53.9	19♑23.2	25♏57.3
2 Th	4 43 24	9 49 9	11♋38 52	18 9 44	3R 2.2	22 35.8	28 44.9	16 33.8	4 26.7	24 39.8	19 56.8	19 25.0	25 59.6
3 F	4 47 20	10 49 58	24 43 58	1♌21 36	3 1.2	24 2.1	0♐ 0.3	17 18.1	4 38.5	24 43.3	19 59.8	19 26.9	26 2.0
4 Sa	4 51 17	11 50 49	8♌ 2 39	14 47 8	3 0.2	25 29.5	1 15.8	18 2.4	4 50.2	24 46.9	20 2.7	19 28.8	26 4.3
5 Su	4 55 13	12 51 41	21 35 4	28 26 24	2 59.2	26 57.6	2 31.2	18 46.8	5 1.8	24 50.6	20 5.7	19 30.7	26 6.6
6 M	4 59 10	13 52 35	5♍21 7	12♍19 9	2D 58.6	28 26.5	3 46.7	19 31.2	5 13.3	24 54.3	20 8.7	19 32.6	26 9.0
7 Tu	5 3 6	14 53 29	19 20 24	26 24 43	2 58.5	29 56.0	5 2.1	20 15.7	5 24.8	24 58.2	20 11.8	19 34.5	26 11.3
8 W	5 7 3	15 54 26	3♎31 53	10♎41 38	2 59.0	1♐26.0	6 17.6	21 0.3	5 36.3	25 2.1	20 14.8	19 36.5	26 13.6
9 Th	5 11 0	16 55 23	17 53 38	25 7 27	2 59.9	2 56.4	7 33.1	21 44.9	5 47.6	25 6.2	20 17.9	19 38.5	26 15.9
10 F	5 14 56	17 56 21	2♏22 38	9♏38 37	3 1.1	4 27.2	8 48.5	22 29.6	5 58.9	25 10.3	20 21.1	19 40.4	26 18.2
11 Sa	5 18 53	18 57 21	16 54 45	24 10 23	3 2.1	5 58.4	10 4.0	23 14.3	6 10.1	25 14.5	20 24.2	19 42.5	26 20.4
12 Su	5 22 49	19 58 22	1♐24 50	8♐37 21	3R 2.6	7 29.8	11 19.5	23 59.0	6 21.2	25 18.7	20 27.4	19 44.5	26 22.7
13 M	5 26 46	20 59 24	15 47 14	22 53 50	3 2.3	9 1.4	12 35.0	24 43.9	6 32.3	25 23.1	20 30.6	19 46.5	26 24.9
14 Tu	5 30 42	22 0 27	29 56 30	6♑54 43	3 0.9	10 33.3	13 50.5	25 28.7	6 43.3	25 27.6	20 33.8	19 48.6	26 27.2
15 W	5 34 39	23 1 30	13♑48 1	20 36 5	2 58.5	12 5.3	15 6.0	26 13.6	6 54.2	25 32.1	20 37.0	19 50.7	26 29.4
16 Th	5 38 35	24 2 34	27 18 40	3♒55 39	2 55.3	13 37.6	16 21.5	26 58.6	7 5.0	25 36.7	20 40.3	19 52.7	26 31.6
17 F	5 42 32	25 3 38	10♒27 5	16 53 2	2 51.9	15 10.0	17 37.1	27 43.6	7 15.7	25 41.4	20 43.6	19 54.8	26 33.8
18 Sa	5 46 29	26 4 43	23 13 45	29 29 33	2 48.6	16 42.6	18 52.6	28 28.7	7 26.4	25 46.1	20 46.9	19 57.0	26 35.9
19 Su	5 50 25	27 5 48	5♓40 49	11♓48 2	2 45.9	18 15.4	20 8.1	29 13.8	7 36.9	25 50.9	20 50.2	19 59.1	26 38.1
20 M	5 54 22	28 6 54	17 51 41	23 52 22	2D 44.2	19 48.3	21 23.6	29 58.9	7 47.4	25 55.8	20 53.5	20 1.2	26 40.2
21 Tu	5 58 18	29 7 59	29 50 39	5♈47 10	2 43.7	21 21.4	22 39.1	0♑44.1	7 57.8	26 0.8	20 56.9	20 3.4	26 42.4
22 W	6 2 15	0♑ 9 5	11♈42 32	17 37 23	2 44.3	22 54.7	23 54.6	1 29.4	8 8.1	26 5.9	21 0.3	20 5.5	26 44.5
23 Th	6 6 11	1 10 11	23 32 22	29 28 3	2 45.8	24 28.1	25 10.1	2 14.7	8 18.3	26 11.0	21 3.7	20 7.7	26 46.5
24 F	6 10 8	2 11 18	5♉25 3	11♉23 54	2 47.7	26 1.8	26 25.6	2 60.0	8 28.4	26 16.2	21 7.1	20 9.9	26 48.6
25 Sa	6 14 4	3 12 24	17 25 8	23 29 14	2 49.4	27 35.7	27 41.1	3 45.4	8 38.4	26 21.4	21 10.5	20 12.1	26 50.7
26 Su	6 18 1	4 13 31	29 36 35	5♊47 34	2R 50.3	29 9.8	28 56.6	4 30.8	8 48.3	26 26.7	21 13.9	20 14.3	26 52.7
27 M	6 21 58	5 14 38	12♊ 2 28	18 21 30	2 50.0	0♑44.1	0♑12.1	5 16.2	8 58.1	26 32.1	21 17.4	20 16.5	26 54.7
28 Tu	6 25 54	6 15 45	24 44 49	1♋12 28	2 48.0	2 18.7	1 27.6	6 1.7	9 7.8	26 37.6	21 20.8	20 18.7	26 56.7
29 W	6 29 51	7 16 53	7♋44 26	14 20 38	2 44.3	3 53.6	2 43.1	6 47.3	9 17.4	26 43.1	21 24.3	20 20.9	26 58.6
30 Th	6 33 47	8 18 0	21 0 52	27 44 56	2 39.1	5 28.7	3 58.6	7 32.9	9 26.9	26 48.7	21 27.8	20 23.1	27 0.6
31 F	6 37 44	9 19 8	4♌32 31	11♌23 18	2 32.9	7 4.1	5 14.1	8 18.5	9 36.3	26 54.3	21 31.3	20 25.4	27 2.5

Astro Data Dy Hr Mn	Planet Ingress Dy Hr Mn	Last Aspect Dy Hr Mn	☽ Ingress Dy Hr Mn	Last Aspect Dy Hr Mn	☽ Ingress Dy Hr Mn	☽ Phases & Eclipses Dy Hr Mn	Astro Data
☽0S 9 15:15	♀ ♏ 9 2:07	31 23:51 ♇ ☍	♊ 1 10:13	30 16:05 ♄ △	♋ 1 2:17	7 6:36 ☽ 14♌52	1 NOVEMBER 1993
☿ D 15 5:39	♂ ♐ 9 5:29	3 17:43 ♃ △	♋ 3 20:25	3 2:22 ♇ △	♌ 3 9:33	13 21:34 ● 21♏32	Julian Day # 34273
☽0N 22 16:28	♃ ♏ 10 8:15	6 2:28 ♃ □	♌ 6 4:06	5 10:33 ☿ □	♍ 5 14:43	13 21:44:49 ✓ P 0.928	Delta T 59.0 sec
	☉ ♐ 22 7:07	8 8:03 ♃ ⚹	♍ 8 8:47	7 11:39 ♇ ⚹	♎ 7 18:03	21 2:03 ☽ 28♒47	SVP 05♓20'31"
☽0S 6 21:55		10 2:44 ♇ ⚹	♎ 10 10:42	9 12:01 ♄ △	♏ 9 20:04	29 6:31 ○ 7♊03	Obliquity 23°26'20"
☽0N 20 0:44	♀ ♐ 2 23:54	12 1:06 ♄ △	♏ 12 11:00	11 15:38 ♇ ☌	♐ 11 21:39	29 6:26 ☍ T 1.087	⚷ Chiron 6♍46.8
	☿ ♐ 7 1:04	14 3:39 ♇ ☌	♐ 14 11:20	13 16:19 ♄ ⚹	♑ 14 0:06		☽ Mean ☊ 4♐19.5
	♂ ♑ 20 0:34	16 3:12 ♄ ⚹	♑ 16 13:34	15 22:35 ♇ ⚹	♒ 16 4:51	6 15:49 ☽ 14♍33	
	☉ ♑ 21 20:26	18 12:05 ☉ ⚹	♒ 18 19:08	18 10:41 ♂ ⚹	♓ 18 12:59	13 9:27 ● 21♐23	1 DECEMBER 1993
	☿ ♑ 26 12:47	21 2:03 ☉ □	♓ 21 4:27	20 22:26 ☉ □	♈ 21 0:19	20 22:26 ☽ 29♓04	Julian Day # 34303
	♀ ♑ 26 20:09	23 7:42 ♇ △	♈ 23 16:30	23 5:24 ♄ ⚹	♉ 23 13:05	28 23:05 ○ 7♋15	Delta T 59.1 sec
		25 17:48 ♄ ⚹	♉ 26 5:14	25 18:39 ♇ ☍	♊ 26 0:46		SVP 05♓20'26"
		28 8:40 ♇ ☍	♊ 28 16:48	28 3:32 ♄ △	♋ 28 9:46		Obliquity 23°26'20"
				30 10:43 ♇ △	♌ 30 15:59		⚷ Chiron 8♍47.5
							☽ Mean ☊ 2♐44.2

LONGITUDE — JANUARY 1994

Day	Sid.Time	☉	0 hr ☽	Noon ☽	True ☊	☿	♀	♂	♃	♄	♅	♆	♇
1 Sa	6 41 40	10♑20 16	18♌16 53	25♌12 56	2♐26.5	8♑39.9	6♑29.6	9♑ 4.2	9♏45.5	27♒ 0.0	21♑34.8	20♑27.6	27♏ 4.4
2 Su	6 45 37	11 21 24	2♍11 2	9♍10 51	2R 20.7	10 16.0	7 45.1	9 49.9	9 54.7	27 5.8	21 38.3	20 29.9	27 6.3
3 M	6 49 33	12 22 32	16 12 0	23 14 13	2 16.3	11 52.4	9 0.6	10 35.7	10 3.8	27 11.6	21 41.8	20 32.1	27 8.1
4 Tu	6 53 30	13 23 41	0♎17 12	7♎20 42	2 13.6	13 29.1	10 16.1	11 21.5	10 12.7	27 17.5	21 45.3	20 34.4	27 10.0
5 W	6 57 27	14 24 50	14 24 32	21 28 30	2D 12.8	15 6.3	11 31.6	12 7.4	10 21.5	27 23.5	21 48.9	20 36.7	27 11.8
6 Th	7 1 23	15 25 59	28 32 27	5♏36 12	2 13.4	16 43.8	12 47.1	12 53.3	10 30.3	27 29.4	21 52.4	20 38.9	27 13.6
7 F	7 5 20	16 27 9	12♏39 36	19 42 28	2 14.7	18 21.7	14 2.6	13 39.2	10 38.8	27 35.5	21 55.9	20 41.2	27 15.3
8 Sa	7 9 16	17 28 18	26 44 34	3♐45 42	2R 15.7	20 0.0	15 18.1	14 25.2	10 47.3	27 41.6	21 59.5	20 43.5	27 17.1
9 Su	7 13 13	18 29 28	10♐45 33	17 43 50	2 15.5	21 38.8	16 33.6	15 11.2	10 55.7	27 47.8	22 3.0	20 45.7	27 18.8
10 M	7 17 9	19 30 38	24 40 10	1♑34 12	2 13.3	23 17.9	17 49.1	15 57.2	11 3.9	27 54.0	22 6.6	20 48.0	27 20.4
11 Tu	7 21 6	20 31 48	8♑25 33	15 13 49	2 8.7	24 57.4	19 4.6	16 43.3	11 12.0	28 0.2	22 10.2	20 50.3	27 22.1
12 W	7 25 2	21 32 57	21 58 38	28 39 42	2 1.7	26 37.3	20 20.0	17 29.5	11 20.0	28 6.5	22 13.7	20 52.6	27 23.7
13 Th	7 28 59	22 34 6	5♒16 42	11♒49 26	1 52.9	28 17.6	21 35.5	18 15.7	11 27.8	28 12.9	22 17.3	20 54.9	27 25.3
14 F	7 32 56	23 35 15	18 17 46	24 41 37	1 43.1	29 58.3	22 51.0	19 1.9	11 35.5	28 19.3	22 20.8	20 57.1	27 26.9
15 Sa	7 36 52	24 36 23	1♓ 1 3	7♓16 11	1 33.3	1♒39.3	24 6.5	19 48.1	11 43.1	28 25.8	22 24.4	20 59.4	27 28.4
16 Su	7 40 49	25 37 30	13 27 12	19 34 26	1 24.6	3 20.6	25 21.9	20 34.4	11 50.5	28 32.2	22 27.9	21 1.7	27 30.0
17 M	7 44 45	26 38 37	25 38 14	1♈39 3	1 17.6	5 2.1	26 37.4	21 20.7	11 57.8	28 38.8	22 31.5	21 4.0	27 31.4
18 Tu	7 48 42	27 39 43	7♈37 24	13 33 50	1 12.9	6 43.9	27 52.8	22 7.0	12 4.9	28 45.3	22 35.0	21 6.2	27 32.9
19 W	7 52 38	28 40 48	19 28 58	25 23 27	1D 10.5	8 25.8	29 8.3	22 53.4	12 11.9	28 52.0	22 38.6	21 8.5	27 34.3
20 Th	7 56 35	29 41 53	1♉17 55	7♉13 3	1 9.9	10 7.7	0♒23.7	23 39.8	12 18.8	28 58.6	22 42.1	21 10.7	27 35.7
21 F	8 0 31	0♒42 56	13 9 34	19 8 7	1 10.6	11 49.6	1 39.1	24 26.2	12 25.5	29 5.3	22 45.7	21 13.0	27 37.1
22 Sa	8 4 28	1 43 59	25 9 22	1♊13 58	1R 11.4	13 31.3	2 54.5	25 12.7	12 32.1	29 12.0	22 49.2	21 15.2	27 38.4
23 Su	8 8 25	2 45 0	7♊22 29	13 35 28	1 11.3	15 12.6	4 9.9	25 59.2	12 38.5	29 18.8	22 52.7	21 17.5	27 39.7
24 M	8 12 21	3 46 1	19 53 24	26 16 38	1 9.5	16 53.4	5 25.3	26 45.7	12 44.8	29 25.6	22 56.2	21 19.7	27 41.0
25 Tu	8 16 18	4 47 1	2♋45 28	9♋20 4	1 5.3	18 33.5	6 40.7	27 32.2	12 51.0	29 32.4	22 59.7	21 22.0	27 42.2
26 W	8 20 14	5 48 0	16 0 28	22 46 33	0 58.4	20 12.5	7 56.1	28 18.8	12 56.9	29 39.3	23 3.2	21 24.2	27 43.5
27 Th	8 24 11	6 48 57	29 38 5	6♌34 41	0 49.1	21 50.2	9 11.4	29 5.4	13 2.8	29 46.2	23 6.7	21 26.4	27 44.6
28 F	8 28 7	7 49 54	13♌35 51	20 40 57	0 38.2	23 26.2	10 26.8	29 52.0	13 8.4	29 53.1	23 10.2	21 28.6	27 45.8
29 Sa	8 32 4	8 50 50	27 49 17	5♍ 0 4	0 26.9	25 0.1	11 42.1	0♒38.7	13 13.9	0♓ 0.1	23 13.7	21 30.8	27 46.9
30 Su	8 36 0	9 51 45	12♍12 31	19 25 50	0 16.3	26 31.5	12 57.4	1 25.4	13 19.3	0 7.1	23 17.1	21 33.0	27 48.0
31 M	8 39 57	10 52 40	26 39 17	3♎52 10	0 7.6	27 59.8	14 12.8	2 12.1	13 24.5	0 14.1	23 20.6	21 35.2	27 49.0

LONGITUDE — FEBRUARY 1994

Day	Sid.Time	☉	0 hr ☽	Noon ☽	True ☊	☿	♀	♂	♃	♄	♅	♆	♇
1 Tu	8 43 54	11♒53 33	11♎ 3 55	18♎14 3	0♐ 1.6	29♒24.4	15♒28.1	2♒58.8	13♏29.5	0♓21.1	23♑24.0	21♑37.3	27♏50.0
2 W	8 47 50	12 54 26	25 22 10	2♏28 1	29♏58.2	0♓44.8	16 43.4	3 45.6	13 34.4	0 28.2	23 27.4	21 39.5	27 51.0
3 Th	8 51 47	13 55 18	9♏31 25	16 32 16	29D 57.1	2 0.1	17 58.7	4 32.4	13 39.1	0 35.2	23 30.8	21 41.7	27 52.0
4 F	8 55 43	14 56 9	23 30 32	0♐26 15	29R 57.2	3 9.8	19 14.0	5 19.2	13 43.6	0 42.3	23 34.2	21 43.8	27 52.9
5 Sa	8 59 40	15 57 0	7♐19 26	14 10 9	29 57.1	4 12.9	20 29.3	6 6.1	13 48.0	0 49.5	23 37.5	21 45.9	27 53.8
6 Su	9 3 36	16 57 50	20 58 26	27 44 19	29 55.5	5 8.8	21 44.5	6 52.9	13 52.2	0 56.6	23 40.9	21 48.0	27 54.6
7 M	9 7 33	17 58 38	4♑27 47	11♑ 8 49	29 51.5	5 56.7	22 59.8	7 39.8	13 56.3	1 3.8	23 44.2	21 50.1	27 55.4
8 Tu	9 11 30	18 59 26	17 47 19	24 23 13	29 44.5	6 35.7	24 15.0	8 26.7	14 0.1	1 11.0	23 47.5	21 52.2	27 56.2
9 W	9 15 26	20 0 13	0♒56 23	7♒26 40	29 34.4	7 5.3	25 30.3	9 13.7	14 3.8	1 18.2	23 50.8	21 54.3	27 56.9
10 Th	9 19 23	21 0 58	13 53 57	20 18 5	29 21.8	7 24.9	26 45.5	10 0.6	14 7.3	1 25.4	23 54.1	21 56.4	27 57.7
11 F	9 23 19	22 1 42	26 38 59	2♓56 34	29 7.9	7R 34.0	28 0.7	10 47.6	14 10.6	1 32.6	23 57.3	21 58.4	27 58.3
12 Sa	9 27 16	23 2 25	9♓10 50	15 21 48	28 53.7	7 32.4	29 15.9	11 34.6	14 13.8	1 39.8	24 0.6	22 0.4	27 59.0
13 Su	9 31 12	24 3 6	21 29 34	27 34 18	28 40.6	7 20.2	0♓31.1	12 21.6	14 16.8	1 47.1	24 3.8	22 2.4	27 59.6
14 M	9 35 9	25 3 46	3♈36 13	9♈35 39	28 29.6	6 57.4	1 46.3	13 8.6	14 19.6	1 54.4	24 7.0	22 4.4	28 0.1
15 Tu	9 39 5	26 4 24	15 32 57	21 28 33	28 21.4	6 24.7	3 1.4	13 55.6	14 22.2	2 1.6	24 10.1	22 6.4	28 0.7
16 W	9 43 2	27 5 0	27 22 57	3♉16 42	28 16.1	5 42.9	4 16.5	14 42.7	14 24.6	2 8.9	24 13.3	22 8.3	28 1.1
17 Th	9 46 58	28 5 35	9♉10 24	15 4 40	28 13.4	4 53.1	5 31.7	15 29.7	14 26.8	2 16.2	24 16.4	22 10.3	28 1.6
18 F	9 50 55	29 6 8	21 0 11	26 57 39	28 12.5	3 56.5	6 46.8	16 16.8	14 28.9	2 23.5	24 19.5	22 12.2	28 2.0
19 Sa	9 54 52	0♓ 6 39	2♊57 45	9♊ 1 13	28 12.5	2 54.8	8 1.8	17 3.9	14 30.8	2 30.8	24 22.5	22 14.1	28 2.4
20 Su	9 58 48	1 7 9	15 8 43	21 20 55	28 12.0	1 49.6	9 16.9	17 51.0	14 32.5	2 38.1	24 25.6	22 16.0	28 2.8
21 M	10 2 45	2 7 36	27 38 26	4♋ 1 50	28 10.0	0 42.7	10 31.9	18 38.1	14 34.0	2 45.4	24 28.6	22 17.9	28 3.1
22 Tu	10 6 41	3 8 2	10♋31 33	17 7 58	28 5.8	29♒35.7	11 46.9	19 25.2	14 35.3	2 52.6	24 31.5	22 19.7	28 3.4
23 W	10 10 38	4 8 26	23 51 17	0♌41 34	27 58.8	28 30.4	13 1.9	20 12.3	14 36.5	2 59.9	24 34.5	22 21.5	28 3.6
24 Th	10 14 34	5 8 48	7♌38 40	14 42 19	27 49.3	27 28.2	14 16.9	20 59.5	14 37.4	3 7.2	24 37.4	22 23.3	28 3.8
25 F	10 18 31	6 9 8	21 52 0	29 7 1	27 38.0	26 30.3	15 31.9	21 46.6	14 38.2	3 14.5	24 40.3	22 25.1	28 4.0
26 Sa	10 22 27	7 9 27	6♍26 33	13♍49 36	27 26.0	25 37.7	16 46.8	22 33.7	14 38.8	3 21.8	24 43.1	22 26.9	28 4.1
27 Su	10 26 24	8 9 43	21 15 4	28 41 50	27 14.7	24 51.3	18 1.7	23 20.9	14 39.1	3 29.1	24 46.0	22 28.6	28 4.2
28 M	10 30 21	9 9 58	6♎ 8 47	13♎34 50	27 5.3	24 11.5	19 16.6	24 8.0	14R 39.3	3 36.4	24 48.8	22 30.3	28 4.3

Astro Data Dy Hr Mn	Planet Ingress Dy Hr Mn	Last Aspect Dy Hr Mn	☽ Ingress Dy Hr Mn	Last Aspect Dy Hr Mn	☽ Ingress Dy Hr Mn	☽ Phases & Eclipses Dy Hr Mn
♄□♇ 2 2:56	☿ ♒ 14 0:25	1 15:14 ♇ □	♍ 1 20:15	1 20:46 ♅ □	♏ 2 7:49	5 0:01 ☽ 14♎25
☽0S 3 3:49	♀ ♒ 19 16:28	3 18:41 ♇ ✶	♎ 3 23:31	4 7:34 ♇ ☌	♐ 4 11:14	11 23:10 ● 21♑31
☽0N 16 10:12	☉ ♒ 20 7:07	5 22:12 ♄ △	♏ 6 2:29	6 1:30 ♀ ✶	♑ 6 16:02	19 20:27 ☽ 29♈33
☽0S 30 11:06	♂ ♒ 28 4:05	8 1:38 ♄ □	♐ 8 5:34	8 18:30 ♇ ✶	♒ 8 22:16	27 13:23 ○ 7♌23
	♄ ♓ 28 23:43	10 5:39 ♄ ✶	♑ 10 9:16	11 2:52 ♀ ☌	♓ 11 6:23	
☿ R 11 8:30		12 9:44 ♇ ✶	♒ 12 14:25	13 12:51 ♇ △	♈ 13 16:49	3 8:06 ☽ 14♏16
☽0N 12 19:16	☿ ♓ 1 10:28	14 19:02 ♄ ☌	♓ 14 22:04	15 23:20 ☉ ✶	♉ 16 5:20	10 14:30 ● 21♒38
☽0S 26 20:39	☊ ♏ 1 9:15	17 3:46 ♇ △	♈ 17 8:42	18 17:47 ☉ □	♊ 18 18:05	18 17:47 ☽ 29♉51
♃ R 28 13:50	♀ ♓ 12 14:04	19 20:27 ☉ □	♉ 19 21:22	20 5:36 ♂ △	♋ 21 4:27	26 1:15 ○ 7♍13
	☉ ♓ 18 21:22	22 8:04 ♄ □	♊ 22 9:35	23 7:24 ♇ △	♌ 23 10:48	
	☿ ♒ 21 15:15	24 18:01 ♄ △	♋ 24 18:55	25 10:16 ♇ □	♍ 25 13:27	
		26 23:00 ♂ ☍	♌ 27 0:38	27 11:00 ♇ ✶	♎ 27 14:06	
		28 23:56 ♇ □	♍ 29 3:39			
		31 1:56 ♇ ✶	♎ 31 5:34			

Astro Data

1 JANUARY 1994
Julian Day # 34334
Delta T 59.1 sec
SVP 05♓20'21"
Obliquity 23°26'19"
⚷ Chiron 9♍11.9R
☽ Mean ☊ 1♐05.8

1 FEBRUARY 1994
Julian Day # 34365
Delta T 59.1 sec
SVP 05♓20'16"
Obliquity 23°26'20"
⚷ Chiron 7♍52.9R
☽ Mean ☊ 29♏27.3

MARCH 1994 — LONGITUDE

Day	Sid.Time	☉	0 hr ☽	Noon ☽	True ☊	☿	♀	♂	♃	♄	♅	♆	♇
1 Tu	10 34 17	10♓10 12	20♎59 1	28♎20 30	26♏58.6	23♒38.6	20♓31.4	24♒55.2	14♏39.4	3♓43.6	24♑51.5	22♑32.0	28♏ 4.3
2 W	10 38 14	11 10 24	5♏38 34	12♏52 44	26R54.7	23R12.9	21 46.3	25 42.4	14R39.2	3 50.9	24 54.3	22 33.7	28R 4.3
3 Th	10 42 10	12 10 34	20 2 35	27 7 56	26D53.3	22 54.2	23 1.1	26 29.6	14 38.8	3 58.2	24 57.0	22 35.3	28 4.3
4 F	10 46 7	13 10 43	4♐ 8 39	11♐ 4 48	26R53.2	22 42.6	24 15.9	27 16.7	14 38.3	4 5.4	24 59.6	22 36.9	28 4.2
5 Sa	10 50 3	14 10 51	17 56 27	24 43 46	26 53.3	22D37.7	25 30.7	28 3.9	14 37.5	4 12.6	25 2.3	22 38.5	28 4.1
6 Su	10 54 0	15 10 57	1♑26 59	8♑ 6 17	26 52.2	22 39.4	26 45.5	28 51.1	14 36.6	4 19.9	25 4.8	22 40.1	28 4.0
7 M	10 57 56	16 11 1	14 41 56	21 14 7	26 49.0	22 47.2	28 0.3	29 38.3	14 35.5	4 27.1	25 7.4	22 41.6	28 3.8
8 Tu	11 1 53	17 11 4	27 43 3	4♒ 8 54	26 43.1	23 0.9	29 15.0	0♓25.5	14 34.2	4 34.3	25 9.9	22 43.2	28 3.6
9 W	11 5 50	18 11 5	10♒31 49	16 51 56	26 34.3	23 20.1	0♈29.7	1 12.7	14 32.7	4 41.4	25 12.4	22 44.7	28 3.3
10 Th	11 9 46	19 11 4	23 9 19	29 24 4	26 23.4	23 44.6	1 44.4	1 59.9	14 31.0	4 48.6	25 14.9	22 46.1	28 3.1
11 F	11 13 43	20 11 2	5♓36 15	11♓45 55	26 11.0	24 13.9	2 59.0	2 47.1	14 29.2	4 55.8	25 17.3	22 47.6	28 2.8
12 Sa	11 17 39	21 10 58	17 53 9	23 58 2	25 58.5	24 47.7	4 13.7	3 34.3	14 27.1	5 2.9	25 19.6	22 49.0	28 2.4
13 Su	11 21 36	22 10 51	0♈ 0 41	6♈ 1 13	25 46.8	25 25.8	5 28.3	4 21.5	14 24.9	5 10.0	25 22.0	22 50.4	28 2.0
14 M	11 25 32	23 10 43	11 59 50	17 56 45	25 36.9	26 7.9	6 42.9	5 8.7	14 22.4	5 17.1	25 24.3	22 51.7	28 1.6
15 Tu	11 29 29	24 10 33	23 52 13	29 46 33	25 29.6	26 53.7	7 57.4	5 55.8	14 19.8	5 24.1	25 26.5	22 53.0	28 1.1
16 W	11 33 25	25 10 20	5♉40 8	11♉33 24	25 24.9	27 42.9	9 12.0	6 43.0	14 17.1	5 31.1	25 28.7	22 54.3	28 0.7
17 Th	11 37 22	26 10 6	17 26 47	23 20 49	25D22.7	28 35.4	10 26.5	7 30.2	14 14.1	5 38.2	25 30.9	22 55.6	28 0.1
18 F	11 41 18	27 9 49	29 16 3	5♊13 6	25 22.4	29 31.0	11 41.0	8 17.3	14 11.0	5 45.1	25 33.0	22 56.9	27 59.6
19 Sa	11 45 15	28 9 31	11♊12 35	17 15 8	25 23.2	0♓29.4	12 55.4	9 4.5	14 7.7	5 52.1	25 35.1	22 58.1	27 59.0
20 Su	11 49 12	29 9 10	23 21 26	29 32 8	25R24.0	1 30.6	14 9.8	9 51.6	14 4.2	5 59.0	25 37.2	22 59.3	27 58.4
21 M	11 53 8	0♈ 8 46	5♋47 54	12♋ 9 19	25 24.0	2 34.2	15 24.2	10 38.7	14 0.5	6 5.9	25 39.2	23 0.4	27 57.8
22 Tu	11 57 5	1 8 21	18 36 58	25 11 20	25 22.3	3 40.4	16 38.6	11 25.8	13 56.7	6 12.8	25 41.1	23 1.6	27 57.1
23 W	12 1 1	2 7 53	1♌52 46	8♌41 31	25 18.6	4 48.7	17 52.9	12 12.9	13 52.7	6 19.6	25 43.0	23 2.7	27 56.4
24 Th	12 4 58	3 7 23	15 37 42	22 41 11	25 12.9	5 59.3	19 7.2	13 0.0	13 48.6	6 26.4	25 44.9	23 3.7	27 55.6
25 F	12 8 54	4 6 50	29 51 42	7♍ 8 45	25 5.6	7 12.0	20 21.4	13 47.1	13 44.2	6 33.2	25 46.7	23 4.8	27 54.9
26 Sa	12 12 51	5 6 15	14♍31 36	21 59 21	24 57.7	8 26.7	21 35.7	14 34.1	13 39.8	6 39.9	25 48.5	23 5.8	27 54.1
27 Su	12 16 47	6 5 38	29 30 55	7♎ 5 8	24 50.1	9 43.2	22 49.9	15 21.2	13 35.1	6 46.6	25 50.2	23 6.7	27 53.2
28 M	12 20 44	7 4 59	14♎40 41	22 16 17	24 43.7	11 1.7	24 4.0	16 8.2	13 30.3	6 53.3	25 51.9	23 7.7	27 52.4
29 Tu	12 24 41	8 4 18	29 50 41	7♏22 44	24 39.3	12 21.9	25 18.2	16 55.2	13 25.4	6 59.9	25 53.6	23 8.6	27 51.5
30 W	12 28 37	9 3 36	14♏51 22	22 15 43	24D37.2	13 43.9	26 32.3	17 42.2	13 20.3	7 6.5	25 55.2	23 9.5	27 50.6
31 Th	12 32 34	10 2 51	29 35 7	6♐49 2	24 36.9	15 7.5	27 46.3	18 29.2	13 15.1	7 13.0	25 56.7	23 10.3	27 49.6

APRIL 1994 — LONGITUDE

Day	Sid.Time	☉	0 hr ☽	Noon ☽	True ☊	☿	♀	♂	♃	♄	♅	♆	♇
1 F	12 36 30	11♈ 2 5	13♐57 10	20♐59 19	24♏37.8	16♓32.9	29♈ 0.4	19♓16.2	13♏ 9.7	7♓19.5	25♑58.2	23♑11.1	27♏48.7
2 Sa	12 40 27	12 1 17	27 55 28	4♑45 42	24 39.1	17 59.8	0♉14.4	20 3.1	13R 4.2	7 26.0	25 59.7	23 11.9	27R47.7
3 Su	12 44 23	13 0 27	11♑30 14	18 9 19	24R39.9	19 28.3	1 28.4	20 50.1	12 58.6	7 32.4	26 1.1	23 12.7	27 46.7
4 M	12 48 20	13 59 35	24 43 16	1♒12 24	24 39.3	20 58.4	2 42.3	21 37.0	12 52.8	7 38.8	26 2.5	23 13.4	27 45.6
5 Tu	12 52 16	14 58 42	7♒37 7	13 57 45	24 37.0	22 30.1	3 56.2	22 23.9	12 46.9	7 45.1	26 3.8	23 14.1	27 44.5
6 W	12 56 13	15 57 46	20 14 40	26 28 12	24 32.9	24 3.3	5 10.1	23 10.8	12 40.8	7 51.4	26 5.1	23 14.8	27 43.4
7 Th	13 0 10	16 56 49	2♓38 41	8♓46 25	24 27.4	25 38.0	6 24.0	23 57.6	12 34.7	7 57.7	26 6.3	23 15.4	27 42.3
8 F	13 4 6	17 55 50	14 51 41	20 54 44	24 20.9	27 14.2	7 37.8	24 44.5	12 28.4	8 3.9	26 7.5	23 16.0	27 41.2
9 Sa	13 8 3	18 54 50	26 55 49	2♈55 10	24 14.2	28 51.9	8 51.6	25 31.3	12 22.0	8 10.0	26 8.6	23 16.5	27 40.0
10 Su	13 11 59	19 53 47	8♈52 59	14 49 31	24 8.0	0♈31.2	10 5.4	26 18.1	12 15.5	8 16.1	26 9.7	23 17.1	27 38.8
11 M	13 15 56	20 52 42	20 44 58	26 39 35	24 2.8	2 12.0	11 19.1	27 4.8	12 8.9	8 22.1	26 10.7	23 17.6	27 37.5
12 Tu	13 19 52	21 51 36	2♉33 35	8♉27 15	23 59.2	3 54.2	12 32.8	27 51.6	12 2.2	8 28.1	26 11.7	23 18.0	27 36.3
13 W	13 23 49	22 50 27	14 20 52	20 14 45	23D57.2	5 38.1	13 46.4	28 38.3	11 55.4	8 34.0	26 12.6	23 18.5	27 35.0
14 Th	13 27 45	23 49 16	26 9 15	2♊ 4 44	23 56.8	7 23.4	15 0.1	29 25.0	11 48.5	8 39.9	26 13.5	23 18.8	27 33.7
15 F	13 31 42	24 48 4	8♊ 1 37	14 0 21	23 57.5	9 10.3	16 13.7	0♈11.6	11 41.5	8 45.8	26 14.3	23 19.2	27 32.4
16 Sa	13 35 39	25 46 49	20 1 25	26 5 18	23 59.1	10 58.8	17 27.2	0 58.2	11 34.5	8 51.5	26 15.1	23 19.5	27 31.1
17 Su	13 39 35	26 45 32	2♋12 32	8♋23 39	24 0.8	12 48.8	18 40.7	1 44.8	11 27.4	8 57.2	26 15.8	23 19.8	27 29.8
18 M	13 43 32	27 44 12	14 39 12	20 59 42	24 2.2	14 40.4	19 54.2	2 31.4	11 20.2	9 2.9	26 16.5	23 20.1	27 28.4
19 Tu	13 47 28	28 42 51	27 25 41	3♌57 37	24R 2.8	16 33.6	21 7.6	3 17.9	11 12.9	9 8.5	26 17.1	23 20.3	27 27.0
20 W	13 51 25	29 41 27	10♌35 53	17 20 50	24 2.4	18 28.3	22 21.0	4 4.4	11 5.6	9 14.0	26 17.7	23 20.5	27 25.6
21 Th	13 55 21	0♉40 1	24 12 40	1♍11 29	24 0.9	20 24.6	23 34.4	4 50.9	10 58.2	9 19.5	26 18.2	23 20.7	27 24.2
22 F	13 59 18	1 38 33	8♍17 11	15 29 33	23 58.6	22 22.4	24 47.7	5 37.3	10 50.7	9 24.9	26 18.6	23 20.8	27 22.7
23 Sa	14 3 14	2 37 2	22 48 8	0♎12 19	23 55.8	24 21.8	26 1.0	6 23.7	10 43.3	9 30.2	26 19.1	23 20.9	27 21.3
24 Su	14 7 11	3 35 30	7♎41 18	15 14 6	23 53.1	26 22.7	27 14.2	7 10.1	10 35.7	9 35.5	26 19.4	23 21.0	27 19.8
25 M	14 11 7	4 33 55	22 49 37	0♏26 37	23 50.8	28 25.0	28 27.4	7 56.4	10 28.2	9 40.7	26 19.8	23R21.0	27 18.3
26 Tu	14 15 4	5 32 19	8♏ 3 53	15 40 8	23 49.4	0♉28.7	29 40.5	8 42.7	10 20.6	9 45.9	26 20.0	23 21.0	27 16.8
27 W	14 19 1	6 30 41	23 14 9	0♐44 51	23D48.9	2 33.7	0♊53.6	9 28.9	10 13.0	9 50.9	26 20.3	23 21.0	27 15.3
28 Th	14 22 57	7 29 1	8♐11 14	15 32 30	23 49.3	4 39.9	2 6.7	10 15.1	10 5.4	9 56.0	26 20.4	23 20.9	27 13.8
29 F	14 26 54	8 27 19	22 47 59	29 57 13	23 50.2	6 47.1	3 19.7	11 1.3	9 57.7	10 0.9	26 20.5	23 20.8	27 12.2
30 Sa	14 30 50	9 25 36	6♑59 55	13♑55 56	23 51.3	8 55.3	4 32.7	11 47.5	9 50.1	10 5.8	26R20.6	23 20.7	27 10.7

Astro Data

	Dy Hr Mn
♇ R	1 10:00
☿ D	5 5:49
♀0N	10 21:16
☽0N	12 2:37
☽0S	26 7:24
☽0N	8 8:18
♄∠♆	10 4:14
☿0N	12 20:26
♂0N	17 20:26
☽0S	22 17:38
♆ R	25 10:37
♃△♄	28 17:56
♅ R	30 22:18

Planet Ingress

	Dy Hr Mn
♂ ♓	7 11:01
♀ ♈	8 14:28
☿ ♓	18 12:04
☉ ♈	20 20:28
♀ ♉	1 19:20
☿ ♈	9 16:30
♂ ♈	14 18:02
☉ ♉	20 7:36
☿ ♉	25 18:27
♀ ♊	26 6:24

Last Aspect / ☽ Ingress (March)

Last Aspect Dy Hr Mn		☽ Ingress Dy Hr Mn
1 6:46	♂ △	♏ 1 14:43
3 13:36	♇ ☌	♐ 3 16:54
5 19:03	♂ ✶	♑ 5 21:24
8 3:09	♀ ✶	♒ 8 4:15
10 9:24	♇ □	♓ 10 13:09
12 20:04	♇ △	♈ 12 23:59
15 6:35	☿ ✶	♉ 15 12:27
18 0:33	☿ □	♊ 18 1:29
20 12:14	☉ □	♋ 20 12:54
22 16:58	♇ △	♌ 22 20:39
24 20:46	♇ □	♍ 25 0:14
26 21:25	♇ ✶	♎ 27 0:46
28 17:43	♅ □	♏ 29 0:15
30 21:07	♇ ☌	♐ 31 0:41

Last Aspect / ☽ Ingress (April)

Last Aspect Dy Hr Mn		☽ Ingress Dy Hr Mn
1 9:35	♂ □	♑ 2 3:37
4 5:36	♇ ✶	♒ 4 9:45
6 14:24	♇ □	♓ 6 18:51
9 4:29	☿ ☌	♈ 9 6:09
11 11:02	♅ □	♉ 11 18:48
14 7:05	♂ ✶	♊ 14 7:48
16 12:23	☉ ✶	♋ 16 19:41
19 2:34	☉ □	♌ 19 4:45
21 5:30	♇ □	♍ 21 9:58
23 7:23	♇ ✶	♎ 23 11:40
25 10:11	☿ ☍	♏ 25 11:18
27 6:24	♇ ☌	♐ 27 10:48
28 3:32	♂ △	♑ 29 12:05

☽ Phases & Eclipses

Dy Hr Mn	
4 16:53	☽ 13♐53
12 7:05	● 21♓29
20 12:14	☽ 29♊40
27 11:10	○ 6♎33
3 2:55	☽ 13♑08
11 0:17	● 20♈53
19 2:34	☽ 28♋49
25 19:45	○ 5♏22

Astro Data

1 MARCH 1994
Julian Day # 34393
Delta T 59.2 sec
SVP 05♓20'13"
Obliquity 23°26'20"
⚷ Chiron 5♍47.7R
☽ Mean ☊ 27♏58.3

1 APRIL 1994
Julian Day # 34424
Delta T 59.2 sec
SVP 05♓20'10"
Obliquity 23°26'19"
⚷ Chiron 3♍40.1R
☽ Mean ☊ 26♏19.8

LONGITUDE — MAY 1994

Day	Sid.Time	☉	0 hr ☽	Noon ☽	True ☊	☿	♀	♂	♃	♄	♅	♆	♇
1 Su	14 34 47	10♉23 52	20♑45 18	27♑28 10	23♏52.3	11♉ 4.1	5♊45.6	12♈33.6	9♏42.4	10♓10.6	26♑20.6	23♑20.5	27♏ 9.1
2 M	14 38 43	11 22 5	4♒ 4 45	10♒35 23	23R52.9	13 13.5	6 58.6	13 19.7	9R34.8	10 15.3	26R20.6	23R20.3	27R 7.5
3 Tu	14 42 40	12 20 18	17 0 29	23 20 27	23 53.0	15 23.1	8 11.4	14 5.7	9 27.1	10 20.0	26 20.5	23 20.1	27 5.9
4 W	14 46 37	13 18 29	29 35 47	5♓46 56	23 52.5	17 32.7	9 24.2	14 51.8	9 19.5	10 24.6	26 20.4	23 19.8	27 4.3
5 Th	14 50 33	14 16 38	11♓54 24	17 58 40	23 51.7	19 42.1	10 37.0	15 37.7	9 11.9	10 29.1	26 20.2	23 19.5	27 2.7
6 F	14 54 30	15 14 46	24 0 12	29 59 26	23 50.5	21 50.9	11 49.8	16 23.6	9 4.3	10 33.5	26 20.0	23 19.2	27 1.1
7 Sa	14 58 26	16 12 53	5♈56 48	11♈52 42	23 49.4	23 58.8	13 2.5	17 9.5	8 56.7	10 37.9	26 19.7	23 18.9	26 59.5
8 Su	15 2 23	17 10 58	17 47 32	23 41 38	23 48.4	26 5.6	14 15.2	17 55.4	8 49.1	10 42.2	26 19.4	23 18.5	26 57.9
9 M	15 6 19	18 9 1	29 35 21	5♉29 0	23 47.7	28 11.0	15 27.8	18 41.2	8 41.6	10 46.4	26 19.0	23 18.0	26 56.2
10 Tu	15 10 16	19 7 3	11♉22 53	17 17 17	23 47.3	0♊14.7	16 40.4	19 26.9	8 34.2	10 50.5	26 18.6	23 17.6	26 54.6
11 W	15 14 12	20 5 4	23 12 28	29 8 43	23D47.2	2 16.3	17 52.9	20 12.7	8 26.8	10 54.6	26 18.1	23 17.1	26 52.9
12 Th	15 18 9	21 3 3	5♊ 6 19	11♊ 5 31	23 47.3	4 15.8	19 5.4	20 58.3	8 19.4	10 58.6	26 17.6	23 16.6	26 51.3
13 F	15 22 5	22 1 0	17 6 37	23 9 53	23 47.4	6 12.9	20 17.8	21 44.0	8 12.1	11 2.4	26 17.0	23 16.1	26 49.6
14 Sa	15 26 2	22 58 56	29 15 39	5♋24 12	23R47.6	8 7.4	21 30.2	22 29.5	8 4.9	11 6.3	26 16.4	23 15.5	26 48.0
15 Su	15 29 59	23 56 50	11♋35 52	17 51 0	23 47.6	9 59.1	22 42.6	23 15.1	7 57.8	11 10.0	26 15.7	23 14.9	26 46.3
16 M	15 33 55	24 54 42	24 9 55	0♌32 59	23 47.6	11 47.9	23 54.9	24 0.6	7 50.7	11 13.6	26 15.0	23 14.3	26 44.6
17 Tu	15 37 52	25 52 33	7♌ 0 26	13 32 53	23 47.4	13 33.7	25 7.2	24 46.0	7 43.7	11 17.2	26 14.2	23 13.6	26 43.0
18 W	15 41 48	26 50 21	20 10 20	26 53 8	23D47.3	15 16.4	26 19.4	25 31.4	7 36.8	11 20.7	26 13.4	23 12.9	26 41.3
19 Th	15 45 45	27 48 9	3♍41 29	10♍35 31	23 47.3	16 56.0	27 31.5	26 16.7	7 29.9	11 24.0	26 12.6	23 12.2	26 39.6
20 F	15 49 41	28 45 54	17 35 17	24 40 40	23 47.5	18 32.2	28 43.6	27 2.0	7 23.2	11 27.3	26 11.7	23 11.4	26 38.0
21 Sa	15 53 38	29 43 38	1♎51 31	9♎ 7 29	23 47.9	20 5.2	29 55.7	27 47.2	7 16.5	11 30.5	26 10.7	23 10.7	26 36.3
22 Su	15 57 34	0♊41 20	16 28 6	23 52 44	23 48.5	21 34.8	1♋ 7.7	28 32.4	7 10.0	11 33.7	26 9.7	23 9.9	26 34.7
23 M	16 1 31	1 39 0	1♏20 38	8♏50 55	23 49.1	23 1.0	2 19.6	29 17.5	7 3.6	11 36.7	26 8.7	23 9.0	26 33.0
24 Tu	16 5 28	2 36 40	16 22 36	23 54 37	23R49.4	24 23.8	3 31.5	0♉ 2.6	6 57.3	11 39.7	26 7.6	23 8.2	26 31.3
25 W	16 9 24	3 34 18	1♐25 53	8♐55 19	23 49.4	25 43.0	4 43.3	0 47.6	6 51.0	11 42.5	26 6.5	23 7.3	26 29.7
26 Th	16 13 21	4 31 54	16 21 51	23 44 31	23 48.9	26 58.8	5 55.1	1 32.6	6 45.0	11 45.3	26 5.3	23 6.4	26 28.0
27 F	16 17 17	5 29 30	1♑ 2 28	8♑15 0	23 47.9	28 10.9	7 6.8	2 17.6	6 39.0	11 48.0	26 4.1	23 5.5	26 26.4
28 Sa	16 21 14	6 27 4	15 21 31	22 21 38	23 46.4	29 19.4	8 18.5	3 2.4	6 33.1	11 50.6	26 2.9	23 4.5	26 24.8
29 Su	16 25 10	7 24 38	29 15 8	6♒ 1 54	23 44.8	0♋24.2	9 30.1	3 47.3	6 27.4	11 53.1	26 1.6	23 3.5	26 23.1
30 M	16 29 7	8 22 10	12♒42 2	19 15 41	23 43.3	1 25.3	10 41.6	4 32.1	6 21.8	11 55.5	26 0.3	23 2.5	26 21.5
31 Tu	16 33 4	9 19 42	25 43 11	2♓ 4 53	23 42.2	2 22.5	11 53.1	5 16.8	6 16.4	11 57.8	25 58.9	23 1.5	26 19.9

LONGITUDE — JUNE 1994

Day	Sid.Time	☉	0 hr ☽	Noon ☽	True ☊	☿	♀	♂	♃	♄	♅	♆	♇
1 W	16 37 0	10♊17 13	8♓21 17	14♓32 52	23♏41.7	3♋15.8	13♋ 4.6	6♉ 1.5	6♏11.0	11♓60.0	25♑57.5	23♑ 0.4	26♏18.3
2 Th	16 40 57	11 14 43	20 40 11	26 43 49	23D41.9	4 5.2	14 15.9	6 46.1	6R 5.8	12 2.1	25R56.1	22R59.3	26R16.7
3 F	16 44 53	12 12 12	2♈44 21	8♈42 22	23 42.8	4 50.5	15 27.3	7 30.7	6 0.8	12 4.1	25 54.6	22 58.2	26 15.1
4 Sa	16 48 50	13 9 41	14 38 26	20 33 7	23 44.3	5 31.7	16 38.5	8 15.2	5 55.9	12 6.1	25 53.0	22 57.1	26 13.5
5 Su	16 52 46	14 7 8	26 26 56	2♉20 25	23 45.8	6 8.6	17 49.7	8 59.6	5 51.1	12 7.9	25 51.5	22 55.9	26 12.0
6 M	16 56 43	15 4 36	8♉14 1	14 8 12	23 47.2	6 41.3	19 0.9	9 44.0	5 46.5	12 9.6	25 49.9	22 54.8	26 10.4
7 Tu	17 0 39	16 2 2	20 3 21	25 59 52	23R47.9	7 9.6	20 12.0	10 28.4	5 42.1	12 11.3	25 48.2	22 53.6	26 8.9
8 W	17 4 36	16 59 27	1♊58 3	7♊58 14	23 47.7	7 33.4	21 23.0	11 12.7	5 37.8	12 12.8	25 46.6	22 52.4	26 7.3
9 Th	17 8 33	17 56 52	14 0 39	20 5 33	23 46.4	7 52.8	22 34.0	11 56.9	5 33.7	12 14.3	25 44.9	22 51.1	26 5.8
10 F	17 12 29	18 54 16	26 13 7	2♋23 31	23 43.8	8 7.6	23 44.9	12 41.1	5 29.7	12 15.6	25 43.1	22 49.9	26 4.3
11 Sa	17 16 26	19 51 40	8♋36 55	14 53 25	23 40.3	8 17.8	24 55.7	13 25.2	5 25.9	12 16.9	25 41.3	22 48.6	26 2.8
12 Su	17 20 22	20 49 2	21 13 9	27 36 13	23 36.1	8R23.4	26 6.4	14 9.3	5 22.3	12 18.0	25 39.5	22 47.3	26 1.3
13 M	17 24 19	21 46 24	4♌ 2 42	10♌32 41	23 31.7	8 24.5	27 17.1	14 53.3	5 18.8	12 19.1	25 37.7	22 46.0	25 59.9
14 Tu	17 28 15	22 43 44	17 6 16	23 43 32	23 27.7	8 21.1	28 27.8	15 37.2	5 15.5	12 20.1	25 35.8	22 44.6	25 58.4
15 W	17 32 12	23 41 4	0♍24 33	7♍ 9 23	23 24.7	8 13.3	29 38.3	16 21.1	5 12.4	12 20.9	25 33.9	22 43.3	25 57.0
16 Th	17 36 8	24 38 23	13 58 6	20 50 44	23D22.9	8 1.3	0♌48.8	17 4.9	5 9.4	12 21.7	25 32.0	22 41.9	25 55.6
17 F	17 40 5	25 35 40	27 47 17	4♎47 44	23 22.5	7 45.2	1 59.2	17 48.6	5 6.6	12 22.3	25 30.0	22 40.5	25 54.2
18 Sa	17 44 2	26 32 57	11♎51 59	18 59 53	23 23.2	7 25.3	3 9.5	18 32.3	5 4.0	12 22.9	25 28.0	22 39.1	25 52.8
19 Su	17 47 58	27 30 13	26 11 12	3♏25 36	23 24.5	7 1.9	4 19.7	19 15.9	5 1.6	12 23.3	25 26.0	22 37.7	25 51.5
20 M	17 51 55	28 27 29	10♏42 42	18 1 57	23R25.8	6 35.4	5 29.9	19 59.4	4 59.3	12 23.7	25 24.0	22 36.3	25 50.1
21 Tu	17 55 51	29 24 43	25 22 45	2♐44 24	23 26.2	6 6.2	6 39.9	20 42.9	4 57.2	12 24.0	25 21.9	22 34.8	25 48.8
22 W	17 59 48	0♋21 57	10♐ 6 5	17 27 0	23 25.2	5 34.7	7 49.9	21 26.4	4 55.3	12 24.1	25 19.8	22 33.4	25 47.5
23 Th	18 3 44	1 19 11	24 46 15	2♑ 2 59	23 22.5	5 1.4	8 59.8	22 9.7	4 53.6	12R24.2	25 17.7	22 31.9	25 46.3
24 F	18 7 41	2 16 24	9♑16 22	16 25 38	23 18.1	4 27.0	10 9.6	22 53.1	4 52.1	12 24.2	25 15.6	22 30.4	25 45.0
25 Sa	18 11 37	3 13 37	23 30 6	0♒29 12	23 12.4	3 51.9	11 19.3	23 36.3	4 50.7	12 24.0	25 13.4	22 28.9	25 43.8
26 Su	18 15 34	4 10 49	7♒22 32	14 9 48	23 6.0	3 16.8	12 28.9	24 19.5	4 49.5	12 23.8	25 11.2	22 27.4	25 42.6
27 M	18 19 31	5 8 2	20 50 52	27 25 45	22 59.8	2 42.4	13 38.4	25 2.6	4 48.5	12 23.5	25 9.0	22 25.9	25 41.4
28 Tu	18 23 27	6 5 14	3♓54 34	10♓17 35	22 54.5	2 9.1	14 47.9	25 45.7	4 47.6	12 23.0	25 6.8	22 24.4	25 40.2
29 W	18 27 24	7 2 26	16 35 8	22 47 42	22 50.7	1 37.6	15 57.2	26 28.6	4 47.0	12 22.5	25 4.6	22 22.8	25 39.1
30 Th	18 31 20	7 59 39	28 55 45	4♈59 53	22D48.6	1 8.4	17 6.5	27 11.6	4 46.5	12 21.9	25 2.3	22 21.3	25 38.0

Astro Data Dy Hr Mn	Planet Ingress Dy Hr Mn	Last Aspect Dy Hr Mn	☽ Ingress Dy Hr Mn	Last Aspect Dy Hr Mn	☽ Ingress Dy Hr Mn	☽ Phases & Eclipses Dy Hr Mn	Astro Data
☽0N 5 13:44	☿ ♊ 9 21:08	1 11:24 ♇ ✶	♒ 1 16:34	2 11:05 ♇ △	♈ 2 18:31	2 14:32 ☽ 11♒57	1 MAY 1994
♄∠♅ 16 7:38	☉ ♊ 21 6:48	3 19:09 ♇ □	♓ 4 0:47	4 22:48 ♅ □	♉ 5 7:14	10 17:07 ● 19♉48	Julian Day # 34454
☽0S 20 2:06	♀ ♋ 21 1:26	6 6:01 ♇ △	♈ 6 12:01	7 12:17 ♇ ☍	♊ 7 20:03	10 17:11:26 ✔ A 6'14"	Delta T 59.3 sec
	♂ ♉ 23 22:37	8 17:20 ♅ □	♉ 9 0:50	9 8:26 ☉ ☌	♋ 10 7:22	18 12:50 ☽ 27♌21	SVP 05♓20'07"
☽0N 1 20:29	☿ ♋ 28 14:52	11 7:25 ♇ ☍	♊ 11 13:43	12 10:08 ♀ ☌	♌ 12 16:29	25 3:39 ○ 3♐43	Obliquity 23°26'19"
☿ R 12 17:49		13 9:47 ♂ ✶	♋ 14 1:27	14 16:01 ♇ □	♍ 14 23:16	25 3:30 ☍ P 0.243	⚷ Chiron 2♍49.6R
☽0S 16 8:52	♀ ♌ 15 7:23	16 4:51 ♇ △	♌ 16 10:58	16 20:46 ♇ ✶	♎ 17 3:48		☽ Mean ☊ 24♏44.4
♄ R 23 3:57	☉ ♋ 21 14:48	18 12:50 ☉ □	♍ 18 17:31	19 2:21 ☉ △	♏ 19 6:20	1 4:02 ☽ 10♓27	
☽0N 29 5:05		20 20:30 ♀ □	♎ 20 20:54	21 0:42 ♇ ☌	♐ 21 7:32	9 8:26 ● 18♊17	1 JUNE 1994
		22 20:32 ♂ ☍	♏ 22 21:51	22 3:45 ♄ □	♑ 23 8:37	16 19:57 ☽ 25♍26	Julian Day # 34485
		24 16:08 ♇ ☌	♐ 24 21:43	25 3:48 ♇ ✶	♒ 25 11:10	23 11:33 ○ 1♑47	Delta T 59.3 sec
		26 18:52 ☿ ☍	♑ 26 22:17	27 8:48 ♇ □	♓ 27 16:44	30 19:31 ☽ 8♈46	SVP 05♓20'03"
		28 19:00 ♇ ✶	♒ 29 1:19	29 20:23 ♂ ✶	♈ 30 2:07		Obliquity 23°26'18"
		31 1:09 ♇ □	♓ 31 8:03				⚷ Chiron 3♍40.0
							☽ Mean ☊ 23♏06.0

JULY 1994 — LONGITUDE

Day	Sid.Time	☉	0 hr ☽	Noon ☽	True ☊	☿	♀	♂	♃	♄	♅	♆	♇
1 F	18 35 17	8♋56 51	11♈ 0 42	16♈58 50	22♏48.2	0♋42.0	18♌15.6	27♉54.4	4♏46.2	12♓21.1	25♑ 0.1	22♑19.7	25♏36.9
2 Sa	18 39 13	9 54 4	22 54 56	28 49 38	22 48.9	0R18.9	19 24.7	28 37.2	4D46.1	12R20.3	24R57.8	22R18.1	25R35.8
3 Su	18 43 10	10 51 16	4♉43 37	10♉37 28	22 50.2	29♊59.5	20 33.6	29 20.0	4 46.2	12 19.4	24 55.5	22 16.5	25 34.8
4 M	18 47 6	11 48 29	16 31 50	22 27 15	22R51.3	29 44.1	21 42.5	0♊ 2.7	4 46.4	12 18.4	24 53.1	22 15.0	25 33.7
5 Tu	18 51 3	12 45 42	28 24 17	4♊23 24	22 51.3	29 33.1	22 51.2	0 45.3	4 46.8	12 17.3	24 50.8	22 13.4	25 32.7
6 W	18 55 0	13 42 56	10♊25 3	16 29 37	22 49.6	29D26.7	23 59.9	1 27.8	4 47.4	12 16.0	24 48.5	22 11.8	25 31.8
7 Th	18 58 56	14 40 9	22 37 25	28 48 43	22 45.8	29 25.2	25 8.4	2 10.3	4 48.2	12 14.7	24 46.1	22 10.2	25 30.8
8 F	19 2 53	15 37 23	5♋ 3 41	11♋22 27	22 39.8	29 28.6	26 16.8	2 52.7	4 49.2	12 13.3	24 43.8	22 8.6	25 29.9
9 Sa	19 6 49	16 34 37	17 45 4	24 11 32	22 31.9	29 37.0	27 25.2	3 35.0	4 50.3	12 11.8	24 41.4	22 7.0	25 29.0
10 Su	19 10 46	17 31 51	0♌41 47	7♌15 41	22 22.7	29 50.7	28 33.4	4 17.3	4 51.7	12 10.2	24 39.0	22 5.3	25 28.2
11 M	19 14 42	18 29 5	13 53 4	20 33 46	22 13.2	0♋ 9.5	29 41.4	4 59.5	4 53.2	12 8.6	24 36.6	22 3.7	25 27.4
12 Tu	19 18 39	19 26 19	27 17 34	4♍ 4 15	22 4.4	0 33.6	0♍49.4	5 41.6	4 54.8	12 6.8	24 34.2	22 2.1	25 26.6
13 W	19 22 35	20 23 33	10♍53 36	17 45 26	21 57.1	1 3.0	1 57.2	6 23.6	4 56.7	12 4.9	24 31.8	22 0.5	25 25.8
14 Th	19 26 32	21 20 47	24 39 33	1♎35 48	21 52.0	1 37.5	3 4.9	7 5.6	4 58.7	12 2.9	24 29.4	21 58.9	25 25.1
15 F	19 30 29	22 18 1	8♎34 3	15 34 10	21 49.3	2 17.3	4 12.5	7 47.5	5 0.9	12 0.9	24 27.0	21 57.2	25 24.3
16 Sa	19 34 25	23 15 15	22 36 3	29 39 35	21D48.5	3 2.2	5 20.0	8 29.3	5 3.3	11 58.7	24 24.6	21 55.6	25 23.7
17 Su	19 38 22	24 12 29	6♏44 38	13♏51 4	21 48.8	3 52.2	6 27.3	9 11.1	5 5.9	11 56.5	24 22.2	21 54.0	25 23.0
18 M	19 42 18	25 9 44	20 58 40	28 7 14	21R49.3	4 47.3	7 34.4	9 52.7	5 8.6	11 54.2	24 19.8	21 52.4	25 22.4
19 Tu	19 46 15	26 6 58	5♐16 25	12♐25 53	21 48.6	5 47.4	8 41.4	10 34.3	5 11.5	11 51.8	24 17.4	21 50.7	25 21.8
20 W	19 50 11	27 4 13	19 35 11	26 43 47	21 45.9	6 52.4	9 48.3	11 15.9	5 14.6	11 49.3	24 15.0	21 49.1	25 21.2
21 Th	19 54 8	28 1 28	3♑51 10	10♑56 43	21 40.7	8 2.2	10 55.0	11 57.3	5 17.8	11 46.8	24 12.6	21 47.5	25 20.7
22 F	19 58 4	28 58 43	17 59 49	24 59 51	21 32.9	9 16.8	12 1.5	12 38.7	5 21.2	11 44.1	24 10.2	21 45.9	25 20.2
23 Sa	20 2 1	29 55 59	1♒56 16	8♒48 31	21 23.1	10 36.1	13 7.9	13 20.0	5 24.8	11 41.4	24 7.8	21 44.3	25 19.8
24 Su	20 5 58	0♌53 15	15 36 11	22 18 54	21 12.2	11 60.0	14 14.1	14 1.3	5 28.5	11 38.6	24 5.4	21 42.7	25 19.3
25 M	20 9 54	1 50 32	28 56 25	5♓28 38	21 1.3	13 28.2	15 20.1	14 42.4	5 32.4	11 35.7	24 3.0	21 41.1	25 18.9
26 Tu	20 13 51	2 47 50	11♓55 33	18 17 15	20 51.5	15 0.8	16 26.0	15 23.5	5 36.4	11 32.7	24 0.6	21 39.5	25 18.5
27 W	20 17 47	3 45 8	24 33 58	0♈46 0	20 43.7	16 37.5	17 31.6	16 4.5	5 40.7	11 29.7	23 58.2	21 37.9	25 18.2
28 Th	20 21 44	4 42 28	6♈53 48	12 57 49	20 38.2	18 18.0	18 37.2	16 45.5	5 45.0	11 26.5	23 55.9	21 36.4	25 17.9
29 F	20 25 40	5 39 48	18 58 36	24 56 45	20 35.1	20 2.3	19 42.5	17 26.4	5 49.6	11 23.3	23 53.5	21 34.8	25 17.6
30 Sa	20 29 37	6 37 10	0♉52 55	6♉47 45	20D33.9	21 50.0	20 47.6	18 7.2	5 54.2	11 20.1	23 51.2	21 33.2	25 17.4
31 Su	20 33 33	7 34 32	12 41 55	18 36 8	20R33.9	23 40.9	21 52.6	18 47.9	5 59.1	11 16.7	23 48.9	21 31.7	25 17.2

AUGUST 1994 — LONGITUDE

Day	Sid.Time	☉	0 hr ☽	Noon ☽	True ☊	☿	♀	♂	♃	♄	♅	♆	♇
1 M	20 37 30	8♌31 56	24♉31 4	0♊27 24	20♏33.9	25♋34.6	22♍57.3	19♊28.5	6♏ 4.1	11♓13.3	23♑46.6	21♑30.2	25♏17.0
2 Tu	20 41 27	9 29 21	6♊25 44	12 26 43	20R33.0	27 30.9	24 1.9	20 9.1	6 9.3	11R 9.9	23R44.3	21R28.6	25R16.9
3 W	20 45 23	10 26 47	18 30 54	24 38 46	20 30.2	29 29.3	25 6.2	20 49.6	6 14.6	11 6.3	23 42.0	21 27.1	25 16.7
4 Th	20 49 20	11 24 14	0♋50 46	7♋ 7 14	20 25.0	1♌29.6	26 10.4	21 30.0	6 20.0	11 2.7	23 39.7	21 25.6	25 16.7
5 F	20 53 16	12 21 42	13 28 28	19 54 35	20 17.2	3 31.3	27 14.3	22 10.3	6 25.6	10 59.1	23 37.5	21 24.1	25D16.6
6 Sa	20 57 13	13 19 11	26 25 41	3♌ 1 42	20 7.0	5 34.1	28 18.0	22 50.6	6 31.4	10 55.3	23 35.3	21 22.6	25 16.6
7 Su	21 1 9	14 16 41	9♌42 29	16 27 46	19 55.2	7 37.8	29 21.5	23 30.8	6 37.3	10 51.6	23 33.0	21 21.2	25 16.7
8 M	21 5 6	15 14 12	23 17 12	0♍10 21	19 42.9	9 41.8	0♎24.7	24 10.8	6 43.4	10 47.7	23 30.9	21 19.7	25 16.7
9 Tu	21 9 2	16 11 45	7♍ 6 45	14 5 53	19 31.4	11 46.1	1 27.7	24 50.8	6 49.6	10 43.8	23 28.7	21 18.3	25 16.8
10 W	21 12 59	17 9 18	21 7 12	28 10 12	19 21.7	13 50.2	2 30.5	25 30.8	6 55.9	10 39.9	23 26.5	21 16.8	25 16.9
11 Th	21 16 56	18 6 52	5♎14 23	12♎19 19	19 14.7	15 54.0	3 33.0	26 10.6	7 2.4	10 35.9	23 24.4	21 15.4	25 17.1
12 F	21 20 52	19 4 27	19 24 36	26 29 55	19 10.4	17 57.2	4 35.2	26 50.3	7 9.0	10 31.8	23 22.3	21 14.0	25 17.3
13 Sa	21 24 49	20 2 3	3♏35 0	10♏39 39	19 8.6	19 59.6	5 37.1	27 30.0	7 15.8	10 27.7	23 20.2	21 12.7	25 17.5
14 Su	21 28 45	20 59 40	17 43 44	24 47 6	19 8.3	22 1.2	6 38.8	28 9.6	7 22.6	10 23.6	23 18.2	21 11.3	25 17.8
15 M	21 32 42	21 57 17	1♐49 40	8♐51 19	19 8.1	24 1.8	7 40.2	28 49.1	7 29.7	10 19.4	23 16.2	21 9.9	25 18.1
16 Tu	21 36 38	22 54 56	15 51 58	22 51 28	19 7.0	26 1.2	8 41.2	29 28.5	7 36.8	10 15.1	23 14.2	21 8.6	25 18.4
17 W	21 40 35	23 52 36	29 49 40	6♑46 20	19 3.7	27 59.5	9 42.0	0♋ 7.8	7 44.1	10 10.9	23 12.2	21 7.3	25 18.8
18 Th	21 44 31	24 50 17	13♑41 15	20 34 8	18 57.6	29 56.4	10 42.4	0 47.0	7 51.6	10 6.6	23 10.3	21 6.0	25 19.2
19 F	21 48 28	25 47 59	27 24 39	4♒12 30	18 48.9	1♍52.1	11 42.5	1 26.1	7 59.1	10 2.3	23 8.4	21 4.8	25 19.6
20 Sa	21 52 25	26 45 42	10♒57 19	17 38 48	18 37.9	3 46.5	12 42.2	2 5.2	8 6.8	9 57.9	23 6.5	21 3.5	25 20.1
21 Su	21 56 21	27 43 26	24 16 38	0♓50 35	18 25.6	5 39.4	13 41.6	2 44.2	8 14.6	9 53.5	23 4.6	21 2.3	25 20.6
22 M	22 0 18	28 41 12	7♓20 27	13 46 6	18 13.3	7 31.1	14 40.6	3 23.0	8 22.5	9 49.1	23 2.8	21 1.1	25 21.1
23 Tu	22 4 14	29 38 59	20 7 30	26 24 41	18 2.1	9 21.3	15 39.2	4 1.8	8 30.6	9 44.6	23 1.0	20 59.9	25 21.7
24 W	22 8 11	0♍36 47	2♈37 47	8♈46 59	17 52.9	11 10.2	16 37.4	4 40.5	8 38.7	9 40.2	22 59.3	20 58.7	25 22.3
25 Th	22 12 7	1 34 37	14 52 35	20 54 58	17 46.2	12 57.7	17 35.2	5 19.1	8 47.0	9 35.7	22 57.6	20 57.6	25 22.9
26 F	22 16 4	2 32 29	26 54 32	2♉51 49	17 42.2	14 43.8	18 32.6	5 57.7	8 55.4	9 31.1	22 55.9	20 56.5	25 23.6
27 Sa	22 20 0	3 30 23	8♉47 20	14 41 42	17D40.4	16 28.7	19 29.6	6 36.1	9 3.9	9 26.6	22 54.2	20 55.4	25 24.3
28 Su	22 23 57	4 28 18	20 35 33	26 29 32	17 40.1	18 12.2	20 26.2	7 14.4	9 12.6	9 22.1	22 52.6	20 54.3	25 25.0
29 M	22 27 54	5 26 15	2♊24 20	8♊20 38	17R40.3	19 54.3	21 22.2	7 52.7	9 21.3	9 17.5	22 51.0	20 53.3	25 25.8
30 Tu	22 31 50	6 24 15	14 19 7	20 20 28	17 40.1	21 35.2	22 17.9	8 30.8	9 30.2	9 13.0	22 49.5	20 52.2	25 26.6
31 W	22 35 47	7 22 15	26 25 20	2♋34 18	17 38.4	23 14.8	23 13.0	9 8.9	9 39.2	9 8.4	22 48.0	20 51.2	25 27.4

Astro Data Dy Hr Mn	Planet Ingress Dy Hr Mn	Last Aspect Dy Hr Mn	☽ Ingress Dy Hr Mn	Last Aspect Dy Hr Mn	☽ Ingress Dy Hr Mn	☽ Phases & Eclipses Dy Hr Mn	Astro Data
♃ D 2 3:33	☿ ♊ 2 23:18	2 4:08 ♅ □	♉ 2 14:23	1 2:34 ☿ ⚹	♊ 1 11:05	8 21:37 ● 16♋29	1 JULY 1994
☿ D 6 19:43	♂ ♊ 3 22:30	4 18:15 ♇ ☍	♊ 5 3:12	3 14:07 ♀ □	♋ 3 22:22	16 1:12 ☽ 23♎18	Julian Day # 34515
☽0S 13 15:03	☿ ♋ 10 12:41	7 13:13 ☿ ☌	♋ 7 14:17	6 3:43 ♀ ⚹	♌ 6 6:31	22 20:16 ○ 29♑47	Delta T 59.3 sec
☽0N 26 14:44	♀ ♍ 11 6:33	9 14:23 ♇ △	♌ 9 22:43	8 3:29 ♇ □	♍ 8 11:42	30 12:40 ☽ 7♉07	SVP 05♓19'58"
	☉ ♌ 23 1:41	11 20:43 ♇ □	♍ 12 4:48	10 7:51 ♂ □	♎ 10 15:07		Obliquity 23°26'18"
♇ D 5 17:07		14 1:19 ♇ ⚹	♎ 14 9:15	12 13:12 ♂ △	♏ 12 17:56	7 8:45 ● 14♌38	⚷ Chiron 5♍59.6
♀0S 7 2:56	☿ ♌ 3 6:09	16 3:04 ♅ □	♏ 16 12:35	14 12:52 ♇ ☌	♐ 14 20:53	14 5:57 ☽ 21♏14	☽ Mean ☊ 21♏30.7
☽0S 9 22:01	♀ ♎ 7 14:36	18 7:32 ☉ △	♐ 18 15:09	16 20:19 ☿ △	♑ 17 0:18	21 6:47 ○ 27♒60	
☽0N 22 23:57	♂ ♋ 16 19:15	19 11:01 ♄ □	♑ 20 17:30	18 20:20 ♇ ⚹	♒ 19 4:34	29 6:41 ☽ 5♊42	1 AUGUST 1994
♃△♄ 28 17:10	☿ ♍ 18 0:44	22 20:16 ☉ ☍	♒ 22 20:38	21 6:47 ☉ ☍	♓ 21 10:27		Julian Day # 34546
	☉ ♍ 23 8:44	24 17:25 ♇ □	♓ 25 1:56	23 10:00 ♇ △	♈ 23 18:55		Delta T 59.4 sec
		27 1:25 ♇ △	♈ 27 10:30	25 16:03 ♅ □	♉ 26 6:13		SVP 05♓19'53"
		29 9:51 ♅ □	♉ 29 22:13	28 9:49 ♇ ☍	♊ 28 19:07		Obliquity 23°26'18"
				30 17:10 ♀ △	♋ 31 7:00		⚷ Chiron 9♍32.7
							☽ Mean ☊ 19♏52.2

LONGITUDE SEPTEMBER 1994

Day	Sid.Time	☉	0 hr ☽	Noon ☽	True ☊	☿	♀	♂	♃	♄	♅	♆	♇
1 Th	22 39 43	8♍20 18	8♋47 56	15♋ 6 43	17♏34.6	24♍53.2	24♎ 7.6	9♋46.8	9♏48.3	9♓ 3.8	22♑46.6	20♑50.3	25♏28.3
2 F	22 43 40	9 18 23	21 31 3	28 1 13	17R28.4	26 30.3	25 1.7	10 24.7	9 57.4	8R59.2	22R45.1	20R49.3	25 29.2
3 Sa	22 47 36	10 16 30	4♌37 23	11♌19 36	17 19.9	28 6.1	25 55.3	11 2.5	10 6.7	8 54.7	22 43.8	20 48.4	25 30.1
4 Su	22 51 33	11 14 38	18 7 45	25 1 37	17 9.9	29 40.7	26 48.3	11 40.1	10 16.1	8 50.1	22 42.4	20 47.5	25 31.1
5 M	22 55 29	12 12 48	2♍ 0 46	9♍ 4 43	16 59.4	1♎14.1	27 40.7	12 17.7	10 25.7	8 45.5	22 41.1	20 46.6	25 32.0
6 Tu	22 59 26	13 11 0	16 12 47	23 24 16	16 49.4	2 46.3	28 32.5	12 55.2	10 35.3	8 41.0	22 39.9	20 45.8	25 33.1
7 W	23 3 22	14 9 14	0♎38 21	7♎54 13	16 41.0	4 17.2	29 23.7	13 32.5	10 45.0	8 36.4	22 38.6	20 45.0	25 34.1
8 Th	23 7 19	15 7 29	15 11 2	22 28 2	16 35.0	5 46.9	0♏14.2	14 9.8	10 54.8	8 31.9	22 37.5	20 44.2	25 35.2
9 F	23 11 16	16 5 46	29 44 31	6♏59 49	16 31.6	7 15.4	1 4.1	14 46.9	11 4.7	8 27.3	22 36.3	20 43.4	25 36.3
10 Sa	23 15 12	17 4 4	14♏13 25	21 24 53	16D 30.5	8 42.7	1 53.3	15 23.9	11 14.7	8 22.8	22 35.3	20 42.7	25 37.5
11 Su	23 19 9	18 2 24	28 33 53	5♐40 10	16 30.9	10 8.6	2 41.7	16 0.8	11 24.8	8 18.4	22 34.2	20 42.0	25 38.7
12 M	23 23 5	19 0 46	12♐43 35	19 44 2	16R31.6	11 33.4	3 29.4	16 37.7	11 35.0	8 13.9	22 33.2	20 41.3	25 39.9
13 Tu	23 27 2	19 59 9	26 41 28	3♑35 52	16 31.5	12 56.8	4 16.2	17 14.4	11 45.3	8 9.5	22 32.3	20 40.7	25 41.1
14 W	23 30 58	20 57 34	10♑27 15	17 15 36	16 29.8	14 18.9	5 2.2	17 50.9	11 55.6	8 5.1	22 31.4	20 40.1	25 42.4
15 Th	23 34 55	21 56 0	24 0 57	0♒43 16	16 25.8	15 39.6	5 47.4	18 27.4	12 6.1	8 0.7	22 30.5	20 39.5	25 43.7
16 F	23 38 51	22 54 28	7♒22 33	13 58 45	16 19.7	16 58.9	6 31.6	19 3.8	12 16.6	7 56.3	22 29.7	20 39.0	25 45.0
17 Sa	23 42 48	23 52 57	20 31 51	27 1 47	16 11.7	18 16.8	7 15.0	19 40.0	12 27.3	7 52.0	22 28.9	20 38.5	25 46.4
18 Su	23 46 45	24 51 28	3♓28 31	9♓51 59	16 2.6	19 33.2	7 57.3	20 16.1	12 38.0	7 47.7	22 28.2	20 38.0	25 47.8
19 M	23 50 41	25 50 1	16 12 11	22 29 7	15 53.5	20 48.1	8 38.6	20 52.2	12 48.8	7 43.5	22 27.6	20 37.5	25 49.2
20 Tu	23 54 38	26 48 36	28 42 47	4♈53 17	15 45.2	22 1.2	9 18.9	21 28.1	12 59.6	7 39.3	22 26.9	20 37.1	25 50.6
21 W	23 58 34	27 47 13	11♈ 0 43	17 5 16	15 38.4	23 12.7	9 58.1	22 3.8	13 10.6	7 35.2	22 26.4	20 36.7	25 52.1
22 Th	0 2 31	28 45 52	23 7 8	29 6 35	15 33.7	24 22.4	10 36.1	22 39.5	13 21.6	7 31.0	22 25.8	20 36.3	25 53.6
23 F	0 6 27	29 44 32	5♉ 3 58	10♉59 38	15D 31.1	25 30.1	11 13.0	23 15.1	13 32.7	7 27.0	22 25.4	20 36.0	25 55.1
24 Sa	0 10 24	0♎43 15	16 54 1	22 47 35	15 30.5	26 35.8	11 48.6	23 50.5	13 43.9	7 23.0	22 24.9	20 35.7	25 56.7
25 Su	0 14 20	1 42 1	28 40 52	4♊34 25	15 31.3	27 39.3	12 23.0	24 25.8	13 55.2	7 19.0	22 24.5	20 35.4	25 58.3
26 M	0 18 17	2 40 48	10♊28 50	16 24 42	15 32.8	28 40.4	12 56.0	25 1.0	14 6.5	7 15.1	22 24.2	20 35.2	25 59.9
27 Tu	0 22 14	3 39 38	22 22 41	28 23 25	15 34.2	29 39.1	13 27.7	25 36.0	14 17.9	7 11.2	22 23.9	20 35.0	26 1.5
28 W	0 26 10	4 38 30	4♋27 34	10♋35 44	15R34.8	0♏35.0	13 57.9	26 10.9	14 29.4	7 7.4	22 23.7	20 34.8	26 3.2
29 Th	0 30 7	5 37 24	16 48 33	23 6 35	15 34.1	1 28.0	14 26.7	26 45.7	14 40.9	7 3.7	22 23.5	20 34.7	26 4.8
30 F	0 34 3	6 36 20	29 30 21	6♌ 0 16	15 31.8	2 17.8	14 53.9	27 20.4	14 52.6	7 0.0	22 23.4	20 34.6	26 6.6

LONGITUDE OCTOBER 1994

Day	Sid.Time	☉	0 hr ☽	Noon ☽	True ☊	☿	♀	♂	♃	♄	♅	♆	♇
1 Sa	0 38 0	7♎35 19	12♌36 41	19♌19 49	15♏27.9	3♏ 4.2	15♏19.5	27♋54.9	15♏ 4.2	6♓56.4	22♑23.3	20♑34.5	26♏ 8.3
2 Su	0 41 56	8 34 20	26 9 44	3♍ 6 22	15R22.8	3 46.8	15 43.5	28 29.3	15 16.0	6R52.9	22D 23.3	20D 34.4	26 10.0
3 M	0 45 53	9 33 23	10♍ 9 28	17 18 37	15 17.1	4 25.4	16 5.8	29 3.5	15 27.8	6 49.4	22 23.3	20 34.4	26 11.8
4 Tu	0 49 49	10 32 29	24 33 15	1♎52 36	15 11.6	4 59.5	16 26.3	29 37.6	15 39.7	6 46.0	22 23.4	20 34.5	26 13.6
5 W	0 53 46	11 31 36	9♎15 50	16 41 56	15 7.1	5 28.7	16 44.9	0♌11.6	15 51.6	6 42.6	22 23.5	20 34.5	26 15.5
6 Th	0 57 43	12 30 46	24 9 54	1♏38 38	15 4.1	5 52.7	17 1.7	0 45.4	16 3.6	6 39.3	22 23.7	20 34.6	26 17.3
7 F	1 1 39	13 29 57	9♏ 7 7	16 34 20	15D 2.7	6 11.0	17 16.5	1 19.0	16 15.6	6 36.1	22 23.9	20 34.7	26 19.2
8 Sa	1 5 36	14 29 11	23 59 25	1♐21 33	15 2.8	6 23.2	17 29.3	1 52.5	16 27.7	6 33.0	22 24.2	20 34.9	26 21.1
9 Su	1 9 32	15 28 26	8♐40 4	15 54 29	15 4.0	6R28.7	17 40.0	2 25.9	16 39.9	6 30.0	22 24.5	20 35.1	26 23.0
10 M	1 13 29	16 27 43	23 4 22	0♑ 9 29	15 5.5	6 27.1	17 48.5	2 59.0	16 52.1	6 27.0	22 24.9	20 35.3	26 24.9
11 Tu	1 17 25	17 27 2	7♑ 9 41	14 4 56	15R 6.7	6 17.9	17 54.8	3 32.1	17 4.4	6 24.2	22 25.3	20 35.6	26 26.9
12 W	1 21 22	18 26 23	20 55 14	27 40 43	15 7.0	6 0.8	17 58.8	4 4.9	17 16.7	6 21.4	22 25.8	20 35.9	26 28.9
13 Th	1 25 18	19 25 45	4♒21 33	10♒57 53	15 6.1	5 35.5	18R 0.6	4 37.6	17 29.1	6 18.6	22 26.4	20 36.2	26 30.9
14 F	1 29 15	20 25 9	17 29 58	23 58 0	15 4.1	5 1.8	17 59.9	5 10.2	17 41.5	6 16.0	22 27.0	20 36.6	26 32.9
15 Sa	1 33 11	21 24 35	0♓22 13	6♓42 51	15 1.1	4 19.8	17 56.9	5 42.5	17 54.0	6 13.5	22 27.6	20 37.0	26 34.9
16 Su	1 37 8	22 24 3	13 0 8	19 14 15	14 57.6	3 29.7	17 51.5	6 14.7	18 6.5	6 11.0	22 28.3	20 37.4	26 37.0
17 M	1 41 5	23 23 32	25 25 26	1♈33 53	14 53.9	2 32.2	17 43.6	6 46.7	18 19.0	6 8.6	22 29.0	20 37.9	26 39.1
18 Tu	1 45 1	24 23 4	7♈39 47	13 43 21	14 50.7	1 28.2	17 33.3	7 18.6	18 31.6	6 6.4	22 29.8	20 38.4	26 41.2
19 W	1 48 58	25 22 37	19 44 47	25 44 25	14 48.2	0 18.9	17 20.6	7 50.3	18 44.2	6 4.2	22 30.6	20 38.9	26 43.3
20 Th	1 52 54	26 22 12	1♉42 5	7♉38 26	14 46.6	29♎ 6.0	17 5.5	8 21.8	18 56.9	6 2.1	22 31.5	20 39.4	26 45.4
21 F	1 56 51	27 21 50	13 33 34	19 27 48	14D 46.1	27 51.4	16 48.0	8 53.1	19 9.6	6 0.1	22 32.5	20 40.0	26 47.5
22 Sa	2 0 47	28 21 29	25 21 27	1♊14 50	14 46.4	26 37.2	16 28.2	9 24.2	19 22.4	5 58.2	22 33.5	20 40.7	26 49.7
23 Su	2 4 44	29 21 11	7♊ 8 21	13 2 23	14 47.4	25 25.6	16 6.2	9 55.2	19 35.2	5 56.4	22 34.5	20 41.3	26 51.9
24 M	2 8 40	0♏20 54	18 57 24	24 53 52	14 48.7	24 18.9	15 42.1	10 25.9	19 48.0	5 54.6	22 35.6	20 42.0	26 54.0
25 Tu	2 12 37	1 20 40	0♋52 16	6♋53 8	14 50.0	23 19.1	15 16.0	10 56.5	20 0.9	5 53.0	22 36.7	20 42.8	26 56.2
26 W	2 16 34	2 20 29	12 57 0	19 4 25	14 51.1	22 27.8	14 47.9	11 26.8	20 13.8	5 51.5	22 37.9	20 43.5	26 58.5
27 Th	2 20 30	3 20 19	25 15 57	1♌32 8	14R51.8	21 46.4	14 18.1	11 57.0	20 26.7	5 50.1	22 39.2	20 44.3	27 0.7
28 F	2 24 27	4 20 12	7♌53 30	14 20 33	14 51.9	21 15.9	13 46.8	12 26.9	20 39.6	5 48.7	22 40.4	20 45.1	27 2.9
29 Sa	2 28 23	5 20 6	20 53 43	27 33 21	14 51.5	20 56.7	13 14.0	12 56.6	20 52.6	5 47.5	22 41.8	20 46.0	27 5.2
30 Su	2 32 20	6 20 3	4♍19 44	11♍13 0	14 50.8	20D 49.1	12 40.1	13 26.2	21 5.6	5 46.4	22 43.2	20 46.9	27 7.5
31 M	2 36 16	7 20 2	18 13 11	25 20 8	14 49.9	20 52.7	12 5.2	13 55.5	21 18.7	5 45.3	22 44.6	20 47.8	27 9.7

Astro Data	Dy Hr Mn
☿0S	4 8:23
☽0S	6 6:36
☽0N	19 7:35
♄∠♅	23 10:52
♅ D	2 1:47
♆ D	2 17:48
☽0S	3 16:36
☿ R	9 6:44
♀ R	13 5:41
☽0N	16 13:30
♃✶♆	28 10:51
♄∠♆	29 18:04
☿ D	30 4:06
☽0S	31 2:53

Planet Ingress	Dy Hr Mn
☿ ♎	4 4:55
♀ ♏	7 17:12
☉ ♎	23 6:19
☿ ♏	27 8:51
♂ ♌	4 15:48
☿ ♎	19 6:19
☉ ♏	23 15:36

Last Aspect Dy Hr Mn		☽ Ingress Dy Hr Mn
2 10:30	☿ ✶	♌ 2 15:37
4 16:05	♀ ✶	♍ 4 20:33
6 15:35	♇ ✶	♎ 6 22:57
8 12:15	♅ □	♏ 9 0:26
10 19:05	♇ ☌	♐ 11 2:25
12 11:34	☉ □	♑ 13 5:44
15 3:04	♇ ✶	♒ 15 10:42
17 9:41	♇ □	♓ 17 17:31
19 20:01	☉ ☍	♈ 20 2:30
22 2:46	☿ ☍	♉ 22 13:47
24 18:28	♇ ☍	♊ 25 2:41
25 17:29	♄ □	♋ 27 15:12
29 19:46	♂ ☌	♌ 30 0:55

Last Aspect Dy Hr Mn		☽ Ingress Dy Hr Mn
2 0:01	♇ □	♍ 2 6:39
4 8:40	♂ ✶	♎ 4 8:56
5 21:09	♅ □	♏ 6 9:22
8 3:51	♇ ☌	♐ 8 9:47
9 12:07	☉ ✶	♑ 10 11:44
12 9:53	♇ ✶	♒ 12 16:09
14 16:52	♇ □	♓ 14 23:18
17 2:24	♇ △	♈ 17 8:56
19 19:15	☿ ☍	♉ 19 20:34
22 3:00	♇ ☍	♊ 22 9:28
24 9:58	☿ △	♋ 24 22:15
27 3:22	♇ △	♌ 27 9:05
29 11:11	♇ □	♍ 29 16:21
31 15:05	♇ ✶	♎ 31 19:46

☽ Phases & Eclipses Dy Hr Mn	
5 18:33	● 12♍58
12 11:34	☽ 19♐29
19 20:01	○ 26♓39
28 0:23	☽ 4♋39
5 3:55	● 11♎41
11 19:17	☽ 18♑15
19 12:18	○ 25♈53
27 16:44	☽ 4♌02

Astro Data

1 SEPTEMBER 1994
Julian Day # 34577
Delta T 59.4 sec
SVP 05♓19'49"
Obliquity 23°26'18"
⚷ Chiron 13♍45.6
☽ Mean ☊ 18♏13.7

1 OCTOBER 1994
Julian Day # 34607
Delta T 59.5 sec
SVP 05♓19'47"
Obliquity 23°26'18"
⚷ Chiron 17♍58.6
☽ Mean ☊ 16♏38.3

NOVEMBER 1994 LONGITUDE

Day	Sid.Time	☉	0 hr ☽	Noon ☽	True ☊	☿	♀	♂	♃	♄	♅	♆	♇
1 Tu	2 40 13	8♏20 3	2♎33 31	9♎52 51	14♏49.0	21♎ 7.3	11♏29.5	14♌24.5	21♏31.8	5♓44.4	22♑46.1	20♑48.7	27♏12.0
2 W	2 44 9	9 20 7	17 17 27	24 46 30	14R48.4	21 32.0	10R53.4	14 53.4	21 44.8	5R43.6	22 47.6	20 49.7	27 14.3
3 Th	2 48 6	10 20 12	2♏18 59	9♏53 48	14D48.1	22 6.2	10 17.0	15 21.9	21 58.0	5 42.9	22 49.2	20 50.7	27 16.6
4 F	2 52 3	11 20 19	17 29 46	25 5 40	14 48.0	22 48.9	9 40.5	15 50.3	22 11.1	5 42.3	22 50.8	20 51.8	27 19.0
5 Sa	2 55 59	12 20 29	2♐40 18	10♐12 30	14 48.1	23 39.3	9 4.3	16 18.4	22 24.3	5 41.8	22 52.5	20 52.8	27 21.3
6 Su	2 59 56	13 20 39	17 41 14	25 5 35	14 48.2	24 36.5	8 28.5	16 46.3	22 37.4	5 41.3	22 54.2	20 54.0	27 23.6
7 M	3 3 52	14 20 52	2♑24 48	9♑38 18	14R48.3	25 39.7	7 53.4	17 13.9	22 50.6	5 41.0	22 55.9	20 55.1	27 26.0
8 Tu	3 7 49	15 21 6	16 45 40	23 46 38	14 48.3	26 48.1	7 19.2	17 41.2	23 3.9	5 40.9	22 57.7	20 56.3	27 28.3
9 W	3 11 45	16 21 22	0♒41 9	7♒29 13	14 48.3	28 1.0	6 46.2	18 8.3	23 17.1	5D40.8	22 59.6	20 57.5	27 30.7
10 Th	3 15 42	17 21 38	14 11 1	20 46 49	14D48.2	29 17.8	6 14.5	18 35.1	23 30.3	5 40.8	23 1.5	20 58.7	27 33.0
11 F	3 19 38	18 21 57	27 16 55	3♓41 44	14 48.3	0♏37.8	5 44.4	19 1.6	23 43.6	5 40.9	23 3.4	20 59.9	27 35.4
12 Sa	3 23 35	19 22 16	10♓ 1 41	16 17 12	14 48.5	2 0.6	5 16.0	19 27.9	23 56.8	5 41.1	23 5.4	21 1.2	27 37.8
13 Su	3 27 32	20 22 37	22 28 45	28 36 46	14 49.0	3 25.7	4 49.4	19 53.9	24 10.1	5 41.5	23 7.4	21 2.5	27 40.2
14 M	3 31 28	21 23 0	4♈41 44	10♈44 2	14 49.7	4 52.7	4 24.9	20 19.6	24 23.4	5 41.9	23 9.5	21 3.9	27 42.6
15 Tu	3 35 25	22 23 24	16 44 6	22 42 18	14 50.4	6 21.3	4 2.5	20 44.9	24 36.6	5 42.4	23 11.6	21 5.2	27 44.9
16 W	3 39 21	23 23 50	28 39 0	4♉34 33	14 51.1	7 51.2	3 42.4	21 10.0	24 49.9	5 43.1	23 13.8	21 6.6	27 47.3
17 Th	3 43 18	24 24 17	10♉29 16	16 23 25	14R51.5	9 22.2	3 24.6	21 34.8	25 3.2	5 43.8	23 16.0	21 8.1	27 49.7
18 F	3 47 14	25 24 45	22 17 19	28 11 12	14 51.4	10 54.1	3 9.2	21 59.3	25 16.5	5 44.7	23 18.2	21 9.5	27 52.1
19 Sa	3 51 11	26 25 15	4♊ 5 22	10♊ 0 4	14 50.8	12 26.6	2 56.3	22 23.5	25 29.8	5 45.6	23 20.5	21 11.0	27 54.5
20 Su	3 55 7	27 25 47	15 55 32	21 52 4	14 49.4	13 59.7	2 45.8	22 47.3	25 43.1	5 46.7	23 22.8	21 12.5	27 56.9
21 M	3 59 4	28 26 20	27 49 56	3♋49 26	14 47.6	15 33.2	2 37.8	23 10.8	25 56.4	5 47.9	23 25.1	21 14.0	27 59.3
22 Tu	4 3 1	29 26 55	9♋50 51	15 54 33	14 45.3	17 7.1	2 32.4	23 34.0	26 9.7	5 49.1	23 27.5	21 15.6	28 1.7
23 W	4 6 57	0♐27 32	22 0 51	28 10 9	14 42.9	18 41.1	2D29.4	23 56.8	26 23.0	5 50.5	23 30.0	21 17.2	28 4.1
24 Th	4 10 54	1 28 10	4♌22 48	10♌39 15	14 40.8	20 15.3	2 28.9	24 19.3	26 36.3	5 52.0	23 32.4	21 18.8	28 6.5
25 F	4 14 50	2 28 50	16 59 52	23 25 5	14 39.3	21 49.7	2 30.8	24 41.4	26 49.5	5 53.6	23 35.0	21 20.4	28 8.9
26 Sa	4 18 47	3 29 31	29 55 18	6♍30 53	14D38.6	23 24.1	2 35.2	25 3.2	27 2.8	5 55.3	23 37.5	21 22.0	28 11.3
27 Su	4 22 43	4 30 14	13♍12 11	19 59 28	14 38.7	24 58.5	2 41.9	25 24.5	27 16.1	5 57.1	23 40.1	21 23.7	28 13.7
28 M	4 26 40	5 30 59	26 52 56	3♎52 42	14 39.7	26 32.9	2 50.9	25 45.5	27 29.3	5 58.9	23 42.7	21 25.4	28 16.1
29 Tu	4 30 36	6 31 45	10♎58 44	18 10 53	14 41.1	28 7.4	3 2.1	26 6.1	27 42.6	6 0.9	23 45.3	21 27.1	28 18.4
30 W	4 34 33	7 32 33	25 28 49	2♏52 3	14 42.5	29 41.8	3 15.5	26 26.3	27 55.8	6 3.0	23 48.0	21 28.9	28 20.8

DECEMBER 1994 LONGITUDE

Day	Sid.Time	☉	0 hr ☽	Noon ☽	True ☊	☿	♀	♂	♃	♄	♅	♆	♇
1 Th	4 38 30	8♐33 22	10♏19 55	17♏51 34	14♏43.3	1♐16.1	3♏31.1	26♌46.0	28♏ 9.0	6♓ 5.2	23♑50.7	21♑30.7	28♏23.2
2 F	4 42 26	9 34 13	25 25 59	3♐ 2 4	14R43.0	2 50.4	3 48.7	27 5.3	28 22.2	6 7.5	23 53.5	21 32.4	28 25.6
3 Sa	4 46 23	10 35 5	10♐38 35	18 14 16	14 41.4	4 24.7	4 8.3	27 24.2	28 35.4	6 9.9	23 56.3	21 34.3	28 27.9
4 Su	4 50 19	11 35 58	25 47 51	3♑18 9	14 38.5	5 58.9	4 29.9	27 42.7	28 48.6	6 12.4	23 59.1	21 36.1	28 30.3
5 M	4 54 16	12 36 52	10♑44 3	18 4 38	14 34.5	7 33.1	4 53.3	28 0.7	29 1.7	6 15.0	24 2.0	21 38.0	28 32.6
6 Tu	4 58 12	13 37 47	25 19 6	2♒26 54	14 30.2	9 7.3	5 18.5	28 18.2	29 14.9	6 17.7	24 4.8	21 39.8	28 35.0
7 W	5 2 9	14 38 43	9♒27 39	16 21 11	14 26.0	10 41.5	5 45.4	28 35.3	29 28.0	6 20.5	24 7.8	21 41.7	28 37.3
8 Th	5 6 5	15 39 40	23 7 29	29 46 43	14 22.8	12 15.6	6 14.0	28 51.9	29 41.0	6 23.4	24 10.7	21 43.6	28 39.6
9 F	5 10 2	16 40 37	6♓19 11	12♓45 16	14D20.8	13 49.7	6 44.2	29 8.0	29 54.1	6 26.4	24 13.7	21 45.6	28 41.9
10 Sa	5 13 59	17 41 35	19 5 27	25 20 18	14 20.3	15 23.9	7 16.0	29 23.5	0♐ 7.1	6 29.4	24 16.7	21 47.5	28 44.2
11 Su	5 17 55	18 42 33	1♈30 23	7♈36 19	14 21.0	16 58.1	7 49.3	29 38.6	0 20.1	6 32.6	24 19.7	21 49.5	28 46.5
12 M	5 21 52	19 43 32	13 38 44	19 38 13	14 22.6	18 32.3	8 24.0	29 53.2	0 33.1	6 35.9	24 22.7	21 51.5	28 48.8
13 Tu	5 25 48	20 44 32	25 35 23	1♉30 48	14 24.5	20 6.6	9 0.1	0♍ 7.2	0 46.0	6 39.2	24 25.8	21 53.5	28 51.1
14 W	5 29 45	21 45 32	7♉25 0	13 18 30	14R25.8	21 41.0	9 37.6	0 20.7	0 58.9	6 42.7	24 28.9	21 55.5	28 53.3
15 Th	5 33 41	22 46 33	19 11 44	25 5 10	14 25.9	23 15.5	10 16.3	0 33.7	1 11.8	6 46.2	24 32.0	21 57.5	28 55.6
16 F	5 37 38	23 47 34	0♊59 9	6♊54 2	14 24.3	24 50.0	10 56.3	0 46.1	1 24.6	6 49.9	24 35.2	21 59.6	28 57.8
17 Sa	5 41 34	24 48 37	12 50 7	18 47 40	14 20.7	26 24.7	11 37.5	0 57.9	1 37.4	6 53.6	24 38.4	22 1.6	29 0.0
18 Su	5 45 31	25 49 39	24 46 52	0♋47 57	14 15.0	27 59.6	12 19.8	1 9.2	1 50.1	6 57.4	24 41.6	22 3.7	29 2.2
19 M	5 49 28	26 50 43	6♋51 5	12 56 23	14 7.7	29 34.5	13 3.2	1 19.8	2 2.8	7 1.3	24 44.8	22 5.8	29 4.4
20 Tu	5 53 24	27 51 47	19 4 1	25 14 5	13 59.3	1♑ 9.7	13 47.7	1 29.9	2 15.5	7 5.3	24 48.0	22 7.9	29 6.6
21 W	5 57 21	28 52 51	1♌26 45	7♌42 7	13 50.6	2 45.0	14 33.3	1 39.3	2 28.2	7 9.3	24 51.3	22 10.0	29 8.8
22 Th	6 1 17	29 53 57	14 0 21	20 21 38	13 42.5	4 20.5	15 19.8	1 48.1	2 40.7	7 13.5	24 54.6	22 12.2	29 10.9
23 F	6 5 14	0♑55 3	26 46 7	3♍14 2	13 35.9	5 56.2	16 7.3	1 56.3	2 53.3	7 17.7	24 57.9	22 14.3	29 13.0
24 Sa	6 9 10	1 56 9	9♍45 35	16 21 2	13 31.2	7 32.1	16 55.6	2 3.8	3 5.8	7 22.0	25 1.2	22 16.5	29 15.1
25 Su	6 13 7	2 57 16	23 0 36	29 44 33	13D28.8	9 8.2	17 44.9	2 10.6	3 18.2	7 26.4	25 4.5	22 18.6	29 17.2
26 M	6 17 3	3 58 24	6♎33 4	13♎26 22	13 28.3	10 44.5	18 35.0	2 16.8	3 30.6	7 30.9	25 7.9	22 20.8	29 19.3
27 Tu	6 21 0	4 59 33	20 24 34	27 27 42	13 29.0	12 21.0	19 25.9	2 22.2	3 43.0	7 35.5	25 11.3	22 23.0	29 21.3
28 W	6 24 57	6 0 42	4♏35 46	11♏48 34	13R30.0	13 57.6	20 17.6	2 27.0	3 55.3	7 40.1	25 14.6	22 25.2	29 23.4
29 Th	6 28 53	7 1 52	19 5 48	26 27 1	13 30.1	15 34.5	21 10.0	2 31.0	4 7.5	7 44.8	25 18.1	22 27.4	29 25.4
30 F	6 32 50	8 3 2	3♐51 36	11♐18 45	13 28.4	17 11.5	22 3.1	2 34.4	4 19.7	7 49.6	25 21.5	22 29.6	29 27.4
31 Sa	6 36 46	9 4 13	18 47 33	26 16 58	13 24.2	18 48.6	22 57.0	2 36.9	4 31.8	7 54.5	25 24.9	22 31.9	29 29.4

Astro Data

	Dy Hr Mn
♃✶♅	7 11:09
♄ D	9 8:36
☽0N	12 19:01
♀ D	23 16:57
☽0S	27 12:01
♃☌♇	2 7:24
☽0N	10 2:01
♄∠♆	21 8:42
☽0S	24 19:25

Planet Ingress

	Dy Hr Mn
☿ ♏	10 12:46
☉ ♐	22 13:06
☿ ♐	30 4:38
♃ ♐	9 10:54
♂ ♍	12 11:32
☿ ♑	19 6:26
☉ ♑	22 2:23

Last Aspect / ☽ Ingress

Last Aspect Dy Hr Mn		☽ Ingress Dy Hr Mn
2 8:51	♅ □	♏ 2 20:19
4 15:33	♇ ☌	♐ 4 19:46
6 12:03	☿ ✶	♑ 6 20:02
8 18:53	☿ □	♒ 8 22:48
11 0:34	♇ □	♓ 11 5:04
13 10:11	♇ △	♈ 13 14:44
15 13:01	♅ □	♉ 16 2:44
18 11:23	♇ ☍	♊ 18 15:41
20 14:20	♂ ✶	♋ 21 4:21
23 11:51	♇ △	♌ 23 15:33
25 20:48	♇ □	♍ 26 0:09
28 2:24	♇ ✶	♎ 28 5:22
30 1:36	♂ ✶	♏ 30 7:21

Last Aspect / ☽ Ingress

Last Aspect Dy Hr Mn		☽ Ingress Dy Hr Mn
2 4:44	♇ ☌	♐ 2 7:13
4 3:07	♂ △	♑ 4 6:42
6 6:42	♃ ✶	♒ 6 7:51
8 12:02	♃ □	♓ 8 12:24
10 18:39	♇ △	♈ 10 21:03
12 21:39	♅ □	♉ 13 8:56
15 19:53	♇ ☍	♊ 15 22:00
18 7:23	☿ ☍	♋ 18 10:25
20 19:33	♇ △	♌ 20 21:13
23 4:34	♇ □	♍ 23 6:01
25 11:13	♇ ✶	♎ 25 12:27
27 8:11	♅ □	♏ 27 16:17
29 16:52	♇ ☌	♐ 29 17:46
30 6:26	♄ □	♑ 31 17:57

☽ Phases & Eclipses

Dy Hr Mn	
3 13:35	● 10♏54
3 13:39:06	☀ T 4'24"
10 6:14	☽ 17♒37
18 6:57	○ 25♉42
18 6:44	☾ A 0.881
26 7:04	☽ 3♍47
2 23:54	● 10♐35
9 21:06	☽ 17♓34
18 2:17	○ 25♊55
25 19:06	☽ 3♎46

Astro Data

1 NOVEMBER 1994
Julian Day # 34638
Delta T 59.5 sec
SVP 05♓19'44"
Obliquity 23°26'18"
⚷ Chiron 21♍56.4
☽ Mean ☊ 14♏59.8

1 DECEMBER 1994
Julian Day # 34668
Delta T 59.6 sec
SVP 05♓19'40"
Obliquity 23°26'17"
⚷ Chiron 24♍50.7
☽ Mean ☊ 13♏24.5

LONGITUDE JANUARY 1995

Day	Sid.Time	☉	0 hr ☽	Noon ☽	True ☊	☿	♀	♂	♃	♄	♅	♆	♇
1 Su	6 40 43	10♑ 5 24	3♑45 53	11♑13 7	13♏17.4	20♑25.8	23♏51.4	2♍38.8	4♐43.9	7♓59.4	25♑28.4	22♑34.1	29♏31.3
2 M	6 44 39	11 6 35	18 37 33	25 58 5	13R 8.6	22 3.0	24 46.5	2R 39.8	4 55.9	8 4.5	25 31.8	22 36.3	29 33.3
3 Tu	6 48 36	12 7 46	3♒13 44	10♒23 43	12 58.7	23 40.2	25 42.2	2 40.1	5 7.9	8 9.6	25 35.3	22 38.6	29 35.2
4 W	6 52 33	13 8 57	17 27 22	24 24 14	12 48.8	25 17.3	26 38.5	2 39.7	5 19.8	8 14.7	25 38.8	22 40.8	29 37.1
5 Th	6 56 29	14 10 7	1♓14 4	7♓56 48	12 40.2	26 54.2	27 35.3	2 38.4	5 31.6	8 20.0	25 42.2	22 43.1	29 38.9
6 F	7 0 26	15 11 18	14 32 32	21 1 32	12 33.6	28 30.7	28 32.7	2 36.4	5 43.3	8 25.3	25 45.7	22 45.3	29 40.8
7 Sa	7 4 22	16 12 28	27 24 11	3♈40 58	12 29.4	0♒ 6.9	29 30.6	2 33.5	5 55.0	8 30.7	25 49.2	22 47.6	29 42.6
8 Su	7 8 19	17 13 37	9♈52 28	15 59 18	12D 27.5	1 42.4	0♐29.0	2 29.9	6 6.6	8 36.1	25 52.8	22 49.9	29 44.4
9 M	7 12 15	18 14 46	22 2 8	28 1 41	12 27.3	3 17.2	1 27.8	2 25.5	6 18.1	8 41.6	25 56.3	22 52.1	29 46.1
10 Tu	7 16 12	19 15 55	3♉58 37	9♉53 39	12R 27.8	4 50.9	2 27.2	2 20.3	6 29.6	8 47.2	25 59.8	22 54.4	29 47.9
11 W	7 20 8	20 17 3	15 47 27	21 40 40	12 28.0	6 23.4	3 27.0	2 14.3	6 41.0	8 52.8	26 3.3	22 56.7	29 49.6
12 Th	7 24 5	21 18 11	27 33 55	3♊27 46	12 26.8	7 54.3	4 27.2	2 7.4	6 52.3	8 58.5	26 6.9	22 59.0	29 51.3
13 F	7 28 2	22 19 18	9♊22 44	15 19 17	12 23.3	9 23.2	5 27.8	1 59.8	7 3.5	9 4.3	26 10.4	23 1.2	29 53.0
14 Sa	7 31 58	23 20 25	21 17 51	27 18 46	12 17.0	10 49.9	6 28.8	1 51.3	7 14.7	9 10.1	26 14.0	23 3.5	29 54.6
15 Su	7 35 55	24 21 31	3♋22 20	9♋28 45	12 7.9	12 13.7	7 30.3	1 42.1	7 25.7	9 16.0	26 17.5	23 5.8	29 56.2
16 M	7 39 51	25 22 37	15 38 11	21 50 44	11 56.4	13 34.1	8 32.1	1 32.1	7 36.7	9 21.9	26 21.0	23 8.1	29 57.8
17 Tu	7 43 48	26 23 42	28 6 27	4♌25 20	11 43.3	14 50.6	9 34.3	1 21.2	7 47.6	9 27.9	26 24.6	23 10.3	29 59.4
18 W	7 47 44	27 24 47	10♌47 19	17 12 21	11 29.6	16 2.5	10 36.8	1 9.6	7 58.4	9 34.0	26 28.1	23 12.6	0♐ 0.9
19 Th	7 51 41	28 25 51	23 40 21	0♍11 13	11 16.7	17 9.0	11 39.7	0 57.2	8 9.2	9 40.1	26 31.7	23 14.9	0 2.4
20 F	7 55 37	29 26 55	6♍44 51	13 21 12	11 5.7	18 9.4	12 42.9	0 44.0	8 19.8	9 46.2	26 35.2	23 17.2	0 3.9
21 Sa	7 59 34	0♒27 58	20 0 12	26 41 50	10 57.4	19 2.8	13 46.4	0 30.0	8 30.4	9 52.5	26 38.8	23 19.4	0 5.3
22 Su	8 3 31	1 29 0	3♎26 7	10♎13 6	10 52.1	19 48.4	14 50.2	0 15.3	8 40.8	9 58.7	26 42.3	23 21.7	0 6.7
23 M	8 7 27	2 30 3	17 2 49	23 55 23	10 49.6	20 25.3	15 54.4	29♌59.9	8 51.2	10 5.0	26 45.8	23 23.9	0 8.1
24 Tu	8 11 24	3 31 5	0♏50 51	7♏49 18	10 48.9	20 52.6	16 58.8	29 43.7	9 1.4	10 11.4	26 49.4	23 26.2	0 9.5
25 W	8 15 20	4 32 6	14 50 45	21 55 11	10 48.9	21 9.7	18 3.5	29 26.8	9 11.6	10 17.8	26 52.9	23 28.4	0 10.8
26 Th	8 19 17	5 33 7	29 2 30	6♐12 30	10 48.1	21R 15.9	19 8.4	29 9.2	9 21.7	10 24.3	26 56.4	23 30.7	0 12.1
27 F	8 23 13	6 34 8	13♐24 53	20 39 15	10 45.3	21 10.8	20 13.7	28 51.0	9 31.7	10 30.8	26 59.9	23 32.9	0 13.3
28 Sa	8 27 10	7 35 8	27 55 3	5♑11 37	10 39.7	20 54.2	21 19.1	28 32.1	9 41.5	10 37.3	27 3.4	23 35.1	0 14.6
29 Su	8 31 6	8 36 7	12♑28 13	19 44 0	10 31.2	20 26.4	22 24.8	28 12.7	9 51.3	10 43.9	27 6.9	23 37.4	0 15.8
30 M	8 35 3	9 37 6	26 58 7	4♒ 9 39	10 20.0	19 47.7	23 30.8	27 52.6	10 1.0	10 50.6	27 10.4	23 39.6	0 16.9
31 Tu	8 39 0	10 38 3	11♒17 47	18 21 43	10 7.4	18 59.2	24 36.9	27 32.0	10 10.5	10 57.2	27 13.9	23 41.8	0 18.1

LONGITUDE FEBRUARY 1995

Day	Sid.Time	☉	0 hr ☽	Noon ☽	True ☊	☿	♀	♂	♃	♄	♅	♆	♇
1 W	8 42 56	11♒39 0	25♒20 47	2♓14 25	9♏54.6	18♒ 2.0	25♐43.3	27♌10.9	10♐19.9	11♓ 4.0	27♑17.4	23♑44.0	0♐19.2
2 Th	8 46 53	12 39 55	9♓ 2 14	15 43 59	9R 43.1	16R 57.9	26 49.8	26R 49.3	10 29.3	11 10.7	27 20.8	23 46.2	0 20.2
3 F	8 50 49	13 40 49	22 19 34	28 49 2	9 33.7	15 48.5	27 56.6	26 27.3	10 38.5	11 17.5	27 24.3	23 48.4	0 21.3
4 Sa	8 54 46	14 41 42	5♈12 37	11♈30 36	9 27.1	14 36.1	29 3.5	26 4.9	10 47.6	11 24.3	27 27.7	23 50.5	0 22.3
5 Su	8 58 42	15 42 34	17 43 25	23 51 36	9 23.3	13 22.8	0♑10.7	25 42.2	10 56.5	11 31.2	27 31.1	23 52.7	0 23.2
6 M	9 2 39	16 43 24	29 55 43	5♉56 24	9D 21.8	12 10.5	1 18.0	25 19.1	11 5.4	11 38.1	27 34.5	23 54.8	0 24.2
7 Tu	9 6 35	17 44 13	11♉54 20	17 50 12	9R 21.6	11 1.1	2 25.4	24 55.8	11 14.1	11 45.0	27 37.9	23 56.9	0 25.1
8 W	9 10 32	18 45 0	23 44 43	29 38 35	9 21.5	9 56.3	3 33.1	24 32.2	11 22.7	11 52.0	27 41.3	23 59.1	0 25.9
9 Th	9 14 29	19 45 46	5♊32 29	11♊27 6	9 20.5	8 57.4	4 40.9	24 8.5	11 31.2	11 59.0	27 44.6	24 1.2	0 26.8
10 F	9 18 25	20 46 30	17 23 3	23 20 58	9 17.6	8 5.4	5 48.8	23 44.7	11 39.6	12 6.0	27 48.0	24 3.3	0 27.6
11 Sa	9 22 22	21 47 13	29 21 22	5♋24 45	9 12.1	7 20.9	6 56.9	23 20.8	11 47.8	12 13.1	27 51.3	24 5.3	0 28.3
12 Su	9 26 18	22 47 54	11♋31 31	17 42 3	9 3.9	6 44.3	8 5.2	22 56.8	11 55.9	12 20.1	27 54.6	24 7.4	0 29.1
13 M	9 30 15	23 48 33	23 56 34	0♌15 15	8 53.2	6 15.8	9 13.6	22 32.8	12 3.9	12 27.2	27 57.9	24 9.4	0 29.8
14 Tu	9 34 11	24 49 11	6♌38 13	13 5 26	8 40.9	5 55.3	10 22.1	22 8.9	12 11.8	12 34.4	28 1.2	24 11.5	0 30.4
15 W	9 38 8	25 49 48	19 36 50	26 12 14	8 27.9	5 42.6	11 30.8	21 45.1	12 19.5	12 41.5	28 4.4	24 13.5	0 31.0
16 Th	9 42 4	26 50 23	2♍51 26	9♍34 7	8 15.6	5D 37.4	12 39.6	21 21.5	12 27.0	12 48.7	28 7.6	24 15.5	0 31.6
17 F	9 46 1	27 50 56	16 19 58	23 8 40	8 5.1	5 39.4	13 48.5	20 58.0	12 34.5	12 55.9	28 10.8	24 17.5	0 32.2
18 Sa	9 49 58	28 51 28	29 59 51	6♎53 11	7 57.2	5 48.2	14 57.6	20 34.8	12 41.8	13 3.1	28 14.0	24 19.4	0 32.7
19 Su	9 53 54	29 51 59	13♎48 22	20 45 9	7 52.2	6 3.2	16 6.8	20 11.8	12 48.9	13 10.3	28 17.2	24 21.4	0 33.2
20 M	9 57 51	0♓52 29	27 43 16	4♏42 33	7D 50.0	6 24.2	17 16.1	19 49.1	12 56.0	13 17.5	28 20.3	24 23.3	0 33.6
21 Tu	10 1 47	1 52 57	11♏42 52	18 44 4	7 49.6	6 50.6	18 25.5	19 26.8	13 2.8	13 24.8	28 23.4	24 25.2	0 34.0
22 W	10 5 44	2 53 24	25 46 5	2♐48 48	7R 50.1	7 22.1	19 35.1	19 4.8	13 9.6	13 32.1	28 26.5	24 27.1	0 34.4
23 Th	10 9 40	3 53 49	9♐52 9	16 55 59	7 50.1	7 58.2	20 44.7	18 43.3	13 16.2	13 39.4	28 29.5	24 29.0	0 34.8
24 F	10 13 37	4 54 14	24 0 10	1♑ 4 29	7 48.5	8 38.7	21 54.5	18 22.3	13 22.6	13 46.7	28 32.6	24 30.8	0 35.1
25 Sa	10 17 33	5 54 37	8♑ 8 39	15 12 23	7 44.6	9 23.2	23 4.4	18 1.7	13 28.9	13 54.0	28 35.6	24 32.7	0 35.4
26 Su	10 21 30	6 54 58	22 15 15	29 16 52	7 38.1	10 11.3	24 14.3	17 41.7	13 35.0	14 1.3	28 38.6	24 34.5	0 35.6
27 M	10 25 26	7 55 18	6♒16 42	13♒14 17	7 29.5	11 2.9	25 24.3	17 22.3	13 41.0	14 8.7	28 41.5	24 36.3	0 35.8
28 Tu	10 29 23	8 55 37	20 9 7	27 0 41	7 19.5	11 57.6	26 34.5	17 3.4	13 46.8	14 16.0	28 44.4	24 38.0	0 36.0

Astro Data	Planet Ingress	Last Aspect	☽ Ingress	Last Aspect	☽ Ingress	☽ Phases & Eclipses	Astro Data
Dy Hr Mn	Dy Hr Mn	Dy Hr Mn	Dy Hr Mn	Dy Hr Mn	Dy Hr Mn	Dy Hr Mn	1 JANUARY 1995
♂ R 2 21:27	☿ ♒ 6 22:17	2 17:57 ♇ ⚹	♒ 2 18:39	1 3:06 ♂ ☍	♓ 1 8:05	1 10:56 ● 10♑33	Julian Day # 34699
☽0N 6 11:25	♀ ♐ 7 12:07	4 21:11 ♇ □	♓ 4 21:49	3 11:21 ♀ □	♈ 3 14:12	8 15:46 ☽ 17♈54	Delta T 59.6 sec
♃∠♆ 19 16:21	♇ ♐ 17 9:58	7 4:24 ♇ △	♈ 7 4:56	5 19:19 ♅ □	♉ 6 0:09	16 20:26 ○ 26♋15	SVP 05♓19'34"
☽0S 21 1:55	☉ ♒ 20 13:00	9 7:51 ♅ □	♉ 9 15:58	8 8:04 ♅ △	♊ 8 12:44	24 4:58 ☽ 3♏44	Obliquity 23°26'16"
☿ R 26 1:16	♂ ♌ 22 23:48	12 4:40 ♇ ☍	♊ 12 4:57	10 12:23 ♂ ⚹	♋ 11 1:17	30 22:48 ● 10♒35	⚷ Chiron 26♍20.1
		13 0:01 ☿ △	♋ 14 17:20	13 7:42 ♅ ☍	♌ 13 11:31		☽ Mean ☊ 11♏46.0
☽0N 2 22:07	♀ ♑ 4 20:12	17 3:36 ♇ △	♌ 17 3:36	15 12:15 ☉ ☍	♍ 15 18:52	7 12:54 ☽ 18♉17	
☿ D 16 5:07	☉ ♓ 19 3:11	18 10:47 ☿ ☍	♍ 19 11:39	17 20:54 ♅ △	♎ 18 0:00	15 12:15 ○ 26♌21	1 FEBRUARY 1995
☽0S 17 9:07		21 11:58 ♅ △	♎ 21 17:54	20 1:04 ♅ □	♏ 20 3:55	22 13:04 ☽ 3♐26	Julian Day # 34730
♄∠♅ 20 15:56		23 22:06 ♂ ⚹	♏ 23 22:32	22 4:34 ♅ ⚹	♐ 22 7:13		Delta T 59.6 sec
♃∠♅ 27 4:14		26 0:11 ♂ □	♐ 26 1:37	23 14:40 ♂ △	♑ 24 10:11		SVP 05♓19'29"
		28 1:00 ♂ △	♑ 28 3:26	26 10:57 ♅ ☌	♒ 26 13:14		Obliquity 23°26'17"
		30 0:21 ♅ ☌	♒ 30 5:03	27 18:44 ♂ ☍	♓ 28 17:16		⚷ Chiron 25♍58.4R
							☽ Mean ☊ 10♏07.5

MARCH 1995 LONGITUDE

Day	Sid.Time	☉	0 hr ☽	Noon ☽	True ☊	☿	♀	♂	♃	♄	♅	♆	♇
1 W	10 33 20	9♓55 53	3♓48 33	10♓32 19	7♏ 9.2	12♒55.3	27♑44.7	16♌45.1	13♐52.5	14♓23.4	28♑47.3	24♑39.8	0♐36.1
2 Th	10 37 16	10 56 8	17 11 40	23 46 22	6R 59.9	13 55.7	28 55.0	16R 27.5	13 58.0	14 30.7	28 50.2	24 41.5	0 36.2
3 F	10 41 13	11 56 22	0♈16 17	6♈41 23	6 52.3	14 58.7	0♒ 5.4	16 10.6	14 3.3	14 38.1	28 53.0	24 43.2	0 36.2
4 Sa	10 45 9	12 56 33	13 1 45	19 17 32	6 47.0	16 4.1	1 15.8	15 54.4	14 8.5	14 45.5	28 55.8	24 44.9	0R 36.3
5 Su	10 49 6	13 56 42	25 29 0	1♉36 30	6D 44.2	17 11.7	2 26.3	15 38.9	14 13.5	14 52.8	28 58.6	24 46.5	0 36.2
6 M	10 53 2	14 56 49	7♉40 26	13 41 19	6 43.5	18 21.4	3 36.9	15 24.1	14 18.4	15 0.2	29 1.3	24 48.2	0 36.2
7 Tu	10 56 59	15 56 55	19 39 40	25 36 5	6 44.2	19 33.1	4 47.6	15 10.0	14 23.1	15 7.6	29 4.0	24 49.8	0 36.1
8 W	11 0 55	16 56 58	1♊31 11	7♊25 36	6 45.5	20 46.8	5 58.3	14 56.7	14 27.6	15 14.9	29 6.7	24 51.4	0 36.0
9 Th	11 4 52	17 56 59	13 20 0	19 15 4	6R 46.4	22 2.2	7 9.1	14 44.2	14 31.9	15 22.3	29 9.3	24 52.9	0 35.8
10 F	11 8 49	18 56 58	25 11 27	1♋ 9 47	6 46.3	23 19.3	8 19.9	14 32.5	14 36.1	15 29.7	29 11.9	24 54.4	0 35.7
11 Sa	11 12 45	19 56 55	7♋10 43	13 14 50	6 44.5	24 38.1	9 30.8	14 21.5	14 40.1	15 37.0	29 14.5	24 56.0	0 35.4
12 Su	11 16 42	20 56 49	19 22 40	25 34 43	6 40.7	25 58.5	10 41.8	14 11.3	14 44.0	15 44.4	29 17.0	24 57.4	0 35.2
13 M	11 20 38	21 56 42	1♌51 23	8♌13 0	6 35.2	27 20.4	11 52.8	14 2.0	14 47.6	15 51.7	29 19.5	24 58.9	0 34.9
14 Tu	11 24 35	22 56 32	14 39 48	21 11 56	6 28.3	28 43.8	13 3.9	13 53.4	14 51.1	15 59.1	29 21.9	25 0.3	0 34.6
15 W	11 28 31	23 56 20	27 49 26	4♍32 11	6 20.8	0♓ 8.6	14 15.1	13 45.5	14 54.4	16 6.4	29 24.3	25 1.7	0 34.2
16 Th	11 32 28	24 56 6	11♍20 1	18 12 35	6 13.6	1 34.9	15 26.2	13 38.5	14 57.6	16 13.7	29 26.7	25 3.1	0 33.8
17 F	11 36 24	25 55 50	25 9 31	2♎10 19	6 7.5	3 2.5	16 37.5	13 32.3	15 0.5	16 21.0	29 29.0	25 4.4	0 33.4
18 Sa	11 40 21	26 55 32	9♎14 26	16 21 15	6 3.1	4 31.5	17 48.8	13 26.8	15 3.3	16 28.3	29 31.3	25 5.7	0 32.9
19 Su	11 44 18	27 55 12	23 30 11	0♏40 35	6D 0.6	6 1.8	19 0.2	13 22.1	15 5.9	16 35.6	29 33.6	25 7.0	0 32.4
20 M	11 48 14	28 54 50	7♏51 53	15 3 30	6 0.0	7 33.5	20 11.6	13 18.2	15 8.3	16 42.9	29 35.8	25 8.3	0 31.9
21 Tu	11 52 11	29 54 26	22 14 56	29 25 44	6 0.8	9 6.5	21 23.0	13 15.0	15 10.6	16 50.1	29 38.0	25 9.5	0 31.4
22 W	11 56 7	0♈54 1	6♐35 31	13♐43 56	6 2.2	10 40.8	22 34.5	13 12.6	15 12.6	16 57.4	29 40.1	25 10.7	0 30.8
23 Th	12 0 4	1 53 34	20 50 43	27 55 38	6R 3.5	12 16.5	23 46.1	13 11.0	15 14.5	17 4.6	29 42.2	25 11.9	0 30.2
24 F	12 4 0	2 53 5	4♑58 29	11♑59 7	6 3.9	13 53.4	24 57.7	13D 10.1	15 16.2	17 11.8	29 44.3	25 13.0	0 29.5
25 Sa	12 7 57	3 52 35	18 57 23	25 53 9	6 3.0	15 31.7	26 9.3	13 9.9	15 17.7	17 19.0	29 46.3	25 14.1	0 28.8
26 Su	12 11 53	4 52 2	2♒46 17	9♒36 40	6 0.6	17 11.2	27 21.0	13 10.5	15 19.0	17 26.1	29 48.3	25 15.2	0 28.1
27 M	12 15 50	5 51 28	16 24 11	23 8 40	5 56.9	18 52.1	28 32.8	13 11.8	15 20.2	17 33.3	29 50.2	25 16.3	0 27.4
28 Tu	12 19 47	6 50 52	29 50 2	6♓28 8	5 52.4	20 34.3	29 44.5	13 13.8	15 21.1	17 40.4	29 52.1	25 17.3	0 26.6
29 W	12 23 43	7 50 15	13♓ 2 51	19 34 7	5 47.8	22 17.9	0♓56.3	13 16.5	15 21.9	17 47.5	29 53.9	25 18.3	0 25.8
30 Th	12 27 40	8 49 35	26 1 51	2♈26 0	5 43.5	24 2.8	2 8.2	13 19.9	15 22.4	17 54.6	29 55.7	25 19.2	0 25.0
31 F	12 31 36	9 48 53	8♈46 34	15 3 36	5 40.2	25 49.0	3 20.0	13 24.0	15 22.8	18 1.6	29 57.5	25 20.2	0 24.1

APRIL 1995 LONGITUDE

Day	Sid.Time	☉	0 hr ☽	Noon ☽	True ☊	☿	♀	♂	♃	♄	♅	♆	♇
1 Sa	12 35 33	10♈48 9	21♈17 10	27♈27 24	5♏38.1	27♓36.7	4♓32.0	13♌28.8	15♐23.0	18♓ 8.6	29♑59.2	25♑21.1	0♐23.2
2 Su	12 39 29	11 47 24	3♉34 30	9♉38 42	5D 37.2	29 25.7	5 43.9	13 34.2	15R 23.0	18 15.6	0♒ 0.8	25 21.9	0R 22.3
3 M	12 43 26	12 46 36	15 40 17	21 39 35	5 37.6	1♈16.1	6 55.8	13 40.3	15 22.8	18 22.6	0 2.4	25 22.8	0 21.4
4 Tu	12 47 22	13 45 46	27 36 59	3♊32 55	5 38.8	3 7.9	8 7.8	13 47.1	15 22.4	18 29.5	0 4.0	25 23.6	0 20.4
5 W	12 51 19	14 44 53	9♊27 52	15 22 20	5 40.4	5 1.1	9 19.8	13 54.4	15 21.9	18 36.4	0 5.5	25 24.3	0 19.4
6 Th	12 55 15	15 43 59	21 16 52	27 12 0	5 42.0	6 55.7	10 31.9	14 2.4	15 21.1	18 43.2	0 7.0	25 25.1	0 18.4
7 F	12 59 12	16 43 2	3♋ 8 21	9♋ 6 30	5 43.3	8 51.7	11 43.9	14 11.0	15 20.2	18 50.1	0 8.4	25 25.8	0 17.3
8 Sa	13 3 9	17 42 3	15 7 4	21 10 39	5R 43.9	10 49.1	12 56.0	14 20.2	15 19.1	18 56.9	0 9.8	25 26.5	0 16.2
9 Su	13 7 5	18 41 2	27 17 49	3♌29 9	5 43.6	12 47.8	14 8.1	14 30.0	15 17.7	19 3.6	0 11.1	25 27.1	0 15.1
10 M	13 11 2	19 39 58	9♌45 9	16 6 18	5 42.7	14 47.8	15 20.3	14 40.4	15 16.2	19 10.3	0 12.4	25 27.7	0 14.0
11 Tu	13 14 58	20 38 52	22 33 1	29 5 36	5 41.1	16 49.1	16 32.4	14 51.3	15 14.6	19 17.0	0 13.6	25 28.3	0 12.9
12 W	13 18 55	21 37 44	5♍44 17	12♍29 11	5 39.3	18 51.6	17 44.6	15 2.8	15 12.7	19 23.6	0 14.8	25 28.8	0 11.7
13 Th	13 22 51	22 36 33	19 20 17	26 17 26	5 37.5	20 55.2	18 56.8	15 14.8	15 10.7	19 30.2	0 16.0	25 29.3	0 10.5
14 F	13 26 48	23 35 20	3♎20 21	10♎28 37	5 35.9	22 59.8	20 9.0	15 27.3	15 8.4	19 36.8	0 17.1	25 29.8	0 9.3
15 Sa	13 30 44	24 34 6	17 41 39	24 58 47	5 35.0	25 5.3	21 21.2	15 40.3	15 6.0	19 43.3	0 18.1	25 30.3	0 8.0
16 Su	13 34 41	25 32 49	2♏19 13	9♏42 7	5D 34.6	27 11.5	22 33.5	15 53.9	15 3.4	19 49.8	0 19.1	25 30.7	0 6.7
17 M	13 38 38	26 31 30	17 6 34	24 31 37	5 34.7	29 18.2	23 45.8	16 7.9	15 0.7	19 56.2	0 20.0	25 31.0	0 5.5
18 Tu	13 42 34	27 30 10	1♐56 23	9♐19 59	5 35.2	1♉25.2	24 58.1	16 22.4	14 57.7	20 2.6	0 20.9	25 31.4	0 4.2
19 W	13 46 31	28 28 47	16 41 37	24 0 36	5 35.8	3 32.3	26 10.4	16 37.4	14 54.6	20 8.9	0 21.8	25 31.7	0 2.8
20 Th	13 50 27	29 27 22	1♑16 17	8♑28 13	5 36.4	5 39.2	27 22.8	16 52.8	14 51.3	20 15.2	0 22.6	25 32.0	0 1.5
21 F	13 54 24	0♉25 58	15 35 59	22 39 21	5 36.8	7 45.7	28 35.2	17 8.7	14 47.9	20 21.5	0 23.3	25 32.2	0 0.1
22 Sa	13 58 20	1 24 31	29 38 6	6♒32 11	5R 37.0	9 51.3	29 47.6	17 25.0	14 44.2	20 27.7	0 24.0	25 32.4	29♏58.7
23 Su	14 2 17	2 23 2	13♒21 36	20 6 24	5 36.9	11 55.8	0♈60.0	17 41.8	14 40.4	20 33.8	0 24.7	25 32.6	29 57.3
24 M	14 6 13	3 21 32	26 46 43	3♓22 40	5 36.7	13 58.9	2 12.4	17 59.0	14 36.5	20 39.9	0 25.2	25 32.8	29 55.9
25 Tu	14 10 10	4 20 0	9♓54 28	16 22 17	5 36.6	16 0.3	3 24.9	18 16.6	14 32.3	20 45.9	0 25.8	25 32.9	29 54.5
26 W	14 14 7	5 18 26	22 46 21	29 6 52	5D 36.5	17 59.6	4 37.4	18 34.6	14 28.0	20 51.9	0 26.3	25 33.0	29 53.0
27 Th	14 18 3	6 16 51	5♈24 2	11♈38 5	5 36.5	19 56.5	5 49.8	18 53.0	14 23.6	20 57.9	0 26.7	25R 33.0	29 51.5
28 F	14 22 0	7 15 13	17 49 14	23 57 39	5 36.6	21 50.9	7 2.3	19 11.8	14 18.9	21 3.7	0 27.1	25 33.0	29 50.1
29 Sa	14 25 56	8 13 35	0♉ 3 35	6♉ 7 13	5R 36.7	23 42.3	8 14.9	19 31.0	14 14.2	21 9.6	0 27.5	25 33.0	29 48.6
30 Su	14 29 53	9 11 54	12 8 47	18 8 31	5 36.7	25 30.6	9 27.4	19 50.6	14 9.2	21 15.3	0 27.8	25 33.0	29 47.0

Astro Data	Planet Ingress	Last Aspect	☽ Ingress	Last Aspect	☽ Ingress	☽ Phases & Eclipses	Astro Data
Dy Hr Mn	Dy Hr Mn	Dy Hr Mn	Dy Hr Mn	Dy Hr Mn	Dy Hr Mn	Dy Hr Mn	1 MARCH 1995
☽0N 2 8:00	♀ ♒ 2 22:11	2 21:25 ♅ ⚹	♈ 2 23:30	1 7:54 ♆ □	♉ 1 16:59	1 11:48 ● 10♓26	Julian Day # 34758
♇ R 4 2:33	☿ ♓ 14 21:35	5 6:51 ♅ □	♉ 5 8:50	3 19:31 ♆ △	♊ 4 4:49	9 10:14 ☽ 18♊23	Delta T 59.7 sec
☽0S 16 17:51	☉ ♈ 21 2:14	7 19:06 ♅ △	♊ 7 20:55	5 18:45 ♄ □	♋ 6 17:40	17 1:26 ○ 25♍59	SVP 05♓19'26"
♂ D 24 17:18	♀ ♓ 28 5:10	9 19:46 ☿ △	♋ 10 9:40	8 20:24 ♆ ☍	♌ 9 5:16	23 20:10 ☽ 2♑44	Obliquity 23°26'17"
☽0N 29 15:40		12 19:10 ♅ ☍	♌ 12 20:28	10 20:11 ☉ △	♍ 11 13:39	31 2:09 ● 9♈54	⚷ Chiron 24♍17.5R
	♅ ♒ 1 12:07	14 0:21 ♃ △	♍ 15 3:54	13 10:38 ♆ △	♎ 13 18:20		☽ Mean ☊ 8♏38.6
♃ R 1 12:03	☿ ♈ 2 7:29	17 7:26 ♅ △	♎ 17 8:18	15 14:13 ☿ ☍	♏ 15 20:13	8 5:35 ☽ 17♋56	
☿0N 4 16:32	☿ ♉ 17 7:54	19 10:10 ♅ □	♏ 19 10:52	17 13:36 ♆ ⚹	♐ 17 20:51	15 12:08 ○ 25♎04	1 APRIL 1995
♅⚹♇ 10 16:08	☉ ♉ 20 13:22	21 12:22 ♅ ⚹	♐ 21 12:57	19 20:46 ☉ △	♑ 19 21:54	15 12:18 ☍ P 0.111	Julian Day # 34789
♃∠♅ 11 7:22	♇ ♏ 21 2:07	23 5:24 ♀ ⚹	♑ 23 15:31	22 0:36 ♇ ⚹	♒ 22 0:38	22 3:18 ☽ 1♒33	Delta T 59.7 sec
☽0S 13 3:41	♀ ♈ 22 4:07	25 18:48 ♅ ☌	♒ 25 19:10	24 5:42 ♇ □	♓ 24 5:51	29 17:36 ● 8♉56	SVP 05♓19'24"
☽0N 25 21:29		27 23:49 ♀ ☌	♓ 28 0:18	26 13:26 ♇ △	♈ 26 13:41	29 17:32:21 ☌ A 6'37"	Obliquity 23°26'17"
♀0N 25 4:46		30 7:19 ♅ ⚹	♈ 30 7:26	28 15:07 ♆ □	♉ 28 23:53		⚷ Chiron 21♍53.4R
♆ R 27 22:14							☽ Mean ☊ 7♏00.0

LONGITUDE — MAY 1995

Day	Sid.Time	☉	0 hr ☽	Noon ☽	True ☊	☿	♀	♂	♃	♄	♅	♆	♇
1 M	14 33 49	10♉10 12	24♉ 6 38	0♊ 3 25	5♏36.4	27♉15.6	10♈39.9	20♌10.5	14♐ 4.2	21♓21.0	0♒28.0	25♑32.9	29♏45.5
2 Tu	14 37 46	11 8 28	5♊59 9	11 54 7	5R35.9	28 57.2	11 52.5	20 30.8	13R59.0	21 26.7	0 28.2	25R32.8	29R44.0
3 W	14 41 42	12 6 42	17 48 39	23 43 8	5 35.2	0♊35.1	13 5.0	20 51.5	13 53.6	21 32.3	0 28.3	25 32.6	29 42.4
4 Th	14 45 39	13 4 54	29 37 55	5♋33 27	5 34.2	2 9.2	14 17.6	21 12.5	13 48.1	21 37.8	0 28.4	25 32.4	29 40.9
5 F	14 49 36	14 3 4	11♋30 10	17 28 32	5 33.1	3 39.5	15 30.2	21 33.9	13 42.5	21 43.2	0R28.5	25 32.2	29 39.3
6 Sa	14 53 32	15 1 12	23 29 3	29 32 13	5 32.2	5 5.7	16 42.8	21 55.6	13 36.7	21 48.6	0 28.5	25 32.0	29 37.7
7 Su	14 57 29	15 59 19	5♌38 35	11♌48 41	5D31.5	6 27.9	17 55.4	22 17.6	13 30.8	21 54.0	0 28.4	25 31.7	29 36.1
8 M	15 1 25	16 57 23	18 3 2	24 22 10	5 31.3	7 46.0	19 8.0	22 39.9	13 24.8	21 59.2	0 28.3	25 31.4	29 34.5
9 Tu	15 5 22	17 55 26	0♍46 34	7♍16 41	5 31.7	8 59.9	20 20.6	23 2.6	13 18.7	22 4.4	0 28.1	25 31.0	29 32.9
10 W	15 9 18	18 53 26	13 52 53	20 35 31	5 32.4	10 9.5	21 33.2	23 25.5	13 12.4	22 9.6	0 27.9	25 30.7	29 31.3
11 Th	15 13 15	19 51 25	27 24 46	4♎20 44	5 33.5	11 14.7	22 45.9	23 48.7	13 6.0	22 14.6	0 27.7	25 30.3	29 29.7
12 F	15 17 11	20 49 22	11♎23 22	18 32 29	5 34.6	12 15.5	23 58.5	24 12.3	12 59.6	22 19.6	0 27.4	25 29.8	29 28.0
13 Sa	15 21 8	21 47 17	25 47 41	3♏ 8 27	5R35.4	13 11.9	25 11.2	24 36.1	12 53.0	22 24.5	0 27.0	25 29.4	29 26.4
14 Su	15 25 4	22 45 10	10♏34 3	18 3 37	5 35.5	14 3.7	26 23.8	25 0.2	12 46.3	22 29.4	0 26.6	25 28.9	29 24.7
15 M	15 29 1	23 43 2	25 36 8	3♐10 28	5 34.8	14 50.9	27 36.5	25 24.5	12 39.6	22 34.2	0 26.1	25 28.4	29 23.1
16 Tu	15 32 58	24 40 53	10♐45 27	18 19 50	5 33.2	15 33.5	28 49.2	25 49.1	12 32.7	22 38.9	0 25.6	25 27.8	29 21.4
17 W	15 36 54	25 38 42	25 52 28	3♑22 13	5 30.9	16 11.3	0♉ 1.9	26 14.0	12 25.8	22 43.5	0 25.1	25 27.2	29 19.8
18 Th	15 40 51	26 36 30	10♑48 6	18 9 17	5 28.2	16 44.4	1 14.6	26 39.1	12 18.8	22 48.1	0 24.5	25 26.6	29 18.1
19 F	15 44 47	27 34 16	25 25 3	2♒34 56	5 25.7	17 12.6	2 27.4	27 4.5	12 11.7	22 52.6	0 23.9	25 26.0	29 16.5
20 Sa	15 48 44	28 32 2	9♒38 34	16 35 49	5 23.7	17 36.1	3 40.1	27 30.2	12 4.5	22 57.0	0 23.2	25 25.3	29 14.8
21 Su	15 52 40	29 29 46	23 26 40	0♓11 13	5D22.7	17 54.6	4 52.9	27 56.0	11 57.2	23 1.3	0 22.4	25 24.6	29 13.2
22 M	15 56 37	0♊27 29	6♓49 42	13 22 27	5 22.7	18 8.4	6 5.7	28 22.1	11 49.9	23 5.6	0 21.7	25 23.9	29 11.5
23 Tu	16 0 34	1 25 11	19 49 49	26 12 14	5 23.7	18 17.3	7 18.4	28 48.5	11 42.6	23 9.8	0 20.8	25 23.1	29 9.8
24 W	16 4 30	2 22 52	2♈30 8	8♈43 58	5 25.2	18R21.4	8 31.2	29 15.0	11 35.2	23 13.9	0 20.0	25 22.3	29 8.2
25 Th	16 8 27	3 20 32	14 54 11	21 1 14	5 26.8	18 20.8	9 44.1	29 41.8	11 27.7	23 17.9	0 19.0	25 21.5	29 6.5
26 F	16 12 23	4 18 12	27 5 33	3♉ 7 30	5R28.0	18 15.7	10 56.9	0♍ 8.9	11 20.2	23 21.8	0 18.1	25 20.7	29 4.9
27 Sa	16 16 20	5 15 50	9♉ 7 29	15 5 50	5 28.2	18 6.2	12 9.7	0 36.1	11 12.6	23 25.7	0 17.1	25 19.8	29 3.2
28 Su	16 20 16	6 13 27	21 2 52	26 58 54	5 27.1	17 52.5	13 22.6	1 3.6	11 5.1	23 29.5	0 16.0	25 18.9	29 1.6
29 M	16 24 13	7 11 2	2♊54 12	8♊49 2	5 24.4	17 34.9	14 35.4	1 31.2	10 57.5	23 33.1	0 14.9	25 18.0	28 59.9
30 Tu	16 28 9	8 8 37	14 43 38	20 38 15	5 20.2	17 13.7	15 48.3	1 59.1	10 49.9	23 36.7	0 13.8	25 17.0	28 58.3
31 W	16 32 6	9 6 11	26 33 7	2♋28 30	5 14.8	16 49.3	17 1.2	2 27.2	10 42.2	23 40.3	0 12.6	25 16.0	28 56.7

LONGITUDE — JUNE 1995

Day	Sid.Time	☉	0 hr ☽	Noon ☽	True ☊	☿	♀	♂	♃	♄	♅	♆	♇
1 Th	16 36 3	10♊ 3 43	8♋20 39	14♋21 50	5♏ 8.6	16♊22.0	18♉14.0	2♍55.5	10♐34.6	23♓43.7	0♒11.4	25♑15.0	28♏55.1
2 F	16 39 59	11 1 15	20 20 20	26 20 29	5R 2.3	15R52.5	19 26.9	3 24.0	10R26.9	23 47.0	0R10.1	25R14.0	28R53.4
3 Sa	16 43 56	11 58 45	2♌22 38	8♌27 7	4 56.5	15 21.1	20 39.8	3 52.7	10 19.3	23 50.3	0 8.8	25 13.0	28 51.8
4 Su	16 47 52	12 56 14	14 34 21	20 44 46	4 51.8	14 48.4	21 52.7	4 21.5	10 11.6	23 53.5	0 7.4	25 11.9	28 50.2
5 M	16 51 49	13 53 41	26 58 48	3♍16 54	4 48.7	14 15.1	23 5.7	4 50.6	10 4.0	23 56.6	0 6.1	25 10.8	28 48.6
6 Tu	16 55 45	14 51 8	9♍39 32	16 7 10	4D47.3	13 41.5	24 18.6	5 19.8	9 56.4	23 59.5	0 4.6	25 9.7	28 47.1
7 W	16 59 42	15 48 33	22 40 15	29 19 10	4 47.4	13 8.4	25 31.5	5 49.2	9 48.8	24 2.4	0 3.2	25 8.5	28 45.5
8 Th	17 3 38	16 45 57	6♎ 4 17	12♎55 52	4 48.4	12 36.3	26 44.5	6 18.8	9 41.3	24 5.3	0 1.7	25 7.4	28 43.9
9 F	17 7 35	17 43 19	19 54 6	26 59 0	4 49.7	12 5.7	27 57.4	6 48.6	9 33.7	24 8.0	0 0.1	25 6.2	28 42.4
10 Sa	17 11 32	18 40 41	4♏10 28	11♏28 12	4R50.4	11 37.1	29 10.4	7 18.5	9 26.3	24 10.6	29♑58.5	25 5.0	28 40.8
11 Su	17 15 28	19 38 2	18 51 44	26 20 23	4 49.6	11 11.1	0♊23.4	7 48.6	9 18.8	24 13.1	29 56.9	25 3.8	28 39.3
12 M	17 19 25	20 35 22	3♐53 15	11♐29 17	4 47.0	10 48.1	1 36.4	8 18.9	9 11.4	24 15.6	29 55.3	25 2.5	28 37.8
13 Tu	17 23 21	21 32 41	19 7 16	26 45 54	4 42.3	10 28.4	2 49.4	8 49.3	9 4.1	24 17.9	29 53.6	25 1.3	28 36.3
14 W	17 27 18	22 29 59	4♑23 47	11♑59 36	4 36.1	10 12.4	4 2.4	9 19.9	8 56.8	24 20.2	29 51.9	24 60.0	28 34.8
15 Th	17 31 14	23 27 17	19 32 2	26 59 57	4 29.0	10 0.4	5 15.5	9 50.6	8 49.6	24 22.4	29 50.1	24 58.7	28 33.4
16 F	17 35 11	24 24 34	4♒22 21	11♒38 27	4 21.9	9 52.5	6 28.5	10 21.5	8 42.5	24 24.4	29 48.3	24 57.3	28 31.9
17 Sa	17 39 7	25 21 51	18 47 42	25 49 44	4 15.9	9D48.9	7 41.6	10 52.5	8 35.4	24 26.4	29 46.5	24 56.0	28 30.5
18 Su	17 43 4	26 19 8	2♓44 24	9♓31 46	4 11.6	9 49.9	8 54.7	11 23.7	8 28.4	24 28.3	29 44.7	24 54.7	28 29.1
19 M	17 47 1	27 16 24	16 12 0	22 45 28	4D 9.2	9 55.4	10 7.8	11 55.0	8 21.5	24 30.0	29 42.8	24 53.3	28 27.7
20 Tu	17 50 57	28 13 39	29 12 35	5♈33 53	4 8.6	10 5.6	11 20.9	12 26.5	8 14.7	24 31.7	29 40.9	24 51.9	28 26.3
21 W	17 54 54	29 10 55	11♈49 54	18 1 15	4 9.1	10 20.4	12 34.0	12 58.1	8 7.9	24 33.3	29 38.9	24 50.5	28 24.9
22 Th	17 58 50	0♋ 8 10	24 8 33	0♉12 22	4R10.1	10 39.8	13 47.2	13 29.9	8 1.3	24 34.8	29 37.0	24 49.0	28 23.5
23 F	18 2 47	1 5 26	6♉13 19	12 11 56	4 10.4	11 3.9	15 0.3	14 1.8	7 54.7	24 36.2	29 35.0	24 47.6	28 22.2
24 Sa	18 6 43	2 2 41	18 8 46	24 4 17	4 9.3	11 32.6	16 13.5	14 33.8	7 48.3	24 37.5	29 33.0	24 46.2	28 20.9
25 Su	18 10 40	2 59 56	29 58 58	5♊53 11	4 6.1	12 5.9	17 26.7	15 6.0	7 42.0	24 38.7	29 30.9	24 44.7	28 19.6
26 M	18 14 36	3 57 11	11♊47 19	17 41 41	4 0.4	12 43.6	18 40.0	15 38.3	7 35.8	24 39.8	29 28.8	24 43.2	28 18.3
27 Tu	18 18 33	4 54 25	23 36 34	29 32 13	3 52.3	13 25.8	19 53.2	16 10.8	7 29.7	24 40.7	29 26.7	24 41.7	28 17.1
28 W	18 22 30	5 51 40	5♋28 51	11♋26 40	3 42.1	14 12.3	21 6.5	16 43.4	7 23.7	24 41.6	29 24.6	24 40.2	28 15.9
29 Th	18 26 26	6 48 54	17 25 50	23 26 32	3 30.7	15 3.2	22 19.7	17 16.1	7 17.8	24 42.4	29 22.5	24 38.7	28 14.7
30 F	18 30 23	7 46 8	29 28 55	5♌33 11	3 19.0	15 58.3	23 33.0	17 49.0	7 12.1	24 43.1	29 20.3	24 37.2	28 13.5

Astro Data Dy Hr Mn	Planet Ingress Dy Hr Mn
♅ R 5 7:48	☿ ♊ 2 15:18
☽0S 10 13:33	☿ ♉ 16 23:22
☽0N 23 3:14	☉ ♊ 21 12:34
☿ R 24 9:02	♂ ♍ 25 16:09
♃∠♆ 3 23:02	♅ ♑ 9 1:46
☽0S 6 22:25	♀ ♊ 10 16:19
☿ D 17 6:58	☉ ♋ 21 20:34
☽0N 19 10:38	
♄✶♆ 27 9:38	

Last Aspect Dy Hr Mn	☽ Ingress Dy Hr Mn	Last Aspect Dy Hr Mn	☽ Ingress Dy Hr Mn
1 11:22 ♇ ☍	♊ 1 11:53	2 17:02 ♇ △	♌ 2 19:17
3 7:38 ♄ □	♋ 4 0:45	5 3:30 ♇ □	♍ 5 5:46
6 12:09 ♇ △	♌ 6 12:55	7 10:58 ♇ ✶	♎ 7 13:13
8 21:43 ♇ □	♍ 8 22:33	9 17:02 ♅ □	♏ 9 17:03
11 3:37 ♇ ✶	♎ 11 4:30	11 17:43 ♅ ✶	♐ 11 17:50
12 23:30 ♆ □	♏ 13 6:53	13 8:09 ♄ □	♑ 13 17:05
15 5:59 ♇ ☌	♐ 15 6:58	15 16:34 ♅ ☌	♒ 15 16:52
17 0:35 ♂ △	♑ 17 6:36	17 16:36 ♇ □	♓ 17 19:13
19 6:26 ♇ ✶	♒ 19 7:39	20 0:53 ♅ ✶	♈ 20 1:29
21 11:36 ☉ □	♓ 21 11:40	22 10:48 ♅ □	♉ 22 11:35
23 17:35 ♇ △	♈ 23 19:13	24 23:03 ♅ △	♊ 25 0:02
25 20:32 ♆ □	♉ 26 5:46	27 2:10 ♄ □	♋ 27 12:56
28 16:06 ♇ ☍	♊ 28 18:07	29 23:43 ♅ ☍	♌ 30 1:02
30 18:08 ♄ □	♋ 31 6:59		

☽ Phases & Eclipses Dy Hr Mn		Astro Data
7 21:44	☽ 16♌52	1 MAY 1995
14 20:48	○ 23♏35	Julian Day # 34819
21 11:36	☽ 29♒58	Delta T 59.8 sec
29 9:27	● 7♊34	SVP 05♓19'21"
		Obliquity 23°26'16"
6 10:26	☽ 15♍16	⚷ Chiron 20♍15.3R
13 4:04	○ 21♐42	☽ Mean ☊ 5♏24.7
19 22:01	☽ 28♓09	
28 0:50	● 5♋54	1 JUNE 1995
		Julian Day # 34850
		Delta T 59.8 sec
		SVP 05♓19'17"
		Obliquity 23°26'15"
		⚷ Chiron 20♍08.5
		☽ Mean ☊ 3♏46.2

JULY 1995 — LONGITUDE

Day	Sid.Time	☉	0 hr ☽	Noon ☽	True ☊	☿	♀	♂	♃	♄	♅	♆	♇
1 Sa	18 34 19	8♋43 21	11♌39 29	17♌48 3	3♏ 8.0	16♊57.6	24♊46.3	18♍22.0	7♐ 6.5	24♓43.7	29♑18.1	24♑35.6	28♏12.3
2 Su	18 38 16	9 40 34	23 59 6	0♍12 53	2R 58.6	18 1.1	25 59.6	18 55.1	7R 1.0	24 44.2	29R 15.9	24R 34.1	28R 11.2
3 M	18 42 12	10 37 47	6♍29 42	12 49 52	2 51.6	19 8.6	27 13.0	19 28.3	6 55.7	24 44.6	29 13.7	24 32.5	28 10.1
4 Tu	18 46 9	11 35 0	19 13 43	25 41 37	2 47.2	20 20.1	28 26.3	20 1.7	6 50.6	24 44.9	29 11.5	24 31.0	28 9.0
5 W	18 50 5	12 32 12	2♎13 56	8♎51 2	2D 45.2	21 35.6	29 39.7	20 35.2	6 45.5	24 45.0	29 9.2	24 29.4	28 7.9
6 Th	18 54 2	13 29 24	15 33 17	22 21 0	2 44.8	22 55.1	0♋53.1	21 8.8	6 40.6	24R 45.1	29 6.9	24 27.8	28 6.9
7 F	18 57 59	14 26 36	29 14 26	6♏13 46	2R 45.0	24 18.4	2 6.5	21 42.5	6 35.9	24 45.1	29 4.6	24 26.2	28 5.9
8 Sa	19 1 55	15 23 47	13♏19 3	20 30 13	2 44.7	25 45.5	3 19.9	22 16.4	6 31.3	24 45.0	29 2.3	24 24.6	28 4.9
9 Su	19 5 52	16 20 59	27 47 0	5♐ 8 59	2 42.8	27 16.4	4 33.3	22 50.3	6 26.9	24 44.8	29 0.0	24 23.0	28 3.9
10 M	19 9 48	17 18 10	12♐35 34	20 5 54	2 38.5	28 51.0	5 46.7	23 24.4	6 22.6	24 44.5	28 57.7	24 21.4	28 3.0
11 Tu	19 13 45	18 15 21	27 39 0	5♑13 42	2 31.5	0♋29.2	7 0.2	23 58.6	6 18.5	24 44.0	28 55.3	24 19.8	28 2.1
12 W	19 17 41	19 12 33	12♑48 45	20 22 50	2 22.4	2 10.8	8 13.7	24 32.8	6 14.6	24 43.5	28 53.0	24 18.2	28 1.2
13 Th	19 21 38	20 9 44	27 54 36	5♒22 51	2 12.0	3 55.8	9 27.2	25 7.2	6 10.8	24 42.9	28 50.6	24 16.6	28 0.4
14 F	19 25 34	21 6 56	12♒46 25	20 4 20	2 1.5	5 44.1	10 40.7	25 41.7	6 7.2	24 42.2	28 48.3	24 15.0	27 59.6
15 Sa	19 29 31	22 4 8	27 15 52	4♓20 27	1 52.2	7 35.4	11 54.2	26 16.4	6 3.8	24 41.4	28 45.9	24 13.3	27 58.8
16 Su	19 33 28	23 1 20	11♓17 45	18 7 40	1 44.9	9 29.5	13 7.8	26 51.1	6 0.5	24 40.5	28 43.5	24 11.7	27 58.0
17 M	19 37 24	23 58 33	24 50 15	1♈25 44	1 40.0	11 26.3	14 21.4	27 25.9	5 57.4	24 39.5	28 41.1	24 10.1	27 57.3
18 Tu	19 41 21	24 55 47	7♈54 29	14 16 59	1 37.5	13 25.5	15 35.0	28 0.8	5 54.4	24 38.4	28 38.7	24 8.5	27 56.6
19 W	19 45 17	25 53 1	20 33 47	26 45 30	1 36.7	15 26.8	16 48.6	28 35.9	5 51.7	24 37.2	28 36.3	24 6.9	27 55.9
20 Th	19 49 14	26 50 16	2♉52 48	8♉56 20	1 36.6	17 29.9	18 2.2	29 11.0	5 49.1	24 35.9	28 33.9	24 5.2	27 55.2
21 F	19 53 10	27 47 32	14 56 46	20 54 46	1 36.2	19 34.5	19 15.9	29 46.2	5 46.7	24 34.5	28 31.5	24 3.6	27 54.6
22 Sa	19 57 7	28 44 49	26 50 57	2♊45 56	1 34.4	21 40.3	20 29.6	0♎21.6	5 44.4	24 33.0	28 29.1	24 2.0	27 54.0
23 Su	20 1 3	29 42 6	8♊40 17	14 34 30	1 30.4	23 46.9	21 43.3	0 57.1	5 42.4	24 31.4	28 26.7	24 0.4	27 53.5
24 M	20 5 0	0♌39 25	20 29 4	26 24 24	1 23.6	25 54.1	22 57.1	1 32.6	5 40.5	24 29.7	28 24.3	23 58.8	27 53.0
25 Tu	20 8 57	1 36 44	2♋20 51	8♋18 45	1 14.1	28 1.5	24 10.8	2 8.3	5 38.8	24 27.9	28 21.9	23 57.2	27 52.5
26 W	20 12 53	2 34 3	14 18 21	20 19 53	1 2.3	0♌ 8.9	25 24.6	2 44.0	5 37.3	24 26.0	28 19.5	23 55.6	27 52.0
27 Th	20 16 50	3 31 24	26 23 29	2♌29 19	0 49.1	2 16.0	26 38.4	3 19.9	5 36.0	24 24.1	28 17.1	23 54.0	27 51.6
28 F	20 20 46	4 28 45	8♌37 28	14 48 1	0 35.5	4 22.6	27 52.2	3 55.9	5 34.8	24 22.0	28 14.7	23 52.4	27 51.2
29 Sa	20 24 43	5 26 7	21 1 1	27 16 32	0 22.6	6 28.4	29 6.1	4 32.0	5 33.9	24 19.9	28 12.3	23 50.8	27 50.8
30 Su	20 28 39	6 23 29	3♍34 38	9♍55 23	0 11.6	8 33.3	0♌19.9	5 8.1	5 33.1	24 17.6	28 9.9	23 49.2	27 50.5
31 M	20 32 36	7 20 52	16 18 54	22 45 17	0 3.2	10 37.2	1 33.8	5 44.4	5 32.5	24 15.3	28 7.6	23 47.6	27 50.2

AUGUST 1995 — LONGITUDE

Day	Sid.Time	☉	0 hr ☽	Noon ☽	True ☊	☿	♀	♂	♃	♄	♅	♆	♇
1 Tu	20 36 32	8♌18 16	29♍14 40	5♎47 16	29♎57.7	12♌39.8	2♌47.7	6♎20.7	5♐32.1	24♓12.9	28♑ 5.2	23♑46.1	27♏49.9
2 W	20 40 29	9 15 40	12♎23 15	19 2 50	29R 54.9	14 41.2	4 1.6	6 57.2	5D 31.9	24R 10.4	28R 2.9	23R 44.5	27R 49.7
3 Th	20 44 26	10 13 5	25 46 16	2♏33 45	29D 54.0	16 41.2	5 15.5	7 33.7	5 31.8	24 7.8	28 0.5	23 43.0	27 49.5
4 F	20 48 22	11 10 31	9♏25 29	16 21 36	29R 54.0	18 39.7	6 29.5	8 10.4	5 32.0	24 5.1	27 58.2	23 41.4	27 49.3
5 Sa	20 52 19	12 7 57	23 22 13	0♐27 19	29 53.7	20 36.7	7 43.4	8 47.1	5 32.3	24 2.4	27 55.9	23 39.9	27 49.1
6 Su	20 56 15	13 5 24	7♐36 46	14 50 21	29 51.9	22 32.3	8 57.4	9 24.0	5 32.8	23 59.6	27 53.6	23 38.4	27 49.0
7 M	21 0 12	14 2 51	22 7 40	29 28 10	29 47.8	24 26.3	10 11.4	10 0.9	5 33.5	23 56.7	27 51.3	23 36.9	27 49.0
8 Tu	21 4 8	15 0 20	6♑51 8	14♑15 44	29 41.1	26 18.8	11 25.4	10 37.9	5 34.4	23 53.7	27 49.0	23 35.4	27D 48.9
9 W	21 8 5	15 57 49	21 41 2	29 5 57	29 32.2	28 9.7	12 39.4	11 15.0	5 35.5	23 50.6	27 46.8	23 33.9	27 48.9
10 Th	21 12 1	16 55 19	6♒29 26	13♒50 24	29 22.0	29 59.0	13 53.5	11 52.2	5 36.7	23 47.5	27 44.6	23 32.5	27 49.0
11 F	21 15 58	17 52 50	21 7 50	28 20 50	29 11.6	1♍46.8	15 7.5	12 29.4	5 38.2	23 44.2	27 42.3	23 31.0	27 49.0
12 Sa	21 19 55	18 50 22	5♓28 36	12♓30 32	29 2.2	3 33.1	16 21.6	13 6.8	5 39.8	23 40.9	27 40.1	23 29.6	27 49.1
13 Su	21 23 51	19 47 56	19 26 10	26 15 15	28 54.7	5 17.9	17 35.7	13 44.2	5 41.6	23 37.6	27 38.0	23 28.2	27 49.3
14 M	21 27 48	20 45 30	2♈57 41	9♈33 33	28 49.7	7 1.1	18 49.8	14 21.8	5 43.5	23 34.1	27 35.8	23 26.8	27 49.4
15 Tu	21 31 44	21 43 7	16 3 4	22 26 33	28 47.0	8 42.8	20 4.0	14 59.4	5 45.7	23 30.6	27 33.7	23 25.4	27 49.6
16 W	21 35 41	22 40 44	28 44 28	4♉57 20	28D 46.3	10 23.1	21 18.1	15 37.1	5 48.0	23 27.1	27 31.6	23 24.0	27 49.8
17 Th	21 39 37	23 38 23	11♉ 5 43	17 10 15	28 46.7	12 1.9	22 32.3	16 14.9	5 50.5	23 23.4	27 29.5	23 22.7	27 50.1
18 F	21 43 34	24 36 4	23 11 35	29 10 23	28R 47.2	13 39.2	23 46.5	16 52.8	5 53.2	23 19.7	27 27.4	23 21.3	27 50.4
19 Sa	21 47 30	25 33 46	5♊ 7 18	11♊ 3 0	28 46.7	15 15.1	25 0.7	17 30.7	5 56.0	23 16.0	27 25.4	23 20.0	27 50.7
20 Su	21 51 27	26 31 30	16 58 7	22 53 14	28 44.5	16 49.5	26 15.0	18 8.8	5 59.1	23 12.2	27 23.4	23 18.7	27 51.1
21 M	21 55 24	27 29 16	28 48 55	4♋45 42	28 40.0	18 22.4	27 29.2	18 46.9	6 2.3	23 8.3	27 21.4	23 17.4	27 51.5
22 Tu	21 59 20	28 27 3	10♋44 3	16 44 24	28 33.3	19 53.9	28 43.5	19 25.2	6 5.6	23 4.4	27 19.5	23 16.2	27 51.9
23 W	22 3 17	29 24 52	22 47 5	28 52 25	28 24.5	21 24.0	29 57.8	20 3.5	6 9.2	23 0.4	27 17.5	23 14.9	27 52.4
24 Th	22 7 13	0♍22 42	5♌ 0 38	11♌11 55	28 14.4	22 52.6	1♍12.1	20 41.9	6 12.9	22 56.3	27 15.6	23 13.7	27 52.9
25 F	22 11 10	1 20 34	17 26 24	23 44 7	28 3.9	24 19.7	2 26.4	21 20.4	6 16.8	22 52.2	27 13.8	23 12.5	27 53.4
26 Sa	22 15 6	2 18 27	0♍ 5 7	6♍29 21	27 54.0	25 45.3	3 40.8	21 59.0	6 20.8	22 48.1	27 11.9	23 11.3	27 54.0
27 Su	22 19 3	3 16 22	12 56 46	19 27 18	27 45.6	27 9.4	4 55.1	22 37.6	6 25.1	22 43.9	27 10.1	23 10.2	27 54.6
28 M	22 22 59	4 14 19	26 0 51	2♎37 20	27 39.3	28 32.0	6 9.5	23 16.4	6 29.5	22 39.7	27 8.4	23 9.1	27 55.2
29 Tu	22 26 56	5 12 16	9♎16 39	15 58 43	27 35.5	29 53.0	7 23.9	23 55.2	6 34.0	22 35.4	27 6.6	23 7.9	27 55.9
30 W	22 30 53	6 10 16	22 43 30	29 30 56	27D 33.9	1♎12.3	8 38.2	24 34.2	6 38.7	22 31.1	27 4.9	23 6.9	27 56.6
31 Th	22 34 49	7 8 16	6♏21 1	13♏13 44	27 34.1	2 30.1	9 52.7	25 13.2	6 43.6	22 26.7	27 3.3	23 5.8	27 57.4

Astro Data	Dy Hr Mn
☽0S	4 5:53
♄ R	6 7:46
☽0N	16 20:03
♂0S	22 23:25
☽0S	31 12:25
♃ D	2 16:44
♅✶♇	8 0:57
♇ D	8 13:33
☽0N	13 6:32
♄✶♆	17 8:05
☽0S	27 19:05
☿0S	27 21:30

Planet Ingress	Dy Hr Mn
♀ ♋	5 6:39
☿ ♋	10 16:58
♂ ♎	21 9:21
☉ ♌	23 7:30
☿ ♌	25 22:19
♀ ♌	29 17:32
☊ ♎	31 12:34
☿ ♍	10 0:13
☉ ♍	23 14:35
♀ ♍	23 0:43
☿ ♎	29 2:07

Last Aspect Dy Hr Mn		☽ Ingress	Dy Hr Mn
2 8:06	♇ □	♍	2 11:35
4 18:49	♀ □	♎	4 19:55
6 23:43	♅ □	♏	7 1:19
9 1:59	♅ ✶	♐	9 3:38
10 19:22	♄ □	♑	11 3:43
13 1:29	♅ ☌	♒	13 3:21
15 1:12	♇ □	♓	15 4:37
17 6:58	♅ ✶	♈	17 9:23
19 15:33	♅ □	♉	19 18:20
22 4:11	☉ ✶	♊	22 6:23
24 8:07	♄ □	♋	24 19:16
27 3:43	♅ ☍	♌	27 7:07
29 13:05	♇ □	♍	29 17:12

Last Aspect Dy Hr Mn		☽ Ingress	Dy Hr Mn
31 21:52	♅ △	♎	1 1:23
3 3:57	♅ □	♏	3 7:29
5 7:43	♅ ✶	♐	5 11:14
7 4:21	☿ △	♑	7 12:52
9 9:55	♇ ✶	♒	9 13:28
11 11:07	♇ □	♓	11 14:46
13 14:47	♇ △	♈	13 18:41
15 21:41	♅ □	♉	16 2:25
18 9:19	♇ ☍	♊	18 13:40
20 21:05	☉ ✶	♋	21 2:24
23 10:02	♇ △	♌	23 14:13
25 19:53	♇ □	♍	25 23:50
28 5:07	☿ ☌	♎	28 7:15
30 7:42	♅ □	♏	30 12:51

☽ Phases & Eclipses Dy Hr Mn	
5 20:02	☽ 13♎20
12 10:49	○ 19♑38
19 11:10	☽ 26♈20
27 15:13	● 4♌08
4 3:16	☽ 11♏18
10 18:16	○ 17♒39
18 3:04	☽ 24♉43
26 4:31	● 2♍29

Astro Data

1 JULY 1995
Julian Day # 34880
Delta T 59.8 sec
SVP 05♓19'12"
Obliquity 23°26'15"
⚷ Chiron 21♍42.3
☽ Mean ☊ 2♏10.9

1 AUGUST 1995
Julian Day # 34911
Delta T 59.9 sec
SVP 05♓19'07"
Obliquity 23°26'15"
⚷ Chiron 24♍45.1
☽ Mean ☊ 0♏32.4

LONGITUDE — SEPTEMBER 1995

Day	Sid.Time	☉	0 hr ☽	Noon ☽	True ☊	☿	♀	♂	♃	♄	♅	♆	♇
1 F	22 38 46	8♍ 6 18	20♏ 9 3	27♏ 6 57	27♎35.1	3♎46.1	11♍ 7.1	25♎52.2	6♐48.7	22♓22.3	27♑ 1.6	23♑ 4.8	27♏58.1
2 Sa	22 42 42	9 4 21	4♐ 7 25	11♐10 21	27R35.9	5 0.3	12 21.5	26 31.4	6 53.9	22R17.9	27R 0.1	23R 3.8	27 58.9
3 Su	22 46 39	10 2 26	18 15 37	25 23 2	27 35.7	6 12.7	13 35.9	27 10.7	6 59.2	22 13.5	26 58.5	23 2.8	27 59.8
4 M	22 50 35	11 0 32	2♑32 19	9♑43 8	27 33.8	7 23.2	14 50.4	27 50.0	7 4.8	22 9.0	26 57.0	23 1.8	28 0.6
5 Tu	22 54 32	11 58 40	16 55 1	24 7 27	27 30.0	8 31.7	16 4.8	28 29.4	7 10.4	22 4.5	26 55.5	23 0.9	28 1.5
6 W	22 58 28	12 56 49	1♒19 50	8♒31 31	27 24.5	9 38.1	17 19.3	29 8.9	7 16.3	21 60.0	26 54.1	22 60.0	28 2.5
7 Th	23 2 25	13 54 59	15 41 48	22 50 0	27 17.9	10 42.2	18 33.8	29 48.4	7 22.3	21 55.4	26 52.7	22 59.1	28 3.4
8 F	23 6 21	14 53 11	29 55 23	6♓57 21	27 11.2	11 44.0	19 48.2	0♏28.1	7 28.4	21 50.9	26 51.3	22 58.2	28 4.4
9 Sa	23 10 18	15 51 25	13♓55 16	20 48 41	27 5.0	12 43.3	21 2.7	1 7.8	7 34.7	21 46.3	26 50.0	22 57.4	28 5.4
10 Su	23 14 15	16 49 40	27 37 11	4♈20 29	27 0.3	13 40.0	22 17.2	1 47.6	7 41.1	21 41.7	26 48.7	22 56.6	28 6.5
11 M	23 18 11	17 47 57	10♈58 26	17 31 0	26 57.3	14 33.9	23 31.7	2 27.5	7 47.6	21 37.1	26 47.5	22 55.8	28 7.6
12 Tu	23 22 8	18 46 16	23 58 15	0♉20 22	26D56.1	15 24.7	24 46.3	3 7.4	7 54.4	21 32.5	26 46.3	22 55.1	28 8.7
13 W	23 26 4	19 44 37	6♉37 37	12 50 21	26 56.5	16 12.3	26 0.8	3 47.4	8 1.2	21 27.9	26 45.2	22 54.4	28 9.8
14 Th	23 30 1	20 43 1	18 59 2	25 4 7	26 57.8	16 56.5	27 15.3	4 27.6	8 8.2	21 23.3	26 44.0	22 53.7	28 11.0
15 F	23 33 57	21 41 26	1♊ 6 10	7♊ 5 45	26 59.5	17 37.0	28 29.9	5 7.7	8 15.4	21 18.6	26 43.0	22 53.0	28 12.2
16 Sa	23 37 54	22 39 53	13 3 27	18 59 55	27R 0.9	18 13.5	29 44.4	5 48.0	8 22.6	21 14.0	26 42.0	22 52.4	28 13.5
17 Su	23 41 50	23 38 23	24 55 45	0♋51 35	27 1.3	18 45.7	0♎59.0	6 28.4	8 30.0	21 9.4	26 41.0	22 51.8	28 14.7
18 M	23 45 47	24 36 55	6♋48 0	12 45 37	27 0.5	19 13.3	2 13.6	7 8.8	8 37.6	21 4.8	26 40.1	22 51.3	28 16.0
19 Tu	23 49 44	25 35 29	18 45 0	24 46 39	26 58.3	19 35.9	3 28.2	7 49.3	8 45.3	21 0.2	26 39.2	22 50.7	28 17.4
20 W	23 53 40	26 34 5	0♌51 4	6♌58 41	26 54.8	19 53.3	4 42.8	8 29.9	8 53.1	20 55.6	26 38.4	22 50.2	28 18.7
21 Th	23 57 37	27 32 43	13 9 53	19 24 57	26 50.4	20 5.0	5 57.4	9 10.6	9 1.1	20 51.0	26 37.6	22 49.7	28 20.1
22 F	0 1 33	28 31 24	25 44 9	2♍ 7 38	26 45.6	20R10.6	7 12.0	9 51.3	9 9.1	20 46.4	26 36.8	22 49.3	28 21.5
23 Sa	0 5 30	29 30 6	8♍35 30	15 7 44	26 41.1	20 9.8	8 26.6	10 32.1	9 17.3	20 41.8	26 36.1	22 48.9	28 23.0
24 Su	0 9 26	0♎28 51	21 44 18	28 25 2	26 37.3	20 2.3	9 41.3	11 13.0	9 25.7	20 37.3	26 35.5	22 48.5	28 24.4
25 M	0 13 23	1 27 37	5♎ 9 45	11♎58 12	26 34.7	19 47.8	10 55.9	11 54.0	9 34.1	20 32.8	26 34.9	22 48.2	28 25.9
26 Tu	0 17 19	2 26 26	18 50 3	25 44 59	26D33.3	19 26.0	12 10.5	12 35.1	9 42.7	20 28.3	26 34.3	22 47.8	28 27.5
27 W	0 21 16	3 25 16	2♏42 38	9♏42 38	26 33.3	18 56.8	13 25.2	13 16.2	9 51.4	20 23.8	26 33.8	22 47.5	28 29.0
28 Th	0 25 13	4 24 8	16 44 36	23 48 11	26 34.1	18 20.3	14 39.8	13 57.4	10 0.3	20 19.4	26 33.4	22 47.3	28 30.6
29 F	0 29 9	5 23 3	0♐53 1	7♐58 46	26 35.5	17 36.5	15 54.5	14 38.7	10 9.2	20 15.0	26 33.0	22 47.1	28 32.2
30 Sa	0 33 6	6 21 59	15 5 6	22 11 44	26 36.8	16 46.0	17 9.1	15 20.1	10 18.3	20 10.7	26 32.6	22 46.9	28 33.8

LONGITUDE — OCTOBER 1995

Day	Sid.Time	☉	0 hr ☽	Noon ☽	True ☊	☿	♀	♂	♃	♄	♅	♆	♇
1 Su	0 37 2	7♎20 56	29♐18 22	6♑24 44	26♎37.7	15♎49.4	18♎23.8	16♏ 1.5	10♐27.5	20♓ 6.4	26♑32.3	22♑46.7	28♏35.5
2 M	0 40 59	8 19 56	13♑30 31	20 35 30	26R37.7	14R47.6	19 38.5	16 43.0	10 36.8	20R 2.1	26R32.1	22R46.6	28 37.2
3 Tu	0 44 55	9 18 57	27 39 21	4♒41 50	26 37.0	13 41.7	20 53.1	17 24.6	10 46.2	19 57.8	26 31.9	22 46.5	28 38.9
4 W	0 48 52	10 18 0	11♒42 38	18 41 28	26 35.5	12 33.3	22 7.8	18 6.2	10 55.7	19 53.6	26 31.7	22 46.5	28 40.6
5 Th	0 52 48	11 17 4	25 38 2	2♓32 2	26 33.6	11 23.9	23 22.4	18 48.0	11 5.3	19 49.5	26 31.6	22D46.5	28 42.4
6 F	0 56 45	12 16 11	9♓23 12	16 11 15	26 31.6	10 15.5	24 37.1	19 29.8	11 15.1	19 45.4	26D31.6	22 46.5	28 44.1
7 Sa	1 0 41	13 15 19	22 55 55	29 37 0	26 29.8	9 9.8	25 51.8	20 11.6	11 24.9	19 41.4	26 31.6	22 46.5	28 45.9
8 Su	1 4 38	14 14 29	6♈14 20	12♈47 46	26 28.6	8 8.8	27 6.4	20 53.6	11 34.8	19 37.4	26 31.6	22 46.6	28 47.8
9 M	1 8 35	15 13 41	19 17 12	25 42 38	26D27.9	7 14.2	28 21.1	21 35.6	11 44.9	19 33.4	26 31.7	22 46.7	28 49.6
10 Tu	1 12 31	16 12 55	2♉ 4 5	8♉21 38	26 27.9	6 27.5	29 35.7	22 17.6	11 55.0	19 29.5	26 31.9	22 46.8	28 51.5
11 W	1 16 28	17 12 12	14 35 28	20 45 45	26 28.3	5 49.9	0♏50.4	22 59.8	12 5.3	19 25.7	26 32.1	22 47.0	28 53.4
12 Th	1 20 24	18 11 30	26 52 47	2♊56 54	26 29.1	5 22.4	2 5.1	23 42.0	12 15.6	19 22.0	26 32.3	22 47.2	28 55.3
13 F	1 24 21	19 10 51	8♊58 26	14 57 51	26 29.9	5 5.6	3 19.7	24 24.3	12 26.1	19 18.3	26 32.6	22 47.5	28 57.2
14 Sa	1 28 17	20 10 14	20 55 35	26 52 8	26 30.6	4D59.8	4 34.4	25 6.7	12 36.6	19 14.6	26 33.0	22 47.8	28 59.2
15 Su	1 32 14	21 9 40	2♋48 2	8♋43 51	26 31.2	5 4.9	5 49.1	25 49.1	12 47.2	19 11.1	26 33.4	22 48.1	29 1.2
16 M	1 36 10	22 9 7	14 40 8	20 37 30	26R31.5	5 20.6	7 3.7	26 31.6	12 58.0	19 7.6	26 33.8	22 48.4	29 3.1
17 Tu	1 40 7	23 8 37	26 36 30	2♌37 44	26 31.5	5 46.6	8 18.4	27 14.2	13 8.8	19 4.1	26 34.4	22 48.8	29 5.2
18 W	1 44 4	24 8 10	8♌41 47	14 49 11	26 31.4	6 22.1	9 33.1	27 56.9	13 19.7	19 0.8	26 34.9	22 49.2	29 7.2
19 Th	1 48 0	25 7 44	21 0 27	27 16 5	26 31.2	7 6.5	10 47.8	28 39.6	13 30.7	18 57.5	26 35.5	22 49.7	29 9.2
20 F	1 51 57	26 7 21	3♍36 28	10♍ 1 59	26D31.1	7 59.0	12 2.4	29 22.4	13 41.7	18 54.3	26 36.2	22 50.1	29 11.3
21 Sa	1 55 53	27 7 0	16 32 54	23 9 23	26 31.2	8 58.7	13 17.1	0♐ 5.3	13 52.9	18 51.2	26 36.9	22 50.7	29 13.4
22 Su	1 59 50	28 6 41	29 51 31	6♎39 16	26 31.3	10 4.8	14 31.8	0 48.2	14 4.2	18 48.1	26 37.7	22 51.2	29 15.5
23 M	2 3 46	29 6 24	13♎32 29	20 30 53	26R31.4	11 16.6	15 46.5	1 31.3	14 15.5	18 45.1	26 38.5	22 51.8	29 17.6
24 Tu	2 7 43	0♏ 6 10	27 34 6	4♏41 36	26 31.5	12 33.2	17 1.2	2 14.3	14 26.9	18 42.2	26 39.3	22 52.4	29 19.8
25 W	2 11 39	1 5 57	11♏52 48	19 7 1	26 31.4	13 54.1	18 15.9	2 57.5	14 38.4	18 39.4	26 40.2	22 53.0	29 21.9
26 Th	2 15 36	2 5 47	26 23 30	3♐41 28	26 31.0	15 18.5	19 30.6	3 40.7	14 50.0	18 36.7	26 41.2	22 53.7	29 24.1
27 F	2 19 33	3 5 38	11♐ 0 8	18 18 42	26 30.3	16 45.9	20 45.3	4 24.0	15 1.6	18 34.1	26 42.2	22 54.4	29 26.3
28 Sa	2 23 29	4 5 31	25 36 28	2♑52 43	26 29.5	18 15.8	21 59.9	5 7.4	15 13.4	18 31.6	26 43.3	22 55.2	29 28.5
29 Su	2 27 26	5 5 26	10♑ 6 54	17 18 28	26 28.6	19 47.7	23 14.6	5 50.8	15 25.2	18 29.1	26 44.4	22 56.0	29 30.7
30 M	2 31 22	6 5 22	24 27 1	1♒32 13	26D28.0	21 21.3	24 29.3	6 34.3	15 37.0	18 26.8	26 45.6	22 56.8	29 32.9
31 Tu	2 35 19	7 5 20	8♒33 51	15 31 45	26 27.9	22 56.2	25 44.0	7 17.9	15 49.0	18 24.5	26 46.8	22 57.6	29 35.1

Astro Data	Planet Ingress	Last Aspect	☽ Ingress	Last Aspect	☽ Ingress	☽ Phases & Eclipses
Dy Hr Mn	Dy Hr Mn	Dy Hr Mn	Dy Hr Mn	Dy Hr Mn	Dy Hr Mn	Dy Hr Mn
☽0N 9 16:29	♂ ♏ 7 7:00	1 13:29 ♇ ☌	♐ 1 16:57	30 8:33 ♄ □	♑ 1 1:10	2 9:03 ☽ 9♐26
♃∠♆ 12 2:21	♀ ♎ 16 5:01	3 15:44 ♂ ⚹	♑ 3 19:45	3 1:41 ♇ ⚹	♒ 3 3:59	9 3:37 ○ 16♓00
♀0S 18 13:58	☉ ♎ 23 12:13	5 20:11 ♂ □	♒ 5 21:47	5 5:21 ♇ □	♓ 5 7:35	16 21:09 ☽ 23♊31
☿ R 22 9:15		7 20:51 ♇ □	♓ 8 0:08	7 10:29 ♇ △	♈ 7 12:41	24 16:55 ● 1♎10
☽0S 24 2:55	♀ ♏ 10 7:48	10 0:52 ♇ △	♈ 10 4:14	9 18:49 ♀ ☍	♉ 9 20:05	
	♂ ♐ 20 21:02	12 5:15 ♅ □	♉ 12 11:21	12 4:02 ♇ ☍	♊ 12 6:10	1 14:36 ☽ 7♑57
♆ D 5 3:56	☉ ♏ 23 21:32	14 18:13 ♇ ☍	♊ 14 21:48	13 22:20 ☉ △	♋ 14 18:20	8 15:52 ○ 14♈54
♅ D 6 12:58		16 21:09 ☉ □	♋ 17 10:16	17 4:58 ♇ △	♌ 17 6:46	8 16:04 A 0.825
☽0N 7 0:41		19 18:59 ♇ △	♌ 19 22:19	19 15:38 ♇ □	♍ 19 17:11	16 16:26 ☽ 22♋50
♃∠♅ 7 16:12		22 4:57 ♇ □	♍ 22 8:01	21 22:56 ♇ ⚹	♎ 22 0:15	24 4:36 ● 0♏18
☿ D 14 0:47		24 12:00 ♇ ⚹	♎ 24 14:50	23 22:27 ♅ □	♏ 24 4:06	24 4:32:31 T 2'10"
☽0S 21 12:13		26 13:25 ♅ □	♏ 26 19:20	26 4:58 ♇ ☌	♐ 26 5:56	30 21:17 ☽ 6♒59
		28 20:01 ♇ ☌	♐ 28 22:30	27 12:23 ♄ □	♑ 28 7:15	
				30 8:39 ♇ ⚹	♒ 30 9:23	

Astro Data

1 SEPTEMBER 1995
Julian Day # 34942
Delta T 59.9 sec
SVP 05♓19'04"
Obliquity 23°26'16"
⚷ Chiron 28♍46.1
☽ Mean ☊ 28♎53.9

1 OCTOBER 1995
Julian Day # 34972
Delta T 60.0 sec
SVP 05♓19'01"
Obliquity 23°26'16"
⚷ Chiron 3♎05.4
☽ Mean ☊ 27♎18.5

NOVEMBER 1995 LONGITUDE

Day	Sid.Time	☉	0 hr ☽	Noon ☽	True ☊	☿	♀	♂	♃	♄	♅	♆	♇
1 W	2 39 15	8♏ 5 20	22♒25 51	29♒16 6	26♎28.2	24♎32.2	26♏58.6	8♐ 1.5	16♐ 1.0	18♓22.3	26♑48.1	22♑58.5	29♏37.4
2 Th	2 43 12	9 5 21	6♓ 2 33	12♓45 15	26 29.0	26 8.9	28 13.3	8 45.2	16 13.1	18R 20.2	26 49.4	22 59.4	29 39.6
3 F	2 47 8	10 5 23	19 24 16	25 59 43	26 30.1	27 46.2	29 27.9	9 28.9	16 25.2	18 18.3	26 50.7	23 0.3	29 41.9
4 Sa	2 51 5	11 5 28	2♈31 43	9♈ 0 21	26 31.3	29 23.9	0♐42.6	10 12.8	16 37.4	18 16.4	26 52.1	23 1.3	29 44.2
5 Su	2 55 2	12 5 34	15 25 45	21 48 1	26R 32.2	1♏ 1.9	1 57.2	10 56.6	16 49.7	18 14.6	26 53.6	23 2.3	29 46.5
6 M	2 58 58	13 5 41	28 7 15	4♉23 34	26 32.5	2 40.1	3 11.9	11 40.6	17 2.0	18 12.9	26 55.1	23 3.3	29 48.8
7 Tu	3 2 55	14 5 51	10♉37 4	16 47 53	26 31.9	4 18.3	4 26.5	12 24.6	17 14.4	18 11.3	26 56.7	23 4.4	29 51.1
8 W	3 6 51	15 6 2	22 56 9	29 2 1	26 30.4	5 56.5	5 41.1	13 8.6	17 26.8	18 9.8	26 58.2	23 5.5	29 53.4
9 Th	3 10 48	16 6 15	5♊ 5 39	11♊ 7 15	26 27.9	7 34.5	6 55.8	13 52.8	17 39.3	18 8.4	26 59.9	23 6.6	29 55.7
10 F	3 14 44	17 6 30	17 7 2	23 5 18	26 24.6	9 12.5	8 10.4	14 37.0	17 51.9	18 7.1	27 1.6	23 7.8	29 58.1
11 Sa	3 18 41	18 6 47	29 2 19	4♋58 26	26 20.9	10 50.3	9 25.0	15 21.2	18 4.5	18 5.9	27 3.3	23 8.9	0♐ 0.4
12 Su	3 22 37	19 7 6	10♋54 2	16 49 31	26 17.2	12 27.8	10 39.6	16 5.5	18 17.2	18 4.8	27 5.1	23 10.2	0 2.8
13 M	3 26 34	20 7 27	22 45 22	28 42 2	26 14.0	14 5.1	11 54.2	16 49.9	18 29.9	18 3.9	27 6.9	23 11.4	0 5.1
14 Tu	3 30 31	21 7 49	4♌40 4	10♌40 1	26 11.7	15 42.2	13 8.8	17 34.4	18 42.7	18 3.0	27 8.8	23 12.7	0 7.5
15 W	3 34 27	22 8 14	16 42 25	22 47 53	26D 10.5	17 19.1	14 23.4	18 18.9	18 55.5	18 2.2	27 10.7	23 14.0	0 9.9
16 Th	3 38 24	23 8 40	28 57 0	5♍10 20	26 10.5	18 55.6	15 38.1	19 3.4	19 8.4	18 1.5	27 12.7	23 15.3	0 12.2
17 F	3 42 20	24 9 8	11♍28 27	17 51 54	26 11.6	20 31.9	16 52.6	19 48.0	19 21.3	18 1.0	27 14.7	23 16.6	0 14.6
18 Sa	3 46 17	25 9 38	24 21 9	0♎56 36	26 13.2	22 8.0	18 7.2	20 32.7	19 34.2	18 0.5	27 16.7	23 18.0	0 17.0
19 Su	3 50 13	26 10 10	7♎38 35	14 27 18	26 14.8	23 43.8	19 21.8	21 17.5	19 47.2	18 0.1	27 18.8	23 19.4	0 19.4
20 M	3 54 10	27 10 44	21 22 49	28 25 3	26R 15.8	25 19.4	20 36.4	22 2.3	20 0.3	17 59.9	27 20.9	23 20.9	0 21.7
21 Tu	3 58 6	28 11 19	5♏33 44	12♏48 27	26 15.5	26 54.8	21 51.0	22 47.2	20 13.4	17D 59.7	27 23.1	23 22.3	0 24.1
22 W	4 2 3	29 11 56	20 8 33	27 33 14	26 13.7	28 29.9	23 5.6	23 32.1	20 26.5	17 59.7	27 25.3	23 23.8	0 26.5
23 Th	4 6 0	0♐12 35	5♐ 1 32	12♐32 23	26 10.2	0♐ 4.8	24 20.2	24 17.1	20 39.7	17 59.8	27 27.6	23 25.4	0 28.9
24 F	4 9 56	1 13 15	20 4 34	27 36 52	26 5.4	1 39.6	25 34.8	25 2.1	20 52.9	17 60.0	27 29.9	23 26.9	0 31.3
25 Sa	4 13 53	2 13 56	5♑ 8 7	12♑37 8	25 59.8	3 14.2	26 49.3	25 47.3	21 6.1	18 0.3	27 32.2	23 28.5	0 33.7
26 Su	4 17 49	3 14 39	20 2 56	27 24 36	25 54.4	4 48.6	28 3.9	26 32.4	21 19.4	18 0.7	27 34.6	23 30.1	0 36.1
27 M	4 21 46	4 15 22	4♒41 25	11♒52 53	25 49.9	6 22.9	29 18.4	27 17.6	21 32.7	18 1.2	27 37.0	23 31.7	0 38.5
28 Tu	4 25 42	5 16 7	18 58 39	25 58 30	25 46.9	7 57.0	0♑33.0	28 2.9	21 46.1	18 1.8	27 39.4	23 33.3	0 40.9
29 W	4 29 39	6 16 53	2♓52 26	9♓40 33	25D 45.7	9 31.0	1 47.5	28 48.2	21 59.4	18 2.5	27 41.9	23 35.0	0 43.2
30 Th	4 33 35	7 17 39	16 23 3	23 0 14	25 46.0	11 5.0	3 2.0	29 33.6	22 12.8	18 3.3	27 44.5	23 36.7	0 45.6

DECEMBER 1995 LONGITUDE

Day	Sid.Time	☉	0 hr ☽	Noon ☽	True ☊	☿	♀	♂	♃	♄	♅	♆	♇
1 F	4 37 32	8♐18 27	29♓32 26	6♈ 0 3	25♎47.3	12♐38.8	4♑16.5	0♑19.0	22♐26.3	18♓ 4.2	27♑47.0	23♑38.4	0♐48.0
2 Sa	4 41 29	9 19 15	12♈23 27	18 43 4	25 48.7	14 12.6	5 31.0	1 4.5	22 39.7	18 5.3	27 49.6	23 40.2	0 50.4
3 Su	4 45 25	10 20 4	24 59 15	1♉12 24	25R 49.5	15 46.3	6 45.4	1 50.0	22 53.2	18 6.4	27 52.2	23 41.9	0 52.7
4 M	4 49 22	11 20 55	7♉22 50	13 30 52	25 48.7	17 19.9	7 59.9	2 35.6	23 6.7	18 7.7	27 54.9	23 43.7	0 55.1
5 Tu	4 53 18	12 21 46	19 36 48	25 40 51	25 45.8	18 53.6	9 14.3	3 21.2	23 20.2	18 9.0	27 57.6	23 45.5	0 57.4
6 W	4 57 15	13 22 38	1♊43 15	7♊44 11	25 40.6	20 27.2	10 28.8	4 6.9	23 33.7	18 10.5	28 0.3	23 47.3	0 59.8
7 Th	5 1 11	14 23 32	13 43 52	19 42 27	25 33.1	22 0.8	11 43.2	4 52.6	23 47.3	18 12.1	28 3.1	23 49.2	1 2.1
8 F	5 5 8	15 24 26	25 40 5	1♋36 58	25 23.8	23 34.3	12 57.6	5 38.4	24 0.9	18 13.7	28 5.9	23 51.0	1 4.5
9 Sa	5 9 4	16 25 22	7♋33 15	13 29 11	25 13.4	25 7.9	14 11.9	6 24.2	24 14.5	18 15.5	28 8.7	23 52.9	1 6.8
10 Su	5 13 1	17 26 18	19 24 57	25 20 49	25 2.8	26 41.5	15 26.3	7 10.0	24 28.1	18 17.4	28 11.6	23 54.8	1 9.1
11 M	5 16 58	18 27 16	1♌17 7	7♌14 9	24 53.1	28 15.0	16 40.7	7 56.0	24 41.7	18 19.4	28 14.5	23 56.8	1 11.4
12 Tu	5 20 54	19 28 14	13 12 18	19 12 0	24 45.1	29 48.5	17 55.0	8 41.9	24 55.3	18 21.4	28 17.4	23 58.7	1 13.7
13 W	5 24 51	20 29 14	25 13 43	1♍17 56	24 39.3	1♑22.0	19 9.3	9 27.9	25 9.0	18 23.6	28 20.4	24 0.7	1 16.0
14 Th	5 28 47	21 30 14	7♍25 13	13 36 7	24 35.9	2 55.4	20 23.6	10 14.0	25 22.6	18 25.9	28 23.3	24 2.6	1 18.3
15 F	5 32 44	22 31 16	19 51 13	26 11 7	24D 34.6	4 28.7	21 37.9	11 0.1	25 36.3	18 28.3	28 26.3	24 4.6	1 20.6
16 Sa	5 36 40	23 32 19	2♎36 23	9♎ 7 35	24 34.9	6 1.9	22 52.1	11 46.2	25 50.0	18 30.8	28 29.4	24 6.6	1 22.8
17 Su	5 40 37	24 33 22	15 45 12	22 29 41	24R 35.7	7 35.0	24 6.4	12 32.4	26 3.7	18 33.4	28 32.4	24 8.7	1 25.1
18 M	5 44 33	25 34 27	29 21 21	6♏20 22	24 35.8	9 7.8	25 20.6	13 18.7	26 17.4	18 36.0	28 35.5	24 10.7	1 27.3
19 Tu	5 48 30	26 35 33	13♏26 45	20 40 21	24 34.3	10 40.3	26 34.8	14 4.9	26 31.0	18 38.8	28 38.6	24 12.8	1 29.5
20 W	5 52 27	27 36 39	28 0 43	5♐27 15	24 30.3	12 12.5	27 49.0	14 51.3	26 44.7	18 41.7	28 41.7	24 14.8	1 31.7
21 Th	5 56 23	28 37 46	12♐59 3	20 35 3	24 23.7	13 44.2	29 3.2	15 37.6	26 58.4	18 44.7	28 44.9	24 16.9	1 33.9
22 F	6 0 20	29 38 54	28 13 57	5♑54 20	24 14.7	15 15.4	0♒17.4	16 24.1	27 12.1	18 47.8	28 48.1	24 19.0	1 36.1
23 Sa	6 4 16	0♑40 3	13♑34 43	21 13 36	24 4.4	16 45.8	1 31.5	17 10.5	27 25.8	18 51.0	28 51.3	24 21.2	1 38.3
24 Su	6 8 13	1 41 12	28 49 34	6♒21 21	23 54.0	18 15.4	2 45.6	17 57.0	27 39.5	18 54.2	28 54.5	24 23.3	1 40.4
25 M	6 12 9	2 42 21	13♒47 52	21 8 13	23 44.8	19 43.9	3 59.7	18 43.5	27 53.2	18 57.6	28 57.8	24 25.4	1 42.5
26 Tu	6 16 6	3 43 30	28 21 48	5♓28 13	23 37.8	21 11.0	5 13.7	19 30.1	28 6.9	19 1.1	29 1.0	24 27.6	1 44.6
27 W	6 20 2	4 44 39	12♓27 18	19 19 6	23 33.4	22 36.6	6 27.7	20 16.7	28 20.5	19 4.6	29 4.3	24 29.8	1 46.7
28 Th	6 23 59	5 45 48	26 3 49	2♈41 46	23D 31.4	24 0.4	7 41.7	21 3.3	28 34.2	19 8.3	29 7.6	24 31.9	1 48.8
29 F	6 27 56	6 46 57	9♈13 26	15 39 17	23 31.0	25 21.9	8 55.6	21 50.0	28 47.8	19 12.0	29 11.0	24 34.1	1 50.9
30 Sa	6 31 52	7 48 6	21 59 55	28 15 52	23R 31.2	26 40.7	10 9.6	22 36.7	29 1.5	19 15.8	29 14.3	24 36.3	1 52.9
31 Su	6 35 49	8 49 15	4♉27 46	10♉36 8	23 30.8	27 56.4	11 23.4	23 23.4	29 15.1	19 19.7	29 17.7	24 38.5	1 54.9

Astro Data	Planet Ingress	Last Aspect	☽ Ingress	Last Aspect	☽ Ingress	☽ Phases & Eclipses	Astro Data
Dy Hr Mn	Dy Hr Mn	Dy Hr Mn	Dy Hr Mn	Dy Hr Mn	Dy Hr Mn	Dy Hr Mn	1 NOVEMBER 1995
☽0N 3 7:05	♀ ♐ 3 10:18	1 12:40 ♇ □	♓ 1 13:17	30 20:45 ♅ ⚹	♈ 1 0:51	7 7:21 ○ 14♉24	Julian Day # 35003
♃□♄ 11 2:30	☿ ♏ 4 8:50	3 18:51 ♇ △	♈ 3 19:21	3 5:34 ♅ □	♉ 3 9:40	15 11:40 ☽ 22♌38	Delta T 60.0 sec
☽0S 17 22:19	♇ ♐ 10 19:39	5 21:42 ♅ □	♉ 6 3:35	5 16:35 ♅ △	♊ 5 20:35	22 15:43 ● 29♏52	SVP 05♓18'58"
♄ D 21 19:48	☉ ♐ 22 19:01	8 13:44 ♇ ☍	♊ 8 13:55	7 20:36 ♃ ☍	♋ 8 8:44	29 6:28 ☽ 6♓33	Obliquity 23°26'15"
☽0N 30 13:07	☿ ♐ 22 22:46	10 2:00 ♄ □	♋ 11 1:57	10 17:50 ♅ ☍	♌ 10 21:24		⚷ Chiron 7♎28.2
	♀ ♑ 27 13:23	13 8:50 ♅ ☍	♌ 13 14:37	12 23:50 ♃ △	♍ 13 9:26	7 1:27 ○ 14♊27	☽ Mean ☊ 25♎40.0
♃⚺♆ 7 3:49	♂ ♑ 30 13:58	15 11:40 ☉ □	♍ 16 2:02	15 16:18 ♅ △	♎ 15 19:09	15 5:31 ☽ 22♍45	
☽0S 15 7:50		18 5:22 ♅ △	♎ 18 10:18	17 22:40 ♅ □	♏ 18 1:07	22 2:22 ● 29♐45	1 DECEMBER 1995
☽0N 27 20:48	☿ ♑ 12 2:57	20 10:13 ♅ □	♏ 20 14:40	20 1:07 ♅ ⚹	♐ 20 3:13	28 19:06 ☽ 6♈34	Julian Day # 35033
♃⚺♅ 31 6:02	♀ ♒ 21 18:23	22 15:43 ☉ ☌	♐ 22 15:56	22 2:22 ☉ ☌	♑ 22 2:46		Delta T 60.1 sec
	☉ ♑ 22 8:17	24 9:33 ♀ ☌	♑ 24 15:48	24 0:08 ♅ ☌	♒ 24 1:52		SVP 05♓18'54"
		26 12:19 ♅ ☌	♒ 26 16:15	25 23:35 ♃ ⚹	♓ 26 2:45		Obliquity 23°26'15"
		28 16:29 ♂ ⚹	♓ 28 18:59	28 5:33 ♅ ⚹	♈ 28 7:06		⚷ Chiron 11♎04.9
				30 13:56 ♅ □	♉ 30 15:21		☽ Mean ☊ 24♎04.7

LONGITUDE — JANUARY 1996

Day	Sid.Time	☉	0 hr ☽	Noon ☽	True ☊	☿	♀	♂	♃	♄	♅	♆	♇
1 M	6 39 45	9♑50 24	16♉41 32	22♉44 29	23♎28.5	29♑ 8.5	12♒37.3	24♑10.2	29♐28.7	19♓23.7	29♑21.0	24♑40.7	1♐56.9
2 Tu	6 43 42	10 51 33	28 45 25	4♊44 46	23R 23.6	0♒16.2	13 51.1	24 57.0	29 42.3	19 27.8	29 24.4	24 42.9	1 58.9
3 W	6 47 38	11 52 41	10♊42 54	16 40 9	23 15.7	1 19.0	15 4.8	25 43.8	29 55.8	19 32.0	29 27.8	24 45.2	2 0.9
4 Th	6 51 35	12 53 50	22 36 48	28 33 5	23 4.8	2 16.1	16 18.5	26 30.7	0♑ 9.4	19 36.2	29 31.2	24 47.4	2 2.8
5 F	6 55 31	13 54 59	4♋29 13	10♋25 21	22 51.4	3 6.6	17 32.2	27 17.6	0 22.9	19 40.6	29 34.7	24 49.6	2 4.7
6 Sa	6 59 28	14 56 7	16 21 41	22 18 21	22 36.6	3 49.7	18 45.8	28 4.5	0 36.4	19 45.0	29 38.1	24 51.9	2 6.6
7 Su	7 3 25	15 57 15	28 15 29	4♌13 15	22 21.5	4 24.5	19 59.4	28 51.4	0 49.9	19 49.5	29 41.6	24 54.1	2 8.5
8 M	7 7 21	16 58 24	10♌11 49	16 11 22	22 7.4	4 50.0	21 12.9	29 38.4	1 3.4	19 54.1	29 45.0	24 56.4	2 10.3
9 Tu	7 11 18	17 59 32	22 12 9	28 14 23	21 55.3	5R 5.5	22 26.4	0♒25.4	1 16.8	19 58.8	29 48.5	24 58.7	2 12.2
10 W	7 15 14	19 0 40	4♍18 24	10♍24 32	21 45.9	5 10.1	23 39.8	1 12.4	1 30.2	20 3.5	29 52.0	25 0.9	2 14.0
11 Th	7 19 11	20 1 48	16 33 11	22 44 46	21 39.7	5 3.3	24 53.2	1 59.5	1 43.6	20 8.3	29 55.5	25 3.2	2 15.8
12 F	7 23 7	21 2 56	28 59 46	5♎18 41	21 36.3	4 44.7	26 6.6	2 46.6	1 57.0	20 13.2	29 59.0	25 5.5	2 17.5
13 Sa	7 27 4	22 4 4	11♎42 1	18 10 19	21 35.1	4 14.3	27 19.9	3 33.7	2 10.3	20 18.2	0♒ 2.5	25 7.7	2 19.2
14 Su	7 31 0	23 5 12	24 44 5	1♏23 49	21 35.0	3 32.5	28 33.1	4 20.8	2 23.6	20 23.3	0 6.0	25 10.0	2 20.9
15 M	7 34 57	24 6 20	8♏ 9 55	15 2 44	21 34.6	2 40.1	29 46.3	5 8.0	2 36.8	20 28.4	0 9.5	25 12.3	2 22.6
16 Tu	7 38 54	25 7 28	22 2 28	29 9 10	21 32.8	1 38.5	0♓59.4	5 55.1	2 50.1	20 33.6	0 13.0	25 14.6	2 24.3
17 W	7 42 50	26 8 35	6♐22 44	13♐42 49	21 28.4	0 29.3	2 12.5	6 42.3	3 3.2	20 38.8	0 16.5	25 16.8	2 25.9
18 Th	7 46 47	27 9 43	21 8 50	28 39 58	21 21.3	29♑14.8	3 25.5	7 29.6	3 16.4	20 44.2	0 20.1	25 19.1	2 27.5
19 F	7 50 43	28 10 50	6♑15 13	13♑53 18	21 11.5	27 57.2	4 38.5	8 16.8	3 29.5	20 49.6	0 23.6	25 21.4	2 29.1
20 Sa	7 54 40	29 11 57	21 32 53	29 12 27	21 0.1	26 39.1	5 51.4	9 4.1	3 42.6	20 55.1	0 27.1	25 23.7	2 30.6
21 Su	7 58 36	0♒13 3	6♒50 32	14♒25 41	20 48.4	25 22.7	7 4.2	9 51.4	3 55.6	21 0.6	0 30.7	25 26.0	2 32.1
22 M	8 2 33	1 14 8	21 56 36	29 22 9	20 37.8	24 10.2	8 17.0	10 38.7	4 8.6	21 6.3	0 34.2	25 28.2	2 33.6
23 Tu	8 6 29	2 15 13	6♓41 24	13♓53 43	20 29.4	23 3.4	9 29.7	11 26.0	4 21.5	21 11.9	0 37.7	25 30.5	2 35.1
24 W	8 10 26	3 16 16	20 58 38	27 55 57	20 23.7	22 3.8	10 42.3	12 13.3	4 34.4	21 17.7	0 41.3	25 32.8	2 36.5
25 Th	8 14 23	4 17 19	4♈45 42	11♈28 4	20 20.8	21 12.3	11 54.9	13 0.7	4 47.3	21 23.5	0 44.8	25 35.0	2 37.9
26 F	8 18 19	5 18 20	18 3 23	24 32 6	20D 19.9	20 29.5	13 7.3	13 48.0	5 0.0	21 29.3	0 48.3	25 37.3	2 39.3
27 Sa	8 22 16	6 19 21	0♉54 46	7♉11 59	20R 20.1	19 55.7	14 19.7	14 35.4	5 12.8	21 35.3	0 51.9	25 39.5	2 40.6
28 Su	8 26 12	7 20 20	13 24 22	19 32 34	20 20.0	19 30.9	15 32.1	15 22.8	5 25.5	21 41.3	0 55.4	25 41.8	2 41.9
29 M	8 30 9	8 21 18	25 37 14	1♊38 59	20 18.5	19 15.0	16 44.3	16 10.2	5 38.1	21 47.3	0 58.9	25 44.0	2 43.2
30 Tu	8 34 5	9 22 15	7♊38 25	13 36 6	20 14.8	19D 7.5	17 56.4	16 57.6	5 50.7	21 53.4	1 2.4	25 46.3	2 44.4
31 W	8 38 2	10 23 11	19 32 34	25 28 15	20 8.4	19 8.1	19 8.5	17 45.0	6 3.2	21 59.6	1 5.9	25 48.5	2 45.6

LONGITUDE — FEBRUARY 1996

Day	Sid.Time	☉	0 hr ☽	Noon ☽	True ☊	☿	♀	♂	♃	♄	♅	♆	♇
1 Th	8 41 58	11♒24 6	1♋23 37	7♋19 2	19♎59.2	19♑16.1	20♓20.5	18♒32.4	6♑15.6	22♓ 5.8	1♒ 9.4	25♑50.7	2♐46.8
2 F	8 45 55	12 24 59	13 14 49	19 11 15	19R 47.8	19 31.1	21 32.3	19 19.8	6 28.0	22 12.0	1 12.9	25 52.9	2 48.0
3 Sa	8 49 52	13 25 52	25 8 34	1♌ 6 58	19 35.0	19 52.5	22 44.1	20 7.2	6 40.4	22 18.3	1 16.4	25 55.1	2 49.1
4 Su	8 53 48	14 26 43	7♌ 6 37	13 7 40	19 21.9	20 19.8	23 55.8	20 54.6	6 52.6	22 24.7	1 19.8	25 57.3	2 50.2
5 M	8 57 45	15 27 33	19 10 14	25 14 27	19 9.5	20 52.5	25 7.3	21 42.1	7 4.8	22 31.1	1 23.3	25 59.5	2 51.2
6 Tu	9 1 41	16 28 21	1♍20 25	7♍28 16	18 59.0	21 30.2	26 18.8	22 29.5	7 17.0	22 37.6	1 26.7	26 1.6	2 52.3
7 W	9 5 38	17 29 9	13 38 9	19 50 15	18 50.9	22 12.3	27 30.2	23 17.0	7 29.0	22 44.1	1 30.2	26 3.8	2 53.2
8 Th	9 9 34	18 29 56	26 4 45	2♎21 53	18 45.7	22 58.6	28 41.4	24 4.4	7 41.0	22 50.6	1 33.6	26 5.9	2 54.2
9 F	9 13 31	19 30 41	8♎41 55	15 5 10	18D 43.1	23 48.7	29 52.6	24 51.9	7 53.0	22 57.2	1 37.0	26 8.1	2 55.1
10 Sa	9 17 27	20 31 25	21 31 55	28 2 33	18 42.6	24 42.2	1♈ 3.6	25 39.3	8 4.8	23 3.9	1 40.4	26 10.2	2 56.0
11 Su	9 21 24	21 32 9	4♏37 24	11♏16 48	18 43.3	25 38.8	2 14.5	26 26.8	8 16.6	23 10.6	1 43.8	26 12.3	2 56.9
12 M	9 25 21	22 32 51	18 1 6	24 50 33	18R 44.1	26 38.4	3 25.3	27 14.2	8 28.3	23 17.3	1 47.1	26 14.4	2 57.7
13 Tu	9 29 17	23 33 32	1♐45 22	8♐45 40	18 43.8	27 40.6	4 36.0	28 1.7	8 40.0	23 24.1	1 50.5	26 16.5	2 58.5
14 W	9 33 14	24 34 13	15 51 26	23 2 30	18 41.8	28 45.3	5 46.6	28 49.1	8 51.5	23 30.9	1 53.8	26 18.6	2 59.2
15 Th	9 37 10	25 34 52	0♑18 34	7♑39 8	18 37.5	29 52.2	6 57.0	29 36.6	9 3.0	23 37.7	1 57.2	26 20.6	2 59.9
16 F	9 41 7	26 35 30	15 3 32	22 30 53	18 31.2	1♒ 1.3	8 7.4	0♓24.1	9 14.4	23 44.6	2 0.5	26 22.7	3 0.6
17 Sa	9 45 3	27 36 7	0♒ 0 14	7♒30 27	18 23.5	2 12.3	9 17.6	1 11.5	9 25.7	23 51.5	2 3.7	26 24.7	3 1.3
18 Su	9 49 0	28 36 42	15 0 21	22 28 43	18 15.3	3 25.2	10 27.6	1 59.0	9 37.0	23 58.5	2 7.0	26 26.7	3 1.9
19 M	9 52 56	29 37 16	29 54 25	7♓16 20	18 7.7	4 39.8	11 37.6	2 46.4	9 48.1	24 5.5	2 10.3	26 28.7	3 2.5
20 Tu	9 56 53	0♓37 48	14♓33 31	21 45 12	18 1.8	5 56.0	12 47.4	3 33.9	9 59.2	24 12.5	2 13.5	26 30.7	3 3.0
21 W	10 0 50	1 38 19	28 50 45	5♈49 44	17 57.9	7 13.8	13 57.0	4 21.3	10 10.1	24 19.5	2 16.7	26 32.6	3 3.5
22 Th	10 4 46	2 38 48	12♈41 57	19 27 20	17D 56.3	8 33.0	15 6.5	5 8.7	10 21.0	24 26.6	2 19.8	26 34.6	3 4.0
23 F	10 8 43	3 39 15	26 5 59	2♉38 8	17 56.4	9 53.6	16 15.9	5 56.1	10 31.8	24 33.7	2 23.0	26 36.5	3 4.4
24 Sa	10 12 39	4 39 40	9♉ 4 10	15 24 31	17 57.7	11 15.6	17 25.1	6 43.5	10 42.4	24 40.9	2 26.1	26 38.4	3 4.8
25 Su	10 16 36	5 40 3	21 39 43	27 50 20	17 59.2	12 38.8	18 34.1	7 30.9	10 53.0	24 48.0	2 29.2	26 40.3	3 5.2
26 M	10 20 32	6 40 25	3♊56 58	10♊ 0 15	18R 0.0	14 3.4	19 42.9	8 18.3	11 3.5	24 55.2	2 32.3	26 42.1	3 5.5
27 Tu	10 24 29	7 40 44	16 0 48	21 59 14	17 59.6	15 29.1	20 51.6	9 5.7	11 13.9	25 2.4	2 35.4	26 44.0	3 5.8
28 W	10 28 25	8 41 2	27 56 9	3♋52 9	17 57.5	16 56.0	22 0.1	9 53.0	11 24.2	25 9.7	2 38.4	26 45.8	3 6.1
29 Th	10 32 22	9 41 17	9♋47 46	15 43 29	17 53.7	18 24.1	23 8.5	10 40.3	11 34.4	25 16.9	2 41.4	26 47.6	3 6.3

Astro Data Dy Hr Mn	Planet Ingress Dy Hr Mn	Last Aspect Dy Hr Mn	☽ Ingress Dy Hr Mn	Last Aspect Dy Hr Mn	☽ Ingress Dy Hr Mn	☽ Phases & Eclipses Dy Hr Mn	Astro Data
☿ R 9 21:51	☿ ♒ 1 18:06	2 1:18 ♅ △	♊ 2 2:29	3 1:34 ♆ ☍	♌ 3 9:46	5 20:51 ○ 14♋48	1 JANUARY 1996
☽0S 11 15:50	♃ ♑ 3 7:22	3 17:53 ♄ □	♋ 4 14:56	5 5:22 ♂ ☍	♍ 5 21:22	13 20:45 ☽ 22♎57	Julian Day # 35064
♃⊻♇ 13 18:32	♂ ♒ 8 11:02	7 2:54 ♅ ☍	♌ 7 3:30	8 5:31 ♀ ☍	♎ 8 7:30	20 12:51 ● 29♑45	Delta T 60.1 sec
☽0N 24 6:55	♅ ♒ 12 7:12	9 0:32 ♀ ☍	♍ 9 15:29	10 8:35 ♆ □	♏ 10 15:35	27 11:14 ☽ 6♉48	SVP 05♓18'49"
☿ D 30 10:17	♀ ♓ 15 4:30	12 1:53 ♅ △	♎ 12 1:55	12 17:09 ♂ □	♐ 12 20:58		Obliquity 23°26'14"
	☿ ♑ 17 9:37	14 7:35 ♀ △	♏ 14 9:30	14 22:47 ♂ ✶	♑ 14 23:29	4 15:58 ○ 15♌07	⚷ Chiron 13♎34.7
☽0S 7 22:33	☉ ♒ 20 18:53	16 5:38 ☉ ✶	♐ 16 13:25	16 18:14 ♆ ☌	♒ 16 24:00	12 8:37 ☽ 22♏55	☽ Mean ☊ 22♎26.2
♀0N 10 1:54		17 23:20 ♄ □	♑ 18 14:07	18 23:30 ☉ ☌	♓ 19 0:09	18 23:30 ● 29♒36	
☽0N 20 18:13	♀ ♈ 9 2:30	20 12:51 ☉ ☌	♒ 20 13:15	20 20:05 ♆ ✶	♈ 21 1:58	26 5:52 ☽ 6♊55	1 FEBRUARY 1996
	☿ ♒ 15 2:44	21 5:01 ♂ ☌	♓ 22 13:02	23 0:56 ♆ □	♉ 23 7:08		Julian Day # 35095
	♂ ♓ 15 11:50	24 7:53 ♅ ✶	♈ 24 15:37	25 9:45 ♆ △	♊ 25 16:14		Delta T 60.1 sec
	☉ ♓ 19 9:01	26 14:04 ♆ □	♉ 26 22:16	27 18:20 ♄ □	♋ 28 4:10		SVP 05♓18'44"
		29 0:14 ♆ △	♊ 29 8:42				Obliquity 23°26'14"
		31 5:00 ♄ □	♋ 31 21:11				⚷ Chiron 14♎19.7R
							☽ Mean ☊ 20♎47.8

MARCH 1996 LONGITUDE

Day	Sid.Time	☉	0 hr ☽	Noon ☽	True ☊	☿	♀	♂	♃	♄	♅	♆	♇
1 F	10 36 19	10♓41 31	21♋39 48	27♋37 8	17♎48.4	19♒53.3	24♈16.6	11♓27.7	11♑44.4	25♓24.2	2♒44.4	26♑49.4	3♐ 6.5
2 Sa	10 40 15	11 41 42	3♌35 51	9♌36 17	17R 42.0	21 23.7	25 24.6	12 15.0	11 54.4	25 31.5	2 47.3	26 51.1	3 6.6
3 Su	10 44 12	12 41 51	15 38 43	21 43 24	17 35.3	22 55.1	26 32.3	13 2.2	12 4.3	25 38.8	2 50.2	26 52.8	3 6.7
4 M	10 48 8	13 41 59	27 50 30	4♍ 0 11	17 29.0	24 27.7	27 39.9	13 49.5	12 14.0	25 46.1	2 53.1	26 54.6	3 6.8
5 Tu	10 52 5	14 42 5	10♍12 34	16 27 45	17 23.7	26 1.4	28 47.2	14 36.7	12 23.7	25 53.5	2 56.0	26 56.2	3R 6.9
6 W	10 56 1	15 42 8	22 45 47	29 6 43	17 19.8	27 36.2	29 54.4	15 24.0	12 33.2	26 0.9	2 58.8	26 57.9	3 6.9
7 Th	10 59 58	16 42 10	5♎30 36	11♎57 28	17D 17.6	29 12.1	1♉ 1.3	16 11.2	12 42.6	26 8.2	3 1.6	26 59.5	3 6.9
8 F	11 3 54	17 42 10	18 27 21	25 0 18	17 17.0	0♓49.1	2 8.0	16 58.4	12 51.9	26 15.6	3 4.4	27 1.2	3 6.8
9 Sa	11 7 51	18 42 9	1♏36 22	8♏15 37	17 17.7	2 27.3	3 14.5	17 45.5	13 1.1	26 23.0	3 7.1	27 2.8	3 6.7
10 Su	11 11 47	19 42 5	14 58 5	21 43 50	17 19.1	4 6.5	4 20.7	18 32.7	13 10.2	26 30.4	3 9.8	27 4.3	3 6.6
11 M	11 15 44	20 42 0	28 32 57	5♐25 26	17 20.7	5 46.9	5 26.7	19 19.8	13 19.1	26 37.8	3 12.5	27 5.9	3 6.4
12 Tu	11 19 41	21 41 54	12♐21 18	19 20 32	17R 21.9	7 28.5	6 32.5	20 6.9	13 28.0	26 45.2	3 15.1	27 7.4	3 6.2
13 W	11 23 37	22 41 46	26 23 1	3♑28 36	17 22.1	9 11.2	7 38.0	20 54.0	13 36.7	26 52.7	3 17.7	27 8.9	3 6.0
14 Th	11 27 34	23 41 36	10♑37 4	17 48 3	17 21.2	10 55.1	8 43.3	21 41.1	13 45.3	27 0.1	3 20.3	27 10.3	3 5.7
15 F	11 31 30	24 41 24	25 1 11	2♒15 55	17 19.3	12 40.2	9 48.3	22 28.1	13 53.7	27 7.6	3 22.8	27 11.8	3 5.5
16 Sa	11 35 27	25 41 11	9♒31 41	16 47 49	17 16.7	14 26.5	10 53.1	23 15.2	14 2.0	27 15.0	3 25.3	27 13.2	3 5.1
17 Su	11 39 23	26 40 56	24 3 35	1♓18 15	17 13.7	16 14.0	11 57.6	24 2.2	14 10.2	27 22.5	3 27.8	27 14.6	3 4.8
18 M	11 43 20	27 40 39	8♓31 2	15 41 13	17 11.0	18 2.7	13 1.8	24 49.1	14 18.3	27 29.9	3 30.2	27 15.9	3 4.4
19 Tu	11 47 16	28 40 20	22 48 6	29 51 3	17 9.0	19 52.6	14 5.7	25 36.1	14 26.2	27 37.4	3 32.6	27 17.3	3 3.9
20 W	11 51 13	29 40 0	6♈49 33	13♈43 8	17D 7.8	21 43.8	15 9.3	26 23.0	14 34.0	27 44.8	3 34.9	27 18.6	3 3.5
21 Th	11 55 10	0♈39 37	20 31 31	27 14 29	17 7.6	23 36.2	16 12.6	27 9.9	14 41.6	27 52.2	3 37.2	27 19.8	3 3.0
22 F	11 59 6	1 39 12	3♉51 58	10♉23 58	17 8.1	25 29.9	17 15.6	27 56.7	14 49.1	27 59.7	3 39.5	27 21.1	3 2.4
23 Sa	12 3 3	2 38 45	16 50 40	23 12 15	17 9.2	27 24.7	18 18.3	28 43.6	14 56.5	28 7.1	3 41.7	27 22.3	3 1.9
24 Su	12 6 59	3 38 16	29 29 5	5♊41 31	17 10.5	29 20.8	19 20.7	29 30.4	15 3.7	28 14.6	3 43.9	27 23.5	3 1.3
25 M	12 10 56	4 37 44	11♊50 2	17 55 6	17 11.6	1♈18.0	20 22.6	0♈17.1	15 10.8	28 22.0	3 46.0	27 24.6	3 0.7
26 Tu	12 14 52	5 37 10	23 57 16	29 57 6	17 12.4	3 16.4	21 24.3	1 3.9	15 17.7	28 29.4	3 48.1	27 25.8	3 0.0
27 W	12 18 49	6 36 34	5♋55 11	11♋52 6	17R 12.7	5 15.9	22 25.5	1 50.6	15 24.5	28 36.8	3 50.2	27 26.9	2 59.3
28 Th	12 22 45	7 35 56	17 48 26	23 44 46	17 12.5	7 16.3	23 26.4	2 37.2	15 31.1	28 44.2	3 52.2	27 27.9	2 58.6
29 F	12 26 42	8 35 15	29 41 40	5♌39 41	17 11.9	9 17.7	24 26.9	3 23.9	15 37.6	28 51.6	3 54.2	27 29.0	2 57.9
30 Sa	12 30 39	9 34 32	11♌39 19	17 41 3	17 11.0	11 19.9	25 26.9	4 10.4	15 44.0	28 59.0	3 56.1	27 30.0	2 57.1
31 Su	12 34 35	10 33 47	23 45 20	29 52 33	17 10.1	13 22.8	26 26.6	4 57.0	15 50.1	29 6.3	3 58.0	27 30.9	2 56.3

APRIL 1996 LONGITUDE

Day	Sid.Time	☉	0 hr ☽	Noon ☽	True ☊	☿	♀	♂	♃	♄	♅	♆	♇
1 M	12 38 32	11♈32 59	6♍ 3 3	12♍17 7	17♎ 9.2	15♈26.1	27♉25.8	5♈43.5	15♑56.2	29♓13.7	3♒59.9	27♑31.9	2♐55.4
2 Tu	12 42 28	12 32 9	18 34 59	24 56 49	17R 8.6	17 29.8	28 24.5	6 30.0	16 2.0	29 21.0	4 1.7	27 32.8	2R 54.6
3 W	12 46 25	13 31 17	1♎22 43	7♎52 44	17 8.3	19 33.5	29 22.8	7 16.4	16 7.7	29 28.3	4 3.4	27 33.7	2 53.7
4 Th	12 50 21	14 30 23	14 26 50	21 4 57	17D 8.1	21 37.1	0♊20.6	8 2.8	16 13.3	29 35.6	4 5.1	27 34.5	2 52.8
5 F	12 54 18	15 29 27	27 46 56	4♏32 37	17 8.2	23 40.2	1 17.9	8 49.2	16 18.7	29 42.9	4 6.8	27 35.3	2 51.8
6 Sa	12 58 14	16 28 29	11♏21 45	18 14 4	17R 8.2	25 42.6	2 14.7	9 35.5	16 23.9	29 50.1	4 8.4	27 36.1	2 50.8
7 Su	13 2 11	17 27 29	25 9 18	2♐ 7 7	17 8.3	27 43.9	3 10.9	10 21.8	16 29.0	29 57.3	4 10.0	27 36.9	2 49.8
8 M	13 6 8	18 26 27	9♐ 7 11	16 9 11	17 8.2	29 43.8	4 6.7	11 8.1	16 33.9	0♈ 4.6	4 11.5	27 37.6	2 48.8
9 Tu	13 10 4	19 25 23	23 12 47	0♑17 38	17 8.0	1♉41.8	5 1.8	11 54.3	16 38.6	0 11.8	4 13.0	27 38.3	2 47.8
10 W	13 14 1	20 24 18	7♑23 26	14 29 51	17D 7.8	3 37.7	5 56.4	12 40.5	16 43.2	0 18.9	4 14.5	27 38.9	2 46.7
11 Th	13 17 57	21 23 11	21 36 34	28 43 17	17 7.7	5 31.1	6 50.4	13 26.7	16 47.6	0 26.1	4 15.9	27 39.6	2 45.6
12 F	13 21 54	22 22 2	5♒49 42	12♒55 30	17 7.9	7 21.6	7 43.7	14 12.8	16 51.8	0 33.2	4 17.2	27 40.2	2 44.5
13 Sa	13 25 50	23 20 52	20 0 23	27 4 2	17 8.2	9 9.0	8 36.5	14 58.8	16 55.9	0 40.3	4 18.5	27 40.7	2 43.3
14 Su	13 29 47	24 19 40	4♓ 6 9	11♓ 6 25	17 8.8	10 52.8	9 28.5	15 44.9	16 59.7	0 47.3	4 19.8	27 41.3	2 42.1
15 M	13 33 43	25 18 26	18 4 31	25 0 7	17 9.5	12 32.8	10 19.9	16 30.8	17 3.4	0 54.4	4 21.0	27 41.7	2 40.9
16 Tu	13 37 40	26 17 10	1♈52 57	8♈42 41	17 10.1	14 8.8	11 10.6	17 16.8	17 7.0	1 1.4	4 22.1	27 42.2	2 39.7
17 W	13 41 36	27 15 52	15 29 5	22 11 54	17R 10.4	15 40.5	12 0.5	18 2.7	17 10.3	1 8.3	4 23.2	27 42.6	2 38.5
18 Th	13 45 33	28 14 33	28 50 57	5♉26 3	17 10.2	17 7.7	12 49.7	18 48.6	17 13.5	1 15.3	4 24.3	27 43.0	2 37.2
19 F	13 49 30	29 13 12	11♉57 7	18 24 6	17 9.4	18 30.2	13 38.1	19 34.4	17 16.5	1 22.2	4 25.3	27 43.4	2 35.9
20 Sa	13 53 26	0♉11 48	24 47 1	1♊ 5 58	17 7.9	19 47.9	14 25.6	20 20.1	17 19.3	1 29.0	4 26.3	27 43.7	2 34.6
21 Su	13 57 23	1 10 23	7♊21 4	13 32 32	17 6.0	21 0.7	15 12.3	21 5.9	17 21.9	1 35.9	4 27.2	27 44.0	2 33.3
22 M	14 1 19	2 8 55	19 40 38	25 45 42	17 3.8	22 8.4	15 58.2	21 51.5	17 24.4	1 42.7	4 28.0	27 44.3	2 31.9
23 Tu	14 5 16	3 7 26	1♋48 8	7♋48 19	17 1.7	23 10.9	16 43.0	22 37.2	17 26.6	1 49.4	4 28.8	27 44.5	2 30.6
24 W	14 9 12	4 5 54	13 46 46	19 43 59	16 60.0	24 8.1	17 27.0	23 22.8	17 28.7	1 56.1	4 29.6	27 44.7	2 29.2
25 Th	14 13 9	5 4 21	25 40 29	1♌36 51	16D 58.9	24 60.0	18 9.9	24 8.3	17 30.6	2 2.8	4 30.3	27 44.9	2 27.8
26 F	14 17 5	6 2 45	7♌33 40	13 31 31	16 58.6	25 46.4	18 51.8	24 53.8	17 32.3	2 9.4	4 31.0	27 45.0	2 26.3
27 Sa	14 21 2	7 1 7	19 31 0	25 32 41	16 59.1	26 27.3	19 32.6	25 39.2	17 33.8	2 16.0	4 31.6	27 45.1	2 24.9
28 Su	14 24 59	7 59 27	1♍37 10	7♍44 59	17 0.3	27 2.7	20 12.2	26 24.6	17 35.2	2 22.6	4 32.1	27 45.2	2 23.5
29 M	14 28 55	8 57 44	13 56 38	20 12 35	17 1.9	27 32.5	20 50.7	27 9.9	17 36.3	2 29.1	4 32.7	27R 45.2	2 22.0
30 Tu	14 32 52	9 56 0	26 33 15	2♎58 58	17 3.4	27 56.8	21 28.0	27 55.2	17 37.3	2 35.5	4 33.1	27 45.2	2 20.5

Astro Data

	Dy Hr Mn
♇ R	5 20:17
☽0S	6 5:14
♅✶♇	8 20:38
♄✶♆	15 16:47
☽0N	19 4:37
☿0N	26 0:59
♂0N	27 2:54
☽0S	2 13:01
☽0N	15 12:50
♃∠♇	24 3:12
♄△♇	28 2:40
☽0S	29 22:06
♆ R	29 9:52

Planet Ingress

	Dy Hr Mn
♀ ♉	6 2:01
☿ ♓	7 11:53
☉ ♈	20 8:03
☿ ♈	24 8:03
♂ ♈	24 15:12
♀ ♊	3 15:26
♄ ♈	7 8:49
☿ ♉	8 3:16
☉ ♉	19 19:10

Last Aspect / ☽ Ingress

Last Aspect Dy Hr Mn	☽ Ingress Dy Hr Mn
1 10:25 ♆ ☍	♌ 1 16:47
3 23:37 ♀ △	♍ 4 4:13
6 7:58 ♆ △	♎ 6 13:40
8 15:42 ♆ □	♏ 8 21:05
10 21:27 ♆ ✶	♐ 11 2:32
13 0:51 ♄ □	♑ 13 6:08
15 3:37 ♆ ☌	♒ 15 8:15
16 2:25 ♀ □	♓ 17 9:50
19 10:45 ☉ ☌	♈ 19 12:15
21 12:11 ♆ □	♉ 21 16:59
24 0:03 ♂ ✶	♊ 24 0:59
26 9:10 ♄ □	♋ 26 12:06
28 22:18 ♄ △	♌ 29 0:37
31 5:45 ♀ □	♍ 31 12:15

Last Aspect / ☽ Ingress

Last Aspect Dy Hr Mn	☽ Ingress Dy Hr Mn
2 20:25 ♄ ☍	♎ 2 21:26
4 23:39 ♆ □	♏ 5 3:57
7 8:21 ♄ △	♐ 7 8:21
8 17:05 ☉ △	♑ 9 11:30
11 10:13 ♆ ☌	♒ 11 14:09
13 6:06 ☉ ✶	♓ 13 17:00
15 16:42 ♆ ✶	♈ 15 20:43
17 22:49 ☉ ☌	♉ 18 2:05
20 5:35 ♆ △	♊ 20 9:54
22 4:35 ♂ ✶	♋ 22 20:25
25 4:11 ♆ ☍	♌ 25 8:44
27 14:32 ♆ □	♍ 27 20:49
30 2:41 ☿ △	♎ 30 6:27

☽ Phases & Eclipses

Dy Hr Mn	
5 9:23	○ 15♍06
12 17:15	☽ 22♐25
19 10:45	● 29♓07
27 1:31	☽ 6♋40
4 0:07	○ 14♎31
4 0:10	T 1.379
10 23:36	☽ 21♑22
17 22:49	● 28♈12
17 22:37:12	P 0.880
25 20:40	☽ 5♌55

Astro Data

1 MARCH 1996
Julian Day # 35124
Delta T 60.2 sec
SVP 05♓18'41"
Obliquity 23°26'15"
⚷ Chiron 13♎21.6R
☽ Mean ☊ 19♎15.6

1 APRIL 1996
Julian Day # 35155
Delta T 60.2 sec
SVP 05♓18'39"
Obliquity 23°26'15"
⚷ Chiron 11♎08.1R
☽ Mean ☊ 17♎37.1

LONGITUDE — MAY 1996

Day	Sid.Time	☉	0 hr ☽	Noon ☽	True ☊	☿	♀	♂	♃	♄	♅	♆	♇
1 W	14 36 48	10♉54 14	9♎29 58	16♎ 6 26	17♎ 4.3	28♉15.4	22♊ 4.0	28♈40.5	17♑38.1	2♈41.9	4♒33.5	27♑45.2	2♐19.0
2 Th	14 40 45	11 52 26	22 48 23	29 35 47	17R 4.4	28 28.6	22 38.7	29 25.6	17 38.7	2 48.3	4 33.9	27R45.1	2R17.5
3 F	14 44 41	12 50 36	6♏28 26	13♏26 3	17 3.3	28R36.3	23 12.1	0♉10.8	17 39.1	2 54.6	4 34.2	27 45.0	2 16.0
4 Sa	14 48 38	13 48 44	20 28 12	27 34 22	17 0.9	28 38.6	23 44.0	0 55.9	17R39.3	3 0.9	4 34.5	27 44.9	2 14.4
5 Su	14 52 34	14 46 51	4♐43 56	11♐56 11	16 57.5	28 35.7	24 14.5	1 40.9	17 39.3	3 7.1	4 34.7	27 44.7	2 12.9
6 M	14 56 31	15 44 56	19 10 25	26 25 50	16 53.4	28 27.9	24 43.4	2 25.9	17 39.1	3 13.3	4 34.9	27 44.5	2 11.3
7 Tu	15 0 28	16 43 0	3♑41 43	10♑57 18	16 49.4	28 15.3	25 10.8	3 10.8	17 38.8	3 19.4	4 35.0	27 44.3	2 9.8
8 W	15 4 24	17 41 2	18 11 57	25 25 4	16 45.9	27 58.2	25 36.5	3 55.7	17 38.3	3 25.5	4R35.0	27 44.0	2 8.2
9 Th	15 8 21	18 39 3	2♒36 7	9♒44 44	16 43.6	27 37.1	26 0.6	4 40.6	17 37.5	3 31.5	4 35.0	27 43.7	2 6.6
10 F	15 12 17	19 37 2	16 50 33	23 53 21	16D42.6	27 12.3	26 22.9	5 25.4	17 36.6	3 37.4	4 35.0	27 43.4	2 5.0
11 Sa	15 16 14	20 35 1	0♓52 58	7♓49 20	16 42.9	26 44.3	26 43.4	6 10.1	17 35.5	3 43.3	4 34.9	27 43.0	2 3.4
12 Su	15 20 10	21 32 57	14 42 25	21 32 12	16 44.1	26 13.6	27 2.1	6 54.8	17 34.2	3 49.2	4 34.8	27 42.7	2 1.8
13 M	15 24 7	22 30 53	28 18 43	5♈ 2 2	16 45.6	25 40.9	27 18.9	7 39.5	17 32.7	3 54.9	4 34.6	27 42.2	2 0.2
14 Tu	15 28 3	23 28 47	11♈42 12	18 19 14	16R46.6	25 6.6	27 33.7	8 24.1	17 31.1	4 0.7	4 34.4	27 41.8	1 58.5
15 W	15 32 0	24 26 41	24 53 13	1♉24 9	16 46.4	24 31.4	27 46.4	9 8.6	17 29.2	4 6.3	4 34.1	27 41.3	1 56.9
16 Th	15 35 57	25 24 32	7♉52 4	14 17 0	16 44.5	23 55.9	27 57.1	9 53.1	17 27.2	4 11.9	4 33.8	27 40.8	1 55.3
17 F	15 39 53	26 22 23	20 38 58	26 57 58	16 40.7	23 20.7	28 5.6	10 37.6	17 25.0	4 17.5	4 33.4	27 40.3	1 53.6
18 Sa	15 43 50	27 20 12	3♊14 3	9♊27 17	16 35.1	22 46.5	28 12.0	11 21.9	17 22.6	4 22.9	4 33.0	27 39.7	1 52.0
19 Su	15 47 46	28 17 59	15 37 43	21 45 29	16 28.1	22 13.9	28 16.0	12 6.3	17 20.0	4 28.4	4 32.5	27 39.1	1 50.3
20 M	15 51 43	29 15 46	27 50 43	3♋53 38	16 20.3	21 43.2	28R17.8	12 50.6	17 17.2	4 33.7	4 32.0	27 38.5	1 48.7
21 Tu	15 55 39	0♊13 30	9♋54 28	15 53 30	16 12.5	21 15.1	28 17.2	13 34.8	17 14.2	4 39.0	4 31.4	27 37.8	1 47.0
22 W	15 59 36	1 11 14	21 51 4	27 47 35	16 5.6	20 50.0	28 14.3	14 19.0	17 11.1	4 44.2	4 30.8	27 37.1	1 45.4
23 Th	16 3 32	2 8 55	3♌43 27	9♌39 11	16 0.0	20 28.3	28 8.9	15 3.1	17 7.8	4 49.3	4 30.1	27 36.4	1 43.7
24 F	16 7 29	3 6 35	15 35 16	21 32 17	15 56.4	20 10.2	28 1.1	15 47.1	17 4.3	4 54.4	4 29.4	27 35.7	1 42.1
25 Sa	16 11 26	4 4 14	27 30 49	3♍31 28	15D54.6	19 56.0	27 50.9	16 31.1	17 0.7	4 59.4	4 28.6	27 34.9	1 40.4
26 Su	16 15 22	5 1 51	9♍34 51	15 41 37	15 54.4	19 46.0	27 38.2	17 15.1	16 56.9	5 4.4	4 27.8	27 34.1	1 38.8
27 M	16 19 19	5 59 27	21 52 23	28 7 44	15 55.3	19D40.3	27 23.1	17 59.0	16 52.9	5 9.2	4 27.0	27 33.3	1 37.1
28 Tu	16 23 15	6 57 1	4♎28 15	10♎54 26	15R56.5	19 39.0	27 5.6	18 42.8	16 48.7	5 14.0	4 26.1	27 32.4	1 35.5
29 W	16 27 12	7 54 34	17 26 42	24 5 25	15 56.9	19 42.2	26 45.8	19 26.6	16 44.4	5 18.7	4 25.1	27 31.5	1 33.8
30 Th	16 31 8	8 52 5	0♏50 47	7♏42 54	15 55.9	19 49.9	26 23.7	20 10.3	16 40.0	5 23.4	4 24.1	27 30.6	1 32.2
31 F	16 35 5	9 49 35	14 41 40	21 46 51	15 52.8	20 2.0	25 59.5	20 54.0	16 35.3	5 27.9	4 23.1	27 29.7	1 30.6

LONGITUDE — JUNE 1996

Day	Sid.Time	☉	0 hr ☽	Noon ☽	True ☊	☿	♀	♂	♃	♄	♅	♆	♇
1 Sa	16 39 1	10♊47 4	28♏57 59	6♐14 28	15♎47.5	20♉18.6	25♊33.1	21♉37.6	16♑30.5	5♈32.4	4♒22.0	27♑28.7	1♐28.9
2 Su	16 42 58	11 44 32	13♐35 29	21 0 7	15R40.3	20 39.6	25R 4.8	22 21.1	16R25.6	5 36.8	4R20.9	27R27.7	1R27.3
3 M	16 46 55	12 41 59	28 27 16	5♑55 50	15 32.0	21 5.0	24 34.6	23 4.6	16 20.5	5 41.2	4 19.8	27 26.7	1 25.7
4 Tu	16 50 51	13 39 25	13♑24 37	20 52 32	15 23.5	21 34.6	24 2.8	23 48.1	16 15.3	5 45.4	4 18.6	27 25.7	1 24.1
5 W	16 54 48	14 36 51	28 18 29	5♒41 34	15 15.9	22 8.5	23 29.6	24 31.5	16 9.9	5 49.6	4 17.3	27 24.6	1 22.5
6 Th	16 58 44	15 34 15	13♒ 0 58	20 16 4	15 10.1	22 46.4	22 55.0	25 14.8	16 4.4	5 53.7	4 16.0	27 23.6	1 20.9
7 F	17 2 41	16 31 39	27 26 25	4♓31 43	15 6.5	23 28.3	22 19.4	25 58.1	15 58.8	5 57.7	4 14.7	27 22.5	1 19.3
8 Sa	17 6 37	17 29 2	11♓31 51	18 26 47	15D 4.9	24 14.1	21 42.9	26 41.3	15 53.0	6 1.7	4 13.4	27 21.3	1 17.7
9 Su	17 10 34	18 26 25	25 16 37	2♈ 1 34	15 4.9	25 3.8	21 5.8	27 24.5	15 47.1	6 5.5	4 11.9	27 20.2	1 16.2
10 M	17 14 30	19 23 47	8♈41 52	15 17 48	15R 5.5	25 57.1	20 28.3	28 7.6	15 41.0	6 9.3	4 10.5	27 19.0	1 14.6
11 Tu	17 18 27	20 21 9	21 49 41	28 17 49	15 5.4	26 54.2	19 50.7	28 50.7	15 34.8	6 13.0	4 9.0	27 17.8	1 13.1
12 W	17 22 24	21 18 30	4♉42 29	11♉ 3 59	15 3.7	27 54.8	19 13.2	29 33.7	15 28.6	6 16.6	4 7.5	27 16.6	1 11.5
13 Th	17 26 20	22 15 51	17 22 33	23 38 26	14 59.7	28 58.9	18 36.0	0♊16.6	15 22.2	6 20.1	4 5.9	27 15.4	1 10.0
14 F	17 30 17	23 13 11	29 51 48	6♊ 2 49	14 52.9	0♊ 6.5	17 59.4	0 59.5	15 15.6	6 23.5	4 4.4	27 14.1	1 8.5
15 Sa	17 34 13	24 10 31	12♊11 39	18 18 25	14 43.5	1 17.4	17 23.6	1 42.4	15 9.0	6 26.9	4 2.7	27 12.8	1 7.0
16 Su	17 38 10	25 7 50	24 23 15	0♋26 14	14 32.0	2 31.7	16 48.8	2 25.2	15 2.3	6 30.1	4 1.1	27 11.5	1 5.6
17 M	17 42 6	26 5 9	6♋27 32	12 27 15	14 19.4	3 49.3	16 15.2	3 7.9	14 55.5	6 33.3	3 59.4	27 10.2	1 4.1
18 Tu	17 46 3	27 2 27	18 25 36	24 22 44	14 6.6	5 10.2	15 43.0	3 50.6	14 48.6	6 36.4	3 57.6	27 8.9	1 2.7
19 W	17 49 59	27 59 44	0♌18 55	6♌14 25	13 54.8	6 34.2	15 12.4	4 33.2	14 41.6	6 39.3	3 55.9	27 7.5	1 1.2
20 Th	17 53 56	28 57 1	12 9 34	18 4 42	13 44.9	8 1.5	14 43.6	5 15.7	14 34.5	6 42.2	3 54.1	27 6.2	0 59.8
21 F	17 57 53	29 54 17	24 0 17	29 56 45	13 37.4	9 31.9	14 16.6	5 58.2	14 27.3	6 45.0	3 52.2	27 4.8	0 58.4
22 Sa	18 1 49	0♋51 32	5♍54 37	11♍54 26	13 32.7	11 5.4	13 51.6	6 40.7	14 20.1	6 47.7	3 50.4	27 3.4	0 57.0
23 Su	18 5 46	1 48 47	17 56 48	24 2 19	13 30.3	12 42.1	13 28.7	7 23.0	14 12.8	6 50.3	3 48.5	27 2.0	0 55.7
24 M	18 9 42	2 46 1	0♎11 38	6♎25 23	13D29.6	14 21.8	13 8.0	8 5.3	14 5.4	6 52.9	3 46.6	27 0.5	0 54.3
25 Tu	18 13 39	3 43 15	12 44 12	19 8 42	13R29.6	16 4.5	12 49.6	8 47.6	13 58.0	6 55.3	3 44.6	26 59.1	0 53.0
26 W	18 17 35	4 40 27	25 39 25	2♏16 51	13 29.3	17 50.2	12 33.4	9 29.8	13 50.5	6 57.6	3 42.6	26 57.6	0 51.7
27 Th	18 21 32	5 37 40	9♏ 1 24	15 53 18	13 27.4	19 38.7	12 19.7	10 11.9	13 43.0	6 59.8	3 40.6	26 56.1	0 50.4
28 F	18 25 28	6 34 52	22 52 39	29 59 23	13 23.3	21 30.1	12 8.3	10 54.0	13 35.5	7 2.0	3 38.6	26 54.7	0 49.2
29 Sa	18 29 25	7 32 3	7♐13 9	14♐33 28	13 16.7	23 24.2	11 59.3	11 36.1	13 27.9	7 4.0	3 36.5	26 53.2	0 47.9
30 Su	18 33 22	8 29 15	21 59 33	29 30 26	13 7.7	25 20.8	11 52.7	12 18.0	13 20.3	7 6.0	3 34.5	26 51.7	0 46.7

Astro Data

	Dy Hr Mn
☿ R	3 22:40
♃ R	4 15:37
♅ R	8 19:36
☽0N	12 19:18
♄✶♅	19 16:50
♀ R	20 6:08
♄0N	25 3:36
☽0S	27 7:48
☿ D	27 19:02
♃∠♇	1 11:50
☽0N	9 1:37
☽0S	23 17:01

Planet Ingress

	Dy Hr Mn
♂ ♉	2 18:16
☉ ♊	20 18:23
♂ ♊	12 14:42
☿ ♊	13 21:45
☉ ♋	21 2:24

Last Aspect / ☽ Ingress

Last Aspect Dy Hr Mn		☽ Ingress Dy Hr Mn
2 12:23	♂ ☍	♏ 2 12:43
4 13:46	☿ ☍	♐ 4 16:05
6 9:29	♀ ☍	♑ 6 17:54
8 15:53	☿ △	♒ 8 19:39
10 17:07	☿ □	♓ 10 22:29
12 22:55	♆ ✶	♈ 13 3:00
15 5:23	♀ ✶	♉ 15 9:25
17 13:20	♆ △	♊ 17 17:48
20 0:54	♀ ☌	♋ 20 4:16
22 11:38	♆ ☍	♌ 22 16:28
25 0:40	♀ ✶	♍ 25 4:58
27 10:53	♆ △	♎ 27 15:33
29 18:06	♆ □	♏ 29 22:30

Last Aspect / ☽ Ingress

Last Aspect Dy Hr Mn		☽ Ingress Dy Hr Mn
31 21:32	♆ ✶	♐ 1 1:43
2 17:58	♀ ☍	♑ 3 2:29
4 22:33	♆ ☌	♒ 5 2:44
6 21:24	♂ □	♓ 7 4:19
9 3:59	♂ ✶	♈ 9 8:23
11 10:07	♆ □	♉ 11 15:11
13 18:56	♆ △	♊ 14 0:16
16 1:36	☉ ☌	♋ 16 11:08
18 17:34	♆ ☍	♌ 18 23:22
20 5:01	♀ ✶	♍ 21 12:07
23 17:49	♆ △	♎ 23 23:37
26 2:22	♆ □	♏ 26 7:53
28 6:49	♆ ✶	♐ 28 12:01
30 6:11	☿ ☍	♑ 30 12:47

☽ Phases & Eclipses

Dy Hr Mn	
3 11:48	○ 13♏19
10 5:04	☽ 19♒49
17 11:46	● 26♉51
25 14:13	☽ 4♍38
1 20:47	○ 11♐37
8 11:06	☽ 17♓56
16 1:36	● 25♊12
24 5:23	☽ 2♎59

Astro Data

1 MAY 1996
Julian Day # 35185
Delta T 60.3 sec
SVP 05♓18'36"
Obliquity 23°26'14"
⚷ Chiron 8♎58.6R
☽ Mean ☊ 16♎01.7

1 JUNE 1996
Julian Day # 35216
Delta T 60.3 sec
SVP 05♓18'32"
Obliquity 23°26'14"
⚷ Chiron 7♎55.0R
☽ Mean ☊ 14♎23.2

JULY 1996 LONGITUDE

Day	Sid.Time	☉	0 hr ☽	Noon ☽	True ☊	☿	♀	♂	♃	♄	♅	♆	♇
1 M	18 37 18	9♋26 26	7♑ 4 57	14♑41 48	12♎57.3	27♊19.8	11♊48.5	12♊59.9	13♑12.6	7♈ 7.8	3♒32.4	26♑50.1	0♐45.5
2 Tu	18 41 15	10 23 36	22 19 35	29 56 53	12R46.6	29 21.1	11D46.6	13 41.8	13R 5.0	7 9.6	3R30.2	26R48.6	0R44.3
3 W	18 45 11	11 20 47	7♒32 20	15♒ 4 42	12 36.8	1♋24.4	11 47.1	14 23.6	12 57.3	7 11.2	3 28.1	26 47.1	0 43.2
4 Th	18 49 8	12 17 58	22 32 53	29 55 58	12 29.1	3 29.4	11 49.9	15 5.3	12 49.6	7 12.8	3 25.9	26 45.5	0 42.1
5 F	18 53 4	13 15 9	7♓13 17	14♓24 22	12 23.9	5 36.0	11 55.0	15 47.0	12 41.9	7 14.2	3 23.7	26 44.0	0 41.0
6 Sa	18 57 1	14 12 20	21 28 57	28 26 59	12 21.2	7 43.8	12 2.3	16 28.6	12 34.2	7 15.6	3 21.5	26 42.4	0 39.9
7 Su	19 0 57	15 9 32	5♈18 32	12♈ 3 50	12 20.3	9 52.6	12 11.7	17 10.2	12 26.5	7 16.8	3 19.3	26 40.8	0 38.8
8 M	19 4 54	16 6 44	18 43 11	25 17 0	12 20.2	12 2.0	12 23.3	17 51.7	12 18.8	7 18.0	3 17.0	26 39.2	0 37.8
9 Tu	19 8 51	17 3 56	1♉45 43	8♉ 9 46	12 19.8	14 11.8	12 36.8	18 33.2	12 11.1	7 19.1	3 14.8	26 37.6	0 36.8
10 W	19 12 47	18 1 9	14 29 38	20 45 46	12 17.7	16 21.6	12 52.4	19 14.6	12 3.5	7 20.0	3 12.5	26 36.0	0 35.8
11 Th	19 16 44	18 58 22	26 58 35	3♊ 8 30	12 13.3	18 31.3	13 9.9	19 56.0	11 55.9	7 20.9	3 10.2	26 34.4	0 34.9
12 F	19 20 40	19 55 36	9♊15 53	15 21 4	12 6.1	20 40.5	13 29.2	20 37.3	11 48.3	7 21.6	3 7.9	26 32.8	0 33.9
13 Sa	19 24 37	20 52 50	21 24 19	27 25 55	11 56.2	22 49.0	13 50.3	21 18.5	11 40.8	7 22.3	3 5.6	26 31.2	0 33.0
14 Su	19 28 33	21 50 5	3♋26 4	9♋25 0	11 44.1	24 56.6	14 13.2	21 59.7	11 33.3	7 22.8	3 3.2	26 29.6	0 32.2
15 M	19 32 30	22 47 20	15 22 53	21 19 53	11 30.7	27 3.2	14 37.7	22 40.8	11 25.8	7 23.3	3 0.9	26 28.0	0 31.3
16 Tu	19 36 26	23 44 35	27 16 11	3♌11 57	11 17.2	29 8.5	15 3.9	23 21.9	11 18.4	7 23.6	2 58.5	26 26.4	0 30.5
17 W	19 40 23	24 41 51	9♌ 7 22	15 2 39	11 4.7	1♌12.5	15 31.6	24 2.9	11 11.1	7 23.9	2 56.2	26 24.7	0 29.7
18 Th	19 44 20	25 39 7	20 58 2	26 53 47	10 54.0	3 15.0	16 0.7	24 43.8	11 3.8	7R24.0	2 53.8	26 23.1	0 28.9
19 F	19 48 16	26 36 23	2♍50 13	8♍47 42	10 45.9	5 15.9	16 31.4	25 24.7	10 56.6	7 24.0	2 51.4	26 21.5	0 28.2
20 Sa	19 52 13	27 33 39	14 46 35	20 47 21	10 40.6	7 15.3	17 3.4	26 5.5	10 49.5	7 24.0	2 49.0	26 19.9	0 27.5
21 Su	19 56 9	28 30 56	26 50 28	2♎56 27	10 37.9	9 13.0	17 36.7	26 46.3	10 42.5	7 23.8	2 46.7	26 18.2	0 26.8
22 M	20 0 6	29 28 13	9♎ 5 51	15 19 14	10D37.1	11 9.0	18 11.3	27 27.0	10 35.5	7 23.5	2 44.3	26 16.6	0 26.2
23 Tu	20 4 2	0♌25 31	21 37 12	28 0 20	10R37.3	13 3.2	18 47.2	28 7.6	10 28.7	7 23.2	2 41.9	26 15.0	0 25.6
24 W	20 7 59	1 22 49	4♏29 11	11♏ 4 16	10 37.4	14 55.8	19 24.2	28 48.2	10 21.9	7 22.7	2 39.5	26 13.4	0 25.0
25 Th	20 11 55	2 20 7	17 46 3	24 34 53	10 36.4	16 46.6	20 2.4	29 28.7	10 15.2	7 22.1	2 37.1	26 11.8	0 24.5
26 F	20 15 52	3 17 25	1♐30 59	8♐34 25	10 33.5	18 35.7	20 41.7	0♋ 9.2	10 8.7	7 21.4	2 34.7	26 10.1	0 23.9
27 Sa	20 19 49	4 14 44	15 45 4	23 2 37	10 28.3	20 23.0	21 22.1	0 49.6	10 2.2	7 20.7	2 32.3	26 8.5	0 23.5
28 Su	20 23 45	5 12 4	0♑26 30	7♑55 54	10 21.0	22 8.6	22 3.5	1 30.0	9 55.9	7 19.8	2 29.9	26 6.9	0 23.0
29 M	20 27 42	6 9 24	15 29 51	23 7 7	10 12.2	23 52.5	22 45.9	2 10.3	9 49.7	7 18.8	2 27.5	26 5.4	0 22.6
30 Tu	20 31 38	7 6 44	0♒46 22	8♒26 11	10 3.1	25 34.7	23 29.3	2 50.5	9 43.6	7 17.8	2 25.1	26 3.8	0 22.2
31 W	20 35 35	8 4 6	16 5 8	23 41 48	9 54.7	27 15.2	24 13.5	3 30.7	9 37.6	7 16.6	2 22.7	26 2.2	0 21.8

AUGUST 1996 LONGITUDE

Day	Sid.Time	☉	0 hr ☽	Noon ☽	True ☊	☿	♀	♂	♃	♄	♅	♆	♇
1 Th	20 39 31	9♌ 1 28	1♓14 55	8♓43 23	9♎48.0	28♌53.9	24♊58.7	4♋10.8	9♑31.8	7♈15.3	2♒20.3	26♑ 0.6	0♐21.5
2 F	20 43 28	9 58 51	16 6 16	23 22 53	9R43.6	0♍31.0	25 44.8	4 50.8	9R26.1	7R14.0	2R17.9	25R59.0	0R21.2
3 Sa	20 47 24	10 56 15	0♈32 45	7♈35 37	9D41.5	2 6.4	26 31.6	5 30.8	9 20.5	7 12.5	2 15.6	25 57.5	0 20.9
4 Su	20 51 21	11 53 41	14 31 23	21 20 11	9 41.3	3 40.1	27 19.3	6 10.8	9 15.0	7 10.9	2 13.2	25 55.9	0 20.7
5 M	20 55 18	12 51 7	28 2 15	4♉37 54	9 42.0	5 12.1	28 7.8	6 50.7	9 9.7	7 9.3	2 10.9	25 54.4	0 20.5
6 Tu	20 59 14	13 48 35	11♉ 7 36	17 31 48	9R42.6	6 42.4	28 57.0	7 30.5	9 4.6	7 7.5	2 8.5	25 52.9	0 20.3
7 W	21 3 11	14 46 4	23 51 2	0♊ 5 50	9 42.2	8 11.0	29 46.9	8 10.3	8 59.6	7 5.7	2 6.2	25 51.3	0 20.2
8 Th	21 7 7	15 43 35	6♊16 43	12 24 14	9 40.1	9 37.9	0♋37.5	8 50.0	8 54.7	7 3.7	2 3.9	25 49.8	0 20.1
9 F	21 11 4	16 41 7	18 28 51	24 31 3	9 35.7	11 3.0	1 28.8	9 29.7	8 50.0	7 1.7	2 1.6	25 48.3	0 20.0
10 Sa	21 15 0	17 38 40	0♋31 16	6♋29 54	9 29.3	12 26.4	2 20.7	10 9.3	8 45.5	6 59.6	1 59.3	25 46.8	0D20.0
11 Su	21 18 57	18 36 14	12 27 19	18 23 51	9 21.1	13 47.9	3 13.3	10 48.8	8 41.1	6 57.4	1 57.0	25 45.4	0 20.0
12 M	21 22 53	19 33 50	24 19 47	0♌15 23	9 11.9	15 7.7	4 6.4	11 28.3	8 36.9	6 55.0	1 54.8	25 43.9	0 20.0
13 Tu	21 26 50	20 31 27	6♌10 55	12 6 34	9 2.5	16 25.5	5 0.1	12 7.7	8 32.8	6 52.6	1 52.5	25 42.5	0 20.1
14 W	21 30 47	21 29 6	18 2 35	23 59 9	8 53.8	17 41.4	5 54.4	12 47.1	8 29.0	6 50.2	1 50.3	25 41.1	0 20.2
15 Th	21 34 43	22 26 45	29 56 28	5♍54 45	8 46.5	18 55.3	6 49.2	13 26.4	8 25.2	6 47.6	1 48.1	25 39.6	0 20.3
16 F	21 38 40	23 24 26	11♍54 15	17 55 12	8 41.1	20 7.2	7 44.5	14 5.6	8 21.7	6 44.9	1 45.9	25 38.2	0 20.5
17 Sa	21 42 36	24 22 8	23 57 51	0♎ 2 33	8 37.9	21 16.9	8 40.3	14 44.8	8 18.3	6 42.2	1 43.7	25 36.9	0 20.7
18 Su	21 46 33	25 19 51	6♎ 9 35	12 19 20	8D36.7	22 24.4	9 36.6	15 23.9	8 15.2	6 39.3	1 41.6	25 35.5	0 20.9
19 M	21 50 29	26 17 35	18 32 11	24 48 33	8 37.1	23 29.6	10 33.4	16 3.0	8 12.1	6 36.4	1 39.5	25 34.1	0 21.2
20 Tu	21 54 26	27 15 20	1♏ 8 51	7♏33 32	8 38.4	24 32.3	11 30.6	16 41.9	8 9.3	6 33.4	1 37.4	25 32.8	0 21.5
21 W	21 58 22	28 13 7	14 3 3	20 37 46	8 39.8	25 32.6	12 28.3	17 20.9	8 6.7	6 30.3	1 35.3	25 31.5	0 21.8
22 Th	22 2 19	29 10 54	27 18 6	4♐ 4 20	8R40.5	26 30.1	13 26.4	17 59.7	8 4.2	6 27.2	1 33.3	25 30.2	0 22.2
23 F	22 6 16	0♍ 8 43	10♐56 43	17 55 22	8 40.0	27 24.8	14 25.0	18 38.5	8 1.9	6 24.0	1 31.2	25 29.0	0 22.6
24 Sa	22 10 12	1 6 33	25 0 15	2♑11 14	8 38.0	28 16.6	15 23.9	19 17.3	7 59.8	6 20.6	1 29.3	25 27.7	0 23.0
25 Su	22 14 9	2 4 24	9♑27 56	16 49 52	8 34.4	29 5.2	16 23.2	19 55.9	7 57.9	6 17.3	1 27.3	25 26.5	0 23.5
26 M	22 18 5	3 2 17	24 16 17	1♒46 18	8 29.8	29 50.5	17 22.9	20 34.5	7 56.2	6 13.8	1 25.4	25 25.3	0 24.0
27 Tu	22 22 2	4 0 11	9♒18 54	16 52 55	8 24.9	0♎32.2	18 23.0	21 13.1	7 54.7	6 10.3	1 23.5	25 24.1	0 24.5
28 W	22 25 58	4 58 6	24 27 8	2♓ 0 18	8 20.3	1 10.2	19 23.5	21 51.6	7 53.3	6 6.7	1 21.6	25 22.9	0 25.1
29 Th	22 29 55	5 56 2	9♓31 13	16 58 46	8 16.7	1 44.2	20 24.3	22 30.0	7 52.2	6 3.1	1 19.7	25 21.8	0 25.7
30 F	22 33 51	6 54 0	24 21 56	1♈39 53	8D14.5	2 13.9	21 25.5	23 8.4	7 51.2	5 59.3	1 17.9	25 20.7	0 26.4
31 Sa	22 37 48	7 52 0	8♈51 57	15 57 40	8 13.9	2 39.1	22 27.0	23 46.7	7 50.4	5 55.6	1 16.1	25 19.6	0 27.0

Astro Data Dy Hr Mn	Planet Ingress Dy Hr Mn	Last Aspect Dy Hr Mn	☽ Ingress Dy Hr Mn	Last Aspect Dy Hr Mn	☽ Ingress Dy Hr Mn	☽ Phases & Eclipses Dy Hr Mn	Astro Data
♀ D 2 6:51	☿ ♋ 2 7:37	2 7:03 ♆ ☌	♒ 2 12:05	2 16:51 ♀ □	♈ 2 23:05	1 3:58 ○ 9♑36	1 JULY 1996
☽0N 6 9:19	☿ ♌ 16 9:56	3 11:26 ♂ △	♓ 4 12:07	5 0:11 ♀ ⚹	♉ 5 3:33	7 18:55 ☽ 15♈55	Julian Day # 35246
♄ R 18 20:29	☉ ♌ 22 13:19	6 8:58 ♆ ⚹	♈ 6 14:42	7 3:50 ♆ △	♊ 7 11:49	15 16:15 ● 23♋26	Delta T 60.3 sec
☽0S 21 0:54	♂ ♋ 25 18:32	8 14:30 ♆ □	♉ 8 20:43	8 20:08 ☉ ⚹	♋ 9 22:57	23 17:49 ☽ 1♏08	SVP 05♓18'27"
		10 23:13 ♆ △	♊ 11 5:52	12 2:50 ♆ ☍	♌ 12 11:29	30 10:35 ○ 7♒32	Obliquity 23°26'13"
☽0N 2 18:54	☿ ♍ 1 16:17	12 23:48 ♂ ☌	♋ 13 17:08	14 7:34 ☉ ☌	♍ 15 0:07		⚷ Chiron 8♎32.7
♇ D 10 12:34	♀ ♋ 7 6:15	16 4:35 ☿ ☌	♌ 16 5:31	17 3:16 ♆ △	♎ 17 11:55		☽ Mean ☊ 12♎47.9
☽0S 17 7:29	☉ ♍ 22 20:23	18 8:05 ♂ ⚹	♍ 18 18:16	19 16:03 ☉ ⚹	♏ 19 21:50	6 5:25 ☽ 14♉02	
☿0S 20 22:25	☿ ♎ 26 5:17	21 3:35 ☉ ⚹	♎ 21 6:14	22 3:36 ☉ □	♐ 22 4:48	14 7:34 ● 21♌47	1 AUGUST 1996
☽0N 30 5:40		23 12:54 ♂ △	♏ 23 15:43	24 5:49 ☿ □	♑ 24 8:22	22 3:36 ☽ 29♏20	Julian Day # 35277
♄0S 30 16:56		25 14:47 ♆ ⚹	♐ 25 21:24	26 1:51 ♆ ☌	♒ 26 9:10	28 17:52 ○ 5♓41	Delta T 60.4 sec
		27 9:43 ♀ ☍	♑ 27 23:17	26 19:01 ♄ ⚹	♓ 28 8:49		SVP 05♓18'22"
		29 16:38 ♆ ☌	♒ 29 22:47	30 1:36 ♆ ⚹	♈ 30 9:15		Obliquity 23°26'14"
		31 19:48 ☿ ☍	♓ 31 22:00				⚷ Chiron 10♎49.7
							☽ Mean ☊ 11♎09.4

LONGITUDE — SEPTEMBER 1996

Day	Sid.Time	☉	0 hr ☽	Noon ☽	True ☊	☿	♀	♂	♃	♄	♅	♆	♇
1 Su	22 41 45	8♍50 2	22♈56 43	29♈48 58	8♎14.5	2♎59.5	23♋28.8	24♋24.9	7♑49.8	5♈51.7	1♒14.4	25♑18.5	0♐27.7
2 M	22 45 41	9 48 5	6♉34 29	13♉13 24	8 15.9	3 14.9	24 31.0	25 3.1	7R 49.4	5R 47.8	1R 12.7	25R 17.4	0 28.5
3 Tu	22 49 38	10 46 10	19 46 1	26 12 42	8 17.5	3 24.8	25 33.5	25 41.2	7D 49.2	5 43.8	1 11.0	25 16.4	0 29.2
4 W	22 53 34	11 44 18	2♊33 54	8♊50 7	8R 18.6	3R 29.2	26 36.3	26 19.2	7 49.2	5 39.8	1 9.4	25 15.4	0 30.0
5 Th	22 57 31	12 42 27	15 1 52	21 9 43	8 18.9	3 27.6	27 39.3	26 57.2	7 49.4	5 35.8	1 7.8	25 14.4	0 30.9
6 F	23 1 27	13 40 39	27 14 13	3♋15 55	8 18.1	3 19.9	28 42.7	27 35.2	7 49.7	5 31.6	1 6.2	25 13.5	0 31.7
7 Sa	23 5 24	14 38 52	9♋15 22	15 13 6	8 16.3	3 5.9	29 46.4	28 13.0	7 50.3	5 27.5	1 4.7	25 12.6	0 32.6
8 Su	23 9 20	15 37 8	21 9 35	27 5 18	8 13.5	2 45.4	0♌50.3	28 50.8	7 51.0	5 23.2	1 3.2	25 11.7	0 33.6
9 M	23 13 17	16 35 25	3♌ 0 42	8♌56 9	8 10.1	2 18.4	1 54.5	29 28.6	7 52.0	5 19.0	1 1.7	25 10.8	0 34.5
10 Tu	23 17 14	17 33 44	14 52 4	20 48 45	8 6.6	1 44.9	2 59.0	0♌ 6.2	7 53.1	5 14.7	1 0.3	25 10.0	0 35.5
11 W	23 21 10	18 32 5	26 46 31	2♍45 39	8 3.4	1 5.2	4 3.7	0 43.8	7 54.4	5 10.3	0 58.9	25 9.2	0 36.5
12 Th	23 25 7	19 30 28	8♍46 22	14 48 55	8 0.8	0 19.6	5 8.7	1 21.3	7 55.9	5 5.9	0 57.6	25 8.4	0 37.6
13 F	23 29 3	20 28 53	20 53 30	27 0 19	7 59.1	29♍28.7	6 13.9	1 58.8	7 57.6	5 1.5	0 56.3	25 7.6	0 38.7
14 Sa	23 33 0	21 27 20	3♎ 9 31	9♎21 18	7D 58.3	28 33.1	7 19.3	2 36.2	7 59.5	4 57.0	0 55.0	25 6.9	0 39.8
15 Su	23 36 56	22 25 49	15 35 50	21 53 18	7 58.4	27 33.9	8 25.0	3 13.5	8 1.5	4 52.5	0 53.8	25 6.2	0 40.9
16 M	23 40 53	23 24 19	28 13 51	4♏37 43	7 59.1	26 32.2	9 30.9	3 50.7	8 3.8	4 48.0	0 52.6	25 5.5	0 42.1
17 Tu	23 44 49	24 22 52	11♏ 5 2	17 36 2	8 0.2	25 29.2	10 37.0	4 27.9	8 6.2	4 43.4	0 51.5	25 4.9	0 43.3
18 W	23 48 46	25 21 26	24 10 53	0♐49 45	8 1.4	24 26.4	11 43.3	5 5.0	8 8.9	4 38.9	0 50.4	25 4.3	0 44.6
19 Th	23 52 42	26 20 1	7♐32 48	14 20 9	8 2.3	23 25.3	12 49.8	5 42.0	8 11.7	4 34.3	0 49.4	25 3.7	0 45.8
20 F	23 56 39	27 18 39	21 11 55	28 8 5	8R 2.8	22 27.5	13 56.5	6 19.0	8 14.7	4 29.7	0 48.4	25 3.1	0 47.1
21 Sa	0 0 36	28 17 18	5♑ 8 39	12♑13 29	8 2.8	21 34.4	15 3.5	6 55.9	8 17.9	4 25.0	0 47.5	25 2.6	0 48.5
22 Su	0 4 32	29 15 58	19 22 21	26 34 56	8 2.3	20 47.4	16 10.6	7 32.7	8 21.2	4 20.4	0 46.6	25 2.1	0 49.8
23 M	0 8 29	0♎14 40	3♒50 49	11♒ 9 27	8 1.6	20 7.9	17 17.9	8 9.4	8 24.8	4 15.7	0 45.7	25 1.7	0 51.2
24 Tu	0 12 25	1 13 24	18 30 11	25 52 18	8 0.8	19 36.7	18 25.4	8 46.1	8 28.5	4 11.1	0 44.9	25 1.2	0 52.6
25 W	0 16 22	2 12 10	3♓14 57	10♓37 18	8 0.1	19 14.7	19 33.1	9 22.7	8 32.4	4 6.4	0 44.1	25 0.8	0 54.1
26 Th	0 20 18	3 10 57	17 58 29	25 17 35	7 59.6	19D 2.5	20 41.0	9 59.2	8 36.4	4 1.7	0 43.4	25 0.5	0 55.5
27 F	0 24 15	4 9 47	2♈33 47	9♈46 20	7D 59.4	19 0.3	21 49.0	10 35.6	8 40.7	3 57.0	0 42.7	25 0.1	0 57.0
28 Sa	0 28 11	5 8 38	16 54 31	23 57 47	7 59.5	19 8.3	22 57.3	11 12.0	8 45.1	3 52.3	0 42.1	24 59.8	0 58.6
29 Su	0 32 8	6 7 31	0♉55 40	7♉47 52	7 59.6	19 26.3	24 5.7	11 48.2	8 49.7	3 47.7	0 41.6	24 59.6	1 0.1
30 M	0 36 5	7 6 27	14 34 11	21 14 32	7R 59.7	19 54.2	25 14.3	12 24.4	8 54.4	3 43.0	0 41.0	24 59.3	1 1.7

LONGITUDE — OCTOBER 1996

Day	Sid.Time	☉	0 hr ☽	Noon ☽	True ☊	☿	♀	♂	♃	♄	♅	♆	♇
1 Tu	0 40 1	8♎ 5 25	27♉49 1	4♊17 46	7♎59.8	20♍31.3	26♌23.0	13♌ 0.6	8♑59.4	3♈38.3	0♒40.6	24♑59.1	1♐ 3.3
2 W	0 43 58	9 4 25	10♊41 4	16 59 16	7R 59.7	21 17.3	27 32.0	13 36.6	9 4.5	3R 33.7	0R 40.1	24R 59.0	1 4.9
3 Th	0 47 54	10 3 27	23 12 47	29 22 5	7 59.6	22 11.4	28 41.0	14 12.6	9 9.7	3 29.0	0 39.8	24 58.8	1 6.6
4 F	0 51 51	11 2 32	5♋27 42	11♋30 11	7D 59.5	23 13.0	29 50.3	14 48.5	9 15.2	3 24.4	0 39.4	24 58.7	1 8.2
5 Sa	0 55 47	12 1 39	17 30 6	23 28 2	7 59.5	24 21.4	0♍59.7	15 24.3	9 20.8	3 19.8	0 39.2	24 58.7	1 9.9
6 Su	0 59 44	13 0 48	29 24 34	5♌20 17	7 59.7	25 35.8	2 9.2	16 0.1	9 26.5	3 15.2	0 38.9	24D 58.6	1 11.7
7 M	1 3 40	14 0 0	11♌15 45	17 11 30	8 0.2	26 55.4	3 19.0	16 35.7	9 32.4	3 10.6	0 38.7	24 58.6	1 13.4
8 Tu	1 7 37	14 59 14	23 8 3	29 5 54	8 0.8	28 19.7	4 28.8	17 11.3	9 38.5	3 6.1	0 38.6	24 58.6	1 15.2
9 W	1 11 34	15 58 30	5♍ 5 30	11♍ 7 15	8 1.7	29 47.9	5 38.8	17 46.8	9 44.8	3 1.6	0 38.5	24 58.7	1 17.0
10 Th	1 15 30	16 57 48	17 11 32	23 18 39	8 2.4	1♎19.4	6 48.9	18 22.2	9 51.1	2 57.1	0D 38.5	24 58.8	1 18.8
11 F	1 19 27	17 57 9	29 28 54	5♎42 29	8R 3.0	2 53.7	7 59.2	18 57.5	9 57.7	2 52.7	0 38.5	24 58.9	1 20.7
12 Sa	1 23 23	18 56 31	11♎59 34	18 20 16	8 3.1	4 30.3	9 9.6	19 32.7	10 4.4	2 48.2	0 38.6	24 59.1	1 22.5
13 Su	1 27 20	19 55 56	24 44 39	1♏12 45	8 2.6	6 8.8	10 20.1	20 7.8	10 11.3	2 43.9	0 38.7	24 59.3	1 24.4
14 M	1 31 16	20 55 22	7♏44 32	14 19 55	8 1.5	7 48.6	11 30.7	20 42.9	10 18.3	2 39.5	0 38.9	24 59.5	1 26.3
15 Tu	1 35 13	21 54 51	20 58 50	27 41 7	7 59.8	9 29.6	12 41.5	21 17.8	10 25.4	2 35.2	0 39.1	24 59.8	1 28.3
16 W	1 39 9	22 54 22	4♐26 39	11♐15 15	7 57.7	11 11.4	13 52.4	21 52.7	10 32.8	2 31.0	0 39.4	25 0.1	1 30.2
17 Th	1 43 6	23 53 54	18 6 45	25 0 56	7 55.7	12 53.7	15 3.4	22 27.4	10 40.2	2 26.8	0 39.8	25 0.4	1 32.2
18 F	1 47 2	24 53 29	1♑57 37	8♑56 37	7 54.0	14 36.4	16 14.5	23 2.1	10 47.8	2 22.6	0 40.1	25 0.8	1 34.2
19 Sa	1 50 59	25 53 5	15 57 42	23 0 41	7D 52.9	16 19.3	17 25.7	23 36.6	10 55.6	2 18.6	0 40.6	25 1.2	1 36.2
20 Su	1 54 56	26 52 42	0♒ 5 19	7♒11 24	7 52.7	18 2.2	18 37.1	24 11.1	11 3.5	2 14.5	0 41.1	25 1.6	1 38.2
21 M	1 58 52	27 52 22	14 18 38	21 26 45	7 53.3	19 45.1	19 48.5	24 45.4	11 11.5	2 10.5	0 41.6	25 2.1	1 40.3
22 Tu	2 2 49	28 52 3	28 35 26	5♓44 21	7 54.5	21 27.7	21 0.1	25 19.7	11 19.6	2 6.6	0 42.2	25 2.6	1 42.3
23 W	2 6 45	29 51 45	12♓53 5	20 1 13	7 56.0	23 10.0	22 11.7	25 53.8	11 27.9	2 2.7	0 42.8	25 3.1	1 44.4
24 Th	2 10 42	0♏51 30	27 8 19	4♈13 54	7R 57.0	24 52.1	23 23.5	26 27.9	11 36.4	1 58.9	0 43.5	25 3.7	1 46.5
25 F	2 14 38	1 51 16	11♈17 28	18 18 33	7 57.3	26 33.7	24 35.3	27 1.8	11 44.9	1 55.2	0 44.3	25 4.3	1 48.6
26 Sa	2 18 35	2 51 4	25 16 38	2♉11 17	7 56.4	28 14.9	25 47.3	27 35.7	11 53.6	1 51.5	0 45.1	25 4.9	1 50.7
27 Su	2 22 31	3 50 54	9♉ 2 5	15 48 41	7 54.1	29 55.7	26 59.3	28 9.4	12 2.4	1 47.9	0 45.9	25 5.6	1 52.9
28 M	2 26 28	4 50 46	22 30 48	29 8 13	7 50.6	1♏36.1	28 11.5	28 43.0	12 11.4	1 44.4	0 46.8	25 6.2	1 55.0
29 Tu	2 30 25	5 50 40	5♊40 49	12♊ 8 34	7 46.2	3 16.0	29 23.7	29 16.6	12 20.5	1 40.9	0 47.7	25 7.0	1 57.2
30 W	2 34 21	6 50 37	18 31 33	24 49 55	7 41.3	4 55.4	0♎36.1	29 50.0	12 29.7	1 37.5	0 48.7	25 7.7	1 59.4
31 Th	2 38 18	7 50 35	1♋ 3 54	7♋13 49	7 36.7	6 34.3	1 48.5	0♍23.3	12 39.0	1 34.2	0 49.8	25 8.5	2 1.6

Astro Data	Planet Ingress	Last Aspect	☽ Ingress	Last Aspect	☽ Ingress	☽ Phases & Eclipses	Astro Data
Dy Hr Mn	Dy Hr Mn	Dy Hr Mn	Dy Hr Mn	Dy Hr Mn	Dy Hr Mn	Dy Hr Mn	1 SEPTEMBER 1996
♃ D 3 14:37	♀ ♌ 7 5:07	1 4:06 ♆ □	♉ 1 12:19	30 21:07 ♀ □	♊ 1 4:01	4 19:06 ☽ 12♊31	Julian Day # 35308
☿ R 4 5:47	♂ ♌ 9 20:02	3 11:44 ♀ ✶	♊ 3 19:08	3 11:46 ♀ ✶	♋ 3 13:14	12 23:07 ● 20♍27	Delta T 60.4 sec
☽0S 13 13:40	☿ ♍ 12 9:32	4 19:06 ☉ □	♋ 6 5:29	5 15:22 ☿ ✶	♌ 6 1:12	20 11:23 ☽ 27♐46	SVP 05♓18'19"
☿0N 18 20:31	☉ ♎ 22 18:00	8 16:26 ♂ ☌	♌ 8 17:54	7 11:22 ♂ ☌	♍ 8 13:49	27 2:51 ○ 4♈17	Obliquity 23°26'14"
♅✶♇ 20 13:16		9 4:38 ♄ △	♍ 11 6:28	10 15:15 ♆ △	♎ 11 1:00	27 2:54 • T 1.240	⚷ Chiron 14♎21.9
☽0N 26 16:12	♀ ♍ 4 3:22	13 15:40 ♀ ☌	♎ 13 17:51	13 0:27 ♆ □	♏ 13 9:46		☽ Mean ☊ 9♎30.9
☿ D 26 17:09	☿ ♎ 9 3:13	15 18:05 ♆ □	♏ 16 3:20	15 7:12 ♆ ✶	♐ 15 16:07	4 12:04 ☽ 11♋32	
	☉ ♏ 23 3:19	18 2:18 ☉ ✶	♐ 18 10:31	17 10:50 ☉ ✶	♑ 17 20:37	12 14:14 ● 19♎32	1 OCTOBER 1996
♆ D 6 15:55	☿ ♏ 27 1:01	20 11:23 ☉ □	♑ 20 15:12	19 18:09 ☉ □	♒ 19 23:51	12 14:02:03 • P 0.758	Julian Day # 35338
☽0S 10 20:48	♀ ♎ 29 12:02	22 17:38 ☉ △	♒ 22 17:39	22 0:30 ☉ △	♓ 22 2:22	19 18:09 ☽ 26♑38	Delta T 60.5 sec
♅ D 10 0:55	♂ ♍ 30 7:13	23 23:52 ♀ ☍	♓ 24 18:43	23 20:29 ♆ ✶	♈ 24 4:50	26 14:11 ○ 3♉26	SVP 05♓18'17"
☿0S 12 0:39		26 11:32 ♆ ✶	♈ 26 19:46	26 5:52 ☿ ☍	♉ 26 8:11		Obliquity 23°26'14"
☽0N 24 1:15		28 13:46 ♆ □	♉ 28 22:24	28 11:44 ♂ □	♊ 28 13:34		⚷ Chiron 18♎30.1
♄△♇ 26 3:16				28 17:08 ♇ ☍	♋ 30 21:56		☽ Mean ☊ 7♎55.6

NOVEMBER 1996 LONGITUDE

Day	Sid.Time	☉	0 hr ☽	Noon ☽	True ☊	☿	♀	♂	♃	♄	♅	♆	♇
1 F	2 42 14	8♏50 35	13♋20 3	19♋23 4	7♎32.9	8♏12.8	3♎ 1.1	0♍56.5	12♑48.4	1♈31.0	0♒50.9	25♑ 9.4	2♐ 3.8
2 Sa	2 46 11	9 50 38	25 23 22	1♌21 30	7R30.3	9 50.8	4 13.7	1 29.5	12 58.0	1R27.8	0 52.0	25 10.2	2 6.1
3 Su	2 50 7	10 50 42	7♌18 3	13 13 38	7D29.1	11 28.3	5 26.4	2 2.5	13 7.7	1 24.8	0 53.2	25 11.1	2 8.3
4 M	2 54 4	11 50 49	19 8 53	25 4 25	7 29.3	13 5.4	6 39.2	2 35.3	13 17.5	1 21.8	0 54.4	25 12.0	2 10.6
5 Tu	2 58 0	12 50 58	1♍ 0 53	6♍58 54	7 30.6	14 42.1	7 52.0	3 8.1	13 27.4	1 18.9	0 55.7	25 13.0	2 12.8
6 W	3 1 57	13 51 9	12 59 5	19 2 0	7 32.4	16 18.4	9 5.0	3 40.6	13 37.4	1 16.0	0 57.0	25 14.0	2 15.1
7 Th	3 5 54	14 51 22	25 8 11	1♎18 7	7 33.9	17 54.2	10 18.0	4 13.1	13 47.5	1 13.3	0 58.4	25 15.0	2 17.4
8 F	3 9 50	15 51 36	7♎32 15	13 50 55	7R34.6	19 29.7	11 31.1	4 45.4	13 57.8	1 10.7	0 59.9	25 16.0	2 19.7
9 Sa	3 13 47	16 51 53	20 14 24	26 42 53	7 33.8	21 4.8	12 44.3	5 17.6	14 8.1	1 8.1	1 1.3	25 17.1	2 22.0
10 Su	3 17 43	17 52 12	3♏16 26	9♏55 3	7 31.0	22 39.6	13 57.5	5 49.7	14 18.6	1 5.6	1 2.9	25 18.2	2 24.3
11 M	3 21 40	18 52 32	16 38 34	23 26 46	7 26.3	24 14.0	15 10.9	6 21.6	14 29.2	1 3.3	1 4.4	25 19.4	2 26.6
12 Tu	3 25 36	19 52 55	0♐19 18	7♐15 44	7 20.0	25 48.1	16 24.2	6 53.4	14 39.8	1 1.0	1 6.1	25 20.5	2 28.9
13 W	3 29 33	20 53 19	14 15 34	21 18 14	7 12.7	27 22.0	17 37.7	7 25.1	14 50.6	0 58.8	1 7.7	25 21.7	2 31.3
14 Th	3 33 29	21 53 44	28 23 8	5♑29 41	7 5.3	28 55.5	18 51.2	7 56.6	15 1.5	0 56.7	1 9.5	25 23.0	2 33.6
15 F	3 37 26	22 54 11	12♑37 17	19 45 22	6 58.7	0♐28.7	20 4.7	8 27.9	15 12.5	0 54.7	1 11.2	25 24.2	2 36.0
16 Sa	3 41 23	23 54 39	26 53 28	4♒ 1 6	6 53.8	2 1.7	21 18.4	8 59.1	15 23.5	0 52.9	1 13.0	25 25.5	2 38.3
17 Su	3 45 19	24 55 9	11♒ 7 56	18 13 39	6 50.9	3 34.4	22 32.0	9 30.2	15 34.7	0 51.1	1 14.9	25 26.8	2 40.7
18 M	3 49 16	25 55 40	25 18 2	2♓20 55	6D49.9	5 6.9	23 45.8	10 1.1	15 46.0	0 49.4	1 16.8	25 28.2	2 43.0
19 Tu	3 53 12	26 56 12	9♓22 8	16 21 38	6 50.5	6 39.2	24 59.5	10 31.8	15 57.3	0 47.8	1 18.7	25 29.6	2 45.4
20 W	3 57 9	27 56 45	23 19 20	0♈15 10	6R51.6	8 11.2	26 13.4	11 2.4	16 8.8	0 46.3	1 20.7	25 31.0	2 47.8
21 Th	4 1 5	28 57 19	7♈ 9 3	14 0 55	6 52.2	9 43.0	27 27.2	11 32.8	16 20.3	0 44.9	1 22.7	25 32.4	2 50.1
22 F	4 5 2	29 57 55	20 50 37	27 38 3	6 51.2	11 14.5	28 41.2	12 3.1	16 31.9	0 43.6	1 24.8	25 33.8	2 52.5
23 Sa	4 8 58	0♐58 32	4♉23 2	11♉ 5 23	6 48.0	12 45.9	29 55.1	12 33.1	16 43.6	0 42.5	1 26.9	25 35.3	2 54.9
24 Su	4 12 55	1 59 10	17 44 54	24 21 23	6 42.2	14 17.0	1♏ 9.2	13 3.1	16 55.4	0 41.4	1 29.0	25 36.8	2 57.3
25 M	4 16 52	2 59 50	0♊54 39	7♊24 30	6 33.9	15 47.8	2 23.3	13 32.8	17 7.2	0 40.4	1 31.2	25 38.4	2 59.6
26 Tu	4 20 48	4 0 31	13 50 48	20 13 28	6 23.7	17 18.4	3 37.4	14 2.4	17 19.2	0 39.6	1 33.5	25 39.9	3 2.0
27 W	4 24 45	5 1 13	26 32 26	2♋47 43	6 12.5	18 48.8	4 51.5	14 31.8	17 31.2	0 38.8	1 35.7	25 41.5	3 4.4
28 Th	4 28 41	6 1 57	8♋59 25	15 7 42	6 1.4	20 18.8	6 5.8	15 1.0	17 43.3	0 38.2	1 38.0	25 43.1	3 6.8
29 F	4 32 38	7 2 42	21 12 46	27 14 57	5 51.5	21 48.5	7 20.0	15 30.1	17 55.5	0 37.6	1 40.4	25 44.8	3 9.1
30 Sa	4 36 34	8 3 29	3♌14 36	9♌12 9	5 43.5	23 17.8	8 34.3	15 58.9	18 7.7	0 37.2	1 42.8	25 46.4	3 11.5

DECEMBER 1996 LONGITUDE

Day	Sid.Time	☉	0 hr ☽	Noon ☽	True ☊	☿	♀	♂	♃	♄	♅	♆	♇
1 Su	4 40 31	9♐ 4 17	15♌ 8 7	21♌ 3 2	5♎37.9	24♐46.7	9♏48.7	16♍27.6	18♑20.0	0♈36.9	1♒45.2	25♑48.1	3♐13.9
2 M	4 44 27	10 5 6	26 57 30	2♍52 7	5R34.8	26 15.1	11 3.1	16 56.0	18 32.4	0R36.7	1 47.7	25 49.8	3 16.3
3 Tu	4 48 24	11 5 57	8♍47 35	14 44 33	5D33.7	27 43.0	12 17.5	17 24.3	18 44.9	0D36.6	1 50.2	25 51.5	3 18.6
4 W	4 52 21	12 6 49	20 43 44	26 45 47	5 34.0	29 10.2	13 31.9	17 52.4	18 57.4	0 36.6	1 52.7	25 53.3	3 21.0
5 Th	4 56 17	13 7 43	2♎51 24	9♎ 1 14	5R34.4	0♑36.6	14 46.4	18 20.2	19 10.0	0 36.7	1 55.3	25 55.1	3 23.3
6 F	5 0 14	14 8 38	15 15 53	21 35 52	5 34.0	2 2.2	16 1.0	18 47.9	19 22.7	0 36.9	1 57.9	25 56.8	3 25.7
7 Sa	5 4 10	15 9 34	28 1 40	4♏33 39	5 31.8	3 26.8	17 15.5	19 15.3	19 35.4	0 37.2	2 0.6	25 58.7	3 28.0
8 Su	5 8 7	16 10 31	11♏12 2	17 56 56	5 27.0	4 50.1	18 30.1	19 42.5	19 48.2	0 37.6	2 3.2	26 0.5	3 30.4
9 M	5 12 3	17 11 30	24 48 16	1♐45 50	5 19.4	6 12.1	19 44.8	20 9.4	20 1.1	0 38.2	2 5.9	26 2.4	3 32.7
10 Tu	5 16 0	18 12 29	8♐49 12	15 57 48	5 9.4	7 32.4	20 59.4	20 36.1	20 14.0	0 38.8	2 8.7	26 4.2	3 35.0
11 W	5 19 56	19 13 30	23 10 55	0♑27 41	4 57.9	8 50.9	22 14.1	21 2.6	20 27.0	0 39.6	2 11.5	26 6.1	3 37.3
12 Th	5 23 53	20 14 32	7♑47 8	15 8 16	4 46.0	10 7.1	23 28.8	21 28.9	20 40.0	0 40.5	2 14.3	26 8.1	3 39.6
13 F	5 27 50	21 15 34	22 30 4	29 51 34	4 35.2	11 20.7	24 43.5	21 54.9	20 53.1	0 41.4	2 17.1	26 10.0	3 41.9
14 Sa	5 31 46	22 16 37	7♒11 49	14♒30 4	4 26.6	12 31.4	25 58.3	22 20.6	21 6.2	0 42.5	2 20.0	26 12.0	3 44.2
15 Su	5 35 43	23 17 40	21 45 38	28 58 1	4 20.7	13 38.5	27 13.1	22 46.1	21 19.4	0 43.7	2 22.9	26 13.9	3 46.5
16 M	5 39 39	24 18 44	6♓ 6 49	13♓11 49	4 17.7	14 41.6	28 27.9	23 11.3	21 32.7	0 45.0	2 25.9	26 15.9	3 48.8
17 Tu	5 43 36	25 19 48	20 12 54	27 10 4	4D16.7	15 40.0	29 42.7	23 36.2	21 45.9	0 46.4	2 28.8	26 17.9	3 51.0
18 W	5 47 32	26 20 52	4♈ 3 22	10♈52 57	4R16.7	16 33.1	0♐57.5	24 0.9	21 59.3	0 48.0	2 31.8	26 20.0	3 53.3
19 Th	5 51 29	27 21 57	17 38 59	24 21 38	4 16.2	17 20.1	2 12.3	24 25.3	22 12.7	0 49.6	2 34.8	26 22.0	3 55.5
20 F	5 55 25	28 23 1	1♉ 1 6	7♉37 31	4 14.1	18 0.1	3 27.2	24 49.4	22 26.1	0 51.3	2 37.9	26 24.0	3 57.7
21 Sa	5 59 22	29 24 7	14 11 3	20 41 49	4 9.3	18 32.4	4 42.1	25 13.2	22 39.6	0 53.2	2 40.9	26 26.1	3 59.9
22 Su	6 3 19	0♑25 12	27 9 52	3♊35 16	4 1.4	18 55.9	5 57.0	25 36.7	22 53.1	0 55.1	2 44.0	26 28.2	4 2.1
23 M	6 7 15	1 26 18	9♊58 3	16 18 11	3 50.5	19R 9.9	7 11.9	25 59.9	23 6.6	0 57.1	2 47.1	26 30.3	4 4.3
24 Tu	6 11 12	2 27 24	22 35 40	28 50 30	3 37.2	19 13.4	8 26.8	26 22.8	23 20.2	0 59.3	2 50.3	26 32.4	4 6.4
25 W	6 15 8	3 28 31	5♋ 2 40	11♋12 11	3 22.7	19 5.7	9 41.8	26 45.4	23 33.8	1 1.5	2 53.4	26 34.5	4 8.6
26 Th	6 19 5	4 29 38	17 19 7	23 23 32	3 8.1	18 46.5	10 56.7	27 7.7	23 47.5	1 3.9	2 56.6	26 36.7	4 10.7
27 F	6 23 1	5 30 45	29 25 34	5♌25 24	2 54.7	18 15.4	12 11.7	27 29.7	24 1.2	1 6.4	2 59.8	26 38.8	4 12.8
28 Sa	6 26 58	6 31 53	11♌23 18	17 19 32	2 43.6	17 32.6	13 26.7	27 51.3	24 14.9	1 8.9	3 3.1	26 41.0	4 14.9
29 Su	6 30 54	7 33 1	23 14 29	29 8 33	2 35.2	16 38.9	14 41.7	28 12.5	24 28.7	1 11.6	3 6.3	26 43.1	4 17.0
30 M	6 34 51	8 34 9	5♍ 2 14	10♍56 3	2 29.8	15 35.4	15 56.7	28 33.5	24 42.5	1 14.3	3 9.6	26 45.3	4 19.1
31 Tu	6 38 48	9 35 18	16 50 34	22 46 26	2 27.1	14 23.9	17 11.7	28 54.0	24 56.3	1 17.2	3 12.9	26 47.5	4 21.1

Astro Data Dy Hr Mn	Planet Ingress Dy Hr Mn	Last Aspect Dy Hr Mn	☽ Ingress Dy Hr Mn	Last Aspect Dy Hr Mn	☽ Ingress Dy Hr Mn	☽ Phases & Eclipses Dy Hr Mn
♀0S 1 12:52	☿ ♐ 14 16:36	1 23:34 ♆ ☍	♌ 2 9:16	1 22:22 ☿ △	♍ 2 6:11	3 7:50 ☽ 11♌10
☽0S 7 5:35	☉ ♐ 22 0:49	3 9:47 ♆ □	♍ 4 21:57	4 10:17 ♆ △	♎ 4 18:23	11 4:16 ● 19♏03
♄⚹♅ 10 16:49	♀ ♏ 23 1:34	7 0:13 ♆ △	♎ 7 9:29	6 20:11 ♆ □	♏ 7 3:39	18 1:09 ☽ 25♒59
☽0N 20 8:28		9 9:23 ♆ □	♏ 9 18:02	9 2:09 ♆ ⚹	♐ 9 8:58	25 4:10 ○ 3♊10
♃∠♇ 30 9:12	☿ ♑ 4 13:48	11 15:19 ♆ ⚹	♐ 11 23:26	10 20:21 ♂ □	♑ 11 11:15	
	♀ ♐ 17 5:34	13 6:18 ♀ ⚹	♑ 14 2:44	13 5:59 ♆ ☌	♒ 13 12:14	3 5:06 ☽ 11♍19
♄ D 3 12:39	☉ ♑ 21 14:06	15 21:32 ♆ ☌	♒ 16 5:14	15 9:56 ♀ □	♓ 15 13:44	10 16:56 ● 18♐56
☽0S 4 15:34		18 1:09 ☉ □	♓ 18 8:00	17 10:31 ♆ ⚹	♈ 17 16:55	17 9:31 ☽ 25♓44
☽0N 17 15:02		20 8:38 ☉ △	♈ 20 11:34	19 18:51 ☉ △	♉ 19 22:10	24 20:41 ○ 3♋20
☿ R 23 19:46		22 15:15 ♀ ☍	♉ 22 16:12	21 22:42 ♆ △	♊ 22 5:17	
		24 14:19 ♆ △	♊ 24 22:20	24 7:29 ♂ □	♋ 24 14:14	
		26 7:22 ☿ ☍	♋ 27 6:37	26 20:02 ♂ ⚹	♌ 27 1:09	
		29 9:01 ♆ ☍	♌ 29 17:30	28 4:38 ♂ △	♍ 29 13:45	

Astro Data

1 NOVEMBER 1996
Julian Day # 35369
Delta T 60.5 sec
SVP 05♓18'14"
Obliquity 23°26'14"
⚷ Chiron 22♎59.2
☽ Mean ☊ 6♎17.1

1 DECEMBER 1996
Julian Day # 35399
Delta T 60.6 sec
SVP 05♓18'09"
Obliquity 23°26'13"
⚷ Chiron 26♎59.8
☽ Mean ☊ 4♎41.8

LONGITUDE — JANUARY 1997

Day	Sid.Time	☉	0 hr ☽	Noon ☽	True ☊	☿	♀	♂	♃	♄	♅	♆	♇
1 W	6 42 44	10♑36 27	28♍44 16	4♎44 46	2♎26.3	13♑ 6.5	18♐26.8	29♍14.2	25♑10.2	1♈20.1	3♒16.2	26♑49.7	4♐23.1
2 Th	6 46 41	11 37 37	10♎48 38	16 56 34	2R 26.3	11R 45.7	19 41.8	29 34.0	25 24.0	1 23.2	3 19.5	26 51.9	4 25.1
3 F	6 50 37	12 38 47	23 9 15	29 27 20	2 26.0	10 24.3	20 56.9	29 53.5	25 38.0	1 26.3	3 22.8	26 54.1	4 27.1
4 Sa	6 54 34	13 39 57	5♏51 26	12♏22 5	2 24.1	9 4.8	22 12.0	0♎12.5	25 51.9	1 29.6	3 26.2	26 56.4	4 29.1
5 Su	6 58 30	14 41 7	18 59 43	25 44 38	2 20.0	7 49.7	23 27.1	0 31.1	26 5.8	1 32.9	3 29.6	26 58.6	4 31.0
6 M	7 2 27	15 42 18	2♐37 0	9♐36 45	2 13.1	6 41.1	24 42.2	0 49.4	26 19.8	1 36.4	3 33.0	27 0.8	4 32.9
7 Tu	7 6 23	16 43 28	16 43 40	23 57 17	2 3.7	5 40.5	25 57.3	1 7.2	26 33.8	1 39.9	3 36.4	27 3.1	4 34.9
8 W	7 10 20	17 44 39	1♑16 57	8♑41 45	1 52.7	4 49.0	27 12.4	1 24.5	26 47.8	1 43.5	3 39.8	27 5.3	4 36.7
9 Th	7 14 17	18 45 50	16 10 39	23 42 26	1 41.1	4 7.3	28 27.6	1 41.5	27 1.9	1 47.3	3 43.2	27 7.6	4 38.6
10 F	7 18 13	19 47 0	1♒15 49	8♒49 30	1 30.4	3 35.5	29 42.7	1 57.9	27 15.9	1 51.1	3 46.6	27 9.9	4 40.4
11 Sa	7 22 10	20 48 10	16 22 12	23 52 44	1 21.7	3 13.6	0♑57.8	2 13.9	27 30.0	1 55.0	3 50.1	27 12.1	4 42.2
12 Su	7 26 6	21 49 20	1♓20 3	8♓43 18	1 15.8	3D 1.4	2 13.0	2 29.5	27 44.1	1 59.0	3 53.6	27 14.4	4 44.0
13 M	7 30 3	22 50 29	16 1 47	23 15 1	1 12.7	2 58.2	3 28.1	2 44.5	27 58.1	2 3.0	3 57.0	27 16.7	4 45.8
14 Tu	7 33 59	23 51 37	0♈22 42	7♈24 41	1D 11.8	3 3.5	4 43.2	2 59.1	28 12.2	2 7.2	4 0.5	27 18.9	4 47.5
15 W	7 37 56	24 52 45	14 21 0	21 11 46	1R 12.1	3 16.7	5 58.4	3 13.1	28 26.3	2 11.5	4 4.0	27 21.2	4 49.2
16 Th	7 41 53	25 53 52	27 57 12	4♉37 36	1 12.4	3 37.1	7 13.5	3 26.7	28 40.4	2 15.8	4 7.5	27 23.5	4 50.9
17 F	7 45 49	26 54 58	11♉13 16	17 44 34	1 11.3	4 4.2	8 28.7	3 39.7	28 54.6	2 20.2	4 11.0	27 25.8	4 52.6
18 Sa	7 49 46	27 56 3	24 11 51	0♊35 26	1 8.1	4 37.1	9 43.8	3 52.2	29 8.7	2 24.7	4 14.5	27 28.0	4 54.2
19 Su	7 53 42	28 57 8	6♊55 40	13 12 48	1 2.3	5 15.5	10 58.9	4 4.2	29 22.8	2 29.3	4 18.0	27 30.3	4 55.8
20 M	7 57 39	29 58 12	19 27 8	25 38 52	0 53.8	5 58.8	12 14.1	4 15.6	29 36.9	2 34.0	4 21.5	27 32.6	4 57.4
21 Tu	8 1 35	0♒59 15	1♋48 14	7♋55 23	0 43.4	6 46.4	13 29.2	4 26.5	29 51.0	2 38.8	4 25.0	27 34.9	4 59.0
22 W	8 5 32	2 0 17	14 0 28	20 3 39	0 31.7	7 38.1	14 44.3	4 36.8	0♒ 5.2	2 43.6	4 28.5	27 37.2	5 0.5
23 Th	8 9 28	3 1 18	26 5 4	2♌ 4 50	0 20.0	8 33.3	15 59.5	4 46.6	0 19.3	2 48.5	4 32.1	27 39.4	5 2.0
24 F	8 13 25	4 2 19	8♌ 3 7	14 0 5	0 9.2	9 31.7	17 14.6	4 55.7	0 33.4	2 53.5	4 35.6	27 41.7	5 3.4
25 Sa	8 17 22	5 3 19	19 55 55	25 50 50	0 0.3	10 33.1	18 29.8	5 4.2	0 47.5	2 58.5	4 39.1	27 44.0	5 4.9
26 Su	8 21 18	6 4 18	1♍45 6	7♍39 1	29♍53.7	11 37.1	19 44.9	5 12.2	1 1.6	3 3.7	4 42.6	27 46.2	5 6.3
27 M	8 25 15	7 5 16	13 32 56	19 27 13	29 49.7	12 43.6	21 0.0	5 19.4	1 15.7	3 8.9	4 46.1	27 48.5	5 7.7
28 Tu	8 29 11	8 6 13	25 22 19	1♎18 43	29D 48.0	13 52.2	22 15.2	5 26.1	1 29.8	3 14.2	4 49.7	27 50.7	5 9.0
29 W	8 33 8	9 7 10	7♎16 56	13 17 31	29 48.2	15 2.9	23 30.3	5 32.1	1 43.9	3 19.5	4 53.2	27 53.0	5 10.4
30 Th	8 37 4	10 8 6	19 21 4	25 28 12	29 49.3	16 15.5	24 45.5	5 37.5	1 58.0	3 24.9	4 56.7	27 55.2	5 11.6
31 F	8 41 1	11 9 2	1♏39 31	7♏55 40	29R 50.6	17 29.7	26 0.6	5 42.1	2 12.0	3 30.4	5 0.2	27 57.5	5 12.9

LONGITUDE — FEBRUARY 1997

Day	Sid.Time	☉	0 hr ☽	Noon ☽	True ☊	☿	♀	♂	♃	♄	♅	♆	♇
1 Sa	8 44 57	12♒ 9 56	14♏17 15	20♏44 50	29♍51.0	18♑45.5	27♑15.8	5♎46.1	2♒26.1	3♈36.0	5♒ 3.7	27♑59.7	5♐14.1
2 Su	8 48 54	13 10 50	27 18 56	3♐59 59	29R 49.9	20 2.9	28 30.9	5 49.4	2 40.1	3 41.6	5 7.2	28 1.9	5 15.3
3 M	8 52 50	14 11 43	10♐48 17	17 44 1	29 46.8	21 21.6	29 46.0	5 52.0	2 54.1	3 47.3	5 10.7	28 4.1	5 16.5
4 Tu	8 56 47	15 12 36	24 47 10	1♑57 35	29 41.9	22 41.6	1♒ 1.2	5 53.8	3 8.1	3 53.1	5 14.2	28 6.3	5 17.6
5 W	9 0 44	16 13 27	9♑14 49	16 38 16	29 35.6	24 2.8	2 16.3	5 55.0	3 22.1	3 58.9	5 17.7	28 8.5	5 18.7
6 Th	9 4 40	17 14 18	24 7 6	1♒40 16	29 28.8	25 25.2	3 31.5	5R 55.4	3 36.1	4 4.8	5 21.1	28 10.7	5 19.8
7 F	9 8 37	18 15 7	9♒16 35	16 54 43	29 22.3	26 48.7	4 46.6	5 55.0	3 50.0	4 10.7	5 24.6	28 12.9	5 20.9
8 Sa	9 12 33	19 15 55	24 33 20	2♓11 3	29 17.1	28 13.3	6 1.7	5 53.9	4 3.9	4 16.8	5 28.1	28 15.1	5 21.9
9 Su	9 16 30	20 16 42	9♓46 34	17 18 42	29 13.7	29 38.8	7 16.8	5 52.0	4 17.8	4 22.8	5 31.5	28 17.2	5 22.8
10 M	9 20 26	21 17 28	24 46 27	2♈ 8 57	29D 12.3	1♒ 5.4	8 31.9	5 49.4	4 31.7	4 28.9	5 34.9	28 19.3	5 23.8
11 Tu	9 24 23	22 18 12	9♈25 35	16 35 53	29 12.5	2 33.0	9 47.0	5 46.0	4 45.5	4 35.1	5 38.3	28 21.5	5 24.7
12 W	9 28 19	23 18 54	23 39 38	0♉36 44	29 13.8	4 1.5	11 2.1	5 41.8	4 59.3	4 41.4	5 41.7	28 23.6	5 25.5
13 Th	9 32 16	24 19 35	7♉27 16	14 11 24	29 15.4	5 30.9	12 17.2	5 36.8	5 13.1	4 47.7	5 45.1	28 25.7	5 26.4
14 F	9 36 13	25 20 13	20 49 27	27 21 44	29R 16.3	7 1.3	13 32.3	5 31.1	5 26.8	4 54.0	5 48.5	28 27.8	5 27.2
15 Sa	9 40 9	26 20 51	3♊48 42	10♊10 47	29 16.2	8 32.5	14 47.4	5 24.5	5 40.5	5 0.4	5 51.9	28 29.9	5 28.0
16 Su	9 44 6	27 21 26	16 28 25	22 42 4	29 14.5	10 4.7	16 2.4	5 17.2	5 54.2	5 6.9	5 55.2	28 31.9	5 28.7
17 M	9 48 2	28 22 0	28 52 12	4♋59 14	29 11.3	11 37.8	17 17.5	5 9.2	6 7.8	5 13.4	5 58.5	28 34.0	5 29.4
18 Tu	9 51 59	29 22 32	11♋ 3 34	17 5 36	29 7.0	13 11.7	18 32.5	5 0.3	6 21.4	5 19.9	6 1.9	28 36.0	5 30.1
19 W	9 55 55	0♓23 3	23 5 41	29 4 9	29 1.9	14 46.6	19 47.6	4 50.7	6 35.0	5 26.5	6 5.1	28 38.0	5 30.7
20 Th	9 59 52	1 23 31	5♌ 1 18	10♌57 24	28 56.7	16 22.4	21 2.6	4 40.3	6 48.5	5 33.1	6 8.4	28 40.0	5 31.3
21 F	10 3 48	2 23 58	16 52 45	22 47 34	28 51.9	17 59.2	22 17.6	4 29.1	7 2.0	5 39.8	6 11.7	28 42.0	5 31.9
22 Sa	10 7 45	3 24 23	28 42 7	4♍36 37	28 48.1	19 36.8	23 32.6	4 17.1	7 15.4	5 46.5	6 14.9	28 44.0	5 32.4
23 Su	10 11 42	4 24 47	10♍31 19	16 26 29	28 45.5	21 15.4	24 47.6	4 4.5	7 28.8	5 53.3	6 18.1	28 45.9	5 32.9
24 M	10 15 38	5 25 8	22 22 20	28 19 11	28D 44.2	22 55.0	26 2.6	3 51.0	7 42.2	6 0.1	6 21.3	28 47.8	5 33.3
25 Tu	10 19 35	6 25 29	4♎17 19	10♎17 3	28 44.1	24 35.5	27 17.5	3 36.9	7 55.5	6 7.0	6 24.5	28 49.7	5 33.8
26 W	10 23 31	7 25 47	16 18 45	22 22 47	28 45.0	26 17.0	28 32.5	3 22.0	8 8.7	6 13.8	6 27.6	28 51.6	5 34.1
27 Th	10 27 28	8 26 4	28 29 33	4♏39 28	28 46.5	27 59.5	29 47.5	3 6.4	8 21.9	6 20.8	6 30.8	28 53.5	5 34.5
28 F	10 31 24	9 26 20	10♏52 59	17 10 33	28 48.1	29 43.1	1♓ 2.4	2 50.1	8 35.1	6 27.7	6 33.9	28 55.3	5 34.8

Astro Data

	Dy Hr Mn
☽0S	1 1:17
♃☌♆	9 11:40
☿ D	12 20:41
☽0N	13 22:50
☽0S	28 9:28
♅✱♇	5 10:48
♂ R	6 0:37
♃✱♄	9 15:32
☽0N	10 8:50
♃✱♇	14 0:41
♄0N	16 5:26
♃☌♅	16 2:22
♄△♇	19 16:43
☽0S	24 16:04

Planet Ingress

	Dy Hr Mn
♂ ♎	3 8:10
♀ ♑	10 5:32
☉ ♒	20 0:43
♃ ♒	21 15:13
☊ ♍	25 0:52
♀ ♒	3 4:28
☿ ♒	9 5:53
☉ ♓	18 14:52
♀ ♓	27 4:01
☿ ♓	28 3:54

Last Aspect / ☽ Ingress (January)

Last Aspect Dy Hr Mn	☽ Ingress Dy Hr Mn
1 1:02 ♂ ☌	♎ 1 2:32
3 7:11 ♆ □	♏ 3 13:02
5 14:12 ♆ ✱	♐ 5 19:27
7 16:43 ♀ ☌	♑ 7 21:55
9 17:33 ♃ ☌	♒ 9 22:00
10 5:25 ♇ ✱	♓ 11 21:51
13 20:16 ♃ ✱	♈ 13 23:22
16 1:19 ♃ □	♉ 16 3:40
18 9:27 ♃ △	♊ 18 10:53
18 20:12 ♇ ☍	♋ 20 20:29
23 3:09 ♆ ☍	♌ 23 7:50
23 17:58 ♇ △	♍ 25 20:26
28 5:01 ♆ △	♎ 28 9:21
30 16:49 ♆ □	♏ 30 20:48

Last Aspect / ☽ Ingress (February)

Last Aspect Dy Hr Mn	☽ Ingress Dy Hr Mn
2 2:24 ♀ ✱	♐ 2 4:51
3 6:22 ☉ ✱	♑ 4 8:44
6 6:29 ♆ ☌	♒ 6 9:21
7 15:06 ☉ ☌	♓ 8 8:34
10 5:46 ♆ ✱	♈ 10 8:29
12 8:10 ♆ □	♉ 12 10:56
14 14:04 ♆ △	♊ 14 16:53
16 22:56 ☉ △	♋ 17 2:13
19 11:09 ♆ ☍	♌ 19 13:52
21 12:17 ♀ ☍	♍ 22 2:38
24 13:00 ♆ △	♎ 24 15:23
27 2:49 ♀ △	♏ 27 2:57

☽ Phases & Eclipses

Dy Hr Mn	
2 1:45	☽ 11♎42
9 4:26	● 18♑57
15 20:02	☽ 25♈44
23 15:11	○ 3♌40
31 19:40	☽ 11♏59
7 15:06	● 18♒53
14 8:58	☽ 25♉43
22 10:27	○ 3♍51

Astro Data

1 JANUARY 1997
Julian Day # 35430
Delta T 60.6 sec
SVP 05♓18'04"
Obliquity 23°26'13"
⚷ Chiron 0♏12.6
☽ Mean ☊ 3♎03.3

1 FEBRUARY 1997
Julian Day # 35461
Delta T 60.6 sec
SVP 05♓18'00"
Obliquity 23°26'13"
⚷ Chiron 1♏54.9
☽ Mean ☊ 1♎24.8

MARCH 1997 LONGITUDE

Day	Sid.Time	☉	0 hr ☽	Noon ☽	True ☊	☿	♀	♂	♃	♄	♅	♆	♇
1 Sa	10 35 21	10♓26 34	23♏32 37	29♏59 39	28♍49.4	1♓27.6	2♓17.4	2♎33.2	8♒48.2	6♈34.7	6♒36.9	28♑57.2	5♐35.1
2 Su	10 39 17	11 26 47	6♐32 2	13♐10 9	28R 50.2	3 13.2	3 32.3	2R 15.6	9 1.2	6 41.8	6 40.0	28 59.0	5 35.3
3 M	10 43 14	12 26 58	19 54 20	26 44 48	28 50.1	4 59.9	4 47.2	1 57.3	9 14.2	6 48.8	6 43.0	29 0.8	5 35.6
4 Tu	10 47 11	13 27 8	3♑41 40	10♑44 57	28 49.3	6 47.6	6 2.1	1 38.5	9 27.2	6 55.9	6 46.0	29 2.5	5 35.7
5 W	10 51 7	14 27 16	17 54 30	25 9 59	28 47.9	8 36.4	7 17.1	1 19.1	9 40.1	7 3.1	6 49.0	29 4.3	5 35.9
6 Th	10 55 4	15 27 22	2♒30 56	9♒56 40	28 46.2	10 26.2	8 32.0	0 59.1	9 52.9	7 10.2	6 52.0	29 6.0	5 36.0
7 F	10 59 0	16 27 27	17 26 22	24 59 3	28 44.6	12 17.1	9 46.8	0 38.6	10 5.6	7 17.4	6 54.9	29 7.7	5 36.1
8 Sa	11 2 57	17 27 30	2♓33 36	10♓ 8 51	28 43.3	14 9.1	11 1.7	0 17.7	10 18.4	7 24.6	6 57.8	29 9.4	5R 36.1
9 Su	11 6 53	18 27 32	17 43 36	25 16 38	28D 42.6	16 2.1	12 16.6	29♍56.2	10 31.0	7 31.9	7 0.6	29 11.0	5 36.1
10 M	11 10 50	19 27 31	2♈46 48	10♈13 5	28 42.5	17 56.2	13 31.4	29 34.4	10 43.6	7 39.1	7 3.5	29 12.7	5 36.1
11 Tu	11 14 46	20 27 28	17 34 35	24 50 32	28 42.8	19 51.2	14 46.3	29 12.2	10 56.1	7 46.4	7 6.3	29 14.3	5 36.0
12 W	11 18 43	21 27 24	2♉ 0 22	9♉ 3 41	28 43.4	21 47.2	16 1.1	28 49.7	11 8.5	7 53.7	7 9.0	29 15.8	5 35.9
13 Th	11 22 40	22 27 17	16 0 16	22 50 4	28 44.1	23 44.1	17 15.9	28 27.0	11 20.9	8 1.1	7 11.8	29 17.4	5 35.8
14 F	11 26 36	23 27 8	29 33 8	6♊ 9 41	28 44.6	25 41.7	18 30.7	28 3.9	11 33.2	8 8.4	7 14.5	29 18.9	5 35.6
15 Sa	11 30 33	24 26 57	12♊40 2	19 4 33	28 45.0	27 40.1	19 45.5	27 40.7	11 45.4	8 15.8	7 17.1	29 20.4	5 35.4
16 Su	11 34 29	25 26 44	25 23 42	1♋37 59	28R 45.1	29 39.0	21 0.3	27 17.4	11 57.5	8 23.2	7 19.8	29 21.9	5 35.1
17 M	11 38 26	26 26 28	7♋47 54	13 54 2	28 45.0	1♈38.4	22 15.0	26 53.9	12 9.6	8 30.6	7 22.4	29 23.4	5 34.9
18 Tu	11 42 22	27 26 10	19 56 54	25 57 3	28 44.9	3 38.1	23 29.7	26 30.4	12 21.6	8 38.0	7 24.9	29 24.8	5 34.6
19 W	11 46 19	28 25 50	1♌55 1	7♌51 18	28D 44.8	5 37.8	24 44.4	26 6.8	12 33.5	8 45.5	7 27.5	29 26.2	5 34.2
20 Th	11 50 15	29 25 27	13 46 22	19 40 42	28 44.8	7 37.3	25 59.1	25 43.3	12 45.4	8 52.9	7 30.0	29 27.5	5 33.9
21 F	11 54 12	0♈25 3	25 34 44	1♍28 50	28 45.0	9 36.3	27 13.8	25 19.9	12 57.1	9 0.4	7 32.4	29 28.9	5 33.5
22 Sa	11 58 8	1 24 36	7♍23 23	13 18 44	28 45.2	11 34.6	28 28.5	24 56.6	13 8.8	9 7.9	7 34.8	29 30.2	5 33.0
23 Su	12 2 5	2 24 7	19 15 10	25 12 59	28R 45.4	13 31.8	29 43.1	24 33.4	13 20.4	9 15.4	7 37.2	29 31.5	5 32.5
24 M	12 6 2	3 23 36	1♎12 27	7♎13 47	28 45.4	15 27.5	0♈57.7	24 10.5	13 31.9	9 22.8	7 39.6	29 32.7	5 32.0
25 Tu	12 9 58	4 23 2	13 17 15	19 23 1	28 45.2	17 21.3	2 12.3	23 47.8	13 43.3	9 30.3	7 41.9	29 34.0	5 31.5
26 W	12 13 55	5 22 27	25 31 19	1♏42 20	28 44.7	19 12.9	3 26.9	23 25.3	13 54.6	9 37.9	7 44.1	29 35.2	5 30.9
27 Th	12 17 51	6 21 50	7♏56 16	14 13 19	28 43.9	21 1.7	4 41.5	23 3.2	14 5.9	9 45.4	7 46.4	29 36.3	5 30.3
28 F	12 21 48	7 21 11	20 33 41	26 57 32	28 42.8	22 47.5	5 56.1	22 41.5	14 17.0	9 52.9	7 48.6	29 37.5	5 29.7
29 Sa	12 25 44	8 20 30	3♐25 6	9♐56 34	28 41.6	24 29.7	7 10.6	22 20.1	14 28.1	10 0.4	7 50.7	29 38.6	5 29.0
30 Su	12 29 41	9 19 48	16 32 8	23 11 57	28 40.5	26 8.0	8 25.2	21 59.2	14 39.0	10 7.9	7 52.8	29 39.7	5 28.4
31 M	12 33 37	10 19 4	29 56 11	6♑44 56	28D 39.8	27 41.9	9 39.7	21 38.8	14 49.9	10 15.5	7 54.9	29 40.7	5 27.6

APRIL 1997 LONGITUDE

Day	Sid.Time	☉	0 hr ☽	Noon ☽	True ☊	☿	♀	♂	♃	♄	♅	♆	♇
1 Tu	12 37 34	11♈18 18	13♑38 19	20♑36 19	28♍39.6	29♈11.1	10♈54.2	21♍18.8	15♒ 0.7	10♈23.0	7♒56.9	29♑41.7	5♐26.9
2 W	12 41 31	12 17 30	27 38 53	4♒45 54	28 40.0	0♉35.4	12 8.7	20R 59.4	15 11.3	10 30.5	7 58.9	29 42.7	5R 26.1
3 Th	12 45 27	13 16 40	11♒57 6	19 12 11	28 40.9	1 54.3	13 23.2	20 40.6	15 21.9	10 38.0	8 0.9	29 43.7	5 25.3
4 F	12 49 24	14 15 49	26 30 39	3♓51 58	28 42.0	3 7.6	14 37.7	20 22.3	15 32.4	10 45.6	8 2.8	29 44.6	5 24.5
5 Sa	12 53 20	15 14 56	11♓15 26	18 40 17	28 43.1	4 15.0	15 52.1	20 4.7	15 42.7	10 53.1	8 4.6	29 45.5	5 23.6
6 Su	12 57 17	16 14 1	26 5 40	3♈30 39	28R 43.6	5 16.5	17 6.6	19 47.7	15 53.0	11 0.6	8 6.4	29 46.4	5 22.7
7 M	13 1 13	17 13 3	10♈54 18	18 15 42	28 43.3	6 11.7	18 21.0	19 31.4	16 3.1	11 8.1	8 8.2	29 47.2	5 21.8
8 Tu	13 5 10	18 12 4	25 33 55	2♉48 9	28 42.0	7 0.6	19 35.4	19 15.8	16 13.2	11 15.6	8 9.9	29 48.0	5 20.8
9 W	13 9 6	19 11 3	9♉57 39	17 1 49	28 39.7	7 42.9	20 49.8	19 0.9	16 23.1	11 23.1	8 11.6	29 48.8	5 19.8
10 Th	13 13 3	20 10 0	24 0 11	0♊52 25	28 36.8	8 18.8	22 4.2	18 46.7	16 32.9	11 30.6	8 13.3	29 49.5	5 18.8
11 F	13 17 0	21 8 55	7♊38 21	14 17 56	28 33.6	8 48.0	23 18.5	18 33.3	16 42.6	11 38.0	8 14.8	29 50.2	5 17.8
12 Sa	13 20 56	22 7 48	20 51 17	27 18 36	28 30.5	9 10.6	24 32.8	18 20.6	16 52.2	11 45.5	8 16.4	29 50.9	5 16.8
13 Su	13 24 53	23 6 38	3♋40 12	9♋56 31	28 28.2	9 26.7	25 47.2	18 8.7	17 1.6	11 52.9	8 17.9	29 51.5	5 15.7
14 M	13 28 49	24 5 26	16 8 0	22 15 13	28D 26.8	9 36.2	27 1.4	17 57.6	17 11.0	12 0.3	8 19.3	29 52.1	5 14.6
15 Tu	13 32 46	25 4 12	28 18 43	4♌19 6	28 26.6	9R 39.3	28 15.7	17 47.3	17 20.2	12 7.8	8 20.8	29 52.7	5 13.4
16 W	13 36 42	26 2 55	10♌17 0	16 13 1	28 27.4	9 36.3	29 30.0	17 37.7	17 29.3	12 15.2	8 22.1	29 53.3	5 12.3
17 Th	13 40 39	27 1 36	22 7 47	28 1 53	28 29.0	9 27.3	0♉44.2	17 29.0	17 38.3	12 22.5	8 23.4	29 53.8	5 11.1
18 F	13 44 35	28 0 15	3♍55 55	9♍50 24	28 30.8	9 12.6	1 58.4	17 21.0	17 47.1	12 29.9	8 24.7	29 54.3	5 9.9
19 Sa	13 48 32	28 58 52	15 45 52	21 42 49	28 32.3	8 52.7	3 12.6	17 13.8	17 55.9	12 37.2	8 25.9	29 54.7	5 8.7
20 Su	13 52 28	29 57 27	27 41 39	3♎42 47	28R 33.0	8 28.0	4 26.8	17 7.4	18 4.5	12 44.5	8 27.1	29 55.1	5 7.4
21 M	13 56 25	0♉55 59	9♎46 33	15 53 15	28 32.3	7 59.1	5 40.9	17 1.8	18 12.9	12 51.8	8 28.2	29 55.5	5 6.2
22 Tu	14 0 22	1 54 30	22 3 6	28 16 18	28 30.2	7 26.4	6 55.1	16 57.0	18 21.3	12 59.1	8 29.3	29 55.8	5 4.9
23 W	14 4 18	2 52 59	4♏32 59	10♏53 12	28 26.4	6 50.7	8 9.2	16 53.0	18 29.5	13 6.4	8 30.3	29 56.1	5 3.6
24 Th	14 8 15	3 51 25	17 17 1	23 44 24	28 21.2	6 12.8	9 23.3	16 49.7	18 37.5	13 13.6	8 31.3	29 56.4	5 2.2
25 F	14 12 11	4 49 50	0♐15 19	6♐49 40	28 15.3	5 33.2	10 37.3	16 47.2	18 45.5	13 20.8	8 32.2	29 56.7	5 0.9
26 Sa	14 16 8	5 48 14	13 27 24	20 8 21	28 9.1	4 52.7	11 51.4	16 45.5	18 53.3	13 28.0	8 33.1	29 56.9	4 59.5
27 Su	14 20 4	6 46 36	26 52 26	3♑39 31	28 3.5	4 12.2	13 5.5	16D 44.5	19 0.9	13 35.1	8 33.9	29 57.1	4 58.2
28 M	14 24 1	7 44 56	10♑29 29	17 22 12	27 59.1	3 32.3	14 19.5	16 44.3	19 8.4	13 42.2	8 34.7	29 57.2	4 56.8
29 Tu	14 27 57	8 43 14	24 17 35	1♒15 30	27 56.4	2 53.7	15 33.5	16 44.8	19 15.8	13 49.3	8 35.4	29 57.3	4 55.3
30 W	14 31 54	9 41 31	8♒15 52	15 18 32	27D 55.5	2 17.0	16 47.5	16 46.1	19 23.0	13 56.4	8 36.1	29 57.4	4 53.9

Astro Data	Planet Ingress	Last Aspect	☽ Ingress	Last Aspect	☽ Ingress	☽ Phases & Eclipses	Astro Data
Dy Hr Mn	Dy Hr Mn	Dy Hr Mn	Dy Hr Mn	Dy Hr Mn	Dy Hr Mn	Dy Hr Mn	1 MARCH 1997
♄✶♅ 1 13:24	♂ ♍ 8 19:50	1 10:06 ♆ ✶	♐ 1 12:01	2 3:30 ♆ ☌	♒ 2 3:59	2 9:38 ☽ 11♐51	Julian Day # 35489
♇ R 8 12:53	☿ ♈ 16 4:13	2 9:38 ☉ □	♑ 3 17:39	3 5:44 ♃ ☌	♓ 4 5:42	9 1:15 ● 18♓31	Delta T 60.7 sec
☽0N 9 20:06	☉ ♈ 20 13:55	5 18:26 ♆ ☌	♒ 5 19:54	6 5:57 ♆ ✶	♈ 6 6:19	9 1:23:50 ● T 2'50"	SVP 05♓17'57"
☿0N 17 5:09	♀ ♈ 23 5:26	6 12:04 ♃ ☌	♓ 7 19:57	8 7:01 ♆ □	♉ 8 7:20	16 0:06 ☽ 25♊27	Obliquity 23°26'14"
☽0S 23 22:16		9 18:59 ♂ ☍	♈ 9 19:33	10 10:10 ♆ △	♊ 10 10:28	24 4:45 ○ 3♎35	⚷ Chiron 1♏52.4R
♀0N 25 19:22	☿ ♉ 1 13:45	11 19:23 ♆ □	♉ 11 20:37	12 7:34 ♀ ✶	♋ 12 17:03	24 4:39 ● P 0.919	☽ Mean ☊ 29♍55.8
	♀ ♉ 16 9:43	13 23:34 ♆ △	♊ 14 0:48	15 3:07 ♆ ☍	♌ 15 3:22	31 19:38 ☽ 11♑08	
☽0N 6 6:52	☉ ♉ 20 1:03	16 3:31 ♂ □	♋ 16 8:51	17 10:51 ☉ △	♍ 17 16:00		1 APRIL 1997
☿ R 15 0:01		18 19:00 ♆ ☍	♌ 18 20:08	20 4:27 ♆ △	♎ 20 4:36	7 11:02 ● 17♈40	Julian Day # 35520
☽0S 20 5:23		19 21:54 ♃ ☍	♍ 21 8:59	22 15:11 ♆ □	♏ 22 15:19	14 17:00 ☽ 24♋47	Delta T 60.7 sec
♂ D 27 19:09		23 20:40 ♆ △	♎ 23 21:35	24 23:26 ♆ ✶	♐ 24 23:32	22 20:33 ○ 2♏45	SVP 05♓17'54"
		26 7:55 ♆ □	♏ 26 8:42	26 9:51 ♃ ✶	♑ 27 5:32	30 2:37 ☽ 9♒48	Obliquity 23°26'14"
		28 16:59 ♆ ✶	♐ 28 17:40	29 9:46 ♆ ☌	♒ 29 9:50		⚷ Chiron 0♏15.9R
		30 19:31 ☿ △	♑ 31 0:07				☽ Mean ☊ 28♍17.3

LONGITUDE — MAY 1997

Day	Sid.Time	☉	0 hr ☽	Noon ☽	True ☊	☿	♀	♂	♃	♄	♅	♆	♇
1 Th	14 35 51	10♉39 47	22♒23 23	29♒30 13	27♍56.0	1♉42.9	18♉ 1.5	16♍48.1	19♒30.1	14♈ 3.4	8♒36.7	29♑57.5	4♐52.5
2 F	14 39 47	11 38 1	6♓38 51	13♓49 0	27 57.1	1R 11.9	19 15.5	16 50.8	19 37.0	14 10.4	8 37.3	29R 57.5	4R 51.0
3 Sa	14 43 44	12 36 13	21 0 20	28 12 28	27R 58.2	0 44.4	20 29.4	16 54.2	19 43.8	14 17.3	8 37.8	29 57.5	4 49.5
4 Su	14 47 40	13 34 24	5♈24 56	12♈37 12	27 58.1	0 20.8	21 43.4	16 58.3	19 50.5	14 24.2	8 38.3	29 57.4	4 48.0
5 M	14 51 37	14 32 34	19 48 41	26 58 46	27 56.2	0 1.3	22 57.3	17 3.1	19 56.9	14 31.1	8 38.8	29 57.3	4 46.5
6 Tu	14 55 33	15 30 42	4♉ 6 47	11♉12 4	27 52.2	29♈46.2	24 11.2	17 8.6	20 3.3	14 38.0	8 39.1	29 57.2	4 45.0
7 W	14 59 30	16 28 48	18 14 1	25 12 0	27 46.0	29 35.7	25 25.1	17 14.7	20 9.4	14 44.8	8 39.5	29 57.1	4 43.5
8 Th	15 3 26	17 26 53	2♊ 5 33	8♊54 13	27 38.3	29D 29.8	26 39.0	17 21.6	20 15.4	14 51.6	8 39.8	29 56.9	4 41.9
9 F	15 7 23	18 24 56	15 37 40	22 15 43	27 29.7	29 28.6	27 52.8	17 29.1	20 21.3	14 58.3	8 40.0	29 56.7	4 40.4
10 Sa	15 11 20	19 22 58	28 48 17	5♋15 24	27 21.4	29 32.1	29 6.7	17 37.2	20 27.0	15 5.0	8 40.2	29 56.4	4 38.8
11 Su	15 15 16	20 20 57	11♋37 12	17 53 57	27 14.1	29 40.3	0♊20.5	17 46.0	20 32.5	15 11.6	8 40.3	29 56.2	4 37.2
12 M	15 19 13	21 18 55	24 6 1	0♌13 48	27 8.5	29 53.0	1 34.3	17 55.4	20 37.8	15 18.2	8 40.4	29 55.8	4 35.6
13 Tu	15 23 9	22 16 51	6♌17 50	12 18 40	27 5.0	0♉10.3	2 48.1	18 5.4	20 43.0	15 24.8	8R 40.4	29 55.5	4 34.0
14 W	15 27 6	23 14 45	18 16 54	24 13 10	27D 3.5	0 32.0	4 1.8	18 16.0	20 48.1	15 31.3	8 40.4	29 55.1	4 32.4
15 Th	15 31 2	24 12 38	0♍ 8 9	6♍ 2 29	27 3.6	0 58.0	5 15.6	18 27.1	20 52.9	15 37.8	8 40.3	29 54.7	4 30.8
16 F	15 34 59	25 10 29	11 56 51	17 51 54	27 4.4	1 28.2	6 29.3	18 38.9	20 57.6	15 44.2	8 40.2	29 54.3	4 29.2
17 Sa	15 38 55	26 8 17	23 48 16	29 46 35	27R 5.1	2 2.5	7 43.0	18 51.2	21 2.1	15 50.5	8 40.1	29 53.8	4 27.6
18 Su	15 42 52	27 6 5	5♎47 25	11♎51 17	27 4.7	2 40.6	8 56.7	19 4.1	21 6.5	15 56.8	8 39.8	29 53.3	4 26.0
19 M	15 46 49	28 3 50	17 58 39	24 9 55	27 2.6	3 22.6	10 10.4	19 17.5	21 10.6	16 3.1	8 39.6	29 52.8	4 24.3
20 Tu	15 50 45	29 1 34	0♏25 26	6♏45 25	26 58.1	4 8.2	11 24.0	19 31.4	21 14.6	16 9.3	8 39.3	29 52.3	4 22.7
21 W	15 54 42	29 59 17	13 10 1	19 39 19	26 51.2	4 57.4	12 37.7	19 45.9	21 18.5	16 15.5	8 38.9	29 51.7	4 21.1
22 Th	15 58 38	0♊56 58	26 13 15	2♐51 43	26 42.2	5 50.1	13 51.3	20 0.9	21 22.1	16 21.6	8 38.5	29 51.1	4 19.4
23 F	16 2 35	1 54 38	9♐34 28	16 21 13	26 31.8	6 46.1	15 4.9	20 16.3	21 25.6	16 27.6	8 38.1	29 50.4	4 17.8
24 Sa	16 6 31	2 52 17	23 11 35	0♑ 5 9	26 21.2	7 45.3	16 18.5	20 32.3	21 28.9	16 33.6	8 37.6	29 49.7	4 16.1
25 Su	16 10 28	3 49 54	7♑ 1 29	14 0 7	26 11.3	8 47.7	17 32.0	20 48.7	21 32.0	16 39.6	8 37.0	29 49.1	4 14.5
26 M	16 14 24	4 47 31	21 0 36	28 2 30	26 3.2	9 53.2	18 45.6	21 5.6	21 34.9	16 45.5	8 36.4	29 48.3	4 12.8
27 Tu	16 18 21	5 45 6	5♒ 5 27	12♒ 9 5	25 57.5	11 1.7	19 59.1	21 22.9	21 37.7	16 51.3	8 35.8	29 47.6	4 11.2
28 W	16 22 18	6 42 41	19 13 7	26 17 20	25 54.3	12 13.0	21 12.6	21 40.7	21 40.2	16 57.1	8 35.1	29 46.8	4 9.6
29 Th	16 26 14	7 40 15	3♓21 31	10♓25 32	25D 53.2	13 27.3	22 26.1	21 58.9	21 42.6	17 2.8	8 34.3	29 46.0	4 7.9
30 F	16 30 11	8 37 47	17 29 15	24 32 32	25R 53.2	14 44.3	23 39.6	22 17.6	21 44.8	17 8.4	8 33.6	29 45.1	4 6.3
31 Sa	16 34 7	9 35 19	1♈35 16	8♈37 19	25 53.3	16 4.2	24 53.1	22 36.7	21 46.8	17 14.0	8 32.7	29 44.3	4 4.6

LONGITUDE — JUNE 1997

Day	Sid.Time	☉	0 hr ☽	Noon ☽	True ☊	☿	♀	♂	♃	♄	♅	♆	♇
1 Su	16 38 4	10♊32 51	15♈38 31	22♈38 38	25♍52.0	17♉26.7	26♊ 6.6	22♍56.2	21♒48.6	17♈19.5	8♒31.9	29♑43.4	4♐ 3.0
2 M	16 42 0	11 30 21	29 37 26	6♉34 38	25R 48.5	18 52.0	27 20.0	23 16.1	21 50.3	17 25.0	8R 30.9	29R 42.4	4R 1.4
3 Tu	16 45 57	12 27 51	13♉29 52	20 22 48	25 42.2	20 19.9	28 33.4	23 36.4	21 51.7	17 30.3	8 30.0	29 41.5	3 59.7
4 W	16 49 53	13 25 19	27 13 2	4♊ 0 12	25 33.2	21 50.5	29 46.9	23 57.2	21 53.0	17 35.7	8 29.0	29 40.5	3 58.1
5 Th	16 53 50	14 22 47	10♊43 56	17 23 53	25 22.1	23 23.7	1♋ 0.3	24 18.3	21 54.0	17 40.9	8 27.9	29 39.5	3 56.5
6 F	16 57 47	15 20 15	23 59 47	0♋31 25	25 9.8	24 59.5	2 13.7	24 39.8	21 54.9	17 46.1	8 26.8	29 38.5	3 54.9
7 Sa	17 1 43	16 17 41	6♋58 39	13 21 26	24 57.6	26 37.9	3 27.0	25 1.7	21 55.6	17 51.2	8 25.7	29 37.5	3 53.3
8 Su	17 5 40	17 15 6	19 39 49	25 53 56	24 46.5	28 19.0	4 40.4	25 23.9	21 56.1	17 56.3	8 24.5	29 36.4	3 51.7
9 M	17 9 36	18 12 30	2♌ 3 59	8♌10 18	24 37.5	0♊ 2.5	5 53.7	25 46.5	21 56.3	18 1.2	8 23.3	29 35.3	3 50.1
10 Tu	17 13 33	19 9 53	14 13 15	20 13 19	24 31.1	1 48.7	7 7.0	26 9.5	21R 56.4	18 6.1	8 22.0	29 34.2	3 48.5
11 W	17 17 29	20 7 16	26 11 0	2♍ 6 52	24 27.2	3 37.3	8 20.3	26 32.8	21 56.4	18 11.0	8 20.7	29 33.0	3 47.0
12 Th	17 21 26	21 4 37	8♍ 1 33	13 55 40	24 25.5	5 28.5	9 33.6	26 56.4	21 56.1	18 15.7	8 19.4	29 31.9	3 45.4
13 F	17 25 22	22 1 57	19 49 56	25 45 0	24 25.1	7 22.1	10 46.9	27 20.4	21 55.6	18 20.4	8 18.0	29 30.7	3 43.9
14 Sa	17 29 19	22 59 16	1♎41 34	7♎40 19	24 25.0	9 18.0	12 0.1	27 44.7	21 54.9	18 25.0	8 16.6	29 29.5	3 42.3
15 Su	17 33 16	23 56 34	13 41 54	19 46 59	24 24.2	11 16.3	13 13.3	28 9.3	21 54.1	18 29.5	8 15.1	29 28.3	3 40.8
16 M	17 37 12	24 53 52	25 56 7	2♏ 9 52	24 21.7	13 16.7	14 26.5	28 34.2	21 53.0	18 34.0	8 13.6	29 27.0	3 39.3
17 Tu	17 41 9	25 51 8	8♏28 39	14 52 52	24 16.8	15 19.2	15 39.7	28 59.4	21 51.8	18 38.3	8 12.1	29 25.8	3 37.8
18 W	17 45 5	26 48 24	21 22 45	27 58 28	24 9.3	17 23.6	16 52.9	29 25.0	21 50.3	18 42.6	8 10.5	29 24.5	3 36.3
19 Th	17 49 2	27 45 39	4♐40 0	11♐27 14	23 59.6	19 29.7	18 6.0	29 50.8	21 48.7	18 46.8	8 8.9	29 23.2	3 34.8
20 F	17 52 58	28 42 54	18 19 54	25 17 36	23 48.4	21 37.4	19 19.1	0♎16.9	21 46.9	18 51.0	8 7.2	29 21.8	3 33.4
21 Sa	17 56 55	29 40 8	2♑19 48	9♑25 52	23 36.7	23 46.3	20 32.2	0 43.3	21 44.9	18 55.0	8 5.6	29 20.5	3 32.0
22 Su	18 0 51	0♋37 21	16 35 6	23 46 43	23 25.8	25 56.3	21 45.3	1 9.9	21 42.8	18 59.0	8 3.9	29 19.1	3 30.5
23 M	18 4 48	1 34 35	0♒59 58	8♒14 4	23 16.7	28 7.0	22 58.4	1 36.9	21 40.4	19 2.9	8 2.1	29 17.8	3 29.1
24 Tu	18 8 45	2 31 48	15 28 19	22 42 3	23 10.3	0♋18.2	24 11.4	2 4.1	21 37.8	19 6.7	8 0.3	29 16.4	3 27.7
25 W	18 12 41	3 29 1	29 54 43	7♓ 5 51	23 6.5	2 29.6	25 24.4	2 31.5	21 35.1	19 10.4	7 58.5	29 15.0	3 26.4
26 Th	18 16 38	4 26 14	14♓15 5	21 22 9	23D 5.1	4 40.9	26 37.4	2 59.2	21 32.2	19 14.0	7 56.7	29 13.6	3 25.0
27 F	18 20 34	5 23 26	28 26 51	5♈29 5	23R 5.0	6 51.9	27 50.4	3 27.2	21 29.1	19 17.5	7 54.8	29 12.1	3 23.7
28 Sa	18 24 31	6 20 39	12♈28 46	19 25 53	23 4.9	9 2.3	29 3.4	3 55.4	21 25.8	19 21.0	7 52.9	29 10.7	3 22.4
29 Su	18 28 27	7 17 52	26 20 25	3♉12 21	23 3.8	11 11.9	0♌16.3	4 23.9	21 22.4	19 24.3	7 51.0	29 9.2	3 21.1
30 M	18 32 24	8 15 5	10♉ 1 42	16 48 25	23 0.5	13 20.4	1 29.3	4 52.6	21 18.7	19 27.6	7 49.0	29 7.7	3 19.8

Astro Data Dy Hr Mn	Planet Ingress Dy Hr Mn
♆ R 1 23:20	☿ ♈ 5 1:48
☽0N 3 15:52	♀ ♊ 10 17:20
☿ D 8 18:05	☿ ♉ 12 10:25
♅ R 13 4:05	☉ ♊ 21 0:18
☽0S 17 13:58	
☽0N 30 23:05	♀ ♋ 4 4:18
	☿ ♊ 8 23:25
♃ R 10 0:24	♂ ♎ 19 8:30
☽0S 13 23:28	☉ ♋ 21 8:20
♄□♇ 16 21:47	☿ ♋ 23 20:41
♂0S 21 6:05	♀ ♌ 28 18:38
☽0N 27 5:39	

Last Aspect Dy Hr Mn	☽ Ingress Dy Hr Mn	Last Aspect Dy Hr Mn	☽ Ingress Dy Hr Mn
30 19:04 ♃ ☌	♓ 1 12:50	2 0:09 ♆ □	♉ 2 0:39
3 14:55 ♆ ✶	♈ 3 14:59	4 4:20 ♆ △	♊ 4 4:55
5 17:00 ♆ □	♉ 5 17:04	6 1:15 ♂ □	♋ 6 11:02
7 20:15 ♆ △	♊ 7 20:21	8 19:24 ♆ ✶	♌ 8 19:58
10 1:22 ♆ ✶	♋ 10 2:13	10 15:27 ♃ ☍	♍ 11 7:43
12 11:24 ♆ ☍	♌ 12 11:33	13 19:34 ♆ △	♎ 13 20:35
14 10:55 ☉ □	♍ 14 23:43	16 6:47 ♆ □	♏ 16 7:51
17 12:14 ♆ △	♎ 17 12:27	18 15:05 ♂ ✶	♐ 18 15:39
19 22:57 ♆ □	♏ 19 23:12	20 19:09 ☉ ☍	♑ 20 20:02
22 6:34 ♆ ✶	♐ 22 6:51	22 21:11 ♆ ☌	♒ 22 22:20
23 21:00 ♃ ✶	♑ 24 11:51	24 10:12 ♃ ☌	♓ 25 0:09
26 15:00 ♆ ☌	♒ 26 15:20	27 1:17 ♆ ✶	♈ 27 2:38
28 4:10 ♃ ☌	♓ 28 18:18	29 4:54 ♆ □	♉ 29 6:23
30 20:51 ♆ ✶	♈ 30 21:18		

☽ Phases & Eclipses Dy Hr Mn	
6 20:47	● 16♉21
14 10:55	☽ 23♌41
22 9:13	○ 1♐19
29 7:51	☽ 7♓59
5 7:04	● 14♊40
13 4:52	☽ 22♍14
20 19:09	○ 29♐29
27 12:42	☽ 5♈54

Astro Data

1 MAY 1997
Julian Day # 35550
Delta T 60.8 sec
SVP 05♓17'51"
Obliquity 23°26'13"
⚷ Chiron 27♎59.1R
☽ Mean ☊ 26♍42.0

1 JUNE 1997
Julian Day # 35581
Delta T 60.8 sec
SVP 05♓17'47"
Obliquity 23°26'13"
⚷ Chiron 26♎08.1R
☽ Mean ☊ 25♍03.5

JULY 1997

LONGITUDE

Day	Sid.Time	☉	0 hr ☽	Noon ☽	True ☊	☿	♀	♂	♃	♄	♅	♆	♇
1 Tu	18 36 20	9♋12 18	23♉32 27	0♊13 43	22♍54.6	15♋27.7	2♌42.2	5♎21.5	21♒14.9	19♈30.8	7♒47.0	29♑ 6.2	3♐18.5
2 W	18 40 17	10 9 32	6♊52 9	13 27 37	22R46.1	17 33.7	3 55.1	5 50.7	21R10.9	19 33.9	7R45.0	29R 4.7	3R17.3
3 Th	18 44 14	11 6 45	20 0 0	26 29 12	22 35.5	19 38.0	5 7.9	6 20.1	21 6.8	19 36.9	7 43.0	29 3.2	3 16.1
4 F	18 48 10	12 3 59	2♋55 5	9♋17 35	22 23.8	21 40.8	6 20.8	6 49.8	21 2.4	19 39.8	7 40.9	29 1.7	3 14.9
5 Sa	18 52 7	13 1 12	15 36 38	21 52 15	22 12.0	23 41.8	7 33.6	7 19.7	20 58.0	19 42.6	7 38.8	29 0.1	3 13.7
6 Su	18 56 3	13 58 26	28 4 27	4♌13 22	22 1.3	25 41.1	8 46.4	7 49.8	20 53.3	19 45.4	7 36.7	28 58.6	3 12.6
7 M	19 0 0	14 55 39	10♌19 7	16 21 58	21 52.6	27 38.5	9 59.2	8 20.1	20 48.5	19 48.0	7 34.6	28 57.0	3 11.5
8 Tu	19 3 56	15 52 52	22 22 11	28 20 8	21 46.3	29 34.0	11 12.0	8 50.6	20 43.5	19 50.5	7 32.4	28 55.5	3 10.4
9 W	19 7 53	16 50 6	4♍16 12	10♍10 52	21 42.5	1♌27.6	12 24.7	9 21.4	20 38.4	19 53.0	7 30.2	28 53.9	3 9.3
10 Th	19 11 50	17 47 19	16 4 38	21 58 4	21D40.9	3 19.2	13 37.4	9 52.4	20 33.1	19 55.3	7 28.0	28 52.3	3 8.3
11 F	19 15 46	18 44 32	27 51 47	3♎46 24	21 40.9	5 9.0	14 50.1	10 23.5	20 27.7	19 57.5	7 25.8	28 50.7	3 7.2
12 Sa	19 19 43	19 41 45	9♎42 33	15 40 57	21R41.6	6 56.7	16 2.8	10 54.9	20 22.1	19 59.7	7 23.6	28 49.1	3 6.2
13 Su	19 23 39	20 38 58	21 42 14	27 47 4	21 41.9	8 42.5	17 15.4	11 26.5	20 16.4	20 1.7	7 21.3	28 47.5	3 5.3
14 M	19 27 36	21 36 11	3♏56 8	10♏10 0	21 41.1	10 26.4	18 28.0	11 58.2	20 10.5	20 3.7	7 19.1	28 45.9	3 4.3
15 Tu	19 31 32	22 33 24	16 29 16	22 54 23	21 38.4	12 8.3	19 40.6	12 30.2	20 4.5	20 5.5	7 16.8	28 44.3	3 3.4
16 W	19 35 29	23 30 38	29 25 46	6♐ 3 41	21 33.6	13 48.3	20 53.1	13 2.3	19 58.4	20 7.3	7 14.5	28 42.7	3 2.5
17 Th	19 39 25	24 27 51	12♐48 17	19 39 35	21 26.9	15 26.4	22 5.6	13 34.7	19 52.2	20 8.9	7 12.2	28 41.1	3 1.6
18 F	19 43 22	25 25 5	26 37 25	3♑41 26	21 18.8	17 2.4	23 18.1	14 7.2	19 45.8	20 10.5	7 9.8	28 39.5	3 0.8
19 Sa	19 47 19	26 22 19	10♑51 8	18 5 51	21 10.1	18 36.6	24 30.5	14 39.8	19 39.4	20 12.0	7 7.5	28 37.8	3 0.0
20 Su	19 51 15	27 19 33	25 24 46	2♒46 59	21 2.1	20 8.8	25 43.0	15 12.7	19 32.8	20 13.3	7 5.2	28 36.2	2 59.2
21 M	19 55 12	28 16 48	10♒11 30	17 37 17	20 55.4	21 39.0	26 55.3	15 45.7	19 26.1	20 14.6	7 2.8	28 34.6	2 58.5
22 Tu	19 59 8	29 14 3	25 3 18	2♓28 37	20 50.9	23 7.2	28 7.7	16 19.0	19 19.3	20 15.7	7 0.5	28 33.0	2 57.8
23 W	20 3 5	0♌11 19	9♓52 18	17 13 37	20D48.5	24 33.4	29 20.0	16 52.3	19 12.4	20 16.8	6 58.1	28 31.3	2 57.1
24 Th	20 7 1	1 8 36	24 31 54	1♈46 37	20 48.1	25 57.6	0♍32.3	17 25.9	19 5.4	20 17.7	6 55.7	28 29.7	2 56.4
25 F	20 10 58	2 5 53	8♈57 23	16 3 57	20 48.9	27 19.8	1 44.6	17 59.6	18 58.3	20 18.6	6 53.3	28 28.1	2 55.8
26 Sa	20 14 54	3 3 12	23 6 9	0♉ 3 55	20R49.9	28 39.8	2 56.8	18 33.5	18 51.1	20 19.3	6 50.9	28 26.5	2 55.1
27 Su	20 18 51	4 0 31	6♉57 18	13 46 20	20 50.3	29 57.8	4 9.0	19 7.5	18 43.8	20 20.0	6 48.5	28 24.9	2 54.6
28 M	20 22 47	4 57 52	20 31 9	27 11 53	20 49.1	1♍13.5	5 21.2	19 41.7	18 36.5	20 20.5	6 46.1	28 23.2	2 54.0
29 Tu	20 26 44	5 55 13	3♊48 42	10♊21 45	20 46.1	2 27.0	6 33.3	20 16.1	18 29.1	20 20.9	6 43.7	28 21.6	2 53.5
30 W	20 30 41	6 52 36	16 51 11	23 17 9	20 41.2	3 38.2	7 45.4	20 50.6	18 21.6	20 21.3	6 41.3	28 20.0	2 53.0
31 Th	20 34 37	7 50 0	29 39 47	5♋59 14	20 34.8	4 47.0	8 57.5	21 25.3	18 14.1	20 21.5	6 39.0	28 18.4	2 52.6

AUGUST 1997

LONGITUDE

Day	Sid.Time	☉	0 hr ☽	Noon ☽	True ☊	☿	♀	♂	♃	♄	♅	♆	♇
1 F	20 38 34	8♌47 24	12♋15 36	18♋29 1	20♍27.5	5♍53.4	10♍ 9.5	22♎ 0.1	18♒ 6.5	20♈21.6	6♒36.6	28♑16.8	2♐52.2
2 Sa	20 42 30	9 44 50	24 39 36	0♌47 28	20R20.2	6 57.2	11 21.5	22 35.1	17R58.9	20R21.6	6R34.2	28R15.3	2R51.8
3 Su	20 46 27	10 42 16	6♌52 46	12 55 40	20 13.6	7 58.3	12 33.5	23 10.3	17 51.2	20 21.6	6 31.8	28 13.7	2 51.4
4 M	20 50 23	11 39 44	18 56 21	24 55 1	20 8.3	8 56.7	13 45.4	23 45.6	17 43.4	20 21.4	6 29.4	28 12.1	2 51.1
5 Tu	20 54 20	12 37 12	0♍51 55	6♍47 20	20 4.7	9 52.2	14 57.4	24 21.1	17 35.7	20 21.1	6 27.0	28 10.5	2 50.8
6 W	20 58 17	13 34 41	12 41 35	18 35 2	20D 2.9	10 44.7	16 9.2	24 56.7	17 27.9	20 20.7	6 24.6	28 9.0	2 50.5
7 Th	21 2 13	14 32 11	24 28 5	0♎21 10	20 2.7	11 34.0	17 21.0	25 32.4	17 20.1	20 20.2	6 22.2	28 7.4	2 50.3
8 F	21 6 10	15 29 42	6♎14 45	12 9 22	20 3.7	12 19.9	18 32.8	26 8.3	17 12.3	20 19.6	6 19.9	28 5.9	2 50.1
9 Sa	21 10 6	16 27 14	18 5 34	24 3 54	20 5.3	13 2.4	19 44.6	26 44.4	17 4.4	20 18.9	6 17.5	28 4.4	2 49.9
10 Su	21 14 3	17 24 47	0♏ 4 59	6♏ 9 24	20 7.0	13 41.1	20 56.3	27 20.5	16 56.6	20 18.1	6 15.2	28 2.8	2 49.8
11 M	21 17 59	18 22 20	12 17 46	18 30 41	20R 8.0	14 16.0	22 7.9	27 56.9	16 48.8	20 17.2	6 12.9	28 1.3	2 49.7
12 Tu	21 21 56	19 19 55	24 48 43	1♐12 25	20 8.1	14 46.8	23 19.5	28 33.3	16 41.0	20 16.2	6 10.5	27 59.8	2 49.7
13 W	21 25 52	20 17 30	7♐42 15	14 18 37	20 6.8	15 13.3	24 31.1	29 9.9	16 33.2	20 15.0	6 8.2	27 58.4	2D49.6
14 Th	21 29 49	21 15 6	21 1 49	27 52 0	20 4.4	15 35.3	25 42.6	29 46.6	16 25.4	20 13.8	6 5.9	27 56.9	2 49.6
15 F	21 33 45	22 12 43	4♑49 13	11♑53 19	20 1.0	15 52.6	26 54.1	0♏23.5	16 17.6	20 12.5	6 3.7	27 55.5	2 49.7
16 Sa	21 37 42	23 10 22	19 4 0	26 20 44	19 57.3	16 4.9	28 5.5	1 0.5	16 9.9	20 11.1	6 1.4	27 54.0	2 49.7
17 Su	21 41 39	24 8 1	3♒42 53	11♒ 9 35	19 53.7	16R12.0	29 16.9	1 37.6	16 2.2	20 9.6	5 59.2	27 52.6	2 49.8
18 M	21 45 35	25 5 41	18 39 51	26 12 36	19 50.8	16 13.8	0♎28.2	2 14.8	15 54.6	20 8.0	5 56.9	27 51.2	2 50.0
19 Tu	21 49 32	26 3 23	3♓46 40	11♓20 52	19 49.0	16 10.1	1 39.4	2 52.2	15 46.9	20 6.3	5 54.7	27 49.8	2 50.2
20 W	21 53 28	27 1 6	18 54 3	26 25 9	19D48.3	16 0.6	2 50.7	3 29.7	15 39.4	20 4.5	5 52.5	27 48.4	2 50.4
21 Th	21 57 25	27 58 51	3♈53 9	11♈17 13	19 48.8	15 45.5	4 1.8	4 7.3	15 31.9	20 2.6	5 50.4	27 47.1	2 50.6
22 F	22 1 21	28 56 37	18 36 39	25 50 54	19 49.8	15 24.5	5 12.9	4 45.0	15 24.5	20 0.6	5 48.2	27 45.7	2 50.9
23 Sa	22 5 18	29 54 25	2♉59 34	10♉ 2 27	19 51.2	14 57.8	6 24.0	5 22.9	15 17.1	19 58.5	5 46.1	27 44.4	2 51.2
24 Su	22 9 14	0♍52 14	16 59 24	23 50 28	19 52.2	14 25.6	7 35.0	6 0.9	15 9.8	19 56.4	5 44.0	27 43.1	2 51.5
25 M	22 13 11	1 50 6	0♊35 44	7♊15 26	19R52.7	13 48.1	8 46.0	6 39.0	15 2.6	19 54.1	5 41.9	27 41.8	2 51.9
26 Tu	22 17 8	2 47 59	13 49 48	20 19 8	19 52.4	13 5.6	9 56.9	7 17.2	14 55.5	19 51.7	5 39.8	27 40.6	2 52.3
27 W	22 21 4	3 45 54	26 43 47	3♋ 4 5	19 51.3	12 18.8	11 7.7	7 55.6	14 48.5	19 49.3	5 37.8	27 39.3	2 52.7
28 Th	22 25 1	4 43 51	9♋20 24	15 33 6	19 49.6	11 28.3	12 18.5	8 34.0	14 41.5	19 46.7	5 35.8	27 38.1	2 53.2
29 F	22 28 57	5 41 49	21 42 31	27 49 0	19 47.6	10 34.8	13 29.3	9 12.6	14 34.7	19 44.1	5 33.8	27 36.9	2 53.7
30 Sa	22 32 54	6 39 49	3♌52 52	9♌54 26	19 45.6	9 39.4	14 40.0	9 51.3	14 28.0	19 41.4	5 31.9	27 35.7	2 54.2
31 Su	22 36 50	7 37 51	15 53 59	21 51 50	19 43.8	8 43.1	15 50.6	10 30.2	14 21.3	19 38.6	5 30.0	27 34.6	2 54.8

Astro Data

	Dy Hr Mn
☽0S	11 8:42
♃⚹♄	14 20:58
☽0N	24 13:02
♄ R	1 16:56
☽0S	7 16:38
♇ D	13 8:30
☿ R	17 19:49
♀0S	18 23:01
☽0N	20 22:07

Planet Ingress

	Dy Hr Mn
☿ ♌	8 5:28
☉ ♌	22 19:15
♀ ♍	23 13:16
☿ ♍	27 0:42
♂ ♏	14 8:42
♀ ♎	17 14:31
☉ ♍	23 2:19

Last Aspect / ☽ Ingress

Last Aspect Dy Hr Mn		☽ Ingress Dy Hr Mn
1 9:57	♆ △	♊ 1 11:35
3 2:02	♃ △	♋ 3 18:33
6 1:45	♆ ☍	♌ 6 3:45
7 20:44	♃ ☍	♍ 8 15:22
11 2:00	♆ △	♎ 11 4:21
13 13:57	♆ □	♏ 13 16:20
15 22:41	♆ ⚹	♐ 16 1:02
17 17:45	♀ △	♑ 18 5:45
20 5:12	♆ ☌	♒ 20 7:29
22 5:24	♀ ☍	♓ 22 7:59
24 6:32	♆ ⚹	♈ 24 9:03
26 10:34	☿ △	♉ 26 11:53
28 14:07	♆ △	♊ 28 17:04
30 7:47	♂ △	♋ 31 0:38

Last Aspect / ☽ Ingress

Last Aspect Dy Hr Mn		☽ Ingress Dy Hr Mn
2 7:01	♆ ☍	♌ 2 10:27
4 10:11	♂ ⚹	♍ 4 22:15
7 7:26	♆ △	♎ 7 11:17
9 19:58	♆ □	♏ 9 23:50
12 5:59	♆ ⚹	♐ 12 9:45
14 9:01	♀ □	♑ 14 15:42
16 16:10	♀ △	♒ 16 17:58
18 10:55	☉ ☍	♓ 18 18:01
20 14:12	♆ ⚹	♈ 20 17:45
22 18:25	☉ △	♉ 22 18:57
24 18:50	♆ △	♊ 24 22:56
26 11:07	♄ ⚹	♋ 27 6:11
29 11:35	♆ ☍	♌ 29 16:19

☽ Phases & Eclipses

Dy Hr Mn	
4 18:40	● 12♋48
12 21:44	☽ 20♎34
20 3:20	○ 27♑28
26 18:28	☽ 3♉47
3 8:14	● 11♌02
11 12:42	☽ 18♏53
18 10:55	○ 25♒32
25 2:24	☽ 1♊56

Astro Data

1 JULY 1997
Julian Day # 35611
Delta T 60.8 sec
SVP 05♓17'43"
Obliquity 23°26'13"
⚷ Chiron 25♎43.7
☽ Mean ☊ 23♍28.1

1 AUGUST 1997
Julian Day # 35642
Delta T 60.9 sec
SVP 05♓17'38"
Obliquity 23°26'13"
⚷ Chiron 27♎00.1
☽ Mean ☊ 21♍49.7

Day	Sid.Time	☉	0 hr ☽	Noon ☽	True ☊	☿	♀	♂	♃	♄	♅	♆	♇
1 M	22 40 47	8♍35 55	27♌48 14	3♍43 28	19♍42.6	7♍47.1	17♎ 1.2	11♏ 9.1	14♒14.8	19♈35.7	5♒28.1	27♑33.5	2♐55.4
2 Tu	22 44 43	9 34 0	9♍37 48	15 31 31	19D41.8	6R52.6	18 11.7	11 48.2	14R 8.4	19R32.7	5R26.2	27R32.3	2 56.0
3 W	22 48 40	10 32 7	21 24 53	27 18 12	19 41.6	6 0.8	19 22.2	12 27.4	14 2.1	19 29.6	5 24.4	27 31.3	2 56.7
4 Th	22 52 37	11 30 16	3♎11 47	9♎ 5 56	19 41.9	5 12.8	20 32.6	13 6.7	13 56.0	19 26.5	5 22.6	27 30.2	2 57.4
5 F	22 56 33	12 28 26	15 1 1	20 57 23	19 42.5	4 29.9	21 42.9	13 46.1	13 50.0	19 23.3	5 20.8	27 29.2	2 58.2
6 Sa	23 0 30	13 26 38	26 55 27	2♏55 36	19 43.2	3 53.1	22 53.2	14 25.6	13 44.1	19 20.0	5 19.1	27 28.1	2 58.9
7 Su	23 4 26	14 24 51	8♏58 17	15 3 58	19 43.8	3 23.2	24 3.4	15 5.2	13 38.4	19 16.6	5 17.4	27 27.1	2 59.7
8 M	23 8 23	15 23 6	21 13 7	27 26 12	19 44.3	3 1.0	25 13.6	15 44.9	13 32.8	19 13.2	5 15.7	27 26.2	3 0.6
9 Tu	23 12 19	16 21 23	3♐43 43	10♐ 6 8	19 44.5	2 47.2	26 23.6	16 24.8	13 27.4	19 9.6	5 14.1	27 25.3	3 1.4
10 W	23 16 16	17 19 41	16 33 53	23 7 24	19R44.6	2D42.1	27 33.6	17 4.7	13 22.1	19 6.0	5 12.5	27 24.3	3 2.3
11 Th	23 20 12	18 18 1	29 47 1	6♑33 2	19 44.6	2 46.0	28 43.5	17 44.8	13 16.9	19 2.4	5 11.0	27 23.5	3 3.3
12 F	23 24 9	19 16 22	13♑25 37	20 24 51	19D44.6	2 59.0	29 53.4	18 25.0	13 12.0	18 58.7	5 9.5	27 22.6	3 4.2
13 Sa	23 28 6	20 14 44	27 30 39	4♒42 48	19 44.6	3 21.1	1♏ 3.1	19 5.2	13 7.2	18 54.9	5 8.0	27 21.8	3 5.2
14 Su	23 32 2	21 13 8	12♒ 0 55	19 24 25	19 44.7	3 52.2	2 12.8	19 45.6	13 2.5	18 51.0	5 6.6	27 21.0	3 6.2
15 M	23 35 59	22 11 34	26 52 36	4♓24 32	19 44.8	4 32.0	3 22.4	20 26.0	12 58.0	18 47.1	5 5.2	27 20.2	3 7.3
16 Tu	23 39 55	23 10 2	11♓59 14	19 35 31	19R45.0	5 20.1	4 31.9	21 6.6	12 53.7	18 43.1	5 3.8	27 19.5	3 8.4
17 W	23 43 52	24 8 31	27 12 13	4♈48 6	19 45.0	6 16.1	5 41.3	21 47.3	12 49.6	18 39.1	5 2.5	27 18.8	3 9.5
18 Th	23 47 48	25 7 2	12♈21 58	19 52 42	19 44.7	7 19.4	6 50.7	22 28.0	12 45.6	18 35.0	5 1.2	27 18.1	3 10.7
19 F	23 51 45	26 5 35	27 19 15	4♉40 46	19 44.2	8 29.6	7 59.9	23 8.9	12 41.8	18 30.8	5 0.0	27 17.4	3 11.8
20 Sa	23 55 41	27 4 11	11♉56 33	19 6 3	19 43.4	9 45.9	9 9.1	23 49.8	12 38.2	18 26.6	4 58.8	27 16.8	3 13.0
21 Su	23 59 38	28 2 48	26 8 54	3♊ 4 57	19 42.5	11 7.9	10 18.1	24 30.9	12 34.8	18 22.4	4 57.7	27 16.2	3 14.3
22 M	0 3 34	29 1 28	9♊54 8	16 36 35	19 41.7	12 34.7	11 27.1	25 12.0	12 31.5	18 18.1	4 56.6	27 15.6	3 15.5
23 Tu	0 7 31	0♎ 0 10	23 12 33	29 42 20	19D41.3	14 5.9	12 36.0	25 53.3	12 28.4	18 13.8	4 55.5	27 15.1	3 16.8
24 W	0 11 28	0 58 55	6♋ 6 21	12♋25 3	19 41.2	15 40.8	13 44.8	26 34.6	12 25.6	18 9.4	4 54.5	27 14.6	3 18.2
25 Th	0 15 24	1 57 41	18 38 58	24 48 36	19 41.7	17 18.9	14 53.4	27 16.1	12 22.9	18 5.0	4 53.5	27 14.1	3 19.5
26 F	0 19 21	2 56 30	0♌54 28	6♌57 8	19 42.7	18 59.6	16 2.0	27 57.6	12 20.4	18 0.5	4 52.6	27 13.7	3 20.9
27 Sa	0 23 17	3 55 21	12 57 5	18 54 49	19 44.0	20 42.4	17 10.5	28 39.3	12 18.0	17 56.0	4 51.7	27 13.3	3 22.3
28 Su	0 27 14	4 54 14	24 50 50	0♍45 34	19 45.3	22 26.9	18 18.9	29 21.0	12 15.9	17 51.5	4 50.9	27 12.9	3 23.8
29 M	0 31 10	5 53 9	6♍39 26	12 32 50	19 46.3	24 12.7	19 27.2	0♐ 2.8	12 14.0	17 46.9	4 50.1	27 12.5	3 25.2
30 Tu	0 35 7	6 52 7	18 26 8	24 19 39	19R46.8	25 59.5	20 35.4	0 44.8	12 12.3	17 42.3	4 49.4	27 12.2	3 26.7

LONGITUDE OCTOBER 1997

Day	Sid.Time	☉	0 hr ☽	Noon ☽	True ☊	☿	♀	♂	♃	♄	♅	♆	♇
1 W	0 39 3	7♎51 6	0♎13 42	6♎ 8 35	19♍46.5	27♍46.9	21♏43.4	1♐26.8	12♒10.7	17♈37.7	4♒48.7	27♑11.9	3♐28.2
2 Th	0 43 0	8 50 8	12 4 32	18 1 49	19R45.1	29 34.7	22 51.4	2 8.9	12R 9.4	17R33.0	4R48.1	27R11.7	3 29.8
3 F	0 46 57	9 49 12	24 0 41	0♏ 1 22	19 42.8	1♎22.6	23 59.2	2 51.1	12 8.2	17 28.4	4 47.5	27 11.4	3 31.4
4 Sa	0 50 53	10 48 17	6♏ 4 5	12 9 5	19 39.7	3 10.6	25 6.9	3 33.4	12 7.3	17 23.7	4 46.9	27 11.3	3 33.0
5 Su	0 54 50	11 47 25	18 16 35	24 26 52	19 36.1	4 58.3	26 14.5	4 15.8	12 6.6	17 19.0	4 46.4	27 11.1	3 34.6
6 M	0 58 46	12 46 34	0♐40 11	6♐56 49	19 32.5	6 45.8	27 22.0	4 58.3	12 6.0	17 14.3	4 46.0	27 11.0	3 36.2
7 Tu	1 2 43	13 45 45	13 17 2	19 41 8	19 29.2	8 32.9	28 29.3	5 40.8	12 5.7	17 9.5	4 45.6	27 10.9	3 37.9
8 W	1 6 39	14 44 59	26 9 26	2♑42 13	19 26.9	10 19.5	29 36.5	6 23.5	12D 5.5	17 4.8	4 45.2	27 10.8	3 39.6
9 Th	1 10 36	15 44 14	9♑19 46	16 2 21	19D25.7	12 5.5	0♐43.5	7 6.2	12 5.6	17 0.1	4 44.9	27D10.8	3 41.3
10 F	1 14 32	16 43 30	22 50 11	29 43 25	19 25.7	13 51.0	1 50.4	7 49.0	12 5.9	16 55.3	4 44.7	27 10.8	3 43.1
11 Sa	1 18 29	17 42 49	6♒42 10	13♒46 26	19 26.6	15 35.8	2 57.1	8 31.9	12 6.3	16 50.6	4 44.5	27 10.9	3 44.9
12 Su	1 22 26	18 42 9	20 56 5	28 10 53	19 28.1	17 19.9	4 3.7	9 14.9	12 7.0	16 45.9	4 44.3	27 11.0	3 46.7
13 M	1 26 22	19 41 31	5♓30 27	12♓54 14	19R29.4	19 3.4	5 10.1	9 58.0	12 7.8	16 41.1	4 44.3	27 11.1	3 48.5
14 Tu	1 30 19	20 40 54	20 21 34	27 51 36	19 30.0	20 46.2	6 16.3	10 41.1	12 8.9	16 36.4	4D44.2	27 11.2	3 50.3
15 W	1 34 15	21 40 20	5♈23 22	12♈55 47	19 29.1	22 28.3	7 22.3	11 24.4	12 10.2	16 31.7	4 44.2	27 11.4	3 52.2
16 Th	1 38 12	22 39 47	20 27 43	27 58 1	19 26.7	24 9.7	8 28.2	12 7.7	12 11.6	16 27.0	4 44.3	27 11.6	3 54.1
17 F	1 42 8	23 39 16	5♉25 32	12♉49 12	19 22.6	25 50.5	9 33.8	12 51.0	12 13.3	16 22.3	4 44.4	27 11.9	3 56.0
18 Sa	1 46 5	24 38 48	20 8 4	27 21 19	19 17.5	27 30.5	10 39.3	13 34.5	12 15.1	16 17.6	4 44.5	27 12.1	3 57.9
19 Su	1 50 1	25 38 22	4♊28 19	11♊28 36	19 11.8	29 10.0	11 44.6	14 18.0	12 17.1	16 13.0	4 44.7	27 12.5	3 59.8
20 M	1 53 58	26 37 58	18 21 54	25 8 8	19 6.5	0♏48.7	12 49.7	15 1.6	12 19.4	16 8.3	4 45.0	27 12.8	4 1.8
21 Tu	1 57 54	27 37 36	1♋47 22	8♋19 49	19 2.3	2 26.9	13 54.6	15 45.3	12 21.8	16 3.7	4 45.3	27 13.2	4 3.8
22 W	2 1 51	28 37 16	14 45 49	21 5 50	18 59.5	4 4.4	14 59.2	16 29.1	12 24.4	15 59.2	4 45.7	27 13.6	4 5.8
23 Th	2 5 48	29 36 59	27 20 23	3♌30 2	18D58.5	5 41.3	16 3.7	17 12.9	12 27.2	15 54.6	4 46.1	27 14.1	4 7.8
24 F	2 9 44	0♏36 44	9♌35 24	15 37 9	18 58.8	7 17.7	17 7.9	17 56.9	12 30.2	15 50.1	4 46.5	27 14.5	4 9.8
25 Sa	2 13 41	1 36 31	21 35 55	27 32 20	19 0.2	8 53.5	18 11.9	18 40.9	12 33.4	15 45.6	4 47.0	27 15.1	4 11.9
26 Su	2 17 37	2 36 21	3♍27 3	9♍20 40	19 1.7	10 28.8	19 15.6	19 25.0	12 36.8	15 41.2	4 47.6	27 15.6	4 14.0
27 M	2 21 34	3 36 12	15 13 45	21 6 51	19R 2.7	12 3.5	20 19.1	20 9.1	12 40.4	15 36.8	4 48.2	27 16.2	4 16.1
28 Tu	2 25 30	4 36 6	27 0 28	2♎55 2	19 2.4	13 37.7	21 22.3	20 53.3	12 44.1	15 32.4	4 48.9	27 16.8	4 18.2
29 W	2 29 27	5 36 2	8♎50 58	14 48 38	19 0.2	15 11.4	22 25.3	21 37.6	12 48.1	15 28.1	4 49.6	27 17.5	4 20.3
30 Th	2 33 23	6 35 59	20 48 19	26 50 17	18 55.7	16 44.6	23 28.0	22 22.0	12 52.2	15 23.9	4 50.4	27 18.1	4 22.4
31 F	2 37 20	7 35 59	2♏54 45	9♏ 1 51	18 49.1	18 17.4	24 30.4	23 6.5	12 56.5	15 19.7	4 51.2	27 18.8	4 24.6

Astro Data	Dy Hr Mn	Planet Ingress	Dy Hr Mn
☽0S	3 23:08	♀ ♏	12 2:17
☿ D	10 1:43	☉ ♎	22 23:56
☽0N	17 8:47	♂ ♐	28 22:22
♄⚼♇	22 10:56		
		☿ ♎	2 5:38
☽0S	1 5:05	♀ ♐	8 8:25
☿0S	4 11:03	☿ ♏	19 12:08
♃ D	8 4:37	☉ ♏	23 9:15
♆ D	9 1:29		
☽0N	14 19:50		
♅ D	14 10:48		
☽0S	28 11:52		

Last Aspect Dy Hr Mn		☽ Ingress Dy Hr Mn
31 7:30	♄ △	♍ 1 4:27
3 12:25	♆ △	♎ 3 17:30
6 1:05	♆ □	♏ 6 6:10
8 11:59	♆ ✶	♐ 8 16:54
10 21:56	♀ ✶	♑ 11 0:23
12 23:45	♆ ☌	♒ 13 4:10
14 13:10	♂ □	♓ 15 4:59
17 0:10	♆ ✶	♈ 17 4:25
18 23:57	♆ □	♉ 19 4:21
21 3:31	☉ △	♊ 21 6:38
22 14:59	♄ ✶	♋ 23 12:33
25 17:50	♂ △	♌ 25 22:12
28 9:43	♂ □	♍ 28 10:27
30 18:08	☿ ☌	♎ 30 23:32

Last Aspect Dy Hr Mn		☽ Ingress Dy Hr Mn
3 6:21	♆ □	♏ 3 11:57
5 17:17	♆ ✶	♐ 5 22:43
7 7:14	♄ △	♑ 8 7:04
10 7:35	♆ ☌	♒ 10 12:29
11 20:00	☉ △	♓ 12 14:59
14 10:56	♆ ✶	♈ 14 15:25
16 10:46	♆ □	♉ 16 15:16
18 11:45	♆ △	♊ 18 16:26
20 15:52	☉ △	♋ 20 20:45
23 4:48	☉ □	♌ 23 5:10
24 17:45	♂ △	♍ 25 16:59
28 0:33	♆ △	♎ 28 6:05
30 12:56	♆ □	♏ 30 18:15

☽ Phases & Eclipses Dy Hr Mn	
1 23:52	● 9♍34
1 0:03:47	P 0.899
10 1:31	☽ 17♐23
16 18:51	○ 23♓56
16 18:47	T 1.191
23 13:35	☽ 0♋33
1 16:52	● 8♎33
9 12:22	☽ 16♑15
16 3:46	○ 22♈49
23 4:48	☽ 29♋49
31 10:01	● 8♏01

Astro Data

1 SEPTEMBER 1997
Julian Day # 35673
Delta T 60.9 sec
SVP 05♓17'34"
Obliquity 23°26'14"
⚷ Chiron 29♎46.0
☽ Mean ☊ 20♍11.2

1 OCTOBER 1997
Julian Day # 35703
Delta T 61.0 sec
SVP 05♓17'32"
Obliquity 23°26'14"
⚷ Chiron 3♏26.0
☽ Mean ☊ 18♍35.8

NOVEMBER 1997 LONGITUDE

Day	Sid.Time	☉	0 hr ☽	Noon ☽	True ☊	☿	♀	♂	♃	♄	♅	♆	♇
1 Sa	2 41 17	8♏36 1	15♏11 44	21♏24 29	18♍40.6	19♏49.7	25♐32.5	23♐51.0	13♒ 1.0	15♈15.5	4♒52.1	27♑19.6	4♐26.8
2 Su	2 45 13	9 36 5	27 40 8	3♐58 45	18R 30.9	21 21.5	26 34.3	24 35.6	13 5.7	15R 11.4	4 53.0	27 20.4	4 28.9
3 M	2 49 10	10 36 10	10♐20 21	16 44 57	18 21.1	22 52.9	27 35.8	25 20.2	13 10.6	15 7.3	4 53.9	27 21.2	4 31.1
4 Tu	2 53 6	11 36 17	23 12 35	29 43 16	18 12.1	24 23.9	28 36.9	26 5.0	13 15.6	15 3.4	4 55.0	27 22.0	4 33.3
5 W	2 57 3	12 36 26	6♑17 5	12♑54 5	18 4.8	25 54.4	29 37.7	26 49.7	13 20.8	14 59.4	4 56.0	27 22.9	4 35.6
6 Th	3 0 59	13 36 36	19 34 22	26 18 0	17 59.8	27 24.5	0♑38.1	27 34.6	13 26.2	14 55.6	4 57.2	27 23.8	4 37.8
7 F	3 4 56	14 36 48	3♒ 5 7	9♒55 50	17D 57.1	28 54.2	1 38.2	28 19.5	13 31.8	14 51.8	4 58.3	27 24.8	4 40.1
8 Sa	3 8 52	15 37 2	16 50 13	23 48 22	17 56.5	0♐23.4	2 37.9	29 4.5	13 37.5	14 48.0	4 59.5	27 25.7	4 42.3
9 Su	3 12 49	16 37 17	0♓50 17	7♓55 56	17 57.0	1 52.1	3 37.1	29 49.6	13 43.4	14 44.4	5 0.8	27 26.7	4 44.6
10 M	3 16 46	17 37 33	15 5 12	22 17 51	17R 57.6	3 20.3	4 36.0	0♑34.7	13 49.5	14 40.8	5 2.1	27 27.8	4 46.8
11 Tu	3 20 42	18 37 50	29 33 33	6♈51 50	17 57.1	4 48.1	5 34.3	1 19.8	13 55.8	14 37.3	5 3.5	27 28.9	4 49.1
12 W	3 24 39	19 38 9	14♈12 6	21 33 38	17 54.5	6 15.3	6 32.3	2 5.1	14 2.2	14 33.9	5 4.9	27 29.9	4 51.4
13 Th	3 28 35	20 38 30	28 55 37	6♉17 7	17 49.3	7 42.0	7 29.7	2 50.4	14 8.7	14 30.5	5 6.4	27 31.1	4 53.7
14 F	3 32 32	21 38 52	13♉37 12	20 54 53	17 41.4	9 8.1	8 26.6	3 35.7	14 15.5	14 27.2	5 7.9	27 32.2	4 56.0
15 Sa	3 36 28	22 39 16	28 9 14	5♊19 22	17 31.5	10 33.5	9 23.1	4 21.1	14 22.4	14 24.0	5 9.4	27 33.4	4 58.4
16 Su	3 40 25	23 39 41	12♊24 31	19 24 4	17 20.5	11 58.3	10 19.0	5 6.6	14 29.4	14 20.9	5 11.0	27 34.6	5 0.7
17 M	3 44 21	24 40 9	26 17 32	3♋ 4 37	17 9.8	13 22.2	11 14.3	5 52.1	14 36.6	14 17.9	5 12.7	27 35.9	5 3.0
18 Tu	3 48 18	25 40 37	9♋45 10	16 19 13	17 0.4	14 45.3	12 9.1	6 37.6	14 44.0	14 14.9	5 14.4	27 37.2	5 5.3
19 W	3 52 15	26 41 8	22 46 55	29 8 35	16 53.2	16 7.5	13 3.2	7 23.3	14 51.5	14 12.1	5 16.1	27 38.5	5 7.7
20 Th	3 56 11	27 41 41	5♌24 39	11♌35 35	16 48.5	17 28.5	13 56.8	8 8.9	14 59.2	14 9.3	5 17.9	27 39.8	5 10.0
21 F	4 0 8	28 42 15	17 41 59	23 44 29	16 46.2	18 48.4	14 49.7	8 54.7	15 7.0	14 6.6	5 19.7	27 41.2	5 12.4
22 Sa	4 4 4	29 42 51	29 43 45	5♍40 29	16D 45.6	20 6.9	15 41.9	9 40.5	15 15.0	14 4.0	5 21.6	27 42.5	5 14.7
23 Su	4 8 1	0♐43 28	11♍35 23	17 29 10	16R 45.8	21 23.9	16 33.5	10 26.3	15 23.1	14 1.5	5 23.5	27 44.0	5 17.1
24 M	4 11 57	1 44 7	23 22 30	29 16 3	16 45.7	22 39.1	17 24.3	11 12.2	15 31.3	13 59.1	5 25.5	27 45.4	5 19.5
25 Tu	4 15 54	2 44 48	5♎10 28	11♎ 6 20	16 44.2	23 52.3	18 14.4	11 58.2	15 39.7	13 56.8	5 27.5	27 46.9	5 21.8
26 W	4 19 50	3 45 31	17 4 11	23 4 31	16 40.4	25 3.2	19 3.7	12 44.2	15 48.3	13 54.6	5 29.5	27 48.4	5 24.2
27 Th	4 23 47	4 46 15	29 7 44	5♏14 12	16 33.8	26 11.5	19 52.2	13 30.2	15 56.9	13 52.5	5 31.6	27 49.9	5 26.5
28 F	4 27 44	5 47 0	11♏24 12	17 37 54	16 24.3	27 16.8	20 39.8	14 16.3	16 5.8	13 50.4	5 33.7	27 51.4	5 28.9
29 Sa	4 31 40	6 47 47	23 55 27	0♐16 52	16 12.4	28 18.8	21 26.5	15 2.5	16 14.7	13 48.5	5 35.9	27 53.0	5 31.3
30 Su	4 35 37	7 48 35	6♐42 7	13 11 6	15 58.9	29 16.8	22 12.4	15 48.7	16 23.8	13 46.7	5 38.1	27 54.6	5 33.6

DECEMBER 1997 LONGITUDE

Day	Sid.Time	☉	0 hr ☽	Noon ☽	True ☊	☿	♀	♂	♃	♄	♅	♆	♇
1 M	4 39 33	8♐49 25	19♐43 40	26♐19 37	15♍45.1	0♑10.4	22♑57.3	16♑34.9	16♒33.0	13♈45.0	5♒40.4	27♑56.2	5♐36.0
2 Tu	4 43 30	9 50 16	2♑58 41	9♑40 38	15R 32.2	0 58.9	23 41.1	17 21.2	16 42.4	13R 43.4	5 42.7	27 57.9	5 38.4
3 W	4 47 26	10 51 7	16 25 13	23 12 11	15 21.5	1 41.6	24 24.0	18 7.6	16 51.9	13 41.9	5 45.0	27 59.6	5 40.7
4 Th	4 51 23	11 52 0	0♒ 1 19	6♒52 27	15 13.6	2 17.9	25 5.7	18 53.9	17 1.5	13 40.5	5 47.4	28 1.3	5 43.1
5 F	4 55 19	12 52 54	13 45 27	20 40 12	15 8.8	2 46.9	25 46.3	19 40.4	17 11.2	13 39.2	5 49.8	28 3.0	5 45.5
6 Sa	4 59 16	13 53 48	27 36 38	4♓34 43	15 6.6	3 7.8	26 25.7	20 26.8	17 21.1	13 38.0	5 52.2	28 4.7	5 47.8
7 Su	5 3 13	14 54 43	11♓34 26	18 35 44	15 6.2	3R 19.7	27 3.9	21 13.3	17 31.1	13 36.9	5 54.7	28 6.5	5 50.1
8 M	5 7 9	15 55 39	25 38 36	2♈42 57	15 6.1	3 21.7	27 40.8	21 59.9	17 41.2	13 35.9	5 57.2	28 8.3	5 52.5
9 Tu	5 11 6	16 56 35	9♈48 38	16 55 29	15 4.9	3 13.3	28 16.3	22 46.4	17 51.4	13 35.1	5 59.8	28 10.1	5 54.8
10 W	5 15 2	17 57 32	24 3 13	1♉11 27	15 1.6	2 53.7	28 50.4	23 33.0	18 1.7	13 34.3	6 2.4	28 11.9	5 57.1
11 Th	5 18 59	18 58 29	8♉19 45	15 27 35	14 55.3	2 22.7	29 23.0	24 19.7	18 12.2	13 33.7	6 5.0	28 13.8	5 59.5
12 F	5 22 55	19 59 28	22 34 21	29 39 26	14 46.1	1 40.3	29 54.2	25 6.4	18 22.8	13 33.1	6 7.7	28 15.6	6 1.8
13 Sa	5 26 52	21 0 27	6♊42 8	13♊41 49	14 34.6	0 46.9	0♒23.7	25 53.1	18 33.4	13 32.7	6 10.4	28 17.5	6 4.1
14 Su	5 30 48	22 1 27	20 37 51	27 29 41	14 21.8	29♐43.6	0 51.6	26 39.8	18 44.2	13 32.4	6 13.1	28 19.4	6 6.4
15 M	5 34 45	23 2 27	4♋16 51	10♋58 58	14 9.0	28 31.9	1 17.8	27 26.6	18 55.1	13 32.2	6 15.9	28 21.4	6 8.7
16 Tu	5 38 42	24 3 28	17 35 48	24 7 14	13 57.6	27 13.8	1 42.2	28 13.4	19 6.1	13D 32.1	6 18.7	28 23.3	6 11.0
17 W	5 42 38	25 4 31	0♌33 17	6♌54 2	13 48.4	25 51.9	2 4.7	29 0.2	19 17.2	13 32.1	6 21.5	28 25.3	6 13.2
18 Th	5 46 35	26 5 34	13 9 46	19 20 49	13 42.0	24 28.9	2 25.4	29 47.1	19 28.4	13 32.2	6 24.3	28 27.3	6 15.5
19 F	5 50 31	27 6 37	25 27 37	1♍30 40	13 38.4	23 7.6	2 44.2	0♒34.0	19 39.7	13 32.4	6 27.2	28 29.3	6 17.7
20 Sa	5 54 28	28 7 42	7♍30 32	13 27 52	13D 37.0	21 50.7	3 0.9	1 20.9	19 51.1	13 32.8	6 30.1	28 31.3	6 20.0
21 Su	5 58 24	29 8 47	19 23 19	25 17 34	13R 36.9	20 40.4	3 15.5	2 7.8	20 2.5	13 33.2	6 33.1	28 33.3	6 22.2
22 M	6 2 21	0♑ 9 53	1♎11 20	7♎ 5 17	13 37.1	19 38.7	3 28.0	2 54.8	20 14.1	13 33.7	6 36.1	28 35.4	6 24.4
23 Tu	6 6 17	1 11 0	13 0 9	18 56 36	13 36.4	18 46.6	3 38.2	3 41.8	20 25.8	13 34.4	6 39.0	28 37.4	6 26.6
24 W	6 10 14	2 12 7	24 55 17	0♏56 49	13 33.9	18 5.1	3 46.3	4 28.9	20 37.6	13 35.2	6 42.1	28 39.5	6 28.8
25 Th	6 14 11	3 13 15	7♏ 1 45	13 10 35	13 28.9	17 34.4	3 52.0	5 15.9	20 49.4	13 36.1	6 45.1	28 41.6	6 31.0
26 F	6 18 7	4 14 24	19 23 44	25 41 33	13 21.2	17 14.4	3R 55.3	6 3.0	21 1.4	13 37.1	6 48.2	28 43.7	6 33.2
27 Sa	6 22 4	5 15 34	2♐ 4 16	8♐32 2	13 11.2	17D 4.7	3 56.3	6 50.1	21 13.4	13 38.2	6 51.3	28 45.8	6 35.3
28 Su	6 26 0	6 16 43	15 4 50	21 42 37	12 59.7	17 4.8	3 54.8	7 37.2	21 25.6	13 39.4	6 54.4	28 47.9	6 37.4
29 M	6 29 57	7 17 54	28 25 11	5♑12 13	12 47.7	17 14.0	3 50.8	8 24.4	21 37.8	13 40.7	6 57.6	28 50.1	6 39.5
30 Tu	6 33 53	8 19 4	12♑ 3 20	18 58 5	12 36.4	17 31.5	3 44.3	9 11.6	21 50.1	13 42.2	7 0.8	28 52.3	6 41.6
31 W	6 37 50	9 20 15	25 55 57	2♒56 24	12 27.0	17 56.6	3 35.4	9 58.8	22 2.4	13 43.7	7 3.9	28 54.4	6 43.7

Astro Data	Planet Ingress	Last Aspect	☽ Ingress	Last Aspect	☽ Ingress	☽ Phases & Eclipses	Astro Data
Dy Hr Mn	Dy Hr Mn	Dy Hr Mn	Dy Hr Mn	Dy Hr Mn	Dy Hr Mn	Dy Hr Mn	1 NOVEMBER 1997
☽0N 11 5:47	♀ ♑ 5 8:50	1 23:22 ♆ ⚹	♐ 2 4:27	30 18:07 ♃ ⚹	♑ 1 18:38	7 21:43 ☽ 15♒31	Julian Day # 35734
♃⚹♄ 15 3:53	☿ ♐ 7 17:42	4 10:49 ♀ ☌	♑ 4 12:31	3 20:29 ♆ ☌	♒ 3 23:58	14 14:12 ○ 22♉15	Delta T 61.0 sec
☽0S 24 20:17	♂ ♑ 9 5:33	6 15:42 ☿ ⚹	♒ 6 18:33	5 6:02 ♃ ☌	♓ 6 4:07	21 23:58 ☽ 29♌43	SVP 05♓17'30"
	☉ ♐ 22 6:48	8 22:11 ♂ ⚹	♓ 8 22:35	8 4:15 ♆ ⚹	♈ 8 7:24	30 2:14 ● 7♐54	Obliquity 23°26'14"
☿ R 7 16:56	☿ ♑ 30 19:11	10 20:34 ♆ ⚹	♈ 11 0:44	10 8:22 ♀ □	♉ 10 10:00		⚷ Chiron 7♏43.8
☽0N 8 13:43		12 21:42 ♆ □	♉ 13 1:45	12 9:39 ♆ △	♊ 12 12:35	7 6:09 ☽ 15♓10	☽ Mean ☊ 16♍57.3
♄ D 16 10:29	♀ ♒ 12 4:39	14 23:00 ♆ △	♊ 15 3:05	14 14:40 ☿ ☍	♋ 14 16:25	14 2:37 ○ 22♊08	
☽0S 22 5:57	☿ ♐ 13 18:06	16 3:35 ♃ △	♋ 17 6:32	16 20:54 ♂ ☍	♌ 16 22:58	21 21:43 ☽ 0♎04	1 DECEMBER 1997
♀ R 26 21:21	♂ ♒ 18 6:37	19 9:10 ♆ ☍	♌ 19 13:38	19 3:34 ☉ △	♍ 19 9:00	29 16:57 ● 8♑01	Julian Day # 35764
☿ D 27 11:41	☉ ♑ 21 20:07	21 23:58 ☉ □	♍ 22 0:33	21 18:42 ♆ △	♎ 21 21:35		Delta T 61.1 sec
		24 8:57 ♆ △	♎ 24 13:29	24 7:29 ♆ □	♏ 24 10:07		SVP 05♓17'25"
		26 21:26 ♆ □	♏ 27 1:43	26 17:47 ♆ ⚹	♐ 26 20:07		Obliquity 23°26'13"
		29 7:30 ♆ ⚹	♐ 29 11:28	28 11:40 ♃ ⚹	♑ 29 2:48		⚷ Chiron 11♏51.5
				31 5:07 ♆ ☌	♒ 31 6:58		☽ Mean ☊ 15♍22.0

LONGITUDE — JANUARY 1998

Day	Sid.Time	☉	0 hr ☽	Noon ☽	True ☊	☿	♀	♂	♃	♄	♅	♆	♇
1 Th	6 41 47	10♑21 25	9♒58 53	17♒ 2 52	12♍20.2	18♐28.5	3♒23.9	10♒46.0	22♒14.9	13♈45.3	7♒ 7.2	28♑56.6	6♐45.8
2 F	6 45 43	11 22 36	24 7 51	1♓13 25	12R 16.2	19 6.6	3R 10.0	11 33.2	22 27.4	13 47.1	7 10.4	28 58.8	6 47.8
3 Sa	6 49 40	12 23 46	8♓19 10	15 24 47	12D 14.8	19 50.2	2 53.5	12 20.4	22 40.0	13 49.0	7 13.7	29 1.0	6 49.9
4 Su	6 53 36	13 24 56	22 30 0	29 34 38	12 15.0	20 38.7	2 34.7	13 7.7	22 52.7	13 50.9	7 16.9	29 3.2	6 51.9
5 M	6 57 33	14 26 6	6♈38 30	13♈41 30	12R 15.8	21 31.5	2 13.5	13 55.0	23 5.4	13 53.0	7 20.2	29 5.4	6 53.9
6 Tu	7 1 29	15 27 15	20 43 31	27 44 27	12 15.9	22 28.2	1 50.1	14 42.2	23 18.3	13 55.2	7 23.5	29 7.6	6 55.8
7 W	7 5 26	16 28 24	4♉44 10	11♉42 33	12 14.2	23 28.4	1 24.5	15 29.5	23 31.1	13 57.5	7 26.9	29 9.9	6 57.8
8 Th	7 9 22	17 29 33	18 39 26	25 34 37	12 10.3	24 31.7	0 56.8	16 16.8	23 44.1	13 59.9	7 30.2	29 12.1	6 59.7
9 F	7 13 19	18 30 41	2♊27 52	9♊18 55	12 4.1	25 37.7	0 27.3	17 4.1	23 57.1	14 2.4	7 33.6	29 14.3	7 1.6
10 Sa	7 17 16	19 31 49	16 7 31	22 53 20	11 55.9	26 46.2	29♑56.1	17 51.4	24 10.2	14 5.0	7 36.9	29 16.6	7 3.5
11 Su	7 21 12	20 32 56	29 36 5	6♋15 31	11 46.6	27 56.8	29 23.3	18 38.7	24 23.3	14 7.7	7 40.3	29 18.8	7 5.3
12 M	7 25 9	21 34 3	12♋51 20	19 23 22	11 37.3	29 9.5	28 49.3	19 26.0	24 36.5	14 10.5	7 43.7	29 21.1	7 7.2
13 Tu	7 29 5	22 35 10	25 51 26	2♌15 28	11 28.9	0♑23.9	28 14.1	20 13.4	24 49.8	14 13.4	7 47.1	29 23.4	7 9.0
14 W	7 33 2	23 36 16	8♌35 25	14 51 21	11 22.2	1 40.0	27 38.1	21 0.7	25 3.1	14 16.4	7 50.6	29 25.6	7 10.8
15 Th	7 36 58	24 37 22	21 3 25	27 11 47	11 17.7	2 57.6	27 1.6	21 48.0	25 16.5	14 19.5	7 54.0	29 27.9	7 12.6
16 F	7 40 55	25 38 28	3♍16 45	9♍18 41	11D 15.5	4 16.5	26 24.7	22 35.3	25 29.9	14 22.7	7 57.4	29 30.2	7 14.3
17 Sa	7 44 51	26 39 33	15 17 58	21 15 5	11 15.2	5 36.6	25 47.7	23 22.7	25 43.4	14 26.0	8 0.9	29 32.5	7 16.0
18 Su	7 48 48	27 40 38	27 10 33	3♎ 4 57	11 16.3	6 57.9	25 10.9	24 10.0	25 56.9	14 29.4	8 4.3	29 34.7	7 17.7
19 M	7 52 45	28 41 42	8♎58 51	14 52 54	11 17.9	8 20.2	24 34.5	24 57.4	26 10.5	14 32.8	8 7.8	29 37.0	7 19.4
20 Tu	7 56 41	29 42 47	20 47 44	26 44 2	11R 19.3	9 43.6	23 58.9	25 44.7	26 24.1	14 36.4	8 11.3	29 39.3	7 21.0
21 W	8 0 38	0♒43 51	2♏42 27	8♏43 38	11 19.7	11 7.8	23 24.2	26 32.0	26 37.8	14 40.1	8 14.8	29 41.6	7 22.6
22 Th	8 4 34	1 44 54	14 48 12	20 56 46	11 18.7	12 33.0	22 50.7	27 19.4	26 51.5	14 43.9	8 18.3	29 43.8	7 24.2
23 F	8 8 31	2 45 57	27 9 53	3♐28 3	11 15.9	13 59.0	22 18.6	28 6.7	27 5.3	14 47.7	8 21.8	29 46.1	7 25.8
24 Sa	8 12 27	3 47 0	9♐51 40	16 21 3	11 11.5	15 25.8	21 48.0	28 54.0	27 19.1	14 51.7	8 25.3	29 48.4	7 27.3
25 Su	8 16 24	4 48 2	22 56 25	29 37 53	11 5.9	16 53.4	21 19.2	29 41.4	27 33.0	14 55.7	8 28.8	29 50.7	7 28.8
26 M	8 20 20	5 49 4	6♑25 23	13♑18 44	10 59.8	18 21.8	20 52.3	0♓28.7	27 46.9	14 59.8	8 32.3	29 52.9	7 30.3
27 Tu	8 24 17	6 50 5	20 17 38	27 21 37	10 54.0	19 50.9	20 27.5	1 16.0	28 0.8	15 4.0	8 35.8	29 55.2	7 31.8
28 W	8 28 14	7 51 5	4♒30 7	11♒42 27	10 49.2	21 20.7	20 4.8	2 3.4	28 14.8	15 8.4	8 39.3	29 57.5	7 33.2
29 Th	8 32 10	8 52 5	18 57 50	26 15 29	10 45.9	22 51.2	19 44.4	2 50.7	28 28.8	15 12.7	8 42.8	29 59.7	7 34.6
30 F	8 36 7	9 53 3	3♓34 33	10♓54 13	10D 44.3	24 22.4	19 26.4	3 38.0	28 42.9	15 17.2	8 46.3	0♒ 2.0	7 36.0
31 Sa	8 40 3	10 54 0	18 13 41	25 32 14	10 44.3	25 54.4	19 10.7	4 25.3	28 57.0	15 21.8	8 49.8	0 4.2	7 37.3

LONGITUDE — FEBRUARY 1998

Day	Sid.Time	☉	0 hr ☽	Noon ☽	True ☊	☿	♀	♂	♃	♄	♅	♆	♇
1 Su	8 44 0	11♒54 56	2♈49 13	10♈ 4 5	10♍45.4	27♑27.0	18♑57.4	5♓12.6	29♒11.1	15♈26.4	8♒53.4	0♒ 6.5	7♐38.6
2 M	8 47 56	12 55 51	17 16 20	24 25 38	10 46.9	29 0.3	18R 46.6	5 59.8	29 25.2	15 31.2	8 56.9	0 8.7	7 39.9
3 Tu	8 51 53	13 56 44	1♉31 42	8♉34 19	10R 48.2	0♒34.4	18 38.3	6 47.1	29 39.4	15 36.0	9 0.4	0 11.0	7 41.1
4 W	8 55 49	14 57 36	15 33 22	22 28 46	10 48.7	2 9.2	18 32.4	7 34.3	29 53.6	15 40.8	9 3.9	0 13.2	7 42.3
5 Th	8 59 46	15 58 26	29 20 30	6♊ 8 35	10 48.0	3 44.7	18D 29.0	8 21.5	0♓ 7.8	15 45.8	9 7.4	0 15.4	7 43.5
6 F	9 3 43	16 59 15	12♊53 2	19 33 54	10 46.2	5 20.9	18 28.1	9 8.7	0 22.0	15 50.9	9 10.9	0 17.6	7 44.7
7 Sa	9 7 39	18 0 3	26 11 13	2♋45 5	10 43.4	6 57.9	18 29.5	9 55.9	0 36.3	15 56.0	9 14.3	0 19.8	7 45.8
8 Su	9 11 36	19 0 49	9♋15 32	15 42 38	10 40.0	8 35.6	18 33.4	10 43.1	0 50.6	16 1.2	9 17.8	0 22.0	7 46.9
9 M	9 15 32	20 1 34	22 6 26	28 27 2	10 36.6	10 14.1	18 39.5	11 30.3	1 4.9	16 6.4	9 21.3	0 24.2	7 47.9
10 Tu	9 19 29	21 2 17	4♌44 28	10♌58 51	10 33.6	11 53.5	18 48.0	12 17.4	1 19.2	16 11.8	9 24.7	0 26.3	7 48.9
11 W	9 23 25	22 2 59	17 10 17	23 18 54	10 31.3	13 33.6	18 58.7	13 4.5	1 33.6	16 17.2	9 28.2	0 28.5	7 49.9
12 Th	9 27 22	23 3 40	29 24 49	5♍28 16	10D 29.9	15 14.5	19 11.6	13 51.6	1 47.9	16 22.7	9 31.6	0 30.6	7 50.9
13 F	9 31 18	24 4 19	11♍29 25	17 28 33	10 29.5	16 56.3	19 26.6	14 38.7	2 2.3	16 28.2	9 35.1	0 32.8	7 51.8
14 Sa	9 35 15	25 4 57	23 25 55	29 21 53	10 30.0	18 38.9	19 43.6	15 25.7	2 16.7	16 33.8	9 38.5	0 34.9	7 52.7
15 Su	9 39 11	26 5 33	5♎16 47	11♎11 2	10 31.0	20 22.4	20 2.6	16 12.7	2 31.1	16 39.5	9 41.9	0 37.0	7 53.5
16 M	9 43 8	27 6 8	17 5 4	22 59 21	10 32.4	22 6.7	20 23.6	16 59.7	2 45.5	16 45.3	9 45.3	0 39.1	7 54.4
17 Tu	9 47 5	28 6 42	28 54 24	4♏50 45	10 33.7	23 52.0	20 46.4	17 46.7	2 59.9	16 51.1	9 48.7	0 41.2	7 55.1
18 W	9 51 1	29 7 15	10♏48 57	16 49 35	10 34.7	25 38.1	21 11.1	18 33.7	3 14.4	16 57.0	9 52.0	0 43.3	7 55.9
19 Th	9 54 58	0♓ 7 47	22 53 13	29 0 28	10R 35.3	27 25.2	21 37.4	19 20.6	3 28.8	17 2.9	9 55.4	0 45.3	7 56.6
20 F	9 58 54	1 8 17	5♐11 53	11♐28 2	10 35.3	29 13.1	22 5.5	20 7.5	3 43.2	17 8.9	9 58.7	0 47.3	7 57.3
21 Sa	10 2 51	2 8 46	17 49 26	24 16 32	10 35.0	1♓ 1.9	22 35.1	20 54.4	3 57.7	17 15.0	10 2.1	0 49.4	7 58.0
22 Su	10 6 47	3 9 14	0♑49 45	7♑29 23	10 34.3	2 51.6	23 6.2	21 41.3	4 12.2	17 21.1	10 5.4	0 51.4	7 58.6
23 M	10 10 44	4 9 40	14 15 38	21 8 34	10 33.5	4 42.2	23 38.9	22 28.1	4 26.6	17 27.3	10 8.7	0 53.4	7 59.2
24 Tu	10 14 40	5 10 5	28 8 8	5♒14 6	10 32.8	6 33.6	24 13.0	23 14.9	4 41.1	17 33.5	10 11.9	0 55.3	7 59.7
25 W	10 18 37	6 10 28	12♒26 4	19 43 29	10 32.3	8 25.7	24 48.4	24 1.7	4 55.5	17 39.8	10 15.2	0 57.3	8 0.2
26 Th	10 22 34	7 10 50	27 5 39	4♓31 42	10D 32.0	10 18.6	25 25.1	24 48.5	5 10.0	17 46.2	10 18.4	0 59.2	8 0.7
27 F	10 26 30	8 11 10	12♓ 0 41	19 31 32	10 31.9	12 12.2	26 3.1	25 35.2	5 24.4	17 52.6	10 21.6	1 1.1	8 1.2
28 Sa	10 30 27	9 11 29	27 3 9	4♈34 26	10 32.0	14 6.3	26 42.3	26 21.9	5 38.9	17 59.1	10 24.8	1 3.0	8 1.6

Astro Data

	Dy Hr Mn
☽0N	4 20:19
☽0S	18 15:28
☽0N	1 3:34
♃⚺♆	5 15:11
♀ D	5 21:26
♃∠♄	9 4:06
☽0S	14 23:37
☽0N	28 12:51

Planet Ingress

		Dy Hr Mn
♀	♑	9 21:03
☿	♑	12 16:20
☉	♒	20 6:46
♂	♓	25 9:26
♆	♒	29 2:45
☿	♒	2 15:15
♃	♓	4 10:52
☉	♓	18 20:55
☿	♓	20 10:22

Last Aspect / ☽ Ingress

Last Aspect Dy Hr Mn		☽ Ingress	Dy Hr Mn
1 21:07	♃ ☌	♓	2 9:56
4 11:08	♆ ⚹	♈	4 12:43
6 14:25	♆ □	♉	6 15:52
8 18:21	♆ △	♊	8 19:42
10 20:45	☿ ☍	♋	11 0:43
13 6:38	♆ ☍	♌	13 7:45
15 8:23	♃ ☍	♍	15 17:31
18 4:54	♆ △	♎	18 5:44
20 17:56	♆ □	♏	20 18:34
23 5:00	♆ ⚹	♐	23 5:25
25 8:26	♃ ⚹	♑	25 12:39
27 16:21	♆ ☌	♒	27 16:27
29 15:54	♃ ☌	♓	29 18:08
31 14:06	☿ ⚹	♈	31 19:21

Last Aspect / ☽ Ingress

Last Aspect Dy Hr Mn		☽ Ingress	Dy Hr Mn
2 20:46	♃ ⚹	♉	2 21:25
4 5:08	♀ △	♊	5 1:09
6 7:58	☉ △	♋	7 6:57
8 17:28	♀ ☍	♌	9 14:57
11 10:23	☉ ☍	♍	12 1:09
13 16:20	♀ △	♎	14 13:17
16 22:14	☉ △	♏	17 2:13
19 10:25	☿ □	♐	19 13:56
21 6:08	♂ □	♑	21 22:30
23 17:00	♀ ☌	♒	24 3:10
25 8:41	♄ ⚹	♓	26 4:42
27 23:25	♀ ⚹	♈	28 4:42

☽ Phases & Eclipses

Dy Hr Mn		
5 14:18	☽	15♈03
12 17:24	○	22♋18
20 19:40	☽	0♏33
28 6:01	●	8♒06
3 22:53	☽	14♉55
11 10:23	○	22♌29
19 15:27	☽	0♐47
26 17:26	●	7♓55
26 17:28:26	● T	4'09"

Astro Data

1 JANUARY 1998
Julian Day # 35795
Delta T 61.1 sec
SVP 05♓17'20"
Obliquity 23°26'13"
⚷ Chiron 15♏31.1
☽ Mean ☊ 13♍43.5

1 FEBRUARY 1998
Julian Day # 35826
Delta T 61.1 sec
SVP 05♓17'15"
Obliquity 23°26'14"
⚷ Chiron 17♏58.8
☽ Mean ☊ 12♍05.0

MARCH 1998 — LONGITUDE

Day	Sid.Time	☉	0 hr ☽	Noon ☽	True ☊	☿	♀	♂	♃	♄	♅	♆	♇
1 Su	10 34 23	10♓11 45	12♈ 4 18	19♈31 45	10♍32.0	16♓ 0.9	27♑22.6	27♓ 8.6	5♓53.3	18♈ 5.6	10♒28.0	1♒ 4.9	8♐ 1.9
2 M	10 38 20	11 12 0	26 55 54	4♉15 59	10R 32.0	17 55.8	28 4.0	27 55.2	6 7.8	18 12.1	10 31.1	1 6.8	8 2.3
3 Tu	10 42 16	12 12 13	11♉31 22	18 41 36	10 31.9	19 50.9	28 46.5	28 41.8	6 22.2	18 18.7	10 34.3	1 8.6	8 2.6
4 W	10 46 13	13 12 23	25 46 21	2♊45 25	10 31.7	21 46.0	29 30.0	29 28.4	6 36.6	18 25.4	10 37.4	1 10.4	8 2.8
5 Th	10 50 9	14 12 32	9♊38 46	16 26 27	10D 31.6	23 40.8	0♒14.5	0♈14.9	6 51.0	18 32.1	10 40.4	1 12.2	8 3.1
6 F	10 54 6	15 12 38	23 8 37	29 45 28	10 31.6	25 35.0	0 59.9	1 1.4	7 5.4	18 38.8	10 43.5	1 14.0	8 3.3
7 Sa	10 58 3	16 12 42	6♋17 18	12♋44 25	10 31.9	27 28.4	1 46.2	1 47.9	7 19.8	18 45.6	10 46.5	1 15.8	8 3.4
8 Su	11 1 59	17 12 44	19 7 10	25 25 53	10 32.5	29 20.7	2 33.4	2 34.3	7 34.2	18 52.5	10 49.5	1 17.5	8 3.6
9 M	11 5 56	18 12 44	1♌40 56	7♌52 40	10 33.2	1♈11.4	3 21.5	3 20.7	7 48.5	18 59.3	10 52.5	1 19.2	8 3.7
10 Tu	11 9 52	19 12 42	14 1 24	20 7 28	10 34.1	3 0.2	4 10.3	4 7.0	8 2.8	19 6.3	10 55.4	1 20.9	8 3.7
11 W	11 13 49	20 12 38	26 11 11	2♍12 50	10 34.8	4 46.5	4 59.9	4 53.3	8 17.1	19 13.2	10 58.3	1 22.6	8R 3.7
12 Th	11 17 45	21 12 32	8♍12 41	14 11 1	10R 35.1	6 30.0	5 50.3	5 39.6	8 31.4	19 20.2	11 1.2	1 24.2	8 3.7
13 F	11 21 42	22 12 23	20 8 5	26 4 8	10 34.9	8 10.1	6 41.3	6 25.8	8 45.7	19 27.2	11 4.1	1 25.8	8 3.7
14 Sa	11 25 38	23 12 13	1♎59 25	7♎54 11	10 34.1	9 46.3	7 33.1	7 12.0	8 59.9	19 34.3	11 6.9	1 27.4	8 3.6
15 Su	11 29 35	24 12 1	13 48 41	19 43 14	10 32.6	11 18.1	8 25.5	7 58.2	9 14.2	19 41.4	11 9.7	1 29.0	8 3.5
16 M	11 33 32	25 11 47	25 38 5	1♏33 35	10 30.5	12 45.0	9 18.6	8 44.3	9 28.3	19 48.5	11 12.5	1 30.5	8 3.4
17 Tu	11 37 28	26 11 31	7♏30 2	13 27 50	10 28.0	14 6.5	10 12.3	9 30.4	9 42.5	19 55.7	11 15.2	1 32.0	8 3.2
18 W	11 41 25	27 11 13	19 27 21	25 29 0	10 25.5	15 22.2	11 6.6	10 16.4	9 56.7	20 2.9	11 17.9	1 33.5	8 3.0
19 Th	11 45 21	28 10 54	1♐33 13	7♐40 29	10 23.3	16 31.7	12 1.5	11 2.4	10 10.8	20 10.1	11 20.6	1 35.0	8 2.7
20 F	11 49 18	29 10 32	13 51 15	20 6 2	10 21.7	17 34.5	12 56.9	11 48.3	10 24.9	20 17.3	11 23.2	1 36.4	8 2.4
21 Sa	11 53 14	0♈10 10	26 25 19	2♑49 34	10D 20.9	18 30.3	13 52.8	12 34.2	10 38.9	20 24.6	11 25.8	1 37.8	8 2.1
22 Su	11 57 11	1 9 45	9♑19 16	15 54 48	10 21.1	19 18.9	14 49.3	13 20.1	10 52.9	20 31.9	11 28.4	1 39.2	8 1.8
23 M	12 1 7	2 9 19	22 36 33	29 24 48	10 22.0	20 0.1	15 46.2	14 6.0	11 6.9	20 39.3	11 30.9	1 40.6	8 1.4
24 Tu	12 5 4	3 8 51	6♒19 43	13♒21 22	10 23.5	20 33.5	16 43.7	14 51.7	11 20.9	20 46.6	11 33.5	1 41.9	8 1.0
25 W	12 9 0	4 8 21	20 29 40	27 44 20	10 24.9	20 59.2	17 41.5	15 37.5	11 34.8	20 54.0	11 35.9	1 43.2	8 0.5
26 Th	12 12 57	5 7 49	5♓ 4 57	12♓30 53	10R 25.7	21 17.0	18 39.8	16 23.2	11 48.7	21 1.4	11 38.3	1 44.5	8 0.1
27 F	12 16 54	6 7 15	20 1 19	27 35 17	10 25.5	21R 27.1	19 38.5	17 8.9	12 2.6	21 8.8	11 40.7	1 45.7	7 59.5
28 Sa	12 20 50	7 6 40	5♈11 39	12♈49 11	10 24.0	21 29.5	20 37.7	17 54.5	12 16.4	21 16.3	11 43.1	1 46.9	7 59.0
29 Su	12 24 47	8 6 2	20 26 34	28 2 31	10 21.2	21 24.5	21 37.2	18 40.1	12 30.1	21 23.7	11 45.4	1 48.1	7 58.4
30 M	12 28 43	9 5 22	5♉35 48	13♉ 5 13	10 17.4	21 12.3	22 37.0	19 25.6	12 43.8	21 31.2	11 47.7	1 49.2	7 57.8
31 Tu	12 32 40	10 4 40	20 29 48	27 48 42	10 13.1	20 53.4	23 37.2	20 11.1	12 57.5	21 38.7	11 49.9	1 50.4	7 57.2

APRIL 1998 — LONGITUDE

Day	Sid.Time	☉	0 hr ☽	Noon ☽	True ☊	☿	♀	♂	♃	♄	♅	♆	♇
1 W	12 36 36	11♈ 3 56	5♊ 1 16	12♊ 7 6	10♍ 9.1	20♈28.2	24♒37.8	20♈56.5	13♓11.1	21♈46.2	11♒52.1	1♒51.5	7♐56.5
2 Th	12 40 33	12 3 10	19 5 55	25 57 41	10R 5.9	19R 57.4	25 38.7	21 41.9	13 24.7	21 53.7	11 54.3	1 52.5	7R 55.8
3 F	12 44 29	13 2 21	2♋42 30	9♋20 36	10D 4.1	19 21.6	26 39.9	22 27.3	13 38.3	22 1.3	11 56.4	1 53.6	7 55.1
4 Sa	12 48 26	14 1 30	15 52 19	22 18 6	10 3.6	18 41.7	27 41.4	23 12.6	13 51.7	22 8.8	11 58.5	1 54.6	7 54.3
5 Su	12 52 23	15 0 37	28 38 27	4♌53 52	10 4.4	17 58.5	28 43.3	23 57.8	14 5.2	22 16.4	12 0.5	1 55.5	7 53.5
6 M	12 56 19	15 59 41	11♌ 4 54	17 12 8	10 5.9	17 12.9	29 45.4	24 43.0	14 18.5	22 23.9	12 2.5	1 56.5	7 52.7
7 Tu	13 0 16	16 58 43	23 16 6	29 17 19	10 7.6	16 25.8	0♓47.8	25 28.2	14 31.9	22 31.5	12 4.4	1 57.4	7 51.9
8 W	13 4 12	17 57 43	5♍16 17	11♍13 30	10R 8.6	15 38.2	1 50.4	26 13.3	14 45.1	22 39.1	12 6.4	1 58.3	7 51.0
9 Th	13 8 9	18 56 40	17 9 24	23 4 22	10 8.5	14 51.1	2 53.4	26 58.3	14 58.3	22 46.7	12 8.2	1 59.1	7 50.1
10 F	13 12 5	19 55 36	28 58 46	4♎52 58	10 6.6	14 5.2	3 56.6	27 43.3	15 11.5	22 54.3	12 10.0	1 59.9	7 49.2
11 Sa	13 16 2	20 54 29	10♎47 13	16 41 50	10 2.8	13 21.3	5 0.0	28 28.2	15 24.6	23 1.9	12 11.8	2 0.7	7 48.2
12 Su	13 19 58	21 53 20	22 37 2	28 33 4	9 57.0	12 40.3	6 3.7	29 13.1	15 37.6	23 9.5	12 13.6	2 1.5	7 47.2
13 M	13 23 55	22 52 9	4♏30 7	10♏28 24	9 49.7	12 2.8	7 7.6	29 58.0	15 50.6	23 17.1	12 15.2	2 2.2	7 46.2
14 Tu	13 27 52	23 50 56	16 28 8	22 29 30	9 41.5	11 29.1	8 11.8	0♉42.8	16 3.5	23 24.7	12 16.9	2 2.9	7 45.2
15 W	13 31 48	24 49 42	28 32 44	4♐38 4	9 33.0	10 59.9	9 16.2	1 27.5	16 16.4	23 32.3	12 18.5	2 3.5	7 44.1
16 Th	13 35 45	25 48 25	10♐45 46	16 56 5	9 25.2	10 35.4	10 20.8	2 12.2	16 29.2	23 39.9	12 20.1	2 4.2	7 43.1
17 F	13 39 41	26 47 7	23 9 21	29 25 53	9 18.9	10 15.8	11 25.6	2 56.9	16 41.9	23 47.5	12 21.6	2 4.8	7 42.0
18 Sa	13 43 38	27 45 47	5♑46 2	12♑10 11	9 14.4	10 1.3	12 30.6	3 41.5	16 54.5	23 55.1	12 23.0	2 5.3	7 40.8
19 Su	13 47 34	28 44 26	18 38 43	25 12 0	9D 12.1	9 51.9	13 35.8	4 26.1	17 7.1	24 2.6	12 24.5	2 5.8	7 39.7
20 M	13 51 31	29 43 2	1♒50 25	8♒34 18	9 11.5	9D 47.7	14 41.2	5 10.6	17 19.6	24 10.2	12 25.8	2 6.3	7 38.5
21 Tu	13 55 27	0♉41 38	15 23 56	22 19 33	9 12.2	9 48.7	15 46.8	5 55.0	17 32.1	24 17.8	12 27.2	2 6.8	7 37.3
22 W	13 59 24	1 40 11	29 21 16	6♓29 3	9R 13.2	9 54.7	16 52.5	6 39.5	17 44.4	24 25.4	12 28.4	2 7.2	7 36.1
23 Th	14 3 21	2 38 43	13♓42 47	21 2 7	9 13.4	10 5.6	17 58.5	7 23.8	17 56.7	24 32.9	12 29.7	2 7.6	7 34.8
24 F	14 7 17	3 37 13	28 26 32	5♈55 22	9 12.0	10 21.3	19 4.6	8 8.1	18 8.9	24 40.5	12 30.8	2 8.0	7 33.6
25 Sa	14 11 14	4 35 41	13♈27 41	21 2 26	9 8.2	10 41.7	20 10.8	8 52.4	18 21.1	24 48.0	12 32.0	2 8.3	7 32.3
26 Su	14 15 10	5 34 8	28 38 26	6♉14 21	9 2.1	11 6.6	21 17.2	9 36.6	18 33.1	24 55.6	12 33.1	2 8.6	7 31.0
27 M	14 19 7	6 32 33	13♉48 54	21 20 45	8 54.1	11 35.8	22 23.8	10 20.8	18 45.1	25 3.1	12 34.1	2 8.9	7 29.6
28 Tu	14 23 3	7 30 56	28 48 42	6♊11 38	8 45.2	12 9.1	23 30.4	11 4.9	18 57.0	25 10.6	12 35.1	2 9.1	7 28.3
29 W	14 27 0	8 29 17	13♊28 41	20 39 7	8 36.4	12 46.3	24 37.3	11 49.0	19 8.8	25 18.1	12 36.0	2 9.3	7 26.9
30 Th	14 30 56	9 27 37	27 42 28	4♋38 26	8 28.7	13 27.4	25 44.2	12 33.0	19 20.5	25 25.5	12 36.9	2 9.5	7 25.5

Astro Data Dy Hr Mn	Planet Ingress Dy Hr Mn	Last Aspect Dy Hr Mn	☽ Ingress Dy Hr Mn	Last Aspect Dy Hr Mn	☽ Ingress Dy Hr Mn	☽ Phases & Eclipses Dy Hr Mn
♂0N 6 16:12	♀ ♒ 4 16:14	2 1:57 ♀ □	♉ 2 5:00	2 12:22 ♀ △	♋ 2 19:10	5 8:41 ☽ 14♊34
☿0N 8 13:09	♂ ♈ 4 16:18	4 6:44 ♀ △	♊ 4 7:15	4 14:34 ♂ □	♌ 5 2:36	13 4:34 ○ 22♍24
♃□♇ 10 1:31	☿ ♈ 8 8:28	6 5:09 ☿ □	♋ 6 12:27	7 4:40 ♂ △	♍ 7 13:25	13 4:20 ☍ A 0.709
♇ R 11 4:53	☉ ♈ 20 19:55	7 23:32 ♄ □	♌ 8 20:46	8 19:30 ♃ ☍	♎ 10 2:04	21 7:38 ☽ 0♑29
☽0S 14 6:15		10 10:05 ♄ △	♍ 11 7:35	12 14:15 ♂ ☍	♏ 12 14:56	28 3:14 ● 7♈15
♃⊻♅ 25 2:17	♀ ♓ 6 5:38	13 4:34 ☉ ☍	♎ 13 19:58	13 23:10 ♃ △	♐ 15 2:52	
☽0N 27 23:47	♂ ♉ 13 1:05	15 12:04 ♄ ☍	♏ 16 8:51	17 7:32 ☉ △	♑ 17 13:05	3 20:18 ☽ 13♋52
☿ R 27 19:42	☉ ♉ 20 6:57	18 16:45 ☉ △	♐ 18 20:56	19 19:53 ☉ □	♒ 19 20:41	11 22:23 ○ 21♎49
		20 12:29 ♄ △	♑ 21 6:43	21 15:31 ♄ ⚹	♓ 22 1:06	19 19:53 ☽ 29♑33
♄⚼♇ 9 9:39		22 20:29 ♄ □	♒ 23 13:02	23 7:34 ♀ ☌	♈ 24 2:30	26 11:41 ● 6♉03
☽0S 10 12:22		25 0:50 ☿ ⚹	♓ 25 15:43	25 18:05 ♄ ☌	♉ 26 2:09	
♃∠♆ 18 21:28		26 11:02 ♃ ☌	♈ 27 15:49	27 14:47 ♀ ⚹	♊ 28 1:55	
☿ D 20 7:31		29 1:59 ♀ ⚹	♉ 29 15:06	29 20:20 ♀ □	♋ 30 3:57	
☽0N 24 10:50		31 5:29 ♀ □	♊ 31 15:37			

Astro Data

1 MARCH 1998
Julian Day # 35854
Delta T 61.2 sec
SVP 05♓17'12"
Obliquity 23°26'14"
⚷ Chiron 18♏47.0
☽ Mean ☊ 10♍36.0

1 APRIL 1998
Julian Day # 35885
Delta T 61.2 sec
SVP 05♓17'10"
Obliquity 23°26'14"
⚷ Chiron 17♏59.8R
☽ Mean ☊ 8♍57.5

LONGITUDE — MAY 1998

Day	Sid.Time	☉	0 hr ☽	Noon ☽	True ☊	☿	♀	♂	♃	♄	♅	♆	♇
1 F	14 34 53	10♉25 54	11♋26 59	18♋ 8 13	8♍23.1	14♈12.1	26♓51.3	13♉16.9	19♓32.2	25♈33.0	12♒37.8	2♒ 9.6	7♐24.1
2 Sa	14 38 50	11 24 9	24 42 24	1♌ 9 56	8R19.7	15 0.4	27 58.5	14 0.8	19 43.7	25 40.4	12 38.6	2 9.7	7R22.7
3 Su	14 42 46	12 22 22	7♌31 19	13 47 6	8D18.3	15 51.9	29 5.9	14 44.7	19 55.2	25 47.8	12 39.3	2 9.8	7 21.3
4 M	14 46 43	13 20 33	19 57 55	26 4 25	8 18.4	16 46.7	0♈13.3	15 28.5	20 6.5	25 55.2	12 40.0	2R 9.8	7 19.9
5 Tu	14 50 39	14 18 42	2♍ 7 16	8♍ 7 6	8R18.9	17 44.6	1 20.9	16 12.2	20 17.8	26 2.6	12 40.7	2 9.8	7 18.4
6 W	14 54 36	15 16 49	14 4 35	20 0 18	8 18.9	18 45.4	2 28.6	16 55.9	20 29.0	26 9.9	12 41.3	2 9.8	7 16.9
7 Th	14 58 32	16 14 54	25 54 50	1♎48 45	8 17.3	19 49.1	3 36.3	17 39.5	20 40.1	26 17.2	12 41.8	2 9.7	7 15.4
8 F	15 2 29	17 12 57	7♎42 31	13 36 36	8 13.5	20 55.6	4 44.2	18 23.1	20 51.0	26 24.5	12 42.3	2 9.6	7 13.9
9 Sa	15 6 25	18 10 59	19 31 23	25 27 13	8 7.1	22 4.8	5 52.2	19 6.6	21 1.9	26 31.8	12 42.8	2 9.5	7 12.4
10 Su	15 10 22	19 8 59	1♏24 25	7♏23 13	7 58.0	23 16.5	7 0.4	19 50.1	21 12.7	26 39.0	12 43.2	2 9.3	7 10.9
11 M	15 14 18	20 6 57	13 23 50	19 26 26	7 46.8	24 30.8	8 8.6	20 33.5	21 23.4	26 46.2	12 43.5	2 9.1	7 9.3
12 Tu	15 18 15	21 4 53	25 31 10	1♐38 8	7 34.2	25 47.6	9 16.9	21 16.9	21 34.0	26 53.4	12 43.8	2 8.9	7 7.8
13 W	15 22 12	22 2 48	7♐47 25	13 59 8	7 21.3	27 6.8	10 25.3	22 0.2	21 44.4	27 0.6	12 44.1	2 8.6	7 6.2
14 Th	15 26 8	23 0 42	20 13 21	26 30 10	7 9.2	28 28.4	11 33.8	22 43.5	21 54.8	27 7.7	12 44.3	2 8.3	7 4.6
15 F	15 30 5	23 58 34	2♑49 40	9♑12 1	6 58.9	29 52.3	12 42.4	23 26.7	22 5.1	27 14.8	12 44.4	2 8.0	7 3.1
16 Sa	15 34 1	24 56 25	15 37 21	22 5 51	6 51.2	1♉18.5	13 51.1	24 9.9	22 15.2	27 21.8	12 44.5	2 7.6	7 1.5
17 Su	15 37 58	25 54 14	28 37 44	5♒13 13	6 46.3	2 47.0	14 59.9	24 53.0	22 25.3	27 28.9	12R44.6	2 7.3	6 59.9
18 M	15 41 54	26 52 3	11♒52 33	18 35 59	6 43.9	4 17.7	16 8.8	25 36.1	22 35.2	27 35.8	12 44.6	2 6.8	6 58.3
19 Tu	15 45 51	27 49 50	25 23 45	2♓16 4	6 43.3	5 50.7	17 17.8	26 19.1	22 45.0	27 42.8	12 44.5	2 6.4	6 56.7
20 W	15 49 47	28 47 36	9♓13 5	16 14 53	6 43.3	7 25.9	18 26.8	27 2.0	22 54.7	27 49.7	12 44.5	2 5.9	6 55.1
21 Th	15 53 44	29 45 21	23 21 28	0♈32 42	6 42.6	9 3.3	19 35.9	27 45.0	23 4.3	27 56.6	12 44.3	2 5.4	6 53.4
22 F	15 57 41	0♊43 5	7♈48 18	15 7 51	6 40.2	10 42.9	20 45.2	28 27.8	23 13.8	28 3.4	12 44.1	2 4.9	6 51.8
23 Sa	16 1 37	1 40 48	22 30 45	29 56 15	6 35.3	12 24.7	21 54.4	29 10.6	23 23.1	28 10.2	12 43.9	2 4.3	6 50.2
24 Su	16 5 34	2 38 29	7♉23 25	14♉51 16	6 27.6	14 8.7	23 3.8	29 53.4	23 32.3	28 17.0	12 43.6	2 3.7	6 48.5
25 M	16 9 30	3 36 10	22 18 38	29 44 25	6 17.7	15 54.9	24 13.2	0♊36.1	23 41.4	28 23.7	12 43.3	2 3.1	6 46.9
26 Tu	16 13 27	4 33 50	7♊ 7 28	14♊26 43	6 6.5	17 43.3	25 22.7	1 18.8	23 50.4	28 30.3	12 42.9	2 2.4	6 45.3
27 W	16 17 23	5 31 28	21 41 12	28 50 9	5 55.2	19 33.9	26 32.3	2 1.4	23 59.2	28 37.0	12 42.4	2 1.7	6 43.6
28 Th	16 21 20	6 29 5	5♋52 54	12♋49 2	5 45.2	21 26.7	27 41.9	2 44.0	24 7.9	28 43.5	12 42.0	2 1.0	6 42.0
29 F	16 25 16	7 26 41	19 38 18	26 20 39	5 37.3	23 21.6	28 51.6	3 26.5	24 16.5	28 50.1	12 41.4	2 0.3	6 40.3
30 Sa	16 29 13	8 24 15	2♌56 11	9♌25 10	5 32.0	25 18.5	0♉ 1.4	4 8.9	24 25.0	28 56.6	12 40.8	1 59.5	6 38.7
31 Su	16 33 10	9 21 48	15 47 59	22 5 7	5 29.1	27 17.6	1 11.2	4 51.3	24 33.3	29 3.0	12 40.2	1 58.7	6 37.1

LONGITUDE — JUNE 1998

Day	Sid.Time	☉	0 hr ☽	Noon ☽	True ☊	☿	♀	♂	♃	♄	♅	♆	♇
1 M	16 37 6	10♊19 20	28♌17 7	4♍24 37	5♍28.1	29♉18.6	2♉21.0	5♊33.7	24♓41.4	29♈ 9.4	12♒39.6	1♒57.9	6♐35.4
2 Tu	16 41 3	11 16 50	10♍28 15	16 28 43	5R28.1	1♊21.5	3 30.9	6 16.0	24 49.5	29 15.7	12R38.8	1R57.0	6R33.8
3 W	16 44 59	12 14 19	22 26 41	28 22 50	5 27.8	3 26.2	4 40.9	6 58.2	24 57.4	29 22.0	12 38.1	1 56.1	6 32.2
4 Th	16 48 56	13 11 47	4♎17 49	10♎12 16	5 26.3	5 32.6	5 51.0	7 40.4	25 5.1	29 28.2	12 37.3	1 55.2	6 30.5
5 F	16 52 52	14 9 13	16 6 47	22 1 54	5 22.7	7 40.4	7 1.1	8 22.6	25 12.7	29 34.4	12 36.4	1 54.3	6 28.9
6 Sa	16 56 49	15 6 39	27 58 9	3♏55 59	5 16.5	9 49.5	8 11.2	9 4.7	25 20.2	29 40.5	12 35.5	1 53.3	6 27.3
7 Su	17 0 45	16 4 3	9♏55 46	15 57 53	5 7.8	11 59.7	9 21.4	9 46.7	25 27.5	29 46.5	12 34.6	1 52.4	6 25.7
8 M	17 4 42	17 1 26	22 2 34	28 10 3	4 56.9	14 10.8	10 31.7	10 28.7	25 34.7	29 52.6	12 33.6	1 51.3	6 24.1
9 Tu	17 8 39	17 58 48	4♐20 30	10♐33 59	4 44.5	16 22.5	11 42.0	11 10.6	25 41.7	29 58.5	12 32.5	1 50.3	6 22.5
10 W	17 12 35	18 56 10	16 50 35	23 10 17	4 31.9	18 34.5	12 52.4	11 52.5	25 48.6	0♉ 4.4	12 31.5	1 49.3	6 20.9
11 Th	17 16 32	19 53 30	29 33 4	5♑58 53	4 20.0	20 46.6	14 2.8	12 34.3	25 55.3	0 10.2	12 30.4	1 48.2	6 19.3
12 F	17 20 28	20 50 50	12♑27 40	18 59 20	4 9.9	22 58.5	15 13.3	13 16.1	26 1.9	0 16.0	12 29.2	1 47.1	6 17.7
13 Sa	17 24 25	21 48 10	25 33 51	2♒11 9	4 2.3	25 9.9	16 23.8	13 57.9	26 8.3	0 21.7	12 28.0	1 46.0	6 16.2
14 Su	17 28 21	22 45 28	8♒51 12	15 34 0	3 57.5	27 20.5	17 34.4	14 39.6	26 14.6	0 27.3	12 26.8	1 44.8	6 14.6
15 M	17 32 18	23 42 47	22 19 35	29 7 59	3D55.2	29 30.2	18 45.0	15 21.2	26 20.7	0 32.9	12 25.5	1 43.6	6 13.0
16 Tu	17 36 15	24 40 4	5♓59 14	12♓53 25	3 54.8	1♋38.7	19 55.7	16 2.8	26 26.6	0 38.4	12 24.2	1 42.4	6 11.5
17 W	17 40 11	25 37 22	19 50 33	26 50 40	3R55.1	3 45.7	21 6.5	16 44.4	26 32.4	0 43.9	12 22.8	1 41.2	6 10.0
18 Th	17 44 8	26 34 39	3♈53 43	10♈59 36	3 55.0	5 51.2	22 17.3	17 25.9	26 38.0	0 49.3	12 21.4	1 40.0	6 8.5
19 F	17 48 4	27 31 56	18 8 10	25 19 7	3 53.4	7 55.0	23 28.1	18 7.3	26 43.5	0 54.6	12 19.9	1 38.7	6 7.0
20 Sa	17 52 1	28 29 13	2♉32 5	9♉46 34	3 49.6	9 57.0	24 39.0	18 48.7	26 48.8	0 59.8	12 18.5	1 37.5	6 5.5
21 Su	17 55 57	29 26 29	17 2 0	24 17 41	3 43.4	11 57.0	25 50.0	19 30.1	26 53.9	1 5.0	12 17.0	1 36.2	6 4.0
22 M	17 59 54	0♋23 46	1♊32 52	8♊46 43	3 35.2	13 55.1	27 1.0	20 11.4	26 58.8	1 10.1	12 15.4	1 34.8	6 2.5
23 Tu	18 3 50	1 21 2	15 58 27	23 7 15	3 25.7	15 51.0	28 12.0	20 52.7	27 3.6	1 15.1	12 13.8	1 33.5	6 1.1
24 W	18 7 47	2 18 18	0♋12 21	7♋13 6	3 16.2	17 44.9	29 23.1	21 33.9	27 8.2	1 20.1	12 12.2	1 32.2	5 59.7
25 Th	18 11 44	3 15 33	14 8 57	20 59 26	3 7.6	19 36.6	0♊34.2	22 15.1	27 12.6	1 25.0	12 10.5	1 30.8	5 58.3
26 F	18 15 40	4 12 48	27 44 16	4♌23 18	3 0.9	21 26.1	1 45.4	22 56.2	27 16.9	1 29.8	12 8.8	1 29.4	5 56.9
27 Sa	18 19 37	5 10 3	10♌56 32	17 24 2	2 56.4	23 13.4	2 56.6	23 37.3	27 21.0	1 34.6	12 7.1	1 28.0	5 55.5
28 Su	18 23 33	6 7 17	23 46 5	0♍ 2 59	2D54.2	24 58.5	4 7.9	24 18.3	27 24.9	1 39.2	12 5.3	1 26.6	5 54.1
29 M	18 27 30	7 4 31	6♍15 10	12 23 8	2 53.8	26 41.4	5 19.2	24 59.3	27 28.6	1 43.8	12 3.5	1 25.2	5 52.8
30 Tu	18 31 26	8 1 44	18 27 25	24 28 39	2 54.6	28 22.1	6 30.5	25 40.2	27 32.1	1 48.3	12 1.7	1 23.7	5 51.4

Astro Data

	Dy Hr Mn
♆ R	4 10:39
♀0N	6 20:40
☽0S	7 19:11
♅ R	17 15:01
☽0N	21 20:27
☽0S	4 3:19
☽0N	18 4:04
♃∠♅	24 15:34
♄□♆	25 22:26

Planet Ingress

	Dy Hr Mn
♀ ♈	3 19:16
☿ ♉	15 2:10
☉ ♊	21 6:05
♂ ♊	24 3:42
♀ ♉	29 23:32
☿ ♊	1 8:07
♄ ♉	9 6:07
☿ ♋	15 5:33
☉ ♋	21 14:03
♀ ♊	24 12:27
☿ ♌	30 23:52

Last Aspect / ☽ Ingress (May)

Last Aspect Dy Hr Mn		☽ Ingress Dy Hr Mn
2 6:37	♀ △	♌ 2 9:49
4 11:49	♄ △	♍ 4 19:47
6 13:11	♃ ☍	♎ 7 8:19
9 14:19	♄ ☍	♏ 9 21:10
11 16:05	♃ △	♐ 12 8:48
14 17:42	☿ △	♑ 14 18:39
16 21:53	♄ □	♒ 17 2:30
19 4:35	☉ □	♓ 19 8:03
21 7:44	♂ ⚹	♈ 21 11:06
23 9:13	♄ ☌	♉ 23 12:06
25 2:15	♃ ⚹	♊ 25 12:25
27 11:43	♄ ⚹	♋ 27 13:58
29 18:09	♀ □	♌ 29 18:38

Last Aspect / ☽ Ingress (June)

Last Aspect Dy Hr Mn		☽ Ingress Dy Hr Mn
1 2:24	☿ □	♍ 1 3:21
3 5:08	♃ ☍	♎ 3 15:17
6 3:28	♄ ☍	♏ 6 4:06
8 7:00	♃ △	♐ 8 15:34
10 17:08	♃ □	♑ 11 0:50
13 1:03	♃ ⚹	♒ 13 8:03
15 2:38	☉ △	♓ 15 13:31
17 11:33	♃ ☌	♈ 17 17:23
19 16:48	☉ ⚹	♉ 19 19:47
21 16:24	♃ ⚹	♊ 21 21:26
23 18:46	♃ □	♋ 23 23:39
25 23:11	♃ △	♌ 26 4:04
28 1:05	♂ ⚹	♍ 28 11:54
30 22:57	☿ ⚹	♎ 30 23:05

☽ Phases & Eclipses

Dy Hr Mn	
3 10:04	☽ 12♌47
11 14:29	○ 20♏42
19 4:35	☽ 28♒01
25 19:32	● 4♊23
2 1:45	☽ 11♍21
10 4:18	○ 19♐06
17 10:38	☽ 26♓03
24 3:50	● 2♋27

Astro Data

1 MAY 1998
Julian Day # 35915
Delta T 61.3 sec
SVP 05♓17'07"
Obliquity 23°26'14"
⚷ Chiron 16♏01.3R
☽ Mean ☊ 7♍22.2

1 JUNE 1998
Julian Day # 35946
Delta T 61.3 sec
SVP 05♓17'03"
Obliquity 23°26'13"
⚷ Chiron 13♏47.5R
☽ Mean ☊ 5♍43.7

JULY 1998 LONGITUDE

Day	Sid.Time	☉	0 hr ☽	Noon ☽	True ☊	☿	♀	♂	♃	♄	♅	♆	♇
1 W	18 35 23	8♋58 57	0♎27 26	6♎24 25	2♍55.5	0♌ 0.6	7♊41.9	26♊21.1	27♓35.4	1♉52.7	11♒59.8	1♑22.3	5♐50.1
2 Th	18 39 19	9 56 9	12 20 15	18 15 35	2R 55.8	1 36.8	8 53.3	27 1.9	27 38.6	1 57.1	11R 58.0	1R 20.8	5R 48.9
3 F	18 43 16	10 53 21	24 11 3	0♏ 7 17	2 54.7	3 10.8	10 4.7	27 42.7	27 41.6	2 1.3	11 56.0	1 19.3	5 47.6
4 Sa	18 47 13	11 50 33	6♏ 4 50	12 4 16	2 51.8	4 42.5	11 16.2	28 23.4	27 44.4	2 5.5	11 54.1	1 17.8	5 46.3
5 Su	18 51 9	12 47 44	18 6 5	24 10 44	2 46.8	6 11.9	12 27.8	29 4.1	27 47.0	2 9.6	11 52.1	1 16.3	5 45.1
6 M	18 55 6	13 44 56	0♐18 36	6♐29 59	2 40.2	7 39.1	13 39.4	29 44.8	27 49.4	2 13.6	11 50.1	1 14.8	5 43.9
7 Tu	18 59 2	14 42 7	12 45 10	19 4 19	2 32.3	9 3.9	14 51.0	0♋25.4	27 51.6	2 17.6	11 48.1	1 13.2	5 42.7
8 W	19 2 59	15 39 18	25 27 32	1♑54 51	2 24.1	10 26.4	16 2.7	1 5.9	27 53.7	2 21.4	11 46.0	1 11.7	5 41.6
9 Th	19 6 55	16 36 29	8♑26 13	15 1 31	2 16.4	11 46.5	17 14.4	1 46.4	27 55.6	2 25.2	11 44.0	1 10.1	5 40.4
10 F	19 10 52	17 33 40	21 40 37	28 23 16	2 9.9	13 4.2	18 26.2	2 26.9	27 57.2	2 28.9	11 41.9	1 8.6	5 39.3
11 Sa	19 14 48	18 30 51	5♒ 9 15	11♒58 18	2 5.3	14 19.4	19 38.0	3 7.3	27 58.7	2 32.5	11 39.8	1 7.0	5 38.2
12 Su	19 18 45	19 28 3	18 50 7	25 44 25	2D 2.7	15 32.1	20 49.8	3 47.7	27 60.0	2 36.0	11 37.6	1 5.4	5 37.2
13 M	19 22 42	20 25 15	2♓40 56	9♓39 25	2 1.9	16 42.2	22 1.7	4 28.0	28 1.1	2 39.4	11 35.5	1 3.8	5 36.1
14 Tu	19 26 38	21 22 27	16 39 37	23 41 17	2 2.6	17 49.6	23 13.6	5 8.3	28 2.0	2 42.7	11 33.3	1 2.3	5 35.1
15 W	19 30 35	22 19 40	0♈44 15	7♈48 17	2 3.9	18 54.2	24 25.6	5 48.5	28 2.7	2 45.9	11 31.1	1 0.7	5 34.1
16 Th	19 34 31	23 16 54	14 53 11	21 58 45	2R 5.0	19 56.1	25 37.7	6 28.7	28 3.2	2 49.1	11 28.8	0 59.0	5 33.2
17 F	19 38 28	24 14 8	29 4 47	6♉11 0	2 5.1	20 54.9	26 49.7	7 8.9	28 3.5	2 52.1	11 26.6	0 57.4	5 32.2
18 Sa	19 42 24	25 11 23	13♉17 9	20 22 55	2 3.9	21 50.8	28 1.9	7 49.0	28R 3.6	2 55.1	11 24.3	0 55.8	5 31.3
19 Su	19 46 21	26 8 38	27 27 57	4♊31 52	2 1.0	22 43.5	29 14.0	8 29.1	28 3.5	2 57.9	11 22.1	0 54.2	5 30.4
20 M	19 50 17	27 5 54	11♊34 16	18 34 42	1 56.9	23 32.9	0♋26.2	9 9.1	28 3.2	3 0.7	11 19.8	0 52.6	5 29.6
21 Tu	19 54 14	28 3 12	25 32 46	2♋28 1	1 51.9	24 18.9	1 38.5	9 49.1	28 2.7	3 3.4	11 17.5	0 51.0	5 28.7
22 W	19 58 11	29 0 29	9♋20 1	16 8 26	1 46.8	25 1.3	2 50.8	10 29.0	28 2.1	3 6.0	11 15.2	0 49.3	5 27.9
23 Th	20 2 7	29 57 48	22 52 55	29 33 13	1 42.2	25 40.0	4 3.1	11 8.9	28 1.2	3 8.4	11 12.8	0 47.7	5 27.2
24 F	20 6 4	0♌55 7	6♌ 9 9	12♌40 34	1 38.7	26 14.8	5 15.5	11 48.8	28 0.1	3 10.8	11 10.5	0 46.1	5 26.4
25 Sa	20 10 0	1 52 26	19 7 28	25 29 54	1D 36.7	26 45.6	6 27.9	12 28.6	27 58.9	3 13.1	11 8.1	0 44.5	5 25.7
26 Su	20 13 57	2 49 46	1♍47 59	8♍ 1 56	1 36.0	27 12.2	7 40.4	13 8.4	27 57.4	3 15.3	11 5.8	0 42.8	5 25.0
27 M	20 17 53	3 47 7	14 12 2	20 18 38	1 36.6	27 34.4	8 52.9	13 48.1	27 55.7	3 17.4	11 3.4	0 41.2	5 24.4
28 Tu	20 21 50	4 44 28	26 22 8	2♎22 59	1 38.0	27 52.0	10 5.4	14 27.8	27 53.9	3 19.4	11 1.0	0 39.6	5 23.7
29 W	20 25 46	5 41 49	8♎21 42	14 18 49	1 39.7	28 4.9	11 18.0	15 7.4	27 51.8	3 21.2	10 58.7	0 38.0	5 23.1
30 Th	20 29 43	6 39 11	20 14 55	26 10 33	1 41.2	28 13.0	12 30.6	15 47.0	27 49.6	3 23.0	10 56.3	0 36.4	5 22.6
31 F	20 33 40	7 36 34	2♏ 6 20	8♏ 2 53	1R 42.1	28R 16.0	13 43.3	16 26.6	27 47.2	3 24.7	10 53.9	0 34.7	5 22.0

AUGUST 1998 LONGITUDE

Day	Sid.Time	☉	0 hr ☽	Noon ☽	True ☊	☿	♀	♂	♃	♄	♅	♆	♇
1 Sa	20 37 36	8♌33 57	14♏ 0 46	20♏ 0 37	1♍42.1	28♌14.0	14♋56.0	17♋ 6.1	27♓44.5	3♉26.3	10♒51.5	0♑33.1	5♐21.5
2 Su	20 41 33	9 31 21	26 2 58	2♐ 8 23	1R 41.1	28R 6.8	16 8.7	17 45.5	27R 41.7	3 27.8	10R 49.1	0R 31.5	5R 21.0
3 M	20 45 29	10 28 45	8♐17 21	14 30 19	1 39.2	27 54.3	17 21.5	18 25.0	27 38.7	3 29.2	10 46.7	0 29.9	5 20.6
4 Tu	20 49 26	11 26 10	20 47 41	27 9 46	1 36.7	27 36.7	18 34.3	19 4.3	27 35.6	3 30.4	10 44.3	0 28.3	5 20.2
5 W	20 53 22	12 23 36	3♑36 50	10♑ 9 1	1 33.9	27 14.1	19 47.2	19 43.7	27 32.2	3 31.6	10 41.9	0 26.8	5 19.8
6 Th	20 57 19	13 21 2	16 46 24	23 28 55	1 31.3	26 46.5	21 0.1	20 23.0	27 28.6	3 32.7	10 39.5	0 25.2	5 19.5
7 F	21 1 15	14 18 30	0♒16 29	7♒ 8 50	1 29.1	26 14.2	22 13.0	21 2.2	27 24.9	3 33.7	10 37.1	0 23.6	5 19.1
8 Sa	21 5 12	15 15 58	14 5 39	21 6 31	1 27.7	25 37.6	23 26.0	21 41.4	27 21.0	3 34.5	10 34.8	0 22.0	5 18.9
9 Su	21 9 9	16 13 28	28 10 58	5♓18 27	1D 27.1	24 57.2	24 39.0	22 20.6	27 16.9	3 35.3	10 32.4	0 20.5	5 18.6
10 M	21 13 5	17 10 58	12♓28 23	19 40 10	1 27.3	24 13.5	25 52.1	22 59.7	27 12.7	3 35.9	10 30.0	0 18.9	5 18.4
11 Tu	21 17 2	18 8 30	26 53 10	4♈ 6 48	1 28.0	23 27.1	27 5.2	23 38.8	27 8.2	3 36.5	10 27.6	0 17.4	5 18.2
12 W	21 20 58	19 6 3	11♈20 29	18 33 41	1 29.0	22 38.9	28 18.4	24 17.9	27 3.6	3 36.9	10 25.3	0 15.9	5 18.0
13 Th	21 24 55	20 3 37	25 45 53	2♉56 39	1 29.9	21 49.7	29 31.5	24 56.9	26 58.9	3 37.3	10 22.9	0 14.4	5 17.9
14 F	21 28 51	21 1 13	10♉ 5 35	17 12 22	1R 30.5	21 0.3	0♌44.8	25 35.9	26 53.9	3 37.5	10 20.6	0 12.9	5 17.8
15 Sa	21 32 48	21 58 51	24 16 43	1♊18 22	1 30.6	20 11.7	1 58.1	26 14.8	26 48.8	3R 37.7	10 18.2	0 11.4	5 17.7
16 Su	21 36 44	22 56 30	8♊17 9	15 12 53	1 30.3	19 25.0	3 11.4	26 53.7	26 43.6	3 37.7	10 15.9	0 9.9	5D 17.7
17 M	21 40 41	23 54 10	22 5 28	28 54 46	1 29.7	18 41.0	4 24.8	27 32.6	26 38.2	3 37.6	10 13.6	0 8.5	5 17.7
18 Tu	21 44 38	24 51 52	5♋40 44	12♋23 16	1 29.0	18 0.6	5 38.2	28 11.4	26 32.6	3 37.4	10 11.3	0 7.0	5 17.8
19 W	21 48 34	25 49 36	19 2 21	25 37 57	1 28.2	17 24.8	6 51.6	28 50.2	26 26.9	3 37.2	10 9.0	0 5.6	5 17.8
20 Th	21 52 31	26 47 21	2♌10 1	8♌38 35	1 27.7	16 54.3	8 5.1	29 28.9	26 21.0	3 36.8	10 6.7	0 4.2	5 18.0
21 F	21 56 27	27 45 8	15 3 40	21 25 17	1 27.3	16 29.8	9 18.7	0♌ 7.6	26 15.0	3 36.3	10 4.5	0 2.8	5 18.1
22 Sa	22 0 24	28 42 56	27 43 32	3♍58 30	1D 27.2	16 11.9	10 32.2	0 46.3	26 8.9	3 35.7	10 2.2	0 1.4	5 18.3
23 Su	22 4 20	29 40 46	10♍10 18	16 19 7	1 27.2	16D 1.1	11 45.9	1 24.9	26 2.6	3 35.0	10 0.0	0 0.0	5 18.5
24 M	22 8 17	0♍38 37	22 25 8	28 28 36	1R 27.3	15 57.7	12 59.5	2 3.5	25 56.2	3 34.2	9 57.8	29♐58.7	5 18.7
25 Tu	22 12 13	1 36 29	4♎29 48	10♎29 1	1 27.3	16 2.1	14 13.2	2 42.0	25 49.7	3 33.2	9 55.7	29 57.3	5 19.0
26 W	22 16 10	2 34 22	16 26 38	22 23 3	1 27.2	16 14.3	15 26.9	3 20.5	25 43.0	3 32.2	9 53.5	29 56.0	5 19.3
27 Th	22 20 6	3 32 17	28 18 40	4♏13 58	1 27.0	16 34.6	16 40.7	3 59.0	25 36.2	3 31.1	9 51.4	29 54.7	5 19.6
28 F	22 24 3	4 30 13	10♏ 9 27	16 5 36	1 26.7	17 2.8	17 54.4	4 37.4	25 29.3	3 29.9	9 49.2	29 53.5	5 20.0
29 Sa	22 28 0	5 28 11	22 3 0	28 2 11	1 26.5	17 39.0	19 8.3	5 15.8	25 22.3	3 28.5	9 47.2	29 52.2	5 20.4
30 Su	22 31 56	6 26 10	4♐ 3 44	10♐ 8 12	1D 26.3	18 22.9	20 22.1	5 54.1	25 15.3	3 27.1	9 45.1	29 51.0	5 20.9
31 M	22 35 53	7 24 10	16 16 9	22 28 9	1 26.4	19 14.3	21 36.0	6 32.4	25 8.1	3 25.6	9 43.0	29 49.8	5 21.3

Astro Data (Dy Hr Mn)	Planet Ingress (Dy Hr Mn)	Last Aspect (Dy Hr Mn)	☽ Ingress (Dy Hr Mn)	Last Aspect (Dy Hr Mn)	☽ Ingress (Dy Hr Mn)	☽ Phases & Eclipses (Dy Hr Mn)	Astro Data
☽0S 1 12:23	♂ ♋ 6 9:00	3 7:34 ♂ △	♏ 3 11:45	2 4:01 ☿ □	♐ 2 7:48	1 18:43 ☽ 9♎44	1 JULY 1998
☽0N 15 10:24	♀ ♋ 19 15:17	5 19:08 ♃ △	♐ 5 23:24	4 12:45 ♃ □	♑ 4 17:18	9 16:01 ○ 17♑15	Julian Day # 35976
♃ R 18 1:49	☉ ♌ 23 0:55	8 4:33 ♃ □	♑ 8 8:27	6 18:59 ♃ ✶	♒ 6 23:31	16 15:13 ☽ 23♈53	Delta T 61.3 sec
☽0S 28 21:21		10 11:15 ♃ ✶	♒ 10 14:52	8 18:47 ☿ ☍	♓ 9 3:04	23 13:44 ● 0♌31	SVP 05♓16'58"
☿ R 31 2:28	♀ ♌ 13 9:20	12 3:48 ♀ △	♓ 12 19:22	11 0:25 ♃ ☌	♈ 11 5:10	31 12:05 ☽ 8♏05	Obliquity 23°26'13"
	♂ ♌ 20 19:16	14 19:25 ♃ ☌	♈ 14 22:45	13 6:52 ♀ □	♉ 13 7:04		⚷ Chiron 12♏31.7R
☽0N 11 17:01	☉ ♍ 23 7:59	16 19:51 ♀ ✶	♉ 17 1:33	15 4:18 ♃ ✶	♊ 15 9:46	8 2:10 ○ 15♒21	☽ Mean ☊ 4♍08.4
♄ R 15 19:09	♆ ♑ 23 0:26	19 1:00 ♃ ✶	♊ 19 4:18	17 7:56 ♃ □	♋ 17 13:55	8 2:25 ☍A 0.120	
♇ D 16 6:07		21 4:19 ♃ □	♋ 21 7:43	19 18:48 ♂ ☌	♌ 19 20:01	14 19:49 ☽ 21♉49	1 AUGUST 1998
☿ D 23 22:35		23 9:13 ♃ △	♌ 23 12:48	22 2:03 ☉ ☌	♍ 22 4:21	22 2:03 ● 28♌48	Julian Day # 36007
☽0S 25 5:19		25 14:56 ☿ ☌	♍ 25 20:34	24 14:58 ♆ △	♎ 24 15:02	22 2:06:09 ☌A 3'14"	Delta T 61.4 sec
		28 3:02 ♃ ☍	♎ 28 7:14	27 3:14 ♆ □	♏ 27 3:25	30 5:07 ☽ 6♐39	SVP 05♓16'53"
		30 16:13 ☿ ✶	♏ 30 19:44	29 15:38 ♆ ✶	♐ 29 15:55		Obliquity 23°26'14"
							⚷ Chiron 12♏46.3
							☽ Mean ☊ 2♍29.9

LONGITUDE — SEPTEMBER 1998

Day	Sid.Time	☉	0 hr ☽	Noon ☽	True ☊	☿	♀	♂	♃	♄	♅	♆	♇
1 Tu	22 39 49	8♍22 11	28♐44 42	5♑ 6 16	1♍26.8	20♌12.9	22♌49.9	7♌10.7	25♓ 0.8	3♉24.0	9♒41.0	29♑48.6	5♐21.8
2 W	22 43 46	9 20 14	11♑33 17	18 6 6	1 27.4	21 18.5	24 3.9	7 48.9	24R 53.4	3R 22.2	9R 39.1	29R 47.4	5 22.4
3 Th	22 47 42	10 18 19	24 44 59	1♒30 5	1 28.2	22 30.5	25 17.9	8 27.0	24 46.0	3 20.4	9 37.1	29 46.3	5 23.0
4 F	22 51 39	11 16 25	8♒21 26	15 18 57	1 29.0	23 48.6	26 31.9	9 5.2	24 38.5	3 18.5	9 35.2	29 45.2	5 23.6
5 Sa	22 55 35	12 14 32	22 22 24	29 31 24	1R 29.5	25 12.3	27 46.0	9 43.3	24 30.9	3 16.5	9 33.3	29 44.1	5 24.2
6 Su	22 59 32	13 12 41	6♓45 26	14♓ 3 49	1 29.6	26 41.1	29 0.1	10 21.3	24 23.2	3 14.4	9 31.4	29 43.0	5 24.9
7 M	23 3 29	14 10 51	21 25 45	28 50 22	1 29.0	28 14.5	0♍14.2	10 59.3	24 15.5	3 12.2	9 29.6	29 41.9	5 25.6
8 Tu	23 7 25	15 9 4	6♈16 42	13♈43 44	1 27.9	29 51.9	1 28.3	11 37.3	24 7.7	3 9.8	9 27.8	29 40.9	5 26.3
9 W	23 11 22	16 7 18	21 10 27	28 35 55	1 26.2	1♍32.8	2 42.5	12 15.2	23 59.9	3 7.4	9 26.0	29 39.9	5 27.1
10 Th	23 15 18	17 5 34	5♉59 12	13♉19 32	1 24.3	3 16.7	3 56.8	12 53.1	23 52.1	3 5.0	9 24.2	29 38.9	5 27.9
11 F	23 19 15	18 3 52	20 36 12	27 48 40	1 22.6	5 3.1	5 11.0	13 31.0	23 44.2	3 2.4	9 22.5	29 38.0	5 28.7
12 Sa	23 23 11	19 2 12	4♊56 32	11♊59 29	1 21.4	6 51.6	6 25.3	14 8.8	23 36.2	2 59.7	9 20.9	29 37.0	5 29.6
13 Su	23 27 8	20 0 35	18 57 23	25 50 12	1D 20.9	8 41.6	7 39.7	14 46.6	23 28.3	2 57.0	9 19.2	29 36.1	5 30.5
14 M	23 31 4	20 59 0	2♋37 58	9♋20 50	1 21.2	10 32.9	8 54.0	15 24.3	23 20.3	2 54.1	9 17.6	29 35.3	5 31.4
15 Tu	23 35 1	21 57 27	15 58 58	22 32 36	1 22.3	12 25.1	10 8.4	16 2.0	23 12.3	2 51.2	9 16.0	29 34.4	5 32.4
16 W	23 38 58	22 55 56	29 2 0	5♌27 27	1 23.8	14 17.7	11 22.8	16 39.7	23 4.3	2 48.2	9 14.5	29 33.6	5 33.4
17 Th	23 42 54	23 54 27	11♌49 13	18 7 35	1 25.2	16 10.7	12 37.3	17 17.3	22 56.3	2 45.1	9 13.0	29 32.8	5 34.4
18 F	23 46 51	24 53 0	24 22 48	0♍35 9	1R 26.2	18 3.7	13 51.8	17 54.9	22 48.3	2 41.9	9 11.6	29 32.1	5 35.5
19 Sa	23 50 47	25 51 35	6♍44 51	12 52 8	1 26.3	19 56.5	15 6.3	18 32.5	22 40.4	2 38.6	9 10.2	29 31.3	5 36.6
20 Su	23 54 44	26 50 12	18 57 13	25 0 18	1 25.1	21 49.0	16 20.9	19 10.0	22 32.4	2 35.2	9 8.8	29 30.6	5 37.7
21 M	23 58 40	27 48 51	1♎ 1 35	7♎ 1 17	1 22.6	23 41.1	17 35.4	19 47.4	22 24.4	2 31.8	9 7.5	29 30.0	5 38.8
22 Tu	0 2 37	28 47 32	12 59 36	18 56 45	1 18.8	25 32.6	18 50.0	20 24.9	22 16.5	2 28.3	9 6.2	29 29.3	5 40.0
23 W	0 6 33	29 46 15	24 52 58	0♏48 32	1 14.1	27 23.4	20 4.6	21 2.2	22 8.7	2 24.7	9 4.9	29 28.7	5 41.2
24 Th	0 10 30	0♎44 59	6♏43 43	12 38 51	1 8.8	29 13.4	21 19.3	21 39.6	22 0.8	2 21.1	9 3.7	29 28.1	5 42.5
25 F	0 14 26	1 43 46	18 34 15	24 30 20	1 3.6	1♎ 2.7	22 34.0	22 16.9	21 53.0	2 17.4	9 2.5	29 27.6	5 43.7
26 Sa	0 18 23	2 42 34	0♐27 30	6♐26 12	0 59.0	2 51.1	23 48.7	22 54.1	21 45.3	2 13.6	9 1.4	29 27.1	5 45.0
27 Su	0 22 20	3 41 25	12 26 55	18 30 11	0 55.5	4 38.7	25 3.4	23 31.3	21 37.7	2 9.7	9 0.4	29 26.6	5 46.3
28 M	0 26 16	4 40 17	24 36 30	0♑46 26	0D 53.5	6 25.4	26 18.1	24 8.5	21 30.1	2 5.8	8 59.3	29 26.1	5 47.7
29 Tu	0 30 13	5 39 10	7♑ 0 32	13 19 23	0 53.0	8 11.2	27 32.9	24 45.6	21 22.5	2 1.8	8 58.3	29 25.7	5 49.1
30 W	0 34 9	6 38 6	19 43 29	26 13 21	0 53.7	9 56.1	28 47.6	25 22.7	21 15.1	1 57.8	8 57.4	29 25.3	5 50.5

LONGITUDE — OCTOBER 1998

Day	Sid.Time	☉	0 hr ☽	Noon ☽	True ☊	☿	♀	♂	♃	♄	♅	♆	♇
1 Th	0 38 6	7♎37 3	2♒49 27	9♒32 8	0♍55.2	11♎40.2	0♎ 2.4	25♌59.7	21♓ 7.7	1♉53.7	8♒56.5	29♑24.9	5♐51.9
2 F	0 42 2	8 36 2	16 21 41	23 18 16	0 56.6	13 23.3	1 17.2	26 36.7	21R 0.4	1R 49.5	8R 55.7	29R 24.6	5 53.4
3 Sa	0 45 59	9 35 3	0♓21 51	7♓32 17	0R 57.3	15 5.6	2 32.1	27 13.6	20 53.3	1 45.3	8 54.9	29 24.3	5 54.9
4 Su	0 49 55	10 34 5	14 49 12	22 12 1	0 56.5	16 47.0	3 46.9	27 50.5	20 46.2	1 41.1	8 54.1	29 24.0	5 56.4
5 M	0 53 52	11 33 9	29 39 59	7♈12 8	0 54.0	18 27.5	5 1.8	28 27.3	20 39.2	1 36.8	8 53.4	29 23.8	5 58.0
6 Tu	0 57 49	12 32 16	14♈47 20	22 24 19	0 49.5	20 7.2	6 16.7	29 4.1	20 32.3	1 32.4	8 52.7	29 23.6	5 59.5
7 W	1 1 45	13 31 24	0♉ 1 47	7♉38 20	0 43.6	21 46.2	7 31.6	29 40.9	20 25.6	1 28.0	8 52.1	29 23.4	6 1.1
8 Th	1 5 42	14 30 34	15 12 42	22 43 40	0 37.0	23 24.3	8 46.5	0♍17.6	20 18.9	1 23.6	8 51.5	29 23.3	6 2.7
9 F	1 9 38	15 29 47	0♊10 10	7♊31 20	0 30.6	25 1.6	10 1.4	0 54.3	20 12.4	1 19.1	8 51.0	29 23.2	6 4.4
10 Sa	1 13 35	16 29 2	14 46 28	21 55 9	0 25.4	26 38.2	11 16.4	1 31.0	20 6.0	1 14.5	8 50.6	29 23.1	6 6.1
11 Su	1 17 31	17 28 20	28 57 5	5♋52 12	0 21.8	28 14.1	12 31.4	2 7.5	19 59.8	1 10.0	8 50.1	29D 23.1	6 7.8
12 M	1 21 28	18 27 39	12♋40 36	19 22 31	0D 20.2	29 49.2	13 46.4	2 44.1	19 53.7	1 5.4	8 49.8	29 23.1	6 9.5
13 Tu	1 25 24	19 27 1	25 58 16	2♌28 16	0 20.2	1♏23.6	15 1.4	3 20.6	19 47.7	1 0.8	8 49.5	29 23.1	6 11.2
14 W	1 29 21	20 26 26	8♌52 59	15 12 55	0 21.2	2 57.3	16 16.5	3 57.1	19 41.9	0 56.1	8 49.2	29 23.2	6 13.0
15 Th	1 33 18	21 25 52	21 28 34	27 40 26	0R 22.3	4 30.3	17 31.5	4 33.5	19 36.2	0 51.4	8 49.0	29 23.3	6 14.8
16 F	1 37 14	22 25 21	3♍49 2	9♍54 48	0 22.6	6 2.7	18 46.6	5 9.8	19 30.7	0 46.7	8 48.8	29 23.4	6 16.6
17 Sa	1 41 11	23 24 52	15 58 11	21 59 34	0 21.2	7 34.4	20 1.7	5 46.2	19 25.3	0 42.0	8 48.7	29 23.5	6 18.4
18 Su	1 45 7	24 24 26	27 59 19	3♎57 45	0 17.5	9 5.4	21 16.8	6 22.4	19 20.1	0 37.2	8D 48.6	29 23.7	6 20.3
19 M	1 49 4	25 24 1	9♎55 9	15 51 45	0 11.2	10 35.8	22 31.9	6 58.6	19 15.0	0 32.5	8 48.6	29 24.0	6 22.2
20 Tu	1 53 0	26 23 38	21 47 48	27 43 30	0 2.4	12 5.6	23 47.0	7 34.8	19 10.1	0 27.7	8 48.6	29 24.2	6 24.1
21 W	1 56 57	27 23 18	3♏39 2	9♏34 34	29♌51.8	13 34.7	25 2.1	8 10.9	19 5.4	0 22.9	8 48.7	29 24.5	6 26.0
22 Th	2 0 53	28 22 59	15 30 19	21 26 27	29 40.1	15 3.1	26 17.3	8 47.0	19 0.9	0 18.1	8 48.8	29 24.9	6 27.9
23 F	2 4 50	29 22 43	27 23 11	3♐20 45	29 28.4	16 30.8	27 32.5	9 23.0	18 56.5	0 13.3	8 49.0	29 25.2	6 29.9
24 Sa	2 8 47	0♏22 28	9♐19 26	15 19 30	29 17.6	17 57.9	28 47.6	9 59.0	18 52.4	0 8.5	8 49.3	29 25.6	6 31.9
25 Su	2 12 43	1 22 15	21 21 19	27 25 14	29 8.7	19 24.3	0♏ 2.8	10 34.9	18 48.4	0 3.7	8 49.5	29 26.1	6 33.9
26 M	2 16 40	2 22 4	3♑31 40	9♑41 6	29 2.2	20 50.0	1 18.0	11 10.7	18 44.6	29♈58.9	8 49.9	29 26.5	6 35.9
27 Tu	2 20 36	3 21 55	15 53 59	22 10 51	28 58.4	22 14.9	2 33.2	11 46.5	18 40.9	29 54.2	8 50.3	29 27.0	6 37.9
28 W	2 24 33	4 21 47	28 32 13	4♒58 38	28D 56.8	23 39.0	3 48.4	12 22.2	18 37.5	29 49.4	8 50.7	29 27.6	6 40.0
29 Th	2 28 29	5 21 41	11♒30 37	18 8 38	28 56.8	25 2.4	5 3.6	12 57.9	18 34.3	29 44.6	8 51.2	29 28.1	6 42.0
30 F	2 32 26	6 21 37	24 53 9	1♓44 28	28R 57.2	26 24.8	6 18.8	13 33.5	18 31.3	29 39.9	8 51.8	29 28.8	6 44.1
31 Sa	2 36 22	7 21 34	8♓42 51	15 48 22	28 56.9	27 46.3	7 34.0	14 9.1	18 28.4	29 35.1	8 52.4	29 29.4	6 46.2

Astro Data Dy Hr Mn	Planet Ingress Dy Hr Mn	Last Aspect Dy Hr Mn	☽ Ingress Dy Hr Mn	Last Aspect Dy Hr Mn	☽ Ingress Dy Hr Mn	☽ Phases & Eclipses Dy Hr Mn	Astro Data
♃∠♅ 4 13:56	♀ ♍ 6 19:24	31 16:57 ♃ □	♑ 1 2:23	2 18:27 ♂ ☍	♓ 2 23:23	6 11:21 ○ 13♓40	1 SEPTEMBER 1998
☽0N 8 1:22	☿ ♍ 8 1:58	3 8:56 ♆ ☌	♒ 3 9:21	4 23:34 ♆ ✶	♈ 5 0:32	6 11:10 ☍A 0.812	Julian Day # 36038
☽0S 21 12:05	☉ ♎ 23 5:37	5 9:55 ♀ ☍	♓ 5 12:48	6 23:26 ♂ △	♉ 6 23:57	13 1:58 ☽ 20♊05	Delta T 61.4 sec
☿0S 26 4:33	☿ ♎ 24 10:13	7 13:22 ♆ ✶	♈ 7 13:52	8 22:44 ♆ △	♊ 8 23:44	20 17:02 ● 27♍32	SVP 05♓16'50"
	♀ ♎ 30 23:13	9 13:43 ♆ □	♉ 9 14:16	10 22:37 ☿ △	♋ 11 1:48	28 21:11 ☽ 5♑32	Obliquity 23°26'14"
♀0S 3 14:29		11 15:02 ♆ △	♊ 11 15:40	13 6:17 ♆ ☍	♌ 13 7:25		⚷ Chiron 14♏37.2
☽0N 5 11:47	♂ ♍ 7 12:28	13 7:47 ♃ □	♋ 13 19:20	14 23:54 ☉ ✶	♍ 15 16:32	5 20:12 ○ 12♈23	☽ Mean ☊ 0♍51.4
♆ D 11 14:04	☿ ♏ 12 2:45	16 0:59 ♆ ☍	♌ 16 1:48	18 2:49 ♆ △	♎ 18 4:02	12 11:11 ☽ 18♋55	
☽0S 18 18:17	☊ ♌ 20 5:51	17 10:57 ♂ ☌	♍ 18 10:52	20 15:24 ♆ □	♏ 20 16:36	20 10:09 ● 26♎49	1 OCTOBER 1998
♅ D 18 21:24	☉ ♏ 23 14:59	20 20:57 ♆ △	♎ 20 21:57	23 4:06 ♆ ✶	♐ 23 5:16	28 11:46 ☽ 4♒51	Julian Day # 36068
	♀ ♏ 24 23:06	23 9:18 ♆ □	♏ 23 10:22	24 18:58 ♃ □	♑ 25 17:05		Delta T 61.5 sec
	♄ ♈ 25 18:41	25 21:58 ♆ ✶	♐ 25 23:05	28 2:24 ♄ □	♒ 28 2:44		SVP 05♓16'47"
		28 3:41 ♀ □	♑ 28 10:30	30 8:20 ♄ ✶	♓ 30 8:58		Obliquity 23°26'15"
		30 18:26 ♀ △	♒ 30 18:53				⚷ Chiron 17♏37.2
							☽ Mean ☊ 29♌16.0

NOVEMBER 1998 LONGITUDE

Day	Sid.Time	☉	0 hr ☽	Noon ☽	True ☊	☿	♀	♂	♃	♄	♅	♆	♇
1 Su	2 40 19	8♏21 33	23♓ 0 55	0♈20 12	28♌54.8	29♏ 6.8	8♏49.3	14♍44.6	18♓25.8	29♈30.4	8♒53.0	29♑30.1	6♐48.4
2 M	2 44 15	9 21 33	7♈45 41	15 16 38	28R50.2	0♐26.2	10 4.5	15 20.1	18R23.3	29R25.7	8 53.7	29 30.8	6 50.5
3 Tu	2 48 12	10 21 35	22 52 1	0♉30 39	28 42.8	1 44.4	11 19.7	15 55.5	18 21.1	29 21.0	8 54.5	29 31.5	6 52.6
4 W	2 52 9	11 21 39	8♉11 10	15 52 7	28 33.3	3 1.4	12 35.0	16 30.8	18 19.0	29 16.4	8 55.2	29 32.2	6 54.8
5 Th	2 56 5	12 21 45	23 31 58	1♊ 9 16	28 22.5	4 16.9	13 50.2	17 6.1	18 17.2	29 11.8	8 56.1	29 33.0	6 57.0
6 F	3 0 2	13 21 52	8♊42 40	16 10 57	28 11.8	5 30.9	15 5.5	17 41.3	18 15.5	29 7.2	8 57.0	29 33.9	6 59.1
7 Sa	3 3 58	14 22 2	23 33 8	0♋48 29	28 2.5	6 43.1	16 20.7	18 16.5	18 14.1	29 2.7	8 57.9	29 34.7	7 1.3
8 Su	3 7 55	15 22 14	7♋56 30	14 56 54	27 55.4	7 53.4	17 36.0	18 51.6	18 12.8	28 58.2	8 58.9	29 35.6	7 3.6
9 M	3 11 51	16 22 27	21 49 40	28 34 55	27 51.0	9 1.5	18 51.3	19 26.6	18 11.8	28 53.7	8 60.0	29 36.6	7 5.8
10 Tu	3 15 48	17 22 43	5♌12 58	11♌44 16	27 48.9	10 7.3	20 6.6	20 1.6	18 11.0	28 49.3	9 1.1	29 37.5	7 8.0
11 W	3 19 45	18 23 0	18 9 18	24 28 40	27 48.5	11 10.3	21 21.9	20 36.5	18 10.3	28 44.9	9 2.2	29 38.5	7 10.3
12 Th	3 23 41	19 23 20	0♍42 59	6♍52 53	27 48.5	12 10.2	22 37.2	21 11.4	18 9.9	28 40.6	9 3.4	29 39.5	7 12.5
13 F	3 27 38	20 23 41	12 59 1	19 2 0	27 47.8	13 6.8	23 52.5	21 46.2	18D 9.7	28 36.3	9 4.7	29 40.6	7 14.8
14 Sa	3 31 34	21 24 5	25 2 26	1♎ 0 51	27 45.2	13 59.4	25 7.8	22 20.9	18 9.7	28 32.0	9 6.0	29 41.7	7 17.1
15 Su	3 35 31	22 24 30	6♎57 46	12 53 39	27 39.9	14 47.8	26 23.1	22 55.6	18 9.9	28 27.9	9 7.3	29 42.8	7 19.4
16 M	3 39 27	23 24 57	18 48 56	24 43 57	27 31.6	15 31.2	27 38.4	23 30.2	18 10.3	28 23.7	9 8.7	29 43.9	7 21.6
17 Tu	3 43 24	24 25 26	0♏39 3	6♏34 28	27 20.4	16 9.2	28 53.8	24 4.7	18 10.9	28 19.7	9 10.1	29 45.1	7 23.9
18 W	3 47 20	25 25 57	12 30 28	18 27 13	27 6.9	16 41.0	0♐ 9.1	24 39.2	18 11.7	28 15.7	9 11.6	29 46.3	7 26.2
19 Th	3 51 17	26 26 29	24 24 54	0♐23 39	26 51.9	17 5.9	1 24.4	25 13.5	18 12.8	28 11.7	9 13.2	29 47.5	7 28.6
20 F	3 55 13	27 27 3	6♐23 36	12 24 52	26 36.8	17 23.3	2 39.8	25 47.8	18 14.0	28 7.9	9 14.7	29 48.8	7 30.9
21 Sa	3 59 10	28 27 38	18 27 36	24 31 56	26 22.8	17R32.3	3 55.1	26 22.1	18 15.4	28 4.1	9 16.4	29 50.1	7 33.2
22 Su	4 3 7	29 28 15	0♑38 3	6♑46 10	26 11.0	17 32.1	5 10.4	26 56.2	18 17.1	28 0.3	9 18.0	29 51.4	7 35.5
23 M	4 7 3	0♐28 53	12 56 30	19 9 20	26 2.0	17 22.2	6 25.8	27 30.3	18 18.9	27 56.7	9 19.8	29 52.8	7 37.9
24 Tu	4 11 0	1 29 32	25 24 59	1♒43 49	25 56.2	17 2.0	7 41.1	28 4.3	18 21.0	27 53.1	9 21.5	29 54.1	7 40.2
25 W	4 14 56	2 30 12	8♒ 6 12	14 32 35	25 53.3	16 31.0	8 56.5	28 38.2	18 23.2	27 49.6	9 23.3	29 55.6	7 42.6
26 Th	4 18 53	3 30 54	21 3 22	27 39 0	25D52.3	15 49.2	10 11.8	29 12.0	18 25.7	27 46.2	9 25.2	29 57.0	7 44.9
27 F	4 22 49	4 31 36	4♓19 53	11♓ 6 24	25R52.3	14 56.9	11 27.2	29 45.7	18 28.4	27 42.8	9 27.1	29 58.4	7 47.3
28 Sa	4 26 46	5 32 20	17 58 51	24 57 26	25 51.9	13 55.0	12 42.5	0♎19.4	18 31.2	27 39.5	9 29.0	29 59.9	7 49.6
29 Su	4 30 42	6 33 4	2♈ 2 15	9♈13 13	25 49.9	12 44.6	13 57.8	0 53.0	18 34.3	27 36.4	9 31.0	0♒ 1.4	7 52.0
30 M	4 34 39	7 33 50	16 30 5	23 52 23	25 45.3	11 27.7	15 13.2	1 26.4	18 37.5	27 33.3	9 33.1	0 3.0	7 54.3

DECEMBER 1998 LONGITUDE

Day	Sid.Time	☉	0 hr ☽	Noon ☽	True ☊	☿	♀	♂	♃	♄	♅	♆	♇
1 Tu	4 38 36	8♐34 36	1♉19 28	8♉50 25	25♌38.1	10♐ 6.6	16♐28.5	1♎59.8	18♓41.0	27♈30.2	9♒35.1	0♒ 4.5	7♐56.7
2 W	4 42 32	9 35 24	16 24 11	23 59 33	25R28.4	8R43.9	17 43.8	2 33.1	18 44.6	27R27.3	9 37.2	0 6.1	7 59.0
3 Th	4 46 29	10 36 12	1♊35 10	9♊ 9 40	25 17.4	7 22.3	18 59.2	3 6.4	18 48.5	27 24.5	9 39.4	0 7.7	8 1.4
4 F	4 50 25	11 37 2	16 41 42	24 9 59	25 6.2	6 4.8	20 14.5	3 39.5	18 52.5	27 21.7	9 41.6	0 9.4	8 3.7
5 Sa	4 54 22	12 37 53	1♋33 24	8♋51 0	24 56.3	4 53.6	21 29.8	4 12.6	18 56.7	27 19.1	9 43.8	0 11.1	8 6.1
6 Su	4 58 18	13 38 45	16 2 3	23 6 2	24 48.6	3 50.9	22 45.1	4 45.5	19 1.1	27 16.5	9 46.1	0 12.7	8 8.4
7 M	5 2 15	14 39 38	0♌ 2 41	6♌51 54	24 43.6	2 58.2	24 0.5	5 18.4	19 5.7	27 14.1	9 48.4	0 14.5	8 10.8
8 Tu	5 6 12	15 40 32	13 33 49	20 8 41	24D41.2	2 16.3	25 15.8	5 51.2	19 10.5	27 11.7	9 50.8	0 16.2	8 13.1
9 W	5 10 8	16 41 28	26 36 54	2♍58 59	24 40.7	1 45.8	26 31.1	6 23.8	19 15.4	27 9.5	9 53.2	0 17.9	8 15.4
10 Th	5 14 5	17 42 25	9♍15 29	15 27 1	24R41.1	1 26.7	27 46.5	6 56.4	19 20.6	27 7.3	9 55.6	0 19.7	8 17.8
11 F	5 18 1	18 43 23	21 34 17	27 37 54	24 41.3	1D18.6	29 1.8	7 28.9	19 25.9	27 5.2	9 58.1	0 21.5	8 20.1
12 Sa	5 21 58	19 44 22	3♎38 33	9♎36 54	24 40.2	1 20.9	0♑17.1	8 1.2	19 31.4	27 3.2	10 0.6	0 23.3	8 22.4
13 Su	5 25 54	20 45 22	15 33 32	21 29 5	24 36.9	1 32.9	1 32.4	8 33.5	19 37.1	27 1.4	10 3.1	0 25.2	8 24.7
14 M	5 29 51	21 46 23	27 24 3	3♏18 58	24 31.1	1 53.8	2 47.8	9 5.6	19 42.9	26 59.6	10 5.7	0 27.0	8 27.0
15 Tu	5 33 47	22 47 25	9♏14 17	15 10 24	24 22.7	2 22.7	4 3.1	9 37.7	19 48.9	26 58.0	10 8.3	0 28.9	8 29.3
16 W	5 37 44	23 48 29	21 7 38	27 6 19	24 12.2	2 58.9	5 18.4	10 9.6	19 55.1	26 56.4	10 10.9	0 30.8	8 31.6
17 Th	5 41 41	24 49 33	3♐ 6 41	9♐ 8 56	24 0.5	3 41.5	6 33.7	10 41.4	20 1.5	26 55.0	10 13.6	0 32.7	8 33.9
18 F	5 45 37	25 50 38	15 13 12	21 19 37	23 48.5	4 29.8	7 49.1	11 13.1	20 8.1	26 53.6	10 16.3	0 34.7	8 36.2
19 Sa	5 49 34	26 51 43	27 28 17	3♑39 15	23 37.3	5 23.2	9 4.4	11 44.7	20 14.8	26 52.4	10 19.1	0 36.6	8 38.5
20 Su	5 53 30	27 52 50	9♑52 36	16 8 22	23 28.0	6 20.9	10 19.7	12 16.1	20 21.6	26 51.3	10 21.8	0 38.6	8 40.7
21 M	5 57 27	28 53 56	22 26 39	28 47 27	23 21.0	7 22.6	11 35.0	12 47.4	20 28.7	26 50.2	10 24.7	0 40.6	8 43.0
22 Tu	6 1 23	29 55 3	5♒10 57	11♒37 14	23 16.8	8 27.7	12 50.3	13 18.6	20 35.9	26 49.3	10 27.5	0 42.6	8 45.2
23 W	6 5 20	0♑56 11	18 6 28	24 38 49	23D15.1	9 35.8	14 5.6	13 49.7	20 43.3	26 48.5	10 30.4	0 44.7	8 47.4
24 Th	6 9 16	1 57 18	1♓14 29	7♓53 41	23 15.2	10 46.5	15 20.9	14 20.6	20 50.8	26 47.9	10 33.3	0 46.7	8 49.6
25 F	6 13 13	2 58 26	14 36 37	21 23 31	23 16.3	11 59.5	16 36.2	14 51.4	20 58.5	26 47.3	10 36.2	0 48.8	8 51.8
26 Sa	6 17 10	3 59 34	28 14 33	5♈ 9 51	23R17.2	13 14.5	17 51.5	15 22.0	21 6.3	26 46.8	10 39.1	0 50.8	8 54.0
27 Su	6 21 6	5 0 42	12♈ 9 29	19 13 26	23 17.1	14 31.4	19 6.8	15 52.5	21 14.3	26 46.5	10 42.1	0 52.9	8 56.2
28 M	6 25 3	6 1 49	26 21 33	3♉33 36	23 15.2	15 49.8	20 22.0	16 22.9	21 22.4	26 46.2	10 45.1	0 55.0	8 58.3
29 Tu	6 28 59	7 2 57	10♉49 11	18 7 45	23 11.3	17 9.6	21 37.3	16 53.1	21 30.7	26D46.1	10 48.2	0 57.1	9 0.5
30 W	6 32 56	8 4 5	25 28 39	2♊51 4	23 5.5	18 30.7	22 52.5	17 23.2	21 39.1	26 46.1	10 51.2	0 59.3	9 2.6
31 Th	6 36 52	9 5 13	10♊14 5	17 36 46	22 58.6	19 53.0	24 7.7	17 53.2	21 47.7	26 46.2	10 54.3	1 1.4	9 4.7

Astro Data Dy Hr Mn	Planet Ingress Dy Hr Mn	Last Aspect Dy Hr Mn	☽ Ingress Dy Hr Mn	Last Aspect Dy Hr Mn	☽ Ingress Dy Hr Mn	☽ Phases & Eclipses Dy Hr Mn
☽0N 1 23:12	☿ ♐ 1 16:03	1 11:00 ♆ △	♈ 1 11:27	2 3:43 ♃ ✶	♊ 2 21:30	4 5:18 ○ 11♉35
♄□♆ 1 1:34	♀ ♐ 17 21:06	3 10:28 ♆ □	♉ 3 11:12	4 17:07 ♄ ✶	♋ 4 21:28	11 0:28 ☽ 18♌24
♃ D 13 13:02	☉ ♐ 22 12:34	5 9:29 ♆ △	♊ 5 10:11	6 19:08 ♄ □	♌ 6 23:55	19 4:27 ● 26♏38
☽0S 15 0:59	♂ ♎ 27 10:10	7 9:01 ♄ ✶	♋ 7 10:39	9 1:01 ♄ △	♍ 9 6:21	27 0:23 ☽ 4♓33
☿ R 21 11:46	♆ ♒ 28 1:08	9 13:52 ♆ ☍	♌ 9 14:33	11 16:30 ♀ □	♎ 11 16:43	
☽0N 29 9:39		11 20:05 ♄ △	♍ 11 22:37	13 23:11 ♄ ☍	♏ 14 5:16	3 15:19 ○ 11♊15
	♀ ♑ 11 18:33	14 9:21 ♆ △	♎ 14 9:58	15 21:33 ♃ △	♐ 16 17:47	10 17:54 ☽ 18♍28
♂0S 4 13:44	☉ ♑ 22 1:56	16 22:10 ♆ □	♏ 16 22:41	18 22:50 ♄ △	♑ 19 4:55	18 22:42 ● 26♐48
☿ D 11 6:30		19 10:49 ♆ ✶	♐ 19 11:13	21 8:18 ♄ □	♒ 21 14:17	26 10:46 ☽ 4♈27
☽0S 12 8:56		21 18:52 ♄ △	♑ 21 22:45	23 15:56 ♄ ✶	♓ 23 21:45	
☽0N 26 17:41		24 8:33 ♆ ☌	♒ 24 8:43	25 11:22 ♃ ☌	♈ 26 3:04	
♄ D 29 15:45		26 12:10 ♄ ✶	♓ 26 16:14	28 0:41 ♄ ☌	♉ 28 6:05	
		28 0:56 ♃ ☌	♈ 28 20:34	29 19:22 ♀ △	♊ 30 7:22	
		30 17:53 ♄ ☌	♉ 30 21:53			

Astro Data

1 NOVEMBER 1998
Julian Day # 36099
Delta T 61.5 sec
SVP 05♓16'45"
Obliquity 23°26'14"
⚷ Chiron 21♏29.7
☽ Mean ☊ 27♌37.5

1 DECEMBER 1998
Julian Day # 36129
Delta T 61.6 sec
SVP 05♓16'41"
Obliquity 23°26'14"
⚷ Chiron 25♏29.3
☽ Mean ☊ 26♌02.2

LONGITUDE JANUARY 1999

Day	Sid.Time	☉	0 hr ☽	Noon ☽	True ☊	☿	♀	♂	♃	♄	♅	♆	♇
1 F	6 40 49	10♑ 6 21	24♊58 4	2♋17 0	22♌51.5	21♐16.2	25♑23.0	18♎22.9	21♓56.4	26♈46.4	10♒57.4	1♒ 3.5	9♐ 6.8
2 Sa	6 44 45	11 7 28	9♋32 39	16 44 8	22R45.1	22 40.4	26 38.2	18 52.6	22 5.3	26 46.7	11 0.6	1 5.7	9 8.9
3 Su	6 48 42	12 8 36	23 50 43	0♌51 50	22 40.2	24 5.3	27 53.4	19 22.1	22 14.3	26 47.1	11 3.7	1 7.9	9 11.0
4 M	6 52 39	13 9 44	7♌47 2	14 36 3	22 37.2	25 31.1	29 8.6	19 51.4	22 23.4	26 47.7	11 6.9	1 10.1	9 13.0
5 Tu	6 56 35	14 10 52	21 18 46	27 55 13	22D36.2	26 57.6	0♒23.7	20 20.5	22 32.7	26 48.3	11 10.1	1 12.3	9 15.0
6 W	7 0 32	15 12 0	4♍25 35	10♍50 7	22 36.8	28 24.7	1 38.9	20 49.5	22 42.1	26 49.1	11 13.3	1 14.5	9 17.0
7 Th	7 4 28	16 13 9	17 9 14	23 23 23	22 38.3	29 52.4	2 54.1	21 18.3	22 51.6	26 49.9	11 16.6	1 16.7	9 19.0
8 F	7 8 25	17 14 17	29 33 6	5♎38 57	22 40.0	1♑20.8	4 9.2	21 47.0	23 1.2	26 50.9	11 19.8	1 18.9	9 21.0
9 Sa	7 12 21	18 15 26	11♎41 31	17 41 28	22R41.2	2 49.7	5 24.4	22 15.5	23 11.0	26 52.0	11 23.1	1 21.1	9 22.9
10 Su	7 16 18	19 16 34	23 39 23	29 35 56	22 41.4	4 19.1	6 39.5	22 43.7	23 20.9	26 53.2	11 26.4	1 23.3	9 24.9
11 M	7 20 14	20 17 43	5♏31 43	11♏27 19	22 40.0	5 49.1	7 54.6	23 11.8	23 31.0	26 54.5	11 29.7	1 25.6	9 26.8
12 Tu	7 24 11	21 18 51	17 23 19	23 20 14	22 37.2	7 19.6	9 9.7	23 39.7	23 41.1	26 55.9	11 33.0	1 27.8	9 28.7
13 W	7 28 8	22 20 0	29 18 34	5♐18 45	22 33.1	8 50.6	10 24.8	24 7.5	23 51.4	26 57.5	11 36.4	1 30.1	9 30.5
14 Th	7 32 4	23 21 8	11♐21 12	17 26 15	22 28.2	10 22.1	11 39.9	24 35.0	24 1.8	26 59.1	11 39.7	1 32.3	9 32.4
15 F	7 36 1	24 22 17	23 34 11	29 45 14	22 23.0	11 54.1	12 55.0	25 2.3	24 12.3	27 0.9	11 43.1	1 34.6	9 34.2
16 Sa	7 39 57	25 23 25	5♑59 34	12♑17 18	22 18.1	13 26.6	14 10.0	25 29.4	24 22.9	27 2.7	11 46.5	1 36.9	9 36.0
17 Su	7 43 54	26 24 32	18 38 30	25 3 11	22 14.0	14 59.6	15 25.1	25 56.3	24 33.6	27 4.7	11 49.9	1 39.2	9 37.8
18 M	7 47 50	27 25 40	1♒31 19	8♒ 2 51	22 11.2	16 33.1	16 40.1	26 22.9	24 44.5	27 6.8	11 53.3	1 41.4	9 39.5
19 Tu	7 51 47	28 26 46	14 37 42	21 15 45	22D 9.9	18 7.1	17 55.1	26 49.4	24 55.5	27 8.9	11 56.7	1 43.7	9 41.2
20 W	7 55 43	29 27 52	27 56 53	4♓40 57	22 9.8	19 41.7	19 10.1	27 15.6	25 6.5	27 11.2	12 0.2	1 46.0	9 42.9
21 Th	7 59 40	0♒28 57	11♓27 52	18 17 27	22 10.7	21 16.8	20 25.1	27 41.5	25 17.7	27 13.6	12 3.6	1 48.3	9 44.6
22 F	8 3 37	1 30 2	25 9 37	2♈ 4 14	22 12.1	22 52.5	21 40.0	28 7.3	25 29.0	27 16.1	12 7.1	1 50.6	9 46.3
23 Sa	8 7 33	2 31 5	9♈ 1 11	16 0 19	22 13.5	24 28.7	22 55.0	28 32.8	25 40.3	27 18.7	12 10.5	1 52.8	9 47.9
24 Su	8 11 30	3 32 7	23 1 29	0♉ 4 33	22R14.5	26 5.5	24 9.9	28 58.0	25 51.8	27 21.4	12 14.0	1 55.1	9 49.5
25 M	8 15 26	4 33 9	7♉ 9 18	14 15 30	22 14.8	27 42.9	25 24.8	29 23.0	26 3.4	27 24.2	12 17.5	1 57.4	9 51.1
26 Tu	8 19 23	5 34 9	21 22 52	28 31 5	22 14.2	29 20.9	26 39.6	29 47.7	26 15.0	27 27.1	12 20.9	1 59.6	9 52.6
27 W	8 23 19	6 35 8	5♊39 47	12♊48 32	22 12.9	0♒59.5	27 54.5	0♏12.2	26 26.8	27 30.1	12 24.4	2 1.9	9 54.1
28 Th	8 27 16	7 36 6	19 56 51	27 4 15	22 11.1	2 38.8	29 9.3	0 36.4	26 38.6	27 33.3	12 27.9	2 4.2	9 55.6
29 F	8 31 12	8 37 3	4♋10 11	11♋14 9	22 9.2	4 18.7	0♓24.1	1 0.4	26 50.6	27 36.5	12 31.4	2 6.5	9 57.1
30 Sa	8 35 9	9 37 59	18 15 36	25 14 1	22 7.5	5 59.3	1 38.8	1 24.0	27 2.6	27 39.8	12 34.9	2 8.7	9 58.5
31 Su	8 39 6	10 38 54	2♌ 8 57	8♌59 59	22 6.3	7 40.6	2 53.5	1 47.4	27 14.7	27 43.2	12 38.4	2 11.0	9 59.9

LONGITUDE FEBRUARY 1999

Day	Sid.Time	☉	0 hr ☽	Noon ☽	True ☊	☿	♀	♂	♃	♄	♅	♆	♇
1 M	8 43 2	11♒39 48	15♌46 47	22♌29 5	22♌ 5.7	9♒22.6	4♓ 8.2	2♏10.5	27♓26.9	27♈46.7	12♒41.9	2♒13.3	10♐ 1.3
2 Tu	8 46 59	12 40 40	29 6 42	5♍39 33	22D 5.7	11 5.2	5 22.9	2 33.3	27 39.2	27 50.3	12 45.4	2 15.5	10 2.6
3 W	8 50 55	13 41 32	12♍ 7 37	18 31 0	22 6.2	12 48.6	6 37.6	2 55.8	27 51.5	27 53.9	12 48.9	2 17.8	10 3.9
4 Th	8 54 52	14 42 23	24 49 52	1♎ 4 28	22 6.9	14 32.7	7 52.2	3 18.0	28 4.0	27 57.7	12 52.4	2 20.0	10 5.2
5 F	8 58 48	15 43 13	7♎15 7	13 22 11	22 7.7	16 17.5	9 6.8	3 39.9	28 16.5	28 1.6	12 55.9	2 22.2	10 6.5
6 Sa	9 2 45	16 44 1	19 26 8	25 27 26	22 8.3	18 3.0	10 21.3	4 1.4	28 29.1	28 5.5	12 59.4	2 24.5	10 7.7
7 Su	9 6 41	17 44 49	1♏26 36	7♏24 12	22 8.8	19 49.2	11 35.8	4 22.6	28 41.7	28 9.6	13 2.9	2 26.7	10 8.9
8 M	9 10 38	18 45 36	13 20 48	19 16 59	22R 8.9	21 36.0	12 50.3	4 43.5	28 54.5	28 13.7	13 6.4	2 28.9	10 10.0
9 Tu	9 14 35	19 46 22	25 13 22	1♐10 30	22 9.0	23 23.5	14 4.8	5 4.0	29 7.3	28 18.0	13 9.9	2 31.1	10 11.2
10 W	9 18 31	20 47 7	7♐ 9 1	13 9 27	22 8.9	25 11.6	15 19.3	5 24.2	29 20.2	28 22.3	13 13.3	2 33.3	10 12.3
11 Th	9 22 28	21 47 52	19 12 22	25 18 15	22D 8.8	27 0.3	16 33.7	5 44.0	29 33.1	28 26.7	13 16.8	2 35.5	10 13.3
12 F	9 26 24	22 48 35	1♑27 35	7♑40 46	22 8.8	28 49.5	17 48.0	6 3.4	29 46.2	28 31.2	13 20.3	2 37.6	10 14.4
13 Sa	9 30 21	23 49 16	13 58 10	20 20 3	22 9.0	0♓39.0	19 2.4	6 22.4	29 59.2	28 35.8	13 23.7	2 39.8	10 15.4
14 Su	9 34 17	24 49 57	26 46 39	3♒18 6	22 9.2	2 28.9	20 16.7	6 41.0	0♈12.4	28 40.4	13 27.2	2 42.0	10 16.4
15 M	9 38 14	25 50 36	9♒54 24	16 35 32	22R 9.4	4 18.9	21 31.0	6 59.3	0 25.6	28 45.2	13 30.7	2 44.1	10 17.3
16 Tu	9 42 10	26 51 14	23 21 21	0♓11 37	22 9.5	6 9.0	22 45.2	7 17.1	0 38.9	28 50.0	13 34.1	2 46.2	10 18.2
17 W	9 46 7	27 51 51	7♓ 6 2	14 4 10	22 9.4	7 58.9	23 59.4	7 34.5	0 52.2	28 54.9	13 37.5	2 48.3	10 19.1
18 Th	9 50 4	28 52 26	21 5 36	28 9 50	22 8.9	9 48.4	25 13.6	7 51.5	1 5.6	28 59.9	13 40.9	2 50.4	10 19.9
19 F	9 54 0	29 52 59	5♈16 18	12♈24 28	22 8.0	11 37.2	26 27.7	8 8.0	1 19.1	29 5.0	13 44.3	2 52.5	10 20.7
20 Sa	9 57 57	0♓53 31	19 33 46	26 43 39	22 7.0	13 25.1	27 41.8	8 24.1	1 32.6	29 10.1	13 47.7	2 54.6	10 21.5
21 Su	10 1 53	1 54 0	3♉53 38	11♉ 3 13	22 6.0	15 11.8	28 55.8	8 39.7	1 46.1	29 15.3	13 51.1	2 56.7	10 22.2
22 M	10 5 50	2 54 28	18 11 59	25 19 33	22 5.2	16 56.8	0♈ 9.8	8 54.8	1 59.7	29 20.6	13 54.5	2 58.7	10 22.9
23 Tu	10 9 46	3 54 54	2♊25 37	9♊29 52	22D 4.8	18 39.7	1 23.7	9 9.5	2 13.4	29 26.0	13 57.8	3 0.7	10 23.6
24 W	10 13 43	4 55 19	16 32 36	23 32 7	22 5.1	20 20.0	2 37.6	9 23.7	2 27.1	29 31.4	14 1.1	3 2.8	10 24.2
25 Th	10 17 39	5 55 41	0♋29 45	7♋24 52	22 5.9	21 57.2	3 51.5	9 37.4	2 40.8	29 36.9	14 4.5	3 4.7	10 24.8
26 F	10 21 36	6 56 1	14 17 20	21 7 5	22 7.0	23 30.8	5 5.3	9 50.6	2 54.6	29 42.5	14 7.8	3 6.7	10 25.4
27 Sa	10 25 33	7 56 19	27 53 58	4♌37 55	22 8.2	25 0.1	6 19.0	10 3.3	3 8.5	29 48.2	14 11.0	3 8.7	10 25.9
28 Su	10 29 29	8 56 36	11♌18 50	17 56 38	22R 9.2	26 24.6	7 32.7	10 15.5	3 22.4	29 53.9	14 14.3	3 10.6	10 26.4

Astro Data	Dy Hr Mn
☽0S	8 18:03
☽0N	22 23:46
♃∠♅	2 16:53
♃⚻♄	3 6:40
☽0S	5 3:20
☽0N	19 6:10
♀0N	23 16:57
♃0N	24 11:40
♃✱♆	27 0:26
☿0N	28 21:15

Planet Ingress		Dy Hr Mn
♀	♒	4 16:25
☿	♑	7 2:04
☉	♒	20 12:37
☿	♒	26 9:32
♂	♏	26 11:59
♀	♓	28 16:17
☿	♓	12 15:28
♃	♈	13 1:22
☉	♓	19 2:47
♀	♈	21 20:49

Last Aspect Dy Hr Mn		☽ Ingress Dy Hr Mn
1 2:57	♄ ✱	♋ 1 8:15
3 7:34	♀ ☍	♌ 3 10:31
5 11:31	☿ △	♍ 5 15:49
7 11:07	♃ ☍	♎ 8 0:53
10 6:32	♀ □	♏ 10 12:49
12 12:53	♃ △	♐ 13 1:23
15 6:43	♄ △	♑ 15 12:29
17 15:49	♄ □	♒ 17 21:11
19 22:44	♂ △	♓ 20 3:40
22 0:34	♃ ☌	♈ 22 8:25
24 10:25	♂ ☍	♉ 24 11:52
26 9:44	♀ □	♊ 26 14:29
28 12:52	♄ ✱	♋ 28 16:57
30 16:16	♄ □	♌ 30 20:16

Last Aspect Dy Hr Mn		☽ Ingress Dy Hr Mn
1 21:40	♄ △	♍ 2 1:37
4 6:18	♃ ☍	♎ 4 9:56
6 17:22	♄ ☍	♏ 6 21:06
9 8:01	♃ △	♐ 9 9:38
11 20:39	♃ □	♑ 11 21:10
14 3:31	♄ □	♒ 14 5:57
16 9:41	♄ ✱	♓ 16 11:40
18 7:42	♀ ☌	♈ 18 15:06
20 16:11	♄ ☌	♉ 20 17:29
21 21:36	☿ ✱	♊ 22 19:54
24 22:28	♄ ✱	♋ 24 23:09
27 3:24	♄ □	♌ 27 3:44

☽ Phases & Eclipses Dy Hr Mn	
2 2:50	○ 11♋15
9 14:22	☽ 18♎52
17 15:46	● 27♑05
24 19:15	☽ 4♉21
31 16:07	○ 11♌20
31 16:17	• A 1.003
8 11:58	☽ 19♏16
16 6:39	● 27♒08
16 6:33:36	• A 0'39"
23 2:43	☽ 4♊02

Astro Data

1 JANUARY 1999
Julian Day # 36160
Delta T 61.6 sec
SVP 05♓16'35"
Obliquity 23°26'14"
⚷ Chiron 29♏18.4
☽ Mean ☊ 24♌23.7

1 FEBRUARY 1999
Julian Day # 36191
Delta T 61.6 sec
SVP 05♓16'30"
Obliquity 23°26'14"
⚷ Chiron 2♐14.0
☽ Mean ☊ 22♌45.2

MARCH 1999

LONGITUDE

Day	Sid.Time	☉	0 hr ☽	Noon ☽	True ☊	☿	♀	♂	♃	♄	♅	♆	♇
1 M	10 33 26	9♓56 50	24♌31 14	1♍ 2 33	22♌ 9.4	27♓43.7	8♈46.4	10♏27.1	3♈36.3	29♈59.7	14♒17.5	3♒12.6	10♐26.9
2 Tu	10 37 22	10 57 3	7♍30 34	13 55 12	22R 8.8	28 56.7	9 59.9	10 38.2	3 50.2	0♉ 5.5	14 20.8	3 14.5	10 27.3
3 W	10 41 19	11 57 14	20 16 30	26 34 27	22 7.0	0♈ 3.0	11 13.5	10 48.8	4 4.2	0 11.4	14 24.0	3 16.4	10 27.7
4 Th	10 45 15	12 57 23	2♎49 9	9♎ 0 41	22 4.3	1 2.2	12 27.0	10 58.7	4 18.3	0 17.4	14 27.2	3 18.2	10 28.1
5 F	10 49 12	13 57 30	15 9 15	21 15 1	22 0.9	1 53.7	13 40.4	11 8.1	4 32.3	0 23.4	14 30.3	3 20.1	10 28.4
6 Sa	10 53 8	14 57 35	27 18 15	3♏19 17	21 57.0	2 37.0	14 53.8	11 16.9	4 46.4	0 29.5	14 33.5	3 21.9	10 28.7
7 Su	10 57 5	15 57 39	9♏18 26	15 16 8	21 53.2	3 11.7	16 7.1	11 25.1	5 0.6	0 35.7	14 36.6	3 23.7	10 28.9
8 M	11 1 1	16 57 42	21 12 49	27 8 59	21 50.0	3 37.7	17 20.3	11 32.7	5 14.7	0 41.9	14 39.7	3 25.5	10 29.2
9 Tu	11 4 58	17 57 43	3♐ 5 9	9♐ 1 53	21 47.8	3 54.7	18 33.5	11 39.7	5 28.9	0 48.1	14 42.8	3 27.2	10 29.3
10 W	11 8 55	18 57 42	14 59 44	20 59 19	21D 46.7	4R 2.6	19 46.7	11 46.0	5 43.1	0 54.5	14 45.8	3 29.0	10 29.5
11 Th	11 12 51	19 57 39	27 1 14	3♑ 6 6	21 46.9	4 1.6	20 59.8	11 51.6	5 57.4	1 0.9	14 48.8	3 30.7	10 29.6
12 F	11 16 48	20 57 35	9♑14 30	15 27 0	21 48.0	3 51.8	22 12.8	11 56.6	6 11.7	1 7.3	14 51.8	3 32.4	10 29.7
13 Sa	11 20 44	21 57 29	21 44 9	28 6 26	21 49.7	3 33.6	23 25.8	12 1.0	6 26.0	1 13.8	14 54.8	3 34.1	10R 29.7
14 Su	11 24 41	22 57 22	4♒34 16	11♒ 8 0	21 51.3	3 7.5	24 38.7	12 4.6	6 40.3	1 20.3	14 57.8	3 35.7	10 29.8
15 M	11 28 37	23 57 13	17 47 52	24 33 58	21R 52.3	2 34.3	25 51.6	12 7.5	6 54.7	1 26.9	15 0.7	3 37.4	10 29.7
16 Tu	11 32 34	24 57 2	1♓26 18	8♓24 42	21 52.0	1 54.6	27 4.4	12 9.8	7 9.1	1 33.6	15 3.6	3 39.0	10 29.7
17 W	11 36 30	25 56 49	15 28 50	22 38 13	21 50.1	1 9.6	28 17.1	12 11.3	7 23.4	1 40.3	15 6.4	3 40.5	10 29.6
18 Th	11 40 27	26 56 34	29 52 14	7♈10 7	21 46.5	0 20.2	29 29.8	12R 12.1	7 37.9	1 47.0	15 9.3	3 42.1	10 29.5
19 F	11 44 24	27 56 17	14♈30 58	21 53 50	21 41.5	29♓27.7	0♉42.4	12 12.1	7 52.3	1 53.8	15 12.1	3 43.6	10 29.3
20 Sa	11 48 20	28 55 58	29 17 44	6♉41 38	21 35.8	28 33.2	1 54.9	12 11.4	8 6.7	2 0.6	15 14.8	3 45.1	10 29.1
21 Su	11 52 17	29 55 37	14♉ 4 34	21 25 40	21 30.2	27 37.9	3 7.4	12 10.0	8 21.2	2 7.5	15 17.6	3 46.6	10 28.9
22 M	11 56 13	0♈55 14	28 44 9	5♊59 20	21 25.4	26 43.0	4 19.8	12 7.8	8 35.7	2 14.4	15 20.3	3 48.0	10 28.6
23 Tu	12 0 10	1 54 48	13♊10 43	20 17 55	21 22.2	25 49.6	5 32.1	12 4.9	8 50.1	2 21.4	15 22.9	3 49.5	10 28.3
24 W	12 4 6	2 54 20	27 20 42	4♋18 56	21D 20.7	24 58.7	6 44.4	12 1.2	9 4.6	2 28.4	15 25.6	3 50.9	10 28.0
25 Th	12 8 3	3 53 50	11♋12 38	18 1 51	21 20.8	24 11.2	7 56.5	11 56.7	9 19.1	2 35.4	15 28.2	3 52.2	10 27.6
26 F	12 11 59	4 53 18	24 46 44	1♌27 29	21 21.9	23 27.7	9 8.6	11 51.5	9 33.6	2 42.5	15 30.8	3 53.6	10 27.3
27 Sa	12 15 56	5 52 43	8♌ 4 18	14 37 26	21 23.2	22 49.0	10 20.6	11 45.5	9 48.1	2 49.6	15 33.3	3 54.9	10 26.8
28 Su	12 19 53	6 52 6	21 7 6	27 33 32	21R 23.9	22 15.5	11 32.6	11 38.8	10 2.7	2 56.7	15 35.8	3 56.2	10 26.4
29 M	12 23 49	7 51 26	3♍56 57	10♍17 30	21 23.0	21 47.4	12 44.4	11 31.3	10 17.2	3 3.9	15 38.3	3 57.4	10 25.9
30 Tu	12 27 46	8 50 45	16 35 22	22 50 42	21 20.1	21 25.1	13 56.2	11 23.0	10 31.7	3 11.1	15 40.7	3 58.6	10 25.4
31 W	12 31 42	9 50 1	29 3 36	5♎14 12	21 14.9	21 8.5	15 7.8	11 14.0	10 46.2	3 18.3	15 43.1	3 59.8	10 24.8

APRIL 1999

LONGITUDE

Day	Sid.Time	☉	0 hr ☽	Noon ☽	True ☊	☿	♀	♂	♃	♄	♅	♆	♇
1 Th	12 35 39	10♈49 15	11♎22 35	17♎28 53	21♌ 7.5	20♓57.7	16♉19.4	11♏ 4.2	11♈ 0.7	3♉25.6	15♒45.4	4♒ 1.0	10♐24.2
2 F	12 39 35	11 48 27	23 33 11	29 35 38	20R 58.4	20D 52.7	17 30.9	10R 53.6	11 15.3	3 32.9	15 47.8	4 2.1	10R 23.6
3 Sa	12 43 32	12 47 37	5♏36 23	11♏35 38	20 48.4	20 53.3	18 42.3	10 42.3	11 29.8	3 40.2	15 50.0	4 3.2	10 23.0
4 Su	12 47 28	13 46 45	17 33 34	23 30 28	20 38.4	20 59.4	19 53.7	10 30.3	11 44.3	3 47.6	15 52.3	4 4.3	10 22.3
5 M	12 51 25	14 45 52	29 26 39	5♐22 27	20 29.3	21 10.8	21 4.9	10 17.5	11 58.8	3 54.9	15 54.5	4 5.4	10 21.6
6 Tu	12 55 22	15 44 56	11♐18 17	17 14 35	20 21.8	21 27.3	22 16.1	10 4.0	12 13.3	4 2.3	15 56.7	4 6.4	10 20.9
7 W	12 59 18	16 43 59	23 11 50	29 10 34	20 16.6	21 48.6	23 27.1	9 49.8	12 27.8	4 9.8	15 58.8	4 7.4	10 20.1
8 Th	13 3 15	17 43 0	5♑11 22	11♑14 48	20 13.6	22 14.6	24 38.1	9 34.9	12 42.3	4 17.2	16 0.9	4 8.3	10 19.3
9 F	13 7 11	18 41 59	17 21 31	23 32 7	20D 12.7	22 45.0	25 48.9	9 19.4	12 56.8	4 24.7	16 2.9	4 9.3	10 18.5
10 Sa	13 11 8	19 40 56	29 47 15	6♒ 7 31	20 13.1	23 19.7	26 59.7	9 3.1	13 11.3	4 32.2	16 4.9	4 10.2	10 17.6
11 Su	13 15 4	20 39 52	12♒33 28	19 5 39	20R 13.8	23 58.3	28 10.4	8 46.2	13 25.7	4 39.7	16 6.9	4 11.0	10 16.8
12 M	13 19 1	21 38 46	25 44 30	2♓30 20	20 13.9	24 40.7	29 21.0	8 28.7	13 40.2	4 47.2	16 8.8	4 11.9	10 15.9
13 Tu	13 22 57	22 37 38	9♓23 22	16 23 36	20 12.3	25 26.7	0♊31.5	8 10.6	13 54.6	4 54.8	16 10.7	4 12.7	10 14.9
14 W	13 26 54	23 36 28	23 30 54	0♈44 54	20 8.4	26 16.1	1 41.8	7 52.0	14 9.1	5 2.4	16 12.5	4 13.4	10 14.0
15 Th	13 30 50	24 35 16	8♈ 5 2	15 30 30	20 2.0	27 8.8	2 52.1	7 32.8	14 23.5	5 9.9	16 14.3	4 14.2	10 13.0
16 F	13 34 47	25 34 3	23 0 18	0♉33 18	19 53.4	28 4.6	4 2.3	7 13.1	14 37.8	5 17.5	16 16.0	4 14.9	10 12.0
17 Sa	13 38 44	26 32 47	8♉ 8 12	15 43 39	19 43.6	29 3.3	5 12.4	6 53.0	14 52.2	5 25.1	16 17.7	4 15.5	10 10.9
18 Su	13 42 40	27 31 30	23 18 18	0♊50 54	19 33.6	0♈ 4.8	6 22.3	6 32.4	15 6.6	5 32.8	16 19.4	4 16.2	10 9.9
19 M	13 46 37	28 30 11	8♊20 14	15 45 20	19 24.9	1 9.1	7 32.2	6 11.4	15 20.9	5 40.4	16 21.0	4 16.8	10 8.8
20 Tu	13 50 33	29 28 49	23 5 21	0♋19 43	19 18.1	2 15.9	8 41.9	5 50.1	15 35.2	5 48.0	16 22.6	4 17.4	10 7.7
21 W	13 54 30	0♉27 26	7♋28 1	14 30 3	19 13.9	3 25.2	9 51.5	5 28.5	15 49.5	5 55.7	16 24.1	4 17.9	10 6.5
22 Th	13 58 26	1 26 0	21 25 48	28 15 22	19D 12.0	4 36.8	11 1.0	5 6.7	16 3.7	6 3.3	16 25.6	4 18.4	10 5.4
23 F	14 2 23	2 24 31	4♌59 0	11♌37 2	19 11.7	5 50.8	12 10.4	4 44.6	16 18.0	6 11.0	16 27.0	4 18.9	10 4.2
24 Sa	14 6 19	3 23 1	18 9 51	24 37 52	19R 11.9	7 7.1	13 19.7	4 22.4	16 32.2	6 18.7	16 28.4	4 19.3	10 3.0
25 Su	14 10 16	4 21 28	1♍ 1 33	7♍21 20	19 11.4	8 25.4	14 28.8	3 60.0	16 46.3	6 26.3	16 29.7	4 19.8	10 1.8
26 M	14 14 13	5 19 54	13 37 38	19 50 51	19 9.2	9 46.0	15 37.7	3 37.5	17 0.5	6 34.0	16 31.0	4 20.1	10 0.5
27 Tu	14 18 9	6 18 17	26 1 22	2♎ 9 30	19 4.4	11 8.5	16 46.6	3 15.0	17 14.6	6 41.7	16 32.3	4 20.5	9 59.3
28 W	14 22 6	7 16 38	8♎15 34	14 19 47	18 56.7	12 33.1	17 55.3	2 52.5	17 28.7	6 49.3	16 33.5	4 20.8	9 58.0
29 Th	14 26 2	8 14 57	20 22 25	26 23 38	18 46.3	13 59.8	19 3.8	2 30.1	17 42.7	6 57.0	16 34.6	4 21.1	9 56.7
30 F	14 29 59	9 13 14	2♏23 37	8♏22 32	18 33.7	15 28.3	20 12.2	2 7.7	17 56.7	7 4.7	16 35.7	4 21.3	9 55.3

Astro Data	Dy Hr Mn
☽0S	4 11:44
☿ R	10 9:11
♇ R	13 21:33
☽0N	18 14:41
♂ R	18 13:41
☿0S	24 19:32
♃△♇	29 13:54
☽0S	31 18:53
☿ D	2 9:19
♄□♆	6 15:07
☽0N	15 1:13
☿0N	23 9:02
♃✶♅	23 16:55
☽0S	28 1:18

Planet Ingress	Dy Hr Mn
♄ ♉	1 1:25
☿ ♈	2 22:50
☿ ♓	18 9:23
♀ ♉	18 9:59
☉ ♈	21 1:46
♀ ♊	12 13:17
☿ ♈	17 22:09
☉ ♉	20 12:46

Last Aspect Dy Hr Mn	☽ Ingress Dy Hr Mn
28 5:18 ♅ ☍	♍ 1 10:04
2 6:59 ☉ ☍	♎ 3 18:34
4 22:43 ♅ △	♏ 6 5:22
7 14:38 ☉ △	♐ 8 17:46
10 10:40 ♀ △	♑ 11 5:54
13 3:33 ♀ □	♒ 13 15:32
15 15:40 ♀ ✶	♓ 15 21:30
17 18:48 ☉ ☌	♈ 18 0:13
19 1:07 ♅ ✶	♉ 20 1:09
21 20:52 ☿ ✶	♊ 22 2:05
23 20:11 ☿ □	♋ 24 4:33
25 21:46 ☿ △	♌ 26 9:22
27 13:45 ♅ ☍	♍ 28 16:34
30 9:02 ☿ ☍	♎ 31 1:49

Last Aspect Dy Hr Mn	☽ Ingress Dy Hr Mn
1 8:38 ♅ △	♏ 2 12:49
4 7:01 ☿ △	♐ 5 1:07
6 21:07 ☿ □	♑ 7 13:39
9 18:06 ♀ △	♒ 10 0:24
12 7:02 ♀ □	♓ 12 7:35
14 4:53 ☿ ☌	♈ 14 10:46
16 4:22 ☉ ☌	♉ 16 11:07
17 12:55 ♅ □	♊ 18 10:39
20 11:21 ☉ ✶	♋ 20 11:27
21 14:32 ♃ □	♌ 22 15:06
23 20:57 ♃ △	♍ 24 22:04
26 4:15 ♀ □	♎ 27 7:46
28 21:07 ♀ △	♏ 29 19:12

☽ Phases & Eclipses Dy Hr Mn	
2 6:59	○ 11♍15
10 8:40	☽ 19♐19
17 18:48	● 26♓44
24 10:18	☽ 3♋20
31 22:49	○ 10♎46
9 2:51	☽ 18♑49
16 4:22	● 25♈45
22 19:02	☽ 2♌12
30 14:55	○ 9♏49

Astro Data

1 MARCH 1999
Julian Day # 36219
Delta T 61.7 sec
SVP 05♓16'27"
Obliquity 23°26'15"
⚷ Chiron 3♐40.7
☽ Mean ☊ 21♌16.3

1 APRIL 1999
Julian Day # 36250
Delta T 61.7 sec
SVP 05♓16'25"
Obliquity 23°26'15"
⚷ Chiron 3♐40.9R
☽ Mean ☊ 19♌37.7

LONGITUDE — MAY 1999

Day	Sid.Time	☉	0 hr ☽	Noon ☽	True ☊	☿	♀	♂	♃	♄	♅	♆	♇
1 Sa	14 33 55	10♉11 30	14♏20 31	20♏17 44	18♌19.9	16♈58.8	21♊20.5	1♏45.5	18♈10.7	7♉12.3	16♒36.8	4♒21.5	9♐54.0
2 Su	14 37 52	11 9 44	26 14 20	2♐10 31	18R 6.0	18 31.3	22 28.6	1R23.5	18 24.6	7 20.0	16 37.8	4 21.7	9R52.6
3 M	14 41 48	12 7 56	8♐ 6 29	14 2 28	17 53.1	20 5.6	23 36.6	1 1.6	18 38.5	7 27.6	16 38.7	4 21.9	9 51.3
4 Tu	14 45 45	13 6 6	19 58 45	25 55 40	17 42.2	21 41.9	24 44.4	0 40.1	18 52.4	7 35.3	16 39.6	4 22.0	9 49.9
5 W	14 49 42	14 4 15	1♑53 34	7♑52 52	17 34.0	23 20.0	25 52.0	0 18.8	19 6.2	7 42.9	16 40.5	4 22.0	9 48.5
6 Th	14 53 38	15 2 23	13 54 1	19 57 32	17 28.6	25 0.1	26 59.5	29♎57.9	19 20.0	7 50.6	16 41.3	4 22.1	9 47.0
7 F	14 57 35	16 0 29	26 3 56	2♒13 49	17 25.7	26 42.1	28 6.8	29 37.3	19 33.7	7 58.2	16 42.1	4R22.1	9 45.6
8 Sa	15 1 31	16 58 33	8♒27 45	14 46 21	17 24.8	28 25.9	29 14.0	29 17.2	19 47.4	8 5.8	16 42.8	4 22.1	9 44.1
9 Su	15 5 28	17 56 37	21 10 13	27 39 54	17 24.7	0♉11.7	0♋21.0	28 57.5	20 1.1	8 13.4	16 43.5	4 22.1	9 42.6
10 M	15 9 24	18 54 38	4♓15 58	10♓58 49	17 24.3	1 59.3	1 27.8	28 38.3	20 14.7	8 21.0	16 44.1	4 22.0	9 41.2
11 Tu	15 13 21	19 52 39	17 48 50	24 46 13	17 22.4	3 48.9	2 34.4	28 19.7	20 28.2	8 28.6	16 44.6	4 21.9	9 39.7
12 W	15 17 17	20 50 38	1♈51 0	9♈ 3 3	17 18.3	5 40.4	3 40.9	28 1.6	20 41.7	8 36.2	16 45.2	4 21.7	9 38.1
13 Th	15 21 14	21 48 36	16 21 58	23 47 9	17 11.5	7 33.8	4 47.2	27 44.1	20 55.2	8 43.7	16 45.6	4 21.5	9 36.6
14 F	15 25 11	22 46 32	1♉17 45	8♉52 41	17 2.4	9 29.1	5 53.3	27 27.2	21 8.6	8 51.3	16 46.0	4 21.3	9 35.1
15 Sa	15 29 7	23 44 27	16 30 41	24 10 23	16 51.8	11 26.2	6 59.2	27 10.9	21 21.9	8 58.8	16 46.4	4 21.1	9 33.5
16 Su	15 33 4	24 42 21	1♊50 17	9♊28 56	16 40.9	13 25.2	8 4.9	26 55.4	21 35.2	9 6.3	16 46.7	4 20.8	9 32.0
17 M	15 37 0	25 40 13	17 4 55	24 36 59	16 31.1	15 26.0	9 10.4	26 40.5	21 48.5	9 13.8	16 47.0	4 20.5	9 30.4
18 Tu	15 40 57	26 38 4	2♋ 4 2	9♋25 12	16 23.5	17 28.6	10 15.7	26 26.4	22 1.7	9 21.2	16 47.2	4 20.2	9 28.8
19 W	15 44 53	27 35 53	16 39 51	23 47 34	16 18.4	19 32.8	11 20.7	26 13.0	22 14.8	9 28.7	16 47.4	4 19.8	9 27.2
20 Th	15 48 50	28 33 40	0♌48 11	7♌41 41	16 15.9	21 38.5	12 25.6	26 0.4	22 27.9	9 36.1	16 47.5	4 19.4	9 25.7
21 F	15 52 46	29 31 26	14 28 16	21 8 12	16D15.2	23 45.7	13 30.2	25 48.5	22 40.9	9 43.5	16R47.6	4 19.0	9 24.1
22 Sa	15 56 43	0♊29 10	27 41 54	4♍ 9 49	16R15.3	25 54.2	14 34.6	25 37.5	22 53.8	9 50.8	16 47.6	4 18.5	9 22.5
23 Su	16 0 40	1 26 52	10♍32 30	16 50 29	16 15.0	28 3.8	15 38.7	25 27.2	23 6.7	9 58.2	16 47.6	4 18.0	9 20.8
24 M	16 4 36	2 24 33	23 4 17	29 14 28	16 13.3	0♊14.4	16 42.6	25 17.7	23 19.5	10 5.5	16 47.5	4 17.5	9 19.2
25 Tu	16 8 33	3 22 12	5♎21 32	11♎25 58	16 9.3	2 25.6	17 46.2	25 9.0	23 32.2	10 12.8	16 47.4	4 16.9	9 17.6
26 W	16 12 29	4 19 50	17 28 12	23 28 40	16 2.6	4 37.2	18 49.5	25 1.2	23 44.9	10 20.0	16 47.2	4 16.3	9 16.0
27 Th	16 16 26	5 17 26	29 27 43	5♏25 40	15 53.5	6 49.1	19 52.6	24 54.1	23 57.5	10 27.2	16 47.0	4 15.7	9 14.4
28 F	16 20 22	6 15 1	11♏22 50	17 19 26	15 42.3	9 0.9	20 55.4	24 47.9	24 10.1	10 34.4	16 46.7	4 15.1	9 12.7
29 Sa	16 24 19	7 12 35	23 15 43	29 11 54	15 30.0	11 12.3	21 57.9	24 42.5	24 22.5	10 41.6	16 46.4	4 14.4	9 11.1
30 Su	16 28 15	8 10 7	5♐ 8 8	11♐ 4 37	15 17.5	13 23.1	23 0.1	24 37.9	24 34.9	10 48.7	16 46.0	4 13.7	9 9.5
31 M	16 32 12	9 7 39	17 1 32	22 59 5	15 6.0	15 33.0	24 2.0	24 34.1	24 47.2	10 55.8	16 45.6	4 13.0	9 7.8

LONGITUDE — JUNE 1999

Day	Sid.Time	☉	0 hr ☽	Noon ☽	True ☊	☿	♀	♂	♃	♄	♅	♆	♇
1 Tu	16 36 9	10♊ 5 9	28♐57 26	4♑56 50	14♌56.3	17♊41.7	25♋ 3.6	24♎31.1	24♈59.5	11♉ 2.9	16♒45.1	4♒12.2	9♐ 6.2
2 W	16 40 5	11 2 38	10♑57 33	16 59 51	14R49.0	19 49.1	26 4.8	24R28.9	25 11.6	11 9.9	16R44.6	4R11.4	9R 4.6
3 Th	16 44 2	12 0 7	23 4 3	29 10 32	14 44.3	21 54.8	27 5.7	24 27.5	25 23.7	11 16.9	16 44.1	4 10.6	9 2.9
4 F	16 47 58	12 57 34	5♒19 41	11♒31 56	14D42.0	23 58.8	28 6.3	24D26.9	25 35.7	11 23.8	16 43.5	4 9.8	9 1.3
5 Sa	16 51 55	13 55 1	17 47 44	24 7 35	14 41.7	26 0.8	29 6.6	24 27.1	25 47.7	11 30.7	16 42.8	4 8.9	8 59.7
6 Su	16 55 51	14 52 27	0♓31 58	7♓ 1 22	14 42.3	28 0.8	0♌ 6.4	24 28.1	25 59.5	11 37.6	16 42.1	4 8.0	8 58.1
7 M	16 59 48	15 49 53	13 36 14	20 17 1	14R42.8	29 58.5	1 5.9	24 29.8	26 11.3	11 44.4	16 41.4	4 7.1	8 56.4
8 Tu	17 3 44	16 47 18	27 4 3	3♈57 36	14 42.4	1♋54.0	2 5.1	24 32.3	26 23.0	11 51.2	16 40.6	4 6.2	8 54.8
9 W	17 7 41	17 44 42	10♈57 47	18 4 36	14 40.2	3 47.1	3 3.8	24 35.6	26 34.6	11 58.0	16 39.8	4 5.2	8 53.2
10 Th	17 11 38	18 42 5	25 17 50	2♉37 6	14 35.8	5 37.8	4 2.1	24 39.6	26 46.1	12 4.7	16 38.9	4 4.2	8 51.6
11 F	17 15 34	19 39 29	10♉ 1 48	17 31 7	14 29.6	7 26.0	5 0.0	24 44.4	26 57.5	12 11.3	16 38.0	4 3.2	8 50.0
12 Sa	17 19 31	20 36 51	25 4 2	2♊39 25	14 22.0	9 11.8	5 57.5	24 49.9	27 8.8	12 17.9	16 37.0	4 2.1	8 48.4
13 Su	17 23 27	21 34 13	10♊15 57	17 52 20	14 14.1	10 55.0	6 54.6	24 56.2	27 20.0	12 24.5	16 36.0	4 1.1	8 46.8
14 M	17 27 24	22 31 35	25 27 10	2♋59 13	14 7.0	12 35.7	7 51.1	25 3.1	27 31.2	12 31.0	16 34.9	3 60.0	8 45.2
15 Tu	17 31 20	23 28 56	10♋27 19	17 50 26	14 1.4	14 13.8	8 47.3	25 10.8	27 42.2	12 37.5	16 33.8	3 58.9	8 43.7
16 W	17 35 17	24 26 16	25 7 46	2♌18 42	13 57.8	15 49.3	9 42.9	25 19.2	27 53.2	12 43.9	16 32.7	3 57.7	8 42.1
17 Th	17 39 13	25 23 35	9♌22 51	16 20 1	13D56.4	17 22.3	10 38.0	25 28.3	28 4.0	12 50.2	16 31.5	3 56.6	8 40.6
18 F	17 43 10	26 20 53	23 10 9	29 53 24	13 56.6	18 52.6	11 32.6	25 38.1	28 14.7	12 56.5	16 30.3	3 55.4	8 39.0
19 Sa	17 47 7	27 18 11	6♍30 2	13♍ 0 26	13 57.7	20 20.3	12 26.6	25 48.5	28 25.4	13 2.8	16 29.0	3 54.2	8 37.5
20 Su	17 51 3	28 15 27	19 25 3	25 44 22	13R58.8	21 45.3	13 20.0	25 59.6	28 35.9	13 9.0	16 27.7	3 52.9	8 36.0
21 M	17 55 0	29 12 43	1♎58 58	8♎ 9 23	13 59.1	23 7.6	14 12.9	26 11.3	28 46.3	13 15.1	16 26.4	3 51.7	8 34.5
22 Tu	17 58 56	0♋ 9 58	14 16 12	20 19 58	13 58.0	24 27.2	15 5.1	26 23.7	28 56.7	13 21.2	16 25.0	3 50.4	8 33.0
23 W	18 2 53	1 7 13	26 21 14	2♏20 31	13 55.0	25 44.0	15 56.7	26 36.7	29 6.9	13 27.2	16 23.6	3 49.1	8 31.5
24 Th	18 6 49	2 4 27	8♏18 19	14 15 4	13 50.4	26 58.0	16 47.7	26 50.3	29 17.0	13 33.2	16 22.1	3 47.8	8 30.0
25 F	18 10 46	3 1 40	20 11 12	26 7 6	13 44.3	28 9.1	17 37.9	27 4.5	29 26.9	13 39.1	16 20.6	3 46.5	8 28.6
26 Sa	18 14 42	3 58 53	2♐ 3 6	7♐59 31	13 37.3	29 17.2	18 27.5	27 19.3	29 36.8	13 44.9	16 19.1	3 45.2	8 27.1
27 Su	18 18 39	4 56 5	13 56 38	19 54 41	13 30.2	0♌22.3	19 16.3	27 34.6	29 46.6	13 50.7	16 17.5	3 43.8	8 25.7
28 M	18 22 36	5 53 17	25 53 54	1♑54 29	13 23.6	1 24.3	20 4.3	27 50.5	29 56.2	13 56.4	16 15.9	3 42.4	8 24.3
29 Tu	18 26 32	6 50 29	7♑56 38	14 0 32	13 18.2	2 23.1	20 51.6	28 7.0	0♉ 5.8	14 2.1	16 14.2	3 41.0	8 22.9
30 W	18 30 29	7 47 40	20 6 23	26 14 21	13 14.3	3 18.7	21 38.0	28 24.0	0 15.2	14 7.7	16 12.6	3 39.6	8 21.6

Astro Data Dy Hr Mn	Planet Ingress Dy Hr Mn
♆ R 7 0:51	♂ ♎ 5 21:32
☽0N 12 12:12	☿ ♉ 8 21:22
♄⚻♇ 18 20:14	♀ ♋ 8 16:29
♅ R 21 22:25	☉ ♊ 21 11:52
☽0S 25 7:58	☿ ♊ 23 21:22
♃⚼♇ 28 4:32	
	♀ ♌ 5 21:25
♂ D 4 6:11	☿ ♋ 7 0:18
☽0N 8 21:53	☉ ♋ 21 19:49
☽0S 21 15:28	☿ ♌ 26 15:39
	♃ ♉ 28 9:29

Last Aspect Dy Hr Mn	☽ Ingress Dy Hr Mn	Last Aspect Dy Hr Mn	☽ Ingress Dy Hr Mn
1 4:35 ♅ □	♐ 2 7:36	31 15:54 ♃ △	♑ 1 2:06
4 10:37 ♀ ☍	♑ 4 20:12	3 8:38 ♀ ☍	♒ 3 13:37
7 6:45 ♂ □	♒ 7 7:40	5 18:26 ☿ △	♓ 5 23:00
9 14:01 ♂ △	♓ 9 16:16	7 4:20 ☉ □	♈ 8 5:08
11 3:51 ☉ ✶	♈ 11 20:53	10 2:27 ♃ ☌	♉ 10 7:44
13 17:59 ♂ ☍	♉ 13 21:56	11 10:34 ♅ □	♊ 12 7:48
15 12:05 ☉ ☌	♊ 15 21:07	14 3:19 ♃ ✶	♋ 14 7:14
17 15:04 ♂ △	♋ 17 20:39	16 4:39 ♃ □	♌ 16 8:07
19 19:51 ☉ ✶	♌ 19 22:37	18 9:10 ♃ △	♍ 18 12:12
21 20:14 ♂ ✶	♍ 22 4:15	20 18:13 ☉ □	♎ 20 20:10
23 10:37 ♀ ✶	♎ 24 13:29	23 5:36 ♃ ☍	♏ 23 7:18
26 14:56 ♂ ☌	♏ 27 1:05	25 17:50 ☿ △	♐ 25 19:51
28 21:08 ♀ △	♐ 29 13:37	28 8:11 ♃ △	♑ 28 8:12
		30 16:36 ♂ □	♒ 30 19:19

☽ Phases & Eclipses Dy Hr Mn	
8 17:29	☽ 17♒41
15 12:05	● 24♉14
22 5:34	☽ 0♍43
30 6:40	○ 8♐26
7 4:20	☽ 16♓00
13 19:03	● 22♊20
20 18:13	☽ 28♍59
28 21:37	○ 6♑45

Astro Data

1 MAY 1999
Julian Day # 36280
Delta T 61.8 sec
SVP 05♓16'22"
Obliquity 23°26'15"
⚷ Chiron 2♐14.9R
☽ Mean ☊ 18♌02.4

1 JUNE 1999
Julian Day # 36311
Delta T 61.8 sec
SVP 05♓16'17"
Obliquity 23°26'14"
⚷ Chiron 0♐02.3R
☽ Mean ☊ 16♌23.9

JULY 1999 LONGITUDE

Day	Sid.Time	☉	0 hr ☽	Noon ☽	True ☊	☿	♀	♂	♃	♄	♅	♆	♇
1 Th	18 34 25	8♋44 52	2♒24 38	8♒37 28	13♌12.2	4♌10.8	22♌23.6	28♎41.5	0♉24.4	14♉13.2	16♒10.9	3♒38.2	8♐20.2
2 F	18 38 22	9 42 3	14 53 3	21 11 39	13D 11.6	4 59.5	23 8.3	28 59.6	0 33.6	14 18.7	16R 9.1	3R 36.8	8R 18.9
3 Sa	18 42 18	10 39 14	27 33 32	3♓58 57	13 12.3	5 44.5	23 52.1	29 18.1	0 42.6	14 24.1	16 7.3	3 35.3	8 17.6
4 Su	18 46 15	11 36 26	10♓28 12	17 1 34	13 13.8	6 25.8	24 34.9	29 37.2	0 51.6	14 29.4	16 5.5	3 33.9	8 16.3
5 M	18 50 11	12 33 37	23 39 19	0♈21 42	13 15.3	7 3.3	25 16.8	29 56.7	1 0.3	14 34.7	16 3.7	3 32.4	8 15.0
6 Tu	18 54 8	13 30 49	7♈ 8 55	14 1 8	13R 16.3	7 36.8	25 57.6	0♏16.7	1 9.0	14 39.8	16 1.8	3 30.9	8 13.7
7 W	18 58 5	14 28 1	20 58 25	28 0 44	13 16.3	8 6.2	26 37.4	0 37.2	1 17.5	14 45.0	15 59.9	3 29.4	8 12.5
8 Th	19 2 1	15 25 14	5♉ 7 59	12♉19 53	13 15.1	8 31.3	27 16.1	0 58.2	1 25.9	14 50.0	15 58.0	3 27.9	8 11.3
9 F	19 5 58	16 22 27	19 36 2	26 55 54	13 12.7	8 52.1	27 53.7	1 19.6	1 34.2	14 55.0	15 56.0	3 26.3	8 10.1
10 Sa	19 9 54	17 19 40	4♊18 48	11♊43 55	13 9.6	9 8.4	28 30.0	1 41.5	1 42.3	14 59.9	15 54.0	3 24.8	8 8.9
11 Su	19 13 51	18 16 54	19 10 21	26 37 7	13 6.3	9 20.1	29 5.2	2 3.8	1 50.3	15 4.7	15 52.0	3 23.2	8 7.8
12 M	19 17 47	19 14 8	4♋ 3 11	11♋27 32	13 3.2	9R 27.1	29 39.1	2 26.6	1 58.1	15 9.4	15 50.0	3 21.7	8 6.6
13 Tu	19 21 44	20 11 22	18 49 11	26 7 13	13 0.9	9 29.4	0♍11.7	2 49.7	2 5.8	15 14.1	15 47.9	3 20.1	8 5.5
14 W	19 25 41	21 8 37	3♌20 51	10♌29 24	12D 59.6	9 26.9	0 42.9	3 13.4	2 13.4	15 18.7	15 45.8	3 18.5	8 4.5
15 Th	19 29 37	22 5 52	17 32 21	24 29 21	12 59.4	9 19.7	1 12.6	3 37.4	2 20.8	15 23.2	15 43.7	3 17.0	8 3.4
16 F	19 33 34	23 3 7	1♍20 10	8♍ 4 44	13 0.1	9 7.7	1 40.9	4 1.8	2 28.0	15 27.6	15 41.6	3 15.4	8 2.4
17 Sa	19 37 30	24 0 22	14 43 7	21 15 29	13 1.4	8 51.0	2 7.7	4 26.6	2 35.1	15 31.9	15 39.4	3 13.8	8 1.4
18 Su	19 41 27	24 57 37	27 42 7	4♎ 3 25	13 2.7	8 29.9	2 32.8	4 51.8	2 42.1	15 36.2	15 37.2	3 12.2	8 0.4
19 M	19 45 23	25 54 52	10♎19 47	16 31 42	13 3.9	8 4.5	2 56.3	5 17.4	2 48.9	15 40.4	15 35.1	3 10.6	7 59.4
20 Tu	19 49 20	26 52 8	22 39 43	28 44 23	13R 4.4	7 35.1	3 18.0	5 43.4	2 55.5	15 44.5	15 32.8	3 8.9	7 58.5
21 W	19 53 16	27 49 23	4♏46 14	10♏45 51	13 4.4	7 2.2	3 38.0	6 9.7	3 2.0	15 48.5	15 30.6	3 7.3	7 57.6
22 Th	19 57 13	28 46 39	16 43 48	22 40 37	13 3.6	6 26.1	3 56.1	6 36.4	3 8.4	15 52.4	15 28.4	3 5.7	7 56.7
23 F	20 1 10	29 43 56	28 36 50	4♐32 58	13 2.3	5 47.3	4 12.4	7 3.5	3 14.5	15 56.2	15 26.1	3 4.1	7 55.9
24 Sa	20 5 6	0♌41 12	10♐29 28	16 26 47	13 0.7	5 6.6	4 26.6	7 30.9	3 20.6	15 60.0	15 23.8	3 2.5	7 55.0
25 Su	20 9 3	1 38 29	22 25 21	28 25 30	12 59.0	4 24.4	4 38.9	7 58.6	3 26.4	16 3.6	15 21.5	3 0.8	7 54.3
26 M	20 12 59	2 35 47	4♑27 35	10♑31 54	12 57.5	3 41.7	4 49.0	8 26.6	3 32.1	16 7.2	15 19.2	2 59.2	7 53.5
27 Tu	20 16 56	3 33 5	16 38 43	22 48 13	12 56.4	2 59.0	4 57.0	8 55.0	3 37.6	16 10.7	15 16.9	2 57.6	7 52.8
28 W	20 20 52	4 30 23	29 0 37	5♒16 4	12 55.7	2 17.1	5 2.9	9 23.7	3 43.0	16 14.1	15 14.6	2 56.0	7 52.0
29 Th	20 24 49	5 27 43	11♒34 40	17 56 32	12D 55.4	1 36.9	5 6.5	9 52.7	3 48.2	16 17.4	15 12.2	2 54.3	7 51.4
30 F	20 28 45	6 25 3	24 21 44	0♓50 18	12 55.5	0 59.2	5R 7.8	10 22.0	3 53.2	16 20.6	15 9.9	2 52.7	7 50.7
31 Sa	20 32 42	7 22 23	7♓22 16	13 57 41	12 55.9	0 24.5	5 6.8	10 51.6	3 58.1	16 23.7	15 7.5	2 51.1	7 50.1

AUGUST 1999 LONGITUDE

Day	Sid.Time	☉	0 hr ☽	Noon ☽	True ☊	☿	♀	♂	♃	♄	♅	♆	♇
1 Su	20 36 39	8♌19 45	20♓36 31	27♓18 47	12♌56.4	29♋53.6	5♍ 3.4	11♏21.5	4♉ 2.7	16♉26.7	15♒ 5.1	2♒49.5	7♐49.5
2 M	20 40 35	9 17 8	4♈ 4 27	10♈53 28	12 56.8	29R 27.1	4R 57.7	11 51.6	4 7.2	16 29.7	15R 2.8	2R 47.8	7R 48.9
3 Tu	20 44 32	10 14 32	17 45 47	24 41 18	12 57.0	29 5.6	4 49.7	12 22.1	4 11.6	16 32.5	15 0.4	2 46.2	7 48.4
4 W	20 48 28	11 11 57	1♉39 56	8♉41 31	12R 57.2	28 49.5	4 39.2	12 52.8	4 15.7	16 35.3	14 58.0	2 44.6	7 47.9
5 Th	20 52 25	12 9 23	15 45 51	22 52 43	12D 57.2	28 39.2	4 26.4	13 23.9	4 19.7	16 37.9	14 55.6	2 43.0	7 47.4
6 F	20 56 21	13 6 51	0♊ 1 47	7♊12 42	12 57.2	28D 35.1	4 11.2	13 55.2	4 23.5	16 40.4	14 53.2	2 41.4	7 47.0
7 Sa	21 0 18	14 4 20	14 25 5	21 38 26	12 57.3	28 37.4	3 53.8	14 26.7	4 27.1	16 42.9	14 50.8	2 39.8	7 46.6
8 Su	21 4 14	15 1 50	28 52 13	6♋ 5 53	12 57.4	28 46.4	3 34.0	14 58.6	4 30.5	16 45.2	14 48.4	2 38.2	7 46.2
9 M	21 8 11	15 59 21	13♋18 50	20 30 25	12 57.7	29 2.0	3 12.1	15 30.7	4 33.7	16 47.5	14 46.0	2 36.7	7 45.9
10 Tu	21 12 8	16 56 54	27 40 2	4♌47 4	12 57.9	29 24.5	2 48.1	16 3.0	4 36.8	16 49.6	14 43.6	2 35.1	7 45.6
11 W	21 16 4	17 54 28	11♌50 56	18 51 6	12R 58.0	29 53.9	2 22.0	16 35.6	4 39.6	16 51.7	14 41.3	2 33.5	7 45.3
12 Th	21 20 1	18 52 3	25 47 8	2♍38 37	12 57.9	0♌30.0	1 54.0	17 8.5	4 42.3	16 53.6	14 38.9	2 32.0	7 45.0
13 F	21 23 57	19 49 39	9♍25 16	16 6 54	12 57.5	1 12.9	1 24.3	17 41.6	4 44.7	16 55.5	14 36.5	2 30.5	7 44.8
14 Sa	21 27 54	20 47 16	22 43 24	29 14 47	12 56.7	2 2.5	0 52.9	18 15.0	4 47.0	16 57.2	14 34.1	2 28.9	7 44.6
15 Su	21 31 50	21 44 55	5♎41 6	12♎ 2 35	12 55.6	2 58.6	0 20.1	18 48.6	4 49.1	16 58.9	14 31.7	2 27.4	7 44.5
16 M	21 35 47	22 42 34	18 19 27	24 32 4	12 54.4	4 1.1	29♌45.9	19 22.4	4 51.0	17 0.4	14 29.4	2 25.9	7 44.4
17 Tu	21 39 43	23 40 14	0♏40 49	6♏46 9	12 53.3	5 9.7	29 10.7	19 56.5	4 52.7	17 1.8	14 27.0	2 24.4	7 44.3
18 W	21 43 40	24 37 55	12 48 35	18 48 37	12 52.5	6 24.1	28 34.6	20 30.8	4 54.2	17 3.1	14 24.6	2 22.9	7 44.2
19 Th	21 47 36	25 35 38	24 46 51	0♐43 50	12D 52.2	7 44.3	27 57.9	21 5.3	4 55.5	17 4.4	14 22.3	2 21.4	7D 44.2
20 F	21 51 33	26 33 21	6♐40 9	12 36 23	12 52.4	9 9.7	27 20.7	21 40.0	4 56.6	17 5.5	14 20.0	2 20.0	7 44.2
21 Sa	21 55 30	27 31 6	18 33 7	24 30 56	12 53.2	10 40.1	26 43.4	22 15.0	4 57.5	17 6.5	14 17.7	2 18.6	7 44.3
22 Su	21 59 26	28 28 52	0♑30 22	6♑31 55	12 54.5	12 15.0	26 6.1	22 50.1	4 58.2	17 7.4	14 15.4	2 17.1	7 44.3
23 M	22 3 23	29 26 38	12 36 5	18 43 18	12 55.9	13 54.2	25 29.2	23 25.5	4 58.8	17 8.2	14 13.1	2 15.7	7 44.5
24 Tu	22 7 19	0♍24 27	24 53 57	1♒ 8 23	12 57.1	15 37.1	24 52.8	24 1.0	4 59.1	17 8.9	14 10.8	2 14.3	7 44.6
25 W	22 11 16	1 22 16	7♒26 52	13 49 35	12R 57.8	17 23.2	24 17.2	24 36.8	4R 59.2	17 9.5	14 8.6	2 13.0	7 44.8
26 Th	22 15 12	2 20 7	20 16 42	26 48 15	12 57.7	19 12.3	23 42.6	25 12.7	4 59.1	17 10.0	14 6.3	2 11.6	7 45.0
27 F	22 19 9	3 17 59	3♓24 13	10♓ 4 30	12 56.7	21 3.7	23 9.2	25 48.9	4 58.9	17 10.4	14 4.1	2 10.3	7 45.2
28 Sa	22 23 5	4 15 53	16 48 56	23 37 16	12 54.7	22 57.1	22 37.2	26 25.2	4 58.4	17 10.6	14 1.9	2 8.9	7 45.5
29 Su	22 27 2	5 13 48	0♈29 12	7♈24 24	12 51.8	24 52.1	22 6.8	27 1.7	4 57.7	17 10.8	13 59.7	2 7.6	7 45.8
30 M	22 30 59	6 11 45	14 22 27	21 22 58	12 48.6	26 48.3	21 38.2	27 38.4	4 56.8	17R 10.9	13 57.5	2 6.4	7 46.2
31 Tu	22 34 55	7 9 44	28 25 29	5♉29 37	12 45.4	28 45.3	21 11.5	28 15.3	4 55.7	17 10.8	13 55.4	2 5.1	7 46.6

Astro Data	Planet Ingress	Last Aspect	☽ Ingress	Last Aspect	☽ Ingress	☽ Phases & Eclipses	Astro Data
Dy Hr Mn	Dy Hr Mn	Dy Hr Mn	Dy Hr Mn	Dy Hr Mn	Dy Hr Mn	Dy Hr Mn	1 JULY 1999
☽0N 6 5:18	♂ ♏ 5 3:59	3 3:21 ♂ △	♓ 3 4:34	1 16:03 ☿ △	♈ 1 16:47	6 11:57 ☽ 13♈59	Julian Day # 36341
☿ R 12 23:33	♀ ♍ 12 15:18	4 7:25 ♄ ✱	♈ 5 11:21	3 19:12 ☿ □	♉ 3 21:09	13 2:24 ● 20♋17	Delta T 61.8 sec
☽0S 18 23:56	☉ ♌ 23 6:44	7 10:06 ♀ △	♉ 7 15:22	5 21:35 ☿ ✱	♊ 5 23:57	20 9:00 ☽ 27♎14	SVP 05♓16'12"
♄□♅ 18 3:54	☿ ♋ 31 18:44	9 14:09 ♀ □	♊ 9 17:00	7 0:43 ♅ △	♋ 8 1:52	28 11:25 ○ 4♒58	Obliquity 23°26'15"
♃□♆ 21 15:54		11 16:37 ♀ ✱	♋ 11 17:27	10 3:01 ☿ ☌	♌ 10 3:55	28 11:34 ☍ P 0.396	⚷ Chiron 28♏14.4R
♀ R 30 1:42	☿ ♌ 11 4:25	13 2:24 ☉ ☌	♌ 13 18:26	11 11:09 ☉ ☌	♍ 12 7:21		☽ Mean ☊ 14♌48.6
	♀ ♌ 15 14:12	14 20:55 ♅ ☍	♍ 15 21:39	13 15:30 ♂ ✱	♎ 14 13:24	4 17:27 ☽ 11♉54	
☽0N 2 11:03	☉ ♍ 23 13:51	17 18:28 ☉ ✱	♎ 18 4:19	16 21:12 ♀ ✱	♏ 16 22:40	11 11:09 ● 18♌21	1 AUGUST 1999
☿ D 6 3:27	☿ ♍ 31 15:15	20 9:00 ☉ □	♏ 20 14:30	19 6:06 ♀ □	♐ 19 10:32	11 11:03:06 ☌ T 2'23"	Julian Day # 36372
☽0S 15 8:46		23 2:28 ☉ △	♐ 23 2:48	21 19:36 ☉ △	♑ 21 22:59	19 1:47 ☽ 25♏40	Delta T 61.9 sec
♇ D 19 1:45		24 9:51 ♅ ✱	♑ 25 15:08	23 22:12 ♂ ✱	♒ 24 9:49	26 23:48 ○ 3♓17	SVP 05♓16'08"
♃ R 25 2:38		26 23:05 ♄ △	♒ 28 1:54	26 9:31 ♂ □	♓ 26 17:50		Obliquity 23°26'15"
☽0N 29 16:55		29 8:56 ♄ □	♓ 30 10:27	28 17:41 ♂ △	♈ 28 23:09		⚷ Chiron 27♏36.5
♄ R 30 1:23				31 0:39 ☿ △	♉ 31 2:41		☽ Mean ☊ 13♌10.1

LONGITUDE SEPTEMBER 1999

Day	Sid.Time	☉	0 hr ☽	Noon ☽	True ☊	☿	♀	♂	♃	♄	♅	♆	♇
1 W	22 38 52	8♍ 7 44	12♉34 55	19♉41 1	12♌42.7	0♍42.9	20♌46.8	28♏52.4	4♉54.5	17♉10.7	13♒53.3	2♒ 3.8	7♐47.0
2 Th	22 42 48	9 5 47	26 47 32	3♊54 7	12D41.0	2 40.6	20R24.3	29 29.6	4R53.0	17R10.4	13R51.2	2R 2.6	7 47.4
3 F	22 46 45	10 3 52	11♊ 0 30	18 6 23	12 40.5	4 38.3	20 4.1	0♐ 7.0	4 51.3	17 10.0	13 49.1	2 1.4	7 47.9
4 Sa	22 50 41	11 1 58	25 11 30	2♋15 39	12 41.1	6 35.8	19 46.1	0 44.6	4 49.5	17 9.6	13 47.0	2 0.2	7 48.4
5 Su	22 54 38	12 0 7	9♋18 36	16 20 7	12 42.4	8 32.8	19 30.5	1 22.4	4 47.4	17 9.0	13 45.0	1 59.1	7 49.0
6 M	22 58 34	12 58 17	23 20 0	0♌18 1	12 43.9	10 29.2	19 17.3	2 0.4	4 45.1	17 8.3	13 43.0	1 57.9	7 49.5
7 Tu	23 2 31	13 56 30	7♌13 56	14 7 30	12R44.9	12 25.0	19 6.4	2 38.5	4 42.6	17 7.5	13 41.0	1 56.8	7 50.1
8 W	23 6 28	14 54 44	20 58 28	27 46 34	12 44.7	14 19.9	18 58.1	3 16.7	4 40.0	17 6.6	13 39.1	1 55.7	7 50.8
9 Th	23 10 24	15 53 1	4♍31 35	11♍13 16	12 43.0	16 13.9	18 52.1	3 55.2	4 37.1	17 5.6	13 37.2	1 54.7	7 51.5
10 F	23 14 21	16 51 19	17 51 23	24 25 46	12 39.6	18 6.9	18 48.5	4 33.8	4 34.1	17 4.5	13 35.3	1 53.6	7 52.2
11 Sa	23 18 17	17 49 39	0♎56 17	7♎22 50	12 34.7	19 59.0	18D47.3	5 12.6	4 30.8	17 3.3	13 33.4	1 52.6	7 52.9
12 Su	23 22 14	18 48 0	13 45 25	20 4 2	12 28.6	21 50.0	18 48.4	5 51.5	4 27.4	17 2.0	13 31.6	1 51.6	7 53.7
13 M	23 26 10	19 46 23	26 18 49	2♏29 57	12 22.1	23 39.9	18 51.8	6 30.6	4 23.8	17 0.5	13 29.8	1 50.7	7 54.5
14 Tu	23 30 7	20 44 48	8♏37 39	14 42 15	12 15.9	25 28.7	18 57.5	7 9.8	4 19.9	16 59.0	13 28.1	1 49.7	7 55.3
15 W	23 34 3	21 43 15	20 44 6	26 43 39	12 10.6	27 16.5	19 5.4	7 49.2	4 15.9	16 57.4	13 26.4	1 48.8	7 56.2
16 Th	23 38 0	22 41 44	2♐41 23	8♐37 49	12 6.8	29 3.2	19 15.5	8 28.8	4 11.8	16 55.7	13 24.7	1 47.9	7 57.1
17 F	23 41 57	23 40 14	14 33 31	20 29 5	12D 4.6	0♎48.8	19 27.7	9 8.5	4 7.4	16 53.8	13 23.0	1 47.1	7 58.0
18 Sa	23 45 53	24 38 45	26 25 9	2♑22 19	12 4.1	2 33.3	19 41.9	9 48.3	4 2.9	16 51.9	13 21.4	1 46.2	7 59.0
19 Su	23 49 50	25 37 19	8♑21 14	14 22 33	12 4.9	4 16.8	19 58.1	10 28.3	3 58.2	16 49.9	13 19.8	1 45.4	7 60.0
20 M	23 53 46	26 35 54	20 26 52	26 34 48	12 6.3	5 59.2	20 16.3	11 8.4	3 53.3	16 47.7	13 18.3	1 44.7	8 1.0
21 Tu	23 57 43	27 34 30	2♒46 52	9♒ 3 37	12R 7.6	7 40.6	20 36.4	11 48.6	3 48.3	16 45.5	13 16.8	1 43.9	8 2.1
22 W	0 1 39	28 33 9	15 25 26	21 52 43	12 7.9	9 21.0	20 58.3	12 29.0	3 43.0	16 43.2	13 15.3	1 43.2	8 3.2
23 Th	0 5 36	29 31 49	28 25 41	5♓ 4 29	12 6.6	11 0.3	21 21.9	13 9.5	3 37.7	16 40.8	13 13.9	1 42.5	8 4.3
24 F	0 9 32	0♎30 31	11♓49 8	18 39 31	12 3.2	12 38.8	21 47.3	13 50.1	3 32.1	16 38.3	13 12.5	1 41.9	8 5.4
25 Sa	0 13 29	1 29 15	25 35 22	2♈36 17	11 57.7	14 16.2	22 14.4	14 30.9	3 26.5	16 35.7	13 11.1	1 41.2	8 6.6
26 Su	0 17 25	2 28 0	9♈41 44	16 51 3	11 50.5	15 52.7	22 43.0	15 11.8	3 20.6	16 33.0	13 9.8	1 40.6	8 7.8
27 M	0 21 22	3 26 48	24 3 29	1♉18 14	11 42.3	17 28.3	23 13.2	15 52.8	3 14.6	16 30.2	13 8.6	1 40.1	8 9.1
28 Tu	0 25 19	4 25 38	8♉34 27	15 51 18	11 34.1	19 3.0	23 44.9	16 33.9	3 8.5	16 27.3	13 7.4	1 39.5	8 10.3
29 W	0 29 15	5 24 30	23 7 58	0♊23 42	11 26.9	20 36.7	24 18.0	17 15.2	3 2.2	16 24.4	13 6.2	1 39.0	8 11.6
30 Th	0 33 12	6 23 24	7♊37 52	14 49 55	11 21.6	22 9.6	24 52.6	17 56.5	2 55.8	16 21.3	13 5.0	1 38.5	8 12.9

LONGITUDE OCTOBER 1999

Day	Sid.Time	☉	0 hr ☽	Noon ☽	True ☊	☿	♀	♂	♃	♄	♅	♆	♇
1 F	0 37 8	7♎22 21	21♊59 25	29♊ 6 3	11♌18.5	23♎41.6	25♌28.5	18♐38.0	2♉49.3	16♉18.2	13♒ 3.9	1♒38.1	8♐14.3
2 Sa	0 41 5	8 21 20	6♋ 9 36	13♋ 9 57	11D17.4	25 12.7	26 5.6	19 19.6	2R42.6	16R15.0	13R 2.9	1R37.7	8 15.7
3 Su	0 45 1	9 20 22	20 7 3	27 0 56	11 17.7	26 43.0	26 44.0	20 1.4	2 35.8	16 11.7	13 1.9	1 37.3	8 17.1
4 M	0 48 58	10 19 25	3♌51 37	10♌39 14	11R18.5	28 12.4	27 23.7	20 43.2	2 28.9	16 8.3	13 0.9	1 37.0	8 18.5
5 Tu	0 52 54	11 18 31	17 23 49	24 5 30	11 18.5	29 40.9	28 4.4	21 25.2	2 21.9	16 4.9	13 0.0	1 36.6	8 20.0
6 W	0 56 51	12 17 40	0♍44 19	7♍20 19	11 16.7	1♏ 8.6	28 46.3	22 7.2	2 14.7	16 1.3	12 59.1	1 36.4	8 21.5
7 Th	1 0 48	13 16 50	13 53 32	20 23 58	11 12.5	2 35.3	29 29.2	22 49.4	2 7.5	15 57.7	12 58.3	1 36.1	8 23.0
8 F	1 4 44	14 16 3	26 51 36	3♎16 23	11 5.5	4 1.2	0♍13.2	23 31.7	2 0.1	15 54.0	12 57.5	1 35.9	8 24.5
9 Sa	1 8 41	15 15 18	9♎38 17	15 57 17	10 56.0	5 26.1	0 58.2	24 14.1	1 52.7	15 50.3	12 56.8	1 35.7	8 26.1
10 Su	1 12 37	16 14 34	22 13 20	28 26 27	10 44.5	6 50.1	1 44.1	24 56.7	1 45.2	15 46.5	12 56.1	1 35.5	8 27.7
11 M	1 16 34	17 13 53	4♏36 41	10♏44 5	10 32.1	8 13.1	2 30.9	25 39.3	1 37.6	15 42.6	12 55.5	1 35.4	8 29.3
12 Tu	1 20 30	18 13 14	16 48 49	22 51 3	10 19.8	9 35.1	3 18.5	26 22.0	1 29.9	15 38.6	12 54.9	1 35.3	8 31.0
13 W	1 24 27	19 12 37	28 51 1	4♐49 2	10 8.9	10 56.0	4 7.1	27 4.8	1 22.1	15 34.6	12 54.4	1 35.3	8 32.6
14 Th	1 28 23	20 12 2	10♐45 27	16 40 42	9 60.0	12 15.8	4 56.4	27 47.8	1 14.3	15 30.5	12 53.9	1D35.3	8 34.3
15 F	1 32 20	21 11 28	22 35 15	28 29 37	9 53.7	13 34.5	5 46.6	28 30.8	1 6.4	15 26.3	12 53.5	1 35.3	8 36.1
16 Sa	1 36 17	22 10 57	4♑24 24	10♑20 11	9 50.0	14 51.9	6 37.5	29 13.9	0 58.5	15 22.1	12 53.1	1 35.3	8 37.8
17 Su	1 40 13	23 10 27	16 17 37	22 17 22	9D48.5	16 8.0	7 29.1	29 57.1	0 50.5	15 17.9	12 52.7	1 35.4	8 39.6
18 M	1 44 10	24 9 59	28 20 8	4♒26 35	9R48.3	17 22.7	8 21.5	0♑40.5	0 42.5	15 13.6	12 52.4	1 35.5	8 41.4
19 Tu	1 48 6	25 9 33	10♒37 24	16 53 13	9 48.5	18 35.9	9 14.5	1 23.9	0 34.4	15 9.2	12 52.2	1 35.7	8 43.2
20 W	1 52 3	26 9 8	23 14 38	29 42 11	9 47.8	19 47.4	10 8.2	2 7.3	0 26.3	15 4.8	12 52.0	1 35.9	8 45.0
21 Th	1 55 59	27 8 45	6♓16 18	12♓57 19	9 45.3	20 57.1	11 2.5	2 50.9	0 18.2	15 0.3	12 51.9	1 36.1	8 46.9
22 F	1 59 56	28 8 24	19 45 25	26 40 37	9 40.3	22 4.8	11 57.5	3 34.6	0 10.1	14 55.8	12 51.8	1 36.3	8 48.7
23 Sa	2 3 52	29 8 5	3♈42 43	10♈51 24	9 32.6	23 10.4	12 53.1	4 18.3	0 2.0	14 51.3	12D51.8	1 36.6	8 50.6
24 Su	2 7 49	0♏ 7 47	18 6 3	25 25 54	9 22.6	24 13.7	13 49.2	5 2.1	29♈53.8	14 46.7	12 51.8	1 36.9	8 52.5
25 M	2 11 46	1 7 32	2♉50 2	10♉17 21	9 11.2	25 14.3	14 45.9	5 46.0	29 45.7	14 42.1	12 51.8	1 37.3	8 54.5
26 Tu	2 15 42	2 7 18	17 46 40	25 16 46	8 59.7	26 12.1	15 43.2	6 30.0	29 37.6	14 37.4	12 51.9	1 37.7	8 56.4
27 W	2 19 39	3 7 7	2♊46 25	10♊14 31	8 49.3	27 6.7	16 41.0	7 14.1	29 29.5	14 32.8	12 52.1	1 38.1	8 58.4
28 Th	2 23 35	4 6 57	17 40 1	25 2 3	8 41.2	27 57.8	17 39.3	7 58.2	29 21.4	14 28.1	12 52.3	1 38.5	9 0.4
29 F	2 27 32	5 6 50	2♋19 56	9♋33 8	8 35.9	28 44.9	18 38.2	8 42.4	29 13.4	14 23.3	12 52.6	1 39.0	9 2.4
30 Sa	2 31 28	6 6 46	16 41 20	23 44 20	8 33.2	29 27.8	19 37.5	9 26.7	29 5.3	14 18.6	12 52.9	1 39.5	9 4.4
31 Su	2 35 25	7 6 43	0♌42 8	7♌34 48	8 32.5	0♐ 5.8	20 37.3	10 11.1	28 57.3	14 13.8	12 53.3	1 40.1	9 6.5

Astro Data Dy Hr Mn	Planet Ingress Dy Hr Mn
☽0S 11 17:14	♂ ♐ 2 19:29
♀ D 11 0:23	☿ ♎ 16 12:53
☿0S 17 19:26	☉ ♎ 23 11:32
☽0N 26 0:40	
	☿ ♏ 5 5:12
☽0S 9 0:49	♀ ♍ 7 16:51
♃□♆ 11 6:45	♂ ♑ 17 1:35
♆ D 14 1:36	☉ ♏ 23 20:52
☽0N 23 10:50	♃ ♈ 23 5:49
♅ D 23 6:12	☿ ♐ 30 20:08

Last Aspect Dy Hr Mn	☽ Ingress Dy Hr Mn
2 4:46 ♂ ☍	♊ 2 5:25
3 15:00 ♀ ⚹	♋ 4 8:10
5 13:23 ♄ ⚹	♌ 6 11:29
7 20:30 ♀ ☌	♍ 8 15:57
10 0:33 ☿ ☌	♎ 10 22:16
12 9:38 ♀ ⚹	♏ 13 7:08
15 15:24 ☿ ⚹	♐ 15 18:35
17 20:06 ☉ □	♑ 18 7:13
20 13:04 ☉ △	♒ 20 18:38
22 10:38 ♀ ☍	♓ 23 2:51
24 8:27 ♄ ⚹	♈ 25 7:34
26 22:33 ♀ △	♉ 27 9:51
29 2:00 ♀ □	♊ 29 11:21

Last Aspect Dy Hr Mn	☽ Ingress Dy Hr Mn
1 6:08 ♀ ⚹	♋ 1 13:31
3 12:53 ☿ □	♌ 3 17:13
5 20:14 ♀ ☌	♍ 5 22:40
7 17:27 ♂ □	♎ 8 5:52
10 5:34 ♂ ⚹	♏ 10 15:01
11 21:42 ♄ ☍	♐ 13 2:18
15 12:49 ♂ ☌	♑ 15 15:04
17 15:00 ☉ □	♒ 18 3:17
20 5:53 ☉ △	♓ 20 12:33
22 4:24 ☿ △	♈ 22 17:42
24 19:05 ♃ ☌	♉ 24 19:25
26 14:22 ☿ ☍	♊ 26 19:33
28 18:55 ♃ ⚹	♋ 28 20:09
30 21:00 ♃ □	♌ 30 22:47

☽ Phases & Eclipses Dy Hr Mn	
2 22:17	☽ 9♊60
9 22:02	● 16♍47
17 20:06	☽ 24♐29
25 10:51	○ 1♈56
2 4:02	☽ 8♋31
9 11:34	● 15♎44
17 15:00	☽ 23♑48
24 21:02	○ 1♉00
31 12:04	☽ 7♌37

Astro Data

1 SEPTEMBER 1999
Julian Day # 36403
Delta T 61.9 sec
SVP 05♓16'04"
Obliquity 23°26'16"
⚷ Chiron 28♏32.6
☽ Mean ☊ 11♌31.6

1 OCTOBER 1999
Julian Day # 36433
Delta T 62.0 sec
SVP 05♓16'02"
Obliquity 23°26'16"
⚷ Chiron 0♐47.6
☽ Mean ☊ 9♌56.3

NOVEMBER 1999 LONGITUDE

Day	Sid.Time	☉	0 hr ☽	Noon ☽	True ☊	☿	♀	♂	♃	♄	♅	♆	♇
1 M	2 39 21	8♏ 6 42	14♌22 31	21♌ 5 33	8♌32.4	0♐38.4	21♍37.5	10♑55.5	28♈49.4	14♉ 9.0	12♒53.7	1♒40.7	9♐ 8.5
2 Tu	2 43 18	9 6 44	27 44 11	4♍18 42	8R31.7	1 5.1	22 38.2	11 40.0	28R41.5	14R 4.2	12 54.2	1 41.3	9 10.6
3 W	2 47 15	10 6 48	10♍49 26	17 16 40	8 29.2	1 25.3	23 39.2	12 24.6	28 33.7	13 59.3	12 54.7	1 41.9	9 12.7
4 Th	2 51 11	11 6 54	23 40 42	0♎ 1 44	8 24.0	1 38.3	24 40.7	13 9.3	28 25.9	13 54.5	12 55.3	1 42.6	9 14.8
5 F	2 55 8	12 7 2	6♎20 1	12 35 43	8 15.6	1R43.5	25 42.6	13 54.0	28 18.2	13 49.7	12 55.9	1 43.3	9 16.9
6 Sa	2 59 4	13 7 12	18 48 59	24 59 56	8 4.4	1 40.2	26 44.9	14 38.8	28 10.6	13 44.8	12 56.6	1 44.1	9 19.1
7 Su	3 3 1	14 7 23	1♏ 8 39	7♏15 15	7 51.0	1 27.9	27 47.5	15 23.6	28 3.1	13 39.9	12 57.3	1 44.9	9 21.2
8 M	3 6 57	15 7 37	13 19 48	19 22 23	7 36.5	1 6.1	28 50.5	16 8.6	27 55.6	13 35.1	12 58.1	1 45.7	9 23.4
9 Tu	3 10 54	16 7 53	25 23 8	1♐22 10	7 22.1	0 34.4	29 53.9	16 53.6	27 48.3	13 30.2	12 58.9	1 46.5	9 25.6
10 W	3 14 50	17 8 10	7♐19 39	13 15 48	7 8.9	29♏52.8	0♎57.5	17 38.6	27 41.0	13 25.4	12 59.8	1 47.4	9 27.8
11 Th	3 18 47	18 8 29	19 10 51	25 5 6	6 58.0	29 1.5	2 1.5	18 23.7	27 33.9	13 20.6	13 0.7	1 48.3	9 30.0
12 F	3 22 43	19 8 49	0♑58 55	6♑52 41	6 50.0	28 1.2	3 5.8	19 8.9	27 26.9	13 15.8	13 1.7	1 49.3	9 32.2
13 Sa	3 26 40	20 9 11	12 46 52	18 41 58	6 44.9	26 53.1	4 10.5	19 54.2	27 19.9	13 11.0	13 2.7	1 50.3	9 34.4
14 Su	3 30 37	21 9 35	24 38 33	0♒37 12	6 42.5	25 38.6	5 15.4	20 39.5	27 13.1	13 6.2	13 3.8	1 51.3	9 36.7
15 M	3 34 33	22 10 0	6♒38 34	12 43 16	6D41.9	24 19.8	6 20.5	21 24.8	27 6.5	13 1.4	13 4.9	1 52.3	9 38.9
16 Tu	3 38 30	23 10 26	18 52 0	25 5 27	6R42.1	22 59.1	7 26.0	22 10.2	26 59.9	12 56.7	13 6.1	1 53.4	9 41.2
17 W	3 42 26	24 10 54	1♓24 15	7♓49 3	6 41.9	21 39.2	8 31.8	22 55.7	26 53.5	12 52.0	13 7.4	1 54.5	9 43.4
18 Th	3 46 23	25 11 23	14 20 24	20 58 47	6 40.3	20 22.7	9 37.8	23 41.2	26 47.3	12 47.3	13 8.6	1 55.6	9 45.7
19 F	3 50 19	26 11 53	27 44 35	4♈38 1	6 36.5	19 12.0	10 44.0	24 26.7	26 41.2	12 42.6	13 10.0	1 56.8	9 48.0
20 Sa	3 54 16	27 12 24	11♈39 8	18 47 46	6 30.2	18 9.3	11 50.5	25 12.3	26 35.2	12 38.0	13 11.3	1 58.0	9 50.3
21 Su	3 58 12	28 12 57	26 3 33	3♉25 52	6 21.5	17 16.4	12 57.3	25 57.9	26 29.4	12 33.4	13 12.7	1 59.2	9 52.6
22 M	4 2 9	29 13 31	10♉53 53	18 26 31	6 11.4	16 34.3	14 4.2	26 43.6	26 23.8	12 28.9	13 14.2	2 0.4	9 54.9
23 Tu	4 6 6	0♐14 6	26 2 32	3♊40 36	6 1.0	16 3.7	15 11.5	27 29.3	26 18.3	12 24.4	13 15.7	2 1.7	9 57.2
24 W	4 10 2	1 14 43	11♊19 17	18 57 10	5 51.6	15 44.9	16 18.9	28 15.1	26 12.9	12 19.9	13 17.3	2 3.0	9 59.5
25 Th	4 13 59	2 15 21	26 32 54	4♋ 5 16	5 44.2	15D37.5	17 26.6	29 0.9	26 7.8	12 15.5	13 18.9	2 4.4	10 1.8
26 F	4 17 55	3 16 1	11♋33 14	18 55 57	5 39.4	15 41.1	18 34.5	29 46.7	26 2.8	12 11.1	13 20.6	2 5.7	10 4.1
27 Sa	4 21 52	4 16 43	26 12 48	3♌23 22	5D37.1	15 55.0	19 42.6	0♒32.6	25 58.0	12 6.8	13 22.3	2 7.1	10 6.5
28 Su	4 25 48	5 17 26	10♌27 26	17 24 57	5 36.9	16 18.3	20 50.9	1 18.5	25 53.3	12 2.6	13 24.0	2 8.5	10 8.8
29 M	4 29 45	6 18 11	24 16 4	1♍ 0 58	5R37.6	16 50.3	21 59.3	2 4.5	25 48.9	11 58.4	13 25.8	2 10.0	10 11.1
30 Tu	4 33 42	7 18 57	7♍40 0	14 13 32	5 38.0	17 29.9	23 8.0	2 50.5	25 44.6	11 54.2	13 27.6	2 11.5	10 13.5

DECEMBER 1999 LONGITUDE

Day	Sid.Time	☉	0 hr ☽	Noon ☽	True ☊	☿	♀	♂	♃	♄	♅	♆	♇
1 W	4 37 38	8♐19 44	20♍42 0	27♍ 5 51	5♌37.2	18♏16.4	24♎16.9	3♒36.5	25♈40.5	11♉50.1	13♒29.5	2♒13.0	10♐15.8
2 Th	4 41 35	9 20 33	3♎25 31	9♎41 26	5R34.2	19 9.0	25 25.9	4 22.6	25R36.6	11R46.1	13 31.4	2 14.5	10 18.1
3 F	4 45 31	10 21 24	15 54 1	22 3 39	5 28.8	20 6.8	26 35.2	5 8.7	25 32.9	11 42.2	13 33.4	2 16.0	10 20.5
4 Sa	4 49 28	11 22 16	28 10 42	4♏15 27	5 21.1	21 9.2	27 44.6	5 54.8	25 29.4	11 38.3	13 35.4	2 17.6	10 22.8
5 Su	4 53 24	12 23 9	10♏18 14	16 19 16	5 11.5	22 15.7	28 54.1	6 41.0	25 26.0	11 34.5	13 37.5	2 19.2	10 25.2
6 M	4 57 21	13 24 3	22 18 47	28 17 1	5 1.0	23 25.6	0♏ 3.8	7 27.1	25 22.9	11 30.7	13 39.6	2 20.9	10 27.5
7 Tu	5 1 17	14 24 59	4♐14 8	10♐10 19	4 50.4	24 38.5	1 13.7	8 13.4	25 20.0	11 27.0	13 41.7	2 22.5	10 29.8
8 W	5 5 14	15 25 56	16 5 46	22 0 39	4 40.8	25 54.0	2 23.7	8 59.6	25 17.2	11 23.4	13 43.9	2 24.2	10 32.2
9 Th	5 9 11	16 26 53	27 55 11	3♑49 36	4 33.0	27 11.7	3 33.8	9 45.9	25 14.7	11 19.9	13 46.1	2 25.9	10 34.5
10 F	5 13 7	17 27 52	9♑44 8	15 39 5	4 27.4	28 31.3	4 44.1	10 32.2	25 12.4	11 16.5	13 48.4	2 27.6	10 36.8
11 Sa	5 17 4	18 28 51	21 34 45	27 31 31	4 24.2	29 52.6	5 54.5	11 18.6	25 10.3	11 13.1	13 50.7	2 29.4	10 39.2
12 Su	5 21 0	19 29 51	3♒29 46	9♒29 57	4D23.1	1♐15.4	7 5.0	12 4.9	25 8.4	11 9.9	13 53.0	2 31.1	10 41.5
13 M	5 24 57	20 30 52	15 32 32	21 38 2	4 23.7	2 39.3	8 15.7	12 51.3	25 6.7	11 6.7	13 55.4	2 32.9	10 43.8
14 Tu	5 28 53	21 31 54	27 47 1	4♓ 0 0	4 25.2	4 4.3	9 26.4	13 37.7	25 5.2	11 3.6	13 57.8	2 34.7	10 46.1
15 W	5 32 50	22 32 55	10♓17 35	16 40 19	4 26.7	5 30.3	10 37.3	14 24.1	25 3.9	11 0.6	14 0.2	2 36.6	10 48.4
16 Th	5 36 46	23 33 58	23 8 44	29 43 20	4R27.3	6 57.0	11 48.3	15 10.5	25 2.8	10 57.7	14 2.7	2 38.4	10 50.7
17 F	5 40 43	24 35 0	6♈24 34	13♈12 44	4 26.6	8 24.5	12 59.4	15 56.9	25 2.0	10 54.8	14 5.3	2 40.3	10 53.0
18 Sa	5 44 40	25 36 3	20 8 3	27 10 36	4 24.1	9 52.5	14 10.7	16 43.4	25 1.3	10 52.1	14 7.8	2 42.2	10 55.3
19 Su	5 48 36	26 37 7	4♉20 14	11♉36 39	4 20.1	11 21.1	15 22.0	17 29.9	25 0.9	10 49.5	14 10.4	2 44.1	10 57.6
20 M	5 52 33	27 38 11	18 59 18	26 27 28	4 14.9	12 50.2	16 33.4	18 16.3	25D 0.6	10 46.9	14 13.0	2 46.0	10 59.8
21 Tu	5 56 29	28 39 15	4♊ 0 11	11♊36 19	4 9.3	14 19.7	17 44.9	19 2.8	25 0.6	10 44.5	14 15.7	2 48.0	11 2.1
22 W	6 0 26	29 40 19	19 14 38	26 53 45	4 4.1	15 49.7	18 56.6	19 49.3	25 0.8	10 42.2	14 18.4	2 50.0	11 4.3
23 Th	6 4 22	0♑41 25	4♋32 19	12♋ 8 58	4 0.1	17 20.0	20 8.3	20 35.8	25 1.2	10 39.9	14 21.1	2 51.9	11 6.6
24 F	6 8 19	1 42 30	19 42 29	27 11 45	3D57.7	18 50.6	21 20.1	21 22.3	25 1.8	10 37.8	14 23.9	2 54.0	11 8.8
25 Sa	6 12 15	2 43 36	4♌35 49	11♌53 56	3 57.0	20 21.6	22 32.0	22 8.8	25 2.6	10 35.7	14 26.7	2 56.0	11 11.0
26 Su	6 16 12	3 44 43	19 5 35	26 10 25	3 57.7	21 52.8	23 44.0	22 55.3	25 3.6	10 33.8	14 29.5	2 58.0	11 13.2
27 M	6 20 9	4 45 50	3♍ 8 17	9♍59 11	3 59.2	23 24.4	24 56.1	23 41.9	25 4.8	10 32.0	14 32.4	3 0.1	11 15.4
28 Tu	6 24 5	5 46 58	16 43 17	23 20 51	4 0.8	24 56.3	26 8.2	24 28.4	25 6.2	10 30.2	14 35.2	3 2.1	11 17.6
29 W	6 28 2	6 48 6	29 52 14	6♎17 53	4R 1.9	26 28.4	27 20.5	25 14.9	25 7.9	10 28.6	14 38.2	3 4.2	11 19.8
30 Th	6 31 58	7 49 14	12♎38 17	18 53 56	4 2.0	28 0.9	28 32.8	26 1.5	25 9.7	10 27.1	14 41.1	3 6.3	11 21.9
31 F	6 35 55	8 50 24	25 5 21	1♏13 4	4 0.9	29 33.6	29 45.2	26 48.0	25 11.7	10 25.7	14 44.1	3 8.4	11 24.0

Astro Data Dy Hr Mn	Planet Ingress Dy Hr Mn	Last Aspect Dy Hr Mn	☽ Ingress Dy Hr Mn	Last Aspect Dy Hr Mn	☽ Ingress Dy Hr Mn	☽ Phases & Eclipses Dy Hr Mn
☽0S 5 7:33	☿ ♏ 9 20:13	2 1:43 ♃ △	♍ 2 4:07	30 19:11 ☿ ⚹	♎ 1 17:29	8 3:53 ● 15♏17
☿ R 5 2:59	♀ ♎ 9 2:19	4 2:03 ♀ ☌	♎ 4 11:57	3 23:03 ♀ ☌	♏ 4 3:35	16 9:03 ☽ 23♒33
♀0S 11 19:37	☉ ♐ 22 18:25	6 18:01 ♃ ☍	♏ 6 21:46	6 2:29 ♃ ☍	♐ 6 15:27	23 7:04 ○ 0♊32
♄□♅ 14 9:36	♂ ♒ 26 6:56	8 5:57 ♂ ⚹	♐ 9 9:15	8 18:35 ♃ △	♑ 9 4:14	29 23:19 ☽ 7♍17
☽0N 19 22:09		11 16:53 ♃ △	♑ 11 22:00	11 7:14 ♃ □	♒ 11 16:59	
☿ D 25 3:55	♀ ♏ 5 22:41	14 5:08 ♃ □	♒ 14 10:46	13 18:46 ♃ ⚹	♓ 14 4:18	7 22:32 ● 15♐22
	☿ ♐ 11 2:09	16 15:31 ♃ ⚹	♓ 16 21:21	16 0:50 ☉ □	♈ 16 12:30	16 0:50 ☽ 23♓36
☽0S 2 14:05	☉ ♑ 22 7:44	18 21:04 ☉ △	♈ 19 3:57	18 10:03 ☉ △	♉ 18 16:45	22 17:31 ○ 0♋25
♃⚼♇ 5 3:45	☿ ♑ 31 6:48	21 0:42 ♃ ☌	♉ 21 6:26	19 22:47 ♂ □	♊ 20 17:39	29 14:04 ☽ 7♎24
☽0N 17 8:16	♀ ♐ 31 4:54	23 2:24 ♂ △	♊ 23 6:14	22 9:03 ♃ ⚹	♋ 22 16:52	
♄⚻♇ 17 8:47		24 23:20 ♃ ⚹	♋ 25 5:29	24 8:31 ♃ □	♌ 24 16:32	
♃ D 20 14:48		26 23:36 ♃ □	♌ 27 6:19	26 10:07 ♃ △	♍ 26 18:34	
☽0S 29 21:21		29 2:43 ♃ △	♍ 29 10:11	28 18:51 ♀ ⚹	♎ 29 0:14	
				31 3:34 ♂ △	♏ 31 9:36	

Astro Data

1 NOVEMBER 1999
Julian Day # 36464
Delta T 62.0 sec
SVP 05♓15'58"
Obliquity 23°26'16"
⚷ Chiron 4♐06.7
☽ Mean ☊ 8♌17.8

1 DECEMBER 1999
Julian Day # 36494
Delta T 62.1 sec
SVP 05♓15'54"
Obliquity 23°26'16"
⚷ Chiron 7♐48.1
☽ Mean ☊ 6♌42.4

LONGITUDE — JANUARY 2000

Day	Sid.Time	☉	0 hr ☽	Noon ☽	True ☊	☿	♀	♂	♃	♄	♅	♆	♇
1 Sa	6 39 51	9♑51 33	7♏17 35	13♏19 25	3♌58.6	1♑ 6.7	0♐57.7	27♒34.5	25♈14.0	10♉24.4	14♒47.0	3♒10.5	11♐26.2
2 Su	6 43 48	10 52 43	19 19 1	25 16 50	3R 55.3	2 40.1	2 10.2	28 21.1	25 16.4	10R 23.2	14 50.1	3 12.7	11 28.3
3 M	6 47 44	11 53 53	1♐13 18	7♐ 8 46	3 51.5	4 13.8	3 22.8	29 7.6	25 19.1	10 22.1	14 53.1	3 14.8	11 30.4
4 Tu	6 51 41	12 55 4	13 3 37	18 58 8	3 47.6	5 47.8	4 35.5	29 54.2	25 21.9	10 21.1	14 56.2	3 17.0	11 32.5
5 W	6 55 38	13 56 14	24 52 39	0♑47 25	3 44.2	7 22.2	5 48.2	0♓40.7	25 25.0	10 20.2	14 59.3	3 19.1	11 34.5
6 Th	6 59 34	14 57 25	6♑42 42	12 38 44	3 41.5	8 56.9	7 1.0	1 27.2	25 28.2	10 19.5	15 2.4	3 21.3	11 36.6
7 F	7 3 31	15 58 36	18 35 45	24 33 59	3 39.7	10 32.0	8 13.9	2 13.8	25 31.7	10 18.8	15 5.6	3 23.5	11 38.6
8 Sa	7 7 27	16 59 46	0♒33 39	6♒35 0	3D 39.0	12 7.5	9 26.8	3 0.3	25 35.3	10 18.3	15 8.7	3 25.7	11 40.6
9 Su	7 11 24	18 0 57	12 38 17	18 43 45	3 39.2	13 43.4	10 39.7	3 46.8	25 39.2	10 17.9	15 11.9	3 27.9	11 42.6
10 M	7 15 20	19 2 7	24 51 42	1♓ 2 25	3 40.1	15 19.7	11 52.7	4 33.3	25 43.2	10 17.6	15 15.1	3 30.1	11 44.6
11 Tu	7 19 17	20 3 16	7♓16 14	13 33 28	3 41.3	16 56.4	13 5.8	5 19.8	25 47.4	10 17.4	15 18.3	3 32.4	11 46.5
12 W	7 23 13	21 4 25	19 54 28	26 19 35	3 42.6	18 33.5	14 18.9	6 6.3	25 51.8	10D 17.3	15 21.6	3 34.6	11 48.4
13 Th	7 27 10	22 5 34	2♈49 10	9♈23 33	3 43.6	20 11.1	15 32.0	6 52.8	25 56.4	10 17.3	15 24.8	3 36.8	11 50.3
14 F	7 31 7	23 6 42	16 3 2	22 47 52	3R 44.1	21 49.2	16 45.2	7 39.3	26 1.2	10 17.5	15 28.1	3 39.1	11 52.2
15 Sa	7 35 3	24 7 49	29 38 16	6♉34 19	3 44.2	23 27.8	17 58.4	8 25.7	26 6.1	10 17.8	15 31.4	3 41.3	11 54.1
16 Su	7 39 0	25 8 55	13♉36 2	20 43 20	3 43.8	25 6.8	19 11.7	9 12.2	26 11.3	10 18.1	15 34.7	3 43.6	11 55.9
17 M	7 42 56	26 10 1	27 55 56	5♊13 28	3 43.0	26 46.4	20 25.0	9 58.6	26 16.6	10 18.6	15 38.1	3 45.8	11 57.8
18 Tu	7 46 53	27 11 6	12♊35 23	20 1 0	3 42.2	28 26.4	21 38.3	10 45.0	26 22.1	10 19.2	15 41.4	3 48.1	11 59.6
19 W	7 50 49	28 12 10	27 29 27	4♋59 48	3 41.6	0♒ 7.0	22 51.7	11 31.4	26 27.8	10 19.9	15 44.8	3 50.4	12 1.3
20 Th	7 54 46	29 13 14	12♋31 1	20 1 59	3 41.1	1 48.1	24 5.1	12 17.8	26 33.7	10 20.7	15 48.2	3 52.7	12 3.1
21 F	7 58 42	0♒14 17	27 31 37	4♌58 50	3D 40.9	3 29.7	25 18.5	13 4.1	26 39.7	10 21.7	15 51.5	3 54.9	12 4.8
22 Sa	8 2 39	1 15 19	12♌22 36	19 42 2	3 40.9	5 11.8	26 32.0	13 50.5	26 45.9	10 22.7	15 54.9	3 57.2	12 6.5
23 Su	8 6 36	2 16 21	26 56 21	4♍ 4 55	3 41.0	6 54.4	27 45.5	14 36.8	26 52.3	10 23.9	15 58.4	3 59.5	12 8.2
24 M	8 10 32	3 17 22	11♍ 7 17	18 3 8	3R 41.1	8 37.5	28 59.1	15 23.0	26 58.8	10 25.2	16 1.8	4 1.8	12 9.9
25 Tu	8 14 29	4 18 22	24 52 21	1♎34 55	3 41.1	10 21.0	0♑12.7	16 9.3	27 5.5	10 26.5	16 5.2	4 4.0	12 11.5
26 W	8 18 25	5 19 22	8♎10 59	14 40 48	3 41.0	12 4.9	1 26.3	16 55.6	27 12.4	10 28.0	16 8.6	4 6.3	12 13.1
27 Th	8 22 22	6 20 21	21 4 44	27 23 12	3 40.8	13 49.2	2 39.9	17 41.8	27 19.4	10 29.6	16 12.1	4 8.6	12 14.7
28 F	8 26 18	7 21 20	3♏36 42	9♏45 46	3D 40.7	15 33.7	3 53.6	18 28.0	27 26.5	10 31.3	16 15.5	4 10.9	12 16.2
29 Sa	8 30 15	8 22 18	15 50 57	21 52 52	3 40.7	17 18.5	5 7.3	19 14.1	27 33.9	10 33.1	16 19.0	4 13.1	12 17.7
30 Su	8 34 11	9 23 15	27 52 5	3♐49 10	3 41.0	19 3.3	6 21.0	20 0.3	27 41.4	10 35.0	16 22.5	4 15.4	12 19.2
31 M	8 38 8	10 24 12	9♐44 44	15 39 17	3 41.6	20 48.2	7 34.8	20 46.4	27 49.0	10 37.1	16 25.9	4 17.7	12 20.7

LONGITUDE — FEBRUARY 2000

Day	Sid.Time	☉	0 hr ☽	Noon ☽	True ☊	☿	♀	♂	♃	♄	♅	♆	♇
1 Tu	8 42 5	11♒25 8	21♐33 23	27♐27 30	3♌42.4	22♒32.8	8♑48.6	21♓32.6	27♈56.8	10♉39.2	16♒29.4	4♒20.0	12♐22.2
2 W	8 46 1	12 26 3	3♑22 7	9♑17 40	3 43.4	24 17.2	10 2.4	22 18.6	28 4.8	10 41.5	16 32.9	4 22.2	12 23.6
3 Th	8 49 58	13 26 58	15 14 31	21 13 1	3 44.2	26 0.9	11 16.2	23 4.7	28 12.9	10 43.8	16 36.4	4 24.5	12 24.9
4 F	8 53 54	14 27 51	27 13 30	3♒16 14	3R 44.7	27 43.9	12 30.1	23 50.7	28 21.1	10 46.3	16 39.9	4 26.7	12 26.3
5 Sa	8 57 51	15 28 44	9♒21 27	15 29 21	3 44.8	29 25.7	13 44.0	24 36.7	28 29.5	10 48.8	16 43.4	4 29.0	12 27.6
6 Su	9 1 47	16 29 35	21 40 6	27 53 50	3 44.1	1♓ 6.2	14 57.8	25 22.7	28 38.1	10 51.5	16 46.9	4 31.2	12 28.9
7 M	9 5 44	17 30 25	4♓10 40	10♓30 41	3 42.8	2 44.8	16 11.7	26 8.7	28 46.7	10 54.3	16 50.4	4 33.5	12 30.2
8 Tu	9 9 40	18 31 13	16 53 58	23 20 35	3 40.8	4 21.1	17 25.7	26 54.6	28 55.6	10 57.1	16 53.8	4 35.7	12 31.4
9 W	9 13 37	19 32 1	29 50 34	6♈23 58	3 38.5	5 54.6	18 39.6	27 40.5	29 4.5	11 0.1	16 57.3	4 37.9	12 32.6
10 Th	9 17 34	20 32 46	13♈ 0 49	19 41 9	3 36.1	7 24.8	19 53.5	28 26.3	29 13.6	11 3.2	17 0.8	4 40.1	12 33.8
11 F	9 21 30	21 33 31	26 25 1	3♉12 25	3 34.0	8 51.2	21 7.5	29 12.2	29 22.8	11 6.4	17 4.3	4 42.3	12 34.9
12 Sa	9 25 27	22 34 14	10♉ 3 21	16 57 49	3D 32.7	10 12.9	22 21.4	29 58.0	29 32.2	11 9.6	17 7.8	4 44.5	12 36.0
13 Su	9 29 23	23 34 55	23 55 45	0♊57 6	3 32.2	11 29.4	23 35.4	0♈43.7	29 41.6	11 13.0	17 11.3	4 46.7	12 37.1
14 M	9 33 20	24 35 34	8♊ 1 43	15 9 24	3 32.7	12 39.9	24 49.4	1 29.4	29 51.2	11 16.5	17 14.7	4 48.9	12 38.2
15 Tu	9 37 16	25 36 12	22 19 54	29 32 54	3 33.9	13 43.7	26 3.4	2 15.1	0♉ 1.0	11 20.1	17 18.2	4 51.1	12 39.2
16 W	9 41 13	26 36 48	6♋47 58	14♋ 4 35	3 35.4	14 40.1	27 17.4	3 0.8	0 10.8	11 23.7	17 21.7	4 53.2	12 40.2
17 Th	9 45 9	27 37 22	21 22 12	28 40 10	3R 36.5	15 28.4	28 31.4	3 46.4	0 20.8	11 27.5	17 25.1	4 55.4	12 41.1
18 F	9 49 6	28 37 55	5♌57 45	13♌14 13	3 36.9	16 8.0	29 45.4	4 32.0	0 30.9	11 31.3	17 28.6	4 57.5	12 42.0
19 Sa	9 53 3	29 38 26	20 28 47	27 40 43	3 36.0	16 38.2	0♒59.5	5 17.5	0 41.0	11 35.3	17 32.0	4 59.6	12 42.9
20 Su	9 56 59	0♓38 55	4♍49 16	11♍53 46	3 33.8	16 58.8	2 13.5	6 3.0	0 51.4	11 39.3	17 35.4	5 1.7	12 43.8
21 M	10 0 56	1 39 23	18 53 39	25 48 26	3 30.2	17R 9.3	3 27.6	6 48.5	1 1.8	11 43.4	17 38.8	5 3.8	12 44.6
22 Tu	10 4 52	2 39 49	2♎37 44	9♎21 19	3 25.6	17 9.6	4 41.6	7 33.9	1 12.3	11 47.6	17 42.2	5 5.9	12 45.4
23 W	10 8 49	3 40 14	15 59 5	22 31 3	3 20.7	16 59.8	5 55.7	8 19.3	1 22.9	11 51.9	17 45.6	5 8.0	12 46.1
24 Th	10 12 45	4 40 38	28 57 19	5♏18 9	3 16.1	16 40.2	7 9.8	9 4.6	1 33.7	11 56.3	17 49.0	5 10.0	12 46.9
25 F	10 16 42	5 40 59	11♏33 53	17 44 57	3 12.3	16 11.2	8 23.9	9 49.9	1 44.5	12 0.8	17 52.4	5 12.1	12 47.5
26 Sa	10 20 38	6 41 20	23 51 48	29 55 1	3 9.9	15 33.7	9 38.0	10 35.2	1 55.5	12 5.3	17 55.7	5 14.1	12 48.2
27 Su	10 24 35	7 41 39	5♐55 11	11♐52 54	3D 8.9	14 48.5	10 52.1	11 20.4	2 6.6	12 10.0	17 59.1	5 16.1	12 48.8
28 M	10 28 32	8 41 57	17 48 48	23 43 34	3 9.3	13 56.9	12 6.2	12 5.6	2 17.7	12 14.7	18 2.4	5 18.1	12 49.4
29 Tu	10 32 28	9 42 13	29 37 48	5♑32 9	3 10.7	13 0.2	13 20.3	12 50.7	2 29.0	12 19.5	18 5.7	5 20.0	12 50.0

Astro Data Dy Hr Mn	Planet Ingress Dy Hr Mn	Last Aspect Dy Hr Mn	☽ Ingress Dy Hr Mn	Last Aspect Dy Hr Mn	☽ Ingress Dy Hr Mn	☽ Phases & Eclipses Dy Hr Mn	Astro Data
♄ D 12 4:59	♂ ♓ 4 3:01	2 19:28 ♂ □	♐ 2 21:32	1 13:08 ♃ △	♑ 1 17:10	6 18:14 ● 15♑44	1 JANUARY 2000
☽0N 13 15:37	☿ ♒ 18 22:20	5 1:06 ♃ △	♑ 5 10:24	4 2:16 ♃ □	♒ 4 5:31	14 13:34 ☽ 23♈41	Julian Day # 36525
☽0S 26 5:57	☉ ♒ 20 18:23	7 14:00 ♃ □	♒ 7 22:53	6 13:34 ♃ ✶	♓ 6 16:02	21 4:41 ○ 0♌26	Delta T 62.1 sec
♃□♇ 26 3:19	♀ ♑ 24 19:52	10 1:41 ♃ ✶	♓ 10 9:59	8 19:46 ♂ ☌	♈ 9 0:17	21 4:44 ☍T 1.325	SVP 05♓15'49"
		12 2:23 ☉ ✶	♈ 12 18:48	11 5:19 ♃ ☌	♉ 11 6:21	28 7:57 ☽ 7♏42	Obliquity 23°26'16"
☽0N 9 20:59	☿ ♓ 5 8:09	14 17:47 ♃ ☌	♉ 15 0:38	12 23:22 ♀ △	♊ 13 10:23		⚷ Chiron 11♐34.0
♂0N 13 14:03	♂ ♈ 12 1:04	16 21:50 ☿ △	♊ 17 3:25	15 5:51 ☉ △	♋ 15 12:45	5 13:03 ● 16♒02	☽ Mean ☊ 5♌04.0
☿ R 21 12:46	♃ ♉ 14 21:39	18 22:21 ♃ ✶	♋ 19 4:01	17 12:51 ♀ ☍	♌ 17 14:11	5 12:49:23 ☌P 0.580	
☽0S 22 15:25	♀ ♒ 18 4:43	20 22:36 ♃ □	♌ 21 3:58	18 19:05 ♅ ☍	♍ 19 15:53	12 23:21 ☽ 23♉33	1 FEBRUARY 2000
	☉ ♓ 19 8:33	23 1:30 ♀ △	♍ 23 5:07	20 20:59 ♅ ☍	♎ 21 19:21	19 16:27 ○ 0♍20	Julian Day # 36556
		24 7:48 ♂ ☍	♎ 25 9:09	23 3:16 ♅ △	♏ 24 1:58	27 3:54 ☽ 7♐51	Delta T 62.0 sec
		27 12:00 ♃ ☍	♏ 27 17:01	25 12:18 ♅ □	♐ 26 12:10		SVP 05♓15'44"
		29 7:11 ♂ △	♐ 30 4:17	28 0:28 ♅ ✶	♑ 29 0:45		Obliquity 23°26'16"
							⚷ Chiron 14♐43.0
							☽ Mean ☊ 3♌25.5

MARCH 2000 LONGITUDE

Day	Sid.Time	☉	0 hr ☽	Noon ☽	True ☊	☿	♀	♂	♃	♄	♅	♆	♇
1 W	10 36 25	10♓42 28	11♑27 15	17♑23 40	3♌12.5	11♓59.9	14♒34.5	13♈35.8	2♉40.3	12♉24.4	18♒ 9.0	5♒22.0	12♐50.5
2 Th	10 40 21	11 42 41	23 21 57	29 22 38	3R 14.0	10R 57.5	15 48.6	14 20.9	2 51.8	12 29.4	18 12.3	5 23.9	12 51.0
3 F	10 44 18	12 42 53	5♒26 9	11♒32 56	3 14.4	9 54.5	17 2.7	15 6.0	3 3.3	12 34.4	18 15.6	5 25.9	12 51.4
4 Sa	10 48 14	13 43 3	17 43 18	23 57 32	3 13.3	8 52.4	18 16.9	15 50.9	3 14.9	12 39.6	18 18.8	5 27.8	12 51.8
5 Su	10 52 11	14 43 11	0♓15 50	6♓38 20	3 10.1	7 52.6	19 31.0	16 35.9	3 26.7	12 44.8	18 22.0	5 29.6	12 52.2
6 M	10 56 7	15 43 18	13 5 3	19 35 58	3 5.0	6 56.2	20 45.2	17 20.8	3 38.5	12 50.0	18 25.2	5 31.5	12 52.5
7 Tu	11 0 4	16 43 22	26 10 59	2♈49 54	2 58.2	6 4.3	21 59.3	18 5.7	3 50.3	12 55.4	18 28.4	5 33.3	12 52.8
8 W	11 4 1	17 43 25	9♈32 31	16 18 32	2 50.4	5 17.6	23 13.5	18 50.5	4 2.3	13 0.8	18 31.6	5 35.1	12 53.1
9 Th	11 7 57	18 43 26	23 7 39	29 59 32	2 42.5	4 36.8	24 27.6	19 35.3	4 14.4	13 6.3	18 34.7	5 36.9	12 53.3
10 F	11 11 54	19 43 24	6♉53 50	13♉50 16	2 35.4	4 2.2	25 41.8	20 20.0	4 26.5	13 11.9	18 37.8	5 38.7	12 53.5
11 Sa	11 15 50	20 43 21	20 48 29	27 48 13	2 29.9	3 34.0	26 55.9	21 4.7	4 38.7	13 17.5	18 40.9	5 40.5	12 53.7
12 Su	11 19 47	21 43 15	4♊49 13	11♊51 16	2 26.5	3 12.5	28 10.0	21 49.4	4 51.0	13 23.2	18 44.0	5 42.2	12 53.9
13 M	11 23 43	22 43 7	18 54 11	25 57 47	2D 25.1	2 57.5	29 24.2	22 34.0	5 3.4	13 29.0	18 47.1	5 43.9	12 54.0
14 Tu	11 27 40	23 42 57	3♋ 1 56	10♋ 6 29	2 25.4	2D 49.0	0♓38.3	23 18.5	5 15.9	13 34.9	18 50.1	5 45.6	12 54.0
15 W	11 31 36	24 42 45	17 11 15	24 16 4	2 26.4	2 46.8	1 52.4	24 3.0	5 28.4	13 40.8	18 53.1	5 47.2	12R 54.1
16 Th	11 35 33	25 42 30	1♌20 43	8♌24 56	2R 27.0	2 50.6	3 6.5	24 47.5	5 41.0	13 46.7	18 56.0	5 48.9	12 54.1
17 F	11 39 30	26 42 14	15 28 25	22 30 49	2 26.3	3 0.3	4 20.7	25 31.9	5 53.6	13 52.8	18 59.0	5 50.5	12 54.0
18 Sa	11 43 26	27 41 54	29 31 44	6♍30 45	2 23.3	3 15.4	5 34.8	26 16.3	6 6.3	13 58.9	19 1.9	5 52.1	12 54.0
19 Su	11 47 23	28 41 33	13♍27 24	20 21 13	2 17.9	3 35.8	6 48.9	27 0.6	6 19.1	14 5.0	19 4.8	5 53.6	12 53.9
20 M	11 51 19	29 41 10	27 11 46	3♎58 38	2 10.0	4 1.1	8 3.0	27 44.9	6 31.9	14 11.2	19 7.6	5 55.2	12 53.7
21 Tu	11 55 16	0♈40 44	10♎41 26	17 19 52	2 0.3	4 31.1	9 17.1	28 29.1	6 44.8	14 17.5	19 10.5	5 56.7	12 53.5
22 W	11 59 12	1 40 17	23 53 43	0♏22 52	1 49.7	5 5.5	10 31.2	29 13.3	6 57.8	14 23.8	19 13.3	5 58.2	12 53.3
23 Th	12 3 9	2 39 47	6♏47 16	13 6 59	1 39.3	5 44.0	11 45.3	29 57.4	7 10.8	14 30.2	19 16.0	5 59.6	12 53.1
24 F	12 7 5	3 39 16	19 22 10	25 33 6	1 30.1	6 26.3	12 59.4	0♉41.5	7 23.9	14 36.7	19 18.8	6 1.1	12 52.8
25 Sa	12 11 2	4 38 43	1♐40 7	7♐43 37	1 22.8	7 12.4	14 13.5	1 25.5	7 37.1	14 43.2	19 21.5	6 2.5	12 52.5
26 Su	12 14 58	5 38 9	13 44 7	19 42 9	1 18.0	8 1.8	15 27.6	2 9.5	7 50.2	14 49.7	19 24.2	6 3.8	12 52.2
27 M	12 18 55	6 37 32	25 38 18	1♑33 14	1 15.4	8 54.6	16 41.7	2 53.4	8 3.5	14 56.3	19 26.8	6 5.2	12 51.8
28 Tu	12 22 52	7 36 54	7♑27 35	13 22 1	1D 14.7	9 50.3	17 55.8	3 37.3	8 16.8	15 3.0	19 29.4	6 6.5	12 51.4
29 W	12 26 48	8 36 14	19 17 16	25 13 58	1 15.1	10 49.0	19 9.9	4 21.2	8 30.2	15 9.6	19 32.0	6 7.8	12 51.0
30 Th	12 30 45	9 35 32	1♒12 49	7♒14 27	1R 15.4	11 50.4	20 24.0	5 5.0	8 43.6	15 16.4	19 34.5	6 9.1	12 50.5
31 F	12 34 41	10 34 49	13 19 29	19 28 27	1 14.8	12 54.3	21 38.1	5 48.8	8 57.0	15 23.2	19 37.0	6 10.3	12 50.0

APRIL 2000 LONGITUDE

Day	Sid.Time	☉	0 hr ☽	Noon ☽	True ☊	☿	♀	♂	♃	♄	♅	♆	♇
1 Sa	12 38 38	11♈34 3	25♒41 53	2♓ 0 11	1♌12.1	14♓ 0.8	22♓52.2	6♉32.5	9♉10.5	15♉30.0	19♒39.5	6♒11.5	12♐49.5
2 Su	12 42 34	12 33 16	8♓23 40	14 52 33	1R 7.0	15 9.6	24 6.3	7 16.1	9 24.0	15 36.9	19 41.9	6 12.7	12R 48.9
3 M	12 46 31	13 32 27	21 26 59	28 6 54	0 59.2	16 20.6	25 20.3	7 59.8	9 37.6	15 43.8	19 44.3	6 13.9	12 48.4
4 Tu	12 50 27	14 31 35	4♈52 10	11♈42 32	0 49.1	17 33.9	26 34.4	8 43.3	9 51.3	15 50.8	19 46.7	6 15.0	12 47.7
5 W	12 54 24	15 30 42	18 37 33	25 36 45	0 37.6	18 49.1	27 48.5	9 26.9	10 4.9	15 57.8	19 49.0	6 16.1	12 47.1
6 Th	12 58 21	16 29 47	2♉39 32	9♉45 13	0 25.7	20 6.4	29 2.5	10 10.4	10 18.6	16 4.9	19 51.3	6 17.2	12 46.4
7 F	13 2 17	17 28 50	16 53 7	24 2 32	0 14.9	21 25.6	0♈16.6	10 53.8	10 32.4	16 11.9	19 53.6	6 18.2	12 45.7
8 Sa	13 6 14	18 27 50	1♊12 47	8♊23 13	0 6.1	22 46.7	1 30.6	11 37.2	10 46.2	16 19.1	19 55.8	6 19.2	12 44.9
9 Su	13 10 10	19 26 49	15 33 19	22 42 34	0 0.0	24 9.7	2 44.7	12 20.5	10 60.0	16 26.2	19 57.9	6 20.2	12 44.2
10 M	13 14 7	20 25 45	29 50 36	6♋57 7	29♋56.7	25 34.4	3 58.7	13 3.8	11 13.8	16 33.4	20 0.1	6 21.1	12 43.4
11 Tu	13 18 3	21 24 39	14♋ 1 54	21 4 49	29D 55.5	27 0.9	5 12.7	13 47.1	11 27.7	16 40.7	20 2.2	6 22.0	12 42.5
12 W	13 22 0	22 23 30	28 5 47	5♌ 4 45	29R 55.4	28 29.0	6 26.7	14 30.3	11 41.6	16 47.9	20 4.2	6 22.9	12 41.7
13 Th	13 25 56	23 22 19	12♌ 1 42	18 56 37	29 55.2	29 58.9	7 40.7	15 13.4	11 55.6	16 55.2	20 6.2	6 23.7	12 40.8
14 F	13 29 53	24 21 6	25 49 28	2♍40 13	29 53.4	1♈30.5	8 54.7	15 56.5	12 9.6	17 2.5	20 8.2	6 24.6	12 39.9
15 Sa	13 33 50	25 19 51	9♍28 47	16 15 4	29 49.2	3 3.7	10 8.6	16 39.5	12 23.6	17 9.9	20 10.1	6 25.3	12 39.0
16 Su	13 37 46	26 18 33	22 58 56	29 40 13	29 42.1	4 38.5	11 22.6	17 22.5	12 37.6	17 17.3	20 12.0	6 26.1	12 38.0
17 M	13 41 43	27 17 13	6♎18 43	12♎54 16	29 32.1	6 15.0	12 36.6	18 5.5	12 51.6	17 24.7	20 13.8	6 26.8	12 37.0
18 Tu	13 45 39	28 15 51	19 26 39	25 55 43	29 20.0	7 53.2	13 50.5	18 48.3	13 5.7	17 32.1	20 15.6	6 27.5	12 36.0
19 W	13 49 36	29 14 28	2♏21 18	8♏43 18	29 6.8	9 33.0	15 4.4	19 31.2	13 19.8	17 39.6	20 17.4	6 28.2	12 35.0
20 Th	13 53 32	0♉13 2	15 1 40	21 16 24	28 53.7	11 14.4	16 18.4	20 14.0	13 33.9	17 47.0	20 19.1	6 28.8	12 33.9
21 F	13 57 29	1 11 34	27 27 36	3♐35 23	28 41.8	12 57.5	17 32.3	20 56.7	13 48.0	17 54.5	20 20.8	6 29.4	12 32.8
22 Sa	14 1 25	2 10 5	9♐40 0	15 41 44	28 32.1	14 42.3	18 46.2	21 39.4	14 2.2	18 2.1	20 22.4	6 29.9	12 31.7
23 Su	14 5 22	3 8 34	21 40 57	27 38 4	28 25.0	16 28.7	20 0.2	22 22.1	14 16.3	18 9.6	20 24.0	6 30.5	12 30.6
24 M	14 9 19	4 7 2	3♑33 34	9♑28 1	28 20.7	18 16.8	21 14.1	23 4.7	14 30.5	18 17.2	20 25.5	6 30.9	12 29.4
25 Tu	14 13 15	5 5 27	15 21 59	21 16 6	28 18.7	20 6.6	22 28.0	23 47.2	14 44.7	18 24.8	20 27.0	6 31.4	12 28.2
26 W	14 17 12	6 3 51	27 11 1	3♒ 7 26	28 18.2	21 58.0	23 41.9	24 29.8	14 58.9	18 32.4	20 28.4	6 31.8	12 27.0
27 Th	14 21 8	7 2 14	9♒ 6 1	15 7 28	28 18.2	23 51.2	24 55.8	25 12.2	15 13.2	18 40.0	20 29.8	6 32.2	12 25.8
28 F	14 25 5	8 0 35	21 12 28	27 21 40	28 17.6	25 46.0	26 9.7	25 54.7	15 27.4	18 47.6	20 31.2	6 32.6	12 24.5
29 Sa	14 29 1	8 58 54	3♓35 41	9♓55 3	28 15.5	27 42.5	27 23.6	26 37.0	15 41.6	18 55.3	20 32.5	6 32.9	12 23.3
30 Su	14 32 58	9 57 12	16 20 16	22 51 42	28 11.0	29 40.7	28 37.5	27 19.4	15 55.9	19 2.9	20 33.7	6 33.2	12 22.0

Astro Data (Dy Hr Mn)	Planet Ingress (Dy Hr Mn)	Last Aspect (Dy Hr Mn)	☽ Ingress (Dy Hr Mn)	Last Aspect (Dy Hr Mn)	☽ Ingress (Dy Hr Mn)	☽ Phases & Eclipses (Dy Hr Mn)	Astro Data
♄⊼♇ 6 11:56	♀ ♓ 13 11:36	1 4:38 ♂ □	♒ 2 13:14	31 12:19 ♅ ☌	♓ 1 8:12	6 5:17 ● 15♓57	1 MARCH 2000
☽0N 8 2:47	☉ ♈ 20 7:35	4 1:12 ♀ ☌	♓ 4 23:30	3 7:44 ♀ ☌	♈ 3 15:22	13 6:59 ☽ 23♊01	Julian Day # 36585
☿ D 14 20:39	♂ ♉ 23 1:25	6 5:17 ☉ ☌	♈ 7 6:54	5 2:04 ♅ ⚹	♉ 5 19:29	20 4:44 ○ 29♍53	Delta T 62.1 sec
♇ R 15 11:49		9 2:34 ♀ ⚹	♉ 9 12:01	7 8:24 ☿ ⚹	♊ 7 21:58	28 0:21 ☽ 7♑38	SVP 05♓15'41"
♃□♆ 16 17:15	♀ ♈ 6 18:37	11 11:31 ♀ □	♊ 11 15:46	9 16:01 ☿ □	♋ 10 0:16		Obliquity 23°26'17"
☽0S 21 0:36	☊ ♋ 9 0:11	13 6:59 ☉ □	♋ 13 18:51	12 0:45 ☿ △	♌ 12 3:16	4 18:12 ● 15♈16	⚷ Chiron 16♐38.2
	☿ ♈ 13 0:17	15 13:43 ☉ △	♌ 15 21:43	13 21:14 ☉ △	♍ 14 7:19	11 13:30 ☽ 21♋58	☽ Mean ☊ 1♌53.3
☽0N 4 10:46	☉ ♉ 19 18:40	17 18:07 ♂ △	♍ 18 0:48	15 13:45 ♄ △	♎ 16 12:36	18 17:42 ○ 28♎59	
♀0N 9 14:17	☿ ♉ 30 3:53	20 4:44 ☉ ☍	♎ 20 4:57	18 17:42 ☉ ☍	♏ 18 19:35	26 19:30 ☽ 6♒51	1 APRIL 2000
☿0N 16 18:11		22 10:26 ♂ ☍	♏ 22 11:17	20 10:36 ♂ ☍	♐ 21 4:58		Julian Day # 36616
♃⊼♇ 16 0:41		23 23:53 ♅ □	♐ 24 20:43	22 21:25 ♅ ⚹	♑ 23 16:47		Delta T 62.1 sec
☽0S 17 8:37		26 11:26 ♅ ⚹	♑ 27 8:51	25 18:12 ☿ △	♒ 26 5:42		SVP 05♓15'38"
		28 23:43 ♀ ⚹	♒ 29 21:34	28 10:44 ♀ ⚹	♓ 28 17:06		Obliquity 23°26'17"
							⚷ Chiron 17♐13.8R
							☽ Mean ☊ 0♌14.8

LONGITUDE — MAY 2000

Day	Sid.Time	☉	0 hr ☽	Noon ☽	True ☊	☿	♀	♂	♃	♄	♅	♆	♇
1 M	14 36 54	10♉55 28	29♓29 35	6♈14 3	28♋ 4.0	1♉40.5	29♈51.3	28♉ 1.6	16♉10.2	19♉10.6	20♒35.0	6♒33.5	12♐20.7
2 Tu	14 40 51	11 53 43	13♈ 5 3	20 2 22	27R54.7	3 41.9	1♉ 5.2	28 43.9	16 24.4	19 18.3	20 36.1	6 33.7	12R19.4
3 W	14 44 47	12 51 56	27 5 38	4♉14 17	27 43.9	5 44.8	2 19.1	29 26.1	16 38.7	19 26.0	20 37.2	6 33.9	12 18.0
4 Th	14 48 44	13 50 7	11♉27 37	18 44 48	27 32.7	7 49.3	3 32.9	0♊ 8.2	16 53.0	19 33.7	20 38.3	6 34.1	12 16.6
5 F	14 52 41	14 48 17	26 4 54	3♊26 55	27 22.4	9 55.0	4 46.8	0 50.3	17 7.3	19 41.4	20 39.3	6 34.2	12 15.3
6 Sa	14 56 37	15 46 25	10♊49 51	18 12 43	27 13.9	12 2.1	6 0.6	1 32.4	17 21.6	19 49.1	20 40.3	6 34.3	12 13.9
7 Su	15 0 34	16 44 31	25 34 37	2♋54 45	27 8.1	14 10.2	7 14.5	2 14.4	17 35.9	19 56.8	20 41.2	6 34.4	12 12.5
8 M	15 4 30	17 42 36	10♋12 25	17 27 5	27 5.0	16 19.3	8 28.3	2 56.4	17 50.2	20 4.5	20 42.1	6R34.4	12 11.0
9 Tu	15 8 27	18 40 39	24 38 18	1♌45 49	27D 4.0	18 29.1	9 42.1	3 38.3	18 4.4	20 12.3	20 42.9	6 34.4	12 9.6
10 W	15 12 23	19 38 39	8♌49 26	15 49 6	27R 4.2	20 39.5	10 55.9	4 20.2	18 18.7	20 20.0	20 43.7	6 34.4	12 8.1
11 Th	15 16 20	20 36 38	22 44 49	29 36 39	27 4.4	22 50.2	12 9.8	5 2.0	18 33.0	20 27.7	20 44.4	6 34.3	12 6.7
12 F	15 20 17	21 34 35	6♍24 43	13♍ 9 7	27 3.5	25 0.9	13 23.5	5 43.8	18 47.3	20 35.5	20 45.1	6 34.2	12 5.2
13 Sa	15 24 13	22 32 30	19 50 0	26 27 31	27 0.5	27 11.4	14 37.3	6 25.5	19 1.5	20 43.2	20 45.7	6 34.1	12 3.7
14 Su	15 28 10	23 30 23	3♎ 1 46	9♎32 52	26 55.0	29 21.3	15 51.1	7 7.2	19 15.8	20 50.9	20 46.3	6 33.9	12 2.2
15 M	15 32 6	24 28 14	16 0 53	22 25 53	26 47.1	1♊30.4	17 4.9	7 48.9	19 30.0	20 58.6	20 46.8	6 33.7	12 0.6
16 Tu	15 36 3	25 26 4	28 47 56	5♏ 7 4	26 37.4	3 38.5	18 18.6	8 30.4	19 44.3	21 6.3	20 47.3	6 33.5	11 59.1
17 W	15 39 59	26 23 52	11♏23 18	17 36 43	26 26.7	5 45.1	19 32.4	9 12.0	19 58.5	21 14.1	20 47.8	6 33.2	11 57.6
18 Th	15 43 56	27 21 39	23 47 20	29 55 16	26 16.0	7 50.2	20 46.2	9 53.5	20 12.7	21 21.8	20 48.1	6 32.9	11 56.0
19 F	15 47 52	28 19 24	6♐ 0 36	12♐ 3 28	26 6.3	9 53.4	21 59.9	10 34.9	20 26.9	21 29.5	20 48.5	6 32.6	11 54.5
20 Sa	15 51 49	29 17 8	18 4 5	24 2 40	25 58.4	11 54.5	23 13.7	11 16.4	20 41.1	21 37.1	20 48.8	6 32.3	11 52.9
21 Su	15 55 45	0♊14 51	29 59 29	5♑54 52	25 52.8	13 53.4	24 27.4	11 57.7	20 55.2	21 44.8	20 49.0	6 31.9	11 51.3
22 M	15 59 42	1 12 33	11♑49 12	17 42 54	25 49.5	15 49.9	25 41.1	12 39.1	21 9.4	21 52.5	20 49.2	6 31.5	11 49.7
23 Tu	16 3 39	2 10 13	23 36 26	29 30 20	25D48.4	17 43.8	26 54.9	13 20.3	21 23.5	22 0.1	20 49.3	6 31.0	11 48.1
24 W	16 7 35	3 7 52	5♒25 8	11♒21 27	25 48.8	19 35.1	28 8.6	14 1.6	21 37.6	22 7.8	20 49.4	6 30.5	11 46.5
25 Th	16 11 32	4 5 31	17 19 53	23 21 4	25 49.9	21 23.6	29 22.4	14 42.8	21 51.7	22 15.4	20R49.5	6 30.0	11 44.9
26 F	16 15 28	5 3 8	29 25 39	5♓34 17	25R50.8	23 9.3	0♊36.1	15 24.0	22 5.8	22 23.0	20 49.5	6 29.5	11 43.3
27 Sa	16 19 25	6 0 44	11♓47 36	18 6 12	25 50.8	24 52.2	1 49.8	16 5.1	22 19.9	22 30.6	20 49.4	6 28.9	11 41.7
28 Su	16 23 21	6 58 19	24 30 37	1♈ 1 21	25 49.2	26 32.1	3 3.6	16 46.2	22 33.9	22 38.2	20 49.3	6 28.3	11 40.1
29 M	16 27 18	7 55 54	7♈38 46	14 23 8	25 45.7	28 9.0	4 17.3	17 27.2	22 47.9	22 45.8	20 49.1	6 27.7	11 38.5
30 Tu	16 31 14	8 53 28	21 14 35	28 13 4	25 40.5	29 42.9	5 31.0	18 8.2	23 1.9	22 53.3	20 48.9	6 27.0	11 36.8
31 W	16 35 11	9 51 0	5♉18 22	12♉30 6	25 34.0	1♋13.8	6 44.8	18 49.2	23 15.9	23 0.9	20 48.7	6 26.3	11 35.2

LONGITUDE — JUNE 2000

Day	Sid.Time	☉	0 hr ☽	Noon ☽	True ☊	☿	♀	♂	♃	♄	♅	♆	♇
1 Th	16 39 8	10♊48 32	19♉47 38	27♉10 13	25♋27.1	2♋41.6	7♊58.5	19♊30.1	23♉29.8	23♉ 8.4	20♒48.4	6♒25.6	11♐33.6
2 F	16 43 4	11 46 3	4♊36 53	12♊ 6 37	25R20.7	4 6.3	9 12.2	20 11.0	23 43.7	23 15.8	20R48.0	6R24.9	11R32.0
3 Sa	16 47 1	12 43 33	19 38 14	27 10 34	25 15.5	5 27.8	10 26.0	20 51.8	23 57.6	23 23.3	20 47.6	6 24.1	11 30.3
4 Su	16 50 57	13 41 3	4♋42 27	12♋12 48	25 12.1	6 46.1	11 39.7	21 32.6	24 11.4	23 30.8	20 47.2	6 23.3	11 28.7
5 M	16 54 54	14 38 31	19 40 35	27 4 57	25D10.6	8 1.3	12 53.4	22 13.4	24 25.2	23 38.2	20 46.7	6 22.5	11 27.1
6 Tu	16 58 50	15 35 58	4♌25 11	11♌40 43	25 10.7	9 13.1	14 7.2	22 54.1	24 39.0	23 45.6	20 46.2	6 21.6	11 25.5
7 W	17 2 47	16 33 23	18 51 9	25 56 14	25 11.9	10 21.6	15 20.9	23 34.8	24 52.7	23 52.9	20 45.6	6 20.8	11 23.9
8 Th	17 6 44	17 30 48	2♍55 50	9♍49 58	25 13.2	11 26.7	16 34.6	24 15.4	25 6.4	24 0.2	20 45.0	6 19.9	11 22.2
9 F	17 10 40	18 28 11	16 38 43	23 22 15	25R13.9	12 28.3	17 48.3	24 56.0	25 20.1	24 7.5	20 44.3	6 18.9	11 20.6
10 Sa	17 14 37	19 25 33	0♎ 0 48	6♎34 36	25 13.4	13 26.4	19 2.0	25 36.5	25 33.7	24 14.8	20 43.5	6 18.0	11 19.0
11 Su	17 18 33	20 22 54	13 3 57	19 29 8	25 11.4	14 20.8	20 15.7	26 17.1	25 47.2	24 22.0	20 42.8	6 17.0	11 17.4
12 M	17 22 30	21 20 15	25 50 27	2♏ 8 12	25 7.9	15 11.5	21 29.5	26 57.5	26 0.8	24 29.2	20 42.0	6 16.0	11 15.8
13 Tu	17 26 26	22 17 34	8♏22 39	14 34 3	25 3.2	15 58.4	22 43.2	27 38.0	26 14.3	24 36.4	20 41.1	6 14.9	11 14.2
14 W	17 30 23	23 14 52	20 42 41	26 48 46	24 57.9	16 41.4	23 56.9	28 18.4	26 27.7	24 43.5	20 40.2	6 13.9	11 12.6
15 Th	17 34 19	24 12 10	2♐52 33	8♐54 14	24 52.6	17 20.4	25 10.6	28 58.7	26 41.1	24 50.6	20 39.2	6 12.8	11 11.1
16 F	17 38 16	25 9 27	14 54 3	20 52 14	24 47.8	17 55.3	26 24.3	29 39.0	26 54.5	24 57.7	20 38.2	6 11.7	11 9.5
17 Sa	17 42 13	26 6 43	26 49 0	2♑44 35	24 44.1	18 26.0	27 38.0	0♋19.3	27 7.8	25 4.7	20 37.2	6 10.6	11 7.9
18 Su	17 46 9	27 3 59	8♑39 16	14 33 18	24 41.6	18 52.4	28 51.7	0 59.6	27 21.1	25 11.7	20 36.1	6 9.4	11 6.4
19 M	17 50 6	28 1 14	20 27 1	26 20 43	24D40.6	19 14.4	0♋ 5.4	1 39.8	27 34.3	25 18.6	20 35.0	6 8.2	11 4.9
20 Tu	17 54 2	28 58 29	2♒14 48	8♒ 9 37	24 40.7	19 32.0	1 19.1	2 19.9	27 47.4	25 25.6	20 33.9	6 7.1	11 3.3
21 W	17 57 59	29 55 43	14 5 37	20 3 14	24 41.8	19 45.0	2 32.8	3 0.1	28 0.6	25 32.4	20 32.7	6 5.8	11 1.8
22 Th	18 1 55	0♋52 57	26 2 58	2♓ 5 18	24 43.4	19 53.5	3 46.5	3 40.2	28 13.6	25 39.2	20 31.4	6 4.6	11 0.3
23 F	18 5 52	1 50 11	8♓10 47	14 19 56	24 44.9	19R57.4	5 0.2	4 20.2	28 26.6	25 46.0	20 30.1	6 3.3	10 58.8
24 Sa	18 9 48	2 47 25	20 33 18	26 51 25	24 46.1	19 56.8	6 14.0	5 0.3	28 39.6	25 52.7	20 28.8	6 2.1	10 57.3
25 Su	18 13 45	3 44 39	3♈14 47	9♈43 53	24R46.6	19 51.6	7 27.7	5 40.2	28 52.5	25 59.4	20 27.4	6 0.8	10 55.9
26 M	18 17 42	4 41 52	16 19 8	23 0 52	24 46.2	19 42.0	8 41.4	6 20.2	29 5.3	26 6.1	20 26.0	5 59.5	10 54.4
27 Tu	18 21 38	5 39 6	29 49 21	6♉44 40	24 45.0	19 28.1	9 55.2	7 0.1	29 18.1	26 12.7	20 24.6	5 58.1	10 53.0
28 W	18 25 35	6 36 20	13♉46 49	20 55 36	24 43.1	19 10.1	11 8.9	7 40.0	29 30.8	26 19.2	20 23.1	5 56.8	10 51.5
29 Th	18 29 31	7 33 34	28 10 41	5♊31 30	24 40.9	18 48.2	12 22.6	8 19.9	29 43.4	26 25.7	20 21.6	5 55.4	10 50.1
30 F	18 33 28	8 30 47	12♊57 21	20 27 20	24 38.9	18 22.8	13 36.4	8 59.7	29 56.0	26 32.2	20 20.0	5 54.0	10 48.7

Astro Data Dy Hr Mn	Planet Ingress Dy Hr Mn	Last Aspect Dy Hr Mn	☽ Ingress Dy Hr Mn	Last Aspect Dy Hr Mn	☽ Ingress Dy Hr Mn	☽ Phases & Eclipses Dy Hr Mn	
☽0N 1 20:44	♀ ♉ 1 2:49	30 21:13 ♂ ⚹	♈ 1 0:55	1 6:08 ♃ ☌	♊ 1 16:34	4 4:12	● 14♉00
♆ R 8 12:30	♂ ♊ 3 19:18	2 12:59 ♅ ⚹	♉ 3 4:54	3 2:03 ♂ ☌	♋ 3 16:30	10 20:01	☽ 20♌27
♄□♅ 13 8:34	☿ ♊ 14 7:10	4 15:07 ♅ □	♊ 5 6:23	5 7:48 ♃ ⚹	♌ 5 16:45	18 7:34	○ 27♏40
☽0S 14 15:22	☉ ♊ 20 17:49	6 16:01 ♅ △	♋ 7 7:14	7 10:22 ♃ □	♍ 7 18:57	26 11:55	☽ 5♓32
♃□♅ 20 13:16	♀ ♊ 25 12:15	8 16:31 ♄ ⚹	♌ 9 9:01	9 15:48 ♃ △	♎ 9 23:59		
♅ R 25 8:21	☿ ♋ 30 4:27	11 0:11 ☿ □	♍ 11 12:41	12 2:15 ♂ △	♏ 12 7:55	2 12:14	● 12♊15
♃☌♄ 28 16:04		13 15:57 ☿ △	♎ 13 18:27	14 11:31 ♃ ☍	♐ 14 18:18	9 3:29	☽ 18♍37
☽0N 29 7:06	♂ ♋ 16 12:30	15 8:55 ♅ △	♏ 16 2:16	17 1:50 ♀ ☍	♑ 17 6:26	16 22:27	○ 26♐03
	♀ ♋ 18 22:15	18 7:34 ☉ ☍	♐ 18 12:09	19 14:46 ♃ △	♒ 19 19:26	25 1:00	☽ 3♈47
☽0S 10 21:37	☉ ♋ 21 1:48	20 5:30 ♅ ⚹	♑ 21 0:01	22 4:25 ♃ □	♓ 22 7:52		
☿ R 23 8:32	♃ ♊ 30 7:34	23 7:31 ♀ △	♒ 23 13:00	24 15:40 ♃ ⚹	♈ 24 17:55		
☽0N 25 16:05		25 9:56 ♄ □	♓ 26 1:07	26 7:23 ♅ ⚹	♉ 27 0:19		
		28 4:17 ☿ □	♈ 28 10:08	29 2:34 ♃ ☌	♊ 29 2:59		
		29 23:15 ♅ ⚹	♉ 30 15:02				

Astro Data

1 MAY 2000
Julian Day # 36646
Delta T 62.2 sec
SVP 05♓15'35"
Obliquity 23°26'17"
⚷ Chiron 16♐20.1R
☽ Mean ☊ 28♋39.5

1 JUNE 2000
Julian Day # 36677
Delta T 62.2 sec
SVP 05♓15'31"
Obliquity 23°26'17"
⚷ Chiron 14♐22.8R
☽ Mean ☊ 27♋01.0

JULY 2000 LONGITUDE

Day	Sid.Time	☉	0 hr ☽	Noon ☽	True ☊	☿	♀	♂	♃	♄	♅	♆	♇
1 Sa	18 37 24	9♋28 1	28♊ 0 27	5♋35 34	24♋37.3	17♋54.2	14♋50.2	9♋39.5	0♊ 8.6	26♉38.5	20♒18.4	5♒52.6	10♐47.3
2 Su	18 41 21	10 25 15	13♋11 28	20 46 58	24D 36.4	17R 22.8	16 3.9	10 19.3	0 21.0	26 44.9	20R 16.8	5R 51.2	10R 46.0
3 M	18 45 17	11 22 29	28 20 52	5♌52 4	24 36.3	16 49.1	17 17.7	10 59.0	0 33.4	26 51.2	20 15.1	5 49.8	10 44.6
4 Tu	18 49 14	12 19 43	13♌19 33	20 42 28	24 36.7	16 13.6	18 31.4	11 38.7	0 45.7	26 57.4	20 13.4	5 48.3	10 43.3
5 W	18 53 11	13 16 56	28 0 6	5♍11 55	24 37.5	15 37.0	19 45.2	12 18.4	0 58.0	27 3.6	20 11.7	5 46.9	10 42.0
6 Th	18 57 7	14 14 9	12♍17 34	19 16 50	24 38.4	14 59.8	20 59.0	12 58.0	1 10.2	27 9.7	20 9.9	5 45.4	10 40.7
7 F	19 1 4	15 11 22	26 9 38	2♎56 4	24 39.1	14 22.6	22 12.7	13 37.6	1 22.3	27 15.7	20 8.1	5 43.9	10 39.5
8 Sa	19 5 0	16 8 34	9♎36 18	16 10 35	24R 39.5	13 46.1	23 26.5	14 17.2	1 34.3	27 21.7	20 6.3	5 42.4	10 38.2
9 Su	19 8 57	17 5 47	22 39 16	29 2 44	24 39.5	13 10.9	24 40.3	14 56.7	1 46.2	27 27.7	20 4.4	5 40.9	10 37.0
10 M	19 12 53	18 2 59	5♏21 25	11♏35 44	24 39.2	12 37.7	25 54.0	15 36.2	1 58.1	27 33.5	20 2.5	5 39.4	10 35.8
11 Tu	19 16 50	19 0 11	17 46 10	23 53 9	24 38.6	12 7.1	27 7.8	16 15.7	2 9.9	27 39.3	20 0.6	5 37.8	10 34.6
12 W	19 20 46	19 57 23	29 57 8	5♐58 32	24 38.1	11 39.5	28 21.5	16 55.1	2 21.6	27 45.1	19 58.7	5 36.3	10 33.4
13 Th	19 24 43	20 54 36	11♐57 47	17 55 16	24 37.5	11 15.6	29 35.3	17 34.5	2 33.2	27 50.8	19 56.7	5 34.7	10 32.3
14 F	19 28 40	21 51 48	23 51 22	29 46 25	24 37.1	10 55.7	0♌49.1	18 13.9	2 44.8	27 56.4	19 54.7	5 33.2	10 31.2
15 Sa	19 32 36	22 49 1	5♑40 46	11♑34 44	24 36.9	10 40.2	2 2.8	18 53.3	2 56.2	28 1.9	19 52.7	5 31.6	10 30.1
16 Su	19 36 33	23 46 14	17 28 37	23 22 42	24 36.9	10 29.6	3 16.6	19 32.6	3 7.6	28 7.4	19 50.6	5 30.0	10 29.0
17 M	19 40 29	24 43 27	29 17 17	5♒12 39	24 36.8	10D 24.0	4 30.4	20 11.8	3 18.9	28 12.8	19 48.6	5 28.4	10 28.0
18 Tu	19 44 26	25 40 40	11♒ 9 4	17 6 50	24 36.8	10 23.7	5 44.1	20 51.1	3 30.1	28 18.2	19 46.5	5 26.8	10 26.9
19 W	19 48 22	26 37 54	23 6 14	29 7 36	24 36.7	10 28.9	6 57.9	21 30.3	3 41.2	28 23.4	19 44.3	5 25.2	10 26.0
20 Th	19 52 19	27 35 9	5♓11 13	11♓17 25	24 36.4	10 39.7	8 11.7	22 9.5	3 52.2	28 28.6	19 42.2	5 23.6	10 25.0
21 F	19 56 15	28 32 24	17 26 34	23 39 0	24 36.0	10 56.1	9 25.4	22 48.7	4 3.2	28 33.8	19 40.0	5 22.0	10 24.0
22 Sa	20 0 12	29 29 40	29 55 6	6♈15 12	24 35.5	11 18.3	10 39.2	23 27.8	4 14.0	28 38.8	19 37.8	5 20.4	10 23.1
23 Su	20 4 9	0♌26 56	12♈39 42	19 8 57	24 35.0	11 46.3	11 53.0	24 6.9	4 24.7	28 43.8	19 35.6	5 18.8	10 22.2
24 M	20 8 5	1 24 14	25 43 15	2♉22 56	24D 34.7	12 20.1	13 6.8	24 46.0	4 35.3	28 48.7	19 33.4	5 17.2	10 21.3
25 Tu	20 12 2	2 21 32	9♉ 8 14	15 59 19	24 34.7	12 59.6	14 20.6	25 25.1	4 45.9	28 53.5	19 31.2	5 15.5	10 20.5
26 W	20 15 58	3 18 52	22 56 16	29 59 7	24 35.1	13 44.8	15 34.3	26 4.1	4 56.3	28 58.3	19 28.9	5 13.9	10 19.7
27 Th	20 19 55	4 16 12	7♊ 7 41	14♊21 44	24 35.8	14 35.7	16 48.1	26 43.1	5 6.6	29 3.0	19 26.6	5 12.3	10 18.9
28 F	20 23 51	5 13 34	21 40 50	29 4 26	24 36.6	15 32.1	18 1.9	27 22.1	5 16.9	29 7.6	19 24.4	5 10.7	10 18.2
29 Sa	20 27 48	6 10 56	6♋31 48	14♋ 2 5	24 37.4	16 34.1	19 15.7	28 1.1	5 27.0	29 12.1	19 22.1	5 9.0	10 17.4
30 Su	20 31 44	7 8 20	21 34 19	29 7 27	24R 37.7	17 41.4	20 29.5	28 40.0	5 37.0	29 16.5	19 19.7	5 7.4	10 16.7
31 M	20 35 41	8 5 44	6♌40 20	14♌11 51	24 37.5	18 54.0	21 43.3	29 18.9	5 46.9	29 20.9	19 17.4	5 5.8	10 16.1

AUGUST 2000 LONGITUDE

Day	Sid.Time	☉	0 hr ☽	Noon ☽	True ☊	☿	♀	♂	♃	♄	♅	♆	♇
1 Tu	20 39 38	9♌ 3 9	21♌40 54	29♌ 6 26	24♋36.7	20♋11.7	22♌57.1	29♋57.8	5♊56.7	29♉25.2	19♒15.1	5♒ 4.1	10♐15.4
2 W	20 43 34	10 0 35	6♍27 31	13♍43 22	24R 35.1	21 34.4	24 10.9	0♌36.7	6 6.4	29 29.3	19R 12.7	5R 2.5	10R 14.8
3 Th	20 47 31	10 58 1	20 53 20	27 56 57	24 33.1	23 1.8	25 24.7	1 15.5	6 15.9	29 33.4	19 10.4	5 0.9	10 14.2
4 F	20 51 27	11 55 28	4♎53 55	11♎44 6	24 31.0	24 33.9	26 38.5	1 54.3	6 25.3	29 37.4	19 8.0	4 59.3	10 13.7
5 Sa	20 55 24	12 52 56	18 27 30	25 4 18	24 29.1	26 10.2	27 52.3	2 33.1	6 34.7	29 41.4	19 5.6	4 57.7	10 13.1
6 Su	20 59 20	13 50 25	1♏34 45	7♏59 13	24 27.8	27 50.6	29 6.1	3 11.8	6 43.9	29 45.2	19 3.3	4 56.1	10 12.7
7 M	21 3 17	14 47 54	14 18 9	20 32 3	24D 27.3	29 34.7	0♍19.9	3 50.6	6 52.9	29 49.0	19 0.9	4 54.5	10 12.2
8 Tu	21 7 13	15 45 24	26 41 28	2♐46 57	24 27.7	1♌22.3	1 33.6	4 29.3	7 1.9	29 52.6	18 58.5	4 52.9	10 11.8
9 W	21 11 10	16 42 55	8♐49 6	14 48 28	24 28.9	3 13.0	2 47.4	5 7.9	7 10.7	29 56.2	18 56.1	4 51.3	10 11.4
10 Th	21 15 7	17 40 27	20 45 39	26 41 10	24 30.5	5 6.3	4 1.2	5 46.6	7 19.4	29 59.7	18 53.7	4 49.7	10 11.0
11 F	21 19 3	18 38 0	2♑35 35	8♑29 22	24 32.1	7 2.0	5 14.9	6 25.2	7 28.0	0♊ 3.0	18 51.3	4 48.1	10 10.7
12 Sa	21 23 0	19 35 33	14 23 0	20 16 56	24R 33.3	8 59.7	6 28.7	7 3.8	7 36.4	0 6.3	18 48.9	4 46.6	10 10.4
13 Su	21 26 56	20 33 8	26 11 32	2♒ 7 12	24 33.7	10 58.9	7 42.4	7 42.4	7 44.7	0 9.5	18 46.5	4 45.0	10 10.1
14 M	21 30 53	21 30 44	8♒ 4 14	14 2 57	24 32.9	12 59.3	8 56.2	8 20.9	7 52.9	0 12.6	18 44.1	4 43.5	10 9.9
15 Tu	21 34 49	22 28 21	20 3 35	26 6 23	24 30.8	15 0.6	10 9.9	8 59.5	8 0.9	0 15.6	18 41.7	4 41.9	10 9.6
16 W	21 38 46	23 25 59	2♓11 33	8♓19 16	24 27.4	17 2.4	11 23.6	9 38.0	8 8.8	0 18.6	18 39.4	4 40.4	10 9.5
17 Th	21 42 42	24 23 38	14 29 41	20 42 58	24 22.9	19 4.4	12 37.4	10 16.5	8 16.6	0 21.4	18 37.0	4 38.9	10 9.3
18 F	21 46 39	25 21 19	26 59 14	3♈18 38	24 17.8	21 6.4	13 51.1	10 54.9	8 24.2	0 24.1	18 34.6	4 37.4	10 9.2
19 Sa	21 50 36	26 19 1	9♈41 17	16 7 19	24 12.7	23 8.0	15 4.8	11 33.4	8 31.7	0 26.7	18 32.2	4 35.9	10 9.1
20 Su	21 54 32	27 16 45	22 36 53	29 10 6	24 8.2	25 9.2	16 18.5	12 11.8	8 39.0	0 29.2	18 29.9	4 34.4	10D 9.1
21 M	21 58 29	28 14 30	5♉47 8	12♉28 6	24 4.8	27 9.8	17 32.2	12 50.2	8 46.2	0 31.7	18 27.5	4 32.9	10 9.1
22 Tu	22 2 25	29 12 17	19 13 8	26 2 21	24D 2.9	29 9.5	18 45.9	13 28.6	8 53.2	0 34.0	18 25.2	4 31.5	10 9.1
23 W	22 6 22	0♍10 6	2♊55 49	9♊53 36	24 2.5	1♍ 8.3	19 59.6	14 6.9	9 0.1	0 36.2	18 22.8	4 30.1	10 9.1
24 Th	22 10 18	1 7 57	16 55 40	24 1 57	24 3.3	3 6.1	21 13.3	14 45.3	9 6.9	0 38.3	18 20.5	4 28.6	10 9.2
25 F	22 14 15	2 5 49	1♋12 15	8♋26 18	24 4.6	5 2.7	22 27.0	15 23.6	9 13.4	0 40.4	18 18.2	4 27.2	10 9.3
26 Sa	22 18 11	3 3 43	15 43 44	23 4 2	24R 5.7	6 58.2	23 40.7	16 1.9	9 19.9	0 42.3	18 15.9	4 25.9	10 9.5
27 Su	22 22 8	4 1 39	0♌26 34	7♌50 37	24 5.8	8 52.5	24 54.3	16 40.2	9 26.1	0 44.1	18 13.6	4 24.5	10 9.7
28 M	22 26 5	4 59 37	15 15 19	22 39 46	24 4.2	10 45.6	26 8.0	17 18.5	9 32.3	0 45.8	18 11.4	4 23.1	10 9.9
29 Tu	22 30 1	5 57 36	0♍ 3 0	7♍24 3	24 0.7	12 37.4	27 21.7	17 56.7	9 38.2	0 47.4	18 9.1	4 21.8	10 10.2
30 W	22 33 58	6 55 37	14 41 59	21 55 53	23 55.3	14 27.9	28 35.3	18 34.9	9 44.0	0 48.9	18 6.9	4 20.5	10 10.4
31 Th	22 37 54	7 53 39	29 5 0	6♎ 8 41	23 48.6	16 17.2	29 49.0	19 13.1	9 49.6	0 50.3	18 4.7	4 19.2	10 10.8

Astro Data	Planet Ingress	Last Aspect	☽ Ingress	Last Aspect	☽ Ingress	☽ Phases & Eclipses	Astro Data
Dy Hr Mn	Dy Hr Mn	Dy Hr Mn	Dy Hr Mn	Dy Hr Mn	Dy Hr Mn	Dy Hr Mn	1 JULY 2000
☽0S 8 4:25	♀ ♌ 13 8:02	30 11:47 ♅ △	♋ 1 3:09	1 12:34 ♄ □	♍ 1 13:27	1 19:20 ● 10♋14	Julian Day # 36707
☿ D 17 13:20	☉ ♌ 22 12:43	2 21:36 ♄ ✶	♌ 3 2:38	3 14:50 ♄ △	♎ 3 15:31	1 19:32:33 ☌ P 0.477	Delta T 62.2 sec
☽0N 22 22:50		4 22:26 ♄ □	♍ 5 3:19	5 18:56 ♀ ✶	♏ 5 21:04	8 12:53 ☽ 16♎39	SVP 05♓15'25"
♃△♆ 27 11:23	♂ ♌ 1 1:21	7 1:57 ♄ △	♎ 7 6:47	8 6:18 ♄ ☍	♐ 8 6:30	16 13:55 ○ 24♑19	Obliquity 23°26'17"
	♀ ♍ 6 17:32	9 4:10 ♀ □	♏ 9 13:48	9 20:15 ♅ ✶	♑ 10 18:44	16 13:56 ☍ T 1.768	⚷ Chiron 12♐22.8R
☽0S 4 12:27	☿ ♌ 7 5:42	11 20:29 ♀ △	♐ 12 0:06	11 6:02 ♀ △	♒ 13 7:43	24 11:02 ☽ 1♉51	☽ Mean ☊ 25♋25.7
☽0N 19 4:01	♄ ♊ 10 2:25	13 16:03 ♅ ✶	♑ 14 12:28	15 5:13 ☉ ☍	♓ 15 19:41	31 2:25 ● 8♌12	
♇ D 20 22:41	☉ ♍ 22 19:49	16 21:48 ♄ △	♒ 17 1:27	16 19:58 ♀ ☍	♈ 18 5:44	31 2:13:04 ☌ P 0.603	1 AUGUST 2000
☽0S 31 21:37	☿ ♍ 22 10:11	19 10:37 ♄ □	♓ 19 13:44	20 9:14 ☉ △	♉ 20 13:31		Julian Day # 36738
	♀ ♎ 31 3:35	21 23:08 ☉ △	♈ 22 0:09	22 18:51 ☉ □	♊ 22 18:55	7 1:02 ☽ 14♏50	Delta T 62.3 sec
		23 22:11 ♂ □	♉ 24 7:44	24 7:57 ♀ □	♋ 24 22:00	15 5:13 ○ 22♒41	SVP 05♓15'20"
		26 10:20 ♄ ☌	♊ 26 12:02	26 14:11 ♀ ✶	♌ 26 23:17	22 18:51 ☽ 29♉58	Obliquity 23°26'17"
		27 20:18 ♅ △	♋ 28 13:30	28 4:44 ♅ ☍	♍ 28 23:55	29 10:19 ● 6♍23	⚷ Chiron 11♐09.5R
		30 12:18 ♄ ✶	♌ 30 13:23	31 1:21 ♀ ☌	♎ 31 1:33		☽ Mean ☊ 23♋47.2

LONGITUDE — SEPTEMBER 2000

Day	Sid.Time	☉	0 hr ☽	Noon ☽	True ☊	☿	♀	♂	♃	♄	♅	♆	♇
1 F	22 41 51	8♍51 43	13♎ 6 24	19♎57 49	23♋41.4	18♍ 5.2	1♎ 2.6	19♌51.3	9♊55.1	0♊51.6	18♒ 2.5	4♒17.9	10♐11.1
2 Sa	22 45 47	9 49 49	26 42 44	3♏21 9	23R 34.6	19 52.0	2 16.3	20 29.5	10 0.3	0 52.8	18R 0.3	4R 16.6	10 11.5
3 Su	22 49 44	10 47 55	9♏53 9	16 19 0	23 29.1	21 37.5	3 29.9	21 7.6	10 5.4	0 53.9	17 58.2	4 15.4	10 11.9
4 M	22 53 40	11 46 4	22 39 3	28 53 45	23 25.2	23 21.7	4 43.5	21 45.7	10 10.4	0 54.8	17 56.0	4 14.2	10 12.4
5 Tu	22 57 37	12 44 13	5♐ 3 38	11♐ 9 17	23D 23.3	25 4.8	5 57.1	22 23.8	10 15.2	0 55.7	17 53.9	4 13.0	10 12.8
6 W	23 1 34	13 42 25	17 11 19	23 10 22	23 23.0	26 46.6	7 10.7	23 1.9	10 19.7	0 56.4	17 51.8	4 11.8	10 13.4
7 Th	23 5 30	14 40 37	29 7 7	5♑ 2 13	23 23.9	28 27.2	8 24.2	23 40.0	10 24.2	0 57.1	17 49.8	4 10.7	10 13.9
8 F	23 9 27	15 38 52	10♑56 19	16 50 3	23 25.0	0♎ 6.7	9 37.8	24 18.0	10 28.4	0 57.6	17 47.7	4 9.6	10 14.5
9 Sa	23 13 23	16 37 7	22 44 1	28 38 47	23R 25.7	1 45.0	10 51.3	24 56.0	10 32.5	0 58.1	17 45.7	4 8.5	10 15.1
10 Su	23 17 20	17 35 25	4♒34 53	10♒32 47	23 25.0	3 22.2	12 4.9	25 34.0	10 36.3	0 58.4	17 43.8	4 7.4	10 15.8
11 M	23 21 16	18 33 44	16 32 56	22 35 40	23 22.2	4 58.2	13 18.4	26 12.0	10 40.0	0 58.6	17 41.8	4 6.3	10 16.4
12 Tu	23 25 13	19 32 4	28 41 20	4♓50 10	23 17.1	6 33.1	14 31.9	26 50.0	10 43.6	0R 58.7	17 39.9	4 5.3	10 17.1
13 W	23 29 9	20 30 27	11♓ 2 20	17 17 59	23 9.7	8 6.9	15 45.4	27 27.9	10 46.9	0 58.7	17 38.0	4 4.3	10 17.9
14 Th	23 33 6	21 28 51	23 37 10	29 59 52	23 0.5	9 39.6	16 58.8	28 5.8	10 50.0	0 58.6	17 36.1	4 3.3	10 18.7
15 F	23 37 2	22 27 17	6♈26 5	12♈55 41	22 50.1	11 11.2	18 12.3	28 43.7	10 53.0	0 58.4	17 34.3	4 2.4	10 19.5
16 Sa	23 40 59	23 25 44	19 28 36	26 4 39	22 39.6	12 41.7	19 25.7	29 21.6	10 55.8	0 58.0	17 32.5	4 1.4	10 20.3
17 Su	23 44 56	24 24 14	2♉43 43	9♉25 40	22 30.0	14 11.1	20 39.2	29 59.5	10 58.3	0 57.6	17 30.7	4 0.5	10 21.2
18 M	23 48 52	25 22 46	16 10 20	22 57 36	22 22.3	15 39.4	21 52.6	0♍37.4	11 0.7	0 57.1	17 29.0	3 59.7	10 22.1
19 Tu	23 52 49	26 21 21	29 47 24	6♊39 39	22 17.0	17 6.6	23 6.0	1 15.2	11 2.9	0 56.4	17 27.3	3 58.8	10 23.0
20 W	23 56 45	27 19 57	13♊34 17	20 31 16	22 14.2	18 32.6	24 19.4	1 53.0	11 4.9	0 55.7	17 25.6	3 58.0	10 24.0
21 Th	0 0 42	28 18 36	27 30 34	4♋32 9	22D 13.4	19 57.6	25 32.8	2 30.8	11 6.7	0 54.8	17 24.0	3 57.2	10 25.0
22 F	0 4 38	29 17 17	11♋35 56	18 41 49	22R 13.7	21 21.4	26 46.1	3 8.6	11 8.4	0 53.8	17 22.4	3 56.5	10 26.0
23 Sa	0 8 35	0♎16 0	25 49 38	2♌59 11	22 13.9	22 44.0	27 59.5	3 46.4	11 9.8	0 52.8	17 20.8	3 55.7	10 27.1
24 Su	0 12 31	1 14 46	10♌10 8	17 22 5	22 12.7	24 5.4	29 12.9	4 24.2	11 11.0	0 51.6	17 19.3	3 55.0	10 28.2
25 M	0 16 28	2 13 34	24 34 34	1♍46 59	22 9.3	25 25.5	0♏26.2	5 1.9	11 12.0	0 50.3	17 17.8	3 54.3	10 29.3
26 Tu	0 20 25	3 12 23	8♍58 42	16 9 1	22 3.0	26 44.4	1 39.5	5 39.6	11 12.8	0 48.9	17 16.4	3 53.7	10 30.4
27 W	0 24 21	4 11 15	23 17 12	0♎22 32	21 54.1	28 1.9	2 52.8	6 17.4	11 13.4	0 47.4	17 15.0	3 53.1	10 31.6
28 Th	0 28 18	5 10 9	7♎24 19	14 21 54	21 43.2	29 18.0	4 6.1	6 55.0	11 13.8	0 45.8	17 13.6	3 52.5	10 32.8
29 F	0 32 14	6 9 5	21 14 44	28 2 24	21 31.3	0♏32.6	5 19.4	7 32.7	11R 14.1	0 44.1	17 12.3	3 51.9	10 34.1
30 Sa	0 36 11	7 8 3	4♏44 35	11♏21 5	21 19.8	1 45.6	6 32.7	8 10.4	11 14.1	0 42.3	17 11.0	3 51.4	10 35.3

LONGITUDE — OCTOBER 2000

Day	Sid.Time	☉	0 hr ☽	Noon ☽	True ☊	☿	♀	♂	♃	♄	♅	♆	♇
1 Su	0 40 7	8♎ 7 3	17♏51 52	24♏17 2	21♋ 9.7	2♏56.9	7♏45.9	8♍48.0	11♊13.9	0♊40.3	17♒ 9.8	3♒50.9	10♐36.6
2 M	0 44 4	9 6 5	0♐36 46	6♐51 25	21R 1.9	4 6.5	8 59.2	9 25.6	11R 13.5	0R 38.3	17R 8.6	3R 50.5	10 37.9
3 Tu	0 48 0	10 5 9	13 1 22	19 7 8	20 56.7	5 14.2	10 12.4	10 3.2	11 12.9	0 36.2	17 7.4	3 50.0	10 39.3
4 W	0 51 57	11 4 14	25 9 17	1♑ 8 26	20 54.0	6 19.8	11 25.6	10 40.8	11 12.1	0 34.0	17 6.3	3 49.6	10 40.7
5 Th	0 55 54	12 3 21	7♑ 5 14	13 0 22	20D 53.0	7 23.2	12 38.7	11 18.4	11 11.1	0 31.7	17 5.2	3 49.3	10 42.1
6 F	0 59 50	13 2 30	18 54 31	24 48 24	20R 53.0	8 24.2	13 51.9	11 55.9	11 9.9	0 29.3	17 4.2	3 49.0	10 43.5
7 Sa	1 3 47	14 1 41	0♒42 42	6♒38 6	20 52.8	9 22.7	15 5.0	12 33.4	11 8.5	0 26.8	17 3.2	3 48.7	10 45.0
8 Su	1 7 43	15 0 54	12 35 13	18 34 41	20 51.2	10 18.3	16 18.1	13 10.9	11 6.9	0 24.2	17 2.3	3 48.4	10 46.5
9 M	1 11 40	16 0 8	24 37 2	0♓42 46	20 47.5	11 10.8	17 31.2	13 48.4	11 5.1	0 21.5	17 1.4	3 48.2	10 48.0
10 Tu	1 15 36	16 59 24	6♓52 20	13 6 4	20 41.1	11 60.0	18 44.3	14 25.9	11 3.1	0 18.7	17 0.6	3 47.9	10 49.5
11 W	1 19 33	17 58 42	19 24 13	25 46 59	20 32.0	12 45.5	19 57.3	15 3.3	11 0.8	0 15.8	16 59.8	3 47.8	10 51.1
12 Th	1 23 29	18 58 2	2♈14 24	8♈46 28	20 20.6	13 26.9	21 10.4	15 40.8	10 58.4	0 12.8	16 59.0	3 47.6	10 52.7
13 F	1 27 26	19 57 24	15 23 2	22 3 53	20 7.8	14 3.9	22 23.4	16 18.2	10 55.8	0 9.8	16 58.3	3 47.5	10 54.3
14 Sa	1 31 23	20 56 48	28 48 44	5♉37 11	19 54.9	14 36.1	23 36.3	16 55.6	10 53.1	0 6.6	16 57.7	3 47.5	10 56.0
15 Su	1 35 19	21 56 14	12♉28 51	19 23 16	19 42.9	15 3.0	24 49.3	17 33.0	10 50.1	0 3.4	16 57.1	3D 47.4	10 57.6
16 M	1 39 16	22 55 42	26 19 58	3♊18 33	19 33.2	15 24.1	26 2.2	18 10.3	10 46.9	0 0.1	16 56.5	3 47.4	10 59.3
17 Tu	1 43 12	23 55 12	10♊18 35	17 19 42	19 26.2	15 38.8	27 15.1	18 47.7	10 43.5	29♉56.7	16 56.0	3 47.5	11 1.0
18 W	1 47 9	24 54 45	24 21 35	1♋23 58	19 22.2	15R 46.7	28 28.0	19 25.0	10 40.0	29 53.2	16 55.6	3 47.5	11 2.8
19 Th	1 51 5	25 54 20	8♋26 41	15 29 32	19D 20.6	15 47.2	29 40.9	20 2.3	10 36.2	29 49.7	16 55.2	3 47.6	11 4.5
20 F	1 55 2	26 53 57	22 32 26	29 35 15	19R 20.4	15 39.9	0♐53.7	20 39.6	10 32.3	29 46.1	16 54.8	3 47.8	11 6.3
21 Sa	1 58 58	27 53 37	6♌37 57	13♌40 23	19 20.2	15 24.1	2 6.5	21 16.9	10 28.2	29 42.4	16 54.5	3 47.9	11 8.1
22 Su	2 2 55	28 53 19	20 42 28	27 44 3	19 18.9	14 59.7	3 19.3	21 54.2	10 23.9	29 38.6	16 54.2	3 48.1	11 10.0
23 M	2 6 52	29 53 3	4♍44 55	11♍44 49	19 15.2	14 26.4	4 32.1	22 31.4	10 19.4	29 34.7	16 54.0	3 48.4	11 11.8
24 Tu	2 10 48	0♏52 49	18 43 27	25 40 28	19 8.6	13 44.2	5 44.9	23 8.7	10 14.7	29 30.8	16 53.9	3 48.6	11 13.7
25 W	2 14 45	1 52 38	2♎35 28	9♎28 3	18 59.3	12 53.3	6 57.6	23 45.9	10 9.8	29 26.8	16 53.8	3 48.9	11 15.6
26 Th	2 18 41	2 52 28	16 17 46	23 4 12	18 47.8	11 54.5	8 10.3	24 23.1	10 4.8	29 22.8	16D 53.7	3 49.2	11 17.5
27 F	2 22 38	3 52 21	29 47 0	6♏25 47	18 35.3	10 48.6	9 23.0	25 0.3	9 59.6	29 18.6	16 53.7	3 49.6	11 19.4
28 Sa	2 26 34	4 52 16	13♏ 0 19	19 30 24	18 22.9	9 37.0	10 35.6	25 37.4	9 54.3	29 14.5	16 53.7	3 50.0	11 21.3
29 Su	2 30 31	5 52 12	25 55 55	2♐16 52	18 12.0	8 21.6	11 48.2	26 14.6	9 48.8	29 10.2	16 53.8	3 50.5	11 23.3
30 M	2 34 27	6 52 11	8♐33 21	14 45 33	18 3.3	7 4.5	13 0.8	26 51.7	9 43.1	29 5.9	16 54.0	3 50.9	11 25.3
31 Tu	2 38 24	7 52 11	20 53 43	26 58 14	17 57.3	5 47.9	14 13.4	27 28.8	9 37.3	29 1.6	16 54.2	3 51.4	11 27.3

Astro Data Dy Hr Mn	Planet Ingress Dy Hr Mn	Last Aspect Dy Hr Mn	☽ Ingress Dy Hr Mn	Last Aspect Dy Hr Mn	☽ Ingress Dy Hr Mn	☽ Phases & Eclipses Dy Hr Mn	Astro Data
♀0S 2 3:34	☿ ♎ 7 22:22	1 12:23 ♂ ✶	♏ 2 5:55	30 22:42 ♅ □	♐ 1 22:50	5 16:27 ☽ 13♐24	1 SEPTEMBER 2000
♃☍♇ 4 10:53	♂ ♍ 17 0:19	4 1:34 ☿ ✶	♐ 4 14:08	3 8:03 ♅ ✶	♑ 4 9:42	13 19:37 ○ 21♓18	Julian Day # 36769
☿0S 8 13:44	☉ ♎ 22 17:28	6 22:26 ☿ □	♑ 7 1:47	5 12:34 ♀ ✶	♒ 6 22:33	21 1:28 ☽ 28♊22	Delta T 62.3 sec
♄ R 12 11:34	♀ ♏ 24 15:26	8 10:27 ☉ △	♒ 9 14:44	8 8:55 ♅ ☌	♓ 9 10:36	27 19:53 ● 5♎00	SVP 05♓15'17"
☽0N 15 9:30	☿ ♏ 28 13:28	11 20:09 ♂ ☍	♓ 12 2:34	11 1:09 ♀ △	♈ 11 19:51		Obliquity 23°26'18"
☽0S 28 7:05		13 19:37 ☉ ☍	♈ 14 12:00	13 8:53 ☉ ☍	♉ 14 2:06	5 10:59 ☽ 12♑30	⚷ Chiron 11♐20.7
♃ R 29 12:52	♄ ♉ 16 0:46	16 18:50 ♂ △	♉ 16 19:05	16 6:18 ♄ ☌	♊ 16 6:19	13 8:53 ○ 20♈19	☽ Mean ☊ 22♋08.7
	♀ ♐ 19 6:18	18 17:31 ☉ △	♊ 19 0:22	18 1:01 ☉ △	♋ 18 9:37	20 7:59 ☽ 27♋14	
☽0N 12 17:00	☉ ♏ 23 2:48	21 1:28 ☉ □	♋ 21 4:16	20 12:15 ♄ ✶	♌ 20 12:42	27 7:58 ● 4♏12	1 OCTOBER 2000
♃☍♇ 13 8:24		23 3:58 ♀ □	♌ 23 7:00	22 15:12 ♄ □	♍ 22 15:52		Julian Day # 36799
♆ D 15 14:12		25 1:33 ☿ ✶	♍ 25 9:02	24 18:34 ♄ △	♎ 24 19:30		Delta T 62.4 sec
☿ R 18 13:41		26 3:44 ♃ □	♎ 27 11:22	26 1:03 ♅ △	♏ 27 0:23		SVP 05♓15'14"
☽0S 25 15:44		28 16:57 ♅ △	♏ 29 15:30	29 6:04 ♄ ☍	♐ 29 7:40		Obliquity 23°26'18"
♅ D 26 15:24				31 13:43 ♂ □	♑ 31 18:02		⚷ Chiron 12♐54.4
							☽ Mean ☊ 20♋33.3

NOVEMBER 2000 — LONGITUDE

Day	Sid.Time	⊙	0 hr ☽	Noon ☽	True ☊	☿	♀	♂	♃	♄	♅	♆	♇
1 W	2 42 20	8♏52 13	2♑59 31	8♑58 5	17♋54.0	4♏34.3	15♐25.9	28♍ 5.8	9♊31.3	28♉57.2	16♒54.4	3♒52.0	11♐29.3
2 Th	2 46 17	9 52 17	14 54 28	20 49 17	17D 52.9	3R 26.0	16 38.4	28 42.9	9R 25.1	28R 52.7	16 54.7	3 52.5	11 31.4
3 F	2 50 14	10 52 22	26 43 11	2♒36 49	17 53.1	2 25.1	17 50.9	29 19.9	9 18.9	28 48.2	16 55.1	3 53.1	11 33.4
4 Sa	2 54 10	11 52 29	8♒30 52	14 26 3	17R 53.6	1 33.3	19 3.3	29 56.9	9 12.5	28 43.7	16 55.5	3 53.8	11 35.5
5 Su	2 58 7	12 52 37	20 23 3	26 22 32	17 53.3	0 52.0	20 15.7	0♎33.9	9 5.9	28 39.1	16 56.0	3 54.5	11 37.6
6 M	3 2 3	13 52 47	2♓25 10	8♓31 33	17 51.4	0 21.9	21 28.1	1 10.9	8 59.2	28 34.5	16 56.5	3 55.2	11 39.7
7 Tu	3 6 0	14 52 58	14 42 15	20 57 46	17 47.2	0 3.4	22 40.4	1 47.8	8 52.4	28 29.8	16 57.0	3 55.9	11 41.8
8 W	3 9 56	15 53 11	27 18 31	3♈44 48	17 40.7	29♎56.5	23 52.6	2 24.7	8 45.5	28 25.1	16 57.6	3 57.5	11 43.9
9 Th	3 13 53	16 53 26	10♈16 50	16 54 42	17 32.1	0♏ 0.9	25 4.9	3 1.6	8 38.5	28 20.4	16 58.3	3 57.5	11 46.1
10 F	3 17 49	17 53 42	23 38 20	0♉27 35	17 22.1	0D 16.0	26 17.0	3 38.5	8 31.3	28 15.6	16 59.0	3 58.3	11 48.2
11 Sa	3 21 46	18 53 59	7♉22 5	14 21 25	17 11.8	0 41.0	27 29.2	4 15.3	8 24.0	28 10.9	16 59.8	3 59.2	11 50.4
12 Su	3 25 43	19 54 19	21 25 1	28 32 13	17 2.3	1 15.2	28 41.2	4 52.1	8 16.7	28 6.1	17 0.6	4 0.1	11 52.6
13 M	3 29 39	20 54 40	5♊42 19	12♊54 35	16 54.5	1 57.5	29 53.3	5 28.9	8 9.2	28 1.2	17 1.4	4 1.0	11 54.8
14 Tu	3 33 36	21 55 3	20 8 14	27 22 32	16 49.2	2 47.2	1♑ 5.3	6 5.7	8 1.7	27 56.4	17 2.3	4 2.0	11 57.0
15 W	3 37 32	22 55 27	4♋36 51	11♋50 32	16D 46.5	3 43.4	2 17.2	6 42.5	7 54.1	27 51.6	17 3.3	4 3.0	11 59.2
16 Th	3 41 29	23 55 54	19 3 46	26 14 2	16 45.9	4 45.2	3 29.1	7 19.2	7 46.4	27 46.7	17 4.3	4 4.0	12 1.4
17 F	3 45 25	24 56 22	3♌23 16	10♌29 56	16 46.6	5 51.9	4 40.9	7 56.0	7 38.6	27 41.8	17 5.4	4 5.0	12 3.7
18 Sa	3 49 22	25 56 52	17 34 24	24 36 22	16R 47.6	7 2.8	5 52.7	8 32.7	7 30.7	27 36.9	17 6.5	4 6.1	12 5.9
19 Su	3 53 19	26 57 24	1♍35 44	8♍32 27	16 47.8	8 17.4	7 4.4	9 9.3	7 22.8	27 32.0	17 7.7	4 7.2	12 8.2
20 M	3 57 15	27 57 58	15 26 29	22 17 48	16 46.2	9 35.1	8 16.1	9 46.0	7 14.9	27 27.1	17 8.9	4 8.4	12 10.4
21 Tu	4 1 12	28 58 34	29 6 22	5♎52 27	16 42.6	10 55.4	9 27.7	10 22.6	7 6.9	27 22.2	17 10.1	4 9.6	12 12.7
22 W	4 5 8	29 59 11	12♎35 1	19 14 59	16 36.9	12 18.0	10 39.3	10 59.2	6 58.8	27 17.3	17 11.4	4 10.8	12 15.0
23 Th	4 9 5	0♐59 50	25 51 55	2♏25 40	16 29.5	13 42.4	11 50.8	11 35.8	6 50.7	27 12.5	17 12.8	4 12.0	12 17.3
24 F	4 13 1	2 0 31	8♏56 21	15 23 40	16 21.3	15 8.4	13 2.2	12 12.4	6 42.5	27 7.6	17 14.2	4 13.3	12 19.6
25 Sa	4 16 58	3 1 13	21 47 37	28 8 9	16 13.1	16 35.8	14 13.6	12 48.9	6 34.4	27 2.7	17 15.6	4 14.6	12 21.9
26 Su	4 20 54	4 1 56	4♐25 16	10♐39 1	16 5.9	18 4.2	15 24.9	13 25.4	6 26.2	26 57.9	17 17.1	4 15.9	12 24.2
27 M	4 24 51	5 2 41	16 49 27	22 56 42	16 0.3	19 33.5	16 36.1	14 1.8	6 18.0	26 53.0	17 18.7	4 17.3	12 26.5
28 Tu	4 28 47	6 3 27	29 0 59	5♑ 2 31	15 56.6	21 3.6	17 47.3	14 38.3	6 9.8	26 48.2	17 20.3	4 18.6	12 28.8
29 W	4 32 44	7 4 15	11♑ 1 37	16 58 38	15D 55.0	22 34.3	18 58.4	15 14.7	6 1.6	26 43.4	17 21.9	4 20.0	12 31.1
30 Th	4 36 41	8 5 3	22 53 58	28 48 5	15 55.1	24 5.5	20 9.4	15 51.1	5 53.4	26 38.7	17 23.6	4 21.5	12 33.4

DECEMBER 2000 — LONGITUDE

Day	Sid.Time	⊙	0 hr ☽	Noon ☽	True ☊	☿	♀	♂	♃	♄	♅	♆	♇
1 F	4 40 37	9♐ 5 53	4♒41 29	10♒34 42	15♋56.4	25♏37.1	21♑20.3	16♎27.4	5♊45.3	26♉34.0	17♒25.3	4♒23.0	12♐35.8
2 Sa	4 44 34	10 6 43	16 28 21	22 23 0	15 58.3	27 9.1	22 31.2	17 3.7	5R 37.1	26R 29.3	17 27.1	4 24.4	12 38.1
3 Su	4 48 30	11 7 34	28 19 18	4♓17 54	15 59.9	28 41.3	23 41.9	17 40.0	5 29.0	26 24.6	17 28.9	4 26.0	12 40.4
4 M	4 52 27	12 8 26	10♓19 27	16 24 34	16R 0.7	0♐13.7	24 52.6	18 16.2	5 20.9	26 20.0	17 30.8	4 27.5	12 42.7
5 Tu	4 56 23	13 9 19	22 33 54	28 48 1	16 0.2	1 46.4	26 3.2	18 52.4	5 12.9	26 15.4	17 32.7	4 29.1	12 45.0
6 W	5 0 20	14 10 13	5♈ 7 29	11♈32 45	15 58.3	3 19.1	27 13.6	19 28.6	5 4.9	26 10.9	17 34.7	4 30.7	12 47.3
7 Th	5 4 17	15 11 7	18 4 13	24 42 10	15 55.0	4 52.0	28 24.0	20 4.8	4 56.9	26 6.4	17 36.6	4 32.3	12 49.7
8 F	5 8 13	16 12 3	1♉26 46	8♉18 2	15 50.7	6 25.0	29 34.2	20 40.9	4 49.0	26 1.9	17 38.7	4 33.9	12 52.0
9 Sa	5 12 10	17 12 58	15 15 50	22 19 53	15 46.1	7 58.1	0♒44.2	21 16.9	4 41.2	25 57.5	17 40.8	4 35.6	12 54.3
10 Su	5 16 6	18 13 55	29 29 44	6♊44 44	15 41.8	9 31.2	1 54.2	21 53.0	4 33.4	25 53.2	17 42.9	4 37.3	12 56.7
11 M	5 20 3	19 14 53	14♊ 4 10	21 27 9	15 38.3	11 4.5	3 4.3	22 29.0	4 25.8	25 48.9	17 45.0	4 39.0	12 59.0
12 Tu	5 23 59	20 15 51	28 52 43	6♋20 43	15 35.6	12 37.8	4 14.1	23 4.9	4 18.2	25 44.7	17 47.3	4 40.7	13 1.3
13 W	5 27 56	21 16 51	13♋47 32	21 14 46	15D 35.4	14 11.2	5 23.8	23 40.9	4 10.7	25 40.5	17 49.5	4 42.5	13 3.6
14 Th	5 31 52	22 17 51	28 40 36	6♌ 4 3	15 35.8	15 44.7	6 33.3	24 16.8	4 3.3	25 36.4	17 51.8	4 44.3	13 5.9
15 F	5 35 49	23 18 52	13♌24 49	20 41 50	15 37.0	17 18.3	7 42.7	24 52.7	3 56.0	25 32.4	17 54.1	4 46.1	13 8.2
16 Sa	5 39 46	24 19 54	27 54 46	5♍ 3 15	15 38.4	18 52.0	8 52.0	25 28.6	3 48.7	25 28.4	17 56.5	4 47.9	13 10.5
17 Su	5 43 42	25 20 57	12♍ 7 3	19 6 2	15 39.6	20 25.8	10 1.1	26 4.4	3 41.6	25 24.5	17 58.9	4 49.8	13 12.8
18 M	5 47 39	26 22 1	26 0 9	2♎49 28	15R 40.1	21 59.8	11 10.1	26 40.1	3 34.6	25 20.6	18 1.3	4 51.6	13 15.1
19 Tu	5 51 35	27 23 6	9♎34 23	16 14 5	15 40.0	23 33.8	12 18.9	27 15.9	3 27.8	25 16.9	18 3.8	4 53.5	13 17.3
20 W	5 55 32	28 24 12	22 50 42	29 21 15	15 38.5	25 8.1	13 27.7	27 51.5	3 21.0	25 13.2	18 6.3	4 55.4	13 19.6
21 Th	5 59 28	29 25 18	5♏48 44	12♏12 31	15 36.3	26 42.5	14 36.1	28 27.2	3 14.4	25 9.6	18 8.8	4 57.3	13 21.9
22 F	6 3 25	0♑26 26	18 32 47	24 49 45	15 34.0	28 17.1	15 44.5	29 2.8	3 7.9	25 6.0	18 11.4	4 59.3	13 24.1
23 Sa	6 7 21	1 27 34	1♐ 3 36	7♐14 33	15 31.7	29 51.9	16 52.7	29 38.3	3 1.6	25 2.6	18 14.0	5 1.2	13 26.4
24 Su	6 11 18	2 28 42	13 22 48	19 28 34	15 29.7	1♑26.9	18 0.7	0♏13.9	2 55.4	24 59.2	18 16.7	5 3.2	13 28.7
25 M	6 15 15	3 29 51	25 32 0	1♑33 19	15 28.4	3 2.1	19 8.6	0 49.3	2 49.3	24 55.9	18 19.3	5 5.2	13 30.9
26 Tu	6 19 11	4 31 1	7♑32 43	13 30 26	15D 27.9	4 37.6	20 16.2	1 24.8	2 43.4	24 52.7	18 22.1	5 7.2	13 33.0
27 W	6 23 8	5 32 10	19 26 43	25 21 49	15 27.5	6 13.4	21 23.7	2 0.1	2 37.7	24 49.6	18 24.8	5 9.3	13 35.1
28 Th	6 27 4	6 33 20	1♒16 2	7♒ 9 40	15 27.9	7 49.4	22 31.0	2 35.5	2 32.1	24 46.6	18 27.6	5 11.3	13 37.4
29 F	6 31 1	7 34 30	13 3 4	18 57 0	15 28.7	9 25.7	23 38.1	3 10.8	2 26.7	24 43.7	18 30.4	5 13.4	13 39.4
30 Sa	6 34 57	8 35 40	24 50 46	0♓45 55	15 29.5	11 2.2	24 44.9	3 46.0	2 21.4	24 40.8	18 33.2	5 15.5	13 41.7
31 Su	6 38 54	9 36 50	6♓42 33	12 41 11	15 30.3	12 39.1	25 51.6	4 21.1	2 16.3	24 38.1	18 36.1	5 17.5	13 43.9

Astro Data — 1 NOVEMBER 2000
Julian Day # 36830
Delta T 62.4 sec
SVP 05♓15'11"
☉ Chiron 15♐38.9
☽ Mean ☊ 18♋54.8

1 DECEMBER 2000
Julian Day # 36860
Delta T 62.5 sec
SVP 05♓15'06"
☉ Chiron 18♐57.5
☽ Mean ☊ 17♋19.5

Astro Data Dy Hr Mn	Planet Ingress Dy Hr Mn	Last Aspect Dy Hr Mn	☽ Ingress Dy Hr Mn	Last Aspect Dy Hr Mn	☽ Ingress Dy Hr Mn	☽ Phases & Eclipses Dy Hr Mn
♂0S 8 23:23	♂ ♎ 4 2:00	3 5:37 ♂ △	♒ 3 6:41	3 0:51 ☿ □	♓ 3 3:23	4 7:27 ☽ 12♒11
☿ D 8 2:28	☿ ♎ 7 7:28	5 16:26 ♄ □	♓ 5 19:13	5 7:26 ♀ *	♈ 5 14:17	11 21:15 ○ 19♉47
☽0N 9 2:42	♀ ♐ 8 21:42	8 2:04 ♄ *	♈ 8 5:02	7 20:22 ♀ □	♉ 7 21:27	18 15:25 ☽ 26♌36
☽0S 21 22:49	☉ ♐ 13 2:14	10 5:07 ♀ △	♉ 10 11:12	9 18:00 ♄ *	♊ 10 0:50	25 23:11 ● 3♐60
	☿ ♐ 22 0:19	12 11:12 ♄ △	♊ 12 14:17	11 14:15 ♂ △	♋ 12 1:48	
☽0N 6 13:06		13 18:51 ♅ △	♋ 14 16:21	13 19:04 ♅ △	♌ 14 2:09	4 3:55 ☽ 12♓18
♃△♀ 9 14:14	♂ ♏ 3 20:26	16 14:30 ♄ △	♌ 16 18:19	15 19:57 ♄ △	♍ 16 3:30	11 9:03 ○ 19♊38
☽0S 19 4:50	☉ ♑ 21 13:37	18 17:03 ♀ □	♍ 18 21:15	18 0:41 ○ △	♎ 18 7:01	18 0:41 ☽ 26♍24
	♀ ♑ 21 21:37	20 23:45 ☉ ※	♎ 21 1:35	20 11:07 ☉ ※	♏ 20 13:12	25 17:22 ● 4♑14
	♀ ♑ 23 2:03	22 18:35 ♅ △	♏ 23 8:33	22 12:28 ♀ *	♐ 23 22:03	25 17:34:57 ♇ P 0.723
	♂ ♏ 23 14:37	25 9:52 ♀ △	♐ 25 15:33	24 10:03 ♀ *	♑ 25 8:54	
		27 0:57 ♅ *	♑ 28 1:57	27 10:52 ♄ △	♒ 27 21:25	
		30 7:34 ♄ △	♒ 30 14:26	29 23:47 ♀ ♂	♓ 30 10:27	